DIRECTORY
OF
AMERICAN
SCHOLARS

DIRECTORY
OF
AMERICAN
SCHOLARS

EIGHTH EDITION

FOREIGN LANGUAGES,
LINGUISTICS AND PHILOLOGY

VOLUME
III

EDITED BY
JAQUES CATTELL PRESS

R.R. BOWKER COMPANY
NEW YORK & LONDON 1982

Copyright © 1982 by Xerox Corporation
Published by R. R. Bowker Co.
1180 Avenue of the Americas, New York, N.Y. 10036

International Standard Book Number
       Set: 0-8352-1476-1
  Volume I: 0-8352-1478-8
  Volume II: 0-8352-1479-6
 Volume III: 0-8352-1481-8
 Volume IV: 0-8352-1482-6
International Standard Serial Number: 0070-5150
Library of Congress Catalog Card Number: 57-9125

CONTENTS

CONTENTS

PREFACE

First published in 1942 under the auspices of the American Council of Learned Societies, the *Directory of American Scholars* remains the foremost biographical reference to American humanities scholars. The directory is arranged for convenient use in four subject volumes: Volume I: History; Volume II: English, Speech and Drama; Volume III: Foreign Languages, Linguistics and Philology; Volume IV: Philosophy, Religion and Law. Each volume contains a geographic index, and Volume IV includes an alphabetic index of scholars listed in all four volumes.

The eighth edition of the *Directory of American Scholars* profiles over 37,500 United States and Canadian scholars currently active in teaching, research and publishing; 3800 appear for the first time. The names of new entrants were obtained from former entrants, academic deans, or citations in professional journals. Each nominee received a questionnaire to complete and selection for inclusion was made based on the following criteria:

1. Achievement, by reason of experience and training, of a stature in scholarly work equivalent to that associated with the doctoral degree, coupled with current activity in such work;

   or

2. Achievement as evidenced by publication of scholarly works;

   or

3. Attainment of a position of substantial responsibility by reason of achievement as outlined in (1) and (2).

Copy proofs were supplied to all seventh edition entrants, and new information was returned to the editors for over 70% of the listings. Entrants who did not return a proof continue to be included only if scholarly activity could be verified in public sources. In addition to unverified non-respondents, previous entrants whose listings are discontinued include those who have entered unrelated fields, and those who are emeritus or retired and have not published within the past ten years.

Volume III: Foreign Languages, Linguistics and Philology profiles approximately 7500 scholars in these fields, including those in comparative literature and the classics. Scholars in fields that cross the discipline grouping, such as classical history, and those with major involvement in several fields, are given a complete entry in one volume with cross references in others, as necessary.

The eighth edition is the first *Directory of American Scholars* to be produced by fully automated methods. The advent of computerized editing and printing has allowed a shorter production cycle and, in consequence, more current information. Other enhancements include italicized section headings and a larger type size for easier reading. Limitations in the new printing method have made it necessary to omit most diacritics and non-English alphabets.

Individual entries can include *primary discipline(s), vital statistics, education, honorary degrees, past and present professional experience, concurrent positions, *membership in international, national and regional societies, honors and awards, *research interest, *publications, and mailing address. Elements preceded by an asterisk are limited as to the number of items included. If the entrant exceeded these limitations the editors selected the most recent information.

The editors have made every effort to include all material submitted as accurately and completely as possible within the confines of format and scope. However, the publishers do not assume and hereby disclaim any liability to any party for any loss or damage caused by errors or omissions in the *Directory of American Scholars* whether such errors or omissions result from negligence, accident, or any other cause.

Thanks are expressed to those who contributed information and submitted nominations for the new edition. Many societies provided membership lists for the research process and published announcements in their journals or newsletters, and their help is appreciated.

Comments and suggestions regarding any aspect of the eighth edition are invited and should be addressed to The Editors, Jaques Cattell Press, P. O. Box 25001, Tempe, Arizona, 85282.

Carol J. Borland, *Editor*
Renee Lautenbach, *Managing Editor*
Terence E. Basom, *General Manager*

JAQUES CATTELL PRESS

November 1982

ABBREVIATIONS

AAAS—American Association for the Advancement of Science
AAUP—American Association of University Professors
abnorm—abnormal
abstr—abstract(s)
acad—academia, academic, academica, académie, académique, academy
accad—accademia
acct—account, accountant, accounting
acoust—acoustical, accoustic(s)
adj—adjunct, adjutant
actg—acting
activ—activities, activity
addn—addition(s), additional
AID—Agency for International Development
adjust—adjustment
admin—administration, administrative
adminr—administrator(s)
admis—admissions
adv—advisor(s), advisory
advan—advance(d), advancement
advert—advertisement, advertising
aerodyn—aerodynamic(s)
aeronaut—aeronautic(s), aeronautical
aesthet—aesthetics
affil—affiliate(s), affiliation
agr—agricultural, agriculture
agt—agent
AFB—Air Force Base
AHA—American Historical Association
akad—akademi, akademia
Ala—Alabama
algem—algemeen, algemen
allergol—allergological, allergology
allgem—allgemein, allgemeine, allgemeinen
Alta—Alberta
Am—America, Americain, American, Americana, Americano, Amerika, Amerikaansch, Amerikaner, Amerikanisch, Amerikansk
anal—analysis, analytic, analytical
analog—analogue
anat—anatomic, anatomical, anatomy
ann—annal(s)
anthrop—anthropological, anthropology
anthropom—anthropometric, anthropometrical, anthropometry
antiq—antiquaire(s), antiquarian, antiquary(ies), antiquities
app—appoint, appointed, appointment
appl—applied
appln—application
approx—approximate, approximately
Apr—April
apt—apartment(s)
arbit—arbitration
arch—archiv, archiva, archive(s), archivio, archivo
archaeol—archaeological, archaeology
archäol—archäologie, archäologisch
archeol—archeological, archéologie, archéologique, archeology

archit—architectural, architecture
Arg—Argentina, Argentine
Ariz—Arizona
Ark—Arkansas
asn—association
asoc—asociación
assoc(s)—associate(s), associated
asst—assistant
Assyriol—Assyriology
astrodyn—astrodynamics
astron—astronomical, astronomy
astronaut—astronautical, astronautics
astronr—astronomer
attend—attendant, attending
atty—attorney
audiol—audiology
Aug—August
auth—author(s)
AV—audiovisual
ave—avenue

b—born
BC—British Columbia
bd—board
behav—behavior, behavioral, behaviour, behavioural
Bibl—Biblical, Biblique
bibliog—bibliografía, bibliographic, bibliographical, bibliography(ies)
bibliogr—bibliographer
bibliot—biblioteca, bibliotec, bibliotek, bibliotheca, bibliothek, bibliothèque
biog—biographical, biography
biol—biological, biology
bk(s)—book(s)
bldg—building
blvd—boulevard
bol—boletim, boletín
boll—bollettino
bor—borough
bot—botanical, botany
br—branch
Brit—Britain, British
Bro(s)—Brother(s)
bull—bulletin
bur—bureau
bus—business
BWI—British West Indies

c—children
Calif—California
Can—Canada, Canadian, Canadien, Canadienne
cand—candidate
cartog—cartografic, cartographical, cartography
cartogr—cartographer
Cath—Catholic, Catholique
CBS—Columbia Broadcasting System
cent—central
Cent Am—Central America

cert—certificat, certificate, certified
chap—chapter
chem—chemical, chemistry
chg—charge
chmn—chairman
Cie—Compagnie
cient—científica, científico
class—classical
clin(s)—clinic(s), clinical
Co—Companies, Company, County
coauth—coauthor
co-dir—co-director
co-ed—co-editor
co-educ—co-educational
col(s)—colegio, college(s), collegiate
collab—collaboration, collaborative, collaborating, collaborator
Colo—Colorado
Comdr—Commander
com—commerce, commercial
commun—communications(s)
comn(s)—commission(s)
comnr—commissioner
comp—comparative, comparée
compos—composition(s)
comput—computer, computing
comt—committee(s)
conf—conference
cong—congress
Conn—Connecticut
conserv—conservación, conservation, conservatoire, conservatory
consol—consolidated, consolidation
const—constitution, constitutional
construct—construction
consult—consultant, consulting
contemp—contemporary
contrib—contribute, contribution
contribr—contributor
conv—convention
coop—cooperation, cooperative
coord—coordinating, coordination
coordr—coordinator
corresp—corresponding
Corp—Corporation
coun—council, counsel, counselling
counr—councillor, counselor
criminol—criminology
Ct—Court
ctr—center
cult—cultra, cultural, culturale, culture
cur—curator
curric—curriculum
cybernet—cybernetics
CZ—Canal Zone
Czech—Czechoslovakia

DC—District of Columbia
Dec—December
Del—Delaware
deleg—delegate, delegations

demog—demographic, demography
demonstr—demonstrator
dent—dental, dentistry
dep—deputy
dept—department
Deut—Deutsch, Deutschland
develop—development
diag—diagnosis, diagnostic
dialectol—dialectology
dig—digest
dipl—diplom, diploma, diplomate, diplôme
dir—director(s), directory
Diss Abstr—Dissertation Abstracts
dist—district
distrib—distributive
distribr—distributors
div—division, divorced
doc—document, documentation
Dom—Dominion
Dr—Doctor, Drive
Drs—Doctorandus

e—east
ecol—ecological, ecology
econ—economic(s), economical, economy
ed—edición, edition, editor, editorial,
    edizione
educ—education, educational
educr—educator(s)
Egyptol—Egyptology
elec—electric, electrical, electricity
elem—elementary
emer—emeriti, emeritus
encour—encouragement
encycl—encyclopedia
employ—employment
Eng—England
environ—environment, environmental
EPDA—Education Professions
    Development Act
equip—equipment
ERIC—Educational Resources
    Information Center
ESEA—Elementary & Secondary
    Education Act
espec—especially
estab—established, establishment
estud—estudante, estudas, estudiante,
    estudio(s), estudo(s)
ethnog—ethnographical, ethnography
ethnol—ethnological, ethnology
Europ—European
eval—evaluation
evangel—evangelical
eve—evening
exam—examination
examr—examiner
except—exceptional
exec—executive(s)
exeg—exegesis(es), exegetic, exegetical,
    exegetics
exhib—exhibition(s)
exp—experiment, experimental, experimentation
exped—expedition(s)
explor—exploration(s)
expos—exposition
exten—extension

fac—faculties, faculty
facil—facilities, facility
Feb—February
fed—federal
fedn—federation
fel(s)—fellow(s), fellowship(s)
filol—filologia, filológico
filos—filosofía, filosófico
Fla—Florida
FLES—Foreign Languages in the Elementary
    Schools
for—foreign
forsch—forschung, forschungen
found—foundation

Fr—Francais(e), French
Ft—Fort

Ga—Georgia
gen—general, générale
geneal—genealogical, genealogy
genoot—genootschap
geod—geodesy, geodetic
geog—geografía, geográfico, geographer(s),
    geographic, geographie, geographical,
    geography
geogr—geographer
geol—geologic, geological, geology
geophys—geophysical
Ger—German, Germanic, Germanisch,
    Germany
ges—gesellschaft
gov—governing, governor(s)
govt—government, governmental
grad—graduate
Gt Brit—Great Britain
guid—guidance
gym—gymnasium

handbk(s)—handbook(s)
Hisp—Hispanic, Hispánico, Hispano
hist—historie, historia, historial, historic,
    historica, historical, historique, historische,
    history
histol—histology, histological
Hochsch—Hochschule
hon—honorable, honorary
hosp(s)—hospital(s)
hq—headquarters
HumRRO—Human Resources Research Office
hwy—highway

Ill—Illinois
illum—illuminating, illumination
illus—illustrate, illustration
illusr—illustrator
imp—imperial
improv—improvement
Inc—Incorporated
incl—include, included, includes, including
Ind—Indiana
indust(s)—industrial, industry(ies)
inform—information
inst—institut, institute(s), institution(s), instituto
instnl—institutional, institutionalized
instr—instruction, instructor(s)
instruct—instructional
int—internacional, international, internazionale
intel—intelligence
introd—introduction
invest—investigación, investiganda,
    investigation, investigative
investr—investigator
ist—istituto
Ital—Italia, Italian, Italiana, Italiano, Italica,
    Italien, Italienisch, Italienne, Italy

J—Journal
Jan—January
jour—journal, journalism
jr—junior
jurisp—jurisprudence
juv—juvenile(s)

Kans—Kansas
koninkl—koninklijk
Ky—Kentucky

La—Louisiana
lab—laboratorie, laboratorio, laboratorium,
    laboratory(ies)
lang—language(s)
lect—lecture(s)

lectr—lecturer
legis—legislación, legislatief, legislation,
    legislative, legislativo, legislature,
    legislazione
lett—letter(s), lettera, letteraria, letteratura,
    lettere
lib—liberal
libr—library(ies), librerio
librn—librarian(s)
lic—license, licencia
ling—linguistic(s), lingüística, linguistique
lit—literary, literatur, literatura, literature,
    littera, literature
Ltd—Limited

m—married
mach—machine(s), machinery
mag—magazine
Man—Manitoba
Mar—March
Mariol—Mariological, Mariology
Mass—Massachusetts
mat—matematica, matematiche, matematico,
    matematik
math—mathematica, mathematical,
    mathematics, mathematik,
    mathématique(s), mathematisch
Md—Maryland
mech—mechanical
med—medical, medicine
Mediter—Mediterranean
mem—member, memoirs, memorial
ment—mental, mentally
metrop—metropolitan
Mex—Mexican, Mexicano, Mexico
mfg—manufacturing
mfr—manufacture, manufacturer
mgr—manager(s)
mgt—management
Mich—Michigan
mid—middle
mil—military
Minn—Minnesota
Miss—Mississippi
mitt—mitteilung
mkt—market, marketing
MLA—Modern Language Association of
    America
Mo—Missouri
mod—modern, moderna, moderne, moderno
monatsh—monatsheft(e)
monatsschr—monatsschrift
monogr—monograph
Mont—Montana
morphol—morphologica, morphologie,
    morphology
mt—mount, mountain(s)
munic—municipal
mus—museum(s)
musicol—musicological, musicology

n—north
nac—nacional
NASA—National Aeronautics & Space
    Administration
nat—nationaal, national, nationale, nationalis,
    naturalized
NATO—North Atlantic Treaty Organization
naz—nazionale
NB—New Brunswick
NC—North Carolina
NCTE—National Council of Teachers of English
NDak—North Dakota
NDEA—National Defense Education Act
NEA—National Education Association
Nebr—Nebraska
Ned—Nederland, Nederlandsch
Nev—Nevada
Neth—Netherlands
Nfld—Newfoundland
NH—New Hampshire
NJ—New Jersey
NMex—New Mexico

no—number
nonres—nonresident
norm—normal, normale
Norweg—Norwegian
Nov—November
NS—Nova Scotia
NSW—New South Wales
NT—Northwest Territories
numis—numismatic, numismático, numismatique
NY—New York
NZ—New Zealand

occas—occasional
occup—occupation, occupational
Oct—October
OEEC—Organization for European Economic Cooperation
off—office, officer(s), official(s)
Okla—Oklahoma
Ont—Ontario
oper—operation(s), operational, operative
ord—ordnance
Ore—Oregon
orgn—organization, organizational
orient—oriental, orientale, orientalist, orientalia
ornithol—ornithological, ornithology

Pa—Pennsylvania
Pac—Pacific
paleontol—paleontological, paleontology
Pan-Am—Pan American
pedag—pedagogia, pedagogic, pedagogical, pedagogico, pédagogie, pedagogik, pédagogique, pedagogy
PEI—Prince Edward Island
penol—penological, penology
phenomenol—phenomenological, phenomenologie, phenomenology
philol—philologica, philological, philologie, philologisch, philology
philos—philosophia, philosophic, philosophical, philosophie, philosophique, philosophisch, philosophical, philosophy, philoszophia
photog—photographic, photography
photogr—photographer(s)
phys—physical
pkwy—parkway
pl—place
polit—politica, political, politicas, politico, politics, politek, politike, politique, politisch, politisk
polytech—polytechnic
pop—population
Pontif—Pontifical
Port—Portugal, Portuguese
postgrad—postgraduate
PR—Puerto Rico
pract—practice
prehist—prehistoric
prep—preparation, preparatory
pres—president
Presby—Presbyterian
preserv—preservation
prev—prevention, preventive
prin—principal(s)
prob—problem(s)
probtn—probation
proc—proceeding
prod—production
prof—professional, professor, professorial
prog—program(s), programmed, programming
proj—project, projective
prom—promotion
prov—province, provincial
psychiat—psychiatria, psychiatric, psychiatrica, psychiatrie, psychiatrique, psychiatrisch, psychiatry
psychol—psychological, psychology
pt—point
pub—public, publique

publ—publication(s), published, publisher(s), publishing
pvt—private

qm—quartermaster
quad—quaderni
qual—qualitative, quality
quart—quarterly
Que—Quebec

rd—road
RD—Rural Delivery, Rural Free Delivery
rec—record(s), recording
rech—recherche
redevelop—redevelopment
ref—reference
regist—register, registered, registration
registr—registrar
rehabil—rehabilitation
rel(s)—relacion, relation(s), relative, relazione
relig—religion, religious
rep—representative
repub—republic
req—requirement(s)
res—research, reserve
rev—review, revised, revista, revue
rhet—rhetoric, rhetorical
RI—Rhode Island
RR—Rural Route
Rt—Right
Rte—Route
Russ—Russian
rwy—railway

s—south
SAfrica—South Africa
SAm—South America, South American
Sask—Saskatchewan
SC—South Carolina
Scand—Scandinavian
sch(s)—school(s)
scholar—scholarship
sci—science(s), scientia, scientific, scientifico, scientifique, scienza
SDak—South Dakota
SEATO—Southeast Asia Treaty Organization
sec—secondary
sect—section
secy—secretary
sem—séminaire, seminar, seminario, seminary
sen—senator, senatorial
Sept—September
ser—serial, series
serv—service(s)
soc—social, sociedad, sociedade, societa, societas, societate, société, societet, society(ies)
soc sci—social science(s)
sociol—sociological, sociology
Span—Spanish
spec—special
sq—square
sr—senior
St—Saint, Street
sta—station
statist—statistical, statistics
Ste—Sainte
struct—structural, structure(s)
subcomt—subcommittee
subj—subject
substa—substation
super—supérieur, superior, superiore
suppl—supplement, supplementary
supt—superintendent
supv—supervising, supervision
supvr—supervisor
supvry—supervisory
surg—surgical, surgery
surv—survey
Swed—Swedish
Switz—Switzerland
symp—symposium
syst—system, systematic

tech—technic(s), technica, technical, technicky, techniczny, techniek, technik, technika, technikum, technique, technisch
technol—technologic, technological, technologicke, technologico, technologiczny, technologie, technologika, technologique, technologisch, technology
tecnol—technología, technológica, technologico
tel—telegraph(y), telephone
temp—temporary
Tenn—Tennessee
Terr—Terrace
teol—teología, teológico
Tex—Texas
textbk—textbook(s)
theol—theological, théologie, théoligique, theologisch, theology
theoret—theoretic(al)
ther—therapy
trans—transactions
transp—transportation
transl—translation, translator(s)
treas—treasurer, treasury
trop—tropical
TV—television
twp—township

u—und
UAR—United Arab Republic
UK—United Kingdom
UN—United Nations
unemploy—unemployment
UNESCO—United Nations Educational, Scientific & Cultural Organization
UNICEF—United Nations Children's Fund
univ(s)—universidad, université, university(ies)
UNRRA—United Nations Relief & Rehabilitation Administration
UNRWA—United Nations Relief & Works Agency
USPHS—United States Public Health Service
USSR—Union of Soviet Socialist Republics

Va—Virginia
var—various
veg—vegetable(s), vegetation
ver—vereeniging, verein, vereingt, vereinigung
vet—veteran, veterinarian, veterinary
VI—Virgin Islands
vis—visiting
voc—vocational
vocab—vocabulary
vol(s)—volume(s), voluntary, volunteer(s)
vchmn—vice chairman
vpres—vice president
Vt—Vermont

w—west
Wash—Washington
wetensch—wetenschappelijk, wetenschappen
WHO—World Health Organization
WI—West Indies
wid—widow, widowed, widower
Wis—Wisconsin
wiss—wissenschaft(en), wissenschaftliche(e)
WVa—West Virginia
Wyo—Wyoming

yearbk—yearbook(s)
YMCA—Young Men's Christian Association
YMHA—Young Men's Hebrew Association
YWCA—Young Women's Christian Association
YWHA—Young Women's Hebrew Association

z—zeitschrift

DIRECTORY OF AMERICAN SCHOLARS

FOREIGN LANGUAGES, LINGUISTICS AND PHILOLOGY

A

AAGAARD-MOGENSEN, LARS, b Randers, Denmark, Mar 30, 44; m 67; c 1. PHILOSOPHY, AESTHETICS. *Educ:* State Univ NY, MA, 71; Aarhus Univ, Mag art, 72, Lic theol, 80. *Prof Exp:* Instr philos, Aarhus Univ, 74-78; lectr, Hellenic Int Sch, 78-79; sr assoc, Rijksuniversiteit-Gent, 79-80; ASST PROF PHILOS, WASHINGTON UNIV, ST LOUIS, 80- *Concurrent Pos:* Asst, J Aesthetics & Art Criticisn, 73-74; ed, Acta Humanistica, 76 & Int Libr Aesthetics & Philos, 76-; lectr philos, Folkeuniversitetet, Aarhus & Copenhagen, 77-78; res assoc, Philos Res Ctr, Athens, 78-79; sr fel, Ministry of Dutch Cult, Brussels, 79-80. *Honors & Awards:* Award, Ministry of Cult, Copenhagen, 77. *Mem:* Am Philos Asn; Am Soc Aesthetics; Brit Soc Aesthetics; Commun & Cognition. *Res:* Epistemology; human rights. *Publ:* Ed, Culture and Art, Humanities Press Inc, 76; coauth, Om Tolerance, Folkeligt Oplysnings Forbund, 78; auth, Cumulative Index I-XXXV JAAC, Am Soc Aesthetics, 79; Aestetisk Kultur, Berlingske Forlag, 79; co-ed, Contemporary Aesthetics in Scandinavia, Bokforlaget Doxa, 80; Auth, Our Art, ICIWO Press, 82; co-ed, Art in Culture I and II, Commun & Cognition, 82; ed, The Museum, Humanities Press Inc, 82. *Mailing Add:* Dept of Philos Washington Univ St Louis MO 63130

AARON, M AUDREY, b Lawton, Okla, Dec 29, 13. ROMANCE LANGUAGES. *Educ:* Mt St Scholastica Col, AB; Johns Hopkins Univ, AM, 50, PhD(Romance lang), 52. *Prof Exp:* Mem fac Romance lang & chmn dept, Mt St Scholastica Col, 53-70, chmn div lang & lit, 65-68; vis assoc prof Span, Western Wash Univ, 70-71; assoc prof Span, Univ Idaho, 71-80. *Honors & Awards:* First Prize, Lope de Vega 4th Centenary Contest, Span Embassy. *Mem:* MLA; Am Asn Teachers Span & Port, Am Benedictine Acad. *Res:* Literature of Spanish Golden Age; Spanish religious lyric poetry; Central American novel and poetry. *Publ:* Auth, Cristo en la Poesia Lirica de Lope de Vega, Ed Cult Hisp, Madrid, 67; Lope de Vega & F Quevedo, In: New Cath Encycl, McGraw, 67; Lope de Vega's El Robo de Dina: Lovers Gentell or Gentile?, Univ Idaho, 77. *Mailing Add:* 6200 Meadowood Circle Reno NV 89502

ABBOTT, JAMES HAMILTON, b High Springs, Fla, Nov 22, 24. SPANISH. *Educ:* Univ Fla, BA, 48, MA, 50; Univ Calif, Los Angeles, PhD(Span), 58. *Prof Exp:* Instr Span, Hope Col, 55; from instr to assoc prof, 56-68, PROF SPAN & ASST CHMN DEPT, UNIV OKAL, 68- *Mem:* MLA; Am Asn Teachers Span & Port; Am Coun Teaching Foreign Lang. *Res:* Nineteenth and 20th century European Spanish literature. *Publ:* Co-translr, Leopoldo Zea, The Latin American Mind, Univ Okla, 63; auth, Azorin and Taine's determinism, Hispania, 9/63; Azorin and death, Bks Abroad, fall 67; Azorin y Francia, Semenarios & Ed, Madrid, 74; Ignacio Aldecoa and the journey to paradise, In: Ignacio Aldecoa, A Collection of Critical Essays, Univ Wyo 77. *Mailing Add:* 780 Van Vleet Oval Room 202 Univ of Okla Norman OK 73019

ABBOTT, KENNETH MORGAN, b Lincoln, Nebr, May 3, 06; m 34; c 3. CLASSICAL PHILOLOGY. *Educ:* Harvard Univ, AB, 28; Univ Ill, PhD, 34. *Prof Exp:* From instr to assoc prof, 34-46, PROF CLASSICS, OHIO STATE UNIV, 46- *Concurrent Pos:* Vis res prof, Univ Ill, 45-46; etymological consult, Merriam Webster, 58-59; Fulbright res fel, Rome, 59-60; Am Coun Learned Soc grant, London, 62; vis prof, Univ Waterloo, 68, Univ Ill, 69-70. *Mem:* Class Asn Mid West & South; Am Philol Asn. *Res:* Textual criticism; Cicero; Latin lexicography. *Publ:* Coauth, Index Verborum Ciceronis Epistularum, Univ Ill, 38; auth, The grammarians and the Latin accent, In: Classical Studies in Honor of W A Oldfather, 43; Ictus, accent and statistics in Latin dramatic verse, Trans Am Philol Asn, 44; coauth, Index Verborum in Ciceronis Rhetorica, Univ Ill, 64; auth, Commodian and his verse, In: Classical Studies Presented to Ben Edwin Perry, 69; Seneca and St Paul, In: Wege des Worts, Festschrift Für Wolfgang Fleischauer, 78; Satira and Satirocus in Late Latin, Ill Class Studies, Vol IV, 79. *Mailing Add:* 159 W Jeffrey Pl Columbus OH 43214

ABBOUD, PETER FOUAD, b Jaffa, Palestine, June 30, 31; m 52; c 1. LINGUISTICS, ARABIC STUDIES. *Educ:* Univ London, BS, 56; Am Univ Cairo, MA, 60; Univ Tex, Austin, PhD(ling), 64. *Prof Exp:* From asst instr to instr English, Am Univ Cairo, 57-61; asst prof, 64-68, ASSOC PROF LING, UNIV TEX, AUSTIN, 68- *Concurrent Pos:* Am Res Ctr is Egypt fel, 71-72. *Mem:* Ling Soc Am; Am Orient Soc; Am Asn Teachers Arabic; Mid E Studies Asn NAm. *Res:* Classical Arabic; Arabic dialectology. *Publ:* Coauth, Beginning Cairo Arabic, Univ Tex, 65; Elementary Modern Standard Arabic, Inter-Univ Comt Near Eastern Lang, 68; auth, The Teaching of Arabic in the United States: The State of the Art, ERIC Clearinghouse for Ling, 68; coauth, Modern Standard Arabic: Intermediate Level, Ctr Near Eastern & N African Studies, Mich, 71; auth, Spoken Arabic, In: Current Trends in Linguistics, Vol VI, Mouton, 71; On Ablaut in Cairo Arabic, Afro-Asiatic Ling, 76. *Mailing Add:* Dept of Orient & African Lang & Lit Univ of Tex Austin TX 78712

ABDEL-MASSIH, ERNEST TAWFIK, b Giza, Egypt; m; c 3. LINGUISTICS. *Educ:* Univ Alexandria, BA, 51, Higher dipl, 56; Univ Mich, Ann Arbor, MA, 65, PhD(ling), 68. *Prof Exp:* Lectr English, Cairo Univ, 61-64; asst prof Arabic lang & ling, 68-71, assoc prof, 71-76, PROF ARABIC & BERBER LANG & LING, UNIV MICH, ANN ARBOR, 76-, DIR CTR NEAR EASTERN & N AFRICAN STUDIES, 80- *Concurrent Pos:* Mem bd gov, Am Res Ctr Egypt, 77-; exec bd mem, Am Asn Teachers Arabic 79-82; Danforth assoc, 79-85. *Honors & Awards:* Ruth M Sinclair Award, 73. *Mem:* Ling Soc Am; Mid E Studies Asn; Am Asn Teachers Arabic. *Res:* Arabic dialects, Berber languages; sociolinguistics; computerized lexical statistics. *Publ:* Auth, A Course in Spoken Tamazight, 71, A reference grammar of Tamazight, 71, A Computerized Lexicon of Tamazight, 71, An Introduction to Egyptian Arabic, 74, rev ed, 82, An Introduction to Moroccan Arabic, 73, Advanced Moroccan Arabic, 74, A Sample Lexicon of Pan-Arabic, 75 & coauth, A Comprehensive Study of Egyptia Arabic Research in Sociolinguistics, Vol I, 76, Vol II, 78, Vol IV, 78, Vol III, 79, Univ Mich; coauth, The Coptic Liturgy According to St Basil, 78 & The divine liturgy of St Basil the Great, 82, Coptic Church. *Mailing Add:* Dept of Near Eastern Studies Univ of Mich Ann Arbor MI 48104

ABEL, ADELINE, b Palmebang, Sumatra, June 26, 31; m 52; c 4. FRENCH. *Educ:* La State Univ, BA, 56, MA, 59, PhD(French), 66. *Prof Exp:* Instr French & Span, St John Fisher Col, 61-62; instr French & Latin, La State Univ, Baton Rouge, 62-66; asst prof French, Calif State Col, Long Beach, 66-67; assoc prof, 67-70, PROF FRENCH, CENT CONN STATE COL, 70- *Mem:* MLA; Am Asn Teachers French. *Res:* French poetry. *Publ:* Coauth, La France: Une Tapisserie, 65, La France: Lanque ecrite et parlee, 66 & La France: Ses grandes heures litteraires, 68, McGraw. *Mailing Add:* Dept of Mod Languages Cent Conn State Col Stanley St New Britain CT 06050

ABEL, RICHARD OWEN, Cinema Studies, Comparative Literature. See Vol II

ABLER, LAWRENCE ANTHONY, b Mt Calvary, Wis, Dec 22, 20. ENGLISH, COMPARATIVE LITERATURE. *Educ:* Univ Wis-Madison, BA, 48, MA, 49; Occidental Col, PhD(comp lit), 58. *Prof Exp:* Instr English & comp lit, Occidental Col, 55-59, vis assoc prof comp lit, 63-65; from asst prof to assoc prof English, Northern Ariz Univ, 59-63; vis assoc prof comp studies, Juniata Col, 65-68; assoc prof, 68-73, chmn dept, 70-75, PROF COMP LIT, SUSQUEHANNA UNIV, 73- *Mem:* MLA; Am Comp Lit Asn. *Res:* Romanticism; 19th century Europe; 20th century European literature. *Publ:* Transl, Three Rilke poems, Monument, winter 60; coauth, A role for aesthetics in the teaching process, J Teacher Educ, winter 67; auth, Angel to Orpheus: Mythopoesis in the late Rilke, In: The Binding of Proteus, Bucknell Univ, 81. *Mailing Add:* Dept of English Susquehanna Univ Selinsgrove PA 17870

ABRAHAM, CLAUDE KURT, b Lorsch, Ger, Dec 13, 31; US citizen; m 56; c 4. FRENCH. *Educ:* Univ Cincinnati, AB, 53, MA, 56; Ind Univ, PhD, 59. *Prof Exp:* From instr to asst prof French, Univ Ill, Urbana, 59-64; from assoc prof to prof French, Univ Fla, 64-75, asst dean grad school, 72-73; PROF FRENCH, UNIV CALIF, DAVIS, 75- *Mem:* MLA; Am Asn Teachers Fr; Rocky Mountain MLA; Philol Asn Pac Coast; 17th Century Fr Lit Conf. *Res:* France in the 17th century. *Publ:* Auth, Gaston d'Orleans et sa Cour, Univ NC, 63; ed, Le Bourgeois Gentilhomme, Prentice-Hall, 66; auth, The Strangers, Univ Fal, 66; co-ed, Pascal, Univ Ala, 69; auth, Engin Malherbe, Univ Ky, 71; Corneille, Twayne, 72; co-ed, Theatre Complet de Tristan L'Hermite, Univ Ala, 75; auth, Racine, Twayne, 77. *Mailing Add:* Dept of French & Ital Univ of Calif Davis CA 95616

ABRAHAM, RICHARD D, b Philadelphia, Pa, Nov 6, 10. FOREIGN LANGUAGES, LINGUISTICS & PHILOLOGY. *Educ:* Univ Pa, BS, 31, MA, 35, PhD, 37. *Prof Exp:* Admin asst & head dept foreign lang, Philadelphia Pub Schs, 40-62; prof Span lang & lit, Rockford Col, 62-65; assoc prof Span, Ill State Univ, 65-66; PROF SPAN, UNIV MIAMI, 66- *Concurrent Pos:* Lectr, Rutgers Univ, 61; Fulbright lectr Inst Caro y Cuervo & coordr ling & English as foreign lang, Colombian Univs, SAm, 63. *Res:* Spanish and Portuguese linguistics; bilingual education; socio-psycholinguistics. *Publ:* Auth, A Portuguese Version of the Life of Barlaam and Josaphat: Paleographical Edition and Linguistic Study, Univ Pa, 38; coauth, Japanese Conversaphone, Cortina Method Lang Bks, 50; ed, General Principles of Language, Heath, 53; auth, An Amsterdam version of the Judeo-Spanish Haftara paraphrase, Romance Philol, 61; Linguistics and modern language teaching in Colombia, Moc Lang J, 64; The vocabulary of the old Judeo-Spanish translation of the Canticles and their Chaldean paraphrase, 73 & Selomoh Proops-corrector or copyist?, 75, Hisp Rev. *Mailing Add:* Dept of Foreign Lang Univ of Miami Coral Gables FL 33124

ABRAHAMSEN, SAMUEL, Modern European History, Scandanavian Languages. See Vol I

ABRAMS, FRED, b New York, NJ, June 4, 33. ROMANCE LANGUAGES. *Educ:* Queens Col, NY, BA, 55; Univ Iowa, MA, 57, PhD(Span lit), 60. *Prof Exp:* Asst prof Span lit, Univ Pittsburgh, 60-62; from asst prof to assoc prof Span lit, George Washington Univ, 62-69; assoc prof, 69-72, PROF SPAN LIT, ST JOHN'S UNIV, NY, 72- *Mem:* Am Asn Teachers Span & Port; MLA; AAUP. *Res:* Onomatology; literary cryptology; comparative literature. *Publ:* Auth, The name Celestina: Why did Fernando de Rojas choose it?, 72, Tremendismo and symbolic imagery in Cela's Marcelo Brito: an analysis & Hurtado de Mendoza's concealed signatures in the Lazarillo De Tormes, 73, Romance Notes; Swift's concealed double signature in Gulliver's Travels, Am Notes & Queries, 73; Unamuno's menendez y pelayo cryptogram in Niebla, Papers Lang & Lit, 75; Pio Baroja and Silvestre paradox: An onomastic tour de force, Revista de Estudios Hispanicos, 75; Cervantes Bepganza-cipion anagrams in El Coloquio De Los Perros, Names, 76; Stockton's The Lady or the Tiger, Word Ways, 76. *Mailing Add:* Dept of Mod Foreign Lang St John's Univ Jamaica NY 11439

ABRAMSON, ARTHUR SEYMOUR, b Jersey City, NJ, Jan 26, 25; m 52; c 2. LINGUISTICS. *Educ:* Yeshiva Univ, AB, 49; Columbia Univ, AM, 50, PhD, 60. *Prof Exp:* Teacher French & English pub schs, Jersey City, NJ, 50-53; lectr English to foreigners, Columbia Univ, 55-59; mem res staff exp phonetics, Haskins Labs, New York, 59-63; assoc prof speech, Queens Col, NY, 63-64, prof, 65-67; head dept ling, 67-74, PROF LING, UNIV CONN, 67- *Concurrent Pos:* Fulbright teaching grant, Thailand, 53-55; lectr, NY Univ, 58-59; assoc phonetics, Columbia Univ, 60-63; lectr speech, Hunter Col, 61-63; mem Permanent Coun for Orgn Int Cong Phonetic Sci, 71-; Am Coun Learned Soc & Ford Found fel, Southeast Asia Fel Prog, 73-74; co-ed, Lang & Speech, 74-78, ed, 79- *Mem:* AAAS; Ling Soc Am (secy-treas, 74-78, vpres, 82); MLA; fel Acoustical Soc Am; Int Phonetic Asn. *Res:* Thai language; experimental phonetics; phonology. *Publ:* Auth, The Vowels and Tones of Standard Thai: Acoustical Measurements and Experiments, Ind Univ, 62; coauth, A cross-language study of voicing in initial stops: Acoustical measurements, Word, 64; coauth, Distinctive features and laryngeal control, Language, 71; Voice-timing perception in Spanish word-initial stops, J Phonetics, 73; auth, Thai tones as a reference system, In: Tai Linguistics in Honor of Fang-Kuei Li, Chulalongkorn Univ, 76; Laryngeal timing in consonant distinctions, J Phonetics, 77; auth, The noncategorical perception of tone categories in Thai, In: Frontiers of Speech Communication Research, Academic Press, 79; coauth, Vowel height and the perception of consonantal nasality, J Acoust Soc Am, 81. *Mailing Add:* Dept of Ling Univ of Conn Storrs CT 06268

ABREU, MARIA ISABEL, b Minas Gerias, Brazil, Oct 8, 19. PORTUGUESE. *Educ:* Univ Minas Gerais, BS, 40, Dr Law, 44; Univ Chile, dipl, 50; Columbia Univ, MA, 57. *Hon Degrees:* Dipl de Merito, Brazilian Prom Ctr, 77. *Prof Exp:* High Sch supvr, Brazilian Ministry Educ, 44-61; from asst prof to assoc prof Port, 61-69, head div, 61-69, PROF & CHMN DEPT PORT, GEORGETOWN UNIV, 69- *Concurrent Pos:* US Dept State fel, 48; Brit Coun fel, 51; prof English, Rio de Janeiro & Guanabara State, 53-61; lectr educ, Loyola Col, Md, 62; consult, Peace Corps Training Prog, Georgetown Univ, 65; section chmn, Vanderbilt Conf High Sch Port, 67 & Mid Atlantic Comt High Sch Port, 67-68; lectr methodology of Port teaching, NDEA Inst, Vanderbilt Univ, 68; consult, selection off to teach Port in US, Brazilian Naval Acad, 70 & Nat Endowment Humanities, 77-; dir rec, Portugues Contemporaneo, 71; mem, Screening Comt, Fulbright-Hays Prog, Inst Int Educ, 69, 71, chmn, 75; Brazilian Ministry of Educ res grant, 75; consult, Wash Ctr for Latin Am Studies, 79- *Honors & Awards:* Cert of Distinguished Serv, Inst Int Educ, 76; Cert of Merit, Speakers Bur, Georgetown Univ, 78; Vicennial Medal, Georgetown Univ, 81. *Mem:* MLA; Am Asn Teachers Span & Port (vpres, 80, pres, 81); Asoc Ling y Filol Am Latina; Am Coun Teaching Foreign Lang; Brazilian Am Cult Inst. *Res:* Brazilian literature and civilization; the Portuguese language in Brazilian cultural structure; the study of history through literature. *Publ:* Auth, O estudo comparativo de padroes estruturais em Portuguese em Espanhol, Luso-Brazilian Rev, winter 64; coauth, Portugues Contemporaneo 1, 66, 67, 71, 72 & 75 & Portugues Contemporaneo 2, 67, 69, 71 & 73, Georgetown Univ; auth, Portugues contemporaneo: principios basicos, Bol Soc Lingua Port, 6/68; O Protesto social na obar de Graciliano Ramos, In: Essays on Brazilian Literature, Simon & Schuster, 71; Brazilian Portuguese influences and characteristics, Mod Lang, 6/75; O Estudo do Portugues na Estrutura Socio-Cultural do Brasil, Hispania, 79; Cultures in contact in the making of Brazilian society, Inter-Am Rev Bibliog, 80. *Mailing Add:* Dept of Port Georgetown Univ Washington DC 20007

ABRIOUX, OLIVIER MARIE, b Oct 16, 21; French citizen. FRENCH LANGUAGE & LITERATURE. *Educ:* Univ Paris, Lic es Lett, 42, dipl etudes super, 45; Univ Aberdeen, PhD(French lit), 49. *Prof Exp:* Lectr French, Univ Aberdeen, 49-59, sr lectr, 59-67; prof & chmn dept mod lang, Univ Sask, Regina, 67-70; PROF FRENCH & HEAD DEPT, UNIV VICTORIA, BC, 70- *Concurrent Pos:* Vis prof, Univ Hamburg, 69; ed, Western Can Studies Mod Lang & Lit, 69- *Mem:* Int Asn Fr Studies; Soc Fr Studies; Asn Can Univ Teachers Fr; Inst Collegial Europ. *Res:* Sixteenth, 17th and 20th century French literature. *Mailing Add:* Dept of French Lang & Lit Univ of Victoria Victoria BC V8W 2Y2 Can

ABRUZZI, GIOVANNA GHETTI, b Rimini, Italy, Jan 20, 22; US citizen, m 59. MODERN ITALIAN LITERATURE. *Educ:* Giivlio Cesare Lyceum, Italy, Dipl, 37; Inst Maestre Pie, Italy, Dipl, 41; Univ Roma, Dr Degree, 57. *Prof Exp:* Asst Ital lit, Univ Roma, 57-58; lectr Ital lit & art, Columbia Univ, 60-61; instr, Rutgers Univ, 62-65 & Hunters Col, 65-67; INSTR & PROF ITAL LANG & LIT, BROOKLYN COL, NY, 67- *Concurrent Pos:* Dir, Prog Studies Abroad, Brooklyn Col, 82. *Mem:* MLA. *Res:* Contemporary Italian novel; Italian XIX century novel; Boccaccio. *Publ:* Auth, Verga Romantico, In: Verga's Romantic Novels, Alla Bottega, 7-8/73; Ghismunda Eroinadel Mondo Cortesee Covalleresco, In: Ghismunda Heroine of the Renteel & Chivalric World, La Parola del Popolo, 3-4/73; A dialogue of love, In: Promessi Spos, La Parola del Popolo, 7-8/73; Leonardo Sciasciae la Sicilia, Bulzoni, Roma, 74; The myth of the hero, 11/75 & Interrelationship of arts & psychoanalysis, 1/77, Nuova Antologia, Roma; L'enigma Landolfi, Bulzoni, Roma, 79. *Mailing Add:* 185 Claremont Ave 2E New York NY 10027

ABU-ABSI, SAMIR, b Hasbaya, Lebanon, Apr 4, 38; nat US; m 68; c 4. LINGUSITICS. *Educ:* Am Univ Beirut, BA, 63; Ind Univ, Bloomington, MA, 66, PhD(ling), 72. *Prof Exp:* Instr ling, Univ Toledo, 68-72; asst prof, Am Univ, Beirut, 72-73; asst prof, 73-76, ASSOC PROF LING, UNIV TOLEDO, 76-, DIR PROG, 73- *Concurrent Pos:* Consult, Ctr Educ Res & Develop, Ministry of Educ, Beirut, 72-73. *Mem:* Ling Soc Am; Am Asn Teachers Arabic. *Res:* Arabic linguistics; English linguistics; applied linguistics. *Publ:* Coauth, Spoken Chad Arabic, Intensive Lang Training Ctr, Ind Univ, 68; auth, Stubborn structures in Arabic-English, In: Al-Kulliyah, Am Univ Beirut, 73; A method for surveying second language teachers, Ohio Univ working papers, Applied Ling, No 6, 79; Language-in-Education in the Arab Middle East, Ann Rev Applied Ling II, 82. *Mailing Add:* Ling Prog Univ of Toledo Toledo OH 43606

ACCAD, EVELYNE, b Beirut, Lebanon, Oct 6, 43; US citizen. FRANCOPHONE STUDIES, AFRICAN STUDIES. *Educ:* Anderson Col, BA, 67; Ball State Univ, MA, 68; Ind Univ, Bloomington, PhD(comp lit), 73. *Prof Exp:* From teaching asst to instr French, Anderson Col, 65-68; teacher English & girl's counr, Int Col, Beirut, 68-70; teaching asst comp lit, Ind Univ, 71-73; asst prof, 71-80, ASSOC PROF FRENCH, UNIV ILL, 80- *Mem:* African Lit Asn (pres, 78); African Studies Asn; MLA. *Res:* Women in literature and society; African and Near Eastern literatures; 20th century French literature. *Publ:* Auth, Entre deux, In: Contes et Nouvelles de Langue Francaise, Cosmos, 76; La longue marche des heroines des romans modernes du Mashreq et du Maghreb, Presence Francophone, 76; Veil of Shame: Role of Women in the Contemporary Fiction of North Africa and the Arab World, Naaman, Sherbrooke, 78; Theme of sexual oppression in the North African novel, In: Women in the Muslim World, Harvard, 78; Women in the Middle East, Ba Shiru, 77; Nadia Tueni, Marguerite Taos-Amrouche, Venus Khoury-Ghata, In: A Critical Anthology of French Women Writers, Stock, 78. *Mailing Add:* 2090 Foreign Lang Bldg Univ Ill Urbana IL 61801

ACHBERGER, FRIEDRICH, b Graz, Austria, June 29, 48; m 75; c 2. GERMAN LITERATURE. *Educ:* Univ Graz, Mag Phil, 73; Univ Wis-Madison, PhD(German), 77. *Prof Exp:* ASST PROF GERMAN, UNIV MINN, MINNEAPOLIS, 78- *Mem:* MLA; Am Asn Teachers German; Western Asn German Studies; Am Coun Study Austrian Lit. *Res:* 20th century German literature; Austrian literature; literature of the German Democratic Republic. *Publ:* Transl, Literatur als Libretto Das deutsche Opernbuch seit 1945, Winter, Heidelberg, 80; auth, Die inflation und die zeitgenössische literatur, Aufbruch und Untergang, Europaverlag, Vienna, 81; Lehrstück Weimar? Österreichische Perspektiven auf den Untergang der Weimarer Republik, Weimar Ende, Suhrkamp, Frankfurt, 82; Image of the Country: Provincial Literature in the Weimar Republic-Political Tendencies in the Literature of the Weimar Republic, Univ Minn Press, 82. *Mailing Add:* German Dept Univ of Minn Minneapolis MN 55455

ACHBERGER, KAREN RIPP, b Madison, Wis, Apr 10, 43; m 75; c 2. GERMAN LITERATURE, WOMEN'S STUDIES. *Educ:* Univ Wis-Madison, BS, 67, MA, 68, PhD(Ger lit), 75. *Prof Exp:* Asst prof, Univ Ore, 74-79; ASST PROF GER, ST OLAF COL, 79- *Mem:* MLA; Am Asn Teachers Ger; Western Asn Ger Studies; Women in Ger; Int Brecht Soc. *Res:* Contemporary German women writers; postwar German opera libretto; literature of the German democratic republic. *Publ:* Auth, A multi-disciplinary synthesis in teaching German culture and civilization, Pac Northwest Coun Foreign Lang Proc, 76; coauth, Irmtraud Morgner's Gospel of Valeska, New Ger Critique, 78; auth, Ingeborg Bachmann's Homberg Libretto: Kleist between humanism and existentialism, Mod Austrian Lit, 79; GDR women's fiction of the 1970's: The emergence of feminism within socialism, ECent Europe, 79; Literatur als Libretto: Das deutsche Opernbuch seit 1945, Heidelberg, winter 80; Bachmann und die Bibel: Gomorrah als weibliche Schöpfungsgeschichte, Ingeborg-Bachmann Band, Löcker, Vienna, 82; co-transl (with Friedrich Achberger), Morgner, White Easter, The Duel, Shoes & The Rope, Wolter, I have married again, In: Women's Voices, State Univ NY Press, 82. *Mailing Add:* 505 Highland Ave Northfield MN 55057

ACKER, ROBERT, b St Paul, Minn. GERMAN LITERATURE & LINGUISTICS. *Educ:* St John's Univ, Minn, BA, 68; Univ Tex, Austin, PhD(Ger), 74. *Prof Exp:* Asst prof Ger, Univ Mo-Columbia, 74-77 & Wash State Univ, 77-78; asst prof Ger, SDak State Univ, 78-79; asst prof, 79-81, ASSOC PROF GER, UNIV MONT, 82- *Concurrent Pos:* Ed, SELECTA: J Pac Northwest Coun Foreign Lang, 82- *Mem:* MLA; Am Asn Teachers Ger; Midwest Mod Lang Asn; Westen Asn Ger Studies; Pac Northwest Coun Foreign Lang. *Res:* Twentieth century German literature; German film. *Publ:* Auth, Gustav Regler and Ramon Sender: A comparative study of their Mexican exile, In: Latin American Exile Writers, Univ Tex, 78; Literature about language in postwar Germany, Perspectives,; The ninth book of Parzival: A structural analysis, Proc of the Pac Northwest Coun Foreign Lang, 79. *Mailing Add:* Dept of Foreign Lang Univ of Mont Missoula MT 59812

ACKERMANN, PAUL KURT, b Bremen, Ger, Sept 5, 19; nat US; m 45; c 2. GERMAN. *Educ:* Colgate Univ, AB, 45; Columbia Univ, MA, 47; Harvard Univ, PhD(Ger), 53. *Prof Exp:* Instr Ger, Amherst Col, 46-48; from instr to assoc prof, 48-65, PROF GER, BOSTON UNIV, 65-, ADJ PROF, GRAD DIV THEOL & RELIG STUDIES, 73- *Concurrent Pos:* Ed, Boston Univ J, 66-; prof, Univ Würzburg, 66. *Mem:* Am Asn Teachers Ger; MLA; Int Ver Ger Sprach- und Literaturwiss; Thomas Mann Ges. *Res:* Contemporary German literature; German literure in the 18th century; Thomas Mann. *Publ:* Ed, Thomas Mann: Felix Krull, 58 & Thomas Mann: Die Bekenntnisse des Hochstaplers, 58, Houghton; co-ed, Rene Schickele, Vol 3, Kiepenheuer-Witsch, 59; ed, Friedrich Dürrenmatt: Der Besuch der alten Dame, 60, Max Frisch: Biedermann und die Brandstifter, 63 & Max Frisch: Homo faber, 73, Houghton; auth, Thomas Mann: Letter to Rene Schickele, Boston Univ J, winter 73; ed, Bertolt Brecht: Die Dreigroschenoper, Suhrkamp, 82. *Mailing Add:* Dept of Modern Languages Boston Univ 718 Commonwealth Ave Boston MA 02215

ADAMS, CHARLES CLINTON, English. See Vol II

ADAMS, CHARLES LINDSEY, b Atlanta, Ga, Dec 30, 23; m 45; c 2. ROMANCE LANGUAGES. *Educ:* Hiram Col, AB, 48; Stanford Univ, MA, 49, PhD(Span), 54. *Prof Exp:* Teacher, Chadwick Sch, Calif, 49-50; actg instr Span, Stanford Univ, 52-53; instr, Bradley Univ, 54; asst prof, Col Wooster, 54-59; dir church rels, 59-61, chmn dept foreign lang, 60-70, dir off int educ, 68-70, PROF SPAN, HIRAM COL, 60-, DIR EXTRAMURAL STUDIES, 70- *Concurrent Pos:* Dir, Madrid Ctr, Inst Europ Study, 69-70. *Mem:* Am Asn Higher Learning; Nat Asn Foreign Student Affairs. *Publ:* Auth, The problem of the motif-index with special reference to Lope de Vega, Bull Comediantes, spring 55; Motivos folkloricos en las comedias de Lope de Vega, Cuadernos Hispanoam, 9/66; Independence for study, Hispania, 9/67. *Mailing Add:* Box 1806 Hiram OH 44234

ADAMS, DUANE A, b Omaha, Nebr, Mar 7, 23; m 49; c 3. ROMANCE LANGUAGE & PHILOLOGY. *Educ:* Univ Nebr, BA, 47, MA, 49; La State Univ, PhD(Romance philol), 63. *Prof Exp:* Dir courses, Binational Ctr, Port-au-Prince, Haiti, 49-51; exec secy, Binational Ctr, Bahia, Brazil, 51-53; asst dir, Inst Latin Am Studies, Univ Southern Miss, 54-58; asst prof French & Span, 60-63, assoc prof French, 63-72, PROF FRENCH, UNIV TEX, ARLINGTON, 72-, COORDR FRENCH SECT, 63- *Mem:* SCent Mod Lang Asn. *Res:* French stylistics; Roland legend and the Provencal epic Ronsasvals. *Publ:* Auth, Materials and techniques in teaching English as a second language, Mod Lang J, 12/57. *Mailing Add:* 1916 Norwood Lane Arlington TX 76010

ADAMS, HOWARD CHAUNCEY, JR, b Pueblo, Colo, Nov 26, 26. FRENCH. *Educ:* Kans State Teachers Col, Emporia, BA, 47; Univ Paris, cert, 56; Univ Kans, MA, 58. *Prof Exp:* Asst French, Yale Univ, 48-50; asst Romance lang, Univ Kans, 53-58, instr French, 58-61; asst prof, Wichita State Univ, 61-62; asst prof, Westminster Col, Pa, 64-66; assoc prof, Univ Wis-Stevens Point, 66-76; asst prof, 76-80, ASSOC PROF ENGLISH, FROSTBURG STATE COL, 80- *Mem:* MLA; Am Asn Teachers Fr; Am Coun Teaching Foreign Lang. *Res:* Marguerite Yourcenar; contemporary French literature; Romance languages. *Mailing Add:* Dept of English Frostburg State Col Frostburg MD 21532

ADAMS, KENNETH R, b Orem, Utah, Sept 2, 30; m 56; c 3. GERMANIC LANGUAGES & LITERATURE. *Educ:* Brigham Young Univ, BA, 59, MA, 65. *Prof Exp:* Teacher Ger, Weber Sch Dist, Utah, 61-63; mem fac, 63-66, ASSOC PROF GER, WEBER STATE COL & CHMN DEPT FOREIGN LANG, 66- *Concurrent Pos:* Foreign lang consult, Utah State Bd Educ, 61; Danforth Found assoc, 71- *Res:* Languages and literature; computers. *Publ:* Contribr, Germany As We Saw It, Stanford Univ, 63; The Importance of Reading in Foreign Languages, 63 & Utah State Foreign Language Guide, 70, Utah State Bd Educ. *Mailing Add:* Dept of Foreign Lang Weber State Col 3750 Harrison Blvd Ogden UT 84403

ADAMS, LEONARD, b Port of Spain, Trinidad, WI, Oct 24, 29; m 62; c 1. FRENCH LANGUAGE & LITERATURE. *Educ:* Univ London, BA, 58, PhD(French lit), 71; Univ Col WI, dipl educ, 59; Royal Schs Music, LRSM, 63; Trinity Col Music, FTCL, 66; McMaster Univ, MA, 67. *Prof Exp:* Foreign lang asst English, Tech Sch, Lyon, France, 59-61; grad master French & Span, Queen's Royal Col, Trinidad, 61-66; teaching fel French, McMaster Univ, 66-67; lectr, 67, 71, asst prof, 71-74, ASSOC PROF FRENCH, UNIV GUELPH, 74- *Mem:* Can Asn Univ Teachers; Am Soc 18th Century Studies; Soc Fr Etude XVIIe Siecle; Can Soc 18th Century Studies. *Res:* Eighteenth century French literature; romance philology; Francophone literature and influence in the West Indies. *Publ:* Auth, Coyer and the Enlightenment, Voltaire Found, 74. *Mailing Add:* Dept of Lang Univ of Guelph Guelph ON N1G 2W1 Can

ADAMSON, HUGH DOUGLAS, b Salt Lake City, Utah, Sept 30, 44; m 69; c 2. LINGUISTICS, TEACHING ENGLISH AS A SECOND LANGUAGE. *Educ:* Univ Calif, Berkeley, AB, 67; San Jose State Univ, MA, 72; Georgetown Univ, PhD(ling), 80. *Prof Exp:* Dir English as second lang, US Peace Corps, 68; instr English as second lang, adult prog, San Jose Metro, 72-73, John Adams Adult Ctr, San Francisco Commun Col Dist, 70-71, Inst Estudies Norteamericanos, 74-75; dir English as second lang, Luther Rice Col, 76-77; prof lectr English as second lang, Am Univ, 77-78; instr English as second lang, George Washington Univ, 78-79; ASST PROF LING, GEORGE MASON UNIV, 79- *Concurrent Pos:* Dir, reading lab, Operation SER, 72; coordr, Econ Inst, Univ Colo, 78; dir, English Lang Inst, George Mason Univ, 81. *Mem:* Ling Soc Am; Teachers English Speakers Other Lang. *Res:* Variation theory; second language acquisition; first lang acquisition. *Publ:* Coauth, Variation theory and second language acquisiton & Variation theory and first language acquisiton, 82, Variation Omnibus. *Mailing Add:* Dept English George Mason Univ Fairfax VA 22030

ADE, WALTER FRANK CHARLES, b Ottawa, Ont, Can, Oct 24, 10; m 41; c 2. FOREIGN LANGUAGES, EDUCATION. *Educ:* Queens Univ, Can, BA, 33; Ont Col Educ, 3 teaching lic, 38; Univ Toronto, MA, 39, BPaed, 43, MEd, 45; Northwestern Univ, PhD, 49; Ind Univ, MSc, 55, EdD, 50; Univ Erlangen, dipl, 55. *Prof Exp:* Lectr French, Ger & English, Ont Agr Col, Univ Toronto, 33-37; specialist, foreign lang, Lisgar Collegiate Inst, Ottawa, Can, 39-49; from asst prof to assoc prof, Valparaiso Univ, Ind, 49-59, travel grant, 58-59; assoc prof mod lang & dept chmn, 59-66, prof mod lang & educ, 67-76, Purdue res found grant, 64, travel grant, 67-68, EMER PROF MOD LANG & EDUC, PURDUE UNIV, CALUMET CAMPUS, 76- *Concurrent Pos:* Fulbright exchange prof, W Ger, 55-56. *Mem:* Mediaeval Acad Am; MLA; Am Asn Teachers Ger; fel Int Inst Arts & Lett, Switz; fel Intercontinental Biog Asn, Eng. *Res:* International folklore and comparative mythology; secondary and comparative education; paroemiology; semantics; etymology. *Publ:* Auth, Voltaire on Education, Ind Univ, 60; The Siren in Literature and Art, 63; Voltaire's Paedagogical Views, Paedagogica Hist, Ghent, Belg, 11/63; Le chant du cygne, essai d'une explication, 70; G E Lessing's Nathan the Wise, 72, Prosper Merimee's Carmen, 73, Moliere's The Physician in Spite of Himself, 75 & Moliere's The School for Husbands, 75, Barrons. *Mailing Add:* 8021 Schreiber Dr Munster IN 46321

ADER, KATHLEEN M JOYCE, b Green Bay, Wis, Apr 26, 15; m 67. SPANISH. *Educ:* Mt Mary Col, BA, 35; Univ Wis, MA, 36, PhD(Span), 43. *Prof Exp:* Assoc prof Span, Lawrence Col, 44-65; assoc prof, 65-71, prof, 71-80, EMER PROF SPAN, NMEX STATE UNIV, 80- *Mem:* MLA; Am Asn Teachers Span & Port. *Res:* Poetry of Miguel de Unamuno; contemporary Spanish theater and novel. *Mailing Add:* Dept of Foreign Lang NMex State Univ Las Cruces NM 88003

ADKINS, ARTHUR WILLIAM HOPE, Classics, Philosophy. See Vol IV

ADLER, SARA MARIA, b Malden, Mass, Sept 14, 46; m 73; c 1. ITALIAN LANGUAGE & LITERATURE. *Educ:* Smith Col, BA, 68; Harvard Univ, MA, 69, PhD(Ital lit), 76. *Prof Exp:* Instr, 74-75, ASST PROF ITAL, SCRIPPS COL, 75- *Mem:* Am Asn Teachers Ital; MLA; Dante Soc; Soc Ital Hist Studies. *Res:* Modern Italian literature. *Publ:* Auth, Calvino: The Author as Fablemaker, Jose Porrua (in press). *Mailing Add:* Scripps Col Balch Hall Claremont CA 91711

ADMUSSEN, RICHARD L, b Topeka, Kans, Apr 16, 34; m 62; c 3. ROMANCE LANGUAGES. *Educ:* Washburn Univ, BA, 56; Univ Kans, MA, 60, PhD(French), 66. *Prof Exp:* Asst d'anglais, Lycee Jean Giraudoux, France, 58-59; commun media technician, AID, Bangui, Cent African Repub, 61; instr French, Univ Kans, 63-64; from asst prof to assoc prof romance lang, Wash Univ, 64-76, prof, 77-80, chmn dept, 78-80. *Concurrent Pos:* Nat Endowment for Humanities fel, 67-68; Camargo Found Residential grant, France, 74; Am Philos Soc res grant, 74. *Mem:* MLA; Am Asn Teachers Fr. *Res:* Avantgarde literary periodicals; Samuel Beckett; 19th and 20th century poetry. *Publ:* Auth, Nord-Sud and cubist poetry, J Aesthet & Art Criticism, fall 68; Les Petites Revues Litteraires, Nizet, Paris, 69; coauth, Vicente Huidobro, Pierre Reverdy and the editio princeps of El espejo de agua, Comp Lit, spring 71; The Samuel Beckett Manuscripts, G H Hall, 78. *Mailing Add:* 6324 Alamo Ave St Louis MO 63105

ADOLF, HELEN, b Vienna, Austria, Dec 31, 95; nat US. GERMANICS. *Educ:* Univ Vienna, PhD, 23. *Prof Exp:* Prof, 46-63, EMER PROF GER, PA STATE UNIV, 63- *Concurrent Pos:* Vis prof, Muhlenberg Col, 63-66. *Mem:* MLA; Mediaeval Acad Am; Ling Soc Am; PEN Club. *Res:* Linguistics; literature; religious psychology. *Publ:* Auth, Visio Holy City and Grail, Pa State Univ, 60; Werden und Sein (poems), F Berger, Horn, 64; Personality in medieval poetry and fiction, Deut Vierteljahrsschrift, 70; Words, Ideas and Reality: Analysis of Ewic Lebende and Durch Tugent in the Prologue of the Younger Titurel, Wahrheit & Sprache, Festschrift Bert Nagel, 72; Mysticism and the growth of personality, a study in Dante's Vita nuova, In: Studies in Honor of Tatjana Fotitch, 73; Y W F Hegel, die Kreuzznge mid Chretiens Conte del Graal, Deut Vierteljahrsschrift, 75. *Mailing Add:* 6807 Lawnton Ave Philadelphia PA 19126

ADORNO, ROLENA, b Muscatine, Iowa, Nov 5, 42; m 66. SPANISH. *Educ:* Univ Iowa, BA, 64; Univ Hartford, MAT, 68; Cornell Univ, PhD(Span lit), 74. *Prof Exp:* Lectr, Univ Hartford, 68-69; instr, Ithaca Col, 69-70; asst prof, 76-80, ASSOC PROF SPAN, SYRACUSE UNIV, 80- *Mem:* MLA; Am Asn Teachers Span & Port. *Res:* Colonial Latin American literature; Spanish Golden Age drama. *Publ:* Co-ed, El condenado por desconfiado de Tirso de Molina, Catedra, Madrid, 74, 2nd ed, 76; auth, Racial scorn and critical contempt, Diacritics, winter 74; Icone et idee: une lecture semiotique du texte visuel de Guaman Poma, Annales: Economies, Soc, Civilisations, 12/78; Las otras fuentes de Guaman Poma: sus lecturas castellanas, Hist, 12/78. *Mailing Add:* 50 Presidential Plaza Syracuse NY 13202

ADRIANOW, GENNADIJ Y, b Rowno, Poland, July 19, 21; Can citizen; m 45; c 1. SLAVIC LANGUAGE & LITERATURE. *Educ:* Univ Montreal, BA, 65; McGill Univ, MA, 71, PhD(Russ & Slavic), 76. *Prof Exp:* Instr Russ lang, Int Civil Aviation Orgn, 72-75; lectr, 75-76, ASST PROF, SLAVIC LANG & LIT, UNIV REGINA, 76- *Concurrent Pos:* Teaching asst & lectr Slavic lang, lit & drama, McGill Univ, 69-75; lectr Russ lang, Univ Montreal & lectr Russ lang, cult & drama, Concordia Univ, 70-74; asst dir, Russ Summer Sch, Norwich Univ, 73-80; founder & dir, Alexandra Tolstoy Russ Summer Sch, 80-82; dir, Cult & Educ Progs, Tolstoy Found, Inc, 80-82. *Mem:* Can Asn Slavists; Cent & East Europ Studies Asn Can; Folklore Asn Can; Am Asn Teachers Slavic & East Europ Lang. *Res:* Russian and Slavic studies; Doukhobors and Leo Tolstoy, Alexandra Tolstoy; Russian performing arts: ballet, choreography, stage craft and design. *Publ:* Auth, The importance of lexical and socio-cultural symbolism in A V Sukhovo-Kobyin's trilogy, McGill Univ, 76; Anthroponyms, their symbolism as a literary device in the trilogy of A V Sukhovo-Kobylin, The Pictures of the Past, Norwich Univ Press, 79. *Mailing Add:* 30 Lincoln Dr Regina SK S4S 2V6 Can

AFFRON, CHARLES M, b Brooklyn, NY, Oct 16, 35; m 61; c 2. ROMANCE LANGUAGES. *Educ:* Brandeis Univ, BA, 57; Yale Univ, PhD(Balzac), 63. *Prof Exp:* From instr to asst prof French & Ital, Brandeis Univ, 62-65; from asst prof to assoc prof, 65-73, actg chmn dept, 68-69, PROF FRENCH, NY UNIV, 73- *Mem:* MLA. *Res:* Nineteenth century French novel and theatre; cinema. *Publ:* Auth, Patterns of Failure in La comediè humaine, Yale Univ, 66; A Stage for Poets: Studies in the Theatre of Hugo and Musset, Princeton Univ, 71; Star Acting: Gish, Garbo, Davis, Dutton, 77. *Mailing Add:* Dept of French & Ital New York Univ 19 University Pla New York NY 10003

AGARD, FREDERICK BROWNING, b Westerly, RI, Sept 23, 07. ROMANCE LINGUISTICS. *Educ:* Brown Univ, AB, 28, AM, 30; Princeton Univ, PhD, 35. *Prof Exp:* Asst, Brown Univ, 28-29; instr mod lang, Princeton Univ, 35-40, asst prof, 40-45; res assoc invest of teaching a second lang, Univ Chicago, 45-46; from asst prof to assoc prof, 46-49, prof, 49-74, EMER PROF LING, CORNELL UNIV, 74- *Concurrent Pos:* Reader French, Col Entrance Exam Bd, 36-40, chief reader, 41, mem exam bd, 41-50; Fulbright lectr ling, Coun Am Studies, Rome, Italy, 56-57; prof, Facolta Magistero, Univ Rome, 63-64; asst dir, Cornell Univ English lang prog in Italy, 63-64, dir, 64-66; vis prof ling, Romanian Acad & Univ Bucharest, 69-70; vis prof appl ling, Univ Konstanz, WGer, 76-77. *Mem:* MLA; Ling Soc Am; Am Asn Teachers Span & Port. *Res:* Romance linguistics; English as a foreign language; contrastive linguistics. *Publ:* Auth, Modern Approach to Spanish, Holt, 63, rev ed, 68; coauth, Corso d'Inglese Parlato, Vol 4, Harcourt, 68; auth, A Review of Modern Structural Linguistics: Lecture Series, Acad RS Romania, 70; Prelegeri de Analiza Contrastiva, Univ Bucuresti, 70; coauth, Spoken Romanian Spoken Lang Serv, 76. *Mailing Add:* 1023 Hanshaw Rd Ithaca NY 14850

AGES, ARNOLD, b Ottawa, Ont, May 17, 35; m 60; c 2. ROMANCE LANGUAGES. *Educ:* Carleton Univ, BA, 56; Ohio State Univ, MA, 58, PhD(French), 63. *Prof Exp:* From asst prof to assoc prof, 63-69, PROF FRENCH, UNIV WATERLOO, 69- *Concurrent Pos:* Can Coun res grants, Bibliot Nat, 64; Musee Voltaire, Geneva, 66, Widener Libr, Harvard Univ, 67 & 68; Univ Waterloo fac fels, Bibliot Nat, 66, Widener Libr, Harvard Univ, 67. *Mem:* MLA; Asn Can Univ Teachers Fr. *Res:* French Enlightenment literature. *Publ:* Auth, Voltaire Calmet and the Old Testament, Inst et Musee Voltaire, 66; French Enlightenment and Rabbinic Tradition, Frankfort, 70; The private Voltaire: Three studies in the correspondence, Vol 81, In: Studies on Voltaire and the Eighteenth Century: The Diaspora Dimension, Nijhoff, The Hague, 73; Voltaire and the Old Testament: The testimony of the correspondence, Studies Voltaire, Vol 55; Voltaire and the rabbis, Romanische Forsch, Vol 79; Voltaire and Horace, Studies Voltaire 18th Century, 74; Lammenais and the Jews, Jewish Quart Rev, 75; Merimee and the Philosophics, Studies Voltaire 18th Century, 76. *Mailing Add:* Dept of Classics & Romance Lang Univ of Waterloo Waterloo ON N2L 3G1 Can

AGGELER, GEOFFREY DONOVAN, English. See Vol II

AGOSIN HALPERN, MARJORIE, b Bethesda, Md, June 15, 55; m 77. LATIN AMERICAN & SPANISH LITERATURE. *Educ:* Univ Ga, BA, 76; Ind Univ, MA, 77, PhD(Latin Am lit), 82. *Prof Exp:* Lectr Span lit, Ind Univ, 77-80; ASST PROF SPAN, WELLESLEY COL, 82- *Concurrent Pos:* Vis prof, Middleburry Col, 79; ed, Midwest East--Midwest West A Journal, 80 & Third Woman Mag, 81-; spec ed, Plaza, Harvard Univ, 82. *Mem:* MLA; Northeast Mod Lang Asn; Am Asn Teachers Span & Port. *Res:* Latin American poetry; Spanish poetry; creative writing. *Publ:* Auth, Chile Gemidos, Ed El Observador, 77; Conchali, Senda Nueva de Ed, 80; transl, Delia Dominguez, The Sun Looks Back, Third Woman Press, 81; Fantasy in Ecade Queiroz, Neophilologus, 81; Latin American women poets, Bread & Roses, 81; A bibliography of Violeta Parra, Inter-Am Rev, 81. *Mailing Add:* Dept of Span Wellesley Col Wellesley MA 02181

AGUDIEZ, JUAN VENTURA, b Santiago, Chile, Dec 12, 33; US citizen. SPANISH, FRENCH. *Educ:* Univ Paris, Lic Lett, 58, D Univ, 60. *Prof Exp:* Instr Span, Univ Calif, Berkeley, 60-62; asst prof, 62-68, ASSOC PROF ROMANCE LANG, HUNTER COL, 69- *Concurrent Pos:* Am Philos Soc scholar, 62; fel, City Univ New York, 72. *Res:* Decadentism in French and Spanish literature; realism in the Spanish novel of the 19th century. *Publ:* Auth, Ganivet en las huellas de Galder y Alarcon, Nueva Rev Filol Hisp, 62; Emma Bovary-Ana Ozores o el si mbolo del amer, Romanic Rev, 2/63; Las tardes de Thereze Lamarck, Ed Iberoam, 64; Inspiracion y estetica en la Regenta de Clarin, Inst Estudios Astunaros, 70; Transfiguraciones, Joaquin Mortiz, 71; Las novelas de Angel Ganivet, Anaya, 72; Angel Ganivet y su correspondencia inedita con Francisco Navarro Ledeswa, Filol Hisp, 72. *Mailing Add:* Hunter Col 695 Park Ave New York NY 10021

AGUERA, VICTORIO GARCIA, b Urcal, Almeria, Spain, Mar 30, 33; US citizen; m 70. SPANISH LITERATURE. *Educ:* Col San Fulgencio, Spain, BA, 54; Col Mayor Teol, Madrid, BS, 58; Cath Univ Am, MA, 70, PhD(Span), 71. *Prof Exp:* Asst prof, 70-73, assoc prof, 73-80, PROF SPAN, GEORGE MASON UNIV, 80- *Concurrent Pos:* Nat Endowment for Humanities fel, 72. *Mem:* MLA; Am Asn Teachers Span & Port; Soc Nac Hisp. *Res:* Spanish literature of the Golden Age; criticism and theory. *Publ:* Auth, Jaume Roig y la tradicion picaresca, Ky Romance Quart, 73; Nueva interpretacion del episodio rey de gallos del Buscon, Hispanofila, 73; Dislocacion de elementos picarescos en el Buscon, In: Studies in Spanish Literature in Honor of Professor Hatzfel, Sola-Sole, 73; Savacion del cristiano nuevo en Guzman, Hispania, 74; Aplicacion del estructuralismo genetico al teatro de Alarcon, Anal Hisp Texts, Bilingual, 75; Mito y realidad en Lugar sin Limites, Explicacion de Textos Literarios, 76; El Examen de Maridos y las pruebas de limpieza, Papeles de Son Armadans, 77. *Mailing Add:* Dept of Foreign Lang George Mason Univ Fairfax VA 22030

AGUIRRE, ANGELA M, b Santa Clara, Cuba; US citizen. MODERN SPANISH LITERATURE. *Educ:* City Univ New York, BA, 70, MPhil, 79, PhD, 80; Queens Col, MA, 75. *Prof Exp:* Adj fac Span, Hunter Col, 73-76; instr, Gettysburg Col, 76-79; asst prof, Lebanon Valley Col, 79-80; ASST PROF SPAN, WILLIAM PATERSON COL, 80- *Concurrent Pos:* Consult, Teachers Col, Columbia Univ, 81. *Honors & Awards:* Prize Excellence in Educ, United Women of the Americas, 81. *Mem:* MLA; Northeast Conf Teaching Mod Lang; Am Asn Span & Port. *Res:* Contemporary Latin American literature and culture; Spanish and Spanish-American romanticism; Spanish mysticism. *Publ:* Auth, Vida y Critica Literaria de Enrique Pineyro, Senda Nueva de Ediciones, 81; Primer Critico del romanticismo espanol, Circulo, 82. *Mailing Add:* 71-A Hinchman Ave Wayne NJ 07470

AGUZZI-BARBAGLI, DANILO, b Arezzo, Italy, Aug 1, 24. ITALIAN. *Educ:* Univ Florence, DLet, 49; Columbia Univ, PhD, 59. *Prof Exp:* Lectr Ital, Vassar Col, 54-55; from instr to asst prof Ital, Univ Chicago, 59-64; assoc prof, Tulane Univ, 64-71; PROF ITAL, UNIV BC, 71- *Mem:* MLA; Am Asn Teachers Ital; Accad Let Arti e Sci Petrarca. *Res:* Renaissance literature in Italy; comparative study of Italian and English Renaissance literature. *Publ:* Ed, Francesco Patrizi, Della Poetica, Ist Naz Stud Rin, Firenze, Vols I, II, III, 69, 70 & 71; auth, Un contributo di F Patrizi alle dottrine rinascimentali sull'amore, Yearbk Ital Studies, 72; Ingegno, acutezza and maraviglia in the sixteenth century great commentaries to Aristotle's Poetics, In: Petrarch to Pirandello, Univ Toronto, 73; ed, Francesco Patrizi, Lettere ed opuscoli inediti, Ist Naz Stud Rin, Firenze, 75. *Mailing Add:* 485 Walsh Rd Atherton CA 94025

AHEARN, EDWARD J, b New York, NY, Oct 31, 37; m 60; c 1. FRENCH & COMPARATIVE LITERATURE. *Educ:* Manhattan Col, BA, 59; Yale Univ, PhD, 63. *Prof Exp:* Asst prof French, 63-68, assoc prof, 68-80, PROF FRENCH & COMP LIT, BROWN UNIV, 80- *Concurrent Pos:* Fel, Ctr Advan Studies, Univ Ill. *Honors & Awards:* Harbison Award for Gifted Teaching, Danforth Found, 70. *Mem:* MLA. *Res:* French, comparative literature of the 19th century. *Publ:* Auth, The childlike sensibility: A study of Wordsworth and Rimbaud, Rev Litt Comparee, 4-6/68; The search for community: The city in Holderlin, Wordsworth and Baudelaire, Tex Studies Lit & Lang, summer 71; Imagination and the real: Rimbaud and the city in 19th century poetry, Rev Litt Comparee, 73. *Mailing Add:* Dept of Comparative Lit Brown Univ Providence RI 02912

AHERN, MAUREEN VERONICA, b Bellows Falls, Vt, July 14, 36; c 3. LATIN AMERICAN LITERATURE, LITERARY TRANSLATION. *Educ:* Univ NH, BA, 58; San Marcos Univ, Lima, Peru, Dr Let(lit), 61. *Prof Exp:* Teaching asst Span, Univ Calif, Berkeley, 61-62; instr, Ariz State Univ, 62-63; dir dept mod lang, Univ Sci & Technol, Lima, 68-69; assoc prof Span lang & lit, Univ Ricardo Palma, Lima, 69-72; asst prof Span, 72-74, asst chairperson dept foreign lang, 72-75, ASSOC PROF SPAN, ARIZ STATE UNIV, 74- *Concurrent Pos:* Co-ed & publ, Haravec, 67-69. *Mem:* MLA; Am Asn Teachers Span & Port; Latin Am Studies Asn; Am Lit Transl Asn; Am Transl Asn. *Res:* Peruvian and Mexican literatures; Latin-American women writers; translation. *Publ:* Auth, Mar, magia y misterio en Valdelomar, Sphinx, 60; co-ed, Peru: The New Poetry, Allan Ross, London, 70; co-ed & co-transl, Cisneros, The Spider Hangs too Far from the Ground, Cape Goliard, London, 70; coauth, A comparison of animal dead metaphors in English and Spanish speech, Bilingual Rev, 5-8/76; co-ed, Homenaje a Rosario Castellanos, Albatros-Hispanofila Editores, 80; Auth, A critical bibliography of and about the works of Rosario Castellanos, Homenaje a Rosario Castellanos, 80; transl, Rosario Castellanos, Looking at the Mona Lisa, 81 & co-transl, A Cisneros, Helicopters in the Kingdom of Peru, 81, Rivelin Ecuatorial. *Mailing Add:* Dept of Foreign Lang Ariz State Univ Tempe AZ 85281

AHL, FREDERICK MICHAEL, b Barrow-in-Furness, England, Sept 5, 41; m 69. CLASSICS, COMPARATIVE LITERATURE. *Educ:* Cambridge Univ, BA, 62, MA, 66; Univ Tex, Austin, PhD(classics), 66. *Prof Exp:* Asst prof Classics, Univ Utah, 66-68; asst prof, Univ Tex, Austin, 68-71; from asst prof to assoc prof, 71-77, chmn dept, 74-77, PROF CLASSICS, CORNELL UNIV, 78- *Honors & Awards:* Clark Award Distinguished Teaching, Cornell Univ, 77. *Mem:* Am Philol Asn; AAUP. *Res:* Greek and Roman epic; drama; Roman imperial history. *Publ:* Coauth, To Read Greek, Univ Tex, Austin, 69; auth, Pharsalus and the Pharsalia, Classica et Mediaevalia, 69; Lucan's De incendio urbis, Trans & Proc Am Philol Asn, 71; Curio and Hercules, Latomus, 72; Lucan: An Introduction, Cornell Univ, 76; coauth, Silius Italicus, Aufstieg und Niedergang der romischen Welt, 78. *Mailing Add:* Dept of Classics Cornell Univ 121 Goldwin Smith Hall Ithaca NY 14853

AHRENS, FREDERICK CHRISTIAN, b Elmira, Ont, Oct 31, 08; US citizen; m 40; c 1. GERMAN LANGUAGE & LITERATURE. *Educ:* Univ Western Ont, BA, 28; Columbia Univ, AM, 30, PhD, 50. *Prof Exp:* Teacher Ger, univ exten, Columbia Univ, 29-31, 34; instr, Univ Maine, 33; prof, Albright Col, 34-35; assoc prof, Univ Richmond, 35-42; from asst prof to assoc prof, Gettysburg Col, 46-63; chmn dept foreign lang, 70-74, prof, 63-75,

EMER PROF GER, MONMOUTH COL, NJ, 63- *Mem:* MLA; Am Asn Teachers Ger. *Res:* Works of Conrad Pellican; chronicle of Conrad Pellican translated from the Latin. *Publ:* Co-translr, Luther's Works, Am ed, Vol 36, Muhlenberg, 59; translr, two short works in: Luther's Works, Am ed, Vols 43 & 46, Fortress, 67, 68. *Mailing Add:* Dept of Ger Monmouth Col West Long Branch NJ 07764

AID, FRANCES MARY, b Burlington, Iowa, June 21, 36. SPANISH, LINGUISTICS. *Educ:* Clarke Col, AB, 60; Univ Iowa, MA, 63; Georgetown Univ, PhD(Span), 72. *Prof Exp:* Instr Span, Clarke Col, 60-62 & 63-68, from asst prof to assoc prof ling & Span, 72-74; ASSOC PROF LING & SPAN, FLA INT UNIV, 74-, CHMN MOD LANG, 76- *Concurrent Pos:* Consult, Res on Lang Instr, Yucatan, Mex, 71-72. *Mem:* Am Asn Teachers Span & Port; Am Coun Teaching Foreign Lang; Ling Soc Am; Teachers English to Speakers Other Lang. *Res:* Spanish structure; semantics; second language instruction. *Publ:* Coauth, MVE, Phase II: The Effect of Oral and Orthographic Stimuli on the Memorization and Pronunciation of Basic Dialogs, US Off Educ Report, 70; auth, Semantic Structures in Spanish: A Proposal for Instructional Materials, Georgetown Univ, 73; contribr, Meaning: A Common Ground of Linguistics and Literature, Univ Northern Iowa, 73; auth, The Semantic Formation of Spanish Copula Sentences, Univ Mich Papers Ling, 73. *Mailing Add:* Dept of Modern Languages Florida Int Univ Tamiami Trail Miami FL 33144

AIKENS, HARRY FORBES, b Stellarton, NS, June 23, 23. FRENCH LINGUISTICS. *Educ:* Dalhousie Univ, BA, 45; Yale Univ, MA, 47. *Prof Exp:* Lectr French, Dalhousie Univ, 47-49; lectr, Prince of Wales Col, PEI, 51-53; from lectr to assoc prof, 53-69, dir lang ctr, 67-79, PROF FRENCH, DALHOUSIE UNIV, 69- *Mem:* Int Phonetic Asn; Nat Asn Self Instructing Lang Prog; Int Soc Phonetic Sci. *Res:* Phonetics; translation. *Mailing Add:* Part-time Studies Dalhousie Univ Halifax NS B3H 3J5 Can

AIKIN, JUDITH POPOVICH, b Los Angeles, Calif, Aug 6, 46. GERMAN LITERATURE & LANGUAGE. *Educ:* Univ Ore, BA, 68, MA, 69; Univ Calif, Berkeley, PhD(Ger), 74. *Prof Exp:* Asst prof, 75-81, ASSOC PROF GER, UNIV IOWA, 81- *Mem:* MLA; Am Soc Ger Lit 16th & 17th Centuries; Women in Ger. *Res:* Seventeenth-century German drama; medieval literature; history and theory of German drama. *Publ:* Auth, The Mission of Rome in the Dramas of Daniel Casper von Lohenstein, Stuttgarter Arbeiten Germanistik, 76; Pseudo-ancestors in the genealogical projects of the Emperor Maximilian I, Renaissance & Reformation, 77; Egyptian captivity and the theme of freedom in Lohenstein's Cleopatra, Argenis, 78; Guarini's Il Pastor Fido in Germany: Allegorical and figural aspects, Studi Germanici, 78; German Baroque Drama, Twayne World Authors Series, 82. *Mailing Add:* Dept of Ger Univ of Iowa Iowa City IA 52242

AKEHURST, F RONALD P, b Stoke-on-Trent, Eng, Apr 29, 38; m 64; c 2. FRENCH. *Educ:* Oxford Univ, BA, 62, MA, 65; Univ Colo, PhD(French), 67. *Prof Exp:* Lectr English, Univ Bordeaux, 60-61; teaching asst French, Univ Colo, 62-65; asst prof, Univ Rochester, 65-68; asst prof, 68-70, chmn, Dept French & Ital, 77-78, assoc prof, 70-82, PROF FRENCH & CHMN, DEPT FRENCH & ITAL, UNIV MINN, MINNEAPOLIS, 82- *Concurrent Pos:* Ed, Encomia, Bibliog Bull Int Courtly Lit Soc, 75- *Mem:* MLA; Mediaeval Acad Am; Int Arthurian Soc; Soc Rencesvals; Int Courtly Lit Soc. *Res:* Old French and Old Provencal literature; computer research in the humanities. *Publ:* Contribr, Hendrik van der Werf: The Chansons of Toubadours and Trouveres, Oosthoek, Holland, 72; auth, Les etapes de l'amour chez Bernard de Ventadour, Cahiers Civilisation Medievale, 73; The Troubadours as Intellectuals, Mosaic, 75; contribr, Comparative Romance Linguistics Newslett, 78-80; The Paragram AMOR in the Troubadours, Romanic Rev, 78; La Folie chez les troubadours, Festschrift Camprous, 78; L'Ordinateur et l'etude des troubadours, Cultura Neolatina, 78; 'Sa Place ... son volume...l'usage qui en est fait! Incantatory Value of Words in the Provencal Troubadours, Court & Poet: Selected Proc 3rd Cong Int Courtly Lit Soc, 80. *Mailing Add:* Dept of French & Ital 200 Folwell Hall Univ of Minn Minneapolis MN 55455

AKEROYD, RICHARD HEWSON, b Youlgrave, England, May 7, 21; m 54; c 3. FOREIGN LANGUAGE, RELIGION. *Educ:* Oxford Univ, BA, 51, MA, 55. *Prof Exp:* Lectr Christian work, Europe, 51-55 & United States, 57-59; chmn dept lang, Stony Brook Sch Boys, 55-57 & Louisville Country Day Sch, 60-63; from asst prof to assoc prof, 64-77, PROF FRENCH, UNIV LOUISVILLE, 77- *Concurrent Pos:* Lectr on spiritual significance of 20th century French authors at var univs & cols. *Res:* Reason and revelation: From Paul to Pascal; principles of the early church. *Publ:* Auth, The Door & The Flock and the Kingdom, Ministry of Life, Ind, 72; The Spiritual Quest of Albert Camus, 76, transl, Madeleine and Andre Gide, 80 & auth, He is Nigh, 80, Portals Press. *Mailing Add:* Dept of Mod Lang Univ of Louisville Louisville KY 40208

AKIELASZEK, STANISLAUS, b Plainfield, NJ, Apr 28, 16; m 47; c 3. CLASSICAL PHILOLOGY. *Educ:* Univ Lwow, Poland, Mag Phil, 39; Fordham Univ, PhD, 51. *Prof Exp:* Instr classics prep sch, Fordham Univ, 45-46, instr col, 46-51, asst prof col & grad sch, 51-60; assoc prof, 60-65, chmn dept, 62-77, PROF CLASSICS, ST JOHN'S UNIV, NY, 65- *Concurrent Pos:* From asst to assoc ed, Class Weekly, 50-53; mgr, Traditio, 53-57; ed newslett, Cath Class Asn, 60-66. *Mem:* Cath Class Asn (pres, 60-63); Am Philol Asn; Brit Class Asn. *Res:* Vergil and Vergilian commentators; ancient Roman history. *Publ:* Coauth, Lingua Latina viva, 66 & auth, four articles, In: Catholic Encyclopedia for Sch and Home, 66, McGraw. *Mailing Add:* Dept of Foreign Lang & Class Studies St John's Univ Jamaica NY 11439

AKLUJKAR, ASHOK NARHAR, b India; Can citizen. SANSKRIT LANGUAGE & LITERATURE. *Educ:* Univ Poona, BA, 62, MA, 64; Harvard Univ, PhD(Sanskrit), 70. *Prof Exp:* Lectr Sanskrit & Pali, Fergusson Col, Poona, India, 64-65; asst prof, 69-73, assoc prof, 73-81, PROF SANSKRIT & INDIAN LIT & DEPT HEAD, UNIV BC, 81- *Concurrent Pos:* Can Coun grant, 70-72; Am Coun Learned Soc fel, 73-74; Soc Sci & Humanities Res Coun & Humbolt fel, 78-79. *Mem:* Am Orient Soc; Asn Asian Studies; Can Asian Studies Asn; Can Asn Sanskrit & Related Studies. *Res:* Sanskrit grammar, poetics and philosophy; Indian literatures. *Publ:* Auth, Appa-sastri: Sahitya-samiksa, Sarada, Poona, India, 65; The authorship of the Vakyapadiyavrtti, Wiener Z Kunde Sudasiens, 72; Stylistics in the Sanskrit tradition, Current Trends in Stylistics, Ling Res, 72; coauth, On santa rasa in Sanskrit poetics, J Am Orient Soc, 72; auth, The concluding verses of Bhartrhari's Vakya-kanda, Ann Bhandarkar Orient Res Inst, 78; Interpreting Vakyapadiya 2.486 historically, Adyar Libr Bull, 81. *Mailing Add:* Dept of Asian Studies Univ BC Vancouver BC V6T 1W5 Can

AKMAJIAN, ADRIAN, b Jersey City, NJ, Sept 14, 44; m 66; c 2. THEORETICAL LINGUISTICS. *Educ:* Univ Ariz, BA, 66; Mass Inst Technol, PhD(ling), 70. *Prof Exp:* Res assoc ling, Lang Res Found, Cambridge, Mass, 68-70; from asst prof to assoc prof ling, Univ Mass, Amherst, 70-75; assoc prof ling, 75-79, PROF & HEAD DEPT LING, UNIV ARIZ, 79- *Concurrent Pos:* Nat Endowment for Humanities younger humanist fel, Mass Inst Technol, 74-75. *Mem:* Ling Soc Am. *Res:* Transformational syntax; Japanese language. *Publ:* Auth, On deriving cleft sentences from pseudo-cleft sentences, Ling Inquiry, 70; The role focus in the interpretation of anaphoric expressions, In: A Festschrift for Morris Halle, Holt, 73; More evidence for an NPcycle, Ling Inquiry, 75; coauth, An Introduction to the Principles of Transformation Syntax, Mass Inst Technol, 75; co-ed, Formal Syntax, Acad Press, 77; coauth, An Introduction to Language and Communication, Mass Inst Technol, 79. *Mailing Add:* Dept of Ling Math Bldg 514 Univ of Ariz Tucson AZ 85721

ALATIS, JAMES EFSTATHIOS, b Weirton, WVa, July 13, 26; m 51; c 3. ENGLISH, LINGUISTICS. *Educ:* WVa Univ, AB, 48; Ohio State Univ, MA, 53, PhD(English & ling), 66. *Prof Exp:* Asst English, Ohio State Univ, 53-55, 57-59; Fulbright lectr English as foreign lang, Univ Athens, 55-57; testing & teaching specialist, Int Educ Exchange Serv, US Dept State, 59-61; res specialist, Lang Develop Br, US Off Educ, 61-65, chief lang sect, Res Br, 65-66; assoc dean sch lang & ling, 66-73, DEAN SCH LANG & LING, GEORGETOWN UNIV, 73-, PROF MOD GREEK & ENGLISH AS SECOND LANG, 76- *Honors & Awards:* Mary Glide Goethe Prize, Am Name Soc, 55. *Mem:* MLA; NCTE; Nat Asn Foreign Students Affairs; Ling Soc Am. *Res:* Teaching and testing English as a second language; contrastive linguistics and the neglected languages; modern Greek. *Publ:* Ed, Studies in Honor of Albert H Marckwardt, Teachers English Speakers Other Lang, 72; auth, Linguistics, TESOL and bilingual education, In: Psycholinguistics and Total Communication: The State of the Art, Am Annals Deaf, 72; Teaching standard English as a second language or dialect: The unanswered questions, the successes, and the promise, In: Essays on Teaching English as a Second Language and as a Second Dialect, NCTE, 73; co-ed, English as a Second Language in Bilingual Education, TESOL, 76; auth, Teaching foreign languages--why?, a new look at an old question, Foreign Lang Ann, 10/76; co-ed (with Ruth Crymes), The Human Factors in ESL, 77; (with Gerli & Brod), Language in American Life, 78; (with Altman & Alatis), The Second Language Classroom: Directions for the 1980's, 81. *Mailing Add:* Sch of Lang & Ling Georgetown Univ Washington DC 20057

ALAZRAKI, JAIME, b La Rioja, Argentina, Jan 26, 34; m 62; c 2. SPANISH & SPANISH AMERICAN LITERATURE. *Educ:* Hebrew Univ, Israel, BA, 62; Columbia Univ, MA, 64, PhD(Span), 67. *Hon Degrees:* MA, Harvard Univ, 77. *Prof Exp:* Instr Span, Columbia Univ, 64-67; from asst prof to prof, Univ Calif, San Diego, 67-75; vis prof, Univ Calif, Los Angeles, 75-76; PROF ROMANCE LANG, HARVARD UNIV, 78- *Concurrent Pos:* Fac res grant, Univ Calif, San Diego, 68-78; Guggenheim fel, 71-72 & 82-83; Nat Endowment for Humanities fel, 75-76. *Honors & Awards:* Huntington Prize, Am Asn Teachers Span & Port, NY, 64; D R Nieto Prize, Junta Hist & Lett, Arg. *Mem:* Inst Int Lit Iberoam; MLA; Arg Soc Writers. *Res:* Twentieth century Spanish American novel, poetry and short story; 19th century Spanish American literature; literary theory. *Publ:* Auth, La Prosa Narrative de Jorge Luis Borges, Gredos, Madrid, 68 & rev ed, 74; Jorge Luis Borges, Columbia Univ, 71; ed, El Escritor y la Critica: Jorge Luis Borges, Tauros, Madrid, 76; co-ed, Homenaje a Andres Iduarte, Am Hispanist, Ind, 76; auth, Versiones, inversiones, reversiones: El Espejo Como Modelo Estructural del Relato, Gredos, Madrid, 77; co-ed, The Final Island: The Fiction of J Cortazar, Univ of Okla, 78; ed, Rayuela, Ayacucho, Caracas, 80; En busca del unicornio: los cuentos de Julio Cortazar (Elementos para una poetica de lo neo-fantastico), Gredos, Madrid, 82. *Mailing Add:* Dept of Romance Lang Harvard Univ Cambridge MA 02138

ALBA-BUFFILL, ELIO, b Havana, Cuba, Apr 25, 30; US citizen; m 55. SPANISH AMERICAN LITERATURE, SPANISH LANGUAGE & GRAMMAR. *Educ:* Havana Inst, BA, 48; Havana Univ, LLD, 53; Rutgers Univ, MA, 67; NY Univ, PhD(Span), 74. *Prof Exp:* Prof law, St John Baptist La Salle Univ, Havana, 57-61; head, Dept Foreign Lang, Carteret Col Prep Sch, West Orange, NJ, 66-69; assoc prof, 69-80, PROF SPAN, KINGSBOROUGH COMMUNITY COL, 69- *Concurrent Pos:* Ed, Circulo Revista de Cultura, 75- *Honors & Awards:* Juan J Remos Award, Cruzada Educatia Cubana, 77. *Mem:* Am Asn Teachers Span & Port; MLA; Pan Am Cult Circle; Int Inst Spanish Am Lit; Conf Ed Learned J Am. *Res:* The works of Enrique Labrador Ruiz; the naturalism in the novels of the Antilles. *Publ:* Auth, Enrique Jose Varona, Critica y creacion literaria, Hispanova de ediciones Madrid, 76; ed, Estudios Literarios, Sobre Hispanoamerica, Pan Am Cult Circle, 76; coauth, Spanish for Nurses and Allied Health Science Students, Arco, 76; auth, Una Novela Puertorriquena: Garduna de Zeno Gandia, Caribe, Univ Hawaii, spring 76; Persona, Vida y Mascara en el teatro Cubano de Montes Huidobro, Anales, Univ Madrid, 76; coauth, Indice de El Pensamiento Cuba 1879-1880, Senda Nueva de Edicionios, 77; auth, Los estudios cervantinos de Varona, 79 & coauth, Festschrift-Jose Cid Peroz, 81, NY Senda Nueva. *Mailing Add:* Dept Foreign Lang Kingsborough Community Col Brooklyn NY 11235

ALBER, CHARLES JULIUS, b Bay Shore, NY, June 11, 38, m 63; c 1. CHINESE LANGUAGE & LITERATURE. *Educ:* Harpur Col, BA, 63; Ind Univ, Bloomington, PhD(Chinese lang & lit), 71. *Prof Exp:* From instr to asst prof, 70-77, ASSOC PROF CHINESE & COORDR MID & FAR EASTERN LANG, UNIV SC, 77- *Concurrent Pos:* Consult, Nat Endowment for Humanities, 75-76, 79 & 82; res grant, Univ SC, 79. *Mem:* SAtlantic MLA; SAtlantic Asn Asian & African Studies; Chinese Lang Teachers Asn; Asian Studies Asn. *Res:* Early 20th century Chinese fiction; Chinese prose fiction in general; Soviet criticism of Lu Hsün, 1881-1936. *Publ:* Auth, Review of William A Lyell's Lu Hsun's Vision of Reality, Lit East & West, 1-12/75; Wild Grass, symmetry and parallelism in Lu Hsun's prose-poems, In: Critical Essays on Chinese Literature, Chinese Univ, Hong Kong, 76; Review of Modern Chinese Literature in the May Fourth Era, Lit East & West, 1-12/77; Review of China: The Enduring Heritage, spring 78 & On the road with Charles Alber, spring 80, SAtlantic Asn Asian & African Studies Rev; transl, V I Semanov's Lu Hsuan and His Predecessors, M E Sharpe, 80; coauth, The Beijing Language Institute: An inside view, J Chinese Lang Teachers Asn, 4/81. *Mailing Add:* 1944 Marley Dr Columbia SC 29210

ALBERT, WALTER E, b Little Rock, Ark, July 31, 30; m 59; c 2. FRENCH. *Educ:* Univ Okla, BA, 55; Ind Univ, MA, 57, PhD, 61. *Prof Exp:* Teaching asst, Ind Univ, 55-57, 58-60; instr French, Brandeis Univ, 60-62, asst prof, 62-67; ASSOC PROF FRENCH, UNIV PITTSBURGH, 67- CHMN DEPT FRENCH & ITAL, 77- *Mem:* MLA; Am Asn Teachers Fr. *Res:* Modern French poetry; detective fiction, film. *Publ:* Ed & transl, Selected works of Blaise Cendrars, New Directions, 66; auth, The metaphor of origins in Horace, Fr Rev, 11/66; Yves Bonnefoy and the architecture of poetry, MLN, 12/67; Structures of revolt in Giraudoux's Electre and Anouilh's Antigone, Tex Studies Lit & Lang, spring 70; Bibliography of secondary sources, Armchair Detective, annually, 72-; Les Fanzines americains et le roman policier: Premiere decade, Enigmatika 9, 78; Reel mysteries: Murder in film, Mystery Fancier, 3-4/82. *Mailing Add:* Dept Fr & Ital Univ of Pittsburgh Pittsburgh PA 15260

ALBIJANIC, ALEKSANDAR, b Hollywood, Calif, Nov 16, 32; m 67; c 3. SLAVIC LANGUAGES & LITERATURE. *Educ:* Univ Calif, Los Angeles, AB, 55, MA, 63, PhD(Slavic), 66; Northwestern Univ, MM, 56. *Prof Exp:* From asst prof to assoc prof Slavic Lang, 65-75, PROF SLAVIC LANG, UNIV CALIF, LOS ANGELES, 75- *Concurrent Pos:* Fulbright & Irex sr fel, 75-76. *Res:* Historical development of the Serbo-Croatian literary language; Macedonian, immigrant bilingualism. *Publ:* Auth, The creation of the Slavenno-Serbski literary language, Savonic and East Europ Rev, XLVIII: 483-491; Ikavizmi u delima pisaca 12 vojuodine u predvukovskoj eposi, Zbornik za filologiju i lingvistiku, XV/Z: 25-41; Imenice na-ba/-idba u makedonskom knjizevnom jeziku, Makedonski jazik, XXIII: 15-20; Jezik novina Stefana Novakovica (1792-94) Matica srpska, Novi Sad, Yugoslavia, 68; A diachronic study of six morphological features characteristic of the Sumadija-Voljvodiha dialect, Zbornik za filologiju i lingvistiku: XVIII/1, 161-177; A Yugoslav Community in San Pedro, California, Gen Ling, XV: 78-94; coauth, The Speech of Yugoslav Immigrants in San Pedro, California, Nijhoff, The Hague, 72; Srpskoslovenski i ruskoslovenski elementi u Sobraniju (1793) Jovana Rajica, Zbornik VI, Medunarodni naucni sastanak slavista u Vukove dane, Referati i saopstenja, 77. *Mailing Add:* Dept of Slavic Lang Univ of Calif Los Angeles CA 90042

ALCALA, ANGEL, b Andorra, Span, Oct 2, 28; m 65; c 2. ROMANCE LANGUAGES, PHILOSOPHY. *Educ:* Univ Salamanca, MA, 48; Univ Rome, MA, 52, PhD, 57; Univ Madrid, MA, 61. *Prof Exp:* Instr philos, Sem Zaragoza, 54-55; assoc prof, Univ Salamanca, 55-57, Zaragoza, 57-62; from asst prof to assoc prof Span lit, 70-76, PROF SPAN LIT, BROOKLYN COL, 76- *Concurrent Pos:* Fulbright grant, 62-63; Elias Ahuja fel, 62-63; res grant, City Univ New York, 72-73; Am Philos Soc grant, 73-74; Juan March grant, 74-76. *Mem:* MLA. *Res:* Spanish literature of the Renaissance; Spanish reformers; history of ideas. *Publ:* Auth, Nuestra deuda conservet, Rev Occid, 72; transl & contribr, Servet, el Hereje Perseguido, 73 & Arias Montano, 73, Taurus, Madrid; auth, Para otro Unamuno a traves de su teatro, Papeles Son Armandans, 75; Tres notas sobre Arias Montano, Cuad Hisp, 75; El neoepicureismo y la intencion de La Celestina, Roamnische Forsch, 76; ed, translr & contribr, Servet: Treinto cartas a Calvino y Apologia, Castalia, Madrid, 78. *Mailing Add:* 185 West End Ave New York NY 10023

ALCOVER, MADELEINE, b Casablanca, Morocco, Oct 27, 38. ROMANCE LANGUAGES. *Educ:* Univ Bordeaux, Lic French, 62, MA, 63, PhD(French lit), 65. *Prof Exp:* Teacher, high sch, Casablanca, 61-64; mem fac French, Lycee Int, NATO, Fontainebleau, 64-67; from asst prof to assoc prof, Ind Univ, Bloomington, 67-75; assoc prof, 75-82, PROF FRENCH, RICE UNIV, 82- *Res:* Philosophical thought in the 17th and 18th centuries, especially French; Cyrano de Bergerac; feminism. *Publ:* Ed, Cyrano de Bergerac, Larousse, 68; La Pensee Philosophique et Scientifique de Cyrano de Bergerac, Droz, Geneva, 70; La casuistique du Pere Tout a Tous et les provinciales, Studies Voltaire & 18th Century, 71; Les lieux et les temps dans L'Illusion comique, French Studies, 10/76; Critical Edition of L'Autre Monde by Cyrano de Bergerac, Champion, Paris, 78; The indecency of knowledge, Rice Univ Studies, winter 78; Furetiere et la stratification sociale, Vol VIII, 81 & Poullain de la Barre: Une aventure philosophique, 81, Papers Fr 17th Century Lit. *Mailing Add:* Dept of French Rice Univ Houston TX 77001

ALDEN, DOUGLAS WILLIAM, b Washington, DC, Sept 11, 12. FRENCH. *Educ:* Dartmouth Col, AB, 33; Brown Univ, AM, 34 PhD, 38. *Prof Exp:* From instr to asst prof, Tex Tech Col, 38-42; instr, Amherst Col, 41-42; from instr to assoc prof French, Princeton Univ, 45-61; prof & head dept foreign lang, Univ Md, 61-64; chmn dept mod lang, 64-66, chmn dept Romance lang, 66-71, PROF FRENCH, UNIV VA, 64-, ACTG CHMN, DEPT FRENCH LIT, 82- *Concurrent Pos:* Ed, Fr XX Bibliog; chmn adv comt, Jr Year Abroad, Sweet Briar Col, 59-; rev ed, Fr Rev, 64-71. *Mem:* Int Asn Fr Studies; MLA; SAtlantic Mod Lang Asn; Am Asn Teachers Fr (pres, 72-77); Soc Fr Prof Am. *Publ:* Auth, Introduction to French Masterpieces, 48 & Premier Manuel, 54, Appleton; Jacques de Lacretelle, Rutgers Univ, 58; coauth, Grammaire et Style, Appleton, 67; Marcel Proust and his French Critics, Russell & Russell, 77; Marcel Proust's Grasset Proofs, Univ NC, 78; ed, A Critical Bibliography of French Literature, 20th Century, Syracuse Univ, 80; ed, French, Columbia Dict of Modern European Literature, 80. *Mailing Add:* Dept of French Lit & Gen Ling Univ of Va Charlottesville VA 22903

ALDERSON, EDWIN GRAHAM, b Lexington, Ky, July 7, 23; m 46; c 7. MODERN FOREIGN LANGUAGES. *Educ:* Transylvania Col, AB, 43; Univ Toulouse, DUniv(comp lit), 51. *Prof Exp:* Dept asst French, Transylvania Col, 46-47, instr, 47-49, asst prof mod foreign lang, 51-55, prof, 55-64, dir admis, 52-58; dean world campus afloat, 69-76, PROF FRENCH, CHAPMAN COL, 64-, CHMN DIV INT STUDIES, 71-, HEAD DEPT MOD & CLASSICAL LANG, 76- *Concurrent Pos:* Partic, Col Entrance Exam Bd Colloquium, Mod Foreign Lang, 63; mem, Alliance Francaise. *Mem:* Am Asn Teachers Fr; MLA; Cent States Mod Lang Teachers Asn. *Res:* French language and literature; linguistics; modern language teacher preparation. *Publ:* Auth, Le Jansenisme dans l'oeuvre de Francois Mauriac, Univ Ky, 49; L'influence Francaise dans l'oeuvre de Herman Melville, Univ Toulouse, France 51. *Mailing Add:* Div of International Studies Chapman College Orange CA 92666

ALDRICH, EARL M, b Portland, Ore, Feb 13, 29; m 51; c 2. SPANISH, PORTUGUESE. *Educ:* Univ Ore, BA, 51; Mexico City Col, MA, 52; Ind Univ, PhD, 61. *Prof Exp:* From instr to assoc prof, 60-68, PROF SPAN, UNIV WIS-MADISON, 68- *Concurrent Pos:* Adv Ind Univ Jr Year to Peru Prog, Univ San Marcos, 59-60; contrib ed, Handbook of Latin Am Studies, 62- *Mem:* Am Asn Teachers Span & Port; MLA. *Res:* Latin American literature and culture. *Publ:* Auth, The Modern Short Story in Peru, Univ Wis, 66. *Mailing Add:* Dept of Span & Portuguese Univ of Wisconsin Madison WI 53706

ALDRIDGE, ADRIANA GARCIA DE, b Ponce, PR, Jan 26, 41; m 63. LATIN-AMERICAN LITERATURE & CRITICISM. *Educ:* Univ Md, BA, 64, MA, 67; Univ Ill, Urbana, PhD(Span), 72. *Prof Exp:* Teaching asst Span, Univ Md, College Park, 63-66; instr, Univ Md, Baltimore, 66-67; teaching asst, Univ Ill, Urbana, 68-70, part-time instr, 71-72; asst prof, 72-74, ASST PROF PUERTO RICAN STUDIES, CITY COL NEW YORK, 76- *Concurrent Pos:* North Am rep, Int Asn Studies & Prom AV & Structuro-Global Methods, 71-; actg chmn, Puerto Rican Studies, City Col New York, 80-82. *Mem:* Am Asn Teachers Span & Port; Fed Int Lang & Lit Mod; Inst Int Lit Iberoam; Latin Am Studies Asn; MLA. *Res:* Historical novel; Latin-American fiction; literary criticism. *Publ:* Auth, Herejia y portento en Carne esferas ojos grises junto al Sena de Carlos Fuentes, Cuadernos Am 5/73; Two Latin-American theorists of the historical novel, Clio, Vol 4: 183-199; Fuentes y la Edad Media, Anales de Literatura Hispanoamericana, Madrid, 4: 191-205; La dialectica contemporanea: tiempo propio total en Cumpleanos, Rev Iberoamericana, 45: 513-535; From sub specie temporis nostri Terra Nostra: James Joyce and Carlos Fuentes, Actes du VIIIe Congres de l'Association Internationale de Litterature comparee, Budapest, Hungary, 80; Some Chinese Influences on Latin-American Writers, Tamkang Rev, autumn & winter 79. *Mailing Add:* Dept Puerto Rican Studies City Col of New Yorkk New York NY 10031

ALEGRIA, FERNANDO, b Chile, SAm, Sept 26, 18; m 43; c 4. SPANISH AMERICAN LITERATURE. *Educ:* Univ Calif, PhD(Romance lit), 47. *Prof Exp:* Ed, Pan Am Union, Washington, DC, 45; prof Span & Port, Univ Calif, Berkeley, 47-67; PROF SPAN, STANFORD UNIV, 67-, PROF PORTUGUESE, 76- *Concurrent Pos:* Guggenheim fel, 47; consult Span Am lit, UNESCO, 68; ed, Rev, Inst Int Lit Iberoam, 53. *Honors & Awards:* Latin Am Prize, 43. *Mem:* Inst Int Lit Iberoam. *Publ:* Auth, Walt Whitman in Hispano America; La poesia Chilena, Univ Calif, 54; Breve historia de la novela Hispano-America, 59 & Historia de la novela Hispanoamericana, 66, Studium, Mex; Literatura chilena del siglo XX, ZigZag, Chile, 67; Gabriela Mistral, genio y figura, EUDEBA, Arg, 67. *Mailing Add:* Div of Span & Portuguese Stanford Univ Stanford CA 90035

ALENT, ROSE MARIE BACHEM, b Cologne, Ger, m 47, 65; c 2. COMPARATIVE LITERATURE. *Educ:* Univ Berlin, Staatsexamen Romance lang; Univ Rochester, MA, 53, PhD(comp lit), 57. *Prof Exp:* From asst prof to assoc prof comp lit, 56-63 PROF COMP LIT, STATE UNIV NY COL GENESEO, 63- *Honors & Awards:* Palmes Academique, 72; Distinguished Teaching Professor, State Univ NY, 75; Deutsches Bundesverdienstkreuz, 77. *Mem:* Am Asn Teachers Ger; Am Asn Teachers Fr; MLA. *Res:* Comparative literature. *Publ:* Auth, Andrea del Sarto by Musset and Browning, 64, Perfectionism of Arnold and Renan, 67 & Rediscovery of Spinoza by Schleiermacher, Arnold and Renan, 68, Rev Lit Comparee. *Mailing Add:* Dept of Lit State Univ of NY Col Geneseo NY 11454

ALEXANDER, DOUGLAS II, b New York, NY, Sept 9, 36; m 58; c 2. ROMANCE LANGUAGES. *Educ:* Hamilton Col, AB, 58; Rice Univ, MA, 61; Univ NC, PhD(Romance lang), 67. *Prof Exp:* Asst prof French, 67-72, ASSOC PROF FRENCH & CHMN DEPT, STATE UNIV NY ALBANY, 72- *Concurrent Pos:* State Univ NY res grant, 68-70; assoc ed, Claudel Newlett, 68-71 & Claudel Studies, 71- *Mem:* MLA; Am Asn Teachers Fr; Northeastern Mod Lang Asn (vpres, 78). *Res:* Twentieth century French literature; Claudel and Renaissance bibliography; Francophone literature of Africa and Caribbean. *Publ:* Auth, A note on the Chacun de Willame, X, 2 & Villon's Autre coing, parody or tradition?, 71, Romance Notes; Stendhal & violence on the Baltimore stage, Md Hist Mag, 71; Le tragique dans les romans de Ferdinand Oyono, Presence Francophone, 73. *Mailing Add:* Dept of French State Univ of NY Albany NY 12210

ALEXANDER, JAMES WAGNER, b Jefferson, Ga, May 4, 14; m 44; c 4. GREEK & CLASSICAL CIVILIZATION. *Educ:* Univ Ga, AB, 34, MA, 35; Univ Va, PhD(English), 40. *Prof Exp:* Instr English, Bethany Col, 40-41; from asst prof to assoc prof, 46-61, prof & head dept, 61-80, FRANKLIN PROF CLASSICS, UNIV GA, 80- *Mem:* Am Philol Asn; Archaeol Inst Am; Class

Asn Mid West & South (pres, 62-64). *Res:* Homer; classical tradition. *Publ:* Auth, Marriage of Megacles, 59, Was Cleisthenes an Athenian Archon?, 60 & More remarks on the Archonship of Cleisthenes, 60, Class J. *Mailing Add:* Dept of Classics Univ of Georgia Athens GA 30601

ALEXANDER, LOREN RAY, b Nashville, Kans, 30; m 51; c 3. GERMAN LANGUAGE & LITERATURE. *Educ:* Southwestern Col, BM, 51; Univ Northern Colo, MA, 54; Mich State Univ, MA, 65, PhD(Ger lang & lit), 70. *Prof Exp:* Teacher music, Sedgwick High Sch, 54-56 & Cimarron High Sch, 56-57; teacher music & Ger, Johnson High Sch, 57-61 & Sedgwick High Sch, 61-63; instr Ger, 65-71, ASST PROF GER & EDUC, KANS STATE UNIV 71- *Mem:* MLA; Am Asn Teachers Ger; Am Coun Teaching Foreign Lang. *Res:* Heinrich Böll; foreign language education; Max Frisch. *Publ:* Auth, Foreign language skills in Kansas business in export, Bull Asn Dept Foreign Lang, 11/75; An introduction to the bilingual method of teaching foreign languages, Foreign Lang Ann, 5/78. *Mailing Add:* Dept of Mod Lang Kans State Univ Manhattan KS 66505

ALEXANDER, THEODOR WALTER, b Vienna, Austria, Aug 1, 19; nat US; m 47; c 2. GERMAN. *Educ:* Tex Tech Col, BS, 46, MS, 47. *Prof Exp:* Instr Ger, 47-48, instr geol, 48-49, from instr to assoc prof Ger, 49-68, PROF GER, TEX TECH UNIV, 68- *Honors & Awards:* Distinguished Teaching Award, Standard Oil Found, 69; Spencer A Wells Award, 81. *Mem:* Am Asn Teachers Ger; MLA; SCent MLA. *Res:* Scientific German; modern German drama; modern Austrian literature. *Publ:* Auth, Schnitzler and the inner monologue: A study in technique, J Int Arthur Schnitzler Res Asn, summer 67; coauth, Maupassant's Yvette and Schnitzler's Fraulein Else, Mod Austrian Lit, fall 71; auth, From the scientific to the supernatural in Schnitzler, S Cent Bull, winter 71; Olga Waissnix: the model for the character of the married woman in the early works of Arthur Schnitzler, Mod Austrian Lit, 74; Arthur Schnitzler's Use of Mirrors, Seminar, 78. *Mailing Add:* Box 4579 Tex Tech Univ Lubbock TX 79409

ALEXANDRENKO, NIKOLAI ALEXEI, b Bryansk, Russia, May 7, 22; US citizen; m 53; c 6. CLASSICAL & SLAVIC LANGUAGES & RELIGION. *Educ:* La Col, BA, 53; New Orleans Baptist Theol Sem, BD, 56, ThD, 64; Tulane Univ, MA, 58, PhD(class lang), 70. *Prof Exp:* Asst prof class lang & relig, 59-63, assoc prof lang & relig, 63-67, chmn dept foreign langs, 70-77, PROF LANG & RELIG, LA COL, 67- *Mem:* Am Class League; Class Asn Mid W & S; Am Asn Teachers Slavic & EEurop Lang; SCent Mod Lang Asn; Am Philol Asn. *Res:* Studies in religious existentialism; experiments in the language laboratory; studies in medieval Latin. *Mailing Add:* Dept of Foreign Languages Louisiana College Pineville LA 71360

ALEXANDROV, VLADIMIR, b Rottweil, West Germany, May 9, 47; US citizen. RUSSIAN & COMPARATIVE LITERATURE. *Educ:* Queens Col, BA, 68; City Col New York, MA, 71; Univ Mass, Amherst, MA, 73; Princeton Univ, MA & PhD(comp lit), 79. *Prof Exp:* Teaching asst geol, City Col New York, 68-70, instr, 70-71; teaching asst comp lit, Univ Mass, 72-73; asst instr Russ lang & lit & mod Europ lit, Princeton Univ, 74-78, lectr Russ lang & lit, 78-79; ASST PROF RUSS LIT, HARVARD UNIV, 79- *Concurrent Pos:* Head tutor, Slavic Dept, Harvard Univ 79-, assoc dir, Slavic & East Europ Lang & Area Ctr, 80-; Am Coun Learned Soc fel, 82. *Mem:* MLA; Am Asn Advance Slavic Studies; Am Asn Teachers Slavic & E Europ Lang (vpres). *Res:* Fictional prose of Andrei Bely; symbolism; 18th-20th century Russian, American and European literatures. *Publ:* Auth, Correlations in Pushkin's Little Tragedies, Can Slavonic Papers, 6/78; Unicorn impaling a knight: The transcendent & man in Andrei Bely's Petersburg, Can-Am Slavic Studies, spring 82; Relative time in Anna Karenina, Russ Rev, spring 82; Belyj subtexts in Pil'njak's Golyj god, Slavic & East Europ J (in press); The narrrator as author in Dostoevskij's Besy, Russ lit (in press). *Mailing Add:* Slavic Dept Harvard Univ Cambridge MA 02138

AL FARUQI, ISMA'IL R A, Islamics, Religion. See Vol IV

ALFIERI, GRACIELA ANDRADE, b Arauco, Chile, July 16, 14; US citizen; m. SPANISH LANGUAGE & LITERATURE. *Educ:* Univ Concepcion, Chile, MA, 40; Univ Ill, MA, 49; State Univ Iowa, MA, 52, PhD, 57. *Prof Exp:* Instr Span, State Univ Iowa, 51-58; asst prof, Ohio Univ, 58-60; LECTR SPANISH, LAWRENCE UNIV, 60- *Mem:* MLA. *Res:* Modern Spanish and Spanish American novel; the language and style of Perez Galdos. *Publ:* Auth, El lenguaje familiar de Perez Galdos, 63 & coauth, El lenguaje familiar de Perez Galdos y sus contemporaneos, 66, Hispanofila. *Mailing Add:* Dept of Modern Languages Lawrence Univ Appleton WI 54912

ALFIERI, JOHN JOSEPH, b Central Nyack, NY, Jan 25, 17; m 60. SPANISH LANGUAGE & LITERATURE. *Educ:* Univ Southwestern La, BA, 50; State Univ Iowa, MA, 52, PhD, 57. *Prof Exp:* Instr Span, 54-57, from asst prof to assoc prof Span & freshman studies, 57-65, supvr, Students in Spain Prog, fall 69, WOLLPERT PROF SPAN LIT & CHMN DEPT SPAN, LAWRENCE UNIV, 65- *Mem:* MLA; Am Asn Teachers Span & Port. *Res:* Medieval Spanish literature; Cervantes; Romance linguistics. *Publ:* Auth, The Double Image of Avarice in Galdos' Novels, 63, coauth, El Lenguaje Familiar de Galdos y sus contemporaneos, 66, Hispanofila; el arte pictorico en las novelas de Galdos, Anales Galdosianos, 68. *Mailing Add:* Dept of Spanish Lawrence Univ Appleton WI 54912

ALFONSI, FERDINANDO PIETRO, b Arquata del Tronto, Italy, Oct 10, 28; m 72. COMPARATIVE LITERATURE, ITALIAN. *Educ:* Villanova Univ, MA, 67; Cath Univ Am, PhD(comp lit), 70. *Prof Exp:* Prof Ital lit, Inst Commercial Technol, Italy, 52-64; asst prof Ital, Sweet Briar Col, 70-74; asst prof Ital comp lit, Baruch Col, City Univ New York, 74-76; ASST PROF ITAL, FORDHAM UNIV, 76- *Concurrent Pos:* Ford Found fac res fels, 72 & 73. *Honors & Awards:* Primo Premio per la Poesia, Concorso di Poesia Viobannitti Calabria Regional Asn, 76. *Mem:* Am Asn Teachers Ital. *Res:* Italian literature; American literature; novel. *Publ:* Auth, Satana nel Paradiso perduto di Milton e nell Inferno di Dante, 11-12/70 & Moravia nel pensiero critico italiano e americano, 1-2/71, Citta di Vita; L'elemento sessuale nelle opere di Moravia secondo la critica americana, Italica, summer 72; Moravia e l'America, Orpheus, 74; Il Vangelo secondo Silone, Le di Igagioni Critiche, 76; coauth, An Annotated Bibliography of Moravia Criticism in Italy and in the English Speaking World, 1929-1975, Garland, 76; auth, Gli Ebrei di Ignazio Silone, Citta di Vita, 3-4/78; Questa Nostra Italia, pontone Ed, Cassino, 81. *Mailing Add:* Dept Ital Fordham Univ Bronx NY 10458

ALFONSI, SANDRA RESNICK, b Mar 1, 43; m 71. MEDIEVAL FRENCH LANGUAGE & LITERATURE. *Educ:* George Washington Univ, BA, 64, MA, 66; Cath Univ Am, PhD(French), 70. *Prof Exp:* Actg asst prof French, Lynchburg Co, 72-73; adj asst prof French & Ital, 74-75, ADJ ASST PROF FRENCH, BARUCH COL, 77- *Honors & Awards:* Distinguished Prof Year Award, Lynchburg Col, 72-73. *Mem:* MLA; Am Asn Teachers Fr; Mediaeval Acad Am; Int Courtly Lit Soc. *Res:* Comparative romance linguistics; history of Italian and Spanish language. *Publ:* Coauth, An Annotated Bibliography of Alberto Moravia Criticism in Italy and in the English Speaking World (1929-1975), Garland, 76. *Mailing Add:* 40-16-217 St Bayside NY 11361

ALGEO, JOHN, English. See Vol II

ALIBERTI, DOMENICO BERNARDINO, b Rodi-Milici, Italy, Feb 19, 28; US citizen; m 58; c 2. ITALIAN & LATIN LANGUAGES & LITERATURE. *Educ:* Univ Messina, DLett(lang), 59. *Prof Exp:* Instr Ital, Univ Ore, 61-62; instr, Univ Mass, 62-65; asst prof Ital & Latin, Kans State Univ, 65-67; asst prof, 67-68, assoc prof, 68-80, PROF ITAL, YOUNGSTOWN STATE UNIV, 80- *Concurrent Pos:* Mem adv bd, Am Latina, 72- *Mem:* Am Asn Teachers Ital; MLA; Midwest Mod Lang Asn; Pedag Sem Romance Philol. *Res:* Linguistics; synchronic Romance syntax; 14th century Italian literature; Dante's influence on Italian and Spanish authors. *Publ:* Auth, Della congiunzione se costruita con il verbo al condizionale, Vol XLIV, No 4 & Lei, La, e il problema della concordanza, Vol XLVIII, No 1, Italica; Il condizionale nella protasi di periodi ipotetici nello spagnolo, nel francese e nell'italiano, Sculorum Gymnasium, Vol XXIV, No 2; Il tema dell'autoritarismo paterno in Manzoni, in Moratin ed in altri, In: La Fusta, Vol II, No 2; L'Equivalente del condizionale remanzo nella protasi di alcuni tipi di periodo ipotetico greco, In: Studi classici in o nore di Q Cataudella Varia, 72. *Mailing Add:* Dept of Foreign Lang Youngstown State Univ Youngstown OH 44555

ALLAIN, MATHE, b Casablanca, Morocco, Nov 15, 28; nat US; m 45; c 3. FRENCH, HISTORY. *Educ:* Univ Southwestern La, BS, 48, BA, 56, MA, 63. *Prof Exp:* INSTR FRENCH, UNIV SOUTHWESTERN LA, 63- *Concurrent Pos:* Dir, Coun Develop French in La, 75-76. *Honors & Awards:* Chevalier, Palmes Academiques, 77. *Mem:* MLA; Am Asn Teachers Fr; Southern Hist Asn; Am Soc 18th Century Studies; Soc Fr Etude XVIIIe Siecle. *Res:* Eighteenth century French thought and 19th century French novel; colonial Louisiana; the abbe Raynal. *Publ:* Ed & translr, The Festival of the Young Corn, 64; auth, Voltaire et la fin de la tragedie classique, Fr Rev, 12/65; The humanist's dilemma: Milton, God and reason, Col English, 2/66; El burlador burlado: Tirso De Molina's Don Juan, Mod Lang Quart, 6/66; co-ed, France and North America: Over Three Hondred Years of Dialogue, Univ Southwestern La, 73; ed, France and North America: The Revolutionary Experience, 76 & Twentieth Century Acadians, In: The Acadians, 78, Lafayette. *Mailing Add:* Dept of Foreign Lang Univ of Southwestern La Lafayette LA 70501

ALLAIRE, JOSEPH LEO, b Detroit, Mich, Feb 23, 29; m 74; c 1. ROMANCE LANGUAGES, FRENCH. *Educ:* Univ Detroit, AB, 52; Wayne State Univ, MA, 57, PhD(mod lang), 66. *Prof Exp:* Teacher French & Latin, pub schs, Mich, 53-62, head dept, 62-67; instr French, Wayne State Univ, 60-67; asst prof, 67-72, assoc chmn mod lang, 69-73, ASSOC PROF FRENCH, FLA STATE UNIV, 72- *Mem:* Am Asn Teachers Fr; MLA; S Atlantic MLA; S Cent MLA; AAUP. *Res:* French Renaissance; pre-Reformation literature; late medieval French literature, especially the 15th century. *Publ:* Ed, Le Miroir de l'Ame Pecheresse de Marguerite de Navarre, Wilhelm Fink, Munich, 72; auth, Foreign languages and the Founding Fathers, S Atlantic Bull, 1/77. *Mailing Add:* Dept of Mod Lang Fla State Univ Tallahassee FL 32306

ALLEE, JOHN GAGE, JR, b Helena, Mont, Feb 28, 18; m 43; c 2. PHILOLOGY, ENGLISH. *Educ:* George Washington Univ, AB, 39, AM, 40; Johns Hopkins Univ, PhD, 55. *Prof Exp:* Jr instr, Johns Hopkins Univ, 45-49; from asst prof to assoc prof, 49-62, dean, Div Univ Students, 62-79, PROF ENGLISH, GEORGE WASHINGTON UNIV, 62- *Concurrent Pos:* Fulbright res grant, Iceland, 61; Fulbright prof English, Univ Iceland, 69-70. *Mem:* Soc Advan Scand Studies; Mediaeval Acad Am; Ling Soc Am; Icelandic Archaeol Soc; Am Name Soc. *Res:* English philology; Old Norse; onomastics. *Publ:* Auth, A study of the place names in Bardar Saga Snaefellsass, In: Germanic Studies in Honor of Edward Henry Sehrt, Miami Ling Ser 1, 68; Placenames in Skaftafell, Iceland, 72-73 & Norwegian and Samish place names from the coast of Finnmark, Norway, 77, ONOMA. *Mailing Add:* Dept of English George Washington Univ Washington DC 20052

ALLEN, DAVID HARDING, JR, b Los Angeles, Calif, June 30, 28; m 52; c 3. SPANISH, PORTUGUESE. *Educ:* Stanford Univ, BA, 51; San Diego State Col, MA, 59; Univ Calif, Los Angeles, PhD(Hisp lang & lit), 68. *Prof Exp:* Teacher, Oceanside-Carlsbad Col, 53-61; teaching asst, Univ Calif, Los Angeles, 61-64; asst prof, 65-69, officer, 69-82, DIR, RELAT WITH SCHS, EDUC OPPORTUNITY PROG, UNIV CALIF, DAVIS, 82- *Mem:* Am Asn Teachers Span & Port. *Res:* Latin American literature, history, and culture. *Publ:* Auth, Ruben Dario frente a la creciente influencia de los Estados Unidos, Rev Iberoam, 12/67. *Mailing Add:* Admissions Univ of Calif Davis CA 95616

ALLEN, EDWARD DAVID, b Perth Amboy, NJ, Jan 29, 23; m 46; c 1. FOREIGN LANGUAGE EDUCATION. *Educ:* Montclair State Col, BA, 43; Univ Wis, MA, 49; Ohio State Univ, PhD(educ), 54. *Prof Exp:* Teacher, Belleville High Sch, 43-45; instr French & Span, Ohio State Univ, 45-55, from asst prof to assoc prof foreign lang educ, 55-62, prof, 62-80. *Concurrent Pos:* Vis lectr, Ohio Wesleyan Univ, 55-56. *Mem:* Am Coun Teaching Foreign Lang; MLA; Am Asn Teachers Fr; Am Asn Teachers Span & Port. *Mailing Add:* 165 W Schreyer Pl Columbus OH 43214

ALLEN, HAROLD BYRON, b Grand Rapids, Mich, Oct 6, 02; m 34; c 2. ENGLISH LANGUAGE. *Educ:* Kalamazoo Col, BA, 24; Univ Mich, MA, 28, PhD, 41. *Prof Exp:* Prof rhet, dir forensics & publ & asst to the pres, Shurtleff Col, 25-34; asst ed, Early Mod English Dict, Univ Mich, 34-39 & Middle English Dict, 39-40; asst prof English, San Diego State Col, 40-43; prof lectr, 44-45, from asst prof to prof English, 45-67, dir commun prog, 45-65, prof English & ling, 67-71, EMER PROF ENGLISH & LING, UNIV MINN, MINNEAPOLIS, 71- *Concurrent Pos:* Dir, Ling Atlas Upper Midwest, 48-; Fund Advan Educ fel, 51-52; Fulbright lectr, Ain Shams Univ & Univ Cairo & ling consult, Ministry Educ, Cairo, 54-55; Smith-Mundt vis prof ling, United Arab Repub Ministry Educ, Cairo, 58-59; mem, Nat Adv Coun Teaching English as Foreign Lang, 62-66 & 69-, chmn, 74-; co-dir, Proj English, Curric Develop Ctr, Univ Minn, 62-67; US Off Educ grant, 64-66; dir Comn English Lang, 64-70; mem, Nat Clearinghouse Comt Social Dialects, 66-71; Nat Endowment for Humanities grant, 67-68; consult English as 2nd lang, Univ Tehran, 71 & 73; Fulbright-Hays prof Am English, Kossuth Lajos Univ, Hungary, 72. *Honors & Awards:* David H Russell Award, NCTE, 72. *Mem:* MLA; Ling Soc Am; NCTE (2nd vpres, 57, 1st vpres, 60, pres, 61); Teachers English to Speakers Other Lang (pres, 66-67); Am Dialect Soc (pres, 71 & 72). *Res:* English linguistics, linguistic geography; English as a second language. *Publ:* Auth, Samuel Johnson and the Authoritarian Principle in Language Criticism; ed, Readings in Applied English Linguistics, Appleton, 58 & 64, 3rd ed, Knopf, 82; auth, The Sound-Structure of English, Amalgamated Publ House, Cairo, 60; ed, English as a Second Language, McGraw, 65, 2nd ed, 71; auth, TENES: a survey of the teaching of English to non-English speakers in the US, NCTE, 66; co-ed, Readings in American Dialectology, Appleton, 71; Auth, Linguistics and English Linguistics: A Bibliography (2nd ed), AHM, 77. *Mailing Add:* 8100 Highwood Dr Bloomington MN 55438

ALLEN, JEFFNER M, Contemporary Continental Philosophy. See Vol IV

ALLEN, JOHN JAY, b Wichita, Kans, May 20, 32; m 56; c 2. SPANISH. *Educ:* Duke Univ, AB, 54; Middlebury Col, MA, 57; Univ Wis, PhD, 60. *Prof Exp:* From asst prof to assoc prof Span, 60-72, PROF SPAN, UNIV FLA, 72- *Concurrent Pos:* Vis prof, Rijksuniversiteit te Utrecht, 77; Mellon vis prof, Univ Pittsburgh, 82; ed, Cervantes, Bull Cervantes Soc Am. *Mem:* Am Asn Teachers Span & Port; MLA; corres mem Hispanic Soc Am. *Res:* Cervantes; Golden Age poetry and drama. *Publ:* Auth, El Cristo de la Vega and La Fuerza de la Sangre, Mod Lang Notes, spring 68; Don Quixote: Hero or Fool? A Study in Narrative Technique, Univ Fla, 69; Melisendra's mishap in Maese Pedro's Puppet Show, Mod Lang Notes, 73; Antipetrarquismo en el Romancero General, Hispano-Italic Studies,No 2, 79; Don Quixote: Hero or Fool? Univ Fla, Part 2, 79; ed, Don Quijote de la Manche, Ed Catedra, Madrid, 2nd ed, 80; auth, Don Quixote and the origins of the novel, In: Cervantes and the Renaissance, 80 & Toward a conjectural model of the Corral del Principe, In: Medieval, Renaissance and Folklore Studies in Honor of John Esten Keller, 80, Juan de la Cuesta Press. *Mailing Add:* Dept of Romance Lang Univ of Fla Gainesville FL 32611

ALLEN, JOHN ROBIN, b Chicago, Ill, Feb 24, 35; m 60; c 2. ROMANCE LANGUAGES, COMPUTATIONAL LINGUISTICS. *Educ:* Univ Buffalo, BA, 57; Syracuse Univ, MA, 64; Univ Mich, PhD(Romance lang), 69. *Prof Exp:* Asst prof French, Dartmouth Col, 69-72; ASSOC PROF FRENCH, UNIV MAN, 72- *Concurrent Pos:* Ed, System, 72- & Olifant, 73-; assoc ed, Comput & Humanities, 73-, Comput & Medieval Data Processing Bull, 73- & Tristania, 78- *Mem:* MLA; Int Arthurian Soc; Asn Int Ling Appliquee; Soc Rencesbals; Int Courtly Lit Soc. *Res:* Medieval French epics; computational analysis of literature; computer-aided instruction. *Publ:* Auth, Lerealisme dans la Religieuse, A D Menut Festschrift, Coronado, 73; On the authenticity of the Baligant episode in the Chanson de Roland, Comput in Humanities, 74; Methods of authorship identification, Fr Rev, 74; L'Enseignement assiste par ordinateur: tendances actuelles, L'Informatique, spring 74; Kinship in the Chanson de Roland, Studies Medieval Lit, 77; Les structures de Mainet, Soc Rencesvals VIIe, Congres Actes, 78. *Mailing Add:* Dept of French & Span Univ of Man Winnipeg MB R3T 2N2 Can

ALLEN, MARCUS, b Pittsburgh, Pa, Mar 2, 24; m 53; c 1. FRENCH LITERATURE. *Educ:* Univ Pittsburgh, Ba, 49, PhD(French), 64; Columbia Univ, MA, 51; Univ Bordeaux, Dipl French, 64. *Prof Exp:* From instr to assoc prof French, Morgan State Col, 52-65; ASSOC PROF FRENCH, UNIV MO, ST LOUIS, 66- *Mem:* MLA; Midwest MLA; Col Lang Asn; Am Asn Teachers Fr. *Res:* Eighteenth century French literature. *Publ:* Auth, The role of the Lache in the theatre of Jean-Paul Sartre, 61 & Voltaire and the theatre of involvement, 67, Col Lang Asn J; The problem of the Bienseances in Voltaire's Oreste, Comp Drama, 71; ed, Articles Abbe to Elie & Enoch from Voltiare's Questions sur l'Encyclopedie. *Mailing Add:* Dept of Mod Lng Univ of Mo St Louis MO 63121

ALLEN, MARY VIRGINIA, b Hebron, Va, Nov 11, 14. FRENCH. *Educ:* Anges Scott Col, AB, 35; Univ Toulouse, dipl, 37; Middlebury Col, MA, 38; Univ Va, PhD(French), 54. *Prof Exp:* Teacher high sch, 38-46; teacher French, Meredith Col, 46-47; teacher Ger, Westhampton Col, 47-48; assoc prof French, 48-51 & 54-68, prof, 68-79, chmn dept, 72-79, EMER PROF FRENCH, AGNES SCOTT COL, 79- *Res:* Medieval French literature; 16th century French literature. *Mailing Add:* Dept of French Anges Scott Col Decatur GA 30030

ALLEN, RICHARD JOHN, b Lethbridge, Alta, June 23, 37; m 61; c 4. GERMAN LANGUAGE & LITERATURE. *Educ:* Brigham Young Univ, BA, 62, MA, 63; Johns Hopkins Univ, PhD(Ger), 69. *Prof Exp:* Asst prof Ger, Brigham Young Univ, 66-70; asst prof, Johns Hopkins Univ, 70-76, assoc prof Ger, 76-80, dir arts & sci, Evening Sch & Summer Session, 74-80. *Mem:* MLA; Am Asn Teachers Ger. *Res:* German satire and comic literature; German drama; aesthetic theory. *Publ:* Auth, Johann Daniel Falk as a Satirist and Critic, Dissertation Abstracts; Johann Daniel Falk and the Theory of Characteristic Art, MLN, 71; Falk, Schelling and a Promethean view of Naturphilosophie, In: Traditions and Transitions: Studies in Honor of Harold Jantz, Delp, Munich, 72. *Mailing Add:* 2120 Tred Avon Rd Essex MD 21221

ALLEN, ROBERT FRANKLIN, b New York, NY Sept 9, 28; m 52; c 3. FRENCH, LINGUISTICS. *Educ:* NY Univ, BA, 51; Middlebury Col, MA, 57; Univ Colo, PhD(Fr), 67. *Prof Exp:* Teacher, Peru Cent Sch, NY, 56-57; asst prof French, Cottey Col, 57-59; dir lang lab, 61-70, dir off instruct serv, 70-76, PROF FRENCH LING, RUTGERS COL, RUTGERS UNIV, 76- *Mem:* MLA; Asn Comput Humanities. *Res:* Stylostatistic study of the 19th century French novel. *Publ:* Auth, L'Atmospher telle qu'elle est evoquee par les adjectifs-clefs de Madame Bovary, Les Amis de Flaubert (2 parts), 12/68 & 5/69; A stylistic study of the adjectives of Le Pere Goriot, Lang & Style, winter 71; Annotated bibliography-grammatical aspects of style-French literature, Style, spring 79; Caracterisation affective de guelgues adjectifs-cles dans Le Rouge et le noir, premier livre, Stenda Club, 10/81. *Mailing Add:* Off of the Dean of Instr Rutgers Col Rutgers Univ New Brunswick NJ 08903

ALLEN, ROBERT LIVINGSTON, b Hamadan, Iran, Mar 22, 16; US citizen; m 51, 68; c 4. LINGUISTICS, ENGLISH. *Educ:* Hamilton Col, BA, 38; Columbia Univ, MA, 51, PhD, 62. *Prof Exp:* Instr English & math, Robert Col, Turkey, 38-41; clerk, mil attache's off, Am Legation, Tehran, Iran, 41-42 & Kabul, Afghanistan, 42-43; instr English, Teacher's Training Sch, Kabul, Afghanistan, 43-45; instr, prep sch, Robert Col, 45-47, prin, 47-50, head dept English, 45-50; instr English as foreign lang, Teachers Col, Columbia Univ, 50-51, 52-53, 54-57, adv foreign students, 51-52; lectr, State Training Col for Teachers, Mandalay, Burma, 53-54; dir English prog, Caltex Pac Oil Co, Rumbai, Sumatra, Indonesia, 57-59; lectr ling & English as foreign lang, 59-63, assoc prof English, 63-66, chmn dept lang, lit, speech & theatre, 65-69, prof English, 66-80, prof ling & educ, 76-80, EMER PROF LING & EDUC, TEACHERS COL, COLUMBIA UNIV, 80- *Concurrent Pos:* Lectr, English teachers, Havana, Cuba, 52, 54; Fulbright lectr English as foreign lang, Mandalay, Burma, 53-54; Mem, English teaching adv panel, US Info Agency, 63- *Mem:* Nat Coun Teachers English; Ling Soc Am; Int Ling Asn; Teachers English to Speakers Other Lang; Int Reading Asny. *Res:* Teaching of English as a foreign or second language; the teaching of English grammar; linguistics and beginning reading. *Publ:* Auth, Read Along with Me, Teachers Col, 64;The Verb System of Present-Day American English, Mouton, Holland, 66; coauth, English Sounds and Their Spellings, Crowell, 66; Discovery: A Linguistic Approach to Writing, 67 & Exploration: A Linguistic Approach to Writing, 67, Noble; auth, Sector analysis: From sentence to morpheme in English, Report 18th Round Table Ling & Lang Studies, 67; English Grammars and English Grammar, Scribner's, 72; Working Sentences, Paideia. *Mailing Add:* Dept of Lang Lit Speech & Theatre Teachers Col Columbia Univ New York NY 10027

ALLEN, ROGER MICHAEL ASHLEY, b Devon, Eng, Jan 24, 42; m 72. ARABIC LANGUAGE & LITERATURE. *Educ:* Oxford Univ, BA, MA & DPhil(mod Arabic lit), 68. *Prof Exp:* Asst prof, 68-73, ASSOC PROF ARABIC LANG & LIT, UNIV PA, 73- *Concurrent Pos:* Fels, Am Res Ctr Egypt, 70-71 & 75-76; organist-choirmaster, St Mary's Episcopal Church, Univ Pa, 74; vis lectr, Oxford Univ, England 76; ed, Edebiyat. *Mem:* Am Orient Soc; Mid E Studies Asn; Am Asn Teachers Arabic (pres, 77-78). *Res:* Second language teaching techniques, specifically Arabic; Arabic literature; translation from Near Eastern literatures. *Publ:* Auth, Mirrors by Mahfuz (2 parts), Muslim World, 72 & 73; coauth, God's World, Bibliotheca Islamica, 73; auth, A Study of Hadith Isa ibn Hisham, Al-Muwaylihi's View of Egyptian Society during the British Occupation, State Univ NY, 74; Egyptian drama and fiction in the 1970s, Edebiyat, 76; contribr, Arabic literature, In: The Study of the Middle East: Research in the Humanities and Social Sciences, Wiley, 76; transl, Nagib Mahfuz, Mirrors, 77 & auth, In the Eye of the Beholder: Tales from . . . Yusuf ldris, 78, Bibliotheca Islamica; The Arabic Novel: An Historical and Critical Survey, Syracuse Univ Press, 82. *Mailing Add:* Dept Orient Studies Univ of Pa Philadelphia PA 19104

ALLEN, SHIRLEY SEIFRIED, English Literature, Theatre History. See Vol II

ALLEN, WALTER, JR, b Meriden, Conn, Nov 12, 11. LATIN. *Educ:* Wesleyan Univ, AB, 32; Yale Univ, PhD, 36. *Prof Exp:* Instr classics, Princeton Univ, 36-40 & Yale Univ, 40-42; from assoc prof to prof Latin, 46-76, EMER PROF LATIN, UNIV NC, CHAPEL HILL, 76- *Mem:* Am Philol Asn. *Res:* Greek and Latin literature; Roman history; John Rainolds. *Mailing Add:* Dept of Latin Univ of North Carolina Chapel Hill NC 27515

ALLENTUCH, HARRIET R, b Rochester, NY, Oct 9, 33; m 56; c 2. FRENCH. *Educ:* Univ Rochester, BA, 55; Radcliffe Col, AM, 56; Columbia Univ, PhD(French), 62. *Prof Exp:* Instr French, Queens Col,61-64; asst prof, 64-70, assoc prof, 70-81, PROF FRENCH, STATE UNIV NY STONY BROOK, 81- *Concurrent Pos:* Woodrow Wilson fel, 55-56; Henry Alfred Todd scholar, 56-57. *Mem:* MLA; Am Asn Teachers Fr; North Am Soc 17th Century French Lit. *Res:* Seventeenth and 20th century French literature. *Publ:* Auth, Madame de Sevigne: A Portrait in Letters, Johns Hopkins Univ, 63 & Greenwood Press, 78; Pauline and the Princess de Cleves, Mod Lang Quart, 6/69; Reflections on women in the theater of Corneille, Ky Romance Quart, 1/74; The will to refuse in The Princesse de Cleves, Univ Toronto Quart, spring 75; Mauron, Corneille, and the unconscious, Fr Forum, 1/79; Caesar's Crime: A psychocriticism of La Mort de Pompee, Gradiva, 80-81; Corneille, Melite, and the comedy of narcissism in Corneille Comique, Biblio 17, 82; My daughter/myself: Emotional roots of Mme de Sevigne's art, Mod Lang Quart, 9/82. *Mailing Add:* 49 Fairview St Huntington NY 11743

ALLISON, DONALD E, b Sioux Falls, SDak, June 8, 22. GERMAN, COMPARATIVE LITERATURE. *Educ:* Univ SDak, AB, 47; Wash Univ, MA, 52, PhD(Ger), 56. *Prof Exp:* Instr Ger, Univ SDak, 47-49; from instr to assoc prof, 53-69, chmn dept Ger & Slavic lang, 66-71, chmn dept mod lang & lit, 71-76, PROF GER, UNIV NEBR, LINCOLN, 69- *Mem:* MLA; Am Asn Teachers Ger. *Res:* German literature of the eighteenth century; German Romanticism; German-Spanish literary relations. *Publ:* Auth, The spiritual element in Schiller's Jungfrau and Goethe's Iphigenie, Ger Quart, 59; Schiller today, Prairie Schooner, 64; German Review Grammar, Ronald, 66. *Mailing Add:* Dept of Ger & Slavic Lang Univ of Nebr Lincoln NE 68508

ALMASOV, ALEXEY, b Novgorod, Russia, May 4, 17, US citizen; m 44; c 3. RUSSIAN, SPANISH. *Educ:* Univ Leningrad, Dipl distinction, 39; Univ Iowa, PhD(Span), 68. *Prof Exp:* Assoc prof Russ & Span, Yankton Col, 61-63; assoc prof, 63-76, PROF RUSS & SPAN, COE COL, 76- *Concurrent Pos:* Instr Russ, NDEA summer inst, Dartmouth Col, 65, Span, Coe Col, 66-68. *Mem:* Am Asn Teachers Span & Port. *Res:* Spanish Golden Age drama; Russian epic poetry; modern Spanish usage. *Publ:* Auth, Textbook of Spanish for Russians, UNRRA Team 616, Munich, Ger, 47; Representation of words written with Cyrillic alphabets, Zool J, 54; Fuenteovejuna y el honor villanesco en el teatro de Lope de Vega, 63 & El concepto de American Spanish en la practica pedagogica de los Estados Unidos, 65, Cuadernos Hispanoam; Special uses of tu and usted, 74 & Vos and vosotros as formal address in modern Spanish, 74, Hispania; contribr, Lope de Vega, Wissenschaftliche Buchgesellschaft, Darmstadt, Ger, 75. *Mailing Add:* Dept of Foreign Lang Coe Col Cedar Rapids IA 52402

ALMEIDA, JOSE AGUSTIN, b Waco, Tex, Aug 28, 33; m 64; c 1. SPANISH LANGUAGE & LITERATURE. *Educ:* Baylor Univ, BA, 61; Univ Mo, Columbia, MA, 64, PhD(Span), 67. *Prof Exp:* Teaching asst, Univ Mo Columbia, 61-66; instr Span, Baylor Univ, 62-63; asst prof, 66-77, chmn, Latin Am studies, 79-81, ASSOC PROF LIT & SPAN, UNIV NC, GREENSBORO, 77- *Concurrent Pos:* Vis prof, Elmira Col, 67; Nat Endowment for Humanities fel, 70; consult, Living Lang Method, Hampton Inst, Va, 76 & 78. *Mem:* Am Asn Teachers Span & Port; Assoc Int Hispanistas; MLA; SAtlantic Mod Lang Asn. *Res:* Poetics: literary criticism & literature, especially poetry of the Golden Age of Literature in Spain. *Publ:* Auth, Garcilaso a traves de los nuevos aspectos del New Criticism, Cuadernos Hispanoam, 11/65; Algunos impactos del existencialismo en la poesia de Miguel de Unamuno, Rev Lit, 66; La Critica Literaria de Fernando de Herrera, Ed Gredos, 76; coauth, Descubrir y Crear & Teacher's Guide for Descubrir y Crear, Harper & Row, 76, 2nd ed, 81; auth, Elementos picarescos en la poesia satirica del Siglo de Oro, In: La picaresca, origenes, textos y estructuras, Madrid: Fundacion Universitaria Espanola, 79; El concepto aristotelico de la imitacion en el Renacimiento de las letras espanolas: Sigo XVI, In: Actas del Sexto Congreso Internacional de Hispanistas, Paul Malak & Son, 80. *Mailing Add:* Dept of Romance Lang Univ NC Greensboro NC 27412

ALPHONSO-KARKALA, JOHN B, b Karkala, India, May 30, 23; m 64; c 3. COMPARATIVE LITERATURE. *Educ:* Univ Bombay, BA, 50, MA, 53; Columbia Univ, PhD(English & comp lit), 64. *Prof Exp:* Conf asst, Indian Deleg to Gen Conf of Gen Agreement on Trade & Tariff, Geneva, Switz, 53-54; mem High Comn of India, London, 54-56; secy to chmn, Indian Deleg to Gen Assembly of World Health Orgn, Geneva, 56; res assoc, Indian Deleg, UN, NY, 56-60; vis lectr Asian lit, City Col New York 62-64; instr Orient humanities, Columbia Univ, 62-64; from asst prof to assoc prof lit, 64-69, PROF LIT, STATE UNIV NY COL, NEW PALTZ, 69- *Concurrent Pos:* Ed, Newslett India Club, Columbia Univ, 62-63; chmn lit comt, Tagore Soc Inc, 64-65; State Univ NY Res Found fels, 66-67 & 69-70; mem Cong Orient; vis prof Orient humanities, Columbia Univ, 69-70; external examr PhD degree English & comp lit, Bangalore Univ, India, 77-78 & Karmatak Univ, India, 81-82. *Mem:* Am Comp Lit Asn: Int Comp Lit Asn; MLA; Am Orient Soc; Asn Asian Studies. *Res:* Indian literature; mythology; comparative literature, east and west. *Publ:* Co-ed, Bibliography of Indo-English Literature, 1800-1966, Popular Bks, Bombay, 74; auth, Jawaharlal Nehru as a Writer and Thinker, Twayne World Authors Series, Boston, 75; contribr, Literature and national character, In: Indo-English Literature, 78 & Myth, Matrix and Meaning in Raja Rao's Kanthapura, 79, Vimala Prakashan, India; Joys of Jayanagara (fiction), 81 & When Night Falls (poems), 81, Mysore, India; ed, Vedic Vision, Heinemann, New Delhi, 81; contribr, Twentieth century Indian literature, a survey, In: Encyclopedia of Twentieth Century World Literature, Frederick Ungar, 82. *Mailing Add:* Dept of English & World Lit State Univ of NY Col New Paltz NY 12562

ALSIP, BARBARA WITTMAN, b San Antonio, Tex, May 27, 38; m 59; c 2. FRENCH LANGUAGE & LITERATURE. *Educ:* Tex Christian Univ, BA, 48, MA, 64; Emory Univ, PhD(French), 71. *Prof Exp:* Instr French, Tarleton State Col, 63-65; instr, NC Wesleyan Col, 63-65; instr, WGa Col, 65-67; asst prof, 69-73, ASSOC PROF FRENCH, WESTERN ILL UNIV, 73- *Mem:* AAUP; Am Asn Teachers Fr; MLA; NAm Soc 17th Century Fr Lit. *Res:* Seventeenth century French literature; French theatre; French phonetics. *Mailing Add:* Dept of Foreign Lang & Lit Western Ill Univ Macomb IL 61455

ALT, ARTHUR TILO, b Batavia, Java, Oct 14, 31; US citizen; m 58; c 1. GERMANIC LANGUAGES. *Educ:* Univ Tex, PhD, 64. *Hon Degrees:* Dipl, (Yiddish lang & lit), Columbia Univ & Yivo Inst, NY, 74. *Prof Exp:* Teaching asst, Univ Tenn, 56-57; humanities res assoc, Univ Tex, 57-58, teaching asst, 58-61, spec instr Ger, NDEA Summer Inst, 60; instr, Duke Univ, 61-65; asst prof Ger lit, Mt Holyoke Col, 65-67; asst prof, 67-78, dir, undergrad studies Ger, 67-68, ASSOC PROF GER & YIDDISH LANG & LIT, DUKE UNIV, 78- *Concurrent Pos:* Consult & rev ed, Oceana Publ, 70-; Deutscher Akademischer Austauschdienst fac fel, 73 & 76. *Mem:* Am Asn Teachers Ger; MLA; Asn Jewish Studies; Theodor Storm Ges; Am Lessing Soc. *Res:* Nineteenth century realism; 20th century literature; Yiddish. *Publ:* Auth, Das Phänomen der Erschütterung bei Theodor Storm, Schriften-Theodor-Storm Ges, 66; Theodor Storm, Twayne, 73; Flucht und Verwandlung: Theodor Storms Verhältnis zur Wirklichkeit, Schriften der Theodor-Storm Ges, 76; Die kritische Rezeption Friedrich Hebbels in den USA, Hebbel-Jahrbuch, 78; co-ed, Creative Encounter: Festschrift for Herman Salinger, Univ NC, 78; auth, Theodor Storm-Ernst Esmarch: Briefwechsel, Erich Schmidt Verlag, Berlin, 79; Zu Storms Kritikan Hebbel: Eine Gedichtreplik, Julian Schmidt und obiterdicta, Hebbel Jahrbuch, 81; Theodor Storm--Hieronymus Lorm: Unveroffentlichte Briefe, Schriften der Theodor-Storm-Ges, 78. *Mailing Add:* Dept of Ger Lang & Lit Duke Univ Durham NC 27706

ALTABE, DAVID FINTZ, b New York, NY, Nov 10, 29; m 58; c 2. SPANISH, SEPHARDIC STUDIES. *Educ:* City Col NY, BBA, 50; Columbia Univ, MA, 55, M Phil, 75. *Prof Exp:* Lectr, Hunter Col, 64-65; ASSOC PROF SPAN, QUEENSBOROUGH COMMUNITY COL, 65- *Mem:* Am Soc Sephardic Studies (pres, 77); Am Asn Teachers Span & Port; Hispanic Inst. *Res:* Judeo-Spanish literature; Spanish literature. *Publ:* Auth, Epitaphs in Judeo-Spanish verse, In: Sephardic Scholar, Yeshiva Univ, 73; Symphony of Love: Las Rimas, Translation of Spanish Poetry of G A Becquer, Regina Publ, 74; Temas y Dialogos, Holt, Toronto, 75; La comunidad Sefardita de Bayona en 1801, Am Hispanist, 76; Knosezo a Tomar: A Haskalah work in Judeo-Spanish, Tradition Mag, 76; The Romanso, 1900-1933: a bibliographical survey, In: Sephardic Scholar, Yeshiva Univ, 78. *Mailing Add:* Queensborough Community Col Bayside NY 11364

ALTER, JEAN VICTOR, b Warsaw, Poland, Oct 7, 25; m 77; c 1. FRENCH LITERATURE. *Educ:* Univ Brussels, MA, 48; Univ Paris, DUniv, 51; Univ Chicago, PhD, 57. *Prof Exp:* From instr to asst prof French, Howard Univ, 52-59; lectr, Univ Md, 59-60, from asst prof to assoc prof, 60-67; prof, Case-Western Univ, 67-70; PROF ROMANCE LANG, UNIV PA, 70- *Concurrent Pos:* Smith-Mundt Grant, 51-52; Fulbright grant, 51-53. *Mem:* MLA; Am Asn Teachers Fr; Acad Lit Studies; Semiotic Soc Am. *Res:* Sociology of literature; 17th and 20th century French fiction. *Publ:* Auth, Apollinaire and two Shakespearean sonnets, Comp Lit, 62; L'Enquete policiere dans le nouveau roman, Rev Langues Mod, 64; Faulkner, Sartre and le nouveau roman, Symposium, summer 66; La Vision du Monde d' Alain Robbe-Grillet, 66, Les Origines de la Satire Anti-Bourgeoise, 66 & L'esprit Anti-Bourgeois sous l'Ancien Regime, 70, Droz; Itineraire d'un Poete: Jean Laugier, Caracteres, 80; Aux limites du marxisme, Esprit Createur, 81; From text to performance: Semiotics of theatrality, Poetics Today, 81. *Mailing Add:* Dept of Romance Lang Univ of Pa Philadelphia PA 19104

ALTER, MARIA POSPISCHIL, b Vienna, Austria; US citizen. GERMAN, FRENCH. *Educ:* Univ Okla, BA, 48, MA, 51; Univ Md, PhD(Ger), 61. *Prof Exp:* From instr to asst prof Ger & gen humanities, Howard Unit, 55-66; asst prof Ger, Case Western Reserve Univ, 66-69; acad consult & dir teachers prog, Am Asn Teachers Ger, 69-73; ASSOC PROF GER, VILLANOVA UNIV, 74- *Concurrent Pos:* Grant conj with sabbatical, Howard Univ, 65. *Mem:* MLA; Am Asn Teachers Ger; Mod Austrian Lit Asn; Lessing Soc. *Res:* Twentieth century literature, Schnitzler, Grass and Kafka; promoting German studies. *Publ:* Auth, The technique of alienation in Bertolt Brecht's The Caucasian Chalk Circle, Col Lang Asn, 9/64; Bertolt Brecht und die rassischen Minderheiten, Ger Quart, 1/64; Bertolt Brecht and the Modern Drama, Mod Drama, 9/68; Schnitzler's physician: An existential character, Mod Austrian Lit, 69; The Role of the Physician in the Works of Arthur Schnitzler and Hans Carossa, Verlag Peter Lang, 71; Monograph: A Modern Case for German, Am Asn Teachers Ger, 71; A modern case for foreign language, Asn Depts Foreign Lang, 9/75; coauth & translr, Only a God can save us: Der Spegel's interview with Martin Heidegger, Philos Today, winter 76. *Mailing Add:* Mod Lang Dept Villanova Univ Villanova PA 19085

ALTIERI, MARCELLE BILLAUDAZ, b Lyon, France, Feb 16, 26; US citizen; m 47; c 1. FRENCH LANGUAGE & LITERATURE. *Educ:* Lycee de Lyon, Baccalaureat, 47; Ecole Normale d'Inst Lyon, Cert d'Aptitude Pedagogique, 57; Hunter Col, BA, 62, MA, 64; NY Univ, PhD(French), 72. *Prof Exp:* Teacher, French Pub Sch Syst, Aca du Rhone, 57-58; teacher French, New York City Bd Educ, 62-63; lectr French & French lit, Hunter Col, 64-66; instr, NY Univ, 66-69; chmn dept, Berkeley Inst, 69-70; instr, Univ Bridgeport, 71-72, asst prof, 72-76, actg chmn, Dept Foreign Lang, 75-76; asst prof, Univ Mass, 76-78; asst prof, Univ Rhode Island, 78-79; CHMN, FOREIGN LANG DEPT, FIELDSTON SCH, 80- *Mem:* Am Asn Teachers Fr; MLA; Am Soc Geoling. *Res:* Medieval romances; influence of society on literature; popular speech and sayings. *Publ:* Auth, Les Romans de Chretien de Troyes, A G Nizet, Paris, 76; Dialects and popular speech in the city of Lyon, France, Vol 3, 77 & Engineering the primacy of the French language in Quebec, Vol 5, 79, Geolinguistics. *Mailing Add:* 2437 Wilson Ave Bronx NY 10469

ALTMAN, CHARLES FREDERICK, b De Ridder, La, Jan 9, 45; m 67. FRENCH LITERATURE, CINEMA. *Educ:* Duke Univ, AB & MA, 66; Yale Univ, PhD(French), 71. *Prof Exp:* Fulbright-hayes fel & lectr Am studies, Univ Paris X, Nanterre, 70-71; asst prof French & comp lit, Bryn Mawr Col, 71-74; asst prof French, 74-77, assoc prof French & Comp lit, 77-82, ASSOC PROF FILM, FRENCH & COMP LIT, UNIV IOWA, 82- *Concurrent Pos:* Fel, Cornell Univ Soc for Humanities, 74-75; dir, Paris Film Ctr, 80-81; vis prof, Univ Paris III-Censier, 80-81. *Honors & Awards:* Russell B Nye Prize, J Pop Cult, 80. *Mem:* MLA; Soc Values Higher Educ; Soc Rencesvals. *Res:* Narrative; 12th century Western culture; film. *Publ:* Two types of opposition and the structure of Latin Saints' Lives, Medievalia et Humanistica New Series, 6: 1-11; Towards a historiography of American film, Cinema J, 16: 1-25 & Cinema Examined, Dutton (in press); Psychoanalysis and Cinema: The imaginary discourse, Quart Rev of Film Studies, 2: 257-72; The medieval marquee: Church portal sculpture as publicity, J Pop Cult, 14: 37-46; Cinema/Sound, Yale French Studies, Vol 60, 80; Genre: The musical, Routledge & Kegan Paul, London and Boston, 81; D W Griffith, Spec Issue Quart Rev of Film Studies, Vol 6, No 2; The American film musical, Ind Univ Press (in press). *Mailing Add:* Dept of French & Ital Univ of Iowa Iowa City IA 52242

ALTMAN, HOWARD BRUCE, b Cambridge, Mass, Oct 11, 42. FOREIGN LANGUAGE EDUCATION. *Educ:* Univ Mass, Amherst, AB, 64; Stanford Univ, MA, 66, PhD(foreign lang educ), 72. *Prof Exp:* Instr Ger, Univ Fla, 66-69; asst prof, Univ Wash, 71-73; assoc prof mod lang, 73-75, PROF MOD LANG, UNIV LOUISVILLE, 75- *Concurrent Pos:* Ed, Innovations in Foreign Lang Educ Ser, Newbury House Publ, Mass, 71-75, asst ed foreign lang educ, Am Foreign Lang Teacher, 72-75; co-ed, New Directions in Lang Teaching, Cambridge Univ Press, 80- *Mem:* Am Asn Teachers Ger; Am Coun Teaching Foreign Lang (pres, 77). *Res:* Individualizing foreign language instruction; psychology of second language learning; foreign language teacher education. *Publ:* Ed, Individualizing the Foreign Language Classroom, 72 & auth, Foreign languages in the community college: A mandate of pluralism, In: Changing Patterns in Foreign Language Programs, 72, Newbury House; The three R's of individualization: Reeducation, responsibility and relevance, Foreign Lang Ann, 72; The language teacher in an age of change, Am Foreign Lang Teacher, 72; coauth, College and university foreign language programs: New forms, new emphases, new content, Change Mag, 78; Faculty development in foreign language departments, ADFL Bull, 78; ed, Foreign Language Teaching: Meeting Individual Needs, Perganon, 80; The Second Language Classroom: Directions for the 1980's, Oxford Univ Press. *Mailing Add:* Dept of Class & Mod Lang Univ of Louisville Louisville KY 40292

AL-TOMA, SALIH JAWAD, b Karbala, Iraq, Sept 23, 29; m 59; c 2. ARABIC, LINGUISTICS. *Educ:* Univ Baghdad, BA, 52; Harvard Univ, MAT, 55, EdD(lang educ), 57. *Prof Exp:* Instr Arabic, Col Educ, Univ Baghdad, 58-60, asst dean 59-60; cult attache, Iraq Embassy, Wash DC, 60-63; res fel Near Eastern studies, Harvard Ctr Mid Eastern Studies, 63-64; assoc prof Arabic, 64-73, PROF ARABIC, IND UNIV, BLOOMINGTON, 73- *Concurrent Pos:* Nat Endowment Humanities fel, 71-72; Am Res Ctr in Egypt fel, 72; ed, Al-Arabiyya: J Am Asn Teachers Arabic, 76-78. *Mem:* Am Asn Teachers Arabic; MidE Studies Asn NAm. *Res:* Arabic linguistics; Arabic literature. *Publ:* Auth, The Problem of Arabic Diglossia, Harvard Univ, 69; A bibliographical Survey of Arabic Dramatic Literature, Baghdad, 69; Language education in Arab countries, Current Trends Ling, 70-71; coauth, Modern Standard Arabic: Intermediate Level, Univ Mich, 71; auth, Problems of Arabic Teaching In Iraqi Secondary Schools, in Arabic, Ministry Higher Educ, Baghdad, 72; Palestinian Themes in Modern Arabic Literature, Anglo-Egyptian, Cairo, 72; Sociopolitical themes in the contemporary Arabic novel, In: The Cry of Home, Univ Tenn, 72; Modern Arabic Literature: A Bibliography of Articles, Books, Dissertations, and Translations, in English, Ind Univ, 75. *Mailing Add:* Dept of Near Eastern Lang & Lit Goodbody Hall Ind Univ Bloomington IN 47401

ALVA, CHARLES (ALLEN), b San Jose, Calif, Nov 26, 19; m 61. LINGUISTICS, LANGUAGE. *Educ:* San Jose State Col, BA, 41; Stanford Univ, MA, 48, EdD(English educ), 60. *Prof Exp:* Teacher high schs, Calif, 49-59, head dept English, 50-59; actg instr, Stanford Univ, 56-57, asst English educ, 59-60, res assoc & lectr educ, 60-61; instr English as second lang, English Lang Sch, Rome, Italy, 61-62; PROF HUMANITIES & CHMN DEPT, ORE COL EDUC, 64- *Concurrent Pos:* Consult English, Stanford Sch Planning Lab for projects in Calif & Utah, 59-61 & Napa County Sec Schs, Calif, 60-61; Fulbright lectr ling, Palazzo Antici Mattei, Rome & dir, English Lang Sch sponsored by Cornell-Fulbright Ling Prog, 62-64. *Mem:* NCTE, Asn Depts English; MLA. *Res:* Teaching of English as a second language; teaching of grammar in secondary schools. *Publ:* Auth, Structural grammar in California schools, English J, 60. *Mailing Add:* Dept of Humanities Oregon College of Education Monmouth OR 97361

ALVAREZ, NICOLAS EMILIO, b Havana, Cuba; US citizen. LATIN AMERICAN STUDIES & LITERATURE. *Educ:* Univ PR, BA, 68; Univ Calif, Berkeley, MA, 70, PhD(romance lang & lit), 73. *Prof Exp:* Lectr Latin Am & Span lit, San Jose State Univ, 72-77; asst prof, Wayne State Univ, 78-81, assoc prof, 81-82; ASSOC PROF LATIN AM STUDIES & LIT, DENISON UNIV, 82- *Mem:* MLA; Instituto Internacional de Literatura Ibero-Americana; Am Asn Teachers Span & Port. *Res:* Literary theory: semiotics and mythopoetics; medieval Spanish literature. *Publ:* Auth, El recibimiento y la tienda de Don Amor en el Libro de buen amor a la luz del, In: Libro de Alexandre, Biuletyn Historii Sztuki, 76; Structuralism and Pedro Paramo: A case in point, Ky Romance Quart, 77; Marti y Manach: Analisis estilistico de un panegirico, Explicacion de Textos Literarios, 78; La Obra Literaria De Jorge Manach-Madrid, Porrua, 79; Agonia y muerte de Juan Preciado, Revista de Estudios Hispanicos, 79; El Epilogo del Libro de buen amor, In: Medieval, Renaissance and Folklore Studies in Honor of John E Keller, 80; Aristoteles y Platon en La escritura del dios, Explicacion de Textos Literarios, 81; Analisis estructuralista del Prefacio del Libro de buen amor, Ky Romance Quart, 81. *Mailing Add:* Dept of Mod Lang Denison Univ Granville OH 43023

ALVAREZ, ROMAN, b Orense, Spain; US citizen; m; c 1. SPANISH & COMPARATIVE LITERATURE. *Educ:* Univ Santiago, Spain, BA, 53; Univ Oviedo, Spain, Licenciado law, 63; Univ Heidelberg, Ger, cert lang, 62; Temple Univ, MA, 68; Univ Pa, PhD(Span), 77. *Prof Exp:* Grad asst, Temple Univ, 66-67; instr, Rutgers Univ, Camden, 67-70; prof scorer, Educ Testing Serv, Princeton, 67-68; teaching fel, Univ Pa, 71-72; instr, 72-80, ASST PROF, SPAN, UNIV DEL, 80- *Mem:* MLA; Am Asn Teachers Span & Port; SAtlantic Mod Lang Asn; ECent Am Soc Eighteenth-Century Studies; AAUP. *Res:* Eighteenth and nineteenth century Spanich literature; Latin American literature; comparative literature. *Publ:* El Anarquismo en Pio Baroja, Ediciones Geminis, Uruguay, 77; Teaching 18th century Spanish literature and history, Eighteenth-Century Life (in press). *Mailing Add:* Dept of Lang & Lit Univ Del Newark DE 19711

ALVAREZ-ALTMAN, GRACE DEJESUS, b Dominican Republic, Apr 9, 26; US citizen; m 45; c 4. LINGUISTICS, SPANISH. *Educ:* Hunter Col, BA, 45; Columbia Univ, MA, 47; Univ Southern Calif, PhD, 62. *Prof Exp:* Instr Span, Pub Sch System, NY & NH, 45-47; instr hist & Span, Greater NY Acad, 48-50; supv teacher, La Sierra Prep Sch, 50-59; asst prof Span, La Sierra Col, 59-62, assoc prof mod lang, 62-67; Assoc prof Span lit, 67-74, PROF SPAN LIT, STATE UNIV NY COL, BROCKPORT, 74- *Concurrent Pos:* Deleg, Onomastic Inst of Onomastic Sci, Vienna, 69, Bulgaria, 72 & Ann Arbor, 81; lectureship, week honoring Garcia Lorca, Univ Iowa, 72; mem, Comn Higher Educ, Mid States Asn Cols & Sec Schs, 72-; ed, Garcia Lorca Rev, 73- & Lit Onomastic Studies, 74-; consult, Census Bur US, 77-81. *Mem:* Philol Asn Pac Coast; Am Name Soc (vpres, 82, pres, 83-); MLA; AAUP; Northeast Mod Lang Asn. *Res:* Literary onomastics; patronymics & toponymics; contemporary Spanish literature: empty-nest syndrome. *Publ:* Auth, Toponymical Aspect in Spanish Onomastics; Toponimos en Apellidos Hispanos, Ed Castalis, 68; The Cuba of New York State, Straight, 70; Charactonyms in Garcia Lorca's House of Bernarda Alba, Onomatica Can, 72; Survey of Lorquian matters in the US, Garcia Lorca Rev, 73; Antonio Buero Vallejo: The first fifteen years (Ruple), 5/74 & Garcia Lorca in United States universities and colleges, 5/74, Hispania; Onomastics as a modern critical approach to literature, Lit Onomastics Studies, 74; Dictionary of Hispanic Surnames in Southwest United States, G K Hall, 6/78. *Mailing Add:* Dept of Foreign Lang State Univ of NY Col Brockport NY 14420

AMAN, REINHOLD ALBERT, b Fuerstenzell, Bavaria, Apr 8, 36; nat US; m 60; c 1. GERMANIC LANGUAGES. *Educ:* Univ Wis-Milwaukee, BS, 65; Univ Tex, PhD(Ger lang), 68. *Prof Exp:* Asst prof Ger, Univ Wis-Milwaukee, 68-74; PRES, MALEDICTA, INT RES CTR FOR VERBAL AGGRESSION, 74-, ED, MALEDICTA PRESS PUBL, 75- *Concurrent Pos:* Dir, Maledicta Arch, 76- *Mem:* Int Arthurian Soc; Ling Soc Am; MLA; Int Maledicta Soc (pres, 75-). *Res:* Verbal aggression; dialectology; philology. *Publ:* Auth, Sinnliches, privately publ, 71; Bayrisch-österreichisches Schimpfwörterbuch, Süddeutscher, Munich, 73; Onomastic questionnaire, 77, Taxonomy of metaphorical terms of abuse, 77, Maledicta research made easy, 78 & Menomini maledicta, 81, Maledicta J; Interlingual taboos in advertising, Ablex Publ, 82. *Mailing Add:* Maledicta 331 S Greenfield Ave Waukesha WI 53186

AMASH, PAUL J, b Lydda, Palestin, Aug 8, 33; US citizen; m 58; c 4. ROMANCE LANGUAGES. *Educ:* Juniata Col, BA, 57; Pa State Univ, MA, 59; Univ NC, PhD(Romance lang), 65; Univ Dijon, dipl enseignement super, 65. *Prof Exp:* Chmn dept foreign lang high sch, Pa, 59-61; asst prof mod lang, Elon Col, 61-65; from assoc prof to prof romance lang, Pfeiffer Col, 65-68, chmn dept mod lang, 65-69; assoc prof, 69-80, PROF MOD LANG, MARIETTA COL, 80- *Mem:* Am Asn Teachers Fr; SAtlantic Mod Lang Asn. *Res:* Medieval French literature; 20th century French literature. *Publ:* Auth, The Algerian Arab in L'Estranger of Albert Camus, Romance Notes, spring 67. *Mailing Add:* Dept of Modern Language Marietta College Marietta OH 45750

AMASTAE, JON EDWARD, b Los Angeles, Calif, July 20, 46. LINGUISTICS. *Educ:* Univ NMex, BA, 68; Univ Ore, PhD(ling), 75. *Prof Exp:* Asst prof English, Pan Am Univ, 75-79; Fulbright lectr ling, Univ de los Andes, Bogota, Colombia, 79-80; ASST PROF LING, UNIV TEXAS, EL PASO, 80- *Concurrent Pos:* Actg dir, Lang & Ling Res Ctr, Pan Am Univ, 76-78. *Mem:* Ling Soc Am; Ling Asn Can & US; Soc Caribbean Ling. *Res:* Phonology; Creoles; language contact. *Publ:* Auth, Abstract and concrete analyses of a Creole language, Ore Acad Sci, 76; coauth, Attitudes toward varieties of Spanish, Proc Fourth LACUS Forum, 78; auth, A note on natural generative phonology and paradigm leveling, Ling Inquiry, 78; Dominican English Creole phonology: An initial sketch, Anthrop Ling, 79; Dominican Creole Phonology; Georgetown Univ, Papers in Lang & Ling, 79; co-ed, Spanish in the US: Sociolinguistic Aspects, Cambridge Univ Press, 82. *Mailing Add:* Dept of Ling Univ of Tex El Paso TX 79968

AMBROSE, JOHN WILLIAM, JR, b Worcester, Mass, Jan 23, 31; m 61; c 1. LATIN & GREEK CLASSICS. *Educ:* Brown Univ, AB, 52, AM, 59, PhD, 62. *Prof Exp:* Teacher Latin, Roxbury Latin Sch, 56-61; instr Latin & Greek, Phillips Acad, 61-64; chmn dept classics, Taft Sch, 64-66; from asst prof to assoc prof, 66-76, PROF CLASSICS, BOWDOIN COL, 76-, CHMN DEPT, 71-, MERRILL PROF GREEK CLASSICS, 77- *Concurrent Pos:* Teaching asst, Brown Univ, 59-60. *Mem:* Am Philol Asn; Class Asn New Eng; Archaeol Inst Am. *Res:* Studies in Horace; Horace and the Latin lyric; the Greek anthology. *Publ:* Auth, The ironic meaning of the Lollius Ode, Trans & Proc Am Philol Asn, 65; coauth, Preparatory Latin (2 Vols), Independent Sch, 69; auth, Horace on foreign policy, Odes 4.4, Class J, 73; coauth, Greek Attitudes, Scribner, 74. *Mailing Add:* Dept of Classics Bowdoin Col Brunswick ME 04011

AMBROSE, ZUELL PHILIP, b Ponca City, Okla, June 9, 36; m 65; c 2. CLASSICAL LANGUAGES. *Educ:* Princeton Univ, BA, 58, MA, 60, PhD(classics), 63. *Prof Exp:* From instr to assoc prof, 62-72, PROF CLASSICS, UNIV VT, 72-, CHMN DEPT, 73- *Concurrent Pos:* Vis assoc prof, Middlebury Col, 67-68; Nat Endowment for Humanities jr fel, 69-70. *Mem:* Am Philol Asn; Vergilian Soc; Class Asn New England (secy-treas, 68-72). *Res:* Greek drama; Greek and Latin epic; translation of J S Bach texts. *Publ:* auth, The Homeric Telos, Glotta, 65; The Lekythion and the Anagram of frogs 1203, Am J Philol, 68; Two textual notes on Plautus' Miles Gloriosus, Class J, 73; The etymology and genealogy of Palinurus, Am J Philol, 80; Weinen, Klagen, Sorgen, Zagen und die antike Redekunst, Bach Jahrbuch, 80. *Mailing Add:* Dept of Classics Univ of Vt Burlington VT 05405

AMELINCKX, FRANS C, b Sint-Niklaas, Belg, Sept 23, 32; US citizen; m 59; c 3. FRENCH LANGUAGE & LITERATURE. *Educ:* Northern State Teacher Col, BS, 64; Univ Iowa, MA, 66, PhD(French), 70. *Prof Exp:* From instr to asst prof, 69-75, ASSOC PROF FRENCH, UNIV NEBR, LINCOLN, 75- *Concurrent Pos:* Mem, Nebr Adv Coun Teaching For Lang, 70-76; Camargo Found fel, 76; dir, Centre du Colorado, Bordeaus, France, 78-79; ed, Studies Twentieth Century Lit, 79. *Honors & Awards:* Univ Nebr distinguished teaching award, 77. *Mem:* Am Asn Teachers Fr; Soc Chateaubriand; MLA; Rocky Mountain Mod Lang Asn. *Res:* Romantic Travel literature, French poetry; F-R de Chateaubriand. *Publ:* Auth, Le volcan et les montagnes dans Rene, Bull Soc Chateaubriand, 75; Image et structures dans Atala, Revue Romane, 75; Dynamisme et polarite des images dans l'itineraire de Paris a Jerusalem, Revue Langues Vivantes, 75; The myth of unity and poetic language, Iowa State J Res, 76; L'Itineraire de Paris a Jerusalem ou la poetique de la desillusion, Nineteenth Century Fr Studies, 77; L'Accueil critique de l'Essai sur la litterature anglaise dans les revues britanniques et americaines, Bull Soc Chateaubriand, 77; co-ed & contribr, Travel, Quest & Pilgrimage as a Literary Theme, Univ Microfilms, 78; Man, machines and moral order: Technology and values in French Romanticism, Iowa State J Res, 79. *Mailing Add:* Dept of Mod Lang & Lit Univ Nebr Lincoln NE 68588

AMMERLAHN, HELLMUT HERMANN, b Germany, May 21, 36; US citizen. GERMAN & COMPARATIVE LITERATURE. *Educ:* Univ Vt, MA, 60; Univ Tex, Austin, PhD(Ger), 65. *Prof Exp:* Instr Ger, Univ Wash, 63-66; lectr, Univ New South Wales, 67-68; asst prof, 69-72, ASSOC PROF GER & COMP LIT, UNIV WASH, 72- *Mem:* MLA; Lessing Soc; Int Ver der Germanisten; Philol Asn Pac Coast; Goethe Soc. *Res:* Goethe; psychology and literature; German and English literature 18th-20 centuries. *Publ:* Auth, Wilhelm Meisters Mignon--ein offenbares Raetsel, Deut Vierteljahrsschrift Literaturwiss, 68; Zur Symbolik der Goetheschen Geniusgestalten, Monatshefte, 72; Goethe und Wilhelm Meister, Shakespeare und Natalie: Die klassische Heilung des kranken Koenigssohns, Jahrbuch des Freien Deutschen Hochstifts, 78; Goethe und Gretchens Lied vom Machandelboom: Zur Symbolik des kuenstlerischen Schaffensprozesses, Akten VI, Int Germanisten-Kongress, 80; Puppe-Taenzer-Daemon-Genius-Engel: Naturkind, Poesiekind und Kunstwerdung bei Goethe, Ger Quart, 81. *Mailing Add:* Dept of Ger Lang & Lit Univ of Wash Seattle WA 98195

AMOR, ROSE TERESA, b Havana, Cuba, Sept 21, 31; US citizen. SPANISH LANGUAGE & LITERATURE. *Educ:* St John's Univ, Brooklyn, BA, 52; St John's Univ, Jamaica, NY, MA, 60; Columbia Uiv, PhD(Span), 69. *Prof Exp:* Teacher math, Span & Latin, St Agnes Acad High Sch, College Point, NY, 54-60; chairperson dept, 64-74, PROF SPAN, MOLLOY COL, 60-, CHAIRPERSON DEPT MOD LANG, 75- *Concurrent Pos:* Dir, Lang Lab, 60-, Span Inst, 69- & English Inst, 73-, Molloy Col. *Mem:* MLA; Am Asn Teachers Span & Port; Teaching English Speakers Other Lang; Asn Dept Foreign Lang. *Res:* Afro-Cuban literature; Latin American short story. *Mailing Add:* Molloy Col 1000 Hempstead Ave Rockville Centre NY 11570

AMOR Y VAZQUEZ, JOSE, b Ribadeo, Spain; US citizen. HISPANIC STUDIES. *Educ:* Inst Havana, Cuba, BA, 38; Univ Havana, LLD, 44; Brown Univ, MA, 52, PhD, 57. *Prof Exp:* Lectr Span, Inst Venezolano-Am, Caracas, 46-47; instr Span lang & lit, Russell Sage Col, 47-49; asst Span, 50-54, instr, 54-57, from asst prof to assoc prof Span lang & lit, 57-61, PROF HISP STUDIES, BROWN UNIV, 71-, HEAD RESIDENT FEL, 69- *Concurrent Pos:* Instr, Duke Univ, 51 & 54-56; Am Coun Learned Soc grant-in-aid, 59; vis lectr, Univ RI, 60; coordr, mod lang instr, Brown Univ, 63-67. *Mem:* MLA; Am Asn Teachers Span & Port; Asoc Int Hispanistas (treas, 68-). *Res:* Hispanic studies, especially 16th, 19th and 20th centuries. *Publ:* Co-ed & contribr, Hernan Cortes en dos poemas del Siglo de Oro, Nueva Rev Filol Hisp, 59; co-ed, El Camino, Holt, 61; co-ed & contribr, Conquista y contrarreforma: La Mexicana de G Lobo Lasso de la Vega, Actas II Congr Asoc Int Hispanistas, 67; Presencia de Mexico en tres escritores: Espanoles: Jarnes, Moreno Villa, Sender, Actas III Congr Asoc Int Hispanistas, 70; ed, Mexicana, Bibliot Autores Espanoles, Madrid, 70; co-ed & contribr, Homenaje a William L Fichter: Estudios Sobre el Teatro Antiguo Hispanico y Otros Ensayos, Castalia, Madrid, 71. *Mailing Add:* Dept of Hisp & Ital Studies Brown Univ Providence RI 02912

AMOS, ASHLEY CRANDELL, b New York, NY, July 6, 51; m 76. OLD ENGLISH PHILOLOGY. *Educ:* Stanford Univ, BA, 72; Yale Univ, PhD(English), 76. *Prof Exp:* JR FEL OLD ENGLISH, PONTIFICAL INST MEDIAEVAL STUDIES, UNIV TORONTO, 76-, ASST ED, DICT OLD ENGLISH, 76- *Mem:* Mediaeval Acad Am; Dict Soc NAm; MLA. *Res:* Old English lexicography. *Publ:* Linguistic means of determining the dates of Old English literary texts, Medieval Acad, Vol 90, 80. *Mailing Add:* Dict of Old English Robarts Res Libr 14285 130 St George St Toronto ON M5S 1A5 Can

AMYX, DARRELL ARLYNN, b Exeter, Calif, Apr 2, 11; m 36; c 1. CLASSICAL ARCHAEOLOGY. *Educ:* Stanford Univ, AB, 30; Univ Calif, AM, 32, PhD(Latin & class archaeol), 37. *Prof Exp:* Instr Latin, Univ Chicago, 37-39; teaching asst, lectr & res assoc classics, Univ Calif, 39-42; officer of dist postal censor, US Off Censorship, San Francisco, 42-45 teacher, A to Z ed Sch, Berkeley, Calif, 45-46; instr Latin, 46, from asst prof to prof art, 46-78, asst dean, Col Lett & Sci, 64-65, chmn, Dept Art, 66-72, EMER PROF HIST OF ART, UNIV CALIF, BERKELEY, 78- *Concurrent Pos:* Travel-aid grants, Am Coun Learned Soc, 41, 62 & sr res fel, 65-66; Am Philos Soc study-aid grants, 56 & 76, Fulbright res grant to Greece, 57-58; Guggenheim fel, 57-59 & 73-74; mem grad group Ancient hist & Metiter archaeol, Univ Calif, Berkeley, 68-; vis prof fine arts, Ind Univ, 79. *Mem:* Archaeol Inst Am; Am Philol Asn; corresp mem Ger Archaeol Inst; corresp mem Ist Studi etruschied Italici. *Res:* History of ancient art; Greek vases; Greek sculpture. *Publ:* Auth, An Amphora with a Price Inscription & Corinthian Vases in the Hearst Collection, Univ Calif; The Attic Stelai, Part III, Hesperia, 58; co-ed, Californai Studies in Classical Antiquity (Vols 1-5), 68-72; coauth, Cypriote Antiquities in San Francisco Bay Area Collections, Studies Mediterranean Archaeology, Göteborg, Seden, 74; ed, Echoes from Olympus: Reflections of Divinity in Small-Scale Classical Art, Univ Art Mus, Berkeley, 74; coauth, Corinth, VII: 2-Archaic Corinthian Pottery and the Anapolga Well, Am Sch Class Studies, Princeton Univ, 75. *Mailing Add:* Dept Hist of Art Univ of Calif Berkeley CA 94720

ANDEREGGEN, ANTON JOSEPH, b Yverdon, Switz, May 20, 36; US citizen; m 63; c 2. ROMANCE LINGUISTICS, FRENCH LITERATURE. *Educ:* Monmouth Col, NJ, BA, 68; Univ Colo, PhD(French & Romance ling), 73. *Prof Exp:* Asst prof French & Ger, Univ Portland, 73-77; asst prof French, 77-80, ASSOC PROF FRENCH, LEWIS & CLARK COL, 80- *Concurrent Pos:* Fulbright fel, 80. *Mem:* Am Asn Teachers Fr; Philol Asn Pac Coast; Pac Northwest Conf Foreign Lang; MLA; Rocky Mountain Mod Lang Asn. *Res:* Provencal philology; French philology. *Publ:* Auth, Etude Philologique du Jutgamen General, Drame Provencal du XVe siecle, PGP; L'allongement en--es au pluriel en rovergat, Rev des Lang Romanes, Vol XXIV, 76; La question jurassienne, Contemp French Civilization, Vol 1, No 2, 77. *Mailing Add:* Dept of Foreign Lang Lewis & Clark Col Portland OR 97219

ANDERLE, MARTIN, b Krems, Austria, Feb 28, 32. GERMAN. *Educ:* Univ Vienna, Austria, PhD, 56. *Prof Exp:* From instr to asst prof Ger, Univ Mass, 59-62; asst prof, 62-69, assoc prof, 69-80, assoc prof Scand, 76-80, PROF GER, SLAVIC & EAST EUROP LANG, QUEENS COL, 80- *Res:* Hölderlin Ges Hölderlin; romanticism; lyric. *Publ:* Auth, Die zeit im gedicht, Ger Quart, 11/71; Hölderlin in der lyrick Gunter Eichs, 6/71 & Sprachbildungen Hölderlins in modernen gedichten, 6/72, Seminar. *Mailing Add:* Dept of German Queens College Flushing NY 11367

ANDERSEN, M, b Magdeburg, Ger, Oct 15, 24; c 3. ROMANCE LANGUAGES, COMPARATIVE LITERATURE. *Educ:* Free Univ, Berlin, Staatsexamen, 58; Univ Montreal, PhD, 65. *Prof Exp:* Asst prof French, Haile Selassie Univ, 61-63; asst prof French & Ger, Univ NDak, 63-65; assoc prof French, Loyola Col, Montreal, 65-73; assoc prof, 73-77, PROF FRENCH, UNIV GUELPH, 77-, CHMN DEPT LANG, 73- *Concurrent Pos:* Can Coun leave fel, 72-73. *Mem:* MLA; Can Asn Univ Teachers. *Res:* Women in 20th century French literature. *Publ:* Claudel et l'Allemagne, Univ Ottawa, 65; coauth, Mecanismes Structuraux, Ctr Psychologie et Pedag, Montreal, 67; ed, Mother was Not a Person, Content, Montreal, 72. *Mailing Add:* Dept of Lang Univ of Guelph Guelph ON N1G 2W1 Can

ANDERSEN, ROGER WILLIAM, b Great Falls, Mont, Sept 30, 40; m 69; c 2. ENGLISH AS A SECOND LANGUAGE, LINGUISTICS. *Educ:* Mich State Univ, BA, 63, MA, 67; Univ Tex Austin, PhD(appl ling), 74. *Prof Exp:* Teacher English as a Second Lang, San Sebastian High Sch, PR, 63-74 & Humacao High Sch, PR, 65; from asst instr to instr, 66-70, ASST PROF ENGLISH AS A SECOND LANG, UNIV PR, HUMACAO, 74- *Concurrent Pos:* Vis asst prof English as a second Lang, Univ Calif, Los Angeles, 78-79. *Mem:* Ling Soc Am; Teachers English to Speakers Other Lang; Am Asn Appl Ling; Am Asn Teachers Span & Port; Am Coun Teaching Foreign Lang. *Res:* Second language acquisition; Pidgin and Creole languages; language treatment and language planning. *Publ:* Auth, The impoverished state of cross-sectional morpheme acquisition/accuracy methodology, In: Proceedings of the Los Angeles Second Language Research Forum, Univ Calif, Los Angeles, 6/77 & Working Papers on Bilingualism/Travaux de rechereches sur le bilinguisme, 10/77; Procesos fonologicos en el desarrollo del papiamentu, Revista de Oriente, PR, 8/78; An implicational model for second language research, Lang Learning, 12/78. *Mailing Add:* Dept of English Univ of California Los Angeles CA 90024

ANDERSEN-FIALA, LINDA RUTH, b Muskegon, Mich, Sept 28, 41. MEDIEVAL & MODERN FRENCH LITERATURE. *Educ:* Kalamazoo Col, AB, 63; Univ Calif, Los Angeles, MA, 66, PhD(French), 71. *Prof Exp:* Asst prof French, 70-74, ASSOC PROF FRENCH, CALIF STATE UNIV, FULLERTON, 74- *Mem:* MLA; Philol Asn Pac Coast; Medieval Asn Pac; Mediaeval Acad Am; Int Soc Study Medieval Theatre. *Res:* Old French romance; early French drama. *Mailing Add:* Dept of Foreign Lang & Lit Calif State Univ Fullerton CA 92634

ANDERSON, ALEXANDER R, b Toronto, Ont, Mar 15, 27; m 52; c 4. GERMAN LANGUAGE & LITERATURE. *Educ:* Univ Toronto, BA, 49; Brown Univ, PhD, 62. *Prof Exp:* Instr Ger, Univ BC, 54-63; asst prof, 63-64, ASSOC PROF GER, UNIV WESTERN ONT, 64- *Concurrent Pos:* Asst, Brown Univ, 49-51, R D G Richardson fel, 51-52; Can Coun fel, 61, grant, 63. *Mem:* Asn Can Univ Teachers Ger (secy-treas, 67-69); Am Asn Teachers Ger; MLA; Humanities Asn Can. *Res:* Nineteenth and 20th century German novel. *Publ:* Coauth, Dauer im Wechsel--A Critical Anthology of German Literature, Heath, 68. *Mailing Add:* Dept of German Univ of Western Ontario London ON N6A 3K7 Can

ANDERSON, CHARLOTTE M, b Vienna, Austria, July 7, 23; US citizen; m 57. GERMAN LITERATURE. *Educ:* Univ Calif, Los Angeles, BA, 43, MA, 49; Yale Univ, PhD(Ger), 55. *Prof Exp:* Asst prof Ger, Conn Col Women, 53-58; instr, Yale Univ, 59-60; asst prof, Haverford Col, 61-66; assoc prof mod lang, 66-68, PROF MOD LANG, MONTGOMERY COUNTY COMMUNITY COL, 68-, CHMN DEPT FOREIGN STUDIES, 67- *Concurrent Pos:* Consult, Nat Endowment Humanities, 74-77; assoc ed, Unterrichtspraxis, 76- *Mem:* MLA; Asn Dept Foreign Lang (pres, 73); Am Asn Teachers Ger. *Res:* German heroic tragedy, 1642-1766; domineering mother in German literature; Turks in German baroque tragedy. *Publ:* Coauth, Structual German, Gilbert Publ, 65; Begegnung mit Deutschland, Dodd, 69; auth, Keeping in Step with the Times, 9/71, Reaching the Student, 3/74, contribr, The Role of Foreign Language in the Total Curriculum, 9/74 & The College and the Non-Academic Community, 11/77, Asn Depts Foreign Lang Bull. *Mailing Add:* Dept of Foreign Studies Montgomery County Community Col Blue Bell PA 19422

ANDERSON, DAVID L, b New York, NY, Dec 4, 37; m 64; c 3. ROMANCE LANGUAGES. *Educ:* Dartmouth Col, AB, 59; Mich State Univ, MA, 65; Univ NC, PhD(Romance lang), 68. *Prof Exp:* Assoc prof Romance lang, Pa State Univ, University Park, 68-75; prof & chmn dept, Univ Denver, 75-81; DEAN LIB ARTS, STATE UNIV NY COL ONEONTA, 81- *Concurrent Pos:* Asst bibliogr, MLA Int Bibliog, 71-75. *Mem:* MLA; Am Asn Teachers Fr; Soc Fr Etude XVIIIe Siecle; Am Soc 18th Century Studies; bibliography; epistolary genres in literature. *Publ:* Auth, Edouard and Jean-Jacques in retrospect, L'Esprit Createur, 69; The stigma of illegitimacy resolved: Food for Diderot, Romance Notes, 71; Abelard and Heloise: Eighteenth century motif, 71 & Aspects of motif in La Nouvelle Heloise, 72, Studies Voltaire & 18th Century; Marie Riccoboni: Some sources and directions, Enlightenment Essays, 73; A Bibliography and Checklist of Symbolism as an International and Interdisciplinary Movement, NY Univ, 75; The stigma of illegitimacy resolved, or Suzanne starved to life, Ky Romance Quart, 77; Graduate research in English: A foreign point of view, Lit Res Newslett, 78; Structural mythology et relig dans le ruman epis du XVIII siecle, Trans 5th Int Cong Enlightment, Vol 13, 80. *Mailing Add:* Dean Lib Arts State Univ NY Col Oneonta NY 13820

ANDERSON, EMMETT H, JR, b Richmond, Va, Mar 4, 17; m 45; c 2. MODERN LANGUAGES. *Educ:* Univ Richmond, BA, 40; Univ Va, MA, 48, PhD(Franco-Am rel), 53. *Prof Exp:* Assoc prof French & Span, Converse Col, 53-55; assoc prof mod lang, 55-60, PROF MOD LANG, SOUTHWESTERN AT MEMPHIS, 60-, CHMN DEPT, 76- *Mem:* MLA. *Res:* French Middle Ages; French 17th century. *Mailing Add:* Dept of Modern Language Southwestern at Memphis Memphis TN 38112

ANDERSON, HELENE MASSLO, b Brooklyn, NY, Apr 26, 27; m 50; c 2. LATIN AMERICAN LITERATURE. *Educ:* Brooklyn Col, BA, 47; Syracuse Univ, MA, 51, PhD(Latin Am lit), 61. *Prof Exp:* Bibliogr, Hisp Found, Libr Cong, 54-56; asst prof Span & Latin Am lit, 66-71, ASSOC PROF SPAN & LATIN AM LIT, NY UNIV, 71- *Mem:* MLA; Inst Int Lit Ibero-Am; Am Asn Teachers Span & Port; Am Transl Asn. *Res:* Latin American 19th and 20th century narrative; Mexican and Argentinian literature of 19th and 20th centuries; Caribbean literature. *Publ:* Transl, Margot Arce de Vazquez' Gabriela Mistral: The Poet and Her Work, NY Univ, 64; co-ed, Masterpieces of Spanish American Literature, Macmillan, 73. *Mailing Add:* Dept of Spanish & Portuguese New York Univ 19 University Pl New York NY 10003

ANDERSON, JAMES CLAYTON, JR, Classical Archaeology, Ancient History. See Vol I

ANDERSON, JAMES MAXWELL, b Seattle, Wash, Apr 9, 33; m 57. LINGUISTICS. *Educ:* Univ Wash, BA, 58, MA, 61, PhD(Romance ling), 63. *Prof Exp:* Asst prof ling, Georgetown Univ, 63-68; assoc prof, Univ Alta, 68-70; assoc prof, 70-76, PROF LING, UNIV CALGARY, 76- *Concurrent Pos:* Fulbright lectr, Univ Valladolid, 64-65, Univ Barcelona, 65-66 & Univ Deusto, 66; Can Coun res grant, 72-73 & Apsin, 76-77. *Mem:* Ling Soc Am; Int Ling Asn. *Res:* Historical and Romance linguistics; transformational grammar. *Publ:* Auth, Morphophonemics of Gender in Spanish Nouns, Lingua, 61; A Study of Syncope, Word, 65; La Fonetica Inglesa--A Handbook for Students and Teachers, Comision Intercambio Cult Espana Estados Unidos Am, 65; coauth, Readings in Romance Linguistics, Mouton, The Hague, 72; auth, Structural Aspects of Language Change, Longman, London, 73; Turma Salluitana: A Study in Ancient Iberian Linguistic Relationships, Neophilologus, 73; Ancient Iberian Inscriptions, Occasional Papers No 3, Univ Calgary, 76. *Mailing Add:* Dept of Ling Univ of Calgary Calgary AB T2N 1N4 Can

ANDERSON, KEITH OWEN, b Lamberton, Minn, Feb 18, 34; m 58; c 3. APPLIED LINGUISTICS. *Educ:* Univ Minn, BS, 59; Univ Colo, MA, 64, PhD(Ger), 70. *Prof Exp:* From instr to asst prof Ger, Univ Colo, 69-72; asst prof, Southern Ill Univ, Carbondale, 72-74; assoc prof, Pa State Univ, 74-78; prof Ger & chmn dept, 78-81, VPRES & DEAN, ST OLAF COL, 81- *Mem:* Am Asn Teachers Ger; MLA; Am Coun Teaching Foreign Lang; Ling Soc Am. *Res:* German-English contrastive linguistics; German dialectology; experimental phonetics. *Publ:* Coauth, Deutsch Unserer Zeit, Holt, 69; ed, Some Aspects of English Language Interference in Learning German Intonation, Proc Int Cong Phonetic Sci, 71; Foreign Language Teaching at the Intermediate Levels, Mod Lang J, 11/72; coauth, Language Loyalty Among the Pennsylvania Germans, Ger Am, 76, Univ Kans, 77; auth, The Foreign Language Field Day, Asn Dept Foreign Lang Bull, 3/78. *Mailing Add:* Dept of Ger St Olaf Col Northfield MN 55057

ANDERSON, ROBERT EDWARD, b Gilmer, Tex, Oct 4, 43; m 69; c 2. FRENCH LITERATURE, FOREIGN LANGUAGE PEDAGOGY. *Educ:* Williams Col, BA, 65; Univ Wis-Madison, MA, 66, PhD(French), 73. *Prof Exp:* Asst prof, 70-79, ASSOC PROF FRENCH, UNIV KANS, 79- *Mem:* MLA; Am Asn Teachers French; Am Soc Eighteenth Century Studies. *Res:* French literature of the 18th century; French classical theatre; the works of Andre Gide. *Publ:* Auth, Foreign language study and the voice major: a model course in French for singers, French Rev, 2/76. *Mailing Add:* Dept of Fr & Ital Univ of Kans Lawrence KS 66044

ANDERSON, ROBERT FLOYD, b Cleveland, Ohio, Mar 7, 35; m 62, c 2. ROMANCE LANGUAGES & LITERATURES. *Educ:* Western Reserve Univ, AB, 56; Univ Mich, AM, 60; Case-Western Reserve Univ, PhD(Romance lang & lit), 69. *Prof Exp:* Teacher Span, French & Ger, Cleveland High Sch, 56-58; teaching fel Span & Ger, Univ Mich, Ann Arbor, 58-60; instr Span & French, Cleveland State Univ, 60-63 & Harpur Col, 63-65; asst prof Span & Ger, Denison Univ, 65-69; assoc prof Span lit, Eastern Mich Univ, 69-72; vis prof Span lang & lit, Univ Mo, St Louis, 72-73; lectr, Univ Tex, El Paso, 77-82. *Concurrent Pos:* Lectr Span, Newark Br, Ohio State Univ, 66-67 & Ger, Zanesville Br, Ohio Univ, 67-69; Denison Univ Res Found res grant, 69; spec lectr, Univ Tex, El Paso, 77-79. *Mem:* MLA. *Res:* Spanish literature, specifically existentialism Unamuno and Vedanta; eastern philosophy in Spanish literature. *Publ:* Auth, A Love Affair with Krishna (poem), 11/73, A Glossary of Sanskrit Words Used in Eastern Philosophy, 11/73 & Ode to Baba Ram Dass, 5/73, Folio; Oceanic Consciousness (poem), 78; The Existentialism of Unamuno in the Perspective of Eastern Mythology, Philosophy and Psychology, 78; Learning Words from Words: Instant Vocabulary Expansion in Spanish through Cognates, 79. *Mailing Add:* 2410 N Stanton El Paso TX 79902

ANDERSON, SAM FOLLETT, b Chanute, Kans, Mar 7, 15. GERMANIC & SLAVIC LANGUAGES. *Educ:* Univ Kans, AB, 38; Harvard Univ, AM, 40. *Prof Exp:* From instr Ger to asst prof, Ger & Slavic lang, 41-66; ASSOC PROF SLAVIC LANG & LIT, UNIV KANS, 66- *Honors & Awards:* Bernard H Fink Award for distinguished teaching, Univ Kans, 64. *Mem:* Am Asn Advan Slavic Studies. *Res:* Indo-European, Germanic and Slavic languages. *Publ:* Auth, A variant specimen of Anton Sorg's Bücheranzeige of 1483-1484, Bibliog Soc Am, 1st quarter, 58. *Mailing Add:* Dept of Slavic Lang & Lit Univ of Kans Lawrence KS 66044

ANDERSON, WARREN DEWITT, b Brooklyn, NY, Mar 19, 20; m 47; c 3. COMPARATIVE LITERATURE, CLASSICAL LANGUAGES. *Educ:* Haverford Col, BA, 42; Oxford Univ, BA, 49; Harvard Univ, MA, 47, PhD(class philol), 54. *Prof Exp:* From instr to asst prof, Latin, Col Wooster, 50-55, from assoc prof Latin & head dept to prof Greek & Latin, 55-67; prof English & comp lit, Univ Iowa, 67-70, chmn dept comp lit, 68-70; chmn dept, 71-74, PROF COMP LIT, UNIV MASS, AMHERST, 70- *Concurrent Pos:* Vis prof classics, Univ Mich, 63 & 65; dir, Transl Ctr, Univ Mass, Amherst, 78-81. *Mem:* Am Comp Lit Asn; Am Lit Transl Asn; Am Musicol Asn. *Res:* Classical influences on modern literature; Greek and Roman music; history and theory of literary translation. *Publ:* Transl, Aeschylus: Prometheus Bound, Lib Arts, 63; Matthew Arnold and the Classical Tradition, Univ Mich, 65; Ethos and Education in Greek Music, Harvard Univ, 66; Types of the classical in Arnold, Tennyson and Browning, In: Victorian Essays, 67, co-ed, Victorian Essays, 67 & transl, Theophrastus, The Character Sketches, 70, Kent State Univ; auth, Matthew Arnold and the grounds of comparatism, Comp Lit Studies, 71; contribr, 72 articles, New Grove Dict of Music and Musicians, 81. *Mailing Add:* Dept of Comp Lit Univ of Mass Amherst MA 01003

ANDERSON, WILDA CHRISTINE, b Temple Tex, Apr 6, 51; m 77. FRENCH LITERATURE. *Educ:* Cornell Univ, AB, 72, MA, 76, PhD(French lit), 79. *Prof Exp:* ASST PROF FRENCH LIT, JOHNS HOPKINS UNIV, 78- *Concurrent Pos:* Ed, Mod Lang Notes, 78- *Mem:* MLA; Am Soc Eighteenth Century Studies. *Res:* Theories of language in the 18th century; relationships between science and literature in 18th century France. *Publ:* Auth, Figurative language and the scientific ideal: The preface to P J Macquer's Dict de Chymie, Neophilologus, 4/81; Translating the language of chemistry: Priestley and Lavoisier, The Eighteenth Century: A J Theory & Interpretation, 22: 1; The rhetoric of scientific language: An example from Lavoisier, Mod Lang Notes, 5/81; Qu'est-ce qu'un fait scientifique?, Critique, summer 82. *Mailing Add:* Dept of Romance Lang Johns Hopkins Univ Baltimore MD 21218

ANDERSON, WILLIAM SCOVIL, b Brookline, Mass, Sept 16, 27; m 54; c 5. CLASSICS. *Educ:* Yale Univ, BA, 50, PhD, 54; Cambridge Univ, BA, 52, MA, 56. *Prof Exp:* Instr classics, Yale Univ, 55-60; from asst prof to assoc prof Latin, 60-65, chmn dept classics, 70-73, PROF LATIN & COMP LIT, UNIV CALIF, BERKELEY, 65- *Concurrent Pos:* Morse fel, 59; prof in charge, Intercol Ctr Class Studies, Rome, 67-68; Am Coun Learned Soc grant to deliver lect at Int Cong Satire, Rostock, Ger, 65; ed Vergilius, 65 & Scholia Satyrica, 73-; Nat Endowment Humanities sr fel, 73-74; classicist-in-residence, Am Acad, Rome, 73-74. *Honors & Awards:* Prix de Rome, 54. *Mem:* Am Philol Asn (pres, 77); Soc Relig Higher Educ; Philol Asn Pac Coast. *Res:* Roman satire and comedy; Vergil; Ovid. *Publ:* Auth, Vergil's second Iliad, Trans Am Philol Asn, 57; The Art of the Aeneid, Prentice-Hall, 69; Ovid's Metamorphoses: Books 6-10, Univ Okla, 72; Ovidius, Metamorphoses, Leipzig: Teubner, 77; Essays on Roman Satire, Princeton Univ, 82. *Mailing Add:* Dept of Classics & Comp Lit Univ of Calif Berkeley CA 94720

ANDERSSON, THEODORE, b New Haven, Conn, Feb 18, 03; m 30; c 2. ROMANCE LANGUAGES. *Educ:* Yale Univ, BA, 25, MA, 27, PhD, 31. *Hon Degrees:* Dipl di Benemerenza, Soc Dante Alighieri, 74. *Prof Exp:* Instr French, Yale Univ, 27-37; prof Romance lang & chmn dept, Am Univ, DC, 37-41; assoc prof, Wells Col, 41-43, prof & chmn dept, 43-45; with US Dept State, 45-46; assoc prof French, Yale Univ, 46-57, dir master of arts teaching prog, 51-54, assoc dir, 54-55, prof Romance lang, 57-68, chmn dept, 59-68, prof, 68-80, EMER PROF SPAN & EDUC, UNIV TEX, AUSTIN, 80- *Concurrent Pos:* Prof in charge, Sweet Briar Col jr year in France, 48-49; dir, Conf Teaching Foreign Lang for World Understanding, UNESCO, Deylon, 53; assoc dir foreign lang prog, MLA, 55-56, dir, 56-57; proj dir, Southwest Educ Develop Lab, Austin, Tex, 68-71; organizer & chmn, Conf Child Lang, 71. *Honors & Awards:* Chevalier, Legion d'honneur, 55; Caballero de la Orden del Merito Civil, 76; Nat Asn for Bilingual Educ Award, 78. *Mem:* MLA; Am Asn Teachers Span & Port; Am Coun Teaching Foreign Lang; Int Asn Appl Ling. *Res:* Bilingual education; Childlanguage acquisition; child bilingualism and multilingualism; preschool biliteracy. *Publ:* Auth, The Teaching of Foreign Languages in the Elementary School, Heath, 53; coauth, The Education of the Secondary School Teacher, Wesleyan Univ, 62; auth, Spanish and Portuguese in the Elementary School, In: A Handbook for Teachers of Spanish and Portuguese, Heath, 68; Foreign Languages in the Elementary School: A Struggle Against Mediocrity, Univ Tex, 69; Coauth, Bilingual Schooling in the United States (2 vols), Southwest Educ Develop Lab, 70, 2nd ed (1 vol), Nat Educ Lab Publ, 78; A Guide to Family Reading in Two Languages: The Preschool Years, Nat Clearinghouse Bilingual Educ, 81. *Mailing Add:* Batts Hall 312 Univ of Tex Austin TX 78712

ANDES, RAYMOND NELSON, b Harrisonburg, Va, Sept 12, 18; m 44; c 2. MODERN LANGUAGES. *Educ:* Bridgewater Col, AB, 40; Univ NC, AM, 44, PhD, 48. *Prof Exp:* Instr, Univ NC, 44-46; acting prof mod langs, 47-48, PROF MOD LANGS, BRIDGEWATER COL, 48-, HEAD DEPT, 46- *Mem:* Am Asn Teachers Fr; S Atlantic MLA; Am Coun Teaching Foreign Lang. *Res:* Old French and 17th century French literature; the American image in France. *Publ:* Auth, Rationalization and realization in the characters of Racine, Romance Studies, Univ NC Press, 50. *Mailing Add:* Dept of Foreign Lang Bridgewater Col Bridgewater VA 22812

ANDINO, ALBERTO, b Camagüey, Cuba; US citizen; c 1. SPANISH LITERATURE & LANGUAGE. *Educ:* Inst Santa Clara, Cuba, BA & BS, 34; Jose Marti Univ, MA, 44; Univ Havana, PhD, 48; Columbia Univ, PhD(Span), 71. *Prof Exp:* Prof Span, Inst Gutierrez, Cuba, 49-50, Sch Prof Bus, 52-53 & Sch Arts & Indust, 53-59; dir, Sec Sch Nieves Morejon, 59-61; lexicographer, Appleton-Century-Crofts, New York, 61-64; asst prof, Duquesne Univ, 65-69; prof, 69-80, chmn dept mod & classic lang, 74-80, EMER PROF SPAN, DRURY COL, 80- *Concurrent Pos:* Dir sec & higher educ, Bd Educ, Havana, Cuba, 52-59; prof Span, Cent Univ, Cuba, 55-59; adv, Comt Curric, Cuba, 56-58; partic, Symp on Fray Bartolome de Las Casas,

Pittsburgh, Pa, 66; panelist, First Cong in the Exterior on Cuban Lit, 73-; adv & reader doctoral dissertations, Walden Univ, 77- *Mem:* Int Inst Iberoam Lit; Hist Inst US; MLA; Col Pedag, Cuba; Fed Maestros Cuba. *Res:* Spanish American short story; 19th century Spanish American literature. *Publ:* Auth, Harlem Rat Exterminating Co, Inc, Insula, Spain, 9/73; Bolivar Olmedo y El canto de Junin, Caudernos Hispanoam, 9/73; Snapshots, Hoy, Spain, 8/76; Notas a proposito de Tabare y del Velatorio de Carace, 7/76 & Reyes desde Madrid: Vision de Anahuac, 8/79, Cuadernos Hispanoam; Pena's Motors, Inc: Carburators Specialists, Insula, Spain, 5/80; Frutos de mi trasplante Ediciones Universal, 80; Los juegos politicos, clasistas y etnicos en las novelas de Mariano Azuela sobre la Revolucion Mexicana, Cuadernos Hispanoam, 4/81. *Mailing Add:* Dept of Mod & Classic Lang Drury Col Springfield MO 65802

ANDRACHUK, GREGORY PETER, b Toronto, Ont, Mar 4, 48; m 77. MEDIEVAL HISPANIC STUDIES. *Educ:* Univ Toronto, BA, 70, MA, 71, PhD(Hisp studies), 75. *Prof Exp:* ASST PROF SPAN & ITAL, LAKEHEAD UNIV, 75- *Mem:* Can Asn Hispanists; MLA; Mediaeval Acad Am; Am Asn Teachers Span & Port. *Res:* Sentimental novel; colonial Latin American Literature. *Publ:* Auth, On the missing third part of siervo libre de amor, Hisp Rev, 77; The function of the estoria de dos amadores within the siervo libre de amor, Can Estud Hisp, 77; Prosa y poesia en el siervo libre de amor, ACTAS, Int Congr Hispanists, 78. *Mailing Add:* Dept of Lang Lakehead Univ Thunder Bay ON P7B 5E1 Can

ANDRADE, LEONOR, b Gallup, NMex, Apr 5, 25. ROMANCE LANGUAGES. *Educ:* Univ NMex, BA, 46; Univ Wis-Madison, MA, 50. *Prof Exp:* Teacher, Radford Sch for Girls, Tex, 48-52 & pub schs, Ind, 53-56; ASSOC PROF & COORDR SPAN, MT MARY COL, 56- *Concurrent Pos:* Proj dir, Wis Humanities Comt, Nat Endowment for Humanities, 73. *Mem:* Am Asn Teachers Span & Port; Am Coun Teaching Foreign Lang; AAUP. *Res:* Latin American literature and civilization; Mexican literature. *Mailing Add:* Dept of Foreign Languages Mt Mary College 2900 Menomonee River Pkwy Milwaukee WI 53222

ANDRESEN, JULIE TETEL, b Evanston, Ill, Oct 16, 50; m 76; c 1. HISTORY & PHILOSOPHY OF LINGUISTICS. *Educ:* Duke Univ, BA, 72; Univ Ill, Urbana, MA, 75; Univ NC, Chapel Hill, PhD(ling), 80. *Prof Exp:* Teaching asst French, Univ Ill, Urbana, 73-75; teaching asst Ger, Univ NC, Chapel Hill, 77-80, vis lectr ling, 79-80. *Mem:* Ling Soc Am; MLA; Southeastern Conf Ling; Soc d'Hist & d'Epistemologie Sci Lang. *Res:* Theories of language in the eighteenth century; structural theory in language and literature; history of language and language change. *Publ:* Auth, Francois Thurot and the first history of grammar, Historiographia Ling, 1/2:45-57; coauth, From Saussureto Chomsky: Linguistics and the human sciences, Innovations Ling Educ, 1,2:3-23; auth, From Condillac to Condorcet: The Algebra of History, In: Studies in the History of Linguistics, John Benjamins, Vol XX, 80; Charles de Brosses's Traite of 1765 and the history of linguistics, Ling Invest, 1:1-24; Langage naturel et artifice linguistique, In: Condillac et les problemes du langage, Slatkine, 81; Systems and signs in Condillac and Saussure & Arbitraire and Contingence in the semiotics of the encyclopedists, Semiotica (in press); Debris et Histoire dans la theorie linquistique au XVIIIe siecle, In: Studies in the History of Linguistics, John Benjamins (in press). *Mailing Add:* 3200 Oxford Dr Durham NC 27707

ANDREU, ALICIA GRACIELA, b Lima, Peru, Sept 7, 40; US citizen; m 80; c 1. SPANISH LITERATURE. *Educ:* Chapman Col, BA, 65; Univ Wis, MA, 68; Univ Ore, PhD(Span lit), 78. *Prof Exp:* Chmn, Span & Ital Dept, 80-81, ASST PROF SPAN, MIDDLEBURY COL, 76- *Concurrent Pos:* Native instr, Nat Defense Educ Act, summer 64 & 65; Nat Endowment for Humanities grant, 79 & 81-82, consult, 81-; consult, D C Heath & Co, 80; Am Coun Learned Soc grant, 81; eval panelist, Nat Endowment for Humanities col teachers fels, 82- *Mem:* MLA; Asoc Galdosistas; Asoc Int Hisp; Asoc Iberoamericana; Latin Am Indian Lit Asn. *Res:* Nineteenth century Spanish literature; 20th century Spanish literature; colonial literature. *Publ:* Auth, Relacion intima entre Galdos y la literatura popular, Actas del Sequndo Congreso Int Estudios Galdosianos, 78; ed, La Cruz del Olivar de Faustina Saez de Melgar, Anales Galdosianos, 80; auth, Galdos y la literatura popular, SGEL, 82; Arte y consumo Angela Grassi y El Correo de la Moda, Nuevo Hisp, winter 82. *Mailing Add:* Span & Ital Dept Middlebury Col Middlebury VT 05753

ANDREWS, JAMES RICHARD, b Birmingham, Ala, Oct 22, 24. SPANISH, PORTUGUESE. *Educ:* Rollins Col, BA, 49; Princeton Univ, MA, 51, PhD, 53. *Prof Exp:* From instr to assoc porf Span & Port, Univ Calif, Los Angeles, 53-66; PROF SPAN & PORT, VANDERBILT UNIV, 66- *Mem:* MLA; Polynesian Soc. *Res:* Renaissance theatre of Spain and Portugal; Malayo-Polynesian languages; Nahuatl. *Publ:* Coauth, On destructive criticism: A rejoinder to Mr Leo Spitzer, Mod Lang Forum, 12/56; auth, Juan del Encino: Prometheus in Search of Prestige, Univ Calif, 59; The harmonizing perspective of Gil Vicente, Bull Comediantes, fall 59; coauth, Patterns for Reading Spanish, Appleton, 64; Two notes for Lope de Vega's El Villano En Su Rincon, Bull Comediantes, fall 66. *Mailing Add:* Dept of Spanish VAnderbilt Univ Nashville TN 37240

ANDREWS, NORWOOD, JR, b Camden, NJ, Oct 2, 34; m; c 2. LUSO-BRAZILIAN & SPANISH LITERATURES. *Educ:* Oberlin Col, BA, 57; Univ Ore, MA, 59; Univ Wis, Madison, PhD(Port), 64. *Prof Exp:* From asst prof to assoc prof Span & Port, Vanderbilt Univ, 64-70; chmn dept class & Romance lang, 70-74, chmn acad prog comp lit, 72-76, PROF ROMANCE LANG, TEX TECH UNIV, 70- *Honors & Awards:* Officer, Order of the Southern Cross, Brazil, 72. *Mem:* Am Asn Teachers Span & Port; MLA; Am Soc 18th Century Studies. *Res:* Nineteenth century Brazilian novel; 18th century Spanish literature. *Publ:* Auth, An essay on Camoes concept of the epic, Rev Letras, Brazil, 3/62; Early anticipations of naturalism in Brazil: The dramatic novels of Bernardo Guimaraes, Papers Lang & Lit, 8/72; Some notes on the mythography of Bernardo Guimaraes, Hispania, 73. *Mailing Add:* Dept of Class & Romance Lang Tex Tech Univ Lubbock TX 79409

ANDREWS, OLIVER, JR, b Montclair, NJ, May 26, 17; m 53; c 4. FOREIGN LANGUAGE. *Educ:* Harvard Univ, BS, 39; Middlebury Col, MA, 47; McGill Univ, PhD, 56. *Prof Exp:* Master French & Span, Gov Dummer Acad, 39-43; asst prof French, Bates Col, 48-52; from asst prof to assoc prof, Purdue Univ, 56-60; prof French & head dept mod lang, St Lawrence Univ, 60-66; head dept Romance & class lang, 66-77, PROF FRENCH, UNIV CONN, 66- *Concurrent Pos:* Nat exam coordr, Am Asn Teachers Fr, 58-60; exec dir, Charles Irwin Travelli Scholar Fund, 60-; consult, NDEA Insts, US Off Educ & MLA, 61-66; rep, Sch-Col Foreign Lang Prog, Conn, 68-74. *Honors & Awards:* Palmes Academiques, 60. *Mem:* Am Asn Teachers Fr; MLA; Am Coun Teaching Foreign Lang; Northeast Conf Teaching Foreign Lang. *Res:* Contemporary French economic and political history; audio-visual foreign language teaching; language laboratory methodology. *Publ:* Auth, Chat with Roger Martin du Gard, 5/59 & Explaining modern France, 2/60, Fr Rev; Foreign language in public shcools, Ind Teacher, 5/60. *Mailing Add:* Dept of Romance & Class Lang Univ of Conn Storrs CT 06268

ANDREWS, WALTER GUILFORD, b Pittsburgh, Pa, May 23, 39; m 62; c 2. NEAR EAST LITERATURE, TURKISH. *Educ:* Carleton Col, BA, 61; Univ Mich, Ann Arbor, MA, 63 & 65, PhD(Turkish lan & lit), 70. *Prof Exp:* Acting asst prof Turkish, 68-70, asst prof, 71-76, ASSOC PROF TURKISH, UNIV WASH, 76- *Concurrent Pos:* Nat Endowment Humanities younger humanist fel, 73-74. *Mem:* Mid E Studies Asn NAm; Am Orient Soc; MLA. *Res:* Critical methodologies and literary theory for the study of Turkish, especially Ottoman literature. *Publ:* Auth, A critical-interpretive approach to the Ottoman Turkish gazel, Int J Med E Studies, 73; Introduction to Ottoman Poetry, Bibliotheca Islamica, 76. *Mailing Add:* Dept of Near E Lang & Lit Univ of Wash Seattle WA 98195

ANDRIAN, GUSTAVE WILLIAM, b Hartford, Conn, Sept 17, 18; m 51; c 3. ROMANCE LANGUAGES. *Educ:* Trinity Col, Conn, BA, 40; Johns Hopkins Univ, PhD, 46. *Prof Exp:* Instr Romance lang, Univ Md, 43-44, asst prof, 45-46; from asst prof to assoc prof, 46-62, chmn dept mod lang, 65-70, prof, 62-80, JOHN J MCCOOK PROF MOD LANG, TRINITY COL, CONN, 80- *Mem:* MLA; Am Asn Teachers Span & Port; Am Asn Teachers Fr. *Res:* Contemporary Spanish literature. *Publ:* Ed, Modern Spanish Prose and Poetry: An Introductory Reader, 64, 2nd ed, 69, 3rd ed, 78 & Fondo y Forma, 70, Macmillan; Early use of the lyric monologue in French drama of the seventeenth century, Mod Lang Notes. *Mailing Add:* Dept of Mod Lang Trinity Col Hartford CT 06106

ANDRONICA, JOHN LOUIS, b Boston, Mass, Oct 6, 42; m 66; c 2. CLASSICAL LANGUAGES. *Educ:* Col of the Holy Cross, AB, 63; Boston Col, MA, 66; Johns Hopkins Univ, PhD(classics), 69. *Prof Exp:* Asst prof classic lang, 69-72, dir, Wake Forest-in-Venice Prog, 71-72 & 81, ASSOC PROF CLASS LANG, WAKE FOREST UNIV, 72- *Mem:* Am Philol Asn; Class Asn Midwest & South; Vergiliam Soc; Petronian Soc. *Res:* Latin love elegy; Latin epic. *Mailing Add:* Dept of Class Lang Wake Forest Univ Winston-Salem NC 27109

ANDRUSYSHEN, CONSTANTINE HENRY, b Winnipeg, Man, July 19, 07. SLAVIC PHILOLOGY. *Educ:* Univ Man, BA, 29, MA, 30; Univ Toronto, PhD, 40. *Prof Exp:* Tutor Ital, Univ Toronto, 40; ed, Can Farmer, Winnipeg, Man, 40-44; res fel, Harvard Univ, 44-45; Simpson prof Slavic studies & head dept, 45-76, EMER PROF SLAVIC STUDIES, UNIV SASK, 76- *Mem:* Fel Ukrainian Sci Soc; Royal Soc Can. *Res:* Anatole France and Ernest Renan; annotations of ten Ukrainian novels summarized in English; cultural relationships between western and eastern Europe. *Publ:* Auth, Ukrainian-English Dict, 55; co-transl & compiler, The Ukrainian Poets & Poetical Works of T Shevchenko, Univ Toronto, 63; ed & transl, Vasyl Stefanyk: The Stone Cross, McClelland & Stewart, Toronto, 72. *Mailing Add:* 1120 Main St Saskatoon SK S7H 0K9 Can

ANGELIS, PAUL J, b Scranton, Pa, Jan 28, 41; m 65; c 3. LINGUISTICS. *Educ:* Univ Scranton, AB, 62; Georgetown Univ, PhD(ling), 68. *Prof Exp:* Asst prof English, Col Mil Royal, 69-72; Fulbright lectr ling & English, Univ Rome, 72-73; training dir, Food & Agr Orgn UN, 73-74; from assoc to asst prof ling & English, Tex A&M Univ, 74-77; prog dir lang, Educ Test Serv, 77-81; ASSOC PROF & CHMN LING, SOUTHERN ILL UNIV, 81- *Mem:* Teachers English Speakers Other Lang; Nat Asn Foreign Student Affairs; Ling Soc Am. *Res:* Language testing; second language acquisition; English as a foreign language. *Publ:* Auth, The importance and diversity of aural comprehension, Mod Lang J, 3/73; Listening comprehension and erroranalysis, AILA Proc, 74; coauth, The performance of non-native speakers of English on Toefl and verbal aptitude tests, 78 & Effects of item disclosure of Toefl performance, 12/80, Educ Testing Serv; Psycholinguistics: Two views, In: Language and Communication, Hornbeam Press, 80. *Mailing Add:* Dept of Ling Southern Ill Univ Carbondale IL 62901

ANGENOT, MARC M, b Brussels, Belgium, Dec 21, 41; m 66; c 2. COMPARATIVE LITERATURE, FRENCH. *Educ:* Free Univ, Brussels, Lic Phil, 62, PhD(Romance philol), 67. *Prof Exp:* Res fel, Nat Belg Fund Sci Res, 63-67; asst prof French, 67-72, assoc prof French, 72-80, PROF COMP LIT, MCGILL UNIV, 80- *Concurrent Pos:* Ed, Genres et discours, Univ Que Press, 73- & Sci Fiction Studies, 78- *Mem:* Can Comp Lit Asn; Can Semiotic Asn. *Res:* Semiotics; theory of literary genres; popular culture. *Publ:* Auth, Glossaire de la Critique Litteraire Contemporaine, Hurtubise, Montreal, 72; Art: Les Traites de L'eloquence du Corps, Semiotica, 73; Le Roman populaire--Recherches en Paralitterature, 75 & Les Champions des Femmes, 77, PUQ, Montreal; Topos/presuppose/ideologeme, Etudes Francaises, 77; Le Paradigme Absent, Poetique, 78; La Parole Pamphletaire, Payot, Paris, 82. *Mailing Add:* Dept of French McGill Univ 3460 McTavish Montreal PQ H3A 1X9 Can

ANGER, ALFRED, b Essen, WGer, Dec 10, 27; US citizen, m 60; c 2. GERMANIC LANGUAGES & LITERATURES. *Educ:* Univ Cologne, PhD(Ger), 54. *Prof Exp:* Lectr Ger, Univ Cologne, 54-55 & Free Univ, Berlin, 55-60; vis prof, City Col New York, 59-60; lectr, Univ Bonn, 60-62; from asst prof to assoc prof, 62-69, PROF GER, CITY UNIV NEW YORK, 70-, EXEC OFF, GRAD PROG GER LANG & LIT, GRAD SCH & UNIV CTR, 74- *Concurrent Pos:* Fulbright fel, 59-60; vis prof ordinarius, Univ Göttingen, 67-68, Ruhr Univ & Univ Cologne, 71-72 & Univ Heidelberg, 73; res grant, Free Univ Berlin, 57-58 & City Col New York, 63 & 65; Ger Nat Res Found travel grant, 67-68; Res Found City Univ New York, res grant, 71-72; Guggenheim fel, 75. *Mem:* Am Asn Teachers Ger; MLA; Soc 18th Century Studies; Lessing Soc; Kafka Soc Am. *Res:* German literature of the 17th and 18th centuries; Goethe. *Publ:* Auth, Landschaftsstil des Rokoko, Euphorion, 57; Literarisches Rokoko, 62, 2nd ed, 68 & Deutsche Rokokodichtung: Ein Forschungsbericht, 63, J B Metzler; Der Leipziger Goethe, Deutsches Hochstift, 72; Europisches Rokoko und deutsche Rokokodichtung, Neues Handbuch der Literaturewissenschaft, Aufklärung, Vol XI, 74; co-ed, Gedichte von L A von Arnim, Max Niemeyer Verlag, 76. *Mailing Add:* Grad Sch & Univ Ctr City Univ of New York Grad Prog in Ger 33 West 42nd St New York NY 10036

ANGIOLILLO, PAUL FRANCIS, b New York, NY, July 1, 17; m 48; c 4. ROMANCE LANGUAGES. *Educ:* Columbia Univ, AB, 38, AM, 39, PhD, 46. *Prof Exp:* Prof Am studies, Ecole Int, Geneva, Switz, 47-48; from asst prof to prof mod lang, Univ Louisville, 48-62, dir res, 53-54; chmn dept mod langs, 62-72 & 73-74, secy fac, 73-75, prof French & Ital, 62-81, CHARLES A DANA EMER PROF ROMANCE LANG, DICKINSON COL, 81- *Concurrent Pos:* Albert Gallatin fel, Inst Int Educ, Geneva, 46-47; Fulbright prof, France, 56-57; Ital Govt studies award, Univ Siena, 66; chmn dept foreign lang, Am Col Switz, 68-69. *Honors & Awards:* First Prize, Geneva-London Press Lit Contest, 47; officier, Palmes Academiques, 61; Lindback Distinguished Teaching Award, 65; Grande Award for Inspirational Teaching, Sr Grad Class, Dickinson Col, 75. *Mem:* Am Asn Teachers Fr; Am Asn Teachers Ital; MLA; Soc Fr Prog Am. *Res:* French language and literature; teacher-training in modern foreign languages; Italian language and culture. *Publ:* Auth, French for the feeble-minded: An experiment, Mod Lang J, 4/42; Armed Forces Foreign-Language Teaching, Vanni, 47; Reflections of a department head, Improving Col & Univ Teaching, winter 64; Cecco Angiolieri, scamp & poet of Medieval Siena, Forum Italicum 9/67; contribr, Studies in Honor of Mario A Pei, Univ NC, 3/72; auth, A Criminal as Hero: Angelo Duca, Regents Press, 79. *Mailing Add:* Dept of Mod Lang Dickinson Col Carlisle PA 17013

ANGRESS, RUTH K, b Vienna, Austria, Oct 30, 31; US citizen; div; c 2. GERMANIC LANGUAGE & LITERATURE. *Educ:* Hunter Col, BA, 50; Univ Calif, Berkeley, MA, 53, PhD(Ger), 67. *Prof Exp:* Asst prof Ger, Calif State Col, Hayward, 65-66; from asst prof to assoc prof, Case Western Reserve Univ, 66-70; assoc prof, Univ Kans, 70-73 & Univ Va, 73-76; prof, Univ Calif, Irvine, 76-79; PROF GER, PRINCETON UNIV, 80- *Concurrent Pos:* Vis prof Ger, Univ Cincinnati, 72-73; ed, Ger Quart, 78-; Am Coun Learned Soc res fel, 78-79. *Mem:* MLA; Am Asn Teachers Ger; Am Lessing Soc. *Publ:* Auth, The Early German Epigram: A Study in Baroque Poetry Univ Ky, 71; Dreams that were more than dreams in Lessing's Nathan, Lessing Yearbk III, 71; Lessing's criticism of Cronegk, Lessing Yearbk IV, 72; Das Gespenst in Grillparzers Ahnfrau, Ger Quart, 72; Women in popular fuction, Women Studies, 75; Schnitzler's Frauenroman Therese, Mod Austrian Lit, 77; Kleist's treatment of Imperialism, Montshefte, 77. *Mailing Add:* Dept of Ger Princeton Univ Princeton NJ 08540

ANTAKI, VIVIAN JANE, b New York, NY, Apr 28, 49; m 77. COMPARATIVE LITERATURE. *Educ:* Mills Col, BA, 70; Univ Colo, Boulder, MA, 72, PhD(comp lit), 78. *Prof Exp:* Instr Span, Univ Colo, 74-77; reasearcher lit, Inst de Inv Filologicas, 78-81; coordr, Lit Dept, 79-80, PROF LIT, DEPT LETRAS, DEPT INTERNACIONAL, UNIV IBEROAMERICANA, 79- *Concurrent Pos:* Vis researcher, Centro de Int Ling & Lit, Col Mex, 79; consult, 79-80. *Mem:* Am Comp Lit Asn; MLA. *Res:* Twentieth century theater; Latin American literature. *Publ:* Auth, Stanislavsky y Brecht, dos metodos de actuacion, Op Cit, Vol II, Mexico City, 1/81; Pirandello y su impacto en el teatro frances, Rev de Letras, 1/82 & Sartre en la literature, Rev de Filosofia, 5/82, Univ Iberoamericana. *Mailing Add:* Dept de Letras Univ Iberoamericana Mexico City DF 04200 Mexico

ANTHONY, DAVID FORSYTH, History. See Vol I

ANTHONY, EDWARD MASON, b Cleveland, Ohio, Sept 1, 22; m 46; c 3. LINGUISTICS. *Educ:* Univ Mich, AB, 44, MA, 46, PhD(ling), 54. *Prof Exp:* Instr English, Univ Mich, 45-55, admis officer, 50-55, from asst prof to assoc prof English, 55-64, prof ling, 64, actg dir, English Lang Inst, 63-64; acmn, Dept Ling, 67-74, actg chmn, Dept Ger, 72-73, dir asian studies prog, 78-82, PROF LING, UNIV PITTSBURGH, 64-, DIR, LANG ORIENT INST, 74- *Concurrent Pos:* Consult, Royal Afghan Ministry Educ, Kabul, 51, Thai Ministry Educ, Bangkok, 55-57, US Oper Mission, Cambodia, 58-61, Philippines, 59 & Burma, 60, 61; dir, Southeast Asian Regional English Proj, 58-61; mem adv comt training teachers, Japan, 63; consult, US Off Educ, 64-, Pittsburgh Bd Educ, 65 & US Agency Int Develop, 66; dir, Rockefeller Found/Univ Pittsburgh Thailand Proj, 67-71; mem nat screening comt, Foreign Area Fel Prog, 72; vis prof ling, Southeast Asian Ministers Educ Orgn, Singapore, 74-75; mem, Fulbright Screening Comn English & Ling, Coun Int Exchange Scholars, 75-; consult English lang teaching, US Dept State, Poland, 77, 78, Yugoslavia, 81. *Mem:* Ling Soc Am; Siam Soc; Asn Asian Studies; Asn Teachers English to Speakers Other Lang (pres, 67-68). *Res:* Teaching of English as a foreign language; Thai language; English linguistics. *Publ:* Auth, A Programmed Course in Reading Thai Syllables, Univ Mich, 62; Approach, method, and technique, English Lang Teaching, 63; coauth, Foundations of Thai (4 vols), Univ Mich/Off Educ, 68; auth, Towards a Theory of Lexical Meaning, Singapore Univ, 75; Lexicon and vocabulary, Regional English Lang Ctr J, 6/75; English for special purposes: A lexical context, Regional English Lang Ctr Anthol, 76; co-ed, Reading: Insights and Approaches, Singapore Univ, 76. *Mailing Add:* Lang and Cult Inst 4E38 Quadrangle Univ of Pittsburgh Pittsburgh PA 15260

ANTOLIN, FRANCISCO, b San Pedro Guardo, Spain, Sept 15, 27; Can citizen; m 64; c 4. SPANISH & SPANISH AMERICAN LITERATURE. *Educ:* Univ Oviedo, BA, 54; Univ Madrid, MA, 59, PhD(hist), 66; MA, Univ Nac Autonoma Mexico City, MA, 75. *Prof Exp:* Lectr Span lit, Col St Maria la Real, Spain, 59-62; lectr French, Inst Ramiro de Maeztu, 62-64; lectr Span lang & lit, Inst St Lazare, France, 64-65; asst prof, Laurentian Univ, 65-68; ASSOC PROF SPAN LANG & LIT, CONCORDIA UNIV, 68- *Concurrent Pos:* Juan March Found fel, 67-69; lectureships, Univ PQ, Montreal, 70 & Cercle Cervantes-Camoens, Laval Univ, 72-73. *Mem:* Am Asn Teachers Span & Port; Can Asn Hispanists; Can Asn Latin Am Studies. *Res:* Mexican literature; Spanish American civilization. *Publ:* Auth, El Valle del Bazton, Univ Madrid, 68; Los escritores del boom, 7/71 & Pablo Neruda, 11/71, Mosotros. *Mailing Add:* Dept of Mod Lang Concordia Univ Montreal PQ H4B 1R6 Can

ANTONSEN, ELMER H, b Glens Falls, NY, Nov 17, 29; m 56; c 2. GERMANTIC LINGUISTICS. *Educ:* Union Col, NY, BA, 51; Univ Ill, MA, 57, PhD(Ger), 61. *Prof Exp:* Instr Ger, Northwestern Univ, 59-61; from asst prof to assoc prof Ger ling, Univ Iowa, 61-67; assoc prof Germ lang, 67-70, head dept Ger lang & lit, 73-82, PROF GER & LING, UNIV ILL, URBANA-CHAMPAIGN, 70- *Concurrent Pos:* Corresp mem overseas, Res Coun Inst Ger Lang, 69-; vis prof Ger & Ling, Univ NC, Chapel Hill, 72-73. *Mem:* Ling Soc Am; MLA; Soc Advan Scand Studies; Selskab for nordisk filologi. *Res:* Historical and structural Germanic linguistics; Runic inscriptions. *Publ:* Contribr, Toward a Grammar of Proto-Germanic, Max Niemeyer, 72; Studies for Einar Haugen, Mouton, 72; auth, Suprasegmentalia im Deutschen, Jahrbuch Int Germanistik, 7/73; A Concise Grammar of Older Runic Inscriptions, Max Niemeyer, 75; Linguistics and politics in the 19th century: The case of the 15th rune, 80 & On the syntax of the older runic inscriptions, 81, Mich Ger Studies; Den aeldre futhark: En gudernes gave eller et hverdagsalfabet?, Maal og Minne, 80. *Mailing Add:* Dept of Ger Lang Univ of Ill at Urbana-Champaign Urbana IL 61801

ANTTILA, RAIMO, b Lieto, Finland, Apr 21, 35; m 59; c 2. INDO-EUROPEAN & HISTORICAL LINGUISTICS. *Educ:* Yale Univ PhD(ling), 66. *Prof Exp:* Acting asst prof, Indo-Europ ling, 65-66, asst prof, 66-70, assoc prof, 70-80, PROF LING, UNIV CALIF, LOS ANGELES, 80- *Concurrent Pos:* Prof gen ling, Univ Helsinki, 71-76; ling ed, J Indo-Europ Studies, 72-; mem adv bd, Historiographia Linguistica & Amsterdam Studies Theory & Hist Ling Sci, 73-; co-ed, Language, 76- *Mem:* Ling Soc Am; Finno-Ugrian Soc; Ling Asn Can; Ling Asn Am. *Res:* General, Indo-European, and historical linguistics. *Publ:* Auth, Proto-Indo-European Schwebeaclaut, Univ Calif, 69; An Introduction to Historical and Comparative Linguistics, Macmillan, 72; The Indexical Element in Morphology, Univ Innsbruck, 75; Analogy, Mouton, The Hague, 77; coauth, Analogy: A Basic Bibliography, John Benjamins, Amsterdam, 78. *Mailing Add:* Dept of Ling Univ of Calif Los Angeles CA 90024

AOKI, HARUO, b Kunsan, Korea, Apr 1, 30. LINGUISTICS. *Educ:* Hiroshima Univ, BA, 53; Univ Calif, Los Angeles, MA, 58; Univ Calif Berkeley, PhD(ling), 65. *Prof Exp:* Instr Orient lang, Univ Calif, Berkeley, 61-62 & Stanford Univ, Ctr Japanese Studies, Tokyo, 62-64; acting asst prof, 64-65, from asst prof to assoc prof, 65-72, PROF ORIENT LANG, UNIV CALIF, BERKELEY, 72- *Concurrent Pos:* Co-dir, Stanford-Univ Calif, NDEA E Asia Lang & Area Ctr, 73-74. *Mem:* Ling Soc Japan; Ling Soc Am; Am Orient Soc; Ling Asn Gt Brit; Ling Circle Copenhagen. *Res:* Japanese linguistics; linguistic prehistory of East Asia and North America; American Indian linguistics. *Publ:* Coauth, The Utility of Translation and Writtern Symbols During the First Thirty Hours of Language Study, 62 & auth, Nez Perce Grammar, 70, Univ Calif; A note on glottalized consonants, Phonetica, 70; A note on language change, Studies Am Indian Lang, 71; Reconstruction of Japanese vowels, Papers Japanese Ling, 72; Nez Perce texts, Univ Calif, 79. *Mailing Add:* Dept of Orient Lang Univ of Calif Berkeley CA 94720

APARICIO-LAURENCIO, ANGEL, b Guantanamo, Cuba, Sept 15, 28; m 61; c 2. FOREIGN LANGUAGES, LAW. *Educ:* Univ Havana, Dr Derecho, 51; Univ Madrid, dipl penitentiary studies, 53, Dr Derecho, 54. *Prof Exp:* Pvt prac law, Havana, Cuba, 55-59; legal adv, Ministry Revolutionary Laws, Cuba, 59; tech adv Presidency, Repub Cuba, 59-60; deleg Cuban revolutionary coun, Rio de Janeiro & Chile, 61-64; prof law, Univ America, Bogota, 65; asst prof Span lit, 66-72, dir prog in Spain, 69-70, 72, prog in San Salvador, 71, assoc prof, 72-80, PROF SPAN LIT, UNIV REDLANDS, 80- *Concurrent Pos:* Tech asst, Comn Penitentiary Reform, Cuba, 59-60; deleg, Inter-Am Bar Asn Conf, Bogota, 61; adv, Cuban Comt Bill of Rights, Orgn Am States, Santiago, Chile, 63; teacher, Berlitz Sch Lang, Los Angeles, 66. *Mem:* AAUP; MLA; Am Asn Teachers Span & Port. *Res:* The poetry of Jose Maria Heredia; the Cuban revolution; Rafael Maria Merchan. *Publ:* Auth, Poesias Completas de Jose Maria Heredia, 70, Cinco Poetisas Cubanas, 70 & Herdia: Selected Poems in English Translations, 70, Ed Universal, Spain; Extrano mundo del amanecer, Azor, 11-12/71; Las cartas sobre la mitologia, Poesia Hist, 9/72; Juan Clemente Zenea, Yelmo, 10-11/72; Trabajos desconocidos y olividados de Jose Maria Heredia, 72 & Juan Clemente Zenea: diario de un martir y otros poemas, 72, Ed Universal, Spain. *Mailing Add:* Dept of Spanish Univ of Redlands Redlands CA 92373

APONTE, BARBARA BOCKUS, b Philadelphia, Pa, July 6, 36; m 63. ROMANCE LANGUAGES. *Educ:* Vassar Col, BA, 57; Nat Univ Mex, MA, 59; Univ Tex, PhD(Span), 64. *Prof Exp:* From asst prof to assoc prof Span, 64-73, chmn dept Span & Port, 75-77, PROF SPAN, TEMPLE UNIV, 73-, ASSOC DEAN, COL LIB ARTS, 77- *Mem:* MLA; Latin Am Studies Asn. *Res:* Contemporary Latin American literature. *Publ:* Auth, El dialogo entre J R Jimenez and Alfonso Reyes, La Torre, winter 66; The dialogue between Alfonso Reyes and Spain, Symposium, spring 68; Alfonso Reyes and Spain, Univ Tex, 72; Lenguaje y metamorfosis en Severo Sraduy, Rio Piedras, 3/73; Entrevista con Ricardo Gullon, Cuadernos Hispanoamericanos, 3/73; La Obra Critica de Ricardo Gullon, Insula, 75; La creacion del espacio en El Recurso del Metoco, Revista Iberoam, 7-12/76; translr, The Docile Puerto Rican, Temple Univ, 76. *Mailing Add:* Dept of Span Temple Univ Philadelphia PA 19122

APPLEGATE, JOSEPH ROYE, b Wildwood, NJ, Dec 4, 25. DESCRIPTIVE LINGUISTICS. *Educ:* Temple Univ, BSc, 45; Univ Pa, AM, 48, PhD(ling), 55. *Prof Exp:* Teacher voc & high schs, Pa, 46-55; res linguist, Mass Inst Technol, 55-56, asst prof mod lang, 56-60, dir lang lab, 57-60; asst prof Berber lang, Univ Calif, Los Angeles, 60-66; prof ling, 66-69, dir African studies prog, 67-69, PROF LING & AFRICAN STUDIES, HOWARD UNIV, 69- *Concurrent Pos:* Lang teaching methodology & lang of Morocco, US Peace Corps, 62-63; consult lang lab prog, Ford Found & Nat Univ Mex, 63; researcher Berber lang, US Off Educ; mem, Groupe Ling Etudes Chamito Semitiques; consult comt, Educ Resources Info Ctr, 67-; consult, Nat Endowment for Humanities, 68- & Nat Geog Soc, 74- *Mem:* African Studies Asn; Ling Soc Am; Am Orient Soc; Nat Asn Foreign Studies Affairs; Ling Soc Paris. *Res:* Berber languages; language learning; sociolinguistics. *Publ:* Auth, A grammar of Shilha: The Berber languages, Current Trends Ling, 70. *Mailing Add:* African Studies & Research Prog Howard Univ Washington DC 20001

APPLEWHITE, JAMES V, b New Orleans, La, Sept 18, 37; m 65; c 1. ROMANCE LANGUAGES. *Educ:* Amherst Col, BA, 59; Tulane Univ, PhD(French), 68. *Prof Exp:* Instr French, Davidson Col, 63-65; spec lectr, La State Univ, New Orleans, 65-66; asst prof Romance lang, State Univ NY Binghamton, 66-69; assoc prof, Notre Dame Col, NY, 69-70; PROF FOREIGN LANG, CHEYNEY STATE COL, 70- *Mem:* MLA; Am Asn Teachers Ital. *Res:* French realism and naturalism; Dante; Italian verismo. *Publ:* Auth, Dante's use of the extended simile in the Inferno, Italica, 9/64. *Mailing Add:* Box 181 Cheyney State Col Cheyney PA 19139

APTE, MAHADEV L, b Devache Gothne, India, Feb 1, 31; m 62; c 2. LINGUISTICS & ANTHROPOLOGY. *Educ:* Bombay Univ, BA, 52, MA, 54; Univ London, MA, 58; Univ Wis-Madison, PhD(ling & anthrop), 62. *Prof Exp:* Res asst Marathi, Sch Orient & African Studies, London, 55-57; res fel ling, Deccan Col Post-Grad & Res Inst, Poona, 58-59; instr Hindi, Univ Wis-Madison, 62-63; reader ling, Univ Poona, 63-65; vis lectr Hindi & ling, 65-66, asst prof ling & anthrop, 66-68, ASSOC PROF ANTHROP, DUKE UNIV, 68- *Concurrent Pos:* Sr fel & grantee, Am Inst Indian Studies, 71-72 & 79-80. *Mem:* Ling Soc Am; fel Am Anthrop Asn; Asn Asian Studies; Ling Soc India; Soc Appl Anthrop. *Res:* Sociolinguistics; ethnography of humor; acculturation and ethnicity. *Publ:* Auth, Reduplication, Echo Formation and Onomatopoeia in Marathi, Deccan Col Post-Grad & Res Inst, Poona, 68; Some Sociolinguistic aspects of interlingual communication in India, Anthrop Ling, 70; Pidginization of a lingua franca: A linguistic analysis of Hindi-Urdu spoken in Bombay, In: Contact and Convergence in South Asian Languages, Trivandrum, India, 74; Thank You and South Asian languages: A comparative sociolinguistic study, Int J Sociol Lang, 74; ed, Contact and Convergence in South Asian Languages, spec issue Int J Dravidian Ling, Trivandrum, India, 74; auth, Language controversies in the Indian parliament: 1952-1960, In: Language and Politics, 76 & Region, religion and language: Parameters of identity in the process of acculturation, In: The New Wind: Changing Identities in South Asia & World Anthropology, 77, Mouton, The Hague; ed, Mass Culture, Language and Arts in India, Popular Prakashan, Bombay. *Mailing Add:* Dept of Anthrop Duke Univ Durham NC 27706

APTER, RONNIE SUSAN, Literary Translation, Opera Libretti. See Vol II

ARAGNO, PIERO, b Turin, Italy, Sept 15, 32; US citizen. ITALIAN LITERATURE. *Educ:* Univ Mich, BA, 63; Rutgers Univ, MA, 66, PhD(Ital), 69. *Prof Exp:* Lectr, Princeton Univ, 66-69; asst prof, 69-73, ASSOC PROF ITAL, UNIV WIS-MADISON, 73- *Concurrent Pos:* Dir jr yr abroad in Bologna, Italy, Univ Wis, 74-75. *Mem:* Am Fedn Teachers Ital; MLA. *Res:* Modern Italian literature, novel, theatre and film. *Publ:* Auth, Il Ramanzo di Silone, Longo, Ravenna, Italy, 75. *Mailing Add:* Dept of Fr & Ital Univ of Wis 1220 Linden Dr Madison WI 53706

ARAKI, JAMES TOMOMASA, b Salt Lake City, Utah, June 18, 25; m 57; c 4. ORIENTAL LANGUAGES. *Educ:* Univ Calif, Los Angeles, BA, 54; Univ Calif, Berkeley, MA, 58, PhD(Orient lang), 61. *Prof Exp:* Lectr Japanese, Stanford Univ, 61; from instr to asst prof Orient lang, Univ Calif, Los Angeles, 61-64; PROF JAPANESE LIT, UNIV HAWAII, MANOA, 64-, CHMN DEPT EAST ASIAN LIT, 71- *Concurrent Pos:* Fulbright res fel, Japan, 64-65; sr specialist grant, East-West Ctr, 67, sr fel, 70-71; Am Coun Learned Soc res fel, 7-; Japan Found fel, 77. *Mem:* Asn Asian Studies; Asn Teachers Japanese. *Res:* Medieval Japanese drama and prose; edo period of Japanese fiction; contemporary Japanese fiction. *Publ:* Auth, The Ballad-Drama of Medieval Japan, Univ Calif, 64, rev ed, Charles E Tuttle, 77; cotranslr, T Muraoka, Studies in Shinto Thought, Japanese Nat Comn UNESCO, 64; auth, Sharebon: Books for Men of Mode, 1/69 & The Dream Pillow in Edo Fiction: 1772-1781, 70, Monumenta Nipponica; translr, The Roof Tile of Tempyo, Univ Tokyo, 75; auth, Yuriwaka and Ulysses, Monumenta Nipponica, 78; cotransl, Lou-lan and Other Stories, Kodansha Int, 79; auth, Otogi-zoshi and Nara-ehon, Monumenta Nipponica, 81. *Mailing Add:* Dept of E Asian Lit Univ of Hawaii Manoa Honolulu HI 96822

ARALUCE, JOSE RAMON, b Madrid, Spain, Sept 25, 33; US citizen;. ROMANCE PHILOLOGY, MEDIEVAL SPANISH LITERATURE. *Educ:* Univ Madrid, Lic Law, 57; Inst Estud Polit, dipl sociol, 58; Univ Bern Dr(Int law), 60; Fla State Univ, MA, 65, PhD(Span), 69. *Prof Exp:* Instr Span, Fla State Univ, 64-67; from instr to asst prof, 67-72, ASSOC PROF SPAN, UNIV SOUTHERN CALIF, 72- *Concurrent Pos:* Guest lectr, CBS TV, Los Angeles, 70; vis lectr Span Medieval lit, Univ Calif, Los Angeles, 71-72; prof lit, Inst de Espana, Cairo, 74-75. *Honors & Awards:* Assoc Award Excellence in Teaching, Univ Southern Calif, 72-73. *Mem:* MLA; AAUP; Am Asn Teachers Span & Port; Philol Asn Pac Coast. *Res:* Syntactic, morphologic, phonetic and etymologic development of Peninsular Romance; Semitic-Arabic influence on Peninsular literature; origins of Arabic, Gallician-Portuguese and Castilian lyric poetry. *Publ:* Auth, El Libro de los Estados: Don Juan Manuel y la Sociedad de su Tiempo, Purrua Turanzas, Madrid, 76; Dos cartas ineditas de M de Unamuno y una nota de M Garcia Blanco, Cuadernos de la Catedra M de Unamuno, 76; Tradicion y originalidad en el Don Rodrigo de Alejandro Casona, Revista Hisp Mod, 77. *Mailing Add:* Dept of Span & Port Univ of Southern Calif University Park Los Angeles CA 90007

ARANA, NELSON G, b Trujillo, Peru, Mar 8, 27; US citizen; div; c 2. SPANISH & LATIN AMERICAN LITERATURE. *Educ:* Nat Normal Sch Educ, Lima, Peru, BA, 56; Tex Christian Univ, BS, 60, MA, 63; St Louis Univ, PhD(Span), 78. *Prof Exp:* Instr English & Span, 63-64, asst prof, 66-77, ASSOC PROF SPAN, UNIV SDAK, VERMILLION, 78- *Mem:* Am Asn Teachers Span & Port. *Res:* Contemporary Spanish American novel and short story; contemporary peninsular novel and medieval peninsular literature. *Publ:* Auth, Liberlad (poem), Germinal, Lima, Peru, 9/48; El simbulismo del Agua en el Popol-Vuh, Revista de la Literatura Hispano Americana, Venezuela, 7-12/74; Notas sobre el Libro de Buen Amor y la Sociedad Medieval Espanola, Cuadernos Americanos, Mex, 7-8/76; Auth, Una satira social: La violencia y el elemento autobiografico, In: La ciudad y los perros, Univ NDak, 3/80. *Mailing Add:* 136 Walker St Vermillion SD 57069

ARANA, OSWALDO, b Cachicadan, Peru, June 14, 25; m 59; c 3. SPANISH, SPANISH AMERICAN LITERATURE. *Educ:* Tex Christian Univ, BA, 55; Univ Colo, MA, 57, PhD(Span), 63. *Prof Exp:* Consult Span, Mod Lang Materials Develop Ctr, New York, 60-61; asst prof, Univ Fla, 62-65; assoc prof, 65-71, PROF SPAN, CALIF STATE UNIV, FULLERTON, 71- *Concurrent Pos:* Consult, Mod Lang Materials Develop Ctr, New York, 62-64. *Mem:* MLA; Am Asn Teachers Span & Port; Am Coun Teaching Foreign Lang; Inst Int Lit Iberoam; Coun Latin Am Studies. *Res:* Contemporary Spanish American novel; the novel of the Chaco War; testing. *Publ:* Coauth, MLA-Cooperative Foreign Language Tests, Spanish Writing, Educ Testing Serv, 63-64; El hombre en la novela de la guerra del Chaco, J Inter-Am Studies, 7/64; MLA-Proficiency Tests for Teachers and Advanced Students, Spanish, Educ Testing Serv, 66; Reading for Meaning: Spanish, Harcourt, 66; La novela de la guerra del Chaco como ensayo antiguerrista, S Eastern Latin Americanist, XIII Nol, 5/69. *Mailing Add:* Dept of Foreign Lang & Lit Calif State Univ Fullerton CA 92631

ARANGO, MANUEL ANTONIO, b Yacopi-Cundinamarca, Colombia, Oct 31, 31; Can citizen, m 64; c 3. LATINOAMERICAN LITERATURE, SPANISH PHILOLOGY. *Educ:* Inst Caro y Cuervo, Colombia, dipl, 66; Univ Toronto, MA, 61; Interamericana Univ, Mexico, PhD(philos & letras), 78. *Prof Exp:* Asst prof, West Indies Univ, 63 & Dist Univ Bogota, 66-68; lectr, 68-71, asst prof, 71-80, ASSOC PROF SPAN, LAURENTIAN UNIV, 80- *Mem:* Am Asn Teachers Span & Port; Can Asn Latin Am Studies; Asoc Int Hisp; Inst Int Lit Iberoamericana; Ctr Etudes Iberiques & Ibero-Americaines XIX Siecle. *Res:* Latinoamerican novel; generacion del 27, peninsular literature Spain; Hispanoamerican poetry. *Publ:* Auth, Tres Figuras Representativas en la Generacion de Vanguardia en Hispanoamerica, Ed Procer, 67; Le social en dos novelas de Mariano Azuela: Mala Yerba y Los de Abajo, Calif State Univ, 73; Aspectos sociales en dos comedias de Lope de Vega, Cuadernos Americanos, Mex, 77; Correlacion Surrealista y social en dos novelas: El reino de este Mundo y Hombres de Maiz, Explicacion des Texto Lit, Calif State Univ, 78; Correlacion Social entre el caciquismo y el aspecto religioso, In: Pedro Paramo, Cuadernos Hispanoamericanos, Madrid, Espana, 78; El Gracioso, Sus cualidades y rasgos distintivos en cuatro dramaturgos del siglo XVII, Thesaurus, Inst Caro y Cuervo, Bogota, Tomo, 80; Relacion social e historica Afro-Espiritual y el Realismo Magico, In: Ecue-Yamba-O, Cuadernos Americanos, Mex, 81; Aspectos sociales en ocho escritores Hispanicos, Ed Tercer,Mundo, Bogota, 81. *Mailing Add:* Span Dept Univ Laurentienne Sudbury ON P3E 2C6 Can

ARANT, PATRICIA MAYHER, b Mobile, Ala, Dec 2, 30. SLAVIC LANGUAGE & LITERATURES. *Educ:* Ala Col, BA, 52; Radcliffe Col, AM, 57; Harvard Univ, PhD(Slavic), 63. *Prof Exp:* Researcher, US Govt, 52-56; asst prof Russ, Vanderbilt Univ, 63-65; asst prof Slavic lang, 65-70, assoc prof, 70-79, PROF SLAVIC LANG, BROWN UNIV, 79-, ASSOC DEAN, GRAD SCH, 81- *Concurrent Pos:* Am Philos Soc grant, 68-; Am Coun Learned Soc grant, 69 & grant for computer-oriented res humanities, 72; Int Res & Exchange Bd grant, 73; assoc, Russ Res Ctr, Harvard Univ, 78-69. *Mem:* Mediaeval Acad Am; Am Asn Advan Slavic Studies; MLA; Am Asn Teachers Slavic & E Europ Lang. *Res:* Slavic oral epic poetry and lament; 18th century Russian literature; early Russian literature. *Publ:* Auth, Formulaic style and the Russian Bylina, Ind Slavic Studies, 67; Concurrenece of patterns in the Russian Bylina, J Folkore Inst, 70; Repetition of prepositions in the Russian oral traditional lament, Slavic & East Europ J, 72; The persistence of narrative patterns: Variants of Dobrynja and Homer's Odyssey, Am Contrib 7th Int Cong Slavists, 74; Figurative and literal coupling in Russian oral traditional genres, Slavis & E Europ J, 75; Russian for reading: A classroom model and strategems, Russ Lang J, 78; Russian for Reading, Slavica Publ, 82. *Mailing Add:* Box E Brown Univ Providence RI 02912

ARAUJO, NORMAN, b New Bedford, Mass, Mar 22, 33. FOREIGN LANGUAGES. *Educ:* Harvard Col, AB, 55; Univ Aix-Marseille, cert, 55-56; Harvard Univ, MA, 57, PhD, 62. *Prof Exp:* Asst prof French & Port, Univ Mass, Amherst, 62-64; asst prof mod lang, 64-68, acting chmn dept, 69-70, ASSOC PROF ROMANCE LANG, BOSTON COL, 68- *Concurrent Pos:* Gulbenkian Found fel, 70; Cape Verdean Govt fel, 78. *Honors & Awards:* Bartolomeu Dias Prize, Acad Int Cult Portuguesa, 68. *Mem:* MLA; Int Conf Group Mod Port. *Res:* Portuguese and French romanticism; Portuguese-African Literature. *Publ:* Auth, A study of Cape Verdean literature, 66; Time and rhythm in Balzac's La Peau de Chagrin, Fr Rev, 70; The role of death in Becque's Les Corbeaux, Rev Langues Vivantes, 70; In Search of Eden: Lamartine's Symbols of Despair and Deliverance, Classical Folia Eds, 76; New Directions in Cape Verdean Literature?, The First Numbers of Raizes, Critical Perspectives on Lusophone African Literature, Three Continents Press, Inc, 81. *Mailing Add:* Dept of Romance Lang Boston Col Chestnut Hill MA 02167

ARBEITMAN, YÖEL, b New York, NY, June 30, 41. LINGUISTIC ARCHEOLOGY. *Educ:* Lehman Col, BA, 72; State Univ NY Buffalo, MA, 75; NY Univ, MA, 79; Univ Mich, PhD, 82. *Prof Exp:* Etymologist, Am Heritage Dict, 67-68; RES & WRITING, 75- *Concurrent Pos:* Dir, Ctr Bibl Onomastics, 78-; guest lectr Anatolians in Canaan, Soc Mediterranean

Studies, Toronto, 80 & 81. *Mem:* Soc Bibl Lit; Asn Jewish Studies; Am Orient Soc; Soc Mediterranean Studies; Int Maledicta Soc. *Res:* Indo-European linguistics; Biblical and targumic philology; comparative covenent terminology. *Publ:* Auth, Cuneiform and Hieroglyphic Luwain -za, Z fur vergleichende Sprachwissenschaft, Vol 90, 76; Look ma, What's become of the sacred tongues, Maledicta, Vol IV/1, 80; The recovery of an Indo-European collocation, proc First Int Conf Armenian Ling, 80; co-ed, Bono Homini Donum: Essays in Historical Linguistics in Memory of J Alexander Kerns, John Benjamins, 81; coauth, Adana revisited, Archiv Orientalni, Vol 49/2, 81; Bible, on Crete, and at Troy, Scripta Mediterranea, Vol III, 82; Transl, Otto Rossler, The Structure and Inflexion of the Verb in the Semito-Hamitic Languages & The Hittite is thy Mother: An Anatolian Approach to Genesis 23 (Ex Indo-Europea Lux), In: Bono Homini Donum. *Mailing Add:* 2741 Hone Ave Bronx NY 10469

ARBOLEDA, JOSEPH R, b New York, NY, Feb 15, 33. MODERN SPANISH LITERATURE. *Educ:* NY Univ, BA, 55; Univ Fla, 56; Princeton Univ, MA, 63, PhD(Span), 69. *Prof Exp:* Asst Span, Princeton Univ, 61-64; ASSOC PROF SPAN, LAFAYETTE COL, 64-, COORDR, SPANISH SECT, 66- *Concurrent Pos:* Jones fac lectr, 73. *Mem:* MLA; Am Asn Teachers Span & Port. *Res:* Spanish language; circulo cultural y casa de Espana; 19th century Spanish literature; 20th century Spanish literature. *Publ:* Auth, Mi conciencia y yo Becquer's first prose work, Studies Romanticism, winter 72; Valera y el Krausismo, Rev Estudios Hisp, 1/76; La Historia de los templos de Espana de Gustavo Adolfo Becquer, Puvill, Barcelona, 79; Derivations of French Hispanisms, Word, Vol 29. *Mailing Add:* 210 N 14th St Easton PA 18042

ARBOUR, ROMEO, b St Simeon, Que, June 26, 19. FRENCH LITERATURE. *Educ:* Univ Ottawa, BA, 42, MA, 43, PhD(arts), 47; Univ Paris, DUniv(lit), 55. *Prof Exp:* Dean students, Oblate Sem, Chambly, Que, 55-64; PROF FRENCH LIT, UNIV OTTAWA, 64- *Honors & Awards:* First Prize of Lit, Que, 57. *Mem:* Soc Can Writers; Int Asn Fr Studies; Asn Can Univ Teachers Fr. *Res:* French literature of the 17th century and the beginnings of the 20th century. *Publ:* Auth, Henri Bergson et les lettres Francaises, 56 & Les revues ephemeres a Paris de 1900 a 1914, 56, Corti, Paris; coauth, Pierre Charron et ses idees sociales, 7/70 & auth, Langage et societe dans les nouvelles francoises de Charles Sorel, 4/71, Rev Univ Ottawa; Bergson, In: Dictionnaire des Lettres Francaises, Fayard, Paris, 72; Critical edition of Du Perier's Les Amours de Pistion et de Fortunie, 73 & Critical edition of Du Hamel's Acoubar, 73, Univ Ottawa; Lere baroque en France: Repertoire chronologique des editions de textes litteraires 1585-1643, Droz, Geneva, No I (2 vols), 77, II, 79 & III, 80. *Mailing Add:* 305 Nelson St Ottawa ON K1N 7S5 Can

ARCHAMBAULT, PAUL JOSEPH, b Webster, Mass, Sept 17, 37; m 65; c 1. FRENCH, LATIN. *Educ:* Assumption Col, AB, 58; Yale Univ, PhD(Romance lang), 63. *Prof Exp:* From instr to asst prof, Amherst Col, 62-68; assoc prof, 68-73, PROF FRENCH, SYRACUSE UNIV, 73- *Concurrent Pos:* Amherst Col fac-trustee fel, 65-66; Nat Found on Arts & Humanities jr scholar, 69. *Mem:* MLA; Medieval Acad Am. *Res:* Mediaeval French and Latin literature; 20th century French literature. *Publ:* Auth, Thucydides in France: Commynes, J Hist Ideas, 1/67; Commynes and the Renaissance idea of wisdom, Humanisme et Renaissance, fall 67; Sallust in France: Thomas Basin, Papers on Lang & Lit, summer 68; Camus' Hellenic Sources (Studies in Romance Lang & Lit Ser), Univ NC, 72; Seven French Chroniclers: Witnesses to History, Syracuse Univ, 74; ed, Syracuse Scholar, 79-82; Medieval romance and language, Symp, spring 81. *Mailing Add:* Dept Foreign Lang & Lit Syracuse Univ Syracuse NY 13210

ARCHBOLD, GEOFFREY JOHN D E, b Vancouver, BC, Oct 8, 15; m 54; c 2. CLASSICS, ANCIENT HISTORY. *Educ:* Univ BC, BA, 50; Univ Cincinnati, MA, 53. *Prof Exp:* Staff mem classics & English, Trinity Col Sch, Port Hope, Ont, 51-52; asst headmaster, Shawnigan Lake Boys' Sch, BC, 54-61; from instr to asst prof, 61-70, actg chmn dept, 69-71, assoc prof, 70-81, EMER ASSOC PROF CLASSICS, UNIV VICTORIA, 81- *Concurrent Pos:* Examr, BC Dept Educ, 65-68, reader, Corresp Sch, 65-69. *Mem:* Class Asn Can; Am Philol Asn; Archaeol Inst Am; Philol Asn Pac Coast; Int Orgn Ancient Lang Anal Computer. *Res:* Concordance to the History of Ammianus Marcellinus; stylistic analysis of the History of Ammianus Marcellinus; Roman Imperial history. *Publ:* Contribr, Lyric and Longer Poems (4 vols), Macmillan, Can, 59; auth, A stylistic analysis of Ammianus Marcellinus' History with the assistance of a computer, Proc Pac Northwestern Conf Foreign Lang, 72; Ammianus Marcellinus, Computers & Humanities, 5/72; A Concordance to the History of Ammianus Marcellinus, Univ Toronto Press, 80. *Mailing Add:* 1442 Wende Victoria BC V8P 3T5 Can

ARCHIBALD, BRIGITTE EDITH, b Kaiserslaufern, Ger, Aug 22, 42; US citizen; m 70; c 1. GERMANIC LANGUAGE & LITERATURE. *Educ:* Kings Col, NY, BA, 64; Univ Mainz, MA, 66; Univ Tenn, Knoxville, PhD(Ger lang & lit), 75. *Prof Exp:* Instr Ger, Western Carolina Univ, 66-67; teacher, Hanover Park High Sch, NJ, 67-68; asst prof Ger lang & lit, Mansfield State Col, Pa, 68-70; dir pub libr, Wallace Pub Libr, NC, 72-73; ASST PROF GER & SPAN, NC A&T UNIV, 76- *Concurrent Pos:* Guest lectr, MIFLC, 77-82. *Mem:* MLA; Northeastern Conf Teaching Foreign Lang; League Women Voter's Int Rel Comt. *Res:* Seventeenth century German literature; Barock literature; the German hymn. *Publ:* Auth, Zwei Evangelische Dichterinnen des 17 Jahrhunderts, Monatsblatt, 6/77. *Mailing Add:* One Bayberry Court Greensboro NC 27405

ARDEN, HEATHER MARLENE, b Ocala, Fla, Dec 24, 43; m 76. MEDIEVAL & FRENCH LITERATURE. *Educ:* Mich State Univ, BA, 65; NY Univ, MA, 67, PhD(Fr), 74. *Prof Exp:* Asst prof French, Wilkes Col, 73-78; asst prof, 78-82, ASSOC PROF FRENCH, UNIV CINCINNATI, 82- *Mem:* Medieval Acad Am; Int Courtly Lit Soc; Soc int pour l'etude Theatre medieval; Soc Rencesvals; Int Arthurian Soc. *Res:* Medieval French literature; criticism and theory of literature; women's studies. *Publ:* Auth, Le Fou, la sottie et Le Neveu de Rameau, Dix-Huitieme Siecle, Vol 7, 75; Fools' Plays: A Study of Satire in the Sottie, Cambridge Univ Press, 80; The false hero of Le Chevalier au Lion, Mythos Papers, 82. *Mailing Add:* Dept of French Univ of Cincinnati Cincinnati OH 45221

ARESU, BERNARD CAMILLE, b Constantine, Algeria. FRENCH & COMPARATIVE LITERATURE. *Educ:* Univ Montpellier, Lic es Lettres, 67; Univ Wash, PhD(comp lit), 75. *Prof Exp:* Asst prof, 77-82, ASSOC PROF FRENCH, RICE UNIV, 82- *Concurrent Pos:* Master, Margarett Root Brown Col, Rice Univ, 82- *Mem:* MLA; AM Comp Lit Asn; Am Asn Teachers French; African Lit Asn. *Res:* Twentieth century French studies; comparative literature; African literatures. *Publ:* Auth, Female characterization in the plays of Kateb Yacine, In: 1977 African Studies Association Papers, Brandeis Univ, 1/78; Algerian theatre of the fifties: Kateb Yacine's Les Ancetres redoublent de ferocite, San Jose Studies, 5/78; Polygonal and arithmosophical motifs in the fiction of Kateb Yacine, Res in African Lit, fall 78; Le theatre de Kateb Yacine devant la critique, Oeuvres et Critiques, Vol 4, No 2; Gilbert Durand and the mythical structure of time in three novels by Faulkner, Simon and Kateb, Proc 9th Cong Int Col Lang Asn, Vol 4, 82; The cult of images: Toward a Durandian reading of Les Petits pemes en prose, Forum (in prep). *Mailing Add:* Dept of French & Ital Rich Univ Houston TX 77001

ARIAS, JOAN ZONDERMAN, b Newark, NJ, Mar 29, 41. SPANISH LITERATURE & LANGUAGE. *Educ:* Douglass Col, AB, 62; Univ Ill, MA, 64; Univ Calif, Los Angeles, PhD(Hisp lang & lit), 75. *Prof Exp:* Instr Span, Georgetown Univ, 70-71; lectr, Calif State Col, San Bernardino, 71-72; ASSOC PROF SPAN, LA VERNE COL, 72- *Mem:* Am Asn Teachers Span & Port; MLA. *Res:* Picaresque novel; Chicano literature. *Publ:* Auth, The Unrepentant Narrator: Guzman de Alfarache, Tamesis, 77. *Mailing Add:* La Verne Col 1950 Third St La Verne CA 91750

ARIAS, RICHARDO, b Leon, Span, Aug 27, 34; US citizen. SPANISH LITERATURE & HISTORY. *Educ:* St Anselmo, Rome, BA(philos), 55, BA(theol), 57; Fordham Univ, MSEd, 62; NY Univ, PhD(Span), 68. *Prof Exp:* Lectr Span, Queens Col, NY, 65-67; asst prof, 70-76, assoc prof, 76-80, PROF SPAN & ASST CHMN DEPT, FORDHAM UNIV, 80- *Concurrent Pos:* Fel, Southeastern Inst Medieval & Renaissance Studies, 68; co-ed, J de Valdivielso, Teatro Completo, Isla, Madrid, 75-77. *Mem:* Am Asn Teachers Span & Port; Asoc Int Hispanistas; Cath Renascence Soc. *Res:* Theatre of Spanish Golden Age; 15th century Spanish. *Publ:* Auth, El Concepto del Destino en la Literatura Medieval Espanola, Gredos, 70; La Poesia de los Goliardos, Insula, 70; El Nacimiento de la Mejor de Valdivielso, BBMP, 76; El Hospital de los Locos de Valdivielso, Homenaje R A Molina, 77; Relacion entre el jardin de las delicias . . ., Cuad Hisp-Am, 78. *Mailing Add:* Dept of Mod Langs Fordham Univ Bronx NY 10458

ARIETI, JAMES ALEXANDER, b New York, NY, May 12, 48; m 76; c 1. CLASSICS, HISTORY. *Educ:* Grinnell Col, BA, 69; Stanford Univ, MA, 72, PhD(classics), 72. *Prof Exp:* Asst prof classics, Stanford Univ, 73-74; asst prof, Pa State Univ, 74-75; asst prof classics & hist, Cornell Col, 75-77; asst prof, 78-81, ASSOC PROF CLASSICS, HAMPDEN-SYDNEY COL, 81- *Concurrent Pos:* Asst bibliographer ling, MLA, 74-75; Nat Endowment Humanities fel, classics, 77-78; chmn bd & sr fel, Hesperis Inst for Humanistic Studies, 77- *Mem:* Am Philol Asn; Hesperis Inst Humanistic Studies. *Res:* Ancient historiography and philosophy; ancient literary criticism; Septuagint. *Publ:* Auth, The vocabulary of Septuagint Amos, J Biblical Lit, 74; Nudity in Greek athletics, Class World, 75; coauth, The Dating of Longinus, Studia Classica, 75; co-ed, MLA Int Bibliography, In; 1974 Vol III, MLA, 76; contrib, Two Studies in Latin Phonology, Studia Ling et Philol, 76; coauth, Love Can Be Found, Harcourt Brace Jovanovich, 77; auth, Epedocles in Rome: Rape and the Roman ethos, Clio, 81; A Heorodtean source for Rasselas, Note & Queries, 81. *Mailing Add:* Dept of Classics Hampden-Sydney Col Hampden-Sydney VA 23943

ARIEW, ROBERT A, b Alexandria, Egypt, Dec 22, 46; US citizen; m 67; c 2. FRENCH LANGUAGE & LITERATURE. *Educ:* Univ Ill, BA, 67, MA, 69, PhD(French), 74. *Prof Exp:* Res assoc French, Computer-based Educ Res Lab & Lang Lab, Univ Ill, 72-74; ASST PROF FRENCH, PA STATE UNIV, 74- *Mem:* Am Coun Teaching Foreign Lang; Asn Comput & the Humanities; Asn Lit & Ling Comput. *Res:* Computer assisted instruction; computer applications in the humanities (literary and linguistic); surrealist French literature. *Publ:* Auth, The teaching of French with PLATO IV, System, 2: 1; Breton's poisson soluble, Asn Lit & Ling Comput Bull, 6: 1; How will developments in technological resources affect teaching and research?, In: The College of Liberal Arts in the 80's: Proceedings of Faculty Conference, Pa State Univ, 78; A diagnostic test for students entering computer-assisted learning curriculum in French, Comput & Educ, 3: 4; A management system for foreign language tests, computers & educ, 6: 1, In: Computer Assisted Learning: Selected Papers from the CAL 81 Symposium, Pergamon Press, 81; The textook as curriculum, In: Curriculum, Competency, and the Foreign Language Teacher, Nat Textbook Co, 82. *Mailing Add:* 316 Burrowes Bldg University Park PA 16802

ARKIN, ALEXANDER HABIB, b New York, NY, Mar 1, 33; m 66; c 2. SPANISH & PORTUGUESE LITERATURE. *Educ:* NY Univ, BA, 57, MA, 59, PhD(Romance lang), 63. *Prof Exp:* Instr Span, Univ Conn, 61-62; instr, Skidmore Col, 62-63; asst prof Span & Port, Rutgers Univ, 63-66; asst prof Span, Fordham Univ, 66-68; assoc prof Span & Port, Franklin Pierce Col, 68-70; assoc prof & co-chmn Span, Port, Hebrew & comp relig, Windham Col, 70-74; PRES, SEPHARDIC ACAD FOR STUDY & ADVAN OF HUMANITIES, 73- *Concurrent Pos:* Off guest Span Govt & deleg, Cong Int Inst Hisp, Madrid, 63 & Cong Mundial Sefardi, Inst Benito Arias Montano Estud Hebraicos y Oriente Proximo & Inst Estud Sefardies, Madrid, 64; vis prof and prof Sephardic & Marrano lit, World Inst Sephardic Studies & mem acad coun & bd adv, 73-76. *Mem:* Smithsonian Inst; Bibl Archeol Soc; MLA; Am Soc Sephardic Studies; Sephardic Acad Studies & Advan Humanities (pres, 73-). *Res:* Iberian semitics; medieval, Renaissance and baroque Spanish and Portuguese literature; Sephardic culture and civilization in all of its past and present manifestations; Latin American and converso literature; Romance linguistics. *Publ:* Auth, La influencia de la exegesis hebrea en los comentarios biblicos de Fray Luis de Leon, Inst Benito Arias Montano Estud Hebraicos y Oriente Proximo, 66; Rabi Abraham b Meir b Ezra-Tudelan Immortel, Consistoire de Asn Cultuelle Israelite de Bayonne,

67; A lenda de Nemrod e a Torre de Babel na Consolacao de Sameul Usque, Studies Am Asn Sephardic Studies, 70; The Sephardic people in the Seyahatname of the 17th century Turkish historian Evliya Celebi Efendi, Sephardic World, 74. *Mailing Add:* Sephardic Acad for Study & Advan of the Humanities 102 Laura Lane Keene NH 03431

ARMAS, JOSEPH R DE, b Havana, Cuba, July 3, 24. ROMANCE LANGUAGES, LATIN AMERICAN AREA STUDIES. *Educ:* Univ Havana, EdD & PhD(lit hist), 59. *Hon Degrees:* Prof d'Honneur, Inst des Hautes Etudes Esonomiques et Sociales, Bruxelles. *Prof Exp:* From asst prof to assoc prof Span, Ashland Col, 63-66; from asst prof to assoc prof Span & Latin Am studies, 66-77, coord Latin Am Comt, 71-78, PROF SPAN & LATIN AM STUDIES, DENISON UNIV, 77- *Honors & Awards:* Sociedad Geografica de Cuba, 57; Academia de Ciencias Humanisticas y Relaciones, Filia de Italia, Miembro de Honor, 81. *Mem:* Asn Latin Am Studies; AAUP; Am Asn Teachers Span & Port. *Res:* Spanish contemporary poetry; Cuban essays from 1902 to 1980. *Publ:* Auth, Articles and papers: La columna, el circulo y sus variantes en la poesia primera de Pedro Salinas, Hispania, 3/70; Nuevas tendencias en la Literatura Social de Latin America, Lorain Community Col & Oberlin Col, Hispanic Heritage Week, 75; Nuevas tendencias en la poesia contemporanea de Centro America, Midwest Mod Lang Asn, 76; El mundo poetico de Rita Geada Congress of Interamerican Women Writers, Toronto Press, 78; Florida Atlantic University, Hispanic Heritage Week, 79; La dicotomia amoraso en la vida de Gertrudis Gomez de Avellaneda, Ediciones Universal, 80; transl, Women Without Eden, Alembic, 81; auth, Dolor en la poesia de Carmen Conde, Congress of Interamerican Women Writers, 81. *Mailing Add:* 104 Stone Hall Granville OH 43023

ARMES, KEITH, b London, England, Feb 4, 36; US citizen. RUSSIAN LITERATURE. *Educ:* Univ Cambridge, BA, 59, MA, 63, PhD(Russ lit), 70. *Prof Exp:* Lectr sci Russ, Univ Cambridge, 64-66; instr Russ, New Col, Sarasota, Fla, 66-67; ASSOC PROF LANG, UNIV MINN, MINNEAPOLIS, 68-, CHMN DEPT SLAVIC, 77- *Mem:* MLA; Am Asn Advan Slavic Studies; Am Asn Teachers Slavic & E Europ Lang. *Res:* Soviet Russian literature of 1920s; Russian emigre literature in France; Russian modernist literature. *Publ:* Transl, A Lenten Letter to Pimen Patriarch of All Russia, Burgess, 72; transl & auth introd, Candle in the Wind, Univ Minn, 73; plus var articles in Survey, Russ Lang J, Relig Communist Lands & Nuova Rivista Musicale Ital. *Mailing Add:* Dept of Slavic Lang Univ of Minn Minneapolis MN 55455

ARMISTEAD, SAMUEL GORDON, b Philadelphia, Pa, Aug 21, 27; m 53. SPANISH LITERATURE & LANGUAGE. *Educ:* Princeton Univ, AB, 50, MA, 52, PhD(Span lit, Romance ling), 55. *Prof Exp:* Instr Span & mod lang, Princeton Univ, 53-56; from instr to assoc prof Span, Univ Calif, Los Angeles, 56-67; prof, Purdue Univ, 67-68; prof Span, Univ Pa, 68-82; PROF SPAN, UNIV CALIF, DAVIS, 82- *Concurrent Pos:* Fac fel, Univ Calif, Los Angeles, 58; Del Amo Found fel & Am Coun Learned Soc fel, Spain, 62-63; Ford Found comp studies grant, 66-67; Guggenheim Found fel, 71-72; Nat Endowment for Humanities fel, 81-83. *Honors & Awards:* Chicago Folklore Prize, 73. *Mem:* Am Asn Teachers Span & Port; MLA; fel Mediaeval Acad Am; Soc Rencesvals. *Res:* Medieval Spanish literature and language especially epic, ballad and historiography; Judeo-Spanish literature and language; Hispanic folk literature. *Publ:* Auth, Romancero Judeo-Espanol en el Archivo Menendez Pidal, 77; coauth, Romances Judeo-Espanoles de Tanger, Caterdra-Seminario Mendendez Pidal, 77; El Romancero hoy, 3 vols, Catedra-Seminario Menendez Pidal, 79; Trea calas en el Romancero, Castalia, Madrid, 80; Bibliography of the Hispanic Ballad in oral tradition, Catedra-Seminario Menendez Pidal, 80; Judeo-Spanish Ballads from New York, Univ Calif, 81; Seis romancerillos de cordel, Castalid, Madrid, 81; En torno al Romancero sefardi, Catedra-Seminarion Menendez Pidal, 82. *Mailing Add:* Dept of Span Univ of Calif Davis CA 95616

ARMITAGE, ISABELLE, b Strasbourg, France, Jan 11, 22; US citizen; c 2. FRENCH LANGUAGE & LITERATURE. *Educ:* Col Santa Fe, BA, 66; Univ Kans, MPhil, 70, PhD(16th century French lit), 72. *Prof Exp:* Teacher French, Loretto Acad, NMex, 64-66; grad asst, Univ NMex, 66-67; asst prof, Pa State Univ, University Park, 71-78; PROF FRENCH, MONTEREY INST INT STUDIES, 78-, CHMN LANG & HUMANITIES, 79- *Mem:* Am Asn Teachers Fr; MLA; AAUP; Soc des Prof Francais et Amerique; Alliance Francaise. *Res:* History of public opinion in France 1570-1580; Pierre de l'Estoile; methodology of second language acquisition. *Publ:* Auth, Sophonisbe: Heroine intraitable?, Papers Seventeenth Century Fr Lit, winter 77; Fragment des Recueils Pierre de l'Estoile, Kans Humanistic Studies, 77. *Mailing Add:* Fr Dept Monterey Inst Int Studies State College PA 16801

ARMSTRONG, DOUGLAS HOLCOMBE, b Rochester, NY, June 12, 28; m 56; c 3. SPANISH LANGUAGE & LITERATURE. *Educ:* Middlebury Col, BA, 49, MA, 55; Univ Mich, Ann Arbor, PhD(Span lit), 67. *Prof Exp:* Instr Span, Univ Md, 62-68; asst prof, 68-71, ASSOC PROF SPAN, ITHACA COL, 71- *Mem:* MLA; AM Asn Teachers Span & Port. *Res:* Post Civil War Spanish novel; Galdos and contemporary novelists; Spanish film as art. *Mailing Add:* Dept of Foreign Lang Ithaca Col Ithaca NY 14850

ARMSTRONG, JAMES, b Princeton, NJ, Apr 20, 19; m 42; c 3. CLASSICS. *Educ:* Princeton Univ, AB, 41, PhD, 49. *Hon Degrees:* LLD, Princeton Univ, 67; LHD, Bates Col, 67; LittD, Grinnell Col, 67 & Middlebury Col, 77; DH, Norwich Univ, 75. *Prof Exp:* Instr classics, Princeton Univ, 47-48 & 50-51 & Ind Univ, 49-50; Scribner preceptor & asst prof, Princeton Univ, 52-60, assoc prof, 60-63, asst dean grad sch, 58-60, assoc dean grad sch, 61-62; pres, Middlebury Col, 63-75; pres & dir, 75-81, CONSULT HIGHER EDUC, CHARLES A DANA FOUND INC, 81- *Concurrent Pos:* Fel Am Acad Rome, 55-56. *Mem:* Am Philol Asn; Class Asn Atlantic States. *Res:* Greek literature; homeric epic. *Publ:* Auth, The Arming Motif in the Iliad, Am J Philol, 58; The Marriage Song in the Odyssey, Trans Am Philol Asn, 58; Introd, The Odyssey, Dodd, 59; translr, John Phillips Responsio, Complete Prose Works of Milton, Yale Univ, Vol IV, Part II, 66. *Mailing Add:* Box 528, Rd 1 South Berwick ME 03908

ARMSTRONG, WILLIAM, b Seattle, Wash, Nov 22, 18. ROMANCE LANGUAGES. *Educ:* Gonzaga Univ, BA, 44, MA, 45; Sorbonne Univ, dipl, Inst French Phonetics, 54; Cath Univ Paris, PhD(philos), 55. *Prof Exp:* Asst prof mod lang, 57-68, ASSOC PROF MOD LANG, SEATTLE UNIV, 68- *Concurrent Pos:* Assoc pastor, St Pius X Church, Mountlake Terrace, Wash. *Res:* Language; music; religious life. *Publ:* Auth, Waiting Room Cartoons, 71, Ecclesiastical Cartoons, 72, Tavern Cartoons, 72; Summer Cabin Cartoons, 72, TV Cartoons, 72, I Ate the Whole Thing, 73, Las Adventuras de Pepito, 74 & Franciscan Cartoons, 74, Jesuit Bks. *Mailing Add:* Dept of Mod Lang Seattle Univ Seattle WA 98122

ARNAUD, DANIEL LEONARD, b New York, NY, May 29, 35; m 67; c 3. CLASSICS. *Educ:* Carleton Col, AB, 57; Univ SDak, MA, 60; Stanford Univ, PhD(classics), 68. *Prof Exp:* Master Latin, Groton Sch, Mass, 57-58; from instr to asst prof classics & chmn dept, Lawrence Univ, 64-72, dir freshman prog, 71-72; exec dir, Thomas J Watson Found, 72-77; vpres, Salzburg Sem, 77-81; MANAGING DIR, EARTHWATCH, 82- *Mem:* Am Philol Asn; Archaeol Inst Am. *Res:* Augustan poetry; Ovid. *Mailing Add:* Earthwatch 10 Juniper Rd Belmont MA 02178

ARNDT, KARL JOHN RICHARD, b St Paul, Minn, Sept 17, 03; m 50; c 2. GERMAN LANGUAGE & LITERATURE. *Educ:* Wash Univ, AM, 28; Johns Hopkins Univ, PhD, 33. *Prof Exp:* Instr Ger & Greek, Concordia Col, Can, 25-26; instr Ger, Univ Mo, 29-31 & Goucher Col, 31-33; prof & head dept, Hartwick Col, 33-35; from asst prof to assoc prof, La State Univ, 35-45; chief relig & univ affairs br, US Off Mil Govt, Württemberg-Baden, 45-50; prof Ger & head dept, 50-76, EMER PROF GER, CLARK UNIV, 76- *Concurrent Pos:* Soc Sci Res Coun award, 41; Am Philos Soc grants-in-aid, 53, 61, 63, 66-67; Guggenheim fel, 57-58; Pabst Found grant to edit microfilm ed, Libr Cong collection of Ger prisoner of war camp papers, 1943-46, 65; Nat Endowment for Humanities grant, 67-68; Lilly Endowment grant, Ind Vol of Doc Hist Harmony Soc, 68-70; ed in chief first complete edition of works of Charles Sealsfield, 28 vols. *Mem:* MLA; Am Asn Teachers Ger; Am Antiq Soc; corresp mem Ges Deut Presseforsch. *Res:* Cultural, historical, religious, literary and political relations between the United States and Germany. *Publ:* Auth, Newly discovered Sealsfield relationships documented, Mod Lang Notes, 4/72; The Pittsburgh leader's analysis of the 1890 crisis, WPa Hist Mag, 10/72; Harmony on the Connoquenessing, 1803-1815, Worcester, 80; Teutonia, Quintessence of German American Idealism, In: The Harold Jantz Collection, Duke Univ, Durham; Smolnikars Beziehungen zu Georg Rapps Harmonie Gesellschaft, In: Acta Neophilologica, Vol XIV, Univ Ljubliana, 81; Schliemann's Excavation of Troy and American Politics, or Why the Smithsonian Institution Lost Schliemann's Great Troy Collection to Berlin, In: 1981 Yearbk of German Americn Studies, Univ Kans; Harmony on the Wabash in Transition, 1824-1826, Worcester, 82; Charles Sealsfield, Die deutsch-amerikanischen Wahlverwandtschaften, Hildesheim, 82. *Mailing Add:* 5 Hazelwood Rd Worcester MA 01609

ARNDT, WALTER WERNER, b Constantinople, Turkey, May 4, 16; US citizen; m 45; c 4. LINGUISTICS, SLAVIC LANGUAGES & LITERATURE. *Educ:* Oxford Univ, Dipl(econ polit), 36; Robert Col, Turkey, BS, 43; Univ NC, PhD, 56. *Hon Degrees:* MA, Dartmouth Col, 68. *Prof Exp:* Instr mech eng, Robert Col, 45-48; instr English, Friendsville Acad, Tenn, 49-50; from instr to asst prof class & mod lang, Guilford Col, 50-56; from asst prof to assoc prof Russ & ling, Univ NC, Chapel Hill, 57-66, chmn dept ling, Slavic & orient lang, 65-66; chmn dept Russ lang & lit, 67-70, PROF RUSS, DARTMOUTH COL, 66- *Concurrent Pos:* Fulbright res prof, Munster Univ, 61-62; Am Philos Soc res grant, Leningrad & Moscow, 66; Rockefeller fel, 75; Guggenheim fel, 77-78; Nat Endowment for Humanities fel, 79; Woodrow Wilson fel, 81-82; Am Coun Learned Soc grant, 82. *Honors & Awards:* Bollingen Prize, 63. *Mem:* Ling Soc Am; Am Asn Advan Slavic Studies; Am Asn Teachers Slavic & E Europ Lang (vpres, 65-67). *Res:* Linguistics; Slavic philology; verse translation. *Publ:* Auth, Alexander Pushkin, Eugene Onegin: A New English Translation, Dutton, 63, 2nd ed, 81; Wilhelm Busch, Clement Dove, The Thwarted Poet: A Verse Translation with the Original, Sigbert Mohn, Gütersloh, 67; coauth, Grundzüge Moderner Sprachbeschreibung, Max Niemeyer, Tübingen, 69; auth, Pushkin Threefold: Narrative, Lyric, Polemic, and Ribad Verse: The Originals with Linear and Metric Translations, Dutton, 72; Alexander Pushkin: Ruslan and Liudmila, 74 & Anna Akhmatova: Selected Poems, 76, Ardis Publ; Goethe's Faust, Parts I and II, A New Verse Translation in the Metrics of the Original, Norton Critical Ed, 76; The Genius of Wilhelm Busch: Comedy of Frustration, Univ of Calif Press, 82. *Mailing Add:* 38 Maple St Hanover NH 03755

ARNOLD, ALBERT JAMES, b Ballston Spa, NY, Nov 8, 39; m 63; c 1. MODERN FRENCH & COMPARATIVE LITERATURE. *Educ:* Univ Paris, Cert phonetics, dipl Fr studies & cert contemp lit, 60; Hamilton Col, AB, 61; Univ Wis, Madison, MA, 64, PhD(French), 68. *Prof Exp:* Instr Romance lang, Hamilton Col, 61-62; asst prof French, 66-71, assoc prof, 71-81, prog chmn comp lit, 71-79, PROF FRENCH, UNIV VA, 81- *Concurrent Pos:* Consult, Bollingen Found, 67; assoc, Ctr for Advan Studies, 70-71, 75-76 & 81-82; exchange prof comp lit, Univ Paris III, 81. *Mem:* MLA; SAtlantic Mod Lang Asn; Am Asn Teachers Fr; Am Comp Lit Asn; NAm Nietzsche Soc. *Res:* Modernism; theory of literature and criticism; negritude. *Publ:* Auth, Paul Valery and His Critics, Univ Va, 70 & Haskell House, 73; La querelle de la poesie pure, Rev Hist Litteraire de France, 70; coauth, Les Mots de Sartre, Minard, Paris, 73; auth, Two tempests: Cesaire and Shakespeare, Comp Lit, 78; auth, Pour une edition critique de Caligula, Albert Camus, 79; A Critical Bibliography of French Literature, Syracuse Univ, 80; The Language of Poetry: Crisis and Solution, Rodopi, 80; Modernism and Negritude: Aime Cesaire, Harvard, 81. *Mailing Add:* Dept of French Lit & Gen Ling Univ of Va 302 Cabell Hall Charlottesville VA 22903

ARNOLD, ARMIN, b Zug, Switz, Sept 1, 31; Can citizen. GERMAN, COMPARATIVE LITERATURE. *Educ:* Univ Fribourg, lic phil, 53, PhD, 56. *Prof Exp:* Instr Ger, Univ Fribourg, 56-57; instr French, Ger & English, Col Fahrwangen, Switz, 57-59; asst prof Ger, Univ Alta, 59-61; from asst prof to assoc prof, 61-68, chmn dept, 65-74, PROF GER, McGILL UNIV, 68-

Mem: Mod Humanities Res Asn; Can Asn Univ Teachers Ger; Am Comp Lit Asn; Can Comp Lit Asn; fel Royal Soc Can. *Res:* Expressionism; modern German, English & American literature; comparative literature. *Publ:* Ed, James Joyce, Ungar, 69; Friedrich Duerrenmatt, Colloquium, Berlin, 69 & Ungar, 72; Prosa des Expressionismus, Kohlhammer, Stuttgart, 72; D H Lawrence, Colloquium, Berlin, 72; coauth (with T Schmidt), Kriminalromanfuehrer, 78, ed, Kriminalgeschichten ans drei Tahrnnderten, 78 & Westergeschichten ans zwei Tahrhunderten, 81, Stuttgart; Sherlock Holmes anf der Hintertreppe, Bonn, 81. *Mailing Add:* Dept of Ger McGill Univ Montreal PQ H3A 1G5 Can

ARNOLD, HERBERT A, b Buchau, Czech, June 23, 35; m; c 3. GERMAN, HISTORY. *Educ:* Univ Würzburg, DrPhil(Ger hist), 66; Wesleyan Univ, MA, 80. *Prof Exp:* From instr to asst prof Ger, 63-71, co-dir col, 71 & 73-76, dir prog in Ger, 67-69 & 72-73, fac fel, Ctr Humanities, 72, assoc prof, 71-80, PROF GER & LETT, COL LETT, WESLEYAN UNIV, 80- *Concurrent Pos:* Reviewer, Choice, 66-67, 69-72, Hist Z, 70, Reprint Bull, 71-, Am Hist Rev, 72 & History, 72-; mem bd consult, Hist & Theory, 66-67, 69-72, transl, 67, 71 & 77; reader & transl, Wesleyan Univ Press, 67, 69 & 72; mem bd trustees, Am Field Serv Int, 72-74 & 80- *Mem:* MLA; AHA; Am Asn Teachers Ger; Northeast Mod Lang Asn. *Res:* German literature of the 17th, 18th and 20th centuries; Modern German history; ideology of the SS. *Publ:* Auth, On E Hölzle: Idee und Ideologie, Hist & Theory, Vol X, No 1; Grimmelshausen and his translators, Monatshefte, winter 67; translr, Bodo Scheurig's Free Germany, 69 & E Jäckel's Hittler's Weltanschauung, 72, Wesleyan Univ & Harvard Univ Press, 81; History & Utopia in Nazi ideology, Intellect, 12/76; Die Rollen du Courasche Frau Zwischen Renaissance & Romantic, Bouvier, Bonn, 80; The other's tradition, Theater J, 3/80; Oral tradition & critical song, J Popular Cult, winter 81. *Mailing Add:* Col of Lett Wesleyan Univ Middletown CT 06457

ARNOLD, RICHARD EUGENE, b Springfield, Mo, Dec 5, 08. CLASSICS. *Educ:* St Louis Univ, AB, 31, AM, 32, PhL, 35, PhD, 36, STL, 41. *Prof Exp:* Instr class lang, Univ High Sch, St Louis Univ, 36-37, asst, Univ, 38-41, instr, 41-46, asst prof, 46; asst prof & head dept, Regis Col, 46-48; from asst prof to assoc prof, 48-53, actg chmn, Dept Classics, 61-62, prof, 53-74, EMER PROF CLASSICS, MARQUETTE UNIV, 74- *Concurrent Pos:* Ed, The Class Bull, 45-46; consult, Nat San Standard Med Vocab, 62- *Mem:* Am Philol Asn; Am Class League; Class Asn Midwest & South. *Res:* Classical languages; theology; symphonic and liturgical music. *Publ:* Ed & introd, Classical essays presented to James A Kleist, SJ, Class Bull, 46; coauth, Iris: A Reading List of Articles Selected from Classical Periodicals, St Louis Univ Bk Store, 42; The Universal Treatise of Nicholas of Autrecourt, Marquette Univ, 71. *Mailing Add:* Dept of Class Marquette Univ Milwaukee WI 53233

ARONOFF, MARK H, b Montreal, Que, Jan 9, 49; m 76; c 1. MORPHOLOGY, ORTHOGRAPHY. *Educ:* McGill Univ, BA, 69; Mass Inst Technol, PhD(ling), 74. *Prof Exp:* Asst prof, 74-80, ASSOC PROF LING, STATE UNIV NY STONY BROOK, 80- *Concurrent Pos:* Adj assoc prof, NY Univ, 77-; vis asst prof, Univ Calif, San Diego, 78. *Mem:* Ling Soc Am; Am Dialect Soc; Can Ling Asn. *Res:* Experimental and theoretical studies of word-formation in various languages; relationship between written and spoken language. *Publ:* Auth, Word-formation in generative grammar, Mass Inst Technol Press, 76; Contextuals, Language, 80; The relevance of productivity, In: Historical Morphology, Mouton, 80; co-ed, Juncture, ANMA Libr, 80; auth, Automobile semantics, Ling Inquiry, 81. *Mailing Add:* 420 Moriches Rd St James NY 11780

ARONSON, HOWARD ISAAC, b Chicago, Ill, Mar 5, 36. LINGUISTICS. *Educ:* Univ Ill, AB, 56; Ind Univ, MA, 58, PhD, 61. *Prof Exp:* Asst prof Slavic lang, Univ Wis, 61-62; from asst prof to assoc prof ling & Slavic lang, 62-73, chmn dept ling, 72-80, PROF LING & SLAVIC LANG, UNIV CHICAGO, 73- *Mem:* Am Asn Teachers Slavic & East Europ Lang; Am Asn Advan Slavic Studies; Bulgarian Studies Group; Am Asn Southeast Europ Studies. *Res:* Georgian linguistics; Bulgarian and Russian linguistics; Yiddish linguistics. *Publ:* Auth, The Gender System of the Bulgarian Noun, Int J Slavic Ling & Poetics, 64; The Grammatical Categories of the Indicative in the Contemporary Bulgarian Literary Language, In: To Honor Roman Jakobson, 67 & Bulgarian Inflectional Morphophonology, 68, Mouton; Towards a Semantic Analysis of Case and Subject in Georgian, Lingua, 70; Grammatical Subject in Old Georgian, Bedi Kartlisa, 76; Interrelationships Between Aspect and Mood in Bulgarian, Folia Slavica, 77; English as an Active Language, Lingua, 77; Georgian: A first-year reading grammar, Slavica, 82. *Mailing Add:* Dept of Ling Univ of Chicago Chicago IL 60637

ARONSON, NICOLE HABATJOU, b Bordeaux, France, Oct 9, 34; m 65; c 1. FRENCH LITERATURE & CIVILIZATION. *Educ:* Univ Bordeaux, Lic es Lett, 58; City Univ New York, PhD(Fr), 70. *Prof Exp:* asst prof French, Marymount Col, NY, 67-69; from asst prof to assoc prof, 70-76, PROF FRENCH, E CAROLINA UNIV, 76- *Mem:* MLA; Women's Caucus Mod Lang; Am Asn Teachers Fr; Les Amis de Montaigne; Societe des Professeurs francais en Amerique. *Res:* Sixteenth century French literature; women in French literature; French civilization. *Publ:* Auth, Les reines et le Cinquieme livre de Rabelais, Studi Francesi, 72; Les idees Politiques de Rabelais, Nizet, 73; Mlle de Scudery et l'histoire romaine, Romanische Forschungen, 76; Deux visages de l'Amerique au XVIIIeme, French Rev, 76; Les Heroines de Mlle de Scudery, Papers on 17th Century Fr Lit, 77; Mlle de Scudery, Twayne, 78; Rome et son histoire dans Les Illustrations de Gaule et Singularites de Troie, Melanges Franco Simone, 81; Moliere, Perrault et la peinture, Papers Fr 17th Century Lit, 82; Les Femmes dans les Conversations morales de Mlle de Scudery, Onze Nouvelles Images de la femme au XVIIeme, 82. *Mailing Add:* 107 S Harding Greenville NC 27834

ARORA, SHIRLEY LEASE, b Youngstown, Ohio, June 3, 30; m 51; c 2. SPANISH-AMERICAN LITERATURE & FOLKLORE. *Educ:* Stanford Univ, BA, 50, MA, 51; Univ Calif, Los Angeles, PhD(Hisp lang & lit), 62. *Prof Exp:* From instr to assoc prof Span, 62-76, PROF SPAN, UNIV CALIF, LOS ANGELES, 76- *Mem:* MLA; Am Asn Teachers Span & Port; Inst Int Lit

Iberoam; Am Folklore Soc; PEN Club. *Res:* Colonial and 19th century Spanish-American literature; Spanish and Spanish-American folklore, especially proverbial speech. *Publ:* Auth, Proverbial Comparisons in Ricardo Palma's Tradiciones Peruanas, Univ Calif, 66; El que nace para tamal, a study in proverb patterning, Folklore Am, 12/68; Proverbial exaggerations in English and Spanish, Proverbium, 72; The El Que Nace proverbs: A supplement, J Latin Am Lore, 75; Proverbial Comparisons and Related Expressions in Spanish, Univ Calif, 77. *Mailing Add:* Dept of Span & Port Univ of Calif Los Angeles CA 90024

ARRINGTON, ROBERT LEE, Philosophy. See Vol IV

ARRINGTON, TERESA ROSS, b Detroit, Mich, July 2, 49; m 73; c 2. SPANISH LINGUISTICS. *Educ:* Univ Detroit, AB, 71; Univ Ky, MS, 73, PhD(Span ling), 77. *Prof Exp:* Teaching asst Span, Dept Span & Ital, Univ Ky, 72-76, instr, Evening Prog, 76-77; asst prof, Dept Mod & Class Lang, Lenoir-Rhyne Col, 77-78; ASST PROF SPAN, DEPT ROMANCE LANG, UNIV TENN, 78- *Mem:* Am Asn Teachers Span & Port; South Atlantic Mod Lang Asn. *Res:* Contemporary Spanish phonology and dialectology; Spanish transformational and generative grammar; teaching methodology: foreign languages. *Publ:* Auth, Prognosis for Zeismo: Argentine dialect or Spanish universal?, Tenn Ling, winter 82. *Mailing Add:* Dept of Romance Lang Univ Tenn Knoxville TN 37996

ARROJO, FERNANDO, b Madrid, Spain, Aug 7, 32; US citizen. SPANISH CULTURE & CIVILIZATION. *Educ:* Univ Complutense Madrid, filos y letras; Univ Hartford, MA, 70; Univ Conn, PhD(Span), 75. *Prof Exp:* Adj Span, Univ Hartford, 68-73; vis asst prof, Trinity Col, Hartford, 74-76; ASST PROF SPAN, OBERLIN COL 76- *Concurrent Pos:* Ed & coordr, Great Lakes Col Asn Speaker's Bur, 77- *Mem:* MLA; Am Asn Teachers Span & Port. *Res:* Creative writing (short stories); 20th century Pennisular literarture. *Publ:* El papel del mar en Gran Sol: realidad y simbolo, In: Ignacio Aldecoa: A Collection of Critical Essays, Univ Wyoming, 77; Transmutacion (contemplacion de un cuadro de Valazquez), Papeles de Son Armadans, 77; El sueno erotico de la senorita Elvira en La Colmena: etica y estetica celianas, Am Hisp, 78; La Decision, Cuaderno Lit, Barcelona, 78; Pintura y literatura en la Expana de posguerra, Hispania, 78; El emigrado, Insula, 80; Sentido de la aventura en dos relatos deportivos de Ignacio Aldecoa, Hispanofila, 81; La sensibilidad literaria de Ignacio aldecoa, Prologo-estudio a la edicion homenaje de Gran Sol, Noguer, 82. *Mailing Add:* Dept of Romance Lang Oberlin Col Oberlin OH 44074

ARROM, JOSE JUAN, b Holguin, Cuba, Feb 28, 10. SPANISH AMERICAN LITERATURE. *Educ:* Yale Univ, AB, 37, AM, 40, PhD, 41. *Prof Exp:* From instr to assoc prof Span, 37-54, cur Latin Am collection, 42-62, Sterling jr res fel, 44-45, dir grad studies Span, 52-68, prof, 54-80, EMER PROF SPAN, YALE UNIV, 80-, FEL, SAYBROOK COL, 42- *Concurrent Pos:* Contrib ed, Handbook Latin Am Studies, 45-52; Guggenheim fels, 47-48 & 64-65; John Gordon Stipe lectr, Emory Univ, 55; vis prof, Univ Ariz, 61; mem Nat Screening Comt, Fulbright-Hays Awards, 62-63; mem, Comt Grad Rec Exam Span, 65-66; Fulbright res fel, Spain, 68; Rockefeller fel, 68-69. *Mem:* Cor fel Acad Artes y Letras, Cuba; Acad Cubana Lengua; Real Acad Cordoba; Inst Hist del Teatro Am; MLA. *Res:* Hispanic-American literature. *Publ:* Auth, Estudios de Literatura Hispanoamericana, Ucar Garcia, Havana, 50; El Principe Jardinero y Fingido Cloridano, Comedia Sin Fama del Capitan don Santiago de Pita, Soc Econ Amigos Pais, Havana, 51, 2nd ed, Consejo Nac Cult, Havana, 63; El teatro de Hispanoamerica en la epoca colonial, Anuario Bibliog Cubano, Havana, 56, 2nd ed, Ed Andrea, Mex, 67; Certidumbre de America, estudios de letras, folklore y cultura, Anuario Bibliog Cubano, 59; Esquema Generacional de las Letras Hispanoamericanas: Ensayo do un Metodo, 63 & Historia de la Inuencion de las Yndias que Escreuia el Maestro Hernan Perez de Oliva, 65, Inst Caro y Cuervo, Bogota; Hispano-America: Panorama Contemporaneo de su Cultura, Harper, 69. *Mailing Add:* 70 High Lane Hamden CT 06517

ARROYO, ANITA, b Milan, Italy, June 17, 14; US citizen; m; c 2. SPANISH AMERICAN LITERATURE, COMMUNICATION. *Educ:* Inst Havana, Bachiller Let y Cie, 34; Univ Havana, Dr Fil y Let, 41; Nat Sch Jour, dipl news writing, 53. *Prof Exp:* Asst prof Hispanoam lit, Univ Havana, 50-52; asst prof psychol of commun, Univ PR, 62-69, prof, 69-80. *Concurrent Pos:* Syndicated writer, Reflejos, Ala Agencia Latinoam, 68- *Honors & Awards:* Lyceum Prize, Lyceum of Havana, Cuba, 54; Gold Medal, Col Archit, Havana, 56. *Res:* Sor Juana Ines de la Cruz, Gongora; Spanish American industrial arts; recent developments in contemporary Spanish American fiction. *Publ:* Auth, Las Artes Industriales en Cuba, Cultural, Havana, 46; El Pajaro de lata, Cultural, Havana, 46 & Ed San Juan, 2nd ed, 73; Razon y Pasion de Sor Juana Ines de la Cruz, Ed Porrua y Obregon, 52, 3rd ed, Porrua y Hermanos, Mex, 80; Raiz y Ala, 54, 2nd ed, Ed San Juan, 79 & coauth, El Caballito Verde, 56; Ed Lex, Havana; auth, Superacion y Aporte de la Mujer Norteamericana, US Dept State, 59; Navidades Para un Nino Cubano, Dir Gen Cult, Ministerio Educ, Havana, 59; America en su Literature, 67, 2nd ed, Aumentada, 78 & Narrativa Hispanoamericana Actual, 80, Ed Univ PR, San Juan. *Mailing Add:* PO Box 21375 Univ of PR Rio Piedras PR 00931

ARTHOS, JOHN, English Philology. See Vol II

ARTINIAN, ARTINE, b Pazardjick, Bulgaria, Dec 8, 07; nat US; m 36; c 3. FRENCH LITERATURE. *Educ:* Bowdoin Col, AB, 31; Harvard Univ, AM, 33; Columbia Univ, PhD, 41. *Hon Degrees:* LittD, Bowdoin Col, 66. *Prof Exp:* Asst French, Bowdoin Col, 30-31; prof, John Marshall Col Law, 35-36; lectr, 35-38, assoc, 38-41, from asst prof to prof, 41-64, chmn div lang & lit, 39-40, 44-45, 56-57, 58-59 & 60-64, head inst French, army specialized training prog unit, 43-44, EMER PROF FRENCH, BARD COL, 64- *Concurrent Pos:* Am Coun Learned Soc fel, 43-44; Fulbright res scholar, France, 49-50; prof-in-charge, Sweet Briar jr year, France, 53-55; Am rep bd dir, Soc Litteraire Emile Zola, 54-65; mem comt French exam, Col Entrance Exam Bd, 62-64; mem, Chancellor's coun, Univ Tex, 81- *Mem:* MLA; Soc Amis de Maupassant (vpres, 50-65); Am Asn Teachers Fr; AAUP. *Res:* Flaubert;

Maupassant; Huysmans. *Publ:* Auth, Maupassant Criticism in France, King's Crown Press, 41, Russell, 69; ed, Correspondance Inedite de Guy de Maupassant, Wapler, 51; Pour et Contre Maupassant, 55 & Flaubert, La Queue de la Poire de la Boule de Monseigneur, 58, Nizet; Huysmans, La-Haut, Casterman, 65; From Victor Hugo to Jean Cocteau, New Paltz Col, 65. *Mailing Add:* Winthrop House 100 Worth Ave Palm Beach FL 33480

ARTINIAN, ROBERT WILLARD, b Rhinebeck, NY, Sept 22, 41; m 64. FRENCH LANGUAGE & LITERATURE. *Educ:* Union Col, BA, 63; Cornell Univ, PhD(Fr lit), 67. *Prof Exp:* Asst prof French lit, Univ Chicago, 67-69; asst prof, Univ Va, 69-75; assoc prof & chmn dept, Sweet Briar Col, 75-79; assoc prof, Univ Nev, 79-81; ASSOC PROF, FRENCH LIT, CONN COL, 81- *Concurrent Pos:* Res dir, Sweet Briar jr year in France prog, 74-75; contrib ed, MLA Int Bibliog, 68-; Univ Va res awards, 70-72; Sweet Briar Col res award, 77. *Honors & Awards:* Fulbright Award, 64. *Mem:* MLA; Northeast Mod Lang Asn; SAtlantic Mod Lang Asn; Am Asn Teachers Fr; AAUP. *Res:* French literature of the late 19th century, especially Maupassant and the Decadents; Dante. *Publ:* Auth, The Bitter Sands: Camus' L'Hote, Notes Comtemp Lit, 71; Foul Winds in Argos: Sartre's les Mouches, Romance Notes, 72; Le heros et les choses dans Madame Bovary, Bull Amis Flaubert, 72; La Technique Descriptive Chez Guy de Maupassant, Belgium, Aelberts, 73; Then venom, to thy work: Pathological representation in Pierre et Jean, Mod Fiction Studies, 73; Literary decadence and the Frisson Nouveau, Nassau Rev, 74; Echos balzaciens: Une lettre de 1831, Studi Francesi, 76; Maupassant Criticism: A Centennial Bibliography, 1880-1979, McFarland, 82. *Mailing Add:* French Dept Conn Col New London CT 06302

ARTISS, DAVID STURGE, b Birmingham, Eng, July 5, 32; Can citizen; m 66, c 2. GERMAN LANGUAGE & LITERATURE. *Educ:* Univ Durham, Eng, BA, 58, dipl educ, 60, MA, 69; Downing Col, Univ Cambridge, PhD(Ger), 75. *Prof Exp:* Asst lectr English, Englisches Sem, Univ Tubingen, 56-57, lectr, 58-59; teacher Ger, Taunton's Col, Southampton, England, 60-65; from lectr to asst prof, 65-74, assoc prof, 74-78, PROF GER, MEM UNIV NFLD, 79-, DEPT HEAD, 80- *Concurrent Pos:* Leave fel German, Can Coun, 78-79. *Mem:* Can Asn Univ Teachers Ger; Am Asn Teachers Ger; Cambridge Soc. *Res:* Theodor Storm; techniques of realism; Hermann Hesse. *Publ:* Auth, Bird motif and myth in Theodor Storm's Schimmelreiter, spring 68, Key symbols in Hesse's Steppenwolf, 6/71 & Theodor Storm's Four Marchen: Early examples of his prose technique, 9/78, Seminar; Theodor Storm: Studies in Ambivalence Symbol and Myth in His Narrative Fiction, J Benjamins, Amsterdam, 78; German Culture Heritage Studies in Atlantic Canada, Mt Allison Univ, 79; The microcosmic view: Techniques of compression in T Storm's Novelle-Openings, Charlotte Jolles, 79. *Mailing Add:* Dept Foreign Lang Mem Univ St John's NF A1B 3X9 Can

ARTMAN, JIM PAINE, b Los Angeles, Calif, May 30, 22; m 47; c 3. SPANISH LITERATURE. *Educ:* Univ Okla, BA, 43; Nat Univ Mex, MA, 49. *Prof Exp:* From instr to assoc prof Span, 49-68, PROF SPAN, UNIV OKLA, 68-, ED UNIV PUBL, 55- *Concurrent Pos:* Fel & teaching asst, Univ Calif, Los Angeles, 51-53. *Res:* Spanish literature of the Golden Age; 19th century Spanish literature; 17th century Spanish prose. *Mailing Add:* Dept of Mod Lang Univ of Okla Norman OK 73069

ASCARI, CLAVIO FERDINANDO, b Mirandola, Italy, Feb 15, 39; m 65; c 1. MODERN LANGUAGES & LITERATURES. *Educ:* Bocconi Univ, Italy, Dr Lett, 62; Univ Vienna, dipl Ger, 63. *Prof Exp:* Asst prof English lit, Bocconi Univ, Milan, 63-65; asst prof Ital, 65-67, assoc prof, 70-78, PROF ITAL, MARY WASHINGTON COL, 78- *Concurrent Pos:* Ed consult, Club del Libro, De Agostini, Novara, Italy, 62-65; Fulbright-Hays grantee, 65-67; prof Ital summer lang schs, Middlebury Col, 66-67, 71-78; ed consult, Am Latina, Parma, 73; dir, The Ital Sch, Middlebury Col, 78-; mem grad fac, Mary Washington Col, 79-; reviewer, Forum Italicum, 79- *Mem:* Am Asn Teachers Ital; MLA. *Res:* Literature of the English and Italian Renaissance; literature of the Italian Ottocento; American narrative. *Publ:* Auth & ed, Ital transl, Sir Francis Bacon, Advancement of Learning Essays and New Atlantis, Club del Libro, De Agostini, Novara, Italy, 65; contribr, New Cambridge Modern History; Ital ed, Garzanti Ed, Milan, 69-70; auth, Realism and Transcendental Fantasy in Moby Dick, Club del Libro, De Agostini, Novara, Italy, 70. *Mailing Add:* 5 Delahay Dr Fredericksburg VA 22401

ASCHER, GLORIA JOYCE, b New York, NY, Apr 2, 39. GERMAN LITERATURE & LANGUAGE. *Educ:* Hunter Col, BA, 60; Yale Univ, MA, 64, PhD(Ger), 66. *Prof Exp:* Asst prof, 66-72, ASSOC PROF GER, TUFTS UNIV, 72- *Concurrent Pos:* Mem, Nat Screening Comt, Inst Int Educ, 72-73. *Mem:* MLA; AAUP; Adelantre. *Res:* Age of Goethe; Sephardic studies; Hugo von Hofmannsthal. *Publ:* Auth, Goethes Torquato Tasso und Hofmannsthals Unterhaltung uber den Tasso von Goethe: Ein magisches Verhaltnis, In: Festschrift for Heinrich Henel, Wilhelm Fink, Munich, 70; Die Zauberflote und Die Frau ohne Schatten: Ein Vergleich zwischen zwei Operndichtungen der Humanitat, Francke, Berne & Munich, 72; Izmirli Proverbs and Songs From the Bronx, Words of the Sephardim, Vol I Adelantre, 76. *Mailing Add:* Dept of German Tufts Univ Medford MA 02155

ASHBY, WILLIAM JAMES, b Detroit, Mich, Sept 27, 43; m 69; c 2. ROMANCE LINGUISTICS, FRENCH. *Educ:* Alma Col, BA, 65; Univ Mich, MA, 66, PhD(Romance ling), 73. *Prof Exp:* Asst prof, 71-80, ASSOC PROF FRENCH, UNIV CALIF, SANTA BARBARA, 80- *Concurrent Pos:* Am Coun Learned Socs res fel, 76. *Mem:* Ling Soc Am; MLA; Am Asn Teachers Fr. *Res:* Sociolinguistics; French language. *Publ:* Auth, Il parle or Iparl?, Prefixed inflection in French, Semasia, 74; Liaison, the rhythmic group, nouns and verbs of French, Studia Ling, 75; The loss of the negative morpheme, ne, in Parisian French, Lingua, 76; Clitic Inflection in French, An Historical Perspective, Rodopi, 77; Interrogative forms in Parisian French, Semasia, 77. *Mailing Add:* Dept of French & Ital Univ Calif Santa Barbara CA 93106

ASHHURST, ANNA WAYNE, b Philadelphia, Pa, Jan 5, 33; m 78. SPANISH AMERICAN & SPANISH LITERATURE. *Educ:* Vassar Col, AB, 54; Middlebury Col, MA, 56; Univ Pittsburgh, PhD(Span), 67. *Prof Exp:* Teacher English, Int Inst in Spain, Madrid, 54-56; teacher English & Spanish, Emmaus High Sch, Pa, 57-58; asst prof Span, Juniata Col, 61-63; instr, Carnegie Mellon Univ, 66-67; asst prof, Franklin & Marshall Col, 68-74, convenor foreign lang coun, 72-74, acting chmn dept Span, 72; assoc prof span, Univ Mo-St Louis, 74-78; RES & WRITING, 78- *Concurrent Pos:* Mellon fel, Univ Pittsburgh, 70-71. *Mem:* Am Asn Teachers Span & Port; MLA; AAUP; Inst Int Lit Iberoam; Int Inst Spain. *Res:* Spanish criticism of Hispanic American literature; modernism; generation of 1898. *Publ:* Auth, El simbolismo en Las Montanas del oro, Rev Iberoam, 6/64; Clarin y Dario: Una guerrilla literaria del modernismo, Cuadernos Hispanoamericanos, 2/72; Miguel de Unamuno y Ruben Dario, Cuadernos Americanos, 5-6/74; Ruben Dario y Salvador Rueda, Cuadernos Hispanoamericanos, 4/75; Sor Juana Ines de la Cruz ante la critica espanola, Dialogos, 1-2/78; La literatura hispanoamerricana en la critica espanola, Gredos, 80. *Mailing Add:* 2105 Barcelona Florissant MO 63033

ASHLEY, GARDNER PIERCE, b Winthrop, Mass. FRENCH. *Educ:* Northwestern Univ, BSEd, 41; Univ Ariz, MA, 49; Middlebury Col, DML, 76. *Prof Exp:* Instr French, Univ Vt, 51-53; lectr, Mt Allison Univ, Can, 54-55; assoc prof, 55-80, chmn, Dept Mod Foreign Lang, 77-82, PROF FRENCH, FRANKLIN COL IND, 80- *Mem:* MLA; Am Asn Teachers French; Am Coun Teaching Foreign Lang. *Res:* Nineteenth and twentieth century French literature. *Mailing Add:* Dept of Mod Foreign Lang Franklin Col of Ind Franklin IN 46131

ASHLEY, JOHN BENEDICT, b St John's, Nfld, Oct 29, 15; m 43; c 4. CLASSICS. *Educ:* Dalhousie Univ, BA, 37; Oxford Univ, BA, 40, MA, 43; Fordham Univ, PhD, 60. *Prof Exp:* Assoc prof classics, Mem Univ Nfld, 50-60, prof, 60-82. *Mem:* Joint Asn Class Teachers. *Res:* Roman history; Roman comedy; ecclesiastical Latin. *Mailing Add:* 63 Pine Bud Ave St John's NF A1C 5S7 Can

ASHLIMAN, DEE L, b Idaho Falls, Idaho, Jan 1, 38; m 60; c 3. GERMAN LANGUAGE & LITERATURE, COMPARATIVE LITERATURE. *Educ:* Univ Utah, BA, 63; Rutgers Univ, New Brunswick, MA, 66, PhD(Ger), 69. *Prof Exp:* Instr Ger, 67-69, asst prof Ger & comp lit, 69-73, ASSOC PROF GER & COMP LIT, UNIV PITTSBURGH, 73-, CHMN DEPT GER LANG, 77- *Concurrent Pos:* Ger Acad Exchange Serv grants, 71 & 74; Ger Fulbright Comn fel, 77. *Mem:* MLA; Am Asn Teachers Ger; Popular Cult Asn Am. *Res:* Nineteenth century German literature; American-German cultural relations; popular culture. *Publ:* Auth, The image of Utah in 19th century Germany, Utah Hist Quart, summer 67; The novel of western adventure in Germany, Western Am Lit, summer 68; Popular culture in foreign-language curricula, Unterrichtspraxis, spring 71; Amalie Schoppe in Amerika, Hebbel-Jahrbuch, 73; coauth, Thomas Mann and Caroline Newton, Mod Austrian Lit, 73; auth, M v Ebner-Eschenbach u der dt Aphorismus, Osterreich in Gesch u Lit, 74; Nikolaus Lenau in America, Bulletin, spring 76; The American Indian in 19th century German literature, J Popular Cult, spring 77. *Mailing Add:* Dept of Ger Lang & Lit Univ of Pittsburgh Pittsburgh PA 15260

ASHWORTH, PETER P, b Provo, Utah, June 10, 32; m 62; c 3. SPANISH LITERATURE. *Educ:* Brigham Young Univ, BA, 61; Univ Okla, PhD(Romance Lang), 67. *Prof Exp:* From instr to asst prof Span, 62-78, ASSOC PROF SPAN, BRIGHAM YOUNG UNIV, 78- *Mem:* Am Asn Teachers Span & Port; Rocky Mountain MLA. *Res:* Nineteenth and twentieth century Spanish novel. *Mailing Add:* 174 FOB Brigham Young Univ Provo UT 84602

ASKINS, ARTHUR L, b Clarksville, Ark, Aug 9, 34. SPANISH & PORTUGUESE LITERATURE. *Educ:* Univ Calif, Los Angeles, BA, 56, MA, 58; Univ Calif, Berkeley, PhD(Romance lang), 63. *Prof Exp:* From asst prof to assoc prof Span & Port, 63-76, PROF SPAN & PORT, UNIV CALIF, BERKELEY, 76- *Mem:* Soc Bibliofilos Espanoles. *Publ:* Auth, The Cancioneiro de Evora: Critical Edition and Notes, Univ Calif, 65; Franklin de Silveira Tavora's Literatura do Norte, Homenaje Rodriquez-Monino, Madrid, 66; Cancioneiro de Corte e de Magnates, Univ Calif, 68; co-ed, Romancero del Cid, Castalia, Madrid, 73; ed, The Hispano-Portuguese cancioneiro of the Hispanic Society of America, Studies Romance Lang, 73; Amargas horas de los dulce dias, Mod Lang Notes, Vol 82. *Mailing Add:* Dept of Span Univ of Calif Berkeley CA 94720

ASPEL, PAULENE VIOLETTE, b Normandy, France, Mar 19, 24; US citizen; m 45. FOREIGN LANGUAGES. *Educ:* Univ Paris, MA, 46, dipl, 50; State Univ Iowa, MA, 57, PhD, 58. *Prof Exp:* Instr French & French lit, Mt Holyoke Col, 48-49 & State Univ Iowa, 52-54 & 56-60; assoc prof, 62-72, ADJ PROF FRENCH & FRENCH LIT, IOWA WESLEYAN COL, 72- *Concurrent Pos:* Organizer & dir, FLEX Prog, Iowa City, Iowa, 59-; Old Gold Develop Fund grant, 60. *Mem:* Am Asn Teachers Fr; MLA. *Res:* Translation of American poetry into French; teaching of French civilization with French language at high school and elementary school levels. *Publ:* Auth, Gout d'une autre terre (poems), Pierre Seghers, France, 55; coauth, Homage to Baudelaire (poems), 57 & Mon premier livre de Francais, Book I, 61, State Univ Iowa. *Mailing Add:* Dept of Languages & Literature Iowa Wesleyan College Mt Pleasant IA 52641

ASPINWALL, DOROTHY BROWN, b Regina, Sask, Oct 21, 10; nat US; m 42; c 1. FRENCH LANGUAGE & LITERATURE. *Educ:* Univ Alta, BA, 33, MA, 39; Univ Wash, PhD, 48. *Prof Exp:* Teacher, high schs, Can, 33-37 & 38-40; asst, Univ Wash, 40-41; head dept French, Col Idaho, 41-47; from asst prof to prof Europ lang, 48-76, chmn dept, 55-58, 59-61 & 64-65, EMER PROF EUROP LANG, UNIV HAWAII, MANOA, 76- *Mem:* Am Asn Teachers French. *Res:* Poetry of Jacques Reda. *Publ:* Transl, The death of Andre Gide, NMex Quart, spring 54; auth, Languages in Hawaii, PMLA, 9/60; transl, The Riddle by Albert Camus, Atlantic Monthly, 63; Charles Peguy,

The Portico of the Mystery of the Second Virtue, 70 & auth, French Poems in English Verse, 1850-1970, 73, Scarecrow; Modern Verse Translations from French, Todd & Honeywell, 82. *Mailing Add:* 2003 Kalia Rd No 9-I Honolulu HI 96815

ASSARDO, M ROBERTO, b Philadelphia, Pa, May 12, 32; m 58; c 2. SPANISH & PORTUGUESE. *Educ:* Ind Univ, BA, 59, MA, 60; Univ Calif, Los Angeles, PhD (Hisp lang & lit), 68. *Prof Exp:* Instr Span, Wabash Col, 60-61; asst prof, Univ Calif, Davis, 68-73; assoc prof, 73-80, PROF SPAN, UNIV WIS-STEVENS POINT, 80- *Mem:* MLA; Am Asn Teachers Span & Port; Inst Int Lit Iberoam; Midwest Mod Lang Asn. *Res:* Contemporary Latin American novel and short story; Luso-Brazilian literature; Latin American folklore and literature. *Publ:* Auth, Cesar Branas, Poeta de la Soledad y la Angustia, Ed San Antonio, Guatemala 66; Semejante a la noche o la contemporaneidad del hombre, Cuadernos Am, 69; El Concepto de Tiempo Circular, Representado en El Camino de Santiago, La Torre, 71; El Nagual en la literatura de Guatemale, Rev Dialectologia y Tradiciones Populares; El efecto de la disgregacion temporal en El Acoso de Alejo Carpentier, Revista de Letras, 3/74; El concepto temporal y la tecnica cinematografica en Viaje a la Semilla, Explicacion de textos Literarios, 10/76; Elementos existencialistas en Nostros somos Dios de Wilberto Canton, Caribe, spring 77. *Mailing Add:* Dept of Foreign Lang Univ of Wis Stevens Point WI 54481

ASTE, MARIO, b Carloforte, Italy, Jan 11, 43; m 70. ITALIAN, SPANISH. *Educ:* Studies Theol Torino, Italy, BA, 67; Cath Univ Am, MA, 69 & 78, PhD(Ital & Romance philol), 71. *Prof Exp:* Asst, Cath Univ Am, 68-69; from instr to asst prof Ital & Latin, 71-75, foreign student advr, 72-76, assoc prof lang & chmn dept, 75-79, PROF LANG, UNIV LOWELL, 79- *Concurrent Pos:* Consult, Lexicon Lang Inst, Mass, 76- & Norton Indust, Mass, 78- *Mem:* MLA; Nat Asn Teachers Ital; Am Asn Teachers Span & Port; Baccacio Asn; Asn Univ Prof Ital. *Res:* Medieval literature; contemporary Italian literature; comparative literature. *Publ:* Auth, Uno, Nessuno e Centomila: Tesi Tematica e Stilistica, Univ Microfilms 71; La Narrativa di Luigi Pirandello: Dalle Novelle at Romanzo Uno Nessuno e Centomila, Studia Humanitatis Jose Porrua Turanzas, 78; Two novels of Pirandello, An Essay, Univ Press Am, 79. *Mailing Add:* 115 Reservoir St Lowell MA 01850

ASTIAZARAN, GLORIA C, b Nogales, Ariz, July 8, 24; div; c 2. SPANISH & ITALIAN. *Educ:* Univ Ariz, BA, 61, MA, 66, PhD(Span, Ital), 66. *Prof Exp:* Asst prof Span & Ital, Univ Nev, 66-67; ASST PROF SPAN & ITAL, UNIV TEX, EL PASO, 67- *Mem:* Am Asn Teachers Span & Port; Inst Int Lit Iberoam; MLA; AAUP. *Res:* Pedagogy; improvement in the teaching of languages; relevancy of old works to some of today's problems. *Mailing Add:* Dept of Modern Languages Univ of Texas El Paso TX 79968

ASTIER, PIERRE ARTHUR GEORGES, b Paris, France, Feb 1, 27; m 60; c 2. ROMANCE LANGUAGES. *Educ:* Univ Paris, Baccalaureate, 45, 1st cert (law), 46; Amherst Col, BA; Brown Univ, MA, 55, PhD(Romance lang), 61. *Prof Exp:* From instr to asst prof French, Dartmouth Col, 57-62; asst prof, Vassar Col, 62-63; from asst prof to assoc prof, 63-71, PROF FRENCH, OHIO STATE UNIV, 71- *Honors & Awards:* Distinguished Teaching Award, Ohio State Univ Alumni Asn, 72. *Mem:* Am Asn Teachers French; MLA. *Res:* Twentieth century French literature, especially the novel and drama; comparative stylistics and translation. *Publ:* Auth, Encyclopedie du Nouveau Roman, Debresse, 69; contribr, Les Critiques de Notre Temps et le Nouveau Roman, Garnier, 72; Ecrivaims francais engages: La Generation litteraire de 1930, Debresse, 78; ed, Samuel Beckett: Humanistic Perspectives, Ohio State Univ Press, 82. *Mailing Add:* Dept of Romance Lang Ohio State Univ Columbus OH 43210

ASTMAN, JOSEPH GUSTAV, b Williamantic, Conn, Nov 8, 16. GERMAN. *Educ:* Trinity Col, Conn, AB, 38; Yale Univ, AM, 42, PhD, 48. *Prof Exp:* Instr Ger, Trinity Col, Conn, 41-42, master, Avon Old Farms, 42-43; instr, St Joseph Col, Conn, 46-48; asst prof & in charge dept, 48-50, from assoc prof Ger to prof foreign lang & chmn dept foreign lang & lit, 50-66, dean col lib arts & sci, 66-72, PROF LANG & COMP LIT, HOFSTRA UNIV, 73- *Mem:* MLA. *Res:* German literature; comparative literature; Asian studies. *Mailing Add:* Dept of Foreign Lang & Lit Hofstra Univ Hempstead NY 11550

ASTMAN, MARINA, b Berlin, Ger, May 12, 24; US citizen; m 43; c 4. SLAVIC LANGUAGES & LITERATURES. *Educ:* Columbia Univ, BS, 56, PhD(Slavic lang & Lit), 69. *Prof Exp:* Head dept lang, St Hilda's & St Hugh's Sch, NY, 55-58; head dept French, Chapin Sch, 58-62; instr, 65-69, asst prof grad fac, 69-73, actg chmn dept Russ, 76-77, assoc prof, 73-79, PROF RUSS LANG & LIT, BARNARD COL, COLUMBIA COL, 79- *Concurrent Pos:* Nat Endowment for Humanities jr fel 74-75. *Mem:* Am Asn Teachers Slavic & East Europ Lang; Am Asn Advan Slavic Studies; Assoc Russ-Am Scholars in US; Dostoevsky Soc; Nabokov Soc. *Res:* Philology of Russian; Russian literature and culture of 19th and 20th century; latest developments of literary language. *Publ:* Auth, The Other Trugenev: From Romanticism to Symbolism, Colloqium Slavicum/Jal-Verlag, Wurtzburg, 73; Avdotya Panaeva: Her salon and her life, Russ Lit Tri Quart, spring 75; Dolly Oblonskaya as a structural device, Can-Am Slavic Studies, winter 78. *Mailing Add:* 112-50 78th Ave Forest Hills NY 11375

ASTON, KATHARINE O, b Cambridge, England, June 25, 17; US citizen. ENGLISH, LINGUISTICS. *Educ:* Univ Kans, BA, 37; Bryn Mawr Col, PhD(Germanic philol), 58. *Prof Exp:* Instr English, Syracuse Univ, 45-50; Inst Int Educ lectr, Oita Univ, Japan, 51-53; Fulbright lectr teaching English as second lang, Bur Educ Phillippines, US Dept State, 54-55; instr, Berlitz Sch Lang, Hamburg, Ger, 56; instr, 58-61, from asst prof to assoc prof English & ling, 61-71, PROF ENGLISH & LING, UNIV ILL, URBANA, 71-, DIR PROG ENGLISH AS SECOND LANG, 64- *Concurrent Pos:* Instr, Berlitz Sch Lang, New York, 50; vis prof, Beppu Women's Col, Japan, 53; consult proj evaluating NDEA insts, Bur Res, US Off Educ, 66; consult teaching English as second lang, ILL Migrant Coun, 67-68; mem English teaching adv panel, US Info Agency, 67-; actg acad dir in field, Univ Ill-Tehran Univ Res Unit, Tehran, 74-75. *Mem:* Am Asn Teachers English as Second Lang (secy, 66-67); Teachers English to Speakers Other Lang; Ling Soc Asn; Nat Asn Foreign Studies Affairs. *Res:* Teaching English as a second language; stylistics; historical linguistics. *Publ:* Auth, English Pronunciation Patterns for Foreign Students, Vol I, Prentice-Hall; Another -eme in language teaching: The grapheme, In: ON Teaching English to Speakers of Other Languages, Nat Coun Teachers English, 65; Grammar: The proteus of the English curriculum, Ill Asn Teachers English, 11/67. *Mailing Add:* Dept of English Univ of Illinois Urbana IL 61801

ASTOUR, MICHAEL CZERNICHOW, Ancient History, Semitic Studies. See Vol I

ASTURIAS, ROSARIO MARIA, b Guatemala City, Guatemala; US citizen. SPANISH. *Educ:* Col of the Holy Names, BA, 48; Univ Calif, Berkeley, MA, 59; Univ Southern Calif, PhD(Span) 63. *Prof Exp:* Asst prof, 63-76, assoc prof, 76-80, PROF SPAN, HOLY NAMES COL, 80- *Mem:* MLA; Am Asn Teachers Span & Port. *Res:* Golden Age theatre of Spain. *Mailing Add:* Dept of Spanish Holy Names College 3500 Mountain Blvd Oakland CA 94619

ASTUTO, PHILIP LOUIS, b New York, NY, Jan 5, 23; m 53; c 2. SPANISH. *Educ:* St John's Univ, NY, BA, 43; Columbia Univ, MA, 47, PhD(Span Am lit), 56. *Prof Exp:* Chmn Dept mod foreign lang, 60-64, PROF SPAN, ST JOHN'S UNIV, 47- *Mem:* MLA; Am Asn Teachers Span & Port. *Res:* Latin American history; Spanish American literature; enlightenment in the Hispanic world. *Publ:* Auth, Eugenio Espejo (1747-1795): reformador ecuatoriano de la ilustracion, Fondo de Cult Econ, Mex, 68; A Latin American spokesman in Napoleonic Spain: Jose Mejia Lequrica, Americas, 5/68; Eugenio Espejo: critico dieciochesco y pedagago qulteno, Revista Hisp Mod Columbia Univ, Fall-winter 68. *Mailing Add:* Dept of Spanish St John's University Graduate School Jamaica NY 11439

ASUNCION-LANDE, NOBLEZA CASTRO, b Philippines; m 65; c 2. SPEECH COMMUNICATIONS, SOCIOLINGUISTICS. *Educ:* Univ Philippines, BSE, 52; Mich State Univ, MA, 56, PhD(speech, ling), 60. *Prof Exp:* Teacher high schs, Philippines, 52-55; asst, Mich State Univ, 56-59; asst prof speech, State Univ NY Col New Paltz, 60-63; instr Tagalog, Yale Univ, 63-65; asst prof ling, Univ Kans, 67; vis lectr speech, Univ Hawaii, 67-68; ASSOC PROF SPEECH COMMUN, UNIV KANS, 68- *Mem:* Ling Soc Am; Speech Commun Asn; Asn Asian Studies; Int Commun Asn; Soc for Intercultural Educ, Training, Res. *Res:* Linguistics; foreign languages, expecially Malayo-Polynesian; intercultural communication. *Publ:* Auth, A bibliography of Philippine linguistics; Speech education in the Philippines, In: International Studies of National Speech Education Systems, Burgess, 71. *Mailing Add:* Dept of Speech & Drama Univ of Kans Lawrence KS 66044

ATHANASSAKIS, APOSTOLOS N, b Astrochorion, Greece, Sept 20, 38; US citizen; m 69. PHILOLOGY. *Educ:* Lincoln Univ, BA, 61; Univ Pa, MA, 62, PhD(classics), 65. *Prof Exp:* Asst prof classics, Claremont Men's Col, 65-68; asst prof, 68-74, assoc prof, 74-78, PROF CLASSICS, UNIV CALIF, SANTA BARBARA, 78-, CHMN CLASSICS DEPT, 82- *Concurrent Pos:* Nat Endowment for Humanities grant, Iceland, 76; Deut Akad Austauschdienst, Univ Würzburg, 76; Ctr Hellenic Studies jr fel, 76-77; Fulbright Found grant, 77; dir, Educ Abroad Prog, Lund, Sweden, 78-79; actg dean, Univ Crete, 79-80. *Mem:* Am Philol Asn; Archaeol Inst Am. *Res:* Homeric language; Greek poetry. *Publ:* Auth, Vita Sancti Pachomii, Scholars, 75; The Homeric Hymns, Johns Hopkins Univ, 76; Antilaloi tes Ziouras, Kedros, Athens, 76; The Orphic Hymns, Scholars, 77; Judaeo-Greek Hymns of Jannina, 78 & 82, Lady of the Vineyards, 78 & Ranka, 78, Pella; transl, R Pagoulatou, Pyrrhichios, 79. *Mailing Add:* Dept of Classics Univ of Calif Santa Barbara CA 93106

ATHERTON, JOHN H, b London, England, Sept 6, 31; US citizen; m 60; c 3. COMPARATIVE LITERATURE, AMERICAN STUDIES. *Educ:* Harvard Univ, BA, 53, MA, 56 PhD(comp lit), 61. *Prof Exp:* Actg instr French, Univ Calif, Berkeley, 60-61, from instr to asst prof, 61-64, asst prof French & comp lit, 64-65; assoc prof French, NY Univ, 66-70; PROF ENGLISH, UNIV TOURS, 70- *Mem:* MLA. *Res:* Intellectual history of France and the United States; contemporary American society; modern novel. *Publ:* Auth, Stendhal, Bowes & Bowes, London, 65; The function of space in Michelet's writing, Mod Lang Notes, 5/65; In praise of folly, Partisan Rev, summer 65; ed, Urban America, Masson, 73. *Mailing Add:* 53 rue de Turenne Paris 75003 France

ATKIN, DENNIS H, b Hurricane, Utah, Jan 8, 27; m 53; c 6. JAPANESE LITERATURE & ASIAN CULTURES. *Educ:* Brigham Young Univ, BA, 55, MA, 59; Univ Wash, PhD(Japanese lit), 70. *Prof Exp:* Asst prof, 67-80, ASSOC PROF HUMANITIES, NORTHERN ARIZ UNIV, 80- *Mem:* Asn Asian Studies; Nat Asn Humanities Educ. *Mailing Add:* Dept of Humanities Northern Ariz Univ Flagstaff AZ 86001

ATKINS, SAMUEL DECOSTER, b Madison, NJ, Oct 25, 10; m 35; c 3. CLASSICAL PHILOLOGY. *Educ:* Princeton Univ, AB, 31, AM, 32, PhD, 35. *Prof Exp:* Asst Prof, Baylor Univ, 35-37; from instr to assoc prof classics & sanskrit, 37-58, chmn dept classics, 61-72, prof, 58-78, EMER PROF CLASSICS & SANSKRIT, PRINCETON UNIV, 78- *Concurrent Pos:* Fulbright res scholar, Thailand, 59-60. *Mem:* Am Philol Asn; Am Orient Soc; Ling Soc India. *Res:* Indo-European philology and linguistics; Vedic religion. *Mailing Add:* 41 Cedar Lane Princeton NJ 08540

ATKINS, STUART, b Baltimore, Md, Mar 8, 14; m 46; c 1. GERMAN & COMPARATIVE LITERATURE. *Educ:* Yale Col, AB, 35; Yale Univ, PhD(Ger philol), 38. *Hon Degrees:* AM, Harvard Univ, 48. *Prof Exp:* Instr Ger, Dartmouth Col, 38-41, Harvard Univ & Radcliffe Col, 41-43 & Princeton Univ, 46; from asst prof to prof, Harvard Univ, 46-65; PROF GER, UNIV CALIF, SANTA BARBARA, 65- *Concurrent Pos:* Guggenheim Found fel Ger, 55 & 68; vis prof, Univ Goettingen, 62. *Honors & Awards:* Medal in Gold, Goethe-Inst, 68. *Mem:* MLA(pres, 72); Am Asn Teachers Ger; Goethe-Gesellschaft; Heinrich Heine-Gesellschaft; Goethe Soc NAm.

Res: German classical literature; Goethe; Heine. *Publ:* Auth, The Testament of Werther in Poetry and Drama, 49 & Goethe's Faust: A Literary Analysis, 58, Harvard Univ; auth & ed, Goethe's Faust: The Bayard Taylor Translation Revised (2 vols), 62 & ed, Goethe's Faust, The Prologues and Part One (biling ed), 63, Collier; auth (Zeitalter der) Authklarung, 2/65 & Zeitalter der Entdeckungen, 2/65, Fischer Lexikon Lit; auth & ed, The Age of Goethe, Houghton Mifflin, 69; Heinrich Heine: Werke, C H Beck (2 vols), 73-78; Goethe: Forquato Tasso, Hamburger Ausgabe, 77. *Mailing Add:* Univ of Calif Santa Barbara CA 93106

ATKINSON, JAMES CARROLL, b Americus, Ga, Aug 29, 31; m 56; c 2. ROMANCE LANGUAGES. *Educ:* Duke Univ, AB, 53, MA, 55; Johns Hopkins Univ, PhD(Romance lang), 63. *Prof Exp:* From instr to assoc prof, 58-73, actg head dept Romance lang, 66-67 & 73-74, PROF FRENCH, UNIV NC, GREENSBORO, 73- *Concurrent Pos:* Nat Endowment Humanities younger scholar fel, 69; trustee, Asn Teachers Fr, 74-80, managing trustee 80- *Mem:* MLA; Am Asn Teachers Fr; Mediaeval Acad Am; Soc Rencesvals. *Res:* Old French literature; romance philology; French syntax. *Publ:* Auth, La chanson de Roland: Laisses 169-170, Mod Lang Notes, 5/67; Eulalia's element or Maximian's Studies Philol, 7/68; The Two Forms of Subject Inversion in Modern French, Mouton, The Hague, 73; Theme, structure and motif in the Mystere d'adams, Philol Quart, winter 77. *Mailing Add:* Dept of Romance Lang Univ of NC Greensboro NC 27412

ATKINSON, MICHAEL, Literary Theory, Archetypal Psychology & Literature. See Vol II

ATKINSON, ROSS W, b San Jose, Calif, Dec 18, 45; m 69; c 1. BIBLIOGRAPHY, GERMAN LITERATURE. *Educ:* Univ Pac, BA, 67; Harvard Univ, PhD(Ger lit), 76; Simmons Col, MS, 77. *Prof Exp:* Scholar librn, 77-80, HUMANITIES BIBLIOGR, NORTHWESTERN UNIV LIBR, 80- *Concurrent Pos:* Lectr, German Dept, Northwestern Univ, 81. *Mem:* MLA; Am Libr Asn. *Res:* Bibliographical theory; German literature bibliography. *Publ:* Auth, Irony and commitment in Heine's Deutschland: Ein Wintermärchen, Germanic Rev, 75; An application of semiotics to the definition of bibliography, Studies Bibliog, 80; The early editions of Hauptmannn's Vor Sonnenaufgang, Papers Bibliog Soc Am, 81. *Mailing Add:* Collection Mgt Div Northwestern Univ Libr Evanston IL 60201

ATLAS, JAY DAVID, Philosophy, Linguistics. See Vol IV

ATLEE, ALFRED F MICHAEL, b Jerome, Ariz, Dec 21, 30; m 59; c 3. SPANISH LITERATURE. *Educ:* Univ Ariz, BA, 57, PhD(Span), 67. *Prof Exp:* Assoc prof Span, 65-77, PROF SPAN, CALIF STATE UNIV, LOS ANGELES, 77- *Concurrent Pos:* Dir, Teatro Espanol Del Amo, 71; Mem adv bd, Plaza de Raza Drama Comt, 73- & Carrascolendas, Univ Tex, 73; Yale Univ vis fel, 77-78. *Mem:* Asoc Int Hisp; Pac Coast Coun Latin Am Studies. *Res:* Cervantes; contemporary Spanish theatre; modernism. *Publ:* Auth, Bending of a Twig, In: Mexican American Writers, Houghton, 71; Antonio Buero Vallejo y Dios, Hispanofila, 72; co-ed, Pacific Coast Council on Latin American Studies Proceedings, San Diego State Univ, 72; And man was made word, In: From the Barrio, Canfield, 73; Unas actitudes religiosas de Cervantes encontradas en unas obras de Buero Vallejo, Papeles de Son Armadass, 74; Aventura en lo gris: Buero Vallejo's political message in black and white, Studies in Honor of Ruth Lee Kennedy, 77. *Mailing Add:* Dept of Foreign Lang & Lit Calif State Univ 5151 State University Dr Los Angeles CA 90032

AUBE, LUCIEN ARTHUR, b Lewiston, Maine, July 7, 22; m 53; c 4. SEVENTEENTH CENTURY FRENCH LITERATURE. *Educ:* Case Western Reserve Univ, AB, 48, AM, 50, PhD(Fr), 70. *Prof Exp:* Lectr French, 48-50, from instr to assoc prof, 50-75, chmn dept mod lang, 73-77, dir lang lab, 65-70, PROF FRENCH, JOHN CARROLL UNIV, 75-, CHMN DEPT CLASSICAL & MOD LANG, 77- *Honors & Awards:* Chevalier, Palmes Academiques, 80. *Mem:* Asn Dept Foreign Lang; Am Coun Teaching Foreign Lang; Am Asn Teachers Fr. *Res:* Seventeenth century French novel; history of ideas in France; teaching of foreign languages. *Mailing Add:* 2441 Loyola Rd University Heights Cleveland OH 44118

AUBERY, PIERRE, b Mt St Aignan, Aug 8, 20; m 50; c 1. FRENCH LANGUAGE & LITERATURE. *Educ:* Lycee du Havre, BA, 39; Univ Toulouse, LicLet, 44; DUniv, Paris, 55. *Prof Exp:* Journaliste Parlementaire, Paris, 47-52; instr romance lang, Duke Univ, 53-57; asst prof French, Mt Holyoke Col, 57-61; vis prof, Univ Alta, 61-62; assoc prof, 62-67, PROF FRENCH, STATE UNIV NY, BUFFALO, 67- *Concurrent Pos:* Guggenheim fel, 64-65; pres, Buffalo Br, Alliance Francaise, NY, 65-68; civilization ed, Fr Rev, 67-74; consult French lit, Encycl Judaica; rev ed, Comtemp Fr Civilization, 76- *Mem:* Soc Ecrivains Normands; Am Asn Teachers Fr; Am Soc 18th Century Studies. *Res:* Jewish literature; romantic Religions and social consciousness; a sociological approach to literature and literary criticism. *Publ:* Auth, Milieux juifs de la France contemporaine, PLON, 62; coauth, Juifs et Canadiens, Ed du Jours, Montreal, 67; auth, Pour une lecture ouvriere de la litterature, Ed Syndicalistes, 69; Mecislas Golbert, Intellectual Biography, Minard, 78. *Mailing Add:* Dept of Mod Lang State Univ of NY Buffalo NY 14260

AUBIN, GEORGE FRANCIS, b Bridgeport, Conn, Jan 31, 39. FRENCH, LINGUISTICS. *Educ:* Assumption Col, Mass, AB, 60, AM, 62; Brown Univ, PhD(ling), 72. *Prof Exp:* Instr French, 63-66, asst prof French & ling, 66-73, chmn dept French, 72-76, assoc prof, 73-78, PROF FRENCH & LING, ASSUMPTION COL, MASS, 78- *Concurrent Pos:* Reviewer, Nat Endowment for Humanities Div of Pub Progs, 78. *Mem:* Ling Soc Am. *Res:* French language; comparative stylistics; Algonquian linguistics. *Publ:* Auth, Roger Williams: Another view, Int J Am Ling, 10/72; contribr, Lexique Americain-Francais de la langue idiomatique, Ed Ophrys, Paris, 72; coauth, Narragansett kinship, Man in the Northeast, 75; auth, Narragansett color terms, Papers Seventh Algonquian Conf, 76; ed, A Proto-Algonquian Disctionary, Nat Mus of Man, Ottawa, 76; auth, Toward the linguistic history of an Algonquian dialect: Observations on the Wood vocabulary, Papers Ninth Algonquian Conf, 78; Golden Lake Algonquin: A preliminary report, Papers Tenth Algonquian Conf, 79; Remarks on Golden Lake Algonquin, Papers Twelfth Algonquian Conf, 81. *Mailing Add:* Div of Foreign Lang Assumption Col 500 Salisbury St Worcester MA 01609

AUCOIN, GERALD EDGAR, b Grand Etang, NS, Nov 24, 28; m 53; c 9. FRENCH. *Educ:* St Francis Xavier Univ, BA, 50; Laval Univ, MA, 61. *Prof Exp:* Prin, Queen's Sch, Sydney, NS, 53-55; assoc prof French, Xavier Univ, Sydney, 55-73, dir lang lab, 59-73, chmn dept French, 68-73; acad vpres, Col Ste-Anne, NS, 73-76, dir prov lang training unit, 76-81; CONSULT MOD LANG, NOVA SCOTIA DEPT EDUC, 81- *Concurrent Pos:* Can Coun fel, Ohio State Univ, 71-73. *Mem:* Am Coun Teachers Foreign Lang; Can Asn Applied Ling; Nat Asn Lang Lab Dirs; Can Asn Second Lang Teachers; Can Asn Immersion Teachers. *Res:* French folklore. *Publ:* L'Oiseau de la verite, Les Zuinze, Montreal, 80. *Mailing Add:* 1649 Hollis St 2nd Floor Halifax NS B3J 1V8 Can

AUGST, BERTRAND P, b Marrakech, Morocco, Oct 9, 32; US citizen; m 56; c 2. FRENCH. *Educ:* DePauw Univ, AB, 55; Univ Colo, MA, 56, PhD, 59. *Prof Exp:* Instr French, Univ Colo, 55-58; from actg instr to asst prof, 58-64, ASSOC PROF FRENCH & COMP LIT, UNIV CALIF, BERKELEY, 64- *Concurrent Pos:* Am Coun Learned Soc award for computer oriented res in humanities, 65-66. *Honors & Awards:* Distinguished Teaching Citation, Univ Calif, Berkeley, 63. *Mem:* MLA; Soc Paul Claudel; Col Pataphysique; Asn Machine Transl & Computational Ling. *Res:* Computational stylistics: 19th and 20th century French poetry; comparative literature. *Publ:* Auth, L'Estetique de Schopenhauer en tant que conduite de mauvaise foi, PMLA, 6/60; L'Otage de Paul Claudel, Romanic Rev, 2/62; Descartes' Compendium on Music, J Hist Ideas, 65; Bibliographical Guide to Modern French Drama, Zanzibar, 68. *Mailing Add:* Dept of French Univ of California Berkeley CA 94720

AULD, LOUIS EUGENE, b Conneaut, Ohio, Nov 12, 35; m 68; c 2. FRENCH LITERATURE, MUSIC. *Educ:* Oberlin Col, BA, 57; Univ Calif, Los Angeles, MA, 59; Bryn Mawr Col, PhD(Fr lit), 68. *Prof Exp:* Instr French, Kenyon Col, 64-65; from instr to asst prof, Smith Col, 65-70; asst prof, 70-74; dir music, rec libr, Duke Univ, 76-80; ASST TO DEAN, YALE SCH MUSIC, 81- *Concurrent Pos:* Founder & ed, Ars Lyrica, Soc for Word-Music Relations, spring, 81. *Mem:* MLA; Am Musicol Soc ; Lyrica Soc. *Res:* French literature; ballet de cour; words and music. *Publ:* Auth, Note Sur Hippolyte Amoureux, Cahiers Raciniens, 64; The music of the spheres in the Comedy-Ballets, Esprit Createur, fall 66; Theatrical illusion as theme in Les Amants Magnifiques, Romance Notes, autumn 74; Music in the secular theatre of Marguerite de Navarre, Renaissance Drama VII, new ser, Northwestern Univ; The Lyric Art of Pierre Perrin, Inst Mediaeval Music, 79. *Mailing Add:* Yale School of Music 96 Wall St New Haven CT 06520

AUSTERLITZ, ROBERT PAUL, b Bucharest, Romania, Dec 13, 23; US citizen; wid; c 2. LINGUISTICS. *Educ:* New Sch Soc Res, AB, 50; Columbia Univ, MA, 50, PhD, 55. *Prof Exp:* From asst prof to assoc prof, 58-65, PROF LING & URALIC STUDIES, COLUMBIA UNIV, 65- *Concurrent Pos:* Vis assoc prof, Yale Univ, 64-65 & Univ Calif, Berkeley, 69; consult lang-family map Asia, Smithsonian Inst, 67; Nat Endowment Humanities sr fel, 72-73; vis prof ling, Univ of Köln/Cologne, Ger, 77; vis prof ling, Univ Hawaii, 79 & Univ Umeau, Sweden, 82. *Honors & Awards:* Knight First Class, Order of the Lion of Finland, Repub Finland, 69. *Mem:* Ling Soc Am; cor mem Finno-Ugrian Soc; Soc Ling de Paris; Am Orient Soc (pres, 81-82). *Res:* General linguistics and phonetics; North-Eurasian languages; metrics and prosody. *Publ:* Auth, Ob-Ugric Metrics, Finnish Acad Sci, Helsinki, 58; Finnish Reader and Glossary, Ind Univ Uralic & Altaic Ser, 63, 2nd ed, 66; co-ed, Readings in Linguistics, Univ Chicago, Vol II, 66; ed, The Scope of American Linguistics, de Ridder Press, Lisse, Netherlands, 75. *Mailing Add:* 404 Philosophy Hall Columbia Univ New York NY 10027

AUSTIN, JOHN NORMAN, b Anshun, China, May 20, 37; US citizen. CLASSICAL LANGUAGES. *Educ:* Univ Toronto, BA, 58; Univ Calif, Berkeley, MA, 60, PhD(classics), 65. *Prof Exp:* Asst prof classics, Oakland Univ, 64-65 & Univ Southern Calif, 65-66; asst prof, Univ Calif, Los Angeles, 66-72, assoc prof, 72-76; prof, Univ Mass, 78-80; PROF CLASSICS, UNIV ARIZ, 80- *Concurrent Pos:* Fel, Ctr for Hellenic Studies, Washington, DC, 68-69; sr co-ed, Calif Studies Class Antiq, 72-; Guggenheim fel, 74-75; vis Aurelio prof, Boston Univ, 76-78. *Mem:* Am Philol Asn. *Res:* Comparative Literature; mythology; cosmology. *Publ:* Auth, Translation as baptism: Dryden's Lucretius, Arion, winter 68; Estotiland, a green thought in a green shade, Shenandoah, summer 71; Name magic in the Odyssey, Calif Studies Class Antiq, 72; Archery at the Dark of the Moon, Univ Calif Press, 74; The marketing of love, 32: 85-101 & Beginning Greek, 29: 47-58, Shenandoah; Odysseus Polytropos, Arche 6: 40-52. *Mailing Add:* Dept of Classics Univ of Ariz Tucson AZ 85721

AUSTIN, JOHN SOUTHERN, JR, b Atlanta, Ga, Apr 16, 39; m 62; c 3. GERMANIC LINGUISTICS, DANISH PHONOLOGY. *Educ:* Emory Univ, BA, 60; Middlebury Col, MA, 66; Cornell Univ, MA, 70, PhD(ling), 71. *Prof Exp:* Instr Ger & French, Ga Inst of Tech, 60-64; from instr to asst prof Ger, Oxford Col, Emory Univ, 64-68; ASST PROF GER, GA STATE UNIV, 72- *Mem:* Ling Soc Am; Am Asn Teachers Ger; MLA; AAUP; Soc Advan Scand Studies. *Res:* Modern German syntax; contrastive linguistics. *Mailing Add:* Dept of Foreign Lang Ga State Univ Atlanta GA 30303

AUSTIN, PAUL MURRAY, b China, May 17, 41; Can citizen; m 64; c 3. RUSSIAN LANGUAGE & LITERATURE. *Educ:* Univ Toronto, BA, 63, PhD(Russ lit), 70; Cornell Univ, MA, 64. *Prof Exp:* Lectr Russ, Brock Univ, 67-68; lectr, 68-70, asst prof, 70-75, ASSOC PROF RUSS, McGILL UNIV, 75-, CHMN DEPT, 81- *Mem:* Can Asn Slavists; Am Asn Advan Slavic Studies; Am Asn Teachers Slavic & E Europ Lang. *Res:* Soviet linguistic policy; Russian romanticism; Soviet Turkic linguistic policy. *Publ:* Auth, The etymology of king in Soviet Turkic languages, Can J Ling, 67; An interview with Ilya Ehrenburg, Soviet Studies, 69; Russian loan words in the proposed reform of Soviet Turkic alphabets, Gen Ling, 73; Russian loans in Uzbek, Nat Papers, 74; Russian views of Lowry, Can Lit, 74; La litterature quebecoise d'apresgue-re vue de Moscou, Rev de L'Univ d'Ottawa, 74; The development of modern literary Uzbek: Some historical analogies, Can Slavonic Papers, 75; Petr Kudrjasev: Russia's first Romantic ethnographer, Studies Romanticism, 76. *Mailing Add:* Dept of Russ & Slavic Studies McGill Univ 1001 Sherbrooke St Montreal PQ H3A 1G5 Can

AUSTIN, TIMOTHY ROBERT, Stylistics, Linguistics. See Vol II

AUSTIN, WARREN BARKER, English. See Vol II

AVALLE-ARCE, DIANE PAMP DE, b Maplewood, NJ, Apr 2, 44; m 69; c 2. SPANISH LITERATURE. *Educ:* Smith Col, BA, 66, PhD(Hisp studies), 75. *Prof Exp:* Instr, Smith Col, 67-69; ASSOC PROF SPANISH, NC CENT UNIV, 69- *Mem:* Int Asn Hispanists; Renaissance Soc; Am Cervantes Soc; Soc Courtly Love; MLA. *Res:* Imperial Spain; golden age drama; Spanish historical novel. *Publ:* Auth, Lope de Vega ante el problema de la limpeza de sangre, Smith Col, 68; Don Francesillo de Zuniga: la cronica burlesca del emperador Carlos V, Ed Critica, 81. *Mailing Add:* 3904 Garrett Rd Durham NC 27707

AVALLE-ARCE, JUAN BAUTISTA, b Buenos Aires, Argentina, May 13, 27; m 52 & 69; c 5. SPANISH. *Educ:* Harvard Univ, AB, 51, MA, 52, PhD, 55. *Prof Exp:* From asst prof to assoc prof Romance lang, Ohio State Univ, 55-61; prof Span, Smith Col, 61-65, Sophia Smith prof Hisp studies, 65-69, chmn dept, 66-69, WILLIAM RAND KENAN JR PROF SPAN, UNIV NC, CHAPEL HILL, 69- *Concurrent Pos:* Fel, Ohio State Univ, 58-59; Am Philos Soc grants, 58 & 63; Guggenheim fel, 60-61; Am Coun Learned Soc grant, 62 & 67-68; mem adv bd, Bryn Mawr Col Centro Estud Hisp, Madrid, 65-68; mem nat bd adv, Inst Cult Hisp, Spain, 66-; Nat Endowment Humanities grant, 67-68; consult, Coun Grad Schs, US, 67-, Univ Toronto Press, Johns Hopkins Univ Press, Univ Ga Press keynote address, Int Colloquium in Contemporary Spanish-American Narrative, Windsor Univ, Can, 74, Spanish Grad Prog, Pa State Univ & Revista Canadiense de Estudios Hispanicos; ed, NC Studies Romance Lang & Lit, 71-76; vis scholar, Univ Ctr Ga, 72 & Univ Ctr Va, 76; Southeastern Inst for Medieval & Renaissance Studies sr fel, 74; mem, Nat Inst Lit & Arts; off consult, PhD Prog, NY State Dept Educ; chmn, Medieval Lit, Asoc Int de Hisp, Toronto, 77; Soc Span & Span-Am Studies hon fel; ed adv coun, Critical Perspectives on Calderon de la Barca; Off Evaluator for Nat Endowment Humanities; contrib ed, Dict of the Middle Ages, Biographic Encycl of the World, Diccionario Enciclopedico Salvat Universal & McGraw-Hill Encycl of World Biography; Nat Endowment for Humanities grant, 78-80. *Honors & Awards:* Premio de Centro Gallego, 48; Potter Lit Prize, 51; Bonsoms Prize; Barcelona, 62. *Mem:* MLA; Renaissance Soc Am; Asoc Int Hisp; Asoc Espanola Bibliofilos; Inst Int Lit Iberoam; Anglo Am Basque Studies Soc. *Res:* History of the Spanish Empire; the Renaissance; Middle Ages. *Publ:* Coauth, Suma Cervantina, Tamesis Bks, 73; Las Memorias de Gonzalo Fernandez de Oviedo (2 vols), Chapel Hill, 74; La Novela Pastoril Espanola, 2nd ed, Madrid, 74; Nuevos Deslindes Cervantinos, Barcelona, Ediciones Ariel, 75; Don Quijote Como Forma de Vida, 76, Cervantes, Don Quijote de la Mancha (2 vols), 78 & Dintorno de una Epoca Dorada, 78, Madrid; Cervantes: Novel as Ejemplares (3 vols), Castalia, 82. *Mailing Add:* Euskaletxea 3904 Garrett Rd Durham NC 27707

AVERY, GEORGE COSTAS, b Philadelphia, Pa, July 27, 26; m 51; c 2. GERMAN. *Educ:* Univ Pa, AB, 51, AM, 55, PhD, 59. *Prof Exp:* From instr to asst prof Ger lang & lit, St Joseph's Col, Pa, 55-60; from instr to asst prof, 60-67, assoc prof Ger, 67-71, PROF GER, SWARTHMORE COL, 71- *Concurrent Pos:* Lectr, Swarthmore Col, 59-60; Fulbright-Hays res grant, Ger, 65-66. *Mem:* MLA; Am Asn Teachers Ger. *Res:* German literature since 1900; Herwarth Walden and Der Sturm; German romanticism. *Publ:* Auth, A poet beyond the pale: some notes on the shorter works of Robert Walser, Mod Lang Quart, 6/63; Die Darstellung des Kunstlers bei Franz Kafka, Weltfreunde, Prague, 67; Das Ende der Kunst Zur Robert Walser's Spatprosa, Schweizer Monatsch, 6/68; Inquiry and Testament: A Study of the Novels and Short Prose of Robert Walser, Univ Pa, 68. *Mailing Add:* Dept of Language Swarthmore College Swarthmore PA 19081

AVERY, HARRY COSTAS, b Philadelphia, Pa, Apr 9, 30; m 62; c 4. CLASSICS. *Educ:* Univ Pa, AB, 53; Univ Ill, MA, 56; Princeton Univ, PhD, 59. *Prof Exp:* Instr Greek, Bryn Mawr Col, 59-61; from asst prof to assoc prof classics, Univ Tex, Austin, 61-67; PROF CLASSICS & CHMN DEPT, UNIV PITTSBURGH, 67- *Concurrent Pos:* Jr fel, Ctr Hellenic Studies, 63-64; chmn adv coun, Comt Sch Class Studies, Am Acad Rome, 70-73, trustee, 75-78; vis res prof Greek hist & lit, Am Sch Class Studies Athens, 71-72, mem exec comt, Managing Comt, 72-76. *Honors & Awards:* Bromberg Award, Univ Tex, 66. *Mem:* Am Philol Asn; Soc Promotion Hellenic Studies; Archaeol Inst Am. *Res:* Greek history and literature; Roman history. *Publ:* Auth, Euripides' Heracleidai, 71 & Herodotus' Picture of Cyrus, 72, Am J Philol; Herodotus 6.112.2, Trans Am Philol Asn, 72; Themes in Thucydides' Account of the Sicilian Expedition, Hermes, 73; Sophocles' political career, Historia, 73; The three hundred at Thasos, 411 BC, Class Philol, 78. *Mailing Add:* Dept of Classics Univ of Pittsburgh Pittsburgh PA 51260

AVERY, WILLIAM TURNER, b East Cleveland, Ohio, Sept 9, 12; m 48; c 1. CLASSICAL LANGUAGES & LITERATURE. *Educ:* Western Reserve Univ, AB, 34, AM, 35, PhD, 37; Am Acad Rome, dipl, 39. *Prof Exp:* Teaching fel, Western Reserve Univ, 39-40; instr, Fenn Col, 40-42; from instr to assoc prof, Dickinson Col, 46-48 from assoc prof to prof class lang, La State Univ, 48-55; PROF CLASS LANG & LIT & CHMN DEPT, UNIV MD, COLLEGE PARK, 55- *Concurrent Pos:* Ling consult, Nat Asn Standard Med Vocab, 63- *Mem:* Am Philol Asn; Class Asn Atlantic States; Dante Soc Am. *Res:* Classical philolgoy; textual criticism of Greek and Latin authors; classical and comparative literature. *Publ:* Auth, Elementos-Dantescos del Quijote, Part I, Anales Cervantines, 63, Part II, 74-75; Annos habere: a Roman idiom, Romance Notes, 74. *Mailing Add:* 4324 Van Buren St University Park Hyattsville MD 20782

AVILA, LILIAN E, b Taunton, Mass. MODERN LANGUAGES. *Educ:* Brown Univ, AB; Middlebury Col, AM; Univ Paris, cert; Univ Laval, PhD. *Prof Exp:* Instr & prof English & Span, Bryant Col, 45-47; from instr to assoc prof foreign lang, Univ Maine, 47-60; from assoc prof to prof & chmn dept, RI Col, 60-77, acting chmn dept, 72-73, chmn dept, 74-77; RETIRED. *Mem:* MLA; Am Asn Teachers Fr; New Eng MLA; Claudel Soc. *Res:* Louis Lefebvre; French poetry from 1850; 20th century French literature, culture and civilization. *Publ:* Auth, Report of committee on the role of foreign languages in American life, Northeast Conf Teaching Foreign Lang, 55; Louis Lefebvre: Son Evolution Jusqu'a sa Conversion, Ed Trinite, 70; Paul Claudel et les amis de Saint Francois, Claudel Newslett, 10/70; Paul Claudel and Saint-John Perse: Parallels and contrasts, L'Esprit Createur, 5/73. *Mailing Add:* Heritage Village 73 D Southbury CT 06488

AVINS, CAROL JOAN, b New York, NY, May 9, 50. RUSSIAN & COMPARATIVE LITERATURE. *Educ:* Univ Pa, BA, 70; Yale Univ, PhD(Slavic lang & lit), 74. *Prof Exp:* Asst prof, 74-80, ASSOC PROF RUSSIAN LANG & LIT & COMP LIT, NORTHWESTERN UNIV, 80- *Mem:* MLA; Am Asn Teachers Slavic & East Europ Lang; Am Asn Advan Slavic Studies; AAUP; Am Coun Teachers Russ. *Res:* Twentieth century Russian literature; 20th century comparative literature. *Publ:* Auth, Border Crossings: The West and Russian Identity in Soviet Literature, 1917-1934, Univ Calif Press (in prep). *Mailing Add:* Dept of Slavic Lang & Lit Northwestern Univ Evanston IL 60201

AVIS, WALTER SPENCER, b Toronto, Ont, June 4, 19; m 49; c 3. ENGLISH, LINGUISTICS. *Educ:* Queen's Univ, Ont, BA, 49, MA, 50; Univ Mich, PhD(English lang & let), 55. *Prof Exp:* Teaching fel English lit, Queen's Univ, Ont, 49-50 & Univ Mich, 51-52; lectr English, Royal Mil Col of Can, 52-54, from asst prof to prof, 55-74, DEAN, CAN FORCES MIL COL, ROYAL MIL COL OF CAN, 74-; ASSOC DIR, LEXICOGRAPHICAL CTR FOR CAN ENG, 63- *Concurrent Pos:* Asst ed journ, Can Ling Asn, 54-56. *Mem:* Am Dialect Soc (Can secy, 54-); Can Ling Asn (secy-treas, 56-60, secy, 60-67, vpres, 66-68, pres, 68-70); Asn Can Univ Teachers English; Int Asn Univ Prof English; Can Coun Teachers English. *Res:* Canadian English; linguistic geography, especially Canadian and North American English; linguistics, especially teaching English as a second language and lexicography. *Publ:* Auth, The New England short o: a recessive phoneme, Language, 61; Speech differences along the Ontario-United States border, J Can Ling Asn; coauth, Dictionary of Canadian English Series, 62, 63, 67, auth, Bibliography of Writings on Canadian English, 65 & ed-in-chief, Dictionary of Canadianisms, 67, W J Gage, Toronto; coauth, An Annotated Bibliography of Writings on Canadian English, Fitzony & Whiteside, Toronto, 78. *Mailing Add:* Off of Dean Can Forces Mil Col Royal Mil Col of Can Kingston ON K7L 2W3 Can

AVITABILE, GRAZIA, b Yonkers, NY, Feb 10, 14. ITALIAN. *Educ:* Smith Col, AB, 37, AM, 38; Bryn Mawr Col, PhD, 42. *Prof Exp:* Instr, Wheaton Col, Mass, 42-47; asst prof, Mt Holyoke Col, 47-48; asst prof Ital & French, Wheaton Col, Mass, 48-52; from asst prof to assoc prof Ital, 52-61, prof, 61-79, EMER PROF ITAL, WELLESLEY COL, 79- *Concurrent Pos:* Ed analyst, Off Strategic Serv, 44-45; fac fel, Found Advan Educ, 54-55. *Mem:* MLA; Am Asn Teachers Ital; Mediaeval Acad Am; Dante Soc Am. *Res:* Romance literature; the controversy on Romanticism in Italy, first phase 1816-1823. *Publ:* Auth, Italian for the English Speaking, Bonacci, Rome, 77. *Mailing Add:* 23 Upland Rd Wellesley MA 02181

AXELROD, JOSEPH, b Kingston, Mass, Jan 15, 18. COMPARATIVE LITERATURE, HUMANITIES. *Educ:* Univ Chicago, BA, 37, MA, 38, PhD(Romance lang), 45. *Prof Exp:* Instr humanities, Chicago City Col, 43-45; from instr to asst prof, Univ Chicago, 45-50; from assoc prof to prof, San Francisco State Col, 50-62, chmn dept comp lit, 61-62, dean sch humanities, Calif State Col, Dominguez Hills, 62-65; dean undergrad studies, 65-66, chmn dept comp lit, 71-74, PROF HUMANITIES & COMP LIT, SAN FRANCISCO STATE UNIV, 65- *Concurrent Pos:* Vis res prof, Univ Calif, Berkeley, 67-69. *Res:* Interdisciplinary programs; history and structure; humanistic studies. *Publ:* Ed, Graduate Study for Future College Teachers, 59 & coauth, Resources for Language and Area Studies, 62, Am Coun Educ; Search for Relevance: The American College in Crisis, 69 & auth, The University Teacher as Artist: Toward an Aesthetics of Teaching for Professors of the Humanities, 73, Jossey-Bass; co-ed, College and Character, Montaigne, 80; Cross-cultural learning: The language connection, Cross-Cultural Learning, Jossey-Bass, 81. *Mailing Add:* Sch of Humanities San Francisco State Univ San Francisco CA 94132

AYCOCK, WENDELL MARSHALL, Comparative Literature. See Vol II

AYERBE-CHAUX, REINALDO, b Popayan, Colombia, Oct 27, 28; US citizen; m 61; c 1. SPANISH LITERATURE. *Educ:* Hofstra Univ, MS, 63; NY Univ, MA, 67, PhD(Span), 70. *Prof Exp:* Teacher Span, Massapequa Pub Sch, NY, 61-70; asst prof, 70-79, PROF SPAN, SYRACUSE UNIV, 80- *Mem:* MLA; AAUP; Mediaeval Acad Am. *Res:* Medieval Spanish literature. *Publ:* Auth, Tres enfoques criticos de la obra del arcipreste, In: El Arcipreste de Hita, 73; Aspectos de la tematica de Hector A Murena, Symposium, 73; Guillermo Valencia, Poeta Comprometido, Estudios Univ Cauca, 73; El ejemplo IV de El Conde Lucanor: su originalidad artistica, Romance Notes, 74; El Conde Lucanor: Materia Tradicional y Originalidad Creadora, 75 & ed, Alfonso X el Sabio: Estoria de Espana, Antologia, 78, Porrua Turranzas, Madrid; Las memorias de Leonor Lopez de Cordoba, J Hisp Philol, 78. *Mailing Add:* Dept of Romance Lang Syracuse Univ Syracuse NY 13210

AYLLON, CANDIDO, b Brooklyn, NY, Oct 3, 29. SPANISH. *Educ:* Brooklyn Col, BA, 51; Univ Wis, MA, 52, PhD, 56. *Prof Exp:* Instr Span lang & lit, Univ Wash, 56-57, asst prof Span, 57-63; instr, 63-64, assoc prof Span lang & lit, 64-69, chmn dept Span & Port, 67-73, PROF SPAN LANG & LIT, UNIV CALIF, RIVERSIDE, 69- *Concurrent Pos:* Dir, Univ Wis-Case Inst Technol Span Prog, Monterrey, Mex, 62 & 63; consult, Peace Corps Span Lang Prog, Univ Wash, 62; fel, Humanities Inst, Univ Calif, 67; dir, Edn

Abroad Prog, Madrid, Spain, 79-81. *Mem:* Am Asn Teachers Span & Port; Renaissance Soc Am; Philol Asn Pac Coast, MLA. *Res:* Spanish literature of the 15th, 16th and 17th centuries. *Publ:* Auth, A survey of 20th century Celestina scholarship, In: M H Singleton's translr, La Celestina, Univ Wis, 58; Petrarch and Fernando de Rojas, Romanic Rev, 63; Sobre Cervantes y Lope: La Novella, Romanische Forschunger, 63; La vision pesimista de La Celestina, Ed Studium, Mex, 65; coauth, Spanish Composition Through Literature, Prentice-Hall, 68. *Mailing Add:* Dept Lit & Lang Univ of California Riverside CA 92507

AYNESWORTH, JANINE CHERY, b Nancy, France, May 10, 32. FRENCH LANGUAGE & LITERATURE. *Educ:* Centre de Preparation au Professorate de Musique, Paris, CAEM, 59; Univ Minn, MA, 72, PhD(French), 75. *Prof Exp:* Teacher music primary sch, Nancy, France, 50-55; prof, Lycee Henri IV, Beziers, France, 59-69; fac mem French, Independant Studies Dept, Univ Minn, 72-75; asst prof, 76-79, ASSOC PROF FRENCH, COL ST TERESA, 80- *Concurrent Pos:* Concertmistress, CST Symphony Orchestra, 76- *Mem:* MLA; Soc des Prof Francais en Am; Alliance Francaise. *Res:* Alain Robbe-Grillet; Claudel's poetry; humanities. *Publ:* Auth, Pesanteur et apesanteur . . ., Claudel Studies, fall 77; coauth, Journal, conjoncture, structure (Bernanos), Lettres Modernes, 77; auth, Approche Rhetorique de la Dialectique des sens (in press) & Approche Rhetorique de la Dialectique des sens (in press), Lettres Modernes. *Mailing Add:* Col of St Teresa Winona MN 55987

AYORA, JORGE RODRIGO, b Zaruma, Ecuador, Feb 1, 39; US citizen; m 60; c 2. SPANISH-AMERICAN LITERATURE. *Educ:* Univ Wash, BA, 62, MA, 64; Vanderbilt Univ, PhD(Span), 69. *Prof Exp:* Asst prof, Univ Hawaii, Manoa, 67-68 & Calif State Univ, Hayward, 68-70; asst prof, 70-75, ASSOC PROF SPAN AM LIT, UNIV ORE, 75- *Honors & Awards:* Horseshoe Award, Univ Ore, 73. *Mem:* Inst Int de Lit Iberoamericana; Am Asn Teachers Span & Port. *Res:* Ideologies and literature; the Avant-Carde; Marxism. *Publ:* Auth, Inauguracion del Realismo Social en el Ecuador: A la Costa, Rev Estud Hist, 1/73; Gnosticism and time in El inmortal, Hispania, 9.73; The concept of the modern and the Spanish-American narrative, Latin-Am Lit Rev, 74; La alienacion marxista enLos pasos perdidos, Hispania, 12/74; Psicologia de lo grotesco en El hombre que parecia un caballo, Explicacion de textos lit, 74. *Mailing Add:* Dept of Romance Languages Univ of Oregon Eugene OR 97403

AYRES, GLENN THOMPSON, b Long Branch, NJ; m 80; c 1. LINGUISTICS. *Educ:* Univ Calif, Berkeley, AB, 68, PhD(ling), 80. *Prof Exp:* Teaching asst ling, Univ Calif, Berkeley, 73-74; prof de ling & asesor tecnico, Proyecto Linguistico Francisco Marroquin, Huehuetenango, Guatemala, 75-78; teaching assoc, Univ Calif, Berkeley, 79; LECTR ENGLISH LANG, UNIV IFE, NIGERIA, 80- *Mem:* Ling Soc Am. *Res:* Mayan languages, especially Ixil; syntactic theory; semantics. *Publ:* Auth, I daresay!, Ling Inquiry 5:3, 74; A note on Mayan reflexives, 80 & On ergativity and aspect in Ixil, 81, J Mayan Ling; The antipassive voice in Ixil, Int J Am Ling (in prep); La conjugacion de los verbos en maya yucateco moderno, Univ de Yucatan Press (in prep). *Mailing Add:* 421 Via la Soledad Redondo Beach CA 90277

AZEVEDO, MILTON MARIANO, b Ouro Fino, Minas Gerais, Brazil, Apr 27, 42. IBERO-ROMANCE & APPLIED LINGUISTICS. *Educ:* Cornell Univ, MA, 71, PhD(ling), 73. *Prof Exp:* Lectr Span & Port, Univ Ill, Urbana-Champaign, 72-73, asst prof, 73-76; ASST PROF SPAN & PORT, UNIV CALIF, BERKELEY, 76- *Concurrent Pos:* Vis asst prof Span & Port, Univ Colo, Boulder, 75-76 & Univ Minn, Minneapolis, 78-79. *Mem:* Ling Soc Am; Am Asn Teachers Span & Port. *Res:* Sociolinguistics; translation theory. *Publ:* Auth, On the semantics of estar and participle sentences in Portuguese, Linguistics, 9/74; On passive-like sentences in Portuguese, Lang Sci, 12/75; Thematic meaning, word order and indefinite actor sentences in Portuguese, Georgetown Univ Round Table on Lang & Ling, 76; O Subjuntivo em Portugues: Um Estudo Transformacional, Ed Vozes, Petropolis, Brazil, 76; coauth, A Practical Guide to the Teaching of Spanish, Oxford Univ Press, 76; auth, Identifying Spanish interference in the speech of learners of Portuguese, Mod Lang J, 1-2/78; Passive Sentences in English and Portuguese, 80 & A Contrastive Phonology of Portuguese and English, 81, Georgetown Univ Press. *Mailing Add:* Dept of Span & Port Univ of Calif Berkeley CA 94720

AZIZE, YAMILA, b Rio Piedras, PR, Nov 29, 53; US citizen. SPANISH & LATIN AMERICAN LITERATURE. *Educ:* Univ PR, BA, 75; Univ Pa, MA, 77, PhD(Am lit), 80. *Prof Exp:* Instr conversational Span, Univ Pa, 76-77 & 78; instr hisp Am lit, PR Jr Col, 77; instr Span lang & PR lit, Sacred Heart Univ, 79-81; ASST PROF SPAN LANG & HISP LIT, INTERAMERICAN UNIV, 81- *Concurrent Pos:* Lectr, Dept of Social Sci, Conf Women Studies, PR, 75, Interamerican Univ, 79, Cath Univ, Ponce, 82; consult, Social Res Ctr, 79; coordr honor students prog, Interamerican Univ, 82- *Mem:* Asn Caribbean Studies; Caribbean Studies Asn. *Res:* Latin American literature--sociological approach; women's studies. *Publ:* Ed, Luchas de la mujer en Puerto Rico, 1898-1919, San Juan, 79; auth, Comentarios a la coestion femeni no puertorrigoena, Pensamiento Critico Ano 3, 3/80. *Mailing Add:* 812 Lince St Dos Pinos Rio Piedras PR 00923

B

BAACKE, MARGARITA I, b Berlin, Ger, July 10, 23. GERMAN, ENGLISH. *Educ:* Univ Marburg, PhD(philos), 53. *Prof Exp:* Instr Ger, Univ Ill, 55; asst prof Ger, Eng & Am lit, Western State Col Colo, 55-57; asst prof Ger, Purdue Univ, 57-65; ASSOC PROF GER, KNOX COL, 65- *Concurrent Pos:* Lectr, NDEA Inst, Scranton, Pa, 68. *Mem:* MLA; Am Asn Teachers Ger. *Res:* Modern German literature; German area studies; German culture. *Mailing Add:* Dept of Mod Lang Knox Col Galesburg IL 61401

BAAK, LEONHARD E, b Ricketts, Iowa, May 20, 09; m 53. GERMAN. *Educ:* Buena Vista Col, AB, 39; Univ SDak, AM, 41; Colo Col, MA, 46; Univ Colo, PhD, 53. *Prof Exp:* Teacher high sch, SDak, 40-42; prin, Minn, 43-47; asst prof Ger, St Olaf Col, 47-51; prof Ger & educ & head dept, Col Emporia, 51-60; head dept mod lang, 60-74, PROF GER, MORNINGSIDE COL, 60- *Mem:* MLA; Am Asn Teachers Ger; Am Coun Teaching Foreign Lang; Asn Dept Foreign Lang. *Res:* Minimum German grammar for the second year reader. *Publ:* Auth, The liberals arts in the modern world, Morningside Rev, 67. *Mailing Add:* Dept of Mod Lang Morningside Col Sioux City IA 51106

BAAY, DIRK, b Vreeland, Neth, Dec 28, 23; US citizen; m 51; c 3. GERMAN & COMPARATIVE LITERATURE. *Educ:* Calvin Col, AB, 51; Univ Mich, MA, 53, PhD, 59. *Prof Exp:* From instr to assoc prof Ger, Grinnell Col, 54-66; PROF GER, COLO COL, 66- *Concurrent Pos:* Fulbright-Hays lectr, Cuttington Col, Liberia, 64. *Res:* Twentieth century German literature; comparative literature of the 19th and 20th centuries; African literature. *Mailing Add:* Dept of Ger & Russ Colo Col Colorado Springs CO 80903

BABB, GEORGIANA, b Troy, Ohio. GERMAN, LINGUISTICS. *Educ:* Ohio State Univ, PhD(ling), 51. *Prof Exp:* Instr English & Ger, Minn State Teachers Col, Mankata, 50-51; asst prof, Murray State Col, 52-53; asst prof Ger & Russ, Kent State Univ, 53-57; lectr English as foreign lang, English Lang Inst, Univ Mich, 57-60; asst prof ling & Ger, Montclair State Col, 60-62; asst prof Ger, Eastern Ill Univ, 62-64; from asst prof to assoc prof Ger & ling, Wright State Univ, 64-77; INSTR ENGLISH AS A FOREIGN LANG, COLUMBUS TECH INST, 77- *Mem:* Int Ling Asn; Teachers English to Speakers Other Lang. *Res:* Germanic and general linguistics; Indo-European linguistics; dialect geography. *Mailing Add:* 226 S James Rd Columbus OH 43213

BABBY, LEONARD HARVEY, b New York, NY, July 29, 39. SLAVIC & GENERAL LINGUISTICS. *Educ:* Brooklyn Col, BA, 62; Harvard Univ, MA, 65, PhD(Slavic ling), 70. *Prof Exp:* Asst prof Slavic ling, Princeton Univ, 69-71; asst prof, 71-79, PROF SLAVIC LING, CORNELL UNIV, 80- *Mem:* Ling Soc Am. *Res:* Russian syntax and the Russian language in general; Slavic syntax. *Publ:* Auth, The deep structure of adjectives and the participles in Russian, Language, 73; A note on agreement in Russian, Glossa, 73; Towards a formal theory of parts of speech, Readings in Slavic Transformational Syntax, 74; A Transformational Grammar of Russian Adjectives, Mouton, The Hague, 74. *Mailing Add:* Dept of Mod Lang & Ling Morrill Hall Cornell Univ Ithaca NY 14850

BABCOCK, ARTHUR EDWARD, b Chicago, Ill, May 15, 46; m 72. FRENCH LANGUAGE & LITERATURE. *Educ:* Univ Mich, AB, 68, MA, 69, PhD(French), 74. *Prof Exp:* Asst prof, 74-80, PROF FRENCH, UNIV SOUTHERN CALIF, 80- *Mem:* AAUP; Am Asn Teachers French; MLA; Philol Asn Pac Coast. *Res:* Twentieth-century French literature; Andre Gide. *Publ:* Auth, La Symphonie pastorale as self-conscious fiction, French Forum, 1/78; Perspective narrative dans Les Thibault, Ky Romance Quart, fall 79; Portraits of Artists: Reflexivity in Gidean Fiction, 1902-1946, York, 81. *Mailing Add:* Dept of French & Ital Univ of Southern Calif Los Angeles CA 90007

BABCOCK, CHARLES LUTHER, b Whittier, Calif, May 26, 24; m 55; c 3. CLASSICS. *Educ:* Univ Calif, Berkeley, AB, 48, MA, 49, PhD(classics), 53. *Prof Exp:* Asst classics, Univ Utah, 49-50; Fulbright scholar & fel, Am Acad Rome, 53-55; instr, Cornell Univ, 55-57; from asst prof to assoc prof class studies, Univ Pa, 57-66, asst dean col arts & sci, 60-62, vdean, 62-64, actg dean, 64; chmn dept classics, 66-68, dean col humanities, 68-70, PROF CLASSICS, OHIO STATE UNIV, 66-, CHMN DEPT, 80- *Concurrent Pos:* Mem exam comt Latin, Advan Placement Prog, Educ Testing Serv, 67-72, chmn exam comt classics, 72-74; McKinley scholar, Mt Union, Malone & Walsh Cols, 72; chmn managing comt, Intercol Ctr Class Studies, Rome, 76-82; trustee, Am Acad Rome, 81- *Mem:* Class Asn Midwest & South (pres, 77-78); Vergilian Soc (vpres, 71-74, pres, 75-76); Am Philol Asn. *Res:* Latin literature; Roman history; Latin epigraphy. *Mailing Add:* Dept of Classics Ohio State Univ Columbus OH 43210

BABCOCK, JAMES CHRISTOPHER, b Hammond, Ind, Oct 14, 39; m 64; c 2. FRENCH LANGUAGE & LITERATURE. *Educ:* Marian Col (Ind), BA, 61; Vanderbilt Univ, MA, 68, PhD(French), 71. *Prof Exp:* Assoc prof, 64-79, PROF SPAN & FRENCH, WESTERN KY UNIV, 80- *Mem:* MLA. *Res:* Nineteenth and 20th century French novel. *Mailing Add:* Dept of Foreign Lang Western Ky Univ Bowling Green KY 42101

BABCOCK, LELAND S, b Sacramento, Calif, Apr 24, 22; m 47; c 3. GERMAN. *Educ:* Univ Calif, PhD(Ger), 56. *Prof Exp:* Teaching asst Ger, Univ Calif, 47-49, 50-52; from asst prof to assoc prof, 52-67, PROF GER, OCCIDENTAL COL, 67- *Concurrent Pos:* Instr, Reed Col, 49- *Mem:* Am Asn Teachers Ger; MLA. *Res:* German literature of the 18th and 19th centuries; German Novelle. *Publ:* Coauth, German and Germany in Review, Van Nostrand, 72. *Mailing Add:* Dept of Lang & Ling Occidental College 1600 Campus Rd Los Angeles CA 90041

BABENKO-WOODBURY, VICTORIA A, b Mar 19, 24; US citizen. RUSSIAN LITERATURE & LANGUAGE. *Educ:* Univ Hamburg, PhD(Russ lit), 59. *Prof Exp:* Instr, US Army Inst, Garmisch, Ger, 64-68; asst prof Russ lit, Ohio State Univ, 68-73; asst prof, 77-78, ASSOC PROF RUSS LIT, COL WILLIAM & MARY, 78- *Concurrent Pos:* Ohio State Univ grant-in-aid, 71-72. *Mem:* MLA; Am Asn Advan Slavic Studies; Am Asn Teachers Slavic & East Europ Lang. *Res:* Women in Russian literature. *Publ:* Auth, Grust' (poems), Baschkirzew, Munich, 72; Struny Serdca (poems), Rossels, Belg, 72; Problems of contemporary Soviet poetry, East Europe, 72; The function of nature descriptions in Vladimir Korolenko's stories, Can Slavic Papers; Themes of Borys Oliinyk, Ukranian Rev, 75; Ed Andr Karamzina: Her reflections in Pushkin's works & Fazil Iskander: An examination of his satire, Russ Lang J, 75; Russian women in Evtushenko's poetry, Russ Rev, 77; Trockij and Tolstoy on art and the future of man: Utopia or reality, Russ Lang J, 82. *Mailing Add:* Dept of Mod Lang Col of William & Mary Williamsburg VA 23185

BABIN, MARIA TERESA, b Ponce, PR, May 31, 10; m 64. SPANISH LITERATURE. *Educ:* Univ PR, BA, 31, MA, 39; Columbia Univ, PhD(Span), 51. *Prof Exp:* Teacher Span & French, high schs, NY, Pa & PR, 32-40; assoc prof Span & chmn dept, Univ PR, 40-45; instr Romance lang, Hunter Col, 46-50; asst prof Span, Wash Sq Col, 51-61; chmn Span prog & coordr spec prog for talented students, Dept Educ, PR, 63-66; prof Hisp studies & chmn dept, Univ PR, 66-69; prof Puerto Rican studies & chmn dept, Lehman Col, 69-72; prof, 70-78, EMER PROF SPAN, GRAD CTR, CITY UNIV NY, 78- *Concurrent Pos:* Dir, Sch of the Air, WIPR, Dept of Educ, 36-38; consult, Pan Am Union, Washington, DC, 52-53; spec consult, Ford Found, 69-74; lectr, Inst PR, NY & univ ctrs, 69-74; consult, Dept Educ, Albany, NY, 70; prof, Ctr Advan Studies PR & Caribbean, San Juan, 77-82. *Honors & Awards:* Lit prizes, Inst Lit Puertorriquena, 54, Ateneo Puertorriqueno, 55 & Union Mujeres Americanas, Guatemala, 62; Lit Prize of Year, Inst PR, NY, 70. *Mem:* Corresp mem Hisp Soc Am; Span Royal Acad Lang. *Res:* Spanish and Latin American literature; Puerto Rican culture. *Publ:* Auth, Panorama de la Cultura Puertoriquena, 58; Siluetas literarias (essays), 67 & Jornadas literarias (essays), 67, La Cultura de Puerto Rico, Inst Cult Puertorriquena, 70; The Puerto Ricans' Spirit, Macmillan, 71; co-ed, Borinquen: An Anthology of Puerto Rican Literature, Knopf, 74; auth, Fantasia Boricura, Fr Estudios Lorguianos, Univ Puerto Rico, 76. *Mailing Add:* Morzagaray 266 San Juan PR 00901

BACH, MAX, b Laupheim, Ger, Jan 24, 21; nat citizen; m 47; c 2. FRENCH. *Educ:* Univ Calif, AB, 42, MA, 48, PhD(Romance lit), 53. *Prof Exp:* From instr to assoc prof French, 52-67, chmn dept French & Italian, 67-76, PROF FRENCH, UNIV CALIF, DAVIS, 67- *Concurrent Pos:* Am Philos Soc fel, 58-59. *Mem:* MLA; Am Asn Teachers Fr; Philol Asn Pac Coast. *Res:* Victor Hugo; Sainte-Beuve; 19th century criticism. *Publ:* Sainte-Beuve and Spanish literature, French Rev; Critique et politique: La reception des Miserables en 1862 & Sainte-Beuve critique du theatre de son temps, 12/66, PMLA. *Mailing Add:* Dept of French & Italian Univ of California Davis CA 95616

BACHMANN, JAMES KEVIN, b Yonkers, NY, Aug 3, 40; m 65; c 2. ENGLISH AS A FOREIGN LANGUAGE, LINGUISTICS. *Educ:* Georgetown Univ, BA, 63, PhD(ling), 70. *Prof Exp:* Instr English, Prog in Santo Domingo, St Louis Univ, 66-68, Am Lang Inst, 69; ASST PROF ENGLISH, COLO STATE UNIV, 69-, DIR INTENSIVE ENGLISH PROG, 75- *Mem:* Teachers English to Speakers Other Lang. *Res:* Foreign language communication; sociolingusitics. *Publ:* Auth, Field techniques in an urban language study, TESOL Quart, 9/70. *Mailing Add:* Dept of English Colo State Univ Ft Collins CO 80521

BACK, ARTHUR WILLIAM, b US, Aug 23, 10. HISTORY, LANGUAGE. *Educ:* Clark Univ, AB, 33; Middlebury Col, MA, 41. *Prof Exp:* Teacher French, Holden High Sch, Mass, 34-41; assoc prof hist & lang, 41-68, prof, 68-79, EMER PROF HIST & LANG, WORCESTER POLYTECH INST, 80- *Mem:* AAUP; MLA; Am Coun Teaching Foreign Lang. *Mailing Add:* 81 Winslow Ave Leicester MA 01609

BACKUS, ROBERT LEE, b Saginaw, Mich, Sept 17, 28. JAPANESE STUDIES. *Educ:* Univ Mich, Ann Arbor, BA, 51; Univ Calif, Berkeley, BA, 55, MA, 60, PhD(Orient lang), 63. *Prof Exp:* Sr lectr Japanese, Australian Nat Univ, 63-66; asst prof, 66-74, ASSOC PROF JAPANESE, UNIV CALIF, SANTA BARBARA, 74- *Mem:* Am Orient Soc; Asn Asian Studies; Asn Teachers Japanese. *Res:* Japanese language and history. *Publ:* Auth, Two modes of counting in Japanese, Vol 1, No 2 & Ordinal expressions in Japanese, Vol 2, No 1, Papers in Japanese Ling; What goes into a haiku, Lit East & West, 72; The relationship of Confucianism to the Tokugawa Bakufu as revealed in the Kansei Educational Reform, Harvard J Asiatic Studies, 74. *Mailing Add:* Dept of Ger & Slavic Lang Univ of Calif Santa Barbara CA 93106

BACON, HELEN HAZARD, b Berkeley, Calif, Mar 9, 19. CLASSICAL LANGUAGES & LITERATURE. *Educ:* Bryn Mawr Col, BA, 40, PhD(classics), 55. *Hon Degrees:* DLitt, Middlebury Col, 70. *Prof Exp:* Instr Greek & English, Bryn Mawr Col, 46-48, instr Greek, 48-49; instr classics, Woman's Col, 51-52; from instr to assoc prof, Smith Col, 53-61; assoc prof, 61-65, PROF CLASSICS, BARNARD COL, COLUMBIA UNIV, 65- *Concurrent Pos:* Mem, Col Bd Latin Comt, 61-64; Am Asn Univ Women Founders fel, 63-64; mem fac, Bread Loaf Sch English, Vt, summers 66, 68, 73 & 75; scholar-in-residence, Am Acad in Rome, 68-69; Blegen Distinguished vis res prof, Vassar, fall 79; consult Latin lang & scholar, Comt Physicians Overseeing Translation of 16th Century Latin Medieval Text, 73- *Mem:* Am Philol Asn; Archaeol Inst Am. *Res:* Greek tragedy; Plato; ancient romances. *Publ:* Auth, Socrates crowned, Va Quart Rev, 59; Barbarians in Greek Tragedy, Yale Univ, 61; The shield of Eteocles, Arion, 64; Woman's two faces: Sophocles' view of woman's relation to the tragedy of Oedipus and his family, Sci & Psychoanal, 66; co-transl, Aeschylus' Seven against Thebes, Oxford Univ, 73; auth, In-and out-door schoolings Robert Frost and the classics, Am Scholar, 74; For girls: From birches to wild grapes, Yale Rev, 77; Aeschylus and early tragedy, In: Ancient Writers: Greece, Scribner's, 82. *Mailing Add:* Dept of Greek & Latin Barnard Col Columbia Univ New York NY 10027

BACON, ISAAC, b Czech, Sept 3, 14; nat US; m 42; c 3. GERMAN PHILOLOGY & LITERATURE. *Educ:* Masaryk Univ, Brno, PhD, 39. *Prof Exp:* From instr to assoc prof mod lang, Univ Colo, 46-60; dean, 60-78, PROF LING, YESHIVA COL, YESHIVA UNIV, 60-, EMER DEAN, 78- *Concurrent Pos:* Ford Found fel, 54-55; consult to vpres acad affairs, Yeshiva Univ, 77-79. *Mem:* MLA; Am Asn Teachers Ger; Mediaeval Acad Am. *Res:* Old High German; early new High German; linguistics. *Publ:* Auth, Pietistic and rationalistic elements in Klopstock's language, J Eng & Ger Philol; A survey of the changes in the interpretation of Ackermann from Bohemia, Studies in Philol; Attemps at classification of Old High German charms and incantations, Mod Lang Notes. *Mailing Add:* Yeshiva Col Yeshiva Univ New York NY 10033

BACON, THOMAS IVEY, b Lubbock, Tex, Aug 15, 40; m 68; c 1. GERMAN LANGUAGE & LITERATURE, SCHOLARLY & LITERARY TRANSLATIONS. *Educ:* Tex Tech Univ, BA, 63; Univ Tex, Austin, MA, 67, PhD(Ger), 70. *Prof Exp:* Asst prof, Furman Univ, 69-74; ASSOC PROF GER & CHMN DEPT, TEX TECH UNIV, 74- *Mem:* Am Asn Teachers Ger; MLA; Western Asn Ger Studies; Am Literary Transl Asn. *Res:* German theater; German expressionism; Dadaism. *Publ:* Translr, Gerald Bisiner, Fragmente Zum Ich, 72 & Herbert Heckmann, Ubuville, The City of the Grand Egg, 73, Dimension; auth, Two from Germany, Furman Studies, 74; translr, Gerald Bisinger, Free and Alone and Other Poems, Dimension, 75; auth, Martin Luther and the Drama, Ed Rodopi, Amsterdam, 76; translr, Martin Roda Becher, No Luck with Women, Dimension, 78. *Mailing Add:* Dept of Germanic & Slavic Lang Tex Tech Univ PO Box 4579 Lubbock TX 79409

BADEN, NANCY TUCKER, b Los Angeles, Calif, Jan 7, 37; m 56; c 2. SPANISH-AMERICAN LITERATURE & LANGUAGE. *Educ:* Univ Calif, Los Angeles, BA, 59, MA, 66, PhD(Hisp lang & lit), 71. *Prof Exp:* Asst prof, 69-73, assoc prof, 73-78, PROF SPAN & PORT, CALIF STATE UNIV, FULLERTON, 78- *Concurrent Pos:* Vis assoc prof, Univ Calif, Santa Barbara, summer, 81. *Mem:* MLA; Am Asn Teachers Span & Port; Latin Am Studies Asn; Pac Coast Coun Latin Am Studies (pres, 78, secy-treas, 72-75). *Res:* Luso-Brazilian literature and language; Portuguese language. *Publ:* Auth, The significance of names in Jorge Amado's Gabriela Cravo e Canela, Proc Pac Coast Coun Latin Am Studies, 74; coauth, Portuguese influence in Swahili and East African languages, J African Studies, 76; Popular poetry in the novels of Jorge Amado, J Latin Am Lore, 76; Portuguese-American literature: Does it exist?, MELUS, 79; Portuguese-American literature: An overview, Gavea-Brown, 80. *Mailing Add:* Dept of Foreign Lang & Lit Calif State Univ Fullerton CA 92634

BAECKER, ANNE, b Essen, Ger, July 12, 14; US citizen. GERMAN. *Educ:* Marygrove Col, BA, 41; Univ Mich, MA, 42; Univ Cincinnati, PhD(Ger), 56. *Prof Exp:* From instr to asst prof Ger, Univ Cincinnati, 45-60; PROF GER & CHMN DEPT GER & RUSS, UNIV NC, GREENSBORO, 60- *Concurrent Pos:* Prof Ger & French, Col Conserv Music Cincinnati, 56-60; mem coun, Jr Year, Heidelberg, 59- *Mem:* MLA; Am Asn Teachers Ger; S Atlantic Mod Lang Asn; Ger Schiller Soc. *Res:* Goethe's Faust; 19th century drama and novelle; works of Gertrud von le Fort. *Publ:* Auth, Hundert Jahre Marienschule, Festschrift, 58; Erzählungen und Hörspiele, Harper, 66. *Mailing Add:* Dept of Ger & Russ Univ of NC Greensboro NC 27412

BAER, JOACHIM THEODOR, b Essen, Ger, Nov 11, 33; US citizen. FOREIGN LANGUAGES. *Educ:* Ind Univ, AB, 57; Harvard Univ, PhD, 63. *Prof Exp:* Asst prof Russ, Vanderbilt Univ, 62-66; asst prof Slavic lang & lit & Jonathan Dickinson Bicentennial preceptor, Princeton Univ, 66-71; assoc prof Russ & Polish lang & lit, NY Univ, 71-73; PROF SLAVIC LANG & LIT, UNIV NC, GREENSBORO, 73- *Concurrent Pos:* NDEA-Fulbright Hays award, Poland, 65-66 & res scholar, Inst Lit Studies, Polish Acad Sci, 69-70; Ger Acad Exchange Serv res awards, 74 & 78. *Mem:* Am Asn Advan Slavic Studies; Am Asn Teachers Slavic & East Europ Lang; Int Asn Slavic Lang & Lit; AAUP; Schopenhauer Ges. *Res:* Nineteenth and early 20th century Russian literature; late 19th and early 20th century Polish literature; Russian and Polish. *Publ:* Auth, Dal' und Leskov als Vertreter des Kunstlerischen Philologismus, Z Slavische Philol, Vol XXXVII, No 1; Nietzsche's Influence in the Early Work of Waclaw Berent, Scando-Slavica, 71; Philologism and Conservatism in Nineteenth-Century Russian Literature, Slavic Studies, Hokkaido Univ, 72; Vladimir Ivanovic Dal' as a Belletrist, Mouton, The Hague, 72; co-ed, Mnemozina: Studia Litteraria Russica in Honorem Vsevolod Setchkarev, Fink, Munich, 74; auth, Waclaw Berent, His Life and Work, Institutum Historicum Polonicum, Rome, 74, Ex Antemurale, XVIII: 75-239; Arthur Schopenhauer und die russische Literatur des späten 19 und frühen 20 Jahrhundert, Sagner, Munich, 80; Schopenhauer und Afanasij Fet, 61 Schopenhauer Jahrbuch für das Jahr 1980, Kramer, Frankfurt, 80. *Mailing Add:* Dept of Ger & Russ Univ of NC Greensboro NC 27412

BAER, KLAUS, b Halle, Ger, June 22, 30. EGYPTOLOGY. *Educ:* Univ Ill, BA, 48; Univ Chicago, PhD, 58. *Prof Exp:* Lectr Egyptol, Univ Calif, Berkeley, 59-60, asst prof, 60-64, assoc prof Egyptol & hist, 64-65; assoc prof Egyptol, 65-70, chmn dept Near Eastern lang & civilizations, 72-75, PROF EGYPTOL, UNIV CHICAGO, 70- *Concurrent Pos:* Adv ed jour, Am Res Ctr Egypt. *Mem:* Egypt Explor Soc, London; Am Orient Soc. *Res:* Ancient Egyptian history and language. *Publ:* Auth, Rank and Title in the Old Kingdom, Univ Chicago, 60; The low price of land in ancient Egypt, J Am Res Ctr Egypt, 62; An 11th dynast farmer's letters to his family, J Am Orient Soc, 63; A deed of the time of Ppjj I?, Z Ägyptische Sprache, 66. *Mailing Add:* Oriental Inst Univ of Chicago 1155 E 58th St Chicago IL 60637

BAEUMER, MAX LORENZ, b Trier, Ger, May 19, 17; US citizen; m 45. GERMAN LITERATURE & HUMANITIES. *Educ:* Philosophic Col, Trier, PhL, 39; Northwestern Univ, PhD, 59. *Prof Exp:* Asst prof, Bowling Green State Univ, 59-61; from asst prof to assoc prof Ger, Univ Kans, 61-65; vis prof, Inst Res Humanities, 69, PROF GER LIT, UNIV WIS-MADISON, 65-, PROF, INST RES HUMANITIES, 72- *Concurrent Pos:* Univ Kans res grant, Univ Frankfurt, 62, 63; E M Watkins scholar, 63; evaluator, NDEA Insts Ger for US Off Educ, 63; Am Philos Soc res fel, Ger, 64-; Fulbright lectr, Univ Stuttgart, 64-65; res fel, Univ Wis-Madison, 68-69 & 72 & 77; chief ed, Wilhelm Heinse's Collected Works & Lett, Fink Verlag, Munich, 75-; res fel, Deutscher Akademischer Austauschdienst, 75 & Herzog August Bibliothek Wolfenbüttel, 76-77; dir, Nat Endowment Humanities Sem col prof on Reformation, 80. *Mem:* Int Archiv für Sozialgeschichte der deutschen Lit; Am Soc Eighteenth-Century Studies; Deutsche Gesellschaft zur Erforschung des 18 Jahrhunderts; MLA; Deutsche Schiller Ges. *Res:* Literature and philosophy of Reformation; classical age; romanticism. *Publ:* Ed & coauth, Toposforschung, Wiss Buchgesellschaft, Darmstadt, 73; ed, W Heinse: Ardinghello, Reclam, Stuttgart, 75; contribr, Nietzsche and the Dionysian tradition, In: Studies in Nietzsche, Univ of NC, 76; Lutherfeiern und ihre ppolitische manipulation, In: Deutsche Feiern, Athenaion, Wiesbaden, 77;

Winckelmann, French classicism, and Jefferson, In: Studies in 18th Century Cult, 78; SozialKritische Literatur Oler Reformationszeit, In: Internationales Archiu Sozialgeschichte Deutscher Literatur, 80; Reformation in Braunschweig, In: Wolfenbütteler Beitrage, 81; Nietzche and Luther, In: Studies in Nietzsche, Univ NC, 82. *Mailing Add:* Inst for Res in the Humanities Univ of Wis Old Observ Madison WI 53706

BAGBY, LEWIS, b Brooklyn, NY, July 24, 44; m 67. RUSSIAN LITERATURE. *Educ:* Pomona Col, BA, 66; Stanford Univ, MA, 69; Univ Mich, Ann Arbor, PhD(Slavic lang & lit), 72. *Prof Exp:* Instr, 70-72, asst prof, 72-78, ASSOC PROF RUSS LANG & LIT, UNIV WYO, 78- *Mem:* Rocky Mountain Mod Lang Asn. *Res:* Prose fiction of Aleksandr Bestuzhev-Marlinjkij; Russian romantic prose fiction; transition from Russian romanticism to realisim. *Publ:* Contribr, Human values, quantification and literary evolution, In: The Architecture of Reading, Ohio State Univ, 76; auth, Narrative double-voicing in Lermontov's A Hero of Our Time, Slavic & East Europ J, 78; transl, The test, Bestuzev-Marlinksij's tale, Russ Romantic Prose, 79; auth, A concurrence of psychological and narrative structures: Anamnesis in Valentin Rasputin's Upstream, Downstream, Can Slavonic Papers, fall 80; Aleksandr Bestuzev-Marlinskij's Roman i Ol'ga: Generation and degeneration, Slavic & East Europ J, winter 81; Mikhail Bakhtin's discourse typologies: Theoretical and practical considerations, Slavic Rev, spring 81; Bestuzev-Marlinskij's Mulla Nur: A muddled myth to rekindle romance, Russ Lit, spring 82; transl, Ammalat-bek, Bestuzev-Marlinskij's tale, Russ Romantic Prose (in prep). *Mailing Add:* Dept of Mod & Class Lang Univ of Wyo Laramie WY 82071

BAGG, ROBERT ELY, English. See Vol II

BAGLIVI, GIUSEPPE, b Italy, Aug 7, 40; US citizen; c 1. MEDIEVAL LITERATURE. *Educ:* Queens Col, BA, 67; NY Univ, MA, 69; Ind Univ, PhD(Ital), 82. *Prof Exp:* Asst prof Ital, Kent State Univ, 70-79; ASST PROF ITAL, LA STATE UNIV, 82- *Mem:* Dante Soc Am. *Res:* Dante's divine comedy; Italian Renaissance. *Publ:* Coauth, Dante, Christ and the fallen bridges, Italica, 77; Salimbene and Il Bel motto, Am Benedictine Rev, 77. *Mailing Add:* Dept of French & Ital La State Univ Baton Rouge LA 70803

BAGNALL, ROGER SHALER, b Seattle, Wash, Aug 19, 47; m 69; c 2. GREEK PAPYROLOGY, ANCIENT HISTORY. *Educ:* Yale Univ, BA, 68; Univ Toronto, MA, 69, PHD(class studies), 72. *Prof Exp:* Asst prof classics, Fla State Univ, 72-74; asst prof Greek & Latin, 74-79, ASSOC PROF CLASSICS & HIST, COLUMBIA UNIV, 74- *Concurrent Pos:* Am Coun Learned Soc grant-in-aid, 75; Am Coun Learned Soc study fel, 76-77; mem bd, Scholars Press, 77-; Am Philos Soc grant-in-aid, 80; pres, Egyptological Sem of NY, 81-83; vis prof, Univ Florence, 81. *Mem:* Am Soc Papyrologists (secy-treas, 74-79); Am Philol Asn (secy-treas, 79-); Asn pour les Etudes Grecques; Egypt Exploration Soc; Asn Ancient Historians. *Res:* Greek papyri; social and economic history of the late Roman Egypt; Hellenistic social and economic history. *Publ:* Coauth, Ostraka in the Royal Ontario Museum (2 vols), Samuel Stevens, Toronto, 71-76; auth, Ptolemaic foreign correspondence in Tebtunis Papyrus 8, J Egyptian Archaeol, 75; The Administration of the Ptolemaic Possessions, Brill, Leiden, 76; coauth, Ostraka in Amsterdam Collections, Terra, Zutphen, 76; auth, The Florida Ostraka: Documents from the Roman Army in Upper Egypt, Duke Univ, 76; Bullion purchases and landholding in the fourth century, Chronique d'Egypt, 77; coauth, The Chronological Systems of Byzantine Egypt, Terra, Zutphen, 78; Columbia Papyri VII, Scholars Press, 78. *Mailing Add:* 606 Hamilton Hall Columbia Univ New York NY 10027

BAGULEY, DAVID, b Leicester, Eng, Apr 28, 40; Can citizen. FRENCH LITERATURE. *Educ:* Univ Nottingham, BA, 63; Univ Leicester, MA, 66; Univ Nancy, DUniv, 69. *Prof Exp:* Asst English, Univ Nantes, 66-67; lectr French, Univ Leicester, 67-68; from lectr to assoc prof, 68-77, PROF FRENCH, UNIV WESTERN ONT, 77- *Mem:* MLA; Soc Fr Studies. *Res:* French literature of the 19th century; the naturalist novel; literary criticism. *Publ:* Auth, Fecondite d'Emile Zola: Roman a These, Evangile, Mythe, 73 & Bibliographie de la Critique sur Emile Zola, 1864-1970, 76, Univ Toronto. *Mailing Add:* Dept of French Univ of Western Ont London ON N6A 5B8 Can

BAHE, BARBARA ANN, b Fargo, NDak, Jan 4, 16. GERMANIC LANGUAGE & LITERATURE. *Educ:* Concordia Col, AB, 37; Univ Mich, AM, 50; Columbia Univ, EdD, 60. *Prof Exp:* Instr high schs, NDak, 37-39 & Minn, 39-47; from instr to assoc prof, 47-62, PROF GER, LUTHER COL, IOWA, 62- *Mem:* Am Asn Teachers Ger; Am Coun Teaching Foreign Lang; MLA; AAUP. *Mailing Add:* Dept of Ger Luther Col Decorah IA 52101

BAHL, KALICHARAN, b Amritsar, India, Nov 19, 27; m 57; c 3. LINGUISTICS. *Educ:* Panjab Univ, India, MA, 55, PhD(ling), 65; Yale Univ, MA, 60. *Prof Exp:* Res assoc & lectr SAsian lang, 61-65, vis asst prof, 66-67, asst prof, 67-68, asst prof Hindi & ling, 68-73, ASSOC PROF HINDI & LING, UNIV CHICAGO, 73- *Concurrent Pos:* Am Inst Indian Studies fac res fel, 70-71. *Mem:* Ling Soc Am; Ling Soc India; Asn Asian Studies. *Res:* Indo-Aryan linguistics; Hindi language and literature; semantic structure of modern Indo-Aryan languages. *Publ:* Auth, The causal verbs in Hindi, Lang & Areas, 67; Panjabi, In: Current Trends in Linguistics, Mouton, The Hague, Vol V, 69; A Skeleton Grammar of Panjabi, Govt India; Studies in Semantic Structure of Hindi, Motilal Banarsidass, India, Vol I, 74; The Rasikapriya of Keshavadasa: An introductory review, J SAsian Lit, 74 ; A Grammar of Modern Rajasthani (in Hindi), Rajasthani Res Inst, 80. *Mailing Add:* SAsian Lang & Civilizations Univ of Chicago Chicago IL 60637

BAHNICK, KAREN KAY, b Waterloo, Iowa, Mar 30, 40; m 62. HISTORICAL LINGUISTICS, GERMANIC LANGUAGES. *Educ:* Cornell Col, BA, 62; Univ Iowa, MA, 64, PhD(Ger), 67. *Prof Exp:* From asst prof to assoc prof Ger, 67-76, assoc prof foreign lang, 76-79, PROF FOREIGN LANG, UNIV WIS-SUPERIOR, 80-, ASST VCHANCELLOR FOR ACAD AFFAIRS, 76- *Mem:* Ling Soc Am; MLA; Am Asn Teachers Ger. *Res:* Historical Germanic linguistics; general linguistics. *Mailing Add:* Dept of Foreign Lang Univ of Wisconsin Superior WI 54880

BAHR, EHRHARD, b Kiel, Ger, Aug 21, 32. GERMAN LITERATURE. *Educ:* Univ Kans, MS, 58; Univ Calif, Berkeley, PhD(Ger), 68. *Prof Exp:* Acting asst prof, 66-68, from asst prof to assoc prof, 68-72, PROF GER, UNIV CALIF, LOS ANGELES, 72-, CHMN DEPT GERMANIC LANG, 81- *Honors & Awards:* UCLA Distinguished Teaching Award, 70. *Mem:* MLA; Am Asn Teachers Ger; Am Soc 18th Century Studies; Am Lessing Soc; Heinrich Heine Soc. *Res:* Eighteenth century German literature; German classicism; modern German literature. *Publ:* Auth, Kafka and the Prague spring, Mosaic, summer 70; Georg Lukacs, Colloquium, 71 (also in English & French translr); Die Ironie im Spätwerk Goethese, Erich Schmidt, Berlin, 72; Goethes Wanderjahre as an experimental novel, Mosaic, spring 72; Ernst Bloch, Colloquium, Berlin, 74; ed, Kant, Was ist Aufklärung, Reclam, Stuttgart, 74; auth, The pursuit of happiness in the political writings of Lessing and Kant, In: Studies on Voltaire and the Eighteenth Century, 151: 167-184, 76; Personenwechselung in Goethes Westöstlichem Divan, Chronik des Wiener Goethevereins, 73: 117-125; Nelly Sachs, H C Beck, 80; ed, Goethe, Wilhelm Meisters Lehrjahre, Reclam, Stuttgart, 82. *Mailing Add:* Dept of Germanic Lang Univ of Calif 405 Hilgard Ave Los Angeles CA 90024

BAHR, GISELA ELISE, b Landsberg, Ger; US citizen. MODERN GERMAN LITERATURE. *Educ:* NY Univ, MA, 61, PhD(Ger), 66. *Prof Exp:* Teacher, Sarah Lawrence Col, 61-63; instr, NY Univ, 63-64; from instr to asst prof, Douglass Col, Rutgers Univ, New Brunswick, 66-73; PROF GER, MIAMI UNIV, 73- *Mem:* MLA; Am Asn Teachers Ger; Int Brecht Soc (ed, 71-77, pres, 77-79); Women in German. *Res:* Bertolt Brecht; literature of the German Democratic Republic; feminist literature. *Publ:* Ed, B Brecht, Im Dickicht der Städte, Erstfassung und Materialien, 69 & B Brecht, Die heilige Johanna der Schlachthöfe, Bühnenfassung, Fragmente, Varianten, 71, Suhrkamp, Frankfurt, WGer; Im Dickicht--zur Veröffentlichung der Erstfassung von 1921-22, Arbeitskreis Bertolt Brecht Nachrichtenbrief, 51: 65-72; Brecht in den siebziger Jahren--Themen und Thesen, In: Brecht Heute, Athenäum, Frankfurt, 71; auth, Roundheads and peakheaads: The truth about evil times, In: Essays on Brecht: Theater and Politics, Chapel Hill, 74; Blitz aus heiterm Himmel: Ein Versuch zur Emanzipation in der DDR, In: Die Frau in der Literatur, Franche, Munich, West Ger, 78; B Brecht, Die Rundköpfe und die Spitzköpfe, Bühnenfassung, Varianten, Fragmente, 79; The teaching of GDR literature: Premises and problems, In: Studies in GDR Culture and Society, Proc Sixth Int Symposium on the German Democratic Republic, Univ Press Am, 81. *Mailing Add:* Dept of Ger Russ & E Asian Langs Miami Univ Oxford OH 45056

BAILEY, CHARLES-JAMES NICE, b Middlesborough, Ky, May 2, 26. COMPARATIVE PHILOLOGY, THEOLOGY. *Educ:* Harvard Univ, AB, 50, ThM, 55; Vanderbilt Univ, DMin, 63; Univ Chicago, AM, 67, PhD(ling), 69. *Prof Exp:* Asst prof ling, Univ Hawaii, 68-71 & Georgetown Univ, 71-73; PROF ENGLISH & GEN LING, INST LINGUISTIK, TECH UNIV BERLIN, 74- *Concurrent Pos:* Fel, Netherlands Inst Advan Res, 80-81. *Honors & Awards:* Medal, Univ Helsinki, 78. *Mem:* Ling Soc Am; Lectological Asn; Int Phonetic Asn; Soc Ling Europe; Acoustical Soc Am; Am Horticultural Soc. *Res:* The application of variation theory to historical linguistics. *Publ:* Auth, Introduction to comparative metatheology, Univ Microfilms, 63; Inflectional Pattern of Indo-European Nouns, Univ Hawaii, 70; co-ed, New Ways of Analyzing Variation in English, Georgetown Univ, 73; auth, Variation and linguistic theory, Ctr Applied Ling, 73; Conceptualizing dialects as implicational constellation, In: Zur Theorie des Dialekts, 80; The yin-and-yang nature of language 1982, English Phonetic Transcription for Teachers (in press); Models Tested and Detested, 83. *Mailing Add:* Tech Univ Berlin Tel-9 Ernst-Reuter-Pl 7 Zi 815 D 1000 Berlin 10 Germany, Federal Republic of

BAILEY, JAMES O, JR, b La Junta, Colo, Sept 28, 29; m 56; c 3. RUSSIAN LITERATURE. *Educ:* Univ Southern Calif, BA, 52; Ind Univ, MA, 58; Harvard Univ, PhD(Slavic), 65. *Prof Exp:* Instr Russ, Univ Southern Calif, 63-64; asst prof, Oakland Univ, 64-67; asst prof Slavic, 67-76, PROF SLAVIC LANG, UNIV WIS-MADISON, 76- *Concurrent Pos:* Int Res & Exchanges Bd sr scholar, Soviet Union, 70; Am Coun Learned Soc fel, 73-74; Nat Endowment for Humanities fel, 82. *Mem:* MLA; Am Asn Teachers Slavic & East Europ Lang. *Res:* Russian versification; Russian folklore. *Publ:* Auth, Toward a Statistical Analysis of English Verse, Lisse, 75; The Metrical and Rhythmical Typology of K K Slucevskij's Poetry, IJSLP, 18: 93-117; The Trochaic song meters of Kol'cov and Kasin, Russ Lit, 12: 5-27; Parallelism or Antiparallelism, Asymmetry, In: An Inquiry into the Linguistic Structure of Poetry, Amsterdam, 76 & Folia Slavica, 1: 244-264; Linguistic givens and their metrical realization in a poem by Yeats, Lang & Style, 8: 21-33; The Metrical Typology of Russian Narrative Folk Meters, Am Contrib to 8th Int Cong of Slavists, 1: 82-103; The aims and accomplishments of the Russian linguistic-statistical method for studying poetic rhythm, SEEJ, 23: 251-261. *Mailing Add:* Dept of Slavic Lang Univ of Wis Madison WI 53706

BAILEY, RICHARD WELD, English. See Vol II

BAIRD, HERBERT LEROY, JR, b Taft, Calif, Aug 19, 23. SPANISH. *Educ:* Pomona Col, AB, 48; Univ Chicago, MA, 49, PhD(Romance ling), 55. *Prof Exp:* Instr Span, Northern Ill State Col, 51-53; asst French, Univ Chicago, 54-55; from instr to asst prof Span, Univ Calif, Riverside, 55-57; asst prof Span & French, Pomona Col, 57-61; assoc prof Romance lang, Claremont Men's Col, 61-64; assoc prof Span, Lewis & Clark Col, 64-67; ASSOC PROF SPAN, WESTERN WASH UNIV, 67- *Concurrent Pos:* Danforth fel, 56. *Mem:* MLA; Am Asn Teachers Span & Port; Am Coun Teaching Foreign Lang. *Res:* Medieval Spanish languages and literature; Spanish dialectology, especially the Leonese dialect of Northwestern Spain. *Publ:* Coauth, Three Spanish poets, Malahat Rev, 10/67 & Reyerta, Kenyon Rev, 11/67; auth, Analisis lingüistico y filologico de Otas de Roma, Real Academia Espanola, 76; contribr, Roots and Wings: Poetry from Spain 1900-1975, Harper & Row, 76. *Mailing Add:* Dept of Foreign Lang and Lit Western Wash Univ Bellingham WA 98225

BAKER, ARMAND FRED, b Marshalltown, Iowa, Oct 8, 33; m 59; c 3. SPANISH & SPANISH AMERICAN LITERATURE. *Educ:* Univ Northern Iowa, BA, 55; Univ Iowa, MA, 64, PhD(Span), 67. *Prof Exp:* Instr Span, Univ Iowa, 65-66; ASST PROF SPAN, STATE UNIV NY COL, ALBANY, 67- *Mem:* Am Asn Teachers Span & Port; Int Asn Hispanists. *Res:* Nineteenth and 20th century Spanish novel; modern Spanish American novel; Generation of '98. *Publ:* Auth, A new look at the structure of Don Quijote, Rev Estud Hisp, 1-73; contribr, Homenaje a Enrique Anderson Imbert, Anaya, 74; auth, Las vidas breves de Juan Carlos Onetti, 10-12/72 & Antonio Machado y las galerias del alma, 10/75 & 1/76, Cuadernos Hispanoamericanos; La vision del mundo en los cuentos de Enrique Anderson Imbert, Revista Iberoamerican, 7-12/76. *Mailing Add:* Dept of Hispanic and Ital Studies State Univ of NY Albany NY 12222

BAKER, CLIFFORD HENRY, b San Diego, Calif, Oct 29, 10; m 49. SPANISH LITERATURE. *Educ:* San Diego State Col, BA, 33; Univ Calif, MA, 35; Univ Southern Calif, PhD, 61. *Prof Exp:* From instr to prof Span, 37-76, EMER PROF SPAN, SAN DIEGO STATE UNIV, 76- *Concurrent Pos:* Prin transl clerk traveler's censorship, US Off Censorship, 42-46. *Mem:* Am Asn Teachers Span & Port; Philol Asn Pac Coast. *Res:* Spanish literature of the Golden Age; 19th and 20th centuries; Unamuno and Ortega y Gassett. *Publ:* Auth, The role of ideas in Ortega's Ontology, Romance Notes, 62. *Mailing Add:* 7148 Murray Park Dr San Diego CA 92119

BAKER, JOHN ARTHUR, b Liverpool, UK, Jan 15, 37; UK & Can citizen; m 64; c 2. PHILOSOPHY, ETHICS. *Educ:* Oxford Univ, BA, 61, MA, 63, BPhil, 63, DPhil, 69. *Prof Exp:* Lectr, Balliol Col, Oxford Univ, 63-64, Exeter & Trinity Col, 64-67; asst prof, 67-72, ASSOC PROF PHILOS, UNIV CALGARY, 72- *Concurrent Pos:* Vis lectr, Trinity Col, Oxford Univ, 76. *Mem:* Can Philos Asn; Humanities Asn Can. *Res:* Decision theory; philosophy of language; classical Greek philosophy. *Publ:* Auth, A Select Bibliography of Moral Philosophy: Oxford Study Aids in Philosophy Series, Vol IX, Oxford Univ, 77. *Mailing Add:* Dept of Philos Univ of Calgary Calgary AB T2L 1B4 Can

BAKER, JOSEPH O, b Murray, Utah, Dec 26, 38; m 61; c 2. GERMAN LANGUAGE & LITERATURE. *Educ:* Univ Utah, BA, 64; Tulane Univ, MA & PhD(Ger), 68. *Prof Exp:* Asst prof, 67-73, ASSOC PROF GER, BRIGHAM YOUNG UNIV, 73-, CHMN DEPT STUDY ABROAD, 77- *Mem:* MLA; Rocky Mountain Mod Lang Asn. *Res:* Heinrich von Kleist; German poetic realism. *Mailing Add:* 223 HRCB Brigham Young Univ Provo UT 84602

BAKER, MARY JORDAN, b Chicago, Ill. FRENCH RENAISSANCE LITERATURE. *Educ:* Stanford Univ, AB, 61; Univ Va, MA, 64; Harvard Univ, PhD(Romance lang), 69. *Prof Exp:* Instr French, DePauw Univ, 64-65; asst prof, 68-75, ASSOC PROF FRENCH, UNIV TEX, AUSTIN, 75- *Mem:* Am Asn Teachers Fr; Renaissance Soc Am; Mod Humanities Res Asn. *Publ:* Auth, Didacticism and the Heptameron: the misinterpretation of the tenth tale as an Exemplum, Fr Rev, 12/71; Fiammetta and the Angiosses douloureuses qui procedent d'amours, Symposium, winter 73; France's first sentimental novel and novels of chivalry, Bibliot Humanisme et Renaissance, 1/74; The sonnets of Louise Labe: a reappraisal, Neophilologus, 76; The role of the moral lesson in Heptameron, Fr Studies, 1/77; coauth, Panache Litteraire, Harper & Row, 78. *Mailing Add:* 2301 Windsor Rd Austin TX 78703

BAKER, ROBERT LAWRANCE, b Denver, Colo, Aug 17, 28; m 62; c 2. SLAVIC LANGUAGES & LITERATURE. *Educ:* Univ Colo, BA, 50; Univ Mich, MA, 59, PhD(Slavic lang & lit), 62. *Prof Exp:* Instr Russ, Univ Colo, 48-52; instr Russ & appl ling, Northwestern Univ, 60; lectr Slavic lang, Ind Univ, 60-62; asst prof Slavic lang & dir, NDEA Russ Lang Inst, 62-67; assoc prof, 67-70, chmn dept, 67-82, dean, 68, dir Russ Summer Sch, 69-82, resident dir, Russ Sch, Moscow, 77-78, PROF RUSS, MIDDLEBURY COL, 70-, ASSOC DIR, LANG SCHS, 81- *Concurrent Pos:* Mem adv comt, NDEA Russ Textbk Proj, Syracuse Univ, 61-63; res assoc Russ Testing, MLA, 66-68. *Mem:* MLA; Am Asn Teachers Slavic & Eastern Europ Lang; Am Asn Advan Slavic Studies; Am Coun Teaching Foreign Lang; Nat Fed Mod Lang Teachers Asn (pres, 76). *Res:* Language teaching methodology; Slavic linguistics. *Publ:* Auth, Mastering Russian Pronunciation and the Russian Sound System, 74 & Mastering Russian, Workbooks I & II, 77, Heinle & Heinle. *Mailing Add:* Lang Sch Middlebury Col Middlebury VT 05753

BAKER, SUSAN READ, b El Dorado, Ark, Dec 15, 42. FRENCH LITERATURE. *Educ:* Univ Tex Austin, BA, 64; Harvard Univ, MA, 65, PhD(French), 70. *Prof Exp:* Asst prof, Harvard Univ, 70-76; ASSOC PROF FRENCH, UNIV FLA, 76- *Mem:* MLA; North Am Soc 17th Century Fr Lit; Am Asn Teaching Fr; Am Soc 18th Century Studies; SAtlantic Mod Lang Asn. *Res:* Comedy in 17th-18th centuries; 17th century French moralists; 17th century philosophy and history of ideas. *Publ:* Auth, La Rochefoucauld and the art of the self-portrait, Romanic Rev, 1/74; Tragic vision in Racine's Iphigenie and Euripides' Iphigenia in Aulis, Degre Second, 7/77; La Rochefoucauld and Jacques Esprit, Rev Hist Lit Fr, Vol 78, No 2; Collaboration et Originalite--Chez la Rochefoucauld, Univ Fla Press, 80; Sentimental feminism in Marivaux's La Colonie, In: To Hold a Mirror to Nature, 82. *Mailing Add:* Dept of Romance Lang & Lit Univ of Fla Gainesville FL 32611

BAKKER, BAREND HENDRIK, b Hilversum, Netherlands, Sept 12, 34; Can citizen; m 58; c 3. FRENCH LITERATURE. *Educ:* Univ Toronto, BA, 56, MA, 58, PhD(French), 68. *Prof Exp:* Instr French, Univ Toronto, 60-63; instr, Ind Univ, 64-65; from asst prof to assoc prof, 65-75, PROF FRENCH, YORK UNIV, 75- *Concurrent Pos:* Dir, Emile Zola Res Prog, Univ Toronto, 71-; ed res grant, Social Sci & Humanities Res Coun Can, 76-80. *Mem:* MLA; Soc Lit Amis D'Emile Zola; fel Japan Soc; Asn Prof Francais Univ Can. *Res:* Preparation of 10-volume critical edition of the correspondence of Emile Zola. *Publ:* Auth, Naturalisme pas Mort: Lettres Inedites de Paul Alexis a Emile Zola (1871-1900), Univ Toronto, 71; Huysmans et la Revolution de 80 aux Pays-Bas, Bull Soc Huysmans, 73; Zola aux Pays-Bas, 1875-1885, Rev Sci Humaines, 75; contribr, Fiction, Form, Experience: The French Novel From Naturalism to the Present, Ed France-Quebec, 76; auth, Zola and the Revolution of the 1880's in the Netherlands, Rev Nat Lit, 78; ed, Emile Zola: Correspondance, Vols, I-III, 78, 80 & 82, Univ Montreal. *Mailing Add:* Zola Res Prog 14038 Robarts Libr 130 St George St Toronto ON M3J 1B3 Can

BALAKIAN, ANNA (MRS STEPHAN NALBANTIAN), b Constaninople, Turkey, July 14, 16; US citizen; m 45; c 2. FRENCH LITERATURE. *Educ:* Hunter Col, AB, 36; Columbia Univ, AM, 38, PhD, 43. *Hon Degrees:* LHD, New Haven Univ, 77. *Prof Exp:* Teacher high sch, Hunter Col, 37-43; from instr to asst prof French lit, Syracuse Univ, 43-44; from adj asst prof French to assoc prof foreign lang educ, 55-64, PROF FRENCH & COMP LIT, WASH SQ COL, NY UNIV, 64- *Concurrent Pos:* Res assoc, MLA, 59-60; vis prof, City Univ New York, 67-68; Guggenheim fel, 69-70; Nat Endowment for Humanities grant, 72-74; dir, Symbolism (vol), In: Comp Hist of Lit in Europ Lang; vis prof comp lit, State Univ NY Stony Brook, 75-76; consult, Nat Endowment for Humanities, 78-79. *Honors & Awards:* Distinguished Scholar Award, Hofstra Univ, 75. *Mem:* MLA; Am Asn Teachers Fr (vpres, 68-71); Am Comp Lit Asn (pres, 77-80); PEN Club; Auth Guild. *Res:* Modern French literature; research in the international repercussions of the surrealist and symbolist movements; origin and development of surrealism in literature. *Publ:* Auth, Literary Origins of Surrealism, Columbia Univ, 47; Span transl, Zig-Zag, Chile, 57; Surrealism: The Road to the Absolute, Noonday, 59; Andre Breton as philosopher, Yale Fr Studies, summer 64; The Symbolist Movement: A Critical Appraisal, Random, 67, rev ed, 77; Andre Breton, Magus of Surrealism, Oxford Univ, 71, Span ed, Monte Avila, Venezuela, 76; Introductory Essay to Anais Nin Reader, Swallow, 73; Mallarme et la Liberte, Europe, 4/76; Ren Char: In search of the Violet Man, World Lit Today, summer 77. *Mailing Add:* Dept of French & Ital NY Univ New York NY 10003

BALBIN, JULIUS FREDERIC, b Cracow, Poland, Jan 12, 17; US citizen. ENGLISH, FOREIGN LANGUAGES & LITERATURES. *Educ:* Jagiellonian Univ, Mag Phil, 39; Univ Vienna, PhD(English, French), 50. *Prof Exp:* Inst English & French, US Merchant Marine Acad, 59-63; researcher ling, Columbia Univ, 63-67; ASSOC PROF GER & ROMANCE LANG, ESSEX COUNTY COL, 69- *Concurrent Pos:* Co-dir, Esperanto Info Ctr, 63-, pres, NY Esperanto Soc, 72- *Mem:* MLA; AAUP; Am Coun Teachers Foreign Lang; Am Asn Teachers Esperanto; Am Asn Teachers Span & Portuguese; World Esperanto Asn. *Res:* Slavic, Germanic and Romance language and literatures; literary translation; interlinguistics and Esperantology. *Publ:* Auth, Edith Wharton and Her Relationship to France, Univ Vienna, 50; co-translr, Ten Contemporary Polish Stories, Wayne State Univ, 58; The Broken Mirror, Random, 58. *Mailing Add:* Dept of Foreign Lang Essex County College Newark NJ 07102

BALCAEN, HUBERT LOUIS, b Steinbach, Man, Nov 14, 39; m 63; c 4. FRENCH LANGUAGE & LITERATURE. *Educ:* Univ Man, BA, 61, MA, 68. *Prof Exp:* Teacher, St Boniface Sch Div, 63-66; PROF FRENCH & DIR, LANG LABS, UNIV MAN, 68- *Mem:* Can Asn Second Lang Teachers; Can Asn Univ Teachers; Asn Professeurs des Univ Can. *Res:* Second-language teaching, French; international development; testing of oral expression in French as a second language. *Publ:* Auth, Le Theme de la Religion dans l'Oeurne d'Antoine de Saint-Exupery, Univ Man, 68; Some observations on a practical handbook of Canadian French, Proc Ling Circle Man & NDak, 11/74; Laborataire de langues et Enseignement traditionnel au niveau universitaire, Syst, 11/74; Ecole francaise et verbe francais, Bull Ctr Etud Franco-Can Ouest, 5/80 & In: Entradiens, P-Hall, 82; Les Francais dans l'Ouest Canadien, Bull Ctr Etud Franco-Can Ouest, 2/81; Teaching oral expression in French at the third-year level, Proc Ling Circle Man & NDak, Vol 21, 81. *Mailing Add:* French & Spanish Dept Univ of Man Winnipeg MB R3T 2M8 Can

BALDASSARO, LAWRENCE A, b Holyoke, Mass. MEDIEVAL & MODERN LITERATURE. *Educ:* Union Col, Schenectady, NY, BA, 65; Ind Univ, MA, 67, PhD(Ital), 72. *Prof Exp:* Asst prof, 72-79, ASSOC PROF ITAL, UNIV WIS-MILWAUKEE, 79- *Mem:* Am Asn Teachers Ital; Dante Soc Am; Am Ital Hist Asn. *Res:* Dante; modern Italian literature. *Publ:* Auth, Dante the pilgrim: Everyman as sinner, Dante Studies, Vol XCII, 74; Structure and movement in Purgatorio X, Lingua e stile, Vol X, 75; Sicily's earthquake zone: Waiting in the wreckage, The Nation, 9/13/75; Pasolini: Revolutionary without an audience?, Film Studies Ann, Vol I, 76; Danilo Dolci and the poetics of commitment, Yale Ital Studies, fall 77; Inferno XII: The irony of descent, Romance Notes, Vol XIX, 78. *Mailing Add:* Dept of French & Ital Univ of Wis Milwaukee WI 53201

BALDINI, PIER RAIMONDO, b Florence, Italy, Sept 6, 41. ITALIAN. *Educ:* San Francisco State Univ, BA, 68; Univ BC, MA, 70; Univ Calif, Los Angeles, PhD(Ital), 76. *Prof Exp:* Asst prof, Univ Witwatersrand, Johannesburg, 71-73; asst prof, Ind Univ, 76-78; ASST PROF ITAL, ARIZ STATE UNIV, 78- *Concurrent Pos:* Reviewer Ital, Nat Endowment for Humanities, 77-; external examr, Dept Ital, McGill Univ, 77-; reviewer Ital, McMillan, Inc. *Mem:* Am Asn Teachers Ital; Pac Coast Philol Soc; SCent Mod Lang Asn; Midwest Mod Lang Asn. *Res:* Nineteenth and twentieth century Italian literature. *Publ:* Auth, O Lombardi's La narrativa italiana nlle crisi del novecento, Caltanisetta-Roma, Sciascia Ed, 71; G Cattaneo's Letteratura e ribellione, 4/74 & coauth, Problemi dell' Umanesimo, fall 75, Ital Quart; auth, Calvino: il piu povero degli uomini?, Forum Italicum, 76; L'ottobre fascista di Vittorini, La Fusta, 78; I primi anni di Vasco Pratolini, Otto-Novecento, vol IV, 80; Pavese e Vittorini sul filo della memoria, Nuova Antologia, 81; Varianti vittoriniane, Critica e Filologia (in press); Varianti vittoriniane: Il Garofano Rosso, Can J Ital Studies (in press). *Mailing Add:* Dept of Foreign Lang Ariz State Univ Tempe AZ 85281

BALDWIN, SPURGEON WHITFIELD, b Pensacola, Fla, Nov 30, 29; m 63; c 4. MEDIEVAL SPANISH LITERATURE, PHILOLOGY. *Educ:* La State Univ, BS, 51, BSEd, 55; Univ NC, MA, 57, PhD(Romance lang), 62. *Prof Exp:* Instr Span & French, Emory Univ, 59-62; from instr to assoc prof, 62-71, dir, year abroad prog, Barcelona, 75-76, PROF SPANISH, UNIV ILL, URBANA-CHAMPAIGN, 71-, CHMN DEPT, 81- *Mem:* MLA; Am Asn Teachers Span & Port; Medieval Soc Am. *Res:* Medieval Spanish literature and Bibles; medieval Romance encyclopedic works. *Publ:* Auth, Two old Spanish versions of the Epistle to the Romans, In: Medieval Studies in Honor of U T Holmes, Jr, Univ NC, 65; En tan pocas palabras (Celestina, Auto IV), Romance Notes, 67; coauth, El Nuevo Testamento Segun el Manuscrito Escurialense I-I-6, Read Acad Espanola, 70; auth, Irregular versification in the Libro de Alexandre and the possibility of a cursus in old Spanish verse, Romanische Forschungen, 73; coauth, Two notes on Barceo's Sacrificio de la Misa, Mod Lang Notes, 74; auth, Narrative technique in Gonzalo de Berceo, Ky Romance Quart, 76; co-ed, Estudis de Llengua, Literatura i Cultura Catalanes, Publ de L'Abadia de Monteserrat, 79. *Mailing Add:* Dept of Span Ital & Port Univ of Ill Urbana-Champaign Urbana IL 61801

BALDWIN, THOMAS PRATT, b Rome, Ga, Feb 25, 41. GERMAN LITERATURE. *Educ:* Univ Heidelberg, Zertifikat, 63; Univ Wis-Madison, MA, 67, PhD(Ger), 72. *Prof Exp:* From instr to asst prof, 68-74, assoc prof, 74-79, PROF GER, WESTERN KY UNIV, 80- *Concurrent Pos:* Consult, Nat Endowment Humanities, 78- *Mem:* Am Asn Teachers Ger; Hugo von Hofmannsthal Ges; Am Coun Studies Austrian Lit. *Res:* Austrian literature; Jahrhundertwende; pedagogy. *Mailing Add:* Dept of Foreign Lang Western Ky Univ Bowling Green KY 42101

BALL, BERTRAND LOGAN, JR, b Los Angeles, Calif, Oct 20, 31; m 59; c 1. FRENCH LANGUAGE & LITERATURE. *Educ:* Univ Redlands, BA, 53; Univ Southern Calif, MSLS, 58, PhD(French), 60. *Prof Exp:* Instr French & Span, Southern Ill Univ, 59-60, asst prof French, 60-62; from asst prof to assoc prof French, Brigham Young Univ, 62-69; ASSOC PROF FRENCH, MURRAY STATE UNIV, 69- *Mem:* Am Asn Teachers French. *Res:* Twentieth century French literature. *Publ:* Auth, Nature, symbol of death in La Voie Royale, French Rev, 2/62; A Dict of French Verbal Expressions, Brigham Young Univ, 64; Estaunie's Naturalistic Period and Spiritual Period, autumn 65 & Saint-Exupery and le culte de passe, summer 68, Brigham Young Univ Studies. *Mailing Add:* Dept of Foreign Lang Murray State Univ Murray KY 42071

BALL, DAVID RAPHAEL, b Feb 27, 37; US citizen, m 67; c 2. FRENCH & COMPARATIVE LITERATURE. *Educ:* Brandeis Univ, BA, 59; Univ Paris, Lic es Lett, 64, Dr(gen & comp lit), 71. *Prof Exp:* Lectr French lang & lit, 69-71, asst prof, 71-75, ASSOC PROF FRENCH, SMITH COL, 75- *Mem:* Soc Fr Etude 18 Siecle; Am Soc 18th Century Studies. *Res:* Eighteenth century studies; irony in political writing; translation. *Publ:* Auth, New Topoi (poems), 72 & The Mutant Daughter (poems), 75, Buffalo; Praise of Crazy (poems), Diana's Bi-Monthly, 75; The Garbage Poems, Burning Deck, 76; contribr articles, In: Revue de Litterature Comparee, 76, Etudes Anglaises, 76, Mass Rev, 79 & Ger Rev, 80; transl, Max Jacob, The Dice Cup (poems), Sun Bks, 79. *Mailing Add:* Dept of French Smith Col Northampton MA 01060

BALL, ROBERT J, b New York, NY, Nov 4, 41. CLASSICAL LANGUAGES. *Educ:* Queens Col, BA, 62; Tufts Univ, MA, 63; Columbia Univ, PhD(class), 71. *Prof Exp:* Asst prof, 72-76, ASSOC PROF CLASS, UNIV HAWAII, 77-, CHMN DEPT, 79- *Mem:* Am Philol Asn; Archaeol Inst Am. *Res:* Latin literature; Augustan poetry; teaching methodology. *Publ:* Auth, The Structure of Tibullus 1.7, Latomus, 75; Tibullus 2.5 and Vergil's Aeneid, Vergilius, 75; Tibullus the Elegist: A Critical Survey, Vandenhoeck & Ruprecht (in prep); ed, The Classical Papers of Gilbert Highet, Columbia Univ Press (in prep). *Mailing Add:* Dept of Europ Lang & Lit Univ of Hawaii Honolulu HI 96822

BALLARD, WILLIAM LEWIS, b Fargo, NDak, Apr 5, 36; m 67; c 1. GENERAL LINGUISTICS, CHINESE LANGUAGE. *Educ:* Tufts Univ, BA, 58; Univ Calif, Berkeley, PhD(ling), 69. *Prof Exp:* Teaching asst Chinese, Univ Calif, Berkeley, 64-65; asst prof ling, 69-73, assoc prof, 73-81, ASSOC PROF LING & ENGLISH AS SECOND LANG, GA STATE UNIV, 81- *Mem:* Ling Soc Am. *Res:* Phonological theory; Amerian Indian languages, literature and linguistics. *Publ:* Auth, Scenarios of change in Chinese dialectology, Acta Ling Hafniensia, 71; Change and the Saussurian paradox, Am Speech; More on Yuchi pronouns, Int J Am Ling, 78; The Yuchi Green Corn Ceremonial: Form and Meaning, Am Indian Studies Ctr, Univ Calif, 78; The literary/colloquial distinction in Wu and Chu, Cahiers Ling Asie Orient, 79; Fact, theory and fantasy in Chinese historical phonology, Comput Anal Asian & African Lang, 80; On some aspects of Wu Tone Sandhi, J Asian & African Studies, 80. *Mailing Add:* Ga State Univ Univ Plaza Atlanta GA 30303

BALOWITZ, VICTOR H, b Brooklyn, NY, June 27, 34; m 68; c 3. PHILOSOPHY OF LANGUAGE. *Educ:* Columbia Univ, PhD(philos), 69. *Prof Exp:* Assoc prof, 71-81, PROF PHILOS, STATE UNIV NY BUFFALO, 81- *Mem:* Am Philos Asn. *Res:* Philosophy of language, metaphysics and logic. *Publ:* Auth, A Method for Testing Validity, APA Newsletter on Teaching Philos, autumn 81. *Mailing Add:* Philos Dept State Univ Col 1300 Elmwood Ave Buffalo NY 14222

BALTZELL, JAMES HENRY, b Sumner, Ill, May 12, 22. FRENCH. *Educ:* Univ Ill, AB, Ind Univ, MA, 49, PhD(French), 52. *Prof Exp:* Instr French, Univ Ill, 51-52; Fulbright fel, Paris, 52-53; instr French & Span, John Burroughs Sch, 53-54; asst prof French & Ital, Col William & Mary, 54-56; asst prof French, Southern Methodist Univ, 56-58; from assoc prof to prof French, Calif State Col, Long Beach, 58-71; PROF FRENCH, SOUTHERN ILL UNIV, EDWARDSVILLE, 71- *Concurrent Pos:* Chevalier, Palmes Academiques, Ministry Nat Educ, France, 67. *Mem:* Am Asn Teachers Fr; MLA. *Res:* Mediaeval French literature; 17th & 20th century French literature Publ Auth, The Octosyllabic Vie de Saint Denis; collabr, The Medieval French Lives of Saint Fiacre & The Old French Lives of Saint Edmund, King of East Anglia; auth, Un poeme sur Saint Denis, Moyan Age, 56; Les Meilleures Nouvelles de Marcel Ayme, Scribner, 64. *Mailing Add:* Dept of Foreign Lang & Lit Southern Ill Univ Edwardsville IL 62025

BANAS, LEONARD NORBERT, b Chicago, Ill, Nov 6, 26. CLASSICAL LANGUAGES. *Educ:* Univ Notre Dame, BA, 49; Pontif Gregorian Univ, STL, 53; Princeton Univ, MA, 62. *Prof Exp:* Instr, 54-57, ASST PROF CLASSICS, UNIV NOTRE DAME, 57- *Mem:* Am Philol Asn. *Mailing Add:* Dept of Mod & Class Lang 304 O'Shaugnessy Hall Notre Dame IN 46556

BAND, ARNOLD J, b Boston, Mass, Oct 20, 29; m 54; c 2. LITERATURE. *Educ:* Harvard Univ, AB, 51, MA, 54, PhD(comp lit), 59; Hebrew Col, Boston, MHL, 51. *Prof Exp:* Teaching fel humanities, Harvard Col, 54-58; asst Greek & Hebrew, Brandeis Univ, 58-59; from asst prof to assoc prof, 59-68, PROF HEBREW, UNIV CALIF, LOS ANGELES, 68- *Concurrent Pos:* Asst prof, Hebrew Col, Boston, 57-59; Am Philos Soc grant, 62; Am Coun Learned Soc-Cos Sci Res Coun joint grant, Mid East, 62; mem, Near Eastern Ctr, Univ Calif, Los Angeles, 62; Warburg fel, Hebrew Univ, Israel, 62; mem, Exam Comt Col Bd Hebrew Achievement Test, 63-68; fel, Inst Creative Arts, Univ Calif, 66-67. *Mem:* MLA; Am Philol Asn: Nat Asn Prof Hebrew; PEN Club; Am Comp Lit Asn. *Res:* Modern Hebrew literature; comedy. *Publ:* Auth, HaRe'i Bo'er Ba'esh, Ogdan, Jerusalem & Ogen, NY, 63; Notstalgia and Nightmare: A Study in the Fiction of S Y Agnon, Univ Calif, Berkeley, 68. *Mailing Add:* Dept of Near Eastern Lang Univ of Calif Los Angeles CA 90024

BANDERA, CESAREO, b Malaga, Spain, Apr 28, 34; c 3. SPANISH LITERATURE, COMPARATIVE LITERATURE. *Educ:* Cornell Univ, MA, 62, PhD(romance lit), 65; Univ Salamanca, Spain, Lic Romance philol, 68. *Prof Exp:* Instr Span, Cornell Univ, 62-65, asst prof Span lit, 65-69; assoc prof, 69-74, PROF SPAN & COMP LIT, STATE UNIV NY BUFFALO, 74- *Concurrent Pos:* Cornell Univ grant Span lit, Madrid, 66-68; fac res fel, Res Found, State Univ NY, 78. *Mem:* MLA; Am Asn Teachers Span & Port; Int Asn Hispanists. *Res:* Spanish literature; critical theory; philosophy. *Publ:* Auth, El itinerario de Segismundo en La Vida es Sueno, Hisp Rev, 67; La Sombra de Bonifacio Reyes en Su Unico Hijo, Bull Hisp Studies, 69; El Poema de Mio Cid: Poesia, Historia, Mito, Gredos, Madrid, 69; El confuso abismo de La Vida es Sueno, Mod Lang Notes, 72; La ficcion de Juan Ruiz, PMLA, 73; Literature and desire: Poetic frenzy and the love potion, Mosaic, 75: Mimesis Conflictiva, Gredos, Madrid, 75; Sacrifical levels in Virgil's Aeneid, Arethusa, 81. *Mailing Add:* Dept of Span & Comp Lit State Univ NY Buffalo NY 14261

BANDY, ANASTASIUS CONSTANTINE, b Philadelphia, Pa, Aug 9, 20; m 57. GREEK & LATIN LANGUAGES & LITERATURES. *Educ:* LaSalle Col, BA, 51; Univ Pa, MA, 54, PhD, 61. *Prof Exp:* Asst instr Ger, Univ Pa, 57-58; from instr to assoc prof, 59-72, chmn dept 68-71, prof, 72-81, EMER PROF CLASSICS, UNIV CALIF, RIVERSIDE, 81- *Concurrent Pos:* Am Coun Learned Soc fel, 71; vis fel, Dumbarton Oaks, 72; mem bd educ, Byzantine Studies, 73-; mem, Ctr Neo-Hellenic Studies. *Mem:* Am Philol Asn; Archaeol Inst Am; Am Soc Papyrologists; Franklin Inst; US Nat Comt Byzantine Studies. *Res:* Christian epigraphy; Greek lexicography, Byzantine Greek language and literature. *Publ:* The Greek Christian Inscriptions of Crete, Christian Archaeol Soc Athens, 70; Early Christian Inscriptions of Crete, Hesperia, 73; Ioannes Lydus de Magistratibus Reipublicae, Am Phil Soc, 82. *Mailing Add:* 9 Appletree Ct Philadelphia PA 19106

BANDY, WILLIAM THOMAS, b Nashville, Tenn, May 11, 03; m 29; c 6. FRENCH LITERATURE. *Educ:* Vanderbilt Univ, AB, 23, AM, 26; George Peabody Col, PhD, 31. *Prof Exp:* Head dept mod lang, Stephens Col, 31-36; from asst prof to assoc prof French, Univ Wis, 36-49, chmn dept French & Ital, 59-66; dir, Ctr Baudelaire Studies & distinguished prof, 68-73, EMER DISTINGUISHED PROF FRENCH, VANDERBILT UNIV, 73-; EMER PROF UNIV WIS, 68- *Concurrent Pos:* Fulbright res award, France, 55-56; mem, Inst Res Humanities, 62-63; fel, Japan Soc, 81. *Honors & Awards:* Laureate, Prix Racine, 56. *Mem:* MLA; Am Asn Teachers French; Soc Hist Lit France; S Atlantic Mod Lang Asn. *Res:* Baudelaire; Edgar Allan Poe; modern French poetry. *Publ:* Auth, Baudelaire Judged by His Contemporaries, NY Inst Fr Studies, 33; Baudelaire en 1848, Emile Paul, Paris, 46; Baudelaire devant Ses Contemporains, Rocher, Monaco, 57; contribr, Deux Annees d'etudes baudelairiennes, Soc Editrice Int, Turin, 70 & Etudes baudelairiennes II, A la Baconniere, Neuchatel, 71; ed, Poe: Seven Tales Schocken Bks, 71 & Baudelaire: Edgar Allan Poe, Sa Vie et Ses Ouvrages, Univ Toronto, 73. *Mailing Add:* Box 1514B Vanderbilt Univ Nashville TN 37235

BANERJEE, MARIA NEMCOVA, b Prague, Czech, Nov 22, 37; US citizen; m 61. RUSSIAN & COMPARATIVE LITERATURE. *Educ:* Univ Paris, Baccalaureat, 55; Univ Montreal, MA, 57; Harvard Univ, PhD(Slavic), 62. *Prof Exp:* Tutor Russ lit, Harvard Univ, 61-62; asst prof, Brown Univ, 62-64; from vis lectr to asst prof, 64-72, assoc prof, 72-79, PROF RUSS LIT, SMITH COL, 79- *Concurrent Pos:* Vis lectr, Wellesley Col, 63-64; Int Res & Exchanges Bd sr scholar, Int Russ Lit, Leningrad, 73-74. *Mem:* Am Asn Advan Slavic Studies; Czech Soc Arts & Sci Am. *Res:* Nineteenth and 20th century Russian and European literatures, especially Dostoevsky and symbolism; Pushkin; Russian and European realism in the novel. *Publ:* Auth, Rozanov on Dostoevsky, Slavic East Europ J, winter 71; The Metamorphosis of an Icon, Female Studies, Vol IX, 75; Pushkin's The Bronze Horseman: An Agonistic Vision, Mod Lang Studies, 78; The Narrator and His Masks in Viacheslew Ivanov's Povest' o Suetomire Tsareviche, Can-Am Slavic Studies, 78; Vitezslov Nezval's Progue with Fingers of Rain: A surrealistic image, Slavic and East Europ J, 79; The American Revolver: An Essay on Dostoevsky's The Devils, Mod Fiction Studies, 81; Pavel Yavor and the Pathos of Exile, In: Far From You, Toronto, 81. *Mailing Add:* Dept of Russ Smith Col Northampton MA 01061

BANGERTER, LOWELL ALLEN, b Ogden, Utah, June 23, 41; m 64; c 5. GERMAN LANGUAGE & LITERATURE. *Educ:* Stanford Univ, BA, 66, MA, 67; Univ Ill, Urbana, PhD(Ger), 70. *Prof Exp:* Asst prof, 70-76, assoc prof, 76-81, PROF GER & HEAD MOD & CLASS LANG, UNIV WYO, 81- *Mem:* MLA; Am Asn Teachers Ger; Asn Ger Lang Auth Am. *Res:* Modern East German literature; Schiller; 18th century German literature. *Publ:* Auth, Narrative usage of Old Norse Maela, J Eng & Germanic Philol, 10/72; A Leftist view of Schiller, Res Stud, 6/73; The nature of separable and inseparable prefixes, Die Unterrichtspraxis, fall 73; Der Bau: Franz Kafka's final punishment tragedy, 3/74 & Schiller in East Germany, 12/74, Res Studies; Die Räuber: Friedrich Schiller and E T A Hoffman, Ger Rev, 3/77; Hugo von Hofmannsthal, Frederick Ungar, 77; The Bourgeois Proletarian, Bouvier, 80. *Mailing Add:* Dept of Mod and Class Lang Univ Wyo Box 3603 Univ Sta Laramie WY 82071

BANKS, SARAH JANE, b Punxsutawney, Pa, Dec 6, 41; m 71. SPANISH LITERATURE. *Educ:* Allegheny Col, BA, 63; Univ Southern Calif, MA, 65, PhD(Span). *Prof Exp:* Teaching asst Span, Univ Southern Calif, 63-65 & 67-68; instr, Immaculate Heart Col, 67; from instr to asst prof, Mary Baldwin Col, 68-73; ASSOC PROF SPAN, JACKSON STATE UNIV, 73- *Mem:* AAUP; Am Asn Teachers Span & Port; Midwest Mod Lang Asn; SCent Mod Lang Asn. *Res:* Colonial Latin American literature; colonial Latin American history; contemporary Latin American literature. *Publ:* A selected bibliography of Fray Toribio de Benavente (Motolina), Archivo Iberoam, 10-12/72; Foreign languages: Frill or foundation? or, How to Grab the Bull by the Horns, Asn Dept Foreign Lang Bull, 11/80. *Mailing Add:* Dept of Mod Foreign Lang Jackson State Univ Jackson MS 39201

BANOUN, MERILEE, b New York, NY, Nov 26, 42. FRENCH, GERMAN. *Educ:* Columbia Univ, AB, 64; Cath Univ Am, MA, 72, PhD(French), 78. *Prof Exp:* Instr French & English, Washington, DC Pub Schs, 66-68; transl, French & Ger, US Internal Revenue Serv, 73-75; ASST PROF FRENCH & GER, UNIV TENN, CHATTANOOGA, 76-, DIR, INST INT STUDIES, 77- *Mem:* MLA, AAUP; SAtlantic Mod Lang Asn. *Res:* French Romantic drama; French Baroque studies; contemporary European drama. *Mailing Add:* Dept of Foreign Lang Univ of Tenn Chattanooga TN 37401

BANTA, FRANK GRAHAM, b Franklin, Ind, May 31, 18. GERMAN, LINGUISTICS. *Educ:* Ind Univ, AB, 39; Univ Md, MA, 41; Univ Berne, PhD, 51. *Prof Exp:* Instr foreign lang, Univ Md, 39-44; from instr to assoc prof Ger, Univ Ill, Urbana, 51-64, chmn dept 55-64; assoc prof, 64-70, PROF GER LING, IND UNIV, BLOOMINGTON, 70- *Concurrent Pos:* Dir, Arts & Sci Teaching Resources Ctr, Ind Univ, 75-77. *Mem:* MLA; Ling Soc Am; Am Asn Teachers Ger (vpres, 71-73); Indoger Ges. *Res:* Middle High German; Germanic and Indo-European linguistics. *Publ:* Auth, Neue Perfekbildungen im Spät und Vulgärlatein, Paulusdruckerie, 52; The arch of action in Meier Helmbrecht, 10/64 & Dimensions and reflections: An analysis of Oswald von Wolkenstein's Fröhlich, zärtlich, 1/67, J English & Ger Philol; Berthold von Regensburg: Investigations past and present, Traditio, 69; Berthold von Regensburg, In: Die deutsche Literatur des Mittelalters: Verfasserlexikon, 78. *Mailing Add:* Dept of Ger Lang Ind Univ Bloomington IN 47401

BANZIGER, HANS, b Romanshorn, Switz, Jan 15, 17; m 43; c 3. GERMAN LITERATURE. *Educ:* Univ Zurich, Dr Phil(Ger lit), 42. *Prof Exp:* Teacher Ger, County Sch, Trogen, Switz, 43-67; docent Ger lit, Col Indust & Social Educ, St Gallen, Switz, 53-67, pvt docent, 65-67; assoc prof, 67-70, chmn dept, 71-72, prof, 71-82, EMER PROF GER, BRYN MAWR COL, 71- *Mem:* MLA; Am Asn Teachers Ger; Int Ger Asn; Swiss Authors Soc; Swiss PEN. *Publ:* Auth, Frisch und Dürrenmatt, 60, 7th ed, 76 & Zwischen Protest & Traditionsbewusstsein: On M Frisch, 75, Francke, Bern; contribr, Glücksfischer und Auswanderer: On Jakob Schaffner, Schweizer Monatshefte, 75; Widerstand gegen Modeströmungen: on R Henz, Festschrift Rudolf Henz, 77; Das namenlose Tier und sein Territorium: On Kafka, Deutsche Vierteljahresschrift, 79; Verzweiflung unf Auferstehungen auf dem Todesbett, Deutsche Vierteljahresschrift, 80; Dürrenmatt in Ungarn, Schweizer Monatshefte, 81; Schloss-Haus-Bau, Studien zu einem Motivkomplex, Francke, Bern/München, 82. *Mailing Add:* Dept of Ger Bryn Mawr Col Bryn Mawr PA 19010

BAR-ADON, AARON, b Kolno, Poland, Mar 3, 23; m 46; c 3. LINGUISTICS, HEBREW & SEMITICS. *Educ:* Hebrew Univ, Jerusalem, MA, 49, PhD(ling, Hebrew), 59. *Prof Exp:* Lectr Hebrew ling, Teachers Col, Haifa, Israel, 49-54 & Univ Wis-Madison, 59-60; asst prof Hebrew & Arabic ling &lit, Wayne State Univ, 60-63; assoc prof ling, 63-67, PROF LING & ORIENT & AFRICAN LANG & LIT, UNIV TEX, AUSTIN, 67- *Concurrent Pos:* Wayne State Univ res grant, 61; Univ Tex Res Inst grants, 64-66 & 67-68; bibliogr, MLA Int Bibliog, 67-; Am Coun Learned Soc fel, 68-69; mem, Col Bd Exam Comt on Hebrew, 68- *Mem:* Asn Jewish Studies; Int Ling Asn; MLA; Int Asn Appl Ling; Ling Soc Am. *Res:* Child language, acquisition of language by children; the revival of Modern Hebrew, socialinguistic background; Modern Hebrew, it's structure and the accelerated processes of developments in it. *Publ:* Auth, Studies in the Revival of Modern Hebrew, Univ Tex, 70; co-ed, Child Language: A Book of Readings, Prentice-Hall, 71; auth, Modern Israeli Hebrew, Pemberton-Jenkins, 71; Primary syntactic structures in Hebrew child language, In: Child Language: A Book of Readings, Mouton, 71; S Y Agnon and the revival of Modern Hebrew, Tex Studies Lit & Lang, 72; On the rise and decline of a Galilean dialect, In: Language Planning: Current Issues and Research, Georgetown Univ, 73; The Rise and Decline of a Dialect: A Study in the Revival of Modern Hebrew, Mouton, The Hague, 74. *Mailing Add:* Dept of Ling & Orient & African Lang & Lit Univ of Tex Austin TX 78712

BARBERA, RAYMOND EDMOND, b Brooklyn, NY, Feb 8, 18; m 43; c 5. ROMANCE LANGUAGES. *Educ:* Brooklyn Col, BA, 47; Univ Ariz, MA, 48; Nat Univ Mex, Dr en Letras, 49; Univ Wis, PhD(Span lit), 58. *Prof Exp:* Instr Span, Williams Col, 51-52; assoc prof romance lang, 53-71, dir comp lit MA prog, 73-77, PROF ROMANCE LANG, CLARK UNIV, 71- *Mem:* MLA; Am Asn Teachers Span & Port. *Res:* Medieval Spanish literature. *Publ:* Auth, Fernando de Rojas, converso, Hispania, 3/68; Medieval iconography in the Celestina, Romanic Rev, 2/70; ed, Cervantes, a Critical Trajectory, Mirage, 71; auth, The source and disposition of wealth in the Poema de Mio Cid, Romance Notes, Vol X, No 2. *Mailing Add:* Dept of Foreign Lang & Lit Clark Univ Worcester MA 01610

BARBERET, GENE JOSEPH, b Oakville, Conn, Jan 11, 20; m 56; c 2. FRENCH LITERATURE. *Educ:* Clark Univ, BA, 41; Princeton Univ, MA, 48, PhD, 52. *Prof Exp:* From instr to assoc prof, 49-68, PROF FRENCH, UNIV CONN, 68- *Concurrent Pos:* Dir, Jr Year in France Prog, Univ Rouen, 69-71. *Honors & Awards:* Chevalier Palmes Acad, 72; Distinguished Teaching Award, Univ Conn, 72. *Mem:* Am Asn Teachers Fr; MLA. *Res:* Contemporary French literature, especially the first half of the 20th century; Colette. *Publ:* Auth, Roger Martin du Gard; recent criticism, Fr Rev, 10/67; Nobel Prize symposium: France and Belgium, Bks Abroad, winter 67. *Mailing Add:* Dept of Romances & Class Lang Univ of Conn Storrs CT 06268

BARCHILON, JACQUES, b Casablanca, French Morocco, Apr 8, 23; nat US; m 60; c 2. ROMANCE LANGUAGES, THE FAIRY TALE. *Educ:* Univ Rochester, AB, 50; Harvard Univ, AM, 51, PhD, 56. *Prof Exp:* Teaching fel, Harvard Univ, 52-55; instr, Smith Col, 55-56; instr, Brown Univ, 56-69; instr, 59-65, assoc prof, 65-71, PROF FRENCH, UNIV COLO, BOULDER, 71-, CHMN, FRENCH & ITAL DEPT, 81- *Concurrent Pos:* Res grants, Coun Res & Creative Work, Univ Colo, 61, 63, 64, 76, 77, 79 & 80 & Am Philos Soc, 63, 64, 71 & 80; fac fel, Univ Colo, 64; exchange prof French & comp lit, Ctr Univ Savole, Chambery, France, 78-79. *Mem:* MLA; Am Asn Teachers French; NAm Soc for 17th Century French Lit. *Res:* French literature; the fairy tale; Charles Perrault. *Publ:* Auth & ed, Perrault's Tales of Mother Goose, Peirpont Morgan, 56; co-ed, The Authentic Mother Goose, Swallow, 60; auth, Charles Perrault, Dix-septieme Siecle, 62; Esprit et Humor chez Perrault, Studi Francesi, 67; Le Conte merveilleux francais, Champion, 75; A Concordance to Charles Perrault's Tales, Prose and Verse (2 vols), Norwood, 77-79, chap, In: La Coherence Ingerieure, Hean-Michel Place, 77; Contes de Perrault, Slatkine Reprints, 80; Charles Perrault, A Critical Biography, G K Hall, 81. *Mailing Add:* Dept of French & Ital Univ of Colo Boulder CO 80309

BAREFOOT, HYRAN E, Religion, Philosophy. See Vol IV

BAREIKIS, ROBERT PAUL, b Boston, Mass, Jan 18, 32; m 62; c 2. GERMANIC LANGUAGES & LITERATURE. *Educ:* Harvard Univ, AB, 59, PhD(Ger), 66. *Prof Exp:* Lectr, 64-65, asst prof, 65-68, ASSOC PROF GER LANG, IND UNIV, BLOOMINGTON, 68- *Concurrent Pos:* Ford W Europ study grant, 68; fel, Humanities Ctr, Johns Hopkins Univ, 69-70; Andrew Mellon Found fel, Univ Pittsburgh, 70-71. *Mem:* MLA; Am Asn Teachers Ger; Am Soc 18th Century Studies; Am Lessing Soc. *Res:* Seventeenth and 18th century German literature; production of educational television films. *Publ:* Ed, The 18th century: An annual bibliography, Philos Quart, 72. *Mailing Add:* Dept of Ger Lang Ind Univ Bloomington IN 47401

BARKER, MUHAMMAD ABD-AL-RAHMAN, b Spokane, Wash, Nov 2, 29; m 59. SOUTH ASIAN LINGUISTICS. *Educ:* Univ Wash, BA, 51; Univ Calif, Berkeley, PhD(ling), 59. *Prof Exp:* Asst prof Arabic, Urdu & ling, Inst Islamic Studies, McGill Univ, 57-59; assoc prof Urdu & regional lang & ling, Oriental Col, Lahore, WPakistan, 59-62; from asst prof to prof Arabic, Urdu-Hindi & ling, Inst Islamic Studies, McGill Univ, 62-70; PROF S ASIAN STUDIES & CHMN DEPT, UNIV MINN, MINNEAPOLIS, 72- *Concurrent Pos:* Dept Health, Educ & Welfare grant, 63-69; Shastri Indo-Can Inst fel, 70-71. *Mem:* Ling Soc Am; Asn Asian Studies; Am Orient Soc; Am Inst Pakistan Studies. *Res:* Urdu and other languages of India and Pakistan; language teaching materials preparation; Indo-Pakistani literature. *Publ:* Auth, Klamath Dictionary, 63 & Klamath Grammar, 64, Univ Calif Publ Ling; A Course in Urdu, 67, An Urdu Newspaper Reader, 68, An Urdu Poetry Reader, 68, An Urdu Newspaper Word Count, 69 & A Course in Baluchi, 69, Inst Islamic Studies, McGill Univ; Classical Urdu Poetry (3 vols), Spoken Lang Serv, NY, 77. *Mailing Add:* Dept of South Asian Studies Univ of Minn Minneapolis MN 55455

BARKIN, FLORENCE, b Jersey City, NJ, May 1, 46; m 68; c 1. SOCIOLINGUISTICS, SPANISH. *Educ:* State Univ NY, Albany, BA, 68; State Univ NY, Buffalo, MA (Latin Am studies), 70, MA (Span/ling), 71, PhD(Hispanic ling), 76. *Prof Exp:* Instr & asst prof, Middlebury Col, 74-75; ASST PROF SPAN, ARIZ STATE UNIV, 76- *Mem:* Am Asn Teachers Span; Am Coun Teachers Foreign Lang; Ling Asn Southwest; Nat Asn Bilingual Educ; Ling Asn Can & US. *Res:* Bilingualism; sociolinguistics; applied linguistics. *Publ:* Auth, Language alternation: linguistic norm awareness, In: LEKTOS, Univ Ky, 12/76; Black slave trade in the 17th century real of San Joseph del Parral 1631-45, In: Proc Ariz Latin Am Conf, 77; Language switching: A multifaceted phenomenon, In: Proc SW Areal Lang & Lit Workshop, 77; Loanshifts: An example of multi-level interference, In: Proc of SW Areal Lang & Lit Workshop, 78; The role of loanword assimilation in gender assignment, Bilingual Rev (in press). *Mailing Add:* Dept of Foreign Languages Ariz State Univ Tempe AZ 85281

BARKSDALE, ETHELBERT COURTLAND, b Arlington, Tex, Apr 9, 44. RUSSIAN LITERATURE. *Educ:* Univ Tex, Arlington, BA, 65; Ohio State Univ, MA, 67, PhD(Russ), 71. *Prof Exp:* Instr Russ, Univ Calif, Irvine, 71-72; asst prof, 72-78, ASSOC PROF RUSS, UNIV FLA, 78- *Mem:* MLA; Am Asn Advan Slavic Studies; Am Asn Teachers Slavic & E Europ Lang. *Res:* Nineteenth Century Russian literature; literary myth and the human mind; structuralism. *Publ:* Auth, The Dacha and the Duchess: An Application of Levi-Strauss's Theory of Myth in Human Creativity to Works of Nineteenth-Century Russian Writers, Philos Libr, 74; Daggers of the Mind: Structuralism and Neuropsychology in an Exploration of the Russian Literary Imagination, Coronado, 79; Cosmologies of Consciousness: Science and Literary Myth in an Exploration of the Beginnings and Development of Mind, Schenkman, 80. *Mailing Add:* Dept of Ger & Slavics Univ Fla Gainesville FL 32611

BAR-LEWAW, ISAAC, b Nriow-Bircza, Poland, Feb 9, 22; Can citizen; m 47; c 3. SPANISH AMERICAN LITERATURE. *Educ:* Hebrew Univ, Israel, MA, 53; Nat Univ Mex, PhD(Span & Latin Am lit), 59. *Prof Exp:* Jr asst prof Romance lang, Hebrew Univ, Israel, 53-55; asst prof, Univ Kans, 61-63; asst prof, Univ Fla, 63-64; assoc prof Span, Univ Sask, 64-67; PROF SPAN & CHMN DEPT FOREIGN LANG, YORK UNIV, 67- *Concurrent Pos:* Lectr, Ind Univ, 64, Carleton Univ, 66, McGill Univ, 67 & Laval Univ, 67; Can Coun fel, 72-73. *Mem:* MLA; Am Asn Teachers Span & Port; Am Soc Sephardic Studies; Soc Ibero-Am Enlightenment. *Res:* Mexican contemporary literature; Sephardic literature. *Publ:* Auth, Placido, Vida y Obra, Ed Botas, Mex; Modernismo e impresionismo, Armas y Letras, 3/61; Temas Literarios Iberoamericanos, B Costa-Amic, Mex, 61; La obra educadora vasconceliana, Norte, Neth, 6/64; Introduccion Critico-Biografica a Jose Vasconcelos, 1882-1959, Ed Latinoam, Madrid, 65; Jose Vasconcelos, Vida y Obra, Clasica Selecta, Ed Librera, Mex, 66; Apuntes sobre la primera traduccion espanola del More Nebujim, Tesoro Judios Sefardies, Israel, 66; La Revista Timon y Jose Vasconcelos, Edimex, Mex, 71. *Mailing Add:* 262 Winters York Univ Toronto ON M3J 1B3 Can

BARLOW, JANE FOX, b Philadelphia, Pa, Sept 3, 26. CLASSICS. *Educ:* Smith Col, AB, 47; Johns Hopkins Univ, MA, 49, PhD(classics), 52. *Prof Exp:* Teacher high sch, Md, 47-48; libr asst, Johns Hopkins Univ, 52-53; teacher Latin, Moravian Sem Girls, Pa, 53-54; from asst prof to assoc prof, 54-62, PROF CLASS LANG, SUSQUEHANNA UNIV, 62- *Mem:* Am Philol Asn; Archaeol Inst Am. *Res:* Latin metrics; Latin literature and grammar; analysis of language by computer. *Publ:* Auth, Metrical word types in the Latin dactylic hexameter, Susquehanna Studies. *Mailing Add:* Dept of Class Lang Susquehanna Univ Selinsgrove PA 17870

BARLOW, JOHN DENISON, b Brooklyn, NY, Sept 28, 34; m 70; c 3. GERMAN LITERATURE, FILM. *Educ:* NY Univ, BA, 58, MA, 61, PhD(Ger), 67. *Prof Exp:* Instr Ger, Univ Col, NY Univ, 61-67; asst prof, 67-72, assoc prof Ger, 72-81, PROF FOREIGN LANG, IND UNIV-PURDUE UNIV, INDIANAPOLIS, 81-, DIR, 82- *Concurrent Pos:* Ottendorfer mem fel, 66-67; Danforth assoc, 70- *Mem:* MLA; Am Asn Teachers Ger. *Res:* Twentieth century literature; film. *Publ:* auth, German Expressionist Film, Twayne, 82. *Mailing Add:* Dept of Ger Ind Univ-Purdue Univ 425 Agnes St Indianapolis IN 46202

BARNARD, SYLVIA EVANS, b Greenfield, Mass, Dec 11, 37; m 68; c 1. CLASSICS. *Educ:* McGill Univ, BA, 59; Cambridge Univ, BA, 62; Yale Univ, PhD(classic), 66. *Prof Exp:* Instr classics, Le Moyne Col, 65-66; asst prof, Kenyon Col, 66-67; ASST PROF CLASSICS, STATE UNIV NY ALBANY, 67- *Concurrent Pos:* Adj asst prof women's studies, State Univ NY, Albany, 81- *Mem:* Am Philol Asn; Am Inst Archaeol; Medieval Acad Am. *Res:* Women in antiquity. *Publ:* Auth, Hellenistic women poets, Class J, 2-3/78. *Mailing Add:* Dept of Classics State Univ of NY Albany NY 12222

BARNES, ALLEN RAY, b Newport, Nebr, June 12, 26; m 50; c 2. SPANISH. *Educ:* Hastings Col, AB, 48; Univ Idaho, MA, 50; Univ Madrid, PhD, 53. *Prof Exp:* Asst, Univ Idaho, 50-51; assoc prof Span & Ger, Nebr State Teachers Col, 53-56; exec dir, Iran-Am Soc, 56-58; vis prof NAm lit, Concepcion Univ & exec dir, Chilean-NAm Inst, 58-61; from assoc prof to prof Span, 61-67, head dept, 61-63, head Span grad prog, 63-67, PROF FOREIGN LANG & DEAN, COL ARTS & SCI, 67- *Concurrent Pos:* Nat consult in teaching of mod foreign lang, 63; biling consult social studies, Region I Educ Serv Ctr, Edinburg, Tex, 70-71. *Mem:* Asn Teachers Span & Port; MLA: Midwest Coun Latin Am Studies. *Res:* Spanish American history; study of idiomatic structures in the Spanish language. *Mailing Add:* Col of Arts & Sci SDak State Univ Brookings SD 57006

BARNES, TIMOTHY DAVID, b Yorkshire, Eng, Mar 13, 42; UK & Can citizen; m 65; c 3. CLASSICS, HISTORY. *Educ:* Oxford Univ, BA, 64, MA, 67, DPhil, 70. *Prof Exp:* Jr res fel classics, Queen's Col, Oxford, 66-70; from asst prof to assoc prof, Univ Col, Toronto, 70-76; assoc chmn grad studies, 79-83, PROF CLASSICS, UNIV TORONTO, 76- *Honors & Awards:* Conington Prize, Oxford Univ, 74. *Mem:* Am Philol Asn; Can Class Asn; Am Soc Papyrologists; Am Asn Ancient Historians; Soc Promotion Roman Studies. *Res:* Roman history; early Christianity; patristics. *Publ:* Auth, Tertullian: A Historical and Literary Study, Clarendon, Oxford, 71; The Sources of the Historia Augusta, Collection Latomus, Brussels, 78; Constantine and Eusebius, 81 & The New Empire of Diocletian and Constantine, 82, Harvard Univ Press. *Mailing Add:* Dept of Classics Univ Toronto 16 Hart House Circle Toronto ON M5S 1A1 Can

BARNETT, ANDREE M-L (PAHEAU), b Thuin, Belgium, Aug 1, 17; m 47. ROMANCE PHILOLOGY. *Educ:* Univ Utah, MA, 48, PhD(French), 56. *Prof Exp:* Instr French & Italian, 49-59, from lectr to assoc prof lang, 59-72, assoc dean, Col Humanities, 76-82, PROF LANG, UNIV UTAH, 72- *Mem:* MLA; Am Asn Teachers Ital; Rocky Mountain Mod Lang Asn. *Res:* Comparative literature of the Middle Ages and Renaissance; Vulgar Latin and Romance philology; French and Italian literatures, philologies, linguistics and stylistics. *Publ:* Auth, A Short Introduction to Romance Philology, Univ Utah, 51; co-ed, Les Carnets du Major Thompson, 59, coauth, Le Langage de la France Moderne, 61, auth, L'Actualite Francaise, 67 & Introduction A V Francais Acutel, 74, Holt. *Mailing Add:* Dept of Lang Univ of Utah Salt Lake City UT 84112

BARNETT, RICHARD LANCE, b New York, NY, Mar 10, 51. FRENCH LANGUAGE & LITERATURE. *Educ:* City Univ New York, BA, 71; Columbia Univ, BA, 71; State Univ NY Albany, MA, 74; Univ Geneve, Maitrise-es-lettres, 75, DES, 76; Brandeis Univ, PhD(French lit), 79. *Prof Exp:* Asst French studies, Univ Geneve, 74-76; fel French, Brandeis Univ, 76-78; asst prof French studies, Case Western Reserve Univ, 78-81; ASST PROF FRENCH STUDIES, PURDUE UNIV, 81- *Concurrent Pos:* Consult, French Div, Ecole Dulac, 72-79, Inst Francais, Alliance Francaise, 75-80 & Humanities Div, Cambridge Adult Educ Ctr, 76-81; guest ed, Studi di Letteratura Francese, 81- & L'Esprit Createur, 82-; co-ed, Text-ure: J Appl Lit Theory, 81- *Honors & Awards:* Frenand Prix Letteraire, Univ Geneve, 80; Gilman-Hachette Prize, Gilman-Hachette, 81. *Mem:* NAm Soc French Seveneenth Century Lit; Soc d'Etude du XVII Siecle; Int Soc French Studies; Soc French Professors Am; MLA. *Res:* Seventeenth century French lit; comtemporary critical theory and practice; French stylistics. *Publ:* Auth, La Plage robbe-frilletienne: vers un dechiffrement intra-textuel, Lit: Ann Fac Lett Sci Humaines de Univ Toulouse, La MIrail, 77; Le Conflit du non-conflict: Egocentrisme et disjonction multi laterale dams Britannicus, Nottingham French Studies, 78; Le Travestissement de la Parole racinienne, Studi di Letterature Francese, 79; The non-ocularity of Racine's Vision, Orbis Litterarum, 80; Tenebreuse(s) Unite(s): L'Ouventure strateguqie des Maximes, Lang Quart, 81; Maxim-al codes of minimal closure: Pascal's sequestered schema, 82 & ed & contribr, The Maxim in French literature, 82, L'Esprit Createur; auth, En Quente de referents: La Semantiquie de manque, Estudes de Lettres, Lausanne (in press). *Mailing Add:* Dept Foreign Lang & Lit Purdue Univ West Lafayette IN 47907

BARNETT, ROBERT JOHN, JR, b White Plains, NY, Oct 7, 36; m 58; c 2. CLASSICS. *Educ:* Roanoke Col, BA, 58; Univ NC, PhD(classics), 64. *Prof Exp:* From instr to asst prof, 63-72, ASSOC PROF CLASSICS, FRANKLIN & MARSHALL COL, 72-, CHMN EUROP STUDIES PROG, 76- *Mem:* Am Philol Asn; Vergilian Soc. *Res:* Palaeography; Latin love poetry. *Publ:* Auth, Anonymous Medieval Commentary on Juvenal, Monographic; Title of Cicero's 1st Catilinarian, Class Outlook, 12-360. *Mailing Add:* Dept of Classics Franklin & Marshall Col Lancaster PA 17604

BARNOUW, JEFFREY, b New York City, NY, Nov 1, 40; m 64; c 1. COMPARATIVE LITERATURE, INTELLECTUAL HISTORY. *Educ:* Yale Univ, BA, 63, PhD(comp lit), 69. *Prof Exp:* Dean, Calhoun Col, Yale Univ, 66-69; asst prof English & comp lit, Univ Calif, San Diego, 69-78; ASST PROF GER, BOSTON UNIV, 80- *Concurrent Pos:* Fel, Alexander von Humboldt Found, 72-74 & Am Coun Learned Soc, 79-80; book rev ed, The Eighteenth Century: A Current Bibliog, 77. *Mem:* Am Comp Lit Asn; Am Soc Eighteenth-Century Studies; MLA. *Res:* Bacon and Hobbes and their influence in the enlightenment; a history of conceptions of natural signs from Chrysippus to Dewey; Freud's metapsychology and 19th century German philosophical psychology. *Publ:* Auth, Das Problem der Aktion und Wallenstein, Jahrbuch der deutschen Schiller-Gesellschaft, 72; Active experience versus wish-fulfilment in Francis Bacon's Moral Psychology of Science, Philos Forum, 77; Hobbes's causal account of sensation, J Hist Philos, 80; The critique of classical republicanism and the understanding of modern forms of polity in Vico's New Science, Clio, 80; Vico and the continuity of science: The relation of his epistemology to Bacon and Hobbes, Isis, 80; The morality of the sublime: Kant and Schiller, Studies in Romanticism, 80; The separation of reason and faith in Bacon and Hobbes, and the Theodicy of Leibniz, J Hist of Ideas, 81; Signification and meaning: A critique of the Saussurean conception of the sign, Comp Lit Studies, 81. *Mailing Add:* 325 Wayland Ave Providence RI 02906

BARNSTONE, WILLIS, b Lewiston, Maine, Nov 13, 27; m 49; c 3. SPANISH & COMPARATIVE LITERATURE. *Educ:* Bowdoin Col, BA, 48; Columbia Univ, MA, 56; Yale Univ, PhD, 60. *Hon Degrees:* DLitt, Bowdoin Col, 81. *Prof Exp:* Teacher French & English, Anavrita Acad, Greece, 49-50; instr French, Univ Md Overseas Prog, Perigueux, France, 55-56; from instr to asst prof Span, Wesleyan Univ, 58-62; assoc prof Span & comp lit, 62-66, prof Span & Port, 66-68, prof EAsian studies, 73-76, PROF COMP LIT, IND UNIV, BLOOMINGTON, 66-, PROF LATIN AM STUDIES, 76- *Concurrent Pos:* Guggenheim fel, Spain, 61-62; Am Coun Learned Soc Studies fel, 68-69; vis prof, Univ Calif, Riverside, 68-69 & Inst Prof, Buenos Aires, 75-; Fulbright teaching fel, Argentina, 75; Nat Endowment for Humanities sr res fel, 79-80. *Honors & Awards:* Cecil Hemley Mem Award, 68; Lucille Medwick Award, 78, Poetry Soc Am; Gustav Davidson Mem Award, 80. *Mem:* MLA. *Res:* Spanish; ancient Greek; English, Greek and Spanish poetry; theory and practice of translation. *Publ:* Auth, New Faces of China, Ind Univ, 73; Egypt: Love, death and magic, Rev, 75; My Voice Because of You, State Univ NY, 76; China Poems, Univ Mo, 76; Portugal: Poet kings and the sea, Sat Evening Post, 77; Real and imaginary history in Borges and Cavafy, Comp Lit, 77; Billy and Meursault: A failure of the senses, Tex Quart, 78; Antonio Machado: a theory of method in his dream, landscape and awakening, Revista Hisp Mod, 78. *Mailing Add:* Dept of Comp Lit Ind Univ Bloomington IN 47401

BARON, DENNIS E, English Literature, Linguistics. See Vol II

BARON, FRANK, b Budapest, Hungary, Jan 13, 36; US citizen; m 64; c 2. GERMAN LITERATURE, RENAISSANCE HISTORY. *Educ:* Univ Ill, BA, 58; Ind Univ, MA, 61; Univ Calif, Berkeley, PhD(Ger), 66. *Prof Exp:* Instr Ger, Univ Notre Dame, 60-61; lectr, Haile Selassie Univ, 67-68; Alexander von Humboldt res fel Renaissance lit & hist, Munich, Ger, 68-70; asst prof Ger, 70-74, assoc prof, 74-80, PROF GER, UNIV KANS, 80- *Honors & Awards:* NSF Award, 80. *Mem:* Renaissance Soc Am; Am Asn Teachers Ger. *Res:* Renaissance intellectual history; 20th century German literature. *Publ:* Auth, Der erste Druck einer Schrift Augustins: Ein Beitrag zur Geschichte des frühen Buchdrucks und des Humanismus, Hist Jahrbuch, 71; Stephen Hoest: Reden und Briefe: Quellen zue Geschichte der Scholastik und des Humanismus im 15 Jahrhundert, Fink, Munich, 71; Plautus und die deutschen Frühhumanisten, In: Studia Humanitatis: Festschrift für Ernesto Grassi, 72; Doctor Faustus From History to Legend, 78 & ed, Joachim Camerarius, 1500-1574, 78, Fink, Munich; co-ed (with Ernst S Dick & Warren R Maurer), Rilke: Alchemy of Alienation, Univ Kans, 80; Fanstus, Geschichte, Sage, Dichtung, Winkler, 82; ed, Rilke and the Visual Arts, Coronado Press, 82. *Mailing Add:* Dept of Ger Univ of Kans Lawrence KS 66044

BARON, HANS, Italian Renaissance History & Literature. See Vol I

BARON, NAOMI SUSAN, b New York, NY, Sept 27, 46. LINGUISTICS. *Educ:* Brandeis Univ, BA, 68; Stanford Univ, PhD(ling), 72. *Prof Exp:* asst prof, 72-78, ASSOC PROF LING, BROWN UNIV, 78-, ASSOC DEAN OF COL, 81- *Mem:* Ling Soc Am. *Res:* Child language acquisition; historical linguistics; functional analysis of linguistic representation. *Publ:* Contribr, Functional motivations for age grading in linguistic innovation, Hist Ling, Vol I, 74; auth, Trade jargons and pidgins: A functionalist approach, J Creole Studies, 77; The acquisition of indirect reference, Lingua, 77; Language Acquisition and Historical Change, North-Holland, 77; coauth, The problem of direct and indirect reference, Semiotica, 78; auth, Speech, Writing and Sign, Ind Univ Press, 81. *Mailing Add:* Box E Dept of Ling Brown Univ Providence RI 02912

BAROOSHIAN, VAHAN DICKRAN, b Chelsea, Mass, Jan 21, 32; m 57; c 2. RUSSIAN ART & LITERATURE. *Educ:* PROF RUSSIAN LANG & LIT, WELLS COL, 63- *Concurrent Pos:* Res fel, Harvard Univ, 71-72 & 77; sr scholar, Int Res & Exchange Bd, 71, 74 & 81; Fulbright-Hays res grant, 82; consult, Nat Endowment for Humanities, 74- *Mem:* AAUP; Am Asn Teachers Slavic & East Europ Lang. *Res:* Russian literature and art of the 20th century; 20th century Armenian history; American and Soviet foreign policy. *Publ:* Auth, Russian Cubo-Futurism 1910-1930, 74 & Brik and Mayakovsky, 78, Mouton Publ. *Mailing Add:* Dept of Russian Lang & Lit Wells Col Aurora NY 13026

BARRACK, CHARLES MICHAEL, b Los Angeles, Calif, Jan 6, 38. GERMANIC LINGUISTICS, GERMAN LITERATURE. *Educ:* San Diego State Col, BA, 61; Univ Wash, MA, 66, PhD(Ger ling), 69. *Prof Exp:* Actg asst prof Ger, 68-69, asst prof, 69-74, ASSOC PROF GERMANICS, UNIV WASH, 74- *Mem:* Ling Soc Am. *Res:* Historical linguistics; epistemology. *Publ:* Coauth, The tragic background to Lessing's Minna von Barnhelm, Bessing Yearbk, 70; auth, Conscience in Heinrich von Ofterdingen: Novalis' metaphysic of the poet, Ger Rev, 71; Mephistopheles: 'Ein Teil von jener Kraft/Die stets das Böse will und stets das Gute Schafft, Seminar, 71; Nietzsche's Dionysus and Apollo: Gods in transition, Nietzsche-Studien, spring 74; A Diachronic Phonology from Proto-Germanic to Old English Stressing West-Saxon Conditions, Mouton, The Hague, 74; Muspilli: A dilemma in restructuring, Folia Ling, 75; Lexical diffusion and the High German Consonant Shift, 76 & The High German Consonant Shift: Polygenetic or monogenetic? (in press), Lingua. *Mailing Add:* Dept of Germanics DH-30 Univ of Wash Seattle WA 98195

BARRATT, GLYNN RICHARD, b London, Eng, May 27, 44; m 68; c 3. RUSSIAN LITERATURE & HISTORY. *Educ:* Cambridge Univ, BA, 66; Univ London, PhD(Russ lit), 68. *Prof Exp:* ASSOC PROF RUSS, CARLETON UNIV, 68- *Concurrent Pos:* Can Coun res fel, 68-69 & 73-74. *Mem:* Can Asn Slavists; Can Comp Lit Asn; Am Soc 18th Century Studies; fel Royal Asiatic Soc. *Res:* Russian literature and literary contacts with the west, 1790-1850; Russian history, 1790-1840; Russian Naval history to 1880. *Publ:* Auth, I I Kozlov: The translations from Byron, Lang, 72; Ivan Kozlov: A Study and A Setting, Hakkert, Toronto, 72; Selected Letters of Yeugenij Baratynskij, 73 & M S Lunin: Catholic Decembrist, Mouton, The Hague, 74; Voices in Exile: The Decembrist Memoirs, McGill Univ-Queens Univ, 74; The Rebel on the Bridge: The Life of the Decembrist Baron Andrei Rozen, Paul Elek, London, 75. *Mailing Add:* Dept of Russ Carleton Univ Ottawa ON K1S 5B6 Can

BARREDA, PEDRO M, b Havana, Cuba, Aug 29, 33; m 65; c 1. LATIN AMERICAN LITERATURE. *Educ:* Univ Havana, Dr Filos y Let, 59; State Univ NY Buffalo, MA, 66, PhD(Spanish), 69. *Prof Exp:* Instr Span, State Univ NY Buffalo, 62-63, lectr, 63-69; asst prof, 69-73, ASSOC PROF SPAN, UNIV MASS, AMHERST, 73- *Concurrent Pos:* Fac res grant, Univ Mass, Am herst, 71-72. *Mem:* Am Asn Teachers Span & Port; MLA; Inst Int Lit Iberoam. *Res:* Latin American poetry and novel; Caribbean literature. *Publ:* Auth, Lo universal, lo nacional y lo personal en el teatro de Rene Marques, Memorias XII Congr Lit Iberoam, 66; Elementos religiosos en la poesia de Ruben Dario, Memorias XIII Congr Lit Iberoam, 70; Alejo Carpentier: Dos visiones del negro, dos conceptos de la novela, Hispania, 72; El teatro de Jose J Milanes, Memoria XV Congr Lit Iberoam, 72; La vision conflictiva de la sociedad Cubana: tema y estructura de Cecilia Valdes, Anales Lit Hispanoam, 76. *Mailing Add:* Dept of Span Univ of Mass Amherst MA 01002

BARRELL, REX ARTHUR, b Christchurch, NZ, May 11, 21; m 52; c 1. COMPARATIVE LITERATURE & LINGUISTICS. *Educ:* Univ Canterbury, BA, 41, BSc & MA, 44; Univ Paris, Dr, 51. *Prof Exp:* Lectr French, Univ Otago, NZ, 52-57, sr lectr, 58-60; sr lectr mod lang, Monash Univ, Australia, 61-63; assoc prof French, Univ Waterloo, 64-65; chmn dept, 65-72, PROF FRENCH, UNIV GUELPH, 65- *Concurrent Pos:* Nuffield Found traveling fel humanities, London, 57-58; hon res asst, Univ Col, London, 57-58; Carnegie travel grant, Can & Am, Brit Coun visitorship, Eng & Can Coun res grant, 66; Can Coun travel grants, 67, 69, 71, 73; Humanities Res Coun res & publ subsidy, 78; Can Coun leave fel, 75 & 82. *Mem:* MLA; Can Ling Asn; Asn Can Univ Teachers Fr; fel, Intercontinental Biog Asn. *Res:* Shakespeare and Musset; Bolingbroke and France. *Publ:* Auth, Chesterfield et la France, NEL, Paris, 68; Der Beitrag Deutscher Artze zum Französischen Wortschatz, Z Deut Sprache, 70; The problem of meaning, Speech J, 70; coauth, Materiaux pour L'histoire du Vocabulaire Francais, Didier, Paris, 71; auth, Horace Walpole and France, Humanities Asn Bull, 72; Horace Walpole and France, Carlton, Vol I, 78; Horace Walpole and France, Borealis, Vol II, 79; French Correspondence of Lord Chesterfield, Borealis (2 Vols), 80. *Mailing Add:* Dept of Lang Univ of Guelph Guelph ON N1G 2W1 Can

BARRENECHEA, ANA MARIA, b Buenos Aires, Arg, Mar 6, 13. HISPANIC LITERATURE, THEORY OF LITERATURE. *Educ:* Instituto Superior del Profesorado de Buenos Aires, Master, 73; Bryn Mawr Col, PhD(Span lit), 56. *Hon Degrees:* Doctor Honoris Causa, Smith Col, 73. *Prof Exp:* Prof Span philol, Univ Buenos Aires, 56-57, prof lit, 58-66; lectr Span lit, Harvard Univ, 68; vis prof, Ohio State Univ, 71-72; vis prof, 73-75, PROF SPAN AM LIT, COLUMBIA UNIV, 76- *Concurrent Pos:* Prof scholar-in-residence, Duke Univ, 67; Guggenheim fel ling, 69. *Mem:* Int De Hispanistas (pres, 77-80); Asoc Ling & Filol Am Latina; Inter Am Prog Ling & Lang Teaching. *Res:* Spanish American literature; linguistics; theory of literature. *Publ:* Auth, La Expresion de La Irrealidad en la Obra de Borges, El Colegio de Mexico, Mex, 57; coauth, La Literatura Fantastica en Argentina, Univ Nac Autonoma, Mex, 57; Domingo Faustino Sarmiento, Ceal, Buenos Aires, 67; Estudios de Gramatica Estructural, Paidos, Buenos Aires, 69; auth, Textos Hispanoamericanos: de Sarmiento a Sarduy, Monte Avila, Buenos Aires, 78; coauth, Estudios Linguisticos y Dialectologicos, Hachotte, Buenos Aires, 79. *Mailing Add:* Columbia Univ 612 W 116 St New York NY 10027

BARRETT, ANTHONY ARTHUR, b Worthing, England, July 30, 41. CLASSICS. *Educ:* Univ Durham, BA, 63; Univ Newcastle, BA, 64; Univ Toronto, MA, 65, PhD(classics), 68; Oxford Univ, dipl class archaeol, 74. *Prof Exp:* Lectr Classics, Carleton Univ, 65-66; asst prof, 68-73, ASSOC PROF CLASSICS, UNIV BC, 73- *Mem:* Class Asn Can (secy, 71-73); Humanities Asn Can; Royal Astron Soc; fel, Soc Antiquaries; Archeol Inst Am. *Res:* Roman history; Romano-British archaeology; Latin literature. *Publ:* Auth, The authorship of the Culex, Latomus, 70; Catullus 52 and the consulship of Vatinius, Trans Am Philol Asn, 72; Sohaemus, king of Emesa and Sophene, Am J Philol, 77; Gaius' policy in the Bosporus, Trans Am Philol Asn, 77; coauth, The Oxford Brygos cup: A new interpretation, J Hellenic Studies, 78; auth, The Literary Classics in Roman Britain, 78 & The Career of Cogidubnus, 79, Britannia; The Epigrams of Janus Pannonius, Corvina Press, Budapest, 82. *Mailing Add:* Dept of Classics Univ of BC Vancouver BC V6T 1W5 Can

BARRETT, MADIE WARD, b Stephenville, Tex, June 3, 20. LINGUISTICS, ROMANCE LANGUAGES. *Educ:* Ala Col, AB, 40; Univ NC, MA, 46, PhD(ling, Fr), 48. *Prof Exp:* Teacher, Pub Schs, Ala, 40-43; asst prof foreign lang, Troy State Col, 43-44; Carnegie grant asst, Univ NC, 46-48; lectr Ger & classics, NC Col Women, 49-53; asst prof French & Span, High Point Col, 51-53; chmn dept, 64-80, PROF FRENCH & SPAN, PLYMOUTH STATE COL, 56- *Concurrent Pos:* Am Asn Univ Women Elizabeth Avery Colton fel, 54-55; Carnegie grant; MLA consult, 63-65; actg dean of col, Plymouth State Col, 81-82 & interim dean, 82-83. *Mem:* Am Coun Teaching Foreign Lang; MLA; Am Asn Teachers Fr. *Res:* American speech, especially dialect geography; phonetics and phonemics; problems of second language teaching. *Publ:* Contribr, Our Changing Language, Phonodisc, McGraw-Hill Rec, 59. *Mailing Add:* 4 Summer St Bristol NH 03222

BARRETT, RALPH P, b Detroit, Mich, Oct 31, 29; m 54; c 3. LINGUISTICS, ENGLISH LANGUAGE. *Educ:* Univ Mich, BA, 52, MA, 53, PhD, 61. *Prof Exp:* Asst prof English lang & ling, 62-70, dir, English Lang Ctr, 73-76, ASSOC PROF ENGLISH LANG, MICH STATE UNIV, 70-, ADV ENGLISH LANG MA PROG, 71- *Concurrent Pos:* Adv English lang, Int Prog at Univ Ryukyus, Okinawa, 60-62; Title VI-B grant, Instr Media Inst, Mich State Univ, 67-68; sr staff mem, Univ Pittsburgh Thailand English Proj, Bangkok, Thailand, 69-71; mem Consortium of Intensive English Prog, 73- *Mem:* Nat Asn Foreign Student Affairs; Teachers English to Speakers Other Lang. *Res:* Computer use in language testing; English language teacher training. *Publ:* Coauth, Let's Learn English, Bk III, Am Bk Co, 66 & 73; auth, Future English: Science Fiction or Fact?, Format, 67; The Thammasat Transparency Reading Program, English Lang Ctr, Bangkok, 71. *Mailing Add:* Dept of English Mich State Univ East Lansing MI 48823

BARRETTE, PAUL EDOUARD, b Fall River, Mass, July 4, 35; m; c 2. ROMANCE LANGUAGES. *Educ:* Univ Miami, BA, 54, MA, 55; Univ Calif, Berkeley, PhD(Old Fr lang & lit), 63. *Prof Exp:* Instr French, Univ Calif, Berkeley, 61-62; instr, Univ Ill, Urbana, 62-63, from asst prof to assoc prof, 63-70; PROF FRENCH, UNIV TENN, KNOXVILLE, 70- *Mem:* Int Arthurian Soc; Am Asn Teachers Fr; SAtlantic Mod Lang Asn; MLA; Soc Rencesvals. *Res:* Old French language and literature, specifically medieval romances; hagiography; French stylistics. *Publ:* Coauth, First French, Le Francais Non sans Peine, 64, rev ed, 70; auth, Tableaux de Huit Siecles, 65 & coauth, Second French, 68, Scott; auth, Robert de Blois's Floris et Lyriope, Univ Calif, 68; coauth, Un-certain Style, Oxford Univ, 69; auth, Les ballades en jargon de Francois Villon, ou la poetique de la criminalite, Romania, 77; La legende de sainte Julienne et ses rapports avec la Chanson de Roland, Charlesmagne et l'epopee romane. *Mailing Add:* Dept of Romance Lang & Lit Univ of Tenn Knoxville TN 37916

BARRICELLI, JEAN-PIERRE, b Cleveland, Ohio, June 5, 24. ROMANCE LANGUAGES, COMPARATIVE LITERATURE. *Educ:* Harvard Univ, BA, 47, MA, 48, PhD(Romance lang & lit), 53. *Prof Exp:* From instr to asst prof Romance lang & lit, Brandeis Univ, 53-63; assoc prof, 63-66, chmn dept French & Ital, 65-68, chmn, Dept Comp Lit, 66-75, chmn, Dept Lit & Lang, 76-81, PROF ROMANCE LANG & COMP LIT, UNIV CALIF, RIVERSIDE, 66- *Concurrent Pos:* Conductor, Cafarelli Opera Co, Cleveland, Ohio & Waltham Symphony Orchestra, Mass, 54-59; dir, Wien Int Scholar Prog, Brandeis Univ, 58-63; Fulbright lectr, Norweg Sch Bus Admin & Univ Bergen, Norway, 62-63; ed, Ital Quart, 72-76 & Heloconian, 75- *Honors & Awards:* Humanities Inst Award, Univ Calif, 68-69; Distinguished Teaching Award, Univ Calif, Riverside, 75. *Mem:* Am Comp Lit Asn; MLA; Dante Soc; Balzac Soc; Am Asn Advan Humanities. *Res:* European Romanticism; Renaissance; literature and music. *Publ:* Coauth, Ernest Chausson, Univ Okla, 55; auth, Balzac and Beethoven: The growth of a concept, Mod Lang Quart, 12/64; Demonic Souls: Three Essays on Balzac, Edda, Oslo, 64; Sogno and sueno: Dante and Calderon, Comp Lit Studies, 72; A Manzoni, Twayne, 76; Machiavelli's Prince, Barron's, 75; Chekhov's Great Plays, Columbia & NY Univ, 81; co-ed & coauth, Interrelations of Literature, MLA, 82. *Mailing Add:* Dept of Lit & Lang Univ of Calif Riverside CA 92521

BARRICK, MAC EUGENE, b Cumberland Co, Pa, July 5, 33; m 54; c 1. SPANISH LANGUAGE & LITERATURE. *Educ:* Dickinson Col, AB, 55; Univ Ill, MA, 57; Univ Pa, PhD(Span), 65. *Prof Exp:* Teaching asst, Univ Ill, 55-57; asst instr, Univ Pa, 58-61; from instr to asst prof Span, Lycoming Col, 61-64; asst prof, Dickinson Col, 64-68; assoc prof, 68-81, PROF SPAN, SHIPPENSBURG STATE COL, 81- *Concurrent Pos:* Assoc ed, Abstr Folklore Studies, Am Folklore Soc, 66-73; fel, Southeast Inst Medieval & Renaissance Studies, 74. *Mem:* Am Asn Teachers Span & Port; Mediaeval Acad Am; Renaissance Soc Am; Am Folklore Soc. *Res:* The Celestina and the early Spanish novel; Spanish proverbs; Pennsylvania folklore. *Publ:* Auth, Central Pennsylvania Fishing Spears, Pa Folklife, 72; ed, Tercera parte de la tragicomedia de Celestina, Univ Pa, 73; auth, Form and function of folktales in Don Quijote, J Medieval & Renaissance Studies, 76; auth, The Folklore of Local History, Pa Folklife, 81. *Mailing Add:* Dept of Foreign Lang Shippensburg State Col Shippensburg PA 17257

BARRIGA, GUILLERMO, b Bogota, Colombia, Sept 18, 14; m 44; c 3. LINGUISTICS. *Educ:* Colombian Naval Acad, BS, 38; Middlebury Col, MA, 56; Univ Madrid, Spain, PhD, 60. *Prof Exp:* From instr to asst prof, 51-57, ASSOC PROF SPAN, GETTYSBURG COL, 60- *Res:* Spanish literature; Cervantes: Don Quijote. *Mailing Add:* Dept of Foreign Lang Gettysburg Col Gettysburg PA 17325

BARRITT, CARLYLE WESTBROOK, b Greensboro, NC, Mar 31, 21; m 49; c 1. LINGUISTICS, SPANISH. *Educ:* Washington & Lee Univ, BA, 43; Univ Va, MA, 50, PhD (ling), 52. *Prof Exp:* Instr Romance lang, Emory Univ, 46; instr, Muhlenberg Col, 46-47; instr Romance lang, 47-48, from instr to assoc prof, 52-72, PROF ROMANCE LANG & LING, WASHINGTON & LEE UNIV, 72-, CHMN DEPT, 79- *Concurrent Pos:* Cooperative Prog in Humanities study grant, Univ NC & Duke Univ, 64-65. *Mem:* Ling Soc Am; Am Asn Teachers Span & Port; SAtlantic Mod Lang Asn. *Res:* Structural linguistics; Spanish literature. *Publ:* Coauth, The Old English short digraphs: Some considerations, Language, 55; auth, The phonemic interpretation of accent in Father Rincon's Arte Mexicana, Gen Ling, 56; Vestiges of an ancient syllabic shape in Basque, Anthrop Ling, 66; Scrimshaw and Other Poems, Vantage, 73. *Mailing Add:* Dept of Romance Lang Washington & Lee Univ Lexington VA 24450

BARRON, CARLOS GARCIA, b Barcelona, Spain, Aug 17, 32; US citizen; m 65; c 2. ROMANCE LANGUAGES, SPANISH LITERATURE. *Educ:* Univ Calif, Berkeley, BA, 55, MA, 61; Univ Calif, Los Angeles, PhD(Hisp lang & lit), 67. *Prof Exp:* From actg asst prof to asst prof Span, 65-76, Humanities Inst appointment, 69-70 & 73-74, dir, Madrid Ctr, 70-72, assoc prof, 76-79, PROF SPAN, UNIV CALIF, SANTA BARBARA, 80- *Concurrent Pos:* On sabbatical res in Spain, 69-70. *Mem:* MLA; AAUP. *Res:* Eighteenth and 19th centuries Spanish penisular literature. *Publ:* Auth, La obra critica y literaria de don Antonio Alcala Galiano, Gredos, Madrid, 69; La Gaceta Patriotica del Ejercito Nacional, Rev de Occidente, 4/71; Antonio Alcala Galianao y la Revue Trimestrielle, Insula, 10/72; Cancionero del 98, Papeles de Son Armandans, 10/72. *Mailing Add:* Dept of Span & Port Univ of Calif Santa Barbara CA 93106

BARROS, EDUARDO ENRIQUE, b Havana, Cuba, Sept 7, 19; US citizen;. SPANISH. *Educ:* Univ Havana, DLaws, 42, DSoc Sci, 45, DEuc, 52. *Prof Exp:* Prof humanities, La Salle Col, Cuba, 50-60; teacher Span, La Salle Acad, NY, 60-64; prof, Manhattan Col, 64-67; teacher, Cardinal Spellman High Sch, NY, 67-71; chmn dept lang, Christian Bros Acad, Syracuse, 71-77; TEACHER SPANISH, SACRED HEART HIGH SCH, NY, 77- *Concurrent Pos:* Prof professional ethics, Univ Soc Cath San Jaun Bautista, 58-59; prof Span, St Joseph's Sem, 64-68. *Mem:* Archdiocesan Mod Lang Coun; MLA; Am Asn Teachers Span & Port. *Res:* Spanish grammar; Spanish and Spanish-American culture and literature. *Mailing Add:* Sacred Heart High Sch 34 Convent Ave Yonkers NY 10703

BARRS, JAMES THOMAS, b Danville, Ga, Sept 2, 04; m 31; c 3. PHILOLOGY. *Educ:* Univ Ga, AB, 27; Harvard Univ, AM, 32, PhD, 36. *Prof Exp:* Teacher, High Schs, Ga, 27-31; registr & teacher English, SGa Col, 37-42, dean, 40-42; asst prof English & acting head dept, Wash Col, 43-45; from asst prof to prof, 45-71, lectr, Grad Sch Arts & Sci, 71-74, EMER PROF ENGLISH, NORTHEASTERN UNIV, 71- *Concurrent Pos:* Lectr, WAYX, 40-42; columnist, Enterprise, Douglas, Ga, 40-42; tester turbo-superchargers & jet engines, Gen Electric Co, Lynn, Mass, 42-43; 44; lectr lang, ling & semantics, WGBH-TV, 58-59, WBZ-WBZA, 59-60, WEEI, 61, Concert Network, 61-64; researcher speech data, grant from Air Force Cambridge Res Lab, Bedford, Mass, 62-63; lectr, WCRB, 65-66, WILD, 66-67. *Honors & Awards:* Charles Swain Thomas Ann Bk Award, New England Asn Teachers English, 80. *Mem:* MLA, NCTE; Col English Asn; Conf Col Compos & Commun. *Res:* Classical and comparative philology; linguistics, specifically the graphic shortening of the word and; the ancient names, local, personal and divine of Dacia and Moesia. *Publ:* Auth, The place of etymology in linguistics, Col English, 11/62; Behind the word (ser of 6 articles), CEA Critic, 62; coauth, Study and Investigation of Speech Data: A Report for Air Force Cambridge Research Laboratories, Dept Psychol, Northeastern Univ, 63; auth, Identification of voiceless initial fricatives versus modification of their duration, In: Linguistics, Mouton, The Hague, 66; Suggested Precollege Reading, The Leaflet, fall 81; Concerning the third edition of suggested precollege reading, The Leaflet, spring 82. *Mailing Add:* 166 Chestnut St West Newton MA 02165

BART, BENJAMIN FRANKLIN, b Chicago, Ill, Dec 21, 17; m 42; c 3. ROMANCE LANGUAGES. *Educ:* Harvard Univ, AB, 38, AM, 46, PhD, 47. *Prof Exp:* Instr Romance lang, Harvard, 47; asst prof, Pomona Col, 47-50; asst prof, Univ Mich, 50-56; from assoc prof to prof, Syracuse Univ, 56-67; PROF FRENCH, UNIV PITTSBURGH, 67-, DIR COMP LIT PROG, 74- *Concurrent Pos:* Ford Found fel, 52-53; Am Coun Learned Socs grants-in-aid, 60, 61, & 63; Am Philol Soc grant, 74; Camargo Found fel, 81; Nat Endowment for Humanities fel, 81. *Mem:* Am Asn Teachers Fr; MLA. *Res:* French 19th century literature; the teaching of French. *Publ:* Auth, Flaubert's Landscape Descriptions, Univ Mich, 56; Madame Bovary and the Critics, Scribner's, 66; Flaubert, Syracuse Univ, 67; The Legendary Sources of Flaubert's Saint Julien, Univ Toronto, 77. *Mailing Add:* Dept of French Univ of Pittsburgh Pittsburgh PA 15260

BARTELEMEZ, ERMINNIE HOLLIS, b Chicago, Ill, May 21, 16. GERMANIC PHILOLOGY. *Educ:* Pomona Col, AB, 37; Univ Chicago, AM, 40; Yale Univ, PhD, 42. *Prof Exp:* Asst prof Ger philol, Univ Idaho, 46-48; asst prof Ger, 48-65, assoc prof Ger philol, 65-72, PROF GER, CASE WESTERN RESERVE UNIV, 72- *Mem:* MLA; Mediaeval Acad Am; Am Asn Teachers Ger. *Publ:* Auth, The Exposito in cantica canticorum of Williram, Abbot of Ebersberg 1048-1085, Am Philos Soc, 67; Willirams's text of the Song of Solomon and its distribution, Manuscripta, Vol XVI: 165-168. *Mailing Add:* Dept of Mod Lang & Lit Case Western Reserve Univ Cleveland OH 44106

BARTELS, ROBERT A, Religion. See Vol IV

BARTELT, HANS GUILLERMO, b Vina del Mar, Chile, Oct 21, 50; US citizen. LINGUISTICS. *Educ:* Univ Wyo, BA, 71, MA, 72; Univ Ariz, MA, 77, PhD(ling), 80. *Prof Exp:* Coordr admin, Sinte Gleska Col, 72-73; INSTR ENGLISH, YAVAPAI COL, 74- *Concurrent Pos:* Adj, Prescott Col, 81. *Mem:* Ling Soc Am. *Res:* Bilingualism; language acquisition; creolization. *Publ:* Auth, Two approaches to acculturation: Bilingual education and ESL, J Am Indian Educ, 18: 15-19 & In: Multicultural Non-sexist Education: A human Relations Approach, Kendall Hunt Publ, 2nd ed, 82; Rhetorical redundancy in Apachean English interlanguage, Papers in Linguistics, Int J Human Commun, 13: 689-704; Semantic overgeneralization in Apachean English interlanguage, J English Ling, 15: 6-10; Some observations on Navajo English, Papers in Linguistics: Int J Human Commun, Vol 14, 81; Mode and aspect transfer in Navajo and Western Apache English narrative technique, Int Rev Appl Ling (in prep); Transfer and implication patterning of rhetorical redundancy in Apachean English interlanguage, In: Language Transfer in Language Learning, Newbury House (in prep); co-ed (with B Hoffer & S Jasper), Studies in American Indian English, Trinity Univ Press (in press); auth, Tense switching in narrative English discourse of Navajo and Western Apache speakers, Studies in Second Lang Acquisition, Vol 4, No 2. *Mailing Add:* Dept of English Yavapai Col Prescott AZ 86301

BARTHOLD, ALLEN JENNINGS, b Philadelphia, Pa, Aug 6, 00; m 37; c 1. ROMANCE LANGUAGES. *Educ:* Lehigh Univ, AB, 31; Yale Univ, PhD, 31. *Prof Exp:* Inst Romance lang, Lehigh Univ, 21-22, 23-24; lectr, Univ Clermont-Gerrand, 22-23; instr French, Yale Univ, 24-36, asst prof, 37-39; prof mod lang & head dept, 39-67, EMER PROF ROMANCE LANG, LEHIGH UNIV, 67- *Concurrent Pos:* Assoc ed, Franco-Am Rev, 36-38; fel, Timothy Dwight Col, 38-39; dir, Inst Cult Dominico-Am, Ciudad-Trujillo, Dominican Repub, 51; prof French, East Stroudsburg State Col, 67-73. *Mem:* Bibliog Soc Am. *Res:* History of the French press in America; French pronunciation; French journalists in the United States. *Mailing Add:* 201 W North St Nazareth PA 18064

BARTLETT, BARRIE EVERDELL, b Jersey, Channel Islands, June 28, 32; m 61. GENERAL LINGUISTICS, HISTORY OF LINGUISTICS. *Educ:* Oxford Univ, BA, 54, dipl educ, 55, MA, 58; Univ BC, MA, 65; Yale Univ, MA, 67; Simon Fraser Univ, PhD(ling), 70. *Prof Exp:* ASSOC PROF FRENCH & LING, SIMON FRASER UNIV, 70- *Res:* Syntax; French grammatical theory; the history of ellipsis. *Publ:* Auth, Preface to facsmilie ed of Beauzee's Grammaire Generale, Fromann, 73-74; Beauzee's Grammaire Generale: Theory and Methodology, Mouton, 74. *Mailing Add:* Dept of Lang Lit & Ling Simon Fraser Univ Burnaby BC V5A 1S6 Can

BARTLEY, DIANA ESTHER, b New York, NY, May 18, 40; c 1. APPLIED LINGUISTICS. *Educ:* Rosemont Col, BA, 61; Middlebury Col, MA, 63; Stanford Univ, AM, 64, PhD (lang educ & appl ling), 70. *Prof Exp:* Res asst, Res Develop Ctr, Stanford Univ, 66-69; from instr to asst prof, 69-73, ASSOC PROF CURRIC & INSTR, UNIV WIS-MILWAUKEE, 73- *Concurrent Pos:* Federal proj dir, Dept Health, Educ & Welfare, 70-78, consult, 74-; Fulbright-Hays sr fel, US Dept State, 78-80; consult, Dept Educ, 80- & Statewide Adult Educ, Teachers English to Speakers Other Lang, Serv Ctr, State Ill, 81- *Mem:* Teachers English to Speakers Other Lang; Adult Educ Asn; MLA; Midwest Mod Lang Asn; AAUP. *Res:* Second language education and cirriculum and teacher training in Russian Republic and Eastern Europe; English as a second language; teacher training in foreign language and bilingual education. *Publ:* Coauth, Practice Centered Teacher Training: Spanish, 70, auth, Soviet Approaches to Bilingual Education, 71 & coauth, Practice Centered Standard English for Speakers of Non-Standard Dialects, 72, Ctr Curric Develop; Microteaching and ABE-TESOL: A model program, Am Foreign Lang Teacher, fall 73; ed, The Latin Child Goes Forth: Bilingual Education Experienced Based Lessons: A Guide for Teachers, United Migrant Opportunity Serv, 75; coauth, A staff development priority, Adult Leadership, fall 75; ed, ABE-TESOL: A Handbook for Educators, Collier Macmillan, 79; Final Reports: 1970-1978, Sch Educ, Univ Wis-Milwaukee; Andragogical look at the adult of limited English proficiency, spring 82. *Mailing Add:* Dept Curric & Instr Univ Wis Sch of Educ Milwaukee WI 53201

BARTOCCI, GIANNI, b Fiuminata, Italy, Sept 2, 25. ROMANCE LANGUAGES. *Educ:* Univ Rome, PhD(philos & hist), 50. *Prof Exp:* Lectr Ital, Trinity Col, Dublin, 51-58; sr lectr Ital lit, Univ Auckland, 58-67; assoc prof, 67-73, PROF ITAL LIT & HUMANITIES, UNIV GUELPH, 73- *Concurrent Pos:* Prof hist Ital civilization, Ital Inst Dublin, 54-58. *Honors & Awards:* Cavaliere, Order of Merit, Italy, 67. *Mem:* Dante Soc NZ (pres, 63-65). *Res:* Philosophy; Italian, Spanish literature, humanities. *Publ:* Auth, Per le vie di Dublino, 56, Addio, vecchia strada (bilingual ed), 59, G Intelisano, Parma; Waiting for you--la tua attesa, Officina Poligrafica Laziale, Rome, 66; Viaggio agli Antipodi, 67 & Equinozio ad Armanderiz, 68, Kursaal, Florence; I Volsci a Dublino, G Intelisano, Parma, 68; Stars and Solitude, Dorrance, Phila, 69; Vento a Guelph, G Intelisano, Parma, 69; In margine a Gauguin, Rebellato, Padova, 70; La Riabilitazione di Galileo, Landi, Firenze, 80. *Mailing Add:* Dept of Lang Univ of Guelph Guelph ON N1G 2W1 Can

BARTON, CHARLES RICHMOND, b New York, NY, Aug 27, 36. LINGUISTICS. *Educ:* Yale Univ, BA, 56; NY Univ, MA, 63, PhD(ling), 65. *Prof Exp:* Instr classics, Drew Univ, 64-65, asst prof, 65-66; asst prof, 66-70, ASSOC PROF CLASSICS & LING, SIR GEORGE WILLIAMS UNIV, 70- *Mem:* Ling Soc Am; Am Orient Soc; Am Philol Asn; Can Ling Asn. *Res:* Indo-European linguistics. *Publ:* Auth, The etymology of Armenian ert'am, Language 63; contribr, Studies in Honor of J Alexander Kerns, Mouton, The Hague, 70; auth, The Armenian storng aroist, Revue Etudes Armeniennes, 73-74; Notes on the Baltic preterite, Indogermanische Forschungen (in press); Greek egera, Glotta (in press). *Mailing Add:* Dept of Classics Ling & Mod Lang Sir George Williams Univ Montreal PQ H3G 1M8 Can

BARY, DAVID A, b San Francisco, Calif, Sept 25, 24; m 48; c 2. HISPANIC LITERATURE. *Educ:* Univ Calif, Berkeley, AB, 48, MA, 50, PhD(Romance lit), 56. *Prof Exp:* Instr Span, Univ Wash, 55-58; from asst prof to assoc prof, 58-71, PROF SPANISH, UNIV CALIF, SANTA BARBARA, 71- *Concurrent Pos:* Del Amo fel, 64-65. *Mem:* Am Asn Teachers Span & Port; Inst Int Lit Iberoam. *Res:* Twentieth Century Hispanic poetry. *Publ:* Auth, Huidobro, o la vocacion poetica, Univ Granada, 63; Sobre el nombrar poetico en la poesia espanola contemporanea, Papeles Son Armadans, Mallorca, 2/67; Sobre la Oda a Juan Tarrea, Cuadernos Am, 8/68; Larrea: Poesia y Transfiguracion, Univ Compluteuse, Barcelona, 76; Sobre la poetica de Juan Tarrea, Cuadernos Hispanoamericanos, 77; El Altazor de Huidobro sequn un texto inedito de Juan Tarrea, 78 & Sobre los origenes de Altazor, 79, Rev Iberoamericana; Vallejo's Obra poetica completo and the technical critique of Juan Tarrea, Hispanic Rev, 79; Poesia y narracion en cuatro novelas mexicanas, Cuadernos Americanos, 81. *Mailing Add:* Dept of Span Univ of Calif Santa Barbara CA 93106

BAS, JOE, b San Juan, PR, Oct 21, 32; m 62; c 2. SPANISH. *Educ:* Calif State Col, Long Beach, AB, 58; Univ Southern Calif, AM, 64, PhD(Span), 66. *Prof Exp:* Teacher, La Mirada High Sch, 59-62; instr Span, Cerritos Col, 62-66; asst prof, San Diego State Col, 66-68; chmn dept foreign lang & lit, 70-73, assoc prof, 68-70, PROF SPAN, CALIF STATE COL, SAN BERNARDINO, 70- *Concurrent Pos:* Peace Corps methodology consult, Colombia proj, San Diego State Col, 67; consult, San Diego City Schs & Macmillan Co, 67. *Mem:* Am Asn Teachers Span & Port; Am Coun Teaching Foreign Lang. *Res:* Golden Age drama; Spanish language. *Publ:* Coauth, Cuentos argentinos de misterio, Appleton, 68; El mejor alcalde, el Rey, a critical edition, Cajica, 74. *Mailing Add:* Dept of Span Calif State Col San Bernardino CA 92407

BASDEKIS, DEMETRIOS, b New York, NY, Dec 12, 30. MODERN SPANISH LITERATURE. *Educ:* Queens Col, NY, BA, 53; Columbia Univ, MA, 60, PhD(Span), 64. *Prof Exp:* Preceptor Span, Columbia Univ, 63-64; instr, State Univ NY, Stonybrook, 64-66; asst prof, Univ Calif, Berkeley, 66-71; PROF SPAN, STATE UNIV NY COL ONEONTA, 71- *Mem:* MLA. *Publ:* Auth, Unamuno and Spanish Literature, Univ Calif, 67; Miguel de Unamuno, Columbia Univ, 69; ed, Tres Novolas de Unamuno, Prentice-Hall, 70; auth, Unamuno and the Novel, Univ NC, 74. *Mailing Add:* Dept of Span State Univ of NY Col Oneonta NY 13820

BASGOZ, MEHMET ILHAN, b Sivas, Turkey, Aug 15, 21; m 53; c 2. FOLKLORE, LANGUAGE. *Educ:* Univ Ankara, PhD(folklore), 49. *Prof Exp:* Asst prof, lang & lit, Univ Ankara, 46-49; lectr educ, Univ Calif, Los Angeles, 61-63; lectr Turkish lang & lit, Univ Calif, Berkeley, 63-65; from asst prof to assoc prof, 65-74, PROF TURKISH STUDIES, IND UNIV, BLOOMINGTON, 74- *Concurrent Pos:* Ford Found grant, 61-63; Am Coun Learned Socs grant, 63; assoc ed, Ural-Altaic Series, Ind Univ, 65-68; Soc Sci Res Coun grant, 67; Minister Health, Educ & Welfare grant, 68-70; ed, Turkish Studies Asn Bull, 76-78; ed, Ind Univ Turkish Studies, 78. *Mem:* Soc Asian Folklore; Am Orient Soc; Am Folklore Soc; Turkish Studies Asn; Mid East Studies Asn. *Res:* Linguistics; comparative education; Turkish and Middle East folklore. *Publ:* Auth, Turkish Folk Poetry(selections), A Halit, Turkey, 56; The functions of Turkish riddles, J Am Folklore, 66; Dream motif in Turkish folk literature, Asian Folklore Stud, 67; Turkish Folklore Reader, 1967, Ind Univ Uralic & Altaic Ser, 67; coauth, Educational Problems in Turkey, Ind Univ Uralic-Altaic Ser, 68; Bilmece; A Corpus of Turkish Riddles, Calif Univ Folklore Studies 22, 75; contribr, The singer and his audience, In: Folklore: Performance and Communication, Pen, 75; ed, Studies in Turkish Folklore, Ind Univ Turkish Studies 1, 78. *Mailing Add:* Dept of Uralic & Altaic Studies Ind Univ Bloomington IN 47401

BASHIRI, IRAJ, b Behbahan, Iran, July 31, 40; m 68; c 3. MODERN IRANIAN LINGUISTICS & LITERATURE. *Educ:* Pahlavi Univ, BA, 63; Univ Mich, Ann Arbor, MA, 68, PhD(Iranian ling), 72. *Prof Exp:* Lectr English, Pahlavi Univ & Brit Coun, 63-64; instr, Imp Iranian Air Forces, 65; lectr Persian, Univ Mich, 67-72; vis asst prof Iranian studies & Turkish, 72-73, asst prof, 73-78, ASSOC PROF IRANIAN STUDIES & TURKISH, UNIV MINN, MINNEAPOLIS, 78-, ASSOC CHMN, DEPT SOUTH ASIAN STUDIES, 81- *Concurrent Pos:* Grad travel grant, Univ Mich, 79. *Honors & Awards:* Col Lang Asn Distinguished teacher award, 80. *Mem:* Soc Iranian Studies; Mid EStudies Asn NAm. *Res:* Iranian linguistics and literature. *Publ:* Auth, Persian for beginners, 72 & To be as the origin of syntax: A Persian framework, 73, Bibliotheca Islamica; Hedayat's Ivory Tower: Structural Analysis of The Blind Owl, Manor House, 74; Hafiz' Shirazi Turk: A structuralist point of view, Muslim World, 7 & 10/79; Hafiz and the sufic Ghazal, Studies in Islam, 1/79; Persian for Beginners: Pronunciation and Writing, 9/80, tape manual with notes on grammar, 11/80, reading texts, 7/81, Persian Syntax, 81, Burgess Publ Co. *Mailing Add:* Dept of Mid Eastern Lang Klaeber Ctr Univ of Minn Minneapolis MN 55455

BASSETT, EDWARD LEWIS, b Marblehead, Mass, Sept 1, 14. CLASSICAL PHILOLOGY. *Educ:* Harvard Univ, AB, 36, AM, 38, PhD, 42. *Prof Exp:* Master, Loomis Inst, 38-47; from instr to asst prof classics, Cornell Univ, 47-51; asst prof Univ Wash, 51-52; from asst prof to assoc prof, 52-67, chmn dept classics, 73-75, prof, 67-79, EMER PROF LATIN, UNIV CHICAGO, 79- *Concurrent Pos:* Fulbright res grant, Italy, 61-62. *Mem:* Am Philol Asn; Class Asn Midwest & South. *Res:* Latin literature, especially of the Empire; Latin stylistics. *Publ:* Auth, Regulus and the serpent in the Punica, 1/55 & Scipio and the ghost of Appius, 4/63, Class Philol; Hercules and the hero of the Punica, In: The Classical Tradition: Literary and Historical Studies in Honor of Harry Caplan, Cornell Univ, 66; coauth, Tiberius Catius Asconius Silius Italicus, In: Vol III, Catalogus Translationeum et Commentariorum, 76. *Mailing Add:* Dept of Classics Univ of Chicago Chicago IL 60637

BASSMAN, MICHAEL FREDERIC, b New York, NY. PHILOLOGY, FOREIGN LANGUAGE. *Educ:* Brooklyn Col, BA, 64; Brown Univ, MAT, 66; Univ Conn, MA, 71, PhD(Romance philol), 73. *Prof Exp:* Teacher French, Burrillville High Sch, 64-65; teaching asst, Univ Conn, 65-71; asst prof, 71-76, ASSOC PROF FOREIGN LANG, E CAROLINA UNIV, 76-, COORDR FRENCH, 77- *Concurrent Pos:* Asst dir prog in France, Univ Conn, 67-68; Fulbright fel, Univ Bucharest, 69-70. *Mem:* MLA; Pedagogical Sem Romance Philol; SAtlatnic Mod Lang Asn; AAUP; Romanian Stuides Asn. *Res:* Romance philology; Romanian language; Yiddish language. *Publ:* Auth, Romanian: A Romance language, 76, Loan-words and the neuter gender in Romanian, 76 & the Romanian lexical system, 76, Romanian Bull. *Mailing Add:* Dept of Foreign Lang ECarolina Univ Greenville NC 27834

BASTIANUTTI, DIEGO LUIGI, b Fiume, Italy, Apr 26, 39; Can citizen; m 62; c 2. FOREIGN LANGUAGES & LITERATURES. *Educ:* Marquette Univ, BA, 61, MA, 66; Univ Toronto, PhD(Span & Ital), 74. *Prof Exp:* Instr Span & Ital, Univ Nebr, 66-67; teaching asst, Univ Toronto, 67-70; lectr, 70-73, asst prof, 74-82, ASSOC PROF SPAN & ITAL, QUEEN'S UNIV, 82- *Concurrent Pos:* Res grant, Queen's Univ, 77-78; hon vconsult Italy, Ital Ministry Foreign Affairs, 78- *Mem:* Can Asn Hispanists; Can Soc Ital Studies; Int Asn Professors Ital; Coun Ital & Latin Am Inst Rome; Can Comp Lit Asn. *Res:* The Spanish Hagiographic Theatre; computer assisted instruction, software development in Italian; modern Italian novel. *Publ:* Contribr, Calderon de la Barca Studies 1951-69: A Critical Survey & Annotated Bibliography, Univ Toronto Press, 71; La funcion de la Fortuna en la primera novela sentimental espanola, Romance Notes, Vol XIV, 73; El Caballero de Olmedo: solo un ejercicio triste del alma, Hispanofila, Vol II, 75; Autobiographical elements in Lope de Vega's La Ninez del Padre Rojas, Bull Comediantes, Vol 28, 76; trans, Oh Buone Maniere, Maccari, Parma, 78; La inspiracion pictorica en el teatro hagiografico de Lope de Vega, Acts of the Congreso sobre Lope de Vega y los origenes del teatro espanol, 81; Giorgio Bassani: The record of a confession, Queen's Quart, Vol 88, 81; Opportunita e adattabilita di un sistema d'istruzione di lingue estere a base di computer, Scuole e Lingue Moderne, Vol 19, 81. *Mailing Add:* Dept of Span & Ital Queen's Univ Kingston ON K7L 3N6 Can

BASTO, RONALD GARY, b Putnam, Conn, Nov 20, 52; m 74. CLASSICAL LANGUAGES. *Educ:* Cornell Univ, Ba, 74, PhD(class lang), 80. *Prof Exp:* Teaching asst classics, Cornell Univ, 78-79; ASST PROF CLASSICS, AMHERST COL, 79- *Mem:* Am Philol Asn; Vergilian Soc. *Res:* Roman literature, Augustan and post-Augustan; Roman history, the Principate. *Publ:* Auth, Caecilius, Attis and Catullus 35, Liverpool Class Monthly, 3/82; Horace's propempticon to Vergil: A re-examination, Vergilus, 82; The grazing of Circe's shore, Class World (in press). *Mailing Add:* 120 Amherst Rd Amherst MA 01002

BATCHELOR, C MALCOLM, b Newark, NJ, Oct 14, 14. ROMANCE LANGUAGES. *Educ:* Rutgers Univ, AB, 37; Yale Univ, MA, 40, PhD, 45. *Prof Exp:* Instr French & Span, Rutgers Univ, 37-38; from asst instr to instr Span, 40-47, from instr to asst prof Span & Port, 47-60, dir undergrad courses Span, 48-53 & Span & Port, 57-62, dir grad studies Span, 58, ASSOC PROF SPAN & PORT, YALE UNIV, 60- *Concurrent Pos:* Mem nat screening comt, Inst Int Educ. *Mem:* Am Asn Teachers Span & Port; New Eng MLA; MLA; hon mem, Soc Brasileira Criminalogia. *Res:* Spanish and Brazilian language and literature. *Publ:* Auth, Cuentos de aca y de ala, Houghton, 53; Horizontes latinoamericanos, Am Bk Co, 55; Ati, Dona Marina, Ucar-Garcia, Havana, 59. *Mailing Add:* Dept of Span & Ital Yale Univ 493 College St New Haven CT 06520

BATEMAN, JOHN JAY, b Elmira, NY, Feb 17, 31; m 52; c 3. CLASSICS, SPEECH. *Educ:* Univ Toronto, BA, 53; Cornell Univ, MA, 54, PhD(classics), 58. *Prof Exp:* Lectr classics, Univ Toronto, 56-57; lectr, Univ Ottawa, 57-58, asst prof, 58-60; from asst prof to assoc prof, 60-68, head, Dept Classics, 66-73, actg dir, Sch Humanities, 73-74, PROF CLASSICS & SPEECH, UNIV ILL, URBANA, 68- *Concurrent Pos:* Chmn, Div Humanities, Univ Ill, Urbana-Champaign, 69-73; consult-panelist, Nat Endowment for Humanities, 75-76. *Mem:* Am Philol Asn (secy-treas, 69-73); Renaissance Soc Am; Class Asn Midwest & South; Int Soc Hist Rhetoric. *Res:* Greek language and literature; classical rhetoric and literary criticism; Neo-latin literature. *Publ:* Auth, Some aspects of Lysias' argumentation, Phoenix, 62; The development of Erasmus' views on the correct pronunciation of Latin and Greek, Studies in Honor of Ben Edwin Perry, 68; The text of Erasmus' De recta Latini Graecique sermonis pronuntiatione dialogus, Acta Conventus Neo-Latini Lovaniensis, 73; Aldus Manutius' Fragmenta Grammatica, Ill Class Studies, 76. *Mailing Add:* Dept of Classics Univ Ill Urbana IL 61801

BATES, BLANCHARD WESLEY, b Portland, Maine, June 19, 08. FRENCH LITERATURE. *Educ:* Bowdoin Col, AB, 31; Harvard Univ, AM, 33; Princeton Univ, PhD, 41. *Prof Exp:* Exchange teacher, Ecole Norm, La Rochelle, France, 31-32; instr lang, Fresnal Ranch Sch, 34-37; instr, 37-39 & 41-42, from asst prof to prof, 46-76, EMER PROF FRENCH, PRINCETON UNIV, 76- *Mem:* MLA. *Res:* Literary portraiture in the historical narrative of the French Renaissance; Montaigne, selected essays. *Mailing Add:* Grasshopper Hill Chebeaque Island ME 04017

BATES, MARGARET JANE, b New York, NY, Jan 27, 18. SPANISH, PORTUGUESE. *Educ:* Hunter Col, AB, 38; Columbia Univ, MLA, 40; Cath Univ Am, PhD, 45. *Prof Exp:* Mem interdept comt orgn of libr in Peru & Brazil, US Dept of State, 41-44; from asst prof to assoc prof Romance lang, 44-55; vdir, Inst Ibero-Am studies, 50-55; PROF ROMANCE LANG,

CATH UNIV AM, 44-, DIR, INST IBERO-AM STUDIES, 55- *Concurrent Pos:* Ford fac fel, 53-54. *Mem:* MLA; Am Asn Teachers Span & Port. *Res:* Spanish and Portuguese linguistics and literature; discretion in the works of Cervantes; Gregorio de Mattos, poet of 17th century Brazil. *Publ:* Ed, Las Poesias Completas de Gabriela Mistral, Aguilar, Madrid, 58, 2nd ed, 62, 3rd ed, 66. *Mailing Add:* 5914 Carlton Lane Bethesda MD 20016

BATES, PAUL ALLEN, English. See Vol II

BATES, SCOTT, b Evanston, Ill, June 13, 23; m 48; c 4. FRENCH, FILM. *Educ:* Carleton Col, BA, 47; Univ Wis, MA, 48, PhD(French), 54. *Prof Exp:* Asst prof, 54-64, PROF FRENCH LANG & LIT, UNIV OF THE SOUTH, 64- *Concurrent Pos:* Ed, Ecol Papers, 70-72. *Mem:* MLA. *Res:* Modern French poetry; modern English and American poetry. *Publ:* Auth, Guillaume Apollinaire, Twayne, 67; ed, Poems of War Resistance, Grossman, 69; Petit glossaire des mots libres d'Apollinaire, Sewane, 75; The ABC of Radical Ecology, Highlander, 82. *Mailing Add:* Dept of Lang & Lit Univ of the South Sewanee TN 37375

BATTS, MICHAEL S, b Mitcham, Eng, Aug 2, 29; m 59; c 1. GERMAN. *Educ:* Univ London, BA, 53, DLit, 73; Univ Freiburg, DPhil, 57; Univ Toronto, MLS, 74. *Prof Exp:* Lectr English lang & lit, Univ Basel, 54-56; lectr, Univ Würzburg, 56-58; instr Ger, Univ Calif, Berkeley, 58-60; from asst prof to assoc prof, 60-67, head dept, 68-80, PROF GER, UNIV BC, 67- *Concurrent Pos:* Can Coun sr fel, 64-65 & 71-72; Alexander von Humboldt scholar, 64-65; ed, Seminar, 70-80; Killam fel, 80-82. *Mem:* Can Asn Univ Teachers Ger; Mod Humanities Res Asn; MLA; Philol Asn Pac Coast; Royal Soc Can; Can Fedn Humanities. *Res:* Medieval literature; bibliography. *Publ:* Auth, Die Form der Aventiuren im Nibelungenlied, Schmitz, Giessen, 61; Bruder Hansens Marienlieder, Niemeyer, Tübingen, 63; Studien zu Bruder Hansens Marienliedern, de Gruyter, Berlin, 64; Hohes Mittelalter (Handbuch der deutschen Literaturgeschichte: Bibliographien Band 2), Francke, 69; Das Nibelungenlied: Paralleldruck der Handschriften, Niemeyer, Tübingen, 71; Gottfried von Strassburg, Twayne, 71; A Check-list of German Literature 1945-75, Can Asn Univ Teachers Ger, 77; The Bibliography of German Literature: An Historical and Critical Survey, Lang, 78. *Mailing Add:* Dept of Germanic Studies Univ of BC Vancouver BC V6T 1W5 Can

BAUDOUIN, DOMINIQUE, b Paris, France, Apr 19, 27. FRENCH LANGUAGE & LITERATURE. *Educ:* Sorbonne Univ, France, Lic es Let, 49, dipl, 50, cert, 51, agrege let-grammaire, 54. *Prof Exp:* Prof French, Latin & Greek, Moslem Col, Tunis, 51-53 & various French Lycees, 54-59; Fulbright vis instr French, Oberlin Col, 59-60; asst prof, Univ Ore, 60-62; from asst prof to assoc prof, 62-77, PROF FRENCH, UNIV BC, 77- *Concurrent Pos:* Can Coun res grant, France, 68-69. *Mem:* MLA; Philol Asn Pac Coast; Asn Studies Dada & Surrealism (secy, 66-68). *Res:* French literature of the 20th century. *Mailing Add:* Dept of French Univ of BC Vancouver BC V6T 1W5 Can

BAUER, GEORGE HOWARD, b Cortez, Colo, Dec 31, 33; m 62; c 2. FRENCH LANGUAGE & LITERATURE. *Educ:* Univ Colo, BA, 55; Ind Univ, MA, 60, PhD(Fr), 67. *Prof Exp:* Instr French, Dartmouth Col, 61-63; lectr, Northwestern Univ, Evanston, 63-64, instr Romance lang, 64-67, asst prof French, 67-70; asst prof, Univ Minn, Minneapolis, 70-73, assoc prof Ital & French, 73-77, acting chmn dept comp lit, 73-74; CHMN, DEPT FRENCH & ITAL, UNIV SOUTHERN CALIF, 77- *Concurrent Pos:* Am Coun Learned Socs study fel, 68-69; distinguished vis prof humanities, Univ Wyo, 76-77. *Mem:* Am Asn Teachers Fr; MLA; Col Art Asn Am; Asn Studies Dada & Surrealism; Am Comp Lit Asn. *Res:* Twentieth century French literature; relation between art and literature; comparative literature. *Publ:* Auth, Interview as autobiography: Jean Paul Sartre, L'Esprit Createur, 77; Caligula: Portrait de l'artiste ou rien, Revue des Lettres Modernes, 75; Duchamp, Delay, Overlay in Mid-America, Uomo di lettere/LHOMME, 78; LETRE/Barthes XYZ Game, New York Literary Forum, 78; Satre, In: Critical Bibliography of French Literature, 79; Eatins, The Other, In: Homosexualities and French Literature, Cornell Univ, 79; Peinture et engagement, In: Sartre et les Arts, Obliques, Paris, 81; Sartre, In: Cabeen Critical Bibliography of French Literature, 79. *Mailing Add:* Dept of French and Ital Univ of Southern Calif Los Angeles CA 90007

BAUERLE, RICHARD F, b Lansing, Mich, Aug 19, 21; m 51; c 2. LINGUISTICS. *Educ:* Mich State Univ, BA, 43; Univ Mich, MA, 47; Western Reserve Univ, PhD(English), 53. *Prof Exp:* Instr English, NC State Col, 49-53; from asst prof to assoc prof, 53-61, PROF ENGLISH, OHIO WESLEYAN UNIV, 61- *Concurrent Pos:* Mem, Citator Staff, Webster's New World Dict, 81- *Mem:* Ling Soc Am. *Res:* American speech. *Publ:* Emblematic opening of Warren's All the King's Men, Papers Lang & Lit, summer 72; Mondialization, Int Lang Reporter, 72; Stafford's Holcomb, Kansas, Contemp Poetry, 73; Salties on the Great Lakes, 74 & Origin of Frisbee and related terms, 75, Am Speech; Whitman's index: A map of his language world, Walt Whitman Rev, 80. *Mailing Add:* Dept of English Ohio Wesleyan Univ Delaware OH 43015

BAUGH, JOHN, b Brooklyn, NY, Dec 12, 49. LINGUISTICS, SOCIOLINGUISTICS. *Educ:* Temple Univ, BA, 72; Univ Pa, MA, 76, PhD(ling), 79. *Prof Exp:* Lectr ling, sociol & anthrop, Swarthmore Col, 75-78, asst prof sociol & anthrop, 78-79; asst prof ling, Univ Tex, Austin, 79-82; VIS SCHOLAR LING, CTR APPLIED LING, 82- *Concurrent Pos:* Ford Found res fel, 82; Am Coun Learned Soc grant, 80. *Mem:* Ling Soc Am; Am Dialect Soc; Am Anthrop Asn. *Res:* Sociolinguistics; applied linguistics; language attitudes and perceptions. *Publ:* Auth, The politics of black power handshakes, Nat hist, 10/78; Black Street Speech: History, Structure and Survival, Univ Tex Press (in press). *Mailing Add:* Ctr for Applied Ling 3520 Prospect St NW Washington DC 20007

BAUKE, JOSEPH P, b Briesen, Ger, May 18, 32; US citizen. GERMANICS. *Educ:* Univ Cincinnati, BA, 57, MA, 58; Columbia Univ, PhD, 63. *Prof Exp:* From instr to assoc prof, 59-69, PROF GER, COLUMBIA UNIV, 69- *Concurrent Pos:* Ed, Ger Rev, 66- *Mem:* Am Asn Teachers Ger; Germanistic Soc Am (pres, 70-). *Mailing Add:* Dept of Germanic Lang Columbia Univ New York NY 10027

BAUMGAERTEL, GERHARD, b Merseburg, Ger, Feb 21, 27; US citizen; m 61; c 2. GERMANIC LANGUAGE & LITERATURE. *Educ:* Brown Univ, MA, 53; Univ Tübingen, PhD, 54. *Prof Exp:* Instr Ger & comp lit, Univ Pa, 55-60, asst prof, 60-62; assoc prof Ger, Univ Wash, 62-68, assoc prof Ger & comp lit, 68-72, PROF GER STUDIES & CHMN DEPT, TRENT UNIV, 72- *Concurrent Pos:* Jusserand fel, 60; co-ed, Mod Lang Quart, 70-72. *Mem:* MLA; Am Asn Teachers Ger; Int Comp Lit Asn; Am Comp Lit Asn; Can Asn Univ Teachers Ger. *Res:* The 18th to 20th centuries. *Mailing Add:* Dept of German Trent Univ Peterborough ON K9J 7B8 Can

BAUMGARTEN, JOSEPH M, Oriental Studies. See Vol IV

BAUMGARTNER, INGEBORG HOGH, b Oberstuben, Czech, Jan 29, 36; US citizen; m 67. GERMAN LITERATURE. *Educ:* Univ Mich, AB, 58, PhD(Ger), 70; Univ Wis, AM, 59. *Prof Exp:* Instr Ger, Loyola Univ Chicago, 65-66; ASSOC PROF GER, ALBION COL, 66- *Mem:* MLA; Am Asn Teachers Ger. *Res:* German drama; 19th and 20th century German literature. *Publ:* Auth, Ambiguity in Büchner's Woyzeck, Mich Ger Studies, fall 75; coauth, A one-semester introduction to literary interpretation, Die Unterrichtspraxis, spring 77. *Mailing Add:* Dept of Ger Albion Col Albion MI 49224

BAUML, BETTY JEAN, b New York, NY, Aug 6, 30; m 58. SPANISH LANGUAGE & LITERATURE. *Educ:* Ohio State Univ, BA, 51, MA, 53; Univ Calif, Berkeley, PhD(Romance lang & lit), 57. *Prof Exp:* Instr foreign lang, Immaculate Heart Col Calif, 58-61; from asst prof to assoc prof, 61-75, PROF FOREIGN LANG, CALIF STATE UNIV, NORTHRIDGE, 75- *Mem:* MLA; Philol Asn Pac Coast. *Res:* Nineteenth and 17th century Spanish literature. *Publ:* Auth, The mundane demon: The bourgeois grotesque in Galdos' Torquemada en la hoguera, Symposium, 70; A Dictionary of Gestures, Metuchen, 75. *Mailing Add:* Dept of Foreign Lang & Lit Calif State Univ Northridge CA 91324

BAUML, FRANZ H, b Vienna, Austria, June 12, 26; US citizen; m 58. LANGUAGES. *Educ:* Univ Berkeley, BA, 53, MA, 55, PhD(Ger), 57. *Prof Exp:* From instr to assoc prof, 57-65, PROF GER, UNIV CALIF, LOS ANGELES, 65- *Concurrent Pos:* Am Coun Learned Soc res grant-in-aid, 59. *Mem:* MLA; Mediaeval Acad Am. *Res:* Mediaeval German literature. *Publ:* Auth, Rhetorical Devices and Structure in the Ackermann aus Böhmen, Univ Calif, 60; Zur mündlichen Überlieferung des Nibelungenliedes, Deut Vierteljahrsschrift, 67; Kudrun: Die Handschrift, W de Gruyter Berlin, 69; Medieval Civilization in Germany: 800-1273, Thames & Hudson, London, 69; coauth, Weiteres zur mündlichen Überlieferung des Nibelungenliedes, Deut Vierteljahrsschrift, 72; A Dictionary of Gestures, Scarecrow, 75; A Concordance to the Nibelungenlied, Maney & Son, Leeds, 76; Varieties and consequences of medieval literacy and illiteracy, Speculum, 80. *Mailing Add:* Dept of Ger Lang Univ of Calif Los Angeles CA 90024

BAUSCHINGER, SIGRID ELISABETH, b Frankfurt, Ger, Nov 2, 34. MODERN GERMAN LITERATURE. *Educ:* Univ Frankfurt, Dr Phil(Ger lit), 60. *Prof Exp:* Instr Ger, Oberlin Col, 62-64, asst prof, 64-68; asst prof, 68-71, assoc prof, 71-79, head dept, 76-79, PROF GER, UNIV MASS, AMHERST, 79- *Mem:* MLA. *Res:* Twentieth century German literature; literature of exile; German-Jewish literature. *Publ:* Contribr, Psychologie in der Literaturwissenschaft, Lothar Stiehm, Heidelberg, 71 & Gedichte der Menschheitsdämmerung, Albin Fink, München, 71; coauth, Elementary German, Van Nostrand Rineholt, 71; coauth & co-ed, Amerika in der Deutschen Literatur, Reclam, 75; auth, Else Lasker-Schuler, Ihr Werk und ihre Zeit, Lothar Stiehm, Heidelberg, 80. *Mailing Add:* Dept of Ger Univ of Mass Amherst MA 01003

BAUSLAUGH, ROBERT ALAN, b Berkeley, Calif, Oct 21, 48; m 72; c 2. CLASSICAL LANGUAGES & HISTORY. *Educ:* Univ Calif, Riverside, BA, 70; Univ Calif, Berkeley, MA, 73, PhD(ancient hist & archeol), 79. *Prof Exp:* Teaching asst Latin, Univ Calif, Berkeley, 73-75; fel civilization & humanities, Columbia Univ, Soc Fels, 79-80; ASST PROF CLASSICS, EMORY UNIV, 81- *Concurrent Pos:* Mem managing comt, Am Sch Class Studies, Athens, 82; Nat Endowment for Humanities grant, 82; Am Coun Learned Soc fel, 82. *Mem:* Am Numis Soc; Am Philol Asn; Archeol Inst Am; AAUP. *Res:* Ancient Greek history and historians; ancient Greek numismatics. *Publ:* Contribr, Echoes from Olympus: Reflections of Divinity in Small Scale Classical Art, Univ Calif Press, 74; auth, The text of Thucydides iv 8.6 and the south channel at Pylos, J Hellenic Studies, 79; The posthumous Alexander coinage of Chios, 79 & The unique portrait tetradrachm of Eumenes II (in press), Am Numis Soc Mus Notes. *Mailing Add:* Dept of Mod Lang & Classics Emory Univ Atlanta GA 30322

BAXTER, GLEN WILLIAM, b Sherman, Tex, Jan 14, 14. FAR EASTERN LANGUAGES. *Educ:* Stanford Univ, AB, 47; Harvard Univ, AM, 49, PhD(Far Eastern lang), 52. *Prof Exp:* Harvard-Yenching Inst traveling fel, Harvard Univ, 52-54, asst dir, 56-61, lectr, EAsian studies, 56-80, actg dir, 61-64, assoc dir, 64-80 . *Mem:* Asn Asian Studies; Am Orient Soc. *Res:* Chinese six dynasties, T'ang and Sung history and literature, especially yueh-fu and Tz'u poetry. *Publ:* Ed, The Chronicle of the Three Kingdos, 52 & auth, Index to the Imperial Register of Tz'u prosody, 56, Harvard Univ; Metrical origins of the Tz'u, Harvard J Asiatic Studies; Chinese literature, In: Encycl Britannica, 56; coauth, Chinese poetry, In: Encycl Poetry & Poetics, Princeton Univ, 65; Poems in irregular meter, In: Anthology of Chinese Literature, Grove, 65. *Mailing Add:* 2 Divinity Ave Cambridge MA 02138

BAXTER, WILLIAM, III, b New York, NY, Mar 3, 49; m 69; c 2. GENERAL & CHINESE LINGUISTICS. *Educ:* Amherst Col, BA, 70; Cornell Univ, MA, 74, PhD(ling), 77. *Prof Exp:* ASST PROF LING, UNIV ALA BIRMINGHAM, 78- *Mem:* Ling Soc Am; Asn Asian Studies. *Res:* Chinese historical phonology; linguistic theory. *Publ:* Contribr, Historical Linguistics, E J Brill Leiden, 80. *Mailing Add:* Dept of English Univ of Ala Birmingham AL 35294

BAYERLE, GUSTAV, Ottoman History, Turkish Philology. See Vol I

BAYERSCHMIDT, CARL FRANK, b Providence, RI, Feb 18, 05; m 35; c 2. GERMANIC PHILOLOGY. *Educ:* Brown Univ, AB, 26; Columbia Univ, AM, 28, PhD, 34. *Prof Exp:* Instr Ger, Rutgers Univ, 34-37, asst prof, 37-40; asst prof, Univ Chicago, 40-41; from asst prof to prof, 41-71, VILLARD EMER PROF GER PHILOL, COLUMBIA UNIV, 71- *Concurrent Pos:* Fulbright prof Ger philol, Univ Hamburg, 62-63 & 69-70. *Honors & Awards:* Knight's Cross, Icelandic Order of Falcon, 71; Officer's Cross, Order of Merit, Fed Repub Ger, 71; Royal Order of North Star, First Class, Sweden, 72. *Mem:* MLA; Am Asn Teacher Ger; Germanistic Soc Am (pres, 61-71); Am-Scand Found(trustee, 61-). *Res:* Low German language and literature; Scandinavian language and literature. *Publ:* Auth, Low German Philology; A Middle Low German Book of Kings; Njals Saga; coauth, Scandinavian Studies, Univ Wash, 65; auth, Sigrid Undset, 70 & Seven Years of My Life, 75, Twayne. *Mailing Add:* 14 Franklin Ave Yonkers NY 10705

BAYHOUSE, ANNA TERESA, b Boise, Idaho, Apr 27, 13. ROMANCE LANGUAGES, LINGUISTICS. *Educ:* Immaculate Heart Col, BA, 38; Western Reserve Univ, MA, 41; Georgetown Univ, PhD(French ling), 66. *Prof Exp:* Chmn dept French, Col St Mary, Utah, 41-53; from asst prof to prof, Dunbarton Col Holy Cross, 62-72, chmn dept mod lang, 62-72; chmn dept mod lang, 72-76, prof, 72-78, EMER PROF FRENCH, ST MARY'S COL, IND, 78- *Honors & Awards:* Spes Unica Medal, St Mary's Col, 77. *Mem:* MLA; Am Coun Teachers Foreign Lang. *Res:* Twentieth century French literature; individualization of instruction in foreign languages on the college level. *Mailing Add:* Regina Hall St Mary's Col Notre Dame IN 46556

BAYS, GWENDOLYN M, b Atlanta, Ga; m; c 2. FRENCH, GERMAN. *Educ:* Agnes Scott Col, BA; Emory Univ, MA; Yale Univ, PhD(Fr), 56. *Prof Exp:* Instr French, Univ Md, 53-54; res assoc, Yale Univ, 57-58; assoc prof French & Ger, Antioch Col, 58-62; PROF FRENCH & GER, CLARION STATE COL, 62- *Mem:* MLA; Am Asn Teachers Fr. *Res:* French literature of the 19th and 20th centuries--symbolism, surrealism, existentialism. *Publ:* Auth, Simone de Beauvoir: Ethics and art, 50 & Balzac as seer, 52, Yale Fr Studies; The Orphic Vision, Univ Nebr, 64; The Orphic vision of Nerval, Baudelaire and Rimbaud, Comp Lit Studies, 67; transl, The Life and Liberation of Padmasambhava (2 vols), Dharma Press, 78. *Mailing Add:* 202 South St Clarion PA 16214

BEALER, RALPH GEORGE, b Allentown, Pa, Mar 5, 08; m 35; c 3. BIBLICAL LANGUAGES & LITERATURE. *Educ:* Moravian Col, AB, 35; Christian Theol Sem, MA, 55. *Hon Degrees:* DD, Huntington Col, 75. *Prof Exp:* From asst prof to assoc prof, 46-77, head dept Bible & relig, 73-76, EMER ASSOC PROF BIBLE LANG & LIT, HUNTINGTON COL, 77- *Mem:* Soc Bible Lit. *Res:* The relationship of New Testament literary forms to meaning; Biblical languages and literature in both the college and school of Christian ministries. *Mailing Add:* Dept of Bible & Relig Huntington Col Huntington IN 46750

BEALL, CHANDLER BAKER, b Northport, NY, Oct 29, 01; m 27. ROMANCE LANGUAGES. *Educ:* Johns Hopkins Univ, AB, 22, PhD, 30. *Prof Exp:* Instr, Univ SC, 22-23; instr, Johns Hopkins Univ, 23-24, 25-26; instr, Amherst Col, 26; instr, Univ Md, 26-27; instr, George Washington Univ, 27-28, asst prof, 28-29; from asst prof to assoc prof, 29-36, PROF ROMANCE LANG, UNIV ORE, 36- *Concurrent Pos:* Am Coun Learned Soc fel, France & Italy, 35-36; vis prof, Princeton Univ, 46; Fulbright res fel, Italy, 58-59; ed, Comp Lit (47-72); vis prof, Univ Calif, Berkeley, 66. *Mem:* MLA; Am Asn Teachers Ital; Ctr Appl Ling; Am Comp Lit Asn (pres, 68-71); Int Comp Lit Asn (vpres, 67-70). *Res:* Franco-Italian literary relations; comparative literature. *Publ:* Auth, Chateaubriand et le Tasse, Johns Hopkins Univ, 34; Un Italofilo Americano de cent' anni fa, Ist Ital d'Arti Grafiche, 39; La Fortune du Tasse en France, Univ Ore, 42; Eugenio Montale's Sarcofaghi, In: Studies in Honor of H A Hatzfeld, 64; Dante's mission, Comp Lit Studies, 78; Dante and His Reader, Forum Italicum, 79. *Mailing Add:* Dept of Romance Lang Univ of Ore Eugene OR 97403

BEAM, C RICHARD, b Lancaster, Co, Pa, Feb 15, 25. GERMAN. *Educ:* Franklin & Marshall Col, AB, 49; Middlebury Col, MA, 57. *Prof Exp:* Instr & grad asst Ger, Pa State Univ, 57-61; asst prof, 61-63, resident dir Jr Year in Marburg, 67-70, ASSOC PROF GER, MILLERSVILLE STATE COL, 63- *Concurrent Pos:* Ed, Pa Ger Dict, Thomas Royce Brendle Collection Pa Ger Folklore & Hist Schaefferstown Rec, 71- *Mem:* Am Asn Teachers Ger; AAUP; Am Name Soc; Am Folklore Soc; Am Dialect Soc. *Res:* Pennsylvania German language, folklore, family and place names; Pennsylvania Germans in Pennsylvania, Ohio and Iowa; the contributions of Thomas Royce Brendle to American regional ethnology. *Publ:* Auth, Abridged Pennsylvania German Dictionary, Heimatstelle Pfalz, Kaiserslautern, Ger, 70; Es Pennsilfaanisch Deitsch Eck, weekly dialect colum, In: Budget, 75-, Press & Jour, 76- & Die Botschaft, 77 & Ephrata Shopping News, 80; Pennsylvania German Dictionary: English to Pennsylvania Dutch, 82. *Mailing Add:* 406 Spring Dr Millersville PA 17551

BEAMISH, ROBERT LALONDE, b Ogden, Utah, Apr 1, 27; m 54; c 2. GERMAN LITERATURE, GERMANIC LANGUAGES. *Educ:* Univ Nev, BA, 53; Univ Wash, MA, 57, PhD, 63. *Prof Exp:* Instr Ger lang, Eastern Wash Col Educ, 56-57; from instr to asst prof, Purdue Univ, 57-61; from asst prof to assoc prof Ger lang & lit & French lang, 61-76, ASSOC PROF FOREIGN LANG & LIT, WASH STATE UNIV, 76- *Mem:* Am Asn Teachers Ger; Pac Northwest Conf Foreign Lang Teachers. *Res:* Middle High German language and literature; Germanic philology. *Mailing Add:* Dept of Foreign Lang Wash State Univ Pullman WA 99163

BEARD, LINDA SUSAN, African Literature, Black American Literature. See Vol II

BEARD, ROBERT EARL, b Fayetteville, NC, Feb 26, 38; m 60; c 2. SLAVIC LINGUISTICS. *Educ:* Univ NC, AB, 59; Univ Mich, MA, 61, PhD(Slavic ling), 66; Moscow State Univ, cert Russ, 69. *Prof Exp:* Lectr Russ lang, Univ Mich, 64-65; asst prof Russ & ling, 65-73, ASSOC PROF RUSS & LING, BUCKNELL UNIV, 73-, DIR PROG, 65- *Concurrent Pos:* Int Res & Exchanges Bd, exchange scholar, 76; Fulbright exchange scholar, Univ Beograd, Yugoslavia, 76-77. *Mem:* Ling Soc Am; Am Asn Teachers Slavic & East Europ Lang; Am Asn Advan Slavic Studies; Int Ling Asn; Am Asn Southeast Europ Studies. *Res:* Teaching of Russian; generative grammar; lexicology. *Publ:* Auth, Dynamic glossing, Slavic East Europ J, 19: 49-57; Semantically based model . . . , Language, 52: 108-20; Once more on ed-adjectives, J Ling, 12: 155-7; Material adjectives, Linguistics, 190: 5-34; On the extent of irregularity, Lingua, 42: 305-41; Derivations within derivations, VIII Int Cong Slavists, Zagreb-Ljubljana, 9/78; The Indo-European Lexicon, North-Holland Publishing Co, 81. *Mailing Add:* Prog in Russ Bucknell Univ Lewisburg PA 17837

BEARDSLEY, THEODORE S, JR, b East St Louis, Ill, Aug 26, 30; m 55; c 3. SPANISH & FRENCH LANGUAGE & LITERATURE. *Educ:* Southern Ill Univ, BS, 52; Wash Univ, MA, 54; Univ Pa, PhD, 61. *Prof Exp:* Asst English, Lycee Wilson, Chaumont, France, 52-53; French interpreter, US Army Intel, Ger, 55-56; asst instr Span, Univ Pa, 56-57; instr foreign lang, Rider Col, 57-59, asst prof & chmn dept, 59-61; asst prof Span, Southern Ill Univ, 61-62 & Univ Wis-Madison, 62-65; DIR, HISP SOC AM, 65- *Concurrent Pos:* Adj prof, NY Univ, 67-; mem bd dirs, Span Inst, 67-; mem adv bd, Hisp Rev, 69-; chmn, Mus Coun New York, 72-73; consult hisp bibliog, Libr Cong, 73-; consult, NJ State Bd Educ; Fulbright lectr, Ecuador, 74. *Honors & Awards:* Premio Bibliofilia, Barcelona, 73. *Mem:* Hisp Soc Am; Acad Norteamericana Lengua Espanola; Asoc Int Hispanistas; Renaissance Soc Am; corresp mem Real Acad Espanola. *Res:* Spanish literature of the Renaissance and Golden Age; Spanish influences in the United States; bibliography. *Publ:* Transl & arranger, Ponce de Leon (music by Leonardo Balada), Jose Ferrer & New Orleans Symphony, 10/73; auth, Bibliografia preliminar de estudios sobre el espanol en los Estados Unidos, Boletin Acad Norte am Lengua Espanola, 76; Hispanic Impact upon the United States, Twayne, 76; Bartolome Jimenez Paton y Marcial: El problema bibliografico, Libro-homenaje Memoria Antonio Perez Gomez, 78; La traduction des auteurs classiques en Espagne de 1488 a 1586, L'Humanisme dans les Lettres Espagnoles, Paris, 79; Spanish Printers and the Classics: 1482-1599, Hispanic Rev, 79; El espanol en Cayo Hueso: Cinco informantes, Les cultures ibériques en devenir, Paris, 79; The Lolands Printings of Celestina (1539-1601), Celestinesca, 81. *Mailing Add:* Hisp Soc Am 613 West 155th St New York NY 10032

BEASLEY, SHUBAEL TREADWELL, b Memphis, Tenn, Dec 13, 19; m 44; c 3. GERMAN LITERATURE. *Educ:* Univ of the South, AB, 40; Cornell Univ, AM, 47, PhD, 48. *Prof Exp:* Asst prof mod lang, Univ Richmond, 48-53; asst prof, Univ of the South, 53-56; assoc prof Ger, Col Charleston, 56-61; head dept foreign lang, 61-72, PROF GER, GA STATE UNIV, 61-, ED FOREIGN LANG BEACON, 73- *Concurrent Pos:* Fulbright exchange teacher, Ger, 59-60. *Mem:* Am Asn Teachers Ger; SAtlantic Mod Lang Asn; Am Coun Teaching Foreign Lang; Southern Conf Teaching Foreign Lang. *Res:* Anglo-Germanic literary relationships of the 18th century; 18th century German literature; German influences in Georgia. *Mailing Add:* Dept of Foreign Lang Ga State Univ Atlanta GA 30303

BEATIE, BRUCE A, b Oakland, Calif, Mar 4, 35; m 56. MEDIEVAL & FOLK LITERATURE. *Educ:* Univ Calif, Berkeley, AB, 59; Univ Colo, MA, 60; Harvard Univ, PhD(comp lit), 67. *Prof Exp:* Asst prof Ger, Univ Colo, 64-67, asst prof Ger & comp lit, 67-68; assoc prof, Univ Rochester, 68-70; chmn, Dept Mod Lang, 70-77, PROF GER, CLEVELAND STATE UNIV, 77- *Concurrent Pos:* Nat Endowment for Humanities younger scholar fel, 70. *Mem:* MLA; Mediaeval Acad Am; Int Arthurian Soc; AAUP; Am Folklore Soc. *Res:* Medieval comparative literature; popular and traditional narrative; folklore. *Publ:* Auth, Saint Katharine of Alexandria: Traditional themes . . ., Speculum, 77; Reading German: A self-tutorial skills-learning package, Mod Lang J, 77; coauth, Story and symbol: Notes toward a structural analysis of Bulgakov's The Master and Margarita, Russ Lit Triquart, 78; auth, Ethnic Heritage and Language Schools in Greater Cleveland: A Directory, Cleveland, 79; A minimum grammar approach to reading technical German, Mod Lang J, 79; Measurement and the study of literature, Computer & the Humanities, 79; Developing reading skills in German, Lesen der freudsprache, Munich, 81; coauth, Bulgakov, Dante and relativity, Can-Am Slavic Studies, 81. *Mailing Add:* Dept of Mod Lang Cleveland State Univ Cleveland OH 44115

BEAUCHAMP, WILLIAM EDWARD, b New York, NY, Dec 9, 34; c 1. FRENCH LITERATURE, SEMIOTICS. *Educ:* St Louis Univ, BA, 55; Middlebury Col, MA, 56; Columbia Univ, PhD(French), 69. *Prof Exp:* Instr French & Span, Hun Sch Princeton, NJ, 57-59; asst prof French & Latin, Notre Dame Col Staten Island, 60-67; asst prof French, Columbia Univ, 67-74; ASSOC PROF FRENCH, SOUTHERN METHODIST UNIV, 74- *Mem:* MLA; Simotic Soc Am. *Res:* Semiotics; 19th century French literature; romanticism. *Publ:* Auth, From astrology to structuralism, Romanic Rev, 5/73; The Style of Nerval's Aurelia, Mouton, 76; An introduction to French poetry: Hugo's Demain, des l'aube, French Rev, 2/76; Three stages in the application of linguistics to literary studies, Lektos, 4/76; From structuralism to semiotics, Romanic Rev, 5/76. *Mailing Add:* Southern Methodist Univ Dallas TX 75275

BEAUCHEMIN, NORMAND J A, b Montreal, Que, Oct 2, 32. PHONETICS, LINGUISTICS. *Educ:* Laval Univ, BA, 53, Lic es Lett, 60; Univ Strasbourg, DUniv, 67. *Prof Exp:* Prof philos, Col Nicolet, Que, 60-62, prof French lit & lang & mod lang, 62-67; prof ling, Univ Que, Trois-Rivieres, 68-70; prof, 69-75, TITULAIRE LING, UNIV SHERBROOKE, 75- *Concurrent Pos:* Can Coun Res Humanities grants, 70-72, 73-75 & 77-78; consult, Off French lang, Que, 71-, Ministry Educ, Que, 72 & Can Coun Res Humanities, 72- *Mem:* Soc Ling Romance; MLA; Can Ling Asn (vpres, 76-78, pres, 78-); Asn que'he'oine de Ling (pres, 81-). *Res:* Sociolinguistics; computerized analysis of French vocabulary; micro-computers in the humanities. *Publ:* Coauth, Le Francais par le Rythme, Univ Laval, 67; co-ed, Collection Amorces (10 bks), & Collection Relances (9 bks), Cosmos, 70-; auth, Recherches Sur L'Accent, Univ Laval & Klincksieck, 71; Un accent de bon aloi: l'accent quebecois, Forces, 71. *Mailing Add:* Dept of Ling Fac of Arts Univ of Sherbrooke Sherbrooke PQ J1K 2R1 Can

BEAUDRY, AGNES PORTER, b Charleston, WVa, Dec 9, 32; m 73. FRENCH LITERATURE. *Educ:* Marshall Univ, AB, 54; Case Western Reserve Univ, MA, 58; Univ Ill, Urbana, PhD(French), 68. *Prof Exp:* Teacher French, Fairfax Hall, Waynesboro, Va, 55-57; teacher, Mansfield High Sch, Ohio, 58-59; instr, Ft Hays State Col, 59-60; instr Muskingum Col, 60-62; asst, Univ Ill, Urbana, 63-65, instr, 65-67; asst prof, 67-72, assoc prof, 72-80, PROF FRENCH, DEPAUW UNIV, 80- *Mem:* MLA; Am Asn Teachers Fr. *Res:* Marcel Proust; 20th century French memoirs; Marguerite Duras. *Publ:* Auth, Proust's final Montesquieu pastiche, In: Marcel Proust, A Critical Panorama, Univ Ill, 73; The treatment of time in Proust's pastiches, Fr Rev, spring 74; Memoirs in Critical Bibliography of French Literature, XX Century, Syracuse Univ Press, 80; Detruire, dit-ellc: Destruction or deconstruction, Int Fiction Rev, 81; A Neophyte in literary semiotics, Am J Semiotics, 82. *Mailing Add:* Dept of Romance Lang DePauw Univ Greencastle IN 46135

BECK, HAMILTON HAMMOND HAGY, b Rochester, NY, Aug 1, 52. GERMAN LITERATURE & LANGUAGE. *Educ:* Hamilton Col, BA, 74; Cornell Univ, MA & PhD(Ger lit), 80. *Prof Exp:* Asst prof Ger, Radford Univ, VA, 80-82. *Mem:* MLA; Lessing Soc; Am Soc 18th Century Studies. *Res:* Eighteenth century literature and philosophy. *Publ:* Auth, Hippel and Stone, J 18th Century Cult, 80. *Mailing Add:* 110 Highland Pkwy Rochester NY 14620

BECK, HARRELL FREDERICK, Old Testament. See Vol IV

BECK, JEAN ROBERT, b Marimont, France, May 10, 03. GERMAN. *Educ:* Miami Univ, AB, 31; Stanford Univ, AM, 33; Univ Chicago, PhD, 53. *Prof Exp:* Instr Ger, Univ Utah, 31-32; teaching asst, Stanford Univ, 32-33; instr, Univ Utah, 33-34 & Morgan Park Jr Col, 34-38; lectr, McGill Univ, 38-42; from asst prof to assoc prof, 46-56, prof, 56-79, EMER PROF GERMAN, UNIV ARIZ, 80- *Mem:* MLA. *Res:* Germanic and Romance languages and literatures; Friedrich Neitzche; early German travel literature. *Mailing Add:* Dept of Ger Univ of Ariz Tucson AZ 85721

BECK, JONATHAN, b Minneapolis, Minn, Aug 28, 47; div; c 1. FRENCH, MEDIEVAL LITERATURE. *Educ:* Columbia Univ, AB, 70; Harvard Univ, AM, 71, PhD(romance lang), 74. *Prof Exp:* Asst prof, 74-80, ASSOC PROF FRENCH, EMORY UNIV, 80- *Concurrent Pos:* Vis assoc prof French, Stanford Univ, 80; Guggenheim fel, 82; vpres, Franco Simone Mem Found, 80- *Mem:* Soc Internationale pour l'etude du Theatre Medieval; Medieval Acad Am; MLA. *Res:* Medieval and 16th century French language and literature. *Publ:* Auth, Pro . . . salvament in the Strasbourg Oaths: Safety or salvation?, Romance Philol, 8/76; coauth (with Graham A Runnalls), Repertoire international des specialistes du theatre francais medieveal: Travaux recents et recherches en cours, Soc Int Study Medieval Theatre, 78; auth, Ideological drama in fifteenth-century France, 15th Century Studies, I: 1-14; Le Concil de Basle, 1434: Les Origines du theatre reformiste et partisan en France, In: Studies in the History of Christian Thought, No 18, E J Brill, Leiden, 79; Dissimilation consonantique et le pseudo-latin esse paly dans Maistre Mimin Estudiant, Zeitschrift fü romanische Philologie, 96: 108-116; Seconda Miscellanea di Studi e Ricerche sul Quattrocento Francese, CEFI, Chambery & Torino, 81. *Mailing Add:* 2737 Garber apt 1 Berkeley CA 94705

BECK, ROGER LYNE, b London, England, Jan 11, 37; Can citizen; m 68; c 1. CLASSICS. *Educ:* Oxford Univ, BA, 61; Univ Ill, MA, 63, PhD(class philol), 71. *Prof Exp:* Lectr Classics, Univ Man, 63-64; lectr, Univ Col, 64-65, asst prof, 68-74, ASSOC PROF CLASSICS, ERINDALE COL, UNIV TORONTO, 74- *Mem:* Class Asn Can (secy, 77-79); Am Philol Asn. *Res:* Homer; Petronius; Mithraism. *Publ:* Auth, Ovid, Augustus, and a Nut Tree, 65, A Principle of Composition in Homeric Verse, 72, Some Observations on the Narrative Technique of Petronius, 73 & Encolpius at the Cena, 75, Phoenix; Interpreting the Ponza zodiac, I and II, 76 & Cautes and cautopates, 77, J Mithraic Studies; Eumolpus poeta, Eumolpus fabulator, Phoenix, 79; Sette Sfere, Sette Porte and the spring equinoxes of AD 172 and 173, Mysteria Mithrae, Brill, 79. *Mailing Add:* Dept of Classics Univ of Toronto Mississauga ON L5L 1C6 Can

BECK, WILLIAM JOHN, b Scotch Plains, NJ, Aug 11, 25. FRENCH THEATRE. *Educ:* Rutgers Univ, New Brunswick, AB, 58, MA, 60, PhD(French), 64. *Prof Exp:* Asst French, Rutgers Univ, 58-63, from instr to asst prof, 63-69; assoc prof, 69-77, PROF FRENCH, VA COMMONWEALTH UNIV, 77-, CHMN DEPT FOREIGN LANG, 70- *Concurrent Pos:* Pres, Va Coun Studies Abroad, 73-74. *Honors & Awards:* Am Nat Red Cross Award, 77. *Mem:* Am Asn Teachers Fr (pres, 72-76); Assoc des Amis de Montaigne. *Res:* Sixteenth century French literature; Moliere. *Publ:* Auth, Arnolphe or Monsieur de la Souche?, Fr Rev, 12/68; Le Cas de Gymnaste, Amis Rabelais & Deviniere, 7/70; The medieval doctrine of hope in the Mystere D'Adam, Fr Rev, fall 71; Montaigne et l'anthropophagie dans la medecine, Les Amis de Montaigne, Paris, 5/76; Tartuffe: Mr Sly Weaselnose, Seventeenth-Century News, winter 76; Flaubert's Felicite; Happy or blessed?, Explicator, summer 77; Flaubert's Tripartite concept of history and Trois Contes, CLA J, 9/77; Rabelais' King Picrochole, Neophilologus, 1/80. *Mailing Add:* 5731 Westower Dr Richmond VA 23225

BECKER, ALTON LEWIS, b Monroe, Mich, Apr 6, 32; m 53; c 3. LINGUISTICS. *Educ:* Univ Mich, BA, 54, PhD(ling), 66; Univ Conn, MA, 56. *Prof Exp:* Instr English, Univ Conn, 54-56 & Ripon Col, 56-58; Fulbright teacher, Kambawsa Col, Burma, 58-61; instr, 61-64, instr English & Thai, 64-65, instr English, 65-68, from asst prof to assoc prof ling, 68-74, PROF LING & ANTHROP, UNIV MICH, ANN ARBOR, 74- *Concurrent Pos:* Assoc mem exec comt, Ctr S & Southeast Asian Studies, Univ Mich, 63-, dir, 72-75; mem Ctr Res on Lang & Lang Behav, 65-; Ford Found vis prof ling, Inst Keguruan dan Ilmu Pendidikan, Malang, Java, 69-71; mem, Inst for Advan Study, Princetown, 81-82. *Mem:* Ling Soc Am; Burma Res Soc. *Res:* Formal description of discourse; history and structure of Southeast Asian languages. *Publ:* Auth, Journey through the night: Some reflections on Burmese traditional theatre Drama Rev, winter 70; coauth, Rhetoric: Discovery and Change, Harcourt, 71; A linguistic image of nature: The Burmese numerative classifier system, Int J Sociol of Lang, 75; co-ed, The imagination of reality, Ablex, 79; auth, Text-building, epistemology and aesthetics in Javanese shadow theatre, 79; coauth, Person in Kawi, Oceanic Ling, 176; auth, The figure a sentence makes, Syntax & Semantics, 12/79; On Emerson on language, Georgetown Univ, 82. *Mailing Add:* Dept of Ling Univ of Mich Ann Arbor MI 48104

BECKER, LUCILLE FRACKMAN, b New York, NY, Feb 4, 29; m 54; c 4. FRENCH LANGUAGE & LITERATURE. *Educ:* Barnard Col, BA, 49; Univ Aix-Marseille, Dipl Etudes Francaises, 50; Columbia Univ, MA, 54, PhD(French), 58. *Prof Exp:* Instr French, Columbia Univ, 54-58 & Rutgers Univ, 58-68; assoc prof, 68-76, PROF FRENCH & CHMN DEPT, DREW UNIV,. *Mem:* MLA; AAUP; Am Asn Teachers Fr. *Res:* Twentieth century French literature; 19th century French literature; French novel. *Publ:* Auth, Pessimism and nihilism in the plays of Henry de Montherlant, Yale Fr Studies, spring-summer 62; coauth, The versification techniques of Louis Aragon, Fr Rev, 5/65; co-ed, Le Maitre de Santiago, Heath, 65; auth, Henry de Montherlant: A Critical Biography, Southern Ill Univ, 70; Louis Aragon, Twayne, 71; Henry de Montherlant, In: Colliers Encycl, 73; Henry de Montherlant and Suicide, Romance Notes, winter 75; Georges Simenon, G K Hall, 77; Louis Aragon, In: Encyclopedia World Literature in 20th Century, Ungar, 81. *Mailing Add:* Dept of French Drew Univ Madison NJ 07940

BECKER-CANTARINO, BARBARA, b Goettingen, Ger, Dec 1, 37; m 60; c 3. GERMAN. *Educ:* Univ NC, MA, 62, PhD(Ger/classics), 67. *Prof Exp:* Instr Ger/classics, NC Col, 62-65; asst prof, 74-77, ASSOC PROF GER, UNIV TEX, 77- *Concurrent Pos:* Ger Acad Exchange Serv, res grant, 78; vis prof, Free Univ Berlin, 80-81; Nat Endowment for Humanities res fel, 79. *Mem:* Am Soc 18th Century Studies; Am Asn Teachers Ger; MLA; Int Arbeitskreis für Barockliteratur; Lessing Soc. *Res:* German literature 1500-1900; women and literature; Spanish-German relations. *Publ:* Auth, Opitz' Lob des Krieges Gottes Martis, Deutsche Vierteljahrschrift, 74; Zum Spanienbild in der dt Literature des 18 Jahrhunderts, Zeitschrift f de Philol, 75; Ideal und idealogie in Schillers Don Carlos, Jahrbuch des Freien Deutschen Hochstifts, 75; Joseph von Sonnenfels and Austrian education, In: Facets of Education in the 18th Century, Oxford Univ, 77; Daniel Heinsius, G K Hall, 78; Die Frau von der Reformation zur Romantik, Bouvier, 80; The rediscovery of Spain in enlightened and romantic Germany, Monatshefte, 80; Die neue literatur und politk der Frauen, In: Propyläen Geschichte der Weltliteratur, Vol 6, Ullstein, 82. *Mailing Add:* Dept of Ger Lang Univ of Tex Austin TX 78712

BECKERS, GUSTAV EUGEN, b Eckernförde, Ger, Nov 12, 19. GERMAN LANGUAGE & LITERATURE. *Educ:* Univ Hamburg, Dr phil(Ger lit criticism), 55. *Prof Exp:* Lectr Ger- Univ Edinburgh, 56-58; lectr Ger lit, Aarhus Univ, 58-62; teacher, Univ Hamburg, 63-64; lectr Ger, Helsingin Yliopisto, Finland, 67-70; assoc prof, 70-76, PROF GER, UNIV MAN, 76- *Concurrent Pos:* Fel, Ger lit, Deutsche Forschungsgemeinschaft, Bonn, 62-65 & 68-69; fel, Ger lit, Can Coun, 76-77. *Mem:* Can Asn Univ Teachers Ger; Am Asn Teachers Ger; MLA; Western Asn Ger Studies; Inst Asn Ger Studies. *Res:* German romanticism, 19th & 20th century German literature. *Publ:* Auth, Georg B Büchners Leonce und Lena, Ein Lustspiel der Langeweile, Carl Winter, 61; Versuche zur Schaffensweise deutscher Romantiker, Ejnar Munksgaard, 61; auth & ed, Conrad Ferdinand Meyer: Die Versuchung des Pescara, Ullstein, 65; auth, Morone und Pescara, Ein Beitrag zur Interpretation von C F Meyes Novelle, Euphorion, 69; C F Meyers Saerspruch, 70 & Der verwindete Baum, Infrastrukturelle Analyse bei Conrad Ferdinant Meyer, 72, Colloquia Germanica; Zur Darstellung des Burgertums in Gottfried Kellers Züricher Novellen, Internationale Germanistik Reihe A, 76. *Mailing Add:* 307-100 Ulster St Winnipeg MB R3T 3A2 Can

BECKER-THEYE, BETTY, b St Joseph, Mo, Oct 10, 35; m 78; c 1. COMPARATIVE LITERATURE, TRANSLATION. *Educ:* Washburn Univ, BA, 63; Emporia State Univ, MA, 67; State Univ NY, Binghampton, PhD(comp lit & Trans), 79. *Prof Exp:* Lectr Span, Washburn Univ, 65-67; instr, 67-71, asst prof, 71-75, assoc prof, 75-81 PROF FRENCH & SPAN & DEAN SCH FINE ARTS & HUMANITIES, KEARNEY STATE COL, 81-, CHMN DEPT FOR LANG, 78- *Honors & Awards:* Chevalier de l'Ordre, Amis de la Courtoise francaise, Paris, 5/81. *Mem:* Am Transl Asn; MLA; Am Comp Lit Asn; Am Asn Teachers French; Int Comp Lit Asn. *Publ:* Contribr, transl, Rosa, In: Spanish American Short Story, Univ Calif, Los Angeles Press, 80; auth, Undergraduate training for translation, In: Global Perspectives for Foreign Language Teaching, 81. *Mailing Add:* Sch Fine Arts & Humanities Kearney State Col Kearney NE 68847

BEDFORD, CHARLES HAROLD, b Toronto, Ont, Oct 31, 29; m 61; c 2. RUSSIAN LITERATURE. *Educ:* Univ Toronto, BA, 51, MA, 52; Univ London, PhD(Russ lit), 56. *Prof Exp:* From lectr to assoc prof Slavic studies, 55-75, assoc chmn dept, 66-71, chmn dept, 71-79, PROF SLAVIC LANG & LIT, UNIV TORONTO, 75- *Concurrent Pos:* Inter-Univ Comt travel grant, USSR, 57; Can Coun res grants-in-aid, 61 & 65. *Mem:* Can Asn Slavists (secy-treas, 57-58); Am Asn Advan Slavic Studies. *Res:* Russian literature, 1880-1917; Russian drama and theatre. *Publ:* Auth, D S Merezhkovsky: The forgotten poet, Slavonic & East Europ Rev, 57; Dmitry Merezhkovsky, the intelligentsia, and the Revolution of 1905, Can Slavonic Papers, 58; Dmitry Merezhkovsky, the third testament and the third humanity, Slavonic & East Europ Rev, 63; The Seeker: D S Merezhkovsky, Univ Kans, 75. *Mailing Add:* Dept Slavic Lang & Lit Univ of Toronto Toronto ON M5S 1A1 Can

BEDRICK, THEORDORE, b Fall River, Mass, Feb 21, 15; m 40; c 2. CLASSICAL LANGUAGES. *Educ:* Brown Univ, AB, 36; Univ Ill, AM, 37, PhD, 40. *Prof Exp:* Asst classics, Univ Ill, 36-40, 41-42; instr, Univ Nebr, 41 & Univ Ill, 42-48; from assoc prof to prof, 48-70, SAMUEL STEELE THOMSON PROF LATIN LANG & LIT, WABASH COL, 70-, REGISTR, 71- *Concurrent Pos:* Dean univ men, Nat Music Camp, Interlochen, Mich,

56- *Mem:* Class Asn Mid W & S; Am Philol Asn; Am Class League. *Res:* Ancient athletics; history of mathematics; teaching of Latin. *Publ:* Auth, The race of athletes, Class J, 12/49; contribr, Shipley's Dictionary of World Literature, Philos Libr, 53; John F Latimer's edition: A Life of George Washington in Latin Prose by F Glass, George Washington Univ, 76. *Mailing Add:* Dept of Classics Wabash Col Crawfordsville IN 47933

BEDWELL, CAROL, b Boston, Mass, May 3, 29; m 56; c 3. GERMAN. *Educ:* Wellesley Col, BA, 52; Ind Univ, MA, 54, PhD(Ger), 62. *Prof Exp:* Instr Ger, Friends Univ, 58-62; from instr to asst prof, Univ Ore, 62-69; assoc prof, 69-76, chmn dept foreign lang, 72-74 & 76-78, PROF GER, UNIV WIS-OSHKOSH, 76- *Mem:* MLA; Am Asn Teachers Ger. *Res:* Kafka; Aichinger; Musil. *Publ:* Auth, The ambivalent image in Aichinger's Spiegelgeschichte, Rev Lang Vivantes, 67; The disappointing miracle in Werner Bergengruen's Die Winderbare Schreibmaschine, Studies in Short Fiction, 9/67; Musil's Grigia: An analysis of cultural dissolution, Seminar, fall 67. *Mailing Add:* Dept of Foreign Lang Univ of Wis Oshkosh WI 54901

BEEBE, JOHN FRED, b Montgomery Co, Ind, July 17, 27; m 56; c 4. SLAVIC LINGUISTICS. *Educ:* Wabash Col, BA, 46; Ind Univ, MA, 54; Harvard Univ, PhD (Slavic ling), 58. *Prof Exp:* Instr Russ, Univ Mass, 58-59; dir Air Force Foreign Lang Russ, Ind Univ, 49-61, asst prof Slavic ling, 61-66; asst prof, Univ Chicago, 66-68; ASSOC PROF RUSS, UNIV ORE, 68- *Mem:* MLA; Am Asn Teachers Slavic & E Europ Lang; Am Asn Advan Slavic Studies. *Res:* Russian language and literature; Spanish language. *Publ:* Coauth, Paleosiberian peoples and languages, Human Relat Area Files, 57. *Mailing Add:* Dept of Russ Univ of Ore Eugene OR 97403

BEECHER, GRACIELA FERNANDEZ, b Havana, Cuba, Jan 16, 17. SPANISH, FRENCH. *Educ:* Memphis State Col, BS, 49; Univ Havana, EdD, 51. *Prof Exp:* Lang instr, community schs, Havana, 47-61; prof Span & chmn dept, St Francis Col, Ind, 61-80. *Concurrent Pos:* Asst lang, Memphis St Col, 49-50; pres, Oxford Com Col, Havana, 54-61; proj dir, Title VII Emergency Sch Aid Act, Dept Span Speaking, 76-78. *Mem:* MLA; Circulo de Cult Panam; NEA; Nat Asn Cuban-Am Women. *Res:* Romance languages; linguistics; pre-Columbian civilization and culture. *Publ:* Auth, Los Totonaca, Span Today, 11/72; Romancillos al estilo medieval (poems), Circulo Poetico, 73; Porque estan desunidos los Latino Americanos?, 10/75, Quien descubrio a America?, 11/75, Plegaria por la union, 11/75, Estableciendo prioridades, 11/75, & El sacerdote y la justicia social, 5/76, El Visitante Dominical. *Mailing Add:* 235 W DeWalt Ft Wayne IN 46804

BEECHHOLD, HENRY FRANK, English Linguistics. See Vol II

BEEKMAN, ERIC MONTAGUE, b Amsterdam, The Netherlands, Sept 25, 39; US citizen. GERMANIC LANGUAGES, COMPARATIVE LITERATURE. *Educ:* Univ Calif, Berkeley, BA, 63; Harvard Univ, PhD(comp lit), 68. *Prof Exp:* Teaching fel Greek lit, Harvard Univ, 67-68; asst prof English, 68-69, assoc prof, 69-79, PROF GERMANIC LANG, UNIV MASS, AMHERST, 80- *Concurrent Pos:* Nat Transl Ctr grant, 69-70. *Res:* Modern Duthc literature. *Publ:* Auth, The Critic and Existence, Contemp Lit, 68; Homeopathy of the Absurd, M Nijhoff, The Hague, 70; Lame Duck, Houghton, 71; Patriotism Inc, 71 & Oyster and Eagle, 74, Univ Mass; Carnal Lent (poems), Pennyroyal, 75; The Killing Jar, Houghton, 76. *Mailing Add:* Dept of Germanic Lang 522 Herter Hall Univ Mass Amherst MA 01002

BEELER, JAMES RUSH, b Pensacola, NC, May 27,21; m 61; c 1. ROMANCE LANGUAGES. *Educ:* Univ NC, AB, 42, MA, 49, PhD(Romance lang), 64. *Prof Exp:* Assoc French, Univ Calif, Los Angeles, 52-57; instr, Univ NC, 60-64; from asst prof to assoc prof, Col William & Mary, 64-69; PROF FRENCH, UNIV NC, WILMINGTON, 69-, CHMN DEPT MOD LANG, 76- *Mem:* Renaissance Soc Am; SAtlantic Mod Lang Asn. *Res:* French language; French literature in the 16th and 17th centuries. *Publ:* Auth, Genealogy in historical Romance, In: Renaissance and Other Studies in Honor of William Leon Wiley, Univ NC, 68; Racine and coffee, Romance Notes, spring 69. *Mailing Add:* Dept of Mod Lang Univ NC Wilmington NC 28401

BEELER, MADISON SCOTT, b Seattle, Wash, Apr 24, 10; m 55. LINGUISTICS. *Educ:* Harvard Univ, AB, 31, AM, 35, PhD, 36. *Prof Exp:* Instr Ger & tutor comp philol, Harvard Univ, 38-41; from instr to asst prof Ger, 41-52, assoc prof Ger & class philol, 52-58, actg chmn dept Near East lang, 58-60, prof Ger & ling, 58-65, chmn dept Ger, 62-65, prof ling, 65-77, actg chmn dept ling, 68, EMER PROF LING, UNIV CALIF, BERKELEY, 77- *Mem:* Ling Soc Am; MLA; Philol Asn Pac Coast; Am Name Soc; Ling Soc France. *Res:* Indo-European Germanic, Italic and California Indian languages. *Publ:* Auth, Saclan, Int J Am Ling, 56; Remarks on the German noun inflection, Lang Learning, 58; The Venetic Language: The Ventureno Confesionario of Jose Senan, OFM, Univ Calif, 67. *Mailing Add:* Dept of Ling Univ Calif Berkeley CA 94720

BEER, JEANETTE MARY AYRES, b Wellington, NZ; c 2. MEDIEVAL FRENCH, LINGUISTICS. *Educ:* Victoria Univ, Wellin-ton, BA, 54, MA, 55; Oxford Univ, BA & MA, 58; Columbia Univ, PhD(French), 67. *Prof Exp:* Asst lectr French, Victoria Univ, Wellington, 56; asst lectr English & French, Univ Montpellier, 58-59; lectr French, Otago Univ, 62-64; instr, Barnard Col, 66-68; from asst prof to asoc prof, Fordham Univ, 68-77, dir medieval studies, 72-80, prof French, 77-80; PROF FRENCH, PUDUE UNIV & CHMN DEPT, 80- *Concurrent Pos:* Actg assoc dean, Thomas More Col, 72-73; Nat Endowment Humanities prog grant, 75-; mem, Nat Bd Consult, Nat Endowment Humanities, 77-; Nat Endowment Humanities res fel, 79-80. *Mem:* MLA; Mediaeval Ac Acad Am; Int Arthurian Soc; Am Asn Teachers Fr; Am Philol Asn. *Res:* Medieval French literature, especially historians; linguistic and stylistic aspects of Old French; comparative literature. *Publ:* Auth, Villehardouin-Epic Historian, Droz, Geneva, 68; Villehardouin and the oral narrative, Studies Philol, 7/70; Explication de texte of a surrealist poem by Paul Eluard, Teaching Lang Through Lit, 5/71; A medieval Cato-virtus or virtue?, Speculum, 1/72; French nationalism under Philip Augustus-an unexpected source, Mosaic, winter, 74; Durative traces in the comencier-plus-infinitive formula of Thirteenth Century French, Romance Philol, 74; A medieval Caesar, Droz, Geneva, 76; Stylistic heterogeneity in the Middle Ages, In: Jean Misrahi Memorial Volume, Fr Lit Publ Co, 77; Narrative Conventions of truth in the Middle Ages, Geneva, 81; Medieval Fables--Marie de France, AH & AW Reed, Ltd, UK & Australia, 80. *Mailing Add:* Dept of Foreign Lang & Lit Purdue Univ West Lafayette IN 47907

BEERMAN, HANS, b Berlin, Ger, Oct 3, 18; US citizen; m 44. ROMANCE & SLAVIC LANGUAGES, PHILOSOPHY. *Educ:* Univ Ill, BS, 44; State Univ Iowa, PhD, 51. *Prof Exp:* Asst prof humanities & lang, Kans Wesleyan Univ, 51-55 & Ft Lewis Agr & Mech Col, 55-58; ASSOC PROF HUMANITIES & LANG, PITTSBURG STATE UNIV, 58- *Concurrent Pos:* NDEA grad fel, Univ Mich, 61; Fulbright fel, 63. *Mem:* MLA. *Res:* Humanities; Oriental philosophy. *Mailing Add:* Dept of Foreign Lang Pittsburg State Univ Pittsburg KS 66762

BEESON, MARGARET E, b Topeka, Kans, Dec 20, 26. SPANISH LANGUAGE & LITERATURE. *Educ:* Wesleyan Col, BA, 48; Emory Univ, MA, 49; Univ Tex, PhD, 57. *Prof Exp:* From instr to assoc prof Span, Baylor Univ, 54-60; asst prof, 60-68; ASSOC PROF SPAN, KANS STATE UNIV, 68- *Mem:* Am Asn Teachers Span & Port; MLA. *Res:* Seventeenth century Spanish prose fictions; drama of Federioco Garcia Lorca. *Publ:* Coauth, Hispanic Writers in French Journals: An Annotated Bibliography, Soc Span & Span Am Studies, 78. *Mailing Add:* Dept of Mod Lang Kans State Univ Manhattan KS 66506

BEHARRIELL, FREDERICK JOHN, b Toronto, Ont, June 5, 18; m 42; c 2. GERMAN & COMPARATIVE LITERATURE. *Educ:* Univ Toronto, BA, 39, MA, 46; Univ Wis, PhD, 50. *Prof Exp:* Instr French, Univ Toronto, 45-46; from instr to prof Ger, Ind Univ, Bloomington, 48-69, actg chmn dept, 54-55, 62-63; PROF GER, STATE UNIV NY ALBANY, 69- *Concurrent Pos:* Guggenheim Found fel & Fulbright sr res fel, Austria, 65-66; vis prof Ger, State Univ NY Albany, 68-69; bk rev ed, Ger Quart; Inst Humanistic Studies sr fel, 77- *Mem:* MLA; Am Asn Teachers Ger (1st vpres, 64-65); Inst Arthur Schnitzler Res Asn; Nat Asn Psychoanal Criticism; Am Goethe Soc. *Res:* History of ideas; modern German literature; literature and psychology. *Publ:* Auth, Arthur Schnitzler's range of theme, Monatshefte, 51; Freud and literature, Queen's Quart, 58; Psychology in the works of Thomas Mann, PMLA, 62; Freud und die Literatur, Lit Kritik Vienna, 66; The hidden meaning of Goethe's Bekenntnisse einer schönen Seele, In: Lebendige Form, Festschrift für Heinrich Henel, Fink, Munich, 70; Kafka, Freud, und Das Urteil, In: Texte und Kontexte: Festschrift für Norbert Fuerst, Francke, 73; Schnitzler's Frl Else, Mod Austrian Lit, 77; Freud's influence on Thomas Mann, In: Thomas Mann in Context, Clark Univ, 78. *Mailing Add:* Dept of Ger Lang State Univ NY Albany NY 12222

BEHLER, DIANA IPSEN, b New York, NY, Dec 6, 38; m 67; c 2. GERMANICS, COMPARATIVE LITERATURE. *Educ:* Univ Wash, BA, 65, MA, 66, PhD (Germanics), 70. *Prof Exp:* Asst prof Germanics, 69-75, asst prof comp lit, 73-75, assoc prof, 75-81, PROF GERMANICS & COMP LIT, UNIV WASH, 81-, CHMN DEPT GERMANICS, 78- *Concurrent Pos:* Nat Endowment for Humanities younger humanist fel, 72-73. *Mem:* MLA; Am Asn Teachers Ger; Lessing Soc. *Res:* European romanticism; the novel; Friedrich Nietzsche. *Publ:* Auth, Lessing's legacy to the romantic concept of the poet-priest, Lessing Yearbk IV, 72; contribr various articles on J W Goethe, F Schlegel & J G Herder, Kindlers Literaturlexikon XI, 73; auth, Thomas Mann as a theoretician of the novel: Romanticism and realism, Colloquia Germanica, 74; Henry Crabb Robinson as a mediator of Lessing and Herder to England, Lessing Yearbk VII, 76; Henry Crabb Robinson as a mediator of German romanticism to England, Arcadia, 77; The Theory of the Novel in Early German Romanticism, Utah Studies Lit & Lang, 78; Nietzsche and Lessing: Kindred thoughts, Nietzsche-Studien, 79. *Mailing Add:* 5525 NE Penrith Rd Seattle WA 98105

BEHLER, ERNST, b Essen, WGer, Sept 4, 28; m 67; c 1. GERMANICS, COMPARATIVE LITERATURE. *Educ:* Univ Munich, PhD, 51. *Prof Exp:* Docent philos, Univ Bonn, 61-63; assoc prof Germanics, Wash Univ, 64-65, prof Ger & comp lit, 65-66; chmn Humanities Coun, 73-78, PROF GER & COMP LIT, UNIV WASH, 66-, CO-DIR HUMANITIES PROG & CHMN COMP LIT, 76- *Concurrent Pos:* Guggenheim Found fel, 67 & 75-76; Am Coun Learned Soc fel, 70-71. *Mem:* MLA; Comite d'honneur de la Societe des Etudes Staëliennes; hon mem, Ovidianum Societas, Bucharest; Am Comp Lit Asn. *Res:* Romanticism; history of ideas and critism. *Publ:* Coauth, Critical Edition of F Schlegel's Works (35 vols), 58 & auth, Die Ewigkeit der Welt, 65, Schoeningh, Paderborn; Friedrich Schlegel, Rowohlt, Hamburg, 66; Madame de Staël a Weimar, Studi Francesi, 69; Techniques of irony in light of the Romantic theory, Rice Univ Studies, 72; Klassische Ironie, Romantische Ironie, Tragische Ironie, Wiss Buchgesellschaft, Darmstadt, 72; Die Geschichte des Bewusstseins, Hegel-Studies, 72; Nietzsche's challenge to Romantic humanism, Can Rev Comp Lit, 5/78; The Reception of Calderon Among the German Romantics, Studies in Romanticism, 81. *Mailing Add:* 5525 NE Penrith Rd Seattle WA 98105

BEICKEN, PETER U, b Wuppertal, Ger, May 16, 43; m 67; c 1. GERMAN LITERATURE & CULTURE. *Educ:* Univ Munich, MA, 68; Stanford Univ, PhD(Ger lit), 71. *Prof Exp:* Asst prof Ger lit, Princeton Univ, 71-76; ASSOC PROF GER LIT, UNIV MD, COLLEGE PARK, 76- *Mem:* Am Asn Teachers Ger; MLA; Int Brecht Soc; Goethe Soc; Kafka Soc Am. *Res:* Modern German literature, Kafka studies, Rezeptionsästhetik. *Publ:* Contribr, Bemerkungen zu Bergs LULU, Fs Motekat Hueber: München, 70; Franz Kafka: Eine kritische Einführung in die Forschung, Athenäum: Frankfurt Main, 74; The judgement in the critics' judgement, In: A Flores The problem of the Judgement, Gordian, 77; Kafka's narrative rhetoric, J of Mod Lit, 77; Berechnung und Kunstaufwand in Kafkas Erzählrhetorik, In: Franz Kafka Symp, Agora, 78. *Mailing Add:* Dept of Ger & Slavic Univ of Md College Park MD 20742

BEIZER, JANET L, b New York, NY, Apr 9, 52. FRENCH LITERATURE. *Educ:* Cornell Univ, BA, 74; Yale Univ, PhD(French), 81. *Prof Exp:* ASST PROF FRENCH, UNIV VA, 81- *Mem:* MLA. *Res:* Nineteenth century narrative, psychoanalysis and literature. *Publ:* Transl, Maria Paganini, Intertextuality and the strategy of desire: Melancolique villegistare de Madame de Breyues, Yale French Studies, 79. *Mailing Add:* Dept of French Univ of Va Charlottesville VA 22903

BEKKER, HUGO, b Neth, Feb 12, 25; US citizen; m 52; c 2. GERMAN. *Educ:* Univ Mich, MA, 56, PhD, 58. *Prof Exp:* Asst prof Ger, Univ Ore, 58-61, res grant, 60; assoc prof, 61-66, PROF GER, OHIO STATE UNIV, 66- *Concurrent Pos:* Vis prof, Univ British Columbia, 71. *Mem:* Am Asn Teachers Ger; MLA; Renaissance Soc Am. *Res:* Minnesang; medieval German epic; baroque literature. *Publ:* Auth, The Nibelungenlied: A Literary Analysis, Univ Toronto, 71; Andreas Gryphius: Poet Between Epochs, Lang Verlag, Bern, 73; The Nibelungenlied: Rüdeger von Bechlaren and Dietrick von Bern, Seminar, 75; Friedrich von Hausen: Inquiries into His Poetry, Univ NC, 77; The Poetry of Albrecht von Johansdorf, Univ Calif, Davis, 78. *Mailing Add:* Dept of Ger Ohio State Univ Columbus OH 43210

BELASCO, SIMON, b Philadelphia, Pa, Dec 21, 18; m 49; c 3. ROMANCE DIALECTOLOGY, FRENCH SYNTAX & PHONOLOGY. *Educ:* Temple Univ, BS, 40; Univ Pa, AM, 48; PhD(French phonology), 53. *Prof Exp:* Fr interpreter & transl, La Mission Navale Francaise & English Div, Philadelphia Naval Base, 42-44; assoc audiology, Med Sch, Univ Pa; dir ling prog, Pa State Univ, 54-79, prof Romance ling, 62-79; PROF FRENCH LING, UNIV SC, 79- *Concurrent Pos:* Res assoc psychoacoustics, Jefferson Med Col, 53-58; dir ling prog, NDEA Summer Lang Inst, Colgate Univ, 59-61, Emory Univ, Basancon, France, 62 & Fla State Univ, 65; vis prof ling, Ling Soc Am Summer Inst, Univ Washington, 63 & Ind Univ, 64; Inst Arts & Humanistic Stuides, fel, Pa State Univ, 78. *Honors & Awards:* Teacher of Year, Pa Mod Lang Asn, 79. *Mem:* MLA; Ling Soc Am; Acoust Soc Am; Am Asn Teachers Fr; Am Coun Teaching Foreign Lang; Int Soc Phonetic Sci. *Res:* Occitan dialectology; French syntax; foreign language acquisition. *Publ:* Auth, The psychoacoustic interpretation of vowel color preference in French rime, Phonetica 3: 167-182; ed & coauth, Applied Linguistics, D C Heath & Co, 61; auth, Nucleation and the audiolingual approach, Mod Lang J, 49: 482-491; coauth & ed (with Albert Valdman & Florence Steiner), Son et Sens, In: Son et Sens Listening Comprehension and Writing Exercises & Scenes et Sejours Listening Comprehension and Writing Exercises, Scott, Foresman & Col, 72; auth, Phonemics as a discovery procedure in synchronic dialectolohy, In, Papers in Linguistics and Phonetics to the Memory of Pierre Delattre, Mouton & Co, Hague, 72; Visible speech cues and Sandhi variation rules in French, Current Issues in Ling Theory, Vol 9 & Amsterdam Studies in Theory & Hist Ling Sci, Vol IV, 79; Aital cal aprene las lengas estrangieras, Comprehension: The key to second language acquisition, In: The Comprehension Approach: An Evolving Methodology in Foreign Language Instruction, Newbury House, 81. *Mailing Add:* Dept Foreign Lang & Lit Univ SC Columbia SC 29208

BELCHER, MARGARET, b Dilke, Sask, Dec 19, 20. FRENCH. *Educ:* Univ Sask, BA, 41; Univ Toronto, MA, 47. *Prof Exp:* Instr French & English, Univ Sask, 45-47; teacher Rosetown High Sch, Sask, 48-49; instr, 49-55; ASSOC PROF FRENCH, UNIV REGINA, 55- *Mem:* Asn Can Univ Teachers Fr. *Res:* Seventeenth century French literature. *Mailing Add:* Dept of French Univ Regina Regina SK S4S 0A2 Can

BELFIORE, ELIZABETH STAFFORD, b Austin, Tex, Jun 21, 44. CLASSICAL LANGUAGES, PHILOSOPHY. *Educ:* Columbia Univ, AB, 66; Univ Calif, Los Angeles, MA, 74, PhD(classics), 78. *Prof Exp:* Asst prof, Scripps Col, 79-80; ASST PROF CLASSICS, UNIV MINN, 80- *Mem:* Am Philol Asn; Philol Asn Pac Coast; Class Asn Mid Western States; Women's Class Caucus; Soc Ancient Greek Philos. *Res:* Ancient philosophy; Greek tragedy. *Publ:* Auth, Epode, Elenchus and magic: Socrates as Silenus, Phoenix, Vol 34, 80; Ovid's encomium of Helen, Class J, Vol 76, 81; Plato's greatest accusation against poetry, Can J Philos (in prep). *Mailing Add:* Dept of Classics Univ of Minn Minneapolis MN 55455

BELGARDT, RAIMUND, b Tolkemit, Ger, Feb 24, 35; US citizen; m 63; c 1. GERMAN, COMPARATIVE LITERATURE. *Educ:* Univ BC, BA, 60; Univ Wash, MA & PhD, 64. *Prof Exp:* Asst prof Ger, Univ Calif, Los Angeles, 64-67; res grant, 66-67, assoc prof, 67-70, PROF GER, MICH STATE UNIV, 71-, CHMN DEPT, 76- *Mem:* Am Asn Teachers Ger; MLA; Philol Asn Pac Coast. *Res:* Concepts and theories of literature from Baroque to the present. *Publ:* Auth, Telheim's honor: flaw or virtue? a reinterpretation, Ger Rev, 1/67; coauth, Essays on German Literature, Univ Toronto, 68; auth, Romantische Poesie: Bergriff und Bedeutung bei Friedrich Schlegel, Mouton, The Hauge, 69; Kleists Weg Zur Wahrheit: Irrtum und Wahrheit als Denkformem und Struckturmoglichkeit, Z Deut Philol, 2/73. *Mailing Add:* Dept of Ger Mich State Univ East Lansing MI 48824

BELKIN, JOHANNA S, b Munich, Ger, Apr 13, 22; US citizen; m 48; c 1. GERMAN, PHILOLOGY. *Educ:* Ohio State Univ, PhD(Ger), 66. *Prof Exp:* Asst prof Ger, Ohio Wesleyan Univ, 62-63; asst prof, 66-69, assoc dean, Col Humanities, 72-73, assoc prof, 69-79, PROF GER, OHIO STATE UNIV, 79- *Concurrent Pos:* Develop Fund fac fel, 67; Am Philos Soc grant, 68-69; NSF res grant, 70-75. *Honors & Awards:* Alumni Distinguished Teaching Award, Ohio State Univ, 71. *Mem:* Am Asn Teachers Ger; MLA; Soc Study Dict & Lexicography NAm; Grimmelshausen Gesellschaft. *Res:* Late medieval scientific prose; German medieval literature and philology; early new high German. *Publ:* Auth, Welt als Raumbegriff, 68 & Uber Otfrid von Weissenburg, 71, Z Deut Sprache; Das mechanische Menschenbild in der Floredichtung Konrad Flecks, Z Deut Altertum und Deut Lit, 71; Otfrid von Weissenburg und der Heliand, Erich Schmidt, Berlin, 74; chapters on minerals and mineral products, In: The Herbal of Eucharius Rösslin, 1535, DeGruyter, 78; Index verborum of Grimmelshausen's Works (in prep). *Mailing Add:* Dept of Ger Ohio State Univ Columbus OH 43210

BELKNAP, ROBERT LAMONT, b New York, NY, Dec 23, 29; m 55; c 3. RUSSIAN LITERATURE. *Educ:* Princeton Univ, AB, 51; Columbia Univ, MA, 54, PhD, 60. *Prof Exp:* From instr to assoc prof Russ lang & lit, 57-69, assoc dean student affairs, Columbia Col, 68-69, chmn dept Slavic lang, 70-76, actg dean, 76-77, dir, Columbia Russ Inst, 77-80, PROF RESS LANG & LIT, COLUMBIA UNIV, 69- *Concurrent Pos:* Inter-Univ Comt Travel Grants study grant, Leningrad, 63; Am Coun Learned Soc & Fulbright-Hays fel study in Moscow, 66-67. *Mem:* Am Asn Advan Slavic Studies. *Res:* Nineteenth century Russian novel. *Publ:* Auth, The Structure of The Brothers Karamazov, Mouton, The Hague, 67; coauth, Tradition and Innovation, General Education and the Reintegration of the University, Columbia, NY, 78. *Mailing Add:* Dept of Salvic Lang Columbia Univ New York NY 10027

BELL, JOHN MARSHALL, b Dumbarton, Scotland, Mar 1, 44; Can citizen; m 68; c 1. CLASSICAL LANGUAGES. *Educ:* Univ Glasgow, MA, 66; Univ Western Ont, MA, 69; Univ Toronto, PhD(classics), 73. *Prof Exp:* Asst prof classics, Univ Calgary, 71-72; asst prof, 72-78, ASSOC PROF CLASSICS, UNIV GUELPH, 78-, CHMN DEPT LANG & LIT, 80- *Mem:* Class Asn Can (treas, 77-79); Am Philol Asn; Soc Promotion Hellenic Studies; Class Asn. *Res:* Greek literature, mythology and religion. *Publ:* Auth, Kimbix Kai Sophos: Simonides in the anecdotal tradition, Quaderni Urbinati di Cultura Classica, 78; Euripides' Alkestis: A reading, Emerita, 80. *Mailing Add:* Dept of Lang & Lit Univ of Guelph Guelph ON N1G 2W1 Can

BELL, ROBERT FRED, b Mount Carmel, Ill, Oct 26, 37; m 62; c 3. GERMAN LANGUAGE & LITERATURE. *Educ:* Univ Ill, BA, 59, MA, 63, PhD(Ger), 69. *Prof Exp:* Instr Ger, Univ Ill, 63-64; instr, Purdue Univ, 64-68; from instr to asst prof, Univ Ky, 68-72; asst prof, 72-75, chmn dept Ger & Russ, 76-78, ASSOC PROF GER, UNIV ALA, 75- *Concurrent Pos:* Fulbright teaching asst, English, Munich, Ger, 59-60. *Mem:* MLA; Am Asn Teachers Ger. *Res:* German exile literature; comparative literature; modern German literature. *Publ:* Auth, German exile literature in the undergraduate curriculum, Die Unterrichtspraxix, 74; Theodor Storm's Die Stadt: An interpretation, SAtlantic Bull, 74; contribr, Und alle fahran mit: The train as symbol and setting in German literature from Hauptmann to Borchert, In: Studies in 19th Cent and Early 20th Cent German Lit, Germanische Forschungsketten, Lexington, Ky APRA, 74; Vicki Baum, In: Deutsche Exilliteratur seit 1933, Bank I: Kalifornien, Teil 1, Francke, 76; Perspectives on witch hunts: Lion Feuchtwanger and Arthur Miller, In: Jahrbuch für Internationale, Peter Lang, 77; auth, The Jewish experience as portrayed in three German exile Novellen, SAtlantic Bull, 77. *Mailing Add:* Dept of Ger Univ of Ala PO Box 1987 University AL 35486

BELL, SARAH FORE, b Roxobel, NC, Aug 21, 20; m 43. ROMANCE LANGUAGES. *Educ:* Univ NC, Chapel Hill, AB, 41, MA, 45, PhD(Romance Lang), 68. *Prof Exp:* From instr to asst prof, 67-78, ASSOC PROF FRENCH, UNIV NC, GREENSBORO, 78- *Mem:* MLA; Am Asn Teachers Fr; S Atlantic MLA; Dante Soc Am. *Res:* French romanticism; Charles Nodier. *Publ:* Auth, Charles Nodier, imitator of Dante, Romance Notes, 69-70; Charles Nodier: His Life and Works: A Critical Bibliography, 1923-1967, Univ NC, 71; Francesca revisited: Dante's most notable successors, In: Studies in Honor of Alfred G Engstrom, 72, Univ NC; Charles Nodier's knowledge of modern foreign languages, Romance Notes, 73-74. *Mailing Add:* Dept of Romance Lang Univ NC Greensboro NC 27412

BELL, WENDOLYN Y, b Memphis, Tenn, Nov 21, 28. ROMANCE LANGUAGES. *Educ:* WVa State Col, BA, 48; Univ Wis, MA, 50; Univ Iowa, PhD(Span), 64. *Prof Exp:* Instr Span, Tenn State Univ, 50-51, Prairie View A&M Col, 51-53; asst prof Span, Fla A&M Univ, 53-59 & summer 60; asst prof Span, Univ Iowa, 60-63 ; assoc prof Span, 63-64, head dept mod foreign lang, 64-79, asst dean sch arts & sci, 76-79, PROF SPAN, TENN STATE UNIV, 64-, ASSOC DEAN ARTS, 79- *Concurrent Pos:* Univ rep, Am Asn Cols Teacher Educ; dir, Peace Corps Intern Degree Prog, 72-76; dir, Instnl Self Study Prog, 76-79 & consult, Southern Asn Cols & Schs, 78- *Mem:* MLA; Col Lang Asn; Am Asn Teachers Span & Port; Am Coun Teaching Foreign Lang; SAtlantic MLA. *Res:* Old Spanish; Golden Age drama; Galdos. *Publ:* Auth, Old and new horizons: Some suggestions for cooperation between English and foreign language departments, 12/70 & Nomemclature and Spanish literary analysis, 9/74, CLA J; Some ingredients for effective living, Tenn State Univ Fac J, 74-75; Tenn State Self Study Manual, 77. *Mailing Add:* Sch of Arts & Sci Tenn State Univ Nashville TN 37203

BELLAMY, JAMES ANDREW, b Evansville, Ind, Aug 12, 25. MEDIEVAL ARABIC LITERATURE, ARABIC PAPYROLOGY. *Educ:* Centre Col, Ky, AB, 46; Univ Pa, PhD(Orient studies), 56. *Prof Exp:* Interim lectr Arabic, Univ Pa, 56-57; asst prof, Wayne State Univ, 58-59; lectr, 59-60, from asst prof to assoc prof, 60-68, PROF ARABIC, UNIV MICH, ANN ARBOR, 68- *Concurrent Pos:* Assoc ed, J Am Orient Soc, 70-75; Am Coun Learned Soc fel. *Mem:* Mid East Inst; MLA; Mid Eastern Studies Asn N Am. *Res:* Arabic literature. *Publ:* Auth, Kitab ar-Rumuz of Ibn Abi Sarh, J Am Orient Soc, 9/61; coauth, Short Stories, Vol IV, 63 & Modern Poetry, Vol V, 66, In: Contemporary Arabic Readers, Univ Mich; ed & auth intro & notes, The Noble Qualities of Character by Ibn Abi d-Dunya, Bibliotheca Islamica, Wiesbaden, 73; auth, The mysterious letters of the Koran: Old abbreviations of the Basmalah, 7-9/73. *Mailing Add:* Dept of Near Eastern Studies Univ Mich Ann Arbor MI 48109

BELLAMY, SIDNEY EUGENE, b Dallas, Tex, Mar 9, 42; m 64. GERMANIC LANGUAGES, LINGUISTICS. *Educ:* Rice Univ, BA, 64; Univ Tex, Austin, MA, 65, PhD(Ger lang), 68. *Prof Exp:* Asst prof, 68-79, ASSOC PROF ENGLISH & MOD LANG, STEPHEN F AUSTIN STATE UNIV, 80- *Concurrent Pos:* Lectr, Univ Cologne, 73-75. *Mem:* Ling Soc Am; Am Asn Teachers Ger; Ver Diederdeutsche Sprachforsch; MLA. *Res:* Germanic dialects; sociolinguistics, psycholinguistics. *Publ:* Coauth, The acquisition of English morphology by children 4 to 10, Lang Learning, 12/70. *Mailing Add:* Box 3007 Stephen F Austin State Univ Nacogdoches TX 75961

BELLERT, IRENA, b Poland. THEORETICAL LINGUISTICS, SEMANTICS. *Educ:* Warsaw Univ, MA, 60, Doctoral, 64, Doctor Habilitatus, 70. *Prof Exp:* Vis res asst ling, Univ Pa, 64-65; asst prof formal ling, Warsaw Univ, 65-70; vis prof ling, Univ Montreal, 70-71; assoc prof formal ling, Warsaw Univ, 71-72; vis prof, 72-74, asst prof, 74-77, ASSOC PROF LING, MCGILL UNIV, 77- *Honors & Awards:* Best Book for 1972 award, Polish Acad Sci, 72. *Mem:* Can Ling Asn; Ling Soc Am; Polish Semiotic Asn; Can Commun Asn; Int Acad Philos Sci. *Res:* Theory of metaphor. *Publ:* Auth, Relational phrase structure grammar, Info & Control, Vol 8, No 5; On a condition of the coherence of texts, Semiotica, No 4, 70; On the semantic interpretation of subject-predicate relations, In: Progress in Ling, 70; On the Logico-Semantic Structure of Utterances, Ossolineum, Poland, 72; Sets of implications as the interpretive component of a grammar, In: Generative Grammar in Europe, 73; On inferences and interpretation of natural language sentences, Theoret Ling, Vol 1, No 3; Sherlock Holmes' interpretation of metaphorical texts, Poetics Today, Vol 2, No 1; coauth (with P Weingartner), On different characteristics of texts, In: Sublanguage, 82. *Mailing Add:* Dept of Ling McGill Univ Montreal PQ H3A 1G5 Can

BELLUGI-KLIMA, URSULA, b Jena, Ger, Feb 21, 31; US citizen; m 68; c 2. LINGUISTICS, COGNITIVE PSYCHOLOGY. *Educ:* Antioch Col, BA, 58; Harvard Univ, EdD, 67. *Prof Exp:* Sr res asst lang acquisition, Harvard Univ. 62-67, res fel soc relat & asst prof lang acquisition, 67-68; res assoc found lang, 68-70, RES PROF, SALK INST, 80-, DIR LAB LANG & COGNITIVE STUDIES, 70- *Concurrent Pos:* Adj prof, 70-77, adj prof, Univ Calif, San Diego, 77- *Honors & Awards:* Outstanding book award, Asn Am Publ, 79. *Mem:* Am Psychol Asn; Ling Soc Am; Int Ling Asn. *Publ:* Coauth, Remembering with and without words, In: Current Problems in Psycholinguistics, Ctr Nat Res Sci, Paris, 74; Aspects of sign language and its structure, In: The Role of Speech in Language, Mass Inst Technol, 75; Perception and production in a visually based language, In: Developmental Psycholinguistics and Communication Disorders, 75 & Two faces of sign: Iconic and abstract, In: The Origins and Evolution of Language and Speech, 76, NY Acad Sci; Poetry and song in a language without sound, Cognition, 76; The Signs of Language, Harvard Univ Press, 79; co-ed, Signed & Spoken Language: Biological Constraints on Linguistic form, Verlag Chemie, 80. *Mailing Add:* 6649 Michael John Dr La Jolla CA 92037

BELL-VILLADA, GENE HAROLD, b Port-au-Prince, Haiti, Dec 5, 41; US citizen; m 75. SPANISH, COMPARATIVE LITERATURE. *Educ:* Univ Ariz, BA, 63; Univ Calif, Berkeley, MA, 67; Harvard Univ, PhD(Romance lang), 74. *Prof Exp:* Instr Span, State Univ NY, Binghamton, 71-73; lectr, Yale Univ, 73-74; ASST PROF SPAN, WILLIAMS COL, 75- *Concurrent Pos:* Nat Endowment for Humanities fel, 7-12/79; Am Philos Soc grant, 82. *Mem:* MLA; Am Asn Teachers Span & Port; Latin Am Studies Asn. *Res:* Spanish-American comparative literature; Latin-American studies; sociology of literature. *Publ:* Au, Ideology and American literary criticism, Sci & Soc, fall 73; Nabokov's world of shiny surfaces, Nation, 5/75; Bruno's castle, or some literary misconceptions, Praxis, spring 75; Fantasy, history and the new fiction, Commonweal, 11/76; The rise of the Latin American novel, Okike, fall 78; Letter from Mexico City, Rev 27, 80; Borges and His Fiction: A Guide to His Mind and Art, Univ NC Press, 81; Names and narrative pattern, In: One Hundred Years of Solitude, Latin Am Lit Rev, spring-summer 81. *Mailing Add:* Dept of Romance Lang Williams Col Williamstown MA 01267

BELMONT, DAVID EUGENE, b Highland Park, Ill, May 9, 37. CLASSICS. *Educ:* Trinity Col, Conn, BA, 59; Princeton Univ, MA, 61, PhD(classics), 62. *Prof Exp:* From instr to asst prof, 62-68, chmn dept, 69-78, ASSOC PROF CLASSICS, WASH UNIV, 68. *Mem:* Am Philol Asn; Archaeol Inst Am. *Res:* Homer and Vergil; Catullus and Horace; ancient theatre. *Publ:* Auth, Twentieth Century Odysseus, 11/66, Telemachus and Nausicaa, 10/67 & Athena and Telemachus, 12/69, Class J; Approaching Greek, Univ Microfilms, Ann Arbor, 76; The Vergilus of Horace, Ode 4.1, Tapa, 80. *Mailing Add:* Dept of Classics Washington Univ St Louis MO 63130

BELTRAMO, ANTHONY FRED, b San Mateo, Calif, July 8, 40; m 62; c 2. SPANISH & APPLIED LINGUISTICS. *Educ:* Univ of the Pac, BA, 62; Stanford Univ, MAT, 67, PhD(ling), 72. *Prof Exp:* Asst prof, 72-77, ASSOC PROF SPAN & LING, UNIV MONT, 77- *Concurrent Pos:* Ed, Mont Asn Lang Teachers Bull, 77- *Mem:* Ling Soc Am; Am Asn Teachers Span & Port: Am Coun Teaching Foreign Lang. *Res:* American Spanish; bilingualism; sociolinguistics. *Publ:* Co-ed, Linguistic Studies Presented to Andre Martinet (3 vols), Clowes, London, 68-70; co-ed & coauth, The awareness of borrowing in San Jose Spanish, In: El Lenguaje de los Chicanos, Ctr Appl Ling, 75; auth, Gender assignment on English loanwords in Spanish, Proc 25th Annual Pac Northwest Conf Foreign Lang, 76. *Mailing Add:* Dept of Foreign Lang Univ Mont Missoula MT 59812

BELTRAN, LUIS, b Salmanca, Spain, Sept 6, 32; m 62; c 2. COMPARATIVE LITERATURE. *Educ:* Univ Salamanca, LLB, 54, lic philos, 56; Univ Mich, MA, 61, PhD(comp lit), 66. *Prof Exp:* From asst prof to assoc prof, 66-77, PROF COMP LIT, SPAN & PORT, IND UNIV, BLOOMINGTON, 77- *Mem:* Mediaeval Acad Am; MLA. *Res:* Comparative medieval literature; Spanish poetry. *Publ:* Auth, Hacia la Tierra (poetry), Alfaguara, Madrid, 70; The poet, the king and the cardinal virtues in Juan de Mena's Laberinto, Speculum, 4/71; La Vieille's past, Romanische Forsch, 1-2/72; Anaya mi Esperanza (poetry), Alfaguara, Madrid, 73; El Fruto de su Vientre, Samo, Mex, 73; Razones de Buen Amor: Oposiones y Convergencias en el Libro del Arcipreste de Hita, Castalia, Madrid, 77. *Mailing Add:* Dept of Compt Lit Ballantine Hall Ind Univ Bloomington IN 47401

BENARDETE, SETH GABRIEL, b New York, NY, Apr 4, 30; m 60. CLASSICS. *Educ:* Univ Chicago, BA, 49, MA, 53, PhD, 55. *Prof Exp:* Teaching intern Greek & humanities, St John's Col, Md, 55-57; jr fel, Harvard Univ, 57-60; asst prof Greek & Latin, Brandeis Univ, 60-65; assoc prof, 65-76, PROF CLASSICS, NY UNIV, 76- *Concurrent Pos:* Vis lectr philos, Grad Fac, New Sch Social Res, 65-; Nat Endowment for Humanities sr fel, 72. *Res:* Greek poetry and philosophy. *Publ:* Transl, Aeschylus II, The Persians and The Suppliant Maidens, Univ Chicago, 56; auth, Achilles and the Iliad, Hermes, 63; The Aristeia of Diomedes and the Plot of the Iliad, Agon, 68; Herodotean Inquiries, M Nijhoff, 69. *Mailing Add:* Dept of Classics NY Univ Washington Sq New York NY 10003

BENARIO, HERBERT W, b New York, NY, July 21, 29; m 57; c 2. CLASSICS. *Educ:* City Col New York, BA, 48; Columbia Univ, MA, 49; Johns Hopkins Univ, PhD(classics), 51. *Prof Exp:* Instr Greek & Latin, Columbia Univ, 53-58; asst prof classics, Sweet Briar Col, 58-60; from asst prof to assoc prof, 60-67, chmn dept, 68-73 & 76-78, PROF CLASSICS, EMORY UNIV, 67- *Concurrent Pos:* Mem Latin achievement test comt, Col Entrance Exam Bd, 63-66; fel, Southeastern Inst Medieval & Renaissance Studies, 65; consult, Nat Endowment for Humanities, 71 & 72; Am Coun Learned Soc fel, 78. *Honors & Awards:* Ovation from Class Asn Midwest & South, 79. *Mem:* Am Philol Asn; Vergilian Soc Am (pres, 80-82); Class Soc Am Acad Rome (pres, 65); Archaeol Inst Am; Class Asn Midwest & South (pres, 71-72). *Res:* Latin literature; Roman history; Roman monuments and topography. *Publ:* Auth Tacitus, Agricola, Germany, Dialogue on Orators, Bobbs, 67; An Introduction to Tacitus, Univ Ga, 75; Gordon's Tacitus, Class J, 12/76; Recent work on Tacitus (1969-73), Class World, 9/77; Agricola's Preconsulship, Rheinisches Museum, 79; A Commentary on the Vita Hadriani in the Historia Augusta, Scholars Press, 80. *Mailing Add:* Dept of Classics Emory Univ Atlanta GA 30322

BENARIO, JANICE MARTIN, b Baltimore, Md, Feb 19, 23, m 57; c 2. CLASSICS. *Educ:* Goucher Col, AB, 43; Johns Hopkins Univ, MA, 49, PhD(classics), 52. *Prof Exp:* Tutor Greek, St John's Col, 53-54; instr Latin, Sweet Briar Col, 54-56, asst prof classics & ancient hist, 56-58, vis lectr hist, 59-60; asst prof English, 60-61, asst prof classics, 61-62, ASSOC PROF CLASSICS, GA STATE UNIV, 62- *Concurrent Pos:* Ford Found internship, 53-54; ed, Vergilius, 60-62 & 74-79. *Mem:* Am Philol Asn; Archaeol Inst Am; Vergilian Soc Am; Class Soc Am Acad Rome (vpres, 68, pres, 69). *Res:* Augustan poetry, especially Horace and Vergil. *Publ:* Auth, The structure of Horace's Odes: Some typical patters, Class J, 12/56; Book IV of Horace's Odes: Augustan propaganda, Trans Am Philol Asn, 60; Dido and Cleopatra, Virgilius, 70; The Roman Centennial, Class Outlook 76. *Mailing Add:* Dept of Foreign Lang Ga State Univ Atlanta GA 30303

BENAVIDES, RICARDO F, b Santiago, Chile, Feb 15, 29; m 54; c 1. ROMANCE LITERATURE. *Educ:* Univ Chile, BA, 47; Univ Madrid, PhD, 54. *Prof Exp:* Prof Span lit, Univ Chile, 54-60, head dept Span, 56-60; prof lang, Univ Utah, 60-69; prof Span, Ind Univ, Bloomington, 69-72; PROF SPAN & DIR DIV FOREIGN LANG, UNIV TEX, SAN ANTONIO, 73- *Mem:* MLA; NAm Catalan Soc; Int Comp Lit Asn; Inst de Proj Exterior Cultura Catalana. *Res:* Theory of literature; peninsular novel; Latin American novel. *Publ:* Auth, Five Novelas Ejemplares by Cervantes, 56, F de Avendano y el Teatro del Renacimiento, 61, coauth, Unamuno, 64, & Dante, 64, Univ Chile; Unamuno y la Metanovela, 65 & Exilio y arraigo en novela Expanola, Homenaje a R Oroz, 67, Ann Univ Chile, auth, Para una Poetica del Mito, Chasqui, 73; contrib, Literary Criticism, Bks Abroad. *Mailing Add:* Div Foreign Lang Univ Tex San Antonio TX 78228

BENAY, JACQUES G, b Bone, Algeria, Mar 9, 25; US citizen; m 50; c 3. FRENCH, ITALIAN. *Educ:* Wayne State Univ, Ga, 53; Brown Univ, MA, 55, PhD(French lit), 59. *Prof Exp:* Instr, Brown Univ, 57-59; asst prof, Univ Nebr, 59-60 & Wayne State Univ, 60-63; assoc prof, 63-68, PROF FRENCH, STATE UNIV NY COL BUFFALO, 68- *Concurrent Pos:* Vis prof studies lit & soc, Univ Calif, Los Angeles, 71 & 72; res dir Grad Res Prog in Paris, State Univ NY, 72-73. *Mem:* MLA; Am Asn Teachers Fr; Soc Fr Professors Am. *Res:* Seventeenth century French classical theatre; 20th century French drama; literature and society--creative writing. *Publ:* Coauth, Le theatre des Enfers, Vol I, Le theatre de la Cruaute, Vol II, Le theatre de la Derision, Vol III & Le theatre de Poesie, Vol IV, In: Panorama du Theatre Nouveau, Appleton, 67-68; auth, Delire pour quatre (play), 72, Le conquerant, 73 & Le defunt, 73, Liberte. *Mailing Add:* Dept of Mod Lang & Lit State Univ NY Buffalo NY 14260

BENDA, GISELA, b Brandenburg-Havel, Ger, Oct 5, 41. GERMAN LANGUAGE & LITERATURE. *Educ:* Univ Münster, BA, 62; Marquette Univ, MA, 64; Northwestern Univ, PhD(Ger), 67. *Prof Exp:* Asst prof, 67-72, ASSOC PROF GER, MARQUETTE UNIV, 72- *Mem:* Am Asn Teachers Ger; MLA; AAUP. *Res:* The works of Heinrich Heine, Friedrich Nietzsche, Rainer Maria Rilke and Franz Kafka. *Publ:* Auth, Dem dichter war so wohl daheime--Heines verborgene Deutschlandliebe, 72 & Düsseldorfer Heimatblätter, 12/72, Heine-Jahrbuch, Düsseldorf: Rebellion oder nicht? Ein Vergleich von Goethes Prometheus und Neitzsches Klage der Ariadne, summer 73 & The fusion of life and death in Rilke's Duino Elegies, fall 73, Univ Dayton Rev; Heines testament in deutscher denktradition, Papers Lang & Lit, 74; Heines stellung in der kritik deutscher dichter an ihrer muttersprache, Ger Notes, 75; Heines Deutschlandkritik aus franzoesischer Sicht, Heine-Jahrbuck, Duessedorf, 82. *Mailing Add:* Dept of Ger Marquette Univ Milwaukee WI 53233

BENDELAC, ALEGRIA, b Caracas, Venezuela, Apr 19, 28; Dutch citizen; m 53; c 2. FRENCH LANGUAGE & LITERATURE. *Educ:* Univ Bordeaux, Baccalaureat, 45; Univ Caen, Lic de Lettres, 69; Columbia Univ, PhD(French lit), 72. *Prof Exp:* Instr elem, Lycee Francais de New York, 64-69; asst prof French & Span, Fordham Univ, 69-76; ASST PROF FRENCH & SPAN, PA STATE UNIV, 76- *Mem:* Soc Amis Montaigne. *Res:* Pascal's Pensees and generally 17th century French literature; espistemological problems in fictional and historical story telling; metaphors in poetry. *Publ:* Auth, Tourmaline II, Jean Grassin, Paris, 73; Structures du reve et de la realite dans Sylvie, Editions de l'Athanor, Paris, 75; Montaigne a la recherche d'un equilibre de relations entre le Moi et Autrui, Bull Soc Amis Montaigne, Cinquieme serie, 17: 31-47; Study Manual for Intermediate French, 79, Study Manual for Elementary French II, Pa State Univ, 80, Pa State Univ; Ombre et lumiere dans le theatre de Corneille: Nicomede l'Epiphane, Nottingham French Studies, 81; Montaigne et les anecdotes: le reel, la verite et l'histoire, Bull Soc Amis Montaigne, 82; Melanthera, Jean Grassin Paris, 82. *Mailing Add:* 139 05 85th Dr New York NY 11435

BENDER, BYRON WILBUR, b Roaring Spring, Pa, Aug 14, 29; m 50; c 5. LINGUISTICS. *Educ:* Goshen Col, BA, 49; Ind Univ, MA, 50, PhD(ling), 63. *Prof Exp:* Asst prof anthrop & ling, Goshen Col, 59-62; English prog supvr, Trust Territory of Pac Islands, 62-64; assoc prof, English Lang Inst, 64-65, assoc prof ling, 65-69, PROF LING & CHMN DEPT, UNIV HAWAII, MANOA, 69- *Concurrent Pos:* US Peace Corps grant, Pac & Asian Ling inst for develop pedag materials on Marshallese lang, 66-67; consult Maori educ, NZ Coun Educ Res, 68-69; dir, Ling Inst of Ling Soc Am, 77. *Mem:* Ling Soc Am; Polynesian Soc. *Res:* Language acquisition; Micronesian languages; Austronesian linguistics. *Publ:* Auth, Marshallese phonology, Oceanic Ling, 68; Spoken Marshallese, Univ Hawaii, 69; contribr, Current Trends in Linguistics: Linguistics in Oceania, Mouton, The Hague, 71; auth, Linguistic factors in Maori education, NZ Coun Educ Res, 71; Parallelisms in the morphophonemics of several Micronesian languages, Oceanic Ling, 73; coauth, A Ulithian Grammar, Australian Nat Univ, 73; Marshallese-English Dictionary, Univ Hawaii, 76; contribr, Studies in Pacific Languages and Cultures in honour of Bruce Biggs, 81. *Mailing Add:* Dept of Ling Univ of Hawaii Manoa 1890 East-West Rd Honolulu HI 96822

BENDER, ERNEST, b Buenos Aires, Arg, Jan 2, 19; US citizen. INDOLOGY. *Educ:* Temple Univ, AB, 41; Univ Pa, PhD(Orient studies), 47. *Prof Exp:* Indo-Aryan linguist, 46-50, asst prof, 50-58, from res assoc prof to assoc prof Indo-Aryan lang & lit, 58-67, PROF INO-ARYAN LANG & LIT, UNIV PA, 67- *Concurrent Pos:* Am Coun Learned Soc fel, 47-48; Rockefeller Found fel, 47-48; Am Philos Soc grant, 50; Guggenheim Found fel, 55-56; assoc ed, J Am Orient Soc, 58-63, actg chief ed, 64-, coordr, Coun Sanskrit Studies, 78-; consult, Nat Endowment for Humanities, 68-69 & 72-, sr fel, 72-73; consult, Inst Advan Studies World Relig, 71-, travel grant, 72; fel, Bhandarkar Orient Res Inst, India, 72-; consult, NDEA; consult & contribr, Merriam Webster, Encycl Britannica & Grolier. *Mem:* Ling Soc Am; Ling Soc India; Asn Asian Studies; fel Royal Asiatic Soc; Int Asn Sanskrit Studies. *Res:* Indo-Aryan languages and literature; language and social structure; medieval Indian illustrated manuscripts and texts. *Publ:* Auth, A lunar illustration occurring in several manuscripts of the Dhanya-Salibhadracarita, an old Gujarati work of the 17-18th century, J Am Orient Soc, Vol 88, No 4; Homage and reminiscences, In: Felicitation Volume for Muni Shri Punyavijayaji, 69; An old Gujarati Dramatic Presentation, Mahfil, 71; coauth, Introductory Hindi Readings, Univ Pa, 71; A gilt-illustrated manuscript of the Gita-Govinda, J Indian Soc Orient Art, 74; A recent manuscript acquisition, Baroda Mus Bull, 74; An early nineteenth century study of the Jain, J Am Orient Soc, 76; coauth, Advanced Course in Bengali, Radiant Press, Calcutta, 78. *Mailing Add:* 820 Williams Hall CU Univ of Pa Philadelphia PA 19174

BENDER, MARVIN LIONEL, b Mechanicsburg, Pa, Aug 18, 34; m 56; c 2. LINGUISTICS, ANTHROPOLOGY. *Educ:* Dartmouth Col, BA, 56, MA, 58; Univ Tex, Austing, PhD(ling), 68. *Prof Exp:* Master math, Adisadel Col, Cape Coast, Ghana, 59-60; res assoc, Educ Res Coun, Greater Cleveland, 60-62; asst prof math, Haile Selassie Univ, 62-65; proj specialist ling, Ford Found 68-69; asst prof math, Haile Selassie Univ, 69-70; vis asst prof ling, Stanford Univ, 70-71; asst prof, 71-76, ASSOC PROF ANTHROP, SOUTHERN ILL UNIV, CARBONDALE, 76- *Concurrent Pos:* Ford Found consult, EAfrica, 69-70; prin investr, NSF grant, 73-75; ed, Nilo-Sahelian Newsletter. *Mem:* Ling Soc Am; fel Am Anthrop Asn; Am Fed Teachers. *Res:* Comparative and historial linguistics; descriptive and theoretical linguistics; Afroasiatic and Ethiopian languages; Nilo-Sahelian languages. *Publ:* Auth, Linguistic indeterminacy: Why you cannot reconstruct protohuman, Lang Sci, 8/73; Omotic: A New Afroasiatic Language Family, Southern Ill Univ, 75; The Ethiopian Nilo- Saharans, Artistic Printers, Addis Ababa, 75; Co-ed, Language in Ethiopia, Oxford, 76; ed, The Non-Semitic Languages of Ethiopia, Mich Univ, 76. *Mailing Add:* Dept of Anthrop Southern Ill Univ Carbondale IL 62901

BENDER, MARY ELEANOR, b Elkhart, Ind, Mar 3, 27. FRENCH, GERMAND. *Educ:* Goshen Col, BA, 50; Ind Univ, MA, 51, PhD, 59. *Prof Exp:* Instr Ger & English, Hesston Col, 53-55; asst prof Ger & English, 55-62, PROF FRENCH, GOSHEN COL, 62- *Mem:* MLA; Am Asn Teachers Fr; Am Coun Teaching Foreign Lang Res. *Res:* Literary treatment of Anabaptism; contemporary literature; Christianity and literary expression. *Mailing Add:* Dept of Mod Lang Goshen Col Goshen IN 46526

BENDOR-SAMUEL, BRIAN LESLIE, b London, Eng, May 17, 35; Can citizen; m 59; c 3. FRENCH LITERATURE. *Educ:* Univ Man, BA, 60; Univ Colo, Boulder, MA, 62; Univ Bordeaux, Dr, 69. *Prof Exp:* Asst dean arts & sci, 70-74, dir & adminr, continuing educ, 74-78, assoc prof, 61-81, PROF FRENCH, UNIV WINNIPEG, 81- *Res:* Seventeenth century theatre and criticism; modern language teaching methods and evaluation techniques. *Mailing Add:* Dept of French Univ Winniped 515 Portage Ave Winnipeg MB R3B 2E9 Can

BENEDICT, COLEMAN HAMILTON, b New York, NY, Nov 20, 11; m 62. GREEK & LATIN LITERATURE. *Educ:* Princeton Univ, BA, 34, MA, 35, PhD(classics), 39. *Prof Exp:* Instr classics, Univ Vt, 39-42 & NY Univ, 46-50; from instr to assoc prof Greek & Latin, Columbia Univ 50-75, prof, 76-80; RETIRED. *Mem:* Am Philol Asn; Archaeol Inst Am; Vergilian Soc. *Res:* Roman history, historians and philosophy; Homer; Greek comedy, especially Aristophanes. *Publ:* Auth, Herodotus confirmed once again, Class J, 40-41; A History of Narbo, Lancaster, 41; The Romans in southern Gaul, Am J Philol, 42; The Olcott collection of ancient coins, Columbia Libr, 59. *Mailing Add:* 360 W 22nd St New York NY 10011

BENESCH, MARLENE, b Utica, NY, July 29, 39. GERMAN STUDIES. *Educ:* Univ Rochester, AB, 61; Middlebury Col, MA, 62; Brown Univ, PhD(Ger), 79. *Prof Exp:* ASST PROF GER & COMP LIT, UNIV RI, 79- *Mem:* MLA; Am Asn Teachers Ger. *Res:* Modern German literature; modern European and American poetry; interdisciplinary studies: the arts of poetry, music and visual arts. *Publ:* Contribr, Women Writers in Translation and Out-of-Print Texts, Garland, 81. *Mailing Add:* Dept of Lang Univ of RI Kingston RI 02881

BENHAMOU, PAUL, b Ain-Fezza, Algeria, Sept 2, 35; m 63. FRENCH LITERATURE. *Educ:* Univ Dijon, Lic es Lett, 59; Univ Iowa, MA, 63, PhD(French), 69. *Prof Exp:* Prof English, Lycee de Garcons, Tlemcen, Algeria, 59-61; instr French, Univ Iowa, 68-69; asst prof, 69-79, ASSOC PROF FRENCH, PURDUE UNIV, WEST LAFAYETTE, 80- *Concurrent Pos:* Am Coun Learned Soc travel grant, 73. *Mem:* MLA; Am Asn Teachers Fr; Soc Fre Etude XVIIIe Siecle. *Res:* Eighteenth century French periodicals; the Encyclopedie of Diderot and D'Alembert; twentieth century French singers. *Publ:* Auth, Elie-Catherine Freron, In: Dixionario critico della letteratura Francese, Unione Tipografico- Ed, Turin, Italy, 72; Un ennemi de L'Encyclopedie: le Pere Berthier, 12/72 & Interview avec George Brassen, 5/73, Fr Rev. *Mailing Add:* Dept of Foreign Lang Purdue Univ West Lafayette IN 47907

BENICHOU, PAUL, b Tlemcen, Algeria, Sept 19, 08; m 29; c 1. FRENCH LITERATURE. *Educ:* Univ Paris, Sorbonne, Lic es Let, 27; Ecole Normale Superieure, Univ Paris, Agrege des Let, 30, Dr es Lett, 71. *Prof Exp:* Prof lettres, Lycee Janson de Sailly, Paris, 37-40; prof French lit, Inst Francais, Buenos Aires, 43-49; prof lettres, Lycee Condorcet, Paris, 49-58; prof French lit, Harvard Univ, 59-79. *Mem:* Soc d'Hist Litteraire de la France; Am Acad Arts & Sci. *Res:* French literature; Spanish literature, especially the romancero. *Publ:* Auth, Morales du Grand Siecle, Gallimard, Paris, 48; L'Ecrivain et ses Travaux, Corti, Paris, 67; Creacion Poetica en el romancero tradicional, Gredos, Madred, 68; Romancero Judeo-espanol de Marruecos, Castalia, Madrid, 68; Nerval et la Chanson Folklorique, 71 & Le Sacre de l'ecrivain (1750-1830), 73, Corti, Paris; Le Temps des Prophetes, Gallimard Paris, 77. *Mailing Add:* 79 rue N-D des Camps 75006 Paris France

BENITEZ, MARIO ANTONIO, b Havana, Cuba, May 4, 26; US citizen; m 54; c 4. ROMANCE LANGUAGES, PHILOSOPHY. *Educ:* Pontif Univ Comillas, Lic philos, 52; Tex Christian Univ, MA, 58; Univ Havana, DLitt, 60; Tex Wesleyan Col, MEd, 62; Claremont Grad Sch, PhD(educ), 67. *Prof Exp:* From asst prof to assoc prof philos, Tex Wesleyan Col, 55-62; teacher, W Covina Unified Sch Dist, 62-64, consult, foreign lang, 64-66; assoc prof, 66-68, chmn dept mod lang, 66-72, vpres & dean, 72-76, dir Bilingual Educ Ctr, 76-80, PROF MOD LANG, TEX A&I UNIV, 68-; DIR DIV BICULTURAL-BILINGUAL STUDIES, UNIV TEX, SAN ANTONIO, 80- *Mem:* MLA; Am Coun Teaching Foreign Lang; Am Asn Teachers Span & Port. *Res:* Scholasticism as an educational philosophy; Miguel de Unamuno; Jose Ortega y Gasset. *Publ:* Auth, Examen psilogico del valor de los clasicos, Humanidades, 5/52; La Poesia Mistica de San Juan de la Cruz, Ed Cult, Havana, 60; Miquel de Unamuno's quest for fulfillment, Peabody J Educ, 5/68; John Dewey's concept of experience, Tex A&I J, 10/68; coauth, The Education of the Mexican American: A Selected Bibliography, Bilingual Dissemination Ctr, Austin, Tex, 78. *Mailing Add:* Box 152 Tex A&I Univ Kingsville TX 78363

BENITEZ, RUBEN A, b Buenos Aires, Arg, July 16, 28; m 51; c 4. SPANISH LITERATURE. *Educ:* Univ Buenos Aires, Lic lit, 50, Dr(Span lit), 71. *Prof Exp:* Prof Span, Nat Sch 4, Buenos Aires, Arg, 51-64, from vprin to prin, 52-59; adj prof lit, Univ Buenos Aires, 59-60, secy sch humanities, 60-64; vis prof Span lit, Western Reserve Univ, 64-65; asst prof, 65-69, PROF SPA N LIT, UNIV CALIF, LOS ANGELES, 70- *Res:* Postromantic poetry; Spanish romanticism; Spanish American modernism. *Publ:* Auth, Ladrones de Luz (novel), Emece Ed, Buenos Aires, 59; Una Historica Funcion de Circo, 59 & Bibliografia Razonada de G A Becquer, 61, Univ Buenos Aires; Becquer Tradicionalista, Ed Gredos, Madrid, 71; Becquer: Leyendas, Apologos y Otros Relatos (critical ed), Labor, Barcelona, 74; Coloma: Pequeneces (critical ed), Catedra, Madrid, 76; Ideologia del folletin espanol Wenceslao Ayguals de Izco, Ed Porrua, Madrid, 79; Maria no Jose de Larra, Ed Taurus, Madrid, 79. *Mailing Add:* 15086 Valley Vista Sherman Oaks CA 91403

BENJAMIN, ANNA SHAW, b Philadelphia, Pa, Aug 6, 25. CLASSICS, ARCHAEOLOGY. *Educ:* Univ Pa, BA, 46, MA, 47, PhD(classics), 55. *Prof Exp:* Instr classics, Juniata Col, 51-53; from asst prof to prof classics & archaeol, Univ Mo-Columbia, 53-64, chmn dept, 59-64; PROF CLASSICS, RUTGERS UNIV, NEW BRUNSWICK, 64-, CHMN DEPT, 69- *Concurrent Pos:* Mem, Inst Advan Studies, Princeton Univ, 60, res fel, 66-67; chmn summer session comt, Am Sch Class Studies, Athens, 65-71; assoc archaeol, excavations at Aprodisias, Turkey, 76- *Mem:* MLA; Archaeol Inst Am; Am Philol Asn. *Res:* Greek literature; industrial remains of ancient Athens. *Publ:* Coauth, St Augustine on Free Choice of the Will, 65 & auth, Zeonphon: Recollections of Socrates . . . , 66, Bobbs; Altars of Hadrian in Athens, 32:57-86 & Two dedications in Athens . . . , 37: 338-344, Hesperia. *Mailing Add:* 208 Cedar Aven Highland Park NJ 08904

BENJAMIN, STEVEN MICHAEL, b Woodbury, NJ, Nov 5, 42; m 70; c 2. GERMAN LANGUAGE & LITERATURE. *Educ:* Univ Houston, BA, 72; Univ Wis-Madison, MA, 76, PhD(Ger ling), 81. *Prof Exp:* Instr Ger, Dept Ger & Russ, Mich State Univ, 78-79; lectr Ger ling & Span, Dept Foreign Lang, WVa Univ, 79-81; asst prof Ger, Dept Mod Lang, Clarion State Col, 82; ASST PROF GER & SPAN, DEPT FOREIGN LANG, RADFORD UNIV, 82- *Concurrent Pos:* Bibliographer, MLA, 78-81; ed, Occassional Papers Soc Ger-Am Studies, 79-; book rev ed newslett, Soc Ger-Am Studies, 80- *Mem:* Am Asn Appl Ling; Am Asn Teachers Ger; Am Asn Univ Supervisors & Coordinators Foreign Lang; MLA; Soc Ger Am Studies. *Res:* Applied linguistics; foreign language pedagogy; German-American studies. *Publ:* Auth, Aftar in the Heliand and the instrumental case in Old Saxon, Niederdeutsches Jahrbuch, 102: 7-14; coauth, German loanwords in American English: A bibliography of studies 1872-1978, American Speech, 54: 210-215; German-American Bibliography for 1979, 80, ed, Papers from the Conference on German-Americana in the Eastern United States, 80, co-ed, Papers from the St Olaf Symposium on German-Americana, 80 & coauth, German-American Bibliography for 1980, 81, Soc Ger-Am Studies; auth, The current state of German-American bibliography, In: Germans in America, 82; coauth, German-American Bibliography for 1981, Soc Ger-Am Studies, 82. *Mailing Add:* Dept of Foreign Lang Radford Univ Radford VA 24142

BENNETT, ALVA W, b El Centro, Calif, Dec 18, 35; m 58; 71; c 6. CLASSICS. *Educ:* Univ Calif, Los Angeles, BA, 57, MA, 59; Univ Calif, Berkeley, PhD(classics), 65. *Prof Exp:* Lectr class lang, Lake Forest Col, 63-64; asst prof, 64-69, ASSOC PROF CLASSICS, UNIV CALIF, SANTA BARBARA, 69- *Mem:* Am Philol Asn. *Res:* Poetry of Sextus Propertius; works of G Sallustius Crispus; Latin and Greek poetry. *Publ:* Auth, The patron and poetical inspiration: Propertius 3, 9, Hermes, 68; Index Verborum Sallustianus, Georg Olms, 69; Propertius 3.24: A new approach, Class Philol, 69; The elegaic lie: Propertius 1, 15, Phoenix, 71. *Mailing Add:* Dept of Classics Univ of Calif Santa Barbara CA 83106

BENNETT, EMMETT LESLIE, JR, b Minneapolis, Minn, July 12, 18; m 42; c 5. CLASSICS. *Educ:* Univ Cincinnati, BA, 39, MA, 40, PhD, 47. *Prof Exp:* From instr to asst prof classics, Yale Univ, 47-58; asst prof, Univ Tex, 58-59; vis lectr, Inst Res Humanities, 59-60, from lectr to assoc prof, Inst Res Humanities & dept classics, 60-62, prof, 62-78, MOSES S SLAUGHTER PROF, CLASSICS, UNIV WIS-MADISON, 78- *Concurrent Pos:* Fulbright res scholar, Athens, 53-54 & Cambridge, 65; Guggenheim fel, Inst Advan Studies, 55-56; mem comt Int Permanent Studies Myceniennes, 56-; ed, Nestor, 57-77; vis prof, Univ Colo, 67 & Univ Cincinnati, 72. *Mem:* Am Philol Asn; Archaeol Inst Am; Ling Soc Am; corresp mem Ger Archaeol Inst, Berlin; hon mem Archaeol Soc Athens. *Res:* Epigraphy and language of the Minoan and Mycenean inscriptions. *Publ:* Auth, The Pylos Tablets, Princeton, 55; coauth, Mycenaean Studies, Univ Wis, 64; coauth (with J P Olivier), The pylos tablets transcribed, Athenaeum, Vol I, 74, Vol II, 76. *Mailing Add:* Inst for Res in the Humanities Univ Wis Madison WI 53706

BENNETT, JACOB, Medieval Literature, Linguistics. See Vol II

BENNETT, JOHN MICHAEL, b Chicago, Ill, Oct 12, 42. SPANISH AMERICAN LITERATURE, CREATIVE WRITING. *Educ:* Wash Univ, BA, 64, cert Latin Am studies & MA, 66; Univ Calif, Los Angeles, PhD(Span), 70. *Prof Exp:* Asst prof Span, Univ, 69-76, ASST LATIN AM BIBLIOGR, OHIO STATE UNIV LIBR, 76- *Mem:* MLA; Comt Small Mag Ed & Publ; Asn Poetry Therapy. *Res:* Contemporary Spanish American poetry; poetry therapy; creative writing, especially poetry. *Publ:* Auth, Las estructuras antiteticas en Galope muerto de Pablo Neruda, Rev Hisp Mod; Found Objects, 73 & White Screen, 76, New Rivers; co-ed, El pensamiento politico latinoamericano, Oxford Univ, 76; Meat Watch, Fireweed, 77; Nips poems, 80; Time Release, 78; Puking Horse, 80; Jerks, Laughing Bear, 80. *Mailing Add:* 137 Leland Ave Columbus OH 43214

BENNETT, ROBERT ERNEST, b Des Moines, Iowa, Nov 7, 42. ANCIENT HISTORY, GREEK & LATIN. *Educ:* Trinity Col, Conn, BA, 64; Yale Univ, MA, 65, PhD(classics), 70. *Prof Exp:* From instr to asst prof, 67-76, chmn dept, 73-75, ASSOC PROF CLASSICS, KENYON COL, 76- *Concurrent Pos:* Nat Endowment Humanities res fel, Univ NC, Chapel Hill, 75-76. *Mem:* Archaeol Inst Am; Asn Ancient Historians. *Res:* Roman prefects and papyrological sources in Egypt; women in antiquity; Plutarch. *Mailing Add:* Dept of Classics Kenyon Col Gambier OH 43022

BENNETT, WINFIELD SCOTT, III, b Paterson, NJ, Sept 15, 46; m 70. GERMANIC LANGUAGES, LINGUISTICS. *Educ:* Univ of South, BA, 68; Univ Tex, Austin, PhD(Germanic lang), 78. *Prof Exp:* Teaching asst, 73-77, asst instr, 77-78, INSTR GER, UNIV TEX, AUSTIN, 78-, INSTR LING, 79- *Mem:* Ling Soc Am; Am Asn Teachers Ger; Asn Comput Ling. *Res:* Syntax in early Germanic dialects, especially Old High German and Old Norse; syntactic study of modern German dialects; linguistic study of Medieval German literature. *Publ:* Auth, Verb complementation in Hrafnkels Saga, J Ling Asn Southwest, 76; The Relative Construction in the Works of Notker III, Folia Linguistica Historica, 2: 265-287; coauth, The Metal System, RADC-TR-80-374, Technical Report, 81. *Mailing Add:* Ling Res Ctr PO Box 7247 Austin TX 78712

BENNETT-KASTOR, TINA LYNNE, b La Mesa, Calif, Feb 8, 54; m 79; c 1. LINGUISTICS, PSYCHOLINGUISTICS. *Educ:* Calif Inst of the Arts, BFA, 73; Univ Southern Calif, AM, 76, PhD(ling), 78. *Prof Exp:* Res assoc, John Tracy Clin, 77; ASST PROF LING & ENGLISH, WICHITA STATE UNIV, 78- *Concurrent Pos:* Teaching asst, Dept English & Ling, Univ Southern Calif, 75-78; res asst, Dept Ling, Univ Southern Calif, 75-77; res consult, Rehabilitation Ctr, Univ Calif, Los Angeles, 77. *Mem:* AAAS; Ling Soc Am; Mod Lang Asn; NCTE. *Res:* Child language; discourse analysis; language disorders. *Publ:* Auth, Tonally irregular verbs in Chishona, Studies in Bantu Tonology, No 3, 76, Interrogatives, Haya Grammatical Structure, No 6, 77, coauth, Communicative distress, Discourse Across Time and Space, 77 & co-ed Discourse Across Time and Space, Southern Calif Occasional Papers in Ling, No 5, 77, Scopil; The speaker-hearer dichotomy in linguistic variation and the linguistic attitudes of second language learners, ITL: Rev Applied Ling, 78; Language and consciousness, Papers in Ling, 79; Noun phrase coherence in child narrative, J Child Lang, 82. *Mailing Add:* Dept English Wichita State Univ Wichita KS 67218

BENOUIS, MUSTAPHA KEMAL, b Descartes, Algeria, May 24, 36; US citizen; m 61; c 3. FRENCH LANGUAGE & LITERATURE. *Educ:* Univ Toulouse, CELG, 60, Lic es Lett, 63, Dipl Etudes Super, 64; Univ Ill, Urbana, PhD(French), 71. *Prof Exp:* Prof hist geog, Course Brossolette, Ain Temouchent, Algeria, 56-57; lectr French, Campbell Col, Belfast, 61-62; prof English, Lycee d'Etat de Mazamet, France, 64-65; teaching asst French, Univ Ill, Urbana, 65-68, instr, 68-69; from instr to asst prof, Univ Tenn, Knoxville, 69-72; asst prof, 72-76, assoc prof & chmn div, 76-81, PROF FRENCH & CHMN EUROP LANG & LIT, UNIV HAWAII, MANOA, 81- *Concurrent Pos:* Assoc ed, Fr Contemp Civilization, 75-; Nat Endowment for Humanities fel, Inst Contemporary Fr Cult, 81. *Mem:* AAUP; Am Asn Teachers Fr; Am Transl Asn; Centre d'Etudes des Litteratures d'Expression Francaise. *Res:* French Renaissance; French civilization, stylistics. *Publ:* Auth, La Francophonie a Tahiti, Presence Francophone, fall 76; Un livre contres les livre (Palissy), Romance Notes, 1/77; contribr, Jean Misrahi Memorial Volume, Fr Lit Publ Co, 77; auth, La Polynesie francaise a l'heure de l'autonomie, Fr Contemp Civilization, spring 78; La polynesie francaise: la menace de l'independance, proc PNCFL, 78; L7envers et l'endroit du Cymbalum Mundi, Romance Notes, Vol 19, No 3; Le cliche, point de repere culturel, Fr Contemporary Civilization, Vol 4, No 3; Le francais economique et commercial, Harcourt Brace Jovanovich, 82. *Mailing Add:* Dept of European Lang & Lit Univ of Hawaii Manoa Honolulu HI 96822

BENSELER, DAVID PRICE, b Baltimore, Md, Jan 10, 40. GERMAN. *Educ:* Western Wash Univ, BA, 64; Univ Ore, MA, 66, PhD(Ger), 71. *Prof Exp:* Instr Ger, Univ Ore, 68-69; from asst prof to assoc prof, Wash State Univ, 69-77; PROF GER & CHMN DEPT, OHIO STATE UNIV, 77- *Concurrent Pos:* Ed, ACTFL Ann Bibliog, 74-82 & Proc Pac Northwest Coun Foreign Lang, 75-77; prog officer, Nat Endowment Humanities, 76-77, admin fel, 76; ed, Mod Lang J, 80- *Honors & Awards:* Pro Lingua Award, Wash Asn Foreign Lang Teachers, 75. *Mem:* MLA; Am Asn Teachers Ger (secy, 75-80); Am Coun on Teaching Foreign Lang; Am Asn Applied Ling; Am Asn Advan Humanities. *Res:* German culture and civilization; bibliographical methodology and pedagogy; 18th century German literature. *Publ:* Auth, Culture, civilization, and the college foreign language curriculum of the future, In: Essays on the Teaching of Culture, Advancement Press, 74; Grant proposals in foreign languages and literatures: Some perspectives, Monatshefte, 77 & ADFL Bull, 78; Teaching the basics in the foreign language classroom: Options and strategies, Nat Textbk Co, 79; coauth, Methodological trends in college foreign language instruction, President's Commission on Foreign Language & International Studies: Background Papers and Studies, Govt Printing Office, 79 & Mod Lang J, 80; auth, The American Language Association: Toward new strength, visibility, and effectiveness as a profession, Reports Northeast Conf Teaching of Foreign Lang, Northeast Conf, 80; Factors affecting German after the requirement, Monatshefte, 81; Survey of US doctoral degrees related to the teaching of German, Unterrichtpraxis, 81. *Mailing Add:* Dept of Ger Ohio State Univ Columbus OH 43210

BENSIMON, MARC JOSEPH, b France, Nov 15, 26. FRENCH. *Educ:* Mont State Univ, BA, 49; Univ Colo, MA, 51; Univ Pa, PhD, 55. *Prof Exp:* Instr French, Univ Colo, 49-51 & Univ Pa, 51-53; from asst prof to assoc prof, Pa Mil Col, 53-56; from instr to asst prof, Univ Calif, Berkeley, 56-61; asst prof, 61-68, chmn dept, 71-72, PROF FRENCH, UNIV CALIF, LOS ANGELES, 68- *Mem:* Am Asn Teachers Fr; MLA; Renaissance Soc Am; Soc Fr Prof Am. *Res:* French Renaissance; comparative arts and literatures; 20th century French drama. *Publ:* Auth, Langue et Critique: Marcel Duchamp, Le Manifeste et le Cashe: Langages Surrealistes et autres, Dada/Surrealisme, Vol 1, 73; Modes of Perception of Reality in the Renaissance, In: The Darker Vision of the Renaissance: Beyond the Fields of Reason, Univ Calif Press, 74; Amour et Vengeance: Reflexions sur quelques images de la Renaissance, Mythology in French Literature, French Literature Series, Univ SC, 3:151-155; Desir, espace et temps: Remarques sur l'art de la litterature du XVIe siecle, Mythes-Symboles-Signes, Revue de Litterature Comparee, 2:289-298; Pierre de Ronsard, Les Amours, 1552-1584, Paris, Garnier-Flammarion, 81; La Porte etroite: Essai sur le manierisme, Le Greco, St Jean de La Croix, Sponde, Chassignet, d'Aubigne, Montaigne, J Medieval & Renaissance Studies, Duke Univ Press, fall 81; Venus et Adonis de Shakespeare: Metamorphose d'une metamorphose, In: La Metamorphose dans la Poesie Francaise et Anglaise, Tubigen, 81. *Mailing Add:* Dept of French Univ Calif Los Angeles CA 90024

BENSKY, ROGER DANIEL, b Perth, Western Australia, Aug 27, 37; US citizen; m 64; c 1. AVANT-GARDE & FRENCH THEATRE. *Educ:* Univ Western Australia, BA, 58, MA, 61; Int Univ Theatre, Paris, dipl, 63; Sorbonne, DUniv(theatre), 68. *Prof Exp:* Instr French lit, Univ Ky, 65-66; from instr to asst prof, 66-73, ASSOC PROF FRENCH LIT & DRAMA, GEORGETOWN UNIV, 73- *Concurrent Pos:* French Ministry Foreign Affairs sabbatical res grant, 75-76. *Mem:* MLA; Am Theatre Asn: AAUP. *Res:* Experimental theatre in France, dramaturgy and aesthetics; world trends in contemporary theatre; influence of occultism on modern literature. *Publ:* Auth, Symbolique de la Marionnette, Nizet, Paris, 71; Dubillard: le regard de l'espace, Lettres Nouvelles, 2-3/74; Lettre de Washington: Beckett et Grotowski aux USA, Quinzaine Litteraire, 9/74; Pour un theatre de Questionnement: Geronimo d'Andre Benedetto, Nouvelle Critique, 3/76; Le theatre aux abois, J de Chaillot, 3-4/76; Relfexions hors trajet sur Passion du General Franco par les Emigres Eux-Memes d'Armand Gatti, Singing in the brain or Gatti to the second power, Sub-stance, 12/77. *Mailing Add:* Dept of French Georgetown Univ Washington DC 20057

BENSON, DOUGLAS KEITH, b Marysville, Calif, June 8, 44; m 65; c 2. SPANISH LITERATURE & CULTURE. *Educ:* NMex State Univ, BA, 66; Univ NMex, MA, 68, PhD(Spanish lit), 73. *Prof Exp:* Chmn mod lang, Hastings Col, 69-80; asst prof, 80-82, ASSOC PROF SPANISH LANG & LIT, KANS STATE UNIV, 82- *Mem:* Am Asn Teachers of Spanish & Portuguese. *Res:* Contemporary Spanish poetry (1950-1970); teaching culture in language classrooms; Spanish American literature and culture. *Publ:* Auth, Torrente de la sangre: La desconstruccion de un poema de Damaso Alonso, Explicacion de textos literarios, fall 79; A select bibliography of sources for the teaching of Hispanic culture, ERIC Document Ed 192 558, 80; La ironia, el hablante y la experiencia del lector en la poesia de Angel Ganzalez, Hispania, 12/81; Linguistic parody and reader response in the worlds of Angel Gonzalez, Anales de la lit espanola contemporanea, fall 82; Angel Gonzalez y Muestra, 1977: Las multiples perspectivas de una sensibilidad ironica, Rev Hisp Mod (in prep). *Mailing Add:* 233 Harvey Dr Manhattan KS 66502

BENSON, EDWARD GEORGE, b New York, NY, Apr 23, 41; m 66. FRENCH. *Educ:* Princeton Univ, BA, 63; Brown Univ, MA, 68, PhD(French), 72. *Prof Exp:* Instr French, Univ RI, 69-70, asst prof, 71-80, asst dean, Col Arts & Sci, 75-80. *Mem:* MLA; Am Asn Teachers Fr; Renaissance Soc Am. *Res:* Sexual conflict in French literature of the Renaissance; Renaissance views of warfare; film. *Publ:* Auth, Engin Mieulx Vault que force: Rabelais' use of war in literary and historical context, Etudes Rabelaisiennes, 76. *Mailing Add:* 659 Hope St Providence RI 02906

BENSON, MORTON, b Newark, NJ, Dec 13, 24; m 55. FOREIGN LANGUAGES, LEXICOGRAPHY. *Educ:* NY Univ, BA, 47; Univ Grenoble, Cert, 48; Univ Pa, PhD(Russ), 54. *Prof Exp:* Asst prof Russ & Ger, Ohio Univ, 54-60; PROF SLAVIC LANG, UNIV PA, 60- *Concurrent Pos:* Vis lectr Princeton Univ, 64 & Columbia Univ, 65; mem joint comt East Europ, Am Coun Learned Soc, 71-73. *Mem:* MLA; Am Asn Teachers Slavic & East Europ Lang (pres, 64); Ling Soc Am. *Res:* Russian; Serbocroatian; Slavic linguistics. *Publ:* Auth, Soviet standardization of Russian, Slavic & East Europ J, fall 61; Dictionary of Russian Personal Names, Univ Pa, 64, rev ed, 67; English loanwords in Serbo-Croatian, Am Speech, 69; Serbocroatian-English Dictionary, Univ Pa, 71, rev ed, 79; Attempts to standardize Russian, English, and Serbocroatian, Juznoslovenski Filolog, 73; English-Serbocroatian Dictionary, Prosveta, Belgrade & Univ Pa, 78, rev ed, 83; The lexicographic treatment of English compound verbs, ITL: Rev Applied Ling, 81. *Mailing Add:* Dept of Slavic Lang Univ of Pa Philadelphia PA 19104

BENSON, RENATE, b Tilsit, Ger, Aug 3, 38; m 68; c 1. GERMAN & COMPARATIVE LITERATURE. *Educ:* Univ Montreal, lic es lett, 65; McGill Univ, PhD(Ger lit), 70. *Prof Exp:* Lectr, 67-70, asst prof, 70-77, ASSOC PROF GER, UNIV GUELPH, 77- *Concurrent Pos:* Comt mem, Can Coun Adjudication, 81- *Mem:* Asn Can Univ Teachers Ger; Humanities Asn Can. *Res:* Modern German and French literature. *Publ:* Transl, G Roy, La Route d'Altamont, Manesse Verlag, Zu6rich; transl & coauth (with Eugene Benson & F Grabberger), Beethoven, der Mann und seine Zeit, Vienna; auth, Erich Ka6stner, Studien Zu Seinem Werk, Bouvier Verlag, Bonn, 2nd rev ed, spring 77; Aspects of love in Anne Hebert's short stories, J Can Fiction, 11/79; Character and symbol in Ann Hebert's Les Invites au proces, 4/80, transl & coauth (with Eugene Bensen), Papineau by Louis-H Frechette, 5/81 & Le theatre de Neptune en Nouvelle-France by Marc Lescarbot, spring 82, Can Drama/L'Art dramatique canadien; German Expressionist Drama, E Toller, G Kaiser, McMillan, London (in press). *Mailing Add:* Dept of Lang Col of Arts Univ of Guelph Guelph ON N1G 2W1 Can

BENSTOCK, BERNARD, English, Comparative Literature. See Vol II

BENTAS, CHRISTOS JOHN, b Lowell, Mass, May 14, 36. CLASSICS, HISTORY. *Educ:* Boston Univ, AB, 58, EdM, 60; Tufts Univ, MA, 61, PhD(classics), 64. *Prof Exp:* Asst, Tufts Univ, 61-64; from instr to assoc prof, 64-71, PROF CLASSICS & HIST, LOWELL STATE COL, 71- *Concurrent Pos:* Assoc mem, Ctr Neo-Hellenic Studies, Austin, Tex, 67-; mem adv comt, Mass Bd Higher Educ, 67-68; US rep, First Int Congr Byzantine Music & Orient Liturgy, Byzantine Abbey of Grottaferrata, Rome, 68. *Mem:* Am Philol Asn. *Res:* Byzantine music, especially the Chrysanthine musical system; ancient, Byzantine and modern Greek literature and history; Latin literature and Roman history. *Publ:* Auth, The First International Congress of Byzantine Music and Oriental liturgy, Orthodox Observer, 11/68; The musical treatise of John Laskaris, In: Studies in Eastern Chant, Vol II, Oxford Univ, 69; The Chrysanthine concept of system in the modes of Byzantine music, In: Acts of First Interantional Congress of Byzantine Music, Grottaferra, Rome. *Mailing Add:* 129 11th St Lowell MA 01850

BENWARD, WILBUR ALAN, b Chicago, Ill, Mar 26, 37. GERMAN, LINGUISTICS. *Educ:* Univ Calif, Berkeley, AB, 62; Union Theol Sem (Va), BD, 67; Univ NC, Chapel Hill, PhD(Ger), 71. *Prof Exp:* Asst prof, 70-78, ASSOC PROF GER & LING, UNIV CALIF, DAVIS, 78- *Mem:* MLA; Ling Soc Am; Am Asn Teachers Ger. *Res:* History of linguistics; history of the German language. *Publ:* Auth, The Study of Indo-European Vocalism in the Nineteenth Century, John Benjamins, Amsterdam, 74; Jacob Frimm's vowel triad, Gen Ling, 74; A persistent proglem of prepositional usage, Unterrichtspraxis, 76; Introduction to the reprint of Adolf Holtzmann's Über den Umlaut, Über den Ablout, John Benjamins, Amsterdam, 77; Zur Dentalepithese im Deutschen, Beitrage Geschichte deutschen Sprache & Lit, 79. *Mailing Add:* Dept of Ger Univ of Calif Davis CA 95616

BERBERI, DILAVER, b Kruja, Albania, July 25, 21; US citizen; m 64; c 2. LINGUISTICS. *Educ:* Ind Univ, Bloomington, MA, 63, PhD(ling), 64. *Prof Exp:* Asst prof ling, Am Univ, Cairo, 64-66; linguist supvr lang teaching, Inst Mod Lang, Washington, DC, 66-67; asst prof ling, 67-76, ASSOC PROF LING & LANG, ST MARY'S COL, IND, 76- *Concurrent Pos:* Dir Arabic prog & lectr, Arabic Intensive Training Ctr, Ind Univ, 64-64. *Mem:* Ling Soc Am. *Res:* Anthropological, theoretical, and applied linguistics. *Publ:* Auth, Arabic in a Nutshell, Cortina & Inst Foreign Lang Studies, NJ, 69. *Mailing Add:* Dept of English St Mary's Col Notre Dame IN 46556

BERGEL, ALICE R, b Berlin, Ger, June 15, 11; US citizen; m 38; c 1. FOREIGN LANGUAGES. *Educ:* Univ Berlin, GPhil, 34. *Prof Exp:* From instr to asst prof foreign lang, Deep Springs Col, 41-47; instr, East Los Angeles Col, 48-61, head dept foreign lang, 56-66; asst prof French & Ger, Orange State Col, 61-62; assoc prof foreign lang, East Los Angeles Col, 62-65, prof, 65-76, chmn dept, 66-72; RETIRED. *Mem:* MLA; Am Asn Teachers Ger. *Res:* Historical French grammar. *Publ:* Auth, Der Ausdruck der passivischen Idee im Altfranzösischen, Berliner Beiträge zur Romanischen Philol, 34. *Mailing Add:* 229 N Shattuck Pl Orange CA 92666

BERGEL, KURT, b Frankfurt, Ger, Aug 22, 11; m 38; c 1. GERMAN LITERATURE & HISTORY. *Educ:* Univ Calif, PhD, 48. *Prof Exp:* Instr, Ger High Schs, 33-38; headmaster, Rowden Hall Sch, Margate, England, 39-40; from instr to asst prof, Deep Springs Col, 41-47; lectr, Univ Calif, Los Angeles, 47-49; dir tours, Europe, 51-80, chmn dept hist, 67-76, PROF GER & HIST, CHAPMAN COL, 49- *Concurrent Pos:* Lectr, Civic groups, Calif, 43-; instr, Army Specialized Training Prog, Stanford Univ, 43-44; guest prof, Univ Sao Paulo, 59, Dan Diego State Col, 62, Calif State Col, Fullerton, 66-67, Calif State Col, Los Angeles, 67-68 & Univ Calif, Irvine, 67-68. *Mem:* MLA; Am Asn Teachers Ger; Philol Asn Pac Coast; AHA. *Res:* Comparative literature. *Publ:* Auth, Rilke's Fourth Duino Elegy and Kleist's essay Ueber das Marionettentheater, Mod Lang Notes, 45; Childhood and love in Rilke's Fourth Duino Elegy, Ger Rev, 46; Albert Schweitzer: Leben and Denken, Henry Holt, 49; George Brandes und Arthur Schnitzler: Ein Briefwechsel, Univ Calif & Francke, Bern 56; A Schnitzlers unveroffentlichte Tragikomodie, In: Studies in Arthur Schnitzler, Univ NC, 63; ed, A Schnitzler, Das Wort, S Fischer, Frankfurt, 66. *Mailing Add:* Dept of Hist Chapman Col Orange CA 92666

BERGEL, LIENHARD, b Arnsdorf, Ger, June 22, 05; US citizen; m 32; c 3. COMPARATIVE LITERATURE. *Educ:* New York Univ, PhD(Ger), 45. *Prof Exp:* Asst French, Ger & Latin, Gymnasium Brieg & Breslau, 30-31; instr Ger, NJ Col Women, Rutgers Univ, 32-35; instr French, Cranford High Sch, NJ, 36-37; from tutor to prof Ger & comp lit, Queens Col, City Univ New York, 38-73, adj prof comp lit, Grad Ctr, 73-75. *Concurrent Pos:* Fulbright res fel Ital lit & cult, 60-62 & 69. *Mem:* MLA; Renaissance Soc Am; Am Asn Teachers Ital. *Res:* European literature, 1500-1800; literary theory and criticism; contemporary literature. *Publ:* Auth, America: Its meaning, In: Franz Kafka Today, Univ Wis, 58; Dopo l'Avanguardia, Vallecchi Editore, Florence, 63; Croce's Storia D'Europa nel Secolo XIX and the concept of Americanism, Rivista di Studi Crociani, 66; The Horatians and the Curiations in the dramatic and political-maralistic literature before Corneille, Renaissance Drama, 70; Semiramis in the Italian and Spanish Baroque, Forum Italicum 73; Shakespeare's Cymbeline and Boccaccio, In: Il Boccaccio nella Cultura Inglese e Anglo-Americana, Olschki, Florence, 74; La Scienza Nuova de Vico et le probleme de la decadence, Arch Philos, 77; L'Estetica del Nichilismo e Altri Saggi, bliopoli, Naples, 80. *Mailing Add:* 54 Richards Rd Port Washington NY 11050

BERGEN, JOHN JOSEPH, b Carbondale, Pa; m 64; c 2. LINGUISTICS, PHILOLOGY. *Educ:* St Bonaventure Univ, BA, 61; Cornell Univ, MA, 63; Univ Calif, Los Angeles, CPhil, 69, PhD(hisp lang & lit), 71. *Prof Exp:* Instr Span, Nazareth Col, 67-68; asst prof, 69-76, ASSOC PROF SPAN LING & PHILOL, UNIV N MEX, 76- *Mem:* Am Asn Teachers Span & Port; Nat Hisp Soc. *Res:* Spanish linguistics; Spanish and Portuguese philology; foreign language teaching methodology. *Publ:* Auth, A practical framework for teaching pronunciation in beginning Spanish Courses, 9/74 & The explored and unexplored facets of questions such as ?Que tu tienes?, 3/76, Hispania; The semantics of Spanish Count and measure entity nouns, Lang Sci, 2/77; One rule for the Spanish subjunctive, Hispania, 5/78; A simplified format for teaching Spanish historical phonology, Romance Notes, autumn 78; A simplified approach for teaching the gender of Spanish nouns, 12/78 & The semantics of gender contrasts in Spanish, 80, Hispania. *Mailing Add:* Dept of Mod & Class Lang Univ of NMex Albuquerque NM 87131

BERGER, MARSHALL DANIEL, b Buffalo, NY, May 22, 20; m 46; c 2. LINGUISTICS. *Educ:* City Col New York, BA, 41; Columbia Univ, PhD(gen ling), 51. *Prof Exp:* Tutor, 46-51, from instr to asst prof, 52-65, assoc prof, 65-78, PROF SPEECH, CITY COL NEW YORK, 79- *Mem:* Int Ling Asn; Ling Soc Am; Int Phonetic Asn; Am Dialect Soc; Am Name Soc. *Res:* English phonology and morphology; North American dialect geography; speech correction. *Publ:* Auth, Neutralization in American English vowels, 12/49, Vowel distribution and accentual prominence in modern English, 12/55 & Accent Accent, pattern and dialect in North American English, 4/68, 8/68, 12/68, & 70, Word; The internal dynamics of a metropolitan New York vocalic paradigm, Am Speech, 70; New York City and the antebellum South: The maritime connection, Word, 4/80 & In: Perspectives on American English, Mouton, The Hague, 80. *Mailing Add:* Dept of Speech City Col of New York New York NY 10031

BERGHAHN, KLAUS L, b Düsseldorf, W Ger, Aug 5, 37; m 67; c 1. GERMAN LITERATURE. *Educ:* Univ Munster, Staatsexamen, 63, PhD(Ger), 67. *Prof Exp:* Tutor Ger, Univ Munster, 64-67; from asst prof to assoc prof, 67-73, PROF GER, UNIV WIS-MADISON, 73- *Concurrent Pos:* Vis prof, Inst Res Humanities, 72-73, Romnes fel, Univ Wis-Madison, 75. *Mem:* Schiller Soc; MLA; Am Lessing Soc; Am Asn Teachers Ger. *Res:* German literature since 1750, literary theory and criticism, methodology and history of Germanistik. *Publ:* Auth, Formen der Dialogfuhrung in Shillers Klassischen Dramen, Aschedorff, Munster, 70; ed, Friedrich Shiller: Vom Pathetischen und Erhabenen, Reclam, Stuttgart, 70; co-ed, Schiller: Zur Theorie und Praxis der Dramen, 73 & Komodientheorie, 74, Darmstadt; ed, Schiller-Körner-Briefwechsel, Winkler, Munich, 73; Friedrich Schiller: Zur Geschichtlichkeit seines Werkes, 75 & coauth, Die Weimarer Klassik: Zur Wissenschaftsgeschichte der Germanistik anhand von Literarischen Peispielen, 78, Kronberg; Dokumentarische Literatur, In: Neues Handbuch der Literaturwissenschaft, Frankfurt, 78. *Mailing Add:* 4118 Hiawatha Dr Madison WI 52711

BERGIN, THOMAS GODDARD, b New Haven, Conn, Nov 17, 04; m 29; c 2. ROMANCE LANGUAGES. *Educ:* Yale Univ, AB, 25, PhD, 29. *Hon Degrees:* LittD, Hofstra Col, 58 & Middlebury Col, 76; LHD, Fairfield Univ, 65. *Prof Exp:* Instr Ital, Yale Col, 25-30; assoc prof Ital & Span Western Reserve Univ, 30-35; prof Romance langs, NY State Teachers Col, Albany, 35-41; prof Romance lang & cur, Dante & Petrarch collections, Cornell Univ, 41-48, chmn div lit & actg chmn dept English, 46-48; prof Romance lang, 48-73, chmn exec comt area studies, 50-52, EMER PROF ROMANCE LANG, YALE UNIV, 73- *Concurrent Pos:* Master, Timothy Dwight Col, 53-68; Fulbright scholar Ital, 55-56; prof, Univ RI, 74-75; prof, Indiana Univ, 81 & Conn Col, 82. *Honors & Awards:* Order of Crown of Italy; Order of St Maurice & St Lazarus, Italy; Order of Civil Merit, Italy; Order of Brit Empire; Dante Medal, Dante Soc Am, 72; Petrarch Medal, Petrarch World Cong, 74. *Mem:* AAUP; Renaissance Soc; MLA; Am Asn Teachers Ital (pres, 47); Mediaeval Acad Am. *Publ:* Auth, Dante, Orion, 65; Petrarch: Sonnets and Odes, Appleton, 66; Perspectives on the Divine Comedy, Rutgers Univ, 67; Vico's New Science, rev ed, Cornell Univ, 68; Petrarch, Twayne, 70; Petrarch's Bucolicum Carmen, Yale Univ, 74; Petrarch's Africa, Yale Univ, 77; Boccaccio, Viking, 81. *Mailing Add:* 48 Wyndybrook Lane Madison CT 06443

BERGMAN, HANNAH ESTERMANN, b Hamburg, Ger, June 17, 25; US citizen; m 53; c 1. SPANISH LITERATURE. *Educ:* Carnegie Inst Technol, BS, 46; Smith Col, MA, 47; Univ Calif, Berkeley, PhD, 53. *Prof Exp:* Instr Span, Smith Col, 47-48, Brandeis Univ, 51-53 & Hunter Col, 53-57; reviewer foreign motion pictures, NY State Dept Educ, 58-59; asst prof Span, 61-68, assoc prof Romance lang, 68-71, chmn dept, 68-69, PROF ROMANCE LANG, LEHMAN COL, 71- *Mem:* Assoc Int Hispanistas; Am Asn Teachers Span & Port; MLA; Renaissance Soc Am; corresp mem Hisp Soc Am. *Res:* Spanish drama and actors of the 17th century. *Publ:* Auth, Luis Quinones de Benavente y sus Entremeses, Castalia, Madrid, 65; ed, Entremeses, Anaya, Salamanca, 68; Ramillete de entremeses, Castalia, Madrid, 70; auth, Luis Quinones de Benavente, Twayne, 72. *Mailing Add:* Dept of Romance Lang Lehman Col Bronx NY 10468

BERG-PAN, RENATA, b Hamburg, Ger; US citizen; m 60; c 1. COMPARATIVE LITERATURE & FILM. *Educ:* Univ Wash, BA, 62, MA, 63; Harvard Univ, PhD(Ger), 71. *Prof Exp:* Instr mod lang, Mass Inst Technol 64-69; asst prof Ger & comp lit, Queens Col, City Univ NY, 71-76; vis asst prof Ger, Ind Univ, Bloomington, 76-77; RES & WRITING, 77- *Concurrent Pos:* Res Found fel, City Univ New York, 72, res grant, 75. *Mem:* Soc Values Higher Educ; Int Brecht Soc; MLA; Int Vereinigung für Ger. *Res:* German literature and film. *Publ:* Auth, Poetry and the party, how Bertolt Brecht revinvented Marxism Soundings, 3/75; Confucius in modern Germany, Ger Life and Letters, 7/75; Gabriele Wohmann, 75 & Rudolf Alexander Schroder, 75, Encycl World Lit; Holderlins Gedicht die wanderung, Neophilogus, 9/75; Bertolt Brecht and Chinese philosophy, Philos & Lit, 77; Brecht and China, Bouvier, 78; The Films of Leni Riefenstahl, Twayne (in press). *Mailing Add:* 143-36 Poplar Ave Flushing NY 11355

BERGQUIST, VIOLET, b Chicago, Ill, Oct 6, 18. SPANISH. *Educ:* Wheaton Col, BA, 39; Univ Chicago, MA, 43. *Hon Degrees:* LittD & DHL, Franklin Col, 72. *Prof Exp:* Teacher lang arts, Oak Park Schs, 43-47; asst prof French & Span, Bethel Col, 47-48; asst prof Span, North Cent Col, 48-51; chmn foreign lang dept, Evanstown Twp High Sch, 41-65, coordr foreign langs, Evanston Pub Schs, 61-68; ASSOC PROF SPAN & CHMN SPAN TEACHER EDUC, UNIV ILL, CHICAGO CIRCLE, 65- *Concurrent Pos:* Mem, Ill Curric Coun, 61-68; mem comn, Nat Found Arts & Humanities, 67-69; mem bd regents, Bethel Col & Sem, 71- *Honors & Awards:* Distinguished Service Award, Wheaton Col, 78. *Mem:* Nat Fed Mod Lang Teachers Asn (pres, 71-); Am Asn Teachers Span & Port (vpres, 61-64); MLA; Asn Supv & Curric Develop. *Res:* Foreign language instruction; foreign language articulation, especially in the elementary and high schs and col. *Publ:* Coauth, The Advanced-Level Course in High School Spanish and Portuguese Handbook, Heath, 68; contribr, Effective Foreign Language Instruction in the Secondary School, Prentice-Hall, 69; coauth, Espana es Asi, 73, Puerto Rico es Asi, 73 & La Guitarra Espanola, 74, Int Film Bur. *Mailing Add:* 1801 N Normandy Ave Chicago IL 60635

BERKOWITZ, LUCI, b Ogdensburg, NY, Feb 23, 38; div. CLASSICS. *Educ:* Ohio State Univ, BA, 60, MA, 61, PhD(classics), 65. *Prof Exp:* Asst prof classics, Ohio State Univ, 65-66 & Univ Wis-Milwaukee, 66-67; asst prof, 67-70, actg chmn dept, 77-78, assoc prof, 70-79, PROF CLASSICS, UNIV CALIF, IRVINE, 79-, RESIDENT SCHOLAR THESAURUS LINGUAE GRAECAE, 72- *Concurrent Pos:* NDEA fel, 67-68; IREX fel, Int Res Exchange Bd, 76. *Mem:* Am Philol Asn; Archaeol Inst Am; Am Class League. *Res:* Pastoral poetry; Greek tragedy; Greek lexicography. *Publ:* Auth, Index Arnobianus, 67, coauth, Index Verborum Quae in Saturis Auli Persi Flacci Reperiuntur, 67 & Index Lucilianus, 68, Georg Olms; The Elements of Scientific and Specialized Terminology, Burgess, 67; Sophocles' Oedipus Tyrannus, Norton, 69; Pollio and the Date of the Fourth Ecologue, Calif Studies Class Antiq, 72; auth, Canon of Greek Authors and Works from Homer to A D 200, 77 & A Concordance to Nicander, 80, Thesaurus Ling Graecae. *Mailing Add:* Dept of Classics Univ of Calif Irvine CA 92717

BERKVAM, MICHAEL LEIGH, b Eau Claire, Wis, Nov 26, 42; c 2. FRENCH LITERATURE. *Educ:* St Olaf Col, BA, 64; Univ Wis-Madison, MA, 67, PhD(French), 73. *Prof Exp:* Lectr English, Lycee Voltaire, Paris, 69-70; lectr, Ecole Normale d'Instituteurs/Auteuil, 70-71; lectr French, 71-73, asst prof, 73-80, ASSOC PROF FRENCH, IND UNIV, BLOOMINGTON, 80- *Concurrent Pos:* Nat Endowment for Humanities res fel, 79; Lilly Endowment teaching fel, 81-82. *Mem:* Societe Francaise d'Etude du XVIIIe Siecle; Am Soc 18th Century Studies; MLA. *Res:* Edition of the correspondence and collected papers of Pierre Michel Hennin; Paris in the 18th century French novel; Montesquieu. *Publ:* Auth, Les Pouvoirs du mot (Sartre), 10-12/72 & Le Paris de Proust, 4-6/74, Revue des Sciences Humanines; Correspondence and Collected Papers of Pierre Michel Hennin, Voltaire Found, Oxford, Vol I, 81. *Mailing Add:* Dept of French & Ital Ind Univ Ballantine Bloomington IN 47401

BERLIN, CHARLES, b Boston, Mass, Mar 17, 36; m 65; c 2. HEBRAIC & JUDAIC LITERATURE. *Educ:* Hebrew Teachers Col, BJEd, 56, MHL, 59; Harvard Univ, AB, 58, AM, 59, PhD, 63; Simmons Col, MS, 64. *Prof Exp:* Lectr mod Hebrew, 62-65, LEE M FRIEDMAN BIBLIOGR IN JUDAICA, COL LIBR, HARVARD UNIV, 62- *Concurrent Pos:* Consult, Univ Fla Libr, 73, Univ Tex Libr, 74, New York Pub Libr, 75 & Emory Univ Libr, 76. *Mem:* Asn Jewish Libr (vpres, 67-68, pres, 68-69); Asn Jewish Studies (treas, 70-72, exec secy, 72-). *Res:* Bibliography of Hebraica and Judaica; Jewish history. *Publ:* Auth, The Judaica collection at Harvard, 68 & Jewish bibliographic journals, 71, Jewish Bk Ann; Index to Festschriften in Jewish Studies, Harvard Col Libr, 71; ed, Studies in Jewish Bibliography, History and Literature in Honor of I Edward Kiev, KTAV, 71; coauth, The Jewish People and Palestine, 73, Hebrew Manuscripts in the Houghton Library, 75, American Jewish Ephemera, 77 & Knesset 9, 78, Harvard Univ Libr. *Mailing Add:* Harvard Col Libr Harvard Univ Cambridge MA 02138

BERLINCOURT, MARJORIE ALKINS, Classical History, Numismatics. See Vol I

BERMAN, LORNA, b Semans, Sask, Nov 17, 26. FRENCH. *Educ:* Univ Toronto, PhD(French lit), 60. *Prof Exp:* Instr French, Victoria Col, Univ Toronto, 60-61; asst prof, 61-65, ASSOC PROF FRENCH, WILFRID LAURIER UNIV, 66- *Mem:* Soc Francaise d'Etude du XVIIIe Siecle. *Res:* French literature; linguistics; adult education. *Publ:* Auth, The problem of evil in Sade, Alphabet, 6/63; The Marquis de Sade and his critics, Mosaic, 1/68; The Marquis de Sade and religion, Revue de L'Univ Ottawa, 12/69; The Thought and Themes of the Marquis de Sade, privately publ, 71. *Mailing Add:* 170 Erb St W Waterloo ON N2L 1V4 Can

BERMAN, RUSSELL, ALEXANDER, b Boston, Mass, May 14, 50. GERMAN LITERATURE. *Educ:* Harvard Univ, BA, 72; Washington Univ, MA, 76, PhD(Ger), 79. *Prof Exp:* ASST PROF GER LIT, STANFORD UNIV, 79- *Concurrent Pos:* ed, Telos, 79-; Mellon fac fel, Harvard Univ, 82-83. *Mem:* Am Asn Teachers Ger; Western Asn Ger Studies; MLA; Pac Northwest Coun Foreign Lang. *Res:* Sociology of modernism; history of literary criticism; Marxist literary theory. *Publ:* Auth, Lukacs' critique of Bredel and Ottwalt, New Ger Critique, winter 77; Adorno, Marxism and art, Telos, winter 77; coauth, Karl Emil Franzos: Des Pojaz, In: Romane und Novellen, Reclam, 80; auth, Literarische Offentlichkeit, Deut Lit: Eine Sozialgeshichte, 82; Faschistische Literature, Lit & Ges, 82; Hans Jurgen Syberberg, New Ger Filmmakers, 82; Recipient as spectator, Ger Quart, 82; From Fontane to Tucholskt, Lang, 82. *Mailing Add:* Dept of Ger Studies Stanford Univ Stanford CA 94305

BERNAL, OLGA, b Czech, July 27, 29; US citizen. NINETEENTH & TWENTIETH CENTURY FRENCH LITERATURE. *Educ:* Columbia Univ, BA, 55, MA, 57, PhD(French), 64. *Prof Exp:* Instr French, Columbia Univ, 57-60; from instr to asst prof, Vassar Col, 60-67; assoc prof, 67-70, PROF FRENCH, STATE UNIV NY BUFFALO, 70- *Concurrent Pos:* Guggenheim & Vassar Col fels, 66-67. *Mem:* MLA; Int Asn Fr Studies. *Res:* Nineteenth century French poetry; twentieth century French novel. *Publ:* Auth, Alain Robbe-Grillet: Le Roman de L'absence, Gallimard, 64; L'oubli des noms, Le Monde, 1/68 & Glissement hors du langage, 10/68, Cahiers Chemin; Langage et Fiction Dans Le Roman de Beckett, Gallimard, 69; George Jacson: les Freres de Soledad, Cahiers Chemin, 1/72; Des fiches et des fluides dans le roman de Nathalie Sarraute, Mod Lang Notes, spring 74; Samuel Beckett: l'e'crivain et Le Savoir, J Beckett Studies, summer 77. *Mailing Add:* Dept of Mod Langs & Lit State Univ NY Buffalo NY 14260

BERNARD, ROBERT WILLIAM, b Detroit, Mich, Sept 15, 35; m 65; c 2. FRENCH, ITALIAN. *Educ:* St Thomas Col, BA, 58, Univ Kans, MA, 62, PhD(French), 68; Dipl civilisation Francaise, Sorbonne, 61. *Prof Exp:* From asst prof to assoc prof, 65-76, PROF FRENCH, IOWA STATE UNIV, 76- *Concurrent Pos:* Res & teaching French & English, Univ Besancon, 75. *Mem:* Am Asn Teachers Fr; Renaissance Soc Am; Midwest Mod Lang Asn. *Res:* French & Italian literature of the Renaissance; feminism in French literature. *Publ:* Auth, Textual analysis in the teaching of literature in advanced foreign languages classes, Proc Univ Northern Iowa Conf Ling & Lit, 73 & Mouton, The Hague, 74; Platonism--myth or reality in the Heptameron?, 16th Century J, 4/74; Noel du Fail's portrait of country life in the Propos Rustiques, Iowa State J Res, 11/74; Apercu historique et moral sur le duel au XVIe siecle, L'Escribe Fr, 6/75. *Mailing Add:* Dept of Foreign Lang & Lit Iowa State Univ 300K Pearson Hall Ames IA 50010

BERNARDO, ALDO SISTO, b Italy, May 17, 20; nat US; m 42; c 3. ROMANCE PHILOLOGY. *Educ:* Brown Univ, AM, 47; Harvard Univ, PhD(Romance philol), 50. *Prof Exp:* Instr French & Ital, Triple Cities Col, Syracuse, 49-50; from asst prof to assoc prof Romance lang, State Univ NY Binghamton, 50-58, prof Ital, 58-73, chmn humanities div, 59-73, co-dir ctr medieval & early Renaissance studies, 66-73; pres, Verrazzano Col, 73-75; PROF ITAL & COMP LIT, STATE UNIV NY BINGHAMTON, 75- *Concurrent Pos:* Fulbright res grant, Rome, 55-56; Am Coun Learned Soc res grant, 58; Guggenheim fel, 64-65; mem nat screening comt, Fulbright-Hays Act, Italy & Greece, 66-67; chmn univ awards comt, Res Found State Univ NY, 68-; sr fel, Ctr Medieval & Early Renaissance Studies, State Univ NY Binghamton, 75-; Distinguished Serv Prof, 79-; Nat Endowment for Humanities transl grant, 79-80. *Mem:* MLA; Am Asn Teachers Ital; Mediaeval Acad Am; Dante Soc Am. *Res:* Computer-aided translations; Petrarch; mediaeval esthetics. *Publ:* Auth, Dante, Petrarch and Boccaccio, dimensions of literary perspective, In: Italian Poets and English Critics, 1755-1859, Univ Chicago, 69; Dante's eighth heaven: Ultimate threshold to salvation, J Medieval & Renaissance Studies, fall 72; Petrarch and the art of literature, In: From Petrarch to Pirandello, Univ Toronto, 73; Petrarch, Laura and the Triumphs, 74, transl, F Petrarca, Rerum Familiarium Libri I-VIII, 75 & auth, A Concordance to Petrarch's Familiares, 77, State Univ NY; ed, E H Wilkins Unpublished Studies on Petrarch and Boccaccio, Antenore, Padua, 78; Petrarch, Citizen of the World, Padua & Albany, 81; Libri IX-XVI, Johns Hopkins, 82. *Mailing Add:* Dept of Romance Lang State Univ NY Binghamton NY 13901

BERNATH, PETER, b Berlin, Ger, Jan 2, 41. GERMAN LITERATURE, EUROPEAN CIVILIZATION. *Educ:* McGill Univ, PhD(Ger lit), 75. *Prof Exp:* Pedag coun continuing educ, Senator für Schulwesen, Berlin, 71; prof Ger, 72-77, DIR, LANG COURSES, UNIV SHERBROOKE, 77- *Concurrent Pos:* Prof Ger, Bishop's Univ, 72-77 U Univ Montreal, 75-76; secy Ger sect, ACFAS Cong, 75-78. *Res:* Brecht; opera as drama; distance education. *Publ:* Auth, Französisch für Touristen, Französisch an Vhs, 3/71; Französisch fur Touristen II, Zielsprache Französisch, 2/72; Wesen und Funktion der Sentenz im Drama von Kleist, Büchner und Brecht, Bouvier, 76. *Mailing Add:* Univ of Sherbrooke Sherbrooke PQ J1K 1R1 Can

BERND, CLIFFORD ALBRECHT, b Bronxville, NY, May 14, 29; m 72; c 2. GERMAN LITERATURE. *Educ:* NY Univ, BA, 50; Univ Md, MFS, 52; Univ Heidelberg, PhD, 58. *Prof Exp:* From instr to asst prof Ger, Princeton Univ, 58-64; assoc prof, 64-68, chmn dept, 65-76, PROF GER, UNIV CALIF, DAVIS, 68- *Concurrent Pos:* German Foreign Off Exchange fel, 54-56; mem, Int Fed Mod Lang & Lit; rev ed, German Quart, 64-68; Am Philos

Soc Grant, 65; Humanities Inst awards, Univ Calif, 66 & 71; Fulbright res scholar, Kiel, Ger, 68-69; Fritz Thyssen Found fel, 72; vis fel Ger lit, Univ Leicester, 77. *Mem:* Schiller Ges; Goethe Ges; Kleist Ges; Hölderlin Ges; corresp mem Storm Ges. *Res:* German literature of the 17th, 18th & 19th centuries. *Publ:* Auth, Theodor Storm's Craft of Fiction, Univ NC, 63, 2nd ed, 66; The Formal Qualities of Hölderlin's Wink für die Darstellung und Sprache, Mod Lang Rev, 7/65; Thomas Mann's Meerfahrt mit Don Quijote, Ger Quart, 11/65; Der Lutherbrief in Kleists Michael Kohlhaas, Z Deut Philol, 12/67; Theodor Storm--Paul Heyse Briefwechsel, Kritische Ausgabe (3 vols), E Schmidt, Berlin, 69-74; Enthüllen und Verhüllen in Annette von Droste-Hülshoffs Judenbuche, Festschrift Benno von Wiese, Erich Schmidt, Berlin, 73; Conscience and passion in Gryphius' Catharina von Georgien, Festschrift Walter Silz, Univ NC, 74; ; German Poetic Realism, G K Hall, 81. *Mailing Add:* Dept of Ger Univ of Calif Davis CA 95616

BERNDT-KELLEY, ERNA, b Coronel Suarez, Arg, Aug 10, 27; US citizen; m 65; c 1. ROMANCE LANGUAGES. *Educ:* Univ Wis, BA, 54, MA, 55, PhD(Span), 59. *Prof Exp:* Instr Span, 59-61, dir jr year Madrid, 61-63, from asst prof to assoc prof, 65-75, PROF SPAN & PORT, SMITH COL, 75- *Concurrent Pos:* Mem bd dirs, Int Inst Spain, 65-67 & 75-78. *Mem:* Renaissance Soc Am; MLA. *Res:* Spanish; early Renaissance. *Publ:* Auth, Algunos aspectos de la obra poetica de Fray Ambrosio Montesino, Archivum, 59; Amor, Muerte y Fortuna en La Celestina, Gredos, Madrid, 63; Popularidad del romance Mira Nero de Tarpeya, In: Estudios Dedicados a James Homer Herriott, Univ Wis, 66; Algunas observaciones sobre la edicion de Zaragoza de 1507 de la Tragicomedia de Calisto y Melibea, In: La Celestina y su Conno Social, Mispam, Barcelona, 77. *Mailing Add:* Dept of Hisp Studies Smith Col Northampton MA 01063

BERNHEIMER, CHARLES CLARENCE, b Bryn Mawr, Pa, Aug 16, 42. COMPARATIVE LITERATURE. *Educ:* Haverford Col, BA, 63; Harvard Univ, MA, 65, PhD(comp lit), 72. *Prof Exp:* Asst prof, 70-77, ASSOC PROF ENGLISH & COMP LIT, STATE UNIV NY, BUFFALO, 77- *Concurrent Pos:* Sr res assoc, Ctr Humanities, Wesleyan Univ, 79; vis assoc prof Fr & comp lit, Univ Calif, Berkeley, 80-81. *Honors & Awards:* Chancellor's Award for Excellence in Teaching, State Univ NY, 75. *Mem:* MLA; Comp Lit Asn. *Res:* Nineteenth and 20th century literary; novel theory; psychoanalysis. *Publ:* Auth, Linguistic realism in Flaubert's Bouvard et Pecuchet, Novel, winter 74; Cloaking the Self: The literary space of Gogol's Overcoat, PMLA, 1/75; Etre la matiere: Origin and difference in Flaubert's La Tentation de Saint Antoine, Novel, fall 76; Grammacentricity and Modernism, Mosaic, fall 77; Letters to an Absent Friend: A structural reading of Kafka's The Judgement, In: The Problem of The Judgement, 77 & Symbolic bond and textual play: The structure of Kafka's Castle, In: The Kafka Debate, 77, Gordian Press; Crossing over: Kafka's metatextual parable, MLN, winter 80; Flaubert and Kafka: Studies in psychopoetic structure, Yale Univ Press, 82. *Mailing Add:* Dept of English State Univ of NY Buffalo NY 14214

BERNIAN, DANIEL, b Baltimore, Md, Sept 10, 16. FRENCH & SPANISH. *Educ:* Cath Univ Am, BA, 38; Univ Pa, MA, 43; Laval Univ, PhD, 52; Villanova Univ, LLD, 59; St Joseph's Col (Pa), LLD, 61; Temple Univ, LLD, 63; La Salle Col, PedD, 69. *Prof Exp:* Teacher lang, West Cath High Sch, Philadelphia, Pa, 38-47; teacher French & Span, La Salle High Sch, 47-49; teacher relig & French, Cath Univ Am, 49-51; from asst prof to assoc prof, 51-61, dean men, 53-54, dean students, 54-58, pres col, 58-80, PROF FRENCH, SPAN & ITAL, LASALLE COL, 61-, EMER PRES COL, 80- *Concurrent Pos:* Exchange teacher, Col St Patrice, Can, 40-41; trustee, Immaculata Col; chmn, Philadelphia Comn Higher Educ; mem bd trustees, Philadelphia Community Col, Philadelphia Educ Nominating Panel Bd Educ & Health Systs Agency. *Mailing Add:* Dept of Foreign Lang La Salle Col Philadelphia PA 19141

BERNSTEIN, ALVIN H, Ancient History. See Vol I

BERNSTEIN, ECKHARD RICHARD, b Grimma, Ger, Aug 5, 38; m 65; c 2. GERMAN & COMPARATIVE LITERATURE. *Educ:* Univ Marburg, Staatsexamen, 65, Assessorexamen, 68; Case Western Reserve Univ, PhD(comp lit), 71. *Prof Exp:* Instr English lit, Youngstown Univ, 65-66; instr Ger lit, Lake Erie Col, 66-67; teaching asst English & Latin, Kirchain Sch, Ger, 67-68; from instr to asst prof, 70-74, assoc prof, 74-81, PROF GER LIT, COL OF THE HOLY CROSS, 81- *Mem:* MLA; Am Asn Teachers Ger. *Res:* German Renaissance and Baroque literature; reception of antiquity; East German literature. *Publ:* Auth, Thomas Murner's Latin: Some notes on the first German Aeneid, Class Folia, 72; Die Erste Deutsche Aeneis, Anton Hain, Meisenhaim, Ger, 74; From Struwwelpeter to Rotfuchs: Suggestions for using children's books in culture classes, Unterrichtspraxis, 76; Daniel Symonis Aneis - ubersetzung, Daphnis, 78; Die Literatur des Fruhhumanismus, Metzler Verlag, Stuttgart, 78; German Humanism, Twayne Publ (in press). *Mailing Add:* Dept of Mod Langs Col of the Holy Cross Worcester MA 01610

BERNSTEIN, HARRY, History. See Vol I

BERNSTEIN, JUTTA, b Berlin, Ger, Jan 6, 38; m 65; c 2. GERMAN LANGUAGE & LITERATURE. *Educ:* Case Western Res Univ, MA, 69, PhD(Ger), 73. *Prof Exp:* Instr Ger, Lake Erie Col, 65-67; vis asst prof, Clark Univ, 72-73; LECTR GER, ASSUMPTION COL, MASS, 74- *Mem:* Am Asn Teachers Ger; MLA. *Res:* Twentieth century German literature. *Publ:* Bewusstwerdung im Romanwerk der Ricarda Huch, Europäische Hochschulschriften, 77. *Mailing Add:* Assumption Col 500 Salisbury Worcester MA 01609

BERRONG, RICHARD MICHAEL, b Milwaukee, Wis, Sept 20, 51. SIXTEENTH CENTURY FRENCH LITERATURE. *Educ:* Univ Va, BA, 73; Stanford Univ, MA, 74; Cornell Univ, PhD(French), 77. *Prof Exp:* ASST PROF FRENCH, UNIV LOUISVILLE, 77- *Res:* Sixteenth century French literature. *Publ:* Auth, Genealogies and the search for an origin in the Oeuvres of Rabelais, SAtlantic Bull, 11/77; Note for the commentary on the Cinquieme livre: un pot auz roses, Romance Notes, fall 78. *Mailing Add:* Dept of Mod Lang Univ Louisville Louisville KY 40208

BERRY, EDMUND GRINDLAY, b Aberdeenshire, Scotland, Mar 12, 15; m 43; c 2. CLASSICAL PHILOLOGY. *Educ:* Queen's Univ (Ont), BA, 36, MA, 37; Univ Chicago, PhD, 40. *Prof Exp:* Lectr, 40-45, from asst prof to assoc prof, 45-58, dir summer session, 46-49, asst dean fac arts & sci, 49-51, prof, 58-80, head dept, 61-78, EMER PROF CLASSICS, UNIV MAN, 80- *Concurrent Pos:* Guggenheim fel, Harvard Univ, 51-52; mem acad panel, Can Coun, 66-71; exec, Humanities Res Coun Can, 71. *Mem:* Am Philol Asn; Class Asn Midwest & South; Hellenic Soc; Class Asn Can (pres, 70-72); Humanities Asn Can (pres, 60-62). *Res:* Greek philosophy and literature; classical background of American literature. *Publ:* Auth, Emerson's Plutarch, Harvard Univ, 61; A First Century Moralist, Trans Royal Soc Can, 66; The Poet of Love and Wine, Mosaic, 70. *Mailing Add:* 310 Dromore Ave Winnipeg MB R3M 0J5 Can

BERRY, THOMAS EDWIN, b Carbondale, Ill, Sept 19, 30; m 65. RUSSIAN LANGUAGE & LITERATURE. *Educ:* Southern Ill Univ, BS, 52; Syracuse Univ, Dipl Russ lang; Univ Ill, MA, 55; Univ Tex, PhD(Russ lit), 65. *Prof Exp:* Asst dir, Ford Found Oper Instep, Univ Chicago, Agra, India, 57-58; instr Russ lang, Long Beach City Col, 58-60; prof Russ lang & lit, Lake Forest Col, 60-61; interpreter Russ, Int Parachute Championship, Mass, 61; asst prof Russ lang & lit, Univ Calif, Irvine, 65-68; assoc prof, San Francisco State Col, 68-69; ASSOC PROF RUSS LANG & LIT, UNIV MD, COLLEGE PARK, 69- *Publ:* Auth, The Seasons Through Russian Literature, Burgess, 69; A K Tolstoy: Russian Humorist, Bethany, 72; Plots and Characters in Major Russian Fiction, Archon Bks, Vol I, Pushkin, Lermontov, Turgenev, Tolstoy, 77 & Vol II, Gogol, Goncharov, Dostoevsky, 78; Russian for Business Typewriting and Documents, Birchbark, 78; Russian English Sports Dict 80 & Information Peking (Beijing), 81, Welt Int; Spiritualism in Tsarist Society and Literature, Nordland Int Press, 82. *Mailing Add:* 6919 Carleton Terr College Park MD 20740

BERSANI, LEO, b New York, NY, Apr 16, 31. FRENCH, CRITICAL THEORY. *Educ:* Harvard Univ, BA, 52, PhD(comp lit), 58. *Prof Exp:* From instr to assoc prof French, Wellesley Col, 57-67; assoc prof Romance lang, Rutgers Univ, 67-69; prof French, 69-73; PROF FRENCH & CHMN DEPT, UNIV CALIF, BERKELEY, 73- *Concurrent Pos:* Guggenheim fel, 67-68; Nat Found for Arts award, 68; Nat Endowment for Humanities sr fel, 79-80; vis lectr, College de France, 82; Am Coun Learned Soc fel, 82-83. *Mem:* AAUP; MLA. *Res:* Nineteenth and 20th century French and American criticism and fiction. *Publ:* Auth, Marcel Proust: The Fictions of Life and of Art, Oxford Univ, 65; From Bachelard to Barthes, spring 67 & The Jamesian lie, winter 69, Partisan Rev; Balzac to Beckett: Center and Circumference in French Fiction, Oxford Univ, 70; Is there a science of literature?, Partisan Rev, 72; Le Realisme et la peur du desir, Poetique, 75; A Future for Astyanax: Character and Desire in Literature, Little, 76; Baudelaire and Freud, Univ Calif, French, Port and Japanese transl; The Death of Stephane Mallarine, Cambridge Univ, 82. *Mailing Add:* Dept of French Univ of Calif Berkeley CA 94720

BERSHAS, HENRY NORTON, b Detroit, Mich, Mar 26, 15; m 40; c 2. SPANISH. *Educ:* Wayne State Univ, AB, 38; Univ Mich, AM, 39, PhD, 46. *Prof Exp:* From instr to assoc prof, 46-66, prof, 66-81, EMER PROF SPAN, WAYNE STATE UNIV, 81- *Res:* Spanish literature of the Renaissance and Golden Age; mediaeval Spanish literature. *Publ:* Auth, Puns on Proper Names in Spanish, Wayne State Univ, 61; Pueblos en Frencia, 66, Investigable, inteligible, 72 & The use of cras in Golden Age texts, 72, Hisp Rev. *Mailing Add:* Dept of Romance & Ger Langs Wayne State Univ Detroit MI 48202

BERTMAN, STEPHEN SAMUEL, b New York, NY, July 20, 37; m 68; c 2. CLASSICS, ART HISTORY. *Educ:* NY Univ, BA, 59; Brandeis Univ, MA, 60; Columbia Univ, PhD(Greek & Latin), 65. *Prof Exp:* From actg asst prof to asst prof classics, Fla State Univ, 63-67; assoc prof, 67-77, PROF CLASS & MOD LANG, LIT & CIVILIZATIONS, UNIV WINDSOR, 77- *Concurrent Pos:* Henry Huntington Powers scholar, Am Sch Class Studies Athens, 62. *Honors & Awards:* NY Univ Founders Day Award, 59. *Mem:* Am Philol Asn; Archaeol Inst Am; Col Art Asn; Class Asn Mid W & S; Class Asn Can. *Res:* Greek and Roman literature and civilization; ancient art and archaeology; humanities. *Publ:* Auth, The Telemachy and structural symmetry, Trans & Proc Am Philol Asn, 66; Fire symbolism in Juvenal's first satire, Class J, 3/68; Art and the Romans, Coronado, 75; ed, The Conflict of Generations in Ancient Greece and Rome, Gruner, Amsterdam, 76; auth, Oral imagery in Catullus 7, Class Quart, 78; Lao-tzu, In: The People's Almanac, Doubleday, 2nd ed, 78; The challenge of coinage, J Soc Ancient Numis, 79; Technology and human values: An audiovisual bibliography, Sci & Soc Newsletter, 82. *Mailing Add:* Dept of Class & Mod Lang Univ of Windsor Windsor ON N9B 3P4 Can

BERTOCCI, ANGELO PHILIP, b Gaeta, Porto Salvo, Italy, May 26, 07; nat US; m 38; c 4. COMPARATIVE LITERATURE. *Educ:* Boston Univ, AB, 27; Harvard Univ, AM, 28; Hautes Etudes Francaises, Univ Grenoble, dipl, 29; Columbia Univ, PhD(French), 47. *Prof Exp:* Instr French, Bates Col, 30-40, prof, 40-48; prof comp lit, Boston Univ, 48-66; prof English, Univ Iowa, 66-75; RETIRED. *Concurrent Pos:* Teacher, Univ Calif, Irvine, 76. *Mem:* Am Comp Lit Asn. *Res:* French and English literature, especially the 19th and 20th centuries; criticism. *Publ:* Auth, Symbolism in Women in Love, In: Modern British Fiction, Oxford Univ, 61; Charles Du Bos and English Literature: From Symbolism to Baudelaire, Southern Ill Univ, 64; contrib, Modern French Criticism, Univ Chicago, 72. *Mailing Add:* Town Hill RRI Wolcott VT 05680

BERTRAND, MARC ANDRE, b Metz, France, July 23, 33; m; c 1. FRENCH LITERATURE. *Educ:* Univ Calif, Berkeley, MA, 61, PhD(French), 66. *Prof Exp:* From instr to asst prof, 65-71, ASSOC PROF FRENCH, STANFORD UNIV, 71- *Concurrent Pos:* Ed-in-chief, Stanford Fr Rev, 76- *Mem:* Int Asn Fr Studies; Am Asn Teachers Fr; Coun Fr Social & Cult Studies. *Res:* Contemporary French novel and criticism; intellectual history between the two World Wars. *Publ:* Auth, L'amour et la sexualite dans Candide, Fr Rev, 5/64; Jean Prevost diciple d'Alain, Mod Lang Notes, 12/65; L'annee litteraire: 1966-1967, Fr Rev, 67-68; L'oeuvre de Jean Prevost, Univ Calif, 68; co-ed, Popular Culture in France, Stanford Fr & Ital Studies, 77; auth, Parole et silence dans les Trois Contes de Flaubert, Stanford Fr Rev, fall 77; Les avatars de Lazare, Fr Rev, 4/78; Roman Counterporain et Historie, Fr Rev, 10/82. *Mailing Add:* Dept of French & Ital Stanford Univ Stanford CA 94305

BERTRAND DE MUNOZ, MARYSE, b Montreal, PQ, Nov 19, 32; m 61; c 3. COMPARATIVE & SPANISH LITERATURE. *Educ:* Univ Montreal, MA, 59, LLs, 59; Univ Paris, PhD (comp lit), 62. *Prof Exp:* Prof French lit, Externat Class Longueuil, 63-66; prof Span lit, 66-78, PROF SPAN LIT, UNIV MONTREAL, 78- *Concurrent Pos:* Investr Span lit, Coun Arts Can, 68-71 & 72-77. *Mem:* MLA; Asn Can Hispanistes; Asn Int Hispanistes; Asn Can Lit Comp; Asn Int Lit Comp. *Res:* Modern Spanish literature; literature about the Spanish Civil War. *Publ:* Auth, Bibliografia de le novela de la guerra civil espanols, La Torre, 7-9/68; La Guerre Civile Espagnole et la Literature Francaise, Didier, 72; Fuentes bibliograficas de la creacion literaria de la guerra civil espanola, Les Dossiers H, spring 75; Les poetes hispano-americains et la guerre civile espagnole Budapest, Actes du Symposium International d'Etudes Hispaniques, 8/76; Paralelo estructural entre El Jarama de Sanchez-Ferlosio y El cortejo de Otaola, Cuadernos Am, 7/77; La Pluma y la Espada La literatura del conflicto (1936-1939), Fasciculos, 77-78 & In: La guerra civil espanola, Urbion, Madrid, VI: 63-93; La Guerra Civil Espanola y la Novela (bibliografia comentada), Porrua, 78. *Mailing Add:* Dept of Span Univ of Montreal Montreal PQ H3C 3J7 Can

BESSASON, HARALDUR, b Skagafjordur, Iceland, Apr 14, 31; m 52; c 2. ICELANDIC LANGUAGE & LITERATURE. *Educ:* Univ Iceland, Cand Phil, 52, Cand Mag, 56. *Prof Exp:* Asst prof, 56-72, assoc prof, 72-79, PROF ICELANDIC, UNIV MAN, 80-, HEAD DEPT, 72- *Mailing Add:* Div of Mod Lang Univ of Man Winnipeg MB R3T 2N2 Can

BESSETTE, GERARD, b Sabrevois, Can, Feb 25, 20. FRENCH. *Educ:* Externat Classique St Croix, BA, 41; Univ Montreal, MA, 46, LittD, 50, Univ Ottawa, 82. *Prof Exp:* From instr to asst prof French, Univ Sask, 46-51; asst prof, Duquesne Univ, 51-60; from asst prof to assoc prof, 60-79, PROF FRENCH, QUEEN'S UNIV, ONT, 79- *Concurrent Pos:* Can rep, poetry sect, Olympic Games, 48. *Honors & Awards:* Prix Litteraire de la Prov de Que, 65; Prix du Gov General, 66 & 72; Prix Athanase David, 80. *Mem:* Royal Soc Can; Sov Ecrivains Can. *Res:* French and French Canadian literature. *Publ:* Auth, Le Libraire, Julliard, Paris, 60; Les Images en poesie canadienne-francaise, Beauchemin, Montreal, 60; L'incubation, Libr Deom, 65; Une Litterature en bullition, Ed du Jour, 68; De Quebec a St-Boniface, Macmillan, 68; Le Cycle, Ed du Jour, 71; La Commensale, Ed Quinze, 75; Les Anthropoides, Ed Presse, 78; Le Semestre, Ed Quebec/Amerique, 79. *Mailing Add:* Dept of French Queens Univ Kingston ON K7L 3N6 Can

BEST, EDWARD EXUM, JR, b Goldsboro, NC, May 28, 27. CLASSICS. *Educ:* Univ NC, AB, 52, MA, 54, PhD, 57. *Prof Exp:* Teaching fel, Univ NC, 55-56; from instr to asst prof classics, Univ Ariz, 56-61; asst prof, 61-71, ASSOC PROF CLASSICS, UNIV GA, 71- *Mem:* Am Philol Asn; Class Asn Mid West & South. *Res:* Latin; Greek. *Mailing Add:* Dept of Classics Univ of Ga Athens GA 30602

BEST, OTTO FERDINAND, b Steinheim, Main, Ger, July 28, 29; m; c 4. GERMAN LITERATURE. *Educ:* Univ Munich, PhD, 63. *Prof Exp:* Asst, Col Hippolyte Fontaine, Dijon, France, 52-53; ed, Insel Verlag, S Fischer Verlag, Verlag Kiepenheuer & Witscher, R Piper & Co, 54-68; lectr Ger philol, Univ Munich, 65-68; prof Ger, Univ NDak, 68-69; assoc prof, 69-71, PROF GER, UNIV MD, COLLEGE PARK, 71- *Mem:* MLA; AAUP; Am Asn Teachers Ger; Lessing Soc. *Res:* European literature of the 18th century; European literature of the 20th century; European philosophy. *Publ:* Co-ed, Die Deutsche Literatur: Ein Abris in Text und Darstellung (16 vols), Philipp Reclam Jun Stuttgart, Ger, 73-77; auth, Peter Weiss, Ungar, English ed, 76; ed, Theorie des Expresionismus, Philipp Reclam Jun Stuttgart, Ger, 76; auth, Das verbotene Glück, R Piper Co, München, Ger, 78; Abenteuer-Wonnetraum aus Flucht und Ferne, Fischer, Frankfurt, Ger, 79; ed, Uber die Dummheit der Menschen, Deutscher Taschenbuchverlag, München, Ger, 79; Das Groteske in der Dechtung, Wissenschaftliche Buchgtesellschaft, Darmstadt, Ger, 80; auth, Bertolt Brecht-Weisheit und Uberleben, Suhrkamp, Frankfurt, Ger, 82. *Mailing Add:* Dept of Ger & Slavic Lang & Lit Univ of Md College Park MD 20742

BEST, THOMAS WARING, b Charlotte, NC, Mar 10, 39; m 61; c 2. GERMAN LITERATURE. *Educ:* Duke Univ, BA, 61; Ind Univ, MA, 63, PhD (Ger), 65. *Prof Exp:* Lectr English, Univ Hamburg, 65-66; asst prof Ger, Duke Univ, 66-67; asst prof, 67-70, chmn dept, 72-74, asst dean, 75-79, ASSOC PROF GER, UNIV VA, 70- *Mem:* MLA; Am Asn Teachers Ger. *Res:* Early Dutch and German literature. *Publ:* Auth, The Humanist Ulrich von Hutten, Univ NC, 69; Eccius Dedolatus, Univ Ky, 71; Macropedius, 72, Jacob Bidermann, 75 & Reynard the Fox (in press), Twayne. *Mailing Add:* Dept of Ger Univ of Va Cocke Hall Charlottesville VA 22903

BETORET-PARIS, EDUARDO, b Lucena del Cid, Spain, Feb 21, 14; nat US; m 43. SPANISH. *Educ:* Univ Valencia, Lic, 45; Univ Kans, MA, 52, PhD, 57. *Prof Exp:* Instr Span, Mt St Scholastica Col, 48-49 & Univ Kans, 49-55; from instr to asst prof, Univ Tenn, 55-60; assoc prof, Univ Rochester, 60-65; assoc prof, 65-71, PROF SPAN, UNIV ILL, CHICAGO CIRCLE, 71- *Mem:* MLA; Am Asn Teachers Span & Port; Midwest MLA. *Res:* Nineteenth and 20th century Spanish literature; Golden Age Spanish literature; Hispanic culture. *Publ:* Auth, Valencian professional types in the works of Vicente Blasco Ibanez, Ky Foreign Lang Quart, 64; Alejandro Casona, Drama Critique, 66; El Padre Fray Bartolome de las Casas, cuatrocientos anos despues, Duquesne Hisp Rev, 67; El caso Blasco Ibanez, Hispania, 69; Mito, Leyenda e historia in El ultimo leon de Vicente Blasco Ibanez, Duquesne Hisp Rev, 71; Torreblanca: Su carta puebla, Bos Soc Castellonense Cult, 73; Introduccion a Manuel Vidal Salvador . . ., Soc Castellonense Cult, 75; Sagunto en Manuel Vidal Salvador: El Fuego de las riquezas y destruizion de Sagunto, Publ Caja de Ahorros y Socorros de Sagunto, 80. *Mailing Add:* Dept of Span Ital & Port Univ of Ill Chicago IL 60680

BETZ, FREDERICK, b New York, NY, June 29, 43; m 70. GERMAN LANGUAGE & LITERATURE. *Educ:* Columbia Univ, BA, 64; Ind Univ, MA, 67, PhD(Ger comp lit), 73. *Prof Exp:* Instr Ger, Univ Ill, Chicago Circle, 69-72; asst prof, Univ Maine, Orono, 74-78; asst prof, 78-80, ASSOC PROF GER, SOUTHERN ILL UNIV, CARBONDALE, 80- *Mem:* MLA; Am Asn Teachers Ger. *Res:* Theodor Fontane; 19th century realism and naturalism, novel and novelle; reception study and literary sociology. *Publ:* Auth, Fontane's VdS in the AAZ: Gutzkow or Roquette?, Modern Lag Notes, 72; Die Zwanglose Gesellschaft: Freundeskreis um Fontane, Jahrbuch f brandenburgische Landesgeschichte, 76; Authorship & source of song & sub-title in Fontane's FJT, German Quart, 76; Strindberg or Stauffer?: The Mann's Misquotation of Fontane, Germanic Notes, 79; contribr, DerZug nach dem Western: Aspects of Paul Lindau's Novel, Sherwood Nottingham, 79; Fontanes Irrungen, Wirrungen: zeitgenössische Rezeption, Nymphenburger Munich, 80; ed, Erläuterungen und Dokumente zu Fontanes Irrungen, Wirrungen, Reclam Stuttgart, 79; Theodor Fontane, L'Adultera, Reclam Stuttgart, 82. *Mailing Add:* Dept of Foreign Lang & Lit Southern Ill Univ Carbondale IL 62901

BEUGNOT, BERNARD, b Paris, France, July 3, 32; Can citizen; m 60; c 3. FRENCH LITERATURE. *Educ:* Sorbonne, Lic es Lett, cert gen philos & cert ancient hist, 65, Agrege, 58, DUniv, 69. *Prof Exp:* Assoc prof, 62-70, chmn dept, 65-69, PROF FRENCH, UNIV MONTREAL, 70- *Concurrent Pos:* Res grants, Ministere de l'Educ, Que, 73-77 & Can Coun, 77-78. *Honors & Awards:* Prix Halphen, Acad Francaise, 72. *Mem:* Soc Texts Fr Mod; Soc Etude XVIIe Siecle; Int Asn Fr Studies; Soc d'Hist Lit de la France. *Res:* French literature of the 17th century; French Neo-Latin literature of the 17th century; Francis Ponge. *Publ:* Auth, L'entretien au XVIIe siecle, Univ Montreal, 71; ed, J L G de Balzac entretiens (2 vols), Soc Mod Fr Texts, 72; coauth, Boileau, visages anciens, visages nouveaux, Univ Montreal, 73; auth, Dialogue, entretien et citation a l'epoque classique, Revue Can de Lit Comparee, 76; Les retraites du monoe dans le miroir Saint-Simonien, Cahiers St Simon, 76; J Anouilh, Critiques de Notretemps, Garnier, Paris, 77; Diffusion et statut de lieu commun a l'epoque classique, Etudes Francaises, 77; twenty articles in various periodicals, 77- *Mailing Add:* Dept of French Univ of Montreal Montreal PQ H3C 3J7 Can

BEVERLEY, JOHN R, b Caracas, Venezuela, Jan 26, 43; US citizen; m 67. HISPANIC & COMPARATIVE LITERATURE. *Educ:* Princeton Univ, BA, 64; Univ Wis, MA, 66; Univ Calif, San Diego, PhD(Span), 72. *Prof Exp:* Asst prof, 72-75, ASSOC PROF HISPANIC STUDIES, UNIV PITTSBURGH, 75- *Concurrent Pos:* Mem adv comt, Mod Lang Asn, 72-75; adv fac area studies, Ctr Latin Am Studies, Pittsburgh, 77-; vis prof Hispanic studies, Univ Minn, 78. *Mem:* MLA; Am Fedn Teachers; Inst Study Ideologies & Lit. *Res:* Sixteenth and seventeenth century Spanish literature and society; Gongora; Marxist literary methods (text and ideology). *Publ:* Auth, Soledad Primera: lines 1-61, Mod Lang Notes, 73; The dramatic logic of El Delinaiente Honrado, Revista Hispanica Moderna, 74; Reflections on Galdos' El Abuelo, Anales Galdosianos, 75; En torno a un libro de Hernan Vidal, Revista Ibero-americana, 78; Structure as figure in the Soledades, Dispositio, 78; The languages of contradiction: aspects of the Soledades, Ideologies & Lit, 78; Soledades: Edicion Critica, Ed Castalia, 78; The Architecture of Time: Gongoras' Soledades, NC Tomance Monogr, 79. *Mailing Add:* Dept of Hispanic Lang & Lit Univ of Pittsburgh Pittsburgh PA 15260

BEVINGTON, GARY LOYD, b Ft Madison, Iowa, Feb 3, 44; c 2. LINGUISTICS. *Educ:* Middlebury Col, AB, 66, MA, 67; Univ Mass, Amherst, PhD(ling), 70. *Prof Exp:* Asst prof ling, Univ Mass Amherst, 70-71; asst prof, 71-75, assoc prof, 75-80, PROF LING, NORTHEASTERN ILL UNIV, 80- *Concurrent Pos:* Humboldt Res fel & lectr, Univ Munich, 75. *Mem:* Ling Soc Am; Soc Albany Studies. *Res:* Albanian language; phonological theory; Balkan linguistics. *Publ:* Auth, Albanian Phonology, Harrassowitz, 74; Die albanische betonung im lichte der generativen phonologie, Akten Int Albanologischen Kolloquiums Innsbruck 1972 Gednachtnis Norbert Jokl, 77; A note on stress reduction in Albanian, CLS Bk Squibs, 77; Relativization in Albanian dialects, Folia Slavica, 79. *Mailing Add:* Dept of Ling Northeastern Ill Univ Chicago IL 60625

BEYE, CHARLES ROWAN, b Iowa City, Iowa, Mar 19, 30. CLASSICAL PHILOLOGY. *Educ:* State Univ Iowa, BA, 52; Harvard Univ, MA, 54, PhD(class philol), 60. *Prof Exp:* Instr classics, Wheaton Col (Mass), 55-57 & Yale Univ, 57-60; asst prof, Stanford Univ, 60-66; assoc prof, 66-68, chmn dept, 68-72, PROF CLASSICS, BOSTON UNIV, 68- *Concurrent Pos:* Olivia James traveling fel, Archaeol Inst Am, 63-64; mem managing comt, Am Sch Class Studies Athens, 66 & Am Acad Rome, 67-; Nat Endowment Humanities sr fel, 71-72; sr res fel, Am Sch Class Studies, Athens, 78-79. *Mem:* Am Philol Asn. *Res:* Homeric epic; later Greek epic; Greek tragedy. *Publ:* Auth, The Iliad, The Odyssey and the Epic Tradition, Doubleday, 66 & MacMillan, England, 68; Euripides Alcestis, Prentice-Hall, 69; Jason as love-hero in Apollonios' Argonautika, Greek, Roman & Byzantine Studies, 69; The rhythm of Hesiod's Works and Days, Harvard Studies Class Philol, 72; Ancient Greek Literature and Society, Doubleday, 75; Epic and Romance in Apollonius' Argonautica, Southern Ill Univ Press, 82. *Mailing Add:* Dept of Classics Boston Univ Boston MA 02215

BEYER, THOMAS R, JR, b Brooklyn, NY, May 6, 47; m 73; c 2. RUSSIAN LITERATURE & LANGUAGE. *Educ:* Georgetown Univ, BS, 69; Univ Kans, MA, 72, MPhil, 73, PhD(Slavic lang & lit), 74. *Prof Exp:* Asst dir, Georgetown Univ Group, Leningrad State Univ, 69; escort & interpreter, Soviet deleg in US, Coun Int Educ Exchange, 69-74; vis asst prof, Univ Ill, Urbana-Champaign, 74-75; dir, Kans Univ Group, Leningrad State Univ, 75; actg chmn, Dept Russ & dean, Russ Sch, 77-78, dir, Middlebury Col in Moscow, 78-79, ASSOC PROF RUSS & COORDR FIRST YR RUSS, RUSS SCH, MIDDLEBURY COL, 75-, DEAN, RUSS SCH, 81-, CHMN, DEPT RUSS, 82- *Concurrent Pos:* Escort & interpreter, Am tourists in USSR, Russian Adventure Tours, 72-75. *Publ:* Auth, Andrej Belyj's The Magic of Words and The Silver Dove, Slavi and East Europ J, winter 78; For those wishing to improve their knowledge of Russian, Russian Lang J, spring 79;

Administering an undergraduate program in Moscow: Roles and responsibilities of the resident director, ADFL Bull, 5/80; Where to find the answers to questions on Russian grammar, Russian Lang J, spring 80; Andrej Belvj's reminiscences of Rudolf Steiner: A review article, Slavic & East Europ J, winter 81; The christened Chinaman, Russian Lit, 81; transl, Andrei Belvi, A Star, fall 81 & Azures, fall 81, J Anthroposophy. *Mailing Add:* 3A College St Middlebury VT 05753

BEYL, DAVID WINDELL, b Portland, Ore, July 28, 45. LINGUISTICS, PORTUGUESE. *Educ:* Portland State Univ, BA, 68; Georgetown Univ, MS, 74, PhD(ling), 78. *Prof Exp:* Comput linguist mach trans, Pan Am Health Orgn, 75-77; ASST PROF LING, UNIV MD, 77- *Concurrent Pos:* Prof lectr English as second lang, Am Univ, 75- *Mem:* MLA; Teachers English as Second Lang; Am Teachers Foreign Lang; Ling Soc Am. *Res:* Computational linguistics; machine translation; photography and linguistics; phonology and poetry. *Publ:* Auth, A distinctive feature analysis of the Portuguese phonological system, Georgetown Univ Working Papers Lang & Ling, 75. *Mailing Add:* Dept of English Univ of Md Taliaferro Hall College Park MD 20742

BEYM, RICHARD, b Oak Park, Ill, June 27, 21; m 47; c 2. LANGUAGE TRAINING & ADMINISTRATION. *Educ:* Univ Ill, AB, 43, AM, 48, PhD(Span ling), 52. *Prof Exp:* Instr Span, Univ Ill, 52-53 & Univ Wis, 53-57; sci linguist, Foreign Serv Inst, US Dept State, 57-60, training off lang, US Agency Int Develop Mission, Arg, 60-62, materials off, English Teaching Div, US Inform Agency, 62-64; educ specialist, Defense Lang Inst, US Dept Army, 64-66; mem fac Span & ling, US Dept Agr Grad Sch, 66-68; Fulbright prog fac adv, 69-75, PROF SPAN & LING, CALIF STATE UNIV, COMINGUEZ HILLS, 68- *Concurrent Pos:* Fulbright lectr, Egypt, 54-55; mem, Nat Fed Mod Lang Teachers Asn; sr scientist, HumRRO, George Washington Univ, 66-68. *Mem:* Am Asn Teachers Span & Port; Ling Soc Am; Teachers English to Speakers Other Lang; Am Coun Teachers Foreign Lang. *Res:* Teacher training; teaching English as a foreign language; self instructional programmed Spanish. *Publ:* Auth, Two Phases of the Linguistics Category of Emphasis on Colloquial Spanish, Orbis, 54; Porteno /s/ and . . . Variants, Lingua, 63; El concepto de persona enfrentado con indicaciones de espacio en espanol, Yelmo, Madrid, 2-3/72; Psycholinguistic and Sociolinguistic Perceptions of Aculturated Morphophoemic Options, Quaderni di Semantica, Bologna, 81. *Mailing Add:* 28 Coraltree Ln Rolling Hill Estates CA 90274

BEYNEN, G(IJSBERTUS) KOOLEMANS, b Surabaya, Indonesia, June 12, 35; US citizen; c 5. SLAVIC BIBLIOGRAPHY & FOLKLORE. *Educ:* Stanford Univ, PhD(Slavic ling), 67; State Univ NY, Geneseo, MLS, 74. *Prof Exp:* Asst prof Russian, Emporia State Univ, 63-66; asst prof Slavic ling, Fordham Univ, 66-69; asst prof Russian ling, Univ Rochester, 69-73; SLAVIC BIBLIOGR, OHIO STATE UNIV, 74- *Mem:* MLA; Am Asn Teachers Slavic & East Europ Lang; Am Libr Asn; Am Anthrop Asn; Am Folklore Soc. *Res:* Courtly literature; Russian linguistics. *Publ:* Auth, Semantic difference between No and Odnoko, Slavic & East Europ J, summer 76; The Slavic animal language tales, Am Contrib 8th Int Congr Slavists, Slavica Publ, 78. *Mailing Add:* 686 Neil Ave Columbus OH 43215

BEZDEK, VALADIMIR, b Rovensko, Czech, Mar 23, 09; m 37; c 2. GERMAN. *Educ:* Charles Univ, Prague, PhD, 39. *Prof Exp:* Prof gymnasiums, Czech, 33-39; lectr, Loyola Univ, Ill, 39-42; asst prof, 46-71, assoc prof, 71-79, EMER ASSOC PROF GERMAN, WAYNE STATE UNIV, 80- *Mem:* Am Asn Teachers Ger; MLA; Int Ver Ger Sprach-und Literaturwiss. *Res:* German & Slavic Philology. *Publ:* Transl: French, Spanish, German, Pergande Publ; German at Sight, Crowell. *Mailing Add:* Dept of German Lang & Lit Wayne State Univ Detroit MI 48202

BEZIRGAN, NAJM A, b Baghdad, Iraq, Apr 12, 31; m 60; c 3. PHILOSOPHY, LINGUISTICS. *Educ:* Univ Baghdad, BA, 56; Univ Manchester, PhD(philos), 65. *Prof Exp:* Asst prof philos, Univ Baghdad, 65-66; asst prof ling & philos, 67-76, PROF AFRICAN & ORIENT LANG & LIT, UNIV TEX, AUSTIN, 76- *Concurrent Pos:* Asst ed, Oxford English-Arabic Dict, Oxford Univ Press, 66-67. *Mem:* Am Asn Teachers Arabic; Mid East Studies Asn; Am Orient Soc. *Res:* Westernization of contemporary Arabic thought. *Publ:* Auth, Some linguistic problems of Arabic students in England, Al-Mu'altim Al-Jadid, winter 66; coauth, Elementary Modern Standard Arabic, Inter-Univ Prog Comt, 68. *Mailing Add:* Dept of African & Orient Lang & Lit Univ of Tex Sta Austin TX 78712

BHATIA, TEJ K, b Multan, Pakistan, Oct 19, 45; India citizen; m 77. LINGUISTICS, INDIA LITERATURE & LINGUISTICS. *Educ:* Univ Delhi, India, BA Hons, 65; Univ Ill, Urbana-Champaign, MA, 72, PhD(ling), 78. *Prof Exp:* Teaching asst ling, Univ Ill, 70-76; lectr Hindi & ling, Univ BC, 76-78; ASST PROF HINDI & LING, SYRACUSE UNIV, 78- *Concurrent Pos:* Assessor res proposals ling, Shastri Indo-Can Inst, McGill Univ, 77; consult, NSF & Nat Endowment for Humanities proj; appointed fel, Inst Appl Ling, Syracuse Univ, 79-82; ed & secy, NY State Coun Ling, 80; guest ed, Progression Second Lang Learning, 81; mem, Nat Planning comt, SAsian Lang Roundtable, 81; dir, Int Conf SAsian Lang & Lit, 82. *Mem:* Ling Soc Am; Ling Soc India; Am Orient Soc; Am Teachers Uncommonly Tuahgt Lang; PEN Club. *Res:* South-Asian linguistics, syntax-semantics and phonology; sociolinguistics; phonetics. *Publ:* Coauth, Nasalization in Hindi: A reconsideration, Papers Ling, 72; auth, A computational investigation on the acquisition of perceptual cues of aspirated consonants in Hindi, Proc Int Conf Comput & Math Ling, Rome, 73; The coexisting answering systems and the role of presuppositions, implications and expectations in Hindi simple yes/no questions, Tenth Regional Meeting, Chicago Ling Soc, 74; Negation through question in modern Hindi: Another look, Lang Sci, 12/75; contribr, On the notion of subjecthood in Hindi, Punjabi and Kashmiri, In: The Notion of Subject in South Asian Languages, Univ Wis-Madison, 76; auth, On the predictive role of the recent theories of aspiration, Phonetica, 76; coauth, The emerging dialect conflict in Hindi, Int J Sociol Lang, 78. *Mailing Add:* Dept Foreign Lang & Lit Syracuse Univ Syracuse NY 13210

BIASIN, BIAN-PAOLO, b Reggio Emilia, Italy, Nov 7, 33. ROMANCE STUDIES. *Educ:* Syracuse Univ, MA, 58; Johns Hopkins Univ, PhD(romance lang), 64. *Prof Exp:* Lectr Ital lit, Syracuse Univ Semester Italy, 39-62; from asst prof to assoc prof, Cornell Univ, 64-73; PROF ITAL LIT, UNIV TEX, AUSTIN, 73- *Concurrent Pos:* Assoc ed, Ital Quart, Univ Calif, 61-74 & Forum Italicum, 78-; mem adv bd, Perspectives Contemp Lit, 75- *Mem:* MLA; Am Asn Teachers Ital; Asn Int Studi Ling & Lit Ital; Am Comp Lit Asn; Semiotic Soc Am. *Res:* Modern and contemporary Italian literature; literary criticism; history of ideas. *Publ:* Auth, The Smile of the Gods: A Thematic Study of Cesare Pavese's Works, Cornell Univ, 68; Literary Diseases: Theme and Metaphor in the Italian Novel, Univ Tex, Austin, 75; Also in Italian: Malattie Letterarie, Milan, Bompiani, 76. *Mailing Add:* Dept of French & Ital Univ of Tex Austin TX 78712

BICKERTON, DEREK, b Bebington, Eng, Mar 25, 26; m; c 3. LINGUISTICS. *Educ:* Cambridge Univ, BA, 49, MA, 68, PhD(ling), 76; Univ Leeds, dipl ling, 67. *Prof Exp:* Lectr English, Univ Col Cape Coast, 64-66; sr lectr ling, Univ Guyana, 67-71; lectr, Univ Lancaster, 71-72; assoc prof, 72-76, PROF LING, UNIV HAWAII, MANOA, 76- *Concurrent Pos:* Prin investr, Nonstandard Hawaiian English Proj, 73-75 & Origins Creole Syntax Proj, 75-78. *Mem:* Caribbean Ling Soc. *Res:* Linguistic variation; pidgin and Creole languages; language universals. *Publ:* Auth, Inherent variability and variable rules, Found Lang, 71; The nature of a Creole continuum, Language, 73; Dynamics of a Creole System, Cambridge Univ, 75; Pidgin and Creole studies, Ann Rev Anthrop, 76; contribr, Pidgin and Creole Linguistics, Univ Ind, 77; Theoretical Orientations in Creole Studies, Acad Press, 80; auth, Roots of Language, Karoma, 81. *Mailing Add:* Dept of Ling Univ Hawaii Manoa HI 96822

BICKNESE, GUNTHER, b Gütersloh, Ger, Feb 16, 26; US citizen; m 57; c 3. LITERATURE & LINGUISTICS. *Educ:* Univ Marburg, DPhil, 53. *Prof Exp:* Instr Ger & English, Graham-Eckes Sch, Palm Beach, Fla, 58-60; asst prof Ger, Southwestern at Memphis, 60-63; assoc prof mod lang, Millersville State Col & resident dir jr year, Marburg, Ger, 63-66; assoc prof, 66-70, PROF GER & CHMN DEPT, AGNES SCOTT COL, 70- *Mem:* SAtlantic Mod Lang Asn; Am Asn Teachers Ger; Am Coun Teachers Foreign Lang. *Res:* Twentieth century German literature; evaluating study abroad programs. *Publ:* Auth, Akademische Programme für undergraduates, 11/65 & Zur Rolle Amerikas in Max Frischs Homo Faber, 1/69, Ger Quart; Study abroad: A comparative test of attitudes and opinions & As the students see it: The junior year abroad reassessed, Foreign Lang Ann, 3/74; coauth, Elementary German, Houghton Mifflin, 3rd ed, 76 & suppl workbk, 77; transl, Widerstand, (Ingrid Greenburger, A Private Treason), Rowohlt, Ger, 81; auth, Persuading participants to speak German, World Higher Educ Communique, Vol 3, No 4. *Mailing Add:* Dept of Ger Agnes Scott Col Decatur GA 30030

BIDA, CONSTANTINE, b Lviv, Ukraine; Can citizen. SLAVIC LINGUISTICS & LITERATURES. *Educ:* Univ Vienna, PhD, 46. *Prof Exp:* Res asst, Inst Slavic Studies, Univ Vienna, 44-45; lectr Slavic lit, 52-57, from asst prof to assoc prof, 57-65, chmn dept Slavic studies, 61-75, PROF SLAVIC LIT & LING, UNIV OTTAWA, 65- *Mem:* Am Comp Lit Asn; Asn Can Slavists (pres, 60-61); MLA; Mod Humanities Res Asn; Can Ling Asn. *Res:* Comparative literature; Shakespeare's influence on Slavic literature, especially translations, interpretation, motifs and bibliography. *Publ:* Auth, Shakespeare in Polish and Russian classicism and romanticism, Slavic & East Europ Studies, 61; Shakespeare and national traits in Slavic literatures, In: Proc Cong Int Comp Lit Asn, Mouton, The Hague, 66; Poesie du Quebec Contemporain, Libr Deom, Montreal, 68; Lesya Ukrainka, Univ Toronto, 68; A quest for the dramatic, In: Symbolae in Honrem, Munich, 71; De joannitio galatovskyj eiusque Clavi Cognitionis, 75, I Galatovsky and his Key of Understanding, 75 & Kievan Grammar of 1705, 78, Ed Univ Cath Ucrainorum S Clementis Popae, Rome. *Mailing Add:* Dept of Slavic Studies & Mod Lang Univ of Ottawa Ottawa ON K1N 6N5 Can

BIEBER, KONRAD FERDINAND, b Berlin, Ger, Mar 24, 16; nat US; m 39; c 1. FRENCH. *Educ:* Univ Paris, LLett, 38; Yale Univ, PhD, 53. *Prof Exp:* Teacher, High Schs, France, 41-43 & 45-47; instr French, Yale Univ, 48-53; from asst prof to prof, Conn Col, 53-68, chmn dept French & Ital, 60-68; PROF FRENCH & COMP LIT, STATE UNIV NY STONY BROOK, 68- *Concurrent Pos:* Guggenheim fel, 57-58; rep United Nations, Movement against Racism & Anti-Semitism, 76- *Honors & Awards:* Chevalier des Palmes Academiques, 70. *Mem:* MLA; Am Asn Teachers Fr; Int Comp Lit Asn; Am Comp Lit Asn. *Res:* Franco-German literary relations; 18th century French thought; literature of two world wars. *Publ:* Auth, L'Allemagne Vue par les Ecrivains de la Resistance Francaise, Droz, Geneva, 54; Resistance literature, In: Dictionary of French Literature, Philos Libr, 58; Jean Gione's Greece: A kinship in distant ages, In: The Persistent Voice, Essays on Hellenism in French Literature in Honor of Professor Henri M Peyre, NY Univ, 71; Simone de Beauvoir, Twayne, 79. *Mailing Add:* Dept of French & Ital State Univ of NY Stony Brook NY 11794

BIEDER, MARYELLEN WOLFE, b Traverse City, Mich, Aug 13, 42; m 65. SPANISH LITERATURE. *Educ:* Lawrence Col, BA, 64; Ind Univ, MA, 66; Univ Minn, PhD(Span), 73. *Prof Exp:* Asst prof, Syracuse Univ, 73-74 & State Univ NY Albany, 74-76; asst prof, 76-82, ASSOC PROF SPANISH, IND UNIV, 82- *Mem:* MLA; Am Asn Teachers Span & Port; Midwest Mod Lang Asn. *Res:* Contemporary 19th-20th century Spanish literature; novel; drama. *Publ:* Auth, A case of altered identity: Two editions of Juan Goytisolo's Senas de identidad, Mod Lang Notes, 3/74; Capitulation: Marriage, not freedom--a study of Emilio Pardo Bazan's Memorias de un solteron and Galdos Tristana, Symposium, summer 76; Narrative Perspective in Two Novels of Francisco Ayala, Studies Roman Lang & Lit, 79; The modern woman on the Spanish stage: The contributions of Gaspar and Dicenta, Estreno, fall 81; De Senas de identidad a Makbara: Estrategias narrativas en las novelas de Juan Goytisolo, 7-8/81 & co-ed, La novela en espanol, hoy, 7-8/81, Rev Iberoamericana; The Woman in the Garden: The Problem of Identity in the Novels of Merce Rodoreda, Actes del Segon Col-loqui d'Estudis Catalans a Nord-America, 82. *Mailing Add:* Dept of Span & Port Ind Univ Bloomington IN 47401

BIELER, ARTHUR, b Vienna, Austria, Aug 1, 21; US citizen; m 42. FRENCH. *Educ:* NY Univ BA, 44; Middlebury Col, MA, 51; Univ Paris, France, DUniv, 53. *Prof Exp:* Instr French, Oglethorpe Col, 54-56, from asst prof to prof, 58-68; assoc prof, 68-74, PROF FRENCH, YORK COL, NY, 74- *Concurrent Pos:* Nat Defense Inst vis prof, Emory Univ Grad Sch, 60-62; Dept Health, Educ & Welfare grant, 67-68; consult, Oglethorpe Col, 68- *Mem:* MLA; Am Asn Teachers Fr. *Res:* History of French language; comparative linguistics; Stendhal. *Publ:* Auth, La mort de l'imparfait du subjunctif, French Rev, 2/57; La bataille de Waterloo vue par Stendhal et par Hugo, Stendhal Club, 63; La couleur dans Salammbo, French, Rev, 2/60; coauth, Perspectives de France, 68, rev ed, 71 & Workbook & Teachers Manual, 68, Prentice-Hall; auth, A Descriptive Study of Subjunctive Usage in Contempory French, ERIC Documents Reprod Serv, 69; coauth, Actualite et avenir, Prentice-Hall, 75. *Mailing Add:* York Col City Univ of New York Jamaica NY 11451

BIEN, GLORIA, b Lanchow, China, Dec 24, 40; US citizen; m 79. COMPARATIVE LITERATURE. *Educ:* Univ Calif, Berkeley, BA, 62, MA, 65, Univ Wash, PhD (comp lit), 73. *Prof Exp:* Teacher French, The Bishop's Sch, 65-67; asst prof Chinese, Conn Col, 74-77; vis asst prof Chinese & comp lit, Ind Univ, Bloomington, 77-78; asst prof Chinese, Conn Col, 78-80; VIS ASST PROF CHINESE, UNIV ORE, 81- *Concurrent Pos:* Am Asn Univ Women fel, 80-81. *Mem:* Am Comp Lit Asn; Chinese Lang Teachers Asn; Asn Asian Studies; MLA; Philol Asn Pac Coast. *Res:* French and Chinese literary relations. *Publ:* Auth, The Shih Ching in French literature, Tamkang Rev, 75; transl, A Bannerman at the teahouse, Renditions, 75; auth, Chinese influence on Victor Segalen's poetics, Tamkang Rev, 76; Aspects of Taoism in Victor Segalen's Steles, Pac Coast Philol, 10/78; contribr, Victor Segalen, Critical Bibliog French Lit, 78; Columbia Dictionary of Modern European Literature, 80; auth, Modern Chinese poetry: Three recent studies, J Chinese Lang Teachers Assoc, 5/81; Images of women in Ping Hsin's fiction, Univ Ore Occasional Papers Ser (in press). *Mailing Add:* Dept of East Asian Lang & Lit Univ of Ore Eugene OR 97403

BIEN, PETER ADOLPH, English. See Vol II

BIETER, FREDERIC ARNOLD, b Heron Lake, Minn, June 6, 05. CLASSICAL PHILOLOGY. *Educ:* Col St Thomas, AB, 26; Cath Univ Am, STB, 30, AM, 33, PhD, 38. *Prof Exp:* Asst prof class lang, Col St Thomas, 35-39, prof, 39-80, chmn dept foreign lang, 41-73; RETIRED. *Mem:* Am Philol Asn; Mediaeval Acad Am; Class Asn Mid West & South. *Res:* Mediaeval Latin studies. *Mailing Add:* Dept of Foreign Langs Col of St Thomas St Paul MN 55105

BIGGS, BRUCE GRANDISON, b NZ, Sept 4, 21; m 45; c 3. LINGUISTICS. *Educ:* Univ NZ, BA, 52, MA, 55; Ind Univ, PhD(ling), 57. *Prof Exp:* Jr lectr Maori studies, Univ Auckland, 52-54, lectr, 54-57, sr lectr, 58-63, assoc prof, 65; sr specialist ling, East-West Ctr, Univ Hawaii, 64; prof, Univ Hawaii, 67-69; head dept anthrop, 72-77, PROF LING, UNIV AUCKLAND, 69- *Concurrent Pos:* Nat Inst Mental Health, Am Philos Soc & Wenner-Gren Anthrop Found grants, 59-60; assoc in anthrop, Bishop Mus, Honolulu, 63; ed, Polynesian Soc J, 63-67; NZ Univ Grants Comt grant, 64; Nat Sci Found grant, 68. *Mem:* Ling Soc Am; Polynesian Soc (pres, 79); fel Royal Soc NZ. *Res:* Descriptive and comparative linguistics in Oceania; anthropology and ethnology of the Maori. *Publ:* Auth, Structure of New Zealand Maori, Anthrop Ling, 61; Direct and Indirect Inheritance in Rotuman, Lingua, 65; coauth, Proto-Polynesian Wordlist I, Ling Soc, NZ, 66; auth, English-Maori Dictionary, Reed, 66; The Past Twenty Years in Polynesian Linguistics, In: Polynesian Culture History, Bishop Mus, Honolulu, 67; Coauth, Readings in Maori, 67 & auth, Let's Learn Maori, Reed, NZ, 68; The Polynesian Languages, Current Trends in Ling, 71; History of Polynesian Phonology, Pac Ling, 78; Complete English-Maori Dict, 81. *Mailing Add:* Dept of Anthrop Univ of Auckland Private Bag Auckland New Zealand

BIGGS, PENELOPE PARKMAN, Classical Languages. See Vol II

BIGGS, ROBERT DALE, b Pasco, Wash, June 13, 34. ASSYRIOLOGY. *Educ:* Eastern Wash State Col, BA, 56, Johns Hopkins Univ, PhD(Assyriol), 62. *Prof Exp:* Res assoc Assyriol, Orient Inst, 63-64, from asst prof to assoc prof, 64-72, PROF ASSYRIOL, UNIV CHICAGO, 72- *Concurrent Pos:* Fel, Baghdad Sch, Am Schs Orient Res, 62-63; assoc ed, Assyrian Dictionary, 64-; ed, J Near Eastern Studies, 71- *Mem:* Am Orient Soc; Archaeol Inst Am. *Res:* Babylonian and Assyrian languages; Sumerian language. *Publ:* Auth, The Abu Salabikh tablets: A preliminary survey, J Cuneiform Studies, 66; Semitic names in the Fara Period, Orientalia, 67; SA ZI GA: Ancient Mesopotamian Potency Incantations, J J Augustin, 67; An esoteric Babylonian commentary, Rev Assyriologie, 68; coauth, Cuneiform Texts from Nippur: The Eighth and Ninth Seasons, Univ Chicago, 69; auth, Inscriptions from al-Hiba-Lagash: The First and Second Seasons, 76 & co-ed, Seals and Sealing in the Ancient Near East, 77, Undena, Malibu; coauth, Nippur II: The North Temple and Sounding E, Univ Chicago, 78. *Mailing Add:* Orient Inst Univ of Chicago 1155 E 58th St Chicago IL 60637

BIHARI, STEPHEN T, b Rev, Hungary, Sept 30, 23; Can citizen; m 59; c 2. FRENCH LITERATURE. *Educ:* Eötvös Lorand, Budapest, MA, 45, LLd, 46, PhD(hist), 49. *Prof Exp:* Instr lang & hist for adults high sch, Hungary, 42-44; lectr hist & lit, mil instr & spec appointments, govt, 46-48; private res, 52-56; teacher high sch, Can, 60-64; PROF FRENCH LIT, ASHLAND COL, 64- *Concurrent Pos:* ed, lit mag, 48-49. *Mem:* Archaeol Inst Am; MLA. *Res:* Literature; history; art. *Publ:* Auth, Literature, History in America (bi-weekly radio prog), Ashland Col, 65-66. *Mailing Add:* Dept of French Ashland Col Ashland OH 44805

BILL, VALENTINE TSCHEBOTARIOFF, b Pavlovsk, Russia, Jan 4, 09. RUSSIAN HISTORY & LITERATURE. *Educ:* Univ Berlin, PhD, 36. *Prof Exp:* Res asst, Inst Advan Studies, Princeton, NJ, 39-44; lectr Russ, Princeton Univ, 46-74; RETIRED. *Concurrent Pos:* Adj asst prof Russ hist, grad sch arts & sci, NY Univ, 48-54. *Mem:* Am Asn Teachers Slavic Lang. *Res:* Circular frontier; national feudalism in Muscovy; Anton Chekhov. *Publ:* Auth, The Dead Souls of Russia's Merchant World; The Forgotten Class--The Russian Bourgeoisie, Praeger, 59; The Russian People--A Reader on Their History and Culture, Univ Chicago, 59, 65 & 74; Introduction to Russian Syntax, Holt, 72; Christian elements in Chekhov's fiction, In: Festschrift Honoring Father G Florovsky, NY Univ, 73. *Mailing Add:* 26 Alexander St Princeton NJ 08540

BILLICK, DAVID JOSEPH, b Toledo, Ohio, May 19, 47; m 73. SPANISH LITERATURE BIBLIOGRAPHY. *Educ:* Univ Toledo, BA, 69, MA, 71; Univ Iowa, PhD(Span), 76. *Prof Exp:* Instr, Univ Iowa, 76-77; asst prof Span, Rutgers Univ, 77-80; ASSOC ED, HISPANIA, 76- *Concurrent Pos:* Libr asst, Univ Mich, 81- *Mem:* Am Asn Teachers Span & Port; MLA; Nat Womens Studies Asn; Am Libr Asn. *Res:* Women in Hispanic literature; Jose de Espronceda; 19th century Spanish literature. *Publ:* Auth, El Duque de Rivas, teorico de la poesia romantica en Espana, Abside, Mexico, 75; Women in Hispanic literature: A checklist of Doctoral dissertations and Master's theses, 1905-1975, Women Studies Abstracts, 77; Espronceda, Ensyista, Abside, Mexico, 78; Angle de saavedra, el duque de rivas, a checklist of criticism, 1927-1978, Bull Bibliog, 79; Graduate research on Alfonso X, La Coronica, 79; Misogyny in eca de Queiroz cousin Bazilio, CLA J, 80; Jose de Espronceda, an annotated bibliography 1834-1980, Garland, 81; Pio Baroja, a checklist of graduate research, 1923-1980, Bull Bibliog, 82. *Mailing Add:* Grad Libr Ref Dept Univ of Mich Ann Arbor MI 48109

BILLIGMEIER, JON-CHRISTIAN, US citizen. PHILOLOGY & LINGUISTICS, ANCIENT HISTORY. *Educ:* Univ Calif, BA, 66, MA, 68, PhD, 76. *Prof Exp:* Teaching asst western civilization, Univ Calif, Santa Barbara, 71-74, lectr, 74-75; instr, Santa Barbara City Col, 77-79; asst prof, Classics Dept, Johns Hopkins Univ, 80-82. *Concurrent Pos:* Jr fel, Ctr Hellenic Studies, Washington, DC, 79-80; mem, Nat Endowment for the Humanities Teaching Sem, 80. *Res:* Epigraphy; Bronze Age civilization and archaeology; mythology. *Publ:* Auth, Toward a decipherment of Cypro-Minoan, AJA, 76; The origin of the dual reflex of initial consonantal (in Greek), J Indo-Europ Studies, 76; Origin of the Greek word Phoinix, 77 & Troy, Taruisa and the Etruscans, 77, Talanta; A contribution toward identification of the language contained in the Cypro-Minoan II inscriptions from Enkomi, Colloguium Mycenaeum, Univ de Neuchatel, Switz, 79; coauth (with J Turner), The Socio-economic roles of women in Mycenaean Greece: A brief survey from evidence of the linear B tablets, Women's Studies, 81; Origin and function of the Naukraroi at Athens: An etymological and historical explanation, TAPA, 81; Kadmos and Danaos: A Study of Near Eastern Influence in Mycenaean Greece, J C Gieben & Co, Neth, 82. *Mailing Add:* 398 Stevens Rd Santa Barbara CA 93105

BILLS, GARLAND DEE, b Hico, Tx, May 2, 38; m 68; c 1. LINGUISTICS. *Educ:* Univ Tex, Arlington, BA, 62; Univ Tex, Austin, PhD(ling), 69. *Prof Exp:* Asst prof Span, 69-74, ASSOC PROF SPAN & LING, UNIV NMEX, 74-, CHMN LING DEPT, 76- *Mem:* Ling Soc Am; AAUP; Am Asn Teachers Span & Port. *Res:* Linguistic theory; Spanish linguistics; American Indian languages. *Publ:* Coauth, An Introduction to Spoken Bolivian Quechua, Univ Tex, 69; contrib, The Quechua directional verbal suffix, Papers Andean Ling, 1/72; ed, Southwest Areal Linguistics, San Diego State Univ, 74; auth, On case in Quechua, Papers Andean Ling, 75; coauth, Spanish and English of United States Hispanos, Ctr Applied Ling, 75; contrib, Studies in Southwest Spanish, Newbury House, 76. *Mailing Add:* Dept of Ling Univ of NMex Albuquerque Albuquerque NM 87131

BILOKUR, BORYS, b USSR, Nov 30, 31; US citizen; m 62; c 2. RUSSIAN & EAST SLAVIC LITERATURE. *Educ:* Temple Univ, BA, 59; Univ Ill, Urbana, MA, 61, PhD(Russ), 68. *Prof Exp:* Asst prof Russ, Northern Ill Univ, 65-66; asst prof, 67-72, ASSOC PROF RUSS, UNIV CONN, 72- *Concurrent Pos:* Consult selected issues, Choice Mag, 68-73. *Mem:* MLA; Northeast Mod Lang Asn; Am Asn Teachers Slavic & E Europ Lang. *Publ:* Auth, Statistical observations on Tiutchev's poetry, fall 70 & Folklore devices in Tiutchev's poetry, 72, Slavic & E Europ J; Concordance to Tyutchevs Poetry, Brown Univ, 75. *Mailing Add:* Dept of Ger & Slavic Langs Univ of Conn Storrs CT 06268

BILYEU, ELBERT E, b Spokane, Mo, May 17, 30; m 52; c 5. SPANISH LITERATURE. *Educ:* Southwest Mo State Col, BSEd, 55; Univ Colo, Boulder, PhD(Span lit), 68. *Prof Exp:* Instr Span, Purdue Univ, 58-61, asst prof, 62-63; lectr, Univ Colo, 63-68, assoc prof, 68-70; chmn dept, 70-80, PROF SPAN, CENT WASH STATE COL, 70- *Mem:* MLA; Am Asn Teachers Span & Port; Am Coun Teaching Foreign Lang. *Res:* Contemporary Spanish drama; the drama of Alfonso Sastre; existentialism and contemporary Spanish drama. *Publ:* Auth, An analysis of the Pimsleur proficiency tests for Spanish, J Educ Measurement, spring 69; Escuadra hacia la muerte--an existentialist interpretation, Proc Pac Northwest Coun Foreign Lang, spring 74. *Mailing Add:* Dept of Foreign Lang Cent Wash State Col Ellensburg WA 98926

BING, JANET MUELLER, b Oak Park, Ill, Jan 18, 37; m 64; c 1. LINGUISTICS. *Educ:* Coe Col, BA, 59; Stanfor Univ, MA, 60; Univ Mass, Amherst, PhD(ling), 79. *Prof Exp:* Assoc dir appl ling, Sch Int Training, 70-74; instr ling, Univ NH, 79-80; asst prof, Univ Minn, 81-82; ASST PROF LING, OLD DOMINION UNIV, 82- *Concurrent Pos:* Consult, Inter-Link Assocs, 81- *Mem:* Ling Soc Am; Teachers English to Speakers Other Lang. *Res:* Theoretical linguistics; applied linguistics; first language acquisition. *Publ:* Auth, A predictable alternation between intonation contours, Cunyforum, Vol 5, 78; Sentence stress reanalysed, In: Parasession on the Elements, Chicago Ling Soc, 79; Intonation and the interpretation of negatives, Nels Proc, Vol X, 79; Aspects of English Prosody, Ind Univ Ling Club, 80; The given/New distinction and the unmarked stress pattern, Nels Proc, Vol XI, 80; coauth, A lexical approach to language acquisition and linguistic theory, Mass Inst Technol press, 81; Linguistic rhythm and grammatical structure in Afghan Persian, Ling Inquiry, Vol XI, No 3; auth, Grammar Guide, Regents Publ Co, 82. *Mailing Add:* 39 Moore St Princeton NJ 08540

BINGER, NORMAN HENRY, b Milwaukee, Wis, June 20, 14; m 49. GERMAN. *Educ:* Univ Wis, BS, 37; Miami Univ, AM, 39; Ohio State Univ, PhD, 42. *Prof Exp:* Instr, Va Mil Inst, 42-43, asst prof, 47-49; asst prof, Univ Mich, 46-47; from instr to assoc prof, 49-72, prof, 72-79, EMER PROF GER, UNIV KY, 79- *Concurrent Pos:* Fulbright res fel, Austria, 57-58. *Mem:* MLA; Am Asn Teachers Ger; SAtlantic Mod Lang Asn. *Res:* Indo-European linguistics. *Publ:* Auth, Bibliography of German Plays on Microcards, Shoe String, 70; Moritz Busch: Travels Between the Mississippi and Hudson, Univ Ky, 71. *Mailing Add:* Dept of Ger Univ of Ky Lexington KY 40506

BINGHAM, ALFRED JEPSON, b New Haven, Conn, Dec 30, 08. FRENCH LITERATURE. *Educ:* Yale Univ, AB, 33; Columbia Univ, PhD, 39. *Prof Exp:* Asst prof Romance lang, Grove City Col, 39-40; asst prof French, Brown Univ, 40-44; assoc prof foreign lang, Univ Md, College Park, 47-64, prof French, 65-78. *Concurrent Pos:* Mem, Int Congr Enlightenment, 63, 67, 71, 75 & 79; collabr, Critical Ed Voltaire's Complete Works, 69-75. *Mem:* Am Soc 18th Century Studies, Int Soc Studies 18th Century; Fr Soc 18th Century Studies. *Res:* Early political life and ideas of Marie-Joseph Chenier; encyclopedia movement in 18th century France; Voltaire. *Publ:* Auth, Voltaire and the New Testament, Proc Congr Enlightenment, 63; Voltaire and Marmontel, 67 & Marie-Joseph Chenier: Ideologue and critic, 73, Studies Voltaire & 18th Century; co-ed, Enlightenment Studies in Honor of Lester G Crocker, 79. *Mailing Add:* 2612 Spencer Rd Chevy Chase MD 20815

BINGHAM, JOHN L, SPANISH. *Educ:* Vanderbilt Univ, BA, 41, MA, 47. *Prof Exp:* Taft teaching fel, Univ Cincinnati, 41; asst, Univ Calif, Los Angeles, 47-50; from instr to asst prof Span & French, 50-62, asst dean, Col Arts & Sci, 55-65, assoc dean, 65-80, ASSOC PROF SPAN, VANDERBILT UNIV, 62- *Mem:* SAtlantic Mod Lang Asn; Conf Acad Deans Southern States. *Res:* Nineteenth and 20th century Spanish literature. *Mailing Add:* Col of Arts & Sci Vanderbilt Univ Nashville TN 37240

BINNICK, ROBERT IRA, b New York, NY, June 11, 45; m 69. LINGUISTICS. *Educ:* Queens Col, BA, 65; Univ Chicago, MA, 68, PhD(ling), 69. *Prof Exp:* Asst prof ling, Univ Mass, Amherst, 69-70 & Univ Kans, 70-72; assoc prof, 72-79, PROF LING, SCARBOROUGH COL, UNIV TORONTO, 79- *Mem:* Ling Soc Am; Can Ling Asn; Mongolia Soc; Am Orient Soc. *Res:* Pragmatics; Mongol syntax. *Publ:* Co-ed, Papers from the Fifth Regional Meeting, Chicago Linguistic Society, Chicago Ling Soc, 69; Studies Out in Left Field: Defamatory Essays Presented to James D McCawley, Ling Res, 71; auth, Bring and come, Ling Inquiry, 71; co-ed, Generative Semantik, Athenaum, 72; auth, On the underlying tense of deverbatives, Language, 78; coauth, Grammatik und Sprachgebrauch, Beck, 78; auth, Modern Mongolian: A Transfformational Syntax, Toronto, 79. *Mailing Add:* Dept of Humanities Scarborough Col West Hill ON M1C 1A4 Can

BINNICKER, CHARLES MATHEWS, JR, b Jacksonville, Fla, Apr 29, 29. CLASSICAL LANGUAGES & LITERATURE. *Educ:* Univ of the South, BA, 50; Fla State Univ, MA, 52; Univ NC, Chapel Hill, PhD(classics), 67. *Prof Exp:* Teacher, Brunswick Sch, Conn, 56-60; from instr to asst prof, 60-72, assoc prof, 72-78, PROF CLASSICS, UNIV OF THE SOUTH, 78- *Mem:* Am Philol Asn; Vergilian Soc. *Res:* Augustan poets, especially Vergil and Ovid; Greek and Roman historians. *Mailing Add:* Dept of Class Langs Univ of the South Sewanee TN 37375

BIONDI, RAYMOND LIBERTY, b San Francisco, Calif, July 4, 16; m 58; c 4. ROMANCE LANGUAGES & LITERATURE. *Educ:* Stanford Univ, AB, 40, AM, 42, PhD, 55. *Prof Exp:* Instr Span & Ital, Univ NMex, 46-53; from instr to assoc prof French & Span, Col St Mary-of-the-Wasatch, 55-59; asst prof, Loyola Univ, Los Angeles, 60-65; asst prof, 65-69, assoc prof, 69-81, chmn dept, 78-81, EMER PROF MOD LANG, UNIV SANTA CLARA, 81- *Mem:* Am Asn Teachers Span & Port; Am Asn Teachers Ital; MLA. *Res:* Spanish peninsular literature; Italian. *Publ:* Auth, Philology and history: A note on Croce's Hispanism, Rivista di Studi Crociani, 69. *Mailing Add:* 834 Rubis Dr Sunnyvale CA 94087

BIRCH, CYRIL, b Bolton, England, Mar 16, 25; m 46; c 2. CHINESE LANGUAGE & LITERATURE. *Educ:* Univ London, BA, 48, PhD(Chinese lit), 54. *Prof Exp:* Lectr Chinese, Sch Orient & African Studies, Univ London, 48-60; assoc prof, 60-66, PROF ORIENT LANG, UNIV CALIF, BERKELEY, 66- *Concurrent Pos:* Vis lectr Chinese, Stanford Univ, 58-59; Rockefeller Found fel, 58-59; Am Coun Learned Soc grant, 63-64; Guggenheim fel, 63-64. *Mem:* Asn Asian Studies. *Res:* Chinese vernacular fiction; 20th century Chinese literature; Ming drama. *Publ:* Auth, Stories From a Ming Collection, Bodley Head, London, 58; ed, English & Chinese metres in Hsu Chih-mo, Asia Major, 61; coauth & ed, Anthology of Chinese Literature, Grove, Vols I & II, 64 & 72; ed, Studies in Chinese Literary Genres, Univ Calif, 73; Peony Pavilion, Ind, 80. *Mailing Add:* Dept of Orient Lang Univ of Calif Berkeley CA 94720

BIRCHER, MARTIN, b Zurich, Switz, June 3, 38. GERMAN LITERATURE. *Educ:* Univ Zurich, DrPhil, 65. *Prof Exp:* Asst prof, 68-71, ASSOC PROF GER, McGILL UNIV, 71- *Concurrent Pos:* Schweizer Nationalfonds fel, 65-68; lectr, Univ Zurich, 71-; Guggenheim fel, NY, 71-72; fel, Janggen-Pöhn-Stiftung, St Gallen, 72-73 & Privatdozenten-Stiftung, Univ Zurich, 72-73; res fel, Alexander von Humboldt Found, 76-77; ed, Wolfenbütteler Barock-Nachrichten, Hamburg, 78-; res dir 17th century, Herzog August Bibliothek Wolfenbüttel, 78- *Mem:* Shakespeare Ges Wes; Int Asn Ger Studies; Swiss-Ger Acad Soc; Int Asn Studies Ger Baroque Lit. *Res:* German literature, 16th to 18th centuries; Swiss Literature; Shakespeare. *Publ:* Ed, Die Fruchtbringende Gesellschaft: Quellen und Dokumente (3 vols), Kösel, Munich, 70-71; coauth, Wolfgang Helmhard von Hohberg: Briefe und frühe Gelegenheitsdichtungen, Literaturwiss, Hahrbuch, 70; Andreas Gryphius: Einige Autographen, Mod Lang Notes, 71; coauth, Shakespeare und die Deutsche Schweiz, Francke, Bern, 71; ed, Salomon Gessner: Sämtlich Schriften (3 vols), 71-74 & co-ed, J H Füssli, Sämtliche Gedichte, 73, Orell Füssli, Zurich; auth, Matthäbus Merian d Ä und die Fruchtbringende, Archiv für Geschichte des Buchwesens, 77; Deutsche Drucke des Barock 1600-1720, Herzog August Bibliothek Wolfenbüttel, KTO Press, Nendeln, Vol I, 77, Vol II, 78. *Mailing Add:* Dept of German McGill Univ Montreal 101 PQ H3A 2T5 Can

BIRD, CHARLES STEPHEN, b New York, NY, Sept 12, 35; m 57; c 3. LINGUISTICS, FOLKLORE. *Educ:* Univ Buffalo, AB, 61; Univ Calif, Los Angeles, MA, 62, PhD(ling), 66. *Prof Exp:* Asst prof int studies, Southern Ill Univ, 66-68; assoc prof ling, 69-76, PROF LING & FOLKLORE, IND UNIV, BLOOMINGTON, 76- *Concurrent Pos:* res fel Ling, Mass Inst Technol, 68-69; mem foreign area fel comt, Soc Sci Res Coun-Am Coun Learned Soc, 72-73, mem comt on Africa, 72-, consult, New Directions in Area Studies, 73; UNESCO consult, Ctr Advan Teaching, Bamako, Mali, 72- *Mem:* Ling Soc Am; WAfrican Ling Soc. *Res:* Syntactic and semantic theory; pragmatic sociolinguistics; theory of poetics. *Publ:* Coauth, Lexique Bambara, Educ de Base, Mali, 68; auth, Relative clauses in Bambara, J WAfrican Lang, 68; coauth, English in Mali, Southern Ill Univ, 70; auth, The development of Mandekan, In: Language and History in Africa, Frank Cass, Ltd, 70; Aspects of prosody in West African epic, In: Current Issues in Stylistics, Ling Res, Inc, 72. *Mailing Add:* Dept of Ling Arts & Sci Ind Univ Bloomington IN 47401

BIRD, HAROLD WESLEY, Ancient History & Literature. See Vol I

BIRD, THOMAS EDWARD, b Rome, NY, Mar 28, 35; m 58; c 2. SLAVIC LANGUAGES & LITERATURES. *Educ:* Syracuse Univ, AB, 56; Middlebury Col, MA, 60; Princeton Univ, AM, 65. *Prof Exp:* Lectr, Russ lang & lit, 65-79, dir, Scholars Prog, 70-72, dir, Ethnic Studies Prog, 79-80, DIR, CTR STUDY ETHICS & PUB POLICY, QUEENS COL, 77-, ASST PROF SLAVIC & EAST EUROP LANG & LIT, 80- *Concurrent Pos:* Ed, Queens Slavic Papers, Queens Col, 72- *Mem:* Am Asn Advan Slavic Studies; Am Asn Teachers Slavic & East Europ Lang; Northeast Conf Teaching Foreign Lang; Polish Inst Arts & Sci. *Res:* Slavic emigre literatures; Silver Age of Russian literature; religion in Eastern Europe and USSR. *Publ:* Auth, Patriarch Maximos IV, 64 & ed, Modern Theologians: Christians and Jews, 67, Univ Notre Dame Press; Foreign Language Learning: Research and Development, Northeast Conf, 68; Modern Polish Writing, Queens Col Press, 73; auth, New interest in old Russian things, Slavic Rev, 32: 1; ed, Pawel Lysek's At the Border, Poets' & Painters' Press, 77; co-ed, The 1863 Uprising in Byelorussia, Byelorussia Inst Art & Sci, 80; coauth, The new turn in church-state relations in Poland, J Church & State, 24: 1. *Mailing Add:* Box 189 Little Neck NY 11363

BIRKENMAYER, SIGMUND S, b Warsaw, Poland, June 5, 23; US citizen; m 51. SLAVIC LANGUAGES & LITERATURES. *Educ:* Univ Wis, BA, 48, MA, 48 & 57, PhD, 61. *Prof Exp:* Teaching asst Polish, Univ Wis, 46-47, teaching asst Russ, 55-56 & 58-59; instr English & Ger, Univ PR, 51-55; asst prof Russ & Span, Lycoming Col, 59-60; from asst prof to assoc prof, 60-72, PROF SLAVIC LANG, PA STATE UNIV, UNIVERSITY PARK, 73- *Concurrent Pos:* Mem Kosciuszko Found, 46-; assoc bibliogr, MLA Bibliog Comt, 62, head Europ sect, 63; mem Russ achievement test comt, Col Entrance Exam Bd, 67-68. *Mem:* Am Asn Teachers Slavic & E Europ Lang; MLA; Am Asn Advan Slavic Studies; Polish Inst Arts & Sci Am; Asn Advan Polish Studies (pres, 79-). *Res:* Near Eastern languages, especially Turkish; English language and literature; N A Nekrasov. *Publ:* Auth, Pattern drills in the teaching of Russian, 63 & The peasant poems of Nikolaj Nekrasov, summer 67, Slavic & East Europ J; An Accented Dictionary of Place Names in the Soviet Union, Pa State Univ, 67, Suppl, 70; A Selective Bibliography of Works on the Teaching of Slavic Languages and Literatures in the United States and Canada, 1942-1967, Am Coun Teaching Foreign Lang, 68; Nikolaj Nekrasov: His Life and Poetic Art, Mouton, The Hague, 68; The party organizer as a fictional hero in the Soviet novel, 1946-1952, Russ Lang J, 70; coauth, A Modern Polish Reader, Pa State Univ, 70; Introduction to the Polish Language, Kosciuszko Found, 78. *Mailing Add:* Burrows Bldg Pa State Univ University Park PA 16802

BIRKMAIER, EMMA MARIE, b Munich, Ger, June 8, 08; nat US; m 30. MODERN LANGUAGES. *Educ:* Col St Catherine, BA, 30; Univ Minn, AM, 38, PhD(educ, mod lang), 49. *Prof Exp:* Instr German, English & music educ, Col St Catherine, 28-30; instr high schs & pub schs, Minn, 36-42; instr German, Spanish & Russian, univ lab, high sch & methods course in mod lang, Col Educ, Univ Minn, Minneapolis, 42-49, assoc prof educ, chmn dept mod lang, lab sch & instr methods & curriculum courses, col educ & supvr teacher training in foreign lang, 49-63, prof English as a second lang, 63-80. *Concurrent Pos:* Ford Found grant, 54; consult foreign lang prof, MLA, 54-76, res grant, Univ Minn; vis prof & lectr, Johns Hopkins Univ, 56. *Mem:* Am Asn Teachers Ger (secy, 49-55); Am Educ Res Asn; Am Asn Teachers Fr; Nat Soc Study Educ; Nat Fedn Mod Lang Teachers Asn (vpres, 52-54). *Res:* Psychology of second language learning; German and Russian language and civilization; curriculum and intruction at the secondary school level. *Publ:* Auth, Foreign Language Education: An Overview, Nat Textbk, 72. *Mailing Add:* 3324 Edmund Blvd Minneapolis MN 55406

BIRMINGHAM, JOHN CALHOUN, JR, b Wilmington, NC, Aug 30, 37; m 69; c 2. SPANISH, ROMANCE LINGUISTICS. *Educ:* East Carolina Univ, BA, 59; Middlebury Col, MA, 63; Univ Va, PHD(Span & Romance ling), 70. *Prof Exp:* Teacher English & Span, Randolph-Macon Acad, Front Royal, Va, 59-61; master Span, St Christopher's Sch, Richmond, Va, 61-63; instr English & Span, Richmond Prof Inst, 63-64; asst Span, Univ Va, 64-66; asst prof, 66-77, ASSOC PROF SPAN, VA COMMONWEALTH UNIV, 77- *Mem:* SAtlantic Mod Lang Asn. *Res:* Spanish grammar and dialectology; pidgin and creole languages; bilingual education. *Publ:* Auth, Papiamentu's West African cousins, 1975 Colloquium Hisp Ling, Georgetown Univ, 11/76; Papiamentu: The long-lost lingua franca?, Am Hisp, 12/76; Papiamentu and Afrikaans: Two black-influenced Creole languages, 3/77 & Lexical decreolization in Papiamentu, 3/78, Kristof; Black English Near Its Roots: The Transplanted West African Creoles, In: Perspectives on American English, Mouton, 80. *Mailing Add:* Dept of Foreign Langs Va Commonwealth Univ Richmond VA 23284

BIRN, RANDI MARIE, b Tromso, Norway, Feb 25, 35; US citizen; m 60; c 2. FRENCH & SCANDINAVIAN LITERATURE. *Educ:* Univ Oslo, Cand Philol, 60; Univ Ill, PhD(French), 65. *Prof Exp:* From asst prof to assoc prof, 65-76, PROF FRENCH, UNIV ORE, 76- *Concurrent Pos:* Am Philos Soc grants-in-aid, 65 & 77. *Mem:* MLA; Soc Advan Scand Studies. *Res:* Proust's influence upon the modern novel; Claude Simon: modern Norwegian literature, especially Johan Borgen and Aksel Sandemose. *Publ:* Auth, The comedy of disrespect in Claudel's Soulier de Satin, Fr Rev, 70; The quest for authenticity in three novels by Johan Borgen, Mosaic, 71; The theoretical background for Proust's personnages prepares, L'Esprit Createur, 71; Johan Borgen, Twayne, 74; Proust, Claude Simon, and the art of the novel, Papers Lang & Lit, 77; Johan Borgen, En Litteraer Biografi, Byldendal, Oslo, 77; co-ed, Orion Blinded: Essays on Claude Simon, Bucknell Univ, 81. *Mailing Add:* Dept of Romance Lang Univ of Ore Eugene OR 97403

BIRNBAUM, HENRIK, b Breslau, Ger, Dec 13, 25; m 65; c 2. SLAVIC LANGUAGES & LITERATURES. *Educ:* Univ Stockholm, Phil Cand, 49, Phil Mag, 52, Phil Lic, 54, PhD, 58. *Prof Exp:* Asst Slavic lang, Russ Inst, Univ Stockholm, 47-53, asst prof, univ, 58-61; instr Russ, Ger & Swedish, High Schs & Jr Cols, Stockholm, 53-58; assoc prof Slavic lang, 61-64, dir Ctr Russ & E Europ Studies, 68-78, PROF SLAVIC LANG, UNIV CALIF, LOS ANGELES, 64- *Concurrent Pos:* Vis lectr, Harvard Univ, 60; consult, Rand Corp, Santa Monica, 62-66; prof Slavic, Baltic & Balkan ling, Univ Munich, 72-73. *Mem:* Am Asn Advan Slavic Studies; Ling Soc Am; corres mem Swedish Royal Acad Lett; Am Med Acad; Asn Scand Slavists. *Res:* Comparative and historical Slavic linguistics; mediaeval and Renaissance Slavic literature and history. *Publ:* Auth, Common Slavic, 75; Doktor Faustus und Doktor Schiwago, 76; Linguistic reconstruction; its potentials and limitations in new perspective, 77; co-ed, The New York Musical, 77; ed & contribr, American Contributions to the Eighth International Congress of Slavists, 78; coauth & co-ed, Fiction and drama in Eastern and Southeastern Europe, 80; Lord Novgorod the Great, 81; Essays in Early Slavic Civilization, 81. *Mailing Add:* Dept of Slavic Lang Univ Calif Los Angeles CA 90024

BIRON, ARCHILLE HENRI, b Pittsfield, Mass, Oct 1, 11; m 40. MODERN FOREIGN LANGUAGES. *Educ:* Clark Univ, BA, 32; Univ Paris, France, dipl, 37; Middlebury Col, AM, 40. *Prof Exp:* Teacher French, Sanborn Sem, NH, 33-34 & high sch, Mass, 34-38; head dept, Riverdale Country Sch, New York, NY, 38-48; lectr Romance lang, Rutgers Univ, 46-48, instr, 48-50; from instr to assoc prof, 50-74, PROF MOD FOREIGN LANG, COLBY COL, 74-, INSTR, SUMMER SCH LANG, 49-, ASST DIR, 55- *Concurrent Pos:* Mem, Maine Adv Comt Teacher Educ & Certification; dir, Sweet Briar Col jr year in France, 64-65, 71-72, 73-74 Honors & Awards, Alliance Francaise Prize, 32. *Mem:* MLA; Am Asn Teachers Fr. *Res:* Phonetics; teaching languages in elementary schools. *Publ:* Auth, Paget in Paräys, 6/60 & Madame Blanc's Le roman de la femme-medecin, 9/67, Colby Libr Quart. *Mailing Add:* Dept of Mod Foreign Lang Colby Col Waterville ME 04901

BIRZNIEKS, ILMARS, b Liepaja, Latvia, Aug 16, 32; US citizen; m 57; c 1. GERMAN. *Educ:* Asbury Col, BA, 58; Tulane Univ, PhD(Ger lang & lit), 68. *Prof Exp:* Instr Ger, Univ NC, 65-66; instr Ger & Slavic lang, Univ Mo, 66-68, asst prof Ger, 68-72; teacher English & Ger, Eve Sch, City of Bonn, Ger, 72-74; asst prof, 75-77, ASSOC PROF GER, BEREA COL, 77-, CHMN DEPT FOREIGN LANGS, 76- *Concurrent Pos:* Hon fel, Inst Advan Studies in Humanities, Univ Edinburgh, 82-83. *Mem:* Am Asn Teachers Ger; SAtlantic Mod Lang Asn; Asn Advan Baltic Studies. *Res:* German language and literature; German culture and civilization; Baltic literature. *Publ:* Auth, Ievads Vernera Bergendrina Prozas Darbos, Jauna Gaita, 69; Die Bedeutung des Baltischen Hintergrunds in Werner Bergengruens Erzahlungen, Acta Baltica, 71; An Approach to Teaching the Modern German Novel, Unterrichtspraxis, 73. *Mailing Add:* Dept of Foreign Langs Berea Col Berea KY 40404

BISHAL, WILSON B, b Minia, Egypt, May 18, 23; US citizen; m 58; c 3. SEMITICS. *Educ:* Columbia Union Col, BA, 53; Seventh Day Adventist Theol Sem, MA, 54; Johns Hopkins Univ, PhD, 59. *Prof Exp:* Instr Semitics, Univ Wis, 59-60; asst prof MidE Studies, Sch Advan Int Studies, Johns Hopkins Univ, 60-66; lectr, 66-76, SR LECTR ARABIC STUDIES, HARVARD UNIV, 76- *Concurrent Pos:* Lectr, Foreign Serv Inst Sem MidE & NAfrica, 62-66; sr consult Arabic, Defense Lang Inst, 72- *Mem:* Am Orient Soc; Ling Soc Am; MidE Inst; MidE Studies Asn; Am Asn Teachers Arabic. *Res:* Syntagmemic analysis of Arabic; advanced Arabic syntax for use with the computer; a student's Arabic-English dictionary. *Publ:* Auth, Modern Literary Arabic (5 vols), Johns Hopkins Univ, 63; Form and function in Arabic syntax, Word, 65; Islamic History oc the Middle East, Allyn & Bacon, 68; Syntagmemic analysis of the noun in Arabic, Gen Ling, 69; A possible coptic source for a Qur'anic text, J Am Orient Soc, 71; Concise Grammar of Literary Arabic--A New Approach, Kendall & Hunt, 71; Humanities in the Arabic Islamic World, W C Brown, 73. *Mailing Add:* Ctr Mid-Eastern Studies Harvard Univ Cambridge MA 02138

BISHOP, GEORGE REGINALD, JR, b Altoona, Pa, Jan 17, 22; m 52; c 3. ROMANCE LANGUAGES & LITERATURE. *Educ:* Princeton Univ, AB, 46, MA, 48, PhD(Romance lang), 52. *Prof Exp:* From instr to prof Romance lang, Rutgers Col, 52-65, asst dean col arts & sci, 60-63, assoc dean, 63-67, dean instruct, 68-74, actg dean col, 73-74, PROF ROMANCE LANG, RUTGERS UNIV, 65- *Concurrent Pos:* Ford fac fel, 54-55; mem exec comt, Northeast Conf Teaching Foreign Lang, 58-61, bd dir, 63-67, conf chmn, 65-66. *Mem:* MLA; Am Asn Teachers Fr; Am Coun Teaching Foreign Lang; AAUP. *Res:* C A Sainte-Beuve as poet and critic; relation of painting and literature in 19th century France; renaissance philosophy of man. *Publ:* Ed, Culture in Language Learning, Northeast Conf Teaching Foreign Lang, 60; The identity of E T de la R in the poetry of Sainte-Beuve, Mod Lang Rev; The capacity of the senses in Diderot's aesthetic theory, Mod Lang Forum. *Mailing Add:* 166 Wilson Rd Princeton NJ 08540

BISHOP, JOHN DAVID, b Wasla, Nicaragua, Sept 10, 18; US citizen; m 45, 62; c 3. CLASSICS. *Educ:* Moravian Col, AB, 40; Univ Pa, AM, 42, PhD(class studies), 64. *Prof Exp:* Instr classics, Colgate Univ, 47-52; asst prof, Scripps Col, 52-53, Col Pac, 56-59 & Boston Univ, 61-64; from assoc prof to prof, 65-78, EMER PROF CLASSICS, WHEATON COL (MASS), 78- *Concurrent Pos:* Consult, Beckwith & Assocs, Stockton, Calif, 56-59; Nat Endowment Arts grant, 77. *Mem:* Am Philol Asn. *Res:* Seneca; Catullus. *Publ:* Auth, Catullus 2, Class Philol, 66; Choral meters in Senecan Tragedy, Rheinisches Mus, 68; The Cleroterium, J Hellenic Studies, 70; Catullus 85, Latomus, 71; ed, Roman Construction in Italy From Nerva Through the Antonines, Am Philos Soc, 73; auth, Seneca's Hercules Oetaeus 884-982, Athenaeum, 73; Seneca's Oedipus: Opposition literature, Class J, 78; coauth, Wheaton College Collection of Greek and Roman Coins, Am Numis Soc, 81. *Mailing Add:* P O Box 368 Norton MA 02766

BISHOP, LLOYD ORMOND, b Portland, Maine, June 11, 33; m 58; c 2. FRENCH LANGUAGE & LITERATURE. *Educ:* Bowdoin Col, BA, 55; Columbia Univ, PhD, 61. *Prof Exp:* Asst prof French, Vanderbilt Univ, 60-62 & Univ Maine, 62-63; assoc prof mod lang & chmn dept foreign lang, Univ NC, Wilmington, 63-67, prof French, 67-69; ASSOC PROF FRENCH, VA POLYTECH INST & STATE UNIV, 69-, COORDR DEPT, 71- *Mem:* MLA; Am Asn Teachers Fr. *Res:* Literary stylistics; drama criticism; the novel. *Publ:* Auth, Marie Meurdrac--first lady of chemistry, J Chem Educ, 6/70; Toward an eclectic methodology in foreign language teaching, fall 71 & Jesus as romantic hero: le Mont des Oliviers, spring 73, Fr Rev. *Mailing Add:* Dept of Foreign Lang Va Polytech Inst & State Univ Blacksburg VA 24060

BISHOP, MICHAEL, b London, England, Apr 19, 38; UK & Can citizen. MODERN FRENCH LITERATURE. *Educ:* Univ Manchester, BA, 59; Univ Man, MA, 68; Univ Kent, PhD(French lit), 77. *Prof Exp:* Asst master mod lang, King's Sch, Cheshire, England, 60-63; chmn mod & class lang, Sisler High Sch, Winnipeg, Can, 63-66 & 67-69; chmn French lit & lang, George Stephenson Sch, Newcastle, England, 69-70; asst prof, 70-79, ASSOC PROF FRENCH LIT & LANG, DALHOUSIE UNIV, 80- *Concurrent Pos:* Mem, Manitoba Comt Develop Univ Entrance Oral Tests, 67-69; assoc ed, Dalhousie French Studies, Dalhousie Univ, 78-80 & Ethos, 81-; actg ed, Dalhousie French Studies, Dalhousie Univ, 80- *Mem:* Soc Fr Studies; Am Asn Teachers Fr. *Res:* Nineteenth and 20th century French literature; contemporary French literature, especially poetry; French art. *Publ:* Auth, Pierre Reverdy: A Bibliography, Grant & Cutler, London, 76; Eyes and seeing in the poetry of Pierre Reverdy, In: Sensibility, and Creation, Croom Helm, London & Harper and Row, 77; Bernard Noël, Sub-Stance, 79; Maximum and minimum: The poetics of Andre Frenaud, Fr Forum, Vol 2, 5/80; Swords above the trees: The poetics of Philippe Jaccottet, Swiss-Fr Studies, 5/80; ed, The Language of Poetry: Crisis and Solution, Studies in Modern Poetry of French Expression, 1945 to the Present, Rodopi, Amsterdam & New York, 80; auth, Jacques Dupin: Art and poetry, Contemp Lit, fall 80; Guillevic: The imperfection of Apotheosis, Neophilolgus, Vol LXV, 10/81. *Mailing Add:* Dept French Dalhousie Univ Halifax NS B3H 4H8 Can

BISHOP, THOMAS W, b Vienna, Austria, Feb 21, 29; US citizen; m 50, 67; c 2. FRENCH & COMPARATIVE LITERATURE. *Educ:* New York Univ, AB, 50; Univ Md, MA, 51; Univ Calif, Berkeley, PhD, 57. *Prof Exp:* From instr to assoc prof, 56-64, PROF FRENCH & COMP LIT, NEW YORK UNIV, 64-, CHMN DEPT FRENCH & ITAL, 66-, FLORENCE GOULD CHAIR FRENCH LIT, 74-, CHMN, INST FRENCH STUDIES, 78- *Concurrent Pos:* Asst chief of protocol, Tenth Commemorative Session UN, San Francisco, 55; Arts & Sci Res Fund grants, 59, 60, 62, 63 & 68; mem bd, La Maison Francaise, 59, dir, 59-64; prof, Ecole Libre des Hautes Etudes, New Yor, 61-; mem adv bd, Alliance Francaise, NY, 61-71, pres, 64-68; French Am Cult Serv & Educ Ais grant, 62; Fulbright sr res scholar, France, 65-66; consult, Nat Endowment for Humanities, 75-; mem bd dirs, French-Am Found, NY, 76. *Honors & Awards:* Chevalier, Palmes Academiques, 65, Officier, 71; Officer, Ordre Nat du Merite, Pres French Repub, 77. *Mem:* MLA; Am Asn Teachers Fr; Mod Humanities Res Asn; Int Asn Fr Studies; Soc Fr Prof Am. *Res:* Modern French theater; European and American theater; modern French novel. *Publ:* Auth, Pirandello and the French Theater, New York Univ, 60; Ionesco on Olympus, Saturday Rev, 5/70; contribr, L'Image de la Creation chez Claude Simon, In: Nouveau Roman: Hier et aujourd'hui, Editions 10/18, Paris, 72; ed, L'Avant-garde Theatrale: French Theatre Since 1950, New York Univ, 75; auth, Huis clos de Sartre, Hachette, 75; co-ed & coauth, Beckett, l'Herne, 76; coauth, Robbe-Grillet: Colloque de Cerisy, Editions 10/18, 76; Camus-Comparative Literature Symposium, Tex Tech Univ, 76. *Mailing Add:* Dept of French & Ital New York Univ 19 University Place New York NY 10003

BISMUTH, RENE, b Aug 20, 18; Can citizen;; m 49; c 1. FRENCH LANGUAGE & LITERATURE. *Educ:* Univ Lille, Lic es Lett, 51, D es Lett, 53. *Prof Exp:* Prof French, Carleton Univ, 57-60 & Univ Witwatersrand, S Africa, 61-64; vis prof, Univ Del, 64-65; prof mod lang & chmn dept, 65-72, chmn dept romance studies, 75-78, PROF ROMANCE STUDIES, BROCK UNIV, 72- *Concurrent Pos:* External examr, Sorbonne at Carleton Univ, 59-60; external supvr grad studies, Rhodes Univ, S Africa, 63-; vis prof Span, Cent Univ Ecuador, 69; appraiser, book publ, Humanities Res Coun Can, 71. *Honors & Awards:* Knight, Palmes Acad, 71. *Mem:* Humanities Res Coun Can; Can Latin Am Studies Asn; Soc Ling Europ; Asn Can Univ Teachers Fr (vpres & pres, 68-72); Int Fedn Teachers Fr. *Res:* Poetry; oral literature; 19th century French literature. *Publ:* Auth, The Story of France, S African radio prog, 63; L'ecole romane, Laurentian Univ Rev, 11/69; Les nouveaux noms de pays, Ed Acad Soc Rep Romania, 9/70; contrib, Delimitation linguistique prose-poesie, Soc Ling Europ, 70; Decadentism in Letters and Arts in Europe, Univ of Nantes, France, 76. *Mailing Add:* Dept of Romance Studies Brock Univ St Catharines ON L2S 3A1 Can

BISZTRAY, GEORGE, b Budapest, Hungary, Oct 2, 38; US citizen. COMPARATIVE LITERATURE, HUNGARIAN STUDIES. *Educ:* Eötvös Univ, Budapest, dipl Hungarian & English, 62; Univ Minn, Minneapolis, PhD(comp lit), 72. *Prof Exp:* Asst prof Scand, Univ Chicago, 72-75; vis asst prof Scand, comp lit & Ger, Univ Alta, 76-78; ASSOC PROF HUNGARIAN, UNIV TORONTO, 78- *Concurrent Pos:* Ed, Hungarian Studies Rev. *Mem:* Can Comp Lit Asn; Am Comp Lit Asn; Int Comp Lit Asn; Am Hungarian Educrs Asn; Soc Advan Scand Study. *Res:* Cultural and literary sociology (especially interactions); literature and other arts; literary theory and methodology. *Publ:* Auth, Literary sociology and Marxist theory, Mosaic, 2/72; The documentary novel in Scandinavia, Scand Studies, 1/76; Man's biological future in Hungarian utopian literature, Can-Am Rev Hungarian Studies, 1/76; Scandinavia: The model of a culture and its applicability to literature, Neohelicon, 3-4/76; Marxism and the pluralism of critical methods, Yearbk Comp & Gen Lit, 77; Marxist Models of Literary Realism, Columbia Univ, 78; contribr, Romantic Irony, Vol I, In: Comparative History of Literatures in European Languages, Ser Romanticism (in prep). *Mailing Add:* Dept of Slavic Lang & Lit Univ of Toronto Toronto ON M5S 1A1 Can

BITTON-JACKSON, LIVIA E, Jewish History, Hebrew Literature. See Vol I

BIVENS, WILLIAM PATTERSON, III, Stylistics, English Linguistics. See Vol II

BIZZARRO, SALVATORE, b Tunis, Tunisia, Apr 15, 39; US citizen. LATIN AMERICAN LITERATURE & STUDIES. *Educ:* Fordham Univ, BA, 64; Stanford Univ, MA, 65, PhD(Span), 69. *Prof Exp:* Asst prof, 68-76, ASSOC PROF SPAN, COLO COL, 76- *Concurrent Pos:* Ed, Latin Am Yearly Rev, Paris, 73- *Mem:* MLA; Latin Am Studies Asn. *Res:* Contemporary Latin American literature; contemporary Chilean politics and history; Brazilian literature. *Publ:* Auth, Chilie, In: Hispanic American Report, 10/64 & 11/64; Lope de Vega, In: Hispania, Fordham Univ, 64; El enigma del tiempo en la obra de Jorge Luis Borges, Humanitas, summer 72; Historical Dictionary of Chile, Scarecrow, 72; Articles on Mexico, 74 & 77 & Articles on Chile, 76 & 78, Current Hist; Pablo Neruda/All Poets The Poet, Scarecrow, 78. *Mailing Add:* Dept of Span Box 72 Colo Col Colorado Springs CO 80903

BIZZICCARI, ALVARO, b Rome, Italy, May 31, 29. ITALIAN. *Educ:* Univ Rome, PhD, 59. *Prof Exp:* From instr to assoc prof, 61-75, PROF ITAL, UNIV CONN, 75- *Mem:* Am Asn Teachers Ital. *Res:* Italian literature of the Middle Ages and Renaissance; mystical literature east and west. *Publ:* Auth, L'Umanesimo Nella Vita e Nelle Opere di S Teresa d'Avila, Ancora, Rome, 68; L'amore mistico nel canzoniere di Jacopone da Todi, Italica, 3/68; Motivi agostiniani nel Pensiero di Dante, Ky Romance Quart, 69; Il cantico delle creature o di frate sole, Italica, 72; Dante e Caterina da Siena: Poesia e misticismo, Rassegna Ascetica Mistica, 74; Linguaggio e stile delle lettere di Caterina da Siena, Italica, 76; Questioni di critica Cateriniana, Nuova Rivista Ascetica Mistica, 78. *Mailing Add:* U-57 Univ of Conn Storrs CT 06268

BJARNASON, LOFTUR L, b Logan, Utah, Aug 16, 13; m 36; c 1. LITERATURE, COMPARATIVE LINGUISTICS. *Educ:* Univ Utah, BA, 34, MA, 36; Harvard Univ, MA, 39; Stanford Univ, PhD(comp Ger ling), 51. *Prof Exp:* Asst Ger & mod lang, Univ Utah, 34-36, asst instr Ger & Gothic, 39-40; asst instr Ger & Icelandic, Stanford Univ, 39-42, instr Ger, 46; asst prof Ger & Scand, Univ Fla, 46-47; mem fac English & lit, Hartnell Col, 54-58; prof, 58-75, EMER PROF LIT, NAVAL POSTGRAD SCH, 75- *Concurrent Pos:* Consult ling, US Marine Corps. *Mem:* Am-Scand Found; Soc Advan Scand Studies (secy, 58-60; 62); MLA. *Res:* Scandinavian literature, especially Kierkegaard and Strindberg; modern Icelandic literature; comparative Germanic linguistics. *Publ:* Auth, Character delineation of women in the Old Icelandic sagas, Scand Studies, 11/76; David Stefansson fra Fagraskogi, Icelandic Can, summer 59; Anthology of Modern Icelandic Literature 1800-1950 (2 vols), Univ Calif, 61; Paul Bjarnason: Poet and translator, Am-Scand Rev, fall 71. *Mailing Add:* 3 Windsor Rise Monterey CA 93940

BJERKE, ROBERT ALAN, b Eau Claire, Wis, Dec 23, 39. GERMANIC LANGUAGES. *Educ:* Univ Wis, BA, 61, MA, 62, PhD(Ger), 66; Univ Minn-Minneapolis, MA, 73. *Prof Exp:* Asst prof Norweg, St Olaf Col, 66-71; LIBRN, UNIV WIS CTR-MANITOWOC COUNTY, 73- *Res:* Genealogy; Norwegian language and literature; bibliography. *Publ:* Auth, The Elkinton Family, private publ, 63; Glossary to Henrik Ibsen's Et Dukkehjem, Norweg Dept, St Olaf, 68; A Contrastive Study of Old German and Old Norwegian Kinship Terms, Ind Univ, 69; Fifteen Modern Norwegian Stories: An Intermediate Norwegian Reader, St Olaf Col, 71; The families of Thomas and Henry Bush, 3/72 & The family of Gilbert and Inga Nelson, 3/72, Minn Geneal; Utvandringen fra Nannestad til Amerika, In: Nannestad Bygdebok, Vol 4. *Mailing Add:* Univ Wis Ctr Univ Wis Ctr Manitowoc WI 54220

BJORK, ROBERT ERIC, Medieval & Scandinavian Literature. See Vol II

BJORKLUND, BERNIEL BETH, b Henning, Minn, Mar 28, 42. GERMAN LANGUAGE & LITERATURE. *Educ:* Wheaton Col, AB, 64; Univ Minn, BA, 66; Ind Univ, PhD(Ger), 75. *Prof Exp:* Lectr Ger, Ind Univ, 74-75; asst prof, Furman Univ, 76-78; ASST PROF GER, UNIV VA, 78- *Concurrent Pos:* Ohio State Univ fel, Ger, 75-76; Univ Minn res grant, Ger, 77; Furman Univ res grant, 77; dir develop, comp lit, W K Kellogg Found, 77-78; Nat Endowment for Humanities grant, 81-82; Columbia Univ Soc of Fels, 82-84. *Mem:* MLA; SAtlantic Mod Lang Asn; Am Comp Lit Asn; Am Asn Teachers Ger. *Res:* German language and literature; comparative literature. *Publ:* Auth, A Study in Comparative Prosody, Stuttgarter Arbeiten zur Germanistik, 78; Elements of poetic rhythm, Poetics, No 8, 79; Cognitive strategies in a text, J Lit Semantics, No 8, 79; Dunkel ist Licht genug, Mod Austrian Lit, No 12, 79; Klopstock's poetic innovations, Germanic Rev, No 56, 81; Tradition and innovation, World Lit Today, No 55, 81; transl & ed, Poetry, interviews, and essays in a special Austrian issue, Lit Rev, No 25, 82. *Mailing Add:* Dept of Ger Lang & Lit Univ of Va Charlottesville VA 22903

BLACK, JOEL DANA, b Boston, Mass, Aug 18, 50. COMPARATIVE LITERATURE, CULTURAL HISTORY. *Educ:* Columbia Univ, BA, 72, MA, 73; Stanford Univ, PhD(comp lit), 79. *Prof Exp:* Asst prof, Hamilton Col, 78-79; vis asst prof, 79-80, ASST PROF COMP LIT, UNIV NC, CHAPEL HILL, 80- *Mem:* MLA; Int Comp Lit Asn; Am Comp Lit Asn; Hist Sci Soc. *Res:* Enlightenment and Romanticism; history of criticism and critical theory; history and philosophy of science. *Publ:* Auth, Rhetorical questions and critical riddles, Poetics Today, summer 80; Probing a post-Romantic paleontology: Thomas Pynchon's Gravity's Rainbow, Boundary 2, winter 80; Levana: Levitation in Jean Paul and Thomas De Quincey, Comp Lit, Vol 32, 42-62; contribr, Fragments: Incompletion and Discontinuity, NY Lit Forum, Vols 8-9, 81; The paper empires and empirical fictions of William Gaddis, Rev Contemp Fiction, summer 82. *Mailing Add:* Curric Comp Lit Univ NC Chapel Hill NC 27514

BLACK, MARGARETTA, b Chicago, Ill, Oct 26, 33. FRENCH LANGUAGE & LITERATURE. *Educ:* Marian Col, BA, 61; Case Western Reserve Univ, MA, 66; Univ Wis-Madison, PhD(French), 72. *Prof Exp:* Teacher Elem Schs, Ind, 54-62; teacher French & hist, Acad Immaculate Conception, Oldenburg, 62-65; instr French, Marian Col, Ind, 66-69, asst prof, 71-80, dean acad affairs, 74-80. *Mem:* Am Asn Higher Educ; Am Conf Acad Deans. *Res:* The French novel since 1950; French cultural history--Middle Ages and Renaissance. *Mailing Add:* 3200 Cold Spring Rd Indianapolis IN 46222

BLACK, ROBERT GREENOUGH, b Rosewell, NMex, Dec 17, 44. SPANISH MEDIEVAL LITERATURE, COMPARATIVE LITERATURE. *Educ:* Univ Calif, Berkeley, AB, 69 MA, 73, PhD(Romance lang & lit), 77. *Prof Exp:* ASST PROF SPAN, BELOIT COL, 77- *Mem:* MLA; Midwest Mod Lang Asn; Int Courtly Lit Soc; Medieval Acad Am. *Res:* Spanish Medieval poetry and prose; Spanish American modernism; early Romance language narrative. *Publ:* Auth, Poetic taste at the Argonese court in Naples, In: Florilegium Hispanicum: Studies in Honor of Dorothy Clotelle Clarke, Hisp Sem Medieval Studies, 82; A further note on the private libraries of Spain, 76-77 & Early Spanish manuscripts in the Chicago area, 79-80, La coronica; ed, Hispanic, Luso-Brazilian & Caribbean magazines, In: Magazines for Libraries, Bowker, 82. *Mailing Add:* Dept of Mod Lang & Lit Beloit Col Beloit WI 53511

BLACKALL, ERIC ALBERT, b London, Eng, Oct 19, 14; m 60; c 1. GERMAN & COMPARATIVE LITERATURE. *Educ:* Cambridge Univ, BA, 36, MA, 40, LittD, 60; Univ Vienna, Austria, DPhil, 38. *Prof Exp:* Lectr English lang & lit, Univ Basel, 38-39; asst lectr & univ lectr Ger, Cambridge Univ, 39-58; vis prof Ger lit, 57-58, chmn dept, 58-65, Avalon Found prof humanities, 64-67, JACOB GOULD SCHURMAN PROF GER LIT, CORNELL UNIV, 67-, DIR HUMANITIES, 80- *Concurrent Pos:* Fel, Gonville & Caius Col, Cambridge Univ, 45-58; Guggenheim fel, 65-66; vis prof, Univ Heidelberg, 68. *Honors & Awards:* J G Robertson Prize, 62; Honor Cross Art & Sci, First Class, Austria, 73. *Mem:* Am Philos Soc; AAUP; Int Arthur Schnitzler Res Asn; MLA; Am Asn Teachers Ger. *Res:* Romanticism; 18th century German language and literature; Austrian literature. *Publ:* Auth, Adalbert Stifter, A Critical Study, Cambridge Univ, 48; The Emergence of German as a Literary Language, Cambridge Univ, 59 & Cornell Univ, 2nd ed, 78; Die Entwicklung des Deutschen zur Literatursprache 1700-1775, Metzler, Stuttgart, 66; Goethe and the Novel, Cornell Univ, 76. *Mailing Add:* Dept of Ger Cornell Univ Ithaca NY 14853

BLACKWELL, FREDERICK WARN , b Spokane, Wash, Sept 9, 36; m; c 1. SOUTH ASIAN CULTURE, LITERATURE. *Educ:* Wash State Univ, BA, 58, MA, 60; Univ Wis, MA, 65, PhD(SAsian lang & lit), 73. *Prof Exp:* Asst prof hist, Wash State Univ, 69-72, asst prof English, 70-72, asst prof foreign lang & lit, 72-76, univ ombudsman, 79-81, ASSOC PROF FOREIGN LANG & LIT, WASH STATE UNIV, 76-, DIR EAST & SOUTH ASIA PROGRAM, 80- *Concurrent Pos:* Exec comt, NIndian Studies Asn, 77-80 & Philol Asn Pac Coast, 78-81; educ consult, Educ Resources Ctr, New Delhi, 80; assoc ed, J SAsian Lit, 81- *Res:* Literature of and about India, in English--especially that of Ruth Prawer Jhabvala, Ruskin Bond, Dina Mehta and Paul Scott; contemporary South Asian religious movements in the United States; translation of contemporary Hindi writers. *Publ:* Auth, Comment on Mohan Rakesh and socialist realism, SAsia Ser Occas Paper, 74; Four plays of Nissim Ezekiel, J SAsian Lit, 76; Experiences of teaching South Asian literature to non-Asians, SAsia Perspectives, 77; ed, Feminine sensibility and characterization issue, J SAsian Lit, Vol 13, No 3 & 4; auth, Perception of the Guru in the fiction of Ruth Prawer Jhabvala, J Indian Writing English, 77; Krishna motifs in the poetry of Sarojini Naidu and Kamala Das, 78 & coauth, Mohan Rakesh's Lahrom Ke Rajhans and Ashvagosha's Saundarananda, 78, J SAsian Lit; auth, In defense of Kaikeyi and Draupadi, Indian Lit, 78. *Mailing Add:* East & South Asia Prog Wash State Univ Pullman WA 99164

BLACKWELL, MARILYN JOHNS, b Cincinnati, Ohio, Aug 1, 48; m 80. SCANDINAVIAN LITERATURE, FILM. *Educ:* Univ Wis, BA, 70; Univ Wash, MA, 73, PhD(Scand lit), 76. *Prof Exp:* Lectr, Univ BC, 75-77; ASST PROF, UNIV VA, 77- *Concurrent Pos:* Mellon fac fel, Harvard Univ, 81-82. *Mem:* Soc Advan Scand Studies; MLA. *Res:* Comparative literature. *Publ:* Auth, Oväder and Smutronstllet: Journey into Autumn, Scand Studies, fall 78; Medieval epic and psychological drama in Bergman's Det sjunde inseglet and Strindberg's Folkungasagan, Scandinavica 18, 5/79; Almqvist's novel The Queen's Jewelpiece and Schlegel's concept of the novel, Monatshefte, summer 80; Friedrich Schlegel and C J L Almqvist: Romantic irony and textual artifice, Scand Studies, summer 80; ed, Structures of Influence: A Comparative Approach to August Strindberg, Univ NC Press, 81. *Mailing Add:* Dept Ger Univ Va Charlottesville VA 22903

BLAIR, ROBERT WALLACE, b Santa Barbara, Calif, Sept 25, 30; m 53; c 5. LINGUISTICS, APPLIED LINGUISTICS. *Educ:* Brigham Young Univ, BA, 55, MA, 57, Ind Univ, PhD(ling), 64. *Prof Exp:* From instr to asst prof English, 59-67, assoc prof ling, 67-72, PROF LING, BRIGHAM YOUNG UNIV, 72- *Concurrent Pos:* Res assoc, Univ Chicago, 64-67. *Mem:* Ling Soc Am; Am Coun Teaching Foreign Lang; Teachers English Speakers Other

Lang; Pac Northwest Conf Foreign Lang. *Res:* Linguistics and language teaching; Amerindian languages--Mayan, Guarani, Quechua, Aymara, Navajo. *Publ:* Coauth, Spoken (Yucatec) Maya, Univ Chicago, 66, Guarani Basic Course, 68, Cakchiquel Basic Course, 68 & Mam Basic Course, 69, Peace Corps; coauth, Navaho Basic Course, 69 & Ecuadorian Quechua Basic Course, 72, Brigham Young Univ; ed, Innovative Approaches to Language Teaching and Learning, Newbury House (in press). *Mailing Add:* Dept of Ling Brigham Young Univ Provo UT 84602

BLAISDELL, FOSTER WARREN, JR, b Omaha, Nebr, Jan 3, 27; m 52; c 3. GERMAN, OLD NORSE. *Educ:* Univ Calif, AB, 50, MA, 51, PhD(Ger ling), 56. *Prof Exp:* From instr to assoc prof, 56-67, PROF GER LANG, IND UNIV, BLOOMINGTON, 67- *Concurrent Pos:* Am Coun Learned Soc grants-in-aid, 60 & 70; Fulbright teacher exchange, Ger, 60-61; vis asst prof, Univ Wash, 62-63. *Mem:* Am Asn Teachers Ger; Ling Soc Am; Soc Advan Scand Studies (pres, 75-77); Int Arthurian Soc (pres, 75-79). *Res:* Old Icelandic; comparative Germanic linguistics; semantics. *Publ:* Ed, Erex Saga Artuskappa, Munksgaard, Copenhagen, 65; auth, Observations on style in the riddarasogur 65 & Ivens Saga: Names, 2/69, Scand Studies; The present participle in the Ivens Saga, In: Studies for Einar Haugen, Mouton, The Hague, 72; co-transl, Erex Saga and Ivens Saga: The Old Norse Versions of Chretien de Troyes's Erec and Yvain, Univ Nebr, 77; ed, Ivens Saga, Reitzel, 79; The Sagas of Ywain and Tristan and Other Tales, Rosenkilde & Bagger, 80. *Mailing Add:* Dept of Ger Lang Ind Univ Bloomington IN 47405

BLAKE, ELIZABETH STANTON, b New York, NY, Apr 28, 30. FRENCH. *Educ:* Columbia Univ, AB, 52, PhD(French), 67; Middlebury Col, AM, 53. *Prof Exp:* Instr French, Barnard Col, Columbia Univ, 56-63; instr, Wellesley Col, 63-67, coordr, spec acad progs, 73-74, asst prof, 67-79, dean acad progs, 74-79; ACAD DEAN & PROF FRENCH, UNIV MINN, MORRIS, 79- *Concurrent Pos:* Fac assoc, Danforth Found, 70-; Wellesley Col & Ford Found res grant, 71-72; consult & evaluator, Nat Coun Arts, 81- *Mem:* Int Ling Asn; AAUP; MLA; Am Asn Teachers Fr; Am Asn Higher Educ. *Res:* French language teaching; French phonetics; French 19th century literature. *Publ:* Auth, Un correspondant Americain de Mallarme, avec deux lettres et un document inedits, Rev Hist Lit Fr, 1-2/68; Inter-language contrast in the teaching of French pronunciation, Fr Rev, 2/73; Classroom and context: An educational dialectic, Acad Bull AAUP, 9/79. *Mailing Add:* Acad Dean Univ Minn Morris MN 56267

BLAKE, JAMES JOSEPH, English & Irish Literature. See Vol II

BLAKEY, JOHN MAWSON, b New York, NY, Dec 16, 42; m 69. CLASSICS. *Educ:* Dartmouth Col, AB, 64; Univ NC, Chapel Hill, MA, 68, PhD(classics), 72. *Prof Exp:* Instr classics, Washington & Lee Univ, 72; asst prof, 73-79, ASSOC PROF CLASS, LENOIR RHYNE COL, 80- *Mem:* Am Philol Asn. *Res:* Greek poetry. *Mailing Add:* Div of Humanities Lenoir Rhyne Col Hickory NC 28601

BLANCHARD, HOMER DISBRO, b Elyria, Ohio, Mar 26, 12; m 34; c 3. LINGUISTICS. *Educ:* Ohio Wesleyan Univ, BA, 33; Ohio State Univ, MA, 34, PhD(Ger), 40. *Prof Exp:* Asst Ger, Ohio State Univ, 34-37; asst prof foreign lang, Geneva Col, 37-38, prof Ger, 38-42; instr, US Naval Acad, 42-46 & Hagerstown Jr Col, 48-51; from assoc prof to prof, 63-77, dir univ Ger studies prog, Austria, 65-67, co-dir, 71 & 72, EMER PROF GER, OHIO WESLEYAN UNIV, 77- *Concurrent Pos:* Asst sales mgr, M P Möller, Inc, Md, 46-52, Ohio sales rep, 52-59; owner, H D Blanchard Pipe Organs, 59-72; lectr, Union Theol Sem, NY, 49-52; ed & publ, Praestant Press, 75- *Mem:* Am Guild Organists; Organ Hist Soc. *Res:* History of organ-building terminology; pipe organ history and construction. *Publ:* Transl, H G Klais & H Steinhaus: The Bamboo Organ, 77 & C W Lindow: Historic Organs in France, 80, Praestant; contribr, The organ in the United States: A study in design, Part II, The Tracker, fall 80; transl, A Wolf: Graphic representation and functional systematics of historic musical temperaments, Internationale Zeitschrift für Orgelbau, 12/80; coauth (with C W Lindow), A Little Organ Lexicon, Praestant, 81; transl, K Hofmann: Georg Philipp Telemann, 1681-1767, Am Organist, 11/81; ed, Organs of Our Time II, 81 & Organs of Our Time--Review, 82, Praestant. *Mailing Add:* 103 Griswold St Delaware OH 43015

BLANCO-AGUINAGA, CARLOS, b Irun, Spain, Nov 9, 26; m 50; c 3. ROMANCE LANGUAGES, SPANISH LITERATURE. *Educ:* Harvard Univ, BA, 48; Nat Univ Mex, PhD(Span), 53. *Prof Exp:* From instr to assoc prof Span lit, Ohio State Univ, 53-62; prof, Johns Hopkins Univ, 62-64; PROF SPAN LIT, UNIV CALIF, SAN DIEGO, 64- *Concurrent Pos:* Guggenheim fel, 58-59. *Mem:* MLA; Asoc Int Hispanistas. *Res:* XIX and XX century literature; Golden Age; poetry; the novel. *Publ:* Auth, Unamuno, teorico de lenguaje, 53 & El Unamuno contemplativo, 58, El Col Mex; Emilio Prado, vida y obra, Rev Hist Mod, 59; Juventud del 98, 72; ed, Emilio Prados obras completas, Aguilar, 74. *Mailing Add:* Dept of Lit Third Col Univ of Calif San Diego La Jolla CA 92093

BLANCO-GONZALEZ, MANUEL, b Cadiz, Spain, Sept 2, 32; US citizen; m 64; c 2. CONTEMPORARY LITERATURE. *Educ:* Univ Chicago, MA, 59. *Prof Exp:* Instr Span, Loyola Univ Chicago, 60-62 & Univ Calif, Riverside, 62-63; vis lectr Latin Am Studies, Univ Chicago, 63-64; instr, 64-69, ASSOC PROF SPAN, UNIV ILL, CHICAGO CIRCLE, 70- *Mem:* MLA; Am Asn Teachers Span & Port; AAUP. *Res:* Latin American contemporary literature; contemporary poetry. *Publ:* Auth, J L Borges, el Tiempo en su Obra, Studium, Mexico, 63; Cancion Desnuda (poetry), 64 Gredos, Spain; co-ed, Revised Spanish-English Dict Velazquez, Follett, 64; auth, Ya no es la Primavera Pasada, 67, Memoria y Tiempo, 69 & Gente, 71, Gredos, Spain; Ritos de Pasaje, Poems and Etchings, private ed, 77; Pantomiuma, Narrations and Woodcuts, Graphicas Condor, 78. *Mailing Add:* Dept of Span Univ of Ill Chicago Circle Chicago IL 60680

BLANEY, BENJAMIN, b Newton, Mass, Sept 6, 40; m 69; c 3. GERMANIC LINGUISTICS. *Educ:* Colby Col, AB, 62; Middlebury Col, MA, 64; Univ Colo, Boulder, PhD(Ger ling), 72. *Prof Exp:* Teacher Ger & English, Woodbridge Jr High Sch, NJ, 62-63; instr Ger, Mich Technol Univ, 64-67; ASST PROF GER, MISS STATE UNIV, 72- *Mem:* Am Asn Teachers Ger; MLA; SAtlantic Mod Lang Asn; Soc Advan Scand Studies. *Res:* Historical linguistics; medieval German literature; Old Norse literature. *Mailing Add:* Dept of For Lang Miss State Univ Mississippi State MS 39762

BLASI, ALBERTO O, b Buenos Aires, Arg, Jan 21, 31. SPANISH AMERICAN LITERATURE, COMPARATIVE LITERATURE. *Educ:* Univ Buenos Aires, PESNE en Let, 57, Lic en Let, 65; Univ La Plata, Dr Let, 76. *Prof Exp:* Prof hist cult, Teacher's Col, Buenos Aires, 58-69; prof Arg lit, Univ Rosario, 69-73; vis assoc prof, 75-76, assoc prof, 76-78, PROF MOD LANG, BROOKLYN COL, 79-, MEM DOCTORAL FAC, GRAD CTR, CITY UNIV NEW YORK, 77- *Concurrent Pos:* Dir, Sem theory lit, Univ Buenos Aires, 65-69; Arg Found for Arts fel, 66; Boursier de Marque comp lit, French Govt, 72; vis writer, Univ Iowa, 74-75, hon fel writing, 76; City Univ New York res award, 80-82. *Honors & Awards:* Munic Literary Prize, Munic Buenos Aires, 67; Nat Literary Prize, Arg Found for Arts, 69. *Mem:* Am Asn Teachers Span & Port; Int Comp Lit Asn; Int Inst Ibero-Am Lit; Asoc Int Hisp; PEN Club. *Res:* Nineteenth century and early 20th century Spanish American narrative; European and Ibero American naturalism and avant-garde movements; Ricardo Güiraldes. *Publ:* Auth, Los Fundadores: Cambaceres, Martel, Sicardi, Ed Cult Arg, 62; Introduccion a Lucio Lopez, 65 & La tarea del cuento en Fin de Siglo, 68, Huemul; Guiraldes y Larbaud: una amistad creadora, Nova, 70; Manuel T Podesta, Acad Arg Let, 76; ed, Manuel Peyrou's El crimen de Don Magin Casanovas, Libr Huemul, 76; co-ed and contribr, Lucio V Mansilla 1831-1981, Univ Calif, Riverside, 81; ed & contribr, Movimientos literarios en Iberoamerica durante el siglo XX: Teoria y practica, Rev Iberoamericana, 82. *Mailing Add:* Span Doctoral Prog Grad Ctr City Univ New York 33 W 42nd St New York NY 10036

BLASZCZYK, LEON THADDEUS, b Warsaw, Poland, Mar 30, 23; US citizen. CLASSICS, SLAVIC LITERATURE. *Educ:* Univ Lodz, Poland, MA, 46; Univ Warsaw, Poland, PhD(classics, Polish cult), 50. *Prof Exp:* Asst classics, Univ Lodz, 45-47; lectr classics, Polish & hist, State Teachers Col, Lodz, 47-52; from asst to assoc prof classics, ancient hist & Polish cult, Univ Lodz, 52-68; vis assoc prof classics, Polish & hist, Jersey City State Col, Columbia Univ & Rutgers Univ, Newark, 71-73; PROF SLAVIC LANG & LIT, NEW YORK UNIV, 73- *Concurrent Pos:* Res fel cult hist, Ecole Pratique des Hautes Etudes, Paris, 61-62; vis prof Polish lang & lit, Hunter Col & State Univ NY Stony Brook, 74-75. *Mem:* Am Philol Asn; Am Asn Advan Slavic Studies; Am Asn Teachers Slavic & E Europ Lang; Polish Inst Arts & Sci Am. *Res:* Roman literature, culture and history, Polish literature, intellectual and artistic culture, especially classical heritage; Polish-Russian literary and cultural relations. *Publ:* Auth, Ancient Rome: A Collection of Sources, Panstwowe Zaklady Wydawnictw Szkolnych, Warsaw, 61; Polish and Foreign-Orchestra Conductors in Poland in the 19th and 20th Centuries, Panstwowe Wydawnictwo Muzyczne, Cracow, 64; Studies on the Roman Senate during the Decline of the Republican Period, Ossolineum, Wroclaw, 65; Polish-Russian musical relations in the Polish Kingdom, In: Miscellanea Muzyczne Polsko-Rosyjskie, Wroclaw, 67; Czech musical emigration to Poland in the 18th and 19th centuries, Promvny, Montreal, 1/76; Polish heroic woman: The motif of the siege of Trembowla in Polish and Russian literature, Polish Rev, 1/78; Mickiewicz's generation and classical heritage: A contribution to the history of neo-humanism in Poland, In: American Contributions to the Eighth International Congress of Slavists, vol 2, Slavica Publ, 78; Jezowski and Bulgarin: A case of plagiarism or collaboration?, Polish Rev, 2/80. *Mailing Add:* 44-15 43rd Ave Apt K4 Long Island City NY 11104

BLATCHFORD, CHARLES H, b Tarrytown, NY, July 15, 36; m 62; c 2. ENGLISH AS A SECOND LANGUAGE. *Educ:* Yale Col, BA, 58; Georgetown Univ, MS, 62; Columbia Univ, PhD(educ psychol & English as a second lang), 70. *Prof Exp:* Tutor English, New Asia Col, Chinese Univ Hong Kong, 58-60, asst lectr, 62-65; asst prof, 69-81, ASSOC PROF ENGLISH AS A SECOND LANG, UNIV HAWAII, MANOA, 81- *Concurrent Pos:* Vis prof, Lanzhou Univ, People's Repub of China, 79-81; vis lectr, Univ Calif, Davis, 82. *Mem:* Teachers English to Speakers Other Lang. *Res:* US teaching English as a second language in adult education programs; the training and education of teachers of English as a foreign language; testing in English as a second language. *Publ:* Auth, A theoretical contribution to ESL diagnostic test construction, 9/71 & Newspapers: Vehicles for teaching ESOL with a cultural focus, 6/73, TESOL Quart; ed, TESOL Training Program Directories, 1971-72, 1972-73, 1973-75, Teachers English to Speakers Other Lang, 73; ed, Directory of Teacher Preparation Programs in TESOL and Bilingual Education, 1976-78, 1978-81, 1981-84, Washington: TESOL, 76, 79 & 82. *Mailing Add:* 3901 Bannister Road Fair Oaks CA 95628

BLATT, GLORIA TOBY, b New York, NY, Oct 21, 24; m 46; c 2. ENGLISH LITERATURE, EDUCATION. *Educ:* Univ Cincinnati, BA, 46; Mich State Univ, MA, 60, PhD(English, educ), 72. *Prof Exp:* Teacher English, Snohomish Publ Schs, Wash, 48-53 & East Lansing Pub Schs, Mich, 60-61; instr Am theol & lang, Mich State Univ, 65-66; assoc educ, Simon Fraser Univ, 72-73; ASST PROF EDUC, OAKLAND UNIV, 74- *Mem:* Nat Coun Teachers English; Int Reading Asn; Children's Lit Asn; Am Educ Res Asn; Adolescent Lit Asn. *Res:* Children's literature; children's developmental responses to literature. *Publ:* Auth, Mexican American in children's literature, Elem English, 4/68; contribr, The Culturally Different Child, Addison-Wesley, 71; auth, Violence in children's realistic fiction, English Quart, spring 73; coauth, Movement: a creative approach to poetry, Elem Sch J, 5/75; auth, Children's books, X or PG?, Top News, 11/75; On beyond veatch, ERIC, 10/76; Playing with language, Reading Teacher, 2/78. *Mailing Add:* Sch of Educ Oakland Univ Rochester MI 48063

BLAYLOCK, CURTIS, b Monroe, Okla, Sept 13, 33; m 56; c 2. ROMANCE PHILOLOGY. *Educ:* Univ Okla, BA, 53; Stanford Univ, MA, 55; Univ Calif, Berkeley, PhD(Romance philol), 64. *Prof Exp:* Instr Span, Univ Tex, 59-62; asst, 62-64, from asst prof to assoc prof, 64-73, PROF SPAN, UNIV ILL, URBANA, 73- *Mem:* Soc Ling Romane; Ling Soc Europe; Ling Soc Am; Am Asn Teachers Span & Port. *Res:* Comparative Romance linguistics; Hispanic philology. *Publ:* Auth, The Monophthongization of Latin AE in Spanish, 8/64 & Latin L-, -LL- in the Hispanic Dialects: Retroflexion and Lenition, 5/68, Romance Philol; The UDO Participles in Old Spanish, In: Homenaje a Antonio Tovar, Ed Gredos, Madrid, 72; Observations on Sound Change, Especially Loss, with Particular Reference to Hispano-Romance, In: Issues in Linguistics, Univ Ill, 73; The Romance Development of the Latin Verbal Augment -SK-, Romance Philol, 5/75; Los Preteritos Fuertes en -SK- del Espanol Medieval, In: Studia Hispanica in Honorem Rafael Lapesa, Vol III, Gredos, Madrid, 75. *Mailing Add:* Dept of Span Ital & Port Univ of Ill Urbana IL 61801

BLEIBERG, GERMAN, b Madrid, Spain, Mar 14, 15; m 36; c 2. SPANISH LITERATURE & HISTORY. *Educ:* Univ Madrid, Lic-Filos-y-Let, 47, PhD(Span lit & hist), 58. *Prof Exp:* Asst prof, Spanish lit, Univ Madrid, 47-53; vis assoc prof Romance lang, Univ Notre Dame, 61-62; prof Span, Vanderbilt Univ, 62-66; prof Romance lang, Univ Mass, 66-67; prof Span, Vassar Col, 67-80, dir, Vassar-Wesleyan Semester in Madrid & chmn dept, 77-80; PROF, DEPT HISP & ITAL STUDIES, STATE UNIV NY ALBANY, 80- *Concurrent Pos:* Lit consult, Rev de Occidente, Madrid, 53; dir, Tamesis Bks Ltd, London, 64; dir & organizer, Int Symp on Unamuno, 64; Am Philos Soc fel, 65; Am Coun Learned Soc fel, 68. *Honors & Awards:* Premio Nac Lit, Spain, 37; Premio Extraordinario, Univ Madrid, 58. *Mem:* Hisp Soc Am; Asoc Int Hispanistas; MLA. *Res:* Mateo Aleman and the picaresque novel; Garcia Lorca; Pablo Neruda. *Publ:* Auth, Mas alla de las ruinas (poetry), Rev de Occidente, 47; Algunas revistas literarias hacia 1898, Arbor, 48; Antologia de elogios de la lengua espanola, Inst Cult Hisp, 51; co-ed, Diccionario de literatura espanola, 3rd ed, 64, auth, Mateo Aleman y los galeotes, 66, Rev de Occidente; co-ed, Twentieth Century Spanish Thought and Letters, Vanderbilt Univ, 66; auth, Nuevos datos biograficos de Mateo Aleman, Actas II Int Congr of Hispanists, 67; ed, Diccionario de historia de Espana, Rev de Occidente (3 vols), 2nd ed, 68. *Mailing Add:* Dept of Hisp & Ital Studies State Univ of NY Albany NY 12222

BLEZNICK, DONALD WILLIAM, b New York, NY, Dec 24, 24; m 52; c 2. ROMANCE LANGUAGES. *Educ:* City Col New York BA, 46; Nat Univ Mex, MA, 48; Columbia Univ, PhD(Span lit), 54. *Prof Exp:* Instr Romance lang, Ohio State Univ, 49-55; from asst prof to prof, Pa State Univ, 55-67; head dept, 67-72, PROF ROMANCE LANG, UNIV CINCINNATI, 67- *Concurrent Pos:* Assoc ed, Hispania, 63-74, ed, 74-; Am Philos Soc grant, 64. *Honors & Awards:* Knight's Cross of the Order of Civil Merit, King Juan Carlos I of Spain, 77; Rieveschl Award, 80. *Mem:* MLA; Am Asn Teachers Span & Port; Renaissance Soc Am; Midwest Mod Lang Asn; Comediantes. *Res:* Political theory of Spain's Golden Age and its influence on literature; history of the Spanish essay; Spanish Golden Age literature. *Publ:* Coauth, La benina misericordiosa: conciliacion entre la filosofia y la fe, Cuadernos Hispanoam, 71; auth, A guide to journals in the Hispanic field, Hispania, 72; Quevedo, Twayne, 72; ed, Variaciones Interpretativas en Torno a la Nueva Narrativa Hispanoamericana, 72; co-ed, Directions of Literary Criticism in the Seventies, Univ Cincinnati, 72; auth, Ver para vivir and paradise regained in the Criticon, In: Studies Dedicated to Helmut Hatzfeld, Porrua, 74; Sourcebook for Hispanic Language and Literature, Temple Univ, 74; Homenaje a Luis Leal, Insula, Madrid, 79. *Mailing Add:* Dept of Romance lang Univ of Cincinnati Cincinnati OH 45221

BLICKENSTAFF, CHANNING B, b Lafayette, Ind, Oct 8, 34; m 56; c 2. SPANISH LANGUAGE & EDUCATION. *Educ:* Purdue Univ, BS, 56, MSEd, 61, PhD(foreign lang educ), 65. *Prof Exp:* From instr to asst prof Span, 60-68, dir lang lab, 62-65, asst head dept mod lang, 65-73, asst dean grad sch, 73-80, ASSOC PROF SPAN, PURDUE UNIV, WEST LAFAYETTE, 68-, EXEC ASST DEAN GRAD SCH, 80- *Res:* Foreign language teaching and learning. *Publ:* Auth, Musical Talents and Foreign Language Learning Ability, Mod Lang J, 12/63; coauth, Teacher Preparation for Language Laboratories, Education, 3/65; A Comparison of the Monostructural and Dialogue Approaches to the Teaching of College Spanish, Mod Lang J, 1/67. *Mailing Add:* Dept of Foreign Lang & Lit Purdue Univ West Lafayette IN 47907

BLIQUEZ, LAWRENCE JOHN, b Des Moines, Iowa, June 12, 41; m 69; c 2. CLASSICAL LANGUAGES, ANCIENT HISTORY. *Educ:* St Mary's Col, Calif, BA, 63; Stanford Univ, PhD(classics), 68. *Prof Exp:* Asst prof classics, San Francisco State Col, 66-69; asst prof, 69-77, ASSOC PROF CLASSICS & ART, UNIV WASH, 77. *Mem:* Am Philol Asn; Archaeol Inst Am; Soc Ancient Med. *Res:* Greek and Roman surgical instruments; Greek history; classical archaeology. *Publ:* Auth, Anthemocritus and the orgas disputes, Greek Roman Byzantine Studies, Vol 10, 69; A new bronze Harpocrates in the De Young Museum in San Francisco, Am J Archaeol, Vol 76, 72; Lions and Greek sculptors, Class World, Vol 68, 75; Cypriot pottery in Washington state, Corpus of Cypriot Antiquities 6, 78; Frogs and mice and Athens, Trans Proc, Am Philol Asn, Vol 107, 77; Greek and Roman medicine, Archaeol, Vol 34, 81; An unidentified Roman surgical instrument in Bingen, J of the Hist of Med, Vol 36, 81; Philip II and Abdera, Eranos, Vol 79, 81. *Mailing Add:* Dept of Classics Univ of Wash Seattle WA 98195

BLISS, FRANCIS ROYSTER, b Big Stone Gap, Va, June 7, 19; m 43; c 3. LATIN, GREEK. *Educ:* Bowdoin Col, AB, 40; Univ NC, PhD(Latin), 51. *Prof Exp:* From instr to asst prof classics, Colby Col, 48-55; assoc prof, Western Reserve Univ, 55-66; assoc prof classics, Univ Vt, 66-70, prof, 70-79; RETIRED. *Mem:* Class Asn Mid W & S; Class Asn New England; Soc Ancient Greek Philos; Vergilian Soc; Am Philol Asn. *Res:* Literary imitation; cultural history. *Publ:* Auth, Roman law and Romand citizenship, In: Law in a Troubled World, Western Reserve Univ, 59; The Plancus ode, Trans & Proc Am Philol Asn, 60; A rogues' gallery, Class Outlook, 63; Unity of Odyssey Eight, Bucknell Rev, 68. *Mailing Add:* RFD 1 Box 240 New Vineyard ME 04956

BLOCH, ARIEL ALFRED KARL, b Heidelberg, Ger, May 14, 33. SEMITIC LANGUAGES, LINGUISTICS. *Educ:* Hebrew Univ, Israel, BA, 57; Univ Munster, Dr Phil(Semitic lang & Arabic), 62. *Prof Exp:* Asst Semitic lang & Arabic, Univs Munster & Erlangen, 62-65; from asst prof to assoc prof, 65-74, PROF SEMITIC LANG & ARABIC, UNIV CALIF, BERKELEY, 74- *Concurrent Pos:* Am Coun Learned Soc res grant, 69-70; Nat Endowment Humanities sr fel, 74-75. *Mem:* Mid E Studies Asn N Am; Am Orient Soc: Ling Soc Am. *Res:* Arabic dialectology; Semitic and general linguistics. *Publ:* Auth, Zur nachweisbarkeit einer hebraischen entsprechung der akkadischen verbalform Iparras, Z Deut Morgenlandischen Ges; coauth, Damaszensich-Arabische texte mit ubersetzung, anmerkungern und glossar, In: Vol 2, 64 & auth, Die hypotaxe im Damaszenisch-Arabischen mit vergleichen zur hypotaxe im klassisch- Arabischen, In: Vol 4, 65; Abhandlungen fur die Kunde des Morgenlandes, F Steiner, Wiesbaden; The vowels of the imperfect preformatives in the old dialects of Arabic, Z Deut Morgenlandischen Ges, 67; Morphological doublets in Arabic dialects, J Semitic Studies, 71; A Chrestomathy of Modern Literary Arabic, Otto Harrassowitz, Wiesbaden, 74. *Mailing Add:* Dept of Near Eastern Lang Univ of Calif Berkeley CA 94720

BLOCH, HERBERT, b Berlin, Ger, Aug 18, 11; nat US; m 43, 60; c 2. CLASSICS, HISTORY. *Educ:* Univ Rome, DLett (ancient hist), 35, dipl, 37. *Hon Degrees:* AM, Harvard Univ, 47. *Prof Exp:* Instr Greek & Latin, 41-42, from fac instr to assoc prof, 42-53, prof, 53-73, Pope prof, 73-82, EMER POPE PROF LATIN LANG & LIT, HARVARD UNIV, 82- *Concurrent Pos:* Guggenheim fel, 50-51; Fulbright res award, Italy, 50-51; mem, Inst Advan Study, 53-54; prof-in-chg, Sch Class Studies, Am Acad Rome, 57-59; sr fel soc fels, Harvard Univ, 64-79; trustee, Loeb Class Libr, 64-73; Nat Endowment for Humanities fel, 76-77. *Mem:* Am Philos Soc; fel Pontifical Roman Acad Archaeol; fel Am Acad Arts & Sci; Am Philol Asn (pres, 69); fel Mediaeval Acad Am. *Res:* Ancient and medieval historiography; Monte Cassino; Latin epigraphy. *Publ:* Auth, I bolli laterizi e la storia edilizia romana, Commune, Rome, 38, 47; Supplement to Corpus Inscriptionum Latinarum XV, Harvard Univ, 47-48; coauth, Scavi di Ostia I, III, Libreria dello Stato, Rome, 53 & 58; ed, F Jacoby, Abhandlungen zur griechischen Geschichtschreibung, Brill, Leiden, 56; Monte Cassino's teachers and library in the Middle Ages, Centro Italiano, Spoleto, 72; auth, The Bombardment of Monte Cassino: A New Appraisal, Montecassino, 76; Monte Cassino in the Middle Ages, Ed Storia e Lett, Rome & Harvard Univ, 82. *Mailing Add:* 524 Pleasant St Belmont MA 02178

BLOCK, ELIZABETH, b Chicago, Ill, June 7, 46. CLASSICAL LANGUAGES, COMPARATIVE LITERATURE. *Educ:* Pomona Col, BA, 68; Univ Calif, Berkeley, PhD(comp lit), 77. *Prof Exp:* ASST PROF CLASSICS, UNIV PA, 77- *Mem:* Am Philol Asn. *Res:* Latin poetry; epic. *Publ:* Auth, Failure to Thrive: The Themes of Parents and Children in the Aeneid, Ramos, 80; Ex Pont 3.9, Class Antiquity, 81; The Effect of Divine Manifestations on the Reader's Perspective in Vergil's Aeneid, Arno Press, 81; The Narrator Speaks: Apostrophe in Homer and Vergil, Tapa, 82. *Mailing Add:* Dept of Classics Univ of Pa Philadelphia PA 19174

BLOCK, HASKELL M, b Chicago, Ill, June 13, 23. COMPARATIVE LITERATURE. *Educ:* Univ Chicago, AB, 44; Harvard Univ, AM, 47; Univ Paris, D Univ, 49. *Prof Exp:* Teaching fel French & humanities, Harvard Univ, 48-49; instr English, Queens Col, NY, 49-52; from asst prof to assoc prof comp lit, Univ Wis, 52-61; prof, Brooklyn Col & Grad Sch, City Univ New York, 61-75; PROF COMP LIT, STATE UNIV NY BINGHAMTON, 75- *Concurrent Pos:* Fulbright res scholar, Univ Cologne, 56-57 & Univ Paris, 68-69; consult ed, Random House, NY, 61-; mem selection comt Western Europe, Foreign Area Fel Prog, 65-68; exec officer, Doctoral Prog Comp Lit, City Univ New York, 68-71; assoc, Sem Theory of Lit, Columbia Univ, 70-; fel, Colloquium Comp Lit, NY Univ, 70-; mem selection comt, Camargo Found, 71-; vis prof English, Univ Düsseldorf, 72-73; chmn exec comt, Eastern Comp Lit Conf, 76-; H Fletcher Brown prof comp lit, Univ Del, 77-78; vis prof comp lit, Univ Antwerp, 81. *Mem:* Inst Comp Lit asn (secy, 58-64); Am Comp Lit Asn (secy, 60-65, vpres. 71-74, pres, 74-77); MLA; Dante Soc Am; Soc Fr Studies. *Res:* Modern drama and novel; symbolist movement. *Publ:* Co-ed, The Creative Vision, Grove, 60 & Masters of Modern Drama, Random, 62; auth, Mallarme and the Symbolist Drama, Wayne, 63; Naturalistic triptych: The fictive and the real in Zola, Mann, and Dreiser, Random, 70; Nouvelles tendances en litterature comparee, Nizet, 70. *Mailing Add:* Dept of Comp Lit State Univ NY Binghamton NY 13901

BLOCK, RALPH HOWARD, b Greensboro, NC, Dec 13, 43; m 71; c 1. FRENCH. *Educ:* Amherst Col, BA, 65; Stanford Univ, PhD(French), 70. *Prof Exp:* Asst prof French, State Univ NY, Buffalo, 70-73; asst prof, 73-76, ASSOC PROF FRENCH, UNIV CALIF BERKELEY, 76- *Mem:* MLA: Mediaeval Acad Am; Soc Roncevals; Int Arthurian Soc. *Res:* Medieval literature; history and law. *Publ:* Auth, Roland and Oedipus, Fr Rev, spring 73; From grail quest to inquest, Mod Lang Rev, 1/74; The death of King Arthur and the waning of the feudal age, Orbis Lit. *Mailing Add:* Dept of French Univ Calif Berkeley CA 94720

BLOCKLEY, ROGER CHARLES, b Leicester, Eng, May 5, 43. ANCIENT HISTORY, CLASSICS. *Educ:* Univ Leicester, BA, 64; McMaster Univ, MA, 66; Univ Nottingham, PhD(classics), 70. *Prof Exp:* Lectr, 66-70, asst prof, 70-75, ASSOC PROF CLASSICS, CARLETON UNIV, 75- *Concurrent Pos:* Can Coun leave fel, 76-77. *Mem:* Class Asn Can; Am Soc Ancient Historians. *Res:* Late Romand and early Byzantine historiolgraphy; political history of the 4th to the 6th century AD; late Romand and early Byzantine coinage. *Publ:* Auth, Internal self-policing in the late Roman administration, Classica et Mediaevalia, 69 & 74; Dexippus and Priscus and the Thucydidean Caesars of Constantius II, Latomus, 72; The panegyric of Claudius Mamertinus on the Emperor Julian, Am J Philol, 72; Tacitean influence upon Ammianus Marcellinus, Latomus, 73; Ammianus Marcellinus: A Study of His Historiography and Politcal Ideas, Bruxelles; Ammianus Marcellinus on the Battle of Strasbury, Phoenix, 77. *Mailing Add:* Dept of Classics Carleton Univ Ottawa ON K1S 5B6 Can

BLODGETT, EDWARD DICKINSON, b Philadelphia, Pa, Feb 26, 35; Can citizen; m 60; c 3. MEDIAEVAL & CANADIAN LITERATURE. *Educ:* Amherst Col, AB, 56; Univ Minn, MA, 61; Rutgers Univ, PhD(comp lit), 69. *Prof Exp:* Lectr French, Inst Am Univs, 61-62; instr English, Rutgers Univ, 63, instr gen lit, 65-66; instr classics, Douglass Col, 66; asst prof English & Romance lang, 66-70, assoc prof comp lit, 70-75, assoc chmn dept, 73-75, PROF COMP LIT & CHMN DEPT, UNIV ALTA, 75- *Concurrent Pos:* Anna von Helmholtz Pehlan scholar creative writing, 60-61; Can Coun grant, 71-72. *Mem:* Can Comp Lit Asn (treas, 73-75); Mediaeval Acad Am; Can Asn Advan Neth Studies; Int Comp Lit Asn. *Res:* Time in medieval literature; modern Canadian literature; modern English and American poetry. *Publ:* Auth, Dante's Purgatory as elegy, In: The Rarer Action, Rutgers Univ, 71; The unquiet heart: Time and the poetry of antiquity and the Middle Ages, Filol Pregled, 71; Mouthful of earth: A word for Edward Thomas, Mod Poetry Studies, 72; The well-wrought void: Reflections on the Ars Amatoria, Class J, 73; The masks of D G Jones, Can Lit, 74; This other Eden: The poetrics of space, In: Horace and Bernart de Ventadorn, Neohelicon, 75; Chaucerian Pryvetee and the opposition to time, Speculum, 76; Cold pastorals: A prolecomenon, Can Rev Comp Lit, 79. *Mailing Add:* Dept of Comp Lit Univ of Alta Edmonton AB T6G 2G2 Can

BLOODWORTH, BERTHA ERNESTINE, English, Linguistics. See Vol II

BLOOM, LEONARD, b Brooklyn, NY, Mar 28, 37; m 64; c 2. MODERN LANGUAGES & LITERATURE. *Educ:* Brooklyn Col, BA, 58; Fla State Univ, MA, 60; Duquesne Univ, MEd, 66; Univ Pittsburgh, PhD(mod lang), 67. *Prof Exp:* Asst prof Span, Duquesne Univ, 64-67; assoc prof, 67-78, PROF SPAN, UNIV BRIDGEPORT, 78- *Concurrent Pos:* Foreign lang consult, Masuk High Sch, Monroe, Conn, 69-70 & Bridgeport Pub Schs, 71. *Mem:* Am Asn Teachers Span & Port; MLA; Royal Soc Friends Basque Country; Inst Americano Estudios Vascos; NE Mod Lang Asn. *Res:* Basque language and studies; medieval Spanish language and literature; Romance linguistics. *Publ:* Auth, Lexical coincidences between Basque and Spanish, Am Soc Geoling, 77; Basque nicknames and related onomastic examples in Pio Baroja'a novels, 77, The name of the game in Hispanic literature, Vol 5, 78, Lit Onomastics Studies; Verbal inflections from Spanish to Basque: Enigma variations, Lang Today, Vol III, 78; Names for God in the Basque language, Lilt Onomastics Studies, Vol 6, 79; Manifestations of early Basque lyric poetry, Vol 1, 80 & Toward an understanding of Cervantes and the Basques, Vol 2, 81, Basque Artistic Expression; Pierre Loti's Homage to Euskalerria: Ramuntcho, Basque Artistic Expression, Vol 4, 82. *Mailing Add:* Dept of Foreign Lang Univ of Bridgeport Bridgeport CT 06602

BLOOMBERG, EDWARD M, b New Rochelle, NY, Dec 23, 37. FRENCH LITERATURE. *Educ:* Yale Univ, BA, 59, PhD(French), 68. *Prof Exp:* Instr French, Yale Univ, 64-66; asst prof, 66-73, ASSOC PROF FRENCH, UNIV CALIF, DAVIS, 74- *Mem:* Am Asn Teachers Fr; MLA. *Res:* Pascal; Proust. *Publ:* Auth, Student Violence, Pub Affairs Press, 70; On the nature of man--who's right?, Wall St J, 12/70; Les Raisons de Pascal, Debresse, 74; Etude semantique du mot raison chez Pascal, 73 & Les sens, la raison et la foi dans la dix-huitiene Provinciale, 75, Orbis Litterarum; Raison et dialectique chez Pascal, Romanic Rev, 75; Coletter et la glycine, Arch Studium Neueren Sprachen u Literaturen, CCZ: 140-143; Les rapports deProust et de son narrateur, Neophilologus, LVII: 238-243. *Mailing Add:* Dept of French & Ital Univ of Calif Davis CA 95616

BLOOMFIELD, MORTON WILFRED, English, History of Ideas. See Vol II

BLUE, BETTY A, b Danville, Ill, Sept 16, 22; m 46; c 2. LINGUISTICS. *Educ:* Univ Ill, AB, 44, MA, 46; Interam Univ, Mex, PhD, 62. *Prof Exp:* Asst Span, Univ Ill, 44-46; instr English & Span, 56-58, from instr to assoc prof Span, 58-69, actg chmn dept foreign lang, 67-68, chmn dept, 69-74, PROF SPAN, SOUTHERN ARK UNIV, 69-, CHMN DIV LANG ARTS, 76- *Concurrent Pos:* Consult, Foreign Lang Elem Schs Prog, 60-63; Fulbright fel, Univ Valladolid, Spain, 66; mem, Nat Comt US Scholars, Spain & Port, 75-76. *Mem:* SCent Mod Lang Asn; MLA; Am Asn Teachers Span & Port; Am Coun Teaching Foreign Lang; Am Asn Cols Teacher Educ. *Res:* Foreign languages in elementary schools; Spanish American civilization; Hispanic civilization: Spain. *Publ:* Auth, Fundamentals of Teaching a Foreign Language, Whitehall, 70; Authentic Mexican Cooking, Prentice-Hall, 77; Authentic Spanish Cooking, Prentice-Hall, 81. *Mailing Add:* Dept of Spn Southern Ark Univ Magnolia AR 71753

BLUE, RHEA C(AMELLIA), Oriental Languages. See Vol IV

BLUE, WILLIAM ROBERT, b Shreveport, La, Apr 2, 43; m 70. SPANISH LITERATURE. *Educ:* Univ Calif, Davis, AB, 65, MA, 67; Penn State Univ, PhD(Span), 71. *Prof Exp:* Asst prof, 70-74, ASSOC PROF SPAN, UNIV KANS, 74- *Concurrent Pos:* Exec Comt 16th & 17th Century Span Drama, MLA, 78-83. *Mem:* MLA; Am Asn Teachers Span & Port; Comediantes. *Res:* Spanish Golden Age theater and literature. *Publ:* Auth, Sol: Image and structure in Lope's La Corona Merecida, Hispania, 73; The functions of the Molinera en Don Gil de las Calzas Verdes, Bull Comediates, 73. *Mailing Add:* Dept of Span & Port Univ of Kans Lawrence KS 66044

BLUHM, HEINZ, b Halle, Ger, Nov 23, 07; nat US. GERMAN LITERATURE. *Educ:* Northwestern Col, Wis, AB, 28; Univ Wis, AM, 29, PhD, 32. *Hon Degrees:* AM, Yale Univ, 50. *Prof Exp:* Instr Ger, Univ Wis, 31-37; from instr to prof, Yale Univ, 37-50, chmn dept Ger lang, 54-63, Leavenworth prof Ger lang & lit, 57-67; chmn dept, 68-76, PROF GER STUDIES, BOSTON COL, 67-; ADJ PROF REFORMATION STUDIES, BOSTON THEOL INST, 76- *Concurrent Pos:* Vis prof, Middlebury Col, 51 & 53 & Dartmouth Col, 64; Guggenheim fel, 57; Newberry Libr fel, 58, 60 & 63, sr fel, 67; Folger Shakespeare Libr fel, 74. *Honors & Awards:* Lyceum lectr, Concordia Theol Sem, 63; Grand Order of Merit, Fed Repub Ger, 71. *Mem:* MLA; Fel Soc Relig Higher Educ. *Res:* Luther; Goethe; Nietzsche. *Publ:* Auth, August von Goethe und Ottilie von Pogwisch: Briefe aus der Verlobungszeit, Böhlau, Weimar, 62; ed, Ottilie von Goethe: Tagebücher und Briefe: Vol I, 1839-1841, 62, Vol II, Briefe an Ottilie von Goethe: 1842-1849, 63, Vol III, Ottilie von Goethe, 1852-1854, 63, Spec Vol, Weimar im Jahre 1832, 64 & Vol IV, Ottilie von Goethe, 1854-1856, 66, Bergland, Vienna & Vol V, Ottilie von Goethe, 1856-1867, Lang, Bern, 78; Essays in History and Literature: Presented to Stanley Pargellis by Fellows of the Newberry Library, Newberry Libr, 65; auth, Martin Luther, Creative Translator, Concordia, 66; Die Entwicklung von Fausts erstem Monolog in der Szene Mitternacht in Faust II, 5, Forschen u Bilden, Mitt Nat Forschungs u Gedenkstätten der Klassischen Deut Lit Weimar, 10/66; The young Nietzsche and the secular city, Mod Lang Notes, 10/69; Bedeutung und Eigenart von Luthers Septembertestament, Luther Jahrbuch, Hamburg, 72. *Mailing Add:* Dept of Ger Studies Boston Col Chestnut Hill MA 02167

BLUM, CAROL KATHLYN, b St Louis, Mo, May 22, 34; m 64; c 2. FRENCH LITERATURE. *Educ:* Wash Univ, BA, 56; Columbia Univ, MA, 60, PhD(French), 66. *Prof Exp:* Lectr French, Columbia Univ, 61-62; instr, 62, ASSOC PROF FRENCH, STATE UNIV NY STONY BROOK, 62- *Concurrent Pos:* Deleg & mem assembly adv comt, Mod Lang Asn; Guggenheim Found fel, 75-76. *Mem:* MLA; Am Soc 18th Century Studies. *Res:* Eighteenth century history of ideas; Dederot; 18th century novel; concept of virtue in the 18th century. *Publ:* Auth, Cognitive style as moral option in La Nouvelle Heloise and Les Liaisons Dangereuses, PMLA, 3/73; Diderot: The Virtue of a Philosopher, Viking, 74. *Mailing Add:* Dept of French & Ital State Univ NY Stony Brook NY 11794

BLUMENTHAL, BERNHARDT GEORGE, b Philadelphia, Pa, Mar 8, 37; m 65. GERMAN. *Educ:* La Salle Col, BA, 59; Northwestern Univ, MA, 61; Princeton Univ, PhD(Ger), 65. *Prof Exp:* Assoc prof, 63-73, PROF GER, LA SALLE COL, 73-, CHMN DEPT FOREIGN LANG & LIT, 69- *Mem:* Am Asn Teachers Ger. *Res:* German and comparative literatures, especially modern. *Publ:* Auth, Gertrud Kolmar: Love's service to the Earth, 9/69 & The play element in the poetry of Else Lasker-Schüler, 9/70, Ger Quart; The poetry class, Unterrichtspraxis, fall 71; Paula Ludwig's poetry: Themes of love and death, Ger Quart, 11/71; The writings of Regina Ullmann, Seminar, 3/73; Original German Lyric Poetry in Lyrical Germanica, 9/74 & Ger Am Studies, 5/77; Imagery in Christine Busta's writing, Seminar, 5/77. *Mailing Add:* Dept of Foreign Lang LaSalle Col Philadelphia PA 19141

BLUMENTHAL, GERDA RENEE, b Berlin, Ger, July 26, 23; US citizen. FRENCH & COMPARATIVE LITERATURE. *Educ:* Hunter Col, BA, 45; Columbia Univ, MA, 47, PhD(French), 55. *Prof Exp:* Lectr French, Columbia Univ, 47-52; instr mod lang, Jamestown Community Col, 52; from asst prof to prof French, Wash Col, 55-68, chmn dept mod lang, 64-68; PROF FRENCH & COMP LIT, CATH UNIV AM, 68- *Concurrent Pos:* Lectr, Juilliard Sch Music, 60-61. *Honors & Awards:* Lindback Award for Distinguished Teaching, 64. *Mem:* MLA. *Res:* Nineteenth and twentieth century French and comparative literature and philosophy; Malraux, Bernanos, Balzac and Dostoevsky; existentialism and modern European literature. *Publ:* Auth, Simone Weil's Way of the Cross, Thought, 52; The Conquest of Dread: A Study of Andre Malraux, 60 & The Poetic Imagination of Georges Bernanos, 65, Johns Hopkins. *Mailing Add:* Dept of Mod Lang Cath Univ of Am Washington DC 20064

BLUMSTEIN, SHEILA ELLEN, b New York, NY, Mar 10, 44. LINGUISTICS, PSYCHOLINGUISTICS. *Educ:* Univ Rochester, AB, 65; Harvard Univ, PhD(ling), 70. *Prof Exp:* Asst prof, 70-76, ASSOC PROF LING, BROWN UNIV, 76- *Concurrent Pos:* Res assoc, Aphasia Res Ctr, Sch Med, Boston Univ, 70-; vis scientist, Mass Inst Technol Res Lab Electronics, 74 & 77-78, consult, 74-; fel, Guggenheim Found, 77-78 & Radcliffe Inst, 77-78; mem, Commun Sci Study Sect, NIH, 76-; bd gov, Acad Aphasia, 78- *Mem:* Acad Aphasia; Ling Soc Am; Acoustical Soc Am. *Res:* Aphasia; speech perception. *Publ:* Auth, A Phonological Investigation of Aphasic Speech, Mouton, 73; co-ed, Psycholinguistics and Aphasica, Johns Hopkins Univ, 73; coauth, The perception and production of voice-onset time in Aphasia, Neuropsychologia, 77; Property detectors for bursts and transitions in speech perception, J Acoustical Soc Am, 77; contribr, The perception of speech in pathology and ontogeny, In: Language Acquisition and Language Breakdown, Johns Hopkins Univ, 78; Segment organization and syllable structure in Aphasia, In: Syllables and Segments, North-Holland, 78. *Mailing Add:* Dept of Ling Box E Brown Univ Providence RI 02912

BLY, PETER ANTHONY, b King's Lynn, England, July 31, 44; Can citizen; m 68; c 2. SPANISH LITERATURE. *Educ:* Univ London, England, BA, 66, MA, 67, PhD(Span), 78. *Prof Exp:* Asst prof, Dalhousie Univ, 68-71; ASSOC PROF SPAN, QUEEN'S UNIV, ONT, 71- *Honors & Awards:* Best Article Award, Can Asn Hispanists, 78, 79 & 80. *Mem:* Can Asn Hispanists (pres, 81-84); Int Asn Hispanists; Int Galdo's Asn; Am Asn Teachers Span & Port; Brit Asn Hispanists. *Res:* works of Benito Perez Galdos; modern Spanish novel; medieval Spanish literature. *Publ:* Auth, From disorder to order: The pattern of arreglar references in Galdo's Tormento and La de Bringas' Neophilologus, 62: 392-405; Sex, egotism and social regeneration in Galdos' El caballero encantado', Hispania, 62: 20-29 ; Sallies and encounters in Torquemada en la hoguera: Patterns of significance, Anales galdosianos, 13: 23-31; Galdos, the Madrid Royal Palace and the September 1868 Revolution, Rev Can Estud Hisp, 5: 1-17; Nazarin: Enigma eterno o triunfo del arte galdosiano?, Cuadernos hispanoam, 224: 286-300; Perez Galdos: La de Bringas, Critical Guides to Spanish Texts, Vol 30, Grant & Cutler & Tamesis Bks, London, 81; History in Benito Perez Galdos's Serie contemporanea, Liverpool Mongr Hisp Studies, Vol 2, Francis Cairns, Liverpool, 82; coauth, Fortunata and Feijoo: Four Studies of a Chapter By Perez Galdos, Tamesis Bks, London, 82. *Mailing Add:* Dept of Span & Ital Queen's Univ Kingston ON K7L 3N6 Can

BOARINO, GERALD L, b Los Angeles, Calif, June 28, 31. ROMANCE LANGUAGES. *Educ:* Univ Calif, Berkeley, BA, 53, MA, 55, PhD(Romance lang & lit), 62. *Prof Exp:* Instr Span, San Francisco State Col, 61-64; asst prof, 64-80, PROF SPAN, CALIF STATE UNIV, FULLERTON, 80- *Concurrent*

Pos: Fulbright fel, Spain, 60-61. *Mem:* Am Asn Teachers Ital. *Res:* Middle Ages; literature of Spain and Italy; contemporary Spanish Peninsular literature. *Publ:* Coauth, Lecturas contemporaneas, Blaisdell, 67 & La actualidad espanola, Plaza Mayor, Madrid, 72. *Mailing Add:* Dept of Foreign Lang Calif State Univ Fullerton CA 92631

BOBETSKY, VICTOR, b New York, NY, Sept 24, 23; m 53; c 2. FOREIGN LANGUAGES. *Educ:* Columbia Univ, BA, 46, AM, 47. *Prof Exp:* From instr to assoc prof, 47-67, PROF GER, POLYTECH INST NEW YORK, 68- *Mem:* MLA; Am Asn Teachers Ger. *Res:* Pedagogical aspects of the teaching and learning of foreign languages. *Publ:* auth, Foreign languages in engineering curricula, Mod Lang J, 5/60; coauth, Literatur für den Deutschunterricht, Erste Stufe, 64, Zweite Stufe & Dritte Stufe, 66. *Mailing Add:* Dept of Mod Lang Polytechnic Inst of New York Brooklyn NY 11201

BODMAN, NICHOLAS CLEAVELAND, b Chicago, Ill, July 27, 13; m 43; c 2. LINGUISTICS. *Educ:* Yale Univ, AB, 47, AM, 48, PhD, 50. *Prof Exp:* From sr instr to assoc prof ling, Foreign Serv Inst, US Dept State, 50-57, head dept Far Eastern lang, 57-61, dir, Chinese lang & area training ctr, Taiching, Formosa, 55-57; assoc prof ling, 62-64, prof, 64-79, dir, China Prog & E Asia Lang Area Ctr, 67-70, EMER PROF LING, CORNELL UNIV, 79- *Concurrent Pos:* Guggenheim fel & Nat Sci Found res grant, 61-62; vis prof, Sch Orient & African Studies, Univ London, 67 & Univ Hawaii, 73. *Mem:* Ling Soc Am; Am Orient Soc; Asn Asian Studies; Chinese Lang Teachers Asn. *Res:* Chinese linguistics, historical and descriptive; Chinese dialects; Sino-Tibetan linguistics. *Publ:* Auth, A Linguistic Study of Shih Ming, Initials and Consonant Clusters, Harvard Univ, 54; Spoken Amoy Hokkien, Vol 2, Am Coun Learned Soc, 58; Chinese historical linguistics, In: Current Trends in Linguistics, Vol 2, Mouton, The Hague, 68; Tibetan sdud fold of a garment, the character--and the st- hypothesis, Inst Hist & Philol, Acad Sinica, Taipei, 69; Some Chinese reflexes of Sino-Tibetan S-clusters, J Chinese Ling, 73; Proto-Chinese and Sino-Tibetan data towards establishing the nature of the relationship, In: Contributions to Historical Linguistics, Brill Leiden, Neth, 80; Evidence for 1 and r medials in old Chinese and associated problems (in press) & A sketch of the Namlong dialect (like Longdu a Northeastern Min Outlier in Zhongshan Xian) and the influence of Cantonese on its lexicon and phonology (in press), F K i Festchrift. *Mailing Add:* 518 Wyckoff Rd Ithaca NY 14850

BODMAN, RICHARD WAINWRIGHT, b New Haven, Conn, Aug 19, 47. CHINESE LANGUAGE, LITERATURE & HISTORY. *Educ:* Harvard Univ, BA, 69; Cornell Univ, MA, 74, PhD(Chinese lit), 78. *Prof Exp:* Instr Chinese, Cornell Univ, 76-77; asst prof, Univ Minn, 78-79 & Univ Wis, 79-80; ASST PROF CHINESE, ST OLAF COL, 80- *Mem:* Asn Asian Studies, Am Orient Soc; Chinese Lang Teachers Asn. *Res:* Chinese poetry; Chinese literary criticism; Chinese bibliography. *Publ:* Coauth, Biography of Cheng Ch'ing-chih, In: Sung Biographies, Münchener Ostasiatishce Studien, 76; reviewer, Wong Yoon-wah, Ssu-K'ung T'u, Chinese Lit: Essays, Articles and Reviews, 7/81; ed, The Beijing Language Institute: An inside view, J Chinese Lang Teachers Asn, 5/81. *Mailing Add:* Asian Studies St Olaf Col Northfield MN 55057

BODON, HAROLD WOLFGANG, b Stuttgart, Ger, May 19, 36; US citizen; m 57; c 2. FRENCH & GERMAN LANGUAGES. *Educ:* Univ Utah, BA, 59; Calif State Univ, Hayward, MS, 66; Brigham Young Univ, PhD(Fr & Ger), 79. *Prof Exp:* ASSOC PROF FRENCH & GERMAN, MO SOUTHERN STATE COL, 71- *Concurrent Pos:* Consult, Holt, Rinehart & Winston Publ, 63-64. *Mem:* Am Asn Teachers Ger; Am Asn Teachers Fr; MLA; Mid West For Lang Asn. *Res:* Twentieth century French literature; Charles-Ferdinand Ramuz, Switzerland; modern language teaching methodology. *Publ:* Auth, A foreign language field day, Sch & Community, 4/77; coauth, Sensory perceptions, In: Aline, Mo Philol Asn, 3/80; auth, Soccer tournaments as culture capsules, Sch & Community, 4/80. *Mailing Add:* 1302 N Duquesne Rd Joplin MO 64801

BODROGLEGETI, ANDRAS J E, b Tiszaigar, Hungary, Aug 5, 25; m 71. TURKIC & IRANIAN PHILOLOGY. *Educ:* Pazmany Peter Univ, Budapest, BA, 49; Eötvös Lorand Univ Budapest, MA, 51, dipl Ger & English, 54, MA & lectr dipl Persian & Turkic, 58; Hungarian Acad Sci, PhD(Iranian & Turkic ling), 63. *Prof Exp:* Teaching asst Turkic & Persian, Eötvös Lorand Univ, Budapest, 58-61, from asst prof to assoc prof, 61-70; assoc prof, 67-68 & 70-72, PROF TURKIC & PERSIAN, UNIV CALIF, LOS ANGELES, 72-, CHMN DEPT, 80- *Concurrent Pos:* UNESCO fel & res grant, Turkey, Iran & Afghanistan, 64-65. *Mem:* Am Orient Soc; Turkish Studies Asn; MidE Studies Asn; Soc Iranian Studies; Am Acad Polit & Soc Sci. *Res:* History of the Turkic languages; Eastern Middle Turkic languages and literatures; Islam among the Turks of Central Asia. *Publ:* Auth, Sadiq Hidayat, Az elet vize, Europa, Budapest, 60; A collection of Turkish poems from the fourteenth century, Acta Orient Hungary, 63; A Fourteenth Century Turkic Translation of Sa di's Gulistan, 69 & The Pursian Vocabulary of the Codex Cumanicus, 71, Akad Kiado, Budapest; coauth, The fragments of the Cavahiru'lasrar, Cent Asiatic J, 72; auth, Ahmad's Baraq-nama: A Central Asian Islamic work in Eastern Middle Turkic, Cent Asiatic J, 74; Classical Islamic heritage of Eastern Middle Turkic as reflected in the lexicon of modern literary Uzbek, Can Slavonic Papers, 75; Halis' Story of Ibrahim: A Central Asian Islamic Work in Late Chagatay Turkic, Brill, Leiden, 75. *Mailing Add:* 4518 Greenbush Ave Sherman Oaks CA 91423

BOE, JOHN M, Medieval & Renaissance Music History. See Vol I

BOEGEHOLD, ALAN LINDLEY, b Detroit, Mich, Mar 21, 27; m 54; c 4. CLASSICS. *Educ:* Univ Mich, AB, 50; Harvard Univ, PhD, 58. *Prof Exp:* From instr to asst prof classics, Univ Ill, 57-60; from asst prof to assoc prof, 60-67, chmn dept, 66-70, PROF CLASSICS, BROWN UNIV, 67- *Concurrent Pos:* Secy managing comt, Am Sch Class Studies Athens, 64-74, Howard fel, 64-65, vis res scholar, 68-69, res fel, 74-75 & 80-81; vis lectr hist, Harvard Univ, 67; vis prof classics, Yale Univ, 71-72 & Univ Calif, Berkeley, 78; mem bd dirs, Am Inst Nautical Archaeol, 73-82; sr fel, Nat Endowment for Humanities, 80-81. *Mem:* Am Philol Asn; Archaeol Inst Am; Class Asn New England. *Res:* Greek history, literature and archaeology. *Publ:* Auth, Ten distinctive ballots: The law court in Zea, Calif Studies Class Antiquity, 76; Thucydides' Representation of Brasidas before Amphipolis, Class Philol, 79; A Lid with Dipinto, Hesperia Suppl XIX, 82. *Mailing Add:* Dept of Classics Brown Univ Providence RI 02912

BOEHNE, PATRICIA JEANNE, b Neuilly, France, Feb 4, 40; nat US; m 60; c 2. MEDIEVAL HISPANO-ARABIC & CATALAN LITERATURE. *Educ:* Ind Univ, Bloomington, BA, 61, MA, 62, PhD(Hisp), 69. *Prof Exp:* Instr Span & French, Bradley Univ, 63-65; asst prof Span, Franklin & Marshall Col, 68-70; assoc prof Romance lang, 70-75, PROF ROMANCE LANG, EASTERN COL, 75-, CHMN LANG DEPT, 74- *Concurrent Pos:* Humanist evaluator Hisp, Pub Comt for Huamnities Pa, 77- *Mem:* NAm Catalan Soc; MLA; Renaissance Soc Am; Am Asn Teachers Span & Port. *Res:* Neoplatonism. *Publ:* Auth, Anselm Turmed's Oriental Garden, MLA, 74; Dream and Fantasy in Early Catalan Prose, Hisp, Barcelona, 75; J V Foix: A Catalan poet's response to reality, Fla State Univ, 76; Ramon Llull: The cultural context of his Opera Latina, Villanova Univ, 76; contribr, Introduction to Catalan Literature, Ind Univ 77; Catalan Studies, Hispam, Barcelona, 77; auth, Ausias March and Maurice Sceve: Eros and caritas, Univ Kans, 78; J V Foix, gran creatiu poetic de la poesia catalana, Univ Ill, 78; J V Foix, Twayne, 80. *Mailing Add:* Dept of Lang Eastern Col St Davids PA 19087

BOENING, JOHN, Comparative Literature. See Vol II

BOERNER, PETER, b Tartu, Estonia, Mar 10, 26; m 59; c 3. COMPARATIVE LITERATURE, GERMAN LITERATURE. *Educ:* Univ Frankfurt, DrPhil, 54. *Prof Exp:* Prog asst, Radio Frankfurt, 48-49; fel, Col Europe, Bruges, Belgium, 54-55; cur, Goethe Mus, Dusseldorf, 55-58; asst prof Ger, Stanford Univ & res dir, Stanford Overseas Studies Ctr, Beutelsbach, Ger, 58-61; from asst prof to assoc prof Ger, Univ Wis, 61-64; assoc prof, State Univ NY Buffalo, 64-66; prof comp lit, Univ Wis-Madison, 66-71, PROF COMP LIT, GER & W EUROP STUDIES, IND UNIV, BLOOMINGTON, 71- *Concurrent Pos:* Vis prof, Univ Mich, 67, Middlebury Col, 68 & Yale Univ, 78; Guggenheim fel, 70-71; fel, Herzog August Bibliothek, Wolfenbuttel, WGer, 76-77; fel, Zentrum für interdiszipliäre Forschung, Bielefeld, WGer, 80-81. *Mem:* Goethe Ges; Int Ver Ger Sprach-u Literaturwiss; Am Soc 18th Century Studies; Am Comp Lit Asn; Soc Etudes Staeliennes. *Res:* International literary relations; 18th century and romanticism. *Publ:* Auth, Taschenbuchverlag, Munich, 61-63; Goethe, Rowohlt, Hamburg, 64 (transl into Japanese, Dutch, Fr, English & Span); Tagebuch, Metzler, Stuggart, 69; National images and their place in literary research, Monatshefte, 75; The great travel collections of the eighteenth century: Their scope and purpose, In: The spread and social impact of books and culture, Voltaire Found, Oxford, 80; Goethes englische Reise oder Gedanken zur Physiognomie des nicht-reisenden Reisenden, In: Die deutsche England-Reise im archtzehnten Jahrhundert, Heidelberg, winter 82; Die deutsche Literatur der Goethezeit in ihrer europäischen Ausstrahlung, In: Neues Handbuch der Literaturwissenschaft, Vol 15, Athenaion, Wiesbaden, 82; Utopia in de Neuen Welt: Von europäischen Träumen zum American Dream, In: Utopieforschung, Metzler, Stuttgart, 82. *Mailing Add:* 1213 E First St Bloomington IN 47401

BOFMAN, THEODORA HELENE, b Chicago, Ill, Nov 19, 47. SOUTHEAST ASIAN LANGUAGE & LITERATURE. *Educ:* Univ Mich, BA, 69, PhD(ling), 78; Yale Univ, MA, 71. *Prof Exp:* Lectr ling & English, Ben Gurion Univ, 78-80; INSTR ENGLISH SECOND LANG, UNIV ILL, CHICAGO, 81- *Res:* Thai literature & linguistics; language acquisition. *Publ:* Auth, Poetics of the Ramakian, Northern Ill Univ (in press). *Mailing Add:* 2448 W Berwyn Chicago IL 60625

BOGGS, RALPH STEELE, b Terre Haute, Ind, Nov 17, 01; m 48; c 1. FOLKLORE, ENGLISH FOR FOREIGNERS. *Educ:* Univ Chicago, PhB, 26, PhD, 30. *Prof Exp:* Instr English, Univ PR, 26-28; prof Span & folklore, Univ NC, 29-48 & 49-50; prof, 48-49 & 50-67, EMER PROF MOD LANG, UNIV MIAMI, 67- *Concurrent Pos:* Am Coun Learned Soc travel grant, 40; vis prof, Univ Santo Domingo, 44, Nat Univ Mex, 45-46, Univ NMex, 48, Ministry Educ, Honduras, 61, Univ Calif, Los Angeles, 63 & Univ Calif, Berkeley, 70; dir & ed, Folklore Americas, 40-65; Fulbright lectr, Mus of Manitoba, Dominican Repub, 81. *Mem:* Fel Am Folklore Soc; Hisp Soc Am. *Res:* Hispanic American folklore. *Publ:* Auth, Bibliography of Latin American Folklore, Wilson, 40 & Ethridge, 71; coauth, Tentative Dictionary of Medieval Spanish, 46; auth, Folklore classification, Folklore Am, 48; Folklore en los Estados Unidos, Raigal, Buenos Aires, 54; coauth, English Step by Step with Pictures, Regents, 56, rev ed, 71 & 81; King of the Mountains, Vanguard, 60; auth, Spanish Word Builder, 63 & Basic Spanish Pronunciation, 71, Regents. *Mailing Add:* 536 Altara Ave Coral Gables FL 33146

BOGOJAVLENSKY, MARIANNA, b Helsinki, Finland, Sept 1, 15; US citizen; m 40; c 2. RUSSIAN LANGUAGE. *Educ:* Univ Helsinki, MA, 39; Univ Pa, PhD, 59. *Prof Exp:* Instr Russ, Bryn Mawr Col, 51-54 & Russ & Ger, Friends Cent Sch, 57-60; asst prof Russ, Mt Holyoke Col, 60-63; assoc prof, 63-70 PROF RUSS & GER, DICKINSON COL, 70- *Concurrent Pos:* Mem Russ comt, Nat Asn Independent Schs, 59-, Russ comt reading tests, Educ Testing Serv, Princeton, NY, 60-62 & Russ comt, Col Bd Entrance Exams, 67- *Mem:* MLA; Am Asn Slavic & EEurop Lang; Am Teachers Slavic & EEurop Lang; AAUP. *Res:* Soviety poetry; contemporary German novel; comparison of Leo Tolstoy's and Albert Schweitzer's thought. *Publ:* Auth, Gogol's Religious Thought, Russkaya Zhizn, 60; Advanced placement in Russia, Independent Sch Bull, 61; coauth, Three New Soviet Poets, Eastgate, 67; auth, The teaching of Russian literature in our secondary schools, Independent Sch Bull, spring 68; The future of Russian studies in our independent schools, Teacher's Notebk, Nat Asn Independent Schs, spring 73. *Mailing Add:* Dept of Russ & Ger Dickinson Col Carlisle PA 17013

BOHN, WILLIARD, b Oakland, Calif, Dec 2, 39. FRENCH & COMPARATIVE LITERATURE. *Educ:* Univ Calif, Berkeley, BA, 64, MA, 67, PhD(French), 73. *Prof Exp:* Asst prof French & comp lit, Brandeis Univ, 72-75; res assoc comp lit, Univ Calif, Berkeley, 75-79; ASST PROF FRENCH, ILL STATE UNIV, 79- *Concurrent Pos:* Am Coun Learned Soc grant-in-aid, 77-78. *Mem:* Am Comp Lit Asn; MLA; Asn Int Amis Guillaume Apollinaire; Asn Studies Dada & Surrealism. *Res:* Guillaume Apollinaire; 20th century French poetry; literature and art. *Publ:* Auth, Apollinaire and de Chirico: the making of the mannequins, Comp Lit, spring 75; Guillaume Apollinaire and the New York avant-garde, Comp Lit Studies, 3/76; Free-word poetry and painting in 1914: Ardengo Soffici and Guillaume Apollinaire, In: Ardengo Soffici, L'Artista e lo Scrittore Nella Cultura del 900, Centro Di, Florence, 76; From surrealism to surrealism: Apollinaire and Breton, J Aesthet & Art Criticism, winter 77; L'imagination plastique des calligrammes, In: Actes, Colloque Int Guillaume Apollinaire, Stavelot, Belgium, 9/77; Two circular poem-paintings by Apollinaire and Carra, Comp Lit, 78; La quatrieme dimension chez Apollinaire, Rev Lett Mod (in press); Apollinaire et L'Homme sans Visage: Aux Sources de son Surrealisme, Minard-Lett Mod, Paris (in press). *Mailing Add:* Dept of French Ill State Univ Normal IL 61761

BOHNING, ELIZABETH EDROP, b Brooklyn, NY, June 26, 15; m 43; c 2. GERMAN LITERATURE. *Educ:* Wellesley Col, AB, 36; Bryn Mawr Col, AM, 38, PhD, 43. *Prof Exp:* Instr, Bryn Mawr Col, 40; asst, Stanford Univ, 40-41 instr, 42-46, asst prof mod lang & lit, 46-57, assoc prof mod lang, 57-67, chmn dept, 71-78, PROF LANG & LIT, UNIV DEL, 67 . *Concurrent Pos:* Mem adv comt, Vienna prog, Cent Col Europ Studies Plan, 69-; trustee, Middle States Asn Cols & Schs, 74-80; res assoc, Nat Endowment for Humanities proj, 75-77; Del Humanities Coun, 79- *Honors & Awards:* Lindback Found Award Distinguished Teaching, 62. *Mem:* Am Asn Teachers Ger; Mid States Mod Lang Asn (pres, 63-64); Am Coun Study Austrian Lit. *Res:* Nibelungen legend; Schiller's aesthetic theories; comparative literature. *Publ:* Auth, Concept Sage in Nibelungen Criticism, Time Publ, 44; The Meaning of Death, 18th Century Life, 79; The lure of the little, Österr, Am Sicht, 81; The Child, The Dacmon & Death, Garcia Lorea Rev, 81. *Mailing Add:* Box 574 Newark DE 19711

BOLINGER, DWIGHT LEMERTON, b Topeka, Kans, Aug 18, 07; m 34; c 2. ENGLISH & SPANISH LINGUISTICS. *Educ:* Washburn Univ, AB, 30, Univ Kans, AM, 32; Univ Wis, PhD, 36. *Prof Exp:* Instr Span, Univ Wis, 36 & Jr Col Kansas City, Mo, 37; assoc prof, Washburn Col, 37-43; asst prof, Univ Southern Calif, 44-46, assoc prof, 47-48, prof, 49-60; prof Univ Colo, 60-63; prof, 63-73, EMER PROF ROMANCE LANG & LIT, HARVARD UNIV, 73- *Concurrent Pos:* Exchange Prof, Col San Luis, Costa Rica, 41; Sterling fel, Yale Univ, 43-44; Haskins Labs fel, 56-67; fel, Ctr Advan Studies Behav Sci, 69-70; Am Acad Arts & Sci fel, 73; vis emer prof ling, Stanford Univ, 78- *Honors & Awards:* Orwell Award, Nat Coun Teachers English, 81. *Mem:* Am Asn Teachers Span & Port (pres, 60); Am Dialect Soc: Ling Asn Can & US (pres, 75-76); MLA; Ling Soc Am (pres, 72). *Res:* Intonation; English and Spanish syntax. *Publ:* Auth, Interrogative Structures of American English, Am Dialect Soc, 57; coauth, Modern Spanish, Harcourt, 60; auth, Forms of English, Harvard Univ, 65; Aspects of Language, Harcourt, 68, 2nd ed, 75; Degree Words, Mouton, The Hague, 72; ed, Itonation, Penguin, 72; auth, Meaning and Form, Longman, 77; Language-The Loaded Weapon, Longman, 80. *Mailing Add:* 2718 Ramona St Palo Alto CA 94306

BOLLETTINO, VINCENZO ZIN, b Italy, Sept 19, 42; US citizen; m 68; c 1. FOREIGN LANGUAGE & LITERATURE. *Educ:* City Col New York, BA, 66; Rutger's Univ, New Brunswick, MA & PhD(Span), 72. *Prof Exp:* Asst prof, 69-80, ASSOC PROF SPAN & ITAL, MONTCLAIR STATE COL, 80- *Res:* Contemporary Spanish; Italian; Latin American literature. *Publ:* Auth, La naturaleza en la literatura hspanoamericana, Envio, 72; Breve estudio de la novelistica de Gabriel Garcia Marquez, Plaza Mayor, Madrid, 73. *Mailing Add:* 7 Florence Pl Caldwell NJ 07006

BOLTON, WHITNEY FRENCH, English Language & Literature. See Vol II

BOMHARD, ALLAN R, b Brooklyn, NY, July 10, 43. INDO-EUROPEAN & SEMITIC LINGUISTICS. *Prof Exp:* RES & WRITING, 73- *Mem:* Ling Soc Am; Am Orient Soc. *Res:* Reconstruction of common ancestor of Indo-European and Semitic; phonological systems as they evolved from this pre-proto-language through the consecutive stages of Indo-European. *Publ:* Auth, An Outline of the Historical Phonology of Indo-European, 75, The Placing of the Anatolian Languages, 76 & The Indo-European Phonological System: New Thoughts about Its Reconstruction and Development, 79, Orbis; co-ed (with Yoël L Arbeitman), Bono Homini Donum: Essays in Historical Linguistics in Memory of J Alexander Kerns, John Benjamins, 81; Indo-European and Afroasiatic: New Evidence for the Connection, Bono Homini Donum, 81; Speculations on the Prehistoric Development of the Proto-Indo-European Vowel System, General Linguistics, 81; Toward Proto-Nostratic (in prep). *Mailing Add:* 520 S Second St Springfield IL 62701

BONADEO, ALFREDO A, b Italy, Dec 19, 28. ITALIAN LITERATURE. *Educ:* Univ Calif, Berkeley, PhD(Romance lit), 65. *Prof Exp:* Instr Ital, Univ Calif, Los Angeles, 64-65; asst prof, Univ Calif, Davis, 65-69; assoc prof, 69-79, PROF ITAL LIT & HIST, UNIV CALIF, SANTA BARBARA, 79- *Publ:* Auth, Corruption, Conflict, and Power in the Works and Times of Niccolo Machiavelli, Univ Calif, 73. *Mailing Add:* 1002 Arbolado Rd Santa Barbara CA 93103

BOND, ZINNY SANS, b Riga, Latvia, Sept 1, 40; US citizen. LINGUISTICS. *Educ:* Univ Akron, BA, 62; Ohio State Univ, MA, 67, PhD(ling), 71. *Prof Exp:* Asst prof ling, Univ Alta, 71-73; asst prof, 74-80, ASSOC PROF HEARING & SPEECH SCI, OHIO UNIV, 80- *Concurrent Pos:* Consult, Wright-Pattersen Air Force Base, 74-77. *Mem:* Ling Soc Am; Acoust Soc Am; Am Speech & Hearing Asn; Asn Advan Baltic Studies. *Res:* Phonetics; phonology; speech perception. *Publ:* Coauth, Slips of the Ear: Errors in Perception of Casual Speech, Papers of 11th Regional Meeting of Chicago Ling Soc, Univ Chicago, 75; auth, On the Specification of Input Units in Speech Perception, Brain & Lang, 76; Identification of Vowels Excerpted from Neutral and Nasal Contexts, 76 & Identification of Vowels Excerpted from /l/ and /r/ Contexts, 76, J Acoust Soc Am; coauth, The Relationship Between Acoustic Information and Semantic Expectation, In: Phonologica, 77; Acquisition of the voicing contrast by language--delayed and normally speaking children, J Speech & Hearing Res, 80; Phenological processes in speech addressed to children, Phonetica, 80; From an acoustic stream to a phonological representation: The perception of fluent speech, Speech & Lang, 81. *Mailing Add:* Dept of Hearing & Speech Sci Ohio Univ Athens OH 45707

BONDANELLA, JULIA CONAWAY, b Torrington, Wyo, Jan 1, 43; m 69. COMPARATIVE LITERATURE, ROMANCE LANGUAGES. *Educ:* Univ Mont, BA, 65; Univ Kans, MA, 67; Univ Ore, PhD(comp lit), 73. *Prof Exp:* Instr English & world lit, Wayne State Univ, 70-73; asst prof hist of ideas & coordr, Freshman Honors Sem, 74-80, ASSOC PROF HIST OF IDEAS, IND UNIV, BLOOMINGTON, 80- *Mem:* MLA; Am Asn Teachers Ital; Am Comp Lit Asn; Am Asn Univ Professors Ital (exec secy, 80-84). *Res:* European Renaissance literature; history of ideas; pastoral literature. *Publ:* Coauth, Two kinds of Renaissance love: Spenser's Astrophel and Ronsard's Adonis, English Studies, 71; The deterioration of the heroic and pastoral ideals in Spenser's Calidore and Pastorella Episode: Book VI, Cantos IX-XII, Erasmus Rev, 71; contribr, Petrarch as visionary, In: Francis Petrarch, Six Centuries Later: A Symposium, Univ NC, Chapel Hill Studies Romance Lang, 75; auth, Petrarch's Visions and Their Renaissance Analogues, Studia Humanitatis, Madrid, 78; coauth & ed, The Dict of Italian Literature, Greenwood, 79. *Mailing Add:* Honors Div 213 Student Bldg Ind Univ Bloomington IN 47401

BONDANELLA, PETER EUGENE, b Pinehurst, NC, Dec 20, 43; m 69. ITALIAN & COMPARATIVE LITERATURE. *Educ:* Davidson Col, AB, 66; Stanford Univ, MA, 67; Univ Ore, PhD(comp lit), 70. *Prof Exp:* Asst prof Ital, Wayne State Univ, 70-72; asst prof Ital, 72-74, assoc prof, 74-79, PROF FRENCH & ITAL, IND UNIV, BLOOMINGTON, 80-, DIR CTR ITAL STUDIES, 79- *Concurrent Pos:* Nat Endowment Humanities younger humanist fel, 72-73 & sr independent res fel, 80-81. *Mem:* MLA; Am Asn Univ Teachers Ital; Am Asn Teachers Ital; Midwest Mod Lang Asn; Am Boccaccio Soc. *Res:* Renaissance literature; Italian cinema; Franco-Italian and Anglo-Italian literary relations. *Publ:* Auth, Machiavelli and the Art of Renaissance History, Wayne State Univ, 73; Francesco Guicciardini, Twayne, 76; co-ed, The Decameron: A Norton Critical Edition, Norton, 77; ed, Federico Fellini: Essays in Criticism, Oxford Univ, 78; co-ed, Dictionary of Italian Literature, Greenwood Press/Macmillan, 79; The Portable Machiavelli, Viking Penguin, 79; The Decameron, New Am Libr, 82; auth, Italian Cinema from Neoreaalism to the Present, Ungar, 82. *Mailing Add:* Ctr for Ital Studies Ind Univ Bloomington IN 47405

BONEBAKKER, SEEGER A, b Wisch, Neth, Sept 21, 23; m 53. ARABIC LANGUAGE & LITERATURE. *Educ:* State Univ Leiden, Drs, 51, PhD(Semitic lang), 56. *Prof Exp:* Mem acad staff, State Univ Leiden, 49-60; from asst prof to assoc prof, Arabic studies, Columbia Univ, 60-69; PROF ARABIC, UNIV CALIF, LOS ANGELES, 69- *Concurrent Pos:* Dir, Concordance et Indices Tradition Musulmane, Union Acad Int, 59-60; Columbia Univ Coun Res Humanities grant, Neth, 63; Nat Found Arts & Humanities sr fel, 67-68; regents fac fel, Univ Calif, 72-73 & 75-76; prin investr, Onomasticon Arabicum Proj, Univ Calif, Los Angeles, 76-; Corresp, Royal Nether Acad Arts & Sci, Amsterdam, 80. *Mem:* Am Orient Soc. *Res:* Medieval Arabic literature and biography; history of medieval Arabic rhetoric and philology. *Publ:* Auth, The Kitab Naqd al-Si'r of Qudama b Ga'far, E J Brill & De Goeje Fund, 56; Some early definitions of the Tawriya and Safadi's Fadd al-Xitam 'an at-Tawriya wa-'l-Istixdam, Near & Mid E Studies, 66; Notes on the Kitab Nadrat al-Ighrid of al-Muzaffar al-Husayni, His Archeol Inst, Univ Neth, 68; Poets and critics in the third century A H, In: Logic Classical Islamic Culture, Wiesbaden, 70; Materials for the history of Arabic rhetoric, Ann de-l' Istituto Orientale di Napoli, 75; Religious prejudice against poetry in Early Islam, Medievalia Humanistica: Studies in Medieval & Renaissance Cult, 76; A Fatimid manual for secretaries, Ann dell' Istituto Orientale di Napoli, 77. *Mailing Add:* Dept of Near Eastern Lang & Cult Univ of Calif Los Angeles CA 90024

BONENFANT, JOSEPH, b St-Narcisse, Champlain, Que, April 29, 34; m 60; c 2. LITERATURE. *Educ:* Univ Laval, BA, 57; Univ Montreal, LLL, 59; Univ Paris, DrUniv, 66. *Prof Exp:* Teacher French, Latin & Greek, Col Brebeuf, Montreal, 59-63; PROF FRENCH LIT, UNIV SHERBROOKE, 66- *Concurrent Pos:* Co-ed, Ellipse, Writers in Transl, 69-; consult, Can Coun Arts, 71- & Humanities Res Coun Can, 72- *Res:* French critics; le mouvement litteraire dans les Cantons de l' Est: 1925-1950; subventionne par le Conseil des Arts du Canada. *Publ:* Ed, Index de Parti Pris, 1963-1968, Celef, Univ Sherbrooke, 75; auth, Dimensions iconiques de la poesie de Rina Lasnier, Liberte, 11-12/76; L'oeuvre de Claude Peloquin, Lettres Quebecoises, 9/77; Masculinarites, La Nouvelle Barre du Jour, Montreal, 12/77; La force illocutionnaire dans la situation de discours pamphletaire, Etudes Lit, 78; Repere (roman), Montreal, Hurtubise HMH, L'Arbre, 79; Divergences de l'essai quebecois, Stanford Fr Rev, Vol IV, spring-fall, 80; Gilles Marcotte, on la pensee critique de l'inachevement, Voix et Images, Vol VI, 80. *Mailing Add:* Dept of French Studies Fac of Arts Univ of Sherbrooke Sherbrooke PQ J1K 2R1 Can

BONEY, ELAINE EMESETTE, b Cairo, Mo, May 26, 21. GERMAN LITERATURE. *Educ:* Univ Kans, AB, 43; Univ Tex, PhD, 58. *Prof Exp:* Chem analyst, Lever Bros, 44-46; instr Ger & Russ, Norfolk High Sch & Jr Col, Nebr, 49-51; res analyst, US Armed Forces, Austria, 53-54; asst prof, Tex Technol Col, 55-63; from asst prof to assoc prof Ger, 63-80, PROF GER, SAN DIEGO STATE UNIV, 80- *Concurrent Pos:* Fulbright grant, Goethe Inst, Ger, 62. *Mem:* MLA; Am Asn Teachers Ger; Kafka Soc; Int Arthur Schnitzler Res Asn. *Res:* Rilke and Kafka. *Publ:* Auth, The concept of being in Rilke's Elegien, Symposium, 61; The role of the paradox in Rilke's Sonette, SCent Mod Lang Asn Bull, 62; Rilke's concept of art, In: Homage to Charles

Balaise Qualia, Tex Technol Press, 62; transl & ed, Rainer Marie Rilke, Duinesian elegies, In: Germanic Languages and Literatures Ser, Univ NC, 74; auth, Love's door to death in Rilke's Cornet and other works, Mod Austrian Lit, 77. *Mailing Add:* Dept of Ger & Slavic Lang & Lit San Diego State Univ San Diego CA 92182

BONFINI, MARIE ROSEANNE, b Philadelphia, Pa, Nov 21, 35. FRENCH LANGUAGE & LITERATURE, COMPARATIVE LITERATURE. *Educ:* Immaculata Col, AB, 58; Univ Paris, dipl French studies, 62; Fordham Univ, MA, 64; Univ Rochester, PhD(French/comp lit), 69. *Prof Exp:* Sec teacher, Norfolk Cath High Sch, Ba, 62-65; acad dean, 71-78, PROF FRENCH, IMMACULATA COL, 68-; COORDR, INST RES, 82- *Concurrent Pos:* Res grant, Univ Rochester in Paris, 67; Fulbright reviewer, State Pa Selection Comt, 74; Nat Endowment for Humanities res grant, 78; Lilly grant medieval studies, 80. *Mem:* Am Asn Teachers Fr; Soc Professeurs de Francais a l'Etranger. *Res:* Middle Ages and French literature; creative leisure; play theory and comparative literature. *Mailing Add:* Immaculata Col Immaculata PA 19345

BONGART, KLAUS HERMAN, b Zeitz, Ger, Apr 9, 21; Can citizen; m 45. GERMAN LITERATURE. *Educ:* Waterloo Lutheran Univ, BA, 62; Univ Wash, MA, 64; Univ Toronto, PhD(Ger lit), 68. *Prof Exp:* Teaching asst Ger lit, Univ Wash, 63-64; from instr to assoc prof & exec asst to pres, Waterloo Lutheran Univ, 64-76; ASSOC PROF GER, WILFRID LAURIER UNIV, 76- *Mem:* Am Asn Teachers Ger; Can Goethe Soc. *Res:* Goethe's classical period; the Age of German Enlightenment; Heinrich Zschokke and the history of popular writers in the 19th century. *Mailing Add:* 670 Dunbar Kitchener ON N2M 2X4 Can

BONGIE, ELIZABETH BRYSON, b Victoria, BC, Sept 28, 30; m 58; c 1. CLASSICS. *Educ:* Univ BC, BA, 51; Univ Ill, Urbana, MA, 52, PhD(class philol), 56. *Prof Exp:* Lectr, 56-57 & 65-67, instr, 57-59 & 67-69, from asst to assoc prof, 69-80, PROF CLASSICS, UNIV BC, 80- *Mem:* Am Philol Asn; Can Class Asn; Mediaeval Acad Am; Humanities Res Asn; Archaeol Inst Am. *Res:* Greek tragedy; Greek paleography; medieval Latin literature. *Publ:* Auth, Analytical index, In: Dated Greek Manuscripts of the Thirteenth and Fourteenth Centuries in the Libraries of Italy, 72 & The daughter of Oedipus, In: Serta Turyniana, 74, Univ Ill, Urbana; Heroic elements in the Medea of Eruipides, Trans Am Philol Asn, 77. *Mailing Add:* Dept of Classics Univ of BC Vancouver BC V6T 1W5 Can

BONGIE, LAURENCE LOUIS, b Turtleford, Can, Dec 15, 29; m 58; c 1. FRENCH LITERATURE. *Educ:* Univ BC, BA, 50; Univ Paris, PhD(comp lit), 52. *Prof Exp:* Lectr French, 53-54, from instr to assoc prof, 54-56, PROF FRENCH & HEAD DEPT, UNIV BC, 66- *Concurrent Pos:* Humanities Res Coun Can fel, 55-56; Can Coun sr res fel, 63-64 & 75-76; Social Sci & Humanities fel, 82-83; Killam sr fel, 82-83. *Mem:* Fr Soc 18th Century Studies; Can Soc 18th Century Studies; Am Soc 18th Century Studies. *Res:* David Hume and eighteenth century history of ideas; Diderot; Condillac. *Publ:* Auth, David Hume and the official censorship of the Ancien regime, 58 & Hume philosophe and philosopher in eighteenth-century France, 61, Fr Studies, Oxford; Crisis and the birth of the Voltairian conte, Mod Lang Quart, 64; David Hume: Prophet of the Counter Revolution, Clarendon, Oxford, 65; Diderot's Femme Savante, Voltaire Found, Oxford, 77; Voltaire's English, high treason and a manifesto for Bonnie Prince Charles, Studies Voltaire & 18th Century, 77; A new Condillac letter and the genesis of the Traite des Sensations, J Hist Philos, 1/78; ed, Condillac, In: Les Monades, Studies Voltaire & 18th Century, 80. *Mailing Add:* Dept of French Univ of BC Vancouver BC V6T 1W5 Can

BONIN, THERESE MARCELLE, b St Andre le Desert, France, Oct 17, 38. FOREIGN LANGUAGE. *Educ:* Univ Lyons, CELG, 61; Univ Grenoble, Lic es Lett, 64; Ohio State Univ, PhD(foreign lang educ), 72. *Prof Exp:* Teacher French, Grangefield Grammar Sch, Eng, 59-60, Am Army Dependent Sch, La Rochelle, France, 60-63 & Evans Jr High Sch, Spartanburg, SC, 64-65; lectr, Univ Fla, 65-66; prof, Adult Lang Inst, Lyon, France, 66-68; lectr & teaching asst, Ohio State Univ, 68-72, asst prof, 72-75; fac French, Evergreen State Col, 75-76; ASSOC PROF FRENCH, OHIO STATE UNIV, 76- *Mem:* Am Coun Teaching Foreign Lang; Am Asn Teachers Fr; Nat Women Studies Asn. *Res:* Language pedagogy. *Publ:* Coauth, Passeport pour la France, 77 & Vivent les Differences, 77, 2nd ed, 81, Holt; Teaching French conversation, a lesson from the fourteenth century, Fr Rev, 77; French women in language textbooks, Contemp Fr Civilization, 77; auth, The role of colloquial French in communication, Mod Lang J, 78; Invitation, 79, Et Vous, 82 & Nous Tous, 82, Holt, Rinehart & Winston. *Mailing Add:* 549 Garden Columbus OH 43214

BONNELL, PETER H, b Vienna, Austria, Oct 13, 17; US citizen; m 64. FOREIGN LANGUAGES. *Educ:* Univ Calif, Berkeley, AB, 52; Harvard Univ, PhD(Slavic lang & lit), 62. *Prof Exp:* Instr French & Russian, Brandeis Univ, 60-61; asst prof Russ, Univ Ore, 62-64; assoc prof Russ & Ger, 64-69, PROF RUSS & GER, ROLLINS COL, 69- *Mem:* Am Asn Teachers Ger; MLA; Am Asn Teachers Slavic & E Europe Lang. *Res:* Aleksandr I Kuprin; Vsevolod Garshin. *Publ:* Coauth, Conversation in German, 69 & Conversation in French, 69, Am Bk. *Mailing Add:* Dept of Foreign Lang Rollins Col Winter Park FL 32789

BONNEVILLE, DOUGLAS, b Greenfield, Mass, Apr 30, 31; m 61; c 3. FOREIGN LANGUAGES. *Educ:* Wesleyan Univ, AB, 55; Ohio State Univ, MA, 58, PhD(Romance lang), 61. *Prof Exp:* Instr French, Kenyon Col, 59-60 & Dartmouth Col, 61-63; from asst prof to assoc prof, 63-76, PROF FRENCH, UNIV FLA, 76- *Honors & Awards:* Younger Humanist Award, Nat Endowment Humanities, 71. *Mem:* MLA; S Atlantic Mod Lang Asn (secy, 73-74); Am Asn Teachers Fr; Soc Fr Etude XVIIIe Siecle; Am Soc 18th Century Studies. *Res:* Eighteenth century French literature and criticism; Denis Diderot. *Publ:* Auth, Diderot's Vie de Seneque: A Swan-Song Revised, Univ Fla, 66; Two examples of time-technique in Jacques le Fataliste, Romance Notes, 67; Candide as symbolic experience, 70 & Glanures du Mercure 1739-1748, 72, Studies Voltaire & 18th Century; Diderot's artist: Puppet and poet, In: Literature and History in the Age of Ideas, Ohio State Univ, 75; Voltaire and the Form of the Novel, Voltaire Found, Banbury, England, 76. *Mailing Add:* Dept Romance Lang Univ of Fla Gainesville FL 32601

BONWIT, MARIANNE, b Duisburg, Ger, Oct 29, 13. LITERATURE. *Educ:* Univ Calif, AB, 40, AM, 41, PhD, 46. *Prof Exp:* From instr to asst prof, 46-53, assoc prof, 54-80, EMER PROF GERMAN, UNIV CALIF, BERKELEY, 80- *Mem:* MLA; Philol Asn Pac Coast. *Res:* Modern German and French literature; 19th century comparative Franco-German. *Mailing Add:* Dept of Ger Univ of Calif Berkeley CA 94720

BOOK, E TRUETT, b Tex, Apr 25, 22; m 49; c 2. FRENCH LANGUAGE & LITERATURE. *Educ:* Baylor Univ, BA, 43; Univ Paris, Frnace, DUniv, 50. *Prof Exp:* Instr French, Agr & Mech Col Tex, 46-48; prof, King Col, 50-53; assoc prof, Univ Tex, 53-60; ASSOC PROF FRENCH, UNIV NMEX, 60- *Mem:* Am Asn Teachers Fr. *Res:* Methods of teaching French; French theater and phonology; theater of Alfred de Musset. *Publ:* Coauth, Oral Drill in French, Univ Coop, Univ Tex, 56 & Elements of French, Holt, 59. *Mailing Add:* 105 Maple St NE Albuquerque NM 87106

BOOKER, JOHN T, b Downingtown, Pa, Oct 30, 42. FRENCH LITERATURE. *Educ:* Dartmouth Col, BA, 64; Univ Minn, MA, 67, PhD(French), 74. *Prof Exp:* Teaching Asst French, Univ Minn, 64-68; asst prof, US Mil Acad, West Point, 69-72; asst prof, 72-78, ASSOC PROF FRENCH, UNIV KANS, 78- *Mem:* MLA; Am Asn Teachers Fr. *Res:* French novel; Stendhal; first-person novel. *Publ:* Auth, The implied Narrataire in Adolphe, Fr Rev, 4/78; The Immoralist and the rhetoric of first-person narration, Studies in 20th Cent Lit, Vol 2, 77; Stendhal's use of the impressionists mode, 19th Cent Fr Studies, Vol 8, 80; Retrospective movement in the Stendhalian narration, Romanic Rev, Vol 72, 81; Mauriac's Le Noeud de viperes: Time and writing, Symposium, Vol 35, 81. *Mailing Add:* Dept of French & Ital Univ of Kans Lawrence KS 66045

BOON, JEAN-PIERRE, b New York, NY, May 10, 29. FRENCH LANGUAGE & NARRATIVE ARTS. *Educ:* Columbia Univ, BA, 55, MA, 57, PhD, 60. *Prof Exp:* Instr French, Adelphi Univ, 59-63; asst prof, Vanderbilt Univ, 63-64; from asst prof to assoc prof French, 64-75, PROF FRENCH LANG, LIT & FILM HISTORY, UNIV KANS, 75- *Mem:* MLA; Am Asn Teachers Fr; Soc Amis Montaigne; Midwest Mod Lang Asn; Soc Cinema Studies. *Res:* Film history; the novel. *Publ:* Auth, Montaigne Gentilhomme et Essayiste, Ed Univ, Paris, 71; Baudelaire, correspondances et le magnetisme animal, PMLA, 5/71; Souvenir et creation chez Baudelaire, Mod Lang Quart, 9/71; Tradition et modernite chez Jean-Jacques Rousseau: la thematique du bonheur, Romanic Rev, 2/73; La chasse, la Reigle et le Mensonge: Elements Structuraux dans La Reigle du jeu, 2/80 & Narrative voices in a nous la libente, 3/82, Fr Rev. *Mailing Add:* Dept of French & Ital Univ of Kans Lawrence KS 66044

BOORMAN, JOAN REA, b New York, NY, Dec 27, 29; m 53, 75; c 4. LATIN AMERICAN & COMPARATIVE LITERATURE. *Educ:* NY Univ, BA, 54; Univ Houston, MA, 64; Univ Tex, Austin, PhD(Span & Port), 70. *Prof Exp:* Instr Span & French, Tex Southern Univ, 61-64; instr Span, Univ Tex, 64-65; from instr to asst prof, 68-75, ASSOC PROF SPAN & PORT, RICE UNIV, 75- *Concurrent Pos:* Consult French, Tex Educ Agency, 65-66, consult Span, 66-67; corp deleg, Am Asn Univ Women, 75- *Mem:* Am Asn Teachers Span & Port; MLA; Latin Am Studies Asn; AAUP. *Res:* Latin American novel; Latin American theatre; comparative literature. *Publ:* Auth, La estructura del narrador y el modo narrativo de La Voragine, Cuadernos Hispanoamericanos, 1/67; A Syllabus for Applied Linguistics in Spanish, Tex Educ Agency, 17; The hero in contemporary Spanish American theatre: A case of diminishing returns, Latin Am Theatre Rev, spring 72; La Ultima Niebla y The House of Mist: Un Estudio Comparativo, Prohemio, Madrid, spring 73; La Estructura del Narrador en la Novela Hispanoamericana Contemporanea, Hispanova, Madrid, 76; Contemporary Latin American women dramatists, Rice Univ Studies, 78; Le roman de Gustavo Sainz, Entretiens, fall 78; The theatre of disruption and reconstruction, Latin Am Theatre Rev, summer 80. *Mailing Add:* Dept of Span & Port Rice Univ Houston TX 77001

BOOT, CHRISTINE, b Bilthoven, Neth, July 14, 29; Can citizen. MEDIEVAL GERMAN, DUTCH LANGUAGE & LITERATURE. *Educ:* McMaster Univ, BA, 61; Univ Tex, Austin, MA, 63, PhD(Ger lang), 68. *Prof Exp:* Asst prof Ger, Drake Univ, 67-71, Univ Wis-Parkside, 71-74 & Univ Wis-Madison, 74-76; asst prof Ger & Dutch, Syracuse Univ, 76-82. *Concurrent Pos:* Vis asst prof, LeMoyne Col, 82. *Mem:* MLA; Am Coun Teaching Foreign Lang; Am Asn Teachers Ger; Int Arthurian Soc; Int Ver Nederlandistiek. *Res:* Arthurian literature; medieval German Fachliterature; medieval Dutch literature. *Publ:* Ed, Cassiodorus' Historia Tripartita in Leopold Stainreuter's German Translation, Vol I & II, Rodopi, Amsterdam, 77; auth, Home and farm remedies and charms in a German manuscript from a Texas ranch, Texas J Folklore, 77; Netherlandic Manuscripts in the Libraries of the State of Massachusetts, Tijdschrift voor Archief-en Bibliotheekwezen, Belgie, 80; Das Buch von guten Pflastern und Salben, Verfasserlexikon, Vol III, 2nd ed, 80. *Mailing Add:* 214 Barrington Rd Syracuse NY 13214

BORCHARDT, FRANK L, b New York, NY, Nov 16, 38. GERMAN. *Educ:* St Peter's Col, AB, 60; Johns Hopkins Univ, MA, 62, PhD(Ger), 65. *Prof Exp:* Asst prof Ger, Northwestern Univ, 65-68; asst prof Ger & comp lit, Queens Col, NY, 68-71; ASSOC PROF GER, DUKE UNIV, 71-, CHMN DEPT, 82- *Concurrent Pos:* Fulbright res fel, Univ Würzburg, 71-72; Am Coun Learned Socs fel, 78-79. *Mem:* Renaissance Soc Am; Medieval Acad Am; Am Asn Teachers Ger. *Res:* Renaissance; Middle Ages; modern German drama. *Publ:* Auth, German Antiquity in Renaissance Myth, Johns Hopkins Univ, 71; Goethe, Schiller, sphinx, centaur and sex, Monatshefte, 72; Trithemius and the mask of Janus, In: Jantz Festschrift, Delp, 72; Petrarch:

The German connection, In: Francis Petrarch: Six Centuries Later, Univ NC, 75; Zur Zeitstruktur der radikalen Sozialkritik, Jahrbuch international Germanistik, 76; First contacts with Italy, In: Renaissance & Reformation in Germany, Ungar, 77; Medievalism in Renaissance Germany, In: Herman Salinger Festschrift, Univ NC, 78; Kleist's Space, SAtlantic Bull, 82. *Mailing Add:* Dept of Ger Duke Univ Durham NC 27706

BORDEN, ARTHUR ROSS, JR, English. See Vol II

BORDIE, JOHN GEORGE, b Chicago, Ill, Apr 3, 31; m 56; c 3. LINGUISTICS, APPLIED LINGUISTICS. *Educ:* Univ Chicago, BA, 49; Univ Tex, Austin, PhD(ling), 58. *Prof Exp:* Asst prof ling & English, Georgetown Univ, 58-60; coordr ling & literacy, Electronic Teaching Labs, 60-63; vol develop trainer & area coordr ling & lang, US Peace Corps, Washington, DC, 63-66; assoc prof ling & curric, 66-73, assoc dir foreign lang educ ctr, 67-74, PROF LING & CURRIC, UNIV TEX, AUSTIN, 73-, DIR FOREIGN LANG EDUC CTR, 74- *Concurrent Pos:* Consult & reader, Adult Basic Educ, US Off Educ, 68; mem Nat Adv Coun Teaching English as Foreign Lang, 72; ed, Jour Ling Asn Southwest, 75 & Newslett 2nd Bull Tex Foreign Lang Asn, 77. *Mem:* Ling Soc Am; Am Coun Teachers Foreign Lang; Asn Teachers English To Speakers Other Lang; Am Orient Soc; Asn Asian Studies. *Res:* Measurement of language proficiency; language teaching of languages of the Northern Middle East; descriptions of Pakistani languages. *Publ:* Ed, The Teaching of African Language, Georgetown Univ, 61; auth, Structural English Drills (with tapes), 62 & Intensive Courses in Krio, Temne and Mende, 63, Electronic Teaching Labs; coauth, An Intensive Dari Course (2 vols), Univ Tex & Peace Corps, 69 & 70; auth, Language tests and linguistically different learners, Elem English, 70; Cultural sensitivity training for the teacher of Spanish speaking children, Teachers English Speakers Other Lang Quart, 70; coauth, Criterion Referenced Tests for English and Spanish Proficiency, Tex Educ Agency, 77. *Mailing Add:* Foreign Lang Educ Ctr Univ of Tex Austin TX 78712

BORENSTEIN, WALTER, b Brooklyn, NY, Mar 31, 27; m 53; c 2. SPANISH. *Educ:* Univ Ill, AB, 48, MA, 49, PhD(Span), 54. *Prof Exp:* From instr to asst prof Span & Latin, La State Univ, 54-61, assoc prof Span, 61-64; assoc prof, Cornell Col, 64-69; assoc prof, 69-71, PROF SPAN & CHMN DIV FOREIGN LANG, STATE UNIV NY COL NEW PALTZ, 71- *Mem:* Am Asn Teachers Span & Port; MLA. *Res:* Generation of 98 in Spain; 19th century Spanish novel; translation into English of 20th century Spanish literature. *Publ:* Auth, Baroja's uncomplimentary stereotype of the Latin American, Symposium, spring 57; The failure of nerve: The impact of Pio Baroja's Spain on John Dos Passos, In: Nine Essays in Modern Literature, La State Univ, 65; The combined and the divided foreign language department in the liberal arts college, ERIC/CLIS, 3/70. *Mailing Add:* Dept of Foreign Lang State Univ of New York Col New Paltz NY 12561

BORG, SAM JOSEPH, b Cospicua, Malta, Oct 12, 30; US citizen. FRENCH. *Educ:* Wayne State Univ, BA, 58, MA, 60; Univ Calif, Berkeley, PhD(Romance lang & lit), 66. *Prof Exp:* From teaching asst to teaching assoc French, Univ Calif Berkeley, 59-64; asst prof, 64-69, ASSOC PROF FRENCH, UNIV CALIF, RIVERSIDE, 69- *Res:* Editing Old French texts; medieval French epic literature. *Publ:* Auth, Aye d'Avignon, Edition Critique, Droz, 67. *Mailing Add:* Dept of Lang & Lit Univ of Calif Riverside CA 92521

BORKER, DAVID, b San Francisco, Calif, Mar 8, 46. SLAVIC LANGUAGE & LITERATURE. *Educ:* Cornell Univ, BA, 68; Yale Univ, MPhil, 71, PhD(Slavic), 75. *Prof Exp:* Mem fac Ger & Russ, Shimer Col, Mt Carroll, Ill, 71-72; instr Russ & Czech, Dept Slavic Lang & Lit, Ohio State Univ, 73-74, asst prof, 75-80. *Concurrent Pos:* Nat Endowment for Humanities grant foreign lang, Col Humanities, Ohio State Univ, 76. *Mem:* Am Asn Teachers Slavic & East Europ Lang; Am Asn Advan Slavic Studies; MLA; Mezdunarodnaja Associacija Prepodavatelej Russkogo jazyka j literatury. *Res:* Russian literature 19th and 20th century, especially poetry; poetics and literary theory; comparative literature. *Publ:* Auth, Annenskij and Maliarme: A case of subtext, Slavic & East Europ Rev, 77; Primenenie individualizirovannogo metoda v prepodavanii russkogo jazyka kak inostrannogo, Russkij Jazyk za Rubezem, 77; Sentential structure in Smert' Ivan Il'ica, In: American Contributions to the VIII International Congress of Slavists: Linguistics and Poetics, Slavica Press, 78; coauth, Sociostylistics: The analysis of literature as verbal interaction, Beiträge 12ten Weltkongress Ling, 78; auth, Annenskij and Pushkin's Osen', Slavic & East Europ J, 78. *Mailing Add:* 175 Meadowpark Lane Columbus OH 43214

BORMANSHINOV, ARASH, b Belgrade, Yugoslavia, Dec 5, 22; US citizen; m 59; c 5. SLAVIC LINGUISTICS. *Educ:* Univ Pa, AM, 56, PhD, 58. *Prof Exp:* Asst prof Russ & Ger, Rensselaer Polytech Inst, 58-59; asst prof Russ, Rutgers Univ, 59-60; asst prof Slavic lang & lit, Princeton Univ, 60-66; asst prof Slavic ling, NY Univ, 66-68 & City Col New York, 68-80. *Concurrent Pos:* John Hay Whitney Found fel, 56-57; lectr Russ, Mohawk Educ TV, Albany, NY, 58-59; Am Coun Learned Soc res grants, Uralic & Altaic Lang, 59-63; Inter-Univ Comt travel grant, 60; consult educ TV, NY Univ, 61; Doris Duke travel grant, 62; fac res grant, NY Univ, 67-68; vis prof, New Sch Soc Res, 68; assoc prof Russ, Univ Okla, 69; vis prof, Yeshiva Univ, 71- *Mem:* MLA; Am Orient Soc; Am Asn Teachers Slavic & East Europ Lang; Mongolia Soc; Asn Asian Studies. *Res:* South Slavic linguistics; Yugoslav literature; Kalmyk-Oirat studies. *Publ:* Auth, Kalmyk Manual, 61 & coauth, Kalmyk-English Dict, 63, Am Coun Learned Soc; co-ed, Kalmyk-Oirat Symposium, Soc Prom Kalmyk Cult, 66. *Mailing Add:* 6811 Gairlock Pl Lanham MD 20801

BOROS AZZI, MARIE-DENISE, b Paris, Frnace, Nov 25, 38; US citizen; m 68; c 2. ROMANCE LANGUAGES. *Educ:* Univ Calif, Los Angeles, BA, 59, MA, 60, PhD(French lit), 64. *Prof Exp:* Instr French lit, Immaculate Heart Col, 59-62; teaching asst French, Univ Calif, Los Angeles, 60-63, assoc, 63-64; asst prof, 64-71, assoc in grad sch, 67-73, ASSOC PROF FRENCH LIT, RUTGERS UNIV, NEW BRUNSWICK, 71-, MEM IN GRAD SCH, 73- *Concurrent Pos:* Res grant, Rutgers Univ, New Brunswick, 67-68. *Mem:* MLA; Am Asn Teachers Fr; Soc Prof Fr Am. *Res:* Contemporary French literature. *Publ:* Auth, La metaphore du crabe dans l'oeuvre litteraire de Jean-Paul Sartre, PMLA, 10/66; L'antinaturalisme des personnages de Jean-Paul Sartre, Fr Rev, 10/66; L'homme sartrien: Un sequestre?, Nizet, France, 68. *Mailing Add:* Dept of Romance Lang Rutgers Univ New Brunswick NJ 08903

BOROVSKI, CONRAD, b Prettin, Ger, Dec 4, 30; US citizen; m 62. FOREIGN LANGUAGES. *Educ:* Univ Strasbourg, LittD, 60. *Prof Exp:* Asst Ger, Univ Strasbourg, 59-60; instr, Univ Md Overseas Prog, 61-62; ASSOC PROF GER & FRENCH, SAN JOSE STATE UNIV, 62- *Concurrent Pos:* Lectr mythology, Univ Santa Clara, 64-68. *Mem:* Am Civil Liberties Union; MLA; Medieval Asn Pac; Int Asn Appl Ling. *Res:* Mediaeval literature, especially German and French; the concept of the lady; courtly love. *Publ:* Auth, Active German Idioms, Hueber, Munich, 73; Toward coherence in the college curriculum, In: New Directions in Teaching, Bowling Green State Univ, 73; Die Dialektik der Flüchtlingsgespräche Brechts, In: Dialoge, Univ Bonn, 82. *Mailing Add:* Dept of Foreign Lang San Jose State Univ San Jose CA 95192

BOROWSKI, ODED, Biblical History, Modern Hebrew. See Vol I

BORRAS, ANGELO AUGUSTO, b Fajardo, PR, Oct 7, 35; US citizen; m 63; c 2. SPANISH. *Educ:* Univ Ky, BA, 57; Ind Univ, MA, 59; Pa State Univ, PhD(Span), 67. *Prof Exp:* From asst prof to assoc prof Span, Mich State Univ, 67-74; PROF SPAN & CHMN, WILFRID LAURIER UNIV, 74- *Mem:* Am Asn Teachers Span & Port; MLA. *Res:* Spanish contemporary literature. *Publ:* Auth, Musical underscoring in the dramas of Casona, Hispania, 64; The ideology of the theatre of the Spanish exile Max Aub, Theatre Ann, 12/69; Buero Vallejo's La Senal que se Espera, 69 & Sound, music and symbolism in Carlos Muniz's theatre, 70, Romance Notes; Exiles in the theatre of Max Aub, Theatre Ann, 12/73; Time, the fourth dimension in Max Aub's theatre of exile, Mosaic, 4/75; El Teatro del Exilio de Max Aub, Univ Seville, 75; ed, The Theatre and Hispanic Life, Wilfrid Laurier Univ Press, 82. *Mailing Add:* Dept of Romance Lang Wilfrid Laurier Univ Waterloo ON N2L 3C5 Can

BORROFF, MARIE, English Language & Literature. See Vol II

BORSAY, LASZLO AARON, b Kolozsvar, Hungary, Feb 14, 15; US citizen; m 40; c 6. CLASSICAL LANGUAGES, LINGUISTICS. *Educ:* Reformed Col, Budapest, dipl Greek, 37; Reformed Col, Nagykoros, MEd, 38; Reformed Sem, Budapest, MTh, 39; Univ Pittsburgh, PhD(classics), 65. *Prof Exp:* Instr classics, Univ Pittsburgh, 57-65; assoc prof, 65-79, PROF CLASSICS, WVA UNIV, 79- *Concurrent Pos:* WVa Univ Sen grant, 68-69. *Honors & Awards:* Best Teacher Award, WVa Univ, 75. *Mem:* Am Philol Asn; Am Class League. *Res:* Languages of Ancient Asia Minor; sound structure of Latin; vulgar Latin in relation to Romance languages. *Mailing Add:* Chitwood Hall WVa Univ Morgantown WV 26505

BORTON, SAMUEL LIPPINCOTT, b Philadelphia, Pa, July 10, 15; m 56; c 1. MODERN LANGUAGES & LITERATURE. *Educ:* Haverford Col, BS, 37; Univ Pa, PhD, 62. *Prof Exp:* Asst instr, dept Romance lang, Univ Pa, 52-56; instr mod lang, Univ Del, 57-60; instr Romance lang, Franklin & Marshall Col, 60-62; ASSOC PROF MOD LANG, UNIV DEL, 62- *Res:* Sixteenth century poetry in French literature. *Publ:* Auth, A tentative essay on Dante and Proust, Del Notes, 58; A note on Prosper Merimee: Not De Clara Gazul, but Delecluze, Mod Lang Notes, 60; Six Modes of Sensibility in Saint-Amant, Univ Pa, 62 & Mouton, The Hague, 66. *Mailing Add:* Dept of Lang & Lit Univ of Del Newark DE 19711

BORYSIUK, MYROSLAV, b Galicia, Ukraine, Sept 4, 12; US citizen; m 38; c 1. LATIN. *Educ:* Univ Lvov, PhM, 36, PhD, 36; Columbia Univ, MA, 54, PhD, 57. *Prof Exp:* Assoc prof Greek, Univ Lvov, 34-36; prof Latin & Greek, State Lyceum Stanislavov, 37-39; supt schs, State Bd Educ, USSR, 40-42; dean Gymnasium-Lyceum, Rimini, Italy, 45-47; from instr to asst prof Greek & Latin, 47-56, assoc prof, 57-80, PROF LATIN, ST BASIL'S COL, 80- *Concurrent Pos:* Mem Ministry Educ & lectr, Ukrainian Acad, USSR, 40-41; lectr, Orient Inst, Rome, Italy, 46-47 & Adult Educ Sch, Greenwich, Conn, 60-68. *Mem:* Class Asn Atlantic States; Class Asn Midwest & South; Class Asn Can. *Res:* Pre-Homeric religion; Alexandrian poetry; works of Plutarch. *Publ:* Auth, The Lives of Famous Men of C Nepos, Filomata, Univ Lvov, 36; The Ancient Beliefs Concerning the Soul, Eos, Univ Lvov, 39. *Mailing Add:* 36 Rippowam Rd Stamford CT 06902

BOSCO, PAUL FRED, b Vasto, Italy, May 14, 14; nat US. ROMANCE PHILOLOGY. *Educ:* Wayne Univ, AB, 34; Harvard Univ, Am, 35, PhD, 42. *Prof Exp:* Teacher High Sch, Mich, 36-39; ASSOC PROF ROMANCE LANG, UNIV NOTRE DAME, 47- *Concurrent Pos:* Fulbright teaching grant, Rome, 55-57; dir, US Inform Agency Binat Ctr, Rosario, Arg, 62-64; dir sophomore year France, Cath Univ Angers, 68-70. *Mem:* MLA; Am Asn Teachers Ital; Am Asn Teachers Span & Port; Cent States Mod Lang Teachers Asn; Am Asn Teachers Fr. *Res:* General linguistics; Italian dialectology; English as a foreign language. *Mailing Add:* Dept of Mod Lang Univ of Notre Dame Notre Dame IN 46556

BOSSIERE, JACQUES P, b Paris, France, May 29, 19; m; c 3. FRENCH, COMPARATIVE LITERATURE. *Educ:* Univ Paris, Lic litt, 43, dipl super, 44; Laval Univ, DUniv(French lit), 66. *Prof Exp:* Instr French, Yale Univ, 58-65, ASSOC PROF FRENCH & CHMN DEPT MOD LANG, HOLLINS COL, 66- *Concurrent Pos:* Danforth fel, Yale Univ, 65-66. *Mem:* MLA. *Res:* Literary critique in France, 1900 to 1940. *Publ:* Auth, Problemes Actuels du Clerge Diocesain, Tongerloo Press, Belgium, 47; coauth, Missa est, Fayard, Paris, 50; Perception Critique et Sentiment de Vivre, Nizet, Paris, 68. *Mailing Add:* Dept of Mod Lang Hollins Col Hollins College VA 24020

BOTTIGLIA, WILLIAM FILBERT, b Bernardsville, NJ, Nov 23, 12. FRENCH LITERATURE, HUMANITIES. *Educ:* Princeton Univ, AB, 34, AM, 35, PhD, 48. *Prof Exp:* Instr French & Ital, Princeton Univ, 37-42; asst prof English, St Lawrence Univ, 48; prof French & Ital & chmn dept Romance lang, Ripon Col, 48-56; assoc prof mod lang, 56-60, prof mod lang & humanities, 60-73, head dept mod lang & ling, 64-73, prof foreign lit, 73-74, PROF HUMANITIES, MASS INST TECHNOL, 73- *Mem:* MLA; Am Hist Asn; Am Polit Sci Asn. *Publ:* Auth, Voltaire's Candide: Analysis of a Classic, Inst et Musee Voltaire, Geneva, 59, 2nd ed, 64; coauth, Voltaire: Twentieth Century Views, Prentice-Hall, 68. *Mailing Add:* 50 Windsor Rd Needham MA 02192

BOTTMAN, PHILIP NATHANIEL, English, Comparative Literature. See Vol II

BOUCHARD, GUY, Philosophy, Literature. See Vol IV

BOUDREAU, HAROLD LAVERNE, b Ashkum, Ill, Mar 15, 28; m 55; c 1. MODERN SPANISH LITERATURE. *Educ:* Univ Ill, Champaign, BA, 48, MA, 50; Univ Wis-Madison, PhD(Span), 66. *Prof Exp:* From instr to prof Span, 58-69, chmn dept Span & Port, 71-77, PROF SPAN, UNIV MASS, AMHERST, 69- *Concurrent Pos:* Consult, Nat Endowment Humanities, 76-78. *Mem:* MLA; Am Asn Teachers Span & Port. *Res:* Modern Spanish novel and poetry; critical theory. *Publ:* Co-ed, Cela, La Familia de Pascual Duarte, Appleton, 61; The circular structure of Valle-Inclan's Ruedo Iberico, PMLA, 67; Banditry and Valle-Inclan's Ruedo Iberico, Hisp Rev, 67; contribr, Zahareas, In: Ramon del Valle-Inclan, Las Americas, 68; Miguel Delibes' Parabola del Naufrago: Utopia redreamed, Studies 20th Century Lit, 76; Cinco Horas con Mario and the dynamics of irony, Anales Novela Posguerra, 77; The salvation of Torquemada, Anales Galdosianos, 80; Span lit ed, Columbia Dictionary of Modern European Literature, 80. *Mailing Add:* Dept of Span & Port Univ of Mass Amherst MA 01003

BOULBY, MARK, b Leeds, England, Mar 7, 29; m 56; c 2. GERMAN & COMPARATIVE LITERATURE. *Educ:* Cambridge Univ, BA, 49, MA, 53; Univ Leeds, PhD(Ger), 52. *Prof Exp:* Res fel, Ger, Univ Birmingham, 54-55; asst lectr, Univ Leeds, 55-58, lectr, 58-61; lectr, Univ Hull, 62-63; vis lectr, City Col New York, 63-64; from assoc prof to prof, Case Western Reserve Univ, 64-70, chmn dept, 68-70; actg head dept, 71-72, PROF GER, UNIV BC, 70- *Concurrent Pos:* Can Coun Humanities res grants, 71 & 74; Guggenheim Found fel, 74. *Mem:* MLA; Am Soc 18th Century Studies; Am Lessing Soc. *Res:* Modern German literature; contemporary French and German novel; 18th century literature. *Publ:* Auth, Gerhart Hauptmann: Die Weber, Harrap, London, 62; Der vierte lebenslauf as a key to Das Glasperlenspiel, Mod Lang Rev, 66; Hermann Hesse: His Mind and Art, Cornell Univ, 67; ed, H and J Hart, Kritische Waffengange, Johnson Reprint, 69; auth, Judgment by epithet in Goethe's Torquato Tasso, PMLA, 72; Uwe Jounson, Frederick Ungar, 74; Karl Philipp Moritz: The Fringe of Genius, Toronto Univ, 78. *Mailing Add:* Dept of Ger Univ of BC Vancouver BC V6T 1W5 Can

BOULLATA, ISSA JOSEPH, b Jerusalem, Palestine, Feb 25, 29; US citizen; m 60; c 4. ARABIC LITERATURE. *Educ:* Univ London, BA, 64, PhD(Arabic lit), 69. *Prof Exp:* Asst prof Arabic & Islam, Hartford Sem, 68-70, assoc prof, 70-75; assoc prof Arabic lang & lit, 75-79, PROF ARABIC LANG & LIT, MCGILL UNIV, 79-, ASST DIR, INST ISLAMIC STUDIES, 82- *Concurrent Pos:* Lectr Islam, St George's Col, Jerusalem, 62-66; ed, Muslim World, 70-80 & Al-'Arabiyya, 77-; co-ed, Mundus Arabicus, 81- *Honors & Awards:* Arberry Mem Prize, Cambridge Univ, 72. *Mem:* Fel Middle East Studies Asn NAm; fel Am Asn Teachers Arabic; Asn Arab-Am Univ Grad; Am Comp Lit Asn; Int Comp Lit Asn. *Res:* The developments in modern Arabic poetry and fiction in the light of social and political change in the Arab world; analyzing the structural and aesthetic innovations in them reflecting content change and embodying it; modern Islam and how it is dealing with modernity and how modern Arab thought is grappling with this issue. *Publ:* Auth, Outlines of Romanticism in Modern Arabic Poetry, Dar al-Thaqafa, Beirut, 60; Badr Shakir al-Sayyab: His Life and poetry, Dar al-Nahar, Beirut, 71, 2nd ed, 78, 3rd ed, 81; Literary form and social structure: Reflections on change in modern Arabic poetry, Islamic Quart, Vol XIX, No 1-2; Encounter between East and West: A theme in contemporary Arabic novels, Mid East J, Vol XXX, No 1; Modern Arab Poets 1950-1975, Three Continents Press & Heinemann, London, 76; Adonis: Revolt in modern Arabic poetics, Edebiyat, II: 1-13; ed, Critical Perspectives on Modern Arabic Literature, Three Continents Press, 80; auth, Verbal Arabesque and mystical union: A study of Ibn al-Farid's al-Ta'iyya al-Kubra, Arab Studies Quart, Vol III, No 2. *Mailing Add:* Inst of Islamic Studies McGill Univ Montreal PQ H3A 2T7 Can

BOULTER, CEDRIC GORDON, b Tryon, PEI, May 9, 12; nat US; m 53; c 2. CLASSICAL ARCHAEOLOGY. *Educ:* Acadia Univ, BA, 33; Univ Cincinnati, PhD, 39. *Prof Exp:* From actg instr to instr, 37-45, from asst prof to prof, 45-72, Charles Phelps Taft prof, 72-82, EMER PROF CLASSICS, UNIV CINCINNATI, 82- *Concurrent Pos:* Vis Prof, Am Sch Class Studies Athens, 65-66. *Mem:* Archaeol Inst Am (secy, 55-57); Am Philol Asn; Soc Promotion Hellenic Studies; Class Asn Can. *Res:* Greek pottery; classical art. *Publ:* Auth, Pottery of the Mid-Fifth Century from a well in the Athenian Agora, Hesperia, 53; coauth, Troy, Vol IV, Princeton Univ, 58; auth, Graves in Lenormant Street, Athens, 63 & The Berlin Painter at Corinth, 66, Hesperia; corpus Vasorum Antiquorum, Cleveland Museum of Art, fascicule 1, Princeton Univ, 71; coauth, Corpus Vasorum Antiquorum, Toledo Museum of Art, fascicule 1, 76, fascicule 2, Zabern Mainz (in press). *Mailing Add:* Dept of Classics Univ of Cincinnati Cincinnati OH 45221

BOULTON, MAUREEN BARRY MCCANN, b Yonkers, NY, June 29, 48; m 72. MEDIEVAL & FRENCH LITERATURE. *Educ:* Col New Rochelle, BA, 70; Univ Pa, MA, 73, PhD(French), 76; Univ Oxford, MLitt, 80. *Prof Exp:* ASST PROF FRENCH & COMP LIT, BRANDEIS UNIV, 79- *Concurrent Pos:* Vis lectr humanities, Davidson Col, 79. *Mem:* Medieval Acad Am; MLA; Northeastern Mod Lang Asn; Soc Textual Studies; Anglo-Norman Text Soc. *Res:* Medieval romances, especially French; medieval apocryphal literature, especially French; textual criticism. *Publ:* Auth, The Evangile de l'Enfance: The Rediscovery of the Didot Manuscript, Romania, 82; The Evangile de l'Enfance, Text and Illustration in Bodleian Library Selden Supra 38, Scriptorium (in press). *Mailing Add:* 99 Channing Rd Watertown MA 02172

BOUMA, LOWELL, b July 13, 30; US citizen; m 47; c 3. GERMANIC LINGUISTICS. *Educ:* Calvin Col, BA, 57; Univ Wis-Madison, MA, 64, PhD(Germanic ling), 68. *Prof Exp:* Instr Ger, Univ Mo-Columbia, 61-63 & Univ Wis-Madison, 67-68; asst prof Ger & ling, Univ Ga, 68-75; assoc prof, 75-80, PROF GER, GA SOUTHERN COL, 80-, CHMN DEPT FOREIGN LANG, 75- *Honors & Awards:* Goethe Inst Award, 79. *Mem:* Ling Soc Am; MLA; Am Asn Teachers Ger; Am Coun Teaching Foreign Lang. *Res:* Germanic linguistics; contrastive grammar; second language acquisition. *Publ:* Auth, The Semantics of the Modal Auxiliaries in Contemporary German, Mouton, The Hague, 73; On contrasting the semantics of the modals in German and English, Linqua, 75; Jakobson's view of grammatical meaning, Lang Sci, 78. *Mailing Add:* Dept of Foreign Lang Ga Southern Col Statesboro GA 30458

BOUR, JEAN-ANTOINE, b Paris, France, Sept 18, 34; US citizen; m 63; c 4. FRENCH LANGUAGE & LITERATURE. *Educ:* Univ Rochester, BA, 61, MA, 62; Princeton Univ, MA, 65, PhD(French lit), 69. *Prof Exp:* Asst prof French, Brown Univ, 66-72; assoc prof, Claremont Men's Col, 72-75; ASSOC PROF FRENCH & HEAD FRENCH & SPAN, MT ALLISON UNIV, 75- *Concurrent Pos:* Asst ed, Fr Rev, 70-74. *Mem:* Am Asn Teachers Fr; Can Asn Fr Univ Prof; Humanities Asn Can. *Res:* The 19th century novel; French social history, 19th and 20th centuries. *Publ:* Auth, Evasions, Jean Grassin, Paris, 70; Quelques themes preromantiques du Rivage des Syrtes, 70 & La caverne d'Ali Baba, 71, Fr Rev; La Belle et la Bete, 71 & Nortre-Dame de Paris, 71, Romance Notes; Histoire et les problemes sociaux dans l'enseignement du francais, Fr Rev, 3/74; La femme et la bourgeoisie d'affaires Bull de l'APFUC, 4/77; Entretien avec Marguerite Michaud, Contemp Fr Civilization, 77; Meandres, Jean Grassin, Paris, 77. *Mailing Add:* Dept of French & Span Mt Allison Univ Sackville NB E0A 3C0 Can

BOURAOUI, HEDI E, b Sfax, Tunisia, July 16, 32; Can citizen. FRENCH & COMPARATIVE LITERATURE. *Educ:* Univ Toulouse, Lic es Lett, 58; Ind Univ, Bloomington, MA, 60; Cornell Univ, PhD(romance studies), 66. *Prof Exp:* Asst prof French, Wells Col, 62-66; from assoc prof to prof, 66-78, MASTER, STONG COL, YORK UNIV, 78- *Concurrent Pos:* Consult, Encycl Britannica Educ Corp, 67-70; Can Coun res grants, 68-69; foreign lang consult, Rand McNally & Co, 72- *Mem:* MLA; Am Asn Teachers Fr; Can Asn Univ Teachers; Asn Can Univ Teachers Fr; Can Comp Lit Asn. *Res:* Twentieth century French and American experimental theater and novel; comparative cultural criticism; Francophone African literature. *Publ:* Auth, Creaculture I and II, Parole et Action, Ctr Curric Develop, Philadelphia & Didier, Montreal, 71; Structure Intentionnelle du Grand Meaulnes: Vers Le Poeme Romance, Nizet, Paris, 76; Vesuviade, Ed St Germain-des-Pres, Paris, 76; The Canadian Alternative, 80, Tales of Heritage, The Upstairs Gallery, 81, The Textual Strategy, & Vers et L'envers, ECW Press, 82; J Gnescent, Silex Editions, 82. *Mailing Add:* York Univ Toronto ON M4N 3M6 Can

BOURCIER, CLAUDE LOUIS, b Paris, France, July 15, 10; m 42; c 2. FRENCH LITERATURE. *Educ:* Univ Paris, Lic es Let, 33, dipl, 34, Agrege, 35. *Prof Exp:* Instr French, Univ Maine, 35-36; from asst prof to prof, 37-75, consult, acad year abroad, 62-63, chmn dept French, 63-69, dir grad sch of French in France, Paris, 69-75, EMER PROF FRENCH, MIDDLEBURY COL, 75- *Concurrent Pos:* Vis lectr, Inst Sci Franco-Can, Montreal, 45. *Mem:* MLA; Am Asn Teachers Fr. *Res:* French poetry at the beginning of the 20th century. *Publ:* Coauth, French Elementary Series, Allyn & Bacon, 60-65. *Mailing Add:* Le Chateau Middlebury Col Middlebury VT 05753

BOURGEOIS, ANDRE M, b Orleans, France, Dec 1, 02; nat US; m 30, 40; c 2. FRENCH LITERATURE. *Educ:* Univ Paris, BA, 21, LLB, 23, PhD, 45; Univ Tex, MA, 34. *Prof Exp:* From asst instr to prof French, 28-68, Favrot prof French lit, 69-72, chmn dept, 70-72, FAVROT EMER PROF FRENCH, RICE UNIV, 72- *Concurrent Pos:* Comdr, Palmes Acad, 72. *Honors & Awards:* Medal Honor, Univ Nancy, France, 45. *Mem:* S Cent Mod Lang Asn. *Res:* Vigny, Balzac and Stendhal. *Publ:* Auth, Boylesve et le Probleme de L'Amour, Droz, Geneva, 50; La Curieuse Helene de Jean Giraudoux, Rice Inst, 57; La Vie de Rene Boylesve, Vil I, Minard, Paris, 58; Le Mythe de Stendhal Immoraliste, Rice Inst, 60; Le gout du naturel chez Musset dramaturge, Rice Univ Studies, 65; Rene Boylesve, Le Poete, 67; L'Emploi de l'analogie dans les romans de Balzac, 71, Le mepris des hommes et de leurs institutions, dans le Journal d'Alfred de Vigny, 77, Rice Univ Studies. *Mailing Add:* Dept of French & Ital Rice Univ Houston TX 77001

BOURGEOIS, LOUIS CLARENCE, b Opelousas, La, May 27, 27; m 56; c 2. ROMANCE LANGUAGES. *Educ:* La State Univ, BA, 49; Univ Calif, Los Angeles, MA, 54, PhD(Span Am lit), 64. *Prof Exp:* Teaching asst Span, Univ Calif, Los Angeles, 53-57; instr, Wayne State Univ, 57-59 & John Carroll Univ, 59-61; from instr to asst prof, Univ Pittsburgh, 62-64; asst prof Span & Port, 64-71, ASSOC PROF SPAN, FLA STATE UNIV, 71- *Concurrent Pos:* Consult, eval Air Force Foreign Lang Inst, CZ, 65. *Mem:* Am Asn Teachers Span & Port; Asn Int Hispanistas; S Atlantic Mod Lang Asn; Latin Am Studies Asn. *Res:* Spanish American literature--Chilean, Argentine, Uruguayan, Mexican literature. *Publ:* Auth, The Tolstoy Colony, a Chilean utopian-artistic experiment, Hispania, 9/63; Augusto d'Halmar en el teatro, Duquesne Hisp Rev, fall 66; Augusto d'Halmar, el Loti Hispanoamericano, Hispanofila; Dos novelistas Hispano-americanos frente a Sevilla (D'Halmar y Reyles), In: Actas Del III Congreso de la Asociacion Internacional de Hispanistas, Mexico City, 69. *Mailing Add:* Dept of Mod Lang Fla State Univ Tallahassee FL 32306

BOURNE, MARJORIE ADELE, b Quincy, Ill, Jan 15, 09. ROMANCE LANGUAGES. *Educ:* Rice Univ, BA, 30; Northwestern Univ, MA, 53; Ind Univ, PhD(Span), 60. *Prof Exp:* Prof, 51-75, EMER PROF SPANISH, UNIV HOUSTON, 75- *Res:* Spanish literature; theatre; comparative literature. *Publ:* Coauth, El Espanol, la teoria y la practica & Workbook, Holt, 68; auth, Don Quixote on the boards in France, Rev Estudios Hisp, 71; The characters behind the voices, 71 & Fatality or free will, 73, Opera Cues. *Mailing Add:* 5707 Northridge Houston TX 77033

BOUSQUET, ROBERT EDWARD, b Medford, Mass, Dec 7, 30. FRENCH NOVEL, LINGUISTICS. *Educ:* Cath Univ Am, AB, 53, MM, 61; Georgetown Univ, PhD(French), 70. *Prof Exp:* Teacher, Mt St Joseph High Sch, Baltimore, Md, 53-58; teacher, St John's Prep Sch, Danvers, Mass, 58-62; prof French lang & lit, Xaverian Col, 62-69; teacher, Malden Cath High Sch, Mass, 69-70; PROF FRENCH LING METHODOLOGY, LOWELL UNIV, 70- *Concurrent Pos:* Mem higher educ comt adv coun, Mass Bd Transitional Biling Educ, 72-; prof English as second lang, Boston Univ, summers. *Mem:* Am Asn Teachers Fr; Am Coun Teaching Foreign Lang. *Res:* French language and literature; applied linguistics; language teaching methodology. *Publ:* Auth, What the English department owes the non-English major, Col English, 3/54; History and structure of the Flemish language, Ryken Quart, spring 66; Michel Butor, le Roman en tant qu' Instrument de Transformation du Reel, Georgetown Univ, 70; French immersion classes in the Montreal region, Fr Rev, Vol LII, No 4; The sixteenth century quest for a reformed orthography: The alphabet of Honorat Rambaud, Bibliotheque D'Humanisme et Renaissance, Vol XLIII, No 3. *Mailing Add:* 99 Crystal St Malden MA 02148

BOUTON, CHARLES PIERRE, b Paris, France, Feb 27, 26; m 46; c 2. LINGUISTICS, HISTORY OF GRAMMAR. *Educ:* Univ Paris, Baccalaureat, 44, Sorbonne, Lic es Lett, 47, Dipl Etudes Super, 49, Dr es Lett(ling), 69. *Prof Exp:* Teacher French lang & lit, French Nat Educ Syst, 47-51; asst lectr, French, Univ Col, Dundee, 51-52; prof Alliance Francaise, Paris, France, 52-58; lectr & actg dir, 58-67; vis prof, Converse Col, 67-69; prof, 69-71; PROF FRENCH & LING, SIMON FRASER UNIV, 71-, CHMN DEPT MOD LANG, 73- *Concurrent Pos:* Prof int summer courses, Dijon Univ, 65-; consult, UNESCO, 70. *Mem:* Can Asn Univ Teachers; Northwestern Conf Lang Teaching (vpres, 74); Can Asn Appl Ling. *Res:* Semantics; development of language. *Publ:* Ed, Le Misanthrope, 62, coauth, Des machines et des hommes, 64, Didier, France; coauth, Regardons, ecoutons et parlons, Hulton, London, 68; auth, Les Mecanismes d'Acquisition du Francais Langue etrangere, chez l'adulte, Klincksieck, France, 69; ed, Madame Bovary, Didier, France, 69; auth, Les Grammaires Francaises de classique Mauger XVIIe siecle, Klincksieck, France, 72. *Mailing Add:* Dept of Mod Lang Simon Fraser Univ Burnaby BC V5A 1S6 Can

BOUYGUES, CLAUDE P, b Tarn, France; m 69; c 1. FRENCH LANGUAGE & LITERATURE. *Educ:* Sorbonne, Lic es Lett, 64, Dipl Etude Super, 65, CAPES, 65; Duke Univ, PhD(French lit), 71. *Prof Exp:* Vis lectr French, Univ NC, Chapel Hill, 65-68 & Univ Victoria BC, 68-69, vis asst prof, 69-71, asst prof Ctr Continuing Educ, 69-73, asst prof, 71-77, PROF FRENCH, UNIV BC, 77- *Concurrent Pos:* Mem scholar comt, Alliance Francaise, Vancouver, 71-72 & Fedn Franco-Colombiens, Vancouver, 71-72; Can Coun fel, 77. *Mem:* Am Soc Interpreters; Am Asn Teachers Fr; Can Asn Univ Teachers; Soc Fr Prof Am; Soc Amis Jean Giono. *Res:* French and Francophone language and literature; French civilization; literary critcism. *Publ:* Auth, Un Sage Bonheur: Un Aspect du Chant du Monde de Jean Giono, Romance Notes, 69; Civilization-Culture, ou Apprentissage d'une Lecture, Fr Rev, 70; Poemes a Miss Ellanie, Oswlad, Honfleur, France, 72; coauth, Pour et Contre, Dodd, 72 & Harper & Row, 79; Colline: Structure et Signification, Fr Rev, 73; Aragon's Les lilas et les roses, Proc PNCFL XXVIII, 77; Colonization from within: An interview with Prof R Lafont, Contemp Fr Civilization, Vol III, 78; Le nouveau texte occitan, Proc PNCFL XXX, 79. *Mailing Add:* Dept French Univ BC Vancouver 8 BC V6T 1W5 Can

BOWEN, BARBARA C, b Newcastle, England, May 4, 37; m 63; c 2. FRENCH. *Educ:* Oxford Univ, BA, 58, MA, 62; Univ Paris, DrUniv, 62. *Prof Exp:* From instr to assoc prof, 62-73, PROF FRENCH, UNIV ILL, URBANA, 73- *Concurrent Pos:* Guggenheim Found fel, 74-75. *Mem:* MLA; Renaissance Soc Am. *Res:* French Renaissance literature; medieval French farce; Renaissance in general. *Publ:* Auth, Towards a definition of the French farce as a literary genre, Mod Lang Rev, 61; Les Caracteristiques Essentielles de la Farce Francaise, Univ Ill, 64; Four Farces, Blackwell, 67; Rabelais and the comedy of the spoken word, Mod Lang Rev, 68; Cornelius Agrippa's De Vanitate: Polemic or paradox?, Bibliot d'Humanisme et Renaissance, 72; The Age of Bluff: Paradox and Ambiguity in Rabelais and Montaigne, Univ Ill, 72. *Mailing Add:* Dept of French Univ of Ill Urbana IL 61801

BOWEN, CHARLES ARTHUR, JR, b Attleboro, Mass, Dec 30, 37; m 63; c 2. CELTIC LITERATURE, ENGLISH. *Educ:* Univ Notre Dame, AB, 59; Yale Univ, MA, 61; Harvard Univ, PhD(Celtic), 72. *Prof Exp:* Instr English, Carnegie Inst Technol, 61-64; from instr to asst prof, 67-77, ASSOC PROF ENGLISH, UNIV MASS, BOSTON, 77- *Mem:* MLA; Am Comt Irish Studies; New England Comt Irish Studies (pres, 82); Celtic Studies Asn (secy-treas, 78). *Res:* Middle Irish philology and literature. *Publ:* Auth, Great-bladdered Medb: Mythology and invention in the Tain Bo Cuailnge, Eire-Ireland, 75; A historical inventory of the Dindshenchas, Studia Celtica, 76; Notes on the Middle Irish word for mermaid, Eriu, 78. *Mailing Add:* Dept of English Univ Mass Harbor Campus Boston MA 02125

BOWEN, JEAN DONALD, b Malad, Idaho, Mar 19, 22; m 48; c 5. LINGUISTICS. *Educ:* Brigham Young Univ, AB, 44, Columbia Univ, MA, 49; Univ NMex, PhD, 52. *Prof Exp:* Instr, Duke Univ, 52-53; assoc prof, Foreign Serv Inst, US Dept State, 53-58; assoc prof, 58-66, PROF ENGLISH, UNIV CALIF, LOS ANGELES, 66- *Concurrent Pos:* Co-dir, Philippine Ctr Lang Study, 58-63; vis assoc prof, Univ Calif, Los Angeles, 58-63; English teaching adv panel, US Info Agency, 64-75; field dir, Surv Lang Use & Lang Teaching in Eastern Africa, 68-70; vis prof, Am Univ Cairo, 74-77. *Mem:* Ling Soc Am; MLA; Teachers English to Speakers Other Lang. *Res:* Contrastive analysis; methodology of language teaching; construction of teaching materials. *Publ:* Coauth, The Sounds of English and Spanish, 65 & The Grammatical Structures of English and Spanish, 65, Univ Chicago; ed, Beginning Tagalog, 65 & Intermediate Readings in Tagalog, 68, Univ Calif; auth, Patterns of English Pronunciation, 75 & ed, Studies in Southwest Spanish, 76, Newbury House; Language in Ethiopia, Oxford Univ, 76; coauth, Adaptation in Langauge Teaching, Newbury House, 78. *Mailing Add:* Dept of English Univ of Calif Los Angeles CA 90024

BOWEN, VINCENT EUGENE, b Stronghurst, Ill, June 12, 24; m 63; c 2. FRENCH. *Educ:* Univ Tex, BA, 48; Univ Wis, MA, 50; Univ Ill, PhD(French), 56. *Prof Exp:* From instr to asst prof French, Univ Colo, 56-61; asst prof, 61-65, ASSOC PROF FRENCH, UNIV ILL, URBANA, 65- *Concurrent Pos:* Am Philos Soc grant, 68. *Mem:* MLA; Am Asn Teachers Fr. *Res:* Eighteenth-century French literature and thought. *Publ:* Auth, Diderot's contributions to the Corr Litt, Romanis Rev, 10/64 & 2/65; Voltaire and tragedy: Theory and practice, L'Esprit Createur, winter 67. *Mailing Add:* Dept of French Univ of Ill Urbana IL 61801

BOWEN, WAYNE SCOTT, b Columbus, Ohio, May 18, 26; m 49; c 2. ROMANCE LANGUAGES. *Educ:* Ohio State Univ, BA, 48, PhD(Romance lang), 58; Emory Univ, MA, 53. *Prof Exp:* Teacher High Sch, Ga, 52-53; instr Span, Ohio State Univ, 55-58; from instr to asst prof, Univ Calif, Davis, 58-64; from asst prof to assoc prof, 64-72, PROF SPAN, CALIF STATE UNIV, FRESNO, 72- *Mem:* Am Asn Teachers Span & Port, Inst Int Lit Iberoamericana. *Res:* Spanish American literature; translation. *Mailing Add:* 4733-110 N Cedar Ave Fresno CA 93726

BOWERSOCK, GLEN WARREN, History, Classics. See Vol I

BOWLING, TOWNSEND WHELEN, b St Louis, Mo, May 2, 39. FRENCH LANGUAGE & LITERATURE. *Educ:* Wash Univ, St Louis, AB, 61; Middlebury Col, AB, 68; Yale Univ, PhD(French), 76. *Prof Exp:* ASST PROF FRENCH, UNIV RICHMOND, 76- *Mem:* Am Soc Eighteenth Century Studies; Soc Francaise E'etude du dix huiteme Siecle; MLA; Am Asn Teachers French. *Res:* Eighteenth century French novel; French preromanticism and romanticism. *Mailing Add:* Dept Mod Foreign Lang Univ Richmond Richmond VA 23173

BOWMAN, ELIZABETH, b Chicago, Ill, Mar 7, 15. LINGUISTICS, ENGLISH. *Educ:* Univ Chicago, MA, 53, PhD(ling), 63. *Prof Exp:* From lectr to asst prof ling, Ind Univ, 61-66; asst prof, 66-68, assoc prof, 68-79, EMER ASSOC PROF ENGLISH & LIT, WESTERN WASH UNIV, 80- *Mem:* Am Dialect Soc. *Publ:* Auth, On the analysis of syllabic resonants in English, Studies Ling, 57; An attempt at an analysis of modern Yucatec from a small spoken corpus, Anthrop Ling, 59; The classification of imperative sentences in English, Studies Ling, 63; The Minor and Fragmentary Sentences of a Corpus of Spoken English, Mouton, 66. *Mailing Add:* Dept of English Western Wash Univ Bellingham WA 98225

BOWMAN, FRANK PAUL, b Portland, Ore, June 12, 27. FRENCH. *Educ:* Reed Col, BA, 49; Yale Univ, MA, 52, PhD(French), 55. *Prof Exp:* Asst prof French, Univ Calif, 54-62; assoc prof, Reed Col, 62-63; assoc prof, 63-65, PROF FRENCH, UNIV PA, 65- *Concurrent Pos:* Guggenheim fel, 68-69; vis prof French, Univ Paris, 73-75; Nat Endowment Humanities fel, 78-79. *Mem:* MLA; Mod Humanities Res Asn; Int Asn Fr Studies; Soc Etudes Romantiques. *Res:* French romanticism; autobiography. *Publ:* Auth, Prosper Merimee: Heroism, Pessimism, Irony, Univ Calif, 62; Montaigne; Essays, Arnold, 65; Eliphas Levi, Visionnaire Romanique, Univ France, 69; Le Christ Romanique, 73 & Le Discours Sur L'eloquence Sacree, 80, Droz. *Mailing Add:* Dept of Romance Lang Univ of Pa Philadelphia PA 19174

BOWMAN, HERBERT EUGENE, b Harrisburg, Pa, Feb 8, 17. SLAVIC & COMPARATIVE LITERATURE. *Educ:* Univ Pa, AB, 38; Univ Lille, France, cert, 39; Harvard Univ, MA, 41, PhD(comp lit), 50. *Prof Exp:* Instr Russ lit, Harvard Univ, 50-53; from asst prof to assoc prof Slavic lang, Univ Ore, 53-61; PROF SLAVIC LANG & LIT, UNIV TORONTO, 61- *Concurrent Pos:* Res fel, Harvard Univ Russ Res Ctr, 50-53. *Mem:* MLA. *Res:* Russian literature and intellectual history; comparative modern European literature. *Publ:* Auth, Vissarion Belinski, Harvard Univ, 54; The nose, Slavonic & E Europ Rev; Art and reality in Russian realist criticism, J Aesthet. *Mailing Add:* Dept of Salvic Lang & LIt Univ of Toronto Toronto ON M5S 1A1 Can

BOWMAN, RUSSELL KEITH, b Poughkeepsie, NY, Aug 27, 12; m 34; c 2. FRENCH, SPANISH. *Educ:* Columbia Univ, AB, 34, AM, 35, PhD(French), 40. *Prof Exp:* From instr to asst prof Romance lang, Carleton Col, 41-47; from assoc prof to prof, Carroll Col, 47-56, chmn dept mod foreign lang, 51-56; chmn dept foreign lang, 56-65, prof Romance lang, 56-78, EMERITUS PROF ROMANCE LANG, ARIZ STATE UNIV, 78- *Mem:* MLA; Am Asn Teachers Fr; Am Asn Teachers Span & Port; Rocky Mt Coun Latin Am Studies; Am Coun Teaching Foreign Lang. *Res:* Old French literature and French semantics. *Publ:* Auth, Connections of the Geste des Loherains With Other French Epics and Medieval Genres, New York Univ, 40. *Mailing Add:* Dept of Foreign Lang Ariz State Univ Tempe AZ 85281

BOYD, JULIAN, b Orlando, Fla, Dec 25, 31; m 57; c 2. ENGLISH LANGUAGE. *Educ:* Williams Col, BA, 52; Univ Mich, MA, 54, PhD(English), 65. *Prof Exp:* From lectr to instr, 56-64; asst prof, 64-71, consult, Navaho Proj, 67, prof humanities, 68, ASSOC PROF ENGLISH, UNIV CALIF, BERKELEY, 71- *Concurrent Pos:* Conslut, Educ Develop Corp, Palo Alto, 67 & Roberts English Ser Harcourt, 68-; Am Coun Learned Soc grant, 68; humanities res fel, Univ Calif, Berkeley, 69; fel, Dept English lang, Univ Edinburgh, 69; legal consult English syntax, numerous firms, 70. *Mem:* Ling Soc Am. *Res:* English syntax; linguistics and literary criticism;

linguistics and philosophy. *Publ:* Coauth, Annotated bibliography of generative grammar, Lang Learning, 61 & Deep grammar of the modals, J Ling, 69; Roberts English Series (6 vols), Harcourt, 70-72. *Mailing Add:* Dept of English Univ of Calif Berkeley CA 94720

BOYD, LOLA ELIZABETH, b Panama City, Panama, Nov 24, 16; US citizen. ROMANCE LANGUAGES. *Educ:* Vassar Col, AB, 36; Univ Panama, prof, 37; Univ Md, MA, 41; Los Angeles Bus Prep Sch, dipl, 44; Columbia Univ, PhD(Span & Port), 65. *Prof Exp:* Instr Span & French, Gunston Hall, Washington, DC, 37-41; instr Span, C Z Jr Col & Balboa High Sch, 41-42; secy to the Foreign Counsel, Pan Am Airways, NY, 44-45; asst to advert mgr & Span-English copywriter, Sterling Prod Int & Sydney Ross Co, NY, 45-47 & Soc Cenacle, 47-54; asst to vpres & pub rel, Toy Guid Coun, NY, 55-56; acad dean, Highland Manor Sch, 56-57; from lectr to asst prof Span, Columbia Univ, 58-66; assoc prof, Case Western Reserve Univ, 66-69; assoc prof Span, assoc dean & dir eve col, Assumption Col, Mass, 69-72; dir, Latin Am Inst, Worcester, Mass, 71-72; assoc prof Span, York Col, NY, 72-77; assoc prof Hisp studies, Vassar Col, 78-82, chmn dept, 79-82; RETIRED. *Mem:* MLA; Am Asn Teachers Span & Port. *Res:* Latin American literature; Spanish language and literature; Latin American civilization. *Publ:* Auth, Dos ninos de Nuestra America, Cuadernos Am, 3-4/59; Lo de dentro in Ruben Dario, Hispania, 12/62; The Image of Emiliano Zapata in the Art and Literature of the Mexican Revolution, Univ Microfilms, 67; Zapata, Americas, English ed, 9/68, Span ed, 10/68 & 20th anniversary ed, 69; Spanish America: Many nations with one voice, In: Annals of the Congress of Federation Internationale des Langues et Litteratures Modernes, Griffin Press, Adelaide, 76; La gloria de 'Miliano, In: Homenaje a Andres Iduarte, Am Hispanist, 76; Emiliano Zapata en las letras y el folklore mexicano, Porrua Turanzas 79. *Mailing Add:* 35 F Sherwood Forest Vassar Col Wappingers Falls NY 12590

BOYD-BOWMAN, PETER (MUSCHAMP), b Matsue, Japan, Oct 29, 24; m 44; c 3. ROMANCE LINGUISTICS. *Educ:* Univ Toronto, BA, 44, MA, 47; Harvard Univ, PhD(Romance ling), 50. *Prof Exp:* Instr Span & ling, Harvard Univ, 49-52; from instr to asst prof Span, Yale Univ, 52-55; from assoc prof to prof foreign lang, Kalamazoo Col, 55-65, chmn dept, 55-65; PROF SPAN LING & DIR CTR CRITICAL LANG, STATE UNIV NY BUFFALO, 65- *Concurrent Pos:* Guggenheim fel, 56-57; Fulbright lectr Hispanic ling, Inst Caro y Cuervo, Bogota, 59-60; dir neglected lang proj, NDEA, 63-65; coordr, NY State Carnegie Prog self-instr neglected lang, 66-; chmn steering comt, Mex Microfilm Proj, 67-68; gen consult, US Off Educ Self-Instructional Lang Prog, 70-72, exec secy, 72- *Mem:* MLA; Am Coun Teaching Foreign Lang; Am Asn Teachers Span & Port; Ling Soc Am; Asn Int Hispanistas. *Res:* Spanish American historical linguistics; self-instruction in non-western languages; Spanish-American colonial history and paleography. *Publ:* Auth, El Habla de Guanajuato, Nat Univ Mex, 60; Indice Geobiografico de 40,000 Pobladores Espanoles de America en el Siglo XVI, Vol I, Inst Caro y Cuervo, Bogota, 64 & Vol II, Ed Jus, Mexico City, 68; Negro slaves in early colonial Mexico, In: The Americas, Vol 26, 69; Lexico Hispanoamericano del Siglo XVI, Tamesis Bks, Madrid, 72; L'exico Hispanoamericano del siglo XVIII: Hisp Sem Medieval Studies, Madison, Wis, 82. *Mailing Add:* Ctr Critical Lang 826 Clemens Hall State Univ of NY Buffalo NY 14260

BOYER, HARRIET P, b Portsmouth, Va, Oct 9, 36; m 65. ROMANCE LANGUAGES. *Educ:* Col William & Mary, BA, 57; Univ NMex, PhD(Span), 67. *Prof Exp:* Asst prof Span, Frederick Col, Va, 61-62 & Col Santa Fe, 64-66; from asst to assoc prof, 67-80, PROF SPAN, COLO STATE UNIV, 80- *Mem:* MLA; Am Asn Teachers Span & Port; Rocky Mt Mod Lang Asn. *Res:* Spanish Golden Age drama; literary feminism and women's studies. *Mailing Add:* Dept of Lang Colo State Univ Ft Collins CO 80521

BOYER, MILDRED (VINSON), b Newport, Tenn, June 1, 26. SPANISH. *Educ:* Baylor Univ, BA, 47, MA, 49; Univ Tex, PhD(romance lang), 56. *Prof Exp:* Instr Span, Baylor Univ, 50-51; instr, Univ Tex, 53-54; instr Span & Ital, Univ Ill, 55-58; asst prof, Univ Ark, 58-59; from asst prof to assoc prof Span, 59-66, PROF SPAN & EDUC, UNIV TEX, AUSTIN, 66- *Concurrent Pos:* Consult, US Off Educ, 60-61; mem, Col Entrance Exam Bd, Span, 61-64, chmn 64-66; adv comt, Foreign Lang Prog, MLA, 62-65 & 65-68, Educ Resources Inform Ctr Bd, 71-73; specialist bilingual educ, Southwest Educ Develop Lab, 68-71. *Mem:* Centro Estud Siglo XVIII Catedora Feijoo; MLA; Am Asn Teachers Span & Port; Am Coun Teaching Foreign Lang; Am Soc 18th Century Studies. *Res:* Eighteenth century Spanish literature; Spanish theater; foreign language. *Publ:* Co-transl, Borges, Dreamtigers, Univ Tex, 63; coauth, Bilingual Schooling in the United States, Southwestern Educ Develop Lab, 70; auth, The Texas Collection of Comedias Sueltas, A Descriptive Bibliography, G K Hall, 78. *Mailing Add:* Dept of Span & Port Univ of Tex Austin TX 78712

BOZON-SCALZITTI, YVETTE PAULINE, b Pimorin, France, Oct 14, 37; m 63. FRENCH LITERATURE. *Educ:* Ecole Normale Superieure and Sorbonne, Lic, 59, dipl d'Etudes Superieures, 60, Agregation, 61. *Prof Exp:* Instr French lit, Univ Chicago, 62-64; asst prof, Sorbonne, 64-66; vis asst prof, Stanford Univ, 66-67; asst prof, Univ Chicago, 67-73; vis asst prof, 76-80, VIS ASSOC PROF FRENCH LIT, ROOSEVELT UNIV, 80- *Mem:* Am Asn Teachers French. *Res:* Modern French literature and criticism; 19th century French literature. *Publ:* Auth, Le Verset Claudelien: Etude de Rythme & Blaise Cendrars et le Symbolisme, 65& 72, Minard; Cendrars et la machine infernale, L'Icosatheque, 77; Blaise Cendrars ou la Passion de L'Ecriture, L'Age D'Homme, 77; Blaise cendrars: L'autre et l'ecriture, Stanford Fr Rev, 79; George Sand: Mauprat ou la belle et la be6te, Nineteenth-Century Fr Studies, 81. *Mailing Add:* 1400 E 56th St Chicago IL 60637

BRADFORD, CAROLE A, b Hammond, Ind, Mar 14, 37. SPANISH & FRENCH. *Educ:* Univ Tenn, BA, 58, MA, 59; Vanderbilt Univ, PhD(Span), 72. *Prof Exp:* Instr romance lang, Univ Tenn, 59-66; instr, 70-72, ASST PROF ROMANCE LANG, BOWLING GREEN STATE UNIV, 72- *Concurrent Pos:* Fel, Nat Endowment Humanities, NY Univ, 78-79. *Mem:* MLA; Am Asn Teachers Span & Port; Am Asn Univ Prof. *Res:* Spanish 20th century poetry; Spanish 19th century novel. *Publ:* Auth, The reuse of identical plot material in some novels of Ramon J Sender, Hispania, 60; The dual personality in the last three novels of Emilia Pardo Bazan, Revista de Estudios Hispanicas, fall 78; Death and rebirth in La Sirena Negra of Emilia Pardo Bazan, Revista Hispanica Mod, 78. *Mailing Add:* Dept of Romance Lang Bowling Green State Univ Bowling Green OH 43403

BRADLEY, BRIGITTE L, b Siemianowice, Poland, Sept 17, 24; US citizen; c 2. GERMANIC & ROMANCE LANGUAGES. *Educ:* Univ Strasbourg, Dr Univ, 60; Columbia Univ, PhD, 65. *Prof Exp:* Lectr, 62-63, from instr to assoc prof, 63-73, PROF GER, BARNARD COL, COLUMBIA UNIV, 73-, CHMN DEPT, 68- *Mem:* MLA; Am Asn Teachers Ger; AAUP; Rilke Soc. *Res:* German literature of the twentieth century. *Publ:* Auth, R M Rilkes Neue Gedichte: Ihr Zyklisches Gefüge, Francke, Bern-Munchen, 67; Analysis of a fragment by Kafka, Ger Rev, 69; Marginalien zur biografie Rilkes, Colloquia Ger, 73; Rilkes Buddha-gedichte, In: Rilke Heute I, 75 & Max Frischs Biografie: ein Spiel, In: Uber Max Frisch II, 76, Suhrkamp, Frankfurt; R M Rilke: Entwicklungsstufen seiner Pariser Lyrik, 76 & Rilkes Malte Laurids Brigge, 80, Francke, Bern-Munchen. *Mailing Add:* Dept of Ger Barnard Col Columbia Univ New York NY 10027

BRADLEY, EDWARD DRAKE, b Jamestown, NY, Dec 23, 20; m 53. FRENCH. *Educ:* Principia Col, BA, 43; Middlebury Col, AM, 50. *Prof Exp:* ASSOC PROF FRENCH, PRINCIPIA COL, 46- *Mem:* Am Asn Teachers Fr. *Res:* Phonetics; dialetology. *Mailing Add:* Dept French Principia Col Elsah IL 62028

BRADLEY, EDWARD MIX, b New Haven, Conn, Apr 3, 36; m 59; c 1. CLASSICS. *Educ:* Yale Univ, BA, 58, MA, 59, PhD(classics), 63. *Prof Exp:* Instr classics, Yale Univ, 60-63; from instr to assoc prof, 63-76, fel, 66-67, PROF CLASSICS, DARTMOUTH COL, 76- *Concurrent Pos:* Am Coun Learned Soc study fel, 66-67. *Mem:* Am Philol Asn; Class Asn New Eng. *Res:* Greek epic and lyric poetry; Roman satire; Lucretius. *Publ:* Auth, Hesiod's Theogony, Symbolae Osloenes, 66; Hector and the simile of the snowy mountain, Trans Am Philol Asn, 67; The hybris of Odysseus, Soundings, spring 68. *Mailing Add:* Dept of Classics Dartmouth Col Hanover NH 03755

BRADLEY, JAMES ROBERT, b Philadelphia, Pa, Mar 28, 35; m 63; c 4. CLASSICS. *Educ:* Trinity Col, Conn, BA, 57; Harvard Univ, MA, 59, PhD(class philol), 68. *Prof Exp:* Instr classics, Hobart & William Smith Cols, 60-62; asst prof, Univ NC, 67-70; asst prof, 70-74, ASSOC PROF CLASSICS, TRINITY COL, CONN, 74- *Mem:* Am Philol Asn; Archaeol Inst Am. *Res:* Greek and Latin literature; classical civilization. *Mailing Add:* Dept of Classics Trinity Col Hartford CT 06106

BRADLEY, KEITH RICHARD, Ancient History, Classical Languages. See Vol I

BRADY, JAMES F, b New York, NY, June 23, 10; m 50; c 3. CLASSICS. *Educ:* Fordham Col, BA, 33; Fordham Univ MA, 38; Columbia Univ, PhD, 58. *Prof Exp:* From instr to assoc prof, 34-71, prof, 71-80, EMER PROF CLASSICS, FORDHAM UNIV, 80- *Concurrent Pos:* Assoc ed, Class World, 59-62, managing ed, 62-63. *Mem:* Am Philol Asn; Class Asn Atlantic States; Am Class League. *Res:* Senecan tragedy; Hellenistin philosophy. *Publ:* Coauth, Cicero's Pro Archia, Fordham Univ, 40. *Mailing Add:* Dept of Classics Fordham Univ New York NY 10458

BRADY, PATRICK, b Broken Hill, NSW, Australia, Oct 27; 33; m 64. FRENCH & COMPARATIVE LITERATURE. *Educ:* Univ Sydney, BA, 57; Univ Paris, DUniv(French), 61. *Prof Exp:* Asst English, Norm Sch, Poitiers, France, 57-58; lectr, Univ Lille, 59-60; asst prof French, Univ Melbourne, 61-64; assoc prof, Univ Queensland, 64-68, reader, 69; from assoc prof to prof, Fla State Univ, 70-72; PROF FRENCH, RICE UNIV, 72- *Concurrent Pos:* Vis prof comp lit, Harvard Univ, 78. *Honors & Awards:* Chevalier Palmes Academiques, 77. *Mem:* Int Comp Lit Asn; Am Comp Lit Asn; Am Soc 18th Century Studies; MLA. *Res:* Aesthetics, especially rococo style in European plastic arts and literature; theory and methodology of literary criticism; formal evolution of the novel. *Publ:* Auth, L'Oeuvre d'Emile Zola, Roman sur les Arts: Manifeste, Autobiographie, Roman a Clef, Droz, Geneva, 68; Toward autonomy and metonymy: The concept of rococo literature from 1859 to 1976, Yearbk Comp & Gen Lit, 76; co-ed, Phenomenology, Structuralism, Semiotics, Bucknell Univ, 76; auth, Marcel Proust, Twayne, 77; Structuralist Perspectives in Criticism of Fiction, Lang, Bern, 78; Rococo Poetry of Europe, Synthesis, 80; Le Bouc Emissaire chez Emile Zola, Carl Winter, Heidelberg, 81; Rococo Style versus Enlightenment Novel, Slatkine, Geneva, 82. *Mailing Add:* Dept of French & Ital Rice Univ Houston TX 77001

BRADY-PAPADOPOULOU, VALENTINI, b Greece; Australian citizen; m 64. FRENCH. *Educ:* Univ Melbourne, Australia, BA, 61; Univ Queensland, Australia, PhD(French), 68. *Prof Exp:* Instr French, Univ Melbourne, 62-64; vis asst prof, Univ Queensland, 64, instr French & Greek, Mod Lang Inst, 67-68; instr, 74-75, vis asst prof, 75-76, assoc prof, 76-81, PROF FRENCH, UNIV HOUSTON, 81- *Concurrent Pos:* Nat Endowment for Humanities summer grant, 79. *Mem:* MLA; Am Soc 18th-century Studies; Paul Claudel Soc; SCent Mod Lang Asn. *Res:* Marivaux and Claudel theatre; thematic and symbolic aspects of the novel; archetypal and psychoanalytical methods of criticism. *Publ:* Auth, Archetypal structure of Tete d'or, Romanic Rev, 76; The blazing firmament: The symbolic substructure of Partage de midi, Claudel Studies, 76; French archetypal criticism: The contribution of Gilbert Durand, Fr Lit Ser, 77; Repetition et difference: Du crime sacre a la punition profrane, Orbis litterarum, 78; Mimesis, artifice, disbelief and the problem of the supernatural: Paul Claudel's Le Soulier de satin, L'Esprit createur, 78; Camus Meursault: A Nocturnal Being in a Diurnal World, Orbis Literarum, 80; The Killing of the Mother in Constant's Adolphe, Neophilologus, 81; Separation, death and sexuality: Diderst's La Religieuse and Rites of Mitiation, Studies on Voltaire and the 18th Century, 81. *Mailing Add:* Dept of French Univ Houston Houston TX 77004

BRAENDLIN, HANS PETER, b Miri, Sarawak, Apr 19, 28; US citizen; m 68; c 1. GERMAN LANGUAGE & LITERATURE. *Educ:* Swiss Fed Inst Technol, BS, 50; Univ Edinburgh, PhD(chem), 55; Univ Southern Calif, PhD(Ger), 76. *Prof Exp:* Fel, Univ Chicago, 55-56; asst prof chem, Purdue Univ, 58-62; teaching asst, Univ Southern Calif, 62-64; asst prof Ger, Calif Lutheran Col, 64-68; asst prof, 68-76, ASSOC PROF GER, FLA STATE UNIV, 76- *Mem:* MLA; Am Asn Teachers Ger; Am Comp Lit Asn. *Res:* Literature and science; comparative literature; 17th century German literature. *Publ:* Coauth, Halogenation, In: Friedel-Crafts and Related Reactions, Interscience, 64; Europaische Tradition und Deutscher Literaturbarock, Francke, 73; auth, The dilemma of luxary and the ironic structures of Lessing's Emilia Galotti and Lenz's The Soldiers, Studies Voltaire & 18th Century, CLI, 76. *Mailing Add:* Dept of Mod Lang Fla State Univ Tallahassee FL 32306

BRAGA, THOMAS, b Fall River, Mass, June 13, 43. FOREIGN LANGUAGES, LITERATURE. *Educ:* Providence Col, AB, 66; Rice Univ, PhD(French lit), 70. *Prof Exp:* Asst prof French, Calif State Col, San Bernardino, 70-72; asst prof, 72-78, ASSOC PROF FRENCH, PORT & SPAN, STATE UNIV COL, PLATTSBURGH, NY, 78- *Concurrent Pos:* NDEA fel, Rice Univ, 66-69. *Mem:* MLA; Am Asn Teachers French; Pan Am Soc New Eng; Am Asn Teachers Span & Port; Int Conf Group Mod Portugal. *Res:* French literature; Luso Brazilian studies; poetry. *Publ:* Auth, Daniel Defoe and the Portuguese, Enlightenment Essays, 73; Madness in the theater of Tristan L'Hermite, French Rev, 2/75; The lyrics of a revolution, J Am Portuguese Soc, Vol XIII, 79; Le depaysement moral dans le theatre de Tristan, Cahiers Tristan, 80; Chants Fugitifs (poem), Carpentras, France: Musee de Poesie, 81; Portin Gales (poem), Providence, RI, Gavea-Brown, 81. *Mailing Add:* Dept of Foreign Lang State Univ Col Plattsburgh NY 12901

BRANCAFORTE, BENITO, b Noto, Italy, Nov 15, 34; US citizen; m 61; c 3. SPANISH LITERATURE OF GOLDEN AGE, LITERARY CRITICISM. *Educ:* Brooklyn Col, BA, 59; Univ Colo, MA, 61; Univ Ill, Urbana, PhD(Span), 65. *Prof Exp:* From instr to asst prof Ital & Span, Univ Ill, Urbana, 64-66; asst prof, 66-69, assoc prof, 69-75, PROF SPAN, UNIV WIS-MADISON, 75- *Concurrent Pos:* Jr vis prof, Inst Res Humanities, Univ Wis, 68-669; vis prof, Univ Wash, 70 & Univ Calif, San Diego, 72. *Mem:* Am Asn Teachers Ital. *Res:* Benedetto Croce; Picaresque novel; Spanish literary criticism and comedia of Golden Age. *Publ:* Auth, Benedetto Croce y su Critica de la Literatura Espanola, Gredos, Madrid, 72; Valor y limites de las Anotaciones de Fernando de Herrera, Revista Arch, Bibliotecas & Museos, 76; Deffensa de la Poesia: An Anonymous Spanish Translation of Sidney's Defense of Poesie, North Carolina Univ, 77; ed, Francisco Cascales' Tablas Poeticas, Clasicos Castellanos, Madrid, 77; coauth, Charlotte Lang Brancaforte, La Primera Traduccion Italiana del Lazarillo de Tormes por Giulio Strozzi, Ravenna, Italy, 77; ed, Guzman de AlFarache (2 vols), Catedra, Madrid, 79; auth, Guzman de AlFarache by Mateo Aleman, Madison, 80; co-ed, Homenaje a A Sanchez Barbudo, Madison, 81. *Mailing Add:* 1727 Summit Ave Madison WI 53706

BRANCAFORTE, CHARLOTTE LANG, b Munich, Ger, July 26, 34; m 61; c 3. GERMAN LITERATURE, GERMAN STUDIES. *Educ:* Univ Denver, BA, 58; Univ Ill, Urbana, PhD(Ger/int rels), 66. *Prof Exp:* Instr, Univ Ill, Urbana, 64-66; asst prof, 66-73, assoc prof, 73-79, PROF GER, UNIV WIS-MADISON, 79-, CHMN, DEPT GER & CHAIR WEST EUROP AREA STUDIES, 80- *Mem:* Am Asn Teachers Ger; Am Soc Ger Lit 16th & 17th Centuries; Midwest Mod Lang Asn; MLA; Am Soc 18th Century Studies. *Res:* Baroque literature; German area studies; German cultural studies. *Publ:* Auth, Daniel Casper von Lohensteins Preisgedicht Venus, W Fink, Munich, Ger, 74; coauth, A new perspective in teamwork in teaching: German lectures in the biological sciences, Unterrichtspraxis, fall 76; auth, Beyond the requirment, In: German Studies in the United States, Univ Wis, 76; coauth, La primera traduccion italiana del Lazarillo de Tormes par Giulio Strozzi, A Longo, Revenna Italy, 77. *Mailing Add:* Univ of Wis-Madison Dept of Ger 844 Van Hise Hall Madison WI 53706

BRANDWEIN, NAFTALI CHAIM, b Jeursalem, Israel, June 22, 21; Can citizen; m 52; c 2. BIBLICAL & MODERN HEBREW LITERATURE. *Educ:* Mizrachi Teachers Training Col, Jerusalem, Israel, teachers dipl, 41; Col Rabbinical Studies, Jerusalem, cert, 47; Jewish Theol Sem Am, DHL, 62. *Prof Exp:* Dean & lectr Hebrew lit, United Jewish Teachers Sem Can, Montreal, 58-60; from instr to asst prof mod Hebrew lit, Jewish Theol Sem Am, 61-66; assoc prof, 66-68, PROF MOD HEBREW LIT, BRANDEIS UNIV, 68-, CHMN COUN SCH HUMANITIES, 67- *Concurrent Pos:* Lectr, Sir George Williams Univ, 59-60; Goodman Found grant, 65; mem comn, Melton Res Ctr, NY, 67; mem examining comt, Col Entrance Exam Bd, Princeton Univ, 67-; vis prof Hebrew lit, Univ Tel Aviv, Israel, 75-76; mem adv bd, Ha Doar, Hebrew Weekly, 75- & Jewish Univ without Walls, 76- *Honors & Awards:* Louis Lamed Prize for Hebrew Lit, 60; Wolfson Prize, Brandeis Univ, 78. *Mem:* Hebrew PEN Club (secy, 65-68). *Res:* Literary approach to Biblical texts; critical analysis of modern Hebrew literature; Biblical literature. *Publ:* Auth, In the Courtyards of Jerusalem, Jewish Publ Soc Am, 67; Asher Barash, Selection and Critical Analysis, Goodman Found, NY, 68; co-ed, transl, S Y Agnon, A Guest for the Night, Shocken Publ, NY, 68; contribr, New Dimensions in Religious Experience, Alba, 71; auth, Leaves of Shattered Prayers (ser of Hebrew poems), Lit Jour in US & Israel, 71-73; contribr, Modern Near East-Literature and Society, NY Univ, 72; Cycle of Hebrew poems, Ha Doar, Hebrew Weekly & Lit Suppl to Ha-Aretz, Tel Aviv, 77. *Mailing Add:* Dept of Near Eastern & Judaic Studies Brandeis Univ South St Waltham MA 02154

BRANTLEY, FRANKLIN OAKES, b Memphis, Tenn, May 20, 26; m 59; c 2. SPANISH. *Educ:* Univ NC, BA, 50; Tulane Univ, MA, 62, PhD(Span), 67. *Prof Exp:* Teacher, Am Sch in Madrid, 57-59; teaching fel Span, Tulane Univ, 59-62; instr, Ohio Univ, 62-64; asst prof, 64-67, assoc prof, 68-69, prof & chmn dept foreign lang, 69-79, PROF SPAN, MEMPHIS STATE UNIV, 79- *Mem:* MLA; Am Asn Teachers Span & Port; AAUP. *Res:* Golden Age literature. *Publ:* Auth, Sancho's ascent into the spheres, Hispania, 3/70. *Mailing Add:* Dept of Foreign Lang Memphis State Univ Memphis TN 38152

BRAS, MARY BENVENUTA, b Mitchell, SDak. FRENCH LANGUAGE & LITERATURE. *Educ:* Univ Wash, BS, 24; Univ Fribourg, PhD, 36. *Prof Exp:* From instr to asst prof French, 35-45, dean women, 38-47, prof, 47-55 & 61-75, dept chmn, 49-55, dir, Jr Year Abroad, Fribourg, Switz, 55-61, chmn dept French & mod lang, 72-75, EMER PROF FRENCH, ROSARY COL, 75- *Mem:* Am Asn Teachers Fr; Am Transl Asn. *Res:* Legends and folklore of Switzerland; 19th century French literature, especially literary criticism; French-Swiss literature. *Publ:* Auth, Gustave Planche: Sa Vie Et Son Oeuvre, E De Boccard, Paris, 36; transl, Bernard Schmitt, Macoreconomcis Theory: A Fundamental Revision, Editions Castilla, Switzerland, 72; The Northeast Province of the Sinsinara Dominican Congregation of the Most Holy Rosary: A commentary by Sister Benvenuta Bros, 80 & transl, Henri Lacordaire, Re-establishment of the Dominican Order in France (in prep), Univ Press. *Mailing Add:* Dept French Rosary Col Oak Park IL 60305

BRAULT, GERARD JOSEPH, b Chicopee Falls, Mass, Nov 7, 29; m 54; c 3. FRENCH. *Educ:* Assumption Col, Mass, AB, 50; Laval Univ, AM, 52; Univ Pa, PhD(Romance lang), 58. *Hon Degrees:* DLitt, Assumption Col, Mass, 76. *Prof Exp:* Teaching fel, Univ, Pa, 54-56; instr French, Bowdoin Col, 57-59, asst prof Romance lang, 59-61; assoc prof, Univ Pa, 61-65, vdean grad sch arts & sci, 62-65; head dept, 65-70, PROF FRENCH, PA STATE UNIV, UNIVERSITY PARK, 65- *Concurrent Pos:* Fulbright fel, Strasbourg, France, 56-57 & res scholar, 68-69; NDEA Lang Res Sect res contracts, 60 & 63; Am Coun Learned Soc travel grants, 60, 66, 70, 73, 76 & grant-in-aid, 63; Am Philos Soc grants-in-aid, 60, 66 & 72; Guggenheim fel, 68-69; fel Inst Arts & Humanistic Studies, Pa State Univ, 76-; bd mem, Medieval Ctr, Univ Lille III, 77- *Honors & Awards:* Ordre des Palmes Acad, 65, Officier, 75; Officer, Ordre Nat du Merite, 80. *Mem:* MLA; Int Arthurian Soc; fel Mediaeval Acad Am; Am Asn Teachers Fr; fel Heraldy Soc London. *Res:* Medieval French literature, especially Song of Roland; medieval heraldic terminology; New England French language and culture. *Publ:* Auth, Celestine: A Critical Edition of the First French Translation (1527) of the Spanish Classic La Celestina, Wayne State Univ, 63; coauth, Cours de Langue francaise destine aux jeunes Franco-Americains, Asn Prof Franco-Am, 65; auth, Early Blazon: Heraldic Terminology in the Twelfth and Thirteenth Centuries, Clarendon, 72; Eight Thirteenth-Century Rolls of Arms in French and Anglo-Norman Blazon, 73 & The Song of Roland: An Analytical Edition (2 vols), 78, Pa State Univ; Les Franco-Americains de la Nouvelle Angleterre, In: Le Francais hors de France, Champion, 78; Fonction et sens de l'episode du Chateau de Pesme Aventure dans l'Yvain de Chretien de Troyes, Melanges Charles Foulon, 80; The Cult of Saint Peter, In: The Cycle of William of Orange, Fr Forum, 81. *Mailing Add:* 402 Burrowes Bldg Pa State Univ University Park PA 16802

BRAUN, ERNST, b Breslau, Ger, Dec 16, 21; US citizen; m 56; c 2. GERMAN. *Educ:* Univ Wis, BA, 47, MA, 48, PhD, 60. *Prof Exp:* Instr German, Univ Tenn, 49-53; asst prof German & comp lit, Queens Col, NC, 55-57, assoc prof & chmn dept foreign lang, 57-59; asst prof German, Bowling Green State Univ, 60-61, chmn dept German & Russian, 61-62; assoc prof German, 62-64, PROF GERMAN, UNIV MO-COLUMBIA, 64-, CHMN DEPT GERMAN & SLAVIC STUDIES, 62-68, 76- *Mem:* MLA; Midwest Mod Lang Asn; Am Asn Teachers Ger. *Res:* German literature; comparative literature. *Mailing Add:* Dept of Germanic & Slavic Lang Univ of Mo Columbia MO 65201

BRAUN, FRANK XAVIER, b Spaichingen, Ger, Dec 4, 04; nat US; m 36; c 2. GERMAN. *Educ:* Wayne Univ, BA, 34; Univ Mich, MA, 35, PhD(Ger), 40. *Prof Exp:* Teaching fel Ger, Univ Mich, 36-40; exp toolmaker, King-Seeley Corp, Ann Arbor, Mich, 40-45; from instr to prof, 45-75, EMER PROF GER, UNIV MICH, ANN ARBOR, 76- *Res:* The German novelle; 19th and 20th century German novel; pedagogy. *Publ:* Auth, Kulturelle Ziele im Werk Gustav Frenssens; H Lons and the modern German animal tale, Monatshefte; German for research, Ger Quart. *Mailing Add:* Dept of Ger Univ of Mich Ann Arbor MI 48109

BRAUN, MICHELINE TISON, b Arras, France, Apr 7, 13; US citizen; m 48. ROMANCE LANGUAGES. *Educ:* Univ Lille, Lic es Let, 36; Sorbonne, Agregepes L, 37, Dr es Lett, 73. *Prof Exp:* Prof French, Latin & Greek, French Inst & Lycee, London, 37-41 & 45-47; ed & transl, Brit Broadcasting Co, London, 41-45 & UN, New York, 47-54; prof French & Latin, Lycee France, New York, 55-61; assoc prof, 61-74, PROF ROMANCE LANG, HUNTER COL, 74-, PROF GRAD CTR, CITY UNIV NEW YORK, 68- *Concurrent Pos:* Guggenheim Found fel, 78-79. *Honors & Awards:* Chevalier, Palmes Acad, 50. *Mem:* Foreign Lang Asn; PEN Club; MLA; Am Asn Teachers Fr; Soc Hist Lit Fr. *Res:* Modern French literature; 20th century French literature. *Publ:* Auth, La Crise de L'Humanisme, le Conflit de L'Individue et de la Societe dans le Litterature Francaise Moderne, Nizet, Paris, Vol I & II, 58 & 67; Nathalie Sarraute ou la Recherche de L'Authenticite, Gallimard, Paris, 72; Dada et Surrealisme, Bordas, Paris, 73; Tristan Tzara, Inventeur de L'Homme Nouveau, Nizet, Paris, 77; Poetique du Paysage, Paris, Nizet, 80; L'introuvable origine, Geneve, Droz, 82. *Mailing Add:* 50 Central Park West New York NY 10023

BRAUN, RICHARD EMIL, b Detroit, Mich, Nov 22, 34; m 71. CLASSICS, LITERATURE. *Educ:* Univ Mich, Ann Arbor, AB, 56, AM, 57; Univ Tex, Austin, PhD(class lang), 69. *Prof Exp:* From lectr to assoc prof, 62-76, PROF CLASSICS, UNIV ALTA, 76- *Concurrent Pos:* Can Coun arts bursary, 69-70. *Mem:* Poetry Soc Am. *Res:* Roman elegy, lyric and satire; Greek tragedy. *Publ:* Contribr, introd & notes to J L Mazzaro, Juvenal: Satires, Univ Mich, 65; auth, translr & notes on Odes of Horace, Arion, 72; translr, with introd, notes, appendix & glossary, Sophocles' Antigone, Oxford Univ, 73; auth, translr & notes on Echoes from the sea (classical motifs in novel of Hemingway, To Have and Have Not), Fitzgerald Hemingway Ann, 75; translr, The problem of purpose (problems of translating Greek and Latin strong emotion and wit into English in 17th and 20th centuries), Mod Lang Notes, 75; translr, with introd, notes & glossary, Euripides' Rhesos, Oxford Univ, 78; with intro & notes, Persius' Satires, Coronado Press, 82. *Mailing Add:* Dept of Classics Univ of Alta Edmonton AB T6G 2E5 Can

BRAUN, SHIRLEY WORCESTER, b New York, NY, Nov 10, 25; m 67. LINGUISTICS, ENGLISH AS A SECOND LANGUAGE. *Educ:* Smith Col, BA, 47; Columbia Univ, MA, 64, EdD(appl English ling), 72. *Prof Exp:* Assoc English as second lang, Am Lang Prog, Columbia Univ, 62-72; TEACHER ENGLISH AS SECOND LANG, NEW YORK UNIV, 73- *Concurrent Pos:* Consult English lang, Puerto Rican Forum, Inc, New York, 70; teacher English as second lang, Hunter Col, 71-72; consult bilingual educ, Intelicor, Inc, New York, 72- *Mem:* Teachers English to Speakers Other Lang; Ling Soc Am; Am Coun Teaching Foreign Lang; NCTE; Int Ling Asn. *Res:* Materials for teaching English as a second language; language teaching; bilingual education. *Publ:* Coauth, An evaluation of the Title VII bilingual education program in District 6, New York, 72 & 73 & An evaluation of the Title VII bilingual education program in District 8, New York, 73, Intelicor. *Mailing Add:* 1701 York Ave New York NY 10028

BRAUN, SIDNEY DAVID, b New York, NY, May 10, 12; m 41. FRENCH LITERATURE. *Educ:* Sorbonne, Dipl, 32; NY Univ, AB, 34, AM, 35, PhD, 45. *Prof Exp:* From assoc prof to prof French, Yeshiva Univ, 36-65; prof, Wayne State Univ, 65-68; mem exec comt PhD Prog French, 68-72, prof, 68-80, EMER PROF FRENCH, LEHMAN COL & GRAD CTR, CITY UNIV NEW YORK, 80- *Concurrent Pos:* Vis assoc prof, Long Island Univ, 45-49; consult ed comn, PMLA, 60-; vis prof, Univ Wash, 63-64; Fulbright res fel, France, 65; asst lit ed, Fr Rev, 70-; mem adv bd, Nineteenth Century Fr Studies, 74- *Honors & Awards:* Chevalier, Palmes Acad, 60; Medaille d'Argent, Ville de Paris, 60. *Mem:* AM Asn Teachers Fr; MLA; Soc Prof Fr Am; Int Asn Fr Studies. *Res:* French theatre; 19th and 20th centuries French literature. *Publ:* Auth, Dictionary of French Literature, Philos Libr, 58; Correspondance Gide-Suares, Gallimared, Paris, 63; Andre Suares and Villiers de l'Isle-Adam, Suares, Gallimard, Paris, 63; Andre Suares and Villiers de l'Isle-Adam, In: Studies in Honor of Professor S M Waxman, Boston Univ, 69; Henri Hertz: L'homme et l'oeuvre, Europe, 1/70; Jean Paulhan, In: Encycl World Lit in Twentieth Century, Ungar, 71. *Mailing Add:* Dept of Romance Lang Lehman Col Bronx NY 10468

BRAUN, THEODORE EDWARD DANIEL, b Brooklyn, NY, Apr 18, 33; m 65; c 1. FRENCH LITERATURE & LANGUAGE. *Educ:* St John's Univ, NY, BA, 55; Univ Calif, Berkeley, MA, 61, PhD(Romance lang & lit), 65. *Prof Exp:* Teacher High Sch, NY, 54-55; asst English, Lycee Emile-Loubet, France, 55-56; from asst prof to assoc prof French, Univ Wis-Milwaukee, 64-70; PROF FRENCH, UNIV DEL, 70- *Concurrent Pos:* Frank L Weil Inst Studies Relig & Humanities, 67; Nat Endowment Humanities grant, 74; pres, Univ Fac Sen, 76-77; Ctr Advan Study, Univ Del, 81-82. *Mem:* MLA; Am Soc 18th Century Studies; Am Asn Teachers Fr; AAUP; E Cent Am Soc 18th Century Studies. *Res:* Voltaire; 18th century French and comparative literature. *Publ:* Coauth, First French, 64 & 70 & Second French, 68, Scott; auth, Un Ennemi de Voltaire: Le Franc de Pompignan, Minard, Paris, 72; ed, Voltaire's Alzire, Olympie and others, In: Complete Works of Voltaire; co-ed, Aeschylus, Voltaire and Le Franc de Pompignan's Promethee, Studies Voltaire, 76; Teaching the eighteenth century, spec issue, Eighteenth Century Life, 79. *Mailing Add:* Dept of Lang & Lit Univ of Del Newark DE 19711

BRAUN, WILHELM, b Vienna, Austria, June 29, 21; US citizen. GERMAN LITERATURE. *Educ:* Univ Toronto, BA, 49, MA, 50, PhD, 53. *Prof Exp:* Lectr Ger, Univ Toronto, 51-53; asst prof, Morehouse Col, 53-56; from instr to assoc prof, 56-66, PROF GER LIT, UNIV ROCHESTER, 66- *Concurrent Pos:* Mem, Vorstand Int Robert Musil Gesellschaft, 76. *Mem:* MLA; Am Asn Teachers Ger. *Res:* Modern German literature; Robert Musil. *Mailing Add:* Dept of For & Comp Lit Univ of Rochester Rochester NY 14627

BRAUNROT, BRUNO, b Warsaw, Poland, Feb 18, 36; Can citizen; m 61; c 2. FRENCH LITERATURE. *Educ:* McGill Univ, BA, 57, MA, 60; Yale Univ, PhD(French), 70. *Prof Exp:* Lectr French, McGill Univ, 64-68; actg asst prof, Univ Va, 68-70, asst prof, 70-74; assoc prof, Wayne State Univ, 74-76; ASSOC PROF FRENCH, GA STATE UNIV, 76- *Concurrent Pos:* Reader French lang & lit, Educ Testing Serv, 74- *Mem:* MLA; S Atlantic Mod Lang Asn; AAUP. *Res:* French literature of the Renaissance; Baroque poetry. *Publ:* Auth, L'Imagination Poetique Chez De Bartas, Univ NC, 73; Une rhetorique de la surprise: Motifs et figures de style dans La Creation du Monde de Du Bartas, Cy Romance Quart, 73; co-ed, Les Aventures D'Arsene Lupin, Scribner's, 76. *Mailing Add:* 1125 Lullwater Rd NE Atlanta GA 30307

BRAUSE, RITA S, US citizen. LINGUISTICS. *Educ:* New York Univ, BS, 62, MA, 65, EdD(ling educ), 75. *Prof Exp:* Teacher English & reading, New York City Bd Educ, 62-69; instr lang & art educ, City Univ New York, 70-73; fel, New York Univ, 73-74, adj instr lang educ, 74-75; asst prof psycholing, Yeshiva Univ, 75; asst prof ling & educ, 75-79, ASSOC PROF APPL LING, LIB ARTS COL, LINCOLN CTR, FORDHAM UNIV, 79- *Honors & Awards:* Promising Res Award, Nat Coun Teachers English, 75. *Mem:* Ling Soc Am; Soc Res Child Develop; Nat Coun Teachers English; Nat Conf Res English; Int Reading Asn. *Res:* Language development; psycholinguistics; relationship between oral and written language. *Publ:* Auth, Developmental aspects of the ability to understand semantic ambiguity, Res Teaching English, 77; Language development: research and implications for teachers, English J (in press); coauth, Another perspective on Edwin Newman's comments, Language Arts (in press). *Mailing Add:* Lincoln Ctr Lib Arts Col Fordham Univ New York NY 10023

BRAVO-ELIZONDO, PEDRO JOSE, US citizen. LATIN AMERICAN THEATER & LITERATURE. *Educ:* Inst Pedagogico Tech, Chile, Bach, 55; Univ Catolica, Valparaiso, Chile, MA, 64; Univ Iowa, MA, 71, PhD(lit), 74. *Prof Exp:* Teacher Span grammar, Educ Pub Syst, Chile, 56-65; counr, Liceo Hombres, Talca, Chile, 66-67 & Univ Chile, 67-69; teacher Span & English, Bellevue High Sch, 69-70; instr Span, Univ Wis-Whitewater, 73-74; asst prof, Augustana Col, 74-75; from asst prof to ASSOC PROF SPAN, WICHITA STATE UNIV, 75. *Concurrent Pos:* Nat Endowment for the Humanities summer fel, Yale Univ, 79. *Mem:* Latin Am Studies Asn; Midwest Asn Latin Am Studies. *Res:* Latin American drama. *Publ:* Auth, Teatro Hispanoamericano, Ed Playor, Spain, 75; Ranquil y Los que van quedando en el camino, Texto Critico, Mex, 78; Lisistrata Gonzalez y una Casa en Lota Alto, Conjunto, Cuba, 78; Latin America and the actual documentary theatre, Cuadernos de Invest Theatral, Venezuela, 80; Teatro Documental Latinoamericano, Univ Mex, 81; On the amateur Chilean theater 1973-1979, Conjunto, No 49, 81; Chile: Worker's theatre in the Nitrate Era, Ann Latin Am Worker's Movement, Univ Guadalajara, 81; Worker's theatre in Chile: Antecedents, Araucaria, No 17, 82. *Mailing Add:* 131 N Chautauqua Wichita KS 67214

BRAWER, ROBERT ALLEN, Medieval English Language & Literature. See Vol II

BREARLEY, DENIS GEORGE, b Chatham, Ont, Nov 8, 40. LATIN PALEOGRAPHY, MEDIEVAL LATIN. *Educ:* Univ Western Ont, BA, 63, MA, 64; Univ Toronto, PhD(Latin), 67. *Prof Exp:* Asst prof, 67-72, chmn dept, 75-80, ASSOC PROF CLASS STUDIES, UNIV OTTAWA, 72- *Concurrent Pos:* Soc Sci & Humanities Res Coun Can leave fel, 81-82. *Mem:* Am Philol Asn; Mediaeval Acad Am; Class Asn Can (treas, 69-73); Brit Class Asn; Soc Etudes Latines. *Res:* Hiberno-Latin texts; medieval civilization. *Publ:* Auth, Two mediaeval postscripts, Classica Mediaevalia, 69; A Union List of Classical Periodicals in the University Libraries of Ottawa, Univ Ottawa, 70; Note de lecture: 227-Lucanus, Pharsal I, 66, Latomus, 70; coauth, Un acte notarie latin de 1543, Rev Univ Ottawa, 73; The British Museum Ms Arundel 43 monochard fragments, Mediaeval Studies, 74 & 75; auth, Commentum sedulii scotti in maiorem donatum grammaticum, Pontif Inst Mediaeval Studies, Toronto, 75; Texts and studies in Latin orthography, Class World, 72: 385-392; A bibliography of recent publications concerning the history of grammar during the Carolingian Renaissance, Studi Medievali, XXI: 917-923. *Mailing Add:* Dept of Class Studies Univ of Ottawa Ottawa ON K1N 6N5 Can

BRECHT, RICHARD DOMENICK, b Jeannette, Pa, July 24, 40; m 65; c 1. LINGUISTICS, SLAVIC LANGUAGE & LITERATURES. *Educ:* Pa State Univ, BA, 65; Harvard Univ, MA, 69, PhD(Slavic lang & lit), 72. *Prof Exp:* Asst prof slavic lang & lit, Harvard Univ, 71-72; asst prof ling, Cornell Univ, 72-73; asst prof, Harvard Univ, 73-76, assoc prof, 76-80; ASSOC PROF SLAVIC LANG & LIT, UNIV MD, COLLEGE PARK, 80- *Mem:* Ling Soc Am; Am Asn Teachers Slavic & East Europ Lang. *Res:* Russian syntax; history and structure of Slavic languages, syntax and semantics. *Publ:* Co-ed, Readings in Slavic transformational syntax, Mich Slavic, 74; auth, Deixis in embedded structures, Found Lang, 74; On the syntax and semantics of the infinitive complement in Russian, In: Readings in Slavic Tranformational Syntax, Mich Slavic, 74. *Mailing Add:* Dept of Ger & Slavic Lang & lit Univ of Md College Park MD 20742

BREE, GERMAINE, b Lasalle, France, Oct 2, 07; US citizen. FRENCH LITERATURE. *Educ:* Univ Paris, Lic es Lett, 30, dipl, 31, Agrege, 32. *Hon Degrees:* LittD, Smith Col, 60, Mt Holyoke Col, 63, Allegheny Col, 63, Duke Univ, 64, Oberlin Col, 66, Dickinson Col, 68, Rutgers Univ, 69, Wake Forest Univ, 69, Brown Univ, 71, Univ Wis-Milwaukee, 73, NY Univ, 75, Univ Mass, Amherst, 76 & Kalamazoo Col, 77; LHD, Wilson Col, 60, Colby Col, 64, Univ Mich, 70 & Davis-Elkins Col, 72; LLD, Middlebury Col, 65. *Prof Exp:* Teacher, Oran, Algeria, 32-36; from lectr to prof French lit, Bryn Mawr Col, 36-52; chmn dept French, Wash Sq Col, NY Univ, 53-60, head dept Romance lang, Grad Sch Arts & Sci, 54-60; Vilas prof French, Inst Res Humanities, Univ Wis-Madison, 60-73; KENAN PROF HUMANITIES, WAKE FOREST UNIV, 73- *Concurrent Pos:* Vis prof French, Wellesley Col, 59 & Am Univ Cairo, Egypt, 70; Fulbright prof, Univ London, Eng, 65-66; mem Fleming Comn Doctoral Coun, State Educ Dept, State Univ NY, 72, chmn French Rating Comt doctoral prog; mem adv bd, Am Coun Learned Soc & Nat Foun Arts & Humanities. *Honors & Awards:* Chevalier, Legion of Honor, 58. *Mem:* MLA (vpres to pres, 73-75); Am Philos Soc; Am Asn Teachers Fr; AAUP; PEN Club. *Res:* Contemporary French literature. *Publ:* Auth, Marcel Proust, 55, Camus, 61 & Andre Gide, 63, rev English ed, Rutgers Univ; The world of Marcel Proust, In: Houghton Mifflin Riverside Series, Houghton, 66; Camus and Sartre: Crisis and Commitment, Delacourt, 72; Women Writers in France, Rutgers Univ, 73; Litterature Francaise, 1920-1970, Parix Arthaud, 78. *Mailing Add:* Dept of French Wake Forest Univ Winston-Salem NC 27106

BREFFORT-BLESSING, JULIETTE, b Wallasey, England; m 55. FRENCH LANGUAGE & LITERATURE. *Educ:* Univ Lille, Lic es Let, 47; Inst D'Etudes Pol, Paris, dipl, 50; Univ Paris, DES, 51; Univ Dijon, Doctorate, 78. *Prof Exp:* Teaching asst French, Stanford Univ, 52-53; instr, Wellesley Col, 55-57; from instr to asst prof, 57-68, assoc prof, 68-79, PROF FRENCH, MARY WASHINGTON COL, 79- *Honors & Awards:* Chevalier, Des Palmes Academiques, French Govt, 81. *Mem:* MLA; Am Asn Teachers Fr; Soc Hist Theatre; Am Soc Theatre Res. *Res:* French civilization; 17th and 20th century French theatre. *Mailing Add:* Dept of Mod Foreign Lang Mary Washington Col Fredericksburg VA 22402

BREGOLI-RUSSO, MAUDA RITA, b Italy; US citizen. ITALIAN RENAISSANCE & MEDIEVAL LITERATURE. *Educ:* Univ Bologna, Italy, Laurea, 63; Univ Chicago, PhD(Romance lang), 78. *Prof Exp:* Lectr, Univ Ill, Chicago Circle, 75-78, asst prof, 78-80; ASST PROF ITALIAN, NORTHWESTERN UNIV, 81- *Concurrent Pos:* Nat Endowment for Humanities fel, Newberry Libr Chicago, 81. *Mem:* MLA; Midwest Mod Lang Asn; Rocky Mountain Mod Lang Asn; Renaissance Soc Am; Am Asn Teachers Italian. *Res:* Italian theater of the Renaissance; Italian poetry of the Renaissance, epic and lyric; Dante. *Publ:* Auth, Per La Figura Di Gerione, L'Alighieri, 77; Tecnica Di Contrasto E Fini Moraleggianti Nel Timone Di M M Boiardo, Quardivium, 78; Boiardo Lirico, J Porrua Turanzas, 79; La Pastorale Del Boiardo Fra Le Egloghe Del Quattrocento, Studi E Problemi Di Critica Testuale, 80; Uno Strumento Interpretativo Degli Amores Di Boiardo, Critica Lett, 81; Un Riscontro Francese Nell'Orlando Innamorato Del Boiardo, Studi E Problemi Di Critica Testuale, 81; ed, Galeotto Del Carretto, Li Sei Contenti E La Sofonisba, J Porrua Turanzas, 82. *Mailing Add:* French & Italian Dept Northwestern Univ Evanston IL 60201

BREITENKAMP, EDWARD CARLTON, b La Porte, Ind, Aug 26, 13; m 41; c 2. GERMANICS. *Educ:* Drake Univ, BA, 36, MA, 38; Univ Iowa, PhD(Ger lang & lit), 52. *Prof Exp:* Ed asst chem, Am Peoples Encycl, 45-46; info control off, US Mil Govt, Ger, 46-49; instr Ger & French, Wartburg Col, 49-50; instr Ger, Univ NDak, 50-53; from asst prof to prof, Tex A&M Univ, 53-76; RETIRED. *Mem:* Am Asn Teachers. *Res:* Contemporary German literature and civilization; German science; Frederick Hermann Seele (1823-1902); German pioneer in old Texas. *Publ:* Auth, United States Information Control Division, 1945-1949, Dieresis, 53; Intermediate Reading in Contemporary German, Shaffers Bk Store, 63; Thema: Deutschland, Prentice-Hall, 67; ed, Deutsche Aufsätze, 71 & German Science Readings, 72, Univ Bookstore; transl, Seele's The Cypress, Univ Texas Press, 79. *Mailing Add:* 313 Fairway Dr Bryan TX 77801

BREKKE, ARNE, b Flam, Norway, Oct 19, 27; m 53; c 4. GERMANIC PHILOLOGY. *Educ:* Luther Col, BA, 50; Univ Colo, MA, 52; Univ Chicago, PhD(Scand philol), 64. *Prof Exp:* Instr Norwegian & head dept, Luther Col, 54-62; asst prof, 62-68, ASSOC PROF NORWEGIAN & GERMAN, UNIV N DAK, 68-, DIR SCAND CULT CTR, 72- *Mem:* Norweg-Am Hist Asn; Soc Advan Scand Studies; MLA. *Res:* Comparative Germanic Philogy; German; place names. *Mailing Add:* Dept of Foreign Lang Univ of NDak Grand Forks ND 58201

BRENCKLE, JOSEPH JOHN, JR, b Providence, RI, June 24, 40; m 64. RUSSIAN & SLAVIC LINGUISTICS. *Educ:* Brown Univ, AB, 62; Stanford Univ, MA, 65, PhD(Slavic ling), 71. *Prof Exp:* Asst prof, 71-77, ASSOC PROF RUSS, UNIV ALASKA, FAIRBANKS, 77-, CHMN RUSS STUDIES COMT, 73- *Concurrent Pos:* Int Res & Exchange Bd, US-USSR exchange fel, 75-76; Shell Oil Co grant, 77. *Mem:* MLA: Am Asn Teachers Slavic & East Europ Lang; Am Asn Advan Slavic Studies; Western Slavic Asn; Ling Soc Am. *Res:* Russian morphology; Russian influence on Alaskan native languages. *Publ:* Auth, Observations on the genitive plural in contemporary standard Russian, 74 & Russian influence on native Alaskan culture, winter 75, Slavic & East Europ J; The Asiatic Eskimo language and Russian since 1917, In: Proc of the Banff 74 International Conference, Vol V, Russ Ling, Slavica, 76. *Mailing Add:* Dept of Ling & Foreign Lang Univ of Alaska Fairbanks AK 99701

BREND, RUTH MARGARET, b Winnipeg, Man; US citizen. LINGUISTICS. *Educ:* Univ Man, BA, 46, dipl social work, 47; Univ Mich, MA, 60, PhD(ling), 64. *Prof Exp:* Social worker, Dept of Health & Pub Welfare, Man, 49-51; transl & linguist, Wycliffe Bible Transl, Mex, 53-57; res assoc ling, Univ Mich, 57-64; lectr, 64-66, from asst prof to assoc prof, 66-76, PROF LING, MICH STATE UNIV, 76- *Concurrent Pos:* Teaching asst phonology, Summer Inst Ling, Univ Ikla, 54-66; consult, ling workshop, Ecuador & Peru, 60-61; lectr ling, San Marcos Univ, Lima, 61; ed, Lang Learning, 64-66; res assoc, Univ Mich, 64-; vis lectr ling, Monash Univ, Australia, 68; Fulbright prof, Norway, 75-76. *Mem:* Ling Soc Am; Int Soc Phonetic Sci. *Res:* General linguistic theory; structure and analysis of unwritten languages; general linguistic, grammatical and phonological description, especially from the tagmemic viewpoint. *Publ:* Auth, A Tagmemic Analysis of Mexican Spanish Clauses, 68 & ed, Kenneth L Pike: Selected Writings, 72, Mouton, The Hague; Advances in Tagmemics, North-Holland, Amsterdam, 74; Studies in Tone and Intonation, Karger, 75; co-ed, Discussion, 76 & The Summer Institute of Linguistics: Its Work and Contributions, 77, Mouton, The Hague. *Mailing Add:* Dept of Ling Wells Hall Mich State Univ East Lansing MI 48824

BRENER, BERNARD J, b New York, NY, Jan 20, 25. MODERN LANGUAGES. *Educ:* NY Univ, BA, 47, MA, 50, PhD, 58. *Prof Exp:* From instr to assoc prof, 50-63, secy, 58-61, PROF MOD LANG, LONG ISLAND UNIV, 63-, CHMN DEPT, 63- *Concurrent Pos:* Instr, Brooklyn Polytech Inst, 55-60; lectr, Hofstra Col, 56. *Mem:* MLA; Am Asn Teachers Ger; Thomas Mann Ges. *Res:* Essays and fiction of Thomas Mann and their interrelationship. *Mailing Add:* Dept of Mod Lang Brooklyn Ctr Long Island Univ Brooklyn NY 11201

BRENGELMAN, FREDERICK HENRY, b Farwell, Nebr, Mar 31, 28; m 48; c 4. LINGUISTICS, ENGLISH LANGUAGE STUDIES. *Educ:* Dana Col, BA, 48; Univ Nebr-Lincoln, MA, 51; Univ Wash, PhD(English lang), 57. *Prof Exp:* Instr English, Wash State Univ, 56-57; from asst prof to assoc prof ling, 57-68, PROF LING, CALIF STATE UNIV, FRESNO, 68- *Concurrent Pos:* Vis dir English as foreign lang, Univ Wis-Madison, 61-62; co-dir, US Off Educ Proj Teaching English to Span-Speaking Kindergarten Children, 64-65; dir, Fulbright English Lang Prog, Athens, Greece, 65-66. *Mem:* MLA; Ling Soc Am; Am Dialect Soc; Teachers English Second Lang. *Res:* English spelling; English as a second language; applied linguistics in teaching. *Publ:* Auth, The English Language: An Introduction for Teachers, Prentice-Hall, 70; coauth, Contemporary English, Silver-Burdett, 72; auth, Homophones and the English spelling system, In: Studies in Language and Linguistics, Univ Tex, El Paso, 73; Beyond phonemes and morphemes: Getting the meaning from English spelling, In: Claremont Reading Conference Yearbook, 73; Dialect and the teaching of spelling, In: Language and the Language Arts, Little, 74. *Mailing Add:* Dept of Ling Calif State Univ Fresno Shaw at Cedar Ave Fresno CA 93726

BRENK, FREDERICK EUGENE, b Milwaukee, Wis, July 18, 29. GREEK & ROMAN CLASSICS. *Educ:* Marquette Univ, BA, 51; St Louis Univ, MA, 58; Univ Ky, PhD(hist), 71; Cambridge Univ, MLitt, 71. *Prof Exp:* Asst prof classics, Marquette Univ, 71-80; VIS LECTR, BOSTON COL & TUFTS UNIV, 80- *Mem:* Am Philol Soc; Class Asn Midwest & South; Vergilian Soc; Am Acad Relig. *Res:* Greek and Roman literature; Greek and Roman religion. *Publ:* Auth, Le Songe de Brutus Actes de VIIIe, Congres Guillaume Bude, 69; A most strange doctrine: Daimon in Plutarch, Class J, 73; Hesiod, how much a male chauvinist, Class Bull, 73; From mysticism to mysticism: the religious development of Plutarch of Chaironeia, Proc Soc Bibl Lit, 75; The dreams of Plutarch's Lives, Latomus, 75; Addendum on Sisyphus, 76 & Aphrodite's girdle, 77, Class Bull; In Mist Apparelled: Religious Themes in Plutarch's Moralia and Lives, Brill, 77. *Mailing Add:* Jesuit Community Boston Col Chestnut Hill MA 02167

BRENNAN, M JOSEPHINE, b Green Bay, Wis. CLASSICAL PATRISTIC LANGUAGES & LITERATURE. *Educ:* Marywood Col, BA, 26; Cath Univ Am, MA, 27, PhD(Latin, Greek, ancient hist, patristics), 47. *Prof Exp:* Instr class & mod lang, St Rosalis High Sch, Pittsburg, Pa, 27-44; prof class lang, hist & lit, 47-71, dean grad sch arts & sci, 70-80, prof Latin & Greek, 71-76, RESIDENT PATRISTIC SCHOLAR, MARYWOOD COL, 76- *Mem:* Class Asn Mid States; AAUP; Am Asn Univ Women; N Am Patristic Soc; Am Philol Asn. *Res:* Classical and Christian Latin, Greek, language, literature and history; modern foreign languages. *Publ:* Auth, Clausulae in the Sermons of St Augustine, 47, transl, Letters of St Jerome (3 vols), Vol I, 52 Letters, CAU Press (in press), Vols II & III (in prep) & Fathers of the Church Series, Cath Univ Am. *Mailing Add:* Off of Patristic Studies Learning Resource Ctr Marywood Col Scranton PA 18509

BRENT, STEVEN TRACY, b San Francisco, Calif, Sept 30, 42; m 68; c 2. FRENCH LANGUAGE & LITERATURE. *Educ:* Pa State Univ, University Park, BS, 65, MA, 68, PhD(French), 71 Am Inst Foreign Studies, Greenwich, dipl Russ, 73. *Prof Exp:* Asst prof French, Valparaiso Univ, 71-80; ASST PROF FOREIGN LANG, US NAVAL ACAD, ANNAPOLIS, 80- *Mem:* MLA; Am Asn Teachers Fr. *Res:* Romanticism and realism in the 19th century French novel; French, Spanish and Italian linguistics. *Publ:* Auth, Concerning the resurrection of Epistemon, Romance Notes, 71. *Mailing Add:* Lang Studies Dept US Naval Acad Annapolis MD 21402

BRESKY, DUSHAN, b Prerov, Czech, Aug 15, 20; m 53; c 2. MODERN FRENCH LITERATURE, COMPARATIVE LITERATURE. *Educ:* Charles Univ, Czech, DrJU, 48; Univ Wash, MA, 58, PhD, 62. *Prof Exp:* Teaching fel, Univ Wash, 55-58; instr French & French lit, Univ BC, 58-61; asst prof, Mont State Univ, 61-62; asst prof, 62-68, assoc prof French lit, 68-73, assoc prof French, 73-75, head dept Romance studies, 75-77, PROF FRENCH, UNIV CALGARY, 75- *Concurrent Pos:* Humanities Res Coun Can grant, 67; Can Coun grant, 67; mem, Pac Northwest Conf Foreign Lang Teachers. *Mem:* Asn Can Univ Teachers Fr; Czech Soc Arts & Sci, US; Rocky Mt Mod Lang Asn. *Res:* French literature; literary aesthetics. *Publ:* Auth, Bez Konce Jsou Lesy, V Petr, Prague, 2 eds, 43; coauth, Hory, Lyze, Snih, J Velat, Prague, 3 eds, 46; auth, The Art of Anatole France, Mouton, The Hague & Paris, 69; Les aventures mystiques de Jean Christophe, Fr Rev, 5/71; Cathedral or Symphony--Essays on Jean-Christophe, Herbert Lang, Bern, Switz, 73; coauth, Le Chanteur de Kyme: Anatole France's Atticism at Its Best, Fr Lit Ser II, The French Short Story, Univ SC, 73; auth, The Style of the impressionistic novel, L'Esprit Createur, winter 73; Nova Filipika Proti Mizomuzum, Orbis, New York, 74. *Mailing Add:* Dept of Romance Studies Univ of Calgary Calgary AB T2N 1N4 Can

BRETZ, MARY LEE, b Biddeford, Maine, Sept 9, 45; m 68; c 2. SPANISH LITERATURE, LITERARY THEORY. *Educ:* Trinity Col, BA, 67; Stanford Univ, MA, 69; Univ Md, PhD(Span), 73. *Prof Exp:* Asst prof, 74-80, ASSOC PROF SPAN, RUTGERS COL, RUTGERS UNIV, 80- *Mem:* Am Asn Teachers Span & Port; MLA; Am Asn Univ Prof. *Res:* Nineteenth century Spanish literature; 20th century Spanish literature. *Publ:* Auth, El humor y la Comicidad en Unamuno, Cuadernos Hisp Am, 4/74; Afirmacion y Repudio del ideal Amoroso en Becquer, Bol Bibliot Menendez Pelayo, 76; Naturalismo y feminismo en Emilia Pardo Bazan, Papeles Son Armadans, 12/77; La Evolucion Novelistica de Pio Baroja, Porrcia Turanzas, 79; Concha Espina, G K Hall, 80; The ironic vision in miau, Am Hispanist, 80; Romantic irony and El Diablo mundo, Rev Estudios Hispanicos, 82; coauth, Pasajes, Random House, 82. *Mailing Add:* Dept of Span & Port Rutgers Univ New Brunswick NJ 08903

BREUGELMANS, RENE, b Antwerp, Belg, Aug 16, 25; m 49; c 1. COMPARATIVE LITERATURE. *Educ:* Univ Ghent, Belg, MA & Agrege, 48, PhD, 53. *Prof Exp:* Res asst social anthrop, Mus Cent Africa, Tervuren, Belg, 48-49; teacher English, Ger, Dutch & French, Royal Atheneum, Elizabethville, Congo, 49-55; prof English, Pre-Univ Inst, Rwanda-Burundi, Africa, 55-56; prof English, Ger, comp lit & African studies, State Univ Congo, 56-61; from asst prof to assoc prof, 61-71, PROF MOD LANG, UNIV CALGARY, 71- *Concurrent Pos:* Can Coun fel, 68-69. *Mem:* MLA; Am Asn Teachers Ger; Am Comp Lit Asn; Int Comp Lit Asn; Can Asn Univ Teachers Ger. *Res:* Comparative literature in English, German, French and Dutch (1880-1914); literature and anthropology, depth psychology and myth; Canadian ethnic studies. *Publ:* Auth, The Dutch and Flemish in Canada, Can Ethnic Studies, 12/70; Jacques Perks mythopoesis und sein verhaltnis zur gesellschaft (dichtung), Sprache Ges, 71; Hofmannsthal und der platonismus der jahrhundertwende, Hofmannsthal-Forschung, 71; Jacques Perk, Twayne, 74; Forschungsbericht: Zur Hofmannsthal-Forschung 1969-1975, Wirkendes Wort, 9-10/77 & 11-12/77; Novalis gewissen and the relevance of the Jungian concepts of his works, Proc Pac Northwest Coun Foreign Lang, 4/78. *Mailing Add:* Dept of Ger & Slavic Studies Univ of Calgary Calgary AB T2N 1N4 Can

BREUNIG, LEROY CLINTON, b Indianapolis, Ind, Mar 29, 15. FRENCH LITERATURE. *Educ:* DePauw Univ, AB, 36; Cornell Univ, AM, 38, PhD, 41. *Prof Exp:* Instr Romance lang, Cornell Univ, 39-41; asst prof, Harvard Univ, 47-53; assoc prof French, 53; chmn dept French, 53-70, dean fac, 70-75, interim pres, 75-76, prof, 53-80, EMER PROF FRENCH, BARNARD COL, COLUMBIA UNIV, 80- *Concurrent Pos:* Guggenheim fel & Fulbright res grant, 59-60; Fulbright teacher, Univ Western Australia, 66. *Mem:* MLA; Am Asn Teachers Fr. *Res:* Early 20th century French poetry. *Publ:* Ed, Chroniques d'Art, Gallimard, Paris, 61; coauth, Forme et Fond, Macmillan, 64; co-ed, Guillaume Apollinarie, Les Peintres Cubistes, Hermann, Paris, 65; Apollinaire, Columbia Univ, 69; Apollinaire on Art, Viking, 72. *Mailing Add:* Dept of French Columbia Univ New York NY 10027

BREVART, FRANCIS B, b Casablanca, Morocco, Oct 17, 45; Can citizen; m 79; c 1. GERMAN MEDIEVAL LITERATURE. *Educ:* McGill Univ, BS, 66, MA, 70, PhD(comp lit), 75. *Prof Exp:* Lectr Ger lang, Loyola Col, Montreal, 70-71; lectr Ger & French lang, Loyola Col, Montreal & Vanier Col, 71-72; asst prof Ger lit Mid Ages, Univ Munich, 75-77 & Univ Münster, 77-81; ASST PROF GER LIT MID AGES, UNIV PA, 81- *Res:*

Astronomical-astrological German literature manuscripts; epigonic heroic German literature: Dietrich epics; the theme of the Enfances. *Publ:* Auth, Eine neue deutsche Übersetzung der lat Sphaera mundi des Johannes von Sacrobosco & Ein neues Fragment von Strickers Karl der Grosse, In: Zeitschrift für deutsches Altertum, Vol 108, 79; Joh von Sacrobosco, Das Puechlein von der Spera Kritische Edition, Glossar, Kümmerle, Göppingen, 79; Zur überlieferungsgeschichte der Deutschen Sphaera Konrads von Megenberg, Beiträge Zur Geschichte der deutschen Sprache u Literatur, Vol 102, 80; Konrad von Megenberg, Die Deutsche Sphaera, Max Niemeyer, Tübingen, 80; Konrad Heinfogel, Sphaera materialis Text und Kommentar, Kümmerle, Göppingen, 81; Ein neues Herzog Ernst-Bruchstück aus dem 16 Jahrhundert, Zeitschrift für deutsches Altertum, Vol 110, 81; articles, In: Verfasserlexikon des Mittelalters, W de Gruyter (in press). *Mailing Add:* 243 S 45th St Philadelphia PA 19104

BREWER, JEUTONNE PATTEN, b Enid, Okla, May 5, 39; m 62. LINGUISTICS, ENGLISH. *Educ:* Harding Col, BA, 60; Univ NC, Chapel Hill, MA, 71, PhD(ling), 74. *Prof Exp:* Instr English & ling, Greensboro Col, 72-73; instr, 73-75, asst prof, 75-79, ASSOC PROF ENGLISH & LING, UNIV NC, GREENSBORO, 79-, ASST DEAN, COL ARTS & SCI, 80- *Mem:* Ling Soc Am; Am Dialect Soc; MLA; Am Name Soc; Asn Comput Ling. *Res:* American English dialects; sociolinguistic theory; Anthony Burgess--bibliography. *Publ:* Auth, Subject Concord of Be in early Black English, Am Speech, 73; coauth, Dialect Clash in America, Scarecrow Press, 77; auth, Nonagreeing Am and invariant Be in early Black English, Southeastern Cong Ling Bull, 79; Anthony Burgess: A Bibliography, Scarecrow Press, 80; coauth, Tokens in the Pocosin, Am Speech, 82. *Mailing Add:* Col Arts & Sci Univ NC Greensboro NC 27412

BREWER, JOHN T, b Palo Alto, Calif, Mar 1, 38. GERMAN. *Educ:* Pomona Col, BA, 59; Univ Tex, PhD(Ger lang), 62. *Prof Exp:* From instr to asst prof Ger, Univ Calif, Riverside, 62-67; asst prof, 68-71, ASSOC PROF GER, WASH STATE UNIV, 71- *Concurrent Pos:* Publ dir, PNCFL, 77-81. *Mem:* MLA; Am Asn Teachers Ger; Western Asn Ger Studies. *Res:* Eighteenth century German literature; Romanticism. *Publ:* Auth, Max Frisch's Biedermann und die Brandstifter as the documentation of an author's frustration, Ger Rev, 3/71. *Mailing Add:* Dept of Foreign Lang & Lit Wash State Univ Pullman WA 99163

BREWER, MARIA MINICH, b Budapest, Hungary; US citizen. FRENCH LITERATURE & THEORY. *Educ:* Univ Witwatersrand, Johannesburg, BA, 66; State Univ NY Buffalo, MA, 70; Yale Univ, PhD(French), 77. *Prof Exp:* Instr, Ohio State Univ, 77-78; ASST PROF FRENCH, UNIV MINN, MINNEAPOLIS, 78- *Mem:* MLA. *Res:* Twentieth century French literature; interdiscursive relations in contemporay literary theory. *Publ:* Co-translr, Louis Marin, Pascal: Text, Author, Discourse . . . , Yale Fr Studies, 75. *Mailing Add:* Dept of French & Ital Univ of Minn 200 Folwell Hall Minneapolis MN 55455

BREWER, WILLIAM BENJAMIN, b Cairo, Ill, Jan 9, 33; m 57; c 2. SPANISH LANGUAGE & LITERATURE, ROMANCE PHILOLOGY. *Educ:* Memphis State Univ, BA, 58; Tulane Univ, MA, 59, PhD(Span), 66. *Prof Exp:* Instr Span, Colo State Univ, 60-61; from instr to assoc prof, 61-70, PROF SPAN, MEMPHIS STATE UNIV, 70- *Mem:* MLA; Am Asn Teachers Span & Port; Mod Humanities Res Asn. *Res:* Old Spanish language; Hispanic dialectology; Hispanic literature. *Publ:* Auth, A loista passage of the Primera Cronicageneral, Hispania, 9/69; A semantic distinction common to Old Spanish and Hopi, Studies Ling, 69-70; Extent of verbal influence and choice between LE and LO in Alphonsine prose, Hisp Rev, 4/70. *Mailing Add:* Dept of Foreign Lang Memphis State Univ Memphis TN 38152

BREWSTER, ROBERT RIGGS, b Salonica, Greece, Dec 7, 18; US citizen; m 51; c 3. GERMAN. *Educ:* Wesleyan Univ, BA, 40; Univ Wis, MA, 46, PhD(Ger), 49. *Prof Exp:* Instr Ger, Univ Ill, 49-53; asst prof, Univ Richmond, 53-58; assoc prof, 58-71, prof, 71-79, EMER PROF GER, EARLHAM COL, 79- *Mem:* MLA; Am Asn Teachers Ger; AAUP; Asn Col Teachers Foreign Lang. *Res:* Nineteenth century German drama and novelle; 20th century German drama, poetry and novelle. *Publ:* Auth, Optic and acoustic phenomena in Rilke's poetry; Visual aspects of muscial sound in Rilke's lyric poetry, Monatshefte. *Mailing Add:* Earlham Col Richmond IN 47374

BRICHANT, COLETTE DUBOIS, b Noisy le Sec, France, July 9, 26; nat; m 55; c 1. FRENCH. *Educ:* Univ Paris, BA, 45, Lic es Let, 47, dipl ES, 48, Dr Univ, 53. *Prof Exp:* Teacher English, Cols Modernes de la Ville de Paris, 45-49; instr French, Ind Univ, 49-50, Russell Sage Col, 50-53 & Middlebury Col, 53-58; LECTR FRENCH, UNIV CALIF, LOS ANGELES, 58- *Concurrent Pos:* Consult, Educ Testing Serv, 67-68. *Mem:* MLA. *Res:* French literature of the 20th century; comparative French and Anglo-American literature; history of the West Indies from 1932 to 1945. *Publ:* Auth, Charles Eliot Norton, An American Scholar; L'Heritage Culturel; Tableaux d'Histoire, La France an Travail, 64 & Arts de France, 64, Am Bk Co; French for the Humanities, 68, French for the Social Sciences, 68, French Grammar, Key to Reading, 68 & French for the Sciences, 68, Prentice-Hall; Charles de Gaulle, Artiste de L'Action, 68 & La France au Cours des Ages Grands Jours et vie Quotidienne, 73, McGraw; Premier Guide de France, Prentice-Hall, 78. *Mailing Add:* Dept of French Univ of Calif Los Angeles CA 90024

BRICHTO, HERBERT CHANAN, b Jerusalem, Palestine, Jan 22, 25; US citizen; m 46; c 3. BIBLE, NEAR EASTERN STUDIES. *Educ:* City Col New York, BSS, 48; Hebrew Union Col, MHL, 50; Univ Pa, PhD(Orient studies), 62. *Prof Exp:* From instr to assoc prof Bible, Hebrew Union Col, NY, 55-66; PROF BIBLE, HEBREW UNION COL, OHIO, 66- *Concurrent Pos:* Annual prof, Bibl & Archaeol Sch, Hebrew Union Col, Jerusalem, 64-66. *Mem:* Soc Bibl Lit; Am Orient Soc; Israel Explor Soc; Cent Conf Am Rabbis. *Res:* Biblical literature; philosophy; theology. *Publ:* Auth, Problem of curse in the Hebrew Bible, Soc Bibl Lit, 62, 2nd ed, 68; On faith and revelation in the Bible, 68 & Kin, cult, land and afterlife, 73, Hebrew Union Col Annual. *Mailing Add:* 1018 Avondale Ave Cincinnati OH 45229

BRIGGS, MORTON WINFIELD, b Millbrook, NY, Mar 11, 15; m 41; c 3. ROMANCE LANGUAGES & LITERATURE. *Educ:* Cornell Univ, AB, 37; Sorbonne, dipl, 36; Harvard Univ, AM, 39, PhD, 44. *Hon Degrees:* MA ad eundem gradum, Wesleyan Univ, 56. *Prof Exp:* Asst English, Lycee Descartes, France, 37-38; tutor Romance lang, Harvard Univ, 40-43; from instr to assoc prof, 43-56, from actg chmn to chmn MA in teaching prog, 64-66 & 68-72, PROF ROMANCE LANG, WESLEYAN UNIV, 56-, SECY FAC, 58-, DIR HONORS COL, 66-, CHMN EDUC STUDIES PROG, 73- *Concurrent Pos:* Advert mgr, Fr Rev, 49-72, managing ed, 68-72; mem foreign lang adv comt, Conn State Dept Educ, 56-72, chmn, 65-72; dir Sweet Briar Col Jr Year in France Prog, 62-63 & 72-73; dir, Wesleyan in Paris prog, 79. *Mem:* Am Asn Teachers Fr; MLA; AAUP. *Res:* Richelieu in the Romantic period of the 19th century. *Publ:* Auth, Spanish Grammar, 61; co-ed, Ottaviano Petrucci, Canti B, No 50, Univ Chicago, 67. *Mailing Add:* Dept of Romance Lang Wesleyan Univ Middletown CT 06457

BRIGGS, WARD W, JR, b Riverside Calif, Nov 26, 45. CLASSICS. *Educ:* Washington & Lee Univ, BA, 67; Univ NC, MA, 69, PhD(classics), 74. *Prof Exp:* Instr, 72-75, asst prof, 75-79, ASSOC PROF CLASSICS, UNIV SC, 79- *Mem:* Am Philol Asn; Class Asn Midwest & South; Vergilian Soc. *Res:* Classical Latin poetry; Greek drama; textual criticism. *Publ:* Auth, Augustan athletics and the games of Aeneid V, Stadion, 76; Narrative and Simile from the Georgics in the Aeneid, Brill, 79; Virgil and Hellenistic Epic, 81 & A Bibliography of Virgil's Eclogues: 1927-1977, 81, ANRW; A Complete Concordance to Varro's De Re Rustica, Olms, 82. *Mailing Add:* Dept of Foreign Lang & Lit Univ of SC Columbia SC 29208

BRIGHT, DAVID F, b Winnipeg, Man, Apr 13, 42; US citizen; m 65; c 2. CLASSICAL LANGUAGES. *Educ:* Univ Man, BA, 62; Univ Cincinnati, MA, 63, PhD(classics), 67. *Prof Exp:* Asst prof classics, Williams Col, 67-70; asst prof, 70-76, chmn dept, 77-81, ASSOC PROF CLASSICS, UNIV ILL, URBANA, 76- *Concurrent Pos:* Semple fel classics, Univ Cincinnati, 74-75; Am Coun Learned Soc fel, 81-82; actg dir, Sch Humanities, 82-83. *Mem:* Am Philol Asn; Archaeol Inst Am; Class Asn Mid West & South Vergilian Soc. *Res:* Latin poetry; ancient literary criticism; later Latin literature. *Publ:* Auth, The myths of Baccgylides III, Class Folia, 76; Confectum carmine munus: Catullus 68, Ill Class Stud, 76; Non bona dicta: Catullus' Poetry of Separation, Quaderni Urbinati, 76; The myths of Bacchylides III, Class Folia, 76; Haec Mihi Fingebam, Tibullus in his World, Brill, Leiden, 78; Elaborate Disarray, The nature of Statius' Silvae, Meisenheim, 80; Ovid vs Apuleius, Ill Class Stud, 81. *Mailing Add:* Dept of Classics Univ of Ill Urbana IL 61801

BRIGHT, WILLIAM OLIVER, b Oxnard, Calif, Aug 13, 28; m 52; c 1. GENERAL LINGUISTICS. *Educ:* Univ Calif, Berkeley, AB, 49, PhD(ling), 55. *Prof Exp:* Jr scholar ling, Deccan Col, India, 55-57; linguist Hindi, US Dept State, DC, 57-58; asst prof speech, Univ Calif, Berkeley, 58-59; from asst prof to assoc prof anthrop, 59-66, PROF LING & ANTHROP, UNIV CALIF, LOS ANGELES, 66- *Concurrent Pos:* Am Philos Soc grant, 63-64; Am Coun Learned Soc res fel, 64-65; Wenner-Gren Found grant, 66-67; consult, Ford Found, India, 67; Guggenheim fel, 71; ed dir, Malki Mus Press, 77-; Nat Endowment for Humanities grant, 80. *Mem:* Ling Soc Am; Ling Soc India. *Res:* Ethnolinguistics; American Indian languages; South Asian languages. *Publ:* Auth, The Karok Language, Univ Calif, 57; An Outline of Colloquial Kannada, Deccan Col, 58; ed, Studies in California Linguistics, Univ Calif, 64; Sociolinguistics, Mouton 66; A Luiseno Dictionary, Univ Calif, 68; auth, North American Indian languages, Encycl Britannica, 74; The Dravidian Enunciative Vowel, Dravidian Phonological Syst, Univ Wash, 75; Variation and Change in Language, Stanford Univ, 76. *Mailing Add:* Dept of Ling Univ of Calif Los Angeles CA 90024

BRIGOLA, ALFREDO, b Shanghai, China, Nov 23, 23; US citizen; m 54; c 2. ROMANCE LANGUAGES. *Educ:* Univ Miss, BA, 53, MA, 54. *Prof Exp:* Lectr Ital, Univ Calif, Los Angeles, 61-64; instr Span, French & Ger, Univ Redlands, 57-61, prof Span, 65-70, prof Romance lang, 70-80, coordr, Dept Foreign Lang, 66-80, dir Europ studies, 75-80. *Concurrent Pos:* Dir Span, Redlands High Sch, 57-61. *Honors & Awards:* Bronze Medal, Ital Govt, 63 & Cavaliere, 76. *Mem:* MLA. *Res:* Spanish and Italian literature; language methodology. *Publ:* Auth, Practicing Italian, Holt, 65, 3rd ed, 77; Magnetic tapes for Italian course, 65; Study program in Italian structured and narrated for Muntz stero pak and keyed for auto-learning, 67. *Mailing Add:* 220 Grandview Dr Redlands CA 92373

BRIND'AMOUR, PIERRE RODRIGUE, Roman History, Ancient Astrology. See Vol I

BRINK, DANIEL THEODORE, b Topeka, Kans, May 26, 40; m 69; c 2. ENGLISH HISTORICAL LINGUISTICS. *Educ:* Lawrence Univ, BA, 62; Univ Wis, MA, 65, PhD(Ger ling), 70. *Prof Exp:* Asst prof Ger ling, Univ Calif, Berkeley, 70-75; asst prof, 75-81, ASSOC PROF ENGLISH LING, ARIZ STATE UNIV, 81- *Concurrent Pos:* Fulbright prof, Univ Amsterdam, 72-73; vis prof, Univ Calif, Berkeley, 79 & 82. *Mem:* Am Asn Netherlandic Studies; MLA; Ling Soc Am; Sem Ger Pedag; Am Name Soc. *Res:* Phonological change; history and structure of Dutch; comparative Germanic philology. *Publ:* Auth, Über die phonologische Analyse eines morphophonemischen Weschsels, Jahrbuch für Int Germanistic, 73; Characterizing the natural order of application of phonological rules, Lingua 34, 74; Voice assimilation in Dutch, Acta Ling Hafniensia 16, 76; On the rule of the syllable in natural generative phonology, J Ling Asn Southwest 2, 77; contribr, Linguistic Method, Mouton, 79; Studies in Dutch Phonology, Nijhoff, 80. *Mailing Add:* English Dept Ariz State Univ Tempe AZ 85281

BRINKMANN, RICHARD A, b Elberfeld, Ger, June 16, 21; m 47; c 3. GERMAN LITERATURE. *Educ:* Univ Tübingen, PhD(Ger lit), 48, Dr Habil, 55. *Prof Exp:* Lectr Ger lit, Univ Tübingen, 55-59, prof, 59; PROF GER LIT, UNIV CALIF, BERKELEY, 59- *Concurrent Pos:* Mem, Comn Ger Forschung Deutsche Forschungsgemeinschaft, 71-; guest prof, Univ Tex, Austin, Columbia Univ & Univ NZ; ed, Deut Viertel-Jahrsschrift Für Literaturwissenschaft & Geistesgeschichte. *Res:* German literature from the eighteenth to the twentieth century. *Mailing Add:* Dept of Ger Univ of Calif Berkeley CA 94720

BRINNER, WILLIAM MICHAEL, b Alameda, Calif, Oct 6, 24; m 51; c 3. PHILOLOGY, ISLAMIC HISTORY. *Educ:* Univ Calif, Berkeley, AB, 48, MA, 50, PhD, 56. *Prof Exp:* From instr to assoc prof, 56-64, chmn dept & dir Near Eastern Lang & Area Ctr, 65-70, dir Ctr Arabic Studies Abroad, 67-70, PROF NEAR EASTERN LANG, UNIV CALIF, BERKELEY, 64- *Concurrent Pos:* Lectr Arabic, Ctr Mid Eastern Studies, Harvard Univ, 61; Am Coun Learned Soc-Soc Sci Res Coun grant Near Eastern studies, 61-62; mem, Am Res Ctr Egypt, 68-70; consult, US Off Educ, 65-68; Guggenheim fel, 65-66; mem joint comt Near & Mid E, Am Coun Learned Soc-Soc Sci Res Coun, 66-70 & chmn, 69-70; mem exec comt, Am Inst Iranian Studies, 68; Fulbright-Hays fac res award, 70-71 & sr consult, Comt Int Exchange Persons, 72-73; dir, Univ Calif Studies Ctr, Jerusalem, 73-75. *Mem:* Am Orient Soc (pres, 76-77); Mediaeval Acad Am; Mid E Studies Asn NAm (pres, 69-70); Am Asn Teachers Arabic (pres, 68-69); Am Prof for Peace Mid E (vpres, 77-). *Res:* Arabic language and literature; Islamic history. *Publ:* Auth, The Banu Sasra: A study in the transmission of a scholarly tradition, Arabica, 5/60; The significance of the Harafish and their sultan, J Econ & Social Hist Quart, 63; A Chronicle of Damascus, 1389-1397 (2 vols), Univ Calif, 63; Sutro Library Hebraica: A Handlist, Calif State Libr, 67; coauth, Readings in Modern Arabic Literature, Brill, Leiden, 72; auth, An Elegant Composition Regarding Releif after Adversity, Yale Univ, 77. *Mailing Add:* Dept of Near Eastern Studies 1229 Dwinelle Hall Univ of Cal Berkeley CA 94720

BRISTER, LOUIS EDWIN, b El Dorado, Ark, July 14, 38; m 66; c 3. GERMAN LANGUAGE & LITERATURE. *Educ:* Miss State Univ, BA, 62; Univ Tex, Austin, MA, 66, PhD(Ger), 68. *Prof Exp:* From instr to asst prof Ger, 66-71, chmn dept mod lang, 71-78, assoc prof, 71-79, PROF GER, SOUTHWEST TEX STATE UNIV, 79- *Mem:* Am Asn Teachers Ger; Am Lessing Soc. *Res:* Eighteenth century German prose; biography and German-Americana. *Publ:* Auth, Unterrichtspraxis for undergraduates, Unterrichtspraxis, 72; The image of Arkansas in the Early German Emigrant Guidebook, Ark Hist Quart, 77; An approach to exploring American culture in the local community, Unterrichtspraxis, 78; J G Zimmermanns Essay Von der Erfahrung in der Arzneikunst: Ein Beitrag zur rationalen Medizin, Schweizerische Medizinische Wochenschrift, 80; William von Rosenberg's Kritik: A History of the Society for the Protection of German Immigrants in Texas, Southwestern Hist Quart, 81-82; Eduard Harkort: Ein Freiheitskampfer in Mexiko und Texas, Beitrage zur Geschichte Dortmunds und der Grafschaft Mark, 82. *Mailing Add:* Dept of Mod Lang Southwest Tex State Univ San Marcos TX 78666

BRITT, CLAUDE HENRY, JR, b St Pauls, NC, Sept 18, 29. HISPANIC LANGUAGE & LITERATURE. *Educ:* Wake Forest Col, BA, 51; Univ Ala, MA, 53; Northwestern Univ, PhD(Span), 66. *Prof Exp:* Teacher Span & hist, A L Brown High Sch, Kannapolis, NC, 55-56; asst prof Span, Gardner-Webb Col, 56-57; instr French, Stetson Univ, 59-60; asst prof Span, Mercer Univ, 60-62; from asst prof to assoc prof, Ga Southern Col, 63-76; Pace prof span, Old Dominion Univ, 77-78; PACE PROF SPAN, FLORIDA JR COL, 78- *Mem:* Am Asn Teachers Span & Port; MLA; Am Name Soc. *Res:* Golden Age literature; 17th century Spanish drama; Moreto. *Mailing Add:* 900 Erwin Rd Dunn NC 28334

BROCKHAUS, HENRICH, b Berlin, Ger, Dec, 31, 32; Can citizen; m 60; c 4. GERMAN LITERATURE. *Educ:* Univ BC, BA, 61, MA, 63; Univ Wash, PhD(Ger lit), 67. *Prof Exp:* Asst prof, 65-68, ASSOC PROF GER LANG & LIT, WESTERN WASH UNIV, 68- *Concurrent Pos:* Corresp ed Ger lang & lit monographs, Amsterdam, 76- *Mem:* Am Asn Teachers Ger. *Res:* German literature of the nineteenth century. *Publ:* Auth, Kellers Sinngedicht im Spiegel Seiner Binnenerzahlunger, Bovier, Nonn, 69; Der berittene Naturforscher in Kellers Sinngedicht, Ger Quart, 69; Schwierigkeiten uber Schwierigkeiten: Wahrigs Deutsches Worterbuch, Monatshefte, 70; Walter Kempowski: Kulture aus dem Zettelkasten, Proc PNCFL, 76. *Mailing Add:* Dept of Foreign Lang & Lit Western Wash Univ Bellingham WA 98225

BROD, RICHARD IRA, b Chicago, Ill, May 18, 33. FOREIGN LANGUAGES. *Educ:* Univ Chicago, BA, 53, MA, 56. *Prof Exp:* Instr German, Yale Univ, 61-66, NY Univ 66-69; prog assoc, 69-72, DIR FOREIGN LANG PROG, MLA, 72- *Honors & Awards:* Nelson H Brooks Award, Northeast Conf on Teaching For Lang, 80. *Mem:* Am Coun Teaching For Lang; Am Asn Teachers German. *Res:* History, status and development of foreign language education in the United States; teaching of language and culture in the context of international studies. *Publ:* Coauth, Foreign languages and careers, Mod Lang J, Vol 58, No 4, 74; ed, Survey of Foreign Language Entrance & Degree Requirements for the BA, 1974-1975, MLA, 75; auth, Correspondence at the crossroads, ADE Bull, No 5, 76; co-ed, Language in American Life, Georgetown Univ Press, 78; ed, Survey of Foreign Languages Course Registrations in US Colleges & Universities, MLA, 78; auth, Options & opportunities: New directions in foreign language curricula, ADFL Bull, Vol 10, No 4, 79; ed, Language Study for the 1980's: Reports of the MLA-ACLS Language Task Forces, MLA, 80; auth, Back to the center: Activism and the humanities, Mod Lang J, Vol 66, No 1, 82. *Mailing Add:* Mod Lang Asn 62 Fifth Ave New York NY 10011

BRODEUR, LEO ARTHUR, b St Boniface, Man, Feb 15, 24; m 56; c 4. FRENCH & COMPARATIVE LITERATURES. *Educ:* Univ Man, BA, 44; Laval Univ, MA, 61, PhD(French), 68. *Prof Exp:* Lectr, Laurentian Univ, 58-62 & Laval Univ, 62-63; dir exten, 63-64, from asst prof to assoc prof, 63-72, PROF, UNIV SHERBROOKE, 73- *Concurrent Pos:* Radio & TV producer, Laurentian Univ, 58-62, lectr polit sci, 64-65; exec, Ctr d'Etude Lit d'Expression Francaise, 69-, dir, 74-77; ed, Presence Francophone, 70-, dir, 74-77; IBM grant, 70; exec, Asn Ed Can, 71-74; dir, Proj Recherche Periodisation Litteratures Francophones, Ministere l'Education, Quebec, 74-77 & Ed Nebuleuse & Atelier-Traduction/Transl Workshop, 74-; lectr Can intellectual & social hist, Bishop's Univ, 76-77; vpres & acad dir, Inst Civilisations Comparees, Montreal, 76-; mem adv coun, Can Sch Mgt, 76-; co-ed, Ecriture Francaise, 78- & Poetry Windsor Sherbrooke Poesie, 78- *Mem:* Asn Can Univ Teachers Fr; Soc Paul Claudel; Can Soc Comp Study Civilizations; Can Int Acad Humanities & Soc Sci (vpres). *Res:* Christianity in French literature; history of English and French Canadian literatures; tradition and original innnvations in literary critique. *Publ:* Auth, Le Corps sphere, clef de la symbolique claudelienne, Ed Cosmos, 70; La Legende du Vent (opera-ballet script), CBC-TB, 47; contribr, Dictionnaire des oeuvres litteraires du Quebec II, 78-; coauth, Bibliographie des theses litteraires canadiennes de 1921 a 1976, Ed Naaman, 78- *Mailing Add:* Fac des Arts Univ de Sherbrooke Sherbrooke PQ J1K 2R1 Can

BRODIN, DOROTHY R, b New York, NY, Dec 26, 17; m 48. ROMANCE LANGUAGES, LINGUISTICS. *Educ:* Bryn Mawr Col, BA, 38; Columbia Univ, MA, 43, PhD, 63. *Prof Exp:* Instr French, Manhattanville Col, 40-41; teacher, Hunter Col High Sch, 43-61; lectr, Hunter Col, 61-63, from instr to assoc prof, 63-68; assoc prof, 68-73, prof, 73-80, EMER PROF FRENCH, LEHMAN COL, 80- *Concurrent Pos:* Teacher, WPIX-TV, Metrop Educ TV Asn, 58-59; consult, Dalton Schs, NY, 60 & 66, ALM Develop Ctr, 61-62, Doubleday & Co, 62-65 & Lycee Francais New York, 64-; Am Asn Teachers Fr deleg, Joint Nat Comt on Lang, 73-76. *Honors & Awards:* Chevalier, Palmes Aca, 59, Off, 70; Distinguished Teacher Award, NY State Asn Foreign Lang Teachers, 74; Bk Prize, Acad Francaise, 74; Medal, City of Paris, France, 75. *Mem:* Int Ling Asn; Am Soc Geolinguistics; Am Asn Teachers Fr (pres, 77-79); Soc Fr Prof Am. *Res:* Twentieth century French literature; medieval French; French linguistics. *Publ:* Transl, The Range of Reason, Scribner, 52; auth, The Comic World of Marcel Ayme, Nouvelles Ed Debresse, Paris, 64; A fabulist for our times, Am Soc Fr Legion Honor Mag, 67; French literature, In: Standard Ref Encycl Yearbk, Funk, 67-77; Marcel Ayme, Columbia Univ, 68; coauth, A frequency Dictionary of French Words, Mouton, The Hague, 70; Presences Contemporaines: Auteurs Francais du XXe Siecle, Fr & Europ Publ, 72; auth, A study of the learned words in the earliest French documents, In: Studies in Honor of Mario Pei, Univ NC, 72. *Mailing Add:* Dept of French Lehman Col Bronx NY 10468

BRODSKY, PATRICIA POLLOCK, b Douds, Iowa, June 22, 41; m 68. COMPARATIVE LITERATURE, GERMAN. *Educ:* State Univ Iowa, BA, 64; Univ Calif, Berkeley, MA, 66, PhD(comp lit), 72. *Prof Exp:* Asst prof, 74-80, ASSOC PROF GER & RUSS, UNIV MO-KANSAS CITY, 80- *Concurrent Pos:* Univ Mo-Kansas City fac res grants, 75 & 76; res assoc, Russ & East Europ Ctr, Univ Ill, Urbana, 76-81; res & travel grants to Ger & Switz, 79. *Mem:* MLA; Am Comp Lit Asn; Am Asn Teachers Slavic & East Europ Lang; Am Asn Advan Slavic Studies; Rilke-Ges. *Res:* Rainer Maria Rilke; literature and culture of the fin de siecle; European Romanticism. *Publ:* Auth, Fertile fields and poisoned gardens: Sologub' s debt to Hoffmann, Pushkin and Hawthorne, Essays Lit, spring 74; Russia in Rilke's Das Buch der Bilder, Comp Lit, fall 77; Rilke and Russian art, Germano-Slavica, 78; Auth, The military school: A shared source in Rilke and Musil, Mod Lang Studies, 79-80; The Russian source of Rilke's Wie der Verrat nach Russland kam, Ger Rev, 79; On daring to be a poet: Rilke and Marina Cvetaeva, Germano-Slavica, 80; Rilke's relation to Russian painting, Innsbrucker Beitrage zur Kulturwissenschaft, 81. *Mailing Add:* Dept of Foreign Lang Univ of Mo Kansas City MO 64110

BRODY, JULES, b New York, NY, Mar 6, 28; m 53; c 3. FRENCH. *Educ:* Cornell Univ, AB, 48; Columbia Univ, AM, 49, PhD(French), 56. *Prof Exp:* Lectr French, Columbia Univ, 50-53, from instr to assoc prof, 53-63; prof French & chmn dept foreign & comp lit, Univ Rochester, 63-68; prof romance lang & assoc dean fac, Queens Col, NY, 68-75; PROF ROMANCE LANG & LIT, HARVARD UNIV, 75-, CHMN DEPT, 80- *Concurrent Pos:* Guggenheim fel & Fulbright res fel, 61-62. *Mem:* Soc Fr Studies; Soc Studies 17th Century; MLA; Am Asn Teachers Fr. *Res:* French literature of the 17th century; classical tradition in France; Montaigne. *Publ:* Auth, Boileau and Longinus, Droz, 58; Platonisme et classicisme, Saggi E Ricerche Di Let Francese, 61; co-ed, Critical Bibliography of French Literature, Syracuse Univ, 61; ed, French Classicism: A Critical Miscellany, Prentice-Hall, 66; auth, Du style a la pensee: Trois etudes sur les Caracteres de La Bruyere, French Forum Monographs, 81; Lectures de Montaigne, French Forum Monographs, 82; (with Leo Spitzer), Approches textuelles de Saint-Simon, Narr, 81. *Mailing Add:* Dept of Romance Lang Queens Col Flushing NY 11367

BRODY, ROBERT, b Jersey City, NJ, June 16, 37; m 61; c 2. SPANISH AMERICAN LITERATURE. *Educ:* Rutgers Univ, BA, 62; Univ Ill, MA, 63; Harvard Univ, PhD(Romance lang & Lit), 71. *Prof Exp:* From instr to asst prof, Columbia Univ, 68-74; asst prof, 74-80, ASSOC PROF SPAN, UNIV TEX AUSTIN, 80- *Honors & Awards:* Outstanding Fac Mem Award, Col Humanities, Univ Tex, 77. *Mem:* MLA; SCent Mod Lang Asn; Am Asn Teachers Span & Port; Asoc Int Hispanistase. *Res:* Contemporary Spanish American prose. *Publ:* Auth, Stream-of-consciousness techniques in Cortazar's Rayuela, Symposium, 75; contribr, The Analysis of Hispanic Texts: Current Trends in Methodology, Bilingual, 76; Julio Cortazar: Rayuela, Grant & Cutler/Tamesis, 76; Mario Vargas Llosa and the totalization impulse, Tex Studies Lit & Lang, 77; Mascaro el cazador americano en la traysctoria novekistica de Haroldo Conti, Revista Iberoamericana, 79. *Mailing Add:* Dept Span & Portuguese Univ of Tex Austin TX 78712

BRODY, SAUL NATHANIEL, English, Comparative Medieval Literature. See Vol II

BROEGE, VALERIE ANNE, b Cleveland, Ohio, Dec 19, 42. CLASSICS. *Educ:* Vassar Col, AB, 63; Bryn Mawr Col, MA, 64, PhD, 68. *Prof Exp:* Lectr classics, Univ Western Ont, 66-69, asst prof class studies, 69-74; PROF HUMANITIES, VANIER COL, 74- *Concurrent Pos:* East-West Communication Inst fel, 76; prof classics, Concordia Univ, 76-77 & 78-79 & 80, McGill Univ, 79. *Mem:* Am Philol Asn; Class Asn Can; MLA; Popular Cult Asn; Sci Fiction Res Asn. *Res:* Canadian studies; science fiction and the occult; women's studies. *Publ:* Auth, Divine polarity in Horace's lyric poetry, 1/72, Ovid's autobiographical use of mythology in the Tristia and Epistulae ex Ponto, 4/72, Archetypal views of women in classical mythology and modern literature, 1/73 & Views of technology in classical mythology and modern literature, 4/73, Class News & Views; The horoscope of the Roman Emperor Augustus and his attitude to astrology, Northern Lights, 3/75; The generation gap in Catullus and the lyric poetry of Horace, In: The Conflict of Generations in Ancient Greece and Rome, Gruner, Amsterdam, 76; The influence of classical heroic models on American concepts of the hero, Helios, 5/76; Margaret Atwood's Americans and Canadians, Essays on Canadian Writing, summer 81. *Mailing Add:* Dept of Humanities Vanier Col Snowdon Campus Montreal PQ H4L 3X9 Can

BROM, LIBOR, b Ostrava, Czech, Dec 17, 23; US citizen; m 61. SLAVIC LANGUAGES & LITERATURE. *Educ:* Czech Inst Technol, MS, 48; Univ Colo, MA, 62, PhD(Slavic lang & lit), 70. *Prof Exp:* Economist Foreign Com, Slovak Magnesite Works, Prague, 48-49; economist budgetory acct, Vodostavba, Prague, 51-53, economist prod planner, 53-56; teacher foreign lang, Jefferson Country Schs, 58-67; asst prof, 67-71, ASSOC PROF FOREIGN LANG, UNIV DENVER, 71- *Concurrent Pos:* Foreign lang translr, Tech Sci, Czech Acad Sci, 49-56; hon teacher Slavic lang, Univ Colo, 63-65. *Mem:* Am Asn Teacher Slavic & E Europ Lang (vpres, 73-75); Comenius World Coun (vpres, 76-); Asn Int Lang & Lit Slaves; Am Asn Advan Slavic Studies; Rocky Mountain Asn Slavic Studies. *Res:* Ivan Bunin's Proteges; lives and works; Russian Emigre literature; modern Czechoslovak civilization and literature. *Publ:* Auth, Ceskoslovensko-polska perspektiva, Denni hlasatel LXXXIV; Nezamestnanost v socialismu, Novy Svet XXV & Hlas domova XXV; K vyvoji novohercenismu, Promeny IX; Nikita I Prutskov Gleb Uspensky, Slavic & E Europ J XVI; Literary profile of Bunin's Protege--Leonid Zurov 1902-72, Manitoba Mod Lang Bol VIII; coauth, Otazky Zemepisu, Publ House Czech Acad Sci, 55; auth, Ve Vichricich Hnevu, Comenius World Coun, 76; Leonid Zurov Ivan Bunin's Proteges, Vol I, Pioneer Publ Co, 73. *Mailing Add:* Univ Denver University Park Denver CO 80208

BROMBERT, VICTOR HENRI, b Nov 11, 23; m 50. FRENCH COMPARATIVE LITERATURE. *Educ:* Yale Univ, BA, 48, MA, 49, PhD(French), 53. *Hon Degrees:* LHD, Univ Chicago, 81. *Prof Exp:* Instr French, Yale Univ, 51-54, from asst prof to prof, 55-70, chmn dept Romance lang & lit, 64-75, Benjamin F Barge prof Romantic lit, 70-75; HENRY PUTNAM UNIV PROF ROMANCE & COMP LIT, PRINCETON UNIV, 75- *Concurrent Pos:* Guggenheim fel, 54-55 & 70; Am Coun Learned Soc fel, 67-68; Nat Endowment Humanities sr fel, 73; Rockefeller Found fel, Am Acad Arts & Sci, 75; chmn, Yale Univ Coun, Comt Humanities & Lit, 78- & Comt Romance Lang, Bd Overseas, Harvard Univ, 78-; bd mem, Nineteenth Century French Studies & Stanford French Studies. *Honors & Awards:* Chevalier, Palmes Acad, 77; Harry Levin Prize for Comp Lit, 78; Howard T Behrman Award for distinguished achievement in humanities, 79. *Mem:* Acad Lit Studies; Am Comp Lit Asn; MLA; Am Asn Teachers Fr; Int Asn Fr Studies. *Res:* The 19th century novel; literary criticism; contemporary literature. *Publ:* Auth, The Criticism of T S Eliot, Yale Univ, 48; Stendhal et la Voie Oblique, Univ France, 54; The Intellectual Hero: Studies in the French Novel, 1880-1955, Lippincott, 61; The Novels of Flaubert: A Study of Themes and Techniques, Princeton Univ, 66; Stendhal: Fiction and the Themes of Freedom, Random 68; Flaubert par Lvi-Meme, Seuil, 71; La Prison Romantique, Corti, 75; The Romantic Prison: The French Tradition, Princeton Univ, 79. *Mailing Add:* Dept of Romance & Comp Lit Princeton Univ 201 E Pyne Bldg Princeton NJ 08540

BRONNER, LUISE HELEN, b Heilbronn, Ger, Feb 22, 12; US citizen. GERMAN. *Educ:* Univ RI, BS, 61; Univ Mass, MA, 64, PhD(Ger), 68. *Prof Exp:* Teacher chem, North Providence High Sch, RI, 61-62; asst Ger, Univ Mass, Amherst, 64-65; from instr to asst prof, 65-74, ASSOC PROF GER, UNIV MASS, BOSTON, 74- *Concurrent Pos:* Chemist textile chem, RI, 39-59. *Mem:* MLA; Am Chem Soc; Am Asn Teachers Ger; Int Brecht Soc; Goethe Soc. *Res:* Regarding the German poets Eduard Mörike and Bertolt Brecht; study of German, combining forms (philological) approaches with present ones. *Publ:* Auth, Brecht Gedichte in Deutschunterricht, Die Unterrichtspraxis, 73; Mosaik, Bläschke Verlag, 78. *Mailing Add:* Univ of Mass Harbor Campus Boston MA 02125

BRONSEN, DAVID, b Columbus, Ohio, June 4, 26. GERMAN, COMPARATIVE LITERATURE. *Educ:* Ohio State Univ, BA, 51; Univ Vienna, Dr Phil, 56; Univ Paris, Dipl, 56-57; Harvard Univ, PhD, 75. *Prof Exp:* Lecteur lit, Univ Lille, 56-57; instr Ger, eve sch, Harvard Univ, 59-60; vis asst prof, Kent State Univ, 61-62; vis asst prof, 62, PROF GER & COMP LIT, WASH UNIV, 62- *Concurrent Pos:* Kennedy res fel, Europe, 60-61; Humboldt Stiftung scholar & Osterreichische Gesellschaft Lit scholar, 68-69; vis prof, Univs Haifa & Tel Aviv, 69-70; Nat Endowment for Humanities sr fel, 73-74. *Mem:* MLA; Am Asn Teachers Ger; Leo Baeck Inst; Am Coun Study Austrian Lit. *Res:* German literature of the 19th and 20th centuries; comparative literature. *Publ:* Auth, Boll's women: Patterns in male-female relationships, Monatshefte, 11/66; Die verhaltnisse dieses planeton in Brechts frühen stücken, In: Festschrift Für Bernhard Blume, Göttingen, 67; A conversation with Henry Roth, Partisan Rev, 69; Der sonderfall as exemplarischer fall: Joseph Roth und die emigration als grenzsituation, In: Exit und Innere Emigration, Athenaum, Frankfurt/Main, 73; Joseph Roth: Eiene Biographie, Kiepenheuer & Witsch, Cologne, 74; contrib ed, Joseph Roth und die Tradition, 75 & contribr, Eine alltägliche Verwirrung: Ein kafkaeskes Paradigm, 78, Agora Verlag; Consuming Struggle vs Killing Time: Preludes to Dying in the Dramas of Ibsen and Beckett, Atlantic Highland, 78. *Mailing Add:* Dept of Ger Lang & Lit Wash Univ St Louis MO 63130

BRONSTEIN, ARTHUR J, b Baltimore, Md, Mar 15, 14; m 41; c 2. SPEECH, LINGUISTICS. *Educ:* City Col New York, AB, 34; Columbia Univ, AM, 36; NY Univ, PhD, 49. *Prof Exp:* Instr, Ohio Univ, 36-37 & City Col New York, 37-38; from tutor to prof speech, Queens Col, NY, 38-68; prof speech & ling, Lehman Col, 68-69; exec off PhD prog in speech, Grad Sch, City Univ New York, 69-72; PROF SPEECH & COORDR INTERDEPARTMENTAL PROG LING, LEHMAN COL, 72-; EXEC OFF PhD PROG IN LING, GRAD SCH, CITY UNIV NEW YORK, 81- *Concurrent Pos:* Ed adv pronunciation, Am Col Dictionary, 47-; ed consult pronunciation & lang, Collier's Encycl, 62; assoc ed, Quart J Speech, 63; vis prof, Univ Hawaii, 63; Fulbright prof English ling, Tel-Aviv Univ, 67-68 & Univ Trondheim, Norway, 79; consult, Random House Dictionary English Lang, 77- & Longman's Dictionary Contemp English, 77- *Mem:* Am Speech & Hearing Asn; Int Phonetic Asn; MLA; Int Ling Asn; Am Asn Phonetic Sci. *Res:* Sociolinguistics; phonetics and phonology; dialectology. *Publ:* Coauth, Phonetic-phonemic symbolization problems, Quart J Speech, 59; auth, Pronunciation of American English, Appleton, 61; coauth, Phonetic-linguistic view of the reading controversy, Speech Monogr, 65; auth, The pronunciation of English, In: The Random House Dictionary, 66; coauth, Your Speech and Voice, Random, 67; co-ed, Essays in Honor of C M Wise, Standard, Mo, 70; ed, Biographical Dictionary of the Phonetic Sciences, Lehman Col, 77. *Mailing Add:* PhD Prog Ling Grad Sch City Col New York New York NY 10036

BRONZNICK, NORMAN MEYER, b Yanova, Lithuania, Sept 20, 20; US citizen; m 53; c 3. HEBRAIC STUDIES, RELIGION. *Educ:* Yeshiva Col, BA, 44; Columbia Univ, MA, 47, PhD, 65. *Prof Exp:* From asst prof to assoc prof, 64-73, PROF HEBRAIC STUDIES, RUTGERS UNIV, 73- *Mem:* World Union Jewish Studies; Nat Asn Professors Hebrew. *Res:* Prophetology; Talmudic and Midrashic literature; Hebrew lexicography. *Publ:* Auth, Qabalah as a metonym for the prophets, Hebrew Union Col Ann, 67; Attributes of prophecy in the rabbinic view, Mirsky Memorial Vol, 70; coauth, Ha-Yesod--Fundamentals of Hebrew, Philipp Feldheim, 72; A theological view of the Holocaust, Jewish Educ, 73; The proselyte as a newborn, Or Hamizrach, 77; The semantics of the Stem HLS, Leshonenu, 77; Calque or semantic parallel, 77 & Metathetic parallelism: An unrecognized subtype of synonymous parallelism, 79, Hebrew Ann Rev. *Mailing Add:* 935 Brady Ave Bronx NY 10462

BROOK, RICHARD, b Winona, Minn, Apr 29, 33; m 57; c 4. ENGLISH LINGUISTICS. *Educ:* St Johns Univ, Minn, BA, 55; Univ Minn, MA, 61; Univ Iowa, PhD(English ling), 70. *Prof Exp:* Asst commun, Univ Minn, 60-61, instr, 61-62; asst prof English ling, Bemidji State Col, 62-64; assoc prof ling, Univ Northern Iowa, 65-71; assoc dean instr, 71-80, PROF LANG & LIT, PLYMOUTH STATE COL, 71-, ACTG DEAN, 80- *Concurrent Pos:* Instr English, Macalester Col, 62. *Mem:* Ling Soc Am. *Res:* Dialectology; sociolinguistics; information retrieval. *Mailing Add:* Off of Assoc Dean of Instr Plymouth State Col Plymouth NH 03264

BROOKE, FRANCIS JOHN, b Charleston, WVa, Mar 4, 29; m 58; c 3. GERMAN LITERATURE. *Educ:* Hampden-Sydney Col, BA, 49; Univ Chicago, MA, 51; Univ NC, PhD(Ger), 54. *Prof Exp:* Teaching fel, Univ NC, 51-53, instr, 53-54; from instr to assoc prof Ger, Univ Va, 56-65, asst dean, Col Arts & Sci, 59-62, dir Echols Scholar Prog, 60-62, actg chmn dept mod lang, 62-63; prof Ger & exec dean col, Centre Col Ky, 65-68; acad vpres, 68-74, provost acad div, 73-79, PROF GER, VA COMMONWEALTH UNIV, 68-, ASST TO PRES, 79- *Concurrent Pos:* Ellis L Phillips Found grant, internship acad admin, Cornell Univ, 63-64. *Mem:* MLA; S Atlantic Mod Lang Asn; Am Asn Teachers Ger. *Res:* German drama and novelle of the 19th and 20th centuries. *Publ:* Transl, Preaching, Confession, The Lord's Supper, John Knox, 60. *Mailing Add:* 910 W Franklin St Richmond VA 23284

BROOKS, BLOSSOM SHEILA, b Worcester, Mass, June 29, 31. FOREIGN LANGUAGE EDUCATION. *Educ:* Clark Univ, AB, 53; Middlebury Col, MA, 55; Rutgers Univ, EdD(foreign lang educ), 75. *Prof Exp:* Lang analyst, Dept Defense, Washington DC, 55-58; teacher Ger, North Syracuse Cent High Sch, 58-59 & Bridgewater- Raritan High Sch, 60-67; assoc prof, 67-77, PROF GER & FOREIGN LANG EDUC, EAST STROUDSBURG STATE COL & CHAIRPERSON DEPT FOREIGN LANG, 77- *Mem:* MLA; Am Coun Teaching Foreign Lang. *Mailing Add:* Dept of Foreign Lang East Stroudsburg State Col East Stroudsburg PA 18301

BROOKS, E BRUCE, b Akron, Ohio, June 23, 36; m 64; c 1. CHINESE LITERATURE. *Educ:* Oberlin Conserv Music, MusB, 58; Univ Wash, PhD(Chinese lang & lit), 68. *Prof Exp:* Lectr Chinese, Harvard Univ, 67-68, instr, 68-69, asst prof, 69-73, lectr, 73-74; asst prof Chinese history, Smith Col, 74-78; pres, Sinfac Minor, 68-80. *Concurrent Pos:* Nat Endowment for Humanities res grant, 71-72; Am Coun Learned Socs, 76-77. *Honors & Awards:* Waring Prize, Western Reserve Acad, 80. *Res:* Prosody; stylistics; evolution of thought. *Publ:* Auth, A Yakamochi sampler, East-West Rev, winter 66-67; A geometry of the Shr Pin, In: Wen-lin, Univ Wis, 68; Literary Chinese Primer, SinFac Minor, 72; Journey toward the West: An Asian prosodic embassy in the year 1972, HJAS, 75; Chinese Character Frequency Lists, SinFac Minor, 78. *Mailing Add:* 39 Hillside Rd Northampton MA 01060

BROOKS, H FRANKLIN, b Greenwood, Miss, May 30, 34. FRENCH. *Educ:* North Tex State Univ, BA, 55, MA, 56; Johns Hopkins Univ, PhD(Romance lang), 66. *Prof Exp:* Instr French, Emory Univ, 61-64; asst prof, Dartmouth Col, 64-69; ASSOC PROF FRENCH, VANDERBILT UNIV, 69- *Res:* Seventeenth century French theater arts; historical novels; espistolary literature. *Publ:* Auth, Encore un fragment des Voeux due Paon, Moyen Age, 58; Taste, perfection and delight in Guez de Balzac&s criticism, Studies Philol, 71; Fulvio Testi juge par J-L Guez de Balzac, Dix-septieme Siecle, 72; Guez de Balzac, eloquence and the life of the spirit, L'Esprit Createur, 75; Un canard du Fils assassine publie en 1644, Revue Litterature Comp, 77. *Mailing Add:* Dept of French Station B Vanderbilt Univ Nashville TN 37235

BROOKS, MARIA ZAGORSKA, b Warsaw, Poland, Jan 11, 33; US citizen; m 58; c 2. SLAVIC LINGUISTICS. *Educ:* Univ Warsaw, MA, 55; Univ Mich, MA, 58 PhD(ling), 63; Univ Pa, MA, 63. *Prof Exp:* Instr English, Univ Warsaw, 55-57; res asst acoustic phonetics, Univ Mich, 57-58; from lectr to instr Slavic lang, 60-65, from asst prof to assoc prof, 65-75, PROF SLAVIC LANG & LING, UNIV OF PA, 75- *Mem:* Ling Soc Am; Int Ling Asn; AAUP; Am Asn Teachers Slavic & E Europ Lang; MLA. *Res:* Acoustic phonetics; syntax and semantics as applied to Slavic languages. *Publ:* Auth, Acoustic-Phonetic Analysis of Polish Nasal Vowels, 68 & Nasal Vowels in

Contemporary Standard Polish, 68, Mouton, The Hague; translr, Generic structures in Russian folklore, Genre, 9/71; auth, Displacement and location in Polish, In: Symbolae in Honorem Georgii Y Shevelov, Munich, 71; Polish Reference Grammar with Exercises, Mouton, The Hague, 73; coauth, An analysis of Polish conjugation, Int J Slavic Ling & Poetics, Vol 15: 127-147. *Mailing Add:* Dept of Slavic Lang Univ of Pa Philadelphia PA 19104

BROOKS, MARY ELIZABETH, b Washington, Ind, Mar 13, 25. SPANISH & LUSO-BRAZILIAN LITERATURE. *Educ:* Purdue Univ, BS, 47; Univ NMex, MA, 51, PhD(Span lit), 60. *Prof Exp:* Instr Span, Purdue Univ, 57-59; from instr to assoc prof, 59-68, PROF SPAN & PORT, UNIV WIS-MADISON, 68- *Concurrent Pos:* Univ Wis Grad Sch gres grant, 61 & 67. *Mem:* Am Asn Teachers Span & Port; MLA. *Publ:* Auth, From defeat to immortality: The birth of Sebastianism, Luso-Brazilian Rev, 64; A King for Portugal: The Madrigal Conspiracy, 1594-1595, Univ Wis, 65. *Mailing Add:* Dept of Span & Port Univ of Wis Madison WI 53706

BROOKS, PETER PRESTON, b New York, NY, Apr 19, 38; m 59; c 3. FRENCH & COMPARATIVE LITERATURE. *Educ:* Harvard Univ, AB, 59, PhD(comp lit), 65. *Hon Degrees:* MAH, Yale Univ, 75. *Prof Exp:* From instr to assoc prof French, 65-75, dir lit major, 74-80, prof French & comp lit, 75-80, dir Div Humanities Ctr, 79-82, CHESTER D TRIPP PROF HUMANITIES, YALE UNIV, 80-, DIR WHITNEY HUMANITIES CTR, 80- *Concurrent Pos:* Morse fel, 67-68; Am Coun Learned Soc grant-in-aid, 67 & 72; contrib ed, Partisan Rev, 72-; Guggenheim fel, 73-74; mem adv comt, Pac Mod Lang Asn, 76-80; Am Counc Learned Soc fel, 79-80; vis prof, Summer Inst in Lit, Univ Texas, Austin, 79-80. *Mem:* MLA; Acad of Lit Studies. *Res:* Romanticism; theory and analysis of narrative; psychoanalysis and literary criticism. *Publ:* Auth, The Novel of Worldliness, Princeton Univ, 69; Nouvelle critique et critique nouvelle aux Etats-Unis, Nouvelle Rev Francaise, 9/69; ed, The Child's Part, Beacon, 72; co-ed, Man and His Fictions, Harcourt, 73; auth, The Melodramatic Imagination, Yale Univ, 76; Freud's masterplot, Yale Fr Studies, 78; co-ed, Jean Genet: A Collection of Critical Essays, Prentice-Hall, 78; Repetition, repression, and return: Great Expectations and the study of plot, New lit Hist, 80. *Mailing Add:* Whitney Humanities Ctr Yale Univ 2968 Yale Sta New Haven CT 06520

BROOKS, RICHARD A, b Brooklyn, NY, Aug 5, 31; m 57. COMPARATIVE LITERATURE. *Educ:* Columbia Col, AB, 53; Harvard Univ, AM, 54; Columbia Univ, PhD(French), 59. *Prof Exp:* Instr French, Columbia Col, 55-59; from instr to asst prof, Rutgers Univ, 59-64; from asst prof to assoc prof, NY Univ, 64-67, dir Maison Francaise, 64-67; from assoc prof to prof humanities, Richmond Col & Grad Ctr, 67-77; chmn dept, 74-77, PROF HUMANITIES, CITY UNIV NEW YORK, COL STATEN ISLAND & GRAD CTR, 77- *Concurrent Pos:* Rutgers Univ Res Coun fel, 62; NY Univ Arts & Sci Res Fund grant, 66-67; City Univ New York travel grant, 67; Nat Endowment Humanities grant, 72; City Univ New York Res Found res grants, 71-77. *Mem:* MLA; Am Soc 18th Century Studies; Am Comp Lit Asn. *Res:* Eighteenth century literature; autobiography; bibliography. *Publ:* Auth, Voltaire and Leibniz, Droz, Geneva, 63; Critical Bibliography of French Literature: The Eighteenth Century, Syracuse Univ, 68; ed, Selected Letters of Voltaire, NY Univ, 73; Rousseau's attitude toward women, In: Essays in Honor of George Havens, Ohio State Univ, 73; co-ed, Critical Bibliography of French Literature: The Twentieth Century, Syracuse Univ, 79. *Mailing Add:* Col of Staten Island City Univ New York Staten Island NY 10301

BROSMAN, CATHARINE HILL SAVAGE, b Denver, Colo, June 7, 34; m 70; c 1. FRENCH. *Educ:* Rice Univ, BA, 55, MA, 57, PhD, 60. *Prof Exp:* Instr French, Rice Univ, 60-62; asst prof, Sweet Briar Col, 62-63 & Univ Fla, 63-66; assoc prof, Mary Baldwin Col, 66-68; assoc prof, 68-72, PROF FRENCH, NEWCOMB COL, TULANE UNIV, 72- *Concurrent Pos:* Fulbright scholar, 57-58; Am Coun Learned Soc grants-in-aid, 62; mem comn status women profession, MLA, 69-70; asst ed, Fr Rev, 74-77, managing ed, 77-80. *Mem:* SCent Mod Lang Asn (vpres, 73-74, pres, 74-75); Am Asn Teachers Fr; Asn Amis Andre Gide; Malraux Soc; SAtlantic Mod Lang Asn. *Res:* French novel and poetry of the 19th and 20th centuries. *Publ:* Auth, Andre Gide, L'Evolution de sa pensee religieuse, Nizet, 62; Malraux, Sartre and Aragon as Political Novelists, Univ Fla, 65; Roger Martin du Gard, Twayne, 68; Watering, Univ Ga, 72; Le monde ferme de Paludes, Andre Gide 6, Minard, 79; Gide, translation, and little gidding, Fr Rev, 4/81; Sartre, the Algerian War, and Les Seguestres d'Altona, Papers in Romance, spring 81; Sartres Kean as self-portrait, Fr Rev (special number), 82. *Mailing Add:* Dept of French & Ital Tulane Univ New Orleans LA 70118

BROSMAN, PAUL WILLIAM, JR, b Macon, Ga, Sept 16, 27; m 50, 70; c 1. HISTORICAL LINGUISTICS. *Educ:* Tulane Univ, BA, 49, MA, 50; Univ NC, PhD(comp ling), 56. *Prof Exp:* From asst prof to assoc prof foreign lang, NTex State Col, 56-58; from asst prof to assoc prof, La State Univ, 58-65; assoc prof Indo-Europ ling, Tulane Univ, 65-66, prof, 66-79. *Mem:* Ling Soc Am; Soc Ling Europaea. *Res:* Comparative Indo-European linguistics; historical romance linguistics. *Publ:* Auth, Proto-Indo-Hittite reduced vowel and the allophones of laryngeals, Language, 1-3/57; The old high German element in French, Studies Philol, 7/63; The neuter plural of Hittite i- and u-stems, J Am Oriental Soc, 10-12/64; The FEW and the High element in Old French, Romania, 7-9/76; Hittite evidence and the i/ya-stem adjective, Idogermanische Forschungen, 4-6/78; The origin of the PIE a-stems, J Indo-Europ Studies, 7-12/81. *Mailing Add:* 7834 Willow St New Orleans LA 70118

BROU, MARGUERITE, b Wallace, La, May 3, 22. ROMANCE LANGUAGES, FRENCH. *Educ:* St Mary's Dominican Col, AB, 42; La State Univ, MA, 55; Laval Univ, PhD(French), 66; La State Univ, Baton Rouge, MS in LS, 71. *Prof Exp:* From instr to prof French, St Mary's Dominican Col, 45-72, chmn dept, 55-61, chmn humanities area, 66-68, chmn dept foreign lang, 68-72, asst librn, 72-73; archivist, Archdiocese New Orleans, La, 71-81; LECTR FRENCH, ST MARY'S DOMINICAN COL, 81- *Mem:* Soc Southwest Arch. *Res:* French literature. *Mailing Add:* 7214 St Charles Ave New Orleans LA 70118

BROUGHTON, THOMAS ROBERT SHANNON, Classics, Ancient History. See Vol I

BROWN, CALVIN SMITH, b University, Miss, Sept 27, 09; m 34; c 1. COMPARATIVE LITERATURE. *Educ:* Univ Miss, AB, 28; Univ Cincinnati, AM, 29; Oxford Univ, BA, 32; Univ Wis, PhD(comp lit), 34. *Prof Exp:* Instr Ger & English, Phillips Exeter Acad, 34-35; assoc prof English, Tenn State Teachers Col, Memphis, 35-38; from asst prof to prof English, 38-58, Alumni Found distinguished prof English, 58-68 & comp lit, 68-76, ALUMNI FOUND DISTINGUISHED EMER PROF COMP LIT, UNIV GA, 76- *Concurrent Pos:* Res analyst, US Mil Intel Serv, 42-46; Am Coun Learned Soc fac fel, 51-52; dir comp lit prog, Univ Ga, 62-68, head, Dept Comp Lit, 68-73. *Honors & Awards:* Rhodes Scholar, 29. *Mem:* MLA; Int Comp Lit Asn; Am Comp Lit Asn. *Res:* Musico-literary relationships; 20th century American literature; 19th century European literature. *Publ:* Auth, Music and Literature: A Comparison of the Arts, 48, Repetition in Zola's Novels, 52 & Tones Into Words: Musical Compositions as Subjects of Poetry, 53, Univ Ga; The Color Symphony Before and After Gautier, Comp Lit, 53; gen ed, The Reader's Companion to World Literature, Dryden, 56; auth, Odysseus and Polyphemus: The Name and the Curse, Comp Lit, 66; Sanctuary: From Confrontation to Peaceful Void, Mosaic, 73; A Glossary of Faulkner's South, Yale Univ, 76. *Mailing Add:* 3902 Coqunia Dr Sanibel FL 33957

BROWN, CAROL PAUL, b Tulsa, Okla, Feb 4, 30; m 51; c 4. ROMANCE LANGUAGES. *Educ:* Southwestern Assemblies of God Col, BA, 50; Phillips Univ, BS, 56; Univ Okla, MEd, 57, PhD(Span), 66. *Prof Exp:* Spec instr Span, Univ Okla, 61-63; asst prof Span & French, Kans State Teachers Col, 63-64; acad vpres & prof, Southwestern Assemblies of God Col, 64-67; assoc prof, 67-70, assoc head dept, 67-68, actg dean, Col Arts & Humanities, 81, PROF FOREIGN LANG, WESTERN KY UNIV, 70-, HEAD DEPT, 68- *Mem:* Am Asn Teachers Span & Port. *Res:* Spanish American novel. *Publ:* Auth, Major Themes in the Works of Ramon Rubin, privately pub, 66. *Mailing Add:* Dept of Foreign Lang Western Ky Univ Bowling Green KY 42101

BROWN, CLARENCE FLEETWOOD, JR, b Anderson, SC, May 31, 29; m 56; c 2. COMPARATIVE LITERATURE. *Educ:* Duke Univ, BA, 50; Univ Mich, MA, 55; Harvard Univ, PhD, 62. *Prof Exp:* Instr Russ, 59-60 & 61-62, asst prof, 62-66, from assoc prof to prof Slavic lang & lit, 66-71, PROF COMP LIT, PRINCETON UNIV, 71- *Concurrent Pos:* Mem exec comt, Nat Transl Ctr, Austin, Tex, 67- *Mem:* Am Asn Advan Slavic Studies; Am Asn Teachers Slavic & E Europ Lang; Am Comp Lit Asn; MLA. *Res:* Modernist movements in Russian literature 1890-1920; Osip Mandelstam; translation theory. *Publ:* Auth, The Prose of Osip Mandelstam, Princeton Univ, 65; Into the heart of darkness: Mandelstam's ode to Stalin, Slavic Rev, 67; Nabokov's Pushkin and Nabokov's Nabokov, Wis Studies Studies Contemp Lit, sping 67; The not quite realized transit of Gogol, In: Setchkarev Festschrift, Mouton, The Hague, 73; Mandelstam, Cambridge Univ, 73; co-ed, Selected Poems of Osip Mandelstam, Oxford Univ, 73. *Mailing Add:* Prog in Comp Lit Princeton Univ Princeton NJ 08540

BROWN, EDWARD GUILLEN, JR, b Del Rio, Tex, May 9, 33. ROMANCE LANGUAGES. *Educ:* Whittier Col, BA, 56; Univ Ariz, MA, 66, PhD(French), 68. *Prof Exp:* Teacher French & Span, High Sch, Calif, 59-63; from asst prof to assoc prof French & Span, WTex State Univ, 67-69; asst, 63-66, asst prof, 69-76, assoc dean, col lib arts, 76-80, ASSOC PROF FRENCH, UNIV ARIZ, 76- *Mem:* Am Asn Teachers Fr; Am Asn Teachers Span & Port. *Res:* Twentieth century French theatre; language teaching methodology. *Mailing Add:* Dept of French & Ital Univ of Ariz Tucson AZ 85721

BROWN, EDWARD JAMES, b Chicago, Ill, July 12, 09; m 41; c 1. RUSSIAN LANGUAGE & LITERATURE. *Educ:* Univ Chicago, AB, 33, AM, 46; Columbia Univ, PhD(Slavic), 50. *Prof Exp:* From instr to prof Russ, Brown Univ, 47-65, chmn dept Slavic lang, 60-65; prof & chmn dept, Ind Univ, Bloomington, 65-69; sr fel, Russ Inst, Columbia Univ, 69-70; prof, 70-80, EMER PROF SLAVIC LANG, STANFORD UNIV, 80- *Concurrent Pos:* Howard fel, 55-56. *Mem:* MLA; Am Asn Advan Slavic Studies (pres, 67-70). *Res:* Russian literature; literary criticism; comparative literature. *Publ:* Auth, The Proletarian Episode in Russian Literature, Columbia Univ, 53 & 71; Russian Literature Since the Revolution, Crowell, 63, rev ed, 69; Stankevich and His Moscow Circle, Stanford Univ, 66; ed, Major Soviet Authors: Essays in Criticism, Oxford Univ, 73; auth, Mayakovsky: A Poet in the Revolution, Princeton Univ, 73. *Mailing Add:* Dept of Slavic Lang Stanford Univ Stanford CA 94305

BROWN, EDWIN LOUIS, b Asheville, NC, Apr 6, 29; m 65; c 2. CLASSICS. *Educ:* Haverford Col, BA, 50; Princeton Univ, MA, 57, PhD(classics), 61. *Prof Exp:* Instr Greek, Duke Univ, 58-60; from instr to assoc prof, 61-76, PROF CLASSICS, UNIV NC, CHAPEL HILL, 76- *Mem:* Archaeol Inst Am; Am Philol Asn; Class Asn Mid West & South. *Res:* Greek myth and religion; attic tragedy; ancient didactic and pastoral poetry. *Publ:* Auth, Numeri Vergiliani: Studies in Eclogues and Georgics, Collections Latomus, 63; Achilles and Deidamia on the Portland vase, Am J Archaeol, 72; Cleon caricatured on a Corinthian cup, J Hellenic Studies, 74; The divine name Pan, Trans Am Philol Asn, 78; Antigonus surnamed Gonatas, In: Arktouros, Festschrift for Bernard Knox; The Lycidas of Theocritus' Idyll VII, Harvard Studies Class Philol, 81; The Origin of the Constellation Name Cynosura, Orientalia 50, 81. *Mailing Add:* Dept of Classics Univ of NC Chapel Hill NC 27514

BROWN, FRANCIS ANDREW, b Lewiston, NY, Aug 19, 15; m 41; c 2. GERMAN. *Educ:* Hamilton Col, BS, 37; Cornell Univ, AM, 38; Univ Calif, PhD, 47. *Prof Exp:* Lectr Ger, Univ Mich, 46-47, instr, 47-48; instr, Univ Calif, Los Angeles, 48-49; asst prof, Univ Mich, 49-55; assoc prof foreign lang, 55-61, prof, 61-80, EMER PROF GER, GRINNELL COL, 80- *Concurrent Pos:* US Govt Fulbright res fel Ger & Am Philos Soc res grant, 59-60; grantee & prin investr, Nat Endowment Humanities res fel, 72-73. *Honors & Awards:* Fulbright-Hays Awards, 62-67. *Mem:* MLA; Am Asn Teachers Ger; Lessing Soc; Am Soc 18th Century Studies. *Res:* English-German literary relations in the 18th century; Lessing; German popular journals of the 18th century. *Publ:* Auth, The conversion of Lessing's Freygeist, J English & Ger Philol, 57; Shakespeare and English drama in German popular journals, 1717-1759, Ky Foreign Lang Quart, 1st quart, 65; Sara Sampson: The dilemma of love, In: Lessing Yearbook II, 70; Gotthold Ephraim Lessing, Twayne, 71; auth & contrib, Lessing in Heutiger Sicht, Seneca and Sara: Parallels and problems, Jacobi Verlag, 77; Reason and Emotion in Lessing's Theory of Tragedy, In: Lessing Yearbook, X11/2, 80. *Mailing Add:* Dept of Ger Grinnell Col Grinnell IA 50112

BROWN, FREDERICK, b New York, NY, Dec 23, 34. FOREIGN LANGUAGES. *Educ:* Yale Univ, BA, 56, PhD, 60. *Prof Exp:* Asst instr French, 59-60; from instr to asst prof, Univ Tex, 60-63; asst prof French & gen lit, State Univ NY Binghamton, 63-65; prof off French desk, African-Am Inst, 64-65; from asst prof to assoc prof French, 65-72, PROF FRENCH, STATE UNIV NY STONY BROOK, 72- *Concurrent Pos:* Guggenheim fel, 70-71. *Mem:* MLA. *Res:* Modern French literature. *Publ:* Auth, An essay on surrealism, Tex Quart, fall 62; On Louis Aragon: Silence and history, Southern Rev, spring 67; An Impersonation of Angels: A Biography of Jean Cacteau, Viking, 68; co-transl, The Essays of Paul Valery, Bollingen Ser, Vol XI, Princeton Univ, 70; auth, Pere-Lachaise: Elysium as Real Estate, Viking, 73. *Mailing Add:* Dept of Romance Lang Univ of NY Stony Brook NY 11790

BROWN, FRIEDA STARLING, b Waterbury, Conn, Mar 13, 29. ROMANCE LANGUAGES & LITERATURE. *Educ:* Univ Calif, Los Angeles, AB, 57; Wash Univ, PhD(Romance lang & lit), 62. *Prof Exp:* From instr to asst prof French, Univ Chicago, 62-68; vis assoc prof, Univ Fla, 67-68, assoc prof, 68-70; PROF FRENCH, MICH STATE UNIV, 70- *Concurrent Pos:* Res grants, Univ Chicago, 64-66; fel, Inst Res Humanities, Univ Wis, 65-66. *Mem:* MLA; Renaissance Soc Am; Soc Amis Montaigne; Am Asn Teachers Fr. *Res:* French Renaissance literature; Montaigne and Andre Gide. *Publ:* Auth, Religious and Political Conservatism in the Essays of Montaigne, E Droz, 63; Montaigne and Gide's La Porte Etroite, PMLA, 3/67; Peace and conflict: A new look at Montaigne and Gide, Fr Studies, 1/71; De la solitude: A re-examination of Montaigne's retreat from public life, In: From Marot to Montaigne: Essays on French Renaissance Literature, Ky Romance Quart, 72; ed, French Renaissance studies in honor of Isidore Silver, Ky Romance Quart, 74; auth, Si le chef d'vne place assiegee doit sortir povr parlementer and L'hevre des parlemens dangerevse: Montaigne's political morality and its expression in the early essays, In: O un amy! Essays on Montaigne in Honor of Donald M Frame, Fr Forum, 77. *Mailing Add:* Dept of Romance Lang & Lit Mich State Univ East Lansing MI 48824

BROWN, GEORGE HARDIN, Medieval English, Philology. See Vol II

BROWN, GERARDO, b Havana, Cuba, Oct 3, 16; m 46; c 3. SPANISH, LATIN AMERICAN STUDIES. *Educ:* Univ Havana, PhD(soc sci), 44. *Prof Exp:* Prof sociol & social studies, Escuela Nac Antropologia e Hist, Mex, 48-52; counsel econ, Tribunal Cuentas, 52-55; prof sociol & social studies, Escuela Nac Antropologia e Hist, Mex, 56-57; counsel econ Junta Nac Planiticacion, 57-59; diplomatic counsel, State Dept, Cuba, 59-60; assoc Spanish, Hartwick Col, 62-64; assoc, St Lawrence Univ, 64-65; ASST PROF SPAN, STATE UNIV NY COL CORTLAND, 65- *Concurrent Pos:* Adv soc sci, UNESCO Round Table, Costa Rica, 54. *Mem:* Latin Am Studies Asn; MLA. *Res:* Social and economic history, Cuba and Mexico; Latin American essay. *Publ:* Auth, Sociology in Brazil, Soc Sci in Mex, 5/47; Estudios de abad y queypo, SEP, Mex, 48; Cuba colonial, J Montero, Havana, 52; Introduccion al ensayo Hispano Americano, Las Americas, 68; several articles, In: Trimestre Economico, Mex & Rev Univ Habana. *Mailing Add:* Dept of Foreign Lang State Univ of NY Col Cortland NY 13045

BROWN, H DOUGLAS, b Tondo, Zaire, July 26, 41; US citizen; m 63; c 2. LINGUISTICS. *Educ:* Linfield Col, BA, 63; Univ Calif, Los Angeles, MA, 68, PhD(educ psychol), 70. *Prof Exp:* Asst prof ling, Univ Mich, Ann Arbor, 70-74, assoc prof, 74-78; assoc prof, 79-82, PROF ENGLISH AS A SECOND LANG, UNIV ILL, URBANA, 82-, DIR DIV, 79- *Concurrent Pos:* Ed, Lang Learning, 70-79; vis assoc prof English second lang, Univ Hawaii, 82. *Mem:* Teachers English to Speakers Other Lang; Nat Asn Foreign Student Affairs. *Res:* Second language acquisition; psycholinguistics; English as a second language. *Publ:* Auth, Children's comprehension of relativized English sentences, Child Develop, 12/71; Cognitive pruning and second language acquisition, Mod Lang J, 4/72; The psychological reality of grammar in the ESL classroom, TESOL Quart, 9/72; Papers in second language acquisition, Lang Learning, 76; A Survey of Applied Linguistics, Univ Mich, 76; Principles of Language Learning and Teaching, Prentice-Hall, 80. *Mailing Add:* Div of ESL Univ of Ill Urbana IL 61801

BROWN, HARCOURT, b Toronto, Ont, May 30, 00; m 27; c 1. FRENCH LITERATURE. *Educ:* Univ Toronto, BA, 25, MA, 26; Columbia Univ, PhD(French lit), 34. *Prof Exp:* Lectr French lang & lit, Queen's Univ, Ont, 26-29; tutor French, Brooklyn Col, 30-31; instr, Univ Rochester, 31-32; Am Coun Learned Soc traveling fel, 34-35; prof French, Wash Univ, 35-37; prof, 37-69, EMER PROF FRENCH LANG & LIT, BROWN UNIV, 69- *Concurrent Pos:* Assoc ed, Ann Sci, 36-74. *Mem:* Hist Sci Soc (vpres, 49; pres, 50-52); MLA; Mod Humanities Res Asn, Gt Brit. *Res:* Relations of literature and science; Maupertuis; Lapland expedition of 1736-1737. *Publ:* Auth, Scientific Organizations in Seventeenth Century France, Russell, 67; The composition of the letters concerning the English nation, In: The Age of the Enlightenment, St Andrews Univ, 67; ed, Science and the Creative Spirit, Univ Toronto, 71; auth, Science and the Human Comedy, Univ Toronto, 76; Scientists in wilderness, Virtanen festschrift, Univ Nebr, 78; Collecting Voltaire, Univ Toronto, 80; ed, The Army's Mister Brown, Olympic, 82. *Mailing Add:* 14 Ave Rd Parry Sound ON P2A 2A7 Can

BROWN, JACK DAVIS, b Memphis, Tenn, Dec 26, 41; m 65; c 2. FRENCH, ROMANCE PHILOLOGY. *Educ:* Southwestern at Memphis, BA, 63; Univ Miss, MA, 66; Univ NC, Chapel Hill, PhD(Romance philol), 71. *Prof Exp:* Instr French, Univ Miss, 65-69; instr, Univ NC, Chapel Hill, 69-71; asst prof, 71-73, ASSOC PROF FRENCH, UNIV MISS, 73-, ACTG CHMN DEPT MOD LANG, 80- *Mem:* Am Asn Teachers Fr; Southern Conf Lang Teaching; Am Coun Teachers Foreign Lang. *Res:* The medieval French lai, old French pholology, effective teaching methods. *Publ:* Auth, Hans Carvel's ring: Elements, literary tradition, Rabelais's source, Romance Notes, 72; Old French estre: A new meaning, Romance Notes, 73; 1975 textbooks for French civilization, ERIC Reports, 76; Georges Franck, Francesco Cavalli and his operas, Opera J, 77; co-ed, Robert W Linker, A Bibliography of Old French Lyrics, Romance Monographs, 79. *Mailing Add:* Dept of Mod Lang Univ of Miss University MS 38677

BROWN, JAMES LORIN, b Hanford, Calif, Sept 26, 20. FRENCH. *Educ:* Univ Calif, Berkeley, PhD, 52. *Prof Exp:* From asst prof to assoc prof, 63-73, PROF FRENCH, CALIF STATE UNIV, CHICO, 73- *Publ:* Auth, Reference to Cunegonde in 1756, Mod Lang Notes, 11/53; Note sur Pataques, 9/54 & Contribution a L'histoire du nom parade, 4/59, Fr Mod. *Mailing Add:* Dept of Foreign Lang Calif State Univ First & Normal St Chico CA 95926

BROWN, JAMES W, b Anderson, Ind, Aug 28, 34; m 57; c 3. SPANISH. *Educ:* Ind Univ, BS, 56, MA, 61, PhD(Span), 67. *Prof Exp:* Teacher, High Sch, Fla, 58-60; asst prof, 64-67, assoc prof, 68-71, PROF SPAN, BALL STATE UNIV, 71- *Concurrent Pos:* Vis asst prof & resident dir, Ind Univ Jr Year in Peru, 67. *Mem:* MLA; Am Coun Teaching Foreign Lang; Am Asn Teachers Span & Port. *Res:* Spanish American novel; foreign language teaching methods and curriculum design. *Publ:* Ed, Tomochic, Porrua, Mexico City, 68; auth, El hermano asno from Fioretti through Freud, Symposium, winter 71; coauth, A testing of the audio active voice reflector in the foreign language classroom, Mod Lang J, 3/72; Gazapo: Modelo para Armar, Nueva Narrativa Hispanoam, 9/73; auth, Expatriate syndrome: Mario Vargas Llosa on Peruvian racism, Essays Lit, spring 76; Heriberto Frias, Twayne, 78; And the Revolution Began, Romance Literary Studies: Homage to Harvey L Johnson, 79; Vargas Llosa's Recent Novels and Expatriate Syndrome, In: Requiem For the Boom, Montclair Symposium Proceedings, 80. *Mailing Add:* Dept of Foreign Lang Ball State Univ Muncie IN 47306

BROWN, JAMES W, b Neptune, NJ, March 10, 42; c 2. ROMANCE LANGUAGES, SEMIOTICS. *Educ:* Univ Miami, AB, 64; Middlebury Col, MA, 65; Univ Pa, PhD(Fr) 73. *Prof Exp:* Instr Fr, The Peddie Sch, 65-68; instr, Radnor Sr High Sch, Pa, 68-69; teaching fel, Univ Pa, 69-72; ASSOC PROF FRENCH, DALHOUSIE UNIV, HALIFAX, 72- *Concurrent Pos:* Assoc ed, Dalhousie Fr Studies, 79- *Mem:* Am Asn Teachers Fr; Can Asn Univ Professors; Can Soc Res Semiotics; Semiotic Soc Am. *Res:* Nineteenth century French literature; semiotics and poetics; second language pedagogy. *Publ:* Auth, Style in Rousseau's contrat social, Ky Romance Quart, 76; Comics in the foreign language classroom: Pedagogical perspectives, For Lang Ann, 77; The ideological and aesthofic functions of food in Paul et Virginie, Eighteenth Century Life, 78; On the use of visual and graphic codes in the production of verbal utterances, Can Mod Lang Rev, 78 & 80; Le Dormeur du val: A cinematic reading, Poetics & Theory of Lit, 79; The Power of the Word in Marie Claire d'Orbaix's Erosion du Silence, In: The Language of Poetry: Crisis and Solution, Rodopoi Amsterdam, 80; Fictional meals and their function in the French novel 1789-1848, Univ Toronto Press (in prep). *Mailing Add:* Dept of French Dalhousie Univ Halifax NS B3H 3J5 Can

BROWN, JANE KURSHAN, b Huntington, NY, Oct 20, 43. COMPARATIVE LITERATURE. *Educ:* Harvard Univ, AB, 65; Yale Univ, MPhil, 69, PhD(Ger), 71. *Prof Exp:* Asst prof, Univ NH, 71-72 & Mt Holyoke Col, 73-77; assoc prof Ger, Univ Va, 77-81; ASSOC PROF ENGLISH, UNIV COLO, 81- *Concurrent Pos:* Vis assoc prof English, Univ Colo, 79-81. *Mem:* MLA; Am Asn Advanc Humanities; Goethe Soc NAm; Annette von Droste, Gesellschaft. *Res:* Goethe; 18th and 19th century novel; nineteenth century poetry. *Publ:* Auth, Goethe's Cyclical Narratives, Univ NC, 75; Die Wahlverwandtschaften and the English novel of manners, Comp Lit, 76; The real mystery in the Judenbuche, MLR, 78; The tyranny of the ideal: The dialectics of art in Goethe's Novelle, Studies in Romanticism, 80; Schiller und die Ironie von Hermann und Dorothea, In: Goethczeit, Festschrift für Stuart Atkins, 81. *Mailing Add:* Dept of English Univ of Colo Boulder CO 80309

BROWN, JOHN LACKEY, b Ilion, NY, Apr 29, 14; m 41; c 2. COMPARATIVE LITERATURE, FRENCH. *Educ:* Hamilton Col, BA, 35; Cath Univ Am, MA, 36, PhD(French, Medieval Latin), 39. *Prof Exp:* Asst prof French, Cath Univ Am, 39-42; asst chief publ sect, Off War Info, 42-43; correspondent Sunday ed, NY Times, Paris, 45-48; cult attache, US Embassies, Paris, Brussels, Rome, Mexico City, 48-68; PROF COMP LIT, CATH UNIV AM, 68- *Concurrent Pos:* Mem, Cath Comn on Intellectual & Cult Affairs, 60-; fel, Ctr Advan Studies, Wesleyan Univ, 62-63; vis prof French & English, Univ Louisville, 66-67; prof Am lit & civilization, Inst Anglo-Am Studies, Nat Univ Mex, 66-68; lectr, Cath Inst Paris, 69, Univs Laval, McGill, Montreal & Toronto, 70; dir gen Am Bicentennial Exposition in Paris and Warsaw, 75; vpres, Int Asn Lit Critics, 73-; sr Fulbright prof Am Lit, Univ Lisbon, 79-80. *Honors & Awards:* Newstadt Prize, 82. *Mem:* MLA; Am Studies Asn; Am Comp Lit Asn; Mediaeval Acad Am; Dante Soc. *Res:* European, especially Franco, American literary relations in the 19th and 20th centuries; Europe avantgarde movements of the 20th century; the problem of expatriation in American literature. *Publ:* Auth, The Methodus of Jean Bodin: A Critical Study, Cath Univ Am, 39; contribr, chap on France, In: Public Opinion and Foreign Policy, Harper, 49; auth, Panorama de la Litterature Contemporaine Aux Etats-Unis, 54 & 2nd ed, 72, Hemingway, 61, Gallimard, Paris, Il Gigantesco Teatro, Opera Nuove, Rome, 63; Dialogos Transatlanticos, Limusa Wiley, Mexico, 66; Valery Larbaud, Twayne, 81; Verse Shards, Proteus, 82. *Mailing Add:* 3024 Tilden St NW Washington DC 20008

BROWN, JOHN MADISON, b Long Beach, Calif, Apr 28, 34; m 64; c 3. GERMAN. *Educ:* Yale Univ, AB, 56; Johns Hopkins Univ, MA, 63, PhD(Ger), 69. *Prof Exp:* Exchange asst English, Robert Koch Schule, Berlin, 60-61; teaching asst Ger, Johns Hopkins Univ, 62-66; from instr to asst prof, Bucknell Univ, 66-70; asst prof, Washington Univ, St Louis, 70-75; asst prof,

75-77, ASSOC PROF GER, VA MILITARY INST, 77- *Mem:* Am Teachers Ger; MLA; SAtlantic Mod Lang Asn; Am Asn Univ Prof. *Res:* German literature; German culture; American-German intellectual relations. *Publ:* Auth, Toward a perspective for the Indian element in Hermann Hesse's Siddhartha, Ger Quart, 3/76; Thomas Jefferson and things German-preliminary findings, Report, 78. *Mailing Add:* Dept of Mod Lang Va Millitary Inst Lexington VA 24450

BROWN, MARICE COLLINS, b Moselle, Miss, May 16, 15; m 38; c 2. LINGUISTICS, ENGLISH. *Educ:* Miss State Col Women BA, 37; Univ Southern Miss, MA, 56; La State Univ, PhD(ling), 68. *Prof Exp:* Instr English & speech, Jones Jr Col, 54-62; from asst prof to assoc prof, 62-72, prof & chmn dept, 72-80, EMER PROF ENGLISH & SPEECH, UNIV SOUTHERN MISS, 80- *Concurrent Pos:* Co-ed, Miss Folklore Register. *Res:* Analysis of the Choctaw language of the Indians of East Central Mississippi. *Publ:* Co-ed & contribr, Frost: Centennial Essays; auth, A re-examination of the Middle Ground, English J, 3/61; The educated man and his language, Word Studies, 10/64; Notes on classical and Renaissance analogues of Mississippi Negro folklore, Miss Folklore Register, summer 68. *Mailing Add:* Dept of English Univ of Southern Miss Hattiesburg MS 39401

BROWN, NORMAN OLIVER, b El Oro, Mex, Sept 25, 13. CLASSICAL PHILOLOGY, HISTORY. *Educ:* Oxford Univ, BA, 36; Univ Wis, PhD, 42. *Prof Exp:* Prof lang, Nebr Wesleyan Univ, 42-43; from asst prof to assoc prof classics, Wesleyan Univ, 45; prof classics & comp lit, Univ Rochester to 71; PROF HUMANITIES, COWELL COL, UNIV CALIF, SANTA CRUZ, 71- *Mem:* Am Philol Asn; Class Asn New Eng. *Res:* Mythology; Hermes. *Mailing Add:* Dept of Humanities Cowell Col Univ of Calif Santa Cruz CA 95060

BROWN, ROYAL SCOTT, b Raleigh, NC, June 20, 40; m 64; c 2. CONTEMPORARY FRENCH LITERATURE. *Educ:* Pa State Univ, BA, 62; Middlebury Col, MA, 63; Columbia Univ, PhD(French), 75. *Prof Exp:* Grad assoc French, Ind Univ, 63-64; lectr romance lang, Queens Col, 64-70; dir, City Univ NY, Prog Study Abroad, Nancy, France, 70-72; lectr, 72-75, asst prof, 75-81, ASSOC PROF ROMANCE LANG, QUEENS COL, 82- *Concurrent Pos:* vis assoc prof, NY Univ, summers 81 & 82. *Mem:* MLA. *Res:* Interdisciplinary studies; cinema; contemporary French literature. *Publ:* Ed, Focus on Godard, Prentice Hall, 72; An interview with Shostakovich, High Fidelity, 10/73; Considering DePalma, Am Film, 7-8/77; Auric speaks of then and now, NY Times, 6/78; Hitchcock's Spellbound: Jung versus Freud, winter/spring 80 & Dressed to kill: Myth and male fantasy in the horror suspense genre, summer/fall 80, Film/Psychol Rev; Music and Vivre sa vie, Quart Rev Film Studies, summer 80. *Mailing Add:* Dept of Romance Lang Queens Col NY Flushing NY 11367

BROWN, RUSSELL E, b New York, NY, Feb 7, 30. GERMAN LITERATURE. *Educ:* Rutgers Univ, BA, 51; Columbia Univ, MA, 59; Harvard Univ, PhD, 62. *Prof Exp:* Instr Ger, Yale Univ, 61-64; asst prof, 64-71, chmn dept, 66-76, ASSOC PROF GER, STATE UNIV NY STONY BROOK, 71- *Mem:* MLA; Am Asn Teachers Ger; Am Comp Lit Asn. *Res:* Modern German and Scandinavian literature. *Publ:* Auth, On Classifying the Setting of the Novel, Neophilologus, 67; Attribute Pairs in the Poetry of Georg Trakl, Mod Lang Notes, 67. *Mailing Add:* Dept Ger State Univ NY Stony Brook NY 11790

BROWN, SYLVIA GRACE, Ware, Mass, Nov 1, 46. CLASSICS. *Educ:* Vassar Col, BA, 68; Univ Mich, Ann Arbor, MA, 69, PhD(class studies), 72. *Prof Exp:* Instr Greek, Vassar Col, 70; asst prof Greek & Latin, Wellesley Col, 72-78; ADJ ASST PROF CLASS STUDIES, UNIV PA, 78- *Concurrent Pos:* Mary Isabel Sibley fel, Phi Beta Kappa, 75-76; fel, Radcliffe Inst, 75-76. *Mem:* AAUP; Am Philol Asn. *Res:* Greek drama; metrics; linguistics. *Mailing Add:* Dept of Class Studies Williams Hall Univ of Pa Philadelphia PA 17174

BROWN, THOMAS HAROLD, b Copperton, Utah, July 23, 30; m 55; c 6. FRENCH LITERATURE, FOREIGN LANGUAGE METHODOLOGY. *Educ:* Brigham Young Univ, BA, 55; Univ Ill, MA, 57, PhD(French), 60. *Prof Exp:* Teaching asst French, Univ Ill, 55-60; teaching asst, 54-55, from asst prof to assoc prof, 60-63, chmn French sect, Dept Lang, 61-63 & 66-67, dir lang lab, 64-65, PROF FRENCH, BRIGHAM YOUNG UNIV, 67-, CHMN DEPT FRENCH & ITAL, 67-69 & 77- *Concurrent Pos:* Fulbright lectr, Univ La, 65-66; mission pres, Church of Jesus Christ of Latter-day Saints, France & Belg, 69-72; mem, Col Entrance Exam Bd, 72- *Mem:* MLA; Rocky Mt Mod Lang Asn; Am Asn Teachers Fr. *Res:* Seventeenth century French literature; teaching English as a foreign language. *Publ:* Auth, French: Listening, Speaking, Reading, Writing, 65 & 71, Writing Exercises for French, 65 & 71, Langue et Litterature, 67 & 74 & Cahier d'Exercices: Langue et Litterature, 67 & 74, McGraw; La Fontaine and Cupid and Psyche Tradition, Merrill Monogr Ser, Brigham Young Univ, 68; coauth, Conversational English, Blaisdell, 69; Themes et Discussions, D C Heath, 82. *Mailing Add:* 1635 N 1550 East Provo UT 84601

BROWN, VIRGINIA, b Vicksburg, Miss. CLASSICS, MEDIEVAL LATIN. *Educ:* Manhattanville Col, AB, 62; Univ NC, Chapel Hill, MA, 64; Scuola Vaticana di Paleografia e Diplomatica, Vatican City, Arch Pal, 68; Harvard Univ, PhD(classics), 69. *Prof Exp:* Lectr, Newton Col of the Sacred Heart, 65-66; res asst paleography, Inst Advan Studies, 68-70; asst prof medieval Latin, Pontifical Inst Mediaeval Studies, Toronto, 70-75; PROF CLASSICS & MEDIAEVAL STUDIES, UNIV TORONTO, 76- *Concurrent Pos:* Pontifical Inst Mediaeval Studies sr fel, 74-; ed, Mediaeval Studies, 74-; Guggenheim Found fel, 75; fel, Harvard Ctr Ital Renaissance Studies, Florence, 75; exec comt, Catalogus Translationum et Commentariorum, 76-; coun, Mediaeval Acad Am, 76-79 & Renaissance Soc Am, 78-81. *Mem:* Mediaeval Acad Am; Renaissance Soc Am; Can Class Asn; Virgilian Soc. *Res:* Editing of Latin texts; Latin paleography; translations of medieval Greek commentators; Beneventan MSS. *Publ:* Auth, The Textual Transmission of Caesar's Civil War, Brill, Leiden, 72; Giovanni Argiropulo on the Agent Intellect, In: Essays in Honour of Anton Charles Pegis, Toronto, 74; Gaius Julius Caesar & Lucius Junius Moderatus Columella, In: Catalogus translationum commentariorum, Vol III, Cath Univ Am, 76; A Second New List of Beneventan Manuscripts, Mediaeval Studies, 40: 239-89; Latin Manuscripts of Caesar's Gallic War, In: Palaeographica, Diplomatica et Archivistica Studies in onore di Giulio Battelli, Vol I, 79; ed, E A Loew, The Beneventan Script, 2nd ed (2 vols), Edizioni di Storia e Letteratura, Rome, 80; auth, The Survival of Beneventan Script: Sixteenth-Century Liturgical Copdices from Benedictine Monasteries in Naples, In: Scritti Raccolti in Memoria del XV Centenario della Nascita di S Benedetto, Vol I, Montecassino, 81. *Mailing Add:* Pontifical Inst Mediaeval Studies 59 Queen's Park Crescent E Toronto ON M5S 2C4 Can

BROWNE, GERALD MICHAEL, b Detroit, Mich, Dec 13, 43; m 75. CLASSICS, LINGUISTICS. *Educ:* Univ Mich, AB, 65, AM, 66, PhD(classics), 68. *Prof Exp:* Instr classics, Harvard Univ, 68-69, lectr, 69-70, asst prof, 70-73; asst prof, 74-75, assoc prof, 75-79, PROF CLASSIC, UNIV ILL, URBANA, 80- *Concurrent Pos:* Ctr Hellenic Studies jr fel, classics, 73-74; ed, Bull Am Soc Papyrologists, 74- *Mem:* Am Philol Asn; Am Soc Papyrologists (vpres, 73-75). *Res:* Papyrology; coptology; Old Nubian studies. *Publ:* Auth, Documentary Papyri from the Michigan Collection, Hakkert, 68; coauth, The Oxyrhynchus Papyri, Vol 38, 71, Vol 41, 72, Vol 47, 80, British Acad; auth, The Papyri of the Sortes Astrampsychi, Anton Hain, Ger, 74; Michigan Papyri (P Mich XII), Hakkert, 75; Michigan Coptic Texts, Barcelona, 79; coauth, Nag Hammadi Codies: Greek and Coptic Papyri from the Cartonnage of the Covers, Leiden, 81; Griffith's Old Nubian Lectionary, 82; Chrysostomus Nubianus: An old Nubian version of Ps-Chrysostom, In venerabilem crucem sermo (in prep), Rome/Barcelona. *Mailing Add:* Dept of Classics Univ of Ill Urbana IL 61801

BROWNE, MAUREEN, b Louisville, Ky, Dec 28, 21. FOREIGN LANGUAGES. *Educ:* Nazareth Col, Ky, AB, 54; Fordham Univ, MA & PhD, 58. *Prof Exp:* Fulbright scholar, Univ Paris, 58-59; PROF ROMANCE LANG & CHMN DEPT, BRESCIA COL, KY, 59- *Concurrent Pos:* Col consult, Foreign Lang Asn of Archdiocese of Louisville, 63-64. *Mem:* Am Asn Teachers Fr; Am Asn Teachers Span & Port. *Res:* Medieval French literature; history of the 14th century as seen in the work of Eustache Deschamps. *Mailing Add:* Dept of Mod Lang Brescia Col Owensboro KY 42301

BROWNING, BARTON W, b Springfield, Ill, Aug 22, 40; m 64; c 2. GERMAN LITERATURE. *Educ:* Wesleyan Univ, BA, 62; Univ Calif, Berkeley, MA, 65, PhD(Ger), 70. *Prof Exp:* Asst prof, 69-76, ASSOC PROF GER, PA STATE UNIV, UNIVERSITY PARK, 76- *Mem:* Am Asn Teachers Ger; MLA; Am Soc Ger Lit 16th & 17th Centuries; Int Arbeitskreis Deutsche Barock-Lit; fel, Herzog August Bibliot Wolfenbüttel. *Res:* German Baroque literature; 19th century German literature; European Renaissance and Baroque literature. *Publ:* Auth, Stifter's Nachsommer and the fourth commandment, Colloquia Germanica, 73; Cooper's influence on Stifter: Fact or scholarly fiction?, Mod Lang Notes, 74; Ein Kleiner Hofmannswaldau fund in Pennsylvanien, Wolfenbüttler Barock-Nachrichten, 75; Joseph Roth's Lengende vom heiligen Trinker: Essence and Elirir, Protest-Form-Tradition, 79. *Mailing Add:* Dept of Ger Pa State Univ University Park PA 16802

BROWNING, ROBERT MARCELLUS, b Centerville, Kans, Apr 1, 11; m 40. GERMAN LITERATURE. *Educ:* William Jewell Col, AB, 37; Princeton Univ, PhD, 48. *Prof Exp:* Instr mod lang, Princeton Univ, 39-41 & 46-49; instr Ger, Wake Forest Col, 41-43; from asst prof to assoc prof, 49-60, prof, 60-79, EMER PROF GER, HAMILTON COL, 79- *Concurrent Pos:* Pub officer, inform Control Div, Mil Govt, Ger, 45-46; vis lectr, Ger Acad Year Inst, Univ Colo, 62-63; bk rev ed, Ger Quart, 63-65, ed, 65-67; Nat Endowment Humanities sr fel, 74-75; vis prof Ger, Colgate Univ, 76-77; ed, The German Library. *Mem:* MLA; Am Asn Teachers Ger; Goethe Soc Am. *Res:* German drama; lyric and novelle; studies on Theodor Storm, Goethe, Mörike, Friedrich Spee, Kleist and Grillparzev. *Publ:* Auth, German Poetry: A Critical Anthology, Appleton, 62; Umgang mit Gedichten, McGraw, 69; German Baroque Poetry: 1618-1723, 71, & German Poetry in the Age of the Enlightenment, 78, Pa State Univ; co-ed, The German Library (4 vols); Translation of Keller, Goethe, Kleist, Brantano, and Chamisgo, In: The German Library, Continuum, 82. *Mailing Add:* 9 Griffin Rd Clinton NY 13323

BRUCE, IAIN ANTHONY FYVIE, b Edinburgh, Scotland, June 1, 37; m 60; c 2. CLASSICAL LANGUAGES, ANCIENT HISTORY. *Educ:* Cambridge Univ, BA, 58, MA, 62; Univ Sheffield, dipl educ, 59, PhD(ancient hist), 63. *Prof Exp:* Asst master, Worthing High Sch, Eng, 59-63; from asst prof to assoc prof, 63-73, PROF CLASSICS, MEM UNIV NFLD, 74-, DEAN ARTS, 74- *Mem:* Class Asn Can; Soc Promotion Hellenic Studies. *Res:* Greek history and historiography. *Publ:* Auth, The Democratic Revolution at Rhodes, Class Quart, 61; Historical Commentary on the Hellenica Oxyrhynchia, Cambridge Univ, 67; Theopompus and Greek historiography, Hist & Theory, 70; The Corcyraean Civil War, Phoenix, 71. *Mailing Add:* Fac of Arts Mem Univ of Nfld St John's NF A1B 3X9 Can

BRUCE, JAMES CHARLES, b Washington, DC, July 15, 29; m 56; c 2. GERMAN. *Educ:* Howard Univ, AB, 52, MA, 56; Univ Chicago, PhD(Ger), 63. *Prof Exp:* Instr Ger, SC State Col, 56-57; from instr to asst prof, 61-69, ASSOC PROF GER, UNIV CHICAGO, 69- *Mem:* MLA; Am Asn Teachers Ger. *Res:* Literary criticism; modern German literature. *Publ:* Auth, The equivocating narrator in Günter Grass's Katz und Maus, Monatshefte, summer 66; The motif of failure and the act of narrating in Günter Grass's Örtlich betäubt, Mod Fiction Studies, spring 71. *Mailing Add:* 916 E 55th St Chicago IL 60615

BRUCE, NOVOA JOHN DAVID, b San Jose, Costa Rica, June 20, 44; US citizen; m 69; c 1. MEXICAN & CHICANO LITERATURE. *Educ:* Regis Col, Colo, BA, 66; Univ Colo, Boulder, MA, 68, PhD(Span & Mex lit), 74. *Prof Exp:* Instr Span, Univ Colo, Denver, 72-74; ASST PROF SPAN, YALE UNIV, 74- *Concurrent Pos:* Mex prose annotator, Mex fiction, Libr Cong, Handbook Latin Am Studies, 77- *Mem:* MLA; Am Asn Teachers Span &

Port; Popular Cult Asn. *Res:* Contemporary Mexican novel; Chicano literature; eroticism. *Publ:* Auth, Mexico en la literatura chicana, Revista, 1/75; Tiempoovillo: Paraguayan experimental theatre, Latin Am Theatre Rev, spring 75; The space of Chicano literature, De Colores, 75; The encounters of Juan Garcia Ponce, Latin Am Lit Rev, spring-summer 75; La voz del silencio: Miguel Mendex, Dialogos, 5-6/76; Appendix to Entry Into Matter by Juan Garcia Ponce: Juan Garcia Ponce in contex, Appl Lit, 76; Pocho as literature, Aztlan, spring 76; Eroticism in the contemporary Mexican novel In: Studies in Romance Languages and Literatures, Coronado, spring 78. *Mailing Add:* Dept of Span & Port Yale Univ New Haven CT 06520

BRUECKNER, HANS-DIETER, b Berlin, Ger, Nov 22, 28; US citizen; m 54. GERMAN. *Educ:* Univ Calif, Berkeley, BA, 55, MA, 57, PhD, 61. *Prof Exp:* Teaching asst Ger, Univ Calif, Berkeley, 56-60; lectr, Harvard Univ, 60-62; from asst prof to assoc prof, 62-74, chmn dept mod Europ lang & lit, 71-74, PROF GER, POMONA COL, 74- *Mem:* MLA; Am Asn Teachers Ger; Philol Asn Pac Coast. *Res:* Nineteenth century German realism; 19th and 20th century German poetry. *Publ:* Auth, Der Bürger im Prosawerk C F Meyers, Seminar, 1/65; Heldengestaltung im Prosawerk Conrad Ferdinand Meyers, Lang & Cie, Berne, 70. *Mailing Add:* Dept of Mod Lang & Lit Pomona Col Claremont CA 91711

BRUGMANS, LINETTE F, b Lille, France, Aug 15, 08; US citizen; m 53. ROMANCE LANGUAGES. *Educ:* Rutgers Univ, MA, 45; NY Univ, PhD(French), 55. *Prof Exp:* Instr French, NJ Col Women, Rutgers Univ, 42-45 & Sacred Heart Convent, 45-47; asst, NY Univ, 47-50; instr, Barnard Col, Columbia Univ, 50-57; from instr to asst prof, Queens Col, NY, 57-64; from assoc prof to prof, 64-75, EMER PROF FRENCH, STATE UNIV NY STONY BROOK, 75- *Concurrent Pos:* Am Philos Soc grant, 57. *Honors & Awards:* Ordre de Palmes Acad, 65. *Mem:* MLA ; Am Asn Teachers Fr; Asn Amis d'Andre Gide; Proust Res Asn; Am Asn Univ Women. *Res:* Correspondence of Andre Gide with English writers; modern French poetry; Waldo Frank and his French correspondants. *Publ:* Auth, The Correspondence of Andre Gide and Edmund Gosse, NY Univ, 59 & Peter Owens, London, 60; Correspondence Andre Gide-A Bennett, Droz, Geneva, 64; Andre Gide and Waldo Frank: Correspondence (1922-1940), Bull Amis d'Andre Gide, 1/77. *Mailing Add:* 40 William Penn Dr Stony Brook NY 11790

BRUHN, GERT ERNST, b Brieskow, Ger, Apr 25, 34; m 57; c 4. GERMAN LANGUAGE & LITERATURE. *Educ:* Univ BC, BA, 60; Princeton Univ MA, 62, PhD(Ger), 66. *Prof Exp:* Teaching fel Ger, Princeton, 61-63; instr, Dartmouth Col, 63-66, asst prof, 66-68; ASST PROF GER, BOSTON COL, 68- *Mem:* MLA; Am Asn Teachers Ger; Goethe Soc New Eng; Thomas Mann Ges. *Res:* Nineteenth and twentieth century German literature; Thomas Mann; Anglo-German literary relations. *Mailing Add:* Dept of Germanic Studies Boston Col Chestnut Hill MA 02167

BRUHN, JOACHIM, b Kiel, Ger, Aug 28, 27; US citizen; m 59; c 4. GERMANIC LANGUAGES & LITERATURE. *Educ:* Univ Kiel, dipl, 49, DPhil & Staatsexamen, 53; Cambridge Univ, dipl, 51. *Prof Exp:* Asst instr Ger, Brown Univ, 56-57; from instr to asst prof Univ Mich, 59-65; vis assoc prof, Duke Univ, 65-66; prof Ger & head dept foreign lang, Va Polytech Inst & State Univ, 66-70; prof Ger & humanities & dean studies, Richmond Col, City Univ New York, 70-74; dean, Col Arts, Sci & Lett, 74-79, PROF GER & HUMANITIES, UNIV MICH-DEARBORN, 74-, DIR, HONORS PROG, 79- *Concurrent Pos:* Mem, Mich State Comt Foreign Lang Instr, 62-65; Univ Mich fac res grant, 63-64 & 80-81; mem, Va State Comt Foreign Lang Instr, 66-70; fel, Inst Higher Educ, Claremont Grad Sch & Univ Ctr, 69-70. *Mem:* MLA; Ling Soc Am; Am Asn Teachers Ger; Int Brecht Soc; AAUP. *Res:* Seventeenth century German literature; German cultural history; the German Democratic Republic. *Publ:* Auth, More freedom for superior students through honors in German at Michigan, Superior Student, 11-12/62; Modern language programs for superior students, Foreign Lang Courier, 1/63; The transition of the Participle ending from -ind(e), to -ing(e), Norsk Tidsskrift Sprogvidenskap, 64; New developments in masters programs, Proc Midwestern Asn Grad Schs, 78. *Mailing Add:* Col of Arts Sci & Lett Univ of Mich Dearborn MI 48128

BRUMFIELD, WILLIAM CRAFT, b Charlotte, NC, June 28, 44. RUSSIAN LITERATURE & ART HISTORY. *Educ:* Tulane Univ, BA, 66; Univ Calif, Berkeley, MA, 68, PhD(Slavic lang), 73. *Prof Exp:* Vis lectr Russ lit, Univ Wis-Madison, 73-74; asst prof Russ lit, Harvard Univ, 74-79; ASST PROF RUSS LIT, TULANE UNIV, 81- *Concurrent Pos:* Res dir, ACTR Moscow, 79-80. *Mem:* Am Asn Advan Slavic Studies; Am Asn Teachers Slavic East Europ Lang; MLA. *Res:* Ideology in the Russian novel of the 1860's; Dostoevsky and the French Enlightenment; Russian architectural history. *Publ:* Auth, Sleptsov redvius, Calif Slavic Studies, 76; Bazarov and Rjazanov: The romantic archetype in Russian nihilism, Slavic East Europ J, winter 77; Petersburg: the imperial design, 11/78, Harvard Mag; Therese philosophe and Dostoevsky's Great Sinner, Comp Lit, summer 80; Ukrainian Churches: Kiev and Chernihiv, Harvard Ukrainian Fund, 81; The Soviet Union: Post-war architecture and planning, Bull Atomic Scientists, 3/82. *Mailing Add:* Dept of Ger & Slavic Lang Tulane Univ New Orleans LA 70118

BRUNEAU, MARIE-FLORINE, b Casablanca, Morocco; Fr citizen. FRENCH LITERATURE. *Educ:* Univ Calif, Berkeley, BA, 73, MA, 75, PhD(Fr lit), 80; Univ Bordeaux, Maitrise, 76. *Prof Exp:* ASST PROF FRENCH LIT, UNIV SOUTHERN CALIF, 80- *Mem:* MLA; Am Asn Teachers Fr; NAm Soc 17th Century Fr Lit; Soc d'etudes du 17 siecle. *Res:* French 17th century literature; women writers; psycho analysis literary theory. *Publ:* Auth, Rhetorique Baroque dans Pyrame et Thisbe de Theophile de vian, 81 & Mysticrome et folie ou l'experience de Jeanne Gwyn, 82, Papers Fr 17th Century Lit. *Mailing Add:* Fr & Ital Dept Univ of Southern Calif Los Angeles CA 90007

BRUNER, CHARLOTTE HUGHES, b Urbana, Ill, May 8, 17; m 39; c 2. FRENCH, COMPARATIVE LITERATURE. *Educ:* Univ Ill, BA, 38; Columbia Univ, MA, 39. *Prof Exp:* Instr English, Mod lang & libr, 42-55, from instr to asst prof, 55-75, assoc prof, 75-79, PROF FRENCH, IOWA STATE UNIV, 80- *Concurrent Pos:* Instr English, Univ Ill, 44-45; fac improvement leave, Iowa State Univ, 73-74. *Mem:* African Lit Asn; Am Asn Teachers Fr. *Res:* Negritude Movement; African literature (Maghreb) and South Saharan; Caribbean literature. *Publ:* Auth, Black French Literature in the Classroom, Fr Rev, 10/72; Make Sure of All Things and Hold Fast to What is Fine, Africa Report, 9-10/73; If It Be Not Sweet, Some You May Take As True..., Iowa State J Res, 11/76; The Meaning of Caliban in Black Literature Today, Comp Lit Studies, 9/76; Been-To or Has-Been: A Dilemma for Today's African Woman, Ba Shiru, 77; Bessie Head: Restless in a Distant Land, In: When the Drumbeat Changes, 3 Continents Press, 81; Biligualism: New ideas about an old concept, Muses, 81; The image of Christ black, CLA Journal, 81; An audio-visual presentation of black Francophone poetry, Fr Rev, 82. *Mailing Add:* Dept Lang Iowa State Univ Ames IA 50011

BRUNET, JEAN PAUL, b Neuilly-Sur-Seine, France, Jan 6, 36; m 66; c 2. FRENCH, AMERICAN LITERATURE. *Educ:* Sorbonne, lic, 60, maitrise, 61, Dr(English), 72. *Prof Exp:* Lectr French, Univ Calif, Riverside, 67-69; asst prof, 69-74, ASSOC PROF FRENCH, UNIV WESTERN ONT, 74- *Mem:* Can Asn Univ Teachers; MLA; Can Asn Teachers Fr. *Res:* Comparative linguistics; French and American civilizations. *Publ:* Auth, L'enseignement et la societe Francaise, Civilisation Fr, 76; La formation pedagogique de l'enseignant du second degre, Can Mod Lang Rev, 77; Deux Annees de Gaillard D'Avant, Chiron, Paris, 78. *Mailing Add:* Univ of Western Ont London ON N6A 3K7 Can

BRUNING, PETER, b Amsterdam, Neth, Mar 23, 23; US citizen; m 50; c 2. GERMAN. *Educ:* Univ Amsterdam, Cand Lit, 47, Dr Lit, 49. *Prof Exp:* Teaching fel Ger, Ind Univ, 50-51; from instr to asst prof Ger & Dutch, Univ Calif, Berkeley, 51-55; asst prof Ger, Rice Univ, 55-56; assoc prof, 56-70, PROF GER, IND STATE UNIV, TERRE HAUTE, 71- *Mem:* Am Asn Teachers Ger. *Res:* German literature from 1750-1850; contemporary Dutch literature; history of art. *Publ:* Auth, E T A HOFFMANN and the Philistine, Ger Quart, 55; Boutens, P C & Heijermans, H, Second Edition of the Encyl of World Literature in the XXth Century, Frederick Ungar. *Mailing Add:* Dept of Foreign Lang Ind State Univ Terre Haute IN 47809

BRUNNER, JOHN WILSON, b Philadelphia, Pa, Oct 5, 24; m 53; c 5. GERMAN. *Educ:* Ursinus Col, BA, 49; Columbia Univ, MA, 50, PhD, 57. *Prof Exp:* Lectr, 54, from instr to assoc prof, 55-66, PROF GER, MUHLENBERG COL, 66-, HEAD DEPT FOREIGN LANG, 60- *Concurrent Pos:* Lectr, Columbia Univ, 50-52 & 54-55. *Mem:* MLA; Ling Soc Am; Am Orient Soc; Am Asn Teachers Ger. *Res:* The writings of Hermann Hesse; the use of electronic aids in foreign language teaching. *Publ:* Auth, The Natur-Geist polarity in Hermann Hesse, In: Helen Adolf Festschrift, Ungar, 68. *Mailing Add:* 328 N 26th St Allentown PA 18104

BRUNNER, THEODORE FRIEDERICH, b Nuremberg, Ger, July 3, 34; US citizen; m 57; c 2. CLASSICS. *Educ:* Univ Wis, Milwaukee, BA, 60; Stanford Univ, MA, 63, PhD(classics), 65. *Prof Exp:* Asst prof classics, Ohio State Univ, 64-66; asst prof, 66-69, fel Humanities Inst, 68, chmn dept, 68-72, assoc dean humanities, 69-72, actg chmn dept hist, 71-72, actg chmn dept classics, 75-76, assoc prof, 69-80, PROF CLASSICS, UNIV CALIF, IRVINE, 80-, DIR THESAURUS LINGUAE GRAECAE PROJ, 72-, CHMN, SCH HUMANITIES FAC, 76- *Concurrent Pos:* NDEA res fel, 68-; consult, Am Class League, 69-; prin investr, var Nat Endowment Humanities grants, 76- *Mem:* Class Asn Pac States; Am Philol Asn; Am Soc Papyrologists; Archaeol Inst Am; Centro Int Per Lo Studio Dei Papiri Ercolanesi. *Res:* Ovid; Roman satire; Greek lexicography. *Publ:* Auth, The function of the simile in Ovid's Metamorphoses, 66 & A new classics program in California, 67, Class J; coauth, The Elements of Scientific and Specialized Terminology, Burgess, 67; Index Verborum Quae in Saturis Auli Persi Flacci Reperiuntur, 67 & Index Lucilianus, 68, Georg Olms; auth, A note on Persius 5 179ff, Calif Studies Class Antiquity, 68; coauth, Oedipus Tyrannus-Critical Edition, Norton, 69. *Mailing Add:* Thesaurus Linguae Graecae Proj Univ of Calif Irvine CA 92717

BRUNSDALE, MITZI MALLARIAN, English, Comparative Literature. See Vol II

BRUSH, CRAIG BALCOMBE, b Manhattan, NY, May 28, 30. FRENCH. *Educ:* Princeton Univ, AB, 51; Columbia Univ, MA, 55, PhD, 63. *Prof Exp:* Instr French, Choate Sch, 51-54; from instr to asst prof, Columbia Univ, 55-66; asst prof, City Col New York, 66-70; assoc prof, 70-73, chmn dept mod lang, 73-79, PROF FRENCH, FORDHAM UNIV, 73- *Mem:* MLA; Soc Amis Montaigne; Renaissance Soc Am. *Res:* French literature in the 16th and 18th centuries. *Publ:* Auth, Montaigne and Bayle, Nijhoff, The Hague, 66; coauth, Bayle: Historical and Critical Dictionary, Bobbs, 67; ed, Selected writings of Pierre Gassendi, Johnson Reprint, 73. *Mailing Add:* 411 W 115th St New York NY 10025

BRUSHWOOD, JOHN STUBBS, b Glenns, Va, Jan 23, 20; m 45; c 2. SPANISH AMERICAN LITERATURE. *Educ:* Randolph-Macon Col, BA, 40; Univ Va, MA, 42; Columbia Univ, PhD, 50. *Hon Degrees:* DLitt, Randolph-Macon Col, 81. *Prof Exp:* Instr Romance lang, Va Polytech Inst, 42-44; from instr to prof Span, Univ Mo, 46-67, chmn dept Romance lang, 53-57 & 58-59; ROY A ROBERTS PROF LATIN AM LIT, UNIV KANS, 67- *Concurrent Pos:* Fund Advan Educ fel, 51-52; Am Philos Soc grant, 57; Am Coun Learned Soc grant, 61; Soc Sci Res Coun grant, 71; Nat Endowment for Humanities, summer 76; Bellagio scholar in residence, 78. *Mem:* Midwest Mod Lang Asn (pres, 62-63); MLA; Am Asn Teachers Span & Port; Inst Int Lit Iberoam. *Res:* Mexican literature; Spanish American novel. *Publ:* Auth, Mexico in Its Novel: A Nation's Search for Identity, Univ Tex, 66; Enrique Gonzales Martinez, Twayne, 69; Los Ricos en la Prosa Mexicana, Diogenes, 70; Mexico en su Novela, Fondo Cult Economica, 73;

The Spanish American Novel: A Twentieth Century Survey, Univ Tex, 75; Genteel Barbarism: New Readings of Nineteenth Century Spanish American Novels, Univ Nebr, 81; cotransl, The Precipice (Galindo), Univ Tex, 69; Don Goyo (Aguilera-Malta), Humana, 80. *Mailing Add:* 2813 Maine Ct Lawrence KS 66044

BRUST, WILLIAM ZOLTAN, b Budapest, Hungary, May 20, 19; US citizen; m 48; c 3. GERMAN, RUSSIAN. *Educ:* Univ Minn, BA, 44, BS & MA, 53, PhD(Ger lit), 68. *Prof Exp:* Instr Ger, Univ Minn, 62-65; from instr to asst prof, 65-70, ASSOC PROF GER & RUSS, CARLETON COL, 70- *Mem:* MLA; Am Asn Teachers Ger. *Res:* Twentieth century German and French literature; modern Russian literature. *Mailing Add:* Dept of Ger Carleton Col Northfield MN 55057

BRYANS, JOHN VICTOR, b London, England, Aug 5, 42; Can & Brit citizen; m 67; c 1. SPANISH & COMPARATIVE LITERATURE. *Educ:* Oxford Univ, BA, 66, MA, 70, PhD(Span), 74. *Prof Exp:* ASST PROF SPAN, UNIV BC, 70- *Mem:* Can Asn Hispanists. *Res:* Spanish Golden Age theatre; archetypal criticism; psychology and literature. *Publ:* Auth, Rosaura liberated or a woman's rebellion, Univ BC Hisp Studies, 74; Calderon de la Barca: Imagery, Drama and Rhetoric, Tamesis, 77. *Mailing Add:* 4424 W 12th Vancouver BC V7S 2T2 Can

BRYANT, LUCIE M, b Cherbourg, France, Jan 12, 28; m 48; c 3. FRENCH LITERATURE. *Educ:* Univ Kans, MA, 67, MPhil, 70, PhD(French lit), 73. *Prof Exp:* Asst instr French, Univ Kans, 66-69, instr, 69-71; asst prof, Wichita State Univ, 71-77; lectr French, NDak State Univ, 77-80; ASST PROF FRENCH, ST OLAF COL, 80- *Mem:* MLA; Am Asn Teachers French. *Res:* Humanism and Renaissance; 16th century French literature; French comic theater of the Renaissance. *Mailing Add:* Dept of French St Olaf Col Northfield MN 55057

BRYANT, MARGARET M, b Trenton, SC, Dec 3, 00. ENGLISH LINGUISTICS. *Educ:* Winthrop Col, AB, 21; Columbia Univ, AM, 25, PhD, 31. *Hon Degrees:* LittD, Cedar Crest Col, 66, Northern Mich Univ, 79; LHD, Winthrop Col, 68; DH, Francis Marroin Col, 79. *Prof Exp:* Prin High Sch, SC, 21-22; teacher, Kans, 22-23, WVa, 23-24 & L'Ecole Francaise, NY, 24-25; head dept English, Chowan Col, 25-26; instr eve session, Hunter Col, 26-30; from instr to prof English, 30-71, prof grad div, 38-71, actg chmn dept English, 40-41, chmn, 41-44, grad sch, City Univ New York, 62-71, EMER PROF ENGLISH, BROOKLYN COL, 71- *Concurrent Pos:* Instr Hunter Col, 27-33; Am Coun Learned Soc fel, Ling Inst, Univ Mich, 39; Int Soc Gen Semantics scholar, NY Univ, 45; vis prof, Univ Vt, 47, Univ Ark, 48, New Sch Social Res, 48-49, Univ Utah, 49, Univ Colo, 50, Stockholm Handelshogskola & Uppsala Univ, 50-51, Univ Stockholm, 51, Columbia Univ, 52-53 & 55-56 & Rutgers Univ, 62; consult, Nat Conf Am Folklore Youth, 49-60; Am-Scand Found hon fel, 50-51. *Honors & Awards:* Distinguished prof, Winthrop Col, 73. *Mem:* English Inst; Int Fedn Mod Lang & Lit; Int Ling Asn (pres, 72-73); Int Cong Ling; Int Assoc Profs English. *Res:* Folklore. *Publ:* Auth, English in the Law Courts, Columbia Univ, 30, Ungar, 2nd ed, 62; Modern English and its Heritage, Macmillan, 48, 2nd ed, 62; A functional English grammar, Kenkyusha, Tokyo, 59 & 71; ed, Current American Usage, Funk, 62; auth, Space exploration terms, Am Speech, 10/68; As they say in Japan--An analysis of Japanese English, Studies Current English, 3/71; Some Indian and Dutch names reflecting the early history of Brooklyn, Names, 6/72; Modern English Syntax, Saibido, Tokyo, 76; coauth, The Development of General to English Linguistics Studies in Japan, NY Univ, 81. *Mailing Add:* 222 Hicks St Brooklyn NY 11201

BRYANT, SHASTA M, b Mt Airy, NC, July 12, 24; m 46; c 2. SPANISH LITERATURE. *Educ:* Univ NC, AB, 50, MA, 56, PhD(Romance lang), 58. *Prof Exp:* Asst prof air sci, NTex State Univ, 51-53; from asst prof to assoc prof Span, Univ Miami, 58-66; assoc prof, 66-75, PROF SPAN, WAKE FOREST UNIV, 75- *Concurrent Pos:* Instr Span, Univ NC, 50-51 & 57-58; resident dir in Madrid, Assoc Mid-Fla Cols Year Abroad Prog, 70-71; assoc ed, S Atlantic Bull, 71-77. *Mem:* S Atlantic Mod Lang Asn; Am Asn Teachers Span & Port; MLA. *Res:* Latin American literary bibliography; Spanish Golden Age. *Publ:* Auth, English translations of Spanish ballads, Hispania, 5/63; coauth, Generales y Doctores, Oxford Univ, 65; auth, A Selective Bibliography of Bibliographies of Hispanic American Literature, Pan Am Union, 66 & Inst Latin Am Studies, Univ Tex, Austin, 2nd ed, 76; The Spanish image of India, In: Images of India, Popular Prakashan, Bombay, 71; The Spanish Ballad in English, Univ Press Ky, 73. *Mailing Add:* Dept of Romance Lang Wake Forest Univ Winston-Salem NC 27109

BRYANT, WILLIAM C, b Pontiac, Mich, Oct 22, 36. ROMANCE LANGUAGES & LITERATURES. *Educ:* Univ Mich, BA, 58, MA, 59; Univ Calif, Berkeley, PhD(Romance lang), 64. *Prof Exp:* Asst prof Romance lang, Dominican Col, Calif, 61-64; asst prof, 64-68, ASSOC PROF SPAN, OAKLAND UNIV, 68- *Concurrent Pos:* Nat Endowment Humanities grant, 67-68; dir, Founder Teatro Libre, 76. *Mem:* Latin Am Studies Asn; Am Asn Teachers Span & Port; MLA; Soc Bibliogilos Espanoles; Renaissance Soc Am. *Res:* Golden Age literature; colonial Latin America; Spanish theatre; Peninsular literatures, especially theatre; colonial Hispanic American literature. *Publ:* Auth, Estudio metrico sobre las dos comedias profanas de Sor Juana Ines de la Cruz, Hispanofila, 63; Reaparicion de una poesia de Sor Juana Ines de la Cruz, perdida desde 1714, 64 & Sor Juana Ines de la Cruz y la literatura de cordel del siglo XVIII: noticias bibliograficas, 75, Anuario Letras; Martin de Leon's Historia del Huerfano, an unpublished narrative of Colonial Peru, Homenaje Prof Irving Leonard, 76; collab, The Mutants: A play for Cafe Teatro by Jose Ruibal, Odyssey, 78; La Relacion de un ciego y su lazarillo, piesz dramatica de la literatura colonial, Revista Iberoamericana, No 104-105, 78; An unpublished narrative of seventeenth-century Spain, Mich Academician, XIV, 81. *Mailing Add:* Dept of Mod Lang Oakland Univ Rochester MI 48063

BRYANT, WILLIAM HOWELL, b Houston, Tex, Feb 19, 32; m 56; c 3. FRENCH & FRENCH-CANADIAN LITERATURE. *Educ:* Univ Hawaii, BA, 58; Univ Mo, PhD(French), 71. *Prof Exp:* Lectr, 70-71, asst prof, 71-74, ASSOC PROF FRENCH, WESTERN WASH UNIV, 74- *Mem:* Am Asn Teachers Fr; Asn Can Studies United States. *Res:* Seventeenth and 19th century French poetry; stylistics. *Publ:* Auth, A comparison of translation styles, Meta, 9/72; French-Canadian literature and the teacher of French, Can Mod Lang Rev, 10/73; Advanced French composition: Organization, articulation and style, Fr Rev, 3/74; Marxist blueprints for Quebec schools, Soc Sci J, 1/78; Publicity: Key to higher enrollment, Foreign Lang Ann, 2/78; Unequivocal passe compose/imparfait contexts for Falloir and Pouvoir, French Rev, 3/80; Rimbaud, disciple of Tristan L'Hermite?, Romance Notes, 5/82. *Mailing Add:* Dept of Foreign Lang Western Wash Univ Bellingham WA 98225

BRYCE, FRANK JACKSON, JR, b Baltimore, Md, Apr 6, 44. CLASSICS. *Educ:* Cath Univ Am, AB, 66; Harvard Univ, AM, 68, PhD(class philol), 74. *Prof Exp:* Instr, 72-73, from asst prof to assoc prof, 73-80, PROF CLASS LING, CARLETON COL, 80- *Mem:* Am Philol Asn; North Am Patristics Soc. *Res:* Latin Christian literature; history of later Roman empire; ancient philosophy and religion. *Mailing Add:* Dept of Class Lang Carleton Col Northfield MN 55057

BRYNER, CYRIL, Russian History. See Vol I

BRYSON, JOSETTE THERESE ST AGNE, b Agen, France, Nov 17, 30. FRENCH LITERATURE, TRANSLATION. *Educ:* Immaculate Heart Col, BA, 67; Univ Calif, Los Angeles, MA, 69, PhD(French), 79. *Prof Exp:* Instr French, Mayfield High Sch, 62-68 & Col VI, St Thomas, summer, 71; instr French, Univ Calif, Los Angeles, 74-76, instr transl, 76-81. *Concurrent Pos:* Co-ed, Ante, 64-68; instr French, Immaculate Heart Col, 67-68; adj prof French, Occidental Col, 77-79; advisor, Ecriture francaise, Quebec, 79-; researcher, Henry E Huntington Libr, 82- *Res:* African literature written in French; French activities in California and Louisiana; the world of translation (French-English, English-French). *Publ:* Contribr, Interview with poet (Charles Bukowski), Southern Calif Lit Scene, 12/70; North African novels in French: A survey of engagee literature, Ufahamu, spring 73; transl, Le tendre continent, Europe, Paris, 3/76; Georges Dumezil, Myth and Epic, Univ Calif Press, 80; contribr, Mohammed Dib: La Grande Maison et sa reception critique, Oeuvres & Critiques, Vol IV, No 2; transl, Jacques Cousteau, Salmons, Beavers & Sea Otters, Petersen Publ Co (in prep). *Mailing Add:* 411 West Ave 42 Los Angeles CA 90065

BUBENIK, VIT MORIC, b Nove Mesto, Czech, Mar 31, 42; m 71; c 2. CLASSICS, LINGUISTICS. *Educ:* Univ Brno, Czech, BA, 66, MA, 67, PhD(classics), 69. *Prof Exp:* Asst prof classics & Hebrew, Univ Brno, Czech, 68-70; lectr ling, 71-73, asst prof, 73-77, ASSOC PROF LING, MEM UNIV NFLD, 77- *Concurrent Pos:* Lang training prog, Shastri Indo-Can Inst, 79; Alexander von Humboldt-Stiftung res grant, 82. *Mem:* Can Ling Asn; Ling Soc Am; Class Asn Can; Ling Asn Can & US; Can Asian Studies Asn. *Res:* General and historical linguistics; classics and Indo-European comparative linguistics; Hebrew and Semitic comparative linguistics. *Publ:* Auth, Evidence for Alasija from Linear B Texts, Phoenix, Toronto, 74; contribr, Consonant length in Ancient Greek phonology, In: Current Progress in Historical Linguistics, North Holland, 76; Contrastive study of middle voice in Germanic languages, In: Proceedings of the XIIth International Congress of Linguist, Innsbrucker Beitrage zur Sprach Wiss, 78; Acquisition of Czech in the English environment, In: Aspects of Bilingualism, Hornbeam, 78 ; auth, Historical development of the ancient Greek accent system, Indogermanische Iorschungen, Berlin, 79; Thematization and passivization in Arabic, Lingua, North-Holland, 79; Some issues in Balto-Slavic accentology, Linguistics, The Hague, 80; The Phonological Interpretation of Ancient Greek, Univ Toronto, 82. *Mailing Add:* Dept of Ling Mem Univ of Nfld Elizabeth Ave St John's NF A1B 3X9 Can

BUCHANAN, JAMES JUNKIN, b Pittsburgh, Pa, Mar 7, 25; m 51; c 5. CLASSICS. *Educ:* Princeton Univ, AB, 46, PhD(Classics), 54; Harvard Univ, MBA, 48. *Prof Exp:* Mem staff, Investment Adv Dept, First Boston Corp, 48-51; from instr to asst prof classics, Princeton Univ, 53-60; prof classics & chmn dept, Southern Methodist Univ, 60-63, dean, Col Arts & Sci, 62-63; prof & chmn dept, Trinity Univ, 63-64; PROF CLASSICS, TULANE UNIV, 64- *Mem:* Am Philol Asn; Class Asn England; Archaeol Inst Am. *Res:* Greek history; Roman law; ancient historiography. *Publ:* Coauth, Zosimus: Historia Nova, Trinity Univ, 67; auth, Theorika, Augustin; transl, Boethius: Consolation of Philosophy, Ungar. *Mailing Add:* Dept of Classics 437 Newcomb Hall Tulane Univ New Orleans LA 70118

BUCK, ARTHUR CHARLES, b Long Island City, NY, Feb 14, 27; div; c 2. COMPARATIVE LITERATURE OF FRANCE & ASIA. *Educ:* Univ Pa, BA, 55, MA, 57; Univ Ark, PhD(comp lit), 80. *Prof Exp:* Instr English, Univ Md, Far East Div, Tokyo, 57-61; instr, 62-70, asst prof, 70-79, ASSOC PROF ENGLISH & CHINESE & JAPANESE LIT IN TRANSL, WVA UNIV, 79- *Concurrent Pos:* Ed, Insights, Dominion-Post Panorama, Morgantown, WVa, 69-71, WVa Poetry Soc, 71 & Perspectives, Sunday Gazette-Mail State Mag, Charleston, 71-77; asst ed, Asian Forum: A Quart Asian Affairs, 72-74. *Mem:* MLA; Am Fedn Teachers; Int Platform Asn; Am Comp Lit Asn. *Res:* Jean Giraudoux; Oriental literature and philosophy; the creative process. *Publ:* Auth, The charisma of Alex Haley, 5/24/70 & Alex Haley's autobiography of Malcolm X, 6/7/70, Insights, Dominion-Post Panorama; A philosophy of education, Pathway II, 3/71; Louise McNeill: West Virginia's Hill-Daughter, In: Poems from the Hills, 1971, Morris Harvey Col Publ, 71; Three poems of Marion Schoeberlein, El Viento, VI, spring 73; Walk softly--but breathe a poem, Scimitar & Song, 6-8/74; Louise McNeill's expanding vision, In: Things Appalachian, Morris Harvey Col Pub, 76. *Mailing Add:* PO Box 112 Morgantown WV 26505

BUCK, GEORGE CRAWFORD, b Meriden, Conn, Mar 26, 18; m 43; c 3. GERMAN LITERATURE. *Educ:* Amherst Col, BA, 42; Yale Univ, MA, 48, PhD(Ger), 54. *Prof Exp:* Asst Ger, Yale Univ, 46-50; instr, Univ Wash, 50-54, lectr, 54-56; Fulbright res scholar, Univ Freiburg, 56-57; asst prof Ger lang, 57-62, assoc dean, Col Arts & Sci, 71-73, ASSOC PROF GER, UNIV WASH, 62-, DIR LANG LAB & CTR PROG INSTR, 63-, CHMN GER LANG, 73- *Concurrent Pos:* Res consult, Pierce County Sch Syst, 61; ling consult, Boeing Aircraft Co, 62. *Mem:* MLA; Am Asn Teachers Ger; Philol Asn Pac Coast; Asn Educ Commun & Technol; Nat Soc Prog Instr. *Res:* Eighteenth century literature, especially Goethe; 20th century literature, especially Rudolf Borchardt; medieval literature. *Publ:* Auth, Goethe and His Stowaways; The pattern of the stowaway in Goethe's works, PMLA; The noncreative prose of Franz Werfel, In: Lore B Foltin: Franz Werfel, 1890-1945, 61; co-transl, Linguistic Variability and Intellectual Development, Univ Miami, 71; transl, Thomas Mann: Artist and Partisan in Troubled Times, Univ Ala, 73. *Mailing Add:* Dept of Ger Denny Hall Univ of Wash Seattle WA 98195

BUCK, ROBERT JOHN, b Vermilion, Alta, July 5, 26; m 55; c 2. CLASSICS. *Educ:* Univ Alta, BA, 49; Univ Ky, MA, 50; Univ Cincinnati, PhD(classics), 56. *Prof Exp:* Instr Greek & Latin, Univ Ky, 55-57, asst prof ancient lang, 57-60; from asst prof to assoc prof, 60-66, head dept, 64-72, PROF CLASSICS, UNIV ALTA, 66- *Concurrent Pos:* Mem managing comt, Am Sch Class Studies, Athens, 66-; fel, Can Inst, Rome, 76; vpres, Can Archaeol Inst, Athens, 78-; mem bd dir, Can Meditterranean Inst, 80- *Mem:* Am Philol Asn; Archaeol Inst Am; Class Asn Can (vpres, 70-73). *Res:* Pre-classical Greek archaeology; ancient history; Italian archaeology. *Publ:* Auth, The Athenian domination of Boeotia, 70 & The formation of the Boeotian League, 72, Class Philol; The Via Herculia, Papers Brit Sch Rome, 73; History of Boeotia, Univ Alta, 78. *Mailing Add:* Dept of Classics Univ of Alta Edmonton AB T6G 2E6 Can

BUCKALEW, RONALD EUGENE, English. See Vol II

BUCKNALL, BARBARA JANE, b Teddington, England, June 8, 33. ROMANCE LANGUAGES. *Educ:* Oxford Univ, BA, 55, MA, 59; Univ London, dipl libr sci, 59; Northwestern Univ, PhD(French), 66. *Prof Exp:* Ed asst, French Chamber Com, London, 55-56; libr asst, Dr Williams' Libr, London, 56-57; cataloguer, libr, Univ Ill, Urbana-Champaign, 58-59, teaching asst French, 59-60; teaching asst, Northwestern Univ, 60-62; from instr to asst prof, Univ Ill, Urbana-Champaign, 62-69; asst prof, 69-71, ASSOC PROF FRENCH, BROCK UNIV, 71- *Concurrent Pos:* Can Coun leave fel, 74-75. *Mem:* MLA; Asn Can Univ Prof Fr; Can Comp Lit Asn; Am Asn Teachers Fr; Can Soc Renaissance Studies. *Res:* Proust; women writers; 20th century French literature. *Publ:* Auth, The Religion of Art in Proust, Univ Ill, 69; From material to spiritual food in A La Recherche du Temps Perdu, Esprit Createur, spring 71; Anne Hebert, Violette Leduc, In: Encycl of World Literature in the Twentieth Century, Ungar, suppl vol, 75; La Belle au bois dormant par Perrault, Humanities Asn Rev, spring 75; La redemption de Phedre chez Proust, 76 & Anne Hebert et Violette Leduc, lectrices de Marcel Proust, 77-78, Bull Soc Amis Marcel Proust; Ursela K LeGuin, Ungar, 81. *Mailing Add:* Dept of Romance Studies Brock Univ St Catharines ON L2S 3A1 Can

BUCSELA, JOHN, b Perth Amboy, NJ, May 3, 19; m 59; c 3. RUSSIAN LANGUAGE & LITERATURE. *Educ:* Univ Wis, BA, 55, MA, 56, PhD(Russ), 63. *Prof Exp:* From instr to asst prof Russ, Kenyon Col, 60-64; asst prof, 64-68, ASSOC PROF RUSS & CHMN DEPT, EMORY UNIV, 68- *Mem:* Am Asn Teachers Slavic & E Europ Lang (vpres, 67-69); MLA. *Res:* Lomonsov and eighteenth century Russian literature. *Publ:* Auth, The birth of Russian syllabo-tonic versification, 65 & Lomonsov's literary debut, winter 67, Slavic & E Europ J; The problems of Baroque in Russian literature, Russ Rev, 7/72. *Mailing Add:* Dept of Russ Emory Univ Atlanta GA 30322

BÜDEL, OSCAR, b Wiesen im Spessart, Bavaria, June 22, 23. ROMANCE LANGUAGES & LITERATURE. *Educ:* Univ Würzburg, PhD(Romance lang & lit), 50. *Prof Exp:* Reader Ger, Univ Rome, 52-54; instr French, Ital & Ger, Univ Omaha, 54-56; from asst prof to assoc prof Ital lang & lit, Univ Wash, 56-65; PROF ITAL, UNIV MICH, ANN ARBOR, 65- *Concurrent Pos:* Reader, Ital Inst Ger Studies, Rome, 51-54; romance ed, Mod Lang Quart, 58-65; vis prof Ital lit, Cornell Univ, 69-70; fel, Newberry Library, Chicago, 80. *Mem:* MLA; Int Asn Fr Studies; Dante Soc Am; Renaissance Soc Am; Am Asn Teachers Ital. *Res:* Italian Renaissance; aesthetics; theater. *Publ:* Auth, Contemporary Theater and Aesthetic Distance, PMLA, 6/61; Pirandello sulla scena tedesca, Quad Piccolo Teatro, Milano, 61; Francesco Petrarca und der Literaturbarock, Scherpe, Krefeld, 63; Das Publikum der Stilnovisti, Ideen und Formen, Festschrift Hugo Friedrich, Frankfurt/Main, 65; Pirandello, Bowes & Bowes, London, 66, rev ed, 69; Illusion Disabused: A Novel Mode in Petrarch's Canzoniere, In: Francis Petrarch, Six Centuries Later: A Symposium, Chapel Hill-Chicago, 75; Die Italienische Literatur 1890-1920, Neues Handbuch Literaturwissenschaft, 76; Castiglione, Twayne, 82. *Mailing Add:* Dept Romance Lang Univ Mich Ann Arbor MI 48104

BUEHNE, SHEEMA Z, b Philadelphia, Pa, Sept 21, 10; m 33; c 2. GERMAN LITERATURE & LANGUAGE. *Educ:* Bryn Mawr Col, AB, 31; Pa State Univ, AM, 50, PhD(Ger & philos), 60. *Prof Exp:* Instr philos, Ger & English, Pa State Univ, 47-55; teacher Latin, Ger, Greek & math, Friends Cent Sch, Philadelphia, 55-57; teacher Latin & Ger & head depts, Baldwin Sch, 57-60; from asst prof to prof, 61-74, res coun fac fel, 71-72, EMER PROF GER, RUTGERS UNIV, CAMDEN, 74- *Mem:* MLA; Am Asn Teachers Ger; Nat Carl Schurz Asn; AAUP; Am Transl Asn (secy, 70). *Res:* Hartmann von Aue; translation from German to English. *Publ:* Auth, Translating Middle High German into Modern English, Babel, 64; transl, Hartmann von Aue, Gregorius, 66; auth, Hermann Hesse's Siddharta, Suppl Parastudies Rev, 1/67; transl, Franz Kafka: A Critical Study Of His Writings, 68 & coed, Helen Adolf Festschrift, 68, Frederick Ungar; auth, A Translation Problem in the German Translation of Three Anglo-American Short Stories, Am Transl, 71; co-transl, No Compromise--Selected Writings of Karl Kraus, 77 & Practical Wisdom-A Treasury of Aphorisms and Reflections from the German, 77. *Mailing Add:* Aaronsburg PA 16820

BUENO, JULIAN LOPEZ, b Arges, Spain, Dec 1, 42; US citizen; m 77. MEDIEVAL SPANISH LITERATURE. *Educ:* Gregorian Univ, Italy, PhB, 65; Pan Am Univ, BA, 74; Tex Tech Univ, MA, 76, PhD(Span), 79. *Prof Exp:* VIS ASST PROF SPAN, WAKE FOREST UNIV, 78- *Concurrent Pos:* Consult, Winston-Salem Forsyth County Sch Dist, 82. *Mem:* Am Asn Teacher Span & Port. *Res:* Contemporary peninsular literature; Spanish teaching methodology. *Publ:* Auth, Serian monjas las duenas de Juan Ruiz?, La Coronica, Vol 9, 80; Los pecados capitales y las armas del cristiano en el Libro de Buen Amor, Critica Hisp, Vol II, No 1; La Troba Cacurra de Juan Ruiz: Parodia Liturgica, Romance Notes, Vol 21, 81. *Mailing Add:* 220 Faculty Dr 8-C Winston-Salem NC 27106

BULATKIN, ELEANOR WEBSTER, b Baltimore, Md, Sept 2, 13; m 46. ROMANCE PHILOLOGY. *Educ:* Johns Hopkins Univ, MA, 51, PhD(Romance Philol), 52. *Prof Exp:* From instr to asst prof foreign lang, Univ Md, 52-61; from assoc prof to prof, 61-76, chmn dept, 66-72, EMER PROF ROMANCE LANG, OHIO STATE UNIV, 76- *Concurrent Pos:* Fulbright lectr Span ling, Inst Carol & Cuervo, Bogota, 60-61. *Mem:* MLA; Medieval Acad Am; Ling Soc Am; Mod Humanities Res Asn; AAUP. *Res:* Romance linguistics; Medieval romance literature. *Publ:* Auth, The Spanish word matiz, Traditio; The arithmetic structure of the O F Vie de Saint Alexis, PMLA, 59; Introduccional poema heroicade Hernando Domingues Comargo, Thesavrvs, 62; Structural arithmetic metaphor in the Oxford Roland, Ohio State, 72. *Mailing Add:* Dept of Romance Lang Ohio State Univ Columbus OH 43210

BULHOF, FRANCIS, b The Hague, Neth, Sept 19, 30; m 57; c 3. DUTCH & GERMAN LITERATURE. *Educ:* Univ Groningen, Drs, 56; Univ Utrecht, LittD(Ger), 66. *Prof Exp:* Asst prof, 66-72, assoc prof, 72-81, PROF GER LANGS, UNIV TEX, AUSTIN, 81- *Concurrent Pos:* Prof Netherlandic studies, Univ Oldenburg, Ger, 81. *Mem:* Metschappij der Nederlandse Letterkunde. *Res:* Dutch literary history. *Publ:* Auth, Transpersonalismus und Synchronizitaet, Groningen, Van Denderen, 66; ed, Wortindex zu Thomas Mann: Der Zauberberg, Xerox Univ Monographs, 76; Nijhoff, Van Ostaijen, De Stijl: Modernism in the Netherlands and Belgium, The Hague, Nijhoff, 76; auth, Over Menno ter Braaks Politicus zonder partij, Amsterdam Wetenschappelijke Uitgeverij, 80; Over Du Perrons Land van herkomst, Amsterdam, Wetenschappelijke Uitgeverij, 80; ed, Menno ter Braaks artikelen over emigrantenliteratuur, The Hague, Bzztoh, 80. *Mailing Add:* Dept of Ger Lang Univ of Tex Austin TX 78712

BULLER, JEFFREY LYNN, b Milwaukee, Wis, Sept 9, 54; m 76. CLASSICAL LANGUAGES, COMPARATIVE LITERATURE. *Educ:* Univ Notre Dame, BA, 76; Univ Wis-Madison, MA, 77, PhD(classics), 81. *Prof Exp:* ASST PROF CLASS STUDIES, LORAS COL, 81-, CHMN, 82- *Mem:* Am Philol Asn; MLA; Am Class League. *Res:* Tragedy of Sophocles; comparative mythology; Greek and Roman art history. *Publ:* Auth, Pempo and Ananeke in the Oresteia, Class Bull, 79; Triple sound patterns in Oedipus Tyrannus, Class World, 80; The pathetic fallacy in Hellenistic pastoral, Ramus, 82. *Mailing Add:* Box 886 Loras Col Dubuque IA 52001

BULLOCK, CLARENCE HASSELL, Old Testament Studies, Classical Hebrew. See Vol IV

BUMPASS, FAYE LAVERNE, b Ft Cobb, Okla, Mar 25, 10. ENGLISH, SPANISH. *Educ:* Tex Technol Col, BA, 32, MA, 34; San Marcos Univ, DLitt, Lima, 47. *Prof Exp:* Teacher English, Span & Latin, High Schs, Tex, 32-41; Tex state supvr Span, Army & Navy air bases, US Dept Educ, 41-43; instr English, Army Air Force pre-flight training, Tex Technol Col, 43-45; dir courses, Bi-Nat Ctr, Lima, 45-50; English teaching consult Latin Am, US Dept State, 50-51; prof Span & English & dir dual lang workshops, 56-69, Horn prof, 69-79, EMER HORN PROF ROMANCE LANG, TEX TECH UNIV, 80- *Concurrent Pos:* Rockefeller Found grant, Bi-Nat-Ctr, Lima, 45; consult sec sch textbooks for English as foreign lang, NCTE, 60; prof, NDEA Instrs, Tex Tech Univ, 61, Brooklyn Col, 66, Univ Tex, El Paso, 66-67, Roosevelt Univ, 67- & St Michael's Col, 68; Govt Guam Head Start Prog, Agana, 67-68; consult, schs, cols & prof asns, US, PR & Mex. *Honors & Awards:* Distinguished Serv Award, Peruvian Ministry Educ, 56. *Mem:* NCTE; Teachers English to Speakers Other Lang; Am Asn Teachers Span & Port; Int Reading Asn. *Res:* Teaching young students English as a foreign language; teaching of reading in the second language. *Publ:* Auth, Don and Betty Hall in High School, Sanmarti, Lima, 50, rev ed, 55, 60, 64, 67; Teaching Young Students English as a Foreign Language, Am Bk, 63; Let's Read Stories, Bks 1-5, McGraw, 65; Adapting The Reading Program to the Needs of Non-English Speaking Children, In: Vistas in Reading, Int Reading Asn, Eastern State Univ, 66; Learning to Read in a Foreign Language, English Teaching Forum, 66; Statement on Bilingual Education in the Southwest, Hearings Spec Senate Comt Bilingual Educ, 67; W Speak English, Bks 1 & 2, 68 & The New We Learn English Series (5 texts), 68, Am Bk. *Mailing Add:* Dept Romance Lang Tex Tech Univ Lubbock TX 79409

BUNDY, BARBARA KORPAN, b Chicago, Ill, May 13, 43; wid; c 1. COMPARATIVE LITERATURE, GERMAN. *Educ:* Univ Ill, BA, 64; Ind Univ, PhD(comp lit), 70. *Prof Exp:* Acting asst prof Slavic & comp lit, Univ Calif, Berkeley, 66-69; lectr Russ & Ger, Univ Calif, Santa Cruz, 69-71; PROF COMP LIT, GER & HUMANITIES, DOMINICAN COL SAN RAFAEL, 80- *Concurrent Pos:* Nat Endowment Humanities younger humanist fel rel between fiction & philos in Renaissance, 73, consult humanities, 75- *Mem:* Am Asn Advan Humanities; Asn Am Col; Am Coun Educ. *Res:* Fiction; literary theory and educational philosophy. *Publ:* Auth, Transcending the limitations of new criticism about later literary theory, 2/69 & Literature as a statement about human experience, 8/72, Romance Philol. *Mailing Add:* Dept of Foreign Lang Dominican Col Grand Ave San Rafael CA 94901

BUNDY, JEAN, b Seattle, Wash, Sept 21, 24; m 57; c 4. FRENCH LANGUAGE & LITERATURE. *Educ:* Wash State Col, BA, 50; Univ Wis, MA, 52, PhD, 57; Colby Col, MA, 63. *Prof Exp:* Instr French, Univ Wis, 56-57; from instr to assoc prof, Univ Tex, 57-63; prof 63-68, chmn dept French, 63-72, DANA PROF FRENCH LIT, COLBY COL, 68- *Concurrent Pos:*

Univ fel, Univ Wis, 51-52, Knapp fel, 55-56; Fulbright grants, France, 53-55, 67-68. *Mem:* MLA; Am Asn Teachers Fr; Int Asn Fr Studies. *Res:* Eighteenth century French literature; French novel. *Publ:* Ed, Three French C Comedies, Dell Laurel Lang Libr, 66. *Mailing Add:* Dept of Mod Lang Colby Col Waterville ME 04901

BUNGE, ROBERT PIERCE, b Oak Park, Ill, Sept 24, 30; m 56; c 2. MODERN LANGUAGES. *Educ:* Roosevelt Univ, MA, 73; DePaul Univ, PhD(philos), 82. *Prof Exp:* Lectr philos, Roosevelt Univ, 71-77 & DePaul Univ, 73-79; ASST PROF FOREIGN LANG, UNIV SDAK, 79- *Concurrent Pos:* Consult, Human Resources Facil, Yankton, 79, States of Nebr & Iowa, SDak Vet Admin Hosp & Indian Affairs, SDak, 81; adj prof, Morningside Col, 81. *Mem:* Am Philos Asn; Rocky Mountain Ling Asn; Soc Siouan & Caddoan Ling. *Res:* Native American languages; philosophy of language; linguistics and philology. *Publ:* Auth, 100 articles on Eastern & Near Eastern religion, Encycl Brittanica's Compton Encycl, 73; The American Indian: A natural philosopher, Intellect Mag, 78; Sioux Collections, Inst Indian Studies, 82. *Mailing Add:* 6 Cherrywood Ct Vermillion SD 57069

BUNGE, WILFRED F, Religion, Classical Languages. See Vol IV

BURDICK, DOLORES MANN, b Milwaukee, Wis, Nov 23, 27; m 56; c 3. FRENCH. *Educ:* Univ Wis, BA, 48, MA, 49; Univ Calif, Berkeley, PhD, 58. *Prof Exp:* Grad asst French, Univ Wis, 48-49; French Govt asst, 49-50; teaching asst French, Univ Calif, Berkeley, 50-54; instr, Smith Col, 54-60; lectr, 62-64, asst prof, 64-68, ASSOC PROF FRENCH, OAKLAND UNIV, 68- *Mem:* MLA; Am Asn Teachers Fr. *Res:* Modern French theatre; French drama and film. *Publ:* Auth, Imagery of the plight in Sartre's Les Mouches, 1/59 & Concept of character in Giroudoux's Electre and Sartre's Les Mouches, 12/59, Fr Rev; Concept of happiness in modern French theatre, Papers Mich Acad Aci, Arts & Lett, 65; The moral function of immoral theatre, Performing Arts Rev, 70; Antigone grows middle-aged: Evolution of Anouilh's Hero, Mich Academician, fall 74; Lola, Lisa, and L: The woman unknown as the woman immortal in Ophuls and Robbe-Grillet, Mich Academician, winter 80; Danger of death: The Hawksian woman as agent of destruction, Post Script, fall 81; Symmetry: Doubles and Doubling in Literature and Film, Univ Press Fla, 81. *Mailing Add:* Dept of Mod Lang & Lit Oakland Univ Rochester MI 48063

BURGESS, ROBERT MILLER, b Mt Crawford, Va, Sept 4, 06,. FRENCH. *Educ:* Bridgewater Col, AB, 28; Univ Paris, cert, 35; Univ Va, AM, 36; Univ Calif, Los Angeles, PhD, 51. *Prof Exp:* Asst prin, High Sch, Va, 29-32; instr French, Black-Foxe Mil Inst, 36-40; asst, Univ Calif, Los Angeles, 40-42 & 46-47; from asst prof to prof, 47-72, chmn dept foreign lang, 52-63, EMER PROF FRENCH, UNIV MONT, 72- *Concurrent Pos:* Pres, Northwest Conf Foreign Lang Teachers, 55-56 & 63-64; evaluator, NDEA Foreign Lang Insts, 63; historian, Mont Asn Lang Teachers J. 74-77; jr warden, Episcopal Church of the Holy Spirit, 78. *Honors & Awards:* Chevalier, Palmes Acad, 59. *Mem:* MLA; Renaissance Soc Am; Am Asn Teachers Fr; Am Comp Lit Asn; Int Comp Lit Asn. *Res:* Platonic and Neoplatonic aspects of French Renaissance. *Publ:* Auth, Platonism in Desportes, Univ NC, 54; Mannerism in Phillippe Desportes, L'Esprit Createur, 66; The sonnet--a cosmopolitan literary form--in the Renaissance, Proc IVth Cong Int Comp Lit Asn, 67. *Mailing Add:* 1547 S Higgins Apt 2 Missoula MT 59801

BURGIN, DIANA LEWIS, b Boston, Mass, Aug 4, 43. SLAVIC LANGUAGES & LITERATURES. *Educ:* Awarthmore Col, BA, 65; Harvard Univ, MA, 67, PhD(Slavic), 73. *Prof Exp:* Teaching fel Russ, Harvard Univ, 70-71; from instr to asst prof, Wellesley Col, 71-75; asst prof, 75-80, ASSOC PROF RUSS, UNIV MASS, BOSTON, 80- *Concurrent Pos:* Corresp, Quincy Patriot Ledger, 72-; assoc Russ lit, Russ Res Ctr, Harvard Univ, 73-; vis lectr Russ, Cambridge Ctr Adult Educ, 74-75. *Mem:* MLA; Am Asn Advan Slavic Studies. *Res:* Nineteenth and 20th century Russian literature; Solzhenitsyn; Dostoevsky. *Publ:* Contribr, The Mystery of The Queen of Spades: A new interpretation, Mnemozina, 74; auth, The fate of modern man: Ideas of fate, justice and happiness in Solzhenitsyn's Cancer Ward, Soviet Studies, 74; Rzevsky's Solzhenitsyn: Creator and Heroic Deed, Western Humanities Rev, 78; Bulgakov's early tragedy of the scientist-creator: An interpretation of Heart of a Dog, Slavic & East Europ J, 78; co-transl, The Invisible Book, Ardis, 78. *Mailing Add:* Dept of Russ Univ of Mass Boston MA 02125

BURGOS, FERNANDO, Chilean citizen. SPANISH-AMERICAN LITERATURE. *Educ:* Univ Chile, BA, 70; Univ Fla, PhD(Span-Am lit), 81. *Prof Exp:* Asst prof Span Am lit, Univ Chile, 71-76; instr Span, Univ Fla, 76-80, res asst Span Am lit, Ctr Latin Am Studies, 78-80; ASST PROF SPAN & SPAN AM LIT, MEMPHIS STATE UNIV, 81- *Mem:* MLA; SAtlantic Mod Lang Asn. *Res:* Spanish-American literature, 19th and 20th centuries; Spanish-American Modernity. *Publ:* Auth, Sarduy: Una escritura en movimento, La Chispa 81 Selected Proc, 81; Conexiones: Barrolo y modenrnidad, Escritura, 1-6/81. *Mailing Add:* Dept of Foreign Lang Memphis State Univ Memphis TN 38152

BURIAN, PETER HART, b Hanover, NH, July 18, 43; m 68; c 2. CLASSICAL STUDIES. *Educ:* Univ Mich, Ann Arbor, AB, 64; Princeton Univ, MA, 68, PhD(Classics), 71. *Prof Exp:* From instr to asst prof, 68-77, ASSOC PROF CLASS STUDIES, DUKE UNIV, 77- *Concurrent Pos:* Nat Endowment Humanities younger humanist fel, 72-73; asst prof, Intercol Ctr Class Studies, Rome, 75-76; Ctr Hellenic Studies fel, Washington, DC, 80-81. *Mem:* Am Philol Asn; Class Asn Mid W & S. *Res:* Greek literature; classical tradition. *Publ:* Auth, Supplication and hero cult in Sophocles' Ajax, Greek, Roman & Byzantine Studies, 72; Suppliant and saviour: Oedipus at Colonus, Phoenix, 74; Pelasgus and politics in Aeschylus' Danaid Trilogy, Wiener Studien, 74; Alcestis resurrected, Am Poetry Rev, 76; Euripides the contortionist, Arion, 76; Euripides' Heraclidae: An interpretation, Class Philol, 77; The play before the prologue, In: Ancient and Modern: Essays in Honor of Gerald F Else, 77; Euripides, The Phoenician Women, Oxford Univ Press, 81. *Mailing Add:* Dept of Class Studies Duke Univ Durham NC 27708

BURKE, JAMES F, b Little Rock, Ark, Aug 26, 39, m 64; c 2. MEDIEVAL SPANISH LANGUAGE & LITERATURE. *Educ:* Univ Ark, BA, 61; Univ NC, MA, 63, PhD(Span), 66. *Prof Exp:* Instr Span, Univ NC, 65-66; from asst prof to assoc prof, 66-76, PROF SPAN, UNIV TORONTO, 76- *Mem:* Mediaeval Acad Am; Am Asn Teachers Span & Port; Can Asn Hispanists. *Res:* Hispano-Arabic language and literature. *Publ:* Auth, History and Vision: Figural Structure of El Caballero Zifar, Tamesis, 72; Four comings of Christ in Berceo's Santa Oria, Speculum, 73; The Estrella De Sevella and saturnine melancholy, Bull Hispanis Tudies, 74; Juan Ruiz, serranas, and the rites of spring, J Medieval & Renaissance Studies, 75. *Mailing Add:* Dept of Ital & Hispanic Studies Univ of Toronto Toronto ON M5S 1A1 Can

BURKE, JOHN MICHAEL, b Boston, Mass, Jan 29, 35; m 58; c 4. RUSSIAN & GERMAN LANGUAGE & LITERATURE. *Educ:* Boston, Col, AB, 56; Fordham Univ, AM, 60; Brown Univ, PhD(Slavic), 71; Univ NH, MA, 75. *Prof Exp:* Instr Russ, Col of the Holy Cross, 60-66; teaching asst, Brown Univ, 67-68; asst prof Russ & Ger, Belknap Col, 68; assoc prof, 69-80, PROF RUSS & GER, FITCHBURG STATE COL, 80- *Mem:* Am Asn Teachers Ger; MLA; Am Asn Teachers Slavic & E Europ Lang. *Res:* Russian literature; German literature. *Mailing Add:* Dept of Foreign Lang Fitchburg State Col Fitchburg MA 01420

BURKE, PAUL FREDERIC, JR, b Arlington, Mass, Feb 11, 44; m 69. CLASSICS. *Educ:* Stanford Univ, AB, 65, PhD(classics), 71. *Prof Exp:* Asst prof classics, McMaster Univ, 71-75; asst prof, 76-79, ASSOC PROF CLASSICS, CLARK UNIV, 79-, CHMN DEPT FOREIGN LANG, 81- *Concurrent Pos:* Fel of Am Acad in Rome, 79-80; Nat Endowment for Humanities fel, 79-80; fel, Am Acad Rome, 79-80; Nat Endowment for Humanities fel, 79-80. *Honors & Awards:* Excellence in teaching award, Am Philol Asn, 79. *Mem:* Am Philol Asn; Class Asn New England; Vergilian Soc Am. *Res:* Virgil; Greek and Roman art and archaeology; disease in ancient history. *Publ:* Auth, The role of Mezentius in the Aeneid, Class J, 74; Mezentius and the first fruits, 74 & Vergil's Amata, 76, Vergilius; Drances Infensus: A study in Vergilian character portrayal, Trans & Proc Am Philol Asn, 78; Roman rites for the dead and Aeneid 6, Class J, 79. *Mailing Add:* Dept Foreign Lang Clark Univ Worcester MA 01610

BURKHARD, MARIANNE, b Zurich, Switz, Feb 1, 39. MODERN GERMAN LITERATURE, COMPARATIVE LITERATURE. *Educ:* Univ Zurich, Switz, PhD(Ger & French lit), 65. *Prof Exp:* Cult ed, Zürichsee-Zeitung (Daily), 65-68; asst prof, 68-76, ASSOC PROF GER, UNIV ILL, URBANA-CHAMPAIGN, 76- *Mem:* Am Asn Teachers Ger; Am Comp Lit Asn; Int Ver ger Sprach und Lit wiss; MLA. *Res:* Post-Goethe 19th century German literature, special emphasis on C F Meyer; symbolism; Swiss literature and women in literature. *Publ:* Auth, C F Meyer und die antike Mythologie, Atlantis, Zurich, 66; Bacchus Biformis; Zu einem Motiv C F Meyers, Neophilologus, 71; Die Entdeckung der form in Huttens letzte Tage, Archiv Studium neueren Sprachen & Lit, 72-73; Hofmannsthals Reitergeschichte, ein Gengenstück zum Chandos-Brief, Amsterdamer Beiträge zur neueren Ger, 75; Ambivalence and fragmentation: structural similarities in C F Meyer and Baudelaire, Nineteenth-Century Fr Studies, 77; Conrad Ferdinand Meyer, Twayne, 78; ed, Gestaltet und gestaltent--Frauen in der deutschen literatur, Amsterdamer Beitrage zur neueren Ger, 80; auth, Gauging Existential Space: The Emergence of Women Writers in Switzerland, World Lit Today, 81. *Mailing Add:* Dept of Ger Lang & Lit 3072 Foreign Lang Bldg Univ Ill Urbana IL 61801

BURKHART, SYLVIA DAVIS, b Cincinnati, Ohio, July 4, 41; m 66; c 1. GERMAN LITERATURE. *Educ:* Univ Ky, BA, 62; Univ Cincinnati, MA, 64, PhD(Ger), 69. *Prof Exp:* From instr to asst prof, 65-71, assoc prof, 72-81, PROF GER, EASTERN KY UNIV, 81- *Mem:* SAtlantic Mod Lang Asn; MLA; Am Asn Teachers Ger. *Res:* Modern German drama. *Mailing Add:* Dept of Foreign Lang Eastern Ky Univ Richmond KY 40475

BURKOT, ALEXANDER ROMAN, b Kaska, Pa, Dec 21, 09; m 33; c 2. ROMANCE & GERMANIC LANGUAGES. *Educ:* Dickinson Col, AB, 30; Univ NC, Chapel Hill, MA, 38. *Hon Degrees:* HHD, Elon Col, 67. *Prof Exp:* Instr, 35-43, chmn dept, 35-61, dean col, 43-73, dean of men, 36-47, provost, 73-79, PROF MOD LANG, CAMPBELL UNIV, NC, 61-, VPRES, 68- *Concurrent Pos:* Comn cols & univs, Southern Assoc Cols, 58-65. *Res:* Origins of surnames, onomastics, comparative etymology. *Mailing Add:* Dept of Mod Lang Campbell Col Buies Creek NC 27506

BURLING, ROBBINS, b Minneapolis, Minn, Apr 8, 26; m 51; c 3. LINGUISTICS. *Educ:* Yale Univ, BA, 50; Harvard Univ, PhD(anthrop), 58. *Prof Exp:* From instr to asst prof anthrop, Univ Pa, 57-63; assoc prof, 63-67, PROF ANTHROP & LING, UNIV MICH, ANN ARBOR, 67- *Concurrent Pos:* Fulbright Found lectr, Rangoon, Burma, 59-60; fel, Ctr Advan Studies Behav Sci, 63-64; Guggenheim Found fel, 71-72; vis prof, Univ Gothenburg, Sweden, 79-80. *Mem:* Am Anthrop Asn; Ling Soc Am; Asn Asian Studies. *Res:* Anthropology. *Publ:* Auth, Rengsanggri, Family and Kinship in a Garo Village, Univ Pa, 63; Hill Farms and Padi Fields, Prentice-Hall, 65; Man's Many Voices, 70 & English in Black and White, 73, Holt; The Passage of Power, Acad Press, 74. *Mailing Add:* Dept of Anthrop Univ of Mich Ann Arbor MI 48109

BURNAM, TOM, American Literature, Creative Writing. See Vol II

BURNE, KEVIN GEORGE, b Los Angeles, Calif, May 22, 25; m 56; c 4. ENGLISH, LINGUISTICS. *Educ:* Univ Calif, Los Angeles, AB, 50; Univ Southern Calif, MS, 55, MA, 59, PhD(ling), 73. *Prof Exp:* From instr to assoc prof, 56-72, PROF ENGLISH, LONG BEACH CITY COL, 72-, CHMN LANG ART DIV, 70-, DEAN LANG ARTS, 75- *Concurrent Pos:* Consult ed English & ser ed, Macmillan Publ Co, 65-70, advising ed & ser ed, Dickenson Publ Co, 65-70. *Mem:* NCTE. *Res:* Grammar and rhetoric for freshman and remedial students, especially junior college; analysis of written syntax of some fourth, fifth and sixth grade Caucasian children. *Publ:* coauth, Functional English for Writers, Scott, 64, 78; Rx: Remedies for Writers, 64 & Limits and Latitudes, 65, Lippincott. *Mailing Add:* Dean Lang Arts Div Long Beach City Col Long Beach CA 90808

BURNETT, ANNE PIPPIN, b Salt Lake City, Utah, Oct 10, 25; m 60; c 2. CLASSICS. *Educ:* Swarthmore Col, BA, 46; Columbia Univ, MA, 47; Univ Calif, Berkeley, PhD(ancient hist & classics), 53. *Prof Exp:* Instr classics, Vassar Col, 57-58; asst prof, 61-66, assoc prof, 67-69, PROF CLASSICS & CHMN DEPT, UNIV CHICAGO, 70- *Concurrent Pos:* Am Asn Univ Women traveling fel, Am Sch Class Studies Athens, 56-57; fel, Am Acad Rome, 58-59; grant, Am Philos Soc, 59-60; Am Coun Learned Soc fel, 68-69. *Res:* Greek tragedy; Greek lyric poetry; Greek history. *Publ:* Auth, Helena Euripides: Wege der Forschung, Bd 89, Darmstadt, 68; Euripides' Ion, Prentice-Hall, 70; Catastrophe Survived, Clarendon, Oxford Univ, 71; Medea's revenge, Class Philol, 73; Curse and dream in Aeschylus' Septem, Greek, Roman & Byzantine Studies, 74. *Mailing Add:* Dept of Classics Div of Humanities Univ of Chicago Chicago IL 60637

BURNETT, DAVID GRAHAM, b Detroit, Mich, Nov 28, 44; m 70; c 2. FRENCH LITERATURE, HUMANITIES. *Educ:* Princeton Univ, BA, 66; Ind Univ, MA, 68, PhD(French), 73. *Prof Exp:* Lectr Am civilization, Univ Pau, France, 69-70; lectr French, Ind Univ, 72-73, vis asst prof, 73-76, asst dean arts & sci, 73-76, asst prof continuing studies, 76-80; MEM FAC, DEPT FRENCH, NC STATE UNIV, 80- *Mem:* Am Asn Higher Educ; MLA; Nat Univ Exten Asn; Am Asn Advan Humanities. *Res:* Nineteenth and 20th century French literature; educational philosophy; humanities policy. *Publ:* Auth, The Living Learning Center of Indiana University, In: Development and Experiement in College Teaching, 74; Thematic function of sexual identity in Gautier's Comedie de la mort, Nottingham Fr Studies, 77; The theme of ocean exploration in the Poetry of Theophile Gautier, Exploration, 77; Movement and stasis in The Flies by Jean-Paul Sartre, Perspectives, 78. *Mailing Add:* Dept of French NC State Univ Raleigh NC 27650

BURNS, ALFRED, b Vienna, Austria, Oct 6, 12; US citizen; m 37; c 1. CLASSICS, GREEK PHILOSOPHY. *Educ:* Univ Wash, BA, 52, MA, 58, PhD(classics), 64. *Prof Exp:* From asst prof to assoc prof, 65-73, PROF CLASSICS, UNIV HAWAII, MANOA, 73- *Mem:* Am Philol Asn; Archaeol Inst Am. *Res:* Classical philology; Roman history; Greek literature. *Publ:* Auth, The fragments of Philolaus and Aristotle's account of Pythagroean theories, 67, The meaning of the Prometheus Vinctus, 68 & Ancient Greek thought and the missing energy concept, 69, Clasica et Mediaevaliea; The tunnel Eupalinus and the problem of Hero of Alexandra, Isis, 70; Ancient Greek water supply and city planning, Technol & Culture, 74; The chorus of Ariadne, Class J, 74; Hippodamus and the planned city, Historia, 76; Athenian literacy in the Fifth century B C, J Hist of Ideas, 81. *Mailing Add:* Dept of Classics Univ of Hawaii at Manoa Honolulu HI 96822

BURNS, JOSEPH M, b Memphis, Tenn, June 26, 28; m 63. GERMAN LANGUAGE & LITERATURE. *Educ:* Memphis State Univ, BS, 52; Univ Tenn, MA, 55. *Prof Exp:* Exchange teacher English, Goethe-Gymnasium, Frankfort, Ger, 56-57; instr Ger & French, Miss State Univ, 58-60; asst prof Ger, Heidelberg Col, 62-63; INSTR GER, OHIO UNIV, 63- *Concurrent Pos:* Fulbright scholar, Univ Freiburg, 55-56, Univ Frankfort, 56-57; Von Schleinitz fel, Univ Wis, 57-58; Woodrow Wilson fel, Princeton Univ, 61-62; adv, Fulbright Prog, 72- *Mem:* MLA; Am Asn Teachers Ger. *Res:* Nineteenth and twentieth century German literature. *Mailing Add:* Dept of Mod Lang Ohio Univ Athens OH 45701

BURNS, MARY ANN T, b Philadelphia, Pa, Jan 24, 28. CLASSICS. *Educ:* Rosemont Col, BA, 49; Univ Pa, AM, 50 & PhD(class studies), 60. *Prof Exp:* Teacher Latin, Wellsboro High Sch, Pa, 50-52 & Springfield High Sch, 52-60; from asst prof to prof classics, Univ Wis-Milwaukee, 60-73, chmn dept, 63-67, actg chmn dept Hebrew studies, 62-63; prof classics & dean, Wilson Col, 73-76; acad dean, Emmanuel Col, 77-; VPRES ACAD AFFAIRS & DEAN, MARY WASHINGTON COL, 79- *Concurrent Pos:* Vis lectr, Marquette Univ, 63, 66, 67 & 69. *Mem:* Am Class League (vpres, 73-78, pres, 80-); Am Philol Asn; Archaeol Inst Am; Am Conf Acad Deans. *Res:* Classical mythology; Roman historical writers. *Publ:* Coauth, Lingua Latina: Liber Primus, 64 & Lingua Latina: Liber Alter, 65, Bruce. *Mailing Add:* Off of Acad Affairs Mary Washington Col Fredericksburg VA 22401

BURQUEST, DONALD ARDEN, b Sarasota, Fla, Jan 28, 39; m 65; c 1. LINGUISTICS, AFRICAN STUDIES. *Educ:* Wheaton Col, BA, 61; Univ Calif, Los Angeles, MA, 65, PhD(ling), 73. *Prof Exp:* Res fel ling, Ahmadu Bello Univ, Nigeria, 68-75; ASST PROF LING, UNIV TEX, ARLINGTON, 75- *Concurrent Pos:* Res linguist & consult, Summer Inst of Ling, 64- *Mem:* Ling Soc Am; West Africa Ling Soc. *Res:* Theoretical linguistics; artificial intelligence; semantics. *Publ:* Auth, A preliminary study of Angas Phonology, Studies Nigerian Lang, 71; coauth, Now the computer can learn Choctaw grammar, Noes Ling, 77; auth, Semantic parameters in Angas kinship terminology, Afroasiatic Ling, 78; ed, Topics in Natural Generative Phonology, Res Papers Tex Summer Inst Ling at Dallas, 78. *Mailing Add:* 7500 W Camp Wisdom Rd Dallas TX 75236

BURR, RONALD LEWIS, Philosophy, Comparative Thought. See Vol IV

BURRELL, PAUL BAKEWELL, b Akron, Ohio, June 16, 28; m 53; c 4. FRENCH. *Educ:* Columbia Univ, AB, 50; Western Reserve Univ, MA, 53, PhD(French), 65. *Prof Exp:* Instr French & English, St Vincent Col, 56-60; instr, 62-63, ASST PROF FRENCH, UNIV CINCINNATI, 63- *Publ:* Auth, Frost's The Draft Horse, Explicator, 3/67; Aubeliere: A note on Rabelais's vocabulary, Etudes rabelaisiennes, IX, 74; co-transl, The Origin of the Idea of Chance in Children, Norton, 75; General Rhetoric, Johns Hopkins Press, 81; auth, Pierre Bayle's dictonnaire historique et critique, In: Notable Encyclopedias in 17th & 18th Centuries, Studies on Voltaire & 18th Cent, Vol 194. *Mailing Add:* 3432 St John's Pl Cincinnati OH 45208

BURROWS, REYNOLD Z, b Boston, Mass, May 19, 21; m 52; c 2. LATIN, GREEK. *Educ:* Harvard Univ, BA, 46; Univ Mich, MA, 49; Princeton Univ, PhD(classics), 56. *Prof Exp:* Instr Latin & hist, Lake Forest Acad, 48-49; instr classics, Univ Utah, 50-54; instr, Princeton Univ, 55-56; asst prof, Miami Univ, 56-59; asst prof, Univ Colo, 59-60; assoc prof, San Francisco State Col, 60-62; assoc prof Greek & Latin, 62-76, chmn dept, 63-73, PROF CLASSICAL STUDIES, SWEET BRIAR COL, 76- *Concurrent Pos:* Vis Prof, Col Year in Athens Prog, Athens, Greece, 64-65; vis lectr Latin, Oxford Univ, 69-70; vis tutor, Somerville Col, 70; vis tutor, Theresian Gym, Munich, 74. *Mem:* Am Philol Asn; Class Asn Mid W & S; Archaeol Inst Am History of Roman Empire; Cicero's philosophical works. *Mailing Add:* Dept of Greek & Latin Sweet Briar Col Sweet Briar VA 24595

BURSILL-HALL, GEOFFREY LESLIE, b Yorkshire, England, May 15, 20; m 47; c 2. LINGUISTICS. *Educ:* Cambridge Univ, BA, 47, MA, 50; Univ London, PhD, 59. *Prof Exp:* Assoc prof French, Univ BC, 49-64; PROF LING, SIMON FRASER UNIV, 64- *Concurrent Pos:* Can Coun sr fel, 67-68; Guggenheim fel, 72-73. *Mem:* Can Ling Asn; Philol Soc England; Mediaeval Acad Am. *Res:* General linguistics; history of linguistics. *Publ:* Speculative grammars of the Middle Ages, Mouton, The Hague; Thomas of Erfurt, Grammatica speculativa, Lingman. *Mailing Add:* Dept of Mod Lang Simon Fraser Univ Burnaby BC V5A 1S6 Can

BURTNIAK, MICHAEL, b Poland; Mar 17, 25; Can citizen. SLAVIC PHILOLOGY. *Educ:* Univ Toronto, AB, 51, Am, 53; Univ Ottawa, PhD(Slavic philol), 72. *Prof Exp:* Lectr mod lang, Brooklyn Col, 59-60; lectr Russ lang, McMaster Univ, 60-61; from instr to asst prof, 61-73, ASSOC PROF MOD LANG, CANISIUS COL, 73- *Mem:* MLA; As Asn Teachers Slavic & E Europ Lang; AAUP. *Res:* Slavic philology and history of modern East Central Europe. *Publ:* Auth, Compiler, Anthology of Early Russian Literature, 62 & coauth, Russian-English Dictionary of Common Literary Terms, 63, Canisius Col. *Mailing Add:* Dept of Mod Lang Canisius Col Buffalo NY 14208

BUSCH, ROBERT LOUIS, b Highland Park, Mich, Aug 14, 39; m 63; c 3. RUSSIAN LITERATURE & LANGUAGE. *Educ:* Univ Mich, BA, 64, MA, 67, PhD(Russ lit), 72. *Prof Exp:* ASST PROF RUSS LANG & LIT, UNIV ALTA, 71- *Mem:* Am Asn Teachers Slavic & East Europ Lang; Can Asn Slavists; MLA. *Res:* Russian Romanticism; Soviet Russian Literature. *Publ:* N A Polefoj's Moskovskij telegraf and junaja francija, Can Rev Comp Lit, spring 74. *Mailing Add:* Dept of Slavic Lang Univ of Alta Edmonton AB T6G 2M7 Can

BUSH, NEWELL RICHARD, b Indianapolis, Ind, Sept, 30, 13; m 59; c 2. FOREIGN LANGUAGES. *Educ:* Miami Univ, BA, 35; Columbia Univ, MA, 37, PhD(French), 49. *Prof Exp:* Instr French, Wheaton Col, 39-42; instr, Swarthmore Col, 47-49, asst prof French & Ital, 49-52; instr French, Univ Ill, Urbana, 52-53; from mgr to ed, Teachers English to Speakers Other Lang, McGraw-Hill Bk Co, New York, 56-67; assoc prof, 67-70, prof, 70-80, EMER PROF FRENCH, UNIV NC, CHARLOTTE, 80- *Concurrent Pos:* Inst Int Educ asst English, Lycee Corneille, Rouen, France, 35-36. *Mem:* S Atlantic Mod Lang Asn; Am Asn Teachers Fr; Fr Soc Studies 18th Century; Am Soc 18th Century Studies. *Res:* The Marquis d'Argens and Voltaire; 18th century French literature. *Publ:* Auth, The Marquis d'Argens and His Philosophical Correspondence, Edwards Bros, 53; ed, English for Today (ser), McGraw, 63-67; auth, Present state of studies on the Marquis d'Argens, Romance Notes, 72. *Mailing Add:* Dept of Foreign Lang Univ of NC Charlotte NC 28213

BUSH, WILLIAM SHIRLEY, b Plant City, Fla, July 21, 29; m 59; c 4. FRENCH LITERATURE. *Educ:* Stetson Univ, BA, 50; State Univ SDak, MA, 53; Univ Paris, DrUniv, 59. *Prof Exp:* From instr to assoc prof Romance lang, Duke Univ, 59-66; assoc prof, 66-67, PROF FRENCH, UNIV WESTERN ONT, 67- *Concurrent Pos:* Fulbright grant, 56, prize award, 57; asst English, Lycee Janson Sailly, Paris, 58-59; Duke Univ res grants, 62-63 & 65-66; Can Coun leave fel, 72-73 & 79-80; ed adv, Studies Twentieth Century Lit, 76- *Res:* Nineteenth and 20th century French literature. *Publ:* Auth, Souffrance et Expiation dans la Pensee de Bernanos, 62 & L'Angoisse du Mystere: Essai sur Bernanos et M Ouine, 66, Minard, Paris; Georges Bernanos, Twayne, 69; ed, Actes du Colloque de London, Canada, Courrier Georges Bernanos, 71; contrib, Georges Bernanos, Plon, 72; auth, Les enfants humilies: composition, themes et titre, Rev Lett Mod, 73; ed, Regards sur Baudelaire, Lett Mod, Paris, 74; auth, Peguy a la lumiere de la theologie mystique de l'Eglise d'orient, Contacts, 77; Georges Bernanos, In: Critical Bibliography of French Literature, Syracuse Univ Press, 80. *Mailing Add:* Dept of French Univ of Western Ont London ON N6A 3K7 Can

BUSHALA, EUGENE WALDO, b Cambridge, Ohio, July 29, 28. CLASSICS. *Educ:* Wayne Univ, BA, 50; Ohio State Univ, MA, 51, PhD(classics), 54. *Prof Exp:* Instr classics, Univ Wis, 56-60; asst prof, Hanover Col, 60-61 & Wesleyan Univ, 61-63; asst prof, 63-69, ASSOC PROF CLASSICS, BOTON COL, 69-, CHMN DEPT CLASS STUDIES, 77- *Mem:* Am Philol Asn. *Res:* Latin poetry; Homer; Greek drama. *Publ:* Auth, Meaning of Togata, 69 & Meaning of Rhoptron, 69, Latomus; Euripides, Hippolytus 1173, Trans & Proc Am Philol Asn, 69. *Mailing Add:* Dept of Classics Boston Col Chestnut Hill MA 02167

BUSOT, ADRIANA B, b Santa Clara, Cuba, Jan 18, 29; m 51; c 4. SPANISH LANGUAGE & LITERATURE. *Educ:* Univ Havana, Dr Filos y Let, 54; Univ Wis-Madison, MA, 70. *Prof Exp:* Asst prof hist, Inst Santa Clara, 54-59 & Univ Santa Clara, 59-61; teacher, Cedar Falls, Pub Schs, 62-63 & Waterloo Pub Schs, 64-65; asst prof Span lang, Univ Northern Iowa, 63-64; ASSOC PROF SPAN LANG & LIT, UNIV WIS-WHITEWATER, 65- *Mem:* MLA; Am Asn Teachers Span & Port; NEA. *Mailing Add:* Dept of Foreign Lang Univ of Wis Whitewater WI 53190

BUSOT, ALDO J, b Cuba, Aug 14, 23; m 51; c 4. SPANISH. *Educ:* Univ Havana, DrLaws, 47; NY Univ, MCJ, 52; Univ Paris, DrLaws, 57; Univ Wis-Madison, MA, 70, JD, 72. *Prof Exp:* Prof Span, Edward Waters Col, 61-62; asst prof Span lang & lit, Univ Northern Iowa, 62-65; PROF SPAN LANG & LIT, UNIV WIS-WHITEWATER, 65- *Mem:* MLA; Am Asn Teachers Span & Port; Am Bar Asn. *Res:* International law; Spanish American literature; linguistics. *Mailing Add:* Dept of Foreign Lang Univ of Wis Whitewater WI 53190

BUSSE, BONNIE BEULAH, b Mandato, Minn, Sept 24, 26. SPANISH LANGUAGE & LINGUISTICS. *Educ:* Macalester Col, BA, 48; Univ Nebr-Lincoln, MA, 50; Ohio State Univ, PhD(foreign lang educ), 70. *Prof Exp:* Transl & interpreter Span, 51-57; teacher Span & chmn foreign lang dept, Chicago Bd Educ, 58-66; asst prof, 67-70, assoc prof, 71-80, PROF SPAN & METHODS TEACHING FOREIGN LANG, NORTHEASTERN ILL UNIV, 80- *Concurrent Pos:* Vis prof, Roosevelt Univ, 69- *Mem:* Am Asn Teachers Span & Port; Am Coun Teaching Foreign Lang. *Res:* Teacher education; methodology; professional laboratory experiences. *Publ:* Auth, Innovation in the professional preparation of foreign language teachers, Bull Ill Foreign Lang Teachers Asn 4/72; Suggestions for preparing material to use with slides, filmstrips and motion picture filsm, Hispania, 3/73; The receptive skills--listening and reading, In: Designs for Language Teacher Education, Newbury House, 73. *Mailing Add:* Dept of Foreign Lang Northeastern Ill Univ Bryn Mawr at St Louis Ave Chicago IL 60625

BUTLER, ROY FRANCIS, b Atlanta, Ga, May 4, 14; m 43; c 2. CLASSICAL PHILOLOGY. *Educ:* Univ Chattonooga, AB, 35; Univ Tenn, AM, 38; Ohio State Univ, PhD, 42. *Prof Exp:* Instr, Univ Tenn, 46 & Ohio State Univ, 46-47; from asst prof to assoc prof, 47-52, PROF CLASSICS, BAYLOR UNIV, 52-, CHMN DEPT, 58- *Mem:* Am Philol Asn; Ling Soc Am; Class Asn Mid W & S; Am Orient Soc; AAAS. *Res:* Etymology of English; classical mythology. *Publ:* Auth, Handbook of Medical Terminology, Baylor Univ, 72; ed consult, Dorland's Illustrated Medical Dictionary, 25th ed, Saunders, 74; auth, The Meaning of Agapao and Phileo in the Greek New Testament, Coronado, 77; transl, Martial 6.82, Helios, Vol VI, No 1; Catullus 10, Classical Outlook, Vol 39, No 1; auth, Sources of the medical vocabulary, J Medical Educ, No 55, 80. *Mailing Add:* Dept of Classics Col of Arts & Sci Baylor Univ Waco TX 76703

BUTLER, THOMAS J, b Detroit, Mich, May 15, 29; m 54; c 3. SLAVIC LANGUAGES & LITERATURE. *Educ:* Harvard Univ, AB, 51, MA, 55, PhD(Slavic lang & lit), 63. *Prof Exp:* Teaching fel Russ, Harvard Univ, 58-60; asst prof, Tufts Univ, 62-67; asst prof slavic lang, Univ Wis-Madison, 68-71, assoc prof, 71-79; vis lectr, 79-80, MEM FAC, RUSS RES CTR, HARVARD UNIV, 80- *Concurrent Pos:* Coun Learned Soc res grant, 72; Am Philos Soc travel grant, Yugoslavia, 73; Fulbright fel, Univ Belgrade, 67-68, 81-82 & Univ Sarajevo, 77-78; rev ed, Slavic & E Eruop J, 70-71; mem rev staff, Books Abroad, 71- *Mem:* Am Asn Teachers Alavic & E Europ Lang; Int Conf Bulgarian Studies; MLA; Am Asn S Slavic Studies (secy-treas, 73-75). *Res:* South Slavic and Russian languages and literatures; Slavic cultural history; preparation of a bilingual anthology of Serbo-Croatian texts. *Publ:* Auth, The Origins of the War for a Serbian Language and Orthography, Harvard Univ, 70; The linguistic heterogeneity of Njegos's Gorski Vijenac, Proc Pac Northwest Conf Foreign Lang, 72; Njegos's early poem on a Russian theme, Mnemozina, 74; Literary style and poetic function in Mesa Selimovic's The Dervish and Death, Slavonic & E Europ Rev, winter 75 & Savremenik, 5/75; Yugoslavia's Slavic languages: A historical perspective, Rev Nat Lit, spring 75; The language of Serbian and Croatian medieval tales, Slavic Ling & Lang, Teaching Slavica, 76; ed, Bulgaria Past and Present, AAAS, 76; Monumenta Serbocroatica: A Bilingual Anthology of Serbian and Croatian Texts, Mich Slavic Publ, 80. *Mailing Add:* 32 Vernon St Nahant MA 01908

BUTTERS, RONALD RICHARD, b Cedar Rapids, Iowa, Feb 12, 40; m 60; c 3. DIALECTOLOGY, LINGUISTIC THEORY. *Educ:* Univ Iowa, BA, 62, PhD(English), 67. *Prof Exp:* Asst prof, 67-74, ASSOC PROF ENGLISH, DUKE UNIV, 75- *Concurrent Pos:* Ed, Am Speech. *Mem:* Ling Soc Am; Am Dialect Soc. *Res:* Speech variation; theory of metaphor. *Publ:* Auth, Acceptability judgments for double modals in southern dialects, In: New Ways of Analyzing Variation in English, Georgetown Univ Press, 73; Black English: Some theoretical implications, 75, Variability in indirect questions, 77 & Narrative go, say, 80, Am Speech; A comment on sociolinguistics and teaching black-dialect writers, Col English, 81; Do conceptual metaphors' really exist?, SECOL Bull, 81; Syntactic change in English propredicates', J English Ling (in prep). *Mailing Add:* Dept of English Duke Univ Durham NC 27706

BUTTREY, THEODORE V, JR, b Havre, Mont, Dec 29, 29; m 53; c 2. CLASSICAL LANGUAGES. *Educ:* Princeton Univ, BA, 50, PhD, 53. *Prof Exp:* From instr to asst prof classics, Yale Univ, 54-64; assoc prof, 64-68, chmn dept, 68-71, PROF CLASS STUDIES, UNIV MICH, ANN ARBOR, 68- *Concurrent Pos:* Fulbright fel, Univ Rome, 53-54; Morse fel, 60-61; Am Philos Soc grant, 62; vis fel, Clare Hall, Cambridge, England, 71-72, assoc, 72- *Mem:* Am Numis Soc; Am Philol Soc; Archaeol Inst Am; Royal Numis Soc; Fr Soc Numis. *Res:* Greek literature; numismatics. *Mailing Add:* Dept of Class Studies Univ of Mich Ann Arbor MI 48104

BUTTRY, DOLORES JEAN, b Bloomington, Ill, Feb 24, 44. SCANDINAVIAN & COMPARATIVE LITERATURE. *Educ:* Ill State Univ, BA, 67, MA, 72; Middlebury Col, MA, 69; Univ Ill, PhD(comp lit), 78. *Prof Exp:* Instr French & German, Ill State Univ, 72-73; asst prof Norwegian & French, Moorhead State Univ, 78-80; Mellon fac fel comp lit, Harvard Univ, 80-81; ASST PROF NORWEGIAN & FRENCH, MOORHEAD STATE UNIV, 81- *Mem:* Soc Adv Scandinavian Studies; MLA. *Res:* The life and works of Knut Hamsun; German, French and Scandinavian literature form 1890-1950. *Publ:* Auth, The Friendly Stone: Hamsun's Pathetic Fallacy, EDDA, Vol III, 79; The autodidact in defense of himself: Jean-Jacques Rousseau and Knut Hamsun, J Gen Educ, spring 80; Knut Hamsun and the Rousseauian soul, Scandinavica, 11/80; Music and the musician in the works of Knut Hamsun, Scandinavian Studies, No 53, 81; Secret suffering: Knut Hamsun's Allegory of the Creative Artist, Studies in Short Fiction, winter 82. *Mailing Add:* Dept of Lang Moorhead State Univ Moorhead MN 56560

BUYNIAK, VICTOR O, b Warsaw, Poland, Oct 12, 25; Can citizen; m 54. SLAVIC LANGUAGES. *Educ:* Univ Alta, BA, 54, MA, 55; Univ Ottawa, PhD(Russ lit), 70. *Prof Exp:* From asst prof to assoc prof, 58-66, actg head dept Ger lang, 75-78, head dept, 75-81, PROF SLAVIC STUDIES, UNIV SASK, 73-, HEAD DEPT GER LANG, 78- *Concurrent Pos:* Humanities Res Coun res grant, Can, 72-73. *Mem:* Can Asn Slavists (pres, 65-66); Far Western Slavic Conf; Inter-Univ Comt Can Slavs (secy-treas, 65-67); Cent & E Europ Studies Asn Can; Can Fedn Humanities. *Res:* Slavic languages and literatures; linguistics; early Slavic history. *Publ:* Auth, Slavic studies in Canada: An hisorical review, Can Slavic Papers, 67; Place Names of the Early Doukhobor Settlements in Saskatchewan, Slavs in Can, 71; Marko Vovchok and Leo Tolstoy, Can Slavic Papers, 72; Hryhory Skovoroda--Spiritual Mentor of the Doukhobors, Iskra, 72. *Mailing Add:* Dept of Slavic Studies, Univ of Sask Saskatoon SK S7N 0W0 Can

BYNUM, DAVID ELIAB, b Louisville, Ky, Jan 26, 36; m 66; c 2. EASTERN EUROPEAN ORAL LITERATURE. *Educ:* Harvard Univ, AB, 58, Am, 62, PhD(Slavic lang & lit), 64. *Prof Exp:* From instr to asst prof Slavic & gen educ & asst cur, Harvard Univ, 64-72, cur, Milman Parry Collection oral lit, 72-78, lectr oral lit, 73-78; prof mod lang & chmn dept, The Citadel, 80-82; PROF MOD LANG & DEAN COL ARTS & SCI, CLEVELAND STATE UNIV, 82- *Concurrent Pos:* Consult, subcomt E Cent & Southeast Europ studies & mem adv comt libr needs, Am Coun Learned Soc, 67-72; assoc bibliogr, MLA, 67-, exec comt, div anthrop approaches to lit, 78-82, deleg assembly, 80-82; chmn bd tutors in folklore & mythology, Harvard Univ, 68-77, managing ed, Publ Milman Parry Collection, 73-, exec officer, Ctr Study Oral Traditions, 74-78, mem, Standing Comt African Studies, 74-78, tutor folklore & myth, John Winthrop House, 77-80; prin investr, Nat Endowment for Humanities Prog Dev Grant, 72-74; Guggenheim fel, 79-80; chmn, Comt to Rev Daniel Lib, 81- *Mem:* MLA; Am Folklore Soc; Am Asn Advan Slavic Studies; Am Asn Southern European Studies; Comp Lit Asn. *Res:* Oral traditions; narrative; East European literatures. *Publ:* Auth, The generic nature of oral epic poetry, Genre, 69; Thematic sequences and transformation of character in oral narrative tradition, Rev Philol, 70; ed, Serbocroatian Heroic Songs, Harvard Univ, Vol 4, 74, Vol 6, 79 & Vol 14, 80; auth, Child's legacy enlarged: Oral literary studies at Harvard since 1856, Harvard Libr Bull, 74; The Daemon in the Wood: A Study of Oral Narrative Patterns, Harvard Univ, 78; The bell, the drum, Milman Parry, and the time machine, Chinese Lit, 79; Myth and ritual: Two faces of tradition, Festschrift for Albert Bates Lord, 81; Formula, theme and critical method, Can-Am Slavic Studies, 81. *Mailing Add:* Dept Mod Lang Cleveland State Univ Cleveland OH 44115

BYRD, SUZANNE WADE, b Macon, Ga. SPANISH, SPANISH THEATER. *Educ:* Univ Ga, AB, 46, PhD(Romance lang), 72; Univ SC, MA, 67. *Prof Exp:* Instr English as second lang & Span, Lang Sch, Ft Gordon, Ga, 67-68; teaching asst Span, Univ Ga, 68-72; instr French, Ga State Univ, 72; asst prof, 72-77, ASSOC PROF SPAN, COL CHARLESTON, 77- *Concurrent Pos:* Participant, Nat Endowment for Humanities Sem, Duke Univ, 76; Col Charleston Found res grants, 76-77; Nat Endowment for Humanities & Am Philos Soc grant, 79. *Mem:* Am Asn Teachers Span & Port; SAtlantic Mod Lang Asn; MLA; Soc Span & Port Hist Studies. *Res:* Theater of Federico Garcia Lorca; Spanish national theater; English as second language. *Publ:* Auth, International Bilingual-Bicultural Conference, 1974, Asn Dept Foreign Lang Quart, 9/74; articles publ, Americas, 74, 77 & 79; La Barraca and The Spanish National Theater, Las Americas, 75. *Mailing Add:* Dept of Span Col of Charleston Charleston SC 29401

BYRUM, C STEPHEN, b Athens, Tenn, June 2, 47; m 67; c 2. PHILOSOPHY, LITERATURE. *Educ:* Tenn Wesleyan Col, BA, 69; Southern Sem, MDiv, 71; Univ Tenn, MA, 73, PhD(philos), 76. *Prof Exp:* ASSOC PROF PHILOS, CHATTANOOGA STATE COMMUNITY COL, 76-, ASST DEAN HUMANITIES, 82- *Concurrent Pos:* Nat bd dir, Inst Advan Philos Res, 82- *Mem:* Robert Hartman Inst; Southern Soc Philos & Psychol; Am Philos Asn. *Res:* Axiological implications in aestheics; Heideggar and Gadamer; the concept of intrinsic value. *Publ:* Auth, Philosophy and play, Man and World, 75; The possibility of a theologic in the Hartman value structure, J Value Inquiry, 76; A selection of eight poems, SCETE Newsletter, 79; The Value Structure of Theology, Univ Press Am, 78; What does it mean to know: Heidegger and teaching philosophy, Imprinting Col & Univ Teaching, 80; David would come, Sequoya Rev, 80; Reflections of the wizard of Earth sea, Philos in Context, 81; Maslow's motivatoinal theory: A clarification, Contemporary Philos, 82. *Mailing Add:* Chattanooga State Community Col 4501 Amnicola Hwy Chattanooga TN 37406

C

CABALLERO, JUAN A, b Ciego de Avila, Cuba, May 5, 21; nat US; m 49; c 2. SPANISH. *Educ:* Univ Havana, Dr en Derecho, 47; Rutgers Univ, MA, 67, PhD(Span), 70. *Prof Exp:* Instr Span, Rutgers Univ, Camden, 62-67; from asst prof to assoc prof, 67-76, PROF SPAN, UNIV W FLA, 76- *Honors & Awards:* Distinguished Teaching Award, Univ WFla, 75. *Mem:* MLA; SAtlantic Mod Lang Asn; Am Asn Teachers Span & Port. *Res:* Latin American literature; Spanish literature; Lorca. *Publ:* Auth, A Disctionary of Spanish Idioms, L A Publ, 69; Functional Spanish, Univ WFla, 74; El teatro de Sebastian Salazar Bondy, Garcia Ribeyro, Lima, Peru, 75; coauth, Espanol: practica intensiva, Educ Ling Publ, 76; co-ed, La casa de Bernarda Alba, 76 & Poema del Cante Jondo/Romancero gitano, 77, Catedra, Madrid. *Mailing Add:* Dept of Span Univ WFla Pensacola FL 32504

CACOSSA, ANTHONY ALEXANDER, b Newburgh, NY, Jan 29, 35; m 69. ROMANCE LANGUAGES & LITERATURES. *Educ:* Johns Hopkins Univ, BA, 55; Syracuse Univ, MA, 56; Univ of the Andes, Colombia, cert Hisp studies, 65; Univ Catania, Dr mod lang, 69. *Prof Exp:* Asst Span Syracuse Univ, 56-57; asst prof French & Span & chmn dept, Coppin State Col, 59-65; from asst prof to assoc prof, 65-75, PROF ROMANCE LANG, TOWSON STATE UNIV, 75-, COORDR ITAL & PORT, 74- *Concurrent*

Pos: Fulbright-Hays teacher, Italy, 68-69 & sr lectr English, Costa Rica, 72-73; cult adv & coordr for Cent Am, Am Latina, 72- *Mem:* AAUP; Mid States MLA; SAtlantic MLA; Col Lang Asn; Am Asn Teachers Span & Port. *Res:* Italian literature of the Renaissance; French literature of the 20th century; foreign language education. *Publ:* Auth, The foreign language laboratory: Not just another comment, 65 & A portrait of Paul Claudel, 66, CLA J; A Bergamask Parody of Giovanni Battista Guarini's Il Pastor Fido, Ed Texto, Costa Rica, 72; Una parodia Bergamasca del Pastor Fido di Giambattista Guarini, Casa Ed Maccari, Italy, 73; A cultural note on Costa Rica, Am Latina, 73. *Mailing Add:* Dept of Mod Lang Towson State Univ Baltimore MD 21204

CADART-RICARD, ODETTE MARIE-HELENE, b Romilly, France, Sept 8, 25; US citizen; m 47; c 2. FRENCH, EDUCATION. *Educ:* Univ Paris, BA & LLB, 45; Dominican Col San Rafael, BA, 47; Sacramento State Col, MA, 59; Univ Ore, PhD(French & educ), 70. *Prof Exp:* Instr French, Dominican Col San Rafael, 47-48; instr French & hist, Sacramento City Sch Dist, 60-65; from asst prof to assoc prof French & educ, 65-76, dir Mod Lang Educ, 65-75, PROF FRENCH, ORE STATE UNIV, 76-, HEAD FRENCH SECT, 81- *Concurrent Pos:* Dir Ore Studies Ctr, Univ Poitiers, 71-73. *Honors & Awards:* Chevalier, Palmes Acad, 72. *Mem:* Am Asn Prof Fr; MLA; Int Courtly Lit Soc; Western Soc Fr Hist. *Res:* Cerveri de Girona and troubadour poetry; non-linear programming of French syntax; French civilization. *Publ:* Auth, L'Elaboration du nouveau vocabulaire technique de la langue courante en France, 68 & Meaning in cross-cultural situations: An application of Vygotsky's unit of analysis to ethnolinguistics, Proc Pac Northwest Conf Foreign Lang, 71; The French verb system: A programed text, Vol I, In: The Indicative, Ore State Univ, 71; Alienor d'Aquitaine, domna de Bernard de Ventadour, Proc Pac Northwest Conf Foreign Lang, 72; Le theme de l'oiseau dans les comparaisons et les dictons chez onze troubadours, Cahiers de Civilisation Medievale, 1/78; coauth, Les Gammas! An Introductory French Text, Macmillan, 82. *Mailing Add:* Dept Foreign Lang & Lit Ore State Univ Corvallis OR 97331

CADORA, FREDERICK JOSEPH, b Jerusalem, Jordan, Feb 21, 37; US citizen; m 60; c 2. ARABIC LANGUAGE & LINGUISTICS. *Educ:* Emory Univ, BA, 59; Univ Mich, MA, 61 & 62, PhD(Near Eastern lang & lit), 66. *Prof Exp:* Instr teaching English as second lang & appl ling, Am Univ Beirut, 62-66, asst prof appl ling, 66-67; dir MidE prog, 71-73, ASSOC PROF ARABIC LANG, LIT & LING, OHIO STATE UNIV, 67-, CHMN DEPT JUDAIC & NEAR EASTERN LANG & LIT, 81- *Mem:* Ling Soc Am; Am Orient Soc; MLA; Am Asn Teachers Arabic (exec secy, 71-); Mid E Studies Asn NAm. *Res:* Arabic dialects; modern Arabic literature; contemporary Arabic culture. *Publ:* Coauth, Contemporary Arabic Readers: III Formal Arabic, Univ Mich, 63; auth, The Concept of Compatibility in the Lexical Study of Language Varieties, Word, 66; Some Linguistic Concomitants of Contactual Factors of Urbanization, Anthrop Ling, 70; Interdialectal Lexical Compatibility in Arabic, Brill, 79. *Mailing Add:* Dept of Judaic & Near East Lang & Lit Ohio State Univ Columbus OH 43210

CAGNON, MAURICE, b Woonsocket, RI, Feb 11, 40. TWENTIETH CENTURY FRANCOPHONE & FRENCH LITERATURE. *Educ:* Providence Col, AB, 59; Middlebury Col, AM, 61; Univ Pa, PhD(Romance lang), 67. *Prof Exp:* Instr French, Providence Col, 61-62; asst prof, Atlanta Univ, 65-68; asst prof Romance lang, Univ Conn, 68-71; assoc prof, 71-77, PROF FRENCH, MONTCLAIR STATE COL, 71- *Mem:* MLA; Am Asn Teachers Fr; Am Coun Teaching Foreign Lang; Northeast MLA; Asn Can Studies in US. *Res:* Contemporary French fiction and poetry; modern Quebecois fiction, poetry and essay. *Publ:* Collab ed, Critical Bibliography of French Literature, Syracuse Univ; J M G Leclezio: l'impossible verite de la fiction, Critique, 72; Les pieces de Nathalie Sarraute: voix et contre voix, Rev Sci Humaines, 74; J M G Le Clezio: Fiction's double bind, In: Surfiction: Fiction Now and Tomorrow, Swallow, 75; Le Palimpsest ou la vision lointaine chez Gilbert Toulouse, Presence Francophone, 76; Parody and caricature in Aquin's L'Antiphonaire, Critique, 77; Palimpsest in the writings of Hubert Aquin, Mod Lang Studies, 78; ed, Ethique et esthetique dans la litterature francaise du XXe siecle, Stanford Univ, 78. *Mailing Add:* Dept of French Montclair State Col Upper Montclair NJ 07043

CAILLER, BERNADETTE ANNE, b Poitiers, France, June 8, 41. AFRICAN & CARIBBEAN LITERATURE. *Educ:* Univ Poitiers, Lic es Lett, 61, Dipl d Etudes Superieures, 64; Univ Paris, CAPES, 68; Cornell Univ, MA, 67, PhD(comp lit), 74. *Prof Exp:* Asst prof, 74-79, ASSOC PROF FRENCH, UNIV FLA, 79- *Mem:* African Lit Asn; Am Asn Teachers of Fr; Asn Caribbean Studies. *Res:* Caribbean and African poetry, novel & music and drama. *Publ:* Auth, proposition poetique: Une lecture de poeuvre, Naaman, 5/76; Saint-John Perse devant la crituque antillaise, Stanford Fr Rev, fall 78; Lefficacite der Vaudou daus un Arc-en-ciel pour l' vccident chretien, Fr Rev, 10/79; Analyse critique de Negritude et negrologues par SAdorevi, Veureset Crituques, fall 79; Un Itineraire poetique: Edouard Glissaant et l' Anti-Anabase Presence Francophone, fall 79; L'Aventure ambiguë de Cheikh Hamidou Kane: Autobiographie ou histoire d' un peuple?, Fr Rev, 5/82; Ti-Jean l' Horizon de S Schwarz-Bart ou la lezon du Royaume des Morts, Stanford Fr Rev, winter 82; Defining the African Aesthetics: 1980 Am Libr Asn Selected Papers, Three Continents Press, fall 82. *Mailing Add:* 470 Grinter Hall Univ Fla Gainesville FL 32611

CAIN, JOAN T, b Chicago, Ill, Nov 2, 29. ROMANCE LANGUAGES. *Educ:* Rosary Col, BA, 51; Univ Wis, MA, 59, PhD(Span), 64. *Prof Exp:* Instr Span, Rosary Col, 64-66; asst prof French & Span, 67-71, assoc prof Span, 71-75, PROF SPAN, UNIV SOUTHWESTERN LA, 75-, HEAD, DEPT FOREIGN LANG, 81- *Concurrent Pos:* Nat Endowment for Humanities foreign lang coordr grant, 76-; Danforth assoc, 77. *Honors & Awards:* Univ Distinguished Prof, Univ Southwestern La, 73. *Mem:* Am Asn Teachers Span & Port; MLA; SCentral Mod Lang Asn; Am Asn Adv Humanities. *Res:* Contemporary Spanish women writers; interdisciplinary studies. *Publ:* Coauth, A Basic French Vocabulary, 68 & A Basic Spanish Vocabulary, 69, Univ Press; co-transl, The Historical Journal of the Establishment of the French in Louisiana, Univ Southwestern La, 71; contribr, Teaching about Women in the Foreign Languages, Feminist Press, 75; auth, A portrait of two women by Marta Portal, SCent Bull, winter 75; Ana Diosdado: Winner of the Fastenrath Prize, Letras Femeninas, spring 79; frequent reviews in World Lit Today and other journals. *Mailing Add:* Dept of Foreign Lang Univ of Southwestern La Lafayette LA 70501

CAIRES, VALERIE ANNE, b Hollywood, Calif, Apr 28, 42. COMPARATIVE LITERATURE, GREEK. *Educ:* Univ Calif, Berkeley, AB, 69, MA, 71, PhD(comp lit), 76. *Prof Exp:* Teaching asst mod Greek, Univ Calif, Berkeley, 72-73, acting instr comp & mod Greek, 74-76; ASST PROF BYZANTINE & MOD GREEK, OHIO STATE UNIV, 76- *Concurrent Pos:* Proj dir mod Greek, Exxon Educ Found, 79-80. *Mem:* Mod Greek Studies Asn; MLA; Mediaeval Acad Am. *Res:* Modern Greek literature; Byzantine Greek literature; Medieval Latin and Old French literature. *Mailing Add:* Dept of Byzan & Mod Greek Ohio State Univ Columbus OH 43210

CALDER, WILLIAM MUSGRAVE, III, b Brooklyn, NY, Sept 3, 32. CLASSICAL PHILOLOGY. *Educ:* Harvard Col, BA, 54; Harvard Univ, MA, 56; Univ Chicago, PhD, 58. *Prof Exp:* From instr to prof Greek & Latin, Columbia Univ, 58-76; chmn dept, 77-78, PROF CLASSICS, UNIV COLO, BOULDER, 76- *Concurrent Pos:* Greek ed, Greek, Roman & Byzantine Studies, 60-80; assoc ed, Class World, 61-68; Guggenheim fel & Fulbright res scholar, Ger, 64-65; vis res scholar, Fondation Hardt, Vandoeuvres, Switz, 64-81; Greek examr, Col Entrance Exam Bd, 66-72; mem managing comt, Am Sch Class Studies, Athens, 66-, vis prof, 73-74; guest prof class philol, Univ Rostock, 68 & English lang, 79; Am Coun Learned Soc grant-in-aid, 71; guest prof classics, Boston Univ, 71-72; distinguished visitor, Haverford Col, 72; adv ed, Philologus, Ger Acad Sci, Berline, 72-; guest prof classics, Univ Colo, 75. *Mem:* Soc Prom Hellenic Studies; Soc Prom Roman Studies; Brit Class Asn; Egypt Explor Soc; Archaeol Inst Am. *Res:* Greek literature and epigraphy; history of classical scholarship. *Publ:* Auth, The inscription from Temple G at Selinus, 63; Index Locorum zu Kühner-Gerth, 65 & coauth, Pindaros und Bakchylides, Wiss Buchges, 70; Sophoclean apologia: Philoctetes, 71 & Schliemann on Schliemann, 72, Greek, Roman & Byzantine Studies; U v Wilamowitz, Valediktionsarbeit, E J Brill, 74; Wilamowitz-Jaeger letters, Harvard Studies Class Philol, 78; ed, Wilamowitz nach 50 Jahren, Wiss Buchges, 82. *Mailing Add:* Dept of Classics Univ of Colo Boulder CO 80309

CALDWELL, HELEN F, b Omaha, Nebr, July 9, 04. CLASSICS. *Educ:* Univ Calif, Los Angeles, AB, 25, MA, 39. *Prof Exp:* Sr lectr, 42-70, EMER SR LECTR CLASSICS, UNIV CALIF, LOS ANGELES, 70- *Concurrent Pos:* Am Asn Univ Women Shirley Farr fel, 59-60; Rockefeller Found grants, 61 & 63. *Honors & Awards:* Order Southern Cross, Brazilian Govt, 59. *Res:* Brazilian fiction; classical drama. *Publ:* Transl, Dom Casmurro by Machado de Assis, 53; The Brazilian Othello, 60, coauth & transl, The Psychiatrist and Other Stories by Machado de Assis, 63, Esau and Jacob, 65, Ancient Poets' Guide to UCLA Gardens, 68, Machado de Assis, the Brazilian Master and His Novels, 70, translr, Machado de assis, Counselor Ayres' Memorial, 72, auth, Michio Ito, the Dancer and His Dances, 77, Univ Calif. *Mailing Add:* 330 Cordova Dr Santa Barbara CA 93109

CALDWELL, RUTH LOUISE, b Wooster, Ohio, Jan 21, 44. FRENCH LANGUAGE & LITERATURE. *Educ:* Univ Southern Calif, BA, 65; Univ Chicago, MA, 68, PhD(Romance lang), 73. *Prof Exp:* Asst prof, 71-80, ASSOC PROF FRENCH, LUTHER COL, 80- *Mem:* Am Asn Teachers Fr; MLA; Asn Study Dada & Surrealism. *Res:* Twentieth century French poetry; 18th century French literature; history of the French language. *Publ:* Auth, Structure de la Lettre Sur les Sourds et Muets, Studies Voltaire & 18th Century, 71; A step on Tzara's road to communication, Dada/Surrealism, 74. *Mailing Add:* Luther Col Decorah IA 52101

CALIN, WILLIAM COMPAINE, b Newington, Conn, Apr 4, 36. FRENCH. *Educ:* Yale Univ, AB, 57, PhD(Romance Philol), 60. *Prof Exp:* From instr to asst prof French, Dartmouth Col, 60-63; from asst prof to prof, Stanford Univ, 64-73; chmn dept Romance lang, 76-78, PROF FRENCH, UNIV ORE, 73- *Concurrent Pos:* Guggenheim Found fel, 63-64; Am Coun Learned Soc grants-in-aid, 63-64 & 68; Am Philos Soc grant-in-aid, 70; Fulbright award, 82; vis prof, Univ Poitiers, 82. *Honors & Awards:* Gilbert Chinard First Literary Prize, 81. *Mem:* MLA; Am Asn Teachers Fr; Soc Rencesvals (pres, Am br); Medieval Asn Pac; Western Soc French Hist. *Res:* Medieval French literature; French poetry, epic and lyric; Black African literature in French. *Publ:* A Muse for Heroes, Univ Toronto (in press). *Mailing Add:* Dept of Romance Lang Univ of Ore Eugene OR 97403

CALINESCU, MATEI ALEXE, b Bucharest, Romania, June 15, 34; m 63; c 2. COMPARATIVE LITERATURE, WEST EUROPEAN STUDIES. *Educ:* Univ Cluj, Romania, Dr(comp lit), 72. *Prof Exp:* From asst prof to assoc prof comp lit, Univ Bucharest, Romania, 63-72; vis assoc prof, 73-75, assoc prof, 76-78, PROF COMP LIT, IND UNIV, BLOOMINGTON, 78- *Concurrent Pos:* Guggenheim Mem Found fel, 75. *Mem:* MLA; Int Comp Lit Asn. *Res:* Modernism; history of modern criticism and aesthetics; modern intellectual history. *Publ:* Auth, Conceptul modern de pozie, Editura Eminescu, Bucharest, 72; Fragmentarium, Editura Dacia, Cluj, 73; Imagination and meaning: Aesthetic attitudes and ideas in Mircea Eliade's work, J Relig, 1/77; Faces of Modernity: Avant-Garde, Decadence, Kitsch, Ind Univ, 77; Hermeneutics or Poetics, J Relig, 1/79; Marxism as a work of art, Stanford Fr Rev, spring 79; Ways of looking at fiction, Bucknell Rev, 80; Persuasion, dialogue, autorite, Cadmos, fall 80. *Mailing Add:* Dept of Comp Lit Ind Univ Bloomington IN 47401

CALLAGHAN, CATHERINE A, b Berkeley, Calif, Oct 30, 31. LINGUISTICS. *Educ:* Univ Calif, Berkeley, BA, 54, PhD(ling), 63. *Prof Exp:* Sci linguist, Smithsonia Inst, 62; asst prof ling, Univ Hawaii, 64; asst prof, 65-69, ASSOC PROF LING, OHIO STATE UNIV, 69- *Concurrent Pos:* Am Asn Univ Women fel, 64-65; NSF grant res Calif Indian lang, 66-80. *Mem:* AAAS; Ling Soc Am. *Res:* Reconstruction of proto languages; anthropological linguistics; occult. *Publ:* Auth, Lake Miwok Dictionary, 65 & Bodega Miwok Dictionary, 70, Univ Calif. *Mailing Add:* Dept of Ling Ohio State Univ Columbus OH 43210

CALLAGHAN, MARY CONSUELA, Latin Amercian History. See Vol I

CALLAHAN, ANNE M, b Philadelphia, Pa, Aug 13, 38; m 80. FRENCH & COMPARATIVE LITERATURE. *Educ:* Chestnut Hill Col, BA, 60; Case Western Reserve Univ, MA, 62, PhD(Romance lang), 70. *Prof Exp:* Asst prof French & chmn dept, Chestnut Hill Col, 65-72; chmn dept, 72-78, ASSOC PROF MOD LANG, LOYOLA UNIV CHICAGO, 72- *Honors & Awards:* Palmes Academiques, 75. *Mem:* MLA; Am Soc 18th Century Studies; Int Soc 18th Century Studies ; Friends of George Sand. *Res:* Erotic love in literature; George Sand; early romanticism. *Publ:* Auth, Erotic Love in Literature: From Medieval Legend to Romantic Illusion, Whitston Publ Co, 82. *Mailing Add:* Dept of Mod Lang Loyola Univ 820 N Michigan Ave Chicago IL 60611

CALLAHAN, JOHN FRANCIS, b Chicago, Ill, May 13, 12. CLASSICAL PHILOLOGY, ANCIENT PHILOSOPHY. *Educ:* Loyola Univ, Ill, AB, 33, AM, 34; Univ Chicago, PhD, 40. *Prof Exp:* From instr to asst prof, Loyola Univ, Ill, 37-40 & 41-43; vis instr, Harvard Univ, 40-41; from assoc prof to prof class lang & philos, Georgetown Univ, 46-77; vis scholar, 77-78, FEL, DUMBARTON OAKS, HARVARD UNIV, 78- *Concurrent Pos:* Rockefeller fel, 47-48 & Fund Advan Educ, 53-54; Fulbright res fel, Italy, 53-54 & 55; Guggenheim Found fel, 58-59; Nat Endowment for Humanities fel, 67, res grant, 72-73 & 81-83; res grants, Am Coun Learned Soc, 70 & 79, Am Philos Soc, 70 & Am Res Ctr Egypt, 71 & 72. *Mem:* Am Philol Asn; Am Philos Asn; Int Inst Arts & Lett. *Publ:* Auth, Four Views of Time in Ancient Philosophy, Harvard Univ, 48 & Greenwood, 68 & 79; Basil of Caesarea--a new source for St Augustine's theory of time, Harvard Studies Class Philol, 58; Greek philosophy and the Cappadocian cosmology, Dumbarton Oaks Papers, 58; Plautus' Mirror for a Mirror, Class Philol, 1/64; Augustine and the Greek Philosophers, Villanova, 67; The serpent and H PAXIA in Gregory of Nyssa, Traditio, 68; coauth, Interpretations of Plato, E J Brill, 77. *Mailing Add:* Dumbarton Oaks 1703 32nd St NW Washington DC 20007

CALLAN, RICHARD JEROME, b Mt Vernon, NY, Jan 4, 32; m 54. ROMANCE LANGUAGES. *Educ:* Iona Col, AB, 57; Fordham Univ, MA, 59; St Louis Univ, PhD(Span), 65. *Prof Exp:* Instr Span, St Michael's Col, Vt, 60-63; assoc prof, St Louis Univ, 65-69; ASSOC PROF SPAN AM LIT, UNIV NH, 69- *Mem:* MLA; Am Asn Teachers Span & Port; Inst Int Lit Iberoam; Midwest Mod Lang Asn. *Res:* Spanish American literature; archetypal approach to literature; Meso-American mythology. *Publ:* Auth, Miguel Angel Asturias, Twayne, 70; Funcion sicologica del mito en Hombres de Maiz, Papeles de Son Armadans, 8/71; ed, America, Fabula de Fabulas y Otros Ensayos de Miguel Angel Asturias, Monte Avila Ed, 72; auth, Sabato's fiction: A Jungian interpretation, Bull Hisp Studies, 1/74; La estructura arquetipica de La Lluvia de Uslar Pietri, Cuadernos Am, 3/74; Some parallels between Octavio Paz and Carl Jung, Hispania, 12/77. *Mailing Add:* Dept of Ancient & Mod Lang Univ of NH Durham NH 03824

CALLAS, JAMES HOWARD, b Beaumont, Tex, Sept 15, 31. CLASSICS, ENGLISH. *Educ:* Univ Texas Austin, BA, 54, PhD(classics), 74; Ariz State Univ, MA, 56. *Prof Exp:* Teacher English, humanities & Latin, Sparks High Sch, Nev, 63-66; Fulbright instr English & Am lit, Aleppo Col, Syria, 66-67; teacher & chmn, Dept English & Latin, Marine Mil Acad, Harlingen, Tex, 67-72; Fulbright prof Am lit, Comenius Univ, Bratislava, Czech, 74-75; Fulbright prof English lit, Aleppo Univ, Syria, 75-76; DIR READING ACAD, TEX A&I UNIV, 76- *Concurrent Pos:* US Dept State Fulbright grants, 66, 74, 75 & 76. *Res:* Curriculum development and testing of reading and English language skills, secondary and university levels; development of alternate language programs to meet needs of university students. *Publ:* Contribr, Critical Essays on Roman Literature, Oxford Univ, 63; auth, Language attitudes at the University of Texas, Asn Dept Foreign Lang, 73; Two Greek Poets, Sterling Swift, 73. *Mailing Add:* Campus Box 147 Tex A & I Univ Kingsville TX 78363

CALO, JEANNE EUGENIE, b Tunis, Tunisian, Jan 6, 16; US citizen; m 38; c 4. FRENCH LANGUAGE & LITERATURE. *Educ:* Univ Paris, degree law, 39; Univ Pa, MA, 65, PhD(French), 71. *Prof Exp:* Teacher French, St Mary's Hall, Burlington, NJ, 58-63; teaching fel, Univ Pa, 67-69; asst prof French & Ital, 69-77, ASSOC PROF FRENCH & ITAL, TRENTON STATE COL, 77- *Concurrent Pos:* Teacher French, Pennington Jr & High Schs, NJ, 62-67. *Mem:* MLA; Am Asn Teachers Fr; Alliance Fr; Societe des Professeurs de Langais en Amerique; Am Coun Teaching Foreign Lang. *Res:* Michelet; 19th century French literature; woman in history. *Publ:* Auth, La Creation de la Femme Chez Michelet, Nizet, Paris, 75; Michelet, la mer, la baleine et la femme, Nineteenth-Century Fr Studies, spring-summer 77. *Mailing Add:* Dept of Mod Lang Trenton State Col Trenton NJ 08625

CALVE, PIERRE JEAN, b Maniwaki, Que, Sept 27, 42. FRENCH LANGUAGE. *Educ:* Univ Montreal, BEd, 64; Georgetown Univ, MS, 69, PhD(ling), 78. *Prof Exp:* Teacher French, Loyola Col High Sch, 64-66; PROF APPLIED LING, UNIV OTTAWA, 69- *Concurrent Pos:* Ed dir, Can Mod Lang Rev, 80- *Mem:* Can Asn Applied Ling; Can Ling Asn. *Res:* Foreign language learning and teaching (French); French linguistics; contrastive analysis--French and English. *Publ:* Coauth, Le Francais International, 2nd Version (series of 6 bks), Ctr Educ & Cult, 72-80. *Mailing Add:* Fac Educ Univ Ottawa Ottawa ON K1N 6N5 Can

CALVERT, LAURA MERLE, b Port Clinton, Ohio, June 29, 22; m 42; c 1. ROMANCE LANGUAGES. *Educ:* Univ NMex, BA, 55, MA, 56; Ohio State Univ, PhD(Romance lang), 66. *Prof Exp:* From instr to asst prof Span, Univ NMex, 61-67; asst prof, Univ Mass, Amherst, 67-68; coordr Span, 69-71, mem grad coun, Univ Md Baltimore County, 71-73, from asst prof to assoc prof, 68-76; RETIRED. *Concurrent Pos:* Coord Span instr, Peace Corps Training Ctr, Univ NMex, 62-63; consult, Peace Corps Training prog, Tex Western Col, autumn, 63. *Mem:* MLA; Am Asn Teachers Span & Port. *Res:* Renaissance and baroque literature; literary criticism; linguistics. *Publ:* Auth, The role of written exercises in an audio-lingual program, Hispania, 5/65; An etymological basis for the Pastor-Amador equation, Romance Notes, 69; The widowed turtledove and the amorous dove of Spanish lyric poetry, J Medieval & Renaissance Studies, 73; Francisco de Osuna and the Spirit of the Letter, Univ NC, 73; The Mode of Incongruity, 78 & Meditation of the Creatures, 81, Studia Mystica; Poemas, Verbana, fall 81. *Mailing Add:* 3420 Mateo Prado NW Albuquerque NM 87107

CALVEZ, DANIEL JEAN, b St Goazec, France, May 24, 40; m 67; c 1. MEDIEVAL FRENCH LITERATURE. *Educ:* Univ Angers, France, Acad Poitiers, Lic Lett English, 65; Univ Ga, Athens, PhD(Romance lang), 80. *Prof Exp:* Instr French, Auburn Univ, Ala, 65-69; ASST PROF FRENCH, CLEMSON UNIV, 70- *Mem:* Am Asn Teachers French; SAtlantic Mod Lang Asn; Int Conf Defense Breton Lang. *Res:* Medieval poetry; Voltaire; grammar and composition. *Publ:* Auth, La structure du Rondeau: Mise au point, French Rev, 3/82. *Mailing Add:* Dept of Lang Clemson Univ Clemson SC 29631

CALVO, JUAN ANTONIO, b Valencia, Spain, Mar 29, 30. SPANISH. *Educ:* Univ Valencia, LLB, 53; Ohio Univ, BA, 57; Mich State Univ, MA, 60, PhD(Span lang & lit), 67. *Prof Exp:* Tecnico instr, Ministerio Info y Turismo, Spain, 60-61; instr Span lang, Ohio Univ, 61-62; from instr to assoc prof, 63-74, PROF SPAN LANG & LIT, MICH STATE UNIV, 74-; DIR SPAN PROG, JUSTIN MORRILL COL, 65- *Concurrent Pos:* Mem, Oficina Int Info y Observacion Espanol, 65- *Mem:* MLA; Midwest MLA; Am Asn Teachers Span & Port. *Res:* Spanish literature of the Golden Age; modern Spanish literature; history of Spain. *Publ:* Coauth, La conversacion al dia, Macmillan, 64; Primera lectura, Odyssey, 66; Historia de la civilizacion espanola, Appleton, 69; auth, Aportacion al estudio de la metrica de El Gran Duque de Grandia, Bull Comediantes, 69; Los puntos sobre las ies, Diario de Barcelona, 5/74; Un laberinto invertido: Mein Fuhrer, Mein Fuhrer, Rev Univ Mex, 11/76; La Espana de hoy, Tropos, 6/78. *Mailing Add:* Dept of Romance Lang Mich State Univ East Lansing MI 48823

CAMARGO, MARTIN JOSEPH, Medieval English Literature. See Vol II

CAMBON, GLAUCO, b Pusiano, Italy, May 7, 21; US citizen; m 52, 61; c 4. COMPARATIVE LITERATURE. *Educ:* Univ Pavia, Italy, DrPhil, 47. *Prof Exp:* Lectr English, Scuola Interpreti, Urbino Univ, 54-57 & prof, Arona Lycee, Italy, 56-57; libero docente, Univ Rome, Italy, 58; vis lectr English & comp lit, Univ Mich, 58-61; prof Romance lang & comp lit, Rutgers Univ, 61-69, res fel, 63; PROF ROMANCE LANG & COMP LIT, UNIV CONN, 69- *Concurrent Pos:* Consult English & Am lit, Arnoldo Mondadori Editore, Milan, Italy, 49-58; contribr, Ital Radio Cult Prog, 55-61; fel, Ind Univ Sch Lett, 60; Fulbright-Hays scholar, Italy, 68. *Honors & Awards:* Del Duca Prize, Milan, 56; Star of Italian Solidarity, 62. *Mem:* MLA; Am Asn Teachers Ital; Dante Soc Am; Am Comp Lit Asn. *Res:* Modern poetry; American prose and poetry; Italian modernism in verse and fiction. *Publ:* Auth, The Waste Land as work in progress, Mosaic, Vol VI, No 1; contribr, William Faulkner: Prevailing verities etc, Tex Tech Comp Lit Symp, 73; auth, Ezra Pound as translator of Italian poetry, Studi Am, 73-74; Ugo Foscolo and the poetry of exile, Mosaic, Vol IX, No 2; La Poesia di Ungaretti, Einaudi, Turin, Italy, 76; contribr, Montale--Profilo di uno scrittore, Rizzoli, Milan, 77; Ugo Foscolo, Poet of Exile, 80 & Eugenio Montale's Poetry, 82, Princeton Univ Press. *Mailing Add:* Dept of Romance Lang Univ of Conn Storrs CT 06268

CAMERON, ALAN (DOUGLAS EDWARD), b Windsor, England, Mar 13, 38; m 61; c 2. CLASSICAL PHILOLOGY, BYZANTINE STUDIES. *Educ:* Oxford Univ, BA, 61, MA, 64. *Prof Exp:* Lectr Latin, Univ Glasgow, 61-64, Bedord Col, Univ London, 64-71 & Kings Col, 72-76; ANTHON PROF LATIN, COLUMBIA UNIV, 77- *Honors & Awards:* N H Baynes Prize, London Univ, 67; J Conington Prize, Oxford Univ, 68; fel, British Acad, 75. *Mem:* Soc Roman Studies; Am Philol Asn; fel Am Acad Arts & Sci. *Res:* Latin literature; Roman history; Byzantine history and literature. *Publ:* Auth, Claudian: Poetry and Propaganda at the Court of Honorius, Clarendon, 70; contribr, Prosopography of the Later Roman Empire, Cambridge univ, 70, auth, Porphyrius the Charioteer, 73 & Circus Factions: Blues and Greens at Rome and Byzantium, 76, Clarendon; The date and identity of Macrobius, J Roman Studies, 76; The last days of the Academy at Athens, Proc Cambridge Philol Soc 69; The authenticity of the correspondence of S Nilus of Ancyra, Greek, Roman & Byzantine Studies, 76; Paganism and literature in late fourth century Rome, Fondation Hardt Entretiens, 78. *Mailing Add:* Columbia Univ 604 Hamilton Hall New York NY 10027

CAMERON, ANGUS FRASER, Old English Language & Literature. See Vol II

CAMERON, HOWARD DON, b Pontiac, Mich, Aug 8, 34. CLASSICS, LINGUISTICS. *Educ:* Univ Mich, AB, 56; Princeton Univ, MA, 58, PhD, 62. *Prof Exp:* From instr to assoc prof Greek & Latin, Univ Mich, Ann Arbor, 59-78, chmn Dept Class Studies, 77-80, prof, 78-80. *Concurrent Pos:* Assoc cur, Mus Zool, Univ Mich, 74- *Mem:* Am Philol Asn. *Res:* Greek drama; Homer; history of zoological nomenclature. *Publ:* Auth, The debt to earth in the Seven against Thebes, 64 & The power of words in the Seven against Thebes, 70, Trans & Proc Am Philol Asn, 70; Studies on the Seven against Thebes, Mouton, The Hague, 71; The history of the name Panorpa Linnaeus (Mecoptera), Great Lakes Entomologist, 75; coauth, Cladistic methods in textual, linguistic, and phylogenetic analysis, Systematic Zool, 77. *Mailing Add:* 3519 Burbank Dr Ann Arbor MI 48105

CAMERON, WALLACE JOHN, b Gladstone, Mich, Sept 7, 26. SPANISH LANGUAGE & LITERATURE. *Educ:* Albion Col, BA, 50; Univ Iowa, MA, 52, PhD(Span), 56. *Hon Degrees:* Dipl de Honor, Centro Cult Anglo Am y Col Anglo Am, Oruro, Bolvia, 60. *Prof Exp:* From asst prof to assoc prof Span, 56-65, chmn dept mod lang, 66-71, PROF SPAN, OHIO UNIV, 66- *Concurrent Pos:* Smith-Mundt vis teacher, Bolivia, 59-60. *Mem:* Am Asn Teachers Span & Port; Midwest Asn Latin Am; Latin Am Studies Asn; Cent States Mod Lang Teachers Asn. *Mailing Add:* Dept of Mod Lang Ohio Univ Athens OH 45701

CAMINOS, RICARDO AUGUSTO, b Buenos Aires, Arg, July 11, 15. EGYPTOLOGY. *Educ:* Univ Buenos Aires, MA, 38; Univ Chicago, PhD(Orient langs), 47; Oxford Univ, DPhil(Egyptol), 52. *Prof Exp:* From asst prof to assoc prof, 52-64, prof, 64-80, chmn dept, 71-80, EMER PROF EGYPTOL, BROWN UNIV, 64- *Concurrent Pos:* Field dir, exped to Semna-Kumma, Sudan, Brown Univ, 62-65; epigraphist, Univ Chicago Orient Inst Exped, Luxor, Egypt, 47-50; field dir, Egypt Explor Soc Exped, Silsilah, Upper Egypt, 55-, Buhen, Sudan, 60-61 & Kasr Ibrim, Egyption Nubia, 61-62; Guggenheim Mem Found fel, Europe & Egypt, 58-59; vis prof, Univ Buenos Aires, 60; consult, NSF, 65-; vis prof, Univ Leningrad, 73; vis lectr, USSR Acad Sci, 73-74; consult, Nat Endowment for Humanities, 75- *Mem:* Egypt Explor Soc; Oxford Soc; Int Asn Egyptologists. *Res:* Papyrology; epigraphy; Oriental studies. *Publ:* Auth, Late-Egyption Miscellanies, 54 & Literary Fragments in the Hieratic Script, 56, Oxford Univ; The Chronical of Prince Osorkon, Pontif Bibl Inst, Rome, 58; Gebel es-Silsilah, Vol I, Egypt Explor Soc, 63; Papyrus Berlin 10453, 63, The Nitocris Adoption Stela, 64 & Papyrus British Museum 10298, 68, J Egyptian Archaeol; The Shrines and Rock Inscriptions of Ibrim, 68 & The New-Kingdom Temples of Buhen (2 vols), 73, Egypt Explor Soc, London; A Tale of Woe from a Hieratic Papyrus in the A S Pushkin Museum of Fine Arts in Moscow, Oxford Univ, 77. *Mailing Add:* Dept of Egyptol Brown Univ Providence RI 02912

CAMP, JOHN B, b Winter Haven, Fla, Mar 31, 38. LINGUISTICS. *Educ:* Fla State Univ, BM, 60, MM, 62, PhD(humanities & music), 64. *Prof Exp:* Asst prof humanities, 64-69, assoc prof interdisciplinary lang & lit, 69-73, dir hist of ideas, 73-75, ASSOC PROF LING & DIR, LIB STUDIES PROG, UNIV SOUTH FLA, 75- *Honors & Awards:* Warren D Allen Citation, 65. *Res:* Psycholinguistics; neuropsychology; lipid metabolism. *Publ:* Auth, A psycholinguistic approach to liberal education, Humanist Educr, 12/76. *Mailing Add:* Col of Arts & Lett Univ of South Fla Tampa FL 33620

CAMPANA, PHILLIP JOSEPH, b Jersey City, NJ, Apr 10, 41; c 2. GERMAN. *Educ:* St Peter's Col, AB, 62; Brown Univ, PhD(Ger), 70. *Prof Exp:* Assoc prof, 70-74, PROF GER, TENN TECHNOL UNIV, 74-, CHMN DEPT, 70- *Concurrent Pos:* Mem evaluation team foreign lang, Southern Asn Cols & Schs, 72-; assoc ed, Schatzkammer, 80-; chmn, Tenn Bd Regents Task Force on Improv Qual in Teacher Educ. *Honors & Awards:* Outstanding Fac Award, Tenn Technol Univ, 76. *Mem:* MLA; AAUP; Am Coun Teaching Foreign Lang; Am Asn Teachers Ger. *Res:* German Romanticism; Heinrich Boell; German novel. *Publ:* Coauth, Prediction of success in college foreign language courses, Educ & Psychol Measurement, 12/73; Foreign language programs in Tennessee public schools, 1978-1979, ERIC Doc, 82; Assessing support for high school foreign language programs: The Tennessee model, Foreign Lang Ann, Vol 15, 82. *Mailing Add:* Dept of Foreign Lang Tenn Technol Univ Cookeville TN 38501

CAMPBELL, DAVID AITKEN, b Killywhan, Scotland, Aug 14, 27; m 56; c 3. CLASSICS. *Educ:* Univ Glasgow, MA, 48; Oxford Univ, BA, 53, MA, 67. *Prof Exp:* From asst lectr to sr lectr classics, Bristol Univ, 53-71; PROF CLASSICS, UNIV VICTORIA, BC, 71- *Concurrent Pos:* Vis asst prof, Univ Toronto, 59-60; external examr, Univ London & Univ Sheffield, 68; vis prof, Univ Tex, Austin, 69-70; res grant, Univ Victoria, BC, 72-82. *Mem:* Am Philol Asn; Class Asn Can; Brit Class Asn; Soc Prom Hellenic Studies; Ovidianum. *Res:* Greek and Latin literature; Greek lyric poetry. *Publ:* Auth, Galliambic poems of the 15th and 16th centuries, Bibliot d'Humanisme et Renaissance, 60; ed, More Essays in Greek History and Literature, Basil Blackwell, Oxford, 62; auth, Flutes and elegiac poetry, J Hellenic Studies, 64; Greek Lyric Poetry, Macmillan, London, 67 & Bristol Class Press, 82; ed, Greek lyric, Loeb Class Libr, 82; auth, The Goldon Lyre, Duckworth, London, 82. *Mailing Add:* Dept of Classics Univ of Victoria Victoria BC V8W 2Y2 Can

CAMPBELL, JAMES MARSHALL, b Warsaw, NY, Sept 30, 95. GREEK. *Educ:* Hamilton Col, AB, 17; Cath Univ Am, AM, 20, PhD, 23. *Hon Degrees:* LLD, Dunbarton Col, 60; LittD, Hamilton Col, 62; LHD, Cath Univ Am, 66. *Prof Exp:* Instr classics, 21-27, assoc prof, 27-32, prof Greek, 32-66, dean col arts & sci, 34-66, EMER PROF GREEK, CATH UNIV AM, 67- *Mem:* Am Philol Asn. *Res:* Greek fathers. *Publ:* Auth, Influence of the Second Sophistic on the style of the sermons of St Basil; coauth, Concordance of Prudentius; co-ed, The confessions of St Augustine; auth, Paul the Mystic, Gordon, 77. *Mailing Add:* Greek Dept Cath Univ Am New York NY 10004

CAMPBELL, LYLE, b American Fork, Utah, Oct 22, 42; m 66; c 4. LINGUISTICS, ANTHROPOLOGY. *Educ:* Brigham Young Univ, BA, 66; Univ Wash, MA, 67; Univ Calif, Los Angeles, PhD(ling), 71. *Prof Exp:* Instr ling, Brigham Young Univ, 67-68; asst prof anthrop & behav res, Univ Mo-Columbia, 71-74; asst prof, 74-77, ASSOC PROF ANTHROP, STATE UNIV NY ALBANY, 77- *Concurrent Pos:* Fulbright lectr ling, Univ Helsinki, 73; NSF res grant ling, Cent Am, 74-75, 75-77 & 78; mem, Int Comt Hist Ling, 76-; consult ed, Hist Ling, Ling Soc Europe, 78- *Mem:* Ling Soc Am; Am Anthrop Asn; Finno-Ugric Soc. *Res:* Mesoamerican linguistics; historical linguistics and phonology; Finnish linguistics. *Publ:* Auth, Is a generative phonology possible?, Orbis, 72; Distant genetic relationships and the Maya-Chipaya hypothesis, Anthrop Ling, 73; Phonological features: Problems and proposals, Language, 74; Theoretical implications of Kekchi phonology, Int J Am Ling, 74; coauth, A linguistic look at the Olmecs, Am Antiquity, 76; auth, Language contact and sound change, Proc 2nd Int Conf Hist Ling, 76; Quichean Linguistic Prehistory, Univ Calif, 77; Native American Languages of North America: A Historical and Comparative Assessment, Univ Tex (in press). *Mailing Add:* Dept of Anthrop State Univ of NY 1400 Washington Ave Albany NY 12222

CAMPION, EDMUND JOHN, b Bronx, NY, Aug 28, 49; m 78. FRENCH LITERATURE. *Educ:* Fordham Univ, AB, 71; Yale Univ, PhD(French), 76. *Prof Exp:* ASST PROF FRENCH, UNIV TENN, KNOXVILLE, 77- *Mem:* Soc Fr Studies; NAm Soc 17th Century Fr Lit; MLA; Soc 17th Century Fr Studies; Medieval Asn Midwest. *Res:* Seventeenth-century French literature; rhetoric; 16th century French literature. *Publ:* Auth, Une structure rhetorique de Pyrame et Thisbe, Rev Pacifique, fall 77; ed, A Critical Edition of Philippe Quinault's Astrate, Univ Exeter, 80; auth, La Rhetorique classique et le Sermon sur la Providence de 1662 de Bossuet, Rev d'Hist Ecclesiastique, 80; Erasmus De Copia, classical learning, and epideictic rhetoric in Montaigne's Essais, 15th Century Studies, 81; Rhetorical theory in La Bruyere's Les Caracteres, Papers French 17th Century Lit, 81; Montaigne as critic of Seneca and St Augustine, Class & Mod Lit, 82; Editing seventeenth-century French plays, TEXT, 82. *Mailing Add:* Dept of Romance Lang Univ of Tenn Knoxville TN 37916

CAMURATI, MIREYA BEATRIZ, b Buenos Aires, Aug 17, 34; US citizen. SPANISH AMERICAN LITERATURE. *Educ:* Univ Buenos Aires, Prof en Letras, 59; Univ Pittsburgh, PhD(Span Am lit), 70. *Prof Exp:* Instr Span lang & lit, Univ Buenos Aires, 59-65, asst prof Span Am lit, 65-68; asst prof Span, Ind Univ Northwest, 70-73; asst prof, 73-75, assoc prof Span Am lit, 75-80, PROF SPAN AM LIT, STATE UNIV NY BUFFALO, 80- *Concurrent Pos:* Prof Span Am lit, Univ Salvador, 64-68. *Mem:* MLA; Am Asn Teachers Span & Port; Inst Int Lit Iberoam; Int Asn Hispanists. *Res:* Spanish American avant garde poetry; Spanish American modernismo; contemporary Spanish American novel. *Publ:* Auth, Funcion literaria del cuento intercalado en D Segundo Sombra, La vorangine y Cataclaro, Rev Iberoam, 4-6/71; Blest Gana, Lukacs, y la novela historica, Cuadernos Americanos, 11-12/74; Un capitulo de versificacion modernista: El poema de clausulas ritmicas, Bull Hispanique, 9-12/74; Una ojeada a la poesia concreta en Hispanoamerica: Dos precursores, y escasos epigonos, Cuadernos Hispanoamericanos, 2/76; La fabula en Hispanoamerica, Universidad Nacional Autonoma de Mexico, 78; Bifurcacion, multiplicacion, ficcion, Hispanofila, 1/79; Poesia y poetica de Vincente Huidobro, Fernando Garcia Cambeiro, Buenos Aires, 80; Enfoques, D C Heath, 80. *Mailing Add:* Dept of Mod Lang & Lit State Univ of NY Buffalo NY 14260

CANCALON, ELAINE DAVIS, b Brooklyn, NY, Mar 23, 39; m 68. FRENCH LITERATURE. *Educ:* Univ Buffalo, BA, 60; Middlebury Col, MA, 62; Univ Calif, Berkeley, PhD(romance lang & lit), 68. *Prof Exp:* Lectr French, State Univ NY Buffalo, 68 & asst prof, 68-71; assoc prof, 72-80, PROF FRENCH, FLA STATE UNIV, 80- *Mem:* MLA; Am Asn Teachers Fr; SAtlantic Mod Lang Asn; Asn Amis Andre Gide. *Res:* Twentieth century French novel; structuralism in literary criticism; comparative literature. *Publ:* Auth, Techniques et Personnages dans les Recits D'Andre Gide, Minard, 70; Symbols of motion and immobility in Gide's twin Recits, Mod Lang Rev, 10/71; L'Inversion de l'amour courtois dan 3 comedies de Moliere, Neophilologus, 4/72; La creation des fantoches dans Les Caves du Vatican, Riv Lett Mod & Comp, 72; Fairy-tale Structures and Motifs in Le Grand Meaulnes, Herbert Lang, Bern, 75; Les Recits d'Andre Gide: essai d'analyse actantielle, Mod Lang Notes, 75; La structure de l'epreuve dans Les Faux-Monnayeurs, Revue des Lett Mod, 75; Spatial structures in the narrative of Dino Buzzati, Forum Italicum, 77. *Mailing Add:* Dept of Mod Lang Fla State Univ Tallahassee FL 32306

CANCEL, ROBERT, b Brooklyn, NY, July 16, 50; m 73; c 2. AFRICAN LITERATURE. *Educ:* State Univ NY New Paltz, BS, 72; Univ Wis-Madison, MA, 77, PhD(African lang & lit), 81. *Prof Exp:* Ed films, African Media Ctr, Mich State Univ, 78-80; ASST PROF AFRICAN & COMP LIT, DEPT LIT, UNIV CALIF, SAN DIEGO, 80- *Mem:* African Lit Asn; MLA. *Res:* African oral narrative traditions, especially from the Tabwa people of Zambia; oral narrative traditions from the New World (Caribbean and the Americas); African and Caribbean written literatures in English, Spanish and Bantu languages. *Publ:* Auth, Inshimi performance techniques of the Zambian Tabwa: Elements and experience, Ba Shiru, Univ Wis (in press). *Mailing Add:* Dept of Lit D-007 Univ Calif San Diego La Jolla CA 92039

CANFIELD, DELOS LINCOLN, b Cleveland, Ohio, Dec 13, 03; m 28, 71; c 3. SPANISH LINGUISTICS. *Educ:* Univ Tex, AB, 26; Columbia Univ, MA, 27, PhD, 34. *Prof Exp:* Instr Span, Univ Rochester, 27-31, from asst prof to assoc prof, 34-46; instr, Columbia Univ, 32-34; prof mod lang & head dept, Fla State Univ, 46-52, chmn bd, 46-47; vis prof Span, Univ Rochester, 52-53 & prof, 54-70, chmn Dept Foreign Lang, 54-62 & Dept Lang & Ling, 62-67; RETIRED. *Concurrent Pos:* Examr Span, Col Entrance Exam Bd, 39-41; consult, US Dept State, Mex & US Off Euc, 45; vis prof, Guatemala, 49; El Salvador, 52 & Univ Ill, 63; Fulbright lectr, Bogota, Columbia, 60; prof ling, NDEA, 61-69; chmn, PhD reading exams, Span, Educ Testing Serv, 66-67; consult prof videotapes for teacher training, lang & ling, San Diego Co, Calif, 66-67; vis prof Span, Southern Ill Univ, 67-68, 70-74 & 80-82. *Mem:* Am Asn Teachers Span & Port (pres, 45); MLA; NEA; Hisp Soc Am; NAm Acad Span Lang. *Res:* Spanish-American dialectology; 16th century Spanish language; Hispanic customs. *Publ:* Auth, Observaciones sobre el espanol salvadoreno, 62; La pronunciacion del espanol en America, 63; auth, East meets West, South of the Border, Southern Ill Univ, 68; coauth, El espanol a traves de sus escritores, Macmillan, 68; University of Chicago Spanish-English, English-Spanish Dictionary, Univ Chicago, rev ed, 72 & 3rd ed, 77; auth, Spanish in Florida, In: Hispanic Influences in the US, Span Inst, New York, 75; coauth, Introduction to Romance Linguistics, Southern Ill Univ Press, 75; auth, Spanish Pronunciation in the Americas, Univ Chicago Press, 81. *Mailing Add:* 1609 Taylor Dr Carbondale IL 62901

CANNON, GARLAND H, b Fr Worth, Tex, Dec 5, 24; m 47; c 4. LINGUISTICS. *Educ:* Univ Tex, BA, 47, PhD, 54; Stanford Univ, MA, 52. *Prof Exp:* Instr English, Univ Hawaii, 49-52, Univ Tex, 52-54 & Univ Mich, 54-55; asst prof speech, Univ Calif, Berkeley, 55-56; acad dir, Am Univ Lang Ctr, Bangkok, 56-57; asst prof ling, Teachers Col, Columbia Univ, 59-62; dir, Columbia Univ English Lang Prog in Afghanistan, 60-62; assoc prof ling, Northeastern Ill State Col, 62-63; assoc prof English, Queens Col, NY, 63-66; assoc prof, 66-67, PROF ENGLISH, TEX A&M UNIV, 67- *Concurrent Pos:* Am Philos Soc grant, England, 64, 66 & 74; vis prof humanities, Univ Mich, 70-71; vis fel, Oxford, summer 74; vis prof ling, Kuwait Univ, 79-81; vis fel, Cambridge, summer 80. *Mem:* Conf Col Compos & Commun; NCTE; Am Dialect Soc; Ling Soc Am; MLA. *Res:* Structure and history of English language; Sir William Jones. *Publ:* Auth, Oriental Jones, Asia Publ House, 64; Linguistics as a science, Quart J Speech, 2/65; ed, The Letters of Sir William

Jones (2 vols), Clarendon, 69; auth, Bilingual problems and developments in the United States, PMLA, 5/71; History of the English Language, Harcourt, 72; Sir William Jones, Sir Joseph Banks, and the Royal Society, Notes & Records Royal Soc London, 3/75; An Integrated Transformational Grammar of English, Rodopi, 78; Japanese borrowings in English, Am Speech, 8/81. *Mailing Add:* Dept of English Tex A & M Univ College Station TX 77843

CANNON, HAROLD CHARLES, b Chapel, England, Dec 26, 30; m 68; c 2. CLASSICS. *Educ:* Cambridge Univ, BA, 53, MA, 57. *Prof Exp:* Teacher Latin & English, St Andrew's Sch, Bahamas, 54-59 & Stevens Acad, Hoboken, NJ, 59-61; teacher classics, Sarah Lawrence Col, 62-64; from assoc prof to prof, Manhattanville Col, 63-72, acad dean, 69-71, dean col, 71-72; dep dir & prog off, Div Educ Prog, 72-76, DIR DIV RES GRANTS, NATIONAL ENDOWMENT FOR HUMANITIES, 76- *Mem:* Am Philol Asn. *Res:* Greek and Latin pastoral poetry. *Publ:* Transl, Ovid's Heroides, Dutton, 71 & Allen & Unwin, 72. *Mailing Add:* 8608 Forest St Annandale VA 22003

CANNON, JOANN CHARLENE, b Cleveland, Ohio, May 6, 49; m 78. ITALIAN. *Educ:* Wellesley Col, BA, 71; Cornell Univ, PhD(Ital), 76. *Prof Exp:* Asst prof, 76-81, ASSOC PROF ITAL, SYRACUSE UNIV, 82- *Mem:* MLA. *Res:* Modern Italian literature; literary criticism. *Publ:* Auth, The image of the city in the novels of Italo Calvino, Mod Fiction Studies, summer 78; The reader as detective: Notes on Gadda's Pasticciaccio, Mod Lang Studies, fall 80; Gadda's critical essays, Can J Ital Studies, fall 81; Todo Modo and the Enlightened Hero of Leonardo Sciascia, Symposium, winter 81; Osservazioni sulla poetica verghiana, Misure Critiche, 81; Italo Calvino: Writer and Critic, Ravenna: Longo Editore, 81. *Mailing Add:* 208 HB Crouse Syracuse Univ Syracuse NY 13210

CANO, CARLOS JOSE, b Havana, Cuba; Aug 27, 42; US citizen; m 64; c 2. SPANISH & LATIN AMERICAN LITERATURE. *Educ:* Univ SFla, Tampa, BA, 64; Ind Univ, Bloomington, MA, 66, PhD(Span), 73. *Prof Exp:* Instr, 70-73, asst prof, 73-77, ASSOC PROF SPAN & LATIN AM LIT, UNIV SFLA, TAMPA, 78- *Concurrent Pos:* Vis prof Span & Latin Am lit, Nat Univ Mex, winter 72. *Mem:* Am Asn Teachers Span & Port; MLA; Inst Int Lit Iberoam. *Res:* Contemporary Latin American novel. *Publ:* Auth, La tecnica narrativa de Carlos Fuentes en Aura, Lang Quart, Vol IX, fall-winter 72; El hombre neuvo de Rayuela: Marx o McLuhan, Ostros mundos--otros fuegos & Fantasia y realismo magico en Iberoamerica, Mich State Univ Latin Am Studies Ctr, 75; Epica y misoginia en Los hombres de a caballo, Revista Iberoamericana, Vol XLII, 76; El tiempo ciclico y el teatro cubano desde la Revolucion, XVII Congreso deo Instituto Internacional de Literatura Iberoamericana, Ediciones Cultura Hispanica, 78. *Mailing Add:* 211 Park Ridge Ave Temple Temple Terrace FL 33617

CANO, VICENTE, b Valencia, Spain, Feb 27, 47; m 70. SPANISH & HISPANIC AMERICAN LITERATURE. *Educ:* Francis Marion Col, BA, 73; Univ Ga, MA, 76, PhD(Romance lang), 80. *Prof Exp:* Teacher French & Span, James F Byrnes Acad, 73-74; teaching asst Span & French, Dept Romance Lang, Univ Ga, 74-80, res asst Span, 78-79, preceptor, 79-80; ASST PROF SPAN, DEPT MOD LANG & LIT, UNIV NEBR-LINCOLN, 80- *Mem:* Am Asn Teacher Span & Port; MLA; SAtlantic Mod Lang Asn. *Res:* Mariano Jose de Larra; the Argentine generation of 1837; 19th century Spanish and Spanish American history of ideas. *Publ:* Auth, Larra y Alberdi: Paralelos y divergencias, Kanina, Revista de Artes y Letras de la Univ Costa Rica, No 1, 6/80. *Mailing Add:* Dept Mod Lang & Lit Univ Nebr Lincoln NE 68588

CANO-BALLESTA, JUAN, b Murcia, Spain, 1932; m 69. SPANISH LITERATURE, PHILOLOGY. *Educ:* Univ Munich, PhD(Romance philol), 61. *Prof Exp:* Lectr Span, Univ Gottingen, 62-65; assoc prof, Univ Kans, 65-66; asst prof Span & philol, Yale Univ, 66-70, assoc prof Span lit, 70-71; assoc prof, Boston Univ, 71-76; PROF SPAN, UNIV PITTSBURGH, 76- *Concurrent Pos:* Morse fel, Spain, 68-69; Sr res fel, ACLS, 75-76. *Mem:* MLA; Am Asn Teachers Span & Port; Asoc Int Hispanistas; North Eastern Mod Lang Asn. *Res:* Literary history. *Publ:* Auth, La poesia de Miguel Hernandez, 62, rev ed, 71 & La poesia espanola entre pureza y revolucion, 1930-1936, 72, Ed Gredos; Miguel Hernandez: El hombre y su poesia, 74, 4th ed, 79; Maestros del cuento espanol moderno, Scribner's, 74; co-ed, Poesia y prosa de guerra y otros textos olvidados de Miguel Hernandez, 77; En torno a Miquel Hernandez, 78; Literatura y tecnologia: Las letras espanolas ante la revolucion industrial 1900-1923, 81; Articulos socialels, politicos y de critica de Mariano Jose de Larra, 82. *Mailing Add:* Dept of Span Univ of Pittsburgh Pittsburgh PA 15260

CANTAROVICI, JAIME, b La Paz, Bolivia, June 22, 42; m 67; c 3. LATIN AMERICAN LITERATURE, CULTURE & CIVILIZATION. *Educ:* Univ Houston, BA, 66, MA, 67; Tulane Univ, PhD((Latin Am lit), 72. *Prof Exp:* ASSOC PROF SPAN, UTAH STATE UNIV, 71- *Mem:* Rocky Mountain Mod Lang Asn; Rocky Mountain Coun Latin Am Studies; SCent MLA. *Res:* Latin American poetry; Latin American drama; Latin American novel. *Publ:* Auth, Retorna soldado, Foreign Lang Speaker, 12/72; The line, Crucible, spring 73; New York, Presencia Lit Bolivia, 9/73; Desde lejos, Barcelona, Spain, 75; Viracocha tenia razon, Arbol de Fuego, Venezuela, 5/75; Al ayer de la luna, Nivel, Mex, 5/76. *Mailing Add:* Dept of Lang & Philos Utah State Univ Logan UT 84322

CANTRALL, WILLIAM RANDOLPH, b Fancy Prairie, Ill, June 30, 24; c 2. LINGUISTICS, RHETORIC. *Educ:* Univ Ill, Urbana, AB, 49, MS, 51, PhD(English educ), 69. *Prof Exp:* Teacher English, Plymouth High Sch, Ill, 52-53 & East Aurora High Sch, Ill, 53-54; teacher reading, Northwestern Mil Acad, 54-59; teacher English, Lyons Twp High Sch, LaGrange, Ill, 59-69; prof, Northern Ill Univ, 69-76; assoc prof & dir writing workshop, Wayne State Univ, 77-81; PROF ENGLISH, COMP COORDR & DIR ENGLISH AS SECOND LANG, CHICAGO STATE UNIV, 81- *Mem:* Ling Soc Am; NCTE. *Res:* Syntax; semantics; writing research. *Publ:* Auth, Pitch, stress and grammatical relatins, Papers Fifth Regional Meeting Chicago Ling Soc, 69; The artistic use of seeming contradiction, In: Current Trends in Linguistics, Ling Res, 72; The incorporation of viewpoint into noun phrases, Proc XI Int Congr Ling, 73; Viewpoint, Reflexives, and the Nature of Noun Phrases, Mouton, 74; Reflexive pronouns and viewpoint, Ling Berichte, 12/73; Favored structures and intonational limitations, In: Papers from the Parassession on Functionalism, 75 & Comparison, and beyond, In: Papers from the Thirteenth Annual Regional Meeting of the Chicago Linguistic Society, 77, Univ Chicago; Good luck with a unified reading program, Ill English Bull, 10/77. *Mailing Add:* Dept of English Chicago State Univ Chicago IL 60628

CANTWELL, WILLIAM RICHARD, b Wilmington, Del, Feb 5, 32; m 55; c 3. GERMAN LANGUAGE & LITERATURE. *Educ:* Princeton Univ, AB, 53; Oxford Univ, BA, 55, MA, 59; Univ Wis, MA, 61, PhD(Ger), 67. *Prof Exp:* Actg instr Ger, Univ Wis, 63-65; from instr to assoc prof, 65-76, chmn dept mod lang, 74-78, PROF GER, CARLETON COL, 76- *Concurrent Pos:* Dir off-campus studies, Carleton Col, 79- *Mem:* MLA; Am Asn Teachers Ger; Popular Cult Asn. *Res:* German literature of the Romantic period and the 19th century; literature and history. *Mailing Add:* Dept of Mod Lang Carleton Col Northfield MN 55057

CAP, BIRUTA, b Riga, Latvia; US citizen. FRENCH LITERATURE & CIVILIZATION. *Educ:* Univ Conn, BA, 60; Rutgers Univ, MA, 61, PhD(Fr), 68. *Prof Exp:* From instr to asst prof Fr, Dunbarton Col, 63-68; asst prof Fr, Lehigh Univ, 69-73; ASST PROF FRENCH, ALLENTON COL ST FRANCIS DE SALES, PA, 79- *Mem:* MLA; Am Asn Teachers Fr; Nat Asn Self-Instruct Lang Prog; Asn Advan Baltic Studies. *Res:* French civilization; Latvian literature and folklore; drama. *Publ:* Auth, A French observer of the Baltic: Jules Verne, J Baltic Studies, summer 72; Stefan Zweig as agent of exchange between French & German literature, Comp Lit Studies, 9/73; O V Milosz and his critics, summer 76 & Tradition and art in the drama of Gunars Priede, 80, Lituanus; contribr O V Milosz & Jean Vilar, In: Critical Bibliography of French Literature VI: Twentieth Century, Syracuse Univ Press, 80; Herve Bazin, Birago Diop, Jean Ricardou, Henri Thomas, In: Columbia Dict Modern European Literature, 2nd ed, Columbia Univ Press, 80; Teaching French civilization in English in a professional continuing educational curriculum, In: Dict Teaching Innovations in Foreign Languages, NY Dept For Lang, 81. *Mailing Add:* 3644 Magnolia Dr Easton PA 18042

CAP, JEAN-PIERRE, b Longueil-Ste-Marie, France, June 2, 34; US citizen; m 62; c 2. FRENCH LANGUAGES & LITERATURE. *Educ:* Temple Univ, BA, 57, MA, 60; Univ Pa, MA, 60; Rutgers Univ, PhD(French), 66. *Prof Exp:* Instr French, Skidmore Col, 61-62; from instr to asst prof, Univ Md, 62-68; assoc prof, 68-80, PROF FRENCH, LAFAYETTE COL, 80- *Concurrent Pos:* Assoc ed, Claudel Studies, 67-80; Humanities enrichment grant, 73-74. *Honors & Awards:* Palmes Academiques, 80. *Mem:* Am Asn Teachers Fr; MLA; AAUP; Soc Fr Prof Am; Claudel Soc. *Res:* The novel; 20th century French literature; literary criticism. *Publ:* Auth, Reprise de la NRF en 1919, Bull Alain-Fournier-Jaques Riviere, 76; A Conrad letter to Gheon, Conradiana, 76; Pierre Benoit, Robert Brasillach, Paul Desjardins, H Gheon, J Lotte, P Claudel, In: Critical Bibliography of French Literature--20th Century, 78; Henri Gheon, Jean Schlumberger, In: Columbia Dict of Mod Europ Lit, 78; Ch Peguy et J Schlumberger, L'Amitie Ch Peguy, 79; M Proust et J Schlumberger, Cahiers Marcel Proust, 79; ed, Jacques Riviere-Jean Schlumberger: Correspondance 1909-1025, Univ Lyon II, 80; A gide and cosmopolitanism, Laurels, 80. *Mailing Add:* Dept of Lang Lafayette Col Easton PA 18042

CAPASSO, HENRY F, b Providence, RI, July 26, 17; m 42; c 4. ITALIAN. *Educ:* Brown Univ, AB, 38, AM, 46; Middlebury Col, DML, 60. *Prof Exp:* From instr to assoc prof, 45-68, PROF ITAL, UNIV RI, 68- *Mem:* MLA; New Eng Foreign Lang Asn; New Eng Am Asn Teachers Ital; Am Asn Teachers Ital. *Res:* Contemporary Italian literature. *Mailing Add:* Dept of Lang Univ of RI Kingston RI 02881

CAPLAN, HARRY, b Hoags Corners, NY, Jan 7, 96. CLASSICS. *Educ:* Cornell Univ, AB, 16, AM, 17, PhD, 21. *Hon Degrees:* LittD, Wesleyan Univ, 67. *Prof Exp:* Instr pub speaking, 19-23, from instr to prof classics, 24-41, Goldwin Smith prof, 41-67, chmn dept, 29-46, EMER GOLDWIN SMITH PROF CLASSICS, CORNELL UNIV, 67- *Concurrent Pos:* Guggenheim fel, Europ libr, 28-29, 56; fel, Ctr Advan Studies, Wesleyan Univ, 62-63; Andrew Mellon vis prof, Univ Pittsburgh, 67-68; vis prof, Univ Ill, 70-71. *Mem:* Am Philol Asn (pres, 55); fel Mediaeval Acad Am; Speech Commun Asn; Renaissance Soc Am; MLA. *Res:* Classical, medieval and Renaissance rhetoric; history of preaching. *Publ:* Ed & transl, Gianfrancesco Pico della Mirandola, On the Imagination, Yale Univ, 30; Mediaeval Artes Praedicandi, 2 vols, Cornell Univ, 34 & 36; auth, Rhetorica ad Herennium, Heinemann, 54; coauth, Pulpit eloquence, 2 vols, Speech Monogr, 55 & 56; contribr, Of Eloquence: Studies in Ancient and Mediaeval Rhetoric, Cornell Univ, 70. *Mailing Add:* 121 Goldwin Smith Hall Cornell Univ Ithaca NY 14850

CAPPS, EDWARD, III, b Oberlin, Ohio, May 28, 35. CLASSICAL PHILOLOGY & LINGUISTICS. *Educ:* Swarthmore Col, BA, 57; Yale Univ, MA, 59, PhD(classics), 64. *Prof Exp:* Instr classics, Emory Univ, 61-64; asst prof, 64-68, ASSOC PROF GREEK & LATIN, UNIV MISS, 68- *Honors & Awards:* Am Coun Learned Soc Award, 59. *Mem:* Am Philol Asn; Archaeol Inst Am. *Res:* Greek and Latin linguistics; stylistic analysis; classical mythology. *Mailing Add:* 804 S Lamar Oxford MS 38655

CAPRETZ, PIERRE JEAN, b Mazamet, France, Jan 30, 25; m 49; c 3. FRENCH. *Educ:* Univ Paris, France, Lic es Let, 47, D Univ, 50. *Prof Exp:* Prof French, Univ Fla, 49-56; PROF FRENCH, YALE UNIV, 56-, DIR LANG LAB, 65- *Concurrent Pos:* Consult cult serv, French Embassy, NY, 56-61, foreign lang proficiency tests, MLA, 60-61 & coop foreign lang tests, 61-62; consult, Harcourt, Brace & World, 61; prof dir, audio lingual tech teaching foreign lang film ser, 61-63; asst coordr, Mod Lang Material Develop Ctr, 61-65; mem, Univ Film Study Ctr. *Mem:* MLA; Am Asn Teachers Fr;

Asn Educ Commun & Technol; Nat Asn Lang Lab Dirs (pres, 73-75); Am Coun Teaching Foreign Lang. *Res:* Nineteenth century French literature; methods for teaching foreign languages. *Publ:* Auth, Cing poemes inconnus de Jules Laforgue, Rev Sci Humaines, 10-12/53; Audio Lingual Techniques for Teaching Foreign Languages, Yale Univ, 62; coauth, Audio Lingual Materials, Harcourt, 62; auth, La France a Travers les Ages, Cult Hist Res, Inc, 66; Du bon usage des exercices structuraux, Appl Ling & Teaching Fr, Montreal, 67. *Mailing Add:* Lang Lab Yale Univ New Haven CT 06511

CAPSAS, CLEON WADE, b Birmingham, Ala, Oct 2, 25. SPANISH & PORTUGUESE. *Educ:* George Peabody Col, AB, 48; Univ NMex, MA, 59, PhD, 64. *Prof Exp:* Assoc prof Span & Port, Univ Kans, 65-68; PROF FOREIGN LANG, UNIV SOUTH FLA, TAMPA, 70- *Concurrent Pos:* Consult, Nat Univ Mex, 66-67 & 69-73; dir, Univ San Francisco Study Prog, Spain, 78- *Mem:* Am Asn Teachers Span & Port; Am Transl Asn. *Res:* Spanish civilization. *Publ:* Auth, Spanish literature, Spanish American literature, Brazilian literature & Peru, In: New International Yearbook, Funk 61-66; coauth, The Spanish Verb, rev ed, McKay, 74. *Mailing Add:* PO Box 16843 Tampa FL 33687

CAPUTO-MAYR, MARIA LUISE, b Trieste, Italy; m 67; c 1. GERMAN LITERATURE. *Educ:* Univ Vienna, Akademischer Übersetzer U Dolmetsch, 63, 64; Lehrämter, 66, DPhil, 66; Rome, Abilitazioni, 72. *Prof Exp:* Teaching asst Ger, Fulham County Sch, Burlington Girls Sch, 65-66; asst lectr, Ger & Ital, Barking Col Technol, England, 66-67; asst prof Ger, 68-75, ASSOC PROF GER COMP LIT, TEMPLE UNIV, 75- *Concurrent Pos:* Various grants, Temple Univ, 70-82; founder & exec dir, Kafka Soc Am, 75-, ed & founder, Newslett, 77-; Leo Baeck Inst grant, 76; Austrian Inst grant, 77; exec secy, Am Comt Study Austrian Lit, 74- *Mem:* Kafka Soc Am (pres, 80-82); MLA; Am Asn Teachers Ger; Am Comt Study Austrian Lit (exec secy, 74-, treas, 77-). *Res:* Bibliography and reception of Franz Kafka; Austrian, German and Italian modern literature. *Publ:* Auth, La funzione della natura e del paesaggio nei romanzi di Guido Piovene, Italica, 73; Hans Leberts Romane: Realismus und Dämonie, Zeitkritik und Gerichtstag, Mod Austrian Lit, 74; German literature in translation, Asn Dept Foreign Lang Bull, 74; Gedanken über die Kafka-Forschung im 50 Todesjahr des Dichters, Lit & Kritik, 75; guest ed, Special Number on Franz Kafka, J Mod Lit, 10/77; ed, Franz Kafka: Eine Aufsatzsammlung Nach Einem Symposium, Agora, 78; Überlieferung aus neuer Sicht: zur jüngsten österreichischen Prosaliteraliteratur, In: Perspectives and Personalities, Heidelberg, 78; co-ed (with Julius M Merz), Franz Kafkas Werke: Eine Bibliographie der Primär Literatur, Francke, Berne, 82. *Mailing Add:* Dept of Ger Temple Univ 339 HB Philadelphia PA 19122

CARDEN, GUY, b Chicago, Ill, July 31, 44. LINGUISTICS. *Educ:* Harvard Univ, AB, 66, AM, 67, PhD(ling) 70. *Prof Exp:* Res scientist ling & artificial intel, Air Force Cambridge Res Lab, 69-71; asst prof ling, Yale Univ, 71-76, assoc prof, 76-80; ASSOC PROF LING, UNIV BC, 80- *Concurrent Pos:* Vis lectr, Yale Univ, 70; consult, Watson Res Ctr, IBM Corp, 73-74; vis scientist ling, Mass Inst Technol, 75-76; res assoc, Haskins Lab, 77-80; vis scholar ling, Harvard Univ, fall, 79. *Mem:* Ling Soc Am; Can Ling Asn. *Res:* Syntax and semantics; data collection methodology; speech perception. *Publ:* Auth, A note on conflicting idiolects, Ling Inquiry, 70; Dialect variation and abstract syntax, In: Some New Directions in Linguistic Variation, 73; coauth, Subject reduplication in Persian, Ling Inquiry, 74; English Quantifiers: Logical Structure and Linguistic Variation, Taishukan, Tokyo and Acad Press, New York, 73 & 76; coauth, Evidence for phonetic processing of cues to place of articulation, Perception & Psychophysics, 81; Backwards anaphora in discourse context, J Ling, 82. *Mailing Add:* 369-1866 Main Mall Univ BC Vancouver BC V6T 1W5 Can

CARDENAS, ANTHONY JOHN, b Los Alamos, NMex, June 29, 46. SPANISH. *Educ:* Univ NMex, BA, 68; Univ Wis-Madison, MA, 69; PhD(Span), 74. *Prof Exp:* Asst prof, 75-81, ASSOC PROF SPAN, WICHITA STATE UNIV, 75- *Concurrent Pos:* Proj assoc, Computerized Medieval Span Dict Proj, Dept Sapn & Port, Univ Wis-Madison, 74-75. *Mem:* Medieval Acad Am; Renaissance Soc Am; MLA; Am Asn Teachers Span & Port; Rocky Mountain Medieval & Renaissance Asn. *Res:* Alfonsine science; Spanish philology; paleography. *Publ:* Auth, Toward an understanding of the astronomy of Alfonso X, el Sabio, winter 78-79 & Alfonso X and the Studium Generale, spring 80, Ind Social Studies Quart; A medieval Spanish collectanea of astronomical instruments: An integrated compilation, J Rocky Mt Medieval & Renaissance Asn, No 1, 80; A new title for the Aflonsine Omnibus on astronomical instruments, L Coronica, No 2, 80; The complete Libro del saber de astrologia and Cod Vat lat 8174, Manuscripta, 4/80; Thirteenth century astronomical technology in the Libro del saber de astrologia of Alfonso X, el Sabio, Scripta: Studies on Medieval Fachliteratur, No 6, 82; Alfonso X: Incest and the scholastic method, Romance Notes (in prep). *Mailing Add:* Dept of Romance Lang Wichita State Univ Wichita KS 67208

CARDENAS, DANIEL NEGRETE, b Williams, Ariz, July 21, 17; m 79; c 3. SPANISH. *Educ:* Park Col, BA, 41; Columbia Univ, MA, 47, PhD, 53. *Prof Exp:* From instr to asst prof Span, Univ Okla, 48-57; from asst prof to assoc prof, Univ Chicago, 57-70; chmn dept, 70-73 & 76-78, PROF SPAN & PORT, CALIF STATE UNIV, LONG BEACH, 70- *Concurrent Pos:* Lectr, Columbia Univ, 47-48; Ford Found fel, 55-56; Fulbright lectr comp ling & English as foreign lang, Univ Madrid, 61-62; assoc ed, Hispania, 69-77. *Honors & Awards:* Academico de numero, Acad Norteam Lengua Espanola, 76. *Mem:* MLA; Am Asn Teachers Span & Port; Ling Soc Am; Int Ling Asn; Am Dialect Soc. *Res:* Spanish American dialectology; literary analysis & criticism; bilingualism. *Publ:* Coauth, Spanish: A Guide for Teachers, Heath, 61; auth, El Espanol de Jalisco, Consejo Super Invest Cient, Madrid, 67; Acoustic vowel loops of a Paraguayan speaker, In: Essays in Romance Philology, Univ Chicago, 68; An introduction to literary analysis, Hispania, 9/68; Dominant Spanish dialects spoken in the United States, Ctr Appl Ling, Educ Resources Info Ctr, 70; Otra interpretacion de Romance Sonambulo, Explicacion de Textos, 73; El arbol de Maria Bombal, Kanina, 80; El proceso creador de lexico espanol, Boletin De La Academia Norteamericana De La Lengua Espanola, 82. *Mailing Add:* Dept of Span & Portuguese Calif State Univ 1250 Bellflower Blvd Long Beach CA 90840

CARDONA, GEORGE, b New York, NY, June 3, 36; m 58; c 2. INDOARYAN & INDO-EUROPEAN LINGUISTICS. *Educ:* NY Univ, BA, 56; Yale Univ, MA, 58, PhD, 60. *Prof Exp:* Asst prof Indo-Aryan lang, 60-65, assoc prof ling, 65-67, PROF LING, UNIV PA, 67- *Concurrent Pos:* US Off Educ grant, 62-64, publ grant, 65; Am Inst Indian Studies fac res grant, 65-66; vis prof, Orient Inst, Baroda, 1/66; vis lectr, Swarthmore Col, spring 67. *Mem:* Ling Soc Am; Am Orient Soc; Am Philol Asn; Ling Soc Europe. *Res:* Indo-Aryan and Indo-European linguistics. *Publ:* Auth, A Gujarati Reference Grammar, 65, On Haplology in Indo-European, 68 & Studies in Indian Grammarians, 69, Univ Pa. *Mailing Add:* Dept of Ling Univ of Pa Philadelphia PA 19104

CARDONA, RODOLFO, b San Jose, Costa Rica, Jan 17, 24; nat US; m 54; c 3. SPANISH LITERATURE. *Educ:* La State Univ, BA, 46; Univ Wash, PhD(Romance lang), 53. *Prof Exp:* Instr Span, Am Inst Foreign Trade, 47-48 & Univ Wash, 48-53; asst prof, Western Reserve Univ, 53-56; from asst prof to assoc prof, Chatham Col, 56-60; prof Span, Univ Pittsburgh, 61-69, chmn dept Hisp lang & lit, 64-69; prof Span & Port & chmn dept, Univ Tex, Austin, 69-78; UNIV PROF MOD FOREIGN LANG & DIR UNIV PROF PROG, BOSTON UNIV, 78- *Concurrent Pos:* Andrew Mellon fel, Univ Pittsburgh, 60-61; consult, Title II & Title IV progs, US Off Educ, 65-67; ed, Anales Galdosianos, Univ Tex, 66-; Am Coun Learned Soc grant-in-aid, 67-68; Nat Endowment for Humanities sr fel, 73-74. *Mem:* MLA; Am Asn Teachers Span & Port. *Res:* Spanish literature of the 19th and 20th centuries. *Publ:* Co-ed, Apostillas a Los Episodios Nacionales de B P Galdos de H Hinterhäuser, Anales Galdosianos, 68; coauth, Vision del esperpento, Castalia, Spain, 70, 2nd ed, 82; Nuevos enfoques criticos a Galdos, 70 & En torno a El mundo es asi de Baroja, 73, Cuadernos Hispanoam; Teatro selecto de Galdos, Escelicer, Madrid, 74; ed, Anaya-Los Americas, 74; auth, Novelistas espanoles de posguerra, Taurusm 76; Greguerias, 80. *Mailing Add:* Dept Mod Foreign Lang Boston Univ Boston MA 02215

CARDUNER, JEAN R, b Carhaix, France, Nov 18, 26; m 52; c 3. FRENCH LANGUAGE & LITERATURE. *Educ:* Sorbonne, Lic es Lett, 49, DES, 50; Univ Minn, PhD, 59. *Prof Exp:* Instr French, Univ Minn, 52-54; from instr to assoc prof, 54-67, assoc dean col lib sci & arts, 74-77, PROF FRENCH, UNIV MICH, ANN ARBOR, 67- *Concurrent Pos:* Dir Mich-Wis jr year, Aixen-Provence, France, Univ Mich, 62-64; NDEA Inst French, 66-69; mem, Col Bd Advan Placement French, 69-73; dir, Middlebury French Sch, 72- *Honors & Awards:* Class of 1923 Award, Univ Mich, 60; Officier des Palmes Academiques, French Govt, 75. *Mem:* MLA; Am Asn Teachers Fr (vpres, 78-); Am Coun Teaching Foreign Lang; Soc Fr Prof Am; AAUP. *Res:* Twentieth century French literature and novel; teaching of French civilization and advanced language courses. *Publ:* Coauth, L'Amerique d'aujourd'hui vue par les Francais, Prentice-Hall, 68; auth, La Creation Romanesque chez Malraux, Nizet, Paris, 68; Les Antimemoires dans l'oeuvre de Malraux, Ky Romance Quart, 69; coauth, Nouvelles et Recits du XXeme Siecle, Appleton, 71; Contextes, Heath, 74; Le Miroir des limbes, l'homme precaire et l'aleatoire, 20th Century Studies, fall 78; Metamorphose et biographic, NY Lit Forum, winter 79; L'Espoir ou la fin de l'imaginaire de roman, Rev Hist Litte'raire de le France, spring 81. *Mailing Add:* Dept of Romance Lang Univ of Mich Ann Arbor MI 48104

CARDWELL, WALTER DOUGLAS, JR, b Gulfport, Miss, Dec 14, 39; m 62; c 2. FRENCH LITERATURE, FRENCH LANGUAGE. *Educ:* Transylvania Col, AB, 61; Yale Univ, PhD(French), 71. *Prof Exp:* Instr French, Ctr Col Ky, 66-69; asst prof, Wittenberg Univ, 69-72; ASSOC PROF FRENCH, SALEM COL, 72- *Mem:* MLA, Am Asn Teachers Fr. *Res:* Nineteenth-century French drama; 19th-century French novel; 17th-century French drama. *Mailing Add:* Salem Col Winston-Salem NC 27108

CARDY, MICHAEL JOHN, b Portsmouth, UK, June 16, 36; m 63; c 2. FRENCH LANGUAGE & LITERATURE. *Educ:* Oxford Univ, BA, 60, BLitt, 70. *Prof Exp:* Instr French, Univ Sask, 64-66; lectr, 66-68; asst prof, 68-71, chmn dept Romance studies, 72-75, ASSOC PROF FRENCH, BROCK UNIV, 71- *Mem:* Asn Can Univ Teachers Fr (secy-treas, 72-74); Can Comp Lit Asn; Can Soc 18th Century Studies; Am Soc 18th Century Studies; Fr Soc 18th Century Studies. *Res:* Jean-Francois Marmontel; aesthetic thought of the 18th century; the quarrel of the ancients and the moderns. *Publ:* Auth, Lettre inedite de Marmontel sur ses droits d'auteur . . ., Rev Laurentian Univ, Vol I, No 3; Marmontel and Boileau, Forum Mod Lang Studies, Vol V, No 3; Rousseau's irreconciliable ennemi, Marmontel, 72 & Discussion of the theory of climate in the querelle des anciens et des modernes, 76, Studies Voltaire & 18th Century; The rehabilitation of a second-rate writer: Jean-Francois Marmontel, Univ Toronto Quart, 78; La trilogie Jean Rezeau: Chef d'oeuvre d'Herve Bazin, Bull Asn Can Univ Teachers Fr, 78; Echos contemporains de La Querrelle des Anciens et des Modernes, Essays in French Lit, 78. *Mailing Add:* Dept of Romance Studies Brock Univ St Catharines ON L2S 3A1 Can

CARENAS, FRANCISCO, b Beniarjo, Valencia, Spain, Dec 23, 38; m 69; c 1. SPANISH. *Educ:* Univ Valencia, MA, 65, PhD(Romance philol), 67. *Prof Exp:* From asst prof to assoc prof Span, Boston Univ, 67-73; assoc prof, 73-82, PROF SPAN & HEAD DEPT, UNIV MO-ST LOUIS, 82- *Mem:* MLA; Am Asn Teachers Span & Port. *Res:* Twentieth century Spanish novel; literature and psychoanalysis; Spanish poets in the United States. *Publ:* Coauth, La figura del sacerdote en la moderna narrativa espanola, Casuz Editores, Caracas, 75; Juan Goytisolo, Ed Fundamentos, Madrid, 75; La vuelta de los cerebros, Plaza & Janes, Barcelona, 76; El mundo pre-preceptivo de Volveras a Region, Norte, 77; El encantador de serpientes, Letras de Deusto, 6/78; La frente en el suelo: Una denuncia, Cuaderno Literario, No XVIII, 78; Juan Goytisolo: Otra concepcion de la moralidad y el arte, Cuadernos Americanos, 9-10/81; Lectura insolita de El Capital: La lucha dialectica entre el antiheroe y su entorno, Soc Basque Studies Am, Vol II-2, 81. *Mailing Add:* Dept of Mod Lang Univ of Mo St Louis MO 63121

CAREY, RICHARD JOHN, b San Francisco, Calif, Mar 30, 25. MEDIEVAL FRENCH LITERATURE. *Educ:* Univ Calif, Berkeley, BA, 47, MA, 49, BLS, 54; Columbia Univ, PhD(French), 65. *Prof Exp:* Teaching asst French & Ger, Univ Calif, Berkeley, 47-49; librn, San Jose State Col, 54-59; instr French, Columbia Univ, 59-65; asst prof, Hunter Col, 66-67; assoc prof, 69-80, PROF FRENCH, EASTERN WASH UNIV, 80- *Concurrent Pos:* Ed, Bull Prof Fr, Pac Northwest, 69- *Honors & Awards:* Concours Oratoire, French Govt, 47. *Mem:* Mediaeval Acad Am; Am Asn Teachers Fr. *Res:* Explication de textes; historical grammar. *Publ:* Contribr, Reader's Encycl, Crowell, 65; critical ed, Jean Le Court, Le Restor du paon, Droz, Geneva, Switz, 66 & Jean de Le Mote, Le Parfait du paon, Univ NC, 71; ed, Juvenel de Carlencas, Bibliotheques, 72 & Bibliographie, 72, J Libr Hist, Univ Fla, 72. *Mailing Add:* Dept of Lang Eastern Wash Univ Cheney WA 99004

CARGO, ROBERT T, b Hanceville, Ala, Nov 20, 33; m 57; c 2. ROMANCE LANGUAGES. *Educ:* Birmingham-Southern Col, AB, 55; Univ Ala, MA, 59; Univ NC, PhD(Romance lang), 65. *Prof Exp:* Instr French, Snead Jr Col, 56-59; Fulbright lectr English & Am Studies, Univ Caen, 60-61; instr French, Univ NC, Chapel Hill, 63-65; from asst prof to assoc prof, 65-72, PROF FRENCH, UNIV ALA, 72- *Mem:* MLA; Am Asn Teachers Fr. *Res:* Baudelaire; French literature of the 19th century; French lyric poetry. *Publ:* Auth, A note on Gide's knowledge of Baudelaire, Romance Notes, Vol VII, No 2; Baudelaire, the military and Paul de Molenes, In: Etudes Baudelairiennes III, Neuchatel, 73; coauth (with Bernerd Weber), Captain Peron and the slave trade, Calcutta Rev, 10-12/75; auth, Baudelaire's L'Etranger as Parlor Game, 19th-century Fr Studies, fall-winter 79-80; Baudelaire, Longfellow, and A Psalm of Life, Rev de Lit Comp, 5-7/80; American Life and Culture in Le Magasin Pittoresque, 1833-1882, French-Am Rev, spring 81; The Flowers of Evil, In: Acad Am Encycl, Arete Publ Co, 81. *Mailing Add:* Dept of Romance Lang Univ of Ala University AL 35486

CARILLA, EMILIO, b Buenos Aires, Arg, May 6, 14; m 46; c 1. ROMANCE LANGUAGES. *Educ:* Univ Buenos Aires, PhD(Span), 42. *Prof Exp:* Prof Span, sec prof, Catamarca, Arg, 43-48, Nat Univ Tucuman, 48, Nat Univ Litoral, 57-61; PROF SPAN, UNIV CALIF, RIVERSIDE, 66- *Concurrent Pos:* Guggenheim Found grant, 59-60; Inst Cult Hisp grant, 65- *Honors & Awards:* Premio Nac Repub Argentine, 46-48; Premio Lorenzo Luzuriaga, Ed Losada, 62, Ricardo Rojas, 64, Buenos Aires. *Mem:* Asoc Inst Hispanistas; Am Asn Teachers Span & Port; Acad Arg Letras; Inst Lit Hispanoamericana. *Res:* Spanish baroque literature; Argentine literature; Romantic movement in Spanish America. *Publ:* Auth, El Barroco Literario Hispanico, Ed Nova, Buenos Aires, 69; Hispanoamerica Y Su Expresion, 69 & Literatura Argentina, Vol I, 69, Ed Eudeba, Beunos Aires; ed, El Persiles, Ed Anaya, Salamanca, 71; auth, Literatura Espanola, Ed Fac Filos, Tucuman, Vols I & II, 71 & 73; ed, Martin Fierro, Ed Labor, Barcelona, 72; La Literatura Barroca en Hispanoamerica, NY, 72; La Creacion Del Martin Fierro, Ed Gredos, Madrid, 73. *Mailing Add:* Dept of Lit & Lang Univ of Calif Riverside CA 92521

CARKEET, DAVID CORYDON, Fiction, English Language. See Vol II

CARL, RALPH FLETCHER, b Jeromesville, Ohio, Nov 7, 16. ROMANCE LANGUAGES. *Educ:* Col of Wooster, BA, 38; Univ Mich, MA, 49, PhD, 56. *Prof Exp:* Instr Span, Col of Wooster, 45-47; instr, 47-48, PROF ROMANCE LANG, DEPAUW UNIV, 52-, CHMN DEPT, 68- *Mem:* MLA; Am Asn Teachers Fr; Am Asn Teachers Span & Port. *Res:* French literature of the 19th and 20th centuries; the petites revues of the period 1900-1915. *Mailing Add:* Dept of Romance Lang DePauw Univ Greencastle IN 46135

CARLOS, ALBERTO J, HISPANIC & ITALIAN STUDIES. *Educ:* Univ Calif, Berkeley, AB, 51, MA, 53; Univ Paris, DUniv, 61. *Prof Exp:* Asst prof Romance lang, Univ Buffalo, 61-62; from asst prof to assoc prof, 62-71, Res Found fac fel, 67, chmn dept Romance lang, 70-71, chmn dept Hisp & Ital studies, 72-75, PROF ROMANCE LANG, STATE UNIV NY ALBANY, 71- *Mem:* MLA; Inst Int Lit Iberoam; Am Asn Teachers Span & Port; Asoc Int Hispanistas; Nat Asn Chicano Studies. *Res:* Latin American and comparative literature. *Publ:* Auth, Rene Werther y La nouvelle Heloise en la primera novela de la Avellaneda, 12/65 & Divagacion: La geografia erotica de Ruben Dario, 12/67, Rev Iberoam; coauth, Bilingual Ed, Martin Fierro, State Univ NY, 67; auth, El anthiheroe en El acoso, Cuadernos Americanos, 1/71; Aproximacion a los cuentos de Garcia Marquez, In: Giacoman: Homenaje a Garcia Marquez, 72; Conversacion en la catedral: Novela politica, In: Homenaje a Vargas Llosa, 73; Pedro Paramo y San Gabriel, In: Actas del sexto congreso internacional de hispanistas, Toronto, 80. *Mailing Add:* Dept of Hisp & Ital Studies State Univ of NY Albany NY 12222

CARLSON, GREGORY IVAN, b Milwaukee, Wis, Nov 11, 41. LATIN & GREEK LITERATURE. *Educ:* St Louis Univ, BA, 65, MA, 66; Univ Heidelberg, DPhil, 72. *Prof Exp:* Instr classics, Marquette Univ, 66-68; asst prof, 74-78, ASSOC PROF CLASSICS, COL OF THE HOLY CORSS, 78- *Concurrent Pos:* Batchelor Fac fel, Col of the Holy Cross, 75, dir, Honors Prog, 76- *Mem:* Am Philol Asn; AAUP. *Res:* Augustan poetry; Homeric poetry; Greek tragedy. *Publ:* Auth, How shall I teach the classics?, Class Bull, 65; coauth, Form and transformation in Vergil's Catalepton, Am J Philol, 71; auth, The two creation accounts in schematic contrast, Bible Today, 73; Spiritual direction and the paschal mystery, Rev Relig, 74; Shepherd and host: A literary look at Psalm 23, Bible Today, 75; Aeneas in thirteen, times three, Reconciliation Quart, 77; From Numantia to necking, Class World, 78; Nova et Vetera, Class Bull, 78. *Mailing Add:* Dept of Classics Col of the Holy Cross Worcester MA 01610

CARLTON, CHARLES MERRITT, b Dec 12, 28; m 57; c 3. FRENCH LANGUAGE, ROMANCE LINGUISTICS. *Educ:* Univ Vt, AB, 50; Middlebury Col, MA, 51; Univ Mich, PhD(Romance ling), 63. *Prof Exp:* Teaching asst French, Univ Mich, 54-58 & teaching asst English as foreign lang, English Lang Inst, 57-58; instr French, Mich State Univ, 58-62; asst prof French & gen ling, Univ Mo, 62-66; assoc prof, 66-77, PROF FRENCH & ROMANCE LING, UNIV ROCHESTER, 77- *Concurrent Pos:* Vis prof, NDEA French Inst, Univ Vt, 64; ed, Comp Romance Ling Newslett, 70-71; lectr English as foreign lang, Babes-Bolyai Univ, Cluj, Romania, 71-72; consult, Nat Endowment for Humanities, 74-; vis prof, Univ Ky, Cluj program, 77; co-ed, Miorita, 77- *Honors & Awards:* Nat Sci Found Award, 65; Nat Defense For Lang Award, 70; Fulbright-Hays Awards, Romania, 74, 78 & 82; Int Res & Exchanges Bd Award, Romania, 82. *Mem:* AAAS; Am Asn Teachers Fr; Ling Soc Am; Soc Romanian Studies; MLA. *Res:* Romanian language; Romance linguistics. *Publ:* Auth, Studies in Romance Lexicology, Univ NC, 65; A Linguistic Analysis of a Collection of Late Latin Documents Composed in Ravenna . . ., Mouton, 73; Defining the Romanian past participle, Linguistics, 74; On Error Analysis, The Romanian-English Contrastive Analysis Project, 74; Romanian and Balkan romance bibliography, Comp Romance Ling Newslett, 74-; The Romanian Numerical System, Italic and Romance: Linguistic Studies in Honor of E Pulgram, 80; Language Teaching: The Romanian Way, Miorita, 81; Some aspects of Romanian as spoken in the US, Yearbk Romanian Studies, 82. *Mailing Add:* 3 Thornfield Way Fairport NY 14450

CARLUT, CHARLES E, b Lyons, France, Mar 8, 11; US citizen; m 53; c 1. ROMANCE LANGUAGES & LITERATURES. *Educ:* Ecole Sci Polit, Paris, dipl, 32; Faculte Droit, Paris & Lyons, lic, 36; Ecole Prep Prof Fr A L'Etranger, Paris, dipl lit, 38; Ohio State Univ, PhD, 48. *Prof Exp:* Instr French, Ohio State Univ, 38-40 & 46-48, from asst prof to assoc prof, 48-65, prof, 65-81. *Concurrent Pos:* Mem ed staff, Fr Rev, 68. *Honors & Awards:* Order of Merit, France, 72; Palmes Academiques, 73 & 78. *Mem:* MLA; Am Asn Teachers Fr; Soc Fr Prof Am. *Res:* French literature of the 19th and 20th centuries; French civilization. *Publ:* Coauth, France de nos jours, 57, 62, 68 & 74 & Recits de nos jours, 64, Macmillan; auth, 19th Century French Short Stories, Dell, 66; coauth, French for Oral and Written Review, Holt, 68 & 75; auth, La correspondance de Flaubert, 68, coauth, Concordance de Madame Bovary, 78 & ed, Essais sur Flaubert pour Don Louis Demorest, 79, Nizet, Paris; coauth, L'Education Sentimentale, Trois Contes Bouvard et Pecuchet La Tentation de Saint Antoine, Garland, 80. *Mailing Add:* Dept of Romance Lang Ohio State Univ Columbus OH 43210

CARMONY, MARVIN DALE, b Richmond, Ind; Feb 27, 23; m 47; c 2. LINGUISTICS, ENGLISH LANGUAGE. *Educ:* Ind State Univ, AB, 50, MA, 51, PhD(ling), 65. *Prof Exp:* Instr English, high schs, Pendleton & Shelbyville, Ind, 53-59; from instr to assoc prof, 59-69, PROF ENGLISH & LING, IND STATE UNIV, TERRE HAUTE, 69-, ASSOC DEAN COL ARTS & SCI, 70- *Concurrent Pos:* Gen ed, Ind Names, 70-75; managing ed, Midwestern J Lang & Folklore, 75- *Mem:* Am Dialect Soc; Am Name Soc; Ling Soc Am; MLA. *Res:* General linguistics; dialectology. *Publ:* Contribr, The First Lincolnland Conference on Dialectology, 70 & Studies in Linguistics in Honor of Raven I McDavid, Jr, 72, Univ Ala; auth, Indiana dialects in their historical setting, Ind Coun Teachers English, 72; coauth, Indiana Place Names, Ind Univ, 75, rev ed, Ind Dialects, 79. *Mailing Add:* Col of Arts & Sci Ind State Univ Terre Haute IN 47803

CARNES, PACK, b Nov, 25, 39; US citizen; m 68; c 1. GERMANIC LANGUAGES & LITERATURES. *Educ:* Wabash Col, BA, 62; Univ Calif, Los Angeles, MA, 70, PhD (Ger lang & lit), 73. *Prof Exp:* Asst prof English & Latin, Toyo Eiwa Col, Tokyo, 65-70; asst prof Ger, Lawrence Univ, 73-74; vis prof Ger, Univ Cincinnati, 74-75; ASST PROF GER, UNIV ARIZ, 75- *Mem:* MLA; Renaissance Soc; Medieval Acad Am; Am Folklore Soc; Am Asn Teachers Ger. *Res:* Medieval love poetry; fables; folklore. *Publ:* Auth, Shakespeare's Small Latine in Titus Andronicus, Toyo Eiwa Studies Humanities, 68; Modern Conversational Japanese (2 vols), Sony Lang Lab, 68 & 70; coauth, Modern Basic English (5 vols), 68-70 & Modern English Patterns (8 vols), 68-70, Sony Lang Lab, Tokyo; auth, Kyushu: The land of Amaterasu, 69, The town that lives a game, In: This is Japan, 70 & English speaken here, In: This is Japan, 70; The fable joke, Southwest Folklore, 81. *Mailing Add:* Dept of Ger Univ of Ariz Tucson AZ 85721

CARNEY, EDMUND JEREMIAH, b Somerville, Mass, Apr 27, 26; m 53; c 2. SPANISH AMERICAN & BRAZILIAN LITERATURE. *Educ:* Dartmouth Col, AB, 46; Univ Cincinnati, MA, 60; Univ Ill, Urbana, PhD(Span Am lit), 71. *Prof Exp:* Teacher Span, Cincinnati Bd Educ, Ohio, 55-59; teacher, Finneytown Bd Educ, 59-65; instr, Ill State Univ, 65-70; assoc prof, 70-77, PROF SPAN, LOCK HAVEN STATE COL, 77- *Mem:* MLA; Am Asn Teachers Span & Port. *Res:* Spanish American novella; Brazilian novella; Latin American fiction. *Mailing Add:* Dept of Foreign Lang Lock Haven State Col Lock Haven PA 17745

CARNICELLI, THOMAS ANTHONY, English. See Vol II

CARON, MARIE THERESE, b Chatham, Ont, Dec 20, 30. FRENCH LANGUAGE & LITERATURE. *Educ:* Univ Ottawa, BA, 56; Laval Univ, MA, 61; Univ Wis, PhD(Fr), 66. *Prof Exp:* Lectr Fr, 64-67, asst prof, 67-72, ASSOC PROF FRENCH, UNIV WINDSOR, 72- *Mem:* MLA. *Res:* Late 16th century French literature; style and content of Jean de Sponde's literary works. *Mailing Add:* 247 Randolph Pl Windsor ON N9B 3P4 Can

CAROZZA, DAVY ANGELO, b Montenerodomo, Italy, Oct 10, 26; US citizen; m 52; c 4. COMPARATIVE LITERATURE, ROMANCE LANGUAGES. *Educ:* Cath Univ Am, BA, 56, MA, 57, PhD(Romance lang), 64. *Prof Exp:* Instr Ital & French, Univ Md, 61-64, asst prof Ital, 64-65; assoc prof, 65-67, chmn dept, 67-69 & 73-76, PROF COMP LIT, UNIV WIS-MILWAUKEE, 68-, COORDR, MA PROG FOREIGN LANG & LIT, 76- *Concurrent Pos:* Lectr, Sch Advan Int Studies, Johns Hopkins Univ, 64-65; Univ Wis-Milwaukee res grant, Rome Italy, 68-69, 74 & 78. *Mem:* Int Comp Lit Asn; MLA; Dante Soc Am; Renaissance Soc Am; Midwest Mod Lang Asn (vpres, 68-69, pres, 69-70). *Res:* Baroque and Renaissance literature; Dante; literary criticism and stylistics. *Publ:* Auth, For a definition of mannerism, the Hatzfeldian thesis, Colloquia Ger, 67; Elements of the Roman courtois in the episode of Paolo and Francesca, Inferno V, Papers on Lang & Lit, fall 67; Delle traduzioni Francesi di Dante: problemi e soluzioni, Trimestre, 6/70;

Converted Venus: A study in thematic transformation, Neohelicon, Budapest, 12/75; European Baroque, 77 & Problems in the identification of European Baroque, 77, Norwood Ed; Requiem for a genre very much alive or il Fu Fiction Pascal, Mod Fiction Studies, 79. *Mailing Add:* Dept of Comp Lit Univ of Wis Milwaukee WI 53201

CARPENTER, CHARLES WHITNEY, II, b New York, NY, Jan 2, 18; m 58; c 2. GERMANIC PHILOLOGY. *Educ:* Cornell Univ, AB, 43; Univ Southern Calif, MA, 52; Indust Col Armed Forces, dipl, 61; NY Univ, PhD(Ger philol), 68; Bucknell Univ, MSEd, 73. *Prof Exp:* Lectr French & Ger, Wagner Col, 54-55; teaching asst Ger, Princeton Univ, 55-56; instr, NY Univ, 56-59; asst prof French & Ger, Bronx Community Col, 59-62; instr Ger, Univ Vt, 62-63 & Univ Hawaii, 63-65; asst prof Ger lang & lit, Buena Vista Col, 65-66; assoc prof, 66-69, PROF GER, BLOOMSBURG STATE COL, 69- *Concurrent Pos:* Instr lang & ling, Adelphi Col, 61-62; mem pres coun, Am Inst Mgt, 66- *Honors & Awards:* Student Coun Award & Spec Fac Award, Bronx Community Col, 62; Silver Order of Merit & Golden Order of Spec Membership, Japanese Red Cross, 65 & Golden Order of Merit; Honors Scholar Award, NY Univ, 69. *Mem:* Am Asn Teachers Ger; Ling Soc Am; MLA; NEA; fel Intercontinental Biog Asn. *Res:* Germanic linguistics; German literature. *Publ:* Auth, Exiled German Writers in America, 1932-1950; The Systematic Exploitation of the Verbal Calque in German, Herbert Lang Verlag, Berne, Switz, 68. *Mailing Add:* Dept of Langs & Cult Bloomsburg State Col Main & Penn Sts Bloomsburg PA 17815

CARR, DENZEL (RAYBOURNE), b West Liberty, Ky, Dec 26, 00; m 51; c 2. LINGUISTICS. *Educ:* Jagiellonian Univ, PhM, 32; Yale Univ, PhD, 37. *Prof Exp:* Lectr English & phonetics, Wakayama Higher Commercial Sch, Japan, 24-29; reader Japanese & Chinese, Jagiellonian Univ, 29-32; instr Romance lang, Univ Hawaii, 33-36, asst prof ling, 37-40; chief lang div, Dept Army, Gen Hq, Supreme Comdr Allied Powers, Japan, 47-48; from lectr to assoc prof, 48-50, prof, 52-68, EMER PROF ORIENTAL LANG, UNIV CALIF, BERKELEY, 68- *Concurrent Pos:* Secy-translr, Eastern Buddhist, Kyoto, Japan, 23; Guggenheim fel, 55-56; resident scholar, East-West Ctr, Univ Hawaii, 62-63. *Mem:* Ling Soc Am; Am Orient Soc; Ling Soc Philippines; Royal Inst Ling, Geor & Ethnol, Neth; Polynesian Soc. *Res:* Relationship of sound to symbol in numerous languages; grammatical analysis in Japanese, Indonesian and Slavic languages; adaptation of developing languages to modern needs. *Publ:* Auth, A characterization of the Chinese national language, Polish Ling Soc, 32; coauth, Gendai Sinago Kagaku, Bunkyudo, Tokyo, 39; co-compiler, English-Indonesian Dict, Dian Rakyat, Jakarta, Indonesia, 74. *Mailing Add:* 924 Contra Costa Dr El Cerrito CA 94530

CARR, DEREK COOPER, b Darlington, England, Feb 26, 44; Can citizen; m 70; c 1. HISPANIC & MEDIEVAL STUDIES. *Educ:* Univ Newcastle, Eng, BA, 65, dipl educ, 66; Univ BC, PhD(Romance studies), 72. *Prof Exp:* Lectr Span, 72-74, asst prof, 74-79, ASSOC PROF SPAN, UNIV BC, 79-, CHMN DEPT, 81- *Mem:* Can Asn Hispanists; MLA; Int Asn Hispanists. *Res:* Medieval & Renaissance Spanish literature; Don Enrique de Villena (1384-1434); editing medieval texts. *Publ:* Auth, Los doze trabajos de Hercules: Fuente posible del Laberinto de Juan de Mena, Hisp Rev, 73; La epistola que enbio don Enrique de Villena a Suero de Quinones y la fecha de la Cronica Serrazina de Pedro de Corral, Univ BC Hisp Studies, Tamesis, London, 74; ed, Enrique de Villena, Tratado de la Consolacion, Clasicos Castellanos, Espasa-Calpe, Madrid, 78; Another look at the metrics of Santillana's sonnets, Hispanic Rev, Vol 46: 41-53; A fifteenth-century Castilian translation and commentary of a Petrarchan sonnet: Biblioteca Nacional, MS 10186, folios 196R-199R, Revista Canadiense de Estudios Hispanicos, Vol 5: 123:43. *Mailing Add:* Dept of Hisp & Ital Studies Univ BC Vancouver BC V6T 1W5 Can

CARR, GERALD FRANCIS, b Pittsburgh, Pa, Dec 29, 30; m 65; c 2. GERMAN, LINGUISTICS. *Educ:* Duquesne Univ, BEd, 58; Univ Wis-Madison, MA, 60, PhD(Ger), 68. *Prof Exp:* Instr Ger & French, Duquesne Univ, 60-62, asst prof, 64-65 & 66-68; from asst prof to assoc prof, 68-75, PROF GER, EASTERN ILL UNIV, 75- *Mem:* MLA; Ling Soc Am; Ling Soc Europe; Am Coun Teaching Foreign Lang; Am Asn Teachers Ger. *Res:* German language; older Germanic languages; medieval poetry. *Publ:* Auth, The prologue to Wace's Vie de Saint Nicholas: A structural analysis, Philol Quart, 1/68; On the Vie de Saint Alexis, Romance Notes, 76; co-ed, Linguistic Method: The Herbert Penzl Festschrift, Peter de Ridder, 78; The Signifying Animal, Ind Univ, 81. *Mailing Add:* Dept of Foreign Lang Eastern Ill Univ Charleston IL 61920

CARR, RICHARD ALAN, b Maplewood, NJ, July 15, 38; , 76. FRENCH & RENAISSANCE LITERATURE. *Educ:* Princeton Univ, AB, 60, MA, 63, PhD(French), 69. *Prof Exp:* Instr, 64-69, asst prof, 69-75, ASSOC PROF FRENCH, IND UNIV, 75- *Mem:* MLA; Am Asn Teachers Fr; Soc Francaise Seiziemistes. *Res:* French Renaissance literature; Renaissance short story. *Publ:* Ed, Histoires tragiques, Champion, Paris, 77; auth, Pierre Boaistuau's Histoires Tragiques: A Study of Narrative, Univ NC, 79. *Mailing Add:* Dept French & Ital Ind Univ Bloomington IN 47405

CARRABINO, VICTOR, b Sicily, Italy, Aug 21, 41; US citizen; m 68; c 1. TWENTIETH CENTURY FRENCH LITERATURE. *Educ:* Univ Hartford, BA, 65; Univ Mass, Amherst, MA, 67; Amherst, Mt Holyoke & Smith Cols & Univ Mass, PhD(Fr), 71. *Prof Exp:* ASSOC PROF FRENCH, FLA STATE UNIV, 69- *Mem:* MLA; SAtlantic MLA; SCent MLA. *Res:* Nouveau roman; black literature of French expression. *Publ:* Auth, Casa Editrice Maccari, Italy; Robbe-Grillet and phenomenological time, Res Studies, 3/73; Phenomenology and the nouveau Roman: A moment of Epiphany, SAtlantic Bull, 11/73; Alain Robbe-Grillet and the phenomenological novel, 74 & Pirandello and Picasso: A pragmatic view of reality, 74, Casa Editrice Maccari, Italy. *Mailing Add:* Dept of Mod Lang Fla State Univ Tallahassee FL 32306

CARRE, JEFFREY JAMES, b Glasgow, Scotland, Jan 16, 19; nat; m 45; c 1. ROMANCE LANGUAGES. *Educ:* Bowdoin Col, AB, 40; Columbia Univ, AM, 42, PhD, 52. *Prof Exp:* From instr to assoc prof Romance lang, Bowdoin Col, 47-62; assoc prof, 62-70, prof, 70-80, WILLIAM LYMAN COWLES PROF ROMANCE LANG, AMHERST COL, 80- *Mem:* MLA; Am Asn Teachers Ital. *Res:* Nineteenth century French literature; Eugene Fromentin; formation of an art critic. *Mailing Add:* Dept of Romance Lang Amherst Col Amherst MA 01002

CARRELL, PATRICIA LYNN, b Chicago, Ill, Sept 22, 40; m 63; c 2. LINGUISTICS. *Educ:* Knox Col, BA, 62; Univ Tex, Austin, MA, 64, PhD(ling), 66. *Prof Exp:* Head English descriptive ling sect, Ling Res Ctr, Univ Tex, Austin, 66-68; asst prof, 68-71, chmn dept, 73-79, ASSOC PROF LING, SOUTHERN ILL UNIV, CARBONDALE, 71- *Mem:* Ling Soc Am; Am Asn Appl Ling; Teachers English to Speakers Other Lang; Soc Res Child Develop. *Res:* Syntax, semantic & progmatics; psycholinguistics; language acquisition. *Publ:* Auth, A Transformational Grammar of Igbo, Cambridge Univ, 70; Empirical investigations of indirectly conveyed meaning: Assertion versus presupposition in first and second language acquisition, Lang Learning, 12/77; Children's understanding of indirect requests: Comparing child and adult comprehension, J Child Lang, 81; coauth (with B Konneker), Politeness: Comparing native and non-native judgments, Lang Learning, 81; auth, Children's requests: A functional-interactional analysis, In: Papers from the 1980 Mid-America Linguistics Conference, Univ Kans, 81; Culture-specific Schemata in L2 comprehension, In: Selected Papers from the Ninth Illinois TESOL/BE Annual Convention and the First Midwest TESOL Conference, 81 & The role of Schemata in L2 comprehension, In: On TESOL 1981, 81, TESOL; coauth (with D Molfese and V Molfese), Early Language Development, In: Handbook of Developmental Psychology, Prentice-Hall, 82. *Mailing Add:* Dept of Ling Southern Ill Univ Carbondale IL 62901

CARRELL, THELMA RUTH, b Mt Carmel, Ill, Oct 24, 13. ROMANCE LANGUAGES. *Educ:* Eureka Col, AB, 35; Univ Ill, AM, 37, PhD(Span), 53. *Prof Exp:* Teacher, high schs, Ill, 38-44 & Mich, 44-46; instr Span, Univ Ill, 46-49; asst prof, NMex Western Col, 51-55; prof mod foreign lang & head dept, Miss Univ Women, 55-80; RETIRED. *Mem:* MLA; Am Asn Teachers Span & Port; Am Asn Teachers Ger; NEA; AAUp. *Res:* Latin-American literature, especially 19th century Mexican; contemporary Spanish literature. *Publ:* Auth, The Role of Ignacio Manuel Attamirano in El Ranacimiento. *Mailing Add:* 114 W 9th St Mt Carmel IL 62863

CARRENO, ANTONIO G, b Parada del Sil, Orense, Spain, July 1, 39; m 62; c 2. SPANISH & SPANISH-AMERICAN LITERATURE. *Educ:* Escuela Normal Superior, BA, 62; Trinity Col, Conn, MA, 69; Yale Univ, PhD (Romance lang), 75. *Prof Exp:* Instr Span, Yale Univ, 74-75; asst prof, Columbia Univ, 75-77; ASST PROF SPAN, UNIV ILL, URBANA, 77- *Honors & Awards:* Don Ramon Menendez Pidal, Royal Span Acad, Madrid, 78. *Mem:* Am Asn Teachers Span & Port; MLA. *Res:* Golden age Spanish poetry, Lope's and Gongora's lyric balladry; contemporary Spanish poetry, Pessoa, Machado, Aleixandre; Spanish American colonial literature, Las Casas. *Publ:* Auth, O fingidor y o fingido: Su significacion en Fernando Pessoa, Cuadernos Hispanoamericanos, 73; Una guerra sine dolo et fraude: El Padre Las Casas y el problema del indio en el siglo XVL, Cuadernos americanos, 74; La verguenza como constante social y narrativa en don Juan Manuel, Thesaurus, 77; Fernao Velloso y Lionardo: La fantasia humoristica e ironica en Los Lusiadas, Hispania, 77; El Romancero Lirico de Lope de Vega, Gredos, Madrid, 78; El romancero espiritual de Lope de Vega, Bol Bibliot Menendez y Pelayo, 78; Perspectivas y dualidades pronominales en el Romancero de Lope de Vega, Revista de Filologia Esp, 78. *Mailing Add:* Dept of Span Ital & Port Univ of Ill Urbana IL 61801

CARRIER, CARL EDWARD, b Lexington, Ky, July 5, 27. GERMAN LITERATURE. *Educ:* Univ Ky, AB, 50; Univ Ill, MA, 52; Ind Univ, PhD(Ger), 62. *Prof Exp:* Instr Ger, Miss Southern Col, 52-55, Vanderbilt Univ, 58-62; asst prof, Purdue Univ, 62-64; asst prof, 64-76, ASSOC PROF GER, OHIO UNIV, 76- *Concurrent Pos:* Asst managing ed Ger, Mod Lang J, 66-70. *Mem:* MLA; Am Asn Teachers Ger; Midwest MLA. *Res:* Twentieth century German literature; German drama of the 19th century. *Mailing Add:* Dept of Mod Lang Ohio Univ Athens OH 45701

CARRINGTON, SAMUEL MACON, JR, b Durham, NC, June 22, 39; m; c 4. ROMANCE LANGUAGES. *Educ:* Univ NC, Chapel Hill, AB, 60, MA, 62, PhD(Romance lang), 65. *Prof Exp:* Instr French, Univ NC, 64-65; asst prof, Univ Colo, 65-67; asst prof, 67-71, assoc prof, 71-79, proctor, 74-80, PROF FRENCH & UNIV LIBRN, RICE UNIV, 79- *Concurrent Pos:* Fel, Southeastern Inst Medieval & Renaissance Studies, 65; res grants, Rice Univ, 67 & Am Philos Soc, 68. *Mem:* Am Asn Teachers Fr; SCent Mod Lang Asn. *Res:* The medieval comic theatre in France; the complete works of Amadis Jamyn; poetry of the Pleiade. *Publ:* Auth, Ronsard's treatment of ignorant poets and the common people, In: Renaissance and Other Studies in Honor of W L Wiley, Univ NC, 68; coauth, Deux pieces comiques inedites du Manuscrit B N fr 904, Romania, 70; auth, Censorship and the medieval comic theatre in France, Rice Univ Studies, 71; ed, Les oeuvres poetiques d'Amadis Jamyn: I Premieres Poesies et Livre I, II, Livres II-IV, ed crit, Librairie Droz, Geneva 73-78; auth, Sainte-Beuve, critic of Ronsard, Rice Univ Studies, 73; Amadis Jamyn's theory of translation, In: Ky Romance Studies in Honor of Isidore Silver, 75. *Mailing Add:* Dept of French Rice Univ Houston TX 77251

CARRINO, FRANK G, b Lima, Ohio, Feb 15, 22; m 50; c 1. HISPANIC STUDIES. *Educ:* Baldwin Wallace Col, AB, 56; Univ Wis, MA, 47; Univ Mich, PhD(Span), 56. *Prof Exp:* Instr Span, Muhlenberg Col, 47-48; from instr to prof, State Univ NY Albany, 48-59; dir Binational Ctr, Paraguayan-Am Cult Ctr, Asuncion, Paraguay, 59-61; asst to pres, foreign student adv & Span teacher, 61-62, dir, Ctr Inter-Am Studies, 62-75, PROF ROMANCE LANG, STATE UNIV NY ALBANY, 62-, CHMN DEPT HISP, ITAL & PORT LANG & LIT, 75- *Concurrent Pos:* Am specialist's grant to Dominican Repub, 62 & 66 & Mex & Cent Am, 64; Fulbright-Hays lectr, Mex, 65; State Univ NY Res Found res grant, prep definitive ed Martin

Fierro, 74-75; mem exec coun, NY State Latin Am Studies Coun. *Mem:* Am Asn Teachers Span & Port. *Res:* Latin American literature; language and area studies; teaching English as a foreign language. *Publ:* Coauth, Every classroom can be a language laboratory, CASD AIDS, spring 53; Let's Speak English II, 60 & Let's Speak English III, 61, US Aid Mission to Paraguay; auth, La dinamica de grupos en el salon de clases, Saber, USIS, Mex, 12/65; ed bilingual version, Martin Fierro, 67 & co-ed & translr, The Gaucho Martin Fierro, 74, State Univ NY. *Mailing Add:* Dept of Hisp Ital & Portuguese Lang & Lit State Univ of NY 1400 Washington Ave Albany NY 12222

CARROLL, CARLETON WARREN, b Rochester, NY, Oct 20, 39. FRENCH LANGUAGE. *Educ:* Ohio State Univ, BA, 61; Univ Wis-Madison, MA, 65, PhD(French), 68. *Prof Exp:* Asst prof French & Ital, Univ Wis-Madison & Univ Wis-Exten, 67-74, chmn dept, 69-74; asst prof, 74-80, ASSOC PROF FRENCH, ORE STATE UNIV, 80- *Mem:* MLA; Am Asn Teachers Fr; Int Arthurian Soc; Soc Rencesvals; AAUP. *Res:* Medieval French literature; medieval Provencal literature; interlinguistics. *Publ:* Co-ed, Chretien de Troyes' Yvain, ou le Chevalier au Lion, Appleton, 68; auth, A comparative structural analysis of Arnau Daniel's Lo ferm voler and Peire Vidal's Mout m'es bon e bel, Neophilologus, 70; coauth, On the generalization of the Sestina, Delta, 75; auth, Medieval romance paleography-a brief introduction, In: Medieval Manuscripts and Textual Criticism, Univ NC, 76; co-transl, Chretien de Troyes, Ywain, the Knight of the Lion, Frederick Ungar, 77. *Mailing Add:* Dept of Foreign Lang & Lit Ore State Univ Corvallis OR 97331

CARROLL, LINDA LOUISE, b Seattle, Wash, June 10, 49. ITALIAN, LINGUISTICS. *Educ:* Princeton Univ, AB, 71; Harvard Univ, MA, 72, PhD (Ital), 77. *Prof Exp:* Instr, Gonzaga Univ, 75-76, asst prof Ital, 76-81, chairperson dept mod lang, 78-81; ASST PROF ITAL, TULANE UNIV, 81- *Concurrent Pos:* Adj asst prof ling, Whitworth Col, 77-79. *Mem:* MLA; Ling Soc Am; Dante Soc Am. *Res:* Italian historical linguistics; Italian Renaissance theater; phonology. *Publ:* Auth, Rassegna bibliografica La Veniexiana, Arch Veneto, 77; Angelo Beolco, Twayne (in press); Language and Dialect in Ruzante and Goldoni, Longo, 81; Ruzante: The natural or the unnatural?, Proc PNCFL, Vol XXXI, 80. *Mailing Add:* Dept of Foreign Lang Tulane Univ New Orleans LA 70118

CARRUBBA, ROBERT WILLIAM, b New York, NY, Aug 1, 34; m 65; c 2. GREEK, LATIN. *Educ:* Fordham Univ, AB, 56, AM, 57; Princeton Univ, AM, 63, PhD(classics), 64. *Prof Exp:* Asst prof classics, Lake Forest Col, 64-66 & City Col New York, 66-67; asst prof Greek & Latin, Columbia Univ, 67-69; assoc prof, 69-74, PROF CLASSICS, PA STATE UNIV, UNIVERSITY PARK, 74- *Concurrent Pos:* Josiah Macy Jr Found res grants, 68-73; ed, The Classical World Ser, 71-73 & Proc Am Philol Asn, 74-76; Am Coun Learned Soc grant, 75. *Mem:* Am Philol Asn (secy-treas, 73-76); Class Asn Atlantic States (pres, 76-77). *Res:* Latin literature; neo-Latin. *Publ:* Co-ed, The curse on the Romans, Trans & Publ Am Philol Asn, 66; auth, The Epodes of Horace: A Study in Poetic Arrangement, Mouton, The Hague, 68; co-ed, Directory of College and University Classicists in the United States and Canada, 73 & Classics and the Classical Tradition, 73, Pa State Univ; coauth, The western world's first detailed treatise on acupunture, J Hist Med, 74. *Mailing Add:* Dept of Classics Pa State Univ University Park PA 16802

CARSON, JANE ISABELLE, b Kingston, NY, June 27, 48. FRENCH NOVEL. *Educ:* Pomona Col, BA; Univ Ore, MA, 76, PhD(French), 79. *Prof Exp:* Asst prof French, St Lawrence Univ, 79-81 & Old Dominion Univ, 81-82; ASST PROF FRENCH & SPAN, IDAHO STATE UNIV, 82- *Mem:* MLA. *Res:* French new novel; contemporary French women writers. *Publ:* Transl, Nino Frank, The shadow that had lost its man, In: Portraits of the Artist in Exile: Recollections of James Joyce by Europeans, Univ Wash Press, 79; auth, Celine: The fire in the night, Symposium, summer 81; transl, Randi Birn's & Karen Gould's Simon on Simon: An interview with the artist, Gerard Roubichou's Histoire, or the serial novel, Karin Holter's Simon citing Simon: A few examples of limited intertextuality, C G Bjurstrom's Composition, repetition, and displacement in Claude Simon's First Three Novels & Serge Doubrovsky's Introduction, In: Orion Blinded: Essays on Claude Simon, Bucknell Univ Press, 81. *Mailing Add:* 1399 NW 14th St Corvallis OR 97330

CARSON, KATHARINE WHITMAN, b Bistol, Tenn, Oct 26, 23. FRENCH LITERATURE. *Educ:* Barnard Col, AB, 45; Columbia Univ, MA, 65, PhD(French), 71. *Prof Exp:* Instr French, Rutgers Univ, 68-71 & lectr, 71-72; asst prof French, Baruch Col, 73-78; RES ASSOC, US ARAB CHAMBER OF COMMERCE, NY, 81- *Concurrent Pos:* Consult educ div, Simon & Schuster, 72-73; consult-evaluator, New York Bd Educ, 74-75; consult-evaluator, NY Bd Educ, 74-75; bibliog-consult, H P Kraus Rare Bks, 79-80; vis assoc prof, Yeshiva Univ, 80 & Fairleigh Dickinson Univ, 79-81. *Mem:* AAUP; MLA, Am Asn Teachers Fr. *Res:* Eighteenth century French novel. *Publ:* Auth, Socrates observed: Three eighteenth century views, In: Vol XIV, Diderot Studies, Droz, Geneva, 71; Aspects of contemporary society in Gil Blas, Vol CX, In: Studies on Voltaire and Eighteenth Century, Voltaire Found, Oxfordshire, 73; transl, The Rohan Master: A book of hours by Marcel Thomas, George Braziller, 73; The Complete Book of Ballet by Genevieve Guillot & Germaine Prudhommeau, Prentice-Hall, 76; contribr, Women's Studies Series (also cassette), Everett/Edwards, 76. *Mailing Add:* 435 W 119 St New York NY 10027

CARTER, ERWIN DALE, JR, b Portales, NMex, Oct 28, 34; c 2. SPANISH-AMERICAN LITERATURE, HISPANIC LINGUISTICS. *Educ:* Calif State Col Long Beach, BA, 58, MA, 59; Univ Southern Calif, MA, 63, PhD(Span), 66. *Prof Exp:* Instr Span, Cerritos Col, 59-66, chmn dept foreign lang, 60-63; asst prof foreign lang, 66-69, assoc prof Span, 69-75, assoc chmn dept foreign lang, 73-76, PROF SPAN, CALIF STATE UNIV, LOS ANGELES, 75- *Concurrent Pos:* Fulbright lectr Am lit, Univ Nacional de Rosario, Argentina, 72. *Mem:* Am Asn Teachers Span & Port; MLA; Inst Int Lit Iberoam. *Res:* Contemporary literature: Argentine, Mexican, and American. *Publ:* Coauth, Cuentos Argentinos De Misterio, Appleton, 68; auth, Antologia Del Realismo Magico, Odyssey, 70; Flight From Vengeance: An Analysis of The Killers by Hemingway and La Espera by Borges, English Lang J, 12/72; El Doble Y La Deformacion Del Tiempo En Dos Ficciones De Anderson Imbert: Fuga y El Grimoria, In: Homenaje a Enrique Anderson Imbert, Las Americas, 73; El Doble En Rayuela: Retrato De Conflicto Siquico, Memorias Del XVI Congr Inst Int De Lit Iber, 77; Adolfo Bioy Casares y la Distorsion del Tiempo, Explicacion Textos Lit, 77; Los Motivos Del Sueno Y Del Doble En Los Cuentos De Silvina Ocampo, Casa Cult de Baja, Calif (in press). *Mailing Add:* Dept Foreign Lang & Lit Calif State Univ Los Angeles CA 90032

CARTER, HENRY HARE, b Staten Island, NY, June 28, 05; m 45; c 2. MODERN LANGUAGES. *Educ:* Univ Pa, BS, 28, AM, 31, PhD, 37. *Prof Exp:* Instr Romance lang, Lehigh Univ, 28-32; prof, Cedar Crest Col, 32-37; from instr to asst prof, Northwestern Univ, 37-42; cult attache, US Dept State, Sao Paulo, Brazil, 46-47; asst prof Romance lang, Univ Pa, 47-51; assoc prof mod lang, De Pual Univ, 51-52; prof & chmn dept foreign lang, Colo Col, 52-56; vis prof gen ling, Univ Recife, Brazil, 56; from assoc prof to prof, 56-70, EMER PROF MOD LANG, UNIV NOTRE DAME, 70- *Concurrent Pos:* US Dept State lectr, Spain & Portugal, 55; Gulbenkian Found fel medieval Port Arthurian Grail, Vienna, Austria, 70. *Honors & Awards:* PMLA Publ Award, 58. *Mem:* MLA; Am Asn Teachers Span & Port; corresp mem, Brazilian Acad Philol & Acad Sci Lisbon. *Res:* Medieval Portuguese and Spanish. *Publ:* Auth, Paleographical Edition Codex Alcobacensis 200, Univ Pa, 38; Paleographical edition Old Portuguese version of the Rule of St Bernard (Codex Alcobacensis 200), PMLA, 40; Cancioneiro da Ajuda, Mod Lang Asn, 41; Contos e anedotas brasileiros, Heath, 42; Medieval Latin-Old Portuguese verb glossary, Romance Philol, 53; The Portuguese Book of Joseph of Arimathea, Univ NC, 67; ed, Cuentos de Espana Hoy, Holt, 74. *Mailing Add:* PO Box 76 Notre Dame IN 46556

CARTER, MARION ELIZABETH, b Jan 25, 15. FOREIGN LANGUAGES & LINGUISTICS. *Educ:* Wellesley Col, BA, 36; Howard Univ, MA, 37; Cath Univ Am, PhD(Romance lang), 45; Middlebury Col, MA, 57; Georgetown Univ, MS, 60, PhD(appl ling), 75. *Prof Exp:* Head dept Romance lang, Wiley Col, 37-38; instr French & Span, Barber-Scotia Col, 38-42; instr French, Howard Univ, 43-46; instr Span, Miner Teachers Col, 46-48, asst prof, 48-52, from assoc prof to prof foreign lang, DC Teachers Col, 52-70; prof foreign lang & ling, Gordon Col, 70-79; RESEARCHER, 79- *Concurrent Pos:* Buenos Aires Convention scholar, Haiti, 51; prof grant, Workshop Asian Cult & Educ Exchange, Duluth, Minn, 63; Fulbright lectr, Univ La Laguna, Spain, 67-68; liaison off, res for DC Teachers Cols, 68-; Gorden Col res grant, 74; reseacher, General Linguistics Textbook for College Students, 79-82. *Mem:* MLA; Am Asn Teachers Span & Port; NEA; Am Asn Teachers French; AAUP. *Res:* Culture patterns in Puerto Rican education; error analysis in the composition of Spanish speakers; genealogical investigations. *Publ:* Auth, The Role of the Symbol in French Romantic Poetry, Murray & Heister, 46; Haitian Normal School Methods and Their Application to Primary and Secondary Education, Libr Pan Am Union, Washington, DC; Human relations in the course offerings of the teacher training program, DC, J Negro Educ; Escollos lingüisticos, Acentos Literarios Americanos. *Mailing Add:* 402 U St NW Washington DC 20001

CARTER, WILLIAM CAUSEY, b Jesup, Ga, Mar 28, 41; m 67; c 3. FRENCH LANGUAGE & LITERATURE. *Educ:* Univ Ga, BA, 63, MA, 67; Ind Univ, PhD(French), 71. *Prof Exp:* Asst prof French, Ohio Univ, 71-74; asst prof, 74-78, PROF FRENCH, UNIV ALA, BIRMINGHAM, 78- *Mem:* MLA; SAtlantic Mod Lang Asn. *Res:* Nineteenth and twentieth century French literature. *Publ:* Auth, A synopsis of Proust's remarks concerning homosexuality, Proust Res Asn Newslett, fall 73; coauth, A Concordance to the Complete Works of Arthur Rimbaud, Ohio Univ, 78; Proust's view on sexuality, Adam Int Rev, 79. *Mailing Add:* 604 Warwick Rd Birmingham AL 35209

CARTIER, FRANCIS ARTHUR, b Sacramento, Calif, July 17, 23; m 47; c 2. SPEECH SCIENCE, COMMUNICATION. *Educ:* Univ Southern Calif, BA, 47, MA, 48, PhD(speech), 51; Univ London, cert phonetics, 50. *Prof Exp:* Lectr phonetics, Trinity Col, Univ London, 49-50; asst prof speech, Fla State Univ, 51-54; from asst prof to prof commun, Air Univ, 54-63; sr res scientist, Am Insts Res, 63-64; chief, Develop Div, English Lang Br, Lackland AFB, Tex, 64-71, chief, Develop Div, Systs Develop Agency, 71-76, chief, Concepts & Syst Div, Directorate of Training Develop, 76-79, DIR EVAL, DEFENSE LANG INST, 79- *Concurrent Pos:* Lectr, Univ Ga, 52-53; ed, J Commun, Int Commun Asn, 52-55; assoc prof lectr, George Washington Univ Resident Ctr, Maxwell AFB, 62-63; ed jour, Nat Soc Performance & Instr, 67-68. *Mem:* Am Educ Res Asn; Am Coun Teachers Foreign Lang; Int Commun Asn (pres, 58-59); Nat Soc Performance & Instr (secy, 64-65); Am Psychol Asn. *Res:* Listening comprehension; foreign-language learning. *Publ:* Auth, The Phonetic Alphabet, 54 & coauth rev eds, 71 & 82, W C Brown; coauth, Foundations of Air Power, 58 & ed & coauth, The Air Force Staff Officer, 61, Air Univ; auth, The Language of the Air Force in English, Regents, 76. *Mailing Add:* Defense Lang Inst Presidio of Monterey CA 93940

CARTIER, NORMAND RAYMOND, b Rochester, NJ, Jan 8, 14; m 46. MEDIEVAL LITERATURE, ROMANCE LANGUAGES. *Educ:* Assumption Col, Mass, BA, 34; Inst Prof de Francais a l'Etranger, Sorbonne, dipl, 35; Columbia Univ, MA, 36; Harvard Univ, MA, 37, PhD(Romance philol), 41. *Prof Exp:* Prof French & Span & chmn dept Romance lang, Marymount Col, 41-42; from instr to asst prof, Romance lang & lit, Harvard Univ, 46-50, coordr lang instr, Romance lang, 46-50, asst prof French & Span, 52-56; assoc prof Romance lang & lit, 56-62, chmn dept mod lang, 64-69, prof, 62-79, EMER PROF ROMANCE LANG & LIT, BOSTON COL, 79- *Mem:* Soc Amis de la Romania; MLA; Mediaeval Acad Am; AAUP. *Res:* Mediaeval literature: chronicles & epic; courtly novels; satire. *Publ:* Auth numerous articles in Romanica, Speculum, Mediaeval Studies & Revue de Litterature Comparee, 46-; ed & contribr, Aquila, Chestnut Hill Studies in Modern Languages (4 vols), Nijhoff, The Hague, 66-; auth, Le Bossu Desenchante, Publ Romanes et Francaises, Geneva, 71; Boccaccio's Revenge, Nijhoff, The Hague, 77. *Mailing Add:* 30 Old Colony Rd Chestnut Hill MA 02167

CARTLEDGE, SAMUEL J, b Atlanta, Ga, Jan 1, 35. FRENCH LINGUISTICS. *Educ:* Univ Paris, Dipl Fr civilization, 54; King Col, AB, 55; Yale Univ, PhD(Romance phil), 66. *Prof Exp:* Instr French, Univ Ga, 62-65; asst prof, 66-71, ASSOC PROF FRENCH, CALIF STATE UNIV, FULLERTON, 71-, CHMN DEPT FOR LANG & LIT, 72- *Res:* History of the French language. *Mailing Add:* 1007 N Martin Lane Fullerton CA 92631

CARTON, MARY JOSEPHA, b Chicago, Ill, Mar 31, 16. LATIN, GREEK. *Educ:* Clarke Col, AB, 53; Loyola Univ, Ill, MA, 63; St Louis Univ, PhD(Latin), 66. *Prof Exp:* Teacher, St Ferdinand Sch, Chicago, 38-43, St Anthony Sch, Casper, Wyo, 44-49 & Cathedral Sch, Rapid City, SDak, 49-54; teacher & counr, Heelan High Sch, Sioux City, Iowa, 54-56; teacher & acad dean, Immaculata High Sch, Chicago, 56-63; asst prof, 66-79, EMER PROF LATIN & GREEK, CLARKE COL, IOWA, 79- *Concurrent Pos:* Asst prof Greek, Aquinas Inst Theol, 68-69; adj prof, Dept English, Clark Col & Loras Col, 79- *Mem:* Am Philol Asn; Class Asn Mid W & S. *Res:* Latin and Greek literature; Greek art and archaeology; Scripture studies. *Publ:* Auth, Va Lat 3417 and its relationship to the text of Macrobius Saturnalia 7, Trans Am Philol Asn, 65; Three Unstudied Manuscripts of Macrobius's Saturnalia, Univ Microfilms, 66; Origin and content of the Rule of St Augustine, Rev for Religious, 9/79. *Mailing Add:* Clarke Col Dubuque IA 52001

CARTWRIGHT, MICHAEL T, b Rothwell, England, May 7, 37. FRENCH LITERATURE & LANGUAGE. *Educ:* Univ Exeter, BA, 60, PhD, 74; Aix-Marseille, D Univ, 64. *Prof Exp:* Asst prof French, Univ Exeter, 63-64 & Stanford Univ, 64-60; ASSOC PROF FRENCH, MCGILL UNIV, 70- *Mem:* MLA. *Res:* French literature of the 18th century; art criticism and aesthetics, 18th century; comparative literature, 18th century. *Publ:* Auth, Diderot et l'expression, Studies Voltaire & 18th Century, 67; Diderot critique d'art et la probleme de l'expression, Droz, Geneva, 68; Gabriel de Saint-Aubin: Interpreter of Diderot's art criticism, Gazette Beaux-Arts, 69; La critique de l'histoire contemporaine dans les Salons de Diderot, Melanges Lit Hurtubis/HMH, 71; Diderot and the idea of performance and the performer, In: Studies in Honour of Robert Niklaus, Univ Exeter, 75; Luxe, gout et l'ivresse de l'objet: un probleme moral et esthetique chez Diderot, Studies Voltaire & 18th Century, 76. *Mailing Add:* Dept of French Lang & Lit Peterson Hall McGill Univ 3460 McTavish St Montreal PQ H3A 1X9 Can

CARVER, GEORGE L, b Austin, Tex, Jan 19, 30. CLASSICAL LANGUAGES. *Educ:* Univ Tex, BA, 51, MA, 60; St Mary's Sem (Md), STB, 57; St Louis Univ, PhD(classics), 65. *Prof Exp:* Asst prof, 65-72, ASSOC PROF LATIN & GREEK, ARIZ STATE UNIV, 72- *Mem:* Am Philol Asn; Am Class League; MLA. *Res:* Lucretius; Terence. *Mailing Add:* Dept of Foreign Lang Ariz State Univ Tempe AZ 85281

CARY, JOHN R, b Baltimore, Md, Oct 28, 23; m 51; c 4. GERMAN. *Educ:* Haverford Col, BA, 47; Johns Hopkins Univ, PhD, 52. *Prof Exp:* Dir, Munich Ctr Univ Studies, Am Friends Serv Comt, 52-54; from instr to assoc prof, 54-69, PROF GER, HAVERFORD COL, 69-, CHMN DEPT, 65- *Concurrent Pos:* Consult, Ger achievement test, Col Entrance Exam Bd, 67. *Mem:* MLA; Am Asn Teachers Ger. *Res:* The Romantic movement; Theodor Fontane; Heinrich von Kleist. *Publ:* A reading of Kleist's Michael Kohlhaas, PMLA, 3/70. *Mailing Add:* Dept of Ger Haverford Col Haverford PA 19041

CASA, FRANK PAUL, b San Lucido, Italy, Nov 18, 32; US citizen; m 57; c 2. ROMANCE LANGUAGES. *Educ:* Univ Ill, BA, 55, MA, 56; Univ Mich, PhD(Span), 63. *Prof Exp:* From instr to asst prof Romance lang, Harvard Univ, 63-69; assoc prof, 69-76, PROF UNIV MICH, ANN ARBOR, 76-, CHMN DEPT, 73- *Concurrent Pos:* Guggenheim fel, 67-68; chief-reader, Educ Testing Serv, 78- *Mem:* MLA. *Publ:* Auth, The Dramatic Craftsmanship of Moreto, Harvard Univ, 66; The dramatic unity of El Caballero de Olmedo, Neophilologus, 66; Toward an understanding of the Arcipreste's lament, Romanische Forsch, 67; En busca de Espana, Harcourt, 68; Crime and responsibility in El medico de su honra, Homenaje a Fichter, Homenaje a Fichter, 71; Affirmation and retraction in Golden Age drama, Neophilogus, 76; Honor and the wife-killers of Calderon, Bull Comediantes, 77; co-ed, Moreto's El lindo don Diego, Catedra, 77. *Mailing Add:* 1410 Hill St Ann Arbor MI 48104

CASADO, PABLO GIL, b Santander, Spain, Aug 17, 31; US citizen; m 67. SPANISH LITERATURE. *Educ:* Inter-Am Univ, Mex, MA, 60; Univ Wis-Madison, PhD(Span), 67. *Prof Exp:* Teacher, Ashland Pub Schs, 55-59 & Wauwatosa Pub Schs, 59-60; instr Span, Univ Northern Iowa, 60-63; teaching asst, Univ Wis-Madison, 63-66; asst prof, 67-70, assoc prof, 71-81, PROF SPAN, UNIV NC, CHAPEL HILL 81- *Concurrent Pos:* Evaluator, Nat Endowment for Humanities, Res Grant Div, 74- *Mem:* MLA; AAUP; PEN Club. *Res:* Nineteenth and 20th century novel. *Publ:* Coauth, Lengua espanola I and II, Scott, 68; auth, La novela social espanola (1941-1968), 68 & rev ed (1920-71), 73, Seix Barral; El paralelepipedo (novel), Joaquin Editor, Mex, 77; Un muchacho en la Puerta del Sol: Entre la ficcion y la realidad, prologue to Jeus Izcaray, Un muchacho en la Puerta del Sol, 3rd ed, Akal Ed, Madrid, 77; Compromiso y novela en la generacion de 1954, Cuadernos Am, 7-8/79; Las novelas de Virgilio Botella Pastor: del exodo y del llanto, Cuadernos Am, 9-10/80; Asi me fecundo zaratustra: Vision y expresion de Joaquin Arderius, Ensayos sobre literatura espanola moderna: Homenaje a Antonio Sanchez Barbudo, Univ Wis-Madison, 81; Makbara es un cementerio, Cuadernos Ame, 11-12/81. *Mailing Add:* Dept of Romance Lang Univ of NC Chapel Hill NC 27514

CASAGRANDE, JEAN, b Oran, Algeria, Aug 19, 38; US citizen; m 63; c 2. FRENCH LANGUAGE & LINGUISTICS. *Educ:* Univ SFla, BA, 63; Ind Univ, MA, 64, PhD(Fr), 68. *Prof Exp:* Lectr French & Ital, Ind Univ, 66-68, asst prof, 68; asst, 68-73, ASSOC PROF FRENCH & LING, UNIV FLA, 73- *Concurrent Pos:* Vis prof, Ling Soc Am Summer Inst, 72 & co-dir, 75; Nat Endowment for Humanities fel, 72-73. *Mem:* Ling Soc Am; Am Asn Teachers Fr; Southeast Conf Ling (pres, 74-75); Int Soc Phonetic Sci. *Res:* French language, syntax and semantics; linguistic theory. *Publ:* Ed & contribr, Generative studies in Romance languages, Newbury House, 72; auth, Sur et certain en French et en angl, Le Fr Mod, 74; French palatal nasal, Krit Lit, 74; contribr, Linguistic studies in Romance languages, Georgetown, 75; Diachronic studies in Romance languages, Mouton, 75; Acts of the XIV international congress on Romance linguistics and philosophy, Johns Benjamins, 79; Proceedings of IX linguistics symposium on Romance languages, Georgetown, 81. *Mailing Add:* 1732 NW Seventh Ave Gainesville FL 32603

CASAS, R ALBERTO, b PR, Mar 23, 19; m 42; c 1. ROMANCE LANGUAGES. *Educ:* Univ Barcelona, Bachiller, 36; Columbia Univ, AM, 47, PhD(Span), 54. *Prof Exp:* From instr to asst prof Span, Dartmouth Col, 47-52; assoc prof, 52-58, PROF SPAN, UNIV NH, 58- *Concurrent Pos:* Mem, Educ Testing Serv-Grad Rec Comt in Span & Port; MLA. *Res:* Spanish literature of the 19th and 20th centuries; modern Catalan literature; Greek literature and visual arts of the 4th and 5th centuries BC. *Publ:* Auth, La Poesia Catalana Moderna, La Prensa, New York, 5/52; El mar en la poesia de Juan Maragall, Res Hisp Mod, 1/54; Joan Maragall: Catalonian poet, Diss Abstr, Vol XIV, No 8. *Mailing Add:* Dept of Span Univ of NH Durham NH 03824

CASCARDI, ANTHONY JOSEPH, b New York, NY, Dec 29, 53; m 78. COMPARATIVE LITERATURE. *Educ:* Princeton Univ, BA, 75; Harvard Univ, MA, 77, PhD(Romance lang), 80. *Prof Exp:* ASST PROF COMP LIT, UNIV CALIF, BERKELEY, 80- *Concurrent Pos:* Soc Fel in the Humanities fel, Columbia Univ, 82- *Mem:* MLA. *Res:* Skepticism and knowledge in the novels of Cervantes, Dostoyevsky and Flaubert. *Publ:* Auth, Lope de Vega, Juan de la Cueva, Giraldi Cinthio and Spanish poetics, Rev Hisp Mod, 76-77 & 80; The rhetoric of defense in the Guzman de Alfarache, Neophilologus, 79; The exit from Arcadia: Reevaluation of the pastoral in Virgil Garcilaso and Gongora, J Hisp Philol, winter 80; Calderon's encyclopaedic rhetoric, Neophilologus, 1/82; Comedia and Trauerspiel: On Benjamin and Calderon, Comp Drama, spring 82; Chronicle towards novel: Bernal Diaz history of the conquest of Mexico, Novel, spring 82; Cervantes and skepticism: The vanishing of the body, In: Studies in Honor of E L King (in press). *Mailing Add:* Dept of Comp Lit Univ Calif Berkeley CA 94704

CASE, THOMAS EDWARD, b Minneapolis, Minn, Feb 27, 34; m 60; c 1. SPANISH. *Educ:* Col St Thomas, BA, 56; State Univ Iowa, MA, 58, PhD(Span), 62. *Prof Exp:* Asst, State Univ Iowa, 56-61; from asst prof to assoc prof, 61-69, PROF SPAN, SAN DIEGO STATE UNIV, 69- *Concurrent Pos:* Fulbright lect grant, Bogota, 65; resident dir, Calif Univ Int Progs, Univ Madrid, Spain, 74-75. *Mem:* Am Asn Teachers Span & Port; Philol Asn Pac Coast; Pac Coast Coun Latin Am Studies. *Res:* Latin American novel; Golden Age literature. *Publ:* Contribr, Vols XXVI, XXVIII, XXX, XXXII & XXXIV, Handbook of Latin American Studies, Libr Congr, 64-72; auth, Paraguay in the novels of Gabriel Casaccia, J Inter Am Studies & World Affairs, 70; Critical and Annotated Edition of Lope de Vega's Las Almenas de Toro, Univ NC, 71; El papel de Ines en Peribanez, Romanische Forsch, 73; Las Dedicatorias de Partes XIII-XX de Lope de Vega, Hispanofila, 75; co-ed, Dictionary of Latin American Authors, Ariz State Univ, 75; auth, Further considerations on Lope's Al triunfo de Judith, Romanische Forsch, 75; Los prologos de Partes IX-XX de Lope, Bull Comediantes, 78. *Mailing Add:* Dept of Span San Diego State Univ San Diego CA 92182

CASERTA, ERNESTO GIUSEPPE, b Montenero, Isernia, Italy, Mar 19, 37; m 68; c 2. ITALIAN LITERATURE. *Educ:* Gannon Col, BA, 60; Tulane Univ, MA, 63; Harvard Univ, PhD(Ital), 69. *Prof Exp:* From instr to asst prof Ital, Boston Univ, 67-70; asst prof, 70-80, ASSOC PROF ITAL, DUKE UNIV, 80- *Concurrent Pos:* Am Philos Soc grant, 76-77. *Mem:* Dante Soc Am; Am Asn Teachers Ital; SAtlantic Mod Lang Asn. *Res:* Nineteenth and twentieth century Italian literature, aesthetics and criticism. *Publ:* Auth, Motivi poetici dominanti nei Paralipomeni del Leopardi, Rev Etudes Ital, 4/71; Primi passi del Croce critico, Rivista Studi Crociani, 1-3/72; Croce Critico Letterario (1882-1921), Giannini, Naples, 72; Manzoni's aesthetic theory, Comp Lit Studies, 3/73; transl, auth & ed, introd, G Leopardi's The War of the Mice and the Crabs, Univ NC, 76; Studi crociani negli Stati Uniti (1964-1979), Rivista Studi Crociani; Manzoni's Christian Realism, Florence, Olschki, 77; L'ultimo Leopardi, Bonacci, Rome, 80. *Mailing Add:* Dept of Romance Lang Duke Univ Durham NC 27706

CASEY, CAMILLUS, b Indian Orchard, Mass, Sept 4, 11. PHILOLOGY. *Educ:* St John's Univ, NY, AB, 40; Fordham Univ, AM, 45; Columbia Univ, PhD, 55. *Prof Exp:* Instr French, St Francis Col, NY, 40-46; prin, St Anthony Juniorate, Smithtown, NY, 46-52; from asst prof to assoc prof, 52-59, acad dean, 55-58, prof, 59-80, EMER PROF FRENCH, ST FRANCIS COL, NY, 80- *Concurrent Pos:* Mem, Nat Fedn Mod Lang Teachers Asn. *Mem:* Mediaeval Acad Am; MLA; Ling Soc Am; Am Asn Teachers Fr; Am Asn Teachers Span & Port. *Res:* Romance philology; Jacques de Longuyon. *Mailing Add:* Dept of Mod Lang St Francis Col 180 Remsen St Brooklyn NY 11201

CASKEY, JOHN LANGDON, b Boston, Mass, Dec 7, 08; m 36. ARCHEOLOGY, CLASSICS. *Educ:* Yale Univ, BA, 31; Univ Cincinnati, PhD, 39. *Prof Exp:* Teaching fel, Univ Cincinnati, 31-36, mem staff univ excavations, Troy, 32-38, acting instr, 37-38, from instr to asst prof, 39-49; from asst dir to dir, Am Sch Class Studies, Athens, 48-59; head dept classics, 59-72, prof class archaeol, 59-80, EMER PROF CLASS ARCHAEOL, UNIV CINCINNATI, 80-, FEL GRAD SCH, 61- *Concurrent Pos:* Mem exec comt, Am Sch Class Studies, Athens, 59-65, vchmn managing comt, 66-; mem, Inst Advan Study, 60 & 65; Am Philos Soc grant, 61; Winner-Gren Found anthrop res grant, 61; NSF grant, 63; Charles Eliot Norton lectr, Archaeol Inst Am, 67-68. *Mem:* Soc Cycladic Studies, Athens; Archaeol Inst Am; Am Philol Asn; Class An Can; Hellenic Soc. *Res:* Classical and pre-classical archaeology; Lerna; Cyclades. *Publ:* Auth, Troy, Princeton Univ; Early Helladic period in the Argolid, 60; chapters on early and middle Bronze Ages in Greece and the Aegean, In: Cambridge Ancient History, rev ed, 64 & 66. *Mailing Add:* Dept of Classics (33) Univ of Cincinnati Cincinnati OH 45221

CASLER, FREDERICK HOWARD, b Mohawk, NY, Nov 14, 40. CLASSICAL LANGUAGES, INDO-EUROPEAN LINGUISTICS. *Educ:* Columbia Univ, BA, 62, MA, 63; NY Univ, PhD(classics), 71. *Prof Exp:* Instr classics, Univ Conn, 65-68; lectr, 68-71, asst prof, 71-74, ASSOC PROF CLASSICS, BROCK UNIV, 74- *Mem:* Am Philol Asn; Am Class League; Class Asn Can; Ling Soc Am; Am Guild Organists. *Res:* Teaching methods of classical languages; Romance linguistics. *Publ:* Auth, Lingua latina at Brock, Class J, 1/70; Adult reading of ancient languages, ERIC, 9/81. *Mailing Add:* Dept of Classics Brock Univ St Catharines ON L2S 3A1 Can

CASSARINO, SEBASTIAN, b Paterson, NJ, Oct 8, 28; m 61; c 2. ITALIAN. *Educ:* City Col New York BA, 53; Univ Calif, Berkeley, PhD(Romance lang & lit), 66. *Prof Exp:* Instr Ital, Stanford Univ, 60-62; from asst prof to assoc prof, 62-77, PROF ITAL, SAN JOSE STATE UNIV, 78- *Mem:* Am Asn Teachers Ital; Am Ital Hist Asn. *Res:* The Italian novel; contemporay Italian literature. *Mailing Add:* Dept of Foreign Lang San Jose State Univ 125 S Seventh St San Jose CA 95114

CASSEDY, STEVEN DENNIS, b Takoma Park, Md, Dec 14, 52; m 75; c 1. COMPARATIVE LITERATURE. *Prof Exp:* ASST PROF SLAVIC & COMP LIT, UNIV CALIF, SAN DIEGO, 80- *Mem:* MLA; Am Asn Teachers Slavic & East European Lang. *Publ:* Auth, Mallarme and Andrej Belyj: Mathematics and the phenomenality of the literary object, Mod Lang Notes, 12/81; Daniil Kharms's parody of Dostevsky: Anti-tragedy as political comment, Can-Am Slavic Studies (in prep). *Mailing Add:* Dept of Lit D-007 Univ of Calif San Diego CA 92093

CASSELL, ANTHONY K, b Reading, Eng, Mar 31, 41; Can citizen. ITALIAN & MEDIEVAL LITERATURE. *Educ:* Univ Toronto, BA, 63; Johns Hopkins Univ, PhD(Ital), 69. *Prof Exp:* Asst prof, 71-76, ASSOC PROF ITAL, UNIV ILL, URBANA, 76- *Concurrent Pos:* assoc ed, Italian Culture & Dante Studies. *Honors & Awards:* Outstanding Book Award, Choice, 76. *Mem:* Am Asn Teachers Ital; Dante Soc Am; Am Boccaccio Asn; MLA; Mediaeval Acad Am. *Res:* Boccaccio; Danta; Petrarca. *Publ:* Auth, The crow of the fable and the Corbaccio, Mod Lang Notes, 70; The Corbaccio and the secundus tradition, Comp Lit, 73; Boccaccio's Corbaccio, 75; Moral and structural conflict in the Corbaccio, Mod Lang Notes, 75; ed & translr, the Corbaccio, Univ Ill, 75; auth, Pride failure and conversion in Inferno I, Dante Studies, 76; Farinata and the image of the Arca, Yale Ital Studies, 77; The Tomb, the Tower and the Pit, Italica, 79; The Lesson of Ylysses, Dante Studies, 81; Pier della Vigna: History and Iconography, Dante, Petrarch and Others, 82. *Mailing Add:* Dept of Span Ital & Port Univ of Ill Urbana IL 61801

CASSIDY, FREDERIC GOMES, b Jamaica, WI, Oct 10, 07; m 31; c 4. ENGLISH & AMERICAN LANGUAGE. *Educ:* Oberlin Col, AB, 30, AM, 32; Univ Mich, PhD, 38. *Prof Exp:* Teaching fel English, Univ Mich, 34-35 & 36-38, instr, 38-39; lectr English lang, Univ Strasbourg, France, 35-36; from instr to assoc prof, 42-49, PROF ENGLISH, UNIV WIS-MADISON, 49-, DIR ENGLISH LANG SURV, 48- *Concurrent Pos:* Res asst & ed, Early Mod English Dict, 31-35 & 36-37, Mid English Dict, 51; field worker, Ling Atlas of US & Can, Ohio & Wis, 39-41; Fulbright res scholar, 51-52 & 58-59; consult, Dialect Surv Brit Caribbean, 54-; first hon fel, Univ Col West Indies, 58-59; vis prof English lit, Stanford Univ, 63-64; consult, Funk & Wagnalls, 64-70; dir & ed, Dict Am Regional English, 65- *Honors & Awards:* Silver Musgrave Medal, Inst Jamaica, 62; Centenary Medal, 80. *Mem:* Ling Soc Am; Am Dialect Soc (pres, 55-57); MLA; Mediaeval Acad Am; Soc Caribbean Ling (pres, 72-76); Am Name Soc (pres, 80). *Res:* Pidgin and Creole languages; English lexicography. *Publ:* Auth, Place names of Dane County, Wisconsin, PADS, 47 & Univ Wis, 68; Jamaica Talk, Macmillan, 61, rev ed, 71; How free was the Anglo-Saxon scop?, In: Franciplegius, NY Univ, 65; coauth, Dictionary of Jamaican English, Cambridge Univ, 67 & rev ed, 80; Toward the recovery of early English-African Pidgin, CSA-CCTA Publ, No 87, 62; The dictionary of American regional English J Lancashire Dialect Soc, 68. *Mailing Add:* 6123 Helen White Hall Madison WI 53706

CASSIRER, THOMAS, b Rome, Italy, Apr 28, 23; US citizen; m 48; c 1. FRENCH & AFRICAN LITERATURE. *Educ:* McGill Univ, BA, 45; Yale Univ, PhD(Fr & comp lit), 53. *Prof Exp:* Asst prof French, Smith Col, 60-65; assoc prof, 65-69, PROF FRENCH & AFRICAN LIT, UNIV MASS, AMHERST, 69- *Mem:* MLA; Am Asn Teachers Fr; African Studies Asn. *Res:* Eighteenth century French literature; modern African literature. *Publ:* Auth, Awareness of the city in the Encycopedia, J Hist Ideas, 63; coauth, Encyclopedia, Selections, Bobbs, 65; auth, Africa's Olympiad of the arts, Mass Rev, 67; Politics and mystique: The predicament of the African writer, African Forum, 67. *Mailing Add:* Dept of French & Italian Univ of Mass Amherst MA 01002

CASSON, RONALD WILLIAM, b Chicago, Ill, July 3, 42; m 69; c 2. ANTHROPOLOGY, LINGUISTICS. *Educ:* Univ Ill, BS, 64; Stanford Univ, MA, 67, PhD(anthrop), 72. *Prof Exp:* Asst prof Anthrop, Duke Univ, 71-78; ASSOC PROF SOCIOL & ANTHROP, OBERLIN COL, 78- *Mem:* Am Anthrop Asn; Ling Soc Am; Am Ethnol Soc; Middle East Studies Asn. *Res:* Anthropological linguistics, cognitive anthropology; Middle East, especially Turkey. *Publ:* Ed, Language, Culture, and Cognition: Anthropological Perspectives, Macmillan, 81. *Mailing Add:* Dept of Social & Anthrop Oberlin Col Oberlin OH 44074

CASTAGNARO, R ANTHONY, b New York, NY, Sept 24, 18; m 55; c 1. ROMANCE LANGUAGES & LITERATURES. *Educ:* City Col New York, AB, 39; NY Univ, AM, 43, PhD(Romance lang & lit), 52. *Prof Exp:* Tutor Romance lang, City Col New York, 41-42; asst Span, 42, from instr to assoc prof, 42-73, PROF SPAN & PORT, NY UNIV, 73- *Concurrent Pos:* Fulbright teaching grant, 53-54; resident dir, NY Univ Jr Year in Spain, 58-60 & Jr Year in Brazil, 61-64; vis prof, Univ Sao Paulo, 62-63. *Mem:* Am Asn Teachers Span & Port; MLA; Am Asn Teachers Ital; AAUP. *Res:* Spanish American literature and history; Portuguese language. *Publ:* Auth, Becquer and Gutierrez Najera--some literary similarities, 5/44 & J Ruben Romero and

the novel of the Mexican Revolution, 8/53, Hispania; As guerras de independencia na Hispano-America, In: Encycl Ambiente, Ed Distribuidora Ambiente, SAm, 63; ed, Contemporary Spanish Readings, 64 & auth, The Early Spanish American Novel, 71, Las Americas; ed, Vinte Contos Brasileiros, Georgetown Univ Press, 80. *Mailing Add:* Dept of Span & Port NY Univ 19 University Pl New York NY 10003

CASTAGNINO, RAUL HECTOR, b Buenos Aires, Arg, Aug 17, 14; Arg citizen; m 40; c 1. SPANISH AMERICAN LITERATURE. *Educ:* Nat Sch Arg, BA, 31; Univ Buenos Aires, MA, 39, PhD(lit), 42. *Hon Degrees:* Academic, Acad Arg Letras, 74. *Prof Exp:* Prof lit, Univ Buenos Aires, 47-55 & Univ La Plata, Arg, 55-68; prof, 68-80, EMER PROF SPAN, STATE UNIV NY ALBANY, 80- *Concurrent Pos:* Ed, Ed Nova SAm, Arg, 58- & La Prensa, Arg, 58-; consult, Revista Nueva Narrativa HispAm, 71-73; fac exchange scholar, State Univ NY, 76. *Honors & Awards:* Carlos O Bunge's Prize, Univ Buenos Aires, 44; Arg's Lit Criticism Nat Award, 58; Arg First Prize, Juan B Alberti Essay National Competition, 65; Ricardo Rojas Award, City Buenos Aires, 66. *Mem:* Int Inst Theatre; Soc Arg Escritores; Int PEN Club; Am Asn Teachers Span & Port; MLA. *Res:* Literary methods; theatre; Spanish American literature. *Publ:* Auth, El teatro en Bs, As, durante la epoca de Rosas, Ministerio Educ, Arg, 44; El analisis literario, 53, ?Que es literatura?, 54 & Teoria del teatro, 56, Ed Nova; Literatura dramatica argentina, Ed Pleamar, 68; Semiotica, ideologia y teatro hispamericano, 74, Sentido y estructura narrativa, 75 & Cuento-artefacto y artificios del cuento, 77, Ed Nova. *Mailing Add:* Olleros 2555 3A Buenos Aries 1426 Argentina

CASTANEDA, JAMES AGUSTIN, b Brooklyn, NY, Apr 2, 33. SPANISH LITERATURE. *Educ:* Drew Univ, AB, 54; Yale Univ, MA, 55, PhD, 58; Univ Paris, cert, 57. *Prof Exp:* From asst prof to assoc prof Span & French, Hanover Col, 58-61; from asst prof to assoc prof, 61-67, chmn dept classics, Ital, Port, Russ & Span, 64-72, PROF SPAN, RICE UNIV, 67- *Concurrent Pos:* Danforth fel, 54-58 & teaching fel, 58-; vis lectr, Univ NC, 62-63, dir Year-at-Lyon, 67-68 & vis prof, 68; pres, Inst Hisp Cult Houston, 72; miembro titular, Inst Cult Hisp Madrid, 72-; mem bd dirs, L'Alliance Francaise Houston, 72-74; vis prof Span, Mt Holyoke Col, 76-77. *Mem:* MLA; Renaissance Soc; Soc Values Higher Educ; Am Asn Teachers Fr; Am Asn Teachers Span & Port. *Res:* Golden Age drama of Spain; French literature. *Publ:* Ed, Lope de Vega's Las Paces de los Reyes, y Judia de Toledo, Univ NC, 62; collabr, The Present State of Lope de Bega Studies: A Critical Survey of the Years 1937-1961, Univ Toronto, 64; auth, El impacto del culteranismo en el teatro de la Edad de Oro, Univ NC Studies Romance Lang & Lit, 66; The Linguistic Dimensions of Cultural Empathy, Prog Educ Interam, 67; Los empenos de un acaso y los empenos de una casa: Calderon y Sor Juana--la differencia de un fonema, Rev Estud Hisp, 67; ed, Anaya, Salamanca, 71; auth, Agustin Moreto, In: No 308, 74 & Mira de Amescua, In: No 449, 77, Twayne World Auth Ser. *Mailing Add:* Dept of Span Portuguese & Classics Rice Univ Houston TX 77001

CASTANIEN, DONALD GARNER, b Dodge City, Kans, Oct 30, 14; m 50. HISPANIC LANGUAGES & LITERATURES. *Educ:* Univ Ore, BA, 40, MA, 41; Univ Mich, PhD(Span), 51. *Prof Exp:* Instr Span, Wayne State Univ, 48-50; from instr to asst prof, Northwestern Univ, 50-50; from asst prof to assoc prof, 60-67, PROF SPAN, UNIV CALIF, DAVIS, 67- *Mem:* MLA; Am Asn Teachers Span & Port; Renaissance Soc Am. *Res:* Colonial Spanish American literature; Spanish literature of the Golden Age. *Publ:* Co-ed, Yo y el ladron, 57 & Moctezuma el de la Silla de Oro, 58, Oxford Univ; auth, El Inca Garcilaso de la Vega, Twayne, 69. *Mailing Add:* Dept of Span & Classics Univ of Calif Davis CA 95616

CASTELLS, MATILDE OLIVELLA, b Santiago, Cuba, Dec 20, 29; m 52; c 3. SPANISH. *Educ:* Univ Havana, PhD(Span lit), 56. *Prof Exp:* Instr Span, Inst Vedado, Havana, Cuba, 56-59; teacher high sch, Pa, 61-63; from instr to asst prof, Rutgers Univ, NB, 63-69; assoc prof, 72-77, PROF SPAN, CALIF STATE UNIV, LOS ANGELES, 77- *Concurrent Pos:* Mem, Span Develop Comt, Col Entrance Exam Bd, 73- *Honors & Awards:* Outstanding Prof Award, Calif State Univ, Los Angeles, 74; Premio Juan J Remos, 80. *Mem:* Am Coun Teaching Foreign Lang; Am Asn Teachers Span & Port; MLA. *Res:* Linguistics. *Publ:* Co-auth, El ramonismo de Zunzunegui, Romance Notes, autumn 67; auth, Note on Hernan Robleto's Y se hizo la Luz, Hispania, 3/68; coauth, Lengua y Lectura: Un Repaso y una Continuacion, Harcourt, 70; La Lengua Espanola: Gramatica y Cultura, Scribner's, 74, 2nd ed, 78; auth, Mundohispano, Wiley, 81. *Mailing Add:* Dept of Foreign Lang & Lit Calif State Univ Los Angeles CA 90032

CASTILLO, RAFAEL FEDERICO, b Bilbao, Spain, Nov 23, 41; Spanish citizen. HISPANIC POETRY, COMPARATIVE LITERATURE. *Educ:* Univ Madrid, lic classics, 67; Ind State Uiv, MA, 71; Univ Ill, PhD(Span), 75. *Prof Exp:* Instr Span, Univ Ill, 74-75; lectr, Univ Calif, Berkeley, 75-76; ASST PROF POETRY, OHIO STATE UNIV, 76- *Concurrent Pos:* Fulbright scholarship, US Govt, 70; Tinker fel, Hisp Soc Am, 74. *Mem:* MLA. *Res:* Poetry; Rhetoric; stylistics. *Publ:* Coauth, Bibliography of semantics, Ill Publ Ling, 74; auth, La universidad alemana, Cuadernos Am, 75; Sobre la lectura poetica, VIA, Berkeley, 78; Los versos de Francisco A Icaza, Fondo de Cult Econ, 78. *Mailing Add:* Romance Lang Dept Ohio State Univ 1841 Millikin Rd Columbus OH 43210

CASTILLO-FELIU, GUILLERMO IGNACIO, b Santiago, Chile, Dec 17, 41; US citizen; m 66. SPANISH LANGUAGE, SPANISH AMERICAN LITERATURE. *Educ:* Mich State Univ, BA, 64, MA, 66, PhD(Span), 72. *Prof Exp:* Asst Span, Mich State Univ, 64-66; instr, Wright State Univ, 66-69; asst prof, 69-73, assoc prof, 73-80, PROF SPAN, WINTHROP COL, 80- *Concurrent Pos:* Nat Asn Foreign Student Affairs grant, Georgetown Univ, 74; Nat Endowment for Humanities award, Princeton Univ, 78. *Mem:* Am Asn Teachers Span & Port; SAtlantic Mod Lang Asn. *Res:* Contemporary Spanish theater; contemporary Latin American literature, especially Jose Donoso. *Publ:* Auth, An interview with Jose Donoso, in Vallvidrera, Spain, Hispania, 12/71; Cuentos y Microcuentos: Una Antologia de la Narrativa Breve, Holt, Rinehart & Winston, 78; Antologia sobre el Teatro Espanol

Contemporaneo, Porrua, 78; Aesthetic Impetus Versus Reality, In: Three Short Stories of Jose Donoso, Studies in Short Fiction, summer 80; Reflexiones sobre el perspectivismo en Coronacion de Jose Donoso, Hispania LXIII, No 4, 12/80; transl, Maleovolent Tales (transl, Cuentos malevolos), Irvington Publ, 82; El obsceno pajaro de la noche: un ejercicio en punto de vista, Revista de Estudios Hispanicos, Enero, 82; ed, The Creative Process in the Works of Jose Donoso, Winthrop Col, 82. *Mailing Add:* Dept of Mod Lang Winthrop Col Rock Hill SC 29730

CASTRO, ALBERT DWIGHT, b Sidney, NY, Aug 27, 44; m 68. CLASSICS, ANCIENT HISTORY. *Educ:* Gettysburg Col, BA, 66; Ind Univ, Bloomington, MA, 70, PhD(classics), 72. *Prof Exp:* Instr, 70-72, asst prof, 72-79, ASSOC PROF GREEK & LATIN, WESTMINSTER COL, 79- *Concurrent Pos:* Nat Endowment for Humanities summer fel, 77. *Mem:* Am Philol Asn; Am Class League; Class Asn Atlantic States. *Res:* Roman historians; Greek and Roman history; early Christianity in Greco-Roman world. *Publ:* Auth, Classics in the Eighties: Obituaries or Opportunities?, PSMLA Bull, 77. *Mailing Add:* Dept Foreign Lang Westminster Col New Wilmington PA 16142

CASTRO-KLAREN, SARA, b Arequipa, Peru, June 9, 40; m 63. MODERN LATIN AMERICAN LITERATURE. *Educ:* Univ Calif, Los Angeles, BA, 61, MA, 65, PhD(Hisp lang & lit), 68. *Prof Exp:* Asst prof Hisp lang & lit, Univ Idaho, 68-70; asst prof, 70-79, PROF SPAN & PORT LANG & LIT, DARTMOUTH COL, 79- *Concurrent Pos:* Mellon fel, Aspen Inst Humanistic Studies, 75-76 & Woodrow Wilson Ctr Int Scholars, 77-78. *Res:* Modern novel; Latin American contemporary literature; pre-Columbian literature. *Publ:* Auth, Critic and public: Directions in literary criticism, Latin Am Res Rev, 79; The word and the world in Jose Maria Arguedas, Review 79, 79; May we not perish: The Incas and Spain, Wilson Quart, 80, reprinted, In: Western Civilization Part I, Pre-History Through the Reformation, 81; Cortazar Lector: Entrevista con Sara Castro-Klaren, Cuadernos Hispano-Americanos, 80; Huaman Poma y el espacio de la Pureza, Rev Iberoam on New Latin American Criticism, 81; Desde el anverso de las cosas: La Poesia de Cobo Borda, Eco, 81; Crimen y Castigo: Sexualidad en Arguedas, Rev Iberoam on Jose Maria Arguedas, 82; Homogeneity and the disappearance of space, Interview with David Vinas, Texto Critico, 82. *Mailing Add:* Dept of Romance Lang & Lit Dartmouth Col Hanover NH 03755

CATALAN, DIEGO MENENDEZ-PIDAL, b Madrid, Spain, Sept 16, 28; m 54; c 7. ROMANCE LANGUAGES, LINGUISTICS. *Educ:* Univ Salamanca, MA, 49; Univ Madrid, PhD(Romance philol), 51. *Prof Exp:* Teaching asst Romance philol, Univ Madrid, 49-51, Univ Edinburgh, 51-52, Univ Madrid, 52-54; catedratico Span Ling, Univ La Laguna, 54-64; prof, Univ Calif, Berkeley, 64-66, Univ Wis-Madison, 66-71; PROF LIT, UNIV CALIF, SAN DIEGO, 71- *Concurrent Pos:* Lectr, Univ Calif, Berkeley, 55-57, Univ Wis, 60-62; guest prof, Univ Bonn, 63-64; mem humanities isnt, Univ Wis, 66-71; Guggenheim fel, 66-67. *Res:* Diachronic phonology; medieval Spanish historiography; Spanish ballads. *Publ:* Auth, La Escuela Linguistica Espanola y Su Concepcion Del Lenguaje, Biblot Romanica Hisp, 55; Un Prosista Anonimo Del Siglo XIV, Univ La Laguna, 55; The End of the Phoneme /Z/ in Spanish, Word, 57; De Alfonso X al Conde de Barcelos, Sem Memendez-Pidal; El taller historiografico Alfonsi, Romania, 63; Por Los Campos Del Romancero, Biblot Romanica Hisp, 69; La Flor de la Maranuela: Romancero General de Las Islas Canarias, Sem Menendez-Pidal, 69. *Mailing Add:* Dept of Lit Univ of Calif San Diego La Jolla CA 92037

CATFORD, JOHN CUNNISON, b Edinburgh, Scotland, Mar 26, 17; m 43; c 2. LINGUISTICS. *Educ:* Univ London, BA, 52. *Prof Exp:* Mem, Brit Coun Overseas Serv, 39-46; broadcaster & ling adv, Brit Broadcasting Corp, 46-52; lectr, Univ Edinburgh, 52-57; sr lectr, Sch Applied Ling, 57-64; dir, English Lang Inst, 64-67, actg dir, Ctr Res Lang & Lang Behav, 67-68, PROF LING, UNIV MICH, ANN ARBOR, 64-, CHMN DEPT, 68-, DIR PHONETICS LAB, 71- *Concurrent Pos:* Mem, Brit Coun Adv Comt Teaching English, 57-64; mem, Steering Comt, World Lang Surv, Ctr Applied Ling, 59-62; Brit deleg, Makerere Conf Teaching English in Commonwealth, 61; mem, Agency Int Develop Survey Teaching English in India, 66. *Mem:* Philol Soc, English; Ling Asn Gr Brit (secy, 59-61). *Publ:* Auth, Vowel systems of Scots dialects, Trans Philol Soc, 57; A Linguistic Theory of Translation, Oxford Univ, 65; Translation and language teaching, Actes I Congr, Int Ling Appl, Nancy, 66; The articulatory possibilities of man, In: Manual of Phonetics, 68. *Mailing Add:* Dept of Linguistics Univ of Mich Ann Arbor MI 48108

CATHEY, JAMES ERNEST, b Bakersfield, Calif, Mar 5, 40. GERMANIC LINGUISTICS, SCANDINAVIAN LANGUAGES. *Educ:* Ore State Univ, BS, 62; Univ Wash, MA, 64, PhD (Ger ling), 67. *Prof Exp:* Asst prof, 67-72, ASSOC PROF GER LING, UNIV MASS, AMHERST, 73-, CHMN DEPT, 79- *Concurrent Pos:* Vis prof, Harvard Univ, 73-74 & Yale Univ, 74-75. *Mem:* Ling Soc Am; Soc Advan Scand Studies (secy-treas, 71-). *Res:* Icelandic phonology; phonological theory; Germanic phonology. *Publ:* Auth, A reappraisal of Holtzmann's law, Studies Ling, 70; Syncopation, i-mutation, and short stem forms in Old Icelandic, Arkiv Nordisk Filol, 72; coauth, The single weak verb class of Old Icelandic, Proc Int Conf Nordic & Gen Ling, 74; On establishing linguistic universals, Lang, 76; Nominal phonology and morphology . . . in Old Icelandic, Nordic Lang & Mod Ling, 78; Vocalic alternations in Old Icelandic, Studia Linguistica, 79; Old Icelandic, Oxford Univ Press, 81. *Mailing Add:* Dept of Ger Lang Herter Hall Univ of Mass Amherst MA 01003

CATHOLY, ECKEHARD KURT, b Lissa/Posen, Ger, Mar 16, 14. GERMAN, DRAMA. *Educ:* Univ Göttingen, DPhil, 50. *Prof Exp:* Asst Ger, Univ Göttingen, 48-50; dir drama, Theatersammlung, Hamburg, 51-53; app prof, Theaterwiss Abtg, Univ Göttingen, 54-56; asst Ger, Deutsches Sem, Univ Tübingen, 56-59, lectr, 59-61; prof, Freie Univ, WBerlin, 61-70; PROF GER, UNIV TORONTO, 70- *Concurrent Pos:* Deutsche Forschungsgemeinschaft fel Ger, 50-51 & 53-54. *Mem:* Can Asn Univ Teachers Ger; Am Soc Ger Lit 16th & 17th Centuries; Can Soc Renaissance Studies; Int Vereinigung Germanische Sprach-und Lit; Heinrich von Kleist-Gesellschaft. *Res:* German comedy; German literature of the 16th and 17th centuries. *Publ:* Auth, Das Fastnachtspiel des Spätmittelalters: Gestalt und Funktion, 61 & Karl Philipp Moritz und die Ursprünge der dt Theaterleidenschaft, 62, Niemeyer, Tübingen; Fastnachtspiel, Metzler, Stuttgart, 66; Die geschichtlichen Voraussetzungen des Illusionstheaters in Deutschld, In: Festschrift für Klaus Ziegler, Niemeyer, 68; Das Deutsche Lustspiel, I: Vom Mittelalter bis zum Ende der Barockzt, Kohlhammer, Stuttgart, 69; Komische Figur u dramatische Wirklichkeit E Vers z Typologie d Dramas, In: Wesen und Formen des Komischen in Drama, Wiss Bchg, 75; Aristoteles u d Folgen Zur Geschichte der deutschen Komödie, In: Die deutsche Komödie in zwanzigsten Jahrhunders, Stiehm, 76; Die deutsche Komödie vor Lessing, In: Die deutsche Komödie vom Mittelalter bis zut Genenwart, Bagel, Düsseldorf, 77. *Mailing Add:* Dept of Ger Lang & Lit Univ of Toronto 97 St George St Toronto ON M5S 1A1 Can

CATLIN, JOHN STANLEY, b Tulsa, Okla, Apr 11, 36; m 64; c 1. CLASSICS. *Educ:* Univ Okla, BA, 58; Univ NC, Chapel Hill, MA, 65, PhD(classics), 69. *Prof Exp:* From instr to asst prof ancient lang, Univ Richmond, 66-69; ASSOC PROF CLASSICS, UNIV OKLA, 69-, ACTING CHMN DEPT, 76- *Mem:* Am Philol Asn. *Res:* Greek historiography, tragedy and epic. *Mailing Add:* Dept of Classics Rm 101 Univ of Okla 780 Van Vleet Oval Norman OK 73069

CAUDET-ROCA, FRANCISCO, b Alcala, Castellon, Spain, July 15, 42; m 69; c 1. TWENTIETH CENTURY SPANISH LITERATURE. *Educ:* Univ Madrid, PhD(20th century lit), 69. *Prof Exp:* Asst Span, Lycee Clemenceau, Reims, France, 66-67; lectr, Univ Nottingham, 67-69; lectr, Univ Sheffield, 69-70; asst prof, San Jose State Col, 70-71; asst prof, 71-76, assoc prof, 76-80, PROF SPAN, CALIF STATE UNIV, LOS ANGELES, 80- *Mem:* MLA; Assoc Int Hispanistas. *Res:* Generation of 1898; letters during the Spanish Republic. *Publ:* Auth, Vida y obra de Jose Maria Salaverria, Consejo Superior Investigaciones Cientificas, 72; Un antecendente del 98: La tierra de campos, 72 & J M Salaverria: el problem y de Espana y del generacion del 98, 73, Rev Estudios Hispanicos; Aproximaciones a Salaverria, Cuadernos Am, 73. *Mailing Add:* Dept of Foreign Lang Calif State Univ Los Angeles CA 90032

CAULKINS, JANET HILLIER, b Sutton, England; US citizen; m 63; c 3. FRENCH LANGUAGE & LITERATURE. *Educ:* Reading Univ, England, BA, 62; Univ Mich, MA, 64; Caen Univ, France, PhD(French), 69. *Prof Exp:* Asst prof, 68-74, asst dean, Col Lett & Sci, 76-79, ASSOC PROF FRENCH, UNIV WIS-MADISON, 74- *Concurrent Pos:* Am Coun Learned Soc fel, 75-76; consult, Educ Sect, UNESCO, 76-80; hon adv, Brit Univ Summer Schs, 79- *Mem:* Int Arthurian Soc; Soc Rencesvals; Medieval Acad Am; Tristania; Int Courtly Soc. *Res:* French medieval literature: Hagiography, epic, romance. *Publ:* Auth, The meaning of Pechie in the Romance of Tristan by Beroul, Romance Notes, Vol 13, No 3; Le jeu du subnaturel et du feodal dans le Tristan de Beroul, In: Melange & Offers A M Charles Rostaing, Univ Liege, 74; Le voyage de Saint Brendan: Precisions numeriques et temporelles, Moyen, Vol 80, No 2; Narrative interventions: The key to the jest of the Pelerinage de Charlemagne, In: Etudes de Philologie Romane et D'Histoire Litteraire Offerts A Jules Horrent, Liege, 80; The case of the University of Wisconsin-Madison and the College of Letters and Sciences, In: Institutional Mechanism of Interaction Between Higher Education and the Community, Orgn Econ Coop & Develop Ctr Educ Res & Innovation, Paris, 80; Beroul's Tristan and Iseult and his expression of youthful pathologies, Vol 1, 82 & The dwarf and treachery in Beroul's Tristan, Vol 2 (in prep), Mythos Papers; Literary and socio-historical perspectives on the Pelerinage de Charlemagne, Studies Medieval Cult (in prep). *Mailing Add:* Dept of French & Ital Univ of Wis Madison WI 53706

CAUSEY, JAMES YOUNG, b Concord, NC, Sept 28, 07; m 34; c 3. SPANISH LITERATURE. *Educ:* Univ Va, AB, 28; Univ Madrid, cert, 30; Univ Dijon, cert, 31; Univ NC, AM, 33; Univ Wis, PhD, 40. *Prof Exp:* Teaching fel Span, Univ NC, 31-33; instr Span & English, Col William & Mary; 33-37; teaching asst Span & Port, Univ Wis, 37-39; instr, Univ Ala, 39-40; asst prof Romance lang, DePauw Univ, 40-46; assoc prof, Emory Univ, 46-48; PROF SPAN, DAVIDSON COL, 48- *Concurrent Pos:* Res asst, Sem Mediaeval Span Studies, Univ Wis, 38-39; Carnegie res grant, Libr Congr, 48; consult, Britannica World Lang Dict, 54; Presby Church Bd Higher Educ fel, 56-57; mem session, Davidson Col Presby Church, 72- *Mem:* MLA; SAtlantic Mod Lang Asn. *Res:* Modern Spanish novel. *Publ:* Auth, Novels and Novelists in Present-Day Spain & Camilo Jose Cela, Bks Abroad; contribr, One decade of the contemporary Spanish novel, Rev Hisp Mod. *Mailing Add:* Box 458 Davidson NC 28036

CAUVIN, JEAN-PIERRE BERNARD, b Casablanca, Morocco, Feb 25, 36; US citizen; m 63; c 2. FRENCH LANGUAGE & LITERATURE. *Educ:* Princeton Univ, BA, 57, PhD(French), 68. *Prof Exp:* Lectr, Harvard Univ, 63-66; asst prof, Princeton Univ, 66-72; ASSOC PROF FRENCH, UNIV TEX AUSTIN, 72- *Concurrent Pos:* Consult French lit, Col Entrance Exam Bd, 76- *Mem:* MLA; SCent Mod Lang Asn; Am Asn Teachers Fr; Soc Professeurs Fr Am. *Res:* Nineteenth and twentieth century French poetry; twentieth century prose fiction. *Publ:* Auth, Henri Bosco et la Poetique du Sacre, Klincksieck, Paris, 74; Les molles vapeurs d'une chaude atmosphere, ou l'espace ideal chez Baudelaire, Bull 1975 SPFA, 76; contribr, Le reel et l'imaginaire dans l'oeuvre de Henri Bosco, Jose Corti, Paris, 76; co-ed, Panache Litteraire: Textes du monde francophone, Harper & Row, 78. *Mailing Add:* Dept of Fr & Ital Univ of Tex Austin TX 78712

CAVALLARI, HECTOR MARIO, b Nueve de Julio, Arg, July 14, 46. LATIN AMERICAN LITERATURE, LITERARY THEORY. *Educ:* San Francisco State Univ, BA, 69; Univ Calif, Irvine, MA, 71, PhD(Romance lang), 77. *Prof Exp:* Assoc Span & Port, Univ Calif, Irvine, 71-73; res teacher bilingual educ, Oakland Pub Schs, 74-75; lectr Span & Port, 75-76, ASST PROF LIT, STANFORD UNIV, 76- *Mem:* MLA; Am Asn Teachers Span & Port; Philol Asn Pac Coast; Semiotic Soc Am; Latin Am Studies Asn. *Res:* Contemporary Latin American narrative; contemporary Latin American poetry; 20th century literary critical theory. *Publ:* Auth, El banquete de severo Arcangelo:

Analisis ideologico-estructural, Vortice, spring 78; El Lunario sentimental: Notas Para una lectura Complice, Proc PNCFL, 79; Savoir and Pouvoir: Michel Foucault's theory of discursive practice, Humanities in Soc, winter 80; Adan Buenosayres: Discurso, texto, significacion, Texto Critico, winter 80; Fernando Alegria y la desconstruccion del fascismo, Texto Critico, fall 81; Discurso humanista, discurso metafisico, Revista de Critica Latinoamericana, 7/81; El Espacio de los Signos, Xalapa, Univ Veracruz Press, 81; Semiotics of confinement and epistemology of madness/sanity, Idologies and Lit, winter 82. *Mailing Add:* Dept of Span & Port Stanford Univ Stanford CA 94305

CAVARNOS, JOHN PETER, History, Classics. See Vol I

CAVAZOS, NELSON AUGUSTO, b Mexico City, Mex, Mar 5, 21; nat US; m 53; c 1. SPANISH. *Educ:* Baylor Univ, AB, 47; Univ Tenn, MA, 49. *Prof Exp:* Teacher, High Sch, 47-48; from instr to asst prof Span, Macalester Col, 49-63; asst prof, Univ Minn, 63-66; chmn dept Span & Ital, 66-77, ASSOC PROF SPAN, CONCORDIA COL, 77- *Concurrent Pos:* Asst pastor, First Baptist Church, St Paul, Minn; assoc prof Span & chmn dept, NDak State Univ, 70-73. *Mem:* Am Asn Teachers Ital; Am Asn Teachers Span & Port. *Res:* Teaching of Romance languages; language arts laboratory. *Publ:* Auth, Una madeja de lana azul celeste, Prentice-Hall, 69. *Mailing Add:* Dept of Span & Ital Concordia Col Moorhead MN 56560

CAVINESS, GEORGE LEWIS, b Silver Springs, Md, Apr 14, 15; m 39; c 3. GERMAN LANGUAGE & LINGUISTICS. *Educ:* Pac Union Col, BA, 37; Univ Calif, Berkeley, MA, 39; Ohio State Univ, Columbus, PhD(Ger), 47. *Prof Exp:* Instr French & Ger, Atlantic Union Col, Mass, 39-46; prof, Pac Union Col, 46-58; acad dean, Union Col, Lincoln, Nebr, 58-66; pres, Newbold Col, Bracknell, Gt Brit, 66-71; prof French & Ger, Walla Walla Col, 71-80; RETIRED. *Concurrent Pos:* Registr, Atlantic Union Col, Mass, 41-45; liaison off for Pac Union Col, Avondale Col, Cooranbong, Australia. *Mem:* MLA. *Res:* Vocabulary study of religious groups; comparative evaluation of educational standards in various countries. *Mailing Add:* 114 NE Cedar College Place WA 99324

CAWS, MARY ANN, b Wilmington, NC, Sept 10, 33; US & Brit citizen; m 52; c 2. FRENCH LITERATURE, POETRY. *Educ:* Bryn Mawr Col, BA, 54; Yale Univ, MA, 56; Univ Kans, PhD(French lit), 62. *Prof Exp:* Vis asst prof French, Univ Kans, 64; from asst prof to assoc prof, 66-74, PROF ROMANCE LANG, HUNTER COL & GRAD CTR, CITY UNIV NEW YORK, 74-, EXEC OFF COMP LIT PHD PROG, 76- *Concurrent Pos:* Asst ed, French Rev, 70-; Guggenheim fel, 72-73; Fulbright-Hays sr travel res scholar, 72-73; ed, Dada/Surrealism, 72-; ed, Le Siecle eclate, 74; mem adv bd Western Europe, Fulbright-Hays Res Prog, 77-; Nat Endowment for Humanities fel, 79-80. *Honors & Awards:* Ordre des Palmes Acad Lit Studies, French Govt, 77. *Mem:* MLA; Asn Studies Dada & Surrealism (treas, 68-70, pres, 71-73); Am Asn Teachers Fr; Am Comp Lit Asn. *Res:* Contemporary poetry; Dada and surrealism; poetics and literary theory. *Publ:* Ed & transl, Tristan Tzara: Approximate Man and Other Writings, Wayne State Univ, 73; auth, Presence of Rene Char & co-ed & co-transl, Poems of Rene Char, 76, Princeton Univ; Surrealist Voice of Robert Desnos, Univ Mass, 77; La Main de Pierre Reverdy, 80; Rene Charj l'oeuvre tilante, 81; Metapoetics of the Passage, New England, 81; The Eye in the Text, Princeton, 81; Selected Poems & Prose of Mallarme, New Directions, 82. *Mailing Add:* Grad Ctr City Univ of New York 33 W 42nd New York NY 10036

CAZELLES, BRIGITTE JACQUELINE, b Rabat, Morroco, Jan 9, 44; French citizen. MEDIEVAL FRENCH LITERATURE. *Educ:* Univ Paris, BA, 66, MA, 67; Univ Calif, Riverside, PhD(French lit), 75. *Prof Exp:* Instr, Pomona Col, 72-75; asst prof, Univ of the Pac, 75-77; ASST PROF FRENCH, UNIV STANFORD, 77- *Concurrent Pos:* Phi Beta Kappa fel, 74-75; Nat Endowment for Humanities fel, 76; Mellon fel, 82- *Mem:* Am Asn Teachers Fr; Medieval Acad Am. *Res:* Medieval French hagiography; medieval French didactic literature. *Publ:* Auth, Un Heros fatigue: Sens et fonction du mot las dens les Miracles de Nostre Dame de Gautier de Coinci, Romance Philol, 77; Jeter Puer: Le traitement de la fuite du monde dans les Miracles de Gautier de Coinci, Le Moyen Age, 77; Ne seit que dire ne que faire: Silence et Passivite dens les Miracles de Gautier de Coinci, Zeitschrift für Romanische Philol, 77; La Faiblesse chez Gautier de Coinci, Stanford Fr Studies, 78; coauth, Le Vain Siecle Guerpir: A Literary Approach to Sainthood in Old French Hagiography, NC, 79; Modele ou mirage: Marie l'Egyptienne, Fr Rev, 79; Alexis et Tristan: les effets de l'enlaidissement, Stanford Fr Rev, 81. *Mailing Add:* Dept of Fr & Ital Stanford Univ Stanford CA 94305

CECCHETTI, GIOVANNI, b Pescia, Italy, June 12, 22; nat US; m 53; c 2. ROMANCE LANGUAGES. *Educ:* Liceo Dante, Dipl, 41; Univ Florence, Litt D, 47. *Prof Exp:* Lectr Ital, Univ Calif, 48-50, from instr to asst prof, 50-57; from assoc prof to prof Ital, Tulane Univ, 57-65; prof, Stanford Univ, 65-69; chmn dept, 69-77, PROF ITAL, UNIV CALIF, LOS ANGELES, 69- *Concurrent Pos:* Tulane Univ, Coun Res grants, 58, 59 & 61-62; Univ Calif grants, 77-82; Nat Endowment for Humanities grant, 82. *Honors & Awards:* Star of Solidarity, 61, Cavaliere, Order of Merit, 66, Cavaliere Ufficiale, 73 & Presidential Gold Medal for Cult Merit, 78, Italy. *Mem:* MLA; Dante Soc Am; Am Asn Teachers Ital; Phil Asn Pac Coast; Leonardo da Vinci Soc. *Res:* Italian literature; relations between English and Italian literature. *Publ:* Auth, La Poesia del Pascoli, Pisa, 54; translr & introd, The She-wolf and Other Stories, Univ Calif, 58, 62 & rev ed, 73 & 82; auth, Leopardi e Verga, 62; Diario Nomade, Padova, 67; Il Verga Maggiore, 68, 71 & 75; Firenze, 68, 70 & 75; Impossibile scendere, Milano, 78; Giovanni Verga, Twayne, 78; Sulle Operette morali, Roma, 78; Villaggio degli inutili, Venezia, 80; Nel cammino dei monti, Firenze, 80; transl & intro, Mastro-don Gesualdo, 79 & Leopardi, Operette morali, 82, Univ Calif. *Mailing Add:* Dept of Ital Univ of Calif 405 Hilgard Ave Los Angeles CA 90024

CELLER, MORTON MARK, b New York, NY, Mar 11, 21; m 46. FRENCH LANGUAGE & LITERATURE. *Educ:* City Col New York, AB, 40, MSEd, 48; Sorbonne, cert, 50; Univ Paris, DUniv, 52. *Prof Exp:* From instr to assoc prof Romance Lang, Wabash Col, 48-66; PROF FRENCH, GA STATE UNIV, 66- *Mem:* MLA; Am Asn Teachers Fr. *Res:* Modern French literature; audiovisual techniques in modern language teaching; evolution of French short story. *Publ:* Auth, Giraudoux et la Metaphore, Mouton, 73. *Mailing Add:* Dept of Foreign Lang Ga State Univ Atlanta GA 30303

CEPAS, KOSTAS VYTAUTAS, b Griskabudis, Lithuania, Mar 21, 11; US citizen; m 37; c 2. FOREIGN LANGUAGES. *Educ:* State Univ Lithuania, LLM, 33, Dr Law, 37, Dr jur habil, 38. *Prof Exp:* Asst prof comp law, State Univ Lithuania, 39-44; lectr econ, Sch Forestry, Vilnius, Lithuania, 44-34; assoc prof comp law, UNRRA, Baltic Univ, Hamburg, 46-49, dean sch law & econ, 46-48; instr Ger & hist, J C Smith Univ, 63-64, from asst prof to assoc prof Ger & French, 64-66; assoc prof Ger & Latin, Elon Col, 66-71, chmn dept foreign lang, 71-76, assoc prof, 76-79; RETIRED. *Concurrent Pos:* Consult, Coun Codification Civil Laws of Lithuania, 38-40. *Mem:* Am Asn Teachers Ger. *Res:* Language laboratory, arrangement and materials in teaching foreign languages. *Publ:* Auth, Codification of Swiss Zivilgetetzbuch, 36 & Codification of German Buergerliches Gesetzbuch, 37, Teise; Tutelage of Adults, State Univ Kaunas, 39; coauth, De la Condition de la Femme en Societe Contemporaine, Inst Droit Compare, Paris, 39. *Mailing Add:* Elon Col PO Box 843 Elon College NC 27244

CERE, RONALD CARL, US citizen. EIGHTEENTH CENTURY SPANISH. *Educ:* City Col New York, BA, 66; Queens Col, MA, 69; NY Univ, PhD(Span), 74. *Prof Exp:* Asst prof Span, City Univ New York, 72-75, State Univ NY, 75-78, Univ Ill, 78-80 & Univ Nebr, 80-82; ASST PROF SPAN, UNIV COLO, 82- *Concurrent Pos:* Managing ed, Independent Press, 79-80; consult, Harper & Row Publ, 79-80, Harcourt Brace Jovanovich, 80, Holt, Rinehart & Winston, 81-82 & Scott Foresman & Co, 82. *Honors & Awards:* James C Healy Award, NY Univ, 75. *Mem:* Am Soc Eighteenth Century Scholars; MLA; Am Asn Teachers Span & Port; Am Coun Teachers Foreign Lang. *Res:* Eighteenth century Spanish literature; applied linguistics; foreign language pedagogy. *Publ:* Coauth, Los fabulistas y su sentido historico, Am Publ Co, 69; Nicolas Fernandez de Moratin & Gergorio Mayans Siscar y Francisco Perez Bayer, The Eighteenth Century: A Current Bibliog (in prep); Las Fabulas literarias de Tomas de Iriarte: Edicion critica, Publ Vanguardia (in prep). *Mailing Add:* Div of Arts & Humanities Univ of Colo Denver CO 80202

CERF, STEVEN ROY, b New York, NY, Oct 9, 45. GERMAN, COMPARATIVE LITERATURE. *Educ:* Queens Col, City Univ New York, BA, 66; Yale Univ, MPh, 71, PhD(Ger), 75. *Prof Exp:* Teaching asst Ger, Yale Univ, 69-70, instr, 70-71; instr, 71-75, asst prof, 75-82, ASSOC PROF GER, BOWDOIN COL, 82- *Concurrent Pos:* Nat Endowment Humanities fel in residence for col teachers, Ind Univ, 78-79. *Mem:* MLA; Am Asn Teachers Ger; Northeast Mod Lang Asn; Arthur Schnitzler Res Asn; Thomas Mann Ges. *Res:* Thomas Mann; Hugo von Hofmannsthal; Georg Brandes. *Publ:* Auth, Bowdoin's contemporary music festival, Musical Am, 4/77; Epistolary novel on stage, Theatrum Mundi (Festschrift), 9/78; Diverse Screenings, Unterricliespraxis, 79; Love in Dokher Faushes, Comp Lit Studies, 81; Georg Braudes and Thomas Mann, Colloquia Germanica, 81; Votes on interdisciplinary team teaching: Music and German, Asn Depts Foreign Lang, 81; Tristram Shandy and Joseph und seine Bruder, Comp Lit Studies, 82; Die schweigsame Frau as a modernistic opera libretto, Mod Austrian Lit, 82. *Mailing Add:* Dept of Ger Bowdoin Col Brunswick ME 04011

CERRETA, FLORINDO V, b New York, NY, July 26; 21; m 55. ROMANCE LANGUAGES. *Educ:* Columbia Univ, MA, 47, PhD(Ital), 54. *Prof Exp:* Newswriter & feature ed, Voice of Am, 51-54; instr Romance lang, Pa State Univ, 54-57; from asst prof to assoc prof, 57-64, PROF ITAL, UNIV IOWA, 64- *Concurrent Pos:* Hon mem, Accad Intronati, Italy, 60. *Mem:* MLA; Am Asn Teachers Ital; Renaissance Soc Am. *Res:* Italian literature, especially mediaeval and Renaissance; Renaissance drama. *Publ:* Auth, Early life of the Accademia degli Infiammati, Romanic Rev, 57; Alessandro Piccolomini: Letterato e Filosofo Senese del Cinquecento, 60 & critical ed, A Piccolomini, L'Alessandro, 66, Accad Intronati, Siena; G Bargagli, La Pellegrina, Olschki, Florence, 71; La Commedia de Gl'Ingannati, Olschki, Florence, 80. *Mailing Add:* Dept of French & Ital Univ of Iowa Iowa City IA 52240

CERVIGNI, DINO SIGISMONDO, b Macerata, Italy, June 13, 41; US Citizen; m. ITALIAN LITERATURE. *Educ:* Univ Louisville, MEd, 71; Ind Univ, Bloomington, MA, 73, PhD(Ital lit), 75. *Prof Exp:* Teaching asst Ital, Ind Univ, Bloomington, 72-74; instr, 74-76, asst prof, 76-80, ASSOC PROF ITAL, UNIV NOTRE DAME, 80- *Mem:* MLA; Renaissance Soc Am; Dante Soc Am; Am Asn Teachers Ital; Am Asn Univ Profs Ital. *Res:* Dante; Renaissance Italian literature; biography and autobiography of the Late Middle Ages and Renaissance. *Publ:* Auth, Demonic and angelic forces in Dante's Second Dream, L'Alighieri, 77; Privacy and concern in Pontormo's Diario, Paragone, 77; Cellini's Vita or the unfinished story of a disillusioned hero, Mod Lang Quart, 78; The Vita of Benvenuto Cellini: Literary Tradition and Genre, Longo, Ravenna, 78; Dante's Poetry of Dreams, 82; Space and Time in the Vita Nuova, 82. *Mailing Add:* Dept of Mod Lang Univ of Notre Dame Notre Dame IN 46556

CHABERT, HENRY L, b Paris, France, May 8, 13. FRENCH CIVILIZATION & LITERATURE. *Educ:* Univ Exeter, cert English, 36; Law Sch Paris, France, LLM, 41; Sorbonne, MA, 43, cert, 52, PhD(comp lit), 65. *Prof Exp:* Prof English lit, Petit Sem Paris, 42-48; mil corresp, Supreme Hdqrs Allied Forces, 44-45; London corresp, Parisien Libere & Carrefour, 45; foreign ed, Carrefour & Terre d'Europe, 46-50; prof English lit, Col Rouen & Lycee Versailles, France, 52-57; translr & prof French, UN, 57-60; asst prof French lit, Ohio Wesleyan Univ, 60-61; assoc prof, 61-66, PROF FRENCH LIT, UNIV NORTHERN IOWA, 66- *Concurrent Pos:* Study grants, Brit Coun, 47, 50, 52 & 56, French Ministry Educ, 48; prof French, NDEA lang insts, Univ Ky, 62 & Univ Idaho, 63; vis lectr, Univ Kans, 64-65. *Mem:* Asn Teachers Fr. *Res:* The influence of Michelet in the United States; the true causes of the French Army collapse in May, 1940; results achieved by various methods of language teaching. *Publ:* Auth, Return from London, Etudes, 3/46; Facts and fictions of foreign language teaching, Fr Rev, 10/70 & Fedn Int Prof, 72; Which French are we to teach?, Fr Rev, 2/72; The myths of conversation classes, Fr Rev, 3/76; Why take a civilization course?, Mod Lang J, 9/76; A possible historical mistake: The 1940 collapse, Mil Rev, 9/76. *Mailing Add:* Dept of Foreign Lang Univ of Northern Iowa Cedar Falls IA 50613

CHADBOURNE, RICHARD MCCLAIN, b Providence, RI, Sept 19, 22. FRENCH & FRENCH-CANADIAN LITERATURE. *Educ:* Brown Univ, AB, 43; Yale Univ, PhD, 50. *Prof Exp:* Asst instr, Brown Univ, 46 & Yale Univ, 46-49; from instr to asst prof French lit, Fordham Univ, 50-57; from assoc prof to prof French, Univ Colo, Boulder, 57-71, chmn dept, 61-71; PROF ROMANCE STUDIES & HEAD DEPT, UNIV CALGARY, 71- *Concurrent Pos:* Am Coun Learned Soc fel, 62-63; vis prof, Univ Calif, Los Angeles, 67-68; Killam fel, 79. *Honors & Awards:* Chevalier, Ordre des Palmes Academiques, 66. *Mem:* Am Asn Teachers Fr; Can Asn Univ Prof; Soc Chateaubriand; Soc Etudes Renaniennes. *Res:* Nineteenth century French literature; French essayists from Montaigne to Sartre; French-Canadian novel. *Publ:* Auth, Ernest Renan as an Essayist, Cornell Univ, 57; Ernest Renan, Twayne, 68; Charles-Augustin Sainte-Beuve, G K Hall-Twayne, 78; co-ed & contribr, The New Land, Wilfrid Laurier Univ, 78; contribr, Symbolism and Modern Literature, Duke Univ, 78; Travel, quest, and pilgrimage as a literary theme, Univ Nebr, 78; Transactions of the Samuel Johnson Society, Univ Calgary, 80; French literature series: The French essay, Univ SC, 82. *Mailing Add:* Dept of Romance Studies Univ of Calgary Calgary AB T2N 1N4 Can

CHAFE, WALLACE L, b Cambridge, Mass, Sept 3, 27. LINGUISTICS. *Educ:* Yale Univ, BA, 50, MA, 56, PhD(ling). 58. *Prof Exp:* Asst prof mod lang, Univ Buffalo, 58-59; linguist, Bur Am Ethnol, Smithsonian Int, 59-62; PROF LING, UNIV CALIF, BERKELEY, 62- *Concurrent Pos:* Vis prof, Cornell Univ, 67-68 & Wellesley Col, 79. *Mem:* Ling Soc Am; Am Anthrop Asn; Am Psychol Asn. *Res:* American Indian linguistics; general linguistic theory; language and cognition; spoken and written language. *Publ:* Auth, Seneca Thanksgiving Rituals, Bur Am Ethnol, 61; Handbook of the Seneca Language, NY State Mus, 63; Seneca Morphology and Dictionary, Smithsonian, 67; Meaning and the Structure of Language, Univ Chicago, 70; The Pear Stories, 80. *Mailing Add:* Dept Ling Univ Calif Berkeley CA 94720

CHAFFEE-SORACE, DIANE, b Worcester, Mass, June 11, 51; m 82. SPANISH GOLDEN AGE LITERATURE. *Educ:* Wells Col, BA, 73; Duke Univ, MA, 75, PhD(Spanish), 79. *Prof Exp:* Lectr, State Univ NY Stony Brook, 77-80; asst prof, Univ Va, 80-82; ASST PROF SPANISH, WASHINGTON UNIV, 82- *Mem:* MLA; South Atlantic Mod Lang Asn; Northeast Mod Lang Asn; Am Asn Teachers of Spanish & Portuguese. *Res:* Spanish Medieval literature; comparative literature. *Publ:* Auth, Imitation as the explanation for chronology: Two versions of a Gongorine Sonnet, Romanische Forschungen, 3/81; The poetic artistry of Gongora's No Son Todos Ruisenores: To end or not to end, Romance Notes, fall 81; The endings of Gongora's Servia en Oran al Rey, Bull Hisp Studies, 1/82; Exphrasis in Juan de Mena and the Marques de Santillana, Romance Philol, 5/82; Pictures and portraits in literature: Cervantes as the painter of Don Quijote, Anales Cervantinos (in prep); Visual art in literature: The role of time and space in exphrastic creation, Rev Canadiense de Estudios Hispanicos (in prep). *Mailing Add:* 7735 Bellstone Rd St Louis MO 63119

CHAIKA, ELAINE OSTRACH, b Milford, Mass, Dec 20, 34; m 60; c 3. LINGUISTICS. *Educ:* RI Col, BEd, 60; Brown Univ, MAT, 65, PhD(ling), 72. *Prof Exp:* Teacher, Mill Sch, Eastbrook, Maine, 54-55, Veteran's High Sch, Warwick, RI, 60-61 & George S West Jr High Sch, Providence, RI, 61-62; instr English, Bryant Col, 66-67; asst prof, 71-74, assoc prof, 75-78, PROF LING, PROVIDENCE COL, 78- *Concurrent Pos:* Nat Endowment for Humanities fel, 82. *Mem:* Am Dialect Soc; Ling Soc Am; MLA. *Res:* Schizophrenic language; deviant linguistic productions; sociolinguistics. *Publ:* Grammars and Teaching, Col English, 78, reprinted, In: Readings in Applied English Linguistics, 82; Response to Bowden, Col English, 40: 370-374; Jargons and Language Change, Anthropological Ling, 2/80; How Shall a discourse be understood, Discourse Proc, 4: 71-87; Review of Zeleman Making Sense of it, Col Commun & Compos, 2/81; Language: The Social Mirror, Newbury House, 10/82; A unified explanation for the deverse structural deviations in the speech of adult schizophrenics, J Commun Disorders, 15: 167-189; Linguistics look at psychiatry: A study in the analysis of discourse, Proc First Del Symposium Lang Studies (in press). *Mailing Add:* Dept Ling Providence Col Providence RI 02918

CHALLIS, DAVID J, b Sewickley, Pa, Aug 23, 39; m 68; c 2. MODERN & CONTEMPORARY SPANISH LITERATURE. *Educ:* Haverford Col, BA, 61; Univ Pittsburgh, MA, 64, PhD(Span), 73. *Prof Exp:* Instr Span, Univ Pittsburgh, Johnstown, 63-65, asst prof humanities & Span & coordr mod lang, 67-70; asst prof Span, Grove City Col, 65-67; asst prof, 70-76, ASSOC PROF SPAN, RANDOLPH-MACON COL, 76- *Mem:* SAtlantic Mod Lang Asn. *Res:* Generation of 1898; Spanish literature and the 20th century; literature and art in the 19th and 20th centuries. *Publ:* Auth, Pio Baroja's reliance upon visual stimuli, Proc Mt Interstate Lang Conf, 73. *Mailing Add:* Dept of Romance Lang Randolph-Macon Col Ashland VA 23005

CHAMBERLAIN, BOBBY JOHN, b Huntington Park, Calif, Oct 30, 46; m 72; c 1. LUSO-BRAZILIAN & SPANISH-AMERICAN LITERATURE. *Educ:* Univ Calif, Los Angeles, BA, 68, MA, 71, PhD(Hisp lang & lit), 75. *Prof Exp:* Teaching assoc Port, Univ Calif, Los Angeles, 69-71; asst prof Port & Span, Mich State Univ, 76-81; ASST PROF PORT & SPAN, UNIV SOUTHERN CALIF, 81- *Concurrent Pos:* Asst dir, Latin Am Studies Ctr, Mich State Univ, 78-80. *Mem:* MLA; Am Asn Teachers Span & Port. *Res:* Portuguese linguistics and philology. *Publ:* Coauth, Brazil: A Working Bibliography in Literature, Linguistics, Humanities and the Social Sciences, Ariz State Univ, Ctr Latin Am Studies, 75; auth, Double perspective in two works of Jorge Amado, Estudos Ibero-Am, 7/78; Unlocking the Roman a Clef: A look at the in-group humor of J Amado, Am Hispanist, fall 78; contribr, Dictionary Contemporary Brazilian Authors, Ariz State Univ, Ctr Latin Am Studies, 81; auth, A consumer guide to developing a Brazilian-literature reference library, 5/81 & Lexical similarities of Lunfardo and Giria, 9/81, Hispania. *Mailing Add:* Dept of Span & Port Univ Southern Calif Los Angeles CA 90007

CHAMBERLIN, VERNON ADDISON, b Topeka, Kans, July 18, 24; m 55; c 2. SPANISH LITERATURE. *Educ:* Washburn Univ, Topeka, AB, 49; Univ Kans, MA, 53, PhD(Span), 57. *Prof Exp:* Instr Span, Fredonia High Sch, Kans, 49-51 & Pembroke Country Day Sch, Kansas City, Mo, 51-53; instr Span, Univ Calif, Los Angeles, 57-59; from asst to prof to assoc prof, Okla State Univ, 59-63; assoc prof, 63-68; PROF SPAN, UNIV KANS, 68- *Mem:* MLA; Am Asn Teachers Span & Port. *Res:* Perez Galdos; 19th century Spanish literature; Hispano-Russian literary relations. *Publ:* Auth, Galdos' use of yellow in character delineation, PMLA, 64; Symbolic green: A time-honored characterizing device in Spanish literature, Hispania, 68; coauth, Galdos' Dona Perfecta and Turgenev's Fathers and Sons: Two interpretations of the conflict between generations, PMLA, 71; auth & translr, A Soviet introduction to Dona Perfecta, In: Anales Galdosianos, 75; auth, El interes sovietico por los Episodios y novelas de Galdos (1935-1940), In: Actas del Primer Congreso Internacional Galdosiano, Las Palmas, 76; coauth, La Revista Illustrada de Nueva York: History, Anthology, and Index of Literary Selections, Columbia Univ & Univ Mo, 76; auth, Galdos and Beethoven: Fortunata y Jacinta, A Symphonic Novel, Tamesis, London, 76; Poor maxi's windmill: Aquatic symbolism in Fortunata y Jacinta, Hisp Rev, 82. *Mailing Add:* Dept of Span & Portuguese Univ of Kans Lawrence KS 66044

CHAMBERLIN, WELLS FENTON, b Peoria, Ill, June 18, 14; m 42; c 5. FRENCH. *Educ:* Oberlin Col, BA, 36; Univ Bordeaux, dipl French, 37; Univ Chicago, MA, 38, PhD(French & Ital), 56. *Prof Exp:* Asst French, Univ Ill, Urbana, 40-42; from instr to assoc prof, 46-76, prof, 76-79, EMER PROF FRENCH, UNIV CHICAGO, 79- *Res:* Balzac; French novel in the 19th century; Proust. *Publ:* Auth, The Zweig manuscript-proof of Une Tenebreuse Affaire, Univ Chicago Studies Balzac, 42; Une Tenebreuse Affaire, roman policier, Ann Faculte Lettres Toulouse, 58. *Mailing Add:* 5735 Dorchester Ave Chicago IL 60637

CHAMBERS, BETTYE THOMAS, b Lynchburg, Va, Apr 17, 41; m 69. FRENCH BIBLIOGRAPHY. *Educ:* Sweet Briar Col, BA, 62; Univ Va, MA, 69; George Washington Univ, PhD(French), 79. *Prof Exp:* LECTR ITAL, GEORGETOWN UNIV, 77- *Concurrent Pos:* Nat Endowment for Humanities grant, 81-82. *Mem:* Bibliog Soc Am. *Res:* Sixteenth century printing and publishing; Reformation and Counter-Reformation; bibliography of 17th century French Bibles. *Publ:* Auth, The first French New Testament printed in England?, 77 & Thomas Gaultier strikes again . . . and again?, 79, Bibl Humanisme & Renaissance; Bibliography of 15th and 16th Century French Language Editions of the Scriptures, Droz (in press). *Mailing Add:* 1237 31 St NW Washington DC 20007

CHAMBERS, FRANK MCMINN, b Tyler, Tex, Aug 2, 10; m 46; c 3. ROMANCE PHILOLOGY. *Educ:* Harvard Univ, AB, 30, AM, 32, PhD, 35. *Prof Exp:* Tutor Romance lang, Harvard Univ, 32-35; from instr to asst prof, Colo Col, 35-45; asst prof, Northwestern Univ, 45-50; assoc head Mod Lang Dept, D C Heath & Co, 50-67; prof French, Univ Ariz, 67-78; RETIRED. *Mem:* MLA; Mediaeval Acad Am. *Res:* Old French; Old Provencal; French Renaissance. *Publ:* Auth, The Poems of Aimeric de Peguilhan, Northwestern Univ, 50; Imitation of form in the old Provencal lyric, Romance Philol, 53; Poems of Raimon de las Salas, In: Essays in Honor of L F Solano, 70 & Proper Names in the Lyrics of the Troubadours, 71, Univ NC; ed, Prosateurs francais du XVIe siecle, Heath, 76; Tentative autobiography, Romance Philol, 81. *Mailing Add:* 245 Calle de la Azucena Tucson AZ 85711

CHAMBERS, LEIGH ROSS, b Kempsey, Australia, Nov 19, 32. FRENCH & COMPARATIVE LITERATURE. *Educ:* Univ Sydney, BA Hons, 53, MA Hons, 59; Univ Grenoble, DUniv, 67. *Prof Exp:* Asst English, Col Mod, France, 53-55; grad asst French, Sydney Boys High Sch, 56; lectr, Univ Queensland, 57-58 & Univ Sydney, 59-63; sr lectr, Univ New South Wales, 64-70, assoc prof, 70-71; McCaughey prof, Univ Sydney, 71-75; PROF FRENCH, UNIV MICH, ANN ARBOR, 75- *Concurrent Pos:* Fel, Australian Acad Humanities, 71. *Res:* Nineteenth century French literature; thematic criticism; theory of literature and theater. *Publ:* Auth, Gerard de Nerval et la Poetique du Voyage, 69 & La Comedie au Chateau, 71, Corti, Paris; L'Ange et l'Automate, 71 & Spirite de Theophile Gautier, 74, Minard, Paris; Meaning and Meaningfulness, Fr Forum, 79. *Mailing Add:* Dept of Romance Lang Univ of Mich Ann Arbor MI 48109

CHAMPIGNEUL, YVONNE, b Paris, France, Oct 14, 18. FRENCH LANGUAGE & LITERATURE. *Educ:* Univ Paris, B es Lett, 36; Univ Toulouse, Lic es Lett, 40; Dipl etudes super, 44; Sorbonne, PhD, 50, DLett, 78. *Prof Exp:* Asst French, King Edward's Grammar Sch, Birmingham, England, 45-46; assoc English & French & pedag adv, Alsace & Lorraine High Sch Teachers, France, 50-52; Fulbright scholar, 52-53; asst prof, 53-67, ASSOC PROF FRENCH, MCGILL UNIV, 67- *Honors & Awards:* Chevalier, Palmes Academiques, 58. *Mem:* Asn Francaise Prof Langues Vivantes. *Res:* Philosophy and poetical rhythms in Shelley; analysis of the musical elements in poetry; La Fontaine and Maucroix. *Publ:* Auth, La Fontaine et les voyages par voie de terre, Rev Hist Lit France, 69; contribr, L'Absolutisme Royal: Une Lecture de La Fontaine, Hurtubise, 71; Le Dialogue dars les Contes, L'Art du Dialogue daus les Fables, SEDES (in prep). *Mailing Add:* Dept of French McGill Univ Peterson Hall Montreal PQ H3C 3G1 Can

CHAMPIGNY, ROBERT JEAN, b Chatellerault, France, Sept 30, 22; m 48. FRENCH. *Educ:* Univ Poitiers, France, Lic es Let, 43; Sorbonne, D es L, 56. *Prof Exp:* From instr to prof, 53-64, RES PROF FRENCH, IND UNIV, BLOOMINGTON, 64- *Concurrent Pos:* Am Coun Learned Soc fel, 64-65. *Mem:* Am Asn Teachers Fr; MLA. *Res:* Modern French literature and philosophy; semantics. *Publ:* Auth, Stages on Sartre's Way, Ind Univ, 59; Le Genre Poetique, 63 & Le Genre Dramatique, 65, Regain; Pour une Esthetique de l'Essai, Minard, 68; Ontologie du Narratif & Humanisme et Racisme Humain, 72 & Le Jeu Philosophique, 76, St Germain des Pres; What Will Have Happened, Ind Univ, 77. *Mailing Add:* Dept of French Ind Univ Bloomington IN 47401

CHAMPLIN, EDWARD JAMES, b New York, NY, June 3, 48; Can citizen; m 72; c 1. ANCIENT HISTORY. *Educ:* Univ Toronto, BA, 70, MA, 72; Oxford Univ, DPhil(literae humaniores), 76. *Prof Exp:* Instr, 75-76, asst prof, 76-81, ASSOC PROF CLASSICS, PRINCETON UNIV, 81- *Mem:* Am Philol Asn; Class Asn Can; Asn Ancient Historians; Soc Prom Roman Studies. *Res:* Roman history; Latin literature. *Publ:* Auth, The chronology of Fronto, 74 & The life and times of Calpurnius Siculus, 78, J Roman Studies; Notes on the heirs of Commodus, Am J Philol, 79; Fronto and Antonine Rome, Harvard Univ, 80; Serenus Sammonicucs, Harvard Studies in Class Philol, 81; Owners and neighbours at Lingures Baebiani, Chiron, 81; Saint Gallicanus (Consul 317), Phoenix, 82; Pliny the Younger, In: Ancient Writers: Greece and Rome, Scribner's, 82. *Mailing Add:* Dept Classics Princeton Univ Princeton NJ 08544

CHAN, SHAU WING, b Canton, China, Apr 4, 07; nat US; m 35; c 2. ENGLISH & ORIENTAL LANGUAGE. *Educ:* Lingnan Univ, China, AB, 27; Stanford Univ, AM, 32, PhD, 37. *Prof Exp:* Instr English, Sun Yat-Sen Univ, China, 27-30; instr Chinese lang & lit, 38-39, asst prof Chinese & English, 39-42, from asst prof to assoc prof Chinese & humanities, 42-50, prof Chinese, 50-72, actg exec head dept Asiatic & Slavic studies, 56-58, exec head dept Asian lang, 58-62, dir Chinese-Japanese Lang Ctr, 59-62, EMER PROF CHINESE, STANFORD UNIV, 72- *Concurrent Pos:* Lectr, Kwangtung Provincial Norm Sch, China, 28-30; consult int secretariat, UN Conf, San Francisco, 45; consult hist sect, Asia Found, Inc, 50-51; dir Human Rel Area Files Chima Proj; mem adv comt, Chinese Lang Instr in Pub Schs, State of Calif, 61; sr lectr hist, Menlo Col, 72-77. *Mem:* Am Orient Soc; MLA; Asn Asian Studies. *Res:* Contemporary Chinese literature; cultural relations between the Orient and the Occident; modern Chinese poetry. *Publ:* Auth, Concise English-Chinese Dictionary; Elementary Chinese; coauth, China's Men of Letters, Green Pagoda, Hong Kong, 62. *Mailing Add:* 751 Live Oak Ave Menlo Park CA 94025

CHANDLER, RICHARD EUGENE, b Kansas City, Mo, Oct 21, 16; m 41; c 2. MODERN FOREIGN LANGUAGES. *Educ:* Univ Mo, AB, 37, MA, 38, PhD(Span,French), 40. *Prof Exp:* Prof foreign lang, Northeastern State Col, Okla, 40-42, head dept, 46-47; prof, 47-50 & 52-81, head dept, 67-81, GABRIELLE HEBRARD PROF FOREIGN LANG, UNIV SOUTHWESTERN LA, 81- *Concurrent Pos:* NDEA fel Port, Univ Wis, 60; chmn acad adv bd, Coun Develop French in La, 75- *Honors & Awards:* Palmes Academiques, Govt France, 77; Order of Isabel la Catolica, King of Spain, 80. *Mem:* Am Asn Teachers Span & Port; SCent Mod Lang Asn. *Res:* Spanish colonial Louisiana; literary history of Spain; medieval Spanish literature. *Publ:* Coauth, Risas y Sonrisas Handbook of Comparative Grammar for Students of Foreign Languages: A New History of Spanish Literature, Am Bk Co, 61; auth, Life in New Orleans in 1798, Rev Louisiane, winter 77; Odyssey continued: Acadians arrive in Natchez, summer 78, Eyewitness history: O'Reilly's arrival in Louisiana, summer 79, The St Gabriel Acadians: The first five months, summer 80, O'Reilly's voyage from Havanna to the Balize, spring 81, Ulloa and the Acadians, winter 80 & O'Reilly and the rebels: Report to Arriaga, winter 82, La Hist. *Mailing Add:* P O Box 4-3331 Univ of Southwestern La Lafayette LA 70504

CHANDLER, STANLEY BERNARD, b Canterbury, Eng, May 31, 21; m 54; c 2. ROMANCE LANGUAGES. *Educ:* Univ London, BA, 47, PhD(Ital), 53. *Prof Exp:* Asst lectr Ital, Univ Col, Univ London, 48-50; lectr, Aberdeen Univ, 50-57; assoc prof, 57-63, PROF ITAL, UNIV TORONTO, 63-, CHMN DEPT ITAL STUDIES, 73- *Mem:* MLA; Am Asn Teachers Ital; Dante Soc Am; Can Soc Ital Studies; Int Asn Ital Lang & Lit (int vpres, 73-82). *Res:* Italian Romanticism; the works and thought of Alessandro Manzoni; Italian literature and society in the 19th century. *Publ:* Auth, The Conte di Carmagnola in the Development of Manzoni's spiritual outlook, 9/70 & Passion, reason and evil in the works of Alessandro Manzoni, 12/73, Italica; contribr, Petrarch to Pirandello, Univ Toronto, 73; auth, Alessandro Manzoni, Univ Edinburgh, 74; Manzoni e William Godwin, Rivista Lett Mod Comparate, 12/75; La memoria melle epere Manzoni, Lettere Italiane, 79; La forma e il significato dei Malavoglia, Espenienze Letterarie, 80; Rassegna sul lieto fine ve I Promessi Sponsi, Critia Letteraria, 80. *Mailing Add:* Dept of Ital Studies Fac of Arts & Sci Univ of Toronto Toronto ON M5S 1A1 Can

CHANDOLA, ANOOP CHANDRA, b Rawatgaon, Pauri, India, Dec 24, 37; m 63. LINGUISTICS. *Educ:* Univ Allahabad, BA, 54; Univ Lucknow, MA, 56; Univ Calif, Berkeley, MA, 61; Univ Chicago, PhD(ling), 66. *Prof Exp:* Tutor Hindi, Sardar Vallabhbhai Vidyapeeth, 56-57, lectr, 57-58; lectr, Univ Baroda, 58-59; res & teaching asst, 59-63, from asst prof to assoc prof Orient studies, 63-71, PROF LING & ORIENT STUDIES, UNIV ARIZ, 71- *Mem:* Ling Soc Am; Asn Asian Studies; Ling Soc India. *Res:* Linguistic theory and method; Hindi language and literature; music and linguistics. *Publ:* Some systems of musical scales and linguistic principles, Semiotica, 70; A Systematic Translation of Hindi-Urdu into English, Univ Ariz, 70; An evolutionary approach to sentence formation, Linguistics, 75; Folk Drumming in the Himalayas, 77 & Situation to Sentence, 79, AMS. *Mailing Add:* Dept of Orient Studies Univ of Ariz Tucson AZ 85721

CHANEY, VIRGINIA M, b Russellville, Ky, Oct 17, 09; m 37; c 2. FOREIGN LANGUAGES. *Educ:* Western Ky State Col, BA, 30, MA, 35; Vanderbilt Univ, PhD, 61. *Prof Exp:* Teacher English & Latin, Russellville High Sch, Ky, 37-39; teacher Scottsville High Sch, 39-41; teacher English & hist, Trezevant High Sch, 41-42; teacher English, Tullahoma High Sch, 42-46; teacher English & Latin, Lebanon High Sch, 46-47, 51-56; assoc prof English French & Latin, Cumberland Univ, 47-51; head dept foreign lang, 64-72, PROF ENGLISH & LATIN, BELMONT COL, 56-, CHMN DEPT ENGLISH & FOREIGN LANG, 72- *Mem:* NCTE; Class Asn Mid W & S. *Res:* Classical and Renaissance periods, especially in the Latin field; the poet Martial. *Publ:* Martial goes out to dinner, Class Bull, 6/73. *Mailing Add:* 5110 Kincannon Dr Nashville TN 37220

CHANG, ALOYSIUS, b China, Oct 14, 30; US citizen; m 72; c 1. EAST ASIAN LANGUAGES & HISTORY. *Educ:* San Jose Sem, BA, 54; Bellarmine Col, STB, 60; St John's Univ, MA, 68, PhD(hist), 70. *Prof Exp:* Asst prof Span, Nagasaki Foreign Lang Jr Col, 64-65; asst prof Chinese, Sophia Univ, Tokyo, Japan, 66-67; asst prof Japanese, St John's Univ, NY, 70-72; assoc prof, 72-80, PROF CHINESE & JAPANESE, WASH STATE UNIV, 80- *Mem:* Am Asn Chinese Studies; Asn Asian Studies; Asn Teachers Japanese; Chinese Lang Teachers Asn; Pac Northwest Coun Foreign Lang. *Res:* Yang Chu; Chinese community in Nagasaki; Asian religions. *Publ:* Auth, The enigmatic decade: Komeito's party building efforts, 1964-1975, Asia Quart, 76; The Taoist concept of God, In: God in Contemporary Thought, Learned Publ, 77; Religious culture in American history, In: The United States in The Third Century, Tamkang Col, 77; A History of Swedish Literature, 78, A History of Norwegian Literature, 80, A History of Danish Literature, 80, A History of Icelandic Literature, 82 & A History of Finnish Literature, 82, Li Ming Cult Enterprise. *Mailing Add:* Dept of Foreign Lang Wash State Univ Pullman WA 99164

CHANG, KANG-I SUN, b Tientsin, People's Repub China, Feb 21, 44; US citizen; m 68. CHINESE LITERATURE. *Educ:* Tunghai Univ, BA, 66; Rutgers Univ, MLS, 71; SD State Univ, MA, 72; Princeton Univ, PhD(Chinese lit), 78. *Prof Exp:* Vis asst prof, Tufts Univ, 79-80; cur, Gest Orient Libr East Asian Collections, Princeton Univ, 80-81; ASST PROF CHINESE LIT, YALE UNIV, 82- *Mem:* Asn Asian Studies. *Res:* Chinese Shih poetry during the Six Dynasties: AD 222-589; Chinese Tz'u poetry from late T'ang to northern Sung; Chinese poetry and cultural history. *Publ:* Auth, The concept of time in the Shih Ching, Tsing Hua J Chinese Studies, 12/79; The Evolution of Chinese Tz'u Poetry from Late T'ang to Northern Sung, Princeton Univ Press, 80; Songs in the Chin-p'ing-mei tz'u-hua, J Orient Studies, Vol 18, 82; Chinese lyric criticism, In: Theories of the Arts in China, Princeton Univ Press (in prep). *Mailing Add:* Dept of East Asian Lang & Lit Yale Univ New Haven CT 06520

CHANG, KUN, b K'ai-Feng, China, Nov 17, 17. CHINESE LANGUAGE & LITERATURE. *Educ:* Nat Tsing-Hua Univ, China, BA, 38; Yale Univ, MA, 49; PhD, 55. *Prof Exp:* Jr res fel, inst hist & philol, Acad Sinica, China, 39-47; instr, Inst Far Eastern Lang, Yale Univ, 47-51; from instr to assoc prof Far Eastern lang & lit, Far Eastern Dept, Univ Wash, 51-63; PROF ORIENT LANG, UNIV CALIF, BERKELEY, 63- *Mem:* Ling Soc Am; Am Orient Soc; Asn Asian Studies; Acad Sinica. *Res:* Comparative Miao-Yao linguistics; comparative study of Buddhistic texts, especially Sanskrit, Tibetan, Chinese; Chinese and Tibetan linguistics. *Publ:* Auth, A Comparative Study of the Kathinavastu; coauth, A Manuel of Spoken Tibetan, Univ Wash, 64; auth, A comparative study of the southern Ch'iang dialects, Monumenta Serica, 67; Wenchow historical phonology, Bull Inst Ethnol, Acad Sinica, 72; coauth, The Proto-Chinese Final System and the Ch'ieh-yün, Inst Hist & Philol, Acad Sinica, 72; The reconstruction of proto-Miao-Yao tones, Bull Inst Hist & Philol, Acad Sinica, 73. *Mailing Add:* Dept of Orient Lang 102 Durant Hall Univ of Calif Berkeley CA 94720

CHANG, RICHARD I-FENG, b Hankow, China, May 20, 21; US citizen; m 57; c 2. CHINESE, LAW. *Educ:* St John's Univ, China, AB, 43; DePaul Univ, JD, 49; George Washington Univ, LLM, 50. *Prof Exp:* Instr Chinese, Army Lang Sch, 53-56 & Yale Univ, 56-67; assoc dir, New Asia Col, Chinese Lang Inst, Hong Kong, 64-66; ASSOC PROF CHINESE, UNIV ILL, URBANA, 67- *Publ:* Auth, Read Chinese II, 58, coauth, Read Chinese III, 59, contribr, Readings on Chinese Culture, 60, Twenty Lectures on Chinese Culture, 67, coauth, Modern Chinese Poetry, 73 & Under the Eaves of Shanghai, 74, Yale Univ. *Mailing Add:* Ctr for Asian Studies Univ of Ill 1208 W California St Urbana IL 61801

CHANG-RODRIGUEZ, EUGENIO, b Trujillo, Peru, Nov 15, 24. ROMANCE LANGUAGES & LITERATURES. *Educ:* San Marcos Univ, Lima, PhB, 46; William Penn Col, BA, 49; Univ Ariz, MA(hist), 53; Univ Wash, MA(Span), 53, PhD(Romance lang), 55. *Hon Degrees:* PhD, Nat Univ Villareal, Lima, 79. *Prof Exp:* Assoc Span, Univ Wash, 51-52; dir La Casa Hispana, 51-56, instr Romance lang, 52-56; asst prof, Univ Pa, 56-61; Chmn Latin Am Studies, 69-78, PROF ROMANCE LANG, QUEENS COL, NY, 61- *Concurrent Pos:* Assoc ed, Hispania, 61-64; vis prof, Univ Miami, 67-68; mem fac, Latin Am Sem, Columbia Univ, 71-; PSC-City Univ New York Res Award, 82-83. *Mem:* Int Ling Asn (pres, 69-72); MLA; Am Asn Teachers Span & Port; Latin Am Studies Asn; Hisp Inst US. *Res:* Hispanic languages and literatures; Spanish American literature and history; linguistics. *Publ:* Auth, La America Latina de Hoy, Ronald, 61; Frequency Dictionary of Spanish, Mouton, The Hague, 64; coauth, Continuing Spanish I & II, Workbook & Instructor's Manual for Continuing Spanish, Am Bk Co, 67; ed, The Lingering Crisis: A Case Study of the Dominican Republic, La Americas, 69; coauth, Collins Spanish-English, English-Spanish Dictionary, Collins, Glasgow, 71; Sobre las alteraciones linguisticas en Vallejo, Rev de Critica Lit Lat, No 5, 77; Mariategui en la redefinicion del indigenismo, Narradores Latinoamericanos, 80. *Mailing Add:* Dept of Romance Lang Queens Col Flushing NY 11367

CHANG-RODRIGUEZ, RAQUEL, b Cardenas, Cuba, Jan 23, 43. SPANISH AMERICAN LITERATURE. *Educ:* Mont State Univ, BS, 65; Ohio Univ, MA, 67; NY Univ, PhD(Span Am lit), 73. *Prof Exp:* From lectr to ASSOC PROF SPAN, CITY COL, CITY UNIV NEW YORK, 68- *Concurrent Pos:* Fac res award, City Univ New York, 74 & 82; co-chairperson, Univ Sem Latin Am, Columbia Univ, 80- *Mem:* Am Asn Teachers Span & Port; Int Ling Asn; Inst Int Lit Iberoam; MLA; Pan Am Women Asn; Asn Peruvian Cult; Lat Am Study Asn. *Res:* Colonial Spanish American literature; Caribbean literature. *Publ:* Auth, Apuntes sobre sociedad y literatura hispanoamericanas en el siglo XVII, Cuadernos Am, Mex, 74; coauth, Tema e imagenes en El mayor monstruo del mundo, Mod Lang Notes, Johns Hopkins Univ, 75; auth, La endiablada, relato peruano inedito del siglo XVII, Revista Iberoam, Univ Pittsburgh, 75; co-ed, Homage to Irving A Leonard: Essays on Hispanic Art, History and Literature, Mich State Univ, 77; Compilation, Introduction and Bibliography, Prosa hispanoamericana virreinal, Hispam, Barcelona, 78; A forgotten Indian chronicle of Peru: Titu Cusi Yupanquis Relacion de la conquista del Peru, Latin Am Indian Literatures, 80; Coloniaje y conciencia nacional: El Inca Garcilaso de la vega y Felipe Guaman Poma de Ayala, Caravelle, 82; auth, Violencia y subversion en la prosa colonial hispanoamericana, Porria (in prep). *Mailing Add:* Dept of Romance Langs City Univ New York New York NY 10031

CHANOVER, PIERRE E, b Paris, France, Dec 10, 32; US citizen. FRENCH, POETRY. *Educ:* Brooklyn Col, BA, 57; Univ Kans, MA, 59; NY Univ, PhD, 74. *Prof Exp:* Instr French, US Armed Forces Inst, Korea, 54-55; asst instr, Univ Kans, 57-59; TEACHER, GARDEN CITY HIGH SCH, NY, 59-, PROF FRENCH, HOFSTRA UNIV, 67- *Concurrent Pos:* Demo teacher, Regents Educ TV Proj, WPIX-TV, 62; reader French, Educ Testing Serv, 62-64 & Col Entrance Exam Bd, Advan Placement Prog, 73-; consult, H W Andersen Prod Inc, 77-; ed & publ, Poesie-USA, 74- *Honors & Awards:* Chevalier, Ordre des Palmes Academiques. *Mem:* MLA; Am Asn Teachers Fr; Am Acad Poets; World Poetry Soc; Comt Small Mag-Press Ed & Publ. *Res:* Poetry in the French language. *Publ:* Auth, Marcel Proust: A Medical and Psychoanalytical Bibliography, Psychoanal Rev, No 4, Vol 56; Martinique and Guadeloupe: A Check List of Modern Literature, New York Pub Libr Bull, 10/70; A Psychological Bibliography of Jean Racine, Am Imago, spring 71; Clapotis d'Outre-Mer (poems), Libr St Germain-des-Pres, Paris, 71; Jean-Jacques Rousseau: A Pedagogical Bibliography, Fr Rev, 5/73; The Marquis de Sade: A Bibliography, Scarecrow Press, 73; Freedom (poem), In: Encycl Poetique, Jean Grassin, 78; Deces (poem), Marginales, Rev Idees et Lett, Belgium, 11-12/78. *Mailing Add:* 599 DeMott Ave Baldwin NY 11510

CHAPIN, PAUL GIPSON, b El Paso, Tex, Dec 27, 38; m 62; c 4. LINGUISTICS. *Educ:* Drake Univ, BA, 60; Mass Inst Technol, PhD(ling), 67. *Prof Exp:* Mem tech staff, Mitre Corp, 65-67; asst prof ling, Univ Calif, San Diego, 67-75, asst provost, John Muir Col, Univ Calif, San Diego, 73-75; dep div dir, behav & neural sci, 77-78, PROG DIR LING, NAT SCI FOUND, 75- *Concurrent Pos:* Am Coun Learned Soc Study fel, 71-72. *Mem:* Asn Comput Ling (pres, 77); Ling Soc Am; Polynesian Soc. *Res:* Theoretical and descriptive syntax; Polynesian linguistics; computational linguistics. *Publ:* Auth, Samoan pronominalization, Language, 70; co-auth, Two factors in perceptual segmentation of speech, J Verbal Learning & Verbal Behav, 72; auth, Quasi-modals, J Ling, 73; Proto-Polynesianai, J Polynesian Soc 74; Easter Island: A VSO language, In: Syntactic Typology, Univ Tex, 78. *Mailing Add:* Ling Prog Nat Sci Found Washington DC 20550

CHAPMAN, GEORGE ARNOLD, b Fresno, Calif, June 26, 17. SPANISH AMERICAN LITERATURE. *Educ:* Fresno State Col, AB, 39; Univ Wis, MA, 41, PhD(Span), 46. *Prof Exp:* Instr Romance lang, Newcomb Col, 42 & Oberlin Col, 45-46; from instr to assoc prof, 46-65, PROF SPAN, UNIV CALIF, BERKELEY, 65- *Mem:* Am Asn Teachers Span & Port; Pac Coast Philol Asn; Inst Int Lit Iberoam. *Res:* Contemporary Spanish-American novel; literature of Argentina; literary relations of the United States and Spanish America. *Publ:* Auth, The Spanish American Reception of United States Fiction, 1920-1940, Univ Calif, 66; Sherwood Anderson and Eduardo Mallea & The Perdido as a literary type in some Spanish-American novels, PMLA; Between fire and ice: A theme in Jack London and Horacio Quiroga, Symposium, 70. *Mailing Add:* Dept of Span & Port Univ of Calif Berkeley CA 94720

CHAPMAN, HUGH HARDING, JR, b Evansville, Ind, Nov 5, 15; m 67; c 1. ROMANCE LANGUAGES. *Educ:* DePauw Univ, AB, 39; Harvard Univ, AM, 40, PhD, 52. *Prof Exp:* Teaching fel Romance lang, Harvard Univ, 46-47; instr Romance lang, Rutgers Univ, 47-49; from instr to assoc prof, 49-62, PROF ROMANCE LANG, PA STATE UNIV, UNIVERSITY PARK, 62- *Mem:* NAm Soc 17th Century Fr Lit (pres, 72-73); Am Asn Teachers Fr; Am Asn Teachers Span & Port; MLA; Am Comp Lit Asn. *Res:* Comparative studies of modern French, Spanish, German and English authors; educational trends; 17th century French literature. *Publ:* Coauth & ed, Bibliography of comparative literature, In: Yearbook of Comparative and General Literature, Univ NC; auth, Two poetic techniques: Lorca's Romance de la luna, luna and Goethe's Erlokönig, Hispania, 12/56; coauth, Educational trends in Romance language departments: Report of a survey, Bull Asn Depts Foreign Lang, 5/73; Maynard and the pride of a poet, Chiers de l'Association des Amis de Maynard, 12/74; Expanding horizons of Phi Sigma Iota, Phi Sigma Iota Forum, summer 76; Faculty advisor and founders, ACHS Spec Report, 77. *Mailing Add:* SS-407 Burrowes Bldg Pa State Univ University Park PA 16802

CHAPMAN, KENNETH G, b East Orange, NJ, June 13, 27; m 58; c 2. SCANDINAVIAN LANGUAGE. *Educ:* Univ Minn, BS, 49, MA, 52; Univ Wis, PhD, 57. *Prof Exp:* Instr Scand Lang, Univ Wis, 58-59; from asst prof to assoc prof, 59-70; PROF SCAND LANG, UNIV CALIF, LOS ANGELES, 70- *Concurrent Pos:* Fulbright res fel, Norway, 67-68. *Mem:* Soc Advan Scand Studies. *Res:* Icelandic linguistic history; West Norwegian dialects; contemporary Norwegian and Icelandic literature. *Publ:* Auth, Icelandic-Norwegian Linguistic Relationships, Univ Oslo, 62; Graded Readings and Exercises in Old Icelandic, Univ Calif, 64; coauth, Spoken Norwegian, Holt, Rinehart & Winston, 64, 3rd ed, 82; co-ed, Norwegian-English Dictionary, Univ Oslo & Univ Wis, 65; auth, Basic Norwegian Reader, Holt, 66; Hovedlinjer i Tarjei Vessas Diktnig, Univ Oslo, 69; Tarjei Vessas, Twayne, 70. *Mailing Add:* Dept of Ger Lang Univ of Calif Los Angeles CA 90024

CHAPPLE, CHRISTOPHER, History of Religions, Sanskrit. See Vol IV

CHAPPLE, CLEMENT GERALD, b Montreal, Que, Nov 15, 37; m 64; c 2. GERMAN & COMPARATIVE LITERATURE. *Educ:* McMaster Univ, BA, 60; Harvard Univ, AM, 62, PhD(Ger), 67. *Prof Exp:* Asst prof, 66-73, ASSOC PROF GER, MCMASTER UNIV, 73- *Concurrent Pos:* Transl consult, Current Soviet Leaders, 76-; vis fel, Harvard Univ, 81. *Mem:* MLA; Can Asn Univ Teachers Ger; Am Asn Teachers Ger; Am Lit Transl Asn. *Res:* End of century literature, especially Hofmannsthal; 20th century literature, German and French; literary criticism and translation. *Publ:* Ed, Rudolf Kassners Briefe an Lili Schalk, Neue Zürcher Zietung, 9/73; co-ed, Thomas Mann: Ein Kolloquium, Bouvier, Bonn, 78; co-transl, Parabola, 5/80 & 7/82; co-ed, The Turn of The Century: German Literature and Art, 1890-1915, Bouvier, Bonn, 81; transl, The Second Voyage, Anthology of Modern Austrian Literature, Wolff, London, 81; auth, Diese drei Jahre Muchen; Rudolf Kassner Writes to Rilke, Mod Austrian Lit, 82. *Mailing Add:* Dept of Ger McMaster Univ Hamilton ON L8S 4M2 Can

CHARLES, JOHN FREDRICK, b Kalamazoo, Mich, Aug 19, 09; m 35; c 2. CLASSICAL PHILOLOGY. *Educ:* Oberlin Col, AB, 32; Univ Chicago, AM, 37, PhD(Greek), 38. *Prof Exp:* Instr lang, Dunkirk Col Ctr, NY, 36-37; asst prof classics & French & dir Jamestown exten, Alfred Univ, 38-40; from asst prof to assoc prof classics, 40-50, chmn dept classics, 40-74, prof class, 50-74, prof hist, 62-74, EMER PROF HIST, WABASH COL, 74- *Concurrent Pos:* Am Coun Learned Soc fel, 42; Ford fac fel, 51-52. *Mem:* Brit Hist Asn; Archaeol Inst Am; Class Asn Mid W & S. *Res:* Ancient history; naval history. *Mailing Add:* Dept of Classics Wabash Col Crawfordsville IN 47933

CHARNEY, BEN LOUIS, b Portland, Ore, Oct 27, 13. CLASSICAL PHILOLOGY. *Educ:* Univ Calif, Los Angeles, AB, 34, AM, 37; Univ Calif, PhD, 40. *Prof Exp:* Instr, Elsinore Naval & Mil Sch, 42; instr, Southern Calif Mil Acad, 43; instr, Flintridge Prep Sch for Boys, 43-44; instr, High Sch, 45-46; instr classics, Univ Calif, 46-48; asst prof, 49-54; teacher, Dept For lang, Merritt Col, 55-78; RETIRED. *Res:* Latin language; text and language of Seneca philosophus. *Publ:* Auth, Survey of Latin Fundamentals; Aesthetics and the teaching of aesthetic values, Sch & Soc. *Mailing Add:* 3309 MacArthur Blvd Oakland CA 94602

CHARNEY, HANNA KURZ, b Vienna, Austria, Jan 8, 31; nat US, m 54. FRENCH. *Educ:* Hunter Col, AB, 51; Smith Col, MA, 52; Columbia Univ, PhD(French), 56. *Prof Exp:* Lectr French & humanities, 52-56, from instr to assoc prof French, 56-69, chmn dept Romance lang, 67-70, PROF FRENCH, HUNTER COL, 69- *Concurrent Pos:* Shirley Farr res fel & Fulbright travel grant, France, 60-61; vis prof, Rutgers Univ, 68-70. *Mem:* MLA; Am Asn Teachers Fr; Soc Fr Prof Am. *Res:* French contemporary literature; modern novel; film and literature. *Publ:* Auth, Quinze, place du Pantheon: la mythologie du verifiable chez Michel Butor, Symposium, summer 65; Le scepticisme de Valery, Didier, Paris, 69; Pourquoi le nouveau roman policier?, Fr Rev, 10/72; Eric Rohmer's Le genou de Claire: Rousseau revisited?, Symposium, summer 73; Monsieur Teste and der Mann ohne Eigenschaften: Homo Possibilis in fiction, Comp Lit, winter 75; Images of Absence in Flaubert and some contemporary films, Style, fall 75; The tide as structure in La Maree by Pieyre de Mandiargues, Dada/Surrealism, 75; The Detective Novel of Manners: Hedonism, Morality, and the Life of Reason, Fairleigh Dickinson Univ Press, 81. *Mailing Add:* 168 W 86th St New York NY 10024

CHARRON, JEAN DANIEL, b Chasseneuil, France, Jan 14, 23; US citizen; m 46, 69; c 6. ROMANCE LANGUAGES. *Educ:* Univ Bordeaux, BA, 40; Univ Paris, BS, 42; Col Stanislas, Paris, MS, 44; Univ NC, MA, 53, PhD, 56. *Prof Exp:* Chemist, Prince Matchabelli, Inc, Bloomfield, NJ, 46-47; instr French & math, Riddle Inter-Am Col, 48-49; math, Univ Miami, 49; instr French conversation & res asst math, Univ Ga, 49-50; part-time instr French, Univ NC, 50-54, Washington Univ, 54-57; asst prof, Romance lang, Univ Tex, 57-61; assoc prof mod lang, Fla State Univ, 61-64, dir grad studies, 66-70, PROF FRENCH, UNIV KY, 64- *Concurrent Pos:* Vis prof, NDEA Summer French Insts, Converse Col, 60, 61 & Univ Miami, 62. *Mem:* MLA; Renaissance Soc Am; Am Asn Teachers Fr. *Res:* History of thought in French literature, 1550-1660. *Publ:* Auth, The Wisdom of Pierre Charron, Univ NC, 61; Quelques rectifications et remarques concernant les Lettres de Gassendi a Peiresc publiees par Tamisey de Larroque dans sa collection: Lettres de Peiresc, XVII3 Siecle, 65; Pierre Charron's view on late Renaissance science, Renaissance Papers, 67; Le theme de la Metamorphose dans l'Astree, XVIIe Siecle, 74. *Mailing Add:* Dept of French Univ of Ky Lexington KY 40506

CHASE, COLIN, English, Medieval Latin. See Vol II

CHASTAIN, KENNETH DUANE, b Salem, Ind, July 20, 34; m 59; c 2. SPANISH. *Educ:* Ind Univ, Bloomington, BS, 56; Ball State Univ, MA, 62; Purdue Univ, Lafayette, PhD(mod lang educ), 68. *Prof Exp:* Teacher Span & English, Seymour Sr High Sch, Ind, 56-57, 58-60; teacher Span, Kokomo High Sch, 61-62; teacher Span & foreign lang coordr, Columbus Sr High Sch, 62-64; from instr Span & methods to asst prof & course chmn, Purdue Univ, Lafayette, 64-72; prof Span & methods, Asbury Col, 72-73; ASSOC PROF SPAN, LING & METHODS, UNIV VA, 73- *Concurrent Pos:* Consult, D C Heath & Co; evaluator manuscripts, Hispania, Mod Lang J & Can Mod Lang Rev. *Mem:* Am Asn Teachers Span & Port; Am Coun Teaching Forign Lang. *Res:* Language learning; theories of learning; linguistic theories and applied linguistics. *Publ:* Auth, Developing Second-Language Skills: Theory to Practice, Rand McNally, 76; Toward a Philosophy of Second-Language Learning and Teaching, Heinle and Heinle, 80; Native speaker reaction to instructor-identified second-language errors, Mod Lang J, 80; Second-

Language Study: Historical Background and Current Status, NSSE, 80 & Yearbook, 80; Native speaker evaluation of student compostition errors, Mod Lang J, 81; Relatos Simbolicos, Heinle and Heinle (in prep). *Mailing Add:* Dept of Span Ital & Port Univ of Va Charlottesville VA 22903

CHATHAM, JAMES RAY, b Caryville, Fla, Nov 11, 31; m 61; c 1. SPANISH PHILOLOGY. *Educ:* Fla State Univ, BA, 53, MA, 56, PhD, 60. *Prof Exp:* Instr mod lang, Miss State Univ, 57-59; assoc prof mod lang, 60-63, assoc prof Romance lang, Univ Ala, 63-64; PROF FOREIGN LANG & HEAD DEPT, MISS STATE UNIV, 64- *Concurrent Pos:* NDEA fel, Univ Tex, 62; mem bd dir, Am Coun Teaching Foreign Lang, 67-68. *Mem:* SAtlantic Mod Lang Asn; Am Asn Teachers Span & Port; Mediaeval Acad Am. *Res:* Mediaeval Spanish language and literature; Golden Age drama. *Publ:* Coauth, The structure of Spanish society in medieval literary and didactic works, Rev Estud Hisp II, 5/68; Dissertations in Hispanic Languages and Literatures, 1876-1966, Univ Ky, 70; A paleographic edition of the Alfonsine collection of prose miracles of the Virgin, In: Oelschläger Festschrift, 76. *Mailing Add:* Drawer FL Miss State Univ Mississippi State MS 39762

CHAVES, TERESA LABARTA DE, b Havana, Cuba, Apr 8, 26; US citizen; m 56; c 4. SPANISH LANGUAGE & LITERATURE. *Educ:* Univ Havana, D Phil y Let, 48; Univ Md, College Park, PhD(Span lang & lit), 70. *Prof Exp:* Teacher Latin, St George's Sch, Havana, Cuba, 47-48, vprin, 49-52; prin, Calvert Sch, Havana, 53-56; auxiliary prof Span, Univ Oriente, Santiago, 56-61; instr & asst prof, Howard Univ, 62-70; assoc prof, 70-72, PROF SPAN, UNIV DC, 72- *Mem:* MLA; Am Asn Teachers Span & Port. *Res:* History of the Spanish language; acquisition of the Spanish Language. *Publ:* Auth, Analisis del lenguaje en la Oda a Salinas, 67 & La forma cerrada y la forma abierta en el uso del espacio y del tiempo en el teatro espanol de los siglos XVI y XVII, 68, Hispanofila; Vida de Sto Domingo de Silos por Gonzalo de Berceo, Ed Castalia, Madrid, 73; Translations of poems by Nicolas Guillen, Latin Am Lit Rev II, 73; El soneto A Cristo crucificado, Explicacion de Textos Lit, 74; coauth, Pedro Ponce de Leon, first teacher of the deaf, 74 & Manuel Ramirez de Carrion and his secret method of teaching the deaf, 75, Sign Lang Studies; auth, Critical ed of Rimado de Palacio by Pero Lopez de Ayala, Espasa-Calpe (in press). *Mailing Add:* 3410 Purdue St Hyattsville MD 20783

CHAVOUS, QUENTIN, b Cleveland, Ohio, Oct 21, 30; c 2. ROMANCE LANGUAGES. *Educ:* Ohio State Univ, BA, 57, MA, 60, PhD, 66. *Prof Exp:* Instr comp lit, Ohio State Univ, 62-63; Hisp studies, Smith Col, 63-67; asst prof Romance lang, Rutgers Univ, New Brunswick, 67-73; ASSOC PROF HUMANITIES, UNIV MASS, BOSTON, 73- *Concurrent Pos:* Assoc provost, Univ Mass, Boston, 78. *Mem:* MLA. *Res:* Modern Spanish Literature. *Mailing Add:* Col of Publ & Community Serv Univ of Mass Boston MA 02116

CHAVY, PAUL, b Saint-Florent, France, July 19, 14; m 38; c 2. FRENCH LANGUAGE & LITERATURE. *Educ:* Univ Paris, Agrege des Let, 42. *Prof Exp:* Head dept, 48-69, prof, 48-80, EMER PROF FRENCH, DALHOUSIE UNIV, 80- *Concurrent Pos:* Officier de l'Instruction Publique, 56; Chevalier, Legion d'Honneur, 65. *Mem:* Can Comp Lit Asn (pres, 71-73). *Res:* History of translations. *Mailing Add:* Dept of French Studies Dalhousie Univ Halifax NS B3H 3J5 Can

CHEEK, JOHN H, JR, b Nashville, Tenn, June 26, 24; m 44; c 2. LINGUISTICS. *Educ:* Yale Univ, BA, 50; Harvard Univ, MA, 57, PhD, 59. *Prof Exp:* Asst prof, 59-71, ASSOC PROF RUSSIAN & CHINESE, VANDERBILT UNIV, 71- *Mem:* Am Asn Advan Slavic Studies; Am Orient Soc; SAtlantic Mod Lang Asn; Am Asn Teachers Chinese Lang & Cult; Chinese Inst Am. *Res:* Slavic linguistics. *Mailing Add:* Dept of Ger & Slavic Lang Vanderbilt Univ Nashville TN 37235

CHELKOWSKI, PETER JAN, b Lubliniec, Poland, July 10, 33; m 61, c 2. NEAR EASTERN LANGUAGES & LITERATURES. *Educ:* Jagiellonian Univ, MA, 58; Univ Tehran, PhD(lit), 68. *Prof Exp:* Assoc prof Near Eastern Lang & Lit, 68-75, prof Persian and Iranian studies & chmn near eastern lang & lit, dir ctr near eastern studies, 75-78, PROF NEAR EASTERN STUDIES, NY UNIV, 78- *Mem:* Mid Eastern Studies Asn; Am Orient Soc; Coun Nat Lit. *Res:* Persian religious drama; Persian literature; theatre, drama and literature in the Near East. *Publ:* Ed, Studies in Art and Literature of the Near East in Honor of Richard Ettinghausen, NY Univ & Univ Utah, 74; The Scholar and the Saint: Studies in Celebration of Abu'l Rayhan al-Biruni and Jalal al-Din Rumi, NY Univ, 75; auth, Mirror of the Invisible World, Metrop Mus Art, NY, 75; coauth, Ayneyeh Jehane Qeyb, Conzett & Huber, Zurich-Tehran, 77; ed & contribr, Ta'Ziyeh: Ritual and Drama in Iran, NY Univ Press, 79. *Mailing Add:* Kevorkian Ctr for Near Eastern Studies NY Univ 50 Washington Sq South New York NY 10003

CHELLAS, BRIAN FARRELL, Philosophy. See Vol IV

CHEN, MATTHEW Y, b Amoy, Fukien, China, Oct 12, 38. LINGUISTICS, CHINESE LINGUISTICS. *Educ:* Univ Hong Kong, BA, 67; Univ Calif, Berkeley, PhD(ling), 72. *Prof Exp:* Instr ling, Stanford Univ, 71; asst prof, 71-76, ASSOC PROF LING, UNIV CALIF, SAN DIEGO, 76- *Concurrent Pos:* Guggenheim fel, 74-75; assoc ed, J Chinese Ling, Proj Ling Anal, Berkeley, Calif, 76- *Mem:* Ling Soc Am; Sino-Tibetan Ling Conf. *Res:* Phonology; linguistic analysis of music and poetry. *Publ:* Auth, Cross-dialectal comparison: A case study and some theoretical considerations, J Chinese Ling, 1: 38-63; Metarules and universal constraints in phonological theory, Proc 11th Int Cong Ling, Bologna, Italy, 8-9/72; On the formal expression of natural rules in phonology, 9: 223-249 & Relative chronology: Three methods of reconstruction, 76, J Ling; From middle Chinese to modern Peking, J Chinese Ling, 76; Hierarchy in metrical structure (in prep). *Mailing Add:* Dept of Ling Univ of Calif San Diego La Jolla CA 92093

CHEN, URSULA F, b Osnabrueck, Ger, Feb 24, 26; US citizen; m 56; c 1. ROMANCE PHILOLOGY & LINGUISTICS. *Educ:* Univ Cologne, BA, 50; Cornell Univ, MA, 58, PhD(Romance ling), 68. *Prof Exp:* Teaching asst French, Cornell Univ, 56-59; instr, Rutgers Univ, 59-64; from instr to asst prof, 64-75, ASSOC PROF ROMANCE PHILOL, UNIV MASS, AMHERST, 75- *Mem:* Ling Soc Am; MLA. *Res:* History of Romance languages. *Publ:* Auth, Essai sur Phonologie Francaise: L'evolution Structurale du Vocalismo, Nizet, Paris, 73. *Mailing Add:* 10 Hills Rd Amherst MA 01002

CHENEY, DONALD, English, Comparative Literature. See Vol II

CHENG, CHIN-CHUAN, b Taiwan, China, Dec 30, 36; US citizen; m 64; c 2. LINGUISTICS. *Educ:* Nat Taiwan Univ, BA, 59, MA, 61; Univ Ill, Urbana, PhD(ling), 68. *Prof Exp:* Lectr Chinese, Harvard Univ, 67-69; lectr ling, Univ Calif, Berkeley, 69-70; asst prof, 70-72, assoc prof, 72-80, PROF LING & CHINESE, UNIV ILL, URBANA, 80- *Concurrent Pos:* Assoc ed, J Chinese Ling, 73-; mem, US Ling Deleg People's Rep China, 74; acad mem, Huazhong Inst Technol, China, 80- *Mem:* Ling Soc Am; Asn Asian Studies; Chinese Lang Teachers Asn. *Res:* Chinese linguistics; computational linguistics; Bantu tonology. *Publ:* Auth, A Synchronic Phonology of Mandarin Chinese, Mouton, The Hague, 73; A quantitative study of Chinese tones, J Chinese Ling, 73; contribr, Language and Linguistics in the People's Republic of China, Univ Tex Press, 75; coauth (with Ching-Hsiang Chen), Computer-assisted instruction in Chinese: An interim report, 76 & auth, In defense of teaching simplified characters, 77, J Chinese Ling; Language reform in China in the seventies, Word, 79; coauth (with Charles W Kisseberth), Ikorovere Makua tonology (part 3), Studies in Ling Sci, 81; auth, Chinese varieties of English, In: The Other Tongue: English across Cultures, Univ Ill Press, 82. *Mailing Add:* Dept of Ling Univ of Ill Urbana IL 61801

CHENG, CHING-MAO, b Taiwan, China, Feb, 4, 33; m 65; c 1. CHINESE & JAPANESE LITERATURE. *Educ:* Nat Taiwan Univ, AB, 56, MA, 59; Princeton Univ, MA, 65, PhD(EAsian studies), 70. *Prof Exp:* Instr Chinese lit, Nat Taiwan Univ, 61-62; vis lectr Chinese, Keio Univ, Japan, 66-67; asst prof orient lang, Univ Calif, Berkeley, 67-73; assoc prof, 73-80, PROF CHINESE LIT, UNIV MASS, AMHERST, 80- *Mem:* MLA; Chinese Lang Teachers Asn. *Res:* Chinese classical poetry; modern Japanese literature; Sino-Japanese literary relations. *Publ:* Auth, A Study of Yuan Drama (in Chinese), Yi-wen, Taiwan, 59; A study of Wang Tz'u-hui (in Chinese), Bull Col Arts, Nat Taiwan Univ, 65; Chinese Literature in Japan (in Chinese), Lit Press, Taiwan, 70; Nagai Kafu's concept of fiction, 71 & Chinese history in the writings of Nakajima Atsushi, 72, Tamkang Rev. *Mailing Add:* Asian Studies Prog Thompson Hall Univ of Mass Amherst MA 01002

CH'ENG, HSI, b Hopei Prov, China, Nov 20, 19; m 39; c 3. CHINESE LANGUAGE & LITERATURE. *Educ:* Yenching Univ, China, BA, 48; Cambridge Univ, MLitt, 63. *Prof Exp:* Res asst hist & philol, Acad Sinica, 48-51; tutor lang, Univ Hong Kong, 51-59; lectr Chinese, Cambridge Univ, 59-60 & Univ London, 60-63; sr lectr, Univ Malaya, 63-66; assoc prof Chinese & Orient studies, 66-73, PROF CHINESE LIT & CIVILIZATION, UNIV IOWA, 73- *Concurrent Pos:* Vis prof Chinese lit & civilization, Univ Wash, 69-70. *Mem:* Asn Asian Studies; Am Theatre Asn; Asn Asian Studies; AAUP. *Publ:* Auth, Chinese Painting--Its Spirit and Cultural Background, 56, Ch'eng's New Dialogue of Zen, 59 & The Chinese Translation of the Tirukkural, 67, Univ Hong Kong; A Study of Some Ming and Ch'ing Paintings in the Mu-Fei Collection, Mu-Fei, 65; 400 Chinese Characters, Univ Malaya, 65; coauth, An Anthology of Chinese Verse, Oxford Univ, 67; auth, Ling-ch'ao'hsüan Shih Tz'u Ch'ü Ho Chi, 71 & Landscape Albums, 72, Ling-ch'ao-hsüan, Hong Kong; Calligraphy of Ming Literatis in Correspondence, Pao-Meng-T'ang, Hong Kong, 78. *Mailing Add:* 205 Gilmore Hall Univ of Iowa Iowa City IA 52240

CHERCHI, PAOLO AGOSTINO, b Oschiri, Italy, May 10, 37; m 68. ROMANCE LANGUAGES. *Educ:* Univ Cagliari, Dr(Romance lang), 62; Univ Calif, Berkeley, PhD(Romance lang), 66. *Prof Exp:* From instr to assoc prof, 65-77, PROF ITAL, UNIV CHICAGO, 77- *Mem:* MLA; Mediaeval Acad Am. *Res:* Middle ages, Italian; Provencal literature; Spanish 18th century. *Publ:* Ed, Tommaso Garzoni--Opere, Fulvio Rossi, Naples, 72; Th Silverstein, Poeti e Filosofi Medievali, Adriatica-Bari, 75; auth, Capitoli di Critica Cervantina (1605-1789), 77 & Andrea Cappellano, I Trovatori e Altri Temi Romanzi, 79, Bulzoni, Rome; Encillopedismo E Politica Della Riscrittura: Tommaso Garzoni, Pacini, Pisa, 81. *Mailing Add:* Dept of Romance Lang Univ of Chicago Chicago IL 60637

CHERNISS, HAROLD FREDRICK, b St Joseph, Mo, Mar 11, 04; m 29. GREEK, ANCIENT PHILOSOPHY. *Educ:* Univ Calif, Berkeley, AB, 25, PhD(Greek), 29. *Hon Degrees:* DHL, Univ Chicago, 50; Johns Hopkins Univ, 65; Brown Univ, 76; Laurea honoris causa, Rome, 78. *Prof Exp:* Assoc Greek, Univ Calif, 28-29; instr classics Cornell Univ, 30-33; assoc Greek, Johns Hopkins Univ, 33-36, assoc prof, 36-46; prof Greek, Univ Calif, Berkeley, 46-48; prof, 48-74, EMER PROF GREEK, INST ADVAN STUDY, 74- *Concurrent Pos:* Lectr, Johns Hopkins Univ, 32. *Honors & Awards:* C J Goodwin Award of Merit, Am Philol Asn, 77. *Mem:* Am Philos Soc; Brit Acad; Am Acad Arts & Sci; Royal Acad Arts & Sci, Sweden; Royal Flemish Acad Sci & Letters Belgium. *Res:* Ancient philosophy. *Publ:* Auth, The Riddle of the Early Academy, Russell; Platonism of Gregory of Nyssa, Univ Calif, 30; Aristotle's Criticism of Plato and the Academy, Johns Hopkins, 44. *Mailing Add:* Inst for Advan Study Princeton NJ 08540

CHERPACK, CLIFTON (CYRIL), b New Britain, Conn, Nov 4, 25; m 48; c 2. ROMANCE LANGUAGES. *Educ:* Trinity Col, Conn, BA, 49; Johns Hopkins Univ, MA, 51, PhD(Romance lang), 53. *Prof Exp:* Asst prof Romance lang, Johns Hopkins Univ, 54-58; from assoc prof to prof Romance lang, Duke Univ, 58-67; prof, Wesleyan Univ, 67-68 & Duke Univ, 68-70; PROF ROMANCE LANG, UNIV PA, 70- *Concurrent Pos:* Fulbright Award, France, 53-54. *Mem:* MLA; Am Asn Teachers Fr; Fr Soc Studies 18th Century; Am Soc 18th Century Studies. *Res:* Critical methodology; 17th and 18th century French literature; theory of literature. *Publ:* Auth, Volney's Les ruines and the age of rhetoric, Studies Philol, 57; The Call of Blood in French Classical Tragedy, Johns Hopkins Univ, 58; Is there any eighteenth century French literature?, Fr Rev, 59; An Essay on Crebillon Fils, Duke Univ, 62; The literary periodization of eighteenth century France, 69 & Paul et Virginie and the myths of death, 75, Publ Mod Lang Asn. *Mailing Add:* Dept of Romance Lang Univ of Pa Philadelphia PA 19174

CHERRY, CHARLES MAURICE, b McCormick County, SC, Sept 16, 44; m 73; c 2. SPANISH GOLDEN-AGE LITERATURE. *Educ:* Furman Univ, BA, 65; Univ of SC, MA, 69; Northwestern Univ, PhD(Spanish), 80. *Prof Exp:* Teacher Spanish, George Washington High Sch, Va, 65-67 & Camden High Sch, SC, 67-69; instr, Furman Univ, 69-71; teaching asst, Northwestern Univ, 71-73; teacher, Niles North High Sch, Ill, 73-74; instr, 74-80, ASST PROF SPANISH, FURMAN UNIV, 80- *Mem:* MLA; The Comediantes; Am Coun Teaching Foreign Lang; Am Asn Teachers Spanish & Portuguese. *Res:* Spanish drama of the golden age; foreign language pedagogy; applied linguistics. *Publ:* Ed, A History of the South Carolina Chapter of the American Association of Teachers of Spanish and Portuguese, Furman Univ, 81. *Mailing Add:* Dept Class & Mod Lang Furman Univ Greenville SC 29613

CHEW, JOHN JAMES, JR, b Philadelphia, Pa, Nov 17, 23; m 49, 62; c 5. LINGUISTICS. *Educ:* Columbia Univ, BA, 50; Yale Univ, MA, 52, PhD(ling), 61. *Prof Exp:* Instr & sci linguist, Foreign Serv Inst, 55, sci linguist Slavic & Germanic lang, 61-63; dir, Japanese Lang & Area Sch, Japan, 55-61; from asst prof to assoc prof ling, State Univ NY, Buffalo, 63-66; assoc prof anthrop, 66-77, PROF ANTHROP, UNIV TORONTO, 77- *Mem:* Can Scoiol & Anthrop Asn; Can Soc Asian Studies; Asn Teachers Japanese. *Res:* Japanese and Indo-European linguistics. *Publ:* Auth, On word boundaries in Japanese, 12/64 & The structure of Japanese baby talk, 4/69, J Asn Teachers Japanese; A Transformational Analysis of Modern Colloquial Japanese, Mouton, 73; Standard Japanese and the Hirara dialect: A case of linguistic convergence, J Asn Teachers Japanese, 76; The prehistory of the Japanese Language in the light of evidence from the structures of Japanese & Korean, Asian Perspectives, 78; The relationship between Japanese, Korean, & Altaic language: In what sense genetic, Bull Int Inst Ling Studies, 81. *Mailing Add:* Dept of Anthropology Univ of Toronto Toronto ON M5S 1A1 Can

CHEYNE, HELEN SWEDIUK, b Ukraine; Can citizen. GERMAN LANGUAGE & LITERATURE. *Educ:* Univ Toronto, BA, 57, MA, 58, PhD(Ger), 66. *Prof Exp:* Instr Ger & French, Goucher Col, 59-60; lectr Ger, 61-64, asst prof, 64-68, res & creativity grant, 68-69, chmn dept, 69-72, coordr world lit maj, 73-76, ASSOC PROF GER, WILFRID LAURIER UNIV, 68-, DIR STUDY ABROAD PROG WITH UNIV WATERLOO, 78- *Concurrent Pos:* Can Coun leave fel, 72-73. *Mem:* Can Asn Univ Teachers Ger; Can Asn Univ Teachers; Carl-Zuckmayer-Gesellschaft; Jean-Paul-Gesellschaft. *Res:* Jean Paul; Carl Zuckmayer; 20th century German literature. *Publ:* Auth, Einkräftigkeit, Jean Paul's term for self-destruction, Ger Life & Lett, 73; co-ed, The correspondence of I U Samarin and Baroness Rahden, Wilfrid Laurier Univ, 74; ed, Die Uhr schlägt Eins, Herbert Lang, Bern, Switz, 77; Hermann Hesse's Steppenwolf as a twentieth century comment on Jean Paul's Three Ways of Becoming Happier, Analecta, Helvetica et Germanica, Bouvier, 79; Derr Rattenfänger Bunting, ein gesteigerter Schinderhannes, Blätter der Carl-Zuckmayer-Gesellschaft, 79; Das Thema 'Von vorne wieder anfagen' als Leitmotiv in den Werken vonCarl Zuckmayer, Blätter der Carl-Zuckmayer-Gesellschaft, 80. *Mailing Add:* Dept of German Wilfrid Laurier Univ Waterloo ON N2L 3C5 Can

CHIAPPELLI, FREDI, b Florence, Italy, Jan 24, 21; c 2. HISTORY OF ITALIAN LITERATURE & LANGUAGE. *Educ:* Univ Florence, DLett(Ital), 45. *Hon Degrees:* DLitt, McGill Univ, 78 & Ariz State Univ, 82. *Prof Exp:* Asst Ital, Univ Florence, 45-46; lectr, Univ Zurich, 46-50; prof, Univ Lausanne, 50-69; PROF ITAL, UNIV CALIF, LOS ANGELES, 69-, DIR, CTR MEDIEVAL & RENAISSANCE STUDIES, 72- *Concurrent Pos:* Vis prof, Univ Calif, Los Angeles, 64-65; Cath Univ Am, 66-67 & Univ Toronto, 70; Swiss Nat Fund Sci Res grant, 68-69; Nat Endowment for Humanities grant, 71-74. *Honors & Awards:* Presidential Gold Medal for Cult Merits, Italy; Grand Officer, Order of Merit, Italy; Commander, Palmes Academiques; Hon Prof, Univ Lausanne, 69; Knight, Order of Merit, Spain, 75. *Mem:* Renaissance Soc Am; Mediaeval Acad Am; Dante Alighieri Soc Am; Acad Crusca; Ling Soc Paris. *Res:* Machiavelli; Petrarch; history of Italian literary language. *Publ:* Auth, Studi sul linguaggio del Tasso epico, Le Monnier, Florence, 69; ed, Le opere di Dante, Mursia, Milan, 65; N Machiavelli, Legazioni, Commissarie e Scritti, Laterza, Bari, 71 & 73; auth, Studi sul linguaggio del Petrarca, Olschki, Firenze, 72; auth, Machiavelli e la lingua fiorentina, Boni, Bologna, 74; ed, First Images of America, Univ Calif, 75; Il conoscitore del caos, Bulzoni, Roma, 81; Commento al Tasso, Rusconi, Milano, 82. *Mailing Add:* Medieval & Renaissance Studies Univ of Calif Los Angeles CA 90024

CHIARENZA, FRANK JOHN, English Literature. See Vol II

CHICK, EDSON MARLAND, b Boston, Mass, May 29, 24; m 53; c 4. GERMAN. *Educ:* Brown Univ, AB, 45; Princeton Univ, PhD(Ger), 53. *Prof Exp:* Instr Ger, Princeton Univ, 51; asst prof, Wesleyan Univ, 52-57 & Univ Calif, Riverside, 57-60; assoc prof, State Univ NY, Binghamton, 61-64; from assoc prof to prof, Dartmouth Col, 64-72; PROF GER, WILLIAMS COL, 72- *Concurrent Pos:* Fulbright res grant, Hamburg, 60-61; mem comt examrs, Ger Col Entrance Exam Bd Advan Placement Prog, 71-74; Fulbright res grant, Berlin, 78-79. *Mem:* MLA; Am Asn Teachers Ger; Mod Humanities Res Asn. *Res:* Twentieth century; satire; censorship. *Publ:* Auth, Ernst Barlach, Twayne, 67; Voices in discord: Some observations on Die Judenbuche, Ger Quart, 69; Sternheim's 1913 as satire, Studies Ger Drama, 74. *Mailing Add:* Dept of German Williams Col Williamstown MA 01267

CHICOY-DABAN, JOSE IGNACIO, b Las Plamas, Spain, Dec 9, 25; Can citizen; m 67; c 2. SPANISH LITERATURE. *Educ:* Sophia Univ, Tokyo, BA, 64; Marquette Univ, MA, 66; Univ Toronto, PhD(Span), 74. *Prof Exp:* Asst prof, 74-78, ASSOC PROF SPAN, UNIV TORONTO, 78- *Mem:* Can Asn Hisp; Mediaeval Acad Am; Int Asn Hisp; Soc Int Rencesvals; Can Soc Renaissance Studies. *Res:* Spanish Medieval literature; French epics; Spanish Golden Age literature. *Publ:* Auth, Un Cantar de Gesta perdue de castille sur le theme de la reine sebile, Actes, 7th Int Cong Soc Rencesvals, Univ Liege, 1976, spring 78; Posibles bases historicas de la Chanson de Sebile, Anales Hist Antigua y Medieval, Univ Buenos Aires, Arg, summer 78, 80; La Historia de Enrrique, fi fe Oliua y la chanson de geste Doon de la Roche, Actes, 8th Int Cong Soc Rencesvals, Roncesvaux-Pamplona-Santiago de Compostela, 8/78; Una edicion incunable desconocida de la hystoria de la reyna sebilla, Explicaion Textos Literarios, Calif State Univ, Sacramento, spring 79; De nuevo sobre la Historia de Emrrique fi de Oliua, Etudes De Philologie Romane Et D'Histoire Litteraire Offertes A Jules Horrent, Liege, 80. *Mailing Add:* Dept of Span & Port Univ of Toronto Toronto ON M5S 1A1 Can

CHIH, YU-JU, b Hopei, China, Nov 14, 17; m 50; c 3. CHINESE LANGUAGE, POLITICAL SCIENCE. *Educ:* Nat Univ Peking, BA, 40; Univ Calif, Berkeley, MA, 50; Ind Univ, PhD(govt), 65. *Prof Exp:* Assoc prof, 65-70, chmn dept, 67-74, PROF E ASIAN LANG, IND UNIV, BLOOMINGTON, 70- *Mem:* Asn Asian Studies; Am Polit Sci Asn; AHA; Chinese Lang Teachers Asn (chmn, 69-70). *Res:* Modern political thought and institutions. *Publ:* Auth, Readings in Modern Chinese History and Social Sciences, Univ Mich, 67; Ch'en Tu-hsiu: A Chronological Study, Lung Men, Hong Kong, 74. *Mailing Add:* Dept of E Asian Lang & Cult Ind Univ Bloomington IN 47401

CHILDERS, JAMES WESLEY, b Emma, Tex, June 21, 06; m 36; c 2. SPANISH. *Educ:* Southern Methodist Univ, AB, 27, AM, 28; Centro de Estud Hist, Madrid, dipl, 30; Univ Chicago, PhD, 39. *Prof Exp:* Instr, Agr & Mech Col, Magnolia, Ark, 28-34, 35-36; instr, DePauw Univ, 36-37, asst prof, 37-41; asst prof Span, State Univ NY, Albany, 41-46, prof mod lang, 46-63, chmn dept, 47-63; prof mod foreign lang & chmn dept, Parsons Col, 63-66 & Pershing Col, 66-67; vis scholar & chmn dept foreign lang, 67-71, prof foreign lang, 72-73, EMER PROF FOREIGN LANG, SOUTHERN ARK UNIV, 72- *Mem:* MLA; Am Asn Teachers Span & Port; Am Folklore Soc. *Res:* Spanish folk literature; Spanish picaresque novel. *Publ:* Auth, Sources and analogues of the cuentos in Alcala Yanez Alonso mozo muchos amos; Motif Index of the Cuentos of Juan Timoneda; Reports of surveys and studies in the teaching of modern foreign languages, Mod Lang Asn, 61; Tales From Spanish Picaresque Novels: Motif Index, State Univ NY, 77. *Mailing Add:* 2010 Brookview Rd Castleton on Hudson NY 12033

CHIN, BEVERLY ANN, English. See Vol II

CHING, EUGENE, b Honan, China, June 1, 21; m 64; c 5. CHINESE. *Educ:* Nat Cheng Chi Univ, BA, 45; Columbia Univ, MA, 50, EdD, 59. *Prof Exp:* Instr Chinese, Nat Defense Lang Inst, 53-58; prof English, Morristown Col, 58; prof hist, Lane Col, 58-60; prof English, Jarvis Christian Col, 60-62; from asst prof to assoc prof Chinese, 62-72, chmn EAsian lang & lit, 63-72, PROF CHINESE, OHIO STATE UNIV, 72- *Concurrent Pos:* Fulbright-Hays Act Off Educ res study grant, 68-69. *Mem:* Asn Asian Studies; Chinese Lang Teachers Asn; Am Asn Chinese Studies. *Res:* Chinese language and culture; teaching of Chinese as a foreign language; Chinese syntax and writing system. *Publ:* Coauth, Papers of the CIC Far Eastern Language Institute, Univ Mich, 65; auth, Translation or transliteration: A case in cultural borrowing, Chinese Cult, 66; Wu Feng: An Annotation of a Chinese Motion Picture Script, 67 & Bisywe Hwanghwa: An Annotation of a Chinese Motion Picture Script, 67, Univ Mich; The difference between two and two in Mandarin Chinese, Papers of CIC Far Eastern Lang Inst, 68 & Kuo-yu, Kyo-wen, yu Yu-wen Chiao-hsueh, Chung-Kuo Yu-wen, 68; coauth, Audio-Visual Materials for Chinese Studies, Am Asn Chinese Studies, 74; 201 Chinese Verbs, Barron's Ed Ser, 77. *Mailing Add:* Dept EAsian Lang & Lit Col of Humanities Ohio State Univ Columbus OH 43210

CHISHOLM, DAVID, b New Rochelle, NY, Aug 30, 40; m 71; c 2. GERMAN LANGUAGE & LITERATURE. *Educ:* Oberlin Col, BA, 62; Univ Chicago, MA, 65; Ind Univ, PhD(Ger), 71. *Prof Exp:* Lectr Ger, Ind Univ, 70-71; postdoctoral fel, Univ Cincinnati, 71-72; asst prof, Univ Ill, Urbana, 72-73; asst prof, 73-76, ASSOC PROF GERMAN, UNIV ARIZ, 77- *Concurrent Pos:* Am Coun Learned Societies grant-in-aid, 73-74; Alexander-Von-Humboldt Found res grant, 79-80 & 81-82; Fulbright selection comt, Bonn, Ger, 81; Fulbright travel grant, 81-82. *Mem:* MLA; Am Asn Teachers Ger; Soc Advan of Scand Studies; Asn Lit & Ling Computing; Lessing Soc. *Res:* German lyric and dramatic verse; linguistic and computational approaches to literature; German-Scandinavian comparative literature. *Publ:* Auth, Phonological patterning in German verse, Computers & Humanities, 76; Generative prosody and English verse, Poetics, 77; A survey of computer-assisted research in modern German language and literature, Computers & Humanities, 78; A Prosodic-Phonological Dictionary for Automatic Transcription of Large Corpora of German Verse, Sprache und Datenverarbeitung, 80; Prosodic approaches to twentieth century verse, J Asn Lit & Ling Comput, Vol 2, No 1; Prosodische Aspekte des Blankversdramas: Eine Untersuchung zu sechs Dramen von Goethe, Schiller, Kleist, Grillparzer und Hebbel, In Literaturwissenschaft und empirische Methoden, Vandenhoeck & Ruprecht, Gottingen, 81; Phonology and style: A computer-assisted approach to German verse, Computers and Humanities, 81, German transl, Max Niemeyer Verlag, Tubingen, 82; coauth (with Steven Sondrup), Konkordanz zu den Gedichten Conrad Ferdinand Meyers, Mit einem VersmaB- und Reimschemaregister, Max Niemeyer Verlag, Tubingen, 82. *Mailing Add:* Dept of German Univ of Ariz Tucson AZ 85721

CHITTENDEN, JEAN STAHL, b Davenport, Iowa, Mar 30, 24; div; c 1. ROMANCE LANGUAGES. *Educ:* Univ Ariz, BA, 44; Univ Ill, MA, 48; Univ Tex, Austin, PhD(romance lang), 64. *Prof Exp:* Instr Span & English, Elmhurst Col, 49-52; instr Span, Univ Tex, Austin, 59-64; from asst prof to assoc prof, 64-74, PROF SPAN, TRINITY UNIV, 74-, CHMN DEPT FOREIGN LANG, 70- *Concurrent Pos:* Consult, Dallas Independent Sch Dist, 62, Tex Educ Agency, 62 & MLA, 62-64; reader, Advan Placement Exam, Educ Testing Serv, 72, 74, 75, 77, 78 & 79; exec comt, Asn Dept For Lang, 78-80. *Mem:* MLA; Am Asn Teachers Span & Port; Am Coun Teaching Foreign Lang; AAUP; Asn Depts Foreign Lang. *Res:* Golden Age drama; contemporary Spanish novel. *Publ:* Auth, The emerging generation of novelists in Latin America, Proc Centennial Conf Lating Am Studies, 69. *Mailing Add:* Dept of For Lang Trinity Univ San Antonio TX 78284

CHOLAKIAN, ROUBEN, b July 9, 32; US citizen; m 55; c 2. FRENCH LITERATURE & LANGUAGE. *Educ:* Bates Col, BA, 54; Columbia Univ, MA, 56, PhD, 63. *Prof Exp:* Master French, Pingry Sch, Elizabeth, NJ, 57-60; instr, Univ Va, 60-63; from asst prof to assoc prof, 63-74, dir, Jr Yr in France, 65-66, 69-70, 73-74 & 77-78, PROF FRENCH, HAMILTON COL, 74- *Concurrent Pos:* Assistantship in English, Inst Int Educ, 55-56. *Mem:* MLA. *Res:* French romanticism; Middle Ages; Renaissance. *Publ:* Auth, A reexamination of the tempest scene in the Quart Livre, Fr Studies, spring 67; An uncensored author of the Second Empire, Rev Lit Comp, 7-9/67; William P Shepard Collection of Provencalia, A Critical Bibliography, Hamilton Col, 70; coauth, The ivory tower: A reader, Librairie Hachette, 70; The Early French Novella: An Anthology, State Univ NY, 71; The year abroad in France: An inside look, Fr Rev, 75; auth, Yvette Guilbert in America, Contemp Fr Civilization, spring 77; Narrative structure in Rabelais & the question of the authenticity of the Cinquieme Livre, Fr Studies, 78. *Mailing Add:* Dept of Romance Lang Hamilton College Clinton NY 13323

CHOLDIN, MARIANNA TAX, b Chicago, Ill, Feb 26, 42; m 62; c 2. RUSSIAN & SOVIET STUDIES. *Educ:* Univ Chicago, BA, 62, MA, 67, PhD(librarianship), 79. *Prof Exp:* Slavic bibliogr, Mich State Univ, 67-79; SLAVIC BIBLIOGR, UNIV ILL URBANA-CHAMPAIGN, 69- *Concurrent Pos:* Res dir, Russ & East Europ Ctr, Univ Ill Urbana-Champaign, 80-, dept affil, Grad Sch Libr & Info Sci, 80-; mem, exec comt, Midwest Slavic Conf, 81-84. *Mem:* Am Asn Advan Slavic Studies; Am Libr Asn; Midwest Slavic Conf. *Res:* Russian and Soviet censorship; Russian bibliography; Russian history, culture and literature. *Publ:* Auth, Three early Russian bibliographers, Libr Quart, 44:1-28; Grigorii Gennadi and Russian bibliography: A reexamination, Libri, 25: 13-33; The Russian bibliographical society: 1889-1930, Libr Quart, 46: 1-19; Some developments in nineteenth century bibliography: Russia, Libri, 27: 108-15; Aleksandr Voeikov's travels in Yucatan, 1874, In: Currents in Anthropology, Mouton, The Hague, 79; coauth (with Mary Stuart), Resources for cooperative reference: The University of Illinois Slavic Reference Service as a model, Ref Quart, 21: 34-39; auth, Censorship: Foreign literature in Russia before 1917, In: The Modern Encycl of Russian and Soviet Literatures (in press); ed, Access to Information in the 80s: Proceedings of the First International Conference of Slavic Librarians and Information Specialists, Russica Publ (in press). *Mailing Add:* 1111 S Pine St Champaign IL 61820

CHOMSKY, AVRAM NOAM, b Philadelphia, Pa, Dec 7, 28; m 49; c 3. LINGUISTICS. *Educ:* Univ Pa, BA, 49, MA, 51, PhD(ling), 55. *Hon Degrees:* DHL, Univ Chicago, 67; DLitt, Univ London, 67; LHD, Loyola Univ, La, 70, Swarthmore Col, 70 & Univ Mass, Amherst, 73; LittD, Univ Delhi, 72. *Prof Exp:* From asst prof to prof ling, 55-66, Ferrari P Ward prof mod lang & ling, 66-76, INST PROF LING & PHILOS, MASS INST TECHNOL, 76- *Concurrent Pos:* Vis assoc prof, Columbia Univ, 57-58; NSF fel, Inst Advan Study, Princeton, NJ, 58-59; Soc Sci Res Coun res grant, 59; Am Coun Learned Soc fel, 64-65; vis Becman prof, Univ Calif, Berkeley, 66-67; Guggenheim fel, 71-72; vis Watson prof, Syracuse, 82. *Honors & Awards:* John Locke lectr ling & philos, Oxford Univ, 69; Whidden lectr, McMaster Univ, 75; Woodbridge lectr, Columbia Univ, 79; Kant lectr, Stanford Univ, 80. *Mem:* Nat Acad Sci; Ling Soc Am; Am Acad Arts & Sci; corresp fel Brit Acad; Deutsche Akademie der Natur forscher Leopolding. *Res:* Linguistics; philosophy; social and political theory. *Publ:* Auth, American Power and the New Mandarins, 69; For Reasons of State, Pantheon, 73; Logical Structure of Linguistic Theory, Plenum, 75; Rules and Representations, Columbia, 80; Lectures on Government and Binding, Foris, 81; Towards a New Cold War, Pantheon, 82. *Mailing Add:* Dept of Ling & Philos Mass Inst Technol Cambridge MA 02139

CHOPYK, DAN BOHDAN, b Ukraine, USSR, Jan 2, 25; US citizen; m 56; c 4. RUSSIAN LANGUAGE. *Educ:* Univ Birmingham, BCom, 53; Univ Colo, Boulder, MA, 62; Ukrainian Free Univ, BLaw, 63, PhD(philol), 70. *Prof Exp:* PROF LANG, UNIV UT, 69- *Mem:* Am Asn Advan Slavic Studies; Rocky Mountain Asn Slavic Studies (pres, 79-80); Am Popular Cult Asn; Ukrainian Hist Asn. *Res:* Slavic phonology and morphophonemics; 17th and 18th century East Slavic literature; Slavic folklore and civilization. *Publ:* Auth, Variant phonemic systems of Ukraine, Ling, Vol 98, 73; Systemy fonem Sulm ta deiaki, 76 & Navchannia movy, 76, Ukrainian Free Univ; Soviet calendar celebrations, J Popular Cult, 77; coauth, Fifty saying of the Lord, J Frank Alcheringa, Ethnopoetics, 77; contribr, Literaturna Zbarazchyna, Zbarazka Zemlja, 79; Hovirka pivnichnykh sil Nadstrypy, Pidhajecka Zemlja, 80; Metr, rytm i tonalnist u katrenax, Lesya Ukrainka Symposium, 80. *Mailing Add:* Dept of Lang Univ of Utah Salt Lake City UT 84112

CHORNEY, STEPHEN, b Lvov, Ukraine, Aug 26, 18; US citizen; m 40; c 2. SLAVIC LANGUAGES & LITERATURES. *Educ:* Univ Lvov, Dipl (Slavic lang & lit), 51; Syracuse Univ, MA, 63; Ukrainian Free Univ, PhD(Slavic lang & lit), 66. *Prof Exp:* Instr Ger sec sch, USSR, 42-44, instr Ukrainian, 52-47; instr Russ, Poland, 58-60; instr Russ & Polish, Syracuse Univ, 61-65; assoc prof Russ, State Univ NY Col Brockport, 65-71, prof Slavic lang & lit, 71-80. *Mem:* Am Asn Teachers Slavic & East Europ Lang. *Res:* Syntax of modern Ukrainian; Slavic philology; 20th century Russian and Ukrainian theatre. *Publ:* Co-ed & coauth, Lesja Ukrajinka--dramaturh--novator, Svoboda, 71; Motyvy patriotyzmu i nacional'noji zrady v dramaturhiji Lesi Ukrajinky, In: Pivnicne Sjajvo, Vol V, Slavuta Publ, Edmonton, 71; Svjato vesny v ukrajins'komu folkljori, Vyzvol'nyj sljax, 1-2/73; auth, Istorija ukrajins'koji literaturnoji movv XX storicca, Ukrainian Free Univ, Munich, 75; Die Philosophisch-Historischen Aspekte im Dramatischen Werk von Ivan Kocerha, Mitteilungen, Munich, 76; Teatral'ni ideji te estetycni pryncypy Lesja Kurbasa, Zapysky Naukovoho Tovarystva im Sevcenka (Memoirs of the Shevchenko Scientific Society), Vol 187 76; Ideen und asthetische Grundsatze des Theaters von Les' Kurbas, Mitteilungen, Munich, 77; Voljovi xaraktery v dramatycnyx Frankovyx tvorax, Vyzvol'nyj Sljax, London, Vol 30 77. *Mailing Add:* 8 Trefoil Lane Brockport NY 14420

CHOW, TSE-TSUNG, b Kiyang Co, Hunan, China, Jan 7, 16; US citizen. CHINESE LITERATURE & LANGUAGE. *Educ:* Cheng-chih Univ, China, BA, 42; Univ Mich, Ann Arbor, MA, 50, PhD(polit sci,), 55. *Prof Exp:* Ed-in-chief, New Understanding, Chungking, Ching, 42-43; dir dept munic planning, res & supvr, city govt Chungking, 43-45; dean educ, City Col Pub Admin, Chungking, 44-45; secy to pres, Repub China, 45-47; vis scholar, Harvard Univ, 54-55; res fel, 56-60, res assoc, 60-63; vis lectr, 63, assoc prof, 64-65, PROF E ASIAN LANG & LIT, UNIV WIS-MADISON, 66-, CHMN DEPT, 73- *Concurrent Pos:* Guggenheim Mem Found fel, 66-67; hon pres, Island Soc Singapore, 67- *Honors & Awards:* Medal of Honor, Chinese Govt, 46. *Mem:* Soc Asian Studies; MLA. *Res:* Chinese philosophy, paleography, and history. *Publ:* Auth, The May Fourth Movement: Intellectual Revolution in Modern China, Harvard Univ, 60; The Stormy Petrel (poems), Chiu-tzu, Hong Kong, 61; Research Guide to the May Fourth Movement: Intellectual Revolution in Modern China, Harvard Univ, 63; On the Chinese Couplet: With 71 Cantos, Union Press, 64; ed, Wen-lin: Studies in the Chinese Humanities, Univ Wis, 68; auth, A new study of The Broken Axes in The Book of Poetry, Island Soc, Singapore, 69; ed, A New Index to Mathew's Chinese-English Dictionary, Based on a New System for Arranging Chinese Characters, Univ Wis, 72; auth, On Wang Kuo-wei's Tz'u Poetry, Universal Bk, Hong Kong, 72. *Mailing Add:* Dept of EAsian Lang & Lit Univ of Wis-Madison Madison WI 53706

CHRISTIAN, CHESTER C, JR, b Albany, Okla, July 18, 26; m 50, 67; c 6. SPANISH, SOCIOLOGY. *Educ:* Univ Tex, Austin, BA, 51, MA, 61, PhD(Latin Am studies), 67; Tex Western Col, MA, 63. *Prof Exp:* Audio-visual librn, Univ Tex, Austin, 52-54; owner, Iconic Prod, Tex, 54-55; field rep venereal disease control, Tex State Dept Health, 55-58; teacher pub schs,Tex, 58-63; instr Span, Univ Tex, El Paso, 63-67, assoc prof & dir Inter-Am Inst, 67-73; PROF SPANISH, TEX A&M UNIV, 73- *Mem:* Am Asn Teachers Span & Port; MLA. *Res:* Dimensions of culturalinguistic reality; sociology of the contemporary Latin American novel; bilingualism. *Publ:* Coauth, Bilingualism in a pluralistic society, In: Foreign Language Education, Nat Textbk, 72; auth, Criteria for cultural-linguistic subdivision in the Southwest, In: Bilingualism in the Southwest, Univ Ariz, 73; Social and psychological implications of bilingual literacy, In: The Bilingual Child, Acad Press, 76; Minority language skills before age three, In: Bilingualism in Early Childhood, Newbury Press, 77; The role of language in multicultural education, Educ Horizons, Vol 55 (summer 77); Preschool literacy in Spanish, Hispania, Vol 60; Language and Culture, In: Language and Communication, Hornbeam Press, 80; Reading in Spanish as a Mode of Language Maintenance in the US, In: Bilingual Education for Hispanic Students in the US, Teachers Col Press, 82. *Mailing Add:* 604 Avondale Bryan TX 77801

CHRISTIANSEN, PEDER GEORGE, b Springfield, Ill, July 21, 34; m 59; c 3. CLASSICS. *Educ:* Carroll Col, BA, 56; Univ Wis, MA, 57, PhD, 63. *Prof Exp:* Asst prof Greek & Latin, 63-66, assoc prof classics, 66-70, PROF CLASSICS, TEX TECH UNIV, 70- *Honors & Awards:* AMOCO Distinguished Teaching Award, 79. *Mem:* Am Philol Asn; Am Class League; Class Asn Mid W & S. *Res:* Late Roman Empire. *Publ:* Auth, The Use of Images by Claudius Claudianus, Mouton, 69; Claudian and the East, Historia, 70; Laus Herculis, Hermes, 71; Claudian and eternal Rome, L'Antiquite Classique, 71. *Mailing Add:* 3609 59th St Lubbock TX 79413

CHRISTOFIDES, CONSTANTINE GEORGE, b Alexandria, Egypt, Mar 31, 28; m 52; c 2. FRENCH, ART HISTORY. *Educ:* Univ Mich, MA, 49 & 50, PhD(comp lit), 56. *Prof Exp:* Instr French, Univ Mich, 54-56; instr, Univ Iowa, 56-57, asst prof, 57-59; from asst prof to assoc prof, Syracuse Univ, 59-66; chmn, Dept Romance Lang & Lit, 66-73, assoc dean humanities, 76-79, PROF ROMANCE LANG & LIT, UNIV WASH, 66-, HEAD ART HIST, 79- *Concurrent Pos:* Rev ed, Symposium, 60-66. *Honors & Awards:* Brit Ambassador's Essay Prize, Cairo, 44; Chevalier of the Order of the Palmes Academiques, Paris, 72. *Res:* French literature; cultural history; Romanesque art. *Publ:* Auth, Four recent Camus studies, Symposium, spring 60; Bossuet; Bachelard's aesthetics, J Aesthet, 62; Gaston Bachelard and the imagination of matter, Rev Int Philos, 63; A Cultural History of Medieval and Renaissance Art, 73, 76 & 79. *Mailing Add:* DM-10 Univ of Wash Seattle WA 98195

CHRISTY, THOMAS CRAIG, b Knoxville, Tenn, May 16, 52; US & French citizen. GERMANIC & GENERAL LINGUISTICS. *Educ:* Univ Tenn, Knoxville, BA, 73, MA, 75; Princeton Univ, MA, 77, PhD(Ger & gen ling), 80. *Prof Exp:* Teaching asst Ger, Univ Tenn, Knoxville, 73-75; teaching asst, Princeton Univ, 77-78, lectr, 79-80; instr, Foreign Lang Inst, Rider Col, 78; ASST PROF GER & GEN LING, UNIV CALIF, LOS ANGELES, 80- *Mem:* MLA; Ling Soc Am; Philol Asn Pac Coast; Soc Hist Epistemologie Sci Lang. *Res:* Historiography of linguistics. *Publ:* Auth, Uniformitarianism in nineteenth century linguistics: Implications for a reassessment of the neogrammarian sound law doctrine, Amsterdam Studies Theory & Hist Ling Sci III: Studies Hist Ling, 20: 249-256; Uniformitarianism in Linguistics, John Benjamins, Amsterdam, 82; The relation of rhetorical and stylistic figures to processes of language change, Proc 2nd Int Conf Hist Lang Sci, 82. *Mailing Add:* Dept of Ger Lang Univ of Calif Los Angeles CA 90024

CHRZANOWSKI, JOSEPH, b Providence, RI, Sept 2, 41. SPANISH & LATIN AMERICAN LITERATURE. *Educ:* Fairfield Univ, BA, 66; Pa State Univ, MA, 67, PhD(Span), 71. *Prof Exp:* Assoc prof, 69-80, PROF SPAN, CALIF STATE UNIV, LOS ANGELES, 80- *Mem:* Am Asn Teachers Span & Port; Latin Am Studies Asn; Int Inst Latin-Am Lit; MLA; Philol Asn Pac Coast. *Res:* Latin American novel, theatre and short story. *Publ:* Auth, La estetica grotesca de Juan Ruiz en El Enxienplo De Los Dos Perezosos,

Romance Notes, 70; La Incomunicacion: Sintoma de Enajenacion en Las Novelas de Juan Carlos Onetti, Maldoror, 73; Juan Carlos Onetti y La Piedra en el Charco, Norte, 74; La estructura de Para Esta Noche, Cuadernos Hispanoamericanos, 74; Consideraciones tematicas y esteticas en torno a Todoes Los Gatos son Pardos, Latin Am Theatre Rev, 75; The double in Las Dos Elenas by Carlos Fuentes, Romance Notes, 77; Theme characterization and structure in Los Invasores, Latin Am Theatre Rev, 78; Psychological motivation in Borge's Emmalunl, Lit & Psychol, 79. *Mailing Add:* Dept of Foreign Lang & Lit Calif State Univ Los Angeles CA 90032

CHU, CHARLES J, CHINESE. *Educ:* Nat Cent Univ, China, BA, 43; Univ Calif, Berkeley, MA, 47. *Prof Exp:* Instr Chinese, Yale Univ, 51-65; from asst prof to assoc prof, 65-74, PROF CHINESE, CONN COL, 74-, CHMN DEPT, 65- *Concurrent Pos:* Trustee, Yale-in-China, 70- *Mem:* Chinese Lang Teachers Asn; Asn Asian Studies; MLA. *Res:* Sino-Soviet relations; Chinese communism; Chinese art history and painting. *Publ:* Auth, Sketch of Chinese Geography, 54 & 63, Chi Pai-shih, His Life and Works, 62 & 67, ed, Contemporary Chinese Writings, 71 & auth, Campus Talks, 74, Far East Publ, Yale Univ. *Mailing Add:* Dept of Chinese Connecticut College New London CT 06320

CHU, CHAUNCEY CHENG-HSI, b Chang-shu, Kiang-su, China, Nov 21, 30; m 66; c 2. LINGUISTICS. *Educ:* Taiwan Normal Univ, BA, 53, MA, 59; Univ Tex, Austin, MA, 64, PhD(ling), 70. *Prof Exp:* Instr English, Taiwan Normal Univ, 59-64, asst prof English & ling, 64-67; asst prof ling & Chinese, 69-74, ASSOC PROF CHINESE & LING, UNIV FLA, 74-, DIR, PROG IN LING, 79- *Honors & Awards:* Distinguished Teaching Award, Univ Fla, 75. *Mem:* Ling Asn Can & US; Ling Soc Am. *Res:* Syntactic theory; historical syntax, with special reference to Chinese; tone phonology. *Publ:* Auth, A Contrastive Phonology of Mandarin Chinese and American English, Taiwan Normal Univ, 65; How relevant is historical information to synchronic linguistic description, 70 & Historical syntax and the Chinese pronominal systems, 72, Papers in Ling; The passive construction: Chinese and English, J Chinese Ling, 73; Semantic aspects of action verbs, Lingua, 76; contribr, The Third and Seventh LACUS Forums, Hornbeam, 77 & 80; A Semantico-Syntactic Approach to Contrastive Analysis, IRAL, 78; Linguistics: Theory, Application & Chinese Syntax, 79. *Mailing Add:* Dept of Romance Lang & Lit Univ of Florida Gainesville FL 32611

CHU, WEN-DJANG (JOHN), b Peking, China, Feb 15, 14; m 54; c 3. ASIAN STUDIES. *Educ:* Cheeloo Univ, China, BA, 35; Nat Peking Univ, MA, 37; Univ Wash, MA, 50, PhD, 55. *Prof Exp:* Instr Chinese, hist & polit sci, Seattle Pac Col, 47-56; instr Chinese lang, Yale Univ, 56-61; from asst prof to assoc prof, Chinese lang & lit, 61-71, PROF CHINESE LANG & LIT, UNIV PITTSBURGH, 71- *Concurrent Pos:* Res assoc, China Proj, Univ Wash, 55-56; vis prof, Nanyang Univ, 67-69. *Mem:* Am Asn Chinese Studies; MLA; Asn Asian Studies. *Res:* Modern Chinese history; modern American history; Chinese language and literature. *Publ:* Coauth, A Regional Handbook on Northwest China, Human Rel Area Files, 56; Ai-shan-lu Shih-ch'ao, Com Press, Taipei, 65; auth, The Moslem Rebellion in Northwest China, 1862-1878, Mouton, The Hague, 66; Selections From the New Testment in Chinese--A Text for the Reading and Oral Drill of Biblical Materials, Far East Publ, Yale Univ, 66; A Theoretical Debate Among the Chinese Communists After Their Break with the Soviet Revisionism, yi-fen-wei-er vs he-er-er-ye, 66 & The Case of Comrade Feng Ting and the Three Main Issues in The Great Proletarian Cultural Revolution, 66, Int Dimensions Prog, Univ Pittsburgh. *Mailing Add:* Dept of East Asian Lang & Lit Univ of Pittsburgh Pittsburgh PA 15260

CHU, YONG-CHEN, b China, Oct 5, 17; US citizen. CHINESE LANGUAGE & CULTURE. *Educ:* Nanking Univ, AB, 39; Univ Calif, Berkeley, MA, 41. *Prof Exp:* Instr Chinese, Calif Col, China, 42-43; instr, US Navy Lang Sch, Boulder, Colo, 44-46; LECTR CHINESE, UNIV CALIF, LOS ANGELES, 47- *Mem:* Asn Asian Studies; Am Orient Soc; Am Polit Sci Asn; MLA. *Res:* International relations, language and culture of China. *Mailing Add:* Dept of Oriental Lang Univ of Calif Los Angeles CA 90024

CHUNG, SANDRA LYNN, b Berkeley, Calif, Sept 25, 48. LINGUISTICS. *Educ:* Harvard Univ, AB, 70, PhD(ling), 76. *Prof Exp:* ASST PROF LING, UNIV CALIF, SAN DIEGO, 74- *Concurrent Pos:* Mellon fac fel, Harvard Univ, 77-78. *Mem:* Ling Soc Am. *Res:* Syntactic theory; Austronesian linguistics; linguistic change. *Publ:* Auth, An object-creating rule in Bahasa Indonesia, Ling Inquiry, 76; On the subject of two passives in Indonesian, In: Subject and Topic, Acad Press, 76; On the gradual nature of syntactic change, In: Mechanisms of Syntactic Change, Univ Tex, 77. *Mailing Add:* Dept of Ling C-008 Univ of Calif at San Diego La Jolla CA 92093

CHURCH, DAN MCNEIL, b Winston-Salem, NC, Apr 30, 39; m 63; c 2. TWENTIETH-CENTURY FRENCH DRAMA. *Educ:* Wake Forest Univ, BA, 61; Middlebury Col, MA, 62; Univ Wis, Madison, PhD(French), 68. *Prof Exp:* Asst prof French, Antioch Col, 65-67; asst prof, 67-70, ASSOC PROF FRENCH, VANDERBILT UNIV, 70- *Mem:* MLA; Am Asn Teachers Fr. *Res:* French theater in general; popular and decentralized theater. *Publ:* Auth, Pere Ubu: The creation of a literary type, Drama Surv, winter 65; Le Malentendu: Search for modern tragedy, Fr Studies, winter 65; Structure and dramatic technique in Gide's Saül and Leroi Candaule, PMLA, 10/69. *Mailing Add:* Dept of French & Ital Vanderbilt Univ Nashville TN 37235

CHURCHILL, FREDERICK J, b Worcester, Mass, July 8, 17; m 44; c 4. GERMAN, FOREIGN LANGUAGES. *Educ:* Clark Univ, BA, 39; Middlebury Col, MA, 47; NY Univ, PhD(Ger), 52. *Prof Exp:* From instr to assoc prof Ger, Hofstra Col, 46-59; dist dir foreign lang, Pub Schs, NY, 59-65; prof Ger & educ, 65-67, chmn dept foreign lang, 66-68, PROF GER, HOFSTRA UNIV, 68- *Concurrent Pos:* Fulbright exchange, Ger, 55-56; dir, NE Conf Teaching Foreign Lang, 65-67 & 70-73; consult, MLA, 66-69. *Mem:* MLA; Am Asn Teachers Ger. *Res:* Contemporary German literature; Friedrich Schiller. *Mailing Add:* Dept of Comp Lit & Lang Hofstra Univ Hempstead NY 11550

CHURMA, DONALD GEORGE, b Pittsburgh, Pa, Sept 12, 46. LINGUISTICS, AFRICAN LANGUAGES. *Educ:* Mich State Univ, BS, 68, MA, 73; Ohio State Univ, PhD(ling), 79. *Prof Exp:* Lectr ling, Ohio State Univ, 80; Fulbright prof, Univ du Benin, Lome, Togo, 81-82. *Mem:* Ling Soc Am. *Res:* Tonology; rule interactions; methodology and argumentation. *Publ:* Auth, Child language acquisition and the justification of linguistic hypotheses, CLS XI, 75; Is Hausa a suprasegmental language?, Ohio State Working Papers Ling, Vol 20, 75; On choosing between linguistic analyses: A reply to Klausenburger, Lingua, 77; Some initial observations on English stress, CLS Bk Squibs, 77; We must argue about rule ordering, Ling Anal, 80; Diachronic evidence for synchronic analyses in phonology & Some further problems for upside down phonology, Ohio State Univ Press Working Papers Ling, Vol 25, 81; Rule inversion in Chadic: A closer look, Studies African Ling, 82. *Mailing Add:* Dept of Ling Ohio State Univ Columbus OH 43210

CHVANY, CATHERINE VAKAR, b Paris, France, Apr 26, 27; US citizen; m 48; c 3. SLAVIC LANGUAGES & LITERATURES. *Educ:* Radcliffe Col, BA, 63; Harvard Univ, PhD(Slavic lang & lit), 70. *Prof Exp:* Instr Russ, Wellesley Col, 66-67; instr, 67-70, lectr, 70-71, asst prof, 71-74, ASSOC PROF RUSS, MASS INST TECHNOL, 74- *Concurrent Pos:* Fel, Harvard Russ Res Ctr, 79- *Honors & Awards:* Lilly Postdoctoral Teaching Award fel, Mass Inst Technol, 75-76. *Mem:* Am Asn Advan Slavic Studies; Ling Soc Am; Am Asn Teachers Slavic & EEurop Lang. *Res:* Syntax; Russian language teaching; Bulgarian. *Publ:* Contribr, Papers from Chicago Linguistic Soc, Univ Chicago, 73; auth, Stylistic uses of affective suffixes in Leskov, In: Festschrift for V Setchkarev, Wilhelm Fink, Munich, 74; co-ed, Slavic Transformational Syntax, Mich Slavic Publ, 74 & 77; auth, On the Syntax Of Be-Sentences in Russian, Slavica, 75; contribr, Slavic & East Europ J, Folia Slavica, Berkeley Ling Soc, 78; coauth, Proc of 8th Int Cong Slavists; co-ed, Morphosyntax in Slavic, Slavica, 80; auth, On the nature of definiteness in Bulgarian, Russian and English, Proc 9th Int Cong Slavists. *Mailing Add:* Dept of Russian Room 14N 216 Mass Inst Technol 77 Massachusetts Ave Cambridge MA 02139

CICCONE DE STAFANIS, STEFANIA, b Rome, Italy, Nov 21, 30; Can citizen; m 56; c 2. ITALIAN LANGUAGE & LITERATURE. *Educ:* Univ Florence, Dr Chimica, 54, Dr Lett, 69; Univ BC, MS, 59, MA, 63. *Prof Exp:* Lectr chem, 58-60, lectr Ital, 60-63, from instr to asst prof, 63-70, ASSOC PROF ITAL, UNIV BC, 70- *Mem:* Am Asn Teachers Ital; MLA; Can Soc Ital Studies; Assoc Int Studies Lingua e Lett Ital. *Res:* Italian literature of the 19th century; history of Italian language. *Publ:* Auth, Boccaccio nelle discussioni linguistiche del primo ottocento, Studies Boccaccio, 70; La Questione Della Lingua nei Periodici Letterari del Primo Ottocento, Olschk, Florence, 71. *Mailing Add:* Dept of Hisp & Ital Studies Univ of BC Vancouver BC V6T 1W5 Can

CIHOLAS, KARIN NORDENHAUG, b Roanoke, Va; m 62; c 2. COMPARATIVE LITERATURE, FRENCH. *Educ:* Westhampton Col, BA, 62; Univ NC, Chapel Hill, MA, 70, PhD(comp lit), 72. *Prof Exp:* Instr comp lit, Univ NC, Chapel Hill, 72-73; instr mod lang, Campbell Col, 72-74; asst prof, 74-78, ASSOC PROF MOD LANG, CENTRE COL, 78-, CHMN, HUMANITIES DIV, 79- *Mem:* MLA. *Res:* Andre Gide; Thomas Mann; 20th century literary criticism. *Publ:* Auth, Gide's Art of the Fugue: A Thematic Analysis of Les Faux-Monnayeurs, Univ NC, 74. *Mailing Add:* Centre Col Danville KY 40422

CIKLAMINI, MARLENE HIEDEWOHL, b Croydon, Eng, July 1, 33; US citizen; m 60. LANGUAGES. *Educ:* Douglass Col, Rutgers Univ, BA, 56; Yale Univ, MA, 58, PhD, 61. *Prof Exp:* From instr to assoc prof Ger, 59-74, PROF GER, DOUGLASS COL, RUTGERS UNIV, NEW BRUNSWICK, 75- *Concurrent Pos:* Res Coun fac fel, Rutgers Univ, 67-68. *Mem:* Mediaeval Acad Am; Folklore Soc London; fel, Medieval Acad Ireland. *Res:* Old Norse. *Publ:* Auth, The old Icelandic duel, Scand Studies, 63; The concept of honor in Valla-Ljotssaga, J English & Ger Philol, 66; Grettir and Ketill hoengr, the giantkillers, ARV, J Scand Folklore, 66; Old Norse epic and historical tradition, Folklore & Traditional History, 73; Ynglinga saga: Its function and its appeal, Mediaeval Scand, 75; Snorri Sturluson, Twayne Publ, 78; A Portrait of a Politician: Erlingr skakki in Heimskringla and in Fagrskinna, Euphorion, 81. *Mailing Add:* Dept of Ger Lang & Lit Douglass Col Rutgers Univ New Brunswick NJ 08903

CIMERHANZEL-NESTLERODE, SAMYE-RUTH MOTT, b Houston, Tex, Jan 25, 35; m 78; c 4. SPANISH LANGUAGE & CULTURE. *Educ:* Univ Houston, BA, 68, MA, 70, EdD, 80; Univ Mex, licenciado, 74. *Hon Degrees:* PhD, Swathmore Univ. *Prof Exp:* Lang lab instr, 64-68, dir, 68-70, teaching fel, 68-70, instr, 70-74, asst prof, 74-76, PROF SPANISH, UNIV HOUSTON, 80-, CHMN DEPT, 76- *Concurrent Pos:* Consult, Tex Educ Agency, 76- & Educ Consult Serv, 80-; lectr, Univ Complutense, Madrid, 77 & Univ Guadalajara, Mex, 78; appointee, Pres comn higher educ, 82. *Mem:* Am Asn Teachers of Spanish & Portuguese; MLA; South Cent Mod Lang Asn; Am Asn Educ Res; Southern Asn Educ Res. *Res:* Foreign language teaching methodology; Spanish language and philology; history, culture and civilization of Mexico. *Publ:* Coauth, Essentials of English Grammar for Foreign Language Students, Hinton Press, 75; Fuentes para conversacion y composicion, 76, auth, Teacher's Manual, El idioma celestial, 77, Workbook, El idioma Celestial, 77 6 El idioma celestial: Un curso fundamental de espanol, 77, Van Nostrand-Reinhold; auth, A study comparing student attitude and achievement in college level Spanish under two instructional approaches: Individualized and lecture recitation, In: Proc of the Second Nat Conf on Individualized Instr in Foreign Lang, Ohio State Univ, 81; coauth, Individualizing instruction in college level Spanish: A study of student achievement and attitude, ERIC Clearinghouse on Lang & Ling, 1/82; auth, Method or madness? It is all a matter of attitude, The Mod Lang J, 11/82. *Mailing Add:* 17414 Swansbury Cypress TX 77429

CIMINI, FRANK A, b Scranton, Pa, Oct 20, 14; m 41; c 2. SPANISH. *Educ:* Univ Scranton, BA, 39; Fordham Univ, MA, 53. *Prof Exp:* Instr, 42-46, asst prof, 47-72, PROF SPAN, UNIV SCRANTON, 72- *Mem:* MLA; AAUP. *Mailing Add:* Dept of Foreign Lang Univ of Scranton Scranton PA 18510

CINTAS, PIERRE FRANCOIS DIEGO, b Sfax, Tunisia, Feb 19, 29; c 2. GENERAL & FRENCH LINGUISTICS. *Educ:* Univ Colo, MA, 62; Ind Univ, PhD(French ling), 69. *Prof Exp:* Teacher French & Latin, Vt Acad, 59-60; teaching asst French, Univ Colo, 60-62; lectr phonetics, Univ Grenoble, 62-63; teaching asst French, Ind Univ, 63-65; lectr, Harvard Univ, 65-70; asst prof French & ling, Univ Va, 70-76; asst prof French & educ, Dalhousie Univ, 76-78; ASST PROF FRENCH, PA STATE UNIV, 78- *Concurrent Pos:* Bibliogr ling, Mod Lang Asn Int Bibliog, 69-80; assoc ed, Bibliog of Am Coun Teaching Foreign Lang, 76-82; instr, French Sch, Middlebury Col, 77- *Honors & Awards:* Chevalier des Palmes Academiques. *Mem:* Am Asn Teachers Fr; MLA; Am Coun Teaching Foreign Lang; Ling Soc Am; Int Phonetic Asn. *Res:* French syntax; applied linguistics; language acquisition. *Publ:* Auth, Self evaluation and a sense of responsibility, Fr Rev, 68; Teacher evaluation, AAUP Bull, 71; Mechant Poete vs Poete Mechant, In: Papers in Linguistics and Phonetics to the Memory of Pierre Delattre, 72; Apprentissage et Maitrise du langage, Bull FIPF, 74; coauth, Aspect in English and German in a semantically based model, Views on Lang, 75; Language acquisition, 1977 Northeast Conf Reports, 77; auth, Aspect, aktionsart and lexicalization, In: Contrastive Linguistics, Hochschul Verlag, Stuttgart, 78. *Mailing Add:* Pa State Univ Ogontz Campus 1600 Woodland Rd Abington PA 19001

CIOFFARI, VINCENZO, b Calitri, Italy, Feb 24, 05; nat US; m 37; c 1. ROMANCE LANGUAGES & LITERATURES. *Educ:* Cornell Univ, AB, 27, AM, 28; Columbia Univ, PhD, 35. *Prof Exp:* Lectr, Col New Rochelle, 31-35; eve session, Hunter Col, 38-43, 45-46; assoc prof, State Univ Iowa, 43-44, mod lang ed, D C Heath & Co, Boston, Mass, 46-67; prof romance lang, 67-71, SCHOLAR-IN-RESIDENCE, BOSTON UNIV, 71- *Concurrent Pos:* Writer, US Armed Forces Inst & US War Dept, 43-45; ling expert & instr army personnel, Brazil; nat chmn, 1965 Dante Centenary Celebration, 63-65. *Honors & Awards:* Nat Foreign Lang Achievement Award, 61; Hon Life Mem Award, Societa Dantesca Italiana, 73; Cavaliere al Merito, Repubblica Italiana, 74. *Mem:* MLA; Mediaeval Acad Am; Dante Soc Am (pres, 67-73); Ling Soc Am; Am Asn Teachers Ital (vpres, 41). *Res:* Dante literature; Dante commentators; fortune and fate through 14th century. *Publ:* Coauth, Spanish Review Grammar, 57, 64, 72 & 79, auth, Beginning Italian Grammar, 58, 65 & 79, coauth, Il Segreto di Luca, 64 & La Nuvola de Smog, 67, Heath; auth, The importance of the commentary of Guido da Pisa, 68 & Canto VIII of the Paradiso, 72, Dante Studies; Fortune, fate and chance, Dictionary Hist Ideas, Scribners, 73; Guido da Pisa's Commentary on the Inferno, Dante Soc Am, 74; coauth, Repaso practico y cultural, Heath, 77. *Mailing Add:* Dept of Mod Lang CLA Boston Univ 718 Commonwealth Ave Boston MA 02115

CIPLIJAUSKAITE, BIRUTE, b Kaunas, Lithuania, Apr 11, 29; Can citizen. ROMANCE LANGUAGES. *Educ:* Lycee Lithuanien, Tubingen, Ger, BA, 47; Univ Montreal, MA, 56; Bryn Mawr Col, PhD(Span lit), 60. *Prof Exp:* From instr Span to prof, 60-73, JOHN BASCOM PROF SPAN, UNIV WIS-MADISON, 73- *Concurrent Pos:* Univ Wis res grants, 62, 66, 68 & 71; Guggenheim fel, 67-68; fel, Inst Res Humanities, Madison, 71-72; consult to pres, State Univ NY Stony Brook, 76-78. *Mem:* Inst Res Humanities; Am Asn Teachers Span & Port; Inst Lithuanian Studies; Asn Int Hispanistas. *Res:* Spanish poetry, contemporary and Golden Age; 19th and 20th century novel; Lithuanian literature, 19th to 20th centuries. *Publ:* Auth, La soledad y la poesia espanola contemporanea, 62 & El poeta y la poesia (Del Romanitcismo a la poesia social), 66, Insula, Madrid; ed, Sonetos completos, Luis de Gongora, Castalia, Madrid, 68, 75 & 80; auth, Baroja, un estilo, Insula, Madrid, 72; Deber de plenitud: La poesia de Jorge Guillen, SepSetentas, Mex, 73; ed, Jorge Guillen (El escritor y la critica), Taurus, Madrid, 76; Sonetos, Luis de Gongora, Hisp Sem Medieval Studies, 81; Los noventayochistas y la historia, Porrua Turanzas, Madrid, 81. *Mailing Add:* Dept of Span Univ of Wis Madison WI 53706

CIRURGIAO, ANTONIO AMARO, b Chaves, Port, Apr 12, 33; US citizen. PORTUGUESE, SPANISH. *Educ:* Inst Filosofico, Port, BA, 55; Assumption Col, MA, 65; Univ Wis-Madison, PhD(Port & Span), 70. *Prof Exp:* Teacher, Salesian High Schs, Port, 55-60; teacher French & Latin, Chester High Sch, Mass, 63-64; teacher Span & Latin, Worcester Acad, Mass, 64-65; instr French & Span, Ft Hays Kans State Col, 65-66; lectr Latin, French & Span, Univ Nev, Reno, 66-68; from instr to asst prof Port & Span, 69-72, assoc prof, 73-79, PROF PORT & SPAN, UNIV CONN, 80- *Concurrent Pos:* Gulbenkian Found fel, 67-; Univ Conn res found fel, 69-; res found fel, Inst de Alta Cultura, Lisbon, Port, 70-71. *Mem:* Am Asn Teachers Span & Port; Soc Lingua Portuguesa; Am Asn Port & Brazilian Cult (pres, 71-). *Res:* Peninsular literature of the Renaissance; poetry of the Renaissance; Portuguese and Brazilian novel. *Publ:* Ed, A estrutura de A ilustre casa de Ramires de Eca de Queiroz, Rev Ocidente, 69; O cancioneiro de D Cecilia de Portugal, 72 & Camonian symposium commemorating the four hundredth anniversay of The Lusiads, 72, Ocidente, Lisbon; auth, Ineditos de Correia Garcao e Basilio da Gama no MS 1842 do ANTT, Biblos, Coimbra, 74; Simbolismo religioso em Dao-lalalas de Guimaraes Rosa, Ocidente, 74; Fernao Alvares do Oriente--O Homem e a Obra, Gulbenkian, Paris, 76; Uma leitura alegorica do Auto dos Anfitrioes de Luis de Camoes, Rev Bracara Augusta, Braga, 80; Frei Agostinho da Cruz e o homo viator, Rev Coloquio-Letras, Lisbon, 81. *Mailing Add:* Dept of Romance & Class Lang Univ of Connecticut Storrs CT 06268

CIRUTI, JOAN ESTELLE, b Ponchatoula, La, Aug 8, 30. FOREIGN LANGUAGES. *Educ:* Southeastern La Univ, BA, 50; Univ Okla, MA, 54; Tulane Univ, PhD(Span), 59. *Prof Exp:* Instr Span, Univ Okla, 57-59, asst prof, 59-63; from asst prof to prof, 63-77, chmn dept, 65-71 & 75-81, dean students, 71-74, PROF ON HELEN DAY GOULD FOUND, MT HOLYOKE COL, 77- *Concurrent Pos:* Res asst lang develop prog, US Off Educ, 59-60; consult, Educ Testing Serv, 68-78; Andrew W Mellon fel, Mt Holyoke Col, 79-80. *Honors & Awards:* Distinguished Alumnus for 1973, Southeastern La Univ, 73. *Mem:* AAUP; Am Asn Univ Women; MLA; Am Asn Teachers Span & Port; Am Coun Teaching Foreign Lang. *Res:* Mexican literature; visual arts. *Publ:* Contrib ed, poetry, In: Handbook of Latin American Studies, Univ Fla, Vol 28 (1966), Vol 30 (1968) & Vol 31 (1970); coauth, Modern Spanish, Harcourt, 2nd ed 66 & Continuing Spanish, Am Bk Co, 67; auth, Leopoldo Lugones: The short stories, Inter-Am Rev of Bibliog, 4-6/75. *Mailing Add:* Dept of Span & Ital Mt Holyoke Col South Hadley MA 01075

CISMARU, ALFRED, b Paris, France, Oct 26, 29; US citizen; m 57; c 2. FRENCH LITERATURE. *Educ:* Fordham Univ, BS, 56; NY Univ, MA, 58, PhD, 60. *Prof Exp:* Instr French & Span, Brooklyn Col, 58-59; from assoc prof to prof French, St Michael's Col (Vt), 59-70, chmn dept lang, 59-70, fac res fund awards, 62-68; PROF CLASS & ROMANCE LANG, TEX TECH UNIV, 70- *Mem:* MLA; Am Asn Teachers Fr. *Res:* French literature of the 18th century; contemporary French literature. *Publ:* Auth, Marguerite Duras, Twayne, 71; Boris Vian, G K Hall, 73; Marivaux and Moliere: A Comparison, Tex Tech Press, 77. *Mailing Add:* Dept of Class & Romance Lang Tex Tech Univ Lubbock TX 79409

CIVIL, MIGUEL, b Sabadell, Spain, May 7, 26; m 60; c 2. ASSYRIOLOGY, LINGUISTICS. *Educ:* Univ Paris, PhD(Orient studies), 58. *Prof Exp:* Res assoc Assyriol, Univ Pa, 58-63; from asst prof to assoc prof Near Eastern Lang & civilizations & ling, 63-70, PROF NEAR EASTERN LANG & CIVILIZATIONS & LING, UNIV CHICAGO, 70- *Concurrent Pos:* Mem ed bd, Chicago Assyrian Dict, 67-; dir d'etudes associe etranger, Sorbonne, 68-70; ed, Materials for the Sumerian Lexicon, 68- *Mem:* Am Orient Soc; Am Sch Orient Res. *Res:* Sumerian grammar and literature; anthropology of Mesopotamia; lexicography. *Publ:* Auth, Prescriptions medicales Sumeriennes, Rev D'Assyriol, 60; The message of Lu-dingirra, J Near Eastern Studies, 64; Notes on Sumerian lexicography, J Cuneiform Studies, 66; coauth, Vol IX, Materials for the Sumerian Lexicon, 67 & auth, Vol XIII, 71, Pontificio Inst Biblico, Rome. *Mailing Add:* Oriental Institute Univ Univ of Chicago Chicago IL 60637

CLACK, JERRY, b New York, NY, July 22, 26. CLASSICS. *Educ:* Princeton Univ, BA, 46; Univ Pittsburgh, MA, 58, PhD(classics), 62; Duquesne Univ, MA, 77. *Prof Exp:* Doc officer, US Nat Comn for UNESCO, 46-51; account exec, Pub Rels Res Serv, 52-53; exec dir, Allegheny County Chap, Nat Found, 53-68; PROF CLASSICS, DUQUESNE UNIV, 69- *Concurrent Pos:* Treas, Pa Class Asn, 76-; ed, Class World, 78- *Mem:* Class Asn Atlantic States (pres, 78-69); Am Philol Asn; Am Class League. *Res:* Alexandrian poetry; Silver Age poetry; Spanish baroque literature. *Publ:* Auth, Vegil engaged, Class World, 72; The Medea similes of Apollonius Rhodius, Class J, 73; Vergil abused, Juvenal amused, Class Outlook, 74; To those who fell on Agrippina's pen, Class World, 75; Otium tibi molestum est, Class Bull, 76; Non ego nunc (Propertius 1 6), 77 & Anthology of Alexandrian poetry, 82, Class World. *Mailing Add:* Dept of Classics Duquesne Univ Pittsburgh PA 15232

CLAESGES, AXEL WALTER, b Zeitz, Ger, Apr 16, 37; US citizen; m 63; c 2. GERMAN LANGUAGE & LITERATURE. *Educ:* Univ Tampa, AB, 61; Vanderbilt Univ, MA, 67, PhD(Ger), 68. *Prof Exp:* Asst prof Ger, Southern Methodist Univ, 69-74; ASSOC PROF GER, WVA UNIV, 74- *Concurrent Pos:* Consult, Salzburg Sem Am Studies, Austria, 79- *Mem:* Am Asn Teachers Ger; Am Coun Teaching Foreign Lang; AAUP. *Res:* Nineteenth century literature; cultural history. *Publ:* Auth, Geistesgeschichte: The rise and decline of an approach to German literature, Taius, 11/76. *Mailing Add:* 809 Cottonwood St Morgantown WV 26505

CLARK, CHARLOTTE, b Brno, Czech, July 19, 10; m 40; c 1. GERMANIC & ROMANCE LANGUAGES. *Educ:* Charles Univ, Prague, BA, MA & PhD(Germanic & Romance lang), 35. *Prof Exp:* Prof Ger, Dept Educ, Czech, 35-40; lang mistress Latin & French, Dept Educ, Sydney, Australia, 48-58; from asst prof to prof Ger, 60-76, head dept, 73-76, EMER PROF GER, UNIV HARTFORD, 76- *Mem:* MLA; Am Asn Teachers Ger. *Publ:* Auth, Origin and Development of German Family Names in the 12th and 13th Centuries, Reichenberg, Czech, 35; German for Medical Practitioners, Prague, Czech, 40. *Mailing Add:* Dept of German Univ of Hartford Bloomfield West Hartford CT 06117

CLARK, EVE VIVIENNE, b Camberley, Eng, July 26, 42; m 67. LINGUISTICS, PSYCHOLINGUISTICS. *Educ:* Univ Edinburgh, MA, 65, dipl, 66, PhD(ling), 69. *Prof Exp:* Res assoc lang, 69-70, lectr, 70-71, asst prof ling, 71-77, ASSOC PROF LING, STANFORD UNIV, 77- *Concurrent Pos:* NSF grant, Stanford Univ, 71-75, 75-79 & 80-83; Spencer Found grant, 79-80 & 80-83; fel, Ctr Adv Study Behavioral Sci, 79-80. *Mem:* Ling Soc Am; Soc Res Child Develop; Int Asn Study Child Lang. *Res:* Language acquisition; semantics; word-formation. *Publ:* Coauth, Psychology and Language, Harcourt Brace Jovanovich, 77; auth, The Ontogenesis of Meaning, Athenaien, 79; Meanings and concepts, In: Carmichael's Manual of Child Psychology (in press); Acquisition of Romance, with special reference to French, In: The Crosslinguistic Study of Language Acquisition (in press); Language Change During Language Acquisition, In: Advances in Child Development, Vol 2 (in press). *Mailing Add:* Dept of Ling Stanford Univ Stanford CA 94305

CLARK, FRED M, b Marianna, Fla, Oct 29, 43. SPANISH GOLDEN AGE LITERATURE. *Educ:* Univ Fla, BA, 64, PhD(Span & Port), 68. *Prof Exp:* From instr to asst prof, 67-68, assoc prof, 68-79, PROF SPAN & PORT, UNIV NC, CHAPEL HILL, 79- *Res:* Brazilian literature; Brazilian novel; Golden Age comedia. *Publ:* Auth, Objective tests of authenticity and the attribution to El toledano vengado to Lope de Vega, Hispanofila, 69; A note on the authorship of a comedia attributed to Lope: Alejandro el segundo, Romance Notes, 69; Objective Methods for Testing Authenticity and the Study of Ten Doubtful Comedias Attributed to Lope de Vega, Univ NC, 71; Galician literature and Salvador Garcia Bodano, SAtlantic Mod Lang Bull, 73; coauth (with Ana Lucia Gazolla de Garcia), Twentieth Century Brazilian Theatre: Essays, Estudios de Hispanofila, 78; transl, The Wedding Dress, Nelson Rodriques' Vestido de noiva, Ediciones Albatros-Hispanofila, 80. *Mailing Add:* Dept of Romance Lang Dey Hall Univ of NC Chapel Hill NC 27514

CLARK, GEORGE RICHARD, English. See Vol II

CLARK, HOOVER W, b Pleasant Grove, Utah, Dec 10, 39; m 52; c 4. FRENCH. *Educ:* Brigham Young Univ, BA, 54, MA, 58; Syracuse Univ, PhD(French), 64. *Prof Exp:* Asst prof French, Univ NDak, 62-64; asst prof, 64-68, ASSOC PROF FRENCH, BRIGHAM YOUNG UNIV, 68- *Res:* Nineteenth century French literature, especially of Gustave Flaubert; interrelationship of the various arts, especially in 19th century France. *Mailing Add:* 236 McKay Bldg Brigham Young Univ Provo UT 84601

CLARK, JOHN RICHARD, b Dayton, Ohio, June 11, 47. CLASSICAL LANGUAGES, MEDIEVAL LATIN. *Educ:* Univ Cincinnati, BA, 69; Cornell Univ, MA, 71, PhD(class), 74. *Prof Exp:* Asst prof, Univ Pa, 75-79; ASST PROF CLASS, MEDIEVAL & PALAEOGRAPHY, FORDHAM UNIV, 80- *Mem:* Am Philol Asn; Medieval Acad Am. *Res:* Marsilio Ficino's De vita(1489); medieval Latin love lyric; Plautus. *Publ:* Auth, Structure and symmetry in the Bacchides of Plautus, Transactions of the Am Philol Asn, 76; Two ghost editions of Marsilio Ficino's De vita, Papers of the Bibliog Soc of Am, 79; Teaching Medieval Latin, Class J, 79; Word play in Plautus' Amphitruo, Class Philol, 80; Marsilio Ficino among the alchemists, Class Bull (in prep). *Mailing Add:* Dept of Class Fordham Univ Bronx NY 10458

CLARK, KATERINA, b Melbourne, Australia, June 20, 41; m 74; c 2. SOVIET LITERATURE & SOCIETY. *Educ:* Melbourne Univ, BA, 63; Australian Nat Univ, MA, 67; Yale Univ, MPhil, 69, PhD(Slavic), 71. *Prof Exp:* Asst prof, State Univ NY, Buffalo, 70-72, Wesleyan Univ, 72-76 & Univ Texas, Austin, 76-80; ASST PROF RUSSIAN, IND UNIV, 81- *Mem:* MLA; Am Asn Advan Slavic Studies; Am Asn Teachers Slavic & East Europ Lang; Am Counc Teachers Russ. *Publ:* Auth, Boy gets tractor and all that: The parable structure of the Soviet novel, Russ & Soviet Lit, 77; Utopian anthropology as a context for Stalinist literature, In: Stalinism: Essays in Historical Interpretation, Norton, 77; Little heroes and big deeds: Literature responds to the first five-year plan, In: Cultural Revolution in Russia, 1928-31, Ind Univ Press, 78; The Soviet Novel: History as Ritual, Chicago Univ Press, 81; Zhdanovist literature and village prose, Proc Sec World Congress of Russ & East Europ Studies, 82; How Konstantin Vaginov's intellectual milieu is refracted in his Kozlinaja pesn, Russian Hist, 82 ; coauth, M M Bakhtin and his circle of the twenties, Esprit, 82. *Mailing Add:* Slavic Dept Ind Univ Bloomington IN 47405

CLARK, MARGARET LOUISE, b Dixie, Ga; m 54. FRENCH LANGUAGE & CULTURE. *Educ:* Univ Ark, Pine Bluff, BA, 52; Univ Paris, cert, 65; Univ Besancon, cert, 65; Univ Ark, Fayetteville, MA, 68, EdD, 78. *Prof Exp:* Vis instr Fr, 69, instr, 69-72, ASST PROF FRENCH & SEC EDUC, UNIV ARK, FAYETTEVILLE, 72- *Mem:* Am Coun Teaching For Lang; Am Asn Teachers Fr; AAUP; Teachers of English to Speakers Other Lang. *Res:* Foreign language study as a component of career training and advancement; foreign language study as a component of global education, particularly French language and culture; French culture, cultural differences in Francophone countries, French influences in America, especially in Arkansas. *Publ:* Coauth, Why or Why Not Foreign Languages, For Lang Annals, 9-10/81; Univ Ark, Dept of Foreign Languages, In: Part Two: Selected Program Descriptions, The Teaching Apprentice Program in Language and Literature, MLA, 81. *Mailing Add:* PO Box 704 Fayetteville AR 72702

CLARK, MARY MORRIS, b Tuscaloosa, Ala, Dec 28, 41; c 3. LINGUISTICS, AFRICAN LANGUAGES. *Educ:* Univ NH, BA, 62; Univ Mass, PhD(ling), 78. *Prof Exp:* Teacher English, math & sci, US Peace Corps, Nigeria, 64-65; instr, Sch for Int Training, 75-78; ASST PROF LING, ENGLISH DEPT, UNIV NH, 78- *Mem:* Ling Soc Am; African Ling Soc; North Eastern Ling Soc; Teachers of English to Speakers of Other Lang; NCTE. *Res:* The use of tone and intonation in languages; the interaction of phonology with other parts of the grammar; applications of linguistics in language teaching. *Publ:* Auth, An analysis of EQUI which suggests that sentences should be put together from the bottom up, 74 & On the distinction between pitch-accent and tone languages, 78, Papers from the Fifth Annual Meeting of the North Eastern Ling Soc, Harvard Univ; On the alternation between isolation and combination tones in Chaochow, Papers from the 14th Regional Meeting of the Chicago Ling Soc, Univ Chicago, 78; On the representation of lexical tone level in a dynamic-tone theory, Cunyforum 5, 6: Papers in Ling Proc of the Ninth Annual Meeting of the North East Ling Soc, City Col of New York, 79; On the treatment of syntactically-distributed downstep, Studies in African Ling, 80; Ewe and the theory of tone spreading, Proc of the 11th Annual Meeting of the African Ling Soc, 82. *Mailing Add:* English Dept Univ of NH Durham NH 03824

CLARK, MARYBETH, b Springfield, Ill, Dec 14, 24; m 74. LINGUISTICS, ENGLISH AS A SECOND LANGUAGE. *Educ:* Wash Univ, BA, 52; Univ Hawaii, MA, 70, PhD(ling), 75. *Prof Exp:* Teacher English lang, Int Vol Serv, Viet-Nam, 64-67; co-organizer & teacher English lang, Vietnamese English Prog, Honolulu, 75-76; instr & curric developer voc English for immigrants, Honolulu Community Col, 76-77; teacher voc English, Indochina Refugee Proj, Hawaii State Dept Educ, 77-80; RES & WRITING. *Concurrent Pos:* Researcher Southeastern Asian langs, 76- *Mem:* Ling Soc Am; Asn Asian Studies, Vietnam Studies Group. *Res:* Southeast Asian languages; syntactic theory; Hmong (Miao) language with speakers from Laos. *Publ:* Auth, Passive and ergative in Vietnamese, 74 & Submissive verbs as adversatives in some Asian languages, 74, Southeast Asian Ling Studies, Pac Ling; Ditransitive goal verbs in Vietnamese, Mon-Khmer Studies, 77; Coverbs and Case in Vietnamese, Pac Ling, 78; Coverbs: Evidence for the derivation of prepositions from verbs--new evidence from Hmong, 79, Source phrases in White Hmong, 80 & Derivation between goal and source verbs in Hmong, 80, Univ Hawaii Working Papers in Ling; Some auxiliary verbs in Hmong, Proc Hmong Res Conf, Univ Minn, 81. *Mailing Add:* 3045 Pualei Circle Apt 111 Honolulu HI 96815

CLARK, PRISCILLA PARKHURST, b Gloversville, NY, Aug 22, 40. FRENCH LITERATURE, SOCIOLOGY OF LITERATURE. *Educ:* Columbia Univ, MA, 64, PhD(French), 67. *Prof Exp:* Asst prof French, 66-72, assoc prof, 72-79, PROF FRENCH, UNIV ILL, CHICAGO CIRCLE, 79- *Concurrent Pos:* Vis lectr comp lit, Univ Chicago, 70; vis lectr French, Yale Univ, 72-73; Nat Endowment for Humanities younger humanist fel, 73; res grants, Univ Ill, Chicago Circle, 75-77, 80; Nat Endowment for Humanities fel, Newberry Libr, 78; Howard Found grant, 79; Am Philol Soc grant, 80. *Mem:* MLA; Am Comp Lit Asn; Int Asn Studies of French; Am Sociol Asn; Am Asn Teachers French. *Res:* Sociology of literature; literary culture; 19th century novel. *Publ:* Coauth, Writers, literature and student movements in France, Sociol Educ, 69; auth, The battle of the Bourgeois: The novel in France, 1789-1848, Libr Marcel Didier, 73; Suicide, societe, sociologie, 19th Century Fr Studies, summer 75; Thoughts for Food I and II, Fr Rev, 10-12/75; Strategies d'auteur au 19e siecle, Romantisme, 77; The sociology of literature: An historical introduction, In Research in Sociology of Knowledge, Sciences and Art, 78; Literary culture in France and the United States, Am J Sociol; Literary and sociology, In: Interrelations of Literature, Mod Lang Asn, 82. *Mailing Add:* Dept of French Univ of Illinois-Chicago Circle Chicago IL 60680

CLARK, RAYMOND JOHN, b Bristol, Eng, July 8, 41; m 64; c 3. CLASSICS. *Educ:* Univ Exeter, BA, 63, cert educ, 64, PhD(classics), 70. *Prof Exp:* assoc prof, 69-80, PROF CLASSICS, MEM UNIV NFLD, 80- *Concurrent Pos:* Can Coun leave fel, 76-77. *Mem:* Class Asn Can (vpres, 80-82); Vergilian Soc Am; Virgil Soc Eng; Am Philol Soc; Brit Class Asn. *Res:* Greek and Latin epic, especially Homeric and Vergilian; classical religion, mythology and folklore, especially mortuary; pre-Socratic philosophy. *Publ:* Auth, Trophonios: the Manner of His Revelation, Trans Am Philol Asn, 68; Parmenides and sense-perception, Rev Etudes Grecques, 69; Two Virgilian similes and the ΗΡΑΚΛΕΟΥ ΚΑΤΑΒΑΣΙΣ, Phoenix, 70; A classical foundation--legend from Newfoundland, Folklore, 70; Christ's resurrection at Avernus, Classica et Mediaevalia, 74; The wheel and Vergil's Eschatology in Aeneid 6, Symbolae Osloenses, 75; Vergil Aeneid 6.40ff and the Cumaean Sybil's cave, Latomus, 77; Catabasis: Vergil and the Wisdom-Tradition, Grüner, Amsterdam, 79. *Mailing Add:* Dept of Classics Mem Univ of Nfld St John's NF A1C 5S7 Can

CLARK, RICHARD C, b Philadelphia, Pa, Oct 12, 19; m 49; c 3. MODERN LANGUAGE. *Educ:* Temple Univ, AB, 42; Univ Pa, MA, 49 PhD, 54. *Prof Exp:* From instr to asst prof Ger, Kans State Univ, 47-62, asst chmn dept, 60-61, undergrad chmn dept, 61-62; prof Ger & head dept mod lang, 62-68; PROF GER & CHMN DEPT, MACALESTER COL, 68- *Concurrent Pos:* Mem bibliog comt, MLA, 56-62. *Mem:* Am Asn Teachers Ger. *Res:* Linguistics; Netherlandic language and literature; German-American relations. *Publ:* Auth, Netherlandic bibliography, PMLA, 56-62; Die clag von Volff eim hage, Mod Lang Notes; Hans Schwarz and the Battle of Our Lady's Castle, Amsterdamer Beitrage, 74. *Mailing Add:* Dept of Ger Macalester Col St Paul MN 55101

CLARK, SUSAN LOUISE, b Canton, Ohio, Apr 21, 48; m 75. MEDIEVAL LITERATURE, WOMEN'S STUDIES. *Educ:* Mount Union Col, BA, 69; Rutgers Univ, MPhil, 72, PhD(Ger), 73. *Prof Exp:* Teaching asst German, Rutgers Univ, 70-73; asst prof, 73-78, ASSOC PROF GERMAN, RICE UNIV, 78- *Concurrent Pos:* Lectr, Houston Grand Opera, Tex Opera Studio, 78-79. *Mem:* MLA; South Cent MLA; Int Courtly Lit Asn; AAUP. *Res:* Medieval literature; women's studies; detective fiction. *Publ:* Coauth, The Poetics of Conversion, Lang, 77; Language, silence and wisdom in Chretien's Erec et Enide, The Michigan Academician, 77; The imagery of The Wanderer, Neophilologus, 79; Jonah and the whale: Narrative perspective in Patience, Orbis Litterarum, 80; auth, Midwest and money in the novels of Mabel Seeley, Great Lakes Rev, 79; Arenas of conflict and resolution in Hartmann's Iwein, Euphorion, 79; Hartmann's Erec: Language, perception and transformation, Germanic Rev, 81; coauth, Give and take: Good, evil and language in Rebhun's Susanna, Euphorion, 82. *Mailing Add:* Dept of Ger & Russ Rice Univ Houston TX 77251

CLARK, VIRGINIA PRESCOTT, Linguistics, English Literature. See Vol II

CLARK, WILLIAM HARRINGTON, b Washington, DC, July 19, 17; m 41; c 5. GERMAN. *Educ:* Haverford Col, SB, 38; Columbia Univ, AM, 40, PhD(Ger), 54. *Prof Exp:* Instr Ger, Columbia Univ, 39-40; from instr to assoc prof, 46-61, assoc prof Ger & educ, 61-69, asst dean col educ, 72-74, assoc dean grad sch educ & human develop, 74-80, PROF GER & EDUC, UNIV ROCHESTER, 69- *Concurrent Pos:* Am Philos Soc grants, 58, 59; US Dept Educ contract, using prog foreign lang courses in sec sch with spec trained teachers, 67-68. *Mem:* Am Asn Teachers Ger; Am Coun Teaching Foreign Lang. *Res:* German literature, 1750-1850; foreign language teacher training. *Publ:* Auth, Wielandbriefe aus der Sammlung Wilhelm Kurrelmeyers, Mod Lang Notes, 12/61 & 10/64; First-year college German through programmed instruction: five years' experience, Unterrichtspraxis, fall 69; ed, Kleine Schriften 1783-1791, Vol 23, In: Wielands gasammelte Schriften, Part I, Akademie, Berlin, 69& 72. *Mailing Add:* 79 Village Lane Rochester NY 14610

CLARKE, HOWARD W, b Waterbury, Conn, June 12, 29; m 55; c 2. COMPARATIVE LITERATURE. *Educ:* Holy Cross Col, AB, 50; Harvard Univ, AM, 51, PhD, 60. *Prof Exp:* Instr classics, Boston Univ, 56-58, lectr, 59-60; from asst prof to prof classics & comp lit, Oakland Univ, 60-72, actg chmn dept classics, 60-64, chmn, 64-69; PROF COMP LIT, UNIV CALIF, SANTA BARBARA, 69-, CHMN PROG, 80- *Mem:* MLA; Am Comp Lit Asn. *Res:* Epic; mythology. *Publ:* Auth, Fire imagery in the Odyssey, Class J, 62; Telemachus and the Telemacheia, Am J Philol, 63; Homer and Mickiewicz, Ind Slavic Studies, 63; transl, The Return of Odysseus, Ind Univ, 66; auth, The Art of the Odyssey, Prentice-Hall, 67; Homer's Readers: An Historical Introduction to the Iliad and the Odyssey, Univ Del, 78. *Mailing Add:* Dept of Comp Lit Univ of Calif Santa Barbara CA 93106

CLAS, ANDRE, b Laning, France, June 1, 33; Can Citizen; m 55; c 2. LEXICOLOGY, TRANSLATION. *Educ:* Univ Strasbourg, BA, 53; Univ Montreal, MA, 60; Univ Tübingen, PhD(ling), 67. *Prof Exp:* Vprin, Protestant Sch Bd Montreal, 57-62; lectr phonetics, 62-67, asst prof, 67-70, assoc prof transl, 70-77, PROF TRANSL, UNIV MONTREAL, 77-, CHMN DEPT, 70- *Mem:* Soc Ling Romane; Conf Int Ecoles Traduction; Asn Int Ling Appl. *Publ:* Coauth, Phonetique appliquee, Beauchemin, Montreal, 67; Le francais, langue des affaires, McGraw-Hill, 69; ed, META, Translators J, 69 & Actes du colloque de linguistique, 70 & 73 & Neologiswes-Canadianiswes, 77, Univ Montreal. *Mailing Add:* Dept of Ling Univ of Montreal Montreal PQ H3C 3J7 Can

CLAUDEL, CALVIN ANDRE, b Goudeau, La, July 7, 09; m 43; c 1. ROMANCE LANGUAGES & LITERATURES. *Educ:* Tulane Univ, BA, 31, MA, 32; Univ NC, PhD, 47; Univ Paris, dipl, 62. *Prof Exp:* Asst French, Tulane Univ, 31-32; instr French, Span & Latin, Orleans Pub Schs, 32-43; instr French, Univ NC, 43-45; instr French & Span, St Louis Univ, 45-46; asst prof, Beloit Col, 46-47 & ECarolina Col, 47-48; instr, Phoenix Col, 48-49; asst prof, Miss State Univ, 49-50; prof & head dept, Ky Wesleyan Univ, 50-51; assoc prof & actg head dept, Norwich Univ, 51-53; instr Latin, French & Span, Orleans Pub Schs, 53-63; instr lang, Metarie Park Country Day Sch, 63-64; asst prof French, Univ Ark, 64-65; assoc prof lang, Univ Southern Miss, 65-66; prof Romance lang & chmn dept, WVa Wesleyan Col, 66-69; prof French & Span, Salisbury State Col, 69-72; asst prof, Eastern Shore Community Col, Wallops Island, Va, 72-76; INSTR SPAN & ENGLISH, DELGADO COL, 77- *Concurrent Pos:* Vpres, Athenee Louisianais, 63-64; life fel, Inst Int Sociol Res, 69; consult reading, NASA, Wallops Sta, Wallops Island, Va, 73-76; fac mem exten courses Span, Va State Col at Eastern Shore Community Col, Melfa, Va, 75-76; assoc ed, Claudel Studies; asst ed, New Laurel Rev. *Honors & Awards:* Medaille of French Govt, 55; Chevalier, Palmes Acad, 63. *Mem:* NEA; MLA; Am Folklore Soc; Am Asn Teachers Fr; Am ASn Teachers Span & Port. *Res:* The teaching of world masterpieces in English; remedial teaching of reading and writing to adults; Louisiana folktales. *Publ:* Auth, Louisiana's Jean Sot in folklore and literature, La Rev, Vol 1, No 1; Stimulating the retarded reader, In: The Slow Reader, Philos Libr, 69; Claudel's Two Faces of Columbus, In: Papers on Romance Literary Relations, Univ Ga, 71; The Negro's contribution to the world of entertainment, In: The Negro Impact on Western Civilization, Philos Libr, 70; transl, Ruben Dario's Margarita, New Laurel Rev, 72, To Postumus (Horace), Class Outlook, 76; auth, Medical Latin in 1644 AD, Class Outlook, 76; Fools & Rascals: Louisiana Folktales, In: Louisiana, 78; Creole Poems, Nagative Capability Press, 81. *Mailing Add:* Dept of Span & English Delgado Col, City Park Campus New Orleans LA 70119

CLAUSEN, WENDELL VERNON, b Coquille, Ore, Apr 2, 23; m 47; c 3. CLASSICAL LANGUAGES. *Educ:* Univ Wash, BA, 45; Univ Chicago, PhD, 48. *Hon Degrees:* MA, Harvard Univ, 59. *Prof Exp:* From instr to assoc prof classics, Amherst Col, 48-59; PROF GREEK & LATIN, HARVARD UNIV, 59- *Concurrent Pos:* Fel, Am Acad Rome, Italy, 52-53; fel commoner, Peterhouse, Cambridge, 62-; Am Coun Learned Soc fel, 62-63; Sather Prof, Univ Calif, Berkeley, 82. *Mem:* Fel Am Acad Arts & Sci; Am Philol Asn. *Res:* Latin poetry; textual criticism; Latin manuscripts. *Publ:* Auth, A Persi Flacci Suturarum Liber: Accedit Vita, 56, Persi et Iuuenalis Saturae, 59 & coauth, Appendix Vergiliana, 66 Oxford; ed & contribr, The Cambridge History of Latin Literature, Cambridge, 82. *Mailing Add:* Dept of Classics Harvard Univ Cambridge MA 02138

CLAUSING, GERHARD, b Ger, Feb 16, 43; US citizen. GERMAN & APPLIED LINGUISTICS. *Educ:* Univ Calif, Berkeley, AB, 66, MA, 68, DPhil, 72, PhD(Ger ling), 74. *Prof Exp:* From instr to asst prof Ger, Univ Minn, Minneapolis, 72-76; asst prof, 76-79, ASSOC PROF GER, UNIV SOUTHERN CALIF, 79- *Concurrent Pos:* Ger Acad Exchange Serv fel, Freiburg, 72; Interim chmn dept Ger, Univ Southern Calif, fall, 81. *Mem:* MLA; Am Asn Teachers Ger; Am Coun Teaching Foreign Lang; Philol Asn Pac Coast. *Res:* The linguistic analysis of texts, including spoken language, and the transmission of language and methods of analysis on all levels of instruction. *Publ:* Coauth, Individualized Instruction Program in Basic German, Random House, 71, 75, 3rd ed, 80; auth, Adding a creative dimension: Writing and interpreting poetry in intermediate German courses, Unterrichtspraxis, 71; coauth, Individualized German instruction at the college level--a first appraisal, Foreign Lang Ann, 72; The tutor in media-aided language programs, Nat Asn Lang Lab Dir J, 74; auth, Replicated spoken German in beginning textbooks-an appraisal and proposal, 74, coauth, Teaching philology today, 74 & auth, On the visualization of German grammar, 75, Unterrichtspraxis; An examination of two methods of generating and scoring Cloze tests, Mod Lang J, 81. *Mailing Add:* Dept of German THH 402 Univ of Southern Calif Los Angeles CA 90089

CLAYMAN, DEE LESSER, b New York. CLASSICAL PHILOLOGY. *Educ:* Wellesley Col, BA, 67; Univ Pa, MA, 69, PhD(classics), 72. *Prof Exp:* Asst prof classics, Brooklyn Col, 72-77, assoc prof, 78-81, PROF CLASSICS, BROOKLYN COL & GRAD CTR, CITY UNIV NEW YORK, 82- *Concurrent Pos:* Grants-in-aid, Am Philos Soc, 75 & Am Coun Learned Soc, 78. *Mem:* Am Philol Asn; Asn Lit & Ling Computing; Asn Computational Linguistics. *Res:* Greek poetry; computer-assisted stylometry; history of literary criticism. *Publ:* Auth, Horace's Epodes VIII and XII, Class World, 75; Callimachus' Thirteenth Lamb: The Last Word, Hermes, 76; The origins of Greek literary criticism and the aitia prologue, Weiner Studien, 77; The meaning of Corinna's Weroia, 78 & Callimachus' Forth Iamb, 78, Class J; coauth, Enjambement in Greek hexameter poetry, Trans & Proc Am Philol Asn, 78; auth, Callimachus' Iambi, Mnemosyne Supplementa, Brill, Leiden, Vol 59, 80; Sentence length in Greek hexameter poetry, Hexameter Studies, Quantitative Ling, Brockmeyer, Bochman, Vol II, 81. *Mailing Add:* Dept of Classics Brooklyn Col City Univ of New York Brooklyn NY 11210

CLAYTON, ALAN J, b Boston, Mass, Dec 1, 37; m 59; c 2. MODERN FRENCH LITERATURE. *Educ:* Brandeis Univ, BA, 59; Harvard Univ, MA, 60, PhD(French). 67. *Prof Exp:* Instr French, Williams Col, 61-62; from instr to asst prof, 65-70, assoc prof, 70-81, PROF FRENCH, TUFTS UNIV, 81- *Concurrent Pos:* Founder & ed, Jean Giono Ann Rev, 74- *Honors & Awards:* Am Coun Learned Soc grant-in-aid, 76. *Mem:* Asn Amis de Jean Giono. *Res:* Modern French fiction. *Publ:* Auth, Etapes d'un itineraire spirituel: Albert Camus de 1937-1944, Lett Modernes-Minard, 71; ed, Jean Giono I, La Revue des lett modernes, 74; auth, Camus ou l'impossibilite dsaimer, Albert Camus 7, 75; Giono et l'attirance de l'abime, In: Jean Giono II, 76; ed, Jean Giono II, La Revue des lett modernes, 76; auth, Pour une poetique de la parole chez Giono, Lett Modernes/Minard, 78; Jean Giono III, La Revue des lett modernes, 81; Prophylaxie de la negation dans Le Hussaard sur le toit, Asn des Amis de Jean Giono, Bull No 15, 81; Pluralite du cholera: Remarques sur le chapitre XIII du Hussard, Actes du Colloque Giono d'Aix-en-Provence (1981), 82. *Mailing Add:* Dept of Romance Lang Tufts University Medford MA 02155

CLAYTON, JOHN DOUGLAS, b Cheshire, Eng, Dec 14, 43; m 68; c 2. RUSSIAN LITERATURE. *Educ:* Univ Cambridge, BA, 65; Univ Ill, Urbana, AM, 67, PhD(Russ), 71. *Prof Exp:* Asst prof Slavic studies, 71-76, ASSOC PROF MOD LANG & LIT, UNIV OTTAWA, 76- *Mem:* Can Asn Slavists; Am Asn Teachers Slavic & East Europ Lang; Am Asn Advan Slavic Studies; Asn Can Theatre History. *Res:* Alexander Pushkin; 20th century Russian theatre. *Publ:* Auth, Considerations sur la chronologie interne de Evenii Onegin, Can Slavonic Papers, 12/79; Pushkin, Faust and the Demons, Germano-Slavica, spring 80; New Directions in Soviet Criticism on Evgenii Onegin, 6/80 & The Russian Minnons: A Study in the poetics of translation, 3/81, Can Slavonic Papers; Evenii Onegin: Symbolism of time and space, Russ Lang J, 81; ed, Poetica Slavica: Studies to honour Zbigniew Folejewski, Ottawa, 81. *Mailing Add:* Dept of Mod Lang & Lit Univ of Ottawa Ottawa ON K1N 6N5 Can

CLAYTON, LAURA BLAND, b Winston-Salem, NC; m 58. CLASSICS, ENGLISH. *Educ:* Salem Col, AB, 38; Univ NC, Chapel Hill, MA, 39, PhD(Latin, hist), 50; Am Acad Rome, Italy, dipl classics, 50. *Prof Exp:* Instr Latin, Salem Acad, NC, 48-50; assoc prof English, drama, jour & speech, Lees-McRae Col, 50-53; from asst prof to assoc prof Latin & English, 63-67, chmn div humanities, 70-73, PROF CLASSICS & ENGLISH, LENOIR-RHYNE COL, 69- *Concurrent Pos:* Secy-treas, Foreign Lang Asn of NC, 75-77, mem exec comt, 77-78. *Mem:* SAtlantic Mod Lang Am Class League; Class Asn Mid W & S; Am Asn Univ Women; Am Asn Higher Educ. *Res:* Classical research on Atlantis, drugs, medicine and music; ancient drama; hagiography. *Publ:* Auth, A survey of ninety-five colleges on academic calendar and the 4-1-4 system, summer employment of faculty and sabbatical leave, Eric, spring 70; Why an interdepartmental major in classics at Lenoir-Rhyne, Profile Mag, 70; ed, Proceedings Foreign Language Association of North Carolina, Lenoir-Rhyne Col, 76-77. *Mailing Add:* Box 482 Lenoir-Rhyne Col Hickory NC 28601

CLAYTON, THOMAS, English. See Vol II

CLEARY, VINCENT JOHN, b Philadelphia, Pa, Aug 13, 32; m 55, 73; c 7. CLASSICS. *Educ:* St Joseph Col, BS, 54; Villanova Univ, AM, 59; Univ Pa, PhD(class studies), 67. *Prof Exp:* Instr classics, Villanova Univ, 60-63, asst prof, 64-68; asst prof, Ohio State Univ, 68-71; assoc prof, 71-76, PROF CLASSICS, UNIV MASS, AMHERST, 77- *Concurrent Pos:* Lectr, Rosemont Col, 66-68. *Mem:* Class Asn Atlantic States; Am Philol Asn; Class Asn New England; Am Class League. *Res:* Latin language and literature. *Publ:* Auth, Aeneas: A study in alternation, Class Bull, 4/64. *Mailing Add:* Dept of Classics Univ of Mass Amherst MA 01002

CLEGG, JOSEPH HALVOR, b Provo, Utah, July 24, 37; m 62; c 5. ROMANCE PHILOLOGY & LINGUISTICS. *Educ:* Brigham Young Univ, BA, 64; Univ Tex, Austin, MA, 67, PhD(Romance philol & ling), 69. *Prof Exp:* Asst prof Span, Univ NMex, 69 & Univ Wis, 69-72; ASSOC PROF SPAN & LING, BRIGHAM YOUNG UNIV, 72- *Mem:* Am Asn Teachers Span & Port. *Res:* Spanish linguistics; general lingustics. *Mailing Add:* Dept of Span & Port Brigham Young Univ Provo UT 84601

CLEMENT, BESSE ALBERTA, b Norman, Okla, Nov 10, 02. FRENCH. *Educ:* Univ Okla, BA, 25, MA, 28; Stanford Univ, PhD(contemp French lit), 47. *Prof Exp:* Asst mod lang, Ouachita Baptist Col, 25-26; asst Romance lang, 26-28, from instr to prof, 28-63, David Ross Boyd prof, 63-73, DAVID ROSS BOYD EMER PROF MOD LANG, UNIV OKLA, 73- *Mem:* MLA; SCent Mod Lang Asn; Am Asn Teachers Fr. *Res:* Contemporary French novel. *Publ:* Transl, Roger Le Tourneau's Fez in the Age of the Marinides, Univ Okla, 61; co-transl (with John J Te Paske), Noticias secretas de America, In: Kingdoms of Peru, Univ Okla Press, 78. *Mailing Add:* 1108 Chautauqua St Norman OK 73069

CLEMENTE, ALICE RODRIGUES, b Pawtucket, RI, July 28, 34. SPANISH & PORTUGUESE. *Educ:* Brown Univ, AB, 56, MA, 59, PhD(Span), 67. *Prof Exp:* Instr Span, Randolph-Macon Woman's Col, 59-61 & Wheaton Col, 64; from instr to asst prof, 64-71, assoc prof, 64-80, PROF SPAN & PORT, SMITH COL, 80- *Mem:* Asoc Int Hispanistas. *Res:* Gil Vicente; Portuguese novel; Jesuits in the Orient. *Mailing Add:* Dept of Hispanic Studies Smith Col Northampton MA 01060

CLEMENTS, ROBERT JOHN, b Cleveland, Ohio, Oct 23, 12; div; c 2. LITERATURE. *Educ:* Oberlin Col, AB, 34; Univ Chicago, PhD, 39. *Hon Degrees:* LittD, Univ Rome, 61. *Prof Exp:* Instr, Univ Chicago, 37-39; instr, Univ Ill, 39-40; from instr to asst prof, Harvard Univ, 40-47; prof Romance lang & lit & chmn dept, Pa State Univ, 47-54; PROF COMP LIT & CHMN DEPT, NY UNIV, 54- *Concurrent Pos:* Co-organizer, Civil Affairs Prog, Harvard Univ, 40-44; mod lang ed, Ginn & Co, Boston, 44-47; vis prof, Univ Madrid, 53; assoc, Columbia Univ, 55-; Fulbright res scholar, Rome, 60-61; corresp ed, Bol Filol Espanola, Madrid & Romantisches Jahrbuch, Hamburg;

assoc ed, Gotham Libr, 62-; comp lit prog, Fulbright Screening Comt, Washington, 65-68; Mellon prof mod lit, Univ Pittsburgh, 68. *Mem:* Int Asn Studies Ital Lang & Lit (vpres, 60-63, pres, 63-); Am Comp Lit Asn; MLA; Mediaeval Acad Am; Am Asn Teachers Ital (pres, 60-62). *Publ:* Auth, Michelangelo's Theory of Art, NY Univ, 60; Picta Poesis: Literary and Humanistic Theory in Renaissance Emblem Books, Ed Storia Lett, Rome 60; Michelangelo a Self-Portrait, 62; The Poetry of Michelangelo, NY Univ, 64; coauth, Michelangelo Sculpture, 64; Renaissance Letters, 76; Anatomy of the Novella, 76; Comparative Literature as Academic Discipline, 78. *Mailing Add:* Dept of Comp Lit Wash Sq Col NY Univ New York NY 10003

CLEYMAET, ROBERT OMER, b Zelzate, Belg, Dec 22, 12; m 44; c 2. GERMANIC & ROMANIC PHILOLOGY. *Educ:* Univ Ghent, PhD(philos, lett), 42. *Prof Exp:* Lectr, Aarhus Univ, Denmark, 39; aspirant, Belg Fonds Nat de la Recherche Sci, Brussels, 41-43; prof hist of Dutch lit & comp Europ lit, St Bavo Hoger Inst, 42-46; Rockefeller Found fel, Harvard Univ, 46-47; instr Ger & French, Boston Univ, 47-48; lectr Ger lang, Univ Calif, Los Angeles, 48-51; prof French, 55-70, chmn dept mod lang & ling, 61-71, PROF MOD LANG & LING, LOYOLA MARYMOUNT UNIV, 70- *Mem:* MLA. *Res:* Asian studies; linguistics; comparative literature. *Publ:* Handelingen van de Koninklijke Commissie voor Toponymie en Dialectologie; Engelsch Memento. *Mailing Add:* Dept of Mod Lang Loyola Marymount Univ Los Angeles CA 90045

CLINTON, JEROME WRIGHT, b San Jose, Calif, July 14, 37; m 66; c 2. PERSIAN LITERATURE. *Educ:* Stanford Univ, AB, 59; Univ Pa, MA, 62; Univ Mich, MA, 67, PhD(Persian lit), 71. *Prof Exp:* Instr Persian lang & lit, Univ Minn, 70-72; dir, Tehran Ctr, Am Inst Iranian Studies, 72-74; ASST PROF PERSIAN LANG & LIT, PRINCETON UNIV, 74- *Concurrent Pos:* Assoc ed, Iranian Studies, 71-76. *Mem:* Soc Iranian Studies; Mideast Studies Asn. *Res:* Persian literature of the 20-12th centuries; contemporary Persian poetry and prose. *Publ:* Coauth, On the feasibility of an automated bibliography of Iranian studies, Iranian Studies, fall 69; auth, The Divan of Manuchihri Damghani: A critical study, Bibliot Islamica, 72; coauth, The Maden Qasida of Xaqani Sharvani, I, Edebiyat, Vol 1, 76; Safa-yi Batin A study of the interrelations of a set of Iranian ideal character types, Psychol Dimensions of Near Eastern Studies, Darwin, 77; Xaqani and al-Buhturi, Edebiyat, Vol 2, 77. *Mailing Add:* 110 Jones Hall Princeton Univ Princeton NJ 08540

CLINTON, KEVIN, New York, NY, Sept 29, 42; m 70. CLASSICS. *Educ:* Boston Col, BA, 64; Johns Hopkins Univ, PhD(classics), 69. *Prof Exp:* Asst prof classics, St Louis Univ, 69-70; asst prof, 70-75, assoc prof, 75-81, PROF CLASSICS, CORNELL UNIV, 81-, CHMN DEPT, 77- *Concurrent Pos:* Am Coun Learned Soc fel, 75; Soc for Humanities fel, Cornell Univ, 76-77; spec res fel, Am Sch Class Studies, Athens, 83-84. *Mem:* Am Philol Asn; Archaeol Inst Am. *Res:* Greek religion, literature and institutions. *Publ:* Auth, Inscriptions from Eleusis, Arkhaiologike Ephemeris, 71; Apollo, Pan and Zeus, avengers of vultures: Agamemnon, 55-9, Am J Philol, 74; The Sacred Officials of the Eleusinian Mysteries, Am Philos Soc, 74; The Hymn to Zeus, Traditio, 79; A Law in the City Eleusinion Concerning the Mysteries, 80 & The Nature of the Late Fifth-Century Revision of the Athenian Law Code, Suppl 19, 80, Hesperia. *Mailing Add:* Dept of Classics Cornell University Ithaca NY 14853

CLIVIO, GIANRENZO PIETRO, b Turin, Italy, Jan 18, 42. LINGUISTICS, LITERATURE. *Educ:* Univ Torino, Italy, BA, 62; Brandeis Univ, MA, 64; Harvard Univ, PhD (ling), 67. *Prof Exp:* From asst prof to assoc prof, 68-77, PROF ITAL, UNIV TORONTO, 77- *Concurrent Pos:* Pres, Can Ctr Ital Cult & Educ, 77-81; pres, Nat Cong Ital Canadians, Ont Region, 80-; assoc ed, Can J Ital Studies, 81-; ed, Il Forneri, Bull Can Soc Ital Ling, 81- *Mem:* Am Asn Teachers Ital; Ling Asn US & Can; Int Soc Phonetic Sci; Can Soc Ital Ling (pres, 81-). *Res:* Romance linguistics; sociolinguistics; Italian literature. *Publ:* Auth, Bibliografia ragionata dei dialetti del Piemonte, 71 & ed, Poesie piemontese e seritti italiani e francesi di Edoardo I Calvo, 73, Centro Studi Piemontesi; contribr, The assimilation of English loanwords in Italo-Canadian, In: The Second Lacus Forum, Hornbeam, 76; auth, Storia linguistica e dialettologia piemontesi, Centro Studi Piemontesi, Torino, 76; ed, Lingue e dialetti nell'arco alpino occidentale, Centro Studi Piemontes, 78; contribr, The development of the Italian language and its dialects, In: The Culture of Italy, Mediaeval to Modern, Griffin House, 79. *Mailing Add:* Dept of Ital Studies Univ of Toronto Toronto ON M5S 1A1 Can

CLOGAN, PAUL MAURICE, English, Comparative Literature. See Vol II

CLOOS, ROBERT IRA, b Crafton, Pa, Aug 4, 22; m 44; c 3. FOREIGN LANGUAGES, EDUCATION. *Educ:* Grove City Col, BA, 43; Univ Calif, Berkeley, MA, 48; Rutgers Univ, EdD, 64. *Prof Exp:* Teacher French & hist, Kane High Sch, Pa, 48-50; teacher Ger & French & chmn dept foreign lang, Plainfield High Sch, NJ, 50-64; teacher, West Essex High Sch, North Caldwell, NJ, 64-68; asst prof Ger & educ, Univ Mo, St Louis, 68-80. *Concurrent Pos:* Mem comt Nat Symp Advan Teaching Ger, 67; mem selection comt, 1969 Overseas Prog for Perspective Teachers Ger, 68; Bibliogr, Annual bibliog Am Coun Teaching Foreign Lang & MLA Int bibliog, 69-73. *Mem:* Am Coun Teaching Foreign Lang; Am Asn Teachers Ger; Asn Teacher Educ. *Res:* The measurement and remediation of aptitude for foreign language learning; foreign language learning theory. *Publ:* Auth, A four year study of foreign language aptitude at the high school level, Foreign Lang Ann, 5/71; contribr, In-service programs in foreign languages at elementary and secondary levels, In: Vol III, Britannica Review of Foreign Language Education, Encycl Britannica, 71. *Mailing Add:* 2842 Clearview Dr St Louis MO 63121

CLOUGH, CARMEN PELLA, b Havana, Cuba, Jan 14, 17; m; c 1. ROMANCE LINGUISTICS. *Educ:* Univ Havana, DEd, 40, cert, 53; Univ Mich, MA, 52. *Prof Exp:* Teacher English, Spec English Ctr 11, Havana, 35-45, prin, 40-45; prof, Mariano Prep Sch, 45-60, head dept, 55-60; instr Span, Georgetown Univ, 60-63; assoc prof, 63-72, PROF SPAN, CALIF STATE UNIV, FRESNO, 72- *Concurrent Pos:* Vis prof, Univ Havana, 48; prof, Univ Villanueva, 56-60; tutor, Int Monetary Fund, Washington, DC, 61, Peace group, English Lang Serv, 62; lectr, Am Univ, 62; consult biling prog, Fresno Unified Sch Dist, 73- *Mem:* Am Asn Univ Women; Am Dialect Soc; Am Asn Univ Women; Am Dialect Soc; Am Asn Teachers Span & Port. *Res:* Linguistics; methods in teaching foreign language; Spanish spoken in the San Joaquin Valley. *Publ:* Auth, Research in linguistic reading lists for teachers of modern languages, Ctr Applied Ling, 63; Sounds in Spanish, English Lang Serv, 64. *Mailing Add:* Dept of Foreign Lang Calif State Univ Fresno CA 93710

CLOUGH, RAYMOND JOSEPH, b Hartford, Conn, May 19, 40; m 62; c 5. FRENCH LANGUAGE & LITERATURE. *Educ:* Holy Cross Col, AB, 62; Cath Univ Am, AM, 64; State Univ NY, Buffalo, PhD(French), 73. *Prof Exp:* Instr French, Gannon Col, 64-67; asst prof, 67-74, ASSOC PROF FRENCH, CANISIUS COL, 74-, CHMN MOD LANG DEPT, 74- *Concurrent Pos:* Fel, Nat Humanities Inst on Cult & Technol, Univ Chicago, 76-77. *Mem:* MLA; Am Asn Teachers French. *Res:* Literature and technology; 19th and 20th century French literature; French novel. *Mailing Add:* Dept of Mod Lang Canisius Col Buffalo NY 14208

CLOUSER, ROBIN A, b Philadelphia, Pa, June 4, 42; m 72. GERMAN LITERATURE. *Educ:* Ursinus Col, AB, 63; Univ Pa, Am, 65; Univ Kans, PhD(Ger), 71. *Prof Exp:* Teaching asst, Univ Pa, 64; asst instr, Univ Kans, 65-69, dir, Elem Ger Prog, 67-68, asst dean, Nunemaker Col, 72-73, ASST PROF GER, URSINUS COL, 74-, CHMN DEPT, 75- *Mem:* MLA; Am Asn Teachers Ger. *Res:* Heinrich von Kleist; Goethe; the Novelle. *Publ:* Auth, Sosias Tritt Mit Einer Laterne Auf: Messenger to Myth in Kleist's Amphitryon, Ger Rev, 11/75; Romeo and Julia auf dem Dorfe: Keller's Variations Upon Shakespeare, J English & Ger Philol, spring 78; Germania, Pan, and the Davidic Kingdom in Goethe's Novelle, Publ English Goethe Soc (in press). *Mailing Add:* Dept of Ger Ursinus Col Collegeville PA 19426

CLOUTIER, CECILE, b Quebec, Que, June 13, 30; m 66; c 1. FRENCH. *Educ:* Laval Univ, BA, 51, Lic es Lett & MA, 53, DES, 54; Sorbonne, DUniv, 62. *Prof Exp:* Asst prof French lit & aesthet, Univ Ottawa, 58-64; assoc prof, 65-78, PROF FRENCH LIT & AESTHET, UNIV TORONTO, 78- *Concurrent Pos:* Can Coun scholars, 64-65, 67-68; lectr, Royal Ont Mus, 66, NY Univ, 66, Univ Toronto, 67, learned socs, Ottawa, 67 & Ctr Continuing Educ. *Honors & Awards:* Prize, Cocteau, 64. *Mem:* Am Soc Aesthet; MLA. *Res:* French avant-garde literature; aesthetics of poetry; French Canadian literature. *Publ:* Auth, Mains de sable, Arc, 60; Cuivre et soies, Ed du Jour, 64; L'Esthetique de la langue Canadienne francaise, Rev Esthet, Paris, 12/64; Le symbole en litterature et en psychanalyse, Rev Univ, Ottawa, 6/65; La machine a poemes, Liberte, 2/67. *Mailing Add:* Dept of French Univ of Toronto Toronto ON M5S 1V4 Can

CLUBB, LOUISE GEORGE, b New York, NY, July 22, 30; m 54. COMPARATIVE LITERATURE. *Educ:* George Washington Univ, AB, 52, MA, 56; Columbia Univ, PhD(comp lit), 63. *Prof Exp:* Instr English, Univ Md, 56-57 & fall 60, instr English & comp lit, 61-62; asst prof English & comp lit, George Washington Univ, 62-64, vis asst prof Ital & comp lit, 64-65, assoc prof, 66-70, PROF ITAL & COMP LIT, UNIV CALIF, BERKELEY, 70- *Concurrent Pos:* Guggenheim fel, 65-66; res fel, Univ Calif, Berkeley, 73; mem nat screening comt, Inst Int Educ, 72; Am Philos Soc grant, 72-73; Am Coun Learned Soc fel, 77. *Mem:* Dante Soc Am; Renaissance Soc Am; Am Asn Advan Humanities; Am Comp Lit Asn; Am Asn Teacher Ital. *Res:* Chivalric epic; Renaissance literature; Renaissance drama in England, Italy, Spain and France. *Publ:* Auth, The virgin martyr and the tragedia sacra, Renaissance Drama, 64; Giambattista Della Porta, Dramatist, Princeton Univ, 65; Italian comedy and The Comedy of Errors, Comp Lit, summer 67; Italian plays, 1500-1700, in the Folger Library: A bibliography with critical introduction, Casa Editrice Leo S Olschki, 68; The making of the pastoral play: Some Italian Experiments from 1573-1590, In: Petrarch to Pirandello, Univ Toronto, 73; La mimesi della realta invisibile nel dramma pastorale italiano e inglese, Misure Critiche, 74; Italian Renaissance comedy, Genre, 76-77; Woman as wonder: A generic figure in Italian & Shakespearean comedy, Studies in the Continental Background of Renaissance English Literature, 77. *Mailing Add:* Dept of Comp Lit Univ of Calif Berkeley CA 94720

CLUBB, MERREL D, JR, English. See Vol II

CLUVER, CLAUS, b Hamburg, Ger, Oct 25, 32; m 59; c 3. COMPARATIVE LITERATURE. *Educ:* Univ Hamburg, DPhil(English, Latin), 72. *Prof Exp:* Asst English, Univ Hamburg, 59-62; cult asst, US Info Serv, Hamburg, 62-63; lectr, 64-71, asst prof, 72-80, ASSOC PROF COMP LIT, IND UNIV, BLOOMINGTON, 80- *Concurrent Pos:* Dir, Ind Univ Overseas Study Prog, Hamburg Univ, 65-66 & Sao Paulo Univ, Brazil, 76-77; consult humanities, Ind Dept Pub Instr, 73-77. *Mem:* Am Comp Lit Asn; Int Comp Lit Asn; Deutsche Gesellschaft Amerikastudien. *Res:* Comparative arts, modern drama; concrete poetry. *Publ:* Co-ed, Amerikanische Dramaturgie, Rowohlt, Hamburg, 63; auth, Teaching comparative arts, In: Yearbook for Comparative and General Literature, 74; Thorton Wilder und Andre Obey: Untersuchungen zum modernen epischen Theater, Bouvier, Bonn, 78; Painting into poetry, In: Yearbook for Comparative and General Literature, 78. *Mailing Add:* Dept of Comp Lit Ind Univ Bloomington IN 47401

COADY, JAMES MARTIN, b Kokomo, Ind, Aug 14, 41; m 66; c 1. LINGUISTICS. *Educ:* St Meinrad Col, BA, 63; Ind Univ, Bloomington, MA, 67, PhD(ling), 73. *Prof Exp:* Teacher hist, Bennett High Sch, Marion, Ind, 63-64; instr English, Am Univ Beirut, 67-69; ASSOC PROF LING, OHIO UNIV, 71-, CHMN DEPT, 80- *Mem:* Ling Soc Am; Teacher English to Speakers Other Lang; Int Reading Asn; Am Asn Applied Ling. *Res:* Reading; teaching English to speakers of other languages; sociolinguistics. *Publ:* Auth, Ewe, An Intermediate Text, Intensive Lang Training Ctr, Ind Univ, Bloomington, 66; Individualizing the teaching of reading in the ESL classroom, Papers in Applied Ling, summer 75; Intonation and syntax in primers, Reading Improvement, Vol 14 (fall 77). *Mailing Add:* Dept of Ling Ohio University Athens OH 45701

COATES, CARROL FRANKLIN, b Oklahoma City, Okla, July 22, 30. FRENCH LITERATURE. *Educ:* Univ Okla, BA, 51, MA, 54; Yale Univ, PhD, 64. *Prof Exp:* Instr French & Russ, Ohio Univ, 60-62; asst prof, Lycoming Col, 62-63; asst prof French, 63-67, ASSOC PROF FRENCH & COMP LIT, STATE UNIV NY, BINGHAMTON, 67- *Concurrent Pos:* Master, College-in-the-Woods, NY, 69-74; exchange lectr Fr, Univ d'Aix-Marseille I, 80-81 & 83-84. *Mem:* Am Asn Teachers French; MLA; Am Comp Lit Asn; Int Asn French Studies; Asn Can Studies in US. *Res:* Semistic analysis of poetry; 19th century French fiction; literature of Quebec. *Publ:* Auth, Daumier and Flaubert: Examples of graphic and literary caricature, 19th Century Fr Studies, spring 76; Patterns of rhyme and narrative in La Fontaine's fables, Les Bonnes Feuilles, fall 78; Le Joual comme revendication quebecoise: D'Amour P Q de Jacques Godbout, Fr Rev, 10/78; Poetic technique and meaning in La Fontaine's Fables, In: Studies in Romance Languages and Literatures, Coronado Press, 80. *Mailing Add:* Dept of Romance Lang & Lit State Univ NY Binghamton NY 13901

COBB, CARL WESLEY, b Yazoo City, Miss, Aug 11, 26; m 58; c 3. SPANISH LITERATURE. *Educ:* George Peabody Col, BA, 50, MA, 52; Tulane Univ, PhD, 61. *Prof Exp:* Mem fac Span, Va Intermont Col, 52-58; asst prof, Mid Tenn State Col, 61-62; assoc prof, Furman Univ, 62-66; assoc prof, 66-79, PROF SPAN, UNIV TENN, KNOXVILLE, 80- *Concurrent Pos:* Ford Found fel, Univ NC, 65-66. *Mem:* MLA; SAtlantic Mod Lang Asn; Am Asn Teachers Span & Port. *Res:* Modern Spanish literature. *Publ:* Auth, Milton and blank verse in Spain, Philol Quart, 4/63; Federico Garcia Lorca and the dedication to La Casada Infiel, Romance Notes, 67; Federico Garcia Lorca, 67 & Antonio Machado, 71, Twayne; Contemporary Spanish Poetry, Twayne, 76. *Mailing Add:* Dept of Romance Lang Univ of Tenn Knoxville TN 37916

COBB, EULALIA BENEJAM, b Barcelona, Spain, Oct 3, 44; US citizen; m 67; c 2. FRENCH, SPANISH. *Educ:* Birmingham-Southern Col, BA, 66; Univ NC, MA, 68; Univ Ala, PhD(Romance lang), 72. *Prof Exp:* Instr French & Span, Univ Ala, 71-72; instr French, Stillman Col, 72-73; inst assoc, Inst Higher Educ, Univ Ala, 73-74; ASSOC PROF FRENCH, WESTERN MD COL, 74- *Concurrent Pos:* Affirmative action officer, Western Md Col, 77-78; writer, 81- *Mem:* AAUP; Southeastern Mod Lang Asn. *Res:* Jean Anouilh; surrealism; French women writers. *Publ:* Love and the feminine ideal in surrealism and in the theater of Jean Anomilh, Romance Notes, Vol XXI, No 2. *Mailing Add:* Dept of Foreign Lang Western Md Col Westminster MD 21157

COBBS, ALFRED LEON, b Pamplin, Va, Sept 12, 43. GERMAN LANGUAGE & LITERATURE. *Educ:* Berea Col, BA, 66; Univ Mo, Columbia, MA, 68; Univ Cincinnati, PhD(German), 74. *Prof Exp:* Instr, Univ Cincinnati, 69-73; asst prof, Univ Va, 73-79; ASST PROF GERMAN, WAYNE STATE UNIV, 79- *Mem:* MLA; Am Asn Teachers German; South Atlantic Mod Lang Asn. *Res:* German-American literary relations; modern German literature; imagology in literature. *Publ:* Auth, Teaching Kafka's Verwandlung on the intermediate level, Unterrichtspraxis, 80; Image of the Black in German literature, The Harold Jantz Collection, Duke Univ Ctr Int Studies, 81; contribr, Articles on Ulrich von Hutten & several lesser-known writers, Deutsches Literatur-Lexikon, 81; auth, The Image of America in Postwar German Literature: Reflections and Perceptions, Peter Lang Verlag, 82. *Mailing Add:* Dept of Romance & Germanic Lang Wayne State Univ Detroit MI 48202

COBB-STEVENS, VEDA ALISON, Philosophy. See Vol IV

COBLIN, WELDON SOUTH, b Lexington, Ky, Feb 26, 44; m 70; c 2. CHINESE & SINO-TIBETAN LINGUISTICS. *Educ:* Univ Wash, BA, 67, PhD(Chinese), 72. *Prof Exp:* Teaching assoc, Univ Wash, 72-73; asst prof, 73-78, ASSOC PROF CHINESE, UNIV IOWA, 78-, CHMN DEPT ASIAN LANG & LIT, 81- *Mem:* Am Orient Soc; Ling Soc Am; Asn Asian Studies, Soc Study Early China. *Res:* Chinese historical linguistics; Tibetan historical linguistics. *Publ:* Auth, An early Tibetan word for Horse, J Am Orient Soc, 74; The initials of the Wei-Chin Period as revealed in the phonological glosses of Kuo P'u and others, Monumenta Serica, 74-75; Notes on Tibetan verbal morphology, T'oung Pao, 76; The initials of Xu Shen's language as reflected in the Shuowen Duruo glosses, J Chinese Ling, 78; The initials of the Eastern Han Period as reflected in phonological glosses, Monumenta Serica, 77-78; The finals of Xu Shen's language as reflected in the Shuowen Duruo glosses, J Chinese Ling, 79; A new study of the Pai-lang songs, Tsing-hua J Chinese Studies, 79. *Mailing Add:* Dept of Asian Lang & Lit Univ of Iowa Iowa City IA 52240

COCCO, MIA (MARIA), b Italy, Oct 30, 46. ITALIAN & FRENCH RENAISSANCE LITERATURE. *Educ:* Calif State Univ, Los Angeles, BA, 68; Univ Southern Calif, MA, 70; Univ Calif, Riverside, PhD(Fr & Ital), 76. *Prof Exp:* Vis instr Romance Lang, Univ Ga, 73-77; asst prof Fr & Ital, State Univ NY Stonybrook, 77-82; ASSOC PROF ROMANCE LANG, UNIV GA, 82- *Concurrent Pos:* Fac res fel & grant-in-aid, State Univ NY Res Found, 78-79; Nat Endowment for Humanities fel, 79-80. *Mem:* MLA; Renaissance Soc Am; Int Courtly Lit Soc; SAtlantic Mod Lang Asn; Am Asn Univ Prof Ital. *Res:* Italian and French Renaissance literature; petrarchism; comparative literature. *Publ:* Auth, La tradizione cortese ed il petrarchismo nella poesia di Clement Marot Biblioteca dell' Archivum Romanicum, Serie I: Storia - Letterature - Paleografia, Vol 135, Olschki, Florence, Italy, 78. *Mailing Add:* Dept of Romance Lang Univ of Ga Athens GA 30602

COCOZZELLA, PETER, b Monacilioni, Italy, Nov 20, 37; US citizen; m 64; c 1. SPANISH LANGUAGE & LITERATURE. *Educ:* R Regis Col (Colo), AB, 59; St Louis Univ, PhD(Span), 66. *Prof Exp:* Teacher high sch, Colo, 59-60; from instr to asst prof Span, Univ Mo-St Louis, 65-67; asst prof, Dartmouth Col, 67-70; asst prof, 70-73, ASSOC PROF SPAN, STATE UNIV NY, BINGHAMTON, 73- *Mem:* MLA; Am Asn Teachers Span & Port; NAmer Catalan Soc. *Res:* Castilian and Catalan literatures of the 15th century. *Publ:* Ed, Francese Moner, Obres Catalanes, Ed Barcino, Barcelona, 70; auth, Recollection and introspection in Salvador Espriu's Cementiri de Sinera, In: Catalan Studies (Estudis sobre et catala), Hispam, Barcelona, 77; Fray Francisco Moner: Billingualism, love, and experience in Spanish pre-Renaissance literature, In: Estudis de llengua, literatura i cultura catalanes: Actes del Primer Col.loqui d'Estudis Catalans a Nord-America, Urbana, 3 & 4/78; Montserrat: Publicacians de l'Abadia de Montserrat, 79; Konilosia and Sepharad: The dialectic of self-realization in twentieth-century Catalan literature, World Lit Today, spring 80; The thematic unity of Juan Rodriguez del Padron's Siervo Libre de Amor, Hispania, 5/81; transl, Salvador Espriu and Ricard Salvat, Death Around Sinera, Mod Int Drama, fall 80. *Mailing Add:* Dept of Romance Lang State Univ NY Binghamton NY 13901

COFFIN, DAVID DOUGLAS, b New York, NY, Nov 26, 22; m 49; c 2. CLASSICAL LANGUAGES. *Educ:* Yale Univ, BA, 42, MA, 47. *Prof Exp:* Instr classics, Smith Col, 50-53; instr, 53-69, chmn dept classics, 66-71, CILLEY PROF GREEK, PHILLIPS EXETER ACAD, 69- *Concurrent Pos:* Exchange teacher, Eton Col, 59-60; advan placement reader Latin, Educ Testing Serv, Princeton, NJ, 63-73; consult Latin, Edward E Ford Found Curric Comt, 65-67; mem Latin comt, Nat Asn Independent Schs, 68-74, chmn, 71-72; mem Latin comt, Col Entrance Exam Bd Advan Placement Prog, 69-77, chmn, 74-77. *Honors & Awards:* Distinguished Sec Sch Teacher Award, Harvard Col, 67. *Mem:* Am Philol Asn; Vergilian Soc Am; Class Asn New England (vpres, 64-65). *Res:* Greek anthology; Latin poetry. *Publ:* Auth, Catullus and the Coda, Ann Bull, Class Asn New England, 66; ed, Ovid: Acis, Galatea and Polyphemus, Phillips Exeter Acad, 68; coauth, A Teacher's Notebook: Latin, Nat Asn Independent Schs, 74; Beginning an Advanced Placement Classics Course, Col Entrance Exam Bd, 75; Respecting the Pupil, Phillips Exeter Acad, 81. *Mailing Add:* Phillips Exeter Academy Exeter NH 03833

COFFIN, EDNA AMIR, b Haifa, Israel, Oct 10, 32; US citizen; m 54; c 2. HEBREW LANGUAGE & LITERATURE. *Educ:* Univ Wash, BA, 53; Univ Mich, MA, 65, PhD(Near Eastern Studies), 69. *Prof Exp:* Res asst China, Univ Wash, 54-56; teaching fel mod Hebrew, 66-68, lectr, 69-70, asst prof, 70-79, ASSOC PROF MOD HEBREW, UNIV MICH, ANN ARBOR, 79- *Concurrent Pos:* Examr, State Univ NY Buffalo, 69-; consult, NY State Dept Higher Educ, 72; pres, Nat Asn Self Instruct Lang Prog, 73- *Mem:* Mid East Studies Asn; Am Orient Soc. *Res:* Hebrew linguistics; modern Hebrew literature; language instructions, methods and theory. *Publ:* Auth, Lessons in Modern Hebrew, Levels I & II, 73 & Introduction to Reading, Writing and Pronunciation of Modern Hebrew, 73, Univ Mich. *Mailing Add:* Dept of Mod Lang Univ of Mich Ann Arbor MI 48109

COHEN, ALVIN PHILIP, b Los Angeles, Calif, Dec 12, 37; c 2. CHINESE PHILOLOGY & CULTURAL HISTORY. *Educ:* Univ Calif, Berkeley, BS, 60, MA, 66, PhD(Orient lang), 71. *Prof Exp:* Lectr Orient lang, Univ Calif, Davis, 70-71; asst prof, 71-78, ASSOC PROF CHINESE, UNIV MASS, AMHERST, 78- *Concurrent Pos:* Actg bibliogr Orient Collection, Univ Mass, Amherst, 71- *Mem:* Am Orient Soc; Chinese Lang Teachers Asn; Soc Study Chinese Relig. *Res:* Chinese historiography; Chinese folk religion. *Publ:* Auth, A bibliography of writings contributory to the study of Chinese folk religion, J Am Acad Relig, 75; Grammar Notes for Introductory Classical Chinese, Chinese Materials Ctr, 75, 2nd ed, 80; Humorous anecdotes in Chinese historical texts & Notes on a Chinese workingclass bookshelf, J Am Orient Soc, 76; Coercing the rain deities in ancient China, Hist Relig, 78; ed, Selected Works of Peter A Boodberg, Univ Calif, Berkeley, 79; Legend, Lore and Religion in China, Chinese Materials Ctr, 79. *Mailing Add:* Asian Lang Dept Univ of Mass Amherst MA 01003

COHEN, ANDREW DAVID, b Washington, DC, Mar 14, 44; m 68; c 2. LANGUAGE TESTING & EDUCATION. *Educ:* Harvard Univ, BA, 65; Stanford Univ, MA, 71, PhD(educ), 73. *Prof Exp:* Teacher community develop, Peace Corps, Altiplano, Bolivia, 65-67; res analyst Latin Am, Stanford Res Inst, Menlo Park, Calif, 68; asst English for foreign students, Stanford Univ, 71-72; asst prof training teachers of English as second lang, Univ Calif, Los Angeles, 72-75; sr lectr appl ling, 75-79, acad head English as foreign lang unit, 77-78, ASSOC PROF APPLIED LING, SCH EDUC, HEBREW UNIV JERUSALEM, 79-, DIR, CENTRE FOR RES IN APPL LING, 80- *Concurrent Pos:* Internal evaluator, bilingual educ prog, Redwood City Sch Dist, Calif, 69-72; consult/investr, Adult Educ Sect, Ministry of Educ, Israel, 77-79; consult Hebrew lang placement testing, Israeli Army, 77-; chair, Israel Asn Appl Ling, 78-, Teachers Eng to Speaker other Lang Res Comt, 81- *Mem:* Am Coun Teaching Foreign Lang; Israel Asn Applied Ling; Teachers English to Speakers Other Lang; Int Asn Appl Ling. *Res:* Bilingual and second-language education; first-and second-language testing; easifying the learning of a second language. *Publ:* Auth, Forgetting a second language, Lang Learning, 25: 127-138; A Sociolinguistic Approach to Bilingual Education: Experiments in the American Southwest, Newbury, 75; co-ed & contribr, El lenguaje de los Chicanos: Regional and social characteristics of the language used by Mexican Americans, Ctr Appl Ling, 75; coauth, Bilingual education: The immersion model in the North American context, TESOL Quart, 10: 45-53; Toward assessing interlanguage performance: The relationship between selected errors, learner's characteristics and learner's explanations, Lang Learning, 26: 45-66; auth, Testing language ability in the classroom, Newbury, 80; coauth, Developing a measure of sociocultural competence: The case of apology, 31: 113-134 & Some uses of mentalistic data in second-language research, 31: 285-313, Lang Learning. *Mailing Add:* Sch Educ Hebrew Univ of Jerusalem Jerusalem 91905 Israel

COHEN, GERALD LEONARD, b New York, NY, Mar 22, 41; m 68; c 2. LINGUISTICS, FOREIGN LANGUAGES. *Educ:* Dartmouth Col, BA, 62; Oxford Univ, dipl Slavonic studies, 63; Columbia Univ, MA, 66, PhD(Slavic ling), 71. *Prof Exp:* From instr to asst prof, 68-77, ASSOC PROF FOREIGN LANG & GEN LING, UNIV MO-ROLLA, 77- *Mem:* MLA; Ling Soc Am. *Res:* Etymology; syntax; Slavic accentology. *Publ:* Comments on etymology (bi-weekly publ), privately publ, 71- *Mailing Add:* Dept of Humanities Univ of Mo-Rolla Rolla MO 65401

COHEN, GETZEL MENDELSON, b Montreal, Que, Aug 4, 42; m 64; c 3. CLASSICS. *Educ:* Univ Pa, BA, 63; NY Univ, MA, 66; Princeton Univ, MA, 69, PhD(classics), 70. *Prof Exp:* Asst instr classics, NY Univ, 65 & Brooklyn Col, 66; asst prof classics & hist, 70-76, ASSOC PROF CLASSICS & HIST, UNIV CINCINNATI, 76- *Mem:* Am Philol Asn; Archaeol Inst Am; Greek Asn Can. *Res:* Greek and Roman history; papyrology. *Publ:* Auth, The Hellenistic Military Colony: A Herodian Example, TAPA, 72; The Seleucid Colonies, Steiner, 78. *Mailing Add:* 7314 Parkdale Cincinnati OH 45237

COHEN, HENRY DAVID, b Long Branch, NJ, Jan 27, 39; m 68; c 1. ROMANCE LANGUAGES. *Educ:* Williams Col, AB, 60; Harvard Univ, AM, 62; Univ Calif, Berkeley, PhD(Romance lang), 68. *Prof Exp:* Asst prof Romance lang, St Mary's Col Calif, 66-69; asst prof French, Amherst Col, 69-70; asst prof Romance lang, St Mary's Col Calif, 70-74; asst prof, 74-78, ASSOC PROF ROMANCE LANG, KALAMAZOO COL, 78- *Res:* Francophone literatures; 19th century literature; comparative literature. *Publ:* Auth, Auguste Barbier, poeta francese del Risorgimento, Rassegna Storica del Risorgimento, 73; History, invention and Cesaire's Roi Christophe, Black Images, 73; The petrified builder: Cesaire's Roi Christophe, Studies in Black Lit, 74; Le role du mythe dans Kamouraska d'Anne Hebert, Presence Francophone, 76; Baudelaire and Auguste Barbier, Romance Notes, 77; Apocalypse on the avenues: The New York poems of Federico Garcia Lorca and Leopold Senghor, US Foreign Lang Quart, 78; Lamartine's Toussaint Louverture (1848) and Glissant's Monsieur Toussaint (1961): A comparison, Studia Africana, 79; Sografi's operatic adaptation of Corneille's Horace for Cimarosa: Gli Orazi e i Curiazi (1797), 18th Century Studies, 79; A French Romantic poet's adaptation of medieval Spanish Romances, WVa Univ Philol Papers, 81; L'art de petrarquiser in Antoni Deschamps' Etudes sur l'Italie (1833), Italica, 81. *Mailing Add:* Kalamazoo College Kalamazoo MI 49007

COHEN, WILLIAM HOWARD, b Jacksonville, Fla, Aug 13, 27; m 52. COMPARATIVE LITERATURE, PHILOSOPHY. *Educ:* Univ Fla, BA, 50, MA, 54; Southern Ill Univ, PhD(philos, Asian studies), 70. *Prof Exp:* Asst prof English & humanities, Oglethorpe Univ, 60-63; from asst prof to prof English, humanities & philos, Alice Lloyd Col, 63-72; vis lectr English & humanities, Fla Jr Col, Jacksonville, 73-77; author-in-residence, Shimer Col, 77-78; VIS PROF ENGLISH & COMP LIT, NAT CHENGCHI UNIV, TAIWAN, 78- *Concurrent Pos:* Consult English & humanities, Prog Develop Insts, Am Asn Jr Cols, 71-72; poet in the schs, Jacksonville Children's Mus, 75-77. *Honors & Awards:* Int Laureate Poet, 69; Dipl Aureum Honoris Causa, Third World Cong Poets, 76. *Mem:* NCTE; Poetry Soc Am; Haiku Soc Am. *Res:* Translation and study of Chinese and Japanese poetry; translation of Rilke, especially the Sonnets to Orpheus and Duino Elegies; children's poetry and teaching language basics. *Publ:* Auth, The Hill Way Home (verse), Alice Lloyd Col, 65; The Calligraphy of the Cosmos: The Essence of Haiku, Lit East & West, 9/65; Education, Transformer of Man, Southern Humanities Rev, fall 67; The Eternal Meets Now: Season in Japanese Haiku, Haiku Mag, Toronto, winter 69; Haiku: The Poetry of Silence, Haiku of Haiku West, Japan Soc, spring 69; The Silent Thunder of Silent Things: Robert Spiess, Haiku West, fall 71; Mexico 68: The New World of Man (Olympic/verse cycle), Southern Ill Univ Int Educ, 71; To Walk in Seasons: An Introduction to Haiku, Tuttle, Tokyo, 72. *Mailing Add:* Dept of Western Lang & Lit Chengchi Univ Taipei Taiwan China, Republic of

COHN, DORRIT, b Vienna, Austria, Aug 9, 24; US citizen; c 2. GERMAN & COMPARATIVE LITERATURE. *Educ:* Radcliffe Col, BA, 45, MA, 46; Stanford Univ, PhD(Ger), 64. *Prof Exp:* From asst prof to prof Ger, Ind Univ, Bloomington, 64-71; actg chmn, Ger Dept, 77-78, PROF GER, HARVARD UNIV, 71- *Concurrent Pos:* Guggenheim Found fel, 70-71; mem adv comt, PMLA, 75-79; chmn div 20th century Ger lit, MLA, 76-77; mem ed adv bd, German Quart, 78-; vis sr fel, Coun of Humanities, Princeton Univ, 82- *Mem:* Am Asn Teachers Ger; Am Comp Lit Asn; MLA; Acad Lit Studies. *Res:* Modern novel; 19th and 20th century German literature; narrative theory. *Publ:* Auth, The Sleepwalkers: Elucidations of Hermann Broch's Trilogy, Mouton, The Hague, 66; Narrated monologue: Definition of a fictional style, Comp Lit, 66; Kafka's Eternal Present, PMLA, 68; K enters the castle, Euphorion, 68; Psyche and space in Musie's Die Vollendung der Liebe, Germanic Rev, 74; Kleist's Marquise von O--: The problem of knowledge, Monatshefte, 75; Transparent Minds: Narrative Modes for Presenting Consciousness in Fiction, Princeton Univ, 78; Als Traum erzählt: The case for a Freudian reading of Hofmannsthal's Märchen der 672 Nacht, Deutsche Vierteljahrsschrift, 80; The Encirclement of Narrative, Poetics Today, 81; transl, Transparent Minds (La transparence interieure), Seuil, Paris, 81. *Mailing Add:* Dept of Germanic Lang Harvard Univ Boylston Hall Cambridge MA 02138

COHN, ROBERT G, b Richmond, Va, Sept 5, 21; m 47; c 2. FRENCH. *Educ:* Univ Va, BA, 43; Yale Univ, MA, 47, PhD, 49. *Prof Exp:* Founding ed, Yale French Studies, 48-49, instr French, Yale Univ, 49-50; Fulbright fel, 50-51; asst prof French, Swarthmore Col, 52-54 & Vassar Col, 54-57; assoc prof, 59-64, PROF FRENCH, STANFORD UNIV, 64- *Concurrent Pos:* Guggenheim fel, 56-57; in charge confs French, Univ NY, 54-57; fels, Am Coun Learned Soc & Nat Endowment for Humanities, 69-70; assoc ed, Stanford Fr Rev & Stanford French & Italian Studies. *Mem:* MLA. *Res:* French poetry; 19th and 20th century French literature. *Publ:* Auth, Mallarme's Un coup de des, Yale Fr Studies, 49; L'Oeuvre de Mallarme: un coup de des, Libr Les Lett, Paris, 51; The Writer's Way in France, Univ Pa, 60; Toward the Poems of Mallarme, Univ Calif, 65; Mallarme's Masterwork, Mouton, The Hague, 67; The Poetry of Rimbaud, Princeton Univ, 74; Modes of art, Stanford Fr & Ital Studies, 75. *Mailing Add:* Dept of French & Ital Stanford Univ Stanford CA 94305

COKE, JAMES WILSON, b Livia, Ky, May 27, 29. FRENCH, ITALIAN. *Educ:* Western Ky State Col, AB, 51; Ind Univ, MA, 53, PhD, 58. *Prof Exp:* From instr to assoc prof French & Ital, 57-76, PROF MOD LANG, COL WILLIAM & MARY, 76- *Concurrent Pos:* vis prof lectr 17th century French theatre, George Washington Univ, 73-74; vis lectr French & Ital, Univ Exeter, UK, 75-76. *Mem:* MLA; Am Asn Teachers Fr; Am Asn Teachers Ital. *Res:* French and Italian baroque literature; 17th and 20th century French theatre. *Mailing Add:* Dept of Mod Lang Col of William & Mary Williamsburg VA 23185

COLANERI, JOHN NUNZIO, b New York, NY, Jan 8, 30; m 67; c 1. ITALIAN LANGUAGES & LITERATURE. *Educ:* City Col New York, BA, 52; Columbia Univ, MA, 54, PhD(Ital), 68. *Prof Exp:* PROF ITAL & CHMN DEPT MOD LANG, IONA COL, 59- *Concurrent Pos:* Part-time lectr Ital, Col New Rochelle, 61- *Mem:* Ital Teachers Asn (pres, 69-71); Am Asn Teachers Span & Port. *Publ:* Auth, Fra Cristoforon and L'innominato: Two of a kind?, J NY State Fed Foreign Lang Teachers, 5/68; translr, Giovannitti, the United Nations silver anniversary, Thought, summer 70; auth, Reflection of a man: Guido Cavalcanti, Paideuma, winter 72; Edition of Lezzioni d'amore, Fink, Munich, 73; co-ed (with G Lipton), Italian English--English Italian Bilingual Dict, 80, 2nd ed, 82. *Mailing Add:* Dept of Mod Lang Iona Col New Rochelle NY 10801

COLARUSSO, JOHN J, JR, b San Diego, Calif, June 30, 45; m 75; c 1. LINGUISTICS, CAUCASIAN LANGUAGES. *Educ:* Cornell Univ, BA, 67; Northwestern Univ, MA, 69; Harvard Univ, PhD(ling), 75. *Prof Exp:* Vertragsasst ling, Univ Vienna, 75-76; asst prof, 76-81, ASSOC PROF LING, MCMASTER UNIV, 81- *Concurrent Pos:* Sr res assoc, Inst Study Human Issues, 79- *Mem:* Ling Soc Am; Can Ling Asn. *Res:* Phonology including phonetics; northwest Caucasian languages and folklore; syntax. *Publ:* Auth, Rightward movement, question formation and the nature of transformational processes: The Circassian case, Papiere zur Ling, 21: 27-73; North-western Caucasian languages, In: The Modern Encycl of Russian and Soviet Literature, Vol 3, Acad Int Press, 79; Phonemic contrasts and distinctive features: Caucasian examples, In: The Elements: A Parasession on Linguistic Units and Levels, Including Papers from the Conference on the Non-Slavic Languages of the USSR, Univ Chicago, 79; A wildman of the Caucasus, In: Manlike Monsters on Trial, Early Records and Modern Evidence, Univ BC Press, 80; Circassian West (Bzhedukh dialect), In: The Modern Encycl of Russian and Soviet Literature, Vol 4, Acad Int Press, 81; Typological parallels between Proto-Indo-European and the Northwest Caucasian languages, In: Bono Homini Donum: Essays in Historical Linguistics in Memory of J Alexander Kerns, Vol 2, John Benjamins B V, Amsterdam, 81; Epic, Nart: North Caucasian, In: The Modern Encycl of Russian and Soviet Literature, Vol 6, Acad Int Press (in press); Western Circassian Vocalism, Folia Slavica, 5, Proc Second Int Conf on Non-Slavic Lang USSR (in press). *Mailing Add:* Dept of Anthrop McMaster Univ Hamilton ON L8S 4L9 Can

COLBY-HALL, ALICE MARY, b Portland, Maine, Feb 25, 32; m 76. MEDIEVAL FRENCH LITERATURE. *Educ:* Colby Col, BA, 53; Middlebury Col, MA, 54; Columbia Univ, PhD(French), 62. *Prof Exp:* Teacher high sch, Maine, 54-55; teacher French, Gould Acad, Bethel, Maine, 55-57; lectr, Columbia Univ, 59-60; from instr to assoc prof Romance lit, 62-75, PROF ROMANCE LIT, CORNELL UNIV, 75- *Mem:* Mediaeval Acad Am; MLA; Soc Rencesvals; Int Arthurian Soc. *Res:* Chretien de Troyes; the style of medieval French literary texts; William cycle epics. *Publ:* Auth, The Portrait in 12th Century French Literature: An Example of the Stylistic Originality of Chretien de Troyes, Droz, 65; Le substrat arlesien, VIII Congreso de la Soc Rencesvals, 81; Orange et Arles: Un royaume pour deux Guillaumes, Bull des Amis d'Orange, 81. *Mailing Add:* Dept of Romance Studies Goldwin Smith Hall Cornell Univ Ithaca NY 14853

COLE, ANDREW THOMAS, JR, b Chilhowie, Va, Aug 22, 33; m 65; c 2. CLASSICS. *Educ:* Harvard Univ, BA, 54, PhD(classics), 60. *Prof Exp:* Instr Latin & Greek, Harvard Univ, 59-62; asst prof, Stanford Univ, 62-65; assoc prof, 65-71, PROF LATIN & GREEK, YALE UNIV, 71- *Mem:* Am Philol Asn. *Res:* Greek political theory, metrics and philosophy. *Publ:* Auth, Democritus and the Sources of Greek Anthropology, Case Western Reserve Univ (APA), 67. *Mailing Add:* Dept of Classics Yale Univ New Haven CT 06520

COLE, HOWARD CHANDLER, English Literature. See Vol II

COLE, PETER, b Miami Beach, Fla, Aug 1, 41; US citizen; m 58; c 2. LINGUISTICS, LANGUAGE TEACHING. *Educ:* Bard Col, AB, 62; Southern Ill Univ, Carbondale, MA, 71; Univ Ill, Urbana, PhD(ling), 73. *Prof Exp:* Instr English, Haifa Univ, Haifa, 67-68 & Southern Ill Univ, Carbondale, 69-73; asst prof, 73-80, ASSOC PROF LING, UNIV ILL, URBANA-CHAMPAIGN, 80- *Mem:* Linguistic Soc Am. *Res:* Syntax and foreign language instruction; semantics; Hebrew and Quechua. *Publ:* Ed, Speech Acts, Vol III, In: Syntax and Semantics, Seminar Press, 74; auth, The synchronic and diachronic status of conversational implicature, In: Syntax and Semantics, Seminar Press, 74; Indefiniteness and anaphoricity, Language; Global grammar vs index grammar: A question of power, Found Lang. *Mailing Add:* Dept of Ling Univ of Ill at Urbana-Champaign Urbana IL 61801

COLE, ROGER L, b Bay City, Mich, Aug 1, 33; m 56; c 6. GERMANIC LANGUAGES & LITERATURES. *Educ:* Univ Mich, BA, 57, MA, 58, PhD(Ger), 63. *Prof Exp:* From instr to assoc prof, 59-71, chmn dept mod & class lang, 70-81, PROF GER LANG & LIT, WESTERN MICH UNIV, 71- *Concurrent Pos:* Fulbright traveling grant & Western Mich Univ res grant, 66; lectr, Pädagogische Hochsch, Berlin, 66; ed, Mich Foreign Lang Newslett, 70-73. *Mem:* MLA; Am Coun Teaching Foreign Lang. *Res:* Das Horspiel--German radio drama; sociolinguistics; American and German literary naturalism. *Publ:* Auth, Foreign language in the residence hall, Mod Lang J, 10/65; European radio drama still lives, 1-2/65 & translr, Radio drama by Hansjorg Schmitthenner, part I, 11-12/65 & part II, 11-12/66, Nat Asn Educ Broadcasters J; The Ethical Foundations of Rudolf Binding's Gentlemen Concept, Mouton, The Hague, 66; Divergent and convergent attitudes toward the Alsatian dialect, Anthrop Ling, 9/75; Radio drama in Germany, Europ Broadcasting Union, 9/80; Un temoignage de soutien pour le theatre radiophonique en Allemagne, Union Europeene De Radiodiffusion, 9/80. *Mailing Add:* Dept of Mod & Classical Lang Western Michigan Univ Kalamazoo MI 49001

COLE, ROGER WILLIAM, b Tampa, Fla, Apr 15, 35; m 60; c 3. LINGUISTICS, ENGLISH. *Educ:* Univ Fla, BA, 56, MA, 62; Auburn Univ, PhD(ling), 68. *Prof Exp:* Instr, English, Auburn Univ, 62-65; asst prof English & dir freshman English, Miss State Univ, 68-69; from asst prof to assoc prof, 69-78, PROF LING, UNIV S FLA, TAMPA, 78- CHMN DEPT, 69- *Concurrent Pos:* Richard M Weaver fel, Intercollegiate Studies Inst, 68-69; dir, Ling Inst of Ling Soc Am, 75. *Mem:* Ling Soc Am; Southeastern Conf Ling; MLA; Southeastern Mod Lang Asn; Asn Dept Foreign Lang. *Res:* Applied linguistics; psycholinguistics; English language. *Publ:* Auth, Indian linguistics in Flordia: A survey of current trends, Lang Quart, 74; ed, Current Issues in Linguistic Theory, Ind Univ, Bloomington, 77; coauth, Language and discourse structure, 77 & Functional sentence perspective in Moore and other languages, 78, Lang Today; Contextual effects of sex-linked variables in spoken discourse, Proc Minn Inst Advan Studies, 79. *Mailing Add:* Dept of Ling Univ of S Fla Tampa FL

COLECCHIA, FRANCES, b Pittsburgh, Pa. MODERN LANGUAGES. *Educ:* Duquesne Univ, BEd, 47; Univ Pittsburgh, MLitt, 49, PhD, 54. *Prof Exp:* Dir lang lab prog, 60-72, PROF SPAN, DUQUESNE UNIV, 47-, CHMN MOD LANG DEPT, 77- *Concurrent Pos:* Assoc ed, Estudios, 51-55; V Cicto Int fel, Cent Univ Eduador, 62; Fulbright lectr grant, Colombia, 63-64; vis prof Span novel, Mt Mercy Col, 68; ed, NALLD Sec Sch Dir Pa, 69; guest lectr Latin Am lit, Educ Prof Develop Assistance Inst, ECarolina Univ, 69; grant, US Off Educ Inst, Crisis: Women in Higher Educ, 71; assoc ed, Garcia Lorca Rev, 73-; coordr res prog, Women Ethnicity and Mental Health, 75-77. *Honors & Awards:* Am-Ital Women of Achievement Award, 69. *Mem:* MLA; Inst Int Lit Iberoam; Am Asn Univ Women; Nat Coun Admin Women Educ; Am Asn Teachers Span & Port. *Res:* Latin American theatre; theatre of Garcia Lorca; contemporary Latin American literature of protest. *Publ:* Auth, Repaso Oral, Heath, 67; Paisajes y Personajes Lationamericanos, Van Nostrand, 71; coauth, Selected Latin-American One-Act Plays, Univ Pittsburgh, 73. *Mailing Add:* Dept of Mod Lang Duquesne Univ Pittsburgh PA 15219

COLEMAN, INGRID ROBERTA HOOVER, b Evanston, Ill, Dec 12, 34; m 58; c 2. FRENCH LITERATURE, DRAMA. *Educ:* Western Col for Women, Oxford, AB, 56; Univ Va, Charlottesville, MA, 59; Emory Univ, PhD(French), 80. *Prof Exp:* ASST PROF FRENCH, MOREHOUSE COL, ATLANTA, 81- *Mem:* MLA; Am Asn Teachers of French; SAtlantic Modern Lang Asn. *Res:* Theatre of the absurd; myth in contemporary French literature. *Publ:* Auth, Conscious and unconscious intent in the creative process: A letter from Eugene Ionesco, French Rev, 81; The professor's dilemma: The absurd comic principle in Ionesco's La Lecon, Perspectives on Contemp Lit, 82. *Mailing Add:* 476 Princeton Way NE Atlanta GA 30307

COLEMAN, JOHN ALEXANDER, b Hartford, Conn, July 11, 35. CONTEMPORARY LATIN AMERICAN & COMPARATIVE LITERATURE. *Educ:* Harvard Col, BA, 57; Middlebury Col, MA, 58; Columbia Univ, PhD(Span), 64. *Prof Exp:* Instr Span, Columbia Col, New York, 60-62; asst prof, Wellesley Col, 64-67; assoc prof, 67-81, chmn Span & Port dept, 78-81, PROF SPAN, NY UNIV, 81- *Res:* Contemporary Latin American fiction; works of Eca de Queiroz. *Publ:* Translr, Jean Grenier, Conversations on the Good Uses of Freedom, Identity Press, 67; auth, Other Voices: A Study of the Late Poetry of Luis Cernuda, Univ NC, 67; ed, Cinco Maestros, Harcourt, 69; Notes on Borges and American Literature, Tri-Quart, fall 72; Eca de Queiros and European Realism, NY Univ Press, 80. *Mailing Add:* Dept of Spanish New York Univ New York NY 10003

COLEMAN, WILLIAM EMMET, English Literature, Medieval Languages & Literature. See Vol II

COLHOUN, EDWARD RUSSELL, b Bayonne, NJ, Mar 13, 39; m 65; c 2. SPANISH, LINGUISTICS. *Educ:* Cornell Univ, AB, 60, PhD(Span & ling), 67. *Prof Exp:* Chmn span, 67-75, ASST PROF SPAN & LING, SIMON FRASER UNIV, 66- *Concurrent Pos:* Latin Am Studies Prog, Simon Fraser Univ. *Mem:* Prog Interam Ling y Ensenanza Idiomas; Asn Ling y Filol Am Latina. *Res:* Spanish-Caribbean dialectology; applied linguistics; bilingualism and biculturalism. *Publ:* Coauth, Generative phonology and historical Romance linguistics, Taegu Rev, 71; auth, Cultural and linguistic pluralism, Etudes de Linguistique Appliquee, Didier, Paris, 74; coauth, English loanwords in Korean--lexical and phonological problems, Appl Ling, Seoul, Korea, 76; auth, A re-evaluation of Cakchiquel phonology--a three village model, Occasional Papers, Latin Am Studies Prog, Cornell Univ, 82. *Mailing Add:* Dept of Lang Lit & Ling Simon Fraser Univ Burnaby BC V5A 1S6 Can

COLIMORE, VINCENT J, Philosophy of Education, Modern Languages. See Vol IV

COLKER, MARVIN LEONARD, b Pittsburgh, Pa, Mar 19, 27. LATIN. *Educ:* Harvard Univ, PhD(classics), 51. *Prof Exp:* Fulbright fel, Univ Paris, 51; Sheldon fel, Harvard Univ, 51-52; from instr to assoc prof classics, 53-67, chmn dept, 63-67, sesquicentennial assoc, 73-74, PROF CLASSICS, UNIV VA, 67- *Concurrent Pos:* Cataloguer mediaeval manuscripts, Univ Dublin, 58-; Am Coun Learned Soc fel, 62-63; mem ed comt, Medievale et Humanitistica, 69-; Nat Endowment for Humanities grants, 70-73; Guggenheim fel, 73-74. *Mem:* Mediaeval Acad Am; NAm Patristic Soc; Am Philol Asn; Archaeol Inst Am; Class Asn Mid West & South. *Res:* Mediaeval Latin literature and paleography; Latin textual criticism. *Publ:* Auth, Latin poems from Paris Codex B N lat 8433, Medievalia et Humanistica, 58; De nobilitate animi, Mediaeval Studies, 61; Richard of Saint Victor and the anonymous of Bridlington, Traditio, 62; Analecta Dublinensia, Mediaeval Acad Am, 75; A Hagiographic polemic, Mediaeval Studies, 77; Galteri De Castellione Alexandreis, Antenore, 78. *Mailing Add:* Dept of Classics Univ of Va Charlottesville VA 22903

COLLET, GEORGES-PAUL, b Biere, Switz, Apr 8, 17; m 42; c 2. FRENCH & COMPARATIVE LITERATURE. *Educ:* Univ Geneva, Lic es Lett, 43, cert pedag, 51, Dr es Lett, 57. *Prof Exp:* Instr, Lemania Sch, Lausanne, 43-47; lectr French, Durham Univ, 48-50; prof, UN, Geneva, 51-59; vis prof French lit, Univ Tex, Austin, 59-60; prof, Tulane Univ, 60-63; vis prof, Fla State Univ, 63-64; chmn French dept, 66-71, PROF FRENCH LIT, McGILL UNIV, 64- *Concurrent Pos:* Publ grant, Univ Geneva, 57, privat docent fac lett, 58-59; Can Coun leave fel, 71-72. *Honors & Awards:* Chevalier, Palmes Academiques, 64. *Mem:* MLA; Am Asn Teachers French; Can Asn Comp Lit; Soc Amis Marcel Proust; Soc Amis Francois Mauriac. *Res:* French and English comparative literature; art history; 19th and 20th century French literature. *Publ:* Auth, George Moore et la France, Droz, Geneva & Minard, Paris 57; ed, Andre Gide, epistolier, Fr Rev, 5/65; Jacques-Emile Blanche, epistolier, Etudes Francaises, 2/67; Marcel Proust et Jacques-Emile Blanche, Bull Amis Marcel Proust, 74; Francois Mauriac-Jacques-Emile Blanche, Correspondance, Grosset, Paris, 76; Andre Gide-Jacques-Emile Blanche, Correspondance, Gallimard, Paris, 78. *Mailing Add:* Dept of French PO Box 6070 McGill University Montreal PQ H3A 1B1 Can

COLLET, PAULETTE F, b Verviers, Belgium, Oct 21, 26. ROMANCE LANGUAGES. *Educ:* Univ London, BA, 49; Laval Univ, MA, 61, PhD(French Can lit), 62. *Prof Exp:* Asst prof French, Kans State Teachers Col, 62-63; from asst prof to assoc prof, St Peter's Col, 63-67; assoc prof, 67-70, PROF FRENCH CAN LIT, UNIV ST MICHAEL'S COL, 70- *Res:* French Canadian drama; French-Canadian women novelists; Canada in the French novel. *Publ:* Auth, L'Hiver dans le roman Canadien-Francais, Laval Univ, 65; Modern French: A Grammar Review, Appleton, 73; Marie Le Franc: deux patries, deux exils, Sherbrooke, Naaman, 76; La notion du bien et du mal chez Louise Maheux-Forcier, Presence francophone, 77; ed, Le Franc, Naric: Grand-Louis L'innocent, Sherbrooke, Naaman, 78; auth, La Quarantaine: Age De L'abdication ou Du Renouveau pour La Pemme Dans Le Theatre De Marcel Dube, L'art Dramatique Canadien, Automne, 79; Les Romancieres Quebeivises Des Amnees Go Face A La Maternite, Atlantis, Vol V, No 2, Printemps, 80; Les Etres Divises Du Monde De Monique Bosco, Etudes Canadiennes, 6/10/81. *Mailing Add:* Dept of French St Michael's Col 81 St Mary St Toronto ON M5S 1J4 Can

COLLIGNON, JEAN HENRI, b Bagneres de Bigorre, France, Nov 23, 18. FRENCH. *Educ:* Univ Toulouse, Lic es Anglais, 42; Univ Paris, Agrege, 44. *Prof Exp:* Instr English, Lycee Faidherbe, France, 45-46; instr French, Yale Univ, 46-50; asst prof, Cornell Univ, 50-56; assoc prof, Douglass Col, Rutgers Univ, 56-59 & 60-61; vis prof, Smith Col, 59-60, prof, 61-69; PROF FRENCH, UNIV MASS, BOSTON, 69- *Concurrent Pos:* Taft lectr, Univ Cincinnati, 56. *Mem:* Am Asn Teachers Fr; Soc Fr Professors Am. *Res:* Contemporary French and comparative literature. *Publ:* Coauth, Patters of French, Harcourt, 57, 2nd ed, 61; transl, Andre Gide et Hamlet, Rev Lett Mod, 71; Number One, Gallimard, Paris; The sincerity of Andre Gide, Yale Fr Studies. *Mailing Add:* Dept of French Univ of Mass Boston MA 02125

COLLINS, DAVID ALMON, b Caribou, Maine, Jan 9, 31; m 51; c 5. FRENCH LANGUAGE & LITERATURE. *Educ:* Univ Maine, BA, 52; Yale Univ, MAT, 53; Brown Univ, PhD, 62. *Prof Exp:* Master French & Span, Denver Country Day Sch, 53-56; teaching asst, Brown Univ, 56-58, instr French, 59-60; instr, Univ NH, 60-63; from asst prof to assoc prof, 63-76, PROF ROMANCE LANG & LIT, KALAMAZOO COL, 76- *Concurrent Pos:* Consult, Choice, 64- *Mem:* MLA. *Res:* French classical theatre; Diderot and Rousseau; history of rationalist thought in France. *Publ:* Auth, Thomas Corneille: Protean Dramaist, Mouton, The Hague, 66. *Mailing Add:* Dept of Romance Lang Kalamazoo Col Kalamazoo MI 49007

COLLINS, PATRICK JOSEPH, b New York, NY, Jan 6, 20. CLASSICS, CREATIVE WRITING. *Educ:* Fordham Univ, BS, 44, AM, 49. *Prof Exp:* Latin instr, Sch Educ, Fordham Univ, 49-51; from instr to asst prof, 58-66, chmn classics dept, 58-67 & 76-79, fac fel, 68-69, ASSOC PROF LATIN, IONA COL, 67- *Concurrent Pos:* Assoc ed, Class Folia, 63-71; mem staff, Univ Utah Writer's Conf, 64; founder & dir, Iona Col Writer's Conf, 64, mem staff, 68 & 70; mem staff, La Salle Col Writer's Conf, 65, 66 & 67. *Mem:* Class Asn Atlantic States; Cath Press Asn; Soc Mag Writers. *Res:* Humanism; non-Western studies; theology. *Publ:* Auth, Work and ecumenism, Friar, 10/67; Non-Western studies in our schools, Our Studies, 5/68; Education for the 21st century, America, 1/69; Today's campus crisis, Cath Educr, 1/69; Secondary schools in the 21st century, Cath Educr, 2/70; Montserrat: Mary's mountain, Cath Digest, 5/70; Priestly celibacy, US Cath-Jubilee, 1/71; Athletes for hire, America, 79. *Mailing Add:* Dept of Classics Iona College New Rochelle NY 10801

COLLINS, RALPH STOKES, b Grifton, NC, Nov 1, 10; m 38; c 4. GERMAN LANGUAGE & LITERATURE, RUSSIAN. *Educ:* Univ NC, AB, 30, MA, 31; Johns Hopkins Univ, PhD (Ger), 38. *Prof Exp:* Instr Ger, Univ NC, 30-32; assoc prof, Maryville Col, 35-45; foreign serv officer, 45-67; prof German & chmn dept mod lang, Maryville Col, 67-79. *Mem:* MLA; Am Coun Teaching Foreign Lang; SAtlantic Mod Lang Asn. *Res:* German classical period; German drama of the 19th century; Thomas Mann. *Publ:* Auth, Hermann Bahr's Die Mutter, Ger Rev, 2/42. *Mailing Add:* 1741 Linda Lane Maryville TN 37801

COLMAN, CHARLES WILSON, b Brookfield, NH, Sept 22, 09; m 35; c 4. FRENCH LITERATURE. *Educ:* Harvard Univ, AB, 30; Cornell Univ, PhD, 38 . *Prof Exp:* Instr, Cornell Univ, 34-37; instr French, Univ Ill, 37-41, assoc, 41-45; assoc prof, Univ Miss, 46-47; from assoc prof to prof Romance lang, Univ Nebr, 47-64, chmn dept, 56-64; prof French, State Univ NY Albany, 64-82, chmn, Dept Romance Lang, 64-68, assoc dean, Col Arts & Sci, 68-71, dir off int prog, 71-82; RETIRED. *Mem:* MLA. *Res:* Vagabond and beggar literature of the nineteenth century. *Mailing Add:* 12 Glenwood McKnownville NY 12203

COLTHARP, LURLINE HUGHES, b Bridgeport, Tex, May 9, 13; m 35; 63; c 2. ENGLISH, LINGUISTICS. *Educ:* Univ Tex, Austin, BA, 35, MA, 51, PhD(English ling), 64. *Prof Exp:* Teacher, Ysleta Grade Sch, 32-34, 45-47, 49-50 & 52-53; from instr to assoc prof English, 54-70, prof, 70-81, EMER PROF LING & ENGLISH, UNIV TEX, EL PASO, 81- *Concurrent Pos:* Training asst, Peace Corps Colombia IV Proj, 62-63; conductor, sem prof English, Univ Durango, 64 & Univ Sinaloa, 64 & 66; vis lectr, Inst Mex Am Resls Cult, Hermosillo, Mex, 66. *Mem:* SCent Mod Lang Asn; Am Name Soc (pres, 78); Ling Soc Am; MLA; Teachers English Speakers Other Lang. *Res:* Dialect study; teaching English as a foreign language. *Publ:* Auth, The Tongue of the Tirilones: A Linguistic Study of a Criminal Argot, Univ Ala, 65; Invitation to the dance, In: Texan Studies in Bilingualism, Walter Gruyter & Co, Berlin, 68; A ditigal classification of place names: A note, Names, 9/72; Bilingual onomastics: A case study, In: Bilingualism in the Southwest, Univ Ariz, 72; A Bilingual dialectology course, Hispania, 3/74; Pachuco, Tirilo and Chicano, Am Speech, spring-summer 75. *Mailing Add:* Dept of English Univ of Tex El Paso TX 79968

COLTON, ROBERT EDWARD, b Portland, Maine, July 7, 22; m 64. CLASSICAL PHILOLOGY, COMPARATIVE LITERATURE. *Educ:* Bowdoin Col, AB, 44; Columbia Univ, AM, 47, PhD(class lang), 59. *Prof Exp:* Instr classics, NY Univ, 49-51 & Univ Okla, 51-53; interim asst prof, Univ Fla, 53-54; asst prof, Cath Univ Am, 55-59, La State Univ, 59-60, Miami Univ, 60-61 & Loyola Univ, La, 61-62; assoc prof, Duquesne Univ, 62-66; RES & WRITING, 66- *Mem:* Am Philol Asn; Class Asn Atlantic States. *Res:* Roman satire and elegy; influence of the classics on modern literature. *Publ:* Auth, Echoes of Martial in Juvenal's Third Satire, 66 & Juvenal and Propertius, 67, Traditio; Philemon and Baucis in Ovid and La Fontaine, Class J, 68; Juvenal 6.398-412, 6.419-433 & Martial, Classica et Mediaevalia, 70; Echoes of Persius in Boileau, Latomus, 76; Echoes of Martial in Juvenal's 14th Satire, Hermes, 77; Martial in Juvenal's 10th Satire, Studies Philol, 77; A note on Juvenal and Pushkin, Class World, 81. *Mailing Add:* 8105 Eastern Ave C311 Silver Spring MD 20910

COMAN, COLETTE M, US Citizen. FRENCH LITERATURE. *Educ:* Fac des Lett l'Univ Paris, BA, 46; Univ Bucarest, dipl Fr, 53; City Univ New York, PhD(Fr), 80. *Prof Exp:* Instr French, Manhattanville Col, 66-67; INSTR FRENCH, CITY UNIV NEW YORK, GRAD CTR, 77- *Mem:* Am Asn Teachers Fr. *Res:* Poetics of fiction; representation of identity and proper names; autobiography. *Publ:* Auth, Noms propres et duree dans La Princesse de Cleves, Fr Rev, 12/77; Le Voyeur dans les romans de Mme de La Fayette et la Recherche, Rev du Pacifique, 2/79; Le Paradoxe de la maxime dans Adolphe, Romanic Rev, 2/82. *Mailing Add:* 4625 Independence Ave Riverdale NY 10471

COMBE, GUY P, b Malo-les-Bains, France, Feb 14, 22; US citizen; m 46; c 2. FRENCH. *Educ:* Univ Algiers, Baccalaureat, 46; Univ Tex, BA, 50, MA, 54; Univ Okla, PhD(Romance lang), 78. *Prof Exp:* Asst prof French, Midwestern Univ, 46-58; asst, Univ Okla, 58-60; asst prof, Okla Col Women, 60-65; chmn dept mod lang, 65-80, ASSOC PROF FRENCH, OKLA BAPTIST UNIV, 65-, DIR MOD LANG, 80- *Mem:* Am Asn Teachers Fr; SCent Mod Lang Asn; Am Coun Teaching Foreign Lang. *Res:* Jules Romains; Robbe-Grillet and the Nouveau Roman. *Mailing Add:* Dept of Mod Lang Okla Baptist Univ Shawnee OK 74801

COMEAU, PAUL T, b New Bedford, Mass, Sept 21, 26; m 53; c 3. ROMANCE LANGUAGES. *Educ:* Assumption Col, Mass, BA, 49; Princeton Univ, MA, 64, PhD(French lang & lit), 68. *Prof Exp:* From instr to assoc prof French, US Air Force Acad, 64-70; dir educ, Air Force Res Off Training Corps Hq, Air Univ, Maxwell Air Force Base, Ala, 70-72; prof aerospace studies, 72-75, PROF FOREIGN LANG & HEAD DEPT, NMEX STATE UNIV, 75- *Concurrent Pos:* Acad coun humanities, US Air Force Acad, 68-70. *Mem:* MLA; Am Coun Teaching Foreign Lang; Am Asn Teachers Fr; Am Transl Asn; Am Lit Transl Asn. *Res:* Pre-Romantic and Romantic periods in French literature; French literature of Southeast Asia; Culture of Franco-Americans of New England. *Publ:* Auth, Le Satyre dans la Legende des siecles de Victor Hugo, Fr Rev, 5/66; Etienne Jouy: His life and his Paris essays, Diss Abstr, 69; Workbook for Wheeloch's Latin: An Introductory Course, Harper & Row, 80; The Love Theme and the Monologue Structure in Armance, 19th Century Fr Studies, fall-winter 81. *Mailing Add:* Dept of Foreign Lang NMex State Univ Las Cruces NM 88003

COMFORT, HOWARD, b Haverford, Pa, June 4, 04; m 31; c 2. LATIN, GREEK. *Educ:* Haverford Col, AB, 24; Princeton Univ, AM, 27, PhD, 32. *Prof Exp:* Teacher Latin, Haverford Sch, Pa, 24-26; asst prof Latin & Greek, Hamilton Col, 29-30; from instr to prof classics & chmn dept, 32-69, EMER PROF CLASSICS, HAVERFORD COL, 69- *Concurrent Pos:* Consult, Prison Industs Reorgn Admin, Washington, DC, 36; dir off, Am Friends Serv Comt, Rome, 40; cult attache, Am Embassy, Italy, 50-51; Am legation, Switz, 51-52; mem, Inst Advan Studies, 56, 60; bd mgr, Moore Col Art, 60-68; Am Philos Soc travel grant, Spain, 61. *Mem:* Am Philol Asn (secy-treas, 46-49, 2nd vpres, 60-61, 1st vpres, 61-62, pres, 62-63); Archaeol Inst Am; corresp mem, Accad Petrarca Lett, Arti e Sci; Rei Cretariae Romanae Fautores (pres, 57-71, hon pres, 71-); fel Soc Antiq London. *Res:* Latin literature; Roman ceramics. *Publ:* Ed, Oxe's Corpus vasorum arretinorum, Habelt, Bonn, 68; Notes on Roman ceramic archeology 1928-1978, RCRF, 8/79. *Mailing Add:* Crosslands 224 Kennett Square PA 19348

COMFORT, THOMAS EDWIN, b Streator, Ill, Apr 15, 21; m 45; c 5. FRENCH. *Educ:* Northwestern Univ, AB, 43; Univ Ill, Urbana, MA, 51, PhD(French), 54. *Prof Exp:* Instr Latin, French & Greek, St Ambrose Col, 47-49; instr French, Univ Ill, Urbana, 49-54; from asst prof to assoc prof, Tex A&M Univ, 54-65; head dept foreign lang, 65-74, PROF FRENCH, ILL STATE UNIV, 74- *Concurrent Pos:* Dir English lang prog, US Info Serv, Morocco, 58-60 & Dept Defense, Turkey, 61-63. *Mem:* Am Asn Teachers Fr; MLA; Am Coun Teaching Foreign Lang. *Res:* Old French; chanson de geste; 18th century French literature. *Mailing Add:* Dept of Foreign Lang Illinois State Univ Normal IL 61761

COMMAGER, STEELE, US citizen. CLASSICS. *Educ:* Harvard Univ, BA, 54. *Prof Exp:* From instr to asst prof classics, Harvard Univ, 58-65; assoc prof Greek & Latin, 65-71, PROF GREEK & LATIN, COLUMBIA UNIV, 71- *Mailing Add:* 618 Hamilton Hall Columbia Univ New York NY 10027

COMPITELLO, MALCOLM ALAN, b Brooklyn, NY, Feb 9, 46; m 77; c 1. SPANISH LANGUAGE & LITERATURE. *Educ:* St John's Univ, BA, 68, MA, 70; Ind Univ, PhD(Span), 77. *Prof Exp:* Asst prof, 77-81, ASSOC PROF SPAN, MICH STATE UNIV, 81- *Concurrent Pos:* Ed, The Am Hisp, 75- & An Annual Bibliog Post-Civil-War Span Fiction, 77-; vis prof, Span Sch, Middlebury Col, 80. *Mem:* Am Asn Teachers Span; MLA. *Res:* Contemporary Spanish literature; literary sociology; contemporary Spanish cultural history. *Publ:* Auth, Juan Benet and hist critics, Anales Novela Posguerra, 78; Teatro en el Metro: Un experimento teatral el Barcelona, Estreno, 79; The novel, the critics and the Civil War, Anales narrativa espanola contemp, 79; Region's Braziliam backlands, Hisp J, 80; Drama and the foreign language classroom, Ram's Horn: J Rassais Found, 82; Volveras a Region, the critics and the Spanish Civil WAr, Am Hisp, 82. *Mailing Add:* Dept Romance Lang Mich State Univ East Lansing MI 48824

COMPTON, BITA HALL, b Waco, Tex, Mar 31, 11. FRENCH, ITALIAN. *Educ:* Tex Christian Univ, AB, 31, MA, 36; Columbia Univ, PhD, 52. *Prof Exp:* Teacher French & Span, Clarendon Jr Col, Tex, 34-36; teacher Ft Worth pub schs, 36-38; prof French, Span & Ital, 38-76, EMER PROF FRENCH & SPAN, TEX CHRISTIAN UNIV, 76- *Mem:* MLA; Am Asn Teachers Fr; Am Coun Teachers Foreign Lang. *Res:* Medieval French literature; history of French language. *Mailing Add:* 3225 Tanglewood Trail Ft Worth TX 76109

COMPTON, MERLIN DAVID, b Ogden, Utah, July 22, 24; m 50; c 5. HISPANIC LANGUAGES & LITERATURE. *Educ:* Brigham Young Univ, BA, 52, MA, 54; Univ Calif, Los Angles, PhD(hisp lang & lit), 59. *Prof Exp:* Asst prof Span, Adams State Col, 59-63; assoc prof foreign lang, Weber Col, 63-64; assoc prof, Span & Port, 64-70, PROF SPAN & PORT, BRIGHAM YOUNG UNIV, 70- *Concurrent Pos:* Asst coord Madrid Sch Prog, For Univ Calif, Los Angeles Grad Sch Bus Admin, Spanish Govt & Int Coop Admin, 57. *Mem:* Am Asn Teachers Span & Port; Rocky Mountain Mod Lang Asn. *Res:* Style of Ricardo Palma; Dona Barbara. *Publ:* Auth, Las Tradiciones peruanas de Richardo Palma, Duquesne Hisp Rev, 69; Colejo de dos versiones de Lida, 74 & Estilo de las Tradiciones peruanas, 74, Fenix; Ricardo Palma, Twayne, 82. *Mailing Add:* Dept of Span Brigham Young Univ Provo UT 84602

CONACHER, DESMOND JOHN, b Kingston, Ont, Dec 27, 18; m 52. CLASSICAL PHILOLOGY. *Educ:* Queen's Univ, Ont, BA, 41, MA, 42; Univ Chicago, PhD, 50. *Prof Exp:* Asst classics, Queen's Univ, Ont, 41-42; spec lectr classics, Dalhousie Univ, 46-47; from asst prof to assoc prof, Univ Sask, 47-58; assoc prof classics, 58-66, head dept, 66-71, intercol chmn classics, 72-75, PROF CLASSICS, TRINITY COL, UNIV TORONTO, 66- *Concurrent Pos:* Class Asn Can univ lectr, 73 & 81; Bonsall vis prof, Stanford Univ, 81; dir, Can Fedn for Humanities, 81-83. *Mem:* Am Philol Asn; Class Asn Can; fel Royal Soc Can. *Res:* Euripidean drama Greek tragedy; Aeschylean tragedy. *Publ:* Auth, A problem in Euripides Hippolytus, Trans Am Philol Asn, 61; Themes in Exodus of Euripides' Phoenissae, Phoenix, 67; Euripidean Drama: Myth, Theme and Structure, Univ Toronto & Oxford Univ, 68; Probability and relevance in Euripidean drama, Maia, 72; Aeschylus, Persae, Serta Turyniana, Univ Ill, 74; Interaction between chorus and character in the Oresteia, Am J Philol, Vol 95, 74; Prometheus as founder of the arts, Greek, Roman & Byzantine Studies, Vol 18, 77; Aeschylus, Prometheus Bound: A Literary Commentary, Univ Toronto Press, 80. *Mailing Add:* Dept of Classics Trinity Col Univ of Toronto Toronto ON M5S 1H8 Can

CONANT, JONATHAN BRENDAN, b Hartford, Conn, Dec 16, 41; m 64; c 1. GERMANIC PHILOLOGY, PEDAGOGY. *Educ:* Yale Univ, AB, 64, MPhil, 68, PhD(Ger), 69. *Prof Exp:* Asst prof Ger, Brown Univ, 69-75, vis assoc prof, Univ Minn, Minneapolis, 75-77, ASSOC PROF FOREIGN LANG & LIT, UNIV MINN, DULUTH, 77- *Concurrent Pos:* Assoc ed, Unterrichtspraxis, 77- *Mem:* Am Asn Teachers Ger. *Res:* Old Icelandic poetry; runology and foreign language pedagogy. *Publ:* Ed, Cochran's German Review Grammar, Prentice-Hall, 74. *Mailing Add:* Dept of Foreign Lang & Lit Univ of Minn Duluth MN 55812

CONANT, JOSEPH M, b New York, NY, Jan 10, 13; m 41; c 3. CLASSICAL LANGUAGES & LITERATURE. *Educ:* Columbia Univ, AB, 34, AM, 36, PhD, 53. *Prof Exp:* Instr Greek, Bates Col, 39-41; instr Greek & Latin, Columbia Univ, 46-50; from asst prof to assoc prof classics, 50-61, chmn dept, 61-68, 73-76, PROF CLASSICS, EMORY UNIV, 61- *Concurrent Pos:* Fund Advan Educ fel, 54-55; mem managing comt, Am Sch Class Studies, Athens, 61, vis prof, 68-69. *Mem:* Am Philol Asn; Archaeol Inst Am; Class Asn Mid W & S; Soc Promotion of Hellenic Studies; Vergilian Soc. *Res:* Greek poetry and philosophy. *Mailing Add:* 447 Emory Dr NE Atlanta GA 30307

CONDOYANNIS, GEORGE EDWARD, b New York, NY, Sept 9, 15. MODERN LANGUAGES. *Educ:* Columbia Univ, AB, 35, AM, 37, PhD, 53. *Prof Exp:* Instr Ger, Columbia Univ, 36-39, Polytech Inst Brooklyn, 40-41 & Union Univ, NY, 41-43; instr Ger, French & Span, Univ Rochester, 43-46; from instr to asst prof mod lang, Mass Inst Technol, 45-46; from asst prof to assoc prof, 56-67, chmn dept, 68-74, PROF MOD LANG, ST PETER'S COL 67- *Mem:* MLA; Am Asn Teachers Ger; Am Asn Teachers Slavic & East Europ Lang. *Res:* German-American literature and prose fiction; German-English lexicography. *Publ:* Auth, Scientific German, 57 & Scientific Russian, 59, Wiley; coauth, Russian Speakit, McGraw, 61. *Mailing Add:* Dept of Mod Languages St Peter's College Jersey City NJ 07306

CONERLY, PORTER PATRICK, b Paterson, NJ, Dec 18, 48; m 72; c 2. SPANISH & ITALIAN LANGUAGE. *Educ:* King's Col, BA, 70; Univ NC, MA, 75, PhD (Romance philol), 79. *Prof Exp:* Instr Span, King's Col, 70; linguist, US Army, 70-73; ASST PROF SPAN & ITALIAN, WEST VA UNIV, 79- *Concurrent Pos:* Instr English, Univ de Sevilla, 77-78; grant, Nat Endowment for Humanities Workshop, Univ Wis, 76, US Dept Educ, 80, National Endowment for Humanities Inst, 81. *Honors & Awards:* Urban T Holmes Award, Univ NC, 79. *Mem:* MLA; Am Asn Teachers Span & Port; Renaissance Soc Am; South Atlantic Mod Lang Asn; North Am Catalan Soc. *Res:* Medieval Spanish literature; Spanish novel; Romance philology. *Publ:* Contribr, Bibliography of Old Spanish Texts, Hisp Semi, Ltd, 77; auth, Cinematografo y el realismo critico de Carranque de Rios, Cuadernos Americanos, 81; co-ed, Texts and Concordances of Juan Fernandez de Heredia, Hisp Sem, Ltd (in press); Largesse of the Epic Hero as a Thematic Pattern in the Cantar de mio Cid, Ky Romance Quart (in prep); contribr, Dictionary of Literature of the Iberian Peninsula, Greenwood Press (in prep). *Mailing Add:* Dept of Foreign Lang WVa Univ Morgantown WV 26506

CONLEY, TOM CLARK, b New Haven, Conn, Dec 7, 43; m 67; c 2. FRENCH LITERATURE. *Educ:* Lawrence Univ, BA, 65; Columbia Univ, MA, 67; Univ Wis-Madison, PhD(French), 71. *Prof Exp:* asst prof, 71-75, assoc prof, 75-79, PROF FRENCH, UNIV MINN, MINNEAPOLIS, 79- *Concurrent Pos:* Univ Minn grantee, 72-73; Am Coun Learned Soc study fel, 75-76; vis assoc prof French, Univ Calif, Berkeley, 78-79. *Mem:* MLA; Am Asn Teachers French; Midwest Mod Lang Asn; Am Soc Study Dada & Surrealism; Renaissance Soc Am. *Res:* Modern literature and criticism; 16th century literature and aesthetics; film. *Publ:* Auth, The radicality of modern art, Diacritics, 3/73; Feminism, ecriture and the closed room: les Angoysses douloureuses qui procedent damours (1538), Symposium, 12/73; Wasted, Diacritics, 76; Montaigne's Gascoingne, Mod Lang Notes, 77; Intervalle et arrachement: Malraux/Focillon, Revue des Lett Mod, 78; A last spending of Rhetoricque: Reading Marot Par Contradictions, L'Esprit createur, 78; Cataparalysis, Diacritics, 78; Les Abords d'vne lettre, Litterature, 81; On some figural problems of flamboyant architecture, Image & Cook, 81; Vigo/Van Gogh, NY Lit Forum, 82. *Mailing Add:* Dept of French & Italian 200 Folwell Hall Univ of Minn Minneapolis MN 55455

CONLON, PIERRE MARIE, b Reefton, NZ, Nov 8, 24; m 54; c 2. FRENCH LANGUAGE & LITERATURE. *Educ:* Univ Auckland, BA, 45, MA, 46; Univ Paris, DUniv, 54. *Prof Exp:* Lectr French, Univ Birmingham, 51-55; prof, Victoria Univ, NZ, 56-61; lectr, Yale Univ, 61-62; assoc prof, 62-64, PROF FRENCH, McMASTER UNIV, 64- *Mem:* Fel Royal Soc Can. *Res:* Voltaire; 18th century French literature. *Publ:* Auth, Voltaire's Literary Career From 1728 to 1750, Inst Voltaire, Switz, 61; Jean Francois Bion et sa relation des tourments soufferts par les Protestants, 66 & Prelude au siecle des lumieres en France (6 vols), 70-75, Droz, Geneva; co-transl, Goethe's Egmont, 76 & Marivaux, Two Plays, 76, Cromlech, Hamilton, 76; Ouvrages francais relatifs a Jean-Jaques Rousseau, Droz, Geneva, 81. *Mailing Add:* Dept of Romance Lang McMaster Univ Hamilton ON L8S 4K1 Can

CONNER, JOHN WAYNE, b Peterson, Utah, Jan 16, 19; m 42; c 4. ROMANCE LANGUAGES. *Educ:* Queen's Univ, Ont, BA, 41, MA, 42; Princeton Univ, PhD(French), 48. *Prof Exp:* From instr to assoc prof romance lang, Wash Univ, 48-62; prof, 62-77, head dept foreign lang, 62-68, dir div humanities, 68-73, chmn dept Romance lang, 68-80, DISTINGUISHED SERV PROF, UNIV FLA, 77- *Concurrent Pos:* Mem selection comt, region VI, Woodrow Wilson Nat Fel Found, 64-66; Camargo Found fel, 81. *Mem:* SAtlantic Mod Lang Asn; MLA; Am Asn Teachers Fr. *Res:* French literature of the 19th century; medieval French literature. *Publ:* Auth, Frame and story in Balzac, L'Esprit Createur, spring 67; Glossaire for the Contes drolatiques, In: Vol XX, Oeuvres Completes d'Honore de Balzac, 69; Loeve-Veimars, Translator of Reality, Rev Lit Comparee, 71; Un aspect de l'onomastique balzacienne: l'elaboration des noms de personnage, Actes 13th Congr Int Ling & Philol Romanes, 76; Une Pluie a Paris: The hidden history of a Balzac text, Ky Romance Quart, 77; Scott and Balzac, Scottish Lit J, 80. *Mailing Add:* Dept of Romance Lang Univ of Fla Gainesville FL 32611

CONNER, MAURICE WAYNE, b Houston, Tex, Aug 20, 38; m 66. GERMANIC LANGUAGE & LITERATURE. *Educ:* Univ Tex-Arlington, BA, 64; Univ Nebr-Lincoln, MA, 66, PhD(Ger), 73. *Prof Exp:* Instr English as second lang, Stuttgarter Fremdsprachenschule, 63-64; instr Ger, Univ Wis-Green Bay, 66-68; Instr, 71-73, asst prof, 73-76, assoc prof, 76-81, asst dean, Col Arts & Sci, 79-80, vchair, Dept Foreign Lang, 81-82, PROF GERMAN, UNIV NEBR, OMAHA, 81- *Concurrent Pos:* Lab dir, Univ Wis-Green Bay, 66-68; co-ed, Schatzkammer der deutschen Sprachlehre, 75-77; consult, Central States Conf Teaching Foreign Lang, 81-82. *Mem:* MLA; Am Coun Teaching Foreign Lang; Am Asn Teachers Ger; Int Arthur Schnitzler Res Asn. *Res:* Austrian literature; German-Americana; foreign language pedagogy. *Publ:* Coauth, A German dialect spoken in South Dakota: Swiss-Volhynian, Ger-Am Studies, 74; Language camp guidelines, Die Unterrichtspraxis, 74; auth, New curricular connections, In: The Language Connection: From the Classroom to the World, 77; From Switzerland to South Dakota: A two century journey, Schatzkammer, 79; Schnitzler's Sterben and Durrenmatt's Der Meteor: Two responses to the prospect of death, Ger Notes, 80; ed, New Frontiers in Foreign Language Education, 80 & A Global Approach to Foreign Language Education, 81, Nat Textbk Co; auth, Teaching global perspectives, Mod Lang J, 81. *Mailing Add:* Dept Foreign Lang Univ Nebr Omaha NE 68182

CONNER, WILLIAM BOUDINOT, b Portland, Ore, Apr 25, 13. ROMANCE LANGUAGES & LINGUISTICS. *Educ:* Oberlin Col, AB, 37; Univ Ill, AM, 39, 41-42. *Prof Exp:* Instr French & Span, Wis State Col, La Crosse, 44-45; instr, Wash State Col, 46-47; lectr French, Northwestern Univ, 56; assoc prof French & Span, Huron Col, SDak, 58-61; asst prof, St Cloud State Col, 61-63; instr Span, Temple Univ, 63-66; assoc prof, 66-76, prof, 76-79, EMER PROF FRENCH & SPAN, KUTZTOWN STATE COL, 79- *Mem:* MLA; Am Asn Teachers Span & Port. *Res:* Medieval French literature, the Tristan legend; Tonalingua-Concordophone system, which enhances coloristic poetry though addition of color light and chordal sound combinations. *Mailing Add:* 117 S Fourth St Allentown PA 18102

CONNOLLY, JULIAN WELCH, b Newburyport, Mass, 49; m 77. SLAVIC LANGUAGES & LITERATURE. *Educ:* Harvard Col, AB, 72; Harvard Univ, AM, 74, PhD(Slavic lang & lit), 77. *Prof Exp:* ASST PROF SLAVIC LANG & LIT, UNIV VA, 77- *Mem:* Am Asn Advan Slavic Studies; Am Asn Teachers Slavic & E Europ Lang; MLA. *Res:* Symbolism; early Soviet prose; Nabokov. *Publ:* Auth, The role of duality in Sologub's Tvorimaja Legenda, Die Welt der Slaven, 74-75; A modernist's palette: Color in the prose fiction of Eugenij Zamjatin, Russ Lang J, 79; Bunin's Petlistye Ushi: The Deformation of a Byronic Rebel, Can-Am Slavic Studies, 80; Desire and renunciation: Buddhist elements in the prose of Ivan Bunin, Can Slavonic Papers, 81; The function of literary allusion in Nabokov's Despair, Slavic and East Europ J, 82; Ivan Bunin, G K Hall & Co, 82. *Mailing Add:* Dept of Slavic Lang & Lit Cocke Hall B-22 Univ of Va Charlottesville VA 22903

CONRAD, CARL WILLIAM, b Washington, DC, July 22, 34; m 59; c 2. CLASSICS. *Educ:* Tulane Univ, BA, 55, MA, 56; Harvard Univ, PhD(classics), 64. *Prof Exp:* Instr French & Ger, Warren Wilson Col, 57-58; from instr to assoc prof classics, 61-73, PROF CLASSICS, WASH UNIV, 73-, CHMN DEPT, 80- *Res:* Greek philosophy and tragedy; Latin poetry. *Publ:* Auth, Traditional patterns of word-order in Latin epic from Ennius to Vergil, Harvard Studies Class Philol, 65. *Mailing Add:* 7222 Colgate Ave St Louis MO 63130

CONRAD, JOSEPH LAWRENCE, b Kansas City, Mo, June 26, 33; m 55; c 3. RUSSIAN LANGUAGE & LITERATURE. *Educ:* Univ Kans, BA, 55; Univ Tex, PhD, 61. *Prof Exp:* From instr to asst prof, Ger & Russ, Fla State Univ, 59-62; asst prof, Univ Tex, 62-66; chmn dept Slavic lang, 66-75, PROF RUSS LANG & LIT, UNIV KANS, 66- *Concurrent Pos:* Int Res & Exchanges Bd scholar, Moscow Univ, spring 74; Fulbright res scholar, Zagreb, Yugoslavia, 81. *Mem:* Am Asn Advan Slavic Studies; Am Asn Teachers Slavic & E Europ Lang; Am Asn S Slavic Studies; Am Asn Southeast Europ Studies. *Publ:* Auth, Cexov's An Attack of Nerves, winter 69, Cexov's Verocka: A polemical parody, winter 70 & Unresolved tension in Cexov's stories, 1886-1888, spring 72, Slavic & East Europ J; Russian Language Study in 1975: A Status Report: MLA & Ctr Applied Ling, 76; Anton Chekhov's literary landscapes, In: Chekhov's Art of Writing: A Collection of Critical Essays, Slavica, 77; Sensuality in Anton Chekhov's prose, Slavic & East Europ J; Metaphorical images of women in South Slavic proverbs, Balkanistica VI; Magic charms and healing rituals in contemporary Yugoslavia, Slavic Studies, special issue (in press). *Mailing Add:* Dept of Slavic Lang Univ of Kans Lawrence KS 66044

CONROY, PETER VINCENT, JR, b New York, NY, Apr 9, 44; m 67. FRENCH LANGUAGE & LITERATURE. *Educ:* Queens Col, NY, BA, 65, MA, 67, Univ Nancy, cert French lit & Philol, 66; Univ Wis, PhD(French), 70. *Prof Exp:* Asst prof, 70-74, ASSOC PROF FRENCH, UNIV ILL, CHICAGO CIRCLE, 74- *Concurrent Pos:* Dir, Ill Year Abroad Prog, Rouen, France, 72-73 & Paris, 73-74. *Mem:* MLA; Am Asn Teachers Fr; Am Soc 18th-Century Studies. *Res:* French novel of the 18th century; Crebillon fils. *Publ:* Auth, Crebillon fils: Techniques of the novel Vol 99, In: Studies on Voltaire and the 18th Century, Voltaire Found, 72; contribr, Songs and sonnets: Patterns of characterization, In: Moliere and the Commonwealth of Letters, Univ South Miss, 73; The Hotel de Balbec as church and theatre, In: Marcel Proust: A Critical Panorama, Univ Ill, 73; auth, The narrative stance in Scarron's Roman comique, Fr Rev (spec issue), spring 74; La Vision schizophrene chez Meursault, La Rev Lett Mod, 76; Deep Throat as Oracle, Southern Quart, 7/77. *Mailing Add:* Dept of French Univ of Ill Chicago IL 60680

CONTRERAS, HELES, b Victoria, Chile, Aug 1, 33; m 55; c 5. SPANISH LINGUISTICS & SYNTACTIC THEORY. *Educ:* Concepcion Univ, Profesor de Estado, 57; Ind Univ, MA, 59, PhD(ling), 61. *Prof Exp:* Prof ling, Concepcion Univ, 61-64; vis asst prof ling & Romance lang, 64-65, asst prof, 65-67, assoc prof, 67-79, PROF LING & ROMANCE LANG, UNIV WASH, 79- *Res:* Spanish grammar. *Publ:* Coauth, The validation of phonological grammar, Lingua, 60; A Phonological Grammar of Spanish, Univ Wash, 62; auth, Sobre el acento en espanol, Bol Filol, Santiago, Chile, 63; Una clasificacion morfosintactica de las lenguas romanicas, Romance Philol, 63; Sobre Gramatica Transformacional, Univ Republica, 66. *Mailing Add:* Dept of Ling Univ of Wash Seattle WA 98105

CONWAY, GEORGE EDWARD, b Philadelphia, Pa, Apr 6, 21. CLASSICS. *Educ:* Cath Univ Am, MA, 44, PhD(classics), 57. *Prof Exp:* From instr to assoc prof, 56-73, PROF CLASSICS, CHESTNUT HILL COL, 73- *Mem:* Am Class League; Am Philol Asn; Class Asn Atlantic States. *Publ:* Auth, De Bono Patientiae (treatise of St Cyrpian), Cath Univ, 57; contribr, St Cyprian, Treatises transl, The Good of Patience, Fathers of the Church, NY, 58; 17 articles in the field of Medieval Latin, In: New Cath Encycl, McGraw, 67. *Mailing Add:* Dept of Classics Chestnut Hill Col Philadelphia PA 19118

CONWELL, MARILYN J, b Philadelphia, Pa, June 28, 33. LINGUISTICS, ROMANCE LANGUAGES. *Educ:* Univ Pa, BS, 54, MS, 55; Univ Pa, PhD, 61. *Prof Exp:* Teacher, Philadelphia Bd Educ, 54-57; from instr to asst prof Romance lang, Pa State Univ, 57-66; from assoc prof to prof, 66-76, PROF FRENCH, ROSEMONT COL, 76- *Concurrent Pos:* Vis lectr Romance lang, Rosemont Col, 64-66. *Mem:* Am Asn Teachers Fr; Ling Soc Am; MLA; Am Coun Teaching Foreign Lang; Nat Asn Lang Lab Dir. *Res:* Applied and descriptive linguistics; Romance language methodology; Diderot's art criticism. *Publ:* Coauth, Louisiana French Grammar, Vol I, 63 & auth, Vol II, 79, Mouton, The Hague. *Mailing Add:* Dept of Romance Lang Rosemont Col Rosemont PA 19010

COOK, ALBERT BALDWIN, III, b Ionia, Mich, Aug 29, 31; m 54; c 4. ENGLISH, LINGUISTICS. *Educ:* Mich State Univ, BA, 53; Western Reserve Univ, MA, 56, PhD(English), 63. *Prof Exp:* Asst prof English, Buena Vista Col, 58-60; from asst prof to assoc prof, Northern Mich Univ, 60-68; ASSOC PROF ENGLISH, UNIV KANS, 68- *Res:* English language structure and history; American dialects; 17th century British prose. *Publ:*

Auth, Introduction to the English Language, Ronald, 69; John Bunyan & John Dunton: A case of plagiarism, PBSA, 71: 11-28; Perspectives for a linguistic atlas of Kansas, Am Speech, 53: 199-210; The De Analogia Anglicani Sermonis of Thomas Tonkis, Leeds Studies English, Vol 13. *Mailing Add:* Dept of English Univ of Kans Lawrence KS 66045

COOK, EUNG-DO, b Seosan, Korea, Feb 3, 35; Can citizen; m 64; c 2. LINGUISTICS. *Educ:* Chungang Univ, Korea, BA, 59, MA, 61; Univ Hawaii, MA, 65; Univ Alta, PhD(ling), 68. *Prof Exp:* Lectr English, Chungang Univ, Korea, 61-63; asst prof ling, York Univ, 68-69; from asst prof to assoc prof, 69-75, PROF LING, UNIV CALGARY, 75-, HEAD DEPT, 76- *Concurrent Pos:* Can Coun res grant, 69-71; Killam sr res scholar, 72-73; vis scholar, Brit Columbia Prov Mus, 75-76; Can Coun leave fel, 75-76; Killam res fel, 79. *Mem:* Ling Soc Am; Can Ling Asn; Ling Asn Gt Brit. *Res:* Generative grammar; Athabaskan languages; Korean. *Publ:* Co-ed (with J D Kaye) & auth, Palatialations and related rules in Sarcee, In: Linguistic Stuudies of Native Canada, Univ BD Press & Peter de Ridder Press, 78; auth, Generative approaches to historical linguistics, In: Approaches to Language: Anthropological Issues, Mouton, 78; Flattening and rounding in Chilcotin velars, In: The Victoria Conference on Northwestern Languages, Heritage Records, No 4, BC Museum, 78; The verb 'be' in Sarcee, Amerindia, 78; The synchronic and diachronic status of Sarcee, Int J Am Ling, 78; Central Indian language, In: The Languages of Canada, Didier, 79; Athabaskan linguistics: Proto-Athabaskan phonology, Annual Rev Anthrop, 81. *Mailing Add:* Dept of Ling Univ of Calgary Calgary AB T2N 1N4 Can

COOK, MARY JANE, b Amsterdam, NY, Apr 17, 21. LINGUISTICS. *Educ:* Univ Chicago, AB, 45; Columbia Univ, MA, 47; Univ Tex, PhD(ling), 61. *Prof Exp:* Instr Ger, Adelphi Col, 47-50; lectr English foreign studies, Columbia Univ, 50-51; instr English compos, George Washington Univ, 54-57; teaching asst English, Univ Tex, 58-61; asst prof, San Jose State Col, 61-63; asst prof, Univ NMex, 63-65; asst prof, 65-68, ASSOC PROF ENGLISH & DIR MASTER'S DEGREE PROG ENGLISH AS SECOND LANG, UNIV ARIZ, 68- *Concurrent Pos:* Columbia Univ grant-in-aid, 46-47; cult affairs asst, US Info Agency, Switz, 51-53; consult, English as second lang, Bur Indian Affairs & Ariz State Dept Educ, Adult Educ Br, 67- *Mem:* Ling Soc Am; AAUP; Teachers English to Speakers Other Lang. *Res:* Structure of English; English as a second language. *Publ:* Coauth, Problems of Navajo speakers in learning English, Lang Learning, 9/66; auth, The need for materials for teaching English to Southwestern Indian speakers, TESOL Quart, 4/67; Manual for Teaching English of Navajo Beginners & Manual for Teaching English to Navajo First Graders, 71, Bur Indian Affairs; Problems of Southwestern Indian speakers in learning English, In: Bilingualism in the Southwest, Univ Ariz, 73. *Mailing Add:* Dept of English Univ of Ariz Tucson AZ 85257

COOK, ROBERT FRANCIS, b Atlanta, Ga, Oct 24, 44. MEDIEVAL FRENCH LANGUAGE & LITERATURE. *Educ:* King Col, AB, 65; Vanderbilt Univ, MA, 68, PhD(French), 70; Univ Pittsburgh, MS, 75. *Prof Exp:* Asst prof French, Univ Pittsburgh, 69-75; ASSOC PROF FRENCH, UNIV VA, 75- *Mem:* MLA; Am Asn Teachers Fr; Mediaeval Acad Am; Int Arthurian Soc; Soc Rencesvals. *Res:* The chansons de geste; textual criticism. *Publ:* Auth, Les manuscrits de Baudouin de Sebourc, Romania, 70; ed, Le batard de Bouillon, chanson de geste, Droz-Minard, 72; coauth, Le deuxieme Cycle de la Croisade, Droz, 72; auth, Foreign language study and intellectual power, ADFL Bull, 5/77; coauth, The Legendary Sources of Flaubert's Saint Julien l'Hospitalier, Univ Toronto, 77; coauth, Chanson d'Antioche, Chanson de geste, 80; Aucassin et Nicolete, a Critical Bibliography, 82. *Mailing Add:* Dept of French Univ of Va Charlottesville VA 22903

COOK, ROBERT GEIGER, b Bethlehem, Pa, Nov 25, 32; div; c 1. ENGLISH, MEDIEVAL LITERATURE. *Educ:* Princeton Univ, BA, 54; Johns Hopkins Univ, MA, 61, PhD(English), 62. *Prof Exp:* From instr to asst prof, 62-69, assoc prof, 69-79, PROF ENGLISH, NEWCOMB COL, TULANE UNIV, 80- *Concurrent Pos:* Fulbright lectr, Univ Iceland, 68-69; Nat Endowment Humanities fel, 70-71; Fulbright res grant, Iceland, 82-83. *Mem:* MLA; Mediaeval Acad Am; Soc Advan Scand Studies; Int Arthurian Soc. *Res:* Icelandic literature; medieval English literature. *Publ:* Auth, Chaucer's Pandarus and the medieval ideal of friendship, J English & Ger Philol, 70; The character of Gunnlaug serpent-tongue, Scand Studies, 71; The structure of romance in Chretien's Erec and Yvain, Mod Philol, 73; co-ed (with Mattias Tveitane), Strengleikar: An Old Norse Translation of Twenty-one Old French Lais, Oslo, 79. *Mailing Add:* Newcomb Col Tulane Univ New Orleans LA 70118

COOK, VERNON, b Columbia, SC, July 31, 26; m 49 c 5. FOREIGN LANGUAGES. *Educ:* Univ Va, BA, 49, PhD, 59. *Prof Exp:* Instr Ger, Univ Va, 50-56; actg prof, Va Mil Inst, 56-57; asst prof Ger & Russ, Clemson Col, 58-61; assoc prof, 61-63, PROF GER & RUSS, COL CHARLESTON, 63- *Res:* Germanic linguistics. *Mailing Add:* Dept of Mod Lang Col of Charleston Charleston SC 29401

COOK, WALTER ANTHONY, b Washington, DC, Feb 17, 22. LINGUISTICS, SOUTH ASIAN LANGUAGES. *Educ:* Woodstock Col, Md, BA, 45, PhL, 46, MAT, 47; St Mary's Col, India, STL, 53; Georgetown Univ, MS, 64, PhD(ling), 65. *Prof Exp:* Instr math & physics, St Joseph's Prep Sch, Philadelphia, Pa, 46-49; social worker, Jamshedpur Mission, Bihar, India, 54-62; from asst prof to assoc prof ling, 65-74, PROF LING, GEORGETOWN UNIV, 74-, CHMN DEPT, 78- *Concurrent Pos:* Consult, Ohio State Univ Res Proj Commun, 70-72 & Proj on Intercult Commun, Yucatan, Merida, 71-72. *Mem:* Ling Soc Am; Teaching English Speakers Other Lang. *Res:* Syntax; semantics; South Asian languages. *Publ:* Auth, On Tagmemes and Transforms, Georgetown Univ, 64; Introduction to Tagmemic Analysis, Holt, 69; A case grammar matrix, 72, Covert case roles, 73, Case grammar and generative semantics, 74, Stylistics: Measuring style complexity, 75 & Durative aspect, 76, In: Languages and Linguistics Working Papers No 6, 7, 8, 11, & 12, Georgetown Univ. *Mailing Add:* Sch of Lang & Ling Georgetown Univ Washington DC 20007

COOKE, JOSEPH ROBINSON, b Muchengpo, China, Apr 29, 26; US citizen; m 51. LINGUISTICS. *Educ:* Biola Col, ThB, 49, BA, 52; Univ Calif, Berkeley, BA, 61, PhD(ling), 65. *Prof Exp:* Missionary, Overseas Missionary fel, Thailand, 54-57; asst prof English & ling, Northern Ill Univ, 65-67; asst prof, 67-69, ASSOC PROF THAI & LING, UNIV WASH, 69- *Res:* Thai sentence-final particles; Thai and Karen linguistics. *Publ:* Auth, Pronominal Reference in Thai, Burmese, and Vietnamese, Univ Calif Publ in Ling, 68; coauth, Phlong, In: Phonemes and Orthography, Pac Ling Series, 76. *Mailing Add:* Dept of Asian Lang & Lit Univ of Wash Seattle WA 98195

COOLEY, MARIANNE, b Oklahoma City, Okla, Mar 16, 44; m 79. ENGLISH LANGUAGE & LINGUISTICS. *Educ:* Okla State Univ, BA, 66; Univ Tex, Austin, MA, 69, PhD(English lang & ling), 72. *Prof Exp:* English teacher, Tulsa Pub High Schs, Okla, 66-68; asst prof English & ling, Univ Calif, Davis, 72-80; ASST PROF ENGLISH, TEX TECH UNIV, 80- *Mem:* MLA; NCTE; Conf Col Compos & Commun; Ling Soc Am; Am Dialect Soc. *Res:* English historical linguistics; English grammar; stylistics. *Publ:* Auth, Opacity and rule loss: A case from English, Pac Coast Philo, 74; coauth, Rule reordering in Middle English, Glossa, 75; auth, Morphological conditioning and the loss of 1x1, J English Ling, 76; Phonological constraints and sound changes, Glossa, 78. *Mailing Add:* Dept of English Tex Tech Univ Lubbock TX 79409

COOMBS, ILONA C, b Smyrna, Turkey, Aug 13, 18; US citizen; m 45; c 1. FRENCH LITERATURE. *Educ:* Drew Univ, BA, 59; NY Univ, MA, 60, PhD(French), 65. *Prof Exp:* From instr to assoc prof French, 59-70, asst to dean, 63-64, chmn dept, 69-78, PROF FRENCH, DREW UNIV, 70-, BALDWIN PROF HUMANITIES, 81- *Concurrent Pos:* Woodrow Wilson fel, New York Univ, 59-60. *Honors & Awards:* Founders Day Award, NY Univ, 66. *Mem:* MLA; Am Asn Teachers Fr. *Res:* French theatre; Renaissance poetry; women studies. *Publ:* Auth, Baroque elements in Jean de Sponde Stances de la mort, L'Esprit Createur, summer 61; Camus homme de theatre, A G Nizet, Paris, 68 & In: Camus et les critiques de son temps, Garnier, 70. *Mailing Add:* Dept of French Drew Univ Madison NJ 07940

COOMBS, VIRGINIA M, b Youngstown, Ohio, Mar 22, 46. GERMANIC LINGUISTICS. *Educ:* Denison Univ, AB, 68; Univ Ill, AM, 70, PhD(Ger ling), 74. *Prof Exp:* Teaching asst, Univ Ill, 68-74; asst prof, Ind Univ, 74-81; ASST PROF GER, BUCKNELL UNIV, 81- *Mem:* MLA; Am Asn Teachers Ger; Ling Soc Am; Am Coun Teaching Foreign Lang; AAUP. *Res:* Modern German linguistics, specific areas; semantics and syntax. *Publ:* Auth, Beowulf negative indefinites: The Klima hypothesis tested, Orbis, 75; A Semantic Syntax of Grammatical Negation in the Older Germanic Dialects, Kümmerle, 76; Magazine advertisements, In: Beginning German Advertisements, Indiana Univ Pa, 78; Die Studen geniesen as speech act, Ger Quart, 53: 199-212; Foreign language in the market place: Busines German, Studies in Language, Learning, 111: 91-96. *Mailing Add:* Mod Lang Dept Bucknell Univ Lewisburg PA 17837

COONS, DIX SCOTT, b Mesa, Ariz, July 11, 30; m 56; c 5. SPANISH; LATIN AMERICAN LITERATURE. *Educ:* Brigham Young Univ, BA, 55, MA, 57; Univ Tex, PhD(Span), 64. *Prof Exp:* Asst Span, Univ Tex, 56-57; asst, St Stephen's Episcopal Sch, 57-63; from instr to asst prof, Brown Univ, 63-66; asst prof, 66-68, ASSOC PROF SPAN, RI COL, 68- *Mem:* Am Asn Teachers Span & Port. *Res:* Latin-American novel and short story; modernismo; Mexican novel. *Mailing Add:* Dept of Span RI Col Providence RI 02908

COOPE, MARIAN GARRISON ROBINSON, b Antwerp, Belgium, June 22, 33; m 66; c 2. SPANISH. *Educ:* Cambridge Univ, BA, 56; Univ London, PhD(mod Span lit), 67. *Prof Exp:* From lectr to instr, 61-66, ASST PROF SPAN, UNIV BC, 67- *Mem:* Can Asn Hispanists; Int Asn Hispanists. *Res:* Modern Spanish novel, especially Gabriel Miro. *Publ:* Auth, Gabriel Miro's image of the garden as Hortus Conclusus and Paraiso Terrenal, Mod Lang Rev, 1/73; Span trans, El hortus conclusus y el Paraiso terrenal en los jardines literarios de Gabriel Miro, In: Homenaje del Instituto de Estudios Alicantinos a Gabriel Miro . . .1879, Alicante: Instituto de Estudios Alicantinos, 79; The critics' view of Nuestro Padre San Daniel and El Obispo leproso by Gabriel Miro, Univ of BC Hisp Studies, 74. *Mailing Add:* Dept of Hisp & Ital Studies Univ of BC Vancouver BC V6T 1W5 Can

COOPER, DANIELLE CHAVY, b Paris, France, Dec 11, 21; US citizen; m 47; c 1. FOREIGN LANGUAGES. *Educ:* Univ Paris, BA, 39, MA, 41, PhD(Am lit), 42; Univ Southern Calif, PhD, 63. *Prof Exp:* Teacher English & Span, Sec Schs, France, 42-44; asst French, Whalley Range High Sch & Univ Manchester, 45-46; Marcelle Parde teaching fel, Bryn Mawr Col, 46-47; lang coordr, Isabelle Buckley Schs, Los Angeles, Calif, 55-56; instr French & Ger, Immaculate Heart Col, 57-60, asst prof French, 60-63; lectr, Univ Colo, 63-65; from assoc prof to prof, Keuka Col, 65-70, chmn dept mod lang, 65-70; chmn div lang & civilizations, 71-73, chmn dept lang & humanities, 75-77, PROF FRENCH, MONTEREY INST INT STUDIES, 70- *Concurrent Pos:* Instr French, Fr Found Calif, Los Angeles, 56-58; bd reviewer, Bks Abroad/World Lit Today, 58-; instr, Univ Southern Calif, 58; mem, Alliance Francaise. *Honors & Awards:* Chevalier, Ordre des Palmes Academiques, 72. *Mem:* Am Asn Teachers Fr; MLA; African Studies Asn; Am Name Soc; Philol Asn Pac Coast. *Res:* French phonetics; African and Caribbean literature of French expression; translation theory and practice. *Publ:* Auth, Le Probleme des Liaisons en Francais, Calgary Bd Educ, 50; coauth, The Isabelle Buckley Plan of Education, Buckley Schs, 55; Les Suites Romanesques de Jean de la Varende, Univ Microfilms, 64. *Mailing Add:* Monterey Inst of Foreign Studies PO Box 1978 Monterey CA 93940

COOPER, GRACE CHARLOTTE WASHINGTON, b Washington, DC, July, 19, 37. PSYCHOLINGUISTICS, SOCIOLINGUISTICS. *Educ:* DC Teachers Col, BS, 62; Fed City Col, MS, 74; Howard Univ, PhD(psycholing commun), 79. *Prof Exp:* Educ pub rels spec, Chesapeake & Potomac Telephone Co of DC, 62-65; res sci educ lang, George Washington Univ, 65-66; instr English, Northern Va Commun Col, 67-69; dep & actg dir, Skills

Ctr, Fed City Col, 69-71; urban planner, Model Cities of Miami-Dade County, 71-72; curric spec, Child Welfare League of Am, 73-74; ASSOC PROF ENGLISH STUDIES, UNIV DC, 74- *Concurrent Pos:* Teacher sec sch eve div, Washington, DC, 65-66; playwright, 66-; Danforth assoc, Danforth Found, 80-86. *Mem:* Ling Soc Am; MLA; SEastern Conf Ling; NCTE; Col Lang Asn. *Res:* Cognitive style; Black language; imagery in writing. *Publ:* Auth, Joseph A Walker: Evolution of a playwright, New Dir, Howard Univ, 10/75; Black stylistic features in student compositions, Resources in Educ, NCTE, 78; Issues in cross-cultural communication, New Directions, Howard Univ, 4/79; Everyone does not think alike, English J, 4/80; A look at our language, New Directions, Howard Univ Mag, 7/80; Different ways of thinking, Minority Educ, 12/80; Black language and holistic cognitive style, Western J Black Studies, fall 81. *Mailing Add:* 6712 West Park Dr West Hyattsville MD 20782

COOPER, HENRY RONALD, JR, b New York, NY, Sept 30, 46. SLAVIC LITERATURES & LANGUAGES. *Educ:* City Col New York, BA, 67; Columbia Univ, MA, 69, PhD(Slavic lit), 74. *Prof Exp:* ASST PROF SLAVIC, NORTHWESTERN UNIV, 74- *Concurrent Pos:* Fel Russ, Nat Endowment Humanities, 78- *Mem:* Am Asn Advan Slavic Studies; Am Asn Teachers Slavic & E Europ Lang; Soc Slovene Studies; Asn Advan Polish Studies; Kosciuszko Found. *Res:* Old Russian literature; Polish literature; Slovene literature. *Publ:* Auth, Torquato Tasso in Eastern Europe, Italica, 74; Poles on Croats, Can-Am Slavic Studies; 76; Tasso and Preseren's Krst Pri Savici, Papers Slovene Studies, 76; The Igor Tale: An Annotated Bibliography, M E Sharpe, 78. *Mailing Add:* Dept of Slavic Northwestern Univ Evanston IL 60201

COOPER, JERROLD STEPHEN, b Chicago, Ill, Nov 24, 42. ASSYRIOLOGY. *Educ:* Univ Calif, Berkeley, AB, 63, AM, 64; Univ Chicago, PhD(Assyriol), 69. *Prof Exp:* Asst prof, 68-74, assoc prof, 74-79, PROF NEAR EASTERN STUDIES, JOHNS HOPKINS UNIV, 79- *Concurrent Pos:* Co-ed, J Cuneiform Studies, 72- *Mem:* Am Orient Soc. *Publ:* Auth, Structure, humor and satire in The Poor Man of Nippur, J Cuneiform Studies, 75; Gilgamesh drams of Enkidu, In: Essays on the Ancient Near East in Memory of J J Finkelstein, 77 & co-ed, Essays on the Ancient Near East in Memory of J J Finkelstein, 77, Archon Bks; auth, The Return of Ninerta to Nippur, Pontif Bibl Inst, 78; Symmetry and repetion in Akkadian narrative, J Am Orient Soc, 78; Apodotic death and the historicity of historical omens, Mesopotamia, Vol 8, 80; Studies in Mesopotamian Lapidary Inscriptions, Vol I & II, J Cuneiform Studies & Rev d'Assyriologie, 80; The Curse of the Agade, Johns Hopkins Press, 82. *Mailing Add:* Dept of Near Eastern Studies Johns Hopkins Univ Baltimore MD 21218

COOPER, ROBIN HAYES, b Shanklin, England, Dec 23, 47. LINGUISTICS. *Educ:* Cambridge Univ, MA, 74; Univ Mass, Amherst, PhD(ling), 75. *Prof Exp:* Asst prof ling, Univ Tex, Austin, 75-76; asst prof, Univ Mass, Amherst, 76-77; ASST PROF LING, UNIV WIS-MADISON, 77- *Concurrent Pos:* Res Assoc ling, Univ Tex, Austin, 77. *Mem:* Ling Soc Am. *Res:* Model theoretic semantics, syntax, transformational grammar. *Publ:* Auth, Montague's semantic theory of adverbs and the VSO hypothesis, In: Proc 5th Meeting N Eastern Ling Soc, 75; coauth, Montague grammar, generative semantics and interpretive semantics, In: Montague Grammar, Acad Press, 76; auth, Lixical and non-lexical causatives in Bantu, In: Syntax & Semantics, Vol 6, Acad Press, 76; Abstract structure and the Indian raga system, Ethnomusicology, XXI.1, 77; coauth, The NP-S analysis of relative clauses and compositional semantics, Ling & Philos, 2.1, 78; auth, The interpretation of pronouns, In: Syntax & Semantics, Vol 11, Acad Press (in press); Variable binding and relative clauses, In: Proc Bad Homburg Workshop on Formal Semantics, Reidel (in press). *Mailing Add:* Dept of Ling Univ of Wis-Madison Madison WI 53706

COOPER, VINCENT O'MAHONY, b Basseterre, St Kitts, Dec 3, 47; m 75; c 2. LINGUISTICS, ENGLISH. *Educ:* Univ Bordeaux, dipl, 67; Col VI, BA, 72; Princeton Univ, MA, 74, PhD(ling), 79. *Prof Exp:* Adj instr English, Borrough of Manhatten Community Col, City Univ New York, 74-75, & Mercy Col, 75-76; adj instr socioling, Hunter Col, City Univ New York, 76; INSTR ENGLISH, COL OF THE VI, 77-, ASST PROF ENGLISH/LING, 79- *Concurrent Pos:* Field reader, Nat Sci Found, 80- *Mem:* Col Lang Asn; Ling Soc Am; Nat Coun Teachers England (pres, 78-81). *Res:* Sociolinguistics; Caribbean Creole languages; Caribbean literatures. *Publ:* Contribr, Aspects of St Kitts-Nevis Creole Phonology, Col of the VI J, 78; Creole languages and national identity: An essay review, Caribbean Res Inst, Microstate Studies, 78; Pronoun/Copuloid co-occurence in SKNC (anthology), Univ of Hawaii (in prep); Runnin down some lines: . . ., J ApplLing (in prep); auth, St Kitts-Nevis Creole, Karowa Publ (in prep); auth, A sociolinguistic profile of the Virgin Isles, In: Educational Issues and Concerns in the US VI, CVI/Teacher Corp Proj (in prep); coauth, An Interdisciplinary Approach to Reading, Heinnemann Publ Serv (in prep). *Mailing Add:* Dept of English Col of VI St Thomas VI 00802

COOPERSTEIN, LOUIS, b Boston, Mass, Apr 4, 12; m 39; c 1. MODERN LANGUAGE. *Educ:* Harvard Univ, AB, 33, AM, 34. *Hon Degrees:* Dr Lett, Northeastern Univ, 79. *Prof Exp:* From asst prof to assoc prof, 46-62, chmn dept, 65-77, PROF MOD LANG, NORTHEASTERN UNIV, 62- *Mem:* New England Mod Lang Asn; MLA; Am Asn Teachers Ger; Goethe Soc. *Res:* German literature of the 18th century. *Publ:* Auth, Frau Gottsched. *Mailing Add:* Dept of Mod Lang Northeastern Univ Boston MA 02115

COPELAND, JAMES EVERETT, b Tex, June 6, 37; m 65; c 1. GENERAL & GERMANIC LINGUISTICS. *Educ:* Univ Colo, BA, 61; Cornell Univ, PhD(ling), 65. *Prof Exp:* Instr Ger, Cornell Univ, 64-65; asst prof ling & Ger, Univ Calif, Davis, 65-66; asst prof, 66-69, chmn ling, 69-82, ASSOC PROF LING & GER, RICE UNIV, 69- *Concurrent Pos:* Vis asst prof ling, Cornell Univ, summer, 67. *Mem:* MLA; Ling Soc Am; SCent MLA; Ling Asn Can & US. *Res:* Disourse analysis; stratificational linguistics; German syntax and semantics. *Publ:* Auth, Two dimensional phonotactics, Studies Ger, 69; A Stepmatricial Generative Phonology of German, Mouton, The Hague, 70; coauth, A stratificational approach to discourse, 6th Ling Asn Can & US Forum, 80; Knowledge, consciousness and language: Sources of discourse, In: Papers in Cognitive Stratificational Linguistics, Vol 66, 80 & co-ed, Papers in Cognitive-Stratificational Linguistics, Rice Univ, Vol 66, 80; The 7th Ling Asn Can & US Forum, Hornbeam Press, 81; coauth, Identification and focal attention in an integrated view of discourse, 7th Ling Asn Can & US Forum, 81; Discourse portmanteaus and the German Satzfeld, Cornell Univ Studies, 82. *Mailing Add:* Dept of Ling & Semantics Rice Univ Houston TX 77252

COPLEY, FRANK OLIN, b Mt Vernon, NY, Aug 11, 07; m 35; c 5. LATIN. *Educ:* Stanford Univ, AB, 30, PhD, 35; Harvard Univ, AM, 31. *Prof Exp:* Instr classics, Stanford Univ, 32-34; from instr to prof, 34-77, EMER PROF LATIN, UNIV MICH, ANN ARBOR, 77- *Mem:* Am Philol Asn; Class Asn Midwest & South. *Res:* Greek and Roman paraclausithyron; Catullus; Roman comedy. *Publ:* Transl, Vergil, The Aeneid, Bobbs, 65; Cicero, On Old Age & On Friendship, 67 & auth, Latin Literature, 69, Univ Mich; contribr, In: Approaches to Catullus, Heffer, 72; auth, Aristotle to Gertrude Stein: The Arts of Poetry, Mosaic, 72; Lucretius, The Nature of Things (transl), Norton, 77. *Mailing Add:* Box 216 Rogers City MI 49779

COPPERUD, ROY HERMAN, b Crystal Falls, Mich, June 28, 15; m 46; c 3. JOURNALISM. *Educ:* Univ Minn, BA, 42. *Prof Exp:* Ed editorial pages, Pasadena Star-News & Independent, 59-64; from asst prof to assoc prof, 64-70, prof, 70-80, EMER PROF JOUR, UNIV SOUTHERN CALIF, 80- *Concurrent Pos:* Mem usage panel, Am Heritage Dict, 64-; consult, Washington Post, 64-65, English Lang Inst Am, 66 & Webster Living Encycl Dict, 70-71. *Res:* English usage; journalism techniques. *Publ:* Auth, Editorial workshop column, Ed & Publ Mag, 52-; Words on Paper, 60 & Dictionary of Usage and Style, 64, Hawthorn; American Usage: The consensus, Van Nostrand, 70; Foreword, A Dictionary of Contemporary and Colloquial Usage, English Lang Inst Am, 71; American Usage and Style: The Consensus, Van Nostrand, 79. *Mailing Add:* Sch of Jour Univ of Southern Calif University Park Los Angeles CA 90007

COPPOLA, CARLO, b Wooster, Ohio, Oct 1, 38; m 81; c 2. COMPARATIVE LITERATURE, LINGUISTICS. *Educ:* John Carroll Univ, BS, 60; Univ Chicago, MA, 61, PhD(comp lit), 75. *Prof Exp:* Lectr Hindi & Urdu lit, 68-70, asst prof, 70-75, assoc prof, 75-82, PROF HINDI & URDU LING, OAKLAND UNIV, 82-, CHMN AREA STUDIES PROG, 76- *Concurrent Pos:* SAsian bibliogr, Publ MLA, 71-76; ed, J SAsian Lit, 63-; asst ed, J Asian Studies, 78- *Mem:* Asn Asian Studies; Philol Asn Pac Coast; N Indian Studies Asn (pres, 75-78); MLA; SAsia Lit Asn. *Res:* Modern Hindi; Urdu literature; Indian writing in English; Marxist aesthetics. *Publ:* Ed, Marxist Influences and South Asian Literature, 2 vols, Asian Studies Ctr, Mich State Univ, 74; auth, The All-India Progressive Writers' Association: The European phase, In: Marxist Influences and South Asian Literature, Mich State Univ, 74; Politics, social criticism and Indian film songs: The case of Sahir Ludhianvi, J Popular Cult, spring 77; Muhammad Iqbal and the Progressive Movement, J SAsian & Mid Eastern Studies, 12/77; Urdu literary reactions to the 1943 Bengal famine, Vagartha, 7/77; The poetry of Ahmed Ali, J Indian Writing in English, 1/80; The Angare Group: The Enfants Terribles of Urdu Literature, Annal of Urdu Studies, 1/81; Asrarul Haq Majaz: The progressive poet as revolutionary romantic, Indian Lit, 5/81. *Mailing Add:* Dept of Mod Lang & Lit Oakland Univ Rochester MI 48063

COR, M ANTONIA, b Berkeley, Calif, Oct 4, 50; m 80; c 1. MEDIEVAL FRENCH LITERATURE. *Educ:* Univ Wyo, BA, 72; Univ Ore, MA, 74; Univ NC, PhD(French), 79. *Prof Exp:* Teaching asst French, Univ Ore, 72-74, Univ NC, 75-79; instr, Univ Ga, 80-81; INSTR FRENCH, UNIV MD, 81- *Mem:* Am Asn Teachers French; MLA; Mediaeval Acad Am. *Res:* Medieval literature; 17th century literature. *Publ:* Auth, Review of J Mandel's The Ethical Context of Erec's Character, Studi Francesi, Vol 21; Games of love and war in La Princesse de Cleves, Ky Romance Quart, Vol 28; The shield of Telemaque, Romance Notes (in prep). *Mailing Add:* 7826 Hanover Pkwy 104 Greenbelt MD 20770

CORBETT, JOHN HARTY, b Kingston, Ont, July 16, 42; m 63. ANCIENT HISTORY, CLASSICS. *Educ:* Queen's Univ, Ont, BA, 64; Univ Toronto, MA, 65, PhD(classics), 68. *Prof Exp:* Lectr, 67-68, asst prof, 68-72, ASSOC PROF CLASSICS, SCARBOROUGH COL, UNIV TORONTO, 72- *Mem:* Class Asn Can; Am Philol Asn; Soc Promotion Roman Studies; Asn Ancient Historians; Medieval Acad Am. *Res:* Roman history, conquest and Romanization of Italy; Jewish history in the Greco-Roman period, with emphasis on ideological and cultural elements; medieval history, especially ideology and social structure in ancient and early medieval worlds. *Publ:* Auth, L Metellus (cos 251, 247 BC), agrarian commissioner?, Class Rev, 69; Rome and the Gauls 285-280 BC, Historia: Z Alte Geschichte, 71; The succession policy of Augustus, Latomus, 74; The world to come; the millenarian tradition in Christianity, its origins and transmission, Papers Can Soc for Church Hist, 75; The foster child: A neglected theme in early Christian life and thought, Proceedings of XIVth Congress of Int Asn Hist Relig, 80; The saints patron in the work of Gregory of Tours, J Medieval Hist, 81. *Mailing Add:* Div of Humanities Univ of Toronto West Hill ON M5S 1A1 Can

CORBETT, NOEL L, b Bowmanville, Ont, Nov 23, 38; m 63. FRENCH LANGUAGE & LINGUISTICS. *Educ:* Univ Toronto, BA, 60, MA, 63, PhD(French), 67. *Prof Exp:* Teaching asst French, Victoria Col, Univ Toronto, 62-66, lectr, 66-67; asst prof, 67-72, prog coordr fac educ, 77-81, ASSOC PROF FRENCH, YORK UNIV, 72- *Concurrent Pos:* Can Coun res fel, 69-70, 73-74 & 81-82; Can Secy of State grant, 72; fac fel, York Univ, 79-80. *Mem:* MLA; Ling Soc Am; Soc Ling Romane; Can Asn Univ Teachers; Can Ling Asn. *Res:* Diachronic study of French and Romance languages; medieval French language and literature; synchronic structure of French and Canadian French. *Publ:* Auth, The French verbal flexion-ons as a result of homonymy, 69 & Reconstructing the diachronic phonology of Romance, 70, Romance Philol; Ancien francais Huis de la porte, huis de la fenestre, Romancia, 70; Critical Edition of La Vie de Saint Louis, Sherbrooke PQ, Naaman, 77; Current trends in Romance linguistics and philology: North America, The Hague: De Gruyter, 78. *Mailing Add:* Dept of French Studies York Univ 4700 Keele St Downsview ON M3J 1P3 Can

CORBITT, ROBERTA DAY, b Bluemound, Kans, Oct 20, 02; m 24; c 1. LANGUAGE. *Educ:* Univ Chicago, AB & MA, 41; Univ Ky, PhD, 55. *Prof Exp:* Instr Span & English, Candler Col High Sch, Havana, Cuba, 37-42, 45-46; instr hist, Columbia Col, SC, 43-45; chmn div, 61-68, PROF SPAN, ASBURY COL, 46- *Mem:* Am Asn Teachers Span & Port; Midwest Coun Latin Am Studies Asn; NEA; AAUP; Caribbean Studies Asn. *Res:* Cuban and Spanish literature; Spanish speaking West Indies. *Publ:* Auth, A survey of Cuban Costumbrismo, Hispania, 2/50; This colossal theater: Jose Marti in the United States, Univ Ky Microfilms, 55; coauth, Papers from the Spanish Archives Relating to Tennessee and the Old Southwest, ETenn Hist Soc, 37-69. *Mailing Add:* 205 E Morrison Wilmore KY 40390

CORCORAN, MARY B, b Pasadena, Calif, May 22, 24; m 56; c 4. GERMAN LITERATURE & PHILOLOGY. *Educ:* Wellesley Col, BA, 46; Radcliffe Col, MA, 49; Bryn Mawr Col, PhD(Ger), 58. *Prof Exp:* Transl, US War Dept, Nürnberg, Ger, 46-47; from instr to assoc prof Ger, 53-76, PROF GER, VASSAR COL, 76-, CHMN, DEPT GER, 78- *Mem:* MLA; Am Asn Teachers Ger. *Res:* German Romanticism and lyric poetry; modern German literature. *Publ:* Transl, Marianne Thalmann, The Romantic Fairy Tale: Sees of Surrealism, Univ Mich, 64. *Mailing Add:* Dept of Ger Vassar Col Poughkeepsie NY 12601

CORCORAN, THOMAS HENRY, b Osborne, Kans, Apr 1, 25; m 50; c 2. CLASSICS. *Educ:* La State Univ, BA, 50; Northwestern Univ, MA, 53, PhD, 57. *Prof Exp:* Asst prof classics, La State Univ, 55-58; asst prof, Miami Univ, 58-60; assoc prof, 62-72, PROF CLASSICS, TUFTS UNIV, 72- *Mem:* Class Asn Mid W & S; Am Philol Asn; Am Class League; Class Asn New England. *Res:* Roman social and economic history; Latin textual criticism. *Publ:* Auth, Seneca Naturales Quaestiones, Harvard Univ, Vols I & II, 71 & 72; Latin Prose & Poetry Book One, 76 & Latin Prose & Poetry Book Two, 77, Univ Microfilms Int. *Mailing Add:* Dept of Classics Tufts Univ Medford MA 02155

CORD, WILLIAM OWEN, b St Louis, Mo, May 1, 21; m 43; c 2. SPANISH AMERICAN LITERATURE. *Educ:* Mo State Col, BS, 43; Wash Univ, MA, 48; Univ Colo, PhD(Romance lang), 60. *Prof Exp:* Instr Span & English, St Louis Univ High Sch, 43-45; lectr Span, Wash Univ, 45-48; instr, St Louis Univ, 48-52; chmn dept foreign lang, Glenbrook High Sch, 52-55; from asst prof to assoc prof Span, Fresno State Col, 58-63; assoc prof, 63-65, chmn div humanities, 70-76, PROF SPAN, CALIF STATE COL, SONOMA, 65- *Concurrent Pos:* Consult, Kerman Sch Dist, Calif, 62, San Marino Sch Dist & Primera Feria del Libro, Ciudad Juarez, Mex, 63. *Mem:* Am Asn Teachers Span & Port; MLA. *Res:* Unedited manuscripts, biography and bibliography of Jose Ruben Romero; contemporary Mexican novel. *Publ:* Auth, Jose Ruben Romero: El autor visto por si mismo, In: Iberoamerica, Libreria Studium, 62; Jose Ruben Romero's image of Mexico, Hispania, 12/62; Jose Ruben Romero--cuentos y poemas ineditos, Libreri a Studium, 63; The Futile Life of Pito Perez, 67 & ed, La vida inutil de Pito Perez, 72, Prentice-Hall. *Mailing Add:* Dept of Foreign Lang Calif State Col Sonoma Rohnert Park CA 94928

CORDARO, PHILIP, b Palermo, Italy, July 5, 18; US citizen; m 48; c 2. ROMANCE LANGUAGES, PHILOSOPHY. *Educ:* State Univ Turin, Dr, 42. *Prof Exp:* Assoc prof Ital & humanity, Univ PR, Mayaguex, 66-70, prof, 70-80. *Honors & Awards:* Cult Prize, Govt of Italy, 62, Cult Gold Medal, 67; Cavaliere, Pres Rep of Italy, 67. *Mem:* Asn Int Studies Lingua e Lett Ital; Dante Alighieri Soc (pres, 61-67); MLA; Am Asn Teachers Ital. *Publ:* Auth, Kennedy, Sciascia, Rome, 61; El Kennedy, Plaza y Janes, Barcelona, 64; El estudio de Dante el las institutiones universitarieas, 12/67, Francesca da Rimini segun Dante y segun la indulgencia de la posteridad, 3/68 & Silvio Pellico y la tragedia de ispiracion Dantesca, 6/68, Atenea; Idioma Italiano, Univ PR, 68; Andrea Angiolli, e l' eredita dell'800, Sciascia, Rome, 69; Cost e se vi pare di L Pirandello, 74 & coauth, Episodios Famosos de la Divina Comedia, 75, Univ PR; El Principe de Maquiauelo, Flozentia, Boston, 76. *Mailing Add:* 57 Miraders Gardens Mayaguez PR 00708

CORDLE, THOMAS HOWARD, b Atlanta, Ga, July 15, 18; m 41. FRENCH. *Educ:* Univ Va, BA, 40; Yale Univ, MA, 48, PhD(French) 51. *Prof Exp:* From instr to assoc prof, 50-71, PROF ROMANCE LANG, DUKE UNIV, 71- *Concurrent Pos:* Fund Advan Educ fel, 55-56. *Mem:* MLA; Am Asn Teacher Fr. *Res:* Contemporary French literature. *Publ:* Auth, The role of dreams, In: A la Recherche du Temps Perdu, Romanic Rev, 12/51; Andre Gide, Twayne, 69; Malruax and Nietzche's Birth of Tragedy, In: Makers of the Twentieth-Century Novel, Bucknell, 76. *Mailing Add:* Dept of Romance Lang Duke Univ Durham NC 27706

CORDOVA, JOSE HERNAN, b Loja, Ecuador; m 70. SPANISH AMERICAN LITERATURE. *Educ:* Iona Col, BA, 69; Univ Hawaii, MA, 72; Cornell Univ, PhD(Hisp studies & comp lit), 76. *Prof Exp:* Instr Span, Univ Hawaii, 70-72; teaching asst intro lit, Cornell Univ, 72-75; asst prof Romance lang & lit, Colgate Univ, 75-80; ASST PROF LATIN AM LIT/HUMANITIES, ST ANSELM'S COL, 80- *Concurrent Pos:* Colgate Humanities Fac Develop grant, 76-77; Nat Endowment for Humanities fel comp lit, 78-79. *Mem:* MLA; Am Asn Teachers Span & Port; Inst Int Lit Iberoam; Am Col Lang Asn; Soc Critical Exchange. *Res:* Modern poetry; comparative literature; criticism and literary theory. *Publ:* Auth, Carrera Andrade: New Steps to the Highest Window, Mid-Hudson Lang Studies, 2:136-147; El Otono Del Patrirca De Garcia Marquez O La Poesia Y La Politica De La Narracion, Requiem for the Boom--Premature?; Cobra de Severo Sarduy: La Narracion y Sus Recursos Poeticos, 10/79 & Severo Sarduy: Theoria y Praxis De La Revolucion Textual: Del Placer Del Texto A Lo Escrito Sobre Un Cuerpo, 10/80, In: Proc Hisp Conf, Ind Univ Pa; Looking for the Indian in Columbua, J & Garcia Marquez's; The Autumn of the Patriarch, In: J Comp Poetics, Am Univ Cairo. *Mailing Add:* Saint Anselm Col Manchester NH 03102

CORGAN, MARGARET M, b Wilkes-Barre, Pa, Aug 24, 36. FRENCH LANGUAGE & LITERATURE. *Educ:* Marymount Col, NY, BA, 58; Univ Rennes, dipl French lang & lit, 59; Fordham Univ, MA, 62, PhD(French), 67. *Prof Exp:* Instr French, Col Misericordia, 59-61; asst, Fordham Univ, 61-63; instr, St John's Univ, NY, 64-65; from asst prof to assoc prof, 65-74, PROF FRENCH, KING'S COL, PA, 74-, CHMN DEPT FOREIGN LANG & LIT, 77- *Mem:* Am Asn Teachers Fr; Am Coun Teaching For Lang; Am Asn Univ Women. *Res:* Twentieth century French literature; bibliography of twentieth century French authors; translation. *Mailing Add:* Dept of For Lang & Lit King's Col Wilkes-Barre PA 18711

CORMIER, LOUIS-PHILIPPE, b Can, Jan 16, 17; nat USl m 46; c 1. ROMANCE LANGUAGES. *Educ:* Laval Univ, AB, 38, Lic es Let, 41; Northwestern Univ, PhD(Romance lang), 54. *Prof Exp:* From instr to prof French, Mich State Univ, 45-68; PROF FRENCH & CHMN DEPT MOD LANG, UNIV LETHBRIDGE, 68- *Mem:* Am Asn Teachers Fr; MLA. *Res:* Renaissance French literature; North American French; Franco-American history. *Publ:* Auth, Lettres de Papineau, LaFontaine, Faillon a Pierre Margry, Laval Univ, 68; coauth, Porte Ouverte, Bellhaven House, 73. *Mailing Add:* Dept of Mod Lang Univ of Lethbridge Lethbridge AB T1K 3M4 Can

CORMIER, RAYMOND JOSEPH, b Bridgeport, Conn, Nov 23, 38; m 60; c 2. MEDIEVAL FRENCH LITERATURE. *Educ:* Univ Bridgeport, AB, 60; Stanford Univ, AM 62; Harvard Univ, PhD(French, Celtic), 67. *Hon Degrees:* DLitt, Univ Bridgeport, 80. *Prof Exp:* Teaching asst French, Stanford Univ, 60-62 & Harvard Univ, 63-65; instr, Tufts Univ, 65-67; asst prof, Univ Va, 67-73; chmn dept French & Ital, 73-75, assoc prof, 73-79, PROF FRENCH, TEMPLE UNIV, 79- *Concurrent Pos:* Instr, Harvard Summer Sch, 66-67; consult foreign lang pedag, Va Union Univ, 72; fel Celtic, Univ Edinburgh, fall 72; reader, Dublin Inst Advan Studies, Celtic Studies, spring, 77; consult, Rassia's Found, 79-; ed, Ram's Horn, 80- *Honors & Awards:* Chevalier des Palmes Academiques, French Gov, 77. *Mem:* MLA; Medieval Acad Am; Int Arthurian Soc; AAUP; Int Courtly Lit Soc. *Res:* Comparative literature, French, Latin and Celtic. *Publ:* Auth, The present state of studies on the Roman d'Eneas, Cult Neolatina, Rome, 71; Tradition and sources: The Jackson-Loomis controversy re-examined, Folklore, 8/72; One heart one mind: The rebirth of Virgil's hero in medieval French romance, Romance Monogr, 73; The problem of anachronism: Recent studies on the medieval French romances of antiquity, Philol Quart, 74; Cu Chulainn and Yvain: The love hero in early Irish and old French lit, Studies Philol, 75; Open contrast: Tristan and Diarmaid, Speculum 76; coauth, Aimer, Sonvenir, Souffrir: Les Chansons d'amour de Thibaut de Champagne, Romania, 78; transl, Jean Frappier, Chretien de Troyer: The Man and His Works, Ohio Univ Press, 82. *Mailing Add:* 761 Millbrook Lane Haverford PA 19041

CORNEJO, RAFAEL ESTEBAN, b Malaga, Spain, Sept 14, 37; US citizen; m 62; c 3. SPANISH LINGUISTICS & LITERATURE. *Educ:* Univ Calif, Santa Barbara, BA, 67, MA, 68, PhD(Span), 74. *Prof Exp:* Assoc Span, Univ Calif, Santa Barbara, 71-72; ASSOC PROF SPAN, HUMBOLDT STATE UNIV, 72- *Mem:* MLA; Am Asn Teachers Span & Port; Soc Espanola Ling. *Res:* Spanish drama, especially the Golden Age; Spanish phonetics; picaresque novel. *Publ:* Auth, Aspectos neocristianos cu el Lazarillo de Tormes, Prohemio, 74; La Celestina y su Contorno Social, Hispam, 77; La nave del Mercader Autoplagio o mejoramiento?, Estud Text Lit, 4/78. *Mailing Add:* Dept of Foreign Lang Humboldt State Univ Arcata CA 95521

CORNETTE, JAMES CLARKE, JR, b Sparta, NC, Feb 27, 18; m 42; c 3. GERMAN LANGUAGE & LITERATURE. *Educ:* Guilford Col, AB, 38; Haverford Col, AM, 39; Univ NC, PhD(Ger), 42. *Prof Exp:* Instr Ger, Univ NC, 42-43; prin elem sch, NC, 43-44; asst prof mod lang, Emory Univ, Oxford Br, 44-46; prof, 46-60, chmn dept mod lang, 47-66, prof, 60-80, EMER PROF GER, AUSTIN COL, 80- *Concurrent Pos:* Vis teacher, State Foreign Lang Sch, Hamburg, Ger, 67-68; mem nat adv bd, Wayne State Univ jr year in Munich & Freilburg, 68-77. *Mem:* Am Asn Teachers Ger; Am Coun Teaching Foreign Lang; Am Coun Studies Austrian Lit. *Res:* German folklore, proverbs and proverbial expressions; 19th and 20th century German literature, especially Adalbert Stifter, Hesse and Kafka. *Publ:* Aut, Luther's attitude toward Wellerisms, Southern Folklore Quart, 45. *Mailing Add:* Dept of Mod Lang Austin Col Sherman TX 75090

CORNGOLD, STANLEY ALAN, b Brooklyn, NY, June 11, 34; div; c 1. GERMAN & COMPARATIVE LITERATURE. *Educ:* Columbia Univ, AB, 57; Cornell Univ, MA, 63, PhD(comp lit), 68. *Prof Exp:* Instr English, Univ Md, Europ div, 59-62; teaching asst, Cornell Univ, 63-64, teaching asst French, 64-65; from lectr to asst prof Ger, 66-72, assoc prof, 72-79, assoc prof Ger & comp lit, 79-81, PROF GER & COMP LIT, PRINCETON UNIV, 81- *Concurrent Pos:* Nat Endowment for Humanities fel, 73-74;Guggenheim fel, 77-78. *Mem:* MLA; PEN Club; Am Comparative Lit Asn. *Res:* European Romanticism; modern German literature; modern poetics. *Publ:* Ed & transl, The Metamorphosis, Bantam, 72; auth, The Commentators' Despair: The Interpretation of Kafka's Metamorphosis, Kennikat, 73; co-ed & contribr, Thomas Mann 1875-1975, Princeton Univ, 75; auth, Sein und Zeit: Implications for poetics, Boundary 2, 76; co-ed, Aspekte der Goethezeit, Vandenhoeck & Ruprecht, 77; contribr, The Problem of The Judgment, Gordian, 77; Mann as a reader of Nietzsche, Boundary 2, 80; Error in Paul de man, Critical Inquiry, 82. *Mailing Add:* Dept of Germanics Princeton Univ Princeton NJ 08540

CORRAL, HELIA MARIA, b Mexico City, Mex, Aug 21, 41. HISPANIC LANGUAGE & LITERATURES. *Educ:* San Diego State Univ, BA, 67, MA, 70; Univ Southern Calif, PhD(Span), 75. *Prof Exp:* asst prof, 74-80, ASSOC PROF SPAN, CALIF STATE COL, BAKERSFIELD, 80- *Honors & Awards:* Alphonsine Festival Award, 77, 78 & 79. *Mem:* MLA; Am Asn Teachers Span & Port; Pac Coast Coun Lat Am Studies; Philol Asn Pac Coast. *Res:* Spanish Golden Age, Cervantes and Lope de Vega; Spanish American essay, Montalvo and Alfonso Reyes. *Publ:* Auth, Alfonso Reyes: humor y pedagogia, 5/78 & Grecia y gracia de Alfonso Reyes, 6/78, Bol Alfonsino; Gastronomia historica, cultural y literaria en Memorias de Cocina y Bodega de Alfonso Reyes, 12/78; Los personajes femeninos en las Nouelas ejemplores de Cervantes, 82; Actas del ier Congreso de Cervantes, Madrid, 78; La moza de cantaro de Lope de Vega, un verdalero caso de esqivez, Actas del ier Congreso Int de Lope de Vega, Madrid, 80. *Mailing Add:* Calif State Col 9001 Stockdale Hwy Bakersfield CA 93309

CORRE, ALAN DAVID, b London, England, May 2, 31; US citizen; m 57; c 4. SEMITIC STUDIES, LINGUISTICS. *Educ:* Univ London, BA, 51; Univ Manchester, MA, 53; Univ Pa, PhD(ling), 62. *Prof Exp:* Minister, Congregation Mikveh Israel, Pa, 55-63; from asst prof to assoc prof, 63-68, PROF HEBREW STUDIES, UNIV WIS-MILWAUKEE, 68-, CHMN DEPT, 80- *Concurrent Pos:* Nat Endowment for Humanities younger scholar fel, Univ Col, Univ London, 67-68. *Honors & Awards:* Res in Humanities Prize, Wis Acad Sci, Arts & Lett, 66; Standard Oil of Ind Award for teaching excellence, 73. *Mem:* Ling Soc Am; Am Orient Soc. *Res:* Semitic linguistics; Sefardic studies; Judeo-Arabic studies. *Publ:* Auth, A Programmed Hebrew Speller for Colleges, Univ Wis-Milwaukee, 70; contribr, Sephardim, Encycl Judaica, Macmillan, 71; auth, Daughter of My People, Brill, Leiden, 71; ed, Understanding the Talmud, Ktav, 74; Waw and digamma & A suprasegmental feature of length, Afroasiatic Ling, 5/75; Two loves in Muslim Cordova, Magreb Rev, 8/77. *Mailing Add:* Dept of Hebrew Studies Univ of Wis-Milwaukee Milwaukee WI 53201

CORREA, GUSTAVO, b San Gil, Colombia, Sept 20, 14; nat citizen; m 47; c 3. SPANISH LINGUISTICS & LITERATURE. *Educ:* Escuela Norm Superior, Colombia, Lic en Filol e Idiomas, 41; Johns Hopkins Univ, PhD, 47. *Prof Exp:* Instr Span, Williams Col, 42-43; asst prof, Univ Md, 43-45; asst prof, Johns Hopkins Univ, 47-48; nat dir sec educ Bogota, Colombia, 48-49; head dept lang, Escuela Norm Superior, 49-50; vis prof Span, Univ Ore, 50-51; assoc prof, Tulane Univ, 51-54; assoc prof, Univ Chicago, 54-58; assoc prof, Univ Pa, 56-59; PROF SPAN, YALE UNIV, 59- *Concurrent Pos:* Guggenheim fel, 59-60; co-ed, Hisp Rev, 58-60. *Mem:* MLA; Am Asn Teachers Span & Port; corresp mem Hisp Soc Am. *Res:* Literary criticism; folklore, linguistics. *Publ:* Auth, La loa en Guatemala; La poesia mitica de Federico Garcia Lorca, Univ Ore, 57; El simbolismo religioso en las novelas de Perez Goldos, Gredos, Madrid, 62; Realidad, ficcion y simbolo en las novelas de Perez Galdo, Inst Caro y Cuervo, Bogota, 67; Antologia de la poesia espanola del siglo XX, Appleton, 72, Prentice-Hall, 73; Antologia de la poesia espanola 1900-1980 (2 vols), Ed Gredos, Madrid, 80. *Mailing Add:* 163 Hepburn Rd Hamden CT 06517

CORRIERE, ALEX, b Easton, Pa, Oct 12, 14; m 42; c 4. FRENCH LANGUAGE & LITERATURE. *Educ:* Lafayette Col, AB, 40; Columbia Univ, MA, 42; Univ Grenoble, cert, 45; Univ NC, PhD, 54. *Prof Exp:* Instr French & Span, Muhlenberg Col, 46-48; instr, Utica Col, 48-50; asst instr French, Univ NC, 52-54; assoc prof, Elon Col, 54-55; supvr French & Span, Northwestern State Col La, 55-56; asst prof, Troy State Col, 57-59; mem fac, Phoenix Jr Col, 59-60; asst prof French & chmn dept, Mass State Col Bridgewater, 60-63; assoc prof, Univ SFla, 63-67; assoc prof, 67-69, PROF FRENCH, W GA COL, 69- *Mem:* SAtlantic Mod Lang Asn. *Res:* Sainte-Beuve as a poet; 19th century French drama; the tragedy in France. *Publ:* Auth, Alexandre Soumet minor dramatist of the early nineteenth century, Ky Foreign Lang Quart, 12/62; Pierre Lebrun's adaptation of La estrella de Sevilla, Xavier Univ Studies, 3/64; Madame de Girardin as a dramatist, Romance Notes, 12/67. *Mailing Add:* Dept of Foreign Lang WGa Col Carrollton GA 30117

CORRO, RAYMOND LOPEZ, b Murieta, Navarra, Spain, Jan 24, 32; US citizen; m 67; c 1. SPANISH. *Educ:* Regis Col, Colo, BA, 63; Univ Utah, MA, 67, PhD(Span), 71. *Prof Exp:* Instr, 70-71, asst prof Span, 71-80, ASSOC PROF FOREIGN LANG, UNIV MONT, 80- *Mem:* AAUP; Pac Northwest Conf Foreign Lang; Rocky Mountain Coun Latin Am Studies; Am Asn Teachers Span & Port. *Res:* Narrative of contemporary Spanish exiles; Spanish culture and language; bilingualism. *Publ:* Auth, Lo mexicano en la narrativa de Max Aub, 72 & La Revolucion Agraria de Mexico en Romula Gallegos, 73, Proc Pac Northwest Conf Foreign Lang. *Mailing Add:* Dept of Foreign Lang Univ of Mont Missoula MT 59801

CORTES, JULIO, b Bilboa, Spain, Jan 23, 24; m 67; c 1. ARABIC LANGUAGE. *Educ:* Univ Madrid, Dr(Semitic philol), 65. *Prof Exp:* Dir, Centro Cult Hispanico, Damascus, Syria, 56-60, 62-67; vis lectr, 67-68, assoc prof, 68-80, PROF ARABIC & SPAN, UNIV NC, CHAPEL HILL, 80- *Concurrent Pos:* Consult, Suppl to Oxford English Dict, 69- *Honors & Awards:* Oficial, Orden Merito Civil, Spain, 59. *Mem:* Am Orient Soc; Am Asn Teachers Arabic; Am Asn Teachers Span & Port; MLA; Union Europeenne d'Arabisants et d'Islamisants. *Res:* Arabic lexicography; Quranic Arabic. *Publ:* Auth, Guia cultural y universitaria de Madrid, Sipe, 52; Articles, In: Arabic Encyclopaedia, 56 & Enciclopedia de la Biblia, 63; coauth, Dun Kijuti fi-l-qarn al-isrin, IHAC, 68; auth, Siria en la Sagrada Escritura, Gran Enciclopedia Rialp, 75; El Coran, Nacional, 79. *Mailing Add:* Dept of Romance Lang Univ of NC Chapel Hill NC 27514

CORTINA, LYNN ELLEN RICE, b Huntington, WVa, March 9, 46; m 70; c 1. SPANISH LANGUAGE & LITERATURE. *Educ:* Siena Heights Col, BA, 67; Case Western Reserve Univ, PhD(Romance lang), 72. *Prof Exp:* Teacher bilingual educ & English as a second lang, Milwaukee Pub Schs, 72-73; teacher Span, Univ Sch, 73-75; lectr, Univ Wis, 75-78; ASST PROF SPAN, CARROLL COL, WIS, 78-, CHAIR, DEPT FOR LANG, 80- *Concurrent Pos:* Lectr for lang methods, Beloit Col, 72; consult, Sch of Educ, Univ Wis, 76-78. *Mem:* MLA; Latin Am Studies Asn; North Cent Coun Latin Americanists. *Res:* Hispanic and Latin American studies; women's studies; medieval studies. *Publ:* Auth, The aesthetics of morality: Two portraits of Mary of Egypt in The Vida de Santa Maria Egipiaca, Hispanic J, Vol II, 41-45; Spanish American Women Writers: A Bibliographical Research Checklist, Garland Press, 82; Composiciony significado de La Vida de Santa Maria Egipciaca, 82. *Mailing Add:* 2976 N Farwell Ave Milwaukee WI 53211

CORTINA, RODOLFO JOSE, b Guantanamo, Cuba, Feb 23, 46; US citizen; m 70. SPANISH LANGUAGE & LITERATURE. *Educ:* Tex A&I Univ, BA, 66; Case Western Reserve Univ, MA, 68, DPhil, 71. *Prof Exp:* Instr Span, Beloit Col, 69-71; asst prof Span & Port, 71-77, assoc dir, Ctr for Latin Am, 75-77, ASSOC PROF SPAN & PORT, 77-, DIR SPAN-SPEAKING OUTREACH INST, UNIV WIS-MILWAUKEE, 78- *Concurrent Pos:* Mem Wis humanities comt, Nat Endowment for Humanities, 77. *Honors & Awards:* League United Latin Am Citizens Distinguished Serv Award, 80. *Mem:* MLA: Am Asn Teachers Span & Port; NCent Coun Latin Americanists (secy-treas, 75-78, vpres, 78-79, pres, 79-); Latin Am Studies Asn. *Res:* Spanish lyric poetry and novel; literary historiography; Latin American studies. *Publ:* Auth, Becquer y la poesia mistica, Rev Estudios Hisp, 70; Blasco Ibanez y la novela evocativa, Ed Maisal, Madrid, 73; coauth, Canes y filosofos: Baroja, Unamuno y Schopenhauer, Abside, 73; auth, Jose Gautier Benitez, poeta esencial, 73 & Toward a literary biogram of the Puerto Rican personality, 74, Revista Chicano Requena, 74; Becquer y Quevedo, Papers Lang & Lit, 76; On dating the Lazarillo, Hisp Rev, 77. *Mailing Add:* Dept of Span & Port Univ of Wis Milwaukee WI 53201

CORTINEZ, CARLOS, b Santiago, Chile, Apr 8, 34; m 76; c 4. SPANISH AMERICAN POETRY, CREATIVE WRITING. *Educ:* Univ Iowa, MA, 70, PhD(Span), 75. *Prof Exp:* Dir cult affairs, Univ Australia, Chile, 62-68; asst Span, Univ Iowa, 69-71; vis prof, Drake Univ, 72-73; asst prof, Univ Maine, 73-77; asst prof, 77-80, ASSOC PROF SPAN, TULANE UNIV, 80- *Concurrent Pos:* Pres, Inst Chileno-Norte Am Cult, 66-68; Int Writing Program fel, Univ Iowa, 68-70. *Mem:* Inst Int Lit Iberoam; MLA; Asn Teachers Span & Port. *Res:* Latin American literature; poetry. *Publ:* Auth, Opus Cero, 64 & co-ed, Poesia Chilena (1960-1965), 66, Universitaria, Santiago; auth, La Estacion de las Fresas, La Rama Fla, Lima, 68; En el Mundo Una Casa, en Mi Casa Una Pieza Con Puertas y Ventanas, La Frontera, USA, 68; Treinta y Tres, La Murally, Madrid, 69; Interpretacion de El Habitante y Su Esperanze de Pablo Neruda, Revista Iberoam, 73; Introduccion a la muerte en Residencia en la Tierra: Ausencia de Joaquin, In: Pablo Neruda, Taurus, Madrid, 78. *Mailing Add:* Dept of Span Tulane Univ New Orleans LA 70118

CORUM, ROBERT TILLMAN, JR, b Great Lakes, Ill, Sept 19, 47; m 66; c 2. FRENCH LITERATURE. *Educ:* Old Dominion Univ, BA, 69; Univ Va, MA, 71, PhD (French lit), 75. *Prof Exp:* Instr, Univ Va, 71-75 & Sweet Briar Col, 75; asst prof, Univ Southern Calif, 75-77; asst prof, 77-81, ASSOC PROF FRENCH, KANS STATE UNIV, 81- *Concurrent Pos:* Assoc ed, Studies Twentieth-Century Lit J, 77- *Mem:* MLA; Am Asn Teachers Fr. *Res:* French literature of the seventeenth century; cirtical methods; Baroque lyric. *Publ:* Auth, Mythic allusions in Saint-Amant: Rhetorical ornament or thematic focus?, Fr Lit Ser, 76; A reading of Tristan l'Hermite's La Mer, Papers Seventeenth-Century Fr Lit, 78; Other Worlds and Other Seas: Art and Vision in Saint-Amant's Nature Poetry, Fr Forum Monogr, 78; coauth, Etat present des etudes sur Saint-Amant: Perceptions sur La Solitude, Oeuvres at Critiques, 79; auth, Perceptions of the External World in Tristan l'Hermite, L'Esprit Createur, 80; Paris as Barrier: Boileau's Satire VI, Papers Seventeenth-Century Fr Lit, 82. *Mailing Add:* Dept of Mod Lang Kans State Univ Manhattan KS 66506

CORY, MARK E, b Carmel, Calif, July 1, 42; m 65; c 2. MODERN GERMAN LITERATURE & LANGUAGE. *Educ:* Dartmouth Col, BA, 63; Ind Univ, MA, 68, PhD(German), 71. *Prof Exp:* Asst prof, 71-76, ASSOC PROF GERMAN, UNIV NEBR, LINCOLN, 76- *Mem:* MLA; Am Asn Teachers Ger; Western Asn Ger Studies. *Res:* German radio drama; concrete poetry; drama. *Publ:* Auth, A neglected aspect of foreign language testing: structuring the review session, Foreign Lang Ann, 5/74; The Emergence of an Acoustical Art Form, Univ Nebr Studies, 6/74; A mini-semester abroad, Die Unterrichtspraxis, 75; The O-Ton Hörspiel: An analysis of Paul Wühr's Preislied, Monatshefte, winter 76; The internalized landscape of Günter Eich's radio plays, Festschrift for Reino Virtanen, 78; Shakespeare and Dürrenmatt: From tragedy to tragicomedy, Comp Lit (in press). *Mailing Add:* Dept of Mod Lang Univ Nebr Lincoln NE 68588

COSENTINI, JOHN WALTER, b Brooklyn, NY, Feb 2, 09; m 51; c 2. FRENCH, ROMANCE PHILOLOGY. *Educ:* St John's Univ, NY, BA, 32; NY Univ, MA, 36; Columbia Univ, PhD(French), 51. *Prof Exp:* From instr to prof French, 35-74, chmn dept mod foreign lang, 57-61, 67-69, EMER PROF FRENCH, ST JOHN'S UNIV, NY, 74- *Publ:* Auth, Fontenelle's Art of Dialogue, King's Crown Press, 52; The literary art of Fenelon's Dialogues des morts, Thought Patterns, 59; Fenelon, In: New Cath Encycl, McGraw, 67. *Mailing Add:* 144-03 71st Ave Flushing NY 11367

COSPER, D DALE, b Plentywood, Mont, Dec 25, 40; m 69; c 1. FRENCH LITERATURE. *Educ:* Univ Wash, AB, 63, MA, 67, PhD(French lit), 73. *Prof Exp:* Asst prof French, 69-80, ASSOC PROF FOREIGN LANG & LIT, WHITMAN COL, 80- *Mem:* MLA. *Res:* Saint-Amant; literature and the visual arts; 17th century French novel. *Mailing Add:* Dept of French Whitman Col Walla Walla WA 99362

COSTA, GUSTAVO, b Rome, Italy, Mar 21, 30; m 63; c 1. ITALIAN, HISTORY. *Educ:* Univ Rome, DPhilos, 54. *Prof Exp:* Asst hist of mod & contemporary philos, Univ Rome, 57-60; lectr Ital, Univ Lyon, 60-61; from instr to assoc prof, 61-72, chmn dept, 73-76, PROF ITAL, UNIV CALIF, BERKELEY, 72- *Concurrent Pos:* Ist Ital Studi Storici, Naples fel, 54-57; French & Belg govt grants, 56; Am Philos Soc grant, 67; Nat Endowment for Humanities fel, 70-71; consult Centro del Lessico Intellettuale Europeo, Univ Rome, 76-77; Guggenheim Mem Found fel, 76-77; ed staff, Romance Philology, Forum Italicum & Nouxelles de la Republique des Lettress. *Mem:* AHA; MLA; AATI; Renaissance Soc Am; Am Soc Aesthet. *Res:* Literary criticism; history; philosophy. *Publ:* Auth, La Critica Omerica di Thomas Blackwell (1701-1757), G C Sansoni, 59; Un Collaboratore Italiano del Conte di Boulainviller: Francesco Maria Pompeo Colonna (1644-1726), Accad Toscana di Sci e Lett La Colombaria, 64; Un Avversario di Addison e Voltaire: John Shebbeare, Alias Battista Angeloni, S J, Contributo allo Studio dei Rapporti Italo-Britannici da Salvini a Baretti (con due inediti addisoniani), Accad Sci di Torino, Classe di Sci Morali, Storiche e Filologiche, 64-65; La Leggenda dei Secoli d'Oro Nella Letteratura Italiana, Laterza, 72; Le Antichita Germaniche Nella Cultura Italiana da Machiavelli a Vico, Bibliopolis, Naple, 77; Vico e Locke, Giornale Critico Filos Ital, XLIX: 344-361; Melchiorre Cesarotti, Vico and the sublime, Italica, 58: 3-15; Longinus's treatise On the Sublime in the age of Arcadia, Nouvelles De La Republique Des Lettres, I: 65-86. *Mailing Add:* Dept of Ital Univ of Calif Berkeley CA 94720

COSTA-ZALESSOW, NATALIA, Kumanovo, Macedonia, Dec 5, 36; US citizen; m 63; c 1. ITALIAN. *Educ:* Univ Calif, Berkeley, BA, 59, MA, 61, PhD(Romance lang & lit), 67. *Prof Exp:* Instr Ital, Mills Col, Oakland, 63; asst prof, 67-74, assoc prof, 74-79, PROF ITAL, SAN FRANCISCO STATE UNIV, 79- *Mem:* Am Asn Teachers Ital; MLA; Renaissance Soc Am; Dante Soc; Croatian Acad Am. *Res:* Eighteenth, 19th and early 20th century European literature. *Publ:* Auth, Italy as a victim: A historical appraisal of a literary theme, Italica, 68; Un autografo in inglese di Gabriele D'Annunzio, 74 & Autografi dannunziani in inglese indirizzati a Kaye Don e Fred Cooper, 74, Ausonia; Su due sonetti del Cinquecento attribuiti a L Terracina, Forum Italicum, 81; Scrittrici italiane dal XIII al XX secolo, Testi e critica, Ravenna, Longo Editore, 82. *Mailing Add:* Dept Foreign Lang & Lit San Francisco State Univ San Francisco CA 94132

COSTE, BRIGITTE MARIE, b Paris, France, Apr 27, 41; French citizen. FRENCH LITERATURE, HISTORY OF IDEAS. *Educ:* Univ Paris, Lic es Lett, 63; Mt Holyoke Col, MA, 67; Univ Mass, PhD(French), 72. *Prof Exp:* Teacher English, Institut Montalembert, Nogent-sur-Marne, France, 67-69; from instr to asst prof French, Mt Holyoke Col, 69-75; asst prof, 75-82, ASSOC PROF FRENCH, MARQUETTE UNIV, 82- *Mem:* Am Asn Teachers Fr; MLA; Women's Caucus Mod Lang; Am Soc Eighteenth Century Studies; Soc Professeurs fr Amerique. *Res:* Eighteenth century French literature; women writers; Utopia. *Publ:* Co-ed, Female Studies IX: Teaching About Women in the Foreign Languages, Feminist Press, 75; auth, Mably: Pour une Utopie du bon sens, Klincksieck, Paris, 76; coauth, La France que je connais, Van Nostrand, 77; Engagements, Harcourt, Brace J, 81. *Mailing Add:* Dept of For Lang Marquette Univ Milwaukee WI 53233

COSTELLO, BONNIE, Modern American Poetry. See Vol II

COSTELLO, JOHN ROBERT, b New York, NY, Sept 12, 42; m 67. LINGUISTICS. *Educ:* Wagner Col, BA, 64; NY Univ, MA, 66, PhD(Ger ling), 68. *Prof Exp:* Instr Ger, Univ Col, 67-68, asst prof, 68-72, ASSOC PROF LING, WASHINGTON SQ COL, NY UNIV, 73- *Concurrent Pos:* Consult, Universe Bks & Lexik Houser Publ. *Mem:* Ling Soc Am; Int Ling Asn (pres, 81-82); Soc Ger-Am Studies. *Res:* Historical linguistics; linguistic reconstruction; language acquisition. *Publ:* Auth, The palcement of crimean gothic by means of abridged test lists in glottochronology, J Indo-European Studies, 74; Vistigial substantival adverbs and prepositionalization in Old Frisian, Neuphilologische Mitteilungen, 75; coauth (with John Chiang & Joseph Chiang), The mastery of complex syntactic structures in first and second language learning, City Univ New York Forum Ling, 77; auth, A generative grammar of Old Frisian, Peter Lang Verlag, Bern, 77; Syntactic change and second language acquisition: The case for Pennsylvania German, Linguistics, 78; Rule simplification and the reconstruction of interdialectal rule borrowing, Word, 78; A lexical comparison of two sister languages: Pennsylvania German and Yiddish, Pa Folklife, 80; The absolute construction in Gothic, Word, 80. *Mailing Add:* Dept of Ling NY Univ 10 Washington Pl Wash Sq New York NY 10003

COSTELLOE, M JOSEPH, b Ames, Iowa, Nov 5, 14. CLASSICAL LANGUAGES. *Educ:* St Louis Univ, AB, 38, MA & PhL, 41; St Mary's Col, Kans, STL, 47; Johns Hopkins Univ, PhD, 58. *Prof Exp:* Instr class lang, St Louis Univ, 52-56; from asst prof to prof, Creighton Univ, 57-70, chmn dept, 61-70; vis scholar res, editing & Jesuit hist, Jesuit Hist Inst, Rome, 71-72; librn, Pontif Bibl Inst, 73-75; LIBRN, CURIA GENERALIZIA DELLA COMPAGNIA DI GESU, 75- *Concurrent Pos:* Vis Prof, Loyola Univ Ctr Humanistic Studies, Rome, 63-64. *Mem:* Am Philol Asn. *Res:* Roman criminal law; Christian archaeology; early church history. *Publ:* Transl, Julian the Apostate (Guiseppe Ricciott, L'imperatore Guiliano l'Apostata), Bruce, 60; Rite and man (Louis Bouyer, Le rite et l'homme), 63 & St Ambrose, His Life and Times (Angelo Paredi, S Ambrogio e la sua eta), 64, Univ Notre Dame; Church and State in the Teaching of St Ambrose (Claudio Morino, Chiesa e Stato nella dottrina di S Ambrogio), Cath Univ Am, 69; Francis Xavier (Georg Schurhammer, Franz Xaver), Jesuit Hist Inst, Vols I & II, 73 & 77. *Mailing Add:* Curia Generalizia della Compagnia di Gesu Borgo S Spirito 5 Rome 00193 Italy

COSTICH, JULIA FIELD, b Lexington, Ky, Aug 20, 49; m 69; c 2. MODERN FRENCH LITERATURE. *Educ:* Duke Univ, BA, 69; Univ Ky, MA, 70, PhD(French), 73, MPA, 80. *Prof Exp:* Instr, 73-76, asst prof French, 76-78, MGT SPECIALIST, UNIV KY, 80- *Mem:* MLA; S Atlantic Mod Lang Asn; Asn Study Dada & Surrealism (secy, 72-74). *Res:* Literature and medicine. *Publ:* Auth, The poem in the world of change: Peret's Quatre a quatre, Romance Notes, fall 74; Antonin Artaup, Twayne, 79; Benjamin Peret, Univ NC, 78. *Mailing Add:* Dept of Family Practice Univ of Ky Lexington KY 40506

COTNAM, JACQUES, b July 20, 41; Can citizen; m 64; c 1. FRENCH & FRENCH-CANADIAN LITERATURE. *Educ:* Laval Univ, BA & BPh, 62, Lic es Lett, 64, Dipl Etudes Super, 66, D es L, 78. *Prof Exp:* From lectr to asst prof, 64-72, ASSOC PROF FRENCH LIT, YORK UNIV, 72- *Concurrent Pos:* Lectr, MLA, 69 & Col de France, Paris, 70; lectr at var foreign univs, 73-; vis prof, Univ de Guenoble III, 80-82. *Mem:* Amis Andre Gide; Can Asn Comp Lit; Can Asn Univ Teachers; Asn Can Univ Teachers Fr. *Res:* Influence of nationalism on literature; Andre Gide and English and American literatures; cosmopolitism and the French symbolist movement. *Publ:* Auth, Andre Gide et le cosmopolitisme litteraire, Rev Hist Lit de France, 3/70; Le Roman Quebecois a l'heure de la Revolution Tranquille, Fides, Montreal, 71; Cultural nationalism and its literary expression in French-Canadian fiction, In: Cry of Home, Univ Tenn, 72; Essai de bibliographie chronologique des ecrits d'Andre Gide, Amis d' Andre Gide, Paris, 72; Contemporary Quebec, McClelland & Stewart, Toronto, 73; Bibliographie chronologique de l'oeuvre d'Andre Gide 1889-1973, 74 & Inventaire bibliographique et Index analytique de la correspondance d'Andre Gide, 75, G K Hall; Le Theatre quebecois, instrument de contestation sociale et politique, Fides, Montreal, 76. *Mailing Add:* Dept of French Lit York Univ 4700 Keele St Downsview ON M3J 1P3 Can

COTTAM, MARTHA LEMAIRE, b St Usage, Aube, France, Feb 5, 19; US citizen; m 41, 68; c 2. FRENCH LITERATURE, PHILOSOPHY OF EDUCATION. *Educ:* Brooklyn Col, BA, 39; Iowa State Univ, MA, 41; Columbia Univ, PhD(French), 58. *Prof Exp:* Asst instr French, Univ Iowa, 40-41; instr, Elmira Col, 42-43; native tutor, Yale Univ, 43-45; asst instr gen studies, Columbia Univ, 51-53; from instr to asst prof, 57-66, ASSOC PROF FRENCH, MILLS COL, 66- *Concurrent Pos:* Vis asst prof, Wellesley Col, 61-62; lectr, Alliance Francaise, San Francisco & Oakland, 65-75. *Mem:* MLA; Am Asn Teachers Fr; AAUP; Ctr Studies Dem Insts. *Res:* Integration of the humanities; French African literature; women in literature. *Mailing Add:* Dept of Foreign Lit & Lang Mills Col Oakland CA 94613

COTTINO-JONES, MARGA, b Torino, Italy, Aug 25, 30; US citizen; m 58; c 2. ITALIAN, HUMANITIES. *Educ:* Univ Torino, Laurea humanities, 54; Univ Wash, MA, 60, PhD(Romance lang), 65. *Prof Exp:* Lectr English, Univ Torino, 58-59; assoc Ital & French, Univ Wash, 59-61; lectr French, San Diego State Col, 61-62; instr Ital, 62-64, actg asst prof, 64-65, from asst prof to assoc prof, 65-76, res grants, 66-68, 68-69, PROF ITAL, UNIV CALIF, LOS ANGELES, 76-, CHMN DEPT, 80- *Concurrent Pos:* Humanities Inst award, 72. *Mem:* MLA; Medieval Soc Am. *Res:* Medieval literature; Baroque literature; literary criticism. *Publ:* Auth, An Anatomy of Boccaccio's Style, Cymba, Naples, 68; Saggio di lettura della Prima Giornata del Decameron, Teoria e Critica, 72; The city/country conflict in the Decameron, Studies Boccaccio, 73; Observations on the structure of the Decameron novella, Romance Notes, 73; Metodi di critica letteraria americana, Palumbo, 73. *Mailing Add:* Dept of Ital Univ of Calif Los Angeles CA 90024

COTTRELL, ALAN P, b New York, NY, Jan 16, 35. GERMANIC LANGUAGES. *Educ:* Ohio State Univ, BSc, 56, PhD(Ger), 63; Univ Wis-Madison, MA, 58. *Prof Exp:* From instr to asst prof Ger, Univ Wash, 62-66; from asst prof to assoc prof, 68-77, PROF GER, UNIV MICH, ANN ARBOR, 77- *Concurrent Pos:* Guggenheim Found fel, 76-77. *Mem:* Am Asn Teachers Ger. *Res:* Scandinavian. *Publ:* Auth, Zoilo-Thersites: Another sehr ernster Scherz in Goethe's Faust II, Mod Lang Quart, 3/68; The significance of the name Johannes in Die Judenbuche, Seminar, 10/70; Wilhelm Muller's Lyrical Song-Cycles, Interpretations and Texts, Univ NC Studies in Ger Lang & Lit, 70; Chalice and skull: A Goethean answer to Faust's cognitional dilemma, Ger Quart, 1/72; Goethe's Faust: Seven Essays, Univ NC Studies in Ger Lang & Lit, 76. *Mailing Add:* Dept of Ger Lang & Lit Univ of Mich Ann Arbor MI 48104

COTTRELL, ROBERT DUANE, b Farmersburg, Iowa, Feb 20, 30; m 65; c 2. FRENCH LITERATURE. *Educ:* Columbia Univ, BS, 57; Yale Univ, PhD(Romance lang), 61. *Prof Exp:* From instr to asst prof Romance lang, Northwestern Univ, 60-65; asst prof, Amherst Col, 65-68; assoc prof, 68-71, chmn dept, 74-78, PROF ROMANCE LANG, OHIO STATE UNIV, 71- *Concurrent Pos:* Vis prof, Univ Pittsburgh, 72. *Mem:* MLA; Am Asn Teachers Fr; Mod Humanities Res Asn; Soc Amis Montaigne. *Res:* French Renaissance literature. *Publ:* Auth, Pernette du Guillet's rymes: An adventure in ideal love, Bibliot Humanisme et Renaissance, 69; Brantome: The Writer as Portraitist of His Age, Droz, 70; coauth, Repondez-moi! Pratique Orale des Verbes Irreguliers Francais, Prentice-Hall, 71; Alain on Happiness, 73, auth, Colette, 74 & Simone de Beauvier, 75, Ungar; Of dialects and goat's blood in an anecdote by Montaigne, Renaissance Quart, 77; Sexuality/Textuality: A Study of the Fabric of Montaigne's Essais, Ohio State Univ Press, 81. *Mailing Add:* Dept of Romance Lang Ohio State Univ Columbus OH 43210

COUGHANOWR, EFFIE, b Konitsa, Greece, Dec 30, 23; US citizen; m 55; c 3. CLASSICS. *Educ:* Univ Thessaloniki, BA, 47; Univ Ill, MA, 53, PhD(classics), 55. *Prof Exp:* Asst prof French, Ind Univ, Kokomo, 66-67; asst prof, 68-80, ASSOC PROF GREEK & LATIN, VILLANOVA UNIV, 81- *Mem:* Am Philol Asn; Class Asn Atlantic States. *Publ:* Auth, The meaning of Telugetos in Homeric poetry, L'Antiquite Classique, 72; Dirke and the sun's course in Sophocles' Antigone, Class Quart, 73; Mastax in Homer, Grazer Beiträge, 75; The meaning of Molouros in Homer, Class Quart, 79. *Mailing Add:* 504 Midland Circle St Davids PA 19087

COUGHLIN, EDWARD V, b Norwood, Mass, Mar 2, 32; m 59; c 2. ROMANCE LANGUAGES. *Educ:* Col Holy Cross, BA, 54; Boston Col, MA, 55; Univ Mich, PhD, 65. *Prof Exp:* Asst prof, 64-74, assoc prof, 74-81, PROF SPAN LIT, UNIV CINCINNATI, 81- *Mem:* Am Asn Teachers Span & Port; Am Soc 18th Century Studies; Ctr Estud del Siglo XVIII. *Res:* Eighteenth and 19th century Spanish literature. *Publ:* Ed, Antologia de la poesia espanola del siglo XVIII, Representaciones Ingenieria, 71; coauth, Bibliografia selecta y critica de Octavio Paz, Univ San Luis Potosi, 73; ed, Habides de Ignacio Lopez de Ayala, Ed Hisp, 74; co-ed, Homenaje a Octavio Paz, Univ San Luis Potosi, 76; auth, Adelardo Lopez de Ayala, Twayne, 77; coauth, Una obra inedita de D Ramon de la Cruz, Bol Bibliot de Menendez Pelayo, 77; ed, Tres obras ineditas de Ramon de la Cruz, Puvill, 79. *Mailing Add:* Dept of Romance Lang Univ of Cincinnati Cincinnati OH 45221

COULET DU GARD, RENE, b Saint-Denis-du Sig, Algeria, Dec 29, 19; US citizen; m 40; c 3. ROMANCE LANGUAGES. *Educ:* Univ Pa, MS, 63; Univ Besancon, PhD(lit), 66. *Prof Exp:* Prin, Ecole d'Apprentissage, Morocco, 46-52; teacher, high sch, NY, 53-57 & Kimberton Sch, Pa, 57-62; teacher French, Ursinus Col, 62-63; asst prof French & Span, West Chester State Col, 63-66; from asst prof to assoc prof, 66-80, PROF FRENCH, UNIV DEL, 80-

Concurrent Pos: Ed, Thursday Page, Maroc Press, Morocco, 47-52; foreign corresp, Echos Monde Roman Inedit, Morocco, 52-55. *Honors & Awards:* Adventure Novel Prize, Soc Arts et Let Algeria, 52; Poetry Award, Acad Jeux Floraux Tunisia, 53; Chevalier, Soc Philanthropique at Culturelle France, 66, Commandeur, 68; Chevalier, Palmes Academiques, 67, Officier, 77; Medaille d'argent, Concours Lit: Acad Int Lutece, Paris, 73; Medaille d'OR Concours Litteraire, Acad Int Lutece, Paris, 74; Prix d'Hist Maritime, Soc Arts et Lettres Acad Bordeaux, France, 80; Prix de la Langue Francaise, Acad Francaise, 80. *Mem:* Am Asn Teachers Fr; Soc des Gens Lett et auteurs France. *Res:* Eighteenth and 19th century French literature; origin of French geographical names in the United States. *Publ:* Auth, L'Arithmosophie de Gerard de Nerval, Ed Deux Mondes, 72; Reine (novel), Ed La Revue Mod, Paris, 73; The Handbook of French Place Names in the USA, Ed Des Deux Mondes, 74 & 77; La France Contemporaine de 1900 a 1976, 76 & L-Oiseau de feu (poetry), 76, Slavuta, Can; Le fruit defendu (poetry), Ed Chantecler, France, 76; Pleure pas P'tit Bonhomme (novel), Ed Du Vent, France, 77; The Handbook of American Counties, Parishes and Independent Cities, Ed Deux Mondes, 81. *Mailing Add:* P O Box 251 Elkton MD 21921

COULTER, GEOFFREY RESTALL, US citizen. LINGUISTICS. *Educ:* Swarthmore Col, BA, 72; Univ Calif, San Diego, MA, 79, PhD(ling), 79. *Prof Exp:* Lang asst Fr, 74-75, teaching asst, 75-76, ling, 76-77, psychol, 77-79, ASST PROF LING, ENGLISH LANG INST, AM UNIV CAIRO, 79- *Mem:* Ling Soc Am. *Res:* Linguistic structure of American sign language of the deaf; Egyptian sign language of the deaf, Cairo dialect. *Publ:* Auth, Continuous representation in American sign language, In: Proceedings of the First National Symposium on Sign Language Research and Teaching, Nat Asn Deaf, 77; Raised eyebrows and wrinkled noses: The grammatical function of facial expression in American sign language, In: Proceedings of the Second National Symposium on Sign Language Research and Teaching, Nat Asn Deaf, 78; A conjoined analysis of American sign language relative clauses, J Discourse Proc, 81. *Mailing Add:* 26 Sunset Blvd Pittsford NY 14534

COULTER, JAMES ALBERT, b New York, NY, Sept 23, 32; div; c 1. CLASSICAL PHILOLOGY. *Educ:* Harvard Univ, BA, 56, MA, 60, PhD(class philol), 62. *Prof Exp:* From instr to asst prof, 60-68, ASSOC PROF GREEK & LATIN, COLUMBIA UNIV, 68- *Concurrent Pos:* Guggenheim Found fel & Am Coun Learned Soc grant-in-aid, 70-71. *Mem:* Am Philol Asn. *Res:* Early Greek literature; Greek philosophy and rhetoric; neo-Platonic literary theory. *Publ:* Auth, The relation of the Apology of Socrates to Gorgias' Defense of Palamedes and Plato's critique of Gorgianic rhetoric, Harvard Studies Class Philol, 64; Phaedrus 279A: The praise of Socrates, Greek, Roman & Byzantine Studies, fall 67; coauth, The middle speech of Plato's Phaedrus, J Hist Philos, 71; auth, The Literary Microcosm: Theories of Interpretation of the Later Neoplatonists, Brill, Leiden 76. *Mailing Add:* Dept of Greek & Latin Columbia Univ New York NY 10027

COULTER, MARY WELLES, b South Pasadena, Calif, July 22, 11. FOREIGN LANGUAGES. *Educ:* Wells Col, BA, 33; Univ Southern Calif, MA, 41, PhD(French), 53. *Prof Exp:* From instr to asst prof French, Univ Redlands, 53-60; from assoc prof to prof, 60-77, EMER PROF FRENCH & SPAN, KUTZTOWN STATE COL, 77- *Mem:* MLA; Am Soc 18th Century Studies; Am Asn Univ Women; Nat Retired Teachers Asn; Am Asn Retired Persons. *Res:* Satire in French literature of the 16th and 17th centuries; Alfred Fouillee, philosophere and educator; contemporary French novel. *Publ:* Auth, Satyres Chrestienes de la Cuisine Papale, Studies Philol, 4/59; Albert Camus' art of satire, Redlands Fac Rev, spring 59; Satyre as a dramatic genre in the French Renaissance, Kutztown State Col Fac Bull, 2/63. *Mailing Add:* 182 C Avenida Majorca Laguna Hills CA 92653

COUNTESS, ROBERT HARVEY, Religion, Philosophy. See Vol IV

COURTEAU, JOANNA, b Lwow, Poland, Apr 15, 39; US citizen; c 2. SPANISH, PORTUGUESE. *Educ:* Univ Minn, Minneapolis, BA, 60; Univ Wis-Madison, MA, 62, PhD(Span & Port), 70. *Prof Exp:* Instr Span, Sullins Col, 63-65; asst prof, Univ Ark, Fayetteville, 67-71; asst prof Span & Port, 71-76, assoc prof, Foreign lang & lit, 76-80, PROF SPAN & PORT, IOWA STATE UNIV, 76- *Concurrent Pos:* Vis prof, Warsaw Univ, Poland, 79; Int Commun grant, 79. *Mem:* AAUP; Am Asn Teachers Span & Port; Midwest Mod Lang Asn; Midwest Asn Latin Am Studies; Latin Am Studies Asn. *Res:* Contemporary Brazilian novel; contemporary peninsular poetry; romantic Spanish poetry. *Publ:* Auth, O Sonho na Poesia Ortonima de Fernando Pessoa, Luso-Brazilian Rev, 2: 206-211; Manuel Vilanova, A young poet of Spain, Poet & Critic, 3: 47-49; The image of woman in the novels of Graciliano Ramos, Revista-Review Interamericana, 4: 162-176; The last poems of Jorge Guillen, 11: 20-21, The pervading unity in the novels of Graciliano Ramos, 12: 31-36 & The Angustia de la Nada as expressed in Antonio Machado's Soledades and Compos de Castilla, 17: 39-51, NAm Mentor; The pronoun lhe in the Cronica de Dom Pedro, Lingua Posnaniensis, 22: 63-74; The mysticism of Juan Ramon Jimenez, NAm Mentor Mag, 29: 63-77. *Mailing Add:* Foreign Lang & Lit Dept Iowa State Univ Ames IA 50011

COURTNEY, ALICE KAAREN, b Pueblo, Colo, July 8, 42; m 73; c 1. FRENCH LITERATURE, WOMEN'S STUDIES. *Educ:* Emporia State Univ, BS, 63; Ohio State Univ, MA, 66, PhD(French), 73. *Prof Exp:* Teacher English, Lowther Jr High Sch, Emporia, Kans, 63-64; instr French, 67-72, asst prof, 73-80, ASSOC PROF ROMANCE LANGS, OHIO WESLEYAN UNIV, 80- *Mem:* AAUP; MLA; Am Asn Teachers Fr; Am Soc 18th Century Studies; Nat Women's Asn. *Res:* Short fiction in French literature (medieval); women writers in contemporary continental fiction. *Publ:* Ed, Great Lakes Colleges Association Women's Studies Resource Handbook, Great Lakes Col Asn, 77 & 78. *Mailing Add:* Ohio Wesleyan Univ Delaware OH 43015

COURTNEY, HUMPHREY J, b Butte, Mont, June 21, 26. CLASSICAL LANGUAGES. *Educ:* St Edward's Sem, AB, 47; St Louis Univ, MA, 55, PhD, 59. *Prof Exp:* From asst prof class lang & head dept to assoc prof, 59-73, PROF CLASS LANG & CHMN DIV ARTS & HUMANITIES, CARROLL COL, CONT, 73- *Mem:* Class Asn Mid W & S; Am Class League. *Res:* Textual criticism; Dares Phrygius. *Mailing Add:* Dept of Class Lang Carroll Col Helena MT 59601

COUSIN, FLORENCE CAMILLE, French citizen. LINGUISTICS, FRENCH. *Educ:* Coun of Europe, PhD(ling), 62. *Prof Exp:* Asst French, Col Maillet, 58-59, Inst Cath Paris, 60-64; asst English, Lycee Buffon Paris, 65-67; asst French & ling, Univ Carleton, 67-73; ASSOC FRENCH & LING, CARLETON UNIV, 73- *Concurrent Pos:* Asst English, Inst ND de Sion Paris, 61-64; asst French, Univ Mex, 65, Mauk Poland, summer, 66 & McGill Univ, summer, 67. *Mem:* Learned Soc. *Res:* Phonetics and phonology; teaching of French as a second language; theoretical French linguistics. *Publ:* Auth, L'Enseignement du Frangais au Carada anglais, FIPF, 74; Le language, dictionnaire du savoir moderne, Sci et Vie, 3/74; Ou en est la tradition automatique en 1975?, CAUT, Vancouer, 75; La significance, function actionnelle du language, A Paraitre dans lcs Actes du Congre's de Simiotique de Vienne, 79; Le systeme semiologique en egyptien ancien, Accepte pjar Canadian, J Res Semiotics, 82. *Mailing Add:* French Dept Carleton Univ Ottawa ON K1S 5B6 Can

COUSSENS, PRUDENT C, b Butler, Minn, Feb 17, 19; m 46; c 2. GERMAN. *Educ:* St Ambrose Col, BA, 46; De Paul Univ, BMus, 49; State Univ Iowa, MA, 51, PhD, 58. *Prof Exp:* From instr to asst prof Ger & Latin, 46-56, assoc prof Ger, 56-60, prof, 60-80, EMER PROF FRENCH & GER, ST AMBROSE COL, 80- *Mem:* Am Asn Teachers Ger. *Res:* Modern German literature, especially expressionism. *Mailing Add:* Dept of Ger St Ambrose Col Davenport IA 52803

COUTANT, VICTOR CARLISLE BARR, b East Orange, NJ, Jan 15, 07; m 40; c 2. FOREIGN LANGUAGES. *Educ:* Columbia Univ, AB, 29, AM, 30, PhD, 36. *Prof Exp:* Instr lang & soc sci, Essex County Jr Col, NJ, 33-36; instr lang, Allentown Prep Sch, 36-37; instr univ sch, Ohio State Univ, 37-42, 46-47; from asst prof to prof foreign lang, Cent Mich Univ, 47-66, head dept, 59-65; prof Ger & Latin, 66-77, EMER PROF CLASS LANG & LIT, WESTERN MICH UNIV, 77- *Mem:* Am Philol Asn. *Res:* Ancient science, period of Aristotle and successors; relation of science to humanities; palaeography. *Publ:* Auth, Alexander of Aphrodisias: Book IV of Aristotle's Meteorologica, Columbia Univ, 36; The firewalk in Theophrastus, Isis, 5/54; Science and the humanities, a symbiosis, J Higher Educ, 6/57; A Glimpse of the USA, Max Hueber, Munich, 64; ed, Theophrastus de Igne, Royal van Gorcum, Netherlands, 71; (with Val Eichenlaub), Theophrastus de Ventis, Notre Dame Univ Press, 75. *Mailing Add:* 803 Dorchester Dr Kalamazoo MI 49001

COVEY, DELVIN, b Ill, May 23, 21. CLASSICAL PHILOLOGY. *Educ:* Greenville Col, BA, 42; Univ Ill, MA, 49, PhD(class philol), 51. *Prof Exp:* Assoc prof creative writing, Wesleyan Col, Ga, 51-55; asst prof classics, Univ Conn, 55-62; chmn dept foreign lang, Montclair State Col, 62-64; chmn div humanities, Spring Arbor Col, 64-72; PROF ENGLISH & CHMN DIV HUMANITIES, GORDON COL, 72- *Concurrent Pos:* Consult, English Workshop, Northeast Mo State Col & Latin Workshops, Univ Conn, 58; consult, Ind Univ, 63, 65; consult mod English grammar, Mich Elem Schs, Jackson, 67- *Mem:* Am Philol Asn; MLA; Northeast Lang Conf. *Res:* Poetry of the Augustan Age. *Mailing Add:* Dept of English Gordon Col Wenham MA 01984

COWAN, GEORGE MCKILLOP, b Kelwood, Man, Feb 23, 16; m 43; c 3. THEOLOGY, LINGUISTICS. *Educ:* McMaster Univ, BA, 36; Dallas Theol Sem, ThM, 41; Univ NDak, MA, 63. *Hon Degrees:* LLD, Biola Col, 70. *Prof Exp:* Dir Can Summer Inst Ling, 44-53; assoc dir, Wycliffe lang course, England, 54-59; pres, 57-81, dep gen dir Europe & Africa, Wycliffe Bible Transl, 63-71. *Concurrent Pos:* Mem bd dir, Summer Inst Ling, Inc, 56-81; dir Sem Sprachmethodik, Ger, 66-72; dir phonol, summer inst ling, Gordon Col, 70-72. *Mem:* Ling Soc Am; Am Soc Missiology. *Res:* Linguistic research in preliterate societies with applied results in field of literary materials and Bible translation; whistled languages. *Publ:* Auth, Mazateco house building, Southwestern J Anthrop; Mazateco whistle speech, Language; The social and political importance of the Mazateco Faena, Am Indigena; coauth, Maria Sabina and her Mazatec Mushroom Velada, Harcourt, 75; auth, Whistled Tepehua, In: Speech Surrogates: A Reader, Vol I, Mouton, The Hague, 76. *Mailing Add:* 2218 W Edinger St Apt 3 Santa Ana CA 92704

COWAN, J MILTON, b Salt Lake City, Utah, Feb 22, 07; m 34; c 3. GENERAL LINGUISTICS. *Educ:* Univ Utah, AB, 31, AM, 32; State Univ Iowa, PhD, 35. *Prof Exp:* Res assoc, State Univ Iowa, 35-38, from asst prof to assoc prof Ger, 38-46; prof ling & dir div mod land, Cornell Univ, 46-72, PRES, SPOKEN LANG SERV, INC, 71- *Concurrent Pos:* Prof, ling instr, Univ Mich, 38, 40, 48, Univ NC, 41 & Univ Wis, 44; dir intensive lang prog, Am Coun Learned Soc, 42-46, ling res fund, bd dir, 46-51; spec consult in charge lang phase, Army Specialized Training Prog, US War Dept & US Dept State, 42-45; ed, A Dictionary of Modern Written Arabic, Cornell Univ-Harrassowitz, 61-71, Spoken Lang Serv Inc, 71-, Arabic-English Dictionary, Spoken Lang Serv Inc, 76-, Harrassowitz-Spoken Lang Serv Inc, 78- *Mem:* MLA; Ling Soc Am (past secy-treas, pres, 66); fel Acoustical Soc Am. *Res:* Phonetics: Monograph in the archieves of speech; pitch and intensity characteristics of stage speech. *Publ:* Ed & coauth, Aramco-Arabic Language Series, 4 vols, 54-56 & auth, English-Arabic Word List, 58, Aramco. *Mailing Add:* Spoken Lang Serv Inc Box 783 Ithaca NY 14850

COWAN, JOHN BAINARD, American & Comparative Literature. See Vol II

COWAN, WILLIAM GEORGE, b St Petersburg, Fla, Nov 17, 29; m 52; c 5. LINGUISTICS. *Educ:* Univ Calif, Berkeley, AB, 51; Cornell Univ, PhD(ling), 60. *Prof Exp:* Sci linguist, foreign serv inst, US Dept State, Beirut, Lebanon, 60-64; assoc prof ling, Brown Univ, 64-71; PROF LING, CARLETON UNIV, 71- *Concurrent Pos:* Lectr, Am Univ Beirut, 61-63; ed, Papers of the Algonquian Conferences, 76- *Mem:* Ling Soc Am; Can Ling Asn. *Res:* Arabic dialectology; Algonquian linguistics. *Publ:* Auth, Workbook in Historical Reconstruction, New York, 71. *Mailing Add:* Dept of Ling Carleton Univ Ottawa ON K1S 5B6 Can

COWEN, ROY CHADWELL, JR, b Kansas City, Mo, Aug 2, 30; m 56. GERMAN LITERATURE. *Educ:* Yale Univ, BA, 52; Univ Göttingen, DrPhil, 61. *Prof Exp:* From instr to assoc prof, 60-71, PROF GER, UNIV MICH, ANN ARBOR, 71-, CHMN DEPT, 79- *Concurrent Pos:* Nat Endowment for Humanities sr fel, 72-73. *Mem:* MLA; Int Asn Germanic Studies. *Res:* German lyrics and drama in 19th century. *Publ:* Ed, Dantons Tod, Blaisdell, 69; auth, Neunzehntes Jahrhundert (1830-1880), Francke, 70; Christian Dietrich Grabbe, Twayne, 72; Naturalismus: Kommentar zu einer Epoche, Winkler, 73, 3rd ed, 81; ed & auth, Christian Dietrich Grabbe, Werke in zwei Bänden mit einem Kommentarband, Hanser, 75-77; auth, Hauptmann Kommentar zum dramatischen Werk, 80, Hauptmann Kommentar zum nichtdramatischen Werk, 81 & ed, Dramen des deutschen Naturalismus: Von Gerhart Hauptmann bis Karl Schonherr in zwei Bänden, 81, Winkler. *Mailing Add:* 2874 Baylis Dr Ann Arbor MI 48104

COWGILL, WARREN CRAWFORD, b Grangeville, Idaho, Dec 19, 29. LINGUISTICS. *Educ:* Stanford Univ, BA, 52; Yale Univ, MA, 53, PhD, 57. *Prof Exp:* From instr to assoc prof, 56-72, PROF INDO-EUROP LING, YALE UNIV, 72- *Concurrent Pos:* Vis lectr classics, Univ Ill, 61-62. *Mem:* Ling Soc Am; Am Orient Soc. *Res:* Indo-European comparative linguistics. *Mailing Add:* Dept of Ling Yale Univ New Haven CT 06520

COWHERD, CARRIE ELIZABETH, b Louisville, Ky, Jan 26, 44. LATIN, GREEK. *Educ:* Ind Univ, Bloomington, BA, 65; Univ Chicago, MA, 67, PhD(classics), 72. *Prof Exp:* Instr classics, Univ SDak, 67-70; asst prof classics, Univ Wis-Milwaukee, 72-80; MEM FAC, HOWARD UNIV, 80- *Mem:* Am Philol Asn; Classics Asn Mid West & South; Classics Asn Atlantic States. *Res:* Latin epic poetry; Ovid; Pindar. *Publ:* Auth, Notes on Pythia II, Classics J, 4-5/73. *Mailing Add:* Howard Univ Washington DC 20059

COX, JERRY LYNN, b Wichita, Kans, Apr 14, 45; m 73; c 2. GERMAN, APPLIED LINGUISTICS. *Educ:* Wichita State Univ, BA, 68; Univ Colo Boulder, MA, 72; Ind Univ Bloomington, MS, 75, PhD(Ger ling), 77. *Prof Exp:* Instr, 76-77, ASST PROF GER & ENGLISH AS A SECOND LANG, FURMAN UNIV, 77- DIR LANG LAB, 76- *Concurrent Pos:* Fulbright fel ling, Univ Hamburg, 72-73. *Mem:* Am Asn Teachers Ger; Ling Soc Am; Teachers English to Speakers of Other Lang; Am Asn Appl Ling; Am Coun Foreign Lang Teachers. *Res:* Foreign language methodology; applied linguistics-language acquisition; comparative Germanic linguistics. *Publ:* Auth, From dream to reality: Towards a psycholinguistically based methodology, 75 & Applying certain features of dependency theory to the teaching of foreign languages, 78, Can Mod Lang Rev. *Mailing Add:* Dept of Mod Foreign Lang Furman Univ Greenville SC 29613

COX, RALPH MERRITT, b Richmond, Va, June 29, 39. ROMANCE LANGUAGES. *Educ:* Univ Richmond, BA, 61; Univ Wis, MA, 62, PhD(Span), 67. *Prof Exp:* Instr Span, Univ Wis, 65-66; from instr to asst prof, Duke Univ, 66-72; assoc prof, 72-77, PROF SPAN, COL WILLIAM & MARY, 77- *Concurrent Pos:* Philos Soc grant, Oxford Univ, 72; Col William & Mary grant, Oxford Univ 73 & Madrid, 76; Busch fel, 79. *Mem:* MLA; Am Asn Teachers Span & Port; Am Soc 18th Century Studies; SAtlantic Mod Lang Asn; Hisp Soc Am. *Res:* Spanish 18th century literature. *Publ:* Auth, The Reverend John Bowle, the Genesis of Cervantean Criticism, Univ NC, 71; Tomas de Iriarte, 72 & Juan Melendez Valdes, 74, Twayne; An English Illustrado: The Reverend John Bowle, Peter Lang, 77; Cervantes and three illustrados: Mayans, Sarmiento, and Bowle, Studies in the Spanish Golden Age, 78; Eighteenth Century Spanish Literature, Twayne, 79; Revelations in English Hispanism: The Library of the Rev John Bowle, Studies in Honor of Gerald Wade, 79; Giuseppe Baretti: A contemporary view of Charles III, La Chispa, 81. *Mailing Add:* Dept of Mod Lang Col of William and Mary Williamsburg VA 23185

COX, ROBERT STURGEON, JR, English, Linguistics. See Vol II

COX, SOREN FRANKLIN, Linguistics, English. See Vol II

COY, SUSANNA PETERS, b Baltimore, Md, July 25, 39; m 73. ITALIAN LITERATURE. *Educ:* Col Notre Dame, Md, BA, 60; Johns Hopkins Univ, MA, 67, PhD(Romance lang), 68. *Prof Exp:* From lectr to asst prof Ital, Univ Toronto, 67-70; asst prof, Rutgers Univ, 70-73 & Univ Ga, 73-76; asst to vpres acad affairs, Eastern Conn State Col, 77-78; ASSOC PROF ITAL & CHMN DEPT, UNIV HARTFORD, 78- *Mem:* Mla. *Res:* Seventeenth century Italian lyric poetry; 17th century poetic theory; medieval Italian literature. *Publ:* Auth, Metaphor and Maraviglia: Tradition and innovation in the Adone of G B Marino, Ling e Stile, 72; The anatomical machine: A representation of the microcosm in the Adone of G B Marino, Mod Lang Notes, 73; A Geometry of Time, Barroco, Brazil, 73; The problem of per in the Cantico di frate Sole of Saint Francis, Mod Lang Notes, 76; Poetic unity in the Cantico di frate Sole of Saint Francis, Ital Quart, 76; The quarrel of the Adone and the crisis of the narrative, Barroco, Brazil, 77. *Mailing Add:* Mansfield Hollow Rd Mansfield Center CT 06250

COZAD, MARY LEE, b Munich, Ger, Jan 2, 47; US citizen; m 76; c 1. SPANISH LITERATURE, LITERARY THEORY. *Educ:* Univ Calif, Davis, AB, 68; Univ Calif, Berkeley, MA, 69, PhD(Romance lang & Span), 75. *Prof Exp:* Instr, Univ Ga, 75-76; ASST PROF SPAN, UNIV VA, 76- *Concurrent Pos:* Grant, Univ Va, 80; Nat Endowment for Humanities fel, 81-82. *Mem:* MLA; Northeastern Mod Lang Asn; Philol Asn Pac Coast; SCent Mod Lang Asn. *Res:* Literature of the Spanish Renaissance, especially romances of chivalry and works influenced by the Byzantine novel; Greek romance; Renaissance poetry and poetics. *Publ:* Auth, Los prologos de Ruben Dario Estudio bibliografico, Thesaurus, 74; Una curiosidad bibliografica: La portada de Lidamarte de Armenia, Revista de Archivos, Bibliotecas y Museos, 76; A facsimile edition of a sixteenth-century Navarrese poem: Jeronimo de Abolanche's Las Abidas, Romance Philol, 80; Experiential conflict and rational motivation in the Diana Enamorada: An anticipation of the modern novel, J Hisp Philol, 81; A Platonic-Aristotelian Linguistic Controversy of the Spanish Golden Age, Florilegium Hispanicum, 82. *Mailing Add:* Dept of Span Univ of Va Charlottesville VA 22903

CRADDOCK, JERRY RUSSELL, b Pueblo, Colo, May 19, 35; m 61. ROMANCE PHILOLOGY, MEDIEVAL HISPANIC LITERATURE. *Educ:* Tex Western Col, BA, 58; Univ Calif, Berkeley, PhD, 67. *Prof Exp:* Asst prof Span, Univ Calif, Davis, 65-68, from asst prof to assoc prof Span & Romance philol, 68-76, PROF SPAN, UNIV CALIF, BERKELEY, 76- *Mem:* Ling Soc Am; MLA; Mediaeval Acad Am. *Res:* Linguistics. *Publ:* Coauth, The Hispanic sound-suffix -ido, 63064, auth, A critique of recent studies in Romance diminutives, 65-66 & Latin diminutive versus Latin-Mediterranean hybrid, 67-68, Romance Philol; Latin Legacy Versus Substratum Residue: The Unstressed Derivational Suffixes in the Romance Vernaculars of the Western Mediterranean, Univ Calif Pub Ling, 69. *Mailing Add:* Dept of Span & Port Univ of Calif Berkeley CA 94720

CRAIG, BARBARA MARY ST GEORGE, b Ottawa, Ont, Feb 24, 14; nat US. FRENCH. *Educ:* Queen's Univ, Can, BA, 37, MA, 39; Bryn Mawr Col, PhD, 49. *Prof Exp:* Postal censorship examr, Can, 41-43; instr French & Ger, Mt Royal Col, 43-46; from instr to assoc prof, 47-64, chmn dept French & Ital, 76-78, PROF FRENCH, UNIV KANS, 64- *Honors & Awards:* Teaching Award, Standard Oil Co, Ind, 73 & Outstanding Educrs Am, 74. *Mem:* MLA; AAUP; Am Asn Teachers Fr. *Res:* Medieval French drama; medieval lyric and didactic poetry; French-Canadian literature. *Publ:* Ed, L'Estoire de Griseldis, 54, La Vie Monseigneur Saint Fiacre, 60 & La Creacion, La Transgression and L'Expulsion of the Mistere du Viel testament, 68, Humanistic Ser Univ Kans; auth, The didactic element in medieval French serious drama, L'Esprit Createur, 62; The moralite du Sacrifice d'Abraham of the Recueil Trepperel, In: Jean Misrahi Mem Vol, Fr Lit Publ, 77; Prefiguration and literary creativity in the Sacrifice d'Abraham of the Mistere du Viel Testament, In: Voices of Conscience, Tempe Univ, 77; The Staging and Dating of the Mystere du Siege d'Orleans, Res Publica Litterarum, Vol 4, 82; The evolution of a mystery play: A critical edition of Le Sacrifice d'Abraham of Le Mistere du Viel Testament, In: La Moralite du Sacrifice d'Abraham and the 1539 version of Le Sacrifice d'Abraham of the Mistere du Viel Testament, Fr Lit Publ Co, 82. *Mailing Add:* Dept of French Univ of Kans Lawrence KS 66045

CRAIG, CHARLOTTE MARIE, b Ostrava, Czech, Jan 14, 29; m 54. GERMAN LANGUAGE & LITERATURE. *Educ:* Univ Puget Sound, BA & teaching cert, 57; Univ Ariz, MA, 60; Rutgers Univ, PhD(Ger), 64. *Prof Exp:* Teacher English & hist, Alaska Pub Schs, 57-59; asst prof Ger, Univ Kans, 64-68; lectr, George Washington Univ, 68-69; prof & chairperson Ger & comp lit, Schiller Col, Heidelberg, Ger, 69-73; PROF GER, KUTZTOWN STATE COL, 74- *Concurrent Pos:* Watkins fac fel Ger lit, Univ Kans, 65. *Mem:* MLA; Asn Teachers Ger; Am Soc 18th Century Studies; Northeastern Am Soc 18th Century Studies. *Res:* Eighteenth century German literature; 18th century comparative literature. *Publ:* Auth, From folk legend to travesty: An example of Wieland's artistic adaptations, Ger Quart, 5/68; Christoph Martin Wieland as the Originator of the Modern Travesty in German Literature, Univ NC, 70; Fiesco's fable: A portrait in political demagoguery, Mod Lang Notes, 71; Do I hear an echo? Reflections of a translator's woes and rewards, Viewpoints, 76; Sophie La Roche's enlightened anglophilia, Ger Notes, 78; Mind and method: Sophie La Roche--a 'praeceptra filiarum Germaniae?, Transactions of the V Int Cong Enlightenment, 79, The Voltaire Found, Oxford, England; Humor in German literature: A rare commodity?, Past MLA Bull, 82. *Mailing Add:* 2 Field Stone Ct Eatontown NJ 07724

CRAIG, HERBERT RUSH, Speech, English. See Vol II

CRAIG, VIRGINIA ROBERTSON, b Ft Worth, Tex, Oct 16, 35; m 54; c 1. SPANISH LANGUAGE & LITERATURE. *Educ:* Bethel Col, Tenn, BA, 56; Univ Mo-Columbia, PhD(Span), 68. *Prof Exp:* Chairperson dept mod foreign lang, 76-80, ASST PROF SPAN, IND UNIV, FT WAYNE, 69- *Concurrent Pos:* Ind Univ grant-in-aid, 70-71; dir, Ind Univ Overseas Study Prog, Madrid, 77-78. *Honors & Awards:* Distinguished Teaching Award, Ind Univ, 75. *Mem:* MLA; Am Asn Teachers Span & Port; Comediantes. *Res:* Seventeenth century Spanish drama; Spanish civilization and culture. *Publ:* Contribr, Manual of Hispanic Bibliography, Univ Wash, 70; Annotated Analytical Bibliography of Tirso de Molina Studies, 1627-1977, Univ Mo, 79. *Mailing Add:* Dept of Mod Foreign Lang Ind Univ Ft Wayne IN 46805

CRAMER, OWEN CARVER, b Tampa, Fla, Dec 1, 41; m 62; c 4. CLASSICS. *Educ:* Oberlin Col, AB, 62; Univ Tex, Austin, PhD(Greek), 73. *Prof Exp:* From instr to asst prof, 65-75, ASSOC PROF CLASSICS, COLO COL, 75-, M C GILE CHAIR, 77- *Mem:* Am Philol Asn; Class Asn Mid W & S. *Res:* Early Greek literature. *Publ:* Auth, Ulysses the Good?, TAPA, 74; Speech and silence in the Iliad, Class J, 76. *Mailing Add:* Dept of Classics Colo Col Colorado Springs CO 80903

CRANE, THEODORE, b New Haven, Conn, Dec 17, 35; m 68. PHILOLOGY, CLASSICS. *Educ:* Colby Col, BA, 58; Univ NC, Chapel Hill, MA, 61, PhD(Latin), 64. *Prof Exp:* Vis instr ancient lang, Col William & Mary, 64-65; res scholar coop prog humanities, Duke Univ, 65-66; asst prof foreign lang, Univ SC, 67-74, dir avt media ctr, col gen studies, 73-74, chmn class studies prog, 69-74, adv group leader & sem leader, Contemporary Univ, 70-73, sen, fac senate, 72-74; staff assoc instrnl technol, Learning Systs Ctr, Off of Vpres for Acad Res & Develop, Univ Southern Calif, 74-75. *Concurrent Pos:* Danforth assoc, Danforth Found, 73- *Mem:* Am Philol Asn; AAUP; Asn Ling & Lit Comput; Asn Educ Commun & Technol. *Res:* Silver Latin literature; computer analysis of Latin epic poetry; Greek art and archaeology. *Publ:* Auth, Times of the night in Cicero's first Catilinarian, Class J, 3/66; Roman country inns, Class Bull, 69; The squalor that was Rome, Nat Hist Mag, 5/73; Hunter and hunted in Aeneid 7-12, Class Bull, 73; A note on Aeneas' Human Sacrifice, Aeneid 10: 517-520, Class World, 74; The apotheosis of Classical architecture, Class Outlook, 74; Ancient Rome: Environmental Pollution Then and Now, Weston Walsh, 78. *Mailing Add:* PO Box 48499 Bicentennial Sta Los Angeles CA 90048

CRANSTON, EDWIN AUGUSTUS, b Pittsfield, Mass, Oct 18, 32; m 60. JAPANESE LITERATURE. *Educ:* Univ Ariz, BA, 54; Stanford Univ, MA, 63, PhD(Japanese lit), 66. *Hon Degrees:* MA, Harvard Univ, 72. *Prof Exp:* Instr Japanese, 65-66, from asst prof to assoc prof, 66-72, PROF JAPANESE LIT, HARVARD UNIV, 72- *Concurrent Pos:* Fulbright-Hays res grant, 69-70. *Mem:* Am Asn Asian Studies; Asn Teachers Japanese. *Res:* Heian literature; Man'yoshu; poetry of Izumi Shikibu. *Publ:* Auth, The Izumi Shikibu Diary: A Romance of the Heian Court, Harvard Univ, 69; The poetry of Izumi Shikibu, Monumenta Nipponica, 70; Water-plant imagery in the Man'yoshu, Harvard J Asiatic Studies, 71; Murasaki's Art of fiction, Japan Quart, 4-6/71; coauth, Nihon Koten Bungei: The Courtly Tradition in Japanese Art and Literature, Kodansha Int, Tokyo, 73; auth, Young Akiko: The literary debut of Yosano Akiko (1878-1942), Lit East & West, 74; The dark path: Images of longing in Japanese love poetry, Harvard J Asiatic Studies, 75; contribr, Toward a reconsideration of Makurakotoba: An analysis of preposited figurative elements in a Choka by Hitomaro, In: Man'yoshu Kenkyu, Hanawa Shobo, Vol V, 76. *Mailing Add:* Dept of E Asian Lang & Civilizations Harvard Univ Cambridge MA 02138

CRANSTON, MECHTHILD, b Berlin, Ger. ROMANCE LANGUAGES & LITERATURES. *Educ:* Univ Calif, Berkeley, BA, 58, PhD(Romance lang & lit), 66. *Prof Exp:* Assoc French, Univ Calif, Berkeley, 64-66, instr, 66; asst prof, Univ San Francisco, 66-68 & Calif State Col Hayward, 68-69; chmn dept foreign lang, Univ NC, Asheville, 71-72, assoc prof French, 72-77; ASSOC PROF FRENCH, CLEMSON UNIV, 80- *Concurrent Pos:* US deleg & Belg Govt grant, Apollinaire Symp, Belg, 68; vis prof, Phillipps-Univ, Marburg, Ger, 70; Am Coun Learned Soc fel, 73-74; Nat Endowment for Humanities grant, 77. *Mem:* Am Asn Teachers Fr; MLA; Amis Rimbaud; Amis Guillaume Apollinaire; SAtlantic Mod Lang Asn. *Res:* Poetry; music; criticism. *Publ:* Auth, Florilege: An Anthology of French Literary Criticism, Assoc Students Univ Calif, Berkeley, 65; Apprendre Le Larron de Guillaume Apollinaire, PMLA, 10/67; Sortir d'Orkenise: Reflexions sur Onirocritique, Le Brasier et Les Fiancailles, In: Guillaume Apollinaire: Images d'un Destin, Minard, Paris, 67; Enfance, mon amour: La Reverie vers l'enfance dans l'oeuvre de Guillaume Apollinaire, Saint-John Perse et Rene Char, 70 & Mains Serrees (poems in three languages), 71, Debresse, Paris; Rene Char 1923-1928: The young poet's struggle for communication, PMLA, 10/72; The light within: The encounter of word and world in the Poem of Martin Heidegger and Rene Char, Rivista di Lett Mod & Comp, 12/76; Orion Resurgent: Rene Char, Poet of Presence, Porrua, Madrid, 79. *Mailing Add:* Dept of Lang Clemson Univ Clemson SC 29631

CRANSTON, PHILIP EDWARD, b Pittsfield, Mass, Mar 22, 29; m 62. ROMANCE LANGUAGES & LITERATURES. *Educ:* Univ Ariz, BA, 51; Univ Calif, Berkeley MA, 58, PhD(Romance lang & lit), 72. *Prof Exp:* Asst prof foreign lang, Calif State Univ, Hayward, 64-69 & Western Carolina Univ, 71-72; asst prof French, 72-82, ASSOC PROF FRENCH, UNIV NC, ASHEVILLE, 82- *Concurrent Pos:* Nat Endowment for Humanities fel, Boston Univ, summer, 76 & Univ Calif, Berkeley, 81. *Mem:* MLA; Am Asn Teachers Fr; SAtlantic Mod Lang Asn; Am Lit Transl Asn; Asn Recherche Poesie. *Res:* Poetry; translation; Voltaire. *Publ:* Auth, Time of the Sun (poems), Vishwavidyalaya Prakashan, Varanasi, India, 68; Rene Char, poete outil: A l'instant du poema, 70 & Jules Supervielle: Livre de fables, 73, Fr Rev Spec Issues; Les Fleurs du Mal translated: A potpourri, SAtlantic Bull, 11/75; Rome, en anglais, se prononce Roum . . . Shakespeare versions by Voltaire, Mod Lang Notes, 12/75; transl & ed, Before Time (poems), Vishwavidyalaya Prakashan, Varanasi, India, 79; auth, In Hoc Signo: An explication of Mallarme's Cygne, Ky Romance Quart, 1/81; transl, Le Sillage, sequence from Les Amis inconnus of Jules supervielle, L'isle Sonante, 1/82. *Mailing Add:* PO Box 8972 Asheville NC 28814

CRAWFORD, KARIS ANN, English, Medieval Studies. See Vol II

CRAWFORD, RONALD LEE, b Warren, Ohio, Mar 28, 39; m 73; c 2. GERMAN LITERATURE. *Educ:* Heidelberg Col, BS, 61; Kent State Univ, MA, 67; Rutgers Univ, PhD(Ger), 74. *Prof Exp:* Temp instr, Hiram Col, 61-63; from instr to asst prof, 66-77, ASSOC PROF GER, KENT STATE UNIV, 77- *Concurrent Pos:* Nat Endowment for Humanities, summer, 80. *Mem:* Am Asn Teachers Ger. *Res:* Classical German literature; Schiller. *Publ:* Auth, Images of Transience in the Poems and Ballads of Friedrich Schiller, Lang, Berne, 77. *Mailing Add:* 1615 Bobwhite Trail Stow OH 44224

CREAN, JOHN EDWARD, JR, b New York, NY, Nov 15, 39. GERMANIC LANGUAGES. *Educ:* Col Holy Cross, BA, 62; Yale Univ, MA, 64, PhD(Ger), 66. *Prof Exp:* Teaching assoc Ger, Yale Univ, 64-65, actg instr, 65-66; asst prof, Univ Wis-Madison, 71; chmn div Ger, 72-74, assoc prof, 71-80, PROF GER, UNIV HAWAII, MANOA, 80- *Mem:* Am Asn Teachers Ger. *Res:* Foreign language methodology; Germanic philology; medieval literature. *Publ:* Auth, Bilden/Beelden in the writings of Eckhard and Ruusbroec, Z Deut Sprache, 69; The extended modifier in American English, Am Speech, 69; coauth, Briefe aus Deutschland, Harcourt, 69; Rhetoric & religion in Der Arme Heinrich, Sprachkunst, 71; Kritische Gespräche, Holt, 72; auth, Obsculta, O File/Hör, O Tochter, Class Folia, 77; Deutsche Sprache und Landeskunde, 81 & coauth, Alles Gute, 82, Random House. *Mailing Add:* 1327-A Moku Pl Apt 3 Honolulu HI 96822

CRECELIUS, KATHRYN JUNE, b New Rochelle, NY. FRENCH LITERATURE. *Educ:* Bryn Mawr Col, BA, 73; Yale Univ, MA, 74, PhD(French), 78. *Prof Exp:* ASST PROF FRENCH, MASS INST TECHNOL, 78- *Mem:* Am Asn Teachers French; Friends George Sand; MLA; Northeast Mod Lang Asn. *Res:* George Sand; French novel; French-Canadian novel. *Publ:* Auth, Feminist magazines: The view from Europe, Sojourner, 79; Fictional history in Merimee's Chronique du regne de Charles IX, Fr Lit Series, 81; French historical monuments revisited, Contemp Fr Civilization, 81; L'histoire et son double dans Pelagie-la-Charrette, Studies Can Lit, 81; Merimee's Federigo: From folktale to short story, Studies in Short Fiction, winter 82. *Mailing Add:* For Lang & Lit Mass Inst Technol Cambridge MA 02139

CREECH, JAMES NARVIN, b Smithfield, NC, July 31, 45; m 75. FRENCH LITERATURE. *Educ:* Univ NC, AB, 68; Cornell Univ, PhD(French), 75. *Prof Exp:* Asst prof, 75-80, ASSOC PROF FRENCH & ITAL, MIAMI UNIV, 80- *Mem:* MLA; Midwest Mod Lang Asn; Am Soc Eighteenth Century Studies; AAUP. *Res:* Denis Diderot; eighteenth century French thought; contemporary French critical theory. *Publ:* Auth, Misreading as triumph: Julia Kristeva's Bataille, Diacritics, spring 75; translr, The supplement of the Copula by J Derrida, Ga Rev, 77; Diderot and the pleasure of the other, Eighteenth Century Studies, summer 78. *Mailing Add:* Dept of French & Ital Miami Univ Oxford OH 45056

CREED, ROBERT PAYSON, English, Comparative Literature. See Vol II

CREEL, BRYANT LAWRENCE, b Berkeley, Calif, Apr 24, 44; m 69; c 2. SPANISH LITERATURE & LANGUAGE. *Educ:* Stanford Univ, BA, 65; Calif State Univ, Sacramento, 68; Univ Calif, Davis, PhD(Span), 78. *Prof Exp:* Grad asst Span, Calif State Univ, Sacramento, 67-68; lectr English, York Col, City Univ NY, 68-70; teaching asst Span, Univ Calif, Davis, 72-73; instr, Univ Calif Exten Total Immersion Prog, 74; assoc teaching, Univ Calif, Davis, 73-75, lectr, 78-79; LECTR SPAN, CALIF STATE UNIV, LONG BEACH, 79- *Mem:* Asn Int Poesia Oral & Romancero; MLA; Philol Asn Pac Coast; Am Asn Teachers Span & Port. *Res:* Renaissance literature of Spain, Portugal and Europe; modern European literature; the study of literature in a cultural-social and historical perspective. *Publ:* Auth, Shadows, un corto paso hacia adelante, No 50, 66, Companadas a medianoche de Orson Welles, No 55, 66 & XIV Festival de San Francisco, 70, Nuestro Cine, Madrid, Spain; The Religious Poetry of Jorge de Montmayor, Tamesis Bks Ltd, London, 81. *Mailing Add:* Dept of Span & Port Calif State Univ Long Beach CA 90840

CREIGHTON, DOUGLAS GEORGE, b Toronto, Ont, July 8, 23; m 53; c 3. FRENCH LANGUAGE & LITERATURE. *Educ:* Univ Toronto, BA, 45, MA, 46; Columbia Univ, PhD(French lit), 52. *Prof Exp:* Instr French, Brown Univ, 47-49; instr, Univ Sask, 50-53; asst d'anglais, Lycee Chaptal, Paris, 53-54; asst prof French, Beloit Col, 55-59; asst prof, 59-66, actg chmn dept, 76-77, assoc prof, 66-81, PROF FRENCH, UNIV WESTERN ONT, 81- *Mem:* MLA; Am Asn Teachers Fr; Am Soc 18th Century Studies; Fr Soc Studies 18th Century; Can Soc Studies 18th Century. *Res:* Eighteenth century French literature. *Publ:* Coauth, A travers les siecles, An Anthology of French Literature, Macmillan, Can, 67; Man and mind in Diderot and Helvetius, PMLA; A Genevan reaction to Diderot's Pensees philosophiques: J F de Luc, In: City and Society in the 18th Century, Hakkert, Toronto, 73; Rouseau and the De Lucs in 1754, Diderot Studies, 78; Jacques-Francois Deluc of Geneva and his friendship with Jean-Jacques Rousseau, Romance Monographs, Univ Miss, 82. *Mailing Add:* Dept of French Univ of Western Ont London ON N6A 3K7 Can

CREORE, ALVIN EMERSON, b Rochester, NY, Mar 24, 14; div; c 3. FRENCH LANGUAGE & LITERATURE. *Educ:* Univ Rochester, AB, 34, AM, 36; Johns Hopkins Univ, PhD, 39. *Prof Exp:* Jr instr Romance lang, Johns Hopkins Univ, 37-39; from instr to asst prof, 40-53, assoc prof, 53-77, prof, 77-79, EMER PROF ROMANCE LANG, UNIV WASH, 79- *Concurrent Pos:* Lectr, Univ Buffalo, 48; Fund Advan Educ fel, France, 54-55; vis prof, Univ Minn, 56-57. *Res:* Renaissance and 17th century; computer assisted studies in 16th century French language and literature. *Publ:* Auth, A Word-Index to the Poetic Works of Ronsard, W S Maney & Sons, Leeds, 72. *Mailing Add:* 1524 NE 62nd St Seattle WA 98115

CREORE, JO ANN DAVIS, b Columbus, Ohio, Feb 16, 37. ROMANCE LANGUAGES, LINGUISTICS. *Educ:* Lake Erie Col, BA, 59; Univ Wash, MA, 63. *Prof Exp:* Actg asst prof French, Univ Calif, Davis, 65-66; asst prof, 66-70, ASSOC PROF ROMANCE LING, UNIV ALTA, 70-, CHMN DEPT, 75- *Concurrent Pos:* Am Coun Learned Soc fel, 63-64. *Mem:* Ling Soc Am; Can Ling Soc. *Res:* Old French; applied linguistics-French; history of French and Italian. *Publ:* Co-ed, Readings in Romance Linguistics, Mouton, The Hague, 73; auth, French phonology revisited, Can J Ling, fall 74. *Mailing Add:* Dept of Romance Lang Univ of Alta Edmonton AB T6G 2M7 Can

CRESSEY, WILLIAM WHITNEY, b Hartford, Conn, June 6, 39; m 64. SPANISH LINGUISTICS. *Educ:* Trinity Col, Conn, BA, 61; Univ Ill, Urbana, MA, 62, PhD(Span), 66. *Prof Exp:* Asst prof Romance ling, Univ Mich, Ann Arbor, 66-71; assoc prof, 71-81, chmn dept, 78-82, PROF LANG & LING, GEORGETOWN UNIV, 81- *Concurrent Pos:* Univ Mich Rackham fac grant-in-aid, 68-69; consult, Lang & Lit Workshop High Sch Span Teachers, Lansing, Mich, 69 & Scott, Foresman & Co, 69 & Prentice-Hall, 70; mem adv coun, Northeast Conf Teaching Foreign Lang & vis asst prof Span, Univ Hawaii, Manoa, 69-70; Acorh award for computer-oriented studies in humanities, Am Coun Learned Soc, 73-74; dir, Summer Inst, Nat Endowment for Humanities, 80. *Mem:* Ling Soc Am; Am Asn Teachers Span & Port; MLA; SAtlantic Mod Land Asn. *Res:* Spanish phonology; phonological theory; computational linguistics. *Publ:* Auth, Relative adverbs in Spanish: A transformational analysis, Language, 9/68; Relatives and interrogatives in Spanish, Linguistics, 70; coauth, Tertulia, libro de conversacion, composicion y repaso gramatical, Appleton, 72; auth, Irregular verbs in Spanish, Generative Studies Romance, 73; Spanish phonology and morphology: A generative view, Georgetown Univ Press, 78. *Mailing Add:* Sch of Lang & Lit Georgetown Univ Washington DC 20057

CRICHTON, MARY CHRISTINA, b Toronto, Ont, Sept 6, 25. GERMAN. *Educ:* Univ Toronto, BA, 47, MA, 50; Univ Wis, PhD(Ger), 54. *Prof Exp:* Sessional lectr Ger, McMaster Univ, 47-50; res asst, Univ Wis, 52-53, instr, 54-55; from instr to asst prof, 55-65, ASSOC PROF GER, UNIV MICH, ANN ARBOR, 65- *Concurrent Pos:* Can Fed Univ Women McWilliams Mem fel, 54-55. *Mem:* AAUP, MLA; Am Asn Teachers Ger; Int Ver Ger Sprachu Literaturwiss. *Res:* German lyric poetry from Goethe through the early 20th century. *Publ:* Auth, Conrad Ferdinand Meyers Hohe Station, Ger Rev, 58; Zur Funktion der Gnade-Episode in C F Meyers Der Heilige, In: Lebendige Form: Festschrift für Heinrich E K Henel, Wilhelm Fink, 70; Heiterkeit und Schatten der Tragik: Gedanken zum Droste-Gedicht Die Schenke am See, In:

Husbanding the Golden Grain: Studies in Honor of Henry W Nordmeyer, Univ Mich, 73; And no birds sing: Lenau's Desolate Urwald, Mich Ger Studies, 75; Es winkt zu Fühlung; Rilke's Response to Goethe's Ganymed?, Ger Rev, 78; Mann, Pferd, Wald und Todesgedanken: Ein kritischer Vergleich zwischen Nikolaus Lenaus Gedicht Der Urwald und Robert Frosts Stopping by Woods on a Snowy Evening, Jahrbuch für Int Germanistik, 80; A Goethean Echo in Mörike's An eine Äolsharfe, Sem, 80. *Mailing Add:* Dept of Ger Lang & Lit Univ of Mich Ann Arbor MI 48109

CRIMINALE, LEONARD REX, b Mobile, Ala, Mar 30, 24. SPANISH, ITALIAN. *Educ:* Washington & Lee Univ, AB, 46; Princeton Univ, AM, 48, PhD, 57. *Prof Exp:* Instr, Rutgers Univ, 47-49; asst prof Romance lang, Washington & Lee Univ, 49-53 & Ohio Wesleyan Univ, 53-58; assoc prof, 58-62, PROF ROMANCE LANG, ELMIRE COL, 62- *Concurrent Pos:* Ed, Ohio Lang Newslett; dir jr year abroad prog, Elmire Col, 60-65. *Mem:* MLA; Am Asn Teachers Span & Port; Renaissance Soc Am; Mod Humanities Res Asn; Am Asn Teachers Ital. *Res:* Spanish language and literature; Anglo-Spanish comparative literature; Italian language. *Publ:* Auth, English themes in Spanish Golden Age literature. *Mailing Add:* Dept of Romance Lang Elmira Col Elmira NY 14901

CRISPIN, JOHN, b Tienen, Belg, May 3, 36; US citizen; m 66; c 1. SPANISH LANGUAGE & CONTEMPORARY LITERATURE. *Educ:* Univ St Thomas, Tex, BA, 60; Univ Wis-Madison, MA, 62, PhD(Span & French), 67. *Prof Exp:* From instr to asst prof, 65-71, ASSOC PROF SPAN, VANDERBILT UNIV, 71-, CHMN SPAN-PORT, 79- *Mem:* MLA; Am Asn Teachers Span & Port. *Res:* Contemporary poetry and novel; intellectual history; comparative literature. *Publ:* Coauth, Progress in Spanish, Scott, 72 & 2nd ed, 78; co-ed, Los Vanguardistas Espanoles: 1925-1935, Alianza, Madrid, 73; auth, Pedro Salinas, Twayne, 74; auth articles in Insula, Hispania, Archivum, Cuadernos Hispanoam, Bks Abroad & J Span Studies; La Residencia de estudiantes 1911-1936, Isla de los Ratsnes, 81; Manuel Altolaquirre, Twayne (in press). *Mailing Add:* Dept of Span & Port Box 1518-B Vanderbilt Univ Nashville TN 37203

CRIST, LARRY S, b Harrisburg, Pa, Jan 16, 34; m 61; c 3. FRENCH. *Educ:* Western Md Col, BA, 55; Princeton Univ, MA, 59, PhD(French), 63. *Prof Exp:* Lectr French, Queens Col, NY, 61-63; from asst prof to assoc prof, 63-75, PROF FRENCH, VANDERBILT UNIV, 75-, CHMN DEPT FRENCH & ITAL, 80- *Mem:* Am Asn Teachers Fr; Mediaeval Acad Am; MLA; AAUP; Soc Rencesvals. *Res:* Medieval French cycle of the Crusade; semiotics of medieval French literature. *Publ:* Coauth, Le Deuxieme Cycle de la Croisade: Deux Etudes sur son Developpement, 72 & ed, Saladin: Suite et fin du Deuxieme Cycle de la Croisade, 72, Droz, Geneva; auth, Le Jeu d'Adam et l'exegese de la chute, Melanges Labande, Poitiers, 74; Deep structures in the Chansons de geste: Hypotheses towards a taxonomy, Olifant, 10/75; coauth, Musica verbis concordet: Medieval French lyric poems with their music, Medievalia, fall 75; auth, Remarques sur la structure de la chanson de geste Charroi de Nimes-Prise d'Orange, Actes et Mem 7th Int Mtg Soc Rencesvals, 78; Roland, heros du/vouloir/, Melanges Wathelet-Willem, Liege, 78; coauth, L'Analyse fonctionnelle des fableaux, Etudes Jules Horrent, Liege, 80. *Mailing Add:* Dept of French Vanderbilt Univ Box 1598 Sta B Nashville TN 37235

CRO, STELIO, b Rome, Italy, Apr 7, 36; m 73. ITALIAN, SPANISH. *Educ:* Univ Buenos Aires, Lic en Let, 63; Univ Venice, DLing e Lett Straniere(Span), 66. *Prof Exp:* Assoc prof Ital, Univ Buenos Aires, 67-69; asst prof Ital & Span, Fla State Univ, 69-72; from asst prof to assoc prof, 72-78, HEAD DEPT, McMASTER UNIV, 76-, PROF ITAL, 78- *Mem:* MLA; Am Asn Teachers Span & Port; Am Asn Teachers Ital. *Res:* Italian 19th century literature; Spanish 19th and 20th century literature; Cervantes. *Publ:* Auth, Borges e Dante, Lett Ital, 68; Jorge Luis Borges, poeta, saggista e narratore, Mursia, 71; Una adivinanza medievalel Indovinello Veronese--en boca de los gauchos, Romance Notes, 72; Cervantes entre Don Quijote y Dulcinea, Hispanofila, 73; Cervantes, el Persiles y la historiografia indiana, Inst de Cult Hispanica, Anales Lit Hispanoam, Madrid, 75; ed, Sinapia A Classical Utopia of Spain, 75 & auth, A Forerunner of the Enlightenment in Spain, 76, McMaster Univ; La busqueda de la Ciudad Encantada de los Cesares y la utopia, In: Oelschläger Festschrift, Estud Hisp, 76. *Mailing Add:* Dept of Romance Lang McMaster Univ Hamilton ON L8S 4M2 Can

CROCKER, LESTER GILBERT, b New York, NY, Apr 23, 13. ROMANCE LANGUAGES. *Educ:* NY Univ, AB, 32, AM, 34; Sorbonne, cert, 33; Univ Calif, PhD, 36. *Hon Degrees:* LittD, Univ Southern Calif, 80. *Prof Exp:* Asst prof, Wittenberg Col, 37-39 & Queens Col, NY, 39-44; dir prod, Eastern Sound Studios, 44-48; assoc prof, Sweet Briar Col, 48-50; prof mod lang & chmn dept, Goucher Col, 50-60; W C Leutner distinguished prof Romance lang, Case Western Reserve Univ, 60-71, chmn dept, 60-63, dean grad sch, 63-67, dean humanities, 67-71; Kenan prof, 71-80, EMER PROF FRENCH, UNIV VA, 80- *Concurrent Pos:* Fulbright res scholar & Guggenheim fel, 54-55; mem, Inst Advan Studies, 58-59; Am Coun Learned Soc grants, 60, 67, 69 & 71-74; vis prof French lit, Univ London, 63 & Univ Paris, Sorbonne, 75-76; chmn regional selection comt younger scholars, Nat Endowment for Humanities, 67 & 68. *Honors & Awards:* Chevalier, Palmes Academiques, 64; Chevalier, Legion d'honneur, France, 69; Medaille de la Ville de Paris, 78. *Mem:* Benjamin Franklin fel Royal Soc Arts; hon mem Societe d'Histoire Litteraire; Soc Lit Hist, France; Am Soc 18th Century Studies (pres, 69-71); Int Soc 18th Century Studies (pres, 71-75). *Res:* Eighteenth century history of ideas; French and comparative literature. *Publ:* Auth, Two Diderot's Studies, Ethics and Esthetics, Johns Hopkins, 53; Diderot, The Embattled Philosopher, Mich State Univ, 54, Free Press, 66; An Age of Crisis, 59 & Nature and Culture, 63, Johns Hopkins; Jean-Jaques Rousseau: The Quest (1712-1758), Macmillan, 68; Rousseau's Social Contract, An Interpretive Essay, Case Western Reserve Univ, 68; ed, The Enlightment, Harper, 71; Diderot's Chaotic Order: Approach to Synthesis, Princeton Univ, 74; auth, Order and disorder in Rousseau's social thought, PMLA, 3/79. *Mailing Add:* Dept of French Univ of Va Charlottesville VA 22093

CROFT, KENNETH, b Ripley, Tex, June 19, 17; m 48; c 3. LINGUISTICS, ENGLISH AS A SECOND LANGUAGE. *Educ:* Univ Okla, BALS, 39, BA, 40; Univ Mich, MALS, 42; Ind Univ, MA, 49, PhD(ling, anthrop), 53. *Prof Exp:* Libr asst, Tex A&M Univ Col Libr, 39-41 & Univ Mich Gen Libr, 41-43; dir courses & teacher English, Mex-Am Cult Inst, 43-44, 46 & 50; teaching officer, US Info Agnecy, 50-53 & 55-56; asst prof, Lang Ctr, Am Univ, 53-54, assoc prof & dir res, 56-61; assoc prof & assoc dir Am Lang Inst, Georgetown Univ, 61-66; PROF ENGLISH & ANTHROP, SAN FRANCISCO STATE UNIV, 66- *Mem:* Nat Asn Foreign Studies Affairs (vpres, 65-66); Ling Soc Am; NCTE; Teachers of English to Speakers of Other Lang. *Res:* Applied linguistics, especially the use of linguistic data for teaching English as a foreign language; American Indian linguistics; linguistic anthropology. *Publ:* Auth, Matlapa Nahuatl, Int J Am Ling, 53-54; Reading and Word Study, Prentice-Hall, 60; Reader's Digest Readings: English as a Second Language, Reader's Digest (bks 5 & 6); coauth, Science Readings: For Students of English as a Second Language, McGraw-Hill, 66; ed, Readings on English as a Second Language: For Teachers and Teacher-Trainees, Winthrop, 72, 2nd ed, Little-Brown, 80. *Mailing Add:* Dept of English San Francisco State Univ San Francisco CA 94132

CROFT, LEE B, b Cut Bank, Mont, Sept 19, 46. SLAVIC LINGUISTICS, RUSSIAN LITERATURE. *Educ:* Ariz State Univ, BS, 68; Univ Ariz, MA, 70; Cornell Univ, PhD(Slavic ling), 73. *Prof Exp:* Asst prof, 73-78, ASSOC PROF RUSS, ARIZ STATE UNIV, 78- *Concurrent Pos:* Special instr Serbo-Croatian, Colgate Univ, 73; campus admis officer, Am Inst Foreign Study, 76- *Honors & Awards:* Dean's Quality of Teaching Award, Ariz State Univ, 78. *Mem:* Am Asn Teachers Slavic & East European Lang; Rocky Mountain Mod Lang Asn; Rocky Mt Asn Slavic Studies. *Res:* Slavic and general linguistics; Russian and Soviet literature; linguistics and poetics (translation). *Publ:* Auth, The method to madness: A poem of Igor Chinnov's, Slavic & E European J, 17:393-408; Russian-to-English homographs in Ozhogov's dictionary, Word Ways, 8: 204-206; The expression of modality in English and in Russian: A contrastive analysis, Russ Lang J, 29: 5-25; Russian Symbolist Poetry: Verse Translations from the Silver Age, Four Continent Bk, 76. *Mailing Add:* Dept of Foreign Lang Ariz State Univ Tempe AZ 85281

CRONE, ANNA LISA, b Brooklyn, NY, June 9, 46; c 1. RUSSIAN LITERATURE, LITERARY THEORY. *Educ:* Goucher Col, BA, 67; Harvard Univ, MA, 69, PhD(Slavic lang & lit), 75. *Prof Exp:* Instr, Goucher Col & Johns Hopkins Univ, 71-74; ASST PROF RUSS, UNIV CHICAGO, 77- *Concurrent Pos:* Fel, Radcliffe Inst Independent Study, 76-77. *Mem:* Am Asn Teachers Slavic & Eastern Europ Lang; MLA. *Res:* Late nineteenth and early twentieth-century Russian; literature and religious thought; Russian poetry and poetics. *Publ:* Auth, The disintegration of the mystical body: The church in Balzac and Rozanov, Die Welt der Slawen, 78; Unnamuno and Dostoevskij: Some thoughts on atheistic humanitarianism, Hispanofila, 78; Blok as Don Juan in Axmatora's Poema bez geoja & Gnosticism in Bely's Fotilc Letaer, 82, Russ Lang J; Axmatora's Imitation of Annenskij, Wiener Slawistiches Jahrbueh, 81; Difference in Saussure and Derrida, Neophilologus, 78; Pasternak's Pushkinien Variations, Die Weit der Slawen, 79; The Presence of Mandelstham in the Dedication to Poema bez geroja, Russ Lit, 82. *Mailing Add:* Dept of Slavic Lang Univ of Chicago 1130 E 59th St Chicago IL 60637

CRONMILLER, BRUCE, b South Hadley Falls, Mass, Apr 14, 23; m 53; c 6. FRENCH. *Educ:* Yale Univ, BA, 47, MA, 49, PhD, 53. *Prof Exp:* Instr French, Oberlin Col, 52; assoc prof, 53-61, PROF FRENCH, LAWRENCE UNIV, 61- *Mem:* Am Asn Teachers Fr. *Res:* Literature of French-speaking Africa. *Publ:* Auth, Fenelon, In: Critical Bibliography of French Literature, 17th Century Educ, Vol III, 61; Disturbed Ground, Women's Lit J, 78; On Leaving Notre-Dame de Paris, spring 76 & Surveying Centaurs, Unicorns, Two People and One Sphinx, 77, Tropos; The Patriarch Philander and Bladder Campion, Wis Acad Rev, Vol 27, No 2; Whistling to himself, 1940, 1976, Out of Wisconsin, Wis Fel Poets, 80. *Mailing Add:* 19 S Meadows Dr Appleton WI 54911

CROSBY, DONALD H, b New York, NY, Apr 3, 27; m 50, 73; c 4. GERMANIC STUDIES. *Educ:* NY Univ, AB, 51; Princeton Univ, AM, 53, PhD, 55. *Prof Exp:* Instr Ger, Princeton Univ, 54-55; asst prof, Union Col, NY, 55-56; from instr to asst prof, Ind Univ, Bloomington, 58-63; vis assoc prof Ger lang, Queens Col, NY, 64-65; from assoc prof to prof, Univ Kans, 65-70; PROF GER LANG, UNIV CONN, 70- *Concurrent Pos:* Consult, US Dept Defense, 56-61; Am Coun Learned Soc studies fel, 63-64; vis prof, Dartmouth Col, 70; Fulbright fel, Univ Munich, 78. *Mem:* Am Asn Teachers Ger; Heinrich von Kleist Ges. *Res:* Literature of the Goethezeit; Heinrich von Kleist; musical-literary relations. *Publ:* Coauth, Der Dichter spricht, Ginn, 62; auth, Heinrich von Kleist: Der Zweikampf and Das Bettelweib von Vocarno, Ginn, 68; Psychological realism in the works of Kleist, Lit & Pyschol, 69; Kleist's Prinz von Homburg: An intensified Egmont?, Ger Life & Lett, 70; co-ed, Studies in the German Drama: A Festschrift for Walter Silz, Univ NC, 73. *Mailing Add:* Dept of Ger Lang Univ of Conn Storrs CT 06268

CROSBY, JAMES O'HEA, b New York, NY, Dec 5, 24. SPANISH LITERATURE. *Educ:* Yale Univ, PhD(Romance lang), 54. *Prof Exp:* Instr Span, Yale Univ, 54-55; from instr to prof, Univ Ill, Urbana, 55-68; prof Dartmouth Col, 68-72; PROF SPAN, FLA INT UNIV, 72- *Concurrent Pos:* Guggenheim fel, 62-63; assoc mem, Ctr Advan Studies, Univ Ill, 66-67; Nat Endowment for Humanities fel, 78-69. *Mem:* Hisp Soc Am; Acad Lit Scholars. *Res:* Spanish literature of the Renaissance and Baroque; dramatic and synaesthesic readings. *Publ:* Auth, Text Tradition of the Memorial Catolica, Sacra, Real Magestad, Univ Kans, 58; A new Sueno wrongly attributed to Quevedo?, Hisp Rev, 62; Quevedo, the Greek anthology and Horace, Romance Philol, 2/66; Politica de Dios, 66 & En torno a la poesia de Quevedo, 67, Ed Castalia; Has Quevedo's poetry been edited?, Hisp Rev, 73; Guia bibliografica para el estudio critico de Quevedo, Res Bibliog, 76; Poesia varia de Quevedo, Ed Catedra, 81. *Mailing Add:* Dept of Mod Lang Fla Int Univ Miami FL 33199

CROSMAN, INGE KARALUS, b Hamm, WGer, Jan 17, 40; US citizen; m 67; c 1. FRENCH LITERATURE. *Educ:* Rutgers Univ, New Brunswick, AB, 62; Columbia Univ, MA, 65, PhD(French), 71. *Hon Degrees:* AM, Brown Univ, 77. *Prof Exp:* Lectr French, Brooklyn Col, 64-65; asst prof, Williams Col, 69-72; asst prof, 73-77, ASSOC PROF FRENCH, BROWN UNIV, 77- *Concurrent Pos:* Humboldt res fel, 79-80. *Mem:* MLA; Northeast Mod Lang Asn; Proust Res Asn; Am Asn Teachers Fr; Semiotics Soc Am. *Res:* Proust; approaches to the novel, theories of reading, narrative. *Publ:* Auth, Metaphoric function in A la recherche du temps perdu, 11/76 & The status of metaphoric discourse, 5/77, Romanic Rev; Metaphoric Narration: The structure and function of metaphorics, In: A la recherche du temps perdu, Univ NC, 78; Metaphor and narrative technique, PTL, 78; The reader in the text: Essays on audience and interpretation, Princeton, 80; Poetique de la lecture romanesque, L'Esprit Createur 21, No 2, summer 81. *Mailing Add:* Dept of French Studies Brown Univ Box E Providence RI 02912

CROSS, FRANK MOORE, JR, b Ross, Calif, July 13, 21; m 47; c 3. BIBLICAL & SEMITIC LANGUAGES & LITERATURE. *Educ:* Maryville Col, AB, 42; McCormick Theol Sem, BD, 46; Johns Hopkins Univ, PhD, 50. *Hon Degrees:* MA, Harvard Univ, 57; DLitt, Maryville Col, 68. *Prof Exp:* Jr instr, Johns Hopkins Univ, 49-50; instr Bibl hist, Wellesley Col, 50-51; from instr to assoc prof, McCormick Theol Sem, 51-57; assoc prof Old Testament, Harvard Divinity Sch, 57-58, cur, Semitic Mus, 58-61, chmn dept Near Eastern langs, 59-65, HANCOCK PROF HEBREW & ORIENT LANGS, HARVARD UNIV, 59- *Concurrent Pos:* Co-ed, Bibl Archaeologist, 52-59; annual prof, Am Sch Orient Res, Jerusalem, 53-54; mem int staff for editing Dead Sea Scrolls, 53-; co-dir archaeol exped, Judaean Buqei'ah, 55; Haskell lectr, Grad Sch Theol, Oberlin Col, 57; vis scholar, Univ Ctr, Ga & Richmond Univ Ctr, Va, 57; assoc ed, Harvard Theol Rev, 63-74; archaeol dir, Hebrew Union Col Archaeol Sch, Jerusalem, 63-64; assoc ed, Bull Am Schs Orient Res, 70-; Am Coun Learned Soc fel, 71-72; dir, Harvard Semitic Mus, 74-; pres, Am Schs Orient Res, 74-76; prin investr, ASOR-Harvard Expedition to Carthage, 75-; dir, Harvard Semitic Mus, 75-; fel, Inst Advan Studies, Hebrew Univ, Jerusalem, 78-79. *Honors & Awards:* Schimmel prize, Israel Mus, 80; Albright Award, Soc Bibl Lit, 80. *Mem:* Am Orient Soc; Soc Bibl Lit (pres, 73-74); Bibl Colloquium (pres, 66-68); Am Acad Arts & Sci; Am Philos Soc. *Res:* Early Hebrew literature; Northwest Semitic epigraphy; history of religion of Israel. *Publ:* Auth, Early Hebrew Orthography, 52; Ancient Library of Qumran, 2nd ed, Doubleday, 61; The development of the Jewish scripts, In: The Bible and the Ancient Near East, Doubleday, 61; The origin and early evolution of Alphabet, Eretz Israel, 67; Canaanite Myth and Hebrew Epic, 73 & co-ed, Qumran and the History of the Biblical Text, 75, Harvard Univ; coauth, Studies in Ancient Yahwistic Poetry, Scholars, 75; co-ed, Magnalia Dei, Doubleday, 76. *Mailing Add:* Dept of Near Eastern Lang Harvard Univ Cambridge MA 02138

CROSS, ROBERT BRANDT, b Stockton, Calif, Dec 9, 14. CLASSICAL LANGUAGE. *Educ:* Univ Calif, Los Angeles, AB, 37; Univ Calif, AM, 39; Univ Southern Calif, PhD(classics), 48. *Prof Exp:* Asst prof class lang, Univ Southern Calif, 48; prof, EMER PROF FOREIGN LANG, UNIV ARK, 80- *Mem:* Class Asn Mid W & S. *Res:* Ancient Egyptian philology; Greek lyric poetry; Latin inscriptions. *Publ:* Transl, Secrets of Voodoo (Milo Rigaud, La tradition vaudou et le vaudou Haitien), Arco, 71. *Mailing Add:* Dept of Foreign Lang Univ of Ark Fayetteville AR 72701

CROSSGROVE, WILLIAM CHARLES, b Archbold, Ohio, June 6, 38; m 65; c 2. GERMAN, MEDIEVAL STUDIES. *Educ:* Ohio Univ, AB, 59; Univ Tex, PhD(Ger ling), 62. *Prof Exp:* From instr to asst prof, 62-69, chmn dept, 73-76, assoc prof, 69-80, PROF GER, BROWN UNIV, 80- *Concurrent Pos:* Res assoc ling, Univ Kiel, 65-66; vis prof, Columbia Univ, 70; Alexander von Humboldt-Stiftung res fel, 70-71 & 80. *Mem:* Ling Soc Am; MLA; Am Asn Teachers Ger; Soc Ling Europaea; Mediaeval Acad Am. *Res:* Comparative Germanic grammar; Middle High German literature; medieval technical literature. *Publ:* Auth, Numerical composition in Gottfried's Tristan: The Petitcreiu episode, Mod Lang Quart, 69; The forms of medieval technical literature: Some suggestions for further work, Jahrbuch Int Germanistik, 72; The use of computers in the study of medieval German: Two suggestions, In: Linguistic and Literary Studies in Honor of A A Hill, Peter de Ridder, Vol I, 76; German language teaching in the United States, In: German Studies in the United States: Assessment and Outlook, Univ Wis, 76; co-ed, Graded German Reader Erste Stufe, Heath, 78; auth, Zur Erforschung des älteren deutschen Macer, Sudhoffs Archiv, 79; The alleged source of the German Macer: A misapplied rule, Res Publica Litterarum, 80; Textual criticism in a fourteenth century scientific manuscript, Scripta, 82. *Mailing Add:* Dept of Ger Brown Univ Providence RI 02912

CROW, JOHN ARMSTRONG, b Wilmington, NC, Dec 18, 06; m 56; c 2. FOREIGN LANGUAGE, HISTORY. *Educ:* Univ NC, AB, 27; Columbia Univ, MA, 30; Univ Madrid, DFilos y Let, 33. *Prof Exp:* Instr Span, Univ NC, 27-38; asst prof, Davidson Col, 28-29; instr, NY Univ, 29-37; from instr to assoc prof, 37-50, PROF SPAN, UNIV CALIF, LOS ANGELES, 50- *Concurrent Pos:* Co-ed, Rev Iberoam, 38-45; ed consult & collabr, Encycl Britannica, Americana, World Book, Collier's & Britannica World Lang Dict, 40-; co-ed, Handbook Latin Am Studies, Libr Congr, 51-52. *Mem:* MLA; Am Asn Teachers Span & Port (vpres, 52-53); Inst Int Lit Iberoam (secy, 38-45). *Res:* Hispanic history of culture; Spanish American literature. *Publ:* Auth, Federico Garcia Lorca, Univ Calif, 46; Spanish American Life, Holt, Rinehart & Winston, 63; Italy: A Journey Through Time, 65 & Greece: The Magic Spring, 67, Harper & Row; Mexico Today, 72 & Spain: The Root and the Flower, 75, Harper & Row; The Epic of Latin America, Univ Calif Press, 81. *Mailing Add:* Dept of Span Univ of Calif Los Angeles CA 90024

CROWDER, ROBERT DOUGLAS, b Nashville, Tenn, June 21, 34. FRENCH. *Educ:* Vanderbilt Univ, BA, 56, MA, 60, PhD(French), 67. *Prof Exp:* Instr French, Vanderbilt Univ, 61-64, dir, Vanderbilt-in-France, Aix-en-Provence, 64-65; from instr to asst prof, 65-72, ASSOC PROF FRENCH, NTEX STATE UNIV, 72-, CHMN, DEPT FOREIGN LANG & LIT, 79- *Concurrent Pos:* Fulbright lectr grant, 58-59. *Mem:* Am Asn Teachers Fr;

MLA. *Publ:* Auth, Jacques Copeau in New York, Studies SCent Mod Lang Asn, winter 69; The Brown, Ervin and McEwen families of Fort Nashborough and Franklin, Williamson County Hist J, 72-73. *Mailing Add:* Dept of Foreign Lang NTex State Univ Denton TX 76203

CROWLEY, CORNELIUS J, b New York, NY, Mar 21, 11; m 48; c 2. LINGUISTICS. *Educ:* City Univ of New York, AB, 38; New York Univ, AM, 41, PhD, 51. *Prof Exp:* Teache English to foreigners, NYC Adult Educ, 38-42; teacher English, Span & Latin, Kohut Sch, Harrison, NY, 42-43; instr Span, Bergen Col, 46-48; asst prof Span & Ger, Univ Wyo, 48-50; assoc prof mod lang, 50-62, prof, 62-75, EMER PROF MOD LANG & LING, ST LOUIS UNIV, 75- *Concurrent Pos:* Sr transl, Off US Naval Censorship, 43-46. *Honors & Awards:* Cert of Merit, US Govt, 45. *Mem:* MLA; Ling Soc Am; Am Asn Teachers Span & Port; Renaissance Soc Am; Am Orient Soc. *Res:* Hispanic and Indo-European linguistics. *Publ:* Auth, On Spanish words of Germanic origin, Hispania, 55; Some remarks on the etymology of the Southwestern words for cat, Int J Am Ling, 62; Old Spanish monculra and odice pcon, In: Studies in Honor of J Alexander Kerns, Mouton, The Hague, 70; The Wanderings of the Spear of Longinus: A Medieval Irish Folk-Tale, 72 & Homage to Dr J Alexander Kerns: A Choice of Propertius, 76, Heartland. *Mailing Add:* 1515 N Sprigg Cape Girardeau MO 63701

CROWLEY, FRANCES G, b Merano, Italy, Mar 22, 21; US citizen; m 48; c 1. MODERN LANGUAGE. *Educ:* Hunter Col, AB, 42; Columbia Univ, AM, 45; Wash Univ, PhD, 62. *Prof Exp:* Lectr mod lang, Univ Mo, St Louis, 60-61, instr, 61-62, asst prof Span, 62-66; assoc prof, Lindenwood Col, 66-68; assoc prof Span, 68-80, PROF FOREIGN LANG & EDUC, SOUTHEAST MO STATE UNIV, 80- *Concurrent Pos:* Lectr, Adult Educ Ctr, St Louis Univ, 50 & Univ, 51-54; spec serv, St Louis Pub Schs, 54-59; consult, NDEA Title IV, 71-72; mem, Nat Fed Mod Lang Teachers Asn. *Mem:* Renaissance Soc Am; MLA; AHA. *Res:* Latin American historian; comparative literature; Renaissance Spanish and Italian literature. *Publ:* Auth, Garcilaso de la Vega, El Inca, Mouton; Sarmiento, Twayne. *Mailing Add:* 515 N Sprigg Cape Cape Girardeau MO 63701

CROWLEY, RUTH, b Minn, Sept 21, 43. GERMAN, COMPARATIVE LITERATURE. *Educ:* Pomona Col, BA, 65; Stanford Univ, MA, 68, PhD(Ger), 75. *Prof Exp:* Instr Ger, Queens Col, NY, 71-73, asst prof comp lit, 75-77; ASST PROF GER, UNIV CALIF, IRVINE, 77- *Concurrent Pos:* Jr fac res fel, City Univ New York, 75-76; jr fac grants, Regents/Univ Calif, 78. *Mem:* MLA. *Res:* Franco-German cultural relations circa 1800; 18th century German aesthetics; theory of literature. *Publ:* Co-translr, The Cognition of the Roman Ingarden, Literary Work of Art, Northwestern Univ, 74; auth, Charles de Villers, Mediator and Comparatist, Lang, 78. *Mailing Add:* Dept of Ger Univ of Calif Irvine CA 92717

CROWNE, DAVID K, b Springfield, Mass, June 22, 29; m 50; c 1. COMPARATIVE LITERATURE, ENGLISH. *Educ:* Univ Calif, Berkeley, AB, 53, MA, 57; Harvard Univ, PhD(comp lit), 63. *Prof Exp:* Instr English, Amherst Col, 61-64; asst prof English & comp lit, 64-70, ASSOC PROF ENGLISH & COMP LIT, UNIV CALIF, SAN DIEGO, 70- *Concurrent Pos:* Alexander von Humboldt-Stiftung study fel, Munich, WGer, 63-64; John Simon Guggenheim Mem Found fel, 70-71. *Res:* Old English poetry; medieval literature: English, Latin, French, German and Welsh; Greek and Roman literature. *Publ:* Auth, The hero on the beach: An example of composition by theme in OE narrative poetry, Neuphilologische Mitt, 61; A date for the composition of Henryson's Fables, J English & Ger Philol, 62. *Mailing Add:* Dept of Lit Univ of Calif San Diego La Jolla CA 92093

CRUM, RICHARD HENRY, Ancient History, Classical Literature. See Vol I

CRUMP, JAMES IRVING, JR, b Newark, NJ, Mar 8, 21; m 42; c 2. CHINESE LANGUAGE & LITERATURE. *Educ:* Columbia Univ, AB, 45; Yale Univ, PhD, 50. *Prof Exp:* Asst, Yale Univ, 46; from instr to assoc prof Chinese, 50-72 PROF CHINESE, UNIV MICH, ANN ARBOR, 72- *Concurrent Pos:* Guggenheim fel, 54; Fulbright fel, 74; Ger Acad Exchange Serv scholar, 81. *Mem:* Asn Asian Studies; Am Orient Soc. *Res:* General sinology; Chinese vernacular literature; Yüan drama. *Publ:* Coauth, Dragon Bones in the Yellow Earth, Dodd, 63; auth, Intrigues: Studies of Chan-Kuo Ts'e, Univ Mich, 64; Chan-Kuo Ts'e, 70 & coauth, Ballad of the Hidden Dragon, 71, Oxford Univ; Chinese Theater in the Days of Kublaic Khan, Arizona, 80. *Mailing Add:* Dept of Far Eastern Lang & Lit Univ of Mich Ann Arbor MI 48104

CRUMPACKER, MARY M, Romance Languages. See Vol IV

CRUZ-SAENZ, MICHELE S DE, b Mt Vernon, NY, Jan 5, 49; m 71; c 2. ROMANCE LANGUAGES, MEDIEVAL STUDIES. *Educ:* Conn Col, AB, 71; Univ Pa, MA, 74, PhD(medieval studies & Romance lang), 76. *Prof Exp:* Lectr Span, Swarthmore Col, 74-76; asst prof foreign lang, Beaver Col, 76-78; adj asst, 78-80, ASST PROF ROMANCE LANG & LIT, GEORGE WASHINGTON UNIV, 80- *Concurrent Pos:* Lectr French & Span, Univ Pa, 74-76; instr Span, Haverford Col, 75-76; Am Philos Soc grant, 79. *Mem:* Am Asn Teachers Span & Port; MLA; Mediaeval Acad Am; Int Arthurian Soc; Northeast Mod Lang Asn. *Publ:* Translr, Accatone, a review by Marc Gervais, Vol I, 77 & The scenario as a sturcture designed to become another structure by Pier Paglo Pasolini, Vol 2, 77, Wide Angle; auth, Two additional instances of Old Walloon Feir, Romance Philol, 11/77; El Romancero de Costa Rica: A report on work in progress, Actas, Second Int Symposium on the Hisp Ballad, Gredos, Madrid, 78; The Life of St Mary of Egypt: An Edition and Study of the Medieval French and Spanish Verse Redactions, Ed Hispam, Barcelona, 79; The Marques de Santillana's Coplas on don Alvaro de Luna and the Doctrinal de Privados, Hisp Rev, Vol 49, 81; El Romancero tradicional de Costa Rica, Madrid, 82. *Mailing Add:* Dept of Romance Lang & Lit George Washington Univ Washington DC 20052

CULLER, JONATHAN DWIGHT, Literary Theory, Comparative Literature. See Vol II

CULLEY, GERALD RAY, b Detroit, Mich, May 25, 34; m 60; c 3. CLASSICAL PHILOLOGY. *Educ:* Univ Ky, BA, 63; Univ NC, Chapel Hill, PhD(classics), 73. *Prof Exp:* Instr, 70-73, asst prof, 73-79, ASSOC PROF CLASSICS, UNIV DEL, 79- *Mem:* Am Philol Asn. *Res:* Greek epigraphy; ancient Greek topography; computer-assisted instruction. *Publ:* Auth, The Restoration of Shrines in Attica: IG 2/3 2 1035, Hesperia, Vol XLIV & XLVI, 74 & 77; coauth, Aeschylus, Voltaire, and Le Franc De Pompignan's Promethee: A critical edition, Studies Voltaire & 18th Century, 76; auth, Computer-assisted instruction and Latin: Beyond flashcards, Class World, 78-79; A computer supplement to individualize the Latin course, Proc 1st Nat Conf Individualized Instr For Lang, 79; When Plato knows Latin: Benefits of letting the computer inflect the forms, Proc Asn for Develop Computer-Based Instruct Systs, 80. *Mailing Add:* Dept of Lang & Lit Univ of Del Newark DE 19711

CUMMINS, PATRICIA WILLETT, b Worcester, Mass, Oct 16, 48; m 75; c 1. FRENCH. *Educ:* Smith Col, BA, 70; Univ Rochester, MA, 71; Univ NC, Chapel Hill, PhD(French), 74. *Prof Exp:* From instr to asst prof, Lafayette Col, 73-74; asst prof, 74-79, actg dean, Grad Sch, 81-82, ASSOC PROF FRENCH, WVA UNIV, 79- *Concurrent Pos:* Fac fel, Nat Endowment for Humanities, 76-77; fac res grants, Lafayette Col & WVA Univ, 73-77 & 79-81; Quebec Govt grant, 79. *Honors & Awards:* Holmes Prize, 74; Gilbert Chinard Prize, 81. *Mem:* MLA; Mediaeval Acad Am; Southeastern Medieval Asn (vpres, 81-82); Int Courtly Lit Soc. *Res:* Medieval French literature; foreign languages and careers; teaching advanced French language. *Publ:* Auth, The pseudo-arnaldian Regimen sanitatis salernitanum: A common sense medical guide, Philol Papers, 75; The first French translation of Regimen sanitatis salernitanum, salernitan regimen of health, Romance Philol, 76; A translation of Regimen sanitatis salernitanum, Allegorica, 76; ed, A Critical Edition of Le Regime Tresutile et Tresproufitable Pour Conserver et Grader la Sante du Corps Humain, Univ NC, 76; Commercial French, Prentice-Hall, 82. *Mailing Add:* Dept Foreign Lang WVa Univ Morgantown WV 26506

CUNLIFFE, WILLIAM GORDON, b Southport, England, Mar 25, 29; m 57; c 2. GERMAN. *Educ:* Univ London, BA, 53; Univ Hamburg, PhD(Ger), 63. *Prof Exp:* Lektor transl & interpretation, Univ Saarlandes, 55-60; lectr Ger, Univ Bradford, 60-62; asst prof, 62-68, ASSOC PROF GER, UNIV WIS-MADISON, 68- *Mem:* MLA. *Res:* Medieval and modern German literature; modern English and American literature. *Publ:* Coauth, Insight I, 62 & Insight II, 64, Hirschgraben, Frankfurt; Advanced German Conversation, Oliver & Boyd, Edinburgh, 67; auth, Günter Grass, Twayne, 68. *Mailing Add:* Dept of Ger Univ of Wis Madison WI 53706

CUNNINGHAM, WILLIAM LEONARD, b Cleveland, Ohio, July 15, 39; m 63; c 2. GERMAN. *Educ:* Oberlin Col, BA, 61; Univ Ill, Urbana-Champaign, MA, 64; Univ Tex, Austin, PhD(Ger), 69. *Prof Exp:* Teaching asst Ger, Univ Ill, 61-64; asst prof, Univ Southern Calif, 68-73; ASSOC PROF GER, UNIV LOUISVILLE, 73- *Mem:* MLA; Am Asn Teachers Ger. *Res:* German Baroque lyrics; German literature in English translation; 19th century German literature. *Publ:* Auth, Baroque literature and American students: Oil and water?, Unterrichtspraxis, 73; Martin Opitz' Poems of Consolation in Adversities of War, Bouvier, Bonn, 74; Johann Christian Günther's Trostaria, Monatshefte, 76; Zur Wassersymbolik in Aquis submersus, Schriften Theodor-Storm-Gesellschaft, 78; Zur wassersymbolik in storms novellen, Germanic Notes, 82. *Mailing Add:* 711 Marengo Dr Louisville KY 40243

CURCIO, LOUIS LEROY, b Walla Walla, Wash, May 1, 11; m 49; c 2. FRENCH, SPANISH. *Educ:* Whitman Col, BA, 32, MA, 33; Columbia Univ, PhD(French), 50. *Prof Exp:* Training specialist, US Off Censorship, 42-44; asst prof French & Span, Eastern NMex Col, 44-45, Carleton Col, 45-46 & Upper NY Col, 46-47; prof, Univ St Thomas, 47-49; dir bi-nat ctrs, US Info Agency, Argentina, 49-52 & Costa Rica, 52-54; prof mod lang, French & Span, Bradley Univ, 54-62; prof French & chmn dept foreign lang, Hollins Col, 60-62; prof French, 62-77, chmn dept foreign lang, 63-77, dir, Cuban Inst, 63-64, EMER PROF FRENCH, IND STATE UNIV, TERRE HAUTE, 77- *Concurrent Pos:* Assoc fac French, Ind Univ & Purdue Univ, Indianapolis, 77-78. *Mem:* MLA; Am Asn Teachers Fr; Dramatists Guild. *Res:* Profile of the French Revolution in the Republican papers. *Publ:* Transl, Gorostiza's The Bridge, Samuel French, 59; auth, Ponce de Leon & De Soto, In: Cultural Graded Readers, 61, Coronado, 66 & Los Caballeros de la Cruz, 66, Am Bk Co; transl, Gorostiza's Neighbors, First Stage, Purdue Univ, 68; coauth, Nouveau Visage du monde francais, Rand McNally, 73, 2nd ed, Houghton-Mifflin, 81. *Mailing Add:* PO Box 992 Brackettville TX 78832

CURRAN, LEO CHRISTOPHER, b Bridgeport, Conn, June 26, 34. CLASSICAL LITERATURE. *Educ:* Yale Col, BA, 56, PhD(classics), 61; Oxford Univ, BA, 58, MA, 63. *Prof Exp:* From instr to asst prof classics, Yale Univ, 58-67; actg chmn dept, 69, chmn, 69-72, ASSOC PROF CLASSICS, STATE UNIV NY BUFFALO, 67- *Concurrent Pos:* Julian Biddle Prize fel, Balliol Col, Oxford Univ, 56; Morse fel from Yale Univ, 66-67. *Mem:* Am Philol Asn. *Res:* Literary criticism; Latin poetry of the Republic and the Empire; Propertius. *Publ:* Auth, Ovid, Amores 1 10, Phoenix, 64; Vision and reality in Propertius 1 3, 66 & Catullus 64 and the heoric age, 69, Yale Class Studies; Satire as poetry: nature, convention, and obscenity in Horace, Satires 1 2, Arion, 70; Transformation and anti-Augustanism in Ovid's Metamorphoses, Arethusa, 72; Nature to Advantage Dressed: Propertius 1 2 Ramus, 75; Rape and rape victims in the Metamorphoses, Arethusa, 78. *Mailing Add:* Dept of Classics State Univ of NY Buffalo NY 14260

CURRAN, MARK JOSEPH, b Abilene, Kans, Aug 30, 41; m 69. SPANISH, PORTUGUESE. *Educ:* Rockhurst Col, BSBA, 63; St Louis Univ, PhD(Span & Latin Am studies), 68. *Prof Exp:* Asst prof, 68-73, ASSOC PROF SPAN & PORT, ARIZ STATE UNIV, 73- *Mem:* Am Asn Teachers Span & Port; Pac Coast Coun Latin Am Studies; Am Folklore Soc. *Res:* Folklore and popular culture of Brazil; Latin American civilization; northeastern literature of Brazil. *Publ:* Auth, Introduction and Selected Bibliography of History and Politics in Brazilian Popular Poetry, Ctr Latin Am Studies, Ariz State Univ, 71; A Pagina Editorial do poeta popular, Rev Brasileira de Folclore, 4/72; A literatura de Cordel, Univ Pernambuco, 73; contribr, A satira e a critica social na literatura de Cordel, In: Literatura popular em verso: Estudos I, Fundacao Casa de Rui Barbosa, 73; Twentieth century Brazilian literature: Influence of the poetry of the masses, In: Memorias: UCLA semana de arte moderna symposium, Univ Calif, Los Angeles, 75; auth, A cultura popular e Grande Sertao: Veredas, In: Portuguese and Brazilian Oral Traditions, Univ Southern Calif, 76; Rodolfo Coelho Cavalcante: Brazilian popular poet and propagandist of the Literatura de Cordel, 76, Proc Pac Coast Coun Latin Am Studies. *Mailing Add:* Dept of Foreign Lang Ariz State Univ Tempe AZ 85281

CURRIE, EVA GARCIA-CARRILLO, b Coahuila, Mex, Aug 28, 12; nat US; m 35; c 1. SPEECH, SOCIOLINGUISTICS. *Educ:* Univ Tex, AB, 33, AM, 44. *Prof Exp:* Instr Romance lang, Univ Tex, Austin, 46-47; instr speech, 47-49, spec instr & acad supvr, Speech Commun Lab, 50-72, dir, 72-80, asst prof speech commun, 72-81; RES ASSOC SOCIOLINGUISTICS, SPAN & ENGLISH, REGIONAL RES ASSOCS, 72- *Concurrent Pos:* Consult regionalism. *Mem:* Int Sociol Asn; Int Soc Ling Sci; Am Dialogue Soc. *Res:* Multilingual communication; sociolinguistics; phonetics and phonology. *Publ:* Auth, Linguistic and social consideration of some populations of Texas, Southern Speech J, 50; Proposal for programs in speech communication using the medium of Spanish, 72 & coauth, Sociolinguistics and two American linguistics orthodoxies, 73 & 75, auth, Regional Res Assocs; An area providing a severe test of linguistic hypotheses and the application of linguistic facts, Sociolinguistic Newsletter, summer 77. *Mailing Add:* Dept of Speech Commun Univ of Tex Austin TX 78712

CURRIE, HAVER CECIL, Philosophy, Sociolinguistics. See Vol IV

CURSCHMANN, MICHAEL JOHANN HENDRIK, b Cologne, Ger, Jan 11, 36; m 61; c 2. GERMANIC LANGUAGES. *Educ:* Univ Munich, PhD(Ger), 62. *Prof Exp:* Res asst Ger, Univ Munich, 60-63; from asst prof to assoc prof, 63-68; PROF GER, PRINCETON UNIV, 68- *Concurrent Pos:* John Simon Guggenheim Mem Found fel, 71-72. *Mem:* MLA; Mediaeval Acad Am. *Res:* Twelfth and 13th century German literature; 15th and 16th century German literature; comparative literature of the Middle Ages. *Publ:* Auth, Der Münchener Oswald und die deutsche spielmännische Epik, C H Beck, Munich, 64; Oral poetry in Mediaeval English, French and German literature, Speculum, 1/67; Spielmannsepik: Wege und Ergebnisse der Forschung, J B Metzler, Stuttgart, 68; ed, Texte und Melodien zur Wirkungsgeschichte eines Spaetmittelaeterlichen Liedes, Francke, Bern, 70; auth, Das Abenteuer des Erzaehlens, Deut Vierteljahrsschrift für Literaturwiss, 71; ed, Der Muenchner Oswald, Niemeyer, Tübingen, 74; co-ed, Herrod of Hohenbourg: Hortus deliciarum, 2 vols, E J Brill, Leiden, 79; auth, Texte-Bilder-Stoukturen: Der Hortus deliciarum und die frühmittelhochdeutsche Geistlichendichtung Deutsche Vierteljahrsschrift für Lieraturwisenschaft, 81. *Mailing Add:* Dept of Ger Princeton Univ 230 E Pyne Princeton NJ 08540

CURTIS, ALEXANDER ROSS, b Tredegar, UK, Aug 6, 31; m 64. ROMANCE LANGUAGES. *Educ:* Univ Wales, BA, 53, MA, 57; Univ Paris, DUniv(French), 66. *Prof Exp:* From instr to asst prof, 57-70, acad secy, 66-70, assoc chmn dept, 70-71, ASSOC PROF FRENCH, UNIV TORONTO, 70- *Mem:* Asn Can Univ Teachers Fr; Can Asn Appl Ling. *Res:* Seventeenth century French theatre; comparative stylistics. *Publ:* Auth, A note on Paul Poisson's wife, Romance Notes, 67; The theatre of an actor-playwright, Australian J French Studies, 67; A propos d'une gravure de 1664, 67 & Raymond Poisson, etait-il pauvre?, 69, Rev d'Hist Theatre; Crispin 1er Le Vie et l'oeuvre de Raymond Poisson, Univ Toronto & Ed Klincksieck, Paris, 72; A pastiche by Houdart de la Motte, Papers French 17th Century Lit, 77; Jean Simonin's Comic World, No 14, 81 & Jean Simonin of the Marais Theatre, No 15, 81, Papers on French 17th Century Lit. *Mailing Add:* Dept of French Univ Col Univ of Toronto Toronto ON M5S 1A1 Can

CURTIS, JAMES MALCOLM, b Florence, Ala, Apr 16, 40; m 62; c 1. RUSSIAN LITERATURE. *Educ:* Vanderbilt Univ, BA, 62; Columbia Univ, MA, 64, PhD(Russ), 68. *Prof Exp:* Actg asst prof Russ, Univ Calif, Berkeley, 66-68; asst prof, 68-72, assoc prof, 72-78, PROF RUSS, UNIV MO-COLUMBIA, 79- *Concurrent Pos:* Am Coun Learned Soc fel, 76-77. *Mem:* Am Asn Teachers Slavic & E Europ Lang; Am Asn Advan Slavic Studies. *Res:* Tolstoy; Dostoevsky; critical theory. *Publ:* Auth, Spatial form in drama: The Seagull, Can-Am Slavic Studies, spring 72; Spatial form as the intrinsic genre of Dostoevsky's novels, Mod Fiction Studies, summer 72; Marshall McLuhan and French structuralism, Boundary 2, fall 72; Bergson and Russian formalism, Comp Lit, spring 76; Solzhenitsyn and Dostoevsky, Mod Fiction Studies, spring 77; Culture as Polyphony, Univ Mo, 78; Marshall McLuhan: The esthete as historian, J Commun, 81. *Mailing Add:* Dept of Ger & Slavic Studies Univ of Mo Columbia MO 65201

CURTIS, JUDITH ANN, b Ottawa, Ont, Apr 12, 42; m 64. FRENCH LANGUAGE & LITERATURE. *Educ:* Univ Toronto, BA, 64, MA, 65, PhilM(French), 67. *Prof Exp:* From lectr to asst prof, 67-75, ASSOC PROF FRENCH, UNIV COL & SCARBOROUGH COL, UNIV TORONTO, 75- *Mem:* Soc Can Etude XVIII Siecle; Am Soc 18th Century Studies. *Res:* Letters of Mme de Graffigny; Seventeenth-18th century French theatre; 18th century French literature. *Publ:* Ed, D'Allainval, L'Ecole des bourgeois, Droz, Geneva, 76; auth, Voltaire, d'Allainval and Le temple du gout, Romance Notes, Vol 15, No 3; A forgotten eighteenth-century dramatist..., Australian J Fr Studies, Vol 14, Part 5. *Mailing Add:* Div of Humanities Scarborough Col West Hill ON M1C 1A4 Can

CUSHING, ANNE HYDE GREET, b New York, NY; m 65; c 2. FRENCH. *Educ:* Bryn Mawr Col, BA, 50; Columbia Univ, MA, 54; Univ Colo, PhD(French), 61. *Prof Exp:* Teacher, Chapin Sch, 52-54; instr French, Univ Colo, 55-58; from asst prof to assoc prof, 58-71, PROF FRENCH, UNIV CALIF, SANTA BARBARA, 71- *Concurrent Pos:* Univ Calif res grant, 61- & Humanities Inst res grant, 71; Guggenheim fel, 72-73; Univ Calif Regents Innovative Teaching grant, 73-74; Univ Calif Instrnl Proj grant, 78; Nat

Endowment for Humanities dir, Apollinaire Centenary Colloquium, 80. *Mem:* MLA; Am Asn Teachers Fr; Am Comp Lit Asn; Int Comp Lit Asn. *Res:* Apollinaire; the illustrated book; the French Art song. *Publ:* Auth, Guillaume Apollinaire's Alcools, Univ Calif & Cambridge Univ, 65; Jacques Prevert's Word Games, Univ Calif, 68; Paul Eluard's Early Poems for Painters, Forum Mod Lang Studies, 1/73; Apollinaire et le livre de peintre, Minard, Paris, 78; Paul Elvard, La Critical Biography of French Literature, 20th Century, 79; Guillaume Apollinaire Calligrammes, Univ Calif, 80; Edovard Manet and his poets: The origins of the Livre de peintre, Symposium, winter 80/81; Iliazd and Max Ernst: Sixty-five Maximiliana or the Illegal practice of astronomy, World Lit Today, winter 82. *Mailing Add:* Dept of French & Ital Univ of Calif Santa Barbara CA 93106

CUTTER, CHARLES RICHARD, III, b Woodward, Okla, Feb 8, 24; m 42; c 2. CLASSICS. *Educ:* Baylor Univ, BA, 53; Southwestern Baptist Theol Sem, ThD, 59, PhD, 79. *Prof Exp:* From assoc prof to prof classics, 58-62, REV JACOB BEVERLEY STITELER PROF GREEK, BAYLOR UNIV, 62- *Mem:* Am Philol Asn; Soc Bibl Lit. *Res:* New Testament Greek. *Publ:* Auth, A Beginning Grammar of Classical and Hellenistic Greek, Baylor Univ, 73. *Mailing Add:* Box 184 Baylor Univ Waco TX 76703

CUTTER, WILLIAM, b St Louis, Mo, Feb 9, 37; m 70. MODERN HEBREW LITERATURE, EDUCATION. *Educ:* Yale Univ, AB, 59; Hebrew Union Col, Ohio, MA, 65; Univ Calif, Los Angeles, PhD(Near Eastern lit), 71. *Prof Exp:* From instr to asst prof Hebrew lit, 65-71, asst dean col, 65-69, dir sch educ, sch Judaic studies, 69-76, assoc prof, 71-76, PROF HEBREW LIT EDUC, HEBREW UNION COL, CALIF, 76- *Mem:* Cent Conf Am Rabbis; AAUP; Asn Jewish Studies; Nat Asn Temple Educr; Nat Comn Jewish Educ. *Res:* Hebrew literature between 1880 and 1940; contemporary Jewish religious education; American Jewish fiction. *Publ:* Auth, A critical analysis of Without a Goal by Y Bershadsky, Hebrew Union Col Ann, 74; co-auth, In Brenner's footsteps on the way to Breakdown and bereavement, Hasifrut, spring 74; auth, An analysis of A Simple Story by S Y Agnon, Critique, spring 74; Rationale for graduate professional training in Jewish education at Hebrew Union College in California, Jewish Educ, 74; Thoughts on Jewish professional training, J Jewish Communal Serv, 76. *Mailing Add:* Sch of Educ Hebrew Union Col Los Angeles CA 90007

CYPESS, SANDRA MESSINGER, b Brooklyn, NY, Jan 5, 43; m 64; c 2. SPANISH, PORTUGUESE. *Educ:* Brooklyn Col, AB, 63; Cornell Univ, MA, 65; Univ Ill, Urbana, PhD(Span), 68. *Prof Exp:* Asst prof Span, Duke Univ, 67-70; assoc prof, Point Park Col, 70-75; asst prof, Carnegie-Mellon Univ, 75-76; asst prof, 76-80, ASSOC PROF SPAN, STATE UNIV NY BINGHAMTON, 80- *Concurrent Pos:* Vis assoc prof, Univ Haifa. *Mem:* MLA; Am Asn Teachers Span & Port; Northeast Mod Lang Asn. *Res:* Latin American drama; narrative technique; feminist criticism. *Publ:* Co-ed, Humor y fantasia de Wenceslao Fernandez Florez, Newberry Sun, SC, 73; auth, The function of myth in the plays of Xavier Villaurrutia, Hispania, Vol 55, No 2; Physical imagery in the plays of Griselda Gambaro, Mod Drama, 75; The plays of Griselda Gambaro, In: Dramatists in Revolt: The New Latin American Theatre, 76; ed, Studies in Romance Literatures: Essays Critical and Contextual, Coronado, 78; Machado de Assis vs Bras Cubas: The narrative situation of Memorias Postumas de Bras Cubas, Ky Romance Quart, 78; auth, Women dramatists of Puerto Rico, Revista/Rev Interam, 79; The Unveiling of a Nation: Puerto Rican Literature in the Twentieth Century, In: The Puerto Ricans, Schenkman, 80. *Mailing Add:* Dept of Romance Lang State Univ NY Binghamton NY 13901

CZERWINSKI, EDWARD J, b Erie, Pa, June 6, 29. SLAVIC DRAMA & THEATRE, COMPARATIVE LITERATURE. *Educ:* Grove City Col, BA, 51; Pa State Univ, MA, 55; Univ Wis, MA, 64, PhD(Russ, Polish), 65. *Prof Exp:* Instr English, Ga Tech, 57-59; asst prof English & drama, McNeese State Col, 59-60; assoc prof Russ & Polish lit, Univ Pittsburgh, 65-66; assoc prof Slavics & chmn dept, State Univ NY, Buffalo & Millard Fillmore Eve Div, 66-67; assoc prof Russ & Polish, Univ Kans, 67-70; PROF RUSS & COMP LIT, STATE UNIV NY, STONY BROOK, 70-, CHMN COMT ACAD EXCHANGE WITH POLAND, 73- *Concurrent Pos:* Special ed & mem ed bd, Comp Drama; ed, Slavic & EEurop Theatre J. *Honors & Awards:* Distinguished Teaching Award, NY State Asn Foreign Lang Teachers, 75. *Mem:* MLA; Am Asn Teachers Slavic & EEurop Lang; Int Fedn Mod Lang & Lit; AAUP; Am Asn Advan Slavic Studies. *Publ:* Auth, Jesters and executioners: The future of East European theatre and drama, Comp Drama, fall 71; co-ed, The Soviet Invasion of Czechoslovakia: The Effects on East Europe, Praeger, 72; auth, The Soviet dream: Nationalism in Soviet prose fiction, In: The Cry of Home: Cultural Nationalism and the Modern Writer, Univ Tenn, 72; The Slavic theatre of the absurd 1956-1968, In: Contributions to the International Conference of Slavists, Mouton, The Hague, 73. *Mailing Add:* Dept of Ger & Slavic Lang State Univ of NY Stony Brook NY 11790

D

DABBS, JACK AUTREY, b Mercury, Tex, Jan 31, 14; c 1. LINGUISTICS. *Educ:* Univ Tex, BA, 35, MA, 36, PhD, 50. *Prof Exp:* Teacher high sch, Tex, 37-38; instr Span & French, St Edward's Univ, 38-40 & 48-50; from asst prof to assoc prof, 50-59, head dept mod lang, 64-73, prof, 59-79, EMER PROF SPAN & RUSS, TEX A&M UNIV, 80- *Concurrent Pos:* Dir Am Lang Inst, Baghdad, Iraq, 57-58; Ford Found grant, 60. *Mem:* Ling Soc Am; Am Name Soc (pres, 62); MLA. *Res:* Onomastics; Latin American bibliography; historical linguistics. *Publ:* Auth, A Short Bengali-English, English-Bengali Dict, Tex A&M Col, 62; History of the Discovery and Exploration of Chinese Turkestan, 63, The French Army in Mexico, 63 & Dei Gratia in Royal Titles, 72, Mouton & Co; The Mariano Riv Palacio Archives (3 vols), Editorial Jus, Mexico City, 67-72. *Mailing Add:* 2806 Cherry Ln Austin TX 78703

DABRINGHAUS, ERHARD, b Essen, Ger, Apr 18, 17; nat US; m 45; c 2. GERMAN. *Educ:* Miami Univ, BA, 39; Wayne State Univ, MA, 53; Univ Mich, PhD, 57. *Prof Exp:* Instr, 54-63, ASST PROF GER, WAYNE STATE UNIV, 63- *Mem:* MLA; Am Asn Teachers Ger. *Res:* Political and intellectual currents of Bavaria as reflected in the works of Oskar Maria Graf, 1900-1938; introduction of foreign languages in elementary schools. *Mailing Add:* Dept of German Wayne State Univ Detroit MI 48202

DA CAL, ERNESTO GUERRA, b El Ferrol, Spain, Dec 19, 11; nat US; m 66; c 1. SPANISH & PORTUGUESE. *Educ:* Inst Gen y Tecnico de San Isidro, Madrid, Spain, AB, 28; Cent Univ, Lic en Filos y Let, 36; Columbia Univ, PhD(romance lit), 50. *Hon Degrees:* Dr, Univ Bahia, 59. *Prof Exp:* Instr, Brooklyn Col, 39-41; from asst prof to prof Span & Port, NY Univ, 41-64, chmn dept, 55-59; prof romance lang, Queens Col, NY, & City Univ NY Grad Div, 64-71; RETIRED. *Concurrent Pos:* Vis lectr, Princeton Univ, 42-43; gen consult, Dict Mod Europ Lit, Columbia Univ, Colliers Encycl & Dicionario das lit, Portugal, 56; vis prof Hisp lit, Univ PR, 58; chmn, Nat Selecting Comt, Fulbright awards, 60-61, mem 61-62. *Honors & Awards:* Officer, Order of Southern Cross, Brazil, 59; Rosalia de Castro Prize, Port, 60; officer, Order of St James of Sword, Port, 62; Knight-Commander, Order of Prince Henry the Navigator, Port, 68. *Mem:* MLA; Am Asn Teachers Span & Port; elected mem Real Academia das Ciencias de Lisboa; hon mem, Sociedade de Escritores Portugueses; Int Acad Port Cult. *Res:* Portuguese, Spanish and Galician literatures; stylistics; modern novel. *Publ:* Auth, Lengua y Estilo de Eca de Queiroz, Univ Coimbra, 54, Lisbon, 66 & Rio, 69; Lua de Alen-Mar, 59 & Rio de Sonho e Tempo, 63, Galaxia, Vigo; coauth, Literatura del Siglo XX, Holt, 68; compiler, A Reliquia, Lisbon, 71; Problema do Roance Cervantino, Rio de Janeiro, 73; Queirosiana, Coimbra, (4 vols), 75-81. *Mailing Add:* Melrose Ave D Nuno Alvares Pereira 33-A Estoril Portugal

DAEMMRICH, HORST, b Pausa, Ger, Jan 5, 30; US citizen; m 62; c 2. GERMAN LITERATURE. *Educ:* Wayne State Univ, BA, 58, MA, 59; Univ Chicago, PhD, 64. *Prof Exp:* Admin asst, Eucom Headquarters, 47-50; instr Ger, Univ Chicago, 61-62; from instr to assoc prof, Wayne State Univ, 62-69, prof, 69-80; PROF GER, UNIV PA, 80- *Concurrent Pos:* Dir jr yr, Univ Freiburg, 72-73. *Honors & Awards:* Wayne State Univ Bd of Gov Fac Recognition Award, 75. *Mem:* Am Soc Aesthet; MLA (secy, 72, 73); Midwest Mod Lang Asn (secy, 67, 68); Am Asn Teachers Ger. *Res:* Enlightenment; age of Goethe; realism; aesthetic theory. *Publ:* Coauth, The Challenge of German Literature, 71 & auth, The Shattered Self, E T A Hoffmann's Tragic Vision, 73, Wayne State Univ; Literaturkritik in Theorie und Praxis, Francke, 74; Die Motivreihe Nebel-Licht im Werk Goethes, PEGS, 72; Fragwürdige Utopie, JEGPh, 76; Thomas Mann's perception of self-insight, PLL, 77; Wiederholte Spiegelungen, Themen und Motive in der Literatur, Francke, 78; Messer und Himmelsleiter Einfuhrung in das werk Karl Krolows, Groos, 80; Wilhelm Raabe, Twayne, 81. *Mailing Add:* Dept of Ger Lang & Lit Univ of Pa Philadelphia PA 19104

DAHLBERG, CHARLES, English. See Vol II

DAHLIN, LOIS ANN, b St Paul, Minn. FRENCH LANGUAGE & LITERATURE. *Educ:* Gustavus Adolphus Col, BA, 67; Univ Iowa, MA, 69, PhD(French), 77; Univ Poitiers, France, Lic-es-Lett, 70. *Prof Exp:* Instr French, Univ Iowa, 74-75; vis instr, 75-77, ASST PROF FRENCH, NC STATE UNIV, 77- *Mem:* MLA; Am Asn Teachers Fr. *Res:* Nineteenth and 20th century French poetry. *Mailing Add:* Dept of Foreign Lang & Lit NC State Univ Raleigh NC 27650

DAIGLE, RICHARD JOSEPH, b Springfield, Mass, May 10, 31; m 47; c 4. LINGUISTICS, RUSSIAN LITERATURE. *Educ:* St Mary's Univ, Tex, BA, 59; Duquesne Univ, MA, 62, PhD(English), 71. *Prof Exp:* Instr English, Duquesne Univ, 61-66; from instr to asst prof, 66-72, assoc prof, 72-80, PROF ENGLISH, UNIV BRIDGEPORT, 80- CHMN DEPT, 76- *Mem:* AAUP; Geoling Soc Am; MLA; Nat Coun Teachers English. *Res:* Contrastive Russian-English linguistics; modern Soviet literature; Dostoevsky and Tolstoy. *Publ:* Auth, The American Heritage dictionary of the English language, Cann English J, fall 70; co-ed, Mentor Dictionary of Mythology and the Bible, New Am Libr, 73; auth, A contrastive study of Russian and English verbs, Geoling, 77. *Mailing Add:* Dept of English Univ of Bridgeport Bridgeport CT 06602

DAIKER, DONALD ARTHUR, Literature, Composition. See Vol II

DAILEY, VIRGINIA FLOOD, b Pittsburgh, Pa, Sept 20, 27; m 49; c 9. LINGUISTICS, ENGLISH. *Educ:* Univ Tex, Austin, BA, 48, MA, 49, PhD(ling), 63. *Prof Exp:* Res assoc Ger lang, Univ Tex, Austin, 58-59, managing ed, The Graduate J, 59-63; instr English, 65-66, from asst prof to assoc prof, 66-78, assoc acad dean, 70-72, acting acad dean, 72-73, PROF ENGLISH & LING, ST EDWARD'S UNIV, 78- *Concurrent Pos:* Dir, Instnl self-study, St Edward's Univ, 74-76; Exec Comt mem, Asn Innovation Higher Educ, 72-75. *Honors & Awards:* Teaching excellence award, St Edward's Univ, 75. *Mem:* Ling Soc Am; Asn Innovation Educ; South Cent Mod Lang Asn; NCTE. *Res:* Old English language and literature; English as a second language; bilingual and bicultural education. *Publ:* Coauth, The Cynewulf Alliterations, Univ Tex, 60. *Mailing Add:* Dept of English & Ling St Edward's Univ Austin TX 78704

DAINARD, JAMES ALAN, b Golden, BC, May 26, 30; m 64. FRENCH. *Educ:* Univ BC, BA, 51, MA, 61, BLS, 62; Univ Alta, PhD(Fr lit), 67. *Prof Exp:* Asst prof Romance lang, Univ Alta, 66-68; asst prof, 68-72, ASSOC PROF FRENCH, UNIV COL, UNIV TORONTO, 72- *Mem:* MLA. *Res:* Seventeenth century French literature. *Mailing Add:* Dept of French Univ Col Univ of Toronto Toronto ON M5S 1A1 Can

DAITZ, STEPHEN G, b New York, NY, Aug 16, 26. CLASSICS. *Educ:* Yale Univ, BA, 47, MA, 48; dipl, Sorbonne, 50; Harvard Univ, PhD, 53. *Prof Exp:* Lectr English, Sorbonne, 49-50; instr classics, Brooklyn Col, 53-56 & NY Univ, 56-57; assoc prof, 57-72, PROF CLASSICS, CITY COL NEW YORK,

72-, CHMN DEPT, 73- *Concurrent Pos:* Vis prof Greek, Univ Paris, Nanterre, 71-73 & 79-80. *Mem:* Am Philol Asn. *Res:* Greek oratory and tragedy; Greek paleography and textual criticism; oral interpretation of Greek poetry. *Publ:* Auth, The relationship of the De Chersoneso and the Philippica Quarta of Demosthenes, Class Philol, 7/57; Tacitus' technique of character portrayal, Am J Philol, 1/60; The Jerusalem Palimpsest of Euripides: A Facsimile Edition with Commentary, de Gruyter, Berlin, 70; Concepts of Freedom and Slavery in Euripides' Hecuba, Hermes, 71; ed, Euripides' Hecuba, Teubner, Leipzig, 73; A recital of ancient Greek poetry, 78, Euripides' Hekabe, 81 & The pronunciation of ancient Greek: A practical guide, 81, Norton. *Mailing Add:* Dept of Classical & Hebrew City Col of New York New York NY 10031

DALBOR, JOHN BRONISLAW, b Erie, Pa, Aug 26, 29; m 51; c 2. SPANISH. *Educ:* Pa State Univ, BA, 51, MA, 53; Univ Mich, PhD, 61. *Prof Exp:* Teaching Asst Span, Pa State Univ, 51-53; teaching fel, Univ Mich, 55-58; from instr to assoc prof, 58-72, PROF SPAN, PA STATE UNIV, UNIVERSITY PARK, 72- *Concurrent Pos:* Mem ling staff group to Philippines, Peace Crops, 61-62. *Mem:* MLA; Am Asn Teachers Span & Port; Am Asn Appl Ling. *Res:* Linguistics, especially Spanish; second language pedagogy. *Publ:* Co-ed, Imaginacion y fantasia, 60, rev ed, 68 & 75; coauth, Oral Spanish Review, 65 & Spanish Pronunciation, 69, Holt, rev ed, 80; Temporal distinctions in the Spanish subjunctive, 69 & A simplified tagmemic approach for teaching Spanish syntax, 72, Hispania; Beginning College Spanish, Random, 72; Spanish in Review, Wiley, 79; Observations on present day seseo and ceceo in Southern Spain, Hispania, 80. *Mailing Add:* Dept of Span Ital & Port Pa State Univ University Park PA 16802

DALE, MARCELLE ESTHER, b Oran, Algeria, Jan 1, 23; US citizen; m 44; c 2. FOREIGN LANGUAGES. *Educ:* Univ Algiers, Lic es Let; Western Mich Univ, MA, 53. *Prof Exp:* Instr Spanish & French, 53-55, asst prof, 55-62, ASSOC PROF FRENCH, KALAMAZOO COL, 63- *Concurrent Pos:* Grant to visit ctr studies for Kalamazoo Col Studies in Fr, Caen-Vichy, spring 65. *Mem:* MLA. *Res:* Languages in the elementary field. *Mailing Add:* Dept of Romance Lang & Lit Kalamazoo Col Kalamazoo MI 49001

DALE, ROBERT CHARLES, b Madison, Wis, June 11, 36; div; c 2. FRENCH LITERATURE. *Educ:* Univ Wis, BA, 58, MA, 60, PhD(French), 63. *Prof Exp:* Asst foreign lang, Lycee Michel-Montiagne, Bordeaux, 58-59; asst prof, 63-67, ASSOC PROF FRENCH, UNIV WASH, 67- *Concurrent Pos:* Ed consult French & cinema, Macmillan Co, 66- *Mem:* Am Asn Teachers Fr. *Res:* Nineteenth century prose-fiction and drama; cinema. *Publ:* Auth, A clash of intelligences: Sound vs image in Rene Clair's A Nous, la Liberte, Fr Rev, 4/65; Chatterton is the essential Romantic drama, fall 65 & Le Colonel Chabert between Gothicism and Romanticism, spring 67, Esprit Createur; The Poetics of Prosper Merimee, Mounton, The Hague, 67; ed, Rene Clair's Cinema Yesterday and Today, Dover, 71. *Mailing Add:* Dept of Romance Lang GN60 Univ of Wash Seattle WA 98195

DALLETT, JOSEPH BIRDSALL, b Bryn Mawr, Pa, May 27, 29; m 66. GERMAN LITERATURE. *Educ:* Harvard Univ, AB, 51, PhD(comp lit), 64; Univ Pa, AM, 53. *Prof Exp:* From instr to asst prof Ger lit, Cornell Univ, 62-71; ASSOC PROF GER, CARLETON UNIV, 71- *Mem:* MLA; Can Asn Univ Teachers Ger; Int Arbeitskreis Deutsche Barocklit; Int Paracelsusgesell Schaft; Renaissance Soc Am. *Res:* German Baroque literature; Grimmelshausen and mysticism, Mörike and the idyll. *Publ:* Auth, Ideas of sight in The Faerie Queen, ELH, 60; Melanchthoniana Funebria in the Cornell University Library, Cornell Libr J, 68; contribr, Hohenheims Labyrinth: Bilder der Resonanz, InP Paracelsus Werk und Wirkung: Festgabe für Kur Goldammer, Verband der wissenschaftlichen Gesellschaften Österreichs, 75; auth, Auf dem Weg zu den Ursprungen: Eine Quellenuntersuchung zu Grimmelschausens Schermesser-Episode, Carleton Ger Papers, 76; Mensch und Tierreich im Simplicissimus: Neue Perspektiven zu den Zuellen, Daphnis, 76; Grimmelshausen und die Neue Welt, Argenis, 77; Symmetry in Mörikes poetry, Carleton Ger Papers, 77. *Mailing Add:* Dept of German Carleton Univ Ottawa ON K1S 5B6 Can

D'ALQUEN, RICHARD J E, b London, England, Aug 19, 33; m 62; c 2. GERMANIC LANGUAGES. *Educ:* Univ Nottingham, BA, 56; Univ Alta, MA, 62; Univ Ill, PhD(Ger), 67. *Prof Exp:* Teacher, Ross Sheppard High Sch, 60-61; asst prof Ger, Northwestern Univ, 66-68; asst prof, 68-72, assoc prof, 72-80, PROF GER, UNIV ALTA, 80- *Mem:* Can Ling Asn; Am Asn Teachers Ger; Can Asn Univ Teachers Ger. *Res:* Linguistics, especially Germanic. *Publ:* Auth, Gothic AI and AU: A Possible Solution, Mouton, 73; The Germanic shift and Verner's Law: A synthesis, Gen Ling, 73; Ein gotisch-griechisch-vulgarlateinisches ratsel, Glotta, 76; Criticism of Germanistik in the light of political trauma, Unterrichtspraxis, 77; Acoustic phonetics and vowel quantity in the history of German, Zeitschrift fur Dialektologie und Linguistik, 79. *Mailing Add:* Dept of Germanic Lang Univ of Alta Edmonton AB T6G 2G2 Can

DALTON, MARGARET, b Nissi, Estonia, Nov 1, 28; US citizen; m 67. SLAVIC LANGUAGES & LITERATURES. *Educ:* Radcliffe Col, BA, 58; Harvard Univ, PhD(Slavic), 64. *Prof Exp:* Instr Russ, Wellesley Col, 63-64; asst prof, Brown Univ, 64-67; asst prof, 69-75, ASSOC PROF RUSS, BRANDEIS UNIV, 75- *Concurrent Pos:* Nat Endowment for Humanities fel, 67-68. *Mem:* MLA; Am Asn Teachers Slavic & E Europ Lang; Am Asn Advan Slavic Studies. *Res:* Nineteenth and 20th century Russian literature. *Publ:* Auth, Nikolai Arzhak, New Leader, 11/65; A K Tolstoy, Twayne, 72; Andrei Siniavskii and Iulii Daniel, two Soviet heretical writers, Yal, Wurzburg, Ger, 73; The art of Georgij Peskov, In: Mnemozina, Fink Verlag, Munchen, 74; co-ed, Georgij Tvanov, Sobraine stikhotvorenij, Yal, Verlag Wurzburg. *Mailing Add:* 72 Scott Rd Belmont MA 02178

DALY, LLOYD WILLIAM, b Plano, Ill, Oct 6, 10; m 35; c 2. CLASSICAL STUDIES. *Educ:* Knox Col, AB, 32, LittD, 55; Univ Ill, AM, 33, PhD, 36. *Prof Exp:* Acting prof classics, Kenyon Col, 37; from asst prof to assoc prof class lang, Univ Okla, 38-47; from assoc prof to prof, 47-77, vdean, grad sch, 51-52, dean col, 52-59, chmn dept, 61-67, EMER PROF CLASS STUD, UNIV PA, 77- *Concurrent Pos:* Guggenheim fel, 59-60. *Mem:* Am Philos Soc; Am Philol Asn; Archaeol Inst Am; Mediaeval Acad Am. *Res:* Greek and Latin literature; medieval Latin literature. *Publ:* Coauth, The Altercatio Hadriani Augusti et Epicteti Philosophi, Univ Ill, 39; auth, Aesop Without Morals, Yoseloff, 61; A History of Alphabetization in Antiquity and the Middle Ages, Latomus, 67; Brito Metricus: A Medieval Verse Treatise on Greek and Hebrew Words, Univ Pa, 68; Summa Britonis, Thesaurus Mundi, 74. *Mailing Add:* 310 Morton Ave Ridley Park PA 19078

DALY, PETER MAURICE, b Bristol, England, June 3, 36; m 58; c 2. GERMAN. *Educ:* Bristol Univ, BA, 58; Univ Zurich, Dr Phil(Ger), 63. *Prof Exp:* Lektor English, Univ Zurich, 60; asst prof Ger, Univ NB, 64-65; assoc prof, Univ Sask, Regina, 65-68; from vis assoc prof to assoc prof, Univ Man, 67-73, prof, 73-80; PROF GER, MCGILL UNIV, 80- *Concurrent Pos:* Can Coun Res grants, 66 & 68. *Mem:* MLA; Asn Can Univ Teachers Ger; Int Ver Ger Sprach-u Literaturwiss. *Res:* Shakespeare in Germany; baroque poetry and emblematics. *Publ:* Auth, Southwell's Burning Babe and the emblematic practice, Wascana Rev, 68; The poetic emblem, Neophilologus, 70; Trends and problems in the study of emblematic literature, Mosaic, 72; Translation as Interpretation: Some observations on three German translations of a Macbeth speech, In: Deutung und Bedeutung, B Schludermann et all, The Hague, 73; The semantics of the emblem--recent developments in emblem theory, Wascana Rev, 74; Goethe and the emblematic tradition, J English & Ger Philol, 74; Zu den denkformen des emblems, In: Akten des V Internationalen Germanisten-Kongressess, Cambridge, 75, Bern, 76; C R v Greiffenberg und Honore d'Urfe: Einige bemerkungen zur frage von Catharinas rezeption der Schäferdichtung, In: Schäferdichtung, Werner Vosskamp, Hamburg, 77. *Mailing Add:* Dept of Ger McGill Univ Montreal PQ H3C 3G1 Can

DALY, SARALYN RUTH, English. See Vol II

DALZELL, ALEXANDER, b Belfast, Northern Ireland, May 8, 25; Can citizen; m 54; c 2. CLASSICS. *Educ:* Trinity Col, Univ Dublin, BA, 50, MA, 53, BLitt, 56. *Prof Exp:* Asst lectr classics, King's Col, Univ London, 51-53 & Univ Sheffield, 53-54 from lectr to assoc prof, 54-68, vprovost, 72-79, PROF CLASSICS, TRINITY COL, UNIV TORONTO, 68- *Concurrent Pos:* Assoc Ed, Phoenix, 61-64, ed, 64-71; Can Coun leave fel, 73-74. *Mem:* Class Asn Can, (treas, 58-60); Am Philol Asn; Virgil Soc; Vergilian Soc; Soc Promotion Roman Studies. *Res:* Latin poetry of Augustan period; Lucretius and Epicureanism; Erasmus. *Publ:* Auth, Maecenas and the poets, 56 & The text of Lucretius, 60, Phoenix; ed, Studies in Honor of G M A Grube, Univ Toronto, 69; auth, Bibliography of work on Lucretius 1945-1972, Class World, 73; Lucretius exposition of the doctrine of images, 74 & Homenc Themes in Propertius, 80, Hermathena. *Mailing Add:* 49 De Vere Gardens Toronto ON M5M 3E6 Can

DAMIANI, BRUNO MARIO, b Pola, Italy, Apr 15, 42; US citizen. SPANISH, ITALIAN. *Educ:* Ohio State Univ, BA, 63, MA, 64; Johns Hopkins Univ, PHD(romance lang & lit), 67. *Prof Exp:* Asst prof, 67-69, ASSOC PROF ROMANCE LANG & LIT, CATH UNIV AM, 69- *Concurrent Pos:* Consult Title VII & prog qual consult, Task Group C, Dept Health, Educ & Welfare, 72; prog off, Nat Endowment for Humanities, 76. *Mem:* Asoc Int Hispanistas; MLA; Am Asn Teachers Span & Port. *Res:* Medieval, Renaissance and Baroque periods; Spanish Renaissance literature; Spanish and Italian medieval literature. *Publ:* Auth, Un aspecto historico de La lozana andaluza, Mod Lang Notes, 87: 178-92; The exordium of Malon de Chaide's La Conversion de la Magdalena, In: Studies in Honor of Helmut Hatzfeld's 80th Year, Hispam, 73; La Celestina, Anaya, Madrid, 73; Francisco Delicado, 74 & Lopez de Ubeda, 77, Twayne; Lo grotesco en La Picara Justina, Romance Notes, 64: 331-337; Caridad en el Quijote, Anales Cervantinos, 81: 176-210; Disfraz en La Picara Justina, Homage Vol in Honor Franco Meregalli, 82. *Mailing Add:* Dept of Mod Long Cath Univ Am Washington DC 20017

DAMROSCH, DAVID N, b Bar Harbor, Maine, Apr 13, 53; m 74. COMPARATIVE & ENGLISH LITERATURE. *Educ:* Yale Univ, BA, 65, PhD(comp lit), 80. *Prof Exp:* ASST PROF COMP LIT, COLUMBIA UNIV, 80- *Concurrent Pos:* Speechwriter & ed, Off Special Asst to the Pres for Health, White House, Washington, DC, 79. *Mem:* MLA; Am Comp Lit Asn. *Res:* The novel; epic and romance; scripture. *Publ:* Auth, Heinrich von Kleist, In: European Writers, Scribners (in prep); The paradox of Peter Bell, Wordsworth Circle (in prep). *Mailing Add:* Dept of English & Comp Lit Columbia Univ New York NY 10027

DANA, MARIE IMMACULEE, b Albany, NY, Oct 28, 31. FRENCH LANGUAGE & LITERATURE. *Educ:* Rosemont Col, BA, 53; McGill Univ, MA, 62; Univ Pa, PhD(French), 68. *Prof Exp:* Teacher, St Agnes Sch, 53-54; teacher French, Latin & hist, Our Lady of Mercy Acad, 55-60 & St Peter High Sch, 60-63; instr, 54-63, asst prof, 67-73, ASSOC PROF FRENCH, CARLOW COL, 73-, CHMN DEPT LANG, 67-, CHMN DEPT EDUC, 75- *Concurrent Pos:* Travel grant, Bibliotheque Nationale, Paris, 66; consult, Duquesne-Carlow Pupil-Personnel Serv Prog; Acad Am Coun Educ Admin fel, 74; consult, Pa Dept Educ, 77-; Adv bd mem, Project 81, 78- *Mem:* MLA; Am Coun Teaching For Lang. *Res:* Twentieth century French literature. *Publ:* Auth, Lope de Vega in the work of Moliere, Hispanofila (in press). *Mailing Add:* Dept of Lang Carlow Col Pittsburgh PA 15213

DANAHY, MICHAEL CHARLES, b Framingham, Mass, Jan 10, 42. FRENCH LANGUAGE & LITERATURE. *Educ:* Fordham Col, AB, 63; Princeton Univ, PhD(French), 69. *Prof Exp:* From instr to assoc prof French, Wesleyan Univ, 67-74; asst prof, 74-78, ASSOC PROF FRENCH, PA STATE UNIV, 78- *Concurrent Pos:* Dir res Prog Paris, Wesleyan Univ, 69-70. *Mem:* MLA; Am Asn Teachers Fr. *Res:* Nineteenth century French novel; French women writers; literary criticism. *Publ:* Auth, The drama of Herodiade, Mod Lang Quart, 73; The nature of narrative norms, Studies Voltaire, 73; Narrative timing and the structures of Sentimental Education,

Romanic Rev, 75; Le Roman, est-il chose femelle, Poetique, 76; Flaubert describes, Ky Romance Quart, 79; Growing up female: George Sand's view, Hofstra Univ Cult Studies, 79; Social, Sexual and Human Spaces in La Princesse de Cleves, Fr Forum, 81; The spatial craft of reading fiction, Nineteenth Century Fr Studies, 82. *Mailing Add:* Dept of French Pa State Univ University Park PA 16802

D'ANDREA, ANTONIO, b Messina, Italy, Nov 22, 16. ITALIAN. *Educ:* Univ Pisa, DPhil, 39. *Prof Exp:* Prof hist & philos, Licei Classici, 40-44; asst prof philos, Univ Pisa, 44-45; dir, Cent Bur Res Social & Educ Probs, Ministry Social Welfare, Rome, 45-49; from vis prof to assoc prof, 49-63, chmn dept, 64-76, PROF ITAL, McGILL UNIV, 64- *Concurrent Pos:* Chmn, Govt of Que Comt on Res Grants for Lit, Ling, Fine Arts & Hist, 71-73; McGill Univ res grants, 72-73; mem, Que Prog Training of Researches & Res Teams, 73; chmn, Sous-Comite D'Evaluation des Programmes, Prov Que, 77-78; vpres, Can Mediter Inst, 80- *Honors & Awards:* Comdr, Merit Ital Repub (Ital Govt), 74, Can Silver Jubilee Medal, Gov Gen Can, 78; Grand 'Ufficiale, Order of Merit, Ital Repub, 82. *Mem:* Nominating Comt Humanities Res Coun; Fel Royal Soc Can; Can Soc Ital Studies; Can Soc Studies Hist & Philos Fr; MLA. *Res:* Renaissance studies; problems of history, aesthetics and literary criticism. *Publ:* Contribr, Studies on Machiavelli and his reputation in the sixteenth century, I, Marlowe's prologue to the Jew at Malta, Mediaeval & Renaissance Studies, 62; co-ed, Yearbook of Italian Studies, 71 & 72 & I Gentillet, Discours Contre Machiavel, Casalini Libr, Florence; auth, Alfieri e il mito dell'Italia, Forum Italicum, Vol X, Petrarca: interpretazione del Secretum & Le rubriche del Decameron, Yearbk Ital Studies, 76; Giraldi Cinthio and the Birth of the Machiavellian Hero, In: Il Teatro Italiano del Rinascimento, 80; The Italian Community and the Myth of Italy, In: Peter Martyr Vermigli and the Italian Reform, 80. *Mailing Add:* Dept of Ital McGill Univ Montreal PQ H3A 1G5 Can

DANE, JOSEPH A, Medieval Literature. See Vol II

DANESI, MARCEL, b Lucca, Italy, Oct 1, 46; Can citizen; m 67; c 1. LINGUISTICS, ITALIAN. *Educ:* Univ Toronto, BA, 69, MA, 71, PhD(Ital ling), 74. *Prof Exp:* Vis lectr ling, Rutgers Univ, 72-73; asst prof, 74-77, ASSOC PROF ITAL, UNIV TORONTO, 78- *Mem:* Ling Soc Am; Ling Asn Can & US; Am Asn Teachers Ital; Can Ling Asn; MLA. *Res:* General linguistics; applied linguistics; problems in Romance linguistics. *Publ:* Auth, Teaching standard Italian to dialect speakers: A pedagogical perspective of systems in contact, Italica, 74; A tagmemic model of Italian verb morphology, Second Lacus Forum, 76; La lingua dei Sermoni Subalpini, Centro Studi Peimontesi, Turin, 76; Early Indoamericanisms in Italian: The Itinerario of Juan de Grijalva, Orbis, 76; Some linguistic observations on mathematical puzzles, Third Lacus Forum, 77; The measurement of interference in old texts, Can J Ling, 77; A note on the palatalization of k in twelfth-century piedmontese, Studia Neophilologica, 77; The case for Andalucismo re-examined, Hisp Rev, 77. *Mailing Add:* Dept of Ital Studies Univ of Toronto Toronto ON M5S 1A1 Can

DANIEL, GEORGE B, JR, b Franklin, Ga, May 17, 27; m 58; c 2. FRENCH LITERATURE. *Educ:* Emory Univ, AB, 49; Univ Paris, dipl, 53; Univ NC, PhD, 59. *Prof Exp:* From instr to asst prof French, Berea Col, 50-55; from instr to assoc prof, 57-68, PROF FRENCH, UNIV NC, CHAPEL HILL, 69- *Concurrent Pos:* Dir NDEA Inst, 61-62; Ed, Romance Notes, 72- *Mem:* Am Asn Teachers Fr; S Atlantic Mod Lang Asn; MLA. *Res:* French literature, 17th century. *Publ:* Auth, Phedre and Britannicus, Laurel Ed, 63; The Development of the Tragedie Nationale in France, 1580-1800, 63 & ed, Renaissance and Other Studies in Honor William L Wiley, 68, Univ NC; coauth, Contes de Plusieurs Siecles, Odyssey, 64; auth, Marcel Proust, Le Moyen Age et Pierre Chastellain, Bull Soc Amis Proust & Amis Combray, spring 68; French national history in dramatic productions from 1550-1600, Fr Rev, 71; Aspects of age and time in El Cid, In: Studies in Honor of Alfred G Engstrom, Univ NC, 72; ed & contribr, Moltiere Studies, Castalia, Madrid, 73. *Mailing Add:* Dept of Romance Lang Univ of NC Chapel Hill NC 27514

DANIEL, MARY L, b Madison, Wis, Sept 1, 36. PORTUGUESE. *Educ:* Univ Wis, BS, 58, MA, 59, PhD(Port), 65. *Prof Exp:* Prof Port, Univ Iowa, 65-77; PROF PORT, UNIV WIS, MADISON, 77- *Concurrent Pos:* Co-ed, Luso-Brazilian Rev, 78- *Mem:* Am Asn Teachers Span & Port; Midwest Mod Lang Asn. *Res:* Portuguese language and literature; contemporary Brazilian literature. *Publ:* Auth, Word formation and deformation in Grande Sertao: Veredas, Luso-Brazilian Rev, 65; Joao Guimaraes Rosa: lingua e estilo, Rev Iberoam, 66; Joao Guimaraes Rosa: travessia literaria, Jose Olympio, Rio de Janeiro, 68; Sao Cristovao and Santo Onofre: Aspects of the mystical expression of Eca de Queiroz, Luso-Brazilian Rev, summer 73; Through the looking glass: Mirror play in two works of Joao Guimaraes Rosa & Osman Lins, Luso-Brazilian Rev, 76; Eico Verissimo: Microcosmo e Macrocosmo, 78 & Esses Guimaraes e a sua bicharada mineira, (Suplemento Literario), 81, Minas Gerais; Berdyaev and Guimaraes Rosa: The paradox of necessity and freedom, Luso-Brazilian Rev, 81. *Mailing Add:* 1012 Van Hise Hall Univ Wis Madison WI 53706

DANIELS, WILLIAM JOHN, b Bristol, Pa, Oct 21, 37; m 67; c 3. SLAVIC LANGUAGES, LINGUISTICS. *Educ:* Lehigh Univ, BA, 59; Univ Ill, Urbana, MA, 66, PhD(Slavic ling), 71. *Prof Exp:* Asst prof Slavic Lang, Ohio State Univ, 68-74; CHIEF LINGUIST, HARRIS CORP, 74- *Mem:* Am Asn Teachers Slavic & East Europ Lang; Ling Soc Am; Bulgarian Studies Group. *Res:* Russian grammar; phonetic bases of phonology; Slavic typology. *Publ:* Auth, Assimilation in Russian consonant clusters, vol I, fall 72 & vol II, 73, Papers in Ling; Natural phonology and the teaching of Russian pronunciation, Slavic & East European J, Vol 19 & contribr, Bulgaria: Past and Present, Am Asn Advan Slavic Studies, 75. *Mailing Add:* 6801 Crest Circle Frederick MD 21701

DANIELSON, J DAVID, b Manistique, Mich, Sept 2, 26; m 60; c 2. HISPANIC STUDIES. *Educ:* Northern Mich Univ, BA, 49; Univ Mich, MA, 50, PhD(comp lit), 60. *Prof Exp:* Instr French, Clark Univ, 57-59 & Oakland Univ, 59-60; asst prof Span, State Univ NY, Albany, 61-62 & Univ Akron, 62-63; assoc prof, Univ SDak, 63-66; acting chmn dept for lang & lit, 68-69 & 74-75, chmn, 69-73, ASSOC PROF SPAN, UNIV HARTFORD, 66-, CHMN LING PROG, 68- *Concurrent Pos:* Fel, English Lang Inst, Univ Mich, 60; teacher English & dir courses, Amicana Binat Ctr, Arg, 61; Nat Endowment Humanities Fel, Yale Univ, 77. *Mem:* MLA; Ling Soc Am; Am Asn Teachers Fr; Am Asn Teachers Span & Port; Am Lit Transl Asn. *Res:* Translation theory; linguistics and literature; Caribbean studies. *Publ:* Auth, Antillean nature and Creole world-awareness in Telumee Miracle, Revue du Pacifique, 1/77; Alejo Carpentier and the United States: notes on the Recurso del Metodo, Int Fiction Rev, 7/77; transl, E Martinez Estrada, Marta Riquelme, SDak Rev, winter, 78-79; transl, From Otherness to Complementation, Quinquereme, 1/82. *Mailing Add:* Dept of For Lang & Lit 411 Auerbach Univ of Hartford West Hartford CT 06117

DANKER, FREDERICK W, b Frankenmuth, Mich, July 12, 20; m 48; c 2. NEW TESTAMENT THEOLOGY, LINGUISTICS. *Educ:* Concordia Sem, BA, 42, BD, 50; Univ Chicago, PhD, 63. *Prof Exp:* From asst prof to prof New Testament exec theol, 54-74; PROF NEW TESTAMENT EXEC THEOL, CHRIST SEM-SEMINEX, 74- *Mem:* Am Philol Asn; Soc Bibl Lit; Am Soc Papyrologists; Societas Novi Testamenti Studiorum; Cath Bibl Asn. *Res:* Greek tragedy; Greek and Latin Epigraphy; Greek Lexicography. *Publ:* Auth, Multipurpose Tools for Bible Study, Concordia Publ House, 60, 2nd rev, 66, 3rd rev, 70; I Peter 1:24-2:17-a consolatory pericope, Z Neutestamentliche Wiss, 67; Jesus and the New Age According to St Luke: A Commentary on the Third Gospel, Clayton, 72; Luke-Proclamation Commentary, Fortress, 76; No Room in the Brotherhood, Clayton, 77; co-ed, A Greek-English Lexicon of the New Testament and other Early Christian Literature, Univ Chicago, 79; auth, Invitation to the New Testament: Epistles IV, A Comentary on Hebrews, James, 1 and 2 Peter, 1, 2, and 3 John and Jude, Doubleday, 80; Benefactor: Epigraphic Study of a Graeco-Roman and New Testament Semantic Field, Clayton, 82. *Mailing Add:* 6928 Plateau Ave St Louis MO 63139

DANLY, ROBERT LYONS, b Hinsdale, Ill, Jan 3, 47. JAPANESE LITERATURE. *Educ:* Yale Univ, BA, 69, MA, 71, PhD(Japanese lit), 80. *Prof Exp:* Asst prof, 79-82, ASSOC PROF JAPANESE LIT, UNIV MICH, 82- *Concurrent Pos:* Reader, Nat Endowment for Humanities, 80-81; consult, The Kenyon Rev, 81-; mem, exec comt, Prog Comp Lit, Univ Mich, 81-, Ctr Japanese Studies, 82- *Honors & Awards:* The Am Bk Award for Translation, 82. *Mem:* Asn Asian Studies; Asn Teachers Japanese; MLA; Pen; Am Lit Transl Asn. *Res:* Premodern Japanese fiction of the 17th and 18th centuries; Japanese novel of the early modern period, 1868-1930. *Publ:* Auth, In the Shade of Spring Leaves: The Life and Writings of Higuchi Ichiyo, A Woman of Letters in Meiji Japan, Yale Univ Press, 81; Translating local color, Transl Rev, summer 82. *Mailing Add:* Dept Far Eastern Lang & Lit Univ Mich Ann Arbor MI 48109

DANNERBECK, FRANCIS J, b Ft Wayne, Ind, Jan 19, 32; m 55; c 1. GERMAN EDUCATION. *Educ:* Ind Univ, AB, 58, MAT, 59; Purdue Univ, PhD(educ), 65. *Prof Exp:* Teacher high sch, Ind, 59-61; from instr to asst prof Ger, Purdue Univ, 61-66; asst prof, US Naval Acad, 66-68; assoc prof, 68-72, PROF FOR LANG & EDUC, UNIV SC, 72-, CHMN DEPT, 77- *Concurrent Pos:* Instr, NDEA Summer Insts, Univ Notre Dame, 62 & Univ Scranton, 66-69. *Mem:* Am Asn Teachers Ger; Am Asn Teachers Fr; Am Coun Teaching For Lang. *Res:* Foreign language teaching including methodology and teacher training. *Publ:* Auth, Toward a methods course requirement at the graduate level, Mod Lang J, 5/66; coauth, Closed-circuit TV--an effective adjunct to modern foreign language teaching, Ger Quart, 11/68; auth, Audio-lingual teaching and reading, Fr Rev, 11/69. *Mailing Add:* Dept Foreign Lang Univ SC Columbia SC 29208

DANON, SAMUEL, b Athens, Greece, Aug 27, 37. ROMANCE LANGUAGES. *Educ:* Brandeis Univ, BA, 58; Johns Hopkins Univ, PhD, 76. *Prof Exp:* From asst prof to assoc prof, 62-77, PROF FRENCH, REED COL, 77- *Mem:* MLA. *Res:* French Romantics and symbolists; 17th century French theater; 18th century French novel. *Mailing Add:* Dept of French Reed Col Portland OR 97202

D'APONTE, MIRIAM G, Theatre, Italian. See Vol II

DARBELNET, JEAN LOUIS, b Paris, France, Nov 14, 04; m 38; c 2. FRENCH LANGUAGE & LITERATURE. *Educ:* Lic es Let, Sorbonne, 25, dipl, 26, Agrege, 29. *Prof Exp:* Asst French, Univ Col Wales, 25-26, Univ Edinburgh, 26-27 & Univ Manchester, 28-30; prof English, Lycee Condorcet, Paris France, 35-37; instr French, Harvard & Radcliffe Col, 38-39; assoc prof & chmn dept, McGill Univ, 39-46, prof French & chmn humanities group, 45-46; prof French, Bowdoin Col, 46-62; prof 62-78, dir MA prog in French, 64-67, assoc dir, grad sch, 67-70, dir BA in transl prog, 69-73, EMER PROF LING, LAVAL UNIV, 75- *Concurrent Pos:* Exec mem, Humanities Res Coun Can 64-71. *Honors & Awards:* Chevalier, Ordre nat du Merite, France, 67. *Mem:* Can Ling Asn (pres, 66-68); MLA; Royal Soc Can. *Res:* French and English stylistics. *Publ:* Coauth, Stylistique Comparee du fransais et de l'anglais, Didier, Paris, 58; auth, Regards sur le fransais actuel, Beauchemin, Montreal, 63; Pensee et Structure, Scribner's, 69, rev 77; Dictionaries bilingues et lexicologie differentielle, Languages, 9/70; Linguistique differentielle et traduction, Meta, 3/71; Accent de phrase et dialectique en anglais et en francais, In: Interlinguistics, Max Niemeyer, Tübingen, 71; coauth, Words in Context, Paris Bordas, 73; auth, Le francais en contact avec l'anglais en Amerique du Nord, Laval Univ, 77. *Mailing Add:* Fac of Lett Laval Univ Quebec PQ G7K 7P4 Can

DARDJOWIDJOJO, SOENJONO, b Pekalongan, Java, Indonesia, July 24, 38; m 68; c 2. INDONESIAN LANGUAGES & LINGUISTICS. *Educ:* English Col, Indonesia, BA, 59; Univ Hawaii, MA, 64; Georgetown Univ, PhD(ling), 67. *Prof Exp:* Teacher English, High Schs, Indonesia, 59-61; lectr Indonesian, Victoria Univ, Wellington, 68-70; asst prof, 70-74, assoc prof Indonesian, 74-80, PROF SOUTHEAST ASIAN LANG, UNIV HAWAII, MANOA, 80- *Mem:* Ling Soc Am; Am Coun Teaching For Lang; Am Coun Teachers Uncommonly Taught Asian Lang, (pres, 72-74). *Res:* Semantic and syntactic features of Indonesian language; honorific features in Javanese; development of teaching materials for Indonesian and Javanese. *Publ:* Auth, The meN-, meN-kan, and meN-i verbs in Indonesian, Philippine J Ling, 71; ed, Cultural-Linguistic Aspects in Asian Language Teaching, Southeast Asian Studies, Univ Hawaii, 73; auth, Honorifics in generative semantics: A Case in Javanese, RELC J, 73; Semantic analysis of datang in Indonesian, Occasional Papers in Southeast Asian Ling, 73; The impact of colonialism in national language development, ASANAL Proceedings, 77; Sentence Patterns of Indonesian, Univ Hawaii, 78; The semantic structures of the adversative ke-an verbs in Indonesian, Fetschrift Alisyahbana, 78; Vocabulary building in Indonesian, an advanced reader, USOE Report, 78. *Mailing Add:* Dept of Indo-Pacific Lang Univ of Hawaii at Manoa Honolulu HI 96822

D'ARMS, JOHN HAUGHTON, b Poughkeepsie, NY, Nov 27, 34; m 61; c 2. CLASSICAL STUDIES. *Educ:* Princeton Univ, BA, 56; Oxford Univ, MA, 59; Harvard Univ, PhD (classics), 65. *Prof Exp:* From asst prof to prof class studies, Univ Mich, Ann Arbor, 65-77, chmn dept, 72-77; Mellon prof class studies & dir, Am Acad Rome, 77-80; PROF CLASSICS & CHMN DEPT, UNIV MICH, ANN ARBOR, 80- *Concurrent Pos:* Asst prof, Intercol Ctr Class Studies, Rome, 67-68, chmn managing comt, 72-; trustee, Princeton Univ, 70-74; Am Coun Learned Soc fel, 71-72; prof classics in residence, Am Acad in Rome, 71-72, trustee, 73-; Guggenheim fel & vis mem sch hist studies, Inst for Advan Study, Princeton, 75-76. *Mem:* Am Philol Asn; Archaeol Inst Am. *Res:* Roman social and economic history; Latin epigraphy and literature; Roman archaeology. *Publ:* Auth, Romans on the Bay of Naples, Harvard Univ, 70; CIL X, 1792: A municipal notable of the Augustan Age, Harvard Studies Class Philol, 72; auth, Eighteen unedited Latin inscriptions from Puteoli and vicinity, Am J Archaeol, 73; auth, Puteoli in the second century of the Roman Empire, J Roman Studies, 74; Municipal notables of Imperial Ostia, Am J Philol, 76; The status of traders in the Roman world, Studies in Honor of G F Else, 77; contribr & co-ed, Ancient and Modern: Studies in Honor of G F Else, 77; auth, Ville marittime sul Golfo di Napoli, Atti Lincei, Rome, 77. *Mailing Add:* Dept of Classics Univ of Mich Ann Arbor MI 48109

DARST, DAVID HIGH, b Greensboro, NC, June 8, 43; m 69; c 2. GOLDEN AGE SPANISH LITERATURE. *Educ:* Univ of the South, AB, 65; Univ NC, Chapel Hill, MA, 67; Univ Ky, PhD(Span), 70. *Prof Exp:* Asst prof, 70-76, assoc prof span, 76-81, asst dir humanities, 78-81, FULL PROF SPAN & ASSOC DIR HUMANITIES, FLA STATE UNIV, 81- *Concurrent Pos:* Nat Endowment for Humantities grants, 74, 78 & 81-82. *Res:* Renaissance and baroque; humanities. *Publ:* Auth, The comic art of Tirso de Molina, Estudios de Hispanofila, The two worlds of La Ninfa del Cielo, Hisp Res & The thematic design of El Condemado por Desconfiado, Kentucky Romance Quart, 74; Tirso de Molina's The Trickster of Seville: A Critical Commentary, Simon & Schuster, 76; Lope de Vega y Cervantes o la modernidad literaria, Arbor, Madrid, 77; Juan Buscan, Twayne, 78; Andrenio's perception of reality and the structure of El Criticon, Hispania, 77; Witchcraft in Spain: The testimony of Martin de Castanega's Treatise on Superstition and Witchcraft, Proc Am Philos Soc, 79. *Mailing Add:* Dept Mod Lang Fla State Univ Tallahassee FL 32306

DA SILVA, HERALDO GREGORIO, b Capelo, Faial, Azores, Dec 24, 37; US citizen; m 67; c 1. PORTUGUESE LANGUAGE & LITERATURE. *Educ:* Univ San Francisco, BS, 65; Vanderbilt Univ, EPDA dipl, 68; Univ Calif, Los Angeles, MA, 73, PhD(hisp lang & lit), 78. *Prof Exp:* Instr Span & French, Riverdale High Sch, 66-68; instr Span & Port, Sunset High Sch, 68-71; lectr Port, San Jose City Col, 74-75; LECTR PORT SAN JOSE STATE UNIV, 74-, COORDR PORT BILING CREDENTIAL, 81- *Concurrent Pos:* Staff writer, Portuguese Tribune Inc, 80-; vis lectr, Univ Calif, Santa Barbara, summer, 82. *Mem:* Am Asn Teachers Span & Port. *Res:* Portuguese literature of 19th and 20th centuries; Brazilian literature of 19th and 20th centuries; Portuguese-American history, California. *Publ:* Contribr, Acorianos no Sul do Brasil, J Port, 73; Bibliography of Instructional Materials for the Teaching of Portuguese, Calif State Dept Educ, 76; Varanda da Universidade, Portuguese Tribune, 79 & 82; Portuguese Religious Celebrations in the Azores and California, The Oakland Museum, 81; A Quadra Popular Portuguesa, Crossroads, Univ Calif, Los Angeles, 81; auth, Acorianidade na Prosa de Vitorino Nemesio, Imprensa Nac Publ, 82. *Mailing Add:* Apt 5 2245 Lanai Ave San Jose CA 95122

DA SILVA, ZENIA S, b New York, NY, Feb 21, 25; m 46; c 2. SPANISH. *Educ:* NY Univ, BA, 44, PhD, 55; Univ Calif, Berkeley, MA, 45. *Prof Exp:* Asst instr Spanish, Univ Calif, 44-46; tutor, Queens Col, NY, 46-50; from instr to asst prof, NY Univ, 55-60; from instr to assoc prof, 60-75, PROF SPAN, HOFSTRA UNIV, 75- *Honors & Awards:* Dona de la Orden del Merito Civil, King Juan Carlos of Spain - Ministerio de Relaciones Exteriores, 77. *Mem:* Am Asn Teachers Span & Port (vpres & pres, 73-74). *Res:* Spanish and Spanish-American literature; linguistic studies. *Publ:* Auth, Usted y Yo, 2nd ed, 74, Nuestro Mundo, 2nd ed, 75 & Vuelo, 2nd ed, 77, Macmillan; Spanish: A Short Course, 76, On with Spanish, 2nd ed, 77, Beginning Spanish, 4th ed, 78 & A Concept Approach to Spanish, 4th ed, 79, Harper & Row; En Espanol, Por Favor, 3 Vols, Macmillan, 79. *Mailing Add:* Dept of Span Hofstra Univ Hempstead NY 11550

DASSONVILLE, MICHEL, b Lille, France, Dec 27, 27; US citizen; m 49; c 3. FRENCH LITERATURE. *Educ:* Univ Lille, BA, 46, Lic es Let, 48; Univ Sacre-Coeur, MA, 51; Laval Univ, DLet, 53. *Prof Exp:* Asst prof French lit, Laval Univ, 53-58; charge de cours, Cath Inst Paris, 58-60; from vis asst prof to assoc prof, 60-63, PROF FRENCH LIT, UNIV TEX, AUSTIN, 63- *Concurrent Pos:* Res grants, French Govt, 53 & 58 & Can Arts Coun, 57; Casgrain Prize, 58, Minnie Stevens Piper prof, 65; cult secy, Alliance Francaise, Paris, 58-60; pres, Alliance Francaise, Austin, Tex, 63-67. *Honors & Awards:* Chevalier des Palmes Academiques, French Govt, 76. *Mem:* S Cent Mod Lang Asn. *Res:* Sixteenth century French literature. *Publ:* Auth, La Dissertation Litteraire, 55; Cremazie, Fides, Montreal, 56; L'Analyse de Textes,Laval Univ, 57; Frechette, Fides, Montreal, 58; Initiation a la Rech Litt, Laval Univ, 59; Definition formelle de l'hymne ronsardien, 62 & Interpretation nouvelle des Amours, 66, Bibliot d'Humanisme et Renaissance; La Dialectique de Pierre de la Ramee, 1555, 63 & Ronards, Vol I, 68, Vol II, 70 & Vol III, 76, Droz, Switz; D'un autre differend entre Ronsard et Du Bellay, Studies Lett Francese, 73. *Mailing Add:* Sutton Hall 215 Univ of Tex Austin TX 78712

DAUER, DOROTHEA W, b Cleve, Ger, June 29, 17; US citizen, m 37; c 1. LANGUAGES & LITERATURE. *Educ:* Univ Paris, MA, 37; Japanese Lang Sch, Tokyo, dipl, 43; Univ Tex, PHD, 53. *Prof Exp:* Asst prof Ger & French, State Music Acad & lectr sci Ger, Meteorol Univ Tokyo, Japan, 40-43; coord & interpreter, inform & educ off, Gen Hq US Armed Forces, Tokyo, 45-46; Civil Serv instr Ger & French, US Army Educ Ctr, Tokyo, 46-48; Civil Ser instr Ger, Univ Md, Overseas Prog, 54-55; asst prof Ger, French, & Japanese, Southwestern Univ, 48-50; asst prof Ger & French, Univ Va, 55-56; assoc prof Ger, French & philos, Tex Lutheran Col, 56-57 & Monmouth Col, NJ, 57-63; prof Ger & French & chmn dept mod lang, Ky Wesleyan Col, 63-64; prof mod lang & chmn dept, Marshall Univ, 64-66; chmn dept, 66-68, prof, 66-80, EMER PROF GER, UNIV HAWAII, MANOA, 80- *Mem:* MLA; Am Asn Teachers Ger (pres Hawaii chap, 67-70). *Res:* Buddhist influence on German literature; Schopenhauer-Wagner-Nietzsche. *Publ:* Auth, German Grammar, Meteorol Univ Tokyo, 42, Richard Wagner--Parsifal, Metrop Opera News, 56; Schopenhauer as Transmitter of Buddhist Ideas, Lange, Bern, 68; Nietzsche and the concept of time, In: The Study of Time-2, Springer Verlag, 74; Richard Wagner and Buddism, Tristan and Isolde and the victors, Eastern Buddist, 10/76. *Mailing Add:* 242 Kaalawai Place Honolulu HI 96816

DAUGHERTY, HOWARD, b Joplin, Mo, July 25, 37; m 65; c 3. SLAVIC LANGUAGES & LITERATURES. *Educ:* Univ Wash, BA, 60, PhD(Slavic), 67. *Prof Exp:* ASST PROF SLAVIC LANG & LIT, UNIV COLO, 67- *Concurrent Pos:* Vis prof, Univ Calif, Riverside, 70. *Mem:* Am Asn Advan Slavic Studies; Am Asn Teachers Slavic & EEurop Lang. *Res:* Nineteenth century Russian literature; contemporary Polish literature. *Mailing Add:* Dept of Slavic Univ of Colo Boulder CO 80302

DAUSTER, FRANK NICHOLAS, b Irvington, NJ, Feb 5, 25; m 49; c 2. SPANISH. *Educ:* Rutgers Univ, AB, 49, MA, 50; Yale Univ, PhD(Span), 53. *Prof Exp:* From instr to asst prof Romance lang, Wesleyan Univ, 50-55; from asst prof to assoc prof, 55-61, PROF ROMANCE LANG, RUTGERS UNIV, NEW BRUNSWICK, 61- *Concurrent Pos:* Mem, Soc Sci Res Coun-Am Coun Learned Soc joint comt Latin Am, 66-68. *Mem:* MLA; Am Asn Teachers Span & Port; Inst Int Lit Iberoam. *Res:* Contemporary Latin America, particularly the theater and poetry. *Publ:* Auth, Breve Historia de la Poesia Mexicana, 56, Ensayos sobre Poesia Mexicana, 63 & Breve Historia del Teatre Hispanoamericano, Siglox XIX-XX, 66, 2nd ed, 73, Studium; co-ed, Literatura de Hispanoamericana, Harcourt, 70; auth, Xavier Villaurrutia, Twayne, 71; co-ed, En un acto, Van Nostrand, 74; Ensayos sobre Teatro Hispanoamericana, Sepsetentas, 75; co-ed, 9 dramaturgos hispanamericanos, Sinol, 79. *Mailing Add:* 159 Lakeside Dr N Piscataway NJ 08854

DAVEY, DONALD WILLIAM, b Omaha, Nebr, Nov 23, 44; m 68; c 2. SPANISH, PORTUGUESE. *Educ:* Univ Notre Dame, BA, 66; Univ Fla, PhD(Span), 74. *Prof Exp:* Interim instr Span, Univ Fla, 69-70; instr, Univ Wis-Whitewater, 70-74; asst prof, 74-78, ASSOC PROF SPAN, OHIO NORTHERN UNIV, 78- *Mem:* MLA. *Res:* Contemporary Spanish American prose; Spanish and Latin American theater. *Mailing Add:* Dept of Foreign Lang Ohio Northern Univ Ada OH 45810

DAVIAU, DONALD G, b Medway, Mass, Sept 30, 27; m 50. GERMAN. *Educ:* Clark Univ, BA, 50; Univ Calif, MA, 52, PhD, 55. *Prof Exp:* From instr to assoc prof Ger, 55-75, chmn dept Ger & Russ, 69-75, PROF GER, UNIV CALIF, RIVERSIDE, 75- *Concurrent Pos:* Ed, Mod Austrian Lit, 71- *Honors & Awards:* Ehrenkreuz für Wissenschaft und Kunst, Austrian Govt, 77. *Mem:* MLA; Am Asn Teachers Ger; Int Arthur Schnitzler Res Asn (pres, 78-); Hugo von Hofmannsthal Gesellschaft; Am Coun for Study Austrian Lit (pres, 80-). *Res:* Modern Austrian and German literature. *Publ:* Co-ed, The Correspondence of Arthur Schnitzler and Raoul Auernheimer, Univ NC, 72; auth, The concept of Zufall in the writings of Friedrich Dürrenmatt, Ger Rev, 72; The correspondence of Hugo von Hofmannsthal and Raoul Auernheimer, Mod Austrian Lit, 74; coauth, The Ariadne auf Naxos of Hugo von Hofmannsthal and Richard Strauss, Univ NC, 76; Hermann Bahr and decadence, Mod Austrian Lit, 77; auth, The Letters of Arthur Schnitzler to Hermann Bahr, Univ NC, 78; Das junge und das jungste Wien, In: Österreichiche Gegenwart, Francke Verlag, 80; Hermann Bahr and the secessionist art movement in Vienna, In: The Turn of the Century, Bouvier Verlag, 81. *Mailing Add:* Dept of Lit & Lang Univ Calif Riverside CA 92521

DAVIDHEISER, JAMES CHARLES, b Reading, Pa; c 1. FOREIGN LANGUAGE, LITERATURE. *Educ:* La Salle Col, BA, 63; Univ Pittsburgh, MA & PhD(Ger lang & lit), 72. *Prof Exp:* Instr English, Univ Mainz, 67-68; instr Ger, Univ Pittsburgh, 68-69; asst prof Ger lang & lit, Univ Del, 69-76, fac res grant, 73; ASSOC PROF GER & CHMN DEPT, UNIV OF THE SOUTH, 76- *Concurrent Pos:* Fulbright grant, 77; Exxon Found grant, 81. *Mem:* Am Asn Teachers Ger; Lessing Soc; Southern Comp Lit Asn. *Res:* Modern German literature; comparative literature; 18th century literature. *Publ:* Auth, Six steps towards more stimulating literature classes, MLAPV Newslett, 74; German literature in translation, Die Unterrichtspraxis, 75; An interdisciplinary approach to the teaching of foreign languages, Mod Lang J, 77; Interim measures for the promotion of foreign language study, Asn Depts Foreign Lang Bull, 78; The role of oaths in the Sturm und Drang drama, Lessing Yearbk, 78. *Mailing Add:* Dept of Ger Univ of the South Sewanee TN 37375

DAVIDSON, DAN E, b Wichita, Kans, Sept 18, 44; m 76; c 2. RUSSIAN LANGUAGE & LITERATURE. *Educ:* Univ Kans, BA, 66; Harvard Univ, AM, 71, PhD(Slavic), 72. *Prof Exp:* Instr Slavic, Harvard Univ, 69-71; asst prof Russ, Amherst Col, 72-75, assoc prof, 75-76; ASSOC PROF RUSS, BRYN MAWR COL, 76- *Concurrent Pos:* Vis assoc prof, Harvard Univ, summer 75, Columbia Univ, summer, 75, Univ Pa, spring 77. *Mem:* Am Coun Teachers Russ (pres, 75-80); MLA; Am Asn Teachers Slavic & East Europ Lang; Am Asn Advan Slavic Studies; Am Coun Teaching Foreign Lang. *Res:* Russian literature, 1780-1840; study and teaching of Russian language. *Publ:* Auth, Karamzin's critical vocabulary, Mnemozina, Fink Verlag, 73; co-ed, Soviet-American Russian Language Contribution, Am Asn Teachers Slavic & East Europ Lang, Inc, 75 & 77; coauth, Russian: Stage One & Russian: Stage One Workbook, Russian Lang Publ, Moscow, 80 & 82; co-ed & contribr, Soviet-American contributions to the study & teaching of Russian: Theory, strategies & tools, Russ Lang J, No 125, 82. *Mailing Add:* Dept Russ Bryn Mawr Col Bryn Mawr PA 19010

DAVIDSON, HUGH MACCULLOUGH, b Lanett, Ala, Jan 21, 18; m 51; c 1. ROMANCE LANGUAGES. *Educ:* Univ Chicago, AB, 38, PhD, 46. *Hon Degrees:* MA, Dartmouth Col, 56. *Prof Exp:* From instr to asst prof French, Univ Chicago, 46-53, asst dean col, 49-52, chmn col French staff, 51-53; asst prof Romance lang, Dartmouth Col, 53-56, prof, 56-62, chmn dept, 57-59; prof French, Ohio State Univ, 62-76; mem fac, 76-79, PROF FRENCH, UNIV VA, 79- *Concurrent Pos:* Carnegie fel, Univ Chicago, 48-49; Fulbright res scholar, France, 59-60; Nat Found Arts & Humanities sr fel, 67-68; mem ed comt, PMLA, 68-73. *Mem:* Am Asn Teachers Fr; MLA; Int Asn Fr Studies. *Res:* Seventeenth and 18th century French literature; methods of literary study and criticism; literature and philosophy. *Publ:* Auth, Conflict and resolution in Pascal's Pensees, 2/58 & Descartes on the utility of the passions, 2/60, Romanic Rev; The literary arts of Boileau and Longinus, In: Studies in 17th Century French Literature, Cornell Univ, 62; Audience, Words and Art, Ohio State Univ, 65. *Mailing Add:* Dept of French Univ of Va Charlottesville VA 22903

DAVIES, MARK INGRAHAM, b Boston, Mass, Feb 4, 44; m 67; c 2. CLASSICAL ART & LITERATURE. *Educ:* Princeton Univ, BA, 65, MA, 69, PhD(class archaeol), 71. *Prof Exp:* Asst prof classics, Davidson Col, 71-73; dir, Iconographical Lexicon Class Mythology Ctr, 73-76; ASST PROF, DAVIDSON COL, 76- *Concurrent Pos:* Am Coun Learned Soc grant-in-aid, 78; Nat Endowment for Humanities summer grant, 82. *Mem:* Archaeological Inst Am; Vereinigung der Freunde Antiker Kunst; Soc Promotion Hellenic Studies; Am Philol Asn; Int Asn Class Archaeol. *Res:* Classical Art, classical literature; classical mythology. *Publ:* Auth, Thoughts on the Oresteia before Aischylos, Bull de Correspondance Hellenique, 69; The suicide of Ajax: A bronze etruscan statuette from the Käppeli collection, 71 & Ajax and Tekmessa: A cup by the Brygos Painter in the Bareiss collection, 73, Antike Kunst; The death of Aigisthos: A fragmentary stamnos by the Copenhagen Painter, Opuscula Romana, 73; The reclamation of Helen, Antike Kunst, 77; Sailing, rowing, and sporting in one's cups on the wine-dark sea, AIA Symposium Athens Comes of Age, 78; Antenor I & II, Iconographical Lexicon Class Mythology, Vol I, 81; The tickle and sneeze of love, Am J Archaeol, 82. *Mailing Add:* Dept of Classics Davidson Col Davidson NC 28036

DAVIES, MICHAEL BRENT, b Salt Lake City, Utah, Apr 15, 46. CLASSICS, INDO-EUROPEAN LINGUISTICS. *Educ:* Univ Utah, BA, 67; Univ Tex, MA, 73, PhD (Greek), 78. *Prof Exp:* Asst instr Latin & Greek, Univ Tex, 74-77; instr Latin & Greek, Univ Utah, 77-78, asst prof, 78-80; MEM FAC, DEPT CLASSICS, FLA STATE UNIV, 80- *Mem:* Am Philol Asn. *Res:* Greek satyr drama; Roman satire. *Mailing Add:* Dept of Classics Fla State Univ Tallahassee FL 32306

DAVIS, ALVA LEROY, b Bicknell, Ind, May 17, 15; m 39. ENGLISH LINGUISTICS. *Educ:* Ind State Univ, AB, 38; Univ Mich, MA, 40, PhD(English ling), 48. *Prof Exp:* Asst prof English, Western Reserve Univ, 48-52; from assoc prof to prof English as foreign lang, Am Univ, 52-59, dir Am lang ctr, 52-59; dir, Turkish Air Force Lang Sch, 60-61; prof humanities & chmn dept, Delta Col, 61-63; prof, 63-80, EMER PROF ENGLISH LING & DIR CTR AM ENGLISH LIT, ILL INST TECHNOL, 80- *Concurrent Pos:* Fel, Ohio State Univ, 51; consult, US Off Educ, 64-66. *Mem:* Nat Asn Foreign Student Affairs (vpres, 55-57); Am Dialect Soc; Ling Soc Am; MLA; NCTE. *Res:* English as a foreign language; American dialectology. *Mailing Add:* Dept of Humanities Ill Inst of Technol Chicago IL 60616

DAVIS, GAROLD N, b Downey, Idaho, Oct 14, 32; m 54; c 5. GERMAN & COMPARATIVE LITERATURE. *Educ:* Brigham Young Univ, BA, 58, MA, 59; Johns Hopkins Univ, PhD(Ger lit), 62. *Prof Exp:* Instr Ger, Univ Pa, 62-63; asst prof, Southern Ore Col, 63-66; asst prof Ger & comp lit, Univ Colo, 66-68; PROF GER, BRIGHAM YOUNG UNIV, 68-, ASSOC DEAN, COL HUMANITIES, 80- *Mem:* MLA. *Res:* Anglo-German literary relations; Romanticism; Austrian Heimat literature. *Publ:* Auth, German Thought and Culture in England 1700-1770, Univ NC Studies Comp Lit, 68; Anglo-German cultural relations and the Thirty Years' War, Bull Rocky Mountain Mod Lang Asn, 6/68; Dei Idee Heimat und ihr forleben in der Österreichischen Literatur, In: Österreichhische Gegenwart: Die moderne Literatur und ihr Verhältnis zur Tradition, Grancke Verlag, Bern, 80. *Mailing Add:* Dept of Ger Lang Brigham Young Univ Provo UT 84602

DAVIS, GIFFORD, b Portland, Maine, June 11, 06; m 30; c 2. ROMANCE LANGUAGES. *Educ:* Bowdoin Col, AB, 27; Harvard Univ, AM, 28, PhD, 33. *Prof Exp:* Tutor Romance lang, Harvard Univ, 29-30; from instr to prof, 30-76, dir undergrad Span studies, 48-57 & 64-76, chmn dept, 57-64, dir sch Span studies, 50-55, EMER PROF ROMANCE LANG, DUKE UNIV, 76- *Mem:* MLA; Am Asn Teachers Span & Port. *Res:* Sentiment of nationality in medieval Spanish literature; sources of the poems of Alfonso Onceno; 19th century novel and criticism. *Publ:* Auth, Reception of naturalism in Spain. *Mailing Add:* Dept of Romance Lang Duke Univ Durham NC 27706

DAVIS, HUGH HAMLIN, b Pomeroy, Ohio, Nov 18, 09. CLASSICAL LANGUAGES, HISTORY. *Educ:* Ohio Univ, AB, 32; Ind Univ, MA, 35; Univ Cincinnati, PhD (classics), 50. *Prof Exp:* Instr class lang, Ohio Univ, 36-37; asst prof, Fordham Univ, 50-53; from asst prof to prof, 53-75, chmn dept, 59-75, lectr classics, 75-78, EMER PROF CLASSICS, LE MOYNE COL, NY, 76- *Concurrent Pos:* Comdr, Order of the Crown of Italy, 46. *Mem:* Am Philol Asn; Mediaeval Acad Am; Renaissance Soc Am; Erasmus of Rotterdam Soc. *Res:* Latin textual criticism; classicl tradition in the Middle Ages; history of the papacy in the Counter Reformation. *Publ:* Auth, Cicero's burial, Phoenix, winter 58; A rosary confraternity charter of 1579 and the Cardinal of Santa Susanna, Cath Hist Rev, 10/62; The De rithmis of Alberic of Monte Cassino: A critical edition, Mediaeval Studies, 66; A few proverbs in distichs, Proverbium, 73; A cache of proverbs alongside Pescetti, Class Folia, 74; Two notes on Erasmus as translator of Plutarch, Erasmus English, 78. *Mailing Add:* Dept of Foreign Lang Le Moyne Col Syracuse NY 13214

DAVIS, J CARY, b Pinckneyville, Ill, May 18, 05; m 36; c 2. ROMANCE LANGUAGES. *Educ:* Southern Ill Univ, BEd, 29; Univ Chicago, AM, 30, PhD(Romance lang), 36. *Prof Exp:* From instr to asst prof French, 30-39, assoc prof French & Span, 39-52, prof Romance lang, 52-71, acting chmn dept for lang, 50-51 & 61, chmn dept, 64-67, EMER PROF FOR LANG, SOUTHERN ILL UNIV CARBONDALE, 71- *Concurrent Pos:* Mem fac, NDEA Insts Span, Univ S Dak, 59, S Dak State Col, 61 & Bradley Univ, 63-65; ed, Latin Am Classics, Southern Ill Univ Press, 64- *Honors & Awards:* Mitre Medal, Hisp Soc Am. *Mem:* MLA; Am Asn Teachers Span & Port. *Res:* Linguistics; Romance literature. *Publ:* Auth, Caminos de Mexico, Heath, 62; Recuerdos de Guatemala, Southern Ill Univ, 70; coauth, An Introduction to Romance Linguistics Southern Ill Univ, 75. *Mailing Add:* 38 Mira Las Olas San Clemente CA 92672

DAVIS, JACK EMORY, b Holland, Mich, May 11, 13; m 71; c 1. SPANISH. *Educ:* Univ Ariz, BA, 47; Tulane Univ, MA, 48, PhD(Span), 56. *Prof Exp:* From teaching asst to instr Span, Tulane Univ, 47-49; from instr to assoc prof, 49-68, prof span, 68-78, EMER PROF ROMANCE LANG, UNIV ARIZ, 78- *Res:* Latin American literature; Latin American Spanish linguistics; Spanish American bibliography. *Publ:* Translr, Aztec Thought and Culture, Univ Okla, 63; auth, Estudio lexicografico de El Periquillo Sarniento, Rev lit Iberoam; The Spanish of Argentina and Uruguay: An Annotated Bibliography for 1940-1978, Mouton Publ, Janua Linguarum Ser, Hague, 82. *Mailing Add:* Dept of Romance Lang Univ Ariz Tucson AZ 85721

DAVIS, JAMES HERBERT, JR, b Durham, NC, Aug 15, 32; m 69. FRENCH LITERATURE. *Educ:* Univ NC, BA, 53, MA, 55, PhD(Romance lang), 63. *Prof Exp:* Instr French, Haw River High Sch, 56-57; instr, Perkiomen Prep Sch, 57-59; instr, Girard Col, 59-60; instr, Univ NC, 62-63; asst prof, 63-67, ASSOC PROF FRENCH, UNIV GA, 67- *Mem:* MLA; Am Soc 18th Century Studies; Am Asn Teachers Fr. *Res:* Eighteenth-century drama; 17th century drama. *Publ:* Auth, Tragic Theory and the Eighteenth-century French Critics, Univ NC, 67; Pierre Corneille and the piece retouchee of the 18th century, Studies Philol, 67; contribr, Renaissance and Other Studies in Honor of William Leon Wiley, Univ NC, 68; auth, Jean-Baptiste Rousseau and the 18th century piece restituee, Ky Romance Quart, 69; ed, Alexandre Hardy, La Force du Sang, Univ Ga, 72; coauth, Calderon's El Alcalde de Zalamea in eighteenth century France, Ky Romance Quart, 76; Fenelon, Twayne, 79; The Stage in the 18th Century, Garland, 81. *Mailing Add:* Dept of Romance Lang Univ of Ga Athens GA 30602

DAVIS, JOE EDWARD, JR, b Sterling City, Tex, Oct 27, 15; m 57; c 1. SPANISH, LATIN AMERICAN STUDIES. *Educ:* Univ Tex, BS, 38, MA, 49, PhD(Latin Am studies & Span lit), 51. *Prof Exp:* Teacher pub schs, Tex, 38-39, 40-41; PROF SPAN, JUDSON COL, 51-, CHMN DIV HUMANITIES, 79- *Mem:* AM Asn Teachers Span & Port; Am Coun Teaching Foreign Lang. *Res:* Tirso de Molino and Moliere on the Don Juan theme; Andres Bello and Lord Byron; teaching Spanish language and literature and Hispanic culture at the undergraduate level. *Mailing Add:* Dept of Span Judson Col Marion AL 36756

DAVIS, JOHN T, b Columbus, Ohio, Dec 15, 42; m 67. CLASSICAL PHILOLOGY. *Educ:* Univ Mich, AB, 64, MA, 65, PhD(clasics), 67. *Prof Exp:* Asst prof, 67-73, ASSOC PROF CLASSICS, OHIO STATE UNIV, 73- *Mem:* Am Philol Asn; Class Asn Midwest & South. *Res:* Roman elegy; Catullus; Orid. *Publ:* Auth, Fides and the Construction of Propertius' Books I and IV, Univ Microfilms, 67; Poetic counterpoint: Catullua 72, Am J Philol, 71; Propertius periculum in I.15, Class J, 74; Dramatic Pairings in the Elegies of Propertius and Orid, Noctes Romanae, 77; Rist Amor: Aspects of literary Burlesque in Orid's Amores, Aufstiegund Niedergang der Romishen Welt, 2.4: 2460-2506. *Mailing Add:* Dept of Classics Ohio State Univ Columbus OH 43210

DAVIS, JUDITH MARY, b St Paul, Minn, Aug 7, 36; m 71; c 2. MEDIEVAL FRENCH, COMPARATIVE LITERATURE. *Educ:* St Louis Univ, BS, 58; Univ Minn, Minneapolis, MA, 68, PhD(French), 72. *Prof Exp:* From instr to asst prof French & comp lit, Univ Wis-Green Bay, 70-73; instr women's studies, Univ Wis Exten, 74; adj asst prof & prog officer tech writing, Sch Pub & Environ Affairs, Ind Univ, 74-77; dir commun, 77-79, DIR SPONSORED PROGS, GOSHEN COL, 79- *Concurrent Pos:* Consult commun & orgn develop for various govt agencies & pvt businesses. *Mem:* MLA; Int Arthurian Soc; Mediaeval Acad Am; Int Courtly Soc; Soc Rencesvals. *Res:* Thirteenth century French romance; poetry of the troubadours; literature of courtly love. *Publ:* Auth, Christine de Pisan and chauvinist diplomacy, Female Studies, 72; coauth, Amour Courtois, the Medieval Ideal of Love: A Bibliography, Univ Louisville, 73; auth, A fuller reading of Guillaume IX's Companho, Faray un Vers . . . , Romance Notes, 75; The elusive Visions d'Oger le Danois, Libr Chronicle, 77. *Mailing Add:* Sponsored Progs Goshen Col Goshen IN 46526

DAVIS, KENNETH WALDRON, English. See Vol II

DAVIS, PHILIP WAYNE, b Ft Worth, Tex, Nov 13, 39; m 68; c 2. LINGUISTICS, RUSSIAN. *Educ:* Univ Tex, Austin, BA, 61; Cornell Univ, PhD(Slavic ling), 65. *Prof Exp:* From instr to asst prof Russ & ling, Simon Fraser Univ, 65-69; asst prof, 69-74, assoc prof, 74-81, PROF LING & ANTHROP, RICE UNIV, 81- *Concurrent Pos:* Co-ed, Glossa, 67- *Mem:* Ling Soc Am; Am Anthrop Asn; Soc Study Indigenous Lang Am. *Res:* Semantics and syntax; Salish languages; dialectology. *Publ:* Auth, A classification of the dissimilative jakan'e dialects of Russian, Orbis, 70; coauth, Lexical suffix copying in Bella Coola, Glossa & auth, Modern Theories of Language, Prentice-Hall, 73; coauth, Bella Coola nominal deixis, Lang, 75; Bella Coola deictic roots, 76 & Bella Coola su, 77, Int J Am Ling; coauth, Knowledge, Consciousness and Language, Rice Univ Studies, 80; Bella Coola Texts, BC Provincial Mus, 80. *Mailing Add:* Dept of Anthrop Rice Univ Houston TX 77001

DAVIS, WILLIAM RICHARD, JR, b East Orange, NJ, June 28, 43; m 65. SPANISH LITERATURE. *Educ:* Rutgers Univ, New Brunswick, BA, 65; Univ NC, Chapel Hill, MA, 67; Univ KY, PhD(Span), 69. *Prof Exp:* Asst prof, 69-76, ASSOC PROF MOD LANG, MERCER UNIV, 76- *Mem:* Mediaeval Acad Am; Southeastern Medieval Asn; Am Folklore Soc; SAtlantic Mod Lang Asn. *Res:* Mediaeval Spanish literature; Renaissance Spanish literature; folklore. *Publ:* Auth, Expanding the language program, Southern Baptist Educr, 2/72; Mary and Merlin: An unusual alliance, Romance Notes, 1/73; Another aspect of the Virgin Mary in the Cantigas de Santa Maria, Rev Estudios Hispanicos, 1/74. *Mailing Add:* Dept of Mod Foreign Lang Mercer Univ Macon GA 31207

DAVISON, ALICE LOUISE, b Washington, DC, Sept 10, 40. LINGUISTICS. *Educ:* Bryn Mawr Col, BA, 62; Univ Chicago, MA, 69, PhD(ling), 73. *Prof Exp:* Prog asst, Div Foreign Studies, US Off Educ, 62-66; asst prof ling, State Univ NY Stony Brook, 70-77; VIS ASST PROF LING, UNIV ILL, CHAMPAIGN-URBANA, 77- *Concurrent Pos:* Res stipend, State Univ NY Stony Brook Res Found, 75; vis lectr, U E R Scientifique de Luminy, Marseille, 78. *Honors & Awards:* Am Inst Indian Studies Award, 80. *Mem:* Ling Soc Am; Can Ling Asn; Ling Asn Gt Brit. *Res:* Syntax and pragmatics; South Asian languages; speech acts. *Publ:* Auth, On the semantic representation of performative verbs, In: J Pragmatics, 79; Linguistics and the measurement of readability: The case of Raising, In: Metatheory III, Application of Linguistic Theory in the Human Sciences, Mich State Univ, 79; Peculiar passives, In: Language, 80; Any as existential or universal?, In: The Semantics of Determiners, Croom Helm, London, 80; Linguistic analysis and the law, In: Language Uses and the Uses of Language, Georgetown Univ Press, 80; Contextual effects on generic idefinites, In: Variation Omnibus, Studies Ling Sci, 80 & Ling Res, 81; Syntactic and semantic indeterminacy resolved: A mostly pragmatic analysis of the Hindi conjunctive participle, In: Radical Pragmatics, Acad Press, 81; Markers of derived illocutionary force and the paradox of speech act modifiers, In: Cahiers de linguistique francaise III, 81. *Mailing Add:* Dept of Ling Univ of Ill Urbana IL 61801

DAVISON, JEAN MARGARET, b Glens Falls, NY, Apr 19, 22. CLASSICAL LANGUAGES, ANCIENT HISTORY. *Educ:* Univ Vt,AB, 44; Yale Univ, AM, 50, PhD(class archaeol), 57; Univ Ital Stranieri, Perugia, dipl, 60. *Prof Exp:* Cryptanalyst, US Dept War, 44-45; foreign serv clerk, US Dept State, Athens, 45-46 & Vienna, 47-49; instr ancient hist, Latin, Greek & Greek art, 55-59, from asst prof to prof, 59-72, ROBERTS PROF CLASS LANG & LIT, UNIV VT, 72- *Concurrent Pos:* Am Philos Asn res grant, 67-68; mem managing comt, Am Sch Class Studies, Athens, 65, mem exec comt, 73, vis prof, 74-75. *Mem:* Archaeol Inst Am; Vergilian Soc Am; Class Asn New England; Am Sch Orient Res; Asn Field Archaeol. *Res:* Greek Archaeology; Homeric studies; pre-Roman Italy. *Publ:* Auth, Attic Geometric Workshops, Yale Univ, 61; Seven Italic tomb groups from Narce, Olschki, Florence, 72. *Mailing Add:* Dept of Classics Univ of Vt Burlington VT 05401

DAVISON, NED J, b Salt Lake City, Utah, Oct 3, 26; m 48, 72. HISPANIC LANGUAGES & LITERATURE. *Educ:* Univ Utah, BA, 49; Univ Calif, Los Angeles, MA, 52, PhD, 57. *Prof Exp:* Instr Romance lang, Col Idaho, 54; from instr to asst prof, Univ Ore, 54-63; from assoc prof to prof Span, Univ NMex, 63-70; PROF SPAN AM LIT, UNIV UTAH, 70- *Concurrent Pos:* Adv ed, Studies in 20th Century Lit, 77. *Mem:* Rocky Mountain Mod Lang Asn; Am Asn Teachers Span & Port; Asn Lit & Ling Comput. *Res:* Spanish American poetry; literary computing. *Publ:* Coauth, Lecturas Intermedias, Harper, 65; auth, Sobre Eduardo Barrios y otros: Estudios y Cronicas, Foreign Bks, 66; The Concept of Modernism in Hispanic Criticism, 66 & coauth, A Student Guide to Critical Spanish, 67, Pruett, auth, Eduardo Barrios, Twayne, 70; Particles: Poems from 1960-1970, Damuir, 71; El concepto de modernismo en la critica hispanica, Nova, 71; Sound Patterns in a Poem of Jose Marti, Damuir, 75. *Mailing Add:* Dept of Lang Univ of Utah Salt Lake City UT 84112

DAVISSON, MARY HELEN THOMSEN, b Baltimore, Md, Dec 5, 52; m 80; c 1. CLASSICAL LANGUAGES. *Educ:* Brown Univ, AB, 74, MA, 74; Univ Calif, Berkeley, PhD(class), 79. *Prof Exp:* Lectr, Univ Calif, Berkeley, 79-81; ASST PROF CLASS, UNIV VA, 81- *Mem:* Am Philol Asn. *Res:* Ovid's exile poetry; Elegy; Latin literature. *Publ:* Auth, Omnia Naturae Praepostera Legibus Ibunt: Adunata, The Class J, 12/80; The functions of openings in Ovid's Exile Epistles, Class Bull, 12/81; Duritia and creativity in exile: Epistulae ex Ponto 4.10, Class Antiquity, 82. *Mailing Add:* Class Dept Univ of Va Charlottesville VA 22903

DAWSON, CLAYTON L, b Seattle, Wash, Mar 25, 21; m 51. SLAVIC LANGUAGES & LITERATURE. *Educ:* Univ Wash, BA, 49; Harvard Univ, MA, 51, PhD(Slavic lang & lit), 54. *Prof Exp:* Asst prof Russ, Syracuse Univ, 53-57; lang adv, Air Force Inst Technol, Ohio, 57-59; prof & chmn dept Slavic lang, Syracuse Univ, 59-66, assoc dir EEurop lang prog, 59-66; head dePt, 66-74, PROF SLAVIC LANG & LIT, UNIV ILL, URBANA, 66- *Concurrent Pos:* Mem subcomt grants Slavic & EEurop studies, Am Coun Learned Soc, 66- *Mem:* Ling Soc Am; Am Asn Teachers Slavic & EEurop Lang (pres, 69-70). *Res:* Modern Russian language; history of the Russian language; modern and historical Slavic languages. *Publ:* Coauth, Modern Russian I, 64, auth, Instructor's Manual to Modern Russian, 64 & coauth, Modern Russian II, 65, Harcourt; auth, Intensive Russian (6 vols), Syracuse Univ. *Mailing Add:* 1106 Sliver St Urbana IL 61801

DAWSON, ROBERT LEWIS, b Buenos Aires, Arg, July 26, 43; US citizen. FRENCH LITERATURE, PORTUGUESE. *Educ:* Trinity Col, BA, 65; Yale Univ, MPhil, 68, PhD(French), 72. *Prof Exp:* Actg asst prof French & Ital, Univ Santa Clara, Calif, 70-72; asst prof, Rol lins Col, Fla, 73-75; asst prof, 75-78, ASSOC PROF FRENCH, UNIV TEXAS, AUSTIN, 79- *Concurrent Pos:* Fel, La Fondation Camargo, Cassis, France, 72-73. *Mem:* Am Soc 18th Century Studies; Soc d-etude dix-huitieme siecle. *Res:* Eighteenth-century French literature. *Publ:* Auth, Baculard d'Arnaud: life & prose fiction, Studies on Voltaire & 18th Century, 76; ed, International Directory of 18th Century Research and Scholars, Int Soc 18th Century Studies, 79; Additions to the Bibliographies of 17th and 18th Century French Prose Fiction, Voltaire Found (in press). *Mailing Add:* Dept of French & Ital Univ of Tex Austin TX 78712

DAY, JAMES H, b Tulsa Co, Okla, Nov 25, 27; m 59; c 3. CLASSICAL LANGUAGES. *Educ:* Univ Okla, BA, 52; Harvard Univ, MA, 55; Univ Chicago, PhD, 60. *Prof Exp:* From instr to assoc prof, 58-76, PROF CLASSICS, VASSAR COL, 76- *Concurrent Pos:* Fulbright fel, Magdalen Col, Oxford Univ, 52-53; Harvard Univ traveling fel, Europe, 55-56. *Mem:* Am Philol Asn. *Res:* Aristotle; Aristophanes; Herodotus. *Publ:* Coauth, Aristotle's History of Athenian Democracy, Univ Calif, 62. *Mailing Add:* Dept of Classics Vassar Col Poughkeepsie NY 12601

DAY, LESLIE PRESTON, b Missoula, Mont, Oct 16, 44; m 76. CLASSICAL ARCHEOLOGY & LANGUAGES. *Educ:* Bryn Mawr Col, AB, 66; Univ Cincinnati, MA, 68, PhD(classics), 72. *Prof Exp:* Asst prof classics, Wilson Col, 72-74; instr, San Diego State Univ & instr Latin, Univ San Diego, 75-76; asst prof classics, Ind Univ, 76-77 & Wabash Col, 77-78; ASST PROF CLASSICS, COL WOOSTER, 78- *Mem:* Archaeol Inst Am; Am Class League. *Res:* Archaeology of Minoan Crete; Greek Dark Age archaeology; ancient Greek antiquarianism. *Publ:* Auth, Four Boiotian ape figurines in the J Paul Getty Museum, J Paul Getty Mus J, 77; contribr, Handbook to the Palace of Minos at Knossos, Ares Press, 79; coauth, Excavations and survey at Kavousi, Crete, 1978-81, Hesperia (in prep). *Mailing Add:* Dept of Class Studies Col of Wooster Wooster OH 44691

DAY, RICHARD MERTON, b Morristown, Minn, Apr 29, 36; m 56; c 1. FRENCH LANGUAGE & LITERATURE. *Educ:* Mankato State Col, BS, 61; Univ Ill, MA, 65; Univ Mo, PhD(Romance lang), 73. *Prof Exp:* Teacher French, Fergus Falls Pub Schs, Minn, 61-63; asst prof, 65-76, ASSOC PROF FRENCH, BEMIDJI STATE COL, 76-, CHMN DEPT MOD LANG, 73- *Mem:* Am Asn Teachers Fr. *Res:* Eighteenth century French novel. *Mailing Add:* Dept of Mod Lang Bemidji State Col Bemidji MN 56601

DAYAG, JOSEPH H, b Vienna, Austria, Mar 15, 10; US citizen; m 43; c 2. FOREIGN LANGUAGES. *Educ:* Class Col, Vienna, BA, 30; Univ Paris, PhD, 37; La State Univ, MS, 58. *Prof Exp:* Res adv, Univ Houston Libr, 58-60; assoc prof Ger & French, Midwestern Univ, 60-61; chief reference div, Boston Univ Libr, 61-63; asst dir, Brandeis Univ Libr, 63; assoc prof Ger, 63-66, chmn dept, 68-80, dir Ger grad studies, 71-80, prof, 66-80, EMER PROF GER LANG & LIT, EMMANUEL COL, MASS, 80- *Concurrent Pos:* Ger Acad Exchange Serv res scholar, 66. *Honors & Awards:* Officers Cross, Order of Merit, Fed Ger Repub, 66. *Mem:* MLA; Am Asn Teachers Ger; Hebrew Lang World Asn; Int Schnitzler Res Asn; Am Coun Studies Austrian Lit. *Res:* Thomas Mann Ges Socio-history of colonization; 18th and early 20th century German literature. *Publ:* Auth, La Colonisation Juive en Palestine, ses Etapes, ses Difficultes, Libr Lipschutz, Paris, 37; Schnitzler in französischer Sicht, In: Studies in Arthur Schnitzler, Univ NC, 63; The independent theater in Vienna against the background of German naturalism; In: Studies in Honor of S M Waxman, Boston Univ, 69. *Mailing Add:* Dept of Ger Lang & lit Emmanuel Col Boston MA 02115

DAYDI-TOLSON, SANTIAGO, b Vina del Mar, Chile, Apr 30, 43; m 77. SPANISH LITERATURE. *Educ:* Cath Univ Valparaiso, Lic, 68; Univ Kans, PhD(Span), 73. *Prof Exp:* Asst prof, Cath Univ Valparaiso, 68-69; vis lectr, Univ Kans, 69-70; asst prof, Fordham Univ, 73-77; ASST PROF SPAN, UNIV VA, 77- *Mem:* MLA; Am Asn Teachers Span & Port. *Publ:* Auth, Poesia Social: Un caso espanol contemporaneo, 69 & Gabriela Mistral y su Poema de Chile, In: Signos, 70, Cath Univ Valparaiso; Caracterization in Los de Abajo, Am Hisp, 76; La poetica de lo social: Sobre el lugar del canto de Jose Angel Valente, J Span Studies, 78; La figura del nino en Poema de Chile de Gabriela Mistral, In: El nino en las literaturas hispanicas, Ind Univ Pa, 79; Drinking: A narrative structural pattern in Mariano Azuela's Los de abajo, Ky Romance Quart, 80; Los efectos de la resonancia en la poesia de Jose Angel Valente, In: The Analysis of Literary Texts, 80 & ed, Vicente Aleixandre: A Critical Appraisal, 81, Bilingual Press. *Mailing Add:* Dept of Spanish Italian & Port Univ of Virginia Charlottesville VA 22903

DEAGON ANN, FLEMING, Classics, Creative Writing. See Vol II

DE AGUERO, EDUARDO, b San Ramon, Costa Rica, Dec 24, 30; US citizen. COMPARATIVE LITERATURE, ROMANCE LANGUAGES. *Educ:* Appalachian State Teachers Col, BS, 53; Cornell Univ, MA, 55, PhD(lit), 66. *Prof Exp:* Instr Span, Appalachian State Teachers Col, 53-54; asst prof, 56-70, ASSOC PROF MOD LANG, ITHACA COL, 70- *Concurrent Pos:* Mem acad adv bd, Ger, Schiller Col, Heidelberg, WGer, 70- *Mem:* MLA; Am Asn Teachers Span & Port; AAUP; Am Coun Teachers Foreign Lang. *Res:* Romance linguistics; philosophy; Spanish and Spanish-American literature. *Publ:* Auth, The Philosophical-Religious Thought of Unamuno (in Span), 68 & A Cultural Approach to Spanish Civilization, 68, Am Press; Dreams and Reality-Suenos y Realidad, Las Americas, 82. *Mailing Add:* Dept of Foreign Lang Ithaca Col Ithaca NY 14850

DEAN, RUTH JOSEPHINE, b New York, NY, Mar 10, 02. MEDIEVAL LITERATURE. *Educ:* Wellesley Col, AB, 22; Oxford Univ, BA, 24, MA, 28, DPhil, 38. *Hon Degrees:* Univ Pa, MA, 76, LHD, 79. *Prof Exp:* Reader English, fac let, Univ Lyon, 24-25; instr Romance lang & lit, Mt Holyoke Col, 34-40, from asst prof to prof French lang & lit, 40-67, Mary Lyon Prof, 66-67; lectr English & Romance lang & medieval bibliogr, Van Pelt Libr & univ, 69-72, vis prof English & Romance lang, 72-75, EMER PROF ENGLISH & ROMANCE LANG, UNIV PA, 75-; EMER MARY LYON PROF FRENCH LANG & LIT, MT HOLYOKE COL, 67- *Concurrent Pos:* Palmer fel, Am Assoc Univ Women, 43-44; mem, Inst Advan Studies, Princeton, NJ, 43-44, 50-51; Guggenheim fel, 48-49; mem grad fac & mem coun, Univ Mass, 61-67; Nat Endowment Humanities sr fel, 67-68; mem fel awards comt, Am Coun Learned Soc, Am Asn Univ Women & Assoc Res Coun. *Honors & Awards:* Officier d'Acad, 49, Officier, Palmes Academiques, 63. *Mem:* Fel Mediaeval Acad Am (vpres, 72-73, pres, 73-74); MLA (1st vpres, 62); Mod Humanities Res Asn; Anglo-Norman Text Soc (Am secy, 74-). *Res:* Anglo-Norman Paleography and literature; life and works of Nicholas Trevet. *Publ:* Coauth, The Rule of St Benedict: A Norman Prose Version, Blackwell, Oxford, 64; auth, The fair field of Anglo-Norman: Recent cultivation, Medievalia et Humanistica, 72; coauth, Un fragment anglo-normand de la Folie Tristan de Berne, Le Moyen Age, 73; Henry of Lancaster's Livre de Seyntz Medicines: New fragments of an Anglo-Norman work, Nat Libr Wales J, 73; A 15th-century Spanish book list, Libr Chronicle, 74; auth, Nicholas Trevet, historian, In: Medieval Learning and Literature, Clarendon, Oxford, 76. *Mailing Add:* 165 W 66th St New York NY 10023

DEANGELI, EDNA SOPHIA, b Philadelphia, Pa, Feb 23, 17; m 39; c 2. CLASSICAL LANGUAGES. *Educ:* Temple Univ, BS, 39; Univ Pa, AM, 60, PhD(classics), 65. *Prof Exp:* Asst instr classics, Univ Pa, 60-61; from instr to asst prof class lang, 62-69, assoc prof classics, 69-75, PROF CLASSICS & CHMN DEPT, LEHIGH UNIV, 75- *Mem:* Class Asn Atlantic States; Soc Am Archaeol. *Res:* Roman poetry of the Republic; literary criticism in antiquity; Medieval Latin poetry. *Publ:* Auth, The unity of Catullus 29, Class J, 11/69; A literary chill: Catullus 44, Class World, 68-69. *Mailing Add:* 246 Maginnes No 9 Lehigh Univ Bethlehem PA 18015

DE ARMAS, FREDERICK A, b Havana, Cuba, Feb 9, 45; nat US. COMPARATIVE LITERATURE, ROMANCE LANGUAGES. *Educ:* Stetson Univ, BA, 65; Univ NC, Chapel Hill, PhD(comp lit), 69. *Prof Exp:* From asst prof to assoc prof, 68-78, actg chmn, 79-80, PROF SPAN, LA STATE UNIV, BATON ROUGE, 78-, DIR GRAD STUDIES, 80- *Concurrent Pos:* Nat Endowment for Humanities summer grant, 79. *Mem:* MLA; Am Comp Lit Asn; Am Asn Teachers Span & Port; Asoc Int Hispanistas; Renaissance Soc Am. *Res:* Spanish Golden Age literature; Spanish-French literary relationships during the 17th century. *Publ:* Auth, Paul Scarron, Twayne, 72; La Celestina: An example of love melancholy, Romanic Rev, 75; ed, El sastre del Campillo, Estud Hispanofila, 75; auth, The Invisible Mistress: Aspects of Feminism and Fantasy in the Golden Age, Bibliot Siglo de Oro, 76; Lope de Vega and Titian, Comp Lit, 78; La Figura del Nino Rey en la Purdencia en la Mujer, Bull Hispanique, 78; Metamorphosis as revolt: Cervantes' Persiles Y Sigismunda & Carpentier's el Reino de este Mundo, Hispanic Rev, 81. *Mailing Add:* Dept Foreign Lang La State Univ Baton Rouge LA 70803

DEBEVEC HENNING, SYLVIE MARIE, b Cleveland, Ohio, Apr 11, 48; m 75. FRENCH. *Educ:* Case Western Reserve Univ, BA, 70, MA, 74, PhD(French), 75. *Prof Exp:* Asst prof French, Univ Wis-Parkside, 75-77; ASST PROF FRENCH, UNIV ROCHESTER, 77- *Concurrent Pos:* Rochester Mellon fac fel, 81. *Mem:* Midwest Mod Lang Asn. *Res:* Nineteenth and 20th century French literature; contemporary drama; literary criticism. *Publ:* Auth, La Lutte entre carnaval et careme: Tripes d'Or de Fernand Cormmelynck et Magie Rouge de Michel de Ghelderode, Rev Lang Vivantes, Vol XLIII; Narrative and textual doubles in the work of Samuel Beckett, Sub-Stance, No 29; Film and La Derniere Bande: Intertextual and intertextual doubles, Symposium, Vol XXXV, No 2; The ritual im-plications of Genet's Les Bonnes, Boundary 2, Vol X, No 2; Le Meuble: Tardieu's Grotesque Con-trap-tion, Stanford French Rev, Vol VI, No 1; La Forme In-formante: A reconsideration of the grotesque, Mosaic, Vol XIV, No 4; Genet's Ritual Play, Rodopi, 81; The Guffaw of the Abderite: Murphy and the democritean universe, J Beckett Studies, No 9. *Mailing Add:* Dept of Foreign Lang Lit & Ling Univ of Rochester Rochester NY 14627

DEBICKI, ANDREW PETER, b Warsaw, Poland, June 28, 34; US citizen; wid; c 2. SPANISH. *Educ:* Yale Univ, BA, 55, PhD, 60. *Prof Exp:* Instr Span, Trinity Col, Conn, 57-60; asst prof, Grinnell Col, 60-62, from assoc prof to prof Span, 62-68; prof, 68-76, DISTINGUISHED PROF SPAN, UNIV KANS, 76- *Concurrent Pos:* Fulbright grant, 66; fels, Am Coun Learned Soc, 66-67, Guggenheim, 71-72, 80 & Nat Humanities Ctr, 80. *Honors & Awards:* Prize, Hispania, 71; Teaching Award, Univ Kans, 72. *Mem:* MLA; Am Asn Teachers Span & Port. *Res:* Spanish and Latin American contemporary poetry; poetics and literary theory. *Publ:* Auth, La poesia de Jose Gorostiza, Andrea, Mex, 62; Estudios sobre poesia espanola: La generacion de 1924-1925, Gredos, Madrid, 68 & 81; Damaso Alonso, Twayne, 70 & Catedra, Madrid, 74; La poesia de Jorge Guillen, 73 & Poetas hispanoamericanos contemporaneos, 76, Gredos, Madrid; ed, Pedro Salinas, Taurus, Madrid, 76; Antologia de la poesia mexicana moderna, Tamesis, London, 77; Poetry of Discovery: The Spanish Generation of 1956-71, Kentucky, 82. *Mailing Add:* Dept of Span & Port Univ of Kans Lawrence KS 66045

DEBRECZENY, PAUL, b Budapest, Hungary, Feb 16, 32; m 59; c 2. RUSSIAN LITERATURE. *Educ:* Eötvös Univ, Hungary, BA, 53, BA, 55; Univ London, PhD(Russ), 60. *Prof Exp:* Res asst Russ lit, Inst Lit Hist, Hungarian Acad Sci, 55-56; transl ed, Pergamon Press, Oxford, England, 59-60; asst prof Russ & chmn dept, Tulane Univ, 60-66, assoc prof, 66-67; assoc prof, 67-74, chmn dept, 74-79, PROF RUSS, UNIV NC, CHAPEL HILL, 74- *Concurrent Pos:* Int Res & Exchanges Bd res fel, 73 & 82; Nat Endowment for Humanities fel, 78 & 79. *Mem:* Am Asn Teachers Slavic & EEurop Lang (vpres, 78-79); Am Asn Advan Slavic Studies; MLA; Southern Conf Slavic Studies (pres, 77). *Res:* Nineteenth century Russian literature; comparative literature; sociology of literature. *Publ:* Auth, Niklolay Gogol and His Contemporary Critics, Am Philos Soc, 66; co-ed, Literature and National Identity: 19th Century Russian Critical Essays, Univ Nebr, 70; ed, 2 special issues devoted to Pushkin, Can-Am Slavic Studies, summer 76 & spring 77; co-ed, Chekhov's Art of Writing: A Collection of Critical Essays, Slavica Publ, 77; translr & ed, Alexander Pushkin: Complete Prose Fiction, 82 & auth, The Other Pushkin: A Study of Alexander Pushkin's Prose Fiction, 82, Stanford Univ Press; auth, Temptations of the Past, historical novel, Hermitage Publ, 82. *Mailing Add:* Dept of Slavic Lang Univ of NC Chapel Hill NC 27514

DECAMP, JOSEPH E, JR, b State College, Pa, Apr 12, 35; m 58; c 3. SPANISH LANGUAGE & LITERATURE. *Educ:* Pa State Univ, BA, 56, MA, 59; Univ Madrid, dipl, 57. *Prof Exp:* Asst Spanish, Pa State Univ, 57-59; asst prof Spanish & French, State Univ NY Col Oswego, 59-66; ASSOC PROF SPANISH, MILLERSVILLE STATE COL, 66- *Mem:* Am Asn Teachers Span & Port. *Mailing Add:* 60 Glen Oak Lancaster PA 17603

DE CAPUA, ANGELO GEORGE, b New Haven, Conn, Jan 31, 24; m 50; c 2. GERMAN LITERATURE. *Educ:* Yale Univ, AB, 48, MA, 51, PhD(Ger lit), 53. *Prof Exp:* Teaching asst Ger, Yale Univ, 49-53; instr, Univ Ill, 53-56; asst prof Ger lit, Cornell Univ, 56-62; assoc prof, 62-66, PROF GER, STATE UNIV NY BUFFALO, 66- *Concurrent Pos:* State Univ NY Res Found grant-in-aid, 62; State Univ NY fac fel, 67, grant-in-aid, 67-69; contrib ed, Colloquia Germanica, 66-75. *Res:* Seventeenth and eighteenth century literature. *Publ:* Co-ed, Benjamin Neukirchs Anthologie: Herrn von Hoffmannswaldau und anderer Deutschen . . . Gedichte, erster Teil, 61, zweiter Teil, 65, dritter Teil, 70 & vierter Teil, 75, Niemeyer, Tübingen; coauth, The so-called Neukirch Sammlung: Some facts, Mod Lang Notes, 10/64; Baroque and mannerism: Reassessment 1965, Colloquia Germanica, 67; auth, German Baroque Poetry, Interpretative Readings, State Univ NY, 73. *Mailing Add:* 142 Countryside Lane Williamsville NY 14221

DECARLO, ANDREW, b Akron, Ohio, July 11, 33; m 62. SPANISH & ITALIAN LITERATURE. *Educ:* Kent State Univ, BS, 55; Univ Tex, Austin, MA, 65; Case Western Reserve Univ, PhD(Romance lang), 69. *Prof Exp:* Instr Span, Southwest Tex State Univ, 62-66; asst prof, Rutgers Univ, New Brunswick, 69-75; assoc prof, Old Dominion Univ, 76; MEM STAFF BILINGUAL & ENGLISH AS A SECOND LANG EDUC, E ORANGE BD EDUC, 77- *Concurrent Pos:* Adj prof English, Kean Col NJ, 79- *Mem:* MLA; AAUP; NEA;; Nat Asn Bilingual Educ. *Res:* Nineteenth and twentieth century Spanish literature; contemporary Italian literature; bilingual and English as a second language education. *Mailing Add:* 1 Haran Circle Millburn NJ 07041

DECHANTAL, RENE CHARLES, b Moose Creek, Ont, June 27, 23; m 51; c 2. FRENCH LITERATURE, LINGUISTICS. *Educ:* McGill Univ, BA, 48; Univ Paris, Lic-es-Lett, 51, dipl, 51, Dr, 60. *Hon Degrees:* Dr, Univ Ottawa, 76. *Prof Exp:* From lectr to assoc prof French lit, Univ Ottawa, 51-61, asst to dean, 62; from assoc prof to prof French lit & head dept, Univ Montreal, 62-66; head cult affairs div, Dept External Affairs, Ottawa, 66-67; dean, Fac Lett, 68-72, dean, Fac Arts & Sci, 71-75, PROF FRENCH, UNIV MONTREAL, 68-, VRECTOR CURRICULAR AFFAIRS, 75- *Concurrent Pos:* Pres nat libr adv bd, Nat Libr Can, 75- *Honors & Awards:* Grand Prix Literaire, Ville de Montreal, 68; Medaille Broquette-Gonin, Academie Francaise, 68. *Mem:* Fel Royal Soc Can; Acad Can-Fr; Soc Gens de Lett, France; Conseil Int Lang Fr. *Res:* Marcel Proust; lexicology. *Publ:* Auth, Chroniques de Francais, Univ Ottawa, 56, rev ed, 61; Marcel Proust, Critique Litteraire (2 vols), Univ Montreal, 67. *Mailing Add:* Dept of French Univ of Montreal Montreal PQ H3C 3J7 Can

DE CHASCA, EDMUND V(ILLELA), b Guatemala, June 17, 03; nat US; m 32; c 2. SPANISH. *Educ:* Col Wooster, AB, 28; Univ Southern Calif, AM, 29; Univ Chicago, PhD(Span lit), 41. *Prof Exp:* Instr, Oberlin Col, 43-44; assoc prof, Univ Southern Calif, 44-47, Univ Toronto, 47-50 & Univ Chicago, 50-53; prof Romance lang & chmn dept, 53-67, prof Span lit, 67-71, EMER PROF SPAN LIT, UNIV IOWA, 71- *Concurrent Pos:* Guggenheim fel, 72; vis prof Span lit, Univ Mo-St Louis, 73- *Mem:* MLA; Am Asn Teachers Span & Port; Asoc Int Hispanistas; Soc Rencesvals; corresp mem Hispanic Soc Am. *Publ:* Auth, Algunos aspectos del Ritmo y del movimiento narrativo del Quijote, Rev Filol Espanol, 66; Rima interna en el Poema de Mio Cid, Homenaje a Rodriguez-Monino, 66; El Arte Juglaresco en el Cantar de Mio Cid, Gredos, Madrid, 67, 2nd ed, 72; Registro de formulas verbales en el Cantar de Mio Cid, 68; Sancho-Sanchuelo, Sancho-Sancho, Sancho-Sanchisimo, Estudios Literarios de Hispanitas Norte Americanos a Helmut Hatzfeld con motivo de su 80 Aniversario, Ediciones Hispam, 74; The Poem of the Cid, Twayne, 76; Lope de Rueda's Comedia de los Enganados; Alarcon's Sombrero de tres picos. *Mailing Add:* 4946 Buckingham Ct St Louis MO 63108

DECKER, DONALD MILTON, b Detroit, Mich, June 16, 23; m 61; c 2. FOREIGN LANGUAGES. *Educ:* Univ Mich, AB, 49, MA, 50; Univ Calif, Los Angeles, PhD, 61. *Prof Exp:* Instr Span, Occidental Col, 60-61; asst prof, Univ Calif, Davis, 61-63; from asst prof to assoc prof, 63-69, PROF SPAN & ENGLISH AS FOREIGN LANG, ELBERT COVELL COL, UNIV PAC, 69- *Mem:* MLA; Am Asn Teachers Span & Port; Am Coun Teaching Foreign Lang; Teachers of English to Speakers Other Lang; Nat Asn Foreign Student Affairs. *Res:* English as a second language; contrastive analysis of English and Spanish; Hispanic American literature. *Publ:* Auth, Eduardo Barrios talks about his novels, Hispania, 5/62; The doctrine of Raul Silva Castro, critic-historian of Chilean letters, Inter-Am Rev Bibliog, 7-9/64; Machado de Assia: Short story craftsman, Hispania, 3/65; Mastering the International Phonetic Alphabet, Simon & Schuster, 70; Luis Durand, Twayne, 71; The Use and Teaching of English in Mexico, Educ Resources Info Ctr, MLA, 72; auth, Drilling English auxiliary verbs in ESL classes, TESL Reporter, winter 75; The specifics of teaching ESL pronunciation, CATESOL Occasional Papers, fall 80. *Mailing Add:* Elbert Covell Col Univ of the Pac Stockton CA 95211

DECKER, EUGENE MOORE, III, b Jacksonville, Tex, Jan 19, 40. ROMANCE LANGUAGES. *Educ:* Southern Methodist Univ, BA, 62; Univ Wis, MA, 64; Univ Tex, Austin, PhD(Fr), 68. *Prof Exp:* Teaching asst French, Univ Tex, Austin, 63-66, acad asst, spring 65; instr, Univ NC, Greensboro, 66-68; asst prof, 68-80, ASSOC PROF FRENCH, UNIV HOUSTON, 80- *Concurrent Pos:* vis res prof humanities & agr, Univ Maine at Orono, 80. *Honors & Awards:* Comini Mod Lang Award, Southern Methodist Univ, 62. *Mem:* SCent Mod Lang Asn. *Res:* French literature and history of the Middle Ages; French literature of the 18th century; humanities and world food problems. *Mailing Add:* 2021 Westcreek Houston TX 77207

DECKER, FRANCES LOUISE, b Macon, Ga, Aug 18, 46. GERMANIC LANGUAGE & LITERATURE, MEDIEVAL STUDIES. *Educ:* Emory Univ, BA, 68; Princeton Univ, MA, 71, PhD(Ger), 75. *Prof Exp:* Lectr, 73-75, ASST PROF GER, IND UNIV, 75- *Mem:* Mediaeval Acad Am; MLA; Int Courtly Lit Soc; Int Arthurian Soc. *Res:* Medieval epic and romance (Old French and Middle High German); Medieval lyric; narrative technique and narrator figures. *Mailing Add:* Dept of Ger Lang & Lit Ballantine Hall Univ Bloomington IN 47401

DECKER, HENRY WALLACE, b Orange, NJ, Sept 3, 23; m 46. FRENCH. *Educ:* Olivet Col, AB, 48; Univ Mich, MA, 50, PhD(Romance lang), 55. *Prof Exp:* Instr French, Univ Mich, 53-55; from instr to asst prof, 55-68, ASSOC PROF FRENCH, UNIV CALIF, RIVERSIDE, 68- *Mem:* MLA; Ling Soc Am. *Res:* French poetic theory; 19th century French poetry; 17th century French drama. *Publ:* Auth, Pure Poetry: Theory and Debate in France, Univ Calif, 62; coauth, Modern French; Intermediate, 3rd ed, 67 & Modern French: First Course, 2nd ed, 68, Am Bk Co. *Mailing Add:* Dept of Lit & Lang Univ of Calif Riverside CA 92502

DE COLOMBI-MONGUIO, ALICIA, b Buenos Aries, Arg; c 1. MEDIEVAL & RENAISSANCE POETRY. *Educ:* Univ Santa Clara, BA, 69; Stanford Univ, MA, 71, PhD(Span & humanities), 73. *Hon Degrees:* Dipl, Univ PR. *Prof Exp:* Scholar in residence humanities, Univ Santa Clara, 72-73; asst prof Span, Mills Col, 73-79, chmn, Div Lett, 75-79; mem fac, Bennington Col, 79-82, chmn, Dept Foreign Lang, 80-82; PROF SPAN, STATE UNIV NY ALBANY, 83- *Concurrent Pos:* Guggenheim Mem Found fel, 78. *Mem:* MLA; Philol Asn Pac Coast; Renaissance Soc Am. *Res:* Medieval, Renaissance and contemporary poetry; petrarchism; golden age literature. *Publ:* Auth, Federico y su doble: Una constante arguetipica en la poesic de Ferderico Garcia Lorca, Sin Nombre, 74; La vision evocada: La cancion de Petrarca en el verso de Fray Luis, Anuario de Letras, 76; De amor y poesia en La Espana Medieval: Prologo a Juan Ruiz, Col Mex, 5/76; El Aguardante, Lima, 79; Las visiones de Petrarca en el Barroco Espanol: Quevedo, Lopez de Vega, Gougora, 79 & Las visiones de Petrarca en el Barroco Espanol: II En la Huella de Fray Luis, 80, Neuva Rev de Filolgia Hisp; Ser al Sesgo y oFras imitaciones, Lima, 81; 31 Sonetos, Madrid, 82. *Mailing Add:* Dept of Span State Univ NY Albany NY 12222

DE COSTA, RENE, b New York, NY, Nov 22, 39; m 64; c 1. SPANISH, SPANISH-AMERICAN LITERATURE. *Educ:* Rutgers Univ, AB, 64; Wash Univ, PhD(Hisp lang & lit), 70. *Prof Exp:* Asst prof, 70-76, assoc prof, 76-80, PROF SPAN, UNIV CHICAGO, 80- *Concurrent Pos:* Consult, Ford Foreign Area Fel Prog, 70-73; joint comt Latin Am studies, Am Coun Learned Soc & Soc Sci Res Coun grant, 71; external examr, Univ Toronto, 72; Nat Endowment for Humanities fel, 74-75; Soc Sci Res Coun grant, 78-79; dir, Ctr Latin Am Studies; vis prof, Stanford Univ, 83. *Mem:* MLA; Am Asn Teachers Span & Port; Inst Int Lit Iberoam; Latin Am Studies Asn. *Res:* Nineteenth and twentieth century Spanish-American literature; later moderism and the European avant-garde; contemporary theatre. *Publ:* Auth, The dramaturgy of Florencio Sanchez, Latin Am Theatre Rev, 74; Del modernismo a la vanguardia, Hisp Rev, 75; Reverdy: en marge de son amitie avec Huidobro, Bull Bibliophile, 75; El cubismo literario y la novela filmica, Revista Critica Lit, 77; Narrative voice in Borges' Early Fiction, Mod Philol, 78; The Poetry of Pablo Neruda, Harvard Univ, 78; En pos de Huidobro, Universitaria, 80; huidobro; Las carreras del poeta, Fondo de Cultura, 82. *Mailing Add:* Dept of Romance Lang Univ of Chicago 1050 E 59th St Chicago IL 60637

DECOSTER, CYRUS COLE, b Leesburg, Va, Sept 21, 14; m 48; c 4. SPANISH. *Educ:* Harvard Univ, AB, 37; Univ Paris, Ecole Prof de Francais a l'Etranger, 38; Univ Chicago, AM, 40, PhD, 51. *Prof Exp:* From instr to assoc prof Romance lang, Carleton Col, 46-57; prof, Univ Kans, 57-69, chmn dept, 62-65; chmn dept Span & Port, 73-76, PROF ROMANCE LANG, NORTHWESTERN UNIV, EVANSTON, 69-, CHMN DEPT, 79- *Concurrent Pos:* Fulbright res fel, Spain, 63-64. *Mem:* Am Asn Teachers Span & Port; MLA. *Res:* Nineteenth and twentieth century Spanish literature. *Publ:* Auth, Correspondencia de Juan Valera, 56, Obras desconocidas de Juan Valera, 65, Articulos de El contemporaneo de Valera 66 & ed, Valera, Las ilusiones del Doctor Faustino, 70, Castalia, Madrid; auth, Bibliografia critica de Juan Valera, CSIC, 70; Juan Valera, Twayne, 74; ed, Valera, Genio y figura, Catedra, Madrid, 75; Pedro Antonio de Alarcon, Twayne, 79. *Mailing Add:* Dept of Span Northwestern Univ Evanston IL 60201

DECSY, GYULA JOZSEF, b Negyed, Hungary, Mar 19, 25; Ger citizen; m 67. URALIC FINNO-UGRIC LINGUISTICS, SLAVIC LANGUAGES. *Educ:* Univ Budapest, PhD(ling), 48. *Prof Exp:* Sci assoc ling, Hungarian Acad, 55-57; lectr Hungarian, Univ Göttingen, 57-59; prof Finno-Ugric studies, Univ Hamburg, 59-77; chmn dept, 69-77, PROF URALIC & ALTAIC STUDIES, IND UNIV, 77- *Concurrent Pos:* Secy gen, Soc Uralo-Alterica, 58-76; ed-in-chief, Ural Altaische Tahrbu6chet, 66-80; vis prof, Univ Calif, Los Angeles, 67. *Mem:* Finno-Ugric Asn, Helsinki. *Publ:* Auth, Eine slowakische medizinische Handschrift aus dem 17 Jahrhundert, Ungarische Akademie Wissenschaften, 56; De Münchener Kodex Bd I Ein Ungarisches Sprachdenkmal aus dem Jahre 1466, 58, Die ungarischen Lehnwörter der bulgarischen Sprache, 59 & Einführung in die finnisch-ugrische Sprachwissenschaft, 65, Otto Harrassowitz, Wiesbaden; Yurak Chrestomathy: Developmental Work on Material in West Siberian Uralic Languages, Ind Univ, Bloomington & Mouton, The Hague, 66; Der Münchener Kodex Bd II Das ungarische Hussiten-Evangeliar aus dem 15 Jahrhundert, 66, Die linguistische Struktur Europas Vergangenheit, Gegenwart, Zukunft, 73 & Sprachherkunfs forschung I-II, 77-81, Otto Harrassowitz, Sprachherkunftsforschung, Wiesbaden. *Mailing Add:* Dept of Uralic & Altaic Studies Ind Univ Bloomington IN 47405

DEE, JAMES HOWARD, b Albany, NY, Dec 30, 43; m 69. CLASSICAL LANGUAGES & LITERATURE. *Educ:* Univ Rochester, BA, 66; Univ Tex Austin, PhD(classics), 72. *Prof Exp:* asst prof, 72-79, ASSOC PROF CLASSICS, UNIV ILL CHICAGO CIRCLE, 79-, CHAIRPERSON CLASSICS, 82- *Concurrent Pos:* Nat Endowment for Humanities residential fel, 77-78. *Mem:* Am Philol Asn; Class Asn Middle West & South; Vergilian Soc. *Res:* Augustan Latin poetry; stylistic qualities in Greek and Latin epic; Roman moral and humanistic values. *Publ:* Auth, Propertius 4 2: Callimachus Romanus at work, Am J Philol, 74; Arethusa to Lycotas: Propertius 4 3, 74 & Elegy 4 8: A Propertian comedy, 78, Trans Am Philol Asn; Levi-strauss at the Theban gates, Class World, 78; Orestes and Electra in the twentieth century, Class Bull, 78; Survey of Recent Bibliographies of Classical Literature, Class World, 80; Catullus 64 and the heroic age: A reply, Ill Class Studies, 81. *Mailing Add:* Dept of Classics Univ of Ill Chicago Circle Chicago IL 60680

DEES, JOSEPH BENJAMIN, b Wilmer, La, Feb 17, 38; m 68. RUSSIAN LITERATURE. *Educ:* La State Univ, BA, 63; Princeton Univ, MA, 66, PhD(Russ lit), 67. *Prof Exp:* Asst prof, Russ lang & lit, Univ Miami, 67-74, assoc prof, 74-80. *Concurrent Pos:* Exchange fel, Int Res & Exchanges Bd/USSR Ministry Educ, 72; Nat Endowment for Humanities res fel, 72. *Mem:* Am Asn Teachers Slavic & EEurop Lang; Am Asn Advan Slavic Studies; MLA. *Res:* Russian poetry of the 1820's. *Publ:* Eugeny Baratynsky, Twayne, 72. *Mailing Add:* 2705 SW 32nd Ave Coral Gables FL 33124

DE FABRY, ANNE SRABIAN, b Marseille, France, Sept 7, 28; US citizen. FRENCH & CANADIAN LITERATURE. *Educ:* Univ Houston, BA, 64; Rice Univ, PhD(French), 67. *Prof Exp:* Teacher French, Kinkaid Sch, Houston, Tex, 57-63; asst prof, San Francisco State Col, 67-69; asst prof, 69-73, ASSOC PROF FRENCH, KING'S COL, ONT, 73- *Honors & Awards:* Int Prix d'Etudes Vigny, 79. *Mem:* Am Asn 18th Century Studies; Am Asn Teachers Fr; Soc Jean-Jacques Rousseau; Asn Amis d'Alfred de Vigny; MLA. *Res:* Jean-Jacques Rousseau; Alfred de Vigny; Flaubert. *Publ:* Auth, L'instruction en proces, Amis Flaubert, 12/73 & 5/74; A la recherche de l'ironie perdue chez Gabrielle Roy et Flaubert, Presence Francophone, autumn 75; Etudes autour de La Nouvelle Heloise, Sherbrooke, Naaman, 77; Le professeur et la litterature Canadienne-Francaise, Can Lit, spring 78; Vigny: Le Rayon interieur ou La Permanence de Stello, Pensee Univ, 78; Jeux de Miroirs: Saint Paul, La Fontaine, Mao Genet et Jean-Jacques Rousseau, 82 & Etudes autour d'Alcods (collective) (in press), Sherbrooke, Naaman. *Mailing Add:* 117 Rollingwood Circle London ON N6G 1R1 Can

DEFINA, FRANK PAUL, Spanish & Latin American History. See Vol I

DEFRANCIS, JOHN, b Bridgeport, Conn, Aug 31, 11; m 38; c 1. CHINESE. *Educ:* Yale Univ, BA, 33; Columbia Univ, MA, 41, PhD(Chinese), 48. *Prof Exp:* Asst prof Chinese, Seton Hall Univ, 62-66; prof, 66-76, EMER PROF CHINESE, UNIV HAWAII, MANOA, 76- *Concurrent Pos:* Assoc ed, J Am Orient Soc, 50-55; Am Philos Soc grant, 51-52; Soc Sci Res Coun & Am Coun Learned Soc grants Chinese math, 59-63; US Off Educ grants, 62-67. *Mem:* Chinese Lang Teachers Asn; MLA; Am Orient Soc. *Publ:* Auth, Biography of the Marquis of Huai-yin, Harvard J Asiatic Studies, 47; Nationalism and Language Reform in China, Princeton Univ, 50; National and minority problems, Ann Am Acad Polit & Soc Sci, 51; coauth, Chinese Social History, Am Coun Learned Soc, 56; auth, Beginning Chinese, 63, Intermediate Chinese, 64 & Advanced Chinese, 66, Yale Univ, Colonialism and Language Policy in Viet Nam, Mouton, 77. *Mailing Add:* Univ of Hawaii at Manoa Honolulu HI 96822

DE GENNARO, ANGELO, b Niagara Falls, NY, Dec 9, 19. ROMANCE LANGUAGES, PHILOSOPHY. *Educ:* Nola Col, Italy, BA, 39; Univ Naples, PhD, 43. *Prof Exp:* From instr to prof Span, 51-70, PROF ROMANCE LANG & PHILOS, LOYOLA MARYMOUNT UNIV, 70- *Mem:* MLA; Am Asn Teachers Ital; Am Asn Teachers Span & Port. *Res:* Literary criticism. *Publ:* Auth, The Philosophy of Benedetto Croce, Citadel, 61; ed & translr, Croce's Essays on Marx and Russia, Ungar, 66; Croce and Herbert Read, J Aesthet & Art Criticism, 68; The Vico-tercentenary, Personalist, 68; The relevance of Vico, Forum Italicum, 68; auth, Heidegger's vision, Christian Century, 76; Benedetto Croce: Some considerations, La Revista di Studi Crociani, 80. *Mailing Add:* 8050 Dunfield Ave Los Angeles CA 90045

DEGH-VAZSONYI, LINDA, b Budapest, Hungary, Mar 18, 21; m 58. FOLKLORE, ANTHROPOLOGY. *Educ:* Pazmany Peter Univ, Budapest, PhD(ethnol & lit), 43; Hungarian Acad Sci, Can Sc, 56. *Prof Exp:* Sci asst, Munic Libr, Budapest, 46-47; res assoc folklore, East Europ Res Inst, Budapest, 47-49; asst prof, Eötvös Lorand Univ, Budapest, 50-58, assoc prof folklore & anthrop, 58-63; vis prof folklore, 64, res assoc, 64-65, assoc prof, 65-68, prof, 68-82, DISTINGUISHED PROF FOLKLORE, FOLKLORE INST, IND UNIV, BLOOMINGTON, 82-, FEL E EUROP FOLKLORE & ETHNOL, RUSS & E EUROP INST, 70- *Concurrent Pos:* Field res grant, Czech, 55-56; res grant, Ger 57 & Finland, 62; Nat Found Arts & Humanities res grant, 67; Guggenheim fel, 70-71; assoc ed, J Am Folklore, 73; ed, Ind Folklore, 68-; Am Coun Learned Soc res fel, 77-78; Int Res & Exchange Bd fel, 80-81; Am Coun Learned Soc grant-in-aid, 80. *Honors & Awards:* Guiseppe Pitre Int Folklore Prize, 63. *Mem:* Fel Am Folklore Soc (1st vpres, 70-72, pres, 81); Am Anthrop Asn; Int Soc Folklore & Ethnol (pres, 67-); Int Soc Folk Narrative Res; AAUP. *Res:* American ethnic groups and immigrant cultures; Hungarian immigrant groups in the United States and Canada; folk belief, legend and other forms of narration in modern western society. *Publ:* Auth, The belief legend in modern society, In: American Folk Legend, Univ Calif, 71; Folk narrative, In: Folklore and Folklife, Univ Chicago, 72; People in the Tobacco Belt: Four Lives, Can Ctr Folk Studies, Ottawa, 75; ed & auth, Studies in East European Folk Narrative, Univ Tex, Austin, 78; Magic for Sale, Fabula, 79; Indiana Folklore, Ind Univ Press, 81; Harvest Festival of Strawberry Fatness, Ethnologia European, The Magic Tale and its Magic, Folklore Int, 81; Does the Word Dog Bite?, From Action to Legend, From Legend to Action, Festa, Nueva Gusraldi, 81. *Mailing Add:* Folklore Inst Ind Univ 504 N Fess St Bloomington IN 47401

DE GOROG, RALPH PAUL, b Montreal, Que, Oct 6, 22; US citizen; m 56. ROMANCE PHILOLOGY, OLD FRENCH. *Educ:* Columbia Univ, AB, 43, PhD(Romance philol), 54. *Prof Exp:* Tutor Romance lang, City Col New York, 47-49, 50-51, from lectr to instr, 53-57; radio script writer, Voice of Am, US Dept State, 51-53; from asst prof to assoc prof Romance lang, 57-67, PROF ROMANCE LANG, UNIV GA, 67- *Mem:* Int Ling Asn; Ling Soc Am; MLA; Am Asn Teachers Fr; Am Asn Teachers Span & Port. *Res:* Romance philology; medieval Spanish; Old French lexicology and lexicography. *Publ:* Auth, The Scandinavian Element in French and Norman, Bookman, 58; La sinonimia en las obras de Gonzalo de Berceo, Bol Real Acad Espanola, 5/66; Una Concordancia del Poema de Fernan Gonzalez, Real Acad Espanola, 69-70; La sinonimia en Berceo y el vocabulario del Libro de Alexandre, Hisp Rev, 70; coauth, La Sinonimia en La Celestina, Real Acad Espanola, 72; auth, Lexique Francais Moderne-Ancien Francais, Univ Ga, 73; Comparer et ses concurrents en francais medieval, Z fur Romanische Philol, 74; coauth, Concordancias del Arcipreste de Talavera, Gredos, 78; Dict inverse de l'ancien francais, Medieval & Renaissance Texts & Studies, State Univ NY, Binghamton, 82. *Mailing Add:* Dept of Romance Lang Univ of Ga Athens GA 30602

DE GRUMMOND, W W, b Centerville, La, July 24, 34; m 61; c 4. CLASSICS, ROMANCE LANGUAGES. *Educ:* La State Univ, BA, 57, MA, 60; Univ NC, Chapel Hill, PhD(Latin), 68. *Prof Exp:* Instr Latin & French, La State Univ, 60-61; instr classics, Univ NC, Chapel Hill, 65-67, res assoc, 67-68; asst prof, 68-73, ASSOC PROF CLASSICS, FLA STATE UNIV, 73- *Honors & Awards:* Standard Oil Award for Excellence in Undergrad Teaching, 73. *Mem:* Am Philol Asn; Brit Class Asn; MLA; Class Asn Midwest & S (secy-treas, 73-75); Class Asn Can. *Res:* Latin poetry, especially Virgil, Ennius and Catullus. *Publ:* Co-ed, L'annee Philologique, Vol XXXVI, 65, Vol XXXVII, 66 & Vol XXXVIII, 67, Les Belles Lettres; auth, Virgil's Diomedes, Phoenix, 67; Ennius' Induta Fuit Saeua Stola, 71, Class Philol; Aeneas Dispairing, Hermes, 77; Hands and tails on the Vapheio Cups, Am J Archaeol, 80; Saevus Dolor: The Opening and the Closing of the Aeneid, Vergilius, 81. *Mailing Add:* 821 Watt Dr Tallahassee FL 32303

DEGUISE, PIERRE EMILE, b Pont-de-Vaux, France, July 6, 15; m 48; c 3. FRENCH. *Educ:* Univ Lyon, Baccalaureat, 33, Lic es Let, 37; Univ Paris, Agrege, 41. *Prof Exp:* From asst prof to assoc prof French, Wellesley Col, 51-57; assoc prof, 58-61, prof, 61-78, B P Ardenghi prof, 78-81, EMER PROF FRENCH, CONN COL, 81- *Concurrent Pos:* Vis prof French lit, Hebrew Univ Jerusalem, 71. *Mem:* MLA; Am Asn Teachers Fr; Int Asn Fr Studies; Soc Etudes Romantiques. *Res:* French Romanticism; Benjamin Constant; contemporary French novel. *Publ:* Auth, Le Carnet de Benjamin Constant Fragments Inedits, Rev Paris, 8/63; Benjamin Constant Meconnu, Droz, Geneva, 66; Benjamin Constant: De la Perfectibilite, L'Age d'Homme, Lausanne, 67; contribr, La bibliotheque de Benjamin Constant, Saggi e Ricerche, Pisa, 69; ed, De la Religion Livre I et Extraits des Autres Livres, avec Postface et Notes, Bibliot Romande, Lausanne, 71; auth, Les Ecrivains de Coppet et la Grece, In: Colloque de Coppet, Champion, Paris, 77; Etat Present des Etudes sur B Constant, In: Annales B Constant Droz, Geneva, 81; B Constant et P de Barante, In: Second Colloque de Lausanne, Oxford, Voltaire Found, 82. *Mailing Add:* Dept of French Conn Col New London CT 06320

DEHON, CLAIRE L, b Uccle, Belg, Dec 17, 41; US citizen. FRENCH. *Educ:* Inst Hist l'Art, Brussels, MA, 64; Univ Kans, MA, 69, PhD(French), 73. *Prof Exp:* Asst prof, 72-78, ASSOC PROF FRENCH, KANS STATE UNIV, 79- *Concurrent Pos:* Assoc ed, Studies in Twentieth Century Lit, 76-; Nat Endowment for Humanities fel, 81-82. *Mem:* MLA; Am Asn Teachers Fr; African Lit Asn. *Res:* Belgian symbolist theater; French literature in Black Africa. *Publ:* Auth, Le theatre d'Emile Verhaeren: quelques interpretations, Le Flambeau, 75; Allegory in E Verhaeren plays, Philol Quart, 7/78; La Dame du photographe: sa structure, son sens, Rev Pacifique, fall 78; Corinne: une artiste heroine de roman, 19th Cent Fr Studies, 80; Colette and Art Nouveau, Colette, the Woman, the Writer, 81. *Mailing Add:* Dept of Mod Lang Kans State Univ Manhattan KS 66506

DEINERT, HERBERT, b Ger, Dec 13, 30; US citizen; m 57; c 2. GERMAN LITERATURE. *Educ:* Yale Univ, PhD(Ger lit), 60. *Prof Exp:* Asst prof Ger lit, Univ Ga, 59-61 & Duke Univ, 61-65; chmn dept, 68-74, PROF GER LIT, CORNELL UNIV, 74- *Concurrent Pos:* Consult, Nat Endowment for Humanities, 74-78. *Mem:* MLA; Am Asn Teachers Ger. *Res:* Baroque; 19th century realism; the 20th century. *Publ:* Auth, Der Ackermann aus Böhmen, J English & Ger Philol, 4/62; Kafka's parable Before the Law, Ger Rev, 5/64; Die Entfaltung des Bösen in Böhmes Mysterium Magnum, PMLA, 9/64. *Mailing Add:* Dept of Ger Lit Cornell Univ Ithaca NY 14853

DEINERT, WALTRAUT, b New York, NY, Aug 25; c 2. COMPARATIVE LITERATURE, GERMAN. *Educ:* Queens Col, NY, BA, 54; Univ Wis, MA, 55; Yale Univ, PhD(comp lit), 62. *Prof Exp:* Instr Ger, Conn Col, 58-59 & Classrooms Abroad, 60-69; asst prof, Ithaca Col, 67-70, asst prof Ger & English, 70-71; asst prof, 71-73, ASSOC PROF GER, WELLS COL, 73-, CHAIRPERSON, DIV FOREIGN LANG & LIT, 77- *Mem:* Am Asn Teachers Ger. *Res:* Literary criticism; drama; literature of 19th and 20th centuries. *Mailing Add:* Dept of Lang Wells Col Aurora NY 13026

DEJEAN, JOAN ELIZABETH, b Opelousas, La, Oct 4, 48. FRENCH. *Educ:* Newcomb Col, BA, 69; Yale Univ, MPhil, 72, PhD(French), 74. *Prof Exp:* Asst prof French, Univ Pa, 74-78; asst prof French, Yale Univ, 78-81; ASSOC PROF FRENCH, PRINCETON UNIV, 81- *Concurrent Pos:* Nat Endowment Humanities res fel French, 77-78; Morse fel, Yale Univ, 80-81. *Mem:* MLA; Northeast Mod Lang Asn; Am Soc 18th Century Studies. *Res:* Seventeenth century French novel; eighteenth-century French novel. *Publ:* Auth, Insertions and interventions in Diderot's Neveu de Rameau, 18th-Century Studies, 76; Scarron's Roman Comique: A Novel of Comedy, a Comedy of the Novel, Bern, Language, 77; Method and madness in Cyrano de Bergerac's Voyage dans la Lune, Fr Forum, 9/77; The author as literary citation, 5/78 & Scarron's Roman Comique: the other side of parody, 12/78, Papers Fr 17th Century Lit; Seventeenth Century Libertine Novels: Autobiographies romancees?, L'Esprit createur, spring, 79; Une autobiographie en proces: L'affaire Theophile de Viau, Poetique, 11/81; Libertine Strategies: Freedom and the Novel in 17th Century France, Ohio State Univ Press, 81. *Mailing Add:* Dept of Romance Lang Princeton Univ Princeton NJ 08540

DE JUBECOURT, GERARD STHEME, b Digoin, France, Apr 28, 21. ROMANCE LANGUAGES, FRENCH. *Educ:* Univ Clermont-Ferrand, BA, 40; Univ Paris, MS, 47; Laval Univ, Paris, PhD(French), 68. *Prof Exp:* Instr French, Mundelein Col, 61-63; from asst prof to assoc prof, 64-76, PROF FRENCH, UNIV CALGARY, 76- *Concurrent Pos:* Can Coun awards, 67-68. *Honors & Awards:* Lit Prize Brasillach, ARB, Lausanne, Switzerland, 72. *Mem:* MLA; Am Asn Teachers Fr; Pac Northwest Conf Foreign Lang; La Societe des Gens de lettres de Fr. *Res:* French literary criticism; the French novel between the two wars; L'Ecole Romane; the French writers and Greece. *Publ:* Auth, Robert Brasillach, Critique Litteraire, Amis de R Brasillach, Lausanne, 72; Polyeucte est-il chretien ou maitre do soi, comme le veut Serge Doubrosvsky?, L'Esprit Createur, Vol XIII, No 3. *Mailing Add:* 2528 Chateau Pl NW Calgary AB T2M 4K7 Can

DE JULIO, MARYANN, b New Rochelle, NY, Nov 1, 50. FRENCH POETRY. *Educ:* State Univ NY Stony Brook, BA, 71; Univ Iowa, MA, 72, PhD(French), 79. *Prof Exp:* Vis lectr, Univ Iowa, 79-81; ASST PROF FRENCH, WASHINGTON UNIV, ST LOUIS, 81- *Mem:* MLA; Women's Caucus Mod Lang. *Res:* Contemporary French poetry; comtemporary literary criticism; French women's studies. *Publ:* Transl, Poids D'Angoisse, Suzanne Paradis, Pour Les Enfants Des Morts, Calyx, 10/80; auth, The drama of self in Apollinaire and Reverdy: Play of light and shadow, French Forum, 9/81. *Mailing Add:* 6334 Southwood Apt 3 Clayton MO 63105

DE LA CAMPA, ANTONIO RADAMES, b Havana, Cuba, Sept 26, 26; US citizen. SPANISH, SPANISH-AMERICAN LITERATURE. *Educ:* Univ Havana, Dr Filos y Let, 57. *Prof Exp:* Instr, 64-70, asst prof, 70-80, ASSOC PROF SPAN, CITY COL NEW YORK, 80- *Mem:* MLA; Am Asn Teachers Span & Port. *Res:* Spanish and Spanish-American poetry. *Publ:* Auth, La Poesia espanola de posguerra, 69. *Mailing Add:* Dept of Romance Lang City Col of New York New York NY 10031

DE LACY, PHILLIP, b Seattle, Wash, May 4, 13; m 36. CLASSICS. *Educ:* Univ Wash, BA, 32, MA, 33; Princeton Univ, PhD, 36. *Prof Exp:* Instr classics, Princeton Univ, 36-38; asst prof, Stanford Univ, 38-40; from instr to asst prof Latin, Univ Chicago, 40-49; prof classics, Wash Univ, 49-61, Northwestern Univ, 61-65 & Cornell Univ, 65-67; prof class studies, 67-78, EMER PROF CLASS STUDIES, UNIV PA, 78- *Concurrent Pos:* Ed, Am Philol Asn, 49-52 & Class Asn Midwest & S, 55-56; vis prof, Cornell Univ, 58-59; fels, Guggenheim, 60-61 & Nat Endowment for Humanities, 75-76; deleg, Am Coun Learned Soc, 71-75. *Mem:* Am Philol Asn (pres, 66-67); Soc Ancient Greek Philos (pres, 58, 63-64). *Res:* Hellenistic philosophy; Plutarch; Galen. *Publ:* Coauth, Philodemus on Methods of Inference, Am Philol Asn, 41, 2nd ed, Naples 78 & Plutarch, Moralia, Vol VII, 59 & Plutarch, Moralia, Vol XVI, 67, Harvard; auth, Galen, On the Doctrines of Plato and Hippocrates, Vol I, 78 & Vol II, 80, Berlin Acad. *Mailing Add:* Box 64 Barnegat Light NJ 08006

DELAKAS, DANIEL LIUDVIKO, b Springfield, Mass, Aug 25, 21. ROMANCE LANGUAGES & LITERATURES. *Educ:* Brooklyn Col, AB, 46; Univ Paris, DrUniv, 48; Univ Florence, dipl, 56, 57. *Prof Exp:* Lectr French, Northwestern Univ, 49, from instr to asst prof, 49-56; consult, Acad Year Abroad, Paris & Madrid, 69-70, PROF ROMANCE LANG, RIPON COL, 56-, CHMN DEPT, 56-59 & 74- *Concurrent Pos:* Co-ed, MLA French 17th Century Studies Ann, 52-78; consult, prog French & Span, Sci Res Assoc, Int Bus Machines Corp, 61-62, foreign lang testing, English grammar lab, jr high English compos text, 63-64, foreign lang ed, 62-63; vis prof appl ling, Stillman Col, 64; nat ed, historian & exec secy, Romance Lang Hon Soc, 64-74; vis prof & assoc dir, NDEA Inst, Tufts Univ, 65; vis prof, Univ Toulouse, 66, 68 & Univ Alaska, 67; mem steering comt, Humanities Inst, Univ Chicago, 70-73; fel Japanese studies, Lib Arts Col, Monmouth Col, 74 & Earlham Col, 75; vis scholar, Harvard Univ, 75, vis fel, 77. *Honors & Awards:* Chevalier, Palmes Academiques, 67. *Mem:* MLA. *Res:* Japanese, French and Italian language and literature. *Publ:* Auth, Franco-American bibliography, In: Yearbook of General and Comparitive Literature; co-founder, co-ed & contribr, MLA Fr III Comt, Fr 17th Century Studies, Ind Univ Press & Colo State Univ Press, 30 Vols, 53-83. *Mailing Add:* 416 Woodside Ave Ripon WI 54971

DE LANCEY, DEVAUX, b New York, NY, Nov 23, 01; m 33; c 1. FRENCH. *Educ:* Harvard Col, SB, 24; Princeton Univ, AM, 27. *Prof Exp:* Instr French & Span, Univ Vt, 24-25; lectr, Univ Wis, 29-32; instr, 32-51, chmn dept Romance lang, 51-58, Donner Found prof, 59-62, Independence Found prof, 62-70, 1959 INDEPENDENCE FOUND PROF EMER, PHILLIPS EXETER ACAD, 70- *Concurrent Pos:* Adv Montgomery Bergen fel, 28-29. *Honors & Awards:* Chevalier, Ordre des Palmes Academiques, 61. *Mem:* MLA. *Res:* Sixteenth century French fabulists; 17th century and contemporary French literature. *Publ:* Ed, Le Premier Livre des Emblemes, Soc Rouennaise Bibliophiles. *Mailing Add:* Drinkwater Rd Exeter NH 03833

DELANCEY, SCOTT CAMERON, b Rochester, NY, June 22, 49; m 75; c 2. LINGUISTICS. *Educ:* Cornell Univ, BA, 73; Ind Univ, MA, 77, PhD(ling), 80. *Prof Exp:* Vis asst prof, Univ Colo, 80-82; ASST PROF LING, UNIV ORE, 82- *Mem:* Ling Soc Am; Am Oriental Soc; Cognitive Sci Soc. *Res:* Language and cognition; historical morphology and syntax; Sino-Tibetan and Tai linguistics. *Publ:* Auth, The category of direction in Tibeto-Burman, Ling of the Tibeto-Burman Area, 81; An interpretation of split ergativity and related patterns, Lang, 81; Parameters of empathy, 81 & Lhasa Tibetan: A case study in ergative typology, 82, J Ling Res; contribr, Tense and Aspect: Between Sematics and Pragmatics, John Benjamins, 82. *Mailing Add:* Dept Ling Univ Ore Eugene OR 97403

DELANEY, JOHN THOMAS, b Chattanooga, Tenn, Oct 13, 27. ROMANCE LANGUAGES. *Educ:* St Ambrose Col, BA, 49; St Mary's Univ, Md, STB, 51; Univ Tenn, MA, 57; Cath Univ Am, PhD(Romance lang), 66. *Prof Exp:* Asst prof, Romance Lang, Lincoln Mem, Univ, 57-58; from asst to assoc prof, 58-66, PROF ROMANCE LANG, GALLAUDET COL, 66-, CHMN DEPT, 72- *Mem:* MLA; SAtlantic Mod Lang Asn; Am Inst of Deaf; Am Asn Teachers Span & Port. *Res:* Romance linguistics; Spanish influence on education of the deaf. *Publ:* Coauth, Intermediate Spanish Exercises, Gallaudet Col, 67. *Mailing Add:* Dept of Romance Lang Gallaudet Col Washington DC 20002

DELANO, LUCILE KATHRYN, b Murphysboro, Ill, July 2 02. SPANISH LITERATURE. *Educ:* Wash Univ, AB, 24, AM, 25; State Univ Iowa, PhD, 34. *Prof Exp:* Prof foreign lang, La Polytech Inst, 25-28; prof, Tex Presby Col, 28-29; instr Span, State Univ Iowa, 29-34; prof mod lang, Queens Col, NC, 34-37; prof, Winthrop Col, 47-66; prof Romance lang, Va Wesleyan Col, 68-69; RETIRED. *Mem:* MLA; Am Asn Teachers Span & Port; Am Asn Univ Women; Soc Descendants Mayflower. *Res:* Seventeenth century Spanish comedia; Latin American literature. *Publ:* Auth, A Critical Index of Sonnets in the Plays of Lope de Vega, Univ Toronto, 35; Spain: History and Legend, privately publ, 63; Morning Rain: Diary of a European Journey on Eve of War, 63 & Oh Lovely Spain, 73; The Joys of Teaching, Christopher, 78. *Mailing Add:* Box 2474 Cherry Rd Sta Rock Hill SC 29730

DE LA NUEZ, MANUEL, b Madrid, Spain, Apr 12, 34; US citizen; m 73; c 2. SPANISH LITERATURE. *Educ:* City Col New York, BBA, 56; Middlebury Col, MA, 62; NY Univ, PhD(Span lit), 71. *Prof Exp:* Lectr Span, 62-71, asst prof, 71-80, ASSOC PROF SPAN, CITY COL NEW YORK, 80- *Mem:* Am Asn Teachers Span & Port; MLA. *Res:* Contemporary Spanish theater. *Publ:* Auth, Eduardo Marquina, Twayne, 76; Eduardo Marquina: Apuntes de una rebeldia olvidada, In: Estudios ofrecidos a Rodrigo Molina, Insula, Madrid, 77. *Mailing Add:* Dept of Romance Lang City Col of New York New York NY 10031

DE LA PENA, CARLOS HECTOR, b Atotoinilco, Jalisco, Mex, June 30, 15 m 60; c 3. SPANISH & SPANISH-AMERICAN CULTURE. *Educ:* Ysleta Col, Tex, BS, 39, MA, 41; Nat Univ Mex, MA, 43, PhD & DLitt, 44. *Prof Exp:* Lectr philos & lit, Cent Cult Univ Mexico City, 43-44, sr lectr, 44-47, head dept Span & Latin Am studies, 47-58; head dept Span, Univ Auckland, 63-66; vis res prof, Univ of the Andes, Venezuela, 67; assoc prof Span, Northern Ariz Univ, 68-70, prof, 70-80; RETIRED. *Mem:* Int Soc Hispanoam Lis; Asn Venezuelan Writers. *Res:* World history of literature; Latin American and Spanish cultures; philosophy of nature. *Publ:* Auth, La Novela Moderna, 44, Antologia de la Literatura Universal (2 vols), 59, El Hipocrita (novel), 59, Historia de la Literatura Universal, 10th ed, 71 & Piel de Matar (novel), 75, Ed Jus, Mex; Nosotros los Muertos (novel), Ed Rep, Mex, 59, Ed Jus, 50, 73; Don Francisco Monterde, UNAM, Mexico, 79. *Mailing Add:* Rte 3 Box 120 Marshall AR 72650

DE LA PORTILLA, MARTA ROSA, b Havana, Cuba, June 24, 27. SPANISH LITERATURE. *Educ:* Univ Havana, PhD(Span lit), 50; Univ Madrid, PhD(class philol), 54. *Prof Exp:* Prof Span lit & art hist, Univ St Thomas Villanueva, 50-61, registrar & dean admis, 54-61; lectr Span, Merrimack Col, 61-62; asst prof, Salve Regina Col, 62-64 & Fordham Univ, 64-65; PROF SPAN & CHMN DEPT, MANHATTANVILLE COL, 65- *Concurrent Pos:* Ed, Noverim, 55-61; prof adv, ARHE, Inc, New York, 71- *Mem:* MLA; Am Asn Teachers Span; Span Inst Am; Am Coun Teachers Foreign Lang. *Res:* Twentieth century Spanish literature; bilingual Spanish education in the United States. *Publ:* Compiler, Bibliography on children's books, UNICEF, 69; Textbooks in Spanish and Portuguese--a descriptive bibliography 1939-1970, MLA, 72; Mejora tu Espanol: Lectura y Redaccion Para Bilingues, 78 & Digalo en espanol: Review grammar for communication, 82, Regents. *Mailing Add:* Dept of Span Manhattanville Col Purchase NY 10577

DELATTRE, GENEVIEVE, b France, Sept 9, 20; US citizen; m 53. FRENCH. *Educ:* Univ Grenoble, Lic es Let, 47; Mt Holyoke Col, MA, 50; Columbia Univ, PhD, 60. *Prof Exp:* Instr French, Mt Holyoke Col, 48-52; vis lectr, Columbia Univ, 52-53, 55; asst prof, Univ Colo, 61-64; from asst prof to assoc prof French, 64-71, PROF FRENCH, UNIV CALIF, SANTA BARBARA, 71- *Concurrent Pos:* French lang test comt, Col Entrance Exam Bd, 68-80; mem exec coun, MLA, 72-76. *Mem:* Am Asn Teachers Fr; MLA; Int Asn Fr Studies, Groupe Etudes Balzaciennes; Groupe Etudes Romantiques. *Res:* Balzac; Romanticism. *Publ:* Auth, Les Opinions Litteraires de Balzac, Presses Univs, France, 61; Le retour en arriere chez Balzac, Romanic Rev, 4/66; The changing aspects of teaching French, In: The Study of Foreign Languages, Philos Libr, 68; De seraphita a la fille aux yeux d'or, L'Annee Balzacienne 1970, 70. *Mailing Add:* Dept of French & Ital Univ of Calif Santa Barbara CA 93106

DELATY, SIMONE, b Valenciennes, France, Jan 17, 39; c 1. FRENCH LITERATURE. *Educ:* Univ Grenoble, France, Baccalaureat, 59, Lic es Lett, 62; Univ Bordeaux, France, PhD(comp lit), 70. *Prof Exp:* Instr French, Bowling Green Univ, 64-67; from instr to asst prof, 68-76, ASSOC PROF FRENCH, UNIV IOWA, 76- *Concurrent Pos:* Develop res assignment, Univ Iowa, 76-77; Am Coun Learned Soc grant-in-aid, 76. *Mem:* AAUP; MLA; Am Asn Teachers French. *Res:* Nineteenth century French literature, poetry, poetics, Quebec literature. *Publ:* Auth, L'Heritage Espagnol de Jose'-Maria de Heredia, Paris, 75. *Mailing Add:* Dept of French & Ital Univ of Iowa Iowa City IA 52242

DE LAURETIS, TERESA, b Bologna, Italy, Nov 29, 38; US citizen. ITALIAN LANGUAGE & LITERATURE. *Educ:* Bocconi Univ, Italy, Laurea, 63. *Prof Exp:* Instr Ital, Univ Colo, Boulder, 64-66; lectr, Univ Calif, Davis, 66-68; from asst prof to assoc prof, 68-77, PROF ITAL, UNIV WIS-MILWAUKEE, 77- *Concurrent Pos:* Sr fel, Ctr 20th Century Studies, Univ Wis-Milwaukee, 76-77. *Mem:* MLA; Am Asn Teachers Ital; Assoc Int Studies Lingua & Lett Ital; Can Semiotics Res Asn. *Res:* Literary theory and criticism; film; semiotics. *Publ:* Auth, Metodi strutturali nella critica letteraria italiana, MLN, 1/71; Narrative discourse in Calvino, PMLA, 5/75; Rebirth, In: The Bell Jar, Women's Studies, 3/76; La sintassi del desiderio, Ravenna: Longo, 76; Cavani's Night Porter: A woman's film?, Film Quart, winter 77; Semiosis unlimited, PTL, 4/77; co-ed, Theoretical perspectives in cinema (special issue), Cine-tracts, summer 77; auth, Semiotic models, invisible cities, Yale Ital Studies, winter 78. *Mailing Add:* Dept of French & Ital Univ of Wis Milwaukee WI 53201

DEL CARO, ADRIAN, b Eveleth, Minn, Dec 29, 52. GERMAN, PHILOSOPHY. *Educ:* Univ Minn, Duluth, BA, 76, Minneapolis, MA, 77, PhD(Ger), 79. *Prof Exp:* Lectr Ger & comp lit, Univ Calif, 79-80; ASST PROF GER, LA STATE UNIV, 80- *Mem:* Am Lit Transl Asn; NAm Nietzsche Soc. *Res:* Friedrich Nietzsche; early German romanticism; literature and philosophy of 19th century. *Publ:* Auth, Ethical aesthetic: Schiller and Nietzsche as critics of the 18th century, The Germanic Rev, 2/80; Notes concerning Nietzsche and Novalis, Germanic Notes, 12/81; Dionysian Aesthetics, Peter Lang, 81; Stefan Zweig's Ungeduld des Herzens, Mod Austrian Lit, 3-4/81; Reception and impact: The first decade of Nietzsche in Germany, Orbis Litterarum, Vol 37, 82; Anti-romantic irony in poetry of Nietzsche, Nietzsche-Studien (in press). *Mailing Add:* Dept Class Ger & Slavic Lang La State Univ Baton Rouge LA 70803

DE LEVIE, DAGOBERT, b Oldenburg, Ger, Sep 1, 14; m 42; c 2. GERMAN. *Educ:* Univ Basel, PhD, 39; Harvard Univ, cert, 44. *Prof Exp:* Inst, 46, from asst prof to assoc prof, 47-63, prof, 63-78, dir foreign studies, 62-78, EMER PROF GER, PA STATE UNIV, UNIVERSITY PARK, 78- *Concurrent Pos:* Hon sen Univ Cologne, 71-; adj prof, Duquesne Univ, 78- *Mem:* MLA. *Res:* Secularization and enlightement in the 18th century; German literature and philology; intellectual history. *Publ:* Auth, Die Menschenliebe im Zeitalter der Aufklärung, Herbert Lang, Bern, 75. *Mailing Add:* Off of Foreign Studies Pa State Univ University Park PA 16802

DE LEY, HERBERT CLEMONE, JR, b Altadena, Calif, Nov 24, 36; m 62; c 1. FRENCH LANGUAGE & LITERATURE. *Educ:* Univ Calif, Los Angeles, BA, 58; Yale Univ, PhD(French), 63. *Prof Exp:* Instr French, Wilson Col, 61-62; from instr to assoc prof, 62-77, PROF FRENCH, UNIV ILL, URBANA, 77- *Concurrent Pos:* Vis assoc prof, Univ Calif, Riverside, 67-68, Univ Chicago, 69 & Univ Calif, Los Angeles, 76-77. *Mem:* Am Asn Teachers Fr; MLA; Soc Amis Saint-Simon; Soc Amis Marcel Proust. *Res:* Marcel Proust; the Duke of Saint-Simon; French classicism. *Publ:* Auth, Marcel Proust et le duc de Saint-Simon, Univ Ill, 66; L'Hopital sans style vant le glorieux portail: Salon Painters in A la recherche du temps perdu, L'Esprit Createur, 71; Two modes of thought in L'Astree, Yale Fr Studies, 74; Organized programs of study in France: Some contributions of stranger theory, Fr Rev, 75; Saint-Simon Memorialist, Univ Ill, 75; Deux erotismes deux modes de pensee dans les galanteries du duc d'Ossonne, In: La Coherence interieure, 77; Dans les regles du plaisir: Transformation of sexual knowledge in seventeenth century France, Paper Fr Seventeenth-Century Lit, 82. *Mailing Add:* Dept of French Univ of Ill Urbana IL 61801

DEL GRECO, ARNOLD ARMAND, b Italy, Oct 11, 08; nat citizen; m 36; c 2. HISPANIC & ITALIAN LITERATURE. *Educ:* NY Univ, BS, 32; Columbia Univ, AM, 34, PhD, 50. *Prof Exp:* Tutor Ital & Span, Brooklyn Col, 37-42; instr Romance lang, Sweet Briar Col, 42-46; asst prof, 47-54, assoc prof Span, 54-67, assoc dir Bolivian Sem, 60, dir foreign lang inst, 60-74, dir grad prog Span, Salamanca, Spain, 65-78, prof, 67-68, EMER PROF SPAN, UNIV VA, 78- *Concurrent Pos:* Ed bull, MLA, 51-62; dir Ibero-Am novel proj, William Faulkner Found, 61-71, exec officer, Span sect, 64-72; dir master of arts prog, Lit Univ Salamanca, 72-81. *Honors & Awards:* Distinguished Teacher & Mem Award, Am Asn Teachers Span & Port, 67; Gold Medal of Honor, Universidad de Salamanca, 74. *Mem:* MLA; Am Asn Teachers Span & Port; Am Asn Teachers Ital; Hisp Inst US; Am-Ital Soc. *Res:* Spanish and Italian literature of the 19th and 20th centuries; new key teaching of foreign languages. *Publ:* Auth, Giacomo Leopardi in Hispanic Literature, S F Vanni, 52; Repertorio bibliografico del mundo de Ruben Dario, Las Americas, 69; Foreign languages in Virginia, facts and figures & Bibliography of useful materials for foreign language teachers, MLA Bull. *Mailing Add:* 12 Canterbury Rd Charlottesville VA 22901

DELLA TERZA, DANTE, b Torella, Italy, May 5, 24; m 53; c 2. ITALIAN LITERATURE. *Educ:* Univ Pisa, DLet, 48, dipl, 49. *Prof Exp:* Asst prof Ital, Univ Calif, Los Angeles, 57-61, assoc prof & chmn dept, 61-63; assoc prof Romance lang, 63-68, chmn dept Romance lang & lit, 70-76, PROF ROMANCE LANG, HARVARD UNIV, 68- *Concurrent Pos:* Co-ed, The Yearbook of Italian Studies, Casalini Libr, 71- *Mem:* Am Asn Teachers Ital; MLA. *Res:* Francesco de Sanctis; T Tasso and the late Italian Renaissance. *Publ:* Ed, E Auerbach's Studi su Dante, Feltrinelli, 63; auth, Renato Poggioli tra solario e inventario, Italica, 69; Galileo as a man of letters, In: Galileo Revised; Tasso and Dante, Belfagor; Forma e memoria, Bulzoni, 79. *Mailing Add:* Dept of Romance Lang & Lit Harvard Univ Cambridge MA 02138

DELLEPIANE, ANGELA B, b Rio Cuarto, Arg, May 13, 26; US citizen; m 62. SPANISH AMERICAN LITERATURE. *Educ:* Univ Buenos Aires, MA, 48, PhD(Romance philol), 52. *Prof Exp:* Prof Latin, Teacher's Col, Buenos Aires, 48-57; asst prof Span lit, Fordham Univ, 61-63; from asst prof to assoc prof philol, phonetics & Span lit, 63-72, PROF SPAN AM LIT, CITY COL NEW YORK, 73-; PROF SPAN AM LIT, GRAD CTR, CITY UNIV NEW YORK, 69- *Concurrent Pos:* Consult & panelist, Fel Div, Nat Endowment for Humanities, 77-79; vis prof, Univ Ky, 78. *Mem:* MLA; Int Inst Ibero-Am Lit; Asn Int de Hispanistas; Am Asn Teachers Span & Port; Latin Am Studies Asn. *Res:* Spanish American narrative; Gauchesca literature; structural stylistics. *Publ:* Auth, Ernesto Sabato: el hombre y su obra, Las Americas, 68; Presencia de America en la obra de Tirso de Molina, Estudios, Madrid, 68; La novela argentina desde 1950 a 1965, Rev Ibero-Am, 7-12/68; Sabato: un analisis de su narrativa, Nova, Buenos Aires, 70; ed, R Güiraldes' Don Segundo Sombra, Prentice-Hall, 71; auth, 62 Modelo para armar: agresion, regresion o progresion?, Nueva Narrativea Hispano-Am, 49-72; Tres novelas de la dictadura, Caravelle, 78; Los folletines gauchescos de E Gutierrez, Rev Iber-Am, 78. *Mailing Add:* Span Doctoral Prog Grad Ctr Univ of New York 33 W 42nd St New York NY 10036

DELONG-TONELLI, BEVERLY JEAN, b Norborne, Mo; m 69. SPANISH LITERATURE, TRANSLATION. *Educ:* Univ Mo-Columbia, BJ, 55; Univ Iowa, MA, 62, PhD(Span), 67. *Prof Exp:* Dir news serv, Univ Northern Iowa, 55-58; instr Span, Univ Iowa, 62-66; from asst prof to assoc prof, 66-74, chmn dept, 73-76, PROF SPAN, CALIF STATE UNIV, LONG BEACH, 75-, CHMN DEPT, 81- *Mem:* MLA; Am Asn Teachers Span & Port; Am Lit Transl Asn. *Res:* Modern Spanish literature; aesthetics. *Publ:* Auth, Mythic unity in Lorca's Camborio Poems, Hispania, 12/69; The lyric dimension in Lorca's Romance sonambulo, Romance Notes, 71; Bicycles and balloons in Arrabal's dramatic structure, Mod Drama, 71; La ambigüedad narrativa en el Lazarillo de Tormes, Rev Estud Hisp, 10/76; The trials and tribulations of Lorca's El publico, Garcia Lorca Rev, 81. *Mailing Add:* Dept of Span Calif State Univ Long Beach CA 90840

DEL PORTO, HERIBERTO, b Havana, Cuba, Apr 10, 46; US citizen; m 68; c 2. SPANISH & LATIN AMERICAN LITERATURE. *Educ:* Auburn Univ, BA, 68; Univ Ga, MA, 72, PhD(Romance lang), 79. *Prof Exp:* Instr Span & French, West Ga Col, 78-79; ASST PROF SPAN & FRENCH, WESTMINSTER COL, MO, 79- *Concurrent Pos:* Vis scholar, Univ Tex, Austin, 80. *Mem:* MLA; Am Asn Teachers Span & Port; Circulo de Cultura Panamericano. *Res:* Latin American literature, new Latin American novel; Spanish literature, 19th and 20th century. *Publ:* Auth, La decadencia de la aristocracia espanola y su reflejo en la novela espanola (in prep) & La decadencia de la aristocracia espanola y su reflejo en novela espanola moderna (in prep), Liberia Universal; La decadencia de la aristocracia espanola y su reflejo en la literatura, Circulo de Cultura Hispanoamericano (in prep); La angustia vital del hombre y su reflejo en jos Cuentos Crises de Jose Sanchez Boudy, In: Jose Sanchez Boudy, Liberia Univeersal (in prep). *Mailing Add:* Westminster Col Fulton MO 65251

DEMAITRE, ANN, b Budapest, Hungary, Nov 23, 21; US citizen; m. FRENCH, COMPARATIVE LITERATURE. *Educ:* Columbia Univ, BA, 50, MS, 52; Univ Calif, Berkeley, MA, 51; Univ Md, PhD(French), 65. *Prof Exp:* Asst librn, Cooper Union, NY, 52-54 & Nat Libr Med, Washington, DC, 54-55; lectr French, libr sci & Ger & chmn dept Romance lang, Univ Md Ctr, Munich, Ger, 55-60; instr French & Ger, 60-61, asst prof French & comp lit, 61-65, ASSOC PROF FRENCH, UNIV MD, 65- *Mem:* Am Asn Teachers Fr. *Res:* Modern literature, Romanticism. *Publ:* Auth, The great debate on realism, Mod Lang J, 66; Ionesco and Brecht, Symposium, 68; Artaud and Le Grand Oeuvre, J Hist Ideas, 73; Artaud and the Occult tradition, In: Literature and the Occult, Univ Tex, 77; (with Edmund Demoitre), The Fire Avalons of the Scythian, History of European Ideas, 82. *Mailing Add:* Dept of French & Ital Univ of Md College Park MD 20742

DE MALLAC, GUY, b Ile Maurice, Mauritius, Nov 1, 36; m 67. COMPARATIVE & RUSSIAN LITERATURE. *Educ:* Univ Paris, CELG, 58; Univ Montpellier, cert philos, 60; Cornell Univ, PhD(Russ & comp lit), 68. *Prof Exp:* Res asst Slavic studies, Cornell Univ, 65-66, instr Romance studies, 66-67; asst prof Romance lang & lit, Dartmouth Col, 67-68, French, Russ & comp lit, 68-70; assoc prof Russ lit, 70-73, dir prog in Russ, 70-75, assoc prof, 73-80, PROF COMP & RUSS LIT, UNIV CALIF, IRVINE, 80- *Concurrent Pos:* Sch Humanities res scholar, Univ Calif, Irvine, 71-72. *Mem:* MLA; Am Asn Teachers Slavic & EEurop Lang; Am Asn Advan Slavic Studies. *Res:* Modern Russian and French literature; literature and society; literature and religion. *Publ:* Auth, Pasternak: Series Classiques de XXe Siecle, Ed Univ, Paris, 63; Brazilian structuralism: Haroldo de Campos, Contemporary Lit, spring 70; coauth, Barthes: Series Psychotheque, Ed Univ, Paris, 71; auth, Kafka in Russia, Russ Rev, 1/72 & 4/72; Pasternak's critical-aesthetic views, Russ Lit Triquart, spring 73; coauth, Che Cosa ha Veramente Detto Barthes, Udaldini, Rome, 73; auth, Pasternak and religion, Russ Rev, Autumn 73; Boris Pasternak: His Life and Art, Univ Okla, 78. *Mailing Add:* Dept of Russ Univ of Calif Irvine CA 92717

DEMAY, ANDREE JEANNE, b Gueret, France, May 22, 22. ROMANCE LANGUAGES. *Educ:* Univ Clermont-Ferrand, Lic es Lett, 48; Univ Paris, CAPES, 49; Univ Poiters, dipl, 51, Agregee, 61. *Prof Exp:* Prof English, Ecole Normale, Chateauroux, France, 50-61; from asst prof to assoc prof French, 62-75, dir jr year in France, 67-68, PROF FRENCH, SMITH COL, 75- *Mem:* MLA; Am Asn Teachers Fr; Soc Agreges. *Res:* French pre-romanticism; translations of Shakespeare in 18th century France; women novelists in 18th century France, especially M J Riccoboni. *Mailing Add:* 35 Spruce Hill Rd Hadley MA 01035

DEMBOWSKI, PETER FLORIAN, b Warsaw, Poland, Dec, 23, 25; US citizen; m 54; c 3. ROMANCE PHILOLOGY. *Educ:* Univ BC, BA, 52; Univ Paris, DUniv, 54; Univ Calif, Berkeley, PhD, 60. *Prof Exp:* Instr French & Russ, Univ BC, 54-56; from asst prof to assoc prof French, Univ Toronto, 60-66; assoc prof French & ling, 66-69, dean students, Div Humanities, 68-70, PROF FRENCH, UNIV CHICAGO, 69-, CHMN DEPT ROMANCE LANG & LIT, 76- *Concurrent Pos:* Guggenheim fel, 70-71; resident master, Smell & Hitchcock Halls, Univ Chicago, 73-79; vis mem, Sch Hist Studies, Inst Advanced Study, Princeton, 79-80. *Honors & Awards:* Chevalier, Acad

Palms, France, 81. *Mem:* MLA; Soc Ling Romane; Mediaeval Acad Am. *Res:* Linguistics; medieval French literature; Old French hagiography. *Publ:* Auth, La Chronique de Robert de Caari, Univ Toronto, 63; Ami et Amile, Chanson de Geste: Classiques Francais du Moyen Age, Champion, Paris, 68; Jourdain de Blaye: Chanson de Geste, Univ Chicago & London, 69; La Vie de Sainte Marie l'Egyptienne: Versions en Ancien et en Moyen Francais, Droz, Geneva-Paris, 77. *Mailing Add:* Dept of Romance Lang Univ of Chicago Chicago IL 60637

DEMERS, RICHARD ARTHUR, b Portland, Ore, Sept 10, 41; c 2. LINGUISTICS. *Educ:* Ore State Univ, BA, 63; Univ Wash, MA, 65, PhD(Ger), 68. *Prof Exp:* Asst prof ling, Univ Mass, Amherst, 68-73, assoc prof, 74-75; assoc prof, 75-80, PROF LING, UNIV ARIZ, 80- *Concurrent Pos:* Fel, Mass Inst Technol, 71-72; reader squibs & arts, Ling Inquiry & mem bd ed, Ling Anal, 74- *Mem:* Ling Soc Am. *Res:* Lummi (structure, syntax, grammar) 1972 to present; Old Icelandic phonology 1973 to present; native American languages of Arizona 1975 to present. *Publ:* Auth, Alternating roots in Lummi, Int J of Am Ling, 74; coauth, The single weak verb class of Old Icelandic, Proc Second Int Conf Nordic & Gen Ling, Umea, Sweden, 75; auth, On establishing linguistic universals: A case for in-depth synchronic analysis, Language, 76; coauth, Vocalic alternations in Old Icelandic, Studia Ling, 78; auth, Stress assignment in Squamish, Int J Am Ling, 7/78; coauth, An Introduction to Language and Communication, Mass Inst Technol, 78; Overcoming inadequacies in the Message Model of linguistic communication, Commun & Cognition, 80; auth, The agent hierarchy and voice in some coast Salish languages, Int J Am Ling (in prep). *Mailing Add:* Dept of Ling Math Univ of Ariz Tucson AZ 85721

DEMETRIUS, JAMES KLEON, b Chicopee Falls, Mass, Aug 23, 24. GREEK, HISTORY OF GRECIAN SCHOLARSHIP. *Educ:* Univ Iowa, Iowa City, dipl, 43; Brooklyn Col, BA, 48; Columbia Univ, MA, 49. *Prof Exp:* Teacher, Poly Prep, NY, 49-51; instr Span, Ital, Greek & educ, Iona Col, 53-58; asst prof Span, English, philos & ancient hist, Pa Mil Col, 59-62, Span, Washington Col, 62-63; ASSOC PROF SPAN, BLOOMFIELD COL, 63- *Concurrent Pos:* Bk rev ed, Chicago Greek Press, 61-73; assoc, Ctr Neo-Hellenic Studies, 66-; vis prof Span, Greek & Ital, St Francis Col, 71-73; mem ed bd, Hellenic Press, NY, 73-; chmn English & foreign lang dept, Luterboro Jr Col, 72-77; fel, Anglo-Am Acad, 80. *Mem:* Mod Humanities Res Asn; Am Asn Teachers Span & Port; Mediaeval Acad Am; Am Class League; AAUP. *Res:* Spanish, Greek and Italian studies. *Publ:* Auth, Los Griegos en Espana, privately publ, 62; Nikos Kanzantzakis in Spain, In: Studies in Honor of M J Benardete, Las Americas, 65; coauth, Spanish Grammar Explained, privately publ, 72; auth, Homer--Europe's first educator, In: Studies in Honor of Dr Quintino Cautadella, Univ Catania, 72; Modern Greek Literature, 74; Modern Greek Poetry, 74 & Grecian Studies in Spain, 78, Barcelona, Spain. *Mailing Add:* New York NY

DEMETZ, PETER, b Prague, Czech, Oct 21, 22; US citizen; m 50; c 2. GERMAN, COMPARATIVE LITERATURE. *Educ:* Charles Univ, Prague, DrPhil(Ger & English), 48; Columbia Univ, MA, 54; Yale Univ, PhD(comp lit), 56. *Prof Exp:* Teaching asst Ger, Columbia Univ, 53-54; from instr to assoc prof, 56-62, chmn dept, 62-69, PROF GER & COMP LIT, YALE UNIV, 62-, CHMN DEPT GER LANG & LIT, 77- *Concurrent Pos:* Yale Morse fel, 59-60; Guggenheim fel, 65-66. *Honors & Awards:* Golden Goethe Medal, Fed Repub Ger, 71. *Mem:* MLA; Am Asn Teachers Ger; corresp mem Akad Künste, Berlin; PEN Club Ger; PEN Club Am. *Res:* Sociology of literature; literary theory; German 18th century thought and literature. *Publ:* Auth, Marx, Engels und die Dichter, Deut Verlags-Anstalt, Stuttgart, 59, Univ Chicago, 67 & Fontanella, Barcelona, 68; Theodor Fontaine: Formen des Realismus, Hanser, Munich, 64; coauth, An Anthology of German Literature 800-1750, Prentice-Hall, 68; auth, Balzac and the zoologists: A concept of the type, In: The Discipline of Criticism, Yale Univ, 68; coauth, German Post-War Literature, Pegasus, NY, 70 & Ger ed, Berlin, 70; auth, Marxist criticism today, Survey, London, 72; Ezra Pound's German studies, Ger Rev, XXXI. *Mailing Add:* Dept of Ger Lang & Lit Yale Univ PO Box 18A Yale Sta New Haven CT 06520

DE MONTMOLLIN, DANIEL-PHILIPPE, b Auvernier, Switz, July 17, 21; m 45; c 3. CLASSICS. *Educ:* Univ Neuchatel, Lic es L, 43, D es L, 51. *Prof Exp:* Lectr French, 46-52, asst prof, 52-55, from asst prof to assoc prof Greek, 55-67, PROF GREEK, VICTORIA COL, UNIV TORONTO, 67- *Mem:* Am Philol Asn; Class Asn Can (treas, 62-64). *Res:* Aristotelian philosophy; ancient aesthetics and rhetoric; Homer. *Publ:* Auth, La Poetique d'Aristote Texte Primitif et Additions Ulterieures, Messeiller, Neuchatel, Switz, 51. *Mailing Add:* Victoria Col Univ of Toronto Toronto ON M5S 1K7 Can

DEMOREST, JEAN JACQUES, b Lille, France, Oct 31, 20. FRENCH. *Educ:* Ohio State Univ, BA & MA, 40; Princeton Univ, PhD(moc lang), 49. *Prof Exp:* From instr to assoc prof Romance lang, Duke Univ, 48-56; assoc prof Romance lit, Cornell Univ, 56-57, prof & chmn dept, 57-66; prof Romance lang, Harvard Univ, 68-75; prof Romance lang, 75-81, PROF FRENCH & ITAL & HEAD DEPT, UNIV ARIZ, 81- *Concurrent Pos:* Guggenheim fel, France, 59-60; Am Coun Learned Soc fel, France, 63-64; co-founder & exec pres, Int Asn Philos & Lit, 74-76; chmn, Col Bd Adv Placement French Lit Comt, 76-78. *Mem:* Am Asn Teachers Fr; MLA; Int Asn Philos & Lit. *Res:* Modern French literature. *Publ:* Ed & coauth, Studies in XVIIth Century French Literature, Cornell Univ, 62; co-ed, Charles de Gaulle's Pour l'avenir, Plon, 73; auth, Dans Pascal, Pascal & Les Passionnes ont vecu, Ed Minuit. *Mailing Add:* Dept of Fr & Ital Univ of Ariz Tucson AZ 85721

DEN ADEL, RAYMOND L, b Pella, Iowa, Apr 23, 32. ANCIENT HISTORY, ARCHEOLOGY. *Educ:* Cent Col, Iowa, BA, 54; State Univ Iowa, MA, 59; Univ Ill, PhD(class philol), 71. *Prof Exp:* Instr high sch, Iowa, 53-55 & Proviso W High Sch, 58-62; asst, Univ Iowa, 62-63; asst, Univ Ill, 64-66, instr classics, 66-67; asst prof classics & ancient civilization, 67-71, assoc prof classics, 71-75, chmn div lang & lit, 71-74, PROF CLASSICS, ROCKFORD COL, 75-, CHMN DEPT, 67- *Concurrent Pos:* Consult classics, Am Class League, 68; Cheek res grant, 73, 75 & 78. *Mem:* Am Philol Asn; Am Class League; Vergilian Soc Am; Archaeol Inst Am; AAUP. *Res:* Vocabulary of Latin for non-articulated sounds. *Publ:* Auth, Schliemann and Troy, Class Outlook, 12/65; A pleas for personal involvement, 5/66 & A word for Caesar, 10/68, Class J; Alexander and the Pella Legacy, Class Outlook, 5/81. *Mailing Add:* Dept of Classics Rockford Col 5050 E State St Rockford IL 61101

DENDLE, BRIAN JOHN, b Oxford, Eng, Mar 30, 36; US citizen; m 62 c 2. ROMANCE LANGUAGES. *Educ:* Oxford Univ, BA, 58, MA, 62; Princeton Univ, MA, 64, PhD(Romance lang), 66. *Prof Exp:* Instr French, Kenyon Col, 61-63; instr Span, Princeton Univ, 66; asst prof, Univ Mich, 66-69; assoc prof, Univ Ala, 69-71; assoc prof, 71-78, PROF SPAN, UNIV KY, 78- *Mem:* MLA; Int Inst Spain. *Res:* Galdos; Spanish Romanticism; Spanish novel on the 19th century. *Publ:* Auth, A romantic voyage to Saturn: Tirso Aguimana de Veca's Una temporada en el mas bello de los planetas, Studies Romanticism, summer 68; The Spanish Novel of Religious Thesis 1876-1936, Castalia, Madrid, 68; Galdos and the death of Prim, Anales Galdosianos, 69; The racial theories of Emilia Pardo Bazan, Hisp Rev, 70; Shipwreck and discovery: a study of imagery in Marianela, Neuphilologische Mitteilungen, 73; Point of view in Nazarin, Anales Galdosianos, 74; Galdos: The mature thought, Univ Ky Press, 80; ed, Galdos, Los articulos politicos en la Revista de Espana, 1871-1872, Lexington, 82. *Mailing Add:* Dept of Span & Ital Univ of Ky Lexington KY 40506

DENGATE, JAMES ANDREW, b Grand Rapids, Mich, July 24, 42; m 67; c 1. CLASSICAL ARCHEOLOGY. *Educ:* Mich State Univ, BA, 63; Univ Pa, MA, 66, PhD(class archaeol), 67. *Prof Exp:* Asst prof classics & class archaeol, Univ Tex, Austin, 67-73; mem, Am Sch Class Studies, Athens, 73-75; ASST PROF CLASSICS & CLASS ARCHAEOL, UNIV ILL, URBANA-CHAMPAIGN, 75- *Concurrent Pos:* Grants, Am Coun Learned Soc, 73 & Am Philos Soc, 74. *Mem:* Asn for Field Archaeol; Am Philol Asn; Archaeol Inst Am; Soc Prom Hellenic Studies; Am Numis Soc. *Res:* Ancient numismatics; Greek archaeology; ancient history. *Publ:* Auth, The coinage of Klazomenai, Univ Microfilms, 67; The triobols of Megalopolis, Mus Notes, 67; Coins from the British excavations at Mycenae, Ann Brit Sch Athens, 74; Material excavated from the undersea sanctuary of Apollo, Am Philos Soc Yr Bk, 75; A site survey along the South shore of the Black Sea, Proc Tenth Int Cong Class Archaeol, 78. *Mailing Add:* Dept of Classics 4072 Foreign Lang Bldg Univ of Ill Urbana IL 61801

DENNING, GERTRUDE R, b St Peter-Au, Austria, Apr 15, 29; US citizen; m 58. PHILOLOGY. *Educ:* Univ Vienna, PhD, 52. *Prof Exp:* Teacher English & Ger, Stadium High Sch, Tacoma, Wash, 54-57; instr, Anchorage Br, Univ Alaska, 57-60; vis asst prof Ger, Kent State Univ, 60-61; asst prof foreign lang, Kans State Teachers Col, 61-63; asst prof Ger, 63-73, ASSOC PROF GER, MUNDELEIN COL, 73- *Mem:* MLA; Am Asn Teachers Ger. *Res:* Modern German literature. *Mailing Add:* Dept of Foreign Lang Mundelein Col 6363 Sheridan Rd Chicago IL 60660

DENNIS, HARRY JOE, b Cisco, Tex, Jan 16, 40; m 62; c 1. SPANISH & PORTUGUESE LANGUAGES & LITERATURES. *Educ:* Univ Ariz, BA, 62, MA, 65; PhD(Span & Port), 70. *Prof Exp:* Instr Span, Tex Col Arts & Indust, 65-66; instr English for foreign studies, English Lang Inst, Univ Ariz, summers 64-69; vis prof Span, Univ Nev, Las Vegas, 69-70; ASST PROF SPAN & PORT, CALIF STATE UNIV, SACRAMENTO, 70- *Concurrent Pos:* Assoc mem bd, Luso Am Educ Found, San Francisco, 72-; dir, Calif State Univ Syst Prog, Guanajuato, Mex, 75-77 & Spain, 81; assoc ed, Los Ensayistas; managing ed, Explicacion de textos literario. *Mem:* Am Asn Teachers Span & Port. *Res:* Contemporary Latin American prose fiction; Brazilian literature of the 20th century. *Publ:* Contribr, Enrique Lafourcade, Hispania, 71; Various poems from the Modernist Period explicated for inclusion in, Antologia comentada Modernismo, 73. *Mailing Add:* Dept of Span & Port Calif State Univ Sacramento CA 95819

DENNIS, NIGEL ROBERT, b London, England, Oct 13, 49; m 71. CONTEMPORARY SPANISH LITERATURE. *Educ:* Univ Cambridge, England, BA, 71, CCK, 72, PhD(Span), 76. *Prof Exp:* ASST PROF SPAN, UNIV OTTAWA, 76- *Concurrent Pos:* Humanities Res Fund fel, 77. *Mem:* Am Asn Teachers Span & Port; Can Asn Hisp. *Res:* Liberal Catholicism in the Second Spanish Republic; Scandinavian volunteers to the International Brigades, Spanish Civil War; cultural periodicals of the 1930s in Spain. *Publ:* Auth, Jose Bergamin y la exaltacion del disparate, Cuadernos Hispam, 6/74; Jose Bergamin y su clavo ardiendo, Insula, 4/75; Curz y Raya: una revista que habla por si misma, Cuadernos Hispam, 7/75; El ensayista Jose Bergamin (de la Irreal Anti-Academia), Camp de l'Arpa, 8-9/75; La intelectualidad escandinava y la guerra civil espanola, Hist Int, 10/75; Ernestto Gimenez Caballero: A reminder, Vida Hispanica, winter 76; El aviso de escarmentados y el futuro de Cruz y Raya, Insula, 7-8/77; Il labirinto di Jose Bergamin, Prospettive Settanta, 4-9/77. *Mailing Add:* 8 Hazel St Ottawa ON K1S 0E9 Can

DENNIS, WARD H, b Boston, Mass, Jan 8, 38; m 62; c 2. SPANISH LANGUAGE & LITERATURE. *Educ:* Middlebury Col, AB, 60; Columbia Univ, MA, 61, PhD(Span), 65. *Prof Exp:* Assoc dean, 69-77, dir, Latin Am Inst, 74-77, asst prof, 67-69, ASSOC PROF SPAN, COLUMBIA UNIV, 70-, DEAN, 77- *Concurrent Pos:* Dir, Span Inst US; Fulbright-Hays fel, 74. *Honors & Awards:* Joint Serv Commendation Medal, 67. *Mem:* MLA; Span Inst US; Am Asn Teachers Span & Port; Latin Am Studies Asn. *Res:* Spanish language, literature and history; Latin American affairs. *Publ:* Auth, Perez Galdos: A Study in Characterization, Sucesores de Rivadeneyra, Madrid, 68; contribr, Spain, Time-Life, 71; auth, Guerrilla warfare in the Episodios Nacionales, In: Homenaje a Andres Iduarte, Am Hispanist, 75; contribr, transl, The Dictionary of Scientific Biography, Am Coun Learned Soc. *Mailing Add:* 416 Lewisohn Hall Columbia Univ New York NY 10027

DENOMME, ROBERT T, b Fitchburg, Mass, May 17, 30. FRENCH. *Educ:* Assumption Col, AB, 52; Boston Univ, MA, 53; Univ Paris, dipl, 59; Columbia Univ, PhD, 62. *Prof Exp:* Instr French & Span, St Joseph's Col, Pa, 56-60; from instr to asst prof French, Univ Va, 60-64; asst prof, Univ Chicago, 64-66; assoc prof, 66-70, PROF FRENCH LIT, UNIV VA, 70-, CHMN DEPT FRENCH, 77- *Concurrent Pos:* Reader French lang & lit, Educ Testing Serv, 71-77; mem adv bd, Nineteenth-Century French studies, 72-; Am Philos Soc grant, 75; vis prof Fr, Univ Orleans, France, 78. *Mem:* MLA; Am Asn Teachers Fr; SAtlantic Mod Lang Asn. *Res:* Romanticism; realism and symbolism; 19th century French literature. *Publ:* Auth, The Naturalism of Gustave Geffroy, Droz, Geneva, 63; Nineteenth-Century French Romantic Poets, 68 & The French Parnassian Poets, 72, Southern Ill Univ; Leconte de Lisle, Twayne, 73; Felicite's view of reality and the nature of irony in Flaubert's Un coeur simple, Studies in Short Fiction, 71; Changing perspectives in Stendhal's Vie de Henry Brulard and-La Chartreuse de Parme, Romanic Rev, 76; Flaubert's Portrayal of Mood and Temperament, In: L'Education Sentimentale, Nineteenth Century Fr Studies, 78; Creation et paternite: Le personnage de Vautrin dana La Comedie humaine de Balzac, Stanford Fr Rev, 81. *Mailing Add:* Dept of French 302 Cabell Hall Univ of Va Charlottesville VA 22903

DE OLIVEIRA, CELSO LEMOS, b Minas Gerais, Brazil, Nov 23, 43; US citizen; m 76; c 2. PORTUGUESE, SPANISH. *Educ:* Univ SC, BA, 70, MA, 74, PhD(comp lit), 76. *Prof Exp:* Instr, 77-79, ASST PROF SPAN & PORT, UNIV SC, 79- *Mem:* Am Asn Teachers Span & Port; Am Lit Transl Asn; SAtlantic Mod Lang Asn. *Res:* Brazilian literature, especially short fiction; Spanish American literature; literary translation. *Publ:* Auth, A literatura no Brasil e na America Espanhola: O Inicio do Periodo Nacional, Revista do Inst Hist e Geografico Brasilero, 4-6/75; A cycle of Brazilian literature, Southern Humanities Rev, winter 75; transl, Joao Cabral de Melo Neto, Landscape by telephone, Chicago Rev, summer 76; Graciliano Ramos, Childhood, Peter Owen Ltd, London, 79; Carlos Drummond de Andrade, A writer is born and dies, Southern Humanities Rev, winter 80; auth, Carlos Fuentes and Henry James: The sense of the past, Ariz Quart, autumn 81; contribr transl, Charles Baudelaire, The Green Table, In: the World of Tragedy, New Am Libr, 81. *Mailing Add:* 11 Dantzler Dr Columbia SC 29209

DEONIS, JOSE, b Oviedo, Spain, Jan 28, 11; m 37; c 2. MODERN LANGUAGES. *Educ:* Univ Ala, AB, 35; Columbia Univ, AM, 37, PhD, 51. *Prof Exp:* Instr Manhattan Col, 38-40, Vassar Col, 40-42; asst prof, Lawrence Col, 42-43, Conn Col, 46-49; assoc prof, 49-55, PROF MOD LANG, UNIV COLO, BOULDER, 55- *Concurrent Pos:* Guggenheim fel, 55-56. *Mem:* Rocky Mountain Mod Lang Asn; Hisp Soc Am; MLA. *Res:* Hispanic culture and literature; the United States as seen by Spanish American writers; Spain and New England. *Publ:* Auth, Alcedo's Bibliotheca Americana; The Americas of Herbert E Bolton; Marti and the United States. *Mailing Add:* Dept of Foreign Lang Univ of Colo Boulder CO 80302

DE PUY, BLANCHE, b San Diego, Calif, May 18, 21. SPANISH. *Educ:* Wellesley Col, BA, 42; Univ Pittsburgh, MLitt, 51; Stanford Univ, PhD, 61. *Prof Exp:* Spec asst to sec gen, Int Telecommun Union, Geneva, 47-50; asst Span, Stanford.Univ, 54-55; instr, Wellesley Col, 55-57, lectr, 58-60, asst prof, 61-64; from asst prof to assoc prof, 64-76, dir Madrid grad sem, 67-72, PROF SPAN, UNIV MASS, AMHERST, 76-, COORDR INT STUDIES, 72- *Mem:* Am Asn Teachers Span & Port; MLA; Int Inst Spain. *Res:* Nineteenth and 20th century Spanish literature; literary criticism; history of ideas. *Publ:* Co-transl, America in the Fifties and the Sixties: Julian Marias on the United States, Pa State Univ, 72. *Mailing Add:* Dept of Hisp Lang & Lit Univ of Mass Amherst MA 01002

DERBYSHIRE, WILLIAM W, b Philadelphia, Pa, Dec 30, 36; c 3. RUSSIAN & SLAVIC LINGUISTICS. *Educ:* Univ Pa, BA, 58, MA, 59, PhD(Slavic ling), 64. *Prof Exp:* Asst instr Russ lang, Univ Pa, 59-61; asst prof Russ lang & lit, Lycoming Col, 61-63; from asst prof to assoc prof, State Univ NY Binghamton, 64-59, chmn dept, 67-69; assoc prof Russ & Slavic ling, 69-76, chmn, Dept Slavic Lang & Lit, 69-80, PROF SLAVIC LING, RUTGERS UNIV, 76- *Concurrent Pos:* Fulbright res fel, Inst Ling, Univ Zagreb, 72-73; mem exec coun, Soc for Slovene Studes, 77- *Mem:* Am Asn Teachers Slavic & East Europ Lang; MLA; AAUP; Am Asn Advan Slavic Studies; Soc for Slovene Studies. *Res:* Russian lexicology and lexicography; homonymy in Slavic languages; Slovene language. *Publ:* Auth, Foreign borrowings as homonyms in Russian, Acts X Int Congr Linguists, 70; Homonymic secondary imperfective verbs in Russian, J Russ Studies, 71; The semantic properties of IK-4, Slavic & East Europ J, 75; The intonational patterns of emotive-evaluatives in Russian In: Slavic Linguistics and Language Teaching, Slavica, 76; Some comments on the origin of homonymy in Slovene, Papers Slovene Studies, 77; A note on some verbal and nominal homographs in Slovenian and English In: Slovansko jezikoslovje: Nahtigalov Zbornik, Ljubljana, 77; Some Comments on the Origin of Homonymy in the Slavic Languages, Linguistica, 78. *Mailing Add:* Dept of Slavic Lang & Lit Lit Rutgers Univ New Brunswick NJ 08903

DEREDITA, JOHN FREDERICK, b Saranac Lake, NY, July 24, 43; m 69; c 2. HISPANIC-AMERICAN LITERATURE. *Educ:* Yale Univ, BA, 65, MPhil, 68, PhD(Span), 72. *Prof Exp:* Asst prof Span, State Univ NY Buffalo, 69-72; lectr, Bryn Mawr Col, 72-73, asst prof, 73-76; asst prof, Columbia Univ, 76-80; asst prof, 80-81, ASSOC PROF HISP STUDIES, CONN COL, 81- *Mem:* MLA; Am Asn Teachers Span & Port; Inst Int de Lit Iberoam; New England Coun Latin Am Studies. *Res:* Modern Latin American writing; critical theory; writing and ideology. *Publ:* Auth, El lenguaje de la desintegracion: Notas sobre El astillero de Onetti, Rev Iberoam, 7-12/71; The Shorter works of Juan Carlos Onetti, Studies Short Fiction, winter 71; El doble en dos cuentos de Onetti, In: El cuento hispanoamericano ante la critica, Castalia, Madrid, 73; Vanguardia, ideologia, mito, Rev Iberoam, 7-12/75; Dream and spatial form, Review, winter 75; contribr, Uruguayan section, In: A Dictionary of Contemporary Latin American Authors, Ariz State Univ, 75; auth, Vallejo interpreted, Vallejo traduced, Diacritics, summer 78; Es propiedad? Indeterminacion generica, intertextualidad, diseminacion en un texto de Ricardo Piglia, In: Texto/Contexto en la literatura iberoamericana, Inst Int Lit Iberoam, Madrid, 80. *Mailing Add:* Dept Hisp Studies Conn Col New London CT 06320

DER-HOUSSIKIAN, HAIG, b Cairo, Egypt, Aug 16, 38; US citizen; m 61. LINGUISTICS. *Educ:* Am Univ Beirut, BA, 61, MA, 62; Univ Tex Austin, PhD(ling), 69. *Prof Exp:* Instr English, Brit Lebanese Training Col, Beirut, 60-62; asst prof Swahili & ling, 67-70, assoc prof foreign lang & ling, 70-77, acting dir ling, Univ, 71-72, dir, Ctr African Studies, 73-79, PROF FOREIGN LANG & LING, UNIV FLA, 77-, CHAIR, DEPT AFRICAN & ASIAN LANG & LIT, 82- *Concurrent Pos:* Res assoc, Univ, Dar es Salaam, 66; Fulbright-Hays res award, EAfrica, 66-67; sr Fulbright lectr, Univ Luanda, Angola, 72-73, Univ Benin, Togo, 79-80 & 81 & Univ Ouagadougou, Upper Volta, 81. *Mem:* Ling Soc Am; MLA; African Studies Asn. *Res:* Bantu linguistics; Swahili and Arabic dialectology; syntax and semantics. *Publ:* Auth, Linguistic assimilation in an urban center of the Kenya Coast, J African Lang, 68; The semantic content of class in Bantu and its syntactic significance, Linguistics, 70; Educated urban Swahili, J Lang Asn EAfrica, 71; The evidence for a Niger-Congo hypothesis, Cahiers d'Etudes Africaines, 72; A Bibliography of African Linguistics, Ling Res, Inc, 72; co-ed, Language and Linguistic Problems in Africa, Hornbeam, 77; Tem Grammar Handbook, Tem: Communication and Culture, Tem: Specials Skills, Peace Corps Lang Handbk Series, 80. *Mailing Add:* Ctr for African Studies 470 Grinter Hall Univ of Fla Gainesville FL 32611

DER-OHANNESIAN, JEANINE NELLY, b Paris, France, Feb 3, 28; US citizen; m 46; c 2. FRENCH, SPANISH. *Educ:* State Univ NY, Albany, BA, 64, MA, 66, PhD(French), 73. *Prof Exp:* Fel French, State Univ NY, Albany, 66-68, instr, 68-73, lectr, 73-76; ASST PROF FRENCH, RUSSELL SAGE COL, 76- *Concurrent Pos:* Russell Sage grant, 77. *Mem:* MLA; Am Asn Teachers Fr; Alliance Francaise; Int Comt for the Defense of Breton Lang. *Res:* Twentieth century theater; phonetique. *Publ:* Contribr, Introduction to Natural Sciences, Acad Press, 68; Developpement de la lanque armenienne au ve's, Harvard Univ, 69. *Mailing Add:* Russell Sage Col Ferry St Troy NY 12180

DERSOFI, NANCY, b Boston, Mass. ITALIAN, COMPARATIVE LITERATURE. *Educ:* Radcliffe Col, AB, 57; Harvard Univ, AM, 59, PhD(comp lit), 66. *Prof Exp:* Asst prof Ital, Conn Col, 66-68 & Queens Col, 68-71; asst prof, 72-80, ASSOC PROF ITAL, BRYN MAWR COL, 80- *Concurrent Pos:* Sibley fel Greek, 65-66; I Tatti fel Ital, Harvard Univ, 76-77. *Mem:* MLA; Renaissance Soc Am. *Res:* Renaissance theater. *Publ:* Auth, Arcadia and the Stage: An Introduction to the Dramatic Art of Angelo Beolco, Called Ruzante, Jose Porrua Turanzas, 78. *Mailing Add:* Bryn Mawr Col Bryn Mawr PA 19010

DERWING, BRUCE LLOYD, b Albany, NY, Jan 3, 38; m 74. LINGUISTICS. *Educ:* Univ Southern Calif, AB, 60, AB, 61; Ind Univ, MA, 65, PhD(ling), 70. *Prof Exp:* Lectr ling, Ind Univ, 62-65; asst prof lang, Acad Instr & Allied Officer Sch, Air Univ, 65-67; lectr ling, Ind Univ, 67; vis prof Slavic lang, 68-70, asst prof, 70-74, assoc prof, 74-79, PROF LING, UNIV ALTA, 79- *Concurrent Pos:* Vis res prof, Nat Cent Univ, Chung-Li, Taiwan, 77; vis prof ling, Univ Calif, Los Angeles, 80. *Mem:* Ling Soc Am; Ling Asn Can & US; Can Ling Asn; Alta Conf Lang; Int Asn for Study Child Lang. *Res:* Psycholinguistics; language acquisition; experimental phonology and morphology. *Publ:* Auth, Transformational Grammar as a Theory of Language Acquisition, Cambridge Univ, 73; Morpheme recognition and the learning of rules for derivational morphology, Can J Ling, 76; coauth, The psychological basis for morphological rules, In: Language Learning and Thought, Acad Press, 77; Psycholinguistic evidence and linguistic theory, In: Perspectives in Experimental Linguistics, John Benjamins, 79; auth, Against autonomous linguistics, In: Evidence and Argumentation in Linguistics, de Gruyter, 80; coauth, Reading rules for Russian evaluation, In: Experimental Linguistics, 80 & co-ed, Experimental Linguistics, 80, Story-Scientia. *Mailing Add:* Dept of Ling Univ of Alta Edmonton AB T6G 2H1 Can

DE RYCKE, ROBERT M, b Antwerp, Belgium, Aug 4, 28; US citizen; m 58; c 1. ROMANCE LANGUAGES. *Educ:* Univ Ill, AB, 61, AM, 62, PhD(Fr), 67. *Prof Exp:* Instr French, Carleton Col, 63-66, asst prof, 67-68; asst prof, 86-69, ASSOC PROF FRENCH, UNIV TENN, KNOXVILLE, 69- *Mem:* MLA; Am Asn Teachers Fr. *Res:* Eighteenth and 20th century French literature. *Mailing Add:* Dept of Romance Lang Univ of Tenn Knoxville TN 37916

DESCHENES, MARTIN OVILA, b Somersworth, NH, Mar 29, 38; m 64; c 2. FRANCOPHONE LITERATURE & CIVILIZATION. *Educ:* Univ Montreal, BA, 59; Rivier Col, MA, 65; Vanderbilt Univ, MA, 68, PhD(French), 77. *Prof Exp:* Teacher, Cent High Sch, Manchester, NH, 63-64; asst prof, Rivier Col, 64-65; asst prof, 68-78, ASSOC PROF FRENCH, TENN STATE UNIV, 78- *Concurrent Pos:* Asst prof & vis evaluator French & teaching English as a second lang in francophone countries of Africa, Peace Corps Intern Degree Prog, 72-76 & 78, assoc dir, Peace Corps Francophone Prog, 78; adj assoc prof foreign lang educ, Vanderbilt Univ, 80- *Mem:* African Lit Asn; Am Coun Teaching Foreign Lang; Am Asn Teachers of French; AAUP; MLA. *Res:* African literature of French expression; North American literature of French expression; twentieth century French literature. *Publ:* Auth, The materials challenge, Tenn Foreign Lang Teaching Asn Newslett, 72; contribr, Section on Foreign Languages, Southern Asn Cols & Sec Schs Eval Study, St Bernard Acad High Sch, 72; Section on Foreign Languages, Southern Asn Cols & Sec Schs Eval Report, McGavock High Sch, 73; Moliere et Ses Contemporains, 73-74 & La Querelle de L'Ecole des femmes, 74-75, Fac J, Tenn State Univ; Placide N'Zala-Backa: Le Tipoye dore, spring 77 & Ousmane Sembene: Xala, winter 78, World Lit Today; African literature: Selected resources, In: Dimension: Languages 77, The New South--Expanding Center of Language Study, 78. *Mailing Add:* Dept of Mod Foreign Lang Tenn State Univ Nashville TN 37203

DESCHNER, MARGARETA N, b Helsinki, Finland, Jan 19, 20; US citizen; m 49; c 3. GERMAN. *Educ:* Univ Helsinki, Phil Mag, 45; Southern Methodist Univ, MA, 59; Univ Colo, Boulder, PhD(Ger), 66. *Prof Exp:* Foreign Secy, Studies Christian Fed Finland, 46-49; lectr, Ger & French, Univ Tex, Arlington, 59-62; from instr to asst prof, 63-72, ASSOC PROF GER, SOUTHERN METHODIST UNIV, 72- *Concurrent Pos:* Mem Gen Comt, World Studies Christian Fed, 46-49, Southern Methodist Univ Humanities Coun Studies grant, 68. *Mem:* AAUP; MLA; SCent Mod Lang Asn; Am Asn Teachers Ger. *Res:* Modern German literature; comparative literature; women's studies. *Publ:* Auth, Friedrich Duerrenmatt's Die Wiedertaufer: What the author has learned, Ger Quart, 3/71; Modern German literature in translation: An experimental course on search for indenity, Die Unterrichtspraxis, fall 71. *Mailing Add:* Dept of Foreign Lang Southern Methodist Univ Dallas TX 75275

DESROCHES, RICHARD HENRY, b Worcester, Mass, Oct 17, 27; m 53; c 3. ROMANCE LANGUAGES. *Educ:* Clark Univ, AB, 47; Yale Univ, PhD(French), 62. *Prof Exp:* Master French, Span & Latin, Tabor Acad, Marion, Mass, 49-51; asst, Yale Univ, 53-57; from instr to asst prof Romance lang, 57-69, asst fir, NDEA French Inst, Tours, France, 62-68, instr, 63-65, 67-68, acting chmn dept Romance lang, Univ, 73-74, ASSOC PROF ROMANCE LANG, UNIV ORE, 69- *Concurrent Pos:* Master Span, Hamden Hall Country Day Sch, Conn, 56-57. *Mem:* Am Asn Teachers Fr; Philol Asn Pac Coast. *Res:* Eighteenth century French novel. *Publ:* Coauth, Guide for French, Curric Publ, Portland Pub Sch, Ore, 62; auth, An eighteenth century philosopher's literary protest against slavery, Proc Pac Northwest Conf Foreign Lang, 4/64; Pre-romantic melancholy and the philosophical mind, Pac Coast Philol, 4/68; Reality behind the myth in Giraudoux's La Guerre de Troie n'aura pas lieu, Rev Langues Vivantes, 6/68. *Mailing Add:* Dept of Romance Lang Univ of Ore Eugene OR 97403

DESSEN, CYNTHIA SHELDON, b New York, NY, May 14, 38; m 63; c 2. ROMAN LITERATURE. *Educ:* Oberlin Col, BA, 60; Johns Hopkins Univ, MA, 62, PhD(classics), 64. *Prof Exp:* Asst prof classics, Univ Wis, 68-69, Northwestern Univ, 70-73; ASST PROF CLASSICS, UNIV NC, CHAPEL HILL, 74- *Mem:* Am Philol Asn. *Res:* Latin literature; Roman satire; classics and English literature. *Publ:* Auth, The poetic unity of Horace's Serm I, 4 67 & The sexual and financial mean in Horace's Serm I, 2, 68, Am J Philol; Iunctura Callidus Acri: A Study of Persius' Satire, Univ Ill, 68; Plautus' satirical comedy: The Truculentus, Philol Quart, 1/77. *Mailing Add:* Dept of Classics Univ of NC Chapel Hill NC 27514

DESTEFANO, JOHANNA SUE, b Toledo, Ore, Sept 14, 39; m 67. LINGUISTICS. *Educ:* Stanford Univ, BA, 61, MA, 62, PhD(English educ & ling) 70. *Prof Exp:* Asst prof lang arts & reading, Univ Wis-Eau Claire, 67-68; from asst prof to assoc prof, 70-76, PROF APPL LING & LANG ARTS, OHIO STATE UNIV, 76-, CO-DIR PROGRAM ON LANG & SOCIAL POLICY, MERSHON CTR, 76- *Concurrent Pos:* Mem comn on English lang, NCTE, 76-; proposal evaluator ling prog, NSF, 760. *Mem:* Am Educ Res Asn; NCTE; Ling Soc Am; fel Nat Conf Res English: Int Sociol Asn. *Res:* Sociolinguistics; applied linguistics; language and social policy. *Publ:* Auth, An analysis of the generative sources of pre-nominal adjectives in a tenth grade writing sample, Linguistics, 11/72; Some parameters of register in adult and child speech, ITL, spring 73; ed, Language, Society and Education: A Profile of Black English, Charles A Jones, 73; auth, Developmental sociolinguistics: Child language in a social setting, Child Language 1975, Word, 76; Language, the Learner and the School, Wiley, 78; coauth, Discourse rules for literacy learning in a classroom, Communication in the Classroom, Acad Press, 82. *Mailing Add:* 200 Ramseyer Hall Ohio State Univ Columbus OH 43210

DESUA, WILLIAM JOSEPH, b Monessen, Pa, Aug 13, 30; m 54; c 1. ITALIAN & COMPARATIVE LITERATURE. *Educ:* Univ Pittsburgh, BA, 52, MLitt, 55; Univ Mich, PhD(comp lit), 63. *Prof Exp:* Instr Ital & English, Tufts Univ, 60-63; from asst prof to assoc prof Ital & comp lit, Univ NC, Chapel Hill, 63-72, chmn curric comp lit, 67-72; chmn dept Romance lang, 72-77, PROF ITAL & COMP LIT, MICH STATE UNIV, 72-, DIR, PROG COMP LIT, 76- *Concurrent Pos:* Fulbright res grant to Rome, Italy, 65-66; ed, Univ NC Studies Comp Lit, 66-72; assoc ed, SAtlantic Bull, 69-72. *Mem:* Am Comp Lit Asn; MLA; Dante Soc Am; Am Asn Teachers Ital; Assoc Int Studies Lingua e Lett Ital. *Res:* Dante; literary theory; modern poetry and poetics. *Publ:* Auth, Dante into English: A study of the translation of the Divine Comedy in Britain and America, Univ NC Studies Comp Lit, 64; co-ed, A Dante symposium, in commemoration of the 700th anniversary of the poet's birth 1265-1965, Univ NC Studies Romance Lang, 65; F T Marinetti, In: Columbia Dictionary of Modern European Literature, rev ed, 78. *Mailing Add:* Dept of Romance Lang Mich State Univ East Lansing MI 48824

DETORRE, EMILIO EDWARD, b New York, NY, June 18, 41; m 67; c 3. SPANISH POETRY, LITERARY THEORY. *Educ:* St John's Univ, BS, 64, MA, 66; City Univ New York, PhD(Spanish), 79. *Prof Exp:* Dir, Lang Lab, Manhattanville Col, 66-69; ASST PROF SPANISH & INDIVIDUALIZED LEARNING RESOURCES, QUEENS COL, CITY UNIV NEW YORK, 69- *Concurrent Pos:* Consult, St John's Univ, 75, State Univ NY Old Westbury, 78. *Mem:* MLA; Nat Asn Learning Lab Dir; Am Asn Teachers of Span & Port; Hisp Inst Columbia Univ. *Res:* Peninsular Spanish poetry (post Civil war); structural literary criticism; inner exile as expressed in the works of the post-war generations. *Publ:* Auth, Bilingual resource centers and federal funding, NALLD Journal, spring/summer 76, Hispania, 3/77; Systems clearinghouse: A rationale, & Results of systems inquiry, Lang & Lang Behav Abstracts, 12/76; Jose Luis Hidalgo: Poeta vital, Hisp Rev, Univ Pa, fall 81; Proel: Revista de compromiso, Revista de Estudios Hispanicos, Puerto Rico, Ano VII, 80; El espacio en la poesia de Jose Hierro, Cuadernos Hispanoamericanos, Madrid (in press). *Mailing Add:* Dept of Romance Lang Queens Col Flushing NY 11367

DEUDON, ERIC HOLLINGSWORTH, b Albertville, France, Sept 19, 50; US citizen; m 81; c 1. FRENCH LITERATURE. *Educ:* Va Commonwealth Univ, BA, 74; Univ Richmond, MA, 75; Univ Va, PhD(French lit), 79. *Prof Exp:* Instr French, Univ Va, 78-79; ASST PROF FRENCH, TEX A&M UNIV, 79- *Mem:* NAm Nietzsche Soc. *Res:* History of ideas and religious motifs in French literature, 18th to 20th century; advanced techniques of literary translations. *Publ:* Auth, Gustave Flaubert et le souci de vraisemblance: La mort d'Emma Bovary, Les Amis de Flaubert, 78; Une renaissance du conte fantastique aujourd'hui: Claude Seignolle, Romance Notes, 80; A Propos de Genevieve Bianquis, 80 & Requiescat in Inferno: La maladie de Nietzsche et les psychiatres Francais, 80, Revue de Litterature Comparee; An immigrant looks at American Church and State, Relig Humanism, 80; Claude Seignolle's The Nightcharmer, Fr-Am Rev, 80; Nietzsche en France; L'Antichristianisme et la critique (1891-1915), Univ Press Am, 82; The Nightcharmer and Other Tales of Claude Seignolle, Tex A&M Univ Press (in prep). *Mailing Add:* Dept of Mod Lang Tex A&M Univ College Station TX 77843

DEUTELBAUM, WENDY, b Chicago, Ill, June 19, 48. COMPARATIVE & FRENCH LITERATURE. *Educ:* Northwestern Univ, BA, 69; NY Univ, PhD(comp lit), 78. *Prof Exp:* ASST PROF FRENCH, UNIV IOWA, 75- *Concurrent Pos:* Am Asn Univ Women fel, 78-79; Andrew W Mellon fac fel, Harvard Univ, 82-83. *Mem:* MLA; Midwest Mod Lang Asn. *Res:* Literary criticism and theory; psychoanalysis. *Publ:* Auth, Teaching reader response, Reader, spring 77; Authorizing authority, Reader, 79 & In: Resources in Education, Nat Inst Educ, 6/79; Two Psychoanalytic Approaches to Reading, In: Theories of Reading, Looking and Listening, Assoc Univ Presses, London & Toronto, 81; Desolation & consolation: The correspondence of George Sand and Gustave Flaubert, Genre (in press); Inheriting class conflict from the patriarchal family: A genealogy of George Sand's Anti-feminism, In: The (M)other Tongue: Essays in Feminist Psychoanalytic Literary Interpretation (in press). *Mailing Add:* Dept of French Univ of Iowa Iowa City IA 52240

DEVELASCO, JOAQUIN FERNANDEZ, b Havana, Cuba, May 20, 20; US citizen. SPANISH LANGUAGE & LITERATURE. *Educ:* Inst de la Habana, Havana, Cuba, BA, 38; Univ de la Habana, Havana, JD, 42; Middlebury Col, MA, 72. *Prof Exp:* Lawyer, pvt pract, Havana, 42-52; chief-lawyer, Bur of Info Tribunal de Cuentas de Cuba, Havana, 52-61; ASSOC PROF SPAN, WOFFORD COL, 63- *Mem:* SAtlantic Mod Lang Asn; Am Asn Teachers Span & Port. *Res:* Nineteenth century Spanish realistic-naturalistic novel; Latin American modernistic poetry. *Publ:* Auth, Essay about administrative law, Havana Bar Asn, 52; La Novela Picaresca, 55 & La Comedia Rural de Benavente, 57, Univ del Aire, Havana. *Mailing Add:* Wofford Col N Church St Spartanburg SC 29301

DEVENY, JOHN JOSEPH, JR, b San Antonio, Tex, Aug 30, 44; c 1. SPANISH LANGUAGE. *Educ:* State Univ NY Buffalo, BA, 66; Univ Fla, PhD(Romance lang), 73. *Prof Exp:* Asst prof, 71-76, ASSOC PROF SPAN, OKLA STATE UNIV, 76- *Concurrent Pos:* Consult, Eirik Borve Inc, 80-81 & John Wiley & Sons Inc, 80; actg dept head Foreign Lang, Okla State Univ, 81-82. *Mem:* MLA; Am Coun Teaching Foreign Lang; Am Asn Teachers Span & Port. *Res:* Intensive language programs; Spanish-American literature. *Publ:* Coauth, The intensive language course: Toward a successful approach, Foreign Lang Ann, 76; auth, Ir vs irse: An elaboration, Hisp, 77; Women in Poema de Mio Cid and El Cantar de los Infantes de Lara, La Coronica, 77. *Mailing Add:* Dept of Foreign Lang Okla State Univ Stillwater OK 74078

DEVETTE, ROBERT OSCAR, b Portland, Mich, Nov 21, 19; m 62. SPANISH LANGUAGE & LITERATURE. *Educ:* Wheaton Col, AB, 41, MA, 49; Escuela Interamericana, Mex, MA, 51; Fla State Univ, PhD(Span), 53. *Prof Exp:* Instr English, hist & Span, Fork Union Mil Acad, 41-42; from instr to assoc prof Span, Wheaton Col, Ill, 47-57, dir admis, 66-69, chmn dept foreign lang, 69-72, prof Span, t7-82; RETIRED. *Concurrent Pos:* Foreign lang supvr, State of Ill, 59-61, mem fac adv comt, Bd Higher Educ, 63-64. *Mem:* Am Asn Teachers Span & Port; Midwest Mod Lang Asn. *Res:* Luis de Carbajal, the elder: Founder of Monterey, Mex. *Mailing Add:* Dept of For Lang Wheaton Col Wheaton IL 60187

DEVITO, ANTHONY J, b Cambridge, Mass, June 27, 13. ROMANCE PHILOLOGY. *Educ:* Harvard Univ, AB, 33, PhD, 37. *Prof Exp:* Asst French, Harvard Univ, 37-38; instr Romance lang, Cath Univ Am, 38-42; instr French, Amherst Col, 46; librn, Cambridge Pub Libr, Mass, 46-68; instr Romance lang, 48-50, from asst prof to assoc prof, 50-63, prof, 63-80, EMER PROF ROMANCE LANG, BOSTON UNIV, 80- *Mem:* MLA; Am Asn Teachers Ital; Dante Soc Am (secy-treas, 57-). *Res:* The struggle for existence in the work of Giovanni Verga; fiction of Naples. *Publ:* Auth, Le novelle di Salvatore di Giacomo, Aspetti Letterari, 12/61; co-ed, A Concordance to the Divine Comedy, Harvard Univ, 65. *Mailing Add:* 23 Alewife Brook Pkwy Cambridge MA 02140

DEVITO, JOSEPH A, Speech. See Vol II

DEVLIN, JOHN JOSEPH, JR, b Brighton, Mass, Sept 24, 20; m 53; c 4. MODERN LANGUAGES, HUMANITIES. *Educ:* Boston Col, AB, 45, MA, 50; Boston Univ, PhD(Romance lang), 56. *Prof Exp:* Instr, Boston Col High Sch, 50-51; instr mod lang, Newman Prep Sch, 51-52; instr Ger & great bks, Newton Col Sacred Heart, 52-53; asst prof mod lang & humanities, St Michael's Col, 53-57, chmn dept mod lang, 54-57; from asst prof to assoc prof Span, 57-70, PROF SPAN, GRAD SCH ARTS & SCI, FORDHAM UNIV, 70-, VCHMN DEPT MOD LANG, 66- *Concurrent Pos:* Grad Sch Arts & Sci, Fordham Univ fac fel, 62-63. *Mem:* MLA; Am Asn Teachers Span & Port; Cath Renascence Soc (vpres, 70-). *Res:* Modern Spanish literature, especially reflections of religious and church-state problems; German-French literary relation; great books. *Publ:* Translr, Sven Stolpe, Night Music, 60 & Otto Semmelroth, Mary Archetype of the Church, 63, Sheed & Ward; auth, Spanish Anticlericalism, Las Americas, 66; Spanish realism, Perez Galdos & Pereda, In: New Cath Encycl, McGraw, 67; Garcia Lorca's basic affirmation in Poet in New York, In: Studies in Honor of Samuel Waxman, Boston Univ, 69; The Celestina: A Parody of Courtly Love, Las Americas, 71. *Mailing Add:* 11 Crescent Rd Larchmont NY 10538

DE VRIES, SIMON JOHN, Old Testament, Hebrew & Cognate Languages. See Vol IV

DEW, JAMES ERWIN, b Belfry, Mont, June 27, 32; m 59; c 2. CHINESE LANGUAGE & LITERATURE, LINGUISTICS. *Educ:* Univ Fla, BA, 53, Univ Mich, MA, 59, PhD(Far Eastern lang & lit), 65. *Prof Exp:* Field dir Chinese lang, Cornell Univ Inter-Univ Prog in Taiwan, 61-62; lectr Chinese, 63-65, asst prof, 65-70, ASSOC PROF CHINESE, UNIV MICH, ANN ARBOR, 70-, ASSOC DIR, CTR FOR CHINESE STUDIES, 71-73 & 75- *Concurrent Pos:* Dir, Stanford Univ Inter-Univ Prog Chinese Lang Studies, Taiwan, 66-67 & 73-75. *Mem:* Ling Soc Am; Chinese Lang Teachers Asn (secy-treas, 68-70); Asn Asian Studies; Am Orient Soc. *Res:* Chinese linguistics; 20th century Chinese fiction; Chinese traditional vernacular literature. *Publ:* Translr, City of Cats, Univ Mich Ctr Chinese Studies, 64; auth, Shu Ch'ing-ch'un, In: Vol III, Biographical Dictionary of Republican China, Columbia Univ, 70. *Mailing Add:* Dept of Far Eastern Lang Univ of Mich Ann Arbor MI 48109

DEWEES, WILL, b Chicago, Ill, July 17, 39. LINGUISTICS, WRITING. *Educ:* Univ Ill, BA, 62; Makerere Univ, Uganda, dipl English lang teaching, 63; Northern Ill Univ, MA, 66; Univ Wis, PhD(ling), 70. *Prof Exp:* Asst prof ling, 70-76, DIR COMPOS, ACAD ADVAN CTR, OHIO UNIV, 76- *Concurrent Pos:* Fulbright-Hays lectr, 74-75; prof appl ling, Poznan Univ, Poland, 74-75. *Mem:* Ling Soc Am; African Studies Asn. *Res:* African historical lintuistics; African sociolinguistics. *Publ:* Auth, Ill formed sentences, Col English, 12/69; Epenthesis or deletion, Papers & Studies in Controlled Ling, 77; Secondary language learning and the uncomitted cortex, Glottodidactica, 77. *Mailing Add:* Dept of Ling Ohio Univ Athens OH 45701

DE WEEVER, JACQUELINE ELINOR, b Georgetown, SAm; US citizen. MIDDLE ENGLISH. *Educ:* New York Univ, BA, 67, MA, 68; Univ Pa, PhD(English), 71. *Prof Exp:* Asst prof English, Pa State Univ, Media, 71-73; ASST PROF ENGLISH, BROOKLYN COL, CITY UNIV NEW YORK, 73- *Mem:* Mediaeval Acad Am. *Res:* Medieval lexicography; literature of the Third World; medieval romance. *Publ:* Auth, The inverted world of Toni Morrison's The Bluest Eve and Sula, Col Lang Asn J, 6/79; Chaucerian onomastics: The formation and use of personal names in Chaucer's works, Names, Vol 28, No 1, 1-31. *Mailing Add:* Dept of English Brooklyn Col City Univ of New York Brooklyn NY 11210

DEWEY, HORACE WILLIAM, Slavic Languages & Literature, Russian History. See Vol I

DIACONOFF, SUELLEN, b Buffalo, NY, Oct 18, 40; m 64; c 2. EIGHTEENTH CENTURY FRENCH NOVEL. *Educ:* Willamette Univ, BA, 62; Ind Univ, PhD(French lang & lit), 78. *Prof Exp:* Lectr, Tufts Univ, 78-80; vis lectr, NC State Univ, 80-81; ASST PROF FRENCH, CASE WESTERN RESERVE UNIV, 81- *Concurrent Pos:* Am Coun Learned Soc fel, 82. *Mem:* MLA; Am Asn Teachers French; Am Soc Eighteenth Century Studies. *Res:* Mask and meaning in 18th century French literature and art; eros in the arts; literature and art. *Publ:* Auth, Eros and Power in Les Liaisons dangereuses: A Study in Evil, Droz, Geneva, 79. *Mailing Add:* Dept of Mod Lang & Lit Case Western Reserve Univ Cleveland OH 44106

DIAL, ELEANORE MAXWELL, b Norwich, Conn; m 59. SPANISH. *Educ:* Univ Bridgeport, BA, 51; Mexico City Col, MA, 55; Univ Mo, PhD(Span), 68. *Prof Exp:* Instr Span, Univ NC, Greensboro, 58-59; instr Span & French, Carroll Col, 61-62; from instr to asst prof Span, Univ Wis-Milwaukee, 63-75; asst prof, Ind State Univ, 75-78; ASST PROF SPAN, IOWA STATE UNIV, 79- *Concurrent Pos:* Nat Endowment for Humanities, summer sem, Univ Calif, Los Angeles, 81. *Mem:* Am Asn Teachers Span & Port; MLA; Midwest Mod Lang Asn. *Res:* Twentieth century Latin American theatre; 20th century Spanish Theatre; modern Hispanic literature. *Publ:* Auth, Spanish classical theatre in Mexico in the 1950's, Latin Am Theatre Rev, spring 71; Critical reaction to Buero Vallejo and Casona in Mexico, Hispania, 9/71; Lorca's impact in Mexico: 1936 and 1957, Hispanofila, 74; contribr, Brechtian aesthetics in Chile: Isidora Aguirre's Los papeleros, In: Latin American Women Writers: Yesterday and Today, Latin Am Lit Rev, 77. *Mailing Add:* Dept of Foreign Lang Iowa State Univ Ames IA 50010

DIAL, JOHN ELBERT, b Batavia, Ohio, Dec 9, 27; m 59. SPANISH. *Educ:* Univ Cincinnati, BS, 50; Univ of the Am, MA, 55; Univ Mo, PhD(Span), 66. *Prof Exp:* Instr Span, Univ Mo, 56-59; from instr to asst prof, 60-77, ASSOC PROF SPAN, MARQUETTE UNIV, 77- *Mem:* MLA; Am Asn Teachers Span & Port. *Res:* Spanish theatre; 20th century Spanish literature. *Publ:* Auth, Benavente: The dramatist on stage, Rev Estudios Hispanicos, 74; Gironella's chronicles revisited: A panorama of fratricide, Papers Lang & Lit, 74; contribr, Un Chien andalou': Notes on the uses of surrealism, In: 1976 Film Studies Annual, Purdue Univ, 76. *Mailing Add:* Dept of Foreign Lang & Lit Marquette Univ Milwaukee WI 53233

DIAS, AUSTIN, b Honolulu, Hawaii, June 12, 41; m 66; c 3. SPANISH LANGUAGES, SPANISH PENNINSULAR LITERATURE. *Educ:* Univ Calif, Santa Barbara, BA, 63, MA, 65; Univ Wis-Madison, PhD(Span), 71. *Prof Exp:* Teaching asst Span, Univ Calif, Santa Barbara, 63-65; teaching asst, Univ Wis-Madison, 67-70, instr, 70-71; asst prof, 71-76, ASSOC PROF SPAN, UNIV HAWAII, MANOA, 76- *Mem:* Am Asn Teachers Span & Port. *Res:* Nineteenth and 20th century Spanish literature. *Publ:* Auth, El desajuste de planos en Martes de Carnaval, Res Estudios Hispanicos, (in prep); La escenografia esperpentica en Martes de Carnaval, Explicacion de Textos Lit, (in prep). *Mailing Add:* Dept of European Lang & Lit Moore 470 Univ of Hawaii at Manoa 1890 East-West Rd Honolulu HI 96822

DIAZ, JANET WINECOFF, b Chicago, Ill, Jan 29, 35; div; c 2. ROMANCE LANGUAGES, CONTEMPORARY SPANISH LITERATURE. *Educ:* Univ Kansas City, AB, 55; Duke Univ, MA, 57, PhD(Romance lang), 61; Univ Oslo, dipl Norweg lang & lit, 57. *Prof Exp:* Instr Span, Duke Univ, 62-64, res coun grant, 63-64; asst prof, Queen's Col, NY, 64-66; assoc prof, 67-75, res coun grants, 68-73, prof Romance lang, Univ NC, Chapel Hill, 75-77; vis prof class & Romance lang, 77-78, PROF CLASS & ROMANCE LANG, TEX TECH UNIV, 78- *Concurrent Pos:* Philos Soc grant, 71-73; ed for Span,

Twayne World Authors Ser, 74- *Honors & Awards:* Lit Award, Am Asn Teachers Span & Port, 68. *Mem:* MLA; Am Asn Teachers Span & Port; Asoc Int Hispanistas; Soc for Iberian & Latin Am Thought. *Res:* Spanish 20th century novel; contemporary Spanish theater; Spanish philosophy. *Publ:* Auth, Spanish peninsular literature, In: Encyclopedia of World Literature in the Twentieth Century, Ungar, 66-71; Luis Martin Santos and the contemporary Spanish novel, Hispanis, 5/68; The Major Themes of Existentialism in the Works of Ortega y Gasst, tniv NC, 70; Theater and theories of Fernando Arrabal, Ky Romance Quart, 71; Ana Maria Matute, 71 & Miguel Delibes, 72, Twayne; ed, Novelistas femeninas de la post-guerra espanola, Porrua, Madrid, 78. *Mailing Add:* Dept of Class/Romance Lang Box 4649 Tex Tech Univ Lubbock TX 79409

DIAZ, LOMBERTO, b Pinar del Rio, Cuba, Apr 16, 14; US citizen; m 40; c 2. SPANISH & SPANISH AMERICAN LITERATURE. *Educ:* Univ Havana, Dr, 38, Dr & Master, 44; Ind State Univ, Terre Haute, BA, 65, MA, 66; Fla State Univ, PhD(philos), 69. *Prof Exp:* Prof polit sci, Interam Ctr Econ & Soc Studies, Dominican Repub, 63; instr Span, Ind State Univ, Terre Haute, 65-66; assoc prof, Northeastern Mo State Col, 66-67; instr, Fla State Univ, 67-69; assoc prof, 69-73, dir summer prog, 71, 72 & 74, prof, 73-80, EMER PROF SPAN, IND STATE UNIV, EVANSVILLE, 80- *Concurrent Pos:* Vis prof, Inst Filologia Hispanica, Saltillo, Mex, 71, Univ San Luis Potosi, 72. *Mem:* Am Asn Teachers Span & Port; Circulo Cult Panam; MLA; AAUP. *Res:* Latin American studies. *Publ:* Auth, Municipal Government, 42, Crimes Against Public Economic, 44 & Budget and Its Functions, 48, Ed the Congr, Cuba; Penal Reform, Jesus Montero, Havana, 59; Jose Maria Heredia and the Spanish American Romanticism, Ed Geminis, Montevideo, 73. *Mailing Add:* Dept of Foreign Lang Ind State Univ 8600 University Blvd Evansville IN 47712

DIAZ-DUQUE, OZZIE FRANCIS, b Guanajay, Cuba, Sept, 17, 51; US citizen. ROMANCE LANGUAGES & LITERATURES. *Educ:* Queens Col, City Univ New York, BA, 73; Univ Iowa, MA, 75, PhD(Romance lang), 80. *Prof Exp:* Instr Span, 73-82, ASST PROF SPAN & PORT, UNIV IOWA, 82- *Concurrent Pos:* Med interpreter Am sign lang, Hosps & Clinics, Univ Iowa, 80-; consult & lectr, Col Nursing, Univ Iowa, 77, lectr, Col Med, 74- *Mem:* MLA; Am Med Writers Asn; Am Transl Asn. *Res:* Foreign language teaching techniques; communication in medical settings; vocal music and literature. *Publ:* Ed, Spanish for Health Professionals, Univ Iowa Press, 74; co-auth, Communicating with the Spanish-speaking patient, Univ Iowa Hosps & Clinics, 76 & 82; auth, Communication barriers in medical settings, Am J Nursing, 6/82. *Mailing Add:* Transl Servs Dept Social Servs Univ Iowa Hosps & Clinics Iowa City IA 52242

DIBLASI, DANIEL F, b Brooklyn, NY, Jan 1, 25. ROMANCE LANGUAGES & LITERATURES. *Educ:* Brooklyn Col, AB, 46; Columbia Univ, MA, 48, PhD(Span), 63. *Prof Exp:* PROF SPAN & ITAL, KING'S COL, PA, 48- *Concurrent Pos:* Chmn dept foreign lang & lit & annual workshop for foreign lang teachers, King's Col, 64-76; vis prof Am civilization, Escuela Normal LaSalle, Madrid, Spain, 70-71. *Mem:* Pac Southwest Mod Lang Asn; Am Asn Teachers Span & Portuguese; Am Asn Teachers Ital. *Res:* Spanish literature, generation of '98 and 20th century; Spanish American civilization; Italian Romanticism. *Publ:* Auth, Italy in the works of Sarmiento and Marti, Scop, 61; La revolucion estudiantil norteamericana, Mimbre, 71. *Mailing Add:* King's Col Wilkes-Barre PA 18711

DIBLASI, SEBASTIANO, b Wilmington, Del, Nov 6, 28; m 66; c 3. ROMANCE LINGUISTICS, LEXICOGRAPHY. *Educ:* Temple Univ, AB, 55; Univ Pa, PhD(Romance ling), 64. *Prof Exp:* Teacher Span & English, South Philadelphia High Sch, Pa, 56-57; asst instr Romance lang, Univ Pa, 57-60; from instr to assoc prof mod lang, 60-69, acting chmn dept, 71-72, PROF MOD LANG, ST JOSEPH'S UNIV, PA, 69- *Concurrent Pos:* Prof French, Philadelphia Col Textiles & Sci. *Honors & Awards:* Cavaliere, Order of Ital Solidarity, 72. *Res:* Monolingual and bilingual lexicography; Italian grammar. *Publ:* Auth, Problems in Italian lexicography, Mod Lang J, 11/59; asst auth, Frequency Dict of Italian Words, Mouton, 73; co-ed, The Scribner Bantam English Dictionary, Scribner, 77; The Treatment of Compound Prepositions in Romance Language Dictionaries, Babel Int J Transl, No 2, 77. *Mailing Add:* Dept of Mod Lang St Joseph's Univ Philadelpha PA 19131

DI BONA, JOSEPH, b July 18, 27; US citizen. INTERNATIONAL & COMPARATIVE STUDIES. *Educ:* Univ Wis-Madison, BA, 51; Univ Calif, Berkeley, PhD(comp educ, SAsian lang & area studies), 67. *Prof Exp:* Lectr educ, Brooklyn Col, 65-67; ASSOC PROF, DUKE UNIV, 67- *Concurrent Pos:* NDEA fel, 62-63; Fulbright-Hays & Am Inst Indian Studies fels, India, 70-71; Fulbright res fel, Delhi & Calcutta, 81-82. *Mem:* Asn Asian Studies; Comp Educ Soc; Am Educ Studies Asn. *Res:* Education in India; student protest and university reform. *Publ:* Auth, Change and Conflict, Lalvani, 72; The New Delinquent in Soviet society, Sch & Soc, 72; Extending the History of Education with Archaeological Data: The Case of the University of Taxila, 72; ed, The Context of Education in Indian Development, Duke Univ, 74; auth, The development of educational underdevelopment in India, Asian Profile, 77; Indigenous virtue and foreign vice, Comp Educ Rev, 81; The professional educator's response to the intellectual repression of the Cold War, Educ Forum, 82; One Teacher, One School, Biblia Impex, 82. *Mailing Add:* Dept of Educ Duke Univ Durham NC 27708

DICESARE, MARIO ANTHONY, English & Comparative Literature. See Vol II

DICK, ERNST SIEGFRIED, b Grabenhof, Ger, Apr 7, 29; m 61. GERMANIC LITERATURE & PHILOLOGY. *Educ:* Univ Munster, PhD, 61. *Prof Exp:* Instr Ger, Univ Mont, 57-58, 61-62; from asst prof to assoc prof, Univ Va, 62-67; prof, Univ Wis-Milwauke, 67-68; PROF GER, UNIV KANS, 68- *Mem:* MLA; Am Asn Teachers Ger; Mediaeval Acad Am; Int Arthur Soc; Wolfram von Eschenbach-Gesellschaft. *Res:* Germanic philology; medieval literature; theory and history of the novelle. *Publ:* Auth, A New Seminar Approach: Germanic Heroic Poetry, PSGP Yearbk, 75; Schlag, Schlagen, Erschlagen: Zur Wort und Begriffssymbolik der Judenbuche, In: Gedenkschrift fur Jost Trier, 75; Katabasis and the Grail Epic: Wolfram von Eschenbach's Parzival, Res Publica Litterarum, 78; Epic Space in Historical Perspective: The Virgilian Argument, Res Publica Litterarum, 79; Fels und Quelle: Ein Landschaftsmodell des höfischen Epos, Wolfram-Studien, 80; Ae dream: Zur Semantik der Verbalbeziehungen in der Dichtung, In: Festschrift für Karl Schneider, 82; Ae dream: Zur Semantik der Verbalbeziehungen in der Dichtung, In: Festschrift für Karl Schneider, 82; co-ed, Rilke: The Alchemy of Alienation, Regents Press, 80; Festschrift für Karl Schneider, Benjamins, Amsterdam, 82. *Mailing Add:* Dept of Ger Lang & Lit Univ of Kans Lawrence KS 66045

DICKERSON, ALBERT INSKIP, JR, English Language and Literature. See Vol II

DICKERSON, GREGORY WEIMER, b Hanover, NH, Mar 8, 37; m 67; c 2. CLASSICAL LANGUAGES & LITERATURE. *Educ:* Harvard Univ, AB, 59; Princeton Univ, MA, 65, PhD(classics), 72. *Prof Exp:* Teaching fel classics, Phillips Acad, Andover, Mass, 59-60; secy, Am Sch Class Studies, Athens, 63-64; instr, Gilman Sch, Baltimore, 64-66; instr Classics, 67-70, asst prof Greek, 70-76, ASSOC PROF GREEK, BRYN MAWR COL, 76- *Mem:* Am Phil Asn. *Res:* Greek drama. *Publ:* Auth, Aristophanes' Ranae 862: A note on the anatomy of Euripidean Tragedy, Harvard Studies Class Philol, 74; coauth, Sophocles' Women of Trachis, Oxford Univ, 78. *Mailing Add:* Dept of Greek Bryn Mawr Col Bryn Mawr PA 19010

DICKERSON, HAROLD DOUGLAS, JR, b Boston, Mass, Oct 19, 33; m 60; c 1. GERMAN LANGUAGE & LITERATURE. *Educ:* Univ Mass, BA, 61, MA, 62; Ohio State Univ, PhD(Ger), 67. *Prof Exp:* Instr Ger, Capital Univ, 65-68; asst prof, 68-71, ASSOC PROF GER, GA STATE UNIV, 71- *Mem:* MLA; Am Asn Teachers Ger; Int Arthur Schnitzler Res Asn. *Res:* Medieval German literature, especially Gottfried von Strassburg; Arthur Schnitzler--early 20th century Austrian; contemporary short story--German and Austrian. *Publ:* Auth, Arthur Schnitzler's Die Frau des Richters: A statement of futility, Ger Quart, 3/70; Water and vision as mystical elements in Schnitzler's Der Gang zum Weiher, Mod Austrian Lit, fall 71; Language in Tristan as a key to Gottfried's conception of God, Amsterdamer Beiträege, 72; Sixty-six voices from German: A thematic approach, Amsterdamer Beiträege zur Neueren Germanistik, 73; Hagen: A negative view, Semasia, 75. *Mailing Add:* Dept of Foreign Lang Ga State Univ Univ Plaza Atlanta GA 30303

DICKIE, MATTHEW WALLACE, b Edinburgh, Scotland, Nov 20, 41; Brit citizen. CLASSICAL PHILOLOGY. *Educ:* Univ Edinburgh, MA, 64; Univ Toronto, PhD(Greek), 72. *Prof Exp:* Instr classics, Swarthmore Col, 67-68; asst prof, 72-78, ASSOC PROF CLASSICS, UNIV ILL, CHICAGO CIRCLE, 78-, CHMN DEPT, 80- *Res:* Early Greek poetry; Greek ethics; Greek history. *Publ:* Auth, Thucydides 1.93.3, Historia, 72; Ovid, Metamophoses 2.760-4, Am J Philol, 75; The meaning of Ephermeros, Ill Class Studies, 76; Thucydides, not Philistus, Greek, Roman & Byzantine Studies, 76; Dike as a moral term in Homer and Hesiod, Class Philol, 78; The argument of Simonides 542 PMG, Harvard Studies Class Philol, (in press). *Mailing Add:* Dept of Classics Univ of Ill Chicago Circle Box 4348 Chicago IL 60680

DICKISON, SHEILA KATHRYN, b Walkerton, Ont, Nov 14, 42. CLASSICS, ANCIENT HISTORY. *Educ:* Univ Toronto, BA, 64; Bryn Mawr Col, MA, 66, PhD(Latin & Greek), 72. *Prof Exp:* From instr to asst prof Greek, Latin & ancient hist, Wellesley Col, 69-76; actg chmn classics, 77-78, ASSOC PROF CLASSICS, UNIV FLA, 76- *Mem:* Archaeol Inst Am; Am Class League. *Res:* Roman historiography; ancient social history. *Publ:* Auth, Abortion in antiquity, Arethusa, 4/72; Women In antiquity: A review-article, Helios, fall 76; A note on matriarchy in early Greece, Arethusa, 9/76; Claudius: Saturnalicius Princeps, Latomus, 77; co-ed, Engineering and Humanities, John Wiley, 82. *Mailing Add:* ASB-3C Univ of Fla Gainesville FL 32611

DIEN, ALBERT E, b St Louis, Mo, July 13, 27; m 59. CHINESE LANGUAGE. *Educ:* Univ Calif, Berkeley, AB, 50, MA, 51, PhD, 61. *Prof Exp:* Asst prof Chinese, Univ Hawaii, 60-62, Stanford Univ, 62-66; dir, Ctr Chinese Studies, 62-63, dir, Inter-Univ prog Chinese lang studies, 63-64; assoc prof, Columbia Univ, 66-68; PROF CHINESE, STANFORD UNIV, 68- *Concurrent Pos:* Inter-Univ field training in Chinese fel, 56-57; Ford Found foreign area training fel, 57-59; Wilson Found Orient lang fel, 59-60; grantee, Am Coun Learned Soc, 68-69. *Mem:* Asn Asian Studies; Am Orient Soc; Chinese Lang Teachers Asn. *Res:* Philology; Chinese history; Chinese medieval history. *Publ:* Auth, Chou Shu ll: Yu-wen Hu, Univ Calif, 62; Yen Chih-tui, a Buddho-Confucian, In: Confucian Personalities, Stanford Univ, 62; The Yuan-hun Chih: A sixth century collection of ghost stories, In: Wen-Lin: Studies in the Chinese Humanities, Univ Wis, 68; The Yeh-Hou Chia-Chuan and its use as an historiographical source, Harvard J Asiatic Studies, Vol 34, 74; Elite lineages and the To-Pa accommodation, J Econ and Social Hist Orient, Vol 19, 75; The Biography of Yen Chih-Tui (Pei Chi Su 45), Würzburger Sino-Japonica, Vol 6, 76; The bestowal of surnames under the western Wei/Northern Chou: A case of counter-acculturation, Tvoung Pao, 77. *Mailing Add:* Dept of Asian Lang Stanford Univ Stanford CA 94305

DIETIKER, SIMONE RENAUD, b Sansais, France, Jan 24, 29; m; c 2. FRENCH. *Educ:* Univ Paris, Lic es Lett, 51, Dipl Prof French l'Etranger, 53, CAPES, 55. *Prof Exp:* Instr French, Smith Col Jr Year Abroad, Geneva, Switz, 55-58; asst, Sorbonne, 58-59; teacher, Punahou High Sch, Honolulu, Hawaii, 59-60; instr, David Douglas High Sch, Portland, Ore, 61-62; instr, Univ Ore, 62-64; asst prof, 64-72, assoc prof, 72-80, PROF FRENCH, SAN JOSE STATE UNIV, 80- *Res:* French Grammar; pronunciation; teaching methods. *Publ:* Auth, En Bonne Forme: Revision de Grammaire Francaise, 73, rev ed, 78 & Franc-Parler-1st Year French Textbook, 75, Heath. *Mailing Add:* Dept of Foreign Lang San Jose State Univ San Jose CA 95114

DIETZ, DONALD T, b Chicago, Ill, Sept 9, 39; m 63; c 6. SPANISH. *Educ:* Univ Notre Dame, BA, 61; Univ Ariz, PhD(Span), 68. *Prof Exp:* Instr Span, Univ Dayton, 65-66; from asst prof to assoc prof & admin asst to chmn dept, Ball State Univ, 66-72; prof Span & chmn dept mod lang, Univ Louisville, 72-76; PROF SPAN & CHAIRPERSON DEPT, TEX TECH UNIV, 76- *Mem:* Am Asn Teachers Span & Port; MLA. *Res:* The Autos Sacramentales; Spanish Renaissance. *Publ:* Auth, The Auto Sacramental and the parable in Spanish Golden Age, Romance Lang & Notes, Vol 132; Literature and relevance: Diary of Spanish novel cause, Mod Lang J, 5/72. *Mailing Add:* Dept of Span Tex Tech Univ Lubbock TX 79413

DIEZ, LUIS ALFONSO, b Aranda, Burgos, Spain, Aug 23, 34. LITERATURE, HISTORY. *Educ:* Univ Valladolid & Univ Zaragoza, Lic law & soc sci, 58; Univ London, BA, 67, PhD(Span Am lit), 70. *Prof Exp:* Asst prof & coordr Hisp studies, Lakehead Univ, 69-71; asst prof Span & Latin Am studies, 71-76, ASSOC PROF SPAN & ROMANCE LANG, QUEENS COL, 76-, GRAD ADV, 75- *Concurrent Pos:* Can Coun res grant, 70-71. *Mem:* MLA; Inst Int Lit Iberoam. *Res:* Spanish American contemporary literature, prose and poetry; Spanish contemporary literature; history and politics of Austral countries. *Publ:* Auth, Mario Vargas Llosa's pursuit of the total novel, CIDOC, Cuadernos, Mex, 70; ed & contribr, Asedios a Vargas Llosa, Univ Chile, Santiago, 72; auth, La muerte y la nina de Onetti, Cuadernos Hispanoam, 10/73; coauth, Aproximaciones a Octavio Paz, Mortiz, Mex, 74; auth, La narrativa fantatica de J E Pacheco, Texto Critico, 9/76; The sources of Vargas Llosa's The Green House, Tex Studies Lit & Lang, winter 78; V Llosa: Three conversations on human failure, World Lit Today, winter 78. *Mailing Add:* Dept of Romance Lang Queens Col Flushing NY 11367

DIEZ DEL RIO, PETER, b Bonar, Spain, Apr 27, 19; US citizen; m 45. ROMANCE LANGUAGES. *Educ:* Immaculate Conception Col, DC, Lic Theol, 43; Columbia Univ, MA, 48; Univ Madrid, PhD(lit & hist), 52. *Prof Exp:* Teacher high sch, NJ, 57-64; ASSOC PROF SPANISH & SPANISH LIT, STATE UNIV NY COL OSWEGO, 64- *Mem:* NEA; Am Asn Teachers Span & Port. *Mailing Add:* Dept of Mod Lang State Univ of NY Col Oswego NY 13126

DILILLO, LEONARD MICHAEL, b Cleveland, Ohio, Oct 31, 35; m 65; c 2. SPANISH LANGUAGE & LITERATURE. *Educ:* Rutgers Univ, BA, 57, MA, 59, PhD(Span), 70. *Prof Exp:* Instr Span, Rutgers Univ, 64-65; instr, Univ Md, 65-66; asst prof, Wash Col, 66-69; asst prof, 69-71, chmn foreign langs, 71-78, assoc prof, 71-77, chmn, Div Humanities, 78-79, PROF SPAN, CENTRE COL KY, 77-, DEAN ACAD AFFAIRS, 79- *Mem:* Am Coun Teaching Foreign Lang; Am Asn Teachers Span & Port. *Res:* Spanish comedia; Spanish Golden Age literature; foreign language pedagogy. *Publ:* Auth, Moral purpose in Ruiz de Alarcon's La verdad sospechosa, Hispania, 4/73; Characterization and Ethics in Ruiz de Alarcon's Las paredes oyen, Hispanofila, 1/79. *Mailing Add:* Centre Col Ky Danville KY 40422

DILKEY, MARVIN CHARLES, b Knightstown, Ind, Aug 13, 11. GERMAN. *Educ:* DePauw Univ, AB, 32; Cornell Univ, PhD(Ger & English), 37. *Prof Exp:* Instr Ger, Blackburn Col, 35-36 & Cornell Univ, 36-41; intel officer, gen staff, US Dept War, 41-46 & Cent Intel Agency, 46-50; private bus, 50-54; asst secy, Mod Lang Asn Am, 54-55; from asst prof to prof Ger, 55-76, EMER PROF GER, LAKE FOREST COL, 76- *Mem:* MLA. *Res:* Charles Sealsfield; E T A Hoffmann; history of the opera. *Publ:* Coauth, Letters by German authors of the eighteenth and nineteenth centuries, Ger Rev; John Mitchell Kemble and the Brothers Grimm, J English & Ger Philol. *Mailing Add:* 725 Birch Rd Lake Bluff IL 60044

DILLER, EDWARD, b Cleveland, Ohio, Dec 14, 25; m 55; c 3. GERMAN. *Educ:* Univ Calif, Los Angeles, BA, 55; Los Angeles State Col, MA, 56; Middlebury Col, DML, 61. *Prof Exp:* Teaching asst, Univ Calif, Los Angeles, 57; teacher Ger & coordr foreign lang, Beverly Hills Unified Sch Dist, Calif, 57-62; asst prof Ger, Colo Col, 6265; assoc prof, 66-72, dir honors col, 72-77, PROF GER, UNIV ORE, 72- *Concurrent Pos:* Foreign lang consult, In-Serv Educ in Foreign Lang, Univ Calif, Los Angeles, 59, Calif State Leadership Conf, 60 & Colo State Foreign Lang Conf, 63; resource consult, Conf Dir Improv Instr in Calif, 61; mem advan placement comt, Educ Testing Serv, NJ, 62; ed, Peals; Fulbright prof, Univ Regensburg, 67-68 & Univ Freiburg, 77-78; vis prof Ger, TAP V-Dortmund, 67-70. *Mem:* MLA; Am Asn Teachers Ger (secy, 72-75, pres, 77-78). *Res:* Twentieth century German literature; linguistics and teaching. *Publ:* Auth, Freidrich Dürrenmatt's theological concept of history, Ger Quart, 5/67; Uwe Johnson's Karsch: Language as a reflection of the two Germanies, Monatschefte, spring 68; coauth, Unterwegs 68 & auth, Meisterwerke Der Deutschen Sprache, 70, Random; Friedrich Dürrenmatt's Chaos and Calvinism, Monatschefte, 71; Günter Grass' Tin Drum: A Mythic Journey, Univ Ky, 74. *Mailing Add:* Dept of Ger Univ of Ore Eugene OR 97403

DILLER, GEORGE THEODORE, b Hanover, NH, Jan 1, 40; m 61; c 3. MEDIEVAL FRENCH. *Educ:* Princeton Univ, AB, 61; Middlebury Col, MA, 63; Stanford Univ, PhD(French), 68. *Prof Exp:* Instr French, Brandeis Univ, 66-68; asst prof, 68-73, ASSOC PROF FRENCH, UNIV FLA, 73- *Mem:* Soc Anciens Textes Francais; SAtlantic Mod Lang Asn; Repertoire Int Medievistes. *Res:* Medieval French historians, especially Froissart; Romans antiques. *Publ:* Auth, La derniere redaction du premier livre des Chroniques de Frossart, une etude du Reg lat 869, Moyen Age, 70; ed, Froissart's Chroniques, Derniere Redaction du Premier Livre, Droz, Geneva, 72. *Mailing Add:* Dept of RLL Univ of Fla Gainesville FL 32611

DILLER, KARL CONRAD, b Wooster, Ohio, Jan 24, 39; m 62; c 2. LINGUISTICS, ENGLISH AS A SECOND LANGUAGE. *Educ:* Univ Pittsburgh, BA, 61; Harvard Univ, EdM, 64, PhD(ling), 67. *Prof Exp:* Teaching fel English as second lang, Harvard Univ, 62-65, teaching fel, freshman composition, 65-66; asst prof English, Royal Mil Col St Jean, 67-68; instr & lectr, Harvard Univ, 68-72; assoc prof, 72-80, PROF ENGLISH, UNIV NH, 80- *Concurrent Pos:* Item writer for Test of English as Foreign Lang, Educ Testing Serv, 66; consult, Arthur D Little, Inc & Harper & Row, 69-70; consult English as second lang, Lawrence Pub Schs, Mass, 71-72. *Mem:* Ling Soc Am; MLA; Int Asn Appl Ling; Teachers English to Speakers Other Lang; Am Coun Teaching Foreign Lang. *Res:* Applied linguistics; theories of language acquisition. *Publ:* Auth, Compound and coordinate bilingualism--a conceptual artifact, Word, 8/70; Resonance and language learning, Linguistics, 6/71; Bilingualism and the lexicon, In: Studies for Einar Haugen, Mouton, The Hague, 72; Some new trends for applied linguistics and foreign language teaching in the United States, TESOL Quart, 9/75; coauth, Neurolinguistic foundations for methods of teaching a second language, Int Rev Appl Ling, 78; auth, The Language Teaching Controversy, 78 & ed, Individual Differences and Universals in Language Learning Aptitude, 79, Newbury House. *Mailing Add:* Dept of English Univ of NH Durham NH 03824

DILLON, GEORGE LEWIS, English, Linguistics. See Vol II

DILLON, JOHN MYLES, b Madison, Wis, Sept 15, 39; m 65. CLASSICS. *Educ:* Oxford Univ, BA, 62, MA, 64; Univ Calif, Berkeley, PhD(classics), 69. *Prof Exp:* From asst prof to assoc prof classics, Univ Calif, Berkeley, 69-77, prof, 77-80; REGIUS PROF GREEK, TRINITY COL, DUBLIN, 80- *Mem:* Am Philol Asn; Soc Ancient Greek Philos; Int Soc Neoplatonic Studies. *Res:* Greek philosophy. *Publ:* Auth, Enn III 5: Plotinus' Exegesis of the Symposium Myth, Agon, 69; Harpocration's commentary on Plato: Fragments of a middle Platonic commentary, Calif Studies Class Antiq, 71; Iamblichus and the origin of the doctrine of Henads, Phronesis, 72; Iamblichi Chalcidensis in Platonis Dialogos Commentariorum Fragmenta, Brill, Leiden, 73; The Middle Platonists, Duckworth, London, 77; coauth (with David Winston), Philo, De Gigantibus and Quaod Deus Sit Immutabilis, A Commentary, 82. *Mailing Add:* Sch of Classics Trinity Col Univ of Dublin Dublin 2 Ireland United Kingdom

DILTS, MERVIN R, b Flemington, NJ, Feb 26, 38. CLASSICS. *Educ:* Gettysburg Col, BA, 60; Ind Univ, MA, 61, PhD(classics), 64. *Prof Exp:* Asst prof classics, Knox Col, 64-65 & Univ Ill, Urbana, 65-69; assoc prof, 69-79, PROF CLASSICS, NY UNIV, 79- *Concurrent Pos:* Am Philol Soc grant, 71; Am Coun Learned Soc grant-in-aid, 77. *Mem:* Am Philol Asn; Class Asn Atlantic States; Soc Textual Scholarship. *Res:* Greek textual criticism; Greek codicology. *Publ:* Auth, The manuscript tradition of Aelian's Varia Historia and Heraclides' Politiae, Trans & Proc Am Philol Asn, 65; Heraclidis Lembi excerpta politiarum, In: Greek, Roman and Byzantine Monograph 5, 71; The manuscripts of Appian's Historia Romana, Rev Hist des Textes, 71; Clandii Aeliani Varia Historia, Teubner, 74; Demosthenic scholia in Codex Laur 59 9, 74 & The manuscript tradition of Scholia Ulpiani on Demosthenis in Timocratem, 75, Trans & Proc Am Philol Asn; Scholia in Demosthenem, Teubner, (in press). *Mailing Add:* Dept of Classics NY Classics Univ Washington Sq New York NY 10003

DI MAIO, IRENE STOCKSIEKER, b New York, NY, Sept 5, 40; c 1. GERMAN STUDIES. *Educ:* Vassar Col, BA, 62; Univ Chicago, MA, 65; La State Univ, PhD(Ger), 76. *Prof Exp:* INSTR GER, LA STATE UNIV, 65- *Mem:* MLA; Am Asn Teachers Ger; Women in Ger; Am Coun Teachers of Foreign Lang; Raabe-Gesellschaft Int. *Res:* Nineteenth century German literature; women's studies; German culture. *Publ:* Auth, The Multiple Perspective, Wilhelm Raabe's Third Person Narratives of the Braunschweig Period, John Benjamins, 81; The Fravenfrage and the reception of Wilhelm Raabe's female characters, In: Studien zu Seinem Leben and Werk, Verlag, 81. *Mailing Add:* Dept of Class Germanic & Slavic Lang La State Univ Baton Rouge LA 70803

DIMIC, COLETTE ANNE MARIE, b Angouleme, France, Feb 9, 34; m 59; c 2. FRENCH LANGUAGE & LITERATURE, GERMANIC PHILOLOGY. *Educ:* Univ Paris, BA, 56, MA, 57; Univ Freiburg in Breisgau, PhD(German), 60. *Prof Exp:* Lectr French, Univ Belgrade, 61-63; prof, French Col Konstanz, WGer, 63-65; lectr Ger philol & French, 66-67, from asst prof to assoc prof, 67-68, PROF FRENCH, UNIV ALTA, 78- *Mem:* Asn Can Univ Teachers Fr; Asn Can Prof French; Can Comp Lit Asn. *Res:* German espressionism; French 19th and 20th century literature. *Publ:* Auth, Andre Gide et le bonheur, 75 & Roger Martin du Gard et le bonheur: dans le sillage de Montaigne, 76, Rev de Philol; Stendhal, W Scott et la legende de Tristan et Iseut: une source inconnue de deux episodes de Rouge et Noir?, Stendhal Club Quart, 77; Roger Martin du Gard, disciple de Montaigne, Australian J French Studies, 77; L'aurore et le matin: une influence de Rimbaud sur Gide, Rev des lettres Mod, 78; Gide et la maladie, Studi Francesi, 79; L'Etique chretiente dans Dominique de Fromentin, Revue de l' Universite d' Ottawa, 80; Dominique de Fromentin dans la perspective du Biedermeier, Romanistische Feitschrift fü Literaturwissenschaft, 81. *Mailing Add:* Dept of Romance Lang Univ of Alta Edmonton AB T6G 2E6 Can

DIMIC, MILAN VELIMIR, b Belgrade, Yugoslavia, Mar 15, 33; m 59; c 2. COMPARATIVE & GERMAN LITERATURE. *Educ:* Univ Belgrade, MA, 56; Univ Vienna, dipl, 56. *Prof Exp:* Instr Ger, Serbian Acad Sci & Inst Exp Phonetics, 56-57; asst prof comp lit, Univ Belgrade, 57-62; from asst prof to assoc prof, 66-72, chmn dept comp lit, 69-75 & 81, PROF GERMAN & COMP LIT, UNIV ALTA, 72-, CHMN COMP LIT PROG, 67- *Concurrent Pos:* Res asst, Inst Theory of Lit & Aesthet, Belgrade, 60-62; mem, Can Coun Acad Panel, 74-78, chmn 76-78; ed, Can Rev Comp Lit, Univ Alta Press & Univ Toronto Press, 74- *Mem:* MLA; Asn Can Univ Teachers Ger; Can Asn Slavists; Am Comp Lit Asn; Can Comp Lit Asn. *Res:* Romanticism; folklore; methods in literary scholarship. *Publ:* Auth, The angel as the Hero's substitute in the South-Slavic cycle about Prince Marko, NedeljKaric, 75; A mediaeval use of the motif of the double: The theme of Amicus and Amelius, Rev de Philol, 75; Le Monde mediterraneen et le romantisme, Actes du vie Cong de l'AILC, 75; co-ed, Actes du vie Congres de l'AILC, 75 & ed, Proceedings of the VII Congress of the ICLA, Kunst und Wissen, Stuttgart, 79/80; auth, Aspects of American and Canadian Gothicism, 78 & The motif of the double in Renaissance literature, 78, Proc VIIIth Cong ICLA; ed, Bibliotheque de la Revue Canadienne de Litterature Comparee, Wilfrid Laurier Univ, 78- *Mailing Add:* Dept of Comp Lit Univ of Alta Edmonton AB T6G 2E6 Can

DIMLER, GEORGE RICHARD, b Baltimore, Md, Oct 21, 31. GERMAN LANGUAGE & LITERATURE. *Educ:* Fordham Univ, AB, 56, MA, 60; Woodstock Col, STB, 62, STL, 64; Middlebury Col, MA, 66; Univ Calif, Los Angeles, PhD(Germanic lang), 70. *Prof Exp:* Asst prof, Loyola Col, Md, 70-71; assoc prof, Fordham Univ, 72-81, ED, THOUGHT: QUART REV CULT & IDEA, FORDHAM UNIV PRESS, 78-, PROF LANG, 82- *Concurrent Pos:* Instr Ger, Marquette Univ, 62-; NDEA fel, 67-70; Nat Endowment for Humanities grant, 74; Am Coun of Learned Socs fel, 75; Ger Acad Exchange Serv fel, 76-77 & 78-79; Herzog August bibliothek, Wolfenbüttek Stipendium, 79. *Mem:* Am Asn Teachers Ger; MLA; Mid Atlantic Lang Asn; Goethe Soc Am (treas, 72); Renaissance Soc Am. *Res:* German baroque literature, Jesuit drama; Jesuit emblematics. *Publ:* Auth, Friedrich Spee's Trutznachtigall, Herbert Lang, Bern, 73; The genesis and development of Spee's love imagery in the Trutznachtigall, Germanic Rev, 73; Don Quixote and Simplicius Simplicissimus: Study in alienation, Thought, 74; Gottfried Von Strassburg's Tristan, Amsterdamer Beitrage, 75; The egg as emblem: Genesis and structure of a Jesuit emblem book, Studies in Iconography, 76; A bibliographical survey of Jesuit emblem books in Early Jesuit colleges, Archivum Hist Soc Jesu, 76; Friedrich Spees Trutznachtigall, Univ Press Am, 81; Imago Primi Saeculi: The secular tradition and the Jesuit emblem book, Thought, 81. *Mailing Add:* Thought c/o Fordham Press Univ Bronx NY 10458

DIMMICK, RALPH EDWARD INGALLS, b Cincinnati, Ohio, Oct 19, 16. ROMANCE LANGUAGES & LITERATURE. *Educ:* Pa State Col, AB, 37; Harvard Univ, AM, 38, PhD, 41. *Prof Exp:* Asst dir English courses, Uniao Cult Brasil-US, Sao Paulo, 43-46; instr & tutor Romance lang, Harvard Univ, 46-49; instr, Northwestern Univ, 49-51; asst to dir, dept cult affairs, 52-58, spec asst to secy gen, 58-68, exec asst to secy gen, 68-76, GEN SECRETARIAT, ORGN AM STATES, PAN AM UNION, 76- *Mem:* Am Asn Teachers Span & Port. *Res:* Portuguese and Brazilian literature; French literature of the 17th century; Portuguese language. *Mailing Add:* 1285 Delaware Ave SW Washington DC 20024

DIMOCK, EDWARD CAMERON, JR, b Boston, Mass, Mar 18, 29; m 52; c 5. MODERN INDIAN LANGUAGES, HISTORY OF RELIGION. *Educ:* Yale Univ, BA, 50; Harvard Univ, STB, 53, STM, 54, PhD, 59. *Prof Exp:* Asst prof, 59-61, assoc prof, 61-66, prof, 77-80, DISTINGUISHED PROF BENGALI, UNIV CHICAGO, 80-, DIR SOUTH ASIAN LANG & AREA CTR, 72-, CHMN COMT SOUTH ASIAN STUDIES, 76- *Concurrent Pos:* US State Dept specialist grant, 61; sr res fel, Am Inst Indian Study, Calcutta, 63-64; US Off Educ res fel, 65. *Mem:* Am Inst Indian Studies (secy, 65-); Am Orient Soc; Asn Asian Studies. *Res:* Medieval Bengali religious texts; Bengali linguistics; modern Bengali literature. *Publ:* Auth, Rabindranath Tagore--The greatest of the Bauls of Bengal, J Asian Studies, 11/59; Manasha--Goddess of Snakes, winter 61 & Manasha--Goddess of Snakes Part II, autumn, 63, Hist Relig; coauth, An Introduction to Gengali (part I), 65 & The Maharashtra Purana, 65, East-West Ctr; auth, The Place of the Hidden Moon, Univ Chicago, 66; coauth, In Priase of Krishna, Doubleday, 67. *Mailing Add:* Dept of SAsian Lang Univ of Chicago Chicago IL 60637

DIMOCK, GEORGE EDWARD, JR, b New Haven, Conn, Dec 19, 17; m 46; c 3. CLASSICAL PHILOLOGY. *Educ:* Yale Univ, AB, 39, AM, 40, PhD(classics), 49. *Prof Exp:* From instr to asst prof classics, Yale Univ, 48-55; assoc prof, 55-60, PROF CLASSICS, SMITH COL, 61- *Concurrent Pos:* Am Coun Learned Soc fel, 60-61; Geggenheim fel, 64-65. *Mem:* Am Philol Asn; Class Asn New Eng. *Res:* Homer; Virgil; Greek tragedy. *Publ:* Auth, The name of Odysseus, Hudson Rev, 56; From Homer to Novi Pazar and back, Arion, winter 63; Oedipus: The religious issue, Hudson Rev, 6/68; Crime and punishment in the Odyssey, winter 71 & The mistake of Aeneas, 75, Yale Rev; Euripides' Hippolytus, or virtue rewarded, Yale Class Studies, 77; God, or not God, or between the two?, Euripides' Helen, Smith Col, 77; co-transl, Euripides' Iphigeneia et Aulis, Oxford Univ, 78. *Mailing Add:* 62 Revell Ave Northampton MA 01060

DI NAPOLI, THOMAS JOHN, b Providence, RI, Oct 2, 44. MODERN & CONTEMPORARY GERMAN LITERATURE. *Educ:* Providence Col, BA, 66; Univ Tex Austin, MA, 68, PhD(Ger), 71. *Prof Exp:* Nat exec secy, Phi Sigma Iota, 78-80; ASST PROF CLASS, GER & SLAVIC LANG, LA STATE UNIV, 80- *Concurrent Pos:* Int Res & Exchanges Bd scholar, 82. *Mem:* Am Asn Teachers Ger; SCent Mod Lang Asn. *Res:* Children's literature in Germany. *Publ:* Auth, Guilt and absolution: The contrary world of Gunter Grass, Cross Currents, winter 77; Problems in defining the German Kurzgeschicte, Studies Short Fiction, 78; In quest of the Messiah: A study of the Christ figure in the Danzig trilogy of Gunter Grass, Centennial Rev, 80; Wolf, Christa, In: Columbia Dict of Modern European Literature, 80; Postage stamps and the teaching of GDR culture and civilization, Unterrichtspraxis, 80; Bertolt Brecht and the no: A comparison of two theaters, The Comparatist, 81; Between laymen and the literati the GDR's Schreibende Arbeiter, GDR Monitor, 81; Brecht's Kaukasische Kreidekreis: A study of form and content, Lit Wiss u Unterricht, 81. *Mailing Add:* Dept of Class, Ger & Slavic Lang La State Univ Baton Rouge LA 70803

DINGWALL, WILLIAM ORR, b Washington, DC, Mar 9, 34. LINGUISTICS. *Educ:* Georgetown Univ, BS, 57, MA & PhD(theoretical ling), 64. *Prof Exp:* Inst Ling, Georgetown Univ, 63-65; asst prof, Ind Univ, 65-66; asst prof, Simon Fraser Univ, 66-67; ASSOC PROF & DIR LING PROG, UNIV MD, COLLEGE PARK, 67- *Mem:* Ling Soc Am; Asn Comput Ling. *Res:* Psycholinguistics; neurolinguistics; scientific method. *Publ:* Auth, Secondary conjunction and universal grammar, Papers Ling, 69; ed, A Survey of Linguistic Science, Univ Md, 71; coauth, Government and concord in Russian: A study in developmental linguistics, In: Kahane Festschrift, Univ Ill, 71; Neurolinguistics, In: Annual Review of Anthropology, vol 3, 74. *Mailing Add:* Linguistics Prog Univ of Md College Park MD 20742

DINNEEN, DAVID ALLEN, b New York, NY, June 24, 31; m 56; c 3. FRENCH, LINGUISTICS. *Educ:* Queens Col, NY, BA, 52; Univ Kans, MA, 54; Harvard Univ, PhD(ling), 63. *Prof Exp:* Instr French, Mass Inst Technol, 58-61; asst prof, 62-68, assoc prof, 68-71, chmn dept ling, 70-81, PROF FRENCH & LING, UNIV KANS, 72- *Concurrent Pos:* Fulbright lectr ling, Barcelona, Spain, 66-67. *Mem:* Am Asn Teachers Fr; Asn Comput Ling; Ling Soc Am; Rocky Mountain Mod Lang Asn. *Res:* Stylistics and linguistics; French syntax; second language aquisition. *Publ:* Auth, A Left-to Right Generative Grammar of French, MIT-RLE, 62; The grammar of specifiers, In: Readings in Automatic Language Processing, Am Elsevier, 66; Tonal value analysis of French poetry, Fr Rev, 5/67; Vous avez la parole, Review and Reference Grammar, Macmillan, 68; ed, Syntax and Semantics: Presupposition, Acad Press, 79. *Mailing Add:* Dept of Fr & Ital Univ of Kans Lawrence KS 66045

DINNEEN, FRANCIS PATRICK, b Philadelphia, Pa, Mar 16, 23. LINGUISTICS. *Educ:* Woodstock Col, Md, AB & PhL, 49, MA, 50, ThL, 55; Univ London, PhD(ling), 61. *Prof Exp:* Teacher high sch, Md, 49-52; from asst prof to assoc prof, 61-70, acting head Ger div, 62-64, acting dean sch lang & lit, 66-68, acting dean grad sch, 72-73, chmn dept ling, 72-75, PROF LING, GEORGETOWN UNIV, 70, HEAD DIV THEORETICAL LING, 61- *Concurrent Pos:* Vis asst prof, Cath Univ Am, 63-64. *Mem:* Ling Soc Am; Int Ling Asn. *Res:* General linguistics; history of linguistics; semantics. *Publ:* Auth, Introduction to General Linguistics, Holt, 67; Analogy, langue and parole, Lingua, 21, 68; Linguistics and the social sciences, In: Interdisciplinary Relations in the Social Sciences, Aldine, 69; Semantic structure, In: Proceedings of the Tenth International Congress of Linguists, Ed Acad Rep Socialiste Roumanie, 70; Linguistic significance of C K Ogden's Basic English, In: Kongressbericht der Gesellschaft für Angewandte Linguistik, Gross Verlag, 74; Basic and normal English, In: Proceedings of IV International Congress on Applied Linguistics, Stuttgart, 75; The teaching of linguistics at Georgetown University, Mouton, Trends in Linguistics, (in press). *Mailing Add:* Dept of Ling Georgetown Univ Washington DC 20007

DINSMORE, JOHN DAVID, b San Francisco, Calif, Sept 27, 49; m 80; c 1. THEORETICAL LINGUISTICS. *Educ:* Sonoma State Univ, BA, 75; Univ Calif, San Diego, PhD(ling), 79. *Prof Exp:* Res fel, Univ Bielefeld, Ger, 79-80 & Univ Calif, Berkeley, 80-82; RES & WRITING, 82- *Mem:* Ling Soc Am. *Res:* Semantics, language and cognition. *Publ:* Auth, On the pragmatic theory of presupposition, Proc Western Col Ling Res Inc, 79; Pragmatics, Formal Theory, and Analysis of Presupposition, Univ Ind Ling Club, 81; The Inheritance of Presupposition, John Benjamins, Amsterdam, 81; Toward a unified theory of presupposition, J Pragmatics, Vol 5, 81; Tense choice and time specification in English, Ling, Vol 19, 82. *Mailing Add:* 18475 Old Monte Rio Rd Guerneville CA 95446

DIORIO, DOROTHY MAY, b York, Pa, Nov 17, 32. FOREIGN LANGUAGES. *Educ:* Bucknell Univ, BA, 54; Univ Paris, dipl, 58; Middlebury Col, MA, 60; Univ Munich, cert, 67; Univ NC, Chapel Hill, PhD(French, Ital & Ger), 71. *Prof Exp:* Teacher Latin & French, Neshaminy High Sch, 54-56; lectr Latin & English, La Chatelaine, St Blaise, Switz, 56-57; teacher Latin & French, Paris Am Sch, France, 57-62 & Munich Am Sch, Ger, 62-65; lectr French, Univ Md Overseas Div Munich Campus, 65-67; instr, Col William & Mary, 67-68; asst prof, WVa Univ, 71-72; assoc prof, 72-77, CASTANOLI PROF ITAL LANG, AUBURN UNIV, 77-, HEAD DEPT FOREIGN LANG, 72- *Honors & Awards:* Chevalier, L'Ordre des Plames Academiques, 77. *Mem:* MLA; SAtlantic Mod Asn; AAUP; Am Asn Teachers Fr; Am Asn Univ Women. *Res:* Dante; 19th century French literature; 19th century German drama. *Publ:* Auth, Leconte de Lisle: A Hundred and Twenty Years of Criticism, Univ Miss, 72; Stendhal's Le Rouge et le Noir: The enigma of a title, 7/72 & Dante's greatness as seen in the fourfold levels of interpretation, 9/73, Philol Papers, WVa; Languages for Profit and Pleasure, Dimensions, Scolt, 10/74. *Mailing Add:* Dept of Foreign Lang Auburn Univ 8030 Haley Ctr Auburn AL 36830

DIORIO, JOSEPH FREDERICK, II, b York, Pa, July 31, 31. FRENCH, LATIN. *Educ:* Dickinson Col, AB, 53; Middlebury Col, MA, 64. *Prof Exp:* Head dept Latin, French & English, Delhaas Sr High Sch, 53-60; teacher French & Latin, Paris-Am High Sch, St Cloud, Paris, 60-62; master, Deerfield Acad, Mass, 62-63; resident dir, Le Foyer Champlain & secy to dean Fr sch, Middlebury Col, 63-64; ASSOC PROF FRENCH & LATIN, UNIV MONTEVALLO, 64- *Concurrent Pos:* Instr Latin & English, La Chatelainie, St Blaise, Switz, 57-58. *Mem:* AAUP; MLA; Am Coun Teaching Foreign Lang; S Atlantic Mod Lang Asn; Am Class League. *Res:* Classicism in the 19th century; classical influence in the writings of Lamartine; Romance philology. *Publ:* Contribr, Le Conte de Lisle: A Hundred and Twenty Years of Criticism, 1850-1970, Romance Monogr, 72. *Mailing Add:* Dept Foreign Lang Univ of Montevallo Montevallo AL 35115

DI PIETRO, ROBERT J, b Endicott, NY, July 18, 32; m 53. LINGUISTICS. *Educ:* State Univ NY Harpur Col, BA, 54; Harvard Univ, MA, 55; Cornell Univ, PhD, 60. *Prof Exp:* Proj linguist, res on anal of Ital & English, Ctr Applied Ling, Wash DC, 60-61; from asst prof to assoc prof ling, Georgetown Univ, 61-68, co-chmn Annual Round Table Conf Lang & Ling, 62, chmn, 63, prof ling & Ital, 69-78, ed, Interfaces: Ling & Psychoanal, Sch Lang & Ling, 74-78; CHMN DEPT LANG & LIT, UNIV DEL 78- *Concurrent Pos:* Fulbright lectr ling, Univ Rome, 60-61; Fulbright lectr ling, Univ Madrid & coordr English Lang Prog in Spain, 63-64; Am Coun Learned Soc travel grant, Madrid, 65; consult ed, Blaisdell Publ Co, 65-72; bk rev ed, Mod Lang J, 72-77. *Honors & Awards:* Andrew W Mellon Distinguished Lectureship Award, Georgetown Univ, 75-77; Cavaliere Ufficiale, Govt Italy, 77. *Mem:* Ling Soc Am; MLA; Am Asn Teachers Ital; AAAS; Am Anthrop Asn. *Res:* Contrastive analysis; language and psychoanalysis; bilingualism. *Publ:* Ed, 16th Monograph on Languages and Linguistics, Georgetown Univ, 63; coauth, The Sounds of English and Italian, 65 & The Grammatical Structures of English and Italian, 65, Univ Chicago; auth, Language Structures in Contrast, Newbury House, 71, rev ed, 78; Alcune riflessioni sulla linguistica applicata all'insegnamento, In: L'Insegnamento dell' Italiano in Italia e all

'Estero, Bulzoni, Rome, 71; Kurze orientierende Bemerkungen zur Untersuchung sprachlicher Verschiedenheit, Reader zur kontrastiven Linguistic, Frankfurt, 72; Language as Human Creation, Georgetown Univ Press, 76; ed, Linguistics and the Professions, Ablex Publ Corp, 82. *Mailing Add:* Dept of Lang Univ of Del Newark DE 19711

DI STEFANO, GIUSEPPE, b Jan 4, 36; Ital citizen; m 68; c 1. ROMANCE PHILOLOGY. *Educ:* Univ Turin, Dr, 61; Sorbonne Univ, Dipl, Ecole Hautes Etudes, 67, Dr 3e cycle, 68. *Prof Exp:* Asst prof Romance philol, Univ Turin, 64-69; researcher, Nat Ctr Sci Res, 63-69; assoc prof French 69-80, PROF FRENCH, MCGILL UNIV, 80- *Concurrent Pos:* Co-ed, Studies Francesi; ed, Le Moyen Francais. *Mem:* Asn Int Etudes Fr; Mediaeval Acad Am. *Res:* French literature of the 14th and 15th centuries. *Publ:* Auth, L'opera Oratoria de Courtecuisse, Giappichelli, Turin, 67; La Decouverte de Plutarque au XIVe Siecle, Acad Sci, Turin, 68; L'oeuvre Oratoire Francaise de Jean Courtecuisse, Giappichelli, Turin, 69; L'edition des textes en moyen francais, XIII Int Congr Ling & Romance Philol, 73; Flexion et Versification en Moyen Francais, Melanges Lecoy, Paris, 73; Essais sur le Moyen Francais, Liviana, Padova, 77. *Mailing Add:* Dept of French McGill Univ Montreal PQ H3A 1B1 Can

DI TOMMASO, ANDREA, b Chicago Heights, Ill, July 7, 38; m 64; c 3. ITALIAN RENAISSANCE LITERATURE, CINEMA. *Educ:* Johns Hopkins Univ, BA, 62, PhD(Romance lang), 70. *Prof Exp:* Asst prof, 66-73, ASSOC PROF ITAL, WAYNE STATE UNIV, 73- *Mem:* MLA; Renaissance Soc Am; Am Asn Teachers Ital. *Res:* Renaissance literature; baroque poetics. *Publ:* Auth, Structure and Ideology in Boiardo's Orlando Innamorato, Univ NC, 72; Nature and the aesthetic social theory of L B Alberti, Medievalia et Humanistica, 72; Insania and furor: A diagnostic note on Orlando's Malady, Romance Notes, 73. *Mailing Add:* Dept of Romance & Ger Lang Wayne State Univ Detroit MI 48202

DI VINCENZO, VITO JOHN, b Cincinnati, Ohio, Nov 4, 16; m 42; c 2. MODERN SPANISH. *Educ:* Pa State Univ, BA, 37; Univ Pa, MA, 47. *Prof Exp:* Teacher English, Santurce Sr High Sch, PR, 37-39; asst prof Span, Pa State Univ, 40-48; assoc prof, 48-80, PROF SPAN, VILLANOVA UNIV, 80- *Concurrent Pos:* Part-time lectr Span, Cabrini Col, Pa, 57- *Mem:* MLA; AAUP; Am Asn Teachers Span & Port. *Res:* Golden Age Spanish literature; Miguel de Cervantes Saavedra. *Publ:* Coauth, Guia para electores, Women's League, Phila, 61; ed & transl, Fernando Chueca Goitia, Guia del Pueblo Espanol de Palma de Mallorca, Ed Everest, Leon, Spain, (in prep). *Mailing Add:* Dept of Mod Lang & Lit Villanova Univ Villanova PA 19085

DIXON, CHRISTA KLINGBEIL, b Essen, Ger, Dec 8, 35; m 62; c 2. GERMAN LANGUAGE & LITERATURE, FOLKLORE. *Educ:* Univ Heidelberg, Staatsexamen I, 59; Univ Bonn, Staatsexamen II, 62, PhD(Negro spirituals), 65. *Prof Exp:* Asst prof Ger lang & lit & philos, La Salle Col, 69-74; ASSOC PROF GER, ILL STATE UNIV, 78- *Concurrent Pos:* Ill Humanities Coun grant, 75-76; adj assoc prof Ger, Western Ill Univ, 76-77. *Mem:* MLA; AAUP(secy-treas, 70-); Am Asn Teachers Ger. *Res:* Contemporary German literature; philosophy; literature of the German Democratic Republic. *Publ:* Auth, Negro Spirituals, Wesen und Wandel Geistlicher Volkslieder, Jugenddienst, Wuppertal, 67; Peter Handke: Die Angst des Tormanns Beim Elfmeter: Ein Beitrag zur Interpretation, Sprachkunst, Vienna, 72; Peter Handke: Kaspar, ein Modell Fall, Ger Quart, 73; Directions of hope in contemporary German literature, Renascence, 73; Negro Spirituals--From Bible to Folksong, Fortress, 76. *Mailing Add:* 202 W Orlando Normal IL 61761

DJAPARIDZE, JUSTINIA BESHAROV, b Batoum, Russia, May 20, 21; US citizen; m 54; c 1. RUSSIAN LANGUAGE & LITERATURE. *Educ:* Vassar Col, AB, 42; Columbia Univ, AM, 49; Harvard Univ, PhD(Russ lit), 53. *Prof Exp:* Instr Russ, Harvard Univ, 50-53; vis asst prof, Ind Univ, 59-60; assoc prof & chmn, Vassar Col, 66-71; assoc prof Russ lit, New York Univ, 71-73; vis prof, Ecole Hautes Etudes, Paris, 77-78; ASSOC PROF RUSS LANG & LIT, TRINITY COL, 79- *Concurrent Pos:* Jr fel, Dumbarton Oaks, 53-54. *Mem:* Am Asn Teachers Slavic & East Europ Lang; Am Asn Russ-Am Scholars; MLA. *Res:* Old Russian literature; comparative literature; Russian culture and civilization. *Publ:* Auth, Imagery of the Igor Tale in the Light of Byzantino-Slavic Poetry Theory, Brill, 56; The Divine & Human Word, St Vladimirs Sem Press, Vol IV, No 1-2; Remarks on the Zadonscina, Yearbk Am Philos Soc, 60. *Mailing Add:* Trinity Col Box 1365 Hartford CT 06106

D'LUGO, MARVIN ALAN, b Brooklyn, NY, July 15, 43; m 66; c 1. MODERN SPANISH AMERICAN LITERATURE. *Educ:* Brooklyn Col, AB, 65; Univ Ill, AM, 67, PhD(Span), 69. *Prof Exp:* Asst prof Span Am lit, State Univ NY, Buffalo, 69-72; asst prof, 72-80, ASSOC PROF SPAN & COMP LIT, CLARK UNIV, 80- *Concurrent Pos:* Dir, Prog of Humanisitc Studies, Nat Endowment Humanities grant, Clark Univ, 77-80. *Mem:* MLA; Inst Int Lit Iberoam; Am Asn Teachers Span & Port; Soc Cinema Studies. *Res:* Contemporary Spanish American narrative; theory of fiction; film theory. *Publ:* Auth, Arte y vida en Fuga de Anderson Imbert, In: Homenaje a Enrique Anderson Imbert, Ed Anaya, 73; The Heritage of Self-Conscious Form, Barroco, 73; Frutos de los frutos prohibidos: la fantaciencia rioplatense, In: Otros Mundos, Otros Fuegos, Mich State Univ, 75; Signs and meaning in Blow-Up: From Cortazar to Antonioni, Lit/Film Quart, 75; Barry Lyndon: Kubrick on the rules of the game, In: Film Studies Annual: Part I: Explorations in National Cinemas, 77; Las babas del diablo, in pursuit of Cortazar's reel world, Rev Estud Hispanicos, 9/77. *Mailing Add:* Dept of Foreign Lang & Lit Clark Univ Worcester MA 01610

DOBSEVAGE, ALVIN P, Philosophy, Foreign Language. See Vol IV

DOBSON, EUGENE, b Dumas, Ark, Aug 9, 36; m 58; c 3. GERMAN, COMPARATIVE LITERATURE. *Educ:* Henderson Col, BA, 57; Univ Ark, MA, 60, PhD(comp lit), 66. *Prof Exp:* Inst English & Ger, Northeast La State Univ, 61-62; instr Ger, Univ Ala, 62-63; lectr English, Univ Hamburg, 63-65; instr Ger, Univ Ark, 65; instr, 65-66, asst prof, 66-71, assoc prof Ger & comp lit, 71-76, ASSOC PROF GER, UNIV ALA, 76-, CHMN DEPT, 71- *Res:* Modern German literature; drama; Thomas Mann. *Publ:* Translr & English ed, Thomas Mann; A Chronicle of His Life, Univ Ala, 69. *Mailing Add:* Dept of Ger Univ of Ala University AL 35486

DOBSON, MARCIA DUNBAR-SOULE, b New York, NY, Aug 28, 41. CLASSICS, HUMANITIES. *Educ:* Bennington Col, AB, 63; Tufts Univ, AM, 64; Harvard Univ, PhD (class philol), 76. *Prof Exp:* Instr, 76-77, ASST PROF CLASSICS, COLO COL, 77- *Mem:* Am Philol Asn. *Res:* Greek religion; semiotics; women's studies. *Publ:* Auth, Herodotus 1 47 1 and the Hymn to Hermes: A solution to the test oracle, Am J Philol, Vol 100, No 3; Derrida, Tantalus and Helen of Troy, Colo Col Studies, no 18. *Mailing Add:* Dept of Class Colo Col Colorado Springs CO 80903

DOENGES, NORMAN ARTHUR, b Ft Wayne, Ind, Aug 23, 26; m 52; c 3. ANCIENT HISTORY, CLASSICS. *Educ:* Yale Univ, BA, 47; Oxford Univ, BA, 49; Princeton Univ, MA, 51, PhD(classics), 54. *Prof Exp:* Instr classics, Princeton Univ, 49-50 & 52-53; from instr to assoc prof, 55-65, chmn dept classics, 59-63 , 67-71 & 78-79, chmn div humanities, 63-67, assoc dean fac, 64-66, prof-in-chg, Intercol Ctr Class Studies, Rome, Italy, 66-67, PROF CLASSICS, DARTMOUTH COL, 65- *Concurrent Pos:* Mem managing comt, Am Sch Class Studies; mem adv coun, Am Acad in Rome. *Mem:* Soc Prom Hellenic Studies; Am Philol Asn; Class Asn Can; Class Asn New Eng(secy-treas, 63-68); Asn of Ancient Historians. *Res:* Greek and Roman history; Greek pseudonymic letters. *Publ:* Auth, The Letters of Themistokles, Arno Press, 81. *Mailing Add:* Dept of Classics Dartmouth Col Hanover NH 03755

DOERING, BERNARD, b St Louis, Mo, Aug 7, 24; m 57; c 4. FRENCH LANGUAGE & LITERATURE. *Educ:* Univ Dayton, BS, 45; Wash Univ, MA, 54; Univ, Colo, PhD(Fr), 67. *Prof Exp:* Instr, 65-67, ASST PROF FRENCH, UNIV NOTRE DAME, 67- *Mem:* Am Asn Teachers Fr. *Res:* Nineteenth and twentieth century French literature; French Catholic literary revival 16th century French poetry. *Mailing Add:* Dept of Mod Lang Univ of Notre Dame Notre Dame IN 46556

DOERKSEN, VICTOR GERARD, b Winnipeg, Man, Jan 9, 34; m 60; c 2. GERMAN LITERATURE & CRITICISM. *Educ:* Univ Man, BA, 58, MA, 60; Univ Zurich, DPhil(Ger), 64. *Prof Exp:* Asst prof Ger, Univ NB, 60-61; lectr, 61-62 & 64-65, from asst prof to assoc prof, 66-74, PROF GER, UNIV COL, UNIV MAN, 74-, HEAD DEPT, 68- *Concurrent Pos:* Can Coun res grant, 67- *Mem:* Asn Can Univ Teachers Ger; Int Germanistenverband. *Res:* Nineteenth century German literature; literary criticism. *Publ:* Auth, Mörikes Elegien und Epigramme, Juris, Zurich, 64; coauth, Texts in German Literature, Copp Clark, 68; Deutung und Bedeutung: Studies in German and Comparative Literature, Mouton, The Hague, 73; auth, Die Mörike-Literatur Seit 1950: Literaturbericht und Bibliographie, DVLG, 73; ed, Eduord Mörike Darmstadt: Wiss Buch, 75. *Mailing Add:* Dept of Ger Univ of Man Winnipeg MB R3T 2N2 Can

DOERR, RICHARD PAUL, b Stillwater, Minn, July 7, 42; m 66; c 3. SPANISH LANGUAGE, LATIN AMERICAN LITERATURE. *Educ:* Macalester Col, AB, 64; Univ Ill, Urbana, MA, 66; Univ Colo, Boulder, PhD(Span), 73. *Prof Exp:* Instr Span, Colgate Univ, 64-66; from instr to asst prof, Allegheny Col, 71-75; asst prof, 75-79, ASSOC PROF SPAN, METROPOLITAN STATE COL, 79- *Mem:* Am Asn Teachers Span & Port; Am Asn Translrs; Rocky Mt Mod Lang Asn. *Res:* Latin American Spanish usage; contemporary Latin American novel; Latin American culture. *Publ:* Auth, Algunos apuntes sobre el lexico de Cundinamarca, Hispania, 5/69. *Mailing Add:* Dept of Mod Lang Metropolitan State Col Denver CO 80204

DOHERTY, THOMAS WILLIAM, b Poplar Bluff, Mo, July 12, 12; m 46; c 2. FRENCH LITERATURE. *Educ:* Westminster Col, Mo, AB, 34; Middlebury Col, AM, 42, DML, 59; Sorbonne, dipl, 50; Inst Phonetique, Univ Paris, cert, 50. *Prof Exp:* Teacher high sch, Mo, 36-42; transl, US Off Censorship, 42-43; asst prof, Evansvile Col, 46-49; assoc prof, 50-63, prof French, 63-77, EMER PROF MOD LANG, LINDENWOOD COL, 63- *Mem:* Am Asn Teachers Fr. *Res:* Contemporary French literature. *Publ:* Auth, Andre Suares et deux musiciens de son temps: Wagner et Debussy, In: Suares et le Symbolisme, 73 & Suares et Bach, Suares et l'Allemagne, 77, Minard. *Mailing Add:* Dept of French Lindenwood Col St Charles MO 63301

DOLEZEL, LUBOMIR, b Lesnice, Czech, Oct 3, 22; m 61; c 4. SLAVIC LANGUAGES & LITERATURE. *Educ:* Charles Univ, Prague, BA, 49; Acad Sci, Prague, PhD, 58. *Prof Exp:* Res fel, Inst Czech Lang, 53-65; prof slavic philol, Univ Mich, 65-68; PROF SLAVIC PHILOL & CHMN DEPT, UNIV TORONTO, 68- *Concurrent Pos:* Can Coun leave fel, 77-78. *Mem:* Can Semiotics Asn; Circle Ling Praque. *Res:* Poetics; narrative structures; Czech and Russian literature. *Publ:* Auth, O stylu moderni ceske prozy, Academia, Prague, 60; co-ed, Statistics and Style, Am Elsevier, 69; coauth, An early Chinese confessional prose: Shen Fu's six chapters of a floating life, T'oung Pao, 72; Narrative Modes in Czech Literature, Univ Toronto, 73; auth, Narrative semantics, PTL, 76; Narrative worlds, Sound, Sign & Meaning, 76; The visible and the invisible Petersburg, Russ Lit, 79; Truth and authenticity in narrative, Poetics Today, 80. *Mailing Add:* Dept of Slavic Lang & Lit Univ of Toronto Toronto ON M5S 1A1 Can

DOLEZELOVA-VELINGEROVA, MILENA, b Prague, Czechoslovakia, Feb 8, 32; Can citizen; m 61; c 2. MODERN & CLASSICAL CHINESE FICTION. *Educ:* Charles Univ, BA, 55; Czechoslovak Acad Sci, PhD(traditional Chinese storytelling), 65. *Prof Exp:* Res asst Chinese lit, Oriental Inst, Czechoslovak Acad Sci, 55-68; assoc prof, 69-72, PROF CHINESE LANG & LIT, DEPT EAST ASIAN STUDIES, UNIV TORONTO, 72- *Concurrent Pos:* Res assoc, Inst Lit, Acad Sinica, Peking, 58-59 & Ctr Chinese Studies, Univ Mich, 67-68; ed, Proj Mod Chinese Lit, Europ Sci Found, 80- *Mem:* Asn Asian Studies; Can Asn Studies Asia; Chinese Lang Teachers Asn. *Res:* Chinese fiction; Chinese storytelling; semiotics. *Publ:* Coauth, Ballad of the Hidden Dragon, Oxford Univ Press, 71;

An early Chinese confessional prose: Shen Fu's Six Chapters of a Floating Life, T'oung Pao, 72; The origins of modern Chinese literature, In: Modern Chinese Literature in the May Fourth Era, 77 & Lu Xun's medicine, In: Modern Chinese Literature in the May Fourth Era, 77, Harvard Univ Press; ed, The Chinese Novel at the Turn of the Century, Univ Toronto Press, 80; auth, Typology of plot structures in late Quing novels & Narrative modes in late Quing novels, In: The Chinese Novel at the Turn of the Century, 80. *Mailing Add:* 308 Carlton St Toronto ON M5A 2L7 Can

DOLIN, EDWIN, b Utica, NY, July 14, 28; m 57; c 2. CLASSICS, COMPARATIVE LITERATURE. *Educ:* Harvard Univ, BA, 50, MA, 53, PhD(class philol), 66. *Prof Exp:* From instr to asst prof classics, Amherst Col, 60-65; lectr classics & comp lit, Univ Calif, Berkeley, 65-66; asst prof, Univ Calif, San Diego, 66-72; assoc prof Greek & Latin, 72-75, PROF GREEK & LATIN, UNIV MISS, 75-, CHMN DEPT CLASSICS, 72- *Mem:* Am Philol Asn; Archaeol Inst Am; Class Asn Mid-West & South. *Res:* Greek drama; Greek and Roman epic poetry. *Publ:* Auth, Parmenides and Hesiod, Harvard Studies Class Philol, 62; Prometheus Psellistes, Calif Studies Class Antiq, 69; co-ed & contribr, An Anthology of Greek Tragedy, Bobbs, 72; Odysseus in Phaeacia, In: The Odyssey: A Critical Edition, Norton, 73; Thycydides on the Trojan War: A Critique of the Text, Harvard Studies Class Philol (in press). *Mailing Add:* Col of Lib Arts Univ of Miss University MS 38677

DOMAN, LARRY WALLACE, b Corvallis, Ore, Oct 18, 38; m 63; c 3. SPANISH LANGUAGE & LITERATURE. *Educ:* Univ Utah, BA, 64; St Louis Univ, PhD(Span & Latin Am studies), 72. *Prof Exp:* Instr Span, Emory Univ, 69-71; asst prof Span & Port, Univ SC, 71-72; asst prof, 72-76, ASSOC PROF SPAN & PORT, WEBER STATE COL, 76- *Concurrent Pos:* Bibliogr, Am Coun Teaching Foreign Lang & MLA. *Mem:* Rocky Mountain Mod Lang Asn; Am Coun Teaching Foreign Lang; Am Asn Teachers Span & Port. *Res:* Latin American and Brazilian literature; Luso-Brazilian studies. *Publ:* Auth, Estudo da epigrafe em Os Dragoes de Murilo Rubiao, Minas Gerais Suppl Lit, 70; Becquer's Rima XXIV, Las Brisas, 70; The Archetypal Feminine in Grande Sertao: Veredas, Bull Rocky Mountain Mod Lang Asn, 73. *Mailing Add:* Dept of Foreign Lang Weber State Col Ogden UT 84408

DOMARADZKI, THEODORE FELIX, b Warsaw, Poland, Oct 27, 10; Can citizen; m 54. SLAVIC & EAST EUROPEAN STUDIES. *Educ:* Acad Polit Sci, Warsaw, dipl, 36; Univ Warsaw, MA, 39; Univ Rome, LittD(Slavic philol & Polish lit), 41. *Prof Exp:* Asst diplomatic hist, Acad Polit Sci, Warsaw, 36-39; lectr Polish lang, Univ Rome, 41-47; dir dept Slavic studies, 48-64, prof Polish lit & Slavic philol, 48-76, ed Slavic & East Europ studies, 56-76, prof & dir, Ctr Polish Doc & Res, 63-76, PROF & PRES, INST COMP CIVILIZATIONS OF MONTREAL, UNIV MONTREAL, 76- *Concurrent Pos:* Rep, Polish Ministry Educ, Italy & dir, Polish Col Rome, 41-45; assoc prof, Pontif Inst Orient Gregorian, 43-47; vis prof, Fordham Univ, 48-50; prof, Univ Ottawa, 49-53; vpres, Paderewski Found, 49-74; consult, Assumption Col, Ont, 50-51; ed, Etudes Slaves et Est-Europeennes, 56-76; vpres, Can Inter-Am Res Inst, 63-; pres, Can World Univ Asn, 68-; pres & Can negotiator int & cult agreements, Can & Polish univs & learned soc, 70; mem ed staff, Can Slavonic Papers & Polish Rev, 76-81; prof & dir, Grad Res Ctr, Northland Open Univ, 78- *Mem:* Hon mem Can Asn Slavists (vpres, 54-64); Can Asn Slav & East Europ Specialists (pres, 50-); Polish Inst Arts & Sci; hon mem Can Soc Comp Studies Civilizations (pres, 72-). *Res:* Polish and French literary and cultural relations in the 19th and 20th century; Polish literature and civilization in Canada; comparative literature and civilization research. *Publ:* Auth, Modlitwa i Poezja w Litanii do N Marii Panny C Norwida, Richerche Slavistiche, 62; La realite du Mal dans deux manifestes poetiques: celui de C Baudelaire et celui de C Norwid, Etudes Slaves et Est-Europeennes, 66; Les considerations de C K Norwid sur la liberte de la parole, Etudes Slaves et Est Euopeennes & Univ Laval, 71; Les post-romantiques polonais, In: Canadian Contributions to the Seventh International Congress of Slavists, Mouton, The Hague, 73; Le Symbolisme et L'Universalisme de C K Norwid, Laval Univ, 74. *Mailing Add:* 5601 Ave des Cedre Montreal PQ H1T 2V4 Can

DOMBROSKI, ROBERT STANLEY, b Providence, RI, Jan 21, 39. ITALIAN & COMPARATIVE LITERATURE. *Educ:* Providence Col, AB, 62; Univ Calif, Berkeley, MA, 66; Harvard Univ, PhD(Romance lang), 69. *Prof Exp:* Asst prof Ital, Univ Chicago, 69-71; asst prof, 71-72, assoc prof, 73-77, PROF ITAL COMP LIT, UNIV CONN, 73- *Mem:* MLA; Dante Soc Am; Am Asn Teachers Ital. *Res:* Modern and contemporary Italian literature; sociology of literature. *Publ:* Auth, Intoduzione allo studio di C E Gadda, Valle Vallecchi, Florence, Italy, 74; Seicento as strategy, MLN, 76; Le Fascime et la creation litteraire, Revue des Etudes Italiennes, 76; Form of chaos in Pirandello's I vecchi e i giovani, Yale Italian Studies, 78; Le totalita dell'aztificio, Liviana, Padua, 78; Ideological question in Manzoni, Studies in Romanticism, 81; Timpunaro's materialism, J Hist Ideas (in prep); L'esistenza ubbidiente: Fascismo e letteratura, Sansoni, Florence (in prep). *Mailing Add:* Dept of Romance Lang & Lit Univ of Conn Storrs CT 06268

DOMINGUEZ, IVO, b Palma Soriano, Cuba, Oct 10, 30; US citizen; m 57; c 2. SPANISH, SPANISH AMERICAN LITERATURE. *Educ:* Univ Oriente, Cuba, JD, 56; Univ SFla, Tampa, BA, 65; Fla State Univ, MA, 68, PhD(Span), 69. *Prof Exp:* Pvt lawyer, Cuba, 56-61; instr Span, Fla state Univ, 67-70; asst prof, 70-77, ASSOC PROF SPAN, UNIV DEL, 77-, COORDR LATIN AM STUDIES, 78- *Mem:* MLA; Am Asn Teachers Span & Port; AAUP. *Res:* Medieval and Renaissance Spanish literature; prose of the Spanish Golden Age; 19th and 20th-century Spanish American literature. *Publ:* Auth, El cuarto centenario: Lepanto y Cervantes, La M Manana, 7/72: El Derecho como recurso literario en las Novelas ejemplares de Cervantes, 72 & ed, Tres novelas moriscas, 74, Inst Estudio Super, Montevideo; auth, En torno a la poesia Afro-Hispanoamericanan, Cuadernos Hispanoam, 1/77; Spanish stylometrics: A beginning, Asn Lit & Ling Computing Bull, 4/77. *Mailing Add:* Dept of Lang & Lit Univ of Del Newark DE 19711

DOMINGUEZ, SYLVIA MAIDA, b Mercedes, Tex; m 59; c 1. SPANISH & LATIN AMERICAN LITERATURE. *Educ:* Our Lady of the Lake Col, BA, 57, MEd, 58; Univ Ariz, MA, 69, PhD(Span), 71. *Prof Exp:* Instr Span & English, Our Lady of the Lake Col, 56-59; instr Span & English, 60-63, from asst prof to assoc prof Span, 63-77, actg head dept foreign lang, 76-77, PROF SPAN, PAN AM UNIV, 77- *Concurrent Pos:* Lectr & consult, biling educ workshops, Tex, 70-78; Samuel la Carretilla researcher, 73-74 Mem; Am Sociol Asn, SCent. *Res:* Spanish language drama; 19th and 20th century Mexican drama; the contemporary Mexican theatre. *Publ:* Auth, Tesoro espanol de obras originales, produced on KRGV-TV, 71; PAU presents: Tesoro espanol de obras originales, a production in Span of original drama, music & lyrics, monologues and poems, 6/71; La comandre Maria (play), Am Universals Artforms, 73; Christmas on the Rio Grande-A Blending of the Old and the New, a one-hour TV production, 73; Samuel la Carretilla, a tragicomedy in Spanish, prodeced in 74; Curanderismo: A Dramatic Portrayal, Foreign Affairs Res Papers Available, Dept of State Publs, 76; The La Comadre Maria Instruction-Production System, (Two audio cassettes, seven books, and one Instruction Production Guide), 76. *Mailing Add:* Dept of Foreign Lang Pan Am Univ Edinburg TX 78539

DOMINICIS, MARIA CANTELI, b Cuba, June 4, 31: div; c 1. SPANISH. *Educ:* Univ Havana, DPhil & Lett, 55; NY Univ, PhD, 74. *Prof Exp:* Instr Span, Ohio Wesleyan Univ, 61-62; asst prof, Sweet Briar Col, 62-64; asst prof, 64-80, ASSOC PROF SPAN, ST JOHN'S UNIV, NY, 80- *Mem:* Am Asn Teachers Span & Port; AAUP. *Res:* Contemporary Spanish theater. *Publ:* Coauth, De Todo un Poco, Macmillan, 78; auth, Don Juan en el Teatro Espanol Contemporaneo, Ed Univ, 78; coauth, Casos y cosas, 81 &; auth, Escenas cotidianas, 82, Scott Foresman. *Mailing Add:* Dept of Mod Foreign Lang St John's Univ Jamaica NY 11432

DONAHUE, FRANCIS J, b Chicago, Ill, Nov 21, 17; m 47; c 1. SPANISH MODERN AMERICAN LITERATURE. *Educ:* Univ Omaha, BA, 41; Univ Wis, MA, 42; Univ Southern Calif, PhD(Latin Am studies), 65. *Prof Exp:* Asst prof Span & English, US Merchant Marine Acad, 48-54; cult attache, US Embassies, Havana, Cuba & Caracus, Venezuela, 54-60; from asst prof to assoc prof, 60-70, PROF SPAN, CALIF STATE UNIV, LONG BEACH, 70- *Honors & Awards:* Commendable Serv Award, US Info Agency, 56; Meritorious Serv Award, 59. *Mem:* Am Asn Teachers Span & Port; Acad Cubana Lengua. *Res:* Spanish and Spanish-American novel; modern Spanish theater; modern American literature. *Publ:* Ed, Leandro Fernandez Moratin's El si de las Ninas y La Comedia Nueva, Ed Plus Ultra, Buenos Aires, 67; auth, Hacia un credo lorquiano, La Torre, summer 70; Afterword of a literary critic, Americas, 6-7/72; The Chicano story, Colo Quart, winter 73; ed, Alfonso Sastre: Dramaturgo y Preceptista, Ed Plus Ultra, Buenos Aires, 73; auth, Cuban de Tocqueville, New Orleans Rev, fall 73; The three faces of Camilo Jose Cela, Contemp Lit Criticism, Detroit, 75; Politica y estetica: el teatro epico, Cuadernos Americanos, Mexico City, 2/77. *Mailing Add:* Dept of Foreign Lang Calif State Univ Long Beach CA 90840

DONAHUE, MORAIMA DE SEMPRUN, b Madrid, Spain, July 2, 33; US citizen; m 68 c 2. SPANISH & LATIN AMERICAN LITERATURE. *Educ:* Assumption Col, Madrid, Spain, BA, 56; Univ Rochester, MA, 68; George Washington Univ, PhD(Span lit), 71. *Prof Exp:* Asst prof Span & French lit, Nazareth Col, 64-68; instr & teaching fel, George Washington Univ, 69-71; asst prof Span, 71-76, PROF SPAN, HOWARD UNIV, 76- *Concurrent Pos:* Consult Span lang & cult, Am Univ, 77, Pan Am Health Orgn, 77-78 & 80-82. *Mem:* Col Lang Asn; Inter-Am Coun; MLA; AAUP; Am Asn Teachers Span & Port. *Res:* Church discrimination against women portrayed in the literature of Spain; Hispanic language and literatures; violence and torture in the contemporary Hispanic novel. *Publ:* Auth, La doble seduccion de La Regenta, Papeles Son Armadans, Mallorca, Spain, 12/73; Las Narraciones de Federico Garcia Lorca: Un Franco Enfoque, Hispam, Barcelona, Spain, 75; El oro y lo amarillo en 100 Anos de Soledad, Cuadernos Americanos, Mex, 4-5/76; Algunos puntos estructurales y tecnicos de La Senorita de Ramon Nieto, Papeles Son Armadans, Mallorca, Spain, 9/76; Algunos indicios sobre el titulo de Niebla, Cuadernos Catedra Miguel Unamuno, Spain, 9/76; Blas de Otero en su Poesia, Univ NC, 77; La Poesia de Manuel Duran, Latin Am Lit Press, 77; Figuras y Contrafigura, en la poesis de Fernando Alegria, Latin Am Lit Press, 81. *Mailing Add:* 7436 Hallcrest Dr McLean VA 22102

DONAHUE, THOMAS JOHN, b Philadelphia, Pa, Jan 9, 43. FRENCH LITERATURE, THEATRE. *Educ:* Univ Pa, AM, 67 PhD(French), 73. *Prof Exp:* Asst prof, 65-80, ASSOC PROF, ST JOSEPH'S UNIV, PA, 80- *Concurrent Pos:* Fel, Camargo Found, 78. *Mem:* MLA; Alliance Francaise. *Res:* Fernando Arrabal; contemporary theatre. *Publ:* The Theater of Fernando Arrabal, New York Univ Press, 80. *Mailing Add:* Dept of French St Joseph's Univ Philadelphia PA 19131

DONALDSON, WEBER DAVID, JR, b Indianapolis, Ind, May 21, 31; m 63; c 2. FRENCH, LINGUISTICS. *Educ:* DePauw Univ, BA, 53; Middlebury Col, MA, 56; Ind Univ, Bloomington, PhD(French), 70. *Prof Exp:* Asst prof, 63-77, ASSOC PROF FRENCH, NEWCOMB COL, TULANE UNIV, 77-, CHMN DEPT FRENCH & ITAL, 76- *Mem:* Am Asn Teachers Fr; Ling Soc Am. *Res:* French linguistics; applied French linguistics. *Publ:* Auth, Code-cognition approaches to language learning, In: Toward a Cognitive Approach to Second Language Learning, Ctr Curric Develop, Philadelphia, 71; French Reflexive Verbs: A Case Grammar Description, Ser Practice, Mouton, The Hague, 73. *Mailing Add:* Dept of French Newcomb Col Tulane Univ New Orleans LA 70118

DONALDSON-EVANS, LANCELOT KNOX, b Newcastle, Australia, July 22, 41; m 68; c 2. FRENCH LITERATURE. *Educ:* Univ New South Wales, BA, 61; Univ Melbourne, MA, 63; Univ Geneva, Dr es Lett, 69. *Prof Exp:* Instr French, Univ Wis-Milwaukee, 66-67; lectr, Univ Md, 67-68; lectr, 68-69, asst prof, 69-72, ASSOC PROF FRENCH, UNIV PA, 72- *Concurrent Pos:* Am Coun Learned Soc grant, 72; Am Philos Soc grant, 81. *Mem:* MLA; Renaissance Soc Am. *Res:* French literature of Renaissance; Renaissance studies; poetry. *Publ:* Auth, Poesie et Meditation chez Jean de la Ceppede,

Droz, Geneva, 69; Poetry and communication in the work of Lazare de Selve, Ky Romance Quart, 71; Montaigne and poetry, Neophilologus, 73; Two Baroque devotional poets: La Ceppede and Alabaster, Comp Lit Studies, 3/75; Love's fatal glance: eye imagery and Maurice Sceve, Neophilologus, 77-78; Love's fatal glance: A study of eye imagery in the poets of the Ecole lyonnaise, Univ Miss, 80; Panurge perplexus: Ambiguity and relativity in the Tiers Livre, Etudes rabelaisiennes, Vol XV; Two stages of Renaissance style: Mannerism and baroque in French poetry, Fr Forum, 82-83. *Mailing Add:* Dept of Romance Lang Univ of Pa Philadelphia PA 19174

DONALDSON-EVANS, MARY PRUDHOMME, b Duluth, Minn, Jan 15, 43; m 68; c 2. FRENCH LANGUAGE & LITERATURE. *Educ:* Marquette Univ, BA, 65; Univ Wis-Milwaukee, MA, 67; Univ Pa, PhD(French), 75. *Prof Exp:* Instr, 69-76, asst prof, 76-82, ASSOC PROF FRENCH, UNIV DEL, 82- *Mem:* MLA; AAUP; Am Asn Teachers French. *Publ:* Auth, The matrical marsh: A symbol of hope in Maupassant's work, Fr Forum, 9/77; The sea as symbol: A key to the structure of Maupassant's Pierre et Jean, Nottingham Fr Studies, 10/78; Nuit de Noel and Conte de Noel: Ironic diptych in Maupassant's work, Fr Rev, 10/80; Auditory comprehension in the French conversation class, Mod Lang J, Vol 65. *Mailing Add:* Dept of Lang & Lit Univ of Del Newark DE 19711

DONEY, RICHARD JAY, b Chicago, Ill, June 24, 16; m 45; c 1. GERMAN. *Educ:* Univ Ill, BA, 40, MA, 47, PhD(Mediaeval studies), 50; Col Steubenville, LittD, 62. *Prof Exp:* Instr Ger, Univ Ill, 49-50; from instr to assoc prof, 50-63, asst dean col arts & sci, 54-65, assoc dean, 66-76, PROF GER, NORTHWESTERN UNIV, EVANSTON, 63- *Concurrent Pos:* Examr & consult, comn cols & univs, N Cent Asn, 57- *Mem:* MLA; Mediaeval Acad Am. *Res:* Mediaeval intellectual history. *Publ:* Auth, A source for one of the Carmina Burana, Speculum; Giraldus Cambrensis and the Carthusian Order, J English & Ger Philol. *Mailing Add:* Dept of Ger Northwestern Univ 111 Kresge Hall Evanston IL 60201

DONLAN, WALTER, b Boston, Mass, July 30, 34; c 4. CLASSICAL LANGUAGES, ANCIENT HISTORY. *Educ:* Harvard Univ, AB, 56; Northwestern Univ, MA, 65, PhD(philol), 68. *Prof Exp:* PROF CLASSICS, PA STATE UNIV, 67- *Concurrent Pos:* Ed, Class World, 74-78. *Mem:* Am Philol Asn; Am Class League; Asn Ancient Historians; Class Asn Atlantic States (pres, 79-80); Int Soc Comp Study Civilizations. *Res:* Greek literature; social and economic history of Greece. *Publ:* Auth, Changes and shifts in the meaning of Demos in the literature of the Archaic period, La Parola del Passato, 70; Archilochus, Strabo and the Lelantine War, Transactions Am Philol Asn, 70; The tradition of anti-Aristocratic thought in early Greek poetry, Historia, 73; The orgin of kalos kagathos, Am J Philol, 73; Social vocabulary and its relationship to political propaganda in fifth century Athens, Quaderni Urbinati, 77; The Aristocratic Ideal in Ancient Greece, Coronado Press, 80; Reciprocites in Homer, Class World, 82. *Mailing Add:* Dept of Classics Pa State Univ University Park PA 16802

DONOHOE, JOSEPH IGNATIUS, JR, b Philadelphia, Pa, June 18, 34; m 60; c 3. ROMANCE LANGUAGES & LITERATURES. *Educ:* La Salle Col, BA, 56; Univ Cincinnati, MA, 57; Princeton Univ, PhD(Romance lang), 66. *Prof Exp:* Instr French, Syracuse Univ, 60-63; from instr to asst prof, 63-70, assoc prof, 70-80, PROF FRENCH, MICH STATE UNIV, 80- *Res:* French drama; the Enlightenment; film studies. *Publ:* Auth, Marivaux's theater: Comic vision and social reality, Univ Microfilms, 67; Ambivalence and anger: The human center of the Chanson de Roland, Romanic Rev, 12/71; Marivaux: The comedy of enlightenment, Studies Voltaire & 18th Century, 72; The death of Manon: A literary inquest, L'Esprit Createur, 72. *Mailing Add:* Dept of Romance Lang Mich State Univ East Lansing MI 48824

DONOVAN, BRUCE E, b Lawrence, Mass, Mar 8, 37; m 59; c 2. CLASSICS. *Educ:* Brown Univ, AB, 59; Yale Univ, MA, 61, PhD(classics), 66. *Prof Exp:* Actg instr classics, Yale Univ, 62-65; from asst prof to assoc prof, 65-76, PROF CLASSICS, BROWN UNIV, 76- *Mem:* Am Philol Asn; Archaeol Inst Am; Am Soc Papyrologists. *Res:* Greek tragedy; papyrology. *Publ:* Auth, An Isaiah fragment, Harvard Theol Rev, 68; A Homer fragment, Bull Am Soc Papyrologists, 68; Studies in the Papyri of Euripides: The Evidence of Oxyrhynchus, Am Soc Papyrologists, 69; Prometheus Bound reconsidered, Harvard Studies Class Philol, 73. *Mailing Add:* Dept of Classics Brown Univ Providence RI 02912

DONOVAN, LEWIS GARY, b Sceptre, Sask, June 5, 36; m 63; c 1. MEDIEVAL FRENCH LITERATURE. *Educ:* Univ Sask, BEd, 58, BA, 61; Univ Montpellier, Lic-es-Lett, 66; Sorbonne Univ, PhD(French lit), 73. *Prof Exp:* Teacher math & French, Walter Murray High Sch, Sask, 61-64; asst prof medieval French, 66-76, ASSOC PROF MEDIEVAL FRENCH, UNIV CALGARY, 76- *Mem:* MLA. *Res:* The first novels in French, 12th century, especially Romans de Thebes, d'Eneas and de Troie. *Publ:* Auth, Recherches sur le Roman de Thebes, Soc D'Etudes Documentation Econ Indust Sociales, 75. *Mailing Add:* 6332 Bow Cres NW Calgary AB T3B 2B9 Can

DONOVAN, WILLIAM P, b St Louis, Mo, Dec 2, 29; m 55; c 2. CLASSICS, ARCHEOLOGY. *Educ:* Wash Univ, AB, 51, MA, 52; Univ Cincinnati, PhD(classics), 61. *Prof Exp:* Instr classics, hist & art hist, Fla State Univ, 58-61; asst prof classics & cur class & Europ cult mus, Univ Ill, 61-66; assoc prof classics, 66-72, chmn dept, 66-75, PROF CLASSICS, MACALESTER COL, 72- *Concurrent Pos:* Ed, Erato, Newsletter for Class ACM & GLCA Col, 80- *Mem:* Archaeol Inst Am. *Res:* Preclassical and classical archaeology; ancient art. *Publ:* Coauth, Palace of Nester, Vol III, Princeton Univ, 73; Excavations at Nichoria, Univ Minn Press, Vol I, 78. *Mailing Add:* Dept of Classics Macalester Col St Paul MN 55105

DONSKOV, ANDREW, b Belgrade, Yugoslavia, Mar 2, 39; Can citizen; m 63; c 2. RUSSIAN LITERATURE. *Educ:* Univ BC, BA, 66, MA, 67; Univ Helsinki, DrPhil(Russ drama), 72. *Prof Exp:* Lectr Russ, Univ Waterloo, 67-70, from asst prof to assoc prof Russ lang & lit 70-71, assoc chmn dept Russ, 74-77; ASSOC PROF RUSS LIT, UNIV VICTORIA, 77- *Concurrent Pos:* Can Coun res grant, 73- *Mem:* Can Asn Slavists; Can Asn Univ Prof. *Res:* Russian drama; 19th century Russian literature; comparative topics in Russian literature. *Publ:* Auth, A fofgotten play devoted to the emancipation or Russian peasants, Russ Lang Rev, 72; An intensive method of language learning, Can Mod Lang Rev, 72; The Changing Image of the Peasant in 19th Century Russian Drama, Finnish Acad Sci, 72; Precursors to Chekhov's The Cherry Orchard, New J, 73; L Tolstoy's sources for his play, The First-Distiller, 73 & Tolstoy and drama, 76, Can Slavonic Papers; Tolstoy and Galsworthy, Ger Slavica, 77. *Mailing Add:* Dept of Slavonic Studies Univ of Victoria Victoria BC V8W 2Y2 Can

DOOLEY, LINDA JEAN RINKER, English Linguistics, Popular Literature. See Vol II

DOOLING, MARGARET, b Buffalo, NY, July 6, 03. MODERN LANGUAGES. *Educ:* D'Youville Col, BA, 24; McGill Univ, MA, 41; Univ Toronto, PhD(mod lang), 45. *Prof Exp:* From instr to prof, 32-76, EMER PROF FRENCH, D'YOUVILLE COL, 76- *Mailing Add:* Dept of Foreign Lang D'Youville Col Buffalo NY 14201

DOOLITTLE, JAMES, b Morristown, NJ, Oct 8, 17; m 44; c 6. ROMANCE LANGUAGES & LITERATURES. *Educ:* Princeton Univ, AB, 39, MA, 42, PhD, 48. *Prof Exp:* Teacher French & English, Thacher Sch, Calif, 39-40; instr French, Princeton Univ, 46-49; from asst prof to prof, Ohio State Univ, 49-61; prof Romance lang & head dept, Univ Cincinnati, 61-65; PROF FRENCH LIT, UNIV ROCHESTER, 65- *Concurrent Pos:* Ohio State Univ fel, 59-60; Guggenheim fel, 62-63 & 65; Am Coun Learned Soc grant, 69-70. *Res:* History of ideas in France, 1600-1900; French literature of the 17th, 18th and 19th centuries; 17th century French memoirs. *Publ:* Auth, The Humanity of Moliere's Don Juan, PMLA, 53; Heroism and passion in Polyeucte, Symposium, 55; Rameau's Nephew, A Study of Diderot's Second Satire, Droz, Geneva, 60; Alfred de Vigny, Twayne, 67; The Deniaisement of the Prince de Marcillac, Ky Romance Quart, 71. *Mailing Add:* Dept of Foreign Lang, Lit & Ling Univ of Rochester Rochester NY 14627

DORENLOT, FRANCOISE, b Paris, France, Mar 28, 34. FRENCH LANGUAGE & LITERATURE. *Educ:* Univ Aix-Marseille, Lic en Droit, 55; Univ Paris, Lic es Let, 57: Univ Cincinnati, MA, 58; Univ Calif, Los Angeles, PhD(French), 66. *Prof Exp:* Lectr French, McGill Univ, 61-65; lectr, 65-66, from instr to asst prof, 66-72, ASSOC PROF FRENCH, CITY COL NEW YORK, 72- *Publ:* Auth, Malrau ou l'unite de pensee, Gallimard. *Mailing Add:* Dept of Romance Lang City Col of New York New York NY 10031

DORESTE, OCTAVIO OSCAR, b Sagua, Cuba; US citizen. SPANISH. *Educ:* Univ Havana, Dr(law), 42 Dr(polit sci), 47; Temple Univ, MA, 69; Univ Complutense, Madrid, lic lett, 72. *Prof Exp:* Legal coun patents, Cuban Patent Off, 45-53; self-employed law, 60-63; exec vpres pharmactcals, Med Infantil, Mex, 63-64; PROF SPAN, BUCKS COUNTY COMMUNITY COL, 67- *Concurrent Pos:* Lectr law, Acad Law SEF, 45-55; sr partner, Law Off Rousseau & Doreste, 50-60; asst prof Span, Rutgers Univ, 67-73. *Mem:* MLA; Am Acad Polit Sci; Am Acad Polit & Soc Sci. *Res:* Legal terminology on Cervantes' works; Ruben Dario's legitimate filiation. *Publ:* Contribr, Magacen de las Tres Americas, P Fernandez & Cia, 40-43; auth, Mensaje literario, Arrendondo & Cia, 43-45; contribr, Principios de Economia Politica, Univ Havana, 43; co-ed, Rescoldo, Publ Universal, 78; auth, Gazapos y Gazapillos, Talleres Leiva, Mex (in press). *Mailing Add:* Dept of Span Bucks County Community Col Newtown PA 18940

DORIAN, NANCY CURRIER, b New Brunswick, NJ, Nov 5, 36. LINGUISTICS, GERMANIC & CELTIC LANGUAGES. *Educ:* Conn Col, BA, 58; Univ Mich, MA, 61, PhD(ling), 65. *Prof Exp:* Lectr, 65-66, from asst prof to assoc prof, 66-78, prof ling, Ger & anthrop, 78-79, WILLIAM R KENAN, JR, PROF LING, BRYN MAWR COL, 80- *Mem:* Ling Soc Am; Int Ling Asn; Celtic Studies Asn; Scottish Oral Hist Group. *Res:* Linguistic change; language death; Scottish Gaelic and Pennsylvania Dutch. *Publ:* Auth, A substitute name system in the Scottish Highlands, Am Anthrop, 70; Grammatical change in a dying dialect, Language, 73; The problem of the semi-speaker in language death, Int J Sociol Lang 12, 77; A hierarchy of morphophonemic decay in Scottish Gaelic language death, Word 28, 77; East Sutherland Gaelic, Dublin Inst Advan Studies, 78; Linguistic lag as an ethnic marker, Lang in Soc 9, 80; Language Death, Univ Pa Press, 81. *Mailing Add:* Dept of Ger & Anthrop Bryn Mawr Col Bryn Mawr PA 19010

DORNBERG, OTTO, b Lwow, Poland, May 16, 30; US citizen; m 64; c 1. GERMAN. *Educ:* Ohio State Univ, BA, 56, MA, 58, PhD(Ger), 66. *Prof Exp:* Instr Ger, Univ Ill, 60-63; from instr to asst prof, 63-73, ASSOC PROF GER, UNIV RI, 73-, CHMN DEPT LANG, 76- *Mem:* MLA; Am Asn Teachers Ger. *Publ:* Auth, How historical is Grillparzer's Rudolf II?, Mod Austrian Lit, 69; Grillparzer's use of historical sources in König Ottokars Glück und Ende, Colloquia Ger, 2/72; The Grillparzer year in Vienna, Mod Austrian Lit, 73. *Mailing Add:* Dept of Lang Univ of RI Kingston RI 02881

DORON, PINCHAS, b Poland, July 5, 33; US citizen; m 69; c 5. HEBREW LANGUAGE, BIBLE. *Educ:* Hebrew Univ, Jerusalem, BA, 62, MA, 64; NY Univ, PhD(Hebrew studies), 75. *Prof Exp:* Instr Hebrew & Talmud, Jewish Theol Sem, 64-65; lectr Hebrew, Hunter Col, 65-66; ASST PROF HEBREW, QUEENS COL, 66- *Concurrent Pos:* Instr, The Ulpan Ctr, 69-70. *Mem:* Asn Jewish Studies; Nat Asn Professors Hebrew. *Res:* Biblical research; Hebrew language and literature; medieval Hebrew literature. *Publ:* Auth, A new look at an old lex, Janes, 70; The war of truth, Hadoar, 77; Motive clauses in Deuteronomy, Hebrew Annual Rev, 78; auth & ed, The War of Truth, KTAV Publ House, 78; auth, Paronomasia in the prophecies to the nations, 80 & The Bible and the ancient near east--comparisons and contracts, 82, Hebrew Studies; The linguistic character of the responsa of Chacham ZVI, Bitzaron, 82; Companion to Rashi, Maznaim Publ, 82. *Mailing Add:* 730 E 7th St Brooklyn NY 11218

DORSEY, DAVID FREDERICK, JR, b Philadelphia, Pa, June 30, 34. AFRICAN LITERATURE, LINGUISTICS. *Educ:* Haverford Col, AB, 56; Univ Mich, AM, 57; Princeton Univ, AM, 65, PhD (classics), 67. *Prof Exp:* Instr classics, Howard Univ, 60-63 & 66-67, asst prof classics & dir introd to humanities, 67-69; asst prof classics, Wash Sq Col, NY Univ, 69-72; ASSOC PROF ENGLISH & AFRO-AM STUDIES, ATLANTA UNIV, 72- *Mem:* MLA; Col Lang Asn; African Lit Asn; Ling Soc Am. *Res:* Hellenistic poetry; African literature; Creoles and black dialects. *Publ:* Contribr, Beyond Black or White, An Alternate America, Little, 71; auth, Formal elements of the black aesthetic, Ctr African & Afro-Am Studies, 72; contribr, Black Aesthetics, EAfrican Lit Bur, 73. *Mailing Add:* Box 263 Atlanta Univ Atlanta GA 30314

DORWICK, THALIA, b McKeesport, Pa, July 4, 44. SPANISH LITERATURE. *Educ:* Case Western Reserve Univ, BA, 66, PhD(Span), 73. *Prof Exp:* Instr Span, Cleveland State Univ & Cuyahoga Community Col, 71-72; asst prof, Allegheny Col, 71-72 & Calif State Univ, Sacramento, 75-79; PUBL FOREIGN LANG, EIRIK BORVE, INC, 79- *Mem:* MLA; Am Asn Teachers Span & Port; Am Coun Teaching Foreign Lang. *Res:* Nineteenth century Spanish literature; the novel; foreign language teaching methodology. *Publ:* Coauth, Puntos de partida, Random House, 81; auth, El Amor y el Matrimonio en la obra de Creacion de Clarin, Inst Estub Astorianos; coauth, Que tal?, Random House (in press). *Mailing Add:* Eirik Borve Inc 703 Market St San Francisco CA 94103

DOSWALD, HERMAN K, b Oakland, Calif, Mar 24, 32; m 56; c 2. GERMAN. *Educ:* Univ Calif, Berkeley, AB, 55; Univ Wash, MA, 59, PhD, 65. *Prof Exp:* Instr Ger, Oberlin Col, 59-60, Univ Wash, 60-61, Seattle Univ, 61-62; actg asst prof, Univ Kans, 64-65, asst prof, 65-67; from asst prof to assoc prof, Fresno State Col, 67-72; prof Ger & chmn dept Ger & Slavic lang & lit, Kent State Univ, 72-79; PROF GER & HEAD DEPT FOREIGN LANG & LIT, VA POLYTECH INST & STATE UNIV, 79- *Mem:* Int Vereinigung für Germanische Sprach-und Literaturwissenschaft. *Res:* Hugo von Hofmannsthal; modern German literature; East German literature. *Publ:* Auth, The reception of Jedermann in Salzburg: 1920-1966, Ger Quart, 3/67; Cristinas Heimreise in Vienna: The history of two versions on the state, Mod Austrian lit, fall 68; Nonverbal expression in Hofmannsthal's Electr Ger Rev, 5/69; Hugo von Hofmannsthal and the Salzburg festivals, Neophilologus, 10/73; Rotating and revolving: A tragicomic popular play, Chemistry, 4/74; Edward Gordon Craig and Hugo von Hofmannsthal, Theatre Res Int, 1/76; A Festival Play in Celebration of the 25th Doctoral Anniversary of Prof Dr A Baeyer, Educ in Chem, Vol 16, 79; Hofmannsthal's Turn to Drama and the Theater, Theatre Res Int, 6/80-81. *Mailing Add:* Dept of Foreign Lang & Lit Va Polytech Inst & State Univ Blacksburg VA 24061

DOTY, EDITH AULTMAN, b St Louis Mo, Aug 15, 99; wid; c 3. SPANISH. *Educ:* Univ Wis, BA, 22; Univ Mich, MA, 50, PhD, 58. *Prof Exp:* Supvr Span, Off Censorship, Miami, 42-45; from instr to assoc prof, 47-72, EMER ASSOC PROF ROMANCE, LANG, MICH STATE UNIV, 72- *Res:* Language and literature of the Philippines. *Mailing Add:* Dept of Foreign Lang Mich State Univ East Lansing MI 48824

DOUBLES, MALCOLM CARROLL, Religion, Philology. See Vol IV

DOUBROVSKY, SERGE, b Paris, Franch, May 22, 28; m 55; c 2. FRENCH. *Educ:* Sorbonne, Lic philos, 49, Lic English, 51, Dd'Etat(Fr lit), 64; Nat Ministry Educ, France, Agrege, 54. *Prof Exp:* Instr French, Harvard Univ, 55-57; asst prof, Brandeis Univ, 57-61; from assoc prof to prof, Smith Col, 61-66; PROF FRENCH, NY UNIV, 66- *Concurrent Pos:* Guggenheim fels, 65-66, 68-69. *Mem:* MLA. *Res:* Seventeenth century literature; contemporary cirticism and fiction. *Publ:* Auth, La morale d'Albert Camus, Preuves, 10/60; Le rire d'Eugene Ionesco, 2/61 & J-P Sartre et le mythe de la raison dialectique, 9, 10, & 11/61, Nouvelle Rev Fr; Le jour S, Mercure de France, 63; Corneille et la dialectique du heros, Gallimard, Bibliotheque des Idees, 64; Pourquoi la nouvelle critique, Mercure de France, 66. *Mailing Add:* Dept of French NY Univ New York NY 10003

DOUCETTE, LEONARD EUGENE, b Chatham Head, NB, Feb 28, 36; m 63; c 1. FRENCH LITERATURE. *Educ:* St Thomas Univ, NB, BA, 55; Univ London, BA, 58; Brown Univ, PhD(French), 67. *Prof Exp:* Asst prof mod lang, St Thomas Univ, NB, 58-61; asst French, Brown Univ, 61-63; prof mod lang, St Thomas Univ, NB, 63-64; from instr to asst prof French, Univ Pa, 65-67; asst prof, Univ Toronto, 67-72, ASSOC PROF FRENCH, UNIV TORONTO, 72- *Mem:* MLA. *Res:* Emery Bigot and his 17th century French contemporaries; 20th century French theatre. *Mailing Add:* Dept of French Scarborough Col Univ of Toronto West Hill ON M5S 1A1 Can

DOUDOROFF, MICHAEL JOHN, b Carmel, Calif, Apr 26, 39; m 63; c 1. SPANISH LANGUAGE & LITERATURE. *Educ:* Stanford Univ, AB, 61, MA, 65, PhD(Span), 69. *Prof Exp:* From acting asst prof to asst prof, 65-76, ASSOC PROF SPAN, UNIV KANS, 76- *Mem:* MLA; Am Asn Teachers Span & Port; Latin Am Studies Asn. *Res:* Hispanic folklore; Spanish American literature. *Publ:* Auth, Tensions and triangles in Al Filo del Agua, Hispania, 74; El auto de los reyes magos en tradicion reciente, Rev Dialectologia y Tradiciones Populares, 74; Coordinate design in a Chilean Nueva Novela, Latin Am Lit Rev, 75; Lectura de La boba y el Buda, In: Aproximaciones a G Alvarez Gardeazabal, Bogota, Plaza Y Janes, 77; N S Momaday y la novela indigenista en ingles, Texto Critico, 79; Moros y Cristianos in Zacatecas, Lawrence, Amadeo Concha, 81. *Mailing Add:* Dept of Span & Port Univ of Kans Lawrence KS 66045

DOUGHERTY, DAVID MITCHELL, b Wilmington, Del, Aug 6, 03; m 27, 64; c 2. FRENCH LANGUAGE & LITERATURE. *Educ:* Univ Del, AB, 25; Harvard Univ, AM, 27, PhD, 32. *Prof Exp:* Head dept French, Manlius Sch, NY, 26-28; instr, Mass Inst Technol, 29-30; instr French & tutor Romance lang, Harvard Univ, 29-31; from asst prof to prof Romance lang, Clark Univ, 31-46, chmn dept, 42-46; dir, Army Specialized Training Prog, 43-44; prof Romance lang, 47-72, head dept foreign lang, 47-64, exec officer, Div Mod & Class Lang, 64-67, head dept Romance lang, 67-69, EMER PROF ROMANCE LANG, UNIV ORE, 72- *Concurrent Pos:* Dir jr year abroad, Paris, France, 39, Geneva, Switz, 46-47. *Honors & Awards:* Chevalier, Legion d'honneur; Medal of the City of Tours, 67. *Mem:* MLA; Mediaeval Acad Am; Philol Asn Pac Coast(pres, 61-62); Am Asn Teachers Fr (pres, 66-70); Am Asn Teachers Span & Port. *Res:* Old French literature; Medieval French epic poems. *Publ:* Coauth, Year Abroad, Ginn, 53; Perspectives de la Litterature Francaise, Oxford Univ, 61; La geste de Monglane, Univ Ore, 66; Le Galien de Cheltenham, Benjamins, 81. *Mailing Add:* 2829 Central Blvd Eugene OR 97403

DOUGHERTY, RAY CORDELL, b Brookly, NY, Sept 18, 40; m 69. LINGUISTICS, PHILOSOPHY OF LANGUAGE. *Educ:* Dartmouth Col, BA, 62, MS, 64; Mass Inst Technol, PhD(ling), 68. *Prof Exp:* Res assoc ling, Mass Inst Technol, 68-69; asst prof, 69-72, ASSOC PROF LING, NY UNIV, 72- *Concurrent Pos:* Fulbright prof ling, Univ Salzburg, Austria, 76-77. *Mem:* Ling Soc Am; Philos Sci Asn. *Res:* Grammar; semantics; history of science. *Publ:* Auth, A grammar of coordination: I,II, Language, 12/70; coauth, Appositive NP constructions, 1/72 & auth, A survey of linguistic methods, 11/73, Found Lang. *Mailing Add:* Dept of Ling NY Univ New York NY 10003

DOUGLAS, ELAINE ELIZABETH, b Chicago, Ill, Dec 7, 18. LINGUISTICS. *Educ:* LeMoyne Col, BA, 38; Atlanta Univ, MA, 40. *Prof Exp:* Teacher pub schs, Memphis Tenn, 40-41; teacher English & Span, Manassas High Sch, Memphis, 41-42; from instr to assoc prof, 42-76, head dept, 59-80, prof, 76-80, EMER PROF ENGLISH, FT VALLEY STATE COL, 80- *Concurrent Pos:* Mem regents acad comt English lang & lit, Univ Syst Ga. *Mem:* Col Lang Asn; NCTA; Conf Col Compos & Commun. *Res:* Modern English structure and stylistics; structural linguistic theory; teaching of English. *Publ:* Auth, A vision in a dream, A fragment: An examination of a possible application of structural linguistic theory to our Johnny's language learning, 5/62 & some practical aspects of the study of literature in general education, 5/63; Ft Valley State Col Bull. *Mailing Add:* Dept of English Ft Valley State Col Ft Valley GA 31030

DOUGLASS, R THOMAS, b Morristown, NY, June 24, 32; m 81. SPANISH, LINGUISTICS. *Educ:* George Washington Univ, BA, 54; Univ Pa, PhD(Romance ling), 64. *Prof Exp:* Teacher high sch, NY, 58-62; from asst prof to assoc prof Span & ling, Millersville State Col, 63-67; assoc prof French, Span & ling & head dept foreign lang, Simpson Col, 67-70; ASSOC PROF SPAN, UNIV IOWA, 70- *Concurrent Pos:* Vis lectr ling, St Joseph's Col, Pa, 64-66; textbk consult, Xerox Col Publ, 72-73; co-ed, Iowa Foreign Lang Bull, 72-; lang arts consult, Scott, Foresman & Co, 73; textbk consult, Holt-Rinehart, Random House & Prentice-Hall, 76- *Mem:* Am Asn Teachers Span & Port; Am Coun Teaching Foreign Lang. *Res:* Spanish spelling; historical Spanish grammar; teaching methods in foreign languages. *Publ:* Auth, Gerundive and non-gerundive forms, 3/67 & More Ph for f, 3/70, Hispania; coauth, Performance objectives teaching, Bull Asn Dept Foreign Lang, 7/72. *Mailing Add:* Univ Of Iowa 218 Schaeffer Hall Iowa City IA 52242

DOW, JAMES RAYMOND, b D'Lo, Miss, Jan 2, 36; m 62. GERMAN FOLKLORE. *Educ:* Miss Col, BA, 57; Univ Iowa, MA, 61, PhD(Ger), 66. *Prof Exp:* Instr Ger, Univ Iowa, 64-66; asst prof, Univ Wyo, 66-70; asst prof, 71-74, assoc prof, 74-81, PROF GERMAN, IOWA STATE UNIV, 81- *Res:* Hermann Hesse's Märchen; Romantic Kunstmärchen; American-German folkloristic studies. *Publ:* Co-ed, Internationale Volkskundliche Bibliographie, 82. *Mailing Add:* Dept of Foreign Lang Iowa State Univ Ames IA 50011

DOWDEY, DAVID, b Birmingham, Ala, June 3, 42; m 75; c 1. GERMAN LANGUAGE & LITERATURE. *Educ:* David Lipscomb Col, BA, 67; Vanderbilt Univ, MA, 70, PhD (Ger), 76. *Prof Exp:* Asstprof, 76-80, ASSOC PROF GER, ABILENE CHRISTIAN UNIV, 80- *Mem:* SCent Mod Lang Asn; Am Asn Teachers Ger; Lessing Soc. *Res:* Eighteenth century German literature; Albrecht von Haller; J W Goethe; Moses Mendelssohn. *Publ:* Auth, The Lyrical Language of Albrecht von Haller and Goethe: A Comparison, Univ Microfilms, 76. *Mailing Add:* Abilene Christian Univ Box 8090 Abilene TX 79699

DOWDLE, HAROLD L, b May 7, 20; US citizen; m 47; c 5. SPANISH. *Educ:* Brigham Young Univ, BA, 48, MA, 49; Stanford Univ, PhD, 54. *Prof Exp:* Asst prof Span, Okla Col Women, 54-56, assoc prof, 56-60, prof Span & chmn dept mod lang, 60-68; PROF SPAN, BRIGHAM YOUNG UNIV, 68- *Mem:* Am Asn Teachers Span & Port. *Res:* Life and writings of Gaspar Melchor de Jovellanos; the Spanish preposition; comparative studies of Spanish and Portuguese. *Publ:* Auth, Observations on the use of a and de in Spanish, 5/67 & Notes on Conocer and Saber, 5/68, Hispania. *Mailing Add:* Dept of Span & Portuguese Brigham Young Univ Provo UT 84602

DOWLING, JOHN CLARKSON, b Strawn, Tex, Nov 14, 20; m 49. SPANISH. *Educ:* Univ Colo, BA, 41; Univ Wis, MA, 43, PhD(Span), 50. *Prof Exp:* Markham traveling fel from Univ Wis, Spain, 50-51; instr Span & Port, Univ Wis, 51-53; prof foreign lang & head dept, Tex Tech Col, 53-63; prof Span & Port & chmn dept, Ind Univ, Bloomington, 63-72; prof span & head dept Romance lang, 72-79, ALUMNI FOUND DISTINGUISHED PROF ROMANCE LANG, UNIV GA, 80-, DEAN GRAD SCH, 79- *Concurrent Pos:* Guggenheim fel, 59-60; Am Philos Soc grants, 71, 74 & 81; dir, Nat Endowment for Humanities Sem Col Teachers, 77. *Honors & Awards:* Award, Acad Alfonson X el SAbio, Spain, 55. *Mem:* MLA; Am Asn Teachers Span & Port; Asoc Int Hispanistas; Am Soc 18th Century Studies; Hispanic Soc Am. *Res:* Spanish Golden Age prose; 18th and 19th century Spanish literature; modern Spanish drama. *Publ:* Auth, El Pensamiento Filosofico de Saavedra Fajardo, Acad Alfonso X el Sabio, 57; Leandro Fernandez de Moratin, Twayne, 69; ed, Leandro Fernandez de Moratin, La Comedia Nueva, Castalia, 70; auth, Jose Melchor Gomis: Compositor Romantico, Castalia, 73; La genesis de El viejo y la Nina, Hisp Rev, spring 76; Diego de Saavedra Fajardo, Twayne, 77; Capricho as style in Spanish life, literature and art, 18th Century Studies, summer 77; Saavedra Fajardo's Republica literaria: The bibliographical history of a little masterpiece, Hispanofila, 79-80. *Mailing Add:* Dept of Romance Lang Univ of Ga Athens GA 30620

DOWLING, LINDA CRABILL, English Literature. See Vol II

DOWNER, JAMES WALKER, English Linguistics. See Vol II

DOWNING, BRUCE THEODORE, b Boise, Idaho, Nov 11, 34; m 60; c 3. LINGUISTICS. *Educ:* Col Idaho, BA, 59; Univ Tex, Austin, MA, 63, PhD(ling), 70. *Prof Exp:* Teacher English, South High Sch, Salt Lake City, 61-62; instr, Robert Col, Turkey, 63-67; asst prof ling, Univ Southern Calif, 70-74; ASSOC PROF LING & CHMN DEPT, UNIV MINN, MINNEAPOLIS, 74- *Mem:* Ling Soc Am; MLA. *Res:* Intonation; English syntax; grammatical theory. *Publ:* Vocatives and third-person imperatives in English, 69 & Parenthesization rules and obligatory phrasing, 73, Papers Ling; Does English have word-level rules?, Gen Ling, 74; contribr, Current Themes in Linguistics, Hemisphere, 77. *Mailing Add:* Dept of Ling Univ of Minn 142 Klaeber Ct 320 16th Ave SE Minneapolis MN 55455

DOWTY, DAVID R, b Sept 12, 45. LINGUISTICS. *Educ:* Austin Col, BA, 68; Univ Tex Austin, PhD(ling), 72. *Prof Exp:* Asst prof, 72-79, ASSOC PROF LING, OHIO STATE UNIV, 79- *Mem:* Ling Soc Am. *Publ:* Auth, Montague grammar and the lexical decomposition of causative verbs, In: Montague Grammar, Acad Press, 76; Toward a semantic analysis of verb aspect and the English imperfective progressive, Ling & Philos, 77; Governed transformations as lexical rules in a Montague grammar, Ling Inq, 78; Applying Montague's views on linguistic metatheory to the structure of the lexicon, In: Papers From the Parasession on the Lexicon, Univ Chicago, 78; World meaning and Montague grammar, 79, coauth (with R Wall & S Peters), Introd to Montague semantics, 81 & auth, Grammatical relations and Montague grammar, In: On the Nature of Syntactic Representation, 82, D Reidel; Tenses, time adverbials, and compositional semantic theory, Ling & Phil, 82. *Mailing Add:* Dept of Ling Ohio State Univ Columbus OH 43210

DOYLE, RAYMOND HAROLD, b Buffalo, NY, Sept 29, 28; m 59; c 3. SPANISH LANGUAGE & LITERATURE. *Educ:* Gonzago Univ, BA, 56; Univ Colo, Boulder, MA, 66; Interam Univ Mex, PhD(Span), 71. *Prof Exp:* Instr English & Span, Salmon Pub High Sch, 57-63; instr Span, Univ Idaho, 59-60; lectr English, Univ Beunos Aires, 64-64; asst prof Span, Univ NDak, 66-68; ASSOC PROF SPAN, STATE UNIV NY COL, PLATTSBURGH, 68- *Concurrent Pos:* Hays-Fulbright grant, 63-64, res grants, 65-66 & 70-71; US State Dept grant, Georgetown Univ, 63. *Mem:* MLA; AAUP; Am Coun Teaching Foreign Lang. *Res:* Jorge Luis Borges; Spanish civilization and literature; Spanish art history. *Publ:* Auth, La Crisis Occidental Vista por el Teatro Extranjero en Madrid, Primer Acto, Madrid, 71; Un Autosacramental Moderno, Lit Suppl, ABC, 3/71; Madrigal de las Atlas Torres, Guidepost, Madrid, 4/71; La Huella Espanola en la Obra de Borges, Playor, Madrid, 77. *Mailing Add:* Dept of Mod Lang & Lit State Univ of NY Col Plattsburgh NY 12901

DOYLE, RICHARD EDWARD, b Brooklyn, NY, Dec 22,29. CLASSICAL LANGUAGES. *Educ:* Bellarmine Col, NY, AB, 53, PhL, 54, MA, 55; Woodstock Col, Md, STB, 59, STL, 61; Cornell Univ, PhD(classics), 65. *Prof Exp:* Instr Greek, Latin & English, Xavier High Sch, New York, 54-57; teaching asst Latin, Cornell Univ, 63-65; asst prof classics, 65-70, ASSOC PROF CLASSICS, FORDHAM UNIV, 70-, DEAN, GRAD SCH ARTS & SCI & DEAN FAC, 79- *Concurrent Pos:* Mem exec comt, Am Acad Rome, 71-77, NY Soc Archaeol Inst Am, 74-; ed, Traditio, 72-; bk rev ed, Class World, 77- *Mem:* Am Philol Asn; Archaeol Inst Am. *Res:* Greek tragedy and history; Greek epic and lyric poetry. *Publ:* Auth, The Use and Meaning of Ate in the Seven Extant Plays of Aeschylus, Cornell Univ, 65; Olbos, Koros, Hybris, and Ate from Hesiod to Aeschylus, 70 & The Objective Concept of Ate in Aeschylean Tragedy, 72, Traditio; Fate in Greek tragedy, Thought, 72; Two novelties in Euripides, In: Prodosis, Fordham Univ, 76; The concept of Ate in Sophoclean tragedy, In: Traditio 32, 76; Phi Beta Kappa: Two thousand years of meaning, Class Folia 31, 77. *Mailing Add:* Dept of Classics Fordham Univ Bronx NY 10458

DOYLE, RUTH LESTHA, b Doylestown, Pa, Dec 13, 44. FRENCH LANGUAGE AND LITERATURE. *Educ:* Univ NC, Chapel Hill, AB, 66, MA, 68, PhD(Romance lang & lit), 76. *Prof Exp:* Asst prof French, Elon Col, 67-71; asst prof French & head dept, Univ Charleston, 72-75; ASST PROF FRENCH & ITAL, CENT MO STATE UNIV, 76- *Mem:* Am Asn Teachers French; MLA. *Res:* French romanticism; computer aided instruction in modern languages; Italian language. *Publ:* Auth, Victor Hugo's Drama: An Annotated Bibliography, 1900-1980, Greenwood Press, 81. *Mailing Add:* Dept of Mod Lang Cent Mo State Univ Warrensburg MO 64093

DOZER, JANE B, FRENCH LANGUAGE & LITERATURE. *Educ:* Principia Col, BA, 69; Middlebury Col, MA, 70; Univ Calif, Los Angeles, PhD(French), 80. *Prof Exp:* Teaching asst, Univ Calif, Santa Barbara, 70-71; teaching fel, Univ Calif, Los Angeles, 73-78 & instr, 78-79; FAC ASSOC, FRENCH, UNIV WASH, 79- *Mem:* Medieval Acad Am; MLA; Philol Asn Pac Coast; Medieval Asn Pac; Soc Int pour l'etude du Theatre Medieval. *Res:* Medieval French drama; Homo Ludens in mediecal French literature; Trobar Clus. *Publ:* Auth, The bawdy games of Adam de la Halle's Jeu de Robin et Marion, 12th Medieval Workshop, Univ BC, 11/81; New perspectives on li jeus de le fuellie, Treteaux Bull Soc Int pour l'etude du Theatre Medieval, Sect francaise, 82. *Mailing Add:* Dept Romance Lang & Lit Univ Wash Seattle WA 98195

DRABKIN, MIRIAM F, b New York NY, Feb, 15; m 41; c 2. CLASSICAL LANGUAGES, HISTORY OF SCIENCE. *Educ:* Hunter Col, BA, 35; Cornell Univ, MA, 36, PhD, 38; Vatican Sch Palaeography & Diplomatics, dipl, 40. *Prof Exp:* From asst prof to assoc prof, 57-69, chmn dept class lang & Hebrew, 65-74, PROF CLASS LANG, CITY COL NEW YORK, 69- *Mem:* Am Philos Asn; Hist Sci Soc; Class Asn Atlantic States; Am Philol Asn; Class Soc Am Acad Rome. *Res:* Latin palaeography. *Publ:* Auth, Select pages from mediaeval medical manuscripts, 42 & A select bibliography of Greek and Roman medicine, 42, Bull Hist Med; coauth, Caelius Aurelianus Gynaecia, Johns Hopkins Univ, 51. *Mailing Add:* Dept of Classics City Col of New York 138th St & Convent Ave New York NY 10031

DRAGHI, PAUL ALEXANDER, b Hartford, Conn, May 15, 49; m 78. COMPARATIVE LITERATURE, ASIAN STUDIES. *Educ:* Univ Conn, Storrs, BA, 72; Ind Univ, Bloomington, MA, 77, MA, 78, PhD (inner Asian lit), 80. *Prof Exp:* Res assoc Tibetan lit, 79-81, ASST PROF INNER ASIAN LIT & ASST DIR, RES INST INNER ASIAN STUDIES, IND UNIV, BLOOMINGTON, 81- *Concurrent Pos:* Coordr, Buddhist Studies Prog, Res Inst Inner Asian Studies, Ind Univ, 81-; peer reviewer, Comt Scholarly Exchange with People's Repub China, Nat Acad Sci, 81- *Res:* Inner Asian epic literature; comparative study of medieval European and Tibetan religious literature; literature of the minority peoples of China (Tibetans, Mongols, Na-Khi). *Publ:* Auth, Tibet: Sacred and Secular, Tibet Soc, 75; co-ed, Aspects of Altaic Civilization II, Louvain, Belgium, 78; auth, The stag and the hunting dog: A Bhutanese religious drama, J Popular Cult, 82. *Mailing Add:* Res Inst for Inner Asian Studies Ind Univ Bloomington IN 47405

DRAGONE, OLINDO, b Pittsfield, Mass, June 11, 24; m 46; c 3. ROMANCE LANGUAGES. *Educ:* Univ NC, AB, 51; Univ Palermo, DLett, 63. *Prof Exp:* Asst prof French & Ital, 64-65, dir sect mod lang, 65-73, ASSOC PROF MOD LANG, AM INT COL, 67-, CHMN DEPT, 73- *Concurrent Pos:* Comnr, Mass Teachers' Corps, 67- *Mem:* Nat Asn Lang Lab Dir. *Res:* Mafia; Italian religious liberals. *Publ:* Auth, The dollar from de Gaulle's point of view, summer 68, The lira, 69 & Gli amici, 70, Am Int Col J; ed, Say it in Italian, Merriam Webster, 71. *Mailing Add:* Dept of Mod Lang Am Int Col 170 Wilbraham Rd Springfield MA 01109

DRAKE, DANA BLACKMAR, b Macon, GA, Dec 18, 26. ROMANCE LANGUAGES, LAW. *Educ:* Davidson Col, AB, 48; Univ Va, LLB, 51; NY Univ, LLM, 52; Middlebury Col, MA, 66; Univ NC, Chapel Hill, PhD(Span), 67. *Prof Exp:* Jr Partner, Young & Hollis, Columbus, Ga, 52-55; attorney, Joint Comt Taxation, 55-59; asst mgr real estate, Trust Dept, Citizens Southern Nat Bank, 59-62; instr Span, Univ NC, Chapel Hill, 62-67; asst prof, 67-71, assoc prof, 71-82, PROF SPAN, VA POLYTECH INST & STATE UNIV, 82- *Mem:* Am Asn Teachers Span & Port; MLA; Cervantes Soc Am. *Res:* Cervantes. *Publ:* Auth, Taxation (annual article), Mercer Law Rev, 53-55; The sales tax in Georgia, Ga Bar J, 55; Cervantes' Novelas Ejemplares, A Critical Bibliography, Va Polytech Inst, 68, 2nd ed, Garland, 81; Don Quijote, A Selective Annual Bibliography, (3 vols), 74, 78, 80. *Mailing Add:* 210 University Club Blacksburg VA 24060

DRAKE, GERTRUDE COYNE, b Que, Can, June 27, 09; US citizen; m 39; c 2. COMPARATIVE STUDY OF LITERATURE. *Educ:* Cornell Univ, AB, 30, PhD, 39; Univ Chicago, MA, 31. *Prof Exp:* Teacher English & classics & prin sec dept, Monticello Col, 38-40; instr English, Mich State Univ, 40-42; from instr to assoc prof & chmn dept lang, Sault Br, Mich Col Mining & Tech, 44-51; head dept classics, New Trier Twp High Sch, 58-63; assoc prof humanities, 66-71, prof, 71-80, EMER PROF HUMANITIES, SOUTHERN ILL UNIV, EDWARDSVILLE, 80- *Concurrent Pos:* Semple-Taft fel, Univ Cincinnati, 63-64; chmn, Latin Curric Revision Comt II, Oxford Conf, 67-68; mem, State Ill Humanities Curric Planning Comt,. *Honors & Awards:* Excellence in Teaching Award, Southern Ill Univ, Edwardsville, 71; Ovatio Award, Class Asn Mid W & S, 72. *Mem:* Am Philol Asn; Am Class League; MLA; Class Asn Mid W & S; Acad Romanis Studiis Provehendis. *Res:* Late and medieval Latin literature; mediaeval literature; Renaissance Latin and English literature. *Publ:* Auth, Latin Readings, 65 & More Latin Readings, 65, Scott; Candidus: a unifying theme in Apuleius' Metamorphoses, Class J, 68; Lucius's business in the Metamorphoses of Apuleius, 69, Ovid's Metamorphoses, the facsimile of the Caxton MS, and Sandy's 1632 version, 71 & The Moon and Venus: Troilus's heavens in eternity, 73, Papers Lang & Lit; coauth, Marco Gerolamo Vida's The Christiad (Latin & English ed), Southern Ill Univ, 77. *Mailing Add:* 416 Shady Lane Edwardsville IL 62025

DRAKE, GLENDON FRANK, b Jackson Co, Ohio, Mar 24, 33; m 55; c 3. LINGUISTICS, AMERICAN STUDIES. *Educ:* Miami Univ, Ohio, BA, 55; Okla State Univ, MA, 59; Univ Mich, PhD(Am studies), 72. *Prof Exp:* From instr to asst prof ling, Wayne State Univ, 60-66; from asst prof to assoc prof ling, San Diego State Univ, 66-78, chmn dept, 74-79, prof, 78-79; PROF ENGLISH & DEAN COL ARTS & SCI, UNIV MICH, 80- *Mem:* Ling Soc Am; MLA; Am Dialect Soc; Int Sociol Asn. *Res:* Sociolinguistics; history of linguistics; American English. *Publ:* Auth, Black English and the American value system, Kans J Sociol, fall 73; Integrity, promise and language planning, Lang Learning, 12/75; Lau vs Nichols vs HEW, CATESOL Occasional Papers, fall 76; The source of American linguistic prescriptivism, Lang Soc, 12/77; The Role of Prescriptivism in American Linguistics, 1820-1970, John Benjamin B V, 77; contribr, Perspectives on Applied Linguistics, Coronado, 78. *Mailing Add:* Col of Arts & Sci Univ of Mich Flint MI 48503

DRAKE, HAROLD ALLEN, Ancient History. See Vol I

DRAZIN, ISRAEL, Religion, Foreign Language. See Vol IV

DRECHSEL, EMANUEL JOHANNES, b St Gallen, Switz, July 5, 49; m 79. LINGUISTICS. *Educ:* Univ Wis-Madison, MA, 74, MA, 76, PhD(anthrop), 79. *Prof Exp:* Vis asst prof, ling & anthrop, Univ Ga, 78-80; asst prof anthrop, Northwestern State Univ La, 80-81; ASST PROF ANTHROP & LING, UNIV OKLA, 81- *Concurrent Pos:* Co-ed, Festschrift, 80-; researcher, An Ethnohistory of 19th Century La Indians, National Park Serv & US Dept Interior, 81-82; jr fac summer res fel, Univ Okla, 82. *Mem:* Am Anthrop Asn; Ling Soc Am; Southern Anthrop Soc; Soc Native Lang Am. *Res:* North American Indian languages, especially those of the southeastern United States; languages in contact, especially pidgin and creole languages; ethnohistory of North American Indians, especially those of the southeastern United States. *Publ:* Auth, Ha, now me stomany that! A summary of pidginization and creolization of North American Indian languages, Int J Soc Lang, Vol 7, 76; Historical problems and issues in the study of North American Indian marginal languages, In: Papers in Southwestern Indian English, Trinity Univ Press, 77; A preliminary sociolinguistic comparison of four indigenous pidgin languages of North America, Anthrop Ling, Vol 23, 81; coauth, Hawaiian loanwords in two native American pidgins, Int J Am

Ling (in press); auth, Towards an ethnohistory of speaking: The case of Mobilian jargon, an American Indian pidgin of the lower Mississippi Valley, Ethnohist (in press); contribr, Structure and function in Mobilian jargon: Indications for its prehistoric existance, Publ 2nd Ann Symp Hist Ling & Philol (in press). *Mailing Add:* Dept of Anthrop Univ of Okla Norman OK 73019

DREISOERNER, CHARLES, Classical Languages & Philosophy. See Vol IV

DRESDEN, MARK J, b Amsterdam, Netherlands, Apr 26, 11; m 37; c 3. PHILOLOGY, HISTORY. *Educ:* Univ Amsterdam, MA, 37; State Univ Utrecht, MA, 37, PhD, 41. *Prof Exp:* prof, 60-80, EMER PROF IRANIAN STUDIES, UNIV PA, 80- *Concurrent Pos:* Guggenheim fel, 54-55; Soc Sci Res Coun fel, 60-61; Fulbright res fel, India, 60-61; Am Coun Learned Soc Near East grant, 65-66; mem comt int exchange of persons, Sr Fulbright-Hays Prog, 73-76. *Mem:* Ling Soc Am; Am Orient Soc (pres, 73-74); Am Inst Iranian Studies; Philol Soc English; Asiatic Soc France. *Res:* Iranian and Indic philology and history. *Publ:* Auth, Manavagrhysutra, 41; Jatakastava, 55; Reader in Modern Persian, Am Coun Learned Soc, 58; Denkart, a Pahlavi text, O Harrassowitz, Wiesbaden, 66. *Mailing Add:* Dept of Oriental Studies 813 Williams Hall Univ of Pa Philadelphia PA 19174

DRESSLER, HERMIGILD, b Belleville, Ill, Feb 3, 08. CLASSICAL PHILOLOGY. *Educ:* Cath Univ Am, AM, 38, PhD, 47. *Prof Exp:* Registr, Quincy Col, 47-50, prof class lang & chmn div humanities, 50-53; from asst prof to assoc prof Greek & Latin, Cath Univ Am, 53-73, chmn dept, 71-73; PROF GREEK & LATIN, QUINCY COL, 73- *Concurrent Pos:* Ed dir, Fathers of the Church, 75- *Mem:* Ling Soc Am; Am Philol Asn; N Am Patristic Soc. *Res:* Translations of papal documents; medieval Latin. *Publ:* Auth, Preaching I, 67, Clement I, pope, saint, 67 & Irenaeus, saint, 67, In: New Cath Encycl, McGraw; Introduction to Medieval Latin Studies: A Syllabus and Bibliographical Guide, Cath Univ Am, 77. *Mailing Add:* Dept of Greek & Latin Quincy Col 1831 College Ave Quincy IL 62301

DRESSMAN, MICHAEL ROWAN, American Literature, Linguistics. See Vol II

DREWS, ROBERT HERMAN, b Juneau, Wis, Mar 26, 36; m 63. CLASSICS, ANCIENT HISTORY. *Educ:* Northwestern Col, Wis, AB, 56; Univ Mo, AM, 57; Johns Hopkins Univ, PhD, 60. *Prof Exp:* Instr Latin & Roman studies, Duke Univ, 60-61; from asst prof to assoc prof, 61-73, chmn dept, 75-80, PROF CLASS STUDIES, VANDERBILT UNIV, 73- *Concurrent Pos:* Jr fel, Ctr Hellenic Studies, 66-67; Am Coun Learned Soc fel, 73-74; Guggenheim Mem fel, 80-81; resident class studies, Am Acad in Rome, 81. *Mem:* Archaeol Inst Am; Am Philol Asn; Soc Promotion Hellenic Studies. *Res:* Ancient history. *Publ:* Auth, Diodorus and his sources, Am J Philol, 10/62; The first tyrants in Greece, Historia, 8/72; The Greek Accounts of Eastern History, Ctr Hellenic Studies, 73; The Babylonian chronicles and Berossus, Iraq, 75; The earliest Greek Settlements on the Black Sea, J Hellenic Studies, 76; Argos and Argives in the Iliad, Class Philos, 79. *Mailing Add:* Dept of Class Studies Vanderbilt Univ Nashville TN 37235

DRIVER, SAMUEL NORMAN, b Neffs, Ohio, Dec 22, 29; m 60; c 3. RUSSIAN. *Educ:* Ohio State Univ, BA, 51; Columbia Univ, MA, 58, PhD(Russ), 67. *Prof Exp:* Instr Russ, Univ Mich, 60-62; from instr to asst prof, 62-72, ASSOC PROF RUSS, BROWN UNIV, 72-, CHMN DEPT SLAVIC, 77- *Concurrent Pos:* Mem, Inter-Univ Comt on Travel Grants, 65-67. *Mem:* Am Asn Teachers Slavic & E Europ Lang; MLA; Am Asn Advan Slavic Studies. *Res:* Russian poetry, symbolist and post symbolist; Pushkin. *Publ:* Auth, Acmeism, summer 68 & The plays of N Gumilev, 69, Slavic & East Europ J; Anna Akhmatova: Early love poems, Romance Lang Tri-Quart, 71; Anna Akhmatova, Twayne, 72; On transition to college Russian, Slavic & East Europ J, 74; Directions in Akhmatova's poetry, Romance Lang J, 75. *Mailing Add:* Dept of Slavic Brown Univ Providence RI 02912

DRYER, MATTHEW S, b Toronto, Ont, Apr 27, 50; m 79. LINGUISTICS. *Educ:* Univ Toronto, BA, 72, MSc, 73; Univ Mich, AM, 75, PhD(ling), 79. *Prof Exp:* Vis asst prof ling, Univ Windsor, 78-79; sessional instr, Univ Calgary, 79; VIS ASST PROF LING, UNIV ALTA, 80- *Res:* Typology and universals; syntactic theory. *Publ:* Auth, Is logical structure necessary?, Papers Annual Meeting Mich Ling Soc & Univ Mich Papers in Ling 2: 2, 76; On explaining the syntactic properties of passive agent noun phrases in universal grammar, Papers 76 Meeting Mich Ling Soc, 77; Some theoretical inplications of grammatical relations in Cebuano, Univ Mich Papers in Ling, Vol 2, No 4; The positional tendencies of sentential noun phrases in universal grammar, Can J Ling, 25: 123-195; Review of syntactic argumentation and structure of English, Lingua, 55: 97-100; Indirect objects in Kinyarwanda revisited, In: Studies in Relational Grammar, Univ Chicago Press, 82; In defense of a universal passive, Ling Analysis 9: 285-292; Passive and inversion in Kannada, Proc Eighth Ann Meeting Berkeley Ling Soc, 82. *Mailing Add:* Dept of Ling Univ Alta Edmonton AB T6G 2E7 Can

DUARTE, JULIO M, b Mantua, Pinar del Rio, Cuba, July 12, 22; US citizen; m 48; c 3. SPANISH GOLDEN AGE LITERATURE. *Educ:* Univ Havana, LLD, 46; Emory Univ, MA, 65, PhD(Span lit), 68. *Prof Exp:* Teacher Span, Westminster Schs, Atlanta Ga, 61; teacher, Lovett Sch, Atlanta, 61-64; spec lectr, Emory Univ, 64-66; spec lectr, 66-68, asst prof, 68-72, assoc prof, 72-80, PROF SPAN, GA STATE UNIV, 80-, DIR GRAD STUDIES, DEPT FOREIGN LANG, 70- *Concurrent Pos:* Mem Urban Life Fac, 77- *Mem:* SAtlantic Mod Lang Asn. *Res:* Novelas ejemplares by Miguel de Cervantes; the theory of revolution and the vital reason in Ortega y Gasset. *Publ:* Auth, Critical and annotated edition of Lope de Vega's La creacion del mundo y primera culpa del homre, 72 & Edition of Cervantes' Novelas ejemplares El celoso extremeno and La fuerza de la sangre (in press), Bibliot Clasica Ebro, Ed Ebro, Zaragoza, Spain. *Mailing Add:* Dept of Foreign Lang Ga State Univ 33 Gilmer St SE Atlanta GA 30303

DUBAN, JEFFREY M, US citizen. CLASSICAL LANGUAGES. *Educ:* Brown Univ, BA & MA, 71; Johns Hopkins Univ, PhD, 75. *Prof Exp:* Asst prof, Boston Univ, 76 & Ohio State Univ, Mansfield, 76-78; ASST PROF, GA STATE UNIV, 78- *Concurrent Pos:* Assoc ed, Classical Outlook, 79-; Ger Acad Exchange Serv fel, summer, 81; Nat Endowment for Humanities grant, 81. *Mem:* Am Philol Asn; Class Asn Mid West & South; Vergillian Soc. *Res:* Republican and Augustan Latin literature; archaic Greek literature. *Publ:* Auth, A place for Lucretius in the secondary school curriculum, Class Outlook, 57: 52-57; Ratio Divina Mente Coorta and the mythological undercurrent in the deification of Epicurus, Prudentia, 11: 47-54; Verbal links and imagistic undercurrent in Catullus 64, Latomus, 39: 777-802; Distortion as a poetic device in the pursuit of Hektor and related events, Aevum, 54: 3-22; Poets and kings in the Theogony invocation, Quaderni Urbinati di Cultura Classica, 33: 7-21; Les Duels Majeurs de L'iliade et le Langage d'Hector, Les Etudes Classiques, 49: 97-124; Venus, Epicurus and Naturae Species Ratioque, Am J Philol, 103: 165-177; transl, Carl Orff's Carmina Burana, Telarc Rec . *Mailing Add:* Dept of Foreign Lang Ga State Univ Atlanta GA 30303

DUBE, PIERRE HERBERT, b Toronto, Ont, Aug 23, 43; m; c 2. FRENCH LITERATURE. *Educ:* Univ Toronto, BA, 67, MA, 68; Ohio State Univ, PhD(Romance lang), 72. *Prof Exp:* ASSOC PROF FRENCH, UNIV WATERLOO, 72- *Mem:* Soc Chateaubriand; MLA; Am Asn Teachers Fr. *Res:* Computer-aided research in literature. *Publ:* Auth, A Concordance of Pascal's Pensees, Cornell Univ, 75; Les aventures du dernier Abencerage: A mirror of time and civilization, Revue Univ Ottawa, 76; Computergerated concordances and their application to explication de texte, Can Mod Lang Rev, 10/76; Les aventures du dernier Abencerage: Etude spatiotemporelle, Travaux Ling & Lit, 77; A Corcordance of Flauber's Education Sentimentale, 78; A Concordance of Flaubert's Madame Bovary, Garland, 78. *Mailing Add:* 583 Rolling Hills Dr Waterloo ON N2L 5A1 Can

DUBOIS, BETTY LOU, b Oklahoma City, Okla, Dec 13, 27. APPLIED LINGUISTICS, ENGLISH AS FOREIGN LANGUAGE. *Educ:* Univ Okla, BA, 49, MA, 54; Univ NMex, PhD(ling & lang pedag), 72. *Prof Exp:* Asst prof, 73-76, assoc prof, 76-80, PROF SPEECH, NMEX STATE UNIV, 80- *Concurrent Pos:* Consult, Southwest Multicult Ethnic Study Ctr, Univ Tex, El Paso, 73-; head ed comt, Papers in Southwest English, Trinity Univ, 76- *Mem:* Ling Asn of Can & US; Int Asn Appl Ling; Int Asn Study Child Lang; Ling Asn of Southwest; Teachers English to Speakers Other Lang. *Res:* Elementary school language arts; nonstandard southwest English; sex-linked communicative behavior. *Publ:* Auth, Cultural and social factors in the assessment of language capabilities, Elem English, 2/74; co-ed, Proceedings of the conference on the sociology of the languages of American women, Trinity Univ, 76; auth, Spanish, English and the Mescalero Apache, In: Studies in Southwest Indian English, 77; A case study of native American child bidialectalism in English, Anthrop Ling, winter 77. *Mailing Add:* Box 3W NMex State Univ University Park NM 88003

DUBRUCK, ALFRED JOSEPH, b Detroit, Mich, Oct 5, 22; m 57; c 1. FRENCH. *Educ:* Univ Mich, AB, 49, MA, 50, PhD(comp lit), 62; Univ Grenoble, cert, 51. *Prof Exp:* Instr French, Kalamazoo Col, 58-62; from asst prof to assoc prof, 62-70, PROF FRENCH, OAKLAND UNIV, 70- *Concurrent Pos:* Ed adv 19th Century French Studies, 72- *Mem:* MLA; AAUP. *Res:* The German heritage and Gerard de Nerval; 18th century French novel; the drama of Ugo Betti. *Publ:* Auth, A Source for Nerval's Benoni, Romance Notes, 63. *Mailing Add:* Dept of Mod Lang Oakland Univ Rochester MI 48063

DUBRUCK, EDELGARD E, b Breslau, Ger, Nov 1, 25; US citizen; m 57; c 1. FOREIGN LANGUAGES. *Educ:* Univ Mich, MA, 55, PhD(Romance lang & lit), 62. *Prof Exp:* Vis lectr French, Oakland Univ, 62-65; from asst prof to assoc prof, 65-75, PROF FRENCH, MARYGROVE COL, 75-, CHMN DEPT FOREIGN LANG, 73- *Concurrent Pos:* US Govt scholar, Mich State Univ, 51-52; vis lectr, Kalamazoo Col, 61. *Mem:* MLA. *Res:* Humor and humorous intent in French literature of the Middle Ages; French poetry of the Baroque. *Publ:* Auth, The Theme of Death in French Poetry of the Middle Ages and the Renaissance, Mouton, The Hague, 64; Three Religious Sonneteers of the Waning Renaissance: Sponde, Chassignet and La Ceppede, Neophilologus, 70; Jean-Antoine de Baif: Poet of the Absurd, Esprit Createur, 72; ed, La Nef des Folz du Monde, 77 & coauth, Fifteenth-Century Studies, Vol 1, 78, Univ Microfilms. *Mailing Add:* Dept of Foreign Lang Marygrove Col Detroit MI 48221

DUCKERT, AUDREY ROSALIND, b Cottage Grove, Wis, Mar 28, 27. ENGLISH PHILOLOGY & LINGUISTICS. *Educ:* Univ Wis, BS, 48, MA, 49; Radcliffe Col, PhD, 59. *Prof Exp:* Res asst, Wis English Lang Surv, Univ Wis, 48-52; ed asst, G&C Merriam Co, Mass, 53-56; from instr to assoc prof, 59-72, PROF ENGLISH, UNIV MASS, AMHERST, 72- *Concurrent Pos:* Assoc ed & columnist, Names, Am Name Soc, 61-65; mem adv bd, Ling Atlas US & Can, 64- & Dict Am Regional English, 65-; vis res assoc, Univ Wis-Madison, 66-67; consult, Oxford English Dict, Suppl II, 68-; Am Coun Learned Soc sr fel, 73-74; vis prof English, Emory Univ, 78; adj ed, Dict Am Regional English, 81- *Mem:* Am Dialect Soc (pres, 74); Am Name Soc (pres, 71); Mediaeval Acad Am; Mod Humanities Res Asn, Gt Brit; Ling Soc Am. *Res:* Lexicography; medieval language and literature; dialectology. *Publ:* Coauth, A Method for Collecting Dialect, Am Dialect Soc, 53; auth, The linguistic atlas of New England revisited, Publ Am Dialect Soc, 4/63; co-ed, Handbook of the Linguistic Geography of New England, AMS, 72; Lexicography in English, NY Acad Sci Annal, 73; auth, The second time around: Methods in dialect revisiting, Am Speech, 74; The winds of change, In: James B McMillan: (festschrift), Essays in Linguistics by His Friends and Colleagues, Univ Ala, 77. *Mailing Add:* Dept of English Univ of Mass Amherst MA 01003

DUCKWORTH, JAMES E, b Maynard, Mass, Feb 12, 32; m 64. ENGLISH. *Educ:* Harvard Univ, AB, 59; Univ Conn, MA, 61, PhD, 65. *Prof Exp:* Res asst epidemiol, Sch Pub Health, Harvard Univ, 59-63; asst prof English, Ft Hays Kans State Col, 63-65; asst prof, Univ Houston, 65-68; asst prof, 68-76, ASSOC PROF ENGLISH, UNIV RICHMOND, 76- *Concurrent Pos:* Lectr, in-serv training course, Spring Branch, Tex, 65, Baytown, Tex, 66 & Tex Educ Agency Ling Inst, 65-66; coord inter-univ coop, Univs Houston, Tex & Ill, 65-66; lectr, NDEA Inst, Prairie View, Tex, 66. *Mem:* Ling Soc Am; Ling Asn Gt Brit; NCTE. *Res:* Highway safety; structural linguistics in English. *Publ:* Coauth, Correlates of physique, Psychol Bull, 12/64; auth, Rhythm of spoken English, Proc 1967 Foreign Studies Adv Conf, 68. *Mailing Add:* Dept of English Univ of Richmond Richmond VA 23173

DUCLOS, GLORIA SHAW, b Boston, Mass, Aug 2, 28; m 63; c 2. GREEK & LATIN. *Educ:* Radcliffe Col, AB, 49, MA, 53; Oxford Univ, AB, 51, MA, 55. *Prof Exp:* Instr Greek & Latin, Wilson Col, 54-55; instr, Wellesley Col, 55-60, foreign studies adv, 57-60; asst prof classics, Univ Maine, Orono, 62-64; from asst prof to assoc prof, 67-76, prof classics, 76-80, WALTER E RUSSELL PROF PHILOS & EDUC, MAINE, PORTLAND, 80- *Mem:* Vergilian Soc Am; Am Philol Asn; Class Asn New Eng (secy-treas, 72-76). *Res:* Virgil; Greek and Latin poetry. *Publ:* Auth, Dido as Triformis Diana, Vergilius, 69; Nemora inter cresia, Class J, 2-3/71; Catullus II, Arethusa, spring 76; Aechylus' Eumenides and Euripides' Bacchae in the Fifth Century Context, Class Outlook, 5-6/81. *Mailing Add:* Dept of Foreign Lang & Class Univ of Maine Portland ME 04103

DUCRETET, PIERRE RAYMOND, b Paris, France, Jan 18, 31; m 66. ROMANCE LANGUAGES & LINGUISTICS. *Educ:* Univ Pa, BA, 57, MA, 59; Univ Paris, DUniv, 68. *Prof Exp:* Asst instr French, Univ Pa, 57-59; instr, Hamilton Col, 59-61; from lectr to asst prof, 61-69, ASSOC PROF FRENCH, UNIV COL, UNIV TORONTO, 69- *Mem:* MLA; Asn Can Univ Teachers Fr; Can Asn Univ Teachers; Alliance Francaise. *Res:* French language and literature; quantitative linguistics and language studies. *Mailing Add:* 9 West Grove Circle Toronto ON M5N 2S7 Can

DUDA, SADIK TUFAN, b Caucasus, USSR, Aug 26, 26; US citizen; m 52; c 2. RUSSIAN, GERMAN. *Educ:* Univ Ankara, BA, 54, lic Ger, 56. *Prof Exp:* Instr Ger, Univ Ankara, 56-57; instr Russ, US Army Sch Ger, 58-61; asst prof Ger, St Augustine's Col, 61-62; asst prof Russ, Duke Univ, 62-66; assoc prof, 66-80, PROF GER & RUSS, ST AUGUSTINE'S COL, 80- *Mem:* MLA; Am Asn Teachers Slavic & E Europ Lang. *Res:* German and Russian literature. *Publ:* Juvenile Delinquency in USSR, Biblos, Munich, 61. *Mailing Add:* Dept of Mod Lang St Augustine's Col Raleigh NC 27611

DUDLEY, EDWARD J, b St Paul, Minn, July 18, 26; m 59; c 2. SPANISH, ENGLISH. *Educ:* Univ Minn, Minneapolis, BA, 49, MA, 51, PhD(Span), 63. *Prof Exp:* Teacher, Am Sch, Managua, Nicaragua, 54-55; instr Span, St John's Univ, Minn, 56-60; asst prof, Univ Calif, Los Angeles, 63-70; chmn & prof Hisp lang & lit & dir comp lit prog, Univ Pittsburgh, 70-74; chmn dept Span, Ital & Port, 74-77, chmn dept French & Dept Ger & Slavic, 76-77, PROF SPAN & COMP LIT, STATE UNIV NY BUFFALO, 74-, CHMN DEPT MOD LANG & LIT, 77- *Concurrent Pos:* Consult, Nat Bd Consult, Nat Endowment for Humanities, 76- *Mem:* MLA; Mediaeval Acad Am; Asn Int Hispanistas; Cervantes Soc Am; Conrad Soc Am. *Res:* Cervantes; early prose fiction; comparative literature. *Publ:* Auth, Three patterns of imagery in Conrad's Heart of Darkness, Rev des Langues Vivantes, 65; coauth, El cuento, Holt, 66; auth, Court and country: The fusion of two images of love in Juan Rodriguez's El siervo libre de amor, PMLA, 67; Don Quixote as magus: The rhetoric of interpolation, Bull Hisp Studies, 72; co-ed, The Wild Man Within: An Image in Western Thought from the Renaissance to Romanticism, Univ Pittsburgh, 72. *Mailing Add:* Dept of Mod Lang & Lit Clemens Hall State Univ of NY Buffalo NY 14260

DUFFEY, FRANK MARION, b SCharleston, Ohio, Apr 22, 15; m 40. SPANISH. *Educ:* Miami Univ, AB, 38; Univ NC, MA, 40, PhD(Span), 50. *Prof Exp:* Teaching fel Span, 38-39, instr, 39-41, from instr to asst prof, 46-54, assoc prof, 59-65, acting dean, 65-66, PROF SPAN, UNIV NC, CHAPEL HILL, 65-, ASSOC DEAN, COL ARTS & SCI, 60- *Concurrent Pos:* Ed, SAtlantic Bull, 50-; chmn dept Romance Lang, Univ NC Chapel Hill, 76- *Mem:* MLA; Am Asn Teachers Span & Port; SAtlantic Mod Lang Asn. *Res:* Spanish American literature; Costumbrismo; phonetics. *Publ:* Auth, The Early Cuadro de Costumbres in Columbia. *Mailing Add:* Col of Arts & Sci 203 South Bldg Univ of NC Chapel Hill NC 27514

DUFFY, KENNETH J, US citizen. SPANISH. *Educ:* Univ Pittsburgh, PhD(Span), 40. *Prof Exp:* Dir student activities, 59-67, auth ser radio prog & bk rev, Hisp cult, WDUQ, 62-72, pres fac senate, 70-72, PROF SPAN, DUQUESNE UNIV, 46-, DIR WDUQ-FM & TV, 72- *Concurrent Pos:* Mem, Mid States Accreditation Team, Cath Univ PR, 63. *Mem:* Col African Studies Asn; Am Asn Teachers Span & Port. *Res:* Trends in East Africa; resources of East Africa; comparative literature, especially Spanish, French, Portuguese, Italian and English. *Publ:* Coauth, Tradiciones de Ricardo Palma, Duquesne Univ, 53; auth, Llorens Torres, poeta de Puerto Rico, Duquesne Hisp Rev, 56. *Mailing Add:* WDUQ-FM Duquesne Univ Pittsburgh PA 15219

DUGAN, JOHN RAYMOND, b Toronto, Ont, Dec 1, 35; m 61; c 2. FRENCH LITERATURE. *Educ:* Univ Toronto, BA, 57, MA, 59; Yale Univ, PhD(French), 67. *Prof Exp:* Instr French, Univ Western Ont, 64-66; asst prof, Univ Guelph, 66-68; asst prof, 68-70, ASSOC PROF FRENCH, UNIV WATERLOO, 70-, CHMN DEPT ROMANCE LANG, 75- *Mem:* MLA; Can Asn Univ Professors Fr. *Res:* The novels of Guy de Maupassant; style in Flaubert. *Publ:* Auth, Illusion and Reality, Mouton, 71; Maupassant's Notre Coeur, a re-evaluation, Rev Univ Ottawa, 76; co-ed, A Concordance of Flaubert's Madame Bovary, Garland, 78. *Mailing Add:* Dept of French Univ of Waterloo Waterloo ON N2L 3G1 Can

DUGGAN, HOYT NOLAN, Medieval Languages & Literature. See Vol II

DUGGAN, JOSEPH JOHN, b Philadelphia, Pa, Sept 8, 38; m 81; c 2. MEDIEVAL LITERATURE, PHILOLOGY. *Educ:* Fordham Univ, AB, 60; Ohio State Univ, PhD(Romance lang), 64. *Prof Exp:* Instr French, 64-65, asst prof, 65-66, asst prof, French & comp lit, 66-71, assoc prof, 71-78, PROF FRENCH, COMP LIT & ROMANCE PHILOL, UNIV CALIF, BERKELEY, 78- *Concurrent Pos:* Nat Humanities Found younger scholar fel, 68-69; Guggenheim fel, 79-80; ed, Romance Philol, 82- *Mem:* Mediaeval Acad Am; Int Arthurian Soc; Soc Rencesvals; Am Comp Lit Asn. *Res:* Medieval French and Spanish literatures; Romance philology. *Publ:* Auth, Formulas in the Couronnement de Louis, Romania, 66; Yvain's good name: The unity of Chretien de Troyes Chevalier au Lion, Orbis Litterarum, 69; A Concordance to the Chanson de Roland, Ohio State Univ Press, 70; The Song of Roland: Formulaic Style and Poetic Craft, Univ Calif Press, 73; ed & contribr, Oral Literature: Seven Essays, Scottish Acad Press, 75; auth, Ambiguity in twelfth and thirteenth-century French and provencal literature: A problem or a value?, In: Studies in Honor of John Misrahi, Fr Lit Publ, 77; The generation of the episode of Baligant, Romance Philol, 77; A Guide to Studies on the Chanson de Roland, Grant & Cutler, 77. *Mailing Add:* Dept of Comp Lit Univ of Calif Berkeley CA 94720

DUISIT, LIONEL ROGER, b Lyon, France, Apr 14, 23; m 53; c 3. FRENCH LANGUAGE & LITERATURE. *Educ:* Sorbonne Univ, Dipl, 46; Yale Univ, PhD, 60. *Prof Exp:* Instr French, Yale Univ, 54-58; asst prof, San Jose State Col, 58-60 & Univ Calif, Berkeley, 60-67; ASSOC PROF FRENCH & GEN LING, UNIV VA, 67- *Mem:* MLA; Am Asn Teachers Fr; Am Soc 18th Century Studies. *Res:* Eighteenth century French literature; theory of literature--rhetorical and structural approaches; translation of modern critical texts. *Publ:* Auth, Mme du Deffand Epistoliere, Droz, Geneva, 63; Satire, Parodie, Calembour: esquisse d'une theorie des modes devalues, Stanford Fr & Ital Studies, 78; transl, Barthers' Introd to Structural Analysis of Narrative, 75 & Green's Unbinding Process, 80, New Lit Hist. *Mailing Add:* Dept of French & Gen Ling Univ of Va Charlottesville VA 22903

DUKAS, VYTAS, b Lithuania, Feb 14, 23; US citizen; m 57; c 2. SLAVIC LANGUAGES. *Educ:* Univ Mich, BA, 54, MA, 55 & 56, PhD(comp lit), 65. *Prof Exp:* Asst prof Russ & Ger, 59-66, assoc prof Russ, 66-69, chmn dept Russ & Ger, 68-71, PROF RUSS, SAN DIEGO STATE UNIV, 69- *Mem:* Am Asn Teachers Ger; Am Asn Teachers Slavic & East Europ Lang. *Res:* Russian literature; Soviet poetry; Russian and German comparative literature. *Publ:* Coauth, Goethe in Dostoevskij's critical works, Ger Quart, 66; Goethe's Werther and Turgenev's Diary of a Superfluous Man, J Comp Lit & Taoistic patterns in War and Peace, Slavic & East Europ J; Twelve Contemporary Russian Stories, Asn Unity Presses, 77. *Mailing Add:* Dept of Ger & Russ San Diego State Univ San Diego CA 92182

DUKE, ELIZABETH ANN FOSTER, b Richmond, Va, Apr 2, 35; m 60. ENGLISH LINGUISTICS. *Educ:* Longwood Col, BA, 58; Univ Va, MA, 60; Univ Iowa, PhD(English), 68. *Prof Exp:* Instr English, Westhampton Col, Univ Richmond, 62-63; asst prof, 66-73, ASSOC PROF ENGLISH, VA COMMONWEALTH UNIV, 73- *Mem:* NCTE; Ling Soc Am. *Res:* English philology and linguistics. *Mailing Add:* Dept of English Va Commonwealth Univ Richmond VA 23284

DULAI, SURJIT SINGH, b Danubyu, Burma, Nov 6, 30; m 65; c 2. COMPARATIVE LITERATURE, SOUTH ASIAN STUDIES. *Educ:* Panjab Univ, BA, 50, MA, 54; Mich State Univ, PhD(comp lit), 65. *Prof Exp:* Lectr English, Urdu, Panjab Univ, 54-59; headmaster, G N High Sch, Partab, Pura, 59-60; asst English & comp lit, Mich State Univ, 62-67, fel, 64-65; asst prof English, Long Island Univ, 65-66; asst prof humanities, 66-70, assoc prof humanities & Asian studies, 70-74, PROF HUMANITIES, MICH STATE UNIV, 74- *Concurrent Pos:* Co-ed, J SAsian Lit, 69-; Fulbright-Hays fel, Off Health, Educ, Welfare, 70-71. *Mem:* Asn Asian Studies; Can Asn SAsian Studies; MLA; Popular Cult Asn; Asn Gen & Lib Studies. *Res:* Interdisciplinary humanities; Indian & comparative literature; Anglo-Indian literature. *Publ:* Auth, Influence of English on Panjabi literature and language, In: Encycl Panjabi Literature, Panjab Univ, 72; Divine drafts in earthen bowls, In: Bhai Vir Singh, 73; Pragtivad in Panjabi Literature, Mich State Univ, 74; Urdu poetry and its advent in English & Enferimentation in Panjabi poetry, J SAsian Lit, 74; Political Novel in Panjabi, Brill, 75; Jawahurlal Nehru as writer, World Lit Written English, 76; Loss of reality and self in contemporary Indian poetry, Intermuse, 77. *Mailing Add:* Dept of Humanities Michigan State Univ East Lansing MI 48824

DUMAS, BETHANY KAY, b Corpus Christi, Tex, Apr 1, 37. LINGUISTICS. *Educ:* Lamar State Univ, BA, 59; Univ Ark, MA, 61, PhD(English ling), 71. *Prof Exp:* Instr English, Southwest Mo State Univ, 64-66; asst prof English, Southern Univ, 66-73; asst prof English ling, Trinity Univ, 73-74; ASSOC PROF ENGLISH LING, UNIV TENN, 74- *Concurrent Pos:* Nat Endowment for Humanities Younger Humanist fel, 72-73; travel grants, Am Coun Learned Socs, 72 & Can Coun, 75. *Mem:* Ling Soc Am; MLA; Nat Coun Teachers English; Conf Col Compos & Commun; Am Dialect Soc. *Res:* Sociolinguistics; dialectology. *Publ:* Auth, E E Cummings: A Remembrance of Miracles, Barnes & Noble & Vision, London, 74; Teaching without textbooks: Let the students write their own, La English J, fall 74; coauth, A broad-gauge pattern for investigating Mexican-American Spanish-English bilinguals: A sociolinguistic approach, In: Research Techniques and Prospects, 75; auth, Elicitation for linguistic diversity: Guidelines for effectiveness, Proc Third Southwest Areal Lang & Ling Workshop, 75; E E Cummings in the twenties, Lit of Twenties, 75; The morphology of Newton County, Arkansas: An exercise in studying Ozark Dialect, Mid-South Folklore, 75; Male-female conversational interaction cues: Using data from dialect surveys, Sociol Lang Am Women, 76; Research needs in Tennessee English, Papers Lang Variation, 77. *Mailing Add:* Dept of English Univ of Tenn Knoxville TN 37916

DUMONT, JEAN-LOUIS, b Liege, Belg, June 25, 31; US citizen; m 57; c 2. FRENCH, SPANISH. *Educ:* Univ Conn, BA, 60, MA, 63, PhD(Romance lang), 67. *Prof Exp:* Instr French, Univ Conn, 62-63 & Cent Conn State Col, 63-67; asst prof, Univ Hawaii, 67-68; assoc prof, 68-74, PROF FRENCH, SOUTHERN CONN STATE COL, 74- *Concurrent Pos:* Foreign corresp, La Rev Gen Belge, 63-66. *Mem:* MLA; Am Asn Teachers Fr; Am Coun Teaching Foreign Lang; Soc Prof Fr Am. *Res:* Belgian literature of French expression; French literature of current period; Spanish language and culture. *Publ:* Auth, The French Novel in Belgium, Bks Abroad, 10/64; Le pragmetisme pedagogique in Amerique, Synthesis, 9/65; coauth, Paroles du Terroir, Am Bk Co, 67; auth, L'Emploi du temps chez Marcel Ayme, La Rev Gen Belge, 5/68; Marcel Ayme et le Merveilleux, Les Nouvelles Ed, Debresse, Paris, 70; Study abroad: How to choose, Am Asn Teachers French Nat Bull, spring 77. *Mailing Add:* Southern Conn State Col 501 Crescent St New Haven CT 06443

DUNAWAY, JOHN MARSON, b Washington, Ga, June 24, 45; m 66; c 2. FRENCH LANGUAGE & LITERATURE. *Educ:* Emory Univ, BA, 67; Duke Univ, MA, 71, PhD(French), 72. *Prof Exp:* Asst prof, 72-77, chmn, Dept Mod Foreign Lang, 76-79, ASSOC PROF FRENCH, MERCER UNIV, 77- *Honors & Awards:* Don Quixote Award, Valdosta State Col, 76. *Mem:* Am Asn Teachers Fr; SAtlantic Mod Lang Asn. *Res:* Twentieth-century French literature, philosophy, and religious thought. *Publ:* Auth, The motive of self-discovery in Julien Green, SAtlantic Bull, 5/77; Jacques Maritain, Twayne, 78; The Metamorphoses of the Self: The Mystic, the Sensualist, and the Artist in the Works of Julien Green, Univ Ky, 78; Maritain and Breton: Common denominators in the aesthetic confrontation of Thomism and surrealism, Fr Lit Ser, Univ SC, 79. *Mailing Add:* Dept of Mod Foreign Lang Box G Mercer Univ Macon GA 31207

DUNBAR, RONALD WILLIAM, b Valparaiso, Ind, Apr 4, 46; m 69; c 2. GERMANIC LINGUISTICS. *Educ:* Valparaiso Univ, BA, 68; Univ Wis, MA, 72, PhD(Ger ling), 79. *Prof Exp:* Lectr ling & English second lang, Univ Tübingen, 75-77; instr Ger, Univ Wis, 78-79; asst prof Ger & ling, WVa Univ, 79-82; ASST PROF GER LING, UNIV WIS-MAIDSON, 82- *Concurrent Pos:* Asst prof English second lang, Summer Intensive English Lang Inst, WVa Univ, 80-82. *Mem:* Am Asn Teacher Ger; Am Coun Teachers Foreign Lang; Soc Ger-Am Studies; Southeastern Conf Ling; MLA. *Res:* German language and linguistics; early Germanic dialects; English as a second language. *Publ:* Contribr, MLA International Bibliography, MLA, 79, 80, 81; German-American Bibliography, Occasional Papers of the Soc Ger-Am Studies, 79, 80, 81; American Reference Books Annual, Libraries Unlimited, 79, 80, 81; The presence of German in the Jargon of the American skier, Occasional Papers of the Soc for Ger-Am Studies, Vol 8, 80; contribr, Annual Bibliography of the ACTFL, Am Conf Teacher Foreign Lang, 80; Audio-lectal Sprach practice: Neurological impress and the acquistion of foreign language fluency, In: Beziehungen Zwischen Sprachrezeption und Sprachproduktion, Geothe Inst, Munich, 81; Context and Syntax, In: Discourse in Sentential Form, 82 & Discourse pragmatic and contrastive analysis, In: Proceedings International Seminar on Contrastive Grammar (in press), Karoma Press. *Mailing Add:* Ger Dept Univ of Wis Madison WI 53706

DUNCAN, ANNELISE MARIE, b Berlin, Ger, May 13, 22; US citizen; m 51; c 7. GERMANICS. *Educ:* Tex Christian Univ, BA, 58; William Marsh Rice Univ, PhD(Ger), 69. *Prof Exp:* Teacher hist jr high, La Feria, Tex Pub Schs, 58-59; asst prof, 68-74, ASSOC PROF GER, TRINITY UNIV, 75- *Mem:* MLA; SCent Mod Lang Asn; AAUP; Am Asn Teachers Ger; Am Literary Translr Asn. *Res:* Cultural history of German settlement in San Antonio and central Texas, 19th century; Icelandic and Old Norse sagas; study abroad for American students of German culture. *Mailing Add:* Trinity Univ PO Box 139 San Antonio TX 78284

DUNCAN, BRUCE, b Bryn Mawr, Pa, Feb 17, 42; m 64; c 2. GERMAN LITERATURE, GERMANIC LINGUISTICS. *Educ:* Williams Col, BA, 64; Cornell Univ, MA, 66, PhD(Ger), 69. *Prof Exp:* Asst prof, 69-75, assoc prof, 75-80, PROF GER, DARTMOUTH COL, 80- *Concurrent Pos:* Vis prof Ger, Univ Cincinnati, 73; Am Coun Learned Socs grant-in-aid fel, 76. *Mem:* Am Asn Teachers Ger; Lessing Soc; MLA; Northeast Am Soc 18th Century Studies. *Res:* Eighteenth century German literature; German Romanticism; second language acquisition. *Publ:* Auth, Hand, heart, and language in Minna von Barnhelm, 72 & The Marchese's story in Wilhelm Meisters Lehrjahre, 72, Seminar; A Cool Medium as social corrective: J M R Lenz's Concept of Comedy, Colloquia Ger, 75; Some correspondences between Arnim's Majoratsherren and Fichte's Concept of the Ich, Monatshefte, 76; Ich Pflanzel Gerstenberg's Ugolino and the mid-life crisis, Ger Rev, 78; Die Versoehnung in der Sommerfrische, eine Erzäehlung Achim von Arnims, Aurora, 78, 80; The implied reader in Lessing's Theory of Comedy, Lessing Yearbk, 78; Die Sprache der Luise Millerin, In: Friedrich Schiller, 82. *Mailing Add:* Dept of Ger Dartmouth Col Hanover NH 03755

DUNCAN, PHILLIP AARON, b Bedford, Ind, Mar 27, 27; m 53; c 2. FRENCH. *Educ:* Ind Univ, AB, 48, MA, 53, PhD(French), 58. *Prof Exp:* From instr to asst prof French, Okla State Univ, 55-60; from asst prof to assoc prof, 60-65, PROF FRENCH, UNIV KY, 65- *Concurrent Pos:* Univ Ky Res Found pub subsidy, 62, grant, 63. *Mem:* Am Asn Teachers Fr; MLA; SAtlantic Mod Lang Asn. *Res:* Nineteenth century French literature and Franco-Russian literary relations. *Publ:* Auth, The fortunes of Zola's Parizhskiie pis'ma in Russia, Slavic & E Europ J, 59; Zola's An Election at Villebranche, Symposium, 61; co-ed, Emile Zola's Lettres de Paris, Droz, 63; auth, Echoes of Zola's experimental novel in Russia, Slavic & E Europ J, spring 74; The equation of Theme and spatial form in Flaubert's Herodias, Studies Short Fiction, spring 77; Chekhov's An Attack of Nerves as experimental narrative, In: Chekhov's Art of Writing, Slavica, 77; Symbols of the benign and the malevolent in Zola's L'Assommoir, Fr Rev, 80. *Mailing Add:* Dept of French Univ of Ky Lexington KY 40506

DUNCAN, ROBERT MANLY, b Estelline, Tex, Sept 12, 03. MODERN LANGUAGES. *Educ:* Oberlin Col, AB, 26, AM, 30; Univ Wis, PhD, 36. *Prof Exp:* Teacher, Inst Ingles, Chile, 27-29; instr, Oberlin Col, 29-31 & Univ Wis, 36-38; from asst prof to prof mod lang, 38-69, acting head dept, 40-41 & 42-45, chmn dept, 51-63, acting chmn dept mod & class lang, 68-69, EMER PROF MOD LANG, UNIV NMEX, 69- *Concurrent Pos:* Fulbright fel, Spain, 63-64. *Mem:* MLA; Am Asn Teachers Span & Port; Am Name Soc; Am Coun Teaching Foreign Lang. *Res:* Spanish philology and lexicography; onomastics. *Publ:* Auth, Apellidos surgidos de los documentos linguisticos de Espana, Folia Humanistica, 64; Impact of Hispanic Culture on the US, Handbk Teachers Span & Port, 68; Adjetivos de color en espanol medieval, Anuari Estudios Medievales, 68; Color words in Medieval Spanish, Studies Honor Lloyd Kasten, 75. *Mailing Add:* Dept of Mod Lang Univ of NMex Albuquerque NM 87131

DUNHAM, LOWELL, b Wellston, Okla, Oct 14, 10. MODERN LANGUAGES. *Educ:* Okla Univ, AB, 32, AM, 35; Univ Calif, Los Angeles, PhD, 55. *Prof Exp:* Instr Latin & Span, high sch, Okla, 35-56; assoc prof foreign lang, Cent State Teachers Col, Okla, 36-40; spec agent, Fed Bur Invest, Washington, DC, 40-46, asst spec agent in charge off, San Juan, PR, 42-46; from asst prof to prof mod lang, 46-73, DISTINGUISHED REGENTS PROF MOD LANG, OKLA UNIV, 73-, CHMN DEPT, 57- *Concurrent Pos:* Bd trustees, Mid-continent Regional Educ Lab. *Honors & Awards:* Andres Bello Prize, Venezuelan Acad Lang, 48; Juan de Castellanos Lit Prize, Miles M Sherover Found, Caracas, 49 & 58; Outstanding Teacher Award, Univ Okla, 54; Knight, Order of the Liberatore Simon Bolivar, Pres Carlos A Perez, Venezuela, 76. *Mem:* MLA; Am Asn Teachers Span & Port; S Cent Mod Lang Asn; Am Coun Teaching Foreign Lang(vpres, 70, pres 71). *Res:* Latin American literature. *Publ:* Co-ed, The Latin American Mind, Univ Okla, 43; auth, Manuel Diaz Rodriguez, maestro del estilo, 48; ed, Una Posicion en la Vida, Ed Humanismo, Mex, 54; auth, Romulo Gallegos: Vida y Obra, 57; ed, The Aztecs: The Poeple of the Sun, Univ Okla, 58; auth, Manuel Diaz Rodriguez: Vida y Obra, 59; co-ed, The Cardinal Points of Borges, 71 & auth, Romulo Gallegos: An Oklahoma Encounter and the Writing of the Last Novel, 74, Univ Okla. *Mailing Add:* Dept of Mod Lang Univ of Okla Norman OK 73069

DUNHAM, VERA S, b Moscow, Russia, Dec 13, 12; US citizen; m 42; c 1. SLAVIC LANGUAGES & LITERATURE. *Educ:* Univ Erlangen, PhD(slavic philol), 35; Univ Brussels, lic-lettres, 38. *Prof Exp:* Prof, Wayne State Univ, 61-75; PROF, QUEENS COL, CITY UNIV NEW YORK, 75- *Concurrent Pos:* Res analyst, Off Strategic Serv, Washington, DC, 44-45; assoc ed, Common Cause, Univ Chicago, 46-47; res consult, Inst Int Social Res, Princeton Univ, 59-60; vis prof, Slavic Dept, Univ Mich, 65 & Columbia Univ, 67. *Mem:* Am Asn Avan Slavic Studies; Am Asn Teachers Slavic & Eastern Europ Lang. *Res:* A Literary study of the worker and the Soviet system--the 1960's & 1970's. *Publ:* Auth, Eduard Moerike: Sein Verhaelnis Zum Biedermeier, Palm & Enke Erlangen, 35; Literary tightrope-walking in the USSR, Antioch Rev, 10: 505-519; The strong woman motif, The Transformation of Russ Soc, 60; Eros in contemporary Russian poetry, Social Prob, 6Ø; In Stalin's Time: Middle Class Values in Soviet Fiction, Cambridge Univ Press, 76; Introd to Moscow To The End of The Line, Taplinger, 80. *Mailing Add:* 15 Stephens Path Port Jefferson NY 11777

DUNKEL, GEORGE EUGENE, b New York, NY, Nov 28, 48. INDO-EUROPEAN LINGUISTICS, SANSKRIT. *Educ:* Trinity Col(Conn), BA, 70; Univ Pa, MA, 71, PhD(ling), 76. *Prof Exp:* Asst prof, Johns Hopkins Univ, 75-78; ASST PROF CLASS LING, PRINCETON UNIV, 78- *Mem:* Ling Soc Am; Am Orient Soc; Am Philol Asn. *Res:* Indo-European syntax; Rig-Vedic philology; Archaic Greek. *Publ:* Auth, Preverb deletion in Indo-European, Kuhn's Zeitschrift, 78; Preverb repetition, Münchener Studien, 79; Reciprocus und verwandtes, Int Forsch, 79; Ennian atque atque, prope, Glotta, 80; Mycenaean and central Greek, Kadmos, 81; Mycenaean kekmeno, kitimeno, Minos, 81; Original syntax of conjunctive k^we, Sprake, 81; Naming-parenthesis in I-I and I-E, Munchener Studien, 82. *Mailing Add:* Dept of Classics Princeton Univ Princeton NJ 08540

DUNKLE, HARVEY I, b Sunbury, Pa, Aug 17, 22; m 49; c 5. GERMAN. *Educ:* NY Univ, AB, 50; Univ Calif, Berkeley, MA, 52, PhD, 56. *Prof Exp:* Instr Ger, Univ Ariz, 56-57; asst prof, Southern Methodist Univ, 57-63; asst prof, 63-70, ASSOC PROF GER, SAN DIEGO STATE UNIV, 70- *Concurrent Pos:* Asst ed, Mod Austrian Lit. *Mem:* MLA; Philol Asn Pac Coast; Am Asn Teachers Ger; Am Soc 18th Century Studies. *Res:* Eighteenth century literature. *Publ:* Auth, Lessing's Die Juden: An Original Experiment, Monatshefte, 11/57; coauth, A German Review Grammar, Odyssey, 65; Stefan Zweig's Schachnovelle, Monatshefte, winter 73; Friedrich Dürrenmatt's Der Besuch der Alten Dame: A parable of Western society in transition, Mod Lang Quart, 9/74; auth, An unpublished letter by Cyprian Leowitz, Manuscripts, summer 75. *Mailing Add:* Dept of Ger & Slavic Lang & Lit San Diego State Univ San Diego CA 92182

DUNMORE, CHARLES WILLIAM, b Albany, NY, Oct 13, 16. CLASSICS. *Educ:* NY Univ, AB, 51, AM, 54, PhD, 61. *Prof Exp:* Asst, Wash Sq Col, 55-57; from instr to asst prof classics, 57-65, ASSOC PROF CLASSICS, UNIV COL, NY UNIV, 65- *Concurrent Pos:* Ed consult, Imperial Rome, Time, 65. *Mem:* Archaeol Inst Am; Am Philol Asn; Soc Prom Roman Studies. *Res:* Greek and Roman history. *Publ:* Auth, Selections From Ovid, McKay, 63; contrib ed, World Bk Encycl Dict, Doubleday, 63; coauth, Medical Terminology, Davis, 77. *Mailing Add:* 1 Christopher St New York NY 10014

DUNN, CHARLES WILLIAM, b Arbuthnott, Scotland, Nov 30, 15; m 41, 74; c 3. MEDIEVAL LITERATURE. *Educ:* McMaster Univ, BA, 38; Harvard Univ, AM, 39, PhD, 48. *Prof Exp:* Tutor English, Harvard Univ, 40-41; instr, Stephens Col, 41-42; Rockefeller fel, NS, Can, 42-43; instr English, Cornell Univ, 43-46; lectr, Univ Col, Univ Toronto, 46-49; from asst prof to prof, NY Univ, 49-63; master, Quincy house, 66-81, PROF CELTIC LANG & CHMN DEPT, HARVARD UNIV, 63- *Concurrent Pos:* Nuffield Found fel, Edinburgh, Scotland, Dublin, Ireland & Aberystwyth, Wales, 54-55; Taft lectr, Univ Cincinnati, 56; Guggenheim fel, Brittany & Edinburgh, 62-63. *Mem:* MLA; Am Folklore Soc; hon pres Celtic Union, Scotland; Mediaeval Acad Am; fel Am Acad Arts & Sci. *Res:* Middle English and Celtic literature; folklore; linguistics. *Publ:* Auth, Chaucer Reader, Harcourt, 52; Highland Settler, 53 & The Foundling and the werwolf, 60, Univ Toronto; Romances derived from English legends, In: Manual of the Writings in Middle English, Conn Acad, 67; coauth, Middle English Literature, Harcourt, 73. *Mailing Add:* Master's Residence Quincy House Cambridge MA 02138

DUNN, ELLEN CATHERINE, English. See Vol II

DUNN, PETER NORMAN, b London, England, Mar 23, 26; m 53; c 6. ROMANCE LANGUAGES. *Educ:* Univ London, BA, 47, MA, 49, DLitt, 73. *Prof Exp:* Asst lectr Span, Aberdeen Univ, 49-50, lectr, 50-66; prof Span lit, Univ Rochester, 66-77; PROF ROMANCE LANG, WESLEYAN UNIV, 77- *Concurrent Pos:* Examr Span, Scottish Univs Entrance Bd, 51-60; Joint Matriculation Bd, Northern Univ, England, 60-66; vis prof Span, Western Reserve Univ, 64-65. *Mem:* MLA; Asn Hispanists Gt Brit; Cervantes Soc Am; Internation Asn Hispanists. *Res:* Spanish literature; medieval, Renaissance and 17th century. *Publ:* Auth, Castillo Solorzano and the Decline of the Spanish Novel, Blackwell, 52; Garcilaso's A la Flor de Gnido, Z Romanische Philol, 7-10/65; Critical Edition of Calderon, El Alcalde de Zalamea, Pergamon, Oxford Univ, 66; Levels of meaning in Poema de Mio Cid, Mod Lang Notes, 70; Fernando de Rojas, Twayne, 75; Pleberio's world, PMLA, 76; The Spanish Picaresque Novel, Twayne, 79; Cervantes De/Reconstructs the Picaresque, Cervantes, 82. *Mailing Add:* Dept of Romance Lang Wesleyan Univ Middletown CT 06457

DUNN, SUSAN, b New York, NY, July 19, 45. FRENCH LITERATURE. *Educ:* Smith Col, BA, 66; Harvard Univ, PhD(Romance lang), 73. *Prof Exp:* Teaching fel Romance lang, Harvard Univ, 67-70, instr French, 70-73; ASSOC PROF FRENCH & CHMN, DEPT ROMANIC LANG, WILLIAMS COL, 73- *Concurrent Pos:* Instr French, Wellesley Col, 71-73; Nat Endowment for the Humanities fel in residence, Princeton Univ, 75-76; fel, Camargo Found, 81. *Mem:* MLA. *Res:* Nerval; the motif of revolution in 19th and 20th century literature. *Publ:* Auth, Nerval et les portraits, Australian J French Studies, 75; Nerval ornithologue, French Rev, 78; Nerval coloriste, Romanische Forschungen, 79; Education and seduction in Les Liaisons Dangereuses, Symposium, 80; Nerval et le Roman Historique, Ed Lett Mod, Minard, Paris, 81; Nerval: Trangression and the amendement riancey, Nineteenth Century French Studies (in press). *Mailing Add:* Dept of Romanic Lang Williams Col Williamstown MA 01267

DUNNHAUPT, GERHARD, b Bernburg, Ger, Aug 15, 27; Can citizen. GERMANIC LANGUAGES & LITERATURES. *Educ:* Univ Toronto, BA, 68; Brown Univ, AM, 70, PhD(Ger), 72. *Prof Exp:* From asst prof to assoc prof Ger, Univ Wash, 72-76; from assoc prof to prof, 76-78, PROF GER & COMP LIT, UNIV MICH, ANN ARBOR, 78- *Concurrent Pos:* Wolfenbüttel Res grants, 75 & 78; vis prof, Univ Mich, 76, Cornell Univ, 80. *Mem:* Asn Hist Printing; Can Soc 18th Century Studies; Int Asn Ger Baroque Lit; Int Asn Renaissance Lit; MLA. *Res:* German Baroque literature; German Renaissance literature. *Publ:* Auth, Diederich von dem Werder: Versuch einer Neuwertung seiner Hauptwerke, Lang, Bern, 73; ed, Tasso, Gottfried oder Erlösetes Jerusalem, translr, D V D Werder 1626, Max Niemeyer, Tubingen, 74; auth, Kleist's Marquise von O and its Literary Dept to Cervantes, 75 & ed, A Gryphius, Horribilicribrifax Teutsch, Philipp Reclam jun, Stuttgart, 76, rev ed, 81; auth, Sebastian Brant: The Ship of Fools, In: The Renaissance and Reformation in Germany, Ungar, 77; Das Oeuvre des Erasmus Francisci und sein Einfluss auf die deutsche Literatur, Daphnis, 78; Bibliographisches Handbuch der Barockliteratur, Stuttgart, (3 vols), 80, 81, 82; ed, A Gryphius, Absurda Comica oder Herr Peter Squentz, Philipp Reclam jun, Stuttgart, 82. *Mailing Add:* Dept of Ger Lang & Lit Univ of Mich 3110 Mod Lang Bldg Ann Arbor MI 48109

DUNSTAN, FLORENE J, b Baxley, Ga, Mar 21, 04; m 26; c 1. FOREIGN LANGUAGES & LITERATURE. *Educ:* Tift Col, BA, 24; Southern Methodist Univ, MA, 32; Univ Tex, PhD, 36. *Prof Exp:* Instr Romance lang, Southern Methodist Univ, 36-41; from instr to assoc prof Span, Agnes Scott Col, 41-66, chmn dept, 64-74, prof, 66-74; RETIRED. *Concurrent Pos:* Carnegie res grant-in-aid, Brazil, 49, Spain, 51. *Mem:* MLA; S Atantic Mod Lang Asn; Am Asn Teachers Span & Port. *Res:* Golden Age in Spain, especially the picaresque novel; Latin American literature, especially the Mexican novel; Brazilian figures, especially Ruy Barbosa, Joaquin Nabuco and Baron Rio Branco. *Publ:* Co-translr, The History of Mexican Literature, Southern Methodist Univ, 3rd ed, 68. *Mailing Add:* 710 Pinetree Dr Decatur GA 30030

DUPRIEZ, BERNARD, b Seraing, Belgium, July 9, 33; m 57; c 3. STYLISTICS, FRENCH LITERATURE. *Educ:* Sorbonne Univ, Dr Univ, 59; Univ Strasbourg, DLett, 69. *Prof Exp:* Assoc prof, 61-73, PROF FRENCH LANG & POETICS, UNIV MONTREAL, 73- *Concurrent Pos:* Animateur group, Deliberations Info Ramifications de l'Expression, 75- *Mem:* Can Ling Asn; Asn Prof Fr Univ Can. *Res:* Rhetorics; French language. *Publ:* Auth, Fenelon et la Bible, Bloud & Gay, 61; Ecrits Spirituels de Fenelon, Larousse, 64; L'Etude des styles on la Commutation en Litterature, Didier, 69, 2nd ed, 71; Cours Autodidactique de Francais ecrit, Univ Montreal, 75, 2nd ed, 76, 3rd ed, 77, 4th ed, 79; Gradus: Les Procedes litteraries (dictionnaire), UGE, Paris, 80. *Mailing Add:* Dept of French Studies Univ of Montreal case Postal 6128 Montreal PQ H3C 3J7 Can

DUQUETTE, JEAN PIERRE, b Valleyfield, Que, June 27, 39. FRENCH & QUEBEC LITERATURE. *Educ:* Univ Montreal, BA, 60, CAPES, 63, Lic es Lett, 63; Univ Nanterre, DL, 69. *Prof Exp:* ASSOC PROF LIT, McGILL UNIV, 73- *Mem:* Int PEN; Soc Ecrivains Can; Asn Ecrivains Lang Francaise; Can Asn Univ Prof Fr. *Res:* French novel, 19th century; Quebec novel, 19th century. *Publ:* Auth, Structure de l'education Sentimentale, Etudes Francaises, 70; Tristesses de Flaubert, Litteratures, 71; Flaubert ou l'Architecture du Vide, 72 & Germaine Guevremont, 73, Univ Montreal; Flaubert, l'histoire et le roman historique, Rev Hist Lit France, 75; Charles Guerin et la fiction au XIXe siecle, Voix et Images, 75; Fernand Leduc, HMH, 80. *Mailing Add:* McGill Univ Peterson Hall 3460 McTavish Montreal PQ H3A 1X9 Can

DURAN, MANUAL EMIL, b Mar 28, 25; nat US; m 49; c 2. SPANISH LANGUAGE & LITERATURE. *Educ:* Nat Univ Mex, MA, 50; Princeton Univ, PhD, 53. *Prof Exp:* Instr Span lit, Nat Univ Mex, 50-51; asst prof, Smith Col, 53-59; assoc prof Romance lang, 59-66, PROF SPAN, YALE UNIV, 66- *Concurrent Pos:* Guggenheim fel, 63-64. *Mem:* Am Asn Teachers Span & Port; MLA; Asoc Int Hispanistas. *Res:* Renaissance poetry; contemporary Spanish poetry; the Baroque styles in Spanish Golden Age poetry and prose. *Publ:* Auth, El Superrealismo en la Posia Espanola Contemporanea, Nat Univ Mex, 50; La Ambigüedad en el Quijote, Univ Veracruz, 60; Lorca: A Critical Anthology, Prentice-Hall, 62; Luis de Leon, Twayne, 71; Genio y figura de Amado Nervo, Eudeba, 72; La Piedra en la Mano (poems), Agora, 72; Triptico Mexicano: Rulfo, Fuentes, Elizondo, Sepsetentas, 73; Camara oscura (poems), Villa Miseria, 73. *Mailing Add:* Dept of Span Yale Univ New Haven CT 06520

DURAN-CERDA, JULIO, b Chile, July 16, 14. SPANISH AMERICAN LITERATURE. *Educ:* Univ Chile, PhD(Span & philos), 44. *Prof Exp:* Prof Span & philos, Nat Inst, Chile, 44-56; prof Span Am lit, Univ Chile, 57-60, res prof, 60-64; vis prof Span Am lit, Univ Ariz, 64-66; PROF SPAN AM LIT, UNIV IOWA, 66- *Concurrent Pos:* Founder & collabr, Inst Lit Chilena, Univ Chile. *Mem:* Am Asn Teachers Span & Port; MLA; Int Inst Iberoam Lit. *Res:* Spanish American theatre, short story; modernism and poetry. *Publ:* Auth, El Movimiento Literario de 1842, 57, Panorama del teatro Chileno, 1842-1959, 59, Repertorio del teatro Chileno Contemporaneo, Aguilar, 70; El cuento chileno contemporaneo, Studies Short Fiction, 71; Esquema de la evolucion del cuento en Chile, In: El Cuento Hispanoamericano ante la Critica, Castalia, 73; Sobre el concepto de cuento moderno, Explicacion de Textos Literarios, 76. *Mailing Add:* Dept of Span & Port Univ of Iowa Iowa City IA 52240

DURAND, FRANK, b Brooklyn, NY, May 12, 32; m 55; c 2. SPANISH LITERATURE & LANGUAGE. *Educ:* NY Univ, BA, 53; Northwestern Univ, MA, 54, Univ Mich, PhD, 62; Brown Univ, MA, 65. *Prof Exp:* Teaching asst Span, Northwestern Univ, 53-54; teaching fel, Univ Mich, 56-60; asst prof, 60-65, assoc prof Span lit, 65-72, PROF HISP STUDIES & CHMN DEPT HISP & ITAL STUDIES, BROWN UNIV, 72- *Concurrent Pos:* Howard Found Fel, 68-69. *Mem:* MLA; Am Asn Teachers Span & Port. *Res:* Nineteenth and 20th century Spanish literature; literary criticism; Latin American novel. *Publ:* Coauth, Oral Drill in Spanish, Houghton, 63; assoc ed, Novel: A Forum of Fiction, 67-; auth, Search for reality in Nada menos que todo un hombre, 3/69 & The reality of illusion: La desheredada, 3/74, Mod Lang Notes; The Apocalyptic vision of Al filo de agua, Symp, winter, 74. *Mailing Add:* Dept of Hisp & Ital Studies Brown Univ Providence RI 02912

DURETTE, ROLAND, b Manchester, NH, May 2, 32; m 58; c 3. FRENCH EDUCATION. *Educ:* St Anselm's Col, BA, 57; Laval Univ, MA, 58; Fla State Univ, PhD(educ admin), 68. *Prof Exp:* Teacher pub schs, Wis, 60-64; asst prof foreign lang educ, 64-65, assoc prof, 65-68, PROF ELEM EDUC & FOREIGN LANG, UNIV WIS-WHITEWATER, 68- DIR FOREIGN LANG EDUC CTR, 67-, CHMN DEPT FOREIGN LANG, 69- *Mem:* Coun Teaching Foriegn Lang; Cent State Mod Lang Teachers Asn. *Publ:* Auth, How to master a language? Out Answer-Grouping?, Know-How, 2-3/62; Language institute for students, Mod Lang J, 2/65; Training and retraining of FLES teachers, Fr Rev, 4/68. *Mailing Add:* Dept of Foreign Lang Univ of Wis Whitewater WI 53190

DURHAM, CAROLYN ANN, b Plainview, Nebr, Feb 13, 47. FRENCH LANGUAGE & LITERATURE. *Educ:* Wellesley Col, BA, 69; Univ Chicago, MA, 72, PhD(French), 76. *Prof Exp:* Lectr French, Univ Chicago, 76; asst prof, 76-80, ASSOC PROF FRENCH, COL WOOSTER, 81. *Concurrent Pos:* Nat Endowment for Humanities seminar, The Problematics of L'Ecriture Feminine, summer 79. *Mem:* MLA; Nat Women's Studies Asn. *Res:* Twentieth-century novel; feminist literary criticism; film. *Publ:* Auth, Language as culture, French Rev, Vol 53, 80; In search of a new novel: Alain Robbe-Grillet's Un Regicide, French Forum, spring 82; Women and La Cage aux Folles, Jump Cut, Vol 27, spring 82; The contradictory become coherent: La Religieuse and Paul et Virginie, Eighteenth Century: Theory & Interpretation, spring 82; L'Art Romanesque de Raymond Roussel, French Literature Publications, Inc, 82; Noman, Everywomen: Claudine Hermann's Les Voleuses de Langue, Bucknell Rev: Lit, Arts & Ideology (in prep). *Mailing Add:* Dept of French Col of Wooster Wooster OH 44691

DURHAM, JOHN I, Old Testament, Hebrew. See Vol IV

DUROCHE, LEONARD LEROY, b Kansas City, Mo, June 3, 33; m 55, 82; c 4. GERMAN, COMPARATIVE LITERATURE. *Educ:* Univ Kans, AB, 55, MA, 57; Stanford Univ, PhD(Ger & humanities), Stanford Univ, 65. *Prof Exp:* Instr Ger, Harpur Col, 61-65; asst prof, Dartmouth Col, 65-70; ASSOC PROF GER & COMP LIT, UNIV MINN, MINNEAPOLIS, 70- *Concurrent Pos:* Soc for Humanities jr fel, Cornell Univ, 67-68; sr res grant, Fulbright-Hays exchange prog, Univ Freiburg, 72-73; dir, Nat Endowment for Humanities summer sem, 75 & 77, consult summer sem prog, 79 & 80; adv, Nat Humanities Ctr, 77-; vis assoc prof, Univ Tex at Austin, 78. *Mem:* MLA; Am Asn Teachers Ger; Am Comp Lit Asn; Soc Phenomenol & Existential Philos; Int Asn Philos & Lit (secy-treas, 76-77). *Res:* German Romanticism; philosophy and literature; comparative literary theory and criticism. *Publ:* Auth, Aspects of Criticism: Literary Study in Present-Day Germany, Mouton, The Hague, 67; Paul Celan's Todesfuge: A new interpretation, MLN, 10/67; Like and look alike; symmetry and irony in Theodor Storm's Aquis submersus, Seminar, 3/71; Heinrich Böll's Ansichten eines Clowns in existentialist perspective, Symposium, winter 71; A landscape approach to teaching poetry, Unterrichtspraxis, spring 78; Reading and seeing with an accent, Jahrbuch fur internationale Germanistik, 9/78; The perception of space in Rilke's Malte Laurids Brigge and Kafka, Perspectives on Contemp Lit, 5/79. *Mailing Add:* Dept of Ger Univ of Minn Minneapolis MN 55455

DURZAK, MANFRED HEINRICH, b Merkstein-Aachen, Ger, Dec 10, 38; m 63; c 1. GERMAN. *Educ:* Free Univ Berlin, PhD(Ger), 63. *Prof Exp:* Asst philos, Free Univ Berlin, 63-64; res scholar Ger, Yale Univ, 64-65; from asst prof to assoc prof, Ind Univ Bloominton, 65-69; prof, Univ Kiel, 69-72; PROF GER, IND UNIV BLOOMINGTON, 72- *Concurrent Pos:* Dozent, Wirtschaftsakademie, Berlin, 63-64; Volkswagen Found fe, 64-65. *Mem:* Hebbel Soc; Am Lessing Soc; MLA; Am Asn Teachers Ger; Int Ver Ger. *Res:* Classical and modern German literature; methods of literary research. *Publ:* Auth, Der junge Stefan George, 68 & ed, Hermann Broch: Perspektiven der Forschung, 71, Fink; auth, Poesie und Ratio: Lessing-Studien, Athenaum, 70; Der deutsche Roman der Gegenwart, Kohlhammer, 71; ed, Die deutsche Literatur der genwart, 71; auth, Dürrenmatt, Frisch, Weiss: deutsches Drama der Genwart, 72 & ed, Die deutsche Exilliteratur 1933-1945, 73, Reclam; co-ed, Texte und Kontexte: Studien zur deutschen und vergleichenden Literaturwissenschraft, Francke, 73. *Mailing Add:* Dept of Ger Ind Univ Bloomington IN 47401

DUTRA, JOHN ANTHONY, b Fall River, Mass, Feb 8, 40; m 63; c 1. CLASSICAL LANGUAGES. *Educ:* Providence Col, BA, 61; Tufts Univ, MA, 63, PhD(classics), 65. *Prof Exp:* Asst prof classics, St Bonaventure Univ, 65-67; asst prof, 65-73, ASSOC PROF CLASSICS, MIAMI UNIV, 73- *Mem:* Am Class League (treas, 73-); Am Philol Asn; Class Asn Midwest & South. *Res:* Greek religion, Greek philosophy, especially epicureanism; classics in translation. *Publ:* Auth, Catullus 13, a translation, Class Outlook, 67. *Mailing Add:* Dept of Classics Miami Univ Oxford OH 45056

DUTSCHKE, DENNIS JOHN, b Sacramento, Calif, Jan 28, 45; m 73; c 1. ITALIAN LITERATURE. *Educ:* San Francisco State Univ, MA, 68; Univ Calif, Los Angeles, PhD(Ital), 76. *Prof Exp:* Asst prof, 74-81, ASSOC PROF ITAL, UNIV CALIF, DAVIS, 81- *Mem:* Dante Soc; Mediaeval Acad Am; Renaissance Soc Am; Am Asn Teachers Ital; Medieval Asn of Pac. *Res:* Petrarch. *Publ:* Auth, The textual situation and chronological assessment of Petrarch's Canzone XXIII, Ital Quart, 74; Boccaccio: A question of love, Humanities Asn Rev, 76; Francesco Petrarca: Canzone XXIII from First to Final Version, Longo Editore, Ravenna, 77. *Mailing Add:* Dept of Fr & Ital Univ of Calif Davis CA 95616

DUVAL, FRANCIS ALAN, b Glenwood, Iowa, Dec 30, 16; m 42; c 1. GERMAN. *Educ:* Simpson Col, AB, 39; State Univ Iowa, AM, 41, PhD, 48. *Prof Exp:* Assoc prof Ger, Cornell Col, 41-42 & 46-60, prof & chmn dept class & mod lang, 60-82. *Concurrent Pos:* Fulbright scholar, Ger, 57; ed, Iowa Foreign Lang Bull, 63; mem exec comt, Iowa Regents Univs Austrian Prog; mem, Fulbright Selection Comt, 73-75. *Mem:* Am Asn Teachers Ger; MLA; Am Coun Teaching Foreign Lang. *Res:* Christian Metz, German American religious leader and pioneer. *Publ:* Coauth, Moderne Deutsche Sprachlehre, 67-75 & auth, Arbeitsheft für Moderne Deutsche Sprachlehre, 3rd ed, 80, Random; Wiederholung und Fortsetzung, Harper, 71. *Mailing Add:* 710 8th Ave N Mt Vernon IA 52314

DUVERLIE, CLAUD A, b Bras, France, May 8, 41; US citizen, m 64; c 2. FRENCH LANGUAGE & LITERATURE. *Educ:* Univ Rochester, MA, 66; Univ Chicago, PhD(Romance lang & Lit), 69. *Prof Exp:* Teacher French, Whitewater High Sch, Wis, 64-65; asst prof & coordr, 69-75, ASSOC PROF FRENCH, UNIV MD, BALTIMORE COUNTY, 75-, CHMN MOD LANG, 77- *Concurrent Pos:* Instr French, Pvt Sch Lang, 64-65; Nat Endowment for Humanities fel, 75-76. *Mem:* MLA; Am Asn Teachers Fr; Soc Paul Valery; Semiotic Soc Am. *Res:* The nouveau Roman; 20th century French literature; semiotics. *Publ:* Auth, Sur deux oeuvres recentes de Claude Simon, Die Neueren Sprachen, 9/72; Pour un Comment j'ai ecrit certains de mes livres de Claude Simon, Romance Notes, winter 72; co-ed, American Short Stories, Hachette, Paris, 74; auth, Eroticism in question in the works of Claude Simon & Interview with Claude Simon, Sub-Stance 8, 74; The crossing of the image, Diacritics, winter 77; Beyond the image: An interview with Alain Robbe-Grillet, New Lit Hist, Vol XI, 79-80; Premises for a graphopictology, In: Orion Blinded: Essays on Claude Simon, Assoc Univ Presses, 81 . *Mailing Add:* Dept of Mod Lang Univ Md Baltimore Co Baltimore MD 21228

DVOICHENKO-MARKOV, DEMETRIUS, History. See Vol I

DVORAK, PAUL FRANCIS, b Queens, NY, May 26, 46; m 69; c 2. GERMAN LANGUAGE & LITERATURE. *Educ:* La Salle Col, BA, 68; Univ Md, MA, 70, PhD(Ger), 73. *Prof Exp:* Instr, Univ Md, 70-74; ASST PROF GER, VA COMMONWEALTH UNIV, 74- *Concurrent Pos:* Res grant, Va Commonwealth Univ, 78-79 & 82-83; Fulbright grant, summer, 81. *Mem:* Am Asn Teachers Ger; Am Coun Teaching of Foreign Lang; Am Coun Study Austrian Lit; Am Transl Asn. *Res:* Post-War German literature; Austrian literature; foreign language pedagogy. *Publ:* Auth, Adapting personalized questions to second-year foreign language courses, Die Unterrichtspraxis, 75; translr, Ezekiel, humanizing the slave laws in Israel, hope in the OT, letter to the Romans, In: Interpreter's Dictionary of the Bible, Suppl, Abingdon, 76; auth, Communication, small groups and the interview in the foreign language classroom, For Lang Annals, 78; Notation for nouns continued, Die Unterrichtspraxis, 81. *Mailing Add:* Dept Foreign Lang Va Commonwealth Univ Richmond VA 23284

DVORAK, TRISHA ROBIN, b Vallejo, Calif, Nov 28, 50. APPLIED LINGUISTICS. *Educ:* Univ Pa, BA, 72; Univ Tex, Austin, MA, 74, PhD(appl ling), 77. *Prof Exp:* Asst prof, Dept Span & Port, Rutgers Univ, 77-80; ASST PROF SPAN METHODS, DEPT ROMANCE LANG, UNIV MICH, ANN ARBOR, 80- *Res:* Second language learning and acquisition; developing reading and listening skills. *Publ:* Coauth, Mary likes fishes: Use of gustar among New York Puerto Ricans, Bilingual Rev, Vol IX, No 1; Composicion: Proceso y Sintesis third year composition text for Spanish, 12/82 & Pasajes: An intermediate program in Spanish, 12/82, Random House. *Mailing Add:* Dept of Romance Lang Univ Mich Ann Arbor MI 48109

DVORETZKY, EDWARD, b Houston, Tex, Dec 29, 30; m 53; c 1. GERMAN LITERATURE. *Educ:* Rice Inst, BA, 53; Harvard Univ, MA, 58, PhD, 59. *Prof Exp:* From instr to assoc prof Ger, Rice Univ, 56-67; chmn dept, 69-79, PROF GER, UNIV IOWA, 67-, . *Mem:* Am Asn Teachers Ger; MLA; Lessing Soc; Goethe Soc; PEN Club. *Res:* Lessing and German literature of the 18th and 19th centuries; poetry. *Publ:* Auth, The Enigma of Emilia Galotti, Martinus Nijhoff, 63; Lessing in Schiller's Kabale und Liebe, Mod Philol, 5/66; ed, Lessing: Dokumente zur Wirkungsgeschichte 1755-1968 (2 vols), Kümmerle, 71 & 72; auth, Lessingsche Anklänge in Goethes Clavigo--ein Prolegomenon zu einer sprachlichen und stilistischen Untersuchung, In: Lessing Yearbk IV, 72; transl, Gotthold Ephraim Lessing: Emilia Galotti, Mary Rosenberg, 79; Philotas, Akademischer Verlag, 79; Thomas Manns Dr Faustus: Ein Rückblick auf die frühe deutsche Kritik, Blätter der Thomas Mann Gesellschaft, 79; ed, Lessing Heute--Beiträge zur Wirkungsgeschichte, Akademischer Verlag, l81; auth, Der Teufel und sein Advokat--Gedichte und Prosa, Stoedtner Verlag, 81. *Mailing Add:* Dept of Ger Univ of Iowa Iowa City IA 52242

DWARIKESH, DWARIKA PRASAD SHARMA, b Agra, India, Jan 10, 25; m 42; c 2. LINGUISTICS. *Educ:* Agra Univ, BA, 50, MA, 53 & 55; Calcutta Univ, MA, 57; Univ Chicago, PhD(ling), 71. *Prof Exp:* Lect Hindi lit, Nagari Pracharini Sabha, Agra, 49-53; asst prof, Agra Univ, 53-55; lectr Hindi-Urdu, Univ Chicago, 59-67; asst prof ling, 68-73, ASSOC PROF LING, WESTERN MICH UNIV, 73-, SUPVR CRITICAL LANG PROG, 69-, CHMN S ASIAN STUDIES, 73- *Concurrent Pos:* Asst prof, Univ Wis-Madison, 65-66. *Honors & Awards:* Univ Merit Award, Western Mich Univ, 77. *Mem:* Ling Soc Am; Int Ling Asn; Indian Ling Soc; SAsian Soc Am; Nat Asn Self Instr Critical Lang. *Res:* Sytax-semantics, cultural; archeaological linguistics; literature & philosophy. *Publ:* Auth, Chitralekha, 49 & Sadhana, 49, Vinod Pustak, Agra; Shandhagupta ek Adhyayan, Sahitya Prakashan, Agra, 52; Uttarkanda, Vinod Pustak, 53; Bhasa Vinjnan Samiksa (introduction to linguistics), 54 & Hindi Bhaska ka Vaijnanik Adhyayan (historical development of Hindi), 55, Reagal Bk Depot, Delhi; Historical Syntax of the Conjunctive Participial Phrase in Western Hindi, Phoolchang Ved Parkash, Delhi, India, 77. *Mailing Add:* Dept of Ling Western Mich Univ Kalamazoo MI 49001

DWORSKI, SYLVIA, b New Haven, Conn, Apr 10, 15. MODERN FOREIGN LANGUAGES. *Educ:* Conn Col, BA, 35; Yale Univ, MA, 37, PhD(Romance lang), 41; Univ Paris, cert, 39. *Prof Exp:* Teacher high sch, Conn, 42-44; instr French & Span, Sweet Briar Col, 44-46 & St Helena exten, Col William & Mary, 46-48; from asst prof to assoc prof French, Wilkes Col, 48-63; chmn dept French & Russ, 63-65, chmn dept French, 65-67, prof, 64-80, EMER PROF MOD LANG, ST MARY'S COL, IND, 80- *Concurrent Pos:* Instr, eve col, Conn State Teachers Col, 41-44; vis fel Romance lang, Yale Univ, 41-42; US grantee, Span Lang Inst, Univ Mex, summer 44; vis fac mem, Univ Notre Dame Grad Sch, summers 67 & 68. *Mem:* AAUP; Am Asn Teachers Fr; Alliance Francaise. *Mailing Add:* 70 Byron Pl New Haven CT 06515

DYCK, J WILLIAM, b Volga, Feb 10, 18; Can citizen; c 2. MODERN LANGUAGES. *Educ:* Bethal Col, AB, 51; Univ Mo, MA, 53; Univ Mich, PhD, 56. *Prof Exp:* Instr mod lang, Hesston Col, 50 & Univ Mo, 51-53; instr, Oberlin Col, 55-57; from asst prof to assoc prof mod lang & lit, 57-60, PROF GERMAN & RUSSIAN & CHMN DEPT GERMAN & SLAVIC LANG & LIT, UNIV WATERLOO, 60- *Concurrent Pos:* Ed, Germano-Slavica. *Mem:* MLA; Can Asn Teachers German. *Res:* Comparative literature. *Publ:* Auth, Doctor Zhivago: A quest for self-realization, Slavic & E Europ J, 62; Mozart, Ginn, 63; Goethes Humanitätsides und Grillparzers Sappho, Grillparzer Jahrbuch, 65; Humboldt, 65, Wagner, 65 & Nietzsche 67, Blaisdell; Kleist and Nietzsche, German Life & Letters, 68; Boris Pasternak, Twayne, 72; Der Instinkt der Verwandtschaft Kleist, Nietzsche, Kafka, Mann, Brecht, Peter Lang, Bern. *Mailing Add:* Dept of German & Slavic Lang & Lit Univ of Waterloo Waterloo ON N2L 3G1 Can

DYCK, MARTIN, b Gruenfeld, Ukraine, Jan 16, 27; Can citizen; c 4. GERMAN LITERATURE, LITERATURE & MATHEMATICS. *Educ:* Univ Man, BA, 53, MA, 54; Univ Cincinnati, PhD, 56. *Prof Exp:* Asst prof Ger & Russ, Mass Inst Technol, 56-58; from asst prof to prof Ger, Univ Mich, 58-65; PROF GER & HUMANITIES, MASS INST TECHNOL, 65- *Concurrent Pos:* Guggenheim & Am Coun Learned Soc fels, 61-62; Am Philos Soc award, 69; assoc ed, Hist Mathematica, 72-76. *Mem:* MLA; Hist Sci Soc; Int Soc Ger Lang & Lit; AAUP; Lessing Soc Am. *Res:* German literature of the 18th and 20th centuries, especially Goethe, Novalis, Schiller and Kafka; theory of poetry, major fiction, and comedy; foundations of literature and mathematics. *Publ:* Auth, Goethe's thought in the light of his pronouncements on applied and misapplied mathematics, PMLA; 58; Novalis and Mathematics, Univ NC, 60; Die Gedichte Schillers, Francke, Bern & Munich, 67; contribr, Relativity in physics and in fiction, In: Studies in 19th and 20th Century German Literature (Festschrift Coenen), Chapel Hill, Univ NC, 70; Tractatus Poetico-Mathematicus, In: Husbanding the Golden Grain (H W Nordmeyer Festschrift), Univ Mich, Ann Arbor, 73; auth, Goethe und Lermontow: Wandrers Nachtlied, Germano-Slavica, 73; contribr, Permutierender Prozess: eine neue Poetik der Moderne, In: Akten des V Kongresses der IVG, Berne, Frankfurt, Munich: H Lang and P Lang, 76; Der Gedichtschluss, In: Akten des VI Kongresses der IVG, Berne, Frankfurt, Munich, Lang, 81. *Mailing Add:* Ger Lit Sect Mass Inst Technol PO Box 281 Cambridge MA 02238

DYE, ROBERT ELLIS, b Mar 21, 36; US citizen; m 59; c 3. GERMAN LANGUAGE & LITERATURE. *Educ:* Univ Utah, BA, 60; Rutgers Univ, MA, 63, PhD(Ger), 66. *Prof Exp:* Teaching asst Ger, Univ Utah, 59-60; teaching asst, Rutgers Col, Rutgers Univ, 61-62, instr, 63-64; instr, Douglass Col, 64-66; asst prof, 66-71, assoc prof, 71-79, PROF GER, MACALESTER COL, 79-, CHMN DEPT GER & RUSS, 77- *Mem:* MLA; Goethe-Gesellschaft. *Res:* Goethe; literature and religion. *Publ:* Auth, Friedrich von Blanckenburg's theory of the novel, Monatshefte, summer 68; Man & God in Goethes Werther, Symposium, winter 75; The Easter Cantata and the idea of mediation of Goethe's Faust, PMLA, 10/77; Zu Gleichem Gleiches: The idea of correspondence in Iphigenie auf Tauris, Germanic Rev, No 53, 78; Blanckenburgs Werther-Rezeption, Goethes und Seiner Zeitgenossen, Francke, Bern, 81. *Mailing Add:* Dept of Ger Lang & Lit Macalester Col St Paul MN 55105

DYEN, ISIDORE, b Philadelphia, Pa, Aug 16, 13; m 39; c 2. LINGUISTICS, AUSTRONESIAN COMPARATIVE GRAMMAR. *Educ:* Univ Pa, BA, 33, MA, 34, PhD(Indo-Europ ling), 39. *Hon Degrees:* MA, Yale Univ, 57. *Prof Exp:* From instr to prof Malayan lang, 42-58, prof Malayopolynesian & comp ling, 58-73, dir, grad studies, Indic & Far Eastern lang & lit, 60-62, S & Southeast Asia, 62-66 & ling, 66-68, PROF COMP LING & AUSTRONESIAN LANG, YALE UNIV, 73- *Concurrent Pos:* Am Coun Learned Soc fel, 41-42; linguist, Coord Invest Micronesian Anthrop, 47; consult, Webster's Geog Dict, 48 & Javanese Dict Proj, Harvard Univ, 65-; Guggenheim fels, 53-54 & 64-65; assoc ed, William Dwight Whitney Ling Ser, Yale Univ, 53- & Current Trends in Ling, Vol 8, Ling in Oceania, 71, Tri-Inst Pac Prog grant, 57, vis prof, Univ Padjadjaran, 60-61; Dept Health, Educ & Welfare grant, 60-62; coordr ling sect, 10th Pac Sci Cong, Honolulu, 61; Nat Sci Found grants, 62-66, 67-69 & 69-77; fel Am Inst Indian Studies, 64; mem orgn comt, Conf Lexicostatist, Yale Univ, 71, 2nd int Conf, Univ Montreal, 73; mem adv comt, 1st Int Conf Comp Austronesian Ling, Univ Hawaii, 74. *Mem:* Royal Inst Ling Geog & Ethnol Netherlands; Ling Soc Am; Am Orient Soc(vpres, 65-66); Am Anthrop Asn; Soc Ling Paris. *Res:* General and comparative linguistics; Austronesian linguistics and lexicostatistics; Indonesian and Malay grammar. *Publ:* Auth, Spoken Malay (2 vols), Holt, 45; The Proto-Malayo-Polynesian Laryngeals, William Dwight Whitney Ling Ser, Yale Univ, 53; A sketch of Trukese grammar, Am Orient Soc, 65; A lexicostatistical classification of the Austronesian languages, Int J Am Ling, 65; A Descriptive Indonesian Grammar, privately publ, 67; Lexicostatistics in genetic linguistics, In: Proceedings of the Yale Conference, Mouton, 73; coauth, Lexical Reconstruction: The Case of the Athapaskan Kinship System, Cambridge Univ, 74; auth, Linguistic Subgrouping and Lexicostatistics, Mouton, 75. *Mailing Add:* Hall of Grad Studies Yale Univ New Haven CT 06520

DYER, NANCY JOE, b Navasota, Tex, Apr 15, 42; m 77. SPANISH LANGUAGE & LITERATURE. *Educ:* Tex Tech Univ, BA, 64; Tulane Univ, MA, 68; Univ Pa, PhD (Span), 75. *Prof Exp:* Asst instr Span, Univ Tex, Austin, 68-70; instr, Univ Pa, 73; vis asst prof, Univ Calif, Los Angeles, 74-75; asst prof, Univ Houston, Victoria, 75-77; ASST PROF SPAN, TEX A&M UNIV, 77- *Mem:* Am Asn Teachers Span & Port; MLA; Mediaeval Acad Am; Ling Soc Am. *Res:* Medieval Spanish language and literature, especially epic, chronicles, historiography and computer-assisted research; Romance philology and linguistics; teaching methodology. *Publ:* Ed, Beginning Spanish Conversation, Univ Tex, 70; auth, A study of the Old Spanish adverb in -mente, Hisp Rev, 72; A note on the use of verso agudo in the Milagros de Nuestra Senora, Romance Notes, 77; Cronicade Veinte Reys Use of the Cid Epic: Perspectives, Method and Rationale, Romance Philol, 80; Human information processing bilingualism and second language reading & implications for classroom use of a cognitive model of second language reading, Cognition & Develop Ling, 82; El Poema de Mio Cid en la Cronica de Veinte Reyed y la Primera Cronica General, Gredos (in press). *Mailing Add:* Dept of Mod Lang Tex A&M Univ College Station TX 77843

DYKEMA, CHRISTINE RHOADES, b Pawtucket, RI, Aug 23, 08; m 31; c 3. FOREIGN LANGUAGES. *Educ:* Columbia Univ, AB, 32; Western Reserve Univ, MA, 51. *Prof Exp:* From instr to asst prof French & English, 38-60, from asst prof to assoc prof French, 60-70, prof, 70-79, EMER PROF FRENCH, YOUNGSTOWN STATE UNIV, 80-, CHMN DEPT FOREIGN LANG, 73- *Concurrent Pos:* Lectr cult sem for physicians, Youngstown Univ & Mahoning County Med Soc, 61 & 62. *Mem:* MLA; Am Asn Teachers Fr; AAUP. *Res:* Seventeenth century French literature; linguistics; pedagogy. *Mailing Add:* Dept of Lang Youngstown State Univ Youngstown OH 44503

DYKSTRA, GERALD, b Kent Co, Mich, Sept 4, 22; m 79; c 4. LINGUISTICS. *Educ:* Univ Mich, AB & AM, 48, PhD(Romance Philol), 55. *Prof Exp:* Instr Span, Eastern Mich Univ, 48-49; instr English & ling, Univ Mich, 48-55; from asst prof to prof, Teachers Col, Columbia Univ, 55-66; PROF COMMUN, UNIV HAWAII, MANOA, 66- *Concurrent Pos:* Lectr English, Columbia Univ, 53-54; dir, Nat English Prog, Kabul, 58-60; fel, Afro-Anglo-Am Prog Teacher Educ, Africa, 61-62; chief of party, Teachers Col Columbia Univ Team, Peru, 63-64; dir, TESL Materials Develop Ctr, 63-67; consult, Ford Found Near East & Africa Prog, 64-66; mem, Nat Adv Coun Teaching English as Foreign Lang, 65-68; chief consult, Hawaii Curric Ctr, 66-75; consult, Dept Educ State Hawaii, 76-79. *Mem:* Int Commun Asn; Ling Soc Am; NCTE; Teachers English Speakers Other Lang; Speech Commun Asn. *Res:* Education; learning systems design; communication systems. *Publ:* Coauth, Ananse Tales: A Course in Controlled Composition, Columbia Univ, 66; Final Report: TESL Materials Development Center (7 vols), US Dept Health, Educ & Welfare, 67; Set I, Pronunciation and contrasts & Set II, Verb structure practice, Lang Master AV Prog English as Second Lang, Bell & Howell, 67; Today's education for tomorrow's world, Hawaii Asn Supv & Curric, 70; Composition, Guided--free (9 vols), Columbia Univ, 74 & 78; coauth, Hawaii English Program for Special Students, 78 & Revised Teachers Manual, 78, State Hawaii. *Mailing Add:* Dept of Commun Univ Hawaii, Manoa Honolulu HI 96822

DYNNIK, ALEXANDER GEORGE, b Libava, Latvia, Dec 14, 19; US citizen. RUSSIAN LANGUAGE & LITERATURE. *Educ:* Univ Montreal, MA, 61, PhD(Russ), 65. *Prof Exp:* Teacher Russ lang & lit, Russ Parochial Sch, Montreal, 54-58; asst Russ, Univ Montreal, 58-61; teacher var high schs, Montreal, 61-66; asst prof Russ lang & lit, 66-70, assoc ed, Russ Lang J, 66-73, assoc prof, 70-78, PROF RUSS LANG & LIT, MICH STATE UNIV, 78- *Mem:* AAAS; Am Asn Teachers Slavic & East Europ Lang; MLA. *Res:* Russian literature of the 20th century; Soviet literature. *Publ:* Auth, A I Kuprin: Life and Work, Baschkirzew, Munich, 69; Origins of Russian Literary

Language, Sovremennik, 66; Zhenskie portrety v tvorchestve Kuprina, New Rev, 68; A I Kuprin in the years of exile: Moods, feelings, ideals, In: Russian Emigre Literature: A collection of articles, Pittsburgh, 72; Formy, Peizazhoy izobrazitel'nosti v tvorchestve Kuprina, Russ Lang J, No 110, Vol XXI; A S Griboyedov: Man of Pathos and Skepticism, Sovremennik, 79; Approaches to Russian literature of the XIX century: Survey and analyses, Russkaia Kniga, 82. *Mailing Add:* Dept of Ger & Russ Mich State Univ East Lansing MI 48824

DYSON, JOHN PAYNE, b Batesville, Miss, Apr 13, 30; m 58; c 3. SPANISH, PORTUGUESE. *Educ:* Kans State Univ, AB, 60; Univ Kans, MA, 62, PhD(Span), 65. *Prof Exp:* Asst prof, 65-68, ASSOC PROF SPAN & PORT, IND UNIV, BLOOMINGTON, 68- *Concurrent Pos:* Fac res grant, Ind Univ, 66-; ed, Span Am & Luso-Brasilian sect, Twayne's World auth Ser, 67- *Mem:* MLA; Am Asn Teachers Span & Port. *Res:* Spanish American literary criticism; Chilean and Medieval Portuguese literature. *Publ:* Auth, Los cuentos de Nicomedes Guzman, 4-6/64 & Tragedia draiana: la princesa de la eterna espera, 1-3/67, Atenea; La evolucion de la critica literaria en Chile, Ed Universitaria, Santiago, Chile, 65; The comedy of the dead, First Stage, spring 67. *Mailing Add:* Dept of Span & Port Ind Univ Bloomington IN 47401

E

EAGLE, EDWIN DOUGLAS, b Hamilton, Ont, June 3, 11; m 36; c 2. CLASSICS, PHILOSOPHY. *Educ:* Univ Toronto, BA Hons, 34, MA, 35; Univ Wis, PhD(classics), 37. *Prof Exp:* Instr Latin, Suffield Acad, 37-38; instr Latin & Greek, Lycoming Col, 38-40; from asst prof to prof & head dept, 40-76, dean fac arts & sci, 60-68, EMER PROF CLASSICS, UNIV WINNIPEG, 76- *Concurrent Pos:* United Col fel, 77. *Mem:* Class Asn Can. *Res:* Ancient humanism; classical mythology and religion. *Publ:* Auth, Catiline and the Concordia Ordinum, Phoenix; In Principio Verbum, Class J. *Mailing Add:* 235 Ashland Ave Winnipeg MB R3L 1L3 Can

EARLE, PETER G, b Yonkers, NY, May 31, 23; m 49; c 3. SPANISH & LATIN AMERICAN LITERATURE. *Educ:* Mexico City Col, BA, 49, MA, 51; Univ Kans, PhD, 59. *Prof Exp:* Instr Span, Princeton Univ, 56-59; asst prof, Wesleyan Univ, 59-63; assoc prof, 63-69, PROF SPAN, UNIV PA, 69- *Concurrent Pos:* Assoc ed, Hisp Rev, 64-73, ed, 73-; adv ed, Latin Am Lit Rev, 72- *Mem:* Am Asn Teachers Span & Port; MLA; Mod Humanities Res Asn; Inst Int Lit Iberoamericana. *Res:* Modern Spanish literature; modern Latin American literature. *Publ:* Auth, Unamuno and English literature, Hisp Inst, 60; Unamuno and the theme of history, Hisp Rev, 10/64; La nacionalidad mexicana, 11-12/64 & Camino oscuro: la novela hispanoamericana contemporanea, 5-6/67, Cuadernos Americanos, Mex; Voces Hispanoamericanas, Harcourt, 66; Prophet in the Wilderness: The Works of Ezequiel Martinez Estrada, Univ Tex, Austin, 71; coauth, Historia del ensayo hispanoamericano, Ed Andrea, Mexico City, 73. *Mailing Add:* Dept of Romance Lang Univ of Pa Philadelphia PA 19174

EASBY, ELIZABETH KENNEDY, b Mar 20, 25; m 49. ART & ARCHEOLOGY OF LATIN AMERICA. *Educ:* Cornell Univ, AB, 47; Columbia Univ, MA, 52. *Prof Exp:* Res assoc, Mus Am Indian, 60-63; actg cur primitive art, Brooklyn Mus, 65-68; consult, pre-Columbian art, Metrop Mus Art, 68-71; RES ASSOC AM SECT, UNIV MUS, UNIV PA, 72- *Honors & Awards:* Order San Carlos, Colombia, 57; Order Merit, Peru, 61 & 65; Order Aztec Eagle, Mex, 70. *Mem:* Fel Am Anthrop Asn; Archaeol Inst Am; Mex Soc Anthrop; Sem Maya Cult; fel Royal Anthrop Inst, Gt Brit. *Res:* Lapidary work. *Publ:* Auth, Pre-Columbian Jade from Costa Rica, Andre Emmerich, 68; coauth, Before Cortes: Sculpture of Middle America, Metrop Mus Art, 70. *Mailing Add:* 2221 Rittenhouse Sq Philadelphia PA 19103

EASTMAN, CAROL M, b Boston, Mass, Sept 27, 41. LINGUISTICS, ANTHROPOLOGY. *Educ:* Univ Mass, BA, 63; Univ Wis, PhD(ling), 67. *Prof Exp:* Asst prof anthrop & ling, 67-73, assoc prof, 73-79, PROF ANTHROP, UNIV WASH, 79- *Concurrent Pos:* Vis prof, Univ Nairobi, 79-80; adj prof ling & women studies, Univ Wash, 79- *Mem:* Ling Soc Am; fel African Studies Asn; Am Anthrop Asn; Current Anthrop. *Res:* Bantu linguistics and literature; Northwest Indian languages; language and culture. *Publ:* Auth, Who are the Waswahili?, Africa, 71; The proverb in modern written Swahili literature, In: African Folklore Ser, 72; Aspects of Language and Culture, Chandler & Sharp, 75; The emergence of an African regional literature: Swahili, African Studies Rev, 77; Linguistic Theory and Language Description, Lippincott, 78; Word order in Haida, Int J Am Ling, 79; Language planning, identity planning and world view, Int J Sociol Lang, 81; The American Indian's language & culture in US education, In: World Yearbook of Education, Educ Minorities, 81. *Mailing Add:* Dept of Anthrop Univ Wash Seattle WA 98195

EASTON, HOWARD TREVELYAN, b Montevideo, Minn, May 8, 05; m 32; c 2. CLASSICAL LANGUAGES. *Educ:* Johns Hopkins Univ, AB, 26, MA, 30. *Prof Exp:* Instr Latin & Greek, Western Md Col, 25-27; asst prof, Ohio Wesleyan Univ, 30-32; instr Latin, 32-69, George Shattuck Morison prof, 69-71, EMER PROF LATIN, PHILLIPS EXETER ACAD, 71- *Concurrent Pos:* Spec lectr Latin, Univ NH, 74 & 77-78. *Mem:* Am Philol Asn; Class Asn New England; Vergilian Soc Am (secy, 60). *Mailing Add:* 12 Pleasant View Dr Exeter NH 03833

EBANKS, GERARDO MACK, b Havana, Cuba, Nov 6, 26; m 51. ROMANCE LANGUAGES & LITERATURE. *Educ:* Marianao Col, Cuba, BS, 46, AB, 47; Morris Brown Col, BD, 52; Middlebury Col, MA, 53; Univ Madrid, PhD, 63. *Prof Exp:* Instr Span, Morris Brown Col, 53-56; assoc prof mod foreign lang, Morehouse Col, 58-68; prof, Fed City Col, 68-77; PROF MOD FOREIGN LANG, UNIV DC, 77- *Concurrent Pos:* Mem, Sch Teachers of Havana & Inst Hisp Cult, Madrid. *Mem:* Am Asn Teachers Span & Port; Am Asn Teachers Fr; Col Lang Asn. *Res:* Spanish and Spanish American literature. *Publ:* Auth, El honor en la Edad de Oro espanola, 55 & Baroja y sus personajes, 61, Col Lang Asn; La novela de la tierra: su concepto, Cuadernos Hispanoam, 57. *Mailing Add:* Dept of Mod Foreign Lang Univ of DC Washington DC 20008

EBBINGHAUS, ERNST A, GERMANIC PHILOLOGY. *Educ:* Univ Marburg, PhD. *Prof Exp:* PROF GER & COMP LIT, PA STATE UNIV, 63- *Concurrent Pos:* Co-ed, Gen Ling, 80- *Res:* Archaeology; paleography. *Publ:* Auth, The origin of Wulfila's alphabet, Gen Ling, 79; The study of Wulfila's alphabet, J Dept English, 79; Gothic names in the menologies, 80 & A preliminary note on the Gothic Nehemiah fragment, 81, Gen Ling; Gotische Grammatik, Niemeyer Verlag, 81; Stabeis in Wulfila's Bible, 81 & The phonetic values of Wulfila's letters g and h, Gen Ling, 81. *Mailing Add:* PO Box 742 Bellefonte PA 16823

EBERSOLE, ALVA VERNON, JR, b Liberal, Kans, June 17, 19; m 49. SPANISH LANGUAGE & LITERATURE. *Educ:* Mexico City Col, BA, 49, MA, 51; Univ Kans, PhD, 57. *Prof Exp:* Instr Span, Pac Sch Lang, 51-52; asst instr, Univ Kans, 52-57; instr, Univ Ill, 57-59; from asst prof to assoc prof, Univ Mass, 59-62; prof & chmn dept, Adelphi Univ, 62-68; PROF SPAN, UNIV NC, CHAPEL HILL, 68- *Mem:* Am Asn Teachers Span & Port; MLA; Asoc Int Hispanistas; AAUP. *Res:* Golden Age Drama in Spain; superstition in 16th century Spain; 18th century pre-Neoclassic drama in Spain. *Publ:* Ed, Juan Ruiz de Alarcon, El Texedor de Segovia, Estud Hispanofila, 74; auth, Jose de Caizares, dramaturgo olvidado del siglo XVIII, Insula, 74; ed, J R de Alarcon, La verdad sospechosa, Catedra, 76; Lope de Vega, Las Ferias de Madrid, 77 & coauth, Perspectivas de la comedia, 78, Coleccion Siglo de Oro; ed, Pedro Ciruelo, Reprovacion de las supersticiones y hechizerias, 78 & coauth, Perspectivas de la comedia, II, 79, Albatros ediciones, Hispanofila; auth, Disquisiciones sobre El burlador de Sevilla de Tirso de Molina, Almar, 80. *Mailing Add:* Dept of Romance Lang Univ of NC Chapel Hill NC 27514

EBLING, BENJAMIN, II, b Grand Rapids, Mich, Apr 29, 33; m 56; c 1. FRENCH, APPLIED LINGUISTICS. *Educ:* Western Mich Univ, BA, 55; Univ Mich, Ann Arbor, MA, 56; Ohio State Univ, PhD(ling, foreign lang, educ & French), 65. *Prof Exp:* Instr French, Coe Col, 59-62; from asst prof to assoc prof, 62-65, PROF FRENCH, WESTERN MICH UNIV, 65- *Mem:* Am Coun Teaching Foreign Lang; Am Asn Teachers Fr; AAUP. *Res:* Foreign-language methodology; teaching of culture. *Publ:* Auth, Cahier de Travail Pratique (to accompany Echelon: On Decouvre), C E Merrill, 72; Toward the teaching of authentic French culture at the secondary level, 4/72 & A mini-French course for fashion-merchandising majors, 12/80, Fr Rev. *Mailing Add:* Dept of Mod & Class Lang Western Mich Univ Kalamazoo MI 49001

ECHARD, GWENDA, Can citizen. FRENCH RENAISSANCE LITERATURE. *Educ:* Univ Wales, BA, 54, MA, 57; Univ Paris, DUP, 60. *Prof Exp:* Asst lectr French, Univ Col, Univ Wales, 58-60; asst prof, Miami Univ, 60-61, Parsons Col, 61-64; ASSOC PROF FRENCH & HUMANITIES & CHMN, DEPT FRENCH STUDIES, YORK UNIV, 64- *Mem:* Renaissance Soc Am; Can Renaissance Studies. *Res:* Christian humanism; humanist notions of kingship; Erasmus, Ronsard and D'Aubigne. *Publ:* Auth, Aspects of Christian humanism in French renaissance prefaces to the classics, Proc Patristic, Mediaeval Renaissance Conf, Vol IV, 79; The Erasmian ideal of kingship as reflected in the work of Ronsard and d'Auigne, Renaissance and Reformation, Vol V, No 1; The humanists and classical poetry--a crisis of conscience, Studi Francesi (in press). *Mailing Add:* 16 Elmridge Acres Rd Thornhill ON L3T 1W3 Can

ECHEVARRIA, EVELIO A, b Santiago, Chile, Mar 28, 26; US citizen; m 57; c 4. SPANISH, SPANISH AMERICAN LITERATURE. *Educ:* Univ Calif, Berkeley, BA, 62, MA, 64; Univ Colo, Boulder, PhD(Span), 69. *Prof Exp:* Teaching assoc Span, Univ Colo, 64-67; instr, Univ Nev, 67-69; asst prof, 69-73, assoc prof, 73-77, PROF SPAN, COLO STATE UNIV, 77- *Concurrent Pos:* Hon mem, Club Andino de Chile. *Mem:* Am Asn Teachers Span & Port; Rocky Mountain Mod Lang Asn; Coun Latin Am Studies. *Res:* Spanish American fiction, 20th century; novel of social protest of Spanish America, its relation with communism; Bolivian 20th century fiction. *Publ:* Auth, La novela social de Bolivia, Ed Difusion, La Paz, Bolivia, 73; The new face of Bolivian fiction, Latin Am Lit Rev, 73; Lider, anglicismo de cambio semantico en la America espanola, Hispania, 4/73; El nuevo cuento hispanoamericano: Bolivia y Uruguay, Rev Estud Hispanicos, Vol VII, No 1; Hispanic Colorado, Centennial Publ, 76; Indice General Repertorio Americano, San Jose, 80 & 81. *Mailing Add:* Dept of Lang Colo State Univ Ft Collins CO 80523

ECHEVERRIA, DURAND, b Short Hills, NJ, Feb 26, 13; m 45, 67; c 3. FRENCH LITERATURE. *Educ:* Princeton Univ, AB, 35, AM, 49, PhD, 50; Middlebury Col, AM, 46. *Prof Exp:* Asst, Princeton Univ, 47-49; from instr to prof French, 49-67, chmn dept French, 64-67, prof French & comp lit, 67-78, EMER PROF FRENCH & COMP LIT, BROWN UNIV, 78- *Concurrent Pos:* Fulbright grant-in-aid, France, 50-51 & res grant, 57-58; Guggenheim fel, 57-58; Nat Endowment for Humanities grant, 78-80. *Mem:* Soc Hist Mod France; Soc Fr Hist Studies; Int Comp Lit Asn. *Res:* French cultural history; comparative literature of 18th century; 18th century French literature. *Publ:* Auth, Mirage in the West, Princeton Univ, 57 & 68; co-transl & ed, Brissot, New Travels in the United States of America, 1788, Harvard Univ, 64; Antoine Jay and the United States. *Mailing Add:* Dept of French Brown Univ Providence RI 02912

ECHOLS, JOHN MINOR, b Portland, Ore, Mar 25, 13; m 41; c 3. LINGUISTICS. *Educ:* Univ Va, BA, 37, MA, 38, PhD(Ger philol), 40. *Prof Exp:* Assoc prof ling & dept dir, Sch Lang & Ling, Foreign Serv Inst, Dept of State, 47-52; assoc prof ling, 52-57, prof ling, 57-78, asoc dir, Southeast Asia Prog, 65-78, actg dir, 73-74, ASSOC DIR, MOD INDONESIA PROJ, CORNELL UNIV, 61- *Concurrent Pos:* Dir & consult, Ford Found & Indonesian Ministry of Educ English Lang Teaching Proj, 52-55; Rockefeller Found fel & Am Coun Learned Soc travel grant, 59-60. *Honors & Awards:* Honor Award, US Dept State, 51. *Mem:* Ling Soc Am; Asn Asian Studies (pres, 77-78); Am Orient Soc; Koninklijk Instituut voor Taal-, Land- en Volkenkunde, Leiden. *Res:* Indonesian-Malay lexicography; Indonesian bibliography; Malayo-Polynesian. *Publ:* Ed, Indonesian writing in translation, Cornell Mod Indonesia Proj, 56; coauth, An Indonesian-English Dictionary, Cornell Univ, 61 & 63; Preliminary checklist of Indonesian imprints during the Japanese period (March 1942-August 1945), 63, Preliminary checklist of Indonesian imprints (1945-1949): With Cornell University holdings, 65 & coauth, A guide to Indonesian periodicals (1945-1970) in the Cornell University Library, 66, Cornell Mod Indonesia Proj; A guide to Indonesian serials (1945-1970) in the Cornell University Library, Cornell Southeast Asian Prog, 73; coauth, An English-Indonesian Dictionary, Cornell Univ, 75. *Mailing Add:* Southeast Asia Prog 120 Uris Hall Cornell Univ Ithaca NY 14853

ECKARD, RONALD D, English as a Second Language. See Vol II

ECKERT, LOWELL EDGAR, b Racine, Wis, Apr 27, 32. CLASSICAL LANGUAGES, BIBLICAL STUDIES. *Educ:* Concordia Sem, Mo, BA, 54, MDiv, 57; Washington Univ, MA, 59; Univ Alta, BEd, 69; Concordia Sem in Exile, STM, 75. *Prof Exp:* Instr Greek, Concordia Sem, Ill, 59-61; from instr to assoc prof, 61-74, registr, 75-79, PROF GREEK, LATIN & CHURCH HIST, CONCORDIA COL, 74- *Mem:* Am Philol Asn; Lutheran Acad Scholar; Lutheran Educ Asn. *Res:* The Septuagint; New Testament studies. *Mailing Add:* Concordia Col 7128 Ada Blvd Edmonton AB T5B 4E4 Can

ECKHARDT, CAROLINE DAVIS, English & Comparative Literature. See Vol II

ECONOMOU, ELLY HELEN, b Thessalonica, Greece. BIBLICAL & MODERN LANGUAGES. *Educ:* Pac Union Col, BA, 66; Andrews Univ, MA, 67; Univ Strasbourg, France, PhD(relig), 75. *Prof Exp:* Instr French, 67-70, instr French & Greek, 70-72, ASST PROF BIBL LANG & RELIG, ANDREWS UNIV, 72- *Mem:* Soc Bibl Lit; MLA; Int Platform Asn; Am Class League. *Res:* Ecumenical studies; religion, the Greek Orthodox church, patristic literature; papyrology. *Publ:* Auth, Beloved Enemy, Pac Press Publ Asn, 68; numerous articles in Youth's Beakon & Children's Friend, 51-72. *Mailing Add:* Dept of Relig Andrews Univ Berrien Springs MI 49104

EDBERG, GEORGE JOHN, b Philadelphia, Pa, Oct 6, 24. SPANISH. *Educ:* Temple Univ, BS, 49; Univ Havana, Cuba, AM, 51; Univ Kans, PhD, 59. *Prof Exp:* Instr English, Univ Havana, Cuba, 49-50; instr, Cuban-N Am Cult Inst, 50-51; asst instr Span, Univ Kans, 53-57; instr, Univ Va, 57-59; asst prof, Purdue Univ, 59-60; asst prof, Dickinson Col, 61-64; NDEA Summer Lang Inst, Univ Pittsburgh, 64; assoc prof, 65-67, PROF SPAN & CHMN DEPT, TEMPLE UNIV, 68- *Concurrent Pos:* Asst prof, NDEA Summer Lang Inst, Univ Fla, 63-; Andrew Mellon fel, Univ Pittsburgh, 64-65. *Mem:* MLA; Am Asn Teachers Span & Port; Nat Fed Mod Lang Teachers Asn (pres, 67); Inst Int Lit Iberoam; Mid States Asn Mod Lang Teachers. *Res:* Nineteenth century Spanish Peninsular and Latin American literature; the Cuadro form; language teaching methods. *Publ:* Auth, Cuadros Guatemaltecos, Macmillan, 65; Articulos de Don Jose Milla no incluidos en sus obras, El Imparcial, Guatemala, 58; Un estudio de Don Manuel del Pez, una creacion literaria Galdosiana, Humanitas, Mex, 61; The Guatemalan Jose Milla and his Cuadros, Hispania, 61. *Mailing Add:* 554 N 18th Philadelphia PA 19130

EDBROOKE, ROBERT OWEN, JR, History, Classical Philology. See Vol I

EDDINGTON, MARILYN LAMOND, b Middletown, Conn, Oct 6, 31; m 60. ROMANCE LANGUAGES, SPANISH. *Educ:* Miami Univ, AB, 52; Univ NC, MA, 54, PhD(Span & French), 58. *Prof Exp:* Instr Span, Moravian Col, 54-55 & Mercer Univ, 55-56; instr Span & French, Western Mich Univ, 58-60; from instr to asst prof, 61-67, ASSOC PROF SPAN, UNIV DETROIT, 67- *Mem:* Am Asn Teachers Span & Port; Am Coun Teachers Foreign Lang; MLA. *Res:* Calderon and the Spanish Golden Age drama; Eugene Scribe and the Spanish drama 1835-1850. *Publ:* Auth, Eugene Scribe and the Comedies-Vaudevilles in the Spanish romantic drama, Romance Notes, 61. *Mailing Add:* 334 Briggs Bldg Univ of Detroit Detroit MI 48221

EDDLEMAN, HENRY LEO, Theology, Philosophy. See Vol IV

EDDY, PETER ARMES, b New Rochelle, NY, May 23, 41; m 72. FRENCH LANGUAGE, APPLIED LINGUISTICS. *Educ:* Haverford Col, BA, 63; Middlebury Col, MA, 66; Ohio State Univ, PhD(foreign lang educ), 70. *Prof Exp:* Teacher French, Montgomery County, Md, Pub Schs, 63-67; asst prof, Western Wash Univ, 70-74, assoc prof French, 74-80; DIR, ERIC CLEARINGHOUSE ON LANG & LING, CTR APPLIED LINGUISTICS, 74- *Concurrent Pos:* Asst ed, Fr Rev, 73-; mem, MLA Task Force on Govt Rels, 77-78; mem exec comt, MLA Div Applied Ling & dir, bd dirs, Northeast Conf on Teaching Foreign Lang, 77- *Mem:* Am Asn Teachers Fr; Am Coun Teaching Foreign Lang; MLA; Ling Soc Am. *Res:* French applied linguistics; transfer of training in foreign language learning; modern French culture. *Publ:* Ed, A Selected Bibliography of Films and Videotapes on Foreign Language Teacher Training, Ctr Applied Ling, 75; auth, Competence-based certification of foreign language teachers: The Bellevue-Western experience, Mod Lang J, 12/75; Foreign language skills and jobs, Proc Pac Northwest Coun Foreign Lang, 76; The 1976 western workshop for language teachers: A report to the profession, Foreign Lang Ann, 5/77; ed, An Idea Book for Language Teachers, Western Wash Univ, 77; contribr, The evaluation of foreign language programs, Nat Textbk Co, 78; auth, The effect of first foreign language acquisition on second language learning, Proc Pac Northwest Coun Foreign Lang, 78. *Mailing Add:* 2315 N Roosevelt St Arlington VA 22205

EDGERTON, MILLS FOX, JR, b Hartford, Conn, June 11, 31; m 57; c 2. ROMANCE PHILOLOGY. *Educ:* Univ Conn, BA, 53; Princeton Univ, AM, 55, PhD, 60. *Prof Exp:* Instr Span, French & Ital, Princeton Univ, 55-57 & Rutgers Univ, 57-60; assoc prof & chmn dept Span, 60-66, chmn dept mod lang, lit & ling, 68-75, PROF MOD LANG & LING, BUCKNELL UNIV, 66- *Concurrent Pos:* Interpreter Span & English, US Depts Labor, Agr & Health, Educ & Welfare, Point 4 Prog, 56-57; lectr, Univ Bonn, 61 & 62 & Univ Florence, 62; chmn comt advan Span tests & grad record exams, Educ Testing Serv, 63-; reviewer proposals, Nat Endowment for Humanities, 67-; Am ed, Nature Method, Charlottenlund, Denmark; reader, Foreign Lang Ann & Mod Lang J; dir intensive lang prog, Middlebury Col, 73; dir press, 76- *Mem:* Northeast Conf Teaching Foreign Lang; MLA. *Res:* Romance philology; general linguistics; sociolinguistics. *Publ:* Auth, L'espace sociolinguistique et les systemes ideolinguistiques: La France et les Francais, Studia linguistica, Vol XXV, No 1, Lund, Sweden; A philosophy for the teacher of foreign languages, Mod Lang J, 1/71; ed, Training the language teacher--rethinking and reform, For Lang Ann, 12/71; The foreign language teacher's predicament, ADFL Bull, 3/73; Some socio-linguistic considerations in the teaching of foreign languages, Proc ACTFL/SCOLT Joint Ann Meeting, 73; On knowing a foreign language, ADFL Bull, 11: 22-26; Six poems, Ital Quart, summer 80 & Piazza Navona, Rome, summer 81; Voces que oigo, Coleccion de poesia al cuidado de Concha Lagos, Madrid, 81. *Mailing Add:* Dept of Mod Lang Bucknell Univ Lewisburg PA 17837

EDGERTON, WILLIAM BENBOW, b Winston-Salem, NC, Mar 11, 14; m 35; c 2. SLAVIC LANGUAGES. *Educ:* Guilford Col, AB, 34; Haverford Col, AM, 35; Russ Inst, cert, 49; Columbia Univ, PhD, 54. *Prof Exp:* Teacher, prep schs, 35-37, 38-39; asst English, Lycee de Belfort, France, 37-38; from asst prof to assoc prof French & Span, Guilford Col, 39-47; asst prof Russ, Pa State Univ, 50-56; from asst prof to assoc prof Slavic Lang, Columbia Univ, 56-58; chmn dept, 58-65, 69-73, PROF SLAVIC LANG & LIT, IND UNIV, BLOOMINGTON, 58- *Concurrent Pos:* Mem, Joint Comt Slavic Studies, Am Coun Learned Soc & Soc Sci Res Coun, 51-62, chmn, 57-60, consult, Ford Found, 53-57, 58-61; vis asst prof, Univ Mich, 54-55; Am rep, Int Comt Slavists, 58-78; Guggenheim fel, 63-64; exchange res scholar, Am Coun Learned Soc & Soviet Acad Sci, Moscow, 63-64; cong liaison work, Friends Comt Nat Legislation in Washington, spring 68; consult, US Off Educ, 69-72, Nat Endowment for Humanities, 69- & Columbia Univ Press, 77-; MLA exec coun, 62-65. *Mem:* MLA; Am Asn Advan Slavic Studies (pres, 61-62); Am Comp Lit Asn; Am Asn Teachers Slavic & EEurop Lang. *Res:* Comparative literature; 18th and 19th century Russian literature; Russian literary relations with the West. *Publ:* Auth, The penetration of nineteenth-century Russian literature into the other Slavic countries, In: Am Contrib 5th Int Cong Slavists, 63 & The artist turned prophet: Leo Tolstoi after 1880, In: Am Contrib 6th Int Cong Slavists, 68, Mouton, The Hague; transl, Satirical Stories of Nikolai Leskov, Pegasus, 69; auth, Cosmic farce or transcendental vision: Modern manifestations of the absurd in Slavic and non-Slavic literature, In: Am Contrib 7th Int Cong Slavists, Mouton, The Hague, 73; Tolstoy and Magalhaes Lima, Comp Lit, 76; The reception abroad of Tolstoy's What is Art?, Am Contrib 8th Int Cong Slavists, 78; ed, Columbia Dict of Modern European Literature, 80; auth, Spanish and Portuguese Responses to Dostoevskij, Revue de Litterature Comparee, 81. *Mailing Add:* 1801 E Maxwell Lane Ind Univ Bloomington IN 47401

EDSON, LAURIE DALE, b Elizabeth, NJ, Oct 3, 49; m 81. FRENCH LANGUAGE & LITERATURE. *Educ:* Univ Wis, Madison, BA, 71; Univ Calif, Irvine, MA, 73; Stanford Univ, PhD(French & humanities), 78. *Prof Exp:* Lectr French & humanities, Stanford Univ, 78-79; ASST PROF FRENCH, HARVARD UNIV, 79- *Concurrent Pos:* Consult, Guggenheim Mus, 81. *Mem:* MLA. *Res:* Modern and contemporary French poetry; 19th and 20th century French literature; relationship between poetry and visual art. *Publ:* Auth, The fantastic travel adventures of Henri Michaux, In: Scope of the Fantastic, Greenwood Press, 81; Henri Michaux: Between center and absence, French Forum, 82; A new aesthetic: Apollinaire's Les Fiancailles and Picasso's Les Demoiselles d'Avignon, Symp, 82; Henri Michaux: Artist and writer of movement, Mod Lang Rev (in prep); Language, style, and narrative technique in Henri Michaux's Miserable Miracle, Ky Romance Quart (in prep); Lautreamont's Les Chants de Maldoror and the dynamics of reading, 19th Century Fr Studies (in prep). *Mailing Add:* Romance Lang & Lit Harvard Univ Cambridge MA 02138

EDWARDS, MARK WILLIAM, b Dorset, England, Sept 22, 29. CLASSICAL PHILOLOGY. *Educ:* Bristol Univ, BA, 53, MA, 56. *Prof Exp:* From instr to asst prof classics, Brown Univ, 55-62; from assoc prof to prof, Queen's Univ, 62-69; chmn dept, 70-76, PROF CLASSICS, STANFORD UNIV, 69- *Mem:* Am Philol Asn; Am Inst Archaeol; Soc Prom Hellenic Studies; Class Asn. *Res:* Word-order in Greek and Latin; style in early Greek epic. *Mailing Add:* Dept of Classics Stanford Univ Stanford CA 94305

EDWARDS, PRIOR MAXIMILIAN HEMSLEY, b Pau, France, Aug 13, 14; Can citizen. LINGUISTICS, MUSIC. *Educ:* Univ BC, BA, 49; Columbia Univ, MA, 53; Harvard Univ, MA, 55; Univ Pa, PhD(Romance ling), 58; FTCL, ARCM & LRAM, London. *Prof Exp:* Instr Russ, Univ BC, 53-55; lectr, Univ Otago, NZ, 59-64; assoc prof mod lang, Univ Victoria, BC, 64-80; RETIRED. *Res:* Slavonic and Romance languages; Russian morphology. *Publ:* Coauth, Frequency Dictionary of Rumanian Words, 65 & Rumanian Verbal Morphology, Mouton; Rumanian Verb System, Humanities, 71. *Mailing Add:* 3835 Clarndon Rd Victoria BC V8N 4A4 Can

EEKMAN, THOMAS, b Middelharnis, Netherlands, May 20, 23; m 46; c 4. SLAVIC LITERATURES. *Educ:* Univ Amsterdam, MA, 46, PhD(Slavic lang), 51. *Prof Exp:* Docent S Slavic lang & lit, Univ Amsterdam, 55-66; vis prof, 60-61, res grants, 66-78, PROF SLAVIC LANG, UNIV CALIF, LOS ANGELES, 66- *Concurrent Pos:* Vis prof Russ lit, Univ Hamburg, 72-73 & Aarhus Univ, 73; Am Coun Learned Soc res grants, 72-73, 73-74 & 78-; Univ Calif Humanities Inst res grant, 73; co-ed, Calif Slavic Studies, 73- *Honors & Awards:* Order of Yugoslav Flag, Yugoslav Govt, 65; Martinus Nijhoff Award, Netherlands, 81. *Mem:* Philol Asn Pac Coast; Am Asn S Europ

Studies; W Slavic Asn; Asn Int des Lang et Litt Slaves. *Res:* Nineteenth and 20th century Russian literature; comparative Slavic literature; poetics. *Publ:* Auth, Anton Chekhov and the Russian Intelligentsia, Van Loghum Slaterus, Arnhem, 51; ed & contribr, A Chekhov 1860-1960, Brill, Leiden, 60; auth, The Realm of Rime: A Study on Rime in Slavic Poetry, Amsterdam, 74; co-ed & contribr, Juraj Krizanic (1618-1683): A Symposium, Mouton, The Hague, 76; auth, Walt Whitman's role in Slavic poetry, Am Contrib VIII Int Congr Slavists, 78; Thirty Years of Yugoslav Literature (1945-1975), Univ Mich, 78; coed & contribr, Fiction and Drama in Eastern and Southeastern Europe, 80, & Russian Poetics, 82, Columbus. *Mailing Add:* Dept of Slavic Lang Univ of Calif 405 Hilgard Ave Los Angeles CA 90024

EFRON, ARTHUR, English. See Vol II

EGAN, RORY BERNARD, b Sutton West, Ont, Feb 6, 42; m 70. CLASSICS. *Educ:* Assumption Univ, Windsor, BA, 63; Univ Western Ont, MA, 65; Univ Southern Calif, PhD(classics), 71. *Prof Exp:* Asst prof classics, Univ Southern Calif, 70-77; ASSOC PROF CLASSICS & DEPT HEAD, UNIV MAN, 77- *Mem:* Am Class League; Am Inst Archaeol; Am Philol Asn; Class Asn Can; Philol Asn Pac Coast. *Res:* Classical mythology; Greek literature; Greek language. *Publ:* Auth, Notes on the text of the Diegeseis of Konon, Class Philol, 73; Aeneas at Aineia and Vergil's Aeneid, Pac Coast Philol, 74; Hisychius on Kadmos, Clotta, 74; Lexical evidence on two Pauline passages, Novum Testamentum, 77; Gothic Hrotheigs, Orbis, 78; The Calchas Quotation and the Hymn to Zeus, Eranos, 79; The assonance of Athena and the sound of the Salpinx: Eumenides 566-571, Class J, 79. *Mailing Add:* Dept of Classics Univ of Man Winnipeg MB R3T 2N2 Can

EGER, ERNESTINA N, b Philadelphia, Pa, Nov 24, 42. SPANISH. *Educ:* Muhlenberg Col, AB, 63; Emory Univ, AM, 65; Univ Jaime Balmes, PhD (Span & Latin Am lit), 75. *Prof Exp:* ASSOC PROF SPAN, CARTHAGE COL, 65- *Concurrent Pos:* Secy bd, United Migrant Opportunity Serv, 76-79. *Mem:* MLA; Am Asn Teachers Span & Port; Nat Asn Interdisciplinary Ethnic Studies; Soc Multi-Ethnic Lit US; Nat Asn Chicano Studies. *Res:* Chicano and Latin American literature. *Publ:* Auth, Los amores de Artemio Cruz, Esfera, Guadalajara, autumn 76; Selected Bibliography of Chicano Criticism, In: The Identification and Analysis of Chicano Literature, Bilingual Press, 79; Conflicto en Academia: Tres cuentos chicanos, In: Flor y Canto IV and V: An Anthology of Chicano Literature from the Festivals Held in Albuquerque, New Mexico, 1977 and Tempe, Arizona, 1978, Pajarito Publs & Flor y Canto Comt, 80; Hacia una nueva bibliografia de revistas y periodicos chicanos, La Palabra, primavera 80; Bibliography of Criticism of Contemporary Chicano Literature, Univ Calif, Berkeley, 82; contribr, Bibliography of Works by and about Alurista, In: Return: Poems Collected and New, Bilingual Press, 82. *Mailing Add:* Dept of Foreign Lang Carthage Col Kenosha WI 53141

EGERT, EUGENE, b Rudnik, Poland, Dec 29, 35; Can citizen; m 61; c 2. GERMANIC LANGUAGES. *Educ:* Univ BC, 58, MA, 61; Univ Tex, PhD(Ger), 77. *Prof Exp:* Instr Ger, Univ Wash, 64-67; from asst prof to assoc prof, 67-77, PROF GER, UNIV ALTA, 77- *Mem:* Am Asn Teachers Ger; Asn Can Univ Teachers Ger; Mediaeval Acad Am. *Res:* Early Middle High German literature; Middle High German lyric; Middle High German courtly epic. *Publ:* Auth, The Votive Mass of the Holy Spirit in Middle High German literature, In: Essays on German Literature in Honour of G Joyce Hallamore, Univ Toronto, 68; The artistic use of didactic excursions in Hartmann von Aues Erec, Proc Pac Northwest Conf Foreign Lang, 69; Notes on the Parable of the Good Samaritan in Hartmann's Gregorius, Peregrinatio, 71; The holy Spirit in German Literature Until the End of the 12th Century, Mouton, The Hague, 73; Walther van der Vogelweide's Attitude to the Clergy, Amsterdamer Beiträge zur älteren Germanistik, 75; Comments on some metaphors and similes in Hartmann's Iwein, Proc Pac Northwest Coun Foreing Lang, 76. *Mailing Add:* Dept of Ger Lang Univ of Alta Edmonton AB T6G 2G2 Can

EHLE, CARL FREDERICK, JR, b Aberdeen, Wash, Mar 14, 27; m 47; c 6. BIBLICAL LANGUAGES, MODERN HEBREW. *Educ:* New Eng Sch Theol, BA, 49; Gordon Col, BD, 53; NY Univ, MA, 61, PhD, 77. *Prof Exp:* Assoc prof, 53-71, PROF BIBL LANG, BERKSHIRE CHRISTIAN COL, 71- *Concurrent Pos:* Ed, Iggeret, Nat Asn Prof Hebrew, 68-73. *Mem:* Nat Asn Prof Hebrew (secy-treas, 67-68, vpres, 69, pres, 73-74); Evangel Theol Soc. *Res:* Christian Zionism; biblical eschatology. *Publ:* Co-ed, Doron: Hebraic studies, Nat Asn Prof Hebrew, 65; auth, Increase Mather's Puritan hope, Hebrew Studies, 76. *Mailing Add:* Berkshire Christian Col Lenox MA 01240

EHRE, MILTON, b New York, NY, Apr 15, 33; m 63; c 2. RUSSIAN LITERATURE, GENERAL HUMANITIES. *Educ:* City Col New York, BA, 55; Columbia Univ, MA, 66, PhD(Russ), 70. *Prof Exp:* Asst prof, 67-72, assoc prof, 72-81, PROF RUSS & HUMANITIES, UNIV CHICAGO, 81- *Concurrent Pos:* Am Coun Learned Soc grant, 70-71; Guggenheim fel, 75-76. *Mem:* Am Asn Advan Slavic Studies; Am Asn Teachers Slavic & East Europ Lang. *Res:* Russian literature of the 19th century; Russian prose fiction; Russian drama. *Publ:* Auth, Oblomov and His Creator: The Life and Art of Ivan Goncharov, Princeton Univ, 73; On August 1914, In: Aleksandr Solzhenitsyn: Critical Essays and Documentary Materials, Nordland, 73; Zamjatin's Aesthetics, Slavic & East Europ J, fall 75; A classic of Russian realism: form and meaning in The Golovlyous, Studies Novel, spring 77; Gusev, Ulbandus Rev, fall 79; ed & transl, The Theater of N Kolay Gogul: Plays and Selected Writings, Univ Chicago, 80; auth, Laughing through the Apocalypse: The comic structure of Gogul's government inspector, Russ Rev, 4/80; Babel's Red Cavalry: Epic and pathos, culture and history, Slavic Rev, 6/81. *Mailing Add:* Dept of Slavic Univ of Chicago Chicago IL 60637

EHRET, CHRISTOPHER, African History, Historical Linguistics. See Vol I

EICHHOLZ, ERICH HERBERT, b Ger, July 28, 10; m 39; c 1. GERMAN LANGUAGE & LITERATURE. *Educ:* Univ Minn, BS, 35, AM, 36; Univ Wis, PhD, 50. *Prof Exp:* Teacher high sch, Wis, 36-39; teacher Ger, Tipton Jr Col, 39-41; from instr to assoc prof, 45-61, chmn lang lab comt, 48-70, PROF GER, UNIV OKLA, 62- *Concurrent Pos:* Assoc ed Ger, S Cent Bull, 75-77. *Mem:* MLA; Am Asn Teachers Ger; SCent Mod Lang Asn. *Res:* Modern German literature; use of audio aids in teaching foreign languages; language laboratories. *Publ:* Auth, Influence of Boccaccio's Decameron on German Literature; Function and equipment of a language laboratory; Have language lab--what now? The effective use of the language lab, Okla Teacher, 61. *Mailing Add:* Dept of Ger 780 Van Vleet Oval Room 202 Univ of Okla Norman OK 73069

EICHLER, BARRY LEE, b Brooklyn, NY, Feb 6, 40; m 62; c 4. ANCIENT NEAR EASTERN CIVILIZATION. *Educ:* Yeshiva Univ, AB, 60; Univ Pa, PhD(ancient Near Eastern), 67. *Prof Exp:* Instr Assyriol, Univ Pa, 65-68; res fel Mesopotamian law, Yale Univ, 68-69; asst prof Assyriol & Jewish studies, 69-76, ASST CUR UNIV MUS, UNIV PA, 69-, ASSOC PROF NEAR EASTERN STUDIES, 76- *Concurrent Pos:* Am Coun Learned Soc fel, 77-78. *Mem:* AM Orient Soc; Soc Bibl Lit; Asn Jewish Studies. *Res:* Legal traditions and institutions of the Ancient Near Eastern, Mesopotamian, Biblical and Rabbinic law; Jewish law. *Publ:* Auth, Indenture at Nuzi, Yale Univ, 73. *Mailing Add:* Dept of Orient Studies Univ of Pa Williams Hall Philadelphia PA 19174

EICHMAN, THOMAS LEE, b Sibley, Iowa, Dec 17, 40; m 66; c 1. LINGUISTICS, INFORMATION SCIENCE. *Educ:* Univ SDak, BA, 62; Univ Iowa, MA, 65; Univ Ill, Urbana, PhD (Ger ling), 71; Univ Md, College Park, MLS, 76. *Prof Exp:* Asst prof Ger, Ind State Univ, 70-75; LANG TECH, US DEPT DEFENSE, 82- *Concurrent Pos:* Instr English as second lang, Temple Sch Md, 80-81; lectr English, Montgomery Col, 81-82; instr English as second lang, Prince Georges Community Col, 81-82; instr English, Univ Md, 82. *Mem:* Ling Soc Am; MLA; Teachers English to Speakers Other Lang; Am Soc Info Sci; Southeastern Conf Ling. *Res:* Applications of linguistic theory; foundations of information science; cognition. *Publ:* Auth, The Development of Germanic kann-, Amsterdamer Beiträge zur älteren Germanistik, 73; Althochdeutsch sinnan streben nach, sanskritisch san-, sagewinnen und hethitisch sanh- erstreben, Z vergleichende Sprachforschung, 73; The complex nature of opening reference questions, RQ: Ref & Adult Serv Div, 78; Subject heading syntax and natural language nominal compound syntax, Proc Am Soc Info Sci, Vol 15, 78; Applied linguistics in librarianship, Del Working Papers Lang Studies, 79; How to make functional-notional notions function with a standard American ESL text, 82 & Subject indexes vs original documents as research sources: A comparative account of text construction and use for academic libraries, 82, ERIC-CIR; Speech action in the library, In: Linguistics and the Professions, Ablex, 82. *Mailing Add:* 3401 Stanford St Hyattsville MD 20783

EICHMANN, RAYMOND, b Posen, Poland, Feb 4, 43; German citizen; m 66; c 2. FRENCH MEDIEVAL LITERATURE. *Educ:* Univ Ark, BA, 65, MA, 67; Univ Ky, PhD(French), 73. *Prof Exp:* Instr, 69-74, asst prof, 74-78, ASSOC PROF FRENCH, UNIV ARK, 78- *Honors & Awards:* Fac Teaching Award, Univ Ark, 80. *Mem:* Andre Malraux Soc; Mediaeval Acad Am; MLA; Am Asn Teachers French. *Res:* Medieval verse narrative (Fabliaux); French culture; linguistic minorities. *Publ:* Auth, The question of the variantes and the Fabliaux, Fabula, 76; The search for originals in the Fabliaux and the validity of textual dependency, Romance Notes, 78; The Fabliau in the first branch of the Roman de Renart, Philol Asn, 78; The anti-feminism in the Fabliaux, French Lit Series, 79; Oral composition: A recapitulatory rev of its nature and impact, Neuphologische Mitteilungen, 79; coauth, Foreign languages at the pre-school level, Res in Educ; Cuckolds, Clerks and Countrymen, Univ Ark Press, 82. *Mailing Add:* Dept of Foreign Lang Univ Ark Fayetteville AR 72701

EICHNER, HANS, b Vienna, Austria, Oct 30, 21; m 57; c 2. GERMAN LANGUAGE & LITERATURE. *Educ:* Univ London, BA, 44, PhD, 49. *Hon Degrees:* LLD, Queen's Univ, Can, 74. *Prof Exp:* Asst lectr, Bedford Col, Univ London, 48-50; from asst prof to prof Ger & head dept, Queen's Univ, Ont, 50-67; chmn grad dept Ger, 67-72, PROF GER, UNIV TORONTO, 67-, CHMN DEPT, 75- *Concurrent Pos:* Hon prof humanities, Univ Calgary, Can, 78. *Honors & Awards:* Gold Medal, Goethe Inst, Ger, 73. *Mem:* Fel Royal Soc Can; MLA; Can Asn Univ Teachers; Can Asn Univ Teachers Ger (pres, 76-78); Acad Lit Studies. *Res:* Goethe; Romanticism. *Publ:* Auth, Thomas Mann, An Introduction to His Works, Francke, Bern, 53; ed, Friedrich Schlegel's Literary Notebooks, 1797-1801, Univ London, 57; co-ed, Critical Edition, Friedrich Schlegel, Schoeningh, Ger, 58-; auth, Four German Writers: Mann, Kafka, Rilke, Brecht, Can Broadcasting Corp, 64; Friedrich Schlegel, Twayne, 70; ed, Romantic and Its Cognates--The European History of a Word, Univ Toronto, 72. *Mailing Add:* Dept of Ger Univ of Toronto Toronto ON M5S 1A1 Can

EIFLER, MARGRET EVA, b Cottbus, Ger, Apr 9, 39. GERMAN LITERATURE. *Educ:* Univ Calif, Berkeley, BA, 62, MA, 64, PhD(Ger), 69. *Prof Exp:* Asst prof, Stanford Univ, 69-73; asst prof, 73-74, ASSOC PROF GER, RICE UNIV, 75- *Concurrent Pos:* ATP mem, Educ Testing Serv, Princeton, 72-79; chair rev bd, Rice Univ Studies, 77-81; vchair coun acad affairs, Col Entrance Exam Bd, 79-82. *Mem:* Am Asn Ger Teachers. *Res:* German novel of 20th century; novel of the DDR; contemporary novel. *Publ:* Auth, Thomas Mann: Das Groteske in drei Parodien, Bouvier, Bonn, 70; Existentielle Verwandlung in Rilkes Aufzeichnungen des Malte L Brigge, Ger Quart, 1/72; Das Geschichtsbewusstsein des Parodisten Friedrich Dürrenmatt, In: Studien zu seinem Werk, Stiehm, Heidelberg, 76; Dialektische Dynamik: Kulturpolitik und Asthetik im Gegenwartsroman der DDR, Bouvier, Bonn, 76; Max Frisch als Zeitkritiker, In: Aspekte des Prosawerkes, Lang, Bern, 78; Forschungsbericht zur DDR-Literatur, Ger Quart, 78; Ingeborg Bachmann: Malina, Mod Austrian Lit, 79; Erik Neutsch: Die Rezeption Scines Romanwerkes, In: Amsterdamer Beitrage zur neueren Germanistik, Bd, 81. *Mailing Add:* Dept of Ger Rice Univ Houston TX 77001

EILER, MARY ANN, b Chicago, Ill, Oct 10, 40. LINGUISTICS. *Educ:* Mundelein Col, BA, 62; Loyola Univ Chicago, MA, 64; Northeastern Ill Univ, MA, 71; Ill Inst Technol, PhD(ling), 79. *Prof Exp:* Lang consult English, Lyons Twp High Sch, LaGrange, Ill, 64-81; PROJ COORDR & TECH WRITER, DEPT DATA RELEASE, AM MED ASN, 82- *Concurrent Pos:* Instr English & ling, Northeastern Ill Univ, 80-81; instr English, Col DuPage, 81- *Mem:* NCTE; Midwest Mod Lang Asn; Teaching English Speakers Other Lang. *Res:* Text linguistics: semiotics of text; technical communications; English as a second language. *Publ:* Auth, Getting to the surface of things: Cohesion as a text-forming strategy in writing of adolescents, Mich Ling Soc Papers, 2: 14-29; On developing a systematics for the field interview, Papers Int Conf Methods Dialectol, 76; Meaning and choice in writing about literature, In: Developmental Issues in Discourse, Ablex Press (in prep). *Mailing Add:* 2836 N Parkside Chicago IL 60634

EISENBEIS, WALTER JOHANNES HEINZ, Religion. See Vol IV

EISENBERG, DANIEL BRUCE, b Long Island City, NY, Oct 4, 46. SPANISH LITERATURE. *Educ:* Univ Madrid, dipl, 66; Johns Hopkins Univ, BA, 67; Brown Univ, MA, 68, PhD(Span), 71. *Prof Exp:* Asst prof Romance lang, Univ NC, Chapel Hill, 70-73 & City Col New York, 73-74; assoc prof mod lang, 74-78, PROF MOD LANG, FLA STATE UNIV, 78- *Concurrent Pos:* Founder & ed, J Hisp Philol, 76-; prof develop leave, Fla State Univ, 78. *Mem:* MLA; Asoc Int Hisp. *Res:* Spanish chivalric literature; Cervantes; sexuality in literature. *Publ:* Ed, Espejo de Principes y Cavalleros (6 vols), Espasa-Calpe, Madrid, 75; Federico Garcia Lorca, Songs, Duquesne Univ, 76; auth, Poeta en Nueva York: Historia y Problemas de un Texto de Lorca, Ariel, 76; Enrique IV and Gregorio Maranon, Ren Quart, 76; Does the Picaresque novel exist?, Ky Romance Quart, 79; Castilian Romances of Chivalry in the sixteenth century, Grant and Cutler, London, 79; Romances of Chivalry in the Spanish Golden Age, Juan de la Cuesta, 82; ed, Alejo Venegas: Primera parte de las diferencias de libros que hay en el universo, Puvill, Barcelona, 82. *Mailing Add:* Dept of Mod Lang & Ling Fla State Univ Tallahassee FL 32306

EISNER, ROBERT ALLEN, b San Francisco, Calif, Sept 23, 28; m 62; c 2. MEDIEVAL & COMPARATIVE LITERATURE. *Educ:* Univ Southern Calif, BA, 52, MA, 56; Univ Lausanne, dipl d'aptitude a l'enseignement du francais, 55; Occidental Col, PhD(comp lit), 70. *Prof Exp:* Instr English, Army & Navy Acad, Carlsbad, Calif, 56-58 & Ecole Lemania, Lausanne, Switz, 58-59; instr English & French, Univ Md, Europ Div, 59-64; instr French, Pasadena City Col, 64-67; assoc prof, 67-80, PROF FRENCH, CALIF STATE UNIV SACRAMENTO, 80- *Mem:* Am Asn Teachers Fr. *Res:* Medieval French literature; philology. *Publ:* Auth, Raoul de Cambrai, ou la tragedie du desordre, Fr Rev, fall 71; In search of the real theme of the Song of Roland, Romance Notes, Vol XIV, No 1. *Mailing Add:* Dept of French Calif State Univ 6000 J St Sacramento CA 95819

EKFELT, NILS ERIK, b Bryan, Tex, July 18, 45; m 67. GERMAN LITERATURE. *Educ:* Harvard Univ, AB, 67; Ind Univ, MA, 68, PhD(German lit), 73. *Prof Exp:* Asst prof, St Bonaventure Univ, 72-74; ASST PROF GERMAN, ST LAWRENCE UNIV, 74- *Mem:* MLA; Int Arthur Schnitzler Res Asn; AAUP. *Res:* German romanticism; German literature circa 1900; stylistics. *Publ:* Auth, Arthur Schnitzler's Spiel im Morgengrauen: Free will, fate, and chaos, German Quart, 78; Arthur Schnitzler's Leutnant Gustl: Inner monologue or inner dialogue?, Sprachkunst, 80. *Mailing Add:* 24 Judson St Canton NY 13617

EKMANIS, ROLF, b Riga, Latvia, Feb 10, 29; US citizen; m 55; c 3. SLAVIC LINGUISTICS & LITERATURES. *Educ:* Univ Wis, BA, 56, MA, 57; Ind Univ, PhD(Slavic lang & lit), 66. *Prof Exp:* Asst, Univ Wis, 57; instr Russ & Ger, Utah State Univ, 58-60 & Univ S Fla, 62-63; from asst prof Russ to assoc prof Russ lit, 63-73, PROF RUSS LIT, ARIZ STATE UNIV, 73- *Concurrent Pos:* Assoc ed, Jauna Gaita, Latvian lang lit rev, 65-; Nat Endowment Humanities fel, 72; ed, Latvija Sodien (Latvia Today, A Yearbook), 79- *Honors & Awards:* Krisjanis Barons Prize for Literary Criticism, 78. *Mem:* Am-Latvian Humanities Asn; MLA; Asn Advan Baltic Studies; Am Asn Teachers Slavic & E Europ Lang; Ramave. *Res:* Russian 20th century literature; literatures of the non-Russian peoples in the Soviet Union; Latvian literature and folklore. *Publ:* Auth, Sowjetlettische Schriftsteller in der Sowjetunion, 68 & Die kulturellen Probleme in Lettland: Ende der sechziger Jahre, 70, Acta Baltica; Soviet attitudes toward pre-Soviet Latvian writers, J Baltic Studies, spring 72; Latvian literature, In: Discordant Voice: The Non-Russian Soviet Literatures, Mosaic, 76; Latvian Communist writers in the Soviet Union, 1941-1945, E Europ Quart, 77; Latvian Literature Under the Soviets, 1940-1975, Nordland, 78; Die Literatur in Lettland in den 60er und 70er Jahren, 79, & Der Sowjetlettische Schriftstellerverband, 80, Acta Baltica. *Mailing Add:* Dept of Foreign Lang Ariz State Univ Tempe AZ 85281

ELARDO, RONALD JOSEPH, b Buffalo, NY, Aug 25, 48; m 72; c 3. GERMAN LANGUAGE & LITERATURE. *Educ:* State Univ NY Buffalo, BA, 70; Purdue Univ, MA, 72; Univ Mich, PhD(Ger lang & lit), 79. *Prof Exp:* Teaching asst Ger, Purdue Univ, 70-72; lectr, Univ Mich, 79-80 & Oakland Univ, 80-81; ASST PROF GER & ENGLISH, ADRIAN COL, 81- *Mem:* MLA; Am Asn Teachers Ger. *Res:* The writings of Friedrich Wilhelm Joseph von Schelling; German romantic fairy tales; Alchemy and the medieval German epics. *Publ:* Auth, Lanzelet, alchemy and individuation, Symp, summer 80; E T A Hoffmann's Klein Zaches, the Trickster, Sem, 9/80; E T A Hoffman's Nussknacker und Mausekönig: The mouse-queen in the tragedy of the hero, Ger Rev, winter 80; The maw as infernal medium in Ritter Gluck and Die Bergwerke zu Falun, New Ger Studies, spring 81. *Mailing Add:* Dept of Foreign Lang Adrian Col Adrian MI 49221

ELBAZ, ANDRE ELIE, b Fez, Morocco, Mar 19, 37; Can citizen; div; c 2. FRENCH & COMPARATIVE LITERATURE. *Educ:* Univ Bordeaux, Lic es Lett, 62; Sorbonne, DUniv(lit), 69. *Prof Exp:* Teacher French, Universal Israelite Alliance, Meknes, Morocco, 56-61; prof English, UNESCO Emergency Prog, Niamey, Niger, 61-63; lectr French, Western Wash State

Col, 63-65; assoc prof, 65-80, PROF FRENCH, CARLETON UNIV, 80- *Concurrent Pos:* Mem bd dirs, Can Serv Overseas Students & Trainees, 66-68; Can Coun & Humanities Res Coun Can grants, 69-78; fac consult, Acad Coun World Inst Sephardic Studies, 73-; guest lectr Sephardic Studies, Yeshiva Univ, 73-; researcher folk lit, Can Ctr Folk Cult Studies, Nat Museum Man, Ottawa, 76-78; Can Coun leave fel, 78-69. *Honors & Awards:* Numerous Res Awards from Can Coun & Carleton Univ. *Mem:* Int Comp Lit Asn; Can Asn Folklore Studies; World Union Jewish Studies; Acad Coun World Inst Sephardic Studies; Int Res Prog Zola & Naturalism. *Res:* French literataure and the Dreyfus affair; French and North-American Jewish literature; Sephardic popular literature. *Publ:* Auth, Les Romanciers Juifs Americains et les Mariages Mixtes, Grassin, Paris, 72; Sephardim today, Chronicle Rev, Toronto, 5/73; Correspondance d'Edmond Fleg Pendant l'Affaire Dreyfus, Nizet, Paris, 76; Folktales of the Canadian Sephardim, Fitzhenry and Whiteside, Toronto, and Nat Museum of Man, Ottowa . *Mailing Add:* Dept of French Carleton Univ Ottawa ON K1S 5B6 Can

ELBERT, SAMUEL HOYT, b Des Moines, Iowa, Aug 8, 07. LINGUISTICS. *Educ:* Grinnell Col, AB, 28; Ind Univ, PhD, 50. *Hon Degrees:* PhD(ling), Univ Copenhagen, 73; HLD, Grinnell Col, 82. *Prof Exp:* From asst prof to prof, 49-72, EMER PROF LANG & LING, UNIV HAWAII, MANOA, 72- *Concurrent Pos:* Coordinated Invest Micronesia grant, 47-48; hon assoc Bernice P Bishop Mus, 55-; Tri-Inst Pac Prog grant, 57-58; Fulbright res grant, Denmark, 64-65; Nat Sci Found grant, 67-68; res fel, Tokyo Gaikokugo Daigaku, 80-81. *Mem:* Ling Soc Am; Am Anthrop Asn; Am Folklore Soc. *Res:* Descriptive and comparative Polynesian studies; Hawaiian folklore and pedagogy. *Publ:* Coauth, Place Names of Hawaii, Univ Hawaii, 66; From the Two Canoes, Traditions of Rennell and Bellona Islands, Univ Hawaii & Danish Nat Mus, 65; auth, Spoken Hawaiian, Univ Hawaii, 70, 71 & 76; Three Legends of Puluwat and a Bit of Talk, 71 & Puluwat Dictionary, 72, Australian Nat Univ; Dictionary of the Language of Rennell and Bellona, Nat Mus Denmark, 75; coauth, Hawaiian Grammar, 79 & Dictionary of the Language of Rennell and Bellona, Part II, English to Rennellese and Bellonese, 81, Univ Press Hawii. *Mailing Add:* 3293 Huelani Dr Honolulu HI 96822

ELDER, JOHN PETERSEN, b Auburn, NY, Aug 1, 13. CLASSICS. *Educ:* Williams Col, Mass, AB, 34; Harvard Univ, AM, 35, PhD(class philol), 40. *Prof Exp:* Instr & tutor Greek & Latin, 40-42, from asst prof to assoc prof, 46-55, PROF GREEK & LATIN, HARVARD UNIV & DEAN GRAD SCH ARTS & SCI, 55- *Concurrent Pos:* Sheldon traveling fel, Europe, 38-39; Guggenheim fel, Europe, 48-49; mem bd trustees, Marlboro Col, 61-, chmn bd, 67-; dir Am Coun Learned Soc, 68-; dir, Ctr Mid Eastern Studies, Harvard Univ, 68- *Mem:* Am Philol Asn; Am Acad Arts & Sci; Mediaeval Acad Am; Class Asn New Eng. *Res:* Latin literature, especially Horace, Catullus and Lucretius; Latin paleography. *Mailing Add:* Apt 634 145 Pinckney St Boston MA 02114

ELDREDGE, LAURENCE MILTON, Middle English & Medieval Latin Literature. See Vol II

ELFE, WOLFGANG DIETER, b Berlin, Ger, Dec 2, 39; WGer citizen; m 64; c 2. MODERN GERMAN LITERATURE. *Educ:* Philipps-Univ, Marburg, WGer, BA, 64; Univ Mass, MA, 66, PhD(Ger), 70. *Prof Exp:* Instr, Williams Col, 66-68; from instr to asst prof, State Univ NY Albany, 68-73; asst prof, 73-76, ASSOC PROF GER, UNIV SC, 76- *Concurrent Pos:* Dir, State Univ NY-Prog in Würzburg, WGer, 72-73. *Mem:* MLA; SAtlantic Mod Lang Asn; Am Asn Teachers Ger; Soc Exile Lit (exec secy, 78-). *Res:* German exile literature; German expressionism; literature of East Germany. *Publ:* Auth, Stiltendenzen im Werk von Ernst Weiss, Herbert Lang, 71; contribr, Das emergency rescue comt, In: Deutsche Exilliteratur, I, Kalifornien, 76; Emil Bernhard (Cohn), Francke; Curt Goetz; co-ed, Deutsches Exildrama und Exiltheater, 77 & Deutsche Exilliteratur--Literatur des Nationalsozialismus, 78 & Deutsche Exilliteratur--Literatur der Nachkriegszeit, 81, Peter Lang. *Mailing Add:* Dept of Foreign Lang & Lit Univ of SC Columbia SC 29210

ELIA, MAURICE, b Alexandria, Egypt, Dec 25, 44; Can citizen; m 74; c 2. FRENCH LANGUAGE & CIVILIZATION. *Educ:* Univ Lyon, France, BA, 62; McGill Univ, MA, 72; PhD(cinema), Univ Paul-Valery, Montpellier, France, 74. *Prof Exp:* Teacher French, Protestant Sch Bd Greater Montreal, 67-70; chmn, Dept French, 73-76, PROF FRENCH & CINEMA, DAWSON COL, 70- *Concurrent Pos:* Film critic, Sequences, 74-; dir, Cinelia, 76- *Mem:* MLA; World Univ Serv Can. *Res:* Film with priority to American cinema; screenwriting. *Publ:* Auth, more than 500 articles, 73- *Mailing Add:* Dept of French Dawson Col 350 Selby St Westmount PQ H3Z 1W7 Can

ELIAS-OLIVARES, LUCIA E, b Iquique, Chile. HISPANIC SOCIOLINGUISTICS, APPLIED LINGUISTICS. *Educ:* Univ Chile, BA, 66; Univ Tex, Austin, MA, 70, PhD(appl ling), 76. *Prof Exp:* Asst prof ling, Pan Am Univ, 75-76; ASST PROF SPAN LING, UNIV ILL, CHICAGO, 77- *Concurrent Pos:* Span consult, Southwest Educ Develop Lab, Austin, 69-70 & 72-73. *Mem:* Ling Soc Am; Asn Am Teacher Span & Port; Ling Asn Southwest. *Res:* United States varieties of Spanish; language attitudes; bilingualism. *Publ:* Coauth, Attitudes toward varieties of Spanish, Fourth LACUS Forum, 78; auth, Language use in a Chicano community: A sociolinguistic approach, In: Sociolinguistic Aspects of Language Learning and Teaching, Oxford Univ Press, 79; Language diversity in Chicano speech communities: Implications for language teaching, In: Bilingual Education for Hispanic Students in the United States, Teachers Col Press, 82; A search for congruency in language proficiency testing: What the tests measure--What the child does, Bilingual Educ Paper Series, Calif State Univ, 82; co-ed, Spanish in the United States: Sociolinguistic Aspects, Cambridge Univ Press, 82; ed, Spanish in the US Setting: Beyond the Southwest, Nat Clearinghouse for Bilingual Educ (in prep). *Mailing Add:* Dept of Span Ital & Port Univ of Ill Chicago IL 60680

ELIASON, LYNN RUSSELL, b Logan, Utah, Oct 21, 36; m 63; c 4. GERMAN LANGUAGE & LITERATURE. *Educ:* Utah State Univ, BS, 61; Univ Colo, PhD(Ger), 70. *Prof Exp:* Asst prof, 68-76, ASSOC PROF GER, UTAH STATE UNIV, 76- *Mem:* Rocky Mountain Mod Lang Asn. *Res:* Nineteenth-century German novel; comparative studies in the 19th-century novel of Russia and Germany. *Publ:* Auth, A nineteenth-century solution to the problem of the generations--Turgenev and Theodor Fontane, Ger-Slavica, fall 73. *Mailing Add:* Dept of Lang & Philos Utah State Univ Logan UT 84321

ELIOT, CHARLES WILLIAM JOHN, Ancient History. See Vol I

ELISON, GEORGE SAUL, History. See Vol I

ELIZONDO, SERGIO (DANILO), b El Fuerte, Mex, Apr 29, 30; US citizen; m 58; c 2. ROMANCE LANGUAGES. *Educ:* Findlay Col, BA, 58; Univ NC, Chapel Hill, MA, 61, PhD(Romance lang), 64. *Prof Exp:* Instr Span, Univ NC, Chapel Hill, 61-62; instr, Univ Tex, Austin, 63-64, asst prof Span lang & lit, 64-72; head dept foreign lang, 72-75, PROF SPAN, NMEX STATE UNIV, 72- *Concurrent Pos:* Cor ed, J Ethnic Studies; Ford Found fel, Cologio de Mexico, 71; dean col ethnic studies, Western Wash State Col, Bellingham, 71-72; dir, Instituto Estudios Chicanos, NMex State Univ, 75- *Mem:* Am Asn Teachers Span & Port; SCent Mod Lang Asn; Rocky Mountain MLA; Rocky Mountain Coun Latin Am Studies; MLA. *Res:* Spanish Golden Age Comedia, Calderon-Lope de Vega; Mexican theatre; Chicano literature. *Publ:* Auth, A note on Lope de Vega's La mayor victoria, Romance Notes, autumn 67; Concerning poetry, Vortice, fall 71; Perros y Antiperros, Quinto Sol Publ, Calif, 72; Myth and reality lit chicana, Latin Am Lit Rev, Vol 10, 76; Die Chicanos und ihre Literatur, Ibero-Americana, No 2, 77; Libro Para Batos, Justa Publ, 77; Rosa, La Flauta, Berkaley, Justa Publ, 80; coauth (with Richard W Tyler), The Characters, Plots, Settings, of Calderon's Comedias, Soc Span & Span Am Studies, 81. *Mailing Add:* 1740 Foster Rd Las Cruces NM 88001

ELKHADEM, SAAD ELDIN AMIN, b Cairo, Egypt, May 12, 32; m 62; c 1. GERMAN & COMPARATIVE LITERATURE. *Educ:* Univ Graz, PhD(Ger & English philol), 61. *Prof Exp:* Press Attache, Embassy of Egypt, Berne, Switz, 61-65; asst prof Ger, Univ NDak, 67-68; assoc prof, 68-74, PROF GER & CHMN DEPT GER & RUSS, UNIV NB, FREDERICTON, 74- *Concurrent Pos:* Founder & ed, Int Fiction Rev, 73-; ed, York PRess, 75- *Mem:* Can Asn Univ Teachers Ger; MLA; Int Fiction Asn. *Publ:* Auth, Rigal wa Khanazir (stories), Elmaria, Cairo, 67; Six Essays Uber den Deutschen Roman, 69 & Defintionen und Begriffe der Deutschen Literatur, 70, Herbert Lang; Angeha Men Rosas (novel), Elmaaref, Cairo, 71; Zur Geschichte des Deutschen Romans, Herbert Lang, 73; Tajarib Laylah Wahida, 75, York Dictionary of Literary Terms, 76 & The York Companion to Themes and Motifs of World Literature, 81, York Press Press; The York Companion to Themes and Motifs of World Literature, York Press, 81. *Mailing Add:* Dept of Ger & Russ Univ of NB Fredericton NB E3B 5A3 Can

ELKINS, ROBERT JOSEPH, b Oregon City, Ore, Oct 15, 30; m 57; c 2. GERMAN, EDUCATION. *Educ:* Univ Ore, BS, 59; Univ Colo, MA, 62; Univ Kans, PhD(Ger & educ), 67. *Prof Exp:* Instr Ger & educ, Univ Kans, 63-67; from asst prof to assoc prof, Univ Ga, 67-73; PROF GER & CHMN DEPT FOREIGN LANG, WVA UNIV, 73- *Concurrent Pos:* Fulbright exchange teacher, Lessing Gym, Frankfurt, Ger, 70-71; Exchange teacher, John F Kennedy Schule, Berlin, 77-78. *Honors & Awards:* Stephen Freeman Award, Northeast Conf Foreign Lang Teaching, 72 & 74. *Mem:* Am Asn Teachers Ger; Am Coun Teaching Foreign Lang; NEA; SAtlantic Mod Lang Asn. *Res:* Second language acquisition and development. *Publ:* Coauth, Teaching culture through the audio-motor unit, Foreign Lang Ann, 10/72; Fusion of the four skills, Mod Lang J, 11/72; contribr, chap, In: Foreign Language Education: A Reappraisal, Nat Textbk Co, 72; coauth, The Audio-Motor Unit: A Listening Comprehension Strategy that Works, Foreign Lang Asn, 5/71; Profile of a job applicant in foreign languages, Asn Dept for Lang Bull, 2/74; Achievement and Attitudes in an Individualized Beginning German Program, Foreign Lang Asn, 4/76. *Mailing Add:* Dept of Foreign Lang WVa Univ Morgantown WV 26505

ELLENBOGEN, MAXIMILIAN, b Vienna, Austria, July 2, 24; US citizen; m 63; c 2. SEMITIC LANGUAGES, BIOETYMOLOGY. *Educ:* Columbia Univ, MA, 53, PhD(Semitic lang), 57. *Prof Exp:* ASSOC PROF HEBREW, QUEENS COL, NY, 60- *Concurrent Pos:* Consult, Random House Dictionary of English Lang, 65 & The Living Webster Encycl Dictionary of the English Lang, 70-71. *Mem:* Am Orient Soc; Soc Bibl Lit; Nat Asn Prof Hebrew. *Res:* The Biblical vocabulary; sound and meaning relationships; sound-motifs and semantic junctions. *Publ:* Auth, Foreign Words in the Old Testament: Their Origin and Etymology, Luzac, London, 62; Dum spiro spero, 12/64 & Gyros and gerys, 9/72, Class Outlook; The common prehistoric origin of certain non-synonymous Semitic roots, J Hebraic Studies, Vol I, No 1. *Mailing Add:* Dept of Class & Orient Lang Queens Col Flushing NY 11367

ELLERMAN, MEI-MEI AKWAI, b New York, NY, Aug 25, 42; m 68; c 2. ITALIAN. *Educ:* Univ Geneva, BA, 65; Boston Univ, MA, 66; Harvard Univ, PhD(Romance lang & lit), 75. *Prof Exp:* Instr, 70-75, ASST PROF ITALIAN, WELLESLEY COL, 75- *Mem:* MLA. *Res:* Contemporary novel; Italian film; women's studies in Italy. *Mailing Add:* Wellesley Col Wellesley MA 02181

ELLING, BARBARA ELIZABETH, b Braunschweig, Ger, July 20, 36; m 58; c 2. GERMAN LITERATURE. *Educ:* Univ Utah, BA, 60; Hofstra Univ, MA, 68; NY Univ, PhD(Ger), 71. *Prof Exp:* ASSOC PROF GER, STATE UNIV NY, STONY BROOK, 73- *Mem:* Am Coun Teaching Foreign Lang; Am Asn Teachers Ger; MLA. *Res:* German Romanticism and realism; cultural studies; sociology of literature; teacher training. *Publ:* Auth, E T A Hoffmann's Der Sandmann, Mitteilungen der E T A Hoffmanngesellschaft, 6/72; Leserintegration im Werk E T A Hoffmanns, 73; Literatursoziologie--ein Beitrag zur Methodik, Unterrichtspraxis, fall 73; Language and Culture:

Heritage and Horizons, Ger Contrib, 76; Der Leser E T A Hoffmanns, J English & Ger Philol, 10/76; Realities facing the German profession, Unterrichtspraxis, fall 77; Foreign languages in the United States--a look into the future, Lang Asn Bull, 1/78. *Mailing Add:* Dept of Ger State Univ of NY Stony Brook NY 11794

ELLIOTT, ALISON GODDARD, b Rochester, NY, Sept 7, 37; div; c 2. CLASSICAL LANGUAGES, MEDIEVAL LITERATURE. *Educ:* Univ Calif, Berkeley, BA, 60, MA, 62, PhD(comp lit), 77. *Prof Exp:* Mellon fel, 77-79, ASST PROF CLASSICS, BROWN UNIV, 77- *Mem:* Am Philol Asn; MLA; Mediaeval Acad Am; Soc Rencesvals; NAm Catalan Soc. *Res:* Hagiography; Ovid and the Ovidian influence in medieval literature. *Publ:* Auth, Amores I.13: Ovid's Art, Class J, 73-74; The martyr as epic hero: Prudentius' Peristephanon and the Old French epic, Pub Patristic, Medieval & Renaissance Conf, 78; The Triumphus sancti Remacli: Latin evidence for oral composition, Romance Philol, 79; Amores I.5: The afternoon of a poet, Latomus, 79; Ovid's Metamorphoses: A critical bibliography, Class World, 80; The emperor's daughter: A catalan version of the adventures of Charlemagne's mother, Romance Philol, 81; The bedraggled cupid: Ovidian satire in Carmina Burana 105, Traditio, 81; The double genesis of Girart de Vienne, Olifant, 81. *Mailing Add:* Dept of Classics Brown Univ Providence RI 02912

ELLIOTT, DALE EUGENE, b Columbus, Ohio, Oct 13, 41; m 71. LINGUISTICS. *Educ:* Ohio State Univ, BSc, 62, MA, 65, PhD(ling), 71. *Prof Exp:* Asst prof, 68-72, assoc prof, 72-80, PROF ENGLISH & LING, CALIF STATE UNIV, DOMINGUEZ HILLS, 80- *Concurrent Pos:* Fel, Dept Psychiat, Univ Calif, Los Angeles, 75-76. *Mem:* Ling Soc Am; Am Asn Ment Deficiency. *Res:* English syntax and semantics; psycholinguistics. *Publ:* Coauth, Syntactic variation as linguistic data, Papers Fifth Regional Meeting of Chicago Ling Soc, 69; auth, Toward a grammar of exclamations, Found Lang, 74; coauth, The syndrome of hyperlexia, Brain & Lang, 76; Workbook in Syntactic Theory and Analysis, Prentice-Hall, 77. *Mailing Add:* Dept of English Calif State Univ Dominguez Hills Carson CA 90747

ELLIOTT, JACQUELINE CECILE, b Paris, France, Dec 31, 20; US citizen; m 46. FRENCH LANGUAGE & LITERATURE. *Educ:* Southern Ill Univ, BS, 49; Univ Ill, MA, 52. *Prof Exp:* Prof math, Cours Compl Maison Blanche, Clamart, Seine, France, 42-45; instr French & Span, Ferndale High Sch, Mich, 51-59; asst prof French, Eastern Mich Univ, 59-61; asst prof, 61-70, dir dept lang educ, 61-73, ASSOC PROF FRENCH, UNIV TENN, 70- *Mem:* Am Coun Teaching Foreign Lang; MLA; Cent States Conf Lang Teaching. *Res:* French culture. *Publ:* Auth, The language laboratory, Tenn Foreign Lang Bull, fall 67; Language and culture: Two for the seesaw, Dimensions Lang, 69, 69; Language and culture in harmonious performances, Bull Ill Foreign Lang Teachers Asn, 4/72; From diapers to diplomas: Current French educational innovations, Int Educ, 73; Analyzing French culture interpreting some of its manifestations, In: The Cultural Revolution in Foreign Language Teaching, Nat Textbk, 75; Rhythms, a base for learning, Dimensions Lang, 73, 75; Poesie et chansons francaises: base pour l'etude de la langue et de la civilisation, 2/77 & Harmonie chez deux maitres: Paul Delvaux et Alain Robbe-Grillet, 3/77, Fr Rev. *Mailing Add:* Dept of Romance Lang Univ of Tenn Knoxville TN 37916

ELLIOTT, JOAN CURL, b Dallas, Tex, June 6, 27; m 52; c 2. GERMAN LITERATURE, LINGUISTICS. *Educ:* Howard Univ, AB, 47; Middlebury Col, MA, 51; Vanderbilt Univ, PhD(Ger-Am lit), 73. *Prof Exp:* Instr in Ger, Southern Univ, Baton Rouge, La, 49-51; asst prof, Fla A&M Univ, 51-57; PROF GER, TENN STATE UNIV, 62- *Concurrent Pos:* Int Prog Nashville Univ Ctr & US State Dept res grant, Univ Köln, Ger, 74. *Mem:* MLA; Am Asn Teachers Ger; South Cent Mod Lang Asn; Southern Regional Honors Coun. *Res:* German 20th century short story; linguistics; non-verbal communication. *Publ:* Auth, The child as protagonist in selected short stories of Marie Luise Kaschnitz, Fac Res J Tenn State Univ, 73; The soul handshake, In: New Directions, Howard Univ, 75; A comparison of Kafka's Heimkehr and the Biblical parable, The Prodigal Son, Fac Res J Tenn State Univ, 76; Lingualisms of students at a Black University, In: New Directions, Howard Univ, 77; The Black handshake, aspects of non-verbal communication, Trinity Univ, 77; A case for the rubber stamped diploma, In: New Directions, Howard Univ, 78; The Dog Care Center, Writer's Circle, 5/78; Rhodesia/Zimbabwe: Disharmony or concord, In: A Two Way Mirror: Differing Perspectives on the World, Phelps Stokes Fund, 78. *Mailing Add:* German Dept Tenn State Univ Nashville TN 37203

ELLIS, CLARENCE DOUGLAS, b Shawville, Que, Dec 6, 23; m 53; c 3. AMERINDIAN LINGUISTICS. *Educ:* McGill Univ, BA, 44, PhD, 54; Univ Toronto, MA, 46; Yale Univ, MA, 49; Cambridge Univ, BA, 51. *Prof Exp:* Vis fel, Cornell Univ, 54-55; field linguist, Anglican Church of Can, 55-58; Can Coun sr fel, Univ Mich, 58-59; lectr, Univ Toronto, 59-61, asst prof, 61-63; assoc prof classics, 63-65, assoc prof ling, 65-71, vdean humanities div, fac arts & sci, 64-68, PROF LING, McGILL UNIV, 71-, CHMN DEPT, 71- *Concurrent Pos:* Ford Found grant, 68-70; Can Coun grant, 77-79. *Mem:* Ling Soc Am; Can Ling Asn. *Res:* Classics; linguistics. *Publ:* Auth, The so-called interrogative order in Cree, Int J Am Ling, 4/61; Spoken Cree, Part I, Dept Missions, Anglican Church of Can, 62; Cultural conditioning as a factor in speech perception, J Ont Speech & Hearing Asn, 1/62; Cree Verb Paradigms, Int J Am Ling, 4/71; coauth, Ancient Greek: A Structural Programme, McGill-Queen's, rev ed, 73; A Bibliography of Algonguian Linguistics, Univ Man Anthrop Papers, 74; auth, Kuujjuamiutitut, McGill Ctr Northern Studies & Res, 78. *Mailing Add:* Dept of Ling McGill Univ Montreal PQ H3A 1M8 Can

ELLIS, JOHN MARTIN, b London, England, May 31, 36; m 78; c 4. GERMAN LITERATURE, LANGUAGE THEORY. *Educ:* Univ London, BA, 59, PhD(Ger), 65. *Prof Exp:* Tutorial asst Ger, Univ Col Wales, 59-60; asst lectr, Univ Leicester, 60-63; asst prof, Univ Alta, 63-66; assoc prof Ger lit, 66-70, PROF GER LIT, UNIV CALIF, SANTA CRUZ, 70-, DEAN GRAD DIV, 77- *Concurrent Pos:* Vis prof Ger lit, Univ Kent, 70-71; Guggenheim found fel, 70-71; Nat Endowment for Humanities sr fel, 75-76. *Mem:* MLA; Am Asn Teachers Ger; AAUP; English Goethe Soc; Heinrich von Kleist Ges. *Res:* German literature; theory of language and literature; aesthetics. *Publ:* Auth, Hoffmann's Das Fraulein von Scuderi, Mod Lang Rev, 69; Schiller's Kalliasbriefe and the Study of His Aesthetic Theory, Mouton, The Hague, 69; Linguistics, literature and the concept of style, Word, 70; Kleist's Prinz Friedrich von Homburg: A Critical Study, Univ Calif, 70; Narration in the German Novelle: Theory and Interpretation, Cambridge Univ, 74; The Theory of Literary Criticism, A Logical Analysis, Univ Calif, 74, paperback, 77; Heinrich von Kleist, Univ NC, 79; Wiltgensteinian thinking in theory of criticism, New Lit Hist, 81. *Mailing Add:* Dept of Ger Crown Col Univ Santa Cruz CA 95060

ELLIS, MADELEINE BLANCHE, Can citizen. FRENCH & LATIN LANGUAGE & LITERATURE. *Educ:* Univ BC, BA, 36, MA, 37; Univ Toronto, PhD(French), 44. *Prof Exp:* Lectr French, Univ Toronto, 44-45, Univ Man, 45-46; chmn dept mod lang, 64-72, PROF FRENCH, MARIANOPOLIS COL, 46- *Concurrent Pos:* Part-time lectr, Inst Pedag, Montreal, 46-54; Humanities Res Coun Can grant-in-aid, 49; reader, MSS, Univ Toronto Press & Univ Calif Press; collabr, Dictionnaire Int des Termes Litteraires, Asn Int de Litt Comparee, 70-; lectr, Int Rousseau Congr, McGill Univ, Montreal, 78. *Mem:* Am Soc 18th Century Studies; Soc Jean-Jacques Rousseau de Geneve; Asn Can Univ Teachers Fr; Soc Fr Etude XVIIIe Siecle, Comite du Montlouis, France. *Res:* French 18th century, especially J-J Rousseau; ancient classics & comparative literature; fine arts. *Publ:* Auth, Robert Charbonneau et la Creation Romanesque, Ed Levrier, 48; Julie or La Nouvelle Heloise: A Synthesis of Rousseau's Thought, Univ Toronto, 49; St-Denys Garneau: Art et Realisme, Ed Chantecler, 49; Rousseau's Venetian Story: An Essay Upon Art and Truth in Les Confessions, Johns Hopkins Univ, 66; Reflections on the value of Rousseau's correspondence, Studi Francesi, 68; In defense of scholarship, Studies in Burke and His Time, 72; Rousseau's Socratic Aemilian Myths: A Literary Collation of Emile and the Social Contract, Ohio State Univ, 77; Le Nouveau Socrate, Diderot Studies, Vol XXI (in press). *Mailing Add:* 2045 Closse St Apt A-8 Montreal PQ H3H 1Z7 Can

ELLIS, MARION LEROY, b Georgetown, SC, March 27, 28. FRENCH. *Educ:* Univ SC, AB, 38, MA, 50; Univ Aix-Marseille, Dr Univ, 55. *Prof Exp:* Asst prof English, Va Polytech Inst, 57-60; prof French & chmn dept lang, Erskine Col, 60-61; assoc prof French & Span, Va Polytech Inst, 61-64; assoc prof French, Lewis & Clark Col, 65-68 & N Tex State Univ, 68-69; prof foreign lang & head dept, 69-79, PROF ENGLISH SECOND LANG & FOREIGN LANG, LAMAR UNIV, 79- *Concurrent Pos:* Acad leader, Exp in Int Living, 64-65. *Honors & Awards:* Chevalier, Palmes Academiques, 67, Officier, 77. *Mem:* Am Asn Teachers Fr. *Res:* Acadian culture in Southeast Texas; contemporary French theater; history of the Russian colony in the department of Alpes-Maritimes, France. *Publ:* La baye russe de Villefranche, Nce Hist, 7-9/64; Prose Classique, Blaisdell, 66; La culture acadienne dans le Sud-Est du Texas, La Rev, summer 73. *Mailing Add:* Dept Foreign Lang Lamar Univ Beaumont TX 77710

ELLIS, WILLIAM RAY, b Terre Haute, Ind, Nov 18, 25; m 48; c 3. RELIGION, GREEK. *Educ:* Howard Payne Col, BA, 50; Southwestern Baptist Theol Sem, BD, 53, Thd(New Testament), 56. *Prof Exp:* Pastor, First Baptist Church, Groveton, Tex, 56-57; chmn dept foreign lang, 69-74, PROF GREEK, HARDIN-SIMMON UNIV, 57-, CHMN DIV HUMANITIES, 66-, DEAN DIV GRAD STUDIES, 73- *Mem:* Am Coun Teaching Foreign Lang; SCent Mod Lang Asn. *Res:* Relation between classical Greek and Koine Gree. *Mailing Add:* Dept of Foreign Lang Hardin Simmons Univ Abilene TX 79601

ELLISON, FRED P, b Denton, Tex, Jan 11, 22; m 47; c 5. PORTUGUESE & SPANISH. *Educ:* Univ Tex, BA, 41; Univ Calif, Berkeley, MA, 48, PhD, 52. *Prof Exp:* Transl Span, French & Port, US Dept Justice, 41-43, spec agent, Fed Bur Invest, 43-44; from instr Span & Span Am lit to assoc prof Span & Port, Univ Ill, 52-61; dir, Lang & Area Ctr Latin Am Studies, 62-63, assoc dean grad sch, 71-73, assoc prof, 61-80, PROF PORT, UNIV TEX, AUSTIN, 80- *Concurrent Pos:* NDEA grant, Univ Ill, 59-61; mem Latin Am joint comt, Am Coun Learned Soc & Soc Sci Res Coun, 60-66; Orgn Am States travel & res grant, Brazil, 62; coordr writing team, mod Port textbk proj, supported by grants from Am Coun Learned Soc, Soc Sci Res Coun & MLA joint comt Latin Am studies, 65-71. *Mem:* MLA; Am Asn Teachers Span & Port; Latin Am Studies Asn; Am Coun Teaching Foreign Lang; Inst Int Lit Iberoam. *Res:* Brazilian literature; Latin American or Spanish American literature. *Publ:* Auth, Brazil's New Novel: Four Northeastern Masters, Univ Calif, 54; La conferencia de Ruben Dario sobre Nabuco, Rev Iberoam, 61; coauth, The Development and Evaluation of Methods and Materials to Facilitate Foreign Language Instruction in Elementary Schools, privately publ, 63; auth, The writer in Latin America, In: Continuity and Change in Latin America, Stanford Univ, 65; translr, Adonias Filho, Memories of Lazarus, Univ Tex, Austin, 69; coauth, Modern Portuguese, With Instructor's Manual, Tapes, Visual Aids, Random, 71; auth, Los amigos brazileros de Alfonso Reyes, Bol Capilla Alfonsina, 71. *Mailing Add:* Dept of Span & Port Univ of Tex 112 Batts Hall Austin TX 78712

ELLRICH, ROBERT JOHN, b Bridgeport, Conn, Jan 15, 31. FRENCH LITERATURE. *Educ:* Harvard Univ, BA, 52, MA, 53, PhD, 60. *Prof Exp:* From instr to asst prof Romance lang, Princeton Univ, 59-64, coordr French sect, NDEA Inst, 63; asst prof, 64-69, dir, arts & sci honors prog, 77-80, ASSOC PROF FRENCH & COMP LIT, UNIV WASH, 69- *Concurrent Pos:* Princeton Univ Coun Humanities res fel, 63-64. *Mem:* MLA; Int Asn Fr Studies; Am Soc 18th Century Studies. *Res:* French literature of the 17th and 18th centuries; development of the novel; Dante. *Publ:* Auth, The rhetoric of La Religieuse, Diderot Studies, 61; The structure of Les Bijoux indescrets, Romanic Rev, 12/61; Rousseau and His Reader, Univ NC, 69. *Mailing Add:* Dept of Romance Lang GN-60 Univ of Wash Seattle WA 98195

ELLSWORTH, JAMES DENNIS, b Los Angeles, Calif, Oct 25, 39. CLASSICAL PHILOLOGY. *Educ:* Univ Calif, Berkeley, BA, 62, PhD(classics), 71. *Prof Exp:* From instr to asst prof classics, Univ Conn, 67-73; asst prof, Southern Ill Univ, Carbondale, 73-74; asst prof, 74-79, ASSOC PROF CLASSICS, UNIV HAWAII, 79- *Mem:* Am Philol Asn. *Res:* Language of Homer; Greek mythology; history of classical scholarship. *Publ:* Auth, Pind Pyth 1-44: Agonos Balein Exo, a new suggestion, Am J Philol, 73; Agon Neon: An unrecognized metaphor in the Iliad, Class Philol, 74; Agonios, Agonarchos, Agonisterion: Three words allegedy formed from Agon Assembyl, Trans Am Philol Asn, 76; Agamemnon's intentions, Agon and the growth of an error, Glotta, 76; Antoninus Liberalis 15-2, Am J Phil, 79; Ovid's Aliad (metamorphases 12-1-13-622), Prudentia, 80. *Mailing Add:* Dept of Europ Lang & Lit Univ of Hawaii Honolulu HI 96822

ELMQUIST, ANNE MARIE, b Vienna, Austria, Mar 29, 21; US citizen; div; c 4. APPLIED LINGUISTICS, FRENCH. *Educ:* Univ Tex, BA, 42, MA, 61; Tex A&M Univ, PhD, 70. *Prof Exp:* Teacher French & Ger & head dept, Allen Acad, 59-62; teacher, Stephen F Austin High Sch, Bryan, Tex, 62-63 instr & dept head, Allen Jr Col, 63-65; asst prof mod lang, 65-73, assoc prof, 73-80, PROF MOD LANG, TEX A&M UNIV, 80-, HEAD DEPT, 73-, DIR, ENGLISH LANG INST, 74- *Concurrent Pos:* Instr Teachers English speakers other lang, Off Int Prog, Tex A&M Univ, 60. *Mem:* MLA; Am Coun Teaching Foreign Lang; Am Asn Teachers Fr; Am Asn Teachers Ger; SCent Mod Lang Asn. *Res:* Bilingualism; comparative literature; foreign language reading. *Publ:* Auth, The foreign language teacher: background and attitudes, Foreign Lang Ann, 5/73. *Mailing Add:* Dept of Mod Lang Tex A&M Univ College Station TX 77843

EL NOUTY, HASSAN M, b Cairo, Egypt, June 14, 25; m. FRENCH & COMPARATIVE LITERATURE. *Educ:* Cairo Univ, Lic es Lett, 46; Univ Paris, certs, 48 & 49, D es Lett, 53. *Prof Exp:* Asst French, Cairo Univ, 47, lectr French lit, 53-56; res scholar, Ctr Nat Sci Res, Paris, 56-57; asst prof French lit, 57-62, assoc prof French & Franco-African lit, 62-67, PROF FRENCH & FRANCO-AMRICAN LIT, UNIV CALIF, LOS ANGELES, 67- *Concurrent Pos:* Fulbright-Hays res rel, 65-66; mem bd ed, African Arts/A rts d'Afrique, 67- *Mem:* MLA; Int Asn Fr Studies; fel African Studies Asn. *Res:* Modern French and Franco-American literatures; 19th century French theater; French science fiction and contemporary theatre. *Publ:* Auth, Le Proche-Orient dans la litterature francaise de Nerval a Barres, Nizet, Paris, 58; Roman et revolution dans Qui se souvient dela mer de Moh Dib, Presence Francophone, 71; contrib, Concise Encyclopedia of the Middle East, Pub Affairs Press, 72; Problemes et perspectives de l'education dans un pays du Tiers-Monde: Le cas du Senegal, CEAN Bordeaux, 72; Theatre et pre-cinema: Essai sur la problematique du spectacle au 19e siecle, Nizet, Paris, 78. *Mailing Add:* Dept of French Univ Calif Los Angeles CA 90024

EL SAFFAR, RUTH SNODGRASS, b New York, NY, June 12, 41; m 66; c 3. SPANISH LITERATURE. *Educ:* Colo Col, BA, 62; Johns Hopkins Univ, PhD(Span), 66. *Prof Exp:* Asst Span, Johns Hopkins Univ, 63-65; asst prof, Univ Md, Baltimore County, 67-68; from asst prof to assoc prof, 68-78, PROF SPAN, UNIV ILL, CHICAGO CIRCLE, 78- *Concurrent Pos:* Nat Endowment Humanities fel, 70-71; Danforth assoc, 73-79; Guggenheim fel, 75-76; Am Coun Learned Soc grant-in-aid, 78; Nat Endowment for Humanities summer sem dir, 79 & 82, Newberry Libr fel, 82. *Mem:* MLA; Am Asn Teachers Span & Port; Cervantes Soc Am. *Res:* Spanish Golden Age; Cervantes; fiction. *Publ:* Auth, Structural and thematic discontinuity in Montemayor's Diana, Mod Lang Notes, 71; Novel to Romance: A Study of Cervantes' Novelas Ejemplares, Johns Hopkins Univ, 74; Distance and control in Don Quixote, In: Studies in Romance Languages and Literatures, Univ NC, 75; El Casamiento Enganoso and El Cologuio de los Perros, by Cervantes, London Grant & Cutler, 76; Tres imagenes claves de lo feminins en el Persiles, Revista Canadiense de estudios hispanicos, 3: 219-236; La Galatea: The Integrity of the Unintegrated Text, Dispositio, 3: 337-351; En busca de Eden: Consideraciones sobre la obra de Ana Maria Matute, Revista iberoamericana, 48: 223-231; On Beyond Conflict, Cervantes, 1: 83-94. *Mailing Add:* Dept of Span Ital & Port Univ of Ill at Chicago Chicago IL 60680

ELSE, GERALD FRANK, b Redfield, SDak, July 1, 08; m 39 & 76. CLASSICAL STUDIES. *Educ:* Harvard Univ, AB, 29, PhD, 34. *Hon Degrees:* LHD, Univ SDak, 75; LLD, Univ Nebr, 76. *Prof Exp:* Instr Greek & Latin & tutor classics, Harvard Univ, 30-32 & 35-38; fac instr & sr tutor, Winthrop House, 38-43; head, Dept Classics, State Univ Iowa, 45-56; chmn, Dept Class Studies, 57-68, dir, Ctr Coordr Ancient & Mod Studies, 69-76, prof, 57-78, EMER PROF GREEK & LATIN, UNIV MICH, ANN ARBOR, 78- *Concurrent Pos:* Fulbright fel, Rome, 56-57; consult, Educ Servs, Inc, 63; mem, Nat Coun Humanities, 66-72, vchmn, 68-71; Mellon vis prof classics, Univ Pittsburgh, 69; Danforth vis lectr, Asn Am Cols, 72; assoc, Nat Humanities Ctr, 80. *Mem:* Am Philol Asn (pres, 64); Class Asn; Archaeol Inst Am; Class Asn Midwest & South (pres, 56). *Res:* Greek literature; Greek philosophy; ancient literary criticism. *Publ:* Auth, The Origin of Tragoidia, Hermes, 57; Aristotle's Poetics: The Argument, 57 & The Origin and Early Form of Greek Tragedy, 65, Harvard Univ; Homer and the Homeric Problem, Cincinnati, 66; translr, Aristotle's Poetics, Univ Mich, 67; auth, The structure and date of book 10 of Plato's Republic, 72 & The madness of Antigone, 75, Abhandlung Heidelberg Akad. *Mailing Add:* 1303 Wlidwood Dr Chapel Hill NC 27514

ELSON, BENJAMIN F, b Burbank, Calif, Dec 8, 21; m 43; c 4. LINGUISTICS. *Educ:* Seattle Pac Col, AB, 50; Cornell Univ, MA, 54, PhD(ling), 56. *Prof Exp:* Field worker study Sierra Populuca, Summer Inst Ling, 42-82, field dir admin, 57-65; dir SIL Prog, Univ Washington, 58-68 & 78-82; exec dir, Summer Inst Ling, 65-75, field dir, 81-82. *Mem:* Ling Soc Am; Int Ling Asn; Ling Asn Can & US. *Res:* General linguistics; Sierra Populuca language. *Publ:* Auth, Gramatica del Populuca de la Sierra, Univ Veracruz, 60; coauth, An Introduction to Morphology and Syntax, Summer Inst Ling, 65. *Mailing Add:* RR 19 Box 106 Tucson AZ 85704

ELSON, MARK JEFFREY, US citizen. SLAVIC & GENERAL LINGUISTICS. *Educ:* Univ Mich, Ann Arbor, BA, 68; Harvard Univ, MA, 72, PhD(ling), 73. *Prof Exp:* Asst prof Russ, Amherst Col, 73-74; asst prof, 75-81, ASSOC PROF SLAVIC LANG & LIT, UNIV VA, CHARLOTTESVILLE, 81- *Mem:* Ling Soc Am; Am Asn Teachers Slavic & E Europ Lang; Southeastern Conf Ling; MLA. *Publ:* Auth, Symmetry in phonology, Language, 6/75; Morphological aspects of Russian spelling, spring 75 & The definite article in Bulgarian and Macedonian, fall 76, Slavic & E Europ J; Observations on Macedonian conjugation, Folia Slavica, 77; On the history of the present tense of byti in West and South Slavic, Scando-Slavica, 77. *Mailing Add:* B-16 Cocke Hall Univ of Va Charlottesville VA 22903

ELSTUN, ESTHER NIES, b Berkshire Heights, Pa, Feb 22, 35; m 56; c 1. GERMANIC LANGUAGES & LITERATURES. *Educ:* Colo Col, BA, 60; Rice Univ, MA, 64, PhD(Ger), 69. *Prof Exp:* Instr Ger, Colo Col, 60-61; from asst prof to assoc prof Ger, 68-76, chmn dept foreign lang, 71-76, PROF GER, GEORGE MASON UNIV, 76- *Mem:* MLA; Am Asn Teachers Ger; AAUP. *Res:* Twentieth-century German literature; the young Vienna circle; German exile literature. *Publ:* Auth, From Decadence to Jewish Destiny: The Life and Work of Richard Beer-Hoffmann, Pa State Univ Press (in press). *Mailing Add:* Dept of Foreign Lang George Mason Univ 4400 University Dr Fairfax VA 22030

EMBEITA, MARIA, b Bilbao, Spain, 29. SPANISH. *Educ:* Univ Madrid, Dr Filos y let, 50; Univ Chicago, MA, 61; Univ Ill, Urbana, PhD(Span lit), 64. *Prof Exp:* Teacher, Col Madrid, Mex, 53-57; teaching asst Span, Univ Ill, Urbana, 61-64; asst prof Span lang & lit, Northwestern Univ, 64-67, grad sch res grant, 65; assoc prof Span lang & Latin-Am lit, Vassar Col, 67-69; CHARLES A DANA DISTINGUISHED PROF SPAN, SWEET BRIAR COL, 69- *Res:* Nineteenth century and contemporary Spanish literature. *Publ:* Auth, Antonio Buero Vallejo: El teatro de la Verdad, 5/73 & Pio Baroja: una interpretacion, 74, Cuadernos Hispanoam; El empresionismo como vision filosofica de La voluntad de Martinez Ruiz, Bull Europ Asn Prof Span, 74; La Celestina, obra del Renacimento, In: Anales del Primer Congreso Internacional del la La Celestina, 75; Tiempo y espacio en la poesia de Antonio Machado, Cuadernos hispanoamericanos, 76; Creacion y critica en Castillo-Puche, Cuadernos Hispanoamericanos, 9/76; La lucha por la vida Pio Baroja, In: Anales del Primer Congreso Internacional de la novela picaresca, 78. *Mailing Add:* Dept of Span Sweet Briar Col Sweet Briar VA 24595

EMENEAU, MURRAY BARNSON, b Lunenburg, Can, Feb 28, 04; nat US; m 40. SANSKRIT, LINGUISTICS. *Educ:* Dalhousie Univ, BA, 23; Oxford Univ, BA, 26, MA, 35; Yale Univ, PhD, 31. *Hon Degrees:* LHD, Univ Chicago, 68; LLD, Dalhousie Univ, 70. *Prof Exp:* Instr classics, Yale Univ, 26-31, researcher, 31-40; from asst prof to prof Sanskrit, gen ling & fac res lectr, 40-71, EMER PROF SANSKRIT & GEN LING, UNIV CALIF, BERKELEY, 71- *Concurrent Pos:* Guggenheim fel, 49 & 56. *Mem:* Am Orient Soc (pres, 53-54); Ling Soc Am (vpres, 48, pres, 49); hon fel Royal Asiatic Soc; Int An Tamil Res (vpres, 66-); hon mem Ling Soc India. *Publ:* Auth, Studies in Vietnamese, 51 & Kolami, a Dravidian Language, 55, Univ Calif; coauth, A Dravidian Etymological Dictionary, Clarendon, 61, supplement, 68; auth, Dravidian Linguistics, Ethnology and Folktales: Collected Papers, Annamalai Univ, Tamilnad, 67; Toda Songs, Clarendon, 71; Language and Linguistic Area: Selected Essays, Stanford Univ Press, 80. *Mailing Add:* Dept of Ling Univ of Calif Berkeley CA 94720

EMERSON, CARYL GEPPERT, b Highland Park, Ill, Aug 30, 44. RUSSIAN LITERATURE & MUSIC. *Educ:* Cornell Univ, BA, 66; Harvard Univ, MA & MAT, 68; Univ Tex, Austin, PhD(comp lit), 80. *Prof Exp:* From instr to asst prof Russ lang, lit & hist, Windham Col, 70-76; asst instr Russ lang, Univ Tex, Austin, 76-80; ASST PROF RUSS LIT, CORNELL UNIV, 80- *Mem:* Am Asn Advan Slavic Studies; MLA; Am Asn Teachers Slavic & East Europ Lang. *Res:* Russian 19th century literature; Mikhail Bakhtin and his circle; 19th and 20th century Russian music, especially Mussorgsky. *Publ:* Auth, Rilke, Russia and the Igor tale, Ger Life & Lett, 4/80; Grinev'sdream: The Captain's Daughter and a father's blessing, Slavic Rev, spring 81; co-transl, The Dialogic Imagination: Four Essays by M M Bakhtin, Univ Tex Press, 81; auth, Translating Bakhtin: Does his theory of discourse contain a theory of translation?, Univ Ottawa Quart, winter 82; The outer word & inner speech: Bakhtin, Vygotsky and the internalization of language, Critical Inquiry (in press). *Mailing Add:* Dept of Russ Lit Cornell Univ Ithaca NY 14853

EMMEL, HILDEGARD, b Frankfurt, Ger, July 23, 11. GERMAN LITERATURE. *Educ:* Univ Frankfurt, DrPhil(Ger lit), 35; Univ Rostock, DrPhil Habil(Ger lit), 51. *Prof Exp:* Teacher & prof Ger lit, Univ Rostock, 51-56; prof, Univ Greifswald, 56-60, Univ Oslo, 60-61 & Univ Ankara, 64-67; PROF GER LIT, UNIV CONN, 67- *Concurrent Pos:* Colleage Goethe Encycl, Acad Res, Berlin, 50-51 & 20th century lit, Ger Soc Res, Bad Godesberg, 61-64. *Honors & Awards:* Award Philos Fakultät Johann Wolfgang Goethe Univ, Frankfurt/Main, 35. *Mem:* Int Soc Ger; MLA; Soc Kleist; Soc Sealsfield; Soc Ger Univ Prof. *Res:* German literature; Middle Ages, time of Goethe, 20th century. *Publ:* Auth, Formprobleme des Artusromans und der Graldichtung--Die Bedeutung des Artuskreises fur das Gefuge des Romans im 12 und 13 Jahrhundert in Frankreich, Deutschland und den Niederlanden, Bern, 51; Mörikes Peregrinadichtung und Ihre Beziehung zum Noltenroman, 52 & Weltklage und Bild der Welt in der Dichtung Goethes, 57, Weimar; Das Gericht in der Deutschen Literatur des 20 Jahrhunderts, 63, Geschichte des Deutschen Romans, Vol I, 72, Vol II, 75, Was Goethe vom Roman des Zeitgenossen Nahm, 72 & Der Weg in die Gegenwart Geschichte des Deutschen Romans, Vol III, 78, Bern & München. *Mailing Add:* 266 Foster Dr Willimantic CT 06226

EMONT, MILTON D, b Paterson, NJ, Apr 11, 23; m 50; c 2. FOREIGN LANGUAGES. *Educ:* NJ State Col, Montclair, BA, 43; Middlebury Col, MA, 48; Univ Wis, PhD, 58. *Prof Exp:* From instr to assoc prof French & Span, 54-65, chmn dept mod lang, 70-74, PROF FRENCH, DENISON UNIV, 65- *Concurrent Pos:* Fulbright scholar, Univ Grenoble, 51-52; Univ

Wis Albert Markham grad traveling fel, Paris, 60-61; Am Philos Soc grant, 60-61; teaching course in French, NDEA summer lang inst, Vanderbilt Univ, 63. *Mem:* Am Asn Teachers Fr; MLA. *Res:* Seventeenth century French literature; Madame de Sevigne. *Publ:* Auth, Instructor's Guides for Beginning French Course, US Armed Forces Inst, 51; Corneille, Tallemant des Reaux and Louis XIV, Fr Rev, 61; Des eclaircissements sur Corbinelli, d'apres des documents inedits, Rev Sci Humaines, 1-3/70; L'Identite de La mousse, ami des Sevigne, XVIIe Siecle, 77. *Mailing Add:* Dept of Mod Lang Denison Univ Granville OH 43023

EMPLAINCOURT, EDMOND ARTHUR, b Roux, Belg, Aug 2, 43; US citizen; m 75; c 1. ROMANCE PHILOLOGY. *Educ:* Col William & Mary, BA, 69; Univ Ala, MA, 72, PhD(French), 75. *Prof Exp:* Asst prof, 75-82, ASSOC PROF FRENCH, MISS STATE UNIV, 82- *Mem:* Soc Rencesvals; Am Philos Soc. *Res:* Epic, especially Old French; textual criticism. *Publ:* Auth, Le Chevalier au Cygne et Godefroi de Bouillon, Romania, 74 & Olifant, 76; La geste du Chevalier au Cygne, a critical edition, In: The Old French Crusade Cycle, Univ Ala Press (in press); two articles on de Chevalier au Cygne, Romania (in press). *Mailing Add:* Dept of Foreign Lang Miss State Univ Mississippi State MS 39762

ENGEL, WALBURGA VON RAFFLER, b Munich, Ger, Sept 25, 20; US citizen; m 57; c 2. LINGUISTICS. *Educ:* Univ Turin, DLitt, 47; Columbia Univ, MS, 51; Ind Univ, Bloomington, PhD(ling), 53. *Prof Exp:* Instr French & Ger, Bennett Col, NC, 53-55; asst prof foreign lang & ling, Morris Harvey Col, 55-56, asst prof foreign lang & ling & chmn dept foreign lang, 56-57; lectr Ger & Ital, NY Univ, Adelphi Univ & City Col New York, 57-59; lectr, Univ Florence, 60-61; lectr phonetics, Univ Turin, 61-62; vis assoc prof ling, 65-66, assoc prof, 66-77, chmn ling comt, Nashville Univ Ctr, 69-79, PROF LING, VANDERBILT UNIV, 77-, DIR, VANDERBILT UNIV LING COMT, 79- *Concurrent Pos:* Foreign lang cataloguer, Ind Univ, 53-55; guide-interpreter, US Dept State; lectr, many insts, US & abroad; vis prof ling, Univ Ottawa, 72-73; vis prof, Inst for Lang Sci, Int Christian Univ, Tokyo, Japan, 78. *Mem:* Int Child Lang Asn (secy, 72-75, vpres, 75-); Ling Soc Am; Int Ling Asn; Int Sociol Asn. *Res:* Nonverbal behavior; development; kinesics. *Publ:* Co-ed, Baby Talk and Infant Speech, Amsterdam: Swets & Zeitlinger, 75; auth, Language Intervention Programs in the US, 1960-1974, Amsterdam: Vangorcum, 75; ed, Child Language, 1975, Int Ling Asn, 76; co-ed, Aspects of Nonverbal Communication, Trinity Univ, 77; Metakinesic behavior in the description of nonverbal behavior, Proc XIIth Int Cong Linguists, 77; ed, Aspects of Nonverbal Communication, Swets & Zeitlinger, 80; co-ed, Language & Cognitive Styles, Swets & Zeitlinger, 82. *Mailing Add:* 372 Elmington Ave Nashville TN 37205

ENGELBERG, EDWARD, Comparative Literature & English. See Vol II

ENGELHARDT, KLAUS HEINRICH, b Würzburg, Ger, Nov 17, 36; m 67; c 1. FRENCH LITERATURE. *Educ:* Univ Munich, Staatsexamen, 62, PhD(Romance lang), 68. *Prof Exp:* Teaching asst Ger, Lycee Descartes, Tours, France, 60-61; asst prof French, Univ Munich, 65-69; asst prof French & Ger, 69-74, acting chmn dept foreign lang, 70-71, assoc prof, 74-82, PROF FRENCH & GER, LEWIS & CLARK COL, 82- *Mem:* MLA; AAUP; Am Asn Teachers Fr. *Res:* French novel; French theatre; Occitan culture. *Publ:* Auth, Contributions on French literature, In: Kindler Literatur Lexikon, Munich, 64-73; Le Langage des yeux dans la Chartreuse de Parme de Stendhal, Stendhal Club, Grenoble, 7/72; Une Source Roumaine du Tueur Sans Gages d'Eugene Ionesco, Neueren Sprachen, Ger, 1/72; coauth, Daten der Franzosischen Literatur, Uoln, Munden, 79. *Mailing Add:* Dept of Foreign Lang Lewis & Clark Col Portland OR 97219

ENGELHARDT, WALTER HENRY, b Garrison, NDak, Mar 23, 09; m 39; c 3. LATIN, GERMAN. *Educ:* Midland Col, BA, 39; Univ Nebr, MA, 43; Univ Minn, MA, 66. *Prof Exp:* Prin, Trinity Lutheran Sch, Schuyler, Nebr, 36-39; instr high sch, 39-42; instr Latin & Ger, Shattuck Sch, Faribault, Minn, 43-54; ASSOC PROF LATIN & GER, CONCORDIA CO, ST PAUL, 54- *Mem:* MLA; Am Asn Teachers Ger. *Res:* German literature and linguistics. *Mailing Add:* Hamline & Marshall Concordia Col St Paul MN 55104

ENGELS, DONALD WHITCOMB, History, Classics. See Vol I

ENGLEKIRK, JOHN EUGENE, b New York, NY, Sept 24, 05; m 31; c 3. SPANISH AMERICAN LITERATURE. *Educ:* St Stephen's Col, AB, 26; Northwestern Univ, AM, 28; Univ Madrid, dipl, 30; Columbia Univ, PhD, 34; Univ Chile, dipl, 38. *Prof Exp:* Asst, Northwestern Univ, 26-28; from instr to assoc prof, Univ NMex, 28-39; from assoc prof to prof Span & head dept, Tulane Univ, 39-58; chmn dept, 59-62, dir, NDEA summer lang inst, 60 & 61, prof, 58-73, PROF EMER SPAN & PORT, UNIV CALIF, LOS ANGELES, 74- *Concurrent Pos:* Asst & instr, Columbia Univ, 31-33; co-ed, Rev Iberoam, 40-50, ed, 59-61; vis prof, Univ Wis, 41-42 & Univ Madrid, 55-56; prin pub off, Off Inter-Am Affairs, Washington, DC, 42-44; spec rep, Inter-Am Educ Found, Rio de Janeiro, 45-46; dir Europ off, Inst Int Educ, Paris, 50-51; Del Amo Found grant, Spain, 62, 70 & 75; Fulbright grant, Spain, 67. *Mem:* MLA; Am Asn Teachers Span & Port (pres, 49); S Cent Mod Lang Asn (vpres, 46, pres, 53); cor mem Ateneo Am Washington, DC; Inst Int Lit Iberoam (treas, 38-40, pres, 40-42, vpres, 55-57, 61-63 & 67-69). *Res:* Contemporary Spanish American literature; Hispanic folk theater; inter-American literary relations. *Publ:* Auth, A literatura norteamericana no Brasil, Rev Iberoam, Mex, 52; El epistolario Pombo-Longfellow Thesaurus, Pogota, 54; El Teatro Folklorica Hispanoamericano, Univ Miami, 57; La literatura 6 la revista literaria en Hispanoamerica (4 parts), Rev Iberoam, Mex, 61-63; ed & coauth, An Outline History of Spanish American Literature, 3rd ed, Appleton, 65, 4th ed, Irvington, 80; auth, De lo Nuestro y lo Ajeno, Ed Cult, Mex, 66; coauth & ed, La Narrativa Uruguaya, Univ Calif, 67; An Anthology of Spanish American Literature, 2nd ed, Appleton, 68. *Mailing Add:* Dept of Span & Port Univ of Calif Los Angeles CA 90024

ENGLER, LEO F, b Cedar Rapids, Iowa, July 7, 25; m 50; c 6. LINGUISTICS. *Educ:* State Univ Iowa, BA, 52; Univ Tex, MA, 53, PhD(ling), 62. *Prof Exp:* Instr English for allied off, Air Univ, Maxwell Air Force Base, Ala, 53-56; coordr English for Turks, Georgetown Prog, Ankara, Turkey, 56-60; from assoc prof to prof speech & ling, Kans State Univ, 62-73; PROF ENGLISH, SALISBURY STATE COL, 73- *Mem:* Ling Soc Am; Speech Asn Am; Teachers English to Speakers Other Lang; NCTE. *Res:* Contrastive analysis; norms for the speech of children; second language teaching. *Publ:* Coauth, Laboratory Handbook for Active German, Holt, 62; Juncture phenomena and the segmentation of alinguistic corpus, Lang & Speech, 67; Once again: American and British intonation systems, Acta Ling Hafniensia, spring 70; Linguistic analysis of speech samples: A practical guide for clinicians, J Speech & Hearing Disorders, spring 73. *Mailing Add:* Dept of English Salisbury State Col Salisbury MD 21801

ENGLERT, DONALD M C, b Allentown, Pa, Oct 10, 09. SEMITIC PHILOLOGY. *Educ:* Muhlenberg Col, AB, 29; Princeton Theol Sem, ThB, 32; Princeton Univ, AM, 32; Dropsie Col, PhD, 47. *Prof Exp:* Pastor, Evangel & Reformed Church, 34-43; prof, 43-80, EMER PROF HEBREW & OLD TESTAMENT SCI, LANCASTER THEOL SEM, 80- *Mem:* Soc Bibl Lit (treas, 47-51). *Res:* Syriac translation of Old Testament books. *Mailing Add:* Lancaster Theological Sem Lancaster PA 17603

ENGSTROM, ALFRED GARVIN, b Rockford, Ill, Oct 11, 07; m 39. FRENCH. *Educ:* Univ NC, AB, 33, AM, 35, PhD, 41. *Prof Exp:* From asst prof to prof French, 42-61, Alumni Distinguished prof, 61-78, EMER PROF FRENCH, UNIV NC, 78- *Concurrent Pos:* Vis scholar, Univ Ctr, Va, 63 & 74 & Piedmont Univ Ctr, 69. *Mem:* MLA; SAtlantic Mod Lang Asn; Southeastern Renaissance Conf; Am Asn Teachers Fr; Mod Humanities Res Asn. *Res:* French literature of the 19th century; Flaubert and Baudelaire; literary criticism. *Publ:* Auth, In defense of synaesthesia in literature, Philol Quart; Flaubert's correspondence and the ironic and symbolic structure of Madame Bovary, Studies Philol; Baudelaire's title for Les fleurs du mal, Orbis Litterarum, 57; a few comparisons and contracts in the word-craft of Rabelais and James Joyce, In: Renaissance Studies Presented to William Leon Wiley, Univ NC, 68; The man who thought himself made of glass and certain related images, Studies Philol, 70; Darkness & Light: Lectures on Baudelaire, Flaubert, Nerval, Huysmans Racine & Time & Its Images in Literature, Romance Monogr Inc, 75. *Mailing Add:* 403 Lake Shore Lane Chapel Hill NC 27514

ENSSLIN, WALTER, b Akkerman, Bessarabia, May 29, 13; US citizen; m 42, c 2. GERMAN. *Educ:* Univ Berlin, PhD, 39. *Prof Exp:* Instr Ger, US Army Lang Sch, 54-57; instr Am govt, hist, hist of civilization, Russ hist & lang, Boise Jr Col, 57-59; asst prof Ger & Russ, 59-67, assoc prof Foreign Lang, 67-71, PROF FOREIGN LANG, CALIF STATE UNIV, FRESNO, 71- *Mem:* Am Asn Teachers Ger. *Res:* German literature and language. *Publ:* Auth, Selections from Albatros--Gedankensplitter (book of aphorisms), 64; Gevatter Tod (play) & Die literarischmusikalische Intuition von Richard Benz, 69, Europäischer; var articles on lang & cult, Goethe-Inst; poems, var periodicals. *Mailing Add:* Dept of Foreign Lang Calif State Univ Fresno CA 93740

ENZ, JACOB JOHN, Religion. See Vol IV

EOYANG, EUGENE CHEN, b Hong Kong, Feb 8, 39; US citizen; m 62; c 2. COMPARATIVE LITERATURE, EAST ASIAN LANGUAGES & CULTURES. *Educ:* Harvard Univ, BA, 59; Columbia Univ, MA, 60; Ind Univ, Bloomington, PhD(comp lit), 71. *Prof Exp:* Assoc ed, Anchor Bks, Doubleday Inc, 60-66; from instr to asst prof comp lit, 69-74, asst chmn prog, 71-73, assoc chmn, 71-74 & 75-76, assoc prof & assoc dean res & grad develop, 74-80, PROF COMP LIT, IND UNIV, BLOOMINGTON, 80- *Concurrent Pos:* Mem comt study Chinese civilization, Am Coun Learned Soc, 73-76; Albert Hodder fel, Princeton Univ, 74-75; consult, Nat Endowment Humanities, 75- *Mem:* Am Comp Lit Asn; Int Comp Lit Asn; MLA; Asn Asian Studies. *Res:* Vernacular Chinese fiction; classical Chinese poetry; theory of literature. *Publ:* Auth, The historical background of the Tun-huang pien-wen, Lit E & W, 72; The solitary boat: Images of self in Chinese nature poetry, J Asian Studies, 8/73; The Confucian Odes: Ezra Pound's translations of the Shih Ching, Paideuma & Proc VIIth Congr Int Comp Lit Asn, Vol II: Comparative Literature Today: Theory and Practice, spring 74; transl, Sunflower Splendor: Three Thousand Years of Chinese Poetry, Anchor, 75; auth, The tone of the poet and the tone of the translator, Yearbk Comp & Gen Lit, 75; The immediate audience: Oral narration in Chinese fiction, In: Critical Essays on Chinese Literature, Chinese Univ, Hong Kong, 76; Audiences for translations of Chinese literature: In: The Art and Profession of Translation, Hong Kong Transl Soc, 76. *Mailing Add:* Comp Lit Prog Ind Univ Bloomington IN 47401

EPPLE, JUAN ARMANDO, b Osorno, Chile, Apr 26, 46; m 67; c 1. SPANISH AMERICAN LITERATURE. *Educ:* Austral Univ Chile, BA, 71; Harvard Univ, MA, 77, PhD(romance lang), 80. *Prof Exp:* Asst prof lit theory, Austral Univ Chile, 72-74; instr Span, Ohio State Univ, 79-80; ASST PROF ROMANCE LANG, UNIV ORE, 80- *Mem:* MLA; Inst Internac Lit Iberoamericana; Midwest Mod Lang Asn; Pac Coast Coun Latin Am Studies. *Res:* Chicano literature; Latin American literary historiography. *Publ:* Auth, Chronologie historique et litteraire du Chili, Europe, 76; coauth, Chile: poesia de la resistencia y del exilio, Ambito Lit, 78; auth, Estos novisimos narradores Hispanoamericanos, Texto Critico, 78; Eugenio Cambaceres y el Naturalismo en Argentina L & I, 80; Aluisio Azevedo y el Naturalismo en Brasil, Revista de Critica Literaria Latinoamericana, 80; Cruzando la Cordillera: el relato chileno del exilio, 80 & Hacia una evaluacion del Naturalismo frances, 81, Cuadernos Americanos; The new territories of Chilean poetry, Third Rail, 82. *Mailing Add:* Dept Romance Lang Univ Ore Eugene OR 94703

EPRO, MARGARET WINTERS, b Brooklyn, NY, Apr 29, 47. ROMANCE LINGUISTICS, FRENCH MEDIEVAL LITERATURE. *Educ:* Brooklyn Col, BA, 67; Univ Calif, Riverside, MA, 70; Univ Pa, PhD(Romance philol), 75. *Prof Exp:* Lectr French, Univ Pa, 73-77; vis asst prof, 77-78, ASST PROF FRENCH, SOUTHERN ILL UNIV, 78- *Concurrent Pos:* Ed, Comp Romance Ling Newslett, MLA, 77-79; Am Philos Soc grant-in-aid, 78 & 82. *Mem:* MLA; Am Asn Teachers French; Mediaeval Acad Am; Ling Soc Am. *Res:* Romance historical verb morphology and syntax; textual edition. *Publ:* Auth, Negative Polarity and the Syntax of Romance Languages, Proc 12th Ling Symp Romance Lang, 82; The Romance of Hunbaut: An Arthurian Poem of the 13th Century, Davis Medieval Texts & Studies, (in press). *Mailing Add:* Dept of Foreign Lang & Lit Southern Ill Univ Carbondale IL 62901

ERAMIAN, GREGORY MICHAEL, b Providence, RI, Feb 28, 42; m 69. RUSSIAN LANGUAGE, SLAVIC LINGUISTICS. *Educ:* Brown Univ, BA, 64, PhD(Slavic lnag), 71; Columbia Univ, MA, 66. *Prof Exp:* Lectr Russ, 69-71, asst prof, 71-77, ASSOC PROF RUSS, UNIV WESTERN ONT, 77-, CHMN DEPT, 77- *Mem:* Can Asn Slavists; Ling Soc Am; Am Asn Teachers Slavic & E Europ Lang. *Res:* Structure of modern Russian; Russian school of phonological theory; Soviet Russian literature. *Publ:* Auth, Solzhenitsyn Like His Ivan, London Free Press, 10/70; Four monographs on Slavic linguistics, Can Slavic Studies, 71; The separation of levels in Shcherba's Phonemic Theory, Can Slavonic Papers, 75; Some notes on Trubekoy's Abandonment of Disjunctive Oppositions, Historiographia Linguistica, 78. *Mailing Add:* Dept of Russ Studies Univ Western Ont London ON N6A 3K7 Can

ERAZMUS, EDWARD T, b Grand Rapids, Mich, Apr 22, 20; m 53; c 4. LINGUISTICS. *Educ:* Aquinas Col, PhB, 42; Univ Mich, MA, 49, PhD(English lang & lit), 62. *Prof Exp:* Asst prof & dir English, English Lang Ctr, Mich State Univ, 61-64; ASSOC PROF LING & DIR INTENSIVE ENGLISH CTR, UNIV KANS, 64- *Mem:* Ling Soc Am; Nat Asn for Student Affairs; Am Coun Teaching Foreign Lang. *Res:* English as a foreign language; modern English grammar. *Publ:* Coauth, English as a Second Language: A Reader, W C Brown, 70. *Mailing Add:* Intensive English Ctr Univ Kans 1200 Louisiana St Lawrence KS 66044

ERHARDT, JACOB, b Sajkas, Yugoslavia, Mar 15, 39; US citizen. GERMAN. *Educ:* Baldwin-Wallace Col, BA, 62; Middlebury Col, MA, 63; Case Western Reserve Univ, PhD(Ger), 68. *Prof Exp:* Instr Ger, Bowling Green State Univ, 64-66 & 67-68; teaching asst, Case Western Reserve Univ, 66-67; asst prof, 68-71, assoc prof, 71-79, PROF GER, WESTMINSTER COL, PA, 79-, CHMN DEPT FOREIGN LANG, 70- *Concurrent Pos:* Westminster Col, Pa res stipends, 70-75; Nat Endowment Humanities grant-in-residence, Univ Cincinnati 75-76; Fulbright grant, 78; Exxon Educ Found workshop award, 81. *Mem:* MLA; Am Asn Teachers Ger; Ger Am Soc. *Res:* Alfred Döblin; German-American literature; bilingualism. *Publ:* Auth, Alfred Döblins Roman Theorie . . ., Univ Dayton Rev, winter 69; . . . Lyrik Rose Ausländers, Ger-Am Studies, 70; coauth, Hilfestellung . . . Zweisprachigkeit, Die Unterrichtspraxis, spring 71; auth, Alfred Döblins Amazonas-Trilogie, Georg Heintz, Worms, Ger, 74; Rose Ausländers neue lyrik, Zt für deutsch-Amerkanische lit, 12/76; Albert Bierstadt..., Univ Dayton Rev, spring 80; German Society of Pennsylvania, Encycl Ger-Am Voluntary Orgn, 82. *Mailing Add:* Dept of Foreign Lang Westminster Col New Wilmington PA 16142

ERICKSON, GERALD M, b Amery, Wis, Sept 23, 27; m 51; c 3. CLASSICAL LANGUAGES. *Educ:* Univ Minn, BS, 54, MA, 56, PhD(classics), 68. *Prof Exp:* Teacher, Edina-Morningside Pub Schs, 56-65 & 66-67; vis lectr Latin, 65-66, asst prof Latin & Greek, 67-70, ASSOC PROF CLASSICS, UNIV MINN, MINNEAPOLIS, 70- *Concurrent Pos:* Consult classics, Am Coun Teaching Foreign Lang Annual Bibliog Foreign Lang Teaching, 69-; reader, Col Entrance Exam Bd, Advan Placement, 75-76, chief reader designate, 77, chief reader, 78. *Mem:* Am Class League; Class Asn Mid W & S; Am Philol Asn. *Res:* Language teaching, methods and materials; madness and deviant behavior in Greece and Rome; computer based instruction for teaching vocabulary development, technical terminology and ancient Greek. *Publ:* Auth, Classics: The Teaching of Latin and Greek and the Classical Humanities, Britannica Rev Foreign Lang Educ, Vol 2, 70; The knowledge explosion and the classics, Class J, 71; A message from a classicist, Class Outlook, 73; co-ed, Social Class in the Contemporary United States, Marxist Educ press, 78; auth, The enigmatic metamorphosis: From divine possession to demonic, J Popular Cult, 78. *Mailing Add:* Dept of Classics 310 Folwell Hall Univ of Minn Minneapolis MN 55455

ERICKSON, JOHN DAVID, b Aitkin, Minn, Jan 9, 34; m 59; c 2. CONTEMPORARY FRENCH & COMPARATIVE LITERATURE. *Educ:* Univ Minn, BA, 58, MA, 61, PhD(French), 63; Harvard Univ, MA, 59. *Prof Exp:* From instr to asst prof French & comp lit, Univ Iowa, 63-65; assoc prof French lit, Univ Kans, 65-70; vis prof French & Am lit, Mohammed V Univ, Morocco, 70-72; prof French lit, Univ Kans, 72-80; PROF & CHMN FRENCH, LA STATE UNIV, 80- *Concurrent Pos:* Founder & ed, L'Esprit Createur, 61-; Fulbright lectr to Morocco, 70-72; vis prof Univ Damascus, 76; Adv bd, Oeuvres et critiques & French lit pubs Fulbright, 61, 70-72 & 81; Mellon fel, spring, 79; Nat Endowment for Humanities, summer, 79. *Mem:* MLA; Am Asn Teachers Fr; Asn Univ Teachers Gr Brit; Soc Fr Studies, Gt Brit; Soc Fr Prof Am. *Res:* Contemporary literature; modern novel; modern criticism. *Publ:* Contribr, Marcel Poust: A Critical Panorama, Univ Ill, 73; auth, The Gyres of Ubu roi, Dada-Surrealism, spring 74; auth, Alientation in Samuel Beckett: The Protagonist as Eiron, Perspectives, 11/75; Cheikh Hamidou Kane's L'Aventure ambigue, Yale French Studies, Vol 53, 76; Nommo: African fiction in French 1920-1970, French Lit, Columbia, SC, 79; La critique, In: Dictionnarie International des termes Litteraires, Vol II, Geneva: Franche, 80; co-ed, Proust et le texte producteur, Guelph Univ Press, 80; auth, Dada: Performance, Poetry and Art, G K Hall, 82. *Mailing Add:* Dept of French & Italian La State Univ Baton Rouge LA 70808

ERICKSON, RICHARD JOHN, New Testament Studies, Linguistics. See Vol IV

ERIM, KENAN T, Archaeology, Classics. See Vol I

ERLICH, VICTOR, b Petrograd, Russia, Nov 22, 14; m 40; c 2. SLAVIC LANGUAGES & LITERATURES. *Educ:* Free Polish Univ, MA, 37; Columbia Univ, PhD, 51. *Hon Degrees:* MA, Yale Univ, 63. *Prof Exp:* Asst lit ed, New Life, Warsaw, 37-39; res writer, Yiddish Encycl, 42-43; from asst prof to prof Slavic Lang & lit, Univ Wash, 48-62; BENSINGER PROF RUSS LIT, YALE UNIV, 62- *Concurrent Pos:* Rockefeller fel, 49; Ford fel, 53-54; Fulbright lectr, 57-58; Guggenheim fel, 57-58, 64 & 76-77; Nat Endowment Humanities sr fel, 68-69. *Mem:* MLA; Am Asn Advan Slavic Studies (vpres, 73-77). *Res:* Methodology of literary scholarship; modern Russian poetry; Soviet criticism. *Publ:* Auth, Gogol and Kafka, In: For Roman Jakobson, Mouton, The Hague, 56; The conception of the poet in Krasinski and the romantic myth of the artist, Studies Romanticism, summer 62; Russian Formalism: The Double Image, Johns Hopkins Univ, 64; Gogol, Yale Univ, 69; Roman Jakobson: Grammar of Poetry and Poetry of Grammar, In: Approaches to Poetics, Columbia Univ, 72; The Writer as Witness: The Achievement of Aleksandr Solzhenitsyn, In: Aleksandr Solzhenitsyn, Critical Essays and Documentary Materials, Nordland Publ, 73; ed, Twentieth Century Russian Criticism, Yale Univ, 75; Pasternak, Twentieth Century Views, Prentice-Hall, 78. *Mailing Add:* Dept of Slavic Lang & Lit Yale Univ New Haven CT 06520

ERMOLAEV, HERMAN, b Tomsk, Russia, Nov 14, 24; US citizen. SOVIET & RUSSIAN LITERATURE. *Educ:* Stanford Univ, BA, 51; Univ Calif, Berkeley, MA, 54, PhD (Slavic lang & lit), 59. *Prof Exp:* Instr Russ, Army Lang Sch, 55; from instr to assoc prof, Russ & Soviet lit, 59-70, McCosh fel, 67-68, PROF RUSS & SOVIET LIT, PRINCETON UNIV, 70- *Mem:* Am Asn Advan Slavic Studies; Am Asn Teachers Slavic & E Europ Lang (pres, 71-73); Asn Russ Am Scholars USA. *Res:* Sholokhov; Soviet censorship; Solzhenitsyn. *Publ:* Auth, Soviet Literary Theories, 1917-1934: The Genesis of Socialist Realism, Univ Calif, Octagon Bks, 63 & 77; The Redrawn Commissars, Mosty, Munich, 66; translr, Maxim Gorky, Untimely Thoughts, Paul Eriksson, 68, Yarnstone, London, 70; ed, Maxim Gorky's Nesvoevremennye mysli, Ed Seine, Paris, 71; auth, The role of nature in The Quiet Don, Calif Slavic Studies, 72; Sozialistischer Realismus, In: Sowjetsystem und Demokratische Gesellschaft: Eine Vergleichende Enzyklopedie, Herder, Freiburg, 72; Who wrote The Quiet Don? Slavic & East Europ J, Vol 20, No 3; Mikhail Sholokhov and his Art, Princeton Univ Press, 82. *Mailing Add:* Dept of Slavic Lang & Lit Princeton Univ Princeton NJ 08540

ERTL, WOLFGANG, b Sangerhausen, Ger, May 27, 46; m 69. GERMANIC LANGUAGES & LITERATURE. *Educ:* Univ Marburg, Ger, BA, 69; Univ NH, MA, 70; Univ Pa, PhD(Ger lang & lit), 75. *Prof Exp:* Lectr, Univ Pa, 74-76; asst prof, Swarthmore Col, 76-77; ASST PROF GER, UNIV IOWA, 77- *Concurrent Pos:* Univ Iowa Old Gold summer fel, 79, 81 & 82. *Mem:* MLA; Am Asn Teachers Ger; Western Asn Ger Studies; Goethe Soc NAm; Int Brecht Soc. *Res:* Twentieth century German literature; literature of the German Democratic Republic; modern poetry. *Publ:* Auth, Stephan Hermlin und die Tradition, Peter Lang, Bern, 77; Der Flug der Taube: Stephan Hermlin's attempts to adjust to the cultural-political demands in the GDR in the early fifties, Univ Dayton Rev, No 2, 78; Wulf Kirstens satzanfang: Überlegungen zu einem poetologischen Programm, No 4, 79 & Walter Werners Verf6hrerische Gedanken der Schmetterlinge: Heimatliebe oder Provinzialismus?, No 4, 80, Germanic Notes; Wulf Kirstens lyrische Landschaft, Neophilologus, No 1, 81; Natur und Landschaft in der Lyrik der DDR: Walter Werner, Wulf Kirsten und Uwe GreBmann, Akademischer Verlag Hans-Dieter Heinz, Stuttgart, 82. *Mailing Add:* Dept of Ger Univ of Iowa Iowa City IA 52242

ERWIN, JOHN FRANCIS, JR, b Brooklyn, NY, Oct 28, 38; m 63; c 3. FRENCH LITERATURE. *Educ:* Boston Col, AB, 60; Columbia Univ, MA, 62, PhD(French), 70. *Prof Exp:* Instr French, Staten Island Community Col, 64-67; from instr to asst prof, 67-78, ASSOC PROF FRENCH, MT HOLYOKE COL, 78- *Mem:* MLA; Am Asn Teachers Fr; AAUP; Paul Claudel Soc. *Res:* French poetry; symbolist movement; 20th century French poetry. *Publ:* Auth, Claudel and the lesson of Mallarme: The theme of absence, L'Esprit Createur, spring 73; Mery Laurent and Mallarmean absence: A new reading of O si chere de loin, Fr Rev, spring 73. *Mailing Add:* Dept of French Mt Holyoke Col South Hadley MA 01075

ERWIN, WALLACE MOORE, b Louisville, Ky, Sept 10, 21; m 54. LINGUISTICS, ARABIC. *Educ:* Princeton Univ, AB, 42; Georgetown Univ, MS, 55, PhD(ling), 64. *Prof Exp:* Res assoc Arabic Res Prog, 61-64, from asst prof to assoc prof Arabic, 64-73, from acting head to head Arabic div, 64-72, chmn dept, 72-73 & 74-80, PROF ARABIC, GEORGETOWN UNIV, 73- *Concurrent Pos:* Concult, US Off Educ, 72- *Mem:* Am Asn Teachers Arabic(pres, 72); Ling Soc Am; AAUP; Middle E Studies Asn. *Res:* Methodology of teaching Arabic; Arabic dialectology; modern Arabic syntax. *Publ:* Auth, A Short Reference Grammar of Iraqi Arabic, 63, co-ed, A Basic Course in Moroccan Arabic, 65 & A Dictionary of Iraqi Arabic, 67, Georgetown Univ; coauth, Elementary Modern Standard Arabic, Inter-Univ Comt Near Eastern Lang, 68; auth, A Basic Course in Iraqi Arabic, Georgetown Univ, 69; coauth, Modern Standard Arabic: Intermediate Level, Ctr Near East & N African Studies, Univ Mich, 71; coauth, Elem Mod Standard Arabic, Univ Mich, rev ed, 75. *Mailing Add:* Arabic Dept Sch of Lang & Ling Georgetown Univ Washington DC 20057

ESAU, HELMUT, b Danzig, Ger, Oct 22, 41; US citizen; c 2. LINGUISTICS, PHILOLOGY. *Educ:* Easter Mennonite Col, BA, 65; Univ Va, MA, 67; Univ Calif, Los Angeles, PhD(Ger ling & philol), 71. *Prof Exp:* Actg asst prof Ger philol, Univ Calif, Los Angeles, 71-72; from asst prof to assoc prof ling, 72-78, PROF LING, TEXAS A&M UNIV, 78- *Mem:* Ling Soc Am; Ling Asn Can & the US. *Res:* Stylistics; lexicon, measuring writing ability. *Publ:* Auth, Nominalization and complementation in modern German, In: North Holland Linguistic Series, 73; The order of elements in the German verb constellation, Linguistics, 73; coauth, Germanic strong verbs: A case of morphological rule extension?, Lingua, 73; The generality principle and the goals of phonological theory, Linguistische Berichte, 73; The medieval German sibilants /s/ and

/z/, J English & Ger Philol, 76; Der status des Lexikons im generativen grammatikmodell, Zeitschrift fur Germanistische Linguistik, 76; coauth, Defining leterariness: an exercise in futility, Poetica, 76; An anlysis of college classroom discourse, In: The Third LACUS Forum: 1976, Hornbeam, 77. *Mailing Add:* Dept of English Tex A&M Univ College Station TX 77843

ESCALERA-ORTIZ, JUAN, b Santurce, PR, July 1, 52. MEDIEVAL SPANISH LITERATURE, ROMANCE LINGUISTICS. *Educ:* Cayey Univ Col, BA, 72; State Univ NY Stony Brook, MA, 74, PhD(Span), 79. *Prof Exp:* Prof Span, State Univ NY Stony Brook, 76, Univ del Estadode, 77, Col Univ de Humacao, 77-78 & Univ InterAm, 79-81; PROF SPAN, PR JR COL, 82- *Res:* Romance philology. *Publ:* Auth, Rasgos juglarescas en tres milagros de los Milagros de Nuestra Senora de Berceo, Revista Oriente: Organo del Col Univ de Humacao, 79; Tecnicas narrativas y discursivas en El Libro del Caballero Zifar, Boletin de la Acad Puetroariquena de la Lengua Espanola, 80; Aproximacion al estilo del cuento La Noche Que Volvimas A Ser Gente de Jose Luis Gonalez, Revista InterAm, 80; Introduccion al Cid, Playor, S A, Madird, Espana, 81; La perspectiva del narrador y la structure bifronte en el cuento Mercedes Benz 220 SL de Rosario Ferre, Talleres, 82. *Mailing Add:* Evaristo Vazquez 107 Cayey PR 00633

ESCANDON, RALPH, b Barranquilla, Colombia, May 21, 28; US citizen; m; c 1. SPANISH. *Educ:* Union Col, Nebr, BA, 57; Univ Nebr, MA, 60; Inter-Am Univ, Mex, PhD(Span), 68. *Prof Exp:* Instr Span, Univ Nebr, Lincoln, 59-60 & Creighton Univ, 60-62; prin, Cali Jr Acad, Colombia, 62-66; asst prof, Univ Omaha, 66-67; assoc prof, 67-77, prof Span & chmn, 77-81, PROF SPAN & HIST MEX, PAC UNION COL, 81- *Publ:* Auth, Intermediate Spanish, Home Study, Washington, DC, 78; Proteja a sus hijos, 79 & Vers la victoire, 80, Pac Press; Ingles para doctores y enfermeras, 81 & Ingles para secretarias, 82, Ed Mex Unidos; Pensamientos involvidables, Diana, Mex, 82; Como alcanzar la victoria, Casa Bautista, 82; Bilingual Vocabulary for the Medical Profession, Southwestern Publ, 82. *Mailing Add:* Dept of Mod Lang Pac Union Col Angwin CA 94508

ESCURE, GENEVIEVE JEANNE, b Perpignan, France, July 7, 42; c 1. LINGUISTICS, SOCIOLINGUISTICS. *Educ:* Univ Paris, Lic Lett, 63, CAPES, 67; Ind Univ, Bloomington, MA(Fr ling) & (ling), 73, PhD(ling), 75. *Prof Exp:* Instr French & ling, Hollins Col, 70-72; vis prof ling, 74-75, asst prof, 75-80, ASSOC PROF LING, UNIV MINN, 80- *Mem:* Ling Soc Am; Am Anthrop Asn; Am Dialect Soc; Soc Caribbean Ling. *Res:* Sociolinguistics, especially creoles and minority dialects; historical linguistics; theoretical phonology, syntax and semantics. *Publ:* Auth, Negation and dialect variation in French, Papers in Ling, 74; Vowel lengthening in French, In: Current Studies in Romance Linguistics, Georgetown Univ Press, 76; Hierarchies and phonological weakening, Lingua, Vol 43, 77; Vocalic change in the Belizean English Creole continuum and markedness theory, BLS IV: 283-292; Linguistic variation and ethnic interaction in Belize: Creole/Carib, In: Language and Ethnic Relations, Pergamon Press, 79; Decreolization in a creole continuum: Belize, In: Historicity and Variation in Creole Studies, Karoma Publ, 81; Contrastive patterns of intragroup and intergroup interaction, Lang In Soc, Vol 11, 82; Belize, In: Western Caribbean Creole English Texts, Julius Grood Verlag, Heidelberg (in press). *Mailing Add:* Dept of English Univ of Minn Minneapolis MN 55455

ESFORMES, MARIA, b Athens, Greece, US citizen. SPANISH LANGUAGE & LITERATURE. *Educ:* Portland State Univ, BA, 66; Univ Wash, MA, 68; Univ Colo, PhD(Span lit), 77. *Prof Exp:* Instr, Univ Victoria, 68-72; ASST PROF SPAN LANG & LIT, UNIV MASS, AMHERST, 78- *Mem:* MLA; Asn Am Teachers Span & Port; AAUP. *Res:* Spanish literature of the Golden Age. *Mailing Add:* Dept Span & Port Univ Mass Amherst MA 01002

ESKEY, DAVID ELLSWORTH, b Pittsburgh, Pa, May 22, 33; m 60; c 3. ENGLISH, LINGUISTICS. *Educ:* Pa State Univ, BA, 55; Columbia Univ, MA, 58; Univ Pittsburgh, MA, 67, PhD(English), 69. *Prof Exp:* Instr English, Carnegie-Mellon Univ, 57-60; instr, Am Inst Lang, Baghdad, Iraq, 60-61; from instr to asst prof, Am Univ Beirut, 61-65; lectr ling, Bangkok English Proj, Univ Pittsburgh, 67-71, asst prof English & ling, 71-76; ASSOC PROF ENGLISH & LING, UNIV SOUTHERN CALIF, 76- *Concurrent Pos:* English adv, Univ Thammasata, 67-71; mem comt examr, TOEFL Exam, Educ Testing Serv, 73- *Mem:* Nat Asn Foreign Students Affairs; Int Reading Asn; Teachers English to Speakers Other Lang. *Res:* English linguistics; reading; linguistics and literary criticism. *Publ:* Auth, Teaching advanced reading: The structural problem, Eng Teaching Forum, 9-10/71; A model program for teaching advanced reading, Lang Learning, 1/74; The case for the standard language, Col Eng, 4/74. *Mailing Add:* Dept of English Univ of Southern Calif Los Angeles CA 90007

ESLER, CAROL CLEMEAU, b Chicago, Ill, May 6, 35; m 61; c 2. CLASSICS. *Educ:* Oberlin Col, BA, 57; Bryn Mawr Col, MA, 58, PhD(Latin), 65. *Prof Exp:* From instr to asst prof classics, Howard Univ, 65-67; asst prof, Univ Ill, Chicago Circle, 68-69; part-time lectr, 73-74, ASST PROF CLASSICS, COL WILLIAM & MARY, 74- *Mem:* Am Philol Asn; Am Class League. *Res:* Latin Lyric; vulgar Latin; epic poetry. *Publ:* Auth, Horace's Soracte ode: Imagery and perspective, Class World, 4/69; ed, Roman Voices: Everyday Latin in Ancient Rome, Advan Press Am, 74; auth, The Ariadne Clue, Scribner's, 82. *Mailing Add:* 1523 Jamestown Rd Williamsburg VA 23185

ESLING, JOHN HENRY, b Chicago, Ill, June 5, 49. LINGUISTICS, PHONETICS. *Educ:* Northwestern Univ, BA, 71; Univ Mich, MA, 72; Univ Edinburgh, PhD(phonetics), 78. *Prof Exp:* Instr English as 2nd lang, Univ Mich, 72-73; lectr phonetics, Univ Leeds, 77-78; instr, English as 2nd lang, Cent YMCA Col, Chicago, 78-80; lectr ling, Loyola Univ & lectr English as 2nd lang, Ill Inst Technol, 80-81; ASST PROF LING, UNIV VICTORIA, 81- *Concurrent Pos:* Consult, Telesensory Systs, Inc, 80-; coordr, English lang prog, Univ Victoria, 81- *Mem:* Ling Soc Am; Teachers of English to Speakers of Other Lang; Int Phonetic Asn; Int Soc Phonetic Sci. *Res:* Phonetic description of voice quality; sociolinguistics; second language teaching. *Publ:* Auth, Sociolinguistic preliminaries to an experimental phonetic study of voice feature, Univ Edinburgh, Work in Progress, 75; Articulatory setting in the community, Research Seminar on Sociolinguistic Variation, 76; Laryngographic waveform and phonation type, Univ Edinburgh, Work in Progress, 77; The identification of features of voice quality in social groups, J Int Phonetic Asn, 78; Methods in voice quality research in dialect surveys, Papers 4th Int Conf Methods in Dialectol, 81; Pronunciation considerations in ESL-voice quality settings, Working Papers Ling Circle, Univ Victoria, 82. *Mailing Add:* Dept of Ling Univ Victoria Victoria BC V8W 2Y2 Can

ESPADAS, ELIZABETH ANNE, b Chicago, Ill, Oct 26, 43; m 66; c 2. SPANISH, SPANISH AMERICAN LITERATURE. *Educ:* Fla State Univ, BA, 64; NY Univ, MA, 65; Uiv Ill, Urbana, PhD(Span lit), 72. *Prof Exp:* Teaching asst Span, Univ Ill, Urbana, 66-69; instr, Univ Del, 70-71, asst prof, 71-78; vis asst prof, Franklin & Marshall Col, 78-79 & Lincoln Univ, 79-81; asst prof, 81-72, PROF SPAN, WESLEY COL, 82- *Mem:* Am Asn Teachers Span & Port; MLA; Assoc Lit Femenina Hisp; Middle Atlantic Conf Latin Am Studies. *Res:* Contemporary Spanish and Spanish American novel; Spanish lexicography; bilingualism. *Publ:* Auth, Ensayo de una bibliograffia sobre la obra de Ramon J Sender (3 parts), 7/74, 8-9/74 & 8-9/75 & Tecnica literaria y fondo social del cuento A ti no te Enterramos de Ignacio Aldecoa, 8-9/76, Papeles de Son Armadans; Una novela ejemplar del mundo moderno: La Terraza de Ramon J Sender, Cuadernos Am, 11/76; Azorin's Prose Style: Theory and Practice, Hispanofila, 1/77; The Short Fiction of Carmen Martin Gaite, Letras Femeninas, spring 78. *Mailing Add:* Dept of Span Wesley Col Dover DE 19901

ESPANTOSO-FOLEY, AUGUSTA, b Lima, Peru, Oct 4, 23; US citizen; m 63. ROMANCE LANGUAGES. *Educ:* Immaculata Col, Pa, BA, 47; Cath Univ Am, MA, 56; Univ Pa, PhD(Romance lang, Span), 62. *Prof Exp:* Asst prof Romance Lang, Pa State Univ, 62-63; lectr, 65-68, from asst prof to assoc prof, 68-77, PROF ROMANCE LANG & GEN LIT, UNIV PA, 77- *Concurrent Pos:* Pa State Univ res grant, 62-63, res fel, 64-65; Am Philos Soc res fel, 74-75. *Mem:* MLA; Asoc Int Hispanistas; Am Asn Teachers Span & Port; Mod Humanities Res Asn; Renaissance Soc Am. *Res:* High Middle Ages and Renaissance in Spain; comparative history of ideas. *Publ:* Auth, Occult arts and doctrine in the theater of Ruiz de Alarcon, In: Travaux de Humanisme et Renaissance, Droz, Geneva, 72; coauth, El Primero Benavides of Lope de Vega: Critical Edition, Introduction and Notes, Univ Pa & Castalia, 73; auth, Critical guides to Spanish Texts: La Lozana of Delicado, Tamesis, London, 77; Petrarchan Patterns in the Sonnets of Garcilaso, Allegorica, 78. *Mailing Add:* Dept of Romance Lang 505 Williams Hall CU Univ of Pa Philadelphia PA 19104

ESQUENAZI-MAYO, ROBERTO, b Havana, Cuba, Apr 22, 20; US citizen; m 46. ROMANCE LANGUAGES, LATIN AMERICAN STUDIES. *Educ:* Univ Havana, DLett, 41. *Prof Exp:* Instr Span, Columbia Univ, 47-49; asst prof Span Am lit, 60-61; instr Span, Sweet Briar Col, 49-50; ed, Americas, Spanish edition, Pan Am Union, 50-51, head sect Span Am lit, 51-52; mem bd ed, Life Mag, Span edition, 52-58; assoc prof, Latin Am lit, Univ Nebr, 61-63; prof Latin Am lit & head Latin Am studies Prog, 63-66, head dept Romance lang, 64-66; prof Romance lang & head dept, Univ Cincinnati, 66-67; prof, 67-76, chmn dept, 64-66 & 68-71, PROF INT COMMUN, UNIV NEBR, LINCOLN, 76-, DIR INST LATIN AM & INT STUDIES, 67- *Concurrent Pos:* Chmn nat comt selection best Span Am novel, William Faulkner Found, 62; dir, NDEA summer lang inst elem & sec sch teachers Span, Univ Nebr, 63; mem nat screening comt Fulbright fels, Am Repub, 65-68; guest lectr, Oxford Univ & Cambridge Univ, 66; Am Coun Learned Soc grant to attend meeting of Int Fed Mod Lang & Lit, Pakistan, 69; mem, NDEA Title IV selection comt, US Dept Health, Educ & Welfare, 73; consult, Nat Endowment Humanities, 75- & Assoc Press, Flow of News from Third World, 77-78; adv Int studies, Univ Simon Bolivar, Ministry Educ, Venezuela, 76-; coordr & dir, Int studies, Univ Nebr, Lincoln, 82. *Honors & Awards:* Cuban Nat Prize Lit, 51; Key to City, San Juan, Puerto Rico, 56; Medal Andres Bello Cult Affairs, Pres Venezuela & Ministry Educ, 75. *Mem:* Midwest Mod Lang Asn; Am Asn Teachers Span & Port; MLA; Latin Am Studies Asn; Midwest Asn Latin Am Studies. *Res:* Latin American novel, essay and history of ideas; news flow from Third World; essays of Latin America. *Publ:* Auth, Panorama de la poesia latioamericana, Vision, 9/67; coauth, El Cristo de Espaldas, Macmillan, Textbk ed, 67; Esencia de Hispanoamerica, Holt, 69; auth, Raices de la novela hispaniamericana, Studi di Lettertura Ispanoamerica, Milan, Italy, 69; coauth, Latin American Scholarship Since World War II, Univ Nebr, 72; auth, Antologia de Mariano Picon-Salas, Cent Romulo Gallegos Caracas, 77; Arciniega, erudito y travieso, Mexico, 79; coauth, Obras Completa de Eugenio Florit, 82. *Mailing Add:* Inst for Int Studies Univ of Nebr Lincoln NE 68588

ESTARELLAS, JUAN, b Nov 22, 18; US citizen; m 58; c 2. SECOND LANGUAGE LEARNING, PSYCHOLINGUISTICS. *Educ:* Harvard Univ, PhD(Span philol), 48, EdD(lang learning), 56. *Prof Exp:* Asst prof Trinity Col, 56-61; assoc prof, Univ Hartford, 61-64; PROF LANG & LING, FLA ATLANTIC UNIV, 64- *Concurrent Pos:* Consult, UNESCO, Spain, 70. *Mem:* Ling Soc Am; Nat Soc Prog Instr; MLA. *Res:* Psycholinguistics applied to language teaching; technological instruction; programmed instruction in languages. *Publ:* Auth, Psycholinguistics, 62 & Spanish Phonological Patterns, 63, Univ Hartford; coauth, Effects of Teaching Sounds and Letters Simultaneously at the Very Beginning of a Foreign Language Course, Learning, 67; auth, The Self-Instructional Foreign Language Program at Florida Atlantic University, 70 & Problems of Teaching Spanish Pronunciation and Writing by the Audio-Lingual Method, 70, Hispania; Psycholinguistics and the Teaching of Foreign Languages, Las Americas, 71; Preparacion y Evaluacion de Objectivos para la Ensenanza, Anaya, Spain, 71; Spanish 1-2-1, Regents, 74. *Mailing Add:* Dept of Lang & Ling Fla Atlantic Univ Boca Raton FL 33432

ETHERIDGE, SANFORD GRANT, b Conroe, Tex, Aug 23, 27; m 53; c 3. CLASSICAL PHILOLOGY. *Educ:* Univ Tex, BA, 48; Harvard Univ, PhD, 61. *Prof Exp:* Instr classics, Conn Col, 59-61; asst prof class lang, 61-72, ASSOC PROF CLASS LANG, TULANE UNIV, 72- *Concurrent Pos:* Ed, Gaeltacht, 74- *Mem:* Am Philol Asn; Celtic Studies Asn; Class Asn Midwest & South. *Res:* Greek literature and philosophy; Celtic linguistics. *Publ:* Coauth, Scepticism, Man, and God: Selections From the Major Writings of Sextus Empiricus, Wesleyan Univ, 64; auth, Aristotle's practical syllogism and necessity, Philologus, 68; Plutarch o peremenach doktriny, Acta Antiqua, 68. *Mailing Add:* Dept of Class Lang Tulane Univ New Orleans LA 70118

ETMEKJIAN, JAMES, b Turkish Armenia, Jan 12, 15; US citizen; m 52; c 2. ROMANCE LANGUAGES, ARMENIAN STUDIES. *Educ:* Harvard Univ, BA, 39, AMT, 42; Brown Univ, PhD, 58. *Prof Exp:* Teacher French & Span, Dana Hall Sch, Wellesley, Mass, 41-50, head dept, 42-50; teacher, Milton High Sch, Mass, 50-51; teacher, Wellesley Sr High Sch, 51-61, head dept foreign lang, Wellesley Sr & Jr High Schs, 54-61; asst prof Romance lang, Queens Col, NY, 61-64; assoc prof, Southern Ill Univ, 64-65; prof French & chmn dept foreign lang, Univ Bridgeport, 65-72; LECTR ARMENIAN STUDIES & ROMANCE LANG, BOSTON UNIV, 75- *Concurrent Pos:* French Govt traveling fel, 47; Am Coun Learned Soc grant, 58; coordr foreign lang in elem sch, Wellesley Elem Schs, Mass, 59-60; foreign lang consult, Surv Peabody Schs, Mass, 61; Dept Health Educ & Welfare grant, 77. *Mem:* Soc Armenian Studies; Nat Asn Armenian Studies & Res; Armenian Lit Soc. *Res:* French 19th century; Spanish novel of the 19th century; the Armenian Renaissance of the 19th century. *Publ:* Auth, Graded West Armenian Reader, Am Coun Learned Soc & Nat Asn Armenian Studies & Res, 63; coauth, Speaking French, 63 & Le Francais Cournat I, 64, Allyn & Bacon; auth, The French Influence on the Western Armenian Renaissance, Bookman Assoc, 64; co-auth, Le Francais Courant II, Allyn & Bacon, 65; auth, Pattern Drills in Language Teaching, NY Univ, 66; coauth, Spoken and Written French in Review, Odyssey, 71; Anthology of Western Armanian Literature, Caravan Bks, 80. *Mailing Add:* 35 Llewellyn Rd West Newton MA 01465

ETNIRE, ELIZABETH LOUISE, b Augusta, Kans, July 8, 16. SPANISH. *Educ:* Munic Univ, Wichita, AB, 38; Nat Univ Mex, MA, 41. *Hon Degrees:* LittD, Univ San Marcos, Peru, 48. *Prof Exp:* Asst instr Span, Univ Kans, 45-46; asst prof, Webster Col, 46-51; from asst prof to assoc prof, 53-62, PROF SPAN, CENT MICH UNIV, 62- *Mem:* Am Asn Teachers Span & Port; Cent States Mod Lang Asn. *Res:* Romantic literature of Spain and South America; Spanish and South American culture and civilization. *Publ:* Auth, Beginning Lessons for Teaching Spanish to Small Children; Spanish in the Second Grade; Revival of Catholic Letters in South America. *Mailing Add:* Dept of Foreign Lang Cent Mich Univ Mt Pleasant MI 48858

EUBANKS, MELVIN O, b Williston, SC, Mar 17, 23; div; c 2. FOREIGN LANGUAGES. *Educ:* Fla A&M Univ, AB, 51; Univ of the Americas, MA, 54; Fla State Univ, PhD(Span), 69. *Prof Exp:* From asst prof to assoc prof foreign lang, 59-75, ASSOC PROF LANG & LIT, FLA A&M UNIV, 75-, CHMN DEPT FOREIGN LANG, 69- *Mem:* Am Asn Teachers Span & Port. *Res:* Use of music in the dramatic works of Tirso de Molina; Tirso de Molina and women; Spanish and English. *Publ:* Coauth, Position Paper of Foreign Language Study in the State of Florida, Fla State Dept Educ, 73; Tirso and Women, Oelschlager Festschrift, Fla State Univ, 76; Omission of conditional and conditional perfect tenses in modern descriptive English grammar, Fla A&M Univ Res Bull, 77. *Mailing Add:* 400 Gaither Dr Tallahassee FL 32304

EUSTIS, ALVIN ALLEN, JR, b Coeur d'Alene, Idaho, June 17, 17; m 42; c 1. FRENCH LITERATURE. *Educ:* Univ Calif, AB, 38, AM, 39, PhD, 47. *Prof Exp:* From instr to assoc prof French, 47-62, PROF FRENCH, UNIV CALIF, BERKELEY, 62- *Concurrent Pos:* Fulbright grant, France, 53-54. *Mem:* MLA. *Res:* French classicism and criticism. *Publ:* Auth, Racine Devant la Critique Francaise, 49 & Hippolyte Taine and the Classical Genius, 51, Univ Calif; Trois Critiques de la Nouvelle Revue Francaise, Nouvelles Ed Debresse, 61; The paradoxes of language: Jean Paulhan, In: Modern French Criticism, Univ Chicago, 72; Miliere as Ironic Contemplator, Mouton, The Hauge, 73. *Mailing Add:* Dept of French Univ of Calif Berkeley CA 94720

EUVRARD, MICHEL, b Paris, France, July 31, 29; m 59; c 1. FRENCH & AMERICAN LITERATURE. *Educ:* Univ Paris, Lic Anglais, 49, dipl Anglais, 50, agrege Anglais, 51. *Prof Exp:* Asst French, Univ Leeds, 50-51; lectr, McMaster Univ, 54-55; asst prof, McGill Univ, 55-59; asst English, Univ Rennes, 60-65; ASSOC PROF FRENCH, CONCORDIA UNIV, 65. *Concurrent Pos:* Contrib ed, Cinema-Quebec, 71- *Res:* Nineteenth century French novel; American novel; cinema. *Publ:* Auth, Zola, Ed Univ, 67; contribr, Les Cinemas Canadiens, Pierre Lherminier, Paris, 78. *Mailing Add:* 5901 Hutchison Montreal PQ H2V 4B7 Can

EVANS, ARTHUR R, JR, b La Crosse, Wis, Aug 27, 25; m; c 2. ROMANCE LANGUAGES. *Educ:* Col St Thomas, AB, 49; Univ Chicago, MA, 52; Univ Poitiers, PhD(French), 60. *Prof Exp:* Instr French, Univ NMex, 60-61; instr, Univ Notre Dame, 61-62, from asst prof to assoc prof French & Ital, 62-66; PROF FRENCH & ITAL, EMORY UNIV, 66- *Res:* Stylistics; the interrelationship of the arts; modern cultural history. *Publ:* Ed & contribr, Balzac's myth of Pygmalion and modern painting, Romanic Rev, 62; Figural art in the Theoremes of Jean de La Ceppede, Mod Lang Notes, 63; coauth, Pieter Bruegel and John Berryman: Two winter landscapes, Tex Studies Lang & Lit, 63; auth, The Literary Art of Eugene Fromentin, Johns Hopkins Univ, 64; ed & contribr, On Four Modern Humanists, Princeton Univ, 70; auth, Erich Auerbach as European critic, 71 & Leonard Olschki, 1885-1961, 77, Romance Philol. *Mailing Add:* Dept of Lang Emory Univ Atlanta GA 30322

EVANS, CHARLOTTE BUFF, b Duesseldorf, Ger, Oct 30, 27; US citizen; m 47; c 2. GERMAN. *Educ:* Univ Wis, BS, 56; Middlebury Col, MA, 59; Ohio State Univ, PhD(Ger lit), 67. *Prof Exp:* From instr to assoc prof Ger, Muskingum Col, 56-69; assoc prof, 69-73, PROF GER, CENT MICH UNIV, 73-, CHMN FOREIGN LANG, 77- *Concurrent Pos:* Mack Found summer grant, 63; Danforth Teacher's grant, 64-65. *Mem:* Midwest MLA; Am Soc 18th Century Studies; Nat Carl Schurz Asn; MLA; Am Asn Teachers Ger. *Res:* German romantic period; German classicism; 18th century women artists. *Publ:* Auth, Wilhelm von Humboldts Sprachtheorie . . . , Ger Quart, 9/67; Das Goethebild in Thomas Manns Lotte in Weimar, Monatshefte, summer 71; coauth, Nicholaus Copernicus: A Renaissance man, E Europ Quart, 9/73; Women artists in eighteenth-century France, Can Soc Eighteenth-Century Studies (in prep). *Mailing Add:* Dept of For Lang Cent Mich Univ Mt Pleasant MI 48858

EVANS, GILBERT EDWARD, b Lynn, Mass, Aug 14, 30; m 54; c 4. SPANISH. *Educ:* Yale Univ, BA, 52, MAT, 56, PhD(Span), 65. *Prof Exp:* Teacher high sch, Conn, 56-58; actg instr Span, Yale Univ, 60-64; lectr, 64-65; asst prof, 65-70, ASSOC PROF SPAN, UNIV ARIZ, 70-, ACTG DIR, LATIN AM LANG AREA CTR, 72- *Res:* Contemporary novel; Mexico; Latin America. *Publ:* Auth, El procedimiento plurifrastico en Agustin Yanez, Rev Mex Cultura, 6/67. *Mailing Add:* Dept of Romance Lang Univ Ariz Tucson AZ 85721

EVANS, HARRY BIRBECK, b Scranton, Pa, Mar 27, 42. CLASSICS. *Educ:* Yale Univ, BA, 64, PhD(classics), 72. *Prof Exp:* ASST PROF GREEK & LATIN, WAYNE STATE UNIV, 72- *Concurrent Pos:* Prix de Rome fel, Am Acad Rome, 72-73; asst prof classics, Intercol Ctr Class Studies, Rome, 76-77, prof-in-chg, 78-79. *Mem:* Am Philol Asn; Am Inst Archaeol. *Res:* Latin poetry; Latin satire; Roman topography. *Publ:* Coauth, A thirteenth century ms of Honorius of Autun's de Cognitione Verae Vitae, Manuscripta, 72; auth, Winter and warfare in Ovid's Tomis (Tr 3.10), Class J, 75; Ovid's apology for Ex Ponto 1-3, Hermes, 76; Horace Satire 2.7: Saturnalia and Satire, Class J, 78. *Mailing Add:* Dept of Greek & Latin Wayne State Univ Detroit MI 48202

EVANS, JAMES ALLAN STEWART, History. See Vol I

EVANS, JOSEPH CLARK, b Emporia, Kans, Mar 15, 31; m 52; c 3. FRENCH LANGUAGE & LITERATURE. *Educ:* Univ Kans, PhD, 63. *Prof Exp:* Instr French, Bethany Col, Kans, 59-60; from instr to asst prof, Kans State Univ, 60-66; ASSOC PROF FRENCH, COLO STATE UNIV, 66- *Concurrent Pos:* Bk rev, Mod Lang J; contribr, Asn Can Teachers Foreign Lang Annual Bibliog. *Mem:* Am Coun Teaching Foreign Lang; Rocky Mountain MLA. *Res:* French journalism of the 18th century; French memoires of the 17th century. *Publ:* Auth, Versions of the Memoires of Mlle de Montpensier, Romance Notes, spring 66; Some current American pencil names, Names, 3/67. *Mailing Add:* Lib Arts 5 Colo State Univ Ft Collins CO 80521

EVANS, MARTHA NOEL, b Philadelphia, Pa, Feb 21, 39; m 64; c 2. FRENCH LITERATURE. *Educ:* Wellesley Col, BA, 60; Yale Univ, PhD(Fr lang & Lit), 67. *Prof Exp:* Instr French, Peace Corps, 62 & 63;; from instr to asst prof, 65-69, asst prof, 74-76, ASSOC PROF FRENCH, MARY BALDWIN COL, 76- *Mem:* AAUP; Am Asn Teachers Fr; SAtlantic Mod Lang Asn. *Res:* Pre-romantic French literature; nineteenth-century French novel; psychoanalysis, Lacan. *Publ:* Auth, Le theme de l'eau chez Senancour, La rev sci humaines, 63; The dream sequence in Oberman, Symposium, 78; Introduction and translation of Le mythe individuel de nevrose by J Lacan, Psychoanal Quart, 79. *Mailing Add:* Dept of French Mary Baldwin Col Staunton VA 24401

EVANS, MARY LEE, b St Louis, Mo, Jan 27, 11; m 42; c 3. HISTORY, FRENCH. *Educ:* Smith Col, AB, 33; Radcliffe Col, MA, 35; Univ Paris, dipl, 37; Ecole du Louvre, Paris, cert, 62; Univ Conn, MA, 71; Trinity Col, Conn, MA, 71. *Prof Exp:* Teacher French, Cambridge Sch, Mass, 37-38; instr, Wheaton Col, 38-41; head dept, Greenwood Sch, Md, 41-42; instr, US Army, 44-45; res asst, Yale Univ, 46-47; teacher French, Milton Acad, 48-52; instr, Tufts Col, 52-58; asst prof, Newton Col Sacred Heart, 58-59; Stonehill Col, 59-64; assoc prof, Salem State Col, 65; dir prog in Paris, Univ Mass, Boston, 73, 74 & 76, asst prof French, 65-81. *Concurrent Pos:* Asst, Univ Conn, 67-68. *Honors & Awards:* Chevalier de L'Ordre des Palmes Academiques Award, French Govt, 75. *Mem:* AHA; Am Asn Teachers Fr; MLA. *Res:* Seventeenth century biography; France and United States; United States colonial and revolutionary biographies; 17th and 19th century literature. *Mailing Add:* 434 Brush Hill Rd Milton MA 02186

EVANS, WILFRED HUGO, b Cardiff, S Wales, Mar 18, 06; m 69. FRENCH. *Educ:* Univ Col, Cardiff, BA, 27; Paris Univ, Dr Univ, 31. *Prof Exp:* Lectr, Univ Liverpool, 34-48; prof & head dept French lang & lit, 48-71, EMER PROF FRENCH LANG & LIT, QUEEN'S UNIV, ONT, 71- *Honors & Awards:* Queen's Silver Jubilee Medal, Govt Can, 77. *Mem:* Asn Can Univ Teachers Fr(pres, 66-69). *Mailing Add:* 175 Helen St Kingston ON K7L 4P5 Can

EVANS, WILLIAM W, English, Philology. See Vol II

EVERETT, AARON B, b Liberal, Kans, May 16, 26; m 49; c 2. ROMANCE LANGUAGES. *Educ:* Univ Idaho, BA, 48; Univ Ore, MA, 50. *Prof Exp:* Instr Span, Grinnell Col, 50-51; instr French & Span, Ariz State Col, 54-55; asst prof Wesleyan Univ, 55-61; Fulbright exchange teacher English, Lycee Garcons, Metz, France, 61-62; assoc prof French & Span, Antioch Col, 62-68; assoc prof, 68-76, PROF FRENCH, GUSTAVUS ADOLPHUS COL, 76- *Concurrent Pos:* Great Lakes Cols Asn grant, 66; prof, Mt Olivet Sch Relig, Minneapolis, 72. *Mem:* MLA; Midwest Mod Lang Asn; Am Asn Teachers Fr. *Res:* Supernatural; innovative teaching methodology; poetry and art. *Publ:* Auth, A new look for intermediate French, Fr Rev, 10/69; All speak of freedom: Rubin, Radelais, Augustine, Wanderer, 9/72; L'argument du serpent (poem & original drawings), Chimeras, spring 73. *Mailing Add:* Dept of Foreign Lang Gustavus Adolphus Col St Peter MN 56082

EVIN, AHMET O, b Izmir, Turkey, Nov 22, 44. TURKISH LITERATURE & CULTURAL HISTORY. *Educ:* Columbia Univ, BA, 66, PhD(Turkish & Comp lit), 73. *Prof Exp:* Lectr Turkish, NY Univ, 70-71; instr, Harvard Univ, 72-73, lectr comp lit, 73-74; lectr, Hacettepe Univ, Ankara, 74-76; asst prof Turkish, 77-80, asst prof comp lit, 80-81, ASST PROF INT REL STUDIES, UNIV PA, 81- *Concurrent Pos:* Contrib ed, Foreign Area Studies, Am Univ, 72-73; partic, econ/cult hist, Ford Proj in Econ Hist of Turkey, 72-73; dir & Bursar, Res Ctr Turkey & Mid East, 76. *Mem:* Mid E Studies Asn NAm; Int Cong Social & Econ Hist of Turkey; Turkish Studies Asn. *Res:* Modern Turkish literature; modernization & social change in Turkey; theory of the novel. *Publ:* Auth, The changing European attitude toward Turkey: 1600-1750, Iktisat Tarihi Semineri, 75; A poem by Nedim: Some thoughts on criticism of Turkish literature and an essay, Edibiyat, Vol 2, 77; Filolojilerde Karsilastirmali Edibiyat Ögretimi, Bati Dil ve Edibiyatlari Arastirmalari Dergisi, Vol 2, 80; The tulip age and definitions of westernization, Social and Economic History of Turkey, Ankara, 80; Yasar Kemal and his work, Vol V, 80 & Seagull and the fiction of Yasar Kemal, Vol V, 80, Edebiyat; Nationalism in Turkish literature, Essays on Nationalism and Asian Literature (in press); Tanzimat and the Turkish Novel, Edebiyat (in press). *Mailing Add:* Dept of Orient Studies Univ of Pa Philadelphia PA 19174

EVJEN, HAROLD DONALD, b Madison, Wis, June 22, 29. FOREIGN LANGUAGES. *Educ:* Univ Ariz, BA, 51; Univ Wis, MA, 53, PhD(classics), 62; Yale Univ, JD, 59. *Prof Exp:* Instr & asst prof foreign lang, Wash State Univ, 59-62; from asst prof to assoc prof, 62-71, PROF CLASSICS, UNIV COLO, 71- *Concurrent Pos:* Mem Roman Law Comt, Am Coun Learned Soc, 70-72; ed, Class J, 73- *Mem:* Am Philol Asn; Classics Asn Midwest & S. *Res:* Legal history and philosophy; Greek drama; Greek rhetoric. *Publ:* Auth, The plague at Athens, J Hist Med, 4/62; Annnnnn and Athenian homicide procedures, Rev Hist Droit, 70; (Dem) 47.68-73 and the nnnn n nnnn, Rev Int Droits de l'Antiquite, 71. *Mailing Add:* Dept of Classics Univ Colo Boulder CO 80302

EWALD, MARIE LIGUORI, b Chicago, Ill, Dec 23, 06. CLASSICAL PHILOLOGY. *Educ:* Northwestern Univ, AB, 28; Cath Univ Am, PhD, 42. *Prof Exp:* Instr, Marygrove Col, 28-30 & St Mary Acad, 31-37; from instr to asst prof hist & Latin , 45-51, foreign student adv, 72-74, PROF LATIN, MARYGROVE COL, 51-, CHMN DEPT HUMANITIES, 66- *Mem:* Class Asn Midwest & South; Am Class League; Am Coun Teaching Foreign Lang; Nat Asn Foreign Student Affairs. *Res:* St Ambrose; St Jerome; St Augustine. *Publ:* Translr, The Homilies of St Jerome, Cath Univ Am, 64. *Mailing Add:* Dept of Latin Marygrove Col Detroit MI 48221

EWTON, RALPH WALDO, JR, b Shawnee, Okla, Jan 4, 38; m 65; c 2. GERMAN LANGUAGE & LITERATURE. *Educ:* Rice Univ, BA, 59, MA, 61, PhD(Ger), 66. *Prof Exp:* Asst hist, Rice Univ, 59-61, instr Ger, 65-66; asst prof, 66-68, ASSOC PROF GER, UNIV TEX, EL PASO, 68-, CHMN DEPT MOD LANG, 77- *Mem:* Am Asn Teachers Ger; MLA; S Cent MLA; Am Coun Teachers Foreign Lang. *Res:* German Romanticism; Thomas Mann. *Publ:* Auth, The chronological structure of Thomas Mann's Die Geschichten Jaakobs, Rice Univ Studies, 64; co-ed, Studies in Language and Linguistics, 69-70 & 72-73, Tex Western Col; coauth, Programmed Instruction and Educational Technology in the Language Teaching Field, Develop, Phila, 71; auth, The Literary Theories of August Wilhelm Schlegel, Mouton, The Hague, 72; Childhood without end: Tieck's Der Bonde Eckbert, Ger Quart, 73; Programmed and individualized foreign language instruction: the prospects for their professional acceptance, Mod Lang J, 74; Life and death of the body in Tiech's Der Runenberg, Ger Rev, 75. *Mailing Add:* Dept of Mod Lang Univ of Tex El Paso TX 79968

EXNER, RICHARD, b Niedersachswerfen, Ger, May 13, 29; US citizen; m 55; c 2. GERMAN & COMPARATIVE LITERATURE. *Educ:* Univ Southern Calif, AB, 51, PhD(Ger), 57. *Prof Exp:* Instr Ger, Univ Rochester, 55-56; from instr to asst prof, Princeton Univ, 56-60; assoc prof, Oberlin Col, 60-65; PROF GER, UNIV CALIF, SANTA BARBARA, 65- *Concurrent Pos:* Fulbright sr res award & Guggenheim fel, 67-68; vis prof humanities, Mass Inst Technol, 69-70; mem comt advan placement in Ger, Col Entrance Exam Bd, 72-, chief reader Ger lit, 76-77; vis prof Ger lit, Stanford Univ, 73-74; mem, Bavarian Acad Fine Arts, 79; vis prof, Univ de Nice, 80. *Mem:* Am Coun Studies Austrian Lit (vpres, 72-); MLA; Inst Compt Lit Asn; Thomas Mann Ges; Am Literary Translr Asn. *Res:* Lyric poetry; German and comparative literature of the 19th and 20th centuries. *Publ:* Auth, Hugo von Hofmannsthal's Lebenslied, Carl Winter, 64; Index nominum zu Hugo von Hofmannsthal's Gesammelten Werken, Lothar Stiehm, Heidelberg, 76; ed, Rudolf Alexander Schroeder: Aphorismen und Reflexionen, Suhrkamp Verlag, Frankfurt am Main, 77; Fast ein Gespräch (poems), 80 & Mit rauchloser Flamme (poems), 82, Schneekluth, München. *Mailing Add:* Dept of Ger & Slavic Lang Univ of Calif Santa Barbara CA 93106

EXUM, FRANCES BELL, b Birmingham, Ala, May 11, 40. SPANISH GOLDEN AGE LITERATURE. *Educ:* Fla State Univ, BA, 62, MA, 63, PhD(Span), 70. *Prof Exp:* Instr Span, NC Wesleyan Col, 63-65 & Greensboro Col, 65-67; asst prof, 70-73, assoc prof, 73-77, PROF SPAN, WINTHROP COL, 77- *Mem:* MLA; Am Asn Teachers Span & Port; Renaissance Soc Am; Asn Int Hispanistas; Cervantes Soc Am. *Res:* Spanish Golden Age literature; Cervantes. *Publ:* Auth, Translation and Critical Analysis of La Loca de la Casa of Benito Perez Galdos, Univ Ky, 63; The Metamorphosis of Lope de Vega's King Pedro, Plaza Mayor, Madrid, 74; Lope's King Pedro: The divine right of kings vs the right of resistance, Hispania, 9/74; Conceptismo as a comic technique in Moreto's El Desden con el Desden, SAtlantic Bull, 11/77; The role of Prince Henry in Calderon's El Medico de su Honra, Bull Comediantes, spring 77; Moreto's Playmakers: The roles of four Graciosos and their plays within the play, Bull Hisp Studies, 10/78; Another look at Polilla's Parable of the Frog, In: El Desden, con el Desden, Romance Notes, fall 80. *Mailing Add:* Dept of Mod & Class Lang Winthrop Col Rock Hill SC 29733

EYKMAN, CHRISTOPH WOLFGANG, b Frankfurt, WGer, Dec 6, 37. GERMAN LITERATURE. *Educ:* Univ Bonn, PhD(Ger), 64. *Prof Exp:* Asst prof Ger, Antioch Col, 64-68; asst prof, 68-72, ASSOC PROF GER, BOSTON COL, 72- *Mem:* MLA. *Res:* Comparative literature; 20th century German literature; theory of literature. *Publ:* Auth, Die Funktion des Hasslichen in der Lyrik G Heyms, G Trakls und G Benns, Bouvier, Bonn, 65; Der Verlust der Geschichte in der Deutschen Literatur des 20 Jahrhunderts, Neophilologus, 70; Geschichtspessimismus in der Deutschen Literatur des 20, Jahrhunderts, Francke, Berne, 70; Zur Sozialphilosophie des deutschen Expressionismus, Z Deut Philol, 72; Denk-und Stilformen des Deutschen Expressionismus, Francke, Berne, 73; Phänomenologie der Interpretation, Francke, Berne, Munich, 77. *Mailing Add:* Dept of Ger Studies Boston Col Chestnut Hill MA 02167

EYZAGUIRRE, LUIS B, b San Carlos, Chile, Dec 15, 26; US citizen; c 1. SPANISH, SPANISH AMERICAN LITERATURES & LANGUAGE. *Educ:* Univ Chile, BA, 46; Yale Univ, PhD(Span), 70. *Prof Exp:* Instr Span, Pub Sch Syst, Chile, 46-58; chmn dept Span & Port, 72-76, assoc prof span, 66-80, PROF ROMANCE LANG, UNIV CONN, 80- *Mem:* MLA; Am Asn Teachers Span & Port; New England Coun Latin Am Studies; Latin Am Study Asn. *Res:* Latin American novel; Latin American poetry. *Publ:* Auth, La gloria de D Ramiro y Don Segundo Sombra: Dos hitos en la novela modernista en Hispanoamerica, Cuadernos Am, 1-2/72; Rayuela, Sobre heroes y tumbas y El astillero, busqueda de la identidad individual, Nueva Narrativa Hispanoam, 9/72; El Heroe en la Novela Hispanoamericana del Siglo XX, Ed Univ Chile, 73; Patologia en La Voragine de J E Rivera, Hispania, 3/73; Tradicion, renovacion y vigencia de Don Segundo Sombra, Revista de Critica Literaria Latinoamericana, Vol V, 79. *Mailing Add:* Dept of Span & Port Univ of Conn Storrs CT 06268

EZELL, RICHARD LEE, b Lawson, Mo, Nov 9, 41; m 65; c 2. SPANISH. *Educ:* La Tech Univ, BA, 63; Univ Okla, MA, 65, PhD(Span), 71. *Prof Exp:* Asst prof Span, 66-73, assoc prof, 73-78, PROF SPAN & CHMN DEPT FOREIGN LANG, LA TECH UNIV, 78- *Concurrent Pos:* Adv bd, Coun Devel Fr in La, 75-78; vis prof, San Luis Potosi, 74, 75, 76 & 79; consult, Educ Serv Am, 79-; vpres, La Foreign Lang Teachers, 73-77. *Mem:* Am Asn Teachers Span & Port; Am Coun Teaching Foreign Lang; S Cent MLA. *Res:* Pedagogy; Spanish theater; interdisciplinary study abroad. *Publ:* Coauth, On translating quechua, Quartet, winter 68; auth, Foreign language teaching in the United States of America, Rassegna Ital Ling, Applicata, fall 72. *Mailing Add:* Dept of Foreign Lang La Tech Univ Ruston LA 71270

EZERGAILIS, INTA MISKE, b Riga, Latvia, Sept 11, 32; US citizen; m 57; c 1. GERMAN LITERATURE. *Educ:* Cornell Univ, MA, 66, PhD(Ger lit), 69. *Prof Exp:* Asst prof Ger lit, 69-78, studies grant Ger & Japanese lit, 72-73, ASSOC PROF GER LIT, CORNELL UNIV, 78- *Mem:* MLA. *Res:* Thomas Mann; modern German novel. *Publ:* Auth, Spinell's Letter: An approach to Thomas Mann's Tristan, Ger Life & Lett, Oxford, 72; Male and female principles: Thomas Mann's Image of Schiller and Goethe, Mosaic, winter 73; Günter Grass's Fearful Symmetry: Dialectic, mock and real in Katz and Die Blechtrommell, Tex Studies Lit & Lang, spring 74; Thomas Mann's Resort, Mod Lang Notes, 75; Musicality in Poetry: The Case of Heine, Heine Jahrbuch, 77. *Mailing Add:* Dept of Ger Lit 178 Goldwin Smith Hall Cornell Univ Ithaca NY 14853

F

FABIAN, DONALD LEROY, b Chicago, Ill, July 5, 19. SPANISH. *Educ:* Univ Chicago, BA & MA, 41, PhD(Romance lang), 50. *Prof Exp:* Instr Span, Tulane Univ, 46-49; instr, Univ Chicago, 49-51, asst prof, 51-52 & 53-58; from assoc prof to prof, Southern Methodist Univ, 58-65; chmn Span dept, 67-76, PROF SPAN, MACALESTER COL, 65-, CHMN SPAN DEPT, 79- *Concurrent Pos:* Vis asst prof, Univ PR, 52-53 & Univ Minn, Minneapolis, 67-70. *Mem:* Am Asn Teachers Span & Port. *Res:* Spanish literature of the 19th and 20th centuries. *Publ:* Auth, Essentials of Spanish, Houghton, 57; The progress of the artist, Hisp Rev, 4/58; Bases de la novelistica de Ramon Perez de Ayala, Hispania, 3/63; Tres ficciones breves, Houghton, 68. *Mailing Add:* Dept of Span Macalester Col St Paul MN 55105

FABIAN, HANS JOACHIM, b Elbing, Ger, Aug 1, 26; US citizen; m 51; c 2. GERMAN. *Educ:* Syracuse Univ, BA, 50, MA, 52, MSLS, 54; Ohio State Univ, PhD(Ger lit), 63. *Prof Exp:* Dir libr, Wilmington Col, 54-61; asst Ger, Ohio State Univ, 61-62, asst prof libr admin, 63-64; instr Ger, Ohio Univ, 62-63; dir jr year abroad, 68-69, ASST PROF GER, UNIV MICH, ANN ARBOR, 64- *Concurrent Pos:* Rackham fel, 67. *Mem:* Am Asn Teachers Ger; MLA. *Res:* German expressionism; Georg Kaiser. *Mailing Add:* Dept of Ger Univ Mich Ann Arbor MI 48104

FABRIZI, BENEDETTO, b San Donato Val di Comino, Italy, Apr 20, 21; US citizen; m 53; c 3. FOREIGN LANGUAGES. *Educ:* Harvard Univ, BS, 44; Middlebury Col, MA, 46, DML, 57. *Prof Exp:* Instr French & English, Waldoboro High Sch, Maine, 47-48; instr French, Ital & Span, Boston Col, 56-65 & dir lang lab, 59-65; ASSOC PROF MOD LANG, NORTHEASTERN UNIV, 65- *Concurrent Pos:* Instr French, Tufts Univ, 50-56; dir workshops teaching foreign lang, Mass Dept Educ, 60-62 & RI Dept Educ, 61-63; vchmn, Mass Adv Comt Foreign Lang, 68-70 & chmn, 70-72. *Mem:* Am Asn Teachers Fr; Am Asn Teachers Ital; Dante Soc Am; Am Coun Teaching Foreign Lang. *Res:* Modern French and Italian literature; 18th century French literature; Dante. *Publ:* Auth, The how's, Why's and where's of language laboratories, Nation's Schs, 6/60; Language laboratory logic, Bay State Foreign Lang Bull, 10/63; Valery Larbaud and the interior monologue, Ky Foreign Lang Quart, 3/66. *Mailing Add:* 889 Watertown St West Newton MA 02165

FAGUNDO, ANA MARIA, b Santa Cruz de Tenerife, Spain, Mar 13, 38. COMPARATIVE LITERATURE, SPANISH & ENGLISH LITERATURE. *Educ:* Univ Redlands, BA, 62; Univ Wash, MA, 64, PhD(comp lit), 67. *Prof Exp:* Asst prof Span lit, 67-76, ASSOC PROF CONTEMP SPAN LIT, UNIV CALIF, RIVERSIDE, 76- *Concurrent Pos:* Ed-in-Chief, Alaluz. *Honors & Awards:* Carabela de Oro poetry prize. *Mem:* Am Asn Teachers Span & Port; Sociedad Colegial de Escritores. *Res:* Contemporary Spanish poetry; contemporary American poetry. *Publ:* Auth, La poesia de Carlos Bousono; entre el ser y la nada, Insula, Madrid, 69; Diario de una Muerte (poems), 70 & Vida y Obra de Emily Dickinson, 72, Ed Alfaguara, Madrid; La poesia de Jose Hierro, Cuadernos Hispanoamericanos, Madrid, 72; Configurado tiempo (poems), Madrid, 74; Invencion de la luz (poems), Bercelona, 78e; Realidad e irrealidad en la poesia de KElena Andres, Cuadernos Hispanoamericanos, Madrid, 79; El tu en la poesia de Rodriquez Argenta, Cuadernos Americanos, Mex, 80. *Mailing Add:* Dept of Span Univ Calif Riverside CA 92502

FAINBERG, LOUISE VASVARI, b Budapest, Hungary, May 13, 43; US citizen; m 64. SPANISH MEDIEVAL LITERATURE. *Educ:* Montclair State Col, BA, 63; Univ Calif, Berkeley, MA, 65, PhD(Romance lang), 69. *Prof Exp:* Teacher Ger, Hackensack Sr High Sch, NJ, 63-64; asst prof, 73-77, ASSOC PROF SPAN, STATE UNIV NY, STONY BROOK, 77- *Honors & Awards:* Chancellor's Award for Distinguished Teacher, State Univ NY, 75-76. *Mem:* MLA; Asoc Int Hispanistas. *Res:* Romance historical linguistics; Spanish Medieval literature; applied linguistics. *Publ:* Auth, The Vida de Santa Oria in light of new Berceo scholarship, Romance Philol Quart, 5/75; El Laberinto de Fortuna: Edicion Critica, Ed Alhambra, 76; Tratado Sobre el Titulo de Duque: Edicion Critica, Tamesis, 76. *Mailing Add:* Dept of Hisp Lang State Univ of NY Stony Brook NY 11790

FAIRBANKS, GORDON HUBERT, b Calgary, Alta, Mar 22, 13; nat US; m 41; c 2. INDO-EUROPEAN LINGUISTICS. *Educ:* Univ Alta, BA, 37, MA, 38; Univ Wis, PhD(comp Indo-Europ philol), 48. *Prof Exp:* Asst Ger, Univ Wis, 38-39 & 40-41; asst prof, Southwestern Univ, 41-45; from instr to prof, Cornell Univ, 45-70; prof, 70-80, EMER PROF LING, UNIV HAWAII, MANOA, 80- *Concurrent Pos:* Vis prof, Deccan Col, India, 55-56 & 58-59; consult ling, Ford Found, New Delhi, 63-64; sr scholar, East West Ctr & vis prof, Univ Hawaii, 67-68. *Mem:* Ling Soc Am. *Res:* Slavic and Indo-European linguistics; Indo-Aryan linguistics. *Publ:* Coauth, Spoken East Armenian, Am Coun Learned Soc, 58; Readings in Russian Popular Science, Columbia Univ, 63; auth, Basic Conversational Russian, Holt, 63; History of Russian Phonology, Deccan Col, 65; coauth, Spoken and Written Hindi, Cornell Univ, 66. *Mailing Add:* 171 Nawiliwili St Honolulu HI 96825

FAIRCHILD, WILLIAM DEFOREST, JR, b Boyne City, Mich, July 23, 22. CLASSICAL LANGUAGES. *Educ:* Northwestern Univ, BA, 47, MA, 48, PhD(classics), 51. *Prof Exp:* Ford Found fel, Northwestern Univ, 51-52; instr class langs, Tufts Univ, 52-53 & Juniata Col, 53-56; asst prof, Univ Ala, 56-64; assoc prof, 64-77, PROF CLASS LANG, MICH STATE UNIV, 77- *Mem:* Am Philol Asn; Class Asn Mid W & S; Am Class League (treas, 67-73); Archaeol Inst Am. *Res:* Constitutional and legal antiquities. *Publ:* Coauth, Isocrates and improvisation, 11/67, Extemporaneous elements in Aeschines, 1/70, Improvisation in Isaeus, 2/72, Extemporaneous elements in some minor Attic orators, 2/72, Andocides and improvisation, 11/72, Antiphon and improvisation, 12/73, On Xenophon, Hellenica 2 3 24-49, 2/75 & auth, Evidence of improvised speaking in Thucydides, 11/75, Argument from probability in lysias, 2/79 & An aspect of Cicero's greatness, 3/82, Class Bull. *Mailing Add:* Dept of Romance & Class Lang 543 Wells Hall Mich State Univ East Lansing MI 48824

FAIRLEY, IRENE R, b Brooklyn, NY, Jan 2, 40. LINGUISTICS, ENGLISH. *Educ:* Queens Col, NY, AB, 60; Harvard Univ, MA, 61, PhD(ling), 71. *Prof Exp:* From instr to asst prof English, C W Post Col, Long Island Univ, 68-73; asst prof English & ling, 73-76, ASSOC PROF ENGLISH, NORTHEASTERN UNIV, 76- *Concurrent Pos:* Am Coun Learned Soc grant-in-aid, 77-78; Guggenheim fel, 79-80. *Mem:* Ling Soc Am; MLA; Semiotic Soc Am; Millay Colony for Arts. *Res:* Linguistic approaches to literature, stylistics, poetics. *Publ:* Auth, Syntax as style: An analysis of three Cummings' poems, In: Studies Presented to Roman Jakobson by His Students, Slavica, 68; Meaning and syntax in E E Cummings' quick i the death of thing, Proc Univ Northern Iowa Conf Meaning, 73; Syntactic deviation and cohesion, Lang & Style, summer 73; E E Cummings and Ungrammar: A Study of Syntactic Deviance in his Poems, Watermill, 75; Cummings' love lyrics: Some notes by a female linguist, J Mod Lit, 4/79; Experimental approaches to language in literature: Reader responses to poems, Style, fall 79; Millay in feminist perspective: Critical trends of the 70's, Tamarack, spring 81; On reading poems: Visual and verbal icons in William Carlos Williams' Landscape With the Fall of Icarus, Studies in 20th Century Lit, fall 81. *Mailing Add:* 34 Winn St Belmont MA 02178

FALB, LEWIS W, b New York, NY, Aug 8, 35. ROMANCE LANGUAGES, DRAMA. *Educ:* Cornell Univ, BA, 56; Yale Univ, MA, 59, PhD(French), 67. *Prof Exp:* Actg instr French, Yale Univ, 62-66; from instr to asst prof, Vassar Col, 66-73; assoc prof, Hunter Col, City Univ New York, 73-74 & Briarcliff Col, 74-77; vis assoc prof French, Boston Univ, 77-78, CHMN, THEATRE PROG, NEW SCH SOC RES, 78- *Mem:* MLA. *Res:* Contemporary French and American drama; reception of American drama abroad. *Publ:* Auth, Le naturalisme de papa, American drama in France, Fr Rev, 10/71; American Drama in Paris, 1945-70, Univ NC, 72; Jean Anouilh, A Study of the Plays, Ungas, 77; Sally Bard Nellie T, Illus London News, 12/79; Jean Anouilh, 80 & Jacques Audiberti, 80, Encycl World Lit; The Entertaining Sarah Bernhardt, Gourmet, 12/81. *Mailing Add:* Carpenter Rd Hopewell Jct New York NY 12533

FALCONER, ALEXANDER GRAHAM, b Dumfries, Scotland, Jan 1, 32; m 57; c 2. FRENCH & COMPARATIVE LITERATURE. *Educ:* Oxford Univ, MA, 53; Univ Aix Marseille, D Univ (French lit), 59. *Prof Exp:* Asst, Ecole Norm Aix-en-Provence, 55-57; lectr English, Folkuniversitet, Sweden, 57-58; tutor French, St John's Col, Oxford Univ, 58-59; from asst lectr to lectr, Glasgow Univ, 59-66; asst prof, 66-67, assoc prof, 67-78, PROF FRENCH, UNIV TORONTO, 78- *Concurrent Pos:* Vis assoc prof, Queen's Univ, Ont, 73. *Mem:* Soc Fr Studies; Mod Humanities Res Asn; MLA. *Res:* French cyclic novel of the 20th century; genetic studies of 19th century French literature, especially fiction; Musset, Flaubert, Balzac, Zola. *Publ:* Auth, La genese de Mardoche, Rev Hist Litt France, 1/65; Le travail de style dans la revisions de la Peau de chagrin, L'Annee Balzacienne, 4/69; co-ed, La lecture sociocritique du texte romanesque, Hakkert, Toronto, 74; auth, Creation et conservation du sens dans Mme Bovary, In: La production du sens chez Flaubert, Paris, 75; Flaubert assassin de Charles, In: Languages de Flaubert, Minard, 76; Folie et sagesse de l'ecriture zolienne, In: Le Naturalisme, Paris, 78; Communication i prose fiction, Queen's Quart, 78; Le role poetique de la doxa bakacienne, Roman de Babzac, Didler Montreal, 80. *Mailing Add:* Dept of French Univ Col Univ of Toronto Toronto ON M5S 1A1 Can

FALEN, JAMES EDWARD, b Philadelphia, Pa, Apr 6, 35; m 63; c 3. RUSSIAN LANGUAGE & LITERATURE, SOVIET AREA STUDIES. *Educ:* Univ Pa, BA, 56, MA, 63, PhD(Russ), 70; US Army Lang Sch, cert, 57; Moscow Univ Prog Teachers Russ, cert, 75. *Prof Exp:* PROF RUSS, UNIV TENN, 65- *Mem:* Am Asn Teachers Slavic & East Europ Langs. *Res:* Nineteenth and 20th century Russian literature. *Publ:* Auth, Isaac Babel: Russian Master of the Short Story, Univ Tenn Press, 74. *Mailing Add:* Dept of Ger & Slavic Langs Univ of Tenn Knoxville TN 37996

FALK, EUGENE HANNES, b Czech, Aug 10, 13; nat US; m 38; c 2. FRENCH LANGUAGE & LITERATURE. *Educ:* Victoria Univ, England, PhD(Fr), 42. *Prof Exp:* Asst & asst lectr Ger, Univ Manchester, 39-42; master French, Alcester Sch, England, 43-46; from asst prof to prof French, Univ Bridgeport, 46-53, chmn dept, foreign lang, 47-53; vis prof French, Univ Minn, 53-54 & assoc prof, 54-57, prof Romance lang, 57-63, chmn comt comp lit, 56-63, chmn Romance lang, 60-63; Edward Tuck prof French lang & lit & chmn Romance lang, Dartmouth Col, 63-67; prof French & comp lit, 67-73, chmn dept, 72-80, MARCEL BATAILLON PROF COMP LIT, UNIV NC, CHAPEL HILL, 73- *Concurrent Pos:* Fund Advan Educ fel, 52-53; fel, Nat Humanities Ctr, 82. *Mem:* MLA; Am Asn Teachers Fr; Am Comp Lit Asn; Int Asn Fr Studies. *Res:* French literature of the 19th and 20th centuries; literary theory and criticism; comparative literature. *Publ:* Auth, Renunciation as a Tragic Focus, Univ Minn, 54; Types of Thematic Structure, Univ Chicago, 67; The Poetics of Roman Ingarden, Univ NC, 81. *Mailing Add:* Curric Comp Lit Univ of NC Chapel Hill NC 27514

FALK, JULIA SABLESKI, b Englewood, NJ, Sept 21, 41; m 67; c 1. LINGUISTICS, ENGLISH. *Educ:* Georgetown Univ, BS, 63; Univ Wash, MA, 64, PhD(ling), 68. *Prof Exp:* From instr to assoc prof, 66-78, PROF LING, MICH STATE UNIV, 78-, ASSOC DEAN COL ARTS & LETT, 79- *Concurrent Pos:* Sr researcher educ, Inst Res on Teaching, 76-77. *Mem:* Ling Soc Am; MLA; Nat Coun Teachers English. *Res:* Language acquisition; implications of linguistics for education. *Publ:* Auth, Equational clauses in Bengali, Language, 65; A Generative Phonology of a Spanish Dialect, 65 & Nominalizations in Spanish, 68, Univ Wash; auth, Linguistics and Language, Wiley, 1st ed, 73, 2nd ed, 78; Child language acquisition, Ling Reporter, 74; Language and linguistics: Bases for a curriculum, In: Language in Education, Ctr Appl Ling, 78; Lang acquisition and the teaching and learning of writing, Col English, 79; coauth, Speaking Black English and reading, J Negro Educ, 82. *Mailing Add:* Dept of Ling Mich State Univ East Lansing MI 48824

FALK, THOMAS HEINRICH, b Frankfurt, Ger, Sept 25, 35; US citizen; m 67; c 1. CONTEMPORARY GERMAN LITERATURE. *Educ:* Wagner Col, BA, 58; Univ Southern Calif, AM, 63, PhD(Ger), 70. *Prof Exp:* Supvr lower div inst, Dept Ger, Univ Southern Calif, 61-64 & dir intensive lang prog, 64-67; instr Ger, NTex State Univ, 64-65; dir Ger prog, 66-68, ASSOC PROF GER, MICH STATE UNIV, 65- *Mem:* MLA; Am Coun Teaching Foreign Lang; Am Asn Teachers Ger. *Res:* Concrete poetry; multimedia literature; German Democratic Republic literature. *Publ:* Auth, Articles on contemporary Ger lit, Bks Abroad & World Literature Today, 73-; auth & translr, Short stories by H V Doderer, Lit Rev, 73. *Mailing Add:* Dept of Ger Mich State Univ East Lansing MI 48824

FALKE, RITA, b Hamburg, Ger, Sept 24, 19. ROMANCE LANGUAGES & LITERATURES. *Educ:* Univ Hamburg, Dr phil (Romance lang & philos), 55. *Prof Exp:* Librn sem Romance lang & lit, Univ Hamburg, 46-56; asst Romance lit, Univ Göttingen, 56-65 & interpreter English, French, Span & Ger, 65-66; assoc prof, 66-67, PROF FRENCH, UNIV ARK, FAYETTEVILLE, 67- *Concurrent Pos:* Deut Forschrngsgemeinschaft, Bad Godesberg grant, 61-64. *Mem:* MLA; SCent Mod Lang Asn. *Res:* Comparative literature; 18th and 20th century French literature. *Publ:* Alfieri and his Autobiography, 1968; Die Confessions Rousseaus und ihr Vorbild, 1968; J'ai vecu plus negligemment--Montaigne in der Deutung Andre Gides, Germ-Romanische Monatsschr, 63; about 60 articles concerning works of French, Spanish, Italian and German authors, from the 16th to the 20th century, In: Lexikon der Welt-literature II, Kroner, Stuttgart, 68; Utopie-logische Kronstruktion und chimere, In: Der Utopische Roman, Wiss Buchgesellscaft, Darmstadt, 73; On Santa Teresa's Vida, 76 & On Cellini's Vita, 77, Hamburg; collabr, Lexikon des Mittelalters, München (in prep). *Mailing Add:* Dept of Foreign Lang Univ of Ark Commun Ctr 514 Fayetteville AR 72701

FALKENSTEIN, HENNING, b Langen, WGer, July 4, 35; m 65; c 1. GERMAN LANGUAGE & LITERATURE. *Educ:* Univ Marburg, State dipl German & English, 61, PhD(Ger lit), 63. *Prof Exp:* Vis lectr, 63-65, from asst prof to assoc prof, 65-76, PROF GER, VALPARAISO UNIV, 77- *Mem:* MLA. *Res:* Twentieth century German literature. *Publ:* Auth, Peter Handke, 74, Alexander Solschenizyn, 75 & Hans Magnus Enzensberger, 77, Colloquium Verlag, Berlin. *Mailing Add:* Dept of Foreign Lang Valparaiso Univ Valparaiso IN 46383

FALLANDY, YVETTE MARIE, b Los Angeles, Calif, Dec 3, 26. FRENCH LANGUAGE & LITERATURE. *Educ:* Univ Calif, Los Angeles, BA, 48, PhD(Romance lang & lit), 57; Univ Ore, MA, 50. *Prof Exp:* Teaching asst French, Univ Ore, 48-49; instr French & math, Kemper Hall, Wis, 49-51; teaching & res asst, Univ Calif, Los Angeles, 51-54; asst prof, Mary Washington Col, Univ Va, 54-59; asst prof, Skidmore Col, 59-60; asst prof, Mills Col, 60-64; assoc prof French, 64-68, chmn div humanities, 68-70, dean fac, 70-71, actg provost, 71-72, dean acad planning, 72-74, PROF FRENCH, CALIF STATE COL, SONOMA, 68-, VPRES ACAD AFFAIRS, 74- *Concurrent Pos:* Chmn accrediting comt, Western Asn Schs & Cols, 65-; consult, Nat Endowment for Humanities, 72-; mem vis comn, Southern Asn Schs & Cols, 73 & vis comn to Strasbourg & Madrid, Fed Regional Asn Accreditation Higher Educ. *Mem:* MLA; Am Asn Teachers Fr. *Res:* Colette; Teilhard de Chardin; contemporary American Catholicism. *Publ:* Auth, A reexamination of the role of the Blessed Virgin in the Miracles de Notre Dame par Personnages, Philol Quart; Everat & Tombel de Chartrose, Dictionnaire Let Francaises, Ed Grente. *Mailing Add:* Off of Acad Affairs Calif State Col Sonoma 1801 E Cotati Ave Rohnert Park CA 94928

FALTZ, LEONARD M, b New York, NY, Oct 11, 40. LINGUISTICS. *Educ:* City Univ New York, BA, 61; Harvard Univ, MA, 62; Univ Calif, Berkeley, PhD(ling), 77. *Prof Exp:* Instr math, Boston Univ, 67-68; instr, Univ Mass, Boston, 68-69; asst prof ling, Univ Calif, Los Angeles, 75-77 & 78-79; ASST PROF LING, ENGLISH DEPT, ARIZ STATE UNIV, 79- *Concurrent Pos:* Res asst, Dept Ling, Univ Calif, Berkeley, 72-74; sr scientist, Operating Syst, Inc, 77-78; asst res linguist, Univ Calif, Los Angeles, summers, 80 & 81. *Mem:* Ling Soc Am; Asn Comput Ling. *Res:* Formal structure of natural language semantics and its connection with natural language syntax; syntactic and semantic language universals; computational linguistics. *Publ:* Auth, Push comes to drag: The reflexive replacement in English, Proc 2nd Ann Conf Berkeley Ling Soc, 76; On indirect objects in universal syntax, Papers from the 14th Regional Meeting Chicago Ling Soc, 78; coauth, Logical types for natural language, In: Univ Calif, Los Angeles Occasional Papers in Linguistics, No 3, 78; A new approach to quantification in natural language, Time, Tense & Quantifiers, Neimeyer, Tubingen, 80; Logical Types for Natural Languages, Reidel (in prep); auth, On the non-bal(l)m(i)er character of Keenan-Faltz grammar, Theoret Ling (in press). *Mailing Add:* English Dept Ariz State Univ Tempe AZ 85287

FAMIRA, HELMUT F, b Eggenburg, Austria, Apr 7, 32; Can citizen; m 68; c 2. GERMAN LITERATURE. *Educ:* McGill Univ, PhD(Ger), 68. *Prof Exp:* Teacher Ger, BR Gym, Landeck, Austria, 60; asst prof Ger, Loyola Col, 68-74; ASSOC PROF GER, CONCORDIA UNIV, 74- *Mem:* Can Asn Univ Teachers Ger. *Res:* Twentieth century novel; late middle ages. *Publ:* Auth, Die Erzählsituation in den Romanen Joseph Roths, H Lang, Bern, Switz, 70; Vergebens wartet der Held auf einen drink, Die Welt, spec ed, Can, 12/71; Diesseits des Kitsch, Die Welt Buches, 8/72; co-ed & transl, Erziehungsprogramm im Zeitalter der Luftfahrt, Wichita, Kans, 76. *Mailing Add:* Dept of Mod Lang & Ling Concordia Univ Montreal PQ H4B 1R6 Can

FANGER, DONALD LEE, b Cleveland, Ohio, Dec 6, 29; m 55; c 3. RUSSIAN & COMPARATIVE LITERATURE. *Educ:* Univ Calif, Berkeley, BA, 51, MA, 54; Harvard Univ, PhD(comp lit), 62. *Prof Exp:* Instr Russ lang & lit, Brown Univ, 60-62; from asst prof to assoc prof Russ lang & lit & dir Slavic Div, Stanford Univ, 66-68; chmn slavic dept, 73-82, PROF SLAVIC & COMP LIT, HARVARD UNIV, 68- *Concurrent Pos:* Mem nat adv comt, Inter-Univ Comt Travel Grants, 67-68; Am Coun Learned Soc res grant, 68-69; mem prog comt, Int Res & Exchanges Bd, 69-73; Guggenheim fel, 75-76; fel, Am Acad Arts & Sci, 80-; res fel, Rockefeller Found Ctr Advan Study, Bellagio, summer 81. *Honors & Awards:* Christian Gauss Award, Phi Beta Kappa, 80. *Mem:* MLA; Am Asn Teachers Slavic & East Europ Lang; Am Comp Lit Asn; Acad Lit Studies. *Res:* Development of the Russian novel. *Publ:* Auth, Dostoevsky today, Survey, 4/61; Romanticism and comparative literature, Comp Lit, spring 62; ed, Brown Univ Slavic Reprint Series, 61-66; auth, Dostoevsky and Romantic Realism, Harvard Univ, 65 & Univ Chicago, 67; The Peasant in 19th Century Russia, Stanford Univ, 68; The Creation of Nikolai Gogol, Harvard Univ, 79. *Mailing Add:* Dept of Slavic Lang & Lit Harvard Univ Cambridge MA 02138

FANSELOW, JOHN FREDERICK, b Chicago, Ill, Oct 24, 38; m 72. TEACHING ENGLISH TO SPEAKERS OF OTHER LANGUAGES. *Educ:* Northern Ill Univ, BA, 60, MA, 61; Columbia Univ, PhD(educ), 71. *Prof Exp:* ASSOC PROF LANG & EDUC, TEACHERS COL, COLUMBIA UNIV, 71- *Res:* Observation and analysis of language classes; English education. *Publ:* Auth, Teaching English in exhilarating circumstances, Washington, DC Peace Corps, 66; Read and look up, Literacy Discussion, 6/72; The responses of ninth grade bilingual students to four short stories, Bilingual Rev, autumn 73. *Mailing Add:* Dept of Lang & Lit Box 185 Teachers Col Columbia Univ 525 W 120th St New York NY 10027

FANTAZZI, CHARLES EMMANUEL, b Yonkers, NY, Aug 27, 30; m 61; c 2. CLASSICAL & ROMANCE LANGUAGES. *Educ:* Cath Univ Am, AB, 53, MA, 56; Harvard Univ, PhD(comp lit), 64. *Prof Exp:* Assoc prof classics & Ital, 63-72, head dept classics, 66-81, PROF CLASSIC & ITAL, UNIV WINDSOR, 72- *Concurrent Pos:* Can Coun fel, Italy, 69-70. *Mem:* Class Asn Can; Can Comp Lit Asn; Renaissance Soc Am; Int Soc Neo-Latin Studies; Int Soc Hist Rhet. *Res:* Pastoral poetry; Renaissance poetry, Latin and Italian; contemporary Italian literature. *Publ:* Auth, Ottiero Ottieri: Involvement Italian style, Symposium, winter 71; Golden Age in Arcadia, Latomus, 4-6/74; Marcabru's Pastourelle: Courtly love uncoded, Studies Philol, 10/74; The revindication of Roman myth in the Pomona-Vertumnus Tale, In: Acta conventus omnium gentium Ovidianis, Univ Bucharest, 76; Juan Luis Vives, In: Pseudodialecticos, A Critical Edition, EJ Brill, Leiden, 79; The Latin lyric poetry of Giovanni Cotta, Acta Conventus Neo-Latini Turonensis, Vol II, Vrin, Paris, 80; Vives More and Erasmus, Wolfenbüttler Abhandlungen zur Renaissanceforschung, Vol 3, 81; transl, The Collected Works of Erasmus (Erasmus De conscribendis epistolis), vol 26, Univ Toronto (in press). *Mailing Add:* Dept of Class Studies Univ of Windsor Windsor ON N9B 3P4 Can

FANTHAM, ROSAMUND ELAINE, b Liverpool, England, May 25, 33; m 58; c 2. CLASSICAL LANGUAGES & LITERATURE. *Educ:* Oxford Univ, BA, 54, BLitt, 57; Univ Liverpool, PhD(Latin lit), 62. *Prof Exp:* Asst lectr classics, Univ St Andrews, 58-59 & 65-66; vis lectr, Ind Univ, 66-68; from asst prof to assoc prof, 68-78, PROF CLASSICS, UNIV TORONTO, 78- *Mem:* Soc Prom Roman Studies; Class Asn Can; Am Philol Asn. *Res:* Hellenistic and Roman comedy; Ciceronian studies; Senecan tragedy. *Publ:* Auth, The Curculio of Plautus: An illustration of Plautine methods in adaptation, Class Quart, 65; Terence Diphilus and Menander: A reexamination of Terence Adelphoe Act II, Philologus, 68; Comparative Studies in Republican Latin Imagery, Univ Toronto, 72; Ciceronian conciliare and Aristotelian ethos, Phoenix, 73; Virgil's Dido and Seneca's tragic heroines, Greece & Rome, 75; Sex status and survival in Hellenistic Athens: Women in new comedy, Phoenix, 75; Philemon's Thesaurus as a dramatisation of peripatetic ethics, Hermes, 77; Imitation and evolution (Cicero de Oratore 2-87-97), Class Philol, 78. *Mailing Add:* 555 Sherbourne Toronto ON M4X 1W6 Can

FARBER, JAY JOEL, b Philadelphia, Pa, Nov 6, 32; m 52; c 2. CLASSICAL LANGUAGES & LITERATURES. *Educ:* Univ Chicago, BA, 52, MA, 54; Yale Univ, PhD(Greek & ancient hist), 59. *Prof Exp:* Instr classics, Univ Chicago, 57-60; asst prof, Rutgers Univ, 60-63; assoc prof, 63-70, chmn dept, 63-79, PROF CLASSICS, FRANKLIN & MARSHALL COL, 70- *Concurrent Pos:* Rutgers Univ Res Coun grants, 61 & 62; vis res assoc, Ctr Int Studies, Princeton Univ, 62-63; examnr, comt advan placement classics, Col Entrance Exam Bd, 71-74. *Mem:* Am Philol Asn; Am Soc Papyrologists; Class Asn Atlantic States. *Res:* Greek myth; Greek tragedy; Greek political theory. *Publ:* The Cropaedia and Hellenistir kingship, Am J Philol, 100: 497-514. *Mailing Add:* Dept of Classics Franklin & Marshall Col Lancaster PA 17604

FARINA, LUCIANO FERNANDO, b Milan, Italy, Jan 3, 43; US citizen; m 82. ITALIAN, COMPUTATIONAL LINGUISTICS. *Educ:* Catholic Univ, BST, 70; Ohio State Univ, MA, 72, PhD(Romance Ling), 77. *Prof Exp:* Teach asst, 70-76, instr, 76-77, ASST PROF ITAL, OHIO STATE UNIV, 77- & DIR ITAL LANG PROG, 76- *Concurrent Pos:* Res dir computer appln Ital, instruct & res computer ctr, Ohio State Univ, 75-, dir individualized lang instr, 77-; res guest, Vocabolario Dialetti Svizzera Italiana, Lugano, Switz, summer 76 & consult, 79; consult, Archivio Storico Ticinese, Bellinzona, Switzerland, 80, Assessorato Cult, Regione Lombardia, Milano, Italy, 80 & Pyramid Serv Corp, Columbus, Ohio, 80- *Mem:* Asn Comput Ling; Asn Ling & Lit Comput; Soc Ling Ital; MLA; Am Asn Applied Ling. *Res:* Lexicography; dialectology; pedagogy. *Publ:* Auth, Realta' e Potenzialita' linguistica della computerizzazione, 81 & Glossario Semantico-Dialettale Luganese, Archivio Storico Ticinese, 82; coauth, Indice Generale dei Volumi-XIII, Forum Italicum, 82. *Mailing Add:* Dept Romance Lang Ohio State Univ Columbus OH 43210

FARMER, EDWARD LEWIS, Chinese History. See Vol I

FARNHAM, ANTHONY EDWARD, English, Philology. See Vol II

FARQUHARSON, ROBERT HOWARD, b Gleichen, Alta, Mar 1, 23; m 58; c 3. GERMAN LANGUAGE & LITERATURE. *Educ:* Univ BC, BA, 49, MA, 56; Univ Calif, Berkeley, MA, 58, PhD(Ger), 61. *Prof Exp:* Lectr Ger, Univ BC, 53-56; lectr, 60-62, asst prof, 62-66, assoc dean Fac Arts & Sci, 74-77, assoc prof, 67-81, PROF GER, VICTORIA COL, UNIV TORONTO, 81- & DEAN FAC ARTS & SCI, 81- *Concurrent Pos:* Ed, Seminar: A J of Ger Studies, 65-70; mem Humanities Res Coun Can, 72-75. *Mem:* MLA; Am Asn Teachers Ger; Asn Can Univ Teachers Ger (vpres, 71-73, pres, 73-75). *Res:* Modern German literature; the German Sturm und Drang. *Publ:* Auth, The identity and significance of Leo in Hesse's Morgenlandfahrt, Monatshefte, 3/62; Hermann Hesse: An Outline of His Life and Works, Forum House, Toronto, 73; Poets, poetry and life in Eichendorff's Ahnung und Gegenwart, Seminar 1/81. *Mailing Add:* Dept of Ger Victoria Col Univ of Toronto Toronto ON M5S 1K7 Can

FARRELL, ANTHONY GORHAM, b South Bend, Ind, Mar 31, 38. CLASSICAL LANGUAGES, THEOLOGY. *Educ:* St Ambrose Col, AB, 60; Univ Notre Dame, South Bend, MA, 64; Aquinas Inst Sch Theol, Univ Dubuque, PhD(theol), 72. *Prof Exp:* From instr to asst prof classics, 64-68, assoc prof, 72-77, PROF THEOL & CLASSICS, ST AMBROSE COL, 78- *Concurrent Pos:* Vis lectr classics, Augustana Col, 67-68 & 70-71; consult, Diocese of Davenport, 70-; vis asst prof, Univ Notre Dame, 73-74. *Mem:* Am Class League; Relig Educ Asn; Class Asn Mid W & S. *Res:* Patristics; sacramental theology; Mediaeval Latin. *Publ:* Auth, Of Bees and Bur Oaks, Desaulnier & Co, 82. *Mailing Add:* Dept of Class Lang St Ambrose Col Davenport IA 52803

FARRELL, CLARENCE FREDERICK, JR, b Stoughton, Mass, Nov 10, 34; m 57; c 2. FRENCH. *Educ:* Univ Mass, BA, 56; Univ Iowa, MA, 56; Univ Pittsburgh, PhD(French), 65. *Prof Exp:* Instr French, Lake Forest Col, 61-65; asst prof, 65-68, assoc prof, 68-78, PROF FRENCH, UNIV MINN, MORRIS, 78- *Mem:* MLA; Midwest Mod Lang Asn; Am Asn Teachers Fr; Am Coun Teachers Foreign Lang; Am Asn Teachers Fr. *Publ:* Ed, Emeric Cruce, The New Cineas, Garland. *Mailing Add:* Div of Humanities Univ Minn Morris MN 56267

FARRELL, MARY MACLENNAN, b New York, NY, Aug 28, 45. FRENCH LANGUAGE & LITERATURE. *Educ:* Bryn Mawr Col, BA, 67; Yale Univ, MPhil, 71, PhD(Romance lang), 76. *Prof Exp:* Instr, 73-76, ASST PROF FRENCH, MOUNT HOLYOKE COL, 76- *Mem:* MLA; Renaissance Soc Am; Northeast Mod Lang Asn. *Res:* Rabelais; Renaissance occultism; Ariosto. *Mailing Add:* Dept of French Mt Holyoke Col South Hadley MA 01075

FASOLD, RALPH WILLIAM AUGUST, b Passaic, NJ, Apr 8, 40; m 64; c 2. LINGUISTICS. *Educ:* Wheaton Col, BA, 62; Univ Chicago, AM, 65, PhD(ling), 68. *Prof Exp:* Res assoc socioling prog, Ctr Applied Ling, 67-70, asst prof, 70-74, ASSOC PROF LING, GEORGETOWN UNIV, 74- *Mem:* Ling Soc Am; Southeast Conf Ling. *Res:* Sociolinguistics; urban social dialectology; linguistic variation theory. *Publ:* Auth, Tense Marking in Black English, 70; coauth, The Study of Social Dialects in American English, Prentice-Hall, 74; auth, Language variation and linguistic competence, Linguistic Variation: Models and Methods, Acad Press, 78; The relation between black and white speech in the South, Am Speech, 81 . *Mailing Add:* Sch of Lang & Ling Georgetown Univ Washington DC 20007

FAULHABER, CHARLES BAILEY, b East Cleveland, Ohio, Sept 18, 41; m 71. MEDIEVAL SPANISH LITERATURE. *Educ:* Yale Univ, BA, 63, MPhil & PhD(Romance philol), 69; Univ Wis-Madison, MA, 66. *Prof Exp:* Actg instr Span, Yale Univ, 68-69; asst prof, 69-75, assoc prof, 75-80, PROF SPAN, UNIV CALIF, BERKELEY, 80- *Concurrent Pos:* Prin investr, Hispanic Soc Am, Nat Endowment for Humanities, 76 & 78-80; Guggenheim fel, 82-83. *Mem:* MLA; Assoc Int Hispanistas; Medieval Acad Am; Hisp Soc Am; Int Soc Hist Rhetoric. *Res:* Medieval rhetoric, medieval Catalonian literature. *Publ:* Auth, Latin Rhetorical Theory in Thirteenth and Fourteenth Century Castile, Univ Calif, 72; Retoricas Clasicos y Medievales en Bibliotecas Castellanas, Abaco, 73; Neo-traditionalism, formulism, individualism, and recent studies on the Spanish epic, Romance Philol, 76; Some private and semi-private Spanish libraries: travel notes, La Coronica, 76; The hawk in Melibea's Garden, Hispanic Rev, 77; ed, Dictaminis Epithalamium, Pisa: Pacini Editore, 78; auth, Las retoricas hispanolatinas medievales, siglos XIII-XV, Repertorio de Historia de los ciencias Eclesiasticas, Espana, 79. *Mailing Add:* Dept of Span Univ of Calif Berkeley CA 94720

FAULKNER, JAMES CLEMENT, b Lola, Ky, Aug 6, 19; m; c 6. FRENCH LANGUAGE, LITERATURE. *Educ:* Univ Poiters, Baccalaureat, 37; Univ Paris, dipl, 38; Western Ky State Univ, BA, 41; Laval Univ, AM, 47, PhD, 50. *Prof Exp:* Teacher French, hist & geog, Col St Francis Xavier, Vannes, France, 38-39; chmn dept, Okinawa Univ, 45-46; instr, Laval Univ, 46-47; asst prof, Miami Univ, 47-48; asst prof French, Univ NH, 48-54 & assoc prof lang, 54-61; chmn div foreign lang, 64-69, PROF LANG, STATE UNIV NY COL NEW PALTZ, 61- *Concurrent Pos:* Prof, Good Neighbor Lang Sch, Washington, DC, 47; vis prof, Univ Richmond, 47; Fulbright scholar, France, 51; dir foreign lang educ, NH State Dept Educ, 59-61; consult foreign lang, Mid-Hudson Sch Study Coun, 61-69; mem, Centre d'Art Dramatique; prof French cult, NDEA Inst, Univ NH, 60, 61 & Bowdoin Col, 62; dir NDEA Inst, State Univ NY New Paltz, 63, 64, 65 & dir Leadership Inst, 66. *Honors & Awards:* Palmes Academiques, 62. *Mem:* MLA; Am Asn Teachers Fr; Am Coun Teaching Foreign Lang; Asn Prof Fr. *Res:* French culture, linguistics and pedagogy. *Publ:* Auth, Charles Le Goffic; The Theatre of Tristan Bernard; Anatole Le Braz. *Mailing Add:* Dept Foreign Lang State Univ of NY Col New Paltz NY 12561

FAUROT, JEANNETTE L, b St Lambert, Que, Mar 1, 43; US citizen. CHINESE LITERATURE, CHINESE LANGUAGE. *Educ:* Harvard Univ, BA, 64; Univ Calif, Berkeley, MA, 67, PhD(orient lang), 72. *Prof Exp:* From instr to asst prof, 71-77, ASSOC PROF CHINESE, UNIV TEX AUSTIN, 77- *Mem:* Asn Asian Studies; Chinese Lang Teachers Asn; Southwest Conf Asian Studies; SCent Mod Lang Asn. *Res:* Modern Chinese fiction; early Chinese thought; Tang and Sung poetry. *Publ:* Ed, Chinese Fiction From Taiwan: Critical Perspectives, Indiana Univ Press, 80. *Mailing Add:* Dept of Orient & African Lang Univ of Tex Austin TX 78712

FAVATA, MARTIN ALFRED, b Tampa, Fla, Jan 16, 43; m 64; c 2. SPANISH, LINGUISTICS. *Educ:* Univ South Fla, BA, 63; Univ NC, Chapel Hill, MA, 66; Fla State Univ, PhD(Span), 73. *Prof Exp:* Instr Span, Univ NC Chapel Hill, 64-65; teaching asst Span & French, Fla State Univ, 65-66; from instr to assoc prof Span, French & ling, Tenn Technol Univ, 66-70, chmn, Dept Foreign Lang, 67-70; teaching asst Span, Fla State Univ, 70-73; asst prof Span, French & methods, Ga Southwestern Col, 73-74; from lectr to ASSOC PROF SPAN, FRENCH & METHODS, ROANOKE COL, 74- *Mem:* Am Asn Teachers Span & Port; Am Coun Teaching Foreign Lang; SAtlantic Mod Lang Asn; Soc Seven Sages. *Res:* Hispanic language and culture in the United States; medieval Spanish language and literature. *Publ:* Contribr, Encycl of the Middle East, Washington DC Pub Affairs Press, 73; auth, Static society in medieval Spanish exempla, Oelschlager Feschrift, Estud Hispanofila, Vol 36, 76. *Mailing Add:* 1700 Margaret Ln No 78 Salem VA 24153

FAZZOLARI, MARGARITA JUNCO, b Havana, Cuba, Aug 20, 33; m 58. SPANISH AMERICAN LITERATURE. *Educ:* Hunter Col, MA, 67; City Univ New York, PhD(Span), 77. *Prof Exp:* Lectr, 66-67, instr, 67-71, asst prof, 71-80, ASSOC PROF, BOROUGH OF MANHATTAN COMMUNITY COL, 80- *Concurrent Pos:* Nat Endowment for Humanities grant, 80. *Mem:* MLA; Northeast Mod Lang Asn. *Res:* Latin American literature; biography. *Publ:* Auth, Paradiso yel sistema poetico de Lezama Lima, Fernando Garcia Cambeiro, 79; coauth, Muerte de Narciso de Jose Lezama Lima, Megafon, 78; auth, Reader's Guide to Paradiso, Review, 81. *Mailing Add:* 66-36 Yellowstone Blvd 1-C Forest Hills NY 11375

FEAGIN, LOUISE CRAWFORD, b Anniston, Ala, Oct 8, 38; m 69. SOCIOLINGUISTICS, ENGLISH LINGUISTICS. *Educ:* Agnes Scott Col, BA, 60; Georgetown Univ, MS, 67; PhD(appl ling), 76. *Prof Exp:* Res assoc, Ctr Appl Ling, 73-74; ADJ MEM FAC, FALLS CHURCH REGIONAL CTR, UNIV VA, 79- *Mem:* Ling Soc Am; Am Dialect Soc; Teachers English to Speakers Other Lang; Southeast Conf Ling. *Res:* Southern white English; English phonology; bilingualism. *Publ:* Auth, Variation and change in Alabama English: A sociolinguistic study of the white community, 79 & Woman's place in nonstandard Southern white English: Not So Simple, In: Language Use and the Uses of Language, 80, Georgetown Univ Press. *Mailing Add:* 2312 N Upton St Arlington VA 22207

FEAL, CARLOS, b La Coruna, Spain, Mar 6, 35; c 2. ROMANCE LANGUAGES, SPANISH. *Educ:* Univ Madrid, PhD(Romance lang), 63. *Prof Exp:* Lectr Span, Univ Lyon, 60-61 & Univ Nantes, 63-66; asst prof, Univ Mich, Ann Arbor, 66-69; assoc prof, 69-75, PROF SPAN, STATE UNIV NY BUFFALO, 75- *Concurrent Pos:* Fac res fels, Univ Mich, 69 & State Univ NY, 70, 74 & 79. *Mem:* MLA; Am Asn Teachers Span & Port. *Res:* Modern Spanish literature; Golden Age Drama. *Publ:* Auth, La poesia de Pedro Salinas, Gredos, Madrid, 65; Simbolos de renacimiento en la obra de Unamuno, Hisp Rev, 10/71; Eros y Lorca, Edhasa, Barcelona, 73; coauth, Calderon's Life is a Dream: From psychology to myth, Hartford Studies Lit, 1/74; auth, El burlador de Tirso y la mujer, Symposium, 10/75; Unamuno: El Otro y Don Juan, Planeta, Madrid, 76; Honory adulterio en Realidad, Anales Galdosianos, 77; Conflicting Names, Conflicting Laws: Zorrila's Don Juan Tenorio, Pac Mod Lang Asn, 5/81. *Mailing Add:* Dept of Mod Lang & Lit State Univ NY Buffalo NY 14260

FEAL, GISELE C, b Froges, France, July 5, 39. SPANISH, FRENCH. *Educ:* Univ Grenoble, France, Lic es Lett, 62; Sorbonne, Agreg l'Univ, 65; Unich Mich, PhD(French), 72. *Prof Exp:* Prof Span, Nantes, France, 65-66; asst prof French, Eastern Mich Univ, 67-68; lectr French, Univ Mich, 68-69; ASSOC PROF SPAN, STATE UNIV COL BUFFALO, 73- *Concurrent Pos:* Dir, NY State Span Hon Soc; fel, Res Found, State Univ NY. *Mem:* MLA; Am Asn Teachers Fr; Am Asn Teachers Span. *Res:* Psychoanalytically oriented criticism of Spanish and French literature. *Publ:* Auth, La Magnificence du Roi Candaule: Comparison d'une piece de Gide et d'une piece de Crommelynck, Romance Notes, 71; La vida es sueno: De la Psicologia al mito, Reflexion 2, Carleton Univ, 72; La Fuite devant 1 amour chez les personnages de Crommelynck, Symposium, 72; L'Ame et le corps dans Le Cocu magnifique de Crommelynck, Rev lang vivantes, 72; Le Balcon de Genet ou le culte matriarcal: Une interpretation mythique, Fr Rev, 75; La Signification de la lepre dans L'Annonce faite a Marie, Claudel Studies, 75; Le Theatre de Crommelynck: Erotisme et spiritualite, Lett modernes Minard, Paris, 76. *Mailing Add:* Dept of Foreign Lang State Univ NY Col Buffalo NY 14222

FEARS, JESSE RUFUS, History. See Vol I

FEAVER, DOUGLAS DAVID, b Toronto, Ont, May 14, 21; m 50; c 4. CLASSICAL LANGUAGES & ARCHAEOLOGY. *Educ:* Univ Toronto, BA Hons, 48; Johns Hopkins Univ, MA, 49, PhD(classics), 51. *Prof Exp:* Seymour fel Greek hist, Am Sch Class Studies, Athens, 51-52; instr classics, Yale Univ, 52-56 & fel, Timothy Dwight Col, 54-56; asst prof classics, 56-60, assoc prof class lang, 60-66, dir humanities perspectives on technol, 72-76, PROF CLASS LANG, LEHIGH UNIV, 66- *Concurrent Pos:* Ctr Hellenic Studies jr fel, 67-68; Nat Humanities scholar, Nat Endowment for Humanities, 71-72, consult, 76-; res prof classics, Am Sch Class Studies, 76-77. *Mem:* Am Philol Asn; Am Inst Archaeol; Class Asn Atlantic States. *Res:* Greek priesthoods; ancient music; ancient technology. *Publ:* Auth, The priest Timokles and the Archon Euandros, Am J Philol, 52; Historical development in the priesthoods of Athens, Yale Class Studies, 57; The musical setting of Euripides' Orestes, Am J Philol, 60; Words and music in ancient Greek drama, I: Essence of Opera, Free Press Glencoe, 64; Classical languages, In: Christ and the Modern Mind, Inter-Varsity Press, 72; El mundo en que vivio Jesus, Ed Caribe, San Jose, 73. *Mailing Add:* 249 Maginnes 9 Lehigh Univ Bethlehem PA 18015

FEDER, LILLIAN, English, Classics. See Vol II

FEDERICO, JOSEPH A, b Cleveland, Ohio, June 3, 49. GERMAN LITERATURE, DRAMA & THEATER. *Educ:* Cleveland State Univ, BA, 71; Ohio State Univ, MA, 72, PhD(German), 76. *Prof Exp:* Teaching assoc, Ohio State Univ, 72-74; ASST PROF GERMAN, COL OF ST THOMAS, 78- *Concurrent Pos:* Mellon fel, Eastman Sch of Music, 77; lectr, Ohio State Univ, 78. *Mem:* Am Asn Teachers of German; Am Coun Teaching of Foreign Lang; Cent States Coun Teaching Foreign Lang; Midwest Mod Lang Asn. *Res:* Contemporary German drama. *Publ:* Auth, The hero as playwright in dramas by Frisch, Dürrenmatt, and Handke, German Life and Letters, 79; Solipsism and Spiel: Dürrenmatt's dramaturgy of the self, Germanic Rev, 79; contribr, Time, play and the terror of history in dramatic works by Dürrenmatt, In: Play Dürrenmatt: Dürrenmatt Symposium, Univ Southern Calif (in prep). *Mailing Add:* 1405 E 40th St apt 15 Minneapolis MN 55407

FEDORCHEK, ROBERT MARION, b New Salem Pa, Dec 8, 38; m 63; c 2. ROMANCE LANGUAGES. *Educ:* Bowling Green State Univ, BA, 60; Univ Conn, MA, 64, PhD, 66. *Prof Exp:* Instr Span, Bowling Green State Univ, 64-65; from asst prof to assoc prof, 66-76, PROF MOD LANG, FAIRFIELD UNIV, 76- *Mem:* MLA; Am Asn Teachers Span & Port. *Res:* The novels of Benito Perez Galdos; 19th century Spanish literature; the novels of J M Eca de Queiroz. *Publ:* Auth, A note on imagery in Becquer's La ajorca de oro, Romance Notes, winter 71; Social reprehension in La desheredada, Rev Estudios Hisp, 10/73; Luisa's dream worlds in O primo Basilio, Romance Notes, 74; On character portrayal in O Crime do Padre Amaro, Hispania, 3/76; En torno a una imagen de La Regenta, Horizontes, 4/76; Aspects of characterization in Os Maias, Hispanofila, (in prep); Presentation of protagonist in Alves & Ca, Ky Romance Quart, (in prep); Rosalia and the rhetoric (in prep). *Mailing Add:* Dept of Mod Lang Fairfield Univ Fairfield CT 06430

FEENY, THOMAS PAUL, b Boston, Mass. SPANISH LANGUAGE & LITERATURE. *Educ:* Boston Univ, BA, 58, MA, 59; Univ Va, PhD(Span), 68. *Prof Exp:* ASSOC PROF MOD LANG, NC STATE UNIV, 68- *Mem:* AAUP; Am Asn Teachers Span & Port; Asn Prof Ital. *Res:* Nineteenth and 20th century Spanish peninsular literature. *Mailing Add:* Dept of Foreign Lang & Lit NC State Univ Raleigh NC 27650

FEHRER, CATHERINE, b Munich, Ger, Feb 8, 12. ROMANCE LANGUAGES. *Educ:* Vassar Col, AB, 34; Bryn Mawr Col, AM, 35, PhD, 42. *Prof Exp:* Asst prof Romance lang, Western Col, 43-45; asst prof French, Wilson Col, 45-47 & Wilkes Col, 47-48; from asst prof to prof Romance lang, 48-77, dir, 3rd Year in Paris, Reid Hall, chmn dept mod lang, 63-68, EMER PROF ROMANCE LANG, SUFFOLK UNIV, 77- *Concurrent Pos:* Asst dir, Sweet Briar Col Jr Year France, 55-56. *Mem:* MLA. *Res:* A history of the French Madrigal through the 17th century. *Publ:* Auth, A search for the Julian Academy, Drawing (in press). *Mailing Add:* Route 3 Old Lyme CT 06371

FEILER, SEYMOUR, b New York, NY, Apr 11, 19. FRENCH. *Educ:* City Col, New York BA, 48; Columbia Univ, MA, 51; Northwestern Univ, PhD, 57. *Prof Exp:* Teacher French & English, Oxford Acad, Pleasantville, NJ, 51-53; teaching asst, Northwestern Univ, 53-55; from instr to assoc prof, 55-67, PROF FRENCH, UNIV OKLA, 67- *Concurrent Pos:* Smith Mundt grant, Fr WIndies, 57-58; lang specialist, US Off Educ, 64-65. *Mem:* MLA; SCent Mod Lang Asn; Am Asn Teachers Fr; Am Coun Teaching Foreign Lang; Am Soc 18th Century Studies. *Res:* Eighteenth century French literature. *Publ:* Transl & ed, Jean Bernard Bossu's Travels in the Interior of North America, 1751-62, 62, transl, Cairo, 64, On the Western Tour with Washington Irving: The Journal and Letters of Count de Pourtales, 68 & Gaston Wiet, Baghdad, 71, Univ Okla. *Mailing Add:* Dept of Mod Lang Univ Ola Norman OK 73069

FEIMAN WALDMAN, GLORIA FRANCES, b New York, NY, Mar 10, 47. SPANISH LANGUAGE, WOMEN'S STUDIES. *Educ:* City Col, BA, 66; Cornell Univ, MA, 68; Grad Sch & Univ Ctr, PhD(foreign lang), 78. *Prof Exp:* ASST PROF SPANISH, YORK COL, 68- *Concurrent Pos:* Regents scholar, NY State, 63-66; NDEA grant, 67-68; journalist, El Nuevo Dia, 79-82; video filmmaker, PR, 79-82; radio commentator, WOSO, San Juan, 79-82; vis prof Span, Interam Univ, Puerto Rico, 80-81; consult, Nat Endowment for the Humanities & Grad Ctr for Advan Study Caribbean & Puerto Rico, 80-81. *Mem:* MLA; Am Asn Teachers Span & Port; AAUP; Women's Caucus Mod Lang Asn. *Res:* Latin American & Puerto Rican studies; theatre of Latin American. *Publ:* Auth, Three female playwrights explore contemporary Latin American reality: Myrina Casas, Griselda Gambaro, Wisa Hofefina Hernandez, In: Latin American Women Writers: Yesterday and Today, Carnegie Mellon Univ Press, 77; An interview with Issac Chocron, Latin Am Theatre Rev, 77; Luis Rafael Sanchez: An interview, Interamericana, 79; coauth, Feminismoante el franquismo: Interview with Spanish Feminists, Edicones Universal, 79; Goodbye Fidel y Swallows: Catenaje chejoviano y musical del Exitio, LATR, 80; La Quarachadel Macho Caluadios as popular culture, Hispamerica, 82. *Mailing Add:* 315 Ave C New York NY 10009

FEIN, DAVID ALAN, b Cambridge, Mass, May 15, 49; m 71; c 2. FRENCH. *Educ:* Brown Univ, BA, 71; Cornell Univ, PhD(French), 76. *Prof Exp:* asst prof, 77-81, ASSOC PROF FRENCH, UNIV NC, GREENSBORO, 82- *Mem:* Am Asn Teachers French; SAtlantic Mod Lang Asn; Southeastern Medieval Asn. *Res:* Medieval French lyric poetry; 15th-century French literature. *Publ:* Evidence supporting attribution of an anonymous song to Colin Muset, Neuphilologische Mitteilugen, 80; The provre villon and other martyred lovers of the Testament, Neophilologus, 80; The conclusion of the Testament: An image in the shroud?, Fifteenth-Century Studies, 82; Verb usage in a ballad of Charles d'Orleans, Romance Philology, 82. *Mailing Add:* Dept of Romance Lang Univ of NC Greensboro NC 27412

FEIN, JOHN MORTON, b Chicago, Ill, Dec 23, 22; m 46; c 4. SPANISH. *Educ:* Harvard Univ, BA, 44, MA, 44, PhD(Romance lang), 50. *Prof Exp:* Tutor Romance lang, Harvard Univ, 44-49 & instr, 49-50; from asst prof to assoc prof, 50-63, chmn dept, 64-73 & 79-81, vprovost & dean, Trinity Col Arts & Sci, 74-79, PROF ROMANCE LANG, DUKE UNIV, 63- *Concurrent Pos:* Fulbright lectr, Chile, 57-58. *Mem:* MLA; Am Asn Teachers Span & Port; S Atlantic MLA. *Res:* Spanish American literature; Portuguese literature. *Publ:* Auth, The Mirror as Image and Theme in the Poetry of Octavio Paz, Symposium, 56; Eugenio de Castro and the Introduction of Modernismo to Spain, PMLA, 58; Modernism in Chilean Literature: The Second Period, Duke Univ, 64; La Estructura de Piedra de Sol, Rev Iberoam, 1-3/72. *Mailing Add:* Dept of Romance Lang 216 Allen Bldg Duke Univ Durham NC 27706

FEINERMAN, JAMES VINCENT, Law, East Asian Literature. See Vol IV

FEINMAN, ROY, b New York City, NY, Feb 10, 43. SLAVIC LINGUISTICS. *Educ:* Rutgers Univ, BA, 64; Univ Wis-Madison, MA, 70; Univ Pa, PhD(Slavic lang), 79. *Prof Exp:* ANALYST, NAT SECURITY AGENCY, 80- *Mem:* Am Asn Teachers of Slavic & East Europ Lang; MLA. *Res:* Orthography; morphology; phonetics. *Publ:* Auth, Russian orthographic reform: A problem of language planning, J Slavic Studies, Vol 1, 7-8. *Mailing Add:* 8759 Contee Rd Laurel MD 20708

FELDMAN, LOUIS H, b Hartford, Conn, Oct 29, 26; m 66; c 3. CLASSICS. *Educ:* Trinity Col, Conn, BA, 46, MA, 47; Harvard Univ, PhD(class philol), 51. *Prof Exp:* Instr, Trinity Col, 52-53 & Hobart Col, 53-55; instr hist & humanities, Yeshiva Col & Stern Col, 55-56, asst prof class lang & civilization, Yeshiva Col, 56-61, assoc prof classics, 61-66, PROF CLASSICS, YESHIVA COL, YESHIVA UNIV, 66- *Concurrent Pos:* Assoc ed, Class Weekly, 55-57; managing ed, Class World, 57-59; Guggenheim fel, 63-64; fel, Mem Found Jewish Cult, 69-70 & 80-81; Am Coun Learned Soc sr fel, 71-72; Am Philos Soc fel, 72-73 & 79-80; Littauer Found fel, 73-74; Wurzweiler Found fel, 74-75. *Honors & Awards:* Award for excellence in teaching, Am Philol Asn, 81. *Mem:* Am Philol Asn. *Res:* Hellenistic Judaism. *Publ:* Auth, The sources of Josephus' Antiquities (bk 19), Latomus, 62; Scholarship on Philo and Josephus, Yeshiva Univ, 63; Josephus, Jewish Antiquities (bks 18-20); Harvard Univ, 65; Hellenizations in Josephus' portrayal of man's decline, Goodenough Mem, 68; coauth, The Biblical Antiquities of Philo, KTAV, 71; auth, Abraham the Greek philosopher in Josephus, 68 & Hellenizations in Josephus' version of Esther, 70, Trans Am Philol Asn; Josephus and Modern Scholarship, de Gruyter, 82. *Mailing Add:* 69-11 Harrow St Forest Hills NY 11375

FELDMAN, THALIA PHILLIES, b Buffalo, NY, Sept 29, 16; m 47, 65; c 2. CLASSICAL LANGUAGES, ANCIENT ART. *Educ:* Columbia Univ, PhD(fine arts, archaeol), 52. *Prof Exp:* Lectr classics, Brandeis Univ, 57-58; vis asst prof, Univ Mich, 58-59; from asst prof classics to assoc prof classics & fine arts, Brandeis Univ, 59-65; assoc prof fine arts, 66-72, PROF CLASSICAL LANG, CANISIUS COL, 72- *Concurrent Pos:* Am Asn Univ Women fel, 56-57; Bollingen grant, 62-63. *Mem:* Am Philol Asn; Archaeol Inst Am; Brit Classical Asn; Vergilian Soc. *Res:* Greek culture and civilization; primitive art and anthropology. *Publ:* Auth, Sophocles, Mikon and the Argonauts, Am J Archaeol, 10/57; The Primitive presence in pre-Classical Greece, In: Culture and History: Studies in Honor of Paul Radin, Columbia Univ, 60; Taboo in the Oedipus Theme, Trans Am Philol Asn, 63. *Mailing Add:* Dept of Classical Lang Cunisius Col Buffalo NY 14208

FELDSTEIN, RONALD FRED, b Newark, NJ, Aug 15, 47; m 75; c 2. SLAVIC LINGUISTICS, RUSSIAN. *Educ:* Princeton Univ, MA, 69, PhD(Slavic lang), 73. *Prof Exp:* Instr Russian & ling, State Univ NY, Binghamton, 69-73, asst prof, 73-76, dir, Critical Lang Prog, 74-76; asst prof, 76-80, ASSOC PROF SLAVIC LING, IND UNIV, 80- *Concurrent Pos:* Co-dir Slavic workshop, Ind Univ, Bloomington, 78-81. *Mem:* Am Asn Teachers of Slavic & East Europ Lang. *Res:* Slavic accentology; Slavic historical phonology; contemporary Slavic phonology. *Publ:* Auth, The prosodic evolution of West Slavic in the context of the neo-acute stress, Glossa, 75; Another look at Slavic liquid diphthongs, Lingua, 76; On the paradigmatic representation of common Slavic prosody, Linguistics, 78; On compensatory and neo-acute lengthening in the dialects of Slavic, Int Rev Slavic Ling, 78; On stress and the vowel-zero alternation in Russian, Russian Lang J, 79; The Polish vowel dispalatalization and its environment, Lingua, 80; The phonological background of Ukrainian consonant dispalatalization, Die Welt der Slaven, 80; On the definition of Russian stress paradigms, Gen Ling, 80. *Mailing Add:* 603 Plymouth Rd Bloomington IN 47401

FELLOWS, OTIS EDWARD, b Sprague, Conn, Nov 6, 08; m; c 2. FRENCH LITERATURE. *Educ:* Am Univ, DC, AB, 30; Univ Dijon, France, dipl, 30; Brown Univ, AM, 33, PhD, 36. *Prof Exp:* Tutor English, Norm Sch, Savenay, France, 30-31; instr French, St Dunstan's Sch, RI, 31-32 & Brown Univ, 35-39; from instr to prof French lit, 40-70, chmn dept Ital, 63-66, Avalon Found prof, 70-77, AVALON FOUND EMER PROF HUMANITIES, COLUMBIA UNIV, 77- *Concurrent Pos:* French Govt grant, 30-31; assoc ed, Romanci Rev, 46- & Symposium, 56-; Am Philos Soc grant, 55; Guggenheim fel, 59; vis prof French, Univ Pa, 64 & 69; mem inst consult comt, Oeuvres de Voltaire, Voltaire Found, England; mem vis comt, Dept Foreign Lit & Ling, Mass Inst Technol, 70-76. *Honors & Awards:* Palmes Academiques, 59; Officier de l'Academie, 65. *Mem:* MLA; Am Asn Teachers Fr. *Res:* History of ideas; Diderot; 18th century French fiction. *Publ:* Auth, French Opinion of Moliere, Brown Univ, 37; The Periodical Press in Liberated Paris; coauth, The Age of Enlightenment, Appleton, 42 & Prentice-Hall, 71; co-ed; Diderot Studies, Vols I-XX, 49-73 & auth, From Voltaire to La nouvelle critique: Problems and Personalities, 70, Droz, Geneva; Look and Learn Italian, Dell, 66; coauth, Buffon, Twayne, 72; auth, Le roman epistolaire francais, Dix-Huitieme Siecle, 72; contribr, Festschrift: Essays on Diderot and the Enlightenment Written in his Honor, 74; auth, Diderot, Twayne, 77. *Mailing Add:* Grad Fac French Columbia Univ New York NY 10027

FELSHER, WILLIAM MUNSON, b Biloxi, Miss, Oct 6, 33; m 58; c 4. FRENCH LANGUAGE & LITERATURE. *Educ:* Miss State Univ, AB, 58, La State Univ, PhD(French, Span, Romance philol), 66; Univ Paris, Dipl Etudes Approfoundies, 81. *Prof Exp:* Asst prof French & Span, Centenary Col La, 62-66; assoc prof French, Univ Southern Miss, 66-67; assoc prof & chmn dept, Western Carolina Univ, 67-69; chmn dept foreign lang, 69-74, PROF FRENCH, UNIV EVANSVILLE, 69- *Concurrent Pos:* Ed, Who's Who Foreign Lang Mid-Am High Sch, Krieger-Ragsdale, 73- *Mem:* Am Asn Teachers Fr; Am Asn Teachers Span & Port; Am Asn Teachers Ital; Am Asn Teachers Ger. *Res:* Nineteenth century French literature; 20th century French literature; Faulkner. *Publ:* Auth, The Flight of Phoenix Phugit, Krieger-Ragsdale, 74; Passeport France, 77, Pasaporte Espana, 77 & Reisepass Deutschland, 77, Graphic Arts. *Mailing Add:* Dept of Lang & Ling Univ of Evansville Evansville IL 47702

FELT, WILLIAM NORCROSS, b Northboro, Mass, Sept 24, 04; m 31; c 1. ROMANCE LANGUAGES. *Educ:* Clark Univ, AB, 26; Univ Bordeaux, cert, 30; Middlebury Col, AM, 31, DML, 51; Univ Grenoble, dipl, 36. *Prof Exp:* Teacher, high sch, Mass, 26-27; instr French & Span, Denison Univ, 27-29 & 30-34, asst prof, 34-35 & 36-47, secy mod lang dept, 37-40; from asst prof to assoc prof, 47-72, EMER ASSOC PROF ROMANCE LANG, UNIV NC, GREENSBORO, 72- *Honors & Awards:* Chevalier, Palmes Academiques, 65. *Mem:* MLA; Am Asn Teachers French; Am Asn Teachers Span & Port; SAtlantic Mod Lang Asn. *Res:* Eighteenth century French literature; Voltaire; foreign language laboratories. *Publ:* Auth, The adaptation of radio to the teaching of foreign languages, Radio & Foreign Lang Lab, 5/61; coauth, Students' works in the laboratory of experimental phonetics in the French school of Middlebury College, French Rev; auth, Articulation in the teaching of French, NC Foreign Lang Teacher, spring 72; Origins and growth of the endowment fund, Am Asn Teachers French Nat Bull, 4-11/77. *Mailing Add:* 1003 Westridge Rd Greensboro NC 27410

FENIK, BERNARD CARL, b Johnstown, Pa, Sept 13, 34; m 64; c 2. CLASSICS. *Educ:* Univ Pittsburgh, AB, 56; Princetown Univ, PhD(classics), 60. *Prof Exp:* From instr to assoc prof classics, Princeton Univ, 60-74; PROF CLASSICS & HEAD DEPT, UNIV CINCINNATI, 74- *Concurrent Pos:* Am Coun Learned Soc fels, 63 & 65-66; Alexander von Humboldt Stiftung fel, 70-71. *Res:* Homeric studies; Silver Latin literature. *Publ:* Auth, Parallelism of theme and imagery in Aeneid II and IV, Am J Philol, 59; Horace's first and sixth Roman odes and the second Georgic, Hermes: Z Klass Philol, 62; Iliad X and the Rhesus: The myth, Latomus, Brussels, 64; Typical Battle Scenes in the Iliad: Studies in the Narrative Techniques of Homeric Battle Description, 68 & Studies in the Odyssey, 74, Franz Steiner, Wiesbaden; Homer and writing, Würzburger Jahrbücher Altertumswissenschaft, 76; contribr, Homer: Tradition and Invention, E J Brill, 78. *Mailing Add:* Dept of Classics 221 Library Univ of Cincinnati Cincinnati OH 45221

FENNER, REST, JR, b East Orange, NJ, July 24, 11; m 37; c 2. ROMANCE LANGUAGES. *Educ:* Colgate Univ, AB, 35; Columbia Univ, AM, 39; Syracuse Univ, PhD, 55. *Prof Exp:* Instr Romance lang, Wilbraham Acad, 35-37 & Upsala Col, 37-39; from instr to asst prof, Colgate Univ, 39-57 & foreign studies adv, 54-57; asst dean Wilbraham Acad, Mass, 57-60 & dean, 60-62; teacher, Newark Acad, NJ, 62-73, head dept, 64-73; RETIRED. *Concurrent Pos:* Instr, Naval Flight Prep Sch, Colgate Univ, 42-44. *Honors & Awards:* Chevalier, Palmes Academiques, 68. *Mem:* Am Asn Teachers Fr. *Res:* French philology; prognosis of aural-oral linguistic abilities. *Mailing Add:* 22 Wynnewood Dr Livingston NJ 07039

FERGUSON, ALBERT GORDON, b Toronto, Ont, Can, Feb 17, 17; nat US; m 42; c 1. SPANISH, FRENCH. *Educ:* Univ Chicago, AM, 50. *Prof Exp:* Prof Span, Nebr Cent Col, 49-51; prof mod lang & chmn dept, Dana Col, 52-64; ASSOC PROF SPAN, ILL STATE UNIV, 64- *Res:* The ideas of Cecillio Benitz de Castro; Spain through her novel; changes and attitudes reflected in the contemporary novel. *Mailing Add:* Dept of Foreign Lang Ill State Univ Normal IL 61761

FERGUSON, CHARLES ALBERT, b Philadelphia, Pa, July 6, 21; div; c 2. LINGUISTICS. *Educ:* Univ Pa, AB, 42, AM, 43, PhD, 45. *Prof Exp:* Sci linguist, Near Eastern lang, Foreign Serv Inst, US Dept State, 46-55; lectr ling, Harvard Univ, 55-59; dir, 59-66, MEM BD DIRS, CTR APPL LING, 67-; PROF LING, STANFORD UNIV, 67- *Concurrent Pos:* Mem bd adv ed, MidE J, 55-; coord, Five-Univ Summer Prog MidE Lang, 56-61; mem comt ling & psychol, Soc Sci Res Coun, 59-61; chmn comt socioling, 64-70. *Mem:* Ling Soc Am (vpres, 68); Am Oriental Soc; Am Anthrop Asn; Ling Circle NY; Am Asn Teachers Arabic. *Res:* Arabic dialects; Bengali: sociolinguistics. *Publ:* Auth, Diglossia, Word, 59; coauth, Phonems of Bengali, Language, 60; auth, Assumptions about nasals, In: Universals of language, Mass Inst Technol, 63; co-ed, Language Problems of Developing Nations, Wiley, 68; auth, Language Structure and Language Use: Essays by Charles A Ferguson, Stanford Univ, 71; co-ed, Studies in Child Language and Development, Holt, 73. *Mailing Add:* Dept of Ling Stanford Univ Stanford CA 94305

FERGUSON, CHARLES ANTHONY, b Ilion, NY, May 25, 33; m 56; c 3. ROMANCE LANGUAGES. *Educ:* Oberlin Col, AB, 55; Ohio State Univ, MA, 57, PhD(French), 63. *Prof Exp:* Instr French, Ohio Univ, 60-63; asst prof, Univ Conn, 63-67; ASST PROF FRENCH, COLBY COL, 67- *Mem:* MLA. *Res:* Seventeenth and 18th century French literature; Italian language; translation. *Mailing Add:* Dept of Mod Lang Colby Col Waterville ME 04901

FERNANDEZ, EUSTASIO, b Tampa, Fla, Dec 11, 19; m 40. SPANISH. *Educ:* Univ Fla, BS, 41; Univ Md, MAE, 47; Middlebury Col, MA, 50; Nat Univ Mex, Dr en Let, 60. *Prof Exp:* From instr to assoc prof Span, 51-66, actg chmn dept mod lang, 58-60, chmn dept, 60-72, PROF SPAN, UNIV TAMPA, 66-, COORDR, 72- *Mem:* MLA; Am Asn Teachers Span & Port, SAtlantic Mod Lang Asn. *Res:* Latin American literature. *Mailing Add:* Dept of Span Univ of Tampa Tampa FL 33606

FERNANDEZ, GASTON J, b Placetas, Cuba, Oct 20, 21; US citizen; m 56; c 2. SPANISH, SPANISH-AMERICAN LITERATURE. *Educ:* Inst Remedios, Cuba, BAS, 38; Univ Havana, LLD, 42; Univ NC, Chapel Hill, MA, 67; Univ Ky, PhD(Span-Am lit), 71. *Prof Exp:* From asst prof to assoc prof, 62-80, PROF SPAN, CLEMSON UNIV, 80- *Res:* Ecuadorian poetry; poetry of Alfonso Moscoso. *Publ:* Ed, Southeastern Latin Americanist, 73; auth, articles in Studies in Language and Literature, Proc 23rd MIFLC, Richmond, Ky, 76; Temas e imagenes en los Versos sencillos de Jose Marti, Ed Universal, Miami, 77; auth article in Circulo: Revista de Cultura, Vol VII. *Mailing Add:* Dept of Lang Clemson Univ Clemson SC 29671

FERNANDEZ, JOSE BENIGNO, b Santiago, Cuba, May 13, 22; m 45; c 2. ROMANCE LANGUAGES, SOCIAL SCIENCES. *Educ:* Univ Havana, Lic en Derecho(diplomatics), Lic en Derecho(admin) & Dr(soc sci), 60; Miami Univ, MA, 64. *Prof Exp:* Instr Span, Miami Univ, 61-64; from asst prof to prof mod foreign lang, Valdosta State Univ, 68-76, head dept, 73-76; asst prof, 76-80, ASSOC PROF SPAN, UNIV COLO, 80- *Concurrent Pos:* Ed, The Guide, 62-64. *Mem:* MLA; SAtlantic Mod Lang Asn. *Res:* Spanish American literature. *Publ:* Coauth, El crimen de la leche, 52 & La Basura, 54, Ministerio Salubridad, Cuba. *Mailing Add:* Dept of Span Univ of Colo Colorado Springs CO 80907

FERNANDEZ, JOSEPH ANTHONY, b Richmond, Va, Apr 15, 21; m 63. ROMANCE LANGUAGES. *Educ:* Univ Pa, AB, 48, MA, 51; Univ Toulouse, dipl French, 49; Univ Madrid, Ds(Romance ling), 53. *Prof Exp:* Instr French & Span, Univ Pa, 53-55 & vis lectr, Span, 60-61; collabr Span phonetics, Coun Span, Georgetown Univ, 64-66; linguist NDEA Span Inst, 65 & 68, asst prof, 66-68, chmn dept Romance lang, 68-73, PROF SPAN & FRENCH, E CAROLINA UNIV, 68- *Concurrent Pos:* Asst ed, Hisp Rev, 53-55 & 60-61; ed board, Collectanea Phonetica, CSIC, Madrid, 64-; res grants, Fulbright Hays, 64, ECarolina Univ Res Counc, 75, 76 & 80. *Mem:* MLA; Am Asn Teachers Fr; Am Asn Teachers Span & Port; SAtlantic Mod Lang Asn; Am Dialect Soc. *Res:* Spanish phonetics; French phonetics; Spanish dialectology. *Publ:* Auth, El habla de Sisterna, Coun Sci Res, Spain, 60; La anticipacion vocalica en espanol, Rev Filol Espanola, 63; Deformaciones populacheras en el dialogo galdosiano, Anale Galdosianos, 78; coauth, Curso de fonetica y fonologia espanolas, 9th ed, Coun Sci Res, Spain, 79; Aportacion al estudio del bable de Occidente: El habla de Villarin (Salas): I Fonologia y morfosintaxis, Rev de Dian y Trad Pop, 79-80. *Mailing Add:* Dept of For Lang & Lit ECarolina Univ Greenville NC 27834

FERNANDEZ, OSCAR, b St Louis, Mo, Mar 22, 16; m 53; c 2. ROMANCE LANGUAGES. *Educ:* Wash Univ, AB, 37, MA, 40; Univ Wis, PhD(Romance lang), 53. *Prof Exp:* Instr English & asst athletic coach, Mo Mil Acad, 37-38; teaching asst & instr Span, Wash Univ, 38-41; teaching asst, Univ Wis, 41-42; prof foreign lang, US Naval Acad, 45-61; prof Romance lang & dir Port prog, NY Univ, 61-67, actg dir Ibero-Am Lang & Area Ctr, 65-67, lang coordr, Peace Corps prog Brazil, 64; chmn dept, 67-75, PROF SPAN & PORT, UNIV IOWA, 67- *Concurrent Pos:* Asst managing ed, Mod Lang J, 64-75; Soc Sci Res Coun study grant, 68; mem Span-Port Doctoral Eval Comt, State NY, 75-76 & 79-80; consult, Span Am & Luso-Brazilian Lit, Nat Endowment for Humanities, 77-78. *Honors & Awards:* Theatre Award, Colonial Players, Inc, Annapolis, Md, 62. *Mem:* MLA; Am Asn Teachers Span & Port Asn; Midwest Mod Lang Asn; Inst Int Lit Iberoam. *Res:* Spanish Golden Age drama; Spanish, Spanish-American and Brazilian theatre and literature. *Publ:* Coauth, De que hablamos?, Appleton, 52; The contemporary theatre in Rio de Janeiro and in Sao Paulo, 1953-55, Hispania, 12/56; auth, The living language Course in Portuguese, Crown, 65; A preliminary listing of foreign periodical holdings in the US and Canada which give coverage to Portuguese and Brazilian language and literature, Univ Iowa, 68; translr, Alfredo Dias Gomes, Payment as Pledged, In: The Modern Stage in Latin America, Dutton, 71; co-ed, Hispanic Studies in Honor of Edmund de Chasca, Univ Iowa, 72; auth, Censorship and the Brazilian theatre, Educ Theatre J, 10/73; El arbol y la hoja en tres cuentos: J R R Tolkien, O Henry y Maria Luisa Bombal, Estudos Ibero-Am, 7/77. *Mailing Add:* Dept of Span & Port Univ of Iowa Iowa City IA 52242

FERNANDEZ, PELAYO HIPOLITO, b Gijon, Spain, Dec 20, 27; US citizen; m 60; c 5. SPANISH LITERATURE. *Educ:* Univ Calif, Berkeley, BA, 57; Wayne State Univ, MA, 59; Lit Univ Salamanca, PhD(philos & lett), 60. *Prof Exp:* PROF SPAN, UNIV N MEX, 73- *Res:* Twentieth century Spanish and Spanish American literature. *Publ:* Auth, Miguel de Unamuno y William James, Un paralelo pragmatico, Cervantes, Salamanca, 61; El problema de la personalidad en Unamuno y en San Manuel Bueno, Mayfe, Madrid, 66; coauth, A Student Guide to Critical Spanish, Pruett, 67; auth, Ramon Perez de Ayala: Tres novelas analizadas, Yepes, Gijon, 72; Estilistica, Porrua, Madrid, 72; Bibliografia critica de Miguel de Unamuno, Porrua, Madrid, 76; Ideario etimologico de Jose Ortega y Gasset, Flores, Gijon, 81; Ideario etimologico de Miguel de Unamuno, Albatros Hispanofila, Chapel Hill, 82. *Mailing Add:* Dept of Mod & Class Lang Univ of NM Albuquerque NM 87131

FERNANDEZ-MORERA, DARIO OSCAR, b Santi-Spiritus, Cuba, US citizen. COMPARATIVE LITERATURE, SPANISH. *Educ:* Stanford Univ, BA, 71; Univ Pa, MA, 72; Harvard Univ, PhD(comp lit), 77. *Prof Exp:* Teaching fel humanities & Span, Harvard Univ, 75-76; ASST PROF SPAN & COMP LIT, NORTHWESTERN UNIV, EVANSTON, 77- *Mem:* Am Comp Lit Asn; MLA; Int Comp Lit Asn; Asn Int Hispanistas; Cervantes Soc. *Res:* Sixteenth and seventeenth century European literature; twentieth century poetry. *Publ:* Auth, La poesia desgarrada, Insula, Madrid, fall 76; Garcilaso's Second Eclogue and the literary tradition, Hisp Rev, winter 79; Vicente Aleixandre in the context of modern poetry, Symposium, summer 79; The dedication of Garcilaso's third eclogue, Rev Canadiense de Estud Hisp, winter 80; El universo cervantino en la comedia Pedro de Urdemalas, Actas del I Congreso Int sobre Cervantes, fall 81; Cervantes and the aesthetics of reception, Comp Lit Studies, winter 81; The Lyre and the Oaten Flute: Garcilaso and the Pastoral, London, 82; Don Quixote and the modern novel, Proc 9th Cong Int Comp Lit Asn, summer 82. *Mailing Add:* Dept of Span Northwestern Univ Evanston IL 60201

FERNANDEZ-TURIENZO, FRANCISCO, b Taranilla, Spain, Sept 12, 29; m 68; c 1. SPANISH HISTORY OF IDEAS. *Educ:* Pontif Univ, Salamanca, lic, 56; Univ Basel, PhD(philos), 65. *Prof Exp:* Asst prof, 69-73, assoc prof, 73-81, PROF SPAN, UNIV MASS, AMHERST, 81- *Concurrent Pos:* Ed, Editorial Herder, 66-69. *Honors & Awards:* Distinguished Teaching Award, Univ Mass, Amherst, 80. *Mem:* Hon mem, Inst Alfonso X el Sabio, Salamanca, 81. *Res:* Renaissance and Baroque studies, especially Spain; history of ideas; modern Spanish essay. *Publ:* Auth, Unamuno, ansia de Dios y creacion literaria, 66 & ed & auth intro, notes & appendices to Unamuno's En torno al casticismo, 71, Alcala, Madrid; ed & auth intro to Unamuno's San Manuel Bueno, martir y tres historias mas, Almar, Salamanca, 78; Americo Castro y Marx, Dieciocho, Vol 1, 30-45; La Novela picaresca, Revista de Lit, Vol 42, 45-53; El Quojote historia verdadera, Anales Cervantinos, Vol 18, 35-48; La evolucion intelectual de Aranguren, Los Ensayistas, 1980; three articles for Columbia Dict of Modern European Literatures, Columbia Univ Press, 1980. *Mailing Add:* Span & Port Dept Univ Mass Amherst MA 01003

FERNANDEZ Y FERNANDEZ, ENRIQUE, b Madrid, Spain, Feb 17, 29; US citizen; m 62. SPANISH LANGUAGE & LITERATURE. *Educ:* Sem Metrop Oviedo, Span, BA, 50, STB, 54; Temple Univ, MA, 68; Univ Pa, PhD(Span), 73. *Prof Exp:* Secular priest, Archdiocese Oviedo, Spain, 54-61; consult Span lit, In de Rechte Straat Found, 61-64; minister, United Church Christ, Reading, Pa, 64-69; assoc prof, 69-80, PROF SPAN, EASTERN COL, PA, 80- *Mem:* Am Asn Teachers Span & Port; MLA; Renaissance Soc Am; AAUP. *Res:* Spanish and Hispanic American culture; Latin American novel; 16th century Spanish literature. *Publ:* Auth, Para Ti, Universitario, Publ Juventud, 65; Las Biblias del Exilio, Ed Caribe, 76; Espana y la Independencia de los Estados Unidos, Circulo Espanol, Philadelphia, Pa, 77; La perspectiva simbolica de Mallea en Los Enemigos del Alma, Studium Ovetense, 77; Contexto religioso y mensaje profetico de Historia de una Pasion Argentina, Cuadernos Hispanoam, 77; Spain's diplomats in Philadelphia, Pa Heritage, 78; 11 articles in Span ed, New International Dictionary of the Christian Church, Ed Caribe, 79; Dos traducciones del Cantar de los Cantar de los Cantares, Studium Ovetense, 79; Spain's contribution to the independence of the United States, Revista/Review Interamericana, 80. *Mailing Add:* 251 W DeKlab Pike D-509 King of Prussia PA 19406

FERRACANE, GERARDO, b Muro Lucano, Italy, Apr 20, 43. ROMANCE LANGUAGES, CLASSICAL HISTORY. *Educ:* Univ Florence, BA, 64, PhD(Ital), 68; Univ Leningrad, cert Russ lang, 76. *Prof Exp:* Instr Ital, Univ Warsaw, 68-69 & Int Inst Madrid, 70-71; asst prof, 72-79, ASSOC PROF ITAL, UNIV PR, MAYAGUEZ, 79- *Concurrent Pos:* Nat Endowment for Humanities summer sem, Stanford Univ, 79. *Mem:* MLA; PR Asn Univ Prof; PR Asn Univ Prof Lang(secy, 74-75). *Res:* Fourteenth century Italian literature; modern Italian novel; Italian Renaissance. *Publ:* coauth, Handbook of Selected Episodes of Inferno, Ed Univ PR, Rio Piedras, 76; introd, transl & commentary of The Prince by Machiavelli, 76 & of On the Dignity of Man by Pico Della Mirandola, 77, Ed Florentia, Boston; auth, Twenty years of Italian filmmaking: 1945-1965, Atenea, Univ PR, 78; Introd, transl & commentary, De Breuitate Vitae, Seneca. *Mailing Add:* Dept of Humanities Univ of PR Mayaguez PR 00708

FERRAN, JAIME, b Cervera, Spain, July 13, 28; m 60; c 1. FOREIGN LANGUAGES. *Educ:* Univ Barcelona, Lic, 51; Univ Madrid, Dr, 66. *Prof Exp:* Prof ayudante, Univ Madrid, 53-54; instr Span, Colgate Univ, 60-62; from asst prof to assoc prof, 63-72, PROF SPAN LIT, SYRACUSE UNIV, 72- *Concurrent Pos:* Prof, Univ Bogota, 65; spec lectr, Vanderbilt Semester in Spain, 66; mem, Inst Estudios Ilerdenses, 67. *Honors & Awards:* Lazarillo Prize, 68. *Publ:* Auth, Descubrimiento de America, Editora Nac, 57; Angel en Espana, 60, Antologia de Juan Maragall, 60, Antologia de Eugenio D'Ors, 60, Doncel, Madrid; Libro de Ondina, Papelas de son Armadans, 64; Nuevas Cantigas, Adonais, madrid, 66; Tarde de Circo, Editora Nac, 67; Angel en Colombia, Doncel, Madrid, 67. *Mailing Add:* Dept of Span Lit Syracuse Univ Syracuse NY 13210

FERRARI, LENA M, b Brooklyn, NY, June 7, 13. FOREIGN LANGUAGES. *Educ:* Brooklyn Col, BA, 34; Columbia Univ, MA, 36, PhD, 62. *Prof Exp:* Lectr Ital, Marymount Col, NY, 54-56; teacher Latin & Ital, Wash Irving High Sch, New York, 56-58; from lectr to asst prof Ital, Columbia Univ, 57-65; asst prof, St John's Univ, 65-67, assoc prof Ital, 67-78; RETIRED. *Mem:* MLA; Am Asn Teachers Ital; Renaissance Soc Am; Classical Asn Atlantic States; Soc Ital Hist Studies Res Italian Renaissance. *Publ:* Antonio Ivani a Volterra, Rassegna Volterrana, Italy, 65. *Mailing Add:* 522 92nd St Brooklyn NY 11209

FERRER, OLGA PRJEVALINSKAYA, b Nice, France, Apr 25, 12; nat US; m 39, 55; c 1. SPANISH, RUSSIAN. *Educ:* Univ Valencia, Lic 33; Sorbonne, Cert de Lic, 37, PhD, 48. *Prof Exp:* Asst in charge Latin & philos, Univ Valencia, 33; asst in charge, Inst Higher Learning, Mataro, Spain, 33-36; res asst to Menendez Pidal, Columbia Univ, 37-38; assoc prof Romance lang, Univ Buffalo, 49-60, La State Univ, New Orleans, 60-68; PROF RUSSIAN & SPAN, UNIV MD, BALTIMORE COUNTY, 68- *Concurrent Pos:* Junta para Ampliacion de Estudios e Investigaciones Cientificas grant, Slavic studies; grant Int Univ Santander, 34-36; consult, Le Club Francais Livre, 47-48; Am Philos Soc grant, 55; reviewer, Books Abroad, World Lit Today, 56- *Mem:* Am Asn Teachers Span & Port; MLA; Am Asn Teachers Slavic & EEurop Lang; Inst Int Lit Iberoam. *Res:* Spanish literature of the 16th and 17th centuries; contemporary Spanish literature; Russian literature. *Publ:* Auth, El Cantar de la Campana de Igor, Samaran, Madrid, 41; El Sistema Estetico de C J Cela, Castalia, Madrid 60; Las almas muertas de Gogoll y el Quijote, Cuadernos de Lit; Theater in the USSR, Bks Abroad, 7/65; La America Latina en la Union Sovietica, Cuadernos Am, Mex, 67; En torno al teatro sovietica actual, Insula, Madrid, 9/59; M A Sholojov, Novedades de Moscin, Moscow, 964. *Mailing Add:* Dept of Foreign Lang Univ of Md Baltimore County Baltimore MD 21228

FERRIGNO, JAMES MOSES, b Lawrence, Mass, Apr 20, 10; m 40; c 4. ROMANCE LANGUAGES. *Educ:* Boston Univ, AB, 32, AM, 34, PhD, 51; Univ Rome, Italy, cert, 35. *Prof Exp:* Asst, Inst Int Educ, Univ Rome, 34-35; instr, high sch, Fitchburg, Mass, 37-46; asst prof Romance lang, Ft Devens Ctr, Univ Mass, 46-48 & Amherst Ctr, 48-53, from assoc prof to prof, 53-63; prof romance lang, Univ Dayton, 63-75, chmn dept lang, 63-71; RETIRED. *Concurrent Pos:* Lectr, Boston Univ, 47-48. *Mem:* MLA; Am Asn Teachers Span & Port; Am Asn Teachers Ital; Am Coun Teaching Foreign Lang. *Res:* Comparative Romance linguistics; influence of Spanish and Catalan in Sicilian and other South Italian dialects; phonology and syntax of Costa Rican Spanish. *Publ:* Coauth, Everyday Spanish for the Language Laboratory, Univ Mass, 58; Continuing Spanish I and II, Am Bk Co, 67 & Van Nostrand, 73. *Mailing Add:* 1145-B S Atlantic Ave Cocoa Beach FL 32931

FERRIS, WILLIAM N, b Bellaire, Ohio, Dec 23, 22; m 50; c 3. FRENCH, SPANISH. *Educ:* Bethany Col, AB, 49; Univ NC, MA, 55, PhD(Romance lang), 63. *Prof Exp:* Instr French & Span, Univ NC, 55-57 & 60-61; from instr to assoc prof, Bethany Col, WVa, 61-65; assoc prof, 65-80, PROF FRENCH & CHMN FOREIGN LANG, MILLIKEN UNIV, 65- *Concurrent Pos:* Fulbright-Hays grant, Nat Univ Mex, 64. *Res:* Mediaeval French literature; Anglo-Norman literature; Mexican drama. *Publ:* Auth, Arthur's golden dragon, 11/60 & The amorphous John of Canterbury, Romance Notes. *Mailing Add:* Dept of Foreign Lang Millikin Univ Decatur IL 62522

FERRUA, PIETRO MICHELE STEFANO, b Sanremo, Italy, Sept 18, 30; Brazil citizen; m 58; c 2. ROMANCE LANGUAGES & LITERATURES. *Educ:* Univ Geneve, Switz, BA, 57; Pontif Univ, Rio de Janeiro, MA, 65; Univ Ore, PhD(Romance lang), 73. *Prof Exp:* Prof French, Alliance Francaise, 64-69; dean instr polycult, Centro Brasileiro de Estudos Int, Rio de Janeiro, 65-67; asst prof Port, Portland State Univ, 70-73, assoc prof, 70-80, PROF FRENCH, ITAL & SPAN, LEWIS & CLARK COL, 80- *Concurrent Pos:* Travel grant, Am Coun Learned Soc. *Honors & Awards:* Gilbert Chinard Award, Inst Francais de Washington. *Mem:* Am Asn French Teachers; Am Asn Ital Teachers; Am Asn Teachers Span & Port; Romanian Study Asn; Am Asn Lang Specialists. *Res:* Romance languages and literatures; social history; film criticism. *Publ:* Auth, Eros chez Thanatos: Essaisur les Romans de Marc Saporta, Avant-Garde, Paris, 79; Le bon et le mauvais gout dans le theatre de Claudel, Berenice, Vol 1 No 1; Incontridi Pirandello col cinema, Can J Ital Studies, Vol 3, No 2; Indagocoes metafisicas na obra de Elisa Lispector, Ky Romance Quart, Vol 26, No 4; Antonioni's Interpretation of Reality and Literature, Forum italicum, Vol 13, No 1; Sur Quelques analogies entre le Futurisme et le Lettrisme cahiers Roumains d'Etudes Litteraires, 78; contribr, A Critical Bibliography of French Literature, Syracuse Univ Press; Columbia Dict Mod Europ Lit, 80. *Mailing Add:* Dept of Foreign Lang & Lit Lewis & Clark Col 0615 SW Palatine Hill Rd Portland OR 97219

FESTLE, JOHN EDWARD, b Chicago, Ill, July 28, 25. CLASSICAL LITERATURE, PHILOSOPHY OF EDUCATION. *Educ:* Loyola Univ, Ill, BA, 47, AM, 49; WBaden Col, PhL, 49; Oxford Univ, BA, 53, MA, 56; Gregorian Univ, Italy, STL, 57. *Prof Exp:* Assoc dean & instr classics, Milford Col Lib Arts, 58-61, asst prof, 61-66; asst prof classic studies, 66-75, assoc dir honors prog, Lewis Towers Campus, 68-74, asst prof classics, Rome Ctr, 69-70, assoc prof & freshman dean, 75-77; assoc dean col arts & sci, Loyola Univ Chicago, Water Tower Campus, 77-82. *Concurrent Pos:* Vis lectr, Loyola Univ, Ill, 62-63. *Mem:* Am Philol Asn; Vergilian Soc; Virgil Soc. *Res:* Classical Greek and Latin poets; history and principles of education. *Mailing Add:* Dept of Class Studies Loyola Univ Chicago IL 60626

FETTING, HANS FREDERICK, Historical Linguistics, Medieval Literature. See Vol II

FETZER, JOHN F, GERMAN. *Educ:* NY Univ, AB, 53; Columbia Univ, MA, 57; Univ Calif, Berkeley, PhD(Ger), 65. *Prof Exp:* Instr Ger, Northwestern Univ, 62-65; from asst prof to assoc prof, 65-76, PROF GER LANG & LIT, UNIV CALIF, DAVIS, 76-, CHMN, DEPT GER & RUSS, 81- *Concurrent Pos:* Am Philos Soc & Humanities Inst fels, 69-70; Guggenheim, 80-81. *Mem:* MLA; Am Asn Teachers Ger; Western Soc Ger Studies. *Res:* German Romanticism; relationships between music and literature; German bibliography. *Publ:* Auth, Ritter Gluck's Unglück: The crisis of creativity in the Age of Epigone, 71, Ger Quart; Schatten ohne Frau: Marginalia on a Werther motif, Ger Rev, 71; The scales of injustice: Comments on Heinrich Böll's Die Waage der Baleks, Ger Quart, 72; Recent trends in Clemens Brentano research (1968-1970), Lit Wiss Jahrbuch, 72; Romantic Orpheus: Profiles of Clemens Brentano, Univ Calif, 74; Paul Elbogen, In: Deutsche Exillliteratur I, Francke, 76; coauth, Bibliographie der Buchrezensionen für deutsche Literatur, Univ Microfilms, 77; Clemens Brentano, Twayne, 81. *Mailing Add:* Dept of Ger & Russ Univ of Calif Davis CA 95616

FETZER, LELAND, b Salt Lake City, Utah, Aug 26, 30; m 50; c 3. RUSSIAN LITERATURE. *Educ:* Univ Utah, BS, 51; Univ Calif, MLS, 56, MA, 62, PhD(Russ lit), 69. *Prof Exp:* Assoc prof Russ, Univ Calif, 65-66; from asst prof to assoc prof Russ & Ger, 66-76, PROF RUSS, SAN DIEGO STATE UNIV, 76- *Res:* The relationship between Russian literature and Russian painting; Russian science fiction. *Publ:* Auth, Tolstoy and Mormonism, spring 71 & Bernard DeVoto and the Mormon tradition, autumn 71, Dialogue; The Bunin-S Koteliansky-D H Lawrence-Leonard Woolf version of The gentleman from San Francisco, Virginia Woolf Quart, summer 73; Russian Air Force in World War II, Doubleday, 73; Art and assassination, Russ Rev, 1/75; The Jewish predicament of Isaac Levitan, Soviet Jewish Affairs, 2/81; An Anthology of Pre-Revolutionary Russian Science Fiction, Ardis, 82. *Mailing Add:* Dept of Ger & Russ San Diego State Univ San Diego CA 92115

FEUERLICHT, IGNACE, b Austria; US citizen. GERMAN, ROMANCE LANGUAGES. *Educ:* Univ Vienna, PhD(Ger), 32. *Prof Exp:* Asst Ger, lycee, St Etienne, 30-31; teacher French & Ger, Realgym, Vienna, 32-38; teacher Ger, Ecole Normale Seine, 38-39; teacher, high schs, NY & NJ, 43-46; asst prof Ger, Sampson Col, 46-47; assoc prof French, Span & Ger, State Univ NY, New Paltz, 47-57, prof, 57-74. *Res:* European literatures of the 19th and 20th centuries. *Publ:* Auth, Vom Wesen der deutschen Idylle, Ger Rev, 47; Camus's L'Etranger reconsidered, PMLA, 12/63; Thomas Mann und die Grenzen des Ich, Winter, Heidelberg, 66; Vom Ursprung der Minne, In: Der Provenzalische Minnesang, Wiss Buchges, Darmstadt, 67; Thomas Mann, Twayne, 68; Alienation: From the past to the future, Greenwood Press, 78; Werther's suicide, 78 & Heine's Lorelei, 80, Ger Quart. *Mailing Add:* 110 W 96th St New York NY 10025

FEUSTLE, JOSEPH A, JR, b Baltimore, Md, Nov 25, 42; m 73; c 1. LATIN AMERICAN LITERATURE. *Educ:* Univ Md, BA, 64, MA, 68, PhD(Latin Am lit), 74. *Prof Exp:* Instr Span, Univ Md, Baltimore County, 66-70; instr, Univ Md, College Park, 70-72; instr, 72-74, from asst to assoc prof, 74-80, PROF SPAN & CHMN FOREIGN LANG, UNIV TOLEDO, 80- *Mem:* MLA; Asn Int Hispanistas; Inst Int Lit Iberoamericana; Am Asn Teachers Span & Port; Midwest & S Atlantic Mod Lang Asns. *Res:* Latin American modernism; Latin American fiction; Latin American poetry. *Publ:* Auth, La metafisica de Amado Nervo, Hispanofila, 70; El concepto del tiempo en el ensayo de Ezequiel Martinez Estrada, Cuadernos Hispanoamericanos, 72; Hacia una interpretacion de Los empenos de una casa de Sor Juana Ines de la Cruz, Explicacion de textos literarios, 73; Mario Vargas Llosa: A labryrinth of solitude, Tex Studies Lit & Lang, 78; Poesia y mistica: Dario, Jimenez y Paz, Univ Veracruzana, 78; Blanco de Octavio Paz: Una sintesis poetica de tres culturas, Cuadernos Hispanoamericanos, 79; Juan Ramon Jimenez: El concepto de la desnudez, Alaluz, 81; Juan Ramon Jimenez y la poesia mexicana, Revista Iberoamericana (in prep). *Mailing Add:* Dept of For Lang Univ of Toledo Toledo OH 43606

FIBER, LOUISE, b Detroit, Mich, Feb 9, 35; m 73. FRENCH LANGUAGE & LITERATURE. *Educ:* Univ Mich, BA, 56; Middlebury Col, MA, 59; Northwestern Univ, PhD(French), 72. *Prof Exp:* Instr French, Ohio Univ, 62-65; from instr to asst prof, 70-75, assoc prof, 75-81, PROF FRENCH, MIAMI UNIV, 81- *Mem:* MLA; Am Asn Teachers Fr; Midwestern Mod Lang Asn; Soc Intercultural Educ, Training & Res. *Res:* Nineteenth century French theater and novel; 20th century French theater; cross-cultural communication. *Publ:* Auth, Ruben Dario's debt to Paul Verlaine in El Reino interior, Romance Notes, 73; A selected guide to journals in the field of French language and literature, Fr Rev, spring 74; The masked avenger: Historical analogue in Eugene Sue's Les Mysteres de Paris, Fr Forum, Vol 1, No 3; Innocents abroad: Foreign language learning and the use of the overseas community, Am Dept Foreign Lang Bull, 76; The mask of language in Musset's Proverbes, Romance Notes, 77; The Voyant in Balzac's Massimilla Donni and La Peau de Chagrin, L'Esprit Createur, 78; Alchemy & the artist in Balzac's Gambara, Centerpoint, 78; co-ed, Towards Internationalism, Newbury House, 78. *Mailing Add:* Dept of French & Ital Miami Univ Oxford OH 45056

FICHTER, ANDREW JOHN, English Renaissance & Comparative Literature. See Vol II

FICHTNER, EDWARD G, b 31; US citizen. GERMANIC PHILOLOGY, GERMAN LINGUISTICS. *Educ:* Univ Ill, AB, 57; Ind Univ, MA, 60; Univ Pa, PhD(Ger), 66. *Prof Exp:* Instr Ger, St Joseph's Col, Pa, 62-63 & Columbia Univ, 63-67; from asst prof to assoc prof, 67-77, PROF GER, 78-, MEM DOCTORAL FAC GER LANG, GRAD CTR, QUEENS COL, CITY UNIV NEW YORK, 73- *Concurrent Pos:* Managing ed, Word, 80. *Mem:* MLA; Ling Soc Am; Int Ling Asn. *Res:* Structure of modern German; medieval German literature; medieval Scandinavian language and literature. *Publ:* Auth, The Trager-Smith stress levels of English: A reinterpretation, Int Rev Appl Ling, 2/72; The pronunciation of the English digraph ng, Int Rev App Ling, 10: 21-33; The calculus of honor: Vengeance, satisfaction, and reconciliation in the Story of Thorstein Staff-Struck, In: Germanic Studies in Honor of Otto Springer, K & S Enterprises, 78; English and German Syntax: A Contrastive Analysis on Generative Tagmemic Principles, Verlag, 79; Gift exchange and initiation in the Audunar Thattr Vestfirzka, Scand Studies, 51: 249-272; Measuring syntactic complexity: The quantification of one factor in linguistic difficulty, Die Unterrichtspraxis, 13: 67-75; Patterns of arithmetical proportion in the Nibelungenlied, In: Essays in the Numerical Criticism of Medieval Literature, Bucknell Univ Press, 80; The position of modal adverbs in German, Word, 31: 73-90. *Mailing Add:* Dept of Germantic & Slavic Langs Queens Col Flushing NY 11367

FICKERT, KURT JON, b Pausa, Ger, Dec 19, 20; US citizen; m 46; c 3. GERMAN, LANGUAGE & LITERATURE. *Educ:* Hofstra Col, AB, 41; NY Univ, MA, 47, PhD, 52. *Prof Exp:* Asst, Ind Univ, 41-42; from instr to asst prof Ger, Hofstra Col, 47-53; asst prof, Fla State Univ, 53-54; asst prof Ger & English, Ft Hays Kans State Col, 54-56; from asst prof to assoc prof Ger, 56-67, chmn dept lang, 70-75, PROF GER, WITTENBERG UNIV, 67- *Honors & Awards:* Citation Meritorious Achievement, Soc Ger-Am Studies, 73. *Mem:* Am Asn Teachers Ger. *Res:* Modern German literature. *Publ:* Auth, The window metaphor in Kafka's Trial, Monatshefte, winter 66; introd, Otto Dix's Der Krieg, Garland, NY & London, 72; To Heaven and Back: The New Morality in the Plays of Friedrich Durenmatt, Univ Ky, 72; Hermann Hesse's Quest: The Evolution of the Dichter Figure in His Work, York Press, 78; Kafka's Doubles, Peter Lang, 79; Signs and Portents: Myth in the Work of Wolfgang Borchert, York Press, 80. *Mailing Add:* Dept of Lang Wittenberg Univ Springfield OH 45501

FIDO, FRANCO, b Venice, Italy, July 15, 31; m 58; c 2. ITALIAN & COMPARATIVE LITERATURE. *Educ:* Univ Pisa, DLett(Ital lit), 53; Ital govt, Lib Doc, 69; Brown Univ, MA, 71. *Prof Exp:* French govt fel, Sorbonne, 53-54; lectr Ital, Faculte des Lett, Dijon, 54-58; instr, Univ Calif, Berkeley, 58-61; lectr, Faculte des Lett, Grenoble, 61-63; from asst prof to prof Ital, Univ Calif, Los Angeles, 63-69, chmn dept, 66-69; prof, Brown Univ, 69-78; R Pierotti prof Ital lit, Stanford Univ, 78-79; UNIV PROF, BROWN UNIV, 79- *Mem:* MLA; Am Asn Teachers Ital; Dante Soc Am; Am Soc 18th Century Studies. *Res:* Italian literature and theatre from the 18th to the 20th century; Boccaccio; Italian Renaissance, especially Machiavelli. *Publ:* Auth, Machiavelli, Storia della Critica, Palumbo, Italy, 65; ed, Baretti, Opere, Rizzoli, Italy, 67; ed, Lettere Sparse, Centro Studi Piemontesi, 76; Scritti Teatrali, Longo, 77; auth, Guida a Goldoni--Teatro e Societa nel Settecento, Einaudi, 77; Le Metamorfosi del Centauro: Studi e Letture da Boccaccio a Pirandello, Bulzoni, 77. *Mailing Add:* Dept of Hisp & Ital Studies Brown Univ Providence RI 02512

FIEDLER, THEODORE, b Altenburg, Mo, Oct 1, 42; m 63; c 1. GERMAN & COMPARATIVE LITERATURE. *Educ:* Washington Univ, AB, 64, MA(Ger) & MA(comp lit), 66; Univ Tübingen, PhD(Ger), 69. *Prof Exp:* Asst prof, Univ Calif, Irvine, 68-75; assoc prof, Univ Tex, San Antonio, 76-77; ASSOC PROF GER, UNIV KY, 77- *Concurrent Pos:* Fulbright fel, 66-68; Am Philos Soc grant-in-aid, 73. *Mem:* MLA; Int Brecht Soc; Semiotic Soc Am. *Res:* Twentieth century German literature and literary theory; poetics; film. *Publ:* contribr, Holderlin: An Early Modern, Univ Mich, 72; Wahrheit und Sprache: Festschrift Bert Nagel, Alfred Kummerle, 72; auth, Brecht and Cavafy Comp Lit, 73; Taking Ingarden seriously: Critical reflection on The Cognition of the Literary Work of Art, J BSP, 75; Hoffmannsthals' Reitergeschichte und ihre Leser, zur Politik der Irmie, Germanisch-Romanische Monatshefte, 76; The Reception of a Socialist Classic: Kunert and Biermann read Brecht, In: Brecht: Political Theory and Literary Practice, Univ Ga, 80. *Mailing Add:* Dept of Ger Univ of Ky Lexington KY 40506

FIELD, GEORGE WALLIS, b Cobourg, Ont, Mar 5, 14; m 49; c 4. GERMAN. *Educ:* Univ Toronto, BA, 35, MA, 46, PhD(Ger), 48. *Prof Exp:* Lectr Ger, 48-50, from asst prof to assoc prof, 50-64, chmn dept, 66-74, prof, 64-79, EMER PROF GER, VICTORIA COL, UNIV TORONTO, 79- *Mem:* MLA; Can Asn Univ Teachers Ger. *Res:* Schiller and 18th century philosophy; contemporary novel; Thomas Mann, Hermann Hesse. *Publ:* Auth, Schiller's theory of the idyl and Wilhelm Tell, Monatshefte, 1/50; Schiller's Maria Stuart, Univ Toronto Quart, 4/60; ed, Heine: A Verse Selection, 65 & Fontane: Irrungen, Wirrungen, 67, Macmillan, London; auth, Hermann Hesse, Twayne, 70 & Hippocrene, 72; A Literary History of Germany: The Nineteenth Century, Ernest Benn, London, 74; Hermann Hesse: Kommentar zu sämtlichen Werken, Akademischer Verlag, Stuttgart, 77, 2nd ed, 79; Idiosyncrasies of Dubslav von Stechlin: A Fontane Original, In: Formen realistischer Erzählkunst, Festschrift für Charlotte Jolles, Nottingham, 79. *Mailing Add:* Dept of Ger Victoria Col Univ of Toronto Toronto ON M5S 1K7 Can

FIELD, THOMAS TILDEN, b Hardwick, Vt, Sept 9, 49; m 77; c 1. ROMANCE & THEORETICAL LINGUISTICS. *Educ:* Wheaton Col, BA, 71; Cornell Univ, MA, 75, PhD(ling), 78. *Prof Exp:* Instr French, State Univ NY Col Oswego, 78-79; ASST PROF LING & FRENCH, UNIV MD BALTIMORE COUNTY, 79- *Concurrent Pos:* Bibliogr, Comp Romance Ling Newsletter, 81-; consult, Charlotte-Mecklenburg Sch, NC, 82. *Honors & Awards:* Gilbert Chinard Prize in Pedagogy, 82. *Mem:* Ling Soc Am; MLA; Am Asn Teachers French; Asn Int d'Etudes Occitanes. *Res:* Occitan and French linguistics; textual analysis; phonology. *Publ:* Auth, The sociolinguistic situation of modern Occitan, French Rev, 80; Language survival in a European context: The future of Occitan, Lang Problems and Lang Planning, 81; contribr, Phonologica 1980, Innsbrucker Beitrage zur Sprachwissenschaft, 82; coauth, A linguistic and semiotic approach to textual analysis, French Rev, 82; contribr, Actes du VIII Congres international de Langue et Litterature d'Oc, Marche Romane (in prep). *Mailing Add:* Dept of Mod Lang & Ling Univ of Md Baltimore County Catonsville MD 21228

FIELD, WILLIAM HUGH W, b Leatherhead, England, Oct 14, 26; m 50; c 2. ROMANCE LANGUAGES. *Educ:* Univ Edinburgh, MA, 51; Univ Chicago, PhD, 65. *Prof Exp:* From instr to asst prof French & Span, Univ Chicago, 58-64; asst prof, 64-78, ASSOC PROF FRENCH, UNIV WASH, 78- *Res:* Old Provencal; Old French language and literature. *Publ:* Auth, The Picard origin of the name Pathelin, Mod Philol, 5/68; Raimon Vidal; poetry and prose, Vol II, Univ NC, 71; Le Roman d'Andrieu de Fransa, Rev Langues Romanes, 76; Raimon Vidal, Vol I, Univ NC (in prep). *Mailing Add:* Dept of Romance Lang Univ of Wash Seattle WA 98195

FIENE, DONALD MARK, b Schenectady, NY, Feb 24, 30; m 56; c 2. SLAVIC LANGUAGES & LITERATURE. *Educ:* Univ Louisville, BA, 59, MA, 61; Ind Univ, PhD(Slavic langs & lit), 74. *Prof Exp:* Instr English & humanities, Eng Col, Univ Louisville, 62-65 & 69-72; asst prof, 74-79, ASSOC PROF RUSSIAN, DEPT GER & SLAVIC STUDIES, UNIV TENN, 79- *Concurrent Pos:* Res awards, Univ Tenn, 75, 76 & 82; rev ed, Mod Lang J, 77-80; rev ed, Dostoevsky Studies, 81- *Mem:* Am Asn Advan Slavic Studies; Am Asn Teachers Slavic & E Europ Lang; Southern Comp Lit Asn; Int Dostoevsky Soc. *Res:* Russian fiction, various authors since 19th century; influence of Russian literature on American authors; reception of American literature in the Soviet Union. *Publ:* Coauth, Bibliographie des oeuvres de M A Ossorguine, Inst d-Etudes Slaves Paris, 73; auth, Alexander Solzhenitsyn: An International Bibliography of Writings By and About Him, 1962-1973, Ardis, 73; ed, translr & article in: Snowball Berry Red and Other Stories, Ann Arbor, 78; Entries on F Gladkov, V Lidin, V Maramzin, M Osorgin, V Shukshin and V Voynovich in Columbia Dict Mod Europ Lit, 2nd ed, Columbia Univ Press, 80; A comparison of the Soviet and Possev editions of The Master and Margarita, with a note on interpretation of the novel, Can Am Slavid Studies, summer-fall 81; R Crumb Checklist of Work and Criticism, Boatner Norton Press, 81; Elements of Dostoevsky in the novels of Kurt Vonnegut, Dostoevsky Studies, 2, 81; M A Osorgin, Selected Stories, Reminiscences & Essays, Ardis, 82. *Mailing Add:* Dept of Ger & Slavic Langs Univ of Tenn Knoxville TN 37916

FIFE, AUSTIN EDWIN, b Lincoln, Idaho, Dec 18, 09; m 34; c 2. FRENCH LANGUAGE & LITERATURE. *Educ:* Stanford Univ, BA, 34, MA, 35, PhD(Romance lang), 39; Harvard Univ, MA, 37. *Prof Exp:* Instr French, Santa Monica City Col, 39-42; from asst prof to prof, Occidental Col, 45-58; Guggenheim fel, 58-59; adv foreign lang, US Off Educ, Washington, DC, 59-60; prof French & head dept lang & philos, Utah State Univ, 60-75; RETIRED. *Concurrent Pos:* Fulbright exchange prof, French Nat Mus, 49-50; Nat Endowment for Humanities sr scholar, 71-72. *Mem:* MLA; fel Am Folklore Soc(vpres, 57-59 & 67-69). *Res:* French literature of Middle Ages, Renaissance and 18th century; American folklore and folk music. *Publ:* Co-ed Latin American Interlude, Utah State Univ, 66, coauth, Songs of the Cowboys, 66 & Cowboy and Western Songs, 69, C N Potter; co-ed, Forms upon the Frontier, 69; coauth, Heaven on Horseback, 70, Utah State Univ; Ballads of the great West, Am West, 70; contribr, Lore of Faith and Folly, Univ Utah, 71; co-ed, Bill Bailey came Home, Utah State Univ, 73. *Mailing Add:* 686 E 10 North Logan UT 84321

FIFE, JAMES DAVID, b Gridley, Calif, Nov 2, 32; m 58; c 7. FRENCH, SPANISH. *Educ:* Brigham Young Univ, BA, 57, MA, 60; Syracuse Univ, PhD(Romance lang), 71. *Prof Exp:* Teacher English, speech & math, Live Oak Union High Sch, Calif, 58-59; teacher French & English, Lincoln High Sch, Stockton, Calif, 60-62; asst & instr French, Syracuse Univ, 62-67; instr, 67-71, actg head French sect, 77-78, ASST PROF FRENCH, UNIV OKLA, 71- *Honors & Awards:* Regents Award Super Teaching, Regents Univ Okla, 76. *Mem:* MLA; Am Asn Teachers Fr; SCent Mod Lang Asn; Am Coun Teaching Foreign Lang. *Res:* Gustave Flaubert; Jules Michelet; 19th century short fiction in France. *Publ:* Auth, A Comparative Study of the Effectiveness of Live and Televised French Instruction, Brigham Young Univ, 66; Aspects of Michelet's Influence on Flaubert, Syracuse Univ, 71; contribr, Modern French Writing, Heinemann, London, 71; translr, That Everything in the World is Bound to End Up as a Book by Francois Chapon, Bks Abroad, 76. *Mailing Add:* Dept of Mod Lang & Lit Univ of Okla 780 Van Vleet Oval Room 202 Norman OK 73019

FIFER, ELIZABETH, b Pittsburgh, Pa, Aug 5, 44; m 70. COMPARATIVE LITERATURE, ENGLISH. *Educ:* Univ Mich, Ann Arbor, BA, 65, MA, 66, PhD(comp lit), 69. *Prof Exp:* Lectr humanities, Res Col, Univ Mich, 69-72; asst prof, 73-80, ASSOC PROF ENGLISH, LEHIGH UNIV, 80- *Mem:* MLA; Asn Theater Res. *Res:* Gertrude Stein; Modern literature; Modern drama. *Publ:* Auth, The confessions of Italo Sveno, Contemp Lit, 73: Sex-stereo typing in Geography & Plays, Univ Mich Papers Women's Studies, 75; Tragedy into melodrama, Lex et Scientia, 77; The interior theater of Gertrude Stein, Signs, 78. *Mailing Add:* Dept of English Lehigh Univ Bethlehem PA 18015

FIGUEROA-CHAPEL, RAMON ANTONIO, b Anasco, PR, Feb 26, 35. COMPARATIVE LITERATURE, MODERN LANGUAGES. *Educ:* Univ PR, BS, 56; Univ Paris, MA, 59; Univ Munich, Dipl, 60 Fordham Univ, PhD(comp lit), 64. *Prof Exp:* Instr physics, 56-57, asst prof humanities, 64-68, assoc prof French & lit, 68-72, PROF COMP LIT, UNIV PR, MAYAGÜEZ, 72-, ASSOC DIR DEPT HUMANITIES, 73- *Concurrent Pos:* Vis prof philos, Inter-Am Univ, 69- *Mem:* MLA; Soc Prof Francais. *Res:* Literary theory; nineteenth century Spanish literature; symbolism in poetry. *Publ:* Auth, Poesia, 69 & Quinto Evangelio (poetry), 70, Vascoamericana, Spain; ed, Readings in Humanities, Vols I & II, 73 & 74 & auth, Theory of the Novel, Rev de Letras, Univ PR. *Mailing Add:* Dept of Humanities Univ of PR College Sta Mayaguez PR 00708

FIGURITO, JOSEPH, b Gaeta, Italy, Nov 24, 22; US citizen; m 56. ROMANCE LANGUAGES, PHILOLOGY. *Educ:* Boston Col, AB, 47; Middlebury Col, MA, 49, DML, 53; Univ Rome, cert, 52. *Prof Exp:* Instr French, 47-48, instr Romance lang, 48-54, asst prof, 55-68, actg chmn dept, 71, ASSOC PROF MOD LANG, BOSTON COL, 68- *Concurrent Pos:* Asst prof, exten, Harvard Univ, 57-68 & assoc prof, 68- *Honors & Awards:* Silver Medal of Culture, Italy, 62; Knight, Order of Merit, Italy, 68. *Mem:* MLA; Am Asn Teachers Ital; Dante Soc Am; Mediaeval Acad Am. *Res:* Dante, Boccaccio, Petrarch and Leopardi; 17th century French literature. *Publ:* Auth, A Student Guide to the Divina Commedia, Eaton, 59; L'Ultimo Baluardo dei Borboni nel Risorgimento, Italica, 9/61; contribr, A Concordance to Dante's Divine Comedy, Harvard Univ, 65; auth, Dante, Divine Comedy, Bk Notes, Barnes & Noble, 69; Leopardi Ribelle, In: Leopardi e l'Ottocento, Acts of II International Congress of Studies on Leopardi, Olschki, Florence, 70. *Mailing Add:* Dept of Romance Lang & Lit Boston Col Chestnut Hill MA 02167

FILER, MALVA ESTHER, b Arg, Feb 25, 33; US citizen; m 64; c 2. SPANISH AMERICAN LITERATURE. *Educ:* Univ Buenos Aires, BA, 58; Columbia Univ, PhD(philos), 66. *Prof Exp:* Lectr Span, 63-66, instr, 66-68, asst prof, 69-72, ASSOC PROF SPAN, BROOKLYN COL, 73- *Mem:* MLA; Hist Inst US; Inst Int Lit Iberoam; Int Assoc Comp Lit. *Res:* Contemporary Spanish American literature. *Publ:* Coauth, Eduardo Mallea y Miguel de Unamuno, Cuadernos Hispanoamericanos, 5/68; auth, Los mundos de Julio Cortazar, 70 & coauth, Homenaje a Julio cortazar, 72, Las Americas; The ambivalence of the hand in Cortazar's fiction, In: The Final Island, Univ Okla Press, 78; Vargas Llosa, the novelist as critic, In: Mario Vargas Llosa, Univ Tex Press, 78; auth, La novela y el dialogo de los textos, In: Aama de A Di Benedetto, Mexico, 82; coauth, A Change of Skin and the shaping of a Mexican time, Carlos Fuentes, Univ Tex Press, 82. *Mailing Add:* Dept of Mod Lang Brooklyn Col Bedford Ave & Ave H Brooklyn NY 11210

FILIPS-JUSWIGG, KATHERINA P, US citizen. RUSSIAN LITERATURE, EUROPEAN LITERATURE. *Educ:* Pedag Inst, Vinnitsa, USSR, BA, 53; Univ Montreal, MA, 55, PhD(Russ lang & lit), 61. *Prof Exp:* Asst prof Russ & Ukrainian lang & lit, Univ Alta, 61-62; assoc prof Russ lang, lit & cult, Ore State Univ, 62-67; assoc prof, 67-71, chmn dept Slavic lang, 68-74, PROF RUSS LANG, LIT & CULT, UNIV WIS-MILWAUKEE, 71- *Concurrent Pos:* Consult Russ lit, Slavic & EEurop J, 78. *Mem:* MLA; Am Asn Teachers Slavic & EEurop Lang; Am Asn Advan Slavic Studies; Asn Russ-Am Scholars US; Int Dostoevsky Soc. *Res:* European novel. *Publ:* Auth, Russian words in the German post-war memoirs, Slavic & EEurop J, 64; Names of poets in the poetry of Georgij Ivanov, Names, 67; Innokentij Volodin in Solzhenitsyn's The First Circle . . . , Trans Asn Russ-Am Scholars, 74; New chapters for Solzenicyn's V Kruge Pervom . . . , Russ Lang J, 75; ed, Boris Singermann (Moskau), Brechts' Zur Aesthetik der Montage, Dreigroschenoper, Brecht-Jahrbuch 1976, 76; auth, Nemtsy o Russkikh (Russians in German Memoirs), Slavica (Volga Bks), 76; Russkaja religioznaja zizn' . . . , 76 & Anglo-American books on L N Tolstoy: A critical bibliography for the 70's, 78, Trans Asn Russ-Am Scholars. *Mailing Add:* Dept of Russ Univ of Wis 3203 N Downer Ave Milwaukee WI 53201

FILOCHE, JEAN-LUC C, b Rouen, France, May 20, 49; m 71. FRENCH LITERATURE. *Educ:* Univ de Rouen, France, Licence, 71; Univ Ill, MA, 72, PhD(French lit), 77. *Prof Exp:* Teaching asst French, Univ Ill, 71-77; ASST PROF FRENCH, UNIV SOUTHERN CALIF, 77- *Mem:* Cercle Francais de Poesie. *Res:* XIXth century literature; intertextuality; the awakening of the subconscious. *Publ:* Coauth, Translation of a poem by Aragon, Contemp Lit in Transl, 77. *Mailing Add:* Dept of French Univ of Southern Calif Los Angeles CA 90007

FIN, ROBERT GEORGE, b Budapest, Hungary, Mar 17, 19; US citizen. SLAVIC & EAST EUROPEAN LANGUAGES, FRENCH. *Educ:* Gregorian Univ, BPh, 40; Studium Gen OP, Budapest, STL, 44; State Teachers Col, Budapest, MEd, 48; Pazmany Peter Univ, STD, 48; Middlebury Col, MA, 58. *Prof Exp:* Instr philos, Divinity Col, Czech, 44-46; instr French High Sch, Hungary, 48-50; ASSOC PROF RUSSIAN, GANNON COL, 53-54, 68- *Res:* Visual aids in Soviet schools. *Mailing Add:* Dept of Lang Gannon Col Erie PA 16501

FINCH, CHAUNCEY EDGAR, b Carmi, Ill, Dec 16, 09; m 32; c 4. PHILOLOGY. *Educ:* Univ Ill, AB, 30, AM, 32; PhD, 37. *Prof Exp:* From instr to prof class lang, 36-78, chmn dept, 72-78, EMER PROF CLASS LANG, ST LOUIS UNIV, 78- *Concurrent Pos:* Ed, Class Bull, 72-80. *Mem:* Am Philol Asn: Class Asn Mid W & S. *Res:* Classical palaeography; linguistics; Russian. *Mailing Add:* Dept of Lang St Louis Univ St Louis MO 63103

FINCO, ALDO, b Asiago, Italy, Jan 5, 21; US citizen; m 58; c 2. FOREIGN LANGUAGES. *Educ:* Collegio Colombo, BA, 49; Boston Univ, BA, 55; Middlebury Col, MA, 63, DML(Ital, French & Span), 67. *Prof Exp:* Teacher French & Latin, Millis High Schs, Mass, 55-60; lectr Ital, Univ NH, 60-64; asst prof Ital, Univ Iowa, 65-68; assoc prof, 68-76, PROF ROMANCE LANG, TEX TECH UNIV, 76- *Concurrent Pos:* Teacher, French, Berwick Acad, Maine, 60-64. *Mem:* Am Asn Teachers Ital; Cent States Mod Lang Asn; Inst Ital Cult. *Res:* Italian trecento and ottocento. *Publ:* Auth, La voce degli esseri nelle liriche di Antonio Fogazzaro, Studies by mem SCent Mod Lang Asn, 69; L'arte di Antonio Fogazzaro, 70 & Letture Italiane per conversazione, 71; Grafica Toscana, Firenze, Italy; Appunti, Tex Tech Univ, 72; Una Donna Fogazzariana: Iole Moschini, Studies by mem SCent Mod Lang Asn, 73; L'umorismo di Antonio Fogazzaro, Romance Notes, 73. *Mailing Add:* Dept of Class & Romance Lang Texas Tech Univ Lubbock TX 79409

FINE, ELLEN SYDNEY, b New York, NY, Sept 30, 39; div. FRENCH LITERATURE & LANGUAGE. *Educ:* Smith Col, BA, 61; Univ Calif, Berkeley, MA, 64; NY Univ, PhD(French), 79. *Prof Exp:* Researcher dept doc, French Embassy Press & Info Serv, 63-64; asst prof, 64-80, ASSOC PROF FRENCH, KINGSBOROUGH COMMUNITY COL, 80- *Concurrent Pos:* Vis lectr, Jack P Eisner Inst Holocaust Studies of the City Univ New York, 81-82. *Mem:* MLA; Northeastern Mod Lang Asn; Am Asn Teachers Fr. *Res:* Holocaust studies; Elie Wiesel. *Publ:* Auth, Gerard de Nerval et le temps dans Sylvie, Nineteenth-Century Fr Studies, spring-summer 74; The journey homeward: The theme of the town in the works of Elie Wiesel, In: Responses to Elie Wiesel, Persea Press, 78; The return, In: Face to Face: An Interreligious Bull, spring 79; co-ed, The Holocaust, In: Centerpoint: A J of Interdisciplinary Studies, fall 80; auth, Witnesses: A tour of remembrance, Shoah, spring 80; The act of listening, Midstream, 8-9/81; Legacy of Night: The Literary Universe of Elie Wiesel, State Univ New York Press, 82. *Mailing Add:* 130 E 18th St New York NY 10003

FINEGAN, EDWARD , b New York, NY, June 25, 40. LINGUISTICS & ENGLISH LANGUAGE. *Educ:* Iona Col, BS, 62; Ohio Univ, MA, 64, PhD(English lang), 68. *Prof Exp:* Instr English, Ohio Univ, 64-66; instr ling, Case Western Reserve Univ, 66-68; asst prof English, 68-69; from asst prof to assoc prof English & ling, 69-76, chmn ling dept, 69-76, dir, Am Lang Inst in Tehran, Iran, 75-76, ASSOC PROF LING, UNIV SOUTHERN CALIF, 76- *Mem:* NCTE; Ling Soc Am; Am Dialect Soc; Law & Soc Asn. *Res:* Sociolinguistics; language attitudes; legal language. *Publ:* Auth, Linguistics, lexicography and attitudes toward usage during the last decade, Pac Coast Philol, 4/71; Attitudes toward English usage: The history of a war of words, NY Teachers Col Press, 80. *Mailing Add:* Dept of Ling Univ of Southern Calif Los Angeles CA 90007

FINELLO, DOMINICK LOUIS, b Mar 17, 44; US citizen. SPANISH RENAISSANCE & BAROQUE LITERATURE. *Educ:* Brooklyn Col, BA, 65; Univ Ill, Urbana-Champaign, MA, 67, PhD(Span), 72. *Prof Exp:* Asst prof, 71-75, ASSOC PROF SPAN, RIDER COL, 75- *Mem:* Inst Asn Hispanists; Cervantes Soc Am; Am Asn Teachers Span & Port; MLA. *Res:* Cervantes; 16th century Spanish literature; southern European Renaissance. *Publ:* Auth, Temas y formas de la literatura espanola, Revista Filol Espanola, 75; Cervantes y lo pastoril a nueva luz, Anales Cervantinos, 77; co-ed, La cornada by Alfonso Sastre, Ed Abra, 78; auth, The Galatea: Theory and practice of the pastoral novel, In: Cervantes, his World and his Art, Fordham Univ, 78; Una olvidada defensa de la poesia del s 16, Anuario de Letras, 78; En la Sierra Morena--Actas del 6th Cong Int de Hisp, Toronto, 77; Don Quijote's Profession and Mark Van Doren's Profession, Actac del I Cong Int Sobre Cervantes, Madrid, 81. *Mailing Add:* Dept of Foreign Lang Rider Col Lawrenceville NJ 08648

FINK, BEATRICE, b Vienna, Austria, Sept 13, 33; US citizen; m 55; c 3. FRENCH LITERATURE, HISTORY OF IDEAS. *Educ:* Bryn Mawr Col, BA, 53; Yale Univ, MA, 56; Univ Pittsburgh, PhD(French), 66. *Prof Exp:* From instr to asst prof French, 64-72, ASSOC PROF FRENCH, UNIV MD, COLLEGE PART, 72- *Concurrent Pos:* Am Philos Soc res grant, 81. *Mem:* MLA; Am Soc 18th Century Studies; Soc Fr Etude XVIIIe Siecle; Int Soc 18th Century Studies (secy, 79-); Asn Benjamin Constant. *Res:* Benjamin Constant; food in 18th century French literature; Sade and utopian thought. *Publ:* Auth, Sade and cannibalism, L'Esprit Createur, 75; The banquet as phenomenon or structure in selected 18th century French novels, Studies Voltaire & 18th Century, 76; A parasitic reading of Diderot's Neveu de Rameau, Forum, 78; Ambivalence in the gymogram: Saed's Utopian Woman, Women & Lit, 79; Narrative techniques and utopian structures in Sade's Aline et Valcour, Sci Fict Studies, 80; Utopian nurtures, Studies Voltaire & 18th Century, 80; Un inedit de Benjamin Constant, Dix-Ruilieme Siecle, 82; Benjamin Constant et la guerre, Actes du Congres de lausanne (in press). *Mailing Add:* 6111 Madawaska Rd Bethesda MD 20816

FINK, KARL J, b Delmont, SDak, Nov 12, 42; m 64; c 3. GERMAN LANGUAGE & LITERATURE. *Educ:* Wartburg Col, BA, 64; Univ Ariz, MA, 66; Univ Ill, PhD(Ger), 74. *Prof Exp:* Asst prof Ger, Univ Ill, 74-77, Southern Ill Univ, 77-78 & Univ Ky, 78-82; ASSOC PROF GER & CHMN DEPT, ST OLAF COL, 82. *Concurrent Pos:* Dir, Ill-Austria exchange prog, Univ Ill, 74-77. *Honors & Awards:* Grawemeyer Award, Univ Louisville, 79. *Mem:* MLA; Am Asn Teachers Ger; Am Soc Eighteenth Century Studies; Goethe Soc NAm. *Res:* Goethe studies; 18th century science; foreign language methodology. *Publ:* Auth, Learning to read German: A search for relevant models, Studies in Lang Learning, 77; The ecospace concept for the bicultural classroom abroad, Int Educ, 79; contribr, The meta-language of Goethe's history of color theory, In: The Quest for the New Science, Southern Ill Univ Press, 79; auth, Atomism: A counterpoint tradition in Goethe's writings, Eighteenth Century Studies, 80; contribr, Herder's theory of origins: From poly to palingenesis, In: Herder: Innovator through the Ages, Bouvier Press, 81; auth, Herder's stages of life as forms in geometric progression, Eighteenth Century Life, 81; Goethe's West-Östlicher Divan: Orientalism restructured, Int J Mid East Studies, 82; Dualisten, Trinitarier, Solitarier: Formen der Autorität in Goethes Geschichte der Farbenlehre, Goethe-Jahrbuch, 82. *Mailing Add:* 715 Orchard Pl Northfield MN 55057

FINK, ROBERT J, b Rochester, NY, Feb 17, 31; Can citizen; m 74; c 1. FRENCH RENAISSANCE, CINEMA. *Educ:* Univ Toronto, BA, 54, MA, 58; Univ Chicago, PhD(Romance lang), 71. *Prof Exp:* From instr to asst prof French, St Michael's Col, Univ Toronto, 65-73; arts officer, Can Coun, 73-77; assoc prof, St Francis Xavier Univ, 78-80; assoc prof, Mt Allison Univ, 80-81; PROF FRENCH, ACADIA UNIV, 81- *Mem:* MLA; Renaissance Soc Am; Can Soc Renaissance Studies. *Res:* French Renaissance humanism; French-Canadian novel and cinema. *Publ:* Auth, la Satire dans la litterature europeenne au XVIe siecle, Neobelicon VIII, 143-159; Une deffense et illustration de la langue francaise avant la lettre: La traduction par Jacques Peletier du mans de l'art poetique d'Horace (1541), Can Rev Comp Lit, spring 81. *Mailing Add:* Dept of Mod Lang Acadia Univ Wolfville NF Can

FINK, ROBERT ORWILL, b Geneva, Ind, Nov 4, 05; m 35. LATIN, ANCIENT HISTORY. *Educ:* Ind Univ, AB, 30; Cornell Univ, AM, 31; Yale Univ, PhD(ancient hist), 34. *Prof Exp:* Instr classics, Yale Univ, 34-41; asst prof, Russell Sage Col, 41-42; from asst prof to assoc prof, Beloit Col, 42-46; from assoc prof to prof, Kenyon Col, 46-66; prof, 66-76, EMER PROF CLASSICS, STATE UNIV NY ALBANY, 76- *Concurrent Pos:* Fulbright res grant, Italy, 56-57; Eli Lilly Found grant, 58-59; Am Coun Learned Soc res fel, 63-64. *Mem:* Am Philol Asn. *Publ:* Coauth, Dura Final Report V: Part I: The Parchments and Papyri, Yale Univ 59; auth, Roman military records on papyrus, Am Philol Asn Monogr, Vol XXVI, 71; Victoria Parthica and Kindred Victoriae & coauth, The Feriale Duranum, Yale Class Studies. *Mailing Add:* PO Box 503 Gambier OH 43022

FINK, STEFAN RICHARD, b Bregenz, Austria, Aug 26, 36. LINGUISTICS, GERMAN. *Educ:* Georgetown Univ, MS, 71, PhD(ling & Ger), 75. *Prof Exp:* Teacher & adminr, Austrian Pub Sch, 55-60; instr Ger, Wagner Col, 60-61; teacher & adminr Ger & English, Austrian Pub Sch, Wagner Col Prog, 61-68; instr Ger, 68-75, asst prof, 75-81, ASSOC PROF GER, GEORGETOWN UNIV, 81- *Concurrent Pos:* Fulbright fel, 60-61. *Mem:* Asn Am Teachers Ger; Am Ling Soc; MLA; Am Asn Appl Ling. *Res:* Foreign language teaching and testing; linguistic theories; semantics. *Publ:* Auth, Dialog memorization in introductory language instruction, AILA Proc, 74; Semantic-pragmatic aspects in foreign language pedagogy, Ling Berichte, 76; Aspects of a Pedagogical Grammar, Niemeyer, 77; Analytical trends in contemporary German, Proc 3rd Lang Asn Can & US Forum, 76. *Mailing Add:* Sch of Lang & Ling Georgetown Univ Washington DC 20057

FINKENTHAL, STANLEY MELVIN, b New York, NY, Apr 4, 33; m 66; c 2. SPANISH DRAMA, COMPARATIVE LITERATURE. *Educ:* City Col New York, BA, 57, MA, 60; NY Univ, PhD(Span lit), 72. *Prof Exp:* Instr Span, NY Univ, 63-66 & Univ Bridgeport, 66-67; from asst prof to assoc prof, 67-77, PROF SPAN, SALEM STATE COL, 77- *Mem:* MLA; Am Asn Teachers Span & Port; Asn Int Hispanistas; Northeast Mod Lang Asn. *Res:* Sociology of literature; 19th century literary movements; Latin American studies. *Publ:* Auth, Santa Juana de Castillo: Galdos' last play, 74 & Regenerating Galdos' theater, 75, Anales Galdosianos; The social dimensions of Galdos' theater, Hispania, 9/76; Galdos en el teatro: La reaccion critica, In: Estudios de Historia, Literatura y Arte Hispanicos Ofredicos a Rodrigo A Molina, 77; El teatro de Galdos, Ed Fundamentos, Madrid, 80; Galdos en 1913, Actas del VI Congreso de la Asn Int de Hispanistas, Univ Toronto Press, 81. *Mailing Add:* PO Box 385 Hodges Way Ipswich MA 01938

FINLEY, JOHN HUSTON, JR, b New York, NY, Feb 11, 04; m 33; c 2. CLASSICS. *Educ:* Harvard Univ, AB, 25, PhD, 33. *Hon Degrees:* LHD, Hamilton Col, 61, LHD, Harvard Univ, 68. *Prof Exp:* Master, Eliot House, 42-68, Eliot prof, 42-74, sr prof, 75-76, EMER PROF GREEK LIT, HARVARD UNIV, 76- *Concurrent Pos:* Eastman prof, Oxford Univ, 54-55; sr fel, Ctr Hellenic Studies, Washington, DC. *Honors & Awards:* Goodwin Award of Merit, Am Philol Asn, 82. *Mem:* Am Philol Asn; Am Acad Arts & Sci. *Publ:* Auth, Pindar and Aeschylus, Harvard Univ, 55; Thucydides, Harvard Univ & Univ Mich, 63; Four Stages of Greek Thought, Stanford Univ, 66; Three Essays in Thucydides, 67, and Homer's Odyssy, 78, Harvard Univ. *Mailing Add:* 1010 Memorial Dr Cambridge MA 02138

FINLEY, THOMAS JOHN, Old Testament, Ancient Semitic Languages. See Vol IV

FINN, JOHN R, b London, Ont, Nov 12, 18. FRENCH. *Educ:* Univ Western Ont, BA, 40; Univ Toronto, MA, 55; Univ Ill, PhD(French), 59. *Prof Exp:* Lectr French, 59-60, from asst prof to assoc prof, 60-72, dean arts, 63-66, pres, 66-72, PROF FRENCH & CHMN DEPT, ST JEROME'S COL, UNIV WATERLOO, 73- *Mem:* Mediaeval Acad Am; MLA. *Res:* Mediaeval French literature. *Mailing Add:* Dept of Romance Lang St Jerome's Col Univ of Waterloo Waterloo ON N2L 3G3 Can

FINN, MARGARET R, b Jersey City, NJ, Aug 3, 16. CLASSICS. *Educ:* Col St Elizabeth, AB, 37; Fordham Univ, MA, 42, PhD, 50. *Prof Exp:* Instr Latin, Col St Elizabeth, 37-38; teacher, St Michael's High Sch, Jersey City, NJ, 38-43; teacher Latin & math, pub high schs, Jersey City, 43-50; asst to prin, Ferris High Sch, 50-62, from vprin to prin, 62-72; coordr non-pub secular educ prog, 72-73, actg dir, 72-80, DIR ADULT EDUC, JERSEY CITY BD EDUC, 80- *Concurrent Pos:* Instr Latin, Seton Hall Univ, 51-54; adj asst prof, Fordham Univ, 55-69. *Honors & Awards:* Women of Achievement, Jersey J, 69. *Mem:* Am Class League; Am Philol Asn. *Res:* History of Latin paleography; medieval Latin literature. *Mailing Add:* 144 Erie St Jersey City NJ 07302

FINNEGAN, ROBERT EMMETT, Old & Middle English, Patristic Theology. See Vol II

FINOCCHIARO, MARY, b New York, NY, Apr 21, 13; m 40; c 2. LINGUISTICS. *Educ:* Columbia Univ, PhD, 48. *Prof Exp:* Teacher foreign lang, New York Bd Educ, 32-47, guid counr, 47-49, curric asst, 49-50, supvr instr PR educ, 50-54, chmn foreign lang, Sec Schs, 54-57, elem sch prin, 57; from assoc prof to prof, 57-72, dir foreign lang inst, 57-72, EMER PROF EDUC, HUNTER COL, CITY UNIV NEW YORK, 72- *Concurrent Pos:* Consult dept educ, PR, 52-62; Fulbright prof, Italy, 54, Spain, 61; consult English lang prog, Georgetown Univ, 61-62; Fulbright lectr, Italy, 68-70; spec consult English speaking lang, Am Embassy, Rome, 75- *Honors & Awards:* Educ Serv Award, 56; Col Asn Bd Educ Award, 61. *Mem:* Am Asn Teachers Fr; Am Asn Teachers Ital; Nat Coun Admin Women Educ; Teachers English to Speakers Other Lang (pres, 70-71). *Res:* Bilingual, educational, functional and notional approaches to foreign language teaching. *Publ:* Auth, Teaching English as a Second Language, Harper, 58; Children's Living Spanish, Crown, 62; Teaching Children Foreign Language, McGraw, 64; coauth, Educators Vocabulary Handbook, Am Bk Co, 66; auth, Learning to Use English, 67; coauth, English as a Second Language: Theory and Practice, 73, The Foreign Language Learner: A Guide for Teachers, 75 & Growing in English Language Skills, 77 Regents. *Mailing Add:* Int Commun Agency APO New York NY 09794

FIORE, ROBERT L, b New York, NY, Aug 2, 35; m 64; c 1. ROMANCE LANGUAGES. *Educ:* Iona Col, BA, 61; Middlebury Col, MA, 62; Univ NC, Chapel Hill, PhD(Romance lang), 67. *Prof Exp:* Instr Span, Univ NC, Greensboro, 62-67; asst prof, 67-68, PROF SPAN & ITAL, MICH STATE UNIV, 68- *Mem:* Am Asn Teachers Span & Port; Am Asn Teachers Ital; MLA. *Res:* Spanich Golden Age drama; Picaresque novel. *Publ:* Auth, Towards a bibliography on Jorge Luis Borges (1923-69), In: The Calderon de la Barca Studies 1951-69, Univ Toronto, 71; El gran teatro del mundo: An ethical interpretation, Hisp Rev, 72; Drama and Ethos: Natural-Law Ethics in Spanish Golden Age Theater, Univ KY, 75; Desire and disillusionment in Lazarillo de Tormes, Studies Lang & Lit, 76; The interaction of motives and mores in La Verdad Sospechosa, Hispanofila, 77; Lazarillo de Tormes: Estructura narrativa de una novela picaresca, In: Actas del 1 Congr Int Sobre la Picaresca, 78; Lazarillo de Tormes and Midnight Cowboy: The Picaresque Model and Myth, In: Studies in Honor of Everett W Hesse, 81. *Mailing Add:* Dept of Romance Lang Mich State Univ East Lansing MI 48824

FIORENZA, NICHOLAS A, b Brooklyn, NY, Nov 18, 14. FOREIGN LANGUAGES, FINE ARTS. *Educ:* St Francis Col, NY, BA, 36; Fordham Univ, MA, 39. *Prof Exp:* Instr French & hist, St Francis Prep Sch, 39-42 & 45-46; instr French, 46-49, from asst prof to assoc prof, 49-66, prof, 66-80, chmn mod lang, 76-80, EMER PROF FRENCH & FINE ARTS, ST FRANCIS COL, NY, 80- *Concurrent Pos:* Div chmn, St Francis Col, NY, 49-62, dir fine arts, 59-60, dir & conductor, Glee Clubs & Chorus, 59-67; Trustee, Community Opera, Inc, New York, 57-58. *Honors & Awards:* Pax et Bonum Medal, St Francis Col, 62. *Mem:* Metrop Mus Art; MLA; Am Asn Teachers Fr; Am Choral Conductors Asn. *Res:* French epic poetry of the 17th century; aesthetics. *Mailing Add:* Dept of Mod Lang St Francis Col 180 Remsen St Brooklyn NY 11201

FIRCHOW, EVELYN SCHERABON, b Vienna, Austria; US citizen; m 69; c 2. GERMANIC LANGUAGES & LITERATURES. *Educ:* Univ Tex, Austin, BA, 56; Univ Man, MA, 57; Harvard Univ, PhD(Ger lang & lit), 63. *Prof Exp:* Teacher math, Balmoral Hall Sch, Winnipeg, Man, 53-55; lectr, Univ Md Br Munich, 61; from instr to asst prof Ger, Univ Wis-Madison, 62-65; assoc prof Ger philol, 65-69, PROF GER & GER PHILOL, UNIV MINN, MINNEAPOLIS, 69- *Concurrent Pos:* NDEA-Fulbright-Hays fac fel, Univ Iceland, 67-68; vis prof Ger philol, Univ Fla, 73; Inst Advan Studies res fel, Univ Edinburgh, 73; Alexander von Humboldt-Stiftung res fel, 60-61, 74 & 81; vis scholar res grant, Austria, 77; Fulbright res prof, Univ Iceland, 80; Nat Endowment for Humanities fel, independent study & res, 80-81; vis res prof, Nat Cheng Kung Univ, Tainan, Taiwan, 82-83. *Mem:* AAUP; Soc Advan Scand Studies; Mediaeval Acad Am; Am Asn Teachers Ger; Asn Lit & Ling Computing. *Res:* Germanic philology; medieval studies; linguistics. *Publ:* Co-ed, Taylor Starck-Festschrift, 64, Studies by Einar Haugen, 72 & Studies for Einar Haugen, 72, Mouton, The Hague; co-transl & ed, Einhard: Vita Karoli Magni, The Life of Charlemagne: The Latin Text with a New English Translation, introduction, notes and illustrations, Univ Miami, 72; co-ed, Was Deutsche Lesen: Modern German Short Stories, McGraw, 73; Deutung und Bedeutung, Mouton, The Hague, 73; ed & transl, Modern Icelandic Short Stories, 74 & East German Short Stories, 79, Twayne; transl, Einland: Da Leben Karl, des Grossen, Reclam, 2nd ed, 81; co-ed (with Kaaren Grimstad), The Old Icelandic Elncidarius, Univ Iceland (in press). *Mailing Add:* Dept of Ger Univ Minn Minneapolis MN 55455

FIRCHOW, PETER EDGERLY, English & Comparative Literature. See Vol II

FIRESTONE, ROBERT T, b Odessa, Mo, Nov 4, 28. GERMAN LINGUISTICS. *Educ:* Cent Methodist Col, BA, 49; Univ Nebr, MA, 51; Ind Univ, PhD(Ger ling), 62. *Prof Exp:* Instr Ger, Univ Mich, 57-60; instr, 60-62, ASST PROF GER, UNIV COLO, 62- *Mem:* MLA; Ling Soc Am; Am Asn Teachers Ger. *Res:* Historical German linguistics; structure of modern German; language teaching. *Mailing Add:* Dept of Ger Lang & Lit Univ of Colo Boulder CO 80309

FIRESTONE, RUTH HARTZELL, b Baltimore, Md, Aug 19, 36; m 70; c 2. GERMAN. *Educ:* Univ Pa, BA, 59; Univ Colo, MA, 65, PhD(Ger), 72. *Prof Exp:* Asst prof Ger, Otterbein Col, 69-70; asst prof, 73-78, ASSOC PROF GER, UNIV MO-COLUMBIA, 78-, CHMN DEPT GER & SLAVIC STUDIES, 81- *Honors & Awards:* Chicago Folklore Prize, Ger Dept, Univ Chicago, 72. *Mem:* Am Asn Teachers Ger; MLA. *Res:* Medieval Ger Literature; comparative literature; linguistics. *Publ:* Auth, Elements of Traditional Structure in the Couplet Epics of the MHG Dietrich Cycle, Kümmerle, 75. *Mailing Add:* Dept of Ger & Slavic Studies Univ Mo Columbia MO 65211

FISCHEL, HENRY ALBERT, Cultural History. See Vol IV

FISCHER, ALEXANDER, Munich, Ger, Aug 6, 31; m 60; c 2. GERMAN LANGUGAGE & LITERATURE. *Educ:* Univ Munich, Staatsexamen, 57, Assessor, 59, Dr Phil, 63. *Prof Exp:* Lectr Ger lang & lit, Univ Clermont-Ferrand, France, 59-60; lectr Ger lang & lit, McGill Univ, 60-62; from lectr to asst prof, 60-67, ASSOC PROF GER LANG & LIT, UNIV MONTREAL, 67. *Mem:* MLA; Can Asn Univ Teachers Ger. *Res:* Comparative literature, James-Proust-Mann; research of motives, fatherson; Musil. *Publ:* Auth, Das Vater -Sohn-Motiv in der franzosischen Literatur des 19 and 20 Jahrhunderts, Salzer, Munich, 63. *Mailing Add:* Dept D'etudes Anicennes et Modernes Montreal PQ HC3 3J7 Can

FISCHER, PETER ALFRED, b Lodz, Poland, Nov 3, 32; US citizen; m 65; c 2. SLAVIC LANGUAGES & LITERATURES. *Educ:* Ind Univ, Bloomington, AB, 56, MA, 57; Harvard Univ, PhD(Slavic), 67. *Prof Exp:* Instr Russ, Univ Mo, Columbia, 57-60, 63-64; asst prof Russ, Univ Mass, Amherst, 68-69; asst prof Russ & actg chmn dept, Amherst Col, 69-73; assoc prof, 73-80, PROF RUSS & DIR LANG & LIT PROG, CLEAR LAKE CITY CTR, UNIV HOUSTON, 80-, DIR HUMANITIES PROJ, 76- *Mem:* Am Asn Teachers Slavic & EEruop Lang; Am Asn Advan Slavic Studies; MLA. *Res:* Soviet literature of 1920's; methodology of language teaching; intellectual and cultural enrichment of foreign language study. *Mailing Add:* Clear Lake City Center Univ of Houston Houston TX 77058

FISCHER, ROBERT ALLEN, b Cincinnait, Ohio, Dec 3, 44; m 66; c 2. LINGUISTICS, FRENCH. *Educ:* Univ Cincinnati, BA, 67, MA, 70; Pa State Univ, PhD(ling & French), 75. *Prof Exp:* ASST PROF LING & FRENCH, SOUTHWEST TEX STATE UNIV, 73- *Mem:* MLA; Ling Soc Am; Am Asn Teachers French. *Res:* Applied linguistics; foreign language methodology; French literature of the sixteenth century. *Publ:* Auth, The role of aural comprehension in the language classroom, SCent Mod Lang Asn, 11/77; Listening comprehension: A cognitive prerequisite for communication, ERIC System, spring 78; Measuring linguistic competence in a foreign language, Int Rev Appl Lings (in press). *Mailing Add:* Dept of Mod Lang Southwest Tex State Univ San Marcos TX 78666

FISCHER, SIMONNE SANZENBACH, b Paris, France; US citizen; m 49, 73 c 3. FRENCH LITERATURE. *Educ:* Univ Paris, Baccalaureat, 41, Lic es Lett, 44, dipl polit sci, 46; Tulane Univ, PhD(French lit), 69. *Prof Exp:* From instr to asst prof, 61-72, ASSOC PROF FRENCH, TULANE UNIV, 72- *Mem:* Am Asn Teachers Fr; MLA. *Res:* Contemporary novel; contemporary drama and cinema. *Publ:* Auth, Les romans de Pierre Jean Jouve, Libr Philos Vrin, 72; Vagadu: Traversee a grand spectacle de L'inconscient et excursion dans la liberte, Cahiers Pierre Jean Jouve, spring 78. *Mailing Add:* Dept of French & Ital Tulane Univ New Orleans LA 70118

FISCHETTI, RENATE MARGARETE, b Berlin, Ger, Jan 10, 38; US citizen; m 66; c 2. GERMAN LITERATURE. *Educ:* Univ Md, College Park, BA, 66, MA, 69, PhD(Ger), 71. *Prof Exp:* Asst Ger, Univ Md, College Park, 67-68; asst prof, 72-77, ASSOC PROF GER, UNIV MD BALTIMORE COUNTY, 77- *Mem:* Brecht Soc. *Res:* New German cinema; feminist cinema; film theory. *Publ:* Ed, Die Deutsche Literatur: Ein Abriss in Text und Darstellung, Phillipp Reclam jun, Stuttgart, 74 & 80; Uber die Grenzen der List oder Der gescheiterte Dreigroschenfilm Anmerkungen zu Brechts expost Die Beule, Brecht J, 76. *Mailing Add:* Div of Humanities Univ Md Baltimore MD 21228

FISCHLER, ALEXANDER, b Reichenberg, Czech, Dec 28, 31; US citizen; m 58; c 2. COMPARATIVE LITERATURE. *Educ:* Univ Wash, BA, 54, PhD(compt lit), 61. *Prof Exp:* Teaching asst & assoc, Univ Wash, 52-56, assoc 57-59; teaching asst, Ind Univ, 56-57; from instr to asst prof English, Whitman Col, 59-62; asst prof foreign lang, Univ Ore, 62-64; asst prof, 64-66, ASSOC PROF FRENCH & COMP LIT, STATE UNIV NY BINGHAMTON, 66- *Mem:* Am Comp Lit Asn; MLA, Am Asn Teachers Fr. *Res:* English-French literature, 19th and 20th centuries. *Mailing Add:* Dept of Romance Lang & Lit State Univ of NY Binghamton NY 13901

FISHER, JOHN C, b Mendon, NY, Nov 27, 27; m 56; c 2. LINGUISTICS, LITERATURE. *Educ:* Champlain Col, BA, 53; Univ Mich, AM, 54, EdD(English lang & lit), 62. *Prof Exp:* From instr to assoc prof, 57-62, dir summer instr, 62-68, chmn dept, 72-74, PROF ENGLISH, STATE UNIV NY COL, OSWEGO, 63- *Concurrent Pos:* Vis lectr, English Lang Inst, Univ Mich, 57-61; instr, State Univ NY, Ford Found Indonesia Proj, 62-63; Fulbright lectr, Univ Rome, 63-64; dir, NEA Inst English, 65; coordr, BA Ling Prog, State Univ NY Col, Oswego, 66-73; exec secy, NY State English Coun, 68-70, fel, 70; vis prof, ling, Univ Hawaii, Hilo, 70; vis prof, English, Inter-Am Univ PR, 70. *Mem:* MLA; NCTE. *Res:* Nineteenth century British literature; linguistics, especially in literary criticism; English as a foreign language. *Publ:* Auth, Mythological concepts in Galsworthy's The Apple-Tree, Col English, 5/62; English language tests for Italians, Coun Am Studies, Rome 64; Linguistics in remedial English, Mouton, 66; Workbooks in Transformational Grammer, Ginn, 70. *Mailing Add:* Perry Hill RD 3 Oswego NY 13126

FISHER, JOHN HURT, English. See Vol II

FISHMAN, JOSHUA AARON, b Philadelphia, PA, July 18, 26; m 51; c 3. SOCIOLINGUISTICS. *Educ:* Univ Pa, BA & MS, 48; Columbia Univ, PhD(social psychol), 53. *Hon Degrees:* PedD, Yeshiva Univ, 68. *Prof Exp:* Res assoc social psychol, Jewish Educ Comt New York, 50-54; res assoc & res dir, Col Entrance Exam Bd, 55-58; assoc prof psychol & Human rels, Univ Pa, 58-60; prof psychol & sociol, 60-66, DISTINGUISHED UNIV RES PROF SOC SCI, YESHIVA UNIV,. *Concurrent Pos:* Soc Sci Res Coun fel, 54-55; fels, Ctr Advan Study Behav Sci, 63-64, Inst for Advan Study, NJ, 75-76 & Nat Inst Educ, 76-77; consult, Ministry Finance, Repub Ireland, 65-; sur sr specialist, East-West Ctr, Univ Hawaii, 68-69; ed, Int J Sociol Lang, 74- *Mem:* Am Psychol Asn; Am Sociol Asn; Am Anthrop Asn; Ling Soc Am; Yivo Inst Jewish Res. *Res:* Sociology of language; bilingual education; applied linguistics. *Publ:* Auth, Language and Nationalism, Newbury House, 72; ed, Advances in Language Planning, Mouton, The Hague, 74; auth, Bilingual Education: An International Sociological Perspective, 76 & coauth, The Spread of English, 77, Newbury House; ed & coauth, Advances in the Revision and Creation of Writing Systems, 77 & Advances in the Study of Societal Multilingualism, 78, Mouton, The Hague; Never Say Die! A Thousand Years of Yiddish in Jewish Life and Letters, Mouton, The Hague, 81; Bilingual Education for Hispanic Students, Teachers Col Press, 82. *Mailing Add:* Soc Sci Div Yeshiva Univ 500 W 185th St New York NY 10033

FISHWICK, DUNCAN, b Ablington, UK, May 12, 29; Can citizen; m 63; c 3. CLASSICAL PHILOLOGY, ANCIENT HISTORY. *Educ:* Univ Manchester, UK, BA, 50; Oxford Univ, BA, 53, MA, 56; Univ Leiden, Holland, DLitt, 77. *Prof Exp:* Lectr classics, McGill Univ, Montreal, 56-57; asst prof, Univ Toronto, 57-64; assoc prof, St Francis Xavier Univ, NS, 64-71; assoc prof, 71-75, PROF CLASSICS, UNIV ALTA, 75- *Concurrent Pos:* Can Coun sr fel, 66-77; leave fel, 76-77. *Mem:* Can Class Asn; Am Philol Asn; Am Asn Ancient Historians; Soc Promotion Roman Studies. *Res:* Hellenistic II; Western Provinces of the Roman Empire; Latin epigraphy. *Publ:* Auth, On the Origin of the Rotas-Sator Square, Harvard Theol Rev, 64; Hastiferi, J Roman Studies, 67; The formation of Africa proconsularis, Hermes, 77; Studies in Roman Imperial History, Leiden, 77; The development of Provincial rule worship in the Western Roman Empire, In: Aufstief und Niedergang der römischen Welt, Tübingen, 78; Die Einrichtung des provinzialen Kaiserkults in r4omischen, Mauretarien, In: Romischer Kaiserkult, Wege der Forschung, Darmstadt, 78; Le Culte federal des Trois Gaules, In: Les Martyrs de Lyon (177 AD), Darmstadt & Paris, 78; The Imperial Cult in the Latin West, Vols I & II, Leiden (in press). *Mailing Add:* Dept of Classics Humanities Ctr Univ of Alta Edmonton AB T6G 2E6 Can

FITCH, BRIAN THOMAS, b London, Eng, Nov 19, 35; m 59; c 3. FRENCH. *Educ:* Univ Durham, BA, 58; Univ Strasbourg, Dr(French), 62. *Prof Exp:* Lectr English, Univ Strasbourg, 60-62; from asst lectr to lectr French, Univ Manchester, 62-66; actg chmn dept, 71-72, chmn dept, 72-75, assoc chmn grad studies French, 77-81, LARKIN PROF FRENCH, TRINITY COL, UNIV TORONTO, 66-, ASSOC CHMN GRAD STUDIES FRENCH, 77- *Concurrent Pos:* Vis assoc prof, Trinity Col, Univ Toronto, 65-66; Can Coun leave fel, 70-71, 76-77 & 82-83; lit dir, Les Lettres Modernes, Paris, 69-; vis sr res fel, Merton Col, Oxford Univ, 70; found & co-ed, Texte, 82. *Mem:* MLA; Can Asn Univ Teachers; Soc Fr Studies, UK; fel Royal Soc Can. *Res:* French 20th century novel; literary theory; critical methodology. *Publ:* Auth, Narrateur et narration dans L'Etranger d'Albert Camus, 60 & 2nd ed, 68; Essai de bibliographie des etudes en langue francaise consacrees a Albert Camus, 1937-62, 65, 2nd ed, 1937-67, 69 & 3rd ed, 1937-70, 72; Dimensions et structures chez Bernanos, Essai d'une methode critique, Lett Modernes, 69; L'Etranger d'Albert Camus: Un texte, ses lecteurs, leurs lectures, Larousse, 72; Dimensions, structures et textualite dans la trilogie de Samuel Beckett, Lett Modernes, 77; ed & coauth, Ecrivains de la modernite, Lett Modernes, 81; The Narcissistic Text: A Reading of Camus' Fiction, Univ Toronto, 82; Monde a l'envers/Texte reversible: la fiction de Bataille, Lett Modernes, 82. *Mailing Add:* Dept of French Trinity Col Univ of Toronto Toronto ON M5S 1H8 Can

FITZ, EARL EUGENE, b Marshalltown, Iowa, Mar 7, 46; m 73; c 1. LUSO-BRAZILIAN STUDIES. *Educ:* Univ Iowa, BA, 68, MA, 70; City Univ New York, MA, 73, PhD(comp lit), 77. *Prof Exp:* Vis lectr Span & Port, Univ Mich, Ann Arbor, 76-77; asst prof, Dickinson Col, 77-78; ASST PROF LUSO-BRAZILIAN STUDIES & SPAN AM LIT, PA STATE UNIV, 78- *Mem:* MLA; Am Asn Teachers Span & Port; Am Translr Asn; Midwest Mod Lang Asn. *Res:* Spanish American literature and culture; comparative literature. *Publ:* Transl, Enrique Lefevre El Elemento Poetico en Grande Sertao: Veredas, Nueva Narrativa Hispano-Am, 1/73; auth, The Black poetry of Jorg de Lima and Nicolas Guillen: A comparative study, Inti Rev Cult Hisp, autumn 76; translr, Mas Alla del Olvido (The Panama Scandal: Why They Hate Us), Pageant-Poseidon, 76; auth, Clarice Lispector and the lyrical novel: A reexamination of A Maca No Escuro, Luso-Braz Rev, winter 77; Gresorio de Matos and Juan del Valle y Caviedes: Two Baroque poets in Colonial Spanish and Portuguese America, Inti Rev Cult Hisp, autumn 77; The New Latin American novel, Intermuse, spring 79; The Leitmotif of darkness in seven novels by Clarice Lispector, Chasqui (in press); contribr, Five critical vignettes, In: Dict Comtemp Braz Auth, Ariz State Univ (in press). *Mailing Add:* Dept of Span Ital & Port Pa State Univ N 357 Burrowes Bldg University Park PA 16802

FITZELL, JOHN, b New York, NY, Mar 22, 22; m 62; c 4. GERMAN LITERATURE. *Educ:* Princeton Univ, AB, 49, MA, 53, PhD(Ger lit), 54. *Prof Exp:* Doc mgr, US War Dept, 45-48; instr Ger & Latin, Peddie Sch, 49-52 & inst mod lang, Princeton Univ, 52-54; instr Ger, Williams Col, 54-57; asst prof, 57-62, assoc prof, 62-80, dept chmn, 74-81, PROF GER, RUTGERS UNIV, 80- *Concurrent Pos:* Ed, Lyrica Germanica. *Mem:* MLA: Am Asn Teachers Ger, Wilhelm Busch Gesellschaft; Lessing Soc; West Asn German Studies. *Res:* Goethe period; lyric poetry and translation; folklore in German literature. *Publ:* Auth, Josef Weinheber: Kammermusik, In: Die deutsche Lyrik, Vol 2, Düsseldorf, 58; The Hermit in German Literature, Univ NC, 61 & AMS Press; contribr, Poem translations of Scheffel, Münchhausen, Busch, Pracht-Fitzell, In: Lyrica Germanica, Skylark, Unio and Wilhelm Busch Jahrbuch, 72-81; auth, Horse's skull and soul-mouse: Folklore in a fairy-tale by Wilhelm Busch, Univ Dayton Rev, 76; Goethe's Faust: A perspective on the mirror-image in Hexenküche and on the eternal-feminine, Ger Notes, 78; World Wide Yyaiku Harvest, Sapporo, Japan, 80; Hermann Sudermann: Feuer und Wassermutivik in dramatischer Werk, In: Hermann Sudermann, Werk und Wirkung, Würzburg, 80; Frauen, Humor und Humanitat in der Gedichten von Wilhelm Busch, In: Wilhelm Busch Jahrbuch, 79-80. *Mailing Add:* 46 Ridgeview Rd Jamesburg NJ 08831

FITZGERALD, ALOYSIUS, b New York, NY, July 3, 32. SEMITIC LANGUAGES. *Educ:* Cath Univ Am, BA, 54, STL, 61; Manhattan Col, MA, 58; Pontif Bibl Inst, Rome, SSL, 64. *Prof Exp:* Asst prof theol, Manhattan Col, 67-69; asst prof, 69-80, ASSOC PROF SEMITIC LANG, CATH UNIV AM, 80-, CHMN DEPT, 72- *Res:* Northwest Semitic philology. *Mailing Add:* Dept of Semitic Lang Cath Univ of Am Washington DC 20064

FITZGERALD, MARIE CHRISTINE, b Feb 13, 16; US citizen. ROMANCE LANGUAGES. *Educ:* D'youville Col, BA, 44; Cath Univ Am, MA, 48; Univ Madrid, PhD(hist), 54; Western Reserve Univ, PhD(Romance Lang), 55. *Prof Exp:* Teacher, Christ the King Elem Sch, Ga, 37-40 & Christ the King High Sch, 40-47; from instr to prof Span, D'Youville Col, 48-53, dean arts & sci, 54-64, vpres acad affairs, 64-65, prof foreign lang & chmn dept, 65-81; PEACE CORPS, OUAGODOUGOU, UPPER VOLTA, AFRICA, 80- *Concurrent Pos:* Fel Span lit, Cath Univ Peru, 66; teaching leave, Pontif Univ Peru, Lima, 75-77. *Honors & Awards:* Annual Achievement Award, Am Asn Univ Women-Buffalo, 68; Brotherhood Award, Nat Conf Christians & Jews, 71. *Res:* The Spanish mystics especially St John of the Cross and St Teresa of Avila; the Irish in Spain; teaching of English as a foreign language. *Mailing Add:* Dept of Foreign Lang D'Youville Col Buffalo NY 14201

FITZGERALD, THOMAS, b Washington, DC, Feb 23, 22. CLASSICAL LANGUAGES. *Educ:* Woodstock Col, BA, 45, MA, 48; St Albert de Louvain, Belgium, STL, 53; Univ Chicago, PhD, 57. *Prof Exp:* Dean of Studies, Wernersville Novitiate, 58-64; dean col arts & sci, Georgetown Univ, 64-66, acad vpres, 66-73; pres, Fairfield Univ & Fairfield Col Prep Sch, 73-79; PRES, ST LOUIS UNIV, 79- *Concurrent Pos:* Vis prof, Georgetown Univ,

60 & Col Philos & Lett, Fordham Univ, 62. *Res:* Greek history; language learning. *Publ:* Auth, The murder of Hipparchus: A reply, Historia, 57; The language revolution, Cath Educ Rev, 60; Freedom of speech in Homer, Class Bull, 61. *Mailing Add:* St Louis Univ St Louis MO 63103

FITZGERALD, WILLIAM HENRY, b New Haven, Conn, Apr 19, 18. CLASSICAL LANGUAGES. *Educ:* Boston Col, BA, 44; Fordham Univ, MA, 48, PhD(class lang), 57; Weston Col, STL, 57. *Prof Exp:* Asst prof class lang, Boston Col 57-67; asst prof, 67-69, ASSOC PROF CLASS LANG, COL HOLY CROSS, 69-, CHMN DEPT CLASSICS, 77- *Mem:* Am Philol Asn; Vergilian Soc; Class Asn New England; Archaeol Inst Am. *Res:* Classical drama; Roman archaeology. *Mailing Add:* Dept of Classics Col of the Holy Cross Worcester MA 01610

FITZGERALD, WILMA L, b Dyer, Wash, Oct 31, 28. LATIN, GREEK. *Educ:* Col Great FAlls, BA, 57; St Louis Univ, MA,62, PhD(Latin & Greek), 67. *Prof Exp:* Teacher, elem & sec schs, Idaho & Mont, 48-60; instr Latin & English, Col Great Falls, 62-63, asst prof, 65-67, assoc prof Latin & Greek, 67-71; res assoc, 71-73, DIR MANUSCRIPT MICROFILM COLLECTION, PONTIF INST MEDIAEVAL STUDIES, 73- *Mem:* Am Coun Teachers Foreign Lang. *Res:* Greek manuscripts catalogues. *Publ:* Auth, Latin tapes, Class Outlook, 65; Nugae Hyginianae In: Essays in Honour of Anton Charles Pegis, Toronto, 74; Notes on the Iconography of Saint Basil the Great, In: Basil of Caesarea Christian, Humanist, Ascetic, Toronto, 81. *Mailing Add:* Pontif Inst of Mediaeval Studies 59 Queen's Park Toronto ON M5S 2C4 Can

FITZMYER, JOSEPH AUGUSTINE, b Philadelphia, Pa, Nov 4, 20. BIBLICAL LITERATURE & LANGUAGES. *Educ:* Loyola Univ, Ill, AB, 43, AM, 45; St Albert Louvain, Belgium, STL, 52; Johns Hopkins Univ, PhD(Semitic lang), 56; Pontif Bibl Inst, Italy, SSL, 57. *Hon Degrees:* LittD, Col Holy Cross, 79; LHD, Univ Scranton, 79, Fairfield Univ, 81; Teol H Dr, Lunds Univ, Lund, Sweden, 81. *Prof Exp:* Instr Latin & Greek, Gonzaga High Sch, Washington, DC, 45-48; asst prof New Testament, Woodstock Col, 58-59, from assoc prof to prof Bibl lit & lang, 59-69; prof Near East lang & civilizations, Univ Chicago, 69-71; prof New Testament, & Bibl lang, Fordham Univ, 71-74 & Weston Sch Theol, 74-76; PROF BIBL LANG & NEW TESTAMENT, CATH UNIV AM, 76- *Concurrent Pos:* Fel, Am Sch Orient Res, Jerusalem, Jordan, 57-58; vis lectr Semitic lang, Johns Hopkins Univ, 58-61; Am Coun Learned Soc fel, 63; vis lectr Semitic lang, Univ Pa, 65-66; vis prof New Testament, Yale Univ Divinity Sch, 67-68; mem int study comn, Lutheran World Fedn & Vatican Secretariate for Promoting Christian Unity, 67-71; ed, J Bibl Lit, 71-76; speaker's lectr Bibl studies, Oxford Univ, 74-75; ed, Cath Bibl Quart, 80- *Mem:* Cath Bibl Asn Am (pres, 69-70); Soc Bibl Lit(pres, 79); Soc Studies New Testament; Cath Comn Intellectual & Cult Affairs; AAUP. *Res:* Aramaic language, Dead Sea Scrolls and their relation to the New Testament; New Testament literature. *Publ:* Auth, The Aramaic Inscriptions of Sefire, 67, Bibl Inst, Rome; Pauline Theology, 67& co-ed, The Jerome Biblical Commentary, 68, Prentice-Hall; Essays on the Semitic Background of the New Testament, Chapman, Longdon, 71; coauth, A Manual of Palestinian Arambaic Texts: Second Century BC-Second Century AD, Bibl Inst, Rome, 78; auth, A Wandering Aramean: Collected Aramaic Essays, Scholars Press, Missoula, 78; Gospel according to Luke I-IX, Doubleday, 81; To advance the gospel, Crossroads, 81. *Mailing Add:* Dept of Bibl Studies Cath Univ of Am Washington DC 20064

FIXLER, MICHAEL, Biblical & English Literature. See Vol II

FIZER, JOHN, b Ukraine, June 13, 25; nat US; m 57; c 4. SLAVIC & COMPARATIVE LITERATURE. *Educ:* Columbia Univ, MA, 52, PhD, 60. *Prof Exp:* Analyst & interviewer, Harvard Univ, 51; asst prof Russ, Univ Notre Dame, 54-60; PROF SLAVIC & COMP LIT, RUTGERS UNIV, NEW BRUNSWICK, 60- *Mem:* MLA. *Res:* Literary aesthetics and theory; aesthetics; psychology. *Publ:* Auth, Philosophy in the Soviet Union: A Survey of the Mid-Sixties, De Reydel, Dordrecht, 67; Conceptual affinities and differences between A A Potebnja's theory of internal form and Roman Ingarden's stratum of aspects, In: American Contributions to the Seventh International Congress of Slavists, Mouton, The Hague, 73; The concept of strata in Roman Ingarden's theory of literary structure, In: The Personality of the Critic, Pa State Univ, 73; Some correlations in the aesthetics of A A Potebnja and Benedetto Croce, In: Sumbolae in Honorarem Georgii Y Shevelov, Logos, Munich, 73; Ingarden's prhases, Bergson's durree reele and William James' stream: metaphoric variants or mutually exclusive concepts on the theme of time, In: Analecta Husserliana, Dortrecht, 76; Psychologism and Psychoaesthetico: A Historical and Critical View of Their Relations, John Benjamin's BV, Amsterdam, 81. *Mailing Add:* Dept of Slavic Lang & Lit Rutgers Univ New Brunswick NJ 08903

FJELSTAD, RUTH NAOMI, b St Paul, Minn, Mar 21, 25. ROMANCE LANGUAGES. *Educ:* St Olaf Col, BA, 47; State Univ Iowa, MA, 49, PhD(Span), 63. *Prof Exp:* Instr Span, St Olaf Col, 52-53; asst prof, 54-59, assoc prof, 61-73, PROF SPAN, LUTHER COL, IOWA, 73- *Mem:* Am Asn Teachers Span & Port. *Mailing Add:* Dept of Span Luther Col Decorah IA 52101

FLAHERTY, MARIE GLORIA, b Kearny, NJ, May 30, 38. GERMAN LITERATURE & LITERARY CRITICISM. *Educ:* Rutgers Univ, BA, 59; Johns Hopkins Univ, MA, 60 PhD(Ger lit criticism), 65. *Prof Exp:* Asst prof Ger, Northwestern Univ, 64-71; ASSOC PROF GER & CHMN DEPT, BRYN MAWR COL, 71- *Mem:* Am Soc 18th Century Studies; Am Lessing Soc; Renaissance Soc Am; Am Asn Teachers Ger; MLA. *Res:* Early German literary criticism; German pre-classicism; German baroque. *Publ:* Auth, Lessing and opera: A re-evaluation, Ger Rev, 3/69; Justus Möser-pre Romantic literary historian, critic and theorist, In: Traditions and Transitions: Studies in Honor of Harold Jantz, 72; Opera and incipient Romantic aesthetics in Germany, Studies 18th Century Cult, 73. *Mailing Add:* Dept of Ger Bryn Mawr Col Bryn Mawr PA 19010

FLAM, BERNARD PAUL, b Brooklyn, NY, Nov 8, 35. SPANISH. *Educ:* NY Univ, AB, 56; Harvard Univ, AM, 57; Univ Wis, PhD(Span lang & lit), 63. *Prof Exp:* Asst prof, 63-76, ASSOC PROF SPAN, LYCOMING COL, 76- *Mem:* MLA; Am Asn Teachers Span & Port. *Res:* Spanish language and literature; Romance philology; linguistics. *Mailing Add:* Dept of Foreign Lang Lycoming Col Williamsport PA 17701

FLANNIGAN, ARTHUR W, b West Indies, Aug 14, 56; US citizen. FRENCH LANGUAGE & LITERATURE. *Educ:* Swarthmore Col, BA, 73; Johns Hopkins Univ, MA, 76, PhD(French), 78. *Prof Exp:* Asst prof, Hampton Inst, 79-80; ASST PROF FRENCH, OCCIDENTAL COL, 80- *Mem:* Asn Am Teachers French; MLA; African Studies Asn. *Res:* Seventeenth century French literature; Francophone African novel; critical theory. *Publ:* Auth, African discourse and the autobiographical novel, French Rev, 5/82; History, Literature, and the Nouvelle Historique, 82 & Les Desordres de l'Amour, A Critical Edition, 82, Univ Press Am. *Mailing Add:* Dept Lang Occidental Col Los Angeles CA 90041

FLAX, NEIL M, b New York, NY, Dec 29, 40. COMPARATIVE LITERATURE, GERMAN. *Educ:* Univ Rochester, BA, 63; Univ Calif, Berkeley, MA, 67; Yale Univ, PhD(comp lit), 78. *Prof Exp:* ASST PROF COMP LIT, UNIV MICH, DEARBORN, 77- *Concurrent Pos:* Vis prof, Univ NC, Chapel Hill, 82- *Mem:* MLA; Am Comp Lit Asn. *Res:* Geothe; semiotics; literature and visual arts. *Publ:* Auth, Goethe's Faust II and the Experimental Theater of His Time, Comp Lit, 79; The Presence of the Sign in Geothe's Faust, PMLA (in prep). *Mailing Add:* Dept of Comp Lit Univ NC Chapel Hill NC 27514

FLAXMAN, SEYMOUR LAWRENCE, b New York, NY, Dec 15, 18; m 44; c 2. GERMANICS. *Educ:* NY Univ, BS, 38; Columbia Univ, AM, 39, PhD, 50. *Prof Exp:* Intr Ger, Univ Col, NY Univ, 46-50, from asst prof to assoc prof, 50-63; prof Ger, State Univ NY Stony Brook & chmn dept foreign lang & lit, 63-66; actg exec off grad prog comp lit, 68-69, exec off grad prog, 69-74, dir summer lang inst, 70-78, PROF GER LANG & LIT, GRAD SCH & CITY COL, CITY UNIV NEW YORK, 67- *Concurrent Pos:* Lectr Ger, Columbia Univ, 47-50; traveling fel, Inst Intercontinental Studies, Scan, 50; Fulbright res scholar, Amsterdam, 54-55, 74-75 & Brussels, 82-83; ed, Neerlandica Am, 62-; consult, Comt Int Exchange Persons, 66-70 & Educ Testing Serv, 68-70; vis prof Dutch, Columbia Univ, 71-72; mem Int Fed Mod Lang & Lit; res grant, Lucius N Littauer Found, 75-76; adj prof Dutch, school of contrib ed, NY Univ, 72- *Mem:* Am Asn Teachers Ger; MLA; Mod Humanities Res Asn; Int Soc Ger Philol & Lit; Int Comp Lit Asn; Am Comp Lit Asn. *Res:* Modern German literature; modern Dutch literature; comparative literature. *Publ:* Auth, Herman Heijermans and his dramas, Nijhoff, 50; The debt of Williams and Miller to Ibsen and Strindberg, Com Lit Studies, 63; The modern novel in the low countries, In: Fiction in Several Languages, Houghton, 68; Thoreau and van Eeden, In: Thoreau Abroad, Shoe String, 71; Vestdijk's Terug tot Ina Damman and Else Böhler Duitsch Dienstmeisje, Nieuwe taalgids, 77; co-ed, Ger sect & auth, all art on Dutch lit, In: Columbia Dictionary of Modern European Literature, Columbia, 80. *Mailing Add:* Grad Sch City Univ New York 33 W 42nd St New York NY 10036

FLECK, JERE, b New York, NY, Apr 2, 35; m 66. GERMANIC LINGUISTICS. *Educ:* Univ Munich, Dr Phil(Ger philol), 66. *Prof Exp:* Asst prof Ger lang, Univ Cincinnati, 66-67 & Vanderbilt Univ, 67-70; asst prof, 70-73, ASSOC PROF GER LANG, UNIV MD, COLLEGE PARK, 73- *Mem:* Pedagog Sem Ger Philol; MLA; Am Asn Teachers Ger; SAtlantic Mod Lang Asn; Mongolia Soc. *Res:* Pre-Christian Germanic religion and cultural history; Germanic, Indo-European and general historic linguistics; language pedagogics and methodology. *Publ:* Auth, Drei Vorschläge zu Baldrs draumar, Arkiv för nordisk filologi, 69; Konr, Ottarr, Geirrodhr: A knowledge criterion for succession to the Germanic sacred kingship, 70 & Odhinn's self-sacrifice: A new interpretation, 71, Scand Studies; The knowledge criterion in the Grimnismal: The case against shamanism, Arkiv för nordisk filologi, 71; Scandinavian Studies and German department enrollments, Unterrichtspraxis, 73; The aventiure divisions of the Nibelungenlied, Monatshefte, 73; The period option in Germanic area studies, PSGP Yearbk, 75; coauth, German studies in America: The expansion potential, Ger Studies USA, 76. *Mailing Add:* Dept of Ger & Slavic Lang Univ Md College Park MD 20742

FLEISCHAUER, CHARLES PAUL, b Lincoln, Nebr, Mar 13, 21; m 43; c 2. FRENCH. *Educ:* Harvard Col, AB, 43; Harvard Univ, AM, 46, PhD, 52. *Prof Exp:* Instr French & Ital, Suffolk Univ, 47-49; from asst prof to assoc prof, 54-70, chmn dept, 55-56, 59-60 & 62-65, PROF FRENCH, CARLETON UNIV, 70- *Concurrent Pos:* Can Coun sr fel, 67-68. *Mem:* Am Asn Teachers Fr; Am Asn Teachers Ital; Am Soc 18th Century Studies; Soc Fr Etude XVIIIe Siecle: Int Asn Fr Studies. *Res:* French rationalism; 18th century; Voltaire. *Publ:* Auth, L'anti-Machiavel, par Frederic II, roi de Prusse, 58 & L'Akakia de Voltaire, 64, Studies Voltaire & 18th Century. *Mailing Add:* Dept of French Carleton Univ Ottawa ON K1S 5B6 Can

FLEISCHHAUER, WOLFGANG, b Kassel, Ger, Aug 6, 10; nat US; m 39; c 2. GERMANIC PHILOLOGY. *Educ:* Univ Cologne, PhD, 36. *Prof Exp:* Asst, 32-33, 36-37, from instr to assoc prof, 37-56, prof, 56-76, EMER PROF GER, OHIO STATE UNIV, 76- *Mem:* MLA; Ling Soc Am; Mod Humanities Res Asn. *Res:* Scandinavian philology; historical semantics; mediaeval studies. *Mailing Add:* Dept of Ger Ohio State Univ Columbus OH 43210

FLEISCHMAN, SUZANNE, b Chicago, Ill, Oct 25, 48. ROMANCE LINGUISTICS, MEDIEVAL LITERATURE. *Educ:* Univ Mich, BA, 69; Univ Lisbon, cert Port, 70; Univ Calif, Berkeley, MA, 71, PhD(Romance philol), 75. *Prof Exp:* Instr Span, Mills Col, 74-75; asst prof, 78-79, lectr, 75-79, ASSOC PROF FRENCH, UNIV CALIF, BERKELEY, 80- *Concurrent Pos:* Am Coun Learned Socs fel, 77; Nat Endowment for Humanities, summer grant, 78; Guggenheim fel, 81-82. *Mem:* Medieval Acad Am; Ling Soc Am; Int Courtly Lit Soc; MLA; Int Arthurian Soc. *Res:* Problems of language growth and culture; Romance courtly literature, specifically Old Provencal.

Publ: Auth, Collision of homophonous suffixes entailing transfer of semantic content: The luso-hispanic action nouns in -on and-dela/-dilla, 73, A fresh approach to the Montanes dialect of Northern Spain, 74 & The suffix -age in Modern French: Language change viewed in a historico-cultural perspective, 76, Romance Philol; Cultural and Linguistic Factors in Word Formation: An Integrated Approach to the Development of Suffix -age, Univ Calif, 77 ; Dialectic structures in Flamenca, Romanische Forschungen, Vol 92: 223-46; Jaufre or chivalry askew: Social overtones of parody in Arthurian Romance, Viator, Vol 12: 101-129; Language and deceit in the farce of Maistre Pathelin, Treteaux Vol 3: 1; The future in thought and language: Diachronic evidence from Romance, Cambridge Studies Ling, Vol 36, 82. *Mailing Add:* French Dept Univ of Calif Berkeley CA 94720

FLEISCHMANN, WOLFGANG BERNARD, Comparative Literature. See Vol II

FLEMMING, LESLIE ABEL, b New York, NY, Oct 4, 43; m 69. SOUTH ASIAN LANGUAGES & LITERATURE. *Educ:* Carleton Col, BA, 65; Univ Wis-Madison, MA, 68, PhD(SAsian lang & lit), 73. *Prof Exp:* Teaching asst Indian civilization, Univ Wis, 68-69, teaching asst Urdu, 70-71; instr, 72-74, asst prof, 74-80, ASSOC PROF HINDI, URDU & INDIAN LIT, UNIV ARIZ, 80- *Concurrent Pos:* Fulbright Fac Res Abroad grant, 82. *Mem:* Asn Asian Studies; Res Comt Runjab; MLA. *Res:* Modern Urdu fiction; teaching methods for Hindi and Urdu Langugage; Indian cinema. *Publ:* Coauth, Another man's drawing room (transl from Urdu), Indian Lit, 9/70; auth, An additional bibliography of English sources for Urdu language and literature, Lit E & W, 3/71; Manto ke Mazamin, Aaj-Kal, Delhi, 7/72; The topical essays of Saadat Hasan Manto, Lit E & W, 73; Recent publications in Urdo literature, J A Asian Studies, 8/74; The post-partition stories of Saadat Hasan Manto & coauth, Open up, By God, J S Asian Lit, fall 77; auth, Another Lonely Voice: The Urdu Short Stories of Saadat Hasan Manto, Univ Calif, 78; coauth, Modern Urdu Literature, Harrassowite, Wiesbaden (in press). *Mailing Add:* Dept of Orient Studies Univ of Ariz Tucson AZ 85721

FLEXNER, STUART BERG, b Jacksonville, Ill, Mar 22, 28; m 67; c 2. AMERICAN LANGUAGE. *Educ:* Univ Louisville, BA, 48, MA, 49. *Prof Exp:* Teaching fel English lang & lit, Cornell Univ, 50-52; exec ed, Verlan Bks, Inc, 52-57; Managing ed, col textbks, Macmillian Co, 57-58; pres, Jugetas, South America, 58-64; div vpres, ref bks, Random House, Inc, 64-72; publ consult & vpres, Hudson Group, Inc, 72-80; CHIEF ED, REF BKS, RANDOM HOUSE, INC, 81- *Concurrent Pos:* Guest lectr, Cornell Univ, NY Univ & Columbia Univ, 72- *Mem:* MLA; Dict Soc North Am; NCTE; Ling Soc Am; Am Acad Social Scientists. *Res:* Lexicography; American history; sociolinguistics. *Publ:* Coauth, The Dict of American Slang, T Y Crowell Publ Co, 60; auth, How to increase your word power, 68 & The family word finder, 75, Reader's Digest; I Hear America Talking, Van Nostrand, 76 & Simon & Schuster, 78; ed, March's Thesaurus, Abbeyville Press, 79; The Oxford-American Dict, Oxford Univ Press, 80; auth, Listening to America, Simon & Schuster, 82. *Mailing Add:* 19C Weavers Hill Greenwich CT 06830

FLIER, MICHAEL STEPHEN, b Los Angeles, Calif, Apr 20, 41; m 73. SLAVIC & GENERAL LINGUISTICS, MEDIEVAL RUSSIAN CULTURE. *Educ:* Univ Calif, Berkeley, AB, 62, MA, 64, PhD(Slavic), 68. *Prof Exp:* From ast prof to assoc prof, 68-79, PROF SLAVIC LANG & LIT & CHMN DEPT, UNIV CALIF, LOS ANGELES, 78- *Concurrent Pos:* Exchange scholar foreign res in USSR, Int Res & Exchanges Bd, 66-67, 78, Czech & USSR, 71. *Mem:* Ling Soc Am; Am Asn Teachers Slavic & East Europ Lang; Int Ling Asn; Am Asn Advan Slavic Studies. *Res:* Slavic linguistics; medieval Slavic culture; Old Russian literature. *Publ:* Auth, The glide shift in Russian deverbal derivation, No 1 & Lightner on Russian phonology, No 3, Russian Ling 1, 74; Aspects of Nominal Determination in Old Church Slavic, Mouton, The Hague, 74; Remarks on Russian verbal prefixation, Slavic & East Europ J, 75; Is kljast' iconclastic?, In: Studia Linguistica Alexandro Vasilii Filio Issatschenko Collegis et Amicis Oblata, De Riddle, Lisse, 77; On the velar infinitive in East Slavic, American Contributions to the Eighth International Congress of Slavists, Zagreb and Ljubljana, 9/3-9/78 & Vol I: Linguistics and Poetics, 78; On Obojansk dissimilative jakan'e: The canonical case of absolute neutralization, Commun and Cognition, 11: 323-82; The sharped geminate palatals in Russian, Russian Ling, 4: 303-28. *Mailing Add:* Dept of Slavic Lang Univ of Calif Los Angeles CA 90024

FLINN, JOHN FERGUSON, b Toronto, Can, Oct 24, 20; m 54. FRENCH LITERATURE & LANGUAGE. *Educ:* Univ Toronto, BA, 42, MA, 47; Univ Paris, D Univ, 58. *Prof Exp:* spec lectr, 59-60, from asst prof to assoc prof, 60-67, PROF FRENCH, UNIV COL, UNIV TORONTO, 67- *Concurrent Pos:* English translr, Dict Can Biog, 62- *Mem:* Asn Can Univ Teachers Fr; Mediaeval Acad Am; Int Asn Fr Studies. *Res:* Medieval French literature, especailly the Roman de Renart and bourgeois literature; iconography, especially of the Roman de Renart; medieval French epic. *Publ:* Auth, Le Roman de Renart dans la Litterature Francaise et dans les Litteratures Etrangeres au Moyen Age, Univ Toronto, 63; La Presiosite dans la litterature neerlandaise: l'oeuvre de Maria Tesselschade, Rev Lit Comp, 1-3/66. *Mailing Add:* Univ Col Univ of Toronto Toronto ON M5S 1A1 Can

FLINT, WESTON, b Boston, Mass, Mar 7, 23; m 51; c 3. ROMANCE LANGUAGES. *Educ:* Harvard Univ, AB, 47; Univ NC, MA, 52, PhD, 57. *Prof Exp:* Instr Span, Dartmouth Col, 54-56; from instr to asst prof, Duke Univ, 56-65; PROF SPAN & ITAL & CHMN DEPT, UNIV WESTERN ONT, 65- *Concurrent Pos:* Coun Hisp Res grant, Spain, 63-64. *Mem:* Am Asn Teachers Span & Port; MLA; Assoc Int Hisp; Can Asn Hisp. *Res:* Spanish prose of the 19th and 20th centuries. *Publ:* Auth, Colon en el teatro espanol, Estud Am, 63; Sounds in the Obra literaria de Jose Gutierrez-Solana, Bull Hisp Studies, 63; Mas sobre la prosa de Solana, Papales Son Armadans, Mallorca, 66; Solana, Escritor, Rev Occidente, 67; More on Galdos' La Fontana de Oro, Romance Notes, 76; Mistica barojiana en Camino de perfeccion (Actas Asoc Int Hispanistas), Univ Toronto, 80. *Mailing Add:* Dept of Span & Ital Univ of Western Ont London ON N6A 3K7 Can

FLORES, ANGEL, b Barceloneta, PR, Oct 2, 00; m 36; c 3. COMPARATIVE LITERATURE. *Educ:* NY Univ, AB, 23; Lafayette Col, AM, 25; Cornell Univ, PhD, 47. *Prof Exp:* Instr, Union Col, NY, 24-25; instr, Rutgers Univ, 25-29; instr, Cornell Univ, 30-33; from asst prof to prof, 45-52, EMER PROF ROMANCE LANG & COMP LIT, QUEENS COL, NY, 70- *Concurrent Pos:* Ed, Alhambra, 29-30, Dragon Press series, 31-33 & Lit World, 34-45; ed asst, Pan Am Union, 39-45; vis prof, Univ Wis, 53-54; prof Latin Am lit, Grad Ctr, City Univ New York, 68- *Mem:* Inst Int Lit Iberoam. *Res:* Latin American literature; 19th and 20th century world literature. *Publ:* Auth, Cervantes across the centuries, Gordian, 69 & Bibliografia de Escritores Hispanoamericanos, 75, Gordian; ed, Masterpieces of Spanish American literature (2 vols), Macmillan, 75; A Kafka bibliography, 76, The problem of the judgement, 77 & The Kafka debate, 78, Gordian; Selecciones espanolas, Macmillan, 80; Narrativa Hispanoamericana, Mexico, Siglo XXI, pages 81-82. *Mailing Add:* 163 Malden Ave Palenville NY 12463

FLORES, JOSEPH S, b Spain, May 10, 08; m 34; c 3. SPANISH. *Educ:* Univ Minn, AB, 32, AM, 33; Univ Ill, PhD, 41. *Prof Exp:* From asst instr to assoc prof, 35-63, prof 63-76, EMER PROF SPANISH, UNIV ILL, URBANA, 76- *Concurrent Pos:* Counsel, coun teacher educ prof, Chanute Field, Rantoul, Ill, 41-44; mem, Natl Fed Mod Lang Teachers Asn; co-dir, NDEA foreign lang instr proj, 59-62; mem Ill curriculum coun, Off Supt Pub Instr, Springfield, 68- *Mem:* Am Asn Teachers Span & Port; Am Coun Teaching Foreign Lang. *Res:* Spanish language and literature; elementary Spanish text books; first and second year Spanish readers. *Publ:* Coauth, The Development and Evaluation of Methods and Materials to Facilitate Foreign Language Instruction in the Elementary Schools, Univ Ill, 63. *Mailing Add:* 4080 Foreign Lang Bldg Univ of Ill Urbana IL 61801

FLOREY, KENNETH, Anglo-Saxon & Medieval Studies. See Vol II

FLORI, MONICA ROY, b Montevideo, Uruguay, Sept 17, 44; m 68. LATIN AMERICAN & SPANISH LITERATURE. *Educ:* Inst Uruguayo de Estudios Prepatorios, 63; Univ Repub Uruguay, Lic Philos, 70; Univ Hawaii, MA, 71; Univ Ore, PhD(Romance lang & lit), 79. *Prof Exp:* Instr Span & Fr, Portland Community Col, 71-74; lectr Span & Fr, 77-79, ASST PROF LANG & LIT, LEWIS & CLARK COL, 79- *Mem:* Am Asn Teachers Span; Pac Northwest Foreign Lang Coun; Pac States Lat Am Studies Asn; Southwestern States Latin Am Studies Asn; MLA. *Res:* Contemporary Latin American fiction; Latin American women writers; fiction of the River Plate area. *Publ:* Auth, Simbolismo existencial en la narrativa de Juan Carlos Onetti, Vol I, 80 & Las ventanas en Paseo de Jose Donoso, Vol II, 81, Selecta; Las imagenes sensoriales en El pozo y El astillero de Juan Carlos Onetti, Explicacion de Textos Literarios, Vol X, 81-82; The Hispanic community as resource for a practical Spanish program, Foreign Lang Ann, spring 82. *Mailing Add:* Foreign Lang Dept Lewis & Clark Col Portland OR 97219

FLORY, STEWART GILMAN, b New York, NY, Oct 28, 41; m 70. CLASSICAL LANGUAGES & LITERATURES. *Educ:* Yale Univ, BA, 64, MA, 67, MPhil, 68, PhD(classics), 69. *Prof Exp:* Asst prof classics, Amherst Col, 69-77; CHMN DEPT CLASSICS, GUSTAVUS ADOLPHUS COL, 79- *Concurrent Pos:* Am Sch Class Studies fel, Athens, 74-75 & sr assoc, 82-83; Nat Endowment for Humanities fel, Rome, summer, 80 & foreign col teachers, 82-83. *Mem:* Am Philol Asn; Archaeol Inst Am. *Res:* Herodotus; Homer; Plato. *Publ:* Auth, The Personality of Herodotus, Arion, 69; Laughter, tears and wisdom in Herodotus, Am J Philol, 78; Medea's right hand, Tapa, 78; Who read Herodotus' histories, Am J Philol, Vol 101. *Mailing Add:* 122 S 7th St St Peter MN 56082

FLOWERS, FRANK C, b Jackson, La, Oct 29, 09; m 35; c 1. LINGUISTICS, SEMANTICS. *Educ:* La Col, AB, 30; Stanford Univ, AB, 32; La State Univ, MA, 38, PhD(Am lit), 41. *Prof Exp:* Asst prof Latin & Greek, La Col, 32-38; asst prof English, Stephen F Austin State Col, 41-43; assoc prof, Univ Southwestern La, 46-48, prof, 48-65; prof written commun, Fla State Univ, 65; dir, remedial English, 75-78, PROF ENGLISH, UNIV SOUTHWESTERN LA, 66- *Mem:* SCent Mod Lang Asn; Ling Soc Am; Ling Asn Southwest; Western Humor & Irony. *Res:* Morphemics; syntax; the teaching of reading. *Publ:* Auth, Practical Linguistics for Composition, Odyssey, 68; Language Patterns, Round Table, 10/67; Discovering truth about words, English J, 2/70; Basic Communication: A Pragmatic Approach to Remedial English, 3rd ed, Contemp Publ, 78. *Mailing Add:* 401 Marilyn Dr Lafayette LA 70503

FLOWERS, MARY LYNNE, b Dover, Ohio, June 12, 42. SEVENTEENTH CENTURY FRENCH LITERATURE. *Educ:* Col Wooster, BA, 64; Ohio State Univ, MA, 67, PhD(French), 73. *Prof Exp:* Lectr French, Ohio State Univ, 67-73; asst prof French, 73-80, DIR, LANG LAB, UNIV KY, 80- *Mem:* SAtlantic Mod Lang Asn; NAm Soc 17th Century Fr Lit; Asn Educ Commun & Technol; Int Asn Learning Labs. *Res:* Epistolary form and style; use of computers in literary studies. *Publ:* Auth, Sentence Structure and Characterization in the Tragedies of Jean Racine, Fairleigh Dickinson Univ, 79. *Mailing Add:* Lang Lab Univ of Ky Lexington KY 40506

FLOYD, EDWIN DOUGLAS, b Prescott, Ariz, May 19, 38; m 67; c 4. CLASSICS. *Educ:* Yale Univ, BA, 58; Princeton Univ, MA, 60, PhD(classics), 65. *Prof Exp:* Instr ancient lang, Col William & Mary, 62-66; asst prof, 66-72, ASSOC PROF CLASSICS, UNIV PITTSBURGH, 72- *Mem:* Am Philol Asn; Archaeol Inst Am; Ling Soc Am; Am Oriental Soc. *Res:* Greek poetry; Greek historical linguistics; Sanskrit poetry. *Publ:* Auth, Sappho's word for sheep, 104 A2 (LP), Class Rev, 68; The singular uses of Hemeteros and Hemeis in Homer, Glotta, 69; Kydos in Pindar, Olympian 1. 107, Hermes, 72; Dissimilation of Nasals in Greek Pephasmai, J Indo-Europ Studies, 75; The etymology of Isasi They Know, Z Vergleichende Sprachforschung, 76; Mycenaean-de-az, they gave, Forschungen, 78; Kleos Aphthiton: An Indo-European Perspective on Early Greek Poetry, Glotta, 80; Levels of phonological restriction in Greek affixes, Bono Homin: Donum, 81. *Mailing Add:* Dept of Classics Univ of Pittsburgh Pittsburgh PA 15260

FLUM, PHILIP NEWTON, b Chicago, Ill, Sept 15, 22; m 44; c 3. ROMANCE PHILOLOGY, LINGUISTICS. *Educ:* Univ NC, MA, 51, PhD(Romance philol), 53. *Prof Exp:* Asst prof mod lang, Western Carolina Col, 52-56; from instr to assoc prof Romance lang, Univ Ark, 56-61; prof, Parsons Col, 61-63; PROF ROMANCE LANG, OHIO UNIV, 63- *Mem:* Am Asn Teachers Fr. *Res:* Medieval French language and literature; comparative Romance linguistics. *Publ:* Auth, Old French Mire: A Neapolitan Borrowing, 10/52 & Aler: An Etymological Defense, 1/62, Philol Quart; Marie de France and the Talbot Family, Romance Notes, Vol 7, No 1. *Mailing Add:* 29 Maplewood Dr Athens OH 45701

FLYNN, GERARD COX, b New York, NY, Aug 14, 24; m 45; c 11. SPANISH. *Educ:* Fordham Col, AB, 47; Columbia Univ, MA, 50; NY Univ, PhD, 59. *Prof Exp:* Asst prof hist, St John's Univ, 49-55; asst prof Span, Rugers Univ, 56-63; assoc prof, 63-69, chmn dept Span & Port, 64-66, 75-78, PROF SPAN, UNIV WIS-MILWAUKEE, 69-, CHMN DEPT, 80- *Concurrent Pos:* Am Philos Soc grant, 61; Rutgers Univ Res Coun Grant, 62; Fulbright-Hays res fel, 68-69. *Mem:* MLA; Am Asn Teachers Span & Port; Midwest Mod Lang Asn. *Res:* Sor Juana Ines de la Cruz, Ramon del Valle-Inclan and Pio Baroja; Mexican novel. *Publ:* Auth, The Alleged Mysticism of Sor Juana, Twayne, 60; Bradomin, 61 & Casanova and Bradomin, 62, Hisp Rev; The Adversary, Bradomin, Sor Juana Ines de la Cruz, 71 & Manuel Tamayo y Baus, 73, Tayne; coauth, Spanish for Urban Workers, Pruett, 73; auth, Manuel Breton de los Herreros, Twayne, 78. *Mailing Add:* Dept of Span & Port Univ of Wis Milwaukee WI 53201

FLYS, MICHAEL JAROSLAW, b Ukraine, Feb 13, 28; m 51; c 4. SPANISH. *Educ:* Univ Madrid, Spain, PhD(Spanish lit), 54. *Prof Exp:* Lectr Spanish lang & lit, Cath Univ Am, 53-54; asst prof, Loyola Univ, 54-61; prof & chmn dept romance lang, Bowling Green State Univ, 61-75; PROF SPAN & CHMN DEPT FOREIGN LANG, ARIZ STATE UNIV, 75- *Mem:* MLA. *Res:* Spanish contemporary poetry; Spanish poetry in general. *Publ:* Auth, El Lenguaje Poetico de F Garcia Lorca, Gredos, Madrid, 55; Problemas de la creacion y originalidad en la poesia, Cuadernos Am, Mex, 1-2/57; Problemas de interpretacion en la poesia contemporaanea espanola, Hispanofila, 1/58; La Poesia Existencial de Damaso Alonso, Gredos, Madrid, 68; Realismo y realidad en la poesia de Damaso Alonso, Prohemio, 9/71; El pensamiento y la imagen en la poesia de Damaso Alonso, Cuadernos Hispanoam, 73; Tres Poemas de Damaso Alonso (comentario estilistico), Gredos, Madrid, 74; A puntes para la cosmovision lorquiana, Bol AEPE, VII, 75. *Mailing Add:* Dept of Foreign Lang Ariz State Univ Tempe AZ 85281

FODY, MICHAEL, III, b Utica, NY, Aug 31, 46; m 73. PORTUGUESE & SPANISH LANGUAGES & LITERATURE. *Educ:* Pan American Univ, BA, 67; Southern Ill Univ, MA, 69; Univ Ariz, MA, 72, PhD(Romance lang), 74. *Prof Exp:* Asst prof, WVa Univ, 74-76; asst prof Port & Span, Univ Southern Calif, 76-81. *Concurrent Pos:* Gulbenkian fel, Fundacao Calouste, 80; Inst de Cult Port fel, 80. *Mem:* Am Asn Teachers Span & Port; MLA. *Res:* The 19th century Portuguese language novel, particularly Machado de Assis and Eca de Queiroz; 20th century Brazilian prose, especially Moacir C Lopes and Origenes Lessa; Nordestino folklore. *Publ:* Auth, The Spanish of the American Southwest and Louisiana: A bibliographical survey for 1954-1969, Orbis, Louvain Univ, 12/70; The relation between distance and morality in some works of Machado de Assis and Eca de Queiroz, WVa Philol Papers, 1/76; Building a Minor language from scratch, Am Depts Foreign Lang Bull, 3/77; La familia de Pascual Durate and L'Etranger: A contrast, WVa Philol Papers, 1/78; contribr, Dictionary of Contemporary Brazilian Authors, Ariz State Univ, 80; auth, O Genio Criativo de Moaicr C Lopes, Editora Catedra, Rio de Janeiro, 78; coauth, Tesserae: An Anthology of 20th Century Brazilian Poetry, Throp Spring, 78; The animal figure in the mature novels of Machado de Assis, Ky Romance Quart, fall 79. *Mailing Add:* Dept of Span & Port Univ of Southern Calif Los Angeles CA 90007

FOGEL, HERBERT, b New York, NY, Apr 24, 31. ROMANCE LANGUAGES. *Educ:* NY Univ, BA, 52, MA, 55, PhD(Romance lang), 63. *Prof Exp:* Instr French, NY Univ, 56-59; instr, Queens Col, NY, 60-61; from instr to asst prof, 61-67, ASSOC PROF FRENCH, LONG ISLAND UNIV, 67- *Concurrent Pos:* Fulbright fel, Sorbonne, 59-60. *Mem:* MLA; Am Asn Teachers Fr. *Publ:* Auth, The Criticism of Cornelian Tragedy, Exposition, 67; L'amour du theatre, Professionnel du Spectacle, 76. *Mailing Add:* Dept of Mod Lang Long Island Univ Brooklyn NY 11201

FOLEJEWSKI, ZBIGNIEW, b Wilno, Poland, Oct 18, 10; m; c 5. SLAVIC LITERATURE & LINGUISTICS. *Educ:* Univ Wilno, MA, 34; Uppsala Univ, Phil Lic, 48, PhD, 49. *Hon Degrees:* PhD, Univ Warsaw, 73. *Prof Exp:* Lectr, Univ Stockholm, 37-47; lectr, Uppsala Univ, 47-49, docent, 49-51; from instr to prof Slavic Lang, Univ Wis, 51-62, chmn dept, 60-62; prof, Pa State Univ, 63-64; prof, Univ Wis, 64-65; prof Slavic & comp lit, Univ Ill, 65-68; prof Slavic & chmn dept comp lit, Univ BC, 67-76; prof & chmn dept Slavic studies & mod lang, 76-81, EMER PROF SLAVIC, UNIV OTTAWA, 81-, ADJ PROF, UNIV VICTORIA, 81- *Concurrent Pos:* Kumlien grant, London & Paris, 51; vis prof, Univ Calif, 56 & Univ Toronto, 62-63; consult, Swedish Acad Nobel Prize Comt, 58; assoc ed, Slavic & East Europ J, 62-; Bks Abroad, 62-; chmn, Can Comt Slavists, 68-; Can rep, Int Comt Slavists, 69- *Mem:* MLA; Am Asn Teachers Slavic & E Europ Lang (pres, 58); corresp mem Royal Sci Soc, Sweden; Can Asn Slavists (pres, 74-75). *Res:* Polish, Russian and comparative Slavic linguistics and literature; comparative literature. *Publ:* Auth, La Fonction des Elements Dialectaux dan les Oeuvres Litteraires, Uppsala Univ, 49; ed, Svio-Polonica; auth, Novelty and convention in futurism, Proc IV Congr Comp Lit, 65; Turgenev in Soviet aesthetics, In: Fathers and Sons, Norton, 65; Maria Dabrowska, Twayne, 67; Short story or novel: Ambiguity of structure in Conrad's The End of the Tether, In: The Novel and Its Changing Form, Univ Man, 72; Futurism and Its Place in Modern Poetry, 80; ed, The Roaring Twenties: The Avantgarde Movements in Europe, 81 & auth intro to, The Roaring Twenties. *Mailing Add:* Dept of Slavonic Studies & Mod Lang Univ Victoria Victoria BC V9A 1L1 Can

FOLEY, JAMES ADDISON, b Bismarck, NDak, Feb 25, 38. LINGUISTICS, PHILOSOPHY OF LINGUISTICS. *Educ:* Univ Nebr, BA, 60; Mass Inst Technol, PhD(ling), 65. *Prof Exp:* Asst prof, 65-72, assoc prof, 72-79, PROF, SIMON FRASER UNIV, 79- *Concurrent Pos:* Can Coun Leave Fel, 77; vis prof, McGill Univ, 79. *Mem:* Ling Soc Am; Philos Sci Assoc. *Res:* Phonological theory; historical change; Indo-European morphology. *Publ:* Auth, Foundations of Theoretical Phonology, Cambridge Univ, 77; Theoretical morphology of the French verb, John Benjamins, 79. *Mailing Add:* Dept of Mod Lang Simon Fraser Univ Burnaby BC V5A 1S6 Can

FOLEY, JOHN MILES, English Literature, Comparative Literature. See Vol II

FOLKERS, GEORGE FULTON, b Joliet, Ill, Aug 27, 19; m 56; c 3. GERMAN LANGUAGE & LITERATURE. *Educ:* Knox Col, Ill, BA, 51; Princeton Univ AM, 60, PhD(Ger), 67. *Prof Exp:* Teaching asst Ger, Rice Inst, 51-52; teaching asst, Princeton, 58-59; instr, Williams Col, 59-61; instr, Phillips Exeter Acad, NH, 61-64; instr, Univ Mass, Amherst, 64-67, asst prof, 67-68; assoc prof, 68-72, PROF GER, BUCKNELL UNIV, 72-, COORDR, GRAD STUDIES, 76- *Mem:* Am Asn Teachers Ger; Am Coun Teaching Foreign Lang; MLA. *Res:* Germanic poetic realism; Conrad Ferdinand Meyer. *Publ:* Ed & coauth, The Complete Narrative Prose of Conrad Ferdinand Meyer, Bucknell Univ, 74. *Mailing Add:* Dept of Mod Lang Lit & Ling Bucknell Univ Lewisburg PA 17837

FOLLINUS, GABOR J, b Budapest, Hungary, Nov 13, 45; stateless; div. RUSSIAN LITERATURE. *Educ:* Eötvös Lorand Univ, Budapest, BA & MA, 70, PhD(Russ lit), 74. *Prof Exp:* Asst prof Russ & lit, Jozef Attila Univ, Szeged, Hungary, 70-71; assoc researcher lit, Inst Lit Studies Hungarian Acad Sci, Budapest, 71-74; ASST PROF RUSS LIT & LANG, UNIV VA, 77- *Concurrent Pos:* Asst ed, Literatura. *Mem:* Am Asn Advan Slavic Studies; MLA. *Res:* Soviet prose of 1920's and 30's; the history and theory of the Russian avant-garde; theory of literature. *Publ:* Auth, In the world of fantasy, Helikon, 72; coauth, The complete works of Turgenev, Studia Slavica, 72, reprint, Filologiai Közlöny, 74; auth, The work of Alexander Blok, Nagyvilag, 74; Avant-garde and utopia, Literatura, 74; co-ed, co-translr & contribr, transl, Literary Analysis, Gondolat Press, Budapest, 74. *Mailing Add:* Dept of Slavic Lang & Lit Univ of Va Charlottesville VA 22903

FOLSOM, MARVIN HUGH, b Vancouver, BC, Mar 12, 29; US citizen; m 56; c 5. GERMANIC LINGUISTICS. *Educ:* Brigham Young Univ, BA, 56, MA, 57; Cornell Univ, PhD(Germanic ling), 61. *Prof Exp:* From asst prof to assoc prof, 61-68, PROF GER, BRIGHAM YOUNG UNIV, 69- *Mem:* MLA; Ling Soc Am; Am Asn Teachers Ger. *Res:* The structure of modern German. *Publ:* Auth, The Syntax of Substantive and Non-Finite Satellites to the Finite Verb in German, Mouton, 66. *Mailing Add:* Dept of Ger Lang Brigham Young Univ Provo UT 84602

FONDA, CARLO, b Zadar, Yugoslavia, Oct 2, 19; Can citizen; m 45; c 3. ROMANCE LANGUAGES, COMPARATIVE LITERATURE. *Educ:* Univ Naples, PhD(polit sci), 44; Univ Paris, MA, 65, PhD(French), 66; McGill Univ, PhD(Ital), 75. *Prof Exp:* From instr to assoc prof French & chmn dept, Lakehead Univ, 58-67; prof, Algoma Col, 67-69; PROF LING, CONCORDIA UNIV, 69- *Concurrent Pos:* Magistero Superiore Venice, Italy fel, 47-49; Univ Trieste fel, 50-53; co-ed, Le Chien d'Or. *Res:* Linguistics. *Publ:* Auth, Le privilege de vivre: Reflexions sur Robert Choquette, Can Lit, summer 68; La liberte contre les hommes, Rev Univ Ottawa, 7-9/68; Narcissus' complex: A critico-psychological interpretation of Carlo Coccioli's The Strings of the Harp, Ital Quart, spring 72; Svevo e Freud: Proposta di interpretazione della Coscienza di zeno, Longo Ed, Ravenna, 78. *Mailing Add:* 6552 Re De Terrebonne Montreal PQ O4B 1B4 Can

FONG, EUGENE ALLEN, b Pittsburgh, Pa, Oct, 48. FRENCH & ITALIAN LINGUISTICS. *Educ:* Univ Calif, Berkeley, AB, 66; Univ Mich, AM, 71, PhD(Romance ling), 76. *Prof Exp:* Asst prof French, Southeastern La Univ, 76-77; ASST PROF FRENCH, UNIV HOUSTON, 77- *Concurrent Pos:* Fulbright-Hays lectr, Bucharest, Romania, 80-82. *Mem:* Am Asn Teachers Fr; Am Coun Teaching Foreign Lang; Ling Soc Am; MLA; Am Asn Appl Ling. *Res:* French syntax; French, Italian and Romanian dialectology; applied linguistics. *Publ:* Auth, On the contributions of applied linguistics to foreign language teaching, In: Studies in Romance Linguistics, 77; Vocalic and consonantal quality in Abruzzese, Orbis, 79; Evidence for the reconstruction of Proto-Abruzzese diphthongs /ie, ia, uo/, In: Contemporary Studies in Romance Languages, 80; Current trends in American Syntactic theory, Univ Bucharest Press, 82; A lexical-interpretivist approach to French causatives, In: Rev Roumaine de Ling (in press). *Mailing Add:* Dept of French Univ of Houston Houston TX 77004

FONSECA, JAMES FRANCIS, b Chicago, Ill, Dec 5, 23; m 57; c 1. SPANISH. *Educ:* Univ Calif, Los Angeles, BA, 44, MA, 45, PhD(Romance lang & lit), 57. *Prof Exp:* Teacher, high sch, Calif, 46-47; instr Span, Ripon Col, 48-50; instr Span & Ger, Willamette Univ, 53-56, asst prof, 57-58; asst prof, Occidental Col, 58-61; asst prof Span, Ger, French, Univ Redlands, 61-65; assoc prof, 65-82, PROF SPAN, CALIF LUTHERAN COL, 82- *Mem:* Am Asn Teachers Span & Port; Universal Esperanto Asn; Am Asn Univ Prof. *Res:* Spanish costumbristas of the 19th century; modern Spanish novel; women in Hispanic literature. *Mailing Add:* Dept of Span Calif Lutheran Col Thousand Oaks CA 91360

FONTANELLA, LEE, b Stafford Springs, Conn, July 23, 41; m 74; c 1. HISPANIC STUDIES, COMPARATIVE LITERATURE. *Educ:* Williams Col, BA, 63; New York Univ, MA, 66; Princeton Univ, MA, 68, PhD(Romance lang & lit), 71. *Prof Exp:* Instr Span, Williams Col, 63-64; asst prof, 70-76, ASSOC PROF SPAN, UNIV TEX, AUSTIN, 76- *Concurrent Pos:* Coun Int Exchange Scholars fel, 77-78 . *Mem:* SCent Mod Lang Asn; SCent Soc 18th Century Studies; Am Asn Teachers Span & Port; MLA; Am Soc 18th Century Studies. *Res:* Spanish romantic literature and essay;

comparative literature; 19th century popular science and photohistory. *Publ:* Auth, Dona Perfecta as historiographic lesson, Anales Galdosianos, 76; contribr, Los peligros de Madrid, In: Poemas y Ensayos para un Homenaje, 76; ed, Los perfumes de Barcelona, 79; auth, La Imprenta y las letras en la Espana romantica, 82; J M Heredia: A case for critical inclusivism, Revista Hispanica Moderna, Vol XXXVII: 162-179; La estetica de las tablas y estampas de El humo dormido, In: Homenaje a Gabriel Miro, Caja de Ahorros Provincial, 79; La historia de la fotografia en Espana, desde sus comienzos hasta 1900, Madrid, 81; Mystical Diction and Imagery in Gomez de Avellaneda and Carolina Coronado, Latin Am Lit Rev (in prep); The Fashion and Styles of Spain's Costumbrismo, Rev Canadiense de Estudios Hispanicos (in prep). *Mailing Add:* Dept of Span & Port Univ of Tex Batts Hall Austin TX 78712

FONTENROSE, JOSEPH, b Sutter Creek, Calif, June 17, 03; m 42; c 3. CLASSICAL PHILOLOGY. *Educ:* Univ Calif, AB, 25, MA, 28, PhD, 33. *Prof Exp:* Instr classics, Cornell Univ, 31-33; asst prof Greek & Latin, Univ Ore, 34; instr, Greek, Univ Calif, 34-35; Am Coun Learned Soc fel, 35-36; Sterling fel, Yale Univ, 36-37; instr Latin, 37-41, from asst prof to prof, 41-70, EMER PROF CLASSICS, UNIV CALIF, BERKELEY, 70- *Concurrent Pos:* Sr fel, Am Acad Rome, 51-52; Guggenheim fel, 58-59; vis prof classics, Brandeis Univ, 71. *Mem:* Am Philol Asn; MLA; Philol Asn Pac Coast; Archaeol Inst Am; Am Folklore Soc. *Res:* Greek and Roman religion; mythology; literature. *Publ:* Auth, Python: A Study of Delphic Myth and Its Origins, 59 & The Cult and Myth of Pyrros at Delphi, 60, Univ Calif; John Steinbeck: An Introduction and Interpretation, Barnes & Noble, 63; The Ritual Theory of Myth, 66 & The Delphic Oracle: Its Responses and Operations, 78, Univ Calif. *Mailing Add:* Dept of Classics Univ Calif Berkeley CA 94720

FORAND, PAUL GLIDDEN, b New Medford, Mass, May 30, 33; m 63; c 2. ARABIC LANGUAGE, ISLAMIC HISTORY. *Educ:* Harvard Univ, AB, 55; Princeton Univ, PhD(Orient studies), 62. *Prof Exp:* Carnegie teaching intern Islamic civilization, Univ Chicago, 61-72; fel, Comt Res Africa & Near E, 62-63; instr hist, Mundelein Col, 63-65; asst prof, 65-70, ASSOC PROF ARABIC, UNIV KY, 70-, CHMN DEPT, 80- *Concurrent Pos:* US Off Educ fac res fel, Cairo, Egypt, 73. *Mem:* Am Orient Soc. *Res:* Social and economic history of medieval Islam; Muslim law. *Publ:* Auth, Early Muslim relations with Nubia, Der Islam, 71; The relation of the slave and the client to the master or patron in medieval Islam, Int J Mid E Studies, 71; The status of the land and inhabitants of the Sawad during the first two centuries of Islan, J Econ & Social Hist Orient, 71. *Mailing Add:* Dept of Slavic & Orient Lang & Lit Univ Ky Lexington KY 40506

FORASTIERI BRASCHI, EDUARDO J, b Caguas, PR, Oct 29, 42; US citizen; m 69; c 1. SPANISH LITERATURE, LINGUISTICS. *Educ:* Fordham Univ, BA, 66; Univ PR, MA, 68, PhD(Span), 75. *Prof Exp:* Instr Span, 68-72, dir Res Ctr & Sem Hisp Studies, 73-74, asst prof, 72-80, ASSOC PROF SPAN, UNIV PR, 80- *Mem:* Asn Int Hispanistas; Asn Ling & Filol Latin Am; MLA. *Res:* Spanish Golden Age theater; Spanish picaresque novel; poetics and theory of literature. *Publ:* Auth, Las Rimas de Becquer a traves de sus imagenes, Sin Nombre, 70; La descripcion de los meses en el Libro de Buen Amor, Revista Filol Espanola, 72; Fuenteovejuna y la justificacion, Revista Estudios Hisp, PR, 72; Aproximacion al tiempo y a un pasaje de Paradiso, Sin Nombre, 74; Sobre el Buscon, Anuario Letras, 75; Aproximaction Estructural al Teatro de Lope de Vega, Hisp Ed, 76; Morfologia e ideologia en el teatro del siglo de oro, Ideologies & Lit, 78; La base hermeneutica del conocimiento literario, Dispositio, 78. *Mailing Add:* Alcala No 1831 College Park Rio Piedras PR 00921

FORBES, CLARENCE ALLEN, b Colebrook, NH, Sept 6, 01; m 24; c 5. CLASSICAL PHILOLOGY. *Educ:* Bates Col, AB, 22; Univ Ill, AM, 24, PhD, 28. *Hon Degrees:* Litt D, Univ Nebr-Lincoln, 71. *Prof Exp:* Instr, Univ Cincinnati, 25-27; prof Classics, Univ Nebr, 27-48; prof, 48-71, EMER PROF CLASSICS, OHIO STATE UNIV, 71- *Concurrent Pos:* Vis prof, Univ Ill, 38 & St Louis Univ, 72-73. *Mem:* NAm Soc Sport Hist; Class League; Am Philol Asn; Class Asn Mid W & S (pres, 50). *Res:* Greek education and athletics; early Christian writers. *Publ:* Auth, Greek Physical Education, Appleton; Neoi, Am Philol Asn; Firmicus Maternus, the Error of the Pagan Religions, Paulist Press, 70; Teachers' Pay in Ancient Greece, Univ Nebr Studies; ed & transl, Vida's Christiad, Southern Ill Univ, 78. *Mailing Add:* 21 E Jeffrey Pl Columbus OH 43214

FORBES, FRANCIS WILLIAM, b Venezuela, Jan 6, 43; US citizen; M 65. SPANISH THEATER. *Educ:* Stanford Univ, BA, 65; Univ Ariz, MA, 67, PhD(Span), 71. *Prof Exp:* Teaching asst Span, Univ Ariz, 66-67, teaching assoc, 68-70; from instr to asst prof, 70-76, asst chmn dept, 72-77, ASSOC PROF SPAN, UNIV NH, 76-, DIR SPAN GRAD PROG, 74- *Mem:* MLA; Am Asn Teachers Span & Port; NEastern Mod Lang Asn. *Res:* Theater of the Spanish Golden Age; modern novel of Latin America; interrelationships of religion and psychology. *Publ:* Ed, A Critical Edition of Antonio Mira de Amescua's Galan, Valiente y Discreto, Plaza Mayor, Madrid, 73; auth, Catalinon, el qu noe ve, Studies Hon Ruth Lee Kennedy, 77; The Gracioso toward a fjntional reevaluation, Hispanis, 3/78. *Mailing Add:* Dept of Ancient & Mod Lang & Lit Span Sect Univ of NH Durham NH 03824

FORCADAS, ALBERTO M, b Barcelona, Spain, Nov 25, 35; m 66. ROMANCE LANGUAGES. *Educ:* Univ Ga, BBA, 62; Univ Mo-Columbia, MA, 64, PhD(Span), 66. *Prof Exp:* Asst prof, 66-70, assoc prof, 70-79, PROF SPAN & CATALAN, UNIV ALTA, 80- *Concurrent Pos:* Univ Alta res grant-in-aid, 67-68; Can Coun res grant Catalan-English dict, 68-69. *Mem:* MLA; Am Asn Teachers Span & Port; Can Asn Hispanists; Can Asn Latin Am Studies; Assoc Int Llenqua & Lit Catalanes. *Res:* Golden Age literature, especially theatre; Catalan language and literature; Ruben Dario and modernism. *Publ:* Auth, La Linguistica en USA, Voz, Badalona, 7/64; Mas Sobre el Gongorismo de Ruben Dario, Papeles Son Armadans, 7/72; Trascendencia de las Lecciones Aprendidas de los Clasicos Espanoles, en el Ruben Dario Post-Azul, Explicacion Textos Literarios, 73. *Mailing Add:* Dept of Romance Lang Arts Bldg Univ of Alta Edmonton AB T6G 2E1 Can

FORCE, EDWARD, b Middletown, NY, Feb 19, 38. GERMAN LANGUAGE & LITERATURE. *Educ:* State Univ NY Albany, AB, 59; Ind Univ, MA, 61, PhD(Ger lit), 64. *Prof Exp:* Instr Ger, DePauw Univ, 63-65; asst prof, Clarkson Col Technol, 65-66; ASSOC PROF GER, CENT CONN STATE COL, 66- *Mailing Add:* Dept of Mod Lang Cent Conn State Col New Britain CT 06050

FORCHHEIMER, PAUL, b Nuremberg, Bavaria, July 25, 13; US citizen; M 43; c 2. LINGUSITCS, GERMAN. *Educ:* NY Univ, MA, 39; Columbia Univ, PhD(ling), 51. *Prof Exp:* From asst prof to assoc prof, 63-76, EMER ASSOC PROF LING & GER, DOWLING COL, 76- *Concurrent Pos:* Vis assoc prof ling, Adelphi Univ, 73- *Mem:* Ling Soc Am; Ling Soc Paris. *Res:* Etymology; nature of primitive languages; theory of language change. *Publ:* Auth, Klar wie Klossbruh, Mod Lang Notes, 11/49; The Category of Person in Language, De Gruyter, Berlin, 53; French glaire, Romance Philol, 8/64; Primitive language(s), In: Studies in Honor of J Alexander Kerns, Mouton, The Hague, 70. *Mailing Add:* Dept of Ger & Ling Dowling Col Oakdale NY 11769

FORCIONE, ALBAN KEITH, b Washington, DC, Nov 17, 38; m 64; c 2. ROMANCE LANGUAGES, SPANISH. *Educ:* Princeton Univ, BA, 60, MA & PhD(Span), 69; Harvard Univ, MA, 61. *Prof Exp:* From instr to assoc prof Span 65-76, Jonathan Edwards bicentennial preceptor, 68-71, PROF ROMANCE LANG & COMP LIT, PRINCETON UNIV, 76- *Concurrent Pos:* Am Coun Learned Soc fel, 73-74. *Mem:* MLA. *Res:* Golden Age Spanish literature; Cervantes; comparative literature. *Publ:* Auth, Melendez Valdes and the Essay on May, 10/66 & Lopes broken clock: Baroque time in the Dorotea, 10/69, Hisp Rev; Cervantes and the freedom of the artist, Romanic Rev, 12/70; Cervantes, Aristotle, and the Persiles, 70 & Cervantes' Christian Romance, 72, Princeton Univ. *Mailing Add:* Dept of Romance Lang Princeton Univ Princeton NJ 08540

FORD, ALVIN EARLE, b Edmonton, Alta, Nov 7, 37. FRENCH LITERATURE. *Educ:* Univ BC, BA, 59, MA, 62; Univ Pa, PhD(French), 71. *Prof Exp:* Instr French, Univ Sask, Regina, 62-65; lectr, 68-71, asst prof, 71-76, assoc prof, 76-81, PROF FRENCH, CALIF STATE UNIV, NORTHRIDGE, 81- *Mem:* MLA; Inst Arthurian Soc; Am Asn Teachers Fr; Am Soc 18th Century Studies Res. *Res:* Medieval apocrypha; enlightenment. *Publ:* Auth, L'evangile de Nicodeme: Les Versions Courtes en Ancien Francais et en Prose, Droz, Geneva, 73; La vengeance de Nostre-Seigneur: The old French prose versions, Vol I: The version of Japheth, Pontifical Inst Mediaeval Studies, 82. *Mailing Add:* Dept of Foreign Lang & Lit Cal State Univ Northridge CA 91330

FORD, GORDON BUELL, JR, b Louisville, Ky, Sept 22, 37. LINGUISTICS, ENGLISH. *Educ:* Princeton Univ, AB, 59; Harvard Univ, AM, 62, PhD(ling), 65. *Prof Exp:* Asst prof Indo-Europ & Baltic ling, Northwestern Univ, 65-72, asst prof anthrop, 71-72; assoc prof English & ling, Univ Northern Iowa, 72-73; PROF LING, SOUTHEASTERN RES & DEVELOP CORP, 73- *Concurrent Pos:* Vis asst prof medieval Latin, Univ Chicago, 66-67 & lectr ling exten, 66-67, 70-72;. *Mem:* Ling Soc Am; Int Ling Asn; Ling Soc Europe Am Asn Teachers Slavic & East Europ Lang; MLA. *Res:* Indo-European and Baltic linguistics; medieval Latin. *Publ:* Transl, Meillet, The Comparative Method in Historical Linguistics, Librairie Honore Champion, 67; auth, Old Lithuanian Texts of the Sixteenth and Seventeenth Centuries, 69 & The Old Lithuanian Catechism of Baltramiejus Vilentas, 69, Mouton, The Hague & Humanities; The Old Lithuanian Catechism of Martynas Mazvydas, Royal Van Gorcum, 71; transl, Mayrhofer, A Sanskrit Grammar, 72 & Meillet, Introduction to the Comparative Study of the Indo-European Languages, 74, Univ Ala; auth, Isidore of Seville: On Grammar, Medieval Latin Press, 80; Readings in Historical Linguistic Methodology, Baltica, 80. *Mailing Add:* PO Box 7847 St Matthews Sta Louisville KY 40207

FORD, JAMES FRANCIS, b Russell County, Ala, Feb 15, 37; m 72; c 4. FOREIGN LANGUAGE EDUCATION, SPANISH. *Educ:* Henderson State Univ, BSE, 62; Univ Cent Ark, MSE, 67; Univ Ark, MA, 68; Ohio State Univ, PhD(for lang educ), 74. *Prof Exp:* Instr Spanish methods, Ark State Univ, 68-69 & Univ Ark, 69-70; asst prof Spanish methods, Okla State Univ, 72-74; asst prof, 74-77, ASSOC PROF SPANISH & CHMN DEPT FOR LANG, 77- *Concurrent Pos:* Bd of dir, Cent State Conf Teaching For Lang, 76-80. *Mem:* MLA; Am Coun Teaching For Lang; Am Asn Teachers Span & Port; Teachers English Speakers Other Lang. *Res:* Language acquisition; sociolinguistics; teacher training. *Publ:* Auth, Language attitude studies: A review of selected research, Fla Foreign Lang Reporter, 74; FLES methods: A proposed course syllabus, Hispania, 75; coauth, A mini-course alternative for level III Spanish, For Lang Annals, 76; auth, A proposal for sharing culture capsules, Span Today, 76; The prospective teacher and non-standard English: An attitudinal study, English Educ, 77; The prospective foreign language teacher and the linguistically and culturally different learner, For Lang Annals, 78; Training graduate assistants: Some basic considerations, SCOLT Dimensions, 78; coauth, TA training and supervision in foreign languages, Teaching Apprentice Prog in Lang & Lit, MLA, 81. *Mailing Add:* Dept For Lang Univ Ark Fayetteville AR 72701

FOREHAND, WALTER EUGENE, b Nashville, Tenn, Feb 17, 43. CLASSICS. *Educ:* Univ Fla, BA, 63, MA, 64; Univ Tex, Austin, PhD(classics), 68. *Prof Exp:* From instr to asst prof, 66-74, ASSOC PROF CLASSICS, FLA STATE UNIV, 74- *Mem:* Am Philol Asn; Archaeol Inst Am; Class Asn Mid W & S. *Res:* Latin literature; Roman Comedy. *Publ:* Auth, Pseudolus 868-872: Ut medea peliam concoxit, Class J, 72; The use of imagery in Plautus' Miles gloriusus, Rev Studies Classici, 73; Plautus' Casina: An explication, Arethusa, 73; Syrus role in Terence's Adelphoe, Class J, 73; Adaptation and comic intent: Plautus' Amphitruo and Moliere's Amphitryon, Comp Lit Studies, 74; Symbolic gardens in Longus' Daphnis and Chloe, Eranos, 76; The retreat to classicism in Robert Frost's Steeple Bush, Class Bull, 78; Truth and reality in Euripide's Ion, Ramus, 8, 79. *Mailing Add:* Dept of Classics Fla State Univ Tallahassee FL 32306

FOREST, JEAN, b Montreal, PQ, Mar 3, 42. FRENCH LITERATURE. *Educ:* Laurentian Univ, BA, 63; Laval Univ, MA, 66, PhD(French lit), 71. *Prof Exp:* ASSOC PROF FRENCH LIT, UNIV SHERBROOKE, 70- *Res:* French 19th century prose and poetry; modern criticism. *Publ:* Auth, L'aristocratie Balzacienne, Libr Jose Corti, Paris, 73; Tessons, Libr Saint-Germaindes-Pres, Paris, 75. *Mailing Add:* 2990 Rue Savard Sherbrooke PQ J1K 1S4 Can

FORGAC, ALBERT, b Mulhouse, France, May 1, 20; US citizen; m; c 1. ROMANCE LANGUAGES. *Educ:* Univ Berlin, dipl Ger, 39; Advan Sch Mod & Orient Lang, Paris, dipl Slavics, 42; Univ Paris, BA, 39, MA, 42, advan dipl int relat, 45, PhD(French), 47; Yale Univ, LLM, 52; Univ London, PhD(Am & English lit & ling), 74 & PhD(bus admin & econ), 74. *Prof Exp:* Prof romance & Ger lang, Univ Col Breguet, France, 45-50; prof, Col Royal Paris, 50-56; assoc prof, Tex Lutheran Col, 56-58; assoc prof, Univ Southwestern La, 58-60; assoc prof, Univ Maine, 60-62; prof, Hartwick Col, 62-66; prof romance lang, Knoxville Col, 66-68; PROF ROMANCE LANG, LIMESTONE COL, 68- *Concurrent Pos:* Brit Coun fel, Oxford Univ, 47-48; Sterling fel, Yale Univ, 51-52; Univ fel & vis prof, Univ State of Mex, 62. *Honors & Awards:* Knight, Order Acad Palsm France, 60, Officer, 73; Int Fel Laureate Arts & Lett, Nobel Comt, 76; Knight, Nat Order of Merit, France, 80. *Mem:* MLA; Am Asn Teachers Fr & Span. *Res:* French, German and Spanish language and literature; Lord Byron influence on Edgar Allen Poe. *Publ:* Auth, La France et la Boheme, Literature Comparee, Univ Paris, 47; Essai sur la Diplomatie Nouvelle, Ed Pedone, Paris, 50; New Diplomacy--French, German, Russian, Pageant, 65. *Mailing Add:* PO Box 651 Gaffney SC 29340

FORMAN, MICHAEL LAWRENCE, b Kansas City, Mo, June 30, 40; m 63; c 4. LINGUISTICS, ANTHROPOLOGY. *Educ:* John Carroll Univ, AB, 61; Cornell Univ, PhD(ling), 72. *Prof Exp:* Asst researcher, Pac & Asian Ling Inst, 68-69, acting asst prof, 69-72, asst prof, 72-73, chmn southeast Asian studies, 77-80, ASSOC PROF LING, UNIV HAWAII, MANOA, 73- *Concurrent Pos:* Nat Endowment for Humanities study fel, 74-75; Soc Sci Res Inst, 80-82. *Mem:* Am Anthrop Asn; Ling Soc Am; Ling Soc Philippines. *Res:* Child language acquisition; pidginization and creolization; Philippine descriptive linguistics. *Publ:* Auth, Kapampangan Grammar Notes, 71 & Kapampangan Dictionary, 71, Univ Hawaii; coauth, Riddles: Expressive models of interrogation, Ethnology, Vol X, Nov 4 & In: Directions in Sociolinguistics, Holt, 72. *Mailing Add:* Dept of Ling Univ of Hawaii Manoa Honolulu HI 96822

FORNARA, CHARLES WILLIAM, b New York, NY, Nov 19, 35. CLASSICS. *Educ:* Columbia Col, AB, 56; Univ Chicago, AM, 58; Univ Calif, Los Angeles, PhD, 61. *Prof Exp:* Instr classics, Ohio State Univ, 61-63; from asst prof to prof, 63-77, PROF CLASS & HIST, BROWN UNIV, 77- *Mem:* Am Philol Asn; Am Hist Asn; Am Asn Ancient Historians; Soc Promotion of Hellenic Studies. *Res:* Greek history; epigraphy and historiography; late antiquity. *Publ:* Auth, Herodotus, an Interpretative Essay, Oxford Univ, 71; The Board of Athenian Generals 501-404 BC, Franz Steiner Verlag, 71; Archaic Times to the End of the Peloponnesian War, Johns Hopkins Univ, 77. *Mailing Add:* Dept of Classics Brown Univ Providence RI 02912

FORSTER, MERLIN HENRY, b Delta, Utah, Feb 24, 28; m 52; c 5. SPANISH & PORTUGUESE. *Educ:* Brigham Young Univ, BA, 56; Univ Ill, MA, 57, PhD, 60. *Prof Exp:* Instr Romance lang, Univ Tex, 60-61, asst prof, 61-62; from asst prof to assoc prof, Univ Ill, Urbana-Champaign, 62-69, prof, 69-78, dir, Ctr Latin Am Studies, 72-78; PROF SPAN & PORT & CHMN DEPT, UNIV TEX, AUSTIN, 79- *Concurrent Pos:* Soc Sci Res Coun res grant, 65-66; Fulbright-Hays res fel, Arg, Uruguay, Chile, Brazil & Peru, 71; res assoc, Ctr Advan Study, Univ Ill, 76. *Mem:* Am Asn Teachers Span & Port; Latin Am Studies Asn; Inst Int Lit Iberoam (pres, 79-81). *Res:* Spanish American poetry and drama; Mexican literature; Brazilian and Portuguese literature. *Publ:* Auth, Los Contemporaneos; 1920-1932, Perfil de un Experimento Vanguardista Mexicano, Ed Andrea, Mex, 64; ed, Index to Mexican Literary Periodicals, Scarecrow, 66; auth, Vicente Huidobro's Altazor: A re-evaluation, Ky Romance Quart, 70; The returning traveler and Portuguese reality in Eca de Queiroz, Luso-Brazilian Rev, 72; Latin American vanguardismo: Chronology and terminology, In: Tradition and Renewal: Essays on 20th Century Latin American Culture and Literature, Univ Ill, 75; Fire and Ice: The Poetry of Xavier Villaurrutia, Univ NC, 76; Pablo Nerude and the Avant-garde, Symposium, 78; Historia de la poesia hispanoamericana, Am Hispanist, 81. *Mailing Add:* Dept of Span & Port Univ Tex Austin TX 78712

FORSYTH, LOUISE H, b Regina, Sask, Oct 11, 35; m 55; c 4. FRENCH. *Educ:* Univ Sask, BA, 52; Univ Western Ont, MA, 63, PhD(French), 66. *Prof Exp:* Lectr, 64-66, asst prof, 66-72, assoc prof, 72-80, PROF FRENCH, UNIV WESTERN ONT, 80- *Mem:* MLA; Nat Women's Studies Asn. *Res:* Women writers of France and French Canada; Canadian theatre history. *Publ:* Auth, Apollinaire's use of Arthurian legend, L'Esprit Createur, spring 72; The Novels of Nicole Brossard: An active voice, In: Room of One's Own, 78; First person feminine singular: Monologues by women in several modern Quebec plays, L'Art Dramatique Canadien, fall 79; L'Ecriture au feminin: L'Euguelionne de Louky Bersianik, L'Absent aigu de Genevieve Amyot, L'Amer de Nicole Brossard, In: Les Romanciers quebecois et leurs oeuvres, J Can Fiction, 79; Three moments in Quebec theatre history: Les Faux Brillants, spring 81 & Theatre history in Canada/Histoire du theatre au Canada, II, spring 81; The radical transformation of the mother-daughter relationship in some Canadian writers, Frontiers: A Journal of Women's Studies, spring-summer, 81; Women reclaim their culture in Quebec--A saga of night cows and wet hens, Spirale, A Women's Art & Cult Quart, autumn 81. *Mailing Add:* Dept of French Univ of Western Ont London ON N6A 5C2 Can

FORT, JANE BENTON, b Jackson, Tenn, Dec 1, 44; m 76; c 1. SPANISH, LATIN AMERICAN STUDIES. *Educ:* Tulane Univ, BA, 66; Vanderbilt Univ, MA, 71, PhD(Span), 75. *Prof Exp:* Teacher English Am Cult Ctr Lisbon, 72-73; instr, 74-75, ASST PROF SPAN, UNIV OF THE SOUIH, 75- *Res:* Modern Spanish American prose. *Mailing Add:* Dept of Span Univ of the South Sewanee TN 37375

FORT, MARRON CURTIS, b Newburyport, Mass, Oct 24, 38. GERMANIC PHILOLOGY, NETHERLANDIC. *Educ:* Princeton Univ, AB, 61; Univ Pa, PhD(Ger philol), 65. *Prof Exp:* Asst prof mod lang, Villanova Univ, 64-69; ASSOC PROF GER LANG, UNIV NH, 69- *Concurrent Pos:* Belgian-Am Found grant, 66-67; vis prof Netherlandic, Univ Pa, 67-68. *Mem:* MLA; Ver Niederdeutsche Sprachforch. *Res:* Frisian; Dutch; Low German. *Mailing Add:* Dept of Ger Lang Univ of NH Durham NH 03824

FORTE, BETTIE LUCILLE, b Columbus, Ga, Apr 7, 33. CLASSICAL LANGUAGES, ANCIENT HISTORY. *Educ:* Anges Scott Col, AB, 55; Bryn Mawr Col, MA, 56, PhD(Greek & Latin, 62. *Prof Exp:* Asst prof Greek & Latin, Sweet Briar Col, 60-66; from asst prof to assoc prof, 66-76, PROF CLASS STUDIES, HOLLINS COL, 76- *Concurrent Pos:* Fel, Ctr Hellenic Studies, Washington, DC & Mary Isabel Sibley fel, Phi Beta Kappa, 67-68; Ford Found Fund improvement teaching humanities grant, 68-72; Mellon Fund grant, 73; Am Coun Learned Soc grant & assoc mem, Am Sch Class Studies, Athens, 74-75. *Mem:* Am Philol Asn; Archaeol Inst Am Soc Roman Studies; Class Asn Mid W & S. *Res:* Greco-Roman relations; Greek literature; Latin literature. *Publ:* Auth, Rome and the Romans as the Greeks Saw Them, Rome, 72. *Mailing Add:* 2755 Brandon Ave Apt 95 Roanoke VA 24015

FORTENBAUGH, WILLIAM WALL, b Philadelphia, Pa, July 10, 36; m 59; c 3. CLASSICS. *Educ:* Princeton Univ, BA, 58; Oxford Univ, BA, 61; Univ Pa, PhD(classics), 64. *Prof Exp:* From instr to asst prof, 64-68, assoc prof, 68-80, PROF CLASSICS, RUTGERS UNIV, 80- *Concurrent Pos:* Ctr Hellenic Studies jr fel, 67-68; Am Coun Learned Soc study fel & hon res fel, Univ Col, London, 72-73. *Mem:* Am Philol Asn. *Res:* Ancient philosophy. *Publ:* Auth, Nicomachean ethics 1096 b26-29, Phronesis, 66; Recent scholarship on Aristotle's psychology, Class World, 67; Aristotle on Emotion, Duckworth, London, 74. *Mailing Add:* Dept of Classics Rutgers Univ New Brunswick NJ 08903

FORTUNE, RICHARD D, b Cleveland Heights, Ohio, Dec 28, 29. RUSSIAN LANGUAGE & LITERATURE. *Educ:* Western Reserve Univ, BA, 55; Ind Univ, MA, 56; Columbia Univ, PhD(Slavic lang), 71; NY Univ, MA, 80. *Prof Exp:* Instr Russ, Pa State Univ, 58-60; instr, Rutgers Univ, New Brunswick, 60-64, lectr, 64-70; PROF FOREIGN LANG, KUTZTOWN STATE COL, 71- *Res:* Russian literature. *Publ:* Coauth, Translation of A P Sumarokov's Dimitrii the Impostor, In: The Literature of Eighteenth Century Russia, Dutton, 67; Selected Tragedies of A P Sumarokov, Northwestern Univ, 70; cotransl, A Child is Born: Twelve Songs for Christmas by ducien Deis, World Libr Publ, Inc, 74. *Mailing Add:* Dept of Foreign Lang Kutztown State Col Kutztown PA 19530

FOSCUE, VIRGINIA ODEN, English Linguistics. See Vol II

FOSTER, BENJAMIN READ, b Bryn Mawr, Pa, Sept 15, 45; m 75; c 2. ASSYRIOLOGY. *Educ:* Princeton Univ, BA, 68; Yale Univ, MA, MPhil, 74, PhD(Near East), 75. *Prof Exp:* Instr Arabic, 73-75, asst prof, 75-81, ASSOC PROF ASSYRIOL, YALE UNIV, 81- *Concurrent Pos:* Instr Arabic, Yale Summer Lang Inst, 73-74. *Mem:* Am Orient Soc. *Res:* Social and economic history of early Mesopotamia; Akkadian literature. *Publ:* Auth, Humor and cuneiform literature, J Ancient Near Eastern Soc of Columbia Univ, No 6, 74; A new look at the Sumerian Temple State, J Econ & Social Hist of the Orient, 1924, 81; Mesopotamia a new look at the Sumerian Temple State, J of the Economic and Social History of the Orient, 1924, 81; An agricultural archive from Sargonic Akkad, Acta Sumerologica, No 4, 82; Umma in the Sargonic Period, Memoirs of Conn Acad of Arts & Sci, No 20, 82; Administration and Use of Institutional Land in Sargonic Sumer, Copenhagen Studies in Assyriology, No 9, 82; coauth, Sargonic Tablets from Telloh in the Istanbul Archeological Museum, Babylonian Sect, Univ Mus, Philadelphia, 82. *Mailing Add:* 318 Sterling Mem Libr Yale Univ New Haven CT 06520

FOSTER, CHARLES WILLIAM, American Literature, Dialect Geography. See Vol II

FOSTER, DAVID WILLIAM, b Seattle, Wash, Sept 11, 40; m 66. ROMANCE LANGUAGES, LINGUISTICS. *Educ:* Univ Wash, BA, 61, MA, 63, PhD(Romance lang), 64. *Prof Exp:* Asst prof Span, Univ Mo, 64-66; from asst prof to assoc prof, 66-71, PROF SPAN, ARIZ STATE UNIV, 71- *Concurrent Pos:* Fulbright prof ling, Inst Nac Lenguas Vivas, Buenos Aires, 67 & 73, Univ Nac La Plata, Arg, 67 & Inst Nac Profesorado Super, 73; Inter-Am Develop Bank prof ling, Cath Univ Chile, 75; chmn, Ariz Coun Humanities & Pub Policy, 78-79. *Mem:* Hisp Inst US; Am Asn Teachers Span & Port; MLA; Ling Soc Am; Latin Am Studies Asn. *Res:* Medieval Romance literature; contemporary Spanish literature; linguistics and literary language and structure. *Publ:* Auth, Nueva narrativa vista por nueva critica, Nueva Narrativa Hispanoam, 74; Currents in the Contemporary Argentine Novel, Univ Mo, 75; Literatura Argentina & realidad politica: David Vinas . . ., Ibero-Am Archiv, 75; Two syntactic approaches to poetry of Garcia Lorca, Lang & Style, 76; Studies on the contemporary Spanish American short story, Univ Mo, 79; Augusto Roa Bastos, Twayne, 79; Mexican literature: A bibliography of secondary sources, Scarecrow, 81; Peruvian literature: A bibliography of secondary sources, Greenwood, 81. *Mailing Add:* Dept of For Lang Ariz State Univ Tempe AZ 85281

FOUGHT, JOHN GUY, b Racine, Wis, Sept 11, 38; c 2. LINGUISTICS, MAYAN STUDIES. *Educ:* Univ Wis, Madison, BA, 60; Yale Univ, MA, 63, PhD(ling), 67. *Prof Exp:* Asst prof, 67-73, ASSOC PROF LING, UNIV PA, 73- *Mem:* Ling Soc Am. *Res:* Descriptive linguistics; Mayan languages; Romance languages. *Publ:* Auth, A phonetic and morphological interpretation of Zimmermann's Affix 61 in the Maya hieroglyphic codices, Estud Cult Maya, 65; Chorti (Mayan) Texts, Univ Pa, Vol I, 72; Rule ordering, interference, and free alternation in phonology, Language, 73; coauth, American Structuralism, Current Trends in Linguistics, Vol 13, Mouton, the Hague, 75. *Mailing Add:* Dept of Ling Univ of Pa Philadelphia PA 19104

FOUILLADE, CLAUDE JEAN, b Neuilly Sur Seine, France, Sept 24, 46; m 74. FRENCH, ROMANCE PHILOLOGY. *Educ:* Univ Paris, Sorbonne, lic es lett, 69; Univ NMex, MA, 71, PhD(Romance lang) 77. *Prof Exp:* Asst French, Univ NMex, 69-71 & 72-74; ASST PROF FRENCH, SOUTHEASTERN OKLA STATE UNIV, 74- *Mem:* Am Asn Teachers Fr; Mediaeval Acad Am; Soc Rencesvals; MLA; SCent Mod Lang Asn. *Res:* Chretien de Troyes; animalia; heraldry. *Publ:* Transl, The Sucker (La poire), Nouvelle Revue Fr, 7/69. *Mailing Add:* Dept of Mod & Class Lang Southeastern Okla State Univ Durant OK 74701

FOWKES, ROBERT ALLEN, b Harrison, NY, Apr 7, 13. LINGUISTICS. *Educ:* NY Univ, AB, 34, AM, 35; Columbia Univ, PhD, 47. *Prof Exp:* Asst Ger, NY Univ, 35-36; asst, Columbia Univ, 37-38, from instr to prof, 38-73, chmn dept Ger lang, 57-68; prof & chmn dept Ger lang, 73-78, EMER PROF LING & GER, NY UNIV, 78- *Concurrent Pos:* Lectr Celtic lang, Univ Pa, 67. *Mem:* Ling Soc Am; MLA; Int Ling Asn. *Res:* Germanic Indo-European and comparative linguistics; Welsh and other Celtic languages; Welsh etymological dictionary. *Publ:* Coauth, The German Lied and Its Poetry, NY Univ, 71. *Mailing Add:* 632 Van Cortland Park Ave Yonkers NY 10705

FOWLER, BARBARA HUGHES, b Lake Forest, Ill, Aug 23, 26; m 56; c 2. CLASSICS. *Educ:* Univ Wis, BA, 49; Bryn Mawr Col, MA, 50 PhD(Greek & Latin), 55. *Prof Exp:* Instr classics, Middlebury Col, 54-56; asst prof Latin, Edgewood Col, 61-63; lectr, 63-71, assoc prof, 71-76, prof, 76-80, JOHN BASCOM PROF CLASSICS, UNIV WIS-MADISON, 80- *Mem:* Am Philol Asn; Archaeol Inst Am; Class Asn Midwest & South. *Res:* Greek tragedy; Greek lyric poets; Hellenistic poetry. *Publ:* Auth, The imagery of the Promethus bound, Am J Philol, 57; Thucydides I 107-108 and the Tanagran federal issues, Phoenix, 57; Demosthenes 54; a topographical note, Class Philol, 58; Aeschylus' imagery, 69 & Plot and prosody in Sophocles' Antigone, 69, Class & Mediaevalia; Story and verse in Oedipus Tyrannus, Symbolae Osloenses, 71; Lyric structures in three Euripidean plays, Dioniso, 78; Thought & Underthought in Three Sophoclean Plays, Eranos, 81. *Mailing Add:* 1102 Sherman Ave Madison WI 53703

FOWLER, CAROLYN, b Lafayette, La. AFRO-FRENCH & AFRO-AMERICAN LITERATURE. *Educ:* Univ Calif, Berkeley, BA, 60, MA, 65; Univ Pa, PhD(French), 72. *Prof Exp:* Instr French & Span, SC State Col, 65-66; assoc prof French, Cheyney State Col, 69-71; ASSOC PROF BLACK LIT, ATLANTA UNIV, 72- *Concurrent Pos:* Lectr, Dominican Repub, 72; Nat Endowment for Humanities res award, 75. *Honors & Awards:* Conrad Kent Rivers Lit Award, Black World, 71. *Mem:* African Lit Asn; First World Found; MLA; Col Lang Asn. *Res:* Haitian literature; periodical literature and the literature of group movements; Blackamerican literary history. *Publ:* Auth, The measure and meaning of the sixties, Black World, 12/69; contribr, In: The Black Aesthetic, Doubleday, 71; auth, Literatura de los Estados Unidos de America, Bloque (Santo Domingo), 74; La Litterature haitienne, Cahiers Dept Lit Africaines, 77-78; Blackamerican literature . . . or the literature of Black Americans?, Abbia (Yaounde, Cameroon), 78; L'oeuvre de Philippe Thoby-Marcelin, Eds Naaman (Sherbrooke) (in press). *Mailing Add:* Atlanta Univ 223 Chestnut St SW Atlanta GA 30314

FOWLIE, WALLACE, b Brookline, Mass, Nov 8, 08. FRENCH LITERATURE. *Educ:* Harvard Univ, AB, 30, AM, 33, PhD, 36. *Prof Exp:* Master French, Taft Sch, 30-31; instr, Harvard Univ, 31-35; prof French & Ital lit, Bennington Col, 35-41; asst prof French, Yale Univ, 41-46; assoc prof, Univ Chicago, 46-50; prof & head dept, Bennington Col, 50-62; prof, Univ Colo, 62-64; JAMES B DUKE PROF FRENCH, DUKE UNIV, 64- *Concurrent Pos:* Guggenheim fel, 48-49; adv ed, Poetry Mag, 50- *Honors & Awards:* Vursell Award, Am Acad & Inst Arts & Lett, 80. *Mem:* MLA; Am Asn Teachers Fr. *Res:* Rimbaud; clowns and angels; Jacob's night. *Publ:* Auth, Rimbaud: A Critical Study, Univ Chicago, 65; Jean Cocteau, Ind Univ, 66; Climate of Violence, Macmillan, 67; The French Critic, Southern Ill Univ, 68; Stendhal, Macmillan, 69; French Literature: Its History and Its Meaning, Prentice-Hall, 73; Journal of rehearsals, Duke Press, 78; A reading of Dante's Inferno, Univ Chicago, 81. *Mailing Add:* Dept of Fr Duke Univ Durham NC 27706

FOX, BERNICE LEE, b Ashland, Ky, Feb 19, 11. CLASSICAL LANGUAGES & LITERATURE. *Educ:* Ky Wesleyan Col, AB, 32; Univ Ky, AM, 34. *Prof Exp:* Instr English, Ky Wesleyan Col, 32-33; asst, Univ Ky, 33-36; asst, Ohio State Univ, 36-41; weather observer, Port Columbus, Ohio, 41-43; teacher, high sch, Ohio, 43-45; asst prof English, 47-50, assoc prof classics, 50-77, actg head dept, 63-64, chmn dept, 70-80, prof, 77-80, EMER PROF CLASSICS, MONMOUTH COL, ILL, 77- *Concurrent Pos:* Lectr classics, Knox Col, 71-74. *Mem:* Class Asn Mid W & S; Vergilian Soc; Am Class League. *Res:* Classical mythology; the Latin poets. *Publ:* Coauth, Paraphrases from the Latin Poets, Kellogg, 61; auth, Dear Ovid, my problem is . . . 66, Latin and the epigram, 3/71 & A Latin poet in the twentieth century, 4/72, Class Outlook; Fabula de Quarto Mago, Wagoner, 76. *Mailing Add:* Dept of Classics Monmouth Col Monmouth IL 61462

FOX, DIAN, b Seattle, Wash, Apr 10, 51. SPANISH LITERATURE. *Educ:* Univ Ore, BA, 75; Duke Univ, MA, 77, PhD(Romance lang), 79. *Prof Exp:* Lectr Span, Duke Univ, 79-80; ASST PROF SPAN & HUMANITIES, COLUMBIA UNIV, 80- *Concurrent Pos:* Am Coun Learned Soc fel, 83; res assoc, Univ Calif, Berkeley, 83. *Mem:* MLA; Am Asn Teachers Span & Port. *Res:* Spanish Golden Age theater, especially political aspects of Calderon; narrative theory of Cervantes; medieval Spanish literature. *Publ:* Auth, A Further Source of Calderon's El principe constante, J Hisp Philol, Vol 4, 80; Kingship and community in La vida es sueno, Bull Hisp Studies, Vol 58, 81; El Medico de su honra: Political considerations, Hispania, Vol 65, 82; Quien tiene al padre alcalde: Conflict of images in Alcalde, RCEH, Vol 6, 82; Pero Vermuez and the politics of the Cid's Exile, Mod Lang Rev (in prep); The critical attitude in Rinconete y Cortadillo, Hispanofila (in prep). *Mailing Add:* 560 Riverside Dr No 10-A New York NY 10027

FOX, EDWARD INMAN, b Nashville, Tenn, Aug 22, 33. FOREIGN LANGUAGES. *Educ:* Vanderbilt Univ, BA, 54, MA, 58; Princeton Univ, MA, 59, PhD, 60. *Prof Exp:* Asst prof Span, Vanderbilt Univ, 60-64, assoc prof, 64-66; assoc prof Romance lang, Univ Mass, 66-67; Prof Hispanic studies & chmn dept, Vassar Col, 67-71, John Guy Vassar prof mod lang, 71-74, dean fac, 71-72, dir long range educ planning, 72-73; pres, Knox Col, Ill, 74-82; PROF SPAN & PORT, NORTHWESTERN UNIV, 82- *Concurrent Pos:* Vis prof, Escuela Verano, Mex, 58-60 & 62; Am Philos Soc grants, 63 & 68; Fulbright res grant, Spain, 65-66; mem exec & nominating comt, Spanish IV, MLA, 65-68, secy, Spanish V, 67, chmn, 68; delivered lect, Spain & Brit Isles, 66, 74 & 77, US, 67-68 & 77-82; vis prof Romance lang, Wesleyan Univ, 71; Miguel de Unamuno prof, Univ Salamanca, 73; chmn, Great Lakes District Rhodes Scholarship Comt, 79-81; mem exec comt, Spanish V, MLA, 80-84; Nat Endowment Humanities fel, 82-83. *Mem:* Asoc Int Hispanistas; MLA. *Res:* Nineteenth and twentieth century Spanish literature and intellectual history. *Publ:* Auth, Azorin, as a Literary Critic, Hisp Inst, 62; coauth, Spanish Thought and Letters in the Twentieth Century, Vanderbilt Univ, 66; ed, La Voluntad, Castalia, 69, 73 & 81 Antonio Azorin, Labor, Barcelona, 70; auth, La Crisis Intelectual Del 78, Cuadernos para el Dialogo, S A, Madrid, 76; coauth, The Poetry of 1936, Crisis and Commitment in Contemporary Spanish Poetry, Tamesis Bks, London, 76; ed, R de Maeztu, Articulos Desconocidos, Castalia, Madrid, 77; El fandolecismo Madrid, Dienga, 82. *Mailing Add:* Northwestern Univ Evanston IL 60201

FOX, EUGENE JACKSON, b Drumright, Okla, July 14, 14; m 42; c 1. FOREIGN LANGUAGES. *Educ:* Cent Okla State Col, BS, 38; Univ Okla, MA, 44; Nat Univ Mex, Dr Lett, 51. *Prof Exp:* From assoc prof to prof Span, 59-76, dir lang lab, 62-76, dean col gen studies, 65-76, actg chmn dept mod lang, 71-76, EMER PROF MOD LANG & DEAN, EASTERN N MEX UNIV, 76- *Concurrent Pos:* Fulbright grant, Colombia, 58. *Mem:* Am Asn Teachers Span & Port; Rocky Mountain Mod Lang Asn. *Res:* Spanish of New Mexico; hearing problems of Spanish speaking children; Latin American grammatical studies. *Publ:* Auth, Roswell, NMex Mag, 59; Summer seminar for Spanish teachers, Hispania, 60; Storm in the Sacramentos, NMex Mag, 61; Guide for college students, 68. *Mailing Add:* Dept of Mod Lang Eastern NMex Univ Portales NM 88130

FOX, LINDA CHODOSH, b Charlottesville, Va, May 20, 43; m 67; c 2. FOREIGN LANGUAGE. *Educ:* Douglass Col, BA, 65; Ind Univ, Bloomington, MA 67; Univ Wis-Madison, PhD(Span), 74. *Prof Exp:* Lectr, 71-74, ASST PROF SPAN, IND UNIV-PURDUE UNIV, FORT WAYNE, 74- *Concurrent Pos:* Newsletter ed, Feministas Unidas: A coalition of feminist scholars in Span, Span-Am, Luso-Brazilian, Afro-Port & Chicano-Riqueno studies. *Mem:* MLA; Am Asn Teachers Span & Port; Assoc Lit Hisp Femenina; Feministas Unidas. *Res:* Power in the family and beyond: Dona Perfecta and Bernarda Alba as manipulators of their destinies; characterization of women in Hispanic literature. *Publ:* Auth, Vision of Cain and Abel in Spain's generation of 1898, CLA J, 6/78; Las lagrimas y la tristeza en el Lazarillo de Tormes, Revista Estudios Hisp, 10/79. *Mailing Add:* Dept of Mod Foreign Lang Ind Univ-Purdue Univ Ft Wayne IN 46805

FOX, ROBERT PAUL, b Troy, NY, Aug 7, 33; m 59; c 1. LINGUISTICS, ENGLISH AS SECOND LANGUAGE. *Educ:* Georgetown Univ, BS, 60, MS, 62; Univ Ill, PhD(ling), 68. *Prof Exp:* Teaching fel English as second lang, Inst Lang & Ling, Georgetown Univ, 59-62; instr English as second lang & English, Univ Ill, Urbana, 62-68, asst prof English as second lang, English & ling, 68-71; assoc prof, 71-75, PROF ENGLISH AS SECOND LANG & LING, AM UNIV, 75-, DIR ENGLISH LANG INST, 71- *Concurrent Pos:* Consult econ terms, Am Lang Inst, Tex, 64; English consult field serv prog, Nat Asn Foreign Student Affairs, 65-; consult, Educ Syst Corp, 69-; consult, Montgomery County Community Col, 72-73. *Mem:* Nat Asn Foreign Student Affairs; Ling Soc Am; AAAS; NCTE. *Res:* Linguistics; contrastive analysis; structure of English and Hindi; problems in second language learning. *Publ:* Coauth, Survey of University and College Programs in English as a Second Language, Nat Asn Foreign Student Affairs, 66; auth, The relative clause in three languages, TESOL Quart, 70; ed, Essays on Teaching English as a Second Language and as a Second Dialect, NCTE, 73. *Mailing Add:* English Lang Inst Rm 200 McKinley Bldg Am Univ Washington DC 20016

FRAJZYNGIER, ZYGMUNT, b Radom, Poland, Apr 3, 38; US citizen; m 71; c 2. LINGUISTICS, AFRICAN LANGUAGES & LINGUISTICS. *Educ:* Univ Warsaw, MA, 63, PhD(philol), 68; Univ Ghana, MA, 65. *Prof Exp:* Doktorant African lang, Univ Warsaw, 65-68, adjunct, 68-69; asst prof, 70-76, assoc prof, 76-82, PROF LING, UNIV COLO, 82- *Concurrent Pos:* Sr lectr, Bayero Col, Ahmadu Bello Univ, Kano, Nigeria, 74-75. *Mem:* Ling Soc Am. *Res:* Semantics; syntax. *Publ:* Auth, An analysis of BE passive, Lingua, 46: 133-156; Notes on the R1R2R2 stems in semitic, J Semitic Studies, Vol 24, No 1; The vowel system of Pero, Studies in African Ling, Vol 11, No 1; Some rules concerning vowels in Chadic, Bull Sch Oriental & African Studies, Vol XLIV, No 2; On the Proto-Chadic syntactic pattern, Proc III Int Hhamito-Semitic Cong (in press); Underlying form of Proto-Chadic verb, Proc Marburg Symp on Chadic Lang (in press); Marking syntactic relations in Proto-Chadic, Studies in Chadic Ling (in press); On the form and function of pre-pronominal markers in Chadic, Bull Sch Oriental & African Studies, Vol 45, No 2. *Mailing Add:* Dept Ling Box 295 Univ Colo Boulder CO 80309

FRAME, DONALD MURDOCH, b New York, NY, Dec 14, 11; m; c 2. FRENCH LITERATURE. *Educ:* Harvard Univ, AB, 32; Columbia Univ, AM, 35, PhD, 41. *Prof Exp:* Teacher, Loomis Sch, Conn, 32-34; from instr to prof, 38-75, MOORE COL PROF FRENCH, COLUMBIA UNIV, 75- *Concurrent Pos:* Guggenheim fel & Fulbright grant, 52-53; Phi Beta Kappa vis scholar, 67-68. *Mem:* MLA; Am Asn Teachers Fr. *Res:* Sixteenth century French literature. *Publ:* Auth, Montaigne in France & Montaigne's Discovery of Man, Columbia Univ; ed & translr, The Complete Works of Montaigne, Stanford Univ, 57; auth, Montaigne: A Biography, Harcourt, 65; translr, Moliere: Tartuffe and Other Plays, 67 & The Misanthrope and Other Plays, 68, New Am Libr; Montaigne's Essais: A Study, Prentice-Hall, 69; Francois Rabelais: A Study, Harcourt, 77; co-ed (with Mary B McKinley), Columbia Montaigne Conference Papers, Fr Forum, 81. *Mailing Add:* 401 W 118th St New York NY 10027

FRANCESCHETTI, ANTONIO, b Padova, Italy, Oct 13, 39; m 65; c 3. ITALIAN. *Educ:* Univ Padova, Dr Lett, 63; Columbia Univ, PhD(Ital), 68. *Prof Exp:* Lectr Ital, Univ Reading, 64; lectr, Barnard Col, Columbia Univ, 64-66, from instr to asst prof, 66-69; asst prof, 69-71, assoc prof, 71-80, PROF ITAL, SCARBOROUGH COL, UNIV TORONTO, 80- *Concurrent Pos:* Can deleg, Asn Int Studi Ling & Lett Ital, 76-; rep Ital, Humanities Res Coun Can, 77- *Mem:* MLA; Am Asn Teachers Ital; Asn Int Studi Ling & Lett Ital; Soc Dante Alighieri. *Res:* Chivalric literature in the Middle Ages and the Renaissance; 18th century poetics and poetry. *Publ:* Auth, Il concetto di meraviglia nell poetiche della prima Arcadia, Lett Ital, 69; L'Orlando Innamorato e le sue Componenti Tematiche e Strutturali, Olschki, 75; coauth, Convegno Internazionale Ludovico Ariosto, Accad Naz Dei Lincei, 75; auth, Appunti sui cantari di milone e Berta e della Nascita di Orlando, Lett Ital, 75; coauth, Petrarca, Venezia e il Veneto, Olschki, 76. *Mailing Add:* Div of Humanities Scarborough Col Univ of Toronto West Hill ON M5S 1A1 Can

FRANCIS, CLAUDE, b Gr Brit. FRENCH LITERATURE. *Educ:* Univ Calif, Los Angeles, PhD(French), 65. *Prof Exp:* PROF FRENCH LIT, SOUTHERN ILL UNIV, 70- *Concurrent Pos:* Hon vis res assoc, Radcliffe Univ. *Mem:* MLA; Am Asn Teachers French. *Res:* Moliere; Cabet and the Icarians; S de Beauvoir; Marcel Proust. *Publ:* Auth, Divertissements Litteraires, 56, L'Evolution de la civilisation Canadienne, 63 & Les metamorphoses di mythe de Phedre, 67, Pelican, Can; coauth, Le Francais de nos jours, Siv, 78; auth, S de Beauvoir et le Cours du Monde, 78, Klincksieck, Paris; coauth, Les Ecrits Feministes de S de Beauvoir, 78 & Les Ecrits de Simone de Beauvoir, 78, Gallimard, Paris; Proust et Les Siens, P Pon, Paris, 82; Marcel Proust, Poemes, Gallimard, Paris, 82. *Mailing Add:* Dept of French Lit Southern Ill Univ Edwardsville IL 62026

FRANCIS, ERIC DAVID, b Sheffield, Eng, Aug 13, 40; m 76; c 3. CLASSICS, LINGUISTICS. *Educ:* Cambridge Univ, BA hons, 62, MA, 65; Yale Univ, MPhil, 67, PhD(ling), 70. *Prof Exp:* Instr ling, Ind Univ, 62-64 & Hofstra Univ, 64-65; instr classics, Yale Univ, 67-68, asst prof, 69-75; vis asst prof ling, Univ Calif, Los Angeles, 69; ASSOC PROF CLASSICS, UNIV TEX, AUSTIN, 75- *Concurrent Pos:* Morse fel, Yale Univ, 72-73; Univ Res Inst fel, 75, 78, 82 & 83; Nat Endowment Humanities grant, 76; Nat Endowment for Humanities summer grant, 82. *Honors & Awards:* Cambridge Philol Soc Dean's Award for Excellence in Teaching, 81; Waynflete lectr, Magdalen Col, Oxford, UK, 83. *Mem:* Royal Asiatic Soc; Philol Soc Gt Brit; Ling Soc Gt Brit; Int Soc Mithraic Studies (secy 71-74); Archaeol Inst Am. *Res:* Greek art and poetry; Indo-European linguistics; comparative religion and mythology. *Publ:* Auth, Menandrian maids and Mithraic lions, 75, Glotta; Franz Cumont: The Dura Mithraeum, 75 & Mithraic graffiti at Dura-Europos, 75, Mithraic Studies; ed, Second International Congress of Mithraic Studies, Brill, 78; contribr, Ancient Persia: The art of an empire, 80; Virtue, folly, and Greek etymology, In: Approaches to Honor, Austin, 82; coauth (with M Vickers), Leagros Kalos, Proc Cambridge Philol Soc, 81; auth, Oense, or a tomb with a view, Class Quart, 82. *Mailing Add:* Dept of Classics Univ of Tex Austin TX 78712

FRANCIS, WINTHROP NELSON, b Philadelphia, Pa, Oct 23, 10; m 39, 67; c 3. LINGUISTICS. *Educ:* Harvard Univ, AB, 31; Univ Pa, AM, 35, PhD, 37. *Prof Exp:* From instr to prof English, Franklin & Marshall Col, 37-62; prof, 62-76, chmn dept ling, 68-75, EMER PROF LING & ENGLISH, BROWN UNIV, 76- *Concurrent Pos:* Fulbright res scholar, Univ Leeds, 56-57; Nat Endowment for Humanities sr fel, 72-73; vis sr lectr, Univ Trondheim, Norway, 76-77. *Mem:* MLA; NCTE; Ling Soc Am; Am Dialect Soc; Int Ling Asn. *Res:* English language; dialectology; mechanolinguistics. *Publ:* Auth, The English Language: An Introduction, Norton, 65; coauth, Computational Analysis of Present-Day American English, Brown Univ, 67; Computer-produced representation of dialectal variation: Initial fricatives in Southern British English, Int Conf Comput Ling, 69; auth, Modal daren't and durstn't in dialectal English, In: Studies in Honour of Harold Orton, Leeds Studies in English, 70; The English language and its history, In: Webster's New Collegiate Dictionary, 8th ed, Merriam, 73; Approaches to grammar, In: Current Trends in Linguistics, Mouton, The Hague 73; coauth, Frequency Analysis of English Usage: Lexicon and Grammar, Houghton, 82; auth, Dialectology: An Introduction, London Longmans (in press). *Mailing Add:* Box E Brown Univ Providence RI 02912

FRANCO, ANDRES, b New York, NY, Feb 7, 32. SPANISH LITERATURE. *Educ:* Brooklyn Col, BA, 53; NY Univ, MA, 60, PhD(Span), 69. *Prof Exp:* Lectr Span, Univ Md, Overseas Prog, Madrid, Spain, 60-62; instr, NY Univ, 62-65; lectr, 65-69, asst prof, 69-75, ASSOC PROF SPAN, QUEENS COL, NY, 75- *Concurrent Pos:* Doctoral Fac, City Univ NY Grad Ctr, 77- *Mem:* MLA; Asoc Int Hispanistas; Am Asn Teachers Span & Port. *Res:* Modern Spanish literature; drama and novel of the Golden Age. *Publ:* Auth, El teatro de Unamuno, Ed Insula, Madrid, 71; contrib ed, McGraw-Hill Encyclopedia of Drama, 2nd ed (in press). *Mailing Add:* Dept of Romance Lang Queens Col Flushing NY 11367

FRANCO, JEAN, b Dukinfield, England, Mar 31, 24. LITERATURE. *Educ:* Univ Manchester, BA, 44, MA, 46; Univ London, BA, 60, PhD(Span), 64. *Prof Exp:* Lectr Span, Queen Mary Col, Univ London, 60-64, reader, King's Col, 64-68; prof lit, Univ Essex, 68-72; PROF SPAN & COMP LIT, STANFORD UNIV, 72- *Concurrent Pos:* Guggenheim fel, 76-77. *Mem:* MLA; Latin Am Studies Asn. *Res:* Latin American literature and society; poetry; social theories of literature. *Publ:* Auth, Modern Culture of Latin America, Praegar, Pall Mall, 67, 70; Introduction to Spanish American Literature, Cambridge Univ, 69; co-ed, Companion to World Literature, Penguin; contribr, Encycl Lit, Cassells; Cesar Vallejo: The Dialects of Poetry and Silence, Cambridge Univ, 76. *Mailing Add:* Dept of Span & Port Stanford Univ Stanford CA 94305

FRANCOIS, CARLO ROGER, b Farciennes, Belgium, May 26, 19; nat US; m 48; c 3. FRENCH LANGUAGE & LITERATURE. *Educ:* Univ Liege, Belgium, lic, 44; Harvard Univ, MA, 51, PhD(French), 53. *Prof Exp:* Teacher, high sch, Belgium, 45; nat secy, Belgian YMCA, 45-50; teaching fel, Harvard Univ, 50-53; from instr to assoc prof, 53-67, chmn dept, 62-68, PROF FRENCH, WELLESLEY COL, 67- *Concurrent Pos:* Mem adv bd, Sweet briar Col Jr Year in Paris, 60. *Honors & Awards:* Harbison Award, 55; Chevalier, Palmes Academiques, 65. *Mem:* MLA; Am Asn Teachers Fr. *Res:* Seventeenth century French literature. *Publ:* Auth, L'Esthetique de Saint-Exupery, Delachaux & Niestle, 57; La Notion de l'Absurde dans la Litterature Francaise du XVIIe Siecle, Klincksieck, Paris, 73; Raison & Deraison dans le Theatre de Pierre Corneille, Fr Lit Publ Co, 79. *Mailing Add:* Dept of French Wellesley Col Wellesley MA 02181

FRANK, ELFRIEDA, b Vienna, Austria, Feb 6, 16; US citizen. LATIN. *Educ:* Univ Milan, LittD, 38; Bryn Mawr Col, MA, 41; Univ Va, PhD(classics), 51. *Prof Exp:* Asst prof classics, Cornell Col, 53-56; from asst prof to assoc prof, Tex Tech Univ, 56-61; from asst prof to assoc prof, 61-70, PROF CLASSICS, UNIV NEW ORLEANS, 70- *Mem:* Am Philol Asn; Class Asn Mid W & S. *Res:* Latin philology; Latin epic poetry; Ovid. *Publ:* Auth, Marius and the Roman nobility, Class J, 55; The structure and scope of Lucan's De bello civili, Class Bull, 70; An Ovidian episode in Valerius Flaccus' Argonautica, Rendiconti Ist Lombardo, 71. *Mailing Add:* Dept of Foreign Lang Univ New Orleans New Orleans LA 70122

FRANK, FRANCINE, b New York, NY, Apr 18, 31; div. LINGUISTICS, SPANISH. *Educ:* NY Univ, BA, 52; Cornell Univ, MA, 53; Univ Ill, Urbana, PhD(Span & ling), 55. *Prof Exp:* Instr Span, Univ Ill, Urbana, 55-57; asst lang training supvr, Inter-govt Comt Europ Migration, 59-66; asst prof, 66-80, asst dean, Col Arts & Sci, 73-74, coordr, curric & interdisciplinary studies, Div Humanities, 75-77, ASSOC PROF SPAN & LING, STATE UNIV NY ALBANY, 80-, DIR LING, 73- *Concurrent Pos:* Consult Span proficiency exam, NY State Educ Dept, 70-80; Fulbright sr lectr appl ling, Rome, Italy, 71-72; lectr, English Lang Off, US Embassy, Yugoslavia, 71-72; mem, Regents External Degree Bachelors Comt, NY State, 73-; Fulbright sr lectr ling & English as a second lang, Buenos Aires, Argentina, 80. *Mem:* Am Asn Teachers Span & Port; Int Ling Asn; Ling Soc Am; MLA; Am Coun Teaching Foreign Lang. *Res:* Spanish linguistics, especially syntax; pidgin and creole languages; sociolinguistics, especially language and gender. *Publ:* Auth, Taxemic redundancy in Spanish, In: Structural Studies on Spanish Themes, Acta Salmanticensia, Filos y Letras, Salamanca, Vol XII, No 3; The training of an English teacher, Lingua & Nuova Didattica, 9/72; Language and education in the Leeward Netherlands Antilles, Caribbean Studies, 1/74; Women's language in America: Myth and reality, In: Women's Language and Style, Studies in Contemporary Language, No 1, Akron, 78; co-ed, Colloquium on Spanish and Luso-Brazilian Linguistics, Georgetown Univ Press, 79. *Mailing Add:* HU 227 Dept of Hisp & Ital Studies State Univ of NY Albany NY 12222

FRANK, LUANNE THORNTON, b Johnstown, Pa, Dec 27, 32; m 66. COMPARATIVE LITERATURE & GERMAN. *Educ:* Univ NC, Chapel Hill, AB, 55; Emory Univ, MA, 59 & 63; Univ Mich, Ann Arbor, PhD(Ger), 70. *Prof Exp:* Teaching asst Ger lit, Univ Mich, 66-69; asst prof Ger, 69-70, asst prof, 70-80, ASSOC PROF COMT LIT & GER, UNIV TEX, ARLINGTON, 80- *Concurrent Pos:* Nat Endowment for Humanities younger humanists fel, 72-73. *Mem:* MLA; Am Soc 18th Century Studies; Int Comp Lit Asn; Int Soc Ger Studies; Am Semiotics Soc. *Res:* Literary criticism; continental literature; German literature. *Publ:* Auth, A scale to measure librarians' attitudes toward librarianship, J Educ Librarianship, 63; Kleist's Achilles: Hilfskonstruktion or hero?, In: Husbanding the Golden Grain, Univ Mich, 73; co-ed, Husbanding the Golden Grain: Studies in Honor of Henry W Nordmeyer, Univ Mich, 73; auth, The 'gott der erde: New key to Kleist's Penthesilea?, J Int Ger, Ser A, Vol 2, 75; ed, Literature and the Occult, Univ Tex, 77; auth, A New Means of Assessing Validity in Interpretation, Proceedings Int Comp Lit Cong, Semiotics Sec, Budapest, (in press). *Mailing Add:* Dept of English Univ of Tex Arlington TX 76019

FRANK, MARGOT KUNZE, b Silesia, Ger, Feb 12, 28; US citizen. MODERN LANGUAGES. *Educ:* Univ Md, College Park, BA, 65; Georgetown Univ, PhD(Russ lang & ling), 70. *Prof Exp:* From instr to asst prof, 69-75, ASSOC PROF RUSS, RANDOLPH-MACON WOMAN'S COL, 75- *Concurrent Pos:* Study Soviet Union, Randolph-Macon Woman's Col Humanities Fund, 73, 76. *Mem:* Am Asn Teachers Slavic & E Europ Lang; Am Asn Advan Slavis Studies. *Res:* Russian formalist school. *Publ:* Auth, Similarity and Theme Arrangement, In: The Inspector General and The Playboy of the Western World, 73, Va Bull Am Asn Teachers Slavic & E Europ Lang; coauth, Absolute rules of stress in Russian grammar, Working Papers Lang & Ling, Georgetown Univ, 74; auth, Women's Lib, Soviet Style, Randolph-Macon Woman's Col Alumnae Bull, 75; A new look at Alyosha Karamazov, Ohio State Univ Slavic Papers, 76; Reviewing Krensler's contemporary Soviet Education, Slavic & E Europ J, 77; Mystery of the master's final destination, Can-Am Slavic Studies, XV, 81. *Mailing Add:* Dept of Russ Studies Randolph-Macon Woman's Col Rivermont Ave Lynchburg VA 24504

FRANK, RICHARD IRA, Ancient History, Latin Literature. See Vol I

FRANK, RICHARD MACDONOUGH, b Louisville, Ky, Dec 4, 27; m 50; c 4. SEMITIC STUDIES, ARABIC. *Educ:* Cath Univ Am, AB, 53. *Prof Exp:* From instr to assoc prof Semitic & Egyptian lang, 55-73, PROF SEMITIC & EGYPTIAN LANG & LIT, CATH UNIV AM, 73- *Mem:* Am Orient Soc; Cath Bibl Asn Am. *Res:* Islamic philosophy and theology. *Publ:* Auth, Theorigin of the Arabic philosophical term al-anniya, Les Cahiers du Byrsa; The Neoplatonism of Gahm ibn Safwan according to al-As'ari, Le Museon, 65; The structure of created causality, Studies Islamica 25, 66; The Metaphysics of Created Being According to abu l-Hudhayl al-'Allaf, Nederlands Hist-Archaeol Inst in Nabije Oosten, 66. *Mailing Add:* Dept of Semitic Lang Cath Univ of Am Washington DC 20017

FRANK, TED EARL, b Ont, Aug 10, 31; m 66. GERMAN LANGUAGE & LITERATURE. *Educ:* Univ Western Ont, BA, 54, MA, 57; Univ Mich, PhD(Ger), 70. *Prof Exp:* Asst English, Elly-Heuss Gym, Wiesbaden, 57-58; instr Ger, Univ Western Ont, 58-62; instr, Univ Mich, 63-69; ASSOC PROF GER, UNIV TEX, ARLINGTON, 70-, GRAD ADV, FOREIGN LANG & LIT, 72- *Concurrent Pos:* Assoc bibliogr, Mod Lang Asn, 73- *Mem:* MLA; Am Asn Teachers Ger; Am Coun Teaching Foreign Lang. *Res:* German literature of 19th and 20th centuries; foreign language pedagody; literature of the German Democratic Republic. *Publ:* Auth, An intensive program in German, Bull Asn Dept Foreign Lang, 5/72; A practical approach to intensive German and its results, Unterrichtspraxis, spring 73; Gerhart Hauptmann and Eugen d'Albert, Mich Germanic Studies, 75; coauth, Deutsch für Amerikaner, 79. *Mailing Add:* Dept of Foreign Lang & Ling Univ of Tex Arlington TX 76019

FRANK, YAKIRA H, Linguistics. See Vol II

FRANKEL, HANS HERMANN, b Berlin, Ger, Dec 19, 16; US citizen; m 48; c 2. CHINESE, COMPARATIVE LITERATURE. *Educ:* Stanford Univ, AB, 37; Univ Calif, Berkeley, MA, 38, PhD(Romance lit), 42. *Prof Exp:* Teaching asst Span, Univ Calif, Berkeley, 38-42, lectr, 45-46, lectr Chinese, 50-51, assoc res historian Chinese hist, 51-59, lectr hist, 57-59; assoc prof Western lang, Nat Peking Univ, China, 47-48; asst prof Chinese, Stanford Univ, 59-61; assoc prof, 61-67, PROF CHINESE LIT, YALE UNIV, 67- *Concurrent Pos:* Guggenheim & Yale Univ sr fac fels, 65-66. *Mem:* Chinese Lang Teachers Asn (pres, 78). *Res:* Chinese literature. *Publ:* Auth, Biographies of Meng Hao-jan, Univ Calif, 52, 61; The plum tree in Chinese poetry, Asiatische Studien, 52; Poetry and painting: Chinese and Western views of their convertibility, Comp Lit, 57; Fifteen poems by Ts'ao Chih, J Am Orient Soc, 3/64; The Flowering Plum and the Palace Lady, Yale Univ, 76. *Mailing Add:* Hall of Grad Studies Yale Univ New Haven CT 06520

FRANKEL, MARGHERITA, b Sao Paulo, Brazil; US citizen; m 63. ITALIAN & FRENCH LITERATURE. *Educ:* Brooklyn Col, BA, 68; NY Univ, PhD(French), 73. *Prof Exp:* Asst prof, 73-76, ASSOC PROF ITAL, NY UNIV, 76- *Honors & Awards:* Gustav O Arlt Award in Humanities, Nat Coun Grad Schs, 75. *Mem:* Dante Soc Am; MLA; Renaissance Soc Am; Mediaeval Acad Am; Am Comp Lit Asn. *Res:* Dante; Renaissance literature; Vico. *Publ:* Auth, Capriccio Italiano: un tentative d'interpretazione, Forum Italicum, 74; Le Code Dantesque dans L'Oeuvre de Rimbaud, Nizet, Paris, 75; Rimbaud illumine par Dante, Revue Lett Mod, Paris, 76; Beckett et Proust: le triomphe de la parole, Cahier Herne, Paris, 76; Rilettura della Mirra: non silenzio ma rivelazione calcolata, Italica, 77; The Dipintura and the structure of the New Science as a mirror of the world, Proc Vico/Venezia Conf 1978, 79. *Mailing Add:* Dept of French & Ital NY Univ 19 University Pl New York NY 10003

FRANKENTHALER, MARILYN ROSENBLUTH, b Bronx, NY, Apr 6, 47; m 70; c 3. LATIN AMERICAN LITERATURE, LAW. *Educ:* City Col New York, BA, 68; Hunter Col, MA, 71; Rutgers Univ, PhD(Span), 75; Seton Hall Univ, JD, 79. *Prof Exp:* Teacher Span, Carey High Sch, 69-70; adj lectr, Hunter Col, 70-71; teaching asst, Rutgers Col, Rutgers Univ, 71-74; instr, Douglass Col, 74-75; asst prof, 75-80, ASSOC PROF SPAN & COORDR PARALEGAL STUDIES, MONTCLAIR STATE COL 80- *Concurrent Pos:* Pvt law pract. *Honors & Awards:* Hispanic Inst Medal, City Col New York, 67; Land Finance Award, NJ Title Insurance, 79. *Mem:* Inst Lit Iberoam; MLA; Am Asn Teachers Span & Port; Am Bar Asn. *Res:* Existentialism in the contemporary Latin American narrative, particularly Jose Revueltas and Juan Carlos Onetti; legal Spanish; translators and interpreters in the legal system. *Publ:* Auth, Complemento a la bibliografia de y sobre Juan Carlos Onetti, Rev Iberoam, 4-6/75; Utilizing the computer to prepare a manuscript, Scholarly Publ, 1/76; El otro Chaves: Un extranjero cosmico, Texto Critico, Xalapa, 5-8/77; J C Onetti: La salvacion por la forma, Abra, 77; contribr, Bibliografia de y sobre Jose Revueltas, In: Conversaciones con Revueltas, Univ Veracruzana, Xalapa, 78; auth, Jose Revueltas: El solitario solidaro, Universal, 79; How to work with court interpreters, NJ Lawyer, 81; ed, Skills for Bilingual Legal Personnel, 82. *Mailing Add:* Dept of Span & Ital Montclair State Col Normal Ave Upper Montclair NJ 07043

FRANKLIN, JAMES LEE, JR, b Dayton, Ohio, July 19, 47. GREEK & LATIN LITERATURE. *Educ:* Denison Univ, BA, 69; Queen's Univ, Ont, MA, 70; Duke Univ, PhD(class studies), 75. *Prof Exp:* Asst prof classics, Barnard Col, Columbia Univ, 75-76; asst prof Greek & Latin, Wellesley Col, 76-77; vis asst prof class studies, Univ Mich, Ann Arbor, 77-80; ASST PROF CLASS STUDIES, IND UNIV, 81- *Concurrent Pos:* fel, Am Acad Rome, 73-75; National Endowment for Humanities fel, 80-81. *Mem:* Am Philol Asn; Archaeol Inst Am; Soc Archit Historians; Class Asn Midwest & South. *Res:* Pompeian studies; Latin prose and poetry; Roman archaeology. *Publ:* Auth, Notes on Pompeian Prosopography: Programmatum Scriptores, Chronache Pompeiane, 78; Notes on Pompeian Prosopography: Two Non-Existent Ancients and the D D Lucretii Valentes, La Parola Del Passato, 79: 405-414; Pompeii: The Electoral Programmata, Campaigns and Politics, AD 71-79, Papers & Monog Am Acad Rome, 80; Street and House in Ancient Pompeii, In: The Ancient City: Its Concept and Expression, 80. *Mailing Add:* Dept of Class Studies Ind Univ Bloomington IN 47405

FRANKLIN, URSULA, b Widdersberg, Ger, July 3, 29; US citizen; m 49. FRENCH LANGUAGE & LITERATURE. *Educ:* Mich State Univ, BA, 64; MA, 66, PhD(French), 71. *Prof Exp:* Instr French, Mich State Univ, 70-71; asst prof, 71-74, assoc prof, 74-80, PROF FRENCH, GRAND VALLEY STATE COL, 80- *Concurrent Pos:* Am Coun Learned Soc fel, 78-69. *Mem:* MLA; Am Asn Teachers Fr; Am Coun Teaching Foreign Lang; AAUP. *Res:* Stephane Mallarme; French symbolism; prose peom in French literature. *Publ:* Auth, Poet and people: Mallarme's Conflict and the thirteen prose poems of Divagations, Fr Rev, spring 73; An Anatomy of Poesis: The Prose Poems of Stephane Mallarme, Univ NC, 76; The Rhetoric of Valery's Prose Aubades, Univ Toronto, 79. *Mailing Add:* Dept of French Grand Valley State Col Allendale MI 49401

FRANZ, THOMAS RUDY, b South Milwaukee, Wis, Apr 7, 42; c 2. SPANISH LITERATURE. *Educ:* Carroll Col, BA, 64; Univ Kans, MA, 67, PhD(Span), 70. *Prof Exp:* Instr Span & English, Plymouth Wis Pub Schs, 65-66; asst prof, 70-75, assoc prof, 75-80, PROF MOD LANG, OHIO UNIV, 80- *Concurrent Pos:* Ohio Univ Res Inst res grant, 74. *Mem:* MLA; Midwest Mod Lang Asn; Am Asn Teachers Span & Port; NAm Nietzsche Soc. *Res:* Miguel de Unamuno; 19th and 20th century Spanish novel; comparative literature. *Publ:* Auth, The figure of the civil guard in the novels of Camilo Jose Cela, Occas Papers Lang, Lit & Ling, 12/71; Ancient rites and the structure of Unamuno's Amor y Pedagogia, Romance Notes, 12/71; Humor in Unamuno's Paz en la Guerra, Horizontes, 4/72; Cela's La familia del heroe, the nouveau roman, and the creative act, Mod Lang Notes, 3/73; Menendez y Pelayo as Antolin S Paparrigopulos of Unamuno's Niebla, Papers Lang & Lit, spring 73; El sentido de humor y adquisicion de autoconciencia en Niebla, Cuadernos Catedra Miguel de Unamuno, 73; The philosophical bases of Fulgencio Entrambosmares in Amor y Pedagogia, Hispania, 9/77; Remaking Reality in Galdos, Strathmore Press, 82. *Mailing Add:* Dept of Mod Lang Ohio Univ Athens OH 45701

FRANZBLAU, DANIEL, b New York, NY. FOREIGN LANGUAGE. *Educ:* Brooklyn Col, BA, 47; NY Univ, MA, 49; Miami Univ, Ohio, PhD(educ admin), 72. *Prof Exp:* Teacher & coordr French, Russ lang prog, Edith A Bogert Sch, NJ, 59-64; state consult foreign lang, WVa Dept Educ, Charleston, 64-68; chief dept adv & prof methodol, 68-78, DIR EARLY SCH CONTACT PROG, MIAMI UNIV, 78-, ASSOC PROF FRENCH EDUC, 80- *Concurrent Pos:* Executor & dir Fulbright proj, Fulbright-Hays Comn & WVa Dept Educ, 65-66 & 67-68; Fulbright-Hays Comn res grant, France, 67-68. *Mem:* Am Coun Teaching Foreign Lang; Am Asn Teachers Fr (vpres, 69-71, pres, 71-72); US Int Sch to Sch Exp; Cent States Conf Foreign Lang Teachers. *Res:* Comparative and teacher education; metrics for foreign language teachers; interdisciplinary approaches to the teaching of metrics. *Publ:* Auth, Is English our passport to the world, WVa Sch J, 11/66; contribr, Teaching--some approaches and strategies, In: From Student to Teacher, Kendall-Hunt, 69; auth, The impact of French educational reforms, J Abstr Int Educ, Univ Toledo, fall-winter 72-73; Les etablissements Superieurs Americains Fabriquentils des Chomeurs?, Le Courrier Union Regionale Paris, 6/74; Secondary education reforms in France, Int Educ, Univ Tenn, 1/75; contribr, Metric shock, In: Teaching for Tomorrow in the Foreign Language Classroom, Nat Textbk, 78. *Mailing Add:* 301 McGuffey Hall Miami Univ Oxford OH 45056

FRAPPIER-MAZUR, LUCIENNE, b Marseilles, France, Apr 1, 32; m 62; c 1. FRENCH LITERATURE. *Educ:* Univ Paris, Agregee, 60, Dr d'Etat es lett & sci humanines, 73. *Prof Exp:* From instr to asst prof, 62-71, assoc prof, 71-79, PROF FRENCH, UNIV PA, 79- *Concurrent Pos:* Vis lectr, Bryn Mawr col; reading consult var acad journals, publishers and organizations; Am Coun Learned Soc grant-in-aid, 79 & travel grant, 80. *Mem:* Soc Hist litt France; Soc Etudes Romantiques; MLA; Am Asn Teachers Fr; Int Asn Fr Studies; Groupe Int de Recherches Balzaciennes. *Res:* Novel, psychoanalysis, semiotics. *Publ:* L'Expression Metaphorique dan La Comedie Humanine, Klincksieck, Paris, 76; Aspects baroques du paysage metaphorique dans La Comedia Humaine, Cahiers l'AIEF, 77; ed, Balzac's Les Chouans, Gallimard, 78; Le Regime de L'Aveu dans le Lys dans la Vallee, Rev Sc Humaines, 79; La description Mnemonique dans le Roman Romantique, Litterature, 80; Semiotique dan Corps Malade dans la Comedie Humaine, In: Balzac L'Invention du Roman, Colloque de Cerisy, 82. *Mailing Add:* Dept of Romance Lang Univ of Pa Philadelphia PA 19174

FRASER, HOWARD MICHAEL, b New York, NY, Nov 11, 43; m 67; c 1. SPANISH AMERICAN LITERATURE. *Educ:* Columbia Univ, BA, 64; Univ NMex, MA, 66, PhD(Span), 70; Harvard Univ, AM, 67. *Prof Exp:* Res asst Span, Hisp Inst US, 63-64; grad asst, Univ NMex, 64-66, instr English, col educ, 67; teaching asst Port, 69-70, instr Span, 70; lab asst Englsih, Southwestern Coop Educ Lab, 68; asst prof Span, Univ Wis-Madison, 70-74; asst prof, 74-77, ASSOC PROF MOD LANG, COL WILLIAM & MARY, 77- *Concurrent Pos:* Reader Span, Columbia Col, 63-64; instr Span, Peace Corps Training Ctr, NMex, 65-66 & Ithaca, NY, 66. *Mem:* MLA; Am Asn Teachers Span & Port; AAUP; Midwest Mod Lang Asn; Inst Int Lit Iberoam. *Res:* Modernist fiction in Spanish America; Spanish American theatre. *Publ:* Auth, Irony in the fantastic stories of Azul, Latin Am Lit Rev, 73; El universo psicodelico de Sangre patricia, Hispanofila, 74; Change is the unchanging: Washington Irving and Manuel Gutierrez Najera, J Span Studies: 20th Century, 74; Magic & Alchemy in Dario's El Rubi, Chasqui, 74; Witchcraft in three stories of Jose Donoso, Latin Am Lit Rev, 75; Theatricality in The Fanlights and Payment as Pledged, Am Hispanist, 77; Points south: Ambrose Bierce, Jorge Luis Borges, and the Fantastic, Studies Twentieth Century Lit, 78; Decadence, Dario and The Nightingale, Romance Notes, 78. *Mailing Add:* Dept of Mod Lang Col of William & Mary Williamsburg VA 23185

FRASER, JAMES BRUCE, b Englewood, NJ, June 27, 38; m 61; c 4. LINGUISTICS. *Educ:* Cornell Univ, BEE, 61; Mass Inst Tech, PhD(ling), 65. *Prof Exp:* Sr scientist, Bolt Berenek & Newman Inc, 67-68; dir, Lang Res Found, 68-72; assoc prof ling, 72-78, PROF LING, BOSTON UNIV, 78- *Concurrent Pos:* Consult, Ctr Appl Ling, 75-81; vis assoc prof, Am Univ, Cairo, Egypt, 77-78; prof, Int Ling Inst, Bourguiba Inst, Tunis, Tunisia, summer, 78. *Mem:* Ling Soc Am. *Res:* Pragmatics; second language acquisition; dispute resolution. *Publ:* Auth, Conversational mitigation, J Pragmatics, Vol 4, 80; On apologizing, In: Conversational Routines, Mounton, 81; coauth (with M Greenbaum), Sexual harrasment in the workplace, Arbitration J, Vol 35, No 3; auth, The use of language: The role of the linguist in the university, In: Linguistics and the University Education, Mich State Univ, 81; Second Language Acquistion: A Synthesis, Newbury House Publ (in prep); The domain of pragmatic theory, In: Conversational Competence, Longman Publ (in press); What is an illocutionary act?, Studies in Lang (in prep). *Mailing Add:* 150 W Canton St Boston MA 02118

FRASER, RALPH SIDNEY, b Ipswich, Mass, July 16, 22; m 46; c 3. GERMAN. *Educ:* Boston Univ, AB, 48; Syracuse Univ, MA, 50. *Prof Exp:* Instr Ger, Univ Tenn, 50-52; from asst prof to assoc prof foreign lang & chmn dept, Ill Col, 54-62; assoc prof Ger, 62-72, PROF GER, WAKE FOREST UNIV, 72- *Mem:* MLA; Am Asn Teachers Ger. *Res:* Seventeenth century literature; modern German literataure. *Mailing Add:* Dept of Ger Wake Forest Univ Winston-Salem NC 27106

FRASSICA, PIETRO, b Messina, Italy, Nov 11, 42. ITALIAN LITERATURE & LANGUAGE. *Educ:* Univ Messina, Italy, DLett, 67; Boston Col, PhD(Ital philol), 77. *Prof Exp:* Prof Ital & Latin, Liceo Scientifico, Milan, 69-70 & Monza-Milan, 70-72; instr Ital, Boston Col, 74-75; vis lectr, Univ Mass, Boston, 75-76; ASST PROF ITAL, PRINCETON UNIV, 76- *Concurrent Pos:* Mem, Medieval Studies Comt, Princeton Univ, 78-79 & 82-83; vis lectr, Rutgers Univ, 81-82; ed, Prometeo. *Honors & Awards:* Premio Calabria, Circolo Cult Villa S Giovanni, Italy, 80. *Mem:* MLA; Dante Soc Am; Am Asn Univ Professors Ital; Int Courtly Love Soc. *Res:* Medieval, Renaissance & 18th century Italian literature; Italian philology; Italian language teaching. *Publ:* Auth, Motivi iconografici del Vespro e della Notte, Forum Ital, 76; Appunti sul linguaggio figurativo del Parini dal Giorno ai Soggetti, Aevum, 76; Una lettera autografa di U Foscolo nella Firestone Library, Giornale Storico Lett Ital, 79; Simillimi of Giangiorgio Trissino: Imitation and experimentation, Aquila, 79; transl, Gian Mario Filelfe, Chroniche de la citta de Anchona, Licosa-Firenze, 79; coauth, Per modo di dire (grammar text), DC Health, 81; auth, Nature and artifice in laying Renaissance tables, Album, 81; Una diversa redazione dell'Oda a Charlotte Lennox de Giuseppe Baretti, Giornale Storico Lett Ital, 82. *Mailing Add:* Dept of Romance Lang Princeton Univ Princeton NJ 08540

FRAUTSCHI, RICHARD LANE, b Rockford, Ill, Nov 14, 26; m 73; c 4. FRENCH. *Educ:* Univ Wis, AB, 49; Harvard Univ, AM, 53, PhD, 58. *Prof Exp:* Instr French, Smith Col, 54-58; from asst prof to prof, Univ NC, Chapel Hill, 58-70; PROF FRENCH & CHMN DEPT, PA STATE UNIV, 70- *Concurrent Pos:* Am Coun Learned Soc grant, 68; vis prof French, St Augustine's Col, NC, 60-70; mem advan placement comt French, Col Entrance Exam Bd, 70-76, consult, 76-; Nat Sci Found-Pa State Univ grant, 71; Am Philos Soc Grant, 72; Int Res & Exchanges Bd grant, Soviet Union, 75; Int Res & Exchange Bd grant, Poland & Czechsloakia, 80-81; Camargo Found grant, 81; res fel, Macquarie Univ, Australia, 82. *Mem:* MLA; Am Asn Teachers Fr; Soc Fr Etude XVIIIe Siecle; Am Soc 18th Century Studies; Asn Computing Machinery. *Res:* French literature of the 16th and 18th centuries; quantitative stylistics; pedagogy. *Publ:* Coauth, Pour et Contre, Manuel de Conversations Graduees, Dodd, 72 & 2nd ed, Harper, 78; auth, The authorship of certain unsigned articles in the Encyclopedie, Computer Studies Humanities & V erbal Behav, 70; Styles de roman et styles de censure dan la 2de moitie du 18e siecle, Studies on Voltaire, 72; A project for computer-assisted analysis of French prose fiction, 1751-1800, In: The Computer and Literary Studies, Edinburgh Univ, 73; coauth, Bibliographie due Genre Romanesque Francais, 1751-1800, Mansell, 77; A Model for Chi-Square Analysis of Regression Vocabularyy in H de Crenne's Les Angoysses douloureuses, Comput & Humanities, 79; Le comportement verbal du narrateur dans Gil Blas: Quelques observations quantitatives, Studies Voltaire, 81; Le jeu des axes de narration dans Les Liaisons dangereuses: Etude de focalisation enonciative, Marche Romane, 82. *Mailing Add:* Dept of Fr Pa State Univ University Park PA 16802

FRAWLEY, WILLIAM JOHN, b Newark, NJ, Sept 17, 53. LINGUISTICS. *Educ:* Glassboro State Col, BA, 75; La State Univ, MA, 77; Northwestern Univ, PhD(ling), 79. *Prof Exp:* Asst prof, 79-82, ASSOC PROF ENGLISH, UNIV DEL, 82-, ASST DIR, PROG IN LING, 80- *Concurrent Pos:* Prof, English Inst, Szolnuk, Hungary & Poznan, Poland, summer, 81 & Pecs, Hungary & Rabat, Morocco, summer, 82. *Mem:* Ling Soc Am; MLA; AAAS; Dict Soc NAm. *Res:* Semantics; text structure; cognitive science. *Publ:* Auth, Topological linguistics, 78 & Topology of texts, 80, Papers in Ling; Instead of Music: Poems by Alain Basquet, La State Univ Press, 80; Discourse analysis of communicative disorders, Lang Sci, 80; co-ed, The First Delaware Symposium on Language Studies: Selected Papers (in press), ed, Literary, linguistic and philosophical perspectives (in press) & auth, Science, discourse and knowledge representation, In: Studies in Science and Culture (in press), Univ Del Press; ed, Linguistics and Literacy, Plenum Publ (in press). *Mailing Add:* Dept of English Univ of Del Newark DE 19711

FRAZER, RICHARD MCILWAINE, JR, b Richmond, Va, Aug 14, 31. CLASSICAL PHILOLOGY. *Educ:* Hampden-Sydney Col, AB, 52; Univ NC, MA, 57, PhD, 59. *Prof Exp:* Instr Latin, Univ NC, 57-59; from instr to asst prof classics, 59-65, assoc prof class philol, 65-77, PROF CLASSICS, TULANE UNIV, 77- *Mem:* Am Philol Asn; Class Asn Mid West & South. *Res:* Latin and Greek literature; Homer and Hesiod. *Publ:* Auth, The Trojan War: The Chronicles of Dictys of Crete and Dares the Phrygian, Ind Univ, 66; The Klismos of Achilles, Iliad, 24 596-98, 71 & Pandora's diseases, Erga 102-04, Greek, Roman & Byzantine Studies, 72; Eurymachus' question at Odyssey 1 409, Class Philol, 73; Hesiod's Titanomachy as an Illustration of Zielinski's Law, Greek, Roman & Byzantine Studies, 81. *Mailing Add:* Dept of Classics Tulane Univ New Orleans LA 70118

FRAZIER, EARLENE FREEMAN, b Ga, m 71; c 1. FOREIGN LANGUAGES, ENGLISH. *Educ:* Savannah State Col, BS, 67; Interam Univ, Mex, MA, 71, PhD(Span & Golden Age lit), 75. *Prof Exp:* Instr English & Span, Duval Co Schs, Jacksonville, Fla, 70-72; ASST PROF SPAN, MORRIS BROWN COL, GA, 72-; ASSOC PROF SPAN, ATLANTA JR COL, GA, 76- *Concurrent Pos:* Assoc prof com Span & English Atlanta Area Tech, Ga, 76-77. *Mem:* Col Lang Asn; NEA; Am Asn Teachers Span; Nat Mental Health Soc. *Res:* Afro-Hispanic literature and culture, an ethnic approach; locating Black authors in the Americas; methods of teaching languages. *Mailing Add:* 1934 Austin Rd SW Atlanta GA 30331

FREDERICKS, SIGMUND CASEY, b Hammond, Ind, May 15, 43; div. CLASSICAL STUDIES, COMPARATIVE LITERATURE. *Educ:* St Louis Univ, BA, 65; Univ Pa, MA, 66, PhD(class studies), 69. *Prof Exp:* Asst prof, 69-73, ASSOC PROF CLASSICS, IND UNIV, BLOOMINGTON, 73- *Concurrent Pos:* Assoc ed & bk rev ed, Helios, 75-; ed consult, Sci-Fiction Studies, 76- *Mem:* Am Philol Asn; Sci Fiction Res Asn; Class Asn Midwest & S. *Res:* Comparative mythology; science fiction; Latin satire. *Publ:* Auth, Rhetoric and morality in Juvenal's Eighth satire, Trans Am Philol Asn, 71; coauth, Roman Satirists and Their Satire, Noyes, 74; auth, Science fiction and the world of Greek myths, Helios, 75; Juvenal's Fifteenth Satire, Ill Class Studies, 76; Lucian's true history as science fiction, 76 & Problems of fantasy, 78, Sci-Fiction Studies; Atlantis, In: Atlantis: Fact or Fiction, 78 & The Future of Eternity: Mythologies of Science Fiction and Fantasy, 82, Ind Univ Press. *Mailing Add:* Dept of Class Studies Ballantine 547 Ind Univ Bloomington IN 47401

FREDMAN, STEPHEN ALBERT, American Literature. See Vol II

FREDRICKSMEYER, ERNST, b Bismarck, NDak, Jan 14, 30; m 57; c 3. CLASSICAL PHILOLOGY. *Educ:* Lakeland COl, BA, 52; Univ Wis, MA, 53, PhD, 58. *Prof Exp:* Teaching fel, Univ Wis, 53-55, res fel, 57-58; instr classics, Cornell Col, 58-59 & Dartmouth Col, 59-60; instr Latin, Bryn Mawr Col, 60-61; asst prof classics, Univ Wash, 61-66; assoc prof, 66-71, PROF CLASSICS, UNIV COLO, BOULDER, 71-, CHMN DEPT, 80- *Concurrent Pos:* Vis prof, Univ Ore, 70 & Univ Wis, 77-78. *Mem:* Am Philol Asn. *Res:* Latin poetry; Greek history and religion. *Publ:* Auth, Alexander, Midas, and the oracle at Gordium, Class Philol, 61; On the unity of Catullus 51, Trans & Proc Am Philol Asn, 65; Octavian and the unity of Vergil's first eclogue, Hermes, 66; Catullus 49, Cicero, and Caesar, Class Philol, 73; Horace C 1 34: the conversion, Trans & Proc Am Philol Asn, 76. *Mailing Add:* Dept of Classics Univ Colo Boulder CO 80302

FREEDMAN, DAVID NOEL, Semitic Languages & Literature. See Vol IV

FREEMAN, BRYANT C, b Richmond, Va, June 26, 31; m 59; c 1. FRENCH LITERATURE. *Educ:* Univ Va, BA, 53; Yale Univ, MA, 54; PhD(French lit), 61. *Prof Exp:* Asst instr French, Yale Univ, 55-57, instr, 57-59; from asst prof to assoc prof, Univ Va, 61-71, actg chmn dept romance lang, 71; PROF FRENCH & CHMN DEPT FRENCH & ITAL, UNIV KANS, 71- *Concurrent Pos:* Danforth fac assoc, 65-; Moliere res grant, Brush Found & Univ Va, 68-71; nat chmn, Conf 17th Century Fr Lit, 70, 75. *Mem:* MLA; Am Asn Teachers Fr; Soc Etude XVIIe Siecle; Asn Amis Alain. *Res:* French literature of the 17th century; Moliere; Racine. *Publ:* Auth, Concordance du theatre et des poesies de Jean Racine, (2 vols), Cornell Univ, 68; contribr to Bull Soc Amis Marcel Proust, 60, 61-63; auth, Why a foreign language requirement?--alternate reasons, Bull Asn Depts Foreign Lang, 5/73. *Mailing Add:* Dept of French & Ital Univ of Kans Lawrence KS 66045

FREEMAN, DONALD CARY, English Linguistics. See Vol II

FREEMAN, MICHELLE ALICE, b Washington, DC, Nov 2, 49; m 74; c 1. FRENCH LITERATURE, FRENCH PHILOLOGY. *Educ:* Bryn Mawr Col, BA, 70; Princeton Univ, MA, 72, PhD(Romance lang), 76. *Prof Exp:* ASST PROF FRENCH, COLUMBIA UNIV, 77- *Concurrent Pos:* Nat Endowment for Humanities fel, 82-83. *Mem:* Medieval Acad Am. *Res:* French literature, especially medieval 12th and 13th century French; poetics. *Publ:* Auth, Problems in Romance composition: Ovid, Chretien de Troyes and the Romance of the Rose, Romance Philol, 8/76; Chretien's Cliges: A close reading of the Prologue, Romanic Rev, 3/76; Froissart's Le Joli Buisson de Jonece: A Farewell to Poetry?, Annals NY Acad Sci, 10/78; The Poetics of Translatio Studii and Conjointure in Chretien de Troyes's Cliges, Fr Forum Publ, 79; Transpositions structurales et Intertextualite: Cliges et son Intertexte, Litterature, 2/81. *Mailing Add:* Dept of French & Romance Philol Philos Hall Columbia Univ New York NY 10027

FREEMAN, THOMAS PARRY, b Chicago, Ill, May 22, 44; m 76; c 2. GERMAN LITERATURE, HUMANITIES. *Educ:* Haverford Col, AB, 65; Stanford Univ, MA, 66, PhD(Ger & humanities), 70. *Prof Exp:* Teaching asst Ger, Stanford Univ, 67-68; instr Ger & humanities, Columbia Univ, 68-71; asst prof Ger, State Univ NY, Brockport, 71-75, assoc prof, 75-81; ASSOC PROF GER, BELOIT COL, 81- *Concurrent Pos:* Mem fac literature, New Sch Social Res, spring 71; Ger Acad Exchange Serv fel, 72; State Univ NY Res Found grants-in-aid, 72-73 & 74-75 & Mellon fel, Ger, Univ Pittsburgh, 76-77; Alexander von Humboldt fel, 79-80. *Mem:* Popular Cult Asn; Northeast Mod Lang Asn; Am Asn Prof Yiddish; MLA. *Res:* Modern German literature; German exile literature; Holocaust studies. *Publ:* Auth, El uso del sueno en la poesia de Benn y Mallarme, Folia Humanistica, 9/69; The lotus and the tigress--symbols of mediation in Hans Henny Jahnn's Perrudja, Genre, summer 74; co-ed, Hans Henny Jahnn--Gesammelte Werke 7 Bänden, Hoffmann und Campe, 74; auth, Zu Hans Henny Jahnns Leben, und Werk, Freie Akademie der Künste in Hamburg, 80; Hans Henny Jahnn, 80 & Hans Erick Nossack, 80, Columbia Dict of Modern European Literature, Columbia Univ Press; Mythische Strukturen in Hans Henny Jahnns Perrudja, text und Kritik, 1/80; Hans Henny Jahnns Schweizerr Aufenthalt, Akten des VI Internationalen Germanisten Kongresses Basel, 80. *Mailing Add:* Dept of Mod Lang Beloit Col Beloit WI 53511

FREERKSEN, JAMES ALBERT, Koine Greek, New Testament Studies. See Vol IV

FREESE, WOLFGANG F O, b Lemförde, Ger, Dec 15, 39; m 69; c 2. GERMAN LANGUAGE & LITERATURE, PHILOSOPHY. *Educ:* Univ Münster, Staatsexamen, 63; Univ Tübingen, Staatsexamen, 66, D Phil(Ger, hist), 68. *Prof Exp:* Asst Ger, Univ Tübingen, 66-67; asst prof, Idaho State Univ, 68-69; asst prof, Ill State Univ, 69-71; assoc prof, 71-75, PROF GER, UNIV MD, BALTIMORE COUNTY, 75- *Concurrent Pos:* Guest prof, Univ Klagenfurt, Austria, 77-78. *Mem:* MLA; Am Asn Teachers Ger; Int Music Soc; Int Brecht Soc; NAm Nietzsche Soc. *Res:* Twentieth century German literature; the novel; comparative literature. *Publ:* Auth, Robert Musil-Thomas Mann: Satirsches Fragment und heilige Form, Lit u Kritik, 66: 372-386; Zur epischen Funktion der Liebe im modernen deutschen Roman, Göppingen, Kümmerle, 69; Min geyst hat sich verwildet; zur literarhistorischen Problematik eines spätmittelalterlichen anonymen Textes, In: Festschrift für Bert Nagel, 72; coauth, Broch-Forschung Rezeptions Problematik, Wilhelm Fink, Munich, 77; auth, Thomas Mann und sein Leser, DVjs, 77; Bejamin and Brecht, Telos, 81; Kawabata and Beckett, Univ Kentucky, 81; Music in Switzerland, Univ NC, Chapel Hill, 82. *Mailing Add:* Dept of Mod Lang Univ of Md Baltimore MD 21228

FREIDIN, GREGORY, b Kuibyshev, USSR, June 25, 46; US citizen. RUSSIAN LITERATURE & INTELLECTUAL HISTORY. *Educ:* Univ Calif, Berkeley, MA, 74, PhD(Slavic lang & lit), 79. *Prof Exp:* Lectr, 77-78, ASST PROF RUSSIAN LIT, DEPT SLAVIC LANG & LIT, STANFORD UNIV, 78- *Concurrent Pos:* Fel, Am Coun Learned Soc, 80-81 & Howard Found, 82-83. *Mem:* MLA; Am Asn Advan Slavic Studies. *Res:* Russian modernism in literature, arts and philosophy; Russian intellectual history; interpretation theory in the human sciences. *Publ:* Auth, The whisper of history and the noise of time in the writings of Osip Mandelstam, The Russian Rev, 10/78; Osip Mandelstam: The poetry of time, 1908-1916, Calif Slavic Studies, 80; Fat Tuesday in Odessa: Isaac Babel's Di Grasso as testament and manifesto, 4/81 & Mandelstam's Ode to Stalin: History and myth, 10/82, The Russ Rev. *Mailing Add:* 769 Vincente Ave Berkeley CA 94707

FREIDIN, ROBERT ALEXANDER, b Los Angeles, Calif, July 20, 45; m 67. LINGUISTICS. *Educ:* Univ Calif, Berkeley, BA, 66; Ind Univ, MA, 69, PhD(English lang), 71. *Prof Exp:* Asst prof English, Purdue Univ, West Lafayette, 70-72, asst prof audiol & speech sci, 72-76; vis scientist, Dept Ling, Mass Inst Technol, 76-79; ASST PROF LING, MCGILL UNIV, 80- *Concurrent Pos:* Am Coun Learned Soc fel, 76; Nat Inst Mental Health fel, 77-78; vis asst prof ling, Brown Univ, 79-80. *Mem:* Ling Soc Am. *Res:* Syntax; semantics; lexical structure. *Publ:* Auth, Review of English transformational grammar, Lang Sci, 12/69; Transformations and interpretive semantics, In: Towards Tomorrow's Linguistics, Georgetown Univ; Semantic Interpretation in Generatuve Grammar, 75, The Analysis of Passives, 75 & A Transformational Approach to English Syntax, 78, Language; Cyclicity & the Theory of Grammer, 78 & coauth (with H Lasnik), Disjoint Reference and W H Trace, 81, Linguistic Inquiry; (with H Lasnik), Core Grammar, Case Theory and Markedness, In: Theory of Markedness in Generative Grammar. *Mailing Add:* Dept of Ling McGill Univ Montreal PQ H3A 1G5 Can

FREIRE, JOSE LUIS, b Leon, Spain, Aug 26, 40; US citizen; m 70. LINGUISTICS, SPANISH. *Educ:* Escuela Magisterio, Spain, BA, 62; Univ Northern Iowa, MA(ling) & MA(Span lit), 69; Univ Mich, PhD(Romance ling), 75. *Prof Exp:* Instr Span & French, Colo State Col, 65-66 & State Col Iowa, 66-67; ASST PROF LING & SPAN, MEMPHIS STATE COL, 75- *Mem:* Am Coun Teaching Foreign Lang. *Res:* New research methods in linguistics; semiotics; acquisition of first and seon and second language. *Publ:* Contribr, Factividad y modo: precesos transformacionales de nominalizacion en el gallego actual, Verba, 76. *Mailing Add:* Dept of Foreign Lang Memphis State Univ Memphis TN 38152

FRENCH, PAULETTE, b Laconia, NH, June 16, 41. COMPARATIVE LITERATURE, FRENCH. *Educ:* Colby Col, BA, 63; Univ Paris at the Sorbonne, cert prof francais, 64; Univ Md, College Park, MA, 67; Univ Colo, Boulder, PhD(comp lit), 71. *Prof Exp:* Instr French & Span, Bowie State Col, 65-66; assoc French, Univ Colo, Boulder, 67-69; asst prof Romance lang, Univ Maine, Orono, 69-72, asst to vpres, 72-73; asst vchancellor acad affairs, Univ Calif, Irvine, 73-76; ASSOC PROF FRENCH & COMP LIT & CHMN LANG & CLASSICS, UNIV MAINE, 76- *Concurrent Pos:* Conf interpreter, US State Dept, Washington, DC, 64-66; instr English as foreign lang, Econ Opportunity COmn, San Jose, Calif, 66-67; Am Coun Educ fel, 73-74. *Honors & Awards:* Prix Litteraire Hachette et Larousse laureate, 63-64. *Mem:* Medieval Acad Am; Am Asn Teacher Fr; MLA; AAUP; Nat Asn Women Deans & Counr. *Res:* Moliere; Medieval lyric poetry; academic administration. *Publ:* Auth, L'Ecrivain Contemporain en France, Larousse, Paris, 63; The Musical Moliere: Six Comedies-Ballets and Their Contribution to French Comic Opera, Univ Md, 67; Moliere: le musicien, Gallimard, Paris, 73; Teaching English as a foreign language to Mexican migrant workers, Econ Opportunity Comn Bull, 66. *Mailing Add:* Dept of Lang & Classics Univ of Maine Orono ME 04473

FRENZEL, PETER MICHAEL JUSTINIAN, b St Paul, Minn, Aug 6, 35; m 61; c 3. GERMAN LITERATURE, MEDIEVAL MUSIC. *Educ:* Yale Univ, BA, 58; Middlebury Col, MA, 61; Univ Mich, PhD, 68. *Prof Exp:* Master Ger, St Paul Acad, Minn, 58-63; instr, Univ Mich, 65-66; from instr to asst prof, 66-73, ASSOC PROF GER, WESLEYAN UNIV, 73- *Concurrent Pos:* Assoc provost & fel, Ctr for Humanities, 73-74. *Mem:* MLA; Am Asn Teachers Ger; Mediaeval Acad Am; Int Courtly Lit Soc. *Publ:* Auth, Function, Order and Convenientia in Walther von der Vogelweide, J English & Ger Philol, 72; Beginning and End in Heinrich von Morungen, Henry Nordmeyer Festschrift, 73; Minnesang: Strophic Order and Sung Presentation, Studies Medieval Cult, 76; Contrary Forces and Patterns of Antagonism in Minnesang, Court & Poet, 81; Minne-Sang: The Conjunction of Singing and Loving in German Courtly Song, Ger Quart, 55. *Mailing Add:* Dept of Ger Wesleyan Univ Middletown CT 06457

FRESCOLN, WILSON LYSLE, b Secane, Pa, June 26, 12; m 46; c 2. FRENCH LITERATURE. *Educ:* Univ Pa, AB, 36, MA, 38, PhD, 61. *Prof Exp:* Asst instr Romance lang, Univ Pa, 41-44, instr, 44-45; copy ed, J B Lippincott Co, 45-52; part-time instr, 47-53, from instr to assoc prof, 53-66, dir dept, 56-60, chmn dept, 61-73, PROF MOD LANG, VILLANOVA UNIV, 66- *Mem:* MLA; Soc Anciens Textes Francais; Int Arthurian Soc; Mediaeval Acad Am. *Res:* Old French Arthurian romance; 18th century French literature. *Publ:* Auth, Voltaire's Letters on the Quakers, Allen, 53; A Study on the Old French Romance of Fergus, Univ Pa, 61; Critical edition of the Romance of Fergus, Allen, 82. *Mailing Add:* Dept of Mod Lang Villanova Univ Villanova PA 19085

FREY, EBERHARD, b Heilbronn, Ger, Oct 12, 34; m 67; c 1. GERMAN LANGUAGE & LITERATURE. *Educ:* Univ Southern Calif, MA, 62; Cornell Univ, PhD(Ger lit & Germanic Ling), 69. *Prof Exp:* Instr Ger, Univ BC, 65-69; asst prof, 69-80, ASSOC PROF GER, BRANDEIS UNIV, 80- *Concurrent Pos:* Assoc ed, Spiel; Am Counc Learned Soc grant, 78. *Mem:* MLA; Am Asn Teachers Ger. *Res:* Stylistics and systematic, including computer-assisted literary analysis; contemporary German literature; German exile literature in United States of America. *Publ:* Auth, Reader reactions to German text samples, Mod Lang J, 5/72; Rezeption literarischer Stilmittel--Beobachtungen am Durchschnittsleser, LiLi, Ger, 9/74; Stil und Leser, Herbert Lang, Bern, 75; Stuttgarter Schwäbisch, Elwert, Marburg, 75; Ethisches theater: B Viertels theatertätigkeit im exil, J Int Ger, 77; Text and Stilrezeption, Athenaum, 80; Franz Kafka's style: Impressionistic and statistical methods of analysis, Lang & Style, 80; Subjective word frequency estimates and their stylistic relevance in literature, Poetics, 10/81. *Mailing Add:* Dept of Ger & Slavic Lang Brandeis Univ Waltham MA 02154

FREY, ERICH A, b Heilbronn, Ger, July 23, 31; US citizen; m 60; c 2. GERMANIC LANGUAGES & LITERATURES. *Educ:* Nebr Wesleyan Univ, BA, 55; Univ Nebr, Lincoln, MA, 57; Univ Southern Calif, PhD(Ger), 63. *Prof Exp:* Teaching asst Ger, Univ Nebr, 55-57; lectr, Univ Southern Calif, 57-60; asst prof, 60-69, chmn dept lang & ling, 72-76, assoc prof, 69-80, PROF GER, OCCIDENTAL COL, 80- *Concurrent Pos:* Fulbright-Hays lectr ling, Univ Saarlandes, 67-68; lectr Ger lit, Calif Inst Technol, 69- *Mem:* MLA; Am Asn Teachers Ger; Schiller Ges; Thomas Mann Ges; AAUP. *Res:* Thomas Mann; German exile literature; modern German literature. *Publ:* Auth, An American prototype in Thomas Mann's Konigliche Hoheit, Ky Foreign Lang Quart, 66; contribr, Thomas Mann in Kalifornien, Francke, Berne, 74. *Mailing Add:* Dept of Lang & Ling Occidental Col 1600 Campus Rd Los Angeles CA 90041

FREY, HERSCHEL J, b Waco, Tex, Dec 27, 35; m 64. SPANISH LINGUISTICS, APPLIED LINGUISTICS. *Educ:* Tex Christian Univ, BA, 57; Univ Wis, MA, 58; Univ NC, PhD(Romance lang), 63. *Prof Exp:* Instr Spanish, Univ NC, 62-63; asst prof Spanish ling, Univ Wash, 63-66; asst prof, Univ Calif, Los Angeles, 66-69; ASSOC PROF SPANISH LING, UNIV PITTSBURGH, 70- *Concurrent Pos:* Chmn Spanish I, Mod Lang Asn Am, 68; Fulbright lectr ling, Buenos Aires, Arg, 69-70. *Mem:* MLA; Am Asn Teachers Span & Port; Am Coun Teaching Foreign Lang. *Res:* Linguistics, especially Spanish; Spanish applied linguistics. *Publ:* Coauth, Spanish for Today, Holt, 64; auth, Audio lingual teaching and the pattern drill, Mod Lang J, 68; coauth, A study of attitudes among elementary Spanish students at UCLA, Hispania, 9/71; auth, Teaching Spanish: A Critical Bibliographic Survey, Newbury House, 74. *Mailing Add:* Dept of Hisp Studies Univ of Pittsburgh Pittsburgh PA 15260

FREY, JOHN ANDREW, b Cincinnati, Ohio, Aug 29, 29. ROMANCE LANGUAGES. *Educ:* Univ Cincinnati, BA, 51, MA, 52; Cath Univ Am, PhD(Romance lang), 57. *Prof Exp:* Assoc prof French, 60-70, chmn dept, 66-69, PROF ROMANCE LANG & LIT, GEORGE WASHINGTON UNIV, 70- *Res:* Nineteenth century French literature; stylistics. *Publ:* Auth, Motif Symbolism in the Disciples of Mallarme, Cath Univ Am, 57 & AMS Press, 69; Linguistic and psychological couplings in the Lais of Marie de France, Studies Philol, 63; The art of the novel and the style of Balzac, In: Studies in Honor of Tatiana Fotitch, Cath Univ Am, 73; The Aesthetics of the Rougon-Macquart, Studias Humanitis, Madrid, 78. *Mailing Add:* Dept of Romance Lang & Lit George Washington Univ Washington DC 20006

FREY, JOHN WILLIAM, b Wilkes-Barre, Pa, July 23, 16; m 39; c 3. MODERN LANGUAGES & LINGUISTICS. *Educ:* Dickinson Col, AB, 37; Univ Ill, AM, 39, PhD, 41. *Prof Exp:* Asst Ger, Univ Ill, 38-41; asst prof Ger & French, Presby Col, 41-43; asst prof, Army Specialized Training Prog, Lehigh Univ, 43-44; from asst prof to prof, Ger & Russ & chmn dept, 44-66, PROF RUSS & CHMN DEPT RUSS & LING, FRANKLIN & MARSHALL COL, 66- *Concurrent Pos:* Ed, Der Pennsylvaanisch Deitsch Eileschpiggel, 43-; co-founder & co-dir, Pa Dutch Folklore Ctr, Kutztown, Pa; vis prof Russ, Dickinson Col, 60-66; dir, Russ area studies, Franklin & Marshall, 66-; dir, Project SLUR, Haas Community Fund grant, 69-72. *Mem:* MLA; Ling Soc Am; Teachers English Speakers Other Lang; Am Asn Advan Slavic Studies; Am Assoc Teachers Slavic & EEurop Lang. *Res:* Pennsylvania Dutch grammar, language, lore and folk music; Amish hymnody; Russian language. *Publ:* Auth, A Simple Grammar of Pennsylvania Dutch, 42 & John Baers & Son, 81; Jake un Johnny, private publ, 43; contribr, Bibliography, Americana Germanica, 44; auth, Amish triple-talk, Am Speech, 4/45; contribr, Amish Hymns as Folk Music, In: Pennsylvania Songs and Legend, Univ Pa Press, 49 & Johns Hopkins Univ Press, 52; Pennsylvania Dutch, In: Encyclopedia Americana, 79. *Mailing Add:* Dept of Russ & Ling Franklin & Marshall Col Lancaster PA 17604

FREY, JULIA BLOCH, b Louisville, Ky, July 25, 43. FRENCH LITERATURE AND CULTURE. *Educ:* Antioch Col, BA, 66; Univ Tex, Austin, MA, 68; Yale Univ, MPhil, 70, PhD(Fr), 77. *Prof Exp:* Instr French, Brown Univ, 72-73; asst lectr law, Univ Paris I, 73-75; lectr French, Yale Univ, 75-76; ASSOC PROF FRENCH, UNIV COLO, 76- *Concurrent Pos:* Prof, Inst Comp & Int Law, Univ San Diego Law Sch, Paris, 79- *Res:* Nineteenth and 20th century French literature and culture; puppet theatre. *Publ:* Auth, Modern puppet theatre and social protest, Cultures, 2:3; contribr, Duchamp/Tradition de la rupture ou rupture de la tradition?, Eds Le Monde en 10/18, 78; auth, George Sand: The Woman and Her World, Univ Colo Publ Serv, 79; George Sand and the Puppet Theatre at Nohant, Col Asn Press, 79; Aime van Rod: Le Dominateur ou l'Ecole des Vierges and Flora en Pension, Am Bk Rev, 2:4; L'Uso Politico delle Marionette, Quaderni di Teatro, 80; Un Inedit de Flaubert: La Lutte du Sacerdoce et de l'Empire (1837), Rev Hist Litt France, 81; Conservative sex: The social implications of the Romam Galant, J Popular Cult, 82. *Mailing Add:* Dept of French & Ital Univ of Colo Boulder CO 80309

FREY, PETER W, b Philadelphia, Pa, June 27, 39; m 70; c 3. FRENCH LANGUAGE & LITERATURE. *Educ:* La Salle Col, BA, 60; Univ Pittsburgh, MA, 62; Temple Univ, EdD, 82. *Prof Exp:* CHMN MOD LANG, HOLY FAMILY COL, PA, 69- *Publ:* Auth, Anguish and absuro in French drama, Gwynedo J, 70; History of Holy Family College, Holy Family Col Press, 79; contribr, The Peoples of Pennsylvania: An Annotated Bibliography, Univ Pittsburgh Press, 81; auth, Voltaire: Closet believer, 81 & Voltaire and the Quakers, 82, Bull Pa Mod Lang Asn. *Mailing Add:* Mod Lang Dept Holy Family Col Philadelphia PA 19114

FREYBURGER, HENRI, b Colmar, France, Aug 24, 27; US citizen. GERMAN, FRENCH. *Educ:* Friends Univ, Kans, BA, 61; Univ Ark, MA, 63; Sorbonne, Dr Univ(French lit), 69. *Prof Exp:* PROF, CHMN DEPT FOREIGN LANG & DIR INT PROGS, PITTSBURG STATE UNIV, KANS, 69- *Mem:* MLA; Am Asn Teachers Fr; Asn Amis Anotre Cejiote. *Publ:* Auth, La Disponibilite Gioienne, Nizet, 70. *Mailing Add:* Pittsburg State Univ Pittsburg KS 66762

FRIEDBERG, MAURICE, b Rzeszow, Poland, Dec 3, 29; US citizen; m 56; c 2. SLAVIC LANGUAGES & LITERATURE. *Educ:* Brooklyn Col, BSc, 51; Russian Inst, cert & Columbia Univ, AM, 53, PhD(Slavic lang & lit), 58. *Prof Exp:* Lectr Russ, Hunter Col, 55-58, from instr to asst prof, 58-62, assoc prof & in charge Russ div, 62-65; prof Slavic lang & lit, Ind Univ, Bloomington, 66-75, dir Russ & E Europ Inst, 67-71; PROF RUSS LIT & HEAD DEPT SLAVIC LANG & LIT, UNIV ILL, URBANA, 75- *Concurrent Pos:* Assoc, Russ Res Ctr, Harvard Univ, 53; lectr, Brooklyn Col, 54, 62, & Middlebury Col, 60, 61; vis asst prof Russ lit, Columbia Univ, 61-62; travel grant, St Antony's Col, Oxford Univ, 62; Inst Study USSR, Munich, Ger, 63, 68; Fulbright vis prof, Hebrew Univ, Israel, 65-66; mem fel comt, Nat Endowment for Humanities, 70: mem bd dirs, Int Res & Exchanges Bd, 70-73; Guggenheim fel, 71 & 81-82; juror, Nat Bk Award, 73. *Mem:* MLA; Am Asn Advan Slavic Studies; Am Asn Teachers Slavic & East Europ Lang; corresp mem Polish Inst Arts & Sci, US. *Res:* Soviet and 19th century Russian literature; Polish literature. *Publ:* Auth, Russian Classics in Soviet Jackets, Columbia Univ, 62: The Part and the Poet in the USSR, NY Univ, 63; ed, A Bilingual Collection of Russian Short Stories, Vols I & II, 64 & 65, Random; auth, The Jew in Post-Stalin Soviet Literature, B'nai B'rith, 70: A Imagem do Judeu na Literatura Sovietica Pos-Stalinista, Ed Grijalbo, Sao Paulo, 71; co-ed & contribr, Encyclopedia Judaica (16 vols), Macmillan, 71-72: ed, Leon Trotsky, The Young Lenin, Doubleday, 72; A Decade of Euphoria: Western Literature in Post-Stalin Russia 1954-64, Ind Univ, 77. *Mailing Add:* Dept of Slavic Lang & Lit 3092 Foreign Lang Bldg Univ Of Ill Urbana IL 61801

FRIEDERICH, WERNER PAUL, b Thun, Switz, June 2, 05; nat US; m 35, 60; c 1. GERMAN & COMPARATIVE LITERATURE. *Educ:* Harvard Univ, AM, 29, PhD, 32. *Prof Exp:* Prof Ger & comp lit, 35-59, Kenan prof comp lit, 59-70, chmn dept, 56-66, EMER KENAN PROF, UNIV NC, CHAPEL HILL, 70- *Concurrent Pos:* Vis prof, Univ Berne, Switz, 38; Fulbright lectr, Australia, 55, 64; vis prof Am & comp lit, Univ Zürich, Switz, 60; vis prof comp lit, Univ Hawaii, 59, Univ Calif, Berkeley, 62, Univ Colo, 63, Duke Univ, 66, 67 & Univ Southern Calif, 68. *Mem:* Int Comp Lit Asn(pres, 58-61); Am Comp Lit Asn(pres, 59-62). *Publ:* Auth, Werden und Wachsen der USA in 300 Jahren, Francke, Berne, 39; coauth, History of German literature, Barnes & Noble, 48; auth, Dante's Fame Abroad, 1350-1850, Storia e Let, Rome, 50; Bibliography of Comparative Literature, 50, Outline of Comparative Literature, 54, Australia in Western Imaginative Prose Writings, 1600-1960 & The Challenge of Comparative Literature and Other Addresses, 70, Univ NC. *Mailing Add:* 112 Carol Woods Chapel Hill NC 27514

FRIEDMAN, ADELE CHARLENE, b New York, NY, May 20, 38; m 60; c 3. FRENCH LANGUAGE & LITERATURE. *Educ:* Barnard Col, BA, 60; Yale Univ, PhD(French), 69. *Prof Exp:* From asst prof to assoc prof French, 70-78, assoc dean undergrad studies, 78-78, PROF FRENCH, SONOMA STATE UNIV, 79-, CHMN, DEPT FOREIGN LANG, 80- *Concurrent Pos:* Nat Endowment Humanities fel in residence, Univ Calif, Los Angeles, 75-76; proj dir foreign regional colt, Calif State Univ & Cols, 77-78. *Honors & Awards:* Quebec Govt Scholar, 78 & 82. *Mem:* Am Asn Teachers Fr; MLA; Western Soc Fr Hist; Am Folklore Soc; Philol Asn Pac Coast. *Res:* French folksongs and British broadside ballads; European popular imagery; women's regional literature and history. *Publ:* Auth, Sterotypes of traditional society in French folksongs and Images Populaires, J Popular Cult, spring 77; Popular imagery and folksongs in Franche-Comte, 1840-1869, Proc Western Soc Fr Hist, 77; Anne Sylvestre et la muse menagere, Fr Rev, 2/78; Emancipated women in British working class literature: Broadside ballard viragos, J Popur Cult, fall 79; Love, sex, and marriage in traditional French society: The documentary evidence of folksong, Fr Rev, 12/78. *Mailing Add:* Dept of Foreign Lang Sonoma State Univ Rohnert Park CA 94928

FRIEDMAN, EDWARD HERBERT, b Richmond, Va, Jan 19, 48; m 74. SPANISH LITERATURE. *Educ:* Univ Va, BA, 70; Johns Hopkins Univ, MA, 71, PhD(Romance lang), 74. *Prof Exp:* Asst prof, Kalamazoo Col, 74-77, asst prof, 77-80, ASSOC PROF SPAN, ARIZ STATE UNIV, 80- *Mem:* MLA, Rocky Mountain Mod Lang Asn: Rocky Mountain Medieval & Renaissance Asn Am Asn Teachers Span & Port. *Publ:* Auth, Dramatic perspective in Calderon's El mayor monstruo los celos, Bull Comediantes, 74; Conceptual proportion in Cervantes' El licenciado Vidriera, SAtlantic Bull, 74; Tragedy and tragicomedy in Ruiz de Alarcon's El dueno de las estrellas and La crueldad por el honor, Ky Romance Quart, 75; La Numancia within structural patterns of sixteenth-century Spanish tragedy, Neophilologus, 76; Dramatic structure in Cervantes and Lope: The two Pedro de Urdemalas plays, Hispania, 77; Poetic duality in Pedro Salinas' Seguro azar, USF Lang Quart, 77; From concept to drama: The other Unamuno, Hispanofila (in press). *Mailing Add:* Dept of Foreign Lang Ariz State Univ Tempe AZ 85281

FRIEDMAN, EVA MARY, b Berlin, Ger, Oct 21, 26; nat US; m. GERMAN. *Educ:* Hunter Col, BA, 49; Johns Hopkins Univ, MA, 51, PhD(German), 54. *Prof Exp:* Instr mod lang, Cedar Crest Col, 52-53; from instr to assoc prof, 53-73, dir Ger prog, 73-74, PROF GER, ADELPHI UNIV, 73- *Honors & Awards:* Senner Prize, 49. *Mem:* MLA; Am Asn Teachers Ger. *Res:* Nineteenth century German literature; foreign languages in the elementary school; Theodor Storm. *Publ:* Auth, Rainer Maria Rilkes Aufzeichmumgen des Malte Laurids Brigge oder das Problem der menschlichen Existenz; T The child in German literature: From marionette through symbol to reality, winter 69 & The generation gap 100 years ago: The father-son conflict in Theodor Storm's novellen, winter 74, Univ Dayton Rev; Existence and alienation in Rainer Maria Rilke's Notebooks of Malte Laurids Brigge, Univ Dayton Rev, 81; Amerikaspiegelung in Theodor Storm's Novelle, Botjer Basch, In: Schriften Der Theodor Storm Gesellschaft (in press). *Mailing Add:* Dept of Lang & Int Studies Adelphi Univ Garden City NY 11530

FRIEDMAN, LIONEL JOSEPH, b Mantua, Ohio, May 6, 21; m 47; c 4. ROMANCE LANGUAGES. *Educ:* Harvard Univ, AB, 43, MA, 46, PhD(Romance philol), 50. *Prof Exp:* Instr Romance lang, Harvard Univ, 50-53; from asst prof to assoc prof French & Ital, Ind Univ, 53-61; assoc prof, 61-68, PROF ROMANCE LANG, UNIV WASH, 68- *Concurrent Pos:* Fulbright res fel, Paris France, 59-60. *Mem:* Mediaeval Acad Am. *Res:* Mediaeval French literature. *Mailing Add:* Dept of Romance Lang & Lit Univ of Wash Seattle WA 98195

FRIEDMAN, MELVIN JACK, English, Comparative Literature. See Vol II

FRIEDRICH, PAUL, b Oct 22, 27; US citizen; m 74; c 4. LINGUISTICS, ANTHROPOLOGY. *Educ:* Harvard Univ, BA, 50, MA, 51; Yale Univ, PhD(anthrop), 57. *Prof Exp:* Res assoc, Russ Res Ctr, 49-50; asst prof anthrop, Harvard Univ, 57-58; asst prof jr ling, Deccan Col, India, 58-59; asst prof anthrop, Univ Pa, 59-62; assoc prof, 62-67, PROF ANTHROP & LING, UNIV CHICAGO, 67- *Mem:* Ling Soc Am. *Res:* Poetry. *Publ:* Auth, Proto-Indo-European Trees, Univ Chicago, 70; The Tarascan Suffixes of Locative Space: Meaning and Morphotactics, Ind Univ, 71; Agrarian Revolt in a Mexican Village, 77 & The Meaning of Aphrodite, 78, Univ Chicago; Bastard Moons, Waite, 79; Language, Context and the Imagination, Stanford, 79. *Mailing Add:* Dept of Anthrop Univ Chicago Chicago IL 60637

FRIEDRICH, RAINER WALTER, b Mannheim, WGer, Sept 25, 37; Can citizen; m 63; c 2. CLASSICS, COMPARATIVE LITERATURE. *Educ:* Univ Goettingen, Dr phil, 72. *Prof Exp:* Lectr classics, 65-70, asst prof, 70-75, assoc prof classics & comp lit, 75-82, PROF CLASSICS & COMP LIT, DALHOUSIE UNIV, 82- *Concurrent Pos:* Guest lectr, Found Year Prog, Univ King's Col, Halifax, 76-79; sabbatical leave fel, Social Sci & Humanities Res Coun Can, 80. *Mem:* Class Asn Can; Can Comp Lit Asn; Int Comp Lit Asn; Int Brecht Soc. *Res:* Classical Greek literature: drama and epic; history and theory of drama; aesthetic theory. *Publ:* Auth, Stilwandel im Homerischen Epos - Studien zur Poetik und Theorie der epischen Gattung, Carl Winter, Heidelberg, 75; On Brecht and Eisenstein, TELOS, 31: 155-164; Reritualisierung und Deritualisierung im Theater Artauds und Brechts, Proc IXth Cong Int Comp Lit Asn, 80; Euripidaristophanizein and Nietzschesokratizein: Aristophanes, Nietzsche and the death of tragedy, DIONYSIUS IV: 5-36; On the compositional use of similes in the Odyssey, Am J Philol, 102: 120-137; contribr, Drama and ritual, In: Themes in Drama, Vol V, Cambridge Univ Press, 82: 159-223; Epeisodion in Drama and Epic, Hermes, 83. *Mailing Add:* 1590 Robie St Halifax NS B3H 3E6 Can

FRIEDRICHSMEYER, ERHARD MARTIN, b Rugby, NDak, Aug 9, 33; c 3. GERMAN. *Educ:* Lakeland Col, BA, 58; Univ Wis, MA, 59; Univ Minn, PhD(German), 64. *Prof Exp:* Instr Ger, Concordia Col, Moorhead, Minn, 59-60; instr, Univ Minn, 61-63; asst prof, Univ Wis-Milwaukee, 63-66; from asst prof to assoc prof, 66-70, PROF GER, MCMICKEN COL, UNIV CINCINNATI, 70- *Res:* Twentieth century German literature. *Publ:* Auth, Schnitzler's Der Grune Kakadu, Z Deutsche Philol, 69; The Dogmatism of Pain-Grass' Local Anaesthetic, Dimension, 71; The Bertram Episode in Hesse's Glass Bead Game, Ger Rev, 74; Hagiography and Humor in Hesse's Glass Bead Game, In: Hermann Hesse Heute, Bouvies, Bonnn, 80; Die satiresihe Kurzprosa Heinrich Bolls, Univ NC Press, 81; The Swan Song of a Male Chauvonist, In: Of The Fisherman and His Wife: Grimbes Grass, The Floundes in Critical Perspective, AMS Press, 82. *Mailing Add:* Dept of Ger Lang & Lit Univ of Cincinnati Cincinnati OH 45221

FRIEMAN, WALTER EDGAR, JR, b Flushing, NY, Sept 10, 13; m 42; c 2. SYSTEMATIC THEOLOGY, CLASSICAL LANGUAGES. *Educ:* NY Univ, BS, 38; Gen Theol Sem, STB, 42; Philadelphia Divinity Sch, STM, 50, ThD, 57. *Prof Exp:* Reactor, St Andrew's Church, Trenton, NJ, 44-46; reactor, Christ Church, Palmyra, NJ, 46-51; vicar, St Ambrose's Church, Philadelphia, 51-65; lectr, class lang, West Chester State Col, 61-62, from instr to assoc prof, 62-68, chmn dept foreign lang, 75-77, prof class lang & coordr class studies, 68-79; RETIRED. *Concurrent Pos:* Dir studies, Diocese Pa, 60-65. *Mem:* Am Class League; Anglican Soc Mary Am(chaplain, 76). *Res:* Comparative grammar and syntax; eucharistic theology and history; medieval Greek and Latin theology. *Publ:* Contribr, Articles in various class & theol periodicals. *Mailing Add:* 827 Mystery Lane West Chester PA 19380

FRIEND, JEWELL ANNE, English, Linguistics. See Vol II

FRIER, BRUCE WOODWARD, b Chicago, Ill, Aug 31, 43. CLASSICAL STUDIES, HISTORY OF LAW. *Educ:* Trinity Col, Conn, BA, 64; Princeton Univ, PhD(classics), 70. *Prof Exp:* Lectr Latin, Bryn Mawr Col, 68-69; ASSOC PROF CLASS STUDIES, UNIV MICH, 69- *Concurrent Pos:* Vis lectr law, Univ Mich, 81- *Mem:* Am Philol Asn. *Res:* Roman legal history; Roman social and economic history; ancient demography. *Publ:* Auth, The rental market of early imperial Rome, J Roman Studies, 77; Tenant's liability for damage to landlord's property, 77 & Law, technology, and social change, 79, Zeitschrift der Savigny-Stiftung, Röman Abstr; Libr Annales Pontificum Maximorum: The Origins of the Annalistic Tradition, Am Acad Rome, 79; Landlords and Tenants in Imperial Rome, Princeton Univ, 80; Roman life expectancy: Ulpian's evidence, Harvard Studies Class Philol, 82. *Mailing Add:* Dept of Class Studies Univ of Mich Ann Arbor MI 48109

FRIES, PETER H, b Ann Arbor, Mich, June 18, 37; m 64. LINGUISTICS, ENGLISH GRAMMAR. *Educ:* Univ Mich, AB, 59; Univ Pa, PhD(ling), 64. *Prof Exp:* Asst prof ling, Univ Wis-Madison, 65-71; from asst prof to assoc prof, 71-76, PROF ENGLISH & LING, CENT MICH UNIV, 76- *Concurrent Pos:* Vis prof, Teachers English to Speakers Other Lang Inst, Columbia Univ, 81; mem, Comn on English Lang, Nat Coun Teachers English, 81-83. *Mem:* Ling Soc Am; MLA; NCTE; Teachers English to Speakers Other Lang; Ling Asn Can & US. *Res:* Text analysis. *Publ:* Auth, Tagmeme Sequences in the English Noun Phrase, Summer Inst Ling, 70; Problems in the tagmemic description of the English noun phrase, In: Proc 11th Int Cong Ling, Bologna, Italy 1972, Soc Ed Mulino Bologna, 74; Some fundamental insights of tagmemics revisited, In: Linguistic and Literary Studies in Honor of Archibald A Hi-l, Peter de Ridder, 77; On surface and underlying structure in tagmemic theory with special reference to phrase, clause, and sentence, In: Tagmemics: Theoretical Discussion, Mouton, The Hague, 76; English predications of comparison, In: The Third Lacus Forum, Hornbeam, 77; Language and the expression of meaning: A linguist looks a literature, English in Australia, 79; On Negation in Comparative Constructions, Festschrift for Jacob Ornstein, Rowley, 80. *Mailing Add:* Dept of English Cent Mich Univ Mt Pleasant MI 48859

FRIESEN, GERHARD KURT, b Wilhelmshaven, WGer, Mar 15, 40; Can citizen; m 69; c 2. MODERN GERMAN LITERATURE. *Educ:* Waterloo Univ Col, BA, 63; Johns Hopkins Univ, MA, 64, PhD(Ger), 68. *Prof Exp:* From instr to asst prof Ger, Johns Hopkins Univ, 67-74; asst prof, 74-75, ASSOC PROF GER, WILFRID LAURIER UNIV, 75- *Mem:* Am Asn Teachers Ger; Am Goethe Soc; MLA; Charles D-Sealsfield Ges; Soc Ger-Am Studies. *Res:* Nineteenth century German literature; American-German literary relations. *Publ:* Auth, Four previously unpublished letters of Gutzkow to Oppermann, 68 & Charles Sealsfield and the German panoramic novel of the 19th century, 69, Mod Lang Notes; Clemens Brenatano's Nachklänge Bethoven'sscher Musik, In: Studies in Honor of Harold Jantz, Delp München, 72; The German Panoramic Novel of the 19th Century, Herbert Lang, Bern, Switz, 72; co-ed, Charles Sealsfield, Das Kajütenbuch (2 vols), Georg Olms, Hildesheim, W Ger; The German Contribution to the Building of the Americas, Studies in Honor of Karl J R Arndt, Clark Univ, 77. *Mailing Add:* Dept of Ger Wilfrid Laurier Univ Waterloo ON N2L 3C5 Can

FRIJTERS, CORNELIS JOSEPH, b Laren, Netherlands, July 15, 20; m 73; c 1. LINGUISTICS, MODERN & CLASSICAL LANGUAGES. *Educ:* St John's Col, Netherlands, Staatsexamen, 41; Sorbonne, cert French lang, 55; Roman Cath Univ Nijmegen, Drs, 57. *Prof Exp:* Instr Dutch & Ger, St John's Col, Netherlands, 48-50; instr Class Greek, Prep Sch Protestant Theol, St Germainen-Laye, France, 55-57; instr, City Sch, Amsterdam, 58-60; vis instr French, Ger & Dutch, 64-65; assoc prof Ger & French, Wilkes Col, 62-64; prof Ger Lang & French lit & chmn dept, Western Md Col, 65-67, assoc prof Ger, 68-69; vis instr Dutch ling & lit, Libanon Lyceum, Rotterdam, 67-68; vis instr French & Ger, Lyceum Alkmaar, Netherlands, 69-70; assoc prof, 70-80, PROF LING & FRENCH, JUNIATA COL, 80- *Mem:* Am Asn Teachers Fr. *Res:* Applied linguistics; literary interpretation. *Mailing Add:* Dept of Lang Studies Juniata Col Huntingdon PA 16652

FRINK, HELEN HILLER, b Portsmouth, NH, July 4, 47; m 73; c 2. GERMAN LITERATURE. *Educ:* Univ NH, BA, 68; Univ Chicago, MA, 70, PhD(Ger), 75. *Prof Exp:* Asst prof French & Ger, Keene State Col, 74-79 & State Univ NY Albany, 79-81; ASST PROF GER, KEENE STATE COL, 81- *Concurrent Pos:* Dir, Humanities Advisement Ctr, State Univ NY, Albany, 80-81. *Mem:* MLA; Am Asn Teachers of Ger; Am Coun Teaching For Lang; Hugo von Hofmannsthal Gesellschaft. *Res:* Hofmannsthal; language teaching; animal symbolism. *Publ:* Auth, The hunting motif in Hofmannsthal's works, Modern Lang Notes, 4/80; Careers for humanities majors, Humanities Report # 3, 11/81; Oral testing for first year language classes, For Lang Ann, 9/82; Hofmannsthal's Knabengeschichten, Mod Austrian Lit, 82. *Mailing Add:* Dept of Modern Lang Keene State Col Keene NH 03431

FRINK, ORRIN, b Bellefonte, Pa, Apr 2, 32; m 73; c 4. SLAVIC LANGUAGES & LITERATURES. *Educ:* Haverford Col, BA, 54; Middlebury Col, MA, 55; Harvard Univ, PhD(Slavic lang & lit), 61. *Prof Exp:* Tutor Russ, Harvard Univ, 56-57, teaching fel, 58-59; asst prof & dir div, Univ Mass, 59-61; asst prof ling & dir intensive lang training ctr, Ind Univ, 61-64; from assoc prof to prof mod lang, Ohio Univ, 64-75, chmn ling comt dept English, 65-66; PROF RUSS & CHMN DEPT FOREIGN LANG & LIT, IOWA STATE UNIV, 75- *Concurrent Pos:* Translr, Peabody Mus, Harvard Univ, 57-59; linguist & programmer, Nat Sci Found math ling & automatic translr studies, Harvard Computation Lab, 58-64; chmn comt publ, mod lang dept, Ohio Univ, 66-68. *Mem:* MLA; Am Asn Teachers Slavic & East Europ Lang; Am Coun Teaching Foreign Lang; Am Transl Asn. *Res:* Slavic languages and literatures; linguistics; teaching methods for modern languages. *Publ:* Auth, On designing an undergraduate Russian program, Mod Lang J, 1/65; Intensive language training, In: The Study of Foreign Languages, Philos Libr, 68; I'd like to have a machine . . . , NALLD J, winter 73; Image and technique in the poetry of Xristo Botev, OPLLL, 75; On the distribution of productive catagories in Russian of the sixties, ERIC, 10/77; The structure of case function in old church Slavonic, Slavia, 9/78. *Mailing Add:* Dept of Foreign Lang & Lit 300 Pearson Hall Iowa State Univ Ames IA 50011

FRISKNEY, THOMAS EDWIN, b Edon, Ohio, Feb 6, 28; m 48; c 6. CLASSICAL GREEK, NEW TESTAMENT. *Educ:* Cincinnati Bible Sem, AB, 51, MA, 52, BD, 55. *Prof Exp:* Instr, 54-59, PROF THEOL, CINCINNATI BIBLE SEM, 59- *Concurrent Pos:* Minister, Church Christ, Pandora, Ohio, 49-52, Columbia Church Christ, Edon, Ohio, 52-56, Church Christ, Hamersville, Ohio, 56-79 & Saltair Church Christ, Bethel, Ohio, 79- *Res:* Greek exegesis; hermeneutics; book of Revelation. *Publ:* Auth, articles, In: Straight Mag, Sem Rev, Bethel J & Bible Teacher & Leader, 56-; Studies in I & II Thessalonians, College Press, 82. *Mailing Add:* 898 State Rte 125 Hamersville OH 45130

FRITSCH, CHARLES THEODORE, b Allentown, Pa, Apr 5, 12; m 46; c 2. ORIENTAL LANGUAGES. *Educ:* Muhlenberg Col, AB, 32; Princeton Theol Sem, ThB, 35: Princeton Univ, PhD(Orient lang), 40. *Prof Exp:* Vis prof, NB Theol Sem, 38: sch theol, Temple Univ, 45; assoc prof, 50-57, prof, 57-59, WILLIAM HENRY GREEN PROF OLD TESTAMENT, PRINCETON THEOL SEM, 80- *Concurrent Pos:* Vis prof, Am Schs Orient Res, Jerusalem, 54; dir, Inst Mediterranean Studies Sem, Educ Div & chief field archaeologist, Link Underwater Exped, Israel, 60; grant, Am Asn Theol Sem, 63-64; adj prof relig, grad sch relig, Temple Univ, 63-; spec lectr, Hankuk Sem, Seoul, Korea & Japan, 65; dir, Negev Archaeol Sem, Israel; trustee, Westminster Found, Princeton Univ & NJ Synod; adj prof Greek, Dropsie Col, 68-78, emer prof, 79- *Mem:* Am Orient Soc; Soc Am Archaeol; Nat Asn Prof Hebrew; Am Schs Orient Res; Int Orgn Septuagint & Cognate Studies. *Res:* Old Testament; theology; Dead Sea Scrolls. *Publ:* Auth, The Anti-Anthropomorphisms in the Greek Pentateuch, Princeton Univ, 43; contribr, Proverbs, In: Interpreter's Bible, Abingdon, 55; auth, The Qumran Community, Its History and Scrolls, Macmillan, 56, 72; Lexical Handbook of the Hebrew Bible (Genesis), 57: contribr, Genesis, In: Layman's Bible Commentary, 59; I & II Chronicles, Ezra, Nehemiah, In: One Volume Interpreter's Bible Commentary, 72; coauth, A Classified Bibliography of the Septuagint, Brill, 73. *Mailing Add:* 314-B Sharon Way Trenton NJ 08650

FROBERG, BRENT MALCOLM, b Baltimore, Md, Apr 8, 43; m 70. CLASSICS. *Educ:* Ind Univ, AB, 64, MA, 65; Ohio State Univ, PhD(classics), 72. *Prof Exp:* Instr Classics, Univ Tenn, Knoxville, 68-69; chmn dept, 70-81, asst prof, 70-74, ASSOC PROF CLASSICS, UNIV SDAK, 74- *Mem:* Am Philol Asn; Am Class League; Class Asn Mid W & S; Vergilian Soc. *Res:* Greek historiography; Greek prose. *Publ:* Auth, Herbert Hoover and Georgius Agricola, Class Bull, 77. *Mailing Add:* Dept of Classics Univ of SD Vermillion SD 57069

FROHOCK, WILBUR MERRILL, b South Thomaston, Maine, June 20, 08. FRENCH LITERATURE. *Educ:* Brown Univ, PhB, 30, AM, 31, PhD, 35. *Prof Exp:* Instr, Brown Univ, 35-37; from instr to assoc prof French, Columbia Univ, 37-53; prof, Wesleyan Univ, 53-56; prof, 56-76, EMER PROF ROMANCE LANG, HARVARD UNIV, 76- *Concurrent Pos:* Vis prof, Lille, 59 & Munich, 62. *Res:* Studies in literary form; picaresque fiction. *Publ:* Auth, Andre Malraux and the Tragic Imagination, Stanford Univ; Strangers to this Ground, Southern Methodist Univ, 62; Rimbaud's Poetic Practice, Harvard Univ, 63; Style and Temper, Blackwell & Harvard Univ, 67. *Mailing Add:* 10 Shady Hill Sq Cambridge MA 02138

FROMKIN, VICTORIA A, b Passaic, NJ, May 16, 23; m 48; c 1. LINGUISTICS, EXPERIMENTAL PHONETICS. *Educ:* Univ Calif, Berkeley, AB, 44, MA, 63, PhD(ling), 65. *Prof Exp:* Asst prof English, Calif State Univ, 65; asst prof speech, 66-67, asst prof ling, 67-69, actg dir phoenetics lab, 68-69, chmn dept, 72-76, PROF LING, UNIV CALIF, LOS ANGELES, 69-, DEAN GRAD DIV, 79- *Concurrent Pos:* Nat Insts Health grant, 63-; asst prof lang sem, Calif State Col Los Angeles, spring 65; Off Naval Res contract, 66-; mem ling panel, Nat Sci Found, 76-78: ling deleg, Nat Acad Sci, China, 74; vis prof, Univ Stockholm, 77. *Mem:* Fel Acoust Soc Am; Ling Soc Am; Int Phonetic Asn; Asn Machine Transl & Computational Ling; Am Assoc Applied Ling. *Res:* Electromyographics studies of speech *Publ:* Coauth (with R Rodman), An Introduction to Language, Holt, Rinehart & Winston, 74, 2nd ed, 78; (with D Van Lancker), Cerebral dominance for pitch contrasts in tone language speakers and in musically untrained and trained English speakers, J Phonetics, No 6, 78; (with J T Gandour), On the phonological representation of contour tones, In: Ling of Tibeto-Burman Area, 78; ed, Tone: A Linguistic Survey, Acad Press, 78; auth, Persistent questions concerning distinctive features, In: Frontiers of Speech Communication Research, Acad Press, 79; Language and the neurosciences, In: Language in Public Life, Georgetown Univ Press, 79; coauth (with Peter Ladefoged), Early views of distinctive features, In: Towards a History of Phonetic, Edinburgh Univ Press, 80; ed, Errors in Linguistic Performance: Slips of the Tongue, Ear, Pen, and Hand, Acad Press, 80. *Mailing Add:* Dept of Ling Univ Calif Los Angeles CA 90024

FRONING, DOROTHY GARDNER, b Cosby, Mo, Apr 8, 14; m 45, 63. FOREIGN LANGUAGES. *Educ:* Park Col, BA, 36; Univ Ala, MA, 47; Univ Calif, Los Angeles, PhD, 61. *Prof Exp:* Teacher English & Span, Boonville High Sch, Mo, 36-41; from instr to assoc prof Span, 47-65, PROF SPAN, WICHITA STATE UNIV, 65- *Mem:* Am Ans Teachers Span & Port. *Res:* Spanish American literature, especially Alfonso Herdandez Cata. *Mailing Add:* Dept of Romance Lang Wichita State Univ Wichita KS 67208

FROST, EDGAR LEE, b Hobart, Okla, May 5, 39; m 72; c 1. RUSSIAN LANGUAGE; RUSSIAN LITERATURE. *Educ:* Univ Okla, BA, 61, MA, 67; Univ Ill, Urbana-Champaign, PhD(Russ lit), 73. *Prof Exp:* Vis lectr Russ lang & cult, Univ Ill, Urbana-Champaign, 74; asst prof, 74-80, ASSOC PROF RUSS LANG, LIT & CULT, UNIV ALA, 80- *Mem:* Am Asn Teachers Slavic & E Europ Lang; Am Asn Advan Slavic Studies. *Res:* Nineteenth century Russian literature; Russian folklore; Soviet cinema. *Publ:* Auth, The function of music in Turgenev's Dvorjanskoe gnezdo, Russ Lang J, spring 74; contribr, Studies in Language and Literature: The Proceedings of the 23rd Mountain Interstate Foreign Language Conference, Eastern Ky Univ, 76; auth, The culture courses as drawing card: Increased enrollments for language departments, Bull Asn Depts Foreign Lang, 5/77; The search for eternity in Cexov's fiction: The Flight from Time as a Source of Tension, Russ Lang J, winter 77. *Mailing Add:* Dept of Ger & Russ Box 1987 Univ Ala University AL 35486

FRYDMAN, ANNE, b New York, NY, May 27, 47; m 82. RUSSIAN & COMPARATIVE LITERATURE. *Educ:* Sarah Lawrence Col, BA, 68; Columbia Univ, MA, 69, PhD(Russ lit), 78. *Prof Exp:* Kenan fel humanities,

Soc Fels in Humanities, Columbia Univ, 77-79; vis asst prof, State Univ NY, Purchase, 79-82; VIS ASST PROF RUSS LIT, STATE UNIV NY, PURCHASE, 79- *Concurrent Pos:* Preceptor Slavic lang, Columbia Univ, 73-76, vis lectr, 79; vis lectr Slavic lang & lit, Princeton Univ, 80; consult, Theatre Dept, State Univ NY, Purchase, 80; vis asst prof Slav lang, Princeton, 80-81. *Mem:* Int Chekhov Soc (exec secy, 80-82); Am Asn Advan Slavic Studies. *Res:* Anton Chekhov's short stories, form and vision; the prose of Isaac Babel. *Publ:* Auth, Enemies: An experimental story, Ulbanous Rev, fall 79; transl, Sergei Dovlatov, The jubilee boy, New Yorker, 6/9/80; auth, Enemies: Chekhov experimenting, Pequod, 11/81; Review of Nabokov's Lectures on Russian Literature, New Leader, 12/14/81; co-transl, Sergei Dovlatov, Straight ahead, New Yorker, 1/25/82; transl, Sergei Dovlatov, The Compromise, Alfred A Knopf (in press). *Mailing Add:* 425 Riverside Dr Apt 7J New York NY 10025

FRYE, RICHARD NELSON, b Birmingham, Ala, Jan 10, 20. IRANIAN. *Educ:* Univ Ill, AB, 39; Harvard Univ, AM, 40, PhD, 46. *Prof Exp:* Exec secy Near East comt, Am Coun Learned Soc, 48-50; from asst prof to assoc prof Mid Eastern studies, 51-57, assoc dir Mid East Ctr, 55-57, AGA KHAN PROF IRANIAN, HARVARD UNIV, 57- *Concurrent Pos:* Asst ed, Speculum, 50-58; vis lectr Iranian archaeol, Hermitage Mus, 66-67; corresp fel, Ger Archaeol Inst, 66-; dir, Asia Inst, Pahlavi Univ, Iran, 69-74, ed bull & monogr ser, 69-74; consult, Pahlavi Libr, Tehran, 76- *Mem:* Hon mem Zorastrian Asn of NAm; Am Orient Soc (vpres, 66); Nat Asn Armenian Studies & Res. *Res:* Iranian studies; middle Persian and central Asian history; archaeology. *Publ:* Auth, The Histories of Nishapur, Harvard Univ, 65; Bukhara the Medieval Achievement, Univ Okla, 65; Persia, London, 68; ed, Middle Iranian inscriptions from Dura Europas, In: Corpus Inscriptionium Iranicarum, Lund Humphries, London, 68; Sasanian Seals in the Collection of Mohsen Foroughi, Lund Humphries, London, 72; Excavations of Qasr-i Abu Nasr, Harvard Univ, 73; auth, Neue Methodologie in der Iranistik, Harrasowitz, Wiesbaden, 74; Opera Minora (2 vols), Asia Inst, Shiraz, 76-77. *Mailing Add:* Harvard Univ 6 Divinity Ave Cambridge MA 02138

FRYE, WENDELL WHITNEY, b Leominster, Mass, Mar 1, 40; m 63; c 3. GERMAN LANGUAGE & LITERATURE. *Educ:* Clark Univ, AB, 63; Middlebury Col, MA, 65; Ind Univ, Bloomington, PhD(Ger), 70. *Prof Exp:* Teacher English, J G Cafter Jr High Sch, Leominster, Mass, 63-64; instr Ger, Wabash Col, 65-70; asst prof, 70-74, assoc prof, 74-80, PROF GER, HARTWICK COL, 80- *Concurrent Pos:* Austauschlehrer, I Bundesgymnasium, Klagenfurt, Austria, 76-77; Liga für Völkerfreundschaft for Fortbildungskurs grant, Karl-Marx Univ, Leipzig. *Mem:* Am Asn Teachers Ger. *Res:* Adalbert Stifter; 19th century German literature in general. *Publ:* Auth, Tradition in Stifters Romanen, Peter Lang Verlas, Bern, Switz, 77. *Mailing Add:* Dept of Mod Lang Hartwick Col Oneonta NY 13820

FRYER, T BRUCE, b Philadelphia, Pa, Jan 21, 41; m 64; c 2. FOREIGN LANGUAGES. *Educ:* Muhlenberg Col, BA, 62; Middlebury Col, MA, 66; Univ Tex, Austin, PhD(foreign lang educ), 70. *Prof Exp:* Teacher Span, Spring-Ford Area Schs, 62-67, head dept foreign lang, 64-67; teaching assoc Span educ, Univ Tex, Austin, 67-70; asst prof, 70-74, ASSOC PROF SPAN, UNIV SC, 74-, COORDR, DIV SPAN & PORT, 75- *Concurrent Pos:* Mem bd dirs, Southern Conf Lang Teaching, 76- *Mem:* Am Asn Teachers Span & Port; Am Asn Teachers Fr; Am Coun Teaching Foreign Lang; Teaching English Speakers Other Lang. *Res:* Foreign language teaching methodology; international business. *Publ:* Coauth, The methods course at the University of South Carolina, 5/73 & An undergraduate experience in self-facing, 10/73, Foreign Lang Ann; Free to explore curricular developments, In: Perspective: A New Freedom, Nat Textbook Co, 76; Foreign languages and business: A lifelong experience, MLA, 77. *Mailing Add:* Dept of Foreign Lang & Lit Univ SC Columbia SC 29208

FRYSCAK, MILAN, b Dobra, Czech, June 27, 32; US citizen; m 65; c 2. SLAVIC LINGUISTICS, CZECH LITERATURE. *Educ:* Palacky Univ, Czech, Promovany filolog, 56; Univ Calif, Berkeley, MA, 62; Ohio State Univ, PhD(Slavic ling), 69. *Prof Exp:* From instr to asst prof Russ lang & lit, Wittenberg Univ, 64-70; asst prof, 70-75, ASSOC PROF SLAVIC LING, NY UNIV, 75- *Concurrent Pos:* Mem fac, Russ Sch, Norwich Univ, Northfield, Vt, summer, 78- *Mem:* MLA; Ling Soc Am; Am Asn Teachers Slavic & E Europ Lang; Am Asn Advan Slavic Studies; Czech Soc Arts & Sci in US. *Res:* Comparative Slavic linguistics; history of the Russian language; Czech literature. *Publ:* Auth, Say it in Czech, Dover, 73. *Mailing Add:* Dept of Slavic Lang & Lit Room 425 NY Univ 19 University Pl New York NY 10003

FUEGI, JOHN B, b London, England, May 9, 36; US citizen; div; c 2. COMPARATIVE LITERATURE. *Educ:* Pomona Col, BA, 61; Univ Southern Calif, PhD(comp lit), 67. *Prof Exp:* Lectr Am lit, Free Univ Berlin, 66-67; from asst prof to prof comp lit, Univ Wis, Milwaukee, 67-76; PROF GER, SLAVIC & COMP LIT & DIR COMP LIT, UNIV MD, 76- *Concurrent Pos:* Vis fel, Wesleyan Ctr for Humanities, 69; Am Coun Learned Soc sr res fel in East Europ Studies, 73-74; Univ Wis, Milwaukee sr res fel in 20th century studies, 73-74; co-ed, Brecht Jahrbuch, 73- *Mem:* MLA; Am Comp Lit Asn; Int Comp Lit Asn; Am Asn Teachers Ger; AAUP. *Res:* Relationship of German, Russian and English literatures; the drama, especially Shakespeare and Brecht; the relationship of literature and film. *Publ:* Auth, producer & dir, The Wall (film), Acme Films, 61; auth, The Essential Brecht, Univ Calif, Studies Comp Lit, 72; ed, Brecht Today: Yearbook of International Brecht Society, 71-79 & 82; auth, Explorations in no man's land: Shakespeare's poetry as theatrical film, Shakespeare Quart, 72; The form and the pressure: Shakespeare's haunting of Bertolt Brecht, Mod Drama, 72; Moliere and Brecht: The authorship of Brecht's Don Juan, Comp Lit Studies, 74. *Mailing Add:* 2701 Curry Dr Adelphi MD 20783

FUENTES, VICTOR FLOREAL, b Madrid, Spain, Mar 25, 33; c 3. LITERATURE. *Educ:* NY Univ, BA, 59, MA,61, PhD(humanities), 65. *Prof Exp:* From instr to asst prof Span, Columbia Univ, 60-64; assoc prof, 65-81, PROF SPAN, UNIV CALIF, SANTA BARBARA, 81- *Mem:* MLA; Int Asn Hispanistas. *Res:* Literary criticism; Spanish and Spanish American literature, 19th and 20th century; relations ideology and literature. *Publ:* Auth, La narrativa espanola de vanguardia, 1923-1931, Romanic Rev, 10-72; La narrativa del primer Sender, Norte, Amsterdam, 3/73; La novelistica de Ana Maria Matute, In: La Novela Espanola de la Postguerra, Taurus, 76; Introduction to Diaz Fernandez El Blocao, Turner, 76; El compromiso en las letras espanolas, 8/77 & Espana, 8/78, Triuno; La marcha al pueblo en las letras espanolas, 1971-1936, Ediuous de la torre, Madrid, 80; El cantico material j espiritual de Cesar Vallejo, Atlantida, Barcelona, 81. *Mailing Add:* Dept Span Univ Calif Santa Barbara CA 93106

FUENTEVILLA, ALBERTO, b Havana, Cuba, Nov 26, 15; US citzen; m 47; c 1. SPANISH LANGUAGE, LATIN AMERICAN HISTORY. *Educ:* Inst Havana, Cuba, BLet y Ciencias, 38; Univ Havana, DLeyes, 45. *Prof Exp:* Instr Span, Fayetteville State Col, 62-64; from instr to asst prof, 64-71, ASSOC PROF SPAN, BEREA COL, 72-, ACTG CHMN DEPT ROMANCE LANG, 71- *Mem:* Mountain Interstate Foreign Lang Conf (vpres, 70-71, pres, 78-); Am Asn Teachers Span & Port; AAUP. *Res:* Spanish-American culture in the United States. *Publ:* Auth, Legislacion Bancaria Cubana, Ed Lex, Havana, 55. *Mailing Add:* Dept of Romance Lang Berea Col Box 627 Berea KY 40403

FUGATE, JOE K, b East St Louis, Ill, Oct 31, 31; m 53; c 3. FOREIGN LANGUAGES. *Educ:* Southern Ill Univ, AB, 54; Princeton Univ, MA, 59, PhD, 62. *Prof Exp:* Instr Ger, Ohio Univ, 59-61; from asst prof to assoc prof, 61-71, chmn dept, 65-74, asst dir foreign studies, 65-72, assoc dir, 72-74, PROF GER, KALAMAZOO COL, 71-, DIR FOREIGN STUDIES, 74- *Concurrent Pos:* Advance placement reader, Educ Testing Serv, 65-66, 68; mem Fulbright selection comt, Ger, 71, chmn, 72; hon fel, Inst Am Univ, Aix-en-Provence, France, 74. *Honors & Awards:* Cross of Merit First Class, Fed Repub Ger, 71; Chevalier dans l'Ordre des Palmes Academiques, France, 81. *Mem:* Am Coun Teaching Foreign Lang; Am Asn Teachers Ger; MLA (mem Bibliog comt, 68-); Am Lessing Soc; Goethe Gesellschaft. *Res:* Aesthetics; 18th century German literature; study abroad. *Publ:* Auth, The Psychological Basis of Herder's Aesthetics, Mouton, The Hague, 66; Confession of an American foreign study enthusiast, Asn Dept Foreign Lang, 11/76; coauth, The foreign study element in German studies, Ger Studies in US, Univ Wis, 76. *Mailing Add:* Dept of Ger Kalamazoo Col Kalamazoo MI 49007

FUHRIG, ANNE MARIE, b Stargard, Ger, July 26, 36; m 62; c 2. GERMAN LANGUAGE & LITERATURE. *Educ:* Pädagogische Hochschule Osnabrück, Ger, BA, 62; Mich State Univ, MA, 65, PhD(Ger lang & lit), 72. *Prof Exp:* Asst instr Ger, Mich State Univ, 62-66; instr, Ill Col, 67-72; ASST PROF GER LANG & LIT, MACMURRAY COL, 71- *Mem:* Am Asn Teachers Ger. *Res:* Agnes Miegel. *Publ:* Auth, Die Sprachgestaltung in den Prosawerken Agnes Miegels: Eine Strukturanalyse, Univ Microfilms, 72. *Mailing Add:* Dept of Foreign Lang MacMurray Col 508 W College Ave Jacksonville IL 62650

FULLER, CLARENCE, b Foxboro, Mass, Jan 17, 27. FOREIGN LANGUAGES. *Educ:* Brown Univ, AB, 50; Middlebury Col, MA, 51. *Prof Exp:* Lectr French, Sch Gen Studies, Columbia Univ, 55-56, instr, Columbia Col, 59-61; asst prof, 61-65, ASSOC PROF FRENCH & SPAN, BLOOMFIELD COL, 65- *Res:* Phonetics; French. *Mailing Add:* Dept of Lang Bloomfield Col Bloomfield NJ 07003

FULLER, HELENE R, b Greenport, NY, Nov 9, 26. LINGUISTICS, ENGLISH. *Educ:* Keuke Col, BA, 48; Colulbia Univ, MA, 55, dipl English, 58. *Prof Exp:* Instr English, Univ PR, 55-57, asst prof, 63-65; lectr, Columbia Univ, 57-61, instr, 61-63; ASST PROF LING, MIAMI UNIV, 65- *Concurrent Pos:* Chmn region VI, English as sec lang, Nat Asn Foreign Student Affairs, 77-78. *Mem:* Ling Soc Am; MLA; Nat Asn Foreign Student Affairs; Teachers English to Speakers Other Lang; Caribbean Studies Asn. *Res:* Applied linguistics; language and culture; contrastive analysis of Luo, Kukuyo and Kamba, Kenyan language. *Publ:* Coauth, Advanced English Exercises, McGraw, 61; auth, Study interest: A study of Puerto Rican and American Students, Univ PR, 6/64; Not always first: The teaching of English as a foreign language, Kiuka Alumnae, 68; Advanced English Essays, Vantage, 69; Contrastive Analysis: Spanish and English Versus Somali and English, 70; Wife Talk, 71; The Generated Essay, 73; The foreign student as a source of cultural enrichment, Nat Asn Foreign Student Affairs Bull, summer 77; Living Language, 79. *Mailing Add:* Dept of English Miami Univ Oxford OH 45056

FULLER, HOMER WOODROW, b Dawn, Mo, Aug 14, 16; m 42; c 2. MODERN GERMAN LITERATURE. *Educ:* Emory Univ, AB, 38; Univ Wis, AM, 40, PhD, 52. *Prof Exp:* Teaching fel Ger, Univ NC, 40-41; instr, Emory Univ, 41-45; grad asst, Univ Wis, 45-47; assoc prof Ger lang, 47-73, PROF GER, UNIV TENN, KNOXVILLE, 73- *Concurrent Pos:* Fulbright res scholar, Vienna & Fund Advan Educ fel, 55-56. *Mem:* MLA; SAtlantic Mod Lang Asn. *Res:* Nineteenth century German literature; the German novelle; Theodor Storm's easthetic theories. *Mailing Add:* Dept of Ger & Slavic Lang Univ of Tenn Knoxville TN 37916

FULLERTON, GERALD LEE, b San Francisco, Calif, Aug 3, 41; m 64. GERMAN LINGUISTICS. *Educ:* Stanford Univ, AB, 63, MA, 65; Univ Mich, Ann Arbor, PhD(Ger), 71. *Prof Exp:* Instr Ger, Meramec Community Col, 64-66; instr, Drake Univ, 66-68; asst prof, State Univ NY Buffalo, 71-75; asst prof, Univ Tex San Antonio, 76-77; ASST PROF GER, UNIV MINN, TWIN CITIES, 77- *Mem:* Am Asn Teachers Ger; Ling Soc Am. *Res:* Comparative Germanic grammar; syntax of modern Ger; teaching German. *Publ:* Auth, The source of the Gothic fourth weak conjugation, Language, 71; The development of obstruents in four Germanic endings, 74 & Grimm's law and WGmc 2sg verb endings -s, 75, Linguistics; Historical Germanic Verb

Morphology, Walter de Grunter, Berlin, 77; On teaching the subjective use of modal auxiliaries, Die Unterrichtspraxis, 77; Subjective modals, assessment adverbs and source phrases, In: Studies in Descriptive German Grammar, Julius Groos, Heidelberg, 82. *Mailing Add:* Dept of Ger Univ of Minn Minneapolis MN 55455

FULTON, NORMAN, b Sedalia, Mo, July 5, 27; m 66. MODERN PHILOLOGY, SPANISH HISTORY. *Educ:* Cent Mo State Col, BA, 49; Univ Rochester, EdM, 54; Univ Madrid, Lic, 65; PhD(mod philol), 66. *Prof Exp:* Master English & Span, Christchurch Sch, Va, 48-49; foreign sales correspondent for SAm, MD, Knowlton Co, NY, 52-54; teacher English, Benjamin Franklin High Sch, Rochester, NY, 54-55; interpreter, liaison & protocol off, Joint Mil Group, Span & Morocco, 56-61; teacher drama & English & chmn dept of English, Madrid High Sch, Torrejon AFB, Spain, 61-65; prof lang, Col Jesuits, Madrid, 65-66; asst prof Span, St Olaf Col, 66-68; assoc prof Span & chmn dept foreign lang, Bradley Univ, 68-72; PROF SPAN & CHMN DEPT SPAN & ITAL, MONTCLAIR STATE COL, 72- *Honors & Awards:* Nat Investr Spain in Hist award, 66. *Mem:* Am Asn Teachers Span & Port. *Res:* History of the Spanish language. *Publ:* Auth, The Heritage of Spain, US Embassy Publ, Madrid, 59; La Musica en la corte de Filipe II, Rev Consejo Investigaciones Cientificas, Madrid, 65; Relaciones Diplomaticas entre Espana y los Estados Unidos, a Finales del Siglo XVIII, Sem Estud Americanistas, Diana Artes Graficas, Madrid, 70. *Mailing Add:* Dept of Span & Ital Montclair State Col Upper Montclair NJ 07043

FULVI, PHILIP ANTHONY, b Malden, Mass, Aug 12, 32; m 60. FRENCH, ITALIAN. *Educ:* Boston Univ, AB, 54, AM, 55; NY Univ, PhD(French & Ital), 72. *Prof Exp:* From instr to asst prof French & Ital, Long Island Univ, 62-67; asst prof, 67-74, assoc prof, 74-82, PROF FRENCH & ITAL, DYSON COL, PACE UNIV, 82-, CHMN FOREIGN LANG, 79- *Concurrent Pos:* Mem bd dir, Pirandello Soc Am, 76-; co-ed, Pirandello Newslett, 76- *Mem:* MLA; Am Asn Teachers Fr; Am Asn Teachers Ital; Soc Fr Prof Am; Pirandello Soc Am. *Res:* Valery; French symbolism; Italian hermeticism. *Mailing Add:* Dept of Foreign Lang Dyson Col Pace Univ Pace Plaza New York NY 10038

FUNKE, FRANCIS JOSEPH, b Indianapolis, Ind, Jun 11, 15; m 41; c 1. SPANISH & FRENCH LITERATURES. *Educ:* Butler Univ, AB, 37; Univ Wis, MA, 38; Fla State Univ, PhD(Span), 64. *Prof Exp:* Teacher, Riverside Mil Acad, 38-41, Evansville Pub Schs, 41-43, Culver Mil Acad, 43-45; transl Span, Eli Lilly Int Corp, 45-50; teacher mod lang, US Civil Serv, 50-55; teacher, Dade County Pub Schs, 55-60; assoc prof French, Miami-Dade Community Col, North Campus, 60-66, prof, 66-80. *Concurrent Pos:* Mod lang observer, MLA, 61; contribr dictionary proj, Am Dialect Soc. *Mem:* SAtlantic Mod Lang Asn; MLA; Am Asn Teachers Span & Port; Am Hist Soc. *Res:* Language methodology; history of literature; Spanish drama. *Publ:* Coauth, Good teaching practices: A survey of high school foreign language classes, MLA, 11/61; auth, Junior College Foreign Language Departments, Miami-Dade Community Col, 62. *Mailing Add:* 7146 Ballantrae Ct Hialeah FL 33014

FUQUA, CHARLES, b Paris, France, Oct 5, 35; US citizen, m 61; c 3. CLASSICS, ANCIENT DRAMA. *Educ:* Princeton Univ, BA, 57; Cornell Univ, MA, 62, PhD(classics), 64. *Prof Exp:* From instr to asst prof classics, Dartmouth Col, 64-66; chmn dept, 66-78, assoc prof, 66-72, GARFIELD PROF ANCIENT LANG, WILLIAMS COL, 72- *Concurrent Pos:* Mem adv coun, Am Acad Rome, 66- & exec comt, 71-74. *Mem:* Am Philol Asn; Class Asn New Eng. *Res:* Greek drama, Sophocles; Latin lyric poetry. *Publ:* Auth, Possible implications of the ostracism of Hyperbolus, Trans Am Philol Asn, 65; Horace, Carmina 1.23-25, 1/68 & Aeschylus: Agamemnon 1446-47, 7/72, Class Philol; Studies in the use of myth in Sophocles' Philoctetes and the Orestes of Euripides, 76, The World of myth in Euripides Ovestes, 78 & Heroism, Heracles, and the Trachiniae, 80, Traditio; Tyrtaeus and the cult of heroes, Greek, Roman & Byzantine Studies, 81; Hector, Sychaeus, and Deiphobus: Three mutilated figures in Aeneid, Class Philol, 1-6/82. *Mailing Add:* Dept of Classics Williams Col Williamstown MA 01267

FURLEY, DAVID JOHN, b Nottingham, England, Feb 24, 22; m 67; c 2. CLASSICS, HISTORY OF PHILOSOPHY. *Educ:* Cambridge Univ, MA, 46. *Prof Exp:* Asst lectr Classics, Univ Col, Univ London, 47-49, lectr, 49-56, reader, 56-66; PROF CLASSICS, PRINCETON UNIV, 66- *Concurrent Pos:* Vis lectr, Univ Minn, 60-61; mem, Inst Advan Studies, 64; ed, Phronesis, 66-72, co-ed, 73-; sr fel, Ctr Hellenic Studies, Washington, DC, 71- *Mem:* Am Philol Asn; Am Philos Asn; Brit Class Asn; Soc Prom Hellenic Studies. *Res:* Greek philosophy; Greek science; Lucretius. *Publ:* Auth, Aristotle: On the Cosmos, Heinemann, 55; Lucretius and the Stoics, Bull Inst Class Studies, 66; Two Studies in the Greek Atomists, Princeton Univ, 67; Variation on themes from Empedocles in Lucretius' Proem, Bull Inst Class Studies, 70; co-ed, Studies in Presocratic Philosophy I, 70 & II, 75, Routledge & Kegan Paul. *Mailing Add:* Dept of Classics Princeton Univ Princeton NJ 08540

FURST, LILIAN RENEE, b Vienna, Austria, June 30, 31; US citizen. COMPARATIVE LITERATURE, GERMAN. *Educ:* Univ Manchester, BA, 52; Univ Cambridge, PhD(Ger), 57; Ital Govt dipl, 65. *Prof Exp:* From asst prof to assoc prof Ger, Queen's Univ Belfast, 55-66; assoc prof & head dept comp lit, Univ Manchester, 66-71; vis prof comp lit & Ger, Dartmouth Col, 71-72; prof comp lit & romance lang & dir grad prog, Univ Ore, 72-75; PROF COMP LIT, UNIV TEX, DALLAS, 75- *Concurrent Pos:* Am Coun Learned Soc res fel, 74-75; hon res assoc comp lit, Harvard Univ, 74-75; Mather vis prof English & foreign lang, Case Western Reserve Univ, 78-79; vis prof Ger, Stanford Univ, 81-82; Guggenheim fel, 82-83; Marta Sutton Weeks fel, Stanford Humanities Ctr, 82-83. *Mem:* MLA; Mod Humanities Res Asn; Am Comp Lit Asn; Int Comp Lit Asn; Western Asn Ger Studies. *Res:* European Romanticism; aspects of narration, 1770-1970; women's studies. *Publ:* Auth, Romanticism in Perspective, Macmillan, 69, 2nd ed, 79 & Humanities, 70; Romanticism, 69, rev ed, 76 & Naturalism, 71, Methuen, London & Harper; Zola's art criticism, In: French Nineteenth Century Painting and Literature, Manchester Univ, 72; co-ed, The anti-hero: Essays, Studies Lit Imagination,

76; auth, Counterparts: The Dynamics of Franco-German Literary Relationships, 1770-1895, Methuen, London & Wayne State Univ, 77; The Contours of European Romanticism, Macmillan, 79 & Nebr Univ Press, 80; European Romanticism: Self-Definition, Methuen, London & NY, 80. *Mailing Add:* 7654 Royal Lane Dallas TX 75230

G

GABRIEL, KARL MICHAEL, b Neukirchen, Austria, July 27, 28; m 62; c 4. GERMAN, ENGLISH. *Educ:* Univ Vienna, cert, 53 & 55, PhD(English), 55. *Prof Exp:* Prof English, Vienna Boys' Choir, 54-56; prof Ger & English, Albertus Magnus Realgymnasium, Vienna, 56-59; instr Ger & Span, John Carroll Univ, 59-61, asst prof Ger, 61-63; from asst prof to assoc prof, 63-76, PROF GER & CHMN DEPT FOREIGN LANG, UNIV NC, CHARLOTTE, 76- *Mem:* Am Asn Teachers Ger; MLA. *Res:* Methods of language teaching; comparative and Austrian literature. *Mailing Add:* Dept of Foreign Lang Univ of NC Charlotte NC 28213

GAEDE, FRIEDRICH WOLFGANG, b Essen, Ger, Feb 20, 37; m 61; c 2. GERMAN LITERATURE, PHILOSOPHY. *Educ:* Univ Freiburg, PhD(Ger lit & philol), 63. *Prof Exp:* Asst prof Ger, 66-69, Can Coun scholar, 69-70, assoc prof, 70-75, PROF GER, DALHOUSIE UNIV, 75-, CHMN DEPT, 79- *Mem:* Int Ver Germanisten; Can Asn Teachers Ger; Grimmelshauser Ges. *Res:* History of literature and thought between 1500 and 1750; aesthetics. *Publ:* Auth, Humanismus-Barock-Aufklaerung, Francke, Berne-Munich, 71; Realismus von Brant bis Brecht, Francke, Munich, 72; Gottscheds Nachahmungs: Theorie und die Logik, Deutsche Vierteljahrsschrift, 75; Grimmelshausen und die Tradition des Skeptizismus, Daphnis, 76; Poetik und Logik, Francke, Berne-Munich, 78; Gryphius und Grimmelshausen als Kritiker des endlichen Verstandes, Simplicana, 80; Buechners Widerspruch, Jahrb f Int Germ, 80; Leibniz' Urteilsreform und das Ende der Barockliteratur, Simpliciana, 81. *Mailing Add:* Dept of Ger Dalhousie Univ Halifax NS B3H 4H6 Can

GAEFFKE, PETER, b Breslau, Silesia, Dec 6, 27; WGer citizen; m 58; c 2. INDOLOGY, COMPARATIVE LITERATURE. *Educ:* Univ Mainz, WGer, MA, 51, PhD(Indoeurop ling), 52. *Hon Degrees:* MA, Univ Pa, 75. *Prof Exp:* Prof Hindi, Univ Utrecht, Netherlands, 64-75; PROF INDIAN LIT, UNIV PA, 75- *Mem:* Ger Orient Soc; Dutch Orient Soc; Am Orient Soc; Am Asn Comp Lit. *Res:* Medieval and modern literatures in Hindi, Urdu and Bengal. *Publ:* Auth, De Hindi literatuur en het indische nationalisme, 66 & Hindiromane in der ersten Hälfte des zwanzigsten Jahrhunderts, 66, Brill, Leiden; Untersuchungen zur Syntax des Hindi, Mouton, The Hague, 67; Grundbegriffe moderner indischer Erzählkunst, 70 & co-ed, India Maior, 72, Brill, Leiden; Tulsidas, Ramcaritmanas, Reclam, Stuttgart, 75; Hindi Literature in the Twentieth Century, Harrassowitz, Wiesbaden, 78. *Mailing Add:* S Asia Regional Studies Dept Univ of Pa Philadelphia PA 19174

GAENG, PAUL A, b Budapest, Hungary, Aug 17, 24; US citizen; m 68. ROMANCE LINGUISTICS & PHILOLOGY. *Educ:* Univ Geneva, Dipl, 47; Columbia Univ, MA, 50, PhD(Romance philol), 65. *Prof Exp:* Chmn dept mod lang, Montclair Acad, NJ, 57-63; from asst prof to prof French & Span ling, Montclair State Col, 64-69; chmn dept, 66-69; assoc prof Romance lang, Univ Va, 69-72; prof Romance philol & head dept Romance lang, Univ Cincinnati, 72-76; assoc, Ctr Advan Studies, 82-83, HEAD, DEPT FRENCH, UNIV ILL, URBANA-CHAMPAIGN, 76- *Concurrent Pos:* Spec lectr, Univ Hofstra, 63-64. *Honors & Awards:* Chevalier, Palmes Academiques, French Govt, 76; Special Citation, Ohio House of Reps, 76. *Mem:* Am Soc Geoling (treas, 65-68); MLA; Soc Ling Romane. *Res:* Vulgar Latin; early Romance. *Publ:* Auth, An Inquiry into the Influences of the Germanic Superstraum on the Vocabulary and Phonetic Structure of Gallo-Romance, Montclair State Col, 68; An Inquiry into Local Variations in Vulgar Latin as Reflected in the Vocalism of Christian Inscriptions, Univ NC, 68; Introduction to the Principles of Language, Harper, 71; ed, Studies in Honor of Mario A Pei, Univ NC, Chapel Hill, 72; contribr, Indo-European Languages in Language and Culture, 74, Northern Mich Univ; coauth, The Story of Latin and the Romance Languages, Harper, 76; auth, A Study of Nominal Inflection in Latin Inscriptions, Univ NC, Chapel Hill, 77. *Mailing Add:* Dept of French FLB 2090 Univ of Ill Urbana IL 61801

GAERTNER, JOHANNES ALEXANDER, Art History, Aesthetics. See Vol I

GAGARIN, MICHAEL, b New York City, NY, Jan 4, 42. CLASSICS. *Educ:* Stanford Univ, BA, 63; Harvard Univ, MA, 65; Yale Univ, PhD(classics), 68. *Prof Exp:* From instr to asst prof classics, Yale Univ, 68-73; asst prof, 73-80, ASSOC PROF CLASSICS, UNIV TEX, AUSTIN, 80- *Concurrent Pos:* Jr fel, Ctr Hellenic Studies, Washington DC, 72-73; vis asst prof classics, Univ Calif, Berkeley, 76-77; Am Coun Learned Soc fel, 80-81. *Mem:* Am Philol Asn; Am Inst Archaeol; Soc Ancient Greek Philos. *Res:* Greek literature; Greek law; Greek philosophy. *Publ:* Auth, Dike in the Works and Days, Class Philol, 73; The vote of Athena, Am J Philol, 75; Aeschylean Drama, Univ Calif, 76; Socrates' hybris and Alchibiades, failure, Phoenix, 77; Self-defense in Athenian homicide law, Greek Roman & Byzantine Studies, 78; The Prosecution of Homicide in Athens, Greek Roman & Byzantine Studies, 79; Drakon and Early Athenian Homicide Law, Yale Univ Press, 81. *Mailing Add:* Classics Dept Univ of Tex Austin TX 78712

GAGE, WILLIAM WHITNEY, b Corning, NY, Feb 8, 25. LINGUISTICS. *Educ:* Cornell Univ, AB, 50, AM, 52, PhD(ling), 58. *Prof Exp:* Proj linguist, Ctr Appl Ling, 59-61, res linguist, 61-67, assoc dir foreign lang prog, 67-71, consult, 74-78. *Mem:* Ling Soc Am; Can Ling Asn; Int Ling Asn; Am Anthrop Asn; Asn Asian Studies. *Res:* Descriptive linguistics; structure of English language of children. *Publ:* Coauth, Verb constructions in Vietnamese, Dept Far Eastern Studies, Cornell Univ, 53; auth, Tieng Anh cho ngu' o' i Viet, Am Coun Learned Soc, 55; Syntax of English stress: Interpretation of three approaches, In: Linguistic Studies in Memory of Richard Slade Harrell, Georgetown Univ, 67; ed, Language in its Social Setting, Anthrop Soc Wash, 74; coauth, The ABC's of Languages and Linguistics, Inst Mod Lang, rev ed, 77; auth, The intermediate state of accent systems, Study Sounds, 78. *Mailing Add:* Ctr Appl Ling 3520 Prospect St NW Washington DC 20007

GAICHAS, LAWRENCE EDWARD, b Chicago, Ill, Mar 30, 42; m 67; c 2. CLASSICS. *Educ:* Xavier Univ, Ohio, AB, 64; Ohio State Univ, MA, 68, PhD(classics), 72. *Prof Exp:* Teaching asst classics, Ohio State Univ, 66-68; instr classics & English, Kalamazoo Col, 70-72; instr Columbus Pub Schs, 72-73; asst prof, 73-77, ASSOC PROF CLASSICS, DUQUESNE UNIV, 77-, CHMN DEPT, 78- *Concurrent Pos:* Circulation mgr, Class World, 78- *Mem:* Am Philol Asn. *Res:* Graeco-Roman historiography; Graeco-Roman epic; etymology. *Mailing Add:* Dept of Classics Duquesne Univ Pittsburgh PA 15259

GAINES, JAMES FREDERICK, b Somerville, Mass, May 31, 49; m 75. FRENCH LITERATURE. *Educ:* Mich State Univ, BA, 71; Univ Pa, MA, 75, PhD(Fr), 77. *Prof Exp:* Asst prof, 77-80, ASSOC PROF FRENCH, SOUTHEASTERN LA UNIV, 80- *Concurrent Pos:* Coordr, Univ Hon Prog, Southeastern La Univ, 80- *Mem:* NAm Soc 17th Century Fr Lit; MLA; Am Asn Teachers Fr. *Res:* Moliere; history and sociology of literature, especially comic theatre; ideologies of French seventeenth century literature. *Publ:* Coauth, Kyd and Garnier: The art of amendment, Comp Lit, 79; auth, The Burlesque Recit in Moliere's Greek Plays, Fr Rev, 79; Political history and moral values in Corneille's Sertorius, Fr Lit Studies, 81; Gambling in the theatre of Moliere's contemporaries, Papers on Fr 17th Century Lit, 81; Menage versus Salon in Les Femmes savantes, L'Esprit Createur, 81; Commentary on Roger Herzel's problems in the original casting of Les Femmes savantges, Biblio 17, 82; L'Ecole des Femmes: Usurpation, dominance and social closure, Papers Fr 17th Century Lit, 82; La Redecouverte de deux pieces de Denis Clerselier, dit Nanteuil, Revue d'Histoire du Theatre, 83. *Mailing Add:* PO Box 724 Southeastern La Univ Hammond LA 70402

GAIR, JAMES WELLS, b Buffalo, NY, Dec 27, 27; m 50; c 2. LINGUISTICS. *Educ:* Univ Buffalo, BA, 49, MA, 56; Cornell Univ, PhD(ling), 63. *Prof Exp:* Instr English, Univ Buffalo, 49-51; instr gen educ, State Univ NY Utica, 51-54; instr commun & lit, Univ Buffalo, 54-57, lectr gen stud & asst to dean, Col Arts & Sci, 57-58; res asst NDEA Sinhalese proj, 61-62, from asst prof to assoc prof, 62-74, dir NDEA SAsia Ctr, 67-69, PROF LING, CORNELL UNIV, 74- *Concurrent Pos:* Instr, Can Ling Inst, Univ Alta, 62-66; Fulbright-Hays res grant, Ceylon, 64-65 & 69-70, lectr award, Sri Lanka, 76-77. *Mem:* Ling Soc Am; Asn Asian Studies; Ling Soc India; Royal Asiatic Soc, Ceylon. *Res:* South Asian languages and linguistics; English linguistics. *Publ:* Auth, The alphabet, Collier's Encycolpedia, 66; coauth, Colloquial Sinhalese, Cornell Univ SAsia Prog, 68; auth, Colloquial Sinhalese Clause Structures, Mouton, 70; Sinhalese digiossia, Anthrop Ling, Vol X, No 8; coauth, Literary Sinhala, Cornell Univ SAsia Prog, 74; auth, Is Sinhala a subject language? In: The Notion of Subject in South Asian Language, Univ Wis, 76; coauth, Spoken Sri Lanka (Jaffna) Taried, Univ Ceylon (in press). *Mailing Add:* Dept of Mod Lang & Ling Cornell Univ Ithaca NY 14853

GAISSER, JULIA HAIG, b Cripple Creek, Colo, Jan 12, 41; m 64; c 1. CLASSICAL PHILOLOGY. *Educ:* Brown Univ, AB, 62; Harvard Univ, AM, 66; Edinburgh Univ, PhD(Greek), 66. *Prof Exp:* Asst prof classics, Newton Col, 66-69, Swarthmore Col, 70-72 & Brooklyn Col, 73-75; ASSOC PROF LATIN, BRYN MAWR COL, 75- *Mem:* Class Asn Atlantic States; Am Philol Asn. *Res:* Greek epic; Latin elegy; Renaissance commentaries and translations of Latin poets. *Publ:* Auth, A structural analysis of the digressions in the Iliad and the Odyssey, Harvard Studies Class Philol, 68; Adaptation of traditional material in the Glaucus-Diomedes episode, Trans Am Philol Soc, 69; Structure and tone in Tibullus 1 6, Am J Philol, 71; Tibullus 1 7: A tribute to Messalla, Class Philol, 71; Noun-epithet combinations in the Homeric hymn to Demeter, Trans Am Philol Soc, 74; coauth, Partons in antiquity, Am J Physics, 77; auth, Mythological Exempla in Propertius 1 2 and , Am J Philol, 77; Tibullus 2 3 and Vergil's Tenth Eclogue, Trans Am Philol, 77. *Mailing Add:* Dept of Latin Bryn Mawr Col Bryn Mawr PA 19010

GALAND, RENE, b France, Jan 27, 23; US citizen. FRENCH. *Educ:* Univ Rennes, Lic es Let, 44; Yale Univ, PhD(French), 52. *Prof Exp:* Instr French, Yale Univ, 49-51; from asst prof to assoc prof, 51-63; chmn dept, 68-72, PROF FRENCH, WELLESLEY COL, 63- *Concurrent Pos:* Asst ed, Fr Rev, 67-74; reviewer Breton Lit, World Lit Today, 78- *Honors & Awards:* Chevalier, Palmes Academiques, French Govt, 71; Xavier de Langlais Prize for Breton Literature, 79. *Mem:* Am Asn Teachers Fr; Soc Fr Prof Am; Soc Inter-Celtic Arts & Cult. *Res:* Nineteenth and twentieth century French literature; Breton language and literature. *Publ:* Auth, L'ame Celtique de Renan, Univ France & Yale Univ, 59; Baudelaire: Poetiques et Poesie, Nizet, Paris, 69; coauth, Baudelaire as a Love Poet and Other Essays, Pa State Univ, 69; auth, Saint-John Perse, Twayne World Auth Ser, 72; coauth, Homosexualities and French Literature, Cornell Univ, 79; The Binding of Proteus, Bucknell Univ, 80; Levr ar Blanedenn (poetry), Al Liamm, 81. *Mailing Add:* Box 45 Wellesley Col Wellesley MA 02181

GALANES, ADRIANA LEWIS, US citizen; c 1. SPANISH & SPANISH-AMERICAN COLONIAL LITERATURE. *Educ:* Siena Heights Col, BPh, 50; Smith Col, MA, 58; Bryn Mawr Col, PhD(Span lit & philol), 70. *Prof Exp:* Instr Span, Univ Hartford, 64-65; from instr to asst prof, 65-72, chmn dept, 77-78, ASSOC PROF SPAN, TEMPLE UNIV, 72- *Honors & Awards:* Distinguished Teaching Citation, Lindback Found, 73. *Mem:* MLA; Cervantes Soc Am. *Res:* Sixteenth and 17th centuries Spanish literature; Spanish American colonial literature; balladry. *Publ:* Auth, El contemplado: El infinito poseido por Pedro Salinas, Rev Hisp Mod, 67; La epopeya de Juan Particular: Primera & segunda series de los Episodios nacionales de Benito Perez Galdos, Ky Romance Quart, 68; El retablo de Mease Valle-Inclan, Rev Estud Hisp, 69; ed, Critical edition of Poesias de Cervantes, Clasicos Ebro, Zaragoza, Spain, 72; auth, Las mocedades del Cid de Guillen de Castro: Corteza y meollo, Hispanofila, 72; Popularismo estilizado: Una travesura cervantina, Mod Lang Notes, 73; Noticias de la comedia anonima llamada El tejedor de Segovia Parte II, Bull Comediantes, 75; El rey-monje y la mujervaron en La campana de Aragon de Lope de Vega, In: Lope de Vega y los origenes del teatro espanol, Madrid, 81. *Mailing Add:* Dept Span & Port Temple Univ Philadelphia PA 19122

GALASSI, BATTISTA J, b Cervarezza Terme, Italy, Nov 11, 39; US citizen; m 65 c 1. SPANISH, ITALIAN. *Educ:* DePaul Univ, BA, 62; Univ Southern Calif, MA, 63, PhD(Span), 67. *Prof Exp:* From instr to asst prof Span, Univ Ill, Chicago, 65-68; asst prof, 68-72, ASSOC PROF & CHMN DEPT, NORTHEASTERN ILL, UNIV, 72- *Mem:* Am Asn Teachers Span & Port; Am Asn Teachers Ital. *Res:* Spanish Golden Age literature; modernismo. *Publ:* Auth, Privar contra su gusto, edicion cirtica de un drama de tirso de molina, Plaza Mayor Ediciones, Madrid, 71. *Mailing Add:* Dept of Foreign Lang Northeastern Ill Univ Chicago IL 60625

GALBIS, IGNACIO RICARDO MARIA, b Havana, Cuba, May 13, 31; US citizen; m 54; c 4. HISPANIC LITERATURES & LANGUAGE. *Educ:* Univ Havana, JD, 52; Miss State Univ, MA, 66; Syracuse Univ, PhD(Romance lit), 72. *Prof Exp:* Instr Span, Miss State Univ, 65-66; instr, Univ Maine, 66-68, asst prof Span lit, 68-72, assoc prof, 73-76; vis assoc prof, Univ Calif, Riverside, 76-78; ASSOC PROF LING, SAN BERNARDINO VALLEY COL, 80- *Mem:* MLA; Mod Humanities Res Asn; Am Asn Teachers Span & Port; Philol Asn Pac Coast. *Res:* Contemporary peninsular Spanish literature; Basque culture and heritage; theory of genres. *Publ:* Auth, Menendez Pidal y el perfil juridico del Cid, Revista Estudios Hispanicos, 5/72; The scope of Ambito: Aleixandre's first cosmic vision, Rev Letras, 6/74; Elaboracion estetica de los ensayos de Alfonso Reyes, Explicacion Textos Lit, 3/75; Tanatologia en la narrativa de Novas-Calvo, Symp, fall 75; Unamuno: Tres Personajes Existenciales, Hispam, Barcelona, 75; Baroja: el Lirismo de Tono Menor, Torres, 76; En torno a la etopeya barojiana, Rev Estudios Hisp, 12/77; La profesion de fe barojiana en La Leyenda de Juan de Alzate, Insula, 6/78. *Mailing Add:* Dept of Ling San Bernardino Valley Col San Bernardino CA 92507

GALINSKY, GOTTHARD KARL, b Strassburg, Alsace, Feb 7, 42; nat US; c 2. CLASSICS. *Educ:* Bowdoin Col, AB, 63; Princeton Univ, MA, 5, PhD(classics), 66. *Prof Exp:* Instr classics, Princeton Univ, 65-66; from asst prof to assoc prof, 66-72, chmn grad assembly, 77-79, chmn fac senate, 81-82, PROF CLASSICS, UNIV TEX, AUSTIN, 72-, CHMN DEPT, 74- *Concurrent Pos:* Am Coun Learned Soc fel, 68-69; mem adv coun Class Sch, Am Acad Rome, 68-, class jury, 70-72, classicist-in-residence, 72-73; Guggenheim Mem Found fel & Fulbright res scholar, Italy, 72-73; lectr, US-UK Educ Comn, 73; consult, Nat Endowment for Humanities, 76-, Univ Fla Syst, 77 & Univ La Syst, 81; dir, Residential Sem, Nat Endowment for Humanities, 77-78; regional dir, Mellon Fels in Humanities, 82- *Honors & Awards:* Teaching Excellence Award, Univ Tex, 70 & 76. *Mem:* Am Philol Asn; Archaeol Inst Am; Class Asn Mid W & S (pres, 80-81); Vergilian Soc Am (vpres, 76-77); Asn Depts Foreign Lang. *Res:* Roman literature; Roman civilization. *Publ:* Aeneas, Sicily and Rome, Princeton & Oxford, 69; co-ed, Albii Tibulli Aliorumque Carminum Libri Tres, Brill, Leiden, 71; auth, The Herakles Theme, Blackwell, 72; ed, Perspectives of Roman Poetry, Univ Tex, 74; auth, Ovid's Metamorphoses, Blackwell & Univ Calif, 75 ; Augustus' Legislation on Morals and Marriage, Philologus, 81; Vergil and the Creation of the Augustan Ethos, Atti del Couvegus Internazionale, Virgiliano, 82. *Mailing Add:* 2729 Trail of Madrones Austin TX 78746

GALLAGHER, EDWARD J(OSEPH), b Philadelphia, Pa, Oct 9, 43; m 77. MEDIEVAL FRENCH LITERATURE. *Educ:* La Salle Col, AB, 65; Brown Univ, AM, 67, PhD(Fr studies), 72. *Prof Exp:* Instr French, Roger Williams Col, 69-70; teaching assoc, Brown Univ, 71-72; asst prof, Washington Univ, 72-74; asst prof, Rosemont Col, Pa, 74-75; asst prof, Washington Univ, St Louis, 75-77; ASST PROF FRENCH, WHEATON COL, MASS, 77-, CHMN DEPT, 82- *Mem:* AAUP; MLA. *Res:* Medieval and Renaisssance French literature; medieval religious drama; social and religious history of late medieval France. *Publ:* Auth, A Critical Edition of La Passion Nostgre Seigneur from MS 1131 from the Bibliotheque Sainte-Genevieve, Paris, NC Studies Romance Lang & Lit, Vol 179, 76; coauth, Novel into film: An experimental course, Lit & Film Quart, 78; auth, Sources and secondary characterization, in the Sainte-Genevieve Passion, Neuphilologische Mitteilungen, 78; A checklist of 19th-century French titles on the Index Librorum Prohibitorum, Romance Notes, 78; Le Roman de Tristan et Iseut: Bedier, renovateur of Beroul and Thomas, Tristania, 80; Political polarities in the writings of Rousseau, NZ J French Studies, 81; Une Reconstitution a la Viollet-le-Duc: More on Bedier's Roman de Tristan et Iseut, Tristania, 82. *Mailing Add:* 117 Fourth St Providence RI 02906

GALLATI, ERNST, b Switz, Oct 12, 34. GERMAN & COMPARATIVE LITERATURE. *Educ:* Engelberg Col, Switz, BA, 54; Univ Zurich, MA, 58; McGill Univ, PhD(ger lit), 66. *Prof Exp:* Tenure Ger, French & hist, Schinznach High Sch, Switz, 59-62; teaching asst Ger, MCGill Univ, 62-64; asst prof, San Diego State Univ, 64-67; lectr, Col Geneva, Switz, 67-70; asst prof 70-75, ASSOC PROF GERMAN, McGILL UNIV, 75- *Concurrent Pos:* Can Coun res fel, 73-74; vis prof, Univ Montreal, 72-73. *Mem:* Swiss Teachers Soc, Swiss Asn Univ Prof Ger; MLA; Can Asn Univ Teachers Ger. *Res:* German and French literature 1815-1850; German poetry 18th to 20th century. *Publ:* Auth, Jeremias Gotthelfs Gesellschaftskritik, H Lang, Bern, 70; Rodolphe Töpffer und die Deutsche Kultur, Bouvier, Bonn, 75; Frederic Soret und Goethe, Francke, Bern, 80. *Mailing Add:* Dept of Ger PO Box 6070 McGill Univ Montreal PQ H3A 2T6 Can

GALLIANI, RENATO, b Pisa, Italy, May 27, 33; Can citizen. FRENCH LITERATURE. *Educ:* Univ Pisa, Laurea(French lit), 60; Univ Bordeaux, Dr(French lit), 65. *Prof Exp:* Instr French & Ital, Univ RI, 65-66; asst prof French, Dalhousie Univ, 66-67; ASSOC PROF FRENCH LIT, CARLETON UNIV, 67- *Concurrent Pos:* Can Arts Coun grant, 72-73. *Res:* Eighteenth century Camus. *Publ:* Auth, Voltaire cite par les brochures de 1789, Studies on Voltaire, 75; Mably, le luxe, le commerce, les manufactures et les ouvriers, Revue Hist Economique Soc, 75; A friend of the American Revolution: Philip Mazzei, Ital-Am, spring 76; Le debat sur le luxe, Voltaire ou Rousseau?, 76, Les notes marginales de Voltaire au Dictionnaire Philosophique, 76 & Quelques notes inedites de Voltaire a l'Esprit des lois, 76, Studies on Voltaire; Mably et la communaute des beins, Revue Sci humaines, 76; La presence de Voltaire dans les brochures de 1790, Studies on Voltaire, 77. *Mailing Add:* 1108-210 Somerset W Ottawa ON K2P 0J4 Can

GALPIN, ALFRED, b Appleton, Wis, Nov 8, 01; m 24, 56. ROMANCE LANGUAGES, MUSICAL COMPOSITION. *Educ:* Univ Wis, AB, 23, PhD, 40; Univ Chicago, AM, 26; Schola Cantorum, Paris, cert, 26; Northwestern Univ, MusM, 30. *Prof Exp:* Instr, Rice Inst, 24-25, Northwestern Univ, 26-31 & Lawrence Univ, 32-38; asst, 38-40; instr, 40-44, 45-47, from asst prof to prof, 47-71, EMER PROF FRENCH & ITAL, UNIV WIS-MADISON, 71- *Honors & Awards:* Cavaliere al Merito Della Repubblica, 74. *Mem:* MLA; Am Asn Teachers Fr; Am Asn Teachers Ital (secy-treas, 50-54, pres, 55); Soc Chateaubriand. *Res:* Balzac; Chateaubriand; Franco-Italian relations since 1800. *Publ:* Auth, Fauriel in Italy, 62; coauth, French Prose: An Intermediate Reader, 65 & Beginning Readings in Italian, 66, Macmillan; auth, Chateaubriand prophete (2 articles), Bull Soc Chateaubriand, 67 & In: Bicentenaire de Chateaubriand, Minard, Paris, 71; A boat in the tower: Rimbaud in Cleveland, 1922, Renascence, fall 72; Hart Crane: Three books, Contemp Lit, winter 72; Protrait of a father, Wis Mag Hist, summer 80. *Mailing Add:* Via Rosselli 8-E 51016 Montecatini Terme Italy

GALT, ALAN BAKER, b Seattle, Wash, Nov 16, 38; m 62; c 2. GERMAN LANGUAGE PEDAGOGY & LITERATURE. *Educ:* Univ Wash, BA, 61; Ind Univ, Bloomington, MA, 63, PhD(Ger), 71. *Prof Exp:* Asst prof Ger, Univ Wash, 66-74; asst prof, 74-78, ASSOC PROF GER, UNIV CINCINNATI, 78- *Concurrent Pos:* Chmn, Am Asn Teachers Ger Comt Bus Ger, 81- *Mem:* Am Asn Teachers Ger; Am Coun Teaching Foreign Lang; AAUP; Mod Lang Asn Am; Am Translor Asn. *Res:* Nineteenth century German literature; foreign language teaching methodology; German area studies. *Publ:* Auth, Sound and Sense in the Poetry of Theodor Storm, Herbert Lang, Bern, 73; Projecting a Better Image: Slides and the Foreign Language Teacher, Ctr Appl Ling, 77; Career directed study abroad: An idea comes of age, Proc Pac Northwest Conf Foreign Lang, 77; coauth, The FL teacher in focus: Creative photography for the classroom, Proc Central States Conf Foreign Lang, 77; ed, Konkordanz zu Wissenschaft und Gesundheit mit Schlüssel zur Heiligen Schrift, Christian Science Publ Soc, 78. *Mailing Add:* Dept of Ger Univ Cincinnati Cincinnati OH 45221

GALTON, HERBERT, b Vienna, Austria, Oct 1, 17; US citizen; m; c 2. SLAVIC LANGUAGES. *Educ:* Univ London, PhD(Slavic ling), 51. *Prof Exp:* Sr monitor, Brit Broadcasting Corp Monitoring Serv, Reading, Eng, 56-62; translr-ed, US Dept State Foreign Broadcase Info Serv, US Embassy, Vienna, 56-62; from asst prof to assoc prof, 62-69, PROF SLAVIC LANG, UNIV KANS, 69- *Concurrent Pos:* Inter-univ comt travel grants exchange scholar, Bulgaria, 65, Czech, 67-68 & Yugoslavia, 70-71. *Mem:* Am Asn Advan Slavic Studies; Am Asn Teachers Slavic & EEurop Lang. *Res:* Comparative Slavic syntax and phonology-synchronic and diachronic; functional morphology; philosophy. *Publ:* Auth, Aorist und Aspekt im Slavischen, Harrassowitz, Wiesbaden, 62; The Evolution of Bulgarian Syntax, Ling Balkanique, Sofia, 67; On the function of the definite article in some Indo-European languages, Folia Ling, 69; The grammatical category of determinacy, Linguistics, 6/73; The Chief Functions of the Slavic Verbal Aspect, Macedonian Acad Sci, Skopje, 76; The meaning of still and already, In: Linguistics and Literary Studies in Honor of A Hill, 76; Freedom from Illusions, Coronado, 77. *Mailing Add:* Dept of Slavic Lang Univ of Kans Lawrence KS 66044

GALVAN, ROBERTO A, b San Antonio, Tex, Feb 25, 23; m 57; c 7. MODERN LANGUAGES. *Educ:* Trinity Univ, BA, 48; Univ Tex, Austin, MA, 49; Tulane Univ, PhD(Span), 54. *Prof Exp:* Instr French & Span & chmn dept, Southwest Tex Jr Col, 57-62, dir commun, 62-64; assoc prof, 64-67, head div, 69-76, PROF SPAN, SOUTHWEST TEX STATE UNIV, 67- *Concurrent Pos:* Dir Foreign Studies, Southwest Tex State Univ, 64-69, mem fac senate, 67-70, lectr & consult bilingual prog, 69-, dir bilingual educ prog, 75-77. *Mem:* Am Asn Teachers Span & Port; Am Coun Teaching Foreign Lang; regular mem Acad norteamericana Espanola Lengua. *Res:* Spanish lexicography; Spanish and Spanish American literature. *Publ:* Auth, Mas observaciones sobre el argot de Barranquilla, 9/66 & More on frito as an English loan-word in Mexican Spanish, 9/71, Hispania; Chicano, vocablo controvertido, Thesaurus, 73; coauth, The Dictionary of the Spanish of Texas, (El diccionario del espanol de Tejas), Inst Mod Lang, 75 & 2nd ed, 77; Poemas en Espanol por un Mexiamericano, Mex Am Cult Ctr Press, 77; Student Study Guide for Contrastive Analysis of Regional and Standars Spanish, ERIC, 79. *Mailing Add:* Dept of Mod Lang Southwest Tex State Univ San Marcos TX 78666

GAMAL, ADEL SULAIMAN, b Cairo, Egypt, Mar 14, 37; Egyptian citizen; m 63; c 2. CLASSICAL ARABIC LITERATURE, ARABIC LANGUAGE. *Educ:* Cairo Univ, BA, 59, MA, 64, PhD(Arabic lang & lit), 70. *Prof Exp:* Instr Arabic lang & lit, Am Univ in Cairo, 62-70; asst prof, Univ Calif, Berkeley, 71-73 & Am Univ in Cairo, 73-75; assoc prof, Univ Ariz, 75-76 & Am Univ in Cairo, 76-78; ASSOC PROF ARABIC LANG & LIT, UNIV ARIZ, 78- *Mem:* MidE Studies Asn Nam; Am Asn Teachers Arabic. *Res:* Classical Arabic literature; Arabic language; classical Arabic manuscripts. *Publ:* Transl, Who's Afraid of Virginia Woolf, In: Majallat al-Masrah, J Theater Art, 3/65; auth, Arabic poetry and the phenomenon of multiple usage of certain verses, 5/66 & The fortitude (Hamäsa) books in classical Arabic literature, 3/68, Al-Majalla; The collected Poetry of Al-Ahwas Al-Ansary, Ministry Cult, Cairo, 70; The dissemination of Arabic language in Egypt after the Arab conquest, Majallat ath-Thaqafa, 3/74; Diwan Hatim al-Ta-i, Cairo, Egypt, 75; The basis of selections in the Hamäsa Collection, J Arabic Lit, Scotland, 11/76; The conception of nobility in Early Arabic literature, J Am Asn Arabic Teachers. *Mailing Add:* Dept of Oriental Studies Univ of Ariz Tucson AZ 85721

GAMEZ, JUAN, b Villanueva de las Torres, Spain, July 30, 26; US citizen; m 65; c 2. CLASSICAL & ROMANCE LANGUAGES. *Educ:* State Univ Granada, Spain, BA, 56; Univ Cartuja, Spain, Lic Theol, 57; Univ Comillas, Spain, Lic Phil, 59; State Univ Madrid, Lic Phil & Let, 61; Univ Jaime Balmes, Mex, DLett, 70. *Prof Exp:* Asst prof Span, Univ Madrid, 60-63; teacher French, Latin & Span, St Paul's Sch, Garden City, NY, 63-65; lectr Span, Bloomfield Col, 65-67; asst prof, Midwestern Col, 67-68; asst prof Span & Latin, Univ SDak, Vermillion, 68-71; examr, lang req for doctoral cand, Span, 72-82, dir, bilingual prog & competency exam prog bilingual cand, 75-79, ASST PROF SPAN, LATIN & GREEK, EAST TEX STATE UNIV, 71- *Mem:* Am Asn Teachers Span & Port; MLA. *Res:* Spanish Golden Age drama; Spanish Romantic drama; writings of Countess of Pardo Bazan;. *Publ:* Ed, Zorrilla's Don Juan Tenorio, 73 & Hartzenbusch's Los amantes de Teruel, 73, Simon & Schuster; auth, El atavismo moruno en La Barraca de Blasco Ibanez, Explicacion Textos Lit, 3/75; La estructura clasica de La Barraca de Blasco Ibanez, 3/77 & La liberacion de la mujer en las obras de la condesa de Pardo Bazan, 11/77, 5/78, 9/78, 1/79 & 5/79, Span Today Mag. *Mailing Add:* Dept of Lit & Lang E Tex State Univ Commerce TX 75428

GAMMON, EDWARD ROY, b Portland, Ore, Sept 11, 28; m 56; c 2. PSYCHOLINGUISTICS, LINGUISTICS. *Educ:* Reed Col, BA, 47; Univ Ore, MA, Univ Calif, Berkeley, MA, 60; Stanford Univ, PhD(ling), 66. *Prof Exp:* Teaching asst math, Univ Ore, 52-53; res engr, Northrop Aircraft Co, 53-56; asst statist, Univ Calif, 56-59; statistician, Lockheed Missiles & Space Co, 59-61, mathematician, Eng & Sci Exten, 61-65; res assoc logic & semantic struct child lang, Inst Math Studies Soc Sci, Stanford Univ, 65-66; from asst prof to assoc prof ling, 66-72, chmn dept, 69-76, PROF LING, CALIF STATE UNIV, FRESNO, 72- *Concurrent Pos:* Lectr math, Univ Calif, 63-65; consult ling, Inst Math Studies Soc Sci, Stanford Univ, 66-68; Nat Sci Found grant, Calif State Univ Fresno, 67-68, Am Coun Learned Soc travel grant, Stockholm, 69. *Mem:* Am Statist Asn; Ling Soc Am; Asn Comput Ling. *Res:* Mathematical linguistics. *Publ:* Auth, A Statistical Study of English Syntax, 64 & Quantitative Linguistic Typologies, 70, Proc Int Cong Ling; Quantitative Approximations to the Word, Tidschrift Inst Toegepaste Ling, 70. *Mailing Add:* Dept of Ling Calif State Univ Shaw & Cedar Ave Fresno CA 93710

GANS, ERIC LAWRENCE, b New York, NY, Aug 21, 41; m 77. FRENCH. *Educ:* Columbia Univ, BA, 60; Johns Hopkins Univ, MA, 61, PhD(French), 66. *Prof Exp:* Instr French, State Univ NY Col Fredonia, 65-66, asst prof 66-67; asst prof, Ind Univ, Bloomington, 67-69; from asst prof to assoc prof, 69-76, chmn dept, 74-77, PROF FRENCH, UNIV CALIF, LOS ANGELES, 76-, CHMN, 81- *Concurrent Pos:* Vis prof, dept Romance lang, Johns Hopkins Univ, 78. *Honors & Awards:* Prix de la langue francaise, Academie Francaise, 77. *Mem:* MLA. *Res:* Sciences humaines; literary theory; 19th century French literature. *Publ:* Auth, The Discovery of Illusion: Flaubert's Early Works 1835-1837, Univ Calif, 71; Un Pari Contre L'Histoire; les Premieres Nouvelles de Merimee (Mosaique), Minard, 72; Musset et le Drame Tragique, Jose Corti, 74; Le Paradoxe de Phedre suivi de Le Paradoxe Constitutif du Roman, Nizet, 75; Essais D'Esthetique Paradoxale, Gallimard, 77; Esthetique de la metaphore, PO & SIE, 77; Differences, MLN, spring 81; The Origin of Language, Univ Calif Press, 81. *Mailing Add:* Dept of French Univ of Calif Los Angeles CA 90024

GANTZ, TIMOTHY NOLAN, b Washington, DC, Dec 24, 45; m 70. CLASSICS, CLASSICAL ARCHEOLOGY. *Educ:* Haverford Col, BA, 67; Princeton Univ, MA, 69, PhD(classics), 70. *Prof Exp:* Asst prof, 70-80, ASSOC PROF CLASSICS, UNIV GA, 80- *Concurrent Pos:* Instr classics, Haverford Col, 70; asst prof archaeol, Intercol Ctr Class Studies, Rome, 71-72. *Res:* Etruscan art; early Roman history; Aeschylus. *Publ:* Auth, Divine triads on an archaic Etruscan frieze from Murlo, Studies Etruschi, 71; Figured friezes from the workshop of Vulca, Opuscula Romana X. *Mailing Add:* Dept of Classics Univ of Ga Park Hall Athens GA 30602

GANZ, DAVID, b Welwyn, UK, May 25, 52. CLASSICAL & MEDIEVAL LATIN. *Educ:* Univ Oxford, BA, 73, DPhil, 80. *Prof Exp:* Res asst hist, Univ St Andrews, Scotland, 79-80; vis asst prof, 80-82, ASST PROF CLASSICS, UNIV NC, CHAPEL HILL, 82- *Concurrent Pos:* Ed, Handlist of Alcuin Manuscripts, 79- *Res:* Latin palaeography; Carotingian Renaissance; Tironian notes. *Publ:* Co-ed, Charles the Bold, court & kingdom, Brit Archaeol Reports, 81; contribr, Church, King & Community, Blackwell, England, 82. *Mailing Add:* Dept of Classics Univ NC Chapel Hill NC 27514

GANZ, MARGARET LEONORE, English & Comparative Literature. See Vol II

GARBATY, THOMAS JAY, English. See Vol II

GARBER, FREDERICK MEYER, b Boston, Mass, Dec 18, 29; m 57; c 3. COMPARATIVE LITERATURE, ROMANTICISM. *Educ:* Boston Univ, BA, 57; Yale Univ, PhD(comp lit), 63. *Prof Exp:* Asst prof English, Univ Wash, 61-66; from asst prof to assoc prof, 66-71, PROF COMP LIT, STATE UNIV NY BINGHAMTON, 71- *Concurrent Pos:* Am Coun Learned Soc fel, 79-80. *Mem:* Am Comp Lit Asn (secy-treas, 70-71-); Int Comp Lit Asn (secy, 71-79); MLA. *Res:* Romanticism; contemporary criticism. *Publ:* Co-ed, Microcosm, Chandler Publ: 68; ed, Ann Radcliffe's The Italian, Oxford Univ, 68; auth, Wordsworth and the Poetry of Encounter, Univ Ill, 71; Thoreau's Redemptive Imagination, NY Univ, 77; The Autonomy of the Self from Richardson to Huysmans, Princeton, 82. *Mailing Add:* Dept of Comp Lit State Univ NY Binghamton NY 13901

GARBER, MARILYN, b Brooklyn, NY. HISTORY, LAW. *Educ:* Univ Calif, Los Angeles, BA, 57, MA, 60, PhD(hist), 67; Southwestern Univ, JD, 77. *Prof Exp:* Assoc prof, 67-80, PROF HIST, CALIF STATE UNIV, DOMINGUEZ HILLS, 80- *Mem:* AHA. *Res:* Utopia; legal history; labor law. *Publ:* Natural Law Liberalism, 67. *Mailing Add:* Dept Hist Calif State Univ Carson CA 90747

GARBRAH, KWEKU ARKU, b Cape Coast, Ghana, Dec 22, 37; m 71; c 3. CLASSICAL LINGUSTICS & PHILOLOGY. *Educ:* Univ London, BA, 61; Oxford Univ, dipl comp philol Indo-Europ lang, 63, BLitt, 66; Univ Cologne, Dr Phil(Greek, Latin & Indo-Europ philol), 72. *Prof Exp:* Asst prof classics, Univ Tex, Austin, 66-67; vis asst prof, Univ Calif, Los Angeles, 67-68; asst prof, 68-73, assoc prof, 73-80, PROF CLASSICS, UNIV ALTA, 80- *Concurrent Pos:* Sr res fel, Alexander von Humboldt Found, Univ Cologne, 76-77. *Mem:* Philol Soc, Eng; Ling Soc Am; Class Asn, Eng; Class Asn Can; Class Asn Pac Northwest. *Res:* Greek and Latin philology and lingustics; Greek epigraphy. *Publ:* Auth, A linguistic analysis of selected portions of the Moderic Odyssey, Glotta, Vol XLVII, 144-170; The Scholia on the ending of the Odyssey, Würzburger J, 77; A Grammar of the Ionic Inscriptions from Erythrae, Anton Hain, Meisenheim/Glan, 78; The scholia on Odyssey XI, Eranos, Vol 76, 1-11; Terence and Scipio: An Echo of Terence in the Oratorical Fragments of Scipio Aemilianus?, Athenaeum, 69: 188-191. *Mailing Add:* Dept of Classics Univ Alta Edmonton AB T6G 2E6 Can

GARBUTT-PARRALES, ERNESTINA FLORENCIA, b Stann Creek, Belize, Jan 19, 36; US citizen. HISPANIC PHILOLOGY, MEDIEVAL SPANISH LITERATURE. *Educ:* Union Col, BS, 59; La Sierra Col, MA, 66; Univ Southern Calif, MA, 72, PhD(Span), 77. *Prof Exp:* Teacher Span, Harrison Mem High Sch, Jamaica, WI, 59-62; cashier-account, Cent Am Union, Costa Rica, 62-64; med records clerk, White Mem Med Ctr, 66-70; asst prof, 76-80, ASSOC PROF SPAN, LOMA LINDA UNIV, 80- *Mem:* MLA; Am Asn Teachers Span & Port; Am Coun Teaching Foreign Lang. *Mailing Add:* Dept of Mod Lang Loma Linda Univ Riverside CA 92515

GARCIA, FREDERICK CHARLES HESSE, b Sao Paulo, Brazil, Jan 15, 28; m 54; c 3. PORTUGUESE LANGUAGE & LITERATURE. *Educ:* Guanabara State Univ, BA, 54, MA, 56; Univ Coimbra, Cert Port, 63; NY Univ, PhD(Luso-Brazilian), 68. *Prof Exp:* From instr to chmn dept Port, Defense Lang Inst W Coast Br, 52-54; chmn dept, Am Sch Rio de Janeiro, 54-59; CIVILIAN PROF PORT, US MIL ACAD, 59- *Concurrent Pos:* Vis prof, Harvard Univ, summer 66 & NY Univ, 82; Nat Endowment for Humanities fel, summer 79. *Honors & Awards:* Fermando Chinaglia Prize, Uniao Brasileira Escritores, 71. *Mem:* MLA; Am Asn Teachers Span & Port; AAUP; Northeast Mod Lang Asn. *Res:* Brazilian literature; literary relations. *Publ:* Auth, Richard Francis Burton e Luis de Camoes: o tradutor e o poeta, Ocidente, 71; Critic turned author, Luso-Brasilian Rev, 72; Ecos de Chateaubriand no Pensamento Critico de M de Assis, Int Colloquium, Rennes, 73; Richard F Burton and Basilio da Gama-the translator and the poet, Luso-Brazilian REv, 75; Aquilino Ribeiro e G Rosa: Duas Visoes da Donzela Guerreira, Tempo Univ, Brazil, 77; Pombal contra Malagrida: Uma Tragedia Francesa de Assunto Portugues, Amsterdam, 81; Um Almocreve na Estrada de Santiago, Lisbon, 81; coauth (with Edward F Stanton), Critical edition of Richard Francis Burton's translation of Jose Basilio da Gama, O Uraguai, Univ Calif, 82. *Mailing Add:* 146 Howard Rd West Point NY 10996

GARCIA, JOSE G, b Valencia, Spain, June 11, 24; US citizen; m 61; c 1. SPANISH. *Educ:* Univ Valencia, BA, 44, MA, 48; Univ Inter-Am Mex, PhD(Span). *Prof Exp:* Instr Span, Andrew Col, 55-56, Colo Mil Acad, 56-57 & Univ Colo, 57-60; asst prof, Univ Hawaii, 60-62 & Cornell Col, 62-63; ASSOC PROF SPAN, CLARION STATE COL, 64- *Concurrent Pos:* Consult & coordr Span curriculum, Inter-Am Univ, Mex, 65-, mem adv bd, 66- *Mem:* Am Asn Teachers Span & Port. *Res:* XIX century century Spanish realism. *Mailing Add:* Dept of Span Clarion State Col Clarion PA 16214

GARCIA-CASTANEDA, SALVADOR, b Zamora, Spain, May 25, 32; m 71. SPANISH LITERATURE. *Educ:* Univ Oviedo, Lic Filos y Let, 56; Univ Calif, Berkeley, PhD(Romance lang), 67. *Prof Exp:* Dir Span Cult Inst, Baghdad, Iraq, 59-62; teaching asst Sp an, Univ Calif, Berkeley, 62-66; asst prof, San Francisco State Col, 66-68 & Univ Mich, Ann Arbor, 68-71; assoc prof, 72-77, PROF ROMANCE LANG, OHIO STATE UNIV, 77- *Mem:* MLA. *Res:* Eighteenth and 19th century Spanish literature; bibliography. *Publ:* Auth, Las ideas literarias en Espana entre 1840 y 1850, Univ Calif, 71; J E Hartzenbusch's Los amantes de Teruel, Castalia, Madrid, 71; Jose Zorilla's Don Juan Tenorio, Labor, Barcelona, 75; Don Telesfora de Trueba y Cosio: Su tiempo, su vida y su obra, Diputacion Provincial, Santander, 78; Miquel de los Santos Alvarez: Romanticismo y poesia, SGEL, Madrid, 79. *Mailing Add:* Dept of Romance Lang Ohio State Univ Columbus OH 43210

GARCIA-GIRON, EDMUNDO, b Albuquerque, NMex, Feb 19, 16; m 47. LATIN AMERICAN LITERATURE. *Educ:* Univ Calif, Berkeley, AB, 40, MA, 47, PhD(Romance lit), 52. *Prof Exp:* Instr Span, Marquette Univ, 52-53; asst prof Latin Am lit, Univ Ore, 53-56; asst prof Span, Western Reserve Univ, 56-57; assoc head mod lang dept, D C Heath & Co, 57-62; dir mod lang dept, Prentice-Hall Inc, 62-72; PROF LATIN AM LIT & CHICANO STUDIES, TEX TECH UNIV, 72- *Concurrent Pos:* Mod lang consult, Prentice-Hall Inc, 72-77. *Mem:* Academia de la Lengua Espanola de las Americas. *Res:* Modernismo; Chicano studies. *Publ:* Co-ed, Chile: A Geographical Extravaganza, Macmillan, Toronto, 43; auth, La azul sonrisa: disquisicion sobre la adjetivacion modernista, Rev Iberoam, 55; El modernismo como evasion cultural, In: Estudios criticos sobre el modernismo, Ed Gredos, 68; Valle-Inclan--modernist poet, In: Ramon del Valle-Inclan, an Appraisal of Life and Works, 67 & translr, Brother Ass, 69, Las Americas; The Chicanos: an overview, Proc Comp Lit Symp, 78. *Mailing Add:* Dept of Class & Romance Lang Tex Tech Univ Lubbock TX 79409

GARCIA-MAZAS, JOSE MANUEL, b Aguada, Cuba, Aug 27, 12; US citizen; m 35; c 5. SPANISH LANGUAGE & CULTURE. *Educ:* Univ Valencia, Lec en Filos y Let, 41; Univ Madrid, Dr Filos y Let, 54. *Prof Exp:* Asst prof hist Spain, Univ Valencia, 41-43; instr Span, NY Univ, 46-49; instr, Teachers Col, Columbia Univ, 49-51; from asst prof to assoc prof, NY Univ, 54-63; assoc prof, 63-69, PROF SPAN, CITY COL NEW YORK, 69- *Concurrent Pos:* Secy, Huntington Found, 54-60. *Mem:* Corresp mem Hisp Soc Am; AAUP. *Res:* Frequency of words in spoken Spanish from recorded conversations; origins of Latin American Spanish. *Publ:* Auth, El poeta y la escultora, Rev Occidente, Madrid, 62; coauth, Primera antologia Sonora . . . , Chilton, Phila, 63; auth, De Spaniae a Al-Andalus, 74, Como se jorjo Espana, 74, Los Siglos de Oro, 74, De la Illustracion al 97, 74 & Espana contemporanea, 74, Guadarrama, Madrid. *Mailing Add:* 150 Ash St Floral Park NY 11001

GARCIA-MOYA, RODOLFO, b Raymondville, Tex, Dec 22, 41; c 2. SPANISH. *Educ:* Bowling Green State Univ, BS, 64; Ind Univ, MA, 67; Ohio State Univ, PhD(foreign lang educ), 73. *Prof Exp:* Teacher Span, Pomona Unified Sch Dist, 64-65; asst prof, Williams Col, 67-69; asst prof educ, Cent Mich Univ, 71-73; dir Study Abroad-Xalape, Mex, 77-78, ASST PROF SPAN, UNIV COLO, 73- *Concurrent Pos:* Dir, Mich Migrant Educ Ctr, 72-73; coordr, BUENO Bilingual Educ Serv Ctr, 81. *Mem:* Am Coun Teaching Foreign Lang; Am Asn Teachers Span & Port; MLA. *Res:* Methodology of teaching foreign languages; teaching Spanish to the Spanish speaking; applied linguistics. *Publ:* Coauth, Vista: Activities for Teaching Social Studies: A Comparative Perspective, Mich State Dept Educ, 73; co-ed, Teaching Spanish to the Spanish-Speaking: Theory and Practice, Trinity Univ, 76; co-ed, Teaching Spanish to the Hispanic Bilingual: Issues, Aims and Methods, Teachers Col Press, Columbia Univ, 81. *Mailing Add:* Dept of Span & Port Univ of Colo Boulder CO 80309

GARCIA-SAEZ, SANTIAGO, b Burgos, Spain, May 1, 32; US citizen; m 65; c 2. SPANISH LITERATURE, FRENCH. *Educ:* Univ Oriente, Cuba, BA, 61; Univ Pittsburgh, MA, 66, PhD(Span), 72. *Prof Exp:* Instr lang, La Salle Col, Cuba, 56-61; instr lang & hist, La Providencia Col, Honduras, 61-62; assoc prof Span & French, Robert Morris Col, 65-74; asst prof Span, Bethany Col, 74-78; ASSOC PROF SPAN, OKLA STATE UNIV, 78- *Concurrent Pos:* Teacher fel Span, Univ Pittsburgh, 64-65; vis prof Span, Case Western Reserve Univ, 64-66. *Mem:* MLA; Am Asn Teachers Span & Port; Inst Int Lit. *Res:* Spanish prerromanticism; the Aztecs civilization. *Publ:* Auth, Don Pedro Montengon, un prerromantico de la Illustracion, Caja de A Alicante, Spain, 74; Philadelphia: Symbol of Freedom in the Literary Movement of 18th century Spain, Folio-Bethany Col, 76; La utopia Americana y el Sentido del Eusebio de Montengon, Revista Estudios Hispanicos-Univ Ala, 78; La vision del indio en La conquista del Megico por Hernan Cortes: poema epico de don Pedro Montengon y Paret, Dieciocho, 82; Reflejos picerescos en el Eusebio de Montengon?, Hispanic J, Vol 3, 82; Toward an interpretation of the Havana's Slang in Jose Sanchez-Boudy and the popular Socio-linguistic languages in the Lilayando of Jose Sanchez-Boudy, In: The Novels and Short Stories of Jose Sanchez-Boudy, Interpretation and Analyses, Ediciones Universal, 82. *Mailing Add:* Dept of Foreign Lang Okla State Univ Stillwater OK 74074

GARCI-GOMEZ, MIGUEL, b Almoharin-Caceres, Spain, Nov 30, 32; US citizen; m 69; c 3. SPANISH LANGUAGE & LITERATURE. *Educ:* Cath Univ Am, MA, 69, PhD(Span), 71. *Prof Exp:* Lectr Span, Univ Md, 70-71; asst prof Gettysburg Col, 71-73; ASSOC PROF SPAN, DUKE UNIV, 73- *Concurrent Pos:* Asst prof, Millersville State Col, 71 & 72. *Honors & Awards:* Premio Internacional, Benalmadena de Ling & Critica Lit, 75. *Mem:* MLA; Am Asn Teachers Span & Port; SAtlantic Mod Lang Asn. *Res:* Medieval epic; 15th century Spanish literature; Spanish refranero. *Publ:* Parafrasis de Cicerron en la definicion de poesia de Santillana, Hispania, 73; Relacion semantica y etimologica entre Latinado y paladino, BRAE, 73; Romance segun los textos esp del prerenacim, JMRS, 74; Mio Cid: Estudios de endocritica, Planeta, Barcelona, 75; The reaction against medieval romances: Its Spanish forerunners, Neophil, 76; ed, Cantar de Mio Cid, CUPSA, 78; Amor Imperuio o Amor improuo, Celestinesca, LC: 94, 80; Hueuos asados: A frodisiaco para el marido de Celestina, Celestinesca, 81. *Mailing Add:* Dept of Romance Lang Duke Univ Durham NC 27706

GARDIOL, RITA MAZZETTI, b Pittsburgb, Pa. SPANISH LITERATURE, LATIN AMERICAN STUDIES. *Educ:* Mt Mercy Col, BA, 59; Middlebury Col, MA, 64; Ind Univ, PhD(Span), 68. *Prof Exp:* Asst prof Span, Mt Mercy Col, 68-69; from asst prof to assoc prof, 69-76, coordr Span, 70-73, PROF SPAN, BALL STATE UNIV, 76-, ADMIN ASST, DEPT FOREIGN LANG, 73-, CHMN DEPT, 76- *Mem:* MLA; Am Asn Teachers Span & Port; Midwest Mod Lang Asn; Midwest Asn Latin Am Studies. *Res:* Works of Ramon Gomez de la Serna; works of Jorge Luis Borges; literary movements in Latin America. *Publ:* Auth, Plurifications in the Work of Ramon Gomez de la Serna, Hispanofila, 5/71; Some comments on the biolgraphical sketches of Ramon de la Serna, Ky Romance Quart, XVII: 275-80; Ramon and Goya: An incident of spiritual kinship, Romance Notes, XIII: 1-6; Ramon and Ortega, Lang Quart, spring-summer, 72; coauth, A testing of the audio-active voice reflector in the foreign language classrooms, Mod Lang J, 3/72; Dios, Obra inedita de Ramon Gomez de la Serna, Razon y Fe, 11/74; Changing Expectations, Women in Management, Univ Col Bus & The Shell Found, 3/81; Planning the Weekend Live-In Foreign Language Workshop, Hispania, 81-82. *Mailing Add:* Dept of Span Ball State Univ Muncie IN 47306

GARDNER, ARTHUR PARCEL, b Scranton, Pa, Apr 18, 22. GERMAN LITERATURE. *Educ:* Duke Univ, AB, 44; Harvard Univ, AM, 45, PhD, 50. *Prof Exp:* Instr Ger, Amherst Col, 50-53; instr, Harvard Univ, 53-55; asst prof, Univ Calif, Riverside, 56-57; asst prof, 58-66, assoc prof, 66-79, PROF GER, LEHIGH UNIV, 79- *Mem:* MLA; Am Asn Teachers Ger; AAUP. *Res:* Nineteenth and twentieth century German literature; German lyric; Renaissance and baroque in German literature. *Publ:* Coauth, Wie sie es sehen, Holt, 52. *Mailing Add:* Dept of Ger Lehigh Univ Bethlehem PA 18015

GAREAU, ETIENNE, b St Jacques, Que, Oct 21, 15. LATIN. *Educ:* Pontifica Univ Gregoriana, Rome, BPh, 38; Univ Ottawa, BA, 40, LTh, 46; Laval Univ, LL, 49; Univ Paris, DUniv(Latin), 52. *Prof Exp:* Prof class studies, Juniorat du Sacre-Coeur, Ottawa, 43-47; head dept class studies, 53-67, PROF CLASS STUDIES, UNIV OTTAWA, 52- *Concurrent Pos:* Fr Govt fel, 49-50; Can Coun fel, 67-68; pres, pre-doctoral awards comt, Can Coun, 66-67, mem, 68-69. *Mem:* Humanities Asn Can; Class Asn Can (pres, 64-66); Soc Etudes Latines; Soc Can Etudes Class (vpres, 60-62, pres, 64-66); Asn Guillaume Bude. *Res:* Roman oratory; Greek and Roman civilization; Roman religion. *Publ:* Auth, L'ironie socratique dans le De Oratore de Ciceron, Bull Humanities Asn Can, 11/60; Le latin pourquoi et pour qui aujourd'jui, Univ Ottawa Rev, 4-6/64; L'importance de l'enseignement scientifique des humanites classiques, Actes de VI Colloquium Soc Studies Greek & Latin, Que, 72; auth, Compte-rendu d'une Experience de Production de Diaporamas sur les Valeurs Dominantes, Dept Ancient Studies, Univ Ottawa, 72; Bene et vere loqui: lactance et la conception ciceronienne de l'orateur ideal, Rev Etudes latines, Paris, 78. *Mailing Add:* Dept of Class Studies Univ of Ottawa 30 rue Stewart Ottawa ON K1N 6N5 Can

GAREY, HOWARD BURTON, b Columbus, Ohio, Aug 29, 17; m 40; c 1. FRENCH, LINGUISTICS. *Educ:* Univ Calif, Los Angeles, MA, 47; Yale Univ, PhD(ling), 53. *Prof Exp:* Teaching asst German, Univ Calif, Los Angeles, 41-42; from instr to asst prof French, 50-60, Morse fel, 54-55, ASSOC PROF FRENCH & ROMANCE PHILOL & FEL, TRUMBULL COL, YALE UNIV, 60- *Mem:* MLA; Am Asn Teachers Fr; Ling Soc Am. *Res:* Historical grammar of French; modern French structure, especially syntax, especially of the verb, Romance linguistics. *Publ:* Auth, The historical development of tenses from late Latin to Old French, Language. *Mailing Add:* Dept of French & Romance Philol Yale Univ New Haven CT 06520

GARFIELD, EVELYN PICON, b Newark, NJ, Aug 23, 40; m 61; c 2. LATIN AMERICAN CONTEMPORARY LITERATURE. *Educ:* Univ Mich, Ann Arbor, AB, 63; Wash Univ, MA, 67; Rutgers Univ, New Brunswick, PhD(Hisp lang & lit), 72. *Prof Exp:* Asst prof Span lang & Latin Am lit, Montclair State Col, 70-74; co-dir affirmative action off, Univ Mass, Boston, 74-76; asst prof, Brown Univ, 76-80; asst prof, 80-81, ASSOC PROF, WAYNE STATE UNIV, 81- *Concurrent Pos:* Chairperson, Affirmative Action Comt on Women, Mont State Co, 72-73, fac consult, Women's Ctr, 72- & Off Affirmative Action, 73; Am Philos Soc res grant, 73; Nat Endowment for Humanities grant, 73-74; corresp mem, Inst Filos Ciencias y Letras, Montevideo, Uruguay, 80; co-dir, Nat Endowment for Humanities summer sem, Concept of Spanish American Modernity, 82. *Mem:* AAUP; MLA; Women's Equity Action League; Nat Orgn Women. *Publ:* Auth, Muerte, Metamorfosis, Modernidad: El gato eficaz de Luisa Valenzuela, Insula, 3-4/80; Lo maravilloso en la realidad cotidiana, In: Julio Cortazar, Taurus, Madrid, 81; coauth (with I A Schulman), Modernismo/Modernidad: Apostillas a la teoria de la Edad Moderna, In: In Honor of Boyd G Carter, Univ Wyo, 81; auth, Tradicion y ruptura: Modernidad en Tres novelas ejemplares de Vicente Huidobro y Hans Arp, Hisp Rev (in press); Del caracol nace una flor amarilla: Sabina de Julieta Campos, Rev Nacional de Cultura, Caracas (in press); Los sistemas de dependencia en la poesia de Ali Chumacero, In: Ensayos criticos sobre poesia mexicana actual, Siglo XXI, Mexico (in press); De sobremesa de Jose Asuncion Silva: El diario intimo y la mujer prerrafaelita, In: Nuevos asedios al modernismo, Grijalbo, Barcelona (in press); coauth (with I A Schulman), El modernismo de ambos mundos: Espana e Hispanoamerica, Ed Taurus, Spain (in press). *Mailing Add:* Dept of Romance & Ger Lang & Lit Wayne State Univ Detroit MI 48202

GARFINKEL, ALAN, b Chicago, Ill, Sept 6, 41; m 65; c 2. SPANISH EDUCATION. *Educ:* Univ Ill, Urbana, BA, 63, MA, 64; Ohio State Univ, PhD(educ), 68. *Prof Exp:* Teacher Span, Waukegan Twp High Sch, Ill, 64-66; asst prof foreign lang educ, Okla State Univ, 69-72; asst prof, 72-74, ASSOC PROF FOREIGN LANG EDUC, PURDUE UNIV, WEST LAFAYETTE, 72-, ASST DIR, DIV SPONSORED PROG, 81- *Concurrent Pos:* Ed notes & news, Mod Lang J, 74- *Mem:* Am Coun Teaching Foreign Lang; MLA; Nat Soc Studies Educ; Am Asn Teachers Span & Port. *Res:* Language teaching methodology and curriculum; language teacher education; continuing education. *Publ:* Auth, Instructional strategies in foreign language, In: The Britannica Review of Foreign Language Education, Encycl Britannica, Vol III, 71; The enrichment oriented radio program: A medium for building listening comprehension, Hispania, 5/72; The public image of language instruction, Mod Lang J, 3/74; coauth, Designs for Foreign Language Teacher Education, 76, Modismos al Momento, 77 & Trabajo y Vida, 82, Newbury House. *Mailing Add:* FLL/SC Purdue Univ West Lafayette IN 47907

GARGANIGO, JOHN F, b Como, Italy, Mar 17, 37; US citizen; m 67. ROMANCE LANGUAGES, LATIN AMERICAN LITERATURE. *Educ:* Iona Col, BA, 59; Univ Ill, MA, 61, PhD(Span), 65. *Prof Exp:* Asst Span & Ital, Univ Ill, 59-62; from instr to asst prof, 64-68, assoc prof, 68-80, PROF SPAN, WASHINGTON UNIV, 80- *Concurrent Pos:* Vis prof Latin Am lit, Latin Am Res Ctr, Univ Florence, 70-71; chmn, Latin Am Studies, 74-; Am Philos Soc res grant, 77. *Mem:* MLA; Inst Int Lit Iberoam. *Publ:* Auth, El perfil del gaucho, Sintesis, 66 & coauth, Antologia de la literatura gauchesca y criollista, Delta, 67, Montevideo; auth, Javier de Viana, Life Works, Twayne, 72; Cintio Vitier: encarnacion de una poetica, Anales Lit Hisp Am, 75; El perfil del negro en la narrativa Rioplatense, Historiografia y Bibliog Americanistas, 77; coauth (with Edward J Mullen), El cuento Hispanico, A Graded Literary Anthology, Random House, 79. *Mailing Add:* Box 1077 Wash Univ St Louis MO 63130

GARIANO, CARMELO, b Nicosia, Mar 4, 22; US citizen; m 53; c 2. FOREIGN LANGUAGES. *Educ:* Univ Catania, Italy, DLet, 46; Univ Buenos Aires, Arg, Prof en Let, 51, Lic en Let, 53; De Paul Univ, MA, 56; Univ Chicago, PhD(Spanish), 64. *Prof Exp:* Lectr Latin Am lit, Univ Buenos Aires, 51-52, aesthet & stylistics, 52-53; instr Span, Univ Detroit, 57-60; asst prof, Roosevelt Univ, 60-62; asst prof, 62-68, PROF ROMANCE LANG, CALIF STATE UNIV, NORTHRIDGE, 68- *Concurrent Pos:* Assoc prof classics, Nat Univ Litoral, Arg, 51-53; mem, Nat Fed Mod Lang Teachers Asn, 59- *Mem:* MLA; Am Asn Teachers Span & Port. *Res:* Diachronic linguistics; Spanish medieval literature; medieval and Renaissance studies. *Publ:* Auth, Spanish For You: Teacher's Guide, 2 vols with 30 educ films, Lingua/Film Inc, 64-67; Analisis estilistico de los Milagros de Berceo, 66, Anhelos, busquedas, encuentros, 66, Anicos del laüd iridiscente, 67 & El mundo poetico de Juan Ruiz, 67, Gredos, Madrid; Saga de Kennedy (verses), Orbe, Inc, 66; La lirica italiana en el siglo XX, Ed La Portena, Buenos Aires, 67; Enfoque estilistico de las obras medievales, Ed Alcala, Madrid, 68. *Mailing Add:* Dept of Foreign Lang Calif State Univ 18111 Nordhoff St Northridge CA 91324

GARIEPY, ROBERT JOSEPH, JR, b Missoula, Mont, Mar 10, 34; c 5. CLASSICS, COMPARATIVE LITERATURE. *Educ:* Gonzaga Univ, BEd, 59; Univ Wash, MA, 62, PhD(classics), 65. *Prof Exp:* From instr to asst prof classics, Gonzaga Univ, 63-68; assoc prof, 68-72, PROF HUMANITIES, EASTERN WASH UNIV, 72-, COORDR DEPT, 70-, DIR, HONORS PROG, 79- *Mem:* Am Philol Asn; Archaeol Inst Am; Medieval Asn Pac; Philol Asn Pac Coast; Class Asn Pac Northwest (pres, 67-68). *Res:* Medieval and Renaissance Latin literature; comparative literature; Ovid. *Publ:* Auth, Lupus of Ferrieres and the classics, Monographic Press, 67; Lupus of Ferrieres: Carolingian scribe and text critic, Mediaeval Studies, 10/68; Recent scholarship on Ovid (1958-68), Class World, 10/70; Animal imagery in the Odyssey, Class Bull, 73; Lupus of Ferrieres' Knowledge of Classical Latin Literature, Hommages a Andre Boutemy, Latomus, Brussels, 76; Beauty unadorned: A reading of Propertius I.2, Class Bull, 80. *Mailing Add:* Dept of Humanities Eastern Wash Univ Cheney WA 99004

GARNER, GARY NEIL, b Prentiss, Miss, Jan 12, 36; m 58; c 2. GERMAN & FRENCH LANGUAGE & LITERATURE. *Educ:* Miss Col, BA, 57; Innsbruck Univ, cert, 57 & 58; Univ Miss, MA, 59; La State Univ, Baton Rouge, PhD(Ger & French), 69. *Prof Exp:* Instr Ger, French & Span, Wayland Baptist Col, 59-62, asst prof Ger & French & actg chmn dept, 64-65; assoc prof & actg chmn dept, La Col, 65-69; from assoc prof to prof & chmn dept, Dallas Baptist Col, 69-77; ACAD DEAN & REGISTR, CLARKE COL, MISS, 77- *Concurrent Pos:* Pres, Multiling Transl Serv, Inc, Dallas, 70-73; pres, Omnilingua, Inc, Dallas, 73-82. *Mem:* MLA; Am Asn Teachers Ger; Int Brecht Soc; Am Transl Asn. *Res:* Professional translating; dramatic works of Bertolt Brecht; teaching foreign languages through the use of videotape facilities. *Mailing Add:* Clark Col PO Box 440 Newton MS 39345

GARNICA, OLGA K, b Shanhai, China, July 19, 45; US citizen. LINGUISTICS. *Educ:* Univ Calif, Berkeley, AB, 67; Stanford Univ, PhD(ling), 74. *Prof Exp:* Psychometrist, Univ Calif, Berkeley, 68-70; instr, 73-74, ASST PROF LING, OHIO STATE UNIV, 74- *Mem:* Ling Soc Am; MLA; Am Anthrop Asn; AAAS. *Res:* Psycholinguistics; sociolinguistics; stylistics, linguistic approaches to literary analysis. *Publ:* Auth, The development of phonemic speech perception, In: Cognitive Development and the Acquisition of Language, Acad Press, 73; coauth, Is he coming or going? A study of the acquisition of deictic verbs, J Verbal Learning & Verbal Behav, 74; Theories of phonological development, In: Foundations of Language Development: A Multidisciplinary Approach, Acad Press, 75; auth, Some prosodic and paralinguistic features of speech to young children, In: Talking to Children, Cambridge Univ, 77; coauth, Phonological variation in children's utterances: The trade-off phenomenon, In: Proceedings of the Fourth International Congress of Applied Linguistics, Hochschul Verlag, 77; auth, Nonverbal concomitants of language input to young children, In: Development of Communication: Social and Pragmatic Factors in Language Acquisition, Wiley & Sons, 78; Rules of verbal interaction and literary analysis, Poetics, 77; co-ed, Language, Children and Society, Pergamon, 78. *Mailing Add:* Dept of Ling Ohio State Univ 1841 Millikin Rd Columbus OH 43210

GAROFALO, SILVANO, b Italy, Aug 22, 34; US citizen; m 64; c 4. ITALIAN & SPANISH LITERATURE. *Educ:* Univ Minn, BA, 57, MA, 61, PhD(Romance lang), 66; Macalester Col, BA, 58. *Prof Exp:* Instr Ital & Span, Univ Minn, 64-66; asst prof, 67-72, assoc prof, 72-79, PROF ITAL, UNIV WIS-MADISON, 79- *Concurrent Pos:* Fulbright teaching & study grant, Univ Pisa, 66-67; dir, Ind-Wis Jr Year Prog, Bologna, 69-70 & 77-78. *Mem:* MLA. *Res:* Nineteenth and 20th century Italian and Spanish literature; the fortune of certain Italian writers in America during the first half of the 19th century. *Publ:* Auth, The moon in the poetry of Leopardi and Unamuno, Symposium, winter 69; coauth, Conversiamo un Po, Appleton, 69; auth, Allesandro Manzoni in the American Literary Scene, 1830-1840, Forum Italicum, 73; L'enciclopedismo Italiano: Gianfrancesco Pivati, Longo, Ravenna, 80. *Mailing Add:* 2909 Oxford Rd Madison WI 53705

GARR, W RANDALL, b Norwalk, Conn, Dec 21, 54. SEMITIC LANGUAGES. *Educ:* Vassar Col, AB, 77; Yale Univ, MA, 79, MPhil, 80, PhD(Near East lit), 82. *Prof Exp:* LECTR NORTHWEST SEMITIC LANG, UNIV PA, 82- *Mem:* Am Orient Soc; Soc Bibl Lit; Am Schs Orient Res; Ling Soc Am; Asn Jewish Studies. *Res:* History of the Hebrew language; comparative semitics; history of Syria-Palestine. *Publ:* Auth, The Qinah: A Study of Poetic Meter, Syntax and Style, Zeitschrift die alttestamentliche Wissenschaft, 82. *Mailing Add:* Dept of Orient Studies Univ of Pa Philadelphia PA 19104

GARRARD, JOHN G, b London, Eng, Aug 28, 34; m 59, 79; c 1. SOVIET STUDIES. *Educ:* Oxford Univ, BA, 58; Columbia Univ, MA, 63, Russ Inst, cert, 64, PhD(Slavic lang), 66. *Prof Exp:* Lectr Russ, Carleton Univ, 58-63, asst prof, 63-64; from asst prof to assoc prof, Dartmouth Col, 64-70; chmn dept, 71-76, PROF SLAVIC LANG, UNIV VA, 71-, DIR CTR RUSS & EAST EUROP STUDIES, 72- *Concurrent Pos:* Vis assoc prof, Ind Univ, 70-71. *Mem:* MLA; Am Asn Advan Slavic Studies; Lang & Literatures Slavs; Am Sociol Asn. *Res:* Russian literature; Soviet media; Soviet society. *Publ:* Ed & contribr, Vladimir Tendryakov: Three Novellas, Pergamon, 67; auth, Mixail Culkov: An Introduction to His Prose and Verse, Mouton, The Hague, 70; ed & contribr, The Eighteenth Century in Russia, Oxford, 73; auth,

Karamzin, Mme de Staël and the Russian Romantics; Am Contrib VII Int Cong Slavists, Mouton, The Hague, 75; auth, Some Thoughts on Gogol's Kolyaska, PMLA, 75; Mikhail Lermontov, G K Hall, 82; ed & contribr, The Russian Novel From Pushkin to Pasternak, Yale Univ Press (in press). *Mailing Add:* Dept of Slavic Lang & Lit Univ of Va Charlottesville VA 22903

GARRISON, DANIEL HODGES, b Hamilton, NY, Dec 24, 37; c 1. CLASSICS, COMPARATIVE LITERATURE. *Educ:* Harvard Col, AB, 59; Univ NC, Chapel Hill, MA, 63; Univ Calif, Berkeley, PhD(comp lit), 68. *Prof Exp:* Instr Latin, Phillips Exeter Acad, 59-60; instr classics, WVa Univ, 62-63; asst prof, 66-73, ASSOC PROF CLASSICS, NORTHWESTERN UNIV, 73- *Mem:* Am Philol Asn; Int Homeric Coun (secy, 74-). *Res:* Hellenistic culture; ancient epic; comparative literature. *Publ:* Auth, Melville's Doubloon and the shield of Achilles, 19th Century Fiction, 71; Mild Frenzy: A Reading of the Hellenistic Love Epigram, Franz Steiner Verlag Hermes-Einzenschrift, 78. *Mailing Add:* Dept of Classics Northwestern Univ Kresge Cent Hall Evanston IL 60201

GARTON, CHARLES, b Yorkshire, England, Aug 13, 26; m 60; c 2. CLASSICS. *Educ:* Cambridge Univ, BA, 49, MA, 53. *Prof Exp:* Asst lectr classics, Univ Hull, 51-53; lectr, Univ Newcastle upon Tyne, 53-65; assoc prof, 65-72, actg chmn dept, 73-74, PROF CLASSICS, STATE UNIV NY BUFFALO, 72- *Concurrent Pos:* Ed, Arethusa, 68-71, assoc ed, 74- *Mem:* Class Asn England & Wales. *Res:* Classical and comparative literature; theatre; educational history. *Publ:* Contribr, The New English Bible Reviewed, Epworth, London, 65; From an Ancient to a Modern Theatre, Univ Man, 72; ed & translr, John Clarke's Orationes et Declamationes, Arethusa Monogr, 72; auth, Personal Aspects of the Roman Theatre, Hakkert, Amsterdam, 72; co-ed & translr, Theophylactus Simocates, On Predestined Terms of Life, 78 & Germans, On Predestined Terms of Life, 79, Arethusa Monogr. *Mailing Add:* Dept of Classics State Univ New York Buffalo NY 14260

GARVIN, PAUL LUCIAN, b Vienna, Austria, Aug 28, 19; m 44; c 1. LINGUISTICS. *Educ:* Ecole Libre des Hautes Etudes, NY, Lic es Let, 45; Ind Univ, PhD(ling), 47. *Prof Exp:* Res assoc, Ind Univ, 47-48; consult, res contemporary cult, Columbia Univ, 48; asst prof anthrop, Univ Okla, 48-51; from asst prof to assoc prof ling, Georgetown Univ, 51-60; mem sr staff, TRW computer div, Bunker-Ramo Corp, 60-64, mgr lang anal & transl, 64-69; PROF LING, STATE UNIV NY, BUFFALO, 69- *Mem:* Ling Soc Am; fel Am Anthrop Asn. *Res:* General linguistics and linguistic theory; semiotics. *Publ:* Ed, Natural Language and the Computer, McGraw, 63; co-ed, Computation in Linguistics, a Case Book, Ind Univ, 66; ed, Cognition, a Multiple View, Spartan, 70; ed, Method and Theory in Linguistics, 70, auth, On Machine Translation, 72 & On Linguistic Method, 2nd ed, 72, Mouton, The Hague. *Mailing Add:* Dept of Ling State Univ NY Buffalo NY 14261

GARY, EDWARD NORMAN, b Borger, Tex, Dec 10, 38; wid. APPLIED & THEORETICAL LINGUISTICS. *Educ:* Okla State Univ, BA, 61; Univ Calif, Los Angeles, MA, 66, MA, 72, PhD(ling), 79. *Prof Exp:* Ed, Curriculum Res & Develop Comp, CITE, 70-71; teaching fel English, Univ Calif, Los Angeles, 72-75; dir English lang training, Sysorex Inst, Comput Training Inst, 75-76; lectr teaching English as second lang & ling, Proj Fac of Educ, Univ Calif, Los Angeles, Ain Shams, 76-79; assoc prof English & ling, Cairo Univ, 80-82; ASSOC DIR, FULBRIGHT COMN, EGYPT, 81- *Concurrent Pos:* Consult lang teaching, 79-; Fulbright scholar, Coun Int Exchange of Scholars, 80-81; adj assoc prof, Am Univ, Cairo, 81-82. *Mem:* Ling Soc Am; Nat Orgn Teachers of English to Speakers of Other Lang. *Res:* Foreign language teaching methodology; foreign language acquisition; English syntax--sentence and discourse. *Publ:* Auth, A Discourse Analysis of Certain Translations, Ind Univ Linguistics Club, 76; coauth, Comp oriented Foreign Language Institute: An overview, The Ling Reporter, 80; Caution: Talking may be dangerous, Int Rev Appl Ling, 81; Comparative-based Language Instruction: Practice, 81 & Comparative-based Language Instruction: Theory, 81, New York Acad Sci; Packaging comparative materials, 82 & Listening recall: Testing list for low professional language (in prep), System. *Mailing Add:* c/o Fulbright/Cairo Dept State Washington DC 20520

GASCON-VERA, ELENA, b Madrid, Spain, Dec 21, 43. SPANISH LANGUAGE & LITERATURE. *Educ:* Univ Madrid, Licenciatura, 66; Yale Univ, MPhil, 70, PhD(Span lit), 74. *Prof Exp:* Vis instr Span, Loras Col, 66-67; instr French & Span, Univ NC, Greensboro, 67-68; instr Span, Yale Univ, 72-73; asst prof, 73-78, ASSOC PROF SPAN, WELLESLEY COL, 78- *Concurrent Pos:* Hubber Award, summer res grant study in Spain, 78; Ford res grant, 79; Mellon res grant, 81. *Mem:* Asoc Int Hispanistas; Medieval Acad Am; Renaissance Soc Am; MLA; Am Asn Teachers Span & Port. *Res:* Fifteenth century Spanish and Portuguese literature and civilization; Golden Age Spanish literature; Spanish novel since the Civil War. *Publ:* Auth, El yema del De Contemptu Mundi en Castilla a mediados del Siglo XV, Bol Bibliot Menendez y Pecayo, Santander, 77; Vida y obra literaria de Don Pedro, Condestable de Portugal, 1429-1466, Fundacion Universitaria Espanola, Madrid, 78; La quema de los libros de don Enrique de Villena: Una maniobra politica y antisemitica, Bull Hisp Studies, 56: 317-324; La ambiguedad en el concepto del amor y de la mujer en la prosa castellana del siglo XV, Bol de la Real Acad Espanola, 59: 119-155; Don Pedro, Condestable de Portugal, Madrid: Fundacion Universitaria Espanola, 79; Homenaje a Jorge Guillen, Insula, Madrid, 79; El concepto de tragedia en los escritores cultos de la corte de Juan II de Castilla, VI Congreso Internacional de Hispanistas, Univ Toronto, 80; New Spanish Cinema/Nuevo cine espanol, Mus Fine Arts, Boston, 80. *Mailing Add:* Dept of Span Wellesley Col Wellesley MA 02181

GASINSKI, THADDEUS ZDZISLAW, b Warsaw, Poland, Oct 26, 31; US citizen; m 61; c 2. SLAVIC LINGUISTICS. *Educ:* Univ Warsaw, Absolutorium, 56; Stanford Univ, MA, 62, PhD(Slavics), 66. *Prof Exp:* Instr Slavic lang & lit, Univ Pittsburgh, 63-65; asst prof Slavic lang, Univ NC, Chapel Hill, 65-70; assoc prof Russ & Polish, Univ Hawaii, Manoa, 70-79; PROF & HEAD DEPT RUSS, UNIV SOUTH AFRICA, PRETORIA, 79- *Mem:* Am Asn Slavic & E Europ Lang; MLA; Polish Inst Aats & Sci Am; Am Asn Advan Slavic Studies; Australia New Zealand Slavists Asn. *Res:* Slavic linguistics and cultures; Russo-African relations. *Publ:* Auth, A new look at the question of Czech influences in the languages of Sime Budinic, J Croatian Studies, 68-69; Existentialist tendencies in recent Polish poetry, Slavic & E Europ J, summer 69; On the functional load of the cont variants of Polish future tenses, Polish Rev, spring 71; Signs of detachment and dissent in resent Polish poetry, Mich Quart Rev, winter 71; A note on Count Strzelecki's visit to Hawaii, Polish Rev, 75; Captain John Dominis and his son Governor John Owen Dominis--Hawaii's Croatian connection, J Croatian Studies, 76; The National Minority Policy of Today's Yugoslavia, Nationalities Papers, 80. *Mailing Add:* Dept of Russ Univ South Africa Pretoria 0001 South Africa

GASIOROWSKA, XENIA Z, SLAVIC LANGUAGES & LITERATURES. *Educ:* Univ Calif, PhD, 49. *Prof Exp:* Lectr, Univ Calif, 48-49; from instr to assoc prof, 49-65, prof, 65-81, EMER PROF SLAVIC LANG & LIT, UNIV WIS-MADISON, 81- *Concurrent Pos:* Vis assoc prof Russ lang & lit, Wellesley Col, 58-59; mem, Int Fedn Mod Lang & Lit, 60-; sr fel, Nat Endowment for Humanities, 80-81. *Mem:* Am Asn Teachers Slavic & E Europ Lang; Polish Inst Arts & Sci Am. *Res:* Russian & Polish twentieth-century literature; historical fiction; women in literature. *Publ:* Auth, Aksin'ia Astakhova of the Quiet Don, In: Studies in Russian and Polish literature, Mouton, 62; Boleslaw the Brave by A Golubiew: A modern Polish epic, Calif Slavic Studies, 67; Women in Soviet Fiction: 1917-1964, Univ Wis, 68; contribr, Solzhenitsyn's women, In: Aleksandr Solzhenitsyn: Critical Essays, Nordland, 73; auth, Two decades of love and marriage in Soviet fiction, Russ Rev, 1/75; Portrait of a lady in Polish positivist fiction, Slavic & E Europ J, fall, 76; The Image of Peter the Great, Univ Wis, 78; Working mothers in recent Soviet fiction, Slavic & E Europ J, summer 81. *Mailing Add:* Dept of Slavic Lang Univ of Wis Madison WI 53706

GASOOL, ANNE, b New York, NY, Aug 26, 06. FRENCH LANGUAGE & LITERATURE. *Educ:* Cornell Univ, AB & AM, 28. *Prof Exp:* Asst French, Univ Wis, 29-30; from instr to asst prof French lang & lit, 30-62, asst dir jrs in France, 36-37 & dir, 56-57, assoc prof French, 62-71, EMER ASSOC PROF FRENCH, SMITH COL, 71- *Mem:* MLA. *Mailing Add:* 82 Green St Northampton MA 01060

GASS, SUSAN MARY, b Boston, Mass, May 21, 43; m 75; c 3. APPLIED LINGUISTICS. *Educ:* Univ Calif, Berkeley, BA, 66; Middlebury Col, MA, 67; Univ Calif, Los Angeles, MA, 74; Ind Univ, PhD(appl ling), 79. *Prof Exp:* Lectr English as second lang, Univ Wis-Milwaukee, 78-79; LECTR ENGLISH AS SECOND LANG, ENGLISH LANG INST, UNIV MICH, 79- *Concurrent Pos:* Lectr, Univ Minn, 80 & Univ Toledo, 82; consult, Ministry Educ, Singapore, 82. *Mem:* Teachers English to Speakers Other Langs; Am Asn Appl Ling; Ling Soc Am; Nat Coun Teachers English. *Res:* Second language acquisition and language universals; language transfer; comprehensibility of non-native speakers speech. *Publ:* Auth, Sentence processing and L2 learning, Studies in Second Lang Acquistion, 2.2: 85-98; Language transfer and universal grammatical relations, Lang Learning, 29.2: 327-344; coauth (with J Ard), L2 Dat: Their relevance for language universals, TESOL Quart, 14: 443-452; Predicting the distribution of relative clause types in discourse, Gen Ling, 21: 1-10; (with E Varonis), The comprehensibility of non-native speech, Studies in Second Lang Acquistion (in press); auth, Pragmatic and semantic contraints in Bikol relativization, Linguistics (in press); coauth (with J Ard), L2 acquisition and the ontology of language universals, In: Second Language Acquisition and Language Universals, John Benjamins Press (in press); auth, Second language acquisition and language universals, In: Selected papers from the Delaware Symposium on Language Studies, Univ Del Press (in press). *Mailing Add:* English Lang Inst Univ of Mich Ann Arbor MI 48109

GATES, HENRY PHELPS, b Los Angeles, Calif, Aug 28, 40; m 73. CLASSICAL LINGUISTICS. *Educ:* Harvard Univ, AB, 61; Princeton Univ, MA, 66, PhD(ling), 71. *Prof Exp:* Lectr classics, Univ Calif, Davis, 65-70; asst prof, 71-73, ASSOC PROF CLASSICS, UNIV NC, CHAPEL HILL, 73- *Mem:* Am Philol Asn; Ling Soc Am. *Res:* History of the Greek language; comparative philology. *Publ:* Auth, The kinship terminology of Homeric Greek, Suppl Int J Am Ling, 71. *Mailing Add:* Dept of Classics 103 Murphey Hall Univ of NC Chapel Hill NC 27514

GATES, JOHN EDWARD, b Chicago, Ill, Feb 2, 24; m 50; c 3. LEXICOGRAPHY. *Educ:* Maryville Col, BA, 45; Yale Univ, BD, 49; Harvard Univ, STM, 53; Hartford Sem Found, PhD(ling), 68. *Prof Exp:* Instr English as foreign lang, Gerard Inst, Sidon, Lebanon, 49-52; asst ed, Merriam Co, Springfield, Mass, 56-62; res assoc, Dict of Ling Terminology, Ctr Ling Studies, Univ Toronto, 68-70; assoc prof, 70-77, PROF ENGLISH, IND STATE UNIV, TERRE HAUTE, 77- *Concurrent Pos:* Vis prof lexicography, Ctr Ling Studies, Univ Toronto, 69-70. *Mem:* Ling Soc Am; Dict Soc NAm (pres, 75-77), MLA; Am Dialect Soc; Ling Asn Can & US. *Res:* Lexicography, principles and practice of dictionary making; grammatical, semantic and distributional characteristics of idiomatic phrases. *Publ:* Co-ed, Dictionary of Idioms for the Deaf, Am Sch Deaf, W Hartford, Conn, 66; auth, Review of glossary of linguistic terminology, Language, 6/68; The function, content and form of a lexicon, Sem Papers Soc Biblical Lit, 71; Idioms, the wild creatures of our talk: Genus and species, Ind English J, fall-winter 72; An Analysis of the Lexicographic Resources Used by American Biblical Scholars Today, Soc Biblical Lit, 72; A bibliography on general and English lexi lexicography, Ann NY Acad Sci, 6/73. *Mailing Add:* Dept of English Ind State Univ Terre Haute IN 47809

GATHERCOLE, PATRICIA MAY, b Erie, Pa, Oct 5, 20. FOREIGN LANGUAGES. *Educ:* Univ BC, BA, 41, MA, 42; Univ Calif, Berkeley, PhD(Romance lang), 50. *Prof Exp:* Teaching asst French, Univ Calif, Berkeley, 45-50; lectr, Univ BC, 50-51, instr, 51-53; instr French & Ital, Univ Ore, 53-56; asst prof French, 56-58, assoc prof mod foreign lang, 58-66, PROF MODERN FOREIGN LANG, ROANOKE COL, 66-, CHMN DEPT FOREIGN LANG, 71- *Concurrent Pos:* Instr Ital, Vancouver Sch Bd,

BC, Can, 52-53; Coop Prog Humanities, Duke Univ & Univ NC fel, 70; panelist, Nat Endowment for Humanities, 75 & 76. *Mem:* MLA; Mediaeval Acad Am; Am Asn Teachers Fr; Am Asn Teachers Ital; Dante Soc. *Res:* Medieval French literature; Boccaccio and the fine arts; medieval French miniature painting on manuscripts. *Publ:* Auth, Selected Poems of Umberto Liberatore, Guanda, Parma, 67; Laurent de Premierfait's Des Cas des Nobles et Femmes, Univ NC, Chapel Hill, 68; Boccaccio and the fine arts, Romance Mongr, 74; contribr to Mod Lang Quart, Fr Rev, Italica, Dante Concordance & World Book Encycl. *Mailing Add:* 423 Highfield Rd Salem VA 24153

GATTI-TAYLOR, MARISA, b Repub San Marino, Apr 18, 46; US citizen; m 73; c 1. COMPARATIVE LITERATURE. *Educ:* Marygrove Col, BA, 67; Wayne State Univ, MA, 70, PhD(French), 73. *Prof Exp:* Instr Ital & French, Wayne State Univ, 73-75, instr humanities, 76; sessional instr Ital, Univ Windsor, 76-77; asst prof French, Bowling Green State Univ, 77-78; lectr French, Carthage Col, 78; LECTR ITAL, UNIV WIS-MILWAUKEE, 79- *Concurrent Pos:* Co-founder, co-producer & co-host, France Internationale, French radio prog aired on WQRS-FM, 75-76. *Mem:* MLA; Mod Humanities Res Asn; Am Asn Teachers Ital; Asn Int des Etudes Francaises. *Res:* Nineteenth century French literature; comparative Romanticism; Jungian criticism. *Publ:* Auth, The myth of the child in Wordsworth and Pascoli, Essays Lit, fall 77; The child as archetypal image in the poetry of Victor Hugo, Mich Academician, Winter 78; Character as Sign: Chant public devant deux chaises electriques, Mich Academician, spring 79; The Sacred Sower in Hugo and D'Annunzio, Saison des Semailles and I seminatori, Romance Notes, 79; Songs as a Linguistic and Cultural Resources in the Intermediate Italian Clss, Foreign Lang Annals, 12/80; Two-light and the Anima: A Jungian Approach to Baudelaire's Two Versions of Le Crepuscule du soir: 19th Century French Studies, fall-winter 82; coauth (with Stephen M Taylor), Eschatological Christianity in Dostoevsky and Silone, Renascence, spring 82; San Marino, In: The Regions of Italy, Societa Dante Alighieri (in press). *Mailing Add:* 4065 S 65th No 4 Greenfield WI 53220

GATTO, LOUIS CONSTANTINE, English Medieval & Renaissance Literature. See Vol II

GAUCHER-SHULTZ, JEANINE S, b Paris, France, June 5, 38; m 60. FRENCH, SPANISH. *Educ:* Univ Nebr, Lincoln, BA, 60; Univ Southern Calif, MA, 62, PhD(French), 65. *Prof Exp:* Instr French & Spanish, Los Angeles Harbor Col, 65; from asst prof to assoc prof French, 65-76, PROF FRENCH, CALIF STATE UNIV, LOS ANGELES, 76- *Mem:* Am Asn Teachers French; Am Asn Teachers Span & Port; Inst Int Lit Iberoam. *Publ:* Auth, Etude Analytique & Critique du Theatre de Samuel Beckett, 62 & La Nature dans le Theatre de F de Curel, 65, Univ Calif; coauth, Three Mexican One-Act Plays, Odyssey, 68. *Mailing Add:* Dept of French Calif State Univ Los Angeles CA 90032

GAUDIANI, CLAIRE LYNN, b Venice, Fla, Nov 10, 44; m 68; c 2. SEVENTEENTH CENTURY FRENCH LITERATURE. *Educ:* Conn Col, BA, 66; Ind Univ, MA, 69, PhD(Fr lit), 74. *Prof Exp:* Asst prof French, Purdue Univ, 77-80 & Emory Univ, 80-81; ASST PROF FRENCH, UNIV PA, 81- *Concurrent Pos:* Am Coun Learned Socs fel, 76-77; Nat Humanities Ctr fel, 80-81. *Mem:* MLA; NAm Soc Seventeenth Century Fr Lit; Am Asn Advan Humanities; Am Coun Teaching Foreign Lang. *Res:* Seventeenth century French literature; Theophile de Viau; scientific revolution and literature in 17th century. *Publ:* Auth, The androgynous vision in the love lyrics of Theophile, Papers in Seventeenth Century Fr Lit, Vol II, 79; Cultivons Notre Jardin: Strategies for building FLL programs, In: Profession, MLA Press, 80; Theophile's subversions of conventional meditative lyrics, Papers in Seventeenth Century Fr Lit, Vol 13, spring 80; The early seventeenth century French lyric, L'Esprit Createur, winter 80; The cabaret poetry of Theophile de Viau: Texts and traditions--Etudes litteraires francaises, Vol 13, Jean-Michel Place, Paris, 80; Foreign languages and humanistic tradition: Outlook for the coming decade, In: Professional Priorities, ACTFL Publ, 81; Teaching compositions in the FL curriculum In: Languages in Education Series, Ctr Appl Ling, 81; La Lumiere cartesienna: Metaphore et phenomine optique, In: Papers on French Seventeenth Century Literature, 82. *Mailing Add:* Dept of Romance Lang Williams Hall Univ of Pa Philadelphia PA 19104

GAUTHIER, GEORGE JOSEPH, b Woonsocket, RI, Dec 5, 36; m 63; c 2. ROMANCE LANGUAGES. *Educ:* Col Holy Cross, AB, 58; Princeton Univ, MA, 62, PhD(French), 66. *Prof Exp:* Instr French, Dartmouth Col, 63-66; asst prof, Case Western Reserve Univ, 66-70; chmn dept, 70-76, ASSOC PROF FRENCH, HIRAM COL, 70- *Mem:* AAUP; Am Coun Teaching Foreign Lang; MLA; Am Asn Teachers Fr. *Res:* Nineteenth century French literature; teaching methods. *Mailing Add:* Dept of Foreign Lang Hiram Col Hiram OH 44234

GAVRONSKY, SERGE, b Paris, France, Aug 16, 32; US citizen; m 60; c 1. ROMANCE LANGUAGES, FRENCH CIVILIZATION. *Educ:* Columbia Univ, BA, 54, MA, 55, PhD(hist), 65. *Prof Exp:* From lectr to assoc prof, 60-75, PROF FRENCH & CHMN DEPT, BARNARD COL, COLUMBIA UNIV, 75- *Concurrent Pos:* Sterling Currier grant, Columbia Univ & Nat Endowment for Humanities Pilot grant, 78; John Simon Guggenheim Found fel, Camargo Found fel, French Govt grant & Mellon Fac grant, 79; Nat Endowment for Humanities implementation grant, 82. *Honors & Awards:* Chevalier dans l'Ordre des Palmes Academiques, French Govt, 81. *Mem:* PEN Club. *Publ:* Auth, The French Liberal Opposition and the American Civil War, Humanities, 68; Poems and texts: Eight contemporary French poets, 10/69; Lectures et Compte-rendu, Poemes, Flammarion, 73; Le Moyen Age, Macmillan, 74; co-ed, Modern French Poetry, Columbia Univ, 75; ed, Francis Ponge: The Sun Placed in the Abyss and Other Texts, State Univ NY, 77. *Mailing Add:* Dept of French Barnard Col Columbia Univ 606 W 120th St New York NY 10027

GAWTHROP, BETTY GEROW, English, Linguistics. See Vol II

GAY, CHARLES WILLIAM, b Jonesboro, Ark, Jan 11, 31. LINGUISTICS. *Educ:* Baylor Univ, BA, 55; Univ Southern Calif, MA, 57, PhD(English), 69. *Prof Exp:* Asst prof English, Wake Forest Col, 57-58; instr, Univ Southern Calif, 58-61; asst prof, Marymount Col, 61-64; asst dir, English Commun Prog, 64-72, dir, Am Lang Inst, 72-78; exec dir, Div Int Progs, Col Continuing Educ, 78-81, PROF LING, AM LANG INST, UNIV SOUTHERN CALIF, 81- *Concurrent Pos:* Chmn, Comn Intensive English Prog, 70-71; consult, Nat Asn Foreign Student Affairs, 71-73; Fulbright scholar, 82-83. *Mem:* Nat Asn Foreign Student Affairs (pres, 79); Teachers English to Speakers Other Lang. *Res:* International education; teaching English as a second language; intercultural communication. *Publ:* Coauth, English at your Fingertips, English Lang Serv, 69. *Mailing Add:* Am Lang Inst Univ of Southern Calif Los Angeles CA 90007

GAY-CROSIER, RAYMOND, b Basel, Switz, Aug 30, 37; nat US; m 63; c 1. FRENCH LITERATURE. *Educ:* Univ Berne, PhD(Romance), 65. *Prof Exp:* Asst Ger lit, Stanislas, Lycee Louis-le-Grand, Paris, 60-61; prof French & philos, Lycee de Berthoud, Switz, 62-66; asst prof French, Trent Univ, 66-67; assoc prof, 67-73, grad coordr, 70-80, fac develop grant, 73-74, PROF FRENCH, UNIV FLA, 73-, CHMN, 80- *Concurrent Pos:* Am Coun Learned Soc grant, 82. *Mem:* MLA; Am Asn Teachers Fr. *Res:* Twentieth-century French literature, criticism and history of ideas. *Publ:* Auth, Les envers d'un echec, Etude sur le theatre d'Albert Camus, Paris, Minard, 67; contribr & ed, Albert Camus, 70, Sherbrooke, Celef, 70; Religious Elements in the Secular Lyrics of the Troubadours, NC Univ Press, 71; Personnage et pronom personnel dans la Modification de Butor Essai sur les modalites de la perspective, Le Roman contemporain d'expression francaise, Sherbrooke Univ, 71; ed, Albert Camus series, Revue des Lettres Modernes, Vol 7, 74, Vol 9, 78, Vol 11 (in press); Albert Camus, Darmstadt, Wissenschaftliche Buchgesellschaft, 76; contribr & ed, Albert Camus 1980, Univ Fla, 80; International Camus Criticism, Critical Bibliography of French Literature, Syracuse Univ, 80. *Mailing Add:* Dept of Romance Lang & Lit Univ of Fla Gainesville FL 32611

GEADA, RITA, b Cuba, Sept 7, 37; US citizen. SPANISH. *Educ:* Univ Havana, MA, 57, PhD(lit), 59; Nat Univ Buenos Aires, dipl, 62. *Prof Exp:* Asst prof lang & lit, Pinar del Rio Inst, Cuba, 57-60; instr sr high sch, Md, 63-64; from asst prof to assoc prof, 66-76, head sect, 74-76, PROF SPANISH, SOUTHERN CONN STATE COL, 76- *Concurrent Pos:* Vis fac fel, Yale Univ, summer, 77. *Mem:* Am Asn Teachers Spanish & Portuguese. *Res:* Spanish and Spanish-American contemporary poetry; Spanish-American contemporary narrative; Cuban literature. *Publ:* Auth, Elsentido de la Evasion en, La poesia de Julian del Casal, Rev Iberoamericana, Inst of Iberoamerican Lit, 1-6/66; Cuando cantan las Pisadas (poems), Americalee, Buenos Aires, 67; Mascarada (poems), Ed Carabela, Barcelona, 70; Lo inasequible como objeto estetico en Gustavo A Becquer, Cuadernos Hispanoam, Madrid, 8/70; Tres agonistas en los enemigos del alma de Eduardo Mallea, La Torre, Univ PR, 72; Vertizonte (poems), Hispanova, Miami, 77; La poesia de Carmen Conde, Los Universitarios, Nacional Autonoma de Mexico, 7/81. *Mailing Add:* Dept of Foreign Lang Southern Conn State Col New Haven CT 06515

GEAGAN, DANIEL JOSEPH, Classics, Ancient History. See Vol I

GEAREY, JOHN E, b Montreal, PQ, July 3, 26; m 55; c 2. GERMAN LANGUAGE & LITERATURE. *Educ:* McGill Univ, BA, 50; Univ Toronto, MA, 52; Columbia Univ, PhD, 60. *Prof Exp:* Instr Ger, Oberlin Col, 56-61; asst prof, Columbia Univ, 61-64; assoc prof, 64-82, PROF GER, CITY COL NEW YORK, 82- *Mem:* MLA; NAm Goethe Soc. *Res:* Goethe's Faust Part II. *Publ:* Ed & contribr, Einführung in die deutsche Literatur, Holt, 63; ed, Heinrich von Kleist: Michael Kohlhaas, Oxford Univ, 67; auth, Heinrich von Kleist: A Study in Tragedy and Anxiety, Univ Pa, 68; Goethe, In: European Writers, the Romantic Century, Scribner's, 82; Faust II and the Darwinian Revolution, Ger Rev, summer 82; Goethe's Faust: The Making of Part I, Yale Univ Press (in press); ed, Goethe's Essays on Art and Literature, Vol II, In: Goethe's Works in English Translation, Suhrkamp (in press). *Mailing Add:* Dept of Lang City Col New York New York NY 10031

GEARY, JOHN STEVEN, b Oakland, Calif, Aug 18, 48; m 78. MEDIEVAL LITERATURE, ROMANCE PHILOLOGY. *Educ:* Univ Calif, Berkeley, AB, 70, MA, 72, PhD(Romance philol), 79. *Prof Exp:* ASST PROF SPANISH LIT, UNIV COLO, BOULDER, 79- *Mem:* MLA; Am Asn Teachers of Spanish & Portuguese. *Res:* Medieval Spanish epic poetry; Medieval Catalan poetry; comparative Romance linguistics. *Publ:* Auth, Formulaic Diction in the Poema de Fernan Gonzalez and the Mocedades de Rodrigo: A Computer-Aided Analysis, Jose Porrua Turanzas, 80; ed, Florilegium Hispanicum: Medieval and Golden Age Studies Presented to Dorothy Clotelle Clarke, Hisp Sem of Medieval Studies, Ltd, 82; auth, A miscellany of old and new problems in Cid studies, Romance Philol (in prep). *Mailing Add:* Dept of Spanish Lit Univ of Colo Boulder CO 80309

GEBHARD, ELIZABETH REPLOGLE, b Oak Park, Ill, Mar 25, 35; m 57; c 2. CLASSICAL ARCHEOLOGY. *Educ:* Wellesley Col, BA, 57; Univ Chicago, MA, 59, PhD(classics), 63. *Prof Exp:* Vis lectr Classics, Roosevelt Univ, 63-67; asst prof, 69-72, chmn dept, 77-79, ASSOC PROF CLASSICS, UNIV ILL, CHICAGO CIRCLE, 72- *Concurrent Pos:* Primary investr, Theater at Stobi, Stobi Excavations, 70-75; cur & dir, Isthmian Res Proj, Isthmia Mus, Greece, 76-; chmn archaeological studies comt, Univ Ill, Chicago, 78-80. *Mem:* Archaeol Inst Am; Am Sch Class Studies at Athens; Am Philol Asn; Asn Field Archaeol; Am Sch Oriental Res. *Res:* Field archaeology; architecture and history of Greek and Roman theatre; materials analysis and techniques of production of artifacts. *Publ:* Contribr, Muses at Work, Mass Inst Technol, 69; auth, The Theater at Isthmia, Univ Chicago, 73; Form of the orchestra in the early Greek theater, Hesperia, 74; Protective devices in Roman theaters, Studies in Antiq of Stobi, 75; coauth (with W Rostaker), The reproduction of rooftiles for the archaic temple of Poseidon at Isthmia, Greece, JFA, 8:211-227; The sanctuary of Poeseidon at Isthmia: Techniques of metal manufacture, Hesperia, 49:347:363; auth, The theatre at Stobi, Studies Antiq Stobi, Vol III, 81. *Mailing Add:* Dept of Classics Univ of Ill at Chicago Circle Chicago IL 60680

GEDNEY, WILLIAM JOHN, b Orchards, Wash, Apr 4, 15. LINGUISTICS. *Educ:* Whitman Col, AB, 35; Yale Univ, PhD(Indic & Far Eastern lang), 47. *Prof Exp:* Res assoc Southeast Asia Prog, Cornell Univ, 55; PROF LING, UNIV MICH, ANN ARBOR, 60-*Concurrent Pos:* Assoc ed, Am Col Dict. *Mem:* Ling Soc Am; Am Orient Soc (pres, 82-83); Asn Asian Studies. *Res:* Thai language and culture; Sanskrit; Pali; Southeast Asian languages. *Publ:* Auth, English for Thais, Am Coun Learned Soc, 56; transl, Life of the Thai Farmer; auth, A comparative sketch of white, black and red Tai, Soc Sci Rev, 64; Yay, a Northern Tai Language in North Vietnam, Lingua, 65. *Mailing Add:* Dept of Ling Univ of Mich Ann Arbor MI 48109

GEFFCKEN, KATHERINE ALLSTON, b Atlanta, Ga, July 24, 27. CLASSICS. *Educ:* Agnes Scott Col, BA, 49; Bryn Mawr Col, MA, 52, PhD(Latin & Greek), 62. *Prof Exp:* Instr Latin, Kemper Hall, Wis, 49-51; asst dean, Bryn Mawr Col, 55-63; from lectr to assoc prof, 63-76, chmn dept, 72-75, PROF LATIN & GREEK, WELLESLEY COL, 76- *Concurrent Pos:* New England ed, Class J, 68-76; trustee, Agnes Scott Col, 75-; prof-in-charge, Intercollegiate Ctr Classical Studies, Rome, 77-78; dir, Am Philol Asn, 79-81; dir summer session, Am Acad, Rome, 80-82. *Mem:* Am Philol Asn; Archaeol Inst Am; Am Classical League; Vergilian Soc. *Res:* Latin literature of the first century BC; Roman comedy. *Publ:* Auth, Comedy in the Procaelio, Brill, 73. *Mailing Add:* Dept of Greek & Latin Wellesley Col Wellesley MA 02181

GEHMAN, HENRY SNYDER, b Lancaster Co, Pa, June 1, 88; m 17; c 2. OLD TESTAMENT. *Educ:* Franklin & Marshall Col, AB, 09, AM, 11; Univ Pa, PhD, 13; Divinity Sch, Protestant Episcopal Church, Philadelphia, Pa, STB, 26, STD, 27. *Hon Degrees:* LittD, Franklin & Marshall Col, 47; Dipl, Lutheran Theol Sem, Buenos Aires, 61. *Prof Exp:* Teacher, pub schs, Pa, 05-06, prin, 09-10; asst Latin, Univ Pa, 13-14; teacher Greek & Latin, Hill Sch, Pa, 14; teacher Ger & Span, high sch, Philadelphia, Pa, 15-29; asst Sanskrit, Univ Pa, 20-21; instr semitic lang, Princeton Univ, 29-35, lectr, 35-38; actg prof Old Testament, 31-34, prof Old Testament lit, 34-58, chmn dept Bibl studies, 42-58, WILLIAM HENRY GREEN EMER PROF, OLD TESTAMENT LIT, PRINCETON THEOL SEM, 58- *Concurrent Pos:* Organizer, Tabor Reformed Church, Philadelphia, 17, pastor, 17-21; vis prof, Dropsie Col, 43-44; Guggenheim fel, 54; vis prof, Presby Theol Sems, Brazil, 55; prof, Lutheran Theol Sem, Arg, 57, 59 & 61; vis prof, Lancaster Theol Sem, 62, Lutheran Theol Sem, Philadelphia, 63 & Gurukul Lutheran Theol Col & Res Inst, Madras, 64. *Mem:* Am Orient Soc; Soc Bibl Lit; Ling Soc Am; Archaeol Inst Am. *Res:* Old Testament studies; linguistics; Septuagint. *Publ:* Auth, Interpreters of foreign languages among the ancients, 14; Westminster Dict of the Bible, Westminster, 44; coauth, Commentary on Books of Kings, International Critical Commentary, Scribner's, 51; The New Westminster Dict of the Bible, Westminster, 70; History of Bergstrasse Evangelical Lutheran Church, 78. *Mailing Add:* 24 Hawthorne Ave Princeton NJ 08540

GEITZ, HENRY, JR, b Philadelphia, Pa, Jan 18, 31; m 52; c 2. GERMAN. *Educ:* Univ Pa, AB, 52; Univ Nebr, MA, 54; Univ Wis, PhD, 61. *Prof Exp:* Asst prof Ger, Univ Richmond, 61-62; from asst prof to assoc prof, 62-72, NAT TEACHERS SEM PROF, UNIV WIS-MADISON, 72-, PROF GER & HUMAN DEVELOP, 76- *Concurrent Pos:* Ed, Ger Serv Bur Notes. *Mem:* MLA; Am Asn Teachers Ger; Nat Univ Exten Asn. *Res:* German seventeenth and nineteenth century literature; pedagogy. *Publ:* Coauth, Foreign language instruction by telephone, Nat Univ Exten Asn Newslett, 63. *Mailing Add:* Dept of Ger Univ of Wis Madison WI 53706

GELB, IGNACE J, b Tarnow, Poland, Oct 14, 07. ASSYRIOLOGY. *Educ:* Univ Rome, PhD, 29. *Prof Exp:* From traveling fel to res assoc, 29-41, from asst prof to prof Assyriology, Orient Inst, 41-65, Frank P Hixon distinguished serv prof, 65-79, EMER PROF ASSYRIOLOGY, ORIENT INST, UNIV CHICAGO, 80- *Concurrent Pos:* Mem expeds, Anatolia & Near East, 32, 35, 47, 65, 66; ed, Chicago Assyrian Dict, 47-; Am Coun Learned Soc fel, 59; Guggenheim fel, 60. *Mem:* Am Orient Soc (pres, 65); Ling Soc Am; Am Name Soc (pres, 64); hon mem Soc Asiatique; fel Am Acad Arts & Sci. *Res:* Assyriology; Hittitology; linguistics. *Publ:* Auth, Hittite Hieroglyphs I-III, 31-42, Inscriptions from Alishar and Vicinity, 35, Hittite Hieroglyphic Monuments, 39, coauth, Nuzi Personal Names, 43, auth, Hurrians and Subarians, 44, Study of Writing, 52, rev ed, 63, Old Akkadian Writing and Grammar, 52, rev ed, 61, Glossary of Old Akkadian, 57, Sargonic Texts in the Louvre Museum, Paris, 69, Sargonic Texts in the Ashmolean Museum, Oxford, 69 & Sequential Reconstruction of Old Akkadian, 69, Univ Chicago. *Mailing Add:* Orient Inst Univ of Chicago Chicago IL 60637

GELBER, LYNNE LEVICK, b Philadelphia, Pa, Feb 6, 39; m 59; c 2. FRENCH & COMPARATIVE LITERATURE. *Educ:* Bryn Mawr Col, AB, 60, MA, 62; Univ Colo, Boulder, PhD(French & comp lit), 71. *Prof Exp:* From instr to asst prof, 68-77, assoc prof, 77-81, PROF FRENCH, SKIDMORE COL, 81-, COORDR, SKIDMORE JR YR ABROAD, 80-, CHAIRPERSON, DEPT FOREIGN LANG & LIT, 79- *Concurrent Pos:* Adj prof, Union Grad Sch, 72-75; Nat Endowment for Humanities teaching fel, Princeton Univ, 75-76. *Mem:* Paul Claudel Soc; MLA; AM Asn Teachers Fr; AAUP; Am Asn Univ Women. *Res:* Modern French literature; French poetry; women in French literature. *Publ:* Auth, The art criticism of Paul Claudel, Claudel Newslett, 2/72; Camille Caludel's art and influence, Caludel Studies, fall 72; Women in France since the revolution, Empire State Col, spring 73; Claudel on Rodin: Sweet vengeance and bitter memory, Claudel Studies, spring 76; ed, Dialogues with the Unseen and the Unknown: Essays in Honor of Andre Malraux, 78; In/Stability: The Shape and Space of Claudel's Art Criticism, UMI Res Press, 80. *Mailing Add:* Dept Mod Lang & Lit Skidmore Col Saratoga Springs NY 12866

GELFAND, ELISSA DEBORAH, b New York, NY, Jan 26, 49. FRENCH STUDIES, WOMEN'S STUDIES. *Educ:* Barnard Col, BA, 69; Brown Univ, MA, 72, PhD(French), 75. *Prof Exp:* Prof English, Ecole Active Bilingue, Paris, 73-75; asst prof, 75-81, ASSOC PROF FRENCH, MOUNT HOLYOKE COL, 81-, DIR, WOMEN'S STUDIES PROG, 82- *Concurrent Pos:* Instr French, Alliance Fr Providence, RI, 71-73; instr English, Int House, Paris, 73; Andrew W Mellon fel interdisciplinary res, 79. *Mem:* Am Asn Teachers Fr; MLA; Northeast Mod Lang Asn; Nat Women's Studies Asn; Women's Caucus Mod Lang. *Res:* Feminist theory, women's and gender studies; prison literature. *Publ:* Auth, Alberline Sarrazin: A control case for femininity in form, Fr Rev, 12/77; A response to the void: Madame Roland's memoires particuliers and her imprisonment, Romance Notes, 79; transl, texts by B Broult, F Pachirier & D Pogg, In: New French Feminisms, Univ Mass Press, 80; auth, Women prison writers in France: Twice criminal, Mod Lang Studies, 80-81; Imprisoned women: Toward a socio-literary feminist analysis, Yale Fr Studie, 81; Studies in monstrosity: Women workers from French prisons, Cornell Univ Press (in press); coauth, French Feminist Criticism: An Annotated Bibliography, Garland Press (in press). *Mailing Add:* Dept of French Mount Holyoke Col South Hadley MA 01075

GELLEY, ALEXANDER, Comparative Literature. See Vol II

GELLINEK, CHRISTIAN JOHANN, b Potsdam, Ger, May 11, 30; US citizen; m 75; c 2. GERMANIC LANGUAGES & LITERATURE. *Educ:* Univ Toronto, BA, 59; Yale Univ, MA, 63, PhD(Ger), 64; Basel Univ, Dr habil(Ger philol), 75. *Prof Exp:* Head, Dept Ger & Latin, Pickering Col, 59-61; instr Ger, Yale Univ, 64-65, from asst prof to assoc prof, 66-70; prof & chmn dept, Conn Col, 70-71; chmn Ger & slavics, 72-77, PROF GER, UNIV FLA, 71-, ASSOC, PROG LING, 72- *Concurrent Pos:* Morse res fel, 65-66; vis prof, Univ Basel, 74; vis prof ling, Adam Mickiewicz Univ, Poland, 76; vis prof Ger, Univ Utah, 77, Ger Den Haag, 80 & vis prof Ger & Dutch, Univ Muenster. *Mem:* MLA; Anglo-Norman Text Soc; Medieval Acad Am; Polish Neophilol Soc; Int Vereinigung Ger Sprach. *Res:* Twelfth and 17th century German literature and poetics; lexicography; linguistics. *Publ:* Auth, König Rother, A Francke, Berne, 68; Programmed German Dict, Prentice-Hall, 68; Die deutsche Kaiserchrinik, Athenaum, Frankfurt, 71; ed, Häufigkeitswörterbuch zum Minnesang des 13 Jhs, 71 & co-ed, Häufigkeitswörterbuch zur deutschen Prosa des 11 und 12 Jhs, 73, Niemeyer, Tübingen; auth, Herrschaft im Hochmittelalter, Ger Studies in America, 80; Elementare Linguistik, H Lang Berne, 80; Hugo Grotius, TWAS 680, Twayne, 82. *Mailing Add:* Dept of Ger & Slavic Lang & Lit Univ of Fla Gainesville FL 32611

GELSON, MARY ALINE, b Brooklyn, NY, Mar 4, 09. LITERATURE, LINGUISTICS. *Educ:* Cath Univ Am, BA, 32, PhD(French lit), 42. *Prof Exp:* Chmn dept mod lang, Col Notre Dame Md, 42-56; dir, high sch, Ft Lee, NJ, 56-61; chmn dept mod lang, Col Notre Dame Wilton, 61-72; SUPV TEACHER SPEC EDUC, YOUTH SERV TRAINING PROG, WESTPORT PUB SCHS, 73- *Res:* French literature and linguistics. *Publ:* Transl, Take This Child, Humphries, 48. *Mailing Add:* 345 Belden Hill Rd Wilton CT 06897

GENDRON, MAURICE C, b Montreal, Can, Apr 27, 40; US citizen; m 66; c 2. FRENCH LITERATURE. *Educ:* Univ Calif, Los Angeles, BA, 63, MA, 65, PhD(French), 70. *Prof Exp:* Instr French, Whittier Col, 66-67 & 68-69; from asst prof to assoc prof, 69-76, PROF FRENCH, CALIF STATE UNIV, FRESNO, 76- *Mem:* Am Asn Teachers Fr; Am Coun Teaching Foreign Lang. *Res:* Nineteenth century French literature; French literature of Quebec. *Publ:* Auth, Henry Monnier: un Jarry avant la lettre, Fr Rev, 4/70; Un'poeme inedit de Henry Monnier, 19th Century Fr Studies, summer 77. *Mailing Add:* Dept of Foreign Lang Calif State Univ Fresno CA 93710

GENDZIER, STEPHEN J, b New York, NY, July 14, 30; m 58; c 1. FRENCH LITERATURE, HISTORY OF IDEAS. *Educ:* Oberling Col, BA, 52; Columbia Univ, MA, 53, PhD(French), 59. *Prof Exp:* Instr French, Columbia Univ, 56-60; asst prof, Mass Inst Technol, 60-62; asst prof, 62-66, ASSOC PROF FRENCH, BRANDEIS UNIV, 66- *Mem:* Am Asn Teachers Fr; MLA; Soc Fr Etude XVIIIe Siecle. *Res:* The French Enlightenment; the English and French novel of the eighteenth century. *Publ:* Auth, L'Interpretation de la figure humaine chez Diderot et chez Balzac, L'Annee Balzacienne, 62; Balzac's changing attitudes toward Diderot, Fr Studies, 4/65; Denis Diderot: The Encyclopedia, Harper, 67 & 69; Diderot and the Jews, Diderot Studis, 73. *Mailing Add:* 36 Hayes Ave Lexington MA 02173

GENNO, CHARLES NORMAN, b Toronto, Ont, Nov 19, 34; m 60; c 1. GERMAN. *Educ:* Univ Toronto, BA, 57, MA, 59, PhD(Ger), 62. *Prof Exp:* From instr to asst prof, 61-68, chmn combined dept Ger, 70-72, ASSOC PROF GER, VICTORIA COL, UNIV TORONTO, 68- *Concurrent Pos:* Exec, Ontario High Sch Ger Contest, 75-; discipline rep, German Victoria Col, 77- *Mem:* MLA; Asn Can Univ Teachers Ger; Am Asn Teachers Ger; Ontario Asn Teachers Ger, (pres, 74-76). *Res:* Sturm und Drang, Aufklärung; Musil; modern German drama. *Publ:* Auth, Peter Weiss's Marat/Sade, Mod Drama, 12/70; Kitsch elements in Horvath's Geschichten aus dem Wiener Wald, Ger Quart, 3/72; Der Dichter als revolutionär: Peter Weiss's Hölderlin, In: Rezeption der deutschen Gegenwarts literatur im Ausland, Kohlhammer Verlag, 76; The Anatomy of Pre-War Society in Robert Musil's Der Mann ohne Eigerschaften, In: The First World War in German Narrative Prose, 80 & co-ed (with Heinz Wetzel), The First World War in German Narrative Prose, 80, Univ Toronto Press; auth, The Importance of Ellen Key's Die Entfaltung der Seele durch Lebenskunst for Musil's Concept of the Soul, Orbis Litterarum, 4/81. *Mailing Add:* Dept of Ger Victoria Col Univ of Toronto Toronto ON M5S 1V4 Can

GENOVESE, EDGAR NICHOLAS, b Baltimore, Md, Sept 18, 42; m 69; c 2. CLASSICS. *Educ:* Xavier Univ, Ohio, AB, 64; Ohio State Univ, PhD(classics), 70. *Prof Exp:* From asst prof to assoc prof, 70-76, PROF CLASSICS, SAN DIEGO STATE UNIV, 76- CHMN DEPT CLASS & ORIENT LANG & LIT, 77- *Mem:* Am Philol Asn. *Res:* Greek and Latin poetry; mythology. *Publ:* Auth, Propertius' tardus Amor, Class J, 1/73; Cicero and Sallust: Catiline's ruina, Class World, 74; Symbolism in the Passer poems, Maia, 74; Deaths in the Aeneid, Pac Coast Philol, 75; Case of the poor preposition, Class Outlook, 76; Serpent Leitmotif in the Metamorphoses, Latomus (in press). *Mailing Add:* Dept of Class & Orient Lang & Lit San Diego State Univ San Diego CA 92182

GENTRY, FRANCIS GERARD, b Boston, Mass, June 8, 42. MEDIEVAL GERMAN LITERATURE, MEDIEVAL STUDIES. *Educ:* Boston Col, BS, 63; Ind Univ, MA. 66, PhD(Ger), 73. *Prof Exp:* From instr to asst prof Ger, State Univ NY, Albany, 69-75; asst prof, 75-80, ASSOC PROF GER, UNIV WIS-MADISON, 80- *Concurrent Pos:* Inst Res in Humanities res fel, 78-69; Alexander Von Humboldt Stiftung fel, 78-79. *Mem:* MLA; Int Arthurian Soc; Int Courtly Lit Soc; Medieval Acad Am; Wolfram von Eschenbach Gesellschaft. *Res:* Medieval literature and culture; social and political aspects of medieval literature. *Publ:* Auth, Trends in Nibelungenlied research since 1949: A critical review, Amsterdamer Beiträge älteren Germanistik 7, 74; Triuwe and Vriunt in the Nibelungenlied, Rodopi, 75; Hagen and the problem of individuality in the Nibelungenlied, Monatshefte 68, 76; Mittelalterfeiern im 19 Jahrhundert, In: Deutsche Feiern, Athenaion, 78; Arbeit in der mittelalterlichen Gesellschaft: Die Entwicklung einer mittelalterlichen Theorie der Arbeit vom 11 bis 14 Jahrhundert, In: Arbeit als Thema in der deutschen Literatur vom Mittelalter bis zur Gegenwart, Athenäum; Vruot... Verdamnot? Memento mori, 108: 299-306; La lotta per le Investiture e la societa medievale tedesca: Per un approccio storico-sociologico alla letteratura medievale, L'immagine riflessa, 3: 3-31; Noker's Memento mori and the Desire for Peace, ABäG, 16: 25-62. *Mailing Add:* Dept of Ger Univ Wis Madison WI 53706

GENUIST, MONIQUE SUZANNE, b St Mihiel, France, May 30, 37; m 58; c 3. FRENCH CANADIAN LITERATURE, FRENCH LANGUAGE. *Educ:* Univ Nancy, Lic es Lett, 58; Univ Rennes, Dipl advan studies, 59, Dr Univ (French Can lit), 65. *Prof Exp:* From lectr to asst prof, 65-73, assoc prof, 73-77, PROF FRENCH, UNIV SASK, 78- *Mem:* Asn Prof French Can Univ; Asn Can Studies; Asn Litt; Can Quebecoise. *Res:* Canadian literature and civilization. *Publ:* Auth, La Creation Romanesque chez Gabrielle Roy, Cercle Livre France, Montreal, 66; Exorcismes (novel), La Pensee Universelle, Paris, 73; Les Grands departs de Jacques Languirand et le theatre de l'absurde, Presence Francophone, spring 76; Quatre essais de theatre national ou variations sur un theme, Can Drama, fall 76; Mille Milles et la femme dans Le nez qui vogue, Atlantis, spring 77; Jacques Languirand et l'obsurde, Cercle du Livre de France, 82. *Mailing Add:* Dept of French Univ Sask Saskatoon SK S7N 0W0 Can

GENUIST, PAUL MARCEL, b Rennes, France, May 24, 36; Can citizen; m 58; c 3. ROMANCE LANGUAGES. *Educ:* Univ Rennes, Lic es Lett, 58, Dipl etudes super, 59, DUniv(French lit), 61. *Prof Exp:* From instr to asst prof, 59-67, assoc prof, 67-74, PROF FRENCH, UNIV SASK, 74- *Publ:* Auth, Alain-Fournier Face a l'Angoisse, Minard, Paris, 65; Alain-Fournier ou la querelle des historiens litteraires, Culture, 12/66; The Quebec Church and the Separatist option, Chelsea J, 7-8/77; Pour une lecture feministe de la Princesse de Cleves, Papers Fr 17th Century Lit, 78; La Faillite du Canada Anglais, Editions Quinze, Montreal, 80. *Mailing Add:* Dept of French Univ of Sask Saskatoon SK S7N 0W0 Can

GENZ, HENRY EDWARD, b Atlanta, Ga, June 8, 23; m 49; c 3. FRENCH. *Educ:* Emory Univ, AB, 48; Univ Wis, MA, 49; Case Western Reserve Univ, PhD(French), 60. *Prof Exp:* From instr to assoc prof & head dept French, 49-59, dean men, 52-59; assoc prof, Miss Col, 59-61; from asst prof to assoc prof, 61-65, PROF FRENCH, ECKERD COL, 65-, CHMN DEPT, 80- *Mem:* AAUP; SAtlantic Mod Lang Asn; Am Asn Teachers Fr; Soc Amis Montaigne. *Res:* Montaigne. *Publ:* Auth, An early reference by Montaigne to coaches and its possible bearing on the meaning of Des coches, Renaissance News, summer 62; First traces of Montaigne's progression toward self-portraiture, Symposium, fall 62; Exaggeration and anger in the Apologie de Raimond Sebond, Romantic Rev, 64; Montaigne's preference for limitations, Fr Rev, 65; The relationship of title to content in Montaigne's essay, Des boyteux, Bibliot Humanisme et Renaissance, 9/66. *Mailing Add:* Dept of French Eckerd Col St Petersburg FL 33733

GEORGACAS, DEMETRIUS JOHN, b Siderokastro, Triphylia, Greece, Jan 30, 08; nat US; m 48; c 4. CLASSICS. *Educ:* Univ Athens, MA, 32; Univ Berlin, PhD(classics & ling), 42. *Prof Exp:* Redactor hist lexicon of Greek lang, Acad Athens, 33-46; Am Friends of Greece fel, 47; lectr classics & ling, Univ Chicago, 48, instr, 48-59; instr Greek, McCormich Theol Sem, 49-51; asst prof classics, Univ Utah, 51-53; from asst prof to prof, 53-78, res & univ prof, 75-78, EMER PROF CLASS LANG, UNIV N DAK & DIR, MOD GREEK DICT CTR, 78- *Concurrent Pos:* Guggenheim fels, 57-58 & 65-66; mem US Comt Int Ctr Onomastic Sci, Louvain, Belg, 58-; dir & ed, Greek-English Dict, 60-; chmn, Int Comt Outer Space Onomastics, 66-; Nat Found on Arts & Humanities sr fel, 67-68; chmn ling comt, Ctr Neo-Hellenic Studies, Austin, Tex, 68-; vis scholar, Harvard Univ Dumbarton Oaks Ctr Byzantine Studies, 68. *Honors & Awards:* Distinguished Univ Prof, Univ N Dak, 75; Certificate of Achievement, Inter-Univ Comt on Mod Greek Lang in the Univ of the English-Speaking World, 80. *Mem:* Ling Soc Am; Am Orient Soc; Am Name Soc (pres, 65); Mediter Ling Atlas (vpres, 77-); hon mem & hon pres, Ling Circle Man & N Dak. *Res:* Indo-European and classic languages; ancient, medieval and modern Greek language; onomastics. *Publ:* Auth, The Names for the Asia Minor Peninsula, Heidelberg, winter, 71; The names for the African continent: Libya, Africa, Aethiopia, and Congeners, Int Cong Onomastic Sci, Vienna, 71; The waterway of Hellespont and Bosporus, 2/71 & Historical and language contacts and the placename Karlovasi, 1/74, Names; Ichthyological terms for the sturgeon and etymology of the intern terms botargo, caviar and congeners, 78, Turkish ichthyonyms (and congeners) and fishing terms of Greek origin, 78 & A Graeco-Slavic controversial problem reexamined: The -Ico suffixes in Byzantine, medieval and modern Greek; Their origin and ethnological implications, 82, Athenian Acad; The First Large Intern Dictionary of Common and Cultivated Modern Greek, Mandatotoros, 11/81. *Mailing Add:* Dir Greek Dict Ctr Montgomery 217 Univ of N Dak Grand Forks ND 58201

GEORGE, EDWARD V, b Buffalo, NY, Dec 10, 37; m 68. CLASSICAL LANGUAGES. *Educ:* Niagara Univ, BA, 59; Canisius Col, MS, 62; Univ Wis, MA, 62, PhD(Classics), 66. *Prof Exp:* Asst prof classics, Univ Tex, Austin, 66-71; assoc prof, 71-78, PROF CLASSICS, TEX TECH UNIV, 78- *Mem:* Am Philol Asn; Class Asn Midwest & South; Class Asn Southwestern US; Vergilian Soc Am; Am Class League (vpres, 80-82). *Res:* Augustan Latin and Hellenistic Greek poetry; teaching classical humanities; Renaissance Latin Lit. *Publ:* Auth, Poet and characters in Apollonius Rhodius' Lemnian episode, Hermes, 69; Latin literature in translation, In: Teaching Classical Subjects in English, Am Class League, 73; Aeneid VIII and the Aitia of Callimachus, Brill, Leiden, 74; Periodical literature on teaching the Classics in translation, 1924-1975, Class World, 75; coauth, Garcilaso's Salicio and Vergil's Eighth Ecologue, Hispania, 80; auth, Imitatio in the Somnium Vivis, Wolfenbuttel, West Ger, 82. *Mailing Add:* 2007 28th St Lubbock TX 79411

GEORGE, EMERY EDWARD, b Budapest, Hungary, May 8, 33; US citizen. GERMANIC LANGUAGES, EAST EUROPEAN STUDIES. *Educ:* Univ Mich, BA, 55, MA, 59, PhD(Ger), 64. *Prof Exp:* Instr Ger, Univ Mich, 62-64; from instr to asst prof, Univ Ill, Urbana, 64-66; from asst prof to assoc prof, 66-75, off res admin res grant, 67-68, PROF GER LANG & LIT, UNIV MICH, ANN ARBOR, 75- *Concurrent Pos:* Assoc ed Russ lit, Triquarterly, 73-; found ed, Mich Ger Studies, 75-76; fel, Int Acad Poets, England, 76-; Int Res & Exchanges Bd fel, 81. *Honors & Awards:* Hopwood Award in Poetry, 60. *Mem:* MLA; AM Soc Aesthet; Hölderlin Ges; Poetry Soc Am; Int Poetry Soc. *Res:* German literature of the Age of Goethe; English literature; Russian and Hungarian literataure. *Publ:* Ed, Friedrich Hölderlin: An Early Modern, Univ Mich, 72; auth, Hölderlin's Ars Poetica, Mouton, The Hague, 73; co-ed, Husbanding the Golden Grain: Studies in Honor of Henry W Nordmeyer, Univ Mich, 73; auth, Black Jesus, a long poem about Dr Martin Luther King, Jr, Kylix, 74; ed & tranlr, Subway Stops: Fifty Poems by Miklos Radnoti, Ardis, 77; auth, A Gift of Nerve: Poems 1966-1977, Kylix, 78; Kate's Death: A Book of Odes, 80 & ed & transl, Miklos Radnoti, The Complete Poetry, 80, Ardis. *Mailing Add:* Dept of Ger Univ of Mich Ann Arbor MI 48109

GERATO, ERASMO GABRIELE, b Formia, Italy, Mar 24, 43; US citizen. ITALIAN & FRENCH LANGUAGE & LITERATURE. *Educ:* City Univ New York, BS, 66; Univ Wis, MA, 68, PhD(Ital-French), 74. *Prof Exp:* Teaching asst Ital, Univ Calif, Los Angeles, 66-67 & Univ Wis, 67-70; asst prof, 70-77, ASSOC PROF ITAL-FRENCH, FLA STATE UNIV, 77- *Concurrent Pos:* COFRS Univ Scholar, 74-75. *Honors & Awards:* Ward Medal, City Univ New York, 66. *Mem:* SAtlantic Mod Lang Asn; SCent Mod Lang Asn; Mountain Interstate Foreign Lang Asn; Am Assoc Teachers Ital. *Res:* Italian and French language, literature and linguistics. *Publ:* Auth, A Critical Study of the Life and Works of Alessandro Poerio, Casa Editrice C Maccari, 75; Thematic fragments in Alessandro Poerio's poetry, La Parola del Popolo, 5/75; La Chartreuse de Parme: A study of its origins A discussion of several possible sources, La Stagione, 1/76; Reality of illusion and illusion of reality in Leopardi's Zibaldone, SAtlantic Bull, 5/76; Un capolavoro della lett italiana del 600: La Reina de Scotia--Studio critico della sua lingua e stile, Neuphilolische Mitteilungen, 6/76; Vittorio Alfieri, the artist and his creation: An exposition of Alfieri's personal nature as reflected in his protagonists, Rocky Mt Rev, 81; Guido Gustavo Gozzano, Hall Publishers (in prep); La nature amante--nature's role in Sand's Le Marquis de Villemer (in prep). *Mailing Add:* Dept of Mod Lang Fla State Univ Tallahassee FL 32306

GERBER, BARBARA LESLIE, b New York, NY, Oct 29, 41. COMPARATIVE LITERAURE, FRENCH. *Educ:* Brooklyn Col, BA, 62; Univ Wis-Madison, MA, 65, PhD(French), 68. *Prof Exp:* Asst prof French, St Lawrence Univ, 68-73; asst prof, 73-77, assoc prof, 77-81, PROF COMP LIT, BROOKLYN COL, 82- *Concurrent Pos:* Dir, St Lawrence Jr Year in France, 71-72; dir, Spec Baccalaureats Degree Prog Adults, 79- *Mem:* AAUP; MLA; Am Asn Teachers Fr; Am Comp Lit Asn. *Res:* Twentieth century French novel and theatre. *Publ:* Contrib, Twentieth Century French Fiction, Rutgers Univ, 75; coauth, Dictionary of Modern French Idioms, Garland, 77; transl, Color of Time (trans, Apollinaire, Couleur du Temps), Zone Press, 80. *Mailing Add:* Apt A 1507 1655 Flatbush Ave Brooklyn NY 11210

GERBER, DOUGLAS EARL, b North Bay, Ont, Sept 14, 33; m 57; c 1. CLASSICS. *Educ:* Univ Western Ont, BA, 55, MA, 56; Univ Toronto, PhD(Greek lyric poetry), 59. *Prof Exp:* Lectr Greek, Univ Col, Univ Toronto, 58-59; from lectr to assoc prof, 59-69, PROF CLASSICS & CHMN DEPT, UNIV WESTERN ONT, 69-, WILLIAM SHERWOOD FOX CHAIR CLASSICS, 77- *Concurrent Pos:* Ed, Transactions, 74-82. *Mem:* Class Asn Can (treas, 60-61); Am Philol Asn; Class Asn Mid W & S; Brit Class Asn. *Res:* Greek lyric poetry; Greek and Roman drama. *Publ:* Auth, A survey of publications on Greek lyric poetry since 1952, Class World, 3-5/68; A Bibliography of Pindar, 1513-1966, Am Philol Asn, 69; ed & auth, Euterpe: An Anthology of Early Greek Lyric, Elegiac and Iambic Poetry, 70 & Emendations in Pindar, 1513-1972, 76, Hakkert, Amsterdam; Studies in Greek lyric poetry: 1967-1975, Class World, 76; Pindar's Olympian One: A Commentary, Univ Toronto Press, 82. *Mailing Add:* Dept of Class Studies Univ of Western Ont London ON N6A 3K7 Can

GERDES, DICK CHARLES, b Corpus Christi, Tex, Jan 17, 43; m 68; c 2. LATIN AMERICAN LITERATURE. *Educ:* Colo State Univ, BA, 65; Tex A&I Univ, MA, 71; Univ Kans, PhD(Span), 76. *Prof Exp:* Asst prof, 75-81, ASSOC PROF LATIN AM LIT, DEPT MOD & CLASS LANG, UNIV N MEX & ASSOC DIR ACAD PROG, 81- *Concurrent Pos:* Fulbright-Hays fac overseas res grant, Lima, Peru, 79-80. *Mem:* Am Asn Teachers Span & Port; MLA; Rocky Mountain Mod Lang Asn. *Res:* Contemporary Latin American literature. *Publ:* Auth, Cronica de San Gabriel y el rito de la iniciacion en la novela de costumbres, J Span Studies: Twentieth Century, 80; Cultural values in three novels of New Mexico, Bilingual Rev/La revista bilingue, 80; Cronica de San Gabriel/Los genericos dominicales, Socialismo y participacion, 80; Point of view in Los de abajo, Hispania, 81; Monologo desde las tinieblas: Oral tradition and ideological silence, Rocky Mountain Rev, 81; El concepto del despojo en tres novelas andinas, Estudios andinos, 82. *Mailing Add:* Dept of Mod & Class Lang Univ of NMex Albuquerque NM 87131

GERICKE, PHILIP OTTO, b Ukiah, Calif, Dec 24, 36; c 4. ROMANCE LANGUAGES & LITERATURE. *Educ:* Univ Calif, Riverside, BA, 58; Univ Calif, Berkeley, MA, 60, PhD(Romance lang & lit), 65. *Prof Exp:* Assoc Span, Univ Calif, Riverside, 62-63, lectr, 63-64; asst prof foreign lang, San Fernando Valley State Col, 64-66; asst prof, 66-71, assoc prof, 71-78, assoc dean, grad div, 75-81, PROF SPAN, UNIV CALIF, RIVERSIDE, 78- *Mem:* MLA; Am Asn Teachers Span & Port; Philol Asn Pac Coast. *Res:* Spanish literature of the Middle Ages and early Renaissance; historical linguistics. *Publ:* Coauth, El Vencimjento del mundo, tratado ascetico del siglo XV: edicion, Hispanofila, 64; auth, El Invencionario de Alfonso de Toledo, Rev Arch, Bibliot & Mus, 1-12/67; The narrative structure of the Laberinto de fortuna, Romance Philol, 5/68; ed & transl, Manuel C Rojo's Historical Notes on Lower California, Dawson's 72; auth, Mucho de bien me fizo con Dios en limpio amor: Dona Garoca, Andreas Capellanus y el amor cortes en el Libro de buen amor, Explicacion Textos Literarios, 77; The turtledove in four sixteenth-century versions of Fontefrida, El Romancero Hoy, 79; On the structure of the Libro de Buen Amor: A question of method, Ky Romance Quart, 2/81. *Mailing Add:* Dept of Lit & Lang Univ of Calif Riverside CA 92521

GERLACH, HANS HARTMUT, b Dresden, Ger, July 30, 29; US citizen; m 76; c 2. GERMAN LANGUAGE & LITERATURE. *Educ:* Ind Univ, PhD(Ger lit), 66. *Prof Exp:* ASST PROF GER, LAWRENCE UNIV, 66- *Mem:* Am Asn Teacher Ger. *Mailing Add:* 536 N Drew Appleton WI 54911

GERLACH, U HENRY, b Berlin, Ger, June 29, 38; US citizen; m 65; c 4. GERMAN LITERATURE. *Educ:* Univ Utah, BA, 64; Cornell Univ, MA, 66, PhD(Ger lit), 68. *Prof Exp:* Teaching asst Ger lang, Cornell Univ, 64-68; asst prof, 68-74, ASSOC PROF GER LANG & LIT & FOREIGN LANG METHODOLOGY, UNIV ILL, URBANA, 74- *Concurrent Pos:* Alexander von Humboldt-Stiftung Dozentenstipendiat, 74-75. *Mem:* MLA; Am Asn Teachers Ger; Am Coun Teaching Foreign Lang; Hebbel-Ges. *Res:* Nineteenth century German drama; literary history; foreign language methodology. *Publ:* Auth, Hebbel as a Critic of His Own Works, A Kummerle, 72; Hebbel-Bibliographie 1910-1970, 73, Friedrich Hebbel: Briefe, 75 & Briefe von und an F Hebbel, 78, C Winter; contribr, Motiv des unterdrueckten Gewissen in Hochwaelders Heiligem Experiment, In: Hebbel-Jahrbuch, Oesterreich in Geschichte und Lit, 80. *Mailing Add:* 3072 Foreign Lang Bldg Univ of Ill Urbana IL 61801

GERLI, EDMONDO MICHAEL, b San Jose, Costa Rica, Sept 11, 46; m 66; c 1. SPANISH LANGUAGE & LITERATURE. *Educ:* Univ Calif, Los Angeles, BA, 68, PhD(Hisp lang & lit), 72; Middlebury Col, Madrid, MA, 69. *Prof Exp:* Asst prof, 72-77, assoc prof, 77-81, PROF SPAN, GEORGETOWN UNIV, 81- *Concurrent Pos:* Co-ed, Hispano-Italic Studies, 76- *Honors & Awards:* Williams Prize, Hispanic Rev, 81. *Mem:* MLA; SAtlantic Mod Lang Asn; Am Acad Res Historians Medieval Spain; Am Asn Teachers Span & Port; Asoc Int Hispanistas. *Res:* Medieval Spanish literature; Renaissance Spanish literature. *Publ:* Auth, Ars Praedicandi and the structure of Arcipreste de Talavera, part I, Hispania, 75; Alfonso Martinez de Toledo, Twayne, G K Hall, 76; Pleberio's Lament and two Medieval Topoi, Romanische Forschungen, 76; The burial place and probable date of death of Alfonso Martinez de Toledo, J Hisp Philol, 77; La picaresca y El licenciado Vidriera: Genero y contagenero en Cervantes, Nueva Revista Filologia Hisp, 78; articles in Hisp Rev, Ky Romance Quart, Neophilologus, Thesaurus Revista Estudio Hisp, Celestinesca, Romance Notes & Romania & Romance Philol; The Spanish Sentimental Romance, 1440-1550, Twayne/G K Hall, 82. *Mailing Add:* Sch Lang & Ling Georgetown Univ Washington DC 20007

GEROW, EDWIN, b Akron, Ohio, Oct 16, 31; m 57, 76; c 2. SANSKRIT. *Educ:* Univ Chicago, BA, 52, PhD, 62. *Prof Exp:* Asst prof Sanskrit, Univ Rochester, 62-64; from asst prof to assoc prof, Univ Wash, 64-72, assoc dir SAsia, Far East & Russ Inst, 70-72; FRANK L SULZBERGER PROF INDIC CIVILIZATION & PROF SANSKRIT, UNIV CHICAGO, 73- *Concurrent Pos:* Lectr, Columbia Univ, 63-64; fac fel, Am Inst Indian Studies, 67-68 & 75. *Mem:* Ling Soc Am; Am Orient Soc; Asiatic Soc France. *Res:* Indian cultural history. *Publ:* Ed & annotator, Sanskrit Poetics as a Study of Aesthetic, Univ Calif, 63; auth, The Quintessential Narayan, Lit E & W, 67; A Glossary of Indian Figures of Speech, Mouton, 71; co-ed, Studies in the Language and Culture of South Asia, Washington, 73; auth, Indian Poetics, Harrassowitz, 77. *Mailing Add:* Dept of S Asian Lang & Civilizations Univ of Chicago Chicago IL 60637

GERRARD, CHARLOTTE FRANKEL, b Stamford, Conn, Mar 20, 28. ROMANCE LANGUAGES. *Educ:* Ohio State Univ, BA, 48, MA, 49; Univ Pittsburgh, PhD(French), 65. *Prof Exp:* Instr French, Western Col, 56-58; teacher English, Fulbright Comn, Japan, 58-59; instr French, Ohio Wesleyan Univ, 59-62; lectr, 65-66, asst prof, 66-75, ASSOC PROF FRENCH, IND UNIV, BLOOMINGTON, 75- *Mem:* Am Asn Teachers Fr; MLA; AAUP. *Res:* Twentieth century French literature; drama; comparative literature. *Publ:* Auth, Anti-militarism in Vian's Minor texts, French Rev, 5/72; Thierry Maulnier's Le profanateur, a Nietzschean tragedy, Sumposium, fall 72; Bergsonian elements in Ionesco's Le Pieton de l'air, Papers Lang & Lit, summer 73; Vian's Priest as showman in Le Dernier des Metiers, French Rev, 5/74; Satirical letters of B Vian & Cyrano de Bergerac, Papers Lang & Lit, 76; Montherlant & Suicide, Studia Humanitatis, 77; Pestilence in contemporary drama, Symposium, winter 77; Religion as a dramatic target in 20th century France, In: Voices of Conscience, Temple Univ, 77. *Mailing Add:* Dept of French & Ital Ind Univ Bloomington IN 47405

GERSHENSON, DANIEL ENOCH, b New York, NY, Mar 27, 35; m 63. GREEK & LATIN. *Educ:* Columbia Univ, AB, 55, PhD, 61; Jewish Theol Sem Am, BHL, 56. *Prof Exp:* From instr to asst prof Greek & Latin, Columbia Univ, 59-68; actg assoc prof classics, Univ Calif, Los Angeles, 68-69; SR LECTR CLASS STUDIES, TEL-AVIV UNIV, 69- *Concurrent Pos:* Nat Sci Found grant, 62. *Mem:* Am Philol Asn. *Res:* Greek mythology. *Publ:* Coauth, Anaxagoras and the Birth of Physics, 63 & auth, Aristotle: Metaphysica, Book A, a new translation, In: The Natural Philosopher, Vol II, 63, Blaisdell; coauth, Aristotle confronts the Eleatics: Two arguments on the One, Phronesis, 63; Averting Baskania in Theocritus, Calif Studies Call Antiq, 69; The reversal of nature theme in Theocritus, Scripta Classica Israelica, 74. *Mailing Add:* Dept of Class Studies Tel-Aviv Univ Ramat-Aviv Tel-Aviv Israel

GERTEL, ZUNILDA AIMARETTI, b Argentina, Dec 21, 26; m 50; c 1. SPANISH AMERICAN LITERATURE, LITERARY CRITICISM. *Educ:* Inst Nac Profesorado, Arg, MA, 47; Univ Iowa, PhD(Romance lang), 66. *Prof Exp:* Prof lang & lit, Nat Col & Norm Sch, Arg, 50-63; from instr to asst prof Span lang & lit, Univ Iowa, 63-68; assoc prof Span Am Lit, Univ Nebr, 68-72; PROF SPAN AM LIT, UNIV WIS-MADISON, 72-, PROF PORT, 76- *Concurrent Pos:* Univ Nebr res grants, 68-69; Int Exchange res fel, Spain, 72. *Honors & Awards:* First Prize for Short Stories, Bibliot Consejo Mujeres Arg, 56; Univ Iowa Grad Sch Award, 67. *Mem:* MLA; Midwest Mod Lang Asn; Asn Int Hispanistas; Latin Am Studies Asn; Inst Int Lit Iberoam. *Res:* Twentieth century Latin American literature. *Publ:* Auth, Borges y su retorno a la poesia, Univ Iowa & Las Americas, 68; La novela hispano-americana contemporanea, Columba, Buenos Aires, 70 & 75; Funcion estructural del leit motiv en Jijo de ladron, de M Rojas, Rev Hisp Mod, Vox XXV, No 4; Heraclito, conjuncion de opuestos, Ky Romance Quart, Vol XIX, No 2; La noche boca arriba, de J Cortazar, disyuncion de la identidad, Nueva Narrativa Hispanoam, Vol III, No 1. *Mailing Add:* Dept of Span & Port Univ of Wis Madison WI 53706

GERTNER, MICHAEL HOWARD, b Cleveland, Ohio, June 29, 44. LINGUISTICS, FRENCH LITERATURE. *Educ:* Columbia Univ, AB, 66, MA, 67, PhD(Fr & Romance philol), 71. *Prof Exp:* Teaching asst French, Columbia Univ, 68-69; asst prof Romance lang, Univ Cincinnati, 71-78; RESEARCHER & ADJ ASST PROF LANG RESOURCES, YESHIVA UNIV, 79- *Mem:* Am Asn Teacher Fr; Int Ling Asn; MLA. *Res:* Modern French linguistics; history of the French language; medieval French Romance. *Publ:* Auth, On the French semiconsonants, Linguistics, 72; The Morphology of the Modern French Verb, Mouton, The Hague, 73; Five comic devices in Zadig, Studies Voltaire & 18th Century Lit, 74; Teaching physics to art students: The philogist's pedagogical predicament, In: Pedagogical Seminar For Romance Philology Yearbook, 75; Maintien des langues, renouveau ethnique et diglossie aux Etats-Unis, La Linguistique, 82; Guide to Non-English-Language Broadcasting (in press) & Guide to Non-English-Language Schools (in press), Nat Clearinghouse for Bilingual Educ. *Mailing Add:* Ferkauf Sch Yeshiva Univ Bronx NY 10461

GERULITIS, RENATE, b Kassel, Ger, Aug 16, 34; m 60. GERMAN LANGUAGE & LITERATURE. *Educ:* Univ Toledo, BA, 59; Univ Mich, MA, 61, PhD(Ger), 69. *Prof Exp:* Instr Ger, Univ Mich, 64-66; asst prof, 66-70, ASSOC PROF GER, OAKLAND UNIV, 70- *Mem:* Am Asn Teachers Ger; AAUP; MLA; Am Soc 18th Century Studies. *Res:* Eighteenth century German literature; German classicism; Marxism and literature. *Publ:* Auth, Ansätze zu einer thematischen anordnung des Deutschen divan, In: Festschrift for Henry W Nordmeyer, 75; Oakland Symposium on Socialist Realism in Literature, Oakland Univ, 76. *Mailing Add:* Oakland Univ Rochester MI 48063

GESELL, GERALDINE CORNELIA, b Evanston, Ill, July 23, 32. CLASSICAL ARCHEOLOGY & LITERATURE. *Educ:* Vassar Col, BA, 53; Univ Okla, MA, 55; Univ NC, Chapel Hill, PhD(class archaeol), 72. *Prof Exp:* Teacher Latin, John Marshall High Sch, Oklahoma City, 55-65 & 66-67; asst prof, 72-79, ASSOC PROF CLASSICS, UNIV TENN KNOXVILLE, 80- *Concurrent Pos:* Mem managing comt, Am Sch Class Studies, Athens, 73-; Adv coun Am Acad Rome. *Mem:* Archaeol Inst Am; Vergilian Soc; Class Asn Mid W & S. *Res:* Minoan shrines and cult objects. *Publ:* The Minoan snake tube: A survey and catalogue, Am J Archaeol, 76; The Town Fresco of Thera: A reflection of Cretan topography, Pepragmena 4th Int Cretological Cong, Athens, 80. *Mailing Add:* Dept of Classics Univ of Tenn Knoxville TN 37916

GESNER, B EDWARD, b Middleton, NS, Sept 22, 42; m 71; c 3. DIALECTOLOGY, APPLIED LINGUISTICS. *Educ:* Univ King's Col, BA Hons, 63; Dalhousie Univ, MA, 67; Univ Toulouse II, Dr 3 cycle ling, 77. *Prof Exp:* Teacher French, Queen Elizabeth High Sch, 65-66; lectr, 67-69, asst prof, 69-80, ASSOC PROF FRENCH, DALHOUSIE UNIV, 80- *Concurrent Pos:* Res assoc, Int Ctr Res Biling, Laval Univ, 80-81. *Mem:* Am Asn Teachers Fr. *Res:* Acadian morphology and syntax; pedagogy of French as second language. *Publ:* Auth, L'emploi des auxiliane avoir et etre dans le parler acadien de la Baie Sainte-Marie, Nouvelle-Ecosse, 78 & La performance linguistique des eleves acadiens neo-ecosais, 79, Acts Reunion Annuelle Asn Ling Prov Atlantiques; Etude morphosyntaxique du parler acadian de la Baie Sainte-Marie (Nouvelle Ecosse), Canada, Int Ctr Biling Res, 79; L'emploi de passe simmple dans le parler acadian de la Baie Sainte-Marie, Nouvelle-Ecosse, Cahier Ling, 79; Bibliographie sur les parlers acadiens, Actes 10th Colloque ACLA, 79; Observations sur le comportenent morphosyntaxique de tout en acadien, Actes Reunion Annuelle Asn Ling Prov Atlantique, 81; Description de la morphologie verbale du parler acadien de pubnico (Nouvelle-Ecosse), Cent Rech Enseignement Francais, 82; Remarques sur les themes verbaux du parler acadien de la Baie Sainte-Marie (Nouvelle-Ecosse), Si Que, 82. *Mailing Add:* French Dept Dalhousie Univ Halifax NS B3H 3J5 Can

GESSEL, VAN C, b Compton, Calif, Aug 1, 50; m 72; c 2. JAPANESE LITERATURE & LANGUAGE. *Educ:* Univ Utah, BA, 73; Columbia Univ, MA, 75, PhD(Japanese), 79. *Prof Exp:* Asst prof, Columbia Univ, 79-80; asst prof Japanese, Univ Notre Dame, 80-82; ASST PROF JAPANESE, UNIV CALIF, BERKELEY, 82- *Honors & Awards:* Transl Award, UNESCO, 79. *Mem:* Asn Asian Studies; Asn Teachers of Japanese. *Res:* Contemporary Japanese fiction; Japanese Christian writers; modern Japanese theatre. *Publ:* Auth, Nihon no gendai shosetsu to dokusha ni tsuite, English Today, 9/78; War and postwar in the writings of Kojima, Yasuoka & Endo, Toho Gakkai Trans, 78; coauth, How to use native informants to learn a foreign language,

79 & auth, Inadequacies of the Japanese syllabary for teaching foreign languages, 79, Western Am Lang Inst; transl, Endo Shusaku, When I Whistle, Peter Owen Ltd, 79; auth, Jakusha no kyusai, Omoshiro Hambun, 1/80; Shimpageki: Bridge between classical & modern theatre in Japan, Proc 3rd Int Symp on Asian Studies, 82; transl, Endo Shusaku, The Samurai, Peter Owen Ltd, 82. *Mailing Add:* 919 Bellevue Ave South Bend IN 46615

GESSMAN, ALBERT MILOSLAV, b Vienna, Austria-Hungary, Dec 12, 16; US citizen; m 40; c 3. LINGUISTICS. *Educ:* State Col, Vienna, VI, AB, 35; Charles Univ, Prague, MA, 39; Rudolf Univ, Vienna, PhD(comp ling & Slavistics), 50. *Prof Exp:* Prof mod lang acad commerce, Mlada Boleslav, Czech, 39-48, head master, inst mod lang, 47-48; prof mod lang & head dept, Talladega Col, 54-61; assoc prof, 61-67, chmn dept, 61-75, prof classics & ancient studies, 67-75, COORDR ANCIENT STUDIES, UNIV SOUTH FLA, TAMPA, 75- *Concurrent Pos:* Ed-in-chief, Univ SFla Lang Quart, 62- *Mem:* Ling Soc Am; Czech Soc Arts & Sci; Nat Georgr Soc. *Res:* Ancient studies; general and comparative linguistics. *Publ:* Auth, The Codes of Language, Univ SFla, 64; The neglected aspects of language kinship, Univ SFla Lang Quart (in installments), 64-67; The tongue of the Romans, Studies Antiqua, 70; The Tongues of the Bible, Univ SFla Bkstore, 71; coauth, Perennial Atlantis, Sea Frontiers, 72; The Spectrum of Language, 73 & The Gift from Thoth, 75, Univ SFa Bkstore; Egyptian as a guest language in Hebrew, Univ SFla Lang Quart, 76; The Riddle of the Single Reed, Univ SFla Lang Quart, 80. *Mailing Add:* 10905 N 19th St Tampa FL 33612

GETHING, THOMAS WILSON, b Jackson, Mich, Mar 30, 39; c 2. SOUTHEAST ASIAN LINGUISTICS. *Educ:* Univ Mich, BA, 61, MA, 63, PhD(ling), 66. *Prof Exp:* Asst prof Thai, Indonesian & ling, Univ Mich, 66-67; asst prof Thai & ling, Univ Hawaii, Manoa, 67-70; assoc prof ling, Ohio Univ, 70-71; PROF THAI, LAO & LING, UNIV HAWAII, MANOA, 71- *Concurrent Pos:* Assoc dean, Grad Div, Univ Hawaii, Manoa, 79- *Mem:* Asn Asian Studies; Ling Soc Am; Am Orient Soc; Siam Soc. *Res:* Thai structure; semantic structure; lexicography. *Publ:* Auth, The Ram Khamhaeng inscription, In: The World of Southeast Asia, Harper, 67; Structural Redundancy in Thai semantics, Language, 68; Aspects of Meaning in Thai Nominals: A Study in Structural Semantics, Mouton, The Hague, 72; Location in Thai and Lao, Thai Ministry Educ, 75; Notes on Lao Personal Pronouns, Chulalongkorn Univ, 76; coauth, Thai Basic Reader, Univ Hawaii, 78; Two types of semantic contrast between Thai and Lao, Australian Nat Univ, 79. *Mailing Add:* Univ of Hawaii Manoa Honolulu HI 96822

GETHNER, PERRY JEFFREY, b Chicago, Ill, June 17, 47. FRENCH LITERATURE, HISTORY OF DRAMA. *Educ:* Carleton Col, BA, 69; Yale Univ, MA, 74, PhD(French), 77. *Prof Exp:* Lectr, Quinnipiac Col, 77-78; ASST PROF FRENCH, UNIV CHICAGO, 78- *Mem:* MLA. *Res:* History of French drama and opera. *Publ:* Auth, Temptation and taboo in two Biblical tragedies of the Romantic Era, Quinquereme, 78; Good and evil heroes in the tragic theatre of Antoine de Montchrestien, Bibliotheque d'humanisme et Renaissance, 78; Andromede--from tragic to operatic discourse, Papers on French Seventeenth Century Lit, 79; Jean de Mairet and poetic justice: A definition of tragicomedy?, Renaissance Drama, 80; The staging of prayer in French theatre of the 17th century, Papers on French 17th Century Lit, 82; co-ed, Du Ryer, Esther, Textes litteraires, Exeter, 82. *Mailing Add:* Dept of Romance Lang Univ of Chicago Chicago IL 60637

GEVIRTZ, STANLEY, b Brooklyn, NY, Jan 27, 29; m 62; c 3. ANCIENT HISTORY, HEBREW PHILOLOGY. *Educ:* Brooklyn Col, AB, 51; Univ Chicago, PhD, 59. *Prof Exp:* From instr to asst prof hist, Univ Chicago, 58-65, assoc prof Palestinian hist, 65-74; PROF BIBLE & ANCIENT NEAR EASTERN CIVILIZATION, HEBREW UNION COL, CALIF, 72- *Mem:* Am Orient Soc; Soc Bibl Lit; Am Sch Orient Res; Asn Jewish Studies. *Res:* History of Palestine and Syria; Biblical Hebrew literature; Northwest Semitic philology. *Publ:* Auth, Jericho and Shechem, Vetus Testamentum, 63; Patterns in the Early Poetry of Israel, Univ Chicago, 63; The reprimand of Reuben, J Near Eastern Studies, 71; On Canaanite Rhetoric: The Evidence of the Amarna Letters From Tyre, Orientalia, 73; The Issachar Oracle, Eretz Israel, 75; Of patriarchs and puns, 75 & Simeon and Levi in the Blessing of Jacob, 81, Hebrew Union Col Annual; Adumbrations of Dan in Jacob's Blessing on Judah, Zeitschrift für die alttestamentliche Wissenschaft, 81. *Mailing Add:* Hebrew Union Col Jewish Inst Relig Los Angeles CA 90007

GEX, ROBERT BERNARD, b New Orleans, La, Aug 7, 34; m 58; c 3. FRENCH LANGUAGE & LITERATURE, LINGUISTICS. *Educ:* Xavier Univ, BA, 56; Univ Ill, MA, 57; Univ Mo, PhD, 78. *Prof Exp:* ASSOC PROF ROMANCE LANG, SOUTHERN UNIV, NEW ORLEANS, 63-, DIR CONTINUING EDUC, 72- *Concurrent Pos:* Asst secy-gen, Nat Sch Law & Admin, Kinshasa, Congo, 65-67. *Mem:* MLA; Nat Asn Prof Continuing & Adult Educ; Asn Univ Eve Cols. *Res:* Computer-based medieval French language studies; Bantu languages and linguistics; 20th century French novel. *Mailing Add:* 7533 Oak St New Orleans LA 70118

GHALI, SAMIR, b Cairo, Egypt; US citizen; m 64; c 3. ROMANCE LANGUAGES & LITERATURES. *Educ:* Univ Geneva, Dip de traducteur, 63; Univ Nebr, Lincoln, PhD(Romance lang & lit), 72. *Prof Exp:* Foreign lang instr French & Span, Int Sch, Geneva, Switz, 62-64; translr & pub rels, Wellcome Found Ltd, London, Eng, 65-66; asst prof French, Creighton Univ, 66-72; asst prof lang & coordr foreign lang & continuing educ, Ark State Univ, 73-77; adminr intensive English lang prog, Univ Nebr, Omaha, 77-80; PRES & DIR, MIDWEST INST INT STUDIES, DOANE COL, 80- *Mem:* Nat Asn Foreign Student Affairs. *Res:* Comparative literature, French, English, Spanish; Lebanese literature and politics. *Publ:* Contribr, Les Grands Traducteurs Francais, Georg, 63; coauth, France and the Lebanese conflict, J South Asian & Mid East Studies, fall 69; auth, La Portee d'Edgar Poe sur la Pensee et l'Oeuvre de Paul Valery, Publ Ark Philol Asn, spring 76; coauth, The Lebanese bloodshed: a modern crusade, or a socioeconomic conflict, Asian Profile, 8/77. *Mailing Add:* Midwest Inst Int Studies Doane Col Omaha NE 68182

GHANOONPARVAR, MOHAMMAD REZA, b Esfahan, Iran, May 11, 43; m 72; c 1. PERSIAN LANGUAGE & LITERATURE. *Educ:* Univ Esfahan, BA, 66; Eastern Mich Univ, MA, 72; Univ Tex, PhD(comp lit), 79. *Prof Exp:* Instr Persian lang, Iran-Am Soc, Iran, 73; instr English lang & lit, Univ Esfahan, Iran, 73-76; consult Persian lang & cult, Persepolis Enterprises, 77-79; ASST PROF PERSIAN LANG & LIT, UNIV VA, 79- *Concurrent Pos:* Vis asst prof Persian, Univ Tex, 80; contrib ed, Iran-e Nu Lit Collection, 81- *Mem:* Mid East Studies Asn; Am Orient Soc; Soc Iranian Studies; Southern Comp Lit Asn; South East Regional Mid East & Islamic Studies Sem. *Res:* Twentieth century Persian literature; comparative literary history and criticism; contemporary Irano-Islamic thought. *Publ:* Coauth, Ahmad Shamlu's The Fairies & auth, Bozorg Alavi's Her Eyes, Lit East & West, 76 & 80; Buf-e Kur as a title, Univ Tex Press, 78; transl, The Fundamental Principles & Precepts of Islamic Government, Mazda Publ, 81; The Patient Stone, Bibl Persica, 82; auth, Genre experimentation and social content in Nader Ebrahimi's Ten Short Stories, Iranian Studies, 82; Persian Cuisine, Albany Press, 82; transl, The tale of the shepherd vizier, Mazda Publ, 82. *Mailing Add:* Orient Lang Dept Univ of Va Charlottesville VA 22903

GHATTAS-SOLIMAN, SONIA REZK, b Kena, Egypt; US citizen; m 81. FRENCH LANGUAGE & LITERATURE. *Educ:* Univ Alexandria, Egypt, BA, 65; Calif State Univ, MA, 73; Univ Calif, Irvine, PhD(Fr lit), 79. *Prof Exp:* Teaching asst French lang & lit, Univ Calif, Irvine, 74-77, assoc, Humanities Core Course, 77-79; LECTR FRENCH LANG & LIT, CALIF INST TECHNOL, 79- *Concurrent Pos:* Transl, transl group & Med Ctr, Univ Calif, Irvine, 75-79, speaker Islamic women, 79; transl, Psychiat Ctr, Julia Ann Singer Presch, 71-74. *Mem:* Am Asn Teachers French; MLA; Am Asn Univ Women; African Lit Asn. *Res:* French speaking literature of Egypt, Lebanon and North Africa; folklore, songs, proverbs and myths; language, culture and society. *Publ:* Auth, Proverbs in the North African lit, Humanities Working Paper, 12/81; Language d culture: Etude Socio linguistique du roman de Out El Kouloub, African Lit Asn, 4/81. *Mailing Add:* Div Humanities & Soc Sci 228-77 Calif Inst Technol Pasadena CA 90039

GHIGO, FRANCIS, b Jan 23, 08; m 38; c 1. ROMANCE LANGUAGES. *Educ:* Davidson Col, BS, 29; Univ NC, AM, 37, PhD, 43. *Prof Exp:* Instr French & Span, Riverside Mil Acad, 29-31; asst prof Span, Hampden-Sydney Col, 32-36, assoc prof, 37-41; teaching fel, French, Univ NC, 36-37, instr, 41-43, actg asst prof army specialized training prog, 43-44; asst prof French & Span, Univ Richmond, 44-45; prof Romance lang & head mod lang dept, Hampden-Sydney Col, 46-59; prof French, 59-74, chmn dept, 63-72, EMER PROF FRENCH, DAVIDSON COL, 74- *Mem:* Am Asn Teachers Fr; SAtlantic Mod Lang Asn; MLA. *Res:* Provencal language and literature; Provencal speech of Waldensian colonists in Valdese, North Carolina; linguistics. *Publ:* Auth, The Provencal Speech of the Waldensial Colonists of Valdese, North Carolina, Valdese: Historic Valdese Found, 80. *Mailing Add:* Box 236 Davidson NC 28036

GHURYE, CHARLOTTE WOLF, b Ger; US citizen; m 53. GERMAN LANGUAGE & LITERATURE. *Educ:* Roosevelt Univ, BA, 59; Northwestern Univ, Evanston, MA, 60, PhD(Ger lit), 67. *Prof Exp:* Teaching assoc Ger lang & lit, Ind Univ, Bloomington, 63-66, instr, 66-67; asst prof Ger, 68-73, ASSOC PROF GER, IND STATE UNIV, TERRE HAUTE, 73- *Mem:* Am Asn Teachers Ger; MLA. *Res:* Contemporary West German literature; prose. *Publ:* The Movement Toward a New Social and Political Consciousness in Postwar German Prose, 71 & The Writer and Society: Studies in the Fiction of Günter Grass and Heinrich Böll, 76, Herbert Lang, Bern. *Mailing Add:* Dept of Foreign Lang Ind State Univ Terre Haute IN 47809

GIAMATTI, VALENTINE, b Conn, Feb 9, 11. ROMANCE LANGUAGES & LITERATURES. *Educ:* Yale Univ, AB, 32; Harvard Univ, PhD, 40. *Hon Degrees:* DLitt, Univ Florence, Italy, 48. *Prof Exp:* Asst dean, Vt Jr Col, 36-39; instr Italian, 39-40, prof, 50-72, EMER PROF ITALIAN, MT HOLYOKE COL, 72- *Mem:* MLA; Am Asn Teachers Ital; Mediaeval Acad Am. *Res:* Italian grammar; hell, purgatory and paradise of Dante. *Publ:* Bibliog illustrated ed of the Divine comedy. *Mailing Add:* 29 Silver St South Hadley MA 01075

GIANGRANDE, LAWRENCE, b New York, NY; m 70; c 2. CLASSICS. *Educ:* NY Univ, BA, 50; St Louis Univ, MA, 59, PhD(classics), 61. *Prof Exp:* Asst classics, NY Univ, 52-53; instr, Univ Tex, 56-57; asst prof, Univ Detroit, 59-65; ASSOC PROF CLASSICS, UNIV OTTAWA, 65- *Mem:* Am Philol Asn; Can Class Asn. *Res:* Greek mythology; Utopia then and now. *Publ:* Auth, Triptych texts, Arion, 70; Spoudaiogeloion, Mouton, Paris & Hague, 72; Peace in Homer, Class, J, 72. *Mailing Add:* Fac of Arts Univ of Ottawa 30 Stewart St Ottawa ON K1N 6N5 Can

GIAUQUE, GERALD S, b Boise, Idaho, Apr 10, 41; m 68; c 5. MEDIEVAL & SEVENTEENTH CENTURY FRENCH. *Educ:* Brigham Young Univ, BA, 65; Univ Ore, MA, 67, PhD(Fr), 71. *Prof Exp:* Teaching asst French, Univ Ore, 67-68; from instr to asst prof French & Span, Univ Mo-Rolla, 69-74; head dept & assoc prof lang, Ga Inst Technol, 74-76; ASSOC PROF LANG, NORTHERN ARIZ UNIV, 76- *Mem:* MLA; Am Asn Teachers Fr. *Res:* Edition of Old French texts; 17th century French drama; French applied linguistics. *Publ:* Auth, An early example of uvular r, Orbis, 75; Using native speakers in the foreign language classroom, Foreign Lang Annals, 5/75; Breaking the foreign language sound barrier by writing, Utah Lang Quart, 4/76; Explication of Brise Marine, Romance Notes, 6/76; Program in individualized instruction in French, Ga Foreign Lang Beacon, fall 76; Increasing conversational ability through stenography, Mod Lang J, 11/76; A forgotten approach to foreign language acquisition: Phonics, DLLS, Brigham Young Univ, 77; The psycho-structure of Britannicus, Rocky Mountain Rev, Vol 31, 77. *Mailing Add:* Dept of Mod Lang Northern Ariz Univ Flagstaff AZ 86011

GIBBON, WILLIAM B, b Harvard, Nebr, Dec 14, 25; m 58; c 3. LINGUISTICS. *Educ:* Georgetown Univ, BS, 49; Univ Pa, MA, 53, PhD(Slavic lang), 60. *Prof Exp:* From instr to asst prof Russ & Ger, 59-67, assoc prof Russ, 67-74, PROF RUSS, UNIV NEBR-LINCOLN, 74- *Concurrent Pos:* Exchange prof for res, Budapest, Hungary, 72-73. *Mem:* MLA; Am Folklore Soc; Am Asn Advan Slavic Studies. *Res:* Folklore. *Publ:* Auth, Asiatic parallels in North American star lore: Ursa Major, 7/64 & Asiatic parallels in North American star lore: Milky Way, Pleiades, Orion, 7/72, J Am Folklore. *Mailing Add:* Dept of Mod Lagn & Lit Univ of Nebr Lincoln NE 68508

GIBBONS, REGINALD, American Poetry, Poetry in Spanish. See Vol II

GIBBS, BEVERLY J, b Cadillac, Mich, Dec 6, 29. SPANISH LANGUAGE & LITERATURE. *Educ:* Univ Mich, BA, 51, MA, 52; Univ Wis, PhD(Span lang & lit), 60. *Prof Exp:* Teaching asst Span, Univ Wis, 52-54, 56-57, res asst, 54-55, 57; from instr to assoc prof Span, Univ Tex, Austin, 57-73, asst to pres, 72-73; asst to pres acad affairs, 73, vpres acad affairs, 73-79, actg dir, Div Foreign Lang, 79-80, PROF FOREIGN LANG, UNIV TEX, SAN ANTONIO, 73- *Concurrent Pos:* Univ res inst asst & mat grant, 70-71; Am Coun Educ Acad Admin Internship Prog fel, 72-73. *Res:* Contemporary Spanish-American novel, essay and short story; modern Spanish novel. *Publ:* Auth, Spatial treatment in the contemporay psychological novel of Argentina, 9/62, El tunel: Portrayal of isolation, 9/65 & Ambiguity in Onetti's El astillero, 4/73, Hispania. *Mailing Add:* Div Foreign Lang Univ of Tex San Antonio TX 78285

GIBIAN, GEORGE, b Prague, Czech, Jan 29, 24; nat US; div; c 5. RUSSIAN, COMPARATIVE LITERATURE. *Educ:* Univ Pittsburgh, AB, 43; Sch Adv Int Studies, AM, 47; Harvard Univ, PhD, 51. *Prof Exp:* Instr English, Smith Col, 51-53, from asst prof to assoc prof English & Russ, 53-61; prof, 61-76, chmn dept, 63-73 & 80-82, chmn comt Soviet Studies, 66-70 & 81-82, GOLDWIN SMITH PROF RUSS LIT, CORNELL UNIV, 76- *Concurrent Pos:* Assoc prof Slavic lit, Univ Calif, Berkeley, fall 59; Guggenheim fel, 60; Fulbright res fel, Paris, fall 60; exchange prof, Soviet Acad Sci, Leningrad, 65-66; exec secy, Masaryk Publ Trust, 67-; nat adv comt, Inter-Univ Travel Grants, 67-69; E Europe selection comt, Foreign Area Fel Prog, 67-68; joint comt Slavic studies, Am Coun Learned Soc & Soc Sci Res Coun, 67-68; sr assoc, Russ Inst, Columbia Univ, 69-70; Nat Endowment Humanities sr grant, 74. *Mem:* MLA; Comp Lit Asn Am; Am Asn Advan Slavic Studies; Am Asn Teachers Slavic & East Europ Lang. *Res:* The novel; Soviet literature. *Publ:* Auth, Tolstoy and Shakespeare, Mouton, The Hague, 57; Interval of Freedom: Soviet Literature during the Thaw, Univ Minn, 60; ed, Crime and Punishment, Norton, 64; coauth, Russian Modern Short Stories, Harper, 65; ed, War and Peace, Norton, 66; Masaryk, Spirit of Russia, Allen & Unwin, London, 67; Anna Karenina, Norton, 70; ed & translr, Russia's Lost Literature of the Absurd, 71 & co-ed & contribr, Russian Modernism, 76, Cornell Univ. *Mailing Add:* Dept of Russ Lit Cornell Univ Ithaca NY 14853

GIBSON, ELSA MARIA PETERSON, b Washington, DC, Nov 28, 43; m 73. CLASSICAL PHILOLOGY, GREEK EPIGRAPHY. *Educ:* Radcliffe Col, BA, 66; Harvard Univ, MA, 67, PhD(class Philol), 74. *Prof Exp:* RES & WRITING, 74- *Mem:* Am Inst Archaeol. *Res:* Greek inscriptions of Roman period in Phrygia, Asia Minor; Montanism. *Publ:* Auth, A unique Christian epitaph from the Upper Tembris Valley, Am Soc Papyrologists Bull, 75; A Montanist community at Usak, Greek, Roman & Byzantine Studies, 75; Dining delights of Tehran, Town & Country, 75; Eating your way around Istanbul, Crossroads, 77-78; Zoorkhaneh: Persian religious gymnastics, Crossroads, 78; The Christians for Christians Inscriptions of Phrygia, Harvard Theol Studies, 78; The Rahmi Koc Collection (series), Zeitschrift Papyrologie und Epigraphik, 78-; Gravestones in the Kutahya Museum, Turk Arkeoloji Dergisi, 80. *Mailing Add:* 181 Summit Ave Upper Montclair NJ 07043

GIBSON, EUGENE M, b Newport, Ark, Jan 6, 15; m 41. FOREIGN LANGUAGES. *Educ:* Univ Okla, AB, 34, MA, 36; Univ Calif, Berkeley, PhD, 52. *Prof Exp:* Teacher French & Span, High Sch & Jr Col, Okla, 36-40; chmn dept French & Span, Panhandle Agr & Mech Col, 40-43; teaching asst French, Univ Calif, Berkeley, 44-49, lectr, 52-53; instr French & Span, Univ Nev, 49-50; instr French, Univ Tex, 54-56; from asst prof to assoc prof, Eastern Mich Univ, 56-61; prof & chmn dept, Albion Col, 61-63; PROF FRENCH, EASTERN MICH UNIV, 63- *Mem:* MLA; Am Asn Teachers Fr. *Res:* Prose fiction of the nineteenth century. *Mailing Add:* 220 S Huron Ypsilanti MI 48197

GIBSON, MOSES CARL, b St Thomas, Nev, May 31, 19; m 44; c 5. ROMANCE LANGUAGES & LITERATURE. *Educ:* Brigham Young Univ, AB, 47, MA, 49; Univ Ore, PhD(Romance lang), 60. *Prof Exp:* Instr lang, 49-54, from asst prof to assoc prof, 54-65, chmn dept Span & Port, 67-79, PROF SPAN, BRIGHAM YOUNG UNIV, 65- *Mem:* MLA; Rocky Mountain Mod Lang Asn; Am Asn Teachers Span & Port. *Res:* Spanish literary historiography; Hispanic culture and civilization; Romance philology. *Publ:* Auth, Background to the theory of Arabic origins, spring 62 & Spanish academies of the Golden Age, spring 64, Brigham Young Univ Studies. *Mailing Add:* Brigham Young Univ Provo UT 84602

GICOVATE, BERNARD, b Santos, Brazil, Apr 21, 22; nat US; m; c 1. ROMANCE LANGUAGES. *Educ:* Nat Univ Buenos Aires, D Filos y Let, 43; Bowdoin Col, AB, 45; Univ NC, AM, 46; Harvard Univ, PhD, 52. *Prof Exp:* Instr Span, Randolph-Macon Women's Col, 46-47 & Boston Univ, 47-49; asst prof Romance lang, Univ Ore, 49-55; from assoc prof to prof Span, Tulane Univ, 55-65, dir ctr Latin Am studies, 62-65; PROF SPAN & PORT & CHMN DEPT, STANFORD UNIV, 65- *Mem:* MLA; Am Asn Teachers Span & Port; Inst Int Lit Iberoam. *Res:* Twentieth century and Spanish American literature; 16th century poetry. *Publ:* Auth, Julio Herrera y Reissig and the Symbolists, Univ Calif, 57; La Poesia de Juan Ramon Jimenez, 59 & Conceptos fundamentales de literatura comparada, 62, Asomante; Ensayos sobre poesia hispanica, Studium, Mex, 67; Saint John of the Cross, Twayne, 71; La Peosia de Juan Ramon Jimenez, Obra en Marcha, Ariel, Barcelona, 73; Garcilaso de la Vega, Twayne, 75. *Mailing Add:* Dept of Span & Port Stanford Univ Stanford CA 94305

GIEBER, ROBERT L, b Clifton, Kans, Jan 22, 44. FRENCH LANGUAGE & LITERATURE. *Educ:* Kans State Teachers Col, BEd, 65; Univ Iowa, MA, 66; Univ Nebr, PhD(Romance lang & lit), 71. *Prof Exp:* Instr French, Ft Hays State Col, 66-69; ASSOC PROF FRENCH, SIMPSON COL, 71-, CHMN DEPT, 74- *Concurrent Pos:* Nat Endowment Humanities res grant, 75. *Mem:* Am Asn Teachers French; Mediaeval Acad Am. *Res:* Medieval hagiography; medieval & Renaissance civilization. *Publ:* Ed, A critical edition of La Vie Saint-Jehan-Baptiste, an old French poem of the early 14th century, Z Romanische Philol, 78; An English-French Glossary of Educational Terminology, Univ Press Am, 81; Poetic elements of rhythm in the ballades, Rondeaux and Virelais of Guillaume de Machaut, Romantic Rev, 82. *Mailing Add:* Dept of Foreign Lang Simpson Col Indianola IA 50125

GIENAPP, NORMAN FRANK, b Chester, SDak, Nov 6, 12; m 42; c 3. CLASSICAL LANGUAGES. *Educ:* Univ Minn, MA, 41; Univ Ill, PhD, 57. *Prof Exp:* Asst prof Latin, Concordia Theol Sem, 39-40; pastor, Knoke, Iowa, 41-44; assoc prof class lang, 44-58, PROF CLASS LANG, ST PAUL'S COL, MO, 58- *Concurrent Pos:* Univ Ill fel, 55-56. *Mem:* Am Philol Asn; Class Asn Mid W & S. *Res:* Versification of Homeric Greek. *Mailing Add:* Dept of Lang St Paul's Col Concordia MO 64020

GIER, NICHOLAS FRANCIS, Modern Philosophy & Philosophy of Religion. See Vol IV

GIES, DAVID THATCHER, b Pittsburgh, Pa, Aug 18, 45; m 67. SPANISH LITERATURE. *Educ:* Pa State Univ, BA, 67; Univ Pittsburgh, MA, 70, PhD(Span), 72. *Prof Exp:* Assoc prof, St Bonaventure Univ, 70-79; ASSOC PROF SPAN, UNIV VA, 79- *Concurrent Pos:* Assoc, Danforth Found, 75-81; vis lectr, Univ Birmingham, England, 78; contrib ed, Purdue Monogr, 77- & Scriblerian, 80- *Mem:* MLA; Northeast Mod Lang Asn; Am Asn Teachers Span & Port; Assoc Int Hispanistas. *Res:* Spanish Enlightenment and Romanticism. *Publ:* Auth, Agustin Duran: A Biography and Literary Appreciation, Tamesis, London, 75; Evolution--Revolution: Spanish Poetry, 1770-1820, Neohelicon, Budapest, 75; Nicolas Fernandez de Moratin en el Arte de las Putas, Actas del 6 Congreso Int de Hispanistas, Toronto, 78; Nicolas Fernandez de Moratin, Twayne, 79; Jose Zorrilla and the betrayal of Spanish Romanticism, Romanistisches Jahrbuch, 80; Don Juan contra don Juan apoteosis del romanticismo espanol, Actas del 7 Congreso Int de Hispanistas, Venice, 81; The plurality of Spanish Romanticisms, Hisp Rev, 81; Vision, ilusion y el sueno romantico en la poesia de Espronceda, Cuadernos de Filologia, Valencia, 82. *Mailing Add:* Dept Span Univ Va Charlottesville VA 22903

GIGNAC, FRANCIS THOMAS, b Detroit, Mich, Feb 24, 33. PHILOLOGY, THEOLOGY. *Educ:* Loyola Univ, Ill, AB, 55, MA, 57, MA, 68; Oxford Univ, DPhil(Greek), 64. *Prof Exp:* Instr Greek, Loyola Univ, Ill, 65-67; from asst prof to assoc prof theol, Fordham Univ, 68-74; ASSOC PROF BIBL STUDIES & CHMN DEPT, CATH UNIV AM, 74- *Concurrent Pos:* NSF travel grant, 67. *Mem:* Cath Bibl Asn; Ling Soc Am; Am Philol Asn; Am Soc Papyrologists. *Res:* The language of the non-literary Greek papyri; the language of the Greek New Testament; textual criticism. *Publ:* Auth, The language of the non-literary Greek papyri, Am Studies Papyrology, 70; The text of Acts in Chrysostom's homilies, Traditio, 70; The pronunciation of Greek stops in the papyri, Trans & Proc Am Philol Asn, 70; An Introductory New Testament Greek Course, Loyola Univ, 73; A Grammar of the Greek Papyri of the Roman and Byzantine Periods (2 vols), Cisalpino-La Goliardica, Milan, 76 & 81. *Mailing Add:* Dept Bibl Studies Cath Univ of Am Washington DC 20064

GIL, ILDEFONSO-MANUEL, b Paniza, Spain, Jan 22, 12; m 43; c 6. ROMANCE LANGUAGES, SPANISH LITERATURE. *Educ:* Univ Madrid, Lic 31; Univ Zaragoza, lic, 47, Dr, 57. *Prof Exp:* Prof Span lit, Rutgers Univ, 62-65; PROF SPAN LIT, BROOKLYN COL, 65- *Concurrent Pos:* Premio Int de Primera Novela, 50. *Mem:* MLA; Am Asn Teachers Span & Port. *Res:* Golden Age and twentieth century Spanish literature. *Publ:* Auth, Las victimas inocentes en Valle-Inclan, Cuadernos Hisp, 7-8/66 & English transl, In: Valle-Inclan Centennial Studies, Univ Tex, Austin, 69; En la base del Esperpento, Cuadernos Hisp, 8-9/69; Los dias del hombre, SUR, Santander, 68; ed, La jura de Santa Gadea, 71 & El Mejor Alcalde, El Rey, 72, Clasicos Ebro, Zoragoza; auth, Luz Sonreida, Goya, Amarga Luz, Col Fuendetodos, 72; ed, Federico Garcia Lorca--el escritor y la critica, Taurus, Madrid, 73; auth, Poemas del Tiempo y del peoma, Curso Super de Filol, Malaga, 73. *Mailing Add:* 19 Sweetbriar Rd Somerset NJ 08873

GILBERT, GLENN G, b Montgomery, Ala, Sept 17, 36; m 64; c 2. SOCIOLINGUISTICS. *Educ:* Univ Chicago, BA, 57; Sorbonne, dipl French grammar, 60; Harvard Univ, PhD(ling), 63. *Prof Exp:* From instr to asst prof Ger lang, Univ Tex, Austin, 63-70; assoc prof, 70-75, PROF LING, SOUTHERN ILL UNIV, CARBONDALE, 75- *Concurrent Pos:* Fulbright lectr ling, Univ Marburg, 66-67; sr Fulbright lectr ling, Univ Mainz, 73-74 . *Mem:* Am Assoc Applied Ling; Soc Caribbean Ling. *Res:* Pidgin and Creole languages; dialectology and linguistic geography of non-English languages spoken in the United States; sociolinguistics. *Publ:* Auth, The German dialect of Kendall and Gillespie Counties, Tex, 31: 138-172 & Dative vs accusative in the German dialects of Central Texas, 32: 288-298, für Mundartforschung; English loan words in the German of Fredericksburg, Texas, Am Speech, 41: 102-112; ed, Texas Studies in Bilingualism, Walter de Gruyter, Ger, 70; The German Language in America, 71 & auth, Linguistic Atlas of Texas German, 72, Univ Tex; ed (with Jacob Ornstein) Problems in Applied Educational Sociolinguistics, Mouton, The Hague, 78; ed & transl, Pidgin & Creole Languages: Selected Essays by Hugo Schuchardt, Cambridge Univ Press, 80. *Mailing Add:* Dept of Ling Southern Ill Univ Carbondale IL 62901

GILBERT, RUSSELL WIEDER, b Emmaus, Pa, Sept 3, 05; m 31; c 2. GERMAN. *Educ:* Muhlenberg Col, AB, 27; Univ Pa, AM, 29, PhD, 43. *Prof Exp:* Asst Ger, Lehigh Univ, 27-29; instr, Muhlenberg Col, 29-30; prof, 30-70, chmn dept mod foreign lang, 59-70, EMER PROF GER, SUSQUEHANNA UNIV, 70- *Concurrent Pos:* Co-ed, Susquehanna Univ Studies; consult,

Britannica World Lang Dictionary, 54, 55. *Res:* The Medieval German novelle; Pennsylvania Germans; Heinrich Heine. *Publ:* Auth, Jacob Appet: Der Ritter underm Zuber, privately publ, 43; Scope of Heine's reading based on his Briefwechsel, Susquehanna Univ Studies, 3/45, 3/46; Pennsylvania German wills, Pa Ger Folklore Soc, 51; Penthesilea als Abbild Kleistischen Wesens, Susquehanna Univ Studies, 5/52; Blooming Grove, the Dunker settlement of Central Pennsylvania, Pa Hist, 1/53; A picture of the Pennsylvania Germans, 3rd ed, Pa Hist Asn, 62 & 70; Bilder un Gedanke, A Book of Pennsylvania German Verse, Pa Ger Soc, 75. *Mailing Add:* 100 Susquehanna Ave Selinsgrove PA 17870

GILBY, WILLIAM REID, b Drumheller, Alta, Feb 13, 40; m 63; c 1. GERMAN LITERATURE. *Educ:* Univ BC, BA, 65; Univ Wash, MA, 66, PhD(Ger), 71. *Prof Exp:* Asst prof, 70-77, ASSOC PROF GER, UNIV CALGARY, 77- *Res:* Classical period of German literature. *Publ:* Auth, Das Bild des Feuers bei Hölderlin: Eine genetische Betrachtung, Bouvier, 73; Eichendorffs Der stille Grund, eine Interpretation, 3/73 & The structural significance of Mignon in Wilhelm meisters Lehrjahre, 3/80, Sem. *Mailing Add:* Dept of Germanic & Slavic Studies Univ of Calgary Calgary AB T2N 1N4 Can

GILDEA, JOSEPH JAMES, b Lawrence, Mass, July 26, 13. MEDIEVAL FRENCH & LATIN LITERATURE. *Educ:* Villanova Col, AB, 36; Cath Univ Am, AM, 40; Univ Pa, PhD, 46. *Hon Degrees:* LLD, Merrimack Col, 60. *Prof Exp:* Instr, Villanova Col, 40-47; prof French & vpres, Merrimack Col, 47-59; vpres acad affairs, 59-64, RES PROF, VILLANOVA UNIV, 64- *Mem:* MLA; Int Arthurian Soc; Soc Anciens Textes Fr. *Res:* Remediarium Conversorum (c 1195), derived from Moralia in Job. *Publ:* Ed, Durmart le Galois: Roman Arthurien du Treizieme Siecle, 65-66, Partonopeu de Blois: A French Romance of the Twelfth Century, 67-70 & L'Hystore Job: An Old French Verse Adaptation of Compendium in Job, 74-79, Villanova Univ; Extant manuscripts of Compendium in Job, Scriptorium, 76; Manuscript tradition of the Treatise on Job, Am Philos Soc Yearbk, 76. *Mailing Add:* The Monastery Villanova PA 19085

GILES, GEOFFREY JOHN, Modern European History. See Vol I

GILES, MARY E, b Missoula, Mont, Sept 18, 34; m 53; c 2. SPANISH LITERATURE, HUMANITIES. *Educ:* Univ Idaho, BA, 55; State Univ Wash, MA, 57; Univ Calif, Berkeley, PhD, 61. *Prof Exp:* Teaching asst, State Univ Wash, 55-57 & Univ Calif, Berkeley, 58-61; from instr to asst prof foreign lang, Calif State Col Hayward, 61-64; from asst prof to assoc prof Span, 64-71, PROF HUMANITIES, UNIV SACRAMENTO, 71- *Concurrent Pos:* Part-time instr, Univ Idaho, 56-57; ed, Studia Mystica, 78- *Mem:* Philol Asn Pac Coast; Am Asn Teachers Span & Port; MLA; Asn Advan Humanities. *Res:* Nineteenth century and contemporary Spanish novel. *Publ:* Auth, Impressionist techniques in descriptions by Emilia Pardo Bazan, Hisp Rev, 10/62; Juan Goytisolo's Juego de Manos: An archetypal interpretation, Hispania, 12/73; transl with critical introduction, Francisco de Osuna's Third Spiritual Alphabet, Paulist, 81; auth, Poetic expressiveness and mystical consciousness: A reading of St John's Dark Night of the Soul, Studia Mystica, fall 79; Emilia Pardo Bazan, Hispania, 5/80; ed, Enter the heart of the Fire, 81 &; auth, Meditations on Teresa, spring, 82, Studia Mystica; The feminist mystic, Crossroad/Continuum, 82. *Mailing Add:* Dept of Humanities Calif State Univ Sacramento CA 95818

GILL, M ROSENDA, b Newton, Mass, Aug 30, 17. FRENCH, ITALIAN. *Educ:* Regis Col, AB, 38; Boston Col, MA, 50; Middlebury Col, DML, 67. *Prof Exp:* Teacher, Archdiocese of Boston, 40-63; from instr to assoc prof French, 63-74, PROF FRENCH, REGIS COL, MASS, 74- *Concurrent Pos:* Fulbright Found fel, 61-62; adjunct assoc prof, Bentley Col, 77- *Mem:* MLA; New Eng Mod Lang Asn; Am Asn Teachers Fr (pres, 65-68). *Res:* Bernanos; Romancier. *Mailing Add:* Dept of French Bentley Col Waltham MA 02193

GILLAIN, ANNE THERESE, b Ay, France, Aug 18, 42. FRENCH LITERATURE, CINEMA. *Educ:* Sorbonne, Lic Lett, 63; Harvard Univ, PhD(French lit), 75. *Prof Exp:* Instr, 73-75, asst prof, 75-80, ASSOC PROF FRENCH, WELLESLEY COL, 80- *Mem:* MLA; Soc Etudes Celiniennes. *Res:* Nineteenth century French novel; works of Louis-Ferdinand Celine. *Publ:* Auth, Le Grotesque chez Celine, Actes Colloque Paris, 78; Feerie pour une autre fois et le cinema, Rev Lett Mod Minard, Paris, 78. *Mailing Add:* Dept of French Wellesley Col Wellesley MA 02181

GILLAN, GARTH J, Philosophy. See Vol IV

GILLE, GISELE CORBIERE, b Clamart, France, Apr 29, 23; US citizen; m 55; c 2. ROMANCE LANGUAGES. *Educ:* Univ Rennes, 3 certs English, 44-46; Columbia Univ, MA, 49, PhD(French), 56. *Prof Exp:* Teacher, Greenwich Acad, Conn, 53-54; instr French, Douglass Col, Rutgers Univ, 54-57; teacher, Spence Sch, NY, 57-60; asst prof, 60-66, ASSOC PROF FRENCH, CITY COL NEW YORK, 66- *Mem:* MLA; Am Asn Teachers Fr. *Res:* French literary criticism and French novel in nineteenth century. *Publ:* Auth, Barbey D'Aurevilly, critique litteraire, Droz, Geneva, 62; coauth, Promenades litteraires it grammaticales, Heath, 66; Etapes Litteraire, Am Bk, 68; auth, Apercus de l'oeuvre critique de Sainte-Bueve Nouvelles ed, Debresse, Paris, 73; Les bas-bleus et le feminisme, Rev Mod Let, 73. *Mailing Add:* Dept of French City Col of New York New York NY 10031

GILLELAND, BRADY BLACKFORD, b Wheeling, WVa, July 12, 22; m 75; c 2. LATIN, GREEK. *Educ:* Washington & Jefferson Col, AB, 44; Univ Okla, MA, 48; Univ NC, PhD(classics), 54. *Prof Exp:* Instr classics, Univ Tenn, 54-55; asst prof, Beloit Col, 54-57; PROF CLASSICS, UNIV VT, 57- *Mem:* Am Philol Asn; MLA; Class Asn New Eng; Int Maledicta Soc; Soc Seven Sages. *Res:* Roman satire; Petroniana; medieval studies. *Publ:* Auth, The date of Cicero's Partitiones Oratoriae, Class Philos, 61; The development of Cicero's ideal orator, In: Classical and Medieval Studies in Honor of B L Ullman, Vol I, 64; co-ed, Petronius: The Satiricon, Appleton, 69; auth, Three stories from the Dolopathos of Johannes de Alta Silva, Allegorica, spring 77; The Dolopathos of Johannes de Alta Silva: A new evaluation, Studies Seven Sages of Rome, 78. *Mailing Add:* Dept of Classics Univ of Vt 481 Main St Burlington VT 05401

GILLESPIE, GERALD ERNEST PAUL, Comparative Literature. See Vol II

GILLESPIE, JOHN KINSEY, b Louisville, Ky, Mar 21, 45; m 77. JAPANESE LITERATURE, THEATRE. *Educ:* Houston Baptist Col, BA, 67; Ind Univ, MA, 70, PhD(comp lit), 79. *Prof Exp:* Asst prof Japanese lang & lit, Raymond-Callison Col, Univ Pac, 75-78; asst prof Japanese lang & lit, Ohio State Univ, 78-80; asst prof Japanese & comp lit, Southern Ill Univ, 80-82; ASST PROF JAPANESE & COMP LIT, CTR ASIAN STUDIES, ST JOHN'S UNIV, 82- *Concurrent Pos:* Nat Endowment for Humanities grant, summer, 81. *Mem:* MLA; Asn Asian Studies; Int Comp Lit Asn; Am Asn Teachers Japanese. *Res:* Aesthetics; drama; Japanese-Western literary and cultural relationships. *Publ:* Auth, Irony of Wu Ch'eng-En and Chaucer, Tea Leaves, 69; Beyond Byzantium: Aesthetic pessimism in Mishima's modern Noh plays, Monumenta Nipponica, 82; Drama as guided dream: The impact of Noh and Paul Clandel's style of playwriting, Theatre J, 82; Interior action: The impact of Noh on Jean-Louis Barrault, Comp Drama, 82. *Mailing Add:* Ctr for Asian Studies St John's Univ Jamaica NY 11439

GILLIAM, B JUNE, b Cleveland, Ohio. FRENCH LANGUAGE & LITERATURE. *Educ:* Univ Chicago, PhB, 47; Western Reserve Univ, MA, 53; Sorbonne, dipl etudes super, 53; Ohio State Univ, PhD(French & teacher educ), 69. *Prof Exp:* Dir jr year in Rouen, France, 73-74, ASSOC PROF FRENCH, UNIV CONN, 68- *Mem:* MLA; Am Asn Teachers Fr; Am Coun Teaching Foreign Lang. *Res:* Teacher education in modern languages. *Publ:* Coauth, Nouveau cours pratique, 3rd ed, 69 & Un peu de tout, 70, Holt. *Mailing Add:* Dept of Romance & Class Lang Univ of Conn Storrs CT 06268

GILLIAM, HARRIET S, English & American Literature. See Vol II

GILLIAM, JAMES FRANK, b Seattle, Wash, Mar 14, 15; m 41; c 3. CLASSICS, ANCIENT HISTORY. *Educ:* San Jose State Col, AB, 35; Stanford Univ, AM, 36; Yale Univ, PhD, 40. *Prof Exp:* Instr classics, Yale Univ, 40-41 & 45-47; asst prof, Wells Col, 47-49; from asst prof to prof, State Univ Iowa, 49-61; prof hist, Univ Ore, 61-62; prof Greek & Latin, Columbia Univ, 62-65; PROF ANCIENT HISTORY, INST ADVAN STUDY, NJ, 65- *Concurrent Pos:* Guggenheim fel, 55-56; staff mem, Inst Advan Studies, 58-59 & 63-64; adj prof Greek & Latin, Columbia Univ, 70-; vis lectr classics, Princeton Univ, 72-75. *Mem:* Am Philol Asn; Archaeol Inst Am; Soc Prom Roman Studies; Int Asn Papryologists; Am Soc Papryologists (pres, 71-73). *Res:* Roman empire; papyrology; epigraphy. *Publ:* Auth, The governors of Syria Coele, Am J Philol, 58; coauth, The Excavations at Dura-Europos: The Parchments and Papyri, Yale Univ, 59; auth, The plague under Marcus Aurelius, Am J Philol, 61. *Mailing Add:* Sch of Hist Studies Inst for Advan Study Princeton NJ 08540

GILLIS, DANIEL J, b New Bedford, Mass, Sept 25, 35. CLASSICS. *Educ:* Harvard, AB, 57; Cornell Univ, MA, 59, PhD(classics), 63. *Prof Exp:* Instr classics, Brown Univ, 59-60; asst prof, Univ Tex, 64-65 & Swathmore Col, 65-66; from ast prof to assoc prof, 66-76, PROF CLASSICS, HAVERFORD COL, 76- *Concurrent Pos:* Ger govt fel, Univ Munich, 63-64; Ford Found humanities res grant, 73. *Mem:* Am Philol Asn. *Res:* Latin poetry; Roman history; Greek politics. *Publ:* Auth, Furtwangler Recalled, DeGraff, 66; Furtwangler and America, Manyland Bks, 70; Vita, Westworks, 79; Collaboration with the Persians, Steiner, 79; Measure of a Man, Iona Fdn, 82; Eros and Death in the Aeneid, Bretschneider, 82. *Mailing Add:* Dept of Classics Haverford Col Haverford PA 19041

GILMAN, DONALD, b Newport News, Va, Feb 24, 45. FRENCH, COMPARATIVE LITERATURE. *Educ:* Univ NC, Chapel Hill, AB, 67, PhD(French, comp lit), 76; Harvard Univ, AM, 70. *Prof Exp:* Instr French, Christopher Newport Col, Col William & Mary, 67-70; asst prof, 74-79, ASSOC PROF FRENCH & HUMANITIES, BALL STATE UNIV, 79- *Concurrent Pos:* Ed, Nuntia: Newslett Medieval Asn Midwest, 78-82. *Mem:* MLA; Renaissance Soc Am; Medieval Asn Midwest; Midwest Mod Lang Asn; SAtlantic Mod Lang Asn. *Res:* Sixteenth-century French literature; Renaissance literature in France and Italy; history of literary criticism, from Plato to French structuralism. *Publ:* Auth, The River of Death: Motif and metaphor in Racine's Phedre, 72 & Le venin qui vous tue: Motif, metaphor, and mode, In: Britannicus, 73, Romance Notes; compiler, Annual critical bibliography in style and stylistics for 1979 and 1980, Style; auth, Ronsard's concept of the Poete Humain, Bibliotheque d'Humanisme et Renaissance (in prep). *Mailing Add:* Dept of Foreign Lang Ball State Univ Muncie IN 47306

GILMAN, SANDER LAWRENCE, b Buffalo, NY, Feb 21, 44; m 69; c 2. GERMAN LITERARY & INTELLECTUAL HISTORY. *Educ:* Tulane Univ, BA, 63, PhD(Ger), 68. *Prof Exp:* Lectr Ger, St Mary's Dominican Col, 63-64; instr, Dillard Univ, 67-68; asst prof, Case Western Reserve Univ, 68-69; from asst prof to assoc prof, 69-76, chmn dept, 74-81, PROF GER LIT, CORNELL UNIV, 76- *Concurrent Pos:* Am Philos Soc grantee, 70-71; Guggenheim Found fel, 72-73; Int Res & Exchanges Bd sr fel, 72-73, 76; Am Coun Learned Soc travel grant, 75-; res fel psychiat, Cornell Med Col, 77-78 & adj prof, 78- *Mem:* Int Soc Germanists; MLA; Am Asn Teachers Ger; Am Lessing Soc; Soc Int Etudes Litt & Psychiat. *Res:* History of ideas; comparative literature; cultural history. *Publ:* Auth, Nietzschean Parody, Bouvier, 76; The Face of Madness: Hugh Diamond and the Rise of Psychiatric Photography, Brunner/Mazel, 76; ed, The City of Sense of Community, Cornell Univ, 76; co-ed, F M Klinger: Werke, Niemeyer, 78; auth, Wahnsinn, Text and Kontext, Peter Lang, 81; ed, Begegnungen mit Nietzsche, Bouvier, 81; auth, On Blackness Without Blacks, G K Hall, 82; Seeing the Insane, Wiley-Interscience, 82. *Mailing Add:* Dept of Ger Lit Cornell Univ Ithaca NY 14853

GILMAN, STEPHEN, b Chicago, Ill, Aug 26, 17; m 43; c 3. SPANISH LITERATURE. *Educ:* Princeton, AM, 40, PhD, 43; Harvard Univ, hon AM, 54. *Prof Exp:* Asst prof Span, Princeton Univ, 46-48; from assoc prof to prof, 48-54; assoc prof, 54-57, PROF SPAN, HARVARD UNIV, 57- *Concurrent Pos:* Vis prof, Columbia Univ, 53. *Mem:* MLA; Am Acad Arts & Sci; Medieval Acad Am; Renaissance Soc Am. *Res:* Spanish novel; contemporary

Spanish poetry; Golden Age theater. *Publ:* Auth, Cervantes y Avellaneda, Nueva Rev Filo Hisp, 51; The Art of La Celestina, Univ Wis, 56; Tiempo u tiempos verbales en el Poema del Cid, Gredos, 61; The Spain of Fernando de Rojas, 72, & Galdos and the Art of the European Novel: 1867-1887, 81, Princeton Univ. *Mailing Add:* Dept of Romance Lang Harvard Univ Cambridge MA 02138

GILROY, JAMES PAUL, b Worcester, Mass, Aug 30, 47. FRENCH LITERATURE, ROMANCE LANGUAGES. *Educ:* Col Holy Cross, BA, 68; Princeton Univ, MA, 70, PhD(French), 72. *Prof Exp:* Asst prof, 72-79, ASSOC PROF FRENCH, UNIV DENVER, 79- *Mem:* Rocky Mountain Mod Lang Asn; Soc Prof Fr Am; Am Asn Teachers Fr; Les Amis Lang Francaise; Philol Asn Pac Coast. *Res:* Romanticism and Pre-Romanticism; French fiction of 18th and 19th centuries; French Enlightenment; nonmetropolitan French literature. *Publ:* Auth, The Theme of Etre and Paraitre in the Works of Agrippa d'Aubigne, Bull Rocky Mountain Mod Lang Asn, 73; Theatricality in the Universe of Balzac's Le Pere Goriot, Degre 2nd, 77; Prevostian themes in the Suite de Manon Lescaut, In: Enlightenment Essays, 77; Peace and the Pursuit of Happiness in the French Utopian Novel, In: Studies on Voltaire and the Eighteenth Century, Voltaire Found, 79; The Romantic Manon and Des Grieux, Naaman, Sherbrooke, 80; The theme of the woman in Balzac's La Cousine Bette, Rocky Mountain Rev, 80; ed, Francophone literatures of the New World, Vol II, In: Occasional Papers, 82. *Mailing Add:* Dept of Foreign Lang Univ of Denver Denver CO 80210

GIMENO, JOAQUIN, b Madrid Spain, Sept 8, 31; US citizen; m 64; c 1. ROMANCE LANGUAGES. *Educ:* Univ Murcia, MA, 54, PhD(Span), 56. *Prof Exp:* Collab, Sem lexicography, Real Acad Lengua, 55-56; instr Span, Harvard Univ, 56-59; from asst prof to assoc prof, Univ Calif, Riverside, 59-65; prof, Case Western Reserve Univ, 65-72; prof, Southern Calif Univ, 72-80; PROF SPAN, UNIV CALIF, LOS ANGELES, 80- *Concurrent Pos:* Am Philos Soc res grants, 59-66. *Mem:* MLA; Int Asn Hispanists; corresp mem Hispanic Soc Am. *Res:* Medieval and 19th century Spanish literature; Golden Age literature. *Publ:* Auth, La imagen del monarca en la Castilla del siglo XIV, Rev Occidente, 72; Extructura y Diseno en la Literatura Castellana Medieval, 75 & La Creacion Literaria de la Edad Media y del Renacimiento, 77, Porrua Turanzas. *Mailing Add:* Dept of Span & Port Univ of Calif Los Angeles CA 90024

GINGERICH, VERNON J, b Kaona, Iowa, Nov 3, 14; m 42. MODERN FOREIGN LANGUAGES. *Educ:* State Univ Iowa, BA, 35, MA, 36, PhD(French), 50. *Prof Exp:* Instr French, William Penn Col, 37; instr French & Ger, Burlington Col, 37-51; chmn dept lang, Sault Ste Marie Br, Mich Col Mining & Technol, 51-59; assoc prof French, Mankato State Col, 59-62; PROF FOREIGN LANG & CHMN DEPT, UNIV WIS-EAU CLAIRE, 62- *Mem:* MLA; Am Asn Teachers Fr; Am Asn Teachers Ger. *Res:* Nineteenth and twentieth century French novel; Flaubert. *Mailing Add:* Dept of Foreign Lang Univ of Wis Eau Claire WI 54701

GINSBERG, ELLEN SUTOR, b South Bend, Ind, Apr 18, 35; m 62. FRENCH LANGUAGE & LITERATURE. *Educ:* Northwest Univ, BA, 55, MA, 56; Univ Chicago, PhD(Fr), 63; Univ Vienna, cert Ger, 63. *Prof Exp:* Lectr English, Ecole Norm Super de Jeunes Filles, France, 61-62; asst prof, 65-69; vis asst prof, Univ Md, 71-72; asst prof, 72-80, ASSOC PROF FRENCH, CATH UNIV AM, 81- *Mem:* MLA; SAtlantic Mod Lang Asn; Northeast Mod Lang Asn; Renaissance Soc Am; Southeast Renaissance Conf. *Res:* French literature of the Renaissance; comparative literature of the Renaissance; drama. *Publ:* Ed, Le Cesar de Jacques Grevin: Edition Critique, Droz, Geneva, 71; auth, The Legacy of Muret's Julius Caesar, Acta Conventus Neo-Latini Lovaniensis, Wilhelm Fink, Munich, 73; coauth, Fictional material and philosophic method, Mod Lang Studies, fall, 73; auth, Genre theory in the French Renaissance, French Lit Ser Vol IV, 77; Joachim du Bellay's Latin poem Patriae Desiderium and his vernacular poetry, In: Acta Conventus Neo-Latini Turonensis, Vrin, Paris, 80. *Mailing Add:* Dept of Mod Lang Cath Univ of Am Washington DC 20064

GINSBERG, JUDITH ELLEN, b New Rochelle, NY; Aug 7, 46; m 80. SPANISH LITERATURE. *Educ:* Brown Univ, BA, 68, MA, 68; City Univ New York, PhD(Span lit), 76. *Prof Exp:* Instr Span, City Col New York, 70-75; asst prof, 75-81, ASSOC PROF SPAN, UNION COL, NY, 81- *Concurrent Pos:* Tutor English as foreign lang, Univ Poznan, Poland, 70-71. *Mem:* MLA; Northeast Mod Lang Asn; Am Asn Teachers Span & Port; Women's Caucus Mod Lang Asn. *Res:* The generation of 1898; 19th and 20th century Latin American literature; feminist criticism. *Publ:* Auth, Los juicios de Jose Marti sobre la inmigracion a los Estados Unidos, Bilingual Rev, 74; From anger to action: The avenging female in two luctas, 80 & In search of a voice: Baroja's early writings and political career, 81, Rev Estudios Hispanicos; Angel Gunivet, Twayne (in press). *Mailing Add:* Humanities Bldg Union Col Schenectady NY 12308

GIONET, ARTHUR JOSEPH, b Feb 9, 25; US citizen; m 50; c 1. FRENCH, LATIN. *Educ:* Univ St Thomas, Tex, BA, 53; Univ Tex, Austin, MA, 57, PhD(French), 68. *Prof Exp:* High sch teacher French & Latin, Galena Park Independent Sch Dist, 53-61; assoc prof, 61-80, PROF FRENCH & LATIN, N TEX STATE UNIV, 80- *Concurrent Pos:* Consult, Col Entrance Exam Bd, Princeton, NJ, 60-61; Danforth Assoc, 79. *Mem:* Am Asn Teachers Fr; Nat Asn Lang Lab Dir; SCent Mod Lang Asn; SCent Renaissance Conf. *Res:* Sixteenth century drama; Montaigne; Renaissance. *Publ:* Coauth, The Texas report on format preferences in publishers' recordings, Nat Asn Lang Lab Dir J, Vol V, No 1; auth, Les systemes philosophiques dans l'essai XX des Essais de Montaigne, SCent Mod Lang Asn Studies, Vol XXXII, No 4; Potpourri, SCent Mod Lang Asn Bull, Vol XXXII, No 2, Vol XXXIII, No 1 & XXXIII, No 3. *Mailing Add:* Dept of Foreign Lang & Lit N Tex State Univ Denton TX 76203

GIORDANETTI, ELMO, b Paterson, NJ, Sept 10, 25. ROMANCE LANGUAGES. *Educ:* Bowdoin Col, AB, 51; Princeton Univ, MA, 54, PhD(Romance lang), 59; Amherst Col, hon MA, 68. *Prof Exp:* Asst English, Ecole Cent, Paris, 54-55; from instr to assoc prof romance lang, 55-68, PROF ROMANCE LANG, AMHERST COL, 68- *Concurrent Pos:* Vis prof French, Mt Holyoke Col, 59-60. *Mem:* MLA; Dante Soc; Am Asn Teachers Ital. *Res:* Eighteenth century history and literature; European romanticism. *Publ:* Auth, Alfieri, Pirandello & Tasso, In: Encycl Americana, Grolier; 54; coauth, Was America a Mistake?, Harper Torchbooks, 67 & Univ SC, 68. *Mailing Add:* Dept of Romance Lang Amherst Col Amherst MA 01002

GIORDANO, JAIME ANIBAL, b Concepcion, Chile, Mar 3, 37; m; c 3. SPANISH-AMERICAN LITERATURE. *Educ:* Univ Chile, BLet, 55, Prof(Span), 61; Univ Concepcion, Chile, Lic, 59. *Prof Exp:* Instr Span-Am lit, Univ Concepcion, Chile, 58-62, assoc prof, 62-66; vis asst prof Span, 66-67, asst prof, 67-70, dir grad studies Span, 72-73, ASSOC PROF SPAN, STATE UNIV NY STONY BROOK, 70- *Concurrent Pos:* Full-time mem 3rd Writers Workshop, Univ Concepcion, Chile 62-63; mem grad fac, Span summer sch, Middlebury Col, 69-71; guest lectr, Univ Chile, Southern Univ Chile, Nat Libr Chile, Middlebury Col, Univ Conn, Haverford Col & Univ Pa. *Honors & Awards:* Municipal Prize for Literature, Santiago, Chile, 72. *Mem:* MLA; Northeastern Mod Lang Asn; Inst Lit Iberoam. *Res:* Spanish-American contemporary novel; Spanish-American essay and poetry. *Publ:* Auth, Notas sobre Jose Vasconcelos y el ensayo hispanoamericano en el siglo veinte, Hispanic Rev, Univ Pa, spring 73; La alegria colectiva y la alegria solitaria en Neruda, Approximaciones a Pablo Neruda, Ocnos, Madrid, 73; El nivel de la escritura en la narrativa hispanoamerica contemporanea, Nueva narrativa hispanoamericana, 1-9/74; El libro del destierro, Cuadernos Americanos, Mexico, 9-10/75; Finis Britannia o el poder de abstraccion de Huidobro, Revista Iberoamericana, 1-6/79; La imaginacion dialectica en Neruda: La fase de los Versos, Pablo Neruda, Publications du Centre de Recherches Latino-Americaines de l'Universite de Poitiers, France, 4/79; Agustin Yanez en el contexto de la escritura contemporanea, Texto/Contexto en la Literatura Iberoamericana, Instituto Internacional de Literatura Iberoamericana, Memoria del XIX Congreso, Madrid, 80; Gabriela Mistral o la ronda extraviada, Gabriela Mistral, Universidad Veracruzana, Mexico, 80. *Mailing Add:* Dept of Hisp Lang & Lit State Univ of NY Stony Brook NY 11790

GIRARD, RENE NOEL, b Avignon, France, Dec 25, 23; US citizen; m 51; c 3. FRENCH. *Educ:* Ind Univ, PhD. *Prof Exp:* Instr French, Ind Univ, 47-52 & Duke Univ, 52-53; asst prof, Bryn Mawr Col, 53-57; from assoc prof to prof, Johns Hopkins Univ, 57-68; prof arts & lett, State Univ NY Buffalo, 68-71, distinguished prof, 71-76; James M Bell prof French, Johns Hopkins Univ, 76-81; ANDREW B HAMMOND PROF FRENCH LANG & LIT, STANFORD UNIV, 82- *Concurrent Pos:* Gen ed, Mod Lang Notes; Guggenheim fel, 60, 67; consult, Nat Endowment Humanities, 71-73. *Mem:* MLA. *Res:* French literature; comparative literature; mythology and religion. *Publ:* Auth, Proust, A Critical Anthology, Prentice-Hall, 62; Dostoievski du double a l'unite, Plon, Paris, 63; Deceit, Desire and the Novel, Johns Hopkins Univ, 66; La violence et le sacre, Grasset, Paris, 72; translr, Violence and the Sacred (La Violence et le sacre), Johns Hopkins Univ, 77; auth, Mensonge romantique et verite romanesque, Livre de Poche, Paris, 78; Des Choses cachees depuis la fondation du monde, Grasset, Paris, 78; To Double Business Bound, Johns Hopkins Univ, 78; Le Bouc Emissaire, Grasset, 82. *Mailing Add:* Andrew B Hammond Prof French Lang & Lit Stanford Univ Stanford CA 94305

GIRARD-CORKUM, JERRIA, b Clay, NY; m 79. SPANISH LITERATURE. *Educ:* Calif State Univ, Northridge, BA, 65; Fullerton, MA, 72; Irvine, PhD(Span lit & ling), 80. *Prof Exp:* EDUCATOR & CHAIR, SPAN, FRENCH & ENGLISH, ANAHEIM UNION HIGH SCH, 66- *Concurrent Pos:* Ed, Brainstorm Books, 80-, consult, 81-; educator English as second lang, Rancho Santiago Community Col Dist, 81-82. *Mem:* Am Asn Teachers Span & Port. *Res:* Linguistics; conditions for learning; Spanish poetry. *Publ:* Auth, The Poetry of Juvencio Valle, Univ Calif, 80; coauth, Spelling Made Sonic, Brainstorm Books, 81. *Mailing Add:* 1641 Garland Ave Tustin CA 92680

GIRAUD, RAYMOND DORNER, b New York, NY, Aug 26, 20; m 48. FRENCH. *Educ:* City Col New York, AB, 41; Univ Chicago, MA, 49; Yale Univ, PhD(French), 54. *Prof Exp:* Instr English, Ill Inst Technol, 46-50; asst in instr French, Yale Univ, 50-51, from instr to prof French, 52-76, chmn dept, 68-71, PROF FRENCH, SOCIAL THOUGHT & INST COMT, STANFORD UNIV, 76- *Concurrent Pos:* Morse fel, 55-56; Guggenheim fel, 61-62. *Mem:* MLA; Am Asn Teachers Fr. *Res:* Nineteenth century French literature. *Publ:* Auth, The Unheroic Hero in the Novels of Stendhal, Balzac and Flaubert, Rutgers Univ; ed, Flaubert, A Collection of Critical Essays, Prentice-Hall. *Mailing Add:* Dept of French & Ital Stanford Univ Stanford CA 94305

GIRO, JORGE ANTONIO, b Havana, Cuba, Oct 21, 33; US citizen; m 61; c 2. SPANISH, SPANISH LITERATURE. *Educ:* Ind State Univ, BA, 64, MS, 65. *Hon Degrees:* LLD, Jose Marti Univ, Cuba, 57; LL D, Univ Villanueva, Cuba, 57. *Prof Exp:* Instr Span, Elkhart Sr High Sch, Ind, 64-66; from instr to assoc prof, 66-73, coordr Latin Am studies, 73-82, PROF SPAN & SPAN LIT, TOWSON STATE UNIV, 76-, CHMN MOD LANG DEPT, 77- *Concurrent Pos:* Vis lectr Span, Coucher Col, 68-; comnr, Comn on Concerns of Span Speaking People in Md, 73 & Comn Ethnics Affairs, 77- *Honors & Awards:* Best Teacher of the Year Award, Towson State Univ, 76. *Mem:* Am Asn Teachers Span & Port; MLA; Am Coun Teaching Foreign Lang. *Res:* The Middle Ages in Spanish literature; the Golden Ages in Spanish literature; Spanish and Latin American short stories. *Mailing Add:* Dept of Mod Lang Towson State Univ Baltimore MD 21204

GIROUX, ROBERT, b Montreal, Que, Jan 29, 44; c 1. FRENCH & FRENCH CANADIAN LITERATURES. *Educ:* Col Ste Croix, BA, 64; McGill Univ, MA, 67; Faculte de Vincennes, Paris, France, PhD(lettres mod), 71. *Prof Exp:* Teaching asst French lit & French second lang, McGill Univ, 65 -67; asst prof, French Can lit, Univ Montreal, 70-71; asst prof French lit & French second lang, Loyola Col, 71-72; PROF FRENCH CAN LIT, UNIV DE SHERBROOKE, 72- *Mem:* Union des ecrivains Quebecois; Asn des auteurs des Cantons de l'est. *Res:* Semiotic and sociology of literature; relations between literature, song and idealogies. *Publ:* Auth, Du va-et-vient horizontal a la circularite de la reverie chez J A Loranger, Voix & images Ellipse, 9-12/76, English, 77; Notion et--ou functions de la litterature, Voix & Images, Vol V, 77; Desir de synthese chez S Mallarme, Ed Naaman, Sherbrooke, 78; Conflit ideologique au milieu du XIX's au Quebec, Presence francophone, printemps, 78; L'appel d'air (poemes), Ed St Germain-des-pris, 80; coauth, Litterature, histoire, ideologie, 80 & auth, Semiotique de la poesie Quebecoise, 81, Univ de Sherbrooke; L'oeuf sans jaune (poems), Ed Moebuis-Triptyque, 82; coauth, L'arbitraire culturel, Univ Sherbrooke, 82. *Mailing Add:* 85 Rue Compton Ouest Waterville PQ J0B 3H0 Can

GISOLFI, ANTHONY M, b San Felice a Cancello, Italy, Nov 13, 09; US citizen; m 35; c 4. ITALIAN. *Educ:* City Col New York, AB, 30; Columbia Univ, AM, 31, PhD (Ital lit), 59. *Prof Exp:* Teacher Span & Ital, High Sch Music & Art, New York, 37-64; assoc prof romance lang, 64-76, EMER ASSOC PROF HISP & ITAL STUDIES, STATE UNIV NY, ALBANY, 76- *Concurrent Pos:* Lectr Ital, div adult educ, City Col Sch Gen Studies, 47-63; adj prof Span, C W Post Col, Long Island Univ, 64. *Mem:* Am Asn Teachers Ital (vpres, 59, 60); MLA; Dante Soc Am. *Res:* Nineteenth and twentieth century Italian literature. *Publ:* Auth, The beach of heaven: Italy 1943-1945 in American fiction, Italica, 9/50; coauth, Classical Italian Songs, S F Vanni, 55; auth, On Classic Ground, Bk Assoc, 62; Ariosto's Prologue to La Cassaria, Theatre Annual 65-66; The Essential Matilde Serao, Las Americas, 68; Rome theatre winter 1971, Italica, 12/71; Giovanni Pascoli's Italia raminga, Ital Am, fall/winter 79; transl, Salvatore Di Giacomo: March, A Little Tavern, In the Garden, Forum Italicum, winter 79. *Mailing Add:* PO Box 225 Bronxville NY 10708

GITLITZ, DAVID MARTIN, b Binghamton, NY, Apr 24, 42; c 2. HISPANIC LITERATURE. *Educ:* Oberlin Col, BA, 63; Harvard Univ, MA, 64, PhD(Span), 68. *Prof Exp:* Dir, Jr Year in Peru, Ind Univ, 69 & Grad Prog in Madrid, 73-74, acting dir, Overseas Study Prog, 74-76, asst to Dean int prpg, 74-76; CHMN DEPT MOD LANG & LIT, UNIV NEBR, LINCOLN, 76- *Mem:* MLA; Asn Teachers Span & Port; Renaissance Soc Am; Comediantes. *Res:* Golden Age Spanish literature; sephardic literature. *Publ:* Auth, Conversos and the Fusion of Worlds in Micael de Carvajal's Tragedia Josephina, Hisp Rev, 72; La ruta alegorica del segundo Quijote, Romanische Forschungen, 72; Hacia una definicion empirica de la aliteracion, Nueva Revista Filologia Hisp, 73; La actitud cristiano nueva en Las Cortes de la Muerte, 74, Segismundo; Ironia e imagines en el Castigo sin venganza, Revista Estudios Hisp, 77; Estructura lirica de la comedia de Lope de Vega, Albatros, 80; Quevedo, Songs of Love and Death, Coronado Press, 80; Critical perspectives on Calderon de la Barca, Soc Span & Span Am Studies, 81. *Mailing Add:* Dept of Mod Lang & Lit Univ of Nebr Lincoln NE 68588

GITTLEMAN, ANNE IKER, b Bois Colombes, France, Aug 17, 28; m 57; c 3. FRENCH MEDIEVAL LITERATURE. *Educ:* Sorbonne, MA, 50, DUniv, 66. *Prof Exp:* Instr classics & French, Col Mayenne, France, 52-53; from instr to asst prof, 54-68, assoc prof, 68-80, PROF FRENCH, VASSAR COL, 80- *Res:* Medieval French literature. *Publ:* Auth, Le Style Epique dans Garin le Loheren, Soc Publ Romanes et Fr, Droz, Geneva, 67. *Mailing Add:* Dept of French Vassar Col Poughkeepsie NY 12601

GITTLEMAN, SOL, b Hoboken, NJ, June 5, 34; m 56; c 2. GERMAN, COMPARATIVE LITERATURE. *Educ:* Drew Univ, AB, 55; Columbia Univ, AB, 56; Univ Mich, 61. *Prof Exp:* From instr to asst prof Ger, Univ Mich, 59-64; from asst prof to assoc prof & chmn dept, 64-72, PROF GER, TUFTS UNIV, 72- *Concurrent Pos:* Consult & reviewer, Choice, 63-; assoc ed, J Int Arthur Schnitzler Soc, 64- *Honors & Awards:* Harbison Award for Gifted Teaching, Danforth Found, 71. *Mem:* Am Asn Teachers Ger; MLA. *Res:* Anglo-German literary relations in 19th century; German expressionism; works of Frank Wedekind. *Publ:* Auth, John Hay as a critic, Victorian Newsletter, autumn 63; Image of America in Wedekind, Ger Quart, 3/66; Wedekind and Brecht: A literary relationship, Mod Drama, 2/68; Frank Wedekind, Twayne, 68; Sholom Aleichem: A Non-Critical Introduction to His Works, Mouton, 74; Thomas Mann and the Jews: A final word, Dayton Univ Rev, spring 76; Sternheim and Wedekind, Ger Quart, 1/76; Shtetl to Suberbia: The Family In Jewish Literary Imagination, Beacon, 78. *Mailing Add:* Dept of Ger Tufts Univ Medford MA 02155

GIULIANO, WILLIAM PAUL, b New York City, NY. SPANISH, ITALIAN. *Educ:* Brooklyn Col, BA, 35; Columbia Univ, MA, 37; Univ Mich, PhD(Romance lang), 52. *Prof Exp:* Instr Span, NY Univ, 47-52; PROF SPAN, QUEENS COL, 58- *Mem:* Am Asn Teacher Span & Port; MLA. *Res:* Twentieth century Spanish theatre. *Publ:* Co-ed, Selections from Italian Poetry, Harvey House, 66; auth, Buero Vallings, Sastre y el teatro de su tiempo, Las Am Publ Co, 71; Lauro Olmo's La casmisa, Rev Estudes Hisp, 1/71; The theatre of Buero Vallejo, Mod Drama, 2/71; Spanish Grammar for Reading, Macmillian, 76; Helping the student of low language ability, Hispanic, 12/21; The defense of Buero Vallejo, Mod Drama, 9/77; coauth, En breve: A Concise Spanish Review Grammar, Holt, Rinehart & Winston, 82. *Mailing Add:* 67-50 188 St Flushing NY 11365

GIUSTINIANI, VITO ROCCO, b Lucca, Italy, June 25, 16; m 45; c 2. ITALIAN LITERATURE, ROMANCE PHILOLOGY. *Educ:* Univ Pisa, PhD(Orient lit), 38. *Prof Exp:* Teacher Latin & Greek, Licei Classici, 55-60; teacher medieval Latin, Univ Pisa, 60-63; prof Romance philol, Univ Freiburg Br, WGer, 63-71; PROF ITAL, UNIV MASS, BOSTON, 71- *Mem:* Dante Soc Am. *Res:* Mediaeval Latin; Romance linguistics. *Publ:* Auth, Sulle traduzioni latine delle Vite di Plutarco, Rinasccimento, 61; Zitat und literarische Anspielung in der modernen italienischen Lyrik, Festschrift Friedrich, 64; Rinucccini: Materialien und Forschunger zur Geschichte des florentinischen Humanismus, 65; Geschichte, Erzahlung und Humor in Manzonis Promessi Sposi, Romanische Forschungen, 74; Altes und Neues in der Dichtung Ungarettis, Festschrift Friedrich, 74; Il testo della Nencia e della Beca secondo le piu antiche stampe, 76; contribr, Neulsteiuische Dichtung in Italien 1850-1950, 79; auth, Il Filelfo el interpreterisue allegonia di Virgilio, Miscellanes Kri Skelter, 80. *Mailing Add:* Dept of Ital Univ of Mass Boston MA 02125

GLADE, HENRY, b Ger, Oct 8, 20; US citizen; m 58. GERMAN, RUSSIAN. *Educ:* Elizabethtown Col, AB, 42; Univ Pa, MA, 48, PhD(Ger), 58. *Prof Exp:* Prof mod lang, Hershey Jr Col, 50-53; instr Ger, Bates Col, 53-54; asst prof French & Ger, 54-55, assoc prof Ger, 55-62, PROF GER & RUSS, MANCHESTER COL, 62-, CHMN DEPT MOD LANG, 67- *Concurrent Pos:* Sr Fulbright fel & Int Res & Exchanges Bd grant, sr exchange scholar, Gorky Inst World Lit, 70-71; Am Philos Soc grant res Moscow, 72; vis prof, Slavisches Inst der Univ zu Koln, 79-80. *Mem:* MLA; Am Asn Teachers Slavic & Europ Lang; Am Asn Teachers Ger. *Res:* Modern German drama; Soviet-German literary relations. *Publ:* Auth, Carl Zuckmayer's The Devil's General as Autobiography, Mod Drama, 9, 54-61; Soviet views of Heinrich Böll, Arcadia, Vol 7, No 1; contribr, Brecht and the Soviet theatre: A 1971 overview, Brecht Heute, 72; auth, Der Gesang im Feurofen: Quintessential Zuckmayer, In: Views and Reviews of Modern German Literature, Delp, Munich, 74; Soviet views of modern and contemporary German literature: A 1973 survey, Germano-Slavica, fall 74; DDR-dramatik in der Sowjetunion, Europäische Ideen, No 13, 47-50; coauth, Heinrich Böll in der Sowjetunion, 1952-1976, Erich Schmidt Verlag, Berlin, 80; auth, Major Brecht Productions in the Soviet Union since 1957: Reception and Adaptation, In: Bertolt Brecht: Politcal Theory and Literary Practice, Univ Tex, Austin, 80. *Mailing Add:* Box 36 Manchester Col North Manchester IN 46962

GLADNEY, FRANK Y, b Mt Vernon, NY, Jan 20, 36; m 58; c 3. SLAVIC LANGUAGES. *Educ:* Harvard Univ, AB, 57, AM, 59, PhD(Slavic lang & lit), 66. *Prof Exp:* ASSOC PROF SLAVIC LANG, UNIV ILL, URBANA-CHAMPAIGN, 63- *Concurrent Pos:* Ed newslett, Am Asn Advan Slavic Studies, 66-69; ed, Slavic & EEurop J, 71-75. *Mem:* Am Asn Teachers Slavic & EEurop Lang; Am Asn Advan Slavic Studies; Ling Soc Am. *Res:* Russian and Polish grammar. *Publ:* Ed, 15-year index to Slavic & EEurop J, Am Asn Teachers Slavic & East Europ Lang, 72; auth, On the structure of nouns with prefixes in Russian, Am Contrib to VII Int Congr Slavists, Vol 1: 117-128; Item and process in Russian verbal inflection, In: American Contributions to the VIII International Congress of Slavists, 78. *Mailing Add:* Dept of Slavic Lang & Lit Univ of Ill Urbana-Champaign Urbana IL 61801

GLAETTLE, WALTER ERIC, b Winterthur, Switz, Aug 23, 20; nat US. GERMAN, FRENCH. *Educ:* Univ Geneva, Switz, cert, 42; Univ Zurich, PhD, 49. *Prof Exp:* Teacher French & Ger, Skerry's Col, Scotland, 47; Instr, Univ Akron, 50 & Northwestern Univ, 50-53; from instr to prof, 53-80, EMER PROF LANG, CENTENARY COL, 80- *Mem:* Am Asn Teachers Fr; Swiss-Am Hist Soc. *Res:* German-French relations in 20th century literature. *Publ:* Auth, Der Affekt der Furcht im Roman des 18 Jarhunderts, Juris, Zurich, 49; co-ed, Cultural Graded Readers, auth, Die Vierte Kurve, 63 & coauth, Conversational German Review Grammar, 66, Am Bk Co; auth, Fontane's Stand on Russia, Monatshefte. *Mailing Add:* Centenary Col Hackettstown NJ 07840

GLASGOW, JANIS M, b Wooster, Ohio, Aug 24, 34. FRENCH. *Educ:* Western Reserve Univ, BA, 45; Univ Wis, MA, 58; Univ Calif, Los Angeles, PhD(French), 66. *Prof Exp:* Teaching fel French & Ital, Univ Wis, 57-58; asst, French, Univ Calif, Los Angeles, 58-62; asst prof, 62-68, assoc prof, 68-80, chmn dept French & Ital, 71-73, PROF FRENCH, SAN DIEGO STATE UNIV, 80- *Concurrent Pos:* Exchange prof, Univ Paris VIII, 73-74; vis prof, Univ Nice, spring 82. *Mem:* MLA; Am Asn Teachers Fr; Int Asn Fr Studies; Friends of George Sand. *Res:* George Sand and Balzac; 19th and 20th century French literature; Romain Gary. *Publ:* Auth, Une Esthetique de Comparaison: Balzac et George Sand, La Femme Abandonree et Metella, A G Nizet, Paris, 78; Balzac and George Sand, In: George Sand Papers, Hofstra Univ, 79 & 82. *Mailing Add:* Dept of French & Ital Lang & Lit San Diego State Univ San Diego CA 92182

GLASS, ELLIOT STEVEN, b Los Angeles, Calif, Jan 28, 40; m 72. LATIN AMERICAN & SPANISH LITERATURE. *Educ:* Univ Calif, Los Angeles, BA, 63; Columbia Univ, MA, 67, PhD(Span & Latin Am lit), 72. *Prof Exp:* Instr Span & Latin Am Lit, Keuka Col, 67-68; asst prof, 68-75, ASSOC PROF SPAN & LATIN AM LIT & CHAIRPERSON DEPT FOREIGN LANG & LIT, QUEENSBOROUGH COMMUNITY COL, 75- *Concurrent Pos:* State Univ NY Res Found grant, 73-74; bilingual evaluator, Dist 1, New York Chinese Bilingual Prog, 77-78; mem bd trustees, Doctoral Asn NY Educr Inc, 77- *Mem:* MLA. *Res:* Language and literature of South America; Effectiveness of video in classroom teaching; culture, politics and economics of Mexico. *Publ:* Auth, La actitud de Mariano Azuela e Isaac Babel hacia le Revolucion, Cuadernos Am, 8/74; Mexico en las Obras de Emilio Rabasa, Ed Diana, 75; Dead souls and the Hispanic picarascuq novel, Revista de Estudios Hispanicos, 1/77; coauth, Video tape: A means to develop the bilingual professional in the community college, Perspectives in Bilingual Educ, 77; auth, The four faces of Castile in the poetry of Antonio Muchado, Homenaje al Profesor Andres l duarte, 77; coauth, Video tape in language instruction: Observations on two TV-VT experiments, Bilingual Rev, fall 77; auth, Puerto Rican obituary: Reflections on the poetry of Pedro Pietri, Cross Country, fall 77; Presencia de Garcia Lorca en la poesia de Andrei Vozenesenki, Homenaje a Humberto Pinera, 78. *Mailing Add:* 15 Buckminster Lane Manhasset NY 11030

GLASS, ERLIS, b Philadelphia, Pa, Dec 24, 41; m 61; c 2. GERMANIC LANGUAGES & LITERATURES. *Educ:* Radcliffe Col, BA, 63; Harvard Univ, MA, 64; Bryn Mawr Col, PhD(Ger), 73. *Prof Exp:* Asst prof Ger, 66-76, dir, Continuing Educ, 76-78, ASSOC PROF GER, ROSEMONT COL,

76- *Concurrent Pos:* Chmn, Placement Info Ctr, Am Asn Teachers Ger, 74-76; vis prof, Ursinus Col, 79-81. *Mem:* Am Asn Teachers Ger (treas, 75-77); Northeast Mod Lang Asn. *Res:* Expressionist drama; comparative Romanticism; age of Goethe. *Mailing Add:* Rosemont Col Montgomery Ave Rosemont PA 19010

GLAUSER, ALFRED CHARLES, b St Imier, Switz, Feb 24, 13. FRENCH LITERATURE. *Educ:* La Chaux-de-Fonds Gymnase, BLitt, 32; Univ Geneva, LLitt, 35; Univ Wis, PhD, 47. *Prof Exp:* Teacher French, Inst Perce-Neige, Switz, 36-37, Ravenscourt Sch, Winnipeg, Can, 38-41 & Bishop's Col Sch Lennoxville, 41-43; lectr Univ Man, 43-46; asst prof, 46-60, PROF FRENCH, UNIV WIS-MADISON, 60- *Concurrent Pos:* Dir jr year France, Aix-en-Provence, 68-69; Guggenheim fel, 65-66; Pickard-Bascom Professorship, 81. *Honors & Awards:* Palmes Academiques Award, 59; Steiger Mem Teaching Award, Univ Wis-Madison, 77. *Mem:* MLA; Am Asn Teachers Fr. *Res:* Victor Hugo; Albert Thibaudet; Rabelais. *Publ:* Auth, Thibaudet et la Critique Creatrice, Boivin, Paris, 51; Hugo et la Poesie Pure, Droz, Paris, 57; Rabelais Createur, 66, Le Poeme-Symbole, 67, Montaigne Paradoxal, 72, Le faux Rabelais, De l'inauthenticite du Cinquieme Livre, 74, La Poetique de Hugo, 78 & Fonctions du nombre chez Rabelais, 82, Nizet, Paris. *Mailing Add:* Dept of French & Ital Univ of Wis Madison WI 53706

GLEAVES, ROBERT MILNOR, b Nashville, Tenn, Mar 18, 38; m 64; c 2. SPANISH LANGUAGE, SPANISH AMERICAN LITERATURE. *Educ:* David Lipscomb Col, BA, 60; Vanderbilt Univ, MA, 63, PhD(Span), 68. *Prof Exp:* From instr to asst prof Span, Univ SFla, 65-69; asst prof, 69-72, ASSOC PROF SPAN, UNIV NC, CHARLOTTE, 72- *Mem:* Am Asn Teachers Span & Port; Int Inst Iberoam Lit; SAtlantic Mod Lang Asn. *Res:* Contemporary Spanish-American prose fiction; Spanish-American poetry. *Publ:* Auth, La emancipacion literaria de Mexico, spring-summer 66 & Los pasos perdidos, Pedro Paramo and the classic novel in Spanish America, fall-winter 69, Lang Quart; co-ed, Hispanoamerica magica 6 misteriosa: once relatos, Holt, 73. *Mailing Add:* Dept of Foreign Lang Univ of NC Charlotte NC 28223

GLECKNER, ROBERT FRANCIS, English. See Vol II

GLENDINNING, ROBERT JAMES, b Deloraine, Man, Can, June 23, 31; m 59; c 5. GERMAN LANGUAGE & LITERATURE. *Educ:* Univ Man, BA, 52, MA, 59; Univ Freiburg, PhD(Ger), 70. *Prof Exp:* Lectr, 62-65, asst prof, 65-69, ASSOC PROF GER, UNIV MAN, 69- *Mem:* Can Asn Univ Teachers Ger; Mediaeval Acad Am. *Res:* Old Icelandic and Middle High German literature; Latin middle ages. *Publ:* Auth, Saints, sinners and the age of the Sturlungs: two dreams from Islendinga saga, 66 & Arons saga and Islendinga saga: A problem in parallel transmission, 69, Scand Studies; Grettis saga and European literature in the late Middle Ages, Mosaic, 71; The dreams in Sturla Thordarson's Islendinga Saga and literary consciousness in 13th century Iceland, Arv, 73-74; co-ed, A History of the Old Icelandic Commonwealth, Univ Man, 74; auth, Träume and Vorbedeutung in der Islendinga saga Sturla Thordarsons: Eine Form-und Stiluntersuchung, Lang, 74; The Archetypal Structure of Hymisqvida, Folklore, Vol 91, 80; transl & coauth, Gragas, The Old Icelandic Lawcode, Univ Manitoba Icelancic Studies, Vol 3, 80. *Mailing Add:* Dept of Ger Univ of Man Winnipeg MB R3T 2N2 Can

GLENN, JERRY, b Little Rock, Ark, Sept 5, 38. GERMAN. *Educ:* Yale Univ, BA, 60; Univ Tex, MA, 62, PhD(Ger), 64. *Prof Exp:* Asst prof Ger, Univ Wis-Milwaukee, 64-67; from asst prof to assoc prof, 67-72, dir hon prog, 77-79, PROF GER, UNIV CINCINNATI, 72-, HEAD DEPT, 80- . *Mem:* MLA; Am Asn Teachers Ger; Am Lessing Soc (secy-treas, 68-74); Am Lit Transl Asn; Mid-E Hons Asn (pres, 79-80). *Res:* German lyric, literature and classics. *Publ:* Auth, An introduction to the poetry of Johanees Bobrowski, Ger Rev, 1/66; ed, Lessing Yearbook, Heuber, Munich, Vols I, II, III, V & X, 69, 70, 71, 73 & 78; auth, Deutsches Schrifttum der Gegenwart, Francke, Berne, 71; Paul Celan, Twayne, 73; Nightmares, dreams, and intellectualization in the poetry of Paul Celan, World Lit Today, 77; Paul Celan in Wien, Die Pestsaeule, Loecker & Woegenstein, 77; Blumenworte/Kriegsgestammel: The poetry of Rose Auslaender, Mod Austrian Lit, 79; Arno Reinfrank: Satirist, Holocaust poet, and poet of facts, Colloquia Germanica, 81. *Mailing Add:* Dept of Ger Univ of Cincinnati Cincinnati OH 45221

GLENN, JUSTIN MATTHEWS, b Little Rock, Ark, Apr 10, 45; m 71; c 2. GREEK & LATIN LITERATURE. *Educ:* Stanford Univ, BA, 67; Princeton Univ, MA, 69, PhD(classics), 70. *Prof Exp:* Asst prof Classics, Univ Ga, 70-72; asst prof, 72-76, ASSOC PROF CLASSICS, FLA STATE UNIV, 76- *Mem:* Am Philol Asn; Class Asn Mid W & S. *Res:* Classical mythology; psychoanalytic criticism; Greek and Latin poetry. *Publ:* Auth, Mezentius and Polyphemus, Am J Philol, 71; The Polyphemus folktale, Trans Am Philol Asn, 71; Psychoanalytic writings on Greek and Latin authors, Class World, 72; Virgil's Polyphemus, Greece & Rome, 72; Psychoananlytic writings on classical mythology and religion, Classical World, 76-77. *Mailing Add:* Dept of Classics Fla State Univ Tallahassee FL 32306

GLENN, KATHLEEN MARY, b Exeter, Calif, June 12, 36. SPANISH LITERATURE. *Educ:* Stanford Univ, BA, 57, MA, 61, PhD(Span), 70; Univ Madrid, dipl Hisp studies, 59. *Prof Exp:* Instr, Univ Victoria, 64-66; instr, Col San Mateo, 67-69; asst prof, Univ Santa Clara, 69-73 & Kans State Univ, 73-74; ASSOC PROF SPAN, WAKE FOREST UNIV, 74- *Concurrent Pos:* Assoc ed, Anales de la literatura espanola contemporanea, 76- *Mem:* MLA; Am Asn Teachers Span & Port; S Cent Mod Lang Asn; SAtlantic Mod Lang Asn; Asn Lit Femenina Hisp. *Res:* Twentieth century Spanish novel; 20th century Spanish theater. *Publ:* Auth, The Novelistic Technique of Azorin, Plaza Mayor, 73; The narrators changing perspective in Azorin's Tomas Rueda, Revista de Estudios Hispanicos, 75; Azorin's Salvadora de Olbena: Reality and the artist, Hispanofila, 76; Animal imagery in Nada, Revista de Estudios Hispanicos, 77; Communication in the works of Carmen Martin Gaite, Romance Notes, 79; Point of view and narrative distance in Las confesiones de un pequeno filosofo, In: Perspectivas de la novela, Albatros Ediciones, 79; Azorin, Twayne, 81; El cuarto de atras: Literature as juego and the self-reflexive text, In: From Fiction to Metafiction: Essays in Honor of Carmen Martin Gaite, Soc Span & Span-Am Studies, 82. *Mailing Add:* Dept of Romance Lang Wake Forest Univ Winston-Salem NC 27109

GLENN, RICHARD FOSTER, b Farmville, Va, June 7, 40. ROMANCE LANGUAGES. *Educ:* Hampden-Sydney Col, BA, 62; Duke Univ, PhD(Span drama), 67. *Prof Exp:* Asst prof, Northwestern Univ, Evanston, 67-75; vis asst prof, Colgate Univ, 76-77; ASSOC PROF ROMANCE LANG, UNIV ALA, 77-, CHMN DEPT, 80- *Mem:* MLA; Am Asn Teachers Span & Port; Renaissance Soc Am. *Res:* Sixteenth and 17th century Spanish. *Publ:* Ed, The moral implications of El abencerraje, Mod Lang Notes, 65; The impact of the Spanish pastoral romance on Lope de Vega's dramatic art, Annali, 71; The loss of identity: Towards a definition of the dialectic in Lope's early drama, Hisp Rev, 73; Juan de la Cueva, Twayne, 73; coauth, Castillo Solorzano, Sala de Recreacion, Estud de Hisp, 77. *Mailing Add:* Dept of Romance Lang Univ of Ala University AL 35486

GLENN, ROBERT BRUCE, b Kalamazoo, Mich, July 9, 27; m 50; c 3. LINGUISTICS. *Educ:* Western Mich Univ, AB, 49; Univ Mich, MA, 53, PhD, 61. *Prof Exp:* Asst prof English, State Univ NY Col Cortland, 56-61, assoc prof, 61-62, admin coord, 62-63, assoc dean, 63-66; assoc dean acad affairs, Univ Mich-Flint, 67-71; PROF ENGLISH & DEAN ARTS & SCI, NORTHERN MICH UNIV, 71-, PROVOST, 74- *Concurrent Pos:* Am Coun Educ fel, Fresno State Col, 66-67. *Mem:* Ling Soc Am; NCTE; MLA; Am Asn Higher Educ. *Res:* Applied linguistics; grammatical theory; college administration. *Publ:* Co-ed, Language and Culture, Northern Mich Univ, 74. *Mailing Add:* Northern Mich Univ Marquette MI 49855

GLIER, INGEBORG JOHANNA, b Dresden, Ger, June 22, 34. GERMAN LANGUAGE & LITERATURE. *Educ:* Univ Munich, Dr Phil(Eng, Ger), 58, Habil Ger, 69. *Hon Degrees:* MA, Yale Univ, 73. *Prof Exp:* Asst & lectr Ger, Univ Munich, 58-69, univ docent, 69-73; vis prof, 72-73, PROF GER, YALE UNIV, 73-, CHMN DEPT, 79- *Concurrent Pos:* Vis prof Ger, Univ Cologne, 70-71. *Mem:* MLA; Mediaeval Acad Am; Int Courtly Lit LSoc. *Res:* Medieval European literature; theory of literature; 20th century German literature. *Publ:* Auth, Struktur und Gestaltungsprinzipien in den Dramen John Websters, Straub, Munich, 58; coauth, Deutsche Metrik, Hueber, Munich, 61; auth, Personifikationen im deutschen Fastnachtspiel des Spätmittelalters, Deut Vierteljahresschrift fuer Lit und Geistesgeschichte 39, 65; Der Minneleich im späten 13 Jahrhundert, In: Werk-Typ-Situation, Metzler, Stuttgart, 69; co-ed, Werk-Typ Situation, Metzler, Stuttgart, 69; auth, Artes Amandi, Beck, Munich, 71; Diener zweier Herrinnen Zu Ulrichs von Lichtenstein Frauen dienst, In: The Epic in Medieval Society, Niemeyer, Tübingen, 77; co-ed, Deutsche Dichtung des Mittelalters (3 volumes), Hanser, München, 81. *Mailing Add:* Dept of Ger Lang Yale Univ New Haven CT 06520

GLOECKNER, NYDIA RIVERA, b Caguas, PR, Nov 12, 36; m 64; c 1. SPANISH MEDIEVAL LITERATURE, PHILOLOGY. *Educ:* Hunter Col, AB, 59; Pa State Univ, MA, 61, PhD(Span), 71. *Prof Exp:* Grad asst Span, Pa State Univ, 59-62, instr, 63-64; teacher, West Orange High Sch, 64-67; ASSOC PROF SPAN LANG & LIT, RIDER COL, 72- *Concurrent Pos:* Co-dir summer workshop, West Orange Sch Syst, 65-; state interviewer for candidates bilingual certification; Nat Endowment for Humanities fel, 79. *Mem:* MLA; Am Asn Teachers Span & Port; AAUP. *Res:* Transcription of unpublished manuscript found in Biblioteca Nacional in Madrid; evidence of the Marian cult in medieval Spanish literature of the Middle Ages. *Publ:* Coauth, Teacher's Manual for the Spanish Program in West Orange Public Schools, West Orange, 66. *Mailing Add:* Dept Foreign Lang & Lit Rider Col Lawrenceville NJ 08648

GLOWKA, ARTHUR WAYNE, Medieval Literature, English Linguistics. See Vol II

GOBERT, DAVID LAWRENCE, b Decatur, Ill, Oct 18, 32; m 56; c 5. FRENCH LANGUAGE & LITERATURE. *Educ:* Millikin Univ, BA, 54; State Univ Iowa, MA, 56, PhD(Fr), 60. *Prof Exp:* Asst prof French & Span, Coe Col, 58-61, assoc prof French, 62-65, actg chmn dept foreign lang, 64-65; assoc prof, 65-70, asst dean, col lib arts & sci, 68-70, assoc dean humanities, 71-74, PROF FRENCH, SOUTHERN ILL UNIV, 71- *Concurrent Pos:* Admin intern, Am Coun Educ, Syracuse Univ, 69-70; French reader, Educ Testing Serv, 77-78. *Mem:* Am Asn Teachers Fr. *Res:* Eighteenth century French literature; French novel; applied French linguistics. *Publ:* Auth, Tense variation in complex hypothetical utterances in contemporary French speech, Iowa Philol Quart, 4/66; Des reflects du beylisme dans la structure episodique du Rouge, Fr Rev, 2/70; ed, Problems of Description and Values in Humanistic Studies, Univ Graphics & Publ, Southern Ill Univ, 71; auth, Merimee revisited, Symposium, spring 72. *Mailing Add:* Dept of Foreign Lang Faner Hall Southern Ill Univ Carbondale IL 62901

GOCHBERG, HERBERT S, b New York, NY, Feb 28, 28; m; c 4. FRENCH. *Educ:* City Col New York, AM, 49; Brown Univ, AB, 51, PhD(Romance lang), 56. *Prof Exp:* Instr French, Brown Univ, 54-56; instr Romance lang, Northwestern Univ, 56-58; asst prof French, Univ Chicago, 58-64; assoc prof, Univ Nebr, 64-65; from assoc prof to prof, Univ Wis-Madison, 65-77; head dept, 77-81, PROF ROMANCE LANG, UNIV NC, GREENSBORO, 77- *Concurrent Pos:* Andrew Mellon fel, Univ Pittsburgh, 62-63; Am Coun Learned Soc study fel, 68-69. *Mem:* MLA; Am Asn Teachers Fr. *Res:* French literature since 1650; French film, poetry and drama. *Publ:* Co-ed, Worldwide French-English Dictionary, Follett, 60; auth, Stage of Dreams, The Dramatic Art of Alfred de Musset, Droz, Geneva, 67; co-ed, Pensee et Litterature Francaises: Anthology, McGraw, 72; auth, Looking out (poems), Dettmann, 74. *Mailing Add:* Dept of Romance Lang Univ of NC Greensboro NC 27412

GODDARD, R H IVES, III, b Providence, RI, June 12, 41. LINGUISTICS, ETHNOHISTORY. *Educ:* Harvard Univ, AB, 63, PhD(ling), 69. *Prof Exp:* Vis res assoc anthrop, Smithsonian Inst, 69-70; vis lectr ling, 70-72, from asst prof to assoc prof, Harvard Univ, 72-76, assoc cur, 76-79, CUR ANTHROP, SMITHSONIAN INST, 79- *Concurrent Pos:* Ling ed, Handbk N Am Indians, 70- *Mem:* Ling Soc Am; Am Anthrop Asn; Am Soc Ethnohist; Ling Soc Paris; Am Ethnol Soc. *Res:* Algonquian linguistics; ethnohistory of North America; Algonquian ethnography. *Publ:* Auth, Algonquian Independent

Indicative, Bull 214, Nat Mus Can, 67; Philological approaches to the study of native North American languages: Documents and documentation, In: Current trends in linguistics, Vol 10, Ling N Am, 73; Historical and philological evidence regarding the identification of the Mascouten, Ethnohistory, Vol 19, No 2; auth, 4 chap & coauth, 1 chap, In: Northeast, Handbook North American Indians Vol 15, Smithsonian Inst, 78; auth, Delaware Verbal Morphology, Garland Press, 79; coauth, Territorial groups of west-central Alaska before 1898, In: Subarctic, Handbook of North American Indians, Vol 6, Smithsonian Inst, 81; auth, The historical phonology of Munsee, Int J Am Ling, Vol 48, No 1. *Mailing Add:* NHB Stop 100 Smithsonian Inst Washington DC 20560

GODDARD, WESLEY (RAWDON), b St Louis, Mo, July 29, 15; m 46; c 3. FRENCH. *Educ:* Swarthmore Col, AB, 37; Univ Calif, MA, 39; Univ Paris, DUniv, 50. *Prof Exp:* Instr English, 39-46, chmn dept foreign lang, 58-69, 75-77, from asst prof to assoc prof, 46-80, PROF MOD LANG, SAN JOSE STATE UNIV, 80- *Concurrent Pos:* Resident dir for France, Calif State Univs Int Progs, 64-65, resident dir for Italy, 69-71. *Mem:* MLA. *Publ:* Coauth, Preface to Compostion, Harper, 48; translr & ed, Racine: Phaedra, Chandler, 62. *Mailing Add:* Dept of Foreign Lang San Jose State Univ San Jose CA 95192

GODFREY, AARON W, b New York, NY, Jan 10, 29; wid 76, m 81; c 7. CLASSICS. *Educ:* Fordham Univ, BA, 58; Hunter Col, MA, 60. *Prof Exp:* Asst Latin-Am rels, Grace Nat Bank, 52-60; instr lang, Newton Col Sacred Heart, 60-61, asst prof hist & class lang, 61-65; dir spec proj, 65-74, DIR UPWARD BOUND PROJ, STATE UNIV NY STONY BROOK, 66-, LECTR CLASSICS, 67- *Concurrent Pos:* Consult, State Educ Dept NY, 67-73; secy-treas, Nat Coord Coun Educ Opportunity, 70-, ed, Review; consult, ESEA Title I, New York Schs, 70-72. *Mem:* AHA; Medieval Acad Am; Liturgical Arts Soc; Class Asn Atlantic States; Asn Equality & Excellence Educ (secy, 77-). *Res:* Ancient and medieval history; compensatory education; classical and medieval Latin. *Publ:* Auth, The Faculty as Enemy, America, 71; Teaching ancient history: A question of relevance, AHA Occasional Paper, 74; Henry Adams revisited, Stained Glass, winter 75; auth various articles in Newsday, NY Times, Liturgy, Stained Glass Quart & Hist Teacher. *Mailing Add:* Thompson Hill Rd St James NY 11780

GODFREY, ROBERT G, b Lexington, Ky, Dec 5, 14; m 57; c 1. LINGUISTICS. *Educ:* Univ Ky, AB, 39, MA, 41, PhD, 56. *Prof Exp:* Asst English, Univ Ky, 39-41, instr, 46-54; instr, SDak State Col, 54-56; from asst prof to prof ling, 56-77, prof, 77-80, EMER PROF ENGLISH, UNIV WYO, 80- *Concurrent Pos:* Huntington Libr grant-in-aid, 65. *Res:* Medieval Latin; Melayo-Polynesian language. *Publ:* Auth, The language theory of Thomas of Erfurt, Studies Philol, 1/60; Late mediaeval linguistic theory and Chomsky' snytactic structures, Word, 8/65; A medieval controversy concerning the nature of a general grammar, Gen Ling, 5/68. *Mailing Add:* Dept of English Univ of Wyo Laramie WY 82070

GODIN, JEAN CLEO, b Petit-Rocher, NB, Aug 13, 36; Can citizen; m 63; c 4. FRENCH & QUEBEC LITERATURE. *Educ:* Boston Col, BA, 61; Univ Montreal, Lic es Lett, 64; Aix-Marseille, D Univ, 66. *Prof Exp:* Chmn dept French studies, 74-77, PROF LIT, UNIV MONTREAL, 66- *Concurrent Pos:* Mem jury Coun Arts, Gov Gen Prize, 71-73. *Mem:* Asn Can Univ Teachers Fr; MLA; Can Lit Asn; Asn Can Theatre Hist. *Res:* French novel of the 19th and 20th centuries; theatre Quebecois. *Publ:* Coauth, Le theatre quebecois, introduction a dix framaturges contemporains, HMH, Montreal, 70; Rebirth in the word, Yale Fr Studies, 11/70; Roch Carrier: une terre entre deux ou trois, soleils, In: Livres et Auteurs Quebecois, 71; Henri Bosco, surrealiste?, Cahiers de l'amitie Henri Bosco, 11/74; Le recif: recit, discours et explorations, In: Le Reel et l'imaginaire dans l'oeuvre de Henri Bosco, Actes du Colloque, 75 & Jose Corti, Paris, 76; Lesgaietes montrealaises: Sketches, revues, Etudes Francaises, 4/79; Theatre quebecois II, HMH, Montreal, 80. *Mailing Add:* Dept of French Studies Univ of Montreal CP 6128 Montreal PQ H3C 3J7 Can

GODOY, GUSTAVO J, b Havana, Cuba, Jan 29, 18; m 42, 53; c 1. SPANISH, FRENCH. *Educ:* Univ Havana, Dr Laws, 41; Univ Miami, PhD(Span), 67. *Prof Exp:* Lectr Span & French, Univ Miami, 62-66; from asst prof to assoc prof, 66-76, PROF SPANISH & FRENCH, JACKSONVILLE UNIV, 76- *Concurrent Pos:* Vis prof, Towson State Univ, Baltimore, summer, 81. *Honors & Awards:* Cuban Nat Prize for grad attorneys, 41; Knight Comdr, Cuban Order of Agr & Indust Merit, 56. *Mem:* MLA; Am Asn Teachers Span & Port; SAtlantic Mod Lang Asn; AAUP. *Res:* Spanish, Spanish-American and French poetry. *Publ:* Auth, Fernando Ortiz, las razas y los negros, J InterAm Studies, 4/66; Dos martires de la fe segun Dostoyewski y Unamuno, Cuadernos de la catedra Miguel de Unamuno, 4/70; Algunos antecedentes en el romanticismo frances de la leyenda de Becquer Las hojas secas, Romance Notes, autumn 70; Becquer en Unamuno, Duquesne Hisp Rev, winter70; A Cuban patriot in Jacksonville politics: Jose Alejandro Huau, Fla Hist Quart, Oct 75; En el cincuentario de Jose Manuel Poveda, poeta ancestral, In: Homenaje a Lydia Cabrera, Ediciones Universal, 78; Jose Martin Jacksonville, autumn 78 & Agustin Acosta o la fidelidad ontologica, autumn 82, Circulo Revista de Cultura. *Mailing Add:* Box 46 Jacksonville Univ Jacksonville FL 32211

GODZICH, WLADYSLAW B, b Germany, May 13, 45; US citizen; m 69; c 2. COMPARATIVE LITERATURE, SEMIOTICS. *Educ:* Columbia Univ MA, 67, PhD(comp lit), 72. *Prof Exp:* Asst prof French, Columbia Univ, 72-73; asst prof French & lit, Yale Univ, 73-78; ASSOC PROF COMP LIT & DIR, UNIV MINN, 78- *Concurrent Pos:* Co-ed, Semiotexta, 74-76; vis assoc prof, Univ Silesia, Poland, 76-77; dir, Minn Ctr for Advan Studies in Lang Style & Libr Theory, 79-81; dir, Off Res Develop, Col Liberal Arts, 80-81; co-ed, Glyph, 80- & series, Theory & Hist of Lit, Univ Minn Press, 81- *Honors & Awards:* Justin O'Brien Prize, Columbia Univ, 72. *Mem:* Int Asn Semiotics Studies; Midwest Mod Lan Asn; MLA; Soc Critical Exchange; Soc Roncesvalles. *Res:* Literary theory; contemporary criticism; semiotics. *Publ:* Auth, Noun proper: Language/Texte, Recherches, 74; Semiotics: The texture of a weaving song, Semiotexte, 75; The construction of meaning, New Lit Hist, 78; Harold Bloom as rhetorician, Centrum, 78; Construction Poetique Chez Rouge Heidegger, Am Muses and Philosophers, 79; De l'oeil a l'oreille: d'alleyorie chez Philonician, In: L'Archeologie du Signe, Pontif Inst Toronto, 82; co-ed, Deconstruction in America: The Yale Critics,Uinv Minn Press, 82. *Mailing Add:* 300 Folwell Hall Univ Minn 9 Pleasant St SE Minneapolis MN 55455

GOEDICKE, HANS, b Vienna, Austria, Aug 7, 26. EGYPTOLOGY. *Educ:* Univ Vienna, PhD, 49. *Prof Exp:* Res Assoc Egyptol, Brown Univ, 52-56; lectr, 60-62, from asst prof to assoc prof, 62-68, prof, 68-79, CHMN NEAR EASTERN STUDIES, JOHNS HOPKINS UNIV, 79- *Concurrent Pos:* Howard fel, 56-57; tech asst, UNESCO-Centre doc l'ancienne Egypte, Cairo, 57-58; asst, Univ Göttingen, 58-60; Am Philos Soc grant, 66; John Simon Guggenheim Mem fel, 66-67; mem, Am Res Ctr Egypt; dir archaeol exped, Giza, Egypt, 72 & 74 & Tell el Rataba, 77, 78 & 81; corresp mem, Ger Archaeol Inst, 74. *Mem:* Egypt Explor Soc, London. *Res:* Egyptian historical and administrative inscriptions. *Publ:* Auth, Die Stellung des Konigliche Dokumente aus dem Alten Reich, 67, Otto Harrassowitz, Ger; Privatrechtliche Inschriften aus dem Alten Reich, Notring, 68; The report about the dispute of a man with his ba, 70; Near Eastern Studies in Honor of William Foxwell Albright, 71 & Nofretari, 71, Graz; Re-used blocks from List, Metrop Mus Art, 71; The Protocal of Neferyt, Baltimore, 76; Die Geschichte des Schiffbrüchijen, Harrassowitz, 74. *Mailing Add:* Dept of Near Eastern Studies Johns Hopkins Univ Baltimore MD 21218

GOERTZ, RICHARD O W, Spanish & Portuguese Literature. See Vol I

GOETCHIUS, EUGENE VAN NESS, b Augusta, Ga, Mar 26, 21; m 55; c 4. BIBLICAL LANGUAGES, NEW TESTAMENT PHILOLOGY. *Educ:* Univ Va, BA, 41, MS, 47, MA, 48, PhD(Ger lang), 49; Episcopal Divinity Sch, BD, 52; Union Theol Sem, ThD(Bibl Greek), 63. *Prof Exp:* Master Ger & math, Woodberry Forest Sch, 47-49; instr math, Tufts Univ, 50-52; instr relig, Trinity Col, 52-54; fel & tutor, Gen Theol Sem, 54-56; head dept math, Am Acad Athens, Greece, 56-57; from asst prof to assoc prof New Testament, 57-63, PROF BIBL LANG, ESPISCOPAL DIVINITY SCH, 63-, PROF NEW TESTAMENT, 78- *Concurrent Pos:* Am Coun Learned Soc Study grants, Ling Inst, 41 & 59; lectr Hellenistic Greek, Harvard Univ, 57-58 & 70-; Am Asn Theol Schs study grant, Univ Zürich, 64-65; vis scholar, Mansfield Col, Oxford Univ, 70-71. *Mem:* Soc New Testament Study; Int Orgn for Septuagint & Cognate Studies. *Res:* Pauline epistles; Biblical languages and linguistics; methods of teaching languages, especially ancient languages. *Publ:* Auth, Jesus, In: Viewpoints, Seabury, 59; Language of Christ, In: Hastings Dictionary of the Bible, Scribner, 63; The Language of the New Testament, Scribner, 64; Postis Iesou Christou, Lux in Lumine, 66; coauth, Teaching the Biblical Languages, Am Asn Theol Schs, 67; translr, O Kaiser & W Kümmel, Exegetical Method, Seabury, 67. *Mailing Add:* Dept of Bibl Lang Episcopal Divinity Sch Cambridge MA 02138

GOETZ, THOMAS HENRY, b Philadelphia, Pa, Feb 9, 36; m 70; c 1. FRENCH LITERATURE. *Educ:* La Salle Col, BA, 61; Syracuse Univ, MA, 63, PhD(humanities), 67. *Prof Exp:* Asst prof French, Ill Wesleyan Univ, 66-67; asst prof, 67-74, assoc prof, 74-78, PROF FRENCH, STATE UNIV NY COL FREDONIA, 78-, CHMN, DEPT FOREIGN LANG & LIT, 79- *Concurrent Pos:* Ed, Nineteenth-Century Fr Studies, 72-; Nat Endowment for Humanities fel, 77 & 79; consult, La Bd Regents, 82. *Honors & Awards:* Chevalier, Ordre des Palmes Academiques, 81. *Mem:* MLA; Am Asn Teachers Fr; Soc Etudes Romantiques; Asn de l'Ordre des Palmes Academiques; Am Soc de l'Ordre des Palmes Academiques. *Res:* Nineteenth-century French literature; Hippolyte Taine. *Publ:* Auth, Taine and the Fine Arts, Ed Playor, 73; Poetry and civilization: An essay on the humanities and the human condition, In: Studies in the Humanities, Indiana Univ, Pa, 6/73; A partially unpublished Taine letter, Romance Notes, 73; Poe and Taine: A neglected French critic, Poe Studies, 73; transl, The Defeat of the armouchiquois Savages, Nat Museum of Man Mercury Ser, Can, 75; Paul Bourget's Le Disciple and the Text-Reader Relationship, Fr Rev, 78. *Mailing Add:* State Univ of New York Col Fredonia NY 14063

GOETZ-STANKIEWICZ, MARKETA, b Liberec, Czech; Can citizen; m 65. GERMAN & COMPARATIVE LITERATURE. *Educ:* Univ Toronto, BA, 54, MA, 55, PhD(Ger & comp lit), 57. *Prof Exp:* From instr to asst prof, 57-65, assoc prof, 65-81, PROF GER STUDIES, UNIV BC, 81-, HEAD GER STUDIES, 81- *Concurrent Pos:* Can Coun fel, 63-64, leave fel, 73-74. *Mem:* Can Asn Univ Teachers Comp Lit; Can Asn Univ Teachers Ger; Am Asn Teachers Slavic Studies. *Res:* Contemporary drama; comparative literature, theory, translation. *Publ:* Co--ed & contribr, Essays in German Literature, Univ Toronto, 68; Der Schneider und der Feger-zwei Grundgestalten bei Wilhelm Raabe, Jahrbuch der Raabe-Ges, 72; The theatre of the absurd in Czechoslovakia, Survey, 75; Pavel Kohout-the Barometer of Czechoslovak Theatre, Mod Drama, 77; The Silenced Theatre--Czech Playwrights without a Stage, Univ Toronto, 78; ed, Special issue of Canadian Review of Comparative Literature, 80; Slawomir Mrozek--the moulding of a Polish playwright, The Temper of Polish Ideals, 81; VacLau Havel: A writer for today's season, World Lit Today, 81. *Mailing Add:* Dept of Ger Studies Univ of BC Vancouver BC V6T 1W5 Can

GOFF, PENRITH BRIEN, b Warren, Pa, Jan 8, 30; m 62. GERMAN LITERATURE. *Educ:* Univ Ky, BA, 53; Univ Calif, Los Angeles, MA, 56, PhD, 61. *Prof Exp:* Instr Ger, Pomona Col, 58-60; from instr to asst prof, Univ Chicago, 60-64; asst prof, Univ Ky, 65-68; assoc prof, 68-72, PROF GER, WAYNE STATE UNIV, 72- *Mem:* Am Asn Teachers Ger; Hugo von Hofmannsthal Ges. *Res:* Early 20th century German literature. *Publ:* Auth, Wilhelminisches Zeitalter, Francke, Bern & Munich, 70; Hugo von Hofmannsthal and W Pater, Comp Lit Studies, 70; Impressionism and expressionism, In: The Challenge of German Literature, Wayne State Univ, 71. *Mailing Add:* Dept of Romance & Ger Lang Wayne State Univ Detroit MI 48202

GOHEEN, JUTTA, b Zwickau, Ger, June 29, 35; m 65. GERMAN. *Educ:* Pädagogische Hochsch Potsdam, Staatsexamen, 56, PhD(Ger), 57; Univ Bonn, Staatsexamen(English), 61. *Prof Exp:* Asst Ger, Pädagogische Hochsch Potsdam, 56-58; lectr, McMaster Univ, 63-64, asst prof, 64-65; asst prof, 65-68, assoc prof, 68-81, PROF GER, CARLETON UNIV, 81- *Res:* Medieval literature: linguistic stylistics; language as means of manipulation. *Publ:* Auth, Tempus und Zeitbegriff in R M Rilkes Aufzeichnungen des Malte Laurids Brigge, Wirkendes Wort, 69; Natur-und Menschenbild in der Lyrik Neidharts, Beiträge zur Geschichte der deutschen Sprache u Lit, 73; Ulrich von Lichensteins Frauendienst, maere und liet, Amsterdamer Beiträge zur Alteren Germanistik, 73; Oswald von Wolkenstein zwischen Mittelalter und Renaissance, 75, Walthers von der Vogelweide gnomisches Lied von Traumglück, 77, Hugos von Montfort Version vom Paradies auf Erden, 79 & Erinnerung als Geste der Lyrik: Das Prateritum im mhd Lied und Spruch, 80, Carleton Ger Papers; Die Rolle der Frau in der deutschen Literatur und Sprache, Jb f Int Germanistik, 81. *Mailing Add:* Dept of Ger Carleton Univ Ottawa ON K1S 5B6 Can

GOIC, CEDOMIL, b Antofagasta, Chile, Mar 3, 28; m 56; c 5. SPANISH AMERICAN & CHILEAN LITERATURE. *Educ:* Univ Chile, Santiago, Profesor de Estado, 53, Dr en Filos(Romance philol), 65. *Prof Exp:* Prof, Dept Span, Univ Chile, 55-76; PROF SPAN AM LIT, DEPT ROMANCE LANG, UNIV MICH, 76- *Concurrent Pos:* Vis prof Span Am lit, Dept Romance Lang, Univ Tex, Austin, 65-67 & Dept Span & Port, Univ Wis, 67-68; res evaluator humanities, Nat Comn Sci Invest, 71 & Cath Univ Chile, 75. *Mem:* Int Inst Iberoam Lit; MLA; Asoc Int Hispanistas. *Res:* Spanish American novel; Spanish American poetry; Spanish American colonial literature. *Publ:* Auth, Historia de la novela hispanoamericana, 72 & co-ed, La novela hispanoamericana, 73, Ed Univ Valparaiso; auth, L'Antipoesie, Etudes Litteraires, 73; ed, Manuel Rojas, Lanchas en la bahia, Ed Zig-Zag, Santiago, 74; Vincente Huidobro, Altazor, Ed Univ Valparaiso, 74; auth, La periodisation dans l'histoire litteraire, Etudes Litteraires, 75; El surrealismo y la literatura iberoamericana, Rev Chilena Lit, 77; El emblema de Amor Tirano en Gabriela Mistral, Mapocho, 77. *Mailing Add:* Dept of Romance Lang Univ of Mich Ann Arbor MI 48109

GOLAB, ZBIGNIEW, b Nowy Targ, Poland, Mar 16, 23; m 47; c 1. SLAVIC LINGUISTICS. *Educ:* Wroclaw Univ, MA, 47; Jagiellonian Univ, PhD(Slavic ling), 58. *Prof Exp:* Adj asst prof Slavic ling, Slavic Inst, Polish Acad Arts & Sci, 55-61; assoc prof, 61-67, PROF SLAVIC LING, UNIV CHICAGO, 67- *Concurrent Pos:* Yugoslav Comt Cult Exchange with Foreign Countries studies fel, 58; Fulbright-Hays res fel, Yugoslavia, 68. *Mem:* Am Asn Teachers Slavic & East Europ Lang; Polish Inst Arts & Sci Am; Macedonian Acad Arts & Sci, Skopje, Yugoslavia. *Res:* Comparative Slavic linguistics; Slavic-Balkan linguistics; Polish syntax. *Publ:* Auth, Conditionalis typu balkanskiego w jezykach poludniowoslowianskich, Polish Acad Arts & Sci, 64; Proba klasyfikacji syntaktycznej czasownikow polskich (Syntactic classification of Polish verbs), Bull Soc Polonaise Ling, 67; The grammar of Slavic causatives, Am Contrib VI Int Congr Slavists, 68; Etnogenezata na Slovenite, Vols I & II, Makedonski Jazik, 68 & 69; coauth, Slownik terminologii jezykoznawczej, Panstwowe Wydawnictwo Naukowe, Warsaw, 68; auth, Subject as a linguistic category, Gen Ling, 69; Za mehanizmot na slovensko-romanskite odnosi na Balkanskiot Poluostrov, Makedonski Jazik, 70; Endocentricity and endocentrization of verbal predicates, Gen Ling, 75. *Mailing Add:* Dept Slavic Univ of Chicago 1130 E 59th St Chicago IL 60637

GOLD, BARBARA KIRK, b Brooklyn, NY, Mar 23, 45; m 67; c 1. CLASSICS. *Educ:* Univ Mich, BA, 66; Univ NC, MA, 68, PhD(classics), 75. *Prof Exp:* Lectr & asst prof, Univ Calif, Irvine, 71-76; asst prof, Univ Richmond, 76-77 & Univ Va, 77-78; ASST PROF CLASSICS, UNIV TEX, 78- *Concurrent Pos:* Andrew Mellon fel, 80. *Mem:* Am Philol Asn; Classics Asn Midwest & South; Philol Asn of Pac Coast; Am Inst Archaeol. *Res:* Latin poetry; Greek poetry; comparative literature. *Publ:* Coauth, The addressees in Horace's first book of Epistles, Studies Philol, 70; Martial: Knight, publisher, poet, Class J, 70; Auth, Eukosmia in Euripides' Bacchae, Am J Philol, 77; A question of genre: Plato's symposium as novel, MLN, 95: 1353-59; Labyrinths in Borges' House of Asterion, Helios, 8: 49-59; Propertius 39: Maecenas asques, dux, fautor, In: Literary & Artistic Patronage in Ancient Rome, 82 & ed, Literary & Artistic Patronage in Ancient Rome, 82, Univ Tex Press. *Mailing Add:* Dept of Classics Univ Tex Waggener Hall Austin TX 78712

GOLDBERG, HARRIET ALICE, b New York, NY, May 26, 26; m 45; c 4. MEDIEVAL SPANISH LITERATURE, HISTORY OF LANGUAGE. *Educ:* City Col New York, BBA, 48; Villanova Univ, MA, 68; Univ Pa, PhD(Romance lang), 71. *Prof Exp:* Asst prof, 69-76, assoc prof, 76-79, PROF SPAN, VILLANOVA UNIV, 80- *Mem:* MLA; Northeast Mod Lang Asn; Am Asn Teachers Span & Port. *Res:* Medieval didactic prose; advices to princes; pro-feminism/anti-feminism controversy in Spain; Folklore and literature. *Publ:* Ed, Jardin de nobles donzellas, Fray Martin de Cordoba: A critical edition and study, In: Studies in the Romance Languages and Literature, Univ NC, 74; Moslem and Spanish Christian literary portraiture, Hisp Rev, 77; Fifteenth century Castilian versions of Boccaccio's Fortune-Poverty Contest, Hispania, 78; Antifeminism and antisemitism in medieval Castilian literature, In: Aspects of Medieval Judaism, State Univ NY, 78; The several faces of ugliness, 79 &; The voice of the author in Berceo, the Poema de Fernan Gonzalez and the Libro de Alexandre, 80, Cor; The literary portrait of the child, KRQ, 81. *Mailing Add:* Dept of Mod Lang & Lit Villanova Univ Lancaster Pike Villanova PA 19085

GOLDBERG, MAXWELL HENRY, b Malden, Mass, Oct 22, 07. MODERN PHILOLOGY. *Educ:* Univ Mass, BS, 28: Yale Univ, AM, 32, PhD, 33. *Prof Exp:* Instr English, 28-30 & 33-34, from asst prof to prof, 34-62, EMER COMMONWEALTH PROF HUMANITIES, UNIV MASS, 62-; EMER PROF HUMANITIES & ENGLISH, PA STATE UNIV, 72-; EMER HELMUS DISTINGUISHED PROF HUMANTIES & LIT, CONVERSE COL, 77- *Concurrent Pos:* Ed, Col English Asn, 50-59, exec dir, 80; Fund Adult Educ fel, 56-57; pres humanities ctr, Lib Educ, Inc, 62-71; assoc dir ctr continuing lib educ, Pa State Univ, 62-72; lectr, Oak Ridge Assoc Univs, 65; mem adv comt technol change & soc, Nat Coun Churches, 65-67; Danforth vis lectr, 68-72; consult, Pub Broadcasting Corp, 72, Nat Endowment for Humanities Col Prog, 72 & Dept Health, Educ & Welfare Prof, 73; educ dir, Wildacres Retreat, 78. *Mem:* MLA; Col English Asn; NCTE. *Res:* Thomas Carlyle and technological change; images of man, telicism and humanities teaching; humanities, technological change and futuristics. *Publ:* Auth, Unity of knowledge, In: The University Today, UNESCO, 60; The humanities, critical issues, and the quest for wholeness, In: Critical Issues and Decisions, USDA Grad Sch, 62; auth & ed, Blindness Research: The Expanding Frontiers, Pa State Univ, 69; auth, Design in Liberal Learning, Jossey-Bass, 71; Thomas Carlyle's Relationships to the Edinburgh Review, Univ Microfilms, 71; Cybernation, systems, and the teaching of English: The dilemma of control, NCTE, 72; The reticulum as epochal image for the technetronic age, In: Yearbook of Comparative Criticism, Pa State Univ, 73; Tocqueville's Futurism, Univ SC, 81. *Mailing Add:* 1865 Fernwood Glendale Rd Spartanburg SC 29302

GOLDBERG, NATHAN, b New York, NY, Apr 13, 24; m 52; c 4. HEBREW LANGUAGE & LITERATURE. *Educ:* Brooklyn Col, BA, 44; Columbia Univ, MA, 47, PhD(Semitic lang), 61; Jewish Theol Sem Am, MHL, 48. *Prof Exp:* Lectr class lang, 48-56, lectr mod lang, 56-62, from instr to asst prof Hebrew, 62-73, ASSOC PROF HEBREW, BROOKLYN COL, 73- *Mem:* Assoc mem Am Sch Orient Res; Nat Asn Prof Hebrew; Am Acad Jewish Res. *Res:* Comparative Semitic linguistics; Biblical literature and history; modern Hebrew literature. *Publ:* Auth, The New Functional Hebrew-English, English-Hebrew Dictionary, 58, The New Illustrated Hebrew-English Dictionary for Young Readers, 58, contrib ed, A New Concise Jewish Encyclopedia, 62 & auth, The Passover Haggadah, 64, KTAV. *Mailing Add:* Dept of Mod Lang & Lit Brooklyn Col Brooklyn NY 11210

GOLDBERG, RITA MARIA, b New York, NY, Oct 1, 33. SPANISH. *Educ:* Queens Col, NY, BA, 54; Middlebury Col, MA, 55; Brown Univ, PhD(Span), 68. *Prof Exp:* Lectr Span, Queens Col, NY, 56-57; from asst prof to prof, 57-71, Harriet Lewis prof mod lang, 71-75, chmn dept, 72-75, CHARLES A DANA PROF MOD LANG & LIT, ST LAWRENCE UNIV, 75- *Concurrent Pos:* Danforth Found grants, 60-61 & 63-64; Assoc Newman Alumni, NY fel, 63; chmn Regional Conf Am Prog in Spain, 71-72, 75-76 & 79-81. *Mem:* MLA; Am Asn Teachers Span & Port; AAUP. *Res:* Romance; 17th century poetry and music; modern novel and theatre. *Publ:* Auth, Una nueva version manuscrita del romance de Lope De pechos sobre uan torre, Hisp Rev, 67; Un modo de subsistencia del romancero nuevo: romances de Gongora y Lope de Vega en bailes del Siglo de Oro, Bull Hisp, 70; Don Fernando Cortes, III Marques de Valle: su boda con dona Mencia de la Cerda y el inventario de bienes de 1602, 70 & Mas datos sobre Don Pedro Cortes, IV Marques del Valle de Oaxaca, 71, Bull Nat Arch Gen, Mex; La Familia de Calderon y la Calle de la Nao o Henao, ABC, Madrid, 9/74; The Impossible Dream of Integration, In: Fornells and Cynthia: Ruiz-Fornells; The United States and the Spanish World, SGEL, Madrid, 79. *Mailing Add:* Dept of Mod Lang & Lit St Lawrence Univ Canton NY 13617

GOLDBERGER, AVRIEL H, b Philadelphia, Pa, Feb 23, 28; m 50; c 2. FRENCH LITERATURE. *Educ:* Univ Pa, BA, 49; Bryn Mawr Col, MA, 51, PhD, 60. *Prof Exp:* Instr French & Span, 60-64, from asst prof to assoc prof French, 64-77, chmn dept, 69-74, assoc provost, Undergrad Educ/Fac Personnel, 74-76, PROF FRENCH, HOFSTRA UNIV, 77- *Mem:* MLA; Am Asn Teachers Fr; Malraux Soc. *Res:* Twentieth century French novel. *Publ:* Auth, Visions of a New Hero, Jean Minard, 65: Andre Malraux's antimemoires, Hofstra Rev, 70. *Mailing Add:* Dept of French Hofstr Univ Hempstead NY 11550

GOLDBLATT, HOWARD CHARLES, b Long Beach, Calif, Feb 21, 39; m 66; c 2. CHINESE LITERATURE & LANGUAGE. *Educ:* Long Beach State Col, BA, 61; San Francisco State Univ, MA, 70; Ind Univ, PhD(EAsian lang), 74. *Prof Exp:* ASST PROF CHINESE, SAN FRANCISCO STATE UNIV, 74- *Mem:* Asn Asian Studies; Chinese Lang Teachers Asn. *Res:* Modern Chinese literature; Taiwan literature. *Publ:* Auth, Hsiao Hung, Twayne, 76. *Mailing Add:* Chinese Prog San Francisco State Univ San Francisco CA 94132

GOLDEN, HERBERT HERSHEL, b Boston, Mass, Nov 1, 19; m 43; c 3. ROMANCE LANGUAGES & LITERATURES. *Educ:* Boston Univ, AB, 41, AM, 42; Harvard Univ, AM, 47, PhD(Romance lang), 51. *Prof Exp:* From lectr to assoc prof, 46-63, PROF ROMANCE LANG, COL LIB ARTS, BOSTON UNIV, 63- *Concurrent Pos:* Asst managing ed, Mod Lang J, 55-59; chmn Ital listening comprehension test, classroom testing proj, MLA, 60-63; Fulbright lectr, Univ Rome, 62-63. *Honors & Awards:* Medaglia d'Oro, Ital govt, 61; Dipl di Benemerenza, Assoc Int Studies Lingua & Lit Ital, 73. *Mem:* Am Asn Teachers Ital (secy-treas, 59-64, pres, 64-66); MLA; Am Asn Teachers Fr; Mod Humanities Res Asn; Am Coun Teaching Foreign Lang. *Res:* Eighteenth century French literature and history of ideas; teaching of Italian language and literature in the United States. *Publ:* Auth, Modern Italian Language and Literature: A Bibliography of Homage Studies, Harvard Univ, 59; ed & contribr, Studies in Honor of Samuel Montefiore Waxman, Boston Univ, 69; contribr, The eighteenth century: A current bibliography, Philol Quart, 71- *Mailing Add:* Dept of Mod Foreign Lang & Lit Boston Univ 718 Commonwealth Ave Boston MA 02215

GOLDEN, LEON, b Jersey City, NJ, Dec 25, 30. CLASSICAL LANGUAGES. *Educ:* Univ Chicago, BA, 50, MA, 53, PhD(class lang & lit), 58. *Prof Exp:* Instr ancient lang, Col William & Mary, 58-61, asst prof, 61-65; assoc prof classics, 65-68, PROF CLASSICS, FLA STATE UNIV, 68-, DIR, HUMANITIES PROG, 77- *Concurrent Pos:* Fel coop prog humanities, Univ NC & Duke Univ, 64-65; Soc Relig Higher Educ fel, 71-72. *Mem:* Am Philol Asn; Class Asn Mid W & S; Archaeol Inst Am; Am Soc Aesthetics. *Res:* Greek tragedy; classical literary criticism. *Publ:* Auth, Catharsis, Trans Am Philol Asn, 63; Is tragedy the imitation of a serious action?, Greek, Roman

& Byzantine Studies, winter 65; In Praise of Prometheus: Humanism and Rationalism in Aeschylean Thought, Univ NC, 66; coauth, Aristotle's Poetics: A Translation and Commentary for Students of Literature, Prentice-Hall, 68; auth, Mimesis and Katharsis, Class Philol, 7/69; The purgation theory of catharsis, J Aesthet & Art Criticism, summer 73; Toward a definition of tragedy, Class J, 10-11/76; The clarification theory of catharsis, Hermes, 76. *Mailing Add:* Prog in Humanities Fla State Univ Tallahassee FL 32306

GOLDEN, MARK, b Winnipeg, Man, Aug 6, 48. CLASSICAL LANGUAGES, ANCIENT HISTORY. *Educ:* Univ Toronto, PhD(classics), 81. *Prof Exp:* Asst prof classics, Univ BC, 80-82; ASST PROF CLASSICS, UNIV WINNIPEG, 82- *Res:* History of childhood. *Publ:* Auth, Demosthenes and the age of majority at Athens, 79 & Demography and the exposure of girls at Athens, 81, Phoenix; Pais in Hipponax fr 13W, QUCC; A pun in Aristophanes Lysistrata, CQ, 82; contribr, Sprot and wage-labour in the Heracles myth, Proc 5th Can Symp Hist Sport & Phys Educ, 82; auth, Pais, child and slave, Antiquite Classique (in press). *Mailing Add:* Dept of Classics Univ of Winnipeg Winnipeg MB R3B 2E9 Can

GOLDEN, PETER BENJAMIN, Turkic History & Philology. See Vol I

GOLDIN, FREDERICK, b Brooklyn, NY, Nov 3, 30; m; c 3. MEDIEVAL & COMPARATIVE LITERATURE. *Educ:* City Col New York, BA, 52; Columbia Univ, MA, 54, PhD(comp lit), 64. *Prof Exp:* Instr English, Brooklyn Col, 60-61; from instr to asst prof, Rutgers Univ, 61-67; from asst prof to assoc prof English & comp lit, 67-76, PROF ENGLISH & COMP LIT, CITY COL NEW YORK, 77-, PROF GER, FRENCH, ENGLISH & COMP LIT, GRAD SCH, CITY UNIV NY, 77- *Concurrent Pos:* Fulbright sr res fel, Vienna, 68-69; Am Coun Learned Soc grant, 68-69; Fulbright sr res scholar, Vienna, 75-76; Am Coun Learned Soc travel grant, 78 & fel, 80-81; City Univ NY Res Found grant, 81. *Mem:* Soc Rencesvals; MLA; Mediaeval Acad Am; Int Arthurian Soc; Int Courtly Lit Soc. *Res:* Medieval courtly literature; medieval and Renaissance epic; medieval and Renaissance drama. *Publ:* Auth, The Mirror of Narcissus in the Courtly Love Lyric, Cornell Univ, 67; The law's homage to grace: Piere Cardenal's Vera vergena, Maria, Romance Philol, 67; Lyrics of the Troubadours and Trouveres, 73 & German and Italian Lyrics of the Middle Ages, 73, Doubleday; coauth, In Pursuit of Perfection, Kennikat, 75; auth, Die rolle Ganelons und das motiv der worte, Z Romanische Philol, 77; The Song of Roland, Norton, 78; Le temps de chronique dans la Chanson de Roland, In: VIII Congreso de la Societe Rencesvals, Inst Principe de Viana, 81. *Mailing Add:* Dept of Comp Lit Grad Sch City Univ NY 33 W 42nd St New York NY 10036

GOLDIN, JUDAH, b New York, NY, Sept 14, 14. ORIENTAL STUDIES. *Educ:* City Col New York, BS, 34; Sem Col Jewish Studies, dipl, 34; Columbia Univ, AM, 38; Jewish Theol Sem, MHL, 38, DHL, 43. *Hon Degrees:* MA, Yale Univ, 59; HLD, Jewish Theol Sem, 68; DD, Colgate Univ, 73. *Prof Exp:* Lectr & vis assoc prof Jewish lit & hist, Duke Univ, 43-45; assoc prof relig, State Univ Iowa, 45-52; assoc prof & dean teachers inst & sem col, Jewish Theol Sem Am, 52-58; prof class Judaica, Yale Univ, 58-73; PROF POST-BIBL HEBREW LIT, UNIV PA, 73- *Concurrent Pos:* Adj prof relig, Columbia Univ, 55-58; Am Philos Soc grant, 57 & 71; Fulbright & Guggenheim fels, 58-59; chmn, Yale Judaica Ser, 62-73; Fulbright res fel, Denmark, 64-65; consult Judaica, Encycl Britannica, 68-73; assoc ed, Yale Judaica Series, 77-; Am Coun Learned Soc grant, 78. *Mem:* Soc Bibl Lit; Archaeol Inst Am; Am Schs Orient Res; Hist Soc Israel; fel Am Acad Jewish Res. *Res:* Midrashic literature; biblical exegesis; Judaism in New Testament times. *Publ:* Auth, Fathers According to Rabbi Nathan, Yale Univ, 55; ed, The Jewish Expression, Bantam, 70; auth, The song at the Sea, Yale Univ, 71; Toward a profile of the Tanna, Aquiba ben Joseph, J Am Orient Soc, 76; ed, The Munich Mekilta, Rosenkilde & Bagger, 80. *Mailing Add:* Dept of Orient Studies Univ of Pa Philadelphia PA 19104

GOLDMAN, EDWARD ARON, Rabbinic Literature. See Vol IV

GOLDMAN, HOWARD ALLEN, b New York, NY, Apr 3, 42; m 67; c 3. RUSSIAN LITERATURE & LANGUAGE. *Educ:* Cornell Univ, AB, 63, AM, 65; Ind Univ, cert Russ area studies, 72, PhD(Russ lit), 75. *Prof Exp:* Vis asst prof Russ, Univ Waterloo, 75-76; asst prof, Bates Col, 76-80; ASST PROF RUSS, TEL AVIV UNIV, 80- *Concurrent Pos:* Orgnr, Maine Slavic Sem, 78- *Mem:* MLA; Am Asn Teachers Slavic & E Europ Lang; Am Asn Advan Slavic Studies; Int Dostoevsky Soc; Can Asn Slavists. *Publ:* Auth & co-ed, articles, In: Soviet Russian Literature in English, Cornell Univ, 67; auth, French literary imagination and Dostoevsky, Germano-Slavica, 76; A Russian in Maine, Bates Col Bull, 4/78; Anna Axmatova's Hamlet: The immortality of personality & the discontinuity of time, 12/78 & ed & translr, Axmatova's Macbeth, 79, Slavic & E Europ J; auth, Ilya Ehrenburg, Vera Inber, Vladimir Soloukhin, Pavel Antokolsky, & Aleksandr Tarasov-Rodionov, In: Columbia Dict of Mod Europ Lits, 79. *Mailing Add:* Ed Transl Russ Tel Aviv Univ Ramat Aviv Israel

GOLDSMITH, EMANUEL SIDNEY, b New York, NY, Aug 15, 35. HEBREW & YIDDISH LITERATURE. *Educ:* City Col New York, BA, 56; Jewish Theol Sem Am, MHL, 60; Brandeis Univ, PhD(Judaic studies), 72. *Prof Exp:* Instr Hebrew & Yiddish lit, Brandeis Univ, 69-70, lectr, 70-71, asst prof Yiddish lang & lit, 71-74; asst prof, 75-78, ASSOC PROF HEBREW & JUDAIC STUDIES, UNIV CONN, 78- *Concurrent Pos:* Assoc prof Judaic studies, Clark Univ, 71-78; res grant, Univ Conn, 75. *Mem:* Asn Jewish Studies; Am Asn Prof Yiddish; MLA. *Res:* Modern Jewish thought. *Publ:* Auth, Modern Trends in Jewish Religion, B'nai B'rith Youth Orgn, 65; Jacob Glatstein: Twentieth Century Poet of Judaism, Reconstructionist, 66; The polarity of Mendele's art, Conservative Judaism, 68; Aaron Zeitlin's Poems of the Holocause, Judaism, 69; Masters of Yiddish Literature: A Study Guide and Syllabus, Brandeis Univ Nat Women's Comt, 72; The spiritual odyssey of Nathan Birnbaum, conservative Judaism, 75; Architects of Yiddishism at the Beginning of the twentieth Century, Fairleigh Dickinson Univ, 76; I love Yiddish: A mini-course in Yiddish, Audio Hertiage, 77. *Mailing Add:* Dept of Romance & Class Lang Univ Of Conn Storrs CT 06268

GOLDSMITH, ULRICH KARL, b Freiburg, Ger, Jan 19, 10; nat US. GERMAN LITERATURE. *Educ:* Univ Toronto, BA, 42, MA, 46; Univ Calif, PhD, 50. *Prof Exp:* Instr, Univ Sask, 44-46; teaching asst, Univ Calif, 46-47; instr, Princeton Univ, 47-50; asst prof Ger lit, Univ Man, 50-51; assoc prof, Univ Mass, 51-55; instr, Yale Univ, 55-57; from asst prof to prof Ger, 57-65, chmn dept Ger, 61-65, chmn dept comp lit, 65-71, prof, 65-79, EMER PROF GER & COMP LIT, UNIV COLO, 79- *Mem:* Western Asn Ger Studies; Am Asn Teachers Ger; MLA; Am Comp Lit Asn; Int Comp Lit Asn. *Res:* Modern German literature; Franco-German studies; translation theory and criticism. *Publ:* Auth, Stefan George: A Study of his Early Work, Univ Colo, 59; contribr, Encycl Poetry & Poetics (10 articles), Princeton Univ, 69; auth, Stefan George, Columbia Essays on modern writers, 70; Dirt or marble? Bertolt Brecht's lyrical poetry, In: Essays in Modern European Literature for Liselotte Dieckmann, Washington Univ, 72; Shakespeare and Stefan George: The sonnets, In: Festschrift Gerhard Loose, Francke, Bern, 74; auth & ed, Briefwechsel F v Unruh-Arthur Schnitzler, In: Modern Austrian Literature, Univ Calif, Riverside, 78; ed, R M Rilke: A verse Concordance of His Complete Lyrical Poetry, Maney & Sons, Ltd, Leeds, England, 80; auth, Ulrich von Wilamawitz-Mollendorff and the Georgekreis: New documents, In: Wilamowitz-Symposium, Wissenschaftl, Buchgesellschaft, Darmstadt, 82. *Mailing Add:* 865 Seventh St Boulder CO 80302

GOLLA, VICTOR KARL, b Santa Rosa, Calif, Feb 10, 39; m 80. ANTHROPOLOGICAL LINGUISTICS. *Educ:* Univ Calif, Berkeley, BA, 60, PhD(ling), 70. *Prof Exp:* Asst prof ling, Univ Alta, 66-67; instr anthrop, Columbia Univ, 67-68; asst prof, 68-74, chmn dept, 77-80, ASSOC PROF ANTHROP, GEORGE WASHINGTON UNIV, 74- *Concurrent Pos:* Nat Endowment for Humanities fel, 74-75; ed, Calif-Ore Lang Newslett, 77- *Mem:* Am Anthrop Asn; Ling Soc Am; Am Folklore Soc; Soc for Study Indigenous Lang Am (secy-treas, 81-). *Res:* American Indian languages & literature. *Publ:* Auth, Proto Yokuts Phonology, Univ Calif, 64; An etymological study of Hupa noun stems, Int J Am Ling, 64; A grammatical sketch of Hupa, In: Handbook of North American Indians, Smithsonian Inst, 76; co-ed, Northern California Texts, Univ Chicago Native Am Texts Ser, 77; coauth, Northern Athapaskan Languages, In: Handbook of North American Indians, Smithsonian Inst, Vol 8, 81. *Mailing Add:* Dept of Anthrop George Washington Univ Washington DC 20052

GOMEZ-GIL, ALFREDO, b Alicante, Spain, Nov 1, 36. POETRY, SPANISH & LATIN AMERICAN LITERATURE. *Educ:* Univ Madrid, Lic Lett & Philos, 65, PhD(educ), 78. *Prof Exp:* Dir Univ progs radio & TV, Univ Madrid, 60-64; lectr Span, Yale Univ, 65-66; COLLAB, SPAN & LATIN AM LIT, HARTFORD COL WOMEN, 65-, PROF SPAN & LATIN AM LIT, 66- *Res:* Problems of the Puerto Ricans and European immigrants in the United States. *Publ:* Auth, Introduccion a la Esperanza, El Toro de Granito, Avila, 71; 24 Poemas de Nieve, 71 & Entre fetiches y amuletos, 74, Cuadernos del Sur, Malaga; A pas cinco de la tarde, 75 & Paisajes y formass de Eberhard Schlotter a traves de un poeta, 75, Ed de Arte S A, Madrid; La frente en el suelo, Inst Estud Alicantinos, Alicante, 76; coauth, La vuelta de los cerebros, Plaza & Janes, Barcelona, 76; auth, The vibrations of silence, Ed Cult Hisp, Madrid, 78. *Mailing Add:* Dept of Span & Latin Am Lit Hartford Col for Women 1265 Asylum Ave Hartford CT 06105

GOMEZ-LOBO, ALFONSO, Philosophy, Classics. See Vol IV

GOMEZ-MARTINEZ, JOSE LUIS, b Soria, Spain, June 1, 43; nat US; m 67; c 3. SPANISH LITERATURE, HISPANIC THOUGHT. *Educ:* Escuela Normal de Bilbao, BA, 63; Roosevelt Univ, MA, 69; Univ Iowa, PhD(Span), 73. *Prof Exp:* Instr hist & lit, Union Espanola, Ger, 65-66; instr Span, Luther Col, 69-70; asst prof, Augustana Col, 72-74; assoc prof, 74-80, PROF SPAN, UNIV GA, 80- *Concurrent Pos:* Fac Growth award, Am Lutheran Church, 73; ed, Los Ensayistas, 76- *Mem:* Asn Int Hispanistas; MLA; Am Asn Teachers Span & Port; SAtlantic Mod Lang Asn; Latin Am Studies Asn; Inst Int de Literatura Iberoam. *Res:* Latin-American and peninsular Spanish essay and thought, 16-20th centuries. *Publ:* Auth, Dilthey en la obra de Americo Castro, Abside, 73; Distancia estetica e identificacion estetica, Revista Ideas Eteticas, 73; Americo Castro y el origen de los Espanoles: Historia de una polemica, Ed Gredos, 75; El ensayo y su funcion social, Dialogos, 76; Los supuestos modelos delas Empresas de Saavedra Fajardo y su caracter ensayistico, Nueva Revista de Filologia Hispanica, 79; Teoria del ensayo, Educ Universidad de Salamanca, 81; ed, Cuadernos Salmantinos de Filosofia, 81. *Mailing Add:* Dept of Romance Lang Univ of Ga Athens GA 30602

GOMEZ-MORIANA, ANTONIO, b Malaga, Spain, Sept 13, 36; m 63; c 3. SPANISH LINGUISTICS & LITERATURE. *Educ:* Lit Univ Salamanca, Lic en Filos y Let, 58, Dr Filos y Let, 62; Univ Munich, MA, 64, PhD(Romance philol), 65. *Prof Exp:* Dozent Span, Inst Span Cult, Munich, 62-65; lectr, Ruhr Univ, 65-71; from assoc prof to prof, Univ Ottawa, 71-74; chmn dept ancient & mod studies, 74-78, TITULAR PROF MOD & ANCIENT LANG, UNIV MONTREAL, 74- *Concurrent Pos:* Assoc ed, Philos Literaturanzeiger, Munich, 66-70; consult, Lexikon Philos, Herder, Munich, 67-70; vis prof, Carleton Univ, 70-71; assoc ed, Revista Canadiense Estudios Hispanicos, Toronto, & Imprevue, France, 81- *Mem:* Can Asn Univ Prof; Can Hispanistas; Asoc Int Hispanistas; Int Comp Lit Asn; assoc mem Patronato Arcipreste de Hita. *Res:* General theory of literature; historical linguistics; Spanish comedia of Golden Age. *Publ:* Auth, Unamuno en su congoja, Cuadernos de Catedra Miguel de Unamuno, 69 & 70; Die sprach und literarhistorische Entwicklung des Spanischen, Klett, Stuttgart, 73; Procedes de veridiction dans le roman picaresque espagnol, Le Vraisemblable et la Fiction, Colloque, Univ Montreal, 74; La subversion del discurso ritual, Imprevue, 80; Pour une semanalyse du roman picaresque, Semiotics on the Novel, Can J Res Semiotics, 80-81; Specificite du texte vs vocation universelle de la litterature, Memoires de la Soc Royale du Can, 80; La evocacion como procedimiento en el Quijote, Revista Canadiense de Estudios Hispanicos, 81-82; Autobiografia y discurso ritual, 2nd Colloque Int l'Autobiographie en Espagne, Aix-en-Provence, 82. *Mailing Add:* 3150 Jean-Brillant Montreal PQ H3T 1N8 Can

GOMMERMANN, ANDREAS, b Mucsi, Hungary, Oct 20, 28; US citizen; m 55; c 2. GERMAN. *Educ:* Marquette Univ, MA, 67; Univ Nebr, Lincoln, PhD(Ger), 75. *Prof Exp:* From asst to assoc personnel dir, Deutsche Bundespost, Fed Repub Ger, 54-65; from instr to asst prof Ger, 67-78, chmn dept, 76-77, COORDR MOD LANG, 77-, ASSOC PROF GER, CREIGHTON UNIV, 78- *Mem:* MLA; Am Asn Teachers Ger. *Res:* Linguistics; German dialects and languages in contact; German literature. *Mailing Add:* Dept of Classics & Mod Lang Creighton Univ Omaha NE 68178

GONTRUM, PETER B, b Feb 13, 32; US citizen; m 56; c 3. GERMAN & COMPARATIVE LITERATURE. *Educ:* Haverford Col, BA, 54; Princeton Univ, MA, 56; Univ Munich, PhD, 58. *Prof Exp:* Instr Ger, Univ Chicago, 58-61; from asst prof to assoc prof, 61-72, PROF GER, UNIV ORE, 72-, HEAD DEPT GER LANG & LIT, 78- *Concurrent Pos:* Am Philos Soc granst, 60, 65-66; Am Coun Learned Soc grant & Alexander von Humboldt fel, 65-66; Alexander von Humboldt fel, 71 & 79; mem Nat Fulbright Selection Comn, 71-73; Fulbright lectr, Univ Mannheim, 74. *Mem:* Am Asn Teachers Ger; MLA; Philol Asn Pac Coast; Am Comp Lit Asn; Int Comp Lit Asn. *Res:* Rilke; modern German literature; Hesse, Brecht, Dürrenmatt and Frisch. *Publ:* Auth, Natur und Dingsymbolik als Ausdruck de Inneren Welt Hermann Hesses, Univ Munich, 58; The legend of Rip van Winkle in Max Frisch's Stiller, Studies Swiss Lit, 71; Max Firsch and the theatre of Bertolt Brecht, German Life and Letters, 1/80. *Mailing Add:* Dept of Ger Lang & Lit Univ of Ore Eugene OR 97403

GONZALEZ, ALAN ANGEL, b Madrid, Spain, Feb 16, 22; m 51; c 4. HISPANIC LANGUAGES & LITERATURE. *Educ:* Edinburg Univ, MA, 46; John Hopkins Univ, PhD(Romance lang), 66. *Prof Exp:* From instr to assoc prof Span, Univ of the Americas, 48-65, co-chmn dept, 60-65; from asst prof to assoc prof, Univ Pittsburgh, 66-72; PROF FOREIGN LANG & LIT, NC STATE UNIV, 80-, CHMN DEPT, 72- *Concurrent Pos:* Catedratico English, Nat Univ Mex, 59-64; investr, Col Mex, 72- *Mem:* Am Coun Teaching Foreign Lang; Asn Depts Foreign Lang; MLA; Am Asn Teachers Span & Port. *Res:* Spanish Civil War literature; literature of exile; Golden Century drama. *Publ:* Auth, Un Best-Seller Mexicano, Hispania, 61; coauth, Emilio en Espana, Britannica, 65; auth, Ida y Vuelta al Confabulario, Rev Iberoam, 68; Relacions Epistolares Entra Maura y Galdos, Anales Galdosianos, 69. *Mailing Add:* Dept of Foreign Lang & Lit NC State Univ Box 5156 Raleigh NC 27650

GONZALEZ, ALFONSO, b Mexico City, Mex, Jan 7, 38; US citizen; m 63; c 3. MEXICAN LITERATURE, SPANISH LANGUAGE. *Educ:* Univ Kans, BA, 67, MA, 68, PhD(Span), 71. *Prof Exp:* Asst prof Span, Ohio Univ, 71-75; asst prof, 75-78, ASSOC PROF SPAN, CALIF STATE UNIV LOS ANGELES, 78- *Concurrent Pos:* Ohio Univ Res Inst grants Mex cult, 72-73 & 73-74; vis prof Lat Am lit, Univ Southern Calif, 75-76. *Mem:* Am Asn Teachers Span & Port; MLA; Philol Asn Pac Coast; Pac Coast Coun Latin Am Studies. *Res:* Latin American literature; Latin American studies. *Publ:* Auth, El novumundismo en la prosa de ficcion de Altamirano, Palabra & Hombre, 10-12/72; Onomasticas and creativity in Dona Barbara and Pedro Paramo, Names, 3/73; Narrative techniques in twentieth-century Spanish American novomundismo, Grad Studies Latin Am, fall 73; Elementos del Quijote en la caracterizacion de La Voragine, Romance Notes, 74; Elementos hispanicos y clasicos en la caracterizacion de La Voragine, Cuadernos Am, 5-6/75; introd to chap on Julieta Campos, In: Mujeres en la Literature, Fleischer Ed, Mex, 78; Indice de la Cultura en Mexico (1962-1971), Univ Microfilms Int, 78. *Mailing Add:* 5151 State University Dr Los Angeles CA 90032

GONZALEZ, BERNARDO ANTONIO, b San Pedro, Calif, June 20, 50; m 76; c 2. MODERN SPANISH LITERATURE. *Educ:* Univ Calif, Berkeley, AB, 72, MA, 74, PhD(Romance lang & lit), 79. *Prof Exp:* ASST PROF SPAN, WESLEYAN UNIV, 79- *Mem:* MLA; Am Asn Teachers of Span & Portuguese; Northeastern MLA. *Res:* Contemporary Spanish fiction; theory of the novel. *Publ:* Auth, Perspective in Fiestas: Towards an understanding of objectivity in neorealism, Anales de la Lit Esp Cont, 81; The character in his time: From Juegos de Manos to Reivindicacion del Conde don Julian, Revista Canadiense de Estudios Hispanicos (in prep); Mimesis and narrative discourse: Juan Goytisolo's search for immediacy, Rev Contemp Fiction (in prep). *Mailing Add:* Dept of Romance Lang Wesleyan Univ Middletown CT 06457

GONZALEZ, EMILIO, b La Coruna, Spain, Nov 13, 03; US citizen; m 31. ROMANCE LANGUAGES. *Educ:* Univ Madrid, MS, 26, Phd(soc sci & law), 28. *Prof Exp:* Adj prof law, Univ Madrid, 29-30; prof law & dean law & soc sci sch, Univ La Laguna, 31-32; prof law, Univ Salamanca, 32-36, Univ Oviedo, 36-37, Univ Valencia, 37 & Univ Barcelona, 38; PROF SPAN, HUNTER COL, 40-; EXEC OFF PHD PROG SPAN, GRAD CTR, CITY UNIV NEW YORK, 67- *Concurrent Pos:* Vis prof, Span Grad Summer Sch, Middlebury Col, 46- & dir, 63-; vis prof, grad schs, Columbia Univ, 56-64, NY Univ, 58-59 & 61 & Brooklyn Col, 60; chmn dept Romance lang, Hunter Col, 63-67. *Mem:* Am Asn Teachers Span & Port; Royal Galician Acad; Euclides da Cunha Soc, Brazil. *Res:* History of Spain; Spanish Golden Age; contemporary Spanish theatre and novel. *Publ:* Auth, Bajo las luves de la ilustracion: Galicia en los reinados de Carlos III y Carlos IV, Ed Castro, La Coruna, 77; El aguila desplumada: Del Mino al Bidasoa, Ed Castrelos, Vigo, 77; El alba flor de lis: Galicia en los reinados de Felipe V, Luis I y Fernando VI, Ed Castro, La Coruna, 78; Grandeza e decadencia do reino de Galacia, Ed Galaxia, Vigo, 78; Canonistas del Noroeste de Espana profesores de Bolonia: Su influencia en el desarrollo del Derecho canonico en Europa y en la formacion de las Universidades espanolas, La Coruna, Academia Gallege de Jurisprudencia y Legislacion, 78; Historia de Galicia, Ed La Voz de Galicia, 80, Entre el antiguo y el nuevo regimen: Absolutistas y liberales el reinado de Fernando VII en Galicia, Ed Castro, 81 & La Galicia de los Austrias, Ed Fundascion Barrie de la Maza, 81, La Coruna. *Mailing Add:* 425 W 57th St New York NY 10019

GONZALEZ, JAIME JOSE, b Matanzas, Cuba, Feb 11, 25; US citizen; m 55; c 1. SPANISH & PORTUGUESE LITERATURES. *Educ:* Matanzas Preuniv Inst, Cuba, BS, 44; Univ Havana, EdD, 62; Univ Tenn, MA, 65; Vanderbilt Univ, PhD(Span & Port), 69. *Prof Exp:* Instr Span, Vedado Pre-Univ Inst, Havana, 46-54; prof & chmn dept, Matanzas Sch Bus Admin, 56-62; from instr to asst prof, Tusculum Col, 63-66, assoc prof Span & chmn dept & dir lang labs, 66-69; assoc prof, 69-74, PROF SPAN, GA COL, 74- *Concurrent Pos:* Int student adv, Ga Col, 78-, coord English as second lang, 82- *Mem:* MLA; Am Asn Teachers Span & Port; SAtlantic Mod Lang Asn; Nat Asn Foreign Student Affairs; AAUP. *Res:* Spanish theater of the Golden Age; Spanish theater of the 20th century; methods in teaching foreign languages. *Publ:* Auth, Estudios genealogicos de varias comedias de Tirso de Molina, Univ Microfilms, 70; coauth, Tirso de Molina and the Gonzagas, Hispania, 5/72; auth, Elementos absurdos en el Teatro de Enrique Jardiel Poncela, privately publ, 74. *Mailing Add:* Dept of Mod Foreign Lang Ga Col Milledgeville GA 31061

GONZALEZ, PABLO, b Aguadas, Colombia, May 11, 39; m 64; c 3. SPANISH & LATIN AMERICAN LITERATURE & CULTURE. *Educ:* Univ Pittsburgh, MA, 66, PhD(lit), 68. *Prof Exp:* Prof Latin, Col Theodor Hertzl Medellin, 62-63; prof English, Univ Antioquia, Columbia, 63-64; instr Span, Carnegie-Mellon Univ, 65-66; asst prof Latin Am Studies 66-77, ASSOC PROF SPAN, WVA UNIV, 77-, CO-DIR, LATIN AM RES GROUP, 72- *Concurrent Pos:* Adv, Regional Coun Int Educ, Pittsburgh, 70-74. *Mem:* Int Inst Latin Am Lit; MLA; Columbian Asn Span Teachers. *Res:* The narrative of Gabriel Garcia-Marquez; the contemporary poetry in Latin America; a cultural approach to Spanish teaching. *Publ:* Auth, El movimiento nadaista en Colombia, Rev Iberoam, 7/66; Huasipungo: una novela ecuatoriana, Anales, Univ Quito, 4/67; Miquel Angel Asturias: El Sr Presidente, Letras Nac, 1/68. *Mailing Add:* 1381 Anderson Ave Morgantown WV 26505

GONZALEZ, RAFAEL A, b Utuado, Puerto Rico, Dec 17, 22; US citizen; m 48; c 2. SPANISH LANGUAGE AND LITERATURE. *Educ:* Univ Puerto Rico, BBA, 53, MA, 56, PhD, 70. *Prof Exp:* From instr to assoc prof Spanish & humanities, Univ Puerto Rico, 56-78, chmn & founder, Spanish Dept Cayey Col, 67-72, prof, 73-82. *Concurrent Pos:* Secy, Sociedad de Autores Puertorriquenos, 77-79. *Honors & Awards:* Premio Bolivar Pagan, 76; Los cuentos de Emilia Pardo Bazan Award, 77. *Mem:* MLA; Sociedad de Autores Puertorriquenos; Sociedad Europea de Profesores de Espanol; PEN Club; Ateneo Puertorriqueno. *Res:* Puertorrican literature; Spanish literature, especially 19th century. *Publ:* Auth, Un hombre se ha puesto de pie (Novela), Edit Anaya-Salamanca, 70; Felix Franco Oppenheimer y su vision metafisica, La Torre, 1-6/72; El Estilo en la prosa de antonio Machado, Asomante, Vol XXVII, 1-3/73; El retrato del otro (Novela), Editorial Edil, 76; Los cuentos de Emilia Pardo Bazan, Florentia Publ, 77; La busqueda de lo absoluto o la Poesia de Francisco Matos Paoli, BAP, 78; La obra poetica de Felix Franco Oppenheimer, Edit Universitaria, 81; El cantaro celeste (poem), Edit Yaurel (in press). *Mailing Add:* Dept of Span Gen Studies Univ of Puerto Rico Rio Piedras PR 00931

GONZALEZ-CRUZ, LUIS F, b Cardenas, Matanzas, Cuba, Dec 11, 43; US citizen. HISPANIC LANGUAGES, LATIN AMERICAN LITERATURE. *Educ:* Inst Jose Smith Comas, Cardenas, Cuba, BS, 60; Univ Pittsburgh, MA, 68, PhD(Hisp lang & lit), 70. *Prof Exp:* Instr chem, Manuel Bisbe PU Sch, Havana, Cuba, 63-65; instr Span, Manter Hall Sch, Cambridge, Mass, 68; part-time instr, Point Park Col, 68-69, from instr to asst prof, 69-73, assoc prof, 73-79, PROF HISP LANG, PA STATE UNIV, NEW KENSINGTON, 79- *Concurrent Pos:* Dir, Publ Consenso, 77- & Consenso Revista Lit, 77-81; mem ed bd, Caribe, 77- & Escolios, 77-81; reviewer for grant proposals, Nat Endowment for Humanities. *Honors & Awards:* Dir Award for outstanding acad achievement, Pa State, 73. *Mem:* MLA; Northeast Mod Lang Asn; Latin Am Studies Asn; Am Asn Teachers Span & Port; Inst Int Lit Iberoam. *Res:* Pablo Neruda; Hispanic poetry; Latin American literatures, cultures and civilizations. *Publ:* Auth, Pablo Neruda y el Memorial de Isla Negra, Ed Universal, 72; Pablo Neruda: Soledad, incommunicacion e individualismo en Memorial de Isla Negra, Rev Iberoam, 1-6/73; Tirando al blanco Poemas/Shooting Gallery Poems (bilingual ed), Ed Universal, 75; Pablo Neruda, Cesar Vallejo y Federico Garcia Lorca: Microcosmos poeticos, 75 & Pablo Neruda De Tentativa a la totalidad, 79, Anaya-Las Am; The art of Julio Matas, Vol I, No I & Poet as God: The resurrection myth and other archetypal motifs in Cesar Vallejo's Ascuas (Embers), Vol I, No 2, Latin Am Lit Rev. *Mailing Add:* Dept of Span Ital & Port Penn State Univ New Kensington PA 15068

GONZALEZ-DEL-VALLE, LUIS TOMAS, b Santa Clara, Cuba, Nov 19, 46; US citizen; m 69; c 2. SPANISH & SPANISH AMERICAN LITERATURES. *Educ:* Wilmington Col, BA, 68; Univ Mass, Amherst, MA, PhD(Span), 72. *Prof Exp:* From asst prof to assoc prof mod lang, Kans State Univ, 72-76; assoc prof, 77-79, PROF MOD LANG & LIT, UNIV NEBR-LINCOLN, 79- *Concurrent Pos:* Bur Gen Res fac grant, Kans State Univ, 72-73, res grant, 74-75, 75-76 & 76-77; ed, J Span Studies Twentieth Century, 72-80, Anales de la novela de posquerra, 75-78 & Studies 20th Century Lit, 75-76, 77-79 (assoc ed, 79-); dir, Soc Span & Span-Am Studies, 75-; Res Coun grant-in-aid, Res Coun, Univ Nebr-Lincoln, 77-78 & 79-80, sr fac res fel, Res Coun, 78, grants-in-aid, Chancellor's Res Initiation Fund, 80-82, res leave, spring 82; adv ed, Critica Hispanica, 78-; ed, Anales de la narrativa espanola contemporanea, 79-80 & Anales de la literatura espanol contemporanea, 81- *Honors & Awards:* Mid-Am State Univ Asn honor lectr, 76-77. *Mem:* MLA; Am Asn Teachers Span & Port; MLA Conf Ed of Learned J; Asoc Int Hisp; Asn Int Critiques Lit. *Res:* Spanish literature of the 19th and 20th centuries; 20th century fiction of Latin America; drama, tragedy. *Publ:* Auth, La nueva ficcion hispano-americana, Torres Libr Lit Studies, 72; La tragedia en el teatro de Unamuno, Valle-Inclan y Garcia Lorca, Torres Libr Lit Studies, 75; La correspondencia comercial, S Western Publ Co, 75, 2nd ed, 81; La ficcion de Luis Romero, 76 & Hispanic Writers in French Journals, 78, Soc Span & Span Am Studies; Novela espanola contemporanea, Soc Gen Espanola de Libreria, 78, 2nd ed, 80; Luis Romero, Twayne, 79; El teatro de Frederico Garcia Lorca y otros ensayos sobre literatura espanola e hispanoamericana, Soc Span & Span-Am Studies, 80. *Mailing Add:* Dept of Mod Lang Univ of Nebr Lincoln NE 68588

GONZALEZ-ECHEVARRIA, ROBERTO, b Sagua la Grande, Cuba, Nov 28, 43; m 64; c 3. SPANISH & MODERN LATIN AMERICAN LITERATURE. *Educ:* Univ SFla, BA, 64; Ind Univ, MA, 66; Yale Univ, MPh, 68, PhD(Span), 70. *Prof Exp:* From instr to asst prof Span, Yale Univ, 69-71; from asst prof to assoc prof Romance studies, Cornell Univ, 71-77; assoc prof, 77-81, PROF SPAN, YALE UNIV, 81-, CHMN LATIN AM STUDIES PROG, 81- *Concurrent Pos:* Contrib ed, Handbook Latin Am Studies, 72-; mem ed comn, Rev Iberoam, 73-77, Mod Lang J & Latin Am Lit Rev; Guggenheim fel, 82-83. *Mem:* MLA; Am Asn Teachers Span & Port; Latin Am Studies Asn; Cervantes Soc Am. *Res:* Golden Age poetry and drama; colonial and modern Latin American fiction; literary and critical theory. *Publ:* Auth, Relecturas: Estudios de literatura cubana, Monte Avila, Caracas, 76; Calderon y la critica; historia y antologia (2 vols), Gredos, Madrid, 77; coauth, Alejo Carpentier: The Pilgrim at Home, Cornell Univ, 77; Historia y ficcion en la narrativa Hispana Americana, Caracas, Monte Avila, 82. *Mailing Add:* Dept of Span & Port Yale Univ New Haven CT 06520

GONZALEZ-MARTIN, JERONIMO PABLO, b Salamanca, Spain, Mar 22, 33; Can citizen. SPANISH LANGUAGE & LITERATURES. *Educ:* Univ Oviedo, Lic en Derecho, 55; Univ Zaragoza, Dr en Derecho, 64. *Prof Exp:* Lectr Span, McMaster Univ, 60-63, asst prof, 63-65; from asst prof to assoc prof Span, 65-76, acting chmn, 67-68, PROF HISPANIC STUDIES, TRENT UNIV, 76- *Concurrent Pos:* Can Coun Arts grant, 68. *Mem:* MLA; Am Asn Teachers Span & Port; Can Asn Hispanists. *Res:* Contemporary Spanish poetry; comparative literature, especially contemporary poetry. *Publ:* Auth, Pude seguir intensamente, 62 & Canto a la desposada y otros versos, 63, Dezir, Zaragoza; Cayeron los Negros, Ed Zaragoza, 65; Cinco poetas francocanadienses actuales, Consejo Super Invest Cient, 66; Andar a Gillos, Poesia, Barcelona, 66; Sinceramente Dedicido, El Bardo, Barcelona, 67; Poesia Hispana de postguerra, El Bardo, Madrid, 69; Ensayo sobre la poesia Gallega Contemporanea, Ed Castro, La Coruna, 72. *Mailing Add:* Dept of Hispanic Studies Trent Univ Peterborough ON K9J 6X3 Can

GONZALEZ-MAS, EZEQUIEL, b Madrid, Spain, July 20, 19; m 54. SPANISH LITERATURE. *Educ:* Univ Madrid, BA, 36, MA, 47; Univ Cuenca, PhD, 58. *Prof Exp:* Prof lit, Univ Guayaquil, 52-62, 64-66; vis prof, 62-64, adv res, 66-73, PROF LIT, UNIV PR, 66- *Mem:* MLA; AAUP. *Res:* Nineteenth century Spanish literature. *Publ:* Auth, Sartre y Camus, Univ Guayaquil, 59; Nivel de sueno, 60 & El Quijote, invitacion a la locura, 60, Senefelder, Guayaquil; Historia de la Literature espanola: Epoca Medieval, 68, Historia de la literatura espanola: Renacimiento, 73 & El retrato literario y Otros Motivos, 73, Univ PR. *Mailing Add:* Dept of Span Univ of PR Mayaguez PR 00708

GONZALEZ-MUELA, JOAQUIN, b Madrid Spain, Dec 21, 15; m 57; c 2. SPANISH LANGUAGE & LITERATURE. *Educ:* Univ Madrid, PhD(Span), 46. *Prof Exp:* Prof Span, Univ Ore, 59-61 & Western Reserve Univ, 61-64; PROF SPAN, BRYN MAWR COL, 64- *Concurrent Pos:* Guggenheim fel, 64. *Res:* Romance philology; Medieval literature; modern Spanish poetry. *Publ:* Auth, El infinitivo en el Corbacho, Univ Granada, 54; El lenguaje poetico de la generacion Guillen-Lorca, 55 & La realidad y Jorge Guillen, 65, Insula, Madrid. *Mailing Add:* Dept of Spn Bryn Mawr Col Bryn Mawr PA 19010

GONZALEZ-PEREZ, ANIBAL, b San German, PR, Aug 25, 56; US citizen. LATIN AMERICAN LITERATURE. *Educ:* Univ PR, BA, 77; Yale Univ, PhD(Span), 82. *Prof Exp:* ASST PROF SPAN, UNIV TEX, AUSTIN, 82- *Mem:* MLA. *Res:* Nineteenth century Spanish American prose; Spanish American colonial literature; Puerto Rican literature. *Publ:* Auth, La cuarterona and slave society in Cuba and Puerto Rico, Latin Am Lit Rev, 80; La escritura modernista y la filologia, Cuadernos Am, 81. *Mailing Add:* Dept of Span & Port Univ of Tex Austin TX 78712

GOOD, ROBERT MCCLIVE, b Covington, Va, Sept 30, 52; m 76; c 1. OLD TESTAMENT, NEAR EASTERN LANGUAGES. *Educ:* Princeton Univ, BA, 74; Yale Univ, MA, 76, PhD(Near Eastern hist), 80. *Prof Exp:* ASST PROF RELIG STUDIES, BROWN UNIV, 80- *Mem:* Am Orient Soc; Soc Bibl Lit; Am Sch Orient Res. *Res:* Old Testament history and religion; Ugaritic studies; comparative Semitic linguistics. *Publ:* Auth, Geminated sonants, word stress, and energic in -nn/-.nn in Ugaritic, Ugarit-Forschungen, Vol 13, 81; co-ed, Love and Death in the Ancient Near East: Essays presented to Marvin H Pope, 4 Quarters Press, 81; auth, Zechariah's second night vision, Bibl, Vol 63, 82. *Mailing Add:* 12 Colonial Rd Providence RI 02906

GOODALE, HOPE K, b New York, NY, Apr 23, 26; m 51. SPANISH. *Educ:* Bryn Nawr Col, AB, 48, MA, 50, PhD(Span), 65. *Prof Exp:* From lectr to assoc prof Span, PMC Cols, 65-72; PROF SPAN, WIDENER COL, 72- *Concurrent Pos:* Dir, Int Inst for Girls in Spain, 67-; chmn, Steering Comt Self-Eval Report for Mid States, 76-78. *Mem:* MLA; Am Asn Teachers Span & Port; AAUP; Am Asn Higher Educ. *Res:* B Perez Galdos; modern Spanish literature; cirricular planning. *Publ:* Auth, Galdos and Shakespeare, Hisp Rev, 68; Gerona and its literary critics, Cong Lit Hisp, 75. *Mailing Add:* Dept of Span Widener Col Chester PA 19013

GOODE, HELEN D, b Lenexa, Kans, Jan 16, 13. ROMANCE LANGUAGES. *Educ:* Univ Kans, AB, 35, BMus, 40, MMus, 45, MA, 57, PhD(Span, French), 62. *Prof Exp:* Asst instr Span, Univ Kans, 57-60; from instr to asst prof Span & French, Bethany Col, Kans, 60-62; from lectr to asst prof, 62-68, assoc prof, 68-80, EMER ASSOC PROF SPAN, SOUTHERN ILL UNIV EDWARDSVILLE, 80- *Mem:* Am Asn Teachers Span & Port. *Res:* Spanish literature of the Renaissance period; stylistics, especially Spanish. *Publ:* Auth, La prosa retorica de Fray Luis de Leon en Los nombres de Cristo, Ed Gredos, Madrid, 69; The unknown De los 9 nombres de Cristo of Jose de Siguenza, Papers Lang & Lit, spring 76. *Mailing Add:* Humanities Div Southern Ill Univ Edwardsville IL 62025

GOODE, WILLIAM OSBORNE, b Chase City, Va, June 22, 39; m 72; c 3. FRENCH LITERATURE. *Educ:* Washington & Lee Univ, BA, 60; Duke Univ, MA, 63, PhD(French), 68. *Prof Exp:* Asst prof French, Univ Md, 67-68 & Univ Pa, 68-73; asst prof, 74-78, ASSOC PROF FRENCH, UNIV NC, GREENSBORO, 78- *Concurrent Pos:* Advert mgr, The Fr Rev, 80- *Mem:* MLA; Am Asn Teachers Fr; SAtlantic Mod Lang Asn; AAUP. *Res:* Seventeenth century French literature; classical theater; tragedy. *Publ:* Auth, Dom Juan and Heaven's spokesmen, Fr Rev, spring 72; The comic recognition scenes in L'Avare, Romance Notes, fall 72; A mother's goals in La princesse de Cleves, Neophilologus, 10/72; Hand, heart and mind: The complexity of the heroic quest in Le Cid, PMLA, 1/76; Medee and Jason: Hero and nonhero in Corneille's Medee, Fr Rev, 5/78. *Mailing Add:* Dept of Romance Lang Univ of NC Greensboro NC 27412

GOODELL, RALPH JEFFERSON, b Hampden, Maine, Nov 21, 25; m 51; c 3. LINGUISTICS. *Educ:* Taylor Univ, BA, 51; Columbia Univ, MA, 52; Univ Edinbrugh, PhD(ling), 65. *Prof Exp:* Instr English as second lang, Habibia Col, Kabul, Afghanistan, 54-56; mem, Columbia Univ Team, Afghanistan, 56-62, dept head, Afghan Inst Technol, 56-57 & Daral Mu'Allemin Teacher's Col, 57-59; dir teachers, English lang prog, inst educ, Kabul Univ, 59-61, dir res, 61-62; assoc prof, 65-69, PROF ENGLISH, CENT CONN STATE COL, 69- *Concurrent Pos:* Danforth Found assoc, 68-70; consult & mem adv bd, Elem & Sec Educ Art Title III proj psycholing res & English lang instr, Westlake High Sch, Thornwood, NY, 68-72; fac mem, Nat Humanities Fac, 77- *Mem:* Ling Soc Am; Ling Soc Gt Brit; Teachers English to Speakers Other Lang; Am Coun Teaching Foreign Lang. *Res:* Cultural differences in second language teaching and learning; semantic space and semantic difference cross-culturally; cultural and semantic differences in a sociolinguistic context. *Publ:* Auth, An ethnolinguistic bibliography with supporting material in linguistics and anthropology, Anthop Ling, 2/64. *Mailing Add:* Dept of English Cent Conn State Col New Britain CT 06050

GOODHAND, ROBERT, b Buffalo, NY, July 5, 32; m 53; c 4. FRENCH. *Educ:* Hamilton Col, BA, 54; Rice Univ, MA, 56, PhD, 61. *Prof Exp:* Teaching asst French, Rice Univ, 54-56, instr, 57-61; instr, Duke Univ, 61-64; from asst prof to assoc prof, 64-72, PROF FRENCH, KENYON COL, 72- *Concurrent Pos:* Resident dir MidE Prog, Great Lakes Col Asn, Beirut, Lebanon, 69-70; vis assoc prof, Am Univ Beirut, 69-70; Nat Endowment for Humanities fel, 77 & 81. *Mem:* MLA; Am Asn Teachers Fr. *Res:* Modern French novel, Giraudoux and Gide. *Publ:* Auth, Psychological development in Giraudoux's Eglantine, Fr Rev, 10/63; The religious leitmotif in L'Immoraliste, Romanic Rev, 12/66; Emma Bovary, the baker's paramour, Rice Univ Studies, summer 73. *Mailing Add:* Dept of French Kenyon Col Gambier OH 43022

GOODRICH, CHAUNCEY SHAFTER, b San Francisco, Calif, Mar 18, 20; m 45; c 4. CHINESE LANGUAGE & LITERATURE. *Educ:* Yale Univ, BA, 42; Univ Calif, MA, 51, PhD, 57. *Prof Exp:* Asst res hist, East Asia Studies, Univ Calif, 59-60; univ lectr, class Chinese, Cambridge Univ, 61-63; pvt res, 63-64; asst prof, 64-66, assoc prof, 66-80, PROF CLASS CHINESE, UNIV CALIF, SANTA BARBARA, 80- *Concurrent Pos:* actg asst ed, Am Orient Soc J, 60-61 & assoc ed, 68-72; prog chmn & dir, Am Orient Soc, 76- *Mem:* Am Orient Soc; Asn Asian Studies; Philol Asn Pac Coast; Soc Study Chinese Religions. *Res:* Ancient Chin ese kingship; early Chinese literature. *Publ:* Transl, Biography of Su Ch'o, Univ Calif, 53 & 61; auth, Two chapters in the life of an empress of the later Han, Harvard J Asiatic Studies, 64-65 & 66; The Ancient Chinese Prisoner's Van, T-oung Pao, Brill, Leiden, 75. *Mailing Add:* Dept of Ger & Russ Univ of Calif Santa Barbara CA 93106

GOODRICH, NORMA LORRE, b Huntington, Vt, May 10, 17; m; c 1. FRENCH, COMPARATIVE LITERATURE. *Educ:* Univ Vt, BS, 38; Univ Grenoble, cert lit, 39; Columbia Univ, PhD(French lit), 65. *Prof Exp:* Teacher English & chmn dept, Newport High Sch, Vt, 39-43; dir, Am Villa Sch, Deauville-Trouville, France, 47-53; teacher, Fieldston Sch, NY, 53-63; from asst prof to assoc prof French & comp lit, Univ Southern Calif, 64-70; dean fac, 70-71, PROF FRENCH & COMP LIT, SCRIPPS COL, 71- *Concurrent Pos:* Univ Southern Calif res grants, 65-68; prof, Claremont Grad Sch, 72-; vis scholar colloquium, Calif Lutehran Col, 75. *Mem:* Am Asn Teachers Fr; Philol Asn Pac Coast; Medieval Asn Pac. *Res:* Arthurian literature. *Publ:* Auth, The dream of Panurge, Etudes Rabelaisiennes, 67; Le Moulin de Pologne: Novel and tragedy, Rev Lit Comp, 67; Vingt contes du jeune Giono, Sud, No 7, 71; Medieval heroes (film), Am Hist Soc Arch, 72; Giono, Master of Fictional Modes, Princton Univ, 73 & London, 73; Studies of women in France (Balzac), Phi Kappa Phi J, 73; Medieval Myths, rev ed, NAL, 77. *Mailing Add:* Dept of French Scripps Col Claremont CA 91711

GOODWIN, REASON ALVA, b Montgomery Co, Kans, Sept 19, 03; m 25; c 2. LINGUISTICS. *Educ:* Univ Chicago, AM, 46, PhD(Slavic ling), 51. *Prof Exp:* Asst prof mod lang, Univ Louisville, 46-48; res assoc Slavic ling, Univ Chicago, 48-50; LING CONSULT, C L BARNHART, BRONXVILLE, NY, 51- *Concurrent Pos:* Legis analyst, US Brewers Asn, 50-62. *Mem:* Ling Soc Am; Am Orient Soc. *Res:* Lexicography. *Mailing Add:* 2634 Virginia St Berkeley CA 94709

GOODWYN, FRANK EPPSE, b Alice, Tex, June 28, 11; m 38; c 3. MODERN LANGUAGES. *Educ:* Tex Col Arts & Industs, BA, 40, MA, 41; Univ Tex, PhD(folklore), 46. *Prof Exp:* Tutor English, Tex Col Arts & Industs, 40-41; adv foreign students, Univ Tex, 42-44, instr English, 44-46; asst prof Span, Northwestern Univ, 46-50; prof, 50-82, EMER PROF SPAN, UNIV MD, COLLEGE PARK, 82- *Mem:* MLA; Am Asn Teachers Span & Port; Am Folklore Soc. *Res:* Folklore; literary techniques; poetry. *Publ:* Auth, Life on the King Ranch; Lone Star Land; The Black Bull, Doubleday, 58; The literary style fof William Hickling Prescott, Inter-Am Rev Bibliog, 59; Garcilaso de la Vega, representative in the Spanish Cortes, Mod Lang Notes, 3/67; Tipos de verso y ritmo en la segunda egloga de Garcilaso, Hispanofila, 68; New light on the historical setting of Garcilaso's poetry, Hisp Rev, winter 78. *Mailing Add:* Dept of Span & Port Univ of Md College Park MD 20742

GOOLD, GEORGE PATRICK, b London, England, May 15, 22; m 44, 74; c 2. CLASSICAL PHILOLOGY. *Educ:* Univ London, BA, 48, PhD(classics), 54. *Prof Exp:* Lectr classics, Univ Hull, England, 48-55; prof, Univ Cape Town, 55-57; assoc prof, Univ Man, 57-60; from assoc prof to prof, Univ Col, Univ Toronto, 60-65; prof Greek & Latin, Harvard Univ, 65-73; prof Latin, Univ Col, Univ London, 73-78; PROF CLASSICS, YALE UNIV, 78- *Concurrent Pos:* Ed, Harvard Studies Class Philol, 66-71; Guggenheim Found fel, 71; gen ed, Loeb Class libr, 74-; Bonsall vis prof humanities, Stanford Univ, 78; dir Am Philol Asn, 81- *Mem:* Class Asn Gt Brit; Class Asn Can (secy, 61-63); Am Philol Asn. *Res:* Textual criticism; Homer; Greek astrology. *Publ:* Ed, Catulli Carmina, 73 & Horati Carmina, 77, Groton Sch; auth, The nature of Homeric composition, Ill Class Studies, 77, co-ed, Ovid, Heroides and Amores, 77, Ovid, Metamorphoses 1-8, 77 & ed, Manilius, Astronomica, 78, Loeb. *Mailing Add:* Dept of Classics Yale Univ New Haven CT 06520

GOPNIK, MYRNA, b Philadelphia, Pa, June 21, 35; Can citizen; m 54; c 6. LINGUISTICS, SEMIOTICS. *Educ:* Univ Pa, BA, 62, MA, 64, PhD(ling), 68. *Prof Exp:* Instr hist & philos sci, Phila Col Arts, 67-68; invited lectr info sci, Drexel Inst Technol, 68; res assoc auto transl, Univ Montreal, 68-69; ASSOC PROF LING, MCGILL UNIV, 69- *Mem:* Ling Soc Am; Can Ling Asn; Ling Asn Can & US; Can Asn Hist & Philos Sci; MLA. *Res:* Linguistic metatheory; textlingusitics; semiotics. *Publ:* Auth, Linguistic Structures in Scientific Texts, Mouton, 72; Philosophical semantics and linguistic semantics, Cahier de Linguistique, 73; What the theorist saw, In: Assessing Ling Arguments, Hemisphere, 76; Semiotic Approaches to Theories, Working Papers of Toronto Semiotic Circle, 76; Scientific theories as meta-semiotic systems, Semiotic, 77; Some metatheoretical considera tions of text theory, Proc Colloquium on Pragmatics of Dialogue (in press); Correctness of judgements in transformational-generative grammar, Proc of XIIth Int Cong Linguists (in press); On differentiating sentence grammars, In: Text vs Sentence (in press). *Mailing Add:* Dept of Ling McGill Univ 1001 Sherbrooke St Montreal PQ H3A 1G5 Can

GORDON, ALAN MARTIN, b Brooklyn, NY, Feb 9, 30; m 59; c 3. ROMANCE LANGUAGES. *Educ:* Harvard Uhiv, AB, 52, AM, 53, PhD, 56. *Prof Exp:* Instr Span, Harvard Univ, 57-60; asst prof, 60-65, ASSOC PROF SPAN, UNIV TORONTO, 65- *Concurrent Pos:* Buenos Aires convention grant to Cuba, 56-57; Can Coun grant, 68-69. *Mem:* MLA; Can Asn Hispanists; Can Asn Latin Am Studies. *Res:* Applied linguistics; American-Spanish dialectology. *Publ:* Auth, Elementary Spanish: An Audio-Lingual Approach, Macmillan, 65. *Mailing Add:* Dept of Hisp Studies Univ Toronto Toronto ON M5S 1A1 Can

GORDON, ALEXANDER LOBBAN, b Grantown-on-Spey, Scotland, Apr 12, 35. FRENCH. *Educ:* Aberdeen Univ, MA, 58; Sorbonne, DUniv (French), 65. *Prof Exp:* Asst English, Univ Rennes, 58-59; from lectr to asst prof French, 61-70, ASSOC PROF FRENCH, UNIV MAN, 70- *Mem:* MLA; Int Soc Hist Rhetoric. *Res:* French poetry of the 16th century; modern French poetry. *Publ:* Auth, Daniel D'Auge, interprete de la poetique d'Aristote, Bibliot Humanisme et Renaissance, 66; Ronsard et la Rhetorique, Droz, Geneva, 70; Things dying, things newborn: The poetry of Yves Bonnefoy, Mosaic, 73; From anti-platon to Pierre ecrite: Bonnefoy's indispensable death, World Lit Today, summer 79; Bonnefoy and 'la conscience dans les pierres', Dalhouse Fr Studies, 10/79; Pierre de Courcelles et sa Rhetorique (1557), Bibliotheque d'humanisme et renaissance, XLIII: 471-485. *Mailing Add:* Dept of French & Span Unif of Mann Winnipeg MB R3T 2M8 Can

GORDON, ARTHUR E, b Marlborough, Mass, Oct 7, 02; m 24, 37; c 1. LATIN. *Educ:* Dartmouth Col, AB, 23; Johns Hopkins Univ, PhD, 29. *Prof Exp:* Instr Latin, Dartmouth Col, 25-27; asst ancient hist, Johns Hopkins Univ, 27-28; assoc prof Latin & ancient hist, Univ Vt, 29-30; asst prof to prof, 30-70, chmn dept classics, 53-59, EMER PROF LATIN, UNIV CALIF, BERKELEY, 70- *Concurrent Pos:* Res fel, Am Acad Rome, 48-49; Guggenheim fel & Fulbright res scholar, Italy, 55-56; vis prof classics, Ashland Col, 70-71 & Ohio State Univ, fall 71; Nat Endowment for Humanities fel, 72-73. *Mem:* Am Philol Asn; Archaeol Inst Am; Class Asn Pac States; Philol Asn Pac Coast(pres, 52); Class Asn Eng. *Res:* Latin epigraphy. *Publ:* Auth, Epigraphica, Vol I, 35, Vol II, 36 Supralineate Abbreviations in Latin Inscriptions, 48, 77; Q Veranius, Coas A D 29, 52; Potitus Valerius Messalla, Cos Suff 29 BC, 54; coauth, Contributions to the Palaeography of Latin Inscriptions, 57, 77; Album of Dated Latin Inscriptions, Parts I-IV, 58-65; auth, The Inscribed Fibula Praenestina, Problems of Authenticity, 75. *Mailing Add:* 125 Camino del Mar Inverness CA 94937

GORDON, CYRUS H, b Philadelphia, Pa, June 29, 08; m 46; c 5. NEAR EAST CULTURE. *Educ:* Univ Pa, AB, 27, AM, 28, PhD, 30. *Hon Degrees:* DHL, Baltimore Hebrew Col, 81. *Prof Exp:* Instr Hebrew & Assyrian, Univ Pa, 30-31; teaching res scholar Semitic langs, Johns Hopkins Univ, 36-38; vis lectr Bible & ancient hist, Smith Col, 38-41; mem, Inst Advan Study, 39-42; prof Assyriol & Egyptol, Dropsie Col, 46-56; prof Mediter studies, Brandeis Univ, 56-73; PROF HEBREW STUDIES, NY UNIV, 73-, DIR, CTR EBLA RES, 82- *Concurrent Pos:* Field archaeologist, Am Schs Orient Res, Jerusalem & Baghdad, 31-35; Am Coun Learned Soc fel, 32-33; Am-Scand Found fel, 39; vis prof, New Sch Social Res, 47 & 54-57 & Jewish Inst Relig, 56-57; trustee, Boston Hebrew Col, 65-; vis fel humanities, Univ Colo, 67; corresp mem, Inst Antiq & Christianity, Claremont Grad Sch & Univ Ctr, 67. *Mem:* Hon fel Royal Asiatic Soc; Am Orient Soc; Soc Bibl Lit; Archaeol Inst Am; fel Am Acad Arts & Sci. *Res:* Glyptic art; classical and Egypto-Semitic interrelations; history of antiquity. *Publ:* Auth, Smith College Tablets, Smith Col, 52; Hammurapi's Code, Holt, 57; Before the Bible, Harper, 63; The Ancient Near East, 65, The Common Background of Greek and Hebrew Civilizations, 65 & Ugarit and Minoan Crete, 66; Norton; Evidence for the Minoan Language, Ventnor, 66; Ugaritic Textbook, Pontif Bibl Inst, Rome, 67; Forgotten Scripts, Basic Bks, 71, rev ed, 82. *Mailing Add:* Dept of Hebrew Cult East Bldg 637 NY Univ Washington Sq New York NY 10003

GORDON, DONALD BISHOP, b Chicago, Ill, Sept 21, 11; m 40; c 2. FRENCH, SPANISH. *Educ:* Westminster Col, Mo, AB, 33; Wash Univ, AM, 37. *Prof Exp:* From instr to prof French, 36-72, registr, 43-72, asst dean, 62-72, distinguished serv prof mod lang & chmn dept, 72-75, dean, 75-76, EMER DEAN, WESTMINSTER COL, MO, 76-, DISTINGUISHED PROF FOREIGN LANG, 72- *Mem:* Am Asn Teachers Fr; MLA. *Res:* Seventeenth century and modern French literature. *Publ:* Auth, Trade secrets of Maupassant, Writer Mag, 48; Improving the church college, Presby Surv, 48. *Mailing Add:* Dept of Mod Lang Westminster Col Fulton MO 65251

GORDON, DONALD KEITH, b St Catherine, Jamaica, Sept 27, 35; Jamaican & Can citizen; m 64; c 2. SPANISH AMERICAN LITERATURE. *Educ:* Univ Toronto, BA, 58, MA, 63, PhD(Hisp studies), 69. *Prof Exp:* Asst prof Span, Univ Guelph, 66-70; asst prof, 70-72, ASSOC PROF SPAN, UNIV MAN, 72- *Concurrent Pos:* Appointed Jamaican honorary consul at Winnipeg, 6/81. *Mem:* Can Asn Hispanists (secy-treas, 72-74); Can Asn Latin Am Studies; Am Asn Teachers Span & Port. *Res:* Contemporary Mexican prose fiction; the contemporary short story in Spain; Costa Rican prose fiction since 1950. *Publ:* Auth, The Green Paper on Immigration Policy, Queen's Printer Can, 75; Review of Sedwick & Azana, In: Conversacion con madrilenos, Can Mod Lang Rev, 76; Los cuentos de Juan Rulfo, Playor, 76; Jamaica's influence on Limon, Jamaica Gleaner, 77; Ticoburocracia, Tico Times, 77; Review of R L Jackson, In: Black Writers in Latin America, Can Mod Lang Rev, 81; Prologo to Marinero del alba, Ed La Alborada, 82; Manifestations of racism in high places, Contrast, 82. *Mailing Add:* Dept of French & Span Univ of Man Winnipeg MB R3T 2N2 Can

GORJANC, ADELE ALEXANDRA, b Italy; nat US; c 2. FRENCH, ITALIAN. *Educ:* Teacher's Col, BS, 49; Lincoln Univ, BA, 62; Univ Mo-Columbia, MA, 63, DPhil(French & Ital), 67. *Prof Exp:* Instr French & Ital, Univ Mo-Columbia, 63-67; assoc prof, 67-80, PROF FRENCH ITAL, WILLIAM WOODS COL, 67-, CHMN JOINT DEPT FOREIGN LANG, WILLIAM WOODS & WESTMINSTER COLS, 75- *Concurrent Pos:* Chmn, Comt Int Studies, Mid-Mo Assoc Cols & Univs, 77- *Mem:* MLA; Am Asn Teachers Ital; Am Asn Teachers Fr. *Res:* Renaissance; foreign languages in commerece and industry; Italian language. *Publ:* Auth, Italian Conversation: A Practical Guide for Students and Travelers, Branden, 76. *Mailing Add:* Dept of Foreign Lang William Woods Col Fulton MO 65251

GORLIN, LALLA E, b Leningrad, Russia, July 11, 13; US citizen. GERMANIC LANGUAGES & LITERATURE. *Educ:* Hunter Col, BA, 56; Columbia Univ, MA, 57, PhD(Ger), 68. *Prof Exp:* Lectr Ger, Barnard Col, Columbia Univ, 61-62, instr, 62-67; lectr, 67-68, instr, 68-71, ASST PROF GER, BROOKLYN COL, 71- *Mem:* MLA; Am Asn Teachers Ger; Int Arthur Schnitzler Res Asn. *Res:* Arthur Schnitzler. *Publ:* Auth, A survey of Russian readers, Mod Lang J, 4/48; Mayakowky, In: Collier's Encycl, Vol XV, 61. *Mailing Add:* 304 W 78th St New York NY 10024

GORMAN, JOHN, b Hoboken, NJ, Aug 28, 38. GERMAN. *Educ:* Manhattan Col, BA, 60; Johns Hopkins Univ, MA, 61, PhD(Ger), 67. *Prof Exp:* Asst prof foreign lang, Lamar State Col, 65-66 & Univ Miami, 67-74; WRITER, 74- *Res:* German-Spanish literary relations; comparative literature. *Publ:* Transl, Lorenz Winter, Heinrich Mann and His Public, Univ Miami, 70; auth, The Reception of Federico Garcia Lorca in Germany, Göppinger Arbeiten für Germanistik, 73; coauth, Federico Garcia Lorca Bibliography, MLA, 78. *Mailing Add:* 4713 NW 7th St Miami FL 33126

GOSSMAN, JEFFREY LIONEL, b Glasgow, Scotland, May 31, 29; m 63. FRENCH. *Educ:* Univ Glasgow, MA, 51; Univ Paris, dipl, 52; Oxford Univ, DPhil, 57. *Prof Exp:* Asst lectr French, Univ Glasgow, 57-58; from asst prof to prof, Johns Hopkins Univ, 58-76; PROF ROMANCE LANG, PRINCETON UNIV, 76- *Concurrent Pos:* Am Coun Learned Soc study fel, 69-70; Nat Endowment for Humanities fel, 78-79. *Mem:* MLA. *Res:* French literature of the 17th and 18th centuries. *Publ:* Auth, Men and Masks: A Study of Moliere, 63 & Medievalism and the Ideologies of Englightenment, 68, Johns Hopkins Univ; French Society and Culture: An Introduction to Eighteenth-Century France, Prentice-Hall, 73; Augustin Thierry and Liberal Historiography, Weleyan Univ, 76; The Empire Unpossess'd: An Essay on Gibbon's Decline and Fall, Cambridge Univ, 81. *Mailing Add:* 206 E Pyne Princeton Univ Princeton NJ 08540

GOSTAUTAS, STASYS, b Kaunas, Lithuania, Jan 3, 39; US citizen; m 66; c 3. LATIN AMERICAN LITERATURE. *Educ:* Fordham Univ, BA, 66; NY Univ, MA, 67, PhD(Span), 71. *Prof Exp:* From instr to asst prof Span, 68-77, Wellesley Col, chmn dept, 73-77; vis asst prof, Boston Univ, 77-81; VIS ASST PROF SPAN, LAFAYETTE COL, 81- *Concurrent Pos:* Consult Latin Am lit, Encycl Britannica, 65-; ed, Vision, 65-68. *Mem:* MLA; Am Asn Teachers Apsn & Port; Inst Int Lit Iberoam; Inst Lithuanian Studies. *Res:* Latin American Colonial literature; Latin American novel; Picaresque novel. *Publ:* Auth, El auge de la nueva narrativa hispanoamericana, In: Encycl Britannica, 71; La evasion de la ciudad en las novelas de R Arlt, Revista Iveroam, 72; Dostoievski en las novelas de Roberto Arlt, Nueva Narrativa Hispanoam, 73; De la vanguardia a la literatura africana, In: Encycl Britannica, 73; Del Arbol de los Veras a La endiablada, In: Estudios . . .ofrecidos a Rodrigo A Molina, 77 U Buenos Aires y Arlt, 77, Insula, Madrid; Dos humanistas espanoles del siglo XVI en Italia, Polonia y Lithuania, In: El Cardenal Albornoz y el Colegio de Espana, Bolonia, 78; co-ed, Homenaje a Jorge Guillen, Wellesley Col, 78. *Mailing Add:* Dept of Lang Lafayette Col Easton PA 18042

GOTH, MAJA JULIA, b Basel, Switz, Aug 5, 23. FOREIGN LANGUAGES. *Educ:* Univ Basel, Dipl, 46, PhD, 55. *Prof Exp:* Teacher, Mädchengym, Basel, 47; asst, dept Ger, Lycee Fenelon, Paris, France, 47-51; teacher, Basel, 51-55; from instr to assoc prof, 56-68, chmn dept, 63-78, PROF GER, WELLESLEY COL, 68-, CHMN DEPT, 81- *Mem:* MLA; AAUP; Int Germanisten Verein. *Res:* Modern French and German literature and philosophy; poetics; Goethe. *Publ:* Auth, Kafka et Les Lettres Francaises, Jose Corti, France, 56; The myth of Narcissus in the works of Rilke and of Valery, Wis Studies Contemporary Lit, winter-spring 66; Existentialism and

Franz Kafka: Sarte, Camus and their relationship to Kafka, Proc Comp Lit Symp, 1/71; Der Surrealismus und Franz Kafka, In: Franz Kafka, Wissenschaftliche Buchgesellschaft, Darmstadt, 73; Rilke und Valery, Aspekte ihrer Poetik, Francke Verlag, Munchen und Bern, 81. *Mailing Add:* Dept of Ger Wellesley Col Wellesley MA 02181

GOTOFF, HAROLD CHARLES, b New York, NY, Apr 19, 36; m 69; c 2. CLASSICAL PHILOLOGY. *Educ:* Amherst Col, BA, 56; Cornell Univ, MA, 58; Cambridge Univ, BA, 62; Harvard Univ, PhD(classics), 65. *Prof Exp:* Instr classics, Univ NC, 65-66; from instr to asst prof, Harvard Univ, 66-73; assoc prof, Univ Mass, Boston, 73-77; ASSOC PROF CLASSICS, UNIV ILL, URBANA, 77- *Mem:* Am Philol Asn; fel Am Acad Rome. *Res:* Textual transmission and criticism; Latin prose style; Greek and Latin literature. *Publ:* Auth, Virgil's Fourth Ecologue, Philogus, 67; The Text of Lucan in the Ninth Century, Harvard Univ, 71; The concept of periodicity in Ad Her, 73 & Tibullus: Nunc Levis est Tractanda Venus, 74, Harvard Studies; Cicero's Elegant Style, Univ Ill, 79; Thrasymachus of Calchedon, Class Philol, 81; Erasmus on Cicero, Univ Ill, 80, 81. *Mailing Add:* 4072 Foreign Lang Univ Ill Urbana IL 61801

GOTTLIEB, MARLENE DIANE, b New York, NY, Sept 13, 45. CONTEMPORARY LATIN AMERICAN LITERATURE. *Educ:* Hunter Col, BA, 65; Columbia Univ, MA, 66, PhD(Span), 71. *Prof Exp:* Asst prof, 67-80, ASSOC PROF SPAN, LEHMAN COL, 80- *Concurrent Pos:* Resident dir, studies abroad in Granada, City Univ New York, 71-72, dir studies abroad in Mex, 73-74; mem, Span Doctoral Fac, City Univ New York Grad Ctr, 77- *Mem:* Am Asn Teachers Span & Port. *Res:* Contemporary Latin American poetry with emphasis on Chile; contemporary Latin American fiction; contemporary Spanish poetry. *Publ:* Auth, Pablo Nervda & Cesar Vallejo, 9-10/67 & Canciones rusas de Nicanor Parra, 1-2/70, Cuadernos Am; Del Antipoema al artefacto al . . . , la trayectoria poetica de Nicanor Parra, Hispamerica, 4/74; Un mundo en crisis: Emrgency Poems de Nicanor Parra, Ind: Am Hispanist, 75; No se termina nunca de nacer: La poesia de Nicanor Parra, Playor, Madrid, 77; El Burlador de Sevilla & Francisco Villaespesa In: Communicaciones del simposia internacional sobre Villaespesay Modernmismo, Almeria, 77. *Mailing Add:* Dept of Romance Lang Herbert H Lehman Col Bedford Park Blvd Bronx NY 10468

GOTTLOB, VICKIE NEELY, b Washington, DC, Dec 4, 49; m 70. FRENCH LITERATURE. *Educ:* Fla State Univ, BA, 69, MA, 70, PhD(French), 73. *Prof Exp:* Asst prof, 73-80, ASSOC PROF FRENCH, CENTENARY COL LA, 80- *Mem:* Am Asn Teachers Fr; MLA. *Res:* Fenelon; religious literature of 17th century in France; 18th century French novel. *Mailing Add:* Dept of Foreign Lang Centenary Col of La Shreveport LA 71104

GOTTSCHALK, GUNTHER H, b Berlin, Ger, Sept 30, 29; US citizen; div; c 1. GERMAN LANGUAGE & LITERATURE. *Educ:* Univ Southern Calif, PhD, 63. *Prof Exp:* Lectr Ger, Univ Southern Calif, 56-59; instr Ger, 59-62, asst prof, 62-66, lectr, 66-69, assoc dean col lett & sci, 69-76, assoc prof, 69-80, chairperson dept, 76-80, PROF GER LANG & LIT, UNIV CALIF, SANTA BARBARA, 80- *Concurrent Pos:* Assoc dir, Univ Calif Studies Ctr, George-August Univ, Goettingen, Germany, 67-69. *Mem:* MLA; Am Asn Teachers Ger; Deutsche Schillergesellschaft. *Res:* General philology; computer studies; selected authors of 20th century literature. *Publ:* Auth, Lion Feuchtwanger, Bouvier, 65; Verb groups: A study in new high German syntax, Lingua, 69; Dichter und ihre Handschriften, Akad Verlag, 79. *Mailing Add:* Dept of Ger & Slavic Lang & Lit Univ of Calif Santa Barbara CA 93106

GOTTSCHALK, MARTIN E, b Winters, Tex, Aug 1, 30; m 63; c 2. GERMAN. *Educ:* Tex Lutheran Col, BA, 51; Univ Tex, Austin, MA, 60,. *Prof Exp:* Instr Ger, Tex A&M Univ, 60-67; asst prof, 67-68, ASSOC PROF GER, HOWARD PAYNE UNIV, 68- *Mem:* Am Asn Teachers Ger. *Res:* Language dialects; language syntax and grammar. *Publ:* Auth, A Beginning in German, Shaffer's Univ Bkstore, 65; A routine for the open hour lab, Nat Asn Lang Lab Dir Newslett, 12/68; German Grammar, 72 & Everyday German for Americans, 73, Quick Print & Specialties. *Mailing Add:* Dept of Ger Howard Payne Univ Brownwood TX 76801

GOTZKOWSKY, BODO KARL, b Fulda, Ger, Jan 26, 35; m 63; c 2. GERMAN LANGUAGE & LITERATURE. *Educ:* La State Univ, BA, 59, MA, 62; Rice Univ, PhD (Ger), 66. *Prof Exp:* Asst Ger, La State Univ, 58-60; instr, Univ Miss, 60-62; instr, Univ Houston, 62-66; asst prof, 67-72, assoc prof, 72-76, chmn, Dept Ger & Russ, 72-78, PROF GER, TULANE UNIV, 76- *Concurrent Pos:* Grantee, Am Philos Soc, 69. *Mem:* Am Asn Teachers Ger; SCent Mod Lang Asn. *Res:* Sixteenth and 17th century German literature; German folklore. *Publ:* Auth, Die verschiedenen Drucke des Volksbuches des Finkenritter und seine Aufnahme in Dänemark und Schweden, Hessische Blätter Volkskunde, 71-72; ed, Barbarossa, Vol I, In: Johannes Adelphus, Selected Works, DeGruyter, 74; auth, Untersuchungen zur Barbarossa Biographie (1520) des Johannes Adelphus und ihr Verhältnis zum Volksbuch (1519) vom Kaiser Friedrich, Daphnis, 74; ed, Hans Wilhelm Kirchhof, Militaris Disciplina, Hiersemann, 76; auth, Hans Wilhelm Kirchhof, Neue Deutsche Biographic, 77; ed, Historia von Rhodis, Turckisch Chronica, Vol II, Das Buch des Lebens, Vol III, In: Johannes Adelphus, De Gruyter, 80; Hans Wilhelm Kirchhof, Kleine Schriften, Hiersemann, 81; auth, Johannes Adelphus Muling, Schaffhause beitrage zur Geschichte, 81. *Mailing Add:* Dept of Ger & Slavic Lang Tulane Univ New Orleans LA 70118

GOUGHER, RONALD LEE, b Allentown, Pa, July 27, 39; m 66; c 1. FOREIGN LANGUAGE, INTERNATIONAL EDUCATION. *Educ:* Muhlenberg Col, BA, 61; Lehigh Univ, MA, 64; Goethe Inst, Adv Cert, 69. *Prof Exp:* Chmn dept foreign lang, Parkland High Sch, Allentown, Pa, 61-65; instr Ger, Lehigh Univ, 65-69; ASSOC PORF GER & DIR INT EDUC, WEST CHESTER STATE COL, 69-, CHMN DEPT FOREIGN LANG, 78- *Concurrent Pos:* Fulbright travel, Ger Govt & US Off Educ, 69; consult, Ctr Curriculum Develop, Chilton Co, Philadlphia, Pa, 69-72; co-ed, Individualization Foreign Lang Learning in Am, 70-; auth, US Off Educ grant, Teacher's Guide for Adapting Mat for Individualizing Instruct, 72-73; consult, Rand McNally Corp, 72-78; treas, Pa Consortium Int Educ, 78- *Mem:* Am Asn Teachers Ger; Am Coun Teaching Foreign Lang; Philos Educ Soc; Northeast Conf Teaching Foreign Lang. *Res:* Philosophy of education. *Publ:* Auth, Issac Habrecht's Janua Linguarum Quadrilingus, 1624, Papers Bibliog Soc; Vol 62, No 1; A Note of the history of Janua Linguarum, winter 69 & A Comparism of English and American views of the German University, winter 69, History Educ Quart; Individualization of instruction, Britannica Rev Foreign Lang Educ, 72; ed, Individualization of Instruction in Foreign Languages, Rand McNally, 72-73; ed, Individualizing instruction, Foreign Lang Ann, 70-74 & co-ed, Northeast Conf Reports. *Mailing Add:* Dept of Foreign Lang West Chester State Col West Chester PA 19380

GOULD, THOMAS FAUSS, b East Liverpool, Ohio, July 15, 27. CLASSICS, PHILOSOPHY. *Educ:* Cornell Univ, BA, 50, MA, 51, PhD, 54. *Prof Exp:* Instr classics, Wash Univ, 53-55; instr, Amherst Col, 55-56, from asst prof to assoc prof classic & philos, 56-63; prof, Univ Tex, Austin, 64-71; PROF CLASSICS, YALE UNIV, 71- *Concurrent Pos:* Trustee res fel, 58; Leverhulme Trust vis fel, St Andrews Univ, Scotland, 61-62; ed, Arion, 64-; Guggenheim fel, 66; fel comnr, Peterhouse, Cambridge, 66 & vis fel, 74; vis prof, Yale Univ, 68. *Mem:* Soc Ancient Greek Philos. *Res:* Plato; Aristotle; Greek tragedy. *Publ:* Auth, Platonic Love, Routledge & Kegan Paul & Free Press of Glencoe, 63; ed, The Discourses of Epictetus, Washington Square, 63, auth, The innocence of Oedipus, Arion, autumn 65, winter 65 & 66; transl & commentary, Oedipus the King, Prentice-Hall, 69; auth, The innocence of Oedipus and the nature of tragedy, Mass Rev, spring 69. *Mailing Add:* Dept of Classics Yale Univ New Haven CT

GOYNE, MINETTA ALTGELT, Germanic Languages, English. See Vol II

GRABOWSKI, YVONNE S, b Poland, Can citizen. RUSSIAN, SLAVIC STUDIES. *Educ:* Univ Lodz, MA, 51; Univ Warsaw, MA, 52; Univ Toronto, MA, 62, PhD(Slavic studies), 69. *Prof Exp:* Lectr, 64-69, asst prof, 69-78, ASSOC PROF RUSS, YORK UNIV, 78- *Concurrent Pos:* Can Coun post grad fel, 59-62; Soc Sci Humanities Res Coun leave, 80-81. *Mem:* Can Asn Slavists; Can Ling Asn; Polish Inst Comp Civilizations; Can Ethnic Studies. *Res:* Languages in contact; Russian and Polish languages and literatures. *Publ:* Coauth, Anthology of American Thought in the Eighteenth Century, Polish Sci Publ, Warsaw, 63; auth, Recent English loans in Polish language, Can Slavonic Papers, XIII: 65-72; English loan words in contemporary Russian, Slavonic-East Europ Studies, XVII: 121-129; English loan words in Polish, Prace Filolgiczne, XXII: 221-233; English language influence on Russian and Polish, Can Contribr VII Cong Slavists, 73; Some features of Polish and other slavic languages in Canada; Polish Rev, 77; Some recent changes in Canadian Polish, Can Contribr Villougress Slavists, 78. *Mailing Add:* Dept of Foreign Lit Stong Col York Univ Downsview ON M3J 1P3 Can

GRACE, GEORGE WILLIAM, b Corinth, Miss, Sept 8, 21; div. LINGUISTICS, ANTHROPOLOGY. *Educ:* Univ Geneva, Lic, 48; Columbia Univ, PhD(anthrop), 58. *Prof Exp:* Asst prof sociol, Women's Col, Univ NC, 58-59; asst prof anthrop, Northwestern Univ, 59-60; asst prof, Southern Ill Univ, 60-63, assoc prof, 63-64; sr specialist, East-West Ctr, 63-64, chmn dept ling, 66-69, PROF LING, UNIV HAWAII, MANOA, 64- *Mem:* AAAS; Am Anthrop Asn; Ling Soc Am. *Res:* Languages of Oceania; language classification; relations between language and culture. *Publ:* Auth, Austronesian linguistics and culture history, Am Anthropologist, 61; On the scientific status of genetic classification in linguistics, Oceanic Ling, 65; Notes on the phonological history of the Austronesian languages of the Sarmi coast, Oceanic Ling, 71; Canala Dictionary (New Caledonia), C-2, 75 & Grand Couli Dictionary (New Caledonia), C-12, 76, Pacific Ling; An Essay on Language, Hornbeam Press, 81. *Mailing Add:* Dept of Ling Univ of Hawaii at Manoa Honolulu HI 96822

GRACE, LEE ANN, b Meadville, Pa. SPANISH, LINGUISTICS. *Educ:* State Univ of NY at Buffalo, BA, 69, MA, 71, PhD(Spanish), 76. *Prof Exp:* Actg assoc dean, 80-81, ASST PROF SPAN & LING, STATE UNIV NY COL BUFFALO, 73-, ASSOC DEAN ARTS & HUMANITIES, 81- *Mem:* MLA; Am Asn Teachers of Span & Port; Am Asn Advan Humanities. *Res:* Bilingualism; applied linguistics, Spanish; language and the sexes. *Publ:* Auth, Multiple symbolism in the Libro de Buen Amor: The erotic in the Forces of Don Carnal, Hispanic Rev, 75; contribr, Indigenisms in Mexican Spanish: A sociolinguistic approach, In: Linguistic Approaches to the Romance Lexicon, Georgetown Univ, 78; auth, Lizardi and linguistic realism in the Picaresque, Bollettino dell'Istituto di Lingue Estere, Genoa, 78; contribr, Los mestizos y los indigenismos, 1550-1600, In: Dialectologia hispanoamericana: Estudios Actuales, Georgetown Univ, 80. *Mailing Add:* Dept of Foreign Lang State Univ NY Buffalo NY 14222

GRADMAN, HARRY LEE, b Louisville, Ky, Dec 14, 42. LINGUISTICS, ENGLISH AS A FOREIGN LANGUAGE. *Educ:* Miami Univ, BA, 64; Ind Univ, Bloomington, MA, 66, cert appl ling, 68, PhD(ling), 70. *Prof Exp:* Lectr ling, Ind Univ, Bloomington, 68-69, Urban & Overseas English Prog, 69-70, asst prof, 71; asst prof ling, Univ NMex, 71-72; asst prof urban & overseas English prog, 72-76, ASSOC PROF EDUC, IND UNIV, BLOOMINGTON, 76-, CHMN, DEPT LING, 79- *Mem:* Teachers English to Speakers Other Lang; Am Coun Teachers Foreign Lang; Nat Asn For Student Affairs; Int Asn Appl Ling; Irish Asn Teachers English as Second or Other Lang. *Res:* Second language acquisition; language testing; contrastive analysis. *Publ:* Auth, The limitations of contrastive analysis prediction, 71 & What methodologists ignore in contrastive teaching, 71, Working Papers in Ling; Reduced redundancy testing: A reconsideration, In: Testing in Second Language Teaching: New Dimensions, Dublin, 73; coauth (with Bernard Spolsky), Reduced redundancy testing: A progress report, In: Language Testing Symposium, Ctr Appl Ling, 75; (with Stephen J Gaies & Bernard Spolsky), Toward the measurement of functional proficiency: Contextualization of the noise test, TESOL Quart, 3/77; (with Edith Hanania), Acquisition of English structures: A case study of an adult native speaker of Arabic in an English speaking environment, Lang Learning, 6/77; English as a foreign language, In: Classroom-Relevant Research in the Language Arts, ACSD, 78. *Mailing Add:* Dept of Ling Ind Univ Bloomington IN 47405

GRAFTON, ANTHONY THOMAS, History, Classics. See Vol I

GRAGG, GENE BALFORD, b Amsterdam, NY, Aug 24, 38; m 69; c 2. LINGUISTICS, SUMEROLOGY. *Educ:* Loyola Univ, Chicago, BA, 60; West Baden Col, Lic Phil, 62; Univ Chicago, PhD(ling), 66. *Prof Exp:* Res assoc Sumerian, Univ Amsterdam, 67-69; asst prof, 69-73, ASSOC PROF LING & SUMERIAN & CHMN DEPT, UNIV CHICAGO, 73- *Mem:* Ling Soc Am; Am Orient Soc. *Res:* Historical linguistics; Sumerian; Cushitic. *Publ:* Auth, The Sumerian Dimensional Infixes, Butzon, 73; The fable of the heron and the turtle, Arch Orient-forschung, 73; Linguistics, method, and extinct languages, Orient-alia, 73; Cleft sentences on Tigrinya, J African Lang, 73; Oromo of Wallagga, In: Non-Semitoc Languages of Ethiopia, 75; Amhara loanwords in Oromo, Vth Int Cong Ethiopian Studies Acts, 77; Morpheme structure conditions in Amharz, Afroasiatic Ling, 78; Polysemy and lexical hedundoney rules, Charles Lamb Soc, 78. *Mailing Add:* Oriental Institute Univ of Chicago 1155 E 58th St Chicago IL 60637

GRAHAM, JOHN, Speech. See Vol II

GRAHAM, ROBERT SOMERVILLE, b Vegreville, Can, May 14, 13; nat US; m 47; c 1. FRENCH. *Educ:* Queens Univ, Can, BA, 38; Univ Colo, MA, 53, PhD(French), 55. *Prof Exp:* Instr French & Span, Upper Can Col, 48-49; asst prof mod lang, Fisk Univ, 49-52; instr French, Univ Colo, 51-55; instr mod lang, Univ Calif, Riverside, 55-57; instr, Univ NDak, 57-58; assoc prof French, Univ Northern Colo, 58-69, prof, 69-78; RETIRED. *Concurrent Pos:* Asst & acting inform officer, Brit Polit Mission, Hungary, 45-48. *Mem:* Can Ling Asn; Am Asn Teachers French. *Res:* French literature; general linguistics; stylistics. *Publ:* Auth, The anglicization of German family names in Western Canada, Am Speech; Bilingualism and the Creative Writer, Word; The transition from German to English in German settlements in Saskatchewan, 3/57; Spanish-language radio in Northern Colorado, Am Speech, 10/62; The music of language and the foreign accent, French Rev, 2/69. *Mailing Add:* 2620 17th Ave Greeley CO 80631

GRAHAM, VICTOR ERNEST, b Calgary, Alta, May 31, 20; m 46; c 4. FRENCH LITERATURE. *Educ:* Univ Alta, BA, 46; Oxford Univ, BA, 48, DLitt, 68; Columbia Univ, PhD, 53. *Prof Exp:* From asst prof to prof French, Univ Alta, 48-58, asst to dir, 52-58; assoc prof, 58-60, chmn grad dept French, 65-67, assoc dean sch grad studies, 67-69, vprin, univ col, 69-70, PROF FRENCH, UNIV TORONTO, 60- *Concurrent Pos:* Vis lectr, Univ Mich, 54-55; Can Coun sr fel, 63; Guggenheim fel, 70-71; Connaught fel, 78-79; vis prof, Univ Victoria, 80-81. *Mem:* Royal Soc Can. *Res:* French literature of the 16th century; relations between poetry, music and art. *Publ:* Ed, Critical editions of the works of Desportes, 7 vols, in ser, 58-63 & Pernette du Guillet, 68, textes litteraires francais, Droz, Geneva; The Imagery of Proust, Blackwell's, Oxford, 66; coauth, Estienne Jodelle, le Recueil des Inscriptions, 72, The Paris Entries of Charles IX and Elizabeth of Austria 1271, 74 & The Royal Tour of France by Charles IX and Catherine de Medicis, 79, Univ Toronto. *Mailing Add:* Dept of French Univ of Toronto Toronto ON M5S 1V4 Can

GRANT, JOHN NEILSON, b Edinburgh, Scotland, May 3, 40; m 62; c 3. CLASSICS. *Educ:* Univ Edinburgh, MA, 62; Cambridge Univ, BA, 64; Univ of St Andrews, PhD(Latin), 70. *Prof Exp:* Lectr classics, Univ Man, 65-67; asst prof, 67-72, assoc prof, 72-80, PROF CLASSICS, UNIV TORONTO, 80-, CHMN, 82- *Concurrent Pos:* Can Coun fel, 77-78. *Mem:* Class Asn Can; Am Philol Asn. *Res:* Roman comedy; transmission of texts; republican Latin literature. *Publ:* Auth, Notes on Donatus' commentary on Adelphoe, Greek, Roman & Byzantine Studies, 12/71; The miniatures of Terence, Class Quart, 73; The ending of Terence's Adelphoe and the Menandrian original, Am J Philol, 75; Contamination in the mixed mass of Terence, Trans Am Philol Asn, 75; Three passages in Terence's Adelphoe, Am J Philol, 76; The commentum Monacense and the MS tradition of Terence, Manuscripta, 78; Propertius 1.18, Phoenix, 79; The beginning of Menander Adelphoe B, Class Quart, 80. *Mailing Add:* Dept Class Univ Toronto Toronto ON M5S 1A1 Can

GRANT, JOHN RATCLIFFE, b Wei Whei Fu, China, Oct 6, 13; Can citizen; m 46. CLASSICS. *Educ:* Univ Toronto, BA, 36; Harvard Univ, AM, 37, PhD, 47. *Prof Exp:* Lectr Classics, Dalhousie Univ, 40-42; assoc prof, Western Reserve Univ, 46-50; assoc prof, 50-67, PROF CLASSICS, VICTORIA COL, UNIV TORONTO, 67- *Mem:* Am Philol Asn; Class Asn Can. *Res:* Greek and Roman history. *Publ:* Auth, Leonidas' last stand, Phoenix, 61; A note on the tone of Greek diplomacy, Class Quart, 65; Toward knowing Thucydides, Phoenix, 74. *Mailing Add:* Victoria Col Univ Toronto Toronto ON M5S 1V4 Can

GRANT, RICHARD BABSON, b Boston, Mass, Jan 18, 25. FRENCH. *Educ:* Harvard Univ, PhD(Romance lang), 52. *Prof Exp:* From instr to prof Romance lang, Duke Univ, 52-71; PROF FRENCH, UNIV TEX, AUSTIN, 71- *Mem:* MLA; Am Asn Teachers Fr. *Res:* French naturalism; French romanticism. *Publ:* Auth, The Jewish question in Zola's L'Argent, PMLA, 12/55; Zola's Son Excellence Eugene Rougon: An Historical and Critical Study, Duke Univ, 60; Imagery as a means of psychological revelation in Maupassant's Une Vie, Studies Philol, 10/63; The Perilous Quest: Image, Myth, and Prophecy in the Narratives of Victor Hugo, Duke Univ, 68; The Goncourt Brothers, Twayne, 72; coauth, Premieres Decouvertes Litteraires, Random, 72; auth, Theophile Gautier, Hall (Twayne), 75; Sequence and theme in Victor Hugo's Les Orientales, PMLA, 10/79. *Mailing Add:* Dept of French & Ital Univ of Tex Austin TX 78712

GRAS, MAURICE MARC, b Draguignan, France, Feb 11, 28; US citizen. ROMANCE LANGUAGES. *Educ:* Univ Aix-Marseille, Lic en Droit, 49; Univ Wis, PhD, 61. *Prof Exp:* Asst prof, 61-67, assoc prof, 67-74, PROF FRENCH, UNIV WIS-MADISON, 74- *Mem:* MLA; Am Asn Teachers Fr. *Res:* Sixteenth century French theatre and conteurs. *Publ:* Auth, R Garnier, Son Art et Sa Methode, Droz, Geneva, 65; coauth, Pensee et Litterature Francais, McGraw-Hill, 71. *Mailing Add:* Dept of French Univ of Wis Madison WI 53706

GRASS, ROLAND LEO, b St Louis, Mo, Oct 20, 25; m 50; c 2. HISPANIC LANGUAGE & LITERATURE. *Educ:* Washington Univ, AB, 50, AM, 55; Columbia Univ, PhD(Span), 68. *Prof Exp:* From instr to asst prof Span, 55-61; asst prof, Okla State Univ, 61-68, assoc prof, 68-69; PROF SPAN, WESTERN ILL UNIV, 71- *Concurrent Pos:* Fel, Nat Humanities Inst Univ Chicago, 76-77. *Mem:* Am Asn Teachers Span & Port; MLA. *Res:* The novel of the Mexican revolution; the Spanish American regional novel and essay; Modernismo. *Publ:* Auth, Como se hace una revolucion segun Emilio Rabasa, Cuadernos Am, 65; contribr, Pikarische Welt: Schriften zum europäischen schelmenroman, Wiss Buchges, Darmstadt, 69; Auth, Jose Lopez-Portillo y Rojas: A Novelist of Social Reform in Mexico Before the Revolution of 1910, Western Ill Univ, 70; contribr, Homenaje a Sherman H Eoff, Ed Castalia, Madrid, 70; ed, Andres Iduarte: un homenaje el escritor y masestro ofrecido por amigos y discipulos, Western Ill Univ, 75; co-ed, Homenaje a Andres Iduarte, 76 & Carlos Reyles and the Impact of the Symbolist-Decadent Novel in Spanish America, 77, Am Hispanist. *Mailing Add:* Dept of Foreign Lang & Lit Western Ill Univ Macomb IL 61455

GRAUPERA, ARTURO AGUSTIN, b Habana, Cuba, Aug 28, 16; m 56; c 3. SPANISH. *Educ:* Col Mimo, Cuba, BAS, 37; Univ Habana, LLD, 43; Univ Iowa, MA, 66. *Prof Exp:* Prof Span lit, Col De Las Americas, Cuba, 43-49; prof, St Joseph Sch, Habana, Cuba, 49-61; instr Span, Eastside Jr High Sch, Council Bluff, Iowa, 63-66; from instr to asst prof, 66-71, assoc prof, 71-79, PROF SPAN, IOWA STATE UNIV, 79- *Mem:* Am Asn Teachers Span. *Res:* Influence of English syntax in Southwest Florida Spanish; Spanish and Latin American civilization; Spanish and Spanish American drama and novel. *Publ:* Coauth, Espanol en Espanol, Van Nostrand, 70; auth, La oracion causativa, 12/77 & The Spanish article with titles, 5/78 & Pejorative connotations of El Tal and Un Tal: A comment, 12/81, Hispania; Latin American Essays, Prentice-Hall (in press). *Mailing Add:* Dept of Foreign Lang & Lit Iowa State Univ Ames IA 50010

GRAVA, ARNOLDS, b Riga, Latvia, Sept 30, 12; m 37; c 1. ROMANCE LANGUAGES & LITERATURE, PHILOSOPHY. *Educ:* Univ Lille, France, BA, 31; Univ Latvia, MA, 43; Univ Nebr, PhD(Romance lang), 54. *Prof Exp:* Instr, High Sch, Latvia, 37-38; expert mod lang, Riga Broadcasting, Latvia, 38-44; instr mod lang, West Ger, 45-51; asst French, Univ Nebr, 53-54; from asst prof mod lang & ling to prof, State Univ NY Albany, 54-75; RETIRED. *Concurrent Pos:* Grant-in-aid, State Univ NY Albany, 60-61; Danforth Found grant, 61; State Univ NY res grant, 68-69. *Mem:* Am Asn Teachers Fr. *Res:* French literature of the 18th and 19th centuries; phenomenological research in the history of ideas, including comparative religions; comparative linguistics. *Publ:* Auth, The Metaphysical Aspect of Evil in the Literary Works of Charles Baudelaire and Edgar Allan Poe, Univ Nebr Studies, 56; coauth, Diderot Studies, Vol IV, Droz, Switz, 63; auth, Molecular or atomic propositions . . ., Linguistics, 3/66; L'intuition baudelairienne de la realite bipolaire, Rev Sci Humaines, 7-9/67; A Structural Inquiry into the Symbolic Representation of Ideas, Mouton, The Hague, 68; L'aspect metaphysique du mal dans l'oeuvre litteraire de Charles Baudelaire et d'Edgar Allan Poe, Slatkine Reprints, Geneva, Switz, 76. *Mailing Add:* 11 South Lake Ave Albany NY 12203

GRAVIT, FRANCIS WEST, b Elkhart, Ind, Nov 1, 04;. FRENCH LITERATURE. *Educ:* Oberlin Col, AB, 28; Univ Mich, AM, 29, PhD, 39. *Prof Exp:* Instr French, Univ Mich, 28-34, 35-42, 45-48; from asst prof to prof, 48-75, from asst chmn dept to assoc chmn, 56-75, dir elem French, 48-70, EMER PROF FRENCH & ITAL, IND UNIV, BLOOMINGTON, 75- *Honors & Awards:* Palmes Academiques, 64. *Mem:* MLA; Mediaeval Acad Am; Am Asn Teachers Fr; Nat Fed Mod Lang Teachers Asn; Cent States Mod Lang Teachers Asn. *Res:* Scepticism; Freron and the Annee litteraire; bibliography. *Mailing Add:* 519 South Fess Ave Bloomington IN 47401

GRAY, EUGENE FRANCIS, b Flint, Mich, Apr 22, 36; m 64; c 2. FRENCH LITERATURE. *Educ:* Univ Mich, Ann Arbor, BSE, 60, MA, 62, PhD(Romance lang), 68. *Prof Exp:* Instr lang & phys sci, Detroit Inst Technol, 62-67; from instr to asst prof, 67-71, acting chmn dept, 71-72, assoc prof, 71-81, PROF FRENCH, MICH STATE UNIV, 81- *Concurrent Pos:* Contribr, The Romantic Movement, 74- *Mem:* Am Asn Teachers Fr; Les Amis de Flaubert. *Res:* Nineteenth century French novel; French literary style; history of science. *Publ:* Auth, Flaubert's esthetics and the problem of knowledge, Nineteenth-Century French Studies, spring 76; Emma by twilight: Flawed perception, In: Madame Bovary, Nineteenth Century Fr Studies, spring-summer 78; The clinical view of life: Gustave Flaubert's Madame Bovary, Med & Lit, 80. *Mailing Add:* Dept of Romance Lang Mich State Univ East Lansing MI 48824

GRAY, FLOYD FRANCIS, b Meadville, Pa, Aug 12, 26. FRENCH. *Educ:* Syracuse Univ, BA, 50; Inst Phonetique, Univ Paris, 51, Ecole Prof Francais a l'Etranger, cert, 51; Univ Wis, MA, 52, PhD, 56. *Prof Exp:* Asst English, Lycee Henri-Martin, Saint-Quentin, 50-51; instr French, Univ Wis, 55-56; from instr to assoc prof, 56-65, univ fel, 58, PROF FRENCH, UNIV MICH, ANN ARBOR, 65- *Concurrent Pos:* Vis prof 16th century French lit, Univ Calif, Santa Barbara, 70-71; managing ed, Mich Romance Studies. *Honors & Awards:* Palmes Academiques, French Govt, 75. *Mem:* Am Asn Teachers Fr; Soc ALmis Montaigne; MLA. *Res:* French 16th century literature, especially Montaigne; Du Bellay; Rabelais. *Publ:* Auth, Le Style de Montaigne, Nizet, Paris, 58; Albert Thibaudet's Montaigne, Gallimard, Paris, 63; ed & transl, Gargantua and Pantagruel, 66 & auth, Anthologie de la Poesie francaise du XVIe siecle, 67, Appleton; Rabelais et l'ecriture, Nizet, Paris, 74; La Poetique de Du Bellay, 78 & ; ed, Textes et Intertextes, Etudes sur le XVIe siecle pour Alfred Glauser, 79, Nizet, Paris; Poetiques: Theorie et critique litteraires, Mich Romance Studies, Vol 1, 80. *Mailing Add:* Dept of Romance Lang Univ of Mich Ann Arbor MI 48109

GRAY, JOSEPH LARUE, III, b Lynchburg, Va, July 31, 29; m 63; c 2. GERMAN LANGUAGE & LITERATURE. *Educ:* Washington & Lee Univ, AB, 53; Univ Chicago, MA, 59, PhD(Ger), 67. *Prof Exp:* Instr Ger, Univ Dubuque, 59-60, Chicago undergrad div, Univ Ill, 60-64; asst prof, Ohio

State Univ, 65-70; asst prof, 70-72, res assoc, 72-77, ASSOC PROF GER & RUSS & CHMN DEPT, BOWLING GREEN STATE UNIV, 77- *Mem:* Am Asn Teachers Ger; Medieval Acad Am. *Res:* Late medieval, Renaissance and Reformation German literature. *Publ:* Auth, New Wine in an Old Jug: Hans Sachs' early experiments in Shrovetide drama, Theatre Annual, 71-72. *Mailing Add:* Dept of Ger & Russ Bowling Green State Univ Bowling Green OH 43403

GRAY, STANLEY EVERTS, b Indianapolis, Ind, Nov 2, 26; m 51; c 2. FRENCH. *Educ:* Univ Colo, BA, 52; Ind Univ, MA, 54, PhD(French), 59. *Prof Exp:* From instr to asst prof, 57-65, ASSOC PROF FRENCH, UNIV ILL, URBANA, 65- *Mem:* Am Asn Teachers Fr. *Res:* Nineteenth and 20th century French literature; comparative literature. *Publ:* Auth, From realism to new realism in the French novel, spring 65 & Phenomenology: Structuralism and Marcel Proust, spring 68, L'Esprit Createur; Beckett and Queneau as formalists, James Joyce Quart, summer 71. *Mailing Add:* 2109 Zuppke Urbana IL 61801

GRAYSON, JOHN D, b Buenos Aires, Arg, July 11, 33. SPANISH, LINGUISTICS. *Educ:* NY Univ, MA, 55, PhD(Indo-Europ ling), 62. *Prof Exp:* Lectr Span, Queen's Col, NY, 57-59, tutor, 59-62; asst prof, 63-69, ASSOC PROF SPAN & LING, SIR GEORGE WILLIAMS UNIV, 69- *Mem:* Am Asn Teachers Span & Port. *Res:* Germanic languages; Arabic & Coptic studies. *Publ:* Auth & Transl, Vera & The mysterious sketch, In: 19th Century French Tales, 59 & Maria Wutz, In: 19th Century German Tales, 60, Anchor; auth, Lunfardo, Argentina's Unknown Tongue, Hispanis, 64; The participle in Afrikaans, Festschriften for J A Kearns, 71. *Mailing Add:* Dept of Span Sir George Williams Univ Montreal PQ H3G 1M8 Can

GREAVES, ANTHONY A, b Sheffield, England, Mar 29, 38; m 62; c 2. ROMANCE STUDIES. *Educ:* Univ Nottingham, BA, 60, PhD(French), 65. *Prof Exp:* Asst prof mod lang, 63-68, ASSOC PROF ROMANCE STUDIES, UNIV CALGARY, 68- *Mem:* Asn Can Univ Teachers Fr; MLA; Mod Humanities Res Asn. *Res:* Naturalism and decadentism in Western Europe; 18th century French literature; modern French novel. *Publ:* Auth, Religion et realite dans l'oeuvre de Zola, Rev Europe, 4/68; Mysticisme et pessimisme dans la Faute de l'Abbe Mouret, Cahiers Naturalistes, 68; Some contradictions in the work of Maupassant, Nottingham Fr Studies, 5/68; Maurice Barres-Twayne World Auth Ser, 77. *Mailing Add:* Dept of Romance Studies Univ of Calgary Calgary AB T2N 1N4 Can

GREBENSCHIKOV, VLADIMIR, b Novorossisk, Russia, May 12, 19; Can citizen; m 41; c 3. LINGUISTICS, LITERATURE. *Educ:* Univ Sofia, Dipl, 43; Univ Montreal, MA, 57, PhD, 60. *Prof Exp:* Instr Russ lang, Dept Nat Defense, Ottawa, 59-61; asst prof Russ ling & lit, Univ Montreal, 61-65; assoc prof Russ lang & lit, Mich State Univ, 65-67, prof Russ & Slavic & ed, Russ Lang J, 67-71; PROF RUSS & CHMN DEPT, CARLETON UNIV, 71- *Concurrent Pos:* Lectr, Univ Ottawa, 60-64; vis prof, McGill Univ, 80-82. *Mem:* Can Ling Asn; Can Asn Slavists; Am Asn Advan Slavic Studies; MLA; Can Comp Lit Asn. *Res:* Slavic linguistics; theory of translation; Russian and comparative literature. *Publ:* Auth, Manuel russe de langue francaise, La vie chretienne, Liege, 48; Traductions, theories et traducteurs en URSS, META, Transl Quart, 67; The infernal circles of Dante and Solzhenitsyn, Can Slavonic Papers, 71; A Transformational Approach to Brunin's and Sholokhov's Prose, In: Canadian Contributions to the VIII International Congress of Slavists, Zagreb, 78. *Mailing Add:* Arts Tower 1301 Carleton Univ Ottawa ON K1S 5B6 Can

GRECO, JOSEPH VITTORIO, b Italy, Nov 16, 12; US citizen; m; c 2. LANGUAGES. *Educ:* Park Col, AB, 39; Univ Pittsburgh, LittM, 41, PhD, 50; Univ Siena, cert, 54. *Prof Exp:* Instr Ital, French & Span, Univ Nev, 46-47; assoc prof, 47-80, PROF ITAL, UNIV PITTSBURGH, 80- *Concurrent Pos:* Senatorial scholar, 40; Fulbright scholar, Italy, 54; Shell Found res grant, Italy, 61. *Honors & Awards:* Neocastrum silver medal, 64; Knight Comdr of the Order of the Star of Solidarity, Ital Govt, 78. *Mem:* Am Asn Teachers Ital; Accad Int Neocastrum, Italy; Associazione Int Studi Ling e Lett Ital; Soc Dante Alighieri. *Publ:* Coauth, Conversational Italian for Beginners, Univ Pittsburgh, 59; auth, La Siciliana e la Poesia Popolare, Battaglia Lett, Italy, 59; La Letteratura Americana Vista Dallo Scrittore Italiano d'oggi, Ky Foreign Lang Quart, 62; Canti e Proverbi Maieratesi, Cimento, Roma, 65; Three Men on the Bridge, Keystone Folklore Quart, 70; Si Dice Cosi--That's How We Say It, Univ Cent, 77; Virgil Cantini, Alla Bottega, 77; Chianti Way (poetry), P L Rebellato, Venice, Italy, 79. *Mailing Add:* Dept of French & Ital Univ of Pittsburgh Pittsburgh PA 15260

GREEN, DAVID ROYLE, b Audubon, Minn, May 20, 31; m 55; c 2. FRENCH LITERATURE & LANGUAGE. *Educ:* Concordia Col, BA, 53; Northwestern Univ, Evanson, MA, 57; Univ Paris, Cert phonetics, 58; Univ Minn, PhD(Fr), 72. *Prof Exp:* Instr French, Concordia Col, 55-56; lectr English, Cent Sch Arts & Indust, Paris, 57-58; from asst prof to assoc prof, 61-73, PROF FRENCH, CONCORDIA COL, 73-, CHMN DEPT MOD LANG, 62- *Concurrent Pos:* Partic, NDEA Inst Col & Univ Trainers Mod Lang Teachers, 66. *Honors & Awards:* Am Lutheran Church fac growth award, 67. *Mem:* Soc 17th Century Fr Lit; Am Asn Teachers Fr; Am Coun Teaching Foreign Lang; Asn Dept Foreign Lang; MLA. *Res:* French Baroque literature; French applied linguistics; foreign language learning methodology. *Publ:* Coauth, New Directions and Dimensions in Foreign Language Learning, Concordia Col, 63. *Mailing Add:* Dept of French Concordia Col Moorhead MN 56560

GREEN, DONALD CHARLES, English, Linguistics. See Vol II

GREEN, EUGENE, ENGLISH LINGUISTICS. *Educ:* Ohio State Univ, BA, 53, MA, 57; Univ Mich, PhD(English lang), 62. *Prof Exp:* Asst prof English, San Diego State Col, 61-64; res asst ling, Columbia Univ, 64-66; from asst prof to assoc prof English, 66-77, PROF ENGLISH, BOSTON UNIV, 77- *Concurrent Pos:* Am Coun Learned Soc grant-in-aid, 75; consult aphasia res, Boston Vet Admin Hosp, 76-; Am Philos Soc Award, 77. *Mem:* Am Name Soc; Ling Soc Am; Am Dialect Soc; MLA. *Res:* Place-names; aphasia; Chaucer. *Publ:* Auth, On accentual variants in the Slavic component of Yiddish, In: The Field of Yiddish (The Third Collection), Mouton, The Hague, 69; Phonological and grammatical aspects of jargon in an aphasic patient: A case study, Lang & Speech, 69; coauth, Generic terms for water and waterways in Algonquin place-names, Anthrop Ling, 69; auth, On the contribution of studies in aphasia to psycholinguistics, Cortex, 70; Place-names and dialects in Massachusetts: Some complementary patterns, Names, 71; The voices of the pilgrims in the general prologue to the Canterbury Tales, Style, 75; On conduction aphasia: A study of its anatomical and clinical features and of its underlying mechanisms, In: Studies in Neurolinguistics, Acad Press, 77; Reading local history; Shattuck's Concord, Emerson's Discourse, and Thoreau's Walden, New England Quart, 77. *Mailing Add:* Dept of English Boston Univ Grad Sch Boston MA 02215

GREEN, GEORGIA MARKS, b Atlanta, Ga, Apr 16, 44. LINGUISTICS. *Educ:* Univ Chicago, BA, 66, MA, 69, PhD(ling), 71. *Prof Exp:* Asst prof, 71-73, ASSOC PROF LING, UNIV ILL, URBANA, 73- *Concurrent Pos:* Fels, Ctr Advan Study, Univ Ill, 70-71 & 78-79. *Mem:* MLA; Ling Soc Am. *Res:* Syntax; semantics; pragmatics. *Publ:* Co-ed, Papers from the 5th Regional Meeting, Chicago Ling Soc, 69; auth, The lexical expression of emphatic conjunction, Found Lang, 73; Semantics and Syntactic Regularity, Ind Univ, 74; How to get people to do things with words, In: Syntax and Semantics 3: Speech Acts, Acad Press, 75; Main clause phenomena in subordinate clauses, Language, 76; coauth, Pragmatics and reading comprehension, In: Theoretical Issues in Reading Comprehension, 79; auth, Some wherefores of English inversion, Lang, 80; Linguistics and the pragmatics of language use, Poetics, 82. *Mailing Add:* Dept of Ling Univ Ill Urbana IL 61801

GREEN, JAMES RAY, JR, b Durham, NC, Sept 15, 48. MEDIEVAL & RENAISSANCE SPANISH LITERATURE. *Educ:* Univ NC, Chapel Hill, BA, 70; Johns Hopkins Univ, MA, 72, PhD(Romance lang), 74. *Prof Exp:* Asst prof Span, Univ Wis-Milwaukee, 74-81; ASST PROF SPAN, BOSTON UNIV, 82- *Mem:* MLA; Medieval Acad AM; Renaissance Soc AM; AM Asn Teachers Span & Port; Asoc Int Hisp. *Res:* Medieval and Renaissance Spanish literature; contemporary Latin American narrative; literary theory. *Publ:* Auth, La forma de la ficcion caballeresca del siglo XVI, Actas VI Congreso, AIH, Univ Toronto, 78; El beso de la mujer arana: Sexual Repression and Textual Repression, La Chispa, 81. *Mailing Add:* Dept of Mod For Lang Boston Univ Boston MA 02215

GREEN, JERALD RICHARD, b Atlantic City, NJ, Nov 28, 33; m 60; c 3. FOREIGN LANGUAGE EDUCATION, SPANISH. *Educ:* Montclair State Col, BA, 56, MA, 57; Columbia Univ, EdD(foreign lang educ), 67. *Prof Exp:* Assoc foreign lang educ, NY State Educ Dept, 62-68; ASSOC PROF SPAN, QUEENS COL, NY, 68- *Mem:* MLA; Am Asn Teachers Span & Port; Am Coun Teaching Foreign Lang. *Publ:* Auth, A Gesture Inventory for the Teaching of Spanish, Chilton, 68; Spanish Phonology for Teachers, 70 & coauth, French Phonology for Teachers, 71, Ctr Curriculum Develop; ed, Foreign Language Education Research, 73, Direccion: Tacuba, 76 & Direccion: Moncloa, Rand McNally. *Mailing Add:* Dept of Romance Lang Queens Col Flushing NY 11367

GREEN, JOHN ALDEN, b Cardston, Alta, Nov 4, 25; US citizen; m 54; c 9. FOREIGN LANGUAGES. *Educ:* Brigham Young Univ, BA, 54, MA, 55; Univ Wash, PhD, 60. *Prof Exp:* Asst prof French, Univ NDak, 60-62, assoc prof, 62-63; assoc prof & chmn dept, Univ Wichita, 63-64; assoc prof, 64-67, chmn dept, French & Ital, 69-71, PROF FRENCH, BRIGHAM YOUNG UNIV, 67- *Mem:* Am Asn Teachers Fr. *Res:* French literature and culture, 19th century; the Third Republic. *Publ:* Coauth, That's the Spirit full length comedy in 3 acts, televised 68-69; transl, The Miser, 74, 77 & 79; Prophecy in Music, DK, Paris, 75; auth, Liberty vs authority In: The Gallant Assault in France, 75 & French Reaction to Shakespeare, 75, Brigham Young Univ; transl, The Would-Be Gentleman, 77; Marcel Schwob, Chroniques, 81; Tartuffe, 82. *Mailing Add:* 623 S 590 E Orem UT 84057

GREEN, MARIA, b Arad, Roumania, Sept 21, 22; Can citizen; m 51, 66; c 2. FRENCH & WORLD LITERATURE. *Educ:* Eötvös Univ, Budapest, BA & BEd, 54; Univ BC, BEd & MA, 59; Univ Wash, PhD(Malherbe), 69. *Prof Exp:* Govt off jr col, Ministry Educ, Budapest, 48-50; ed world lit, Hungarian Broadcasting Corp, Budapest, 50-54; ed juvenile bks, Ifjusagi Könyvkiado, Budapest, 54-56; librn asst, Oeuvres Catholiques, Paris, 56-57; lectr French, Univ BC, 59-62; assoc prof, 62-78, PROF FRENCH LIT & WORLD LIT, UNIV SASK, 78- *Concurrent Pos:* Can Coun res grant, Paris, 67 & 70; Nat Res Coun grant, Xth Int Congr Ling, Bucharest, 67; Can Coun grant, XIV Int Cong Romance Ling Philol, Naples, 74. *Honors & Awards:* Educ & cult medal, Hungarian Govt, 77. *Mem:* Pac Northwestern Conf Foreign Lang; Philol Asn Pac Coast; Can Soc 18th Century Studies; Int Soc Hungarian Philol; Soc for Textual Scholar. *Res:* Malherbe's poetry; Max Jacob's prose; Baudelaire's poetry. *Publ:* Auth, Quelques problemes du langage actes, X-e Cong Int Ling, 70; Snobbery as a pursuit and disease in Proust and Jane Austen, Proc Pac Northwestern Conf Foreign Lang, 70; Le vocabulaire de Guillaume Apollinaire, Actes XIIe Int Cong Romance Ling & Philol, Bucarest, 71; L'image de l'Hydre dans la poesie officielle de Malherbe, Actes XIIIe Int Cong Romance Ling & Philol, Quebec, 73; coauth, Reactions the odes of Malherbe, Oeuvres et Critiques, 76; auth, The Unlimited and the Circumscribed, Terre-Neuve, 79; Les regles et le roi, Actes XIVe Int Congr Romance Ling and Philol, Naples, 80; contribr, Max Jacob, Les litteratures de langues Europeennes au tournant du Siecle, Ottawa, 82. *Mailing Add:* 207 Lake Cresent Saskatoon SK S7H 3A1 Can

GREEN, PETER MORRIS, b London, Eng, Dec 22, 24; English citizen; m 51, 75; c 3. CLASSICS, HISTORY. *Educ:* Cambridge Univ, Eng, BA, 50, MA, 54, PhD(classics), 54, Royal Soc Lit, UK, FRSL, 56. *Prof Exp:* Dir Studies, Selwyn Col, Cambridge, 51-3; freelance critic, novelist, ed & publ, Daily Telegraph, London, Times Lit Suppl, Hodder & Stoughton, publ & Bk Soc, 54-63; scholar, historian & translr Greek hist & lit, Roman lit & French & Ital lang, var UK & US Publ, 63-71; PROF CLASSICS, UNIV TEX,

AUSTIN, 72- *Concurrent Pos:* Lectr Greek hist & lit, Athens, Greece, 67-71; vis prof classics, Univ Tex, Austin, 71-72 & Univ Calif, Los Angeles, 76. *Honors & Awards:* Heinemann Award, Royal Soc Lit, 57. *Mem:* Royal Soc Lit, UK; Soc Promotion Hellenic Studies, UK; Class Asn, UK; Am Philol Asn; Am Asn Ancient Historians. *Res:* Greek history, 6th-1st centuries, BC; Roman elegy and satire; the ancient and modern topography and cultural continuity of Greece. *Publ:* Auth, Essays in Antiquity, World/Murray, 60; Juvenal: The Sixteen Satires, Penguin, 67; The Year of Salamis, 480-479 BC, Weidenfeld & Nicolson/Praeger, 70; Armada from Athens: The Failure of the Sicilian Expedition, 415-413 BC, Hodder/Doubleday, 71; The Shadow of the Parthenon, Univ Calif, 72; A Concise History of Classical Greece, Thames & Hudson/Praeger, 73; Alexander of Macedon, 356-323 BC: A Historical Biography, Penguin, 74; Ovio: The Erotic Poems, Penguin, 82. *Mailing Add:* Dept Classics Univ of Texas Austin TX 78712

GREENBAUM, SIDNEY, English Linguistics. See Vol II

GREENBERG, IRWIN L, b New york, NY, Mar 25, 33; m 62; c 1. ROMANCE LANGUAGES. *Educ:* Long Island Univ, BA, 54; NY Univ, MA, 57; Univ Mo, PhD(French), 66. *Prof Exp:* Instr French, Univ Ariz, 61-65; asst prof, 66-74, ASSOC PROF FRENCH, UNIV CINCINNATI, 74- *Mem:* Am Asn Teachers Fr. *Res:* Eighteenth century French novel; 17th and 18th century French theatre; Denis Diderot. *Publ:* Auth, The Supplement au voyage de Bougainville and chapter XVIII of the Bijoux indiscrets, Ky Romance Quart, 70; Narrative technique and literary intent in Diderot's Les bijoux indescrets and Jacques le fataliste, 71 & Destination in Jacques le fataliste, 74, Studies Voltaire & 18th Century; Manipulation in Dederot's Jacques le Fataliste, Romance Notes, XVI, 3. *Mailing Add:* Dept of French Univ of Cincinnati Cincinnati OH 45221

GREENBERG, JOSEPH HAROLD, b Brooklyn, NY, May 28, 15; m 40. ANTHROPOLOGY, LINGUISTICS. *Educ:* Columbia Col, BA, 36; Northwestern Univ, PhD(anthrop), 40. *Prof Exp:* Instr & asst prof anthrop, Univ Minn, 46-48; from asst prof to prof, Columbia Univ, 48-62; PROF ANTHROP & LING, STANFORD UNIV, 62- *Concurrent Pos:* Dir, African Studies Ctr, Stanford Univ, 69- *Mem:* Nat Acad Sci; Am Acad Arts & Sci; Ling Soc Am (pres, 77); Am Anthrop Asn. *Res:* Historical linguistic classifications; language universals; African culture history. *Publ:* Auth, Influence of Islam on a Sudanese Religion, J J Ausgustin, 46; Essays in Linguistics, Chicago Univ, 57; ed & contribr, Universals of Language, Mass Inst Technol, 63 & Stanford Univ, 78; auth, Language Universals, 66 & Languages of Africa, 66, Mouton; Language, Culture and Communication, Stanford Univ, 71; Language Typology, Mouton, 73; New Invitation to Linguistics, Doubleday, 77. *Mailing Add:* Dept of Anthrop Stanford Univ Stanford CA 94305

GREENBERG, MITCHELL DAVID, b New York, NY, Oct 4, 46; m 75. ROMANCE LANGUAGES & LITERATURE. *Educ:* Queens Col, BA, 67; Univ Calif, Berkeley, MA, 69, PhD(Romance lang & lit), 73. *Prof Exp:* Asst prof, 75-80, ASSOC PROF FRENCH, MIAMI UNIV, 80- *Concurrent Pos:* Fondation Camargo fel French, 73-74. *Mem:* MLA. *Res:* Renaissance and Baroque literature; comparative Romance literature; French Renaissance and Baroque literature. *Publ:* Auth, Agrippa d'Aubigne's Histoire Universelle: Theatrical Rhetoric and Protestant propaganda, KRQ, 78; D'Aubigne's Tableaux Celestes: The poetics of Trompe-l'oeil, Mod Lang Notes, 79. *Mailing Add:* Dept of French Miami Univ Oxford OH 45056

GREENBERG, MOSHE, b Philadelphia, Pa, July 10, 28; m 49; c 3. SEMITICS. *Educ:* Univ Pa, AB, 49, PhD(Orient studies), 54; Jewish Theol Sem Am, MHL, 54. *Prof Exp:* Asst prof Hebrew, Univ Pa, 54-58, assoc prof, 58-61, prof Bibl studies, 61-65, Ellis prof Hebrew, 65-70; PROF BIBLE, HEBREW UNIV JERUSALEM, 70- *Concurrent Pos:* Ed, monogr ser, J Bibl Lit, 60-66; fel, Guggenheim Found, 61; vis lectr, Hebrew Univ, Jerusalem, 61; vis lectr, Swarthmore Col, 63; vis prof Bible, Jewish Theol Sem Am, 64-70; mem, Bible Transl Comt, Jewish Publ Soc Am, 66-; Danforth Found Harbison award, 68; acad adv Bible curriculum, Israel ministry educ, 72- *Mem:* Am Orient Soc; Soc Bible Lit; Bible Colloquium; fel Am Acad Jewish Res. *Res:* Biblical philology and religion. *Publ:* Auth, The Hab/piru, Am Orient Ser, 55; coauth, The Religion of Israel, Univ Chicago, 60; auth, Introduction to Hebrew, Prentice-Hall, 65; Understanding Exodus, Behrman House, 69. *Mailing Add:* Dept of Bible Hebrew Univ of Jerusalem Jerusalem Israel

GREENBERG, NATHAN ABRAHAM, b Boston, Mass, Aug 23, 28; m 52; c 3. CLASSICAL PHILOLOGY. *Educ:* Hebrew Teachers Col, Boston, BJEd, 48; Harvard Univ, AB, 50, AM, 52, PhD, 55. *Prof Exp:* From instr to assoc prof, 56-69, assoc dean humanities, 67-68, chmn dept, 70-76, PROF CLASSICS, OBERLIN COL, 69- *Concurrent Pos:* Fulbright scholar, Italy, 55-56; Rockefeller Found study grant, 62-63; Am Coun Learned Soc study grant, 68; Fulbright sr res fel, Belgium, 69-70; vis fel, Wolfson Col, Oxford Univ, 76-77; Am Coun Learned Soc res fel, 76-77. *Mem:* AAUP; Am Philol Asn; Archaeol Inst Am; Vergilian Soc. *Res:* Ancient poetics; political philosophy; computer use in literary study. *Publ:* Auth, Socrates' choice in the Crito, Harvard Studies Class Philol, 65; Vergil and the computer: Fourth foot texture in Aeneid I, 67 & The hexametrical maze, 70, Revue; Success and failure in the Adelphoe, Class World, 80; Aspects of alliteration, Latomus, 80. *Mailing Add:* Dept of Classics Oberlin Col King Bldg Oberlin OH 44074

GREENBERG, WENDY, b Philadelphia, Pa, Dec 31, 51. FRENCH, COMPARATIVE LITERATURE. *Educ:* Columbia Univ, BA, 73, MA, 74, PhD(Fr), 79. *Prof Exp:* Preceptor, Columbia Univ, 74-77; ASST PROF FRENCH, PA STATE UNIV, FOGELSVILLE, 79- *Concurrent Pos:* Nat Endowment for Humanities fel, Harvard Univ, 81. *Mem:* MLA; Am Asn Teachers Fr; Alliance Francaise. *Res:* Theory of metaphor; Victor Hugo; 19th century French romanticism. *Publ:* Auth, Hugo and Whitman: Poets of totality, Whitman Rev, 3/78; coauth & transl, The object-event, Yale French Studies, No 59; auth, Is there a text in this class?, Teaching Lang Through Lit, spring 82. *Mailing Add:* French Dept Pa State Univ Fogelsville PA 18051

GREENE, NAOMI, b New York, NY, June 28, 42. FRENCH. *Educ:* Brown Univ, BA, 63; NY Univ, PhD(Romance lang & lit), 67. *Prof Exp:* Asst prof, 67-76, ASSOC PROF FRENCH, UNIV CALIF, SANTA BARBARA, 76- *Mem:* MLA. *Res:* Modern and 17th century French literature; comparative literature; film. *Publ:* auth, Art and ideology in Pasolini's films, Yale Ital Studies, 77; transl, The theater of Pirandello by Antonio Gramsci, Praxis, winter 77; auth, Letter from Pesaro, Yale Ital Studies, summer 78; auth, Sartre, sexuality and The Second Sex, Philos & Lit, fall 80; Fascism in recent Italian cinema &; Notes on Edinburgh Festival, Film Criticism, 81; Godard and surrealism, Dada & Surrealism, fall 73; Esthetic and political structures in cinematic language, Sub-stance, No 9. *Mailing Add:* Dept of French Univ of Calif Santa Barbara CA 93106

GREENE, ROBERT WILLIAM, b Boston, Mass, Jan 3, 33; m 59; c 2. ROMANCE LANGUAGES. *Educ:* Boston Col, AB, 54; Middlebury Col, MA, 58; Univ Pa, PhD(Romance lang), 63. *Prof Exp:* From instr French to asst prof, Univ Calif, Berkeley, 63-69; assoc prof, Univ Iowa, 69-74; vis prof, 74-75, PROF FRENCH, STATE UNIV NY, ALBANY, 75- *Concurrent Pos:* Am Coun Learned Soc grant-in-aid, 73; Am Philos Soc grant, 75; Nat Endowment for Humanities res fel, 80-81. *Mem:* MLA; Am Asn Teachers Fr; Northeastern Mod Lang Asn. *Res:* Modern French poetry and fiction. *Publ:* Auth, The Poetic Theory of Pierre Reverdy, Univ Calif, 67; Six French Poets of Our Time: A Critical and Historical Study, Princeton Univ, 79; Fluency, Muteness and Commitment in Camus's La Peste, Fr Studies, Vol 34: 422-433. *Mailing Add:* Dept of French State Univ of NY Albany NY 12222

GREENE, TATIANA W, b Paris, France, May 13, 20; US citizen; m 44; c 1. FRENCH LITERATURE. *Educ:* Univ Brussels, Cand in Law, 39; Columbia Univ, MA, 46, PhD, 57. *Prof Exp:* Lectr, Sch Gen Studies, 43-46, from instr French to assoc prof, 46-78, PROF FRENCH LANG & LIT, BARNARD COL, COLUMBIA UNIV, 78- *Concurrent Pos:* Columbia Univ, fac grants, 53 & 58; Am Asn Univ Women Eileen C Sabin fel, 53-54. *Honors & Awards:* Chevalier, Ordre des Palmes Academiques, 72. *Mem:* Soc Fr Prof Am; Am Asn Teachers Fr; MLA. *Res:* French poetry; 16th and 17th century poetry and prose; French composition and grammar. *Publ:* Auth, Les Bottes de Sept Lieues de Robert Desnos: Son Language Poetique, Symposium, winter 71; Palme de Paul Valery et le 4e Cantique de Racine, Ky Romance Quart, 72; Max Jacob et le Surrealisme, French Forum, 9/76; De J Sand a George Sand: Rose et Blanche, Nineteenth-Century French Studies, spring 76; Transfuges (poems in French and English), Saint-Germain-des-Pres, Paris, 77; Le chef d'oeuvre de Louise de Vilmozni: Sainte-Unefois, Symposium, 80; Dire (poems), Saint-germain-des-pres, Paris, 82; Women and Madness in the Works of George Sand, Hofstra Univ George Sand Papers, 82. *Mailing Add:* Dept of French Barnard Col Columbia Univ New York NY 10027

GREENE, THOMAS MCLERNON, b Philadelphia, Pa, May 17, 26; m 50; c 3. ENGLISH. *Educ:* Yale Univ, BA, 49, PhD(comp lit), 55. *Prof Exp:* From instr to asst prof English, 54-62, assoc prof English & comp lit, 62-66, chmn dept comp lit, 72-78, PROF ENGLISH & COMP LIT, YALE UNIV, 66-, CHMN RENAISSANCE STUDIES PROG, 80- *Concurrent Pos:* W I Morse fel, 58-59; Am Coun Learned Soc grant, 63-64; Guggenheim fel, 68-69; mem adv bd, Yale Ital Studies, 77-; Nat Endowment for Humanities res grant, 78-79. *Honors & Awards:* Danforth Found Harbison Prize, 68. *Mem:* Renaissance Soc Am (pres, 82-); Dante Soc Am; Mediaeval Acad Am; Spenser Soc; Am Comp Lit Asn (vpres, 80-). *Res:* Continental and English literature of the Renaissance; epic poetry; theory of literary history. *Publ:* Auth, Descent from Heaven: A Study in Epic Continuity, Yale Univ, 63; co-ed & contribr, The Disciplines of Criticism, Yale Univ, 68; Rabelais: A Study in Comic Courage, Prentice-Hall, 70; Ben Jonson and the centered self, Studies English Lit, spring 70; Love's Labor's Lost: The grace of society, Shakespeare Quart, fall 71; auth, Styles of experience in Sceve's Delie, Yale Fr Studies, 72; contribr, Petrarch and the humanist hermeneutic, In: Italian Literature: Roots and Branches, Yale Univ, 78; The Light in Troy: Imitation and Discovery in Renaissance Poetry, Yale Univ, 82. *Mailing Add:* 125 Livingston St New Haven CT 06511

GREENFIELD, JONAS CARL, b New York, NY, Oct 30, 26; m 50; c 3. HEBREW & SEMITIC LANGUAGES. *Educ:* City Col New York, BSS, 49; Yale Univ, MA, 51, PhD(Near Eastern lang), 56. *Prof Exp:* Instr Semitics, Brandeis Univ, 54-56; from asst prof to assoc prof Hebrew, Univ Calif, Los Angeles, 56-65; prof, Univ Calif, Berkeley, 65-71; PROF ANCIENT SEMITIC LANG, HEBREW UNIV JERUSALEM, 71- *Concurrent Pos:* Lectr grad sch, Univ Judaism, 57-68; Guggenheim fel & Fulbright travel fel, 63-64; Am Coun Learned Soc/Soc Sci Res Coun fel, 68-69; Fulbright-Hays fel, 68-69; trustee, W F Albright Inst Archaeol Res, 69-; mem transl comt, Psalms, Jewish Publ Soc, 73; vis prof, Brandeis Univ, 74-75; ed, Israel Exploration J, 76- *Mem:* Am Orient Soc; Soc Bible Lit; Am Acad Jewish Res; Am Schs Orient Res; Ling Soc Am. *Res:* Semitic philology; Iranian studies; history and culture of ancient Near East. *Publ:* Co-ed, New Directions in Biblical Archaeology, 69 & assoc ed, Anchor Bible Commentary, 72-77, Doubleday; Prologomenon to reprint of H Odeberg's 3 Enoch, KTAV, 73; coauth, Jews of Elephantine, Aramaeans of Syene, Akademnon, Hebrew Univ Jerusalem, 74 & 76. *Mailing Add:* Dept of Semitic Lang Hebrew Univ Jerusalem Israel

GREENFIELD, SUMNER M, b Boston, Mass, Dec 13, 21; m 46; c 2. SPANISH. *Educ:* Boston Col, AB, 44; Boston Univ, AM, 47; Harvard Univ, AM, 51, PhD(Romance lang), 57. *Prof Exp:* From instr to assoc prof, 51-67, PROF SPAN, UNIV MASS, AMHERST, 67- *Mem:* MLA; Am Asn Teachers Span & Port; New England Coun Latin Am Studies. *Res:* Twentieth century Spanish literature; the modernist movement. *Publ:* Assoc ed & contribr, Ramon del Valle-Inclan: an Appraisal of his Life and Works, Las Americas, 68; auth, Valle-Inclan: anatomia de un teatro problematico, Ed Fundamentos, 72; co-ed, Valle-Inclan, Divinas Palabras and Luces de Bohemia, Anaya-Las Americas, 72; auth, Lorca's theatre: a synthetic reexamination, J Span Studies: Twentieth Century, 77; Bradomin and the Ironies of Evil: A Reconsideration of Sonata de primavera, Studies in 20th Century Lit, 77; La Iglesia terrestre de San Manuel Bueno, Cuadernos

Hispanoamericanos, 79; ed, La Generacion de 1898 ante Espana: Antologia de literatura de temas nacionales y universales, Soc Span & Span-Am Studies, 81; auth, Yerma, the Woman and the Work: Some Reconsiderations, Estreno, 81. *Mailing Add:* Dept of Span & Port Univ of Mass Amherst MA 01003

GREENGUS, SAMUEL, b Chicago, Ill, Mar 11, 36; m 57; c 3. SEMITIC PHILOLOGY. *Educ:* Univ Chicago, MA, 59, PhD, 63. *Prof Exp:* From instr to assoc prof, 63-71, PROF SEMITIC LANG, HEBREW UNION COL, OHIO, 71-, DEAN SCH, 79- *Mem:* Am Orient Soc. *Res:* Cuneiform studies; ancient law; Bible. *Publ:* Auth, Old Bablonian marriage ceremonies and rites, J Cuneiform Studies, 66; The old Babylonian marriage contract, J Am Orient Soc; A textbook case of adultery in ancient Mesopotamia, Hebrew Union Col Annual, Vol 40-41 (1970); Sisterhood adoption at Nuzi and the Wife-Sister in genesis, HUCA, Vol 46 (1975); Law in the O T, IDB suppl vol. *Mailing Add:* 3976 Beechwood Ave Cincinnati OH 45229

GREENLEE, JACOB HAROLD, b Charleston, WVa, May 12, 18; m 49; c 3. NEW TESTAMENT GREEK. *Educ:* Asbury Col, AB, 39; Asbury Theol Sem, BD, 43; Univ Ky: MA, 44; Harvard Univ, PhD, 47. *Prof Exp:* Prof New Testament lang, Asbury Theol Sem, 47-65; prof New Testament Greek, Grad Sch Theol, Oral Roberts Univ, 65-69; prof New Testament, Sem Biblico Unido, Medellin, Colombia, 70-74; CONSULT, WYCLIFFE BIBLE TRANSL, 73- *Concurrent Pos:* Fulbright grant, Oxford Univ, 50-51; res assoc transl dept, Am Bible Soc, 55-65; Chirstian Res Found award, 61; vis prof, Sem Bibl, Colombia, 63 & 65; Am Philos Found res grant, 67; missionary, OMS Int, 69-; adj prof ling, Univ Tex, Arlington, 76- *Res:* New Testament textual criticism; New Testament Greek grammar; evangelical missionary work. *Publ:* Auth, Hina substantive clauses in the New Testament, Asbury Seminarian, winter 47; The Gospel Text of Cyril of Jerusalem, Ejnar Munksgaard, Copenhagen, 55; Texts and versions, In: The New Pictorial Dictionary, Zondervan, 63; Concise Exegetical Grammar of New Testament Greek, 63 & Introduction to New Testament Textual Criticism, 64, Eerdmans; coauth, How to Build Expository Sermons, Beacon Hill, 65; auth, Nine Uncial Palimpsests of the Greek New Testament, Univ Utah, 68; The catena of Codex Zacynthius, Biblica, Vol XL, No 4. *Mailing Add:* 715 Kennedy Ave Duncanville TX 75116

GREGG, ALVIN LANER, b Littlefield, Tex, Sept 29, 33; m 58; c 3. ENGLISH LANGUAGE & LINGUISTICS. *Educ:* Tex Tech Univ, BA, 56, MA, 57; Univ Tex, Austin, PhD(English ling), 69. *Prof Exp:* ASST PROF ENGLISH, WICHITA STATE UNIV, 68- *Mem:* Ling Soc Am; NCTE. *Res:* English syntax; linguistic analysis of literature; American dialects. *Publ:* Auth, Is that ever a relative pronoun, In: Mid-American Linguistics Conference Papers, 1972, Okla State Univ, 73. *Mailing Add:* Dept of English Wichita State Univ Wichita KS 67208

GREGG, RICHARD ALEXANDER, b Paris, France, Aug 22, 27; US citizen; m 53; c 1. RUSSIAN LITERATURE. *Educ:* Harvard Univ, AB, 51, MA, 52; Columbia Univ, PhD(Russ), 61. *Prof Exp:* Instr Russ, Amherst Col, 57-58; instr, Brown Univ, 59-60; from instr to assoc prof, Columbia Univ, 60-68; Am Coun Learned Soc fel, 68-69; PROF & CHMN DEPT, VASSAR COL, 69- *Concurrent Pos:* Guggenheim fel, 65-66. *Mem:* Am Asn Advan Slavic Studies. *Res:* Russian 19th century literature, especially Gogol, Pushkin and Dostoevsky; Russian poetry; comparative literature in the 19th century. *Publ:* Auth, F I Tiutchev: The Evolution of a Poet, Columbia Univ, 65; Tat'yana's Two dreams: The unwanted spouse and the demonic lover, Slavonic & E Europ Rev, 10/70; Apollo underground: His master's still, small voice, Russ Rev, 1/73; contribr, Major Soviet writers: Essays in criticism, Oxford Univ, 73; The eudaemonic theme in Puskins Little Tragedies, In: Alexander Puskin: A Symposium on the 175th Anniversary of His Birth, NY Univ, 76. *Mailing Add:* Dept of Russ Vassar Col Poughkeepsie NY 12601

GREGG, ROBERT JOHN, b Larne Co, Antrim, Ireland, July 2, 12; Can citizen; m 33; c 4. LINGUISTICS. *Educ:* Queen's Univ, Ireland, BA, 33, dipl, 42; Univ Edinburgh, PhD, 63. *Prof Exp:* Sr master mod lang, Regent House, Ireland, 34-39; head dept, Mercantile Col, Belfast, 39-54; sr master mod lang & English, N Vancouver High Sch, BC, 54-55; from asst prof to assoc prof French & ling, 55-66, dir lang lab, 59-66, prof, 66-78, head dept, 72-78, EMER PROF LING, UNIV BC, 78- *Concurrent Pos:* Nuffield Trust grant, 60-61; Brit Coun bursary & Can Coun fel, 63; Can Coun res grant, 64, travel grant, Int Phonology Conf, Vienna, 66, sr fel, 67-68; scholar, Can Cult Inst, Rome, 67; consult, Collins English Dict, 73-; Can Coun Res grant, 79-82. *Mem:* Int Phonetic Asn; Can Ling Asn (pres, 72-74); Am Dialect Soc; Ling Asn Gt Brit; Dict Soc NAm. *Res:* General phonetics; dialectology; phonology. *Publ:* Auth, Phonology of Scotch-Irish Dialect, Orbis, Louvain, 58 & 59; A Students' Manual of French Pronunciation, Macmillan, 60; coauth, Dictionary of Canadian English, I-III, W J Gage, Toronto, 62-66; Ulster dialects, Ulster Folk Mus, 64; Patterns in the folk speech of the British Isles, Athlone, 72; Canadian English: Origins and Structure, Methuen, 75, Japanese translation, 81; contribr, Proc of Fourth Int Conf on Dialectology, Victoria, BC, 82. *Mailing Add:* Dept of Ling Univ of BC Vancouver BC V6T 1W5 Can

GREGORY, JUSTINA WINSTON, b Brattleboro, Vt, Sept 24, 46; m 69; c 2. CLASSICS. *Educ:* Smith Col, BA, 67; Harvard Univ, MA, 72, PhD(classics), 74. *Prof Exp:* Asst prof classics, Yale Univ, 74-75; asst prof, 75-80, PROF CLASSICS, SMITH COL, 80- *Concurrent Pos:* Am Coun Learned Socs fel, 76. *Mem:* Am Philol Asn; Class Asn New England. *Res:* Greek tragedy. *Publ:* Co-translr, Aesop's Fables, Gambit, 75; auth, Euripides' Heracles, Yale Class Studies, 77; Euripides, Alcestis, Hermes, Vol 107, 79; The ancients' concept of antiquity, Smith Col Studies in Hist, Vol 48, 80. *Mailing Add:* Dept of Classics Smith Col Northampton MA 01063

GREIS, NAGUIB A F, b Ayyat, Egypt, Oct 6, 24. ENGLISH, ARABIC. *Educ:* Cairo Univ, MA, 45; Ain Shams Univ, Cairo, dipl educ, 48; Univ Exeter, dipl English, 54; Univ Minn, PhD(educ & English), 63. *Prof Exp:* Asst prof English Teachers' Col, Cairo, 56-59; instr commun & Arabic, Univ Minn, 59-63; from instr to assoc prof, 63-76, PROF ENGLISH & ARABIC,

PORTLAND STATE UNIV, 76-, DIR CTR ENGLISH AS SECOND LANG, 67- *Mem:* Ling Soc Am; Teachers English to Speakers Other Lang; MLA; Am Asn Teachers Arabic; AAUP. *Res:* English as a second language; applied linguistics; Arabic. *Publ:* Coauth, Writing Arabic, 65, Beginning Arabic, 66 & Introducing Literary Arabic, 68, Univ Utah; auth, Basic Concepts in the Teaching of English as a Foreign Language, Ser I, 65 & The Implications of Contrastive Studies for the Teaching of English to Arabic Speakers, Ser II, 68, TESOL; Aspects of Arab culture, Al-Lisan Arabi Morocco, 1/69; coauth, The teaching of Arabic as a living language, ERIC, spring 70; auth, Dialectical variations and the teaching of Arabic as a living language, For Lang Ann, 12/70. *Mailing Add:* Ctr for English as a Second Lang Portland State Univ Portland OR 97207

GRENEWITZ, RAINER VADIM, b Leningrad, USSR, Feb 26, 34; US citizen; m 60; c 2. RUSSIAN LITERATURE & HISTORY. *Educ:* Syracuse Univ, BA, 63; Cornell Univ, MA, 65, PhD(Russ lit), 71. *Prof Exp:* Instr Russ, Syracuse Univ, 59-63; teaching asst, Cornell Univ, 63-67; asst prof, Univ Calif, Irvine, 67-76; PROF RUSS & GER, US ARMY RUSSIA INST, 76- *Concurrent Pos:* Consult comput transl, Russ-English & English-Russ, Latsec, Inc, 72-; fel, Humanities Inst, Univ Calif, 74-75. *Mem:* MLA; Am Asn Advan Soviet Studies; Am Asn Teachers Slavic & E Europ Lang. *Res:* Dostoevsky and Russian Orthodox theology; the quest for imagination in Russian fiction; the politcal structure in the Soviet Union and its impact on the arts. *Mailing Add:* Dept of Russ & Ger US Army Russia Inst APO New York NY 09053

GREPPIN, JOHN AIRD COUTTS, b Rochester, NY, Apr 2, 37. LINGUISTICS. *Educ:* Univ Rochester, AB, 61; Univ Wash, MA, 66; Univ Calif, Los Angeles, PhD(Indo- Europ studies), 72. *Prof Exp:* Interim asst prof class ling, Univ Fla, 71-72; stazhor armenian, Yerevan State Univ, Armenia, USSR, 74-75; asst prof, 75-80, ASSOC PROF LING, CLEVELAND STATE UNIV, 80- *Concurrent Pos:* Nat Endowment for Humanities fel, 78-79; ed, Ann Armenian Ling. *Honors & Awards:* Silver medal, Melchiatarist Congregation, Venice, Italy. *Mem:* Am Philol Asn; Am Oriental Soc; Soc Armenian Studies. *Res:* Classical and Middle Armenian Linguistics; Classics; Indo-European linguistics. *Publ:* Auth, Initial vowel and aspiration in classical Armenian, 73 & Classical Armenian nominal suffixes, 75, Mekhitarists; Classical and Middle Armenian Bird Names, 78 & Proceedings, First International Congress on Armenian Linguistics, 81, Caravan. *Mailing Add:* Program in Ling Cleveland State Univ Cleveland OH 44115

GRESSETH, GERALD K, b Portland, Ore, Sept 7, 18; m 58; c 4. CLASSICS, MYTHOLOGY. *Educ:* Reed Col, BA, 41; Univ Calif, Berkeley, MA, 48, PhD(classics), 51. *Prof Exp:* Instr classics, Stanford Univ, 49-55; from asst prof to assoc prof, 55-66, PROF CLASSICS, UNIV UTAH, 66- *Mem:* Am Philol Asn; Philol Asn Pac Coast; Am Orient Soc. *Res:* Classics, especially Greek. *Publ:* Auth, The Myth of Alcyone, Trans Am Philol Asn, 64; Linguistics and Myth Theory, Western Folklore, 69; The Homeric Sirens, Trans Am Philol Asn, 70. *Mailing Add:* Dept of Lang Univ of Utah Salt Lake City UT 84112

GRIBANOVSKY, PAUL V, b St Petersburg, Russia, Nov 12, 12; US citizen; m 35. RUSSIAN LANGUAGE & LITERATURE. *Educ:* Univ Wash, BA, 63, MA, 65, PhD(Russ lang & lit), 68. *Prof Exp:* Instr Russ, US Army Lang Sch, 50-60; from instr to lectr, 60-68, asst prof, 68-74, ASSOC PROF ADVAN RUSS, UNIV WASH, 74- *Mem:* Am Asn Advan Slavic Studies; West Slavic Asn. *Res:* Russian language and literature of the 19th century. *Publ:* Auth, Literary work of Boris Zaisev (essay in Russ), In: Russian Emigree Literature, Collection of Articles, Univ Pittsburgh, 72; Lubov Andreevna Ranevskaia (essay in Russ), Vozrozhdenie, Paris, 6/72; Strange foreigner (essay in Russ), New Rev, 3/74; Fifty years of Russian emigre criticism on B Zaitsev, Russkaia Mysl, 2/74; B Zaitsev on monasteries (essay in Russ), Vestnik, Paris, 1/76. *Mailing Add:* Dept of Slavic Lang & Lit Univ of Wash Seattle WA 98195

GRIBBLE, CHARLES EDWARD, b Lansing, Mich, Nov 10, 36. SLAVIC LANGUAGES. *Educ:* Univ Mich, BA, 57; Harvard Univ, AM, 58, PhD(slavic), 67. *Prof Exp:* From lectr to asst prof Russ, Brandeis Univ, 61-68; asst prof Slavic, Ind Univ, Bloomington, 68-75, asst chmn dept Slavic lang & lit & dir Slavic Workshop, 68-70; asst prof, 75-80, PROF SLAVIC LANG, OHIO STATE UNIV, 80- *Concurrent Pos:* Pres, Slavica Publ, 68-; mem, E Europ libr resources comt, Am Coun Learned Soc, 70-73, Slavic area fel, 72; partic sr scholar exchange to USSR, Int Res & Exchanges Bd, 72. *Mem:* Ling Soc Am; Am Asn Teacher Slavic & East Europ Lang; Am Asn Advan Slavic Studies; Am Asn Southeast Europ Studies; Ling Soc Europe; MLA. *Res:* History and structure of Russian; comparative Slavic linguistics; South Slavic languages. *Publ:* Ed, Studies Presented to Professor Roman Jakobson by His Students, 68, auth, Russian Root List with a Sketch of Russian Word Formation, 73, Medieval Slavic Texts, vol I, 73 & A Short Dictionary of 18th Century Russian, 76, Slavica. *Mailing Add:* Dept of Slavic Lang Ohio State Univ 1841 Millikin Rd Columbus OH 43210

GRIEBSCH, HEINZ-JURGEN, b Angerburg, Ger, May 7, 26; US citizen; m 55; c 1. MODERN LANGUAGES. *Educ:* Albertina Univ, Konigsberg, BA, 44; Univ Halle, MA, 49. *Prof Exp:* Asst prof Ger, Nasson Col, 63-66, head dept, 65-66; assoc prof Ger, Franklin Col, 66-67; assoc prof mod lang & chmn dept, Mackinac Col, 67-70; ASSOC PROF FOREIGN LANG, BAPTIST COL CHARLESTON, 70- *Concurrent Pos:* Dir studies abroad prog, Nasson Col, 64-66. *Mem:* MLA; Am Asn Teachers Ger. *Mailing Add:* Dept of Foreign Lang Baptist Col Charleston SC 29411

GRIES, FRAUKE, b Berlin, Ger, Sept 6, 22; US citizen; m 45. GERMAN LANGUAGE & LITERATURE. *Educ:* San Francisco State Col, BA, 62; Stanford Univ, MA, 64, PhD(Ger & humanities), 67. *Prof Exp:* From asst prof to assoc prof, 66-75, PROF GER & HIST WEST CULT, CALIF STATE UNIV, HAYWARD, 75- *Concurrent Pos:* Mem, liaison comt foreign lang, Calif Articulation Conf, 70-74; Am Coun Learned Soc grant-in-aid, 73-75; Am Philos Soc res grant, 73-74. *Mem:* MLA; Philol Asn Am; Am Asn Teachers Ger; Int Asn Germanic Studies. *Res:* German romanticism;

contemporary and modern drama; sociology of literature. *Publ:* Auth, A model for in-service education, Am Foreign Lang Teacher, 70; Eine unbeachtet gebliebene Rezension von Ludwig Tieck: Belisar, Trauerspiel in fünf Akten Ed von Schenk, Zeitschrift für deutsche Philologie, 71; Two critical essays by Ludwig Tieck: On literature and its sociological aspects, Monatshefte, 74. *Mailing Add:* Dept of Foreign Lang Calif State Univ Hayward CA 94542

GRIES, KONRAD, b New York, NY, Feb 17, 11; m 33; c 4. CLASSICAL PHILOLOGY. *Educ:* City Col, New York, AB, 31; Columbia Univ, AB, 33; PhD(class ling), 47. *Prof Exp:* Teacher, High Sch, NY, 31-32, 34-37; from tutor to prof, 37-77, supvr instr, Sch Gen Studies, English Lang Inst, 50-69, EMER PROF CLASS LANG, QUEENS COL, NY, 77- *Concurrent Pos:* Assoc ed, Class Outlook, 47-57, ed, 57-77. *Mem:* Am Class League; Am Philol Asn; Class Asn New England. *Res:* Livy, the teaching of English as a second language; Augustan poetry. *Mailing Add:* Dept Class Lang Queens Col Flushing NY 11367

GRIFFEN, TOBY DAVID, b Washington, DC, May 12, 46. LINGUISTICS, GERMAN. *Educ:* The Citadel, BA, 68; Univ Va, MA, 69; Univ Fla, PhD(ling). *Prof Exp:* Asst prof Ger, Wichita State Univ, 75-77; ASST PROF GER, SOUTHERN ILL UNIV, EDWARDSVILLE, 77- *Concurrent Pos:* Res scholar award, Southern Ill Univ, Edwardsville, 78. *Mem:* Ling Asn Can & US; Int Ling Asn; Int Soc Phonetic Sci; Am Asn Teachers Ger. *Res:* Nonsegmental model of phonology; Germanic/Indo-European sound shifting; methodology of teaching pronunciation. *Publ:* Auth, The development of Welsh affricates, a change through borrowing, 74, Toward a nonsegmental phonology, 76 & German (x), 77, Lingua; Lenition, provection, and the Indo-European sound shift, Forum Linguisticum, 79; On phonological stress in Welsh, Bull Bd Celtic Studies, 79; German Affricates, 81 & German (R), 82, Lingua; On the position of Germanic in the Indo-European sound shift, Colloquia Germanica, 82. *Mailing Add:* Dept Foreign Lang Southern Ill Univ Edwardsville IL 62026

GRIFFIN, DAVID ALEXANDER, b Buffalo, NY, Jan 25, 19; m 42; c 5. ROMANCE LANGUAGES. *Educ:* Univ Chicago, AB, 47, AM, 49, PhD(Span), 56. *Prof Exp:* Instr Romance lang, Oberlin Col, 52-56; vis asst prof Span, Newcomb Col, Tulane Univ, 56-57; asst prof mod lang, Univ Okla, 57-59; sci linguist & asst head dept Southwestern Europ & Latin Am lang, Foreign Serv Inst, US Dept State, 59-61; assoc prof Romance lang, 61-74, acting chmn dept, 71-72, PROF ROMANCE LANG, OHIO STATE UNIV, 74-, CHMN DEPT, 72- *Mem:* Ling Soc Am; Int Ling Asn; Ling Soc Europe. *Res:* General linguistics; Romance linguistics; Spanish dialectology. *Publ:* Auth, Los Mozarabismos del Vocabulista, Escuela Estudios Arabes, Madrid, 61; El Castellano Ralea, Bol Real Acad Espanola, 1-4/64; Rotacismo y Aspiracion: Una Nota Sobre Cronologia Dialectal, Univ Chile Bol Filol, 65; Arcaismos Dialectales Mozarabes, Actas Segundo Congreso Int Hispanitas, 67. *Mailing Add:* Dept of Romance Lang Ohio State Univ 190 N Oval Dr Columbus OH 43210

GRIFFIN, ROBERT BERRY, b Riverside, Calif, June 20, 36; m 58; c 2. ROMANCE LANGUAGES & LITERATURES. *Educ:* Univ Calif, Riverside, BA, 58; Yale Univ, PhD, 62. *Prof Exp:* Instr French, Carleton Col, 62-63; from asst prof to assoc prof, 63-71, assoc dean humanities & soc sci, 76-80, PROF FRENCH, UNIV CALIF, RIVERSIDE, 71- *Concurrent Pos:* Asst ed, French Rev, 76-, Oeuvres & Critiques, 76- & Rev Pacifique, 77-, French forum, 78- *Mem:* MLA; Am Asn Teachers Fr; fel Soc Relig Higher Educ. *Res:* French Middle Ages; Renaissance literature; psychocriticism. *Publ:* Auth, The rebirth motif in Agrippa d'Aubigne's Le Printemps, Fr Studies, 7/65; Aucassin et Nicolette and the Albigensian Crusade, Mod Lang Quart, 6/65; The presence of Saint Paul in the religious works of Jean de Sponde, Bibliot Humanisme et Renaissance, 65; Coronation of the Poet: Joachim du Bellay's Debt to the Trivium, 69 & Clement Marot and the Inflections of Poetic Voice, 73, Univ Calif; Ludovico Ariosto, Twayne, 73. *Mailing Add:* Dept of Lang & Lit Univ of Calif Riverside CA 92502

GRIFFITHS, DAVID A, b Vancouver, Can, Sept 13, 24; m 50; c 2. FRENCH LANGUAGE & LITERATURE. *Educ:* Univ BC, BA, 45, MA, 48; Univ Paris, Dr(Fr), 55. *Prof Exp:* Sessional lectr French, McMaster Univ, 55-57, lectr, 57-59, asst prof, 59-62; asst prof, Royal Roads Mil Col, 62-63, assoc prof, 63-65; actg head dept, 68-69, assoc prof, 65-76, PROF FRENCH, UNIV VICTORIA, BC, 76- *Concurrent Pos:* Can Coun grants, 58, 60 & fel, 71-72; mem, Felibrige, France, 64; grant-in-aid, Ctr Nat Recherche Sci, Paris, 65; Prix Bordin, Acad Fran, Paris, 66. *Mem:* Soc Lit Hist France. *Res:* Nineteenth Century French literature. *Publ:* Auth, Les Caprices de Rachel, Rev Hist theatre, 59; Un confrere de Victor Hugo a l'Academie: Ernest Legouve, Rev Sci Humaines, 60; Victor Hugo et Victor Schoelcher au ban de l'Empire, Rev Hist Litteraire France, 63; Jean Reynaud, Encyclopediste de l'Epoque Romantique, Marcel Riviere, Paris, 65. *Mailing Add:* Dept of French Univ of Victoria Victoria BC V8W 2Y2 Can

GRIGGS, SILAS, b Ft Worth, Tex, Apr 13, 28; m 56; c 2. LINGUISTICS, ENGLISH LANGUAGE. *Educ:* Univ Tex, Austin, BA, 50, MA, 57, PhD(English lang), 63. *Prof Exp:* Instr English, Univ Tex, Austin, 58-62; from asst prof to assoc prof, 62-71, PROF ENGLISH, NTEX STATE UNIV, 71- *Concurrent Pos:* Vis assoc prof English, Southern Methodist Univ, 65-66. *Mem:* Ling Soc Am; MLA. *Res:* Structure of modern English; theory of grammars; history of the English language. *Publ:* Coauth, English Verb Inflection: A Generative View, Mouton, The Hauge, 74. *Mailing Add:* Dept of English NTex State Univ Denton TX 76203

GRIGSBY, JOHN LAMBERT, b Kansas City, Mo, July 19, 28; m 56. FRENCH. *Educ:* Univ Kans, 51, MA, 55; Univ Paris, dipl Fr, 53, Univ Pa, PhD(Fr), 60. *Prof Exp:* Asst English, Lycee Jacques-Amyot, Melun, France, 51-52; asst prof French, Univ Okla, 60-62; asst prof, Univ Calif, Berkeley, 62-67; assoc prof, 67-69, chmn dept Romance lang, 68-72, 80-82, PROF FRENCH, WASHINGTON UNIV, 69-, CHMN LING PROG, 78-, CHMN MEDIEVAL & RENAISSANCE STUDIES, 79- *Concurrent Pos:* Am Philos Soc grants, 66 & 72; Am Council of Learned Soc travel grants, 75 & 79. *Mem:* Int Arthurian Soc (NAm secy-treas); MLA; Am Asn Teachers Fr; Soc Rencesvals: Asn Int Fr Studies. *Res:* Old French literature and language. *Publ:* Auth, The Middle French Liber Fortunae, Univ Calif, 67; co-ed, Joufroi de Poitiers, Roman D'Aventures du XIIIe Siecle, Droz, Geneva, 72; auth, Sign, symbol and metaphor: Todorov and Chretien de Troyes, Esprit Createur, 78; Narrative voices in Chretien de Troyes, Romance Philol, 79; The ontology of the narrator in medieval French romance, In: The Nature of Medieval Narrative, 81; L'Empir des signes chez Beroul et Thomas, Melanges Foulon, II, Liege, 81; A Note on the Genre of the Voyage de Charlemagne, Studies in Honor of Barbara M Craig, Fr Publ, 82. *Mailing Add:* Dept of Romance Lang Washington Univ St Louis MO 63130

GRILK, WERNER HANS, b Davenport, Iowa, Jan 9, 28. GERMAN LITERATURE. *Educ:* Northwestern Univ, BS, 51; Univ Mich, MA, 60, PhD(Ger), 66. *Prof Exp:* Teacher pub schs, Ohio, 53-58; instr, 62-65, lectr, 65-66, ASST PROF GER, UNIV MICH, ANN ARBOR, 66- *Mem:* MLA; Am Asn Teachers Ger. *Res:* German 19th and 20th century drama. *Publ:* Coauth, MLA International Bibliography, PMLA, 65- *Mailing Add:* Dept of Ger Univ of Mich Ann Arbor MI 48109

GRIMALDI, WILLIAM A, b New York, NY, Oct 24, 17. CLASSICAL LANGUAGES. *Educ:* Georgetown Univ, AB, 40; St Louis Univ, MA, 42; Woodstock Col, PhL, 41, STL, 48; Princeton, PhD, 55. *Prof Exp:* Instr Classs lang, Canisius Col, 42-44; instr, Fordham Univ, 49-50; asst prof & chmn dept, Canisius Col, 54-55; asst prof, Bellarmine Col, 55-59; asst prof, 59-65, dir hon prog, Thomas More Col, 64-69, assoc prof, 65-71, PROF, CLASS LANG, FORDHAM UNIV, 71- *Concurrent Pos:* Mem, managing comt, Am Sch Class Studies, Athens, 64-; vis fel classics, Princeton Univ, 74-75 & 80-81; sr fel classics, Nat Endowment for Humanities, 81-82; vis scholar classics, Stanford Univ, 81. *Mem:* Am Philol Asn; Vergilian Soc Am; Vergilian Soc Eng; AAUP. *Res:* Aristotelian rhetoric; Euripidean drama. *Publ:* Auth, The Aristotelian Topics, Traditio, 58; Aristotle's Rhetoric 1391 b 29 and 1396 b 29, 61 & The Lesbia love lyrics, 65, Class Philol; Studies in the Philosophy of Aristotle's Rhetoric, Steiner, 72; Aristotle, Rhetoric I A Commentary, Fordham Univ Press, 80; Semeion Eikos, Tekmerion in Aristotle's Rhetoric, AJP, 80. *Mailing Add:* Dept of Classics Fordham Univ New York NY 10458

GRIMAUD, MICHEL ROBERT, b Edinburgh, Scotland, Nov 25, 45; French citizen; m 73. DISCOURSE ANALYSIS. *Educ:* Univ Aix-Marseille, BA, 67, MA, 69; Univ Wis-Madison, MA, 73, PhD(French), 76. *Prof Exp:* ASST PROF FRENCH, WELLESLEY COL, 76- *Concurrent Pos:* Co-ed, Empirical Studies of Arts; ed, Serie Victor Hugo (Lettres Modernes). *Mem:* Semiotic Soc Am; Cognitive Sci Soc; Soc Philos & Psychol. *Res:* Semiotics; psychology; discourse analysis, including natural language processing in artificial intelligence. *Publ:* Auth, Prosopopee de Sainte Sophie, Patronne des Poeticiennes: Vers une Science des Textes, Poetique, 80; Preliminaires pour une psycholinguistique des discours, Langue Francaise, 81; contribr, Theorie de la litterature, A & J Picard, Paris, 81; coauth, Saint/Oedipus: Psychocritical Approaches to Flaubert, Cornell Univ Press, 82; auth, Delusion and dream in literary semiotics, 82, Frameworks for a science of texts: The compleat semiotician, 82 & Mindless or mindful rhetorics? (in prep), Semiotica. *Mailing Add:* Dept of French Wellesley Col Wellesley MA 02181

GRIMES, JOSEPH EVANS, b Elizabeth, NJ, Dec 10, 28; m 52; c 3. LINGUISTICS. *Educ:* Wheaton Col, Ill, BA, 50; Cornell Univ, MA, 58, PhD(ling), 60. *Prof Exp:* Vix assoc prof, 67-68, assoc prof, 69-76, PROF LING, CORNELL UNIV, 76- *Concurrent Pos:* Transl Bible, Wycliffe Bible Transl, Inc, 50-; field investr, Summer Inst Ling, Inc, 50-, lectr descriptive ling, 56-, consult comput, 64-; Inter-Am prof ling & lang teaching, 63- *Mem:* Ling Soc Am; Asn Ling y Filol Am Latina; Asn Comput Ling; Asn Comput Machinery. *Res:* Aboriginal languages; linguistic theory; computational linguistics. *Publ:* Coauth, Semantic distinctions in Huichol kinship, Am Anthrop, 2/52; auth, Measures of linguistic divergence, In: Ninth International Congress of Linguists, Mouton, 64; Huichol Synta, Mouton, 64; translr, Cacaüyari Niuquieya, Soc Biblica Mex, 68; auth, Descriptive linguistics, In: Current Trends in Linguistics, Vol IV, Mouton, The Hague, 68; The Thread of Discourse, Mouton, 75; ed, Network Grammars, Summer Inst Ling, 75. *Mailing Add:* Dept of Mod Lang & Ling Morrill Hall Cornell Univ Ithaca NY 14853

GRIMM, REINHOLD, b Nuremberg, Ger, May 21, 31; m 54; c 1. GERMAN & COMPARATIVE LITERATURE. *Educ:* Univ Erlangen, DPhil(Ger), 56. *Prof Exp:* Vis prof Ger, NY & Columbia Univs, spring 67; Alexander Hohlfeld prof, 67-80, VILAS PROF, UNIV WIS, MADISON, 80- *Concurrent Pos:* Guggenheim Found fel, 69-70; distinguished vis lectr, Can Asn Teachers Ger, winter 70; Nat Endowment for Humanities Coun on Res Tools, 77, Panel on Transl, 77-78; summer stipend, 79; Inst Res Humanities fel, Madison, 81. *Honors & Awards:* Förderungspreis der Stadt Nürnberg, 64. *Mem:* Am Asn Teachers Ger (pres, 74-); MLA; Am Lessing Soc; Int Brecht Soc (pres, 69-70); Büchner Gesehschaft. *Res:* Modern German and comparative literature; 19th century German literature; drama and theater. *Publ:* Auth, Bertolt Brecht: Die Struktur seines Werkes, Hans Carl, Nuremberg, 59, 6th ed, 72; Strukturen: Essays zur deutschen Literatur, Athenäum, 63 & ed, Deutsche Dramentheorien (2 vols), Athenäum, 71, 3rd ed, 81, Frankfurt; auth, Brecht, Artaud e il teatro contemporaneo, Studi Tedeschi, 76; From Collot to Butor: E T A Hoffman and the tradition of the Capriccio, Mod Lang Notes, 78; Nach dem Naturalismus: Essays zur modernen Dramatik, Athenäum, Kronberg, 78; Brecht and Nietzsche oder Geständnisse eiucs Diditers, Suhrkamp, Frankfurt, 79; Von der Arwut und vom Regen: Rilkes Antwort auf die soziale Frage, Athenäum, Königstein, 81. *Mailing Add:* 3983 Plymouth Circle Madison WI 53705

GRIMM, RICHARD E, b Urbana, Ind, Aug 31, 26; m 58. CLASSICS. *Educ:* Ind Univ, AB, 49, MA, 51; Princeton Univ, PhD, 59. *Prof Exp:* From instr to asst prof classics, Univ Ore, 58-60; asst prof, 60-67, ASSOC PROF CLASSICS, UNIV CALIF, DAVIS, 67- *Concurrent Pos:* Fulbright scholar,

Italy, 51-52, sr travel grant, 66-67; fel classics, Am Acad Rome, 54-56; Ford teaching intern, Brown Univ, 56-57. *Mem:* Am Philol Asn; Philol Asn Pac Coast; Class Soc Am Acad Rome (pres, 68). *Res:* Greek and Roman lyric poetry, especially Pindar; Vergilian epic; medieval Latin mathematical literature. *Publ:* Auth, Pindar and the beast, Class Philol, 1/62; Catullus 5 again, Class J, 10/63; Aeneas and Andromache in Aeneid III, Am J Philol, 4/67. *Mailing Add:* Dept of Classics Univ of Calif Davis CA 95616

GRISE, CATHERINE MARGARET, b Midland, Ont, Apr 30, 36. FRENCH LANGUAGE & LITERATURE. *Educ:* Univ Toronto, BA, 59, MA, 60, PhD(French), 64. *Prof Exp:* Lectr, 64-65, from asst prof to assoc prof, 65-77, PROF FRENCH, ST MICHAEL'S COL, UNIV TORONTO, 77- *Concurrent Pos:* Can Coun res grant, 66, leave fel, 71-72. *Mem:* Asn Can Univ Teachers Fr; Int Asn Fr Studies; MLA. *Res:* French poetry of the 17th century; La Fontaine; rhetoric. *Publ:* Ed, Tristan L'Hermite, Les Vers Heroiques, Droz, 67; Tristan L'Hermite est-il l'auteur de ballet du triomphe de la beaute?, Rev Hist Fr Lit, 10-12/67; Italian sources of Tristan L'Hermite's poetry, Studies Fr, Italy, 1/70; The religious poetry of Tristan L'Hermite, Mosaic, 4/71; Tristan L'Hermite, Lettres Meslees, Droz, 72; John-Baptiste Chassignet's debt to Seneca, Bibliotheque d'Humanisme & Renaissance, 76; Jean-Baptiste Chassignet and Guevara, Fr Studies, 77; Jean-Baptiste Chassignet and Diego de Estella, Mod Lang Rev, 77. *Mailing Add:* Dept of French St Michael's Col Univ of Toronto Toronto ON M5S 1V4 Can

GRITTNER, FRANK MERTON, b Ashland, Wis, Feb, 12, 27; m 49; c 5. FOREIGN LANGUAGES. *Educ:* Northland Col, BA, 50; Univ Wis, MA, 52, PhD(foreign lang educ), 72. *Prof Exp:* Teacher Ger, Fond du Lac Pub Schs, Wis, 52-56; teacher Ger & Span, Madison Pub Schs, 56-60; STATE SUPVR FOREIGN LANG, WIS DEPT PUB INSTR, 60- *Concurrent Pos:* Comt mem, MLA studies of effectiveness of NDEA Title XI Foreign Lang Summer Inst Prog, 67; ed, Cent States Conf Teaching Foreign Lang publ, 68-74; educ auditor, Milwaukee Biling Prog, & State Off Educ ESEA Title VII grant, 69-72. *Mem:* Am Coun Teaching Foreign Lang (pres, 75); Am Asn Teachers Ger (pres, 84); Cent States Conf Teaching Foreign Lang; Asn Dept Foreign Lang (secy, 65-68); Nat Coun State Supvr Foreign Lang (pres, 64-65). *Res:* History of foreign language acquisition. *Publ:* Contribr, Britannica Review of Foreign Language Education, Encycl Britannica, 71; auth, Behavioral objectives, Skinnerian rats and Trojan horses, Foreign Lang Ann, 10/72; coauth, Individualized Foreign Language Instruction, 73 & ed, Student Motivation and the Foreign Language Teacher, 74, Nat Testbk; auth, Teaching Foreign Languages, Harper, 77; ed, Yearbook on Second Language Education, Nat Soc Study Educ, 81. *Mailing Add:* Dept Pub Instr PO Box 7841 Madison WI 53707

GRONICKA, ANDRE VON, b Moscow, Russia, May 25, 12; nat US; m 36; c 2. GERMAN. *Educ:* Univ Rochester, AB, 33, AM, 35; Columbia Univ, PhD(Ger), 42. *Prof Exp:* Instr Ger, Univ Kans, 37-40; instr Ger & Russ, Univ Chicago, 40-44; asst prof, Columbia Univ, 44-49, from assoc prof to prof Ger, 49-62; chmn dept, 62-72, prof, 62-80, EMER PROF GER, UNIV PA, 80- *Concurrent Pos:* Soc Sci Res fel, 57; Guggenheim & Fulbright fels, 57-58; Am Coun Learned Soc grant, 65; Guggenheim fel, 68-69; Nat Endowment for Humanities senior res fel, 76-77. *Honors & Awards:* Festschrift, Probleme der Komparatistik und Interpretation, Bouvier, 78. *Mem:* Acad Lit Studies; MLA; Am Asn Teachers Ger. *Res:* Russo-German literary relations; Thomas Mann; modern German drama and novelle. *Publ:* Coauth, Essentials of Russian, Prentice-Hall, 4th ed, 64; auth, Myth plus psychology: A stylistic analysis of Death in Venice, In: Twentieth century views: Thomas Mann, Prentice-Hall, 64; The Russian Image of Goethe, Univ Pa, 68; Thomas Mann: Profile and Perspectives, Random, 70; Der Unbehauste Mensch im Drama G Büchners, In: Festschrift for W Silz: Studies in the German Drama, Univ NC, 72; A Russian Revolutionary and the Cavalier von Goethe, In: Festschrift for A Klarmann: Views and Reviews of Modern German Literature, Delp, Munich, 74; Goethe and Chernyshevski, Ger Rev, 1/74; Ivan S Turgenev's Faust essay, Germano-Slavica, spring 79. *Mailing Add:* Dept of Ger Lang & Lit Univ of Pa Philadelphia PA 19104

GROOS, ARTHUR BERNHARD, JR, b Fullerton, Calif, Feb 5, 43. GERMAN LITERATURE. *Educ:* Princeton Univ, BA, 64; Cornell Univ, MA, 66, PhD(Ger), 70. *Prof Exp:* Asst prof Ger, Univ Calif, Los Angeles, 69-73; asst prof, 73-76, assoc prof, 76-82, PROF GER, CORNELL UNIV, 82-, DIR MEDIEVAL STUDIES, 74- *Concurrent Pos:* John Simon Guggenheim Mem fel, 79-80; Sr Fulbright res fel to Ger, 79-80. *Mem:* MLA; Mediaeval Acad Am; Am Asn Teachers Ger; Wolfram von Eschenbach Gesellschaft. *Res:* Medieval German literature; 18th-century German literature. *Publ:* Auth, Wolfram's Bow metaphor and the narrative technique of Parzival, Mod Lang Notes, 72; Time reference and the liturgical claendar in Parzival, Deut Vierteljahrsschrift, 75; Parzival's Swertleite, Ger Rev, 75; Walther von der Vogelweide and his lady, PMLA, 76; The two loves in Heinrich von Veldeke's Eneit, Traditio, 76; Kurenberg's Dark Star, Speculum, 79; Studien zum Problem der Sprache bei Friedrich Schiller, Bouvier, Bonn, 80; Trevrizent's Retraction, Deut Vierteljahrsschrift, 81. *Mailing Add:* Dept of Ger Lit Cornell Univ Ithaca NY 14853

GROSE, DAVID DEANE FREDERICK, Ancient History, Classical Archaeology. See Vol I

GROSS, CHARLES J, JR, b Medford, Mass, Aug 13, 31. CLASSICAL LANGUAGES. *Educ:* Tufts Col, AB, 53, AM, 54; Univ NC, PhD, 60. *Prof Exp:* Asst classics, Tufts Col, 53-54; instr, Univ NC, 54-57 & Univ Ariz, 57-60; asst prof, Pa State Univ, 60-61 & Tufts Univ, 61-62; teacher Latin, Malden High Sch, 62-65 & Berwick Acad, 66-67; assoc prof, State Univ NY Col Potsdam, 68-76; MASTER LATIN, BERKSHIRE SCH, 76- *Mem:* Am Class League; Am Philol Asn; Class Asn New England; Nat Asn Independent Schs. *Res:* Latin poetry; Roman satire; medieval studies. *Publ:* Auth, The Gracchi of the 1960's, 69, The Vergilian Brand, 70 & The Hostility of Statius and Martial, 71, Class Outlook. *Mailing Add:* Berkshire Sch Sheffield MA 01257

GROSSBERG, LAWRENCE, Philosophy of Communication. See Vol II

GROSSFELD, BERNARD, b Vienna, Austria, June 13, 33; nat US; m 64; c 3. HEBREW LANGUAGE & LITERATURE. *Educ:* Univ Calif, Los Angeles, BA, 59, Berkeley, MA, 62; Johns Hopkins Univ, PhD(Near Eastern studies), 68. *Prof Exp:* Chaplain, US Air Force, 62-64; grad student Near Eastern studies, Johns Hopkins Univ, 64-68; asst prof, 69-73, chmn dept, 70-73, assoc prof, 73-80, PROF HEBREW & ARAMAIC, UNIV WIS-MILWAUKEE, 80-, CHMN DEPT, 76- *Mem:* Soc Biblical Lit; Am Orient Soc; Asn Jewish Studies; Asn Targumic Studies; Nat Asn Prof Hebrew. *Res:* Targum, Aramaic Bible translation; Bible language and literature; Rabbinic language and literature. *Publ:* Auth, Bible versions--Aramaic: The Targumim: 841-851, Encyclopaedia Judaica, 72; A Bibliography of Targum Literature Bibliographica Judaica, KTAV Publ House, 72; Targum Onkelos and Rabbinic interpretation to Genesis 2: 1-2, J Jewish Studies, 73; A critical note on Judges 4: 21, Z Alttestamentliche Wiss, 73; Targum Neofiti 1 to Deuteronomy 31: 7, the problem re-analyzed, Australian Biblical Rev, 76; coauth, Targum Onkelos on Genesis 49; Translation and Analytical Commentary, Scholars Press, 76; auth, Targum Literature Vol II: Bibliographica Judaica, KTAV Publ House, 77. *Mailing Add:* Dept of Hebrew Studies Univ of Wis Curtin Hall 904 Milwaukee WI 53201

GROSSMAN, EDITH MARIAN, b Philadelphia, Pa, Mar 22, 36; m 64; c 2. LATIN AMERICAN & SPANISH LITERATURE. *Educ:* Univ of Pa, BA, 57; MA, 59; NY Univ, PhD(Span), 72. *Prof Exp:* Lectr Span, Hunter Col, 64-67 & Queens Col, 68-69; from instr to asst prof, NY Univ, 69-72; asst prof, 72-80, ASSOC PROF SPAN, DOMINICAN COL, 80-, DIR, DIV ARTS & SCI, 72- *Concurrent Pos:* Fels, Woodrow Wilson & Fulbright. *Mem:* MLA; PEN Club; Am Counc Teaching For Lang; Hisp Inst; Am Assoc Teachers Span & Port. *Res:* Contemporary Latin American poetry; comtemporary Latin American fiction; contemporary Spanish poetry. *Publ:* Auth, Myth and madness in Carlos Fuentes A Change of Skin, Latin Am Rev, fall-winter 74; The Antipoetry of Nicanor Parra, NY Univ, 75; transl, Julio Cortazar, Julia, Fiction, 76; Manuel Scorza, Drums for Rancas, Harper, 77; Jorge Edwards, Experence, Fiction, 78; Nicanor Parra, Sermones y predicas del Cristo de Elqui, New Directions in Prose and Poetry 41, New Directions, 80; Ariel Dorfman, Missing, Amnesty Int British Sect, London, 81; auth, Truth is stranger than fact, Garcia Marquez' Cronica de una muerte anunciada, Review 30, 82. *Mailing Add:* Dept of Spanish Dominican Col Orangeburg NY 10962

GROSSMAN, JOAN DELANEY, b Dubuque, Iowa, Dec 12, 28. SLAVIC LANGUAGES. *Educ:* Clarke Col, AB, 52; Columbia Univ, MA, 62; Harvard Univ, PhD(Slavic lang & lit), 67. *Prof Exp:* Asst prof Russ, Mundelein Col, 67-68; asst prof, 68-80, ASSOC PROF SLAVIC LANG & LIT, UNIV CALIF, BERKELEY, 80- *Concurrent Pos:* Consult, US-USSR summer lang teachers enchange, Int Res & Exchanges Bd, 69-72; Am Coun Learned Soc fel, 71-72; Guggenheim fel, 78-79. *Mem:* Am Asn Advan Slavic Studies; Western Slavic Asn; Mod Lang Asn. *Res:* Russian literary and cultural trends at the end of the 19th and the early 20th century; Russian novel. *Publ:* Auth, Turgenev's Sportsman: Experiment in unity, Slavic & E Europ J, 64; Edgar Allan Poe in Russia: A Study in Legend and Literary Influence, Jal, Würzburg, 73; Genius and madness: Return of the Romantic concept of the poet in late nineteenth-century Russia, In: American Contributions to the Seventh International Congress of Slavists, Vol II, Mouton, The Hague, 74; Tolstoy's Portrait of Anna: Keystone in the arch, Criticism, winter 76; Feminine images in Old Russian literature and art, California Slavic Studies XI, Univ Calif, 78; Dostoevsky and Stendhal's Theory of Happiness, American Contributions to the Eighth International Congress of Slavists, Vol II, Columbus: Slavica, 78. *Mailing Add:* Dept of Slavic Lang Univ of Calif Berkeley CA 94720

GROSSMAN, KATHRYN MARIE, b New York, NY, Dec 6, 45. FRENCH LITERATURE, UTOPIAN STUDIES. *Educ:* Bryn Mawr Col, AB, 67; Yale Univ, MPhil, 70, PhD(Romance lang), 73. *Prof Exp:* Asst prof, 73-80, ASSOC PROF FRENCH LANG & LIT, PA STATE UNIV, 81-, ACTG ASST DEAN, COL LIB ARTS, 82- *Mem:* MLA; Am Asn Teachers Fr; Am Coun Teaching Foreign Lang; Soc Utopian Studies; Am Asn Advan Humanities. *Res:* Victor Hugo (prose fiction); romanticism; utopias. *Publ:* Auth, Gautier's Dream of Stone: The plastic aesthetics of Emaux et camees, Les Bonnes Feuilles, spring 75; Jean Valjean and France: Outlaws in search of integrity, Stanford Fr Rev, winter 78; Playing surrealist games: Parataxis and creativity, Fr Rev, 4/79; Monsieur Teste as modern parable, Dalhousie Fr Studies, 10/79; Hugo's romantic sublime: Beyond chaos and convention in Les Miserables, Philol Quart, fall 82. *Mailing Add:* 215 W Fairmont Ave Apt 709 State College PA 16801

GROSSVOGEL, DAVID I, b San Francisco, Calif, June 19, 25; div; c 2. FRENCH, ROMANCE STUDIES. *Educ:* Univ Calif, BA, 49; Univ Grenoble, cert, 50; Columbia Univ, MA, 51, PhD(French), 54. *Prof Exp:* Instr French lang & lit, Columbia Univ, 53-56; vis lectr, Harvard Univ, 56-57, asst prof Romance lit, 57-60; assoc prof Romance Studies, 60-64, prof, 64-70, GOLDWIN SMITH PROF COMP LIT & ROMANCE STUDIES, CORNELL UNIV, 70- *Concurrent Pos:* Fulbright fel, Paris, 59-60; Guggenheim fel, 63-64; found & ed, Diacritics, 71- *Mem:* MLA. *Res:* Criticism; cinema; modern European literature. *Publ:* Auth, Self-Conscious Stage, Columbia Univ; Anouilh's Antigone, Integral Ed, 58; Four Playwrights and a Postscript, Cornell Univ, 62; Sagan's Bonjour Tristesse, Integral Ed, 64; Limits of the Novel, Cornell Univ, 68; co-ed, Divided We Stand: Reflections on the Crisis at Cornell, Doubleday, 70; Mystery and Its Ficitons: From Oedipus to Agatha Christie, Johns Hopkins Univ, 79. *Mailing Add:* Dept of Romance Studies Cornell Univ Ithaca NY 14853

GROTEGUT, EUGENE K, b Clark, Nev, Apr 8, 27; m 50; c 3. GERMANIC LANGUAGE & LITERATURE. *Educ:* Univ Nev, BA, 49; Univ Calif, Los Angeles, MA, 52, PhD, 59. *Prof Exp:* Fac asst Ger, Univ Calif, Los Angeles, 53-56; instr Ger & Scandinavian, Univ Mich, 56-59; asst prof Ger, Univ Calif, Berkeley, 59-62; assoc prof, Univ Ky, 62-65; prof Ger lang, Univ Kans, 65-69; prof Ger, Univ Nev, Reno, 69-76; chmn dept, 72-76, PROF FOREIGN LANG & LIT, UNIV NEV, RENO, 76-, CHMN DEPT, 82- *Concurrent Pos:*

Mem rev comt, Inst Int Educ, 73. *Mem:* MLA; Am Asn Teachers Ger. *Res:* German literature of the 18th and 20th centuries; Norwegian literature of the 19th and 20th centuries. *Publ:* Auth, Freedom in Hagedorn's Seifensieder, Monatshefte, 3/60; Bodmer Contra Gellert, Mod Lang Quart, 12/62; Wilhelm Tell: A Dramatic Triangle, Mod Lang Notes, 12/65; coauth, Auflklarung, Francke, 73. *Mailing Add:* Dept Foreign Lang & Lit Univ Nev Reno NV 89507

GROTEN, FRANK JOHN, JR, b New Haven, Conn, July 28, 28; m 57. GREEK, LATIN. *Educ:* Princeton Univ, AB, 50, MA, 52, PhD, 55. *Prof Exp:* Teacher Latin & Greek, Groton Sch, Mass, 53-55 & Lawrenceville Sch, NJ, 55-56; Fulbright teacher, Leighton Park Sch, Reading, England, 56-57; TEACHER LATIN & GREEK, HILL SCH, 57-, CHMN DEPT CLASSICS, 68- *Concurrent Pos:* Fulbright award, Am Acad Rome, 56; asst prof, Haverford Col, 60-61; asst master, Rugby Sch, Rugby, Eng, 72. *Mem:* Am Philol Asn; Class Asn Can. *Res:* Tradition of the Helen legend in Greek literature. *Publ:* Auth, Herodotus' use of variant versions, Phoenix, summer 63; Homer's Helen, Greece & Rome, 4/68; Latin: A Course for Schools and Colleges, 80 & A Basic Course for Reading Greek, 82, The Bill Sch. *Mailing Add:* Hill Sch Pottstown PA 19464

GROTHMANN, WILHELM HEINRICH, b Osnabrück, Ger, Jan 18, 31; US citizen; m 64; c 2. MODERN GERMAN LITERATURE. *Educ:* Brigham Young Univ, BA, 60; Univ Kans, MA, 62, PhD(Ger), 68. *Prof Exp:* Instr Ger, Purdue Univ, 63-65; from instr to asst prof, 66-73, ASSOC PROF GER, UNIV S FLA, TAMPA, 73- *Mem:* Am Asn Teachers Ger. *Res:* Post World War II German literature. *Publ:* Auth, Die Rolle der Religion im Menschenbild Heinrich Bölls, Ger Quart, 3/71; Die Uberwindung des Krieges: eine Interpretation von Gerd Gaisers Der Hund von Scholm, fall-winter/71 & Rilke: Ausgesetzt auf den Bergen des Herzens Eine unterrichtliche Darstellung, fall-winter/74, Lang Quart; Zur Struktur des Humors in Heinrich Bölls Gruppenbild mit Dame, Ger Quart, 3/77. *Mailing Add:* Dept of Foreign Lang Univ of SFla Tampa FL 33620

GROVER, FREDERIC JOHN, b Paris, France, June 25, 20; nat US; m 49, 79; c 4. FRENCH. *Educ:* Sorbonne, Lic es Let, 40; Univ Strasbourg, Lic d'Anglais, 45; Univ Calif, PhD(Romance lit), 54. *Prof Exp:* From asst prof to prof French, Swarthmore Col, 54-67; PROF FRENCH, UNIV BC, 67- *Concurrent Pos:* Guggenheim fel, 59-60; Am Coun Learned Soc res fel, 64-65; Can Coun fel, 72-73; Univ BC sr Killam fel, 78. *Mem:* MLA. *Res:* Contemporary French literature; Canadian literature. *Publ:* Auth, Drieu la Rochelle and the Fiction of Testimony, Univ Calif, 58; Drieu la Rochelle, 62 & ed, Sur les Ecrivains, 64, Gallimard, Paris; Six Entretiens Avec A Malraux, Gallimard, Paris, 78; (with Pierre Andreu), Drieu La Rochelle, Hachette, Paris, 79. *Mailing Add:* 3995 W 19th Ave Vancouver BC V6S 1C9 Can

GRUBE, FRANK WILLIAM, English. See Vol II

GRUBER, LOREN CHARLES, Medieval Studies, English Literature. See Vol II

GRUBER, VIVIAN M, b Salerno, Fla, May 12, 25; m 48; c 1. LANGUAGES. *Educ:* Fla State Col Women, BA, 47; Fla State Univ, MA, 48, PhD, 60. *Prof Exp:* Instr Spanish, Okla Col Women, 48-49; from instr to prof Span & French, Wayland Baptist Col, 50-64, head dept, 56-60; prof Ky Southern Col, 64-65; assoc prof, 65-67, PROF SPAN & FRENCH, STEPHEN F AUSTIN STATE UNIV, 67-, CHMN DEPT MOD LANG, 79- *Concurrent Pos:* Am Asn Univ Women fel, 47-48; teaching asst Span, Univ Tex, 55-56; mem ad hoc comt fels & awards, Charles E Merrill Found, 60-63. *Mem:* Am Asn Teachers Fr; Am Asn Teachers Span & Port; MLA; Am Coun Teaching Foreign Lang; Latin Am Studies Asn. *Res:* Comparative literature. *Publ:* Auth, Origins of a new world pronunciation, Fla State Univ Studies, 50; Rabelais & Cervantes, novelists of transition, Diss Abstr, 60; Rabelais' didactics of modernation, L'Esprit Createur, summer 63; The use of the grotesque in literature as social protest (contemporary European), Proc VIth Cong Int Comp Lit, 72; The search for identity: The adolescent in representative Latin American novels, Proc VIIIth Cong Int Comp Lit, 75; The general and the lady: Two views of religion in the Mexican Revolution, Relig in Latin Am Life & Lit, 80. *Mailing Add:* Dept of Mod Lang Sch Lib Arts Stephen F Austin State Univ Nacogdoches TX 75961

GRUMMEL, WILLIAM CHARLES, b St Louis, Mo, May 26, 14; m 39; c 2. CLASSICAL LANGUAGE & LITERATURE. *Educ:* St Louis Univ, AB, 37; Wash Univ, AM, 40, PhD(classics), 48. *Prof Exp:* Instr classics, NY Univ, 40-45; chmn dept, 56-71, asst prof, 45-49, assoc prof, 49-80, PROF CLASSICS, UNIV WASH, 80- *Concurrent Pos:* Ford Found fel, Yale Univ, 49-50. *Mem:* Soc Am Archaeol. *Res:* Roman republican history and literature; linguistics. *Publ:* Auth, Life and political career of L Calpurnius Piso. *Mailing Add:* 12015 Exeter NE Seattle WA 98125

GRUN, RUTH DOROTHEA, b Dreihausen, Ger, June 14, 27. GERMAN LANGUAGE, ROMANCE LANGUAGES. *Educ:* Univ Marburg, PhD(Romance philol), 64. *Prof Exp:* Instr mod lang, Bradley Univ, 60-62; mem staff Romance lang, Univ-Bibliot, Marburg, 65-66; ASSOC PROF MOD LANG, IND STATE UNIV, TERRE HAUTE, 66- *Mem:* Am Asn Teachers Ger; MLA. *Res:* German and Romance languages. *Publ:* Auth, Hommes-Copies, Dandies und Fausses Passions, Droz, Geneve & Minard, Paris, 67. *Mailing Add:* Dept Foreign Lang Ind State Univ Terre Haute IN 47809

GRUNDLEHNER, PHILIP, b New York, NY, July 24, 45; US & Swiss citizen; m 72; c 1. GERMAN. *Educ:* Univ Pa, BA, 67; Tufts Univ, MA, 68; Ohio Stat Univ, PhD(Ger), 72. *Prof Exp:* Asst prof Ger, Middlebury Col, 71-72; asst prof, Univ Ill, Urbana, 72-78; ASST PROF GER, JOHNS HOPKINS UNIV, 78- *Mem:* MLA; Am Asn Teachers Ger. *Res:* Lyric poetry; late 19th and early 20th century German literature. *Publ:* Auth, Kafkas Uhren und sein Begriff der Zeit, Litt & Kritik, 8/77; Kraus vs George: Shakespeare's Sonnets, Jahrbuch Deutschen Shakespeare Gesellschaft, 77; The Lyrical Bridge: Essays from Hölderlin to Benn, Fairleigh Dickinson Univ, 78; Sprich Deutsch, Holt, 79, 2nd ed (in press); Points de Vue, Holt, 81; Manual Gesture in Kafka's Prozess, German Quart, 3/82. *Mailing Add:* Dept of Ger Johns Hopkins Univ Baltimore MD 21218

GRUNDSTROM, ALLAN WILBUR, b Gary, Ind, Sept 17, 37; m 59; c 3. FRENCH LANGUAGE & LINGUISTICS. *Educ:* DePauw Univ, AB, 59; Univ Kans, AM, 61; Univ Mich, PhD(Romance ling), 66. *Prof Exp:* Asst instr French, Univ Kans, 59-61; instr, DePauw Univ, 61-64; asst prof, 66-71, assoc prof, 71-77, PROF FRENCH & LING, BUCKNELL UNIV, 77-, CHMN DEPT MOD LANG, 75- *Mem:* Am Asn Teachers Fr; Ling Soc Am; Am Asn Phonetic Sci; MLA. *Res:* Foreign language teaching; experimental phonetics and phonology; French-Canadian language and culture. *Publ:* Auth, An Experimental Study of Interrogative Intonations in French, speech Commun Res Lab; A new model for present tense verbs, Fr Rev, 10/73; co-ed (with P R Leon), Intonation et interrogation, Studia Phonetica, 73; auth, Listener reconstruction of the prosodies, In: Problemes de prosodie, Studia Phonetica, 80; L'Analyse du francais (manuscript), 82. *Mailing Add:* Dept Mod Lang Bucknell Univ Lewisburg PA 17837

GRUPP, WILLIAM JOHN, b Rochester, NY, June 3, 22; m 45; c 5. SPANISH LITERATURE. *Educ:* Univ Toronto, BA, 46; Cornell Univ, PhD, 49. *Prof Exp:* From instr to assoc prof span lit, Univ Notre Dame, 49-64, head dept mod land, 59-63; assoc prof span, Valparaiso Univ, 64-65; chief inst assistance sect, Div foreign studies, US Off Educ, 65-67; prof Span & Port & chmn dept, 67-77, PROF SPAN, UNIV COLO, 77- *Concurrent Pos:* Cult attache, US Embassy, Buenos Aires, 61- *Mem:* MLA; Am Asn Teachers Span & Port. *Res:* Contemporary Spanish literature; Spanish literature since 1936; contemporary Spanish American literature. *Mailing Add:* Dept Span & Port McKenna 126 Univ Colo Boulder CO 80302

GRUZINSKA, ALEKSANDRA, b Poznan, Poland, US citizen. FRENCH LANGUAGE & LITERATURE. *Educ:* State Univ NY, Buffalo, BA, 64, MA, 66; Pa State Univ, PhD(French), 73. *Prof Exp:* Instr, Rosary Hill Col, 65-68; instr, Sweet Briar Col, 71-73; ASST PROF FRENCH, ARIZ STATE UNIV, 73- *Mem:* MLA; AAUP. *Res:* E M Cioran; the French short story in the nineteenth century; Octave Mirbeau. *Publ:* Auth, Octave Mirbeau antimilitariste, Nineteenth Century Fr Studies, spring 76; Un Roumain grand moraliste francais: E M Cioran, Yearbook of Romanian Studies, 77; Le Conte enchasse de Modierra Villiers de l'Isle-Adam, Zagadnienia Rodzajow literackich, 79; Ovid in exile in Vintila Horia's Dieu est ne en exil, Miorita, 7/79; Stucture in Octave Mirbeau's Le Jardin des supplices, Zagadnienia Rodzajow Literackich (in press). *Mailing Add:* Dept of Foreign Lang Ariz State Univ Tempe AZ 85281

GRYTING, LOYAL ANSEL THEODORE, b Thief River Falls, Minn, Sept 16, 16. ROMANCE LANGUAGES. *Educ:* Bowling Green State Univ, AB & BS, 38; Univ Mich, MA, 39, PhD(Romance lang), 49; Univ Grenoble, cert, 45. *Prof Exp:* Teaching asst French, Univ Grenoble, 45; teaching fel, Univ Mich, 46-49; from instr to assoc prof, 49-60, PROF FRENCH, UNIV ARIZ, 60- *Mem:* MLA; Am Asn Teachers Fr; Mediaeval Acad Am; Philol Asn Pac Coast; Soc Rencesvals. *Res:* Old French literature and language; Romance linguistics; French literature of the 16th century. *Publ:* Auth, The Oldest Version of the Twelfth-Century Poem La Venjance Nostre Seigneur, Univ Mich, 52; The Venjance Nostre Seigneur as a Medieval composite, Mod Lang J, 1/54; La Venjance Nostre Seigneur in Dictionnaire des Lettres Francaises, 64; The flowering of an epic, In: Romance Studies in Memory of Edward Billings Ham, Calif State Col, Hayward, 67; Epic Themes in the Venjance Nostre Seigneur, In: Proceedings of the VIII Congreso de La Societe Rencesvals, Pamplona, Spain, 81. *Mailing Add:* Dept of French & Ital Univ of Ariz Tucson AZ 85721

GUARINO, GUIDO, b Castellamare di Stabia, Italy, Jan 18, 25; US citizen; m 55; c 2. ITALIAN LITERATURE. *Educ:* Columbia Univ, BS, 49, MA, 51, PhD(Ital), 54. *Prof Exp:* Instr Ital, Long Island Univ, 49-54; instr Romance lang, Lehigh Univ, 54-55; instr, 55-58, from asst prof to assoc prof, 58-66, PROF ROMANCE LANG, RUTGERS UNIV, 66-, CHMN, DEPT ITAL, 71- *Concurrent Pos:* Gen ed, Renaissance Texts in Translation, Bucknell Univ, 70- *Mem:* MLA; Am Asn Teachers Ital; Renaissance Soc Am. *Res:* Italian humanism; Renaissance. *Publ:* Auth, Leon Battista Alberti's Vita S Potiti, Renaissance News, 55; Two views of a Renaissance tyrant, Symposium, 56; Boccaccio--Concerning Famous Women, Rutgers Univ, 63 & Allen & Unwin, 64; Hans Baron's The crisis of the early Italian Renaissance, Mod Lang J, 68; The Albertis of Florence: L B Alberti's Della Famiglia, Bucknell Univ, 71; Humanism, In: Dict of Italian Literature, Greenwood Press, 79; ed, Giovanni di Conversino da Ravenna, Dragmalogia, Bucknell Univ, 80. *Mailing Add:* Dept Ital Rutgers Univ New Brunswick NJ 08903

GUBERN, SANTIAGO, b Barcelona, Spain, Feb 25, 33; m 59; c 4. SPANISH. *Educ:* Univ Barcelona, Lic Derecho, 55, Dr Derecho, 67; NY Univ, MA, 70; Inst Estudios Iberoam, PhD(Romanic philol), 71. *Prof Exp:* Lectr Span lang & lit, Univ Barcelona, 56-58; transl & interpreter, Hamburg Am Line, Hamburg, 59-61; prof & dir Span lang & lit, Inst Eurolingua, Barcelona, 62-65; head dept mod lang, 69-70, lectr Span lang & lit, 65-67, asst prof, 67-71, ASSOC PROF SPAN LANG & LIT, LAURENTIAN UNIV, 71- *Mem:* Asn Can Hispanistas: Am Asn Teachers Span & Port; MLA; Can Asn Univ Teachers. *Publ:* Auth, Sobre los origenes de El Conde Lucanor, Inst Estudios Iberoam, Mex, 71; Cuentos de sol y luna, Coches Ed, Barcelona, 72; Mexico: Coleccion audiovisual, 72 & Don Quijote de la Mancha: Coleccion audiovisual, 72, Goldsmith; Pintores espanoles: Coleccion audiovisual, Goldsmith-Playette, 72; Poesia satirico--politica hasta la corte del cuarto Felipe, NY Univ & Cochs Ed, Barcelona, 72; Motivos en Los siete infantes de Lara, NY Univ & Cochs Ed, Barcelona, 72; Ed, Moneda y Credito, Madrid, 72. *Mailing Add:* Dept of Span Lang & Lit Laurentian Univ Sudbury ON P3E 2C6 Can

GUBLER, DONWORTH VERNON, b La Verkin, Utah, Aug 11, 15; m 45; c 9. SLAVIC LANGUAGE & LITERATURE. *Educ:* Brigham Young Univ, BA, 48, MA, 49, PhD, 71. *Prof Exp:* Instr Ger, 50-51, instr Russ, 54-62, from asst prof to assoc prof, 62-76, chmn dept, 62-71, chmn dept Asian & Slavic, 71-76 & 77-80, prof, 76-80, EMER PROF RUSS, BRIGHAM YOUNG UNIV, 80- *Concurrent Pos:* NDEA fel, Ind Univ, 59-62. *Mem:* Rocky Mountain Mod Lang Asn; Pac Northwest Coun Foreign Lang. *Res:* Lev Tolstoy; Thomas Mann. *Mailing Add:* 250 FB Brigham Young Univ Provo UT 84602

GUDDAT, KURT HERBERT, b Berlin, Ger, July 13, 24; nat US. GERMAN. *Educ:* Paedag Inst, Ger, Dipl, 47; Eastern NMex Univ, BA, 52; Ohio State Univ, MA, 53, PhD, 59. *Prof Exp:* Teacher pub schs, Ger, 47-50; res asst Ger, Ohio State Univ, 51-54; from asst prof to assoc prof, 54-63, PROF GER, OHIO WESLEYAN UNIV, 63-, CHMN DEPT, 61- *Mem:* Am Asn Teachers Ger; Am Coun Teaching Foreign Langs. *Res:* Nineteenth and twentieth century German literature. *Publ:* Coauth, Writings of the Young Marx on Philosophy and Society, Doubleday, 67. *Mailing Add:* Dept of Ger Ohio Wesleyan Univ Delaware OH 43015

GUEDENET, PIERRE, b Vesoul, France, Feb 2, 14; m 39; c 1. FRENCH. *Educ:* Sorbonne, France, Dipl, 37. *Prof Exp:* Asst prof French, Mt Holyoke Col, 39-44; asst cult counsel, French Embassy, 44-54; lectr French, Hunter Col, 54-55; assoc prof, Kenyon Col, 55-59; assoc prof, 59-80, PROF FRENCH, HUNTER COL, 80- *Concurrent Pos:* Mem Int Educ Comt for Award of French Govt Fel, 59- *Mem:* Am Asn Teachers Fr; MLA. *Res:* French literature of the 19th and 20th centuries. *Publ:* Auth, Valery et la Prevision; Les Souvenirs de Vienne dans l'oeuvre de Gerard de Nerval; Le Plan de Paix Perpetuelle de Saint Simon. *Mailing Add:* Dept of Romance Lang Hunter Col 695 Park Ave New York NY 10003

GUENTHER, PAUL FELIX, b Berlin, Ger, Oct 15, 13; nat US; m 41; c 3. COMPARATIVE LITERATURE. *Educ:* Univ Denver, BA, 46; Univ Colo, MA, 48; Univ NC, PhD(comp lit), 54. *Prof Exp:* Instr Ger & Span, Univ Colo, 46-49; instr Ger, Vanderbilt Univ, 49-50 & Univ NC, 50-51; asst prof, Vanderbilt Univ, 60-66; PROF MOD LANG & LIT, SOUTHERN ILL UNIV, EDWARDSVILLE, 66-, CHMN DEPT, 80- *Mem:* MLA; Midwest Mod Lang Asn; Am Asn Teachers Ger. *Res:* German; translation; contemporary literature. *Publ:* Transl, E Morwitz' The Theory of Blood Coagulation, C C Thomas, 58; auth, Faithful ugliness or faithless beauty--the translator's problem, Ger Quart, 11/62; Heinito von Daderers Magnun Opus Austriacum, winter 66 & coauth, Little magazines and the cosmopolitan tradition, winter 70, Papers Lang & Lit. *Mailing Add:* Sch of Humanities Dept of Mod & Foreign Lang Southern Ill Univ Edwardsville IL 62025

GUENTHER, PETER, b Dresden, Ger, Mar 29, 20; US citizen; m 47; c 4. ART HISTORY. *Educ:* Univ Tex, Austin, MA, 60, PhD(Ger lang), 68. *Prof Exp:* From instr to asst prof art & Europ hist, Ger lang & chmn dept art, St Mary's Univ, Tex, 57-61; from asst prof to assoc prof, 62-77, chmn, Dept Art, 63-73, PROF ART HIST, UNIV HOUSTON, 77- *Concurrent Pos:* Hon trustee, Houston Mus Fine Arts; scholar-in-residence, R G Rifkind Col, Beverly Hills, 78; fel, Ctr Advan Study Visual Arts, Nat Gallery, Washington, DC, 80; vis scholar, Germanisches Nat Mus Nürnberg, 81. *Honors & Awards:* Scholarship Award, Art Libr Soc NAm, 77. *Mem:* Col Art Asn Am; Archaeol Inst Am; SCent Renaissance Conf (pres, 71-72); Int Ctr Medieval Art; Renaissance Soc Am. *Res:* Mannerism in the Holy Roman Empire; interrelationship of literature and the visual arts; German expressionism. *Publ:* Auth, Karl Schmidt-Rottluff and Karl Rossing, Am-Ger Rev, 61; Hans Hartung, Forum, 69; The aesthetics of the Bauhaus, Tex Quart, 73; Concerning the destruction of works of art during the Reformation, Explorations in Renaissance Cult, 75; Edvard Munch 76 & German Expressionism: Toward a New Humanism, 77, Sarah Campbell Blaffer Gallery; Edvard Munch und der Symbolismus, In: Munch, Liebe, Angst, Tod, Kunsthalle Bielefeld, 80; Bemerkungen zum Jungen Felixmüller, Germanisches Nationalmuseum, Archiv für Bildende Kunst, Nürnberg, 81. *Mailing Add:* Art Dept Univ of Houston Houston TX 77004

GUERS-VILLATE, YVONNE, b Senas, France, June 22, 24; m 63. ROMANCE LANGUAGES. *Educ:* Univ Aix-Marseille, Lic es Lett, 44; Bryn Mawr Col, MA, 51, PhD(French), 60. *Prof Exp:* Instr French, Mt Holyoke Col, 53-55; head dept, Chapin Sch, 55-59; asst prof, Syracuse Univ, 59-65; from assoc prof to prof, Univ Wis-Milwaukee, 65-74; PROF MOD LANG, FLA INT UNIV, 74- *Mem:* MLA; Am Asn Teachers Fr. *Res:* Twentieth century novel, drama and French literature. *Publ:* Auth, C F Ramuz, Essai, Buchet-Chastel, Paris, 66; Revolt and submission in Camus & Bernanos, Renascence, summer 72; Structures antithetiques chez Bernanos, Rev Lett Mod, fall 73; Comparison des procedes stylistiques dans deux romans de M Duras, In: Albert Menut Festschrift, Coronado, 73; L'imaginaire et son efficacite chez Marguerite Duras, Les Lett Romanes, 75; Structure dans 2 romans de Duras, USF Lang Quart, winter 78; Continuite/ Discontinuite chez M Duras, Revue du Pacifique, 79; From Hiroshima to India-Song, Philol Papers, 80. *Mailing Add:* Dept of Mod Lang Fla Int Univ Miami FL 33199

GUEST, JOHN LEMUEL, b Haskell, Tex, May 17, 21. GERMAN. *Educ:* Univ Tex, BA; Columbia Univ, MA. *Prof Exp:* Instr Ger, NY Univ, 49-51 & Rutgers Univ, 53-57; ASSOC PROF GER & CHMN DEPT, MILLSAPS COL, 57- *Mem:* Am Asn Teachers Ger; MLA. *Res:* Modern German literature; modern drama. *Mailing Add:* Dept of Ger Millsaps Col Jackson MS 39210

GUGLI, WILLIAM V, b Providence, RI, Oct 8, 32. ROMANCE LANGUAGES. *Educ:* Brown Univ, AB, 54, AM, 59; Syracuse Univ, PhD(French & Ital), 67. *Prof Exp:* Teaching asst French, Syracuse Univ, 59-

61, instr, 61-66; asst prof, 66-80, ASSOC PROF FRENCH & ITAL, UNIV MASS, AMHERST, 80- *Mem:* Am Asn Teachers Fr. *Res:* The journal as literature. *Publ:* Transl, Letter to an Arab friend, (transl, A Chouraqui, Lettre a un ami arabe), Univ Mass, 73; Multi-track options for French study, Fr Rev, 5/73. *Mailing Add:* 138 E Pleasant Ave Amherst MA 01002

GUIDER, ELIZABETH GRIER, Renaissance Drama, Italian Literature. See Vol II

GUIEU, JEAN-MAX, b Marseille, France, Oct 24, 43. FRENCH LITERATURE. *Educ:* Univ Aix en Provence, Lic es Lett, 67, Maitrise de lett, 68; Univ Md, PhD(French), 75. *Prof Exp:* Instr ling & phonetics, Univ Aix en Provence, 67-68; instr French, Univ Md, 68-73; prof, Lycee Francais Int Wash, 73-76; ASST PROF FRENCH, SCH FOREIGN SERV, GEORGETOWN UNIV, 76- *Concurrent Pos:* Collabr res comt, Complete Corresp of Emile Zola, 75- *Mem:* Am Asn Teachers Fr. *Res:* Emile Zola's lyric dramas; literature and politics. *Publ:* Coauth, Aux Sources de la verite der Theatre Moderne, Minard, 74; auth, Le Beau reve de T Nore, Prix Marcel Pagnol 1975, Le Meridional-La France, 2/75. *Mailing Add:* Dept of French Sch Foreign Serv Georgetown Univ Washington DC 20067

GUILLERMO, EDENIA, b Bolondron, Matanzas, Cuba, Mar 28, 15; US citizen; m 42; c 2. SPANISH & SPANISH AMERICAN LANGUAGE & LITERATURE. *Educ:* Inst Matanzas, Cuba, Bachiller, 35; Univ Havana, DEduc, 39, PhD, 49. *Prof Exp:* Prof Span & soc sci, Inst Pre-Univ Vedado, 40-61; instr Span, Lander Grade Sch, Wyo, 62-64 & Morrisville High Sch, Pa, 64-65; from asst prof to assoc prof, Monmouth Col, Ill, 65-74; PROF SPAN, HOOD COL, 74- *Concurrent Pos:* Lectr & assoc dir, Univ Aire, Sta CMQ, Havana, 56-60; dir educ, Prov Havana, 60-61. *Mem:* MLA; Am Asn Teachers Span & Port; AAUP; Am Asn Univ Women; Circulo de Cult. *Publ:* Auth, Dario y Americas, Int Rev Bibliog, 67; La primera epopeya americana en su cuarto centenario, Inter-Am Rev Bibliog, 70; coauth, Novelistica Espanola de los Sesenta, Torres, 71; Quince Novelas Hispanoamericanas, Las Americas, 72; El Teatro Hispanico, Nat Textbk, 72; auth, Paradiso, culminacion del barroco cubano, Papeles de Son Armadans, Madrid-Palma de Mallorca, 6/74. *Mailing Add:* Dept of Span Hood Col Frederick MD 21701

GUILLOTON, DORIS STARR, b Stuttgart, Ger, July 2, 29; US citizen; m 62. GERMAN LANGUAGE & LITERATURE. *Educ:* NY Univ, BA, 56, PhD(Ger lit), 62; Middlebury Col, MA, 57. *Prof Exp:* Instr Ger, NY Univ, 61-62 & Rutgers Univ, 63-74; asst prof, 64-68, assoc prof, 68-81, PROF GER & COMP LIT, NY UNIV, 81-, DIR DEPT, 69- *Concurrent Pos:* Chmn, Nat Teachers Training Comt, Am Asn Teachers Ger, 73-76; mem pedagogical publ comt, MLA, 73-74; assoc ed, Teaching Lang Through Lit, 67- *Mem:* Am Asn Teachers Ger; MLA; Am Asn Comp Lit; Goethe Soc North Am; Faustgesellschaft. *Res:* European romanticism; literary theory; women's studies. *Publ:* Auth, Uber den Begriff des Symbols, Hutzler, Reutlingen, Ger, 64; Friedrich Schlegel und die französ Schriftsteller seiner Zeit, NY Univ Studies Ger Lang & Lit, 67; coauth, Deutsche Literatur von Heute, Holt, 74; auth, Rahel Varnhagen und die frauenfrage in der dt Romantik . . ., Monatshefte, 77; Motifs in German Faust texts, Teaching Lang through Lit, 78; Trends and Innovations in German Studies, Nat Conf Int Studies, 79; coauth, Faustische Elemente in M Frischs Don Juan, M F Aspekte des Bühnenwerks, Bern, 79; ed, Geographische Aspekte deutschsprachiger Länder, New York Univ-Deutscher Akademischer Austauschdienst, 81. *Mailing Add:* Dept of Ger NY Univ 19 University Pl New York NY 10003

GUINAGH, KEVIN JOSEPH, b New Castle, Pa, June 3, 97. CLASSICAL PHILOLOGY. *Educ:* St Vincent Col, AB, 19, AM, 21; Cath Univ Am, STB, 23; Univ Pittsbrugh, PhD, 31. *Prof Exp:* Instr, Antioch Col, 30; from instr to assoc prof, 31-34, prof foreign lang, 34-64, head dept, 34-62, EMER PROF FOREIGN LANG, EASTERN ILL UNIV, 64- *Concurrent Pos:* Prof, Antioch Col, 47-48; vis prof, Univ PR, 64-68; lectr, Univ SFla, 68-69. *Mem:* Am Philol Asn; Am Asn Teachers Span & Port. *Res:* Latin literature; Roman philology. *Publ:* Transl, Vergil's Aeneid, Holt, 52; coauth, Latin Literature in Translation, 42 & Greek and Roman Classics in Translation, 47, McKay; ed, Dictionary of Foreign Phrases and Abbreviations, Wilson, 82. *Mailing Add:* 424 Dunedin Circle Temple Terrace FL 33617

GUINEY, MORTIMER MARTIN, b Boston, Mass, Jan 27, 30; m 53; c 4. FRENCH, COMPARATIVE LITERATURE. *Educ:* Colby Col, BA, 52; Middlebury Col, MA, 56. *Prof Exp:* Teacher high sch, Conn, 52-53; master French & Ger, Choate Sch, 53-54; bus mgr, Aiglon Col, Switz, 54-55; from instr to asst prof French, Univ NC, Greensboro, 58-65; asst prof, 65-72, ASSOC PROF FRENCH & COMP LIT, UNIV CONN, 72- *Concurrent Pos:* Ed French lang texts, Prentice-Hall, Inc, 65-67; vis prof comp lit, Univ Rouen, France, 67-68; dir prog in France, Univ Conn, 67-69 & 76-77. *Mem:* Am Asn Teachers Fr; MLA; Eastern Comp Lit Conf (pres, 77). *Res:* Contemporary French poetry; relationship between plastic arts and literature. *Publ:* Auth, La poesie de Pierre R Reverdy, Libr Univ Georg, Geneva, 66; ed, Un Crime de Bernanos, Prentice-Hall, 64; Cubisme, litteraire et plastique, Rev Sci Humaines, 7/71; auth, Cubisme et litterature, Libr Univ, Georg, Geneva, 72; contribr, Lire Milosz, A Silvain, Paris, France, 77. *Mailing Add:* U 57 Univ of Conn Storrs CT 06268

GUINN, LAWRENCE, b Jacksonville, Tex, Aug 22, 30; m 53; c 1. LINGUISTICS, PHILOLOGY. *Educ:* Univ Ark, BM, 51, MA, 55; Univ Pa, PhD(English philol), 59. *Prof Exp:* Instr English, 59-61; from asst prof to assoc prof English & foreign lang, 61-71; acting chmn dept, 67-68; chmn dept foreign lang, 68-77, PROF FOREIGN LANG, UNIV ARK,

FAYETTEVILLE, 71- *Mem:* MLA; SCent Mod Lang Asn. *Res:* Germanic philology and linguistics; Germanic medieval literature. *Mailing Add:* Dept of Foreign Lang Univ of Ark Fayetteville AR 72701

GUIRAGOSSIAN CARR, DIANA, b Cyprus, July 11, 30; m 76; US citizen. FRENCH LITERATURE. *Educ:* Univ Paris, B es L, 49, lic libr, 55; Columbia Univ, MA, 53, PhD, 62. *Prof Exp:* Lectr French, Columbia Univ, 53-54; instr & dir French house, Rutgers Univ, 54-55; lectr French, Columbia Univ, 57-60, from instr to asst prof, 60-66; assoc prof, 66-70, PROF FRENCH LIT, IND UNIV, BLOOMINGTON, 70- *Concurrent Pos:* Coun Res Humanities grant, Columbia Univ, 63; Am Coun Learned Soc grant, 66; Nat Endowment Arts & Humanities proj grant, 67-68; Am Coun Learned Soc fel, 78-79. *Mem:* MLA; Am Soc 18th Century Studies; Soc Etude XVIIIe Siecle; Soc Lit Hist France. *Res:* French Enlightenment; French and English novel of the 18th century. *Publ:* Auth, Voltaire's Faceties, 63 & co-ed, Diderot Studies, 65-, Droz, Geneva; contribr, Manon Lescaut et la justice criminelle sous l'ancien regime, Studies Voltaire & 18th Century, 67; contribr, Complete Works of Voltaire, Voltaire Found, 68-; auth, Subterfuges et strategemes, ou les romanciers malgre-eux, In: Literature and History in the Age of Ideas, Ohio Univ, 75; Le Pere de famille et sa descendance anglaise, In: Enlightenment Studies in Honour of Lester G Crocker, Voltaire Found, 799. *Mailing Add:* Dept of French & Ital Ind Univ Bloomington IN 47401

GUITART, JORGE MIGUEL, b Havana, Cuba, Sept 15, 37; US citizen; m 69; c 2. SPANISH, LINGUISTICS. *Educ:* George Washington Univ, BA, 67; Georgetown Univ, MS, 70, PhD(Span & Ling), 73. *Prof Exp:* Teaching fel, Georgetown Univ, 69-71, instr Span, 71-73; asst prof, 73-77, ASSOC PROF SPAN LING, STATE UNIV NY AT BUFFALO, 77-, DIR SPAN LANG INSTR, 74- *Concurrent Pos:* Dir State Univ NY at Buffalo/Univ of Salamanca summer prog, 75-76; vis assoc prof, Univ Pittsburgh, summer 78 & 79. *Mem:* Ling Soc Am; MLA; Am Asn Teachers Span & Port. *Res:* Spanish linguistic theory; Caribbean Spanish dialectology. *Publ:* Auth, Markedness and a Cuban Dialect of Spanish, Georgetown Univ, 76; Aspects of Spanish aspect: A new look at the imperfect/preterit distinction, In: Contemp Studies in Romance Ling, 78; Conservative vs radical dialects of Spanish: Implications for language instruction, Bilingual Rev, 78; Aspectos del consonantismo habanero: Reexamen descriptive, Bol de la Academia Puertorriquena de la Lengua Espanola, 78; co-ed, La estructura fonica de la lengua castellana, Anagrama, 80; auth, on loanword phonology as distinctive feature phonology in Cuban Spanish, In: Linguistics Symposium on Romance Languages, Georgetown Univ, Vol 9, 81; Sobre la silaba como entidad fonematica en los dialectos del Caribe Hispanico, Thesaurus, 81; coauth, Dialectologia Hispanoamericana, Almar, 82. *Mailing Add:* Dept Mod Lang & Lit State Univ NY 910 Clemens Hall Buffalo NY 14260

GUITE, HAROLD FREDERICK, b Clayworth, UK, Mar 12, 20; m 51; c 2. CLASSICS. *Educ:* Univ London, BA, 44, MA, 46, MA, 52. *Prof Exp:* Asst master, Keil Sch, Scotland, 45-46; col supvr classics, St Catharine's Col, Cambridge, 46-47; asst lectr, Univ Manchester, 47-48, lectr Latin, 48-56; lectr classics, Univ Ibadan, 56-58, sr lectr, 58-63; prof & chmn dept, Univ Col Rhodesia & Nyasaland, 63-67, mem exec coun, 65-67; PROF CLASSICS, McMASTER UNIV, 67- *Concurrent Pos:* Chmn youth comt, Int Fel Reconciliation, 50-56; hon inspector educ western region, Nigeria, 57-63; ed, Proc African Class Asn, 63-66; mem, Joint Comt Churches Teacher Training, Rhodesia, 64-67; govt adv, Comt Teacher Training, Rhodesia, 65-67; secy Christian citizenship comt, Methodist Church, Rhodesia, 65-67; pres, McMaster Univ Fac Asn, 77-78. *Mem:* Soc Prom Roman Studies; Am Philol Asn; Class Asn Can. *Res:* Elegy; metre; satire. *Publ:* Auth, European education in West Africa, Univ Rev, Dublin, 61; Cicero's attitude to the Greeks, Greece & Rome, 10/62; What Kind of Classics?, Oxford Univ, 65; One Man's Classics, Class Asn Cent Africa, 65; An 18th century view of Roman satire, In: The Varied Pattern, Studies in the 18th Century, Hakkert, Toronto, 71; Culture and mission, Theol Bull, 5/75. *Mailing Add:* Dept of Class McMaster Univ Hamilton ON L8S 4M2 Can

GUITTON, JEAN MARIE, b Jugon, France, Apr 11, 29; m 63; c 2. FOREIGN LANGUAGES. *Educ:* Univ Caen, MA, 59; Emory Univ, MA & PhD(French), 69. *Prof Exp:* Asst prof French, Ga Col, 62-63 & Valdosta State Col, 63-66; assoc prof, 69-71, PROF FRENCH, GA COL, 72-, CHMN DEPT, 69- *Mem:* MLA; Am Asn Teachers Fr. *Res:* The French novel. *Mailing Add:* Dept of French Ga Col Milledgeville GA 31601

GULLACE, GIOVANNI, b Italy, Apr 4, 14; nat US; m 49; c 1. FRENCH, ITALIAN. *Educ:* Univ Naples, Italy, LittD, 47; Univ Rochester, MA, 50; Syracuse Univ, PhD, 52. *Prof Exp:* Instr French, Liceo, Italy, 47-48; teacher Ital, high sch, NY, 51-52; instr French & Ital, Syracuse Univ, 52-53; from asst prof to assoc prof Romance lang, Le Moyne Col, 53-59, prof & chmn 59-60; assoc prof French, Tulane Univ, 60-63; prof, 63-70, chmn dept, 67-70, PROF FRENCH & COMP LIT, STATE UNIV NY BINGHAMTON, 70-, CHMN DEPT ROMANCE LANG, 72- *Concurrent Pos:* Assoc ed, Symposium, 61- *Honors & Awards:* Star of Solidarity, Italy, 62. *Mem:* MLA; Am Asn Teachers Fr; Am Asn Teachers Ital. *Res:* Italian literature; literary criticism; 18th and 19th century French literature. *Publ:* Auth, Gentile versus Croce: A comparison of two rival aesthetic systems, Symposium, 57; Pensee et poesie dans les Destinees d'Alfred de Vigny, Rev Univ Laval, 63; Gabriele D'Annunzio in France: A Study in Cultural Relations, Syracuse Univ, 66; Voltaire's idea of progress and Candide's conclusion, Personalist, 67; transl, Giovanni Gentile, The Philosophy of Art, Cornell Univ, 72. *Mailing Add:* Dept of Romance Lang State Univ of NY Binghamton NY 13901

GULLON, GERMAN, b Santander, Spain, May 21, 45; m 70; c 1. SPANISH & SPANISH AMERICAN LITERATURE. *Educ:* Lit Univ Salamanca, Lic, 69; Univ Tex, Austin, PhD(Romance lang), 73; Univ Pa, MA, 79. *Prof Exp:* Asst prof, 73-80, ASSOC PROF SPAN, UNIV PA, 80- *Concurrent Pos:* Assoc ed, Hisp Rev, 73- *Honors & Awards:* Lindback Award, 78. *Mem:* MLA; Am Asn Teachers Span & Port. *Res:* Modern Spanish novel; literary criticism; comparative literature. *Publ:* Auth, Simultaneidades ambientales, 4-6/71; La retorica de Cortazar en Rayuela, Insula, 10/71; El narrador y la narracion en Los pasos perididos, Cuadernos Hispanoam, 5-6/72; co-ed, Teoria de la Novela, 74, auth, El narrador en la Novela del Siglo XIX, 76 & coauth, El Exilio de 1939, 77, Taurus; co-ed; Surrealismo/Surrealismos Espana y Hispanoamerica, Univ Pa, 77; auth, Poesia Espanola de Vunguardia, Taurus, 81. *Mailing Add:* Dept of Romance Lang Univ of Pa Philadelphia PA 19104

GULLON, RICARDO, b Astorga, Spain, Aug 31, 08. SPANISH & SPANISH AMERICAN LITERATURE. *Educ:* Inst Leon, Spain, BA, 23; Univ Madrid, Lic Leyes, 29. *Prof Exp:* Prof Span, Int Univ Satander, 46-52, 56-58 & Univ PR, 53-55, 58-60; from vis prof to prof, Univ Tex, Austin, 60-72, Ashbel Smith prof, 72-76; PROF SPAN, UNIV CHICAGO, 76- *Concurrent Pos:* Vis prof, Univ Calif, Los Angeles, Stanford Univ, NY Univ, Columbia Univ, Univ Colo, Univ Iowa & Univ PR, 61-68; Guggenheim fel, 70. *Mem:* Hist Soc Am; MLA; Hisp Soc Am. *Publ:* Auth, Estudios sobre Juan Ramon Jimenez, Ed Losada, Buenos Aires, 60; Direcciones del modernismo, 63 & 71, Autobiografias de Unamuno, 64 & Una poetica para Antonio Machado, 70, Ed Gredos, Madrid; Relaciones entre Antonio Machado y Juan Ramon Jimenez, Univ Pisa, 64; Tecnicas de Galdos, 71 & 80 & Psicologias del autor y logicas del personaje, 80, Ed Taurus, Madrid; Espacio y Novela, Ed Bosch, Barcelona, 81. *Mailing Add:* Dept of Span Univ of Chicago Chicago IL 60637

GULSOY, J, b Ordu, Turkey, Aug 15, 25; Can citizen; m 59; c 2. ROMANCE LANGUAGES, HISPANIC LINGUISTICS. *Educ:* Univ BC, BA, 53; Univ Toronto, MA, 55; Univ Chicago, PhD, 61. *Prof Exp:* From instr to assoc prof, 58-70, PROF SPAN, UNIV TORONTO, 70- *Concurrent Pos:* Can Coun grant, 67-68. *Mem:* MLA; Am Asn Teachers Span & Port; Soc Ling Romane; Medieval Acad Am. *Res:* Lexicographical compilations; Catalan and Spanish linguistics; Hispanic dialectology. *Publ:* Auth, La lexicografia valenciana, Rev, Valenciana Filol, 59-62; ed, Diccionario Valenciano--Castellano de M J Sanelo, Soc Castellonense de Cult, Castellon, 64; The descendants of Old Catalan and Provencal ab with, Rev Ling Romane, 29/65; The -i words in the poems of G de Berceo, Romance Philol, 69. *Mailing Add:* Dept of Hispanic Studies Univ of Toronto Toronto ON M5S 1A1 Can

GULSTAD, DANIEL E, b Bottineau, NDak, Sept 26, 33; m 57; c 2. SPANISH, LINGUISTICS. *Educ:* Mexico City Col, BA, 57, MA, 60; Univ Ill, PhD(Span), 69. *Prof Exp:* Teacher high sch, Ill, 59-63; from instr to assoc prof, 67-72, PROF SPAN, UNIV MO-COLUMBIA, 78- *Mem:* MLA; Ling Soc Am; Am Asn Teacher Span & Port; Int Ling Asn; Int Soc Phonetic Sci. *Res:* Romance linguistics; linguistic semantics; Spanish literature through the 16th century. *Publ:* Auth, A Modern Theory of Langue, Mouton, The Hague, 73; Parody in Valle Inclan's Sonata de Otono, Revista Hisp Mod, 73; A generatuve discourse model, Linguistics, 3/73; Antithesis in a novel by Ruben Romero, Hispania, 4/73; Reconstruction in syntax, Proc First Int Conf Hist Ling, 74; La lingusitica y el texto de La Celestina, Actas del Vo Congreso Internacional de Hispanistas, Asociacion Internacional de Hispanistas, 77; co-ed, Papers from the 1977 Mid-America Linguistics Conference, Univ Mo, 78; auth, On the Function of Focus in Some English Verbs, Transactions of the Mo Acad Sci, 80. *Mailing Add:* Dept of Romance Lang Univ of Mo Columbia MO 65201

GUMPEL, LISELOTTE, b Berlin, Ger; US citizen. HUMANITIES, GERMAN. *Educ:* San Francisco State Col, BA, 64; Stanford Univ, MA, 66, PhD(Ger lang & lit), 71. *Prof Exp:* Asst prof, 68-73, assoc prof, 73-80, PROF GER LANG & LIT, UNIV MINN, MORRIS, 80- *Concurrent Pos:* Helen Cam res fel, 77-78. *Mem:* MLA; AAUP. *Res:* German literature; semantics; esthetics. *Publ:* Auth, The essence of reality as a construct of language, Found Lang, 3/74; The structure of idioms: A phenomenological approach, Semiotica, J Int Asn Semiotic Studies, 12-1/74; Metaphor as nominalized meaning: A phenomenological analysis of the lyrical genre, Jarhbuch Int Germanistik, 76; Concrete Poetry from East and West Germany: The Language of Exemplarism and Experimentalism, Yale Univ, 76. *Mailing Add:* Div of Humanities Univ of Minn Morris MN 56267

GUMPERT, GARY, Communications. See Vol II

GUMPERZ, JOHN J, US citizen. LINGUISTICS, ANTHROPOLOGY. *Educ:* Univ Cincinnati, BA, 47; Univ Mich, PhD(Ger ling), 54. *Prof Exp:* Instr ling, Cornell Univ, 52-54; from instr to assoc prof S Asian lang & ling, 56-67, PROF ANTHROP, UNIV CALIF, BERKELEY, 67- *Concurrent Pos:* Ford Found fel ling, India, 54-56; mem comt socioling, Soc Sci Res Coun, 66-73; Trainers of Teachers of Teachers comt, Berkeley sch bd, 69-71. *Mem:* Ling Soc Am; Am Anthrop Asn; Ling Soc India; AAAS. *Res:* Sociolinguistics; linguistics and cognitive anthropology; applied linguistics. *Publ:* Auth, Language in Social Groups, Stanford Univ, 71; co-ed, Directions in Sociolinguistics, Holt, 72; coauth, Bilingualism, bidialectism and classroom interaction, In: Functions of Language in Classroom, 72; Social meaning in natural conversations, a study of classroom interaction, In: Sociolinguistics: Current Trends and Prospects, 72; auth, Sociolinguistics and communication in small groups, In: Reader in Sociolinguistics, 73. *Mailing Add:* Dept of Anthrop Univ of Calif 232 Kroeber Hall Berkeley CA 94720

GUNDERSON, LLOYD L, b Whitehall, Wis, Aug 24, 31; m 58; c 3. CLASSICAL LANGUAGES, ANCIENT HISTORY. *Educ:* St Olaf Col, BA, 53; Luther Theol Sem, BTh, 57; Univ Wis, MA, 59, PhD(classics), 66. *Prof Exp:* Asst prof hist & classics, Concordia Col, 62-67; PROF CLASSICS & CHMN DEPT, ST OLAF COL, 67- *Mem:* Am Philol Asn. *Res:* Alexander historians and the Alexander Romance-Hellenistic history; Sallust. *Publ:* Auth, The human situation in the Gilgamesh epic and Prometheus bound,

Discourse, fall 64; Early elements in the Alexander romance, In: Ancient Macedonia, Inst Balkan Studies, 70; Alexander the Great in the Sybilline oracles, Ancient Macedonia, 77. *Mailing Add:* Dept of Class Lang St Olaf Col Northfield MN 55057

GUNTERMANN, GAIL, b Miles City, Mont, Oct 9, 38. SPANISH, FOREIGN LANGUAGE EDUCATION. *Educ:* Univ Mont, BA, 60, Univ NMex, MA, 69; Ohio State Univ, PhD(foreign lang educ), 77. *Prof Exp:* Teacher Span, Whitefish Schs, Mont, 60-62 & Albany Union High Sch, Ore, 62-65; lang coordr & instr Span, Brockport State Col, New York, 69-71; lang coordr, Avance, SA, El Salvador, 74-76; methods instr & supvr student teachers Span & French, Fredonia State Col, New York, 77; ASST PROF SPAN & METHODS, ARIZ STATE UNIV, 77- *Mem:* Am Coun Teaching Foreign Lang; Am Asn Teachers Span & Port; MLA. *Res:* Error analysis and perception. *Publ:* Auth, A suggested approach to determining cultural objectives, Hispania, 3/76; How important are errors? A study of frequency, comprehensibility, and evaluational effects of errors in Spanish Mod Lang J, 78. *Mailing Add:* Dept of Foreign Lang Ariz State Univ Tempe AZ 85281

GURALNIK, DAVID BERNARD, b Cleveland, Ohio, June 17, 20; m 42; c 1. LEXICOGRAPHY. *Educ:* Western Reserve Univ, BA, 41, MA, 47. *Prof Exp:* Asst ed, William Collins & World Publ Co, Inc, 41-73, vpres & dict ed-in-chief, 73-80; VPRES & DICT ED-IN-CHIEF, SIMON & SCHUSTER, 80- *Concurrent Pos:* Mem bd dirs, Yiddish Sci Inst Jewish Res, 67. *Honors & Awards:* Ohioana Libr Award, 54. *Mem:* PEN; NCTE; Conf Col Compos & Commun; Am Name Soc; Dictionary Soc NAm. *Res:* American language. *Publ:* Gen ed, Webster's New World Dictionary, col ed, 53, ed-in-chief, concise ed, 56, elem ed, 61, 2nd col ed, 70, 2nd concise ed, 75, students ed, 76 & Young Readers Dict, 79, World Publ. *Mailing Add:* Simon & Schuster 850 Euclid Ave Cleveland OH 44114

GURTTLER, KARIN R, b Guben, Ger, Apr 13, 35. MODERN LANGUAGES. *Educ:* Univ Freiburg, MA(French) & MA(English), 61; McGill Univ, PhD(Ger), 72. *Prof Exp:* PROF GER, UNIV MONTREAL, 65- *Concurrent Pos:* Ed, Bull d'info, de l'Asn des Prof d'Allemand du Quebec, 77- *Mem:* MLA; Asn Can Univ Teachers Ger; Fr-Can Asn Advan Sci. *Res:* Medieval literature; German-Canadian studies; applied linguistics to the teaching of German. *Publ:* Coauth, Les Sons Allemands, 68, auth, Petite Grammaire Pratique de l'Allemand, 69 & coauth, Deutsch-Einfach, Schnell und Sicher, I & II, 69 & 70, Univ Montreal, auth, Künec Artus der Guote Das Artusbild der Höfischen Epik des 12 und 13 Jahrhunderts, Bouvier, Bonn, 76; coauth, Dialog Deutsch, Didier Can, 76; co-ed & contribr, Annalen 1-Deutschkanadische Studien, Presses Elite, Montreal, 76; auth, Texte und Themen, Univ Montreal, 76. *Mailing Add:* Dept of Ancient & Mod Studies Univ of Montreal Montreal PQ H3C 3J7 Can

GUSS, EVELYN GRACE, b West York, Pa, June 21, 28. CLASSICS. *Educ:* Gettysburg Col, AB, 49; Univ Pittsburgh, MA, 51, PhD(classics), 62. *Prof Exp:* From instr to asst prof classics, Maryville Col, 50-60; from asst prof to prof, Juniata Col, 61-77; MEM STAFF, DIV WORLD MISSIONS & ECUMENISM, LUTHERAN CHURCH AM, 77- *Mem:* Am Philol Asn; Archaeol Inst Am. *Res:* Aristophanes; Greek and Roman religion; Greek and Latin language. *Mailing Add:* Div for World Missions & Ecumenism Lutheran Church of Am 231 Madison Ave New York NY 10016

GUSTAFSON, DONNA J, b Duluth, Minn, Aug 1, 30. SPANISH LITERATURE. *Educ:* Col St Scholastica, BA, 52; Mexico City Col, MA, 55; Stanford Univ, PhD(Span), 67. *Prof Exp:* Instr Romance lang, Col St Scholastica, 53-54 & Hiram Col, 55-57; teaching asst Span, Stanford Univ, 57-61; from instr to assoc prof, 62-74, PROF SPAN, SAN JOSE STATE UNIV, 74-, DEPT CHAIRPERSON, 81- *Mem:* Am Coun Teaching Foreign Lang; Am Asn Teachers Span & Port. *Res:* Pre-Lopean drama; foreign language teaching methodology. *Publ:* Auth, The role of the shepherd in the pre-Lopean drama of Diego Sanchez de Badajoz, Bull Comediantes, spring 73; Towards the auto sacramental: Eucharistic prefiguration in the Farsas of Diego Sanchez de Badajoz, Hispanofila, 75. *Mailing Add:* Dept of Foreign Lang San Jose State Univ San Jose CA 95192

GUSTAFSON, MARJORIE LILLIAN, b Galesburg, Ill, Apr 17, 20. FOREIGN LANGUAGE. *Educ:* Knox Col, BA, 42; Univ Ill, MA, 53. *Prof Exp:* Teacher French & Span, Wayland Acad & Jr Col, 42-45, 47-50 & 51-52; teacher lang & head of residence, Holland Hall Sch, Tulsa, Okla, 45-47; teacher English, Cours Complementaire, Paris & Lycee Guingamp, Bretagne, 50-51; asst French, Univ Ill, 52-53; teacher & dean, Estherville Jr Col, Iowa, 53-54; head dept lang, Milwaukee-Downer Sem, 54-57; asst prin, Tudor Hall Sth, Indianapolis, Ind, 57-62; dean students, St Katharine's Sch, Davenport, Ill, 62-63; asst prof French & dean of women, 63-66, ASSOC PROF FOREIGN LANG & DIR LANG LAB, MACMURRAY COL, 66- *Concurrent Pos:* Fulbright Exchange Teacher, France, 50-51. *Honors & Awards:* Ref Source in Libr of Human Resources, Am Bicentennial Res Inst, 76. *Mem:* Am Asn Univ Women; Am Asn Teachers Fr; Nat Asn Lang Lab Dirs; Intercontinental Biog Asn. *Publ:* Auth, Le Cornemuseur et Son Chien, Carleton, 69. *Mailing Add:* 1419 Lakelawn Jacksonville IL 62650

GUSTAFSON, RICHARD FOLKE, b Hartford, Conn, June 17, 34. RUSSIAN LANGUAGE & LITERATURE. *Educ:* Yale Univ, AB, 56; Columbia Univ, PhD(Russ poetry), 63. *Prof Exp:* Instr Russ, Brown Univ, 60-62; from lectr to asst prof, Yale Univ, 62-65; assoc prof, 65-72, PROF RUSS, BARNARD COL, COLUMBIA UNIV, 72-, CHMN DEPT, 65- *Mem:* MLA; Am Asn Advan Slavic Studies; Am Asn Teachers Slavic & East Europ Lang. *Res:* Russian poetry; 19th century fiction; Tolstoy. *Publ:* Auth, The Upas Tree: Pushkin and Erasmus Darwin, PMLA, 1/60; Tjutcev's Imagery and What It Tells Us, 6/60 & The Suffering Usurper: Gogol's Diary of a Madman, 3/65, Slavic & East Europ J; The Imagination of Spring: The Poetry of Afanasy Fet, Yale Univ, 66. *Mailing Add:* Dept of Russ Barnard Col Columbia Univ New York NY 10027

GUTERMUTH, MARY ELIZABETH, b Columbia, Mo, Aug 27, 38. FRENCH. *Educ:* St Louis Univ, BS, 60; Univ Mo, MA, 61, PhD(French), 65; Univ Paris, cert langue francaise, 62. *Prof Exp:* Asst French, Univ Mo, 61-62, instr, 62-65; asst prof, Loyola Univ, Ill, 65-67; assoc prof, 67-81, PROF FRENCH, SAM HOUSTON STATE UNIV, 81- *Concurrent Pos:* Consult educ filmstrips of Huntsville, 70-; res grant studies Marie Claire Blais, 73; consult filmstrip, Eleven centuries of French literature. *Mem:* Am Asn Teachers Fr; MLA; AAUP; SCent Mod Lang Asn; Am Asn Univ Women. *Res:* Marie Claire Blais and Francophone American literature; Aragon; 20th century French literature. *Publ:* Triangular schizophrenia in Aragon's Execution, Ky Romance Quart, fall 68; Aragon's Collages, SCent Mod Lang Asn Bull, winter, 69; contribr, On Louis Aragon to the twentieth century section, In: Critical Bibliography of French Literature, 77. *Mailing Add:* Dept of For Lang Sam Houston State Univ Huntsville TX 77340

GUTHKE, KARL SIEGFRIED, b Lingen, Ger, Feb 17, 33; US citizen; m 65; c 1. GERMAN LITERATURE. *Educ:* Univ Tex, MA, 53; Univ Göttingen, PhD, 56. *Hon Degrees:* MA, Harvard Univ, 68. *Prof Exp:* From instr to prof Ger lit, Univ Calif, Berkeley, 56-65; prof Ger, Univ Toronto, 65-68; PROF GER, HARVARD UNIV, 68- *Concurrent Pos:* Am Philos Soc grant-in-aid, 61-62; vis prof, Univ Colo, 63 & Univ Mass, 67; Guggenheim fel, 65; Am Coun Learned Soc fel, 72-73. *Honors & Awards:* Walter C Cabot Prize, Harvard Univ, 77. *Mem:* MLA; Am Lessing Soc (pres, 71-72); Acad Lit Studies; Lessing Akad Schiller Ges. *Res:* Anglo-German literary relations; 18th century German literature; Gerhart Hauptmann. *Publ:* Co-ed, J H Fuessli, Saemtliche Gedichte, Orell, Zurich, 73; auth, G E Lessing, Metzler, Stuttgart, 73; Literarisches Loben im 18 Jahrhundert, Francke, Berne, 75; Der glücksspieler als autor, Euphorion, 77; Franz Werfels Anfänge, Deut Viertaljahresschrift, 78; Schillers Kabale u Liebe, In: Schiller Neue Interpretationen, 79; Das Abenteuer der Literatur, 81; Haller im Halblicht, 81. *Mailing Add:* Dept of Ger Harvard Univ Cambridge MA 02138

GUTHRIE, JOHN RICHARD, JR, b Newport News, Va, Nov 11, 39. FRENCH, GERMAN. *Educ:* Col William & Mary, AB, 62; Middlebury Col, AM, 66; Univ NC, Chapel Hill, PhD(French), 78. *Prof Exp:* Teacher French & Ger, US Air Force Inst, Ft Eustis, Va, 62-65; instr French, Wake Forest Univ, 66-67; from instr to asst prof French & Ger, 67-78, ASSOC PROF FRENCH & GER, CHRISTOPHER NEWPORT COL, 78- *Concurrent Pos:* Teacher French & Ger, Homer L Ferguson High Sch, Newport News, Va, 62-64 & Kecoughtan High Sch, Hampton, Va, 64-65. *Mem:* Am Asn Teachers Ger; MLA; SAtlantic Mod Lang Asn. *Res:* French and German literature since 1945; development of language among the deaf. *Publ:* Auth, An analysis of style and purpose in the first episode of the Histoire Comique de Francion, Romance Notes, 74. *Mailing Add:* Christopher Newport Col Box 6070 Newport News VA 23606

GUTIERREZ, GREGORIA VIOLETA, b Havana, Cuba; US citizen. SPANISH. *Educ:* Inst Habana, Bachelor, 38; Univ Havana, Cuba, Dr Pedag, 42; Univ Calif Los Angeles, MA, 64, PhD(Hisp lang), 72. *Prof Exp:* Prof Span, Teachers Col Havana, 45-60, prin, 45-48; teacher, Villa Cabrini Acad High Sch, 61-68; ASSOC PROF SPAN, CALIF STATE UNIV, NORTHRIDGE, 68- *Concurrent Pos:* Prof Span & prin, Col Cubano Arturo Montori, 45-60; consult, Cruzada Educ Cubana, 68- & Southern Calif Chap Am Asn Teachers Span & Port. *Mem:* MLA; Mod & Class Asn Am; Am Asn Teachers Span & Port. *Res:* Spanish civilization; Latin American civilization; Spanish and Spanish-American literature. *Publ:* Auth, Reforma de la ensenanza secundaria, Univ Havana Mag, 58; La ensenanza en Cuba, Selva Habanera, 59; La Celestina en las Comedias de Lope de Vega, Calif State Univ Sacramento Lit; Ideas Esteticas y Poesia, de Fernando de Herrera, Ed Universal Miami, 77; El modernismo en la prosa de Jose Marti, Caribe, 78. *Mailing Add:* Calif State Univ 11188 Nordoff St Northridge CA 91324

GUTIERREZ, JESUS, b Santander, Spain, Oct 31, 28. SPANISH LANGUAGE & LITERATURE. *Educ:* Univ Comillas, PhBach, 49; Inst Cath, Paris, Dipl, 59; Fordham Univ, MA, 63; Hunter Col, MA, 70; City Univ New York, PhD(Span & Span Am), 73. *Prof Exp:* Asst prof Span lang & lit, Col Guizar Valencia, 52-57; instr sociol & Span, Marymount Manhattan Col, 65-68; lectr Span, Queens Col, NY, 70-73, asst prof, 73-74; asst prof, Hofstra Univ, 74-76; vis prof, Wellesley Col, 76-77; assoc prof, Douglass Col, Rutgers Univ, 77-78 & York Col, City Univ New York, 78-81; ASSOC PROF SPAN GOLDEN AGE, WAYNE STATE UNIV, 81- *Concurrent Pos:* Examr NY Reg Interviewing Comt Teacher Exchange Prof, Europe & Latin Am, 66-68; consult, Bilingual Educ Prog Girl Scouts Am, 73-75. *Mem:* MLA; Asoc Int Hispanistas; Am Asn Teachers Span & Port; Soc Menendez Pelayo. *Res:* Spanish literature and thought of the Renaissance and Golden Age; the 18th century. *Publ:* Auth, La pasion de Santa Juana de Castilla de Perez Galdos, Rev Estud Escenicos, 74; Modalidades estilisticas e ideologicas en la prosa de Gutierrez Najera, In: Estudios Criticos Sobre la Prosa Modernistica, Torres, 75; La Fortuna Bifrons en el Teatro del Siglo de Oro, Soc Menendez Pelayo, 75; Armas, letras y estoicismo en una vida espanola del XVII, Dieciocho, 79; Don Francisco de Moncada, el Hombre y el Embajador, Bol Bibliot Menendez Pelayo, 80; El poligrafo Martin A del Rio y su relacion con Justo Lipsio, In: Vol I, Homenaje a Ignacio Aguilera y Santiago, Santander, 81; Modernidad y tradicion en El hombre practico del Conde de Fernan Nunez, 81 & Mayans y la Elocuencia espanola, 82, Dieciocho. *Mailing Add:* Dept of Span Lang & Lit Wayne State Univ Detroit MI 48202

GUTIERREZ DE LA SOLANA, ALBERTO, b Havana, Cuba; US citizen; m 44; c 2. SPANISH AMERICAN & SPANISH LITERATURE. *Educ:* Inst Segunda Ensenanza, Havana, BA & BS, 37; Univ Havana, LLD, 41; NY Univ, PhD, 67. *Prof Exp:* Instr, Columbia Univ, 64-65; vis lectr, St John's Univ, 65-66; vis asst prof, Hunter Col, 71-72; ASSOC PROF SPAN, NY UNIV, 64- *Concurrent Pos:* Span adv, Romanica, NY Univ Learned J, 76-; assoc ed, Circulo: Rev Cult, 77- *Mem:* Am Asn Teachers Span & Port; AAUP; MLA; Conf Ed Learned J. *Res:* Spanish American theatre; Spanish American novel; Cuban literature. *Publ:* Auth, En torno a Fernando Ortiz, lo afrocubano y otros ensayos, In: El Ensayo y la critica Literaira en Iberoamerica, Univ Toronto, 70; Maneras de narrar: Contraste de Lino Novas Calvo y Alfonso

Hernandez Cata, Torres, 72; En torno al siboneyismo y la poesia cubana alusiva a la emancipacion, In: Literatura de la emancipacion y otros ensayos, Univ Mayor de San Marcos, 72; La novela cubana escrita fuera de Cuba, Anales de la Lit Hispanoamericana, 73-74; Ideas morales, politicas y sociales en dos novelas cubanas del siglo XIX, In: La literatura Iberoamericana del Siglo XIX, Univ Ariz, 74; Jose Marti: Prefiguracion de su vida en Abdala y Patria y Libertad, Latin Am Theatre Rev, spring 78; Investigacion y critica literaria y lingüistica cubana, Senda Nueva, 78; Ruben Dario: Prosa y poesia, Senda Nueva, 78. *Mailing Add:* Dept of Span NY Univ New York NY 10003

GUTIERREZ-VEGA, ZENAIDA, b Union del Reyes, Cuba, June 23, 24. SPANISH, SPANISH AMERICAN LITERATURE. *Educ:* Inst Sec Educ, Matanzas, Cuba, BA, 45; Univ Havana, PhD(Span lit), 50; Univ Madrid, PhD(Romance philol), 66. *Prof Exp:* Prof Span & lit, Inst Sec Educ Velado, Havana, 52-62; prof, Univ Las Villas, Cuba, 59-62; asst prof Span & Span Am lit, Univ Mo, St Louis, 67-68; asst prof, State Univ NY Col Oswego, 68-72; ASSOC PROF SPAN, HUNTER COL, 72- *Concurrent Pos:* Mem, Ministry Educ, Cuba, 56-57; mem, Inst Hisp Cult, Madrid, 62-66. *Honors & Awards:* Lit Prize, Inst Hisp Cult, Madrid, 66. *Mem:* MLA; Am Asn Teachers Span & Port. *Res:* Hispanic American literature; poets, essayists, novelists of the twentieth century of Spain and Latin America. *Publ:* Auth, Jose Maria Chacon y Calvo en las letras hispanicas, 4/67; La obra poetica de Hopkins, Cuadernos Hisp Am, Madrid, 9/68; Jose Maria Chacon y Calvo, hispanista cubano, Ediciones, Cult Hisp, 68. *Mailing Add:* 220 E 63rd Apt 4L New York NY 10021

GUTMANN, ANNI, b Nuremburg, Ger, Jan 3, 19; US citizen. GERMAN LANGUAGE & LITERATURE. *Educ:* NY Univ, BA, 54; Univ Ill, Urbana, MA, 56; Yale Univ, PhD(Ger), 62. *Prof Exp:* Lectr, 61-62, from instr to asst prof, 62-71, ASSOC PROF GER LANG & LIT, HUNTER COL, 72-, CHAIRPERSON DEPT, 77- *Mem:* MLA; Am Asn Teachers Ger (treas, 63-65, vpres, 65-67); Int Arthur Schnitzler Res Asn; Am Soc 18th Century Studies; NEastern Mod Lang Asn. *Res:* The dramatist Friedrich Schiller; the German classics, Lessing, Goethe, Schiller, literature and the Bible. *Publ:* Auth, Grillparzers der arme Spielmann: Erlebtes und Erdichtetes, spring 67 & Das Schicksal des Auserwählten in R Beer-Hofmanns David-Zyklus, winter, 67, J Int Arthur Schnitzler Res Asn; Schillers Jungfrau von Orleans: Das wunderbare und die schuldfrage, Z Deut Philol, 69; Der bisher unterschätzte Einfluss von Voltaires Pucelle auf Schillers Jungfrau von Orleans, In: Voltaire und Deutschland, 78; Ein bisher unbeachtetes Vorbild zu Schillers Maria Stuart, Ger Quart, Vol LIII, 80; Tronchins Marie Stuart und Schillers Maria Stuart: Parallelen und Kontraste, Neophilologus (in press). *Mailing Add:* Dept of Ger Hunter Col 695 Park Ave New York NY 10021

GUTSCHE, GEORGE J, b St Paul, Minn, Nov 29, 42; m 66; c 2. RUSSIAN & SERBO-CROATIAN LITERATURE. *Educ:* Univ Wis, BA, 64, MA, 66, PhD(Slavic lang), 72. *Prof Exp:* From instr to asst prof Russ, Univ Ill, Chicago Circle, 69-76; asst prof, Univ Tenn, 76-77; asst prof, 78-81, ASSOC PROF RUSS, NORTHERN ILL UNIV, 81- *Mem:* Am Asn Teachers Slavic & E Europ Lang; Am Asn Advan Slavic Studies; MLA; Midwest Mod Lang Asn. *Res:* Russian Romanticism; Croatian Renaissance; literature and philosophy. *Publ:* Auth, Classical antiquity in Marulic's Judita, 75 & Pushkin's revisions of his Lyceum poems for his first collection of poems, 76, Slavic & E Europ J; Pushkin's Andrei Shen'e and Poetic Genres in the 1820's, Can-Am Slavic Studies, 76; contribr & translr, Vasily Shuksin, The Bastard (short story), In: Snowball Berry Red and Other Stories, Ardis, 78; auth, Sound and significance in Pasternak's Leto, Slavic and E Europ J, 81; Pushkin's Boldino Elegy, Russ Lang J, 81. *Mailing Add:* Dept of Foreign Lang & Lit Northern Ill Univ De Kalb IL 60115

GUTWIRTH, MADELYN, b Brooklyn, NY, Jan 4, 26; m 48; c 3. FRENCH LITERATURE, WOMEN'S STUDIES. *Educ:* Brooklyn Col, BA, 47; Bryn Mawr Col, MA, 49, PhD(French), 58. *Prof Exp:* Instr French, Haverford Col, 50-51; assoc prof, 66-69, PROF FRENCH, WEST CHESTER STATE COL, 69-, FAC COORDR, ARTS & SCI, 79- *Concurrent Pos:* Vis lectr French, Univ Pa, 67-68; Am Coun Learned Soc fel, 71-72. *Mem:* MLA; Northeast Mod Lang Asn (pres, 73-74); Am Soc 18th Century Studies; Soc d'Etudes Staëliennes; AAUP. *Res:* Madame de Staël; Romanticism; the 18th century. *Publ:* Auth, Madame de Staël's debt to Phedre: Corinne, Studies Romanticism, spring 64; Madame de Staël, Rousseau and the woman question, PMLA, 1/71; co-ed, Sources et Reflets de l'Histoire de France, Oxford Univ, 71; auth, Corinne et l'esthetique du camee, Acta Collogue de Clermont sur le preromantisme, 72; Madame de Staël, Novelist, Univ Ill, 78; Laclos and le sexe: The rack of ambivalence, Studies Voltaire & 18th Century, 80; Femme, Revolution et mode epistolaire, Cahiers Staeliens, 81. *Mailing Add:* Dept of Foreign Lang West Chester State Col West Chester PA 19380

GUTWIRTH, MARCEL MARC, b Antwerp, Belgium, Apr 11, 23; US citizen; m 48; c 3. FRENCH LITERATURE. *Educ:* Columbia Univ, AB, 47, AM, 48, PhD, 50. *Prof Exp:* Asst French, Columbia Univ, 47-48; from instr to assoc prof French lit, 48-61, chmn dept romance lang, 59-72, prof French Lit, 61-76, WILLIAM R KENAN JR PROF, HAVERFORD COL, 77- *Concurrent Pos:* Fulbright res fel, 53-54; Am Coun Learned Soc fel, 63-64; Guggenheim fel, Paris, 71-72; vis prof, Johns Hopkins Univ; Mellon vis prof, Tulane Univ. *Mem:* MLA; Am Asn Teachers Fr. *Res:* Moliere; Racine; Montaigne. *Publ:* Co-ed, The Unity of Moliere's L'Avare, PMLA, 9/61; Problematic innocence in Racine's plays, Rev Sci Humanaires, 4/62; auth, Moliere ou l'invention comique, Minard, Paris, 66; Jean Racine: Un Itineraire poetique, Univ Montreal, 70; Stendhal, Twayne, 71; La Bible de Combray, Rev Sci Humaines, 7/71; co-ed, Sources et Reflets de l'Histoire de France, Oxford Univ, 72; auth, Michel de Montaigne ou le pari d'exemplarite, Univ Montreal, 77. *Mailing Add:* Dept of French Haverford Col Haverford PA 19041

GUY, BASIL JAMES, b Lynn, Mass, Apr 12, 26. FRENCH. *Educ:* Bowdoin Col, BA, 49; Yale Univ, MA, 51, PhD(French), 55. *Prof Exp:* From instr to assoc prof, 54-68, PROF FRENCH, UNIV CALIF, BERKELEY, 68- *Concurrent Pos:* Comn Relief Belgium fel, 60-61; Guggenheim fel, 64-65; actg chmn, Dept French, Univ Calif, Berkeley, 63-64 & 68-69, fac res prof, 71-72. *Mem:* MLA; Philol Asn Pac Coast. *Res:* French literature of the 18th century; Prince de Ligne; Peguy. *Publ:* Ed, Oeuvres Choisies dur Prince de Ligne, Stanford Univ, 78; Domestic Correspondence of D M Varlet, Brill, Leiden (in prep); Prince de Ligue--Coup d'Oeiv sur Beloeil, Univ Calif press (in press). *Mailing Add:* Dept of French Univ of Calif Berkeley CA 94720

GUYER, LELAND ROBERT, b Palestine, Tex, Dec 30, 46. PORTUGUESE & BRAZILIAN LITERATURE. *Educ:* San Diego State Univ, AB, 68, MA, 72; Univ Calif, Santa Barbara, PhD(Hispanic lang & lit), 79. *Prof Exp:* Grad assoc Span, Univ Calif, Santa Barbara, 72-76; ASST PROF PORT, UNIV CHICAGO, 79- *Concurrent Pos:* Instr Port, Santa Barbara City Col, 78; instr Span, Oxnard Col, 78-79. *Mem:* MLA; Northeast MLA; Pac Northwest Coun Foreign Lang. *Res:* Modern Portuguese and Brazilian poetry and narrative; modern Spanish American narrative. *Publ:* Auth, A viagem do heroi na ode maritima, Persona, 80; In search of self-identity: House imagery in the poetry of Fernando Pessoa, 80, Arcane numbers and Fernado Pessoa's Passos da Cruz, 81, Selecta; Spatial Imagery of Enclosure in the Poetry of Fernando Pessoa, Imprensa Nacional de Portugal, 82. *Mailing Add:* Univ of Chicago Chicago IL

GUYLER, SAMUEL LERERT, b Sealy, Tex, Nov 6, 39; div; c 1. SPANISH & ITALIAN LITERATURE. *Educ:* Univ Tex, BA, 62; Cornell Univ, PhD(Romance lit), 68. *Prof Exp:* Teaching asst Span & Ital, Univ Tex, 63-65; asst prof, Univ Pa, 68-70; ASST PROF SPAN & ITAL, UNIV N MEX, 70- *Concurrent Pos:* Am Coun Learned Soc grant-in-aid, 73. *Mem:* Dante Soc; Renaissance Soc Am. *Res:* Spanish Golden Age literature; Latin American colonial literature; Italian Renaissance literature. *Mailing Add:* Dept of Mod & Class Lang Univ of N Mex Albuquerque NM 87131

GUZZARDO, JOHN JOSEPH, b San Jose, Calif, Dec 20, 49; m 77. ITALIAN LANGUAGE & LITERATURE. *Educ:* Univ Calif at Santa Cruz, BA, 72; Johns Hopkins Univ, MA, 74, PhD(Ital), 76. *Prof Exp:* ASST PROF ITAL, UNIV VA, 76- *Mem:* MLA; SAtlantic Mod Lang Asn; Am Asn Teachers of Ital; Renaissance Soc Am. *Res:* Dante; medieval and renaissance Italian literature. *Publ:* Auth, The noble castle and the eighth gate, Mod Lang Notes, (in press). *Mailing Add:* Dept of Span Ital & Port Univ of Va 301 Cabell Hall Charlottesville VA 22903

GWATKIN, WILLIAM EMMETT, JR, b Troy, Ohio, Dec 25, 00; m 26; c 2. CLASSICAL PHILOLOGY, ANCIENT HISTORY. *Educ:* William Jewell Col, AB, 21; Ind Univ, AM, 23; Princeton Univ, PhD, 30; Univ Mo, LLB, 49. *Prof Exp:* Tutor Latin & Greek, Ind Univ, 21-23; instr classics, Princeton Univ, 24-26; lectr Greek, McMaster Univ, 26-28; from asst prof to prof class langs & archaeol, Univ Mo, 28-60; prof, 60-67, EMER PROF CLASSICS, WILFRID LAURIER UNIV, 68- *Concurrent Pos:* Am Coun Learned Soc res fel, 35-36; annual prof, Am Sch Class Studies, Athens, Greece, 55-56. *Mem:* Am Philol Asn; Archaeol Inst Am; Class Asn Midwest & South (pres, 53); Class Asn Can. *Res:* Latin and Greek literature; Greek and Roman history; Roman provincial government. *Publ:* Cappadocia as a Roman procuratorial province, Univ Mo Studies, Vol 4, 30. *Mailing Add:* 49 Cardinal Crescent S Waterloo ON N2J 2E6 Can

GYURKO, LANIN ANDREW, b Litchfield Co, Conn; m 73; c 1. LATIN AMERICAN & COMPARATIVE LITERATURE. *Educ:* Yale Univ, BA, 64; Harvard Univ, MAT, 65, PhD(Romance lang), 69. *Prof Exp:* Instr exten studies, Harvard Univ, 66-67 & 68-69; from instr to assoc prof Span, Yale Univ, 69-77, dir, grad studies, 76-77; chmn dept mod lang, Tex Christian Univ, 77-78; head dept Romance lang, 78-81, PROF SPAN, UNIV ARIZ, 78- *Concurrent Pos:* Teaching fel Span, Harvard Univ, 65-66 & 67-68; Yale Univ Concilium Int & Area Studies grant, 70; res comt vis fel Span, Univ Wis Grad Sch, 72-73; Morse fel, Yale Univ, 74-75. *Mem:* MLA; Am Asn Teachers Span; Inst Int Lit Iberoam; Southwestern Coun Latin Am Studies. *Res:* Latin American modern and Colonial literature; Romance philology and linguistics; Peninsular Spanish literature. *Publ:* Auth, Borges and the Machismo Cult, Rev Hisp Mod, 70-71; El yo y su imagen en Cambio de Piel de Carlos Fuentes, Rev Iberoam, 7-12/71; Affixal negation in Spanish, Romance Philol, 11/71; Truth and deception in Cortazar's Las Babas del Diablo, Romanic Rev, 5/73; Destructive and ironically redemptive fantasy in Cortazar, Hispania, 12/73; Self, mask, and double in Fuentes' La Muerte de Artemio Cruz, Tex Studies Lit & Lang, summer 74; Social satire and the ancient Mexican Gods in the narrative of Fuentes, Ibero-Am, Archiv, 75; The artist manque in Fuentes, Cambio del Piel, Symposium, summer 77. *Mailing Add:* Dept of Span Univ of Ariz Tucson AZ 85721

H

HAAC, OSCAR ALFRED, b Frankfurt, Ger, Jan 28, 18; nat US. ROMANCE LANGUAGES. *Educ:* Yale Univ, AB, 39, AM, 42, PhD, 48. *Prof Exp:* Head mod lang dept, Adirondack-Fla Sch, 39-40; asst instr French, Yale Univ, 45-47; asst prof Romance lang, Pa State Univ, 48-54; from assoc prof to prof, Emory Univ, 54-65; dir NDEA French inst, Insts, 60-63; prof Romance lang, 65-71, PROF FRENCH, STATE UNIV NY STONY BROOK, 71- *Concurrent Pos:* Am Philos Soc grants, 49 & 55; fels, Pa State Univ, 49-53, Nat Ctr Sci Res, France, 52, Univ Ctr, Ga, 55, Emory Univ, 56-63 & Guggenheim, 57-58; Emory Univ grants, 63-65; State Univ NY Res Found grants, 66-68, 71 & 73; Am Coun Learned Soc grant, 77. *Honors & Awards:*

Ordre de Palmes Acad, 63. *Mem:* MLA; Am Asn Teachers Fr; Soc Fr Prof Am; AAUP; Am Soc 18th & 19th Century Studies. *Res:* French and comparative literature; eighteenth and nineteenth century literature. *Publ:* Coauth, Perspectives de France, Prentice-Hall, 68, 2nd ed, 72 & 3rd ed, 82; auth, Voltaire and Plato, In: The Persistent Voice, NY Univ, 71; Deism in Marivaux, Romanic Rev, 72; Theories of literary criticism, Studies on Voltaire, 72; Marivaux, Twayne, 73; Rousseau and Marivaux, Studies on Voltaire, 74; The Literature of History: Midielet, 19th Century Fr Studies, 76; Toward a Definition of Utopia, Studies in 18th Century Cult, 77 & Michelet, 82. *Mailing Add:* Dept of French & Ital State Univ of NY Stony Brook NY 11794

HAAS, MARY ROSAMOND, b Richmond, Ind, Jan 23, 10; div. LINGUISTICS. *Educ:* Earlham Col, AB, 30; Yale Univ, PhD(ling), 35. *Hon Degrees:* DLit, Northwestern Univ, 75; DHumL, Univ Chicago, 76, Earlham Col & Ohio State Univ, 80. *Prof Exp:* Res worker, Yale Univ, 36-38; comt res Am native lang, Am Coun Learned Soc, 38, 39-41, res fel, comt res mod Orient lang, 41-43, 44-46; lectr Siamese, 43-44, 46-47, from asst prof to assoc prof Siamese & ling, 47-57, prof ling, 57-77, acting head dept, 56-57, head dept, 58-64, EMER PROF LING, UNIV CALIF, BERKELEY, 77- *Concurrent Pos:* Res fel, Am Philos Soc, 38-39; Walker-Ames vis prof ling, Univ Wash, 61; Guggenheim fel, 64-65; fac res lectr, Univ Calif, Berkeley, 65; Nat Endowment for Humanities sr fel, 67-68; Ctr Advan Studies Behav Sci fel, 67-68. *Honors & Awards:* Berkeley Citation, Univ Calif, Berkeley & Wilbur Cross Medal, Yale Grad Asn, 77. *Mem:* Ling Soc Am (vpres, 56, pres, 63); Am Anthrop Asn; Am Orient Soc; Am Acad Arts & Sci; Nat Acad Sci. *Res:* Linguistic prehistory; American Indian linguistics; areal linguistics. *Publ:* Auth, Thai-English Student's Dict, Stanford Univ, 64; The Prehistory of Languages, 69, American Indian linguistic prehistory, In: Current Trends in Linguistics, 73 & The Northern California linguistic area, In: Hokan Studies, 76, Mouton, The Hague; Language, Culture, and History, Stanford Univ, 78. *Mailing Add:* 1065 Keith Ave Berkeley CA 94708

HAAS, SAMUEL SHERIDAN, Old Testament. See Vol IV

HAAS, WERNER, b Graz, Austria, Mar 26, 28; m 55; c 2. GERMAN, HISTORY. *Educ:* Univ Graz, PhD & Staatsexamen, 51. *Prof Exp:* Studienassessor Ger & phys educ, Bundesrealgym, Graz, 52-54; studienassessor hist & phys educ, Hopkins Grammar Sch, 54-55; studienassessor Ger & phys educ, Akad Gymn, Graz, 55-56; from asst prof to assoc prof Ger & hist, Springfield Col, 56-64; asst prof Ger, Univ Mass, Amherst, 64-67; assoc prof, 67-77, dir lang instr, 67-78, PROF GER, OHIO STATE UNIV, 77- *Concurrent Pos:* Fulbright fel, Springfield Col, 51-52; dir studies, Middlebury Col Grad Sch Ger, Univ Mainz, 62-63; vis lectr Ger, Am Int Col, 63; asst dir, Deut sommerschule, Middlebury Col, 67; mem nat screening comt, Fulbright Prog, Hays Inst Int Educ, 74-75. *Honors & Awards:* Distinguished Visiting Professor Award, US Air Force Acad, 80-81. *Mem:* Am Asn Teachers Ger; MLA. *Res:* Cultural graded readers in German; German civilization and culture; computer assisted instruction in foreign language teaching. *Publ:* Auth, Is the four-skills approach obsolete?, Unterrichtspraxis, 70; DECU/TUCO Computer Assisted Interactive Tutorial Program, Ohio State Univ, 72-73; Bismarck, Scribner's, 73; coauth, Fortschritt Deutsch, Holt, 76; auth, The potential and limitation of computer assisted instruction in the teaching of foreign languages, ERIC/Clearing House Lang & Ling, 76; Das dritte reich-von der vision Moeller van den Brucks zur realität des Hitlerrreiches, Unterrichtspraxis, 77; coauth, Perspektiven zu Aktuellen Fragen, Holt, 78; Deutsch für alle, Wiley, 80. *Mailing Add:* Dept of Ger Ohio State Univ Columbus OH 43210

HAASE, DONALD PAUL, b Cincinnati, Ohio, Mar 20, 50; m 72; c 2. GERMAN & COMPARATIVE LITERATURE. *Educ:* Univ Cincinnati, BA, 72, MA, 73; Univ NC, Chapel Hill, PhD(comp lit), 79. *Prof Exp:* Vis asst prof, Miami Univ, 79-81; ASST PROF GER, WAYNE STATE UNIV, 81- *Mem:* MLA; Lessing Soc; Am Asn Teachers of Ger; SAtlantic Modern Lang Asn; Southern Comp Lit Asn. *Res:* Novalis; European romanticism; Franco-German literary relations. *Publ:* Auth, Kafka's Der Jaegerr Gracchus: Fragment or figment of the imagination, Modern Austrian Lit, 78; Romantic facts and critical myths: Novalis' early reception in France, The Comparatist, 79; Coleridge and Henry Boyd's translation of Dante's Inferno: Toward a demonic reading of Kubla Khan, English Lang Notes, 80; Nerval's knowledge of Novalis: A reconsideration, Romance Notes, 81; Gerard de Nerval's magnum opus: Alchemy in literature and life, Ky Romance Quart, 82; Romantic theory of fantastic & Novalis: Heinrich von Oftendingen, In: Survey of Modern Fantasy Literature, Salem Press, 82. *Mailing Add:* Dept of Romance & Ger Lang Wayne State Univ Detroit MI 48202

HABERL, FRANZ P, b Nürnberg, Ger, Mar 8, 35; Can citizen; div. GERMAN LANGUAGE & LITERATURE. *Educ:* Ursinus Col, BA, 59; Cornell Univ, MA, 61, PhD(Ger & comp lit), 64. *Prof Exp:* Instr Ger, Ohio Univ, 62-63; from instr to asst prof, C W Post Col, Long Island Univ, 63-65; asst prof, Univ Md, 65-66; asst prof, Brooklyn Col, 66-69; assoc prof & chmn dept, Mt Allison Univ, 69-73; PROF GER, DAWSON COL, 73- *Mem:* MLA; Can Asn Univ Teachers Ger. *Res:* German literature especially the Age of Goethe; modern drama and modern novel. *Publ:* Auth, Im Stil Unserer Zeit, Macmillan, 67; The water imagery in Doderer's novels, 7/68, Peter Weiss' documentary theater, summer 69, Peter Weiss: A progress report, summer 72 & Recent trends in East German drama, winter 75, Bks Abroad; Max Frisch: A retrospective, spring 77, Young German dramatists, spring 78 & Social issues and l'art pour l'art in contemporary West German Drama, autumn 81, World Lit Today. *Mailing Add:* Dept of Mod Lang Dawson Col 535 Viger Ave Montreal PQ H2L 2P3 Can

HABERLAND, PAUL MALLORY, b Milwaukee, Wis, Sept 24, 35; m 62; c 2. GERMAN LITERATURE & LANGUAGE. *Educ:* Haverford Col, BA, 57; Johns Hopkins Univ, MA, 60, PhD(Ger), 69. *Prof Exp:* Actg asst prof Ger, Univ Calif, Riverside, 64-66; from instr to asst prof, Lawrence Univ, 66-72; lectr English, Univ Göttingen, Ger, 72-73; assoc prof, 74-79, PROF GER, WESTERN CAROLINA UNIV, 79-, HEAD DEPT MOD LANG, 81- *Concurrent Pos:* Fulbright scholar, US Govt, 62-63; Am Philos Soc res grant, 78. *Mem:* MLA; Am Asn Teachers Ger; SAtlantic Mod Lang Asn. *Res:* Eighteenth century German literary criticism; 19th century German literature; 20th century Austrian literature. *Publ:* Auth, The Development of Comic Theory in Germany during the Eighteenth Century, Göppinger Arbeiten Ger Alfred Kümmerle, 71; The reception of German literature in Baltimore's literary magazines 1800-1875, Ger-Am Studies, 74; Number symbolism: The father-daughter relationship in E T A Hoffmann's Rat Krespel, 75 & A Fabian's view of Goethe--an unpublished letter from Sidney Webb to Beatrice Potter, 76, Lang Quart; Duality, the artist, and Wolfgang Bauer, Mod Austrian Lit, 78; The role of art in the writings of Barbara Frischmuth, Mod Austrian Lit, 81. *Mailing Add:* Dept of Mod Foreign Lang Western Carolina Univ Cullowhee NC 28723

HABERLY, DAVID T, b Tucson, Ariz, Dec 11, 42; m 63; c 2. ROMANCE LANGUAGES. *Educ:* Harvard Univ, AB, 63, AM, 64, PhD(Romance lang), 66. *Prof Exp:* From instr to asst prof romance lang, Harvard Univ, 66-73; chmn, Dept Span, Ital & Port, 73-78, ASSOC PROF PORT, UNIV VA, 73- *Mem:* MLA; Am Asn Teachers Span & Port. *Res:* Brazilian and Portuguese literature; Spanish American and North American literature. *Publ:* Coauth, Brazil, Portugal and other Portuguese-Speaking Lands: A Bibliography, Harvard Univ, 69; auth, Abolition in Brazil: Anti-slavery and anti-slave, Luso-Brazilian Rev, 72; Edward Morris and linguistic nationalism, Australian Lit Studies, 74; Eugenia Camara, Luso-Brazilian Rev, 75; The literature of an invisible nation, J Black Studies, 76; Women and Indians: The captivity tradition and The Last of the Mohicans, Am Quart, 76; Captives and infidels: The cautiva in Argentine literature, Am Hispanist, 78; Three sad races: Racial identity and national consciousness in Brazilian literature, Cambridge Univ Press, 82. *Mailing Add:* Dept of Span Ital & Port Cabell Hall Univ of Va Charlottesville VA 22903

HACKE, ROBERT E L, b Athens, Ga, Jan 18, 31; div; c 2. ENGLISH, LINGUISTICS. *Educ:* Univ Ariz, BA, 55; McCormick Theol Sem, MDiv, 58; Univ St Andrews, PhD, 63. *Prof Exp:* Asst pastor, Presby Church, Ill, 58-59; instr Greek & Bible, Trinity Univ, Tex, 61-62; univ Presby pastor, Univ Ariz, 62-64; prof English, Pikeville Col, 64-67; asst prof, Morehead State Univ, 67-70; dir external educ, 70, assoc prof, 70-80, PROF ENGLISH, KEAN COL NJ, 80- *Mem:* MLA; Ling Soc Am; Col English Asn (exec secy, 78-81). *Res:* Linguistics; Dead Sea scrolls; literature. *Mailing Add:* Dept of English Kean Col of NJ Union NJ 07083

HACKEL, ROBERTA JOYCE, b New York, NY, Dec 5, 43; m 72; c 1. EIGHTEENTH CENTURY FRENCH PROSE FICTION. *Educ:* Oakland Univ, BA, 64; Univ Wis-Madison, MA, 65; Univ NC, Chapel Hill, PhD(Romance lang & lit), 70. *Prof Exp:* Asst prof French, St Michael's Col, 71-74; ASST PROF FRENCH, CASTLETON STATE COL, 77- *Concurrent Pos:* Mem, Vt Gov's French Cult Comn, 75-76. *Mem:* Am Soc Eighteenth Century Studies; Fr Soc Eighteenth Century Studies. *Res:* Narrative theory and linguistics. *Publ:* Auth, Dehumanization through style (A note on Flaubert's L'Education sentimentale), 69, The irreducible tension in Stances de la mort, 69 & The depersonalized world of the Roman Bourgeois, 69, Romance Notes; The final ambiguity of El Medico de su honra, Studies Philol, 70; coauth, Did Diderot author La Marquise de Claye et le Comte de Saint--Alban and Cinqmars et Derville?, Romance Notes, 72; auth, De Sade's Quantitative Moral Universe of Irony, Rhetoric and Boredom, Mouton, 76; coauth (with R Frautschi), Le Compartement Verbal Chez Gil Blas: Quelues Observations Quantitatives, Voltaire Fondation, summer 81. *Mailing Add:* Dept of French Castleton State Col Castleton VT 05735

HACTHOUN, AUGUSTO, b Cuba, Dec 17, 45; US citizen. SPANISH, PORTUGUESE. *Educ:* Univ SFla, AB, 67, PhD(Romance lang), 77. *Prof Exp:* Asst prof Span & Port, Univ Ala, 71-77; ASST PROF SPAN, WHEATON COL, 77- *Concurrent Pos:* Nat Endowment for Humanities summer fel, 80; Mellon Found res fel, Harvard Univ, 80-81. *Mem:* MLA; Cervantes Soc Am; Asoc Int Hisp. *Res:* Literary theory of XVI and XVII centuries; Cervantes, translation theory and practice. *Publ:* Auth, Estado de los estudios sobre el genero chico, Revista de estudios Hisp, 75; La doble figuracion de la realidad, revelaciones textuales en a reliquia, Luzo-Brazilian Rev, 75; Papillons, clises, El cuento, 76; Perfil del genero chico, South Atlantic Bull, 77; Perfil poetico-espiritual de Camoes, Univ SFla Lang Quart, 78; Imagen, emblema cifra (poem), Rushlight, 79; Los mecanismos del humor en el habla de Sancho Panza, Actas del Sexto Congreso Int de Hisp, 80; Lugar de encuentros (poem), Rushlight, 81. *Mailing Add:* Box 174 Norton MA 02766

HADDED, ELAINE, b Willimantic, Conn, Aug 28, 30. ROMANCE LANGUAGES. *Educ:* Univ Conn, BA, 52; Univ Wis,MA, 53, PhD(Span), 62. *Prof Exp:* Asst prof Span, Univ Wis-Milwaukee, 60-63; asst prof, Univ Mass, Amherst, 63-70; asst prof, 70-80, ASSOC PROF SPAN, SOUTHERN CONN STATE COL, 80- *Concurrent Pos:* Univ Wis Markham traveling fel, 64-65. *Mem:* Am Asn Teachers Span & Port. *Res:* Contemporary Spanish literature. *Publ:* Auth, Maximiliano Rubin, Archivum, Oviedo, 58; The structure of Al filo del agua, Hispania, 64. *Mailing Add:* Dept of Foreign Lang Southern Conn State Col 501 Crescent St New Haven CT 06515

HADEN, ERNEST FABER, b Mohkanshan, China, Aug 14, 04; US citizen; m 28; c 2. ROMANCE LINGUISTICS. *Educ:* Southwestern Presby Univ, AB, 24; Univ Chicago, PhD, 36. *Prof Exp:* Asst prof French & Ger, Ark Col, 24-26; asst prof French, Southwestern Col, 26-28; from instr to asst prof, Univ Chicago, 28-34; prof & head dept, McMaster Univ, 34-43; prof, 47-79, EMER PROF ROMANCE LANG, UNIV TEX, AUSTIN, 80- *Concurrent Pos:* Fulbright lectr, Univ Rome, Italy, 54-55. *Honors & Awards:* Chevalier de l'Ordre des Palmes Acad, French Govt, 75. *Mem:* MLA; Ling Soc Am; SCent Mod Lang Asn (pres, 67-68). *Res:* General and Romance linguistics; application of linguistics to teaching. *Publ:* Coauth, Modern Spanish, Harcourt, 60; A Resonance-Theory for Linguistics, Mouton, The Hague, 62; Oral Drill in Spanish, Houghton, 63. *Mailing Add:* Dept of French & Ital Univ of Tex Austin TX 78712

HADERLEIN, KUONRAT GEORG JOSEF, b Berlin, Ger, Feb 25, 32; Can citizen; m 66; c 1. COMPARATIVE LITERATURE, CONTEMPORARY GERMAN THEATRE. *Educ:* Univ Alta, MA, 61, PhD(comp lit), 70. *Prof Exp:* Lectr Ger, Univ Alta, 61-62, non-teaching fel comp lit, 62-64; lectr Ger lit, 65-72, asst prof Ger & comp lit, 73-77, ASSOC PROF GER, UNIV SASK, 78- *Concurrent Pos:* Ed, Can-Mongolia Rev, 76-80. *Mem:* Can Comp Lit Asn; Can Scholars Inner Asia; Can-Mongolia Soc; MLA; Can Assoc Univ Teachers Ger. *Res:* Contemporary Mongolia: history, politics and diplomacy; classical Mongolian literature; European Romanticism. *Publ:* Auth, In memory of Ryambyn Rinchen, 5/77 & Scholarship in the early editions, 5/77, Can-Mongolia Rev; The Burgfestspiele at Jagsthausen, Prisma, summer 77. *Mailing Add:* Dept of Ger Lang & Lit Univ of Saskatchewan Saskatoon SK S7K 0W0 Can

HADLEY, MICHAEL LLEWELLYN, b Campbell River, BC, Apr 6, 36; m 59; c 4. GERMAN LANGUAGE & LITERATURE. *Educ:* Univ BC, BA, 59; Univ Man, MA, 64; Queen's Univ, Ont, PhD(Ger), 71. *Prof Exp:* Foreign Serv officer, Can Govt, 59-62; lectr Ger, St John's Col, Univ Man, 62-64; asst prof, Univ Winnipeg, 65-70; asst prof, 70-73, chmn dept, 74-80, ASSOC PROF GER LANG & LIT, UNIV VICTORIA, 74- *Concurrent Pos:* Chmn, External Rels Comt, Humanities Res Coun Can, 78- *Mem:* Can Asn Univ Teachers Ger (vpres, 76-78, pres, 78-80); Am Asn 18th Century Studies; Can Asn 18th Century Studies; Am Lessing Soc ; Maritime Defense Asn Can. *Res:* Eighteenth-century literature; Deutsche Schauerromantik; U-Boat warfare in Canadian waters. *Publ:* Auth, Johann Beer's approach to the novel, Seminar, 3/71; Ideology and fiction: A case for Christian realism in Germany and Russia in the thought of Willy Kramp, Germano-Slavica, 12/73; The German Novel in 1790: A Descriptive Account and Critical Bibliography, Lang, 73; Education and Alienation in Dyck's Verloren in der Steppe: A novel of cultural crisis, Ger Can Yearbk, 76; Die deutsche Sprache in Britisch-Kolumbien, In: Deutsch als Muttersprache in Kanada, Wiesbaden Steiner Verlag, 77; Romanverzeichnis: Bibliographie der swischen 1750-1800 erschienenen Erstausgaben, 77 & The Undiscovered Genre: A Search for the German Gothic Novel, 78, Lang, Bern; U-Boat Begegnung Vor Halifax, Marine-Rundschau, 3/82 & 4/82. *Mailing Add:* Dept of Ger Lang & Lit Univ of Victoria Victoria BC V8W 2Y2 Can

HADLICH, ROGER LEE, b St Paul, Minn, Jan 10, 30; m 52; c 2. LINGUISTICS. *Educ:* Yale Univ, BA, 51; Univ Madrid, dipls, 56; Middlebury Col, MA, 57; Univ Mich, PhD(Romance ling), 61. *Prof Exp:* Instr Span, Univ Mich, 60-61; asst prof ling, Cornell Univ, 61-65; assoc prof Span, 65-69, from asst dean to assoc dean, 68-77, PROF SPAN, UNIV HAWAII, 69- *Concurrent Pos:* Ed, Comp Romance Ling Newslett, MLA, 63; vis prof ling, Univ Rome, 64-65. *Res:* Comparative Romance linguistics; language teaching pedagogy; Spanish language and linguistics. *Publ:* Coauth, A Structural Course in Spanish, Macmillan, 63; auth, The Phonological History of Vegliote, Univ NC, 65; coauth, A Drillbook of Spanish Pronunciation, Harper, 68; auth, A Transformational Grammar of Spanish, 71 & coauth, A Spanish Review Grammar: Theory and Practice, 77, Prentice-Hall. *Mailing Add:* Dept of Europ Lang Univ of Hawaii Honolulu HI 96822

HAEFER, JOHN RICHARD, Ethnomusicology, Musicology. See Vol I

HAENICKE, DIETHER HANS, b Hagen, Ger, May 19, 35; m 62; c 2. GERMAN LITERATURE & PHILOLOGY. *Educ:* Univ Munich, DrPhil, 62. *Prof Exp:* From asst prof to assoc prof, Wayne State Univ, 63-72, dir, Jr Year Abroad Prog, 70-75, chmn dept Romance & Ger lang & lit, 71-72, assoc dean, Col Lib Arts, 72-75, provost, 75-77, prof Ger, 72-78, vpres & provost, 77-78; PROF GER & DEAN COL OF HUMANITIES, OHIO STATE UNIV, 78- *Concurrent Pos:* Fulbright scholar, 63-65; resident dir, Jr Year in Frieburg, Ger, Univ Mich, Mich State Univ & Univ Wis, 65-66 & 69-70. *Mem:* MLA; Am Asn Teachers Ger; Int Ver Ger Sprach- und Literaturwiss. *Res:* Romanticism; 19th and 20th century literature; post-war poetry. *Publ:* Auth, Untersuchungen zum Versepos des 20 Jahrhunderts, Munich, 62; ed, Liebesgeschichte der schönen Magelone, 69, Der blonde Eckbert und andere Novellen, 69 & Franz Sternbalds Wanderungen, 70, Goldmann; co-ed & coauth, The Challenge of German Literature, Wayne State Univ, 71. *Mailing Add:* Dean Col of Humanities Ohio State Univ Columbus OH 43210

HAFTER, MONROE Z, b New York, NY, June 28, 26; m 57; c 2. SPANISH LITERATURE. *Educ:* Harvard Univ, PhD, 56. *Prof Exp:* Teaching fel Span, Harvard Univ, 51-56; from instr to asst prof Romanic lang, Williams Col, 56-60; from asst prof to assoc prof, 60-67, PROF SPAN, UNIV MICH, ANN ARBOR, 67- *Concurrent Pos:* Am Philos Soc grant, 58; Williams Col Class of 1900 Fund grant, 58; grant, Rackham Sch Grad Studies, Univ Mich, Ann Arbor, 62; Fulbright & Guggenheim Found res grants, 67-68. *Mem:* MLA; Am Soc 18th Century Studies. *Res:* Transition in Spanish literature from Golden Age to nineteenth century; moralist literature, satire and novel. *Publ:* Auth, Ironic reprise in Galdos' novels, PMLA, 61; Gracian and Perfection, Harvard Univ, 66; The Enlightenment's interpretation of Saavedra Fajardo, Hisp Rev, 73; Toward a history of Spanish imaginary voyages, 18th Century Studies, 75; Heroism in Alas and Carlyle's On Heroes, Mod Lang Notes, 80. *Mailing Add:* Dept of Romance Lang Univ of Mich Ann Arbor MI 48109

HAGIWARA, MICHIO PETER, b Tokyo, Japan. ROMANCE LANGUAGES. *Educ:* Univ Kansas City, BA, 56; Wash Univ, MA, 58; Univ Mich, PhD(French lang & lit), 66. *Prof Exp:* Instr, 62-64, lectr, 64-66, asst prof, 66-72, ASSOC PROF FRENCH, UNIV MICH, ANN ARBOR, 72- *Concurrent Pos:* Foreign lang prof consult Mich, MLA, 65-; consult ling, Hawaii Curric Ctr, 66-68; NDEA, Univ Hawaii, 66-69; asst prof French, Harvard Univ, 69-70; dir, Mich-Wis jr year in France, 79-80. *Mem:* MLA; Am Asn Teachers Fr; Ling Soc Am; Am Coun Teaching Foreign Lang; Am Asn Applied Ling. *Res:* Applied linguistics; foreign language curriculum and instruction; French literature. *Publ:* Coauth, Active Review of French: Selected Patterns, Vocabulary and Pronunciation Problems for Speakers of English, Ginn, 63; L'Echelle: Structures Essentielles du Francais, 66 & Continuons a Parler, 67, Blaisdell; French Epic Poetry in the 16th Century, Mouton, The Hague, 72; ed, Studies in Romance Linguistics, 77; coauth, Mosaique, 77; Theme et Variations, 2nd ed, 81; D'accord: La prononciation du francais international, acquisition et perfectionnement, 82. *Mailing Add:* Dept of Romance Lang Univ of Mich Ann Arbor MI 48109

HAGSPIEL, ROBERT, b Innsbruck, Austria, Nov 19, 25; m 51. LANGUAGES. *Educ:* Innsbruck Univ, PhD, 53. *Prof Exp:* Instr French, English, Ger & world hist, Massanutten Mil Acad, 55-57; from asst prof to assoc prof French & Ger, 57-73, chmn dept mod lang, 62-65, PROF MOD LANG, CANISIUS COL, 73- *Concurrent Pos:* Regular consult, Bks Abroad, Choice & Southern Humanities Rev, 65- *Mem:* Am Asn Teachers Fr. *Res:* Twentieth century French literature; French, German, English and American comparative literature. *Publ:* Ed, Port-Royal by Montherlant, Prentice-Hall, 67. *Mailing Add:* 190 Campus Dr Snyder NY 14226

HAHM, DAVID EDGAR, b Milwaukee, Wis, Sept 30, 38; m 64; c 4. CLASSICAL LANGUAGES, INTELLECTUAL HISTORY. *Educ:* Northwestern Col, Wis, BA, 60; Univ Wis-Madison, MA, 62, PhD(classics), 66. *Prof Exp:* Asst prof class lang, Univ Mo-Columbia, 66-69; from asst prof to assoc prof class, 69-78, PROF CLASSICS, OHIO STATE UNIV, 78- *Concurrent Pos:* Fel, Ctr Hellenic Studies, Wash, DC, 68-69. *Mem:* Am Philol Asn; Hist Sci Soc; Class Asn Midwest & South. *Res:* Ancient philosophy, science and medicine; Greek and Roman intellectual history; Stoicism. *Publ:* Auth, Roman Nobility and the Three Major Priesthoods, 218-167 BC, Trans Am Philol Asn, 63; Plato's Noble Lie and political brotherhood, Classica Mediaevalia, 69; Chrysippus' Solution to the Democritcan Dilemma of the Cone, Isis, 72; contribr, Motion and Time, Space and Matter: Interrelations in the History of Philosophy and Science, 76, auth, The Origins of Stoic Cosmology, 77 & contribr, Studies in Perception: Interrelations in the History and Philosophy of Science, 78, Ohio State Univ; auth, The fifth element in Aristotle's De Philosophia: A critical reexamination, J Hellenic Studies, 82. *Mailing Add:* Dept of Classics Ohio State Univ Columbus OH 43210

HAHN, OSCAR, b Iquique, Chile, July 5, 38; m 71; c 1. SPANISH AMERICAN POETRY, LITERARY THEORY. *Educ:* Univ Chile, Profesor Span, 63; Univ Iowa, MA, 72; Univ Md, PhD(Span), 77. *Prof Exp:* Prof Hisp lit, Univ Chile Arica, 65-73; instr, Univ Md, 74-77; asst prof Span Am poetry, 77-79, ASSOC PROF SPAN AM LIT, UNIV IOWA, 79- *Concurrent Pos:* Hon fel writing, Int Writing Prog, Univ Iowa, 72; contrib ed Span Am poetry, Handbook of Latin American Studies, Libr Cong, 77- *Mem:* MLA; Inst Lit Iberoam. *Res:* Spanish American literature; literary theory. *Publ:* Auth, El motivo del golem en Las ruinas circulares, Rev Chilena de Lit, 4/71; El Motivo de los mundos comunicantes, Texto Critico, 5-8/77; Borges y el arte de la dedicatoria, Rev Iberoam, 7-9/77; Vicente Huidobro o la voluntad inaugural, Revista Ibero-americana, Vol 78: 104-105; Herrera y Reissig o el indiscreto encanto de lo cursi, Texto Critico, 12/79; El cuento fantastico hispanoa-mericano en el siglo XIX, Mexico, Premia, 78; Vicente Huidobro, poeta mariano, Hispamerica, Vol 29, 81; Borges: De los meros simulacros a los coincidentes puntuales, Rev Chilena de Lit, Vol 18, 81. *Mailing Add:* Dept of Span Univ of Iowa Iowa City IA 52240

HAHN, THOMAS GEORGE O'HARA, English Literature & Language. See Vol II

HAHN, WALTER LUCIAN, b Berlin, Ger, Jan 5, 23; US citizen; m 51; c 3. GERMAN LITERATURE. *Educ:* Pädag Hochsch, Berlin, dipl, 49; Rice Univ, MA, 54; Univ Tex, PhD (Ger lit), 56. *Prof Exp:* From instr to asst prof Ger, Purdue Univ, 56-61; asst prof Ger, 61-65, assoc prof Ger lit, 65-73, PROF GER LIT, UNIV ORE, 73- *Mem:* Am Asn Teachers Ger; Philol Asn Pac Coast; Am Asn Univ Prof; Pac Northwest Coun Foreign Lang; Am Gioethe Soc. *Res:* German Romanticism; poetic realism; German novelle. *Publ:* Auth, Zu Stifters Konzept der Schönheit: Brigitta, Adalbert-Stifter-Institut Vierteljahrschrift, 70; Zum Erzählvorgang in Raabes Akten des Vogelsangs, Jahrbuch der Raabegesellschaft, 72; Hölderlins Einsamkeit und Dichtertum, Rice Univ Studies, Vol 55, No 3. *Mailing Add:* Dept of Ger & Russ Univ of Ore Eugene OR 97403

HAIDU, PETER, b Paris, France, Mar 7, 31; US citizen; c 2. FRENCH. *Educ:* Univ Chicago, BA, 52; Columbia Univ, MA, 59, PhD(French), 66. *Prof Exp:* From instr to asst prof French, Columbia Univ, 61-68; from asst prof to assoc prof, Yale Univ, 68-72; assoc prof, Univ Va, 72-74; PROF FRENCH & SCH HUMANITIES, UNIV ILL, 74- *Concurrent Pos:* Morse fel, Yale Univ, 70-71; Nat Endowment for Humanities fel, 77-78; Camargo Found fel, 77-78. *Res:* Semiotics; French and medieval literature; theory of literature. *Publ:* Auth, Aesthetic Distance in Chretien de Troyes: Irony and Comedy in Cliges and Perceval, 68 & Lion-queue-coupee: L'Ecart symbolique chez Chretien de Troyes, 72, Droz, Geneva; ed, Approaches to Medieval Romance, 75 & auth, Narrativity and Style in some XIIth Century Romances, 75, Yale Univ Fr Studies; Repetition: Modern reflections on medieval aesthetics, Mod Lang Notes, 77; Toward a socio-historical semiotics: Power and legitimacy in the Couronnement de Louis, Kodikas/Code, 80; Text and history: The semiosis of XIIth century lyric as socio-historical phenomenon, 80-81 & Semiotics and history, 82, Semiotica. *Mailing Add:* Dept of French Univ of Ill Urbana IL 61801

HAIG, IRVINE REID STIRLING, b Washington, DC, May 20, 36; m 60; c 2. FRENCH. *Educ:* Univ NC, BA, 58; Yale Univ, PhD(French), 64. *Prof Exp:* Instr French, Yale Univ, 62-64; from instr to asst prof, Princeton Univ, 64-67; from asst prof to assoc prof, 67-73, PROF FRENCH, UNIV NC, CHAPEL HILL, 73- *Concurrent Pos:* Mem grad sch foreign lang test in French, Educ Testing Serv, 67-69, chmn, 69-73; asst ed, Fr Rev, 68, managing ed & advert mgr, 72-74, ed-in-chief, 74-; secy-gen & treas, Inst Francais, Washington, 72-77, trustee, 72-; vis prof, Univ Mich, 74. *Honors & Awards:* Palmes Academiques, French Government, 78. *Mem:* MLA; Am Asn Teachers Fr; Int Asn Fr Studies; Conf 17th Century Fr Lit. *Res:* French classicism and romanticism; French novel. *Publ:* Co-ed, Contes et Nouvelles D'Aujourd'hui, Harper, 66; auth, Madame de Lafayette, Twayne, 70; The Madame Bovary blues, Romanic Rev, 2/70; The identities of Fabrice del Dongo, Fr Studies, 4/73; Hugo's Portrait of the Artist in Notre-Dame De Paris & Parlez-vous Quebecois?, 6/80, Stanford Fr Rev. *Mailing Add:* Dept of Romance Lang Univ of NC Chapel Hill NC 27514

HAILE, GETATCHEW, b Apr 19, 31; Ethiopian citizen; m 64; c 4. LINGUISTICS, RELIGION. *Educ:* Am Univ Cairo, BA, 57; Coptic Theol Col Cairo, BD, 57; Univ Tübingen, PhD(semitic philol), 62. *Prof Exp:* Lectr, Amharic, Ge'ez & Arabic, HSI Univ, Ethiopia, 62-64, asst prof Amharic, Ge'ez & Arabic & chmn dept Ethiopian lang, 64-69; exchange scholar ling, Univ Calif, Los Angeles, 69-70; vis prof African studies, Okla State Univ, 70-71; assoc prof Amharic, Ge'ez & Arabic, HSI Univ, Ethiopia, 71-75; CATALOGUER, HILL MONASTIC MANUSCRIPT LIBR, ST JOHN'S UNIV, MINN, 76- *Concurrent Pos:* Contrib ed, Northeast African Studies, Mich State Univ. *Res:* Ge'ez literature; Amharic grammar. *Publ:* Auth, Archaic Amharic forms, Proc Third Int Conf Ethiopian Studies, 66; The suffix pronouns in Amharic, Papers in African Ling, 71; coauth, The dialect of Gojjam, J Ethiopian Studies, 7/73; auth, A Catalogue of Ethiopian Manusripts Microfilmed for EMML/HMML, Vol 4, Collegeville, 79; The martyrdom of St Peter, Archbishop of Alexandria, Analecta Bollandiana, Bruxelles, 98: 85-92; A preliminary investigation of the tomara Tesbe't of Emperor Zar'a Ya'ezob of Ethiopia, Bull Sch Oriental and African Studies, Univ London, 43: 207-235; A new Ethiopic version of the Acts of St Mark, Analecta Bollandiana, Bruxelles, 99: 117-134; Religious controversies and the growth of Ethiopic literature in the fourteenth and fifteenth centuries, Oriens Christianus, Wiesbaden, 65: 102-136. *Mailing Add:* Hill Monastic Ms Libr St John's Univ Collegeville MN 56321

HAILE, HARRY G, b Tex, July 31, 31; m 52; c 3. GERMAN LITERATURE. *Educ:* Univ Ark, BA, 52, MA, 54; Univ Ill, PhD, 57. *Prof Exp:* Instr Ger, Univ Pa, 56-57; from asst prof to assoc prof, Univ Houston, 57-63; assoc prof, 63-65, chmn dept, 64-67, head dept, 67-73, assoc mem, Ctr Advan Studies, 69-70, PROF GER, UNIV ILL, URBANA, 65- *Concurrent Pos:* Am Coun Learned Soc grant, 60; Deut Forschungsgemeinschaft grant, 62-63; vis prof Ger, Univ Mich, 78. *Mem:* MLA; Am Asn Teachers Ger; Goethe Soc; Wiener Goethe Verein. *Res:* Humanities education and higher education in the United States; pre-industrial German literature; Martin Luther biography. *Publ:* Auth, The History of Johann Faustus, Univ Ill, 65; Teaching and basic research in literature, 68 & Teaching about language, 70, Mod Lang J; Artist in Chrysalis: A Biographical Study of Goethe in Italy, Univ Ill, 73; Invitation to Goethe's Faust, Univ Alabama, 73; Luther and literacy, PMLA, 77; The great Martin Luther spoof, Yale Rev, 78; Forces Shaping Technology: Martin Luther and the Book, Univ Ill, 79. *Mailing Add:* 1001 W White St Champaign IL 61820

HALE, THOMAS ALBERT, b Boston, Mass, Jan 5, 42; m 68; c 1. AFRICAN & FRENCH LITERATURE. *Educ:* Tufts Univ, BA, 64, MA, 68; Univ Rochester, PhD(French), 74. *Prof Exp:* Agr co-op asst, Peace Corps, Union Nigerienne de Credit et de Cooperation, 64-66; admin asst, NDEA French Inst, Tufts Univ, 67; ASSOC PROF FRENCH & COMP LIT, PA STATE UNIV, 73- *Concurrent Pos:* Co-ed, Cahiers Cesairiens, 74- & African Lit Asn Newsletter, 74-78; Fulbright sr lectr, Univ de Niamey, Niger, 80-81. *Mem:* MLA; African Lit Asn (secy-treas, 74-79, press, 81-82); Am Asn Teachers French; African Studies Asn; Am Comp Lit Asn. *Res:* Caribbean literature; French literature outside France. *Publ:* Auth, Sur Une tempete d'Aime Cesaire, Etudes Lit, 4/73; Aime Cesaire: A bio-bibliography, Africana J, spring 74; From Afro-America to Afro-France: The literary triangle trade, French Rev, 5/76; Structural dynamics in a Third World classic: Aime Cesaire's Cahier d'un retour au pays natal, Yale French Studies, No 53, 76; co-ed, The Teaching of African Literature, Univ Tex Press, 77; auth, Les Ecrits d'Aime Cesaire: Bibliographie commentee, Univ Montreal Press, 78; co-ed, Artist and Audience: African Literature as a Shared Experience, Three Continents Press, 79; auth, From written literature to the oral tradition and back: Camara Laye, Babou Conde, and Le Maitre de la Parole: Kouma Lafolo Kouma, French Rev, 5/82. *Mailing Add:* French Dept Pa State Univ University Park PA 16802

HALEY, GEORGE, b Lorain, Ohio, Oct 19, 27. SPANISH LITERATURE. *Educ:* Oberlin Col AB, 48; Brown Univ, AM, 51, PhD, 56. *Prof Exp:* Chmn dept Romance lang, 70-73, PROF SPAN LIT, UNIV CHICAGO, 68- *Concurrent Pos:* Guggenheim fel, 62-63 ; Bol De La Biblioteca De Menendex Pelayo, 80- *Mem:* MLA; Hisp Soc Am. *Res:* Spanish poetry of the Golden Age; Spanish prose fiction; Spanish theatre of the 17th Century. *Publ:* Auth, Vicente Espinel and Marcos de Obregon: A Life and its Literary Representation, Brown Univ, 59; The narrator in Don Quixote, Mod Lang Notes, 65; The earliest dated manuscript of Quevedo's Sueno del juicio final, Mod Philol, 70; Lope de Vega y el repertorio de Gaspar de Porras en 1604 y 1606, In: Homenaje a William L Fichter, 71; Diario de un estudiante de Salamanca, Univ Salamanca, 77; El Escritor Y La Critica: Don Quijote, Madrid (in press). *Mailing Add:* 1050 E 59 Chicago IL 60637

HALL, CLIFTON D, b Somerville, Mass, Oct 8, 31; m 56; c 2. MEDIEVAL GERMAN LITERATURE. *Educ:* Queens Col, NY, BA, 53; Columbia Univ, MA, 65; Univ Mich, PhD(Ger), 66. *Prof Exp:* Instr Ger, Univ Mich, 65-66; from instr to asst prof, Univ Iowa, 66-68; asst prof, 68-71, ASSOC PROF GER, UNIV COLO, 71- *Concurrent Pos:* Univ Iowa Grad Col grant, 67-68. *Mem:* MLA; Mod Humanities Res Asn. *Res:* Medieval German literature; computer-aided lexicography for medieval manuscripts. *Publ:* Coauth, Rolandslied concordance with indexes and reverse indexes, In: Compendia, W S Maney & Son, Leeds, England; auth, Kleist, Catholicism and the Catholic Church, fall 67 & The Saelde-Group in Das Rolandslied and Karl der Grosse, winter 69, Monatshefte. *Mailing Add:* Dept of Ger Lang & Lit Univ of Colo Boulder CO 80302

HALL, ROBERT ANDERSON, JR, b Raleigh, NC, Apr 4, 11; m 36, 76; c 3. ROMANCE & GENERAL LINGUISTICS. *Educ:* Princeton Univ, AB, 31; Univ Rome, Italy, DLitt, 34; Univ Chicago, AM, 35. *Prof Exp:* Asst prof foreign lang, Univ PR, 37-39; instr Romance lang, Princeton Univ, 39-40; from instr to asst prof Ital, Brown Univ, 40-46; from assoc prof to prof, 46-76, EMER PROF LING, CORNELL UNIV, 76- *Concurrent Pos:* Consult, US Armed Forces Inst, 43; assoc, Columbia Univ, 43-44; vis asst prof, Yale Univ, 43-44; consult, US Dept War, 44-45; lectr ling inst, Univ Mich, 45 & assoc prof, 49; consult fundamental educ proj, UNESCO, Haiti, 49; Fulbright lectr, Rome, 50-51 & sr lectr ling, 57-58; prof, ling inst, Ind Univ, 53; Guggenheim fel, Australia & New Guinea, 54; vis prof ling, Univ Rome, 62-63; prof, Primer Inst Ling Latino-Am, Montevideo, 65-66; dir, Cornell-Ford English Lang Prog, Rome, 66-67; prof, Cuarto Inst Panam Ling, PR, 71. *Mem:* Dante Soc Am; MLA; Ling Soc Am (vpres, 61); Am Asn Teachers Ital (vpres, 45). *Res:* History of Italian language; comparative Romance linguistics; Pidgin and creolized languages. *Publ:* Auth, Short history of Italian Literature, Linguistica, 51; Bibliografia Della Linguistica Italiana, Sansoni, 58 & 69; Cultural Symbolism in Literature, Linguistica, 63; Introductory Linguistics, Chilton, 64; Pidgin and Creole Languages, Cornell Univ, 66; La Struttura dell'italiano, Armando, Rome, 71; Comparative Romance Grammar, Elsevier, 74-; Antonio Fogazzaro, Twayne, 78; The Kensington Rune-Stone Is Genuine, Horbeam, 82. *Mailing Add:* 308 Cayuga Heights Rd Ithaca NY 14850

HALL, THOMAS W, b Bel Air, Md, Mar 3, 16; m 45; c 2. FRENCH, ITALIAN. *Educ:* Univ Md, BA, 38, PhD(French), 58; Middlebury Col, MA, 50. *Prof Exp:* Chmn mod lang, Presby Jr Col, NC, 45-51; ASSOC PROF FRENCH & ITAL & ASST CHMN DEPT, UNIV MD, COLLEGE PARK, 51- *Mem:* MLA; Am Asn Teachers Fr. *Res:* Roger Martin du Gard; French novel of the 20th century. *Publ:* Auth, A note on the so-called clevage in Les Thibault of Roger Martin du Gard, Fr Rev, 12/53. *Mailing Add:* Dept of French & Ital Univ of Md College Park MD 20742

HALLE, MORRIS, b Liepaja, Latvia, July 23, 23; nat US; m 55. MODERN LANGUAGES, LINGUISTICS. *Educ:* Univ Chicago, MA, 48; Harvard Univ, PhD(Slavic lang & lit), 55. *Prof Exp:* Teaching fel Russ & Ger, Univ Chicago, 47-48; teaching fel Russ, Harvard Univ, 49-51; from asst prof to prof, 51-76 Ferrari P Ward prof, 76-81, INST PROF MOD LANG & LING, MASS INST TECHNOL, 81- *Concurrent Pos:* Guggenheim fel, 60-61; fel, Ctr Advan Studies Behav, 60-61. *Mem:* Fel Am Acad Arts & Sci; Ling Soc Am (vpres, 73, pres, 74). *Res:* Phonetics; general linguistics; Slavic languages and linguistics. *Publ:* Auth, The Sound Pattern of Russian, Mouton, The Hague, 59; coauth, Preliminaries to Speech Analysis, Mass Inst Technol, 63; The Sound Pattern of English, Harper, 68; auth, The accentuation of Russian words, Language, 9/73. *Mailing Add:* 20C132 Mass Inst of Technol Cambridge MA 02139

HALLER, HERMANN WALTER, b Aarau, Switz, June 2, 45. ITALIAN LINGUISTICS, ROMANCE PHILOLOGY. *Educ:* Univ Bern, Switz, PhD(Romance philol), 71. *Prof Exp:* Sci asst Romance philol, Univ Bern, 70-72; instr, 73-74, asst prof, 74-80, ASST PROF, PROG COMP LIT, GRAD CTR, QUEENS COL, CITY UNIV NEW YORK, 78-, ASSOC PROF ROMANCE LANG, 80- *Concurrent Pos:* Res award, Res Found, City Univ New York, 76 & 78; vis prof, New York Univ, 80 & Brown Univ 80-81. *Mem:* MLA; Am Asn Teachers Ital; Int Ling Asn; Ling Soc Am. *Res:* Early Italian texts; history of Italian language; Italian stylistics; Italian dialectology. *Publ:* Auth, Der Deiktische Gebrauch des Demonstrativums im Altitalienischen, Lang, Bern, 73; Stylistic trends in the making of Pirandello's Novelle per un Anno, Italica, 75; Il volgarizzamento del Panfilo in antico veneziano, Studi grammatica ital, Florence, 76; Da Le Storie ferraresi al Romanzo di Ferrara: varianti nell' opera di Bassani, Can J Ital Studies, 77; Linguistic Interference in Il Progresso Italo-Americano, Italian Americana, 79; contribr, Columbia Dictionary of European Literature, 80; Cronostilistica nei romanzi d'esilio di Ignazio Silone, Mod Lang Studies, 82; ed & auth, Il Panfilo veneziano, Edizione critica, Olschki, Firenze (in press). *Mailing Add:* Dept of Romance Lang Queens Col Flushing NY 11367

HALLERAN, MICHAEL ROS, b New York, NY, Oct 31, 53; m 81. CLASSICS. *Educ:* Kenyon Col, AB, 75; Harvard Univ, AM, 78, PhD(Class philol), 81. *Prof Exp:* Vis lectr, Col Holy Cross, 81; ASST PROF CLASSICS, CONN COL, 81- *Mem:* Am Philol Asn; Class Asn New England. *Res:* Greek drama; archaic Greek poetry; Latin poetry. *Publ:* Auth, Alkestis redux, Harvard Studies in Class Philol, 82. *Mailing Add:* Conn Col Box 1543 New London CT 06320

HALLETT, JUDITH PELLER, b Chicago, Ill, Apr 4, 44; m 66; c 2. CLASSICAL PHILOLOGY. *Educ:* Wellesley Col, AB, 66; Harvard Univ, MA, 67, PhD(class philol), 71. *Prof Exp:* Lectr classics, Clark Univ, 72-73, asst prof, 73-74; asst prof class studies, Boston Univ, 74-82, asst dean, Col Lib Arts, 77-79; ASST PROF, SCH HUMANITIES, MELLON FOUND, BRANDEIS UNIV, 82- *Concurrent Pos:* Mem, Inst Class Studies, London, Eng, 75-76; Nat Endowment for Humanities fel, 81. *Mem:* Am Philol Asn; Asn Ancient Historians. *Res:* Latin literature; women in classical antiquity; Roman and Greek civilization. *Publ:* Auth, Fathers and Daughters: women in Roman Kinship and Society, Princeton Univ Press (in prep). *Mailing Add:* Dept of Class & Oriental Studies Brandeis Univ Waltham MA 02254

HALLOCK, ANN HAYES, b Los Angeles, Calif, May 13, 41. ITALIAN LITERATURE. *Educ:* Stanford Univ, BA, 63; Middlebury Col, MA, 66; Harvard Univ, PhD(Romance lang & lit), 74. *Prof Exp:* Asstprof Ital lang & lit, Univ Calif, Rkiverside, 71-72; asst prof, 72-80, ASSOC PROF ITAL LANG & LIT, TULANE UNIV, 80- *Concurrent Pos:* Consult, Nat Bilingual/Bicultural Resource Ctr Southern US, 75-77 & Nat Endowment for Humanities, 76- *Honors & Awards:* Cultural Achievement Award, Greater New Orleans Ital Cult Soc, 77; Cavaliere Ufficiale nell'Ordine di Merito, Repub of Italy, 77. *Mem:* Dante Soc; MLA; Am Asn Teachers Ital; SCent Mod Lang Asn; SAtlantic Mod Lang Asn. *Res:* Dante and Italian literature from 13th to 14th centuries; poetry of Michelangelo. *Publ:* Auth, Dante's Selva Oscura and other obscure Selvas, Forum Italicum, 3/72; The pre-eminent role of Babilonia in Petrarch's Theme of the Two Cities, Italica, 77; Ugo Foscolo and the critics of Michelangelo's Rime, SAtlantic Bull, 11/77; Ensuring an Italian Renaissance, Asn Dept Foreign Lang Bull, 3/78; Michelangelo the Poet, Page-Ficklin, 78; Explication of Michelangelo's obscure pastoral poem, Rom Notes, spring 79; The origin of Michelangelo's poetic expression, Ital Quart, summer 80; Fantasticheria: Verga's declaration of transition, Ital Cult, 3/82. *Mailing Add:* Dept of French & Ital Tulane Univ New Orleans LA 70118

HALLOWELL, ROBERT EDWARD, b Charleston, Ill, Aug 30, 18; m 49; c 1. FRENCH LITERATURE. *Educ:* Eastern Ill State Col, AB, 39; Univ Ill, MA, 40, PhD(French), 42; Univ Poitiers, dipl, 60. *Prof Exp:* Spec agent, Counter Intel Corps, US Dept Army, France & Ger, 45-47; from instr to asst prof French, Univ Ill, 48-60; assoc prof, Univ Wis-Milwaukee, 60-62, prof & chmn dept, 63-68; PROF FRENCH, UNIV ILL, CHICAGO, 68- *Concurrent Pos:* French ed, Mod Lang J, 60-63, asst managing ed, 63; fel, Ctr Renaissance Studies, Newberry Libr, 80. *Mem:* MLA; Renaissance Soc Am; Am Asn Teachers Fr; Int Asn Fr Studies; Soc Fr des Seiziemistes. *Res:* Renaissance mythology and iconography; aesthetics of Pleiade poets; the education of the Prince as a popular literary genre. *Publ:* Auth, Ronsard and the Conventional Roman Elegy, Univ Ill, 54; L'Hercule gallique: Expression et image politique, In: Lumieres de la Pleiade, Vrin, 66; Matthäus Greuter's Hercules Tri-Mysticus, Renaissance Papers, 67; Une ode retrouvee de Jodelle, Bibliot d'Humanisme et Renaissance, 68; The role of French writers in the royal entries of Marie de' Medici in 1600, Studies Philol, 4/69; contrib, Myth and mythography in French Renaissance literature, In: Literature, the Visual Arts and Music, Univ Cincinnati, 75; Prince Humaniste ou Prince Chevaleresque, Ky Romance Quart, 76. *Mailing Add:* Dept of French Univ of Ill Chicago Circle Chicago IL 60680

HALPERIN, DAVID M, b Chicago, Ill, Apr 2, 52. CLASSICAL & COMPARATIVE LITERATURE. *Educ:* Oberlin Col, BA, 73; Stanford Univ, MA, 77, PhD(classics & humanities), 80. *Prof Exp:* Teaching asst classics, Oberlin Col, 71-73; teaching fel classics & humanities, Stanford Univ, 74-76; actg instr classics, Intercol Ctr Class Studies, Rome, 77-78; ASST PROF LIT, DEPT HUMANITIES, MASS INST TECHNOL, 79- *Concurrent Pos:* Assoc dir archaeol, Sch Class Studies, Am Acad, Rome, 77-78; teaching asst humanities, Stanford Univ, 78. *Mem:* Am Acad Rome; Am Philol Asn; Women's Class Caucus; Petronian Soc; Joseph Conrad Soc Am. *Res:* Bucolic and pastoral poetry; Russian literature; platonic love. *Publ:* Auth, The role of the lie in The First Circle, In: Aleksandr Solzhenitsyn: Critical Essays and Documentary Materials, 2nd ed, Collier Bks, 75; Lord Jim and the pear tree caper, Am Notes & Queries, Vol 14, No 8, 76; Man's fate in the Aeneid, Va Quart Rev, Vol 53, No 1, 77; Solzhenitsyn, Epicurus and the ethics of Stalinism, Critical Inquiry, Vol 7, 80/81; Continuities in Solzhenitsyn's ethical thought, In: Solzhenitsyn in Exile, 82; Before Pastoral: Theocritus and the Ancient Tradition of Bucohe Poetry, Yale Univ Press (in press). *Mailing Add:* 14N-316 Mass Inst Technol 77 Massachusetts Ave Cambridge MA 02139

HALPERN, ABRAHAM MEYER, b Boston, Mass, Feb 20, 14: m 41, 68; c 2. ANTHROPOLOGY, LINGUISTICS. *Educ:* Harvard Col, AB, 33; Univ Chicago, PhD(anthrop), 47. *Prof Exp:* From instr to asst prof anthrop, Univ Chicago, 41-46; adv lang revision, Supreme Comdr Allied Powers, Japan, 46-48; from staff mem to sr staff mem, Rand Corp, 49-62; res assoc, Ctr Int Affairs, Harvard Univ, 65-68; sr staff mem, Ctr Naval Analyses, 68-72; prof Asian studies, Sch Advan Int Studies, Johns Hopkins Univ, 73-74; adj prof int affairs, George Washington Univ, 74-78; res assoc, Dept Ling, Univ Calif, San Diego, 77-78; RETIRED. *Concurrent Pos:* Res assoc, Hist Div, Carnegie Inst Washington, 41-46; dir lang prog, Civil Affairs Training Sch, Univ Chicago, 43-52; mem joint comt contemp China, Soc Sci Res Coun-Am Coun Learned Socs, 59-63; lectr polit sci, Univ Calif, Berkeley, 61-62; res fel, China Proj, Coun Foreign Rels, NY, 63-65; Morrison lectr, Australian Nat Univ, 66: lectr, Sch Advan Int Studies, Johns Hopkins Univ, 70 & 72-73; res fel grant, Earhart Found, Ann Arbor, Mich, 75; Nat Endowment for Humanities fel for independent students, 78-79. *Mem:* Am Anthrop Asn. *Res:* American Indian languages and cultures. *Publ:* Auth, Yuma, I-VI, Int J Am Ling, 46-47; Changing Japanese Attitudes Toward Atomic Weapons, Rand Corp, 54; China in the postwar world, China Quart, 65: ed, Policies Toward China, McGraw, 66; auth, Contemporary China as a problem for political science, World Polit, Vol 15, No 3; Peking and the Problem of Japan 1968-72, Ctr Naval Anal, Prof Paper, No 99, 72; co-ed, The Future of the Korean Peninsula, Praeger, 77. *Mailing Add:* 629 Calle de Valdez Santa Fe NM 87501

HALPERN, JOSEPH DAVID, b New York, NY, June 25, 46; m 68; c 1. FRENCH, LITERATURE. *Educ:* Harvard Univ, BA, 67; Stanford Univ, PhD(Fr & comp lit), 72. *Prof Exp:* Asst prof French, Yale Univ, 72-78, assoc prof, 78-80. *Concurrent Pos:* Morse fel humanities, Yale Univ, 76-77. *Mem:* MLA. *Res:* Modern literature and criticism. *Publ:* Auth, Critical Fictions: The Literary Criticism of Jean-Paul Sartre, Yale Univ, 76; ed, Mallarme, Yale Univ Fr Studies, 77; co-ed, Genet: A Collection of Critical Essays, Prentice-Hall, 78. *Mailing Add:* 175 Lawrence New Haven CT 06511

HALPERT, INGE D, b Berlin, Ger, Aug 5, 26; US citizen; m 48; c 2. FOREIGN LANGUAGES. *Educ:* Hunter Col, BA, 48: Columbia Univ, MA, 50, PhD(Ger lit, Hesse & Goethe), 57. *Prof Exp:* From instr to assoc prof Ger, 50-73, PROF GER LANG & LIT, COLUMBIA UNIV, 73-, CHMN DEPT GER LANG, 79- *Concurrent Pos:* Res grant, Columbia Univ, 60-61, Columbia Coun Res Humanities grant, 62; Am Philol Soc grant, 64-65; consult, Eval Foreign Lang Depts West Point Mil Acad, US Dept Army, 77. *Mem:* Am Asn Teachers Ger; Am Coun Teaching Foreign Lang; MLA. *Res:* Modern German literature. *Publ:* Auth, Hermann Hesse and Goethe, Monatshafte, 60 & 61, Ger Quart, 61; Annotated Rilke Text, Appleton, 61; coauth, See it and Say it in German, New Am Libr, 62; auth, Goethe, In: Einführung in die Deutsche Literatur, Holt, 64; Auditory Reading Comprehension Exercises in German, Latin Am Inst, 66; coauth, In Wort und Schrift (advan Ger conversation & compos), Appleton, 72; contribr, Hermann Hesse, Columbia Dict Mod Europ Lit, 79. *Mailing Add:* 445 Riverside Dr New York NY 10027

HALPORN, JAMES WERNER, b New York, NY, Jan 4, 29; m 51, 60; c 2. GREEK, LATIN. *Educ:* Columbia Univ, AB, 49, MA, 50; Cornell Univ, PhD(Greek, Latin), 53. *Prof Exp:* Instr Greek & Latin, Columbia Col, 54-58; vis lectr classics, Carleton Univ, 58-59; vis asst prof, Univ Mo, 59-60; asst prof, 60-64, assoc prof, 64-68, PROF CLASS STUDIES & COMP LIT, IND UNIV, BLOOMINGTON, 68- *Concurrent Pos:* Fulbright fel, Univ Vienna, 53-54; rep adv coun, Am Acad Rome, 62-, mem class jury Rome Prize fels, 70-71; Am Coun Learned Soc/Int Bus Mach Corp fel, 66-67; chmn region IX, Woodrow Wilson Nat Fel Found, 69-; vis prof classics & comp lit, Univ Calif, Berkeley, 71-72; mem comt on placement, Am Philol Asn, 80-83; vis scholar classics, Harvard Univ, 81-82. *Mem:* Am Philol Asn; NAm Patristic Soc; Class Asn Gt Brit; Soc Promotion Roman Studies; Soc Promotion Hellenic Studies. *Res:* Late Latin literature; Latin palaeography; Greek and Latin metrics. *Publ:* Coauth, Römische Metrik, Vandenhoeck & Ruprecht, 62, 2nd ed, 80; Meters of Greek and Latin Poetry, Methuen & Bobbs, 63, 2nd ed, Univ Okla Press, 80; auth, Lateinische Metrik und Prosarythmus, In: Lexikon der Alten Welt, Artemis, Zurich, 65; Agido, Hagesichora, and the chorus: Alcman 1.37ff PMG, In: Antidosis: Festschrift Walter Kraus, 72: ed, Cassidorus De anima, Vol CVI, In: Corpus Christianorum Ser Latina, 73; auth, St Augustine and the Epulae Venerales, Jahrbuch für Antike und Christentum, 76; Methods of reference in Cassiodorus, In: Libraries and Culture, Univ Texas Press, 81; The skeptical Electra (Euripides Electra 508H), Harvard Studies in Classical Philol (in press). *Mailing Add:* 702 Ballantine Rd Bloomington IN 47401

HALSEY, MARTHA T, b Richmond, Va. ROMANCE LANGUAGES. *Educ:* Goucher Col, AB, 54; State Univ Iowa, MA, 56; Ohio State Univ, PhD(Span), 64. *Prof Exp:* Instr Span & French, Iowa State Univ, 56-59; asst instr Span, Ohio State Univ, 59-64; asst prof, 64-70, assoc prof, 70-79, PROF SPAN, PA STATE UNIV, UNIVERSITY PARK, 79- *Concurrent Pos:* Ed assoc, Mod Int Drama, Ky Romance Quart & Estreno. *Mem:* Am Asn Teachers Span & Port; MLA; Northeast Mod Lang Am; SAtlantic Mod Lang Asn. *Res:* Nineteenth and twentieth century Spanish literature. *Publ:* Auth, Light and darkness as dramatic symbols in two tragedies of Buero Vallejo, 3/67 & Buero Vallejo and the significance of hope, 3/68, Hispania; The dreamer protagonist in the tragic theater of Buero Vallejo, Rev Estud Hisp, 11/68; Reality versus illusion: Ibsen's The Wild Duck and Buero Vallejo's En la ardiente oscuridad, Contemp Lit, 12/70; Goya en the theater: Buero Vallejo's El sueno de la razon, Ky Romance Quart, 71; El traguluz: A tragedy of contemporary Spain, Romanic Rev, 12/72; auth, Antonio Buero Vallejo, Twayne, 73; co-ed, Jose Martin Recuerda's El enganao, Caballos des bocaos, Catedra, 81. *Mailing Add:* Dept of Span Pa State Univ University Park PA 16802

HALTON, THOMAS, b Cavan, Ireland, Feb 6, 25. GREEK, LATIN. *Educ:* Maynooth Col, Ireland, BA, 46, STB, 49; Univ Col, Dublin, MA, 58; Cath Univ Am, PhD, 63. *Prof Exp:* Assoc prof, 60-75, PROF GREEK & LATIN, CATH UNIV AM, 75- *Res:* Early Christian Greek. *Mailing Add:* Dept of Greek & Latin Cath Univ of Am Washington DC 20064

HAM, GALIA M, b Russian, Aug 30, 11; US citizen; m 55. FRENCH. *Educ:* Col Ste-Marie, BA, 27, BA, 28; Univ Calif, Los Angeles, MA, 39, PhD(Romance lang), 47; Univ Mich, MLA, 53. *Prof Exp:* From teaching asst to asst French, Univ Calif, Los Angeles, 39-47; from instr to asst prof, Wayne State Univ, 47-56; vis asst prof, Mills Col, 64-66; actg chmn dept, 67-70, ASSOC PROF FRENCH, CALIF STATE UNIV, HAYWARD, 66- *Publ:* Auth, Les Empereurs de Rome de Calendre, Univ Mich, 57. *Mailing Add:* Dept of French Calif State Univ 25800 Hillary St Hayward CA 94542

HAMBLET, EDWIN JOSEPH, b Portland, Maine, Feb 15, 37. ROMANCE LANGUAGES. *Educ:* Bowdoin Col, BA, 59; Middlebury Col, MA, 64; Univ Pa, PhD(Romance lang), 67. *Prof Exp:* Asst prof French, Emory Univ, 67-68; ASSOC PROF FRENCH, STATE UNIV NY COL PLATTSBURGH, 68- *Concurrent Pos:* Vis prof French-Can lit, McGill Univ, 71-72; State Univ NY fel, 73. *Mem:* MLA; Am Asn Teachers Fr. *Res:* Seventeenth century French drama; French-Canadian literature. *Publ:* Auth, Marcel Dube and the French-Canadian Drama, Exposition, 70; Quebec's theatre of liberation, Comp Drama, spring 71; Michel Tremblay et le joual Quebecois, Mod Lang Asn Fr Bull, 12/72. *Mailing Add:* Dept of Mod Lang State Univ of NY Col Plattsburgh NY 12901

HAMILTON, CARLOS D, b Santiago, Chile, Oct 20, 08; US citizen. SPANISH LITERATURE & HISTORY. *Educ:* Univ Chile, Bachiller, 23; Pontif Gregorian Univ, JCD, 31. *Prof Exp:* Prof legal hist & philos, Univ Chile, 41-51; lectr Span-Am lit, Columbia Univ, 52-56; assoc prof Span, Vassar Col, 56-61; prof mod lang, Brooklyn Col, 61, prof Span, 61-78; EMER PROF, CITY UNIV NEW YORK, 78- *Concurrent Pos:* Fel, Inst Cult Hisp, Madrid, 50-; Fulbright lectr, Inst Caro y Cuervo, Bogota, 63-64; mem, Nat Fulbright Comn, 65-67. *Mem:* Latin Am Studies. *Res:* Justice and human rights; history of Spanish-American literature. *Publ:* Auth, Historia de la literatua Hispanoamericana, Epesa, Madrid, 2nd ed, 66; Ruben Dario en la Isla de Oro, Cuadernos Hisp-Am, Madrid, 9/67; Lirica Hispanica, McGraw, 69; El ensayo Hispanoamericano, Eisa Madrid, 72; La novela actual de Hispanoamerica, Cuadernos Americanos, Mex, 73; Pablo Neruda, poeta Chileno universal, Lord Chochrane, Santiago, Chile, 73; Origen Hispanico de las ciencias politicas, Thesaurus, Bogota, 78; El Lujo de la Libertad, Acad Americanos, Mexico, 81 & 82- *Mailing Add:* City Univ New York NY 10021

HAMILTON, JAMES FRANCIS, b Cleveland, Ohio, Dec 9, 39; m 63; c 2. FRENCH LITERATURE & LANGUAGE. *Educ:* Kent State Univ, BSEd, 62; Ohio State Univ, MA, 65, PhD(Romance lang), 70. *Prof Exp:* Teacher French, Lincoln High Sch, Cleveland, Ohio, 62-63; instr & asst supvr, Ohio State Univ, 63-69; asst prof, Denison Univ, 69-70; asst prof, 70-76, assoc prof, 76-81, PROF FRENCH, UNIV CINCINNATI, 81- *Concurrent Pos:* Taft fac grant, 72. *Mem:* Am Asn Teachers Fr; MLA; Soc Fr Etude VIIIe Siecle; Am Soc Eighteenth Century Studies. *Res:* Rousseau and romanticism; Montesquieu to Zola. *Publ:* Auth, The novelist an historian: A contrast between Balzac's Les Chouans and Hugo's Quatrevingt-treize, Fr Rev, 6/76; From art to nature in George Sand's La Mare au Diable, Fr Lit Ser: Fr Lit & Arts, 78; Rousseau's Theory of Literature: The Poetics of Art and Nature, Fr Lit Publ Co, 79; The anti-Rousseauism of Madame Bovary, Romance Notes, fall 80; Zola's Nana and Jeanne d'arc: Contrary myths and the creative process, USF Lang Quart, fall-winter, 80; Two psychodramatic scenes in Stendhal's Armance, Ky Romance Quart, 81; Pagan ritual and human sacrifice in Merimee's Mateo Falcone, Fr Rev, 10/81; The impossible return to nature in Maupassant's Bel-Ami, Nineteenth-Century Fr Studies, spring-summer, 82. *Mailing Add:* Dept of Romance Lang Univ of Cincinnati Cincinnati OH 45221

HAMILTON, JOHN DANIEL BURGOYNE, b Los Angeles, Calif, Oct 19, 39. CLASSICAL LANGUAGES, GREEK MYTHOLOGY & RELIGION. *Educ:* St Louis Univ, AB, 63; AM, 64; Weston Col, Cambridge, Mass, MDiv, 69; Univ Minn, PhD(classics), 73. *Prof Exp:* Instr classics, Univ Santa Clara, 65-66; asst prof, 72-76, ASSOC PROF CLASSICS, COL OF THE HOLY CROSS, 77- *Concurrent Pos:* Assoc, Danforth Found, 77-; Grad Studies Adv, Col of Holy Cross, 81- *Mem:* Am Philol Asn; Class Asn New England; Soc Promotion Hellenic Studies; Class Asn Gt Brit. *Res:* Greek tragedy; mythology; Roman satire. *Publ:* Auth, Justin's Apology 66: A review of scholarship, 72 & The church and the language of mystery, 77, Ephemerides Theol Lovanienses; transl (with B Nagy), L Gernet, The Anthropology of Ancient Greece, Johns Hopkins, 81. *Mailing Add:* Dept of Calssics Col of the Holy Cross Worcester MA 01610

HAMILTON, MARY P, b Mass, Sept 26, 14. GERMAN LITERATURE. *Educ:* Regus Col, AB, 36; Radcliffe Col, AM, 37; Heidelberg, cert, 36. *Prof Exp:* From instr to assoc prof Ger, Col Mt St Vincent, 37-48; PROF GER, REGIS COL, MASS, 48- *Mem:* MLA; Am Asn Teachers Ger; AAUP; Am Coun Teaching For Lang. *Res:* The Kinderlied in German literature; Romanticism. *Mailing Add:* Div of Lang & Lit Regis Col Weston MA 02193

HAMILTON, RICHARD, b Bryn Mawr, Pa, Dec 19, 43; m 65; c 2. GREEK LITERATURE. *Educ:* Harvard Col, AB, 65; Univ Mich, PhD(class), 71. *Prof Exp:* Asst prof, 71-76, ASSOC PROF GREEK, BYRN MAWR COL, 77- *Mem:* Am Philol Asn; Am Class League. *Res:* Greek lyric; tragedy. *Publ:* Epinikion: General Form in the Odes of Pindar, Mouton, The Hague, 74; Objective evidence for actors' interpolations in Greek tragedy, Greek, Roman & Byzantine Studies, 74; Neoptolemos' story in the Philoctetes, Am J Philol, 75; Solon 13.74 ff (West), Greek, Roman & Byzantine Studies, 77; Prologue, prophecy and plot in four plays of Euripides, Am J Philol, 78; Euripides' Cyclopean Symposium, Phoenix, 79; Bryn Mawr commentaries: Euripides' Hippolytus, Bryn Mawr, 80 & 82; Hesiod's Theogony, Bryn Mawr, 81. *Mailing Add:* Dept of Greek Bryn Mawr Col Bryn Mawr PA 19010

HAMILTON, THOMAS EARLE, b Savannah, Ga, June 10, 05; m 33; c 3. SPANISH. *Educ:* Southern Methodist Univ, AB, 27, AM, 29; Univ Tex, PhD, 40. *Prof Exp:* From assoc prof to prof, 40-72, EMER PROF CLASS & ROMANCE LANG, TEX TECH UNIV, 72- *Concurrent Pos:* Consult foreign lang, Houston Pub Sch Syst, 53 & Angelo State Univ, 67-68; ed, SCent Mod Lang Asn Bull, 55-60; vis prof Span & classics, Austin Col, 62-63; councilman, Asn Col Honor Soc, 66-, mem comt standards, 67-, chmn, 70- *Mem:* Emer mem MLA; emer Am Asn Teachers Span & Port; hon mem SCent Mod Lang Asn. *Res:* Spanish literature of the Golden Age. *Publ:* Auth, Spoken letters in Lope, Tirso and Alarcon, PMLA, 47; Paleographic Edition of Lope de Vega's El cardenal de Belen, Tex Technol Col, 48; Comedias attributed to Alarcon examined in the light of his known epistolary practices, Hisp Rev, 49 & In: Critical Essays on the Life & Works of Ruiz de Alarcon, Madrid, 72; The aside in the Comedias of Alarcon, Hispania, 9/63; The audio-lingual method in the University: Fad or panacea?, Ky Foreign Lang Quart, 65, Hispania, 9/66 & In: The Teaching of German-Problems and Methods, Nat Carl Schurz, 71; coauth, Graduate Reading Exams (Span), Educ Testing Serv, Princeton, NJ, 66-67; auth, What Happened in the Cave of Montesinos?, Tech Press, 68. *Mailing Add:* 2303 N Celia Dr Cedar Park TX 78613

HAMILTON, WILLIAM SELDEN, JR, b Cincinnati, Ohio, Dec 11, 41; m 69; c 2. SLAVIC LINGUISTICS, RUSSIAN. *Educ:* Yale Univ, BA, 63, MA, 68, PhD(Slavic Ling), 71. *Prof Exp:* Asst prof, 70-76, ASSOC PROF RUSS, STATE UNIV NY BUFFALO, 76- *Honors & Awards:* Chancellor's Award, State Univ NY, 75. *Res:* Russian linguistics; phonology and morphology; Slavic linguistics. *Publ:* Auth, Deep and surface changes in four Slavic noun systems, Linguistics, 74; Phonemic hard-soft oppositions before soft consonants in Russian, Studies Ling, 75; Vowel power vs consonant power in Russian morphophonemics, Russ Ling, 76; Introduction to Russian Phonology and Word Structure, Slavica, 80; On the future of soft consonants in Russian, Russ Lang J, 82. *Mailing Add:* Dept of Mod Lang & Lit State Univ of NY Buffalo NY 14260

HAMLIN, CYRUS, b New Haven, Conn, Aug 26, 36; m 58. COMPARATIVE LITERATURE. *Educ:* Harvard Univ, BA, 58; Yale Univ, PhD, 63. *Prof Exp:* From instr English to asst prof Ger & comp lit, Yale Univ, 62-70; ASSOC PROF ENGLISH, VICTORIA COL, UNIV TORONTO, 70-, CHMN COMP LIT, 71- *Concurrent Pos:* Nat Humanities Found jr fel, 67-68; Can Coun res fel, 72-73. *Mem:* MLA; Am Comp Lit Asn; Can Comp Lit Asn. *Res:* European romanticism; theories of literature and criticism. *Publ:* Auth, Hölderlin in perspective, Seminar, 71; Hölderlins mythos der heroischen Freundschaft, Hölderlin-Jahrbuch, 71-72; The poetics of self-consciousness, Genre, 73. *Mailing Add:* 93 Bernard Ave Toronto ON M5R 1R8 Can

HAMLIN, FRANK RODWAY, b Wolverhampton, England, Apr 10, 35; m 68; c 2. ROMANCE LINGUISTICS. *Educ:* Univ Birmingham, BA, 57, PhD(French), 59 Cambridge Univ, MA, 61. *Prof Exp:* Lectr mediaeval French, Queen's Univ, Belfast, 60-61; res fel French, Gonville & Caius Col, Cambridge, 61-63; asst prof, 63-68, assoc prof, 68-78, PROF FRENCH, UNIV BC, 78- *Concurrent Pos:* Can Coun fel, 68-69, 76-77 & 82-83. *Mem:* Soc Ling Romane; Soc Fr Onomastique; English Place-Name Soc; Can Soc Study Names; Am Name Soc. *Res:* Toponymy, especially of Southern France; Old Provencal language and literature. *Publ:* Auth, Le Suffixe -acum dans la Toponymie de l'Herault, privately pub, 61; coauth, Introduction a l'etude de l'Ancien Provencal, Droz, 67; Bibliographie des etudes romanes en Amerique du Nord, Rev Langues Romanes, annually, 69-78; auth, Les noms de domaines en -anum dans le departement de l'Herault, Rev Int d'Onomastique, 71, 72 & 74; Les noms de lieux en chante- et leur origine, a la lumiere de la cartographie, Actes XIII Congr Int Ling & Philol Romanes, 76; Les Toponymes gallo-romains en -anicum dans le departement de l'Herault, Rev Int d'Onomastique, 77; La Toponymie gallo-romaine de l'Herault: Une mise au point, Melanges, Offert a Charles Camproux, 78; Les Noms de lieux du departement de l'Herault: Nouveau dictionnaire topographique et etymologique (in press). *Mailing Add:* Dept of French Univ of BC Vancouver BC V6T 1W5 Can

HAMLIN, FRANKLIN GRANT, b Old Town, Maine, June 23, 15; m 67; c 4. FRENCH. *Educ:* Bowdoin Col, AB, 36; Middlebury Col, AM, 46, DML, 55; Sorbonne, France, Dipl, 48. *Prof Exp:* Teacher & coach, Berwick Acad, 36-38; head dept French, Salisbury Sch, 38-42; from asst prof to assoc prof, 48-58, PROF FRENCH, HAMILTON COL, 58- *Concurrent Pos:* Dir, jr yr in France, Hamilton Col, 58-78. *Mem:* Am Asn Teachers Fr; Am Asn Teachers Ital. *Res:* Nineteenth and 20th century French literature. *Publ:* Auth, L'Aventure de Poesie Dans L'oeuvre de Jean Giraudoux, Homme de Lettres. *Mailing Add:* Dept Foreign Lang Hamilton Col Clinton NY 13223

HAMMER, CARL, JR, b Salisbury, NC, 10; m 39; c 2. GERMAN. *Educ:* Catawba Col, AB, 34; Vanderbilt Univ, AM, 36; Univ Ill, PhD, 39. *Prof Exp:* Teaching fel Ger, Univ NC, 34-35 & Vanderbilt Univ, 35-36; teaching asst, Univ Ill, 36-39; from instr to asst prof, Vanderbilt Univ, 39-47; from assoc prof to prof, La State Univ, 47-64; prof Ger, 64-67, Horn prof Ger & chmn dept Ger & Slavic Lang, 67-77, EMER PROF GER, TEX TECH UNIV, 78- *Concurrent Pos:* Guest lectr, Southern Ill Univ, 49; Ford fac fel, Columbia Univ & Princeton Univ, 53-54; vis prof, Mont State Univ, 62 & 67. *Honors & Awards:* Ky Foreign Lang Conf Award, 72. *Mem:* MLA; Am Asn Teachers Ger; S Cent Mod Lang Asn. *Res:* Goethe and world literature; German-American literary relations; comparative literature. *Publ:* Auth, Goethe's Dichtung und Wahrheit, Univ Ill, 45; Longfellow's Golden Legend and Goethe's Faust, 52 & ed, Studies in German Literature in Honor of John T Krumpelmann, 63, La State Univ; auth, Rhinelanders on the Yadkin, 2nd rev ed, Rowan, 65; The current re-emergence of Gottsched, winter 66 & A final break between Goethe and Herder?, 72, SCent Bull; Goethe and Rousseau: Resonances of the Mind, Univ Press Ky, 73; Moliere's Tartuffe and Goethe's Grosskophta, Romance Notes, 78. *Mailing Add:* Dept of Ger & Slavic Lang Tex Tech Univ Lubbock TX 79409

HAMMERBACHER, GEORGE HENRY, British Literature, Linguistics. See Vol II

HAMMERLY, HECTOR MARCEL, b Buenos Aires, Arg, Oct 12, 35; Can citizen; m 56; c 1. APPLIED LINGUISTICS, SECOND LANGUAGE TEACHING. *Educ:* Columbia Union Col, BA, 61; Univ Tex, Austin, PhD(foreign lang educ), 70. *Prof Exp:* Instr Span, Foreign Serv Inst, Washington, DC, 58-61 & Ohio State Univ, 64-65; from instr to asst prof, 65-76, ASSOC PROF APPL LING & SPAN, SIMON FRASER UNIV, 76- *Concurrent Pos:* Simon Fraser Univ Pres res grant, 73. *Mem:* Am Asn Teachers Span & Port; Am Coun Teaching Foreign Lang; Am Asn Applied Ling; Am Asn Teachers Fr; Nat Asn Learning Lab Dirs. *Res:* Second language methodology. *Publ:* Auth, Recent methods and trends in second language teaching, 71 & The correction of pronunciation errors, 73, Mod Lang J; Teaching pronunciation and generative phonology, Foreign Lang Ann, 73; The Articulatory Pictorial Transcriptions: New Aids to Second Language Pronunciation, Second Lang Publ, 74; Primary and secondary associations with visual aids as semantic conveyors, Int Rev Appl Ling, 74; auth, The teaching of ser/estar by a cognitive audiolingual approach, Hispania, 77; Synthesis in second language teaching: An intoduction to languistics, 2nd Lang Publ, 82. *Mailing Add:* Dept of Lang Lit & Ling Simon Fraser Univ Burnaby BC V5A 1S6 Can

HAMMOND, JOHN HAYS, b Ft Worth, Tex, Nov 8, 12; m 39; c 4. ROMANCE LANGUAGES, LATIN AMERICAN LITERATURE. *Educ:* Tex Christian Univ, BA, 33; Univ Tex, MA, 35, PhD(Span), 48. *Prof Exp:* Instr Span, Tex Christian Univ, 34-36, Univ Nebr, 37-41 & Princeton Univ, 41-42; instr Span & French, US Naval Acad, 42-45; from instr to asst prof Span, Univ Tex, 45-50; assoc prof, 50-60, prof, 60-80, EMER PROF SPAN & FRENCH, TEX CHRISTIAN UNIV, 80- *Concurrent Pos:* Am Coun Learned Soc fel, 51-52; Ford Found Fund for Advan Educ fel, 53-54; Span ed, SCent Mod Lang Asn Bull, 68-70. *Honors & Awards:* Accesit Prize, Span Embassy, 62. *Mem:* Am Asn Teachers Span; SCent Mod Lang Asn. *Res:* Spanish literature, especially 17th century fiction; Mexican literature; Spanish American literature. *Publ:* Auth, Jose Maria Roa Barcena: Champion of Catholicism, The Americas, 7/49; Francisco Santos' Indebtedness to Gracian, 50 & Universal pursuit, In: Tex Quart Studies, 65, Univ Tex; Concha Urquiza: Mexican poetess, SCent Mod Lang Asn Bull Studies Issue, winter 72. *Mailing Add:* Dept of Span Tex Christian Univ Ft Worth TX 76129

HAMMOND, MASON, b Boston, Mass, Feb 14, 03; m 35; c 3. ROMAN HISTORY, LATIN LITERATURE. *Educ:* Harvard Univ, AB, 25; Oxford Univ, BA, 27, BLitt, 30. *Hon Degrees:* LHD, St Bonaventure Univ, 78. *Prof Exp:* From instr to Pope prof, 28-73, EMER POPE PROF, LATIN LANG & LIT, HARVARD UNIV, 73- *Concurrent Pos:* From instr to prof, Radcliffe Col, 28-42; prof in charge class studies, Am Acad Rome, 37-39 & 55-57, vis prof, 51-52 & 63; actg dir, Villa I Tatti, Harvard Ctr Renaissance Studies, Florence, Italy, 72 & 73; vis prof classics, Univ Wis-Madison, 74; emer trustee, Am Acad Rome & St Mark's Sch; trustee, Isabella Stewart Gardner Mus, Boston. *Mem:* Am Philol Asn; Archaeol Inst Am; Am Acad Arts & Sci; hon mem Ger Archaeol Inst. *Res:* Roman history; Latin literature. *Publ:* Auth, The Augustan Principate, 33 & Russell, 68, co-ed, Plautus, Menaechmi, 33 & rev ed, 68, auth, City-State and World State, etc, 51 & Biblo & Tannen, 66, Harvard; The Antonine Monarch, Am Acad Rome, 57; coauth, From Aeneas to Augustus, 62 & 2nd ed, 67, ed, Plautus, Miles, 63 & rev ed, 69, coauth, The City in the Ancient World, 72 & auth, Latin: A Historical and Linguistic Handbook, 76, Harvard. *Mailing Add:* Widener Libr H Cambridge MA 02138

HAMMOND, ROBERT M, b July 22, 43; US citizen. LINGUISTICS, PHONETICS. *Educ:* Univ Wis, BA, 67; Fla Atlantic Univ, MA, 73; Univ Fla, PhD(ling), 76. *Prof Exp:* Asst prof Span ling & English, Univ Interam San German, PR, 75-77; asst prof Span & ling, Univ Fla, 77-80 & Boston Univ, 80-81; ASST PROF LANG & LING, MIAMI-DADE COMMUNITY COL, 81- *Mem:* Ling Soc Am; Asoc Ling Filol Am Latina; Asn Can Ling; MLA; Am Asn Phonetic Sci. *Res:* Phonological theory; Spanish linguistic; second language acquisition. *Publ:* Auth, Phonemic restructuring of voiced obstruents in Miami-Cuban Spanish, 1975 Colloquium Hisp Ling, 76; An experimental verifiction of the phonemic status of open and closed vowels in Caribbean Spanish, Corrientes actuales en la Dialectologia del Caribe Hispanico, 78; The velar nasal in rapid Cuban Spanish, Colloquium Hisp Luso-Brazilian Ling, 79; Restricciones semanticas y/o sintacticas en la elision de /s/ en el espanol cubano, Boletin Acad Puertorriquena lengua espanola, 7-2: 41-57; The stratifiation of the velar R in the Spanish of Puerto Rico, Secol Rev, 4-2: 60-71; Weakening chains and relative syllable strength postion in Caribbean Spanish, Contemp Studies Romance Lang, 80; Las variantes foneticas del fonema /s/ en el habla rapida del espanol cubano, Dialecotlgia hispanam-estudios contemp, 80; Dequera la yuta: Capia la bufosina!, Kanina, 4-1: 119-25. *Mailing Add:* Div de Estudios Bilingues Miami-Dade Community Col Miami FL 33135

HAMMOND, ROBERT MORRIS, b New York, NY, Dec 29, 20; m 43; c 2. LANGUAGE & LITERATURE. *Educ:* Univ Rochester, BA, 42; Yale Univ, MA, 47, PhD, 52. *Prof Exp:* From instr to asst prof French, Univ Ariz, 50-63, assoc prof romance lang & lit, 63-67; vis prof French lit & cinema, Wells Col, 67-68; chmn dept int commun & cult, 68-77, PROF FRENCH LIT & CINEMA, STATE UNIV NY COL CORTLAND, 68- *Concurrent Pos:* Cur, Hammond Collection French & Mex Filmscripts, 68-; Nat Endowment for Humanities grants, 70-72; NY State res scholar, 71-72. *Mem:* MLA; Northeast Mod Lang Asn; Univ Film Asn; Soc for Cinema Studies; Am Asn Teachers Fr. *Res:* Eighteenth century French literature; filmscripts as literature and for language learning; Cocteau as cineaste. *Publ:* Coauth, Creative French, Harper, 68; ed, Beauty and the Beast, NY Univ, 70; auth, The bride wore black, Kans Quart, spring 72; The mysteries of Cocteau's Orpheus, Cinema J, spring 72; Jensen's Gradiva: A clue to the composition of Cocteau's Orpheee, Symposium, spring 72; co-ed, Macario, Blanchard, 73; auth, The authenticity of the filmscript: Cocteau's Beauty and the Beast, Style, fall 75; The father of Cousin, Cousine, and interview with Jean-Charles Tacchella, Film & Lit, winter 78. *Mailing Add:* Dept of Int Commun & Cult State Univ of NY Cortland NY 13045

HAMP, ERIC PRATT, b London, England, Nov 16, 20; nat US; m 51. LINGUISTICS. *Educ:* Amherst Col, BA, 42; Harvard Univ, MA, 48, PhD(ling), 54. *Hon Degrees:* LHD, Amherst Col, 72. *Prof Exp:* Chief lend-lease, Govt Union SAfrica, 42-46; from instr to assoc prof, 50-62, chmn, Dept Ling, 66-69, PROF INDO-EUROP LING, UNIV CHICAGO, 62-, PROF BEHAV SCI, 71-, PROF SLAVIC LANG, 80-, DIR, CTR BALKAN & SLAVIC STUDIES, 65- *Concurrent Pos:* Vis lectr, Univ Mich, 53, Univ Wash, 62, Europe, 65-67 & 73-78 & US cult exchange lectr, Univ Bucharest, USSR, 75 & 76; Fulbright res scholar, Greece, 55-56 & Fulbright-Hays fel, Copenhagen Univ, 66-67; mem staff, Gaelic Dialect Surv, Edinburgh, 56-58; secy comt lang prog, Am Coun Learned Soc, 59-63, chmn, 63-69; Am Coun Learned Soc-Soc Sci Res Coun grant Albanian res, Greece & Yugoslavia, 60-61; mem, Nat Sci Found Sem Comput Ling, Rand Corp, 63; mem, Comt Automatic Lang Processing, Nat Acad Sci-Nat Res Coun, 64- & Comt Ling Info, Ctr Appl Ling, 64-68; vis prof, Ind Univ, 64, Univ Belgrade, 64 & 67, Univ Ill, 68 & Univ Salzburg, 79 & 82; mem, Comt Hist & Theory Ling, Ind Univ Press, 65-73, Adv Comt East Europ Coun Int Exchange Scholars, 66-78, Comt Lang & Lit, Ctr Neo-Hellenic Studies, 67-78, US Nat Comn, UNESCO, 72-78 & Phillips Fund Comt, Am Philos Soc, 77-; chmn, Comt Ill Place-Name Surv, 66-; consult, US Off Educ, 66-72, Harper & Row, 71-, Nat Endowment for Humanities, 76-82, Nat Sci Found Subcomt Linguistics, 77-79 & Am Printing House for Blind, 77-; adv, Encycl Britannica, 69-; assoc ed, Int J Am Ling, 69-; vis scholar, Inst Arts & Humanistic Studies, Pa State Univ, 69; Guggenheim fel, 73-74. *Honors & Awards:* Ling Soc Am Collitz prof, Univ Tex, 60; Vernam Hull lectr Celtic studies, Harvard Univ, 71; Innaugural lectr, Ctr Celtic Studies, Aberystwyth, 79. *Mem:* Fel Am Acad Arts & Sci; Am Philos Soc; Ling Soc Am (vpres, 63 & 70, pres, 71); MLA; fel Am Anthrop Asn. *Res:* General linguistics; Indo-European language and culture; Celtic, Balkan and Amerindian languages. *Publ:* Auth, A Glossary of American Technical Linguistic Usage 1925-1950, Spectrum, Ultrecht, 57, 63 & 3rd rev ed, 66; coauth, Readings in Linguistics II, Univ Chicago, 66; auth, Albanian, In: Vol IX, Current Trends in Linguistics, 72; Problems of Multilingualism in Small Linguistic Communities, Georgetown Round Table, 78; A Glance from Here On, The Languages of Native America, 79; Indo-European *g^{w}en-H_a, Kuhns Zeitschrift, 79; Imbolc, Oimelc, Studia Celtica, 80; IE *( )kuon-dog, Indogermanische Forschungen, 80. *Mailing Add:* Dept of Ling Univ of Chicago Chicago IL 60637

HAMPARES, KATHERINE J, b Grand Rapids, Mich, May 24, 32. SPANISH LANGUAGE, LATIN AMERICAN LITERATURE. *Educ:* Univ Mich, BA, 55, MA, 56; Univ Vallodolid, Dipl de Espanol, 63; Columbia Univ, PhD(Latin Am lit), 68. *Prof Exp:* Assoc prof Span & French & chmn dept, Jersey City State Col, 61-67; asst prof Span & undergrad coordr, NY Univ, 67-69; chmn mod lang, Finch Col, 69-72; asst prof, 72-76, chmn Romance lang dept, 75-77, ASSOC PROF SPAN, BARUCH COL, 76- *Concurrent Pos:* Span lang & cult instr, Anti-poverty Prog, State of NJ, 65-67; Nat Endowment for Humanities grant, 76. *Mem:* MLA; Am Asn Teachers Span & Port; Am Coun Teaching Foreign Lang; Am Asn Univ Women; AAUP. *Res:* Spanish linguistics; Latin American literature; Spanish literature. *Publ:* Coauth, Spanish Graduate School Foreign Language Test Book, 68, Graduate Reading Examination in Spanish, 69 & Spanish: 3100 Steps to Master Vocabulary, 70, Arco; auth, Spanish 2400: A Programmed Review of Spanish Grammar, Harper, 71, rev ed, 80; Miguel Angel Asturias and Romulo Gallegos: Two Views of the North American Businessman, Inter-Am Rev, 72; coauth, Spanish: A Modular Approach (3 vols), Harper, 76, rev ed, 81; Paso a Paso, Holt, 78; contribr, Der Nordamerikanische Geschaftsmann im Sudamerikanischen Roman, In: Die Historischen und Kulturellen Ursachen Eines Stereotyps, Vanenhoeck & Ruprecht, 78. *Mailing Add:* Dept of Romance Lang Baruch Col 17 Lexington Ave New York NY 10011

HAMPLE, DALE J, Speech, Communication. See Vol II

HAMPTON, WARREN REED, b Havana, Cuba, Oct 30, 26; US citizen; m 64; c 2. SPANISH & PORTUGUESE. *Educ:* Tulane Univ, BA, 47, PhD(Span), 71 Univ Miss, MA, 65. *Prof Exp:* Prof English & bus, Havana Bus Univ, 54-60; instr English & Span, Jefferson Mil Col, Natchez, 61-62, 63-64; asst mgr, Cordell Hull Found, New Orleans, 62-63; instr Span & Port, Tulane Univ, 68-69; instr, 69-71, asst prof, 71-80, ASSOC PROF SPAN, UNIV SFLA, 80- *Mem:* MLA; Am Asn Teacher Span & Port. *Res:* Modern Spanish peninsular literature; general literary criticism; methods of language instruction. *Publ:* Auth, La critica literaria de Ortega y Gasset, 71 & La teoria de la novela en las Meditaciones del Quijote, 73, Lang Quart. *Mailing Add:* Dept of Mod Lang Univ of SFla Tampa FL 33620

HAN, MIEKO SHIMIZU, b Tokyo, Japan, Mary 28, 29; m 55; c 1. LINGUSITICS, ORIENTAL LANGUAGES. *Educ:* Tsuda Col, Japan, BA, 50; Austin Col, BA, 53; Univ Tex, MA, 59, PhD, 61. *Prof Exp:* Instr French & Japanese, Univ Tex, 60-61; asst prof Orient lang, Univ Calif, Los Angeles, 61-64; assoc prof Asian studies & ling, 64-70, PROF E ASIAN LANG & CULT, UNIV SOUTHERN CALIF, 70- *Concurrent Pos:* Sr fel, Japan Found, 73. *Mem:* Ling Soc Am; Am Orient Soc; MLA; Phonetic Soc Japan; Asn Teachers Japanese. *Res:* Teaching English as a second language; phonetics; teaching Japanese as a foreign language. *Publ:* Auth, Modern Japanese, Mikado Publ, 61; Japanese Phonology, An Analysis Based Upon Sound Spectrograms, Kenkyusha, Tokyo, 62; coauth, A Resonance Theory for Linguistics, Mouton, 62. *Mailing Add:* Dept of E Asian Lang & Cult Univ of Southern Calif Los Angeles CA 90007

HAN, PIERRE, English, Comparative Literature. See Vol II

HANAK, MIROSLAV JOHN, b Plzen, Czech, May 16, 26; US citizen. ROMANCE LANGUAGES, COMPARATIVE LITERATURE. *Educ:* Univ Ill, Urbana, BA, 51; Univ Southern Caif, MA, 64; Univ Madrid, PhD(Span, philos), 65. *Prof Exp:* Instr Span, French & English, Mt St Mary's Col, 62-63; asst prof Span, Ger & comp lit, Nev Southern Univ, 65-68; assoc prof foreign lang, 68-73, PROF SPAN & PHILOS, E TEX STATE UNIV, 73- *Mem:* MLA; Am Comp Lit Asn. *Res:* Comparative literature studies, especially European Baroque; Nietzche's philosophy and Spanish thought of the late 19th and 20th centuries; Faulkner and the thought of Schopenhauer and Bergson. *Publ:* Auth, The Symbolic Drama of Maurice Maeterlinck: A Leap into Transcendence, Peeters, Louvain, Belg, 74; An English Prose Version of Gongora's Polifemo, In: Allegorica, Univ Tex, Arlington, 76; Dostoevsky's Diary of a Writer: A Vision of Plato's Erotic Immortality, Beartracks, 12/77; Dostoevsky Versus Tolstoy: The Problem of Subjective Nihilism, Canadian-American Studies, Vol 12, No 3; Move Over, Android, Realia, Inst Advanced Philosphic Res, Univ Colo, 11/79; An Answer to A A Anderson's Modest Proposal, Relia, 3/80; The Jaianz de Malprose in the Chanson de Roland, Academia de Buenas Artes, Barcelona, Spain, spring 82; The Lyrical Poetry of Heine and Becquer, Third Louisiana Conf Hispanic Studies, 2/82. *Mailing Add:* Dept of Foreign Lang E Tex State Univ Commerce TX 75429

HANAN, PATRICK DEWES, b NZ, Jan 4, 27; m 51; c 1. CHINESE LITERATURE. *Educ:* Univ NZ, BA, 48, MA, 49; Univ London, BA, 53, PhD(Chinese lit), 60. *Prof Exp:* Lectr Chinese, Sch Orient & African Studies, Univ London, 54-63; from assoc prof to prof, Stanford Univ, 63-68; PROF CHINESE LIT, HARVARD UNIV, 68- *Mem:* Asn Asian Studies; Am Orient Soc. *Res:* Chinese literature; comparative literature. *Mailing Add:* Dept of Far Eastern Lang Harvard Univ 2 Divinity Ave Cambridge MA 02138

HANAWALT, EMILY ALBU, b Canton, Ohio, Nov 21, 45; m 68; c 1. MEDIEVAL LITERATURE & HISTORY. *Educ:* Col Wooster, BA, 67; Univ Calif, Berkeley, MA, 69, PhD(comp lit), 75. *Prof Exp:* Instr lit, Chaminade Col Honolulu, 72-73; instr class studies, 74-75, ASST PROF CLASS STUDIES, BOSTON UNIV, 75-, ACAD COORDR, DIV RELIG STUDIES, 82- *Concurrent Pos:* Fac fel, Bunting Inst, Radcliffe Col, 77-79. *Mem:* Am Philol Asn; Byzantine Studies Conf; Class Asn New England; Mediaeval Acad Am. *Res:* Norman historiography; classical language and literature; 12th century. *Publ:* Auth, A note on William IX, Arion, 76; A review of Empress Athenais-Eudoica by Jeanne Tsatsos, Greek Orthodox Theol Rev, fall 77; Norman historiography, 78 & The medieval world: The Norman view, 79, Bunting Inst Working Papers; The Suda on the pagan gods, East Europ Quart, winter 79; An annotated bibliography of Byzantine sources in English translation, Byzantine Studies & Etudes Byzantines, 82; Vita: Anna Comnena, Harvard Mag, 3-4/82. *Mailing Add:* Div of Relig Studies Boston Univ Boston MA 02215

HANAWAY, WILLIAM LIPPINCOTT, JR, b New York, NY, Sept 22, 29; m 59; c 1. PERSIAN LANGUAGE & LITERATURE. *Educ:* Amherst Col, BA, 51; Columbia Univ, MS, 59, MA, 66, PhD(Iranian studies), 70. *Prof Exp:* Instr Persian & Isalmic civilization, Columbia Univ, 68-70, asst prof Persian lang & lit, 70-71; asst prof, 71-76, ASSOC PROF PERSIAN LANG & LIT, UNIV PA, 76-, CHMN, ORIENT STUDIES DEPT, 81- *Concurrent Pos:* Ed, Edebiyat, 76- *Mem:* Royal Asiatic Soc; Am Inst Iranian Studies (secy, 71-73, vpres, 77-79, pres, 79-); Am Orient Soc; Mid E Studies Asn NAm; Soc Iranian Studies. *Res:* Persian popular literature; pre-Safavid Persian inscriptions. *Publ:* Auth, Formal elements in the Persian popular romances, Rev Nat Lit, 71; The concept of the hunt in Persian literature, Bull Boston Mus Fine Arts, 71; contribr, The Nationality Question in Soviet Central Asia, Praeger, 73; auth, Love and War, Scholars' Facsimiles & Reprints, 74; conbribr, The Islamic Garden, Dumbarton Oaks, 76; The Study of the Middle East, John Wiley, 76; auth, The Pre-Safavid Inscriptions of Khorasan, Vol I, Lund Humphries, London, 77; contribr, The Heroic Epic, Ind Univ, 78. *Mailing Add:* Dept of Oriental Studies 841 Williams Hall CU Univ of Pa Philadelphia PA 19104

HAND, WAYLAND D, b Auckland, NZ, Mar 19, 07; US citizen; m 32, 57; c 3. GERMAN, FOLKLORE. *Educ:* Univ Utah, AB, 33, MA, 34; Univ Chicago, PhD, 36. *Prof Exp:* Ger examr, Univ Chicago, 34-36; instr Ger, Univ Minn, 36-37; from instr to prof, 37-74, chmn dept Ger lang, 47-50, chmn folklore group, 54-59, dir ctr comp folklore & mythology, 60-74, EMER PROF GER & FOLKLORE, UNIV CALIF, LOS ANGELES, 76- *Concurrent Pos:* Guggenheim fel, 52-53, 60-61; ed, Am Folklore Soc J, 47-51; ed, Western Folklore, 54-66; collabr, Int Volkskundliche Bibliog; trustee, Am Folklife Ctr, 76-82, chmn, 76-77. *Honors & Awards:* SIV Int Folklore Prize, 65; Knight First Class, Order of the Lion of Finland, 72. *Mem:* Am Folklore Soc (pres, 57-59); MLA; Am Dialect Soc; hon mem Brit Folklore Soc. *Res:* American popular beliefs and superstitions; folk medicine; American mining folklore. *Publ:* Auth, American folklore after seventy years, J Am Folklore, 59; co-ed, Humaniora: Essays in Literature, Folklore and Bibliography Honoring Archer Taylor on his Seventieth Birthday, 60; ed, Popular Beliefs and Superstitions from North Carolina (2 vols), 61-64; American Folk Legend, 71, American Folk Medicine, 76, Magical Medicine, 80 & co-ed (with Anna Casetta and Sondra Thiederman), Popular Beliefs and Superstitions: A Commpendium of American Folklore from the Ohio Collection of Newbell Niles Puckett (3 vols), 81, Univ Calif Press. *Mailing Add:* Ctr Comp Folklore & Mythology Kinsey Hall 76 Univ of Calif Los Angeles CA 90024

HANDELMAN, SUSAN ANN, Literary Criticism, Jewish Literature. See Vol II

HANDELSMAN, MICHAEL H, b Weehawken, NJ, May 11, 48; m 71; c 1. SPANISH. *Educ:* Gettysburg Col, AB, 70; Univ Fla, MA, 73, PhD(Span), 76. *Prof Exp:* ASST PROF SPAN, UNIV TENN, 76- *Mem:* MLA; Am Asn Teachers Span & Port; Latin Am Studies Asn; Inst Int Lit Iberoam; S Atlantic Mod Lang Asn. *Res:* Ecuadorian women writers; Latin American narrative. *Publ:* Auth, Amazonas y Artistas: Un Estudio de Las Escritoras de Prosa del Ecuador, Casa de la Cult Ecuatoriana, 78; coauth, La Cultura Hispana: Dentro y Fuera de los Estados Unidos, Random House, 81; auth, El Modernismo en las Revistas Literarias del Ecuador: 1895-1930, 81 & ed, Diez Escritoras Ecuatorianas y sus Cuentos (in press), Casa De La Cultura Ecuatoriana. *Mailing Add:* Dept of Romance Lang Univ of Tenn Knoxville TN 37916

HANDSCOMBE, RICHARD JAMES, English. See Vol II

HANGIN, JOHN GOMBOJAB, b Inner Mongolia, Chahar, China, Apr 3, 21; US citizen; m 44; c 3. MONGOLIAN LANGUAGE & CIVILIZATION. *Educ:* Hokkaido Univ, Dipl, 41; Columbia Univ, MA, 63; Ind Univ, Bloomington, PhD(Altaic studies), 70. *Prof Exp:* Instr gen sci, Mongolian Reconstruct Sch, Kalgan, 42-44; secy, Pres Off, Inner Mongolia, 44-45; rep to Nat Assembly, Repub China, Nanking, 47; res assoc Mongolian, Georgetown Univ, 52-54; res linguist, Univ Calif, Berkeley, 56-59; lectr Mongolian, Columbia Univ, 60-63; asst prof, 64-75, assoc prof Mongolian, 75-81, PROF URALIC & ALTAIC STUDIES, IND UNIV, BLOOMINGTON, 82-, DIR MONGOLIA STUDIES PROG, 78- *Concurrent Pos:* Exec dir, Mongolia Soc, Inc, 61- *Mem:* Asn Asian Studies; AAUP; Mongolia Soc Inc. *Res:* Mongolian linguistics; Mongolian literature and civilization; Sino-Mongol, Soviet-Mongol relations. *Publ:* Coauth, Mongolia-English Dictionary, Univ Calif, 60; auth, Basic Course in Mongolian, 68 & English-Mongolian Dictionary, 70, In: Uralic and Altaic series, Ind Univ; Tumed manuscript of the Koke Sudar, Cent Asiatic J, 71; Analecta Mongolica, Mongolia Soc, 72; Köke Sudar (the Blue Chronicle), a study of the first Mongolian historical novel by Injannasi, In: Asiatische Forschungen Series Band 38, Otto Harrassowitz, Wiesbaden, 73; Intermediate Mongolian, In: Uralic and Altaic series, Ind Univ, 73; ed & contrib, Köke Sudor Nova, Part I, (Injannasi's manuscript of the expanded version of his Blue Chronicle), Otto Harrassowitz, Wiesbaden (in prep). *Mailing Add:* 101 Goodboy Hall Ind Univ Bloomington IN 47401

HANKAMER, JORGE, b Alvin, Tex, Sept 12, 40. LINGUISTICS. *Educ:* Rice Univ, BA, 62, MA, 66; Yale Univ, PhD(ling), 71. *Prof Exp:* Fel ling, Mass Inst Technol, 71-73; asst prof, Tufts Univ, 72-73; asst prof, Harvard Univ, 73-78, assoc prof ling, 78-80; ASSOC PROF LING, UNIV CALIF, SANTA CRUZ, 80- *Concurrent Pos:* Ed, Ling Inquiry, squibs & discussions, 75-77 & Dissertations in Ling ser, Garland Publ Co, 75-; vis asst prof ling, Bogazici Univ, Istanbul, 76-77; assoc ed, Language, 81- *Mem:* Ling Soc Am; New Eng Ling Soc. *Res:* Syntax and semantics of natural language; Turkish syntax. *Publ:* Auth, Unacceptable ambiguity, 73 & coauth, Deep and surface anaphora, 76, Ling Inquiry; auth, On the interpretation of anaphoric expressions, Georgetown Univ Round Table, 76; Multiple analysis, In: Mechanisms of Syntactic Change, 77; coauth, Ambiguity, Encycl Einandi, 78. *Mailing Add:* Bd Studies in Ling Stevenson Col Santa Cruz CA 95064

HANKEY, CLYDE THOMAS, Linguistics, English Language. See Vol II

HANKS, JOYCE MAIN, b St Louis, Mo, Oct 11, 35; m 61; c 2. FRENCH RENAISSANCE POETRY. *Educ:* Washington Univ, St Louis, AB, 57, PhD(French), 77; Univ Wis, MA, 59. *Prof Exp:* Prof French, Wheaton Col, 59-61; ASSOC PROF FRENCH, UNIVERSIDAD DE COSTA RICA, 70- *Mem:* MLA; Am Asn Teachers Fr. *Res:* Ronsard; Bible in French literature; image of women in French literature. *Publ:* Auth, Ronsard's debt to Marot in L'Hymne de la Mort, L'Esprit Createur, 72; Una sorpresa en los poemas de amor de Ronsard, 72, Los primeros poemas biblicos de Ronsard, 72 & L'Attitude de Ronsard vis-a-vis de Marot, 73, Revista la Universidad de Costa Rica; Ronsard and Biblical Tradition, Jean Michel Place/Gunter Narr, Tubingen, 82. *Mailing Add:* Apt 10250 1000 San Jose Costa Rica

HANLEY, MARY ESTHER, b Kenora, Ont, June 14, 18. CLASSICS. *Educ:* Univ Toronto, BA, 41, MA, 52; Cornell Univ, PhD(classics), 59; Rosary Col, MALS, 74. *Prof Exp:* Lectr classics, Univ St Michael's Col, 52-56 & 59-60, from asst prof to assoc prof, 60-73; librn & admin asst, Cath Theol Union, 74-75; LIBRN-CATALOGER, UNIV ST MICHAEL'S COL LIBR, 75- *Mem:* Class Asn Can; Am Philol Asn; Am Theol Libr Asn. *Res:* The poet Prudentius. *Publ:* Auth, Prudentius and Juvenal, Phoenix, 61; auth introd & transl, Lorenzo Valla, In Praise of St Thomas Aquinas, In: Renaissance Philosophy, Mouton, The Hague, 73; auth, The Newman Collection of St Michael's College Library, Univ St Michael's Col Libr, 77. *Mailing Add:* Loretto Col 70 St Mary St Toronto ON M5S 1J3 Can

HANLIN, TODD CAMPBELL, b Buchanan, Mich, Nov 9, 41; m 69; c 2. GERMANIC LANGUAGES & LITERATURE. *Educ:* Wabash Col, AB, 64; Univ Kans, AM, 67; Bryn Mawr Col, PhD(Ger), 75. *Prof Exp:* Instr, Col Wooster, 67-71; asst prof, Univ Pa, 75-81; ASST PROF GER, UNIV ARK, FAYETTEVILLE, 81- *Concurrent Pos:* Danforth assoc, Danforth Found, 79-; vis asst prof Haverford Col, 81; Fulbright Comn grant, Ger, 82. *Mem:* MLA; Am Asn Teachers Ger; Deutsche Schillergesellschaft; Int Arthur Schnitzler Res Asn; Kafka Soc Am. *Res:* Twentieth century German literature and culture; comtemporary prose; Franz Kafka. *Publ:* Auth, Franz Kafka: Kunstprobleme, Peter Lang Verlag, 77; Franz Kafka's Landarzt: Und heilt er nicht, Mod Austrian Lit, 78; Kafka as the Hieronymus Bosch of our century, Newslett Kafka Soc, 80; Literature and political prejudice, 81 & Demonic eroticism in Jugendstil, 82, Jahrbuch für Int Germanistik. *Mailing Add:* Foreign Lang Dept Univ of Ark Fayetteville AR 72701

HANNA, BLAKE THOMPSON, b Boston, Mass, Aug 2, 27; m 50; c 3. LINGUISTICS, MODERN LANGUAGES. *Educ:* Bowdoin Col, BA, 48; Univ Montreal, MA, 53, PhD(French), 64. *Prof Exp:* Instr English, Col Stanislas, Montreal, 53-57; from asst prof to assoc prof, 57-69, PROF LING, UNIV MONTREAL, 69- *Concurrent Pos:* Can Coun res grant, 66. *Mem:* MLA; Soc Transl & Interpreters Can (vpres, 67-68); Soc Fr Etude XVIIIe Siecle; Am Soc 18th Century Studies; Can Soc 18th Century Studies. *Res:* Translating and interpreting; 18th century French literature; teaching English as a second language. *Publ:* Auth, Oral comprehension, 6/66 & Patterns of thought in English translation, 9/72, Meta; contribr, Eighteenth century studies presented to Arthur M Wilson, Univ Press New Eng, 72; contribr, Diderot, Oeuvres Completes (vol I), Hermann, Paris, 75; auth, Diderot theologien, Rev His Lit France, 1-2/78; contribr, Vingt-cing ans de linguistique au Canada, Montreal Ctr Educ et Culturel, 79. *Mailing Add:* Sch of Transl Univ Montreal PO Box 6128 Br A Montreal PQ H3C 3J7 Can

HANNA, SAMI A, b Al-Fayum, Egypt, Oct 3, 27; m 63; c 2. FOREIGN LANGUAGES, COMPARATIVE EDUCATION. *Educ:* Cairo Univ, BA, 48; Ain Shams Univ, Cairo, BEd, 50; Hunter Col, MS, 56; Columbia Univ, MA, 58; Univ Utah, PhD(educ & Mid E studies), 64; Univ Ill, EdCA, 64. *Prof Exp:* From instr to asst prof, 63-68, ASSOC PROF LANG, UNIV UTAH, 68-, DIR N AFRICA PROG & ASST DIR MID E CTR, 67- *Concurrent Pos:* Consult Ann Arabic Teachers Workship, Univ Mich, 65, Columbia Univ, 66, Princeton Univ, 67, State Dept Tunisian Prog, 67 & Weidner Commun; admin, Mod Lang Div, Porta Plants, Inc. *Mem:* Am Asn Teachers Arabic (exec secy, 63-); Am Acad Arts & Sci; Am Coun Teaching For Lang. *Res:* Contemporary changes in the Middle East; methods of teaching foreign languages; comparative education. *Publ:* Auth, First Year Arabic Qualifying Examination, College Level, 64, ed & translr, Issues in University Education: Commentaries by Arab University Educators, 64 & 66 & auth, Laboratory Handbook, 65, Univ Utah; Writing Arabic, A Linguistic Approach from Sounds to Script, Univ Utah, 65 & Leiden, 69; Beginnning Arabic, Univ Utah, 65 & Leiden, 69; Education and Arab Socialism, Proc Phi Delta Kappa, 67; The Mawwal in Egyptian folklore, J Am Folklore, 67; Al-Afghani: A pioneer of Islamic socialism, Muslim World, Vol LVII, No 1; Arab Socialism: A Documentary Survey, Leiden, 69. *Mailing Add:* Mid E Ctr Univ of Utah Salt Lake City UT 84112

HANNAH, RICHARD WARREN, b Seattle, Wash, July 7, 50; m 76. GERMAN LITERATURE, PHILOSOPHY. *Educ:* Stanford Univ, MA, 72, MA, 77, PhD(Ger), 79. *Prof Exp:* Asst prof Ger, Ohio State Univ, 79-81; RES & WRITING, 81- *Honors & Awards:* Publ Award, Ohio State Univ, 81. *Mem:* MLA; Ling Soc Am; Am Asn Teachers Ger; Am Lit Transl Asn. *Res:* Romanticism; German idealism; literary theory. *Publ:* Auth, the Fichtean Dynamic of Novalis' Poetics, Peter Lang, Bern, 81; The Tortures of the Idyll: Jean Paul's Wutz and the loss of presence, Ger Rev, fall 81; A translation course for science majors, Die Unterrichts praxis, fall 81; A broken heart and the accusing flame: The tension of imagery and the ambivalence of political commitment in Heine's Deutschland ein Wintermärchen, Colloquia Germanica, 82; Carlyle Novalis and the metaphysics of semeiosis, Proc Univ Houston, 3rd Symp Lit, 82. *Mailing Add:* 231 Manitoba Ave Wayzata MN 55391

HANRAHAN, THOMAS G, b Petersburg, Va, Dec 26, 26; m 74. SPANISH LITERATURE. *Educ:* Gonzaga Univ, MA, 54; San Francisco de Borja, Barcelona, STL, 61; Univ Madrid, lic Romance philol, 63, Dr Romance philol, 66. *Prof Exp:* Asst prof, 66-70, assoc prof, 70-80, PROF SPAN, LOYOLA MARYMOUNT UNIV, 80-, CHMN DEPT MOD LANG, 71- *Concurrent Pos:* Vis prof Span, Calif State Univ, Northridge, 73-74. *Mem:* MLA; Conf Latin Am Hist; Philol Asn Pac Coast; AAUP. *Res:* Spanish picaresque novel; Spanish Jesuit school drama 16th and 17th centuries; Mexican Jesuit school drama 17th century. *Publ:* Auth, La mujer en la novela picaresca de Mateo Aleman, 64 & La mujer en la novela picaresa espanola (2 vols), 67, Porrua, Madrid; Sin, the Celestina and Inigo Lopez de Loyola, Romance Notes, 3/69; El Tocotin expresion de identidad, Rev Iberoam, 3/70; Dos Desconocidas Comedias des Siglo XVII, In: Los Jesuitas en Mexico: Cuatro Siglos de Labor Cultural, 72-73. *Mailing Add:* Dept of Mod Lang Loyola Marymount Univ Los Angeles CA 90045

HANREZ, MARC, b Brussels, Belgium, Aug 15, 34. ROMANCE LANGUAGES. *Educ:* Free Univ Brussels, Lic en Philos et Lett & Agrege, 58; Univ Paris, VsI, Dr 3e Cycle(lett mod), 73. *Prof Exp:* Asst prof Romance lang, Univ Mass, Amherst, 67-70; assoc prof, 70-76, PROF FRENCH, UNIV WIS-MADISON, 76- *Concurrent Pos:* Guggenheim fel, 72-73. *Mem:* MLA; Am Asn Teachers Fr; AAUP. *Res:* Contemporary French literature, especially Abellio, Celine, Drieu la Rochelle, Malraux, Proust; the war fiction, ideology and fine arts. *Publ:* Auth, Le dernier Drieu, Fr Rev, 70; Malraux L'Espoir Goya, Rev Belles-Lett, 72; poetry, Lett Nouvelles, 72 & Rev Belles-Lett, 72; Champs des signes/Chant du cygne, In: Marcel Proust: A Critical Panorama, 73; ed, Les ecrivains et la guerre d'Espagne, Dossiers H, Paris, 75; auth, Sous les signes d'Abellio, L'Age d'Homme, Lausanne, 76; poetry, Tel quel, 77. *Mailing Add:* Dept of French & Ital Univ of Wis Madison WI 53706

HANSEN, CARL VICTOR, b West Haven, Conn, May 16, 19; m 45; c 4. GERMAN. *Educ:* Yale Univ, PhD(Ger), 52. *Prof Exp:* Instr Ger, Ind Univ, 50-53; asst prof, Univ RI, 53-56; asst prof Ger, 56-62, ASSOC PROF MOD LANG, TRINITY COL, CONN, 62- *Concurrent Pos:* Fulbright exchange teacher, 2nd Bundesreal gymnasium, Innsbruck, Austria, 59-60; consult Ger teaching, St Joseph Col, Conn, 69-70. *Mem:* Am Asn Teachers Ger. *Res:* Germanic philogy; general linguistics; the German Novelle. *Publ:* Coauth, Tourists' English, Pädagogisches Inst für Tirol, 60; auth, German Review Grammar with Exercises, Trinity Col, 63; The death of first Sergeant Anton Lerch in Hofmannsthal's Reitergeschichte: A military analysis, Mod Austrian Lit, Vol 13, 80. *Mailing Add:* Box 1328 Trinity Col Summit St Hartford CT 06106

HANSEN, ELAINE TUTTLE, Old English Language & Literature. See Vol II

HANSEN, THOMAS SVEND, b New Haven, Conn, Feb 1, 47; m 74. GERMAN LANGUAGE & LITERATURE. *Educ:* Tufts Univ, BA, 69, MA, 71; Harvard Univ, PhD(Ger), 77. *Prof Exp:* ASST PROF GER, WELLESLEY COL, 77- *Mem:* MLA; Northeast Mod Lang Asn; Schiller-Gesellschaft. *Res:* Twentieth century German literature; German exile literature, 1933-1945; history of publishing and the book trade. *Publ:* Auth, Kurt Bauchwitz: Exilautor sucht einen Charakter & Rudolf Kayser, In: Duetsche Exilliterature, Francke, Bern, 79. *Mailing Add:* Dept of Ger Wellesley Col Wellesley MA 02181

HANSEN, WILLIAM FREEMAN, b Fresno, Calif, June 22, 41; m 72; c 1. CLASSICAL STUDIES, FOLKLORE. *Educ:* Univ Calif, Berkeley, BA, 65, PhD(classics), 70. *Prof Exp:* Asst prof, 70-77, ASSOC PROF CLASSICS, IND UNIV, BLOOMINGTON, 77- *Concurrent Pos:* Fel, Folklore Inst, Ind Univ, Bloomington, 70-, Younger Humanist, Nat Endowment Humanities, 72-73 & Am Coun Learned Soc, 77-78. *Mem:* Am Philol Asn; Class Asn Mid West & South; Am Folklore Soc; Int Soc Folk-Narrative Res. *Res:* Early Greek epic; classical mythology; comparative study of the folktale. *Publ:* Auth, The Conference Sequence: Patterned Narration in the Odyssey, Univ Calif Publ Class Studies, Vol 8, 72; contribr, Folklore Today: A Festschrift for Richard M Dorson, Res Ctr Lang & Semiotic Studies, Ind Univ, 76; auth, Odysseus' Last Journey, Quaderni Urbinati di Cult Classica, Vol 24, 77; An oral source for the Menaechmi, Class World, Vol 70, 77; contribr, The Heroic Epic and Saga, Ind Univ Press, 78; Folklore on Two Continents: Essays in Honor of Linda Degh, Trickster Press, 80; auth, Saxo Grammaticus and the Life of Hamlet, Univ Nebr Press (in press). *Mailing Add:* Dept of Class Studies Ind Univ Bloomington IN 47405

HANSON, BLAIR, b Bloomington, Ill, Nov 2, 15. ROMANCE LANGUAGES. *Educ:* Wash Univ, AB, 35; Univ Wis, AM, 36, PhD, 39. *Prof Exp:* Asst French, Univ Wis, 37-39; instr French & Span, Allegheny Col, 39-43, asst prof Romance lang, 43-49, assoc prof mod lang, 49-55, chmn dept, 54-81, prof mod lang, 55-81; RETIRED. *Honors & Awards:* Ordre de Palmes Academiques, 63. *Mem:* Am Asn Teachers Fr; MLA. *Res:* Eighteenth and 20th century French literature; evaluation techniques of Foreign Language in the Elementary School programs and the methodology training of teachers. *Mailing Add:* 7724 Chateau House Meadville PA 16335

HANSON, JOHN ARTHUR, b Charleston, WVa, Mar 5, 31; m 57; c 1. CLASSICS. *Educ:* Univ Mich, Ann Arbor, AB, 51; Princeton Univ, MA, 53, PhD(classics), 56. *Prof Exp:* Instr classics, Univ Mich, 55-58, asst prof, 58-64; assoc prof, 64-73, PROF CLASSICS, PRINCETON UNIV, 73- *Concurrent Pos:* Hodderfel, Coun Humanities, Princeton Univ, 58-59; vis asst prof, Swarthmore Col, 63-64; classicist in residence, Am Acad Rome, 70-71. *Mem:* Am Philol Asn. *Res:* Latin literature; Roman archaeology. *Publ:* Auth, Roman Theatre-Temples, Princeton, 59; Plautus as a source book for Roman religion, Trans Am Philol Asn, 59; contrib, Roman Drama, Routledge & Kegan Paul, London, 65. *Mailing Add:* Dept of Classics 103 E Pyne Bldg Princeton Univ Princeton NJ 08540

HANSON, KLAUS DIETER, b Berlin, Ger, Oct 14, 39. GERMAN LITERATURE & THEATRE. *Educ:* Muskingum Col, BA, 63; Univ Ill, MA, 67, PhD(Ger), 73. *Prof Exp:* Asst prof Ger, Schiller Col, Ger, 70-71; high sch teacher Ger & English, Lingen/Ems, Ger, 71-73; asst prof Ger, 73-80, ASSOC PROF GER, UNIV WYO, 80- *Mem:* MLA; Rocky Mountain Lang Asn; Pac Northwest Coun Foreign Lang; Am Asn Teachers Ger. *Res:* Baroque literature; modern drama. *Publ:* Auth, Theobald Höck, Schönes Blumenfeld (1601), Bouvier, Bonn, 75. *Mailing Add:* Dept of Mod & Class Lang Univ Wyo Laramie WY 82071

HANZELI, VICTOR EGON, b Hungary, Oct 21, 25; US citizen; m 47; c 5. FRENCH LINGUISTICS, HISTORY OF LINGUISTICS. *Educ:* Univ Budapest, LLB, 47; Ind Univ, MA, 55, PhD, 61. *Prof Exp:* From instr to asst prof, 57-66, assoc prof, 66-82, PROF ROMANCE LANG & LIT, UNIV WASH, 82- *Concurrent Pos:* Asst linguist, Air Force Lang Training Prog, Ind Univ, 55-56; rev ed ling, Mod Lang J, 70-80. *Mem:* Ling Soc Am; Can Cath Hist Asn; Am Coun Teaching Foreign Lang; Int Asn Hungarian Studies; Am Asn Appl Linguists. *Res:* History of linguistic studies in 17th and 18th centuries; French applied linguistics. *Publ:* Auth, The Hungarians: An Area Study, Human Rels Area Files, New Haven, 56; coauth, A Comparative Evaluation of Two Modern Methods for Teaching a Spoken Language, Univ Wash, 60; The Algonkin R-dialect in historical records, Proc Tenth Int Congr Ling, Bucarest, 67; auth, Missionary Linguistics in New France, Mouton, 69; co-ed, Essays on the Teaching of Culture, Heinle & Heinle, 74; English for Academic and Technical Purposes, Newbury House, 81; ed & translr, S Gyarmathi's Affinitas, Benjamins, Amsterdam, 82. *Mailing Add:* Dept of Romance Lang & Lit Univ of Wash Seattle WA 98195

HARARI, JOSUE V, b Cairo, Egypt, 44; US citizen. FRENCH & COMPARATIVE LITERATURE. *Educ:* Brooklyn Col, BA, 67; State Univ NY Buffalo, PhD(comp lit), 74. *Prof Exp:* Instr French & comp lit, Stanford Univ, 71-74; asst prof French, Cornell Univ, 74-79; ASSOC PROF FRENCH, JOHNS HOPKINS UNIV, 79- *Concurrent Pos:* Am Coun Learned Soc fel, 77; Wesleyan Univ sr res fel, 78. *Res:* Eighteenth century French literature; contemporary criticism. *Publ:* Auth, Structuralists and structuralisms: A selected bibliography of French contemporary thought, Diacritics, 71; ed, Textual Strategies: Perspectives in Post-Structuralist Criticism, Cornell Univ, 79; ed, Hermes, Literature, Science, Philosophy, Johns Hopkins Univ, 82. *Mailing Add:* Dept Romance Lang Johns Hopkins Univ Baltimore MD 21218

HARDEE, A MAYNOR, b Conway, SC, Mar 10, 23; m 43; c 1. FRENCH LANGUAGE & LITERATURE. *Educ:* Univ Sc, BA, 47, MA, 48; Univ Calif, Los Angeles, PhD, 63. *Prof Exp:* Instr French & Span, Clemson Col, 48-51; instr French, Duke Univ, 56-60; asst prof, Rollins Col, 60-63; from assoc prof to prof, Tex Technol Col, 63-69; PROF FRENCH, UNIV SC, 69- *Concurrent Pos:* Mem Advan French Test comt, Grad Record Exam, 72; ed, Fr Lit Ser, Univ SC, 75- *Mem:* MLA; Am Asn Teachers Fr; Soc des Amis de Montaigne; SAtlantic Mod Lang Asn. *Res:* Sixteenth century prose fiction and drama; 17th century novel and epistolary art. *Publ:* Auth, Classification of Narrative Motifs in Cent Nouvelles Nouvelles, In: Motif-Index of Folk Literature, Univ Ind, 2nd ed, 55-56; Jean de Lannel and the Pre-Classical French Novel, Droz, 67; Toward a Definition of the French Renaissance Novel, Studies Renaissance, 68; Anthoine de Montchrestien: La Reine d'Escosse (edition critique avec introduction et notes), Cisalpino, Milan, 75; Sur l'art narratif dans lex anecdotes de Montaigne, Bull Soc Amis de Montaigne, 82. *Mailing Add:* Dept of Foreign Lang & Lit Univ of SC Columbia SC 29208

HARDEN, ARTHUR ROBERT, b Folkestone, Kent, England, Apr 29, 19; Can citizen; m 51. FRENCH LITERATURE. *Educ:* Univ Toronto, BA, 49; Columbia Univ, AB, 54; Univ NC, PhD, 58. *Prof Exp:* Asst prof French, Duquesne Univ, 58-60 & Univ BC, 60-63; PROF FRENCH, VICTORIA COL, UNIV TORONTO, 63- *Res:* Anglo-Norman language and literature; Medieval French literature. *Publ:* Auth, Francois Villon and his monetary bequests, Speculum, 58; The coins in Don Quixote, 62 & Aucassin et Nicolette as parody, 66, Studies Philol; La vie in Seint Auban, Anglo-Norman Text Soc, 68. *Mailing Add:* Dept of French Victoria Col Univ of Toronto Toronto ON M5S 1A1 Can

HARDEN, ELIZABETH MCWHORTER, English. See Vol II

HARDER, JAYNE CRANE, English as a Second Language. See Vol II

HARDIN, JAMES NEAL, b Nashville, Tenn, Feb 17, 39. GERMAN & COMPARATIVE LITERATURE. *Educ:* Washington & Lee Univ, AB, 60; Univ NC, Chapel Hill, MA, 64, PhD(Ger & comp lit), 67. *Prof Exp:* Asst Ger, Univ NC, 62-67; from asst prof to assoc prof, 69-73, Ger Acad Exchange Serv grant, 73, PROF GER, UNIV SC, 73- *Concurrent Pos:* Fulbright fel, 60-61; Alexander von Humboldt fel, 74-75. *Mem:* MLA; SAtlantic Mod Lang Asn; Am Asn Teachers Ger; Am Soc Ger Lit 16th & 17th Centuries. *Res:* Sixteenth and 17th century German literature; German Baroque novel; descriptive bibliography. *Publ:* Auth, Theme of salvation in the novels of Hermann Broch, PMLA, 70; George B Shaw's Saint Joan, Diesterweg, 74; Hermann Broch's theories of mass psychology, Ger Quart, 74; Johann Beers Parodie Printz Adimantus, Jahrbuch int Ger, 75; Descriptive bibliography and the works of Johann Beer, Wolfenbütteler Barocknachrichten, 77; ed, Der verliebte Oesterreicher von Johann Beer, Lang, Bern, 78; auth, Eine Beschreibende Bibliographie der Werke Johann Beers, Francke Verlag, 78; Johann Beer, Twayne Series (in press). *Mailing Add:* Dept of Foreign Lang Univ of SC Columbia SC 29208

HARDIN, ROBERT JOSEPH, b Ralls, Tex. ROMANCE LANGUAGES. *Educ:* N Tex State Univ, BA, 50, MA, 56; Univ Ill, PhD(French), 63. *Prof Exp:* From instr to assoc prof, 59-69, PROF FRENCH, N TEX STATE UNIV, 69- *Concurrent Pos:* Fulbright grant, France, 64. *Mem:* MLA; Am Asn Teachers Fr; Am Coun Teachers For Lang. *Res:* French novel. *Mailing Add:* Box 5612 N Tex State Univ Denton TX 76203

HARDMAN-DE-BAUTISTA, MARTHA JAMES, US citizen; m 62; c 2. ANTHROPOLOGICAL LINGUISTICS, ANDEAN LANGUAGES. *Educ:* Univ Utah, BA, 55; Univ NMex, MA, 57; Stanford Univ, PhD, 62. *Prof Exp:* Instr English, Univ de San Marcos, 58; instr ling, Cornell Univ, 61-63, asst coordr, Quechua Prog, 62; trainer of Peace Corps volunteers for Peru, Univ Calif, Los Angeles, 63; asst prof Spanish, Univ Santa Clara, 63-65; prof ling, Univ Nacional Mayor de San Andres, 65-67; dir & founder, Inst Nat Studies Ling, Bolivia, 65-67; vis prof anthrop, Ind Univ, 68; assoc prof, 69-72, PROF ANTHROP & LING, UNIV FLA, 73- *Concurrent Pos:* Dir, Amyara Lang Mat Proj, Ctr Latin Am Studies, 73. *Mem:* Am Anthrop Asn; Ling Soc Am; Soc Humanism & Anthrop; Latin Am Studies Asn. *Res:* Jaqui languages; language contact in the Andes; applied anthropological linguistics. *Publ:* Auth, Jaqaru: Outline of Phonological and Morphological Structure, Mounton, The Hague, 66; Aymara Women, Hanover, 75; coauth, Aymar Ar Yatiqanataki (3 vols), 75; ed, Actas del XXV Congreso Anual Latinoamerican Los Autoctonos American Opinan, State Univ Press Fla, 76; auth, Linguistics postulates and applied anthropoligical linguistics, In: Ruth Hirsch Weir Memorial Volume: Papers on Linguistics & Child Language & co-ed, Ruth Hirsch Weir Memorial Volume: Papers on Linguistics & Child Language, Mouton, The Hague, 76; ed, Aymara Language in its Cultural and Social Context, Univ Fla, 81. *Mailing Add:* Dept of Anthrop Univ Fla Gainesville FL 32601

HARDRE, JACQUES, b Dinan, France, Jan 10, 15; nat US. FRENCH LITERATURE. *Educ:* Guilford Col, AB, 37; Univ NC, Chapel Hill, MA, 42, PhD, 48. *Prof Exp:* Instr Ger & French, Guilford Col, 37-39; from instr to Kenan prof French, 45-77, EMER KENAN PROF FRENCH, UNIV NC, CHAPEL HILL, 77- *Concurrent Pos:* Ed-in-chief, Fr Rev, 68-74. *Honors &*

Awards: Chevalier, Legion d'Honneur, 67; Officer, Order of the Lion, Repub of Senegal, 73; Officer, Palmes Academiques, French Govt, 74. *Mem:* MLA; Am Asn Teachers Fr (pres, 62-67); Soc Fr Prof Am; Mod Humanities Res Asn; Int Fed Prof Fr (pres, 62-67). *Res:* Existentialism; contemporary French literature and civilization; surrealism. *Publ:* Auth, The Letters of Louvois, Univ NC, 49; co-ed, Huis Clos, Appleton, 62; Le Malentendu, Macmillan, 64; ed, Les Enfants Terribles, Blaisdell, 64; La France et sa Civilisation, Dodd, 69. *Mailing Add:* Dept of Romance Lang Univ of NC Dey Hall Chapel Hill NC 27514

HARDY, WILLIAM GEORGE, b Oakwood, Ont, Feb 3, 95; m 19; c 3. LATIN & GREEK LITERATURE. *Educ:* Univ Toronto, BA, 17, MA, 19; Univ Chicago, PhD, 22. *Hon Degrees:* LLD, Univ Alta, 73. *Prof Exp:* Lectr classics, Univ Toronto, ; from lectr to prof, 20-64, head dept, 38-64, EMER PROF CLASSICS, UNIV ALTA, 64- *Honors & Awards:* Nat Award in Lett, 62; Mem, Order Can, 73. *Mem:* Class Asn Can; Can Auth Asn (pres, 50-52 & 68-70); fel Int Inst Arts & Lett. *Res:* Greek and Roman history, especially archaeological findings. *Publ:* Auth, The City of Libertines, Appleton, 57, McClelland & Stewart & Heinemann, Gt Brit, 57; From Sea unto Sea, Doubleday, 60; The Greek and Roman World, Schenkman, US & McClelland & Stewart, 62; ed-in-chief, Alberta: A Natural History, Mismat Corp, Edmonton, 67; auth, Origins and Ordeals of the Western World, Schenkman, US & Copp Clark, Can, 68; The Scarlet Mantle, Macmillan, 78. *Mailing Add:* 9429 83 St Edmonton AB T6C 2Z8 Can

HARKINS, PAUL WILLIAM, b New York, NY, June 17, 11; m 41; c 9. CLASSICAL LANGUAGES. *Educ:* Woodstock Col, AB, 36; Fordham Univ, MA, 42; Univ Mich, MA, 43, PhD, 48. *Hon Degrees:* LLD, St Ambrose Col, 60. *Prof Exp:* Asst prof classics & English, Loyola Col, Md, 37-39 & Sacred Heart Sem, 40-46; asst prof classics & philos, Col Mt St Joseph-on-the-Ohio, 46-49; from asst prof to prof, 49-77, chmn dept, 64-69, EMER PROF CLASS LANG, XAVIER UNIV, OHIO, 77- *Concurrent Pos:* Am Coun Learned Soc grant-in-aid, 62; mem, Int Patristic Conf, Oxford Univ, 63 & 67; prof, Cath Univ Am, 69-70. *Mem:* Int Asn Papyrologists; Am Philol Asn. *Publ:* Auth, St John Chrysostom: Baptismal Instructions, Longmans Green & Newman, 63; coauth, Galen: On the Passions and Errors of the Soul, Ohio State Univ, 63; auth, St John Chrysostom: Discourses Against Judaizing Christians, Cath Univ Am, 78. *Mailing Add:* 820 Yorkhaven Rd Cincinnati OH 45240

HARKINS, WILLIAM E, b State College, Pa, Nov 10, 21. PHILOLOGY, LITERARY HISTORY & CRITICISM. *Educ:* Pa State Univ, BA, 42; Columbia Univ, MA, 46, PhD, 50. *Prof Exp:* Instr Slavic lang, Univ Pa, 48-49; from instr to assoc prof, 49-63, chmn dept Slavic lang, 63-70, dir, Russ Inst, 74-76, PROF SLAVIC LANG, COLUMBIA UNIV, 63- *Concurrent Pos:* Guggenheim Mem fel, 59-60; consult, Nat Endowment for Humanities, 72-75. *Mem:* Am Asn Teachers Slavic & East Europ Lang (pres, 74-76); Am Asn Advan Slavic Studies (treas, 69); Masaryk Inst (pres, 70-73); Ukiyo-E Soc Am (pres, 81-). *Res:* Old Russian literature; Russian folk literature; Czechoslovakian literature. *Publ:* Auth, The Russian Folk Epos in Czech Literature, Kings Crown, 51; Dictionary of Russian Literature, Philos Libr, 56 & Allen & Irwin, 57; Karel Capek, Columbia Univ, 62. *Mailing Add:* Dept of Slavic Lang Sch of Int Affairs Columbia Univ 420 W 118th St New York NY 10027

HARMAN, GILBERT H, Philosophy, Linguistics. See Vol IV

HARMAN, MARK, b Dublin, Ireland; Mar 6, 51. GERMAN & COMPARATIVE LITERATURE. *Educ:* Nat Univ Ireland, MA, 74; Yale Univ, MPhil, 77, PhD(German), 80. *Prof Exp:* ASST PROF GERMAN, DARTMOUTH COL, 79- *Mem:* MLA; Am Asn Teachers German. *Res:* Kleist and romanticism, Kafka and Jahrhundertwende; postwar German literature; stream of consciousness prose. *Publ:* Contribr, An Echo of Kafka in Kleist, Heinrich von Kleist Studies, AMS/Erich Schmidt, 80. *Mailing Add:* German Dept Dartmouth Col Hanover NH 03755

HARMON, DANIEL PATRICK, b Chicago, Ill, May 3, 38. CLASSICAL LANGUAGES & LITERATURE. *Educ:* Loyola Univ Chicago, AB, 62; Northwestern Univ, MA, 65, PhD(classics), 68. *Prof Exp:* From actg asst prof to asst prof, 67-75, ASSOC PROF CLASSICS, UNIV WASH, 75-, CHMN DEPT, 76- *Mem:* Class Asn Pac Northwest (pres, 74, secy-treas, 75-77); Am Philol Asn; Soc Etudes Latines, Paris; Archaeol Inst Am. *Res:* Latin poetry; Greek & Roman religion. *Publ:* Auth, Catullus 72, 3-4, Class J, 70; Nostalgia for age of heroes in Catullus 64, Latomus, 73; Myth and Fantasy in Propertius I, 3, Trans Am Philol Asn, 75; Myth and proverb in Propertius II, 8, Class World, 75; The family festivals of Rome, 78 & The public festivals of Rome, 78, Aufstieg und Niedergang der Römischen Welt; The poet's initiation and the Sacerdotal imagery of Propertius 3.1-5, Collection Latomus, 79; Religion in the Latin Elegists, Aufstief und Niedergang der Römischen Welt (in prep). *Mailing Add:* 3149 NE 83rd St Seattle WA 98115

HARMS, ROBERT THOMAS, b Peoria, Ill, Apr 12, 32; m 56; c 4. LINGUISTICS. *Educ:* Univ Chicago, AB, 52, AM, 56, PhD, 60. *Prof Exp:* From instr to asst prof Russ & ling, 58-65, assoc prof ling & Slavic lang, 65-67, actg chmn, 72-73, chmn dept, 73-77, PROF LING, UNIV TEX, AUSTIN, 67- *Concurrent Pos:* Grant, Inter-Univ Comt Travel Grants, Leningrad State Univ, USSR, 62-63; res grant, Hungarian Acad Sci, Budapest & Univ Szeged, 67-68; Fulbright res scholar, Univ Helsinki, 68; res grant, USSR Acad of Sci, Tallinn & Syktyvkar, 78. *Mem:* Ling Soc Am. *Res:* Phonology; historical linguistics; Uralic linguistics. *Publ:* Auth, Estonian Grammar, 62 & Finnish Structural Sketch, 64, Uralic & Altaic Ser, Ind Univ; The measurement of phonological economy, Language, 66; Introduction to Phonological Theory, Prentice-Hall, 68; coauth, How do languages get crazy rules, In: Linguistic Change and Generative Theory, Ind Univ, 72; auth, Uralic languages, In: Encycl Britannica, 74. *Mailing Add:* Dept of Ling Univ of Tex Austin TX 78712

HARPER, HUBERT HILL, JR, b Mobile, Ala, Apr 27, 28. CLASSICAL LANGUAGES, ENGLISH. *Educ:* Birmingham Southern Col, BA, 48; Univ NC, Chapel Hill, PhD(Latin & Greek), 52. *Prof Exp:* Instr classics, Univ Tenn, Knoxville, 52-53; asst prof, Xavier Univ, Ohio, 53-59; lectr, Exten Ctr, 61-63, asst prof, 63-67, ASSOC PROF CLASSICS & ENGLISH, UNIV ALA, BIRMINGHAM, 67-, ASSOC DEAN GRAD SCH, 71- *Concurrent Pos:* Latin consult, Int Anat Nomenclature Comt, 71-73; consult, Delphi Proj Undergard Educ, Univ Tex, Dallas, 73. *Mem:* Am Philol Asn; AAUP; MLA; Coun Grad Schs US. *Res:* Homeric studies; Greek tragedy; Latin palaeography. *Publ:* Auth, Translations of Horatian odes, Carolina Quart, 50; contribr, Catalogue of the Reynolds Historical Medical Library, Univ Ala, 69; Nomina Anatomica, Am Asn Anat, 72. *Mailing Add:* Grad Sch Univ of Ala University Station Birmingham AL 35294

HARPER, KENNETH E, b Moberly, Mo, Oct 6, 18; m 44; c 2. LITERATURE. *Educ:* Univ Southern Calif, MA, 41; Columbia Univ, PhD, 50. *Prof Exp:* PROF SLAVIC LANG, UNIV CALIF, LOS ANGELES, 49- *Mem:* MLA. *Res:* Nineteenth century Russian novel. *Mailing Add:* Dept of Slavic Lang Univ of Calif Los Angeles CA 90024

HARPER, SANDRA NADINE, b Fostoria, Ohio, June 28, 38; m 59. ROMANCE LANGUAGES. *Educ:* Ohio State Univ, BS, 59, MA, 65, PhD(Span theater), 68. *Prof Exp:* Teacher pub schs, Ohio, 59-62; instr, 68-69, asst prof, 69-79, ASSOC PROF ROMANCE LANG, OHIO WESLEYAN UNIV, 79-, CHAIRPERSON, 80- *Concurrent Pos:* Mellon grant, Ohio Wesleyan Univ, 72-73, 76 & 80. *Mem:* MLA; Am Asn Teachers Span & Port; AAUP. *Res:* Contemporary Spanish theater, especially Alfonso Sastre; developing real communication in the foreign language classroom; the works of Rosario Castellanos. *Publ:* Auth, A teaching strategy for developing real communication in the foreign language classroom, Hispania, 9/80; Meaning and Structure of Dramatic Symbol in Guillermo tell tiene los ojos tristes, Estreno (in press). *Mailing Add:* Dept of Romance Lang Ohio Wesleyan Univ Delaware OH 43015

HARRIGAN, RENNY K, b New York, NY, May 17, 43. GERMAN LANGUAGE & LITERATURE. *Educ:* Conn Col, BA, 65; Brown Univ, MA, 69, PhD(Ger), 73. *Prof Exp:* From instr to asst prof Ger, Simmons Col, 72-74; ASST PROF GER, UNIV WIS-MILWAUKEE, 74- *Mem:* MLA; Women in German; Women's Caucus Mod Lang Asn. *Res:* Nineteenth century realism; Weimar Republic Neue Sachlichkeit; women's literature 20th century. *Publ:* Auth, Effi Briest, Marquise of O (the Fassbinder and Rohmer films), Jump Cut: A Review of Contemp Cinema, 7/77; Stereotyp der emanzipierten Frau in der Weimarer Republik, Beiheft, Literaturwissenschaft Und Linguistik, summer 78 & English version of same, Proceeding of 2nd Annual Women in German Symposium, 77; co-ed, Special Feminist Issue, New Ger Critique, winter 78; auth, The limits of female emancipation: Fontane's lower class women, Monatshefte, summer 78. *Mailing Add:* Dept of German Box 413 Univ of Wis Milwaukee WI 53201

HARRINGTON, RONALD VERN, b Salamanca, NY, Sept 21, 25; m 54; c 3. SLAVIC LANGUAGES, GENERAL LINGUISTICS. *Educ:* Cornell Univ, BA, 52; Harvard Univ, MA, 57, PhD(Slavic lang & lit), 64. *Prof Exp:* Training off Russ, Nat Security Agency, Washington DC, 54-56 & 57-60; teaching fel, Harvard Univ, 63-64; asst prof, 64-69, ASSOC PROF RUSS, UNIV ROCHESTER, 69- *Mem:* Ling Soc Am; Am Asn Advan Slavic Studies; Am Asn Teachers Slavic & E Europ Lang. *Res:* History of the Slavic languages; semantics; social systems. *Publ:* Coauth, A basic circularity in traditional and current linguistic theory, Lingua, Vol 22, No 4; Toward consistent definitions of some psycholinguistics terms, Linguistics, 70. *Mailing Add:* Dept of Foreign Lang Lit & Ling Univ of Rochester Rochester NY 14627

HARRIS, CARL VERNON, b Morganton, NC, Dec 29, 22; m 55. CLASSICAL LANGUAGES & LITERATURE. *Educ:* Wake Forest Col, AB, 44; Yale Univ, BD, 46, STM, 47; Duke Univ, PhD, 52. *Prof Exp:* Instr relig & Greek, Mars Hill Col, 47-50; asst prof relig & social studies, East Carolina Univ, 53-54; assoc prof relig & Greek, Univ Dubuque, 54-56; assoc prof, 56-68, PROF CLASS LANG & LIT, WAKE FOREST UNIV, 68- *Mem:* Class Asn Mid W & S; Am Class League; Am Soc Church Hist; Am Acad Relig; Am Philol Asn. *Res:* Linguistics; translation from Greek of works of Origen of Alexandria, Egypt; patristic theology and philosophy. *Publ:* Auth, Origen of Alexandria's Interpretation of the Teacher's Function in the Early Christian Hierarchy and Community, Am Press, 68. *Mailing Add:* PO Box 7402 Reynolda Sta Winston-Salem NC 27109

HARRIS, EDWARD PAXTON, b Greenville, Miss, Sept 12, 38; m 63. GERMAN LANGUAGE & LITERATURE. *Educ:* Millsaps Col, BA, 63; Tulane Univ, PhD(Ger), 67. *Prof Exp:* From asst prof to assoc prof, 67-77, PROF GER, UNIV CINCINNATI, 77- *Concurrent Pos:* Taft res award, Hamburg & Munich, 68; dir, Nat Work-Study Prog in Ger, 69 & 70; mem adv comt, Mainz Akademie Wissenschaften und Literatur, 71-; managing ed, Lessing Yearbk, 75-; Humboldt Found sr fel, 77. *Mem:* Am Asn Teachers Ger; Midwest Mod Lang Asn; MLA; Lessing Soc (asst secy-treas, 68-70, secy-treas, 73-77, exec secy, 77-); Int Brecht Soc (secy-treas, 70-77). *Res:* German drama of the 18th century; German drama of the 20th century; German civilization. *Publ:* Coauth, Think German, Levl I, Visual-Educ Asn, 68; auth, Structural unity in J M R Lenz's Der Hofmeister: A revaluation, Seminar, 72; An unknown early version of F M Klinger's Damocles, Archiv Studium Neueren Sprachen, 74; J M R Lenz in German literature: From Büchner to Bobrowski, Colloquia Ger, 74; The liberation of flesh from stone: Pygmalion in Frank Wedekinds Erdgeist, Ger Rev, 77; co-ed, Lessing in heutiger Sicht, Jacobi Verlag, 77; co-ed, Humanitat und Dialog, Wayne State Univ Press, 82. *Mailing Add:* Dept of Ger Univ of Cincinnati Cincinnati OH 45221

HARRIS, FREDERICK JOHN, b New York, NY, July 29, 43. FRENCH, COMPARATIVE LITERATURE. *Educ:* Fordham Univ, BA, 65; Columbia Univ, MA, 66, PhD(French), 69. *Prof Exp:* ASST PROF FRENCH & COMP LIT, COL LINCOLN CTR, FORDHAM UNIV, 70-, CHMN DIV

HUMANITIES, 79- *Mem:* MLA; Am Asn Teachers Fr; Soc des Amis d'Andre Gide. *Res:* Twentieth century French literature; 19th century French literature; 19th and 20th century comparative literature. *Publ:* Auth, Andre Gide and Romain Rolland: Two Men Divided, Rutgers Univ, 73; Andre Gide et la guerre: Deux apercus, Fr Rev, 10/74; Tonio Kröger: An explication de texte, In: Teaching Language Through Literature, 12/73; Annotated bibliographical listings on Gide and the novel, In: A Critical Bibliography of French Literature, Syracuse Univ Press, 80. *Mailing Add:* Col at Lincoln Ctr Fordham Univ New York NY 10023

HARRIS, JANE GARY, b New York, NY. SLAVIC LANGUAGES & LITERATURES. *Educ:* Stanford Univ, BA, 59; Columbia Univ, MA & PhD(Russian and Polish Lang & Lit), 69. *Prof Exp:* Instr, Univ Pittsburgh, 67-69; asst prof, Indiana Univ, Bloomington, 73-74; ASSOC PROF & CHAIRPERSON DEPT SLAVIC LANG & LIT, UNIV PITTSBURGH, 75- *Concurrent Pos:* Corresp ed, Canadian-American Slavic Studies, 73-; dir summer sem, Nat Endowment for Humanities, 81. *Mem:* AAAS; MLA; Am Asn Teachers Slavic & East Europ Lang; Am Soc Eighteenth Century Studies; Asn Dept Foreign Lang. *Publ:* Auth, History of a feminine image: Towards an analysis of Boris Pasternak's esthetic vision, Russian Lit Triquart, 74; transl, Osip Mandelstam's poetry, In: The Silver Age of Russian Culture, Ardis, 75; Osip Mandelstam's prose fiction, Russian Lit Triquart, 75; Osip Mandelstam's critical essays, In: Modern Russian Poets on Poetry, Ardis, 76; auth, An inquiry into the use of autobiography as a stylistic determinant of the modernist aspect of Osip Mandelstam's literary prose, In: American Contributions to the VIIIth International Congress of Slavists, Slavica Publ, 78; Osip Mandelstam: The Complete Critical Prose and Letters, Ardis, 79; Mandelstamian Zlost: A new acmeist esthetic?, Ulbandus Rev, 82; G R Derzhavin: The Poetic Imagination in Evolution (in prep). *Mailing Add:* Dept of Slavic Lang Univ of Pittsburgh Pittsburgh PA 15260

HARRIS, JULIAN EARLE, b Henderson, NC, Sept 3, 96; m 28; c 1. OLD FRENCH. *Educ:* Univ NC, AB, 17; Columbia Univ, AM, 20, PhD, 30; Sorbonne, Dipl, 24. *Prof Exp:* Master English, Va EpiscopalSch, 17-18; instr French, exten, Columbia Univ, 20-22; instr Romance lang, 24-29, from asst prof to prof French, 30-67, chmn dept French & Ital, 42-59, instr, Army Specialized & Civil Affairs Training Prog, 43-44, EMER PROF FRENCH, UNIV WIS, 67- *Concurrent Pos:* Ed, Fr Rev, 55-62; vis prof, Inst Res Humanities, Univ Wis, 64-65. *Honors & Awards:* Chevalier, Legion d'honneur, 49, Officier, 58; Officier, Palmes Academiques, 67. *Mem:* MLA; Am Asn Teachers Fr (pres, 50-54); Ling Soc Am. *Res:* Old French epic and romance; teahing French by intensive method; language laboratory and computer aids in French. *Publ:* Auth, The Humanities: An Appraisal, Univ Wis, 50; coauth, Basic French Reader, Holt, 56 & 70; Three French Books for Children, Heath, 56-62; auth, Munjoie and Reconuisance in Chanson de Roland, line 3620, Romance Philol, 57; coauth, Intermediate Conversational French, Holt, 60-72; ed, Modern French Translation of Chretien de Troyes' Yvain, Dell, 63; auth, How old was Charlemagne in the Chanson de Roland?, Romance Philol, 71; Basic Conversational French, Hold, 6th ed, 78. *Mailing Add:* 1309 Edgehill Dr Madison WI 53705

HARRIS, KATHLEEN, b Huddersfield, England, July 25, 27. GERMAN STUDIES. *Educ:* Univ Leeds, BA, 48, dipl educ, 49; Univ Göttingen, Dr phil(Ger studies), 61. *Prof Exp:* From instr to asst prof Ger, Univ Calif, Berkeley, 60-68; assoc prof, Univ Saskatchewan, 68-70; vis assoc prof, Brock Univ, 74-76; RES & WRITING, 76- *Concurrent Pos:* Res scholar, Ger Acad Exchange Serv, 73; mgr, Fr serv, Harlequin Bks, 80- *Mem:* Am Asn Teachers Ger; Can Asn Univ Teachers Ger; Mod Humanities Res Asn; MLA. *Res:* Age of Goethe, Bibliography; editing of texts, preparation of editions. *Publ:* Auth, Das Problem der Spiegelbildlichkeit im Rolandslied, Neophilologus 48, 64; Stiller (Max Frisch): Ich oder nicht-Ich? Ger Quart, 68 & Materialien zu Max Frisch, Stiller, Frankfurt/Main, Suhrkamp, 78; Die Sprache der menschilichen Beziehungen bei Max Frisch, In: Dichtung, Sprache, Gesellschaft, Athenäum Verlag GmbH, Frankfurt, 71; Studien zur Goethezeit: Blendet noch deas Epochenetikett? In: Akten des 5, Int Ger Kongr Cambridge 1975, Herbert Lang & Cit, 76; Goethe Studies 1947-77: New Ways (f)or Old?, Seminar, 79; coauth (with Richard M Sheirich), Richard Beer-Hofmann: A Bibliography, Mod Austrian Lit, 82. *Mailing Add:* 1533-20 Carlton St Toronto ON M5B 2H5 Can

HARRIS, MARVYN ROY, b West Monroe, La, May 15, 35; m 70; c 2. ROMANCE PHILOLOGY & LINGUISTICS. *Educ:* La State Univ, BA, 55, MA, 59; Univ Calif, Berkeley, PhD(Romance philol), 66. *Prof Exp:* From instr to asst prof French, Univ Ill, Urbana, 63-67; asst prof Romance lang, Univ Pa, 67-72; ASSOC PROF ROMANCE LING, UNIV VA, 72- *Res:* Old French and Old Provencal philology; Romance etymology. *Publ:* Auth, Hispanic barda and Occitanian barta, a Romance word family of pre-Latin stock, 69-70 & Studies in Old Valencian phytonymy, 72-73, Romance Philol; Cofe pourquoi, un africanisme parmi d'autres en Creole louisianais, Rev Lou/La Rev, 73; Old Provencal caira haircloth, reflex of a Gaulish borrowing from Germanic, Semasia, Beiträge zur germanisch-romanischen Sprachforschung, 74; La etimologia de barruntar, problema estructural, In: Studia hispanica in honorem R Lapesa, Vol III, 75; Index inverse du Petit dictionnaire provencal-francais, Heidelberg: Carl Winter, 81; Occitan fruc fruit: Etude etymologique d'un regionalisme, Romania, 82; Les Cenelles: Meaning of a French Afro-American title from New Orleans, Rev Lou/La Rev, 82. *Mailing Add:* Dept of French Lit & Gen Ling Univ of VA Charlottesville VA 22903

HARRIS, RODNEY ELTON, b Mt Vernon, Ohio, Mar 15, 26; m 67. FRENCH LITERATURE. *Educ:* Kenyon Col, AB, 47; Ohio State Univ, MA, 49; Univ Mass, Amherst, PhD(French), 71. *Prof Exp:* Asst prof Romance lang, Ashland Col, 48-56; asst prof French, Hillsdale Col, 56-58, Bradley Univ, 58-60 & Carroll Col, 60-63; instr, Univ Mass, Amherst, 63-70; asst prof French lit, Univ Mass, Boston, 70-75; sr lectr, 75-79, READER FRENCH, AHMADU BELLO UNIV, 79- . *Concurrent Pos:* Ed & consult, Ecriture Fn dans moide, Cahiers Cesairiens. *Mem:* MLA; Am Asn Teachers Fr; African Studies Asn. *Res:* African and Antillean poetry and theater. *Publ:* Co-ed, Palabres . . ., Scott, Foresman, 73; auth, Humanisme dans le theatre d'Aime Cesaire, Ed Naaman, Sherbrooke, 73; plus articles in Fr Rev, Nineteenth Century Fr Studies, Rev Litt Comp & Res in African Lit; Cahiers cesaines, Nigerian J Fr Studies. *Mailing Add:* Dept of French Ahmadou Bello Univ Zaria 84327 Nigeria

HARRIS, ZELLIG, b Balta, Russia, Oct 23, 09; nat US. MATHEMATICAL LINGUISTICS. *Educ:* Univ Pa, BA, 30, MA, 32, PhD(ling), 34. *Prof Exp:* From instr to prof ling, 31-66, BENJAMIN FRANKLIN PROF LING, UNIV PA, 66- *Concurrent Pos:* Lectr, Ling Inst, Univ Mich, 37; Guggenheim fel, 39-40; res assoc, Am Philos Soc, 45-47; lectr, Ind Univ, 52 & 53. *Mem:* Nat Acad Sci; Ling Soc Am (pres, 55); Am Philol Soc; AAAS. *Res:* Structural linguistics; language and culture; transformational linguistics. *Publ:* Auth, Methods in Structural Linguistics, Univ Chicago, 51; String Analysis of Sentence Structure, 62 & Discourse Analysis Reprints, 63, Mouton, The Hague; Mathematical Structures of Language, Interscience Publ, 68; Papers in Structural and Transformational Linguistics, Reidel, Dordrecht, 70; A theory of language structure, Am Philol Quart, 76; Notes du Cours de Syntaxe, Seuil, Paris, 76; Grammar on mathematical principles, J Ling, 78; Papers on Syntax, Reidel, Dordrecht, 81; Grammar of English on Mathematical Principles, Wiley, 82. *Mailing Add:* Dept of Ling Univ Penn Philadelphia PA 19104

HARRISON, ANN TUKEY, b Geneva, NY, Apr 19, 38. ROMANCE LANGUAGES, LINGUISTICS. *Educ:* Mich State Univ, BA, 57; Univ Mich, MA, 58, PhD(Romance ling), 62. *Prof Exp:* Teaching asst French, Univ Mich, 57-61; instr, Univ Wis, 61-63, asst prof French & ling, 63-65; from asst prof to assoc prof Romance lang, 65-73, PROF FRENCH, MICH STATE UNIV, 73- *Honors & Awards:* Ruth Dean Annual Lectr, Mt Holyoke Col, 76. *Mem:* MLA; AAUP; Medieval Acad; Am Asn Teachers French. *Res:* French medieval language and literature; French linguistics. *Publ:* Auth, Notes on Involuntary Memory in Proust, Fr Rev, 69; Medieval French literature and women's studies, Proc Conf of Women's Studies Asn, 74; Charles d'Orleans and the Allegorical Mode, Univ NC, 75; The theme of authority in Francois Villon, The Centennial Rev, 79; Orleans and Burgundy, The literary relationship, The Stanford French Rev, 81; Aude and Bramimunde: Their importance in the Chanson de Roland, The French Rev, 81; The nitty-gritty: The president's commission report at the local leval, Am Asn Teachers French Nat Bull, 81; Echo and her medieval sisters, The Centennial Rev, 82. *Mailing Add:* 277 Maplewood Dr Lansing MI 48823

HARRISON, KEITH EDWARD, Modern Poetry. See Vol II

HARRISON, REGINA L, b Washington, DC. LATIN AMERICAN LITERATURE. *Educ:* Univ Mass, Amherst, BS, 65; Univ Ill, Urbana, AM, 73, PhD(Span), 79. *Prof Exp:* Instr, 77-79, ASST PROF SPAN, BATES COL, 79- *Concurrent Pos:* Consult, Maine Coun for Humanities & Pub Policy, 78; actg assoc dean, Bates Col, 80; vis asst prof Quechua, Ctr Latin Am Studies, Univ Conn, Storrs, 81. *Mem:* MLA; Latin Am Studies Asn; Latin Am Indian Lit Asn. *Res:* Andean symbolism and literary expressiion; Quechua poetics and discourse; cultural symbols and Latin American literature. *Publ:* Auth, The order of things: An analysis of the ceramics from Santarem, Brazil, J Steward Anthrop Soc, fall 72; Rosario Castellanos: On language, In: Homenaje a Rosario Castellanos, Hispanofila, No 11, 80; The Quechua oral tradition: From Waman Puma to contemporary Ecuador, Rev, 1-4/81; Modes of discourse in the Relacion by Pachacvti Yamqui Salcamaygua, In: From Oral to Written Expression, Syracuse Univ, 82; La influencia de la poesia quechua en Los riso profundos, Proc V Ann Hisp Lit Conf (in prep); Jose Maria Arguedas: El sustrato quechua, Rev Iberoam (in prep). *Mailing Add:* Dept of Foreign Lang & Lit Bates Col Lewiston ME 04240

HARRISON, STEPHEN GEORGE, b Doncaster, England, Sept 14, 42. HISPANIC STUDIES. *Educ:* Oxford Univ, BA, 65, MA, 76; Univ Toronto, PhD(Span), 78. *Prof Exp:* LECTR SPAN, UNIV WATERLOO, 74- *Mem:* Can Asn Hispanists; Int Asn Hispanists. *Res:* Golden Age literature; Cervantes. *Publ:* Auth, Magic in the Spanish golden age: Cervantes' Second Thoughts, Renaissance & Reformation, 79. *Mailing Add:* 653-P Albert Waterloo ON N2L 3V5 Can

HARRIS-SCHENZ, BEVERLY, b Detroit, Mich, July 20, 48. GERMAN LITERATURE. *Educ:* Univ Mich, BA, 70; Stanford Univ, MA, 71, PhD(German), 77. *Prof Exp:* Asst prof, Univ Pittsburgh, 74-79 & Rice Univ, 79-80; ADJ ASST PROF & ASST DEAN, UNIV PITTSBURGH, 80- *Concurrent Pos:* Consult, Nat Endowment for the Humanities, 78- *Mem:* MLA; Col Lang Asn; Western Asn German Studies. *Res:* The image of Blacks in German literature and culture. *Publ:* Auth, Der Sklave: Ein Bild des Schwarzen in der deutschen lit des 18. Jahrhunderts, Int Ger Congr Basel, 80; Black Images: Depictions of the Black in 18th Century German Literature, Akademischer Verlag Hans-Dieter Heinz, 81. *Mailing Add:* 3323 Shady Ave ext Pittsburgh PA 15217

HARSH, WAYNE C, b WaKeeney, Kans, Nov 13, 24; div. ENGLISH, LINGUISTICS. *Educ:* Colo State Col, BA, 50; Denver Univ, MA, 53; Univ Calif, Berkeley, PhD(English), 63. *Prof Exp:* Teacher high sch, Calif, 53-57; asst prof English, Ohio Univ, 62-64; from asst prof to assoc prof, 64-73, chmn ling comt, 70-76, PROF ENGLISH & LING, UNIV CALIF, DAVIS, 73- *Concurrent Pos:* NDEA consult, Calif districts & counties, 66-68; consult, state depts educ, Calif & Nev, 66-68; actg chmn dept English, Univ Athens, 68-69; Fulbright sr lectr, USEF, Greece, 68-69 & 71; consult, Calif State Dept English Assessment, 74-78; guest prof English, Sch Philos, Aristotelian Univ, Greece, 76-77; dir 13 county writing proj, Area III Writing Ctr, 77-; dir, Univ Calif Study Ctr, Hong Kong, 79-81. *Mem:* NCTE; MLA; Teaching English as Foreign Lang. *Res:* Historical grammar; stylistics; teaching English as foreign language. *Publ:* Auth, The Subjunctive in English, Univ Ala, 68; Introduction to Linguistics: A Guidebook for Teachers, Grade K-12, McCutchan, 68; Linguistics and the Teaching of Literature, Eric Ctr Appl Ling, 68; coauth, Laidlaw Linguistics Program, Grade 7-8, 69 & Laidlaw Language Experiences Program, Grades 3-9, 72, Laidlaw Bros; auth, Three Approaches to Grammar, Anniversary Volume, English Teaching Forum,

USIS, 76; coauth, English Structure and Usage, Efstathiadis Group, Athens, Greece, 77; The Good English Series K-8, Laidlaw Bros, 78; Linguistics and TESOL: A turbulent twenty years, English Teaching Forum, 1/82. *Mailing Add:* Dept of English Univ of Calif Davis CA 95616

HART, PIERRE ROMAINE, b Baraboo, Wis, May 6, 35; m 58; c 2. RUSSIAN LITERATURE. *Educ:* Antioch Col, BA, 57; Univ Wis-Madison, MS, 60, MA, 66, PhD(Russ lit), 68. *Prof Exp:* Asst prof Russ, State Univ NY Buffalo, 67-72, assoc prof, 72-79; PROF RUSS, LA STATE UNIV, 80- *Concurrent Pos:* Am Coun Educ fel, 78-79. *Mem:* Am Asn Teachers Slavic & E Europ Lang. *Res:* Russian 18th century poetry; symbolist prose; fictional representations of childhood. *Publ:* Auth, Gavriil Derzavin's ode God and the Great Chain of Being, Slavic & E Europ J, spring 70; Looking over Reskol'nikov's shoulder: The narrator in Crime and Punishment, Criticism, spring 71; Psychological primitivism in Belyj's Kotik Letaev, Russ Lit Triquart, fall 72; The Master and Margarita as creative process, Mod Fiction Studies, summer, 73; Aspects of Anacreontea in Derzhavin's verse, Slavic & E Europ J, winter, 73; contribr, Continuity and change in the Russian ode, In: Russian Literature in the Age of Catherine the Great, Meeuws, Oxford, 76; auth, Nature as the norm in Fathers and Sons, Russ Lang J, fall, 77; G R Derzhauin: A Poet's Progress, Slavica, 78. *Mailing Add:* Dept of Class, Ger & Slavic Lang La State Univ Baton Rouge LA 70808

HART, THOMAS ELWOOD, b Rochester, NY, July 5, 39; m 62, 74; c 3. GERMANIC LITERATURE & LANGUAGE. *Educ:* Boston Col, BA, 61; Middlebury Col, MA, 62; Univ Wis, PhD(Germanics), 66. *Prof Exp:* Asst prof, 71, assoc prof, 71-80, PROF GERMANIC PHILOL, SYRACUSE, UNIV, 80- *Concurrent Pos:* Fulbright-Hays res grant, Austria, 68-69; Nat Endowment for Humanities res fel, 73-74; Am Coun Learned Soc res fel, 80-81. *Mem:* MLA, Int Courtly Lit Soc; Medieval Acad Am; Soc Microcomput Appln Lang & Lit; Int Arthur Schnitzler Res Asn. *Res:* Medieval literature, especially Germanic; language esthetics. *Publ:* Auth, Linguistic patterns, literary structure, and the genesis of C F Meyer's Der roemische Brunnen, Lang & Style, Vol IV, 83-115; Zu den Abschnitten in den Hartmann-Handschriften, Z fuer deutsche Philol, Vol XCI, 17-19; Twelfth-century Platonism and the geometry of textual space in Hartman's Iwein, Res Publica Litterarum, Vol II, 81-107; Tectonic methodology and an application to Beowulf, In: Essays in the Numerical Criticism of Medieval Literature, Bucknell Univ Press, 80; Werkstruktur in Stricker's Daniel? A critique by counterexample, Colloquia Germanica, Vol XIII, 106-141, 156-159; Chrestien, Macrobius and Chartrean science: The allegorical robe as symbol of textual design in the Old French Erec, Mediaeval Studies, Vol XLIII, 250-296; Calculated casualties in Beowulf: Geometrical scaffolding and verbal symbol, Studia Neophilolgica, Vol LIII, 1-33; Medieval structuralism: Dulcarnoun and the five-book design of Chaucer's Troilus, Chaucer Rev, Vol XVI. *Mailing Add:* Dept of Ger Lang Syracuse Univ Syracuse NY 13210

HART, THOMAS ROY, b Raleigh, NC, Jan 10, 25; m 45; c 2. ROMANCE LANGUAGES & LITERATURE. *Educ:* Yale Univ, BA, 48, PhD, 52. *Prof Exp:* Instr Span, Amherst Col, 52-53; instr Romance lang, Harvard Univ, 53-55; asst prof, Johns Hopkins Univ, 55-60; assoc prof, Emory Univ, 60-64; PROF ROMANCE LANG, UNIV ORE, 64- *Concurrent Pos:* Fulbright res grants, Univ Montpellier, 50-51 & Univ Madrid, 66-67; ed, Comp Lit, 72- *Mem:* Assoc Int Hispanistas. *Res:* Spanish literature of the Middle Ages and Golden Age; Portuguese literature. *Publ:* Ed, Gil Vicente's Obras dramaticas castellanas, Clasicos castelanos, 62; auth, The literary criticism of Jorge Luis Borges, Mod Lang Notes, 63; The literary criticism of Mario de Andrade, In: The Disciplines of Criticism, Yale Univ, 68; ed, Gil Vicente: Farces and Festival Plays, Univ Ore, 72; auth, The author's voice in the Lusiads, Hisp Rev, 76; The pilgrim's role in the first Solitude, Mod Lang Notes, 77; Versions of pastoral in three Novelas ejemplares, Bull Hispanic Studies, 81. *Mailing Add:* Dept of Romance Lang Univ of Ore Eugene OR 97403

HART, WILLIAM ROBERT, b Harrisburg, Ill, Apr 21, 29; m 56; c 3. LINGUISTICS, ENGLISH. *Educ:* Wash Univ, AB, 51; Univ Mich, MA, 53, PhD(English, educ & Ger grammar), 63. *Prof Exp:* Asst English, Univ Mich, 54-55, teaching asst English lang, 55-56; instr English, Univ Mo, 57-60; from asst prof to assoc prof, 60-68, PROF ENGLISH, GROVE CITY COL, 68- *Mem:* Ling Soc Am; MLA; Teachers English to Speakers Other Lang. *Res:* English literature, especially the beginnings to 1800; English language; modern English grammar. *Mailing Add:* Dept of English Grove City Col Grove City PA 16127

HARTER, HUGH A, b Columbus, Ohio, Dec 13, 22; m 70. FOREIGN LANGUAGES. *Educ:* Ohio State Univ, BA, 47, PhD, 58; Univ of the Americas, MA, 51. *Prof Exp:* Asst, Ohio State Univ, 46-47 & 51-53; from instr to asst prof Span, French & humanities, Wesleyan Univ, 53-59; assoc prof, Elmira Col, 59-60; from asst prof to assoc prof, Chatham Col, 61-64; assoc prof Span & French, Loyola Univ, Ill, 64-66; prof Romance lang, 66-77, chmn dept, 66-80, ROBERT HAYWARD PROF ROMANCE LANG, OHIO WESLEYAN UNIV, 77- *Concurrent Pos:* Mellon fel, Univ Pittsburgh, 60-61, lectr, 61-63; mem bd dir, Regional Coun Int Educ, 62-; dir Programas Americanos, Segovia, Spain, 68-; pres, Asoc Fundacion Juan Ruiz, 71-; US-Span Joint Comt grant, 79. *Mem:* MLA; Am Asn Teachers Span & Port; AAUP; Col Lang Asn; Am Transl Asn. *Res:* Becquer and 20th century Spanish poetry; Quevedo and the Spanish novel of the 17th century; the picaresque tradition. *Publ:* Co-ed, Rinconete y Cortadillo, Las Americas, 60; auth, A First Spanish Handbook for Teachers in Elementary Schools, Univ Pittsburgh, 61; transl with introd, The Scavenger, Las Americas, 62; auth, A History of Spanish Literature, NY Univ, 71; Introduction to Paul Verlaine's Femmes/Hombres, Chicago Rev Press, 77; Gertudis Gomez de Avellaneda, G K Hall, 81. *Mailing Add:* Dept of Romance Lang Ohio Wesleyan Univ Delaware OH 43015

HART-GONZALEZ, LUCINDA, b Oakland, Calif, Mar 31, 50; m 78. LINGUISTICS. *Educ:* Univ Mass, Boston, BA, 75; Georgetown Univ, MS, 77, PhD(socioling), 80. *Prof Exp:* Lectr English as foreign lang, Georgetown Univ, 76-81; ASST PROF LING, SOCIOL & ANTHROP, OAKLAND UNIV, 81- *Mem:* Ling Soc Am; Am Anthrop Asn; Middle Atlantic Coun Latin Am Studies; Asn Latin Am Indian Lit; Soc Intercult Educ, Training & Res. *Res:* Quechua language, music and literature; Spanish-English bilingualism in the United States; language change and variation. *Publ:* Auth, Commentary on Albo's review of Lastra's Cochabamba Quechua Syntax, Int J Am Ling, 1/79; contribr, Speaking, Singing and Teaching: A Multidisciplinary Approach to Language Variation, Anthrop Res Papers No 20, Ariz State Univ, 80; Latin American Indian Literatures, Northwestern Pa Inst Latin Am Studies, 80; auth, Bolivian contribution to Quechua study: Two reviews, Int J Am Ling, 82; contribr, El Espanol en los Estdos Unidos, Newbury House (in prep). *Mailing Add:* Dept of Ling Oakland Univ Rochester MI 48063

HARTH, DOROTHY EVE, b New York, NY, Dec 28, 25; m 51; c 2. FOREIGN LANGUAGES. *Educ:* Queens Col, NY, BA, 47; Columbia Univ, MA, 48; Syracuse Univ, PhD(Span), 58. *Prof Exp:* Instr Span, Syracuse Univ, 48-51; admin asst Latin Am, US Inter-Am Coun, 51-53; instr Span, Duke Univ, 53-57 & Syracuse Univ, 57-62; PROF SPAN, ONONDAGA COMMUNITY COL, 62- *Concurrent Pos:* Bd dir, Span Action League, 75-78. *Mem:* MLA; Am Asn Teachers Span; Multi-Ethnic Lit US; Am Indian Lit Soc. *Res:* Latin American literature; Chicano literature; native American literature. *Publ:* Auth, Ariel y Caliban, 2/48, La picaresca espanola y Mejicana, 48 & La literatura de Ramon Sender, 2/49, Rev Nac Cuba; Jorge Carrera Andrade: A Bibliography, Bibliotheca Hisp Novissima, 73; co-ed, Voice of Aztlan, New Am Libr, 74. *Mailing Add:* Onondage Community Col Rte 173 Syracuse NY 13215

HARTH, ERICA, b New York, NY. FRENCH LITERATURE. *Educ:* Barnard Col, BA, 59; Columbia Univ, MA, 62, PhD(French), 68. *Prof Exp:* Instr French, NY Univ, 64-66; from instr to asst prof, Columbia Univ, 67-71; lect, Tel-Aviv Univ, Israel, 71-72; asst prof, 72-75, ASSOC PROF FRENCH, BRANDEIS UNIV, 75- *Concurrent Pos:* Fels, Nat Endowment Humanities, 70 & Am Coun Learned Socs, 78. *Mem:* MLA. *Res:* Seventeenth century French literature; sociology of literature. *Publ:* Auth, Cyrano de Bergerac and the Polemics of modernity, Columbia Univ, 70; The tragic moment in Athalie, Mod Lang Quart, 12/72; Exorcising the beast: Attempts at rationality in French classicism, MLA Publ, 1/73; Classical innateness, Yale Fr Studies, 6/73; The creative alienation of the writer: Sartre, Camus and Simone de Beauvoir, Mosiac, spring 75; Classical disproportion: La Bruyere's Caracteres, L'Esprit Createur, spring-summer 75; Sur des vers de Virgile (III, 5): Antinomy and totality in Montaigne, Fr Forum, 1/77. *Mailing Add:* Dept of Romance & Comp Lit Brandeis Univ Waltham MA 02154

HARTIGAN, KARELISA VOELKER, b Stillwater, Okla, Mar 5, 43. CLASSICS. *Educ:* Col Wooster, BA, 65; Univ Chicago, AM, 66, PhD(classics), 70. *Prof Exp:* Asst prof classics, St Olaf Col, 69-73; asst prof humanities, 73-75; ASSOC PROF CLASSICS, UNIV FLA, 75- *Concurrent Pos:* Fac Develop Ford Found grant, St Ofaf Col, 71; Fac Develop grant, Univ Fla, 75; Aegean Inst staff, 79, 81 & 83; co-dir, Ctr Greek Studies, 80-; Nat Endowment Humanities summer grant, 82. *Mem:* Am Philol Asn; Archaeol Inst Am; Class Asn Mid West & South; Mod Greek Studies Asn. *Res:* Classical literature; comparative literature; ancient cities. *Publ:* Auth, He rose like a lion: Animal similes in Homer and Virgil, Acta Antiqua, 73; Sophocles: Oedipus Tyrannus 293, Class J, 75; Dramatic dialogue in Theocritus, Ziva Antika Antiquite Vivante, 76; The Poets and the Cities, Anton Hain, 78; The Ancient City: Concept and Expression, Ginn, 81; Myth and the Helen, Eranos, 81; coauth (with W C Terry), Vigiles and men in blue: Police authority in Imperial Rome and 19th century England, Law and Human Behavior, 82; Ancient myth in modern poetry: Odysseus' reappearance in modern Greek verse, Classical Outlook, 82. *Mailing Add:* Dept of Classics ASB 3-C Univ of Fla Gainesville FL 32611

HARTLE, ROBERT WYMAN, b Kongmoon, China, Sept 1, 21; US citizen; m 41; c 2. MODERN LANGUAGES & LITERATURES. *Educ:* Univ Tex, BA, & MA, 47; Princeton Univ, AM, 49; PhD(French), 51. *Prof Exp:* Instr French & Span, Univ Tex, 46-48; instr French, Princeton Univ, 50-53, asst prof French & Europ lit, 53-60; asst prof Romance lang, Queens Col, NY, 60-61; assoc prof, Univ Ore, 61-63; prof & chmn dept, 63-65, assoc dean fac, 65-66, dean, 66-70, PROF ROMANCE LANG, QUEENS COL, NY, 72- *Concurrent Pos:* Dir, City Univ New York Prog Study Abroad, 65-70, French Doctoral Prog in Paris, 70-73; mem bd dir, Coun Int Educ Exchange, 66-70, mem exec comt, 67-70; mem bd dir, Alliance Francaise, New York, 68-70; Am Ctr for Students & Artists, Paris, 70-, mem exec comt, 71-72. *Honors & Awards:* Chevalier, Ordre des Palmes Academiques, 66, Officier, 76; Cavaliere, Order of Merit, Italy, 68; Officer's Cross, Order of Merit, Fed Ger Repub, 72. *Mem:* MLA. *Res:* Seventeenth century French literature; iconography of Alexander the Great. *Publ:* Auth, Index du vocabulaire du theatre classique; transl, Moliere's Le Tartuffe; auth, Le Brun's Histoire d'Alexander and Racine's Alexandre le Grand, Romance Rev, 57; The image of Alexander the Great in seventeenth century France, In: Ancient Macedonia, Vols I & II, 70-77. *Mailing Add:* Dept of Romance Lang Queens Col Flushing NY 11367

HARTMAN, ALEXANDER PAUL, b Grosschoenau, Ger, Sept 17, 10; nat US. FRENCH, GERMAN. *Educ:* Univ Leipzig, PhD(Romance & Ger land & lit), 37. *Prof Exp:* Asst, Romance Inst, Univ Leipzig, 36; instr Ger lang & lit, Royal Sch, Armagh, Northern Ireland, 38-39; from lectr to prof, 39-76, head dept French, 47-49 & dept foreign lang, 49-74, EMER PROF FRENCH & GER, UNIV S DAK, 76- *Mem:* Am Asn Teachers Fr; Am Asn Teachers Ger; Am Coun Teaching Foreign Lang. *Res:* Contemporary French literature; contemporary German language; classical German literature. *Publ:* Auth, C F Ramuz, Mensch, Werk und Landschaft. *Mailing Add:* Dept of Mod Lang Univ of S Dak Vermillion SD 57069

HARTMAN, GEOFFREY H, English & Comparative Literature. See Vol II

HARTMAN, JAMES WALTER, b Newark, Ohio, Jan 28, 39; m 59; c 2. ENGLISH LANGUAGE, LINGUISTICS. *Educ:* Ohio Univ, BA, 61; Univ Mich, MA, 62, PhD(English lang), 66. *Prof Exp:* Instr English, Eastern Ill Univ, 63-64; asst prof English & ling, Ohio Univ, 66-67; asst prof English lang, Univ Wis-Madison, 67-70; ASSOC PROF ENGLISH & LING, UNIV KANS, 70- *Concurrent Pos:* Asst dir, Dict Am Regional English, 67-70, assoc ed, 70-; assoc ed, Am Speech, 72-; ed publ, Am Dialect Soc. *Mem:* Am Dialect Soc; MLA. *Res:* Dialectology; structure and history of English; sociolinguistics. *Publ:* Auth, Preliminary findings from Dare, Am Speech, fall 70; Dare in 1970, J English Ling, spring 71; co-ed, Sociolinguistics (spec issue), Kans J Sociol, 73. *Mailing Add:* Dept of English Wescoe Hall Univ of Kans Lawrence KS 66045

HARTMAN, STEVEN LEE, b Lexington, Va, May 4, 46. SPANISH, LINGUISTICS. *Educ:* Univ Wis, BA, 66, MA, 68, PhD(Span), 71. *Prof Exp:* ASST PROF SPAN, SOUTHERN ILL UNIV CARBONDALE, 71- *Concurrent Pos:* Vis prof, Univ Veracruzana, Mexico, 73. *Mem:* Am Asn Teachers Span & Port; MLA; Ling Soc Am; Asn Comput Ling. *Res:* Historical linguistics; generative phonology; computational linguistics. *Publ:* Auth, Alfonso el Sabio and the varieties of verb grammar, Hispania, 3/74; An outline of Spanish historical phonology, Papers Ling, spring-summer, 74; La etimologia de dulce, Nueva Rev de Filol Hispanica, 80; A universal alphabet, Comput & Humanities, 81. *Mailing Add:* Dept of Foreign Lang & Lit Southern Ill Univ Carbondale IL 62832

HARTNETT, CAROLYN GREEN, English Composition. See Vol II

HARTOCH, ARNOLD J, b Chicago, Ill, Mar 26, 15. GERMAN. *Educ:* Northwestern Univ, BA, 36, MA, 37, PhD(Ger, educ), 52; Chicago Teachers Col, MEd, 40. *Prof Exp:* Teacher, pub sch, Ill, 37-42; PROF GER, UNIV ILL, CHICAGO CIRCLE, 46- *Mem:* Am Asn Teachers Ger (pres, 52-54); MLA; Cent States Mod Lang Asn; Am Asn Higher Educ; NEA. *Res:* Germanic philology; German grammar and language; problems of modern education. *Publ:* Factors in the success of pre-medical students; The academic history of remedial English students; Characteristics of drop-out students. *Mailing Add:* Dept of Ger Univ of Ill Chicago Circle Box 4348 Chicago IL 60680

HARVEY, CAROL JOSEPHINE, b Apr 18, 41; Can citizen; m 64; c 2. FRENCH LANGUAGE & LITERATURE. *Educ:* Univ Edinburgh, MA, 63, PhD(Anglo-Norman lyric poetry), 69; Univ Caen, Lic es Lett, 64. *Prof Exp:* Lectr English, Univ Caen, 63-64; asst prof French, 70-76, ASSOC PROF FRENCH, UNIV WINNIPEG, 76- *Concurrent Pos:* Chmn, Jr High Fr Curric Comt, Dept of Educ, Man, 77- *Mem:* Asn Prof Francais Univ Can; Int Courtly Lit Soc; Mediaeval Acad NAm. *Res:* Contemporary French novel; Anglo-Norman lyric poetry. *Publ:* Auth, Macaronic techniques in Anglo-Norman verse, L'Esprit createur, summer 78; Au fil des mots, Ampiboufe, 4/80, 3/82, 6/82 & 4/82; Manitoba de Michel Desgranges, Centre d'Etudes franco canadienues de l'ouest, 10/82; Jean-Paul Sartre's L'Enfance d'um Chef: The Use of Obscenity, Romance Notes, 82. *Mailing Add:* Dept of French Univ of Winnipeg 515 Portage Ave Winnipeg MB R3B 2E9 Can

HARVEY, GINA CANTONI, b Gorizia, Italy, 1922; US citizen. LINGUISTICS, LANGUAGE PEDAGOGY. *Educ:* Univ Rome, Dr(hist, lang), 44. *Prof Exp:* Asst prof French & English, Ft Lewis Col, 65-70; assoc prof educ, Univ NMex, 70-74; assoc prof, 74-80, PROF ENGLISH, NORTHERN ARIZ UNIV, 80- *Concurrent Pos:* Chmn bd, Southwest Educ Assoc Res, 73-; ed, Ariz Bilingual Coun Newsletter, 75- *Mem:* Nat Coun Teachers English; Teachers English to Speakers of Other Lang; AAUP; Native Am Bilingual Educ Conf; Nat Bilingual Educ Asn. *Res:* Interlanguage; conceptual development among minority children; native American education. *Publ:* Auth, The Italian Verb, McKay, London, 65; coauth, Helpful hints for new BIA teachers, Bur Indian Affairs, 68; auth, Dormitory English, In: Southwest Areal Linguistics, 74 & co-ed, Southwest Languages and Linguistics in Educational Perspective, 75, Inst Cult Pluralism; auth, Some observations on Red English and Standard English in the classroom, Southwest Studies Indian English, 77. *Mailing Add:* Southwest Educ Assoc Res Box 181 Flagstaff AZ 86002

HARVEY, JOHN EDMOND, b New York, NY, Oct 22, 32; m 62; c 1. FRENCH, DRAMA. *Educ:* Johns Hopkins Univ, BA, 53, MA, 54; Yale Univ, PhD(French), 62. *Prof Exp:* Instr French, Univ Mass, 60-62; asst prof, Smith Col, 62-65; assoc prof, Univ Colo, 65-67 & Va Polytech Inst, 67-68; assoc prof, 68-73; PROF FRENCH, UNIV UTAH, 73- *Mem:* MLA; Am Asn Teachers Fr. *Res:* Drama; 20th century literature. *Publ:* Auth, Anouilh, a Study of Theatrics, Yale Univ, 64; translr, Episode from an author's life by Jean Anouilh, Educ Theater, J, 3/64. *Mailing Add:* Dept of Lang Univ of Utah Salt Lake City UT 84112

HARVEY, JOHN EDWARD, JR, b Lewiston, Maine, Mar 14, 17; m 39; c 3. ROMANCE LANGUAGES. *Educ:* Bates Col, AB, 37; Middlebury Col, AM, 46; Harvard Univ, MA, 46, PhD, 52. *Prof Exp:* Asst English, Lycee, Angers, France, 37-38; from asst prof to assoc prof mod lang, 48-58, chmn dept mod lang, 54-57, dept French, 58-67, dept Romance lang, 68-74 & dept mod foreign lang & lit, 74-78, SAMUEL MATHER PROF FRENCH, KENYON COL, 58- Concurrent POs: Mem Fr comt, advan placement prog, Col Entrance Exam Bd, 54-61; asst managing ed Fr, Mod Lang J, 64-69; prof-in-charge, Sweet Briar Jr Year in France, 66-67, mem adv bd, 74-77. *Concurrent Pos:* Mem Fr comt, advan placement prog, Col Entrance Exam Bd, 54-61; asst managing ed Fr, Mod Lang J, 64-69; prof-in-charge, Sweet Briar Jr Year in France, 66-67. *Mem:* MLA; Am Asn Teachers Fr; Cent States Mod Lang Teachers Asn (vpres, 62-64). *Res:* Seventeenth and 19th century French literature; Edouard Estaunie and his times; Jack Kerouac. *Mailing Add:* Dept of Mod Foreign Lang & Lit Kenyon Col Gambier OH 43022

HARVEY, LAWRENCE ELLIOT, b Denver, Colo, Feb 13, 25; m 51; c 4. ROMANCE LANGUAGES. *Educ:* Western Reserve Univ, BA, 48; Harvard Univ, MA, 51, PhD(Romance lang & Lit), 55. *Prof Exp:* Interpreter French, US Army, 46; cult affairs off, US Inform Serv, Turin, Italy, 52; from instr to prof Romance lang, 55-72, fac fel, 64-65, chmn dept comp lit, 66-68, chmn div humanities & assoc dean fac, 67-68, dean, 69-71, EDWARD TUCK PROF FRENCH & ITAL, DARTMOUTH COL, 72- *Concurrent Pos:* Guggenheim fel & Am Coun Learned Sco grant-in-aid, 61-62; sr res Fulbright scholar, Florence, Italy, 68-69. *Mem:* MLA; Acad Lit Studies; Am Asn Teachers Fr. *Res:* Pierre Corneille and 17th century French theatre; Samuel Beckett and 20th century French theatre; Italian poetry. *Publ:* Auth, The Aesthetics of the Renaissance Love Sonnet, Droz, Geneva, 62; The role of emulation in Corneille's Polyeucte, PMLA, 67; Art and nothingness in Anouilh's Antigone and Giraudoux's Odine, Esprit Createur, 69; Samuel Beckett: Poet and Critic, Princeton Univ, 70; Corneille's Horace: A study in tragic and artistic ambivalence, In: Studies in 17th Century French Literature, Cornell Uiv, 72. *Mailing Add:* 3 Tyler Rd Hanover NH 03755

HARVEY, MARIA-LUISA ALVAREZ, b Torreon, Coahuila, Mex; US citizen; c 1. TWENTIETH CENTURY SPANISH LITERATURE. *Educ:* Tex Western Col, BA, 65; Univ Tex, El Paso, MA, 66; Univ Ariz, PhD(Span), 69; Jackson State Col, MSci in Ed, 72. *Prof Exp:* Teaching assoc Span, Univ Ariz, 69; asst prof & head dept mod lang, Col Artesia, 69-70; assoc prof, 70-74, prof span, 74-80, PROF MOD FOREIGN & DIR, HONS PROG, JACKSON STATE UNIV, 81- *Mem:* Am Asn Teachers Span & Port; MLA; Col Lang Asn; S Cent Mod Lang Asn; Int Readin g Asn; Nat Collegiate Hons Coun. *Res:* Twentieth century Spanish poetry; bilingual education; human development. *Publ:* Auth, Cielo y tierra en la poesia lirica de Manuel Altolaguirre, Univ & Col Press Miss, 72; Where is the critical period of development for the disadvantaged, fall-winter, 73 & Is teaching selection the answer, fall, 74, Ill Schs J; Teach Spanish to Black students? Make it relevant! Make it Black!, J Negro Educ, summer 74; A good teacher and an eclectic approach: The hopeful answer to successful reading instruction, fall 74 & Teach them reading while you teach them Spanish . . . or French . . . or any other subject, summer 75, Reading Horizons; One egg has the subject, another has the predicate: A Spanish (or English) teaching game, Elem English, 4/75; Lorca's Yerma: Frigid . . . or mismatched?, Col Lang Asn J, 6/80. *Mailing Add:* Dept of Mod Foreign Lang Jackson State Univ Jackson MS 39217

HARVEY, PAUL BENJAMIN, JR, Ancient History, Classical Philology. See Vol I

HARVEY, WILLIAM JOURNEAUX, b Racine, Wis, 38; m 62; c 2. GERMANIC LANGUAGES & LITERATURES. *Educ:* Wabash Col, BA, 59; Univ Tex, Austin, MA, 64, PhD(Ger lang), 72. *Prof Exp:* Instr Ger, Lamar State Col, 62-63 & Univ Mo-Columbia, 63-66; from instr to asst prof, 66-76, ASSOC PROF GER & PHILOS & DIR TITLE VII BILING EDUC PORJ, E TEX STATE UNIV, 76- *Concurrent Pos:* Consult, Tex Educ Agency, 69-; Am Asn Teachers Ger deleg & chmn state proj task force, Joint Nat Comt Lang, 72-78; consult, Calif Biling Educ Study, 78. *Honors & Awards:* Cert of Merit, Goethe House-New York, 77. *Mem:* MLA; Am Asn Teachers Ger (vpres, 73-74); Am Coun Teaching Foreign Lang; Nat Asn Biling Educ; Ling Soc Am. *Res:* Kafka; Dürrenmatt; bilingual education. *Publ:* Auth, Visual Aids for German Classroom Instruction, a Handbook, E Tex State Univ, 67; transl, H Piontek, Play for a dark room (radio play), Dimension, II: 386-439; auth, The problem of a literary relevance, Unterrichtspraxis, V: 106-108; Helping guidance counselors see the value of foreign languages, Asn Depts Foreign Lang Bull, 5/74. *Mailing Add:* East Tex Station Box 3316 Commerce TX 75428

HARWOOD, SHARON ELIZABETH, b Memphis, Tenn, July 18, 45. FOREIGN LANGUAGES. *Educ:* Memphis State Univ, BA, 66, MA, 67; Tulane Univ, MA, 72, PhD(French), 73. *Prof Exp:* Instr French, 67-69, asst prof French & Ital, 72-76, ASSOC PROF FRENCH & ITAL, MEMPHIS STATE UNIV, 76- *Mem:* MLA; SCent Mod Lang Asn; Am Asn Teachers Fr; NAm Soc 17th Century Fr Studies; Dante Soc Am. *Res:* Seventeenth century French literature; medieval and Renaissance Italian literature; medieval French literature. *Publ:* Auth, Moral blindness and freedom of will: A study of light images in Dante's Divina Commedia, Romance Notes, 74; Logic and emotion: The structure of orations in Corneille, Papers 17th Century Fr Lit, 75; Rhetoric and the Tragedies of Corneille, Tulane Univ, 77; Italian critical antecedents of Boileau's Art Poetique, Proc Pac Northwest Coun Foreign Lang, 78; three articles, In: Columbia Dict of Modern European Literature, 2nd ed, 80. *Mailing Add:* Dept of Foreign Lang Memphis State Univ Memphis TN 38152

HASKA, TADEUSZ LEON, b June 30, 19; US citizen; m 46; c 1. SLAVIC LANGUAGES & LITERATURES. *Educ:* Univ Calif, Berkeley, BA, 62, PhD(Educ), 76; San Jose State Univ, MA, 67. *Prof Exp:* Instr Polish lang & civilization, Army Lang Sch, 51-56, supvr instr, 56-63; assoc prof, 63-65, PROF POLISH LANG & CIVILIZATION, DEFENSE LANG INST, 65- *Mem:* Ling Soc Am; MLA; Am Coun Teaching Foreign Lang; AAUP; Am Educ Res Asn. *Res:* Development of curricula for language courses; second language acquisition; second language teaching methodology. *Publ:* Coauth, Polish Comprehensive Course, Vols I, II, II & V, 52-64 & Polish, Basic Course, Vols I & II, 63-69 (textbooks), Defense Lang Inst, Foreign Lang Ctr. *Mailing Add:* 550 Dry Creek Rd Monterey CA 93940

HASSEL, JON BRIAN, b Fargo, NDak, Jan 28, 39; m 60; c 1. FRENCH. *Educ:* Amherst Col, BA, 61; Brown Univ, MA, 64, PhD(French), 67. *Prof Exp:* Asst prof, 66-76, ASSOC PROF FRENCH, UNIV ARK, FAYETTEVILLE, 76- *Mem:* MLA. *Res:* French Romanticism. *Mailing Add:* Dept of Foreign Lang Univ of Ark Fayetteville AR 72701

HASSELBACH, INGRID TIESLER, b Rabishau, Ger; m 72. GERMAN LITERATURE. *Educ:* Goethe Univ, Ger, Staatsexamen; Tulane Univ, PhD(German), 78. *Prof Exp:* Asst prof German, Fla State Univ, 65-73; LECTR GERMAN, LOYOLA UNIV, 75-; LECTR GERMAN, TULANE UNIV, 78- *Mem:* Mod Foreign Lang Asn. *Res:* Modern German literature (Günter Grass); women in German literature of the 19th century; medieval German literature. *Publ:* Auth, Günter Grass Katz u Maus Interpretation, Oldenbourg Verlag Munchen, 2nd ed, 71. *Mailing Add:* 7325 Maple St New Orleans LA 70118

HASSELBACH, KARL HEINZ, b Giessen, Ger. GERMAN LANGUAGE & LITERATURE. *Educ:* Univ Marburg, DPhil(Ger), 71. *Prof Exp:* Actg asst prof, Fla State Univ, 65-72; asst prof, 72-74, ASSOC PROF GER, TULANE UNIV, 74- *Mem:* AAUP; MLA; Am Asn Teachers Ger. *Res:* Nineteenth century German literature; German dialectology; modern German novel. *Publ:* Auth, Die Mundarten des zentralen Vogelsbergs, Deutsche Dialektgeographie, Vol 76, Elwert, Marburg, 71; Tendenzen neuerer Mundartentwicklung, Z Deutsche Philol, 75; Ortsspott im Vogelsberg, Z Hessischen Heimatbundes, 77; Thomas Mann, Doktor Faustus, Oldenbourg, Munich, 78; Der leitmotivische Gebrauch von Sprachschichten und Sprachpartikeln, In: Thomas Manns Doktor Faustus, Sprache und Brauchtum, 80. *Mailing Add:* Dept Ger & Slavic Lang Tulane Univ New Orleans LA 70118

HASSELL, JAMES WOODROW, JR, b Kobe, Japan, July 5, 15; US citizen; m 47; c 5. FOREIGN LANGUAGES. *Educ:* Davidson Col, AB, 36; Univ NC, AM, 37, PhD(Romance lang), 41. *Prof Exp:* Instr, Univ NC, 39-41; from instr to asst prof foreign lang, Va Polytech Inst, 41-46; from adj prof to prof, Univ SC, 46-62; head dept French, 62-68, PROF FRENCH, UNIV GA, 62- *Concurrent Pos:* Russell res award, Univ SC, 59; Fulbright advan res grant, France, 60-61. *Honors & Awards:* Chevalier, Palmes Academiques, 71. *Mem:* Am Folklore Soc; S Atlantic Mod Lang Asn; Renaissance Soc. *Res:* The short story; French and Italian literature of the Renaissance; Middle French literature. *Publ:* Auth, Sources and Analogues of the Nouvelles Recreations et joyeux devis of Bonaventure des Periers, Vol I, Univ NC, 57; critic ed, Bonaventure des Periers, the Mirrour of Mirth and Pleasant Conceits, Univ SC, 59; auth, Sources and Analogues of the Nouvelles Recreations et joyeux devis of Bonaventure des Periers, Vol II, Univ Ga, 69; The French editions of Des Periers' Tales: A bibliographical study, Ky Romance Quart, 74; ed, Amorous Games: A Critical Edition of Les Adevineaux amoureux, Univ Tex, 74; auth, Middle French Porverbs, Sentences, and Proverbial Phrases, Pontifical Inst Mediaeval Studies, 82. *Mailing Add:* Dept of Romance Lang Univ of Ga Athens GA 30602

HASSELMO, NILS, b Kola, Sweden, July 2, 31; m 58; c 3. LINGUISTICS, SCANDINAVIAN. *Educ:* Univ Uppsala, Fil Mag, 56, Fil Lic, 62; Augustana Col, Ill, AB, 57; Harvard Univ, PhD(ling), 61. *Prof Exp:* Asst Swed, Augustanta Col, Ill, 57, asst prof Scand, 58-63, dir Swed area studies, Augustant summer sch, Swed, 59-63; vis asst prof Scand, Univ Wis, 64-65; assoc prof, 65-71, chmn dept Scand & dir ctr NW Europ lang & area studies, 70-73, assoc dean, Col Lib Arts, 73-78, PROF SCAND & LING, UNIV MINN, MINNEAPOLIS, 71-, VPRES ADMIN & PLANNING, 80- . *Concurrent Pos:* NSF res grant, 63-65; Fulbright-Hays Area Ctr fac fel, 68-69; Thord-Grey fel, UMEA Univ, Sweden, 77; vis prof Scand lang, Uppsala Univ, Sweden, 80. *Mem:* Ling Soc Am; Soc Advan Scand Studies (vpres, 67-69, pres, 71-73); MLA; Am Dialect Soc. *Res:* Scandinavian linguistics; sociolingistics; bilingualism. *Publ:* Auth, Amerika Svenska, Esselte Studium, 74; Swedish America: An Introduction, Swed Info Serv, 76; contribr, De Nordiska Sprakens Framtid, Esselte Studium, 77; Det Moderna Skandinaviens Framvort, Acta Univ Upsoliensis, 78; ed, Perspectives on Swedish immigration, Swed Pioneer Hist Soc, 78; contribr, Ord och Struktur, Lundequistska Bokhandeln, 80; auth, Some Problems in immigrant Bilingualism: Quantitative and qualitative contraints, J Intercult Studies, 80; contribr, Languages in Conflict, Univ Nebr Press, 80. *Mailing Add:* 516 Westwood Dr S Minneapolis MN 55416

HASTINGS, HESTER, b Providence, RI, Sept 15, 09. ROMANCE LANGUAGES. *Educ:* Brown Univ, AB, 31; Johns Hopkins Univ, PhD(Romance lang), 34. *Prof Exp:* Instr Romance lang, Wells Col, 37-38; instr French, Elmira Col, 38-39; asst prof, Marshall Col, 40-41; from asst prof to prof Romance lang, Randolph-Macon Woman's Col, 41-57, prof, 57-78, chmn dept, 62-68; RETIRED. *Mem:* MLA; AAUP. *Res:* Romanticism; W E Channing in France; liberal Christian movement in France, 1820-1870. *Publ:* Ed, Man and Beast in French Thought of the 18th Century, Hopkins Studies Romance Lit & Lang, 37; L'Amusement Philosophique sur le Language des Betes, Droz, Geneva, 57; auth, W E Channing & L'Academie des Sciences Morales et Politiques, Brown Univ, 59. *Mailing Add:* Dept of Romance Lang Randolph-Macon Woman's Col Lynchburg VA 24503

HATCH, MARY GIES, b Omaha, Nebr, Feb 17, 13; m 40; c 4. GERMANIC LANGUAGES. *Educ:* Vassar Col, AB, 35; Univ Mich, MA, 37; Syracuse Univ, PhD(Ger lang), 52. *Prof Exp:* Teacher English, Lincoln High Sch, Detroit, Mich, 37-38, Montclair High Sch, NJ, 38-40 & Dana Hall Sch, Wellesley, 40-42; assoc prof, 60-63, PROF GER & CHMN DEPT, COLUMBIA COL, SC, 63- *Concurrent Pos:* Columbia Col res grant, 68. *Mem:* MLA; SCent Mod Lang Asn; Am Asn Teachers Ger; Am Sociol Asn; Nat Coun Family Rels. *Res:* Middle High German literature; Goethe; Old Frisian language and literature. *Publ:* Auth, Development of Goethe's concept of the calling in Wilhelm Meister's Lehrjahre and the Wanderjahre, Ger Quart, 59; An unhappy family, Marriage & Family Living, 62; coauth, Problems of married working women, In: Woman in a Man-Made World, Ran McNally, 72. *Mailing Add:* Dept of Ger Columbia Col Columbia SC 29205

HATCHER, PAUL GILLIAM, b Sylvia, Tenn, July 1, 22; m 46; c 1. SPANISH, FRENCH. *Educ:* George Peabody Col, BS, 42; Univ Mich, AM, 46, PhD(Romance lang), 56. *Prof Exp:* Instr mod for lang, Delta State Col, 46-47; assoc prof, King Col, 47-49; from asst prof to assoc prof, Furman Univ, 52-56; assoc prof, Carson-Newman Col, 56-59, actg head dept, 58; head dept for lang, 59-77, dean, Potter Col Lib Arts, 65-74, PROF MODERN LANG, WESTERN KY UNIV, 59- *Concurrent Pos:* Charter mem, Ky Arts Comm. *Mem:* Am Asn Teachers Span & Port; Am Asn Teachers Fr. *Res:* Spanish 20th century drama; Spanish American literature; French Romantic drama. *Publ:* Auth, Ideas and opinions of Manuel Linares Rivas. *Mailing Add:* Dept of Modern Lang Western Ky Univ Bowling Green KY 42101

HATFIELD, HENRY CARAWAY, b Evanston, Ill, June 3, 12; m 37; c 2. GERMAN. *Educ:* Harvard Univ, AB, 33; Columbia Univ, AM, 38, PhD, 42. *Prof Exp:* From instr to asst prof, Williams Col, 38-46; from asst prof to assoc prof Ger, Columbia Univ, 46-54; from assoc prof to prof Ger, Harvard Univ, 54-68, Kuno Francke prof, 67-78, sr res prof, 78-82 . *Concurrent Pos:* Gen ed, Ger Rev, 47-52; Guggenheim & Fulbright fesl, 52-53; Am Coun Learned Soc grants, 62 & 75; Nat Endowment for Humanites grant, 75. *Mem:* MLA; Am Asn Teachers Ger. *Res:* German literature of the classical period and the 20th century; myth in 19th and 20th century German literature. *Publ:* Auth, Winckelmann and His German Critics, Columbia Univ, 43; Thomas Mann, rev ed, 62 & Goethe, 63 New Directions, 2nd ed, Harvard Univ, 64; Thomas Mann (anthology), Prentice-Hall, 64; Aesthetic Paganism in German Literature, Harvard Univ, 64; Modern German Literature, E Arnold, London, 66; Crisis and Continuity in Modern German Fiction, Cornell Univ, 69; Clashing Myths in German Literature, Harvard Univ, 74. *Mailing Add:* Widener Libr Harvard Univ Cambridge MA 02138

HATHAWAY, LUISE H, b Hohenaltheim, Ger. GERMANIC LINGUISTICS. *Educ:* Univ Calif, Berkeley, BA, 68, MA, 70, PhD(Ger ling), 76. *Prof Exp:* ASST PROF GER LING, UNIV ILL, CHICAGO, 78- *Concurrent Pos:* Lectr, Univ Calif, Berkeley, 76-77. *Mem:* MLA; Ling Soc Am; Lang Soc; Philol Asn Pac Coast; Am Coun Teaching of Foreign Lang. *Res:* Historical linguistics; sociolinguistics; dialectology. *Publ:* Auth, Some aspects of semantic change in a speech community, Berkeley Ling Soc, 77; The development of sociol dialects in a speech community, Int Cong Ling, 78; Mundartwandel in Imst in Tirol Zwischen 1897 und 1973, Braumuller Verlag: Wein, 79; Style shifting as metaphorical change in point of view, Chicago Ling Soc, 82; Language manipulation by modern totalistic groups, In: Language Policy, Univ Tex Press, 82. *Mailing Add:* German Dept Univ Ill Box 4348 Chicago IL 60680

HATHAWAY, ROBERT LAWTON, b Fall River, Mass, Jan 20, 32. SPANISH GOLDEN AGE LITERATURE. *Educ:* Williams Col, BA, 53; Georgetown Univ, MS, 57; Brown Univ, MA, 62, PhD(Span lit), 69. *Prof Exp:* Instr Span lang & lit, Oakwood Sch, 57-59 & Monon Acad, 59-61; PROF SPAN LIT, COLGATE UNIV, 64- *Mem:* Cervantes Soc Am; Comediantes; Asn Int Hispanistas; MLA; Am Asn Teachers of Span & Port. *Res:* Golden Age theatre; Cervantes' Quijote; Spanish Renaissance. *Publ:* Auth, The art of the epic epithet in the Cantar de Mio Cid, Hisp Rev, 74; Love in the Early Spanish Theatre, Ed Playor, 75; ed, The Villancicos from the Cancionero of Pedro Manuel Jimenex de Urrea, Univ Exeter, 76; La Egloga de Calixto y Melibea de Ximenez de Urrea, Nueva Revista de Filologia Hisp, 78; auth, A hypothetical ancestry for Alonso Quijano, Anales Cervantinos, 78. *Mailing Add:* PO Box 123 Hamilton NY 13346

HATHORN, RICHMOND YANCEY, b Alexandria, La, July 31, 17; m 47; c 3. CLASSICAL LANGUAGES. *Educ:* La Col, BA, 37; La State Univ, MA, 40; Columbia Univ, PhD, 50. *Prof Exp:* Asst prof class lang, La Col, 44-46; lectr Greek & Latin, Columbia Univ, 47-53; prof English & Latin, Northwestern State Col La, 53-62; assoc prof class lang, La State Univ, 62-63; head dept classics, Univ Ky, 63-66; prof Europ lang, Am Univ Beirut, 66-69; PROF CLASSICS & COMP LIT, STATE UNIV NY STONY BROOK, 69- *Concurrent Pos:* Vis assoc prof class lang, Univ Mich, 59; adv ed class lang & lit, Encycl Am, 67- *Mem:* Am Philol Asn. *Res:* Greek tragedy; Homer; classical mythology. *Publ:* Auth, Lear's equations, Centennial Rev, 60; The ritual origin of pastoral, Trans Am Philol Asn, 62; Tragedy, Myth, and Mystery, Ind Univ, 62; Crowell's Handbook of Classical Drama, Crowell, 67; Greek Mythology, Am Univ Beirut, 77. *Mailing Add:* Dept of Classics State Univ of NY Stony Brook NY 11794

HATTON, ROBERT WAYLAND, b Columbus, Ohio, Feb, 5, 34; m 54; c 3. ROMANCE LANGUAGES. *Educ:* Capital Univ, AB, 57; Middlebury Col, AM, 59. *Prof Exp:* Teacher pub schs, Ohio, 58-60; Binat Cult Ctr Grantee, US Info Agency, Colombia, 60-62; instr Span, Ohio Wesleyan Univ, 62-63; from asst prof to assoc prof, 63-70, PROF MOD LANG, CAPITAL UNIV, 70- *Concurrent Pos:* Escort interpreter, US Dept State, 66-70. *Mem:* Am Asn Teachers Span & Port; Taurine Bibliophiles Am; Am Coun Teaching Foreign Lang; Midwest Asn Lang Studies. *Res:* Editing of student texts. *Publ:* Co-ed, La gloria de Don Ramiro, Heath, 66; ed, Hombre hispanico, C E Merrill, 70; Los clarines del miedo, Xerox, 71; coauth, The Bullfight: A Teaching and Study Guide, Advan Press Am, 74; ed, Just a little bit of the Civil War as seen by W J Smith, Co M, 2nd OVC, Ohio Hist, Parts I & II, summer-autumn 75; coauth, A day at the bullfight: A viable alternative to the language fair, Foreign Lang Ann, 2/77; auth, The sideline show, NAWDAC J, fall 78; Louis Bromfield revisited, Ohioana Quart, summer 80. *Mailing Add:* Dept of Mod Lang Captial Univ 2199 E Main St Columbus OH 43209

HATZANTONIS, EMMANUEL S, b Symi, Greece, May 20, 25; US citizen; m 59; c 3. ROMANCE LANGUAGES. *Educ:* City Col New York, BA, 52; Columbia Univ, MA, 53; Univ Calif, Berkeley, PhD, 58. *Prof Exp:* Assoc Ital, Univ Calif, Berkeley, 57-59; from instr to asst prof Ital & French, Univ Ore, 59-61; asst prof Ital, San Jose State Col, 61-62; from asst prof to assoc prof, Univ Ore, 62-65; dir, Ital Studies Ctr, Pavia, 65-67; assoc prof, 67-71, PROF ITAL, UNIV ORE, 71- *Concurrent Pos:* Vis assoc prof, Univ Colo, 68-69; mem adv bd, Forum Italicum, 68-; mem exec comt & regional rep, Am Assoc Teachers Ital; Faculty grant for res overseas. *Mem:* Am Asn Teachers Ital; Dante Soc Am; AAUP. *Res:* Italian Renaissance literature; literary relations between Italy and Greece; nineteenth century Italian fiction. *Publ:* Auth, La Circe della Divina commedia, Romance Philol, 5/60; Lope de Vega's treatment of a Homeric theme, Hispania, 9/65; Circe, redenta d'amore, nel Roman de Troie, Romania, 73; La resa omerica della fimminilita di Cirece, Antiquite Classique, 74; L'affettivita verghiana ne I Malavoglia, Forum Italicum, 74; Una costante della ritrattistica del Verga premalavogliano, Italica, 75; The dimensions of tragedy in Verga's I Malavoglia, Neophilologus, 78; Spain and the genesis of Neohellenic literature, Hispanofila, 80. *Mailing Add:* Dept of Romance Lang Univ of Ore Eugene OR 97403

HAUBER, ROSE MARIE, b St Marys, Pa, Sept 13, 97. CLASSICAL LANGUAGES. *Educ:* Duquesne Univ, AB, 34; Cath Univ Am, AM, 36, PhD, 38. *Prof Exp:* Instr class lang & lit, 38-42, PROF CLASSICS, CARLOW COL, 42- *Mem:* Am Class League; Class Asn Atlantic States; Am Philol Asn. *Res:* Late Latin vocabulary of the moralia of Saint Gregory the Great. *Mailing Add:* Dept of Classics Carlow Col 5th Ave Pittsburgh PA 15213

HAUGEN, EINAR INGVALD, b Sioux City, Iowa, Apr 19, 06; m 32; c 2. SCANDINAVIAN & GENERAL LINGUISTICS. *Educ:* St Olaf Col, AB, 28; Univ Ill, AM, 29, PhD(English & Scand), 31. *Hon Degrees:* LittD, Univ Mich, 53; DHL, St Olaf Col, 58; MA, Harvard Univ, 60; DPhil, Univ Oslo, 61; DrHum, Univ Wis, 69; DPhil, Univ Reykjavik, 71, Univ Trondheim, 72 & Univ Uppsala, 76; DLit, Luther Col, 75, Morningside Col, 78. *Prof Exp:* From asst prof to prof Scand lang, Univ Wis, 31-38; Thompson prof, 38-62, dir ling inst, 43-44, Vilas res prof, 62-64, Thomas Prof Scand & ling, 64-75, EMER PROF SCAND & LING, HARVARD UNIV, 75- *Concurrent Pos:* Vis lectr, Univ Oslo, 38; Guggenheim fel, 42; US Cult Off, Oslo, 45-46; lectr, Univ Minn, 48, 58 & 81, Univ Mich, 49; Fulbright res prof, Univ Oslo, 51-52; lectr, Georgetown Univ, 54; US Dept State lectr, Univ Iceland, 56; lectr, Harvard Univ, 60-61; pres, Int Congr Linguists, 62; res fel, Ctr Advan Studies Behav Sci, 63-64; lectr, Ind Univ, 64; Nat Endowment for Humanities fel, 67-68; NSF res grant, 67-69; lectr, Univ Uppsala, 76-77. *Honors & Awards:* Order of St Olaf, Norway, 40; Order of North Star, Sweden, 61; Nansen Award, Oslo Acad Sci, 70; Jancke Award, 77, Royal Gustavus Adolphus Acad, Sweden; Mjoen Award, 79. *Mem:* MLA; Ling Soc Am (pres, 50); Am Dialect Soc (pres, 65-67); Soc Advan Studies (pres, 47); hon mem Royal Norweg Soc Sc. *Res:* Scandinavian languages, textbooks and linguistics; bilingualism; American-Scandinavian cultural relations. *Publ:* Auth, Norwegian-English Dictionary, Univ Wis & Univ Oslo, 65; Language Conflict and Language Planning, Harvard Univ, 66; Ecology of Language, Stanford Univ, 72; Studies, Mouton, 72; The Scandinavian Languages, Faber & Faber, Harvard Univ, 76; Ibsen's drama, Univ Minn, 79; Oppdalsmaalet, Tanum, 82; Scand Lang Structures, Niemeyer & Univ Minn, 82. *Mailing Add:* 45 Larch Circle Belmont MA 02178

HAUSER, ALAN JON, Old & New Testament. See Vol IV

HAUSER, RONALD, b Stuttgart, Ger, Feb 7, 27; US citizen; m; c 1. NINETEENTH CENTURY & CURRENT GERMAN LITERATURE. *Educ:* Univ Calif, Berkeley, AB, 51, MA, 54, PhD(Ger), 57. *Prof Exp:* Instr Ger, Northwestern Univ, 55-58; instr, Smith Col, 58-60; asst prof, Univ Mass, Amherst, 60-66; assoc provost arts & lett, 68-70, ASSOC PROF GER, STATE UNIV NY BUFFALO, 66- *Res:* Nineteenth and twentieth century German literature; literature and science. *Publ:* Auth, The concept of social necessity in Hebbel's Moloch, Germanic Rev, 61; Georg Buchner's Leonce und Lena, Monatshefte, 61; Einführung in die Deutsche Literatur, Hold, 64; Critic on a razor edge, Nation, 66; Georg Büchner, Twayne, 74. *Mailing Add:* Dept of Ger & Slavic Lang State Univ of NY Amherst Campus Buffalo NY 14214

HAVELOCK, ERIC ALFRED, b London, England, June 3, 03; US citizen; m 27, 62; c 3. ANCIENT PHILOSOPHY. *Educ:* Cambridge Univ, BA, 26, Emmanuel Col, MA, 29. *Hon Degrees:* MA, Harvard Univ, 47 & Yale Univ, 63. *Prof Exp:* From asst to prof classics, Acadia Univ, 26-29; assoc prof, Victoria Col, Univ Toronto, 29-47; assoc prof, Harvard Univ, 47-51, prof Greek & Latin, 51-63, chmn dept Classics, 55-60; Sterling prof, 63-71, chmn dept, 63-68, EMER PROF CLASSICS, YALE UNIV, 71- *Concurrent Pos:* Guggenheim fel, 41-43; sr tutor, Leverett House, 47-50; vis prof, Princeton Univ, 60-61; Nat Endowment for Humanities sr fac fel, 68-69. *Mem:* Am Philol Asn; Am Acad Arts & Sci; Eastern Div Am Philos Asn; Can Class Asn (1st pres). *Res:* Ancient philosophy; Latin poetry; Greek epic and drama. *Publ:* Auth, The Liberal Temper in Greek Politics, 57, reissued, 64; Preface to Plate, Blackwell, 63, reissued, 67 & 82; transl, Cultura Orale e Civilta della Scrittura, Rome, 73; auth, The Greek Concept of Justice, 78; transl, Dike: La Nascita della Coscienza, Rome, 81; The Literate Revolution in Greece and its Cultural Consequences, Princeton, 82. *Mailing Add:* Route 5 Merryall New Milford CT 06776

HAWLEY, DONALD C, b Platteville, Colo, June 18, 30; m 53; c 3. SPANISH. *Educ:* Nebr State Col, AB, 52; Univ Iowa, MA, 56, PhD, 61. *Prof Exp:* Instr Span & Ger, Sacramento State Col, 57-60; from asst prof to assoc prof Span, Univ Wyo, 61-66; assoc prof Span, 66-70, head dept foreign lang, 66-77, PROF SPAN, UNIV NORTHERN IOWA, 70- *Mem:* MLA; Am Asn Teachers Span & Port. *Res:* Spanish literature, especially Golden Age and poetics; translation. *Mailing Add:* Dept of For Lang Univ of Northern Iowa Cedar Falls IA 50613

HAWLEY, WHEELER, b Hartford, Conn, Sept 20, 04; m 25, 51; c 3. MODERN LANGUAGES. *Educ:* Trinity Col, Conn, AB, 24; Harvard Univ, MA, 25; Univ Tex, PhD(Romance lang), 48. *Prof Exp:* Instr Romance lang, Univ Minn, 26-28; teacher, Blake Sch, Minneapolis, Minn, 28-29; instr French, Trinity Col, Conn, 29-30; instr Romance lang, Univ Buffalo, 30-31; teacher, McBurney Sch, New York, 31-34; instr Romance lang, Univ Tex, 45-48; from asst prof to assoc prof French, Tex Christian Univ, 48-52; assoc prof mod lang, 52-55, prof for lang, 55-78, head dept, 62-74, chmn div humanities, 66-69, EMER PROF FOREIGN LANG, SAMFORD UNIV, 78- *Mailing Add:* 219 Dixon Ave Birmingham AL 35209

HAWORTH, MARCUS A, b Manitowoc, Wis, Sept 10, 15. CLASSICAL LANGUAGES. *Educ:* St Louis Univ, AB, 39, MA, 41; Fordham Univ, PhD(Latin), 53. *Prof Exp:* From asst prof to assoc prof, 51-68, PROF CLASS LANG, ST LOUIS UNIV, 68- *Concurrent Pos:* St Thomas More proj grants, Yale Univ, 60 & 62. *Mem:* Am Philol Asn; Class Asn Mid W & S. *Res:* Correspondence of Thomas More; epistles of Erasmus; the Jesuit Latin drama Zeno. *Publ:* Transl, Latin epistles, In: St Thomas More: Selected Letters, 61 & St Thomas More: Selected Letters, 67, Yale Univ; Erasmus and His Age: Selected Letters of Desiderius Erasmus, Harper, 70. *Mailing Add:* Dept of Class Lang St Louis Univ St Louis MO 63103

HAWS, GARY LEWIS, b Vernal, Utah, Apr 12, 35; m 59; c 3. IBERO-AMERICAN STUDIES. *Educ:* Brigham Young Univ, AB, 59; Univ NMex, PhD(Ibero-Am studies), 68. *Prof Exp:* Mem Peace Corps staff area studies, Univ NMex, 63; chmn dept mod lang, Adams State Col, 63-64; asst prof, Weber State Col, 64-67; univ found res grant, 67-68, PROF SPAN, MURRAY STATE UNIV, 67-, DIR LATIN AM STUDIES PROG, 70- *Mem:* Inst Lit Iberoam; MLA; Latin Am Studies Asn; Am Asn Teachers Span & Port. *Res:* Contemporary Latin American literature; Uruguyan literature; cultural anthropology. *Publ:* Auth, Carlos Sabat Ercasty y la poesia Uruguaya del siglo XX, 67; El Prometeo Uruguayo, Impresora Uruguaya Colombino, Montevideo, 69; Florencio Sanchez y el drama vioplatense, Montevideo: Siglo Ilustado, 82. *Mailing Add:* Box 3187 University Station Murray KY 42071

HAYAKAWA, SAMUEL ICHIYE, b Vancouver, BC, July 18, 06; nat US; m 37; c 3. SEMANTICS, ENGLISH LITERATURE. *Educ:* Univ Man, BA, 27; McGill Univ, MA, 28; Univ Wis-Madison, PhD(English), 35. *Hon Degrees:* DFA, Calif Col Arts & Crafts, 56; DLitt, Grinnell Col, 67; LHD, Pepperdine Univ, 72; LLD, The Citadel, 72. *Prof Exp:* Instr English, Univ Wis-Exten, 36-39; from instr to assoc prof, Ill Inst Technol, 39-47; lectr semantics, Univ Col, Univ Chicago, 50-55; prof English, 55-68, from actg pres to pres, 68-73, EMER PRES, SAN FRANCISCO STATE UNIV, 73- *Concurrent Pos:* US Senator, 77-82. *Mem:* Fel Am Asn Advan Sci. *Res:* Psycholinguistics. *Publ:* Coauth, Oliver Wendell Holmes, Am Bk Co, 39; auth, Language in Action, 41 & Language in Thought and Action, 49, 63, 72 & 78, Harcourt; ed, Language, Meaning and Maturity, 52 & Our Language and Our World, 59, Harper; Use and Misuse of Language, Fawcett, 62; Modern Guide to Synonyms, Funk & Wagnalls, 68; Through the Communication Barrier, Harper, 79. *Mailing Add:* 225 Eldridge Ave PO Box 100 Mill Valley CA 94941

HAYCOCK, BEVAN ORLANDO, b Ogden, Utah, Oct 18, 28; m 56; c 6. SPANISH LANGUAGE & LITERATURE. *Educ:* Brigham Young Univ, BA, 50, MA, 61. *Prof Exp:* Instr Span, Brigham Young Univ, 61-62; asst prof, 64-69, ASSOC PROF SPAN, NMEX STATE UNIV, 70- *Concurrent Pos:* Lang coordr, Training for Latin Am, US Peace Corps Ctrs, Escondido, Calif & Detroit, Mich, 66-68. *Mem:* Am Asn Teachers Span & Port; Rocky Mountain Mod Lang Asn. *Res:* Spanish Golden Age drama; Mexican literature. *Mailing Add:* Dept of Foreign Lang NMex State Univ Box 3L Las Cruces NM 88003

HAYES, ADEN WILLIAM, b Idaho Falls, Idaho, Sept 4, 43. LATIN AMERICAN & HISPANIC LITERATURE. *Educ:* Rutgers Univ, BA, 65; Princeton Univ, MA, 67, PhD(Romance lang), 77. *Prof Exp:* Asst prof Romance lang, Wesleyan Univ, 73-81; ASST PROF MOD LANG, ST LAWRENCE UNIV, 81- *Mem:* MLA; Am Asn Univ Professors; Am Asn Teacher Span & Port. *Res:* Latin American fiction; autobiography; Jorge Luis Borges. *Publ:* Auth, Arlt's confessional fiction: The aesthetics of failure, Vol 5, No 3 & Rulfo's counter-epic: Pedro Paramo and the stasis of history, Vol 7, No 3, J Span Studies, Twentieth Century; Reality and the novel--The case of Roberto Arlt, Romance Notes, Vol 21, No 1; Narrative errors in Rinconete y Cortadillo, Bull Hisp Studies, 57: 13-20; Fiton's Aleph, Ercilla's world, Rev Estudios Hisp, Vol 15, No 3; coauth (with Khachig Tololyan), The cross and the compass: Patterns of order in Chesterton and Borges, Hisp Rev, 49; 395-405; auth, Roberto Arlt--La estrategia de su ficcion, Tamesis Books Ltd, London, 81. *Mailing Add:* Dept of Mod Lang St Lawrence Univ Canton NY 13617

HAYES, CURTIS W, b Long Beach, Calif, Sept 13, 37; m 65; c 2. ENGLISH, LINGUISTICS. *Educ:* Calif State Univ, Long Beach, BA, 59, MA, 60; Univ Tex, PhD, 64. *Prof Exp:* Asst prof English, Univ Nebr-Lincoln, 64-73; PROF ENGLISH & COORDR ENGLISH LANG PROG, UNIV TEX, SAN ANTONIO, 73- *Concurrent Pos:* Consult, Nebr Curriculum Ctr, 64- & tri-univ proj, Univ Nebr, 64-73; Nebr Univ Res Coun fels, 65, 67 & 69-70; Japanese Ministry Educ prof & adv chmn English Prog, Kumamoto Univ, 71-72; vpres, TEX-TESOL, 77-78, pres, 78-79 & 81-82. *Mem:* NCTE; Teachers English to Speakers Other Lang; Ling Soc Am; Ling Asn Southwest; Nat Asn Biling Educ. *Res:* Bilingualism; literary analysis and linguistics; medieval English. *Publ:* Auth, The rise and fall of the foreign language teacher, linguistically, In: From Meaning to Sound, Univ Nebr Press, 76; coauth, The ABC's of Languages and Linguistics, Inst Mod Lang, 77; The role of handwriting in TESOL, Teachers English Speakers Other Lang Newslett, 2/79; Japan: Languages in contact, In: Sociolinguistic Studies in Language Contact, Mouton, The Hague, 79; What do I do on Monday?, In: An ESL Institute Provides the Answer, TESL Reporter, 13: 56-57; co-ed, Talking Purposefully, Vol I of Teacher Idea Series, Inst Mod Lang, 81; coauth, The business of selling foreign languages, Tex Foreign Lang Asn Bull, 12/81; ESL: Now it's the law in Texas, Teachers English Speakers Other Lang Newslett, XVI: 3-4. *Mailing Add:* 3017 Charter Crest San Antonio TX 78230

HAYES, FRANCIS CLEMENT, b Buncombe Co, NC, Dec 14, 04; m 31. SPANISH, FOLKLORE. *Educ:* Univ NC, AB, 28, PhD, 36; Columbia Univ, AM, 30. *Prof Exp:* Instr Span, Univ NC, 27-28, 30-31 & 32-40 & NY Univ, 28-30; assoc prof Span & French, Charleston Col, 31-32; prof foreign lang & chmn dept, Guilford Col, 40-44; prof Am civilization, Univ Chuquisaca, Bolivia, 44-45; from assoc prof to prof, 46-73, EMER PROF SPAN, UNIV FLA, 73- *Concurrent Pos:* Assoc ed, SAtlantic Bull, 48-72; mem adv comt, Mod Span, publ by Foreign Lang Prog, MLA, through Harcourt. *Mem:* SAtlantic Mod Lang Asn; Am Asn Teachers Span & Port; MLA; Southern Humanities Conf (pres, 55-56); Am Asn Advan of Humanities. *Res:* Spanish proverbs and folk gestures; Spanish drama. *Publ:* Auth, The Use of Proverbs as Titles and Motifs in the Siglo de Oro Drama, Univ NC, 36; The collecting of proverbs as titles and motifs in the Siglo de oro drama: Lope de Vega, Hisp Rev, 38; Gesture, In: Encycl Americana, Grolier, 41 & 58; co-ed, Stephen Vincent Benet, America, US Dept State, 45; coauth, Beginning Spanish, Houghton, 49; auth, Gestures: A Working Bibliography, Univ Fla Libr & Southern Folklore Quart, 57; Lope de Vega, Twayne, 67; The great dismal swamp of amateur Freudian literary criticism, Mod Lang J, 74. *Mailing Add:* 2035 NW Seventh Lane Gainesville FL 32703

HAYES, WALTER MARTIN, b Detroit, Mich, Sept 4, 22. CLASSICS, BYZANTINE GREEK. *Educ:* Loyola Univ Chicago, AB, 45, AM, 50; West Baden Col, PhL, 47, STL, 54; Harvard Univ, AM, 60 PhD(class philol), 69. *Prof Exp:* Instr Latin, Xavier Univ, 55-57; asst prof classics, Univ Detroit, 61-67 & John Carroll Univ, 69-70; res assoc, 70-71, FEL GREEK, PONTIF INST MEDIAEVAL STUDIES, 72-, DIR AUTHOR, TITLE, INDEX CATALOGUES GREEK MANUSCRIPTS, 74- *Concurrent Pos:* Assoc prof Byzantine Greek, Ctr Medieval Studies, Univ Toronto, 71-74; mem, Creative Educ Found. *Mem:* Int Asn Byzantine Studies; Am Philol Soc; Nat Soc Prog Instr. *Res:* Greek codicology. *Publ:* Auth, Introductory Greek Program (5 vols), 66 Introductory Latin Program (5 vols) & coauth, Introductory French Program (2 vols), 70, Loyola Univ; auth, Greek Manuscript Tradition of Basil's Adversus eunomium, Brill, Leiden, 72; Pontifical Institute Greek MSI, Mediaeval Studies, 77. *Mailing Add:* 21 Sultan Toronto ON M5S 1L8 Can

HAYMES, EDWARD RANDOLPH, b Lynchburg, Va, Dec 15, 40; m 63; c 2. GERMAN COMPARATIVE LITERATURE. *Educ:* Lynchburg Col, BA, 65; Univ Va, MA, 66; Univ Erlangen, Ger, PhD(Ger), 69. *Prof Exp:* Asst prof Ger Va Commonwealth Univ, 69-72; asst prof, 73-76, ASSOC PROF GER, UNIV HOUSTON, 76- *Mem:* MLA; SCent Mod Lang Asn; Am Asn Teachers Ger; Medieval Acad; SAtlantic Mod Lang Asn. *Res:* Oral Epic poetry; Medieval German poetry; Medieval narrative poetry. *Publ:* Auth, Mündliches Epos in mittelhochdeutscher Zeit, Kümmerle, Göppingen, 69, 2nd ed, 75; A bibliography of studies relating to Parry's and Lord's Oral Theory, Ctr Study Oral Lit, 73; Das mündliche Epos, Metzler, Stuttgart, 77. *Mailing Add:* Dept of Ger Univ of Houston Houston TX 77004

HAYNE, DAVID MACKNESS, b Toronto, Ont, Aug 12, 21; m 55. FRENCH. *Educ:* Univ Toronto, BA, 42; Univ Ottawa, MA, 44, PhD, 45. *Prof Exp:* From lectr to assoc prof, 45-61, registr univ col, 56-61, PROF FRENCH, UNIV TORONTO, 61- *Concurrent Pos:* Mem, Nat Res Coun Can, 42-43; Dir Mil Intel, Dept Nat Defence, 43-45; gen ed, Dictionary Can Biog, 65-69; assoc ed, Univ Toronto Quart, 65-76. *Mem:* Fel Royal Soc Can; Asn Can Univ Teachers Fr; Bibliog Soc Can; Can Ling Asn; Can Comp Lit Asn. *Res:* French-Canadian literature; 17th century French literature. *Publ:* Auth, Les Origines du roman canadien-francais, Arch Lett Can, 64; Les grandes options de la litterature canadienne-francaise, Etudes Francaises, 2/65; coauth, Bibliographie critique du roman canadien-francais, 1837-1900, 68 & ed, Dictionary of Canadian Bibliography, Volume II: 1701-1740, 69, Univ Toronto; auth, La Poesie romantique au Canada Francais, 1860-1890, Arch Lett Can, 69. *Mailing Add:* Rm 143 Univ of Toronto Toronto ON M5S 1A1 Can

HAYNES, MARIA SCHNEE, b Rankweil, Austria, Feb 10, 12; US citizen; m 47; c 1. ENGLISH, GERMAN. *Educ:* Innsbruck Univ, MA, 38, MA, 40, MA, 42; Univ Calif, Los Angeles, PhD(English), 56. *Prof Exp:* Asst prof, German Instituto Sant'Anna, Lugano, Switz, 35-36; from instr to assoc prof German & Italian, teachers' cols, Austria, 37-45; interpreter German & English, special serv, US Army, Salzburg, Austria, 45-47; PROF GERMAN & ENGLISH, CALIF STATE UNIV, CHICO, 56- *Mem:* Geront Soc. *Publ:* Auth, Henry Handel Richardson, Bull Bibliog, 55; The supposedly golden age for the aged in ancient Greece, 62 & The supposed golden age for the aged in ancient Rome, 63, Gerontologist; Deutsch in Drei Ländern, Odyssey, 68; coauth, Kultur and Alltag, Scribner, 73. *Mailing Add:* 2 Marvin Cir Chico CA 95926

HAYS, DAVID GLENN, b Memphis, Tenn, Nov 17, 28; m 50, 76; c 3. LINGUISTICS. *Educ:* Harvard Univ, BA, 51, MA, 53, PhD(sociol), 56. *Prof Exp:* Soc scientist, Rand Corp, 55-68; PROF LING, STATE UNIV NY BUFFALO, 68- *Concurrent Pos:* Stagiaire qualifie, Europ Atomic Energy Comn Res Ctr, Ispra, Italy, 62-63; mem automatic lang processing adv comt, nat acad sci, 64-66; mem, Math Soc Sci Bd, 67-72; adv comt soc sci, Nat Sci Found, 70-72, chmn, 72. *Mem:* Asn Comput Ling (pres, 64); Int Comt Comput Ling. *Res:* Cognitive structure in relation to language; cross-cultural linguistics. *Publ:* Auth, Dependency theory, Language, 10/64; ed, Readings in Automatic Language Processing, 66 & auth, Introduction to Computational Linguistics, 67, Am Elsevier; coauth, Color term salience, Am Anthropologist, 12/72; auth, Language and interpersonal relationships, Daedalus, 6/73; Linguistics as a focus for intellectual integration, In: Linguistics: Teaching and Interdisciplinary Relations, Georgetown Univ, 74; On alienation: An essay in the psycholinguistics of science, In: Theories of Alienation, Nijhoff, 76; Types of processes on cognitive networks, Comput & Math Ling, 77. *Mailing Add:* Dept of Ling State Univ NY Buffalo NY 14222

HAYWARD, EARL FRANKLIN, b Cheboygan, Mich, Feb 2, 32; m 58; c 4. FRENCH LANGUAGE & LITERATURE. *Educ:* Alma Col, BA, 53; Univ Mich, Ann Arbor, MA, 54. *Prof Exp:* From instr to asst prof French, 61-70, assoc prof, 70-78, PROF FRENCH & CHMN DEPT, ALMA COL, 78-, DIR STUDIES IN FRANCE, 69- *Mem:* MLA; Am Asn Teachers Fr; Am Coun Teaching Foreign Lang. *Res:* Development of reading materials in French outside area of literature; international programs. *Mailing Add:* Dept of French Alma Col Alma MI 48801

HAYWOOD, BRUCE, b York, England, Sept 30. 25; US citizen; m 47; c 2. GERMAN. *Educ:* McGill Univ, BA, 50, MA, 51; Harvard Univ, PhD, 56. *Prof Exp:* From asst prof to assoc prof Ger, Kenyon Col, 54-60, dean col, 63-67, prof, 60-80, provost, 67-80; PRES, MONMOUTH COL, 80- *Concurrent Pos:* Consult ed, Studies Romanticism, 62-; consult, Nat Endowment for Humanities, 75- *Mem:* Am Asn Teachers Ger. *Res:* Romanticism; modern German literature, 20th century. *Publ:* Auth, Novalis: The Veil of Imagery, Harvard Univ, 58. *Mailing Add:* Kenyon Col Gambier OH 43022

HAZERA, LYDIA DELEON, b Pueblo, Colo. SPANISH AMERICAN LITERATURE. *Educ:* Univ Colo, BA, 45, MA, 49; George Washington Univ, PhD(Span Am lit), 71. *Prof Exp:* Instr Span, Sch Advan Int Studies, Johns Hopkins Univ, 63-70; lectr, 70-72, asst prof, 72-76, ASSOC PROF SPAN, GEORGE MASON UNIV, 76- *Mem:* MLA; AAUP; Am Asn Teachers Span & Port. *Res:* Spanish American novel. *Publ:* Auth, La novel de la selva hispanoamericana, Instituto Caro y Cuervo, Bogota, Columbia, 71; Narrative technique in Manuel Puig's Boquitas Pintadas, Latin Am Lit Rev, fall 73; Tema y estructura de La mala hora de Gabriel Garcia Marquez, Thesaurus, Tomo XXVIII, 73. *Mailing Add:* Dept of Foreign Lang George Mason Univ Fairfax VA 22030

HEAD, GERALD L, b Artesia, Calif, Mar 27, 36; m 56; c 3. SPANISH, PORTUGUESE. *Educ:* Univ Calif, Los Angeles, BA, 59, PhD(hisp, lang & lit), 64. *Prof Exp:* Assoc prof, 64-72, PROF SPANISH & PORTUGUESE, SAN DIEGO STATE UNIV, 72- *Mem:* Inst Int Lit Iberoam. *Mailing Add:* Dept of Span & Portuguese San Diego State Univ San Diego CA 92115

HEALEY, ROBERT FISHER, b Medford, Mass, May 21, 24. CLASSICS. *Educ:* Boston Col, BA, 47, MA, 48; Oxford Univ, AB, 52, MA, 55; Harvard Univ, PhD(classics), 61. *Prof Exp:* From instr to asst prof classics, Boston Col, 60-66, chmn dept, 61-66; asst prof, Fairfield Univ, 66-67; ASSOC PROF CLASSICS, COL OF THE HOLY CROSS, 68- *Concurrent Pos:* Vis prof, Brandeis Univ, 70. *Mem:* Class Asn New England; Class Teachers New England; Am Philol Asn; Archaeol Inst Am; Vergilian Soc. *Res:* Greek epigraphy; ancient religions. *Publ:* Auth, A sacrifice without a deity in the Athenian state calendar, Harvard Theol Rev, 7/64; coauth, A sacred calendar of Eleusis, Harvard Theol Studies, 12/65. *Mailing Add:* Dept of Classics Col of the Holy Cross Worcester MA 01610

HEATH, DALE E, b Newcastle, Pa, Nov 23, 17; m 40. ANCIENT LANGUAGE & HISTORY. *Educ:* Mich State Univ, PhD(medieval hist), 65. *Prof Exp:* PROF ANCIENT LANG & HIST, TAYLOR UNIV, 60- *Res:* Hellenistic Greek. *Publ:* Auth, Manuscript Vatican Greek 2061, Taylor Univ, 65. *Mailing Add:* Dept of Ancient Lang Taylor Univ Upland IN 46989

HEATH, JAMES MAGUIRE, b Beckenham, England, July 2, 33; US citizen; m 65; c 3. CLASSICS. *Educ:* Princeton Univ, AB, 54, MA, 59, PhD(classics), 64. *Prof Exp:* Instr classics, Kenyon Col, 59-61; from instr to asst prof, Rice Univ, 61-65; asst prof, 65-72, ASSOC PROF CLASSICS, BUCKNELL UNIV, 72- *Mem:* Am Philol Asn; Archaeol Inst Am. *Res:* Greek philology; Roman history. *Publ:* Assoc ed, The arts and their interrelations, 79, Romanticism, Modernism, Postmodernism, 80 & Literature, arts and religion, 81, Bucknell Rev. *Mailing Add:* Dept of Classics Bucknell Univ Lewisburg PA 17837

HECHT, LEO, b Vienna, Austria, Mar 16, 27; US citizen; m 54 c 1. RUSSIAN LANGUAGE & LITERATURE. *Educ:* Columbia Univ, BS, 60, MA, 61 PhD(Slavic langs), 73. *Prof Exp:* Instr polit sci, US Govt Sch, Dept Defense, 56-60; instr Ger, Univ Md, 69-70; assoc prof Russ & chmn dept foreign lang & lit, 72-80, CHMN RUSS STUDIES, GEORGE MASON UNIV, 80- *Concurrent Pos:* Fulbright fel to Moscow Univ, 82; ed, Newsnotes on Soviet & E Europ Drama & Theatre. *Mem:* Am Asn Teachers Slavic & E Europ Lang; MLA. *Res:* Russian cultural history; contemporary Soviet affairs. *Publ:* Auth, Cagliostro in Russian, 18th Century Life, 6/75; Tolstoy the Rebel, Revisionist Press, 12/76; Lermontov and the German poets, Can-Am Slavic Studies, fall 77; The place of literature in the foreign language instruction of non-majors, Reading Improvement, fall 78; The Biggest and the Best: Moscow State University, Col Student J, fall 78; The Dementia of I-330, TOPIC, 80; The USSR Today: Facts and Interpretations, Scholasticus Publ, 2nd ed, 5/82. *Mailing Add:* Dept of Foreign Lang & Lit George Mason Univ Fairfax VA 22030

HECK, FRANCIS S, b Morristown, NJ, Apr 14, 24; m 52; c 2. FRENCH. *Educ:* Manhattan Col, BA, 50; Univ Louvain, Cert, 51; NY Univ, MA, 55, PhD(French lit), 64. *Prof Exp:* From instr to asst prof French & Ger, Manhattan Col, 52-64; from asst prof to assoc prof French, Univ Scranton, 64-66; asst prof, 66-71, assoc prof, 71-81, PROF FRENCH, UNIV WYO, 81- *Mem:* MLA. *Res:* French new novel; symbolist poets; 19th century French literature. *Publ:* Auth, Spiritual Isolation in French Literature, 71 & Essays on the French New Novel, 75, Dos Continentes, Madrid; Montaigne's liberalism and conservatism, Romanic Rev, 75; Baudelaire's La Fanfarlo: Romantic irony, Fr Rev, 76; Sabato, Robbe-Grillet, new novel, Rev Estud Hispanicos, 78; La Beaute: Enigma of irony, 19th-Century Fr Studies, 81; Baudelaire's Chacun sa Chimere, Romance Notes, 81; Evolution in Baudelaire's later poetry, Nottingham Fr Studies, 81. *Mailing Add:* Dept of Mod Lang Univ of Wyo Laramie WY 82070

HEDGES, INEZ KATHLEEN, b Washington, DC. COMPARATIVE LITERATURE, FRENCH LITERATURE. *Educ:* Harvard & Radcliffe Cols, BA, 68; Univ Wis, Madison, PhD(comp lit), 76. *Prof Exp:* ASST PROF ROMANCE LANG, DUKE UNIV, 76- *Mem:* MLA; Am Comp Lit Asn; Soc for Cinema Studies. *Mailing Add:* Dept of Romance Lang Duke Univ Durham NC 27706

HEDGES, JAMES STOY, b Posey Co, Ind, Nov 27, 33; m 63; c 2. LINGUISTICS, AMERICAN LITERATURE. *Educ:* Purdue Univ, BS, 60, MA, 64; Univ Nebr, Lincoln, PhD(English), 70. *Prof Exp:* Teacher English, Span & hist, Clarksville Jr/Sr High Sch, Ind, 60-64; teacher English, Mt Vernon High Sch, Ind, 64-67; instr, Ind State Univ, Evansville, 65-67 & Univ Nebr, Lincoln, 67-70; asst prof, 70-75, ASSOC PROF ENGLISH, UNIV NC, CHARLOTTE, 75- *Concurrent Pos:* Consult English, Ind English Curric Develop Ctr, Ind Univ, 64-67. *Mem:* Mid-Am Ling Conf; SAtlantic Mod Lang Asn; Popular Cult Asn South; Southeastern Am Studies Asn. *Res:* American linguistics; 19th century American literature; American folklore. *Publ:* Auth, Phrasal verbs: Elements of folk-language, In: From Meaning to Sound, Univ Nebr, 75; Towards a Case for Isodinomous Verse, Proc 1975 Mid-Am Ling Conf, Univ Kans, 76; Nouns with Stressed Final Syllables in Midwestern Folk Speech, Proc 1976 Mid-Am Ling Conf, Univ Minn, 77; Correlation of Line and Syntax in Shaped Poems, Proc 1977 Mid-Am Ling Conf, Univ Mo, 78; The cricket in Thoreau's Journals, Thoreau J Quart, 4/79; Towards formal boundaries for the act in popular culture, Studies Popular Cult, spring 81; Sidney Lanier's The Science of English Verse: A linguistic rereading, Proc 1981 Mid-Am Ling Conf, Wichita State Univ, 82; ed introd, James F Cooper's The Monikins, Col & Univ Press (in press). *Mailing Add:* Dept of English Univ NC Charlotte NC 28223

HEER, NICHOLAS LAWSON, b Chapel Hill, NC, Feb 8, 28. ARABIC & ISLAMIC STUDIES. *Educ:* Yale Univ, BA, 49; Princeton Univ, PhD(Orient lang), 55. *Prof Exp:* Transl analyst, Arabian Am Oil Co, Dhahran, Saudi Arabia, 55-57; cur MidE Collection, Hoover Inst & asst prof Arabic, Stanford Univ, 58-62; vis lectr, Yale Univ, 62-63; asst prof, Harvard Univ, 63-65; assoc prof, 65-76, PROF ARABIC, UNIV WASH, 76- *Concurrent Pos:* Alexander Kohut fel, Yale Univ, 62-63. *Mem:* Am Orient Soc; Am Asn Teachers Arabic (treas, 65-76, pres, 81); MidE Studies Asn. *Res:* Arabic language; Islamic philosophy and theology. *Publ:* Ed, Al-Hakim al-Tirmidki: Bayan al-Farq bayn al-Sadr wa al-Qalb wa al-Fu'ad wa al-Lubb, Cairo, 58; auth, Some biographical and bibliographical notes on al-Hakim al-Tirmidhi, In: The World of Islam, London, 59; A Sufi psychological treatise, Muslim World, 61; transl, The Precious Pearl, State Univ NY, 79; ed, Jami: al-Durrah al-Fakhirah, Tehran, 80. *Mailing Add:* Dept of Near Eastern Lang & Lit DH-20 Univ of Wash Seattle WA 98195

HEESEN, PHILIP T, b Philadelphia, Pa, Mar 7, 26; m 52; c 6. CLASSICAL LANGUAGES, LATIN & GREEK. *Educ:* St Charles Sem, Pa, BA, 47; Villanova Univ, MA, 56; Univ Pa, MA, 60, PhD(class studies), 65. *Prof Exp:* Teacher high schs, Pa, 48-67; assoc prof, 67-72, asst chmn, Dept For Lang, 70-79, PROF CLASSICS, MILLERSVILLE STATE COL, 72- *Concurrent Pos:* Lectr classics, Villanova Univ, 60-67. *Mem:* Am Philol Asn; Am Class League; Class Asn Atlantic States. *Res:* Latin linguistics and pedagogy; Ciceronian studies. *Publ:* Auth, Further thoughts on teaching Latin as a language: A rejoinder, Pa Class Asn Bull, 2/73; coauth, Cicero and Diodotus, Class Bull, 1/76; auth, Inventory of specialized competencies for the training of teachers of foreign languages, Bull Pa State Mod Lang Asn, spring 77. *Mailing Add:* Dept Foreign Lang Millersville State Col Millersville PA 17551

HEGEL, ROBERT EARL, b Goodrich, Mich, Jan 9, 43. CHINESE LITERATURE. *Educ:* Mich State Univ, BA, 65; Columbia Univ, MA, 67, PhD(Chinese), 73. *Prof Exp:* From instr to asst prof Asian studies & ling, Case Western Reserve Univ, 72-74; asst prof, 75-79, ASSOC PROF CHINESE, WASHINGTON UNIV, ST LOUIS, 79- *Mem:* Asn Asian Studies; MLA; Chinese Lang Teachers Asn. *Res:* Chinese vernacular fiction and drama; Chinese social values. *Publ:* Auth, Sui T'ang yen-i: Its date, sources and structure (in Chinese), Yu-shih yüeh-k'an, 9/74; A brief study of Sui shih i-wen, Yuan Yü-ling, Sui Shi i-wen, 75; contribr, Sui T'ang yen-i and the aesthetics of the seventeenth century Suchow elite, In: Chinese Narrative, 77; co-ed, A Guide to Library Resources for Chinese Studies, Wash Univ Libr, 78; contribr, Maturation and conflicting values, In: Critical Essays on Chinese Fiction, 80; auth, The Novel in Seventeenth Century China, 81, co-ed, Expressions of Self in Chinese Literature (in press). *Mailing Add:* Dept of Chinese & Japanese Box 1111 Wash Univ St Louis MO 63130

HEGYI, OTTMAR, b Sopron, Hungary, Mar 25, 29; Can citizen. SPANISH LANGUAGE & LITERATURE. *Educ:* Univ London, BA, 58; Middlebury Col, MA, 63; Univ Toronto, PhD(Span), 69. *Prof Exp:* From lectr to asst prof, 67-78, ASSOC PROF SPAN, ERINDALE COL, UNIV TORONTO, 78- *Mem:* Asn Int Hispanistas; Can Asn Hispanists; Am Asn Teachers Span & Port; Soc Mediter Studies; Am Oriental Soc. *Res:* Spanish historical linguistics; Aljamiada literature; impact of Islam on Spanish culture. *Publ:* Auth, Maurische kultur, Spanien, Reconquista & Mozaraber, In: Lexikon der Islamischen Welt, Kohlhammer, Stuttgart, 75; Algunos aspectos del sistema de escritura aljamiado-espanol, Iberoromania, 11/78; El uso del alfabeto arabe por minorias musulmanas y otros aspectos de la literatura aljamiada resultantes de circumstancias historicas y sociales analogas, in Actas del Coloquio Internacional sobre Literatura Aljamiada y Morisca, Gredos, Madrid, 78; Observaciones sobre el lexico arabe en los textos aljamiados in Al-Andalus, XLIII: 303-321; The Aljamiado Phenomenon, J Am Oriental Soc, 79; La leyenda de Sarjil ibn Sarjon y otros relatos moriscos, Gredos, Madrid, 81; Cinco leyendas y otros relatos moriscos, Gredos, Madrid, 81. *Mailing Add:* Erindale Col Univ of Toronto Mississauga ON L5L 1C6 Can

HEIBGES, URSULA MARGARETE, b Paderborn, Ger, Dec 17, 28; US citizen. CLASSICS. *Educ:* Cath Univ Am, BA, 54; Columbia Univ, MA, 55; Bryn Mawr Col, PhD, 62. *Prof Exp:* Teacher Latin, Shipley Sch, Bryn Mawr, Pa, 55-57; from instr to asst prof, 61-69, ASSOC PROF CLASSICS, MIDDLEBURY COL, 69- *Concurrent Pos:* Prix de Rome, Am Acad Rome, 65-66; Nat Endowment for Humanities fel, 67-68. *Mem:* Am Philol Asn. *Publ:* Auth, Cicero, a hypocrite in religion?, Am J Philol, 4/69. *Mailing Add:* Dept of Classics Middlebury Col Middlebury VT 05753

HEIDINGER, MAURICE M, b Kulm, NDak, Nov 2, 30. GERMAN LANGUAGE & LITERATURE. *Educ:* Valley City State Col, BA & BS in Educ, 53; Ind Univ, Bloomington, MA, 62, PhD(Ger), 65. *Prof Exp:* Asst prof Ger, Idaho State Univ, 65-67; assoc prof, Rockford Col, 67-69; assoc prof, 69-73, PROF GER & HEAD DEPT FOREIGN LANG, EASTERN MONT COL, 73- *Mem:* MLA; Am Asn Teachers Ger; Am Coun Teaching Foreign Lang; Western Asn Ger Studies. *Res:* Twentieth century German literature; German romanticism. *Mailing Add:* Dept of Foreign Lang Eastern Mont Col Billings MT 59101

HEIDSIECK, ARNOLD, b Leipzig, Ger, Feb 20, 37. GERMAN LITERATURE. *Educ:* Free Univ Berlin, Staatsexamen, 64, PhD(Ger), 66. *Prof Exp:* Asst prof Ger, NY Univ, 66-73; asst prof, Stanford Univ, 73-74; asst prof, 75-79, ASSOC PROF GER, UNIV SOUTHERN CALIF, 79- *Mem:* AAUP; Lessing-Soc; MLA. *Res:* Twentieth century literature; literary theory; intellectual history. *Publ:* Auth, Das Groteske und das Absurde im Modernen Drama, W Kohlhammer, 69 & 71; Travestie des tragischen, In: Tragik und Tragödie, 71; Zum amerikanischen drama, Literaturwiss und Geschichtsphilosophie, 75; Psychologische strukturen bei Brecht, Ideologiekritische Studien zur Literatur II, 75; Lessing und Mendelssohn, Lessing Yrbk, 79; Kritische theorie und exil, Das Exilerlebnis, 82; Kafka as outsider, The Anxious Subject, 82; Motivation and rights in Durrenmatt, Play Durrenmatt, 82. *Mailing Add:* Dept of Ger Univ of Southern Calif Los Angeles CA 90007

HEIEN, LARRY G, b Mt Olive, Ill, Jan 18, 37; m 61; c 2. CONTEMPORARY RUSSIAN & FOREIGN LANGUAGE PEDAGOGY. *Educ:* Eastern Ill Univ, BSEd, 59, BA, 61; Ind Univ, Bloomington, MAT, 63, MA, 67, Cert Russ & PhD(Russ & higher educ), 69. *Prof Exp:* Asst prof, 69-72, chmn Grad Studies Russ & Russ Area Studies, 75-78 & Russ Div, Dept Europ Lang & Lit, 76-78, ASSOC PROF RUSS, UNIV HAWAII, MANOA, 73- *Mem:* MLA; Am Asn Teachers Slavic & EEurop Lang; Am Coun Teachers Foreign Lang. *Res:* Foreign language learning theory; applied linguistics; foreign language methodology. *Publ:* Auth, The usage of Pocemu, Otcego, Zacem, Slavic & EEurop J, 71; Foreign language teaching in different keys, Mod Lang J, 73; Principy organizacii grammaticeskogo materiala pri programmirovannom obucenii, Russ Lang J, 73; Rol' rodnogo jazyka v razvittii slusanija i ponimanija zvucascej reci (nacal'nyj etap obucenija jazyku kak inostrannomu), Russkij jazyk za rubezom, Moscow, 74; Towards a systematic development of listening comprehension, Russ Lang J, spring 75. *Mailing Add:* Dept of Europ Lang & Lit Univ of Hawaii Manoa Honolulu HI 96822

HEIER, EDMUND, b May 7, 26; Can citizen; m 54; c 2. FOREIGN LANGUAGES. *Educ:* Univ BC, MA, 55; Univ Mich, PhD, 61. *Prof Exp:* Instr Ger & Russ, Grinnell Col, 58-60; from asst prof to assoc prof, 60-66, PROF GER & RUSS, UNIV WATERLOO, 66- *Concurrent Pos:* Acad Exchange Serv travel grant & Am Coun Learned Soc grant, 61. *Mem:* MLA; Can Asn Slavists. *Res:* Russo-German literary relations. *Publ:* Auth, Wieland and Nicolay, Monatshefte, 62; L H Nicolay (1737-1820) and His Contemporaries, M Nijhoff, The Hague, 65; The Second Hero of Our Time, 67 & Religious Schism in the Russian Artist, 70, SEEJ, The Hague; Turgenev and Lavater, Slavist Beiträge, 77. *Mailing Add:* Dept of Ger & Russ Univ of Waterloo Waterloo ON N2L 3G1 Can

HEILBRONN, DENISE MARTIN, b Ger, July 31, 25; US citizen; m 51; c 3. ITALIAN LANGUAGE & LITERATURE, FRENCH. *Educ:* Barnard Col, BA, 47; Bryn Mawr Col, MA, 48; Ind Univ, PhD(Ital), 71. *Prof Exp:* Instr French, Hampton Inst, 60-65; instr French & Ital, Col William & Mary, 65-67; asst prof, 71-77, ASSOC PROF ITAL, NORTHERN ILL UNIV, 77- *Mem:* Dante Soc Am; Mediaeval Acad Am; Renaissance Soc Am; Am Asn Teachers Ital; Midwest Mod Lang Asn. *Res:* Dante; Medieval Italian literature. *Publ:* Auth, Dante's Valley of the Princes, Dante Studies, 72; Dante's Gate of Dis and the Heavenly Jerusalem, Studies Philol, 75; The prophetic role of statius in Dante's Purgatory, 77 & Io Pur Sorrisi: Dante's Lesson on the Passions, 78, Dante Studies. *Mailing Add:* Dept of Foreign Lang & Lit Northern Ill Univ De Kalb IL 60115

HEILBRONNER, WALTER LEO, b Memmingen, Ger, May 10, 24; nat US; m 48; c 2. GERMAN. *Educ:* Univ Mich, AB, 49, MA, 50, PhD(Ger), 55. *Prof Exp:* Instr Ger & humanities, Univ WVa, 53-56; from asst prof to assoc prof Ger, Univ Va, 56-66, actg chmn dept mod lang, 63-64, asst dean col arts & sci, 64-65; prof Ger & vpres acad affairs, State Univ NY Col Cortland, 66-70; vpres acad affiars, 70-73, PROF GER, MONTCLAIR STATE COL, 70- *Concurrent Pos:* Univ Mich fel, Ctr Studies Higher Educ, 65-66. *Mem:* MLA; Am Asn Teachers Ger; Am Asn Higher Educ; Am Acad Polit & Soc Sci; AAUP. *Res:* Social and political implications of literature; higher education. *Publ:* Auth, The graduate foreign language requirement-an exercise in futility, Grad Comment, 66; Printing and the Book in Fifteenth Century Englnad, Univ Va, 67. *Mailing Add:* 8 Van Breemen Ct Upper Montclair NJ 07043

HEIM, MICHAEL HENRY, b New York, NY, Jan 21, 43; m 75. SLAVIC LANGUAGES & LITERATURES. *Educ:* Columbia Univ, AB, 64; Harvard Univ, MA, 66, PhD(Slavic), 71. *Prof Exp:* Asst prof Slavic, Univ Wis-Madison, 70-72; asst prof, 72-79, ASSOC PROF SLAVIC, UNIV CALIF, LOS ANGELES, 79- *Res:* Czech language and literature; Russian literature of the 18th and 19th centuries; comparative literature. *Publ:* Auth, Moravian folk music: a Czechoslovak novelist's view, J Folklore Inst, 6/72; co-ed, Letters of Anton Chekhov, Harper, 73; auth, Two approaches to translation: Trediakovskij and Sumarokov, Mnemozina: Studies Litteraria Russica in Honorem Vsevolod Setchkarev, 74; La litterature sovietique et la guerre d'Espagne, Les Ecrivains et la guerre d'Espagne, 75; Lomonosov's La Fontaine, Slavic & EEurop J, fall 76; Contemporary Czech, Mich Slavic Materials, 76; The Russian Journey of Kavel Havlicek Borovsky, Univ Munich, 79; Chekhov and the Moscow Art Theater, Chekhov's Great Plays, NY Univ Press, 81. *Mailing Add:* Dept of Slavic Lang Univ of Calif Los Angeles CA 90024

HEIMANN, DAVID FRANCIS, b Aurora, Ill, Mar 31, 32; m 67; c 3. LATIN, GREEK. *Educ:* Pontifical Col Josephinum, AB, 54; Ohio State Univ, PhD(classics), 65. *Prof Exp:* Asst prof, 65-77, ASSOC PROF CLASSICS, UNIV COLO, BOULDER, 77- *Concurrent Pos:* Univ Colo Res Coun res grant, 67-70;. *Mem:* Am Philol Asn; Archaeol Inst Am; Class Asn Midwest & South; Rocky Mountain Mod Lang Asn. *Res:* Patristics, especially St Jerome; word order studies and analysis; satire. *Mailing Add:* Dept of Classics Univ of Colo Boulder CO 80302

HEINE, RONALD EUGENE, Religion, Classical Languages. See Vol IV

HEINEMANN, EDWARD ARTHUR, b New York, NY, Sept 16, 41; m 64; c 2. FRENCH. *Educ:* Hamilton Col, AB, 63; Princeton Univ, MA, 66, PhD(French), 70. *Prof Exp:* From lectr to asst prof, 66-74, ASSOC PROF FRENCH, UNIV TORONTO, 74- *Mem:* MLA; Soc Rencesvals; Medieval Acad Am. *Res:* Chanson de geste; history of the French language. *Publ:* Auth, Composition stylisee et technique litteraire dans la Chanson de Roland, 73 & La place de l'element brandir la lance dans la structure du motif de l'attaque a la lance, 74, Romania; Sur la valeur des manuscrits rimes pour l'etude de la tradition rolandienne: tentative pour trouver les filiations des manuscrits TLP, Le Moyen Age, 74; Some Reflections on the Laisse and on Echo in the Three Versions of the Prise d'Orange, Olifant, 75; Sur l'art de la laisse dans le Couronnement de Louis, Charlemagne et l'epopee romane, Belles Lettres, Paris, 78; Langage metrique, la variante et la chanson de geste, La Pratique des ordinateurs dans la critique des textes, Editions du CNRS, Paris, 79;

Apercus sur quelques rythmes semantiques dans les versions A, B et D du Charroi de Nimes, VIII Cong Soc Rencesvals, Institucion principe de Viana, PampTona, 81. *Mailing Add:* Dept of French Univ of Toronto Toronto ON M5S 1A1 Can

HEINEN, HUBERT, b Houston, Tex, Mar 5, 37; m 59; c 3. GERMAN LANGUAGE & LITERATURE. *Educ:* Univ Tex, BA, 58, PhD(Ger), 64. *Prof Exp:* Instr Ger, Univ Pa, 63-64; from asst prof to assoc prof, Univ Pittsburgh, 64-69; ASSOC PROF GER, UNIV TEX, AUSTIN, 69- *Mem:* MLA; Am Asn Teachers Ger; SCent Mod Lang Asn; Medieval Acad Am. *Res:* Middle and Early New High German language and literature; German-American cultural history. *Publ:* Auth, Interwoven time in Keats's poetry, Tex Studies Lit & Lang, 61; Die rhythmischmetrische Gestaltung des Knittelverses bei Hans Folz, Elwert, 66; coauth, Paths to German Poetry, Harper, 69; auth, Observations on the Role in Minnesang, J English & Ger Philol, 76; Lofty and Base Love in Walther von der Vogelweide, Ger Quart, 78; co-ed, Bertolt Brecht, Univ Ga, 80; contribr, Vox feminae, Medieval Inst, 81; auth, Konvention und höfische Haltung in den Kürenbergliedern, Z für deutsche Philol, 81. *Mailing Add:* Dept of Ger Lang Univ of Tex Austin TX 78712

HEINRICH, ALBERT CARL, b Columbia, Ill, Feb 2, 22; m 57; c 1. ANTHROPOLOGY, LINGUISTICS. *Educ:* New Sch Soc Res, BA, 50, 50; Univ Alaska, Fairbanks, MEd, 55; Univ Wash, PhD(anthrop), 63. *Prof Exp:* Govt teacher Alaska Native Serv, 44-48; instr educ, Univ Alaska, 55-57; teaching asst anthrop, Univ Wash, 57-60; asst prof anthrop & ling, Mont State Univ, 60-63; from asst prof to assoc prof, 64-70, PROF ANTHROP, UNIV CALGARY, 70- *Concurrent Pos:* NSF fac fel, Cornell Univ, 63-64; vis prof anthrop & ling, Karnatak Univ, India, 68-69; vis scholar, Cent Inst Indian Lang, Mysae, India, 75-76. *Mem:* AAAS; Am Anthrop Asn; Inst Human Ideas on Ultimate Reality & Meaning; Can Asn Univ Teachers; Ling Soc India. *Res:* Social anthropology; ethnosematics of the Arctic, South Asia and South America. *Publ:* Auth, A short history of linguistics science, J Karnatak Univ, 70; Some borrowings from German into Eskimo, Anthrop Ling, 71; Divorce as an integrative factor among Eskimos, J Comp Family Studies, 72; Changing anthropological perspectives on color naming behavior, J Psych Anthrop, 78; The colours of Kannada, SAAN, 81. *Mailing Add:* Dept of Anthrop Univ of Calgary Calgary AB T2N 1N4 Can

HEINRICH, AMY VLADECK, b New York, NY, June 5, 45; m 65; c 2. JAPANESE & COMPARATIVE LITERATURE. *Educ:* Columbia Univ, BA, 67, MA, 76, PhD(Japanese lit), 80. *Prof Exp:* LECTR EAST ASIAN STUDIES, COLUMBIA UNIV, 80- *Concurrent Pos:* Res assoc, East Asian Inst, Columbia Univ, 80-81; consult, Nat Humanities Fac, 80-81. *Mem:* Asn Asian Studies; Am Comp Lit Asn. *Res:* Modern Japanese poetry; women's literature: Japanese & English; comparative literature: Japanese, Chinese, English. *Publ:* Auth, My mother is dying: Saito Mokichi's Shinitamau haha, Monumenta Nipponica, winter 78; Ame furihajimu: 5 poems, 2/79, Furusato: 6 poems, 8/79, & Hyakuendama no tsuki: 15 poems, 80, Uchufu; ed, Contemporary Japan: A Teaching Workbook, East Asian Inst, Columbia Univ, 81; auth, Tanka no kozo o megutte, Uchufu, 10-12/81; Blown in flurries: The role of Waka in Ukifune, In: Ukifune: Love in The Tale of Genji, 82 & Fragements of Rainbows: The Life and Poetry of Saito Mokichi (in press), Columbia Univ Press. *Mailing Add:* 250 W Broadway New York NY 10013

HEINY, STEPHEN BROOKS, b Muncie, Ind, Nov 25, 44; m 68. CLASSICS. *Educ:* Wabash Col, AB, 66; Ind Univ, MA, 67, PhD(classics), 73. *Prof Exp:* Instr, 70-72, asst prof, 72-80, ASSOC PROF CLASSICS, EARLHAM COL, 80- *Mem:* Am Philol Asn; Japan Soc. *Res:* Greek prose style; early Greek literature. *Mailing Add:* Dept of Lang Earlham Col Richmond IN 47374

HEIPLE, DANIEL L, b Oregon City, Ore, Dec 22, 42; div; c 1. SPANISH LITERATURE, COMPARATIVE LITERATURE. *Educ:* Univ Ore, BA, 66; NY Univ, MA, 71; Univ Tex, Austin, PhD(Spanish), 77. *Prof Exp:* ASST PROF SPANISH, TULANE UNIV, 77- *Res:* Spanish golden age literature, music and art; medieval courtly love tradition. *Publ:* Auth, The tradition behind the punishment of the rebel soldier in La vida es sueno, Bull Hisp Studies, 73; Renaissance medical psychology in Don Quijote, Ideologies and Lit, 79; El apellido picaro se deriua de picar, La Picaresca, 79; Gutierre's witty diagnosis in El medico de su honra, Critical Perspectives on Calderon, 81; El licenciado Vidriera y el humor tradicional del Loco, Hispania (in prep); Lope de Vega and the early conception of metaphysical poetry, Comp Lit (in prep); The Accidens Amoris in lyric poetry, Neophilologus (in prep); Tirso's Esto si que es negociar and the marriage negotiations of 1623, Bull of the Comediantes (in prep). *Mailing Add:* Spanish Dept Tulane Univ New Orleans LA 70118

HEISER, MARY MARGARET, b Freeport, Ill, Apr 3, 34. LINGUISTICS, FRENCH LANGUAGE. *Educ:* Univ Wis, BA, 56, MA, 57; Univ Mich, PhD(Romance ling), 58. *Prof Exp:* Teacher English, Col Jeunes Filles, Chateauroux, France, 57-58; teacher French, Am Community Sch, Beirut, 58-60; asst prof Romance ling, Univ Wash, 64-65; asst prof French & ling, Univ Southern Calif, 66-70 & Brown Univ, 70-72; ASSOC PROF FRENCH & LING, CLEVELAND STATE UNIV, 72- *Mem:* MLA; Ling Soc Am; Int Ling Asn; Am Coun Teaching Foreign Lang; Am Dialect Soc. *Res:* The linguistic structure of modern French; dialectology; the linguistic structure of Ohio Amish English. *Publ:* Coauth, Teaching evaluation checklist for foreign language instructors, Bull Prof Francais, 5/67; Linguistic atlases and phonological interpretation, Linguistics, 3/72; A diasystem of four southcentral French dialects, Word, 72; auth, The French adverb: A feature analysis of syntactic function, Orbis, 79. *Mailing Add:* Dept of Mod Lang Cleveland State Univ Cleveland OH 44115

HEITNER, ROBERT RICHARD, b St Louis, Mo, Feb 1, 20. GERMAN. *Educ:* Washington Univ, AB, 41, AM, 42; Harvard Univ, PhD(Ger), 49. *Prof Exp:* Asst prof Ger, Washington Univ, 50-55; from asst prof to assoc prof, Univ Calif, Los Angeles, 55-64, chmn dept Ger lang, 61-64; prof Ger, Univ Tex, Austin, 64-66, asst dean grad sch, 65-66; head dept Ger, 66-76, PROF GER, UNIV ILL, CHICAGO, 66- *Concurrent Pos:* Ed, Ger Quart, 67-70. *Mem:* MLA; Lessing Soc (pres, 77-79). *Res:* Lessing; 18th century drama and theater. *Publ:* Auth, German Tragedy in the Age of Enlightenment, Univ Calif, 63; The Iphigenia in Tauris theme in drama of the 18th century, Comp Lit, fall 64; Real life or spectacle? A conflict in 18th century drama, PMLA, 12/67; Rationalism and irrationalism in Lessing, In: Lessing Yearbook, 73; Goethe's natural creatures: A typological study, In Vistas and Vectors: Essays Honoring the Memory of Helmut Rehder, 79; Goethe's ailing women, Mod Lang Notes, 4/80; Notes on audience reception of German Calssicist tragedies, In: Lessing Yearbook, 80. *Mailing Add:* Dept of German Univ of Ill Chicago Circle Chicago IL 60680

HELBIG, LOUIS FERDINAND, b Liegnitz, Silesia, Sept 2, 35; Can citizen; m 65; c 2. GERMAN STUDIES. *Educ:* Univ Alta, BA, 66, MA, 67; Univ Waterloo, PhD(Ger), 69. *Prof Exp:* Asst prof, 69-72, dir, Inst Ger Studies, 69-76, ASSOC PROF GER, IND UNIV, BLOOMINGTON, 72- *Mem:* MLA; Am Asn Teachers Ger; Can Asn Univ Teachers Ger; Conf Group Ger Polit. *Res:* Modern German literature and culture; Buechner. *Publ:* Auth, Hermann Brochs Roman der Tod des Vergil als Dichtung des Gerichtes über die Dichtung, Mod Austrian Lit, spring 69; Der Einzelne und die Gesellschaft in Goethe's Wahlverwandtschaften, Bouvier, Bonn, 72; ed & introd, A Bibliography of German Studies, 1945-1971 . . ., Ind Univ, Bloomington, 72; co-ed & contribr, Teaching Postwar Germany in American, Inst Ger Studies, Ind Univ, 72; auth, Das Geschichtsdrama Georg Büchners; Zitatprobleme und historische Wahreit in Dantons Tod, Lang & Cie, Bern, 73. *Mailing Add:* Dept of Ger Lang Ind Univ Bloomington IN 47401

HELBLING, ROBERT E, b Lucerne, Switz, May 6, 23; US citizen; m 56. GERMAN & FRENCH LITERATURE. *Educ:* Univ Utah, MA, 49; Stanford Univ, PhD, 59. *Prof Exp:* Instr Ger & French, Univ Utah, 50-53; asst, Stanford Univ, 53-55; from instr to assoc prof, 55-66, traveling scholar, 61 & 63, honrs dir, 64-66, chmn dept lang, 65-77, PROF GER & FRENCH, UNIV UTAH, 66- *Mem:* MLA; Asn Depts Foreign Lang (pres, 74). *Res:* Modern German and French literature, especially existentialist literature; Heinrich von Kleist. *Publ:* Coauth, Le language de la France moderne, Holt, 61; ed, Dürrenmatt: The Physicists, Oxford, 64; coauth, L'Actualite francaise, Holt, 67; co-ed, The Intellectual Tradition of the West, Scott, Vol I & II, 67 & 68; ed, Heinrich von Kleist, Novellen und aesthetische Schriften, Oxford, 68; coauth, Introduction au francais actuel, 73 & First Year German, 75, 79 & 83, Holt; auth, The Major Works of Heinrich von Kleist, New Directions, 75; auth & ed, Orei Erzahlunger von Heinrich von Kleist, Suhrkamp Insel, 82. *Mailing Add:* Dept of Lang Univ of Utah Salt Lake City UT 84112

HELD, CHARLES ROBERT, b Pittsburgh, Pa, Jan 26, 25. PHILOLOGY. *Educ:* Gettysburg Col, BA, 49; Princeton Univ, MA, 51. *Prof Exp:* Instr Latin, St John's Sch, Houston, Tex, 52-53, Greek & English, Gettysburg Col, 54-55 & Latin, Iolani Sch, Honolulu, Hawaii, 55-56; instr classics, 56-58, ASST PROF CLASSICS, GETTYSBURG COL, 58- *Mem:* Class Asn Atlantic States; Am Philol Asn; Am Class League; Archaeol Inst Am. *Res:* Greek tragedy; Greek archaeology. *Mailing Add:* Dept of Classics Gettysburg Col Gettysburg PA 17325

HELD, DIRK TOMDIECK, Ancient Philosophy, Intellectual History. See Vol IV

HELD, MOSHE, b Warsaw, Poland, Nov 1, 24; m 58. SEMITIC LANGUAGES. *Educ:* Hebrew Univ, Israel, MA, 52; Johns Hopkins Univ, PhD, 57. *Prof Exp:* Instr Hebrew philol & Bible, Hebrew Univ, Israel, 52-53; from asst prof to prof Assyriol, Dropsie Col, 57-66; assoc prof, 66-70, PROF SEMITIC LANG & CULT, COLUMBIA UNIV, 70- *Concurrent Pos:* Res fels, Columbia Univ, 66-69, chmn, Sem Studies Hebrew Bible, 68-69; Guggenheim Found fel, 72-73. *Mem:* Am Orient Soc; Am Schs Orient Res; Soc Bibl Lit. *Res:* Akkadian language and literature; Biblical philology; northwest Semitic languages. *Publ:* Auth, MHS/MHS in Ugaritic and other Semitic languages, 59 & The root ZBL/SBL in Akkadian, Ugaritic and Biblical Hebrew, E A Speiser Mem Vol, 68, J Am Orient Soc; Philolgical notes on the Mari Covenant rituals, Bull Am Schs Orient Res, 70. *Mailing Add:* 605 Kent Hall Columbia Univ New York NY 10027

HELD, WARREN HOWARD, JR, b Allentown, Pa, Oct 9, 28; m 51; c 2. LINGUISTICS. *Educ:* Princeton Univ, BA, 50; Yale Univ, MA, 52, PhD, 55. *Prof Exp:* From instr to assoc prof English, Fairleigh Dickinson Univ, 56-67, chmn dept humanities, 60-67, admin asst to dean lib arts, 63-67; assoc dean lib arts, 67-71, PROF CLASSICS, UNIV NH, 67- *Mem:* Ling Soc Am; Am Orient Soc; Class Asn New England. *Res:* Classical linguistics; Hittitology. *Publ:* Auth, The Hittite relative sentence, suppl to Language, 57; transl, The Brothers, In: Roman Drama, Laurel Class Ser, Dell, 67; coauth, Some comments on the Hittite phonemic system, Gen Ling, Vol 9, No 2; More still on the Trojan horse, Class J, 73. *Mailing Add:* 1 Woodrige Rd Durham NH 03824

HELLER, ERICH, b Komotau, Bohemia, Mar 27, 11. GERMAN. *Educ:* Charles Univ, Prague, Djur, 35; Cambridge Univ, PhD, 48. *Hon Degrees:* DLett, Emory Univ, 65. *Prof Exp:* Lectr Ger, London Sch Econ, 43-45; dir studies mod lang, Peterhouse, Cambridge Univ, 45-48; prof Ger, Univ Col Swansea, 48-60; prof, 60-67, AVALON PROF GER, NORTHWESTERN UNIV, 67- *Concurrent Pos:* Vis lectr, Univs Hamburg, Göttingen & Bonn, 47-48 & Harvard Univ, 53-54; Ziskind vis prof, Brnadeis Univ, 57-58; vis prof, Heidelberg, 63; Carnegie vis prof humanities, Mass Inst Technol, 63; mem, Ger Acad Lang & Lit, Darmstadt, 64-; vis prof, Munich, 65; Tübingen, 66; Columbia Univ, 66; mem, Bavarian Acad Arts, Munich, 66- *Honors & Awards:* Kulturkreis Bund Deut Indus Lit Prize, 58; JH Merck Prize for Essay & Lit Criticism, 68; Goethe Inst Gold Medal, 68. *Mem:* MLA fel AAAS; PEN Club. *Res:* Modern German and European literature. *Publ:* Auth, The disinherited mind, In: Essays in Modern German Literature and Thought, Bowe, Cambridge & London, 52, 71, Ger ed, Juhrhamr, 54; The Ironic German, A Study of Thomas Mann, Little, 58 & Meridian Books, 62; Ger ed,

Suhrkamp, 59; The Artist's Journey into the Interior, Random, 65, Secker & Warburg, London, 66 & Vintage, 68; Die Reise der Kunst ins Innere, Frankfurt, 66; Essays über Goether, Frankfurt, 70; Franz Kafka, Viking & Fontana, London, 74; The Poet's Self and the Poem, Athone, London, 76; Die Wiederkehr der Unschuld, Suhrkamp, 77. *Mailing Add:* Dept of Ger Northwestern Univ Evanston IL 60201

HELLER, JOHN LEWIS, b Riegelsville, Pa, Oct 06; m 36; c 2. CLASSICAL PHILOLOGY. *Educ:* Haverford Col, AB, 27; Princeton Univ, AM, 28, PhD(classics), 33. *Prof Exp:* Instr Greek & Latin, Wesleyan Univ, 28-29; instr Latin, Haverford Col, 29-31; instr classics, Allegheny Col, 33-37; from asst prof to assoc prof class lang, Univ Minn, 37-47, prof & chmn dept, 47-49; prof, 49-75, EMER PROF CLASSICS, UNIV ILL, URBANA, 75- *Concurrent Pos:* Vis Mellon prof, Univ Pittsburgh, 69-70. *Mem:* Am Philol Asn (pres, 66-67); Archaeol Inst Am; Soc Bibliog Natural Hist. *Res:* Latin lexicography; classical literature; neo-Latin natural science. *Publ:* Coauth, To draw a labyrinth, In: Classical Studies Presented to B E Perry, Univ Ill, Urbana, 69; auth, Linnaeus's Bibliotheca botanica, Taxon, 19: 363-411; Classical poetry in the Systema naturae of Linnaeus, Trans Am Philol Asn, 102: 183-216; Bibliotheca Zoologica Linnaeana, Yearbk Swed Linn Soc, 78. *Mailing Add:* Dept of Classics Univ of Ill Urbana IL 61801

HELLER, PETER, b Vienna, Austria, Jan 11, 20; US citizen; m 51; c 5. GERMAN & COMPARATIVE LITERATURE. *Educ:* McGill Univ, BA, 44; Columbia Univ, MA, 45, PhD, 51. *Prof Exp:* Instr Ger, Columbia Univ, 48-51 & Harvard Univ, 51-54; from assoc prof to prof, Univ Mass, 54-61, Commonwealth prof, 61-68, dir Inst Atlantic Studies, Freiburg, Ger, 67-68; chmn dept Ger & Slavic, 68-71, PROF GER & COMP LIT, STATE UNIV NY COL BUFFALO, 73- *Concurrent Pos:* Fulbright res grants, Ger, 54-56; dir, Inst Atlantic Studies, Freiburg, Ger, 68; vis prof, Univ Wuerzburg, Ger, 78; ed, Mod Ger Studies, 78-; dir, Nat Endowment for Humanities summer sem, 79; vis prof, State Univ New York Binghamton, spring 81; Guggenheim fel, 82. *Mem:* MLA; Am Asn Teachers Ger. *Res:* German literature, 1750-1950; comparative literature; philosophy. *Publ:* Auth, Dialectics and Nihilism, Univ Mass, 66; Von den ersten und letzten Dingen: Studien und Kommentar zu einer Aphorismenreihe von Friedrich Nietzsche, De Gruyter, Berlin, 72; Prosa in Versen, Blaeschke, Darmstadt, 74; Emigrantenlitaneien, Blaeschke, St Michael, 78; Probleme der zivilisation: Versuche Ueber Goethe, Mann, Nietzsche und Freud, 78, Studies on Nietzsche, 80 & A Quarrel over bisexuality, In: The Turn of the Century (German Literature and Art, 1890-1915), 81, Bouvier, Bonn; Lessing's historical dialectic, In: Lessing Yearbook XIII, Wayne State Univ Press, 82. *Mailing Add:* Dept of Mod Lang State Univ of NY Buffalo NY 14216

HELLERSTEIN, NINA SALANT, b New York, NY, March 29, 46; m 70; c 2. MODERN FRENCH LITERATURE, FRENCH CIVILIZATION. *Educ:* Brown Univ, BA, 68; Univ Chicago, MA, 69, PhD(Fr), 74. *Prof Exp:* Adj asst prof Fr, Bernard Baruch Col, 74-75; vis asst prof, Vassar Col, 75-76; instr, Rosary Col & Roosevelt Univ, 76-78; ASST PROF FRENCH, UNIV GEORGIA, 78- *Mem:* SAtlantic Mod Lang Asn; MLA; Paul Claudel Soc; Societe Paul Claudel France; Asn des Amis de la Fondation St John Perse. *Res:* Paul Claudel; Modern French poetry; The French new novel. *Publ:* Auth, The oriental legends and their role in Claudel's Connaissance de l'Est, Claudel Studies, 73; Paul Claudel and Guillaume Apollinaire as visual poets: Ideogrammes occidentaux and Calligrammes, Visible Lang, 77; The poet as linguist: Motivation and poetry in the theories of Paul Claudel, Australian J Fr Studies, 78; Connaissance de l'Est et l'Orient Claudelien, Saggi e Ricerche di Letteratura Francese, 78; Reality and its absence in the French new novel: Butor, Sarraute, Ricardou, USF Lang Quart, 81; Paul Claudel et l'Autobiographie, Les Lettres Romanes, Belgium, 81. *Mailing Add:* Dept of Romance Lang Moore Hall Univ Ga Athens GA 30602

HELM, JAMES JOEL, b Chicago, Ill, Dec 17, 37; m 60; c 2. CLASSICAL STUDIES. *Educ:* Elmhurst Col, BA, 59; Union Theol Sem, MDiv, 63; Univ Mich, Ann Arbor, MA, 65, PhD(class studies), 68. *Prof Exp:* Instr class studies, Univ Mich, Ann Arbor, 66-68; asst prof, 68-74, chmn dept, 76-82, ASSOC PROF CLASSICS, OBERLIN COL, 74- *Concurrent Pos:* Vis assoc prof classics, Scripps Col, 78-79. *Mem:* Am Philol Asn; Archaeol Inst Am; Class Asn Mid West & South. *Res:* Greek paleography; computer applications in classical studies; poetry of Catullus. *Publ:* Auth, The lost manuscript tau of Aeschylus' Agamemnon and Eumenides, Trans & Proc Am Philol Asn, 72; Poetic structure and humor: Catullus 13, Class World, Vol 74, 80-81; Plato's Apology: Text and Grammatical Commentary, Bolchazy-Carducci Publ, 81. *Mailing Add:* Dept of Classics Oberlin Col Oberlin OH 44074

HELM, PEYTON RANDOLPH, Ancient History, Classical Studies. See Vol I

HELMBOLD, NANCY PEARCE, b Abilene, Tex, Dec 16, 18; m 38; c 1. CLASSICS. *Educ:* Univ Tex, AB, 39; Univ Calif, MA, 53, PhD(classics), 57. *Prof Exp:* Asst prof classics, Mt Holyoke Col, 57-59; vis asst prof, Univ Ore, 61-63; vis asst prof, 63-64, asst prof, 64-70, dean students, Div Humanities, 70-73, ASSOC PROF CLASSICS, UNIV CHICAGO, 70- *Mem:* Am Philol Asn. *Res:* Political history of late Roman republic; Ovid; Catullus. *Mailing Add:* Dept of Classics Univ of Chicago Chicago IL 60637

HELMETAG, CHARLES HUGH, b Camden, NJ, Apr 7, 35; m 59; c 2. GERMAN. *Educ:* Univ Pa, BA, 57; Univ Ky, MA, 59; Princeton Univ, PhD(Ger), 68. *Prof Exp:* Instr, Ger Purdue Univ, 60-62; asst prof, 64-75, assoc prof, 75-80, PROF GER, VILLANOVA UNIV, 80-, CHMN DEPT MOD LANG, 73- *Mem:* Am Asn Teachers Ger; MLA; AAUP; Northeast Mod Lang Asn. *Res:* Nineteenth and 20th century German literature; German film. *Publ:* Auth, Paul Heyse-Bibliographie, Börsenblatt deut Buchhandel, 10/69; The image of the automobile in Max Frisch's Stiller, Ger Rev, 3/72; Penthesilea's hair: A note on Kleist's imagery, In: Studies in 19th and Early 20th Century German Literature Essays in Honors of Paul K Whitaker, APRA, 74; Bibliographical outline for a course in humanism and reformation, Die Unterrichtspraxis, 75; Mother courage and her American cousins in the skin of our teeth, Mod Lang Studies, fall 78; Walter Hasenclever in Hollywood, Seminar, 5/80. *Mailing Add:* Dept of Mod Lang & Lit Villanova Univ Villanova PA 19085

HELMKE, HENRY CONRAD, b New York, NY, Aug 8, 31; m 57; c 4. GERMAN LANGUAGE & LITERATURE. *Educ:* Duke Univ, BA, 56, MA, 57; Ohio State Univ, PhD(Ger), 70. *Prof Exp:* From instr to asst prof, 59-70, ASSOC PROF GER, AUBURN UNIV, 71- *Mem:* Am Asn Teachers Ger; Int Arthur Schnitzler Res Asn; Nat Carl Schurz Soc; Nat Fedn Studies Ger. *Res:* Modern German literature. *Mailing Add:* Dept of Foreign Lang Auburn University AL 36849

HELSTEN, ROBERT LOUIS, Bible, German. See Vol IV

HELWIG, FRANK SCOTT, b Topeka, Kans, May 16, 33; m 58; c 2. SPANISH & SPANISH-AMERICAN LITERATURE. *Educ:* Kans State Teachers Col, BS, 59, MS, 63; Univ Kans, PhD(Span), 73. *Prof Exp:* Instr Span, Kans State Teachers Col, 61-63; asst prof, 65-80, ASSOC PROF SPAN, WESTERN ILL UNIV, 80- *Mem:* AAUP; Am Asn Teachers Span & Port. *Res:* Modern Spanish and Spanish-American prose fiction. *Publ:* Auth, Narrative techniques in the rural novels of Enrique Amorim, Grad Studies Latin Am, 73. *Mailing Add:* Dept of Foreign Lang Western Ill Univ Macomb IL 61455

HENDERSON, CHARLES, JR, b Lynchburg, Va, Aug, 22, 23; div; c 5. CLASSICS. *Educ:* Davidson Col, AB, 42; Univ NC, MA, 47, PhD, 55. *Prof Exp:* Part time instr classics, Univ NC, 48-50; instr, Washington Square Col, NY Univ, 50-55; from asst prof to assoc prof, Univ NC, 55-64; chmn dept, 66-76, asst to pres, 71-76, PROF CLASSICS, SMITH COL, 64- *Mem:* Am Philol Asn (secy-teas, 63-66); Mediaeval Acad Am; Renaissance Soc Am; Am Class League. *Res:* Ancient rhetoric. *Publ:* Auth, Cato's pine cones and Seneca's plums, Trans & Proc Am Philol Asn, 55; ed, Classical Mediaeval and Renaissance Studies in Honor of B L Ullman, Storia e Lett, Rome, 64; coauth, Latin for Americnas, Macmillan, Books I & II, 68. *Mailing Add:* Dept of Classics Smith Col Northampton MA 01060

HENDERSON, JEFFREY JAMES, b Verona, NJ, June 21, 46. CLASSICAL PHILOLOGY. *Educ:* Kenyon Col, BA, 68; Harvard Univ, MA, 70, PhD(classics), 72. *Prof Exp:* From instr to asst prof classics, Yale Univ, 72-78; ASSOC PROF CLASSICS, UNIV MICH, ANN ARBOR, 78- *Concurrent Pos:* Morse fel classics, Yale Univ, 76-77; vis prof, Univ Southern Calif, 82-83. *Mem:* Am Philol Asn. *Res:* Aristophanes; archaic Greek poetry; ancient religion and textual criticism. *Publ:* Auth, The Maculate Muse, Yale Univ, 75; The Cologne epode, Arethusa 9, 76; Coniecturarum in Aristophanes' Lysistratam Repertorium, Harvard Studies Class Philol, 78; ed, Aristophanes: Essays in Interpretation, Cambridge Univ, 79. *Mailing Add:* Dept of Classics Studies Univ Mich Angell Hall Ann Arbor MI 48109

HENDERSON, JOHN STANTON, b Bath, Maine, Jan 25, 39; m 68. FRENCH. *Educ:* Bates Col, AB, 61; Brown Univ, MA, 63, PhD(Fr), 67. *Prof Exp:* Vis lectr French, Providence Col, 65-66; asst prof, 66-72, ASSOC PROF FRENCH, DICKINSON COL, 72-, DIR, OFF CAMPUS STUDIES, 73- *Mem:* MLA. *Res:* Voltaire, 18th Century France. *Publ:* Auth, Voltaire's Tancrede: Author and Publisher, Inst Musee Voltaire, GEneva, 68. *Mailing Add:* Dept of French Dickinson Col Carlisle PA 17013

HENDRICK, RANDALL JAMES, b Chico, Calif, Apr 29, 51. LINGUISTICS, LITERARY CRITICISM. *Educ:* Univ Calif, Irvine, BA, 73; Univ Toronto, MA, 74; Univ Calif, Los Angeles, PhD(ling), 79. *Prof Exp:* Vis asst prof ling, 79-81, ASST PROF LING & ENGLISH, UNIV NC, CHAPEL HILL, 81- *Mem:* Ling Soc Am. *Res:* Syntactic theory; conditions on logical form; linguistics and literary criticism. *Publ:* Auth, The phrase structure of adjectives and comparatives, Ling Anal, 78; An argument that adjectives leave traces, Ling Inquiry,, 78; An essay on passives and core grammar, Cahier Ling d'Ottawa, 80; Extensions of subjacency, In: Current Research in Romance Languages, Ind Univ Ling Club, 82; Construing relative pronouns, Ling Anal, 82; Reduced questions and their theoretical implications, Lang, 82. *Mailing Add:* 738 5th St Manhattan Beach CA 90266

HENDRICKSON, RICHARD H, English Linguistics. See Vol II

HENDRICKSON, WILLIAM LEE, b Denver, Colo Feb 13, 36; m 76; c 1. FRENCH, MEDIEVAL LITERATURE. *Educ:* Ariz State Univ, BA, 59; Univ Kans, MA, 62; Princeton Univ, PhD(French), 69. *Prof Exp:* Instr French, Brown Univ, 65-68, asst prof, 69-72; asst prof Washington Univ, 72-76; asst prof, 76-78, ASSOC PROF FRENCH, ARIZ STATE UNIV, 78- *Concurrent Pos:* Nat Endowment for Humanities younger humanist grant, 73-74. *Mem:* MLA; Am Asn Teachers Fr; Int Arthurian Soc; Soc Rencesvals; Mediaeval Acad Am. *Res:* Chanson de geste, Medieval theatre, Jean de Meun. *Publ:* Coauth, Quinze Lecons de Francais, Holt, 72; Les sources litteraires de Garin de Monglane, Soc Rencesvals VIe Conr Int, Univ Aix-en-Provence, 74 & Quelques aspects due vers orphelin dans Garin de Monglane, Soc Rencesvals Ve Congr Int, Univ Salford, 77; auth, Un nouveau fragment de Garin de Monglane, Romania, 96: 163-192; co-ed & auth, Toward an edition of Garin de Monglane, In: Jean Misrahi Memorial Vol, Fr Lit Publ Co, 77; co-ed, Studies on the Seven Sages of Rome and other essays in medieval literature, Ed Res Assoc, 78; coauth, Roland and Oliver: Prowess and wisdom, the ideal of the epic hero, Romance Philol XXXIII: 357-72. *Mailing Add:* Dept of Foreign Lang Ariz State Univ Tempe AZ 85287

HENDRIKSEN, DANIEL P, b Zeeland, Mich, Feb 12, 29; m 54; c 3. LINGUISTICS, ENGLISH AS A SECOND LANGUAGE. *Educ:* Calvin Col, AB, 51; Univ Mich, MA, 57, MA, 58, PhD(appl ling), 63. *Prof Exp:* Instr English to foreign born, Univ Mich, 59-63; asst prof English, Ball State Univ, 63-66; asst prof ling, 66-69, ASSOC PROF LING, WESTERN MICH UNIV, 69- *Concurrent Pos:* Acad dir, Career English Lang Ctr for Int Students, 75-81. *Mem:* Teaching English to Speakers Other Lang; Ling Soc Am. *Res:* Teaching English to speakers of other languages; psycholinguistics; philosophy and language. *Publ:* Auth, From paradigm to practice in linguistics, Papers Mich Ling Soc, 71; Reshaping inquiry into the perception of sounds, Papers Mich Ling Soc, 76; Shifing questions, partial answers and the Teaching of English to Asians, In: Bilingual Education for Asian Americans, 80. *Mailing Add:* Dept of Ling Western Mich Univ Kalamazoo MI 49001

HENKELS, ROBERT MACALLISTER, JR, b Philadelphia, Pa, Sept 20, 39. FRENCH LITERATURE. *Educ:* Princeton Univ, AB, 62; Brown Univ, MA, 65, PhD(French), 67. *Prof Exp:* Teacher English & French, Noble & Greenough Sch, 62-63; teacher French, Phillips Acad, Andover, 66-67; asst prof, Williams Col, 68-73 & Emory Univ, 73-77; ASST PROF FRENCH, WESTERN MICH UNIV, 77- *Mem:* MLA; Am Asn Teachers Fr. *Res:* Novel of the 19th and 20th centuries; French new novel; Robert Pinget. *Publ:* Auth, The House metaphor in L'Inquisitoire, Critique, spring 73; Graal Flibuste's curious voyage, Studies Mod Fiction, spring 74; Using graphic symbols in explicating the French new novel, In: Forme, Fiction et Experience, 77; Using a computer-generated concordance to analyze and document stylistic devices in Robert Pinget's Fable, Comput & Humanities, spring 78; Robert Pinget: The Novel as Quest, Univ Ala, 78. *Mailing Add:* Dept of Mod & Class Lang Western Mich Univ Kalamazoo MI 49008

HENLE, JANE ELIZABETH, b Cleveland, Ohio, July 14, 13. ARCHEOLOGY, LITERATURE. *Educ:* Smith Col, AB, 34; Columbia Univ, MA, 35, PhD(archaeol), 54. *Prof Exp:* Lectr fine arts, Columbia Univ, 55-71; instr, 71-74, ASST PROF ART HIST, MARYMOUNT COL, NY, 74- *Concurrent Pos:* Instr Greek & transl, New Sch Soc Res, 55-60. *Mem:* Archaeol Inst Am. *Res:* Minoan-Mycenaean script; Greek and pre-Greek art. *Publ:* Auth, A study in word structure in Minoan Linear B; Greek Myths: A Vase Painter's Notebook, Ind Univ, 73. *Mailing Add:* Dept of Art Marymount Col Tarrytown NY 10591

HENLEY, NORMAN, b Auburndale, Mass, Nov 7, 15; m 54; c 1. RUSSIAN LANGUAGE & LITERATURE. *Educ:* Boston Univ, AB, 38; Pac Sch Relig, BD, 42; Univ Paris, Dipl, 49; Harvard Univ, MA, 59, PhD, 67. *Prof Exp:* LECTR HUMANITIES, JOHNS HOPKINS UNIV, 59- *Mem:* Am Asn Teachers Slavic & EEurop Lang. *Publ:* Ed, Russian Prose Reader, Van Nostrand, 63; A N Ostrovsky's Groza, 63 & A S Pushkin's Povesti Belkina, 65, Bradda, England; auth, Ostrovskij's play-actors, puppets and rebels, Slavic & East Europ J, fall 70. *Mailing Add:* Box 452 Johns Hopkins Univ Baltimore MD 21218

HENNING, WILLIAM ANDREW, b Blantyre, Ont, July 1, 35; US citizen; m 57; c 2. FRENCH LINGUISTICS. *Educ:* Wheaton Col Ill, AB, 55; Ind Univ, MA, 61, PhD(French ling), 64. *Prof Exp:* Lectr French ling, Ind Univ, 63-64, asst prof French, Concordia Col, Moorhead, Minn, 64-66; from asst prof to assoc prof, 66-77, PROF FRENCH, WHEATON COL ILL, 77-, DEAN ARTS & SCI, 80- *Mem:* Am Coun Teaching Foreign Lang; Am Asn Teachers Fr. *Res:* Phonology of French. *Publ:* Auth, Discrimination training and self-evaluation in the teaching of pronunciation, Int Rev Applied Ling, 66; coauth, You shouldn't say that, Discourse, 66; auth, Toward programmed instruction in reading, Fr Rev, 2/72. *Mailing Add:* Dept of Foreign Lang Wheaton Col Wheaton IL 60187

HENRY, ERIC PUTNAM, b Greensboro, NC, Mar 15, 43; m 76; c 2. CHINESE LITERATURE & HISTORY. *Educ:* Amherst Col, BA, 72; Yale Univ, MPh, 76, PhD(Chinese lit), 79. *Prof Exp:* Vis asst prof Chinese lang & lit, Dartmouth Col, 80-82; LECTR CHINESE LANG, UNIV NC, CHAPEL HILL, 82- *Mem:* Asn Asian Studies. *Res:* Chinese drama and fiction; Chinese legendary history; Chinese social history. *Publ:* Auth, Chinese Amusement: The Lively Plays of Li Yü, Shoe String Press, 80. *Mailing Add:* Dept Slavic & Oriental Lang Univ NC Chapel Hill NC 27514

HENRY, FREEMAN GEORGE, b Pontiac, Mich, Sept 8, 42; c 1. FRENCH LITERATURE. *Educ:* Ashland Col, BA, 64; Wash State Univ, MA, 66; Univ Colo, PhD(French), 73. *Prof Exp:* Asst English, Lycee Janson de Sailly, Paris, 67-68; from instr to asst prof French, Univ Ga, 70-77; asst prof, 77-80, ASSOC PROF FRENCH, UNIV SC, 80-, GRAD DIR, 82- *Concurrent Pos:* Assoc ed, Fr Lit Ser, 79- *Mem:* MLA; Am Asn Teachers Fr; SAtlantic Mod Lang Asn. *Res:* Nineteenth century French literature; French poetry and theatre. *Publ:* Auth, Rousseau et Dewey: Restritution de l'homme oublie au moyen de l'education pragmatiste, Rev Sci Humaines, 1/70; Baudelaire: The Plato controversy, Romance Notes, 1/74; L'Onomastique des Fleurs du Mal, Rev Int d'Onomastique, 4/74; Commentary on the Bible and Les Fleurs du Mal, PMLA, 5/74; Myth & anguish in Les Fleurs du Mal, Fr Lit Ser, 76; Baudelaire's Satan Trismegistus, Lit & Occult, 77; Baudelaire's Chanson d'apres-midi, Ky Roman Quart, 79; Les Fleurs du Mal and the Exotic, 19th Century Fr Studies, 80. *Mailing Add:* Dept of Foreign Lang & Lit Univ of SC Columbia SC 29208

HENSEY, FREDERICK GERALD, b Albany, NY, Oct 30, 31; m 56; c 2. LINGUISTICS, ROMANCE LANGUAGES. *Educ:* Univ Am, Mex, BA, 56; Univ Texas, Austin, PhD(ling), 67. *Prof Exp:* Teaching asst English, Univ Nacional Autonoma, Mex, 60-62; vis prof ling, Pontificia Cath Univ, Brazil, 65; ASSOC PROF SPAN & PORT, UNIV TEXAS AUSTIN, 66- *Concurrent Pos:* Vis prof ling, Vanderbilt Univ, Nashville, 68, Tulane Univ, New Orleans, 69 & Univ los Andes, Bogota, 77; Fulbright Comn sr lectr, Colombia, 77. *Mem:* Am Asn Teachers Span & Port; Ling Soc Am; Asoc Latinoam Ling Filol; Universala Esperanto-Asocio; North Am Catalan Soc. *Res:* Sociological linguistics; general Romance linguistics; translation. *Publ:* Coauth, Modern Portuguese: A Project of the Modern Language Association (and Accompanying Teacher's Guide), Random House & Knopf, 70; auth, Portuguese inflectional morphology, Lang Quart, 71; The Sociolinguistics of the Brazilian Uruguayan Border, Mouton, 72; Portuguese Vowel Alternations in Casagrande and Saciuk: Generative Studies in Romance Linguistics, Newbury House, 72; Grammatical variation in Southwestern United States Spanish, Linguistics, The Hague, 73; Toward a grammatical analysis of Southwestern Spanish, In: Studies in Southwestern Bilingualism, Newbury House, 76; coauth, Three Essays on Linguistic Diversity in the Spanish-Speaking World, Mouton, 76; co-ed, Contemporary Studies in Romance Linguistics, Georgetown Univ, 77. *Mailing Add:* Dept of Span & Port Univ Tex Austin TX 78712

HENSHAW, RICHARD AUREL, Old Testament, Assyriology. See Vol IV

HENSLEY, GORDON, b Levelland, Tex, May 22, 30. ROMANCE LANGUAGES. *Educ:* Tex Technol Col, BA, 52; Univ Tex, Austin, MA, 56; Inter-Am Univ, Mex, PhD(Span), 62. *Prof Exp:* Teacher, high sch, Tex, 52-53; instr Span & French & chmn dept foreign lang, Alvin Jr Col, 54-64; from assoc prof to prof Span, Lamar State Col Technol, 64-68; prof & dir Span prog, Windham Col, 68-69; chmn dept foreign lang, 72-75, PROF SPAN, EDINBORO STATE COL, 69- *Concurrent Pos:* Lang consult, Lamar Area Sch Studies Coun, Tex, 64-68; consult in-serv training, Beaumont Independent Sch Dist, 66-67; title III teaching demonstration films, S Park Independent Sch Dist, 67-68. *Mem:* MLA; Am Asn Teachers Span & Port; Am Coun Teaching Foreign Lang. *Res:* Contemporary Latin American novel; comparative literature, especially the Don Juan character type; generation of 1898 in Spain. *Mailing Add:* Dept of Foreign Lang Edinboro State Col Edinboro PA 16412

HERBERT, KEVIN BARRY JOHN, b Chicago, Ill, Nov 18, 21; m 46; c 2. CLASSICAL LANGUAGES. *Educ:* Loyola Univ, Ill, BA, 46; Harvard Univ, MA, 49, PhD, 54. *Prof Exp:* Instr classics, Marquette Univ, 48-52 & Indiana Univ, 52-54; master, St Paul's Sch, Concord, NH, 54-55; from instr to asst prof, Bowdoin Col, 55-62; assoc prof, 62-68, PROF CLASSICS & CUR WULFING COLLECTION ANCIENT COINS, WASHINGTON UNIV, 68-, CHMN DEPT CLASSICS, 82- *Concurrent Pos:* Wilbour fel, Brooklyn Mus, 67-68; chief reader advan placement Latin, Educ Testing Serv, 69-73; mem test comt Latin, Col Entrance Exam Bd, 69-73; dir, Nat Endowment for Humanities adult educ prog, Wash Univ, 71-76; dir, Archaeol tours mus & ancient sites of Europ & Mid East, 74- *Mem:* Am Numis Soc; Int Asn Egyptologists; Am Philol Asn; Am Sch Orient Res; Class Asn Mid W & S. *Res:* Epigraphy; ancient history; Greek and Latin prose. *Publ:* Transl, Hugh of St Victor: De Arrha Animae, Marquette Univ, 56; auth, Ancient Art in Bowdoin College: A Handbook of the Warren and Other Collections, Harvard Univ, 64; Greek and Latin Inscriptions in the Brooklyn Museum, Brooklyn Mus, 72; contribr, Great Events From History: Ancient and Medieval Series, Vol I, Salem, 72; co-ed, Ancient Collections in Washingtonington University, Wash Univ, 73; The Wulfing Collection in Washington University: Ancient Coins in North American Collections, Am Numismatic Soc, 79. *Mailing Add:* Dept of Classics Washington Univ St Louis MO 63130

HERIN, CHRISTOPH ABRAHAM, b Ger, Dec 5, 27; m 52. GERMAN. *Educ:* Univ Bonn, PhD(Ger), 50. *Prof Exp:* From instr to asst prof Greek & Latin, Midland Col, 53-55; prof Ger, Washinton & Jefferson Col, 55-58; assoc prof, 58-67, chmn dept, 68-75, PROF GER & SLAVIC LANG, UNIV MD, COLLEGE PARK, 67- *Mem:* MLA; Am Asn Teachers Ger. *Res:* Modern and contemporary poetry; history of German drama and the stage; 18th century novel. *Publ:* Auth, Genesis of an abstract poem, 1/61 & Klinger's Romane, 10/64, Mod Lang Notes; Gestaltungsprinzipien im Lyrisch-Dramatischen Werk August Stramms; Friedrich Maximilian Klinger, De Gruyter, Berlin, 67; Novalis und die lyrische Chiffre, In: Das Nachleben der Romantik, L Stiehm, Heidelberg, 68. *Mailing Add:* Dept of Ger & Russ Univ of Md College Park MD 20742

HERINGTON, CECIL JOHN, b Isleworth, England, Nov 23, 24; US citizen; m 49; c 3. CLASSICS. *Educ:* Oxford Univ, Dipl & BA, 49, MA, 60; Yale Univ, MA, 72. *Prof Exp:* From asst lectr to lectr Greek & Latin, Manchester Univ, England, 49-55; lectr classics, Exeter Univ, 56-60; vis lectr, Smith Col, 60-62; assoc prof, Univ Toronto, 62-65; from assoc prof to prof & chmn dept, Univ Tex, Austin, 65-70; prof classics, Stanford Univ, 70-72; PROF CLASSICS & TALCOTT PROF GREEK, YALE UNIV, 72-, CHMN DEPT, 77- *Concurrent Pos:* Guggenheim fel, 68-69; Sather prof class lit, Univ Calif, Berkeley, 78. *Honors & Awards:* Cromer Prize for Greek, Brit Acad, 58. *Mem:* Am Philol Asn; Class Asn Can; Soc Prom Hellenic Studies. *Res:* Greek archaeology and tragedy; Senecan tragedy. *Publ:* Auth, Athena Parthenos and Athena Polias, Manchester Univ, 55; The Temple of Zeus at Cyrene: Part II, Papers Brit Sch Rome, 58; Senecan Tragedy, Arion, 66; The Author of Prometheus Bound, Univ Tex, 70; The older scholia on the Prometheus Bound, Brill, Leiden, 72; coauth, Aeschylus' Prometheus Bound, Oxford Univ, 75; Aeschylus' Persians, Oxford Univ, 81; Seneca the Younger, In: Cambridge History of Classical Literature II, 82. *Mailing Add:* Dept of Classics Yale Univ New Haven CT 06520

HERKSTROETER, LYNN H, b St Louis, Mo, Jan 22, 45. FRENCH, GERMAN. *Educ:* Washington Univ, St Louis, AB, 66; Middlebury Col & Univ Paris, MA, 67; Univ Wis-Madison, PhD(French), 75. *Prof Exp:* Instr French, William Woods Col, 67-69; asst prof, 73-80, ASSOC PROF FRENCH & GER, SAGINAW VALLEY STATE COL, 80-, CHAIRPERSON MOD FOREIGN LANG, 73- *Mem:* Am Asn Teachers Fr; MLA. *Res:* Eighteenth century French novel; contemporary European drama; women's studies. *Mailing Add:* Saginaw Valley State Col 2250 Pierce Rd University Center MI 48710

HERMAN, ARTHUR LUDWIG, Philosophy, Indian Philosophy. See Vol IV

HERMAN, GERALD, b Wiesbaden, Ger, Apr 4, 36; US citizen; m 60. FRENCH, MEDIEVAL LITERATURE. *Educ:* San Francisco State Col, BA, 58, MA, 62; Stanford Univ, PhD(French), 67. *Prof Exp:* Asst prof, 66-73, ASSOC PROF FRENCH, UNIV CALIF, DAVIS, 73- *Mem:* MLA; Mediaeval Acad Am; Am Asn Teachers Fr. *Publ:* Auth, Unconventional arms as a comic device in some Old French chansons de geste, Mod Lang Quart, 9/69; Nationality groups in the Old French epic, Ann Mediaevale, 69; Is there humor in La chanson de Roland?, Fr Rev, fall 71. *Mailing Add:* Dept of French & Italian Univ of Calif Davis CA 95616

HERMAN, JACK CHALMERS, b New Orleans, La, July 20, 14; m 44; c 2. SPANISH, FRENCH. *Educ:* Tulane Univ, BA, 35, MA, 37; Univ Kans, PhD(Span), 50. *Prof Exp:* Instr Span, Tulane Univ, 35-38 & 45-46, asst Span & French, 39-41; postal censor, Off Censorship, Cristobal, CZ, 42-45; instr Span, Univ Kans, 46-50, asst prof, 50-52; prof & chmn dept, 52-80, EMER PROF FOREIGN LANG, E CENT OKLA STATE UNIV, 80- *Concurrent Pos:* Vis prof Span, Univ Ariz, 54 & San Diego State Col, 57; assoc ed,

Hispania, 55-73; assoc prof, Kans State Teachers Col, 61-62. *Mem:* Am Asn Teachers Span & Port (secy-treas, 64-65); Am Coun Teaching Foreign Lang. *Res:* Modern Spanish novel; Spanish American literature. *Publ:* Co-ed, El asesino desvelado, Houghton, 52; auth, Galdos' expressed appreciation of Don Quijote, Mod Lang J, 1/52; Quotations and locutions from Don Quijote in Galdos' novels, Hispania, 5/53; Don Quijote and the Novels of Perex Galdos, E Cent State Col, 55; An historical account of the AATSP chapter movement, Hispania, 12/67. *Mailing Add:* Dept of Mod Lang E Cent Okla State Univ Ada OK 74820

HERMAND, JOST, b Kassel, Ger, Apr 11, 30; m 56. MODERN GERMAN LITERATURE. *Educ:* Univ Marburg, PhD, 55. *Prof Exp:* From asst prof to prof Ger, 58-67, VILAS RES PROF, UNIV WIS-MADISON, 67- *Concurrent Pos:* Am Coun Learned Soc fel, 65-66; vis prof, Harvard Univ, 67, Univ Tex, Austin, 70, Free Univ WBerlin, 77, Univ Bremen, 78 & Univ Giessen, 81. *Mem:* MLA; Int Brecht Soc; Heine Soc. *Res:* Cultural and intellectual history of Germany between 1870-1914; Heinrich Heine; literature after 1945. *Publ:* Auth, Literaturwissenschaft und Kunstwissenschaft, Metzler, Stuttgart, 65; Stilkunst um 1900, Akademie, Berlin, 67; Synthetisches Interpretieren, Nymphenburger, Munich, 68; Pop International, Athenaum, Frankfurt, 71; ed, Heine's Reisebilder, Hoffmann & Campe, Hamburg, 73; auth, Streitobjekt Heine, Athenaum, Frankfurt, 75; Orte Irgendwo Formen utopischen Denkens, Athenaum, Koenigstein, 81; Konkretes Hoeren Zum Inhalt der Instrumentalmusik, Argument, Berlin, 81. *Mailing Add:* Dept of Ger Univ of Wis Madison WI 53706

HERMINGHOUSE, PATRICIA ANNE (BURKE), b Melrose Park, Ill, Mar 13, 40; m 64; c 2. GERMAN, WOMEN'S STUDIES. *Educ:* Knox Col, BA, 62; Washington Univ, MA, 65, PhD(Ger), 68. *Prof Exp:* Asst prof Ger, Univ Mo-St Louis, 66-67, vis lectr, 68-69; asst prof, 67-78, ASSOC PROF GER, WASH UNIV, 78- *Concurrent Pos:* Lectr Ger, Fontbonne Col, 65-66; coordr, Coalition Women Ger, 74-75, mem Nat Steering Comt, 76-; Int Res & Exchanges Bd ad hoc grant, 76; ed, GDR Bull: Newslett Lit & Cult in Ger Dem Repub, 75- *Mem:* MLA; Am Asn Teachers Ger; Soc Study Multi-Ethnic Lit US; Coalition Women Ger. *Res:* German Democratic Republic literature; German-American studies; women as writers. *Publ:* Co-ed, Literatur und Literaturtheorie in der Deutschen Demokratisch en Republik, Suhrkamp, 76; auth, German-American studies in a new vein: Resources and possibilities, Unterrichtspraxis, 76; From Deutsche Turner to American Turners-- an immigrant institution and the process of Americanization, Am Asn Teachers Ger, 76; Vorbemerkung und materialien zu Jurek Beckers Jakob der Lügner, Suhrkamp Lit Zeitung, 77. *Mailing Add:* Dept of Ger Lang & Lit Washington Univ St Louis MO 63130

HERNADI, PAUL, English, Comparative Literature. See Vol II

HERNANDEZ, JUAN EDUARDO, b Herradura, Cuba, Oct 15, 08; nat US; m 36; c 5. MODERN LANGUAGES. *Educ:* Ky Wesleyan Col, AB, 33; Univ Ky, AM, 34, PhD(psychol), 38. *Prof Exp:* Head commercial dept, Pinson Col, Cuba, 28-29; from instr to head dept, Ky Wesleyan Col, 33-36; from instr to assoc prof romance lang, 36-59, actg head dept, 49-50, PROF ROMANCE LANG, UNIV KY, 59-, ASST DEAN COL ARTS & SCI, 67- *Concurrent Pos:* Asst dean admis, US Air Force Inst Technol, Wright- Patterson Air Force Base, Ohio, 52-53; consult higher educ in Guatemala, Int Coop Admin, 56 & US Pub Health Serv Hosp, Lexington, Ky, 59. *Mem:* Am Asn Teachers Span & Port. *Res:* Proverbs in Spanish literature; the Spanish-American novel. *Publ:* Auth, Practical Spanish grammar; Monochromatic perception of light. *Mailing Add:* 236 Clay Ave Lexington KY 01826

HERNANDEZ, JUANA AMELIA, b Havana, Cuba; US citizen. SPANISH & SPANISH AMERICAN LITERATURE. *Educ:* Univ Havana, BA, 54, Dr Filos y Let (Span), 59. *Prof Exp:* Prof Span, Loyola Mil Acad, Cuba, 57-60; prof Span & hist, Preuniv Inst Vedado, Cuba, 59-61; prof Span, Loyola Sch, Miami, Fla, 61-62; instr, Tri- Ctr Community Sch Dist, Iowa, 62-63 & Riverton Sch Dist, Wyo, 63-65; from asst prof to assoc prof, 65-74, dir, Span House, 65-68, CHMN DEPT MOD & CLASS LANG, HOOD COL, 72-, PROF SPAN, 74- *Concurrent Pos:* Ed Crucero, 59-60; mem exam comt, Span Achievement Test, Col Entrance Exam Bd, 68-76; consult, Am Asn Jr Cols, 70-; mem comt, Span Proficiency Test, Defense Lang Inst, 72-73; mem, Span Lang Develop Comt, Col Entrance Bd Exam, 76-80; dir, Am Asn Teachers Span & Port Nat Span Exams, 80-; Hodson Beneficial fel, 82. *Mem:* North East Conf Teaching Foreign Lang; Am Asn Teachers Span & Port; Int Inst Iberoam Lit; AAUP. *Res:* Contemporary Spanish novel; Spanish American fiction; foreign language testing. *Publ:* Auth, Primera Constancia (poems), Grafica Comercial, Madrid, 66; coauth, Novelistica Espanola de los Sesenta, Eliseo Torres & Sons, NY, 71; Quince novelas Hispanoamericanas, Las Americas, 71; Tres tristes tigres (essay), Papeles de Son Armadans, spring 72; Paradiso (essay), Papeles de Son Armadans, 6/74; co-ed, Selecciones de Ana M Matute, FFH Publ, 82. *Mailing Add:* Dept of Mod & Class Lang Hood Col Frederick MD 21701

HERNANDEZ-ARAICO, SUSANA, b Ensenada, Baja Calif, Mex, Dec 19, 47; m 76; c 1. SPANISH DRAMA, SPANISH AMERICAN LITERATURE. *Educ:* Mt St Mary's Col, BA, 68; Univ Calif, Los Angeles, MA, 70, PhD(hisp lang & lit), 76. *Prof Exp:* Assoc Span lang & lit, Univ Calif, Los Angeles, 71; lectr Span lang, Santa Monica Col, 73-75; PROF SPAN LANG & LIT, CALIF STATE POLYTECH UNIV, POMONA, 72- *Concurrent Pos:* Vis scholar, Latin Am Ctr, Univ Calif, Los Angeles, 82. *Mem:* MLA; Am Asn Teaachers Span & Port; Pac Coast Coun Latin Am Studies; Comediantes; Instituto Literario Cultural Hispanico. *Res:* Spanish Golden Age drama, Calderon de la Barca; Spanish American contemporary women authors, Syria Poletti; Mexican literature. *Publ:* Auth, Redondeo de arbol y mo en Piedra de sol, Cuadernos Americanos, 11-12/78; Memoing el determinismo tragico en La lija del aire, In: Approaches to the Theater of Calderon, Univ Press, 82; contribr, An Annotated Bibliography of Women Authors Whose Works Have Been Translated into English Since 1945, Garland Press, 82; auth, Tres voces semeninas en la poesia hispenoamericano de hoy, Alba de America, fall 82; Texto y espectaculo en La lija del aire: Escenificacion triangular de un metadrama tragico, In: Proc For II Annual Golden Age Span Drama Symp (in press); Chato, gracioso singular en La lija del aire, Bull Comediants (in press); German and English Romanticism: The Schlegels, Shelley and Calderon, Comp Lit (in press); El espiritu sensual de Ruben Dario, Letras de Buenos Aires (in press). *Mailing Add:* 3922 Minerva Ave Los Angeles CA 90066

HERNANDEZ-DANIEL, OSCAR F, b La Habana, Cuba, Apr 28, 24; US citizen; m 51; c 1. SPANISH LITERATURE, APPLIED LINGUISTICS. *Educ:* Instituto Pre-Universitario del Vedado, BA, 41; Univ Nacional La Habana, LLD, 46; Univ Fla, Gainesville, PhD(Span lit), 75. *Prof Exp:* Law practice, Havana-Colon, Cuba, 46-62; prof polit sci, Colon Inst of Technol, 51-59; pres, Colon Bus Col, Cuba, 59-62; PROF SPAN, EMPORIA STATE UNIV, 64- *Concurrent Pos:* Adv econ, Nat Bank, Cuba, 55-62; Danforth assoc humanities, 78- *Honors & Awards:* Ricardo Dolz y Arango, President of Cuba, 46; Miguel Angel Asturias, Ministry of Educ, Guatemala, 68. *Mem:* Am Asn Teachers Span & Port; MLA; Am Writers Asn (secy, 76). *Res:* Literature and plastic arts; Spanish Renaissance and Golden Age literature; Latin America contemporary novel. *Publ:* Auth, Estructura cosmica del Popol Vuh en dos novelas de Miguel Angel Asturias, El Imparcial, Guatemala, 67; Dinamismo en la Marcha Trinfal de Dario, Rev Unv Ind Santander, 68; El Lazarillo de Tormes y la pintura, Hispanofila, 69; El negro y el azucar en la novelistica cubana, Nuevos Rumbos, 74; Don Quixote's structural center, Essays in Criticism, 75; Acercamiento al Quijote a traves de los Principios del Arte de Heirich Wölfflin, Espasa-Calpe, 77; El comercio hispanico: Teoria y practica, Emporia Univ, 77; Ironia en las poesias pastoriles del Quijote, Anales Cervantinos, 78. *Mailing Add:* Dept of Foreign Lang Emporia State Univ Emporia KS 66801

HERNANDEZ-MIYARES, JULIO ENRIQUE, b Santiago, Cuba, July 15, 31; US citizen; m 57; c 4. SPANISH, HISPANIC LITERATURES. *Educ:* Colegio de Belen, Cuba, BA, 48; Univ of Havana, LLD, 54; NY Univ, MA, 66, PhD(Hisp lit), 72. *Prof Exp:* Jr attorney, Nunez Mesa-Machado Law Office, 54-57; attorney-partner, Fabre Law Office, Havana, 57-61; prof Span U Span lit, 66-71, CHMN DEPT FOREIGN LANG, KINGSBOROUGH COMMUNITY COL, 71- *Honors & Awards:* Diploma of Honor Lincoln-Marti, Dept Health Educ & Welfare, 73; Juan J Remos Award, Cruzada Educativa Cubana- Miami, Fla, 72. *Mem:* MLA; Am Asn Teachers of Span & Port; Inst Int Lit Iberoamericana; Circulo de Cultura Panamericana (pres, 74-76). *Res:* Spanish for occupational careers, orthography, semantics; Cuban narrative abroad; Spanish American modernismo. *Publ:* Auth The Cuban short story in Exile: A selected bibliography, Hispania, 71; La poesia cubana del exterior: Testimonio y recuento, Norte, Amsterdam Ano XII, 6-8/71; Antillana Rotunda (poems), Editorial Vosgos, Barcelona, 74; coauth, Julian del Casal: Estudios Criticos sobre su obra, 74 U auth, Narradores cubanos de hoy, 75, Ediciones Universal, Miami; coauth, Spanish for Nurses, Arco, 77; auth, Prologue to Jaula de sombras of Pablo Le Riverend, Ediciones Rondas Barcelona, Spain, 77; coauth, Ortografia en accion, S Western, 78. *Mailing Add:* Dept of Foreign Lang Kingsborough Community Col Brooklyn NY 11235

HERRERA Y SANCHEZ, FRANCISCO, b Belmez, Spain, July 27, 11; nat US; m 39; c 5. ROMANCE LANGUAGES. *Educ:* WVa Univ, AM, 37. *Prof Exp:* From asst prof to assoc prof Romance lang, 50-64, prof Span & dir Latin Am area studies prog, 64-78, assoc dir NDEA Lang Inst, 60-67, EMER PROF SPAN, WVA UNIV, 78- *Concurrent Pos:* Mem Inter-Am comt methodology teaching foreign lang, Inter-Am Prog Ling & Teaching Lang, 68; chmn, State Comt Sec Educ, 69-; chmn, WVa Adv Coun Teacher Educ & Prof Standards, 71. *Mem:* Am Asn Teachers Span & Port; Nat Fedn Mod Lang Teachers Asn. *Res:* Spanish folklore; the Golden Age. *Publ:* Auth, Andalcismos y Gitanismos de los cantos flamencos; Sources and characteristics of flamenco music; coauth, Selected Spanish Short Stories, T Y Crowell, 57; auth, Caracteristicas de la filosofia barroca calderoniana en los del pueblo, Ky Foreign Lang Quart, 63. *Mailing Add:* Dept of Romance Lang WVa Univ Morgantown WV 26506

HERRERO, JAVIER, b Murcia, Spain, Aug 12, 26; m 62; c 3. ROMANCE LANGUAGES. *Educ:* Univ Madrid, LLB, 49, BA, 51, PhD(philos), 56. *Prof Exp:* Asst philos, Univ Madrid, 54-55; asst Span, Univ Edinburgh, 56-60, lectr, 60-66; assoc prof, Duke Univ, 66-67, prof, 67-68; prof, Univ Pittsburgh, 68-74, Mellon prof, 74-79; WILLIAM R KENAN JR PROF SPAN, UNIV VA, 79- *Concurrent Pos:* Univ Edinburgh res grant, 62; Sir Ernest Cassel res grant, 65; Guggenheim fel, 68; Am Philos Soc grant, 73; Nat Endowment for Humanities grant, 73. *Mem:* MLA; SAtlantic Mod Lang Asn; Asoc Int Hispanistas. *Res:* Spanish and comparative literature, 17th to 20th centuries; literary criticism. *Publ:* Auth, El Schlosser, de Fernan Caballero, Romanische Forsch, 62; Fernan Caballero, un nuevo planteamiento, Gredos, 63; El elemento biografico en Pio Cid, Hisp Rev, 65; Angel Ganivet, un iluminado, Gredos, 66; Ganivet, cartas familiares, Anel, 67; The image of the centaur in A Machado, Bull Hisp Studies, 68; Los origenes del pensamiento reaccionario espanol, Cuadernos para Dialogo, 71. *Mailing Add:* Dept of Span Univ of Va Charlottesville VA 22903

HERRON, ROBERT DEUPREE, b Roanoke, Va, June 29, 35; m 64; c 3. SPANISH, PORTUGUESE. *Educ:* Univ Richmond, BA, 57; Univ Wis, MA, 59, MA, 63, PhD(Span), 68. *Prof Exp:* Instr Span & Port, Miami Univ, 63-68; asst prof Port, Univ NMex, 68-73, actg dir, lang & area ctr Latin Am, 69-70; assoc prof Span & Port, 73-76, chmn dept, 73-82, PROF MOD LANG, ST LOUIS UNIV, 76- *Concurrent Pos:* Dir, Andean Studies & Res Ctr, Univ NMex in Quito, Ecuador, 71-72. *Mem:* MLA; Am Asn Teachers Span & Port; Midwest Mod Lang Asn. *Res:* Brazilian and Portugues prose fiction of 19th and 20th centuries; Spanish American literature; Chicano literature. *Publ:* Auth, Lima Barreto's Isias Caminha as a psychological novel, Luso-Brazilian Rev, winter 71; Personajes y paises en Adalberto Ortiz, Suplemento Domincal, El Comercio, Quito, Ecuador, 4/72; O tema da amizade em O amanuense Belmiro, de Cyro dos Anjos, Suplemento lit, Minas Gerais, Belo Horizonte, Brazil, 9/72; Three Fables: Translations from A Dor da Bruxa e outras Fabulas by Robert Reis, Vol VI, Webster Rev, spring 81. *Mailing Add:* Dept of Mod & Class Lang St Louis Univ St Louis MO 63103

HERSHBELL, JACKSON PAUL, b Northampton, Pa, Nov 27, 35; m 63; c 2. PHILOSOPHY, CLASSICS. *Educ:* Lafayette Col, BA, 55; Univ Pa, MA, 56; Gen Theol Sem, STB, 63; Harvard Univ, PhD(philos & classics), 64. *Prof Exp:* Asst prof philos & coord humanities, Univ NDak, 66-69; assoc prof, 70-78, PROF CLASSICS, UNIV MINN, MINNEAPOLIS, 78- *Concurrent Pos:* Inst Res Humanities, Univ Wis-Madison fel, 69-70; Alexander von Humboldt fel, Univ Munich, WGer, 77-78. *Mem:* Am Class Asn; Am Philol Asn; Am Philos Asn; Class Asn; Soc Ancient Greek Philos. *Res:* Ancient philosophy, especially the presocratics; classical influences; especially the 18th century; the Epic tradition. *Publ:* Auth, Plutarch as a source for Empedocles re-examined, Am J Philol, 71; Plutarch and Parmenides, Greek, Roman & Byzantine Studies, 72; Hippolytus' Elenchos as a Source for Empedocles re-examined, Phronesis, 2 parts, 73-74; Empedoclean Influences on the Timaeus, Phoenix, 74; Plutarch and Heraclitus, Hermes, 77; Nietzsche and Heraclitus, Nietzsche Studien, 79; co-ed (With E A Harelock), Communication Arts in the Ancient World, 78; Psuedo Plato, Axiochus, Soc Bibl Lit, 81. *Mailing Add:* 1313 Como Ave SE Minneapolis MN 55414

HERSHBERG, DAVID RALPH, b Boston, Mass, June 17, 35; m 57; c 3. SPANISH, ITALIAN. *Educ:* Univ Mich, BA, 57, PhD(Span), 66; Harvard Univ, MA, 64. *Prof Exp:* Teaching asst Ital, Harvard Univ, 57-58; teaching asst Span & Ital, Univ Mich, 58-62; asst prof, Wayne State Univ, 62-65; from instr to assoc prof, Univ Ill, Urbana, 65-76; PROF MOD LANG & CHMN DEPT, UNIV LOUISVILLE, 76- *Mem:* Am Asn Teachers Span & Port; Am Coun Teaching Foreign Lang; Am Asn Teachers Ital. *Res:* Spanish Golden Age literature. *Publ:* Auth, Otium and the Epitaph of Sulpicius Similis, Romanische Forsch, 68; Porcia in the Golden Age literature: Echoes of a classical theme, Neophilologus, 70; ed, Los Errores Celebrados de Juan de Zabaleta, Espasa-Calpe, Madrid, 72. *Mailing Add:* Dept of Mod Lang Univ of Louisville Louisville KY 40208

HERTLING, GUNTER H, b Pasadena, Calif, June 14, 30; m 53; c 2. GERMAN. *Educ:* Univ Calif, Berkeley, BA, MA, PhD(Ger), 61. *Prof Exp:* Assoc Ger, Univ Calif, Berkeley, 60-61; from instr to assoc prof, 61-74, Grad Sch res Fund grant, 65, sen, fac senate, 72-74, PROF GERMANIC, UNIV WASH, 74- *Honors & Awards:* Österreichische Gesll Lit, Vienna, 80. *Mem:* MLA; Am Asn Teachers Ger; Philol Asn Pac Coast; Stifter-Gesellschaft. *Res:* Eighteenth and 19th century German literature, literary theories, aesthetics and culture. *Publ:* Auth, Wandlung der Werte im dichterischen Werk der Ricarda Huch, In: Abhandlunger zur Kunst-, Musik- und Literaturwissenschaft, H Bouvier, Bonn, 66; Grenzubergang und Raumverletzung: Zur Zentralthematik in Adalbert Stifters Studien, Vierteljahressschrift des Adalbert Stifter Inst, 67; Zur Funktion und Bedeutung der Traumerinnerung bei CF Meyer: Nachweis an einem Beispiel aus dem Jürg Jenatsch, Etudes Germaniques, 70; Religiosität ohne Vorurteil: Zum Wendepunkt in CF Meyers Das Amulett, Zeitschrift Für deutsche Philol, 71; Conrad Ferdinand Meyers Epik: Traumbeseelung, Traumbesinnung und Traumbesitz, Franke, Bern & Munich, 73; Theodor Fontanes Stine: Eine Entzauberte Zauberflöte?, Zum Humanitäts Gedanken Am Ausklang Zweier, Bern, Jahrhumderte, 82. *Mailing Add:* Dept of Germanics Univ of Wash Seattle WA 98195

HERTZ-OHMES, PETER DONALD, b Berlin, Ger, June 2, 33; m 77; c 3. GERMAN LITERATURE, PHILOSOPHY. *Educ:* Stanford Univ, AB, 57, PhD(Ger), 67; Columbia Univ, MA, 64. *Prof Exp:* Instr Ger, Univ Redlands, 60-61; assoc prof, 65-71, dir int educ, 72-76, PROF GER, STATE UNIV NY COL OSWEGO, 71- *Concurrent Pos:* Admin fel, Am Coun Educ, 71-72; vis prof, Calif State Univ, Sacramento, 79-80. *Mem:* Am Asn Teachers Ger; MLA. *Res:* Theory of interpretation and translation; poetics. *Publ:* Auth, Language and the poetic process, Topic, fall 69; Minimal poetry, Western Humanities Rev, winter 70; Steppenwolf as a Bible, Ga Rev, winter 71; translr, Martin Heidegger: On the Way to Language, Harper, 71 & 82; Cross-cultural communication and Geman literature, Selecta PNCFL, 80; The public lie and the truth of fiction, Pac Coast Philol, 81. *Mailing Add:* 162 W Fourth St Oswego NY 13126

HERUM, JOHN MAURICE, b Bismarck, NDak, Jan 1, 31; m 58; c 3. RHETORIC, APPLIED ENGLISH LINGUISTICS. *Educ:* Carroll Col, Mont, BA, 51. *Prof Exp:* Tech writer & ed, comput, Nat Security Agency, 55-58; assoc prof, 62-80, PROF ENGLISH, CENT WASH UNIV, 80- *Mem:* NCTE. *Res:* Rhetorical theory and practice; ethnography of literacy. *Publ:* Coauth, Metrical boundaries and rhythm-phrases, Mod Lang Quart, 67; Semantic recurrence and rhetorical form, Lang & Style, 71; Writing Random, 71; co-ed, Tempo: Life, Work, and Leisure, Houghton, 74; Transactional writing, In: The Whys of Teaching Writing, WSCTE, 78. *Mailing Add:* Dept of English Cent Wash Univ Ellensburg WA 98926

HERZ, JULIUS MICHAEL, b Vienna, Austria, Feb 4, 26. GERMAN. *Educ:* Univ Vienna, PhD(Ger); Vanderbilt Univ, MA, 58. *Prof Exp:* Teacher, Austria, 49-50; instr English, Austro-Am Inst Educ, 52, Western civilization, Ithaca Col, 55-56 & Ger & French, Univ Maine, 56-57; asst prof, 57-75, ASSOC PROF GER, TEMPLE UNIV, 75- *Mem:* MLA; AAUP; Int Arthur Schnitzler Res Asn. *Res:* German and Austrian literature; bibliography; German-American studies. *Publ:* Contribr, MLA International Bibliography, MLA, 69-78; coauth, The Friedens-Bate: A major German language newspaper of the Lehigh Valley, Proc Lehigh County Hist Soc, 74; auth, Eli Keller: Pennsylvania-German Pact, Ger-Am Studies, 75. *Mailing Add:* Dept of Ger & Slavic Lang Temple Univ Philadelphia PA 19122

HERZFELD, ANITA, b Buenos Aires, Arg; US citizen. LINGUISTICS, ENGLISH AS A SECOND LANGUAGE. *Educ:* Teacher's Col, Arg, BSc, 53, BA, 61; Univ Kans, MA, 65, MPhil, 74, PhD(ling), 78. *Prof Exp:* Asst coordr lang develop, KU Cent Am & Ford Found Prog, 63-67; chmn, English Dept, Univ Buenos Aires, 67-68; dir jr yr abroad & prof ling, Univ Kans at Univ Costa Rica, 68-70 & 75; foreign study adv & asst to dean col, 71-74, instr ling, 71-75, FULBRIGHT ADV & DIR, OFF STUDY ABROAD, UNIV KANS, 76- *Concurrent Pos:* Lectr ling, NDEA Summer Insts, 62-64; dir jr yr in Ger, Univ Erlangen-Nürnberg, 73; Fulbright fac develop res grant, Panama, 79; Fulbright specialists grant, Ger, 79; Admin internship, Off Acad Abb Ku, 80-; Tinker grant, Cent Am, 82. *Mem:* Soc Caribbean Ling; Ling Soc Am; Nat Asn Foreign Student Affairs; Coun Int Educ Exchange; Latin Am Studies Asn. *Res:* Caribbean Creoles; higher education in the Americas; Costa Rican theater. *Publ:* Co-ed, Metodologia de la Evaluacion Universitaria: Teoria y practica, Univ Kans, 69; coauth, Notas y Ejercicios de Composicion, Prentice Hall, 69; transl, Mary Lester, Un viaje a traves de Honduras, Educa, 71; co-ed, Planificacion, Coordinacion, Autonomia, Innovaciones: Perspectivas Latinoamericanas, Univ Kans, 72; coauth, El Teatro de Hoy en Costa Rica, Ed Costa Rica, 73; co-ed, La Universidad y los Universitarios: Carrera docente, investigacion, estudios postgraduos, Univ Kans, 74; auth, Towards the description of Creoles, In: Proceedings of the Mid-Am Ling Conf, Univ Minn, 76; Second language Acrolect replacement, In: Working Papers in Linguistics, Univ Kans, 77. *Mailing Add:* Off Study Abroad Univ of Kans Lawrence KS 66045

HERZOG, MICHAEL B, Comparative Literature. See Vol II

HESS, WILLIAM HUIE, b Arkadelphia, Ark, Dec 24, 33; m 54; c 2. CLASSICS. *Educ:* Univ Tex, BA, 55, MA, 59; Princeton Univ, MA, 62, PhD(classics), 63. *Prof Exp:* Spec instr class, 59-60, from instr to asst prof classics, Univ Tex, 62-68; assoc prof, 68-78, PROF LANG & CHMN DEPT, UNIV UTAH, 78- *Mem:* Am Philol Asn. *Res:* Greek comedy; ancient religion; history of ideas. *Mailing Add:* Dept of Lang Univ of Utah Salt Lake City UT 84112

HESTER, RALPH M, b Ft Worth, Tex, Dec 22, 31; m 66; c 2. ROMANCE LANGUAGES & LITERATURE. *Educ:* Univ Calif, Los Angeles, BA, 54, MA, 56, PhD(Romance lang), 63. *Prof Exp:* Asst French, Univ Calif, Los Angeles, 54-56, assoc, 56-57, asst 58-59, assoc, 59-60, lectr, 61-63; from asst prof to assoc prof, 63-78, PROF FRENCH, STANFORD UNIV, 78-, CHMN, DEPT FR & ITAL, 79- *Mem:* MLA; Am Asn Teachers Fr; Renaissance Soc Am. *Res:* French Renaissance literature; methodology in teaching of French. *Publ:* Coauth, L'art de la Conversation, 67 & ed & contribr, Teaching a Living Language, 70, Harper; auth, A Protestant Baroque Poet: Pierre Poupo, Mouton, 70; coauth, Decouverte et Creation, Rand McNally, 74 & 2nd ed, 77, 3rd ed, Houghton Mifflin, 81; auth, From reading to the reading of literature, Mod Lang J, 5/72. *Mailing Add:* Dept Fr & Ital Stanford Univ Stanford CA 94305

HETZRON, ROBERT, b Budapest, Hungary, Dec 31, 37; div; c 3. GENERAL LINGUISTICS, AFRO-ASIATIC LANGUAGES. *Educ:* Sch Orient Lang, Paris, Dipl Hebrew, 59, Dipl Amharic, 60; Hebrew Univ, Israel, MA, 64; Univ Calif, Los Angeles, PhD(Near Eastern lang), 66. *Prof Exp:* From asst prof to assoc prof, 66-73, PROF HEBREW, UNIV CALIF, SANTA BARBARA, 73- *Concurrent Pos:* Ed, Afroasiatic Ling, 73-; Guggenheim Mem Found fel, 76-77; NSF res, 80-82. *Mem:* Ling Soc Am; Groupe Linguistique d'Etudes Chamito-Semitiques. *Res:* General linguistics; Semitic and Cushitic linguistics; Hungarian linguistics. *Publ:* Auth, The Verbal System of Southern Agaw, Univ Calif, 69; Ethiopian Semitic, Studies in Classification, Manchester Univ, 72; Surfacing, From Dependency Relations to Linearity, Liviana, 75; The Agaw languages, Afroasiatic Ling, 76; The Gunnän-Gurage Languages, Inst Orient di Napoli, 77; The Limits of Cushitic, Sugia, 81. *Mailing Add:* Dept of Ger & Slavic Univ of Calif Santa Barbara CA 93106

HEWITT, HELEN-JO JAKUSZ, b Ind. APPLIED LINGUSTICS. *Educ:* State Univ Iowa, BA, 48; Purdue Univ, West Lafayette, MS, 61; Univ Tex, Austin, PhD(appl ling), 72, MLS, 75. *Prof Exp:* RES ASSOC LING, LING RES CTR, UNIV TEX, AUSTIN, 70- *Mem:* Ling Soc Am; Ling Soc NZ; MLA. *Res:* Oceanic linguistics; computer assisted indexing; lexicography. *Publ:* Coauth, Selected Measurements in American English Speech, Univ Tex, 65; auth, Aneityum of the New Hebrides: Anejom Phonology and Word List, Te Reo, NZ, 66; Linguistics of Australasia and Oceana, 68-77 & Composite and derivative languages: Other communicative behavior, 69-73, In: MLA International Bibliography. *Mailing Add:* 2511 Pearl Austin TX 78705

HEWITT, LEAH DIANNE, b Carbondale, Ill. CONTEMPORARY FRENCH LITERATURE. *Educ:* Kent State Univ, BA, 72; Univ Calif, Berkeley, MA, 74, PhD(Fr), 79. *Prof Exp:* Asst prof French, Mich State Univ, 79-81; ASST PROF FRENCH & SPAN, CARLETON COL, 81- *Mem:* MLA. *Res:* Contemporary French literature and theory; 17th century French literature. *Publ:* Auth, Les Reliques d'un desabuse of Jean Pierre Mulot, Fr Rev, 78; Historical intervention in Leiris' Bif(f)ur(e)s, Fr Forum, 82. *Mailing Add:* Dept of Mod Lang & Lit Carlton Col Northfield MN 55057

HEWSON, JOHN, b Tugby, Eng, Dec 19, 30; Can citizen; m 54; c 3. LINGUISTICS. *Educ:* Univ Col, London, BA, 52; Inst Educ, London, Cert, 53; Laval Univ, MA, 58 & 60, DUniv, 64. *Prof Exp:* From asst prof to assoc prof, 60-68, PROF LING, MEM UNIV NFLD, 68- *Mem:* Can Ling Asn (pres, 80-82); Ling Soc Am; Ling Asn Gt Brit; Philol Soc; Int Ling Asn. *Res:* Psychomechanics of language; comparative Algonkian linguistics; computerized reconstruction of protolanguages. *Publ:* Auth, Oral French Pattern Practice, 63 & La Pratique du francais, 66, W J Gage; Article and Noun in English, Mouton, The Hague, 72; contribr, Comparative Reconstruction on the Computer, Hist Ling, 74; Derivation and inflection in English, In: Studies in English Grammar, Univ de Lille, 75; auth, Langue and parole since Saussure, Historiographia Ling, 76; The Beothuk Vocabularies, Nfld Mus, 78; La notion de regle en linguistique, Modeles Linguistiques, Vol 3, 81. *Mailing Add:* Dept of Ling Mem Univ of Nfld St John's NF A1B 3X9 Can

HEYER, ELFRIEDE ANNEMARIE, b Frankfurt, WGer; US citizen. GERMAN LITERATURE & LANGUAGE. *Educ:* Millikin Univ, BA, 68; Wash Univ, St Louis, MA, 72, PhD(Ger), 77. *Prof Exp:* ASST PROF GER, STATE UNIV NY, BINGHAMTON, 77- *Mem:* MLA; Am Asn Teachers Ger. *Res:* Eighteenth century literature and aesthetics; history of ideas; Thomas Mann. *Mailing Add:* Dept of Ger State Univ of NY Binghamton NY 13901

HIATT, MARY LANE CHARLES, b Richmond, Ind, Feb 26, 07. FRENCH LANGUAGE & LITERATURE. *Educ:* Earlham Col, AB, 27; Bryn Mawr Col, AM, 28, PhD(French & Ital), 39. *Prof Exp:* Instr French, Hollins Col, 29-34; asst English, Sorbonne, 36-38; prof lang, Wilmington Col, Ohio, 41-46; prof French, Western Col Women, 46-55, actg chmn dept lang, 54-55; from assoc prof to prof, 55-72, actg chmn dept lang, 55-56 & 63, EMER PROF MOD LANG, EARLHAM COL, 72- *Concurrent Pos:* Asst dir, Sweet Briar Col jr year in France, 49-51. *Res:* Contemporary French literature; Romanesque architecture in France. *Publ:* Auth, Growth of Diderot's Fame in France from 1784-1875, Edwards Bros, 42; coauth, French Tachistoslides with Manual, Translation and Tapes, Keystone View Co, 59; auth, Diderot and the Goncourt as critics of eighteenth century French art, Ky Foreign Lang Quart, 64; The art of the theatre by Henri Cheon, Relig Theatre, fall 64. *Mailing Add:* 312 Henley Rd Richmond IN 47374

HIBBETT, HOWARD SCOTT, b Akron, Ohio, July 27, 20; m 46; 60; c 3. JAPANESE LITERATURE. *Educ:* Harvard Univ, AB, 47, PhD(Far Eastern lang), 50. *Prof Exp:* From instr to asst prof Orient lang, Univ Calif, Los Angeles, 52-58; assoc prof, 58-63, chmn dept Far Eastern lang, 65-70, PROF JAPANESE LIT, HARVARD UNIV, 63- *Concurrent Pos:* Jr fel, Soc Fels, Harvard Univ, 49-52; Fulbright res scholars, 56-57, 64-65; Guggenheim fel, 64-65. *Mem:* Asn Asian Studies; Am Acad Arts & Sci. *Res:* Japanese language and literature. *Publ:* Auth, The Floating World in Japanese Fiction, Oxford Univ, 59; coauth, Modern Japanese: A Basic Reader, Harvard Univ, 65; ed, Contemporary Japanese Literature, Knopf, 77. *Mailing Add:* Dept of E Asian Lang & Civilizations Harvard Univ Cambridge MA 02138

HIEBEL, FREDERICK, b Vienna, Austria, Feb 10, 03; nat US; m 45; c 2. GERMAN LANGUAGE & LITERATURE. *Educ:* Univ Vienna, PhD, 28. *Prof Exp:* Instr Ger, Princeton Univ, 45-46; assoc prof & chmn dept, Upsala Col, 46-47; asst prof, Rutgers Univ, 47-53; from assoc prof to prof, Wagner Col, 53-63; DEAN & COUN MEM, GOETHEANUM COL, 63-, ED, DAD GOETHEANUM WEEKLY, 66- *Mem:* MLA. *Res:* Goethe; Romanticism; modern German literature. *Publ:* Auth, Albert Steffen, 60, I Goethe, 61, Rudolf Steiner im Geistesgang des Abendlandes, 65, Biographik und Essayistik, 70, & Novalis, Deutscher Dichter, Europäischer Denker, Christilicher Seher 2; Überarbeitete und stark vermehrte Auflage, 72, Francke, Bern & Munich; Campanella, Geschichte eines Schicksals, Der Sucher nach dem Sonnenstaat, 72 & Der Tod des Aristoteles, Roman, 77, Freies Geistesleben, Stuttgart; Im Stillstand der Stunden, Gedichte, Rudolph Geering Verlag, Basel, 78; Goethe's Message of Beauty in Our Twentieth Century World, AMS Press, 79. *Mailing Add:* The Goetheanum CH 4143 Dornach Switzerland

HIEKE, ADOLF E F, US citizen. LINGUISTICS, ENGLISH AS A SECOND LANGUAGE. *Educ:* Univ Colo, BA, 64, MA, 67; Univ Kans, MPhil, 74, PhD(ling), 80. *Prof Exp:* Instr ling, Inter-Am Univ, PR, 67-68; instr English & ling, Univ Northern Iowa, 68-73 asst prof, 73-75; lectr ling, Univ Tuebingen, West Ger, 75-81; ASSOC LING, UNIV BAYREUTH, WEST GER, 81. *Concurrent Pos:* Nat teaching fel, Inter-Am Univ, PR, 67-68; dir ling & teaching English as a foreign lang, Univ Northern Iowa, 73-74; coordr English as a foreign lang, Univ Bayreuth, 81. *Mem:* Ling Soc Am; Teachers English to Speakers Other Lang. *Res:* Oral fluency acquisition and assessment; complexity of text; methodology and technique of teaching English as a foreign language and teachers of English of other languages. *Publ:* Master Locator Booklet for Materials in Teachers of English to Speakers of Other Languages, Educ Resources Info Ctr Clearinghouse for Lang & Ling, 76; Integrative uses of the language lab for intermediate & advanced students, Anglistik & Englischunterricht, 77; Competence-performance distinctions in translation errors, Int Rev of Appl Ling in Lang Teaching, 80; Suntactic contrast between American and British English, In: Tuebingen Studies in Literature and Language, Soc for New Lang Study, 80; A content-processing view of hesitation phenomena, Lang & Speech, 81; Audio-lectal practice and fluency acquisition, Foreign Lang Annuals, 81; Semantic cohesion in textbook construction, In: New Linguistic Impulses in Foreign Language Teaching, Guenther Narr, 81. *Mailing Add:* 1131 Lafayette St Denver CO 80218

HIGGINBOTHAM, VIRGINIA, b Dallas, Tex, Nov 6, 35. ROMANCE LANGUAGES, CONTEMPORARY SPANISH LITERATURE. *Educ:* Southern Methodist Univ, BA, 57, MA, 62; Tulane Univ, PhD(Span & Port), 66. *Prof Exp:* Teaching asst Span, Southern Methodist Univ, 60-62 & Tulane Univ, 62-66; asst prof, 66-73, ASSOC PROF SPAN & PORT, UNIV TEX, AUSTIN, 73- *Mem:* Am Asn Teachers Span & Port; MLA. *Res:* Contemporary Spanish literature. *Publ:* Auth, Reflejos de Lautreamont en Poeta en Nueva York, Hispanofila, 9/72; The Comic Spirit of Federico Garcia Lorca, Univ Tex, 74; Luis Bunuel, Twayne (in press). *Mailing Add:* Dept of Span & Port Univ of Tex Austin TX 78712

HIGGINS, LYNN ANTHONY, b Ann Arbor, Mich, July 21, 47. FRENCH LANGUAGE & LITERATURE. *Educ:* Oberlin Col, BA, 69; Univ Minn, Minneapolis, MA, 73, PhD(French), 76. *Prof Exp:* ASST PROF FRENCH, DARTMOUTH COL, 76- *Concurrent Pos:* Nat Endowment for Humanities fel, 79 & Camargo fel, 81. *Mem:* MLA; Nat Women's Studies Asn. *Res:* French novel; literary theory; women and autobiography. *Publ:* Auth, Nouvelle nouvelle autobiography: Monique Wittig's Le Corps Lesbien, Sub-Stance, 77; coauth, Conversahon w Christiane Rochefort, Esprit Createur, 79; Godard and Rochefort: Two or three things about prostitution, Fr Rev, 75; auth, Typographical eros: Reading Ricardou in the third demension, Yale Fr Studies, 79; Literature a la lettre: Ricardou and the poetics of Anagram, Romanic Rev, 82; Barthes' imaginary voyages, Studies in Twentieth Century Lit, 82. *Mailing Add:* Dept of Romance Lang & Lit Dartmouth Col Hanover NH 03755

HIGHNAM, DAVID ELLIS, b Bellingham, Wash, Oct 24, 41; m 63; c 1. FRENCH LITERATURE. *Educ:* Western Wash State Col, BA, 63; Univ Minn, Minneapolis, MA, 65, PhD(French), 68. *Prof Exp:* Asst prof French, Univ Wis, 68-70; ASST PROF FRENCH, UNIV BC, 70- *Mem:* MLA; Am Asn Teachers Fr; Soc Int Etudes XVIII Siecle; Can Soc 18th Century Studies. *Res:* Eighteenth century French literature; aesthetics of the rococo movement in France; French novel of the 17th through 19th centuries. *Publ:* Auth, Lettres Portugaises: Passion in search of survival, Mod Lang Quart, 12/72; Le libraire de Bessette: heros malgre lui, Co-Incidences, 3-4/73; Crebillon Fils in context: the rococo ethos in French literature in the early 18th century, Fr Lit Ser, 4/73; L'Ingenu: Flawed masterpiece or masterful innovation, Studies Voltaire & 18th Century, 75. *Mailing Add:* Dept of French Univ of BC Vancouver BC V6T 1W5 Can

HIGHTOWER, JAMES ROBERT, b Sulphur, Okla, May 7, 15; m 40; c 4. CHINESE LITERATURE. *Educ:* Univ Colo, AB, 36; Harvard Univ, AM, 40, PhD(Far Eastern lang),46. *Prof Exp:* From instr to assoc prof, 46-58, prof Chinese lit, 58-81, EMER VICTOR S THOMAS PROF CHINESE LIT, HARVARD UNIV, 82- *Concurrent Pos:* Vis lectr, Oxford Univ, 58-59; Guggenheim fel, 58-59; guest prof, Univ Hamburg, 59, 61, 62; Fulbright-Hays res award, Taiwan, 65-66; sr Killam fel, Univ BC, 76-77. *Mem:* Fel Am Acad Arts & Sci. *Res:* Poetry; criticism. *Publ:* Auth, The Han Shih Wai Chuan, Harvard Univ, 50; The Fu of T'ao Ch'ien, Harvard J Asiatic Studies, 54; Some characteristics of parallel prose, Studia Serica Bernhard Karlgren Dedicata, 59; Topics in Chinese Literature, Harvard Univ, 63; T'ao Ch'ien's drinking wine poems, In: Wen-ling, Univ Wis, 68; The songs of Chou Pang-Yen, 77, Yuan Chen and the story of Ying-Ying, 77 & The Songwriter Liu Yung, 81, Harvard J Asiatic Studies. *Mailing Add:* Dept of East Asian Lang Harvard Univ 2 Divinity Ave Cambridge MA 02138

HILARY, RICHARD BOYD, b Freeport, NY, Aug 15, 41. ITALIAN LITERATURE. *Educ:* Cornell Univ, AB, 63; Univ Wis-Madison, MA, 65, PhD(Ital), 69. *Prof Exp:* Instr Ital, Univ Wis-Milwaukee, 68-70; asst prof, 70-77, ASSOC PROF ITAL, FLA STATE UNIV, 77- *Mem:* MLA; Am Asn Teachers Ital; Renaissance Soc Am; SAtlantic Mod Lang Asn. *Res:* Italian Renaissance literature; Renaissance Papal history. *Publ:* Auth, Biblical exegesis in Alfieri's Saul, SAtlantic Bull, 9/73; Sources for a biography of Pier Candido Decembrio, Romance Notes, spring 75; The Secretaries of Pope Pius II, Oelschläger Festschrift, Estudios de Hispanofila, 36: 211-213; The Nepotism of Pope Pius II, 1458-1464, Cath Hist Rev, 1/78. *Mailing Add:* Dept of Mod Lang Fla State Univ Tallahassee FL 32306

HILDEBRAND, JANET ELIZABETH, b Washington, DC, Nov 10, 49. FOREIGN LANGUAGE. *Educ:* Hope Col, BA, 71; Univ Tex, Austin, MA, 74, PhD(foreign lang educ), 77. *Prof Exp:* Teaching asst Ger, Univ Tex, Austin, 71-72 & 73-74; teacher Ger & English, Bay City High Sch, Tex, 74; teaching asst Ger & English, Univ Tex, Austin, 72-76, asst instr & student teacher supvr, 76-77; instr, 77-78, ASST PROF GER, TEX WESLEYAN COL, 78- *Concurrent Pos:* Instr, Univ Tex, Arlington, 79 & 80-81, lectr, 81-; coordr pre-prof studies, Tex Wesleyan Col, 81- *Mem:* MLA; Am Asn Teachers Ger; Teachers Foreign Lang Asn; AAUP. *Res:* Foreign language pedagogy; teacher education; honors programs. *Publ:* Auth, Optimal sequencing of vocabulary and grammar in language teaching, J Ling Asn Southwest, 8/76; A university simulation in the German class, Schatzkarnes der deutschen, Sprache und Literatures, fall 79; Faculty meetings: A simulation for secondary teacher candidates, Kappa Delta Phi Rec, fall 81; Part-timers in the humanities, are we living in the 1820's? in proc of Conf on part-time employment, Orlando, Fla, 4/82. *Mailing Add:* 3000 Harlanwood Dr Ft Worth TX 76109

HILDEBRANDT, BRUNO FRANZ, b Goerlitz, Ger, Sept 26, 26; US citizen; m 49. GERMANISTICS, LINGUISTICS. *Educ:* Univ Hamburg, PhD(phonology), 63. *Prof Exp:* Asst phonetics, Univ Hamburg, 60-63; asst prof Ger, Univ Colo, 63-65; assoc prof, Univ Ill, Chicago Circle, 65-69; dir grad studies, 69-82, PROF GER, UNIV N DAK, 69- *Concurrent Pos:* Numerous vis positions at Am col & univ, 61- *Mem:* Ling Soc Am; Verein Fuer Niederdeutsche Sprachforschung. *Res:* German phonology; experimental phonetics; Germanic philology. *Publ:* Auth, Die Arithmetische Bestimmung der Durativen Funktion, Z Phoetik, Sprachwiss u Kommunikationsforsch, 4/61; coauth, Drills in German Pronunciation, Pruett, 64; auth, Fontanes Altersstil in Seinem Roman der Stechlin, Ger Quart, 3/65; Language Communication and Linguistics, Chicago Circle Studies, 6/68; Diachronic Aspects in Synchronic Linguistics, Proc Ling Circle Manitoba & NDak, 74; The Significance of Coherent Terminologies in Phonetics and Phonemics, Proc Mid Am Ling Conf, 76-77; Strukturelemente der Deutschen Gegenwartschochsprache: Phone und Phonaden, Mouton, 76; Linguistic Analysis of Sound and Rhyme in Poetry, Proc Mid Am Ling Conf, 77-78. *Mailing Add:* Grad Studies Ger Univ NDak Grand Forks ND 58202

HILGAR, MARIE-FRANCE, b St Palais, France, June 19, 33; US citizen; m 54; c 4. FRENCH LITERATURE. *Educ:* Indiana Univ Pa, BA, 63; San Francisco State Col, MA, 66; Univ Calif, Davis, PhD(French), 71. *Prof Exp:* Prof French, Peace Corps, 66; lectr, San Francisco State Col, 67; PROF FRENCH, UNIV NEV, LAS VEGAS, 71- *Concurrent Pos:* Nat chmn, NAm Soc for 17th Century Fr Lit, 77; ed, Tape Hiss, Nev Foreign Lang Newslett, 77-; conf chmn, Pacific Northwest Conf Foreign Lang, 79. *Mem:* MLA; Int Asn Fr Studies; Asn Caracterologie; Am Soc 17th Century; Soc Fr Etude XVIIe Siecle. *Res:* French theater of the 17th century; women authors; Madame Deshoulieres. *Publ:* Auth, La Mode des Stances dans le Theatre Tragique Francias 1610-1687, Nizet, 73; Un nerveux par excellence: Theophile de Viau, Caracterologie, 73; La mort d'Agis, Proc Pacific Northwest Conf Foreign Lang, 74; La folie dans le theatre du XVIIe siecle en France, Romance Notes, winter 75; La condition d'une heroine feminine: Medee, Papers in 17th Century Fr Lit, 77-78; Grandeur et decadence d'Hercule, Australian J Fr Studies, 78. *Mailing Add:* Dept of Foreign Lang Univ of Nev Las Vegas NV 89154

HILL, ARCHIBALD ANDERSON, b New York, NY, July 5, 02; m 28. LINGUISTICS. *Educ:* Pomona Col, AB, 23; Stanford Univ, AM, 24; Yale Univ, PhD, 27. *Prof Exp:* Instr English, Univ Mich, 26-29, asst prof, 29-30; assoc prof English & English lang, Univ Va, 30-39, prof, 39-52; vdir, Inst Lang

& Ling, Sch Foreign Serv, Georgetown Univ, 52-55; prof, 55-72, EMER PROF ENGLISH, LING & EDUC, UNIV TEX, AUSTIN, 72- *Mem:* Ling Soc Am (secy-treas, 52, pres, 69); MLA; Mediaeval Acad Am; Ling Asn Southwest (pres, 73). *Res:* History of the English Language; English manuscript studies; linguistic approaches to literature. *Publ:* Auth, Introduction to linguistic Structures, Harcourt, 58; The Oral Approach to English (2 vols), Kenkyusha, Tokyo, 62; ed, Linguistics Today, Basic Bks, 69; auth, Juncture and syllable division in Latin, Lang; Some postulates for the distributional studies of manuscript readings, studies Bibliog; Constituent and Pattern in Poetry, Univ Tex, 76. *Mailing Add:* Box 8120 Univ Station Austin TX 78712

HILL, CHARLES GRAVES, b Flushing, NY, May 29, 25. FRENCH. *Educ:* Wesleyan Univ, BA, 46; Yale Univ, PhD(French), 55. *Prof Exp:* Instr French, Univ RI, 51-52; from instr to asst prof, Skidmore Col, 53-62; from asst prof to assoc prof, 62-74, chmn dept mod lang & lit, 74-79, PROF FRENCH, BROOKLYN COL, 74- *Honors & Awards:* Chevalier dans l'ordre des Palmes Academiques, French Govt, 78. *Mem:* MLA; Am Asn Teachers Fr. *Res:* Nineteenth and 20th century French and comparative literature. *Publ:* Auth, Camus and Vigny, PMLA, 3/62; Andre Gide and Blake's Marriage of Heaven and Hell, Comp Lit Studies, 66; Walter Pater and the Gide-Du Bos dialogue, Rev Lit Comp, spring 67. *Mailing Add:* Dept of Mod Lang Brooklyn Col Brooklyn NY 11210

HILL, CLAUDE, b Berlin, Ger, July 28, 11; Nat US; m 38; c 1. GERMAN. *Educ:* Univ Jena, Ger, PhD(Ger), 37. *Prof Exp:* Instr comp lit & drama, Asheville Col, 40-43; prog dir & commentator, Ger Broadcasts, Voice of Am, 43-45; from asst prof to assoc prof, Rutgers Univ, New Brunswick, 46-61, prof Ger & grad dir, 61-79. *Concurrent Pos:* Hon fel, Yale Univ, 40; Am Coun Learned Soc fac study fel, 51-52; gen ed, Harper's Deutsche Bibliot, 68-73. *Mem:* MLA; Am Asn Teachers Ger; AAUP. *Res:* Modern German literature and civilization; comparative literature. *Publ:* Auth, Drama der deutschen Neuromantik, Halle, Ger, 38; Drei Nobelpreistraeger, Harper, 48; coauth, Drama of German Expressionism, Univ NC, 60; auth, Zwei Hundert Jahre Deutscher Kultur, Harpers, 66; Lesen mit Gewinn, Harper & Row, 72; Bertolt Brecht, World Auth Ser 331, Twayne, 75; Bertolt Brecht (rev ed in Ger), Francke, Bern, Switzerland, 78; Perspectives and Personalities: Studies in Modern German Literature Honoring Claude Hill, Carl Winter, Heidelberg, 78. *Mailing Add:* 245 Varsity Ave Princeton NJ 08540

HILL, EMITA B, b Baltimore, Md, Jan 31, 36; m 60; c 3. FRENCH LITERATURE. *Educ:* Cornell Univ, BA, 57; Middlebury Col, MA, 58; Harvard Univ, PhD(French), 67. *Prof Exp:* Asst prof French, 70-73, chmn, Dept Romance Lang, 70-75, assoc prof, 73-78, PROF ROMANCE LANG, LEHMAN COL, 78- *Concurrent Pos:* Mem vis comt lib arts, Case Western Reserve Cols; City Univ New York Res Emergency award 71 & 73-74, fac res awards, 75-76 & 77-78; Nat Endowment for Humanities Younger Humanist fel, 74-75; prog dir, The City and the Humanities, Lehman Col, 77-; dir, Bronx Community History Inst, Lehman Col, 82- *Honors & Awards:* George M Shuster Award, 71. *Mem:* Am Asn 18th Century Studies; Soc Int d'etude 18e siecle; MLA; Am Asn Teachers French. *Res:* Eighteenth century French novel; Diderot's Correspondence; community history. *Publ:* Auth, Materialism and monsters in the Reve de d'Alembert, Diderot Studies, 68; Theophe, a modern Greek: Virtue on trial, 69 & The Role of le Monstre, in Diderot's Thought, 72, Studies on Voltaire & Eighteenth Century; The art of the actor in the Liaisons dangereuses, Romanic Rev, 4/72; Sincerity and self-awareness in the Paysan parvenu, Studies on Voltaire & Eighteenth Century, 72; The Neveu de Rameau: A moral monster, Diderot Studies, 73. *Mailing Add:* Dept of Romance Lang Herbert H Lehman Col Bronx NY 10468

HILL, EMMA MAY, b Madison, Ind, Apr 4, 21. SPANISH LITERATURE. *Educ:* Hanover Col, AB, 42; Univ Wis, AM, 46, PhD, 57. *Prof Exp:* Teacher high schs, Ind, 42-45; from instr to assoc prof, 46-56, asst registr, 46-47, PROF SPAN, HANOVER COL, 56- *Mem:* Am Asn Teachers Span & Port; MLA. *Res:* Portuguese novelist Eca de Queiroz. *Mailing Add:* Dept of Span Hanover Col Hanover IN 47243

HILL, HAROLD CLINTON, b Durham, NC, Aug 27, 26; m 52. GERMAN, CHINESE. *Educ:* George Washington Univ, BA, 66; Johns Hopkins Univ, PhD(Ger), 70. *Prof Exp:* Asst prof Ger, Chinese & Russ, 70-77, ASSOC PROF GER & CHINESE, WASHINGTON & LEE UNIV, 77- *Honors & Awards:* Cert, Chinese Lang & Lit Asn, Taipei, Taiwan, 75. *Res:* Medieval German literature; Chinese drama; Ukrainian literature. *Publ:* Auth, Johann Bissel's Argonauticon Americanorum (1647): A reexamination, Vol 85, No 5 & Astrology and friendship: The net of commitment in Wallenstein, Vol 91, Mod Lang Notes. *Mailing Add:* Dept of Ger Washington & Lee Univ Lexington VA 24450

HILL, JANE HASSLER, b Berkeley, Calif, Oct 27, 39; m 61; c 3. LINGUISTICS, ANTHROPOLOGY. *Educ:* Univ Calif, Berkeley, BA, 60; Univ Calif, Los Angeles, MA, 62, PhD(anthrop), 66. *Prof Exp:* Asst prof, 67-73, assoc prof, 73-80, PROF ANTHROP, WAYNE STATE UNIV, 80-, DEPT CHAIRPERSON, 78- *Concurrent Pos:* Nat Endowment for Humanities res grant, 74-75. *Mem:* Am Anthrop Asn; Ling Soc Am; Royal Anthrop Inst Gt Brit & Ireland. *Res:* American Indian languages; language origins, evolution and functions; language shift. *Publ:* Auth, On the evolutionary foundations of language, Am Anthropologist, 72; Subordinate clauses and language function, In: You Take the High Node and I'll Take the Low Node, Chicago Ling Soc, 73; coauth, Mulu-wetam: The First People, Malki Mus, 73; auth, Possible continuity theories of language, Language, 74; contribr, Language death and relexification in Tlaxcalan Nahuatl, Ling & Int J Sociol Ling, 77; Honorific usage in modern Nahuatl, Language, 78; auth, Mixed grammar, purist grammar and language attitudes in modern Nahuatl, Lang in Society 9. *Mailing Add:* Dept of Anthrop Wayne State Univ Detroit MI 48202

HILL, KENNETH CUSHMAN, b Orange, NJ, Oct 3, 38; m 61; c 3. LINGUISTICS. *Educ:* Georgetown Univ, BS, 60; Univ Calif, Los Angeles, MA, 62, PhD(ling), 67. *Prof Exp:* Acting asst prof ling, Univ Calif, Berkeley, 64-65; lectr, 65-67, asst prof, 67-70, ASSOC PROF LING, UNIV MICH, ANN ARBOR, 70-, CHMN DEPT, 77-,. *Mem:* Ling Soc Am; Int Phonetic Asn; AAAS; AAUP; Am Anthrop Asn. *Res:* General linguistics; Uto-Aztecan languages; phonology. *Publ:* Auth, Some notes on English vowel morphophonemics, Lang Learning, 6/68; coauth, Stress in the Cupan languages, Int J Am Ling, 10/68; A note on Uto-Aztecan color terminologies, Anthrop Ling, 10/70; Honorific usage in modern Nahuatl, Lang, 3/78. *Mailing Add:* Dept of Ling Univ of Mich Ann Arbor MI 48109

HILL, STEVEN PHILLIPS, b Estherville, Iowa, Apr 25, 36. SLAVIC LANGUAGES & LITERATURES. *Educ:* Stanford Univ, BA, 57; Univ Mich, Ann Arbor, MA, 58, PhD(Russ), 65. *Prof Exp:* From instr to asst prof, 61-69, ASSOC PROF RUSS, UNIV ILL, URBANA, 69- *Mem:* MLA; Am Asn Teachers Slavic & EEurop Lang; Soc Cinema Studies. *Res:* Russian film history; East European film history; Russian 20th century drama. *Publ:* Translr, V S Rastorgueva's Short Sketch of Persian Grammar, Ind Univ, 64; auth, Kuleshov--prophet without honor?, Film Cult, spring 67; The Soviet film today, Film Quart, summer 67; coauth, Russian drama after Chekhov: A guide to English translations, 1900-1969, Theatre Doc, fall 69; A quantitative view of Soviet cinema, Cinema J, spring 72; Ilia Frez and Russian children's films, Film Cult, 74; The N-Factor and Russian Prepositions, Mouton, The Hague, 77. *Mailing Add:* Dept of Slavic Univ of Ill Urbana IL 61801

HILLEN, GERD, b Ehren, Ger, Oct 18, 35; m 65; c 1. GERMAN LITERATURE. *Educ:* Stanford Univ, PhD(Ger), 68. *Prof Exp:* Asst prof, 65-71, assoc prof & chmn dept, 71-77, PROF GER, UNIV CALIF, BERKELEY, 77- *Mem:* Lessing Soc; Philol Asn Pac Coast; MLA; Int Arbeitskreis für Barockliteratur. *Res:* Seventeenth and 18th century German literature. *Publ:* Auth, Andreas Gryphius' Cardenio und Celinde, Mouton, The Hague, 71; co-ed, G E Lessing Werke II, Hanser, Munich, 71; auth, Reisemotive in den Romanen von Max Frisch, Wirkendes Wort, 19: 126-133; Ideologie und Humanitat in Lessings Dramen, I; 150-161 & Die Halsstarrigkeit der Tugend: Bemerkungen zu Lessings Trauerspielen, II: 83-97, Lessing Jahrbuch; Lessings theologische Schriften im Zusammenhang seines Werks, In: Lessing in Heutiger Sicht, Bremen und Wolfenbüttel, 76; Lessing Chronik, Hanser, Muchen, 79; Allegorie im kontext, form und funktion der allegorie in Lit texten des 17, Jhds, 592-604, Formen und Funktionen der Allegorie, Metzler, Stuttgart, 79. *Mailing Add:* Dept of Ger Univ Calif Berkeley CA 94720

HILLER, ROBERT LUDWIG, b Unionville, Conn, May 17, 15; m 42; c 2. GERMANIC LANGUAGES & LITERATURE. *Educ:* Cornell Univ, BA, 50, PhD, 59. *Prof Exp:* Asst prof Ger lang & lit, Univ Chicago, 58-63; assoc prof, Univ Nebr, 63-66; prof, 66-82, EMER PROF GER LANG & LIT, UNIV TENN, KNOXVILLE, 82- *Mem:* MLA; Am Asn Teachers Ger; SAtlantic Mod Lang Asn. *Res:* Seventeenth century German literature; contemporary German drama. *Publ:* Auth, A Protestant answer to Spee's Trutznachtigall, J English & Ger Philol, 4/62; The symbolism of Gestus in Brecht's drama, In: Myth and Symbol, Univ Nebr, 63; The Sutler's cart and the lump of gold, Ger Rev, 3/64; co-transl, Hans Jacob Christoffel's The Runagate Courage, Univ Nebr, 65; co-transl, The Runagate Courage, Univ Nebr, 65; The Singular Life Story of Heedless Hopalong, Wayne State Univ, 81. *Mailing Add:* Dept of Ger & Slavic Lang Univ of Tenn Knoxville TN 37916

HILLERS, DELBERT ROY, b Chester, SDak, Nov 7, 32; m 58; c 2. OLD TESTAMENT, SEMITIC LANGUAGES. *Educ:* Concordia Sem, BA, 54, BD, 57; Johns Hopkins Univ, MA, 58, PhD(Semitic studies), 63. *Prof Exp:* Instr Hebrew, Concordia Sr Col, 58-60; from asst prof to assoc prof Hebrew & Old Testament, 63-70, PROF SEMITIC LANG, JOHNS HOPKINS UNIV, 70- *Concurrent Pos:* Ann prof, Am Sch Orient Res, Jerusalem, 68-69; Am Philos Soc grant, 68-69. *Mem:* Soc Bibl Lit; Am Orient Soc. *Res:* Northwest Semitic languages; Old Testament. *Publ:* Auth, Treaty-Curses and the Old Testament Prophets, Pontif Bibl Inst, Rome, 64; An alphabetic cuneiform tablet from Taanach, Bull Am Schs Orient Res, 64; Delocutive verbs in Biblical Hebrew, J Bibl Lit, 68; Covenant: The History of a Biblical Idea, Johns Hopkins Univ, 69; Lamentations, Anchor Bible, Doubleday, 72. *Mailing Add:* Dept of Near Eastern Studies Johns Hopkins Univ Baltimore MD 21218

HILLMANN, MICHAEL CRAIG, b Baltimore, Md, May 5, 40; m 67; c 1. PERSIAN LITERATURE, MIDDLE EASTERN STUDIES. *Educ:* Loyola Col, Baltimore, BA, 62; Univ Chicago, MA, 69, PhD(Persian), 74. *Prof Exp:* Lang officer Persian, Am Peace Corps in Iran, 71-73; cataloger Persian, Univ Chicago Libr, 74; ASSOC PROF PERSIAN, UNIV TEX, AUSTIN, 74-; PRES, EDUC CONSULT, PERSEPOLIS ENTERPRISES, 77- *Concurrent Pos:* Reviewer Persian, World Lit Today, 77-; bibliogr Persian, PMLA, 78- *Mem:* Soc Iranian Studies. *Res:* Contemporary Persian prose fiction and lyric verse; modern Persian art; applied linguistics--Persian. *Publ:* Auth, Unity in The Ghazals of Hafez, Bibliot Islamica, 76; The Fundamentals of Persian Reading and Writing, Persepolis, 77; ed, Hedayat's The Blind Owl forty years after, Univ Tex Mid Eastern Studies, 78; ed, Major voices in contemporary Persian literature, Lit East & West, 80; Iranian Society: An anthology of writings by Jalal Al-e Ahmad, Mazda, 82. *Mailing Add:* 3404 Perry Lane Austin TX 78731

HILTON, RONALD, International Relations, Romance Languages. See Vol I

HILTS, MARGARETE AMBS, b Otsego, Mich, Dec 4, 12; m 56. FRENCH LANGUAGE & LITERATURE. *Educ:* Emmanuel Missionary Col, BA, 35; Univ SC, MA, 40; Western Reserve Univ, PhD, 56. *Prof Exp:* Teacher French & English, Fletcher Acad, NC, 35-38; instr French & Span, Southern Calif Jr Col, 38-40, chmn dept, 40-80, PROF MOD LANG, LOMA LINDA UNIV, LA SIERRA CAMPUS, 40-, DIR INT DIMENSIONS, 77- *Concurrent Pos:* Mem nat screening comt, Fulbright-Hays grants, 73-75.

Honors & Awards: Loma Linda Univ Service Award, 80. *Mem:* MLA; Am Asn Teachers Fr; Am Asn Teachers Span & Port; Am Coun Teaching Foreign Lang; Nat Asn Language Learning Lab Directors. *Res:* Education of children as depicted in French literature of the 19th and 20th centuries; psychological aspects of French literature; literature of French-speaking Africa. *Mailing Add:* Dept of Mod Lang Loma Linda Univ La Sierra Campus Riverside CA 92515

HIMELSTEIN, MORGAN YALE, English. See Vol II

HINCKLEY, LOIS VIVIAN, b Kalamazoo, Mich, Dec 23, 43. CLASSICAL LANGUAGES & LITERATURE. *Educ:* Wellesley Col, AB, 63; Univ NC, Chapel Hill, PhD(classics), 72. *Prof Exp:* Instr Latin & Greek, Dana Hall Schs, Mass, 63-66; instr classics, Princeton Univ, 72-74, asst prof, 74-80; ASST PROF CLASSICS, WVA UNIV, 80- *Concurrent Pos:* Assoc master, Princeton Inn Col, 76-78; Danforth assoc, 76- *Mem:* Am Philol Asn; Class Asn Midwest & South. *Res:* Greek epic, lyric and tragedy; Latin epic and elegy; classics in translation. *Publ:* Auth, Regulus & Odysseus (Horace odes III 5), Class Bull, 1/78. *Mailing Add:* 218 Chitwood Hall WVa Univ Morgantown WV 26506

HINDERER, WALTER HERMANN, b Ulm, WGer, Sept 3, 34; m 66. GERMAN LITERATURE & CRITICISM. *Educ:* Univ Munich, PhD, 60. *Prof Exp:* Chief ed sci, R Piper & Co, Munich, 61-66; asst prof Ger, Pa State Univ, 66-69; assoc prof, Univ Colo, 69-71; prof, Univ Md, College Park, 71-78; PROF GER, PRINCETON UNIV, 78- *Concurrent Pos:* Vis prof, Stanford Univ, 70-71; Inst Res in the Humanities fel, Univ Wis, Madison, 76-77; mem ed comt, NY Univ Ottendorfer Series, 76-; ed, Ger libr, 80- *Mem:* Am Asn Teachers Ger; MLA; Schiller Ges; Lessing Soc; Int Buechner Ges. *Res:* German literature of the 18th, 19th and 20th centuries; library theory. *Publ:* Auth, Elemente der Literaturkritik, Kronberg, 76; Buechner Kommentar, Muenchen, 77; Der Mensch in der Geschichte, Koenigstein/Ts, 80; Uber deutsche Literatur und Rede, Muenchen, 81; ed, Geschichte der politischen lyrik in Deutschland, 78, Schillers Dramen, 79, Goethes Dramen, 80 & Kleists Dramen, 81, Stuttgart. *Mailing Add:* Dept of Ger Princeton Univ Princeton NJ 08540

HINDS, JOHN VAN, III, b Perth Amboy, NJ, Aug 24, 43; m 76; c 3. LINGUISTICS, JAPANESE LANGUAGE. *Educ:* Trenton State Col, BA, 65; Western Ill Univ, MA, 68; State Univ NY Buffalo, PhD(ling), 73. *Prof Exp:* Inst ling, State Univ NY Col Brockport, 71-72; asst prof ling, Univ of the Sacred Heart, Tokyo, 72-75; asst prof Japanese, Univ Hawaii, Manoa, 75-80; vis prof, Univ MN, 80-81; ASSOC PROF & DIR ENGLISH SECOND LANG, PA STATE UNIV, 81- *Concurrent Pos:* Fulbright fel ling/Korean, Fulbright-Hays Coun Int Exchange of Scholars, 76. *Mem:* Ling Soc Am; Asn Teachers Japanese; Ling Asn Can & US; Int Cirlce Korean Linguists; Am Educ Res Asn. *Res:* Discourse analysis; Japanese language; second language acquisition. *Publ:* Contribr, Third person pronouns, In: Japanese Language in Japanese Society, Tokyo Univ, 75; auth, Aspects of Japanese Discourse Structure, Kaitakusha Publ, 76; Paragraph structure and pronominalization, Papers Ling, 77; ed, Anaphora in Discourse, Ling Res, 78; co-ed, Problems in Japanese Syntax and Semantics, Kaitakusha Publ, 78; auth, Ellipsis in Japanese, Papers Japanese Ling, 78; Levels of structure within the paragraph, Berkeley Ling Soc Fourth Ann Proc, 78; Ellipsis in Japanese, Ling Res Inc, 82. *Mailing Add:* Dept of English PA State Univ University Park PA 16802

HINES, SAMUEL PHILIP, JR, English. See Vol II

HINES, THOMAS MOORE, b Columbia, SC, June 28, 36; m 70. FRENCH LITERATURE. *Educ:* Univ Ga, AB, 58; Johns Hopkins Univ, MA, 60; Emory Univ, PhD(French), 73. *Prof Exp:* Instr French, Va Mil Inst, 61-64 & Univ Sc, 64-71; teaching fel French, Emory Univ, 71-73; asst prof French, Univ Ala Birmingham, 73-80. *Concurrent Pos:* Consult ed, French Lit Publ Co, 78-; res grant, Univ of Ala, Birmingham, 77- *Mem:* Am Asn Teachers of Fr; MLA; Am Coun on Teaching Foreign Lang; SAtlantic Mod Lang Asn. *Res:* Twentieth century French novel and theatre; contemporary French civilization. *Publ:* Auth, A new look at Drieu la Rochelle's La Comedie de Charleroi, French Lit Series, spring 75; Le regard misogyne ou le refus de soi, Les Lettres Romanes, fall 78; Myth, misogyny and fascism in the works of Drieu la Rochelle, Mod Fiction Studies, August 78; Le Reve et l'action: Une etude de L'Homme a Cheval de Drieu la Rochelle, French Lit, 78; The concept of friendship in Drieu la Rochelle, SAtlantic Bull, contribr, Critical Bibliography of French Literataure, 20th Century volume, Syracuse Univ & transl, The Man on Horseback by Drieu la Rochelle, French Lit, (in press). *Mailing Add:* 1801 Mission Rd Birmingham AL 35216

HINKLE, DOUGLAS PADDOCK, b Stamford, Conn, June 9, 23; m 66; c 2. SPANISH LITERATURE, ROMANCE LINGUISTICS. *Educ:* Univ Va, BA, 52, MA, 54. *Prof Exp:* Teacher pub schs, Va, 48-49; instr Span, Univ Va, 53-55; dir Am Binat Ctr, La Paz, 55-57; asst prof Span & French, Sweet Briar Col, 57-62; asst prof Span, Southwestern at Memphis, 62-63; col ed mod lang dept, D C Heath & Co, 63-65; assoc prof mod lang, Eastern Ky Univ, 65-67; dir acad yr in Spain, 70-71, grad adv Span, 72-73, LECTR MOD LANG, OHIO UNIV, 67- *Concurrent Pos:* Off campus fac, Sephardic Studies, Yeshiva Univ, 75- *Honors & Awards:* Citations, Teachers English in Bolivia, 55 & Newspapermen of La Paz, 56; Caballero, Order of Condor of Andes, Bolivia, 57. *Mem:* MLA; Am Soc Sephardic Studies; Am Watercolor Soc. *Res:* Medieval Spanish literature; historical Romance linguistics; comparative arts, especially the relationship between contemporary poetry and the plastic arts. *Publ:* Auth, The Impact of India on Medieval Spanish Fiction, Sweet Briar, 62; Onomastics and The Book of Good Love, Names, 3/68; contribr, American Surnames, Chilton, 69; auth, The Impressionist Aesthetic and the Poetry of Machado and Jimenez, Northwestern Univ, 70; Advanced literature: A creative method, Mod Lang J, 70; Some Jarchas of Moses ibn 'Ezra, Sephardic Studies Ser, Yeshiva Univ, 70; Literary and Pictorial Mannerism in the Spanish Golden Age, Eastern Ky Univ, 76; Poetry is You, St Luke's, Memphis, 77. *Mailing Add:* Dept of Mod Lang Ohio Univ Athens OH 45701

HINOJOSA-SMITH, R R, b Mercedes, Tex, Jan 21, 29; m 63; c 2. ENGLISH, SOUTHWESTERN LITERATURE. *Educ:* Univ Tex, BA, 53; NMex Highlands Univ, MA, 63; Univ Ill, PhD(Span), 69. *Prof Exp:* Instr Span, Univ Ill, 66-68; asst prof, Trinity Univ, 68-70; assoc prof & chmn dept, Tex A&I Univ, 70-74, dean Col Arts & Sci, 74-76, vpres acad affairs, 76-77; chmn Chicano dept, Univ Minn, 77-80, prof English, 80-81; PROF, DEPT ENGLISH, UNIV TEX, AUSTIN, 81- *Concurrent Pos:* Consult, Crystal City Independent Sch Dist, Tex, 71- & Dallas Independent Sch Dist Multicult Ctr, 73- *Honors & Awards:* Nat Lit Award, Quinto Sol Publ, 72. *Mem:* MLA; NAm Acad Span Lang; Hisp Soc. *Res:* Chicano literature; Mexican American culture. *Publ:* Auth, Estampas del Valle, 73; Klail City y sus alrededores, 76; Korean Love Songs, 78; Mi querido Rafa, 81. *Mailing Add:* Dept of Mod Lang Tex A&I Univ Box 2201 Kingsville TX 78363

HINTZE, S JAMES, b Idaho Falls, Idaho, Sept 24, 38; m 63; c 2. OLD GERMANIC PHILOLOGY. *Educ:* Univ Idaho, BA, 60; Graz Univ, Dr phil(Ger), 67. *Prof Exp:* From instr to asst prof Ger philol, 67-77, ASSOC PROF GER, LA STATE UNIV, 77- *Concurrent Pos:* Stipendium, Oesterreichisches Bundesministerium für Wissenschaft und Forschung, 73-74. *Mem:* SCent Mod Lang Asn; Ling Soc Am. *Res:* Germanic Philology and Semantics. *Publ:* Auth, Onomasiologische und semasiologische Paradigmen in einem mittelhochdeutschen Text, Z für Dialektologie und Linguistik, 76; coauth, On defining the term creole in Louisiana, J Ling Asn Southwest, 78. *Mailing Add:* Dept of Class Ger & Slavic Lang La State Univ Baton Rouge LA 70803

HINZE, DIANA ORENDI, b Frankfurt, Ger, Oct 23, 41; nat US; m 67; c 2. GERMAN. *Educ:* Washington Univ, MA, 66, PhD(Ger), 72. *Prof Exp:* Instr Ger, Cleveland State Univ, 67-71; instr English, Staatl Gyn, Porz, Ger, 72-73; vis asst prof Ger, John Carroll Univ, 77; RES & WRITING, 77- *Mem:* MLA; Am Asn Teachers Ger; Women's Caucus Mod Lang; Women in Ger. *Res:* Reception history; German-American studies; women's literature. *Publ:* Auth, Trakl, Kokoschka und Kubin, Ger-Romanische Monatsschrift, 71; coauth, Doctor als Kellner, Die Zeit, 72; auth, Heidegger und Trakl, Orbis Litterarum, 77; Rahel Sanzara: Das Verlorene Kind, In: New Edition of the Novel, Nachdrucke, Stuttgarter, 80; Rahel Sanzara: Eine Biographie, Fischer Taschenbuchverlag, 81; Frauen um Trakl, In: Festschrift zum 75 Geburtstag I Zangerles, Otto Müller, Salzburg, 82. *Mailing Add:* 2233 S Overlook Cleveland Heights OH 44106

HINZE, KLAUS-PETER WILHELM, b Berlin, Ger, Sept 6, 36; m 67; c 1. GERMAN & COMPARATIVE LITERATURE. *Educ:* Free Univ Berlin, Staatsexamen, 65; Wash Univ, MA & PhD(Ger), 69. *Prof Exp:* Asst prof Ger, Case Western Reserve Univ, 67-71; assoc prof, 71-78, PROF GER & COMP LIT, CLEVELAND STATE UNIV, 78-, ASST DEAN ARTS & SCI, 80- *Concurrent Pos:* Lit agent, Kreisselmeier Publ, Munich, 76-; scholar, Austrian govt, 76, W Ger Govt, 77, Akad Wiss, 78 & Stifler Soc, 79. *Honors & Awards:* Scholar, Austrian govt, 76. *Mem:* MLA; Am Asn Teachers Ger; Int Arthur Schnitzler Res Asn; Goethe Soc; Wiener Goethe-Soc. *Res:* Goethe; German 20th century literature. *Publ:* Auth, Goethes Spiegelungstechnik im Bereich seiner Erzählungen, Orbis Litterarum, 70; Goethes Dialogerzählung Die Guten Weiber, Neophilologus, 71; Neue Aspekte zum Kafka-Bild, Mod Austrian Lit, 71; Kom Strukt Goethes Erzähl, Boehlau, Cologne, 75; Ernst Weiss Bibliographie, Engel, Hamburg, 77; ed, Der Andere Augenzeuge: Ich der Augenzeuge, Heyme, Munich, 79; auth, Die Gruppe 1925, Dvjs, Der Zweite Augenzeuge, GRM, 81. *Mailing Add:* Dept of Mod Lang Cleveland State Univ Euclid Ave Cleveland OH 44115

HIPPISLEY, ANTHONY RICHARD, b London, Eng, May 9, 38; m 64; c 6. RUSSIAN LANGUAGE & LITERATURE. *Educ:* Oxford Univ, BA, 62, MA, 67, D Phil(Russ), 69. *Prof Exp:* Asst prof Russ, State Univ NY Stony Brook, 65-72; asst prof, Wheaton Col, Mass, 72-74; LECTR RUSS, UNIV ST ANDREWS, SCOTLAND, UK, 74- *Mem:* Asn Teachers Russ; Am Asn Teachers Slavic & East Europ Lang; Brit Univ Asn Slavists. *Res:* Seventeenth century Russian literature; symbolism in Russian literature. *Publ:* Auth, The emblem in the writings of Simeon Polotsky, Slavic & East Europ J, summer 71; Symbolism in Olesa's Love, Studies Short Fiction, summer 73; Carmen echicum u Simeona Polotskogo, Trudy Otdela drevnerusskoi Literatury, Moscow, 74; Gogol's The Overcoat: A further interpretation, Slavic & East Europ J, summer 76; Cryptography in Simeon Polotsky, Russ Lit, fall 77; Leo Tolstoy: Sevastopol' v mae, Exeter Russ Tapes, 78. *Mailing Add:* Dept of Russ Univ of St Andrews Fife KY16 9AL Scotland United Kingdom

HIRAOKA, JESSE, b Fowler, Calif, Jan 2, 27; m 52; c 3. FRENCH LANGUAGE & LITERATURE, ETHNIC STUDIES. *Educ:* Roosevelt Univ, BA, 50; Univ Chicago, MA, 55; Northwestern Univ, PhD, 62. *Prof Exp:* Lectr French, Roosevelt Univ, 52-55, from instr to assoc prof, 56-62, chmn dept, 60-62; assoc prof, Portland State Col, 62-65; prof, Calif State Col, San Bernardino, 65-72, chmn div humanities, 66-69; dean, Col Ethnic Studies, 72-77, dir human serv, 77-81, PROF GEN STUDIES, WESTERN WASHINGTON UNIV, 72-, DIR ETHNIC STUDIES, 77- *Concurrent Pos:* Vpres, Coun Standards Human Ser Educ, 79-81; ed, Journal of Ethnic Studies, 73- *Mem:* Nat Asn Interdisciplinary Ethnic Studies; Am Asn Teachers French; Am Asn Higher Educ. *Res:* Minority literature and literary systems; Asian American studies; French literature. *Publ:* Auth, The foundation of multicultural education, Educ Horizons, 77; A sense of place, J Ethnic Studies, 77. *Mailing Add:* Dept Foreign Lang Western Washington Univ Bellingham WA 98225

HIRSCH, MARIANNE, b Timisoara, Rumania, Sept 23, 49; US citizen; c 1. COMPARATIVE LITERATURE, FRENCH. *Educ:* Brown Univ, BA, & MA, 70, PhD(comp lit), 75. *Prof Exp:* Vis instr French, Dartmouth Col, 74-75, asst prof, 75-77; Mellon asst prof humanities, Vanderbilt Univ, 77-78; ASST PROF FRENCH & COMP LIT, DARTMOUTH COL, 78- *Mem:* MLA; NE Mod Lang Asn; Am Comp Lit Asn; Am Asn Teachers French; Southern Comp Lit Asn. *Res:* Contemporary fiction; history and theory of narrative; women's studies. *Publ:* Auth, An interview with Michel Butor, Contemp Lit, summer 78; coauth, A conversation with Christiane Rochefort,

L'Esprit Createur, summer 79; Godard and Rochefort: Two or three things about prostitution, French Rev; auth, Beyond the Single Vision: Henry James, Michel Buton, Uwe Johson, Fr Lit Publ Co, 81; The Novel of Formation as Genre: Between Great Expectations and Lost Illusions, Genre, 79; Michel Buton: The decentralized vision, Contemp Lit, summer 81; Mothers and daughters: A review essay, Signs, fall 81; A mother's discourse: Incorporation and repetition in La Princesse de Cleves, Yale Fr Studies, Vol 62, 81. *Mailing Add:* Dept Romance Lang Dartmouth Col Hanover NH 03755

HIRSCHBACH, FRANK DONALD, b Berlin, Ger, May 13, 21; US citizen. FOREIGN LANGUAGES. *Educ:* Southern Conn State Col, BA, 46; Yale Univ, MA, 49, PhD, 52. *Prof Exp:* Instr Ger, Yale Univ, 52-57; asst prof, Clark Univ, 57-58; from asst prof to assoc prof, 58-66, PROF GER, UNIV MINN, MINNEAPOLIS, 66-, DIR HONORS DIV, COL LIB ARTS, 71-, CHMN DEPT, 82- *Concurrent Pos:* Morse fel, 54-55; Ger Acad Exchange Serv grant, 74-75; Int Res & Exchanges Bd res fel, 79. *Mem:* MLA; Am Asn Teachers Ger. *Res:* Modern German literature; literature of German Democratic Republic. *Publ:* Auth, The Arrow and the Lyre: A Study of the Role of Love in the Works of Thomas Mann, Nijhoff, The Hague, 55; Doderer's Strudlhofstiege, Publ Lang & Lit, 67; Alfred Kerr and expressionism, Ger Quart, 67; Alfred Kerr and opera, Wirkendes Wort, 67; The German democratic republic, an introduction, Am Asn Teachers Ger, 77. *Mailing Add:* Dept of Ger Univ of Minn Minneapolis MN 55455

HIRSH, JOHN CAMPION, Medieval & American Literature. See Vol II

HIRTLE, WALTER HEAL, b Lunenburg, NS, Aug 23, 27; m 59; c 4. LINGUISTICS. *Educ:* Univ BC, BA, 48; Dalhousie Univ, MA, 50; Laval Univ, MA, 59, PhD(ling), 63. *Prof Exp:* From asst prof to assoc prof, 59-69, PROF ENGLISH LING, LAVAL UNIV 69- *Mem:* Can Ling Asn; Can Asn Appl Ling; Ling Asn Can-US. *Res:* English grammar; psychomechanics of language; Guillaumean linguistics. *Publ:* Auth, The Simple and Progressive Forms, Laval Univ, 67; Adjectives like verandahed and blue-eyed, J Ling, 69; Time, Aspect & the Verb, Lavel Univ, 75; Already, still and yet, Archivum Linguisticum, 77; Meaningful grammar teacher, Bull CILA, 80; ed, Language et psychomicanique du langage, Etudes dediees a Roch Valin, Univ de Lille, 81; auth, Meaning and form in when clauses, In: Langage et psychomiecanique du langage, 81; Number and Inner Space: A Study of Grammatical Number in English, Univ Laval, 82. *Mailing Add:* Dept of Lang & Ling Laval Univ Quebec PQ G1K 7P4 Can

HITCHCOCK, DONALD RAYMOND, b Baltimore, Md, Oct 31, 30. SLAVIC LANGUAGES & LITERATURES. *Educ:* Univ Md, BA, 52; Harvard Univ, MA, 54, PhD(Slavic lang & lit), 65. *Prof Exp:* Lectr Russ, 54, from instr to asst prof 60-72, ASSOC PROF SLAVIC LANG & LIT, UNIV MD, COLLEGE PARK, 72- *Mem:* AAUP; Ling Soc Am; Am Asn Teachers Slavic & E Europ Langs; Am Asn for Advan Slavic Studies; Philol Soc. *Res:* Church Slavonic; Old Russian language and literature; modern Russian language and literature. *Publ:* Auth, N V Gogol', Zapiski sumasshedshego: Memoirs Of a Madman, Letchworth, England, 74; Reading the Russian Text of The Memoirs of a Madman of N V Gogol', Kamkin, 75; ed, F M Dostoevskii, Krotkaia: Gentle Spirit, Libr of Russ Classics, 77 & A P Chekhov, Vishnëvvi sad: The Cherry Orchard, Libr of Russ Classics, (in press), Bradda, Letchworth, England; auth, The Appeal of Adam in Hell to Lazarus, Slavic Printings & Reprintings, 104, Mouton, The Hague (in press). *Mailing Add:* Dept of Ger-Slavic Langs Univ of Md College Park MD 20742

HITT, JAMES ALFRED, b Dallas, Tex, Sept 3, 27; m 53; c 3. CLASSICS. *Educ:* Southern Methodist Univ, BA, 49; Princeton Univ, PhD, 54. *Prof Exp:* Instr classic studies, Univ Pa, 53-54; from instr to asst prof, 54-75 assoc dean div gen & comp studies, 70-77, acting dean, div gen & comp studies, 77-79, ASSOC PROF CLASSICS, UNIV TEX, AUSTIN, 75-, . *Mem:* Am Philol Asn; Archaeol Inst Am; Am Orient Soc; Vergilian Soc Am; Classics Asn Mid West & South. *Res:* Ancient mythology and religion; comparative linguistics. *Mailing Add:* Dept of Classics Waggener Hall 105 Univ of Tex Austin TX 78712

HOAR, LEO JEROME, JR, b Worcester, Mass, May 19, 31; m 76; c 2. ROMANCE LANGUAGES & LITERATURES. *Educ:* Spring Hill Col, AB, 53; Harvard Univ, AM, 56, PhD(Romance lang), 65. *Prof Exp:* Instr, 63-65, asst prof, 65-70, ASSOC PROF SPAN LANG & LIT, FORDHAM UNIV, 70- *Concurrent Pos:* Consult & lectr Span phonetics, Iona Col Summer Lang Inst, 64; exec coun, Cervantes Soc Am, 80-84. *Mem:* Cervantes Soc Am; Asoc Int Hispanistas; Asoc Int Galdosistas. *Res:* Benito Perez Galdos and the modern Spanish novel; 18th century Spanish literature; comparative literature (Western and Far Eastern poetry). *Publ:* Auth, Benito Perez Galdos y la Revista de Movimiento Intelectual de Europa, Madrid, 1865-67, Madrid, Insula, 68; Mi Calle, another lost article by Galdos, and a further note on his indebtedness to Mesonero Romanos, Symp, Vol XXIV, 70; Dos de mayo de 1808, dos de septiembre de 1870 por Benito Perez Galdos, un cuento extraviado y el posible prototipo de sus Episodios Nacionales, Cuadernos Hispanoam, No 250-52, 70-71; Politics and poetry: More proof of Galdos' work for Las Cortes, Mod Lang Notes, Vol LXXXVIII, 73; Galdos y Aureliano de Beruete: Vision renovada de Orbajosa, Anuario de Estud Atlanticos, Madrid-Las Palmas, No 20, 74; More on the pre- (and post-) history of the Episodios Nacionales: Galdos lost(?) article, El Dos de Mayo (1874), Anales Galdosianos, Vol VIII, 73; Rompecabezas, Galdos', lost cuento: A pre-98 esperpento, Neophilologus, 11/75; Galdos' counter-attact on his critics: The lost short-story, El Portico de la Gloria, Symposium, winter 76. *Mailing Add:* Dept of Mod Lang Fordham Univ Bronx NY 10458

HOBSON, IRMGARD WAGNER, b Waiblingen, Ger. GERMAN. *Educ:* Tufts Univ, MA, 65; Harvard Univ, PhD(Ger), 70. *Prof Exp:* Asst prof, 71-76, ASSOC PROF GER, GEORGE MASON UNIV, 76- *Mem:* MLA; Am Asn Teachers Ger. *Res:* Eighteenth century German literature; Kafka; German culture and civilization. *Publ:* Auth, Oranien and Alba: The two political dialogues in Egmont, Germanic Rev, 75; contribr, The Kafka Debate, Gordian, 77; auth, The Kafka problem compounded: Trial and Judgment in English, Mod Fiction Studies, 78; Holderlin Our Contemporary: Empedokles and German intellectuals of the 70's, J Europ Studies, 78; Updating the classics: Faust and Iphigenie in Stuttgart, 1977, Ger Studies Rev, 80. *Mailing Add:* Dept of Ger George Mason Univ Fairfax VA 22030

HODDIE, JAMES HENRY, b Attleboro, Mass, Jan 16, 36; m 65; c 2. ROMANCE LANGUAGES. *Educ:* Boston Univ, AB, 58; Univ Wis, MA, 59; Brown Univ, PhD(Span lit), 65. *Prof Exp:* From instr to asst prof Span, Univ Pittsburgh, 62-65; asst prof, Yale Univ, 65-67; asst prof, 67-69, ASSOC PROF SPANISH, COL LIB ARTS, BOSTON UNIV, 69- *Mem:* MLA. *Res:* Spanish biography in the 20th century, especially Maranon and Gomez de la Serna; Spanish novel. *Publ:* Auth, El concepto de la labor del historiador y biografo en las obras de Gregorio Maranon, Bull Hisp, 1-6/67; El liberalismo de Gregorio Maranon, La Torre, 69; En torno a cuatro prologos desaparecidos de Gregorio Maranon, Bull Hisp, 1-6/72; Sentido y forma de la primera biografia de Ramon Gomez de la Serna, Cuadernos Hispanamericanos, 11/78; El programa solipsista de Ramon Gomez de la Serna, Revista de Literatura, 7-12/79; The Genesis of Galdos' La desheredada: Beethoven, Plato and the Picaresque, Anales galdosianos, 79; Some ovservations on the sources of Galdos' Gloria, Revista de Estudios Hispanicos, 1/80. *Mailing Add:* Dept of Lang Boston Univ Charles River Campus 718 Commonwealth Ave Boston MA 02215

HODGE, A TREVOR, b Belfast, Northern Ireland, June 30, 30. CLASSICS. *Educ:* Cambridge Univ, BA, 51, Dipl, 52, MA, 55, PhD, 56. *Prof Exp:* Instr classics, Stanford Univ, 57-58; asst prof, Cornell Univ, 58-59; asst prof, Univ Pa, 59-60; from asst prof to assoc prof, 60-66, actg chmn dept, 61-62, chmn, 67-72, PROF CLASSICS, CARLETON UNIV, 66- *Mem:* Hellenic Soc; Archaeol Inst Am. *Res:* Classical Greek architecture, especially construction techniques; the campaign of Marathon. *Publ:* Auth, The Woodwork of Greek Roofs, Cambridge Univ, 60. *Mailing Add:* 18 Madawasha Dr Ottawa ON K1S 3G6 Can

HODGE, CARLETON TAYLOR, b Springfield, Ill, Nov 27, 17; m 43; c 4. LINGUISTICS. *Educ:* DePauw Univ, AB, 39; Univ Pa, PhD, 43. *Prof Exp:* Instr, Ind Univ, 43-44; instr, UNRRA Training Ctr, Md, 44; instr, Univ Pa, 45-46; instr lang, US Dept State 46; from asst prof to assoc prof ling, Foreign Serv Inst, 47-55, head dept, Near East & African Lang, 55-62, prof ling, 62-64, prof ling & dir, Intensive Lang Training Ctr, Ind Univ, 64-68; PROF LING & ANTHROP, IND UNIV, BLOOMINGTON, 68- *Concurrent Pos:* Intensive lang prog fel, Univ Pa, 44-45 & 46; vis prof, Brandeis Univ, 63-64; consult, US Off Educ, 64-; mem, Am Res Ctr Egypt; vis prof, Univ Mich, summer 65 & Northern Ariz Univ, summers 68 & 69. *Mem:* Ling Soc Am; Ling Soc India; Am Orient Soc; Am Sch Orient Res; African Studies Asn. *Res:* Descriptive and comparative linguistics; Lisramic family of languages. *Publ:* Auth, An Outline of Hausa Grammar, Ling Soc Am, 47; coauth, Hausa Basic Course, 63 & Serbo-Croatian Basic Course (2 vols), 65-69, US Govt Printing Off; ed, Afroasiatic: A Survey, Mouton, 71; auth, Sources of historical linguistic evidence, In: Studies in Linguistics in Honor of George L Trager, Mouton, 72; Egyptian and survival, In: Hamito-Semitica, Mouton, 75; Lisramic (Afroasiatic): An overview, In: The Non-Semitic Languages of Ethiopia, 76; Lislakh Labials, Anthrop Ling, 81. *Mailing Add:* Dept of Ling Ind Univ Bloomington IN 47401

HODGE, JAMES LEE, b Harrisburg, Pa, Sept, 18, 35; m 58; c 1. GERMAN. *Educ:* Tufts Univ, AB, 57; Pa State Univ, AM, 60, PhD(Ger), 61. *Prof Exp:* From instr to assoc prof, 61-74, PROF GER, BOWDOIN COL, GEORGE TAYLOR FILES CHAIR OF MOD LANG, 77-, CHMN DEPT, 68- *Concurrent Pos:* Nat Defense Educ Act study & res grant, Vienna, Austria, 66-67; ed staff, Ger Quart, 75- *Mem:* MLA; Am Asn Teachers Ger. *Res:* Nineteenth century German and Austrian literature; history of comedy and drama; mythology and culture of the early Celts and Germans. *Publ:* Auth, Rhodope: By any other name?, Mod Lang Notes, 10/64; The marriage group: A precarious equilibrium, English Studies, 8/65; co-ed, Helen Adolf Festchrift, Ungar, 68; auth, The Portable German Tutor, Prentice-Hall, 69; Symmetry and tension in Der arme Spielmann, Ger Quart, 3/75; The dramaturgy of Bahnwärter Thiel, Mosaic, spring 76; An experiment in creating language, Foreign Lang Ann, 5/76; The parable in Nathan as a gambit, Germanic Rev, winter 80. *Mailing Add:* Dept of Ger Bowdoin Col Brunswick ME 04011

HODGSON, PETER CALVERT LEARY, JR, b Greenville, SC, Oct 25, 37; m 61; c 4. RUSSIAN & EUROPEAN LITERATURE. *Educ:* Yale Univ, AB, 59, PhD(Slavic), 69. *Prof Exp:* Asst instr Russ, Yale Univ, 59-62 & 65-66; asst prof, 66-74, ASSOC PROF SLAVIC, UNIV CALIF, LOS ANGELES, 74- *Res:* The Russian novel; 18th century Russian prose; literary parody. *Publ:* Auth, From Gogol to Dostoevsky, Fink, 74; Metaliterature and knowledge, In: Studies in Comparative Literature, Vol VII, Univ Southern Calif, 74. *Mailing Add:* Dept of Slavic Lang & Lit Univ of Calif Hilgard Ave Los Angeles CA 90024

HOEFERT, SIGFRID, b Poland, Aug 14, 25; Can citizen; m 54; c 3. GERMAN. *Educ:* Univ Toronto, BA, 58, MA, 60, PhD(Ger), 63. *Prof Exp:* Lectr, 61-63, from asst prof to assoc prof, 63-69, PROF GER, UNIV WATERLOO, 69- *Concurrent Pos:* Soc Sci & Humanities Res Coun Can awards & fac res grants. *Mem:* Am Asn Teachers Ger; Can Asn Univ Teachers Ger; Can Comp Lit Asn Int Ver Ger Sprach-u Literaturwiss; MLA. *Res:* Naturalism; literature of the German Democratic Republic. *Publ:* Auth, West-Östliches in der Lyrik Johannes Bobrowskis, UniDruck, München, 66; Das Drama des Naturalismus, Metzler, Stuttgart, 68; Einige unveröffentlichte Briefe aus Rilkes Frühzeit, Euphorion, 67; Kunst und literatur: die ikonengedichte Johannes Bobrowskis, Monatshefte, 72; Gerhart Hauptmann, Metzler, Stuttgart, 74; Russische Literatur in Deutschland, Texte zur Rezeption von den Achtziger Jahren bis zur Jahrhundertwende, Niemeyer, Tübingen, 74; Aufnahme und wirkung W M Garschins im deutschen sprachraum-besonders im hinblick auf Gerhart Hauptmann, Mich Ger Studies, 75; Naturalism as an international phenomenon: The state of research, Yearbk of Comp & Gen Lit, 78. *Mailing Add:* Dept of Ger & Russ Univ of Waterloo Waterloo ON N2L 3G1 Can

HOELZEL, ALFRED, b Vienna, Austria, Feb 21, 34; US citizen; m 57; c 3. GERMANIC LANGUAGES. *Educ:* Univ Mass, Amherst, BA, 55; Northwestern Univ, MA, 56; Boston Univ, PhD(Ger), 64. *Prof Exp:* Teacher, Boston Pub Latin Sch, 57-64; dir foreign lang, Brookline Pub Schs, 64-65; from asst prof to assoc prof, 65-75, chmn dept, 65-70, PROF GER, UNIV MASS, BOSTON, 75- *Concurrent Pos:* Vis prof, Bar-Ilan Univ, Israel, 78-79. *Mem:* MLA; Am Asn Teachers Ger; Lessing Soc; Goethe Soc NAm. *Res:* Faust traditon; Lessing; Holocaust literature. *Publ:* Coauth, German One, 70 & German Two, 70, Houghton; Soma Morgenstern, 1890-1976, Midstream, 3/77; Truth and Honesty in Minna von Barnhelm, Lessing Yearbook, IX, 77; Faust, the plague, and theodicy, Ger Quart, 1/79; Betrayed rebels in German literature, Orbis Litterarum, No 34, 79; The conclusion of Goethe's Faust: Ambivalence and ambiguity, Ger Quart, 1/82; Walter Hasenclever's Humanitarianism: Themes of Protest in His Works, Peter Lang Inc, 82. *Mailing Add:* Dept of Ger Univ of Mass Harbor Campus Boston MA 02125

HOENIGSWALD, HENRY M, b Breslau, Ger, Apr, 17, 15; nat US. LINGUISTICS. *Educ:* Univ Florence, D Litt, 36. *Hon Degrees:* LHD, Swarthmore Col, 81. *Prof Exp:* Mem staff, Inst Studies Etruschi, 36-38; lectr ling, Yale Univ, 39-42, res asst, 45-46; lectr phonetics & ling, Hartford Sem Found, 42-43, instr, 45-46; in charge army specialized training in Hindustani, Univ Pa, 43-44; mem staff, foreign serv inst, US Dept State, 46-47; assoc prof classic lang, Univ Tex, 47-48; assoc prof, 48-59, chmn dept, 63-70, PROF LING, UNIV PA, 59- *Concurrent Pos:* Am Coun Learned Soc fel, 42-43, 44-45; lectr, Hunter Col, 42-43 & 46; Guggenheim fel, 50-51; vis assoc prof, Georgetown Univ, 52-53 & 54; assoc ed, J Am Orient Soc, 52-54, ed, 54-58; sr linguist, Deccan Col, India, 55; Newberry Libr fel, 56; chmn Am comt, SAsian Lang, 56; vis assoc prof, Princeton Univ, 59-60; vis prof, Yale Univ, 61-62; Nat Sci Found sr fel, Ctr Advan Study Behav Sci, 62-63; mem comt lang prog, Am Coun Learned Soc, 63-70; mem univ sem, Columbia Univ, 64-; mem corp vis comt, Mass Inst Technol, 68-74; Fulbright lectr, Oxford Univ, 76-77; fel, St John's Col, Oxford, 76-77; chmn, overseers comt to vis Dept of Ling, Harvard Univ, 78- *Mem:* Ling Soc Am (pres, 58); Am Orient Soc (pres, 66-67); Am Philos Soc; Am Acad Arts & Sci; Philol Soc. *Res:* History of linguistics; Indo-European comparative linguistics; theory of change and reconstruction. *Publ:* Auth, The principal step in comparative grammar, Lang, 50; Language Change and Linguistic Reconstruction, Univ Chicago, 60; Graduality, sporadicity and sound change, Phonetica, 64; co-ed, Studies in Formal Historical Linguistics, Reidel, 73; Linguistics, In: Dictionary of the History of Ideas, 73; Intentions, assumptions, and contradictions in historical linguistics, Current Issues in Ling Theory, 77; ed, The European Background of American Linguistics, Foris, 79; 1876 and posterity, Transactions Philol Soc, 78. *Mailing Add:* 618 Williams Hall Univ of Pa Philadelphia PA 19104

HOERBER, ROBERT GEORGE, b St Louis, Mo, Aug 25, 18; m 44; c 1. CLASSICAL PHILOLOGY. *Educ:* Concordia Theol Sem, AB, 41; Wash Univ, AM, 42, PhD, 44. *Prof Exp:* Prof Greek & Latin, Bethany Col, Minn, 44-47; prof, 47-72, distinguished serv prof, 72-74, DISTINGUISHED SERV EMER PROF CLASSICS, WESTMINSTER COL, 74-; PROF EXEGETICAL THEOL, CONCORDIA SEM, 74- *Concurrent Pos:* Vis prof, Univ Mo, 56, Concordia Sem, 58-60 & St Olaf Col, 65-67. *Mem:* Am Philol Asn; Soc Ancient Greek Philos; Am Class League; Class Asn Midwest & S; Soc New Testament Studies. *Res:* Platonism; Greek New Testament. *Publ:* Auth, The Theme of Plato's Republic, Eden, 44; A Grammatical Study of Romans 16, 17, Northwestern Publ House, 47, 2nd ed, Lutheran Synod Bk Co, 63; Saint Paul's Shorter Letters, Ovid Bell, 54. *Mailing Add:* Dept of Exegetical Theol Concordia Sem St Louis MO 63105

HOERMANN, ROLAND, b Highland Park, Ill, Sept 12, 23; m 51; c 2. MODERN GERMAN LITERATURE, COMPARATIVE LITERATURE. *Educ:* Univ Wis, AB, 48, PhD(Ger lit), 56; Univ Mich, MA, 51. *Prof Exp:* Instr Ger, Univ Wis, 53-55, from instr to asst prof, 55-63, assoc dean col lett & sci, 64-76, ASSOC PROF GER LIT, UNIV CALIF, DAVIS, 63- *Concurrent Pos:* Mem, textbk div, US Armed Forces Inst Educ Panel, 60- *Mem:* MLA; Am Asn Teachers Ger. *Res:* German Romanticism; Franz Kafka; modern comparative European drama. *Publ:* Coauth, Spoken German, US Govt Printing Off, 55; auth, Historicity and art in Tieck's Sternbald, 5/55, The Romantic Golden Age in Arnim's writings, 1/58 & Symbolism and mediation in Arnim's View of the Romantic Phantasy, 5/62, Monatshefte; Achim von Arnim, Twayne, 69. *Mailing Add:* Dept of Ger Univ of Calif Davis CA 95616

HOFACKER, ERICH PAUL, JR, b New Haven, Conn, Mar 23, 28; m 59; c 2. GERMANIC LANGUAGES. *Educ:* Wash Univ, BA, 50, MA, 53; Univ Chicago, MA, 59; Univ NC, Chapel Hill, PhD(Ger), 67. *Prof Exp:* Instr Ger, Univ NC, Chapel Hill, 59-65; lectr, 65-67, ASST PROF GER, UNIV MICH, ANN ARBOR, 67- *Res:* The German baroque novel; German literature of the 17th and 18th centuries; East German literature. *Publ:* Auth, Günter Kunert and the East German Image of man, Monatshefte, winter 74; Günter Kunert's Orpheus Cycle: In support of the integrity of the poet, Symp, summer 76; Günter Kunert's Geschichte: Man's struggle with history, Ger Rev, 11/76; ed, Christian Morgenstern, Twayne, 78; auth, Faltering Steps: Günter Kunert's Unterwegs nach Utopia, Ger Rev, winter 82. *Mailing Add:* Dept of Ger Lang & Lit Univ of Mich Ann Arbor MI 48104

HOFF, PETER, b Berlin, Ger, June 13, 22; US citizen; m 52; c 2. FOREIGN LANGUAGES & PHILOLOGY. *Educ:* Middlebury Col, BA, 44; Harvard Univ, MA, 46. *Prof Exp:* Instr Span, Boston Univ, 48-51; from instr to asst prof Romance lang, Bowdoin Col, 56-61; asst prof Romance lang & Ger, Ripon Col, 61-65; master Span, St Mark's Sch, Mass, 65-67; ASSOC PROF FOREIGN LANG, NORTHERN MICH UNIV, 67- *Mem:* MLA; Am Asn Teachers Span & Port. *Res:* Modern Spanish prose; modernism and post-modernism in Latin America. *Mailing Add:* Dept of Foreign Lang Northern Mich Univ Marquette MI 49855

HOFF, ROMA B, b Madison, Wis, May 4, 26; m 58; c 3. SPANISH EDUCATION. *Educ:* Univ Wis, BA, 48, MA, 51, PhD(educ), 56. *Prof Exp:* Teaching asst & instr Span, Univ Wis, 46-48, 49-51, 52-54 & 55-58; asst prof, 58-65 PROF SPAN & EDUC, UNIV WIS-EAU CLAIRE, 65- *Mem:* MLA; Am Asn Teachers Span & Port; AAUP; Am Coun Teaching Foreign Lang. *Res:* Foreign language in the elementary school; TV teaching; adult education Spanish. *Publ:* Auth, Spanish for Travelers, 54 & Spanish in Action for the Elementary School, 56, Univ Wis; Foreign language study: Fluency, fun, careers, Phi Kappa Phi J, fall 77. *Mailing Add:* Dept of Foreign Lang Univ of Wis Eau Claire WI 54701

HOFFMANN, CHARLES WESLEY, b Sioux City, Iowa, Nov 25, 29; m 54; c 2. GERMAN LITERATURE. *Educ:* Oberlin Col, BA, 51; Univ Ill, Urbana, MA, 52, PhD(Ger), 56. *Prof Exp:* Teaching asst Ger, Univ Ill, 55-56; from instr to asst prof, Univ Calif, Los Angeles, 56-64; assoc prof, 64-66; chmn dept, 69-77, PROF GER, OHIO STATE UNIV, 66- *Concurrent Pos:* Fulbright fel, 53-55 & 81. *Mem:* MLA; Am Asn Teachers Ger; Brecht Soc; AAUP; Am Asn Advan Humanities. *Res:* Twentieth century German literature. *Publ:* Ed, Brecht, Kalendergeschichten, Norton, 60; auth, Opposition Poetry in Nazi Germany, Univ Calif, 62; The search for self, inner freedom and relatedness in the novels of Max Frisch, In: The Contemporary Novel in German, Univ Tex, 67; coauth, Brecht, Schweyk, and Commmunism, In: Festschrift für Detlev W Schumann, Delp, 70; auth, Opposition und innere emigration: Zwei aspekte des anderen Deutschlands, In: Exil und Innere Emigration, Vol II, 73; Survey of Research Tool Needs in German Language and Literature, Ohio State Univ Res Found, 78; Survey of German research tool needs, Vol 70, 78 & German research tool needs: An update, Vol 71, 79, Monatshefte. *Mailing Add:* Dept of Ger 1841 Millikin Rd Ohio State Univ Columbus OH 43210

HOFFMANN, ERNST FEDOR, b Munich, Ger, Sept 25, 28; US citizen. GERMAN LANGUAGE & LITERATURE. *Educ:* Yale Univ, MA, 59, PhD(Ger), 62. *Prof Exp:* From instr to asst prof Ger, Yale Univ, 59-64; asst prof, Columbia Univ, 64-66; assoc prof, 66-70, PROF GER, HUNTER COL, 71- *Concurrent Pos:* Mem fac grad sch, City Univ New York, 68-; John Simon Guggenheim Mem Found fel, 71-72; vis prof, Yale Univ, fall 80. *Mem:* MLA; Am Asn Teachers Ger. *Mailing Add:* Dept of Ger Hunter Col 695 Park Ave New York NY 10016

HOFFMANN, GISELA ELISE, b Hamburg, Ger, June 24, 22; Can citizen; m 65; c 1. GERMAN LANGUAGE & LITERATURE. *Educ:* Univ Alta, BEd, 63, MA, 65, PhD(Ger), 71. *Prof Exp:* Teacher elem & jr high sch, Hamburg Sch Bd, Ger, 42-51; teacher English & social studies, Prov Alta, 52-63; asst prof Ger, Rutgers Univ, 69-73; asst prof, 75-81, ASSOC PROF GER, CONCORDIA COL, ALTA, 81- *Mem:* Am Asn Teachers of Ger; Can Asn Univ Teachers of Ger; Can Comp Lit Asn. *Res:* Modern German literature, especially Thomas Mann; age of Goethe. *Publ:* Auth, Das Motive des Auserwählten bei Thomas Mann, Bouvier, Bonn, 74. *Mailing Add:* Concordia Col 7128 Ada Blvd Edmonton AB T5B 4E4 Can

HOFFMANN, LEON-FRANCOIS, b Paris, France, Apr 11, 32; US & Fr citizen; m 60; c 2. FRENCH LITERATURE. *Educ:* Yale Univ, BA, 53; Princeton Univ, MA, 55, PhD(French), 59. *Prof Exp:* From instr to assoc prof, 57-68, PROF FRENCH, PRINCETON UNIV, 68- *Concurrent Pos:* Guggenheim fel, 65; Nat Endowment for Humanities fel, 80-81. *Honors & Awards:* Academie Francaise Prize, 74. *Mem:* MLA; Soc Fr Prof Am; Inst Asn Fr Studies; Ctr Etudes Romantiques. *Res:* French romanticism; Balzac; black French literature. *Publ:* Auth, Romantique Espagne, 61 La peste a Barcelone, 64, Presses Univs France; auth, L'Essentiel de la Grammaire Francaise, Scribner, 64; Repertoire Georgraphique de La Comedie Humaine (2 vols), Jose Corti, Paris, 65-68; ed, Latouche et L'Heritier Dernieres lettres de deux amants de Barcelone, Presses Univs France, 66; auth, Le Negre Romantique, Payot, Paris, 73; La Pratique du Francais Parle, Scribner, 73; ed, Alexandre Dumas Georges, Folio-Gallimard, Paris, 74. *Mailing Add:* Dept of Romance Lang Princeton Univ Princeton NJ 08540

HOFFMANN, URSULA F, b Berlin, Ger, Aug 4, 33; US citizen. GERMAN LITERATURE. *Educ:* Smith Col, AB, 56; Yale Univ, PhD(medieval Ger), 64. *Prof Exp:* From asst to instr Ger, Smith Col, 56-58; instr, Yale Univ, 58-64; instr, Hunter Col, 64-68; chmn dept, 68-72, asst prof, 68-79, ASSOC PROF GER, LEHMAN COL, 80- *Mem:* MLA; Am Asn Teachers Ger. *Publ:* Ed, Wolfram's Parzival, Cornell Univ, 69. *Mailing Add:* Dept of Ger & Slavic Herbert H Lehman Col Bronx NY 10468

HOFFMEISTER, DONNA L, b Pontiac, Mich, June 13, 43. GERMAN LITERATURE. *Educ:* Univ Mich, BA, 65; Brown Univ, MA, 67, PhD(German), 79. *Prof Exp:* Vis lectr German, Jackson State Univ, 70; Brown Univ, 79-80; ASST PROF GERMAN, UNIV PITTSBURGH, 80- *Mem:* Am Asn Teachers of Ger; MLA; Northeastern Modern Lang Asn; Am Comp Lit Asn. *Res:* Modern German literature. *Publ:* Auth, Zamhaltn muB man dan: Reassurance display in Franz Xaver Kroetz's Oberosterreich, German Quart, 11/81; The Theater of Confinement: Language and Survival in the Milieu Plays of Marieluise Fleiber & Franz Xaver Kroetz, Camden House, 82. *Mailing Add:* Dept of Ger Lang & Lit Univ Pittsburgh Pittsburgh PA 15260

HOFFMEISTER, GERHART, b Giessen, Ger, Dec 17, 36; m 66; c 1. GERMAN & COMPARATIVE LITERATURE. *Educ:* Univ Md, College Park, PhD(Ger), 70. *Prof Exp:* Referendar English & Ger, Cologne Sch Syst, 64-66; instr Ger, Univ Md, 66-70; asst prof, Univ Wis-Milwaukee, 70-74; assoc prof, Wayne State Univ, 74-75; assoc prof, 75-79, PROF GER, UNIV CALIF, SANTA BARBARA, 79- *Concurrent Pos:* Am Philos Soc grant, 75. *Mem:* MLA; Am Asn Teachers Ger; Philol Asn Pac Coast. *Res:* German baroque; German-Hispanic relations; European romanticism. *Publ:* Auth, Die spanische Diana in Deutschland, Erich Schmidt, Berlin, 72; Petrarkistische Lyrik, Metzler, Stuttgart, 73; ed, Europäische Tradition und deutscher Literaturbarock, Francke, Bern, 73; auth, Spanien und Deutschland, Erich Schmidt, 76: ed, Kuffstein, Gefängnis der Liebe, Lang, 76; The Renaissance and Reformation in Germany, Ungar, 77; auth, Deutsche und europäische Romantik, Metzler, 78; ed, Goethezeit, Festschrift für Stuart P Atkins, Francke, Bern, 81. *Mailing Add:* Dept of Ger & Slavic Lang Univ of Calif Santa Barbara CA 93106

HOFFMEISTER, WERNER GEORG, b Rotterdam, Netherlands, Jan 20, 31; US citizen. GERMAN LANGUAGE & LITERATURE, COMPARATIVE LITERATURE. *Educ:* Brown Univ, AM, 58, PhD(Ger), 62. *Prof Exp:* Jr teacher Ger & English, Gym, Neuss, Ger, 58-59; instr Ger, Conn Col, 60-62; instr, Brown Univ, 62, from asst prof to prof, 63-74; PROF GER & COMP LIT, DARTMOUTH COL, 77- *Concurrent Pos:* Alexander von Humboldt Found res fel, 67-68; assoc ed, Novel: Forum on Fiction, 67-70. *Mem:* MLA; Am Asn Teachers Ger; Am Comp Lit Asn; Am Coun for Study Austrian Lit. *Res:* Nineteenth and 20th century German literature and comparative literature. *Publ:* Coauth, Practice and Progress, A German Grammar for Review and Reference, Ginn, 63; auth, Studien Zur Erlebten Rede bei Thomas Mann und Robert Musil, Mouton, 65; Beispiele: Deutsche Prosa des 20 Jahrhunderts, Prentice-Hall, 68; contribr, biographical articles on German authors, In: World Bk Encycl, Field, 70. *Mailing Add:* Dept of Ger Dartmouth Col Hanover NH 03755

HOFFNER, HARRY A, JR, b Jacksonville, Fla, Nov 27, 34; m 58; c 3. HISTORY, ANCIENT NEAR EAST LANGUAGES. *Educ:* Princeton Univ, BA, 56; Dallas Theol Sem, ThM, 60; Brandeis Univ, MA, 61, PhD(Hittite), 63. *Prof Exp:* Instr Semitics & Old Testament, Wheaton Col, Ill, 63-64; asst prof Anatolian studies, Brandeis Univ, 64-69; assoc prof Hittitology & Assyriology, Yale Univ, 69-74; PROF HITTITOLOGY, ORIENTAL INST, UNIV CHICAGO, 74- *Concurrent Pos:* Co-dir, Hittite Dict proj, Oriental Inst, 74-; Nat Endowment for Humanities grant, Hittite Dict Proj, 76-82. *Mem:* Am Orient Soc; Soc Bibl Lit; Ger Orient Soc; Archeol Inst Am. *Res:* History and civilization of ancient Near East; Indo-European and Semitic linguistics; interpretation of the Old Testament. *Publ:* Auth, The Elkunirsa myth reconsidered, Rev Hittite et Asianique, 65; Composite nouns, verbs and adjectives in Hittite, Orientalia, 66; Second millennium antecedents to Hebrew Obh, J Bibl Lit, 67; An English-Hittite Glossary, Klincksieck, Paris, 68; Alimenta Hethaeorum, Am Orient Soc, 74; contribr, Hittite Dict, Oriental Inst, Univ Chicago, 80. *Mailing Add:* Oriental Inst 1155 East 58th St Chicago IL 60637

HOFMANN, MARGARET MEADER, b Camden, NJ, Jan 30, 26; div; c 1. FRENCH. *Educ:* Wellesley Col, AB, 47; Univ NH, MA, 49; Univ Kans, PhD(French), 68. *Prof Exp:* Teacher, Moorestown Friends Sch, NJ, 49-51; asst to dir admis, Univ Md Overseas Div, 54-55; instr French, Univ Kans, 55-56; teacher, Kingswood Sch, Cranbrook, 57-59, 62-63; from instr to assoc prof French, 63-73, PROF FRENCH, MARY WASHINGTON COL, 73-, CHAIRPERSON, DEPT MOD FOREIGN LANG, 81- *Mem:* Am Asn Teachers Fr. *Res:* French Arthurian romances. *Mailing Add:* 918 Grove Ave Fredericksburg VA 22401

HOFMANN, TH R, b Chicago Ill, Nov 18, 37; c 3. LINGUISTICS, MATHEMATICS . *Educ:* Univ Ill, BS, 59, MA, 62; Nouvelle Sorbonne, Dr 3 cycle ling, 78. *Prof Exp:* Teaching asst English, Univ Ill, 61-62; mathematician, Res Found, Ill Inst Technol, 62-63 & Univ Chicago, 63-64; lectr English lang, Col mil royal St-Jean, 67-69; asst prof ling, Univ Ottawa, 69-79; PROF ENGLISH & LING, JAPAN MINISTRY EDUC, SHIMANE & TOYAMA UNIV, 79- *Concurrent Pos:* Res asst, Inst Except Children, Univ Ill, 60-61; Mass Inst Tech, 64-66 & Aitken Comput Lab, Harvard Univ, 65-66; mathematician, US Air Force Cambridge Res Lab, 65-66; lectr & res, Univ Montreal, 68-72; ed, Cahiers Ling d'Ottawa, 72-76; res assoc, Univ Sci & Med Grenoble, 75-77; vis prof, Fudan Univ, Shanghai, 80- *Mem:* Ling Soc Am; Asn Comput Ling; Can Ling Asn; English Philol Soc Japan. *Res:* The semantic and pragmatic structure of natural language, especially as regards the interpretation and integration of sentences in their context; the decoding of sequences of words, primarily sentences, into their meaning; sytems of writing, especially non-phonetic systems, ideographic and pasigraphic. *Publ:* Auth, Past tense replacement & the modal system, NSF, Vol 17, 66 & In: Syntax & Semantics, Vol 7, Acad Press, 77; Descriptions in natural language, Lang Sci, Vol 30, 74; Interpretation & integration of sentences into a C-network, Am J Comput Ling, Vol 29, 75; Experimental lexicography & semantics: An empirical basis for semantic research, Commun & Cognition, Vol 10, 77; Description sematique & dynamique du discours, Univ Sci & Med Grenoble, 78; Equational sentence structure in Eskimo, Ling Studies Native Can, 78; Modality in English & other languages, Papers Ling, Vol 12, 79; The law of denotation & notions of antonymy, Prague Bull Math Ling, Vol 36, 81. *Mailing Add:* Fac of Humanities Toyama Univ 3190 Gofuku Toyama City Toyama 930 Japan

HOFMANN, THOMAS KARL, b Berlin, Germany, Aug 30, 42; Can citizen. GERMAN BAROQUE LITERATURE. *Educ:* McGill Univ, BSc, 67, MA, 70, PhD(Ger), 78. *Prof Exp:* Lectr, Univ Alta, 71-72; ASST PROF GER, UNIV MANITOBA, 78- *Mem:* Can Asn Univ Teachers Ger. *Res:* Early German journal; methodology. *Publ:* Auth, Die frühe Zeitschrift als Faktor im bürgerlichen Emanzipationsprozess, Sem, Vol XVII, 81. *Mailing Add:* 379 Hargrave St #302 Winnipeg MB R3B 2K4 Can

HOGAN, JAMES CHARLES, b Hydro, Okla, Jan 10, 36; m 59; c 2. CLASSICS. *Educ:* Univ Okla, BA, 58; Cornell Univ, MA, 61, PhD(classics), 66. *Prof Exp:* Asst prof classics & acting chmn dept, Converse Col, 61-63; asst prof, Wash Univ, 65-66; assoc prof, Univ Okla, 66-69; FRANK T McCLURE PROF CLASSICS, ALLEGHENY COL, 69- *Mem:* Am Philol Asn. *Res:* Greek literature, epic and drama. *Publ:* Auth, Thucydides 3, 52-68 and Euripides' Hecuba, Phoenix, 72; Aristotle's criticism of Homer in the Poetics, Class Philol, 4/73; The temptation of Odysseus, Trans Am Philol Asn, 76; A Guide to the Iliad, Doubleday, 79. *Mailing Add:* Dept of Classics Allegheny Col Meadville PA 16335

HOGE, MIRIAM ELOISE BOWES, b South Avis, Pa, July 2, 18; m. ROMANCE LANGUAGES. *Educ:* Randolph-Macon Woman's Col, AB, 40; Univ Pa, MA, 49, PhD, 52. *Prof Exp:* Instr French, Univ Kans, 52-56; from asst prof to assoc prof, 56-67, PROF FRENCH, MARY WASHINGTON COL, 67- *Mem:* MLA; Am Asn Teachers Fr. *Res:* Nineteenth century French, especially George Sand; contemporary French fiction. *Mailing Add:* Dept of Mod Lang Mary Washington Col Fredericksburg VA 22401

HOGSETT, CHARLOTTE, b Jackson, Tenn, June 1, 38. ROMANCE LANGUAGES. *Educ:* Southwestern at Memphis, BA, 60; Univ Toronto, MA, 62; Harvard Univ, PhD(Romance lang), 65. *Prof Exp:* From instr to asst prof Romance lang, Duke Univ, 64-70; assoc prof, 70-76, PROF FRENCH, MARY BALDWIN COL, 76- *Mem:* MLA; Am Asn Teachers Fr; Am Soc 18th Century Studies; Fr Soc Studies 18th Century. *Res:* Eighteenth and early nineteenth century French literature and literary theory. *Publ:* Auth, Jean-Baptiste Due Bos on art as illusion, Studies Voltaire & 18th Century, 70; On facing artificiality and frivolity: Theories of pastoral poetry in eighteenth century France, 18th Century Studies, 71. *Mailing Add:* Dept of French Mary Baldwin Col Staunton VA 24401

HOHENDAHL, PETER U, b Hamburg, Ger, Mar 17, 36; m 65. GERMAN. *Educ:* Univ Hamburg, PhD(Ger), 64. *Prof Exp:* Asst prof Ger, Pa State Univ, 65-68; assoc prof, Wash Univ, 68-70, prof, 70-77, chmn dept, 72-77; PROF GER & COMP LIT, CORNELL UNIV, 77-, CHMN DEPT, 81- *Concurrent Pos:* Fel, Harvard, 64-65; assoc ed, Ling u Literaturwiss, 71-74; vis prof, Univ Hamburg, Ger, 74; Merton vis prof, Free Univ Berling, 76; Fel, Ctr Interdisciplinary Res, Bielefeld Univ, 81. *Mem:* MLA; Am Asn Teachers Ger; Brecht Soc. *Res:* Theory of literature; 18th and 19th century European literature; modern German literature. *Publ:* Auth, Das Bild der buergerlichen Welt im expressionistischen Drama, C Winter, 67; ed, Benn--Wirkung wider Willen, 71 & co-ed, Exil und innere Emigration, Vol II, 72, Athenäum; ed, Sozialgeschichte und Wirkungsästhetick, Fischer-Athenäum, 74; auth, Literaturkritik und Offen tlichkeit, Piper, 74; ed, Literatur und Literaturtheorie in de DDR, Suhrkamp, 76; auth, Der europäische Roman der Empfindsamkeit, Athenaion, 77; ed, Legitimationskrisen des deutschen Adels, Metzler, 79; auth, The Institution of Criticism, Cornell Univ Press, 82. *Mailing Add:* Dept of Ger Lit Cornell Univ Ithaca NY 14853

HOKENSON, JAN WALSH, b Calif, Sept 13, 42. MODERN EUROPEAN & FRENCH LITERATURE. *Educ:* Univ Calif, Berkeley, BA, 64; San Francisco State Univ, MA, 69; Univ Calif, Santa Cruz, PhD(comp lit), 74. *Prof Exp:* Lectr French & comp lit, Univ Calif, Davis, 75-78; ASSOC PROF FRENCH, FLA ATLANTIC UNIV, 78- *Concurrent Pos:* Asst ed, Fantasy Newsletter, 81- *Mem:* MLA. *Res:* Forms of the comic; comparative fiction. *Publ:* Auth, Biblical paradigms in Beckett's trilogy, James Joyce Quart, summer 71; Celine: Impressionist in language, L'Esprit Createur, winter 73; Proust in the Palace of Sheriar, Far-Western Forum, 5/74; Three novels in large black pauses, In: Beckett: A Collection of Criticism, McGraw-Hill, 75; Norman Mailer, In: Contemp Novelists of the English Language, St Martin's Press, 79; Todorov and the existentialists, In: Scope of the Fantastic, Greenwood Press (in press); W H Auden, In: Contemporary Poets of the English Language, St Martin's Press, 80. *Mailing Add:* Dept of Lang Fla Atlantic Univ Boca Raton FL 33431

HOLCOMB, GEORGE L, b Tex, Sept 10, 11; m 37; c 1. FOREIGN LANGUAGES. *Educ:* Trinity Univ, AB, 31; US Mil Acad, BS, 37; Middlebury Col, MA, 56; Univ Tex, PhD, 58. *Prof Exp:* Asst prof Span, US Mil Acad, 46-49; prof Span & French & head dept foreign lang, US Air Force Acad, 58-60; assoc prof, Trinity Univ, 60-64, chmn dept foreign lang, 62-71, prof Span & French, 64-77; RETIRED. *Mem:* Am Asn Teachers Fr. *Res:* Spanish theatre. *Publ:* Coauth, Moliere, Resumes, Trinity Univ, 71. *Mailing Add:* 2802 Woodcrest San Antonio TX 78209

HOLDHEIM, WILLIAM WOLFGANG, b Berlin, Ger, Aug 4, 26; US citizen; m 54; c 2. COMPARATIVE & FRENCH LITERATURE. *Educ:* Univ Calif, Los Angeles, BA, 49, MA, 51; Yale Univ, PhD(French lit), 56. *Prof Exp:* Instr French, Ohio State Univ, 55-57; from instr to assoc prof Europ Lang & lit, Brandeis Univ, 57-64; prof French & comp lit, Washington Univ, 64-69; PROF COMP LIT & CHMN DEPT, CORNELL UNIV, 69- *Concurrent Pos:* Guggenheim fel, 62-63; Fulbright lectr, Free Univ Berlin, 68-69; Nat Endowment for Humanities sr fel, 72-73. *Mem:* Am Comp Lit Asn; MLA; AAUP. *Res:* Modern novel; literature and history. *Publ:* Auth, Gide's Caves du Vatican and the illusionism of the novel, Mod Lang Notes, 5/62; Theory and Practice of the novel, Droz, Geneva, 68; Der Justizirrtum als literarische Problematik, De Gruyter, Berlin, 69; Das Asthetische und die Zeitlichkeit, 71 & Komparatistik und Literaturtheorie, 72, Arcadia; The concept of poetic estrangement, Comp Lit Studies, 74; The history of art in Victor Hugo's Notre-Dame de Paris, 19th Century Fr Studies, 76/77; Die Suche nach dem Epos, Winter, Heidelberg, 78. *Mailing Add:* Dept of Comp Lit Goldwin Smith Hall Cornell Univ Ithaca NY 14853

HOLDSWORTH, CAROLE A, b Oak Park, Ill, Dec 3, 36. ROMANCE LANGUAGES. *Educ:* Elmhurst Col, BA, 58; Northwestern Univ, MA, 59, PhD(Romance lang), 65. *Prof Exp:* From asst to asst prof Span, 59-71, assoc prof, 71-80, PROF MOD LANG, LOYOLA UNIV CHICAGO, 80- *Concurrent Pos:* Loyola Univ res grant, 68; grant reader, Nat Endowment for Humanities, 78- *Mem:* MLA; Am Asn Teachers Span & Port, Am Asn Univ Prof; AAUP; Am Asn Teachers Fr. *Res:* Hispanic modernism: comparative literature; cervantes and pynchon. *Publ:* Auth, White symbolism in selected Revista Moderna authors, Rev Estud Hisp, 11/68; Characterization in the stories of Ruben M Campos, 12/68 & Some modernist manias verbales and their connotations, 3/72, Hisp; Ideas religiosas en las novelas maduras de Ramon Perez de Ayala, Rev Estud Hisp, 5/72; Two trains of war, two doves of peace, Revista de Letras, 12/73; Temporal preoccupations in the Chansons of J Brel, J Popular Cult, Fall 74; Modern Minstrelsy: Miguel Hernandez and Jacques Brel, Peter Lang, Bern, 80. *Mailing Add:* Dept of Mod Lang Loyola Univ 820 N Michigan Ave Chicago IL 60611

HOLLAND, HENRY, b Calais, Maine, June 15, 23. SPANISH LITERATURE. *Educ:* Univ Maine, BA, 44; Harvard Univ, MA, 48; Univ Madrid, PhD, 52. *Prof Exp:* Instr Span, Univ Maine, 48-50; from instr to assoc prof, 52-66, PROF SPAN, COLBY COL, 66-, CHMN DEPT MOD FOREIGN LANG, 72- *Concurrent Pos:* Consult, Span & Port lit, Am People's Encycl, 62- & Ford Found, 65-66; dir, Latin Am Scholar Prog Am Univs, 66-69; mem Comt Latin Am Student Affairs, 67- *Mem:* MLA; Am Asn Teachers Span & Port; Nat Asn Foreign Student Affairs. *Res:* Latin-American and Portuguese literature; teaching of Spanish in elementary school. *Publ:* Auth, Literature of Spain & Literature of Portugal, In: Book of Knowledge, 62; Manuel Diaz Rodriguez, estilista del modernismo, Iberoamerica Collecion Studium, 62. *Mailing Add:* Dept of Mod Foreign Lang Colby Col Waterville ME 04901

HOLLAND, JOHN GILL, English & American Literature. See Vol II

HOLLANDER, ROBERT B, JR, b New York, NY, July 31, 33. LITERATURE. *Educ:* Princeton Univ, AB, 55; Columbia Univ, PhD, 62. *Prof Exp:* Instr English, Columbia Col, 58-62; from lectr to assoc prof, 62-74, PROF EUROP LIT, PRINCETON UNIV, 74- *Concurrent Pos:* Guggenheim fel, 70-71; Nat Endowment for Humanities sr fel, 74; vchmn, Nat Coun on Humanities, 74-80. *Mem:* Dante Soc Am (pres, 79-82); MLA; Am Boccaccio Asn; Am Asn Advan Humanities. *Res:* Fourteenth century Italian literature; Dante; Boccaccio. *Publ:* Auth, The apocalyptic framework of Dostoevsky's Idiot, Mosaic, winter 74; Vita Nuova: Dante's perceptions of Beatrice, Dante Studies, 74; Purgatorio II: Cato's rebuke and Dante's scoglio, Italica, 75; Dante Theologus-Poeta, Dante Studies, 76; Boccaccio's Two Venuses, Columbia Univ, 77; Typology and secular literature: Some medieval problems and examples, Lit Uses of Typology, 77; The validity of Boccaccio's self-exegesis, Medievalia et Humanistica, fall 77; Studies in Dante, Longo, 80. *Mailing Add:* Dept of Comp Lit 326 E Pyne Princeton Univ Princeton NJ 08540

HOLLER, WILLIAM MCFALL, b Anderson, SC, Mar 4, 36. ROMANCE PHILOLOGY, FRENCH LITERATURE. *Educ:* Wofford Col, AB, 59; Middlebury Col, MA, 62; Univ NC, Chapel Hill, PhD(Romance philol), 72. *Prof Exp:* Instr French & Span, Perkiomen Sch, Pa, 59; teaching asst French, Middlebury Col, 61, lectr, 62; teaching asst, Univ NC, Chapel Hill, 63-67; instr, 67-72, ASST PROF MOD LANG, NC STATE UNIV, 72- *Concurrent Pos:* Mem, Alliance Francaise. *Mem:* MLA; SAtlantic Mod Lang Asn; Am Asn Teachers Fr; Mediaeval Acad Am; AAUP. *Res:* Romance philology, particularly Old French language and literature; paleography. *Publ:* Auth, The ordinary man's concept of nature as reflected in the thirteenth century French Book of Sydrac, Fr Rev, 2/75; Unusual stone lore in the thirteenth century lapidary of Sydrac, Romance Notes, spring 79. *Mailing Add:* Dept of Foreign Lang & Lit NC State Univ Raleigh NC 27607

HOLLERBACH, WOLF, b Cologne, Ger, Nov 30, 35; m 62; c 3. ROMANCE LANGUAGES. *Educ:* Univ Bonn, State dipl (French, English), 62; Univ Rennes, PhD(stylistics), 61. *Prof Exp:* Asst Ger, Lycee Garcons, Rennes, 59-60; lectr French, Univ Bonn, 62; lectr Ger, Ger Acad Exchange & prof French, Univ Cuenca, Ecuador, 62-65; dir lang dept, univ, 63-65; asst prof French, 65-67, assoc prof French & Span, 67-73, PROF FRENCH & SPAN, UNIV ALASKA, FAIRBANKS, 73- *Concurrent Pos:* Vis prof lit theory, Univ Hamburg, 76-77. *Mem:* Am Asn Teachers Fr; Am Asn Teachers Span & Port; Philol Asn Pac Coast; Am Coun Teaching Foreign Lang. *Res:* Literary theory; structural analysis of literary texts; structural approach to French syntax. *Publ:* Auth, Ensayo de teoria literaria, Prohemio, 12/71; Quelques observations sur l'etude de la structure de l'oeuvre litteraire, Die Neueren Sprachen, 1/73; A model for the teaching of advanced syntax in a foreign language, Mod Lang J, 75; Disjointed noun modifiers in French, Proceedings Pac Northeast Conf Foreign Lang, 76; Le point de vue narratif du Nouveau Roman, Proc Pac Northwest Conf, Foreign Lang, 78; Bewusstsein und Literatur, Zeitschr fuer franz, Sprache und Literatur, Vol XC, No 2; Once Again: The French Subjunctive and the Question of Meaning, Selecta 1, 80; The French Subjunctive Revisited: Questions of Structure, Selecta 2, 81. *Mailing Add:* Dept of French & Span Univ of Alaska Fairbanks AK 99701

HOLLERER, WALTER FRIEDRICH, b Sulzbach-Rosenberg, Ger, Dec 19, 22; m 65; c 2. GERMAN LANGUAGE & LITERATURE. *Educ:* Univ Erlangen, Dr phil, 49; Dr habil, Univ Frankfurt AM, 58. *Prof Exp:* Dozent, German Lit, Univ Frankfurt AM, 58-59 & Univ Munster, 59; PROF GER & COMP LIT, TECH UNIV WEST BERLIN, 59-; PROF GER & COMP LIT, UNIV ILL, URBANA-CHAMPAIGN, 73- *Concurrent Pos:* Actg dir, Lit Colloquium, Berlin, 63- *Honors & Awards:* Fontane Prize, Akademie der künste, West Berlin, 66; Merck Prize, Akademie Sprache & Dichtkunst, Darmstadt, 75. *Mem:* Akademie fur Sprache und Dichtkunst; Pen-Club, Bundesrepublik Deutschland. *Res:* Modern comparative literature; German literature of the 19th and 20th century; Jean Paul. *Publ:* Die Elephantenuhr (novel), 73; Hier, wo die Welt anfing, 74; Geschichte, die nicht im Geschichtsbuch steht, 76; Trotz allem die schonste Gegend der Welt, 77; Alle vogel alle (play), 78; ed, Akzente Zeitschrift für Dichtung; Sprache im technischen Zeitalter; Übern Damm und lurch die Dörfer (essays), 78. *Mailing Add:* Dept German Univ Ill Urbana IL 61801

HOLLIDAY, VIVIAN LOYREA, b Manning, SC, Feb 25, 35. CLASSICS, ANCIENT HISTORY. *Educ:* Winthrop Col, AB, 57; Univ Mo, MA, 59; Univ NC, PhD(classics), 61. *Prof Exp:* Instr classics, 61-63, from asst prof to assoc prof, 63-69, AYLESWORTH PROF LATIN, COL WOOSTER, 69-, DEAN FAC, 77- *Concurrent Pos:* Mem managing comt, Am Sch Class Studies, Athens, 67. *Mem:* Am Philol Asn; Am Inst Archaeol. *Res:* Republican Rome; comparative literature; modern Greek literature. *Publ:* Auth, Pompey in Cicero's Letters and Lucan's Civil War, Mouton, The Hauge, 69; Kazantzakis, Odyssey, Neo-Hellenika, Vol III, 78; Jos Satisfaction for the Faculty, Academic Job Satisfaction: Varieties and Values, 80. *Mailing Add:* Dept of Classics Col of Wooster Wooster OH 44691

HOLLOWAY, JAMES EDWARD, JR, b Seattle, Wash, Oct 14, 42; m 64. SPANISH AMERICAN LITERATURE. *Educ:* Univ Northern Colo, BA, 64; Univ Wyo, MA, 68; Duke Univ, PhD(Romance lang), 75. *Prof Exp:* Asst prof Span, Univ Va, 72-74; asst prof, 75-80, PROF SPAN, DALHOUSIE UNIV, 80- *Concurrent Pos:* Mellon fel, Duke Univ, 80-81; Soc Sci & Humanities Res Coun Can leave fel, 82-83. *Mem:* MLA; Asoc Can Hispanistas; Am Asn Teachers Span & Port; Ctr Inter-Am Rel. *Res:* Jorge Luis Borges; contemporary Spanish-American prose. *Publ:* Auth, Lope's Neoplatonism: La Dama Boba, Bull Hisp Studies, 72; Everness: Una Clave para el Mundo Borgiano, Rev Iberoam, 7-12/77; Anatomy of Borges' El Acercamiento a Almotaism, Revista Canadiense de Estudios Hispanicos, Vol V, 80. *Mailing Add:* Dept of Span Dalhousie Univ Halifax NS B3H 3J5 Can

HOLM, JOHN ALEXANDER, b Jackson, Mich, May 16, 43. LINGUISTICS, ENGLISH. *Educ:* Univ Mich, BA, 65; Columbia Univ, MA, 68; Univ London, PhD(ling), 78. *Prof Exp:* Instr English & ling, Univ los Andes, Bogota, 65-66; lectr English, Volkshochschule Zürich, 69-70; instr, Int Inst, Detroit, 70-71; instr English & Ger, Detroit Inst Technol, 71-73; instr English, Kol Sarnen, Switz, 73-75; lectr Engl ling & Ger, Col Bahamas, Nassau, 78-80; ASST PROF ENGLISH, HUNTER COL, CITY UNIV NEW YORK, 80- *Mem:* Soc Caribbean Ling; Ling Soc Am; Am Dialect Soc; Dict Soc North Am. *Res:* The interrelationship of American Black English, creole and West African languages; lexicography; sociolinguistic history. *Publ:* Auth, Copula variability on the Afro-American continuum, Soc Caribbean Ling, Georgetown, Guyana, 76; The Creole copula that highlighted the world, In: Perspectives on American English, Mouton, 80; African features in white Bahamian English, English World-Wide, 1:1; Sociolinguistic history and the Creolist, In: Historicity and Variation in Creole Studies, Karoma Press, 81; ed & contribr, Central American English: Creole Texts from the Western Caribbean, Groos Verlag, Heidelberg, 82; auth, The Creole English of Nicaragua's Miskito Coast, Univ Microfilms Int, 82; coauth (with A Shilling), Dict of Bahamian English, Lexik House Publ, 82; auth, Creole Languages, Lang Surv Ser, Cambridge Univ Press (in prep). *Mailing Add:* Dept of English Hunter Col New York NY 10021

HOLM, LYDIA, b Howard, SDak, Dec 1, 05. SPANISH, LATIN. *Educ:* Sioux Falls Col, BA, 26; State Univ Iowa, MA, 34, PhD(Span), 47. *Prof Exp:* Asst dir English & educ, Col Bautista, Managua, Nicaragua, 36-39; asst prof Span, Bucknell Univ, 47-48; asst prof, Denison Univ, 48-53; asst prof & dean of women, Eastern Wash Col Educ, 54-56; chmn dept foreign lang, Glenbrook High Sch, Ill, 56-65; prof & chmn dept foreign lang, Ill Wesleyan Univ, 65-71; RETIRED. *Concurrent Pos:* Evaluator, MLA Selective Materials for Sec Schs, 61-64. *Mem:* MLA; Cent States Mod Lang Teachers Asn; Am Asn Teachers Span & Port (third vpres, 61-62, second vpres, 62-63, first vpres, 63-64). *Res:* Spanish American literature; teaching of foreign languages. *Publ:* Auth, How do you rate?, 9/63 & coauth, American Association of Teachers of Spanish and Portuguese committee report on articulation in Illinois, 5/65, Hispania; Foreign Languages and the Schools, W C Brown, 67. *Mailing Add:* 4538 Fourth St NE Minneapolis MN 55421

HOLMES, GLYN, b Sheffield, England, Mar 25, 45; Can citizen; m 67; c 3. FRENCH. *Educ:* Leeds Univ, Eng, BA, 67, PhD(French), 75. *Prof Exp:* Lectr French, 69-74, asst prof, 74-81, ASSOC PROF FRENCH, UNIV WESTERN ONT, 81-, ACAD DIR, LANG LABS, 77- *Mem:* Am Asn Teachers of Fr; Nat Asn of Learning Lab Dir; Ont Mod Lang Teachers Asn; Am Coun Teaching Foreign Lang; Asn Develop Comput-Based Instructional Systs. *Res:* Educational technology; computer-assisted learning; language teaching and learning. *Publ:* Auth, The problem of Anglicized French at the university, Can Mod Lang Rev, 33: 520-31; The use of the humorist in the language laboratory, Mod Lang J, 64.2: 197-202; Serving learner needs, System, 9-2: 125-32; The evolving case for computers in the study of modern languages, ALLC Jour, 1/80; A contextualized vocabulary learning drill, Computers and the Humanities, 14: 105-11; Video--aided written/oral assignments, Foreign Lang Annals, 14: 325-31; Second language learning and computers, Can Mod Lang Rev, summer 82; Courseware design: Exploiting the colour micro, Computers and Education, summer 82. *Mailing Add:* Dept of French Univ of Western Ont London ON N6A 5B8 Can

HOLOKA, JAMES PAUL, b Rochester, NY, Jan 19, 47; m 68; c 2. CLASSICAL LANGUAGES & LITERATURES. *Educ:* Univ Rochester, BA, 69; State Univ NY, Binghamton, MA, 72; Univ Mich, PhD(comp lit), 74. *Prof Exp:* Lectr, 74-76, asst prof, 76-81, ASSOC PROF CLASSIC & HUMANITIES, EASTERN MICH UNIV, 81- *Mem:* Am Philol Asn; Class Asn Middle West & South; Am Class League. *Res:* Greek literature, especially Homer; Latin literature, especially Virgil and Catullus; epic tradition: Homer, Virgil, Dante, Milton. *Publ:* Auth, Homeric originality: A survey, Class World, 66: 257-293 & In: The Classical World Bibliography of Greek Drama and Poetry, Garland Publ, NY & London, 78; Horace, Carm, 3.4: The place of the poet, Class Bull, 52: 41-46; Thick as autumnal leaves--The structure and generic potentials of an epic simile, Milton Quart 10: 78-83; Purgatorio, 9.19-39: Syncretism in the dream sequence, Class Folia, 30: 203-208; A Neoplatonic simile in Vida's Christiad, 4: 10-15, Romance Notes, 18: 243-246; Homer Studies 1971-1977, Class World, 73: 65-150; A chariot scene from Mycenae, Kadmos, 19: 38-40; Iliad 13.202-5: Aias Sphairistes, Am J Philol, 102: 351-352. *Mailing Add:* 283 Hurd St Milan MI 48160

HOLQUIST, JAMES MICHAEL, b Rockford, Ill, Dec 20, 35; div; c 3. RUSSIAN LITERATURE. *Educ:* Univ Ill, BA, 63; Yale Univ, PhD(Slavic lang & lit), 68. *Prof Exp:* From lectr to assoc prof Russ Lit, Yale Univ, 67-76; chmn slavic dept, 76-81, prof Russ lit, Univ Tex, Austin, 78-80; PROF SLAVIC & CHMN DEPT, IND UNIV, 81- *Concurrent Pos:* Morse res fel, 69-70; Inter- Univ Comt Travel Grants fel, Leningrad Univ, 69-70; Am Philos Soc fel, 78. *Mem:* MLA; Am Asn Advan Slavic Studies; Am Asn Teachers Slavic & EEurop Lang. *Res:* Nineteenth century Russian literature; theory of novel; semiotics of culture. *Publ:* Auth, Whodunit and other questions: Metaphysical detective stories, New Lit Hist, fall 71; What is a boojum? nonsense and modernism, In: Alice in Wonderland, Norton, 71; Dostoevskian standard time, Diacritics, fall 73; coauth, Man and His Fictions, Harcourt, 73; Dostoevsky and the Novel, Princeton Univ, 78; The politics of representation, In: Allegory and Representation, John Hopkins, 81. *Mailing Add:* Dept of Slavic Ind Univ Bloomington IN 47405

HOLS, EDITH JONES, b Farmington, Iowa, wid; c 2. LINGUISTICS, MEDIEVAL ENGLISH LITERATURE. *Educ:* Iowa Wesleyan Col, BA, 64; Western Ill Univ, MA, 65; Univ Iowa, PhD(ling), 70. *Prof Exp:* Instr English, Western Ill Univ, 65-66; asst prof, 70-74, ASSOC PROF LING & COORDR PROG, UNIV MINN, DULUTH, 74- *Mem:* Ling Soc Am; Am Name Soc; Int Ling Asn; Teachers English to Speakers Other Lang; Poetics & Ling Asn. *Res:* Humor; determiners; stylistics. *Publ:* Auth, Humor and calculated rule breaking, Papers Mid-Am Ling Conf Iowa, 73; coauth, Review of J L Mitchell's Computers in the Humanities, Am J Comput Ling, 74; The rhetoric of humor, Rhetoric, 78. *Mailing Add:* 408 Lakeview Ave Duluth MN 55812

HOLSCHUH, ALBRECHT, b Völklingen, Ger, Feb, 28, 37; m 68; c 5. GERMANIC STUDIES. *Educ:* Princeton Univ, AM, 61, PhD(Ger), 64. *Prof Exp:* Instr Ger, Princeton Univ, 62-64; asst prof, 64-68, ASSOC PROF GER, IND UNIV BLOOMINGTON, 68-, CHMN DEPT, 78- *Concurrent Pos:* Am Coun Learned Soc fel, 81. *Mem:* MLA; Am Asn Teachers Ger; Midwest Mod Lang Asn; Am Coun Teaching Foreign Lang; AAUP. *Res:* Twentieth century German literature. *Mailing Add:* Dept of Ger Studies Ind Univ Ballantine Hall 644 Bloomington IN 47405

HOLTON, JAMES S, b Madison, SDak, May 3, 24; m 44; c 3. FOREIGN LANGUAGES. *Educ:* San Diego State Col, BA, 48; Univ Calif, Berkeley, MA, 50, PhD, 56. *Prof Exp:* Teacher Span, Coronado High Sch, 48-49; from instr to assoc prof foreign lang, Sacramento State Col, 53-63; assoc prof, 63-76, PROF SPAN, UNIV HAWAII, MANOA, 76- *Concurrent Pos:* Consult, Calif State Dept Educ, 60; vis lectr, Univ Wash, 62-63. *Mem:* MLA; Am Asn Teachers Span & Port; Am Coun Teaching Foreign Lang. *Res:* Spanish grammar; foreign language pedagogy. *Publ:* Coauth, Portuguese for Spanish speakers, 12/54 & Placement of object pronouns, 12/60, Hispania; Sound Language Teaching, Univ Publ, 61; Continuing Spanish, Am Bk, 68; A Drillbook of Spanish Pronunciation, Harper, 68; Spanish Review Grammar, Prentice-Hall, 77; Espanol: Curso Primero, Norton, 78. *Mailing Add:* Dept of Europ Lang Univ of Hawaii at Manoa Moore Hall Honolulu HI 96822

HOLTSMARK, ERLING BENT, b Tangier, Morocco, May 19, 36; US citizen; m 61; c 3. CLASSICS. *Educ:* Univ Calif, Berkeley, BA, 59, PhD(classics), 63. *Prof Exp:* Asst prof, 63-69, ASSOC PROF CLASSICS, UNIV IOWA, 69- *Mem:* Am Philol Asn; Classics Asn Midwest & South. *Res:* Greek and Latin poetry. *Publ:* Auth, Spiritual rebirth or the hero: Odyssey V, Classics J, 2/66; Poetry as self-enlightenment: Theocritus II, Trans Am Philol Asn, 66; Quintilian on status: A Progymnasma, Hermes: Z Klassissche Philol, fall 68. *Mailing Add:* Dept of Classics Univ of Iowa Iowa City IA 52240

HOLTZ, AVRAHAM, b New York, NY, May 26, 34. MODERN HEBREW LITERATURE. *Educ:* Brooklyn Col, BA, 55; Jewish Theol Sem Am, MHL, 59, DHL, 62. *Prof Exp:* Dean acad develop, 72-80, PROF MOD HEBREW LIT, JEWISH THEOL SEM AM, 73- *Publ:* Ed, The Holy City: Jews on Jerusalem, Norton/Viking, 71; auth, Isaac Dov Berkowitz: Voice of the Uprooted, Cornell Univ, 73. *Mailing Add:* Jewish Theol Sem of Am New York NY 10027

HOLTZMAN, PAUL D, Speech Communication. See Vol II

HOLUB, ROBERT C, b Neptune, NJ, Aug 22, 49. GERMAN LITERATURE, LITERARY THEORY. *Educ:* Univ Pa, BA, 71; Univ Wis-Madison, MA, 73, MA, 76, PhD(German), 79. *Prof Exp:* Teaching asst, Univ Wis-Madison, 72-78; ASST PROF GERMAN, UNIV CALIF, BERKELEY, 79- *Mem:* MLA; Am Asn Teachers of German; Heinrich Heine Soc. *Res:* Literary theory; oppositional literature in Germany from 1750 to present; literature of the German restoration period (1815-1848), especially Heinrich Heine. *Publ:* Auth, The rise of aesthetics in the eighteenth century, Comp Lit Studies, Vol 40, No 3, 271-283; Spiritual opium and consolatory medicine: A note on the origin of opium des volks, Heine-Jahrbuch, Vol 19, 222-226; coauth, Reappropriation of the democratic bourgeois heritage: Leftist research on Jacobinism, Vormärz and Naturalism in the Federal Republic, Jahrbuch für Int German, Vol 11, No 2, 102-120; auth, Reception theory and Russian formalism, Germano-Slavica, fall 80; Heine's sexual assaults: Towards a theory of the total polemic, Monatshefte, winter 81; Heinrich Heine's Reception of German Grecophilia: The Function and Application of the Hellenic Tradition in the First Half of the Nineteenth Century, Carl Winter, Heidelberg, 81; The American reception of reception theory, German Quart, 1/82; co-ed (with Jost Hermand), Selected Works of Heinrich Heine, Continuum Press (in press). *Mailing Add:* Dept German Univ Calif Berkeley CA 94720

HOLZAPFEL, ROBERT, b Baxter, Iowa, July 2, 31. MODERN GERMAN DRAMA. *Educ:* Univ Iowa, BA, 54, MA, 62, PhD(Ger), 65. *Prof Exp:* Instr Ger, Univ Iowa, 62-64; asst prof, 64-71, asst chmn dept, 72-74, ASSOC PROF GER, UNIV NMEX, 71- *Mem:* Am Asn Teachers Ger; MLA; Am Coun Teaching Foreign Lang. *Res:* Modern German drama; history of ideas. *Publ:* Auth, The divine plan behind the plays of Friedrich Dürrenmatt, Mod Drama, 12/65. *Mailing Add:* Dept of Mod Lang Univ of NMex Albuquerque NM 87106

HOLZAPFEL, TAMARA, b USSR, Oct 25, 35; US citizen; m 60. SPANISH. *Educ:* Univ NC, Greensboro, BA, 57; Univ Iowa, MA, 60, PhD(Span), 64. *Prof Exp:* Instr Span, Univ Iowa, 63-64; from asst prof to assoc prof, 64-78, PROF SPAN, UNIV NMEX, 78- *Mem:* Am Asn Teachers Span & Port; Inst Int Lit Iberoam; MLA. *Res:* Spanish American dialectology; contemporary Spanish American novel and theatre. *Publ:* Auth, Sobre heroes y tumbas, novela del siglo, Rev Iberoam, 4-6/68; Dostoevsky's Notes from the Underground and Sabatos el tunel, Hispania, 9/68; A Mexican Medusa, Mod Drama, 69; Griselda Gambaro's theatre of the absurd, Latin Am Theatre Rev, Fall 70; El informe sobre ciegos o el optimismo de la voluntad, 72 & Soledad y rebelion en La Vida Inutil de Pito Perez, 74, Revista Iberoamericana; The theatre of Rene Marques: In search of identity and form, In: Dramatists in Revolt, Univ Tex, 76; Pueblo rechazado: Educating the public through reportage, Latin Am Theatre Rev, fall 76. *Mailing Add:* Dept of Mod Lang Univ of NMex Albuquerque NM 87131

HOLZHAUSER, EMIL K, b Frankfurt, Ger, Mar 22, 05; US citizen; m 48; c 2. CLASSICAL & MODERN LANGUAGES, PHILOSOPHY. *Educ:* Univ Dubuque, BA, BD & STM, 29; Univ Chicago, PhD, 34. *Prof Exp:* Prof lang, Dakota Wesleyan Univ, 37-43; master ancient & mod civilization, Breck Mil Sch, 43-47; prof lang & philos, Muskingum Col, 47-54; minister, Presby Church, Norwalk, Ohio, 54-58; prof lang, Carthage Col, 58-62; prof lang & philos, Findlay Col, 62-70; pres, Winebrenner Theol Sem, 70-72; dir Res Credit Ctr, Northwest Technol Col, 73-; RETIRED. *Mem:* Soc Bibl Lit; MLA. *Res:* German and Greek; Graeco-Roman philosophy and literature; religion. *Publ:* Auth, The Georgius Gospels, Univ Chicago, 37; Seven reasons for studying foreign languages, Mod Lang J, 42. *Mailing Add:* 1925 N Main Findlay OH 45840

HOMANN, HOLGER, b Haltern, Ger, Mar 27, 37; m 63; c 2. MEDIEVAL GERMAN LANGUAGE & LITERATURE. *Educ:* Univ Göttingen, PhD(Ger), 65. *Prof Exp:* From asst prof to assoc prof Ger, Johns Hopkins Univ, 65-75; assoc prof Ger, Georgetown Univ, 75-82. *Concurrent Pos:* Ed, MLN, Ger, 67-77; ed, SAR, For Lang Bk Rev, 78-80; ed, Emblematik u Literaturwissen-Schaft, JIG, 81- *Mem:* SAtlantic Mod Lang Asn; MLA; Am Asn Teachers Ger. *Res:* Medieval German literature, especially heroic epics; pagan relics in the Germany of the eighth and ninth centuries; German linguistics. *Publ:* Auth, Der indiculus superstitionum et paganiarum und verwandte Denkmäler, Dissertationsdruck, 65; Emblematisches in Sebastian Brants Narrenschiff?, Mod Lang Notes, 66; Prolegomena zu einer Geschichte der Emblematik, Colloquia Ger, 68; Studien zur Emblematik des 16 Jahrhunderts, Haentjens, Utrecht, 71; co-ed & contribr, Das Ludwigslied--Dichtung im Dienste der Politik?, In: Traditions and Transitions, Studies in Honor of Harold Jantz, Delp, Munich, 72; contribr, Reallex d germ Altertumskunde, de Gruyter, Berlin, 73; auth, Die Heldenkataloge in der historischen Dietrichsepik und die Theorie der mündllichen Dichtung, Mod Lang Notes, 77. *Mailing Add:* 6210 Green Meadow Pkwy Georgetown Univ Baltimore MD 21209

HOMBERGER, CONRAD PAUL, b Munich, Ger, Oct 12, 00; nat US; m 31. MODERN LANGUAGES. *Educ:* Univ Munich, PhD, 24. *Prof Exp:* Instr, Amherst Col, 43; master, St Paul's Sch for Boys, Concord, NH, 44; master, Trinity Sch, NY, 45-48; from instr to assoc prof, 48-64, prof, 64-69, EMER PROF MOD LANG, POLYTECH INST BROOKLYN, 69- *Mem:* Ling Soc Am; MLA; Am Asn Teachers Ger. *Res:* Modern languages and linguistics; German and American history. *Publ:* Auth, Foundation Course inGerman, Heath, Mass, 58, rev ed, 64, mod ed (in press); Die Sprache, Max Hueber, München, 61, 72; Foundation Course in German, D C Heath, 58, 64, 2nd ed (in prep); Monarch German phonetic dictionary, New Am Libr, 67; Rückschau und Fortschritt, Heath, 69; The teaching of German, In: How to Study a Language, Nat Carl Schurz Asn, 70; coauth, German for Research, Biological and Physical Sciences, 71 & German for Research, Humanities and Social Science, 73, Random House. *Mailing Add:* Furstenallee 9 Salzburg A 5020 Austria

HONEYCUTT, BENJAMIN LAWRENCE, b Cliffside, NC, Aug 30, 38; m 65; c 2. MEDIEVAL FRENCH LANGUAGE & LITERATURE. *Educ:* Wake Forest Univ, BA, 60; Ohio State Univ, MA, 62, PhD(French & Romance Ling), 69. *Prof Exp:* From instr to asst prof French, Ohio State Univ, 64-70; asst prof, 70-74, ASSOC PROF FRENCH, UNIV MO-COLUMBIA, 74- *Mem:* MLA; Am Asn Teachers Fr; Medieval Acad Am. *Res:* Medieval French lais and fabliaux; computer oriented research in literature and language. *Publ:* Co-ed, Humor in the Fabliaux: A Collection of Critical Essays, Univ Mo, 74; auth, The interaction of structure, description, and symbol in Yonec of Marie de France, Lang Quart, 74; An example of comic cliche in the old French fabliaux, Romania, 75. *Mailing Add:* Dept of Romance Lang Univ of Mo Columbia MO 65201

HONSA, VLADIMIR, b Netolice, Czech, Dec 28, 21; US citizen; m 48; c 2. SPANISH & LINGUISTICS. *Educ:* Charles Univ, Czech, AB, 47; Univ Mich, MA, 53, PhD, 57. *Prof Exp:* From instr to asst prof Span, Marquette Univ, 56-58; asst prof Span & ling, Univ Southern Calif, 58-62, acting chmn ling, 61-62; assoc prof, Ind Univ Bloomington, 62-70; PROF SPAN & LING, UNIV NEV, LAS VEGAS, 70- *Concurrent Pos:* US del, Symp Inter-Am Prog Ling & Lang Teaching, Bloomington, 64, Montevideo, 66, Mexico City, 68, Sao Paulo, 69 & San Juan, 71; Fulbright lectr, Inst Caro Cuervo, Bogota, 64-65 & Univ Uruguay, 65; prof, Latin Am Ling Inst, Montevideo, 66; Ind Univ Found grants, SAm countries, Mex, 67-68 & Panama, 68-69; consult, Tinker Found, 82- *Honors & Awards:* Hispania Award, 67. *Mem:* MLA; Ling Soc Am; Am Asn Teachers Span & Port; Philol Asn Pac Coast (secy, 59-61, chmn, 72-74); Rocky Mountain Mod Lang Asn Csecy, 73-74, chmn, 74-75). *Res:* Modern Spanish linguistics and dialectology; Spanish historical linguistics and mediaeval literature; romance general and applied linguistics. *Publ:* Auth, A study of the contamination of XIIIth century Spanish prose by dialects and foreign languages, Orbis, 61; Old Spanish paragogic 'e', Hispania, 62; The phonemic systems of Argentinian Spanish, Hispania, 65; La extension de la influencia francesa sobre la estructura del castellano medieval, Annuario de Estudios Medievales, 65; Alois Richard Nykl (1885-1958), Arabist and Hispanist: A biography and bibliography, Orbis, 67; Clasificacion de los dialectos espanoles de America y la estructura de los dialectos de Colombia, Actas del Simposio de Montevideo, Mexico Ed Galache, 75; co-ed, Papers on Linguistics and Child Language: Ruth Hirsch Weir Memorial Volume, The Hague, Mouton, 78; auth, A Grammar of Old Spanish, Based on a Critical Edition and Linguistic Study of L gran conquesta de Ultramar, the Medieval Spanish Chronicle of the Crusades, Bk 4, Chaps 126-193, Peter Lang, Bern (in press). *Mailing Add:* Dept of Foreign Lang Univ of Nev Las Vegas NV 89154

HOOK, DONALD DWIGHT, b Charlotte, NC, Dec 16, 28; m 54; c 2. LINGUISTICS, GERMAN. *Educ:* Emory Univ, BA, 50; Duke Univ, MA, 58; Brown Univ, PhD(ling), 61. *Prof Exp:* Asst, Univ NC, 57-58; asst, Brown Univ, 58-60; from asst prof to assoc prof, 61-68, PROF GER & LING, TRINITY COL, CONN, 78-, CHMN DEPT MOD LANG & LIT, 77- *Concurrent Pos:* Vis assoc prof, Chadron State Col, 66 & Cent Conn State Col,

67; lectr, St Joseph Col, Conn 67-68. *Mem:* Am Asn Teachers Ger; MLA; AAUP. *Res:* Gothic and other Germanic languages; pedagogy; sociolinguistics. *Publ:* Coauth, Fahrt ins Weiss-Blaue, Harrap, 70; Conversational German One, 70, 2nd ed, 76, Stimmen aus deutschen Landen, 72 & Intermediate Conversational German, 73, Van Nostrand; contribr, Kultur und Alltag, Scribner, 73; Book of Insults & Irreverent Quotations, 80. *Mailing Add:* Dept Mod Lang & Lit Trinity Col Hartford CT 06106

HOOK, JULIUS N, b Bunker Hill, Ill, Dec 25, 13. ENGLISH. *Educ:* Univ Ill, AB, 33, AM, 34, PhD, 41. *Prof Exp:* Teacher high sch, Ill, 34-36; assoc prof English, Minn State Teachers Col, Mankato, 41-46; from assoc prof to prof English & coun teacher educ, 46-71, dir, English Curric Studies Ctr, 64-69, EMER PROF ENGLISH UNIV ILL, URBANA-CHAMPAIGN, 71- *Concurrent Pos:* Coordr, Proj English, US Off Educ, 62-63. *Honors & Awards:* Distinguished Lectr Award, NCTE, 67; Ill Author of the Year, Int Asn Teachers English, 81. *Mem:* NCTE (exec secy, 53-60). *Res:* History of English language; teaching of high school English; family names. *Publ:* Auth, The Story of American English, Harcourt, 72; History of the English Language, Ronald, 75; My love song, English J, 10/77; Competence in English, 77 & Two-Word Verbs, 80, Harcourt; The Grand Panjandrum, 80 & Family Names, 82, Macmillan; Teaching of High School English, Wiley, 5th ed, 82. *Mailing Add:* RR1 Box 62 Waveland IN 47989

HOOKER, ALEXANDER CAMPBELL, JR, b Detroit, Mich, Mar 24, 21; m 45; c 2. ROMANCE LANGUAGES. *Educ:* Dartmouth Col, AB, 42; Harvard Univ, MA, 47; Middlebury Col, DML, 54. *Prof Exp:* From instr to assoc prof, 50-62, chmn dept Romance lang & lit, 69-74, PROF ROMANCE LANG, RIPON COL, 62- *Concurrent Pos:* Assoc Col Midwest Cent Am fac fel, 62; Inst for Latin Am Hamline Univ fac fel, 72. *Mem:* MLA; Am Asn Teachers Span & Port; AAUP; Latin Am Studies Asn; NCent Coun Latin Am (pres, 72-73). *Res:* Contemporary Spanish-American novel. *Publ:* Auth, La novela de Federico Gambo, Plaza Mayor Ed, 71; annotator, Twentieth century literature; transl, Nueva Rev de Filologia Hisp. *Mailing Add:* Dept of Romance Lang Ripon Col Ripon WI 54971

HOOVER, MARJORIE LAWSON, b New York, NY, Feb 1, 10. GERMAN & RUSSIAN LITERATURE. *Educ:* Smith Col, AB, 30; Univ Bonn, PhD, 34; Yale Univ, MA, 62. *Prof Exp:* Instr Ger, St Xavier Col, 35-36 & Swarthmore Col, 36-38; from instr to lectr, Oberlin Col, 38-53, lectr, 55-59, from assoc prof to prof Ger & Russ, 59-76; RETIRED. *Concurrent Pos:* Campbell prof Ger & Russ, Wells Col, 77. *Mem:* MLA; Am Asn Teachers Slavic & E Europ Lang; Am Asn Advan Slavic Studies; Int Brech Soc. *Res:* Contemporary German literature; Russian theater. *Publ:* Ed, Das Tagebuch der Anne Frank, 57 & Kafka, Die Verwandlung, 59, Norton; auth, Das deutsche Drama der 60 -er Jahre, In: Revolte und Experiment, 5th Amherst Colloquium, Lothar Stiehm, Heidelberg, 72; Brecht's Soviet connection: Tretiakov, Brecht Heute, 10/73; Meyerhold: The Art of Conscious Theater, Univ Mass, 74; Aufstieg und Fall Amerikas im Werk Bertolt Brechts, In: Amerika in der deutschen Literatur, Reclam, Stuttgart, 75; Alexander Ostrovsky, Twayne World Auth Ser, GK Hall, 81; Dada und das russische theater, In: Sinn aus Unsinn, 12th Amherst Colloquium, Francke Verlag, Bern, 82. *Mailing Add:* 704 Washington St Apt 2A New York NY 10014

HOPE, QUENTIN MANNING, b Stamford, Conn, Jan 25, 23; m 44; c 3. FRENCH LITERATURE. *Educ:* Harvard Univ, BA, 42, MA, 46; Columbia Univ, PhD, 56. *Prof Exp:* Instr French, Wesleyan Univ, 53-56; from asst prof to assoc prof, 56-66; chmn dept French & Ital, 65-77, PROF FRENCH, IND UNIV, BLOOMINGTON, 66- *Concurrent Pos:* Fulbright res fel, 62-63; chmn advan French test, grad record exam, Educ Testing Serv, 72-; pres, Asn of Dept Foreign Lang, 76. *Mem:* MLA; Am Asn Teachers Fr; AAUP; Am Counc Teaching Foreign Lang. *Res:* Seventeenth century French literature; language teaching; thematic studies. *Publ:* Auth, Saint-Evremond: The Honnete Homme as Critic, Ind Univ, 62; Spoken French in Review, 63, rev ed, 68 & 74; Moliere's curtain lines, French Studies, 72; Place and setting in Tartuffe, PMLA, 74; Snow imagery in love poetry, Arcadia, 78; Winter pastoral and winter reverie, Comp Lit Studies, 78; Pierre Lemoyne's glorious and lofty hymns, L'Esprit createur, 80; Snow as deformity, decoration and disguise, Orbis litterarum, 81. *Mailing Add:* Dept of French & Ital Ind Univ Bloomington IN 47401

HOPE-SIMPSON, RICHARD, b St Albans, England, May 12, 30; m 58; c 2. ANCIENT HISTORY & ARCHEOLOGY, CLASSICAL LANGUAGES. *Educ:* Oxford Univ, BA, 54, MA, 59; London Univ, PhD(class archaeol), 63. *Prof Exp:* Asst prof class archaeol, Dept Fine Art, Univ Toronto, 63-64; asst prof classics, 64-66, assoc prof, 66-77, PROF CLASSICS, QUEEN'S UNIV, ONT, 77- *Mem:* Brit Sch Archaeol Athens; Soc Prom Roman Studies; Archaeol Inst Am; Class Asn Can; Can Mediter Inst. *Res:* Prehistoric Greek archaeology; Homeric studies; Greek historiography. *Publ:* auth, A Gazetteer and Atlas of Mycenaen Sites, Inst Class Studies, Univ London, 65; coauth, The Catalogue of Ships in Homer's Iliad, Clarendon Press, Oxford, 70; Kythera, Excavations and Studies, Faber & Faber & Noyes Press, 72; auth, Leonidas' Decision, Phoenix, 72; coauth, The Minnesota Messenia Expedition, 72 & Excavations at Nichoria in Southwest Greece, Vol I, 78, Univ Minn Press; coauth, A Gazetteer of Aegean civilization in the Bronze Age, Vol I, Studies Mediter Archaeol, Vol LII, 79; auth, Mycenaen Greece, Noyes Press, 81. *Mailing Add:* Dept of Classics Queen's Univ Kingston ON K7L 3N6 Can

HOPKINS, EDWIN ARNLEY, b Hartford, Conn, Sept 22, 38; m 63; c 2. GERMANIC LANGUAGES, LINGUISTICS. *Educ:* Harvard Univ, BA, 60, MAT, 61; Stanford Univ, PhD(Ger), 67. *Prof Exp:* Instr Ger, Stanford Univ, 62-67; asst prof, Princeton Univ, 67-72; chmn dept, 73-74, PROF FOREIGN LANG LEARNING RES, SEM FOR FOREIGN LANG LEARNING RES, RUHR UNIV, 72- *Concurrent Pos:* Reader advan placement exam Ger, Educ Testing Serv, Princeton, NJ, 67 & 68; ed, Quantitative Ling. *Mem:* Am Coun Teaching Foreign Lang; Am Asn Teachers Ger. *Res:* English syntax; contrastive grammar of English and German; error analysis. *Publ:* Auth, Some thoughts on the um-zu construction and its deep structure, spring 70 & coauth, Jener in modern standard German, spring 72, Die Unterrichtspraxis; co-ed, Empirical Research on Language Teaching and Language Acquisition, 80 & Studies in Language Teaching and Language Acquisition, 81, Brockmeyer; coed & auth, The article and learner strategy in the English IL of German speakers, In: Contrastive Grammar, 82 & auth, Contrastive Analysis, Interlanguage and the Learner, 82, Karoma; Abweichende Konzessiv- und Konditionalsatze: fossilisierte Aspekte der Interimsprache erwachsener Deutscher Lerner, Linguistik und Didaktik, 82. *Mailing Add:* Sem for Foreign Lang Learning Res Ruhr Univ PO Box 102148 4630 Bochum Germany, Federal Republic of

HOPPE, MANFRED KARL ERNST, b Ger, 32. GERMAN LITERATURE. *Educ:* Univ Zurich, PhD, 67. *Prof Exp:* Asst, Univ Zurich, 62-68; asst prof, Ind Univ Bloomington, 69-70; assoc prof, 70-80, PROF GER, UNIV CHICAGO, 80- *Mem:* MLA; Goethe-Ges; Schillerr-Ges; Hofmannsthae-Ges. *Res:* German literature of the eighteenth and nineteenth centuries. *Publ:* Auth, Literatentum, Magie und Mystik im Fruehwerk Hugo von Hofmannsthals, DeGruyter, Berlin, 68; ed, Otto Ludwig: Shakespeare Studien, Reclam, 71; auth, Schillers schauspiel Wilhelm Tell, In: Tell, Werden und Wandern eines Mythos, Hallswag, Bern, 73; Wilhelm Lehmann, In: Deutsche Lyrik 1945-1975, Bagel Verlag, Dusseldorf, 81. *Mailing Add:* Dept of Ger Lang & Lit Univ of Chicago 1050 E 59th St Chicago IL 60637

HOPPER, EDWARD WARREN, b Macon, Mo, Sept 12, 39; div. SPANISH LANGUAGE & LITERATURE. *Educ:* NTex State Univ, BA, 61; Univ Mo, MA, 64, PhD(Romance lang), 73. *Prof Exp:* Instr Span, Univ Mo, 66-67; from instr to asst prof, 67-77, ASSOC PROF SPAN, UNIV NC, CHARLOTTE, 77- *Mem:* MLA; SAtlantic Mod Lang Asn; AAUP. *Res:* Seventeenth century Spanish drama; 19th century Spanish literature. *Publ:* MLA Tirso Bibliography, 78. *Mailing Add:* Dept of Foreign Lang Univ of NC Charlotte NC 28223

HOPPER, PAUL JOHN, b Croydon, England, Oct 23, 39. LINGUISTICS. *Educ:* Univ Reading, BA, 62; Wash Univ, MA, 65; Univ Tex, PhD(ling), 67. *Prof Exp:* Asst prof, Washington Univ, 67-72; assoc prof ling, 72-80, dir ling prog, 72-76, PROF LING, STATE UNIV NY BINGHAMTON, 80-, DIR LING PROG, 81- *Mem:* Ling Soc Am. *Res:* Historical linguistics; typology. *Publ:* Auth, The Syntax of the Simple Sentence in Proto-Germanic, Mouton The Hague, 72; Glottalized and murmured occlusives in Indo-European, Glossa, 73; The typology of the Proto-Indo-European segmental inventory, J Indo-European Studies, 77; ed, Indo-European and Typological Studies, J Indo-European Studies, 77; coauth (with S Thompson), Transitivity in grammar and discourse, Language, 80; ed, Tense and Aspect: Between Semantics and Pragmatics, Benjamins, Amsterdam, 82; co-ed (with S Thompson), Transitivity, Studies in the Verb-Object Relationship, Academic Press, 82. *Mailing Add:* Ling Prog State Univ of NY Binghamton NY 13901

HORAN, WILLIAM DAVID, b Jackson, Miss, July 1, 33. ROMANCE LANGUAGES, GERMAN. *Educ:* Tulane Univ, BA, 55; La State Univ, MA, 57, PhD(Romance lang, Ger), 63. *Prof Exp:* Instr & chmn foreign lang dept, La State Univ at Alexandria, 60-63; asst prof Romance lang, Millsaps Col, 63-64, asst prof & actg chmn dept, 64-66, prof & chmn dept, 66-67; assoc prof, 67-70, chmn dept, 69-76, PROF FOREIGN LANG, ST MARY'S DOMINICAN COL, 70- *Concurrent Pos:* Prof lectr, Dept Russ, Loyola Univ, La, 72-73. *Mem:* MLA; Am Asn Teachers Fr; AAUP; Am Asn Teachers Slavic & EEurop Lang. *Res:* Troubadour poetry, Provencal and Portuguese; French Romantic poetry. *Publ:* Auth, The Poems of Bonifacio Calvi, A Critical Edition, Mouton, 66. *Mailing Add:* Dept of Mod Lang St Mary's Dominican Col New Orleans LA 70118

HORGAN, DANIEL JAMES, b Jan 2, 26; US citizen; m 53; c 3. MODERN LANGUAGES, HISTORY. *Educ:* Yale Univ, BA, 47; Middlebury Col, MA, 56; Univ Madrid, PhD(hist), 67. *Prof Exp:* Instr English, 48-51, from instr to assoc prof mod lang, 53-67, asst chmn lib arts div, 67-76, asst dean col, 69-73, vpres acad affairs, 73-80, PROF MOD LANG, SIENA COL, NY, 67- *Concurrent Pos:* Lectr Span, Col of St Rose, 58-60. *Mem:* MLA; Am Conf Acad Deans. *Res:* Mexican Independence, 1808-1821; Church and state in Mexico; Spanish civilization. *Mailing Add:* Off of VPres for Acad Affairs Siena Col Loudonville NY 12211

HORN, PIERRE LAURENCE, b Paris, France, Oct 13, 42; US citizen; m 68. FRENCH, COMPARATIVE LITERATURE. *Educ:* Brooklyn Col, City Univ New York, BA, 64; Columbia Univ, MA, 65, PhD(French), 74. *Prof Exp:* Instr French, Columbia Univ, 68-69; asst prof, Clark Univ, 69-75; asst prof, 75-78, ASSOC PROF FRENCH, WRIGHT STATE UNIV, 78- *Concurrent Pos:* Contact escort & interpreter, US Dept State, 64-68; mem, bd dirs, Am Soc Interpreters, 72-77. *Honors & Awards:* Chevalier de l'Ordre Palmes academiques, French Govt, 78. *Mem:* MLA; Am Asn Teachers Fr; Am Soc Interpreters; Popular Cult Asn. *Res:* Nineteenth-century French literature; 20th century French literature; comparative novel. *Publ:* Auth, On a Whitman quotation in Les Caves du Vatican, Fr-Am Rev, winter 76; Un correspondant oublie de Victor Hugo: George J Harney, Revue Hist Lit France, 3-4/77; Isabelle: a detective novel by Andre Gide, Romance Notes, fall 77; Reflections on Mme de Renal's first name, Nineteenth-Century Fr Studies, fall-winter 77; L'epiode des banquiers dans Cesar Birotteau et Jerome Paturot, L'Anne Balzacienne, 78; Marguerite Yourcenar's Le Labyrinthe du Monde: A Modern Autobiography In: The Writer and the Past, Ind State Univ Press, 81; Victor Hugo's theatrical royalties during his exile years, Theatre Res Int, spring 82. *Mailing Add:* Wright State Univ Dayton OH 45435

HORNE, ELINOR CLARK, b Winnetka, Ill, June 22, 18; m 48; c 3. LINGUISTICS, ENGLISH. *Educ:* Denison Univ, BA, 39; Yale Univ, MA, 44. *Prof Exp:* Instr Japanese & Korean, Yale Univ, 44-50, teacher English as foreign lang, 55-64, res asst Javanese, 59-62; res assoc Javanese, Harvard Univ, 65-72; LECTR ENGLISH, DARTMOUTH COL, 77-, ACAD COUNR, 78-, ACTG DIR, READING & STUDY SKILLS CTR, 82- *Mem:* Ling Soc Am; Teachers of English to Speakers of Other Languages. *Res:*

Descriptive linguistics of Javanese language; analysis of English language for teaching purposes; the teaching of writing. *Publ:* Auth, Introduction to Spoken Korean, Vols I & II, 50, Beginning Javanese, 61, Intermediate Javanese, 63 & Javanese-English Dictionary, 74, Yale Univ. *Mailing Add:* Dept of English Dartmouth Col Hanover NH 03755

HORNER, WINIFRED BRYAN, English, Linguistics. See Vol II

HORNIK, HENRY, b Austria, Jan 5, 27; nat US. ROMANCE LANGUAGES. *Educ:* Univ Pa, BA, 49, MA, 51, PhD, 55. *Prof Exp:* Instr French lang & lit, Haverford Col, 53-56; instr, Hunter Col, 56-57; instr French & Ger lang & lit, Mass Inst Technol, 57-59; asst prof French, Johns Hopkins Univ, 60-62; res abroad, 62-63; assoc prof, 64-69, PROF ROMANCE LANG, QUEENS COL, NY, 69- *Concurrent Pos:* Part-time instr, Univ Pa, 50-52, 53-54; managing ed, Mod Lang Notes, 60-62; exec off PhD prog French, City Univ NY Grad Ctr, 68-72. *Mem:* Am Asn Teachers Fr; MLA; Renaissance Soc Am. *Res:* The Hermetica in Renaissance France; concomitants of literary metamorphoses; French Renaissance and aesthetic theory. *Publ:* Auth, Le Tempe d'Honneur et de Vertus, Droz, Paris, 57; On change in literature, J Aesthet & Art Criticism, 57; Three interpretations of the French Renaissance, Studies Renaissance, 61; Rabelais and idealism, Studi Francesi, 69; The Philosophical Hermetica, Turin, Acad of Sci, 76; Studies on French Renaissance Theory and Idealism, Geneva, 81. *Mailing Add:* Dept Romance Lang Queens Col Flushing NY 11367

HORNSBY, JESSIE GILLESPIE, b Algiers, French NAfrica, Oct 18, 17; Can citizen. ROMANCE LANGUAGES. *Educ:* Univ Toronto, BA, 39, MA, 49, PhD, 56. *Prof Exp:* Intel asst, Brit Broadcasting Corp, 40-45, Ministry Info, 45-46; instr French, Univ Toronto, 47-52 & 53-56; from instr to asst prof, Univ Iowa, 55-59; asst prof, Univ Toronto, 59-60; from asst prof to assoc prof, 60-73, PROF FRENCH, UNIV IOWA, 73-, CHMN DEPT FRENCH & ITALIAN, 81- *Concurrent Pos:* Can Govt Overseas award, 52-53; Royal Soc Can publ grant, 60. *Mem:* MLA; Am Asn Teachers Fr. *Res:* French literature of the twentieth century; Marcel Proust; new novel. *Publ:* Auth, Le Tragique Dans L'oeuvre de Georges Bernanos, Droz, Geneva, 60; Bernanos, Columbia, Buenos Aires, 65; Le Nouveau Roman De Proust, L'Esprit Createur, summer 67; Monsieur Ouine: Roman Nouveau Ou Nouveau Roman?, Courrier Georges Bernanos, 2/71; Vide Spirituel et Technique Lacunaire Dans Monsieur Ouine, In: Georges Bernanos, Entre, Paris, 72. *Mailing Add:* Dept French & Ital Univ Iowa Iowa City IA 52242

HORNSBY, ROGER ALLEN, b Nye, Wis, Aug 8, 26; m 60. CLASSICS. *Educ:* Western Reserve Univ, BA, 49; Princeton Univ, MA, 51, PhD(classics), 52. *Prof Exp:* Instr Latin & Greek, 54-58, from asst prof to assoc prof classics, 58-67, chmn dept, 66-81, PROF CLASSICS, UNIV IOWA, 67- *Concurrent Pos:* Coun Learned Soc fel, 70-71; consult, Nat Endowment for Humanities, 71-72; ed, Text Book Series APA, 75-81, Am Acad Rome resident, 83. *Honors & Awards:* Ovatio, Classic Asn Midwest & South, 80. *Mem:* Am Philol Asn; Classic Asn Midwest & South (pres, 68-69); Archaeol Inst Am; Am Numis Soc; Mediaeval Acad Am. *Res:* Latin poetry; stoicism; Greek poetry. *Publ:* Auth, The Vergilian Simile as Means of Judgement, 60: 337-344, Classics J; The Armor of the Slain, Philol Quart, 4/66; The Works of Luther; Reading Latin Poetry, Okla Univ, 67; The Pastor in the Poetry of Vergil, Classics J, 1/68; Patterns of Action in the Aeneid, Univ Iowa, 70. *Mailing Add:* Dept Classics Univ Iowa Iowa City IA 52242

HORNSTEIN, NORBERT R, b Montreal, Que, Dec 29, 51; m 79. PHILOSOPHY, LINGUISTICS. *Educ:* McGill Univ, BA, 75; Harvard Univ, PhD(philos), 79. *Prof Exp:* Mellon fel humanities, 79-81, ASST PROF PHILOS, COLUMBIA UNIV, 81- *Mem:* Am Philos Asn. *Res:* Philosophy of language; linguistic theory; ethics and political philosophy. *Publ:* Auth, Sand the X Concentia, Ling Analysis, 76; Toward a theory of tense, 77 & coauth, Trace theory and P Maerent, 79, Ling Theory; On some supposed contributions of artificial intellignece to the scientific theory language, Cognition, 79; Case theory and preposition stranding, Ling Inquiry, 80; co-ed, Explanation in Linguistics, Longmans, 81; auth, Foundationalism and the indeterminancy of Trans Kitica, Social Res, 82; The problem of meaning in natural language, In: Explanation in Linguistics, Longmans, 82. *Mailing Add:* Philos Dept Columbia Univ New York NY 10027

HOROWITZ, LOUISE KAHAN, b New York, NY, Dec 20, 45; m 70. FRENCH LITERATURE. *Educ:* Univ Mich, AB, 67; NY Univ, MA, 69; City Univ New York, PhD(French lit), 73. *Prof Exp:* Asst prof French, Univ Rochester, 73-77; asst prof, 77-80, ASSOC PROF FRENCH, RUTGERS UNIV, 80- *Concurrent Pos:* Am Coun Learned Socs res fel, 76. *Mem:* Am Asn Teachers French; MLA; NAm Soc Seventeenth- Century French Lit; Soc Professeurs Fr Amerique; Northeast Mod Lang Asn. *Res:* Seventeenth century French literature; surrealism. *Publ:* Auth, Eluard's postcards, Dada-Surrealism, 75; La Bruyere: The limits of characterization, Fr Forum, 5/76; Love and Language: A Study of the Classical French Moralist Writers, Ohio State Univ, 77; Justice for dogs: The triumph of illusion in Racine's Les Plaideurs, Fr Rev, 12/78; The Correspondence of Mme de Seuigne: Letters or Belles-Lettres, Fr Forum, 1/81; Honore d'Wife, Twayne (in press). *Mailing Add:* Dept of French Rutgers Univ 406 Penn St Camden NJ 08102

HORRY, RUTH NAOMI, b Bryan, SC. FRENCH LITERATURE. *Educ:* Talladega Col, AB, 36; Howard Univ, MA, 37; NY Univ, PhD(French), 48. *Prof Exp:* Instr French & Span, Rust Col, 38; instr & chmn dept, Allen Univ, 39-49; prof French, NC Cent Univ, 49-79; RETIRED. *Concurrent Pos:* Ford Found fel, Univ Chicago, Univ Paris, 53-54 & Univ NC-Duke Coop rog Humanities, 64-65. *Mem:* MLA; Am Asn Teachers Fr; Col Lang Asn (pres, 71-73); Paul Claudel Soc. *Res:* Nineteenth and 20th century French literature; Black poets of French expression. *Publ:* Auth, Claudel's Tete d'Or, French Rev, 1/62; Paul Claudel and Saint-John Perse, Univ NC, 71; The uses of scholarship, 6/72 & The teacher as futurist, 9/73, CLA J. *Mailing Add:* 211 Pekoe Ave Durham NC 27707

HORSLEY, RITTA JO, US citizen. GERMAN LANGUAGE & LITERATURE. *Educ:* Radcliffe Col, AB, 62; Harvard Univ, MA, 64, PhD(Ger lang & lit), 70. *Prof Exp:* Asst prof Ger, 69-76, assoc dean spec prog & interdisciplinary studies, Col Arts & Sci, 76-77, ASSOC PROF GER, UNIV MASS, BOSTON, 76- *Mem:* Am Asn Teachers Ger; MLA; Women in Ger. *Res:* Age of Goethe; 20th century German fiction; women in literature. *Mailing Add:* Dept of Ger Univ of Mass Harbor Campus Boston MA 02125

HORTON, MARGARET, b Plumerville, Ark, Nov 11, 12. ROMANCE LANGUAGES. *Educ:* Ark State Teachers Col, BSE, 35; Univ NC, AM, 45. *Prof Exp:* Teacher high sch, Ark, 35-39, SC, 39-43; teaching fel Romance lang, Univ NC, 44-45; instr French & Span, Salem Col, 45-48; from asst prof to assoc prof, 48-76, prof, 76-80, EMER PROF FRENCH & SPAN, ERSKINE COL, 80- *Honors & Awards:* Southern Fels Fund Award, Laval Univ, 56. *Mem:* SAtlantic Mod Lang Asn; Am Asn Teachers Span & Port. *Res:* Beginning and intermediate French and Spanish; elements of Romanticism, Parnassianism and Impressionism in the poetry of Albert Samain. *Mailing Add:* Dept of Mod Lang Erskine Col Due West SC 29639

HORVATH, VIOLET M, b New York, NY, July 5, 24. FRENCH & ITALIAN LITERATURE. *Educ:* Stanford Univ, BA, 53; Sorbonne, Deg Sup, 54; Radcliffe-Harvard Univ, MA, 57; Columbia Univ, PhD(French), 67. *Prof Exp:* Instr French, Tex Tech Col, 56-59; lectr French & Span, Bronx Community Col, 59-60; from lectr to instr, Baruch Sch Bus, 60-68; asst prof French, Span & Ital, 68-70, assoc prof Romance lang, 76-80, PROF FRENCH, SPAN & ITAL, BARUCH COL, 70-, CHMN DEPT, 69- *Concurrent Pos:* Mem Fr Inst & Alliance Francaise. *Mem:* MLA; Malraux Soc; Am Asn Teachers Fr. *Res:* Andre Malraux; contemporary French theatre and literature. *Publ:* Auth, Andre Malraux: The Human Adventure, NY Univ & Univ London, 69; Alba della Fazia's Jean Anouilh, J Mod Lit, 71. *Mailing Add:* Dept of Romance Lang Baruch Col New York NY 10010

HORVAY, FRANK DOMINIC, b Budapest, Hungary, July 2, 16; US citizen; m 44; c 2. FOREIGN LANGUAGES. *Educ:* Univ Ala, BA, 39, MA, 40; Wash Univ, PhD, 49. *Prof Exp:* Prof Latin & soc sci, Jefferson Mil Col, 42-43; assoc prof Ger, Wabash Col, 47-52; prof Ger & head dept foreign lang, Ill State Univ, 60-64; prof Ger & head dept, Heidelberg Col, 64-81. *Mem:* MLA; AAUP; Am Asn Teachers Ger; Am Coun Teaching Foreign Lang. *Res:* Nineteenth and twentieth century German literature; Austrian literature; foreign language education at college level. *Publ:* Auth, Goethe and Grillparzer, Ger Rev, 50; Grillparzer as a critic of European literature, Studies Ger Lang & Lit, 63; Attempt of relevance in discussing Goethe's Faust, Unterrichtspraxis, 71. *Mailing Add:* Dept of Ger Heidelberg Col Tiffin OH 44883

HORWATH, PETER, b Petrovgrad, Yugoslavia, June 27, 29; US citizen; c 3. NINETEENTH CENTURY GERMAN LITERATURE, AUSTRIAN LITERATURE. *Educ:* Ind Univ, BA, 52, MA, 53; Univ Mich, PhD(Ger), 59. *Prof Exp:* From asst prof to assoc prof Ger, Univ Ariz, 60-67; from assoc prof to prof Ger & humanities, Prescott Col, 67-73; assoc prof, 73-76, PROF GER, ARIZ STATE UNIV, 76- *Concurrent Pos:* Actg chair, Dept Foreign Lang, summer & fall, 81. *Mem:* MLA; Am Asn Teachers Ger; Am Soc Eighteenth-Century Studies; Int Fedn Teachers Mod Lang & Lit. *Publ:* Auth, Arthur Schnitzlers Professor Bernhardi: Eine Studie ueber Person und Tendenz, Lit und Kritik, 67; Auf den Spuren Vouets, Teniers und Rephaels in Kleists Werk, Sem, 69; Ueber den Fatalismus in Clemens Brentanos Geschichte vom braven Kasperl . . ., Ger Quart, 71; Zur Namengebung des nussbraunen Mädchens in Wilhelm Meisters Wanderjahre, Goethe-Jahrbuch, 72; Strom und Idylle bei Kleist im Spiegel seiner Briefe, Etudes Germaniques, 73; ed, Arno Holz: Deutsches Dichterjubiläum, Ardis, 77; auth, Der Kampf gegen die geistige Tradition: Die Kulturkampfliteratur Oesterreichs, 1780-1918, Peter Lang, 78; The Erosion of Gemeinschaft: German Literature of Prague, 1840-1924, Ger Studies Rev, 2/81. *Mailing Add:* Dept of Foreign Lang Ariz State Univ Tempe AZ 85287

HORWEGE, RONALD EUGENE, b St Francis, Kans, Mar 5, 44; m 70; c 2. GERMANIC LINGUISTICS. *Educ:* Univ Kans, BA, 66; Ind Univ, Bloomington, MA, 68, PhD(Ger ling), 71. *Prof Exp:* Asst prof, 71-79, ASSOC PROF GER, SWEET BRIAR COL, 79-, CHMN, DEPT MOD LANG, 81- *Concurrent Pos:* Guest lectr, Cent Va Community Col, 72-; Fulbright Sem on Ger Cult fel, 76; Sweet Briar Col res grant, 77-78, 81 & 82; Danish teacher, Gen Electric Plant, Lynchbung, 78-79; consult, Nat Endowment for Humanties grant, 79. *Mem:* Am Asn Teachers Ger; Am Coun for Study Austrian Lit. *Res:* Early New High German; German literature and German nationalism; Old Icelandic. *Publ:* Auth, Marquard von Lindau: De nabuchodonosor, Jahrbuch für internationale Germanistik, 76, 79. *Mailing Add:* Dept of Mod Lang Sweet Briar Col Sweet Briar VA 24595

HORWITZ, WILLIAM JAMES, b St Louis, Mo, Jan 10, 46; m 71. ANCIENT NEAR EASTERN CIVILIZATIONS. *Educ:* Harvard Univ, BA, 67; Yale Univ, MPhil, 69, PhD (Near Eastern lang & lit), 71. *Prof Exp:* Asst prof, 71-77, ASSO ASSOC PROF CLASSICS, UNIV OKLA, 77- *Concurrent Pos:* Treas, Bridis House. *Mem:* Soc Bibl Lit; Am Orient Soc; Asn for Jewish Studies. *Res:* Old Testament; ancient languages; paleography. *Publ:* Auth, Audience reaction to Jeremiah, Cath Bibl Quart, 10/70; Discrepancies in an important publication of Ugaritic, 72, A study of Ugaritic scribal practices and prosody in CTA 2:4, 73, Some possible results of rudimentary scribal training, 74, Our Ugaritic mythological texts: Copied or dictated, 77, Ugarit-Forschungen: Int Jahrbuch Altertumskunde Syrien-Palästinas; The significance of the Rephaim, J Northwest Semitic Lang, VII, 78; The Ugaritic Scribe, Schaeffer Festschrift: Ugarit Forschungen, 11/79; contribr, Motifs (part of chap), In: Ras Shamra Parallels, Vol 4, Pontifical Biblical Inst (in press). *Mailing Add:* Dept of Classics Univ of Ila Norman OK 73019

HOSTETTLER, AGNES FREUDENBERG, b Mar 13, 18; US citizen; m 42; c 5. GERMAN LANGUAGE & LITERATURE. *Educ:* Lenoire Rhyne Col, BA, 61; Middlebury Col, MA, 63, DML(Ger), 71. *Prof Exp:* Asst prof Ger, Queens Col, NC, 63-72, assoc prof Ger & folklore, 72-76; chmn dept foreign lang, Carmel Acad, NC, 76-78; assoc prof Ger, Univ NC, Charlotte, 77-79; lectr, Winthrop Col, 79-80; LECTR, EAST CAROLINA UNIV, 80- *Honors & Awards:* Order of Knights of WGer, 79. *Mem:* Am Asn Teachers Ger; Am Folklore Soc; Swiss-Am Hist Soc. *Res:* European folklore especially German, Swiss and Austrian; German literature of the 19th and 20th century. *Publ:* Auth, Symbolic Tokens in a Returned Lover Ballad, Western Folklore, 1/73; Christmas Baking in Southern Germany and Switzerland, NC Folklore, J/11/73; The Natives Costumes of the Oberwallis in Woman and Folklore, Univ Tex, 75. *Mailing Add:* Box 280 Route 13 Statesville NC 28677

HOUGH, JOHN NEWBOLD, b New York, NY, Nov 10, 06; m 30; c 2. CLASSICAL PHILOLOGY. *Educ:* Dartmouth Col, AB, 27; Princeton Univ, AM, 28, PhD, 31. *Prof Exp:* Instr Greek & Latin, Dartmouth Col, 28-29; from instr to assoc prof classic lang, Ohio State Univ, 31-45, prof 46; prof, 46-72, EMER PROF CLASSICS, UNIV COLO, 72- *Concurrent Pos:* Fulbright prof, Univ Sydney, 52; vis prof, Univ SFla, 71 & Univ Va, 73-74. *Mem:* Am Philol Asn; Classic Asn Mid W & S (secy-treas, 51-59, pres, 61). *Res:* Roman comedy; ancient history. *Publ:* Auth, The composition of the Pseudolus of Plautus; Scientific terminology. *Mailing Add:* 250 Ponca Pl Boulder CO 80303

HOULIHAN, KATHLEEN, US citizen. LINGUISTICS, HISPANIC LINGUISTICS. *Educ:* Univ Tex, Austin, BA, 69, PhD(ling), 75. *Prof Exp:* Instr, 72-75, asst prof, 75-79, ASSOC PROF LING, UNIV MINN, 79- *Concurrent Pos:* Vis scholar, Univ Calif, Los Angeles, 80-81. *Mem:* Ling Soc Am; Acoust Soc Am; Acad Forensic Appln Commun Sci; Am Asn Phonetic Sci; Int Soc Phonetic Sci. *Res:* Phonology; phonological universals; phonetics. *Publ:* Coauth, Syllable shaping in Lapp, From Soundstream to Discourse, 72; auth, On a universal rule for syllabic segments, 73 & coauth, Phonological markedness and neutralization rules, 77, Minn Working Papers Ling & Philos Lang; auth, On aspiration and deaspiration processes, Current Themes Ling, 77; co-ed, Proceedings of the 1976 Mid-America Linguistics Conference, Univ Minn, 77; coauth, Functionally-constrained phonology, Current Approaches to Phonological Theory, 78; auth, The effect of disguise on speaker identification from sound spectrograms, Current Issues in Phonetic Sci, 79; On assimilatory and non-assimilatory phonological rules, Glossa, 79. *Mailing Add:* Dept Ling Univ Minn Minneapolis MN 55455

HOUPERT, JEAN, b Paris, France, May 29, 07; Can citizen; m 37; c 5. FRENCH. *Educ:* Univ Ill, BA, 33, MA, 34; Univ Montreal, DLitt, 43. *Prof Exp:* Instr French, Morgan Park Mil Acad, Chicago, 30-31; lectr, Univ Toronto, 35-43; from asst prof to prof & head dept, Univ Montreal, 43-62, dir exten, 62-67; dean arts, Univ Sherbrooke, 67-72; RETIRED. *Mem:* Union des Alliances Francaises Can (vpres, 66-69); Academie Nationale of Metz. *Res:* French literature of the 19th century, especially Maurice Barres and Francois de Curel; history of Lorraine. *Publ:* Auth, La Prevote D'Insming Au Lendemain De La Guerre De Trente Ans, Naaman, Sherbrooke, 74; The Houppert Family in America, 80. *Mailing Add:* C P 493 Sutton PQ J0E 2K0 Can

HOUSEHOLDER, FRED WALTER, JR, b Tex, Feb 1, 13; m 35; c 2. CLASSICS, GENERAL LINGUISTICS. *Educ:* Univ Vt, AB, 32; Columbia Univ, AM, 34, PhD, 41. *Prof Exp:* Lectr, Columbia Univ, 38-46; assoc prof, Allegheny Col, 46-48; from asst prof to assoc prof, 48-56, prof, 56-65, chmn ling, 59-62, acting chmn classics, 62-63, acting chmn ling, 68-69, RES PROF CLASSICS & LING, IND UNIV, BLOOMINGTON, 65-, CHMN LING, 74- *Concurrent Pos:* Vis asoc prof, Cornell Univ, 55-56; vis prof ling, Univ Mich, 58, Univ Hawaii, 65-66 & Univ Colo, 70; Guggenheim fel, Eng & Greece, 58-59; gen ed, Cambridge Studies Ling, Cambridge Univ Press, 69- *Mem:* Am Philol Asn; fel AAAS; Ling Soc Am; Int Phonetic Asn; Am Asn Phonetic Sci. *Res:* Structure of Greek, Latin, Azerbaijani, Turkish and English; acoustic phonetics; linguisitic theory. *Publ:* Auth, Linguistic Speculations, Cambridge Univ, 71; coauth, Universe-scope relations in Chinese and Japanese, Hawaiian Asn Lang Teachers J, 71; ed, Syntactic Theory 1, Structuralist, Penguin, 72; auth, The principal step in linguistic change, Lang Sci, 72; coauth, Greek: A Survey of Recent Work, Mouton, The Hague, 73; auth, On arguments from asterisks, Found Lang, 73. *Mailing Add:* Dept of Ling Lindley Hall Ind Univ Bloomington IN 47401

HOUSTON, GEORGE WOODARD, b New York, NY, Nov 15, 41; m 62; c 2. LATIN LITERATURE, ROMAN HISTORY. *Educ:* Haverford Col, AB, 63; Univ NC, Chapel Hill, PhD(classics), 71. *Prof Exp:* From instr to asst prof, 69-76, ASSOC PROF CLASSICS, UNIV NC, CHAPEL HILL, 76- *Concurrent Pos:* Dir, Class Summer Sch Am Acad, Rome, 77-79 & Vergilian Soc Study Prog, Itlay, 76 & 82. *Mem:* Am Philol Asn; Soc Promotion Roman Studies; Vergilian Soc (pres, 79-80). *Res:* Roman imperial administration; Latin prose; Roman historians. *Publ:* Auth, M Plancius Varus and the events of AD 69-70, Trans & Proc Am Philol Asn, 72; Vespasian's Adlection of Men in Senatum, Am J Philol, 77; Nonius Flaccus: A new equestrian career from Firmum Picenum, Class Philol, 77; Administration of Italian seaports during the first three centuries AD, Memoirs Am Acad Rome, 80. *Mailing Add:* Dept of Classics Univ of NC Chapel Hill NC 27514

HOUSTON, JOHN PORTER, b Wilmar, Calif, Apr 21, 33; m 59; c 2. FRENCH. *Educ:* Univ Calif, Berkeley, AB, 54; Yale Univ, PhD(French), 59. *Prof Exp:* Instr French, Yale Univ, 58-62; from asst prof to assoc prof, 62-69, PROF FRENCH, IND UNIV, BLOOMINGTON, 69- *Concurrent Pos:* Morse fel, Yale Univ, 61-62. *Mem:* MLA. *Res:* Nineteenth century literature. *Publ:* Auth, The Design of Rimbaud's Poetry, Yale Univ, 63; The Demonic Imagination: Style and Theme in French Romantic Poetry, 69 & Fictional Technique in France, 1802-1927, 72, La State Univ, Victor Hugo, Twayne, 74; French Symbolism and the Modernist Movement: A Study in Poetic Structures, La State Univ, 80; The traditions of French prose style: A rhetorical study, La State Univ, 82; The shape and style of Proust's Novel, Wayne State Univ Press, 82; Genera Dicendi: Rhetoric and poetry in the renaissance and seventeenth century, La State Univ (in press). *Mailing Add:* Dept of French & Ital Ind Univ Bloomington IN 47401

HOUSTON, MONA TOBIN, b New York, NY, May 20, 35; m 59; c 2. FRENCH LITERATURE. *Educ:* Barnard Col, AB, 56; Yale Univ, PhD(neoclassic dramatic theory), 64. *Prof Exp:* Instr French, Conn Col, 59-61; lectr, 62-64, asst prof, 64-75, ASSOC PROF FRENCH & ITAL, IND UNIV, BLOOMINGTON, 75- *Mem:* MLA. *Res:* Seventeenth century French literature. *Publ:* Co-ed, Genitrix, Prentice-Hall, 66; coauth, The onomastics of Pasinetti, Ital Quart, fall 66; auth, The Sartre of Madama de Beauvoir, Yale French Studies, No 30. *Mailing Add:* Dept of French & Ital Ind Univ Bloomington IN 47401

HOWARD, CATHERINE MONTFORT, b Marseille, France; m 64; c 1. FRENCH LITERATURE. *Educ:* Univ Aix-Marseille, lic, 64; San Jose State Univ, MA, 69; Stanford Univ, PhD(French), 77. *Prof Exp:* Lectr, Stanford Univ, 76-77; LECTR FRENCH, UNIV SANTA CLARA, 77- *Mem:* MLA; Am Coun Teaching For Lang; North Am Soc 17th Century Fr Lit; Centre Meridional Rencontres XVIIe Siecle. *Res:* Madame de Sevigne; epistolary genre; French women writers. *Publ:* Auth, Quelques reflexions sur les fortunes de Mme de Sevigne au XVIIe et au XVIIIe siecle, Actes de Berkeley, Papers on Fr 17th Century Lit, 15: 153-62; les fortunes de Mme Sevigne au XVIIe et au XVIIIe siecle, In: Collection: Etudes Litteraires Francaises, Jean-Michel Place, Paris, 82; coauth, Appel, Harcourt Brace, 82. *Mailing Add:* Dept of Mod Lang Univ of Santa Clara Santa Clara CA 95053

HOWARD, IRWIN JAY, b Trenton, NJ, Mar 10, 41; div; c 2. LINGUISTICS. *Educ:* Univ Hawaii, BA, 62-64; Mass Inst Technol, PhD(ling), 72. *Prof Exp:* Anthrop field res, Fiji & Rotuma, 60-61, New Guinea, 64; acting asst prof, 69-72, asst prof, 72-73, ASSOC PROF LING, UNIV HAWAII, MANOA, 73- *Concurrent Pos:* Ling res, New Guinea, 76. *Mem:* Ling Soc Am. *Res:* Phonological theory; Japanese syntax; Polynesian linguistics. *Publ:* Coauth, culture and Personality in the Pacific Islands: A Bibliography, Anthrop Soc Hawaii & Univ Hawaii Libr, 63; auth, A directional theory of rule application in phonology, Ind Univ Ling Club, 73; coauth, Recent developments in the study of the Japanese passive, In: Japanese Generative Grammar, Acad Press, 76; auth, Can the elsewhere condition get anywhere? Lang (in press). *Mailing Add:* Dept of Ling Univ of Hawaii Manoa Honolulu HI 96822

HOWARD, JOHN ANDERSON, b Phillipsburg, Pa; m 66; c 1. MEDIEVAL GERMAN LANGUAGE & LITERATURE, YIDDISH LANGUAGE & LITERATURE. *Educ:* Univ Ore, BA, 66; Univ Ill, Urbana, MA, 68, PhD(Ger), 72. *Prof Exp:* Asst prof, 74-80, ASSOC PROF GER, UNIV GA, 80- *Mem:* MLA; Yidishe Vissenshaftlekhe Organizatsie; Int Courtly Lit Soc; SAtlantic Mod Lang Asn; Medieval Inst. *Res:* Medieval German literature; early Yiddish literature. *Publ:* Auth, Ueber die Echtheit eines althochdeutschen Wiegenliedes, Studia Neophilologica, 76; Der Bärmuttersegen--Ein mittelhochdeutscher Spruch, Colloguia Germanica, 78; Bemerkungen zu einem Aspekt altjiddischer Literaturgeschichte, Archiv für das Studium der neueren Sprachen und Literaturen, 78; Ms Orient Ag 31: 'ein deitsch bet büechlin mit hebraischen buoch staben', Deutsche Vierteljahrsschrift, 78. *Mailing Add:* Dept of Ger & Slavic Lang Univ of Ga Athens GA 30602

HOWDEN, MARCIA S, b Rochester, NY. FRENCH LINGUISTICS, STRUCTURAL SEMANTICS. *Educ:* Univ Rochester, AB, 64; Middlebury Col, MA, 66; Cornell Univ, PhD(ling), 79. *Prof Exp:* Asst prof French, Tufts Univ, 78-79; lectr, Mass Inst Technol, 79-80; asst prof, Brown Univ, 80-81; ASST PROF FRENCH LANG & LING, OHIO STATE UNIV, 81- *Mem:* Ling Soc Am; MLA; Int Ling Asn; Am Asn Teachers French. *Res:* Semantics of modern French; morphological structure of modern French; word formation. *Publ:* Auth, Structure in the Lexicon: The French adjectives Neuf and Nouveau, Cornell Linguistic Contributions, Vol II: Contrib to Grammatical Studies, E J Brill, Leiden, 79; Structural analysis and text revision: A linguistic sketch of two versions of a sonnet by Charles Baudelaire, Lang and Style (in press). *Mailing Add:* Dept of Romance Lang & Lit Ohio State Univ Columbus OH 43210

HOWE, EVELYN MITCHELL, b Ilford, England, Aug 27, 15; US citizen; m 41; c 3. ENGLISH, ART HISTORY. *Educ:* Univ London, BA, 36, MA, 38; Univ Wis, PhD(English), 46. *Prof Exp:* LECTR LIT & ART HIST, UNIV WIS, 58- *Res:* Sir George Beaumont, artist and patron, 1753-1827; nineteenth century children's literataue. *Publ:* Auth, Lady Beaumont, Wordsworth's friend, Studies Romanticism, 65; Amateur theatre in Georgian England, Hist Today, 70; Amateur theatricals, Jane Austen Soc Report, 71; Coal, art, and the Beaumonts, Hist Today, 74. *Mailing Add:* Integrated Lib Studies Dept Univ of Wis 228 N Charter St Madison WI 53706

HOWE, HERBERT MARSHALL, b Bristol, RI, Mar 21, 12; m 41; c 3. CLASSICS. *Educ:* Harvard Univ, AB, 34; Univ Wis, MA, 41, PhD, 48. *Prof Exp:* Teacher, Brooks Sch, North Andover, Mass, 34-40; teacher, Pomfret Sch, Conn, 42-48; from instr to assoc prof, 48-56, chmn dept, 55-68, PROF CLASSICS, UNIV WIS-MADISON, 56-, CHMN INTEGRATED LIB STUDIES, 76- *Mem:* Am Philol Asn; Archaeol Inst Am. *Publ:* Coauth, Medical Greek and Latin & auth, Ancient Religion and the Early Church, 69, Am Printing; co-ed, Classics in Translation, Univ Wis. *Mailing Add:* Dept of Classics Univ of Wis Madison WI 53706

HOWELL, RICHARD WESLEY, b Berkeley, Calif, Sept 6, 26; m 48; c 4. ANTHROPOLOGY, LINGUISTICS. *Educ:* Univ Calif, Berkeley, AB, 49, PhD,(anthrop), 67; Univ Hawaii, MA, 51. *Prof Exp:* Asst prof anthrop, Richmond Col, NY, 67-69; assoc prof sociol, Univ Sask, 69-70; ASSOC PROF ANTHROP, UNIV HAWAII AT HILO, 70- *Concurrent Pos:* Vis assoc prof E Asian Lang, Univ Hawaii, Manoa, 75-76; vis assoc prof ling, Int Christian Univ, Tokyo, 76-77. *Mem:* Am Anthrop Asn; Southern Anthrop Asn. *Res:* Japanese ethnology; sociolinguistics; social conflict. *Publ:* Coauth, Contrasting du/Sie patterns in a Mennonite community, Anthrop Ling, 71; Theories of language acquisition, J Psycholing Res, 71; Teasing Relationships, Addison-Wesley, 73; War, Its Causes and Origins, Mouton, 75; Language in Behavior, Human Sci, 76. *Mailing Add:* Dept of Anthrop Univ Hawaii at Hilo Hilo HI 96720

HOWER, ALFRED, b New York, NY, Jan 1, 15. ROMANCE LANGUAGES & LITERATURE. *Educ:* Univ Mich, AB, 39; Northwestern Univ, AM, 40; Harvard Univ, PhD, 54. *Prof Exp:* Instr Romance lang, Rutgers Univ, 47-48, asst prof, 48-55, lectr, 55-56; mem part-time fac Span, Wayne State Univ, 61-62; PROF PORT & SPAN, UNIV FLA, 62- *Mem:* MLA; Am Asn Teachers Span & Port; SAtlantic Mod Lang Asn. *Res:* Brazilian, Portuguese and Spanish literature. *Publ:* Co-transl, A O Pereira, Marcore, Univ Tex, 70; coed, Cronicas Brasileiras, Univ Fla, 71, 6th printing, 80. *Mailing Add:* Dept Romance Lang Univ Fla Gainesville FL 32611

HOWIE, JOHN MARSHALL, b Indianapolis, Ind, Nov 7, 31; m 56; c 1. FRENCH, LINGUISTICS. *Educ:* Ohio State Univ, BA, 55; Univ Colo, MA, 59; Ind Univ, P hd(ling), 70. *Prof Exp:* Lectr French, Univ Winnipeg, 59-60; instr, Purdue Univ, 60-61; instr French & ling, Univ Mo-Columbia, 66-70, prof, 70-82. *Mem:* Am Asn Teachers Fr; Asn Comput Ling; Int Soc Phonetic Sci. *Res:* Linguistic phonetics; French phonetics; acoustic analysis of prosodic features. *Publ:* Coauth, An experimental study of the effect of pitch on the intelligibility of vowels, Bull Nat Asn Teachers Singing, 5/62; Acoustical measurements of distinctive vowel quantity in Malayalam, Lang & Speech, 3/74; auth, On the domain of tone in Mandarin: Some acoustical evidence, Phonetica, 74; Acoustical studies of Mandarin Vowels and Tones, Cambridge Univ, 76. *Mailing Add:* 503 Crestland Ave Columbia MO 65201

HOWREN, ROBERT, b Rome, Ga, Aug, 6, 29; m 50; c 2. LINGUISTICS. *Educ:* Wake Forest Col, BA, 50; Univ Conn, MA, 52; Ind Univ, PhD(English ling), 58. *Prof Exp:* Instr English, Wake Forest Col, 56-58, asst prof, 58-62; from assoc prof to prof, Univ Iowa, 62-76, chmn dept ling, 70-75; PROF LING & CHMN DEPT, UNIV NC, CHAPEL HILL, 76- *Concurrent Pos:* Fulbright lectr, Univ Mandalay, 60-61; Nat Mus Can res grants, 65-67; Nat Sci Found res grant, 67-69, 69-74. *Mem:* Ling Soc Am; Am Dialect Soc. *Res:* Phonological theory; northern Athapaskan languages. *Publ:* Auth, Stem phonology and affix phonology in Dogrib, Papers Fourth Regional Meeting Chi Ling Soc, 68; A formalization of the Athapaskan D-effect, Int J Am Ling, 71; coauth, Some Problems in the Syntax of the Optative in a Northern Athapaskan Language, Univ Mo, 71. *Mailing Add:* Dept of Ling 338 Dey Hall Univ of NC Chapel Hill NC 27514

HOY, CAMILLA, b Clinton, SC, Jan 3, 25. FRENCH, SPANISH. *Educ:* Univ SC, AB, 43, MA, 44; Bryn Mawr Col, PhD(French & Span), 54. *Prof Exp:* Instr French & Span, Sweet Briar Col, 48-50; mem fac, St Mary's Jr Col, NC, 52-59; from asst prof to assoc prof French, Birmingham-Southern Col, 59-66; assoc prof, ECarolina Univ, 66-67; assoc prof, 67-69, PROF FRENCH, GREENSBORO COL, 69-, CHMN DEPT FOREIGN LANG, 67- *Mem:* Am Asn Teachers Fr; MLA; SAtlantic Mod Lang Asn; Am Asn Teachers Span & Port. *Res:* Twentieth century French literature. *Mailing Add:* Dept of Foreign Lang Greensboro Col Greensboro NC 27401

HOY, LOUISE PRICE, b Mullins, WVa, Nov 11, 20; m 50; c 3. FOREIGN LANGUAGES. *Educ:* Duke Univ, AB, 43; Bryn Mawr Col, MA, 45, PhD, 52. *Prof Exp:* Instr Latin & Greek, Western Reserve Univ, 47-50; asst prof, 63-68, PROF CLASS STUDIES, MARSHALL UNIV, 68-, CHMN DEPT, 63- *Mem:* Am Philol Asn; Class Asn Midwest & S; Am Class League. *Res:* Politics in ancient Rome. *Mailing Add:* Dept of Class Studies Marshall Univ Huntington WV 25701

HOYT, GILES REID, b Binghamton, NY, July 28, 43; m 65; c 1. GERMAN LITERATURE. *Educ:* Harpur Col, BA, 65; State Univ NY, Binghamton, MA, 68; Univ Ill, PhD(Ger), 73. *Prof Exp:* Instr English, Jamestown Community Col, 71-73; lectr Ger, Univ Wis-Milwaukee, 74-75; asst prof, 76-81, ASSOC PROF GER, IND UNIV-PURDUE UNIV, INDIANAPOLIS, 81- *Concurrent Pos:* Nat Endowment Humanities grant-in-residence Ger, Univ Cincinnati, 75-76. *Mem:* Am Asn Teachers Ger; MLA; Int Arbeitskreis Barockliteratur; Midwest Mod Lang Asn. *Res:* Seventeenth century German literature; the German novel. *Publ:* Auth, The Development of Anton Ulrich's Narrative Prose on the Basis of Surviving Octavia Manuscripts and Prints, Bouvier Verlag, 77; Guilt in absurdity: Wolfgang Hildesheimer's Tynset, Seminar, 5/78; The Babel of genre in the 17th century German novel, Colloquia Germanica, 80. *Mailing Add:* Dept of Ger Lang & Lit Ind Univ-Purdue Univ Indianapolis IN 46202

HRUBY, ANTONIN, b Vienna, Austria, June 7, 20; US citizen; m 44; c 2. GERMAN. *Educ:* Charles Univ, Prague, PhD, 46; Univ Paris & Clermont-Ferrand, Lic es Lett, 50. *Prof Exp:* Lectr, Ger & asst dept Slavics, Charles Univ, Prague, 45-48; asst Ger, Col Colbert, Paris, 48-49; lectr, Univ Clermont, 49-51; dir studies, Free Europe Univ, Strasbourg, 52-55; from instr to asst prof, Lafayette Col, 56-61; from asst prof to assoc prof, 61-68, PROF GER LANG & LIT, UNIV WASH, 68- *Concurrent Pos:* Asst Ger, Lycee Blaise Pascal, Clermont, 49-51; res fel, Centre Nat Rech Sci, Paris, 51-52, 55-56. *Mem:* Philol Asn Pac Coast; Am Asn Teachers Ger; Int Arthurian Soc; Int Ver Germanisten. *Res:* Mediaeval literature; textual criticism. *Publ:* Ed, Critical Edition, Works of K M Capek-Chod, (4 vols), Borovy, Prague, 47-48; auth, Die Problemstellüng in Chretiens und Hartmanns Erec, Deütsche Vierteljahressehrift, 64; A quantitative solution of the ambiguity of three texts, Studies Bibliog, 65; Historische Semantik in Morungens Narzissusleid und die Interpret des Textes, Deütsche Vierteljahressehrift, 68; Der Ackermann und seine Vorlage, C H Beck, Munich, 71; contribr, The epic in med society, Max Niemeyer Verlog, 77; The Renaissance and reformation in Germany, Frederik Ungar, 77; Deutsche dit im Miffelalter, Hugo Kuhn zum Gedenken, J B Metzler, 79. *Mailing Add:* Dept of Ger Lang & Lit Univ of Wash Seattle WA 98105

HSIA, ADRIAN RUE CHUN, b Chungking, China, Nov 25, 38; Ger citizen; m 60; c 1. GERMAN, COMPARATIVE LITERATURE. *Educ:* Free Univ Berlin, PhD(English & Ger lit), 65. *Prof Exp:* Lectr Ger, Albertus Magnus Univ, 65-68; from lectr to asst prof, 68-72, ASSOC PROF GER, MCGILL UNIV, 72- *Concurrent Pos:* Can Coun res fel, 72-73, leave fel, 78-79 & res awards, Can Coun, 69, 71, 72 & 80. *Mem:* MLA; Can Asn Univ Teachers Ger; Can Comp Lit Asn (treas, 69-71). *Res:* Sino-German literary relationships; 18th and 20th century German literature; novel. *Publ:* ed, Hesses esoterisches Glasperlenspiel, Deut Vierteljahrsschrift Literaturgeschichte & Geistesgeschichte, 70; auth, Die chinesische Kulturrevolution: Zur Entwicklung der Widersprüche in der chinesischen Gesellschaft, Hermann Luchterhand, 71, English ed, Orbach & Chambers, 72, Dutch ed, Het Sprectrum, 72, Am ed, McGraw Hill, 73; Hermann Hesse und China, Suhrkamp, 74, 2nd ed, 82; La mimesis a l'epoque de l'Aufklärung, Ann de l'ACFAS, 74; ed, Hermann Hesse im Spiegel der zeitgenössischen Kritik, Francke, 75; auth, Die Eindeutschung des Kreidekreismotivs, Festschrift für Rolf Badenhausen, 77; Werther in soziologischer Sicht, Festschrift für Hermann Boeschenstein, 78/79; ed, Hermann Hesse Heute, Bouvier, 80. *Mailing Add:* Dept of Ger McGill Univ 1001 Sherbrooke St W Montreal PQ H3A 1G5 Can

HSIA, CHIH-TSING, b Kiangsu, China, Jan 11, 21; m 69; c 2. CHINESE LITERATURE. *Educ:* Shanghai, BA, 42; Yale Univ, MA, 49, PhD(English), 51. *Prof Exp:* Assoc prof English, State Univ NY Col Potsdam, 57-61; assoc prof Chinese, Univ Pittsburgh, 61-62; assoc prof, 62-69, PROF CHINESE, COLUMBIA UNIV, 69- *Concurrent Pos:* Fulbright-Hays fel, 66-67; Guggenheim Found fel, 69-70; Nat Endowment for Humanities fel, 82- *Mem:* MLA; Asn Asian Studies; Am Orient Soc. *Res:* English and comparative literature. *Publ:* Auth, A History of Modern Chinese Fiction, Yale Univ, 61, rev ed, 71; On the scientific study of modern Chinese literature, T'oung Pao, 63; The Classic Chinese Novel: A Critical Introduction, Columbia Univ, 68, Indiana Univ, 80; The travels of Lao Ts'an: An exploration of its art and meaning, Tsing Hua J Chinese Studies, 69; Pope, Crabbe and the tradition, Tamkang Rev, 71; ed, Twentieth-Century Chinese Stories, 71 &; co-ed, Modern Chinese stories and novellas, 1919-1949, Columbia Univ Press. *Mailing Add:* 420 Kent Hall Columbia Univ New York NY 10027

HSIEH, HSIN-I, b Taiwan. LINGUISTICS, CHINESE. *Educ:* Taiwan Univ, BA, 63, MA, 66; Univ Calif, Berkeley, PhD(ling), 71. *Prof Exp:* Asst prof Chinese, Univ Detroit, 70-71; asst res linguist, Univ Calif, Berkeley, 72; asst prof, 72-76, ASSOC PROF CHINESE, UNIV HAWAII, 76- *Mem:* Ling Soc Am; Am Orient Soc. *Res:* Application of logic and mathematics to linguistics; Chinese linguistics; philosophy of language. *Publ:* Auth, The psychological reality of Taiwanese tone Sandhi rules, In: Papers from the Sixth Regional Meeting of Chicago Ling Soc, 70; coauth, The time variable in phonological change, J Ling, 7 1:1-13, 71; auth, Lexical diffusion: Evidence from child language acquisition, Glossa, 6 1:89-104, 72 & In: The Lexicon in Phonological Change, Mouton, 77; A new method of dialect subgrouping, J Chinese Ling, 1 1:64-92, 73 & In: The Lexicon in Phonological Change, Mouton, 77; Time as a cause of phonological irregularities, Lingua, 33 3:253-264, 74; contribr, How generative is phonology?, In: The Transformational-Generative Paradigm and Modern Linguistic Theory, John Benjamins, Amsterdam, 75; auth, On the unreality of some phonological rules, Lingua, 38 1:1-19, 76; Set theory as a meta-language for natural languages, Papers in Ling, 13 3:529-542, 80. *Mailing Add:* Dept E Asian Lang Univ Hawaii Honolulu HI 96822

HSU, KAI-YU, b Szechwan, China, July 5, 22; US citizen; m 50; c 2. LITERATURE, HUMANITIES. *Educ:* Nat Tsing Hua Univ, China, BA, 44; Univ Ore, MA, 48; Stanford Univ, PhD(mod Chinese lit & thought), 59. *Prof Exp:* Liaison off, US Army, China-Burma-India Theater, 43-45; chief interpreter, Chinese Air Force Detachment & lang expert, US War Dept, 45-46; mil aid, Chinese Embassy, Washington, DC, 46-47; reporter, foreign news ed & assoc ed, Chinese World Daily, San Francisco, Calif, 48-52; asst analyst, China proj, Human Rels Area Files, Stanford Univ, 55-56, lectr & instr Asian lang, 56-59; assoc prof humanities, 59-63, chmn dept foreign lang, 60-65, dir area study, 63-67, chmn dept world lit, 68-69; PROF HUMANITIES, FOREIGN LANG & COMP LIT, SAN FRANCISCO STATE UNIV, 63- *Concurrent Pos:* Dir Chinese-Mandarin teaching materials develop proj, San Francisco State Univ, 61-66, Carnegie Chinese proj, 62-, foreign lang insts, 62-65, Chinese cult text proj, 66-70; ed newslett, MLA-Chinese Conf, 61-65, secy, 62, chmn, 63; Nat Endowment for Humanities sr fel, 73-74. *Mem:* Asn Asian Studies; MLA; Philol Asn Pac Coast; Chinese Lang Teachers Asn; Pac Area Intercol Coun Asian Studies; Am Coun Teaching Foreign Lang. *Res:* Modern Chinese literature and thought; journalism. *Publ:* Auth, The teacher as an architect of learning, Foreign Lang Annals, 3/70; Modern Chinese poetry, In: Ting: The Caldron, Chinese Art and Identity in San Francisco, Glide Urban Ctr, 70; Chou En-lai, Longanesi, Milan, 70 & Toko Shoin, Tokyo, 71; Asian-American Authors, Houghton, 72; From Dragon to Man, 72, Chinese Civilization, A Syllabus, 72 & Twentieth Century Chinese Poetry, Chinese ed, 72, Asian Lang. *Mailing Add:* Dept of Comp Lit San Francisco State Univ San Francisco CA 94132

HSUEH, FENG-SHENG, b Kiangsu, China, Oct 9, 31; m 65; c 2. CHINESE. *Educ:* Taiwan Univ, BA, 57, MA, 60; Ind Univ Bloomington, PhD(ling), 68. *Prof Exp:* From instr to asst prof Chinese, Univ Iowa, 66-69; vis assoc prof Chinese ling, Nat Taiwan Univ, 69-70; ASSOC PROF CHINESE LING, OHIO STATE UNIV, 70- *Mem:* Ling Soc Am; Asn Asian Studies. *Res:* History of Chinese phonology; grammar of classical Chinese; Chinese dialectology. *Publ:* Auth, Elements in the metrics of T'ang poetry, Bull Inst Hist & Philol, Acad Sinica, 71; coauth, The Lin-ch'i dialect and its relation to Mandarin, J Am Orient Soc, 6/73; auth, The P'ing-tu dialect as a variant of Mandarin, Twinghua J Chinese Studies, 6/73; Phonology of Old Mandarin, Mouton, the Hague, 74. *Mailing Add:* Dept of EAsian Lang & Lit Ohio State Univ Columbus OH 43210

HUBBARD, LOUISE JONES, b Chambersburg, Pa, Aug 10, 19; m 46. ROMANCE LANGUAGES. *Educ:* Howard Univ, BA, 40; Columbia Univ, MA, 41; Cath Univ Am, PhD(Romance lang), 55. *Prof Exp:* Instr Romance lang, Butler Col, 41-42; instr, Bluefield State Col, 42-44, asst prof, 44-49; teacher high sch, Wash, 49-62; from asst prof to assoc prof, 62-67, supvr student teaching foreign lang, 63-71, chmn div foreign lang, 68-71, PROF FRENCH, UNIV DC, 67- *Concurrent Pos:* Eugene and Agnes Meyer fel, 66; lectr, English as Foreign lang, Fulbright-Hays fel, Univ Benin, Togo, 76-77. *Mem:* MLA; Am Coun Teaching Foreign Lang; NEA; Teachers of English to Speakers Other Lang. *Res:* Contemporary French literature; foreign language teacher education; African literature of French expression. *Publ:* Auth, The Individual and the Group in French Literature Since 1914, Cath Univ Am, 55; Student teaching and the fundamental skills method force a change, Dept Foreign Lang Bull, NEA, 3/67; Modern foreign languages for the racially disadvantaged, Mod Lang J, 3/68; Aptitude, attitude and sensitivity, Foreign Lang Ann, 3/75; Foreign lang study and the Black student, Col Lang Asn J, 6/75; Women in Beti's Perpetue, Ann de l'Universite du Benin, 12/77; English teaching news from Togo, English Teaching Forum, 10/78. *Mailing Add:* Div of Foreign Lang Univ of DC 1100 Harvard ST NW Washington DC 20009

HUBBARD, THOMAS KENT, b Oklahoma City, Okla, July 19, 56. CLASSICAL LANGUAGES. *Educ:* Univ Santa Clara, BA, 75; Univ Calif, Berkeley, MA, 77; Yale Univ, MA, 78, MPhil, 79, PhD(classics), 80. *Prof Exp:* Vis asst prof classics, Bard Col, 80-81; fel, Northwestern Univ, 81; ASST PROF CLASS STUDIES, SKIDMORE COL, 82- *Mem:* Am Philol Asn; Class Asn Can. *Res:* Early Greek poetry and philosophy; Roman poetry of the Republican and Augustan periods; critical theory. *Publ:* Auth, The structure and programmatic intent of Horace's First Satire, Latomus, 80; Pindaric Haromonia: Pythian 8.67-69, Mnemosyne, 82; Catullus 68: The text as self-demystification, Arethusa (in press). *Mailing Add:* Dept of Foreign Lang & Lit Skidmore Col Saratoga Springs NY 12866

HUBBE, ROLF OSKAR, b Brooklyn, NY, Dec 3, 25. CLASSICS. *Educ:* Hamilton Col, AB, 47; Princeton Univ, AM & PhD(classics), 50. *Prof Exp:* Asst prof classics, Univ NMex, 50-53; instr, Univ NC, 53-54; instr, Univ Cincinnati, 55-56; asst prof, 56-69, ASSOC PROF CLASS LANG & LIT, UNIV MD, COLLEGE PARK, 69- *Mem:* Am Philol Asn; Archaeol Inst Am; Classics Asn Atlantic States; Am Classics League, AAUP. *Res:* Methods of teaching Greek; Greek history and civilization; Greek epigraphy. *Publ:* Auth, Decrees From the Precinct of Asklepios at Athens, Hesperia, 59; A Guide to the Grammar of Attic Greek, privately publ, 74. *Mailing Add:* Dept of Classical Lang Univ of Md College Park MD 20742

HUBBLE, THOMAS N, b Pasadena, Calif, Oct 15, 27; m 52; c 2. COMPARATIVE LITERATURE. *Educ:* Univ Southern Calif, BA, 51, MA, 54, PhD(comp lit), 62. *Prof Exp:* Teaching asst comp lit, Univ Southern Calif, 55-58; PROF COMP LIT, CALIF STATE UNIV, LONG BEACH, 58- *Concurrent Pos:* Fulbright lectr, Greece, 63-64, Tunisia, 67-68 & Univ Zaire, 76-77. *Mem:* Am Comp Lit Asn. *Res:* The work of Albert Camus. *Mailing Add:* Dept of Comp Lit Calif State Univ Long Beach CA 90801

HUBBS, VALENTINE CHARLES, b New York, NY, Dec 19, 25; m 48; c 1. GERMAN. *Educ:* Hofstra Col, BA, 50; NY Univ, MA, 52, PhD, 58. *Prof Exp:* Instr Ger, Notre Dame Col Staten Island, 52-56; instr, Hofstra Col, 53-58; from asst prof to assoc prof, 59-69, chmn dept Ger lang & lit, 71-76, PROF GER, UNIV MICH, ANN ARBOR, 69- *Concurrent Pos:* Univ Mich, Ann Arbor res fel, 62. *Mem:* MLA; Am Asn Teachers Ger. *Res:* German literature of the 19th and 20th centuries. *Publ:* Coauth, German Essays (4 vols), 64 & German in Review, 66, Macmillan; auth, Obwohl es keine Vollkommenheit gibt, Ger Quart, 68; Tieck's Romantic Fairy Tales and Shakespeare, Studies Romanticism, 69; The plus and minus of Penthesilea and Käthchen, Seminar, 70; Eichendorff's Marmorbild, Ger Rev, 77; Unified Vision, Kleist Studies, 80; Hessian Journals: Unpublished Documents of the American Revolution, Camden House, 81. *Mailing Add:* 2317 Easy St Ann Arbor MI 48104

HUBER, THOMAS, b Berlin, Ger, Mar 23, 37; US citizen; m 62; c 2. GERMAN LANGUAGE & LITERATURE. *Educ:* Univ Vt, MA, 62; Princeton Univ, MA, 64, PhD (Ger), 65. *Prof Exp:* Instr Ger, Univ Vt, 61-62 & Princeton Univ, 64-65; lectr philol, Univ Bergen, Norway, 65-66; from asst prof to assoc prof Ger, 66-77, dir studies, Sch Ger, 66-67, 69-70 & 72-73, PROF GER, MIDDLEBURY COL, 77-, DEAN, SCH GER & CHMN DEPT, 73- *Concurrent Pos:* Consult int educ, Inst Int Educ, 67-68; bd men, Coun Int Educ Exchange, 76-81. *Mem:* MLA; Deutsche Schillergesellschaft; Goethe Gesellschaft; Freies Deutsches Hochstift. *Res:* Period of enlightenment in Germany; contemporary German novel; popular European fiction. *Publ:* Auth, Studien zur Theorie des Ubersetzens, Hain: Meisenheim, 67; US Programs in Germany: Problems and Perspectives, IIE, New York; coauth, Modern German, Harcourt Brace Jovanovich, 71, 2nd ed, 78; auth, Studium in den USA, 74 & Studium in den USA--a case study, 74, aspekte, Frankfurt; coauth, Thomas Mann's Tonio Kröger, Harcourt Brace Jovanovich, 78. *Mailing Add:* Sch of Ger Middlebury Col Middlebury VT 05753

HUBERMAN, EDWARD, English. See Vol II

HUBERT, CLAIRE MARCOM, b Jacksonville, Fla, Sept 10, 35; m 57; c 4. COMPARATIVE LITERATURE. *Educ:* Duke Univ, BA, 57; Emory Univ, MA, 59, PhD(comp lit), 65. *Prof Exp:* Asst prof humanities, Oglethorpe Col, 63-64; from instr to asst prof French, 65-71, ASSOC PROF FRENCH, AGNES SCOTT COL, 71- *Mem:* MLA; Am Asn Teachers Fr. *Res:* French and English comparative literature. *Mailing Add:* Dept of French Agnes Scott Col Decatur GA 30030

HUBERT, JUDD DAVID, b Toledo, Ohio, Jan 17, 17; m 50. FRENCH LITERATURE. *Educ:* Univ Lille, France, B es L, 37; Middlebury Col, BA, 41; Columbia Univ, MA, 42, PhD, 51. *Prof Exp:* Instr French & Hist, US Merchant Marine Acad, 46-47; instr French, Rutgers Univ, 47-50; from instr to asst prof, Harvard Univ, 52-57; from assoc prof to prof, Univ Calif, Los Angeles, 57-65; prof, Univ Ill, Urbana, 65-67, PROF FRENCH, UNIV CALIF, IRVINE, 67- *Concurrent Pos:* Fulbright res fel, France, 56-57; Guggenheim fel, 60-61. *Mem:* MLA; Int Fedn Mod Lang & Lit; Int Asn Fr Studies; Soc Study Seventeenth Century, France. *Res:* Symbolist poetry; seventeenth century French drama; baroque poetry. *Publ:* Auth, L'Esthetique des Fleurs du mal, Cailler, Geneva, 53; Essai d'exegese Racinienne, Nizet, Paris, 56; Moliere and the Comedy of Intellect, Univ Calif, 62; Les nouvelles francaises de Sorel et de Segrais, Cahiers Asn Int Etudes Fr, 3/66; La Fontaine et Pellisson ou le mystere des deux Acante, Rev Hist Litteraire France, 6/66. *Mailing Add:* Dept of Foreign Lang Univ of Calif Irvine CA 92664

HUBERT, MARIE LOUISE, b New York, NY, June 25, 14. FRENCH. *Educ:* St Joseph's Col NY, AB, 36; Columbia Univ, AM, 39; Yale Univ, PhD(French), 50. *Hon Degrees:* LLD, Albertus Magnus Col, 72. *Prof Exp:* Pres, 56-71, PROF FRENCH, ALBERTUS MAGNUS COL, 42-, DIR INST RES, 72- *Concurrent Pos:* Pres, Conn Coun Higher Educ, 65-67. *Mem:* Am Asn Teachers Fr; Asn for Inst Res. *Publ:* Auth, Pascal's Unfinished Apology, Yale Univ & Presses Univs de France, 52; coauth, Pascal, In: The Seventeenth Century, Vol 4, A Critical Bibliography of French Literature, Syracuse Univ, 62; contribr, New Structures of Campus Power, Jossey-Bass, 78. *Mailing Add:* Dir Inst Res Albertus Magnus Col New Haven CT 06511

HUBERT, RENEE RIESE, b Wiesbaden, Ger, July 2, 16; US citizen; m 50. FRENCH, COMPARATIVE LITERATURE. *Educ:* Univ Lyon, BedL, 36; Columbia Univ, MA, 45, PhD, 51. *Prof Exp:* Instr French & German, Wilson Col, 45-47; instr French, Columbia Univ, 48-49; mem fac, Sarah Lawrence Col, 49-53; instr, Harvard Univ, 53-55; asst prof, Suffolk Univ, 55-56; asst prof French & German, San Fernando Valley State Col, 58-62, assoc prof French & chmn dept foreign lang, 62-65; assoc prof French, Univ Ill, Urbana, 65-66, prof, 66-67; PROF FRENCH & COMP LIT, UNIV CALIF, IRVINE, 67- *Concurrent Pos:* Guggenheim fel, 64-65; Nat Endowment for Humanities, 79. *Mem:* MLA; Am Asn Teachers Fr; Int Fed Mod Lang & Lit; Int Asn Studies Fr. *Res:* Modern Poetry; relation of literature and fine arts; surrealism. *Publ:* Auth, Le Berceau d'Eve, Ed Minuit, 57; Plumes et Pinceaux, Dervy, 60; L'Amour et la feerie chez Madame d'Aulnoy, Romanische Forschungen, 63; Chants funebres, Ed Subervie, 64; Apollinaire et Picasso, Cahiers du Sud, 66; Fromentin's Dominique, the confessions of a man who judges himself, Pac Mod Lang Asn, 12/67; Enchainement, Ed Subervie, 68; Natures mortes, Ed Oswald, 72. *Mailing Add:* Dept of French & Comp Lit Univ of Calif Irvine CA 92664

HUCK, GEORGINA M, b Jersey City, NJ, June 13, 16. GERMANIC STUDIES, ARCHEOLOGY. *Educ:* Vassar Col, BA, 37; Boston Col, PhD(Ger), 72. *Prof Exp:* Teacher, Chapin Sch, 55-65; teacher ancient hist & Ger, Abbott Acad, 65-69; instr Ger, Boston Col, 69-70, res Luther, 70-72; teacher ancient hist & Ger, Winsor Sch, 72-74; RES & WRITING, 78- *Concurrent Pos:* Mem Area Ment Health Bd, State & Fed Comn, Mass, 77- *Mem:* Am Inst Archaeol; Am Asn Teachers Ger. *Res:* Schiller; Greek influence on archaeology as evidence of ancient history; Beatrice Lillie. *Publ:* Translr, Hans Hofmann, A Painter's Primer, Metrop Mus Art, 78; auth, Wanted: no experience, Vassar Quart, winter 78. *Mailing Add:* Box 77 Barnstable MA 02630

HUCKER, CHARLES OSCAR, Chinese History & Language. See Vol I

HUDON, LOUIS JOFFRE, b Sanford, Maine, Dec 14, 17; m 48; c 1. FRENCH LITERATURE. *Educ:* Bowdoin Col, AB, 38; Yale Univ, AM, 42, PhD, 43. *Prof Exp:* Asst instr, Yale Univ, 40-42; instr, US Army Univ, France, 45; instr, Yale Univ, 46-47; asst prof Romance lang, Wesleyan Univ, 47-53; from asst prof to assoc prof French, Wellesley Col, 54-57; assoc prof Romance lang, Vanderbilt Univ, 57-61; chmn dept French & Ital, 65-67, 69-72, PROF FRENCH, UNIV NH, 61- *Mem:* Am Asn Teachers Fr; MLA. *Res:* Montaigne and the late seventeenth century in France; modern French novel. *Mailing Add:* Dept of French & Ital Univ of NH Durham NH 03824

HUDSON, ALFRED BACON, b Hilo, Hawaii, Jan 6, 32; m 56; c 2. ANTHROPOLOGY, LINGUISTICS. *Educ:* Univ Calif, Berkeley, AB, 58; Cornell Univ, PhD(anthrop), 67. *Prof Exp:* From asst prof to assoc prof anthrop, Mich State Univ, 65-71; ASSOC PROF ANTHROP, UNIV MASS, AMHERST, 71- *Concurrent Pos:* Am Coun Learned Soc fel, E Malaysia, Indonesia, 69-70. *Mem:* Fel Am Anthrop Asn; Soc Ethnomusicol; Asn Asian Studies. *Res:* Ethnology of Indonesian Borneo; ethnolinguistic classification of Bornean peoples; national language problems in multi-lingual states. *Publ:* Auth, Death ceremonies of the Padju Epat Ma'anjan Dajaks, Sarawak Mus J, 11/66; Barito Isolects of Borneo: Comparative Reconstruction and Lexicostatistics, Cornell Southeast Asia Prog Data Paper, 67; coauth, Telang: a Ma'anjan village of central Kalimantan, In: Villages in Indonesia, Cornell Univ, 67; Padju Epat: The Ma'anyan of Indonesian Borneo, Holt, 72; A note of Selako: Malayic Dayak and Lang Dayak languages in western Borneo, Sarawak Mus J, 70. *Mailing Add:* Dept of Anthrop Univ of Mass Amherst MA 01002

HUDSON, BENJAMIN F, b Selma, Ala, Aug 30, 17; m 43; c 1. ROMANCE LANGUAGES. *Educ:* Fisk Univ, BA, 46; Univ Mich, MA, 47, PhD(French), 58; Univ Paris, cert, 52. *Prof Exp:* From instr to asst prof French, NC Col, 48-59; prof mod foreign lang & chmn dept, Southern Univ, 59-61; PROF FRENCH & CHMN DEPT, ATLANTA UNIV, 61-, DEAN GRAD SCH, 71- *Mem:* MLA; Am Asn Teachers Fr; Am Coun Teaching Foreign Lang; CLA J. *Mailing Add:* Dept of French Atlanta Univ Atlanta GA 30314

HUEBERT, CATHERINE MUDER, b New Castle, Pa, July 31, 41; div. FRENCH, ENGLISH. *Educ:* Allegheny Col, BA, 63; Middlebury Col, MA, 64; Univ Pittsburgh, PhD(French), 70. *Prof Exp:* Res asst English, Shakespeare Inst, Eng, 70-71; asst prof French, New Univ Ulster, Northern Ireland, 71-72; asst prof, Grove City Col, 76-77 & Westminster Col, Pa, 77-81; ASST PROF FRENCH, GROVE CITY COL, 81- *Concurrent Pos:* Nat Endowment for Humanities fel, NY Univ, summer, 79. *Mem:* Am Asn Teachers Fr; MLA; Pac Mod Lang Asn; Am Coun Teacher For Lang. *Res:* French theatre; 17th-century French literature; 20th-century French literature. *Publ:* Auth, Racine et le Labyrinthe de Versailles, Cahiers Raciniens, spring 72; The Quest for evil: Lorenzaccio and Caligula, Romance Notes, fall 77. *Mailing Add:* 156 E Pine St Grove City PA 16127

HUEBNER, MADELENE CODINA, b Jersey City, NJ, Jan 8, 21. FOREIGN LANGUAGES, SPANISH LANGUAGE & LITERATURE. *Educ:* Mt Holyoke Col, BA, 43; Columbia Univ, MA, 47. *Prof Exp:* Commun clerk, Am Embassy, Lisbon, Port, 47-48; chmn dept mod lang & lit, 77-80, ASSOC PROF LANG, FAIRLEIGH DICKINSON UNIV, 58- *Concurrent Pos:* Ed, Acorn & Oak. *Mem:* Am Coun Teaching Foreign Lang; Am Asn

Teachers Span & Port; AAUP; MLA. *Res:* George Borrow in Spain; ornithological references in the novels of Benito Perez Galdos; modern language teaching innovations. *Mailing Add:* Dept of Lang Fairleigh Dickinson Univ Madison NJ 07940

HUELSBERGEN, HELMUT ERNEST, b Krefeld-Linn, Ger, Feb 14, 29; m 62; c 3. GERMAN, COMPARATIVE LITERATURE. *Educ:* Bethel Col, Kans, BA, 50; Univ Cologne, Dr phil(Ger & English), 56, state dipl Ger & English, 57; Staatl Studiensem Köln I, Ger, state dipl Ger & English, 60. *Prof Exp:* Eiss asst English, Univ Cologne, 57-58; instr Ger, Univ Kans 58-59; Studienreferendar Ger & English, Albertus-Magnus Gym Köln, 59-60; from asst prof to assoc prof, 60-69, asst chmn dept, 63-65, actg chmn, 65-66, chmn, dept Germanic lang & lit, 72-76, PROF GER, UNIV KANS, 69- *Concurrent Pos:* Res grant, Univ Cologne, 57, lectr, 59-60; Studienassessor, Neusprachliches Gym Porz, 60; res grants, Univ Kans, 65, 66; mem nat screening comt grad study in Ger, Inst Int Educ, 70-71, chmn, 71-72. *Mem:* MLA; Am Comp Lit Asn; Renaissance Soc Am; Am Asn Teachers Ger. *Res:* Seventeenth century literature; German-English and German-American literary relations; expressionism. *Publ:* Auth, Studien zu den amerikanischen Neologismen des 19 Jahrhunderts, Univ Cologne, 56; coauth, Alexander von Humboldt, 65 & Wagner, 65, Blaisdell; contribr, chap, In: Europäische Tradition und deutscher Literaturbarock, Francke, 73. *Mailing Add:* Dept of Foreign Lang Unif Kans Lawrence KS 66044

HUEPPE, FREDERICK ERNST, b New York, NY, July 19, 33. GERMANIC PHILOLOGY. *Educ:* St John's Univ, NY, BA, 55; Dolmetscher Inst, Heidelberg, certif, 56; NY Univ, MA, 58, PhD(Ger lang & lit), 69. *Prof Exp:* Asst prof Ger, 60-70, asst foreign studies adv, 63-69, assoc prof, 70-79, PROF GER, ST JOHN'S UNIV, NY, 79-, CHMN DEPT MOD FOREIGN LANG & CLASSICAL STUDIES, 75- *Concurrent Pos:* Mem, Inst Int Educ; pres, NY State Conf of AAUP; fel, Morgan Libr, 81- *Mem:* Am Asn Teachers Ger; MLA; Am Coun Teaching Foreign Lang; Asn Dept Foreign Lang. *Res:* Germanic linguistics; medieval German; Berthold von Regensburg. *Publ:* Auth, The Radiant Light, New City Press, 55; contribr, Faculty Unions and Collective Bargaining, Jossey-Bass, 73; Unity and Synthesis in the Work of Heinrich Heine, Lang, 79. *Mailing Add:* Dept of Mod Foreign Lang St John's Univ Jamaica NY 11432

HUET, MARIE-HELENE JACQUELINE, b St Ciers sur Gironde, France, Jan 30, 44. FRENCH LITERATURE. *Educ:* Univ Bordeaux, Lic es Lett, 64, Dipl es Lett, 65, Dr es Lett(French), 68. *Prof Exp:* Asst prof, 68-75, assoc prof, 75-80, PROF FRENCH, UNIV CALIF, BERKELEY, 80- *Concurrent Pos:* Humanities res fel, Univ Calif, Berkeley, 73-74. *Mem:* Soc Fr Etude XVIII Siecle; Am Soc 18th Century Study; MLA. *Res:* Social rise in 18th century French novels; satire and political writings in 18th century literature. *Publ:* Auth, Lecture du Paysan Perverti, Rev Sci Humaines, 10/70; Roman libertin et reaction aristocratique au XVIII siecle, XVIII Siecle, 5/74; L'Histoire des Voyages Extraordinaires: Essai Sur l'Oeuvre de Jules Verne, Minard, 73; Le Heros et son Double, Jose Corti, 75. *Mailing Add:* Dept of French Univ of Calif Berkeley CA 94720

HUEY, F B, JR, Old Testament, Hebrew. See Vol IV

HUFF, ROBERT, English. See Vol II

HUFFINES, MARION LOIS, b Chester, Pa, Oct 1, 45. GERMAN, SOCIOLINGUISTICS. *Educ:* Maryville Col, Tenn, BA, 67; Ind Univ, Bloominton, MA, 69, PhD(Ger), 71. *Prof Exp:* ASSOC PROF GER & LING, BUCKNELL UNIV, 71- *Concurrent Pos:* Nat Endowment for Humanities fel, 80. *Mem:* Am Asn Teachers Ger; Ling Soc Am; Am Dialect Soc; MLA. *Res:* Sociolinguistics; American dialects; Pennsylvania German. *Publ:* Auth, Sixteenth century printers and standardization of new high German, J English & Ger Philol, 74; OE aglaeca: Magic and moral decline of monsters and men, Semasia, 74; The original manuscript of Ulrich Schmidt: Chivalry and Peasantry of the Late Middle Ages, Gordon, 77; English in contact with Pennsylvania German, Ger Quart, 53: 352-366; Pennsylvania German: Maintenance and shift, Int J Soc Lang, 25: 43-57. *Mailing Add:* Dept of Mod Lang Bucknell Univ Lewisburg PA 17837

HUFFMAN, CLAIRE, b New York, NY; m 67. ITALIAN, COMPARATIVE LITERATURE. *Educ:* Barnard Col, BA, 66; Harvard Univ, MA, 67, PhD(Romance lang), 72. *Prof Exp:* Instr, Harvard Univ, 70-71; instr, 71-72, asst prof, 72-77, assoc prof, 77-81, PROF ITAL, BROOKLYN COL, 82- *Concurrent Pos:* Nat Endowment for Humanities fel, mod poetry, 74-75; City Univ New York fac res grant, Anglo-Ital poetry, 74 & 78; Andrew Mellon fel humanities, Anglo-Ital poetry, Harvard Univ, 77-78; vis fac fel, Brooklyn Col, 77-78. *Mem:* MLA; Dante Soc Am. *Res:* Eugenio Montale; modern poetics, 1870-1970; Renaissance literature in Europe. *Publ:* Auth, Farfalla di Dinard of Eugenio Montale, 69 & Vitaliano Brancati: A reassessment, 72, Forum Ital; T S Eliot, Eugenio Montale and the vagaries of influence, Comp Lit, 75; Eugenio Montale: Questions, answers and contexts, Yrbk Ital Studies, 77; coauth, Firenzuola, Surrey and Thomas Watson once more, Rev lang vivantes, 76; auth, Structuralist literary criticism, Mod Lang Rev, 77; Montale, Eliot and the poetic object, Ital Quart, 80; Montale and the Poetry of Occasions, Princeton Univ Press, 82. *Mailing Add:* Dept of Mod Lang City Univ New York Brooklyn NY 11210

HUFFMAN, FRANKLIN EUGENE, b Harrisonburg, VA, Jan 28, 34; div; c 2. GENERAL LINGUISTICS, SOUTHEAST ASIAN LANGUAGES. *Educ:* Bridgewater Col, BA, 55; Cornell Univ, PhD(gen ling), 67. *Prof Exp:* Interpreter French, Int Voluntary Serv Inc, Community Develop, Laos, Indochina, 56-58; teacher, Augusta County Schs, Va, 58-60; asst prof Thai & Cambodian, Yale Univ, 67-72; assoc prof southeast Asian ling, 72-79, PROF LING & ASIAN STUDIES, CORNELL UNIV, 79- *Concurrent Pos:* Guggenheim Found res fel, Mon-Khmer lang in Thailand, Laos & Cambodia, 70-71; Ford Found Southeast Asia res fel, 76; NSF res grant, 79-81. *Mem:* Ling Soc Am; Asn Asian Studies; Siam Soc; Am Orient Soc; Am Conf Teachers Uncommon Asian Lang. *Res:* Grammatical analysis of Southeast Asian languages; language textbook preparation in Southeast Asian languages; linguistic affiliation in Southeast Asian languages. *Publ:* Auth, Cambodian System of Writing and Beginning Reader, 70, Modern Spoken Cambodian, 70 & ed, Intermediate Cambodian Reader, 72, Yale Univ; Cambodian Literary Reader and Glossary, 77 & English-Khmer Dict, 78, Yale Univ Press; Intermediate Spoken Vietnamese, Cornell Univ, 80; Thai and Cambodian: A case of syntactic borrowing?, J Am Orient Soc, 73; Lexical correspondences between Vietnamese and some other Austroasiatic languages, Lingua, 43. *Mailing Add:* Dept Mod Lang & Ling Cornell Univ Ithaca NY 14850

HUFFMAN, JAMES LLOYD, American Law, Legal Philosophy. See Vol IV

HUGHES, GEORGE ROBERT, b Wymore, Nebr, Jan 12, 07. EGYPTOLOGY. *Educ:* Univ Nebr, AB, 29; McCormick Theol Sem, BD, 32, Univ Chicago, PhD, 39. *Prof Exp:* Res asst, Orient Inst, 34-42, res assoc & epigrapher, Luxor, Egypt, 46-48, field dir epigraphic surv, 49-64, from asst prof to prof, 48-72, actg field dir Sudan excavations, 61-62, dir, Orient Inst, 68-72, EMER PROF EGYPTOL, UNIV CHICAGO, 75- *Concurrent Pos:* Mem, Ger Archaeol Inst; Wilbour fel, Brooklyn Mus, 66; vpres, Am Res Ctr Egypt, 67-72; mem, Fondation Egyptol Reine Elisabeth, Brussels; mem, Smithsonian Foreign Currency Prog Adv Coun, 76-79. *Mem:* Am Orient Soc; Egypt Explor Soc, London. *Res:* Egyptian Demotic language. *Publ:* Coauth, Reliefs and inscriptions at Karnak III, the Bubastite Portal; Medinet Habu V-VII, 57-63 & The Beit el-Wali Temple of Rameses II, 67, Univ Chicago; Demotic Legal Code of Hermopolis West, Fr Inst Cairo, 75; auth, Demotic texts in the Brooklyn Museum, Brooklyn Mus, 78. *Mailing Add:* Oriental Inst 1155 E 58th St Chicago IL 60637

HUGHES, SHAUN FRANCIS DOUGLAS, b Te Puke, NZ, Oct 8, 44. MEDIEVAL ENGLISH LANGUAGE & LITERATURE. *Educ:* Victoria Univ Wellington, BA, 66, MA, 67; Univ Wash, PhD(English), 72. *Prof Exp:* Jr lectr English, Massey Univ, NZ, 67-68; teaching asst, Univ Wash, 68-71, assoc 71-72; asst prof, 72-78, ASSOC PROF ENGLISH, PURDUE UNIV, WEST LAFAYETTE, 78- *Concurrent Pos:* Vis lectr Scand, Dept Ger Lang & Lit, Harvard Univ, 78; corresp ed, Ger Lang & Lit Monogr, 78-; Am Coun Learned Soc fel, 79-80; humanities grant, Icelandic Sci Found, 80-81; guest ed, Mod Fiction Studies, 81. *Mem:* Soc Advan Scand Studies; Australian & NZ Asn Mediaeval & Renaissance Studies; Viking Soc Northern Res; Ling Soc Am; Mediaeval Acad Am. *Publ:* Auth, The last frontier: The Renaissance in Iceland 1550-1750, Parergon, 75; John Cleland's role in the history of Sanskrit studies in Europe, Archivum Linguisticum, 76; The literary antecedants of Ans Saga Bogsvergis, Mediaeval Scand, 76; The ideal of kingship in the Riddarasogur, Mich Acad, 78; Mrs Elstob's defence of antiquarian learning in her Rudiments of Grammar for the English-Saxon Tongue, 1715, Harvard Libr Bull, 79; Report on Rimur 1980, J English & Germanic Philol, 80; Maori and Pakeha behind the tattooed face: The emergence of a Polynesian voice in New Zealand fiction, Mod Fiction Studies, 81; The Anglo-Saxon Grammars of George Hickes and Elizabeth Elstob, In: Anglo-Saxon Scholarship: The First Three Centuries, G K Hall, 82. *Mailing Add:* Dept of English Purdue Univ West Lafayette IN 47907

HUGHES, WILLIAM NOLIN, b Raymond, Wash, May 21, 18; m 53; c 3. GERMAN. *Educ:* Univ Wash, BA, 41; Northwestern Univ, MA, 52, PhD(Ger lit), 55. *Prof Exp:* Personnel supvr, Boeing Aircraft Co, Seattle, Wash, 41-46; asst to labor adv, Allied Comn for Austria, 46-49; asst, Econ Coop Admin Mission to Austria, 49-50; instr, Univ Mich, 55-60; asst prof, Columbia Univ, 60-63; assoc prof, 63-66, chmn dept, 65-75, asst dean, Col Arts & Sci, 75-80, PROF GER, MICH STATE UNIV, 66- . *Concurrent Pos:* Ed, Ger Lit Sect, MLA Intern Bibliog, 81- *Mem:* MLA; Am Asn Teachers Ger; Thomas Mann Gesellschaft. *Res:* Modern literature; German literature of the 17th century. *Mailing Add:* 513 Ardson Rd East Lansing MI 48823

HUHNKE, GERALDINE MAE, b New Rockford, NDak, Oct 29, 20. SPANISH GERMAN. *Educ:* Northwest Nazarene Col, AB, 42; State Univ Iowa, MA, 48. *Prof Exp:* Teacher, High Sch, Minn, 42-46, Univ Wyo, 46-47 & High Sch, Mont, 49-50; asst prof, 50-63, ASSOC PROF SPAN & GER & HEAD, DEPT MOD LANG, BETHANY NAZARENE COL, 63- *Concurrent Pos:* Fulbright grant, Ger, 56; Teacher, Bi-Nat Ctr, Cali, Colombia, SAm, 58; Nat Carl Schurz Asn-Am Asn Teachers Ger scholar, Ger, 70. *Honors & Awards:* Hayes Award, 42. *Mem:* Am Asn Teachers Ger; Am Asn Teachers Span & Port; Am Coun Teaching Foreign Lang; SCent Mod Lang Asn. *Res:* Interdisciplinary humanities course for underclassmen; the computer in teaching foreign languages; comparative Spanish, German and British literature. *Mailing Add:* Dept of Mod Lang Bethany Nazarene Col Bethany OK 73008

HULANICKI, LEO SERGIUS, b St Peterburg, Russia, June 5, 07; US citizan. RUSSIAN LINGUISTICS & LITERATURE. *Educ:* Azerbaijan State Univ, BA, 29; Univ Brussels, Lic econ, 47; Univ Calif, Berkeley, MA, 62; Stanford Univ, PhD(Slavic lang & lit), 69. *Prof Exp:* Lectr land econ, Advan Inst Applied Urbanism, Brussels, 49-50; instr Russ, Defense Lang Inst, W Coast Br, 50-62; from asst prof to assoc prof, 62-73, prof 73-74, EMER PROF RUSS LANG & LIT, SAN JOSE STATE UNIV, 74- *Concurrent Pos:* Lectr Russ lang & lit & comp lit, Monterey Inst Foreign Study, 62-, chmn dept Russ, 63-68; mem adv bd, Russ Lang J, 76- *Mem:* Am Asn Teachers Slavic & East Europ Lang. *Res:* Theory of literature; grammatical semantics. *Publ:* Auth, Actional perfect in Russian, Slavic & East Europ J, 73; A comment on Toward a Generative Account of Aspect in Russian, Russ Ling, summer 74; co-ed & contribr, Anton Cexov as Master of the Short Story, Mouton, The Hauge, 74; auth, The carriage by N V Gogol, Russ Lit, 75; The verbs of reversible actions, 76 & Written conversation, 77, Russ Lang J. *Mailing Add:* 151 Carmel Ave Pacific Grove CA 93950

HULES, VIRGINIA THORNDIKE, b New York, NY, July 2, 48; m 68. FRENCH LANGUAGE & LITERATURE. *Educ:* Wellesley Col, BA, 70; Harvard Univ, MA, 71, PhD(French), 76. *Prof Exp:* ASST PROF FRENCH, WELLESLEY COL, 76- *Mem:* MLA; Northeast Mod Lang Asn; Am Asn

Teachers of French; Am Coun Teaching Foreign Lang. *Res:* Twentieth century French women writers; twentieth century theatre; foreign language pedagogy. *Publ:* Coauth, Adapting Aerodrame for Teaching Oral/Aural Skills: The Experience at Wellesley College, French Rev, 10/78. *Mailing Add:* Dept French Wellesley Col Wellesley MA 02181

HULET, CLAUDE LYLE, b Pontiac, Mich, Dec 22, 20; m 42; c 3. SPANISH & PORTUGUESE. *Educ:* Univ Mich, AB, 42, MA, 47, PhD(Romance lang & lit), 54. *Prof Exp:* Dir, Am Inst Guatemala, 46; res asst Span, Univ Mich, 47, teaching fel, 47-50, instr, 50-51; from instr to asst prof Span & Port, Washington Univ, 51-58; from asst prof to assoc prof, 58-72, PROF SPAN & PORT, UNIV CALIF, LOS ANGELES, 72- *Concurrent Pos:* Orgn Am States fel, Brazil, 60; asst coordr, Univ Calif, Los Angeles-Brazil Studies Leader Sem, 63-66, coordr, 66-73; Fulbright-Hays res cholar, Brazil, 64; assoc ed, Hispania, 64- *Honors & Awards:* Machado de Assis Medal, Brazilian Acad Lett, 68; Cavaleiro, Ordem de Rio Branco, 69. *Mem:* MLA; Am Asn Teachers Span & Port; Philol Asn Pac Coast; Inst Int Lit Iberoam. *Res:* Brazilian literature; Spanish American literature; history of ideas in Ibero-America. *Publ:* Auth, Algumas reminiscencias do Brasil em Carlos Guido y Spano, Memoria del XI Congreso, Inst Int Lit Iberoam, 62; El sustituto: interpretacion filosofico-literario, Atenea, 63; Bibliography of Latin American prose in English translation, 64 & Bibliography of Lating American poetry in English translation, 65, Pam Am Union; A beata Maria do Egito: uma nova tragedin pro Rachel de Queiroz, Memoria del XI Congreso, Inst Int Lit Iberoam, 65. *Mailing Add:* Dept of Span & Port Univ of Calif Los Angeles CA 90024

HULL, ALEXANDER, b Portland, Ore, July 17, 28; m 52. FRENCH. *Educ:* Univ Wash, BA, 45, MA, 47, PhD(Romance ling), 55. *Prof Exp:* From instr to asst prof French, Univ Mass, 54-60; vis asst prof, Univ Mich, 60; assoc prof, St John's Col, Man, 60-62; asst prof, 62-66, ASSOC PROF ROMANCE LANG, DUKE UNIV, 66- *Concurrent Pos:* Fulbright grant, France, 49-50. *Mem:* MLA; Am Asn Teachers Fr; Ling Soc Am; Asn Can Studies in US; Am Coun Teaching For Lang. *Res:* North American French dialects; history of the French language; applied linguistics. *Publ:* Coauth, La France: Une Tapisserie, McGraw, 65; auth, The structure of the Canadian French consonant system, Linguistique, 66; coauth, Le Francais: Langue Ecrite et Langue Parlee, 67 & La France: Ses Grandes Heures Litteraires, 68, McGraw; auth, The origins of New World French phonology, Word, 68; coauth, Premieres Decouvertes Litteraires, Random, 72; auth, The Americanization of French in Windsor, In: The Influence of the United States on Canadian Development, Duke Univ, 72; On the origin and chronology of the French-based Creoles, In: Readings in Creole Studies, Story-Scientia, 79. *Mailing Add:* Dept of Romance Lang Duke Univ Durham NC 27706

HULL, ALEXANDER POPE, JR, b Charlottesville, Va, Apr 12, 23. GERMANIC LANGUAGES. *Educ:* Univ Va, PhD(Ger & English philol), 55. *Prof Exp:* Instr Ger, Univ Va, 49-54; from instr to asst prof, 56-63, assoc prof, Tex Tech Univ, 63-76. *Res:* German linguistics. *Mailing Add:* 113 Maywood Lane Charlottesville VA 22903

HULLEY, KARL KELCHNER, b Factorville, Pa, Apr 11, 98; m 22; c 2. CLASSICAL PHILOLOGY. *Educ:* Bucknell Univ, AB, 18; Harvard Univ, AM, 27, PhD, 41. *Hon Degrees:* LittD, Bucknell Univ, 57; DH, Alderson-Broaddus Col, 71. *Prof Exp:* Registr & instr Latin, Alderson-Broaddus Col, 19-26; from instr to assoc prof, 27-48, prof, 48-66, student coun, 37-66, actg head dept, 43-45, 45-47, chmn, 47-49, 51-53, 55-57 & 59-61, chmn comt student English 46-60, ed, Univ Press, 47-63, EMER PROF CLASSICS, UNIV COLO, 66- *Mem:* Am Philol Asn; Classic Asn Mid West & South; Am Classic League; Vergilian Soc Am; Archaeol Inst Am. *Res:* St Jerome; Aristophanes; Horace. *Publ:* Coauth, The Oresteia-story in the Odyssey, Trans of Am Philol Asn, 46; auth, Principles of textual criticism known to St Jerome, Harvard Univ; sr ed, George Sandys' Ovid's Metamorphosis (1632 ed), Univ Nebr, 70; auth, Intensive language courses and the classics, Classic J; Prologue of the Ecclesiazousae, Classic Weekly; A note on Aristophanes' Clouds, Classical J, 74. *Mailing Add:* 1331 Marshall St Boulder CO 80302

HUME, DAVID RAYMOND, b Morrisville, Pa, July 20, 29; m 52; c 4. GERMANIC LANGUAGES & LITERATURES. *Educ:* King's Col, NY, AB, 52; Southern Baptist Theol Sem, MDiv, 67; Univ La, MA, 69; Univ Ky, PhD(Ger), 72. *Prof Exp:* Asst prof Ger, Ky Southern Col, 6869-; instr, 69-72, asst prof, 72-80, ASSOC PROF GER, UNIV LOUISVILLE, 80- *Mem:* Am Asn Teachers Ger; Am Coun Teaching Foreign Lang; AAUP. *Res:* Middle High German literature; late nineteenth century German literature; Swedish-German literary relationship. *Publ:* Coauth, The Rediscovery of Bethesda, Vanderhoeck & Ruprecht, 66; auth, The German Literary Achievements of Ola Hansson, Univ Microfilms, 73; Qoheleth: Fritz Grasshoff's The New Solomon, Resonance, 73; The first five years of Ola Hansson's literary exile, In: Facets of Scandinavian Literature, APRA, 74. *Mailing Add:* Dept of Mod Lang Univ of Louisville Louisville KY 40208

HUMESKY, ASSYA ALEXANDRA, b Kharkov Ukraine, USSR, May 23, 25; US citizen; m 53; c 2. RUSSIAN & UKRANIAN LITERATURE & LANGUAGE. *Educ:* Albertus Magnus Col, BA, 50; Radcliffe Col, MA, 51, PhD(Slavic), 55. *Prof Exp:* From instr to assoc prof, 53-66, PROF RUSS, UNIV MICH, 67- *Concurrent Pos:* Vis prof, Syracuse Univ, 62 & 64; Am Coun Leanred Socs publ grant, 62 & 72: res assoc, Wayne State Univ, 65-67; chmn, Listening Comprehension Comt, Educ Testing Serv, Princeton; consult, Defense Lang Inst, WCoast Br, Monterey, 68 & 72. *Mem:* Am Asn Advan Slavic Studies; Am Asn Teachers Slavic & EEurop Lang; Am Asn Ukrainian Univ Prof. *Res:* Russian poetics, neologisms and rhyme; Ukrainian Baroque; stylistics. *Publ:* Auth, Majakovskij and His Neologisms, Rausen, 64; coauth, Modern Russian I, 64 & Modern Russian II, 65, Harcourt, Brace & World; auth, Some observations on the neologisms of Igor' Severjanin and Majakovskij, Symbolae in honorem Georgii Mirtaly Kardynalovs'koji), 7/74, Suchasnist'; Pam' jati S V Pylypenka, Novi Dni, 1-2/76; Grammatical rhymes in N Jazykov's poetry, Papers Slavic Philol I, Ann Arbor, 77. *Mailing Add:* Slavic Dept 3008 MLB Univ of Mich Ann Arbor MI 48109

HUMMEL, JOHN HULL, b Passaic, NJ, June 16, 35; m 68; c 3. FRENCH, COMPARATIVE LITERATURE. *Educ:* Univ Tex, BA, 61, PhD(French), 69. *Prof Exp:* Assoc prof Romance lang, Southwestern Univ, Tex, 66-69; assoc prof French, Univ Calif, Santa Cruz, 69-80. *Mem:* MLA. *Res:* Eighteenth century French literature; translation. *Publ:* Coauth, Sainte-Beuve on classics and classicists, Arion, summer 67; auth, Ezra Pound: The Provencal translations, Tex Quart, winter 67; Rousseaus's Pygmalion and the Confessions, Neophilologus, winter 73. *Mailing Add:* 901 Walnut Ave Santa Cruz CA 95060

HUMPHREY, GEORGE, b New York, NY, Nov 19, 23; m 48; c 3. COMPARATIVE LITERATURE. *Educ:* Union Col, NY, BA, 48; Harvard Univ, MA, 52, PhD, 62. *Prof Exp:* Asst humanities, Harvard Univ, 52; instr French & lit, Tulane Univ, 55-59; lectr French, Conn Col Women, 59-60; from instr to asst prof foreign lang, Univ Conn, 60-67; assoc prof Romance & classical lang, Univ Utah, 67-70; ASSOC PROF FRENCH & COMP LIT, TEMPLE UNIV, 70- *Concurrent Pos:* Am correspondent, Asia mag, Takoyo, 49-65; asst ed, Rev Pensee Fr, 49-50; lectr, Ecole Libre des Hautes Etudes, NY, 50-; asst ed & reader Far Eastern hist, Harvard Univ Press, 52-55; dean, Westminster Sch Summer Lang Study Prog, 63; Temple Univ res grant, 71. *Mem:* MLA; Am Asn Teachers Fr; Comp Lit Conf. *Res:* Nerval; Baudelaire; surrealism. *Publ:* Auth, Victor ou l'enfant de la foret, Fr Rev, 59; Gerard de Nerval, 60 & Notre Baudelaire, 63, Le Bayou; L'esthetique de la poesie de G de Nerval, Nizet, Paris, 69; Barrault, arrabal, sarraute, Cult Francaise, fall 73. *Mailing Add:* Dept of French Temple Univ Philadelphia PA 19122

HUMPHREYS, RICHARD STEPHEN, Medieval Islamic History. See Vol I

HUMPHRIES, JOHN JEFFERSON, b Tuscaloosa, Ala, Aug 24, 55. FRENCH & AMERICAN LITERATURE. *Educ:* Duke Univ, AB, 77; Yale Univ, MA, 78, MPhil, 80, PhD(French lit), 81. *Prof Exp:* Actg instr French, Yale Univ, 80-81, instr, Summer Lang Inst, summers 80 & 81, lectr, Univ, 81; ASST PROF FRENCH & ITAL, LA STATE UNIV, BATON ROUGE, 82- *Mem:* MLA. *Res:* Psychoanalysis and literature; literature of the American South. *Publ:* Auth, The machine as metaphor: Jarry's Pompe a Merdre, Romanic Rev, fall 82; The self-devouring self: Montaigne's anti-influential model of identity, Sub-stance, fall 82; Manners without morals: From La Rochefoucauld's Mot Juste to Chamfort's Mot Fou, L'Esprit createur, fall 82; Mourning Becomes Desire: Gnosticism as an Aesthetic Principle in the Works of Proust, Flannery O'Connor, and Francois Villon, La State Univ Press (in prep). *Mailing Add:* Dept of French & Ital La State Univ Baton Rouge LA 70803

HUNG, MING SHUI, b Silo, Taiwan, Apr 30, 38; US citizen; m 67; c 2. CHINESE LITERATURE. *Educ:* Tunghai Univ, BA, 61; Univ Wis-Madison, MA, 66, PhD(E Asian lang), 74. *Prof Exp:* Res asst Chinese lit, Tunghai Univ, 62-63; teaching asst Chinese lang, Univ Wis, 67-68; instr Chinese lang & lit, 72-75, asst prof, 75-80, ASSOC PROF CHINESE LANG & LIT, BROOKLYN COL, 80- *Mem:* Am Asian Studies; Am Orient Soc; MLA. *Res:* Late Ming literary and intellectual history; Chinese literary criticism. *Publ:* Contribr, Dictionary Ming Biography, Columbia, Univ, 76. *Mailing Add:* 1072 E 29th St Brooklyn NY 11210

HUNT, JOEL ANDREWS, b Ramsey, Ill, June 29, 21; m 45: c 3. FRENCH. *Educ:* Wayne Univ, AB, 46; Yale Univ, MA, 50, PhD, 53. *Prof Exp:* Spec instr French, Wayne Univ, 46-47; asst instr, Yale Univ, 48-50, 51-52; lectr, Northwestern Univ, 50-51; instr, Princeton Univ, 52-55; from asst prof to assoc prof, 55-67, assoc dean grad sch, 65-69, PROF FRENCH, IND UNIV, BLOOMINGTON, 67-, PROF ITAL, 76- *Mem:* MLA; Am Asn Teachers Fr. *Res:* French and comparative literature. *Publ:* Contribr, Comp Lit; Ger Rev; Fr Rev. *Mailing Add:* Dept of French Ind Univ Bloomington IN 47401

HUNT, JOHN MORTIMER, JR, b Bryn Mawr, Pa, Sept 21, 43. CLASSICAL PHILOLOGY. *Educ:* Lafayette Col, AB, 65; Bryn Mawr Col, MA, 68, PhD(classics), 70. *Prof Exp:* Asst prof classics, Villanova Univ, 70-76, lectr classics & mod lang, 76-78; vis assoc prof classics, Univ Calif, Santa Barbara, 78-80; LECTR CLASSICS, VILLANOVA UNIV, 80- *Res:* Latin literature and textual criticism. *Mailing Add:* 251 Hillcrest Rd Wayne PA 19087

HUNTER, WILLIAM ARTHUR, b Hammond, La, Jan 22, 15; m 42; c 4. SPANISH LANGUAGE & LITERATURE. *Educ:* Centenary Col, BA, 39; Tulane Univ, MA, 49, PhD(Span), 54. *Prof Exp:* Instr Span, Tulane Univ, 49-54; instr romance lang, Emory Univ, 54-55; assoc prof mod lang, Columbia Col, SC, 55-58; asst prof foreign lang, Bowling Green State Univ, 58-61: assoc prof & head dept, Bradley Univ, 61-67; prof mod lang, Univ SFla, 67-72, chmn dept, 67-70; assoc prof, 74-80, PROF FOREIGN LANG, EAST TEX BAPTIST COL, 80- *Mem:* Univ Prof for Acad Order (pres, 79); Am Asn Teachers Span & Port; Coun Basic Educ. *Res:* Spanish literature of the Golden Age; literature in the Nahuatl language. *Publ:* Auth, The Calderonian auto sacramental, El gran teatro del mundo: An edition and translation of a Nahuatl version, Mid Am Res Inst, 60; The Alva manuscripts in Nahuatl in the Bancroft Library, Ky Foreign Lang Quart; The American Indian languages as literary vehicles, Renaissance Papers; Modern Language Association: An example of our academic problems, 6/75, Bicentennial era should be time for corrective measures, 9/75 & UPAO meets in St Louis, 1/78, Human Events. *Mailing Add:* E Tex Baptist Col 1209 N Grove St Marshall TX 75670

HUNTER-LOUGHEED, ROSEMARIE, b Koenigsberg, Ger; Can citizen. GERMAN & COMPARATIVE LITERATURE. *Educ:* Univ Alta, BA, 63, PhD(Ger), 70; Univ Calgary, MA, 65. *Prof Exp:* Instr Ger, St Malachy's Col, Belfast, 57-60; instr, Univ Alta, 62-63; lectr Ger & French & chmn dept mod lang, Mt Royal Jr Col, Calgary, 65-66; lectr Ger, Univ Sask, 71-72; ASSOC PROF GER, QUEEN'S UNIV, ONT, 72- *Concurrent Pos:* Univ Calgary fel, 70-71; Can Coun leave fel, 78-79. *Mem:* Can Asn Univ Teachers Ger; Adalbert Stifter Ges; Int Vereiningung der Ger; E T A Hoffmann Ges. *Res:*

Nachtwachen von Bonaventura; German and comparative literature of the 18th and 19th centuries; Verfasserschaft der Nachtwachen von Bonaventura. *Publ:* Auth, Clemens Brentanos Wenn der lahme Weber träumt und das problem der sprachverfremdung, Germanisch-Romanische Monatsschrift, 69; Kinderlosigkeit und eschatologie bei Stifter, Neophilologus, Vol 57, 73; Nachtwachen Von Bonaventura and Tristram Shandy, Can Rev Comp Lit, Vol 1, 74; Warum eigentlich nicht E T A Hoffmann? Ein Beitrag zur Verfasserfrage der Nachtwachen, Mitteilungen der E T A Hoffmann-Ges, Vol 23, 77; Das thema der liebe im Armen Spielmann, Jahrbuch der Grillparzer-Ges, 77; E T A Hoffmann: Der Verfasser der Nachtwachen?, Jahrbuch für Int Germanistik, Vol 3, 80; Der Prolog des Hanswurstes: Zur Entstehunggeschichte und Datierung der Nachtwachen, Sem: J of Ger Studies, Vol 18, 82; Bonaventura und E T A Hoffmann, unter besonderer Berücksichtingung de Plozker Tagebuches, Germanisch-Romanische Monatsschrift, 82. *Mailing Add:* Dept of Ger Queen's Univ Kingston ON K7L 3N6 Can

HUNTLEY, MARTIN ADRIAN, b Dover, Eng, May 14, 45. LINGUISTICS, PHILOSOPHY. *Educ:* Univ Sussex, BA, 66; Banaras Hindu Univ, India, MA, 68; Univ Minn, PhD(philos), 72. *Prof Exp:* Asst prof philos, Univ Wis-Madison, 72-79; ASST PROF LING, BROWN UNIV, 79- *Mem:* Am Philos Asn; Linguistics Soc Am. *Res:* Semantics; Pragmatics; philosophy of linguistics. *Publ:* Auth, Presupposition and implicature, Semantikos, 76; Propositions and the Imperative, Synthese, 80. *Mailing Add:* Dept of Ling Box E Brown Univ Providence RI 02912

HUNTSMAN, JEFFREY FORREST, Celtic & Germanic Linguistics, Native American Literature. See Vol II

HUPPE, BERNARD FELIX, English Literature. See Vol II

HURSKY, JACOB P, b Zholdaky, Ukraine, Nov 4, 23; US citizen; m 53; c 2. SLAVIC PHILOLOGY. *Educ:* Ukrainian Free Univ, PhM, 50; Univ Pa, AM, 53, PhD(slavic & Baltic studies), 57. *Prof Exp:* From asst prof to assoc prof, 56-72, PROF SLAVIC LANG & LIT, SYRACUSE UNIV, 72-, CHMN DEPT, 76- *Concurrent Pos:* Vis prof, Harvard, summer 72 & Ukrainian Free Univ, summers, 74-82. *Mem:* MLA; Am Asn Teachers Slavic & East Europ Lang; Am Name Soc; Ukrainian Acad Arts & Sci in US; Shevchenko Sci Soc. *Res:* Slavic languages and comparative grammar, modern and historical; Slavic civilization. *Publ:* Ed, The Administrative and Economic Structure of Bulgaria, Syracuse Univ, 60; auth, Survey of Bulgarian Literature and the Works of Christo Ognjanoff, Ukrainian Lit Mag, 6/60; Bulgarian-English Glossary to Basic Bulgarian, Syracuse Univ, 63, Linguistic Studies of Professor George Y Shevelov, Ukrainian Quart, summer 60; coed, Symbolae in Honorem Georgii Y Shevelov, Munchen, 71; auth, Phonetic Peculiarities in Ukrainian Patronymic Surnames of the Fourteenth-Seventeeth Centuries, Names, 12/71; ed, Tribute to Hryhorij Kytasty on his Seventieth Birthday, 80. *Mailing Add:* 208 Easterly Terrace De Witt NY 13214

HURVITZ, LEON NAHUM, b Boston, Mass, Aug 4, 23; Can citizen; m 58; c 3. FAR EASTERN LANGUAGES, FAR EASTERN BUDDHISM. *Educ:* Univ Chicago, BA, 49; Columbia Univ, MA, 52, PhD, 59. *Prof Exp:* From actg asst prof to prof Far Eastern Lang, Univ Wash, 55-71; PROF ASIAN LANG, UNIV BC, 71- *Concurrent Pos:* Res grants, Am Coun Learned Socs, 69-70 & Can Coun, 76-77. *Mem:* Am Orient Soc; Can Soc Study Relig; Int Asn Buddhist Studies. *Res:* The transmission of Indian Buddhist ideas to China and their development there in the fourth, fifth and sixth centuries. *Publ:* Translr, Miura Baien, Samidare-sho (Musings During the Early Summer Rain), Monumenta Nipponica, 52 & 53; Wei Shou, Shih Lao chih (transl of original Chinese text and of Japanese annotation of Tsukamoto Zenryu), Yunkang XVI, 56; The Buddha of Seiroji, Artibus Asiae 19, 56; Render unto Caesar in Early Chinese Buddhism, Sino-Indian Studies, 57; Chih-yi (538-597): An Introduction to the Life and Ideas of a Chinese Buddhist Monk, Inst Belge Hautes Etudes Chinoises, 63; coauth, Catalogue of the Manchu-Mongol Section of the Toyo Tunko, Toyo Bunko & Univ Wash, 64; The path to Buddhist salvation as described by Vasubhadra, J Am Orient Soc, 69; The Lotus of the True Dharma, Columbia Univ, 76. *Mailing Add:* Dept of Asian Lang Univ BC Vancouver BC V6T 1W5 Can

HUTCHINSON, JOSEPH CANDLER, b Hazlehurst, Ga, Jan 10, 20; m 50; c 2. ROMANCE LANGUAGES. *Educ:* Emory Univ, AB, 40, MA, 41; Univ NC, PhD(Romance lang), 50. *Prof Exp:* Instr Romance lang, Emory Univ, 46-47; instr French Univ NC, 47-50; asst prof French & Ital, Sweet Briar Col, 50-51, 53-54; asst prof French & chmn freshmen & sophomore French, Univ NC, 54-57, assoc prof, 57; assoc prof French & dir lang lab, Tulane Univ, 57-59; Specialist foreign lang, Instr Resources Br, US Off Educ, 59-64; chief res & standards div, Hq, 64-68, acad adv to dir, 68-77, DIR TRAINING DEVELOP, FOREIGN LANG CTR, DEFENSE LANG INST, 77- *Concurrent Pos:* Vis lectr, Univ Va, 66-67; US deleg, Bur Int Lang Coord, NATO, 67-82; lectr, Sch Lang & Ling, Georgetown Univ, 68-69; vis prof, Northern Va Ctr, Univ Va & adj prof, Am Univ, 70-71; vis prof, Grad Sch, US Dept of Agr, 72-73. *Mem:* MLA; NEA; Nat Asn Lang Lab Dirs; Am Coun Teaching Foreign Lang. *Res:* Training of foreign language teachers; instructional technology in language learning; research in second language learning. *Publ:* Auth, Modern Foreign Languages in High School: The Language Laboratory, US Off Educ, 61; The technology of modern language learning, In: Curricular Changes in the Foreign Languages, Col Entrance Exam Bd, 63; Using the language laboratory effectively, In: School Executive's Guide, Prentice-Hall, 64; The language laboratory: Equipment and utilization, In: Trends in Language Teaching, McGraw, 66; Planning for language laboratory facilities, In: Foreign Language Teaching: An Anthology, Macmillan, 67; The language laboratory: How effective is it?, In: Foreign Languages and the Schools: A Book of Readings, Brown, 67: DLI Policy Guidelines, Defense Lang Inst, 70; coauth, Criteria for selecting language laboratory facilities, MLA/ERIC Focus Reports on Teaching Foreign Lang, 70. *Mailing Add:* PO Box OJ Pacific Grove CA 93950

HUTTER, ALBERT DAVID, English, Comparative Literature. See Vol II

HUTTON, LEWIS J, b New York, NY, July 26, 21; m 48; c 4. ROMANCE LANGUAGES, RELIGION. *Educ:* Columbia Univ, AB, 42, MA, 46; Princeton Theol Sem, BD, 44; Princeton Univ, MA, 48, PhD(Romance lang, Span), 50; Union Theol Sem, STM, 50. *Prof Exp:* Instr Span, Princeton Univ, 45-48; instr, NY Univ, 48-49; minister, First Presby Church, Gowanda, NY, 51-55; sr minister, Capitol Hill Presby Church, Wash, DC, 55-62; sr minister, First Presby Church, Kirksville, Mo, 62-64; from asst prof to assoc prof Span, Drake Univ, 64-66; assoc prof, 66-72, PROF SPAN, UNIV RI, 72- *Concurrent Pos:* Assoc Span, George Washington Univ, 57-62. *Mem:* MLA; Am Asn Teachers Span & Port; Am Soc Church Hist; Soc Bibl Lit. *Res:* Sixteenth and seventeenth century Spanish literature; contemporary intellectual thought; sixteenth century ecclesiastical history. *Publ:* Auth, Teresa de Cartagena: An example of Castilian spirituality, Theol Today, 56; Cipriano de Valera: The Spanish heretic, Church Hist, 58; La historia de las sagradas escrituras en Espana, Cuadernos Teol Buenos Aires, 61; Teresa de Cartagena: Arboleda de los Enfermos, Admiracion Operum Dey, La Real Acad Espanola, Madrid. *Mailing Add:* Dept of Span Univ of RI Kingston RI 02881

HUVOS, KORNEL, b Budapest, Hungary, Apr 25, 13; US citizen; m 45; c 1. ROMANCE LANGUAGES & LITERATURES. *Educ:* Univ Budapest, JSD, 38; Univ Cincinnati, PhD(French lit), 65. *Prof Exp:* From instr to assoc prof, 61-73, prof, 73-75, head dept, 77-81, CHARLES PHELPS TAFT PROF ROMANCE LANG & LIT, UNIV CINCINNATI, 75- *Concurrent Pos:* Taft res grant, 69, 74, 78 & 80. *Honors & Awards:* George Rieveschl, Jr Award Excellence in Scholarly Work, 78. *Mem:* AAUP; MLA; Am Asn Teachers fr. *Res:* Franco-American literary relations; 20th century French literature; French-German-Hungarian bilingual lexicography. *Publ:* Coauth & managing ed, German-Hungarian Dictionary, 51, French-Hungarian Dictionary, 57, Hungarian Acad Sci; coauth, Impressions d'Amerique: Les Etats-Unis dans la Litterature Francaise Contemporaine, St Martin's 70; auth, Elements pour une bibliographie de la poesie francaise americaniste au XXe siecle, Comp Lit Studies, 12/71; Cinq Mirages Americains: Les Etats-Unis dans l'Oeuvre de G Duhamel, J Romains, A Maurois, J Maritain et S de Beauvoie, Marcel Didier, Paris, 72; L'erotisation de l'Americaine dans la litterature francaise, Fr Rev, 76; G Duhamel & L Durtain, Columbia Dict of Modern European Literature, Columbia Univ Press, 80. *Mailing Add:* Dept of Romance Lang & Lit Univ of Cincinnati Cincinnati OH 45221

HUXLEY, HERBERT H, b Brooklands, England, July 29, 16; m 41, 75; c 2. GREEK & LATIN LITERATURE. *Educ:* Cambridge Univ, BA, 38, MA, 42; Trinity Col, Dublin, MA, 61. *Prof Exp:* Asst lectr Latin, Univ Leeds, 44-47, lectr classics, 47-51; sr lectr Latin, Univ Manchester, 51-62, reader, 62-68; chmn dept classics, 71-72, PROF CLASSICS, UNIV VICTORIA, BC, 68- *Concurrent Pos:* Vis assoc prof, Brown Univ, 66-67; ed, Classic Asn Pac Northwest Bull, 69-70; vis fel classics, Univ Col, Cambridge Univ, 70-71; Can Coun fel, 70-71. *Mem:* Ovidianum, Romania; Asn for Reform Latin Teaching; Orbilian Soc (pres, 69); Am Philol Asn; fel Inst Arts & Lett. *Res:* Latin poetry, classical, medieval and humanistic; composing Latin poetry, quantitative and accentual. *Publ:* Auth, Claudian: The Rape of Proserpine, Univ Liverpool, 59; Virgil: Georgics I and IV, Methuen, 63, 65; ed, Carmina: MCMLXII, Wilding, Shrewsbury, 63 & Corolla Camenae, Univ Victoria, 69; Aeneid 6 and the English poets, 73 & Fortuante Ambo: Raid and reputation, 74, Proc Pac Northwest Conf Foreign Lang; Martial, Encycl Britannica, 74; De Die Judicii, Classica et Iberica, 75; The Latin Poems of George Herbert, Acta Amstelodamensia, 78. *Mailing Add:* Dept of Classics Univ Victoria Victoria BC V8W 2Y2 Can

HUZAR, ELEANOR GOLTZ, Ancient History. See Vol I

HWANG, HI SOOK, b Seoul, Korea, Dec 5, 29; US citizen. FRENCH LANGUAGE & LITERATURE. *Educ:* Seoul Nat Univ, BA, 52; Univ Tampa, BA, 57; Emory Univ, MAT, 59; State Univ NY Buffalo, PhD(French), 71. *Prof Exp:* Instr French, State Univ NY Col Fredonia, 62-69; ASSOC PROF FRENCH, MOORHEAD STATE UNIV, 69- *Mem:* Am Asn Teachers Fr. *Res:* Nineteenth century French novel. *Mailing Add:* Dept of Lang Moorhead State Univ Moorhead MN 56560

HYATTE, REGINALD L, b LaPorte, Ind, May 9, 43. MEDIEVAL FRENCH LITERATURE. *Educ:* Ind Univ, AB, 65, AM, 66; Univ Pa, PhD(Romance lang), 71. *Prof Exp:* Teaching asst French, Univ Pa, 67-69; instr, Bowling Green State Univ, 70-71; asst prof French, Valley Forge Mil Acad & Jr Col, 77-80; ASST PROF FRENCH, RIPON COL, 80- *Res:* Medieval French didactic literature. *Publ:* Contribr, Review of J M Ferrante, The Conflict of Love and Honor: The Medieval Tristan Legend in France, Germany and Italy, Romanic Rev, 1/77. *Mailing Add:* Dept of French Ripon Col Ripon WI 54971

HYDE, JAMES FRANKLIN, b Corning, NY, June 6, 33. GERMAN LITERATURE. *Educ:* Princeton Univ, AB, 55; Ind Univ, AM, 57, PhD, 60. *Prof Exp:* Instr Ger lit, Univ Calif, 59-61; asst prof, Stanford Univ, 61-64; PROF GER, RIPON COL, 64- *Concurrent Pos:* Consult archit acoustics, Univ Calif, Davis, 59-61 & Stanford Univ, 62- *Mem:* MLA; Am Asn Teachers Ger; Acoustical Soc Am; Organ Hist Soc; Brit Organ Soc. *Res:* Baroque and mediaeval literature. *Mailing Add:* Dept of Ger Ripon Col Ripon WI 54971

HYDE, JOHN KENNETH, Hyde/John Kenneth. FRENCH LANGUAGE & LITERATURE. *Educ:* Univ Mich, BA, 55; Ind Univ, MA, 59, PhD, 63. *Prof Exp:* Lectr French, Ind Univ, 61-62; instr, Oberlin Col, 62-67; asst prof French & Italian, 67-72, ASSOC PROF FRENCH & ITAL, IND UNIV, BLOOMINGTON, 72- *Mem:* MLA. *Res:* Modern French Poetry and Novel. *Mailing Add:* Dept French & Italian Ind Univ Bloomington IN 47401

HYE, ALLEN EDWARD, b New Brunswick, NJ, Dec 1, 44; m 67; c 2. GERMAN & SCANDINAVIAN LITERATURE. *Educ:* Franklin & Marshall Col, BA, 66; Middlebury Col, MA, 67; Univ Conn, PhD(Ger), 72. *Prof Exp:* Instr Ger, Franklin & Marshall Col, 72-73; asst prof, Lehigh Univ, 73-78; ASSOC PROF GER, WRIGHT STATE UNIV, 78- *Mem:* Am Asn

Teachers Ger; Soc Advan Scand Studies. *Res:* Modern German drama; modern Danish drama; science and literature. *Publ:* Auth, Den herskende Klasse, Berlingske Tidende, 4/71; Brecht: aesthetics and the loss of identity in the technological age, In: Philosophers Speak on Aesthetics in Education, Interstate, 75; Kjeld Abell følte med øjne, ører, hele personen, Berlingske Tidende, 9/76; ed, Modernes Deutschland im Brennpunkt, W W Norton, 78; auth, Brecht and atomic physics, Sci-Technol & the Humanities, 5/78; A Tennessee morality play: Notes on Inherit the Wind, Markham Rev, fall 79; The world of Robert Storm Petersen, Bridge, 2/80. *Mailing Add:* Dept of Mod Lang Wright State Univ Dayton OH 45435

HYLAND, JEAN SCAMMON, b Minneapolis, Minn, Jan 12, 26; m 66; c 1. ROMANCE LANGUAGES. *Educ:* MacMurray Col Women, BA, 48; Western Reserve Univ, MA, 53; Univ Kans, PhD(Romance lang), 59. *Prof Exp:* Instr French & Span, St Mary's Hall, Minn, 48-52; lectr Span, Western Reserve Univ, 52-53; instr French, Univ Kans, 54-59; from instr to asst prof French & Span, Col William & Mary, 59-63; assoc prof, Christopher Newport Col, 63-64; asst prof, 64-68, ASSOC PROF FRENCH, UNIV RI, 68-, STUDY ABROAD COORDR, 81- *Concurrent Pos:* Mem Nat Screening Comt for France, Fulbright-Hays Prog, Inst Int Educ, NY, 77; ed, RI Foreign Lang Gazette. *Mem:* MLA; Am Asn Teachers Fr; New Eng Foreign Lang Asn. *Res:* French 19th and 20th century novel Publ; Auth, Reading Proficiency in French (4 vols), Am Bk Co, 69; The contemporary French novel, Va Mod Lang J, 65. *Mailing Add:* 967 Kingstown Rd Peace Dale RI 02879

HYMAN, LARRY MICHAEL, b Los Angeles, Calif, Sept 26, 47. LINGUISTICS, AFRICAN LANGUAGES. *Educ:* Univ Calif Los Angeles, BA, 69, MA, 69, PhD(ling), 72. *Prof Exp:* Asst prof, 71-74, assoc prof, 74-81, PROF LING, UNIV SOUTHERN CALIF, 81-, CHMN DEPT, 74- *Concurrent Pos:* Miller Inst for Basic Research in Sci, Univ Calif, Berkeley, fel, 73-75; principal investigator, Nat Sci Found grant on the Bantu Languages of Cameroon, Africa, 77-79. *Mem:* Ling Soc Am; Studies African Ling; J African Lang & Ling. *Res:* Tonology; language change; linguistic inquiry. *Publ:* Auth, How concrete is phonology?, Language, 70; ed, Consonant Types and Tone, Southern Calif Occas Papers in Ling, No 1, 73; coauth, Hierarchies of natural topic in Shona, Studies in African Ling, 74; Universals of tone rules, Ling Inquiry, 74; auth, On the change from SOV to SVO: Evidence from Niger-Congo, In: Word Order & Word Order Change, Univ Tex, 75; Phonology: Theory and Analysis, Holt, Rinehart & Winston, 75; ed, Studies in Stress and Accent, Southern Calif Occas Papers in Ling No 4, 77; Aghem Grammatical Structure, 79; Tonal Accent in Somali, 81. *Mailing Add:* Dept of Ling Univ Southern Calif Los Angeles CA 90007

HYMES, DELL HATHAWAY, b Portland, Ore, June 7, 27; m 54; c 4. FOLKLORE, LINGUISTICS. *Educ:* Reed Col, BA, 50; Ind Univ, Bloomington, MA, 53, PhD(ling), 55. *Hon Degrees:* MA, Univ Pa, 72. *Prof Exp:* From instr to asst prof social anthrop, Harvard Univ, 55-60; from assoc prof to prof anthrop, Univ Calif, Berkeley, 60-65; prof anthrop, 65-71, PROF FOLKLORE & LING, UNIV PA, 72-, PROF SOCIOL, 73-, PROF EDUC, 75-, DEAN EDUC, 75- *Concurrent Pos:* Ctr Advan Study in Behav Sci fel, 57-58; Am Coun Learned Soc fel, 63-64; dir Soc Sci Res Coun, 65-67 & 68-71; fel, Clare Hall, Cambridge, 68-69; Guggenheim Found fel, 69; Nat Endowment for Humanities sr fel, 72-73; trustee, Ctr for Appl Ling, 73-75 & 76-78; ed, Lang Soc J, 72- *Mem:* Am Anthrop Asn (pres, 83); Am Folklore Soc (pres, 73-74); Ling Soc Am (pres, 82); Coun for Anthrop & Educ (pres, 78). *Res:* American Indian languages and folklore; history of linguistics, folklore and anthropology; ethnography of speaking. *Publ:* Ed & contribr, Language in Culture and Society, Harper, 64; Pidginization and Creolization of Languages, Cambridge Univ, 71; Reinventing Anthropology, Pantheon, 72; Studies in the History of Linguistics: Traditions and Paradigms, Ind Univ, 74; auth, Foundations of Sociolinguistics, Univ Pa, 74; Soziolinguistik, Subrkamp, 79; Language in Education, Ctr Applied Ling, 80; In Vain I Tried to Tell You, Univ Pa, 81; coauth (with John Fought), American Structuralism, Mouton, 81; Essays in the History of Linguistic Anthropology, Benjamins, 82. *Mailing Add:* Grad Sch of Educ Univ of Pa Philadelphia PA 19104

HYSLOP, LOIS BOE, b Baltic, SDak, Apr 3, 08; m 48. ROMANCE LANGUAGES. *Educ:* Augustana Col, BA, 30; Univ Wis, MA, 31, PhD(French), 35. *Prof Exp:* Prof French, Susquehanna Univ, 35-44; prof French & Span, Skidmore Col, 44-48, head dept Romance lang, 47-48; assoc prof, 48-58, prof, 58-74, acting head dept French, 63-65, EMER PROF FRENCH & SPAN, PA STATE UNIV, 74- *Concurrent Pos:* Fel, Inst Arts & Humanities Studies, Pa State Univ, 71. *Mem:* MLA; Am Asn Teachers Fr. *Res:* Nineteenth century French literature; Baudelaire; Henry Becque. *Publ:* Auth, Baudelaire on Poe, Bald Eagle Press, 52; Baudelaire: A Self Portrait, Oxford Univ Press, 57 & Greenwood Press, 78; Baudelaire as a Literary Critic, Pa State Univ Press, 64 & 19th Century Lit Criticism, 81 & 82; coauth & ed, Baudelaire as a Love Poet and Other Essays, Pa State Univ Press 69; auth, Henry Becque, Twayne Press, 72; Baudelaire: Man of his Time, Yale Univ Press, 80. *Mailing Add:* 326 Hillcrest Ave State College PA 16801

HYTIER, ADRIENNE DORIS, b Teheran, Iran, Mar 25, 31; French citizen. FRENCH. *Educ:* Barnard Col, BA, 52; Columbia Univ, MA, 53, PhD, 58. *Prof Exp:* From instr to assoc prof, 59-70, chmn dept, 71-75, PROF FRENCH, VASSAR COL, 70-, LICHTENSTEIN-DALE CHAIR, 74- *Concurrent Pos:* Guggenheim fel, 67-68; vis assoc prof, Univ Calif, Davis, 68-69; asst ed, French Rev, 67-73; ed, Fr Lit 18th Century: A Current Bibliog since 1970. *Honors & Awards:* Chevalier des Palmes Acad, French Govt, 75. *Mem:* MLA; Am Asn Teachers Fr; Int Asn Fr Studies; Soc Fr Prof Am; Am Soc 18th Century Studies. *Res:* French 18th century literature. *Publ:* Auth, Two Years of French Foreign Policy: Vichy 1940-1942 & 1974, 58 & ed, Les Depeches diplomatiques du Comte de Gobineau en Perse, 59, Droz, Switz; auth, Diderot et Frederic II, Diderot Studies, 65; Joseph II, la Cour de Vienne et les philosophes, 73 & Les philosophes et le probleme de la Guerre, 74, Studies on Voltaire & 18th Century; La Guerre, Bordas, Paris, 75; Le Peau-Rouge: est-il bon? est-il mechant?, Fr Rev, 76; The theme of the deserter in 18th century French literature, Studies 18th Century Cult, 82. *Mailing Add:* Dept of French Vassar Col Poughkeepsie NY 12601

I

IACCARINO, PIETRO LUIGI, b Naples, Italy, Mar 2, 26; m 60; c 3. ROMANCE LANGUAGES & LITERATURES. *Educ:* Ist Univ Orient, Naples, Dr lang & lit, 60. *Prof Exp:* From instr to assoc prof, 63-74, PROF ITAL LANG & LIT, SAN FRANCISCO STATE UNIV, 74- *Mem:* Am Asn Teachers Ital; Ist Storia Risorgimento Ital. *Res:* The Italian Renaissance; linguistics; medieval studies. *Mailing Add:* Dept of Foreign Lang San Francisco State Univ San Francisco CA 94132

IANNACE, GAETANO ANTONIO, b Nov, 1927; US citizen; m 62; c 1. ITALIAN LANGUAGE & LITERATURE, HUMANITIES. *Educ:* NY Univ, BA, 56, MA, 62, PhD(Ital), 64. *Prof Exp:* Instr Ital, NY Univ, 60-64, asst prof, 64-67; assoc prof, 67-71, PROF ITAL & HUMANITIES, CENT CONN STATE COL, 71- *Concurrent Pos:* Instr, Fordham Univ, 65-66; adj asst prof, Pace Col, 65-66; instr French, Mt Vernon Adult Educ High Sch, 65-67. *Mem:* MLA; Am Asn Teachers Ital; Ital Hist Soc Am. *Res:* Twentieth century Italian novel; Dante-Joyce, an interdisciplinary approach; 20th century European theater. *Publ:* Auth, La Tragedia dei Fratelli Gamba in Tre Croci, Delta, Napoli, 63; Aspetti del mondo artistico di Giovanni Verga, Forum Ital, Am Asn Teachers Ital, Vol I, Nov 2; Ugo reale: un-altra misura, Forum Ital, State Univ NY, Buffalo, Vol VI, No 2. *Mailing Add:* Dept of Mod Lang Cent Conn State Col New Britain CT 06050

IANNI, LAWRENCE ALBERT, b New Kensington, Pa, Apr 19, 30; m 53; c 2. ENGLISH LINGUISTICS, LITERARY CRITICISM. *Educ:* Clarion State Col, BS, 52; Western Reserve Univ, MA, 57, PhD(English), 62. *Prof Exp:* Teacher, Conneaut Valley Joint Schs, 52-54 & Mentor Pub Schs, 54-59; from assoc prof to prof English, Ind Univ, Pa, 60-75, assoc dean grad sch, 71-75; dean fac affairs & prof English, 75-78, PROVOST, SAN FRANCISCO STATE UNIV, 78- *Concurrent Pos:* Mem comn English English, Col Entrance Exam Bd, 67. *Mem:* Ling Soc Am. *Res:* English linguistics; the relationship of literature and science; psycholinguistics and language games. *Publ:* Auth, An answer to doubts about the usefulness of the new grammar, English J, 11/64; Lawrence Ferlinghetti's fourth person singular and the theory of relativity, Wis Studies Contemp Lit, summer 67; A linguistic approach to rhetoric, Col Entrance Exam Bd, 68; Sinclair Lewis as a prophet of black pride, Sinclair Lewis Newsletter, 71; Language is imprecisely reliable, Conf Col Compos & Commun J, 78. *Mailing Add:* San Francisco State Univ 1600 Holloway Ave San Francisco CA 94132

IANNUCCI, AMILCARE ALFREDO, b Casalvieri, Italy Mar 13, 46; Can citizen; m 70. ITALIAN LITERATURE. *Educ:* Univ Toronto, BA, 70; Harvard Univ, AM, 72, PhD(Ital lit), 77. *Prof Exp:* From instr to asst prof, 73-78, ASSOC PROF ITAL, UNIV TORONTO, 78- *Mem:* Mediaeval Acad Am; Dante Soc Am; Can Soc Ital Studies; Can Soc Renaissance Studies; Humanities Asn Can. *Res:* Dante; Medieval and Renaissance Italian literature. *Publ:* Auth, Dante's theory of genres and the Divina Comedia, Dante Studies, 73; Ulysses' folle volo: The burden of history, Medioevo Romanzo, 76; L'Elegia Di Madonna Fiammetta and the first book of the Asolani: The eloquence of unrequited love, Forum Ital, 76; Brunetto Latini: come l'uom s'etterna, Nemla Ital Studies, 77; Beatrice in limbo: A metaphoric harrowing of hell, Dante Studies, 79. *Mailing Add:* 38 Marianfeld Toronto ON M6B 3W1 Can

IANNUCCI, JAMES EMANUEL, b Philadelphia, Pa, May 20, 14. ROMANCE LINGUISTICS. *Educ:* Temple Univ, AB, 36; Univ Pa, MA, 38, PhD, 51. *Prof Exp:* Instr, 36-42, assoc prof, 42-50, chmn dept, 42-80, prof, 50-80, EMER PROF MOD LANG, ST JOSEPH'S COL, 80- *Concurrent Pos:* Consult & prof ling, Airlangga Univ, Indonesia, 64-65; Nat Defense Foreign Lang fel, Univ Hawaii, 68-69. *Mem:* MLA. *Res:* Gemination of inital consonants and its semantic function in Neapolitan. *Publ:* Auth, Lexical Number in Spanish Nouns with Reference to Their English Equivalents, Univ Pa, 52; contribr, Romance Philol, Mod Lang J, Babel & Hispania. *Mailing Add:* Dept of Mod Lang St Joseph's Col Philadelphia PA 19131

ICAZA, ROSA MARIA, b Mexico City, Mex, Apr 24, 25; US citizen. SPANISH CULTURE & LINGUISTICS. *Educ:* Cath Univ AM, BA, 52, MA, 53, PhD(Span, Latin, French), 57, MA, 81. *Prof Exp:* Chmn, Dept Foreign Lang, 64-70, PROF SPAN, INCARNATE WORD COL, 57-, CHMN, DEPT FOREIGN LANG, 76- *Concurrent Pos:* Consult Span, Trinity Univ, MacArthur & Alamo High Schs, 64-74 & consult lang, San Antonio & New Orleans High Schs, 67-68; dir summer sch, Univ Iberno-Am, 66, 66 & 68, dir summer study & travel in Europe, 70, 73, 75; lectr cult, relig & theol topics, & mem Pastoral Team, Mex Am Cult Ctr, 78- *Honors & Awards:* Moody Found Chair Prof, 75. *Mem:* Am Asn Teachers Span & Port; Class Asn Mid West & South; Int Educ Asn; Int Inst Latin Am Lit; Latin Am Studies Asn. *Res:* Theological foundation for practices in popular piety; meanings in the Guadalupe event and painting; Spanish literature and languages. *Publ:* Auth, Stylistic Relationship in Poetry and Prose in the Cantico esperitual of San Juan de la Cruz, Cath Univ Am, 57; Epiphany: Divine revelation, Dialogo, 1/76; Points of contact between St John of the Cross and Jonathan Livingston, The Logos, 76; translr, Escoge la Vida: An essay, Leadership Conf of Women Relig, 77; contribr, Bilingual/Bicultural Education for Elementary School Teachers, Nat Educ Lab, 78; translr, Modo de Cocinar y Recetas para Usar en Horno de Microonda, Trandway Printer, 78; The cross in Mexican American popular piety, Liturgy, 79; transl, La Morenita: Evangelizadora de las Americas, Ligouri, 80. *Mailing Add:* Dept of Foreign Lang Incarnate Word Col 4301 Broadway San Antonio TX 78209

IFTIKHAR, SAMUEL, South Asian History, Higher Education. See Vol I

IGEL, REGINA, b Sao Paulo, Brazil, Apr 26, 42. PORTUGUESE, SPANISH. *Educ:* Univ Sao Paulo, BA, 64; Univ Iowa, MA, 70; Univ NMex, PhD(Port), 73. *Prof Exp:* Instr Port, Univ Iowa, 68-70 & Univ NMex, 70-73; asst prof, 73-77, ASSOC PROF PORT, UNIV MD, 78- *Mem:* MLA; Am Asn Teachers Span & Port (secy, 76); Mid-Atlantic Asn Port High Sch (vpres, 75). *Res:* Brazilian literature of the 19th and 20th centuries. *Publ:* Contribr to Chasqui, Estudos Iberoam, Inter Bibliography Review, Letras Femeninas & Hispania. *Mailing Add:* Dept of Span & Port Univ of Md College Park MD 20740

IGGERS, WILMA ABELES, b Mirkov, Czech, Mar 23, 21; US citizen; m 48; c 3. MODERN GERMAN & CZECH LITERATURES. *Educ:* McMaster Univ, BA, 42; Univ Chicago, AM, 43, PhD, 52. *Prof Exp:* Instr French & Ger, Univ NB, 46; asst prof mod lang, Philander Smith Col, 50-55; asst prof Ger, Dillard Univ & Tulane Univ, 57-63; asst prof, Loyola Univ, Ill, 63-65; from asst prof to assoc prof Ger, 65-75, actg chmn mod lang, 76-77, PROF GER, CANISIUS COL, 75- *Honors & Awards:* DAAD Award, Ger Acad Exchange Serv, 78. *Mem:* MLA; AAUP; Mod Humanities Res Asn; Czech Soc Arts & Sci in US; Soc Hist Czech Jews. *Res:* Cultural History of the Jews in Boehmia and Moravia; recent Czech literature; Karl Kraus. *Publ:* Auth, Carl Kraus, A Viennese Critic of the Twentieth Century, Nijhoff, 67; The Bohemian Jewish writers: Their attitudes toward their roots, Vol III, In: Czechoslovakia Past and Present, Czech Soc Arts & Sci; Leopold Kompert, romancier of the Bohemian ghetto, Mod Austrian Lit, 73; Vojtech Rakous, A Forgotten Czech Story Teller, In: Czechoslovakia, Past and Present, Vol II, The Hague, Mauton, 66; Karl Kraus Then and Now, In: Kankrete Reflexion Festschrift in Honor of Prof Herman Wein, The Hague, Nijhoff, 75; Karl Kraus and his critics, Mod Austrian Lit, Vol 8, No 1/2; From Socialist to Realism to New Individualism: Some Trends in Recent East German Literature, In: East Central Europe, III:69-83. *Mailing Add:* Dept of Mod Lang Canisius Col Buffalo NY 14208

IGLESIAS, MARIO, b Havana, Cuba, Sept 8, 24; m 50; c 2. SPANISH LANGUAGE & LITERATURE. *Educ:* Univ Havana, Dr Pedag, 49; Western Reserve Univ, MA, 67. *Prof Exp:* Teacher, Inst Urquiza, Havana, 42-46; adult educ, San Jose de las Lajas, 45-52; Special Ctr English 16, Havana, 52-56, prin, 56-61; teacher, supvr & prin, Ruston Acad, Cuba, 47-61; teacher high sch, Ohio, 61-64; asst prof Span, Elmira Col, 64-67; asst prof, 67-73, ASSOC PROF ROMANCE LANG, OHIO STATE UNIV, 73- *Mem:* Am Asn Teachers Span & Port. *Res:* Spanish applied linguistics; methods for teaching foreign languages; college teacher preparation. *Publ:* Contribr, Espanol Moderno I & II, 70 & auth, Spanish Testing Program: Level I, 71, C E Merrill; coauth, Cuaderno de ejercicios, In: Beginning Spanish Series, Houghton, 72 & 79; Spanish for Oral and Written Review, Holt, 75 & 81; auth, Spanish Today, Houghton, Vol 2, 82. *Mailing Add:* Dept of Romance Lang Ohio State Univ 1841 Millikin Rd Columbus OH 43210

IHRIE, MAUREEN E, b Seattle, Wash. PENINSULAR SPANISH LITERATURE. *Educ:* Bryn Mawr Col, BA, 71, PhD(Span), 80. *Prof Exp:* Asst prof Span, Union Col, 80-82; vis lectr, Bryn Mawr Col, 82-83. *Mem:* MLA; Cervantes Soc Am. *Res:* Golden Age prose of Spain; ideological currents of Golden Age Spain. *Publ:* Auth, Skepticism in Cervantes, Tamesis Books Ltd, 82. *Mailing Add:* 743 N Ringgold St Philadelphia PA 19130

IKEDA, HIROKO, b Tokyo, Japan, May 23, 14; US citizen. JAPANESE FOLKLORE. *Educ:* Tokyo Woman's Univ, BA, 36; Ind Univ, PhD(folklore), 56. *Prof Exp:* Bibliogr Japanese, East Asiatic Libr, Univ Calif, Berkeley, 51-57; asst prof Japanese & curator Orient Libr, 57-64, assoc prof Asian & Pac lang, 65-70, prof Japanese lit, 70-80, EMER PROF JAPANESE LIT, UNIV HAWAII, MANOA, 81- *Concurrent Pos:* Res mem, Inst Japanese Folklore Studies, 38-48; Am Coun Learned Soc res grant, 62-64; Am Philos Soc grant, 65; Japan Found res fel, 72-73. *Mem:* Am Folklore Soc; Folklore Soc Japan; Japanese Soc Ethnol. *Res:* Comparative study of folk narratives; Konjaku Monogatari; comparative study of English and Scottish ballads with Japanese folk and traditional literature. *Publ:* Auth, A type and motif index of Japanese folk literature, F F Commun 209, Finland, 71. *Mailing Add:* Dept of East Asian Lit Univ Hawaii Manoa Honolulu HI 96822

IKNAYAN, MARGUERITE, b Charleston, Ill, July 17, 17. FRENCH LANGUAGES & LITERATURE. *Educ:* Univ Chicago, AB, 38, AM, 39; Columbia Univ, PhD(French), 56. *Prof Exp:* Teacher French & Span, Monticello Col, 45-47; lectr French, Wellesley Col, 55-58; asst prof, 59-63, ASSOC PROF FRENCH, UNIV IOWA, 63- *Mem:* MLA; Am Asn Teachers Fr. *Res:* French literature of Romantic period; French novel and criticism. *Publ:* Auth, The Idea of the Novel in France: The Critical Reaction 1815-1848, Droz, Geneva, 61. *Mailing Add:* Dept of French & Ital Univ of Iowa Iowa City IA 52242

ILIE, PAUL, b Brooklyn, NY, Oct 11, 32. ROMANCE LANGUAGES. *Educ:* Brooklyn Col, BA, 54; Brown Univ, MA, 56, PhD, 59. *Prof Exp:* Instr Span, 59-62, from asst prof to assoc prof romance lang, Univ Mich, Ann Arbor, 62-68, prof, 68-82; PROF SPAN & COMP LIT, UNIV SOUTHERN CALIF, LOS ANGELES, 82- *Concurrent Pos:* Rackham res grant, 60-61, 64, 66-67, 76; Guggenheim fel, 65-66; Am Coun Learned Soc fel, 69-70; adv ed, Hisp Rev, 69-; vis prof Span lit, Hebrew Univ Jerusalem, 70; mem Centro Estudios Siglo XVIII, Oviedo; Nat Endowment Humanities fel, comp lit, 78. *Mem:* Am Asn Teachers Span & Port; Am Soc 18th Century Studies; MLA; Am Comp Lit Asn. *Res:* Modern Spanish literature; comparative studies in Spanish, French and English literature from 1700 onward. *Publ:* Auth, La Novelistica de Camilo Jose Cela, Gredos, Madrid, 63; Nietzche in Spain, PMLA, 64; Unamuno: An Existential View of Self and Society, Univ Wis, 67; The Surrealist Mode in Spanish Literature, Univ Mich, 68; Becquer and the Romantic grotesque, PMLA, 6/68; Documents of the Spanish Vanguard, Univ NC, Chapel Hill, 69; French image of Spain, Eighteeenth-Century Studies, 76; Literature and inner exile, Johns Hopkins Univ, 81. *Mailing Add:* Dept of Romance Lang Univ of Mich Ann Arbor MI 48109

ILIESCU, NICOLAE, b Romania, May 21, 19; m 53; c 2. LANGUAGES. *Educ:* Univ Padua, Dr in Lett, 47; Harvard Univ, PhD, 58. *Prof Exp:* From instr to asst prof Italian, 58-63, assoc prof, 63-68, PROF ROMANCE LANG & LIT, HARVARD UNIV, 68- *Concurrent Pos:* UNESCO grant, Fiesole, Italy, 50-51; Guggenheim fel, Rome, 61-62. *Mem:* MLA; Renaissance Soc Am; Mediaeval Acad Am; Dante Soc Am; Am Asn Teachers Ital. *Res:* Nineteenth century Italian literature; medieval Italian literature and Dante; Renaissance Italian literature, especially Petrarch. *Publ:* Auth, Da Manzoni a Nievo (considerazioni sul romanzo ital), 59 & Il Canzoniere petrarchesco e Sant Agostine, 62, Soc Acad Romena, Rome. *Mailing Add:* Deerhaven Rd Lincoln MA 01773

ILLIANO, ANTONIO, b Monte di Procida, Italy, Apr 21, 34; m 62; c 1. ROMANCE LANGUAGES & LITERATURES. *Educ:* Pozzuoli, Liceo, 52; Univ Naples, DottL, 58; Univ Calif, Berkeley, PhD(Romance lang & lit), 66. *Prof Exp:* Asst Ital, Univ Ill, 59-60 & Univ Calif, Berkeley, 60-63; assoc, Univ Calif, Santa Barbara, 63-66; asst prof Romance lang, Univ Tex, Austin, 66-68, res & acad excellence prog fel, 66; vis asst prof Romance Lang, Univ Ore, 68-69; asst prof, 69-71, assoc prof, 71-82, PROF ROMANCE LANG, UNIV NC, CHAPEL HILL, 82- *Concurrent Pos:* Pogue leave, Univ NC, Chapel Hill, 77; mem fac, Ital Sch, Middlebury Col, summer 81, Univ Ga Cortona Prog, summer, 82. *Mem:* MLA; Am Asn Teachers Ital; Dante Soc Am; Pirandello Soc Am. *Res:* Modern literature; comparative literature; history of criticism. *Publ:* Auth, Pirandello in England and the United States, Bull New York Pub Libr, 2/67; Da scelus a innocenza: Osservazioni sulla genesi e problematicita della Mirra di Alfieri, Studi Piemontesi, 3/72; Per una definizione della vena cosmogonica di Calvino, Italica, fall 72; Italian without a master, Mark Twain J, 74; Introduzione alla Critica Pirandelliana, 76; Pirandello and Theosophy, Mod Drama, 12/77; Metapsichica e Letteratura in Pirandello, 82. *Mailing Add:* Dept of Romance Lang Univ of NC Chapel Hill NC 27514

ILNYTZKYJ, OLEH STEPAN, b Furth, WGer, Feb 2, 49; US citizen; m 79. SLAVIC LANGUAGES & LITERATURES. *Educ:* City Univ New York, BA, 71; Harvard Univ, MA, 75. *Prof Exp:* Ed-in-chief, Recenzija: A Review of Soviet Ukrainian Publications, Ukrainian Res Inst, Harvard Univ, 73-74; teaching fel, Harvard Univ, 78-79; LECTR UKRAINIAN & RUSSIAN LANG & LIT, UNIV MANITOBA, 79- *Concurrent Pos:* Dir Ukrainian Summer Inst, Harvard Univ, summer, 80. *Res:* Ukrainian avant-garde literary movements; Ukrainian-Russian literary relations in the early 19th century; Russian formalism and futurism. *Publ:* Auth, Mykola Bazhan: His poetry and his critics, Recenzija, Vol V, No 2, 75; Antonych: Intimations of mortality, J of Ukrainian Grad Studies, Vol 1, No 1, 76; Anatomy of a literary scandal: M Semenko and the origins of Ukrainian futurism, Harvard Ukrainian Studies, Vol II, No 4, 78. *Mailing Add:* Slavic Studies Univ of Manitoba Winnipeg MB R3T 2N2 Can

IMAMURA, SHIGEO, b San Jose, Calif, Aug 14, 22; Japanese citizen; m 63. LINGUISTICS, ENGLISH AS A SECOND LANGUAGE. *Educ:* Matsuyama Univ Commerce, Dipl, 43; Univ Mich, Ann Arbor, BA, 53, MA, 64. *Prof Exp:* Teacher supvr English as second lang, Ehime State Bd Educ, Japan, 49-55; asst prof, Ehime Univ, Japan, 55-61, assoc dir English teaching inst, 56-61; asst prof English as second lang, Mich State Univ, 61-62; asst prof, Ehime Univ, 62-63; asst prof, 63-64, dir English lang ctr, 64-73, ASSOC PROF ENGLISH AS A SECOND LANG, MICH STATE UNIV, 66-, DIR SPEC PROGS, ENGLISH LANG CTR, 78- *Concurrent Pos:* Dir, Konan-Ill Ctr, Kobe, Japan, 77-78. *Mem:* Nat Asn Foreign Student Affairs; Asn Teachers English as Second Lang; Teachers English to Speakers Other Lang. *Res:* Pronunciation and grammar in teaching English as a second language; teaching Japanese as a second language, especially grammar; inter-cultural understanding. *Publ:* Coauth, Readings from Samuel Clemens, 69 & Readings on American Society, 69, Blaisdell; auth, Basic knowledge for Studies in the United States, Kenkyusha, Tokyo, 72; Teaching of English in the Middle East and Indonesia, 7/72 & Cultural interference in language learning, 7/73, English Lang Educ Coun Bull, Tokyo; International Understanding and the Teaching of English, Lang Educ Coun Tokyo, 74. *Mailing Add:* English Lang Ctr Mich State Univ East Lansing MI 48824

IMBERT, PATRICK LOUIS, b Paris, France, Feb 4, 48; Can citizen. FRENCH LITERATURE, SEMIOTICS. *Educ:* Univ Ottawa, MA, 70, PhD(semiotics), 74. *Prof Exp:* Lectr French, Univ Ottawa, 69-74; asst prof, McMaster univ, 74-75; asst prof, 75-79, ASSOC PROF SEMIOTICS & FRENCH, UNIV OTTAWA, 79- *Concurrent Pos:* Can Coun fel, 78; social sci & humanities res coun Can, 81. *Mem:* Can Semiotics Res Asn; Am Semiotic Asn; Asn Can Studies; Can Fedn for Humanities. *Res:* Semiotics; French Canadian literature; French literature. *Publ:* Semiotique et description balzacienne, Univ Ottawa, 78; Anththeses et bouleversement culturel dans La nuit de Ferron, Rev du Pacifique, spring 78; Improving the teaching of literature with the use of linguistic and semiotic approaches, In: Improving University Teaching, 79; Revolution, culturelle et cliches chez Ducharme, J Can Fiction, 25/26: 227-236; Semiostyle: la description chez Balzac, Flaubert, Zola, Revue Litterature, 80; Pastiche, lecture, ideologie, In: Lecture et lecteurs de l'ecrit moderne, Carleton Univ, 80; Multidisciplinarity, semiotics and pedagogy, J Benjamins, Amsterdan, Ars Semeiotica, III: 275-281. *Mailing Add:* 821 Eastbourne Ave Ottawa ON K1K 0H8 Can

IMERTI, ARTHUR D, b New York, NY, July 2, 15; m 51. ROMANCE LANGUAGES. *Educ:* City Col New York, BA, 39; Fordham Univ, MA, 45; Columbia Univ, PhD(Ital), 69. *Prof Exp:* Teacher Romance Lang & dir, Imerti Mod Lang Inst, 43-50; prof, New Sch Social Res, 51-71, chmn dept foreign lang, 60-64; adj assoc prof Span, City Univ NY, 73-74; RETIRED. *Concurrent Pos:* Asst prof Romance lang, Marshall Col, 47; asst prof speech, Yeshiva Univ, 50-59; educ consult, Vet Admin Hosp, 66-68. *Mem:* MLA; Renaissance Soc Am; Am Asn Teachers Ital; Am Ital Soc. *Res:* Italian and comparative Renaissance; Risorgimento. *Publ:* Auth, A blind teacher speaks, Occupations, 3/45; Mexico's lost tribe, Pan-Am, 10/47; translr & ed, The Expulsion of the Triumphant Beast (Giordano Bruno), Rutgers Univ, 64; auth, Vincenzo Catalani: Neopolitan Jacobin, Jurist, Reformer, Coronado, 76. *Mailing Add:* 69 Fifth Ave New York NY 10003

IMMERWAHR, HENRY RUDOLPH, b Breslau, Ger, Feb 28, 16; US citizen; m 44; c 1. CLASSICS. *Educ:* Univ Florence, Italy, DLitt, 38; Yale Univ, PhD(classics), 43. *Prof Exp:* From instr to asst prof classics, Yale Univ, 47-57; from asst prof to prof, 57-76, Kenan prof, 70-71, alumni distinguished prof, 76-77, EMER PROF GREEK, UNIV NC, CHAPEL HILL, 77- *Concurrent Pos:* Guggenheim Mem Found fel, 46-47; Morse fel, Yale Univ, 55-56; Am Coun Learned Soc grant-in-aid, 57-59; mem managing comt, Am Sch Classic Studies, Athens, 65-; sr fel, Ctr Hellenic Studies, DC, 65-; mem adv bd, Greek, Roman & Byzantine Studies, 68-; vis prof, Am Sch Classic Studies, Athens, 70-71, dir, 77-82; mem adv bd, Iconographic Lexicon Classic Mythology, 72- *Mem:* Am Philol Asn; Soc Promotion Hellenic Studies; Class Asn Midwest & S; Archaeol Inst Am; Mod Greek Studies Asn. *Res:* Greek literature; epigraphy and archaeology. *Publ:* Auth, Aspects of historical causation in Herodotus, Trans & Proc Am Philol Asn, 56; Bookrolls on attic vases, Studies . . . B L Ullman, Rome, 63; Form and Thought in Herodotus, Am Philol Asn, 66; Pathology of power and the speeches in Thucydides, In: The Speeches in Thucydides, Univ NC, Chapel Hill, 73. *Mailing Add:* Dept of Classics Univ of NC Chapel Hill NC 27514

IMMERWAHR, RAYMOND MAX, b Chicago, Ill, May 11, 13; m 43; c 2. GERMAN & COMPARATIVE LITERATURE. *Educ:* Swarthmore Col, AB, 34; Northwestern Univ, AM, 35; Univ Calif, PhD, 41. *Prof Exp:* Instr, Swarthmore Col, 38; assoc, Univ Calif, Los Angeles, 38-41; from asst prof to assoc prof Ger, Wash Univ, 47-60; prof Ger lit, Univ Wash, 60-71; prof, 70-78, EMER PROF GER, UNIV WESTERN ONT, 78- *Concurrent Pos:* Guggenheim fel, 56-57; Am Coun Learned Soc grant-in-aid, 65-66. *Mem:* MLA; Asn Can Univ Teachers Ger; Int Ver Germanistik; Asn Ger Studies. *Res:* German and comparative literature of 18th and 19th centuries; critical theory of romanticism; Friedr Schlegel. *Publ:* Tieck's Fantastic Comedy, Wash Univ, 53; Romantisch: Genese und Tradition einer Denkform, In: Republica Literaria Series, Frankfurt, 72; Romantic and its cognates in England, Germany and France between 1790, In: Romantic: The History of a Word, Univ Toronto, 72; Friedrich Schlegel: Der Dichter als journalist und essayist, Jahrbuch Int Germanistik, 77-78; Diderot Herder, and the dichotomy of touch and sight, Seminar, 78; Sublime manliness and lovely femininity in the age of Goethe, In: Tradition and Creation, Essays in Honor of E M Wilkinson, 78. *Mailing Add:* 3545 NE 96 St Seattle WA 98115

IMPEY, OLGA TUDORICA, b Constanta, Romania, Sept 25, 37; m 67; c 2. SPANISH MEDIEVAL & RENAISSANCE LITERATURE. *Educ:* Univ Bucharest, BA, 61; Univ Ky, PhD(Span), 72. *Prof Exp:* Asst prof Span & romance ling, Univ Bucharest, 61-67; teaching asst, Univ Ky, 68-72; instr, Princeton Univ, 72-74; asst prof, 75-80, ASSOC PROF SPAN, IND UNIV, 80- *Concurrent Pos:* Lectr Span & Romance ling, Princeton Univ, 74-75. *Mem:* MLA; Midwest Mod Lang Asn; Asociacion Internacional de los Hispanistas; Soc Romanian Studies. *Res:* Spanish and European medieval prose and poetry; Spanish Renaissance poetry; rhetoric and stylistics (theory and practice). *Publ:* Coauth, Quelques remarques sur la flexion nominale romane, Societe Roumaine de Linguistique Romane, Bucharest, 70; auth, Alfonso de Cartagena, traductor de Seneca y precursor del humanismo espanol, Prohemio, Madrid, Vol 3, 72; Apuntes sobre el estilo romancistico del Duque de Rivas, In: Acta, Cong Romance Ling & Philol, Acta, Quebec, 76; Los topoi y los comentarios literarios en el Libro de buen amor, Nueva revista de filolgia hispanica, Vol 25, 76; La estructura unitaria de Razon feyta d'amor, J Hisp Philol, Vol 4, No 1; Ovid, Alfonso X and Juan Rodriguez del Padron: Two Castilian Translations of the Heroides and the Beginnings of Spanish Sentimental Prose, Bull Hisp Studies, Vol 57, 80; The Literary Emancipation of Juan Rodriguez del Padron: From the Fictional Cartas to the Siervo libre de amor, Speculum, Vol 55, No 2; Un dechado de la prosa literaria alfonsi: el relato cronistico de los amores de Dido, Romance Philol, Vol 34, 80. *Mailing Add:* 1033 Hawthorne Bloomington IN 47401

INAL, HALIMAT, b St Petersburg, Russia, Oct 23, 13; m 34. FRENCH LANGUAGE & LITERATURE. *Educ:* Istanbul Univ, MA, 42; Univ Paris, PhD(French lit), 51. *Prof Exp:* Mem fac French, lycees, Turkey, 42-47, norm training cols, Turkey, 51-58, Vanderbilt Univ, 58-60, teachers cols, Turkey, 60-61 & Istanbul Tech Univ, 61-66; assoc prof, 66-76, PROF FRENCH, SPELMAN UNIV, 76- *Res:* Comparative language study and instruction in French, Turkish, Polish, Russian and English; comparative literature. *Publ:* Auth, La Turquie chez Chateaubriand et Lamartine, 68 & Les ambassadeurs francais en Turquie et les ambassadeurs Turcs en France dans la seconde moitie du XVIII siecle, 68, Istanbul: Key to French grammar, Atlanta Univ, 69. *Mailing Add:* 3660 Peachtree Rd NE Atlanta GA 30319

INCLEDON, JOHN S, b New York, NY, Feb 5, 48; m 75; c 1. LATIN AMERICAN LITERATURE. *Educ:* State Univ NY Binghamton, MA, 73, PhD(comp lit), 79. *Prof Exp:* ASST PROF SPAN, ALBRIGHT COL, 77- *Mem:* MLA; Inst Int Lit Iberoam. *Res:* Literary theory and criticism. *Publ:* Auth, Una clave de Cortazar sobre 62. Modelo para armar, 4-6/75 & La obra invisible de Pierre Menard, 7-12/77, Rev Iberoam; Salvador Elizonda's Farabeuf: The reader as victim, In: Latin American Fiction Today: A Symposium, Hispamerica, 80; La ejecucion silenciosa en Libro de Manuel, Cuadernos Hispanoam, 10-12/80; Octavio Paz y los origenes de la literatura Latinoamericana, In: Texto/Contexto en la literatura Iberoamericana, Madrid, 80. *Mailing Add:* Dept of Mod Lang Albright Col Reading PA 19604

INFANTE, DOMINIC A, Communication. See Vol II

INGALLS, DANIEL HENRY HOLMES, b New York, NY, May 4, 16. SANSKRIT. *Educ:* Harvard Univ, AB, 36, AM, 38. *Prof Exp:* Asst prof Indian studies, 49-54, assoc prof Sanskrit & Indian Studies, 54-58, WALES PROF SANSKIRT & CHMN DEPT SANSKIRT & INDIAN STUDIES, HARVARD UNIV, 58- *Concurrent Pos:* Curator Sanskirt manuscripts, 49-54; ed, Harvard Orient Ser, 49- *Mem:* Am Orient Soc (pres, 58); Asn Asian Studies. *Res:* Sanskrit literature; Indian history and philosophy. *Publ:* Auth, Materials for the Study of Nayva-Nyaya Logic, 51, An Anthology of Sanskrit Court Poetry, 65 & Sanskrit Poetry, 68, Harvard Univ. *Mailing Add:* Widener Libr 273 Harvard Univ Cambridge MA 02138

INGALLS, WAYNE BARRITT, b Vancouver, BC, July 14, 39; c 3. CLASSICS. *Educ:* Univ BC, BA, 62; Univ Toronto, MA, 64, PhD(classics), 71. *Prof Exp:* Asst prof classics, Bishop's Univ, 67-72; asst prof classics & humanities, Champlain Regional Col, 72-73; asst dean, 73-79, ASSOC PROF HIST, MT ST VINCENT UNIV, 73-, DIR RES & SPEC PROJ, 79- *Mem:* Class Asn Can; Am Philol Asn. *Res:* Greek literature; Latin literature; mythology. *Publ:* Auth, The structure of the Homeric hexameter 24: 1-12, Repetition in Lucretius, 25: 227-236 & Another dimension of the Homeric formula, 26: 111-122, Phoenix; The Analogical formula in Homer, 106: 211-226 & Formular density in the similes of the Iliad, 109: 87-109, Trans Am Philol Asn. *Mailing Add:* Off Res & Spec Proj Mt St Vincent Univ Halifax NS B3M 2J6 Can

INGEMANN, FRANCES, b Trenton, NJ, Oct 25, 27. LINGUISTICS. *Educ:* NJ State Col, Montclair, BA, 49; Columbia Univ, MA, 50; Ind Univ, PhD(ling), 56. *Prof Exp:* Instr English, Univ PR, 50-52; instr, Columbia Univ, 50, 51, 56; linguist, Haskins Labs, 56-57; asst prof English, 57-61, assoc prof English & ling, 61-66, PROF LING, UNIV KANS, 66- *Concurrent Pos:* Lectr phonetics, Univ Edinburgh, 59-60. *Mem:* Ling Soc Am; Acoust Soc Am; Am Asn Phonetic Sci. *Res:* Acoustic phonetics; New Guinea languages; Liberian languages. *Publ:* Coauth, Studies in Cheremis, the Supernatural; Eastern Cheremis Manual, Ind Univ, 61. *Mailing Add:* Dept of Ling Univ of Kans Lawrence KS 66045

INGERSOLL, ROSS HOMER, b Eureka, Utah, Oct 16, 14. LINGUISTICS. *Educ:* Univ Colo, BA, 37; Northwestern Univ, MA, 38, PhD, 41. *Prof Exp:* Asst instr Romance lang, Northwestern Univ, 38-41; instr, Univ Colo, 41-43; with US Dept State, 46-52; private bus, 52-62; dir div gen educ, 68-75, PROF FOR LANG, WOODBURY UNIV, 62-, DIR AM ENGLISH LANG PROG, 81- *Mem:* MLA; AAUP. *Mailing Add:* Div of Gen Educ Woodbury Col Los Angeles CA 90017

INGERSOLL, SHEILA MOST, English Language & Linguistics. See Vol II

INGHAM, NORMAN WILLIAM, b Holyoke, Mass, Dec 31, 34. SLAVIC LANGUAGES & LITERATURES. *Educ:* Middlebury Col, AB, 57; Univ Mich, MA, 59; Harvard Univ, PhD(Slavic), 63. *Prof Exp:* Inter-Univ Comt Travel Grants study & res grant, Charles Univ, Prague, 63-64; asst prof Slavic lang & lit, Ind Univ, 64-65; asst prof, Harvard Univ, 65-71; ASSOC PROF & CHMN, DEPT SLAVIC LANG & LIT, UNIV CHICAGO, 71-, CHMN COMT ON SLAVIC & EAST EUROP STUDIES, 82- *Concurrent Pos:* Am Coun Learned Soc grant, Sixth Int Congr, Slavists, Prague, 68; vis fel, Dumbarton Oaks Ctr Byzantine Studies, 72-73. *Mem:* MLA; Am Asn Teachers Slavic & East Europ Lang; Am Asn Advan Slavic Studies; Czech Soc Arts & Sci. *Res:* Medieval Russian and Slavic literature; 19th century Russian literature. *Publ:* Auth, The limits of secular biography in Med-Slavic literature, particularly Old Russian, In: American Contributions to the Sixth International Congress of Slavists, Mounton, The Hague, 68; The sovereign as martyr, East and West, Slavic & East Europ J, 73; E T A Hoffman's Reception in Russia, Jal, 74; co-ed, Mnemozina: Studia Litteraria Russica in Honorem Vsevolod Setchkarev, Wilhelm Fink, 74; auth, Irony in Povest' o Gore: Zlocastii, Slavic & East Europ J, 80; The Martyred Prince and the Question of Slavic Cultural Continuity in the Early Middle Ages, Calif Slavic Studies, 82. *Mailing Add:* Dept of Slavic Lang & Lit Univ of Chicago 1130 E 59th St Chicago IL 60637

INGRAM, DAVID, b Baltimore, Md, Apr 25, 44; m 68; c 1. LINGUISTICS. *Educ:* Georgetown Univ, BS, 66; Stanford Univ, PHD(ling), 70. *Prof Exp:* Res assoc lang disorders, Inst Childhood Aphasia, Stanford Univ, 70-72; asst prof, 72-77, assoc prof, 77-82, PROF LING, UNIV BC, 82- *Mem:* Ling Soc Am; Int Assoc Study Child Lang (pres, 81-). *Res:* Language acquisition in children; language universals. *Publ:* Auth, Transitivity in child language, Language, 71; coauth, The development of base syntax in normal and linguistically deviant children, J Speech & Hearing Res, 73; auth, Phonological rules in young children, J Child Lang, 74; If and when transformations are acquired by children, Monogr Georgetown Round Table, 75; Phonological Disability in Children, Edward Arnold, 76; Procedures for the Phonological Analysis of Children's Language, Univ Park Press, 81. *Mailing Add:* Dept of Ling Univ BC Vancouver BC V6T 1W5 Can

INGRAM, FRANK LEQUELLEC, b Cincinnati, Ohio, Mar 7, 34; m 59; c 3. SLAVIC LANGUAGES & LITERATURES. *Educ:* US Naval Acad, BS, 56; Ind Univ, AM, 63, PhD(Slavic lang), 67. *Prof Exp:* Asst prof Slavic lang & lit, Ind Univ, Bloomington, 67-68; asst prof, 68-72, ASSOC PROF RUSS, MICH STAE UNIV, 72- *Concurrent Pos:* Assoc ed, Russ Lang J, 69-74. *Mem:* Am Asn Teachers Slavic & E Europ Lang; Am Asn Advan Slavic Studies. *Res:* Russian area studies; 19th century Russian verse parody, especially Kozma Prutkov; Russian reading and vocabulary acquisition. *Publ:* Auth, Pushkin's Skazka o zolotom petushke and Washington Irving's The Legend of the Arabian Astrologer, 2/69 & Kozma Prutkov is more alive than ever, spring 71, Russ Lang J; coauth, A program for listening comprehension, Slavic & E European J, spring 75. *Mailing Add:* Dept of Ger & Russ Mich State Univ East Lansing MI 48823

INGWERSEN, NIELS, b Horsens, Denmark, May 18, 35; m 61. SCANDINAVIAN LITERATURE. *Educ:* Copenhagen Univ, Cand Mag, 63. *Prof Exp:* Adj Danish lit & lang, Hellerup Seminaruim, Denmark, 64-65; from asst prof to assoc prof, 65-73, PROF SCAND LIT, UNIV WISMADISON, 73- *Concurrent Pos:* Res assoc, Odense Univ, Denmark, 71-72; assoc ed, Scand Studies, 71-; vis prof, Aarhus Univ, Denmark, 78-79. *Mem:* Soc Advan Scand Studies (pres, 69-71); Dansklaerer-foreningen; MLA. *Res:* Danish novel; Danish prose of 1890's; theory of the novel. *Publ:* Auth, Forfatterens Mange Stemmer i Blichers Sildig Opvaagnen, Danske Stud, 71; Tendenser i amerikansk romankritik, Edda, 74; contribr, The Hero in Scandinavian Literature, Univ Tex, 75; auth, The impact of Structuralism on Danish literary criticism, Bks Abroad, 75; coauth, Martin A Hansen, Twayne, 76; contribr, Nordisk Litteratur Historie, Univ Odensen, 78; ed, Seventeen Danish Poets, Lincoln, 81; The inevitable confrontation: Literary history vs critical schools, World Lit Today, 82. *Mailing Add:* Dept of Scand Studies 1302 Van Hise Hall Univ of Wis Madison WI 53706

INNIS, ROBERT EDWARD, Philosophy, Linguistics. See Vol IV

INSLER, STANLEY, b New York, NY, June 23, 37. INDO-IRANIAN LINGUISTICS. *Educ:* Columbia Col, AB, 57; Yale Univ, PhD(Sanskrit), 63. *Prof Exp:* From instr to asst prof, 63-70, assoc prof, 70-80, PROF SANSKRIT & CHMN DEPT, GRAD SCH, YALE UNIV, 80- *Concurrent Pos:* Morse fel, 67-68. *Mem:* Am Orient Soc; Ling Soc Am; fel Royal Asiatic Soc; Deut Morganläandische Ges. *Res:* History of Sanskrit language; comparative Indo-Iranian linguistics; Zoroastrianism. *Mailing Add:* Dept of Eastern & Southern Asian Lang Yale Univ New Haven CT 06520

IODICE, DON ROBERT, b Providence, RI, May 22, 28; m 61; c 2. FOREIGN LANGUAGES. *Educ:* Yale Univ, AB, 49, MA, 56. *Prof Exp:* Co-owner & mgr, advert agency, 49-54; stockholder & off, Corp Radio, New Rochelle, NY, 53-55; asst English as foreign lang, Col Jules-Ferry, Versailles, France, 56-57; master French, St Albans Sch, Washington, DC, 57-59; instr & dir lang lab, Handon High Sch, Conn, 59-60; asst to dir, teaching res & tech div, Electronic Teaching Lab, Washington, DC, 60-61; asst prof French & dir lang lab, Univ Hawaii, 61-62; chmn dept foreign lang, Hinsdale Twp High Sch, 62-64; asst prof French, ling & educ, 64-69, ASSOC PROF FRENCH & LING, OAKLAND UNIV, 69- *Concurrent Pos:* Ford Found fel, Yale Univ, 55-56; Fulbright grant, 56-57; French Govt asst, 56-57; instr, Cent Conn State Col, 59; lectr, Northeastern Ill Univ, 62-; consult, MLA, 63-65; dir spec French proj, Chrysler Corp, 75-77 & Am Motors, 79-; pres, Innovative Lang Prog Inc, 78- *Mem:* Am Asn Teachers Fr; Nat Asn Educ Broadcasters; AAUP; Am Coun Teaching Foreign Lang. *Res:* Linguistics and teaching of French; development of testing techniques for evaluations of foreign language achievement; development of instructional material in French. *Publ:* Auth, Guidelines to Language Teaching in Classroom and Laboratory, Electronic Teaching Lab, 61; contribr, Effective Foreign Language Instruction in the Secondary School, Prentice-Hall, 69; Getting it Done in French & Getting More Done in French, Oakland Univ, 77. *Mailing Add:* 796 Wilwood Rd Rochester MI 48063

IRBY, JAMES EAST, b Bowie, Tex, May 19, 31; m 56; c 2. LATIN AMERICAN LITERATURE. *Educ:* Univ Kans, BA, 52; Nat Univ Mex, MA, 57; Univ Mich, PhD, 62. *Prof Exp:* From instr to asst prof, 59-67, assoc prof, 67-80, PROF SPAN LANG & LATIN AM LIT, PRINCETON UNIV, 80- *Mem:* MLA. *Res:* Avant-garde literature in Latin America. *Publ:* Co-ed & translr, Labyrinths: Selected Stories and Prose Writings of Jorge Luis Borges, New Directions, 62. *Mailing Add:* Dept of Romance Lang Princeton Univ Princeton NJ 08540

IRIZARRY, ESTELLE DIANE, b Paterson, NJ, Nov 13, 37; m 63; c 3. HISPANIC LITERATURE. *Educ:* Montclair State Col, BA, 59; Rutgers Univ, New Brunswick, MA, 63; George Washington Univ, PhD(Span), 70. *Prof Exp:* Instr English as second lang, Univ PR, 63-66; instr Span, Howard Univ, 66-68; instr, George Washington Univ, 68-70; asst prof, 70-75, assoc prof, 75-78, PROF SPAN, GEORGETOWN UNIV, 78- *Concurrent Pos:* Lectr, Foreign Serv Inst, US State Dept. *Mem:* Asn Int Hispanistas; Am Asn Teachers Span & Port. *Res:* Twentieth century Spanish literature; 20th century Spanish-American literature; Puerto Rican literature. *Publ:* Auth, Los hechos y las cultura en los EE UU, monthly sect: In Nivel, Mex, 70-; Teoria y Creacion Literaria en Francisco Ayala, Ed Gredos, 71; Francisco Ayala, Twayne, 77; La Broma Literaria en Nuestros Dias, Eliseo Torres, 79; La inventiva surrealista de E F Granell, Insula, 76; Rafael Dieste, Twayne, 79; La creacion literaria de Rafael Dieste, do Castro, 80; Enrique A Laguerre, Twayne, 82. *Mailing Add:* 3401 Wessynton Way Alexandria VA 22309

IRVING, EVELYN UHRHAN, b Buffalo, NY, Feb 14, 19; m. SPANISH. *Educ:* Fla State Univ, BA, 41, MA, 47; Univ Ill, PhD(Span & ling), 50. *Prof Exp:* Instr physics, Ind Univ, 43-44, instr math, 46-47; instr French & math, Leelenau Schs, Glen Arbor, Mich, 45-46; asst Span, Univ Ill, 47-48; from assoc prof to prof foreign lang & head dept, SDak State Col, 50-61; vis prof Span & foreign lang teaching methods, Macalester Col, 63-65; prof Span & dir lang lab, NCent Col, Ill, 65-67; sessional prof Span, Univ Guelph, 67-69; consult foreign lang & vis prof Span, Carson-Newman Col, 69-71; vis prof French, Maryville Col, Tenn, 71-72; assoc prof, 72-75, prof, 75-81, EMER PROF SPAN & ENGLISH AS SECOND LANG, TENN TECHNOL UNIV, 81- *Concurrent Pos:* Delta Kappa Gamma scholar, Spain, 56-57; Soc Sci Res Coun grant, 62-63. *Mem:* Emer mem, Am Asn Teachers Span & Port; emer mem, Ling Soc Am; Int Asn Learning Lab Dirs (vpres, 67-69, pres, 69-71); Int Asn AV Methods. *Res:* Spanish language and literature; teaching English as a second language; Ruben Dario in Guatemala. *Publ:* Auth, Linguistic analysis of Gongoras baroque style, In: Descriptive Studies in Spanish Grammar, Univ Ill, 54; Short Stories of Rafaela Contreras de Dario, Univ Miami, 65; Ruben Dario en Guatemala, In: Estudios sobre Ruben Dario, Fondo Cult Econ, Mex, 68; A final examination in the language laboratory, Nat Asn Land Lab Dirs, 3/69; coauth, Let's Learn the Spanish Language (Aprendamos la lengua espanola), Ctr Edit el Arte, Guatemala, 75; contribr, A Dictionary of Contemporary Latin American Authors, Ariz State Univ Ctr Latin Am Studies, 75; auth, Rafael Arevalo Martinez: Un hombre fantastico y su literatura fantastica, In: Otros mundos otros fuegos: Fantasia y Realismo Magico en Iberoamerica, Mich State Univ, 75; The woman experience in North Africa, Monitor, London, 11/81. *Mailing Add:* 2508 Glen Elm Dr N E Cedar Rapids IA 52402

IRVING, JOHN S, b Oakland, Calif, Jan 14, 32; m 58; c 1. GERMANIC LANGUAGES. *Educ:* Stanford Univ, BA, 53; Univ Calif, Los Angeles, MA, 59, PhD(German), 64. *Prof Exp:* Asst prof, 61-72, assoc prof, 72-80, PROF GERMAN, CALIF STATE UNIV, NORTHRIDGE, 80- *Res:* Goethe; European Romanticism. *Mailing Add:* Dept of Ger Calif State Univ Northridge CA 91330

IRVING, THOMAS BALLANTINE, b Cambridge, Ont, July 20, 14; nat US, m 50; c 3. CONTEMPORARY ISLAMIC WORLD, CENTRAL AMERICAN CULTURE. *Educ:* Univ Toronto, BA, 37; Univ Montreal, M es L, 38; Princeton Univ, PhD, 40. *Prof Exp:* Instr Span, Univ Calif, 40-42; dir, Col Nueva Granada, Bogota, Colombia, 44-45; asst prof Romance lang, Wells Col, 45-46; vis prof hist & lit & dir summer sch, Univ San Carlos, 46-48; from asst prof to prof Span & Arabic, Univ Minn, Minneapolis, 48-65; prof mod lang & chmn dept Span, N Cent Col (Ill), 65-67; prof Span, Univ Guelph, 67-69; prof Span, Univ Tenn, Knoxville, 69-80; RETIRED. *Concurrent Pos:* Consult, export div, Minneapolis-Moline Co, 53-54; Fulbright fel, Col Arts & Sci, Baghdad, 56-57; NDEA insts, Brookings, SDak, 61 Peoria, Ill, 62, Guatemala, 63, Stockton, Calif, 64; vis prof, Univ Libya, 73; mem bd trustees & chmn exec coun, Am Islamic Col, Chicago, 81- *Mem:* Am Asn Teachers Span & Port; Am Orient Soc; Geog & Hist Soc Guatemala; Latin Am Studies Asn; Mid E Studies Asn NAm. *Res:* Contemporary translation of the Qur'an; Guatemalan literature; Hispanic-Arabic culture. *Publ:* Auth, Falcon of Spain, Ashraf, Lahore, 54, 2nd ed, 62; coauth, Paisajes del Sur, Ronald, 54; auth, San Marcos de Colon, 9/55 & Preceptos historiales, 12/59, Rev Iberoamericana; The process of Arab thought in Spain, Stud Islam, Delhi, 4/67; Selections from the Noble Reading, a Qur'anic anthology, Unity Publ, 68, rev ed, 80; Polished Jade, 82 & The Tide of Islam, 82. *Mailing Add:* 2508 Glen Elm Dr NE Cedar Rapids IA 52402

ISAACSON, LANAE, b Salt Lake City, Utah, June 13, 45. SCANDINAVIAN LITERATURE, FOLKLORE. *Educ:* Willamette Univ, BA, 67; Univ Calif, Los Angeles, MA, 74, PhD(Scandinavian & folklore), 80. *Prof Exp:* Lang lab asst, Willamette Univ, 63-67; ref asst I-II, Univ Calif, Los Angeles, 68-69; doc librn, Univ Santa Clara, 69-73; res asst, 77-78, RES INTERN, UNIV CALIF, LOS ANGELES, 80- *Concurrent Pos:* Lectr, Folklore Ctr, Univ Calif, Los Angeles, 76-78, ed asst, Ctr Comp Study of Folklore & Mythol, 77-78 & bibliographer, Folklore Ctr, 78; res grant, Am Philos Soc & Norweg Info Serv, 82-83. *Mem:* Soc Advan Scandinavian Studies; Philol Asn Pac Coast; Univ-Jubilaets danske Samfund; MLA. *Res:* Scandinavian ballad, folklore and literature; Arne Garborg. *Publ:* Auth, Peter Dass: Story-teller, moralist, and student: The changing narrator of nordlandstrompet, Edda: Nordisk Tidsskrift for Litteratureforskning, Vol 5, 297-306; Draumkvaedet: The structural study of an oral variant, Jahrbuch für Volksliedforschung, Vol 25, 51-66; Haugtussa: Interweaving tradition theme, character and motif, Edda: Nordisk Tidsskrift for Litteraturforskning, 10/81; Rev of Torunn Eriksen, To Skilling for en Sang: Folkelige Viser i Nord-Norge, Et Utvalg Skillingstrykk, Jahrubuch für Volksliedforschung (in prep); Kolbovnbrev: Poetic Prelude to Haugbussa, Edda: Nordisk Tidsskrift für Littraturfoskning (in press). *Mailing Add:* 50 Glen Eyrie Ave #1 San Jose CA 95125

ISLAM, A K M AMINUL, b Dacca, Bangladesh, Dec 21, 33; m 60; c 2. ANTHROPOLOGY, LINGUISTICS. *Educ:* Univ Dacca, BA, 52; Univ Toronto, MA, 64; McGill Univ, PhD(anthrop), 69. *Prof Exp:* Prof Bengali, Gaffargaeon Col, Mymensigh, 54-55; lectr, Dacca Univ, 55-59; prin, Bhuapur Col, E Pakistan, 62; asst prof sociol, St Cloud State Col, 67; sociol & anthrop, State Univ NY Col Plattsburgh, 68-69; assoc prof, 69-77, PROF ANTHROP, WRIGHT STATE UNIV, 77- *Concurrent Pos:* Prof Bengali, M M Col, Sylhet, 55; vis prof anthrop, Maxwell Sch Citizenship & Pub Affairs, Syracuse Univ, 69; assoc Current Anthrop, 70- *Mem:* Fel Royal Anthrop Soc; fel Am Anthrop Asn; Philol Soc, England; AAUP. *Res:* National ideology versus liberation movement: the Bengali case; socio-economic transformation in developing nations; religion and politics in a secular state: the Bangladesh case. *Publ:* Auth, Jasim Uddin: Kavi O Kavya: 1955, Eden, Dacca, 55; Bangle Shahittye Muslim Kavi O Kavya, Bk Stall, Dacca, 59; Some prosodic aspects of inter-word relations, Pakistani Ling, 64; Cultural patterns of prehistoric Pakistan, Anthrop Quart, 69; ed, An introduction to cultural anthropology, MSS Educ Publ, 73; auth, A Bangladesh Village: Conflict and Cohesion, 74 & Victorious Victims: Political Transformation in American Traditional Society, 78, Schenkman. *Mailing Add:* Dept of Anthrop Wright State Univ Colonel Glenn Highway Dayton OH 45431

ISSACHAROFF, MICHAEL, b Hove, Eng, Oct 6, 42. FRENCH LANGUAGE & LITERATURE. *Educ:* Univ London, BA, 63; Univ Strasbourg, DUniv(French), 67. *Prof Exp:* Lectr English, Univ Lyon, 63-64; lectr, Univ Strasbourg, 64-68; asst prof French, Univ Chicago, 68-71; vis assoc prof, Wash Univ, 71-72; assoc prof, 72-78, PROF FRENCH, UNIV WESTERN ONT, 78- *Concurrent Pos:* Vis prof, Hebrew Univ, Jerusalem, 81. *Mem:* MLA; Am Asn Teachers Fr; Can Asn Univ Teachers; Int Asn Fr Studies; Semiotic Soc Am. *Res:* French literature of 19th and 20th centuries; semiotics of drama; poetics of fiction. *Publ:* Auth, J-K Huysmans devant la critique en France (1874-1960), Klincksieck, 70; L'Espace et la nouvelle, J Corti, 76; ed & coauth, Langages de Flaubert, Lettres Modernes, 76; auth, Narcisse locuteur: Le je(u) d'Adolphe, Travaux de Linguistique et de Litterature, XVIII, 2, 80; Space and Reference in Drama, Poetics Today, Vol 3, No 3; Texte theatral et didascalecture, Mod Land Notes, Vol 96, No 4; co-ed & coauth, Sartre et la mise en signe, Klincksieck & Fr Forum, 82; auth, Sur Nekrassov et le discours de la farce, In: Sarte Colloque de Cerisy, Belfond, 82. *Mailing Add:* Dept of French Univ of Western Ont London ON N6A 3K7 Can

IVASK, IVAR VIDRIK, b Dec 17, 27; nat US; m 49. GERMAN, COMPARATIVE LITERATURE. *Educ:* Univ Minn, MA, 50, PhD(Ger), 53. *Prof Exp:* Assoc prof Ger & chmn dept, St Olaf Col, 52-64, prof, 64-67; PROF MOD LANG & DIR WORLD LIT TODAY, UNIV OKLA, 67- *Mem:* MLA; Southwestern MLA; Am Asn Teachers Ger; PEN Club; Asn Adv Baltic Studies (pres, 78-). *Res:* Austrian literature; modern European poetry; Baltic literatures. *Publ:* Auth, Gespiegelte Erde, Ungar, 67; co-ed, Luminous Reality, 69 & The Cardinal Points of Borges, 71, Univ Okla; Moderne Weltliteratur, Kröner, Stuttgart, 72; World Literature Since 1945, Ungar, 73; ed, The Perpetual Present: The Poetry and Prose of Octavio Paz, 73, co-ed, The Final Island: The Fiction of Julio Cortazar, 78 & ed, Odysseus Elytis: Analogies of Light, 81, Univ Okla. *Mailing Add:* World Lit Today Univ of Okla Norman OK 73019

IVENTOSCH, HERMAN, b Oakland, Calif, May 30, 19; m 54; c 2. SPANISH. *Educ:* Univ Calif, Berkeley, AB, 48; Harvard Univ, PhD, 58. *Prof Exp:* Instr Span, Amherst Col, 50-52; asst prof, Lafayette Col, 59-61; from asst prof to assoc prof, Univ Kans, 61-64; assoc prof, State Univ NY, Stony Brook, 64-68; PROF SPAN, UNIV ARIZ, 68- *Concurrent Pos:* Am Philos Soc grant, 61. *Mem:* Am Name Soc; Am Asn Teachers Span & Port. *Res:* Sixteenth and

J

17th century Spanish literature. *Publ:* Auth, Dulcinea, nombre pastoril, Nueva Rev Filol Hisp, 66; The Renaissance pastoral and the Golden Age, Mod Lang Notes, Vol 85, No 2; Cervantes and courtly love, PMLA, Vol 88, No 3; Los Nombres Bucolicos de Sannazaro y la Pastoral Espanola: Un Ensayo Sobre el Sentido de la Bucolica en el Renacimiento, Castalia, Madrid, 75. *Mailing Add:* Dept of Romance Lang Univ of Ariz Tucson AZ 85721

IVERSON, GREGORY KEITH, b Williston, NDak, Feb 2, 46; m 72. LINGUISTICS, GERMANIC LANGUAGES. *Educ:* Concordia Col Moorhead, Minn, BA, 68; Rice Univ, MA, 70; Univ Minn, PhD(ling), 74. *Prof Exp:* Instr Swedish, Univ Minn, 74-75; asst prof & chmn ling, Univ Wis-Milwaukee, 76-78; asst prof, 78-80, ASSOC PROF LING, UNIV IOWA, 80- *Mem:* Ling Soc Am; Soc Advan Scand Studies; Nordic Asn Ling. *Res:* Phonological theory; language variation; Germanic languages. *Publ:* Auth, On the directionality of paradigm regularization, In: Minnesota Working Papers in Linguistics and Philosophy of Language, 2:32-40 & Phonology in the 1970's, Ghent: E Story-Scienta (in press); Angles on Finnish gradation, In: Minnesota Working Papers in Linguistics and Philosophy of Language, 3:23-33 & In: Vol 3, The Nordic Languages and General Linguistics (in press); The strong alternation condition and Yawelmani phonology, Chicago Ling Soc, 11:303-312; A guide to sanguine relationships, In: The Application and Ordering of Grammatical Rules, The Hague: Mouton, 76; coauth, Icelandic u-umlaut: An exchange of views, Lang Sci, 42:28-34; On constraining the theory of exceptions, In: Proc of 1976 Mid-America Ling Conf, Univ Minnesota, 77; auth, Synchronic umlaut in old Icelandic, Publ Ind Univ Ling Club, 77; coauth, Functionally constrained phonology, In: Current Phonological Theories, Ind Univ (in press). *Mailing Add:* Dept of Ling Univ of Iowa Iowa City IA 52242

IVES, DAVID SCOTT, b Hancock, Mich, Sept 16, 09; m 46; c 1. CLASSICS, COMPARATIVE LITERATURE. *Educ:* Baldwin-Wallace Col, AB, 33; Western Reserve Univ, AM, 35. *Prof Exp:* Instr Greek, Latin & ancient history, Baldwin-Wallace Col, 39-40; asst prof English, Greek & humanities, 47-60, assoc prof class lang, humanities, English & art, 60-78, chmn dept class studies, 65-67, supvr class studies, 67-70, assoc prof English & art & adv class studies, 70-78, EMER ASSOC PROF ENGLISH & ART, YOUNGSTOWN STATE UNIV, 78- *Mem:* Am Philol Asn; Am Class League; Class Asn Midwest & S; AAUP. *Res:* Greek tragedy; comparative literature. *Mailing Add:* Off of Class Studies Youngstown State Univ Youngstown OH 44503

IVY, ROBERT HENRY, JR, b Philadelphia, Pa, May 13, 15; m 50; c 3. FRENCH. *Educ:* Univ Pa, AB, 36, AM, 38, PhD, 49. *Prof Exp:* Res asst Romance lang, Univ Pa, 45-49; from instr to asst prof French, Bowdoin Col, 49-59; assoc prof, Northwestern Univ, 59-62; prof lang, Roosevelt Univ, 62-80; RETIRED. *Mem:* Int Arthurian Soc. *Res:* Medieval French literature; Arthurian romance. *Publ:* Co-ed, Continuations of the Old French Perceval of Chretien de Troyes, 50 & auth, The Manuscript Relations of Manessier's Continuation of the Old French Perceval, 51, Univ Pa; An analytical bibliography of the works of Prof Charles H Livingston, Romance Philol, 2/59; co-ed, Philippe de Vigneulles, Les cent nouvelles nouvelles, Vol CXX, In: Travaux d'Humanisme et Renaissance, Droz, Geneva. *Mailing Add:* 620 Appletree Ct Deerfield IL 60015

IWAMOTO, YOSHIO, b New Westminster, BC, Nov 25, 31. MODERN JAPANESE LITERATURE. *Educ:* Univ Mich, BA, 58, MA, 59, PhD(Japanese lit), 64. *Prof Exp:* Asst prof Japanese lang & lit, Univ Mich, 64-68; asst prof, Univ Ill, 68-69; ASSOC PROF JAPANESE & COMP LIT, IND UNIV, BLOOMINGTON, 69- *Concurrent Pos:* Vis assoc prof Japanese lit, Univ Hawaii, 71. *Mem:* Asn Asian Studies; Am Orient Soc; MLA; Asn Teachers Japanese. *Res:* Modern Japanese novel; politics and literature in modern Japan; Japanese-Western literary relations. *Publ:* Auth, Sanso to Tenko (War and conversion), Hihyo (criticism), winter 66; The changing hero image in Japanese fiction of the thirties, J Newslett Asn Teachers Japanese, 8/66; Suehiro Tetcho: a Meiji political novelist, Monumenta Nipponica, 9/68; Oe Kenzaburo's existentialist novel: A Personal Matter, Papers CIC Far Eastern Lang Inst, Vol IV, 71; Aspects of the proletarian literary movement in Japan, In: Japan in Crisis: Essays on Taisho Democracy, Princeton Univ, 74; coauth, Yukio Mishima; dialectics of mind and body, Contemp Lit, winter 75; The last sad sigh: Time and Kawabata's The Master of Go, Lit E & W, Vol XVIII, 78. *Mailing Add:* Dept of EAsian Lang & Lit Goodbody Hall Ind Univ Bloomington IN 47401

IZZO, HERBERT JOHN, b Saginaw, Mich, July 17, 28; m 58, 71; c 4. ROMANCE LINGUISTICS. *Educ:* Univ Mich, BA, 50, MA, 51, BS, 53, PhD(ling), 65. *Prof Exp:* Charge cours English, Univ of Hue, 58-59; instr Span, Univ Ariz, 60-61; instr Span & ling, Stanford Univ, 61-64; asst prof Span, San Jose State Col, 64-68; assoc prof, 68-76, head dept, 70-72, PROF LING, UNIV CALGARY, 76- *Concurrent Pos:* Asst prof appl ling, NDEA Inst San Jose State Col, 65; Fulbright lectr ling, Univ Cluj, 66-67 & Univ Bucharest, 75-76; asst prof appl ling, NDEA Inst Ital, State Univ NY Buffalo, 68; vis prof Romance ling, Univ Mich, 77-78; Soc Sci & Humanities Res Coun Can fel, 81-82. *Mem:* Ling Soc Am; Am Asn Teachers Ital; Am Asn Teachers Span & Port; Can Asn Latin-Americanists. *Res:* Spanish language and dialects; Italian language and dialects; history of linguistics. *Publ:* Auth, Tuscan and Etruscan, Univ Toronto, 72; The layer-cake model in historical linguistics, Gen Ling, 73; The linguistic philosophy of Benedetto Varchi, Lang Sci, 76; Pre-Latin languages and sound changes in romance: Old Spanish, In: Studies in Romance Linguistics, 77; Influence of Amerindian on American Spanish, LACUS Forum, 77; Intervocalic /p, t, k/ in Italian, Italic and Romance: FS Pulgram, 80; ed, Italic and Romance: FS Ernst Pulgram, John Benjamins, 80. *Mailing Add:* Dept of Ling Univ of Calgary Calgary AB T2N 1N4 Can

JABLON, KENNETH, b Brooklyn, NY, Apr 7, 36; m 57; c 3. SPANISH. *Educ:* Queens Col, NY, AB, 56; Univ Iowa, AM, 58, PhD, 62. *Prof Exp:* From instr to asst prof Span, Univ Iowa, 59-63; asst prof, Hamilton Col, 63-67; head dept mod foreign lang, 67-76, PROF SPAN, FROSTBURG STATE COL, 67-, VPRES ACAD AFFAIRS, 69- *Concurrent Pos:* Instr ling, US Off Health, Educ & Welfare Summer Inst Cuban Refugees, 63; Fulbright lectr, Univ Valladolid, 65-66; instr, NDEA Inst, Hamilton Col, 65, Coe Col, 67 & 68. *Mem:* MLA; Am Asn Teachers Span & Port; Am Coun Teaching For Lang. *Res:* Spanish mediaeval and Golden Age literature; linguistics; English as a foreign language. *Mailing Add:* Dept of Span Frostburg State Col Frostburg MD 21532

JACKENDOFF, RAY SAUL, b Chicago, Ill, Jan 23, 45. LINGUISTICS. *Educ:* Swarthmore Col, BA, 65; Mass Inst Technol, PhD(ling), 69. *Prof Exp:* Lectr ling, Univ Calif, Los Angeles, 69-70; asst prof, 71-73, assoc prof, 73-78, PROF LING, BRANDEIS UNIV, 78- *Concurrent Pos:* Special ling, Rand Corp, 69-70. *Honors & Awards:* Gustave Arlt Humanities Award, 75. *Mem:* Ling Soc Am. *Res:* Semantics; syntactic theory; musical cognition. *Publ:* Auth, An interpretative theory of negation, Found Lang, 69; Gapping and related rules, 71 & Modal structure in semantic representation, 72, Ling Inquiry; Semantic Interpretation in Generative Grammar, 72, X-Bar Syntax, 75, coauth (with Fred Lerdahl), A Generative Theory of Tonal Music, 82 & Semantics and Cognition (in press), Mass Inst Technol Press. *Mailing Add:* Dept of English Brandeis Univ Waltham MA 02154

JACKLE, FRANK ROBERT, b Winchester, Ill, Mar 31, 09; m 38. SPANISH, PORTUGUESE. *Educ:* Southwest Mo State Col, BS, 31; Univ Mo, MA, 35; Stanford Univ, PhD(Port & Luso-Brazilian studies), 67. *Prof Exp:* Teacher, Lamar High Sch, 31-34; High Sch, Mo, 34-38, Okla, 38-45; dir bi-nat ctr, San Jose, Costa Rica, 45-46; teacher, High Sch, Okla, 46-49; assoc prof, 49-55, prof Span & Port, 55-80, chmn Dept Mod Lang, 61-80, TEACHER ENGLISH, AM GRAD SCH INT MGT, 80- *Mem:* MLA; Am Coun Teaching Foreign Lang; Am Asn Teachers Span & Port. *Res:* Portuguese and Luso-Brazilian studies; life of John Casper Branner; language methodology. *Publ:* Auth, Effective language learning-the Thunderbird approach, Mod English Teaching, Tokyo, 3/73. *Mailing Add:* 59 Ave & Greenway Rd Glendale AZ 85306

JACKSON, DONALD FRANCIS, b Niagara Falls, NY, Dec 5, 37. CLASSICAL LANGUAGES & LITERATURE. *Educ:* Niagara Univ, AB, 62; Ind Univ, Bloomington, MA, 64, PhD(classics), 67. *Prof Exp:* Asst prof, 67-73, ASSOC PROF CLASSICS, UNIV IOWA, 73- *Mem:* Am Philol Asn. *Res:* Greek paleography; Greek epigraphy; ancient religion and athletics. *Publ:* Auth, Varia paleographica, Class J, 69; Papyri of Xenophon's Hellenica, Bull Am Soc Papyrologists, 69; coauth, Demosthenes 1915-1965, Lustrum, 69; The TDLV manuscripts of Xenophon's Hellenica and their descendants, Trans Am Philol Asn, 75. *Mailing Add:* Dept of Classics Univ of Iowa Iowa City IA 52240

JACKSON, ELIZABETH R, b Boston, Mass, May 13, 26; m 70; c 2. FRENCH LITERATURE. *Educ:* Reed Col, BA, 47; Univ Toulouse, cert philos, 51; Wellesley Col, MA, 59; Univ Paris, DUniv(French lit), 63. *Prof Exp:* Statist asst, Nat Bur Econ Res, 47-48; teacher, Putney Sch, 48-49; tutor French, Goddard Col, 53-55; vis lectr, Knox Col, 63-65; assoc, humanities & French, Univ Calif, San Diego, 65-66; chmn, Dept French & Ital, 75-80, PROF FRENCH, SAN DIEGO STATE UNIV, 69- *Concurrent Pos:* Fr Govt grant & Fulbright travel grant, 60-62; Am Philos Soc grant-in-aid, 63; grant, Centre national de la recherche scientifique, 65. *Mem:* MLA; Am Asn Teachers Fr; Asn Studies Dada & Surrealism. *Res:* Modern French poetry; Chenier; modern French novel. *Publ:* Auth, L'Evolution de la Memoire Involontaire dans L'Oeuvre de Marcel Proust, Nizet, Paris, 66; The crystallization of A la recherche du temps perdu, Fr Rev, 12/64; Proust et les preraphaelites, Rev Humane Sci, 1-3/65; Poesie activitie de l'esprit: A study of Atout trefle by B Peret, 5/71 & Sense & sensitivity in Valery's poetry: a study of Les Pas, 10/76, Fr Rev; Worlds Apart: Structural Parallels in the Poetry of Valery, S-J Perse, Peret, Char, Mouton, 76; Eloges: Cadre et Recit, Fr Forum, 9/81. *Mailing Add:* Dept of French & Ital San Diego State Univ San Diego CA 92182

JACKSON, ERNEST, b Saugus, Mass, Mar 5, 25; m 56. FRENCH. *Educ:* Boston Univ, AB, 48; Yale Univ, MA, 51; Univ Mich, PhD, 52. *Prof Exp:* Assoc prof, 58-71, chmn dept Europ lang, 61-66 & 75-81; chmn grad div, 67-81, PROF FRENCH, UNIV HAWAII, MANOA, 71- *Concurrent Pos:* French Govt scholar, 51; vis prof, Centre d'Etudes superieures, Brazzaville, Congo, 64-65. *Mem:* MLA; Am Asn Teachers Fr; African Lit Asn. *Res:* French novel; Flaubert; American criticism. *Publ:* Auth, The Critical Reception of Gustave Flaubert in the United States, Mouton, The Hague, 66. *Mailing Add:* Dept of Lang Univ of Hawaii Manoa Honolulu HI 96822

JACKSON, HERBERT HUGH, b Vienna, Austria, Nov 1, 14; m 42; c 2. MODERN LANGUAGES. *Educ:* Univ Vienna, LLD, 38; Univ London, BA, 50. *Prof Exp:* PROF MOD LANG, MEM UNIV NFLD, 51-, HEAD DEPT GER & RUSS, 67- *Concurrent Pos:* Lectr, Col Spec & Continuation Studies, Univ Md, 53; vpres, Can-Ger Acad Exchange Asn, 67. *Mem:* Can Asn Univ Teachers Ger; Mod Humanities Res Asn; Humanities Asn Can; Am Asn Univ Teachers Ger, MLA. *Mailing Add:* 20 Glenridge Crescent St St John's NF A1C 5S7 Can

JACKSON, IRENE DOBBS, b Atlanta, Ga, Feb 16, 08; m 33; c 6. FRENCH, LATIN. *Educ:* Spelman Col, AB, 29; Univ Toulouse, dipl Fr lit & lang, 33, DUniv(English as foreign lang), 58. *Prof Exp:* Instr French & Latin, Spelman Col, 29-34, piano, 45-46; instr French, Clark Col, 47-49; assoc prof French

& Latin, Spelman Col, 50-56, assoc prof French & acting chmn dept, 58-60; assoc prof, Jackson State Col, 60-61; chmn dept Romance lang, 61-68, PROF FRENCH, NC CENT UNIV, 61-, CHMN DEPT MOD FOREIGN LANG, 68- *Concurrent Pos:* Lectr, Libr, Atlanta Univ, 67, consult, Ctr on African Studies, 68; lectr, Senghor Colloquium, Univ Vt, spring 71; consult, SC State Col, 72, Ill State Univ, fall 72; Sem on African Materials in French, Am Coun Teaching Foreign Lang--Southeastern Conf Lang Teaching, fall 72. *Mem:* Southeastern Conf Lang Teaching; Am Coun Teaching Foreign Lang; Am Asn Teachers Fr; Col Lang Asn. *Res:* Psychology of language learning; foreign languages on the elementary school level; the negritude of black poets of French expression. *Publ:* Auth, Negritude in full bloom: A study in outline, Col Lang Asn J, 9/63; Senghor's debt to Teilhard de Chardin, Varia, NC Col Durham, spring 65; coauth, Negritude: Essays and studies with Berrian and Long, Hampton Inst Centennial Publ, 4/67. *Mailing Add:* 1927 Cecil Durham NC 27707

JACKSON, KENNETH DAVID, b Henderson, Tex, July 21, 44. LUSO-BRAZILIAN LITERATURE, COMPARATIVE LITERATURE. *Educ:* Univ Ill, BA, 66; Univ Wis, MA, 67, PhD(Span & Port), 73. *Prof Exp:* Instr English, Ill Wesleyan Univ, 68-70; teaching asst Port, Univ Wis, Madison, 70-71; asst prof, Univ NMex, 73-74; asst prof, 74-79, ASSOC PROF PORT & SPAN, UNIV TEX, AUSTIN, 80- *Concurrent Pos:* Gulbenkian Found fel, 76; Am Inst Indian Studies fel, 82. *Mem:* Am Asn Teachers Span & Port; Royal Asiatic Soc; SCent Mod Lang Asn; Pac Northwest Conf Foreign Lang. *Res:* Contemporary Brazilian literature; Portuguese literature; Portuguese oral & folk traditions in Asia. *Publ:* Auth, Vanguardist prose in Brazilian literature--1912-1929, Auf sätze zur Portugiesischen Kulturgeschichte, 74-75; Bela Infanta of Sri Lanka: Ballad fragments in Portuguese Creole communities, J Royal Asiatic Soc, 75; Rediscovering the rediscoverers: Joao Miramar and Serafim Ponte Grande, Tex Quart, fall 76; Literature and criticism of the Brazilian concrete poets, Proc PNCFL, 78; A Prosa Vanguardista na Literatura Brasileira: Oswald de Andrade, Editora Perspectiva, 78; Patricia Galvao e o Realismo Social Brasileiro dos Anos 30, Jornal do Brasil, 5/78; co-transl, Seraphim Grosse Pointe by Oswald de Andrade, New Latin Quart, 79; Bibliography for Oswald de Andrade, Obras Escogidas, Biblioteca Ayacucho, 81. *Mailing Add:* Dept of Span & Port Univ of Tex Austin TX 78712

JACKSON, KENNETH LEROY, b Sheridan, Wyo, May 7, 34; m 59; c 2. ENGLISH AS A SECOND LANGUAGE. *Educ:* Hendrix Col, BA, 56; Columbia Univ, MA, 60, prof dipl English as a second lang, 62, EdD(English as second lang), 67. *Prof Exp:* Instr English as second lang, Palmore Inst, JaPan, 56-59, Labor Temple, NY, 60-61, Teachers Col, Columbia Univ, 61-62; asst prof appl ling, Doshisha Univ, Japan, 63-67; consult ling, Missionary Orientation Ctr, NY, 67-68; ASSOC PROF ENGLISH AS SECOND LANG, UNIV HAWAII, MANOA, 68- *Concurrent Pos:* US Off Educ res grant, 70-71; consult, Community Col of Am Samoa, 71-72. *Mem:* AAUP; Am Coun Teaching Foreign Lang; Asn Teachers English as Foreign Lang; Ling Soc Am; Teachers English to Speakers Other Lang. *Res:* Language interference; error analysis; history of language teaching. *Publ:* Auth, TESOL Journals in Japan, TESOL Quart, 70; Nichi-Eigo No Taishoo Kenkyuu, Taishukan, Tokyo, 70; coauth, Evaluation of the predictive power of contrastive analyses of Japanese and English, US Off Educ, 71; co-ed, The PCCLLU papers, In: Working Papers in Linguistics, Univ Hawaii, 71; coauth, The unpredictability of contrastive analysis, Lang Learning, 6/72. *Mailing Add:* Dept of English Second Lang Univ of Hawaii Manoa Honolulu HI 96822

JACKSON, KENT PHILLIPS, b Salt Lake City, Utah, Aug 9, 49; m 75; c 5. ANCIENT NEAR EASTERN LANGUAGES. *Educ:* Brigham Young Univ, BA, 74; Univ Mich, MA, 76, PhD(Near Eastern studies), 80. *Prof Exp:* Teaching asst world hist, Brigham Young Univ, 74-75; ed, Am Schs Orient Res, 76-80; ASST PROF ANCIENT SCRIPTURE, BRIGHAM YOUNG UNIV, 80- *Concurrent Pos:* Teaching asst world relig, Univ Mich, 78; Old Testament area dir, Brigham Young Univ, 82- *Mem:* Mormon Scripture Soc; Soc Bibl Lit; Am Schs Orient Res. *Res:* Canaanite inscriptions; West Semitic personal names; Biblical history. *Publ:* Auth, The Ammonite Language of the Iron Ages, Harvard Semitic Mus (in prep); Ammonite personal names in the context of the West Semitic Onomasticon, In: Studies in Honor of David Noel Freedman, Am Schs Orient Res (in prep); The marriage of Hosea and Jehovah's covenant with Israel, In: Isaiah and the Prophets, Brigham Young Univ (in prep); The Book of Mormon as a Holy Book, In: The Holy Book, Am Acad Relig (in prep). *Mailing Add:* Dept of Anicent Scriptures Brigham Young Univ Provo UT 84602

JACKSON, MARY HELEN, b Maryville, Mo, Dec 9, 11. SPANISH. *Educ:* Univ Mo, BA, 32; Univ Kans, MA, 63. *Prof Exp:* Asst instr Span, Univ Kans, 61-62; assoc prof, Northwestern Mo State Univ, 62-77, chmn dept, 76-77; RETIRED. *Publ:* Auth, Let's make foreign language study more relevant, Today's Educ, 71; Must dialogs be memorized?, Mod Lang J, 72; co-ed, Teatro Hispanico, 72 & auth, Manual de Correspondencia Espanola, 73, Nat Textbk; Que Facil!, 77 & Que Divertido!, 78, Allyn & Bacon. *Mailing Add:* 930 S Walnut St Maryville MO 64468

JACKSON, ROBERT LOUIS, b New York, NY, Nov 10, 23; m 51; c 2. SLAVIC LANGUAGES & LITERATURES. *Educ:* Cornell Univ, BA, 44; Columbia Univ, MA, 49; Univ Calif, PhD(Slavic lang & lit), 56. *Prof Exp:* Asst prof Russ lang & lit, 59-62, assoc prof, 62-67, PROF RUSS LIT, YALE UNIV, 67- *Concurrent Pos:* Morse fel, 61-62; Inter-Univ Comt grant to participate in US-USSR Cult Exchange, Moscow, 67; Guggenheim fel, 67-68. *Mem:* MLA; Am Asn Teachers Slavic & EEurop Lang; Am Asn Advan Slavic Studies; Int Dosteovsky Soc (vpres, 71-); NAm Dostoevsky Soc (pres, 70-). *Res:* Interaction of aesthetic and philosophical thought in the 19th century Russian literature; chance and fate in 19th century literature; tragedy and the Brothers Karamazov. *Publ:* Auth, Dostoevsky's Quest for Form: A Study of His Philosophy of Art, Yale Univ, 66; The Testament of F M Dostoevsky, Russ Lit, 73; Miltonic Imagery and Design in Pushkin's Mozart and Salieri: The Russian Satan, Am Contributions to Seventh Int Congr Slavists, 73; auth, introd & ed, Crime and Punishment, a collection of critical essays, In: Twentieth Century Interpretations, Prentice-Hall, 74. *Mailing Add:* Hall of Grad Studies Yale Univ New Haven CT 06520

JACKSON, WILLIAM EDWARD, b Creedmoor, NC, Dec 1, 36; m 61; c 3. GERMAN LANGUAGE & LITERATURE. *Educ:* NC Col, BA, 58; NY Univ, MA, 61; Univ Pa, PhD(Ger), 72. *Prof Exp:* Lectr Ger, City Col New York, 61-64; acting instr, 70-71, from instr to asst prof, 71-75, assoc prof Ger, Yale Univ, 75-80; prog officer, Gen Res Prog, Nat Endowment for Humanities, 80-81; ASSOC PROF GER & ASSOC DIR, CARTER G WOODSON INST, UNIV VA, 81- *Mem:* Am Asn Teachers Ger; MLA; Medieval Acad Am. *Res:* Medieval German language; medieval German literature; medieval Austrian culture. *Publ:* Auth, Helmbrecht the father, Neophilologus, 72; Reinmar der Alte in literary history, Colloquia Germanica, 75; Honor of Otto Springer, 78; Zur Dichtuung Neidharts als Quelle für Wernnhers Helmbrecht, Sprachkunst, 80; Reinmar's Women, Benjamins, Amsterdam, 81; The Woman's Song in Medieval German Poetry, Vox Feminnae, 81. *Mailing Add:* Dept of Ger Lang Univ of Va Charlottesville VA 22903

JACKSON, WILLIAM THOMAS HOBDELL, b Sheffield, England, Apr 2, 15; m 45; c 3. MEDIEVAL LITERATURE. *Educ:* Univ Sheffield, BA, 35, MA, 38; Univ Wash, PhD(Ger), 51. *Prof Exp:* Classics master, High Sch, England, 35-40, 46-48; part-time instr Ger, Univ Wash, 48-50; asst prof Ger & classics, Coe Col, 50-52; asst prof Ger, 52-55, assoc prof Ger & comp medieval lit, 55-58, prof, 58-73, VILLARD PROF GER & COMP LIT, COLUMBIA UNIV, 73- *Concurrent Pos:* Ed, Ger Rev, 54-66; vis lectr, Princeton, Univ, 57; Am Coun Learned Soc grants, 58, 72 & 80; Guggenheim fels, 58-59 & 67-68; vis prof, Rutgers Univ, 63-; ed, Columbia Rec of Civilization Ser, 63-; mem comput fel selection comt, Am Coun Learned Soc, 64-68; vis prof, Duke Univ, 65; Phi Beta Kappa vis scholar, 65-66; vis lectr, Yale Univ, 66; mem fel selection comt, Nat Found Humanities, 66-71; lectr, US Mil Acad, 70-72; Medieval Acad Am fel, 76; vis prof, Fordham Univ, 77, Medieval Inst City Univ New York, 75, 76 & 77 & State Univ NY, 79. *Mem:* Acad Lit Studies; Mediaeval Acad Am. *Res:* Medieval lyric and satire; medieval epic. *Publ:* Auth, The Literature of the Middle Ages, Columbia Univ, 60; The epic center as structural determinant in medieval narrative poetry, In: Studies in Germanic Languages and Literature in Honor of Ernst Rose, Reutlingen, Hutzler, 67; The Anatomy of Love: The Tristan of Gottfried von Strassburg, Columbia Univ, 71; The Nature of Romance, In: Approaches to Medieval Romance, Yale Univ, 74; Persona and audience in two Medieval love-lyrics, Mosaic, 75; The Politics of a Poet: The Political Ideas of the Archipoeta as Seen Through His Imagery, In: Philosophy and Humanism, Brill, 76; The Interpretation of Medieval Lyric, Columbia Univ & Macmillan, 80; The Hero and the King, An Epic Theme, Columbia Univ, 82. *Mailing Add:* 90 Morningside Dr New York NY 10027

JACKSON, WILLIAM VERNON, b Chicago, Ill, May 26, 26. SPANISH, LATIN AMERICAN STUDIES. *Educ:* Northwestern Univ, BA, 45; Harvard Univ, AM, 48, PhD, 52; Univ Ill, MSLS, 51. *Hon Degrees:* Dipl, Cent Univ Venezuela, 68. *Prof Exp:* Teacher high sch, Ill, 46-47; spec recruit, Libr Congr, 51-52; from asst prof to assoc prof libr sci, Univ Ill, 52-62, librn, Undergrad Libr, 52-58; assoc prof Span & Port, Univ Wis-Madison, 63-65; prof libr sci & dir int libr inform ctr, Univ Pittsburgh, 66-70; prof Span & Port, Vanderbilt Univ, & prof libr sci, George Peabody Col, 70-76; PROF LIBR SCI, UNIV TEX, AUSTIN, 76- *Concurrent Pos:* Consult libr, US Dept State, Arg, 56, Brazil & Ecuador, 59, Latin Am, 61, 67 & 77, Latin Am & Europe, 62; Fulbright res scholar, France, 56-57; Fulbright lectr, Nat Univ Cordoba, 58, adv, 70; deleg, US Nat Comn, UNESCO Conf, 59 & 61; vis prof, Inter-Am Libr Sch, Univ Antioquia, 60 & 68, adv, Int Exec Coun, 61-63; vis lectr, Sch Libr Sci, Syracuse Univ, 62; adv, Univ San Marcos, Lima, Peru, 62 & 75; consult, Peace Corps Training Prog for Brazil, Univ Wis-Milwaukee, 64; bibliogr, Hisp Found, Libr Congr, 64-65; consult, regional off, Agency Int Develop, Cent Am & Panama, 65-66, mission to Brazil, 67-72 & mission to Columbia, 70-71; consult, res libr, NY Pub Libr, 65-70, Orgn Am States, 70-71 & Coun of Rectors of Brazilian Univs, 72; external examr, Univ West Indies, 74-78; consult, Int Commun Agency, Dominican Republic, 79, France, 79, Latin Am, 80; consult, Bibliotheque Nationale, France, 79, 81 & 82; lectr, Univ Zulia, Maraccaibo, Venezuela, 80; vis lectr, Grad Sch Libr Sci, Rosary Col, 81. *Mem:* Asn Am Libr Schs; MLA; Am Asn Teachers Span & Port; Am Libr Asn; Sem Acquisition of Latin Am Libr Materials (pres, 77-78). *Res:* Library science and resources; Latin American studies; contemporary Spanish literature. *Publ:* Auth, Studies in Library Resources, 58; A Handbook of American Library Resources, 2nd ed, 62; Aspects of Librarianship in Latin America, 62; Library Guide for Brazilian Studies, Univ Pittsburgh, 64; contrib, Encycl Libr & Inform Sci, Dekker, 69-; ed, Latin American Collections, Vanderbilt Univ, 74; Catalog of Brazilian Acquisitions of the Library of Congress, 1964-74, GK Hall, 77; Resources for Brazilian Studies at the Bibliotheque Nationale, 80. *Mailing Add:* Univ of Tex Box 7576 Univ Sta Austin TX 78712

JACOBS, CAROL FRANCES, English & Comparative Literature. See Vol II

JACOBS, RODERICK ARNOLD, b London, Eng, May 29, 34; US citizen; m 62; c 2. COMPARATIVE & DIACHRONIC LINGUISTICS, STYLISTICS. *Educ:* Univ London, BA, 56; Harvard Univ, EdM, 62; Univ Calif, San Diego, MA, 70, PhD(ling), 71. *Prof Exp:* Teacher English & French, Pub Schs, London, England, New Brunswick, Can & Newton, Mass, 56-64; curric supvr English & reading, Tuxedo Pub Schs, NY, 64-66; assoc prof lit, State Univ NY Col Oneonta, 66-68; res fel ling, Univ Calif, San Diego, 68-72; teacher & researcher Amerindian lang & cult, Pala Indian Band, Calif, 72-73; PROF LING & ENGLISH LANG, UNIV HAWAII, MANOE, 73- *Concurrent Pos:* Consult, Peace Corps Training Div, 70-71; consult bilingual educ, Trust Territory Micronesia, 78-; dir bilingual studies, Dept English Second Lang, Univ Hawaii, Manoa, 77- *Mem:* Ling Soc Am; NCTE. *Res:* Syntactic change; comparative syntax; stylistics. *Publ:* Co-ed, Vanity Fair, 64 & Wuthering Heights, 65, Harper; coauth, English Transformational Grammar, Ginn-Blaisdell, 68; auth, On Transformational Grammar, NCTE, 69; coauth, Transformations, Style, and Meaning, 71 & auth, Studies in Language, 73, Xerox; Syntactic Change, Univ Calif, 75. *Mailing Add:* Dept of Ling Univ of Hawaii Manoa Honolulu HI 96822

JACOBSEN, THOMAS WARREN, b Mankato, Minn, Mar 18, 35; m 56 & 81; c 2. CLASSICAL ARCHEOLOGY & LANGUAGES. *Educ:* St Olaf Col, BA, 57; Univ Minn, MA, 60; Univ Pa, PhD (class archaeol), 64. *Prof Exp:* Asst prof classics, Vanderbilt Univ, 64-66; from asst prof to assoc prof, 66-75, chmn dept, 75-78, PROF CLASSICS, IND UNIV, BLOOMINGT8N, 75-, DIR ARCHAEOL EXCAVATIONS IN GREECE, 67-, CHMN PROG CLASS ARCHAEOL, 70- *Concurrent Pos:* Nat Endowment for Humanities proj grants, 67-68, 70-72 & 78-80; Olivia James traveling fel, 68-69; Am Coun Learned Soc & NSF fels, 73-74; prin investr res grant, Am Philos Soc, 73-74; mem rev panel, Smithsonian Foreign Currency Prog, 76-79; NSF proj grants, 77-79; Am Sch Class Studies, Athens Du Pont Spec res fel, 80-81. *Mem:* Prehistoric Soc, England; Archaeol Inst Am; Asn Field Archaeol (vpres, 70-72); Brit Inst Archaeol, Turkey; Soc Am Archaeoloey. *Res:* Archaeology of Greece, especially the prehistoric archaeology of the Aegean. *Publ:* Coauth, Prehistoric Euboia; Contributions toward a Survey, Ann Brit Sch Archaeol, Athens, 66 & Two Kimolian Dikast Decrees from Geraistos in Euboia, 68, Hesperia; auth, A group of early Cycladic vases in the Benaki Museum, Athens, Archaologischer Anzeiger, 69; coauth, Excavations at Porto Cheli and Vicinity, II, 69 & Excavations in the Franchthi Cave, 1969-1971, Parts I II, 73, Hesperia; auth, 17,000 years of Greek Prehistory, Sci Am, 76; Franchthi Cave and the Beginning of Settled Village Life in Greece, Hesperia, 81. *Mailing Add:* Dept of Class Studies Ind Univ Bloomington IN 47401

JACOBSEN, THORKILD, b Copenhagen, Denmark, June 7, 04; US citizen; m 66; c 4. ASSYRIOLOGY. *Educ:* Univ Copenhagen, MA, 27, Dr Phil(Assyriol), 39; Univ Chicago, PhD(Syriac), 29. *Hon Degrees:* MA, Harvard Univ, 63. *Prof Exp:* Field Assyriologist, Orient Inst, Univ Chicago, 29-37, res assoc Assyriol, 37-42, from asst prof to prof soc insts, 42-62, chmn dept Near Eastern lang & lit & dir Orient Inst, 46-48, dean div humanities, 48-51; prof Assyriol, Harvard Univ, 63-74. *Concurrent Pos:* Haskell lectr, Oberlin Col, 52; Am Coun Learned Soc lectr hist relig, 66-67; Guggenheim fel, 68-69. *Mem:* Am Philos Soc; Am Acad Arts & Sci; corresp mem Royal Danish Acad Arts & Sci, Brit Acad; Am Soc Studies Relig. *Res:* Ancient Mesopotamian languages; archaeology; civilization. *Publ:* Auth, The Sumerian Kinglist, Univ Chicago, 39; Cuneiform Texts in the National Museum Copenhagen, Brill, Leiden, 39; coauth, Before Philosophy, Penguin, 49; auth, Primitive democracy in ancient Mesopotamia, J Near Eastern Studies, 49; Early political development in Mesopotamia, Z Assyriol, 57; About the Sumerian verb, In: Studies in Honor of Benno Landsberger, Univ Chicago, 65; Toward the Image of Tammuz, Harvard Univ, 70; The Treasures of Darkness, Yale Univ, 76. *Mailing Add:* E Washington Rd Bradford NH 03221

JACOBSEN, WILLIAM HORTON, JR, b San Diego, Calif, Nov 15, 31; c 1. LINGUISTICS. *Educ:* Harvard Univ, AB, 53; Univ Calif, Berkeley, PhD(ling), 64: *Prof Exp:* Teaching asst ling, Univ Calif, Berkeley, 57-59, res linguist machine trans proj, 59-61; actg asst prof anthrop, Univ Wash, 61-62, linguist, 62-64; from asst prof to assoc prof, 65-74, PROF ENGLISH, UNIV NEV, RENO, 74- *Concurrent Pos:* Vis assoc prof ling, Univ Calif, Bekeley, 71. *Mem:* Ling Soc Am; Can Ling Asn; Int Ling Asn; Am Anthrop Asn; Soc Study the Indigenous Lang Am. *Res:* Descriptive and historical linguistics; American Indian languages; Basque. *Publ:* Auth, Washo and Karok: An approach to comparative Hokan, Int J Am Ling, 58; Switch-reference in Hokan-Coahuiltecan, In: Studies in Southwestern Ethnolinguistics, Mouton, The Hague, 67; On the prehistory of Nez Perce vowel harmony, Language, 68; Origin of the Nootka pharyngeals, Int J Am Ling, 69; Nominative-ergative syncretism in Basque, Anuario del Seminario de Filologia Vasca Julio de Urquijo, 72; Observations on the Yana stop series in relationship to problems of comparative Hokan phonology, Hokan Studies, Mouton, 76; A glimpse of the pre-Washington pronominal system, Proc Third Ann Meeting Berkeley Ling Soc, 77; Noun and verb in Nootkan, In: The Victoria Conference on Northwestern Languages, BC Provincial Mus, Victoria, 79. *Mailing Add:* Dept of English Univ of Nev Reno NV 89557

JACOBSON, HOWARD, b Bronx, NY, Aug 21, 40; m 65; c 3. CLASSICAL LITERATURE. *Educ:* Columbia Col, NY, BA, 62; Univ Chicago, AM, 63; Columbia Univ, PhD(Greek, Latin), 67. *Prof Exp:* Instr Greek & Latin, Columbia Univ, 66-68; asst prof, 68-73, assoc prof, 73-80, PROF CLASSICS, UNIV ILL, URBANA, 80- *Mem:* Am Philol Asn. *Res:* Latin literature; Hellenistic Judaism; comparative literature. *Mailing Add:* Dept of Classics Univ of Ill Urbana IL 61801

JACOBSON, JOHN WESLEY, b Gillet Grove, Iowa, May 12, 23; m 55; c 2. GERMAN. *Educ:* Morningside Col, AB, 44; Ind Univ, PhD(Ger), 63. *Prof Exp:* Instr English, Syracuse Univ, 46-51; instr Ger, Wyo Sem, 55-59; from instr to asst prof, Purdue Univ, 59-62; asst prof, Univ Calif, Los Angeles, 63-67; PROF GER, CARROLL COL, WIS, 67- *Mem:* Am Asn Teachers Ger; MLA; Am Coun Teaching Foreign Lang. *Res:* Baroque and 19th century German literature; French-German literary relations. *Publ:* Auth, The culpable male: Grimmelshausen on women, 3/66 & A defense of Grimmelshausen's Courasche, 1/68, Ger Quart. *Mailing Add:* Dept of Foreign Lang Carroll Col Waukesha WI 53186

JACOBSON, LEON CARL, b Thief River Falls, Minn, Nov 16, 42. LINGUISTICS, AFRICAN LANGUAGES. *Educ:* Univ Calif, Los Angeles, BA, 65, MA, 75, PhD(ling), 79. *Prof Exp:* Lectr ling, Univ Nairobi, Kenya, 73-74; asst lectr, Univ Idadan, Jos Campus, Nigeria, 75-76; lectr, Univ Maiduguri, Nigeria, 78-80; vis scholar, Univ Port Harcourt, Nigeria, 80-81; RES & WRITING, 82- *Mem:* WAfrican Ling Soc; Int African Inst. *Res:* Nilo-Saharan languages; instrumental phonetics; linguistic universals. *Publ:* Co-ed, Papers in African Linguistics in Honor of William E Welmers, Studies in African Ling, Suppl 6, 76; Dholuo vowel harmony: A phonetic investigation, Working Papers Phonetics, Vol 43, 78; Voice-quality harmony in Western Nilotic languages, In: Issues in Vowel Harmony, John Benjamins, Amsterdam, 80. *Mailing Add:* 2633 16th St NW Washington DC 20016

JACOBSON, RODOLFO, US citizen; m 44; c 4. LINGUISTICS, BILINGUAL EDUCATION. *Educ:* Univ Panama, AB, 52; Univ Mich, MA, 64, PhD(ling), 66. *Prof Exp:* Teacher, Escuela Prof, Panama, 52-62; instr English as foreign lang, English Lang Inst, Univ Mich, 65, lectr, 65-66; assoc prof English, State Univ NY Col Cortland, 66-69, prof English & dir English socioling prog, 69-74; PROF LING, UNIV TEX, SAN ANTONIO, 74- *Concurrent Pos:* Consult, Ministry Educ, Panama, 60-62; lectr, Am Univ Beirut & Am Univ Cairo, 73; consult, United Independent Sch Dist, Laredo, Tex, 75-79; dir, Title VIII Training fel, demonstration proj, 77-; interpreter & examr, Adm US Courts, Washington, DC, 80-81. *Mem:* Teachers English to Speakers Other Lang; Nat Asn Bilingual Educ; Int Sociol Asn; Ling Asn Southwest; Am Educ Res Asn. *Res:* Sociolinguistics; Spanish language varieties and use; methods in bilingual instruction. *Publ:* Auth, Incorporating sociolinguistic norms into an EFL program, TESOL Quart, 76; La reinvindicacion de parole, Estudios Filol, 76; The social implications of intrasentential codeswitching, In: Chicano Scholarship (The New Scholar), 77; Anticipatory embedding and imaginary content, In: SWALLOW VI Proc, 78; Semantic compounding in the speech of Mexican American bilinguals, In: Bilingualism & Bilingual Educ, 79; Beyond ESL: The teaching of content other than language arts in bilingual education, Southwest Educ Development Lab, Austin, Tex, 79; Can bilingual teaching techniques reflect bilingual community behavior?, In: Bilingual Educ and Public Policy, Ypsilanti, Mich, 79; Can and should the Laredo experiment be duplicated elsewhere?, In: NABE Proc, 81. *Mailing Add:* 14222 Golden Woods San Antonio TX 78249

JACOBUS, EVERETT FRANKLIN, JR, b Neptune, NJ, July 8, 45; m 65; c 4. FRENCH. *Educ:* Duke Univ, BA, 67; Cornell Univ, PhD(French), 71. *Prof Exp:* Instr, 71-72, asst prof, 72-80, ASSOC PROF FRENCH, DAVIDSON COL, 80-, DIR SELF-INSTRNL LANG PROG, 75- *Concurrent Pos:* Resident dir, Davidson Col jr yr in Montpellier, France, 73-75; jr yr abroad coordr, Davidson Col, 75-; Danforth assoc, 77; Nat Endowment Humanities fel col teacher French poetry, 78-79. *Mem:* MLA; Am Asn Teachers French, Coun Int Educ Exchange; Am Coun Teaching Foreign Langs. *Res:* French poetry; foreign language pedagogy; international education. *Mailing Add:* Dept of French Davidson Col Davidson NC

JACOBY, FRANK RAINER, b Berlin, Ger, Sept 25, 25; US citizen; m 64; c 2. GERMANIC LANGUAGES. *Educ:* Univ Chicago, AB, 50; Columbia Univ, MA, 62, PhD(Ger), 68. *Prof Exp:* From instr to asst prof Ger, Univ Mass, Amherst, 64-71; asst prof, Univ NH, 72-74; lectr, Brandeis Univ, 76-80; FOREIGN LANG ED, DATA GEN CORP, 80- *Mem:* Mediaeval Acad Am; MLA; Am Asn Teachers Ger. *Res:* Medieval German literature; the medieval beast epic; representations of the law in medieval literature. *Publ:* Auth, Van der Vos Reinaerde: Legal Elements in a Netherlands Epic of the 13th Century, 70 & contrib, Gedichte der Menschheitsdämmerung Interpretationen expressionistischer Lyrik, 71, Wilhelm Fink; auth, The conflict between legal concepts and spiritual values in the MHG Reinhart Fuchs, Rev Langues Vivantes, 2/73; Ecbasis Captivi & Ysengrimus, In: Dict of the Middle Ages, Scribner's (in press); Historical method and romantic vision in Jacob Grimm's writings, Studies Medievalism (in press). *Mailing Add:* 14 Glencrest Ave Dover NH 03820

JACQUART, EMMANUEL CLAUDE, b Lille, France, May 11, 38; US citizen; c 2. FRENCH LITERATURE & LANGUAGE, FRENCH CIVILIZATION. *Educ:* Univ Bordeaux, France, DES, 64, CAPES, 66; Pa State Univ, PhD(contemp French lit), 70. *Prof Exp:* Lectr French, Rosemont Col, Pa, 63-64; prof prin English, High Sch, Bazas, France, 66-67; asst prof French, Harvard Univ, 70-75; assoc prof French & dir, Lang Lab, 76-77, PROF FRENCH, UNIV HOUSTON, 77- *Concurrent Pos:* Consult cult & lang, D C Heath, 75-77; Andrew Mellon vis prof, La Fayette Col, Pa, Spring, 79; vis prof, Univ Strasbourg, France, 81-82. *Mem:* MLA; SCent Mod Lang Asn; Am Asn Teachers French; Semiotic Soc Am; Beckett Soc. *Res:* Contemporary French literature; culture and civilization; stylistics. *Publ:* Coauth, Cours de langue francaise destine aux jeunes Franco-Americains, Assoc Professeurs Franco-Am, 65; auth, Soixante-dix ans d'avant-garde et de refus, Studi Francesi, 5/73; Le Theatre de Derision: Beckett, Ionesco, Adamov, Gallimard, 74; Can literature convey knowledge? Fr Rev, 12/74; Jean Cocteau or Mr Hide-and-Seek, Am Soc Fr Legion Honor Mag, 75; Entretien avec Roman Jakobson: Autour de la Poetique, Critique, 5/76; contribr, Ethique et Esthetique dans la litterature francaise du XX siecle, Stanford Univ, 78; Ionesco aux prises avec la Culture, Ionesco: Situation et Perspectives, Belfond, Paris, 80. *Mailing Add:* 9330 Benning Dr Houston TX 77031

JAEGER, CHARLES STEPHEN, b Hanford, Calif, Sept 1, 40; m 68; c 2. GERMAN LITERATURE OF THE MIDDLE AGES. *Educ:* Univ Calif, Berkeley, BA, 63, MA, 65, PhD(Ger), 70. *Prof Exp:* Asst prof Ger, Univ Chicago, 68-70 & Northwestern Univ, 71-76; assoc prof, 76-82, PROF GER, BRYN MAWR COL, 82- *Concurrent Pos:* Am Coun Learned Soc fel, 74; Fulbright sr res fel, 79-80. *Mem:* Int Arthurian Soc; MLA; Am Asn Teachers Ger. *Res:* Middle High German literature; Middle Latin literature. *Publ:* Auth, The testing of Brangaene: Cunning and innocence in Gottfried's Tristan, J English & Ger Philol, 71; The 'Strophic' Prologue to Gottfried's Tristan und Isolde, Ger Rev, 72; The crown of virtues in the cave of lovers allegory of Gottfried's Tristan, Euphorion, 73; Medieval Humanism in Gottfried von Strassburg's Tristan und Isolde, Carl Winter, Heidelberg, 77; Der Schöpfer der Welt und das Schöpfungswerk als Prologmotiv in der MHD Dichtung, Zeitschrift deutsches Altertum, 78; The Prologue to the Historia Calamatitum and the Authenticity Question, Euphorion, 80; Grimmelshausen's Jupiter and the Figure of the Learned Madman in the 17th Century, Simpliciana, 81; The Image of the Courtier Bishop in Vitae from the 10th to the 12th Century, Speculum (in press). *Mailing Add:* Dept of Ger Bryn Mawr Col Bryn Mawr PA 19010

JAEN, DIDIER TISDEL, b Santiago, Panama, May 12, 33. SPANISH LITERATURE. *Educ:* Univ Tex, Austin, BA, 56, MA, 59, PhD(Span lit), 65. *Prof Exp:* Assoc prof Span lit, Tex Southern Univ, 65; PROF SPAN LIT, UNIV CALIF, DAVIS, 65- *Mem:* Am Asn Teachers Span & Port; MLA; Inst

Int Lit Iberoam. *Res:* Spanish American essay; Spanish American novel and short story; Borges. *Publ:* Auth, Le generacion romantica Argentina y el problema de Hispanoamerica, J Inter-Am Studies, 10/66; Borges y Whitman, Hispania, 3/67; La estructora lirica de Pedro Parano, Revisist Hispanica Moderna, XXXII, 67; Homage to Walt Whitman: A Collection of Poems from the Spanish, translated and annotated, Univ, Ala, 69; ed & transl, Jose Vasconcelos: La Raza Cosmica (transl, The Cosmic Race), Centro de Publicaciones, 79; John II of Castile and the Grand Master Alvgro de Luna, Madrid. *Mailing Add:* Dept of Span Univ of Calif Davis CA 95616

JAHN, GARY ROBERT, b Minneapolis, Minn, Sept 9, 43; m 68; c 3. RUSSIAN LITERATURE. *Educ:* Univ Minn, BA, 65; Univ Wis, MA, 68, PhD(Russ Lit), 72. *Prof Exp:* Asst prof Russ lang & lit, St Olaf Col, 71-72 & State Univ NY, Buffalo, 72-77; asst prof, 77-82, ASSOC PROF RUSS LANG & LIT, UNIV MINN, 82- *Mem:* Am Asn Teachers Slavic & East Europ Lang; Am Asn Advan Slavic Studies. *Res:* Nineteenth century Russian literature, in particular the prose fiction of the second half of the 19th century; the life and work of L N Tolstoy. *Publ:* Auth, A structural analysis of Leo Tolstoy's God Sees the Truth, But Waits, Studies Short Fiction, 75; The aesthetic theory of Leo Tolstoy's What Is Art?, J Aesthet & Art Criticism,, 75; Thematic development in Fathers and Sons, Col Lit, 77; L N Tolstoj's Narodnye rasskazy, Russ Lang J, 77; L N Tolstoj's Vision of the power of death and How Much Land Does a Man Need?, 78 & The image of the railroad in Anna Karenina, 81, Slavic & East Europ J; The unity of Anna Karenina, Russ Rev, 82; Tolstoj and Kant, In: New Perspectives on 19th Century Russian Prose, Slavica Press, 82. *Mailing Add:* Dept of Russ & East Europ Studies Univ of Minn Minneapolis MN 55455

JAHN-RUSCONI, CARLO, b Rome, Italy, Jan 1, 17. FRENCH & ITALIAN LANGUAGE & LITERATURE. *Educ:* Univ Calif, Berkeley, MA, 38; Univ Florence, PhD(soc sci), 42. *Prof Exp:* Exec secy, Olivetti Corp, Ivrea, Italy, 43-44; asst prof Ital, Univ Florence, 45-46; lector, Cambridge, 49-52, transl lit, 52-59; teaching asst Ital, Univ Calif, Berkeley, 59-62; instr Ital & Span, Univ Conn, 62-64; prof comp cult, Goddard Col, 64-66; asst prof Ital, Univ Colo, Boulder, 67-68; ASSOC PROF ITAL, FRENCH & SPAN, HOBART & WILLIAM SMITH COLS, 68- *Mem:* MLA; Am Asn Teachers Ital; Col Art Asn Am. *Res:* Twentieth century Italian literature; 19th and 20th century French literature. *Mailing Add:* Dept of Mod Lang Hobart & William Smith Cols Geneva NY 14456

JAINI, PADMANABH S, b Mangalore, India, Oct 23, 23; m 56; c 2. LINGUSITICS, SOUTH & SOUTHEAST ASIAN RELIGIONS. *Educ:* HPT Col, India, BA, 47; BJ Inst Res, Ahmedabad, MA, 49; Vidyodaya Pirivena, Ceylon, Tripitakacarya, 51; Univ London, PhD(Sanskrit lit), 59. *Prof Exp:* Lectr Sanskrit & Pali, Benaras Hindu Univ, 52-56; Pali & Buddhist Sanskrit, Univ London, 56-64, reader, 65-67; vis lectr Buddhism, Univ Mich, Ann Arbor, 64-65, Prof Indic lang, 67-72; PROF BUDDHISM, UNIV CALIF, BERKELEY, 72- *Res:* Pali and Buddhist Sanskrit language and literature; Abhidharma stuides; comparative study of Indian religions. *Publ:* Ed, Abhidharmadipa, K P Jayawal Inst, 52; auth, On the theory of two Vasubandhus, 58 & The Vaibhasika theory of words, 59, Bull Sch Orient & African Studies, Univ London, ed, Milinda-Tika, Pali Text Soc London, 61; auth, The story of Sudhana and Manohara, 66, Aloka of Haribhadra and the Saratama of Ratnakarasanti: A comparative study of the two commentaries of the Astasahasrika, 72 & Jina Rsabha as an avatara of Visnu, 77, Bull Sch Orient & African Studies, Univ London; The Jaina Path of Purification, Univ Calif, 78. *Mailing Add:* Dept of Southeast Asian Lang & Lit Univ of Calif 246 Dwinelle Berkeley CA 94720

JAKOBSH, FRANK KONRAD, b Emsville, Man, Feb 19, 37; m 61; c 2. GERMAN LANGUAGE, MODERN LITERATURE. *Educ:* United Col, Man, BA, 59; Univ Man, MA, 63; Univ Waterloo, PhD(Ger), 71. *Prof Exp:* Teacher hist & English, Winnipeg Sch Bd, 60-62; lectr Ger, Univ Man, 62-64; lectr, 70-72, ASST PROF GER, UNIV WATERLOO, 72- *Concurrent Pos:* Lectr, Univ Windsor, 71 & 72. *Mem:* Can Asn Univ Teachers Ger. *Res:* Radio drama and related media literature; ethnic culture of German-Canadians; German literature since 1920. *Publ:* Auth, Adaptation and the German Radio Play, Univ Waterloo, 71; Radio plays in the teaching of German, Can Mod Lang Rev, 10/72. *Mailing Add:* 215 Parklawn Pl Waterloo ON N2L 4V5 Can

JAKOBSON, ROMAN, b Moscow, Russia, Oct 11, 96; nat US; m 62. LINGUISTICS. *Educ:* Lazarev Inst Orient Lang, Moscow, AB, 14; Moscow Univ, dipl, 18; Univ Prague, PhD, 30. *Hon Degrees:* Numerous degrees from American and foreign univs. *Prof Exp:* Res assoc, Moscow Univ, 18-20; prof, Masaryk Univ, 33-39; prof gen ling & Czech studies, Ecole Libre des Hautes Etudes, NY, 42-46; Masaryk prof Czech studies, Columbia Univ, 46-49; CROSS PROF SLAVIC LANG & LIT & GEN LING, HARVARD UNIV, 49-; INST PROF, MASS INST TECHNOL, 57- *Concurrent Pos:* Vis lectr, Univs Copenhagen, Oslo & Uppsala, 39-41; vis prof, Columbia Univ, 43-46; vpres, Int Comt Slavists, 58; vis fel, Salk Inst Biol Studies, 66-69; hon pres, Tokyo Inst Advan Studies Lang, 67-; vis prof, Yale Univ, 67, Princeton Univ, 68, Brown Univ, 69 & 70, Brandeis Univ, 70 & Col France, 72; Francqui prof, Cath Univ Louvain, 72; vis prof, NY Univ, 73 & Bergen Univ, 76; foreign mem, Brit Acad & Finnish Acad. *Honors & Awards:* Buslaev Prize, Moscow Univ, 16; Chevalier, Legion d'honneur; Am Coun Learned Soc Award, 60; Award Nat Slavic Honor Soc, 67; Medal Slovak Acad Sci, 68; Award Am Asn Advan Slavic Studies, 70; Antonio Feltrinelli Int Prize for Philol & Ling, 80. *Mem:* Ling Soc Am (pres, 56); Int Asn Semiotics (vpres, 69-); Inst Soc Phonetic Sci (vpres, 70-); Am Anthrop Asn; Mediaeval Acad Am. *Res:* Poetics, semoitics. *Publ:* Auth, Phonolgocial studies, Vol I, 62, 2nd ed, 71, Word and language, Vol II, 71, Early Slavic Paths and Crossroads, Vol III, 81, Slavic epic studies, Vol IV, 66 & Verse, its masters and explorers, Vol V, 78, In: Selected Writings, Studies on Child Language and Aphasia, Mouton, The Hague; Les fondations du langage, Vol I, 63 & Rapports internes et externes du langage, Vol II, 73, In: Essais de Linguistique Generale, Ed Minuit, Paris; Questions de Poetique, Ed Seuil, Paris, 73, vols translated into Czech, Ger, Hungarian, Ital, Japanese, Port, Serivan, Span & Swed; Six Lecons sur le Son et le Sens, Ed Minuit, 76. *Mailing Add:* Boylston Hall 301 Harvard Univ Cambridge MA 02138

JAMES, EDWARD FOSTER, b Hagerstown, Md, Mar 17, 27. LINGUISTICS, ENGLISH. *Educ:* Univ Md, BA, 54, MA, 55; Cath Univ Am, PhD(ling), 69. *Prof Exp:* Lectr English & Foreign lang, 55-69; asst prof educ, 69-80, ASST PROF ENGLISH, UNIV MD, 69- *Concurrent Pos:* Consult Afro-Am dialectology, EPDA Inst Appl Ling, Mt St Agnes Col, Baltimore, 69; consult, Md State Dept Educ, 79-80. *Mem:* Nat Coun Teachers English; Southeastern Conf Ling. *Res:* Afro-American dialectology; transformational sentence combining; Frederick Douglass. *Publ:* Auth, Soviet linguistic policy and the international language movement, 55 & An analytical study and evaluation of the four principal systems of international language, 56-57, Int Lang Rev; ed, The Office of the Akathist, Montfort Fathers, 60; A rhetoric bound grammar: Legacy of the ancients, 66 & Focus on Africa: Oral narrative in the English curriculum, 73-74, Md English J (reprinted in, African Directions, 77); Listening for soul, English Educ, 75; Getting Grammer Out of Storage: Grammer Teacher's Bookshelf, Md English J, 80. *Mailing Add:* Dept of English Univ of Md College Park MD 20742

JAMES, JOSEPH ALSTON, b Columbia, SC, Dec 4, 36; m 60; c 1. ROMANCE LANGUAGES. *Educ:* Univ Ga, AB, 59, PhD(Romance lang), 71; Middlebury Col, MA, 60. *Prof Exp:* Instr French & Span, Ga State Col, 65-67; instr French, Univ Ga, 69-71; asst prof, 71-75, ASSOC PROF FRENCH, FRANCIS MARION COL, & CHMN DEPT, 75- *Mem:* Am Asn Teachers Fr. *Res:* Medieval French literature. *Publ:* Auth, Octarien de Saint-C-elais's use of legend and mythology in Le Sejour d'honneur, SAtlantic Bull, 5/76 & NC Studies Romance Lang & Lit, 77. *Mailing Add:* Dept of Mod Lang Francis Marion Col Florence SC 29501

JAMESON, MICHAEL HAMILTON, b London, Eng, Oct 15, 24; US citizen; m 46; c 4. CLASSICAL STUDIES, ANCIENT HISTORY. *Educ:* Univ Chicago, AB, 42, PhD(Greek), 49. *Prof Exp:* Asst prof class lang & archaeol, Univ Mo, 50-53; from asst prof to assoc prof class studies, 54-62, dean grad sch arts & sci, 66-68, prof class studies, Univ Pa, 62-66; PROF CLASSICS & CROSSETT PROF HUMANISTIC STUDIES, STANFORD UNIV, 77- *Concurrent Pos:* Fulbright fel, Greece, 49-50, res fel Italy, 58-59 & 77-78; Fund Advan Educ fel, Inst Soc Anthrop, Oxford, 53-54; vis assoc prof Greek, Bryn Mawr Col, 57-58; Am Coun Learned Soc fel, 58-59; sr fel, Am Acad Rome, 58-59; res assoc class archaeol, Univ Mus & dir Argolid exploration proj, Univ Pa, 61-, chmn grad group ancient hist, 68-76; Guggenheim fel, 65-66; vis prof class studies, Am Sch Class Studies, 65-66; Nat Endowment for Humanities sr fel, 71-72. *Mem:* Archaeol Inst Am; Am Acad Arts & Sci; Am Philos Soc; Am Philol Asn (pres, 80). *Res:* Greek history; religion and archaeology. *Publ:* Auth, A Decree of Themistokles from Troizen, Hesperia, 60; Greek mythology, In: Mythologies of Ancient World, Anchor, 60; Excavations at Porto Cheli and vicinity, Hesperia, 69; Agriculture and slavery, Classics J, 77. *Mailing Add:* Dept of Classics Stanford Univ Stanford CA 94305

JAMIESON, JOHN CHARLES, b Boston, Mass, June 30, 33; m 60; c 2. CHINESE LITERATURE, MEDIEVAL CIVILIZATION. *Educ:* Univ Calif, Berkeley, AB, 59, MA, 64, PhD(Orient lang), 69. *Prof Exp:* Instr orient lang, 66, acting asst prof, 66-68, asst prof, 68-72, assoc prof, 72-80, PROF ORIENT LANG, UNIV CALIF, BERKELEY, 80- *Concurrent Pos:* Dir, Inter-Univ Prog Chinese Lang Studies, 69-70; Nat Endowment for Humanities younger humanist award & Soc Sci Res Coun grant, 73-74. *Mem:* Asn Asian Studies; Am Orient Soc. *Res:* Literature; culture of medieval China, East Asia. *Publ:* Auth, Collapse of the Tang-Silla alliance, In: Northing Concealed, 70; Na-Tang Tongmaeng ui Wahae, Yoksahakpo, 70. *Mailing Add:* Dept of Orient Lang Univ of Calif Berkeley CA 94720

JAMME, ALBERT W F, b Senzeille, Belgium, June 27, 16. ENGLISH, FRENCH. *Educ:* Cath Univ Louvain, DTheol, 47, DOr, 52; Pontif Bibl Comm, Rome, Lic, 48. *Prof Exp:* RES PROF SEMITICS, CATH UNIV AM, 55- *Concurrent Pos:* Epigraphical adv, Govt Saudi Arabia, 68-69. *Mem:* Cath Bibl Asn Am; Am Orient Soc. *Res:* Pre-Islamic Arabian science. *Publ:* Auth, Pieces Epigraphiques de Heid bin Aqil, la Necropole de Timna, (Hagr Kohlan), Biblio Mus, Louvain, 52; La Kynastie de Sarahbiil Yakuf et la documentation epigraphique sud-arabe, Ned Hist Archaeol Inst, Istanbul, 61; Sabaean inscriptions from Mahram Bilquis (Marib), Johns Hopkins Univ, 62; Miscellanees d'ancient arabe, I-VII, Washington, 71-74; Carnegie Museum 1974-1975 Yemen Expedition, Carnegie Natural Hist Spec Publ No 2, Pittsburgh, 76. *Mailing Add:* Dept of Semitics Cath Univ Am Washington DC 20064

JANKOWSKY, K R, b Löwen, Ger, Apr 23, 28; m 60; c 2. GERMANIC LANGUAGES. *Educ:* Univ Münster, PhD(English, Ger & philos), 56; Staatliches Studiensem Bochum, Ger, Assessorenexamen, 58. *Prof Exp:* Lectr Ger, Univ Poona, 58-62; from asst prof to assoc prof, 62-72, PROF GERMANIC LING & CHMN DEPT GER, GEORGETOWN UNIV, 72- HEAD DIV, 64- *Concurrent Pos:* Founding mem prep comt Advan Ger in Indian, 59-62. *Mem:* Ling Soc India; Ling Soc Am; MLA; Am Asn Teachers Ger; Ling Asn Can & US. *Res:* Germanic versification and lexicology; 19th century linguistics. *Publ:* Auth, The Neogrammarians, Janua Linguarum Ser, Mouton, The Hague, 72; Language and International Studies, Georgetown Univ, 73; The psychologocial component in the work of the early neogrammarians, Sec Int Conf Hist Ling, fall 76; The European engagement of William D Whitney, Third LACUS Forum 1976, 77; On the role of presupposition in the interrelationship of sentences, Orbis, 78; Typological studies in the 19th century and the Neogrammarian sound law principle, Forum Linguisticum, 79; Max Mueller and the development of linguistic science, Historigraphia Linguistica VI, 79; The mising link in the interrelationship of sectences, In: Lacun Forum, Hormbeam Press, 80. *Mailing Add:* Dept of Ger Georgetown Univ Washington DC 20057

JANMOHAMED, ABDUL RAHEMAN, Commonwealth Literature. See Vol II

JANSEN, LAWRENCE FREDERICK, b St Louis, Mo, Mar 2, 19. CLASSICAL LANGUAGES. *Educ:* St Louis Univ, AB, 42, MA & PhL, 44; St Mary's Col, STL, 51. *Prof Exp:* Instr class lang, Regis Col Colo, 44-47; asst prof class lang & asst dean, Col Arts & Sci, Creighton Univ, 52-58; from asst prof to assoc prof class lang, 58-71, asst dean Col Arts & Sci, 58-60, assoc dean, 60-73, dir 1-8-1-8 prog, 73-80, PROF CLASS LANG, ST LOUIS UNIV, 71- *Mem:* Cath Press Asn; Am Personnel & Guid Asn; Asn Am Med Cols; Class Asn Midwest & S; Nat Asn Acad Affairs Adminr (pres, 73-). *Publ:* Auth, Divine Ideas in St Augustine, Mod Schoolman, 45. *Mailing Add:* Col of Arts & Sci St Louis Univ St Louis MO 63103

JANTZEN, JOHN BENJAMIN, b Paso Robles, Calif, Nov 17, 14; m 45; c 3. FRENCH, HIGHER EDUCATION. *Educ:* Whitworth Col, Wash, AB, 48; Ball State Univ, MA, 61; Ind Univ, Bloomington, PhD, 68. *Prof Exp:* Teacher sec mission schs, Belgian Congo, 51-53, dir elem schs, 55-59; from instr to assoc prof French, Taylor Univ, 59-70; assoc prof, 70-72, PROF FRENCH, WESTMONT COL, 72- *Mem:* MLA; Am Asn Teachers Fr; Am Coun Teaching Foreign Lang. *Res:* Effectiveness of language study abroad of Indiana University honors program for high school students. *Mailing Add:* Dept of Foreign Lang Westmont Col 955 La Paz Rd Santa Barbara CA 93108

JARAMILLO, SAMUEL, b Manizales, Colombia, Oct 25, 25. LANGUAGES. *Educ:* Nat Univ Colombia, PhD, 50. *Prof Exp:* Pub admin, Colombian Govt, 50-58; instr Span, Worcester Acad, 59-62; from asst prof to assoc prof Span & Latin Am lit, 62-73, PROF MOD LANG, NORTHEASTERN UNIV, 72- *Publ:* Auth, Morrogacho, Talleres Modelo Mexico DF, 63; Nadaismo Diplomatico, 65, Gurropin, 66 & Santos en El Infierno, 67, Ed Suramerica Ltda, Bogota; Voz en grito, Colombia Nueva, Bogota, 70; Un negro para montrar, Ed Apolo, Manizales, 73; America sin norte, 74 & Los Cobardes, 78, Ed Cosmos, Bogota. *Mailing Add:* Dept of Mod Lang Northeastern Univ Boston MA 02115

JARKA, HORST, b Klosterneuburg, Austria, Aug 9, 25; m 53; c 2. GERMAN PHILOLOGY. *Educ:* Univ Vienna, dipl, 49, PhD, 55. *Prof Exp:* Prof Ger & English, Commercial High Sch, Vienna, 52-59, 61-62; asst prof, 59-61, 62-64, assoc prof, 64-68, PROF GER, UNIV MONT, 68- *Honors & Awards:* Theodor-Körner-Preis, Theodor Körner Found, Vienna, Austria, 77. *Mem:* Am Asn Teachers Ger; Int Arthur Schnitzler Res Asn; Western Asn Ger Studies. *Res:* Nineteenth and 20th century German literature. *Publ:* Ed, Theodor Storm: Gedichte/Hans und Heinz Kirch, McGraw, 72; Politik und Zauberei: Jura Soyfer, Mod Austrian Lit, 72; Odön v Horvath und das Kitschige, Zeitschrift für deutsche Philol, 72; Soldatenbriefe und nationale Bildungsideologie, Monatshefte, 75; ed & translr, The Legacy of Jura Soyfer, Engendra, Montreal, 77; ed, Jura Soyfer-Gesamtausgabe, Europa Verlag, Vienna, 80; Zur Literaturpolitik im Staendestaat, In: Aufbruch und Untergang, Vienna, 81. *Mailing Add:* Dept of Foreign Lang Univ of Mont Missoula MT 59801

JARLETT, FRANCIS GRENIER, b Watertown, Conn, Oct 16, 16; m 44; c 5. FRENCH. *Educ:* Yale Univ, BA, 39, MA, 42, PhD(French), 50. *Prof Exp:* Instr French, Wayne State Univ, 47-51, instr Span, Col Educ, 54-55; from instr French & acting chmn dept to assoc prof French & chmn dept, Chestnut Hill Col, 56-65; dir lang lab, 65-72, ASSOC PROF FRENCH, CENT CONN STATE COL, 65- *Concurrent Pos:* Lectr French & Span, Villanova Univ, 60-64; asst prof French, NDEA Lang Inst, Univ Fla, 61; lectr French & English, St Joseph's Col, Pa, 63-65. *Mem:* Am Asn Teachers Fr; MLA; Nat Asn Lang Lab Dir. *Res:* Francisque Sarcey and French dramatic criticism; 19th century French theatre. *Publ:* Auth, Bibliography for Francisque Sarcey-Cabeen bibliography. *Mailing Add:* Dept of Mod Lang Cent Conn State Col New Britain CT 06050

JARVI, RAYMOND, b Seattle, Wash, Nov 10, 42. MODERN SWEDISH LITERATURE, SWEDISH THEATER. *Educ:* Univ Wash, BA, 64, MA, 66, PhD(drama arts), 70. *Prof Exp:* Instr Scand, Univ Wash, 68-70, asst prof, 70-78; ASSOC PROF SWEDISH, NORTH PARK COL, 79- *Mem:* Soc Advan Scand Studies; Swed Pioneer Hist Soc. *Res:* August Strindberg; Swedish literature, 1890-1914; Swedish-American place-names. *Publ:* Co-translr, Swedenhielms, In: Four Plays by Hjalmar Bergman, Univ Wash, 68; auth, Strindberg's Ghost Sonata and sonata form, Mosaic, summer 72; Ett Drömspel: A symphony for the stage, Scand Studies, winter 72; Svarta handsken: A lyrical fantasy for the stage, Scandinavica, 5/73; contribr, Encyclopedia of World Literature in the 20th Century, F Ungar, 75, rev ed, 81; coauth, Strindberg: Alive in the blue tower, Scand Rev, 9/76; contribr, Academic American Encyclopedia, Princeton: Arete, 80; auth, Strindberg at the opera, In: Structures of Influence: A Comparative Approach to August Strindberg, NC Press, 81. *Mailing Add:* North Park Col 5125 N Spaulding Chicago IL 60625

JARVIS, BARBARA MEACHAM, b Monroe, Ark, Jan 4, 37; m 66; c 3. SPANISH LITERATURE. *Educ:* Univ Ark, Fayetteville, BA, 58, MA, 59; Univ Wis-Madison, PhD(Span), 66. *Prof Exp:* Instr Span, Univ Tex, Austin, 62-65; asst prof, 65-71, ASSOC PROF SPAN, UNIV ARK, FAYETTEVILLE, 71- *Concurrent Pos:* Nat Found Arts & Humanities fel, 67-68. *Mem:* Am Asn Teachers Span & Port; MLA; AAUP. *Res:* Spanish literature, 16th-17th centuries; Gongora, Cervantes. *Mailing Add:* Dept of Foreign Lang Univ of Ark Fayetteville AR 72701

JARVIS, DONALD KARL, b Ithaca, NY, Apr 6, 39; m 65; c 6. FOREIGN LANGUAGE EDUCATION. *Educ:* Brigham Young Univ, BA, 64; Ohio State Univ, PhD(foreign lang educ), 70. *Prof Exp:* Teacher foreign lang, Beaver Pub Schs, 65-66; teacher Russ, Salt Lake City Pub Schs, 66-67; assoc prof, 70-80, chmn dept Asian & Slavic lang, 76-79, PROF RUSS, BRIGHAM YOUNG UNIV, 80-, ASSOC DIR GEN EDUC, 81-, COODR, LANG TEACHING RES, 81- *Concurrent Pos:* Ed, Newslett, Am Asn Teachers Slavic & E Europ Lang, 72-74. *Mem:* Am Asn Teachers Slavic & E Europ Lang (vpres, 76-77); Am Coun Teaching Russ, (bd dirs, 77-, vpres, 79-). *Res:* Language teaching; Russian linguistics; Russian culture. *Publ:* Auth, Teaching foreign etiquette in the foreign language class: Student involvement techniques, Foreign Lang Ann, 5/75; coauth, Russian Language Study in 1975: A Status Report, MLA, 76; The Langugage Connection: From the Classroom to the World, Nat Textbk, 77; ed, Techniques for increasing Slavic program enrollments: A collection of success stories, Am Asn Teachers Slavic & E Europ Lang, 78; auth, Krazvitiiu kommunikativinoi sposobnosti uchashchixsia (obsor amerikanskix eksperimentov i metodov) Russkii iazyk za rubezhom, 1/78; coauth, Viewpoints: A Listening and Conversation Course in Russian, Brigham Young Univ Press, 79; A study of the effect of parallel translations on second language reading and syntax acquisition, Mod Lang J, 82; co-ed, Russian Language Teaching, Slavica, 82. *Mailing Add:* Dept of Asian & Slavic Lang 250 FB Brigham Young Univ Provo UT 84602

JARVIS, GILBERT ANDREW, b Boston, Mass, Feb 13, 41; m 63; c 2. FOREIGN LANGUAGE EDUCATION. *Educ:* St Norbert Col, BA, 63; Purdue Univ, West Lafayette, MA, 66, PhD(foreign lang educ), 70. *Prof Exp:* Teacher French & English, Mineral Point High Sch, Wis, 63-65; instr French & educ, Purdue Univ, 65-70; from asst prof to assoc prof, 70-76, PROF FOREIGN LANG EDUC, OHIO STATE UNIV, 76-, CHMN HUMANITIES EDUC, 80- *Honors & Awards:* NY State Nat Foreign Language Leadership Award, 81. *Mem:* Am Coun Teaching Foreign Lang; Am Educ Res Asn. *Res:* Foreign language learning and curricula development and measurement. *Publ:* Ed, Review of Foreign Language Education, Nat Texbk, Vols V, VI, VII & VIII, 73, 74, 75 & 76; coauth, Connaitre et se Connaitre, 76, Passeport pour la France & Vivent les Differences, 77, Invitation, 79, Et Vous (in prep) & Nous Tous (in prep), Holt. *Mailing Add:* Dept of Foreign Lang Educ Ohio State Univ Columbus OH 43210

JASANOFF, JAY HAROLD, b Brooklyn, NY, June 12, 42; m 68; c 2. LINGUISTICS, GERMANIC PHILOLOGY. *Educ:* Harvard Univ, AB, 63, PhD(ling), 68. *Prof Exp:* Asst prof ling, Univ Calif, Berkeley, 69-70; asst prof, Harvard Univ, 70-74, asst prof ling & Ger philol, 74-75, assoc prof, 75-78; assoc prof, 78-81, PROF LING & CHMN DEPT MOD LANGS & LING, CORNELL UNIV, 81- *Concurrent Pos:* Am Inst Indian Studies fac res fel, 68-69. *Mem:* Ling Soc Am; Soc Ling Paris, Innsbrucker Sprachwissenschaftliche Gesellshaft. *Res:* Indo-European linguistics, Germantic linguistics, historical linguistics. *Publ:* Auth, The Hittite ablative in -anza, Münchener Studien Sprachwissenschaft, 73; The Germanic third weak class, Language, 73; Gr ampho, lat ambo et le mot indo-europeen pour 'l' un et l'autre, Bull Soc Ling, 76; The r-endings of the IE middle, Die Sprache, 77; Stative and Middle in Indo-European, Innsbrucker Beiträge Sprachwissenschaft, 78; Observations on the Germanic Verschärfung, Münchener Studien Sprachwissenschaft, 78; Notes on the Armenian personal endings, Zeitschrift Vergleichende Sprachforschung, 78; The position of the hi-conjugation, In: Hethitisch und Indogermanisch, 79. *Mailing Add:* Dept of Ling Cornell Univ Ithaca NY 14853

JASENAS, ELAINE FRANCINE CHARLOTTE, b Saorge, France, Dec 5, 22; nat US; m 45, 60. FRENCH. *Educ:* Univ Ill, BA & MA, PhD(French lit), 54. *Prof Exp:* Instr French, Univ Ill, 54-55; instr French & dir French House, Douglass Col, Rutgers Univ, 55-56; from instr to assoc prof French, Wells Col, 56-64; assoc prof French lit, 64-77, PROF FRENCH & COMP LIT, STATE UNIV NY, BINGHAMTON, 77- *Concurrent Pos:* Fulbright Scholar, Franco-Am Comn for Educ Exchange, 76; Exchange Prof, Univ Aix-en-Provence, France, 76-77. *Mem:* MLA; Am Asn Teachers Fr; Int Asn Fr Studies; Soc Fr Prof Am; Soc Baudelairienne. *Res:* Comparative literature; French literature of the 19th century; new criticism. *Publ:* Auth, Marceline-Desbordes-Valmore Devant la Critique, Droz, Switz, 62; Saint-Simon et Maurepas, Rev Hist Lit Fr, 1/64; Pascal educateur, Rev Univ Laval, 1/66; Le theme de la chasse au monstre dans la Phedre de Racine, Symposium, summer 67; Le Poetique: Desbordes-Valmore et Nerval, Ed Univ, Paris, 75; The French influence in Kate Chopin's The Awakening, Nineteenth Century Fr Studies, spring 76; Stendhal et les industriels, Degre Second, 7/77; Prosper Merimee and Lithuania, J Baltic Studies, summer 77. *Mailing Add:* Dept of French State Univ NY Binghamton NY 13901

JASINSKI, RENE, b Montcy St Pierre, France, July 28, 98; m 53. FRENCH LITERATURE. *Educ:* Univ Paris, Baccalaureat, 16, Lic es Lett, 17, Ecole Normale Super, 19, Agrege, 22, DLett, 29. *Hon Degrees:* MA, Harvard Univ, 53. *Prof Exp:* Preparateur, French lit, Ecole Normale Super, 23-26; maitre conf, Univ Lille, 29-33, prof 33-42; maitre conf, Sorbonne, 42-43, prof, 43-53; prof, 53-65, EMER PROF FRENCH LIT, HARVARD UNIV, 65- *Concurrent Pos:* Dir, Rev Hist Philos & Hist Gen Civilisation, 33-44; dir collection, Connaissance des Lettres, 46-; co-ed, Rev Hist Lit France, 47-53; vis prof French lit, Univ Ariz, 66. *Honors & Awards:* Chevalier, Legion d'honneur, 48, Off, 53. *Mem:* MLA; Soc Hist Lit France; Soc Hist Theatre; Soc Studies 17th Century; Soc Theophile Gautier (hon pres, 80). *Res:* French literature of the 17th and 19th centuries. *Publ:* Auth, Les annies romantiques de Theophile Gautier, Histoire de la Litterature Francaise, Moliere et le Misanthrope, Vers le Vrai Racine (2 vols), Libr Armand Colin, 58; La Fontaine et les Jix Premiers Livres des Fables (2 vols), Nizet, 66; Moliere, Hatier, 69; Deux acces a la Bruyere, 71 & A Travers le XIXe siecle, 75, Minard; A travers le XVII siecle (2 vols), Nizet, 81. *Mailing Add:* 1716 Cambridge St Cambridge MA 02138

JASPER, SUSAN D PENFIELD, b Los Angeles, Calif, Jan 19, 46; m 77; c 2. APPLIED LINGUISTICS, ANTHROPOLOGY. *Educ:* Univ Ariz, BA, 68, MA, 70; PhD(ling), 80. *Prof Exp:* Teaching assoc anthrop & ling, Univ Ariz, 69-72; dir Indian educ, publ schs, Parker, Ariz, 73-74; res early children's educ, Papago Proj, Univ Ariz, 74-75; consult Indian Educ, Ventura County Sch, Calif, 82; MEM FAC ENGLISH LANG PROG, UNIV CALIF, SANTA BARBARA, 82- *Concurrent Pos:* Instr, Ariz Western Col & Parker High Sch, Ariz, 70-71; recorder archaeol excavations, Colorado River Indian tribes, fall 71. *Res:* American Indian language and education; dialect study; applied linguistics and anthropology. *Publ:* Auth, Chemehuevi basketry, Smoke Signals, spring 71; A historical sketch of the Colorado rive Indian Reservation (pamphlet), Colorado River Indian Tribes, 71; Suggestions for dealing with Mohave English: A grant proposal, In: Southwest Languages and Linguistics in Educational Perspectives, San Diego Inst Cult Pluralism, 75;

Some examples of Southwestern Indian English compared, In: Studies in Southwestern Indian English, Trinity Univ Press, 77; Mohave English and tribal identity & Some comments on negation in Mohave English, In: More Studies In Southwestern Indian English, Trinity Univ Press (in press). *Mailing Add:* 136 Kenneth St Camarillo CA 93010

JASZCZUN, WASYL, b Snyriv, Ukraine, Jan 24, 15; US citizen; m 48; c 2. SLAVIC PHILOLOGY. *Educ:* Graz Univ, PhD(Slavic philol), 48. *Prof Exp:* Teacher high sch, Ukraine, 39-41; pvt teacher, 41-44; lectr Polish lang & lit, Univ Pa, 56-58, lectr Russ & Polish lang, 58-59; asst prof Russ, State Univ Iowa, 59-60; asst prof Russ, 60-61, actg chmn dept Slavic lang & lit, 60-62, assoc prof, 61-65, prof, 65-81, EMER PROF RUSS & SLAVIC PHILOL, UNIV PITTSBURGH, 81- *Concurrent Pos:* Charles E Merrill fac fel humanities, 63; Fac Allocation res fel, 69. *Mem:* Ukrainian Am Asn Univ Prof; Am Asn Teachers Slavic & E Europ Lang; Am Name Soc; Shevchenko Sci Soc. *Res:* East Slavic onomatology; Russian and Ukrainian dialects and historical grammar; history of the Ukrainian literary language. *Publ:* Auth, Phonetic, Morphological and Lexical Peculiarities of the Snyriv Dialect, 64 & The Term and Name Brody, 65, Ukrainian Free Acad Sci; coauth, Russian Pattern Drills, Prentice-Hall, 65; A Dictionary of Russian Idioms and Colloquialisms, Univ Pittsburgh, 67, auth, Vowel/zero Alternations in the Nominal System of Contemporary Standard Ukrainian. Ukrainian Dialect of the District of Brody in Western Ukraine, Philol Sect Shevchenko Sci Soc, 72; Some Problems in the Formation of Neologisms in Modern Ukrainian, Word on Guard, 73; Suffixless Nouns in-a Correlative with Prefixed Verbs in Modern Ukrainian, Memoirs Shevchenko Sci Soc, 76. *Mailing Add:* Dept Slavic Lang & Lit Univ Pittsburgh Pittsburgh PA 15260

JASZI, ANDREW OSCAR, b Budapest, Hungary, Mar 1, 17; nat US; m 44; c 2. GERMAN. *Educ:* Oberlin Col, AB, 38; Harvard Univ, AM, 39, PhD, 47. *Prof Exp:* Instr Harvard Univ, 47-48; from asst prof to assoc prof, 48-63, PROF GERMAN, UNIV CALIF, BERKELEY, 63- *Mem:* MLA. *Res:* German literature; aesthetics; Hofmannsthal's youthful works. *Mailing Add:* Dept of Ger Univ of Calif Berkeley CA 74720

JAVENS, CHARLES, b Orlando, Fla, Nov 13, 27; m 55; c 2. SPANISH, PORTUGUESE. *Educ:* Univ NC, AB, 51, MA, 58, PhD(Romance lang). 65. *Prof Exp:* Asst prof Span, Birmingham-Southern Col, 59-62; asst prof, Univ SC, 62-65; ASSOC PROF SPAN & PORT, UNIV MIAMI, 65- *Mem:* MLA; Am Asn Teachers Span & Port; SAtlantic Mod Lang Asn. *Mailing Add:* Dept of Foreign Lang Univ of Miami Coral Gables FL 33124

JAVITCH, DANIEL GILBERT, b Cannes, France, June 13, 41; m 68. ENGLISH, COMPARATIVE LITERATURE. *Educ:* Princeton Univ, AB, 63; Cambridge Univ, BA, 65, MA, 70; Harvard Univ, MA, 66, PhD(comp lit), 70. *Prof Exp:* Asst prof, Columbia Univ, 70-78; ASSOC PROF COMP LIT, NEW YORK UNIV, 78- *Concurrent Pos:* Dir, New Directions Publ Corp, 72-; fel, Harvard Ctr Ital Renaissance Studies, Florence, Italy, 76-77; Am Coun Learned Socs fel, 77; mem exec comt, Mod Lang Asn Div Comp Studies Renaissance & Baroque Lit, 80-; vis prof comp lit & Ital, Univ Calif, Berkeley, 82; Vis prof comp lit, Univ Calif, Berkeley, 82-; exec comt, Comp Renaissance & Baroque Lit, MLA, 81-; chmn colloquium comp lit, New York Univ, 79- *Mem:* MLA; Renaissance Soc Am; Am Comp Lit Asn; Int Comp Lit Asn. *Res:* Renaissance Europe; English, French, Italian literatures of the Renaissance. *Publ:* Auth, Rescuing Ovid from the allegorizers, Comp Lit, 78; Poetry and Courtliness in Renaissance England, Princeton Univ, 78; Cantus Interruptus in the Orlando Furioso, Mod Lang Notes, 80; Influence of Orlando Furioso on Ovid's Metamorphoses in Italian, J Medieval & Renaissance Studies, 81. *Mailing Add:* 19 University Place New York Univ New York NY 10003

JAVOR, GEORGE, b Nyiregyhaza, Hungary; US citizen; m 44; c 2. PHILOLOGY. *Educ:* Pazmany Peter Univ, Budapest, PhD, 44. *Prof Exp:* Teacher high schs, Calif & Wash, 54-61; asst prof French, Wis State Univ, Superior, 61-63; asst prof foreign lang, Ball State Univ, 64-68; assoc prof, 68-73, PROF FOREIGN LANG, NORTHERN MCIH UNIV, 73-, SUPVR STUDENT TEACHERS, 68- *Concurrent Pos:* Fel, Univ Wash, 51-53. *Mem:* MLA; Midwest Mod Lang Asn. *Res:* Present day American usage; Seneca. *Publ:* Auth, On the ambivalence of verbs expressing sensations, 41; Affluential--a word in (the wrong) Webster, 43: 238-239, Sissy bar: The word that made good, 44: 237-238, From Sundown to Moonlight, 47: 299-301, Divided usage on a divided country, 49: 154-55, White hour happines, 49: 305, Mad money--a semantic change, 50: 155-58, Am Speech; A Senecan echo in Luther's table talk, Harvard Theol Rev, 62: 430. *Mailing Add:* Dept of Foreign Lang Northern Mich Univ Marquette MI 49855

JAZAYERY, MOHAMMAD ALI, b Shushtar, Iran, May 27, 24. LINGUISTICS. *Educ:* Univ Tehran, Iran, Lic, 50; Nat Teachers Col, Iran, Lic, 50; Univ Tex, PhD(English), 58. *Prof Exp:* Teacher English, Ahwaz Norm Sch & Ahwaz Agr Norm Sch, Iran, 50-51; coauth & co-ed, Am Coun Learned Socs, Washington, DC, 54-55; instr English, Univ Tex, 55-57, lectr, 57-58; assoc prof, Univ Tehran, 58-59; lectr Persian, Univ Mich, 59-62; vis assoc prof Persian, English & ling, 62-65, from assoc prof to prof ling, 65-70, asst dir, Mid E Ctr, 66-73, PROF, DEPT ORIENT & AFRICAN LANG & LIT, UNIV TEX, AUSTIN, 70-, CHMN, 76-, DIR MID EAST CTR, 81- *Concurrent Pos:* Univ fel, Univ Tehran, 47-50; asst to US Cult Attache, Tehran, 58-59; lectr Persian, Harvard Univ, 58; vis assoc prof ling, Univ Tex, 61; sr linguist & dir lang training Persian & English, Peace Corps, Utah State Univ, 62; vis lectr, Princeton Univ, 67; vis assoc prof, NY Univ, 68; vis prof, Portland State Univ; chmn, Comt Persian Lang Instr in US & Can, 72- *Mem:* Mid East Studies Asn NAm; Am Orient Soc; Ling Soc Am; Soc Iranian Studies; Teachers English to Speakers Other Lang. *Res:* Sociolinguistics; applied linguistics; Persian linguistics. *Publ:* Coauth, English for Iranians, Am Coun Learned Socs, 55; co-ed, Modern Persian Reader (3 vols), Univ Mich, 62; Western influence in contemporary Persian: A general view, Bull Sch Orient Studies, 66; Observations on loanwords as an index to cultural borrowing, In: Studies in Language, Literature and Culture of the Middle Ages and Later, Univ Tex, 69; Observations on stylistic variation in Persian, In: Proceedings of the 10th International Congress of Linguists, Vol 3, Roumanian Acad, Bucharest, 70; Ahmad Kasravi and the controversy over Persian poetry, Int J Mid E Studies, 73; co-ed, Linguistic and Literary Studies in Honor of Archibald A Hill, 4 vols, Mouton, The Hague, 78-79; Farhangesta: La Academia Irania de la Lengua, Univ Nacional Autonoma de Mexico, 79. *Mailing Add:* Dept of Orient & African Lang & Lit 2601 University Univ of Tex Austin TX 78712

JEANNET, ANGELA MARIA, b Pergine, Arezzo, Italy, Aug 8, 31; c 5. FRENCH. *Educ:* Univ Florence, DLet, 54. *Prof Exp:* Teaching asst, Lycee Fenelon, Lille, France, 52-54; instr Ital & French, Univ Colo, 56-62; asst prof Romance lang, Pa State Univ, 62-67; asst prof French, 67-71, ASSOC PROF ITAL & FRENCH, FRANKLIN & MARSHALL COL, 71- *Concurrent Pos:* Danforth assoc. *Mem:* AAUP; MLA; Am Asn Teachers Ital; Asn Ital Studies. *Res:* Contemporary literature; women's studies. *Publ:* Auth, Nell officina carducciana, Italica, IXIII: 3; The poet as magician, Symposium, spring 68; From Florence, Italy: on Zabriskie Point, Ital Quart, fall 70; co-ed, New World Journeys, Greenwood, 77; Italo Calirno's Invisible City, Perpectives Contemp Lit, 5/77; If America did not exist . . .: Italian writings on America from 1925-1970, Ital Am, fall-winter/80. *Mailing Add:* Dept of French & Ital Franklin & Marshall Col Lancaster PA 17604

JEDAN, DIETER, b Weruschau, Ger, Oct 1, 44; m 71; c 3. GERMAN LANGUAGE & LITERATURE. *Educ:* Carthage Col, BA, 69; Univ Kans, MA, 71, PhD(educ), 73. *Prof Exp:* Asst prof foreign lang pedag & Ger lang & lit, Ill Wesleyan Univ, 72-76; ASST PROF GER, UNIV CALIF, LOS ANGELES, 76- *Concurrent Pos:* Textbk consult, Holt, 77-; *Mem:* Am Asn Teachers Ger; Am Coun Teaching Foreign Lang; Western Asn Ger Studies; Philol Asn of Pac Coast. *Res:* Foreign language pedagogy and methodology; cultural anthropology and foreign language teaching; German philosophy. *Publ:* Auth, Pestalozzis Einfluss auf die Methodische Umgestaltung des Fremdsprachlichen Unterrichts in Amerika, Pestalozzianum, Zurich, 6/74; Pestalozzi and oral Latin, Class Outlook, 12/74; Advertisements--an index to German culture in the classroom, Unterrichtspraxis, fall 78; Teaching the silent language visually in the German classroom, In: Language Acquisition Through Cultural Awareness, Cumberland, 78; coauth, First Year German, Holt, Rinehart, Winston, 79; Arts and Letters, 79 & Current Issues, 79, Holt; auth, Johann H Pestalozzi and the Pestalozzian Method of Language Teaching, Stanford Ger Studies, 81. *Mailing Add:* Dept of Ger Lang Univ of Calif Los Angeles CA 90024

JEEVES, WILLIAM NORMAN, b Leicester, UK, July 13, 21; m 49; c 3. ROMANCE LANGUAGES. *Educ:* Cambridge Univ, BA, 43, MA, 51; Univ Brodeaux, Lic est Let, 48. *Prof Exp:* Lectr English, Univ Bordeaux, 45-47; lectr, Sorbonne, 47-48; lectr, Univ Saarland, 48-50, assoc prof, 50-53; lectr French, King's Col, Univ London, 53-65; ASSOC PROF FRENCH, MCMASTER UNIV, 65- *Mem:* MLA; Am Coun Teaching Foreign Lang; Can Asn Appl Ling. *Res:* French poetics and stylists; translation. *Mailing Add:* Dept of Romance Lang McMaster Univ Hamilton ON L8S 4M2 Can

JEFFERS, COLEMAN REYNOLDS, b Frankfort, Ky, Feb 12, 27. SPANISH. *Educ:* Berea Col, BA, 49; State Univ Iowa, MA, 51, PhD, 54. *Prof Exp:* Instr Span, Dartmouth Col, 54-57; from instr to asst prof, Purdue Univ, 57-65; ASSOC PROF SPAN, UNIV IOWA, 65- *Mem:* Am Asn Teachers Span & Port; MLA. *Res:* Nineteenth century drama of Spain. *Publ:* Coauth, Spanish Readings for Conversation, Houghton, 69. *Mailing Add:* Dept of Span & Portuguese Univ of Iowa Iowa City IA 52240

JEFFRIES, ELNA LOUISE, b Greenville, Ky, July 12, 11. ROMANCE LANGUAGES. *Educ:* Univ Mich, AB, 34, MA, 35; Univ Dijon, PhD(French lit), 58. *Prof Exp:* Teacher pub schs, Mich, 36-47; from instr to prof French, 47-76, EMER PROF MOD LANG, KNOX COL, ILL, 76- *Mem:* Am Asn Teachers Fr; MLA. *Mailing Add:* Dept of Mod Lang Knox Col Galesburg IL 61401

JEGERS, BENJAMIN, b Jelgava, Latvia, Jan 16, 15; US citizen: m 37. LINGUISTICS. *Educ:* Univ Latvia, Mag Phil, 44; Univ Göttingen, Dr Phil (comp ling), 49; Columbia Univ, MSLS, 53. *Prof Exp:* Librn, Middlebury Col, 53-55; subj specialist mod lang & lit, Yale Univ Libr, 55-61; instr Slavic philol, Univ Lund, 61-62; asst prof Ger lang & lit, Centre Col, 63-68; assoc prof, 68-76, PROF GER, NORTHERN ILL UNIV, 76- *Mem:* MLA; Am Asn Teachers Ger. *Res:* Etymology and semasiology of East European languages; bibliography. *Publ:* Auth, Bedeutungsverwandtschaften baltischer Wörter, Z Vergleichende Sprachforsch, 66; Bibliography of Latvian Publications Published Outside Latvia, 1940-1970 (3 vols), Daugava, Stockholm, 68-77; co-transl, J Endzelins' Comparative Phonology and Morphology of the Baltic Languages, Mouton, The Hague, 71; ed, J Reuter, Eine Übersetzungsprobe Riga 1675 (facsimile ed), Daugava, Stockholm, 76. *Mailing Add:* Dept of Foreign Lang & Lit Northern Ill Univ De Kalb IL 60115

JEHENSON, YVONNE MYRIAM, b Belize, Brit Honduras, June 2, 37; nat US; m 68; c 1. COMPARATIVE LITERATURE, HISTORY OF IDEAS. *Educ:* Salve Regina Col, BA, 61; Cath Univ Am, MA, 63; Columbia Univ, PhD(comp lit & English), 74. *Prof Exp:* Asst prof French & Span, Salve Regina Col, 63-67; ASSOC PROF COMP LIT, UNIV ALBUQUERQUE, 73- *Concurrent Pos:* Co-dir Honors prog, Univ Albuquerque, 73-, coordr integrated Sem adult educ, 73-; Danforth fel-assoc prog, 75-81; Nat Endowment for Humanities summer fel bibl studies, Ind Univ, 79, fel, Cornell Univ, 80-81. *Mem:* MLA; Comp Lit Asn; Dante Soc Am; Nat Women's Studies Asn; Rocky Mountain Mod Lang Asn. *Res:* History of pastoral literature from classical antiquity to Renaissance; the inter-relationship of European Renaissance and cultures of Americas, Aztecs, Mayas and Incas; a feminist perspective applied to the history of ideas. *Publ:* Auth, Realism in L'Astree, Papers in French Seventeenth Century Lit, 12/78; Hannah Arendt: On acting and thinking, Folio, 8/78; The Golden World of Pastoral: A Comparative Study, 81; Four Women in Search of Freedom: Alfonsina Storni, Delmira Agustini, Juana de Ibarbourou, Gabriela Mistral, Hisp J, 3/81. *Mailing Add:* 1233 Monroe NE Albuquerque NM 87110

JELINSKI, JACK BERNARD, b Wisconsin Rapids, Wis, Oct 1, 43; m 68; c 2. SPANISH LITERATURE. *Educ:* Univ Wis-Madison, BA, 67, PhD(Span), 74; Ind Univ, Bloomington, MA, 69. *Prof Exp:* Teaching assoc Span, Ind Univ, Bloomington, 68-69; lectr, Univ Wis-Madison, 71-72; asst prof, 73-77, ASSOC PROF SPAN & HEAD DEPT MOD LANG, MONT STATE UNIV, 77- *Concurrent Pos:* Prog consult lang & ethnic studies, Nat Endowment Humanities, 78-79, reviewer/panelist, Div Res Prog. *Mem:* Am Asn Teachers Span & Port; MLA; AAUP. *Res:* Twentieth-century novel; literary criticism. *Publ:* Auth, Unamuno: Descubridor de Don Quijote y Sancho Panza, 4/75 & Unamuno: Su ensayo como poesia, 4/76, Proc Pac Northwest Conf Foreign Lang; La vida de Don Quijote y Sancho: Nueva interpretacion y analisis, Revista Estudios Hispanicos, 1/76; contribr, Ignacio Aldecoa: A Forgotten Master: A Critical Re-examination of Gran Sol, Univ Wyo, 77; auth, A new look at teaching the Spanish subjunctive, Hispania, 5/77; The institutional bias: Where does the buck really stop?, ADFL Bull, 5/80. *Mailing Add:* Dept of Mod Lang Mont State Univ Bozeman MT 59715

JEMBER, GREGORY KIRK, Old & Middle English. See Vol II

JENKINS, FREDERIC MAGILL, b Oakland, Calif, Jan 28, 30; m 56; c 2. CONTEMPORARY FRENCH, LINGUISTICS. *Educ:* Swarthmore Col, BA, 52; Univ Calif, Berkeley, MA, 57, PhD(ling), 63. *Prof Exp:* Asst prof French, San Diego State Col, 61-64; asst prof, 64-67, resident dir, Study Abroad Prog in France, 74-75, ASSOC PROF FRENCH & LING, UNIV ILL, 67- *Concurrent Pos:* Ling bibliogr, Am Coun Teaching Foreign Lang, 71-74. *Mem:* Am Asn Teachers Fr; Am Coun Teaching Foreign Lang; Can Ling Asn. *Res:* Contemporary French linguistics; normative French grammar. *Publ:* Auth, Bally's masterpiece in critical retrospect, Romance Philol, 65; Ambiguity of meaning with post-head modifiers of French nominals, Linguistics, 67; The phonetic value of mute-e, 10/71 & Double-noun compounds in contemporary French, 10/72, Fr Rev; Encore le cas de deux ou plusieurs adjectifs epithetes postposes, Rev Romane, 2/72; Cinema-verite, golf bijou and sandwich beurre in contemporary French, Studies Ling Sci, 76; Allophonic range of French oral vowels, Studies Fr Ling, 78; Government-decreed bionomial compounds in French, Papers in Romance, 80. *Mailing Add:* Dept of French Univ of Ill Urbana IL 61801

JENKINS, MICHAEL FREDERICK OWEN, b London, Eng, Jan 1, 29; US citizen; m 62; c 3. FRENCH LANGUAGE & LITERATURE. *Educ:* Univ London, BA, 54; Laval Univ, MA, 65; Cornell Univ, PhD(French), 71. *Prof Exp:* Lectr English, Fac Lett, Univ Lyons, 54-55; instr French, St Thomas More Col, Univ Sask, 61-67; asst prof, State Univ NY Col Oswego, 67-68; asst prof, 71-75, assoc prof, 75-81, PROF FRENCH, ANGELO STATE UNIV, 81- *Concurrent Pos:* Fac res grants, Angelo State Univ, 75, 76, 78, 81 & 82; Nat Endowment for Humanities summer fel, 79 & 80. *Mem:* Am Asn Teachers Fr; South Central Mod Lang Asn; Col Teachers English. *Res:* Renaissance literature; translation. *Publ:* Translr, Tales of the Early Franks, from Augustin Thierry's Recits des Temps Merovingiens, Univ Ala, 77; Artful eloquence: Jean Lemaire de Belges and the rhetorical tradition, NC Studies in Romance Lang & Lit, 80; translr, Lion of the North: Charles XII of Sweden, 81 & Russia Under Peter the Great (in press), from the French of Voltaire, Assoc Univ Presses, Fairleigh Dickinson UP. *Mailing Add:* 1332 S Madison San Angelo TX 76901

JENKINS-BLANCO, JACINTO, b Dallas, Tex, Nov 23, 26; m 50; c 2. SPANISH. *Educ:* Univ Tex, Austin, BA, 48; Univ Houston, MEd, 53; Stanford Univ, MA, 66, PhD(ling, Span & educ), 69. *Prof Exp:* Elem sch teacher Span & English, Hidalgo Common Sch Dist, Edinburg, Tex, 48-50; teacher, Clearcreek Sch Dist, League City, Tex, 50-52; high sch teacher Span, Dallas Independent Sch Dist, Tex, 52-60; teacher, Pasadena City Schs, Calif, 60-62; dir foreign lang prof Span, Santa Barbara Co Schs, Calif, 63-64; asst prof, Tex Arts & Indust Univ, Kingsville, 64-65; consult English as second lang, Chicago City Schs, Ill, 65-66; biling coordr Span & English, Redwood City Schs, Calif, 69-70; asst prof, 70-73, ASSOC PROF SPAN, CALIF STATE UNIV, SACRAMENTO, 73- *Mem:* Am Asn Teachers Span & Port; Am Coun Teachers Foreign Lang. *Res:* Hispanic & Hispanic American civilization & culture; foreign language methodology; English as a second language for the Spanish speaking. *Publ:* Auth, Utilizing community resources to improve the teaching of modern languages, Calif J Elem Educ, 11/61; Impactual Teaching for Conceptual Learning of a Foreign Language, 63 & Aprendamos la Lengua Linda, 64, Santa Barbara Co Schs; Come wombats and worship, 3/64 & In-service training of Spanish teachers in Santa Barbara, 12/64, Hispania; coauth, El Cancionero Espanol, 73 & Fascinating Facts About the Amazing Americas, Calif State Univ, Sacramento, 77. *Mailing Add:* Dept of Span Calif State Univ 6000 J St Sacramento CA 95819

JENNINGS, L CHANTAL, b Auxerre, France, Nov 21, 39; m 62; c 1. FRENCH LITERATURE & LANGUAGE. *Educ:* Univ Paris, Lic es Lett, 63; Wayne State Univ, PhD(French lit), 69. *Prof Exp:* Instr French, Wayne State Univ, 66-67; lectr, Univ Ottawa, 67-68; asst prof, State Univ NY Buffalo, 69-72; asst prof, 72-73, ASSOC PROF FRENCH, SCARBOROUGH COL, UNIV TORONTO, 73- *Concurrent Pos:* Can Coun of Arts, res fel, 74-75 & leave fel, 77-78. *Mem:* Can Asn Univ Teachers, Soc Etudes Romantiques; Am Asn Teachers Fr; MLA; Soc Lit Amis Emile Zola. *Res:* Nineteenth century French literature; Emile Zola; women studies. *Publ:* Auth, La dualite de Maupassant: son attitude envers la femme, Rev Sci Humaines, 10/70; L'amour-passion de Tristan - Proust: vicissitudes d'un mythe, Symposium, summer 71; Zola feministe?, Les Cahiers Naturalistes, 12/72 & 6/73; La symbolique de l'espace dans Nana, Mod Lang Notes, 5/73; Perspective feministe sur un romancier 'pour dames': Alphonse Daudet, 8/73; Therese Raquin ou le peche originel, Litterature, 10/76; Lecture ideologique de Nana, Mosaic, 7/77; L'Eros et la Femme chez Zola, Klincksieck, 77. *Mailing Add:* Dept of French Scarborough Col Univ of Toronto Toronto ON M5S 1A1 Can

JENNINGS, LEE B, b Willard, Ohio, May 3, 27; m 74. GERMAN. *Educ:* Ohio State Univ, BA, 49; Univ Ill, Urbana, MA, 51, PhD(Ger), 55. *Prof Exp:* Instr Ger, Univ Colo, 56; instr Harvard Univ, 56-57; from instr to asst prof, Univ Calif Los Angeles, 57-62; assoc prof, Univ Tex, 62-68; PROF GER, UNIV ILL, CHICAGO CIRCLE, 68- *Concurrent Pos:* Alexander von Humboldt Found res fel, Munich & Marbach, Ger, 65-67; Ger Acad Exchange Serv res fel, fall 73; Nat Endowment for Humanities grant, 82. *Mem:* MLA Am Asn Teachers Ger. *Res:* German 19th century literature; psychology and literature; the absurd and the grotesque in literature. *Publ:* Auth, Gottfried Keller and the grotesque, Monatshefte, 58; Mörike's grotesquery, J English & Ger Philol, 60; The Ludricrous Demon: Aspects of the Grotesque in German Post-Romantic Prose, Univ Calif, 63; Der aufgespiesste Schmetterling: Justinus Kerner und die Frage der psychischen Entwicklung, Antaois, 68; Justinus Kerners Weg nach Weinsberg, Camden House, 82. *Mailing Add:* Dept of Ger Box 4348 Univ of Ill Chicago Circle Chicago IL 60680

JENSEN, CHRISTIAN ANDREW EDWARD, b Hamburg, Ger, Dec 22, 20; Can citizen; m 47; c 3. ROMANCE LANGUAGE & LITERATURE. *Educ:* Univ Western Ont, BA, 41; Univ Toronto, MA, 46; Univ Chicago, PhD, 57. *Prof Exp:* Lectr French, 46-47, from asst prof to assoc prof, 47-60, acting chmn dept French, 53-54, head dept, 68-70, PROF FRENCH, UNIV MAN, 60-, HEAD DEPT ROMANCE LANG, 70- *Concurrent Pos:* Can Coun fel, 59, 62; vpres, Alliance Francaise, 61-63; chmn ed bd, Mosaic, 72- *Mem:* MLA; Asn Can Univ Teachers Fr; Humanities Asn Can (pres, 75-77). *Res:* Evolution of French Romanticism; evolution of the novel; contemporary literature. *Publ:* Auth, L'Evolution de Romantisme, Droz, Geneva, 59; Stendhal: The Novelist as Critic, L'Esprit Createur, winter 64; The romanticism of Ferdinand d'Eckstein, Rev Lit Comp, 65; coauth, Les Lettres en France, Macmillan, Can, 67. *Mailing Add:* Dept of French & Span Univ of Man Winnipeg MB R3T 2N2 Can

JENSEN, FREDE, b Auning, Denmark, Feb 17, 26. FRENCH & PROVENCAL PHILOLOGY. *Educ:* Univ Copenhagen, MA, 53; Univ Salamanca, dipl, 55; Univ Calif, Los Angeles, PhD, 61. *Prof Exp:* Asst prof French, Univ Alta, Calgary, 61-64, Univ Calif, Los Angeles, 64-67; assoc prof, 67-73, PROF FRENCH, UNIV COLO, BOULDER, 73- *Concurrent Pos:* Mem ed bd, Semasia, 73- *Mem:* MLA; Rocky Mountain Mod Lang Asn; Centre Guillaume IX, Assoc Int d'Etudes Occitanes (pres, 81-). *Res:* Old Provencal morphology, phonology and syntax; troubadour poetry. *Publ:* Auth, The Italian Verb, a Morphological Study, 71 & From Vulgar Latin to Old Provencal, 72, Univ NC; coauth, The Syntax of the Old Spanish Subjunctive, 73 & auth, The Syntax of the Old French Subjunctive, Mouton, The Hague; The old Provencal noun and adjective declension, 76 & The earliest Portuguese lyrics, 78, Odense Univ Press. *Mailing Add:* Dept of French Univ of Colo Boulder CO 80309

JENSEN, HARVEY JAMES, English & Comparative Literature. See Vol II

JENSEN, JOHN BARRY, b Provo, Utah, Dec 30, 43; m 69; c 4. PORTUGUESE, LINGUISTICS. *Educ:* Brigham Young Univ, BA, 65; Harvard Univ, AM, 68, PhD(Port & ling), 71. *Prof Exp:* Vol educr, Peace Corps, Brazil, 65-67; asst prof Port, Univ Va, 70-78; ASSOC PROF MOD LANG, FLA INT UNIV, 78-, CHAIRPERSON, 80- *Concurrent Pos:* Nat Endowment for Humanities younger humanist fel, 74-75; vis lectr Span & Port, State Univ NY Albany, 77-78; Fulbright lectr, Columbia, 81. *Mem:* Am Asn Teachers Span & Port; Ling Soc Am; Am Coun Teaching Foreign Lang; Southeast Coun Ling; Asn Brasileira Ling. *Res:* Portuguese and Brazilian sociolinguistics; Spanish linguistics; applied linguistics. *Publ:* Auth, The Portuguese immigrant community of New England: A current look, Studia, Lisbon, 6/72; The feature human as a constraint on the occurrence of third-person subject pronouns in Spanish, Hispania, 3/73; A linguistica contrastiva: Onde esta hoje?, Littera, Rio de Janeiro, 3/75; A investigacano de formas de tratamento e a telenovela: A Escalada, part I, Revista Brasileira de Linguistica, 9/78; Brazilian Portuguese forms of address: Oriental honorifics or standard European?, In: Studies in Honor of Francis M Rogers, Benjamins, Amsterdam, 12/81; Portuguese, Contrastive Romance Ling Newslett, 4/81 & 4/82; Coming and going in English and Spanish, In: Readings in Spanish-English Contrastive Linguistics, Inter-Am Univ Press, 7/82; Dona Flor and her five forms of address, Luso-Brazilian Rev (in press). *Mailing Add:* Dept of Mod Lang Fla Int Univ Miami FL 33199

JENSEN, JOHN T, b Philadelphia, Pa, June 23, 44; m 72. PHONOLOGY, ENGLISH LINGUISTICS. *Educ:* Univ Pa, BA, 66; McGill Univ, PhD, 72. *Prof Exp:* Mem fac, Univ Colo, Boulder, 73-76; MEM FAC, UNIV OTTAWA, 76- *Concurrent Pos:* NIH fel, Mass Inst Technol, 72-73; ed, Cahiers Linguistiques d'Ottawa, 76-82. *Mem:* Ling Soc Am; Can Ling Asn. *Res:* Syntax; morphology. *Publ:* Auth, A constraint on variables in phonology, Language, 50, 675-686; Stress accent in Swedish, Hamburger Phonetische Beiträge, 17, 9-30; On pruning S-bar, Papers Ling, 9, 187-193; Reply to theoretical implications of Hungarian vowel harmony, Ling Inquiry, 8, 89-97; The relevancy condition and variables in phonology, Ling Anal, 79; X̄ Morphology, Proc NELS, XI, 155-172; Stress and accent in Swedish, Nordic J Ling, 3, 25-58; The metrical structure of Swedish accent, Proc NELS X, Cahiers Ling d'Ottawa 9, 271-282. *Mailing Add:* Dept of Ling Univ of Ottawa Ottawa ON K1N 6N5 Can

JENSEN, RICHARD CARL, b Lone Rock, Iowa, Feb 29, 36; m 58; c 3. CLASSICS. *Educ:* Univ Ariz, BA, 58; Univ NC, PhD(Latin), 61. *Prof Exp:* From instr to asst prof, 61-68, ASSOC PROF CLASSICS, UNIV ARIZ, 68- *Mem:* Am Philol Asn; Class Asn Pac States. *Res:* Latin literature. *Publ:* Auth, Coluccio Salutati's lament of Phyllis, Studies Philol, 4/68; The Latin Poetry of Domenico Silvestri, Wilhelm Fink, Munich, 73; coauth, The fox and the crab: Coluccio Salutati's unpublished fable, 4/76 & Giovanni Moccia on Zanobi da Strada and other Florentine notables, 10/76, Studies Philol. *Mailing Add:* Dept of Classics Univ of Ariz Tucson AZ 85721

JENSEN, THEODORE WAYNE, b Sacramento, Calif, Aug 31, 44. HISPANIC LANGUAGES & LITERATURE. *Educ:* Univ Mont, BA, 66, MA, 70; State Univ NY Buffalo, PhD(Hisp lang & lit), 76. *Prof Exp:* Instr, State Univ NY Buffalo, 70-74; lectr, Canisius Col, 72-73; ASSOC PROF SPAN, EASTERN MONT COL, 74- *Concurrent Pos:* Nat Endowment for Humanities fel, Duke Univ, summer, 76; Am Coun Learned Soc res grant, 78. *Mem:* Inst Int Lit Iberoamericana; Am Asn Teachers Span & Port. *Res:* Spanish American modernismo; contemporary short fiction of Latin America; Spanish Theatre of the Golden Age. *Publ:* El pitagorismo en Las fuerzas extranas de Lugones, In: Fantasia y Realismo Magico en Iberoamerica, Mich State Univ, 75; Modernista Pythagorean literature: The symbolist inspiration, In: Waiting For Pegasus: Studies of the Presence of Symbolism and Decadence in Hispanic Letters, West Ill Univ, 79; The Phoenix and folly in Lope's La noche de San Juan, Forum for Mod Lang Studies, 80; Christian-Pythagorean dualism in Nervo's El donador de almas, Ky Romance Quart, 81; Ruben Dario's final profession of Pythagorean Faith, Latin Am Lit Rev, 82; Contexto Fantastico en el realismo de Omnibus, Revista Iberoamericana, 82. *Mailing Add:* Dept For Lang & Lit Eastern Mont Col Billings MT 59101

JEREMIAH, MILFORD ASTOR, b Antigua, WI, Nov 8, 43. LINGUISTICS, READING INSTRUCTION. *Educ:* Hampton Inst, BA, 69; Brown Univ, MA, 71, PhD(ling), 76. *Prof Exp:* ASST PROF ENGLISH, READING & LANG ART, MORGAN STATE UNIV, 72- *Mem:* Int Reading Asn; Ling Soc Am; Col Reading Asn; Nat Coun Teachers English; Asn Black Anthropologists. *Res:* Linguistic theory and its application to reading and semantics; Creole language studies; language in society. *Publ:* Auth, Another look at Black vernacular English, Spokesman, 4/73; Linguistic and Sociolinguistic Parallels in Antiguan Creole and Black English, Abstracts Am Anthropol Asn, 11/73; On being a competent reader, Morgan Rev, 5/76; A survey of college text books for freshman students' English in Tex, spring 76; Linguistic roots: A study of verbs, Asn Black Anthropologists, 5/77; Aspects of Semantic theory and reading comprehension, Morgan J Educ Res, winter 77; A short note on summarizing, Vol 24, No 1 & Teaching vocabulary in social context, Vol 24, No 2, J Reading. *Mailing Add:* Morgan State Univ Box 353 Coldspring Lane & Hillen Rd Baltimore MD 21239

JERUSALMI, ISAAC, b Istanbul, Turkey, Nov 1, 28; m 62; c 1. BIBLE, SEMITICS. *Educ:* Univ Istanvul, Lic es Let, 51; Hebrew Union Col-Jewish Inst Relig, MHL, 56; Ecole Nat Langues Orient, Paris, France, Dipl, 62; Sorbonne, PhD, 63. *Prof Exp:* Lectr liturgy & Semitics, Inst Int Etudes Hebraïques, Paris, 58-63; from instr to assoc prof, 63-71, PROF BIBLE & SEMITICS, HEBREW UNION COL, OHIO, 71- *Mem:* Cent Conf Am Rabbis. *Res:* Classical Hebrew; Bible; classical Arabic. *Publ:* Auth, Auxiliary Materials for the Study of Semitic Languages, No 1-10, 65-68. *Mailing Add:* Hebrew Union Col-Jewish Inst of Relig Cincinnati OH 45220

JESSUP, FLORENCE L REDDING, b Indianapolis, Ind, Apr 8, 34; m 58; c 3. SPANISH LANGUAGE & LITERATURE. *Educ:* Wellesley Col, BA, 56; Ind Univ, MA, 58, PhD(Span), 75. *Prof Exp:* Teacher Span & English, Howe High Sch, Indianapolis, 59-60; teacher hist & English, Orchard Country Day Sch, Indianapolis, 60-61; instr span, 62-76, asst prof, 76-80, ASSOC PROF SPAN, BUTLER UNIV, 80-, ACTG HEAD DEPT MOD FOR LANG, 82- *Mem:* Am Asn Teachers Span & Port; Mod Foreign Lang Asn; AAUP; Am Coun Teaching For Lang. *Res:* Contemporary Spanish literature; contemporary Latin American literature; generation of 1898. *Mailing Add:* Dept of Span Butler Univ Indianapolis IN 46208

JIMENEZ, FRANCISCO, b Jalisco, Mex, June 29, 43; US citizen; m 68; c 3. LATIN AMERICAN LITERATURE. *Educ:* Univ Santa Clara, BA, 66; Columbia Univ, MA, 69, PhD(Latin Am lit), 72. *Prof Exp:* Precepter Span & Port, Columbia Univ, 69-70, assoc, fall 70, instr 71-72, asst prof, spring 73; asst prof, 73-77, assoc prof, 77-80, PROF MOD LANG & LIT, UNIV SANTA CLARA, 77-, DIR ARTS & HUMANITIES, 81- *Concurrent Pos:* Mem, Western Asn Schs & Cols Accrediting Comn, 74-; consult & mem, WNET-TV Nat Adv Comt proj, 75-77; vchmn, Calif State Comn Teacher Prep & Lic, 76-77, chmn, 77-79; West Coast ed, Bilingual Rev. *Honors & Awards:* Ariz Quart Ann Award, Univ Ariz, 73; Pres Special Recognition Award for Fac, 78. *Mem:* MLA; Am Asn Teachers Span & Port; Hispanic Inst US; Pac Coast Coun Latin Am Studies; Nat Chicano Counc Higher Educ. *Res:* Mexican literature; Chicano literature; Latin American literature. *Publ:* Contribr, Encycl of World Literature in the 20th Century, Vol IV, Ungar, 75; coauth, Viva la Lengua?, 75 & Spanish Here and Now, 78, Harcourt; ed, Identification and Analysis of Chicano Literature, 78 & co-ed, Hispanics in the United States: An Anthology of Creative Literature, 80, Bilingual Press; Mosaico de la vida: Prosa chicana, cubana y puertorriquena, Harcourt, 81; co-ed, Hispanics in the United States: An Anthology of Creative Literature, Vol II, Bilingual Press, 82; contribr, Dict of Mexican American History, Greenwood Press, 82. *Mailing Add:* Dept of Mod Lang Univ Santa Clara Santa Clara CA 95053

JIMENEZ, JOSE, b Santa Clara, Cuba, July 19, 26; US citizen. SPANISH & SPANISH AMERICAN POETRY. *Educ:* Univ Havana, DFilos y Let, 53; Univ Madrid, DFilos y Let, 55; Univ Salamanca, Dipl Hisp filol, 55. *Prof Exp:* Prof Span lit, Villanueva Univ, 56-60; asst prof Span, Merrimack Col, 60-62; from asst prof to assoc prof, 62-67, PROF SPAN, HUNTER COL, 67- *Concurrent Pos:* Vis Prof, NY Univ, 64-65. *Mem:* MLA; Am Asn Teachers Span & Port; Hisp Inst US. *Res:* Spanish contemporary and Spanish-American poetry. *Publ:* Auth, Estudios Sobre Poesia Cubana Contemporanea, Las Americas, 67; coauth, La Poesia Hispanoamericana Desde el Modernismo, Appleton, 68; ed, Antologia de la Poesia Hispanoamericana Contemporanea, 1914-1970, Alianza Ed, Madrid, 71 & Grandes Poetas de Hispanoamerica, Salvat, Barcelona, 72; auth, Diez Anos de Poesia espanola, 1960-1970, Insula, Madrid, 72; Realidad y misterio en la poesia de Francisco Brines, Cuadernos Hispanoam, Madrid, 3/72; Una version realista de la irrealidad: la posia de Jaime Gil de Biedma, Insula, Madrid, 3/72; Poesia de hoy: Espana, hispanoamerica, modernidad, Rev de Occidente, Madrid, 6/73. *Mailing Add:* Dept of Romance Lang Hunter Col 695 Park Ave New York NY 10021

JIMENEZ, ONILDA ANGELICA, b Cuba; US citizen. SPANISH AMERICAN LITERATURE. *Educ:* Inst Vedado, Havana, BA, 48; Univ La Habana, Lic Derecho, 54, PhD(humanities), 55; Columbia Univ, MA, 68; NY Univ, PhD(Spanish), 79. *Prof Exp:* ASST PROF SPAN, JERSEY CITY STATE COL, 68- *Concurrent Pos:* Consult, Ministry Foreign Rel Cuba, 60-61. *Mem:* MLA; Inst Int Lit Iberoamericana; Am Asn Teachers Span & Port; Circulo Cult Panamericano. *Res:* Spanish American novel; contemporary Cuban poetry; Cuban novelists. *Publ:* Auth, La critica literaria en la obra de Gabriela Mistral, DAI, 80 & Ediciones Universl, 82; Un nuevo fenomeno de la literatura cubana: la novela policial, Circulo, Revista Cult, 80; Los perros jibaros, 7-8/81 & Symposium sobre teatro, 6/82, Noticias de Arts. *Mailing Add:* Dept Mod Lang Jersey City State Col Jersey City NJ 07305

JIMENEZ, REYNALDO LUIS, b La Habana, Cuba, July 13, 46; US citizen; m 68; c 1. SPANISH AMERICAN LITERATURE. *Educ:* Univ Ill, BA, 69, MA, 70, PhD(Span Am lit), 74. *Prof Exp:* Instr Span, Dept Foreign Lang, Univ Ill, 72-74; asst prof & MA adv, Dept Romance Lang, Ohio State Univ, 74-81; ASST PROF & SUPVR SPAN, DEPT ROMANCE LANG, UNIV FLA, 81- *Mem:* Latin Am Studies Asn; MLA; Am Asn Teacher Span & Port; Am Coun Teachers Foreign Lang. *Res:* Latin American literature; Spanish linguistic and pedagogy. *Publ:* Auth, Marcha Triunfal, In: Antologia Comentada del Modernismo, Calif State Univ Press, 74; Literatura mejicana, In: Diccionario Enciclopedico Universal, 77; Guillermo Cabrera Infante y Tres Tristes Tigres, Ediciones Universal, 77; Cuban women writers and the revolution, In: Folio, State Univ NY, 78. *Mailing Add:* Dept of Romance Lang Univ of Fla Gainesville FL 32605

JIRGENSONS, LEONID AURELIJS, b Riga, Latvia, Aug 1, 22; m 46; c 3. CLASSICAL LANGUAGES. *Educ:* Univ Hamburg, dipl, 48; Univ Minn, MA, 61, PhD, 81. *Prof Exp:* Instr Latin, Baltic High Sch, Itzehoe, Ger, 45-47, Latin & Ger,Portland Jr High Sch, Bloomington, Minn, 59-60; asst prof, 61-74, ASSOC PROF CLASSICS, TEX TECH UNIV, 74- *Concurrent Pos:* Univ Minn grad sch fel, 67-68. *Honors & Awards:* Distinguished Teaching Award, Standard Oil, Ind Found, 72. *Mem:* Am Philol Asn; Class Asn MidW & S; Am Class League. *Res:* Indo-European philology; Augustan poets. *Mailing Add:* Dept of Class & Romance Lang Tex Tech Univ Lubbock TX 79409

JOCHNOWITZ, GEORGE, b Brooklyn, NY, Aug 1, 37; m 62; c 2. LINGUISTICS, ROMANCE LANGUAGES. *Educ:* Columbia Univ, AB, 58, MA, 60, PhD(ling), 67. *Prof Exp:* Instr French & Ital, Temple Univ, 61-63; instr French, NY Univ, 63-65; lectr Romance lang, Queens Col, NY, 65-68; asst prof ling, 68-72, ASSOC PROF LING, COL STATEN ISLAND, CITY UNIV NEW YORK, 72- *Concurrent Pos:* Nat Sci Found grant, 68-69; vis lectr Yiddish, Yale Univ, 72-73. *Mem:* Ling Soc Am; MLA; Soc Ling Romane; Am Dialect Soc. *Res:* French dialects; Judeo-Italian dialects. *Publ:* Auth, Bilingualism and dialect mixture among Lubavitcher Hasidic children, Am Speech, 10/68; Forme meridionali nei dialetti degli ebrei dell'Italia centrale, Rassegna Mensile di Israel, 9/72; Dialect Boundaries and the Question of Franco-Provencal, Mouton, The Hague, 73; Parole di origine romanza ed ebraica in giudeo-italiano, XIV Cong Int Ling & Filologia Romanza, 77. *Mailing Add:* 54 E Eighth St New York NY 10003

JOERES, RUTH-ELLEN BOETCHER, b Baltimore, Md, May 20, 39; m 62; c 2. GERMAN LITERATURE, WOMEN'S HISTORY. *Educ:* Goucher Col, BA, 61; George Washington Univ, MA, 66; Johns Hopkins Univ, PhD(Ger), 71. *Prof Exp:* Fel, Inst Res Humanities, Univ Wis, 73-74; asst prof, Univ Mo, 74-76; asst prof, 76-79, ASSOC PROF GER, UNIV MINN, 79- *Concurrent Pos:* Humboldt fel, Univ Munich, 75-76 & 79. *Mem:* MLA; Am Asn Teachers Ger; Am Asn Lit Transl; Midwest Mod Lang Asn. *Res:* Women's history and literature, expecially in 19th century Germany; the novel in 19th century German; 20th century German literature. *Publ:* Auth, Karl Gutzkow's Wally the Skeptic, Lang Verlag, 74; The triumph of the woman: Johanna Kinkel's Hans Ibeles in London, Euphorion, 76; Ein Dichter: An introduction to the world of Luise Büchner, Ger Quart, 79; Louise Otto and her journals: A chapter in Nineteenth century German feminism, Internationales Arch Sozialgeschichte dt Lit, 79; coauth, Three unpublished letters from Robert Schweichel to Louise Otto, Monatsh, 80; The ambiguous world of Hedwig Dohm, Amsterdamer Beiträge zur neueren Germanistik, 80; 1848 from a distance: German women writers on the Revolution, Mod Lang Notes, 82; Die Anfänge der deutschen Frauenbewegung: Louise Otto-Peters, Fischer, 82. *Mailing Add:* Dept of German Univ of Minn Minneapolis MN 55455

JOFEN, JEAN, b Vienna, Austria, Nov 13, 22; US citizen; m 44; c 4. GERMAN LITERATURE. *Educ:* Brooklyn Col, BA, 43; Brown Univ, Ma, 45; Columbia Univ, PhD, 53; Yeshiva Univ, MS, 60, cert psychol, 62. *Prof Exp:* Assoc prof Ger, Stern Col for Women, Yeshiva Univ, 53-60; chmn dept, 60-78, PROF GER & SLAVIC LANG, BARUCH COL, 60-, CHMN DEPT MOD LANG, 77- *Concurrent Pos:* Littaure res fel, 63-64; univ scholar spec fund, 65-66; univ res fel, 68; Am Asn Univ Women fel, 68-69; Ford Found grant, 70; Population Coun grant, 71-72; Nat Endowment for Humanities fel, 74. *Mem:* MLA; Am Psychol Asn; Col Yiddish Asn; Marlowe Soc Am (pres, 75-); Am Asn Yiddish Prof (vpres). *Res:* Yiddish linguistics and general philology; literature and psychology. *Publ:* Auth, Yiddish for Beginners, 55 & A Linguistics Atlas of Eastern European Yiddish, 60, Edwards Bros; A Freudian interpretation of Freud's Moses, Brit Ivrit Olamit, 74; The Yiddish idiom and proverb as mirror of Jewish cultural values, Mosaic; Traces of the book of Esther in the works of Shakespeare, Studies Cult Life of Jews in England, Vol V, 75; Yiddish Literature for Beginners, 75, coauth, Hebrew for Beginners, 76 & Chinese for Beginners, 77, Edwards Bros; Das letzte Geheimnis, Francke Verlag, Bern, 72. *Mailing Add:* 1684 52nd St Brooklyn NY 11204

JOHANNES, WILFRED CLEMENS, b Dyersville, Iowa, Jan 19, 24. PHILOLOGY. *Educ:* Loras Col, BA, 45; Cath Univ, Am, MA, 51; Univ Mich, PhD, 63. *Prof Exp:* Instr Latin, 48-59, assoc prof, 63-70, CHMN DEPT CLASS STUDIES, LORAS COL, 68-, PROF, 70- *Concurrent Pos:* Nat Endowment for Humanities fel in residence, Univ Pa, 76-77. *Mem:* Am Philol

Asn; Class Asn Mid W & S; Vergilian Soc; Asn Int Papyrologues; Asn Ancient Historians. *Res:* Menander and new comedy; Greek and Roman historians; Koine language and literature. *Mailing Add:* Dept of Class Studies Loras Col Dubuque IA 52001

JOHN, DAVID GETHIN, b Wales, Mar 24, 47; Can citizen; m 72; c 3. GERMAN LITERATURE & LANGUAGE. *Educ:* Univ Toronto, BA, 67, MA, 70, PhD(Ger), 75. *Prof Exp:* ASST PROF GER, UNIV WATERLOO, 74- *Mem:* Can Asn Univ Teachers Ger; Can Soc 18th Century Studies; Am Soc 18th Century Studies; Lessing Soc; Deutsche Ges für die Erforschung des 18 Jahreshundert. *Res:* German theatre, especially 18th century; German language pedagogy. *Publ:* Auth, Johna Elias Schlegel's ally: Johann Christian Krüger, Ger Rev, 77; Marivaux's Harlequin: His influence of Johann Christian Krüger and German comedy, Seminar, 78; Johann Christian Krüger and the development of German Comedy, Neophilologus, 79; Johann Michael von Loen's Ideal City: A reflection of eilghteenth century currents in Germany, J Urban Hist, 79; Ulrich Plenzdorf's Die neuen Leiden de jungen W: The death of a fool, Mod Drama, 80; The Sperber in Hesse's Demian, In: The First World War in German Narrative Prose, Univ Toronto Press, 80. *Mailing Add:* Dept of Ger Univ of Waterloo Waterloo ON N2L 3G1 Can

JOHNSON, ALFRED MARION, JR, Religion, Social Anthropology. See Vol IV

JOHNSON, BARBARA ELLEN, b Boston, Mass, Oct 4, 47. FRENCH & COMPARATIVE LITERATURE. *Educ:* Oberlin Col, BA, 69; Yale Univ, MPhil, 73, PhD(French), 77. *Prof Exp:* Asst prof, 77-80, ASSOC PROF FRENCH & COMP LIT, YALE UNIV, 80- *Mem:* MLA. *Res:* Nineteenth and 20th century French, American and English literature; critical theory. *Publ:* Auth, La Verite tue, 10/73 & Defigurations, 5/75, Litterature; Quelques consequences de la difference anatomique des textes, Poetique, 12/76; Poetry and performative language, 77 & The frame of reference: Poe, Lacan, Derrida, 78, Yale Fr Studies; Crise de prose, Po & sie, spring 78; The critical difference, Diacritics, summer 78; Defigurations: du Langage Poetique, Flammarion, 79. *Mailing Add:* Dept of French Yale Univ W L Harkness Hall New Haven CT 06520

JOHNSON, CARL LEONARD, b Iowa, June 3, 02. ROMANCE PHILOLOGY. *Educ:* State Univ Iowa, AB, 24, AM, 25; Harvard Univ, AM, 28, PhD, 33. *Prof Exp:* Asst, State Univ Iowa, 24-25, res assoc, 34-35; instr, WVa Univ, 25-27, 28-30; asst, Harvard Univ, 30-32; from asst prof to prof, 35-72, EMER PROF ROMANCE LANG, UNIV ORE, 72- *Honors & Awards:* Mem de l'Ordre des Palmes Academiques, 62. *Mem:* MLA; Philol Asn Pac Coast; Am Asn Teachers Fr. *Res:* Longfellow and France; Baudelaire; Mallarme. *Publ:* Auth, French Pronunciation, Edwards Bros, 36; Professor Longfellow of Harvard, Univ Ore, 44; First Year French, Heath, 55; Longfellow's studies in France, J Am Renaissance, 70. *Mailing Add:* 1080 Patterson Apt 1104 Eugene OR 97401

JOHNSON, CARROLL B, b Los Angeles, Calif, Jan 9, 38. SPANISH LITERATURE. *Educ:* Univ Calif, Los Angeles, BA, 60, MA, 61; Harvard Univ, PhD(Romance lang), 66. *Prof Exp:* Acting asst prof, 64-66, from asst prof to assoc prof, 66-75, vchmn dept, 72-75, chmn dept Span & Port, 75-81, PROF SPAN, UNIV CALIF, LOS ANGELES, 75- *Mem:* MLA; Renaissance Soc Am; Cervantes Soc Am; Asn Int Hisp. *Res:* Seventeenth century Spanish prose fiction; 16th century Spanish drama; literature and psychoanalysis. *Publ:* Auth, A propos of Lope de Rueda's Las Aceitunas, 67 & Lope de Rueda's Comedia Eufemia, 68, Bull Comediantes; Montemayor's Diana: A novel pastoral, Bull Hisp Studies, 71; Matias de los Reyes and the Craft of Fiction, Univ Calif, 73; El Buscin: D Pablos, D Diego y D Francisco, Hispanofila, 74; A second look at Dulcinea's ass, Hisp Rev, 75; Inside Guzman de Alfarache, Univ Calif, 78; Madness and Lust: Don Quixote the Man, Univ Calif (in press). *Mailing Add:* Dept of Span & Port Univ of Calif Los Angeles CA 90024

JOHNSON, DALE RALPH, b Heber City, Utah, Dec 24, 33; m 69; c 2. CHINESE POETRY & DRAMA. *Educ:* Univ Utah, BM, 59; Univ Mich, MA, 62, PhD(Chinese lang & lit), 68. *Prof Exp:* ASST PROF CHINESE LANG & LIT, OBERLIN COL, 68-, DIR E ASIAN STUDIES PROG, 70- *Concurrent Pos:* Trustee, Shansi Mem Asn, 73-; Am Coun Learned Socs Chinese Civilization fel, 74-75. *Mem:* Asn Asian Studies; Am Orient Soc; Chinese Lang Teachers Asn. *Res:* Chinese poetry, drama & music. *Publ:* Auth, One Aspect of form in the arias of Yuan opera, Mich Papers Chinese Studies, 68; The prosody of Yuan drama, T'oung-Pao, 70; contribr, Dictionary of Oriental Literatures, Vol 1, Basic Bks, 74; Traditional Chinese Stories, Columbia Univ, 78; Yuarn Music Dramas: Studies in Prosody and Structure and a Complete Catalogue of Northern Arias in the Dramatic Style, Michigan Papers in Chinese Studies, No 40, Univ Mich, 80; Born of the Same Roots, Ind Univ Press, 81. *Mailing Add:* E Asian Studies Prog Oberlin Col Oberlin OH 44074

JOHNSON, DAVID DONOVAN, b Horton, Kans, Nov 13, 29; m 55; c 5. ROMANCE LANGUAGES. *Educ:* Univ Kans, BS, 54, MA, 58; Univ NC, PhD(Romance lang), 64. *Prof Exp:* Asst prof Span, Presby Jr Col, 57-58; instr Univ NC, 64; asst prof Span, Presby Jr Col, 57-58; instr Univ NC, 61-63; asst prof, Univ SC, 63-67; assoc prof, 67-72, PROF SPAN, THE CITADEL, 72- *Mem:* MLA; Am Asn Teachers Span & Port. *Res:* Medieval Spanish literature; Spanish-American novel. *Mailing Add:* Dept of Foreign Lang The Citadel Charleston SC 29409

JOHNSON, DONALD BARTON, b Indianapolis, Ind, June 15, 33; m 75. RUSSIAN LITERATURE. *Educ:* Ind Univ, BA, 54; Univ Calif, Berkeley, MA, 58; Univ Calif, Los Angeles, PhD(Slavic ling), 66. *Prof Exp:* Asst prof Russ & Slavic ling, Ohio State Univ, 65-66; asst prof, 66-72, assoc prof, 72-80, PROF RUSS & SLAVIC LING, UNIV CALIF, SANTA BARBARA, 80- *Concurrent Pos:* Consult, Rand Corp, 67-69; Inter-Univ Comt Travel Grants grant, Bulgaria & Russia, 68-69; prof & actg chmn dept Russ, Monash Univ, Australia, 75-76. *Mem:* Am Asn Teachers Slavic & E Europ Lang; Am Asn Advan Slavic Studies; Philol Asn Pac Coast; MLA. *Res:* Literary structuralism; Nabokov; Russian modernism. *Publ:* Auth, Toward a typology of the Slavic verb: The verbs of body position, In: American Contributions to the Sixth International Congress of Slavists, Mouton, 68; Transformations and Their Use in the Resolution of Syntactic Homomorphy, Mouton, 69; coauth, Russian Derivational Dictionary, Elsevier, 70; Synesthesia, polychromatism and Nabokov, Russ Lit Triquart, 72; translr & ed, Analysis of the Poetic Text, Ardis, 76; A Structural Analysis of Sasha Sokolou's School for Fools: A Paradigmatic Novel, In: Fiction and Drama in Eastern and Southeastern Europe, Columbus, 80; The Scrabble Game in Ada or Taking Nabakov Clitorally, J Mod Lit, 4/82. *Mailing Add:* Dept of Ger & Russ Univ of Calif Santa Barbara CA 93106

JOHNSON, ERNEST ALFRED, b Methuen, Mass, Sept 3, 17; m 40; c 4. ROMANCE LANGUAGES. *Educ:* Amherst Col, BA, 39; Univ Chicago, MA, 40; Harvard Univ, PhD, 50. *Prof Exp:* PROF ROMANCE LANG, AMHERST COL, 48- *Mem:* Am Asn Teachers Span & Port; MLA. *Res:* Spanish American literature; modern Spanish; Cervantes. *Publ:* auth, Juan Antonio Perez Bonalde: Los anos de formacion-documentos, 1846-1870, Univ de los Andes, Venezuela, 71; transl, Smoke on the Ground, Doubleday, 72; auth, Perez Bonalde, Romulo Gallegos, Manuel Carreno y la Urbanidad, Relectura de Romulo Gallegos, Caracas, 80. *Mailing Add:* Dept of Romance Lang Amherst Col Amherst MA 01002

JOHNSON, FALK SIMMONS, b Wake Forest, NC, Oct 17, 13; m 40; c 3. ENGLISH LINGUISTICS. *Educ:* Wake Forest Col, BA, 35, MA, 36; Univ Chicago, PhD(ling), 56. *Prof Exp:* Instr English, Campbell Col, 36-37; asst dir pub rels, Northwestern Univ, 37-38; instr English, Mars Hill Col, 38-40 & Northwestern Univ, 45-49; from instr to assoc prof, 49-66, PROF ENGLISH, UNIV ILL, CHICAGO, 66- *Mem:* Ling Soc Am; Am Dialect Soc. *Res:* Modern American English; transformational grammar; linguistics and literature. *Publ:* Auth, A Spelling Guide and Workbook, Rinehart, 59; How to Organize What You Write, 64 & Improving What You Write, 65, Houghton; A Self-Improvement Guide to Spelling, Holt, 65; Improving Your Spelling, 3rd ed, Holt, 79. *Mailing Add:* 7624 Maple St Morton Grove IL 60053

JOHNSON, HARVEY LEROY, b Cleburne, Tex, Sept 12, 04; m 50; c 2. SPANISH. *Educ:* Howard Payne Col, BA, 25; Univ Tex, Am, 28; Univ Pa, PhD, 40; Univ San Andres, Bolivia, DLit, 48. *Prof Exp:* Instr high sch, N Mex, 25-26; instr, Victoria Jr Col, Tex, 29-30; instr, Rice Inst, 30-36; prof, Cedar Crest Col, 37-40; prof Romance lang, Northwestern Univ, 40-51; prof Span & Port, Ind Univ, Bloomington, 51-65; prof, 65-75, EMER PROF SPAN & PORT, UNIV HOUSTON, 75- *Concurrent Pos:* US Dept State vis lectr, cols & prof groups, Uruguay, Arg, Paraguay, Bolivia & Peru, 48; consult, US Dept Health, Educ & Welfare, 61-; Hispanic Found, Libr Congr, 62-; contribr ed, Handbook of Latin Am Studies, 62-78; Newberry Libr sr res fel, 73; Am Philos Soc grant, 73. *Mem:* Life fel Int Inst Arts & Lett; Am Asn Teachers Span & Port; MLA; Inst Int Lit Iberoam; Southwestern Coun Latin Am Studies (pres, 69). *Res:* Spanish American and Spanish literature; Portuguese and Brazilian literatures; colonial Mexican theatre. *Publ:* Ed, Triunfo de los Santos, Univ Pa, 41; El Diablo Nocturno, Andrea, 56; auth, Aprende a Hablar Espanol, Ginn, 63; Longfellow and the Portuguese language and literature, Comp Lit, 65; Longfellow translates some verses at Sarmiento's request, Symposium, 66; Latin American literature, 19th and 20th centuries, In: Handbook of Latin American Studies, Univ Fla, 70; auth introd & notes & ed, La Navidad en las Montanas, Libr de Manuel Porrua, Mex, 72; auth introd & co-ed, Contemporary Latin American Literature, Univ Houston, 73. *Mailing Add:* 5307 Dumfries Houston TX 77096

JOHNSON, JANET HELEN, b Everett, Wash, Dec 24, 44. EGYPTOLOGY. *Educ:* Univ Chicago, BA, 67, PhD(Egyptol), 72. *Prof Exp:* Instr, 71-72, asst prof, 72-79, assoc prof, 79-81, PROF EGYPTOL, UNIV CHICAGO, 81- *Concurrent Pos:* Res assoc dept anthrop, Field Mus, Chicago, 80- *Res:* Demotic; history of Egyptian language; dynasties 28-30. *Publ:* Auth, The demotic chronicle as an historical source, Enchoria, 74; The demotic magical spells of Leiden 1384, OMRO, 75; Louvre E3229 a demotic magical text, Enchoria, 77; Remarks on Egyptian verbal sentences, AAL, 77; Private name seals of the Middle Kingdom, Seals & Sealing Ancient Near E, 77; The demotic verbal system, Univ Chicago, 77; co-ed & contribr, Studies in Honor of George R Hughes, Univ Chicago, 77; coauth (with Donald Whitcomb), Quseir al-Qadim, 78 & 80, Preliminary Report, 79 & 80. *Mailing Add:* Orient Inst Univ Chicago Chicago IL 60637

JOHNSON, JEAN (LEE), b St Thomas, Ont, Oct 30, 17; m 54; c 1. COMPARATIVE INDO-EUROPEAN LINGUISTICS. *Educ:* Univ Western Ont, BA, 39; Univ NC, MA, 47, PhD, 50. *Prof Exp:* From assoc prof to prof, 50-76, EMER PROF MOD FOREIGN LANG, NMEX HIGHLANDS UNIV, 76- *Concurrent Pos:* Fund Advan Educ fel, Spain, 54-55. *Mem:* MLA; Rocky Mountain MLA; AAUP; Am Asn Univ Women; Alliance Francaise. *Res:* Romance and Germanic linguistics; French literature; bilingual education. *Mailing Add:* Dept of Mod Foreign Lang NMex Highlands Univ Las Vegas NM 87701

JOHNSON, JOHN THEODORE, JR, b New York, NY, June 8, 36; m 62; c 2. ROMANCE LANGUAGES. *Educ:* San Jose State Col, AB, 58; Univ Wis, MA, 61, PhD(French & art hist), 64. *Prof Exp:* From inst to asst prof French, Princeton Univ, 64-68; assoc prof, 68-75, chmn dept French & Ital, 69-71, dir jr year abroad prog, Centre Colo, Univ Bordeaux, 72-74, PROF FRENCH, UNIV KANS, 75- *Concurrent Pos:* Asst ed, Fr Rev, 68-; ed, Proust Res Asn Newslett, 69; contrib, Critical Bibliog Fr Lit, 20th Century, 72-; Nat Endowment for Humanities sr fel, 76-77. *Mem:* MLA; Am Asn Teachers Fr; Midwest Mod Lang Asn; Int des Etudes Francaises. *Res:* Marcel Proust; interrelations of literature and other arts, especially painting in France; French poetry and artistic prose since 1850. *Publ:* Auth, The Painter and His Art in the Works of Marcel Proust, Univ Wis, 64; Proust and Giotto: Foundations for an Allegorical Interpretation of A la recherche du temps perdu, In: Marcel Proust: A Critical Panorama, Univ Ill, 73; Debacle sur la

Seine de Claude Monet: Source du Degel a Briseville d'Elstir, Etudes Proustiennes, Gallimard, Paris, 73; Literary Impressionism in France: A Survey of Criticism, L'Esprit Createur, winter 73; Proust's Impressionism Reconsidered in the Light of the Visual Arts of the Twentieth Century, In: Twentieth Century French Fiction, Essays for Germaine Bree, Rutgers Univ, 75; Marcel Proust et l'architecture: Considerations sur le probleme du roman-cathedrale, Bull Amis de Marcel Proust et Amis de Combray, 75 & 76; Against Saint Proust, In: The Art of the Proustian Novel Reconsidered, Winthrop Col, 79; Orpheus and the orphic mode in literture and the arts, In: The Register of the Spencer Museum of Arts, fall 81. *Mailing Add:* Dept of French & Ital Univ of Kans Lawrence KS 66045

JOHNSON, JOHN WILLIAM, b Abilene, Tex, Mar 14, 42; m 69; c 2. FOLKLORE, AFRICAN FOLKLORE. *Educ:* Univ Tex, Austin, BA, 65; Univ London, MPh, 71; Ind Univ, PhD(folklore), 78. *Prof Exp:* Assoc instr Bamana lang, Ind Univ, 76-77; instr African Lit & Folklore, Mich State Univ, 77-79; ASST PROF FOLKLORE, IND UNIV, 79- *Concurrent Pos:* Assoc ed, Northeast African Studies, Mich State Univ, 79- *Mem:* Am Folklore Soc; African Studies Asn; Somali Studies Int Asn; African Lit Asn; MLA. *Res:* Mandekan epic poetry; Somali oral poetry. *Publ:* Contribr, Research in Somali folklore, Res in African Lit, 4: 1; Folklore in Achebe's novels, Newlet, 40: 3; auth, Heellooy Heelleellooy: The Development of the Genre Heello in Modern Somali Poetry, Ind Univ, 74; contribr, Etiological legends based on folk etymologies of Manding surnames, Folklore Forum, 9: 3-4; Somali prosodic systems, Horn of Africa, 2: 3; ed & transl, The Epic of Sun-Jata According to Magan Sisoko, Folklore Publ Group, 79; contribr, Yes Virgina, there is an epic in Africa, Res in African Lit, 11: 3; Somalia, In: The New Grove Dict of Music and Musicians, Macmillan, 80. *Mailing Add:* Folklore Dept Ind Univ Bloomington IN 47405

JOHNSON, JULIE GREER, b Hartford, Conn, Sept 6, 45. SPANISH AMERICAN LITERATURE. *Educ:* Memphis State Univ, BA, 67; Ind Univ, MA, 70, PhD(Span lit), 75. *Prof Exp:* From instr to asst prof Span, Univ NC, Asheville, 74-77; ASST PROF SPAN, UNIV GA, 77- *Mem:* MLA; Am Asn Teachers Span & Port; Latin Am Studies Asn; SAtlantic Mod Lang Asn; Am Soc 18th Century Studies. *Res:* Colonial Spanish American literature. *Publ:* Auth, Feminine satire, In: Concolorcorvo's El Lazarillo de Ciegos Caminantes, SAtlantic Bull, 80; The art of characterization, Quinquenarios Ky Romance Quart, 80; Picaresque elements, In: Los infortunios de Alonso Ramirez, Hispania, 81; Three Celestinesque figures of Colonial Spanish American literature, Celestinesca, 81; A caricature of Spanish women in the New World, Latin Am Lit Rev, 81; Three dramatic works, Hispania J, 82. *Mailing Add:* Dept Romance Lang Univ of Ga Athens GA 30602

JOHNSON, LEONARD WILKIE, b Oakland, Calif, Sept 1, 31. FOREIGN LANGUAGES. *Educ:* Dartmouth Col, AB, 53; Harvard Univ, AM, 55, PhD(Romance lang & lit), 62. *Prof Exp:* Acting instr French, 61-62, from instr to asst prof, 62-71, ASSOC PROF FRENCH, UNIV CALIF, BERKELEY, 71- *Concurrent Pos:* Asst dir, studies ctr, Univ Calif in Bordeaux, France, 63-65. *Mem:* MLA; Am Asn Teachers Fr; Renaissance Soc Am. *Res:* Neo-Platonism in French literature, especially 16th and 17th centuries; emblem literature. *Publ:* Auth, Tristan l'Heromite and emblem literature, Renaissance Quart, winter 69; Literary Neo-Platonism in five French treatises of early 17th century, Romantic Rev, 12/69. *Mailing Add:* Dept of French Univ of Calif Berkeley CA 94720

JOHNSON, MARK LEONARD, Philosophy of Language, Aesthetics. See Vol IV

JOHNSON, PHILLIP, b Kemmerer, Wyo, Mar 25, 47; m 68; c 3. SPANISH AMERICAN FICTION. *Educ:* Univ Utah, BA, 71, PhD(Span), 76. *Prof Exp:* Instr Span, Dept Lang, Univ Utah, 76-77; ASST PROF SPAN, BAYLOR UNIV, 77- *Mem:* Am Asn Teachers Span & Port; SCent Mod Lang Asn; Rocky Mountain Mod Lang Asn. *Res:* Contemporary urban novel in Spanish America; novels of the Cuban Revolution; cultural history of the early civilization of Spanish America. *Publ:* Auth, Conversacion en la Catedral: A study of frustration and failure in Peru, Symposium, fall 76; The shadow of the city: Society and disorder in La ciudad y los perros, Am Hispanist, 76. *Mailing Add:* Dept of Mod Foreign Lang Baylor Univ Waco TX 76703

JOHNSON, PHYLLIS ANNE, b Grantsburg, Wis, May 7, 37. MEDIEVAL & MODERN FRENCH LITERATURE. *Educ:* Pomona Col, BA, 59; Univ Calif, Los Angeles, MA, 63, PhD(French), 67. *Prof Exp:* From instr to asst prof, 63-74, assoc prof, 74-81, PROF FRENCH, POMONA COL, 81- *Mem:* MLA; Philol Asn Pac Coast; Mediaeval Acad Am; Medieval Asn Pac. *Res:* Twelfth century Old French hagiography; medieval French narrative poetry; medieval epic poetry. *Publ:* Auth, Dolor, Dolent, sor doloir: le Vocabulaire de la Douleur et la Conception de l'Amour Chez Beronl et Thomas, Romance philol, 72; Huon de Bordeaux et la Semantique de l'Enfes, Z Romanische Philol, 74; coauth (with B Cazelles), Le vain siecle guerpir: A Literary Approach to Sainthood Through Old French Vernacular Saint's Lives of the Twelfth Century, Univ NC Press, 80. *Mailing Add:* Dept of Mod European Lang Pomona Col Claremont CA 91711

JOHNSON, ROBERTA LEE, b Reno, Nevada, Feb 15, 42; m 81. PENINSULAR SPANISH & COMPARATIVE LITERATURE. *Educ:* Univ Calif, Davis, AB, 63, MA, 65; Univ Calif, Los Angeles, PhD(Span lang & lit), 71. *Prof Exp:* Teaching asst Span, Univ Calif, Davis, 63-65, assoc, 65-66; teaching asst, Univ, Calif, Los Angeles, 66-68; instr Span lang & Golden Age lit, Pomona Col, 68-69; lectr Span & comp lit & dir lang lab, Claremont Men's Col, 69-71; Fulbright lectr hist English lang, Univ Valladolid, 71-72; asst prof Span & comp lit, Claremont Men's Col, 72-74; asst prof Span & comp lit, Wartburg Col, 74-77; asst prof, Duke Univ, 77-78; Nat Endowment for Humanities fel, Kans State Univ, 78-80; ASST PROF SPAN, SCRIPPS COL, 80-, ASSOC PROF HISP STUDIES, 80- *Mem:* Am Asn Teachers Span & Port; MLA; Assoc De Pensim Femininas. *Res:* Twentieth century Spanish novel; Ortega y Gasset; Spanish women writers. *Publ:* Auth, William Faulkner and Miguel Delibes: the art of the story teller, English Studies, 9/72; El obispo leproso: echoes of Pauline theology in Alicante, Hispania, 76; Carmen Lafuret, Twayne, 81. *Mailing Add:* Dept of Hisp Studies Scripps Col Claremont CA 91711

JOHNSON, ROGER BARTON, JR, b Columbus, Miss, Nov 28, 42; m 63; c 2. COMPARATIVE LITERATURE, GERMAN. *Educ:* Univ Southern Miss, BA, 63; Univ Ill, Urbana, AM, 65, PhD(comp lit), 68. *Prof Exp:* Asst prof foreign lang, Univ Southern Miss, 67-68; instr English, US Mil Acad, 68-70; assoc prof, 70-73, chmn, Dept Foreign Lang, 70-77, PROF FOREIGN LANG, UNIV SOUTHERN MISS, 73-, DIR CURRIC IN COMP LIT, 77- *Mem:* Am Asn Teachers Ger; MLA; Am Comp Lit Asn. *Res:* Literary realism; Moliere; modern European literature. *Publ:* Coauth, Remarks on Egyptian poetry, Southern Quart, 4/71; auth, L'Apre Verite and Le style emphatique in Le Rouge et le noir, Tex Studies Lit & Lang, fall 71; co-ed, Moliere and the Commonwealth of Letters, Miss Univs, 75. *Mailing Add:* Dept of Foreign Lang Univ of Southern Miss Hattiesburg MS 39401

JOHNSON, SHILDES (RISDON VAIL), Bible, Biblical Languages. See Vol IV

JOHNSON, SIDNEY MALCOLM, b New Haven, Conn, Aug 17, 24; m 45; c 3. GERMAN. *Educ:* Yale Univ, BA, 44, MA, 48, PhD, 53. *Prof Exp:* Asst instr Ger, Yale Univ, 46-51; from instr to prof, Univ Kans, 51-65; prof & chmn dept, Emory Univ, 65-72; chmn dept, 72-78, PROF, IND UNIV, BLOOMINGTON, 78- *Mem:* MLA; Am Asn Teachers Ger; Int Asn Ger Studies; Wolfram von Eschenbach Ges. *Res:* Medieval German literature, especially Wolfram von Eschenbach; Hermann Hesse. *Mailing Add:* Dept of Ger Lang Ind Univ Bloomington IN 47401

JOHNSON, TERESA HERRERA, b San Luis Potosi, Mex, Nov 11, 34; m 55; c 4. SPANISH LANGUAGE & CULTURE, PSYCHOLINGUISTICS. *Educ:* St Louis Univ, BS, 55, MA, 63, PhD(psycholing), 76. *Prof Exp:* Fac, 63-78, ASSOC PROF SPAN & LING, ST LOUIS UNIV, 78- *Concurrent Pos:* Lang coordr Span, Peace Corps Training Prog, St Louis Univ, 64-69; Span coordr, Advan Col Prog, St Louis Univ, 71-, dir, Lang Learning Ctr, 80-; Beaumont Fund res grant, 78; Nat Endowment for Humanities grant, 80; media consult, Japan, 81. *Mem:* Ling Soc Am; MLA; Am Coun Teaching Foreign Lang; Int Asn Lang Lab Dirs. *Res:* Psychology of language; applied linguistics; media in development of language skills. *Publ:* Auth, El Socio Industrial: Spanish for Business Level I, 76 & El Socio Industrial: Spanish for Business Level II, 77, privately publ; Foreign languages in the real world, Foreign Lang Ann, 9/78; Temporal analysis of English & Spanish narratives, Bull Psychol Soc, 10/78; Monolingual and bilingual development at age five, Occas Papers in Ling, Oklahoma Univ, 79; Language Learning Center Internships, Asn Dept Foreign Lang Bull, 11/80; Achiles heel: Foreign languages in USA, Dutchtown Mag, summer 81; Translation: Ecclessial Communities, Social Justice Rev, 1 & 3/82. *Mailing Add:* Dept of Mod Lang St Louis Univ St Louis MO 63103

JOHNSON, VAN LORAN, b Medford, Wis, Jan 18, 08; m 34; c 2. CLASSICAL PHILOLOGY. *Educ:* Univ Wis, AB, 30, AM, 31, PhD, 35; Oxford Univ, BA, 34, MA, 38. *Prof Exp:* Instr classics, Univ Wis, 36-37; from instr to assoc prof Latin, 37-52, prof Classics, 52-73, chmn dept, 52-69, EMER PROF CLASSICS, TUFTS UNIV, 73- *Concurrent Pos:* Vis prof classics, Univ Minn, spring 73; founder, New Eng Latin Workshop,. *Mem:* Fel Int Inst Arts & Lett; Am Class League (pres, 53-60, hon pres, 60-); Archaeol Inst Am (gen secy, 48-51, ed, bull); Class Asn New Eng (secy-treas, 47-49); Am Philol Asn. *Res:* Classical thought, literature and art; history of the calendar. *Publ:* Auth, Tenuis Musa, Tufts Univ, 2nd ed, Am Class League, 78; transl, Andromache, In: Six Greek Plays, Holt, 55; auth, Roman Origins of Our Calendar, Am Class League, 58, 3rd ed, 74. *Mailing Add:* 1056 Hedley Dr San Luis Obispo CA 93401

JOHNSON, WALTER, b Taylors Falls, Minn, Feb 24, 05; m 35; c 1. SCANDINAVIAN LITERATURE. *Educ:* Augsburg Col, AB, 27; Univ Minn, AM, 29; Univ Ill, PhD, 35. *Hon Degrees:* PhD, Univ Uppsala, 73. *Prof Exp:* Instr English, Augsburg Col, 27-31; from asst to asst prof, Univ Ill, 31-47; prof, Univ SDak, 47-48; assoc prof, 48-56, PROF SCAND, UNIV WASH, 56- *Concurrent Pos:* Mem ed staff, Scand Studies, 47-, from assoc managing ed to managing ed, 49-69; Guggenheim fels, 57-58 & 64-65; mem ed staff, Swedish Pioneer Hist Quart, 74- *Honors & Awards:* Order of the North Star, 62; Gold Medal Swed Acad, 72. *Mem:* MLA; Soc Advan Scand Studies; Swed Pioneer Hist Soc; Strindberg Soc; Norweg-Am Hist Asn. *Res:* Strindberg and modern drama; Scandinavian emigrant literature; the Scandinavian heritage. *Publ:* Auth, Strindberg and the Historical Drama, 63, Strindberg's Open Letters to the Intimate Theater, 67, Four Plays by Hjalmar Bergman, 68 & Preinferno Plays, 70, translr, A Dream Play and Four Chamber Plays, 73 & translr & ed, Strindberg Dramas of Testimony, 75, Univ Wash; auth, August Strindberg, G K Hall, 76; translr & ed, Strindberg Plays of Confession and Therapy, Univ Wash, 78. *Mailing Add:* PO Box 442 Clinton WA 98236

JOHNSTON, MARK DAVID, b Puyallup, Wash, Nov 23, 52; m 74. MEDIEVAL & RENAISSANCE STUDIES, ROMANCE LANGUAGES & LITERATURES. *Educ:* Univ Ore, BA, 74; Johns Hopkins Univ, MA, 75, PhD(Romance lang), 77. *Prof Exp:* Asst prof Span, Univ Puget Sound, 77-78; asst prof Romance lang, Washington Univ, 78-81; ASST PROF ENGLISH, ILL STATE UNIV, 82- *Concurrent Pos:* Am Coun Learned Soc grant-in-aid, 79, fel, 82; Nat Endowment for Humanities grant, 80. *Mem:* MLA; Midwest Mod Lang Asn; Am Catalan Soc; Int Soc Hist of Rhetoric; Medieval Asn Midwest. *Res:* Medieval and Renaissance literary and linguistic theories; medieval Catalan literature. *Publ:* Auth, Scholastic psychology as literary tradition in Ausias March, Romance Notes, 78; Bernardo Aldrete and sixteenth century historical linguistics, Revista Estudios Hispanicos, 78; Literary tradition and the ideas of language in the artes de trobar, Dispositio, 78; Antonio de Torquemada y la retorica del saber en el Jardin de flores curiosas, J Hispanic Philol, 78; The translation of the Troubadour tradition in the Torcimany of Lluis d'Avergo, Philol Quart, Vol 60, 81; The reception of the Lullian Art, 1450-1530, 16th Century J, Vol 12, 81; Mateo Aleman in a New World: The Ortografia castellana (1609), Dispositio, 82. *Mailing Add:* 917 E Chestnut Bloomington IL 61701

JOHNSTON, OTTO WILLIAM, b Staten Island, NY, Feb 26, 42; m 66; c 1. GERMANIC LANGUAGES & LITERATURES, PHILOLOGY. *Educ:* Wagner Col, BA, 63; Columbia Univ, MA, 66; Princeton Univ, PhD(Ger lang & lit), 69. *Prof Exp:* Instr English & Ger, Berlitz Sch Lang, 61-62; Instr Ger, Columbia Univ, 63-64; PROF GER, UNIV FLA, 69-, CHMN DEPT GER & SLAVIC LANG & LIT, 78- *Concurrent Pos:* Alexander von Humboldt fel, 74 & 82; Exxon Impact grant, 78. *Mem:* MLA; Am Asn Teachers Ger; Am Coun Teachers Foreign Lang; SAtlantic Mod Lang Asn. *Res:* Nineteenth century German literature; literary sociology; philology. *Publ:* Auth, Schiller, Diderot and the Dalberg Manuscript, Ger Rev, 71; The quest for Bonaparte in Heine's Harzreise, Rev Lang Vivantes, 71; Heinrich Heine and the 13th of December, Colloquia Germanica, 72; Signaturn temporis ur Herrie's Lutezia, Ger Quart, 74; The emergence of the Napoleonic cult in German Lit, Revue belge de Phil et d'hist,74; Joseph Roth's Bu6ste Jes Kaisers, Mod Lang Notes, 74; Lit influence as provocation, Scottish Lit Rev, 80; Napoleon and the Germans, Consortium on Rev Europ, 80. *Mailing Add:* Dept Ger & Slavic Lang & Lit Univ of Fla Gainesville FL 32611

JOHNSTON, PATRICIA ANN, b Chicago, Ill. CLASSICAL LANGUAGES. *Educ:* Univ Calif, Los Angeles, AB, 67; Univ Calif, Berkeley, MA, 72, PhD(classics), 75. *Prof Exp:* Asst prof, 75-82, ASSOC PROF CLASSICS, BRANDEIS UNIV, 82- *Concurrent Pos:* Vis asst prof, Univ Southern Calif, 78-79. *Mem:* Am Philol Asn; Class Asn New England; Vergilian Soc. *Res:* Latin language and literature; Greek language and literature. *Publ:* Auth, Vergil's conception of Saturnus, Calif Studies Class Antiquity, 77; Eurydice and Proserpina in the Georgics, 77 & Poenulus, I, 2 and Roman women, 80, Trans & Proc Am Philol Asn; Vergil's Agricultural Golden Age: A Study of the Georgics, E J Brill, 80; The storm in Aeneid VII, Vergilius, 27: 23-30; An echo of Sappho in Catullus 65, Latomus, 82. *Mailing Add:* Dept Class & Oriental Studies Brandeis Univ Waltham MA 02254

JOHNSTON, ROBERT T LEE, JR, b Spearman, Tex, June 10, 22; m 46; c 5. CLASSICAL LANGUAGES. *Educ:* Abilene Christian Univ, BA, 53, MA, 55. *Prof Exp:* Asst English, Abilene Christian Univ, 53-54, instr, 56-57, instr Bible & Greek, 57-61, asst prof, 61-66, assoc prof, 66-80. *Concurrent Pos:* Univ fel, Univ Tex, 58-60; Southern Fel Fund grant, 61-62. *Mem:* Am Philol Asn; Class Asn Midwest & South. *Res:* Biblical and patristic Greek. *Mailing Add:* 565 E N 23rd St Abilene TX 79601

JOLIAT, EUGENE A, b St Hyacinthe, Que, May 31, 10; m 35; c 2. FRENCH & COMPARATIVE LITERATURE. *Educ:* McGill Univ, BA, 31; Univ Paris, D de l'Univ, 35; BA, Ryerson Tech, 79. *Prof Exp:* Instr French, McMaster Univ, 35-36; instr Romance lang, Wesleyan Univ, 36-37; from asst prof to assoc prof, State Univ Iowa, 37-42; asst to dir, Nat Coun Private Schs, Washington, DC, 42-46 ; from asst prof to assoc prof French, Univ Toronto, 46-57, chmn grad dept, 67-72, prof, 57-76; RETIRED. *Honors & Awards:* Silver Medal, Alliance Francaise, 31. *Mem:* MLA; Int Comp Lit Asn (treas, 58-63). *Res:* Anglo-French literary relations in the 18th century; Victor Hugo; Saint-Evremond. *Publ:* Auth, Smollett et la France, H Champion, Paris; collabr, French individualist poetry, 1686-1760, Univ Toronto, 71; co-ed, Saint-Evremond: Sir Politick Would-be and Les opera, Droz, Paris, 78-79. *Mailing Add:* 64 Astley Ave Toronto ON M4W 3B4 Can

JOLLY, WILLIAM THOMAS, b Helen, Ark, Apr 8, 29. LINGUISTICS, CLASSICAL LANGUAGES. *Educ:* Southwestern at Memphis, 52; Univ Miss, MA, 58; Tulane Univ, PhD(classics), 68. *Prof Exp:* Assoc prof class lang, Millsaps Col, 59-65; assoc prof, 65-75, PROF CLASS LANG, SOUTHWESTERN AT MEMPHIS, 75-, CHMN DEPT FOREIGN LANG, 76- *Mem:* Am Philol Asn; Ling Soc Am; Archaeol Inst Am; Class Asn Midwest & S. *Res:* Greek and Latin literature and history; comparative and historical linguistics. *Mailing Add:* Dept of Foreign Lang Southwestern at Memphis Memphis TN 38112

JONAS, ILSEDORE B, b Stettin, Ger, Aug 31, 20; US citizen; m 45. GERMAN. *Educ:* Univ Heidelberg, dipl Ital & French, 42; Rutgers Univ, MA, 55; Univ Pittsburgh, PhD(Ger), 67. *Prof Exp:* Instr Ger, Douglass Col, Rutgers Univ, 56; from instr to assoc prof, 58-72, PROF GER, CARNEGIE-MELLON UNIV 72- *Concurrent Pos:* Fels, Ger Acad Exchange Serv, 74 & 78, Am Coun Learned Soc, 75 & Am Philos Soc, 76. *Mem:* Am Asn Teachers Ger; MLA; Hugo von Hofmannsthal Ges; Int Arthur Schnitzler Res Asn; Thomas Mann Soc. *Publ:* Ed, Erich Kästner, Holt, 60; coauth, Thomas Mann Studies, Univ Pa, Vol II, 67; auth, Thomas Mann und Italien, Carl Winter, 69; Thomas Mann and Italy, Univ Ala Press, 79. *Mailing Add:* Dept of Mod Lang & Lit Carnegie-Mellon Univ Pittsburgh PA 15213

JONAS, KLAUS WERNER, b Stettin, Ger, June 22, 20; US citizen; m 45. GERMAN LANGUAGE & LITERATURE. *Educ:* Rutgers Univ, MLS, 55; Univ Münster, PhD, 55. *Prof Exp:* Instr Ger, Douglass Col, Rutgers Univ, 50-55; librn Ger lit, Yale Univ Libr, 55-57; from asst prof to assoc prof, 57-65, chmn dept, 59-61, PROF GER, UNIV PITTSBURGH, 65- *Concurrent Pos:* MLA res grants, 56 & 60; Caroline Newton grant, Yale Univ, 57; Am Coun Learned Soc res grant, 58; cur Thomas Mann Arch, Deut Akad Wiss Berlin, 60-; Bollingen Found res grants, 61 & 63; Charles E Merrill Found fac fel, 63; Ford Found fels, 66 & 67; Guggenheim Mem Found fel, 73-74. *Mem:* MLA; Rilke Soc; Am Asn Teachers Ger; Bibliog Soc Am; Int Ver Ger Sprach-u Literaturwiss. *Res:* Modern German literature and culture; bibliography; Anglo-German literary relations. *Publ:* Auth, Fifty Years of Thomas Mann Studies, Univ Minn, 55; The World of Somerset Maugham, Peter Owen, London, 59; Der Kronprinz Wilhelm, H Scheffler, Frankfurt & Univ Pittsburgh, 62; Thomas Mann Studies, Univ Pa, Vol II, 67; ed, Deutsche Weltliteratur von Goethe bis Ingeborg Bachmann, Max Niemeyer, Tübingen, 72; Die Thomas Mann--Literatur, Erich Schmidt, Berlin, Vols I & II, 72 & 78. *Mailing Add:* Dept of Ger Lang & Lit Univ of Pittsburgh Pittsburgh PA 15260

JONES, ANNE PRIOLEAU, b Urbana, Ill, Aug 22, 11. FRENCH MEDIEVAL LITERATURE. *Educ:* Univ Ill, AB, 32, AM, 34. *Prof Exp:* Instr, Knox Sch, Cooperstown, NY, 35-37; from instr to prof, 37-63, chmn dept, 54-62, 64-68, Bergstrom prof, 63-76, EMER PROF FRENCH, LAWRENCE UNIV, 76- *Concurrent Pos:* Ford Found Advan Educ fel, 53-54; Uhrig Found Award, 63. *Honors & Awards:* Chevalier, Palmes Academiques, 67. *Mem:* MLA; Am Asn Teachers Fr. *Res:* Modern French literature. *Publ:* Auth, Freshman studies, an experimental course at Lawrence College, Educ Rec, 7/54; coauth, Hier et Aujourd'hui, Ronald, 59; auth, Andre Malraux: Lectures Choisies, Macmillan, 65. *Mailing Add:* 620 N Owaissa St Appleton WI 54911

JONES, CHRISTOPHER PRESTIGE, b Chislehurst, England, Aug 21, 40. CLASSICAL LITERATURE, ANCIENT HISTORY. *Educ:* Oxford Univ, BA, 62; Harvard Univ, PhD(class philol), 65. *Prof Exp:* Lectr, 65-66, from asst prof to assoc prof, 66-75, PROF CLASSICS, UNIV TORONTO, 75- *Concurrent Pos:* Vis lectr, Harvard Univ, 68-69; leave fel, Can Coun, 71-72; vis mem, Inst Advan Studies, Princeton; vis prof, Ecobe normale superieure de jeunes filles, Paris, 79; Connaught humanities fel, Univ Toronto, 82-83; vis mem, Inst Advan Studies, Princeton, 82-83. *Mem:* Am Philol Asn; Class Asn Can (secy-treas jour, 67-70). *Res:* Roman history; Latin literature; Hellenistic Greek literature. *Publ:* Coauth, Philostratus, Life of Apollonius, Penguin, 70; auth, Plutarch and Rome, Clarendon, Oxford Univ, 71; The Roman World of Dio Chrysostom, Harvard Univ, 78. *Mailing Add:* Dept of Classics Univ of Toronto Toronto ON M5S 1A1 Can

JONES, CLELLAND EVANS, b Salt Lake City, Utah, Jan 31, 17; m 43; c 2. FRENCH. *Educ:* Brigham Young Univ, BA, 42; Univ Utah, MA, 47; State Univ Iowa, PhD(French), 55. *Prof Exp:* Instr French, Army Univ of Oahu, 45-46; asst prof, 49-67, asst chmn dept lang, 65-72, assoc prof, 68-75, PROF FRENCH, UNIV UTAH, 75- *Mem:* Am Coun Teaching Foreign Lang; Am Asn Teachers French. *Res:* French stylistics and phonetics. *Publ:* Auth, L'Art de la Phrase de J J Rousseau dans La Nouvelle Heloise; Manual of French Pronunciation, 61 & coauth, Improve Your French, 62, Deseret News Press; French Verbs and Idioms, Univ Utah, 73. *Mailing Add:* Dept of Foreign Lang Univ Utah Salt Lake City UT 84112

JONES, CYRIL MEREDITH, b Newport, England, Apr 17, 04; m 40; c 3. MEDIEVAL ROMANCE LITERATURE. *Educ:* Univ Wales, UK, BA, 23, MA, 27; Univ Paris, DUniv, 36. *Prof Exp:* Teacher, Brecon Grammar Sch, Wales, 25-28; lectr, 28-31, from asst prof to prof, 31-72, dir, Eve Inst, 34-54, head, Dept French, 43-72, chmn, Div Mod Lang, 62-72, EMER PROF FRENCH, UNIV MANITOBA, 73- *Concurrent Pos:* Royal Soc Can fel, 53-54; pres, Can Mil Intel Asn, 62-64, vis fel, St John's Col, 74- *Honors & Awards:* Can Centennial Medal; Jubilee Medal. *Mem:* Mediaeval Acad Am; Soc Romanistes; MLA; Asn Can Univ Teachers Fr (pres, 64-66). *Res:* Medieval religious life reflected in popular literature; medieval heroic romance; Santiago de Compostela. *Publ:* Auth, La Chronique du Pseudo-Turpin, Droz, Paris 36; Conventional Sarrasin in the songs of Geste, Speculum, 40; Poesie orale Chansons de Geste, In: Thought from the Learned Societies of Canada, Gage, 61; coauth, Senior French, Ginn, Toronto, 63; Vis baptizari?, Culture, Quebec, 64; Les Lettres en France, Macmillan, Toronto, 67; auth, Historia Karoli Magni et Rotholandi, Slatkine, Geneva, 72. *Mailing Add:* 347 Niagara St Winnipeg MB R3N 0V3 Can

JONES, EDWARD ALLEN, b Indianola, Miss, Nov 10, 03. FRENCH LITERATURE. *Educ:* Morehouse Col, AB, 26; Middlebury Col, AM, 30; Univ Paris, dipl, 36; Cornell Univ, PhD, 43. *Prof Exp:* Instr French, Edward Waters Col, 26-27; from instr to assoc prof, 27-36, prof French, 37-70, chmn, Dept Mod Foreign Lant, 37-70 & 73-77, PROF FRENCH, MOREHOUSE COL, 73- *Concurrent Pos:* Ford Found grant, 68; hon consult, Repub Senegal, W Africa, 70-; ed, Col Lang Asn J, 78- *Honors & Awards:* Corson Fr Essay Prize, Cornell Univ, 43. *Mem:* Am Coun Teaching Foreign Lang; Southern Conf Foreign Teaching; MLA; Am Asn Teachers Fr; Col Lang Asn (pres, 50-52). *Res:* Literary creations of contemporary French Negro writers, with special emphasis on the French West Indies and French Africa; Moliere; negritude and Afro-French literature. *Publ:* Auth, A Candle in the Dark: A History of Morehouse College, 67 & Voices of Negritude, 71, Judson. *Mailing Add:* Dept of Mod Foreign Lang Morehouse Col Atlanta GA 30314

JONES, EDWIN HARVIE, b Decatur, Ala, June 10, 07; m 41; c 2. FRENCH. *Educ:* Hampden-Sydney Col, 32; Univ Nancy, dipl, 33; Duke Univ, AM, 41; Univ Va, PhD, 54. *Prof Exp:* Assoc prof, Henderson State Teachers Col, 45-48; asst prof French, 49-60, assoc prof mod foreign lang, 60-69, prof, 69-77, EMER PROF MOD FOREIGN LANG, MARY WASHINGTON COL, UNIV VA, 77- *Mem:* Am Asn Teachers French. *Res:* Spain in the works of Victor Hugo. *Mailing Add:* Dept of Mod Foreign Lang Mary Washington Col Fredericksburg VA 22401

JONES, GEORGE FENWICK, b Savannah, Ga, Apr 3, 16. MEDIEVAL LITERATURE, GERMAN LANGUAGE. *Educ:* Emory Univ, AB, 38; Oxford Univ, BA, 40, MA, 43; Columbia Univ, PhD, 50. *Prof Exp:* From instr to asst prof Mod Lang, Princeton Univ, 50-59, Ellsworth preceptor, 54-55; assoc prof, Goucher Col, 59-62; PROF MOD LANG, UNIV MD, COLLEGE PARK, 62- *Concurrent Pos:* Vis prof Ger lit, Univ Munich, 70 & Univ Ruhr, Bochum, 77. *Honors & Awards:* Austrian Cross of Honor for Sci & Lit. *Mem:* MLA; Mediaeval Acad Am; Am Asn Teachers Ger. *Publ:* Auth, Oswald von Wolkenstein, Twayne, 72; coauth, Konkordanz zu den Liedern Oswalds von Wolkenstein, 73, Verskonkordanz zu den Geistlichen Liedern des Mönchs von Salzburg, 75 & Verskonkordanz zu den geistlichen Liedern des Mönchs von Salzburg, 75, Alfred Kümmerle, Göppingen; Verskonkordanz zu MS A, 78, Verskondordanz zur Weingartner-Stuttgarter Liederhandschrift, 78 & Verskonkordanz zu den Liedern Hugos von Montfort, 81, Kümmerle Verlag, Göppingen. *Mailing Add:* Dept of Ger & Slavic Lang Univ of Md College Park MD 02742

JONES, HAROLD GROVER, b Miami, Fla, Jan 4, 41; m 66. SPANISH LITERATURE. *Educ:* Brown Univ, AB, 62; Princeton Univ, MA, 64, PhD(Romance lang), 68. *Prof Exp:* Instr Span, Macalester Col, 67-68; asst prof, Univ Mo-Columbia, 68-71-71, assoc prof, 71-79; PROF SPAN, UNIV HOUSTON, CENT CAMPUS, 79- *Concurrent Pos:* Nat Endowment for Humanities younger humanist fel, 72-73; Am Coun Learned Socs grant-in-aid, 77; ed, La Coronica, MLA Newslett, 77-79; Guggenheim fel, 79-80; mem exec comt, Cervantes Soc Am, 82- *Mem:* MLA; corresp mem Hispanic Soc Am; Am Asn Teachers Span & Port; AAUP; Asn Int Hisp. *Res:* Old Spanish literature; Spanish literature of the Golden Age; bibliography. *Publ:* Auth, Las rimas moduladas del arcipreste, In: El arcipreste de Hita, el autor, la tierra y la epoca, Actas I Congr Int Arcipreste de Hita, Madrid, 73; El cancionero espanol da la Biblioteca Vaticana, Nueva Rev Filologia Hisp, 72; The epitaph of Fernan Gudiel: An anomaly of Thirteenth Century castilian versification, Hisp Rev, 75; Calderon's El gran teatro del mundo: Two possible sources, J Hisp Philol, 76; Hispanic Manuscripts and Printed Books in the Barberini Collection (2 vols), Biblioteca Apostolica Vaticana, 78; A Cristo Crucificado: Fray Hernando de Camargo y Salgado, Ky Romance Quart, 78; Dos fuentes del primer soliloquio de Segismundo, Nueva Revista de Filologia Hispanica, 79; Grisostomo and Don Quixote: Death and imitation, Revista Canadiense de Estudios Hispanicos, 79. *Mailing Add:* Dept of Romance Lang Univ of Mo Columbia MO 65211

JONES, HARRIMAN, b Orange, NJ, Aug 8, 16; m 41; c 1. ROMANCE LANGUAGES. *Educ:* Dartmouth Col, AB, 39; Harvard Univ, AM, 48, PhD, 51. *Prof Exp:* Instr French lang & lit, Westbrook Jr Col, 39-42; from instr to asst prof, Brandeis Univ, 50-57; from asst prof to assoc prof French lang & lit, St Lawrence Univ, 57-67, prof, 67-81; RETIRED. *Honors & Awards:* Fr Order Acad Palms, 78. *Mem:* Am Asn Teachers Fr. *Res:* French literature of the 19th century. *Mailing Add:* Dept of Mod Lang St Lawrence Univ Canton NY 13617

JONES, HENRI, French Literature. See Vol IV

JONES, HOWARD, Classics. See Vol IV

JONES, JAMES FLEMING, JR, b Atlanta, Ga, Apr 9, 47; m 69; c 3. ROMANCE LANGUAGES. *Educ:* Univ Va, BA, 69; Emory Univ, MA, 72; Columbia Univ, MPhil, 74, PhD(Fr lit), 75. *Prof Exp:* Chmn, Dept Foreign Lang, Woodward Acad, 69-72; asst prof, 75-79, ASSOC PROF FRENCH, WASHINGTON UNIV, 80-, CHMN, DEPT ROMANCE LANG, 82- *Concurrent Pos:* Fels, Nat Endowment for Humanities, 76, Folger Inst Renaissance and Eighteenth-Century Studies, 82. *Mem:* MLA; Am Asn Teachers Fr; Am Soc Eighteenth-Century Studies. *Res:* Eighteenth-century European literature. *Publ:* Auth, Visual communication in Les Egarements du coeur et de l'esprit, 74 & Du Bos and Rousseau: A question of influence, 74, Studies on Voltaire & the Eighteenth Century; Narrative technique in Verga's Le storie del castello di Trezza, Italica, 75; Rousseau's answer to crime: The Utopia at Clarens, Eighteenth Century Life, 76; La Nouvelle Heloise: Rousseau and Utopia, Droz, 77; Montesquieu and Jefferson revisited: Aspects of a legacy, Fr Rev, 78; Adventures in a strange paradise: Utopia in Holberg's Nicolai Klimii Iter subterraneum, Orbis Litterarum, No 35, 80; Washington University and the Centre d'Echanges Internationaux, Bull Am Asn Teachers Fr, 11/81. *Mailing Add:* Dept of Romance Lang Wash Univ St Louis MO 63130

JONES, JOSEPH RAMON, b San Angelo, Tex, May 3, 35. SPANISH. *Educ:* Univ of the South, BA, 56; Univ Wis, PhD, 62. *Prof Exp:* Tex State Good Neighbor Com scholar, Mexico City Col, 54-55; instr, Univ of the South, 56; Buenos Aires Convention scholar, Peru, 58; from instr to assoc prof Span, Univ NC, Chapel Hill, 62-67; assoc prof, 67-72, PROF SPAN, UNIV KY, 72- *Mem:* MLA; Mediaeval Acad Am; Renaissance Soc Am; Am Asn Teachers Span & Port. *Res:* Golden Age prose; Neo-Latin. *Publ:* Auth, Fragments of Antonio de Guevara's Lost Chronicle, Studies Phil, 66; Una Decada de Cesares, Univ NC, 66; coauth, The Scholar's Guide, Pontif Inst Medieval Studies, 69. *Mailing Add:* Dept of Span & Ital Univ of Ky Lexington KY 40506

JONES, LARRY BERT, b Kansas City, Mo, Nov 11, 53; m 77; c 1. LINGUISTICS. *Educ:* Brown Univ, AB, 76; Univ Tex, Arlington, MA, 78, PhD(ling), 80. *Prof Exp:* TRANSL & CONSULT, SUMMER INST LING, INDONESIA BR, 77- *Concurrent Pos:* Vis consult, Summer Inst Ling, Mex Br, 77; vis consult & lectr, Summer Inst Ling, Philippine Br, 81-82; vis lectr, Nat Ctr Indonesian Lang, Jakarta Indonesia, 82. *Mem:* Ling Asn Can & US. *Res:* Prag and the context of speech as it relates to linguistic and translation theory; Papuan languages; discourse analysis. *Publ:* Coauth, Levels of significant information in discourse, Mid-Am Linquistics Conf Okla, Univ Okla, 79; A discourse particle in Cajonos Zapotec & Multiple levels of information in discourse, In: Discourse Studies in Mesoamerican Languages, Summer Inst Lings, summer 79; auth, Pragmatic information in the fourth Gospel, Summer Inst Ling, Dallas, 79; Pragmatic influences on English written discourse, In: The Sixth Lacus Forum 1979, Hornbeam Press, 80; Pragmatic Aspect of English Text Sucture, Summer Inst Ling, 82; coauth, Verb morphology and discourse structure in Mesoamerican languages, In: Paper in Text Ling, Buske Press, 82. *Mailing Add:* 1009 J St La Porte IN 46350

JONES, LAWRENCE GAYLORD, b Scranton, Pa, July 8, 22. LINGUISTICS. *Educ:* Lafayette Col, BA, 43; Columbia Univ, MA, 48; Harvard Univ, PhD(Slavic lang), 52. *Prof Exp:* Res Assoc, Northeastern Univ, 51-54; instr ling, Harvard Univ, 52-55, instr gen educ, 54-55, lectr ling & asst dean grad sch arts & sci, 55-60; PROF SLAVIC LANG & LING, BOSTON COL, 60- *Mem:* Ling Soc Am; Int Ling Asn; Am Asn Teachers Slavic & EEurop Lang. *Res:* Phonetics; Phonemics; symbolism. *Publ:* Auth, Graphic Russian Grammar, C E Merrill, 62; The vowels of English and Russian, Word; Tonality structure of Russian verse, Int J Slavic ling & Poetics, 65; coauth, Shakespeare's Verbal Art in The Expense of Spirit, Mouton, The Hague, 70. *Mailing Add:* Dept of Slavic & Eastern Lang Boston Col Chestnut Hill MA 02167

JONES, LOWANNE ELIZABETH, b New Orleans, La, June 19, 43; c 2. OLD FRENCH LITERATURE & LANGUAGE. *Educ:* Miami Univ, BA, 64; Ohio State Univ, MA, 66, PhD(Romance lang), 72. *Prof Exp:* ASSOC PROF COMP LIT, OHIO STATE UNIV, 76-, ASST DIR, MEDIEVAL & RENAISSANCE STUDIES, 77- *Concurrent Pos:* Fulbright res fel Provencal, Montpellier, France, 71-72. *Mem:* MLA; Mod Humanities Res Asn; Int Courtly Lit Asn; Int Arthurian Soc. *Res:* Allegory in medieval art and literature; Provencal and Old French narrative; 12th and 13th century lyric poetry. *Publ:* Auth, The Cort d'Amor a 13th Century Allegorical Art of Love, Univ NC, 77; Guiraut de Calanso's lyric allegory of Lady Love, Malanges Camproux, 78; Narrative transformations of twelfth century troubadour lyric, In: Transformations of Courtly Literature, Univ Ga (in press); Le Saber dons les gnatres allegories occitanes du treizieme siecle, Actes du Collogne sur la litt narrative medievale en langue d'oc, (in press). *Mailing Add:* Div of Comp Studies in Humanities Ohio State Univ 230 W 17th Ave Columbus OH 43210

JONES, MALCOLM BANCROFT, b Salem, Mass, Mar 23, 02. ROMANCE PHILOLOGY. *Educ:* Harvard Univ, AB, 24, AM, 30, PhD, 35. *Prof Exp:* Tutor & instr, Harvard Univ, 30-34 & Radcliffe Col, 30-35; vis instr, Ohio Univ, 36-37; asst prof, Kenyon Col, 37-38; from instr to prof Romance Lang, 38-70, EMER PROF FRENCH & SPAN, CONN COL, 70- *Res:* French authors in American translation. *Publ:* Auth, Spanish idioms. *Mailing Add:* 15 Shermor Pl New London CT 06320

JONES, MARGARET E W, b New York, NY, Feb 4, 38; m 64. SPANISH. *Educ:* State Univ NY Albany, BA, 59; Univ Wis, MA, 61, PhD(contemp Span), 63. *Prof Exp:* Asst prof Span, Salem Col, 63-64; from asst prof to assoc prof, NC Col Durham, 64-67; from asst prof to assoc prof, 67-75, assoc dean grad sch, 77-79, PROF SPAN, UNIV KY, 75- *Mem:* Am Asn Univ Women; Women's Caucus Mod Lang; MLA; Am Asn Teachers Span & Port. *Res:* Modern and contemporary Spanish literature. *Publ:* Auth, The Literary World of Ana Maria Matute, Univ Ky, 70; Dolores Medio, Twayne, 74; coauth, Spanish Literature: A Brief Survey, Littlefield, Adams, 74; auth, A positive geometry: structural patterns and symbols in Epitalamio del Prieto Trinidad, Symposium, 75; Ana Maria Moix: literary structures and the enigmatic nature of reality, J Span Studies: 20th Century, 76; The modern Spanish theater: the historical perspective, Rev Estud Hisp, 77; contribr, Dialectical movement as feminist technique in the works of Carmen Laforet, In: Studies in Honor of Gerald E Wade, Porrua, 78; Sender, Dramatist, Studies in Honor of Antonio Sanchez Barbudo, Univ Wis Press, 81. *Mailing Add:* Dept of Span Univ of Ky Lexington KY 40506

JONES, MARILYN SCARANTINO, b Jamestown, NY, Oct 27, 48; m 72. SPANISH & COMPARATIVE LITERATURE. *Educ:* Chatham Col, BA, 70; Brown Univ, MA, 71, PhD (Hisp studies), 73. *Prof Exp:* Asst prof Span, Hiram Col, 73-80; ASSOC PROF SPAN, LAKE ERIE COL, 80- *Mem:* MLA. *Res:* Modern poetry. *Publ:* Auth, Verbilization motiviation, ERIC, 3/76; Pessoa's poetic coterie, Luso-Brazilian Rev, winter 77. *Mailing Add:* Dept of Span & Port Lake Erie Col Painesville OH 44077

JONES, MORGAN EMORY, b Devol, Okla, Aug 1, 22; m 49; c 4. LINGUISTICS & ENGLISH LANGUAGE. *Educ:* William Jewell Col, AB, 46; State Univ Wash, MA, 48; Univ Mich, PhD(gen ling), 62. *Prof Exp:* Assoc prof phonetics & phonemics, Univ PR, 50-67; PROF LING & ENGLISH LANG, STATE UNIV NY COL NEW PALTZ, 67- *Concurrent Pos:* Res assoc ling, Mass Inst Technol, 63-64. *Mem:* Am Dialect Soc; Int Ling Asn; Ling Soc Am. *Res:* English grammar; bilingualism; English for speakers of other languages. *Mailing Add:* 6 Lincoln Pl New Paltz NY 12561

JONES, NICHOLAS FRANCIS, b Lynwood, Calif, Aug 22, 46; m 71; c 2. ANCIENT HISTORY, CLASSICAL PHILOLOGY. *Educ:* Univ Southern Calif, BA, 68; Univ Calif, Berkeley, MA, 72, PhD(classics), 75. *Prof Exp:* Instr, 75-76, asst prof 76-81, ASSOC PROF CLASSICS, UNIV PITTSBURGH, 82- *Concurrent Pos:* Am Coun Learned Soc res fel hist, 78-79. *Mem:* Am Philol Asn; Archaeol Inst Am; Asn Ancient Historians. *Res:* Greek city-state organization; the city-state under Roman rule; archaeology, epigraphy, numismatics, topography. *Publ:* Auth, The topography and strategy of the Battle of Amphipolis in 422 BC, Calif Studies Class Antiq, 77; The Autonomous Wreathed Tetradrachmns of Magnesia-on-Maeander, In: American Numismatic Society Museum Notes, Vol 24, 79; The Order of the Dorian Phylai, Class Philol, Vol 75, 197-215; The Civic Organization of Corinth, Trans Am Philol Asn, Vol 110, 161-193. *Mailing Add:* Dept of Classics 207 Hillman Libr Univ Pittsburgh Pittsburgh PA 15260

JONES, RANDALL LEE, b Cedar City, Utah, Feb 21, 39; m 62; c 4. LINGUISTICS, GERMANIC LANGUAGES. *Educ:* Brigham Young Univ, BA, 63, MA, 65; Princeton Univ, MA, 66, PhD(ling), 70. *Prof Exp:* Asst prof ling, Cornell Univ, 68-72; ling consult, Cent Intel Agency Lang Sch, 72-74; asst prof ling, Cornell Univ, 74-78; assoc prof, 78-82, PROF GER, BRIGHAM YOUNG UNIV, 82- *Mem:* Ling Soc Am; MLA; Asn Comput Ling; Am Asn Teachers Ger; Am Coun Teaching Foreign Lang. *Res:* German syntax; language testing. *Publ:* Co-ed, Testing Language Profiency, Ctr Appl Ling, 75; coauth, Word-Indices and Word-Lists to the Gothic Bible and Minor Fragments, Brill, Holland, 76; Testing: A vital connection, In: The Language Connection, Nat Textbk, 77; co-ed, Concordance to the Psychological Works of Sigmund Freud, G K Hall, 80. *Mailing Add:* Dept of Ger Brigham Young Univ Provo UT 84602

JONES, ROBERT ALSTON, b Charleston, SC, Oct 10, 38; m 61; c 3. MODERN GERMAN LITERATURE. *Educ:* Duke Univ, AB, 60; Univ Tex, MA, 62, PhD(Ger), 66. *Prof Exp:* Asst prof Ger, Tufts Univ, 65-66; asst prof, 66-71, ASSOC PROF GER, UNIV WIS, MILWAUKEE, 71- *Concurrent Pos:* Alexander von Humbolt Found res fel, Ger, 77-78. *Mem:* Brecht Soc; Am Asn Teachers Ger; Kafka Soc; MLA. *Res:* Elementary language instruction; German literature, especially of the modern period; modern German drama. *Publ:* Auth, German drama on the American stage: The case of Georg Kaiser, Ger Quart, 1/64; Frank Wedekind: Circus fan, Monatshefte, summer 69; Frank Wedekind: A German dramatist of the absurd?, Comp Drama, winter 70-71. *Mailing Add:* Dept of Ger Univ of Wis Milwaukee WI 53201

JONES, ROBERT BURTON, JR, b Dallas, Tex, Jan 31, 20. LINGUISTICS. *Educ:* Univ Calif, AB, 47, AM, 49, PhD, 58. *Prof Exp:* Asst prof ling, Foreign Serv Inst, US Dept State, Wash, DC, 50-53, Georgetown Univ, 53-55; from asst prof to assoc prof, 55-71, PROF LING, CORNELL UNIV, 71- *Res:* General linguistics; languages and cultures of southeast Asia and Japan. *Publ:* Coauth, Burmese Writing System, 53 & Introduction to Spoken Vietnamese, rev ed, 60, Am Coun Learned Soc; auth, Karen Linguistic Studies, Univ Calif, 61. *Mailing Add:* Southeast Asia Prog Cornell Univ Ithaca NY 14850

JONES, ROBERT EMMET, b New York, NY, Sept 16, 28. FRENCH. *Educ:* Columbia Univ, AB, 48, PhD,54; Sorbonne, cert phonetics, 49. *Prof Exp:* Asst prof French, Univ Ga, 54-61, Univ Pa, 61-67; assoc prof, 67-70, PROF FRENCH & HUMANITIES, MASS INST TECHNOL, 70- *Concurrent Pos:* Am Philos Soc grant, 63. *Mem:* MLA; Am Asn Teachers Fr. *Res:* Contemporary and comparative literature; drama; American 19th century art and culture. *Publ:* Auth, Desire and death in the plays of Lenormand, French Rev, 56; The early heroines of Tennessee Williams, Mod Drama, 59; The Alienated Hero in the Modern French Drama, Univ Ga, 62; Parade de Rimbaud--une nouvelle interpretation, Les Lett Romanes, 67; La Nouvelle Critique, CDU-SEDES, Paris, 68; Gerard de Nerval, Twayne, 74. *Mailing Add:* Dept of Mod Foreign Lang Mass Inst of Technol Boston MA 02116

JONES, STANLEIGH HOPKINS, JR, b Norfolk, Va, Mar 11, 31; m 58; c 2. JAPANESE LANGUAGE & LITERATURE. *Educ:* Va Mil Inst, BA, 53; Columbia Univ, cert, EAsian Inst & MA, 58, PhD(Japanese lang & lit), 68. *Prof Exp:* Lectr Japanese lang & lit, Yale Univ, 61-63; asst prof, Univ Southern Calif, 63-67, Univ Ky, 67-68; ASST PROF JAPANESE LANG & LIT, CLAREMONT GRAD SCH, 68- *Concurrent Pos:* Nat Endowment for Humanities fel, 72, grant, 80-82. *Mem:* Asn Asian Studies; Asn Teachers Japanese. *Res:* Japanese literature; Japanese drama; Japanese history. *Publ:* Auth, The No Plays Obasute and Kanehira, Monumenta Nipponica, 63 & In: Twenty Plays of the No theatre, Columbia Univ, 70; Hamlet on the Japanese puppet stage, J Asn Teachers Japanese, 1/76; Miracle at Yaguchi Ferry: A Japanese puppet play and its metamorphosis to Kabuki, Harvard J Asiatic Studies, 6/78; Experiment and tradition, New plays in the Bunraku Theatre, Monumenta Nipponica, summer 81. *Mailing Add:* Dept Asian Studies Claremont Grad Sch Claremont CA 91711

JONES, TOBIN H, b Minneapolis, Minn, Apr 13, 39; m 62. FRENCH LITERATURE. *Educ:* Univ Minn, Minneapolis, BA, 62, MA, 65, PhD(French), 69. *Prof Exp:* Instr French, Univ Minn, Minneapolis, 66-68; asst prof, Univ Chicago, 68-74; ASSOC PROF FRENCH, COLO STATE UNIV, 74- *Mem:* MLA; Asn Am Teachers Fr; Rocky Mountain Mod Lang Asn; Midwest Mod Lang Asn. *Res:* Novel; 20th century French literature. *Publ:* Auth, The alchemical language of Paul Claudel's L'Announce faite a Marie, Symposium, spring 73; In quest of a newer new novel: Ricardou's La Prise de Constantinople, Contemp Lit, summer 73; Toward a more primitive reading: aesthetic response to radical form in the new French novel, Essays in Lit, fall 76. *Mailing Add:* Dept of Foreign Lang Colo State Univ Ft Collins CO 80521

JONSSON-DEVILLERS, EDITH, FRENCH, SPANISH & COMPARATIVE LITERATURE. *Educ:* Sorbonne, France, Lic es lett, 57; Laerarhoegskolan, Uppsala, Sweden, teacher cert French & Span, 65; Univ Calif, San Diego, PhD(comp lit), 76. *Prof Exp:* Instr French, Univ San Diego, 69-70 & US Int Univ, 70-71; assoc, French-Span, Univ Calif, San Diego, 71-75; asst prof Span, Occidental Col, 76-79. *Concurrent Pos:* Lectr, San Diego State Univ; transl, Nat Transl Cert Serv. *Mem:* MLA; Asn Teachers Fr; Inst Estudios Iberamericanos; Am Transl Asn. *Res:* French literature; Spanish American literature; Octovio Paz. *Publ:* Contribr & transl article, In: Jorge Luis Borges, Taurus, Madrid, 76; auth, Octavio Paz and poems of humor in black, purple and green, J Span Studies 20th Century, winter 76; co-ed & transl, La Voie des Maitres, Dervy-Livres, Paris, 78; Vueltas y revueltas a Veulta: Esbozo para un analisis de la intertextualidad, In: Texto/Contexto en la Literatura Iberoamericana, Vol XIX, Inst Int de Lit Iberoamericana, Madrid, 80. *Mailing Add:* 5148 Enelra Place San Diego CA 92117

JORDAN, CHARLES F, b Salem, Mass, Jan 16, 18; m 43. FOREIGN LANGUAGES. *Educ:* Univ Ala, AB, 39, Loyola Col, Md, MA, 54. *Prof Exp:* Instr, 47-54, ASST PROF MOD LANG, LOYOLA COL, MD, 54- *Mem:* Mid States Asn Mod Lang Teachers (secy-treas, 63); Am Asn Teachers Ger; Am Asn Teachers Span & Port; MLA. *Mailing Add:* Dept of Foreign Lang Loyola Col Baltimore MD 21210

JORDAN, EMIL LEOPOLD, b Russ, Ger, Oct 2, 00; nat US; m 33; c 1. GERMAN LITERATURE. *Educ:* Univ Koenigsberg, PhD, 22. *Prof Exp:* From instr to assoc prof, 31-50, prof, 60-67, chmn dept & mem grad fac, univ, 43-67, EMER PROF GER, DOUGLASS COL, RUTGERS UNIV, 67- *Mem:* MLA; Am Asn Teachers Ger. *Publ:* Auth, History of German Civilization & Cultural Geography of Germany, Appleton; History of the Peoples Who Settled the America, Norton; A Biography of Charles Sealsfield, Prentice-Hall, 69; The Nature Atlas of America, 76 & Travel Atlas of Scenic America, Hammond. *Mailing Add:* Rte 1 Box G18 Blowing Rock NC 28605

JORDAN, GERDA PETERSEN, b Hamburg, Ger, Nov 14, 27; US citizen. GERMAN, COMPARATIVE LITERATURE. *Educ:* Univ SC, BA, 64, MA, 67, PhD(comp lit), 71. *Prof Exp:* Instr Ger, Univ SC, 67-72; asst prof Ger & English, Francis Marion Col, 72-73; asst prof, 73-78, ASSOC PROF GER & COMP LIT, UNIV SC, 78- *Mem:* Am Asn Teachers Ger (secy-treas, 70-73); SAtlantic Mod Lang Asn; Am Coun Teachers Foreign Lang; Southern Comp Lit Asn. *Res:* Richard Wagner. *Publ:* Auth, Reading German, privately publ, 69; transl, Thirteen Uncanny Stories, Peter Lauq, Bern, 78; Biedermann und Die Brandstifter, Moritz Diesterweg, Frankfurt, 78. *Mailing Add:* Dept of Foreign Lang & Lit Univ of SC Columbia SC 29208

JORDAN, GILBERT JOHN, b Mason Co, Tex, Dec 23, 02; m 26; c 2. GERMAN LANGUGAGE & LITERATURE. *Educ:* Southwestern Univ, AB, 24; Univ Tex, AM, 28; Ohio State Univ, PhD, 36. *Prof Exp:* Teacher & adminstr schs, Tex, 24-30; asst prof Ger, Southern Methodist Univ, 30-35 & 36-38, assoc prof, 38-44, prof & chmn dept, 44-68; prof, Sam Houston State Univ, 68-73; RETIRED. *Honors & Awards:* Order of Merit, Fed Ger Repub, 60. *Mem:* MLA; Am Asn Teachers Ger; S Cent Mod Lang Asn. *Publ:* Auth, Southwest Goethe Festival, Southern Methodist Univ, 49; Four German One-Act Plays, Holt, 51; transl, Schiller's Wilhelm Tell, Bobbs, 64; coauth, Ernst and Lisette Jordan: German Pioneers in Texas, Von Boeckmann-Jones, 71; auth, The Morning is Not Far: Some Poems, privately publ, 74; auth & transl, Steinert's View of Texas in 1849, Southwestern Hist Quart, Vols 80 & 81, 76 & 77; auth, The Texas German language . . . , Rice Univ Studies, 77; Texas German Methodism in a rural setting, Perkins J, 78; Yesterday in the Texas Hill Country, Texas A&M Univ Press, 79; German Texana, Eakin Press. *Mailing Add:* 3228 Milton Ave Dallas TX 75205

JORDAN, ROBERT MAYNARD, English. See Vol II

JORDEN, ELEANOR HARZ, LINGUISTICS. *Educ:* Bryn Mawr Col, AB, 42; Yale Univ, MA, 43, PhD(linguistics), 50. *Prof Exp:* Instr Japanese, Yale Univ, 43-46 & 47-48; linguist and dir Japanese lang prog, 49-53, dir, Foreign Serv Inst Japanese Lang Sch, Am Embassy, Tokyo, 53-55; Sci ling for Japanese, 59, for Japanese and Russian, 59-61, chmn Dept EAsian Lang, 61-67, 69, Vietnamese Lang Div, 67-69, Foreign Serv Inst, Dept of State, Washington, DC; vis prof, 69-70, prof ling, 70-74, MARY DONLON ALGER PROF LING, CORNELL UNIV, 74- *Concurrent Pos:* Supvr full-year Asian lang concentration prog in (FALCON) Japanese, 72-; consult and examiner for Japanese, Nat Asn Self-Inst Lang Progs, 65-; coordr Soc Sci Res Coun of Joint Japanese-American Sociolinguistics Res Proj, 70-74; comt on Int Exchange Scholars (Sr Fulbright Hays Prog), 72-75; chmn, Task Force on Japanese Lang Training, Soc Sci Res Coun, 76-; Japan Found & Soc Sci Res Coun sr fel, 75-76; Toyota 20th Anniversary Fund Grantee, 78. *Honors & Awards:* Superior Honor Award, Dept State, 76. *Mem:* Asn Asian Studies (pres, 80-81); Asn Teachers Japanese (pres, 78-); Nat Asn Self-Instr Lang Prog (pres, 77-); Ling Soc Am; Am Coun Teachers Foreign Lang. *Res:* Sociolinguistic study of Japanese attitudes toward language and their effect on intercultural communication; women's speech in Japanese; Japanese language pedogogy. *Publ:* Auth, Syntax of modern colloquial Japanese, Ling Soc Am, 55; Gateway to Russian, Ottenheimer, 60; Beginning Japanese, Part 1 and 2, Yale Univ, 62-63; Basic Vietnamese, Vol I and II, 67 & coauth, Vietnamese Familiarization Course, 69, US Govt Printing Off; Presidential address: Language and area studies--In search of a meaningful relationship, J Asian Studies, 11/81. *Mailing Add:* Dept of Mod Lang & Lint Morrill Hall Cornell Univ Ithaca NY 14853

JORGENSEN, PETER ALVIN, b Jersey City, NJ, July 31, 41; m 70; c 2. GERMANIC PHILOLOGY, GERMAN. *Educ:* Princeton Univ, AB, 63; Harvard Univ, MA, 71, PhD(Ger philol), 72. *Prof Exp:* Asst prof Ger philol, Univ Calif, Riverside, 71-76; ASSOC PROF GER PHILOL, UNIV GA, 76- *Mem:* Soc Advan Scand Stuides; MLA; Mediaeval Acad Am; Medieval Asn Pac Coast; SAtlantic Mod Lang Asn. *Res:* Old Norse manuscripts and paleography; saga forgeries; Old English and Old Norse folklore. *Publ:* Auth, Ten Icelandic exempla and their Middle English Source, Opuscula, 70; The Icelandic translations from Middle English, In: Studies for Einar Haugen, Mouton, The Hague, 72; Four Aeventyri, Opuscula, 75; The two-troll variant of the Bear's Son folktale in Halfdanar Saga Brönufostra and Grims Saga Lodinkinna, Arv, J Scand Folklore, 75; Hafgeirs Saga Flateyings: An eighteenth-century forgery, J English & Ger Philol, 77; St Julian and Basilissa in Medieval Iceland, Jakob Benediktsson Festschrift, 77; Beowulf's Swimming Contest with Breca: Old Norse Parallels, Folklore, 78; The gift of the useless weapon in Beowulf and the Icelandic sagas, Arkiv Nordisk Filol, 79; Thiostolfs Saga Hamramma: The case for forgery, Gripla, 79. *Mailing Add:* Dept of Ger & Salvic Lang Univ of Ga Athens GA 30602

JOSEPH, BRIAN DANIEL, b New York, NY, Nov 22, 51; m 75; c 1. LINGUISTICS, INDO-EUROPEAN STUDIES. *Educ:* Yale Univ, AB, 73; Harvard Univ, AM, 76, PhD(ling), 78. *Prof Exp:* Lectr, Univ Alta, 78-79; ASST PROF LING, OHIO STATE UNIV, 79- *Concurrent Pos:* Izaak Walton Killam fel, Univ Alta, 78-79. *Mem:* Ling Soc Am; Can Ling Asn; Mod Greek Studies Asn; Am Asn Teachers Slavic & East Europ Lang; Am Asn Southeast Europ Studies. *Res:* Indo-European linguistics; relational grammar and the syntax of Modern Greek; Balkan linguistics. *Publ:* Auth, Envy--a functional analysis, Ling Inquiry, 76; Morphology and Universals in Syntactic Change: Evidence from Medieval and Modern Greek, Ind Univ Ling Club, 78; Linguistic universals and syntactic change, Lang, 80; Locatives and obviation in Cree, Int J Am Ling, 80; Recovery of information in relative clauses: Evidence from Greek and Hebrew, J Ling, 80; A new convergence concerning the Balkan loss of the infinitive, Indogermanische Forschungen, 80; On the synchrony and diachrony of Modern Greek na, Byzantine & Mod Greek Studies, 81; The Synchrony and Diachrony of the Balkan Infinitive, Cambridge Univ Press (in press). *Mailing Add:* Dept Ling Ohio State Univ Columbus OH 43214

JOSEPH, GEORGE L, b Louisville, Ky, June 8, 44; m 67; c 2. FRENCH. *Educ:* Oberlin Col, BA, 66; Ind Univ, Bloomington, MA, 68, PhD(French), 73. *Prof Exp:* Asst prof French, Yale Univ, 74-78; ASST PROF FRENCH, BRANDEIS UNIV, 78- *Mem:* MLA; African Lit Asn. *Res:* French Renaissance literature; African oral poetry. *Publ:* Auth, Rhetoric and the structure of Malherbe's Odes celebrating royalty, Papers Fr 17th Century Lit, 74; The Wolof oral Praise Song for Semu Coro Wende, Res African Lit, 79; Early Cameroonian literature, African Lit Europ Lang, (in press); Ronsard's Ode versus Marot's Epistle in HoNor of Frenchancois de Bourbon, Fr Rev, Vol 54, no 6; Rhetoric, Intertextuality, and Genre, In: Elegies deploratives, Romanic Rev, Vol 72, No 1. *Mailing Add:* Dept of Romance & Comp Lit Brandeis Univ Waltham MA 02154

JOSEPH, JOHN EARL, b Monroe, Mich, Oct 30, 56. LINGUISTICS & LITERATURE. *Educ:* Univ Mich, BA, 77, MA, 78, PhD(Romance lang), 81. *Prof Exp:* Lectr ling, Univ Paul Valery, Montpellier, 80-81; ASST PROF FOREIGN LANG & DIR, APPL LANG STUDY CONF, OKLA STATE UNIV, 81- *Mem:* Ling Soc Am; MLA. *Res:* French and Italian literature; historical linguistics; language standardization. *Publ:* Auth, Linguistic classification in Italy: Problems and predictions, summer 80, Review of Heinz Kloss, Die Engwickling ser never germanischer Kultursprachen, summer 80 & Compte render d'A Valdman, Le Francais Hors De France, summer 81, Lang Probs & Lang Planning; Generative poetics, Proc of the Mid-Am Ling Conf, 81. *Mailing Add:* Dept of Foreign Lang Okla State Univ Stillwater OK 74078

JOSEPH, LAWRENCE ALEXANDER, b Des Moines, Iowa, May 30, 35. FRENCH LITERATURE. *Educ:* Harvard Univ, AB, 57, AM, 60, PhD(Romance lang), 69. *Prof Exp:* From instr to asst prof, 63-73, assoc prof, 73-79, PROF FRENCH, SMITH COL, 80- *Mem:* MLA. *Res:* Nineteenth and 20th century French literature. *Publ:* Auth, Mallarme et son amie anglaise, Rev Hist Lit France, 9/65; Coco Barroil et la Prose pour Cazalis de Mallarme, Rev Sci Humaines, 12/71; Henri Cazalis, sa vie, son oeuvre, son amitie avec Mallarme, Nizet, 72; Max Jacob, Lettres a Michel Levanti, Rougerie, 75; Documents Stephane Mallarme VI, Corrependance avec Henri Cazalis, Nizet, 77; Documents Stephane Mallarme VII, Nizet, 80. *Mailing Add:* Dept of French Lang & Lit Smith Col Northampton MA 01060

JOSEPHS, ALLEN, b Charlotte, NC, Nov 20, 42; c 3. MODERN SPANISH LITERATURE, MODERN LITERATURES. *Educ:* Univ NC, Chapel Hill, BA, 65; NY Univ, MA, 66; Rutgers Univ, PhD(Span), 73. *Prof Exp:* Asst prof, 69-76, assoc prof, 76-79, PROF SPAN, UNIV W FLA, 79- *Concurrent Pos:* Consult, Westinghouse Elec Corp, Spain, 74-75; Nat Endowment for Arts fel, 79-80. *Mem:* MLA; SAtlantic Mod Lang Asn; Am Asn Teachers Span & Port. *Res:* The work of Federico Garcia Lorca; Spanish culture and civilization; Hemingway and other writers on Spain. *Publ:* Co-ed, F G Lorca's La Casa de Bernarda Alba, Catedra, 76;; F G Lorca Poema del Cante Jondo/ Romancero Gitano, Catedra, 77; auth, At the heart of Madrid, Atlantic Monthly, 7/79; Homage to Andalucia, Va Quart Rev, summmer 79; The Andaluian Picasso, New Boston Rev, 11-12/80; F G Lorca Antologia poetica, Plaza y Janes, 81; auth, Terra Nostra: Whose land?, Secolas Annals, 3/82; Hemingway's poor Spanish: Chauvinism and the loss of credibility in For Whom the Bell Tolls, In: Hemingway: A Revaluation, Whitson, 82. *Mailing Add:* Dept Foreign Lang Univ W Fla Pensacola FL 32504

JOSEPHS, HERBERT, b New York, NY, Nov 11, 32; m 58; c 1. ROMANCE LANGUAGES. *Educ:* Brooklyn Col, BA, 53; Fordham Univ, MA, 57; Princeton Univ, MA, 59, PhD(French), 63. *Prof Exp:* Instr French, Amherst Col, 60-62; from instr to assoc prof, 62-72, PROF FRENCH LIT, MICH STATE UNIV, 72- *Concurrent Pos:* Nat Endowment for Humanities, summer grant, 75 & 81; Am Coun Learned Soc grant-in-aid, 76. *Mem:* AAUP; Am Soc 18th Century Studies; MLA. *Res:* Literature of the French Enlightenment; Denis Diderot; French novel of the Enlightenment. *Publ:* Auth, Manon Lescaut: A rhetoric of intellectual evasion, Romanic Rev, 10/68; Le Neveu de Rameau: Diderot's Dialogue of Language and Gesture, Ohio State Univ, 69; Metaphor and discovery in Diderot's Lettre sur les Sourds et Muets, Ky Romance Quart, Vol XX, No 2; La Religieuse: The dark cave of the Libertine soul, Mod Lang Notes, 76; The Marquis de Sade and women: Exorcising the awe of the sacred, Studies in Burke & His Time, 77; Diderot's Eloge de Richardson: A Paradox on Praising, In: Essays on the Age of Enlightment in Honor of Ira O Wade, Droz, 77; At the frontiers of the real: Forms and shadows of Diderot's narrative art, Forum, XVI, 78; Le paysan parvenu: Satire and the fiction of innocence, Fr Forum, Vol V, 80. *Mailing Add:* Dept of Romance & Class Lang Mich State Univ East Lansing MI 48824

JOST, DAVID ARTHUR, Medieval English Language & Literature. See Vol II

JOST, DOMINIK, b Lucerne, Switz, July 26, 22; m 53. GERMAN LITERATURE. *Educ:* Univ Fribourg, PhD(Ger lit), 46. *Prof Exp:* Prof Ger lang & lit, Kantonssch St Gallen, Switz, 53-67; assoc prof Ger lit, Univ Rochester, 67-69; PROF GER LANG & LIT, ST GALLEN COL ECON & SOC SCI, 70- *Concurrent Pos:* Vis prof, McGill Univ, 69-70; mem bd, Erasmus, Int Bull Comtemp Scholar, 72- *Mem:* akademische Ges Schweizerischer Germanisten; Asn Suisse Litt Gen & Comp. *Res:* Ludwig Derleth, 1870-1948; German literature since 1890; Goethe. *Publ:* Auth, Stefan George und seine Elite, Speer, Zürich, 49; Ludwig Derleth, Kohlhammer, Stuttgart, 65; Literarischer Jugendstil, Metzler, Stuttgart, 69 & 80; ed, Ludwig Derleth: Das Werk (6 vols), Hinder & Deelmann, Behhnhausen/Gladenbach, 71-72; auth, Henry D Thoreau in Switzerland, In: Thoreau Abroad, Shoe String, 71; Deutsche Klassi: Goethes Römische Elegien, Verlag Dokumentation, Munich, 74 & 78; Die Dichtung Ludwig Derleths Einführung in Das Werk, Hinder & Deelmann, Bellnhausen, 75; Die Wirklichkeit des Dichters, Ed Interfrom, Zürich, 77. *Mailing Add:* Schneebergstr 27 9000 St Gallen Switzerland

JOST, FRANCOIS, b Lucerne, Switz, July 10, 18; m 48; c 3. LANGUAGES. *Educ:* Col Villefranche-sur-Saone, France, BA, 40; Univ Fribourg, PhD(French lit), 47; Univ Paris, PhD(comp lit), 56. *Prof Exp:* Asst prof French lit, Univ Fribourg, 52-59; assoc prof comp lit, Univ Zurich, 60-61; prof French & comp lit, Univ Colo, 61-65; assoc Ctr Advan Studies, 68-69, PROF FRENCH & COMP LIT, UNIV ILL, URBANA, 65- *Concurrent Pos:* Ford Found travel grant to 2nd Congr Int Comp Lit Asn, Chapel Hill, NC, 58, 4th Congr, 64; fel, Fonds Nat Suisse rech Sci, 55, 59, 62; Am Philos Soc res grant, 64; vis prof comp lit, Innsbruck Univ, 69 & Univ Maine, 72. *Mem:* Am Comp Lit Asn; Int Comp Lit Asn; MLA. *Res:* Eighteenth century French literature; theory of literature; European literatures. *Publ:* Auth, Alexandre Vinet, Interprete de Pascal, Payot, Lausanne, 50; La Suisse dans les Lettres Francaises, 56 & Jean-Jacques Rousseau (2 vols), 62, Univ Press, Fribourg; Essais de Litterature Comparee: Vol I, Helvetica, 64, Vol II, Europaeana, 68; ed, Proceedings of the IV Congress of the International Comparative Literature Association (2 vols), Mouton, The Hague, 66; auth, Introduction to Comparative Literature, Bobbs, 74; Major German and French Themes in Early American Drama, J Gen Educ, 76; Critical Edition of Le Paysan Perverti Par Restif de la Bretonne (2 vols), Lausanne, 77. *Mailing Add:* Dept Comp Lit Univ Ill Urbana IL 61801

JOUBERT, ANDRE, b Lyon, France, July 1, 24. FRENCH. *Educ:* Sorbonne, Lic, 46, dipl, 47, cert, 56. *Prof Exp:* Lectr, French-German Inst, Ludwigsburg, 56-57, Tech Univ, Hannover, 58; lectr, 58-59, from asst prof to assoc prof, 59-72, PROF FRENCH, UNIV MAN, 72- *Res:* Contemporary French novel; literary criticism in France; philosophy of time. *Publ:* Auth, Colette et Cheri, Ed Nizet, Paris, 72. *Mailing Add:* Dept of French Univ of Man Winnipeg MB R3T 2N2 Can

JOUBERT, INGRID, b Heidelberg, WGer, Feb 17, 42; m 68; c 2. FRENCH, GERMAN. *Educ:* Univ Man, BA, 64; Univ Ore, MA, 65, PhD(mod lang), 70. *Prof Exp:* Lectr, Univ Winnipeg, 70-71; PROF FRENCH, ST BONIFACE COL, UNIV MAN, 73- *Res:* Sartre; Romain Rolland; Hermann Hesse. *Publ:* Auth, Alienation et Liberte dans les Chemins de la Liberte de Jean-Paul Sartre, Marcel Didier, Paris, Montreal, Brussels, 73. *Mailing Add:* 184 Ash St Winnipeg MB R3N 0P7 Can

JOVICEVICH, ALEXANDER, b Yugoslavia, Sept 19, 23; US citizen. FRENCH LITERATURE. *Educ:* Columbia Univ, BS, 53, MA, 55; Univ Paris, DUniv, 59. *Prof Exp:* Teacher French, Choate Sch, 56-57; teacher, Horace Mann Sch, 59-63; from asst prof to assoc prof, 63-69, PROF MOD LANG, SETON HALL UNIV, 69-, CHMN DEPT FOREIGN LANG, 78- *Concurrent Pos:* Corresp mem, Inst Voltaire Belgium, 60; grants, Am Philos Soc, 63, 66, 67, Caisse Nat Lett, 65-, Shell Chem Co, 66, 67, Nat Endowment for Humanities, 68 & Seton Hall Univ, 76. *Mem:* Am Asn Teachers Fr; Am Soc 18th Century Studies; MLA; Soc Fr Etude XVIIIe Siecle. *Res:* Voltaire; Jean-Francois La Harpe; Montesquieu's theory of education. *Publ:* Auth, Les Lettres D'Amabed de Voltaire, Ed Universitaires, 61; A propos d'une Pamela de Voltaire, Fr Rev, 1/63; Sur la Date de composition de l'homme aux quarante ecus, Symposium, fall 64; Correspondance inedite de Jean-Francois de La Harpe, Ed Universitaires, 65; Le Royaliste La Harpe en Vendemiaire, Ann IV, Ann Hist de la Revolution Francaise, 71; A forgotten text by Diderot: A review of the Traite de Musique . . . of Antoine Bemetzrieder, Fr Rev, 73; Jean-Francois de La Harpe, Adepte et Renegat des Lumieres, Seton Hall Univ, 73; Voltaire and La Harpe--l'affaire des manuscrits: A reappraisal, Studies Voltaire & 18th Century, 78. *Mailing Add:* Dept of Mod Lang Seton Hall Univ South Orange NJ 07079

JOYAUX, GEORGES JULES, b Nice, France, Mar 1, 23; nat US; m 47; c 6. FRENCH LANGUAGE & LITERATURE, COMPARATIVE LITERATURE. *Educ:* Univ Aix-Marseille, BM, 43, PhB, 43; Mich State Univ, MA, 47, PhD, 51. *Prof Exp:* Teacher elem sch, France, 45-46; from instr to asst prof French, 46-57, assoc prof French lang & lit, 57-60, PROF FRENCH & COMP LIT, MICH STATE UNIV, 60-, CHMN DEPT, 80- *Concurrent Pos:* Guggenheim fel, 57-58; vis prof French lit, Univ Ariz, 64-65. *Mem:* Am Asn Teachers Fr; MLA; Am Studies Asn; African Studies Asn. *Res:* French-American cultural relationships in the 19th and 20th century; contemporary French literature; French-language literatures of Africa and Canada. *Publ:* Auth, The French-language press in North Africa, Centennial Rev, winter 59; Prince Napoleon in America, 1861, Ind Univ, 59 & Galley Press, London, 60; coauth, Aspects de la France, Scribner, 60. *Mailing Add:* Dept of Romance Lang Mich State Univ East Lansing MI 48823

JOYCE, DOUGALS A, b Carbonear, Nfld, July 20, 22; m 60. GERMANIC LANGUAGES. *Educ:* McGill Univ, BA, 43; Harvard Univ, AM, 44, PhD, 52. *Prof Exp:* Lectr Ger, 50-54, from asst prof to assoc prof, 54-67, PROF GER & HEAD DEPT, TRINITY COL, UNIV TORONTO, 67- *Concurrent Pos:* Founding mem & asst ed, Seminar: J Ger Studies, 64-; Can Coun grant, 73-74. *Mem:* MLA; Asn Can Univ Teachers Ger (secy, 60-62); Hofmannsthal Soc. *Res:* Literary criticism of the post-romantic period in Germany; German drama of the nineteenth century; Hugo von Hofmannsthal. *Publ:* Auth, Some uses of irony in Hofmannsthal's Der Schwierige, Mod Lang Quart, 9/69. *Mailing Add:* Dept of Ger Trinity Col Univ of Toronto Toronto ON M5S 1H8 Can

JUDD, ELLIOT L, b Brooklyn, NY, Mar 19, 48; m 76. LINGUISTICS, ENGLISH AS A SECOND LANGUAGE. *Educ:* New York Univ, BA, 69, MA, 71, PhD(teaching English as second lang), 77. *Prof Exp:* Asst prof English & ling, State Univ NY Cortland, 73-76; asst prof ling, Ohio Univ, 76-80. *Concurrent Pos:* Consult, Syracuse Pub Sch Syst, 73-76 & Athens Pub Sch Syst, 76- *Mem:* Am Asn Appl Ling; Teachers English to Speakers Other Lang; Nat Asn Foreign Student Adv. *Res:* Applied linguistics; sociolinguistics. *Publ:* Auth, Language Media and Society: A Sociolinguist's View of the Effects of Media, Proc Conf Perspectives Mass Commun, Mohawk Valley Community Col, 75; The Role of Sociolinguistics in a TESOL Teacher's Training Program, Working Papers Appl Ling, Vol 5; Vocabulary Teaching In TESOL: A need to reevaluate existing assumptions, TESOL Quart, 78. *Mailing Add:* 6544 N Fairfield Chicago IL 60645

JUDOVITZ, DALIA, b Transylvania, Romania, Sept 23, 51; US citizen. FRENCH LITERATURE. *Educ:* Brandeis Univ, BA, 73; Johns Hopkins Univ, MA, 76, PhD(French), 79. *Prof Exp:* Lectr French lit, Univ Pa, 78-79, asst prof, 79-82; ASST PROF FRENCH, UNIV CALIF, BERKELEY, 82- *Concurrent Pos:* Mellon fel, Columbia Univ, 81-82. *Honors & Awards:* Special Commendation, Soc Fel in the Humanities, Columbia Univ, 82. *Mem:* MLA; NAm Asn Seventeenth Century French Lit; Int Asn Philos & Lit; Am Asn Aesthetics. *Res:* French seventeenth century philosophy; French seventeenth century novel (ethics and aesthetics); critical theory. *Publ:* Auth, Freud: Translation and/or interpretation, Sub-Stance, Univ Wis, spring 79; Autobiographical discourse and critical praxis in Descartes, Philos and Lit, spring 81; Le Discours de la methode: Theorie du sujet comme pratique litteraire, Papers on French Seventeenth Century Lit, spring 82; Rationality, representation and the question of humanism: Descartes and Heidegger, Annals of Scholarship (in prep); coauth, The figure in writing, Sub-Stance, Univ Wis (in prep). *Mailing Add:* French Dept Univ of Calif Berkeley CA 94720

JUHL, P D, b Hamburg, West Ger, Mar 8, 46. GERMANIC LANGUAGES & LITERATURES, LITERARY THEORY. *Educ:* Columbia Univ, BA, 69; Stanford Univ, MA & PhD(Ger & philos), 71. *Prof Exp:* Kellett fel Ger lit, Oxford Univ, 71-72; asst prof, Kenyon Col, 72-74, Univ Fla, 74-76; ASSOC PROF GERMAN LIT, PRINCETON UNIV, 76- *Mem:* MLA; Int Asn Philos & Lit. *Res:* The philosophy of literature and criticism; European intellectual history; 18th century German literature. *Publ:* Auth, Zur Interpretation eines literarischen Werkes und ihrer Begrenzung durch die Anschauungen seines Autors, LiLi, Zeitschrift fur Literaturwissenschaft und Linguistik, 73; Can the meaning of a literary work change?, In: The Uses of Criticism, Herbert Lang, Bern, 76; Can we exclude an interpretation of a literary work on the basis of the rules of the language?, Mod Lang Notes, 12/77; Eugene O'Neill's The Hairy Ape: Bemerkungen zu Sinn und Struktur des Dramas, In: Theater und Dramas in Amerika, Erich Schmidt, Berlin, 78; Do computer poems show that an author's intention is irrelevant to the meaning of literary work?, Critical Inquiry, spring 79; Life, literature, and the implied author, In: Deutsche Vierteljahrsschrift fur Literaturwissenschaft und Geistesgeschichte, 80; Interpretation: An Essay in the Philosophy of Literary Criticism, Princeton Univ Press, 1/81; On the logical status of sentences in fiction, In: Funktionen des Fiktiven, Poetik und Hermeneutik, Fink, Munchen, 82. *Mailing Add:* Dept of Ger Lang & Lit Princeton Univ Princeton NJ 08540

JUNG, ANTHONY, b Speyer, Ger, Dec 11, 41; US citizen. GERMAN LITERATURE & CULTURE. *Educ:* Univ Ill, Urbana, BA, 64, MA, 67, PhD(Ger), 72. *Prof Exp:* ASSOC PROF GER, UNIV NEBR, OMAHA, 69-, CHMN DEPT, 80- *Mem:* MLA; Midwest Mod Lang Asn; Am Asn Teachers Ger; Am Coun Teachers Foreign Lang. *Res:* German literary history; German, Austrian and Swiss cultural history. *Mailing Add:* Dept of Foreign Lang Univ of Nebr 60th & Dodge Sts Omaha NE 68101

JUNGEMANN, FREDRICK HENRY, b Chicago, Ill, Nov 26, 11. SPANISH, HISPANIC LINGUISTICS. *Educ:* Univ Tex, BA, 33, MA, 40; Columbia Univ, PhD(Romance philol), 52. *Prof Exp:* Teacher Span & hist, High Sch, Falfurrias, Tex, 34-35, teacher, Span, Ger & English, New Braunfels, 35-41; instr Span & Ger, Tex Agr & Mech Col, 41-43; teaching fel Span, Stanford Univ, 47-49; instr, NY Univ, 53-55, Queens Col, NY, 55-57; from asst prof to assoc prof Span, Columbia Univ, 57-71, prof, 71-80; RETIRED. *Mem:* Int Ling Asn. *Res:* Spanish language; Hispanic dialectology; Brazilian Portuguese. *Publ:* Auth, La Teoria del Sustrato y Los Dialectos Hispano-Romances y Gascones, Gredos, Spain, 56. *Mailing Add:* 355 Riverside Dr New York NY 10025

JUNIPER, WALTER HOWARD, b Nelsonville, Ohio, Oct 25, 11. CLASSICS. *Educ:* Ohio State Univ, AB & BS, 33, AM, 34, PhD, 37. *Prof Exp:* Instr class langs, Ohio State Univ, 33-34; prof langs & dean men, Cumberland Col, 37-38; asst prof Latin, Baylor Univ, 38-41, prof Latin & asst dean, 46-49; dean, WTex State Univ, 49-66, acad vpres, 66-71, prof English, 71-74, emer prof, 74-79; RETIRED. *Mem:* Am Philol Asn. *Mailing Add:* Dept English W Tex State Univ Canyon TX 79016

JUNOD, ALFRED E, b Union City, NJ, Feb 23, 16; m 44; c 1. FRENCH. *Educ:* NY Univ, BCS, 36, MA, 47; Univ Buffalo, EdD, 55. *Prof Exp:* Assoc prof French, US Air Force Acad, 59-63; assoc prof, 67-80, EMER ASSOC PROF FRENCH, CLARION STATE COL, 80- *Mailing Add:* Dept of French Clarion State Col Clarion PA 16214

JUNTUNE, THOMAS WILLIAM, b Astoria, Ore, May 27, 40; m 68; c 1. GERMANIC LINGUISTICS. *Educ:* Stanford Univ, AB, 63, MA, 64; Princeton Univ, MA, 66, PhD(ling), 68. *Prof Exp:* Asst prof, 67-71, assoc prof, 71-80, PROF GER, MICH STATE UNIV, 80- *Concurrent Pos:* Res grant, Alexander von Humboldt Found, Ger, 74-75; resident dir jr yr, Freiburg, Ger, 82-83. *Mem:* MLA; Ling Soc Am; Am Asn Teachers Ger; Sem Germanic Philol; Soc Advan Scand Studies. *Res:* Germanic syntax; Germanic phonology; old Icelandic. *Publ:* Auth, The informational value of Germanic loanwords into Finnish, Amsterdamer Beiträge zur älteren Germanistik, 73; Reflexivization and reflexive verbs in old Icelandic, Nordic Lang & Mod Ling, Vol 3, 78; Using parallel Bible translations in teaching the history of the German language, Yrbk Sem Germanic Philol, 80. *Mailing Add:* Dept of Ling & Lang Mich State Univ East Lansing MI 48824

JURADO, JOSE, b Madrid, Spain, Dec 22, 25; m 61; c 1. SPANISH LITERATURE. *Educ:* Univ Madrid, Bachiller, 49, lic, 56, Dr(philos & lett), 63. *Prof Exp:* Asst Latin philol, Univ Madrid, 58-59; prof Span philol & lit, Univ Caldas, Colombia, 60-62; vis asst prof, Univ Chicago, 62-63; asst prof, Univ Va, 63-64; from asst prof to assoc prof, 64-73, PROF SPAN LIT, CARLETON UNIV, 73- *Concurrent Pos:* Can Coun grant, 67. *Mem:* Am Asn Teachers Span & Port. *Res:* Eighteenth century and Old Spanish literature. *Publ:* Auth, Versus: nota filologica, Bol Acad Hist Valle Cauca, Colombia, 65; La imitacion en la poetica de Luzan, Torre, XVII: 113-124; Repercusiones del Pleito con Iriarte en la obra literaria de Forner, Thesaurus, XXIV: 1-53; Fuentes Griegas del De Amicitia, Imp Langa, 68; auth prologue & notes & ed, Los Gramatiocs: Historia Chinesca, Espansa-Calpe, Madrid, 69; El Concepto de la amistad en las obras de Ciceron, Bol Bibly Univ Zulia, 71-72; Dos sonetos espirtuales de Jose de Villarroel imitaciones del No me mueve mi Dios . . ., Bull Hisp, 75; La refundicios final en el Fray gerundiode Campazas, BRAE, LXI: 123-140. *Mailing Add:* Dept of Span Carleton Univ Ottawa ON K1S 5B6 Can

JURICIC, ZELIMIR BOB, b Zagreb, Yugoslavia, Apr 1, 35; Can citizen. RUSSIAN & CROATO-SERBIAN LANGUAGES & LITERATURE. *Educ:* Univ BC, BA, 64, MA, 66; Univ Nottingham, PhD(Russ, Yugoslav drama), 72. *Prof Exp:* Lectr, 66-72, asst prof, 72-81, chmn dept Slavonic & Orient studies, 75-78, ASSOC PROF RUSS & CROATO-SERBIAN LANG & LIT, UNIV VICTORIA, 81- *Mem:* Can Asn Slavists; Am Asn Teachers Slavic & East Europ Lang; Western Slavic Conf; Croatian Philol Soc; Pac Northwest Conf Foreign Lang. *Res:* Russian drama in Yugoslavia; Ivo Andric. *Publ:* Auth, Andric's visions of women in Ex Ponto, Slavic and East Europ J, 23: 233-239; Nasa knjizevnost u svijetu: Americki dio Andriceve sudbine, OKO, VI: 20; O Ruskom utjecaju na razvitak Hrvatskog Narodnog Kazalista i Drame 1874-1914, Kronika, V: 127-135; coauth (with Dr J Kess), Indirect imperatives: An example of indirect speech acts in Serbo-Croatian, Indian J Appl Ling, Vol V, No 2; auth, Osvrt na premijeru drame U Agoniji u Kanadi, In: Dani Hvarskog Kazalista, Miroslav Krleza, 81; Andric's doctorate: A retrospection, Zeitschrift für Balkanologie, XVIII: 21-35; Andric's artistic deformation of the legend: The two faces of Alija Derzelez, Zbornik radova o Ivi Andricu, 81; M Gorki i L Andrejev na pozornici hrvatskog Narodnog Kazalista, Forum, XX: 552-576. *Mailing Add:* Dept of Slavonic Studies Univ of Victoria PO Box 1700 Victoria BC V8W 2Y2 Can

JUSZCZAK, ALBERT S, b Heidelberg, Ger, Sept 24, 47; US citizen; m 68; c 2. SLAVIC LANGUAGES & LITERATURES. *Educ:* Univ Chicago, BA, 68, MA, 69, PhD(Polish lit), 78. *Prof Exp:* Asst to Pres, Kosciuszko Found, 70-74; adjunct lectr Polish & Russ, Hunter Col, 75-77; ASST TO ACAD DEAN ADMIN, MEDGAR EVERS COL, 77- *Mem:* Polish Inst Arts & Sci. *Res:* History of Polish Emigre literature (post-world war two); comparative Slavic literature. *Publ:* Auth, Theater, and Polish theater in the United States, Poetic Press, London, 5/73; transl, Kazimierz Sowinski, Monograms, Sigma Press, 74; auth, A glance at the poetry of Tadeusz Sulkowski, Antemurale, Rome, summer 78. *Mailing Add:* 45 Lancaster Ave Brooklyn NY 11223

K

KABAKOFF, JACOB, b New York, NY, Mar 20, 18; m 44; c 3. HEBREW LANGUAGE & LITERATURE. *Educ:* Yeshiva Univ, BA, 38; Jewish Theol Sem, MHL, 44, DHL, 58. *Hon Degrees:* DD, Jewish Theol Sem, 72. *Prof Exp:* Asst rabbi, Har Zion Temple, Philadelphia, 44-46; rabbi, B'nai Israel of Olney, 44-48; educ dir, Flatbush Jewish Ctr, 48-50; mem ed staff, Encycl Hebraica, Jerusalem, 50-52; prof Hebrew & dean, Cleveland Col Jewish Studies, 52-68; assoc prof Hebrew, 68-72, PROF HEBREW, LEHMAN COL, 72- *Concurrent Pos:* Am Philos Soc grant, 67; Mem Found Jewish Cult grant, 67-68; ed, Jewish Bk Annual, Jewish Bk Coun, 77-; Asn Prof of Hebrew (pres, 74-76). *Mem:* Am Acad Jewish Res; Am Jewish Hist Soc; World Union Jewish Studies; Nat Orgn Hebrew Cult (vpres, 77-). *Res:* Current Israeli literature; American Hebrew literatary and cultural history. *Publ:* Auth, Pioneers of American Hebrew Literature (in Hebrew), Yavneh, Tel Aviv, 66; contribr, Hebrew Sources of American Jewish History, In: A Bicentennial Festschrift for Jacob Rader Marcus, Ktav, 76; The Arab Image in Hebrew Fiction, Hebrew Studies, 77; auth, Seekers and Stalwarts (in Hebrew), Mass, Jerusalem, Israel, 78; Judah David Eisenstein's Me'ah Sefarin Muvharim, Hebrew Studies, 81; co-ed, Sefer Hadoar (in Hebrew), 82. *Mailing Add:* Div Hebraic & Judaic Studies Lehman Col Bronx NY 10468

KAC, MICHAEL BENEDICT, b Ithaca, NY, Oct 19, 43. LINGUISTICS. *Educ:* Haverford Col, BA, 65; Univ Pa, AM, 67; Univ Calif, Los Angeles, PhD(ling), 72. *Prof Exp:* Asst prof, 72-77, ASSOC PROF LING, UNIV MINN, 77- *Concurrent Pos:* Assoc ed, Language, Ling Soc Am J, 76-80. *Mem:* Ling Soc Am; Asn Comput Ling; Cognitive Sci Soc; NY Acad Sci. *Res:* Syntax; semantics; linguistic metatheory. *Publ:* Auth, Action and result: Two aspects of predication in English, In: Syntax and Semantics I, Acad Press, 72; Clauses of saying and the interpretation of because, Language, 72; On composite predication in English, In: Syntax and Semantics VI, Acad Press, 76; Corepresentation of Grammatical Structure, Univ Minn, 78; Corepresentational grammar, Syntax and Semantics 13, Acad Press, 80; On grammatical ambiguity, Evidence and Argumentation in Linguistics, DeGruyter, 80. *Mailing Add:* Dept of Ling Univ of Minn 320 16th Ave SE Minneapolis MN 55455

KACHRU, BRAJ BEHARI, b Srinagar, Kashmir, May 15, 32; m 65; c 1. NON-NATIVE ENGLISHES, SOCIOLINGUISTICS. *Educ:* Jammu & Kashmir Univ, BA, 52; Allahabad Univ, MA, 55; Edinburgh Univ, dipl, 59, PhD(ling), 61. *Prof Exp:* Lectr ling, Lucknow Univ, 62-63; res assoc, 63-64, from asst prof to assoc prof, 64-70, head dept, 69-79, PROF LING, UNIV ILL, URBANA, 70-, COORDR, DIV APPLIED LING, 74- *Concurrent Pos:* Mem SAsia lang comt, Comt Instnl Coop, 65-; consult, Dict English Lang, Random House, 66; Am Inst Indian Studies fac fel, 67-68; chmn comt varieties English, Asn Commonwealth Lit & Lang Studies, 68; assoc Ctr Advan Studies, Univ Ill, 71-72; ed, Papers on SAsian Ling, 73; consult, Ford Found, 74 & 75; mem lang comt, SAsia Regional Coun, 77-; dir, Ling Inst Ling Soc Am, 78; chmn, Int Conf SAsian Lang & Ling, 80- *Mem:* Philol Soc, Eng; Ling Soc Am, Ling Soc India; Ling Asn Can & US. *Res:* South Asian English and linguistics; Kashmiri language and literature; varieties of English. *Publ:* Auth, English in South Asia, Current Trends in Ling, 69; co-ed, Current Trends in Stylistics, Ling Res, 72; Issues in Linguistics: Papers in Honor of Henry and Renee Kahane, Univ Ill, 73; ed, Dimensions of bilingualism, Unit Foreign Lang Study & Res, Univ Ill, 76; co-ed, Aspects of sociolinguistics in South Asia, Int J Sociol Lang, 78; Kashmiri Literature, 81; The Indianization of English: The English Language in India, 82; ed, The Other Tongue: English Across Cultures, 82. *Mailing Add:* Dept of Ling Univ of Ill Urbana IL 61801

KACHRU, YAMUNA, b Purulia, WBengal, India, Mar 5, 33; m 65; c 2. LINGUISTICS. *Educ:* Bihar Univ, BA, 53; Patna Univ, MA, 55; Univ London, PhD(ling), 65. *Prof Exp:* Lectr Hindi, Ranchi Women's Col, India, 56-58; lectr, Sch Orient & African Studies, Univ London, 59-65; asst res prof ling, 65-66, asst prof ling & English, 67-68, assoc prof ling, English & Hindi, 68-71, PROF LING & ENGLISH AS SECOND LANG, UNIV ILL, URBANA, 71- *Concurrent Pos:* Rockefeller fel, Deccan Col, 58-59; Am Inst Indian Studies fac fels, 67-68 & 71-72; assoc, Ctr Advan Study, Univ Ill, 75. *Mem:* Ling Soc Am; Am Asn Appl Ling. *Res:* Generative grammars of South Asian languages; applied linguistics; contrastive analysis. *Publ:* Auth, On the semantics of the causative construction in Hindi-Urdu, In: The Grammar of Causative Constructions, Syntax and Semantics ser VI, Acad Press, 76; On relative clause formation in Hindi-Urdu, Ling, 207: 5-26; Conjunct verbs: Verbs or verb phrases?, In: Proceeding of the XIIth Interntional Congress of Linguists, Innsbruck, 79; Notes on grammatical categories and participant roles in Hindi-Urdu sentences, In: Vol IV, Linguistic and Literary in honor of Archibald A Hill, Mouton, The Hague, 79; The quotative in South Asian languages, South Asian Lang Anal, 1: 63-78; Pragmatics and verb serialization in Hindi-Urdu, In: Studies in the Linguistic Sciences, 9:2; Aspects of Hindi Grammar, Manohar Publ, India, 80; The syntax of Dakhini: A study in language variation and language change, In: South Asia as a Linguistic Area, Osmania Univ Publ Ling (in press). *Mailing Add:* Dept of Ling Univ of Ill Urbana IL 61801

KADIC, ANTE, b Poljica, Groatia, Dalamtia, Jan 18, 10; US citizen. SLAVIC LANGUAGES & LITERATURE. *Educ:* Gregorian Univ, PhD, 35; Univ Geneva, MA, 45; Ecole Hautes Etudes Int, Geneva, Switz, dipl, 47. *Prof Exp:* Admin & finance officer, UN Relief & Works Agency, Beirut, 49-52; lectr Serbo-Croatian, Univ Calif, Berkeley, 53-59; assoc prof Slavic lang & lit, 60-68, prof, 68-80, EMER PROF SLAVIC LANG & LIT, IND UNIV, BLOOMINGTON, 80- *Res:* Contemporary South Slavic literature. *Publ:* Auth, Croatian Reader with Vocabulary, 60, Contemporary Croatian Literature, 60, Contemporary Serbian Literature, 64, From Croatian Renaissance to Yugoslav Socialism (essays), 69 & co-ed, Krizanic Russophile and Ecumenic Visionary, 76, Mouton, The Hague; auth, Domovinska rijec (lit & hist essays), Barcelona, 78. *Mailing Add:* Dept of Slavic Lang & Lit Ind Univ Bloomington IN 47401

KADIR, DJELAL, b Cyprus, Jan 21, 46; m 69; c 1. LATIN AMERICAN & COMPARATIVE LITERATURE. *Educ:* Yale Univ, BA, 69; Univ NMex, PhD(Ibero-Am studies), 72. *Prof Exp:* Vis instr Port, Univ Nev, Reno, 71-72; vis lectr Span, Univ NMex, 72-73; asst prof, 73-76, chmn, Dept Span, 73-80, ASSOC PROF SPAN & COMP LIT, PURDUE UNIV, WEST LAFAYETTE, 76- *Concurrent Pos:* Contribr ed, Handbook Latin Am Studies & assoc ed, Purdue Univ Monographs Romance Lang, 77- *Mem:* Am Comp Lit Asn; Int Comp Lit Asn; MLA. *Res:* Spanish American literature; 20th century prose fiction--comparative; literary theory and criticism. *Publ:* Auth, Nostalgia or nihilism: pop art and the new Spanish American novel, J Span Studies: XX Century, 75; Stalking the oxen of the sun and felling the sacred cows: Joyce's Ulysses and Cabrera Infante's Three Trapped Tigers, Latin Am Lit Rev, 76; ed, Triple Espera: Novelas Cortas de Hispanoamerica, Harcourt, 76; auth, Another sense of the past: Henry James' The Aspern Papers and Carlos Fuentes' Aura, Rev de Litt Comparee, 76; Same voices, other tombs: structures of Mexican Gothic, Studies 20th Century Lit, 77; Juan Carlos Onetti, Twayne, 77; Intimations of terror in Borges' Metaphysics, Symposium, 77; The architectonic principle of Cien anos de soledad and the Vichian theory of history, Ky Romance Quart, 78. *Mailing Add:* Dept of Foreign Lang & Lit Purdue Univ West Lafayette IN 47907

KADLER, ERIC H, b Pilsen, Czech, May 17, 22; US citizen; m 52; c 2. FOREIGN LANGUAGES. *Educ:* Ger Acad Commerce, Pilsen, dipl, 42; Univ Prague, dipl, 48; Univ Mich, MA, 56, PhD, 59. *Prof Exp:* Instr French, St Christopher's Sch, Hove, Eng, 48-51; asst prof French & Span, Ohio Univ, 59-60; assoc prof French & Russ, Lycoming Col, 60-62, prof French lit, 63-70; PROF FRENCH LIT & CHMN DEPT, CENT MICH UNIV, 70- *Mem:* MLA; Am Asn Teachers Fr; NEA; Am Coun Teaching Foreign Lang. *Res:* French literature of the 18th century; applied linguistics; French theater since the 17th century. *Publ:* Auth, Literary figures in French plays, Fr Rev, 1/61; coauth, Some notes on foreign language teaching in other countries, Mod Lang J, 11/64; auth, Linguistics and Teaching of Foreign Languages, Am Bk Co, 69; Literary Figures in French Drama, 1784-1834, Nijhoff, The Hague, 69; L'Utilisation des theorie linguistiques dans l'enseignement des langues, Etudes Ling Appliquee, 73; Articulatory economy in present-day-Spanish, Can Mod Lang Rev, 10/79; Vowel reduction in French, Spanish, and German, 6th Lang Forum, 79. *Mailing Add:* Dept of Foreign Lang Cent Mich Univ Mt Pleasant MI 48858

KAEGI, WALTER EMIL, JR, Byzantine & Roman History. See Vol I

KAES, ANTON J, b Eggenfelden, WGer, Feb 4, 45; Ger citizen; m 71; c 1. GERMAN LITERATURE, COMPARATIVE LITERATURE. *Educ:* Univ Munich, MA, 70; Stanford Univ, PhD(Ger, comp lit), 73. *Prof Exp:* Asst prof Ger & comp lit, Univ Calif, Irvine, 73-77, assoc prof, 77-81; ASSOC PROF GER, UNIV CALIF, BERKELEY, 81- *Concurrent Pos:* Vis prof Ger, Univ Calif, Berkeley, 78; Rockefeller Found Humanities fel, 78-79. *Mem:* MLA; Am Asn Teachers Ger; Lessing Soc. *Res:* Modernism; literary theory and criticism; interdisciplinary and comparative studies of drama and film. *Publ:* Auth, Expressionismus in Amerika: Rezeption und Innovation, Max Niemeyer, Tübingen, 75; co-ed, Literatur für viele 1, Vandenhoeck & Ruprecht, 75; auth, Brecht und der Amerikanismus im Theater der 20er Jahre: Unliterarische Tradition und Publikumsbezug, Sprache im technischen Zeitalter, 75; contribr, Dokumentarismus-Fiktionalität-Politik: Anmerkungen zum deutschen und amerikanischen, Amerikanisches Drama und Theater, Erich Schmidt, 78; ed, Kino-Debatte: Literatur und Film 1909-1929, Max Niemeyer, Tübingen & Deutscher Taschenbuchverlag, 78. *Mailing Add:* Dept of Ger Univ of Calif Berkeley CA 94720

KAGAN-KANS, EVA, b Tientsin, China, Dec 23, 28; US citizen; div; c 1. RUSSIAN LITERATURE. *Educ:* NY Univ, BA, 61; Univ Calif, Berkeley, MA, 63, PhD(Slavic lang & lit), 68. *Prof Exp:* Assoc Russ, Univ Calif, Berkeley, 64-65; asst prof Russ lit, Univ Rochester, 66-68; asst prof Slavic lang & lit, 68-71, dean women's affairs, 72-75, ASSOC PROF SLAVIC LIT, IND UNIV, BLOOMINGTON, 71- *Concurrent Pos:* Mem fel selection comt, Woodrow Wilson Found, 70-; Int Res & Exchange Found sr scholar grant, USSR, 73; Am Coun Learned Soc & Soviet Acad Sci grants, 78 & 82. *Mem:* Am Asn Advan Slavic Studies; Am Asn Teachers Slavic & EEurop Lang. *Res:* Russian and West European literary relations; 19th century Russian lyric poetry; 19th century Russian novel. *Publ:* Auth, Fate and fantasy: A study of Turgenev's fantastic stories, Slavic Rev, 12/69; Metaphysics of an artist, Cahiers Monde Russe & Sovietique, winter, 72; Hamlet and Don Quixote: Turgenev's Ambivalent Vision, Mouton, The Hague, 74, 2nd ed, 79; Lermonfor and Constant, Neohelicon, IX, 82; Turgener and Flaubert, Acted du Congres aur Turgenieff, 3/82. *Mailing Add:* Dept of Slavics Ind Univ Bloomington IN 47401

KAHANE, HENRY, b Berlin, Ger, Nov 2, 02; US citizen; m 31; c 2. GENERAL & ROMANCE LINGUISTICS. *Educ:* Univ Berlin, PhD, 30. *Hon Degrees:* DLitt, Univ Ill, 77. *Prof Exp:* Asst, Univ Berlin, 32; lectr, Univ Florence, 35-38; teaching fel comp lit, Univ Southern Calif, 39-41; from instr to assoc prof, Span & ling, 41-49, dir univ prog ling, 60-62, acting dir Ctr Advan Studies, 71-72, PROF SPAN & LING, UNIV ILL, URBANA, 49-, CTR ADVAN STUDIES, 68- *Concurrent Pos:* Guggenheim fels, 55-56, 62-63; mem, Am Sch Class Studies, Athens; assoc ed, Romance Philol; consult spec proj, Nat Found for Humanities. *Honors & Awards:* Silver Award, Acad Athens, 76. *Mem:* MLA; Ling Soc Am; Int Arthurian Soc; Am Name Soc; Wolfram von Eschenbach Gesellschaft. *Res:* Mediterranean linguistics; cultural linguistics; Hellenistic survivals in Western culture. *Publ:* Auth, Byzantium and the West, In: Language, 76 & Graeca et Romanica: Scripta Selecta, 2 vols, 79 & 81, Hakkert, Amsterdam. *Mailing Add:* Dept of Ling Univ of Ill Urbana IL 61801

KAHN, ARTHUR DAVID, b South Norwalk, Conn, Sept 21, 20. CLASSICAL LITERATURES, HISTORY. *Educ:* Trenton State Col, BS, 40; Rutgers Univ, New Brunswick, MA, 42; NY Univ, PhD(comp lit), 63. *Prof Exp:* Instr English & classics, NY Univ, 62-63; asst prof English, State Univ NY Col Buffalo, 63-65; asst prof classics, State Univ NY Col Buffalo, 65-66; chmn dept classics, Brock Univ, 66-73, prof, 66-72; DIR, SULMONA INST ITAL CIVILIZATION, 81- *Concurrent Pos:* O'Connor prof lit, Colgate Univ, 72; prof, Col Yr in Athens, Greece, 73. *Mem:* Am Philol Asn; Archaeol Inst Am. *Res:* Fifth century drama; late Republican Rome; Byron. *Publ:* Ed, Writer and Critic: An Anthology of Essays by Gyorgy Lukacs, Grosset, 71. *Mailing Add:* 41 Pierrepont St Brooklyn NY 11201

KAHN, LISA M, b Berlin, Ger; nat US; c 2. GERMAN. *Educ:* Univ Wash, BS, 51; Univ Heidelberg, Ger, PhD(psychol, Ger), 53. *Prof Exp:* Asst prof, 68-76, assoc prof, 76-81, PROF GER, TEX SOUTHERN UNIV, 81- *Concurrent Pos:* Guest lectr Ger, Univ NMex, 75; res stipend, Tex Consortium Int Studies, 77; Fulbright Hays Travel grant, 80, Nat Endowment for Humanities grant, 81 & Alexander von Humboldt res grant, 82. *Mem:* MLA; Am Asn Teachers Ger; Soc Ger Am Studies; Western Asn Ger Studies. *Res:* Women in German; GDR-literature; German-American culture and literature. *Publ:* Auth, Klopfet an so Wird euch nicht aufgetan, Bläschke, Darmstadt, 75; The proletariat in literature and art, Tex State Univ Res J, 76; Orpheus in the East, Mod Lang Quart, 1/77; auth, Feuersteine, Strom, Zurich, 78; . . . and remember the ladies, Schatzkammer, Univ Tex Arlington, 7/78; ed, Deutschameri Kanische Autorinnen, Fink, Munich, 79; auth, Denver im Fruhling, 80 & Utahs Geheimnisse, 81, Berlin; Mother's tongue, In: Women Writer in the US, Soc Ger-Am Studies, 82. *Mailing Add:* Dept of Foreign Lang & Lit Tex Southern Univ 3201 Wheeler Ave Houston TX 77004

KAHN, LOTHAR, b Rehlingen, Saar, June 1, 22; US citizen; m 45; c 2. FOREIGN LANGUAGES. *Educ:* City Col New York, BA, 43; Columbia Univ, MA, 45 PhD(French), 54. *Prof Exp:* Instr French, Ger & Latin, Ohio State Univ, 45-46; from asst prof to assoc prof mod lang, 46-57, PROF MOD LANG, CENT CONN STATE COL, 57- *Honors & Awards:* Col Distinguished Serv Award, 74. *Mem:* Am Asn Teachers Ger. *Res:* The Jew in literature; German-Jewish literature and history during emancipation era; Weimar literature and German literature in exile. *Publ:* Auth, Mirrors of the Jewish Mind, A S Barnes, 68; coauth, Elementary Conversational German, Am Bk Co, 69; Stimmen aus deutschen Landen, Van Nostrand, 72; auth, Der arge Weg der Erkenntnis, In: Lion Feuchtwanger, Hennessey & Ingalls, 72; G Hauptmann--der Ketzer von Soana, Holt, 73; Insight and Action: The Life of Lion Feuchtwanger, Fairleigh Dickinson Univ, 75; Liou Feuchtwanger, Deutsche Exilliteratur seit 1933, (Kalifornien), Francke, 76; Liou Feuchtwanger: The hazards of exile, Exile: The Writer's Experience, Univ NC Press, 82. *Mailing Add:* Dept of Mod Lang Cent Conn State Col New Britain CT 06050

KAHN, LUDWIG WERNER, b Berlin, Ger, Oct 18, 10. GERMAN & COMPARATIVE LITERATURE. *Educ:* Univ London, MA, 36; Sorbonne, dipl, 31; Univ Berne, PhD, 34. *Prof Exp:* Asst lectr, Univ Col, Univ London, 34-36; instr, Univ Rochester, 37-40; instr, Bryn Mawr Col, 40-42; mem staff, Strategic Index Latin Am, Yale Univ, 42-43; from instr to asst prof, Vassar Col, 43-47; from asst prof to prof & chmn dept Ger, City Col New York, 47-67; prof, 67-73, Gebhard prof, 73-79, EMER GEBHARD PROF GER, COLUMBIA UNIV, 79- *Concurrent Pos:* Goethe Bicentennial lectr, Smith Col & Am Int Col, 49; Fund Advan Educ fel, 51-52; Fulbright lectr & guest prof, Tech Univ Stuttgart, 59-60; vis prof, Yale Univ, 68-69 & 78; Guggenheim Found fel, 69-70; Fulbright-Hays sr res fel, Ger, 69-70; assoc ed, Germanic Rev; vis prof, Grad Ctr, City Univ New York, 71. *Honors & Awards:* Grand Cross Order of Merit, Ger Fed Repub, 75. *Mem:* MLA; Am Asn Teachers Ger; Germanistic Soc Am. *Res:* Comparative literature of the 18th century; classical and Romantic period in Germany. *Publ:* Auth, Shakespeare's Sonette in Deutschland, Gotthelf, Berne, 35; Social Ideals in German Literature, Columbia Univ, 38; coauth, Syllabus and Guide, Social Humanities, City Col New York, 62; auth, Literatur und Glaubenskrise, Kohlhammer, Stuttgart, 64 & Ital transl, Citta nuova editrice, Roma, 78. *Mailing Add:* Dept of Ger Columbia Univ New York NY 10027

KAIL, ANDREE FOURCADE, b Carpentras, France, Jan 23, 20; nat US; m 48; c 2. FRENCH. *Educ:* Univ Paris, Lic es Lett, 41, dipl, 43, Agregee, 45; Tulane Univ, PhD, 55. *Prof Exp:* Prof hist & geog, Lycee de Metz, France, 45; instr French, Southwestern La Inst, 45-47; instr, Tulane Univ, 55-56; from asst prof to assoc prof, 56-67, chmn dept, 66-70, fac fels, 61, 70-71, dir jr year abroad in Bordeaux, France, 63-64 & 71-72, PROF FRENCH, UNIV COLO, 67-, CHMN DEPT, 72- *Concurrent Pos:* Fulbright travel grant, 81. *Honors & Awards:* French Govt Award, 53. *Mem:* MLA; Am Asn Teachers Fr; Rocky Mountain Mod Lang Asn; Soc Rencesvals; Alliance Francaise. *Res:* Medieval theatre. *Publ:* Auth, The transformation of Comus' heroes . . . , Educ Theatre J, 10/61; Note sur un passage de La vengeance Jhesuchrist d'Eustache Marcade, Rev Etudes Juives Hist Judaica, 7-12/62; Note sur le theatre de Fontenelle, Fr Rev, 12/62; The Sophoclean myth in Henri Gheon's Oedipe, Fr Lit Ser, Vol III, Univ SC, 76. *Mailing Add:* Dept of French Univ Univ of Colo Boulder CO 80302

KAISER, GRANT E, b Kitchener, Ont, Aug 6, 26; m 50; c 2. ROMANCE LANGUAGES. *Educ:* Waterloo Col, BA, 49; Univ Western Ont, MA, 50; Brown Univ, PhD, 57. *Prof Exp:* Lectr, Carlton Univ, 55-56; from instr to assoc prof, 56-65, acting chmn, 59-60, chmn dept, 62-71, PROF ROMANCE LANG, EMORY UNIV, 65- *Concurrent Pos:* Am Philos Soc res grant, 65. *Mem:* Am Asn Teachers Fr; MLA; Am Coun Teaching Foreign Lang. *Res:* French novel since the Revolution; French-Canadian novel; Roger Martin du Gard. *Publ:* Auth, Roger Martin du Gard's Jean Barois: An experiment in novelistic form, Symposium, summer 60; Giono's Solitude de la pitie, Explicator, 4/61; Form and substance in language teaching, Fr Rev, 1/64; Rogert Martin eu Gard devant la critque, Studi Francesi, 5/76; The anti-cartesian context of Gilbert Durand, In: French Literary Criticism, Univ SC, 77; ed, Fiction, Form, Experience, Ed France-Quebec, Montreal, 77. *Mailing Add:* Dept of Romance Lang Emory Univ Atlanta GA 30322

KAISER, GUNDA S, b Chicago, Ill, Oct 30, 22. FOREIGN LANGUAGES. *Educ:* Northwestern Univ, BA, 44; Univ Wis, MA, 49, PhD, 58; Univ Madrid, dipl, 50; Univ Valencia, dipl, 60; Univ Santander, dipl, 62 & 80. *Prof Exp:* Instr Span & Ger, Wilson Col, 44-45, from instr to asst prof Span, 45-54; assoc prof Span & Ger, 58-59, assoc prof Span, 59-62, chmn dept mod lang, 63-65, chmn dept Span, 65-77, chmn div lang & lit, 73-77, PROF SPAN, ALMA COL, 62-, CHMN DEPT FOREIGN LANG, 77- *Concurrent Pos:* Transl, Chambersburg English Co, 44-51; textbook consult, Ginn & Co, 62. *Mem:* MLA; Am Asn Teachers Span & Port; Comediantes; Cent States Mod Lang Asn; Midwest Mod Lang Asn. *Res:* Spanish and German language and literature; Golden Age drama; 20th century Spanish literature. *Publ:* Auth & transl, Several Poems of Gabriela Mistral, Greenriver Press, 75; The Penquin Book of Women Poets, 78; News of the Universe, Bly, 80. *Mailing Add:* Chmn Dept of Foreign Lang Alma Col Alma MI 48801

KAISER, HARTMUT MICHAEL, b Quezaltenango, Guatemala, Sept 27, 33; US citizen; m 68; c 2. GERMAN LANGUAGE & LITERATURE. *Educ:* Brown Univ, PhD(Ger), 68. *Prof Exp:* From instr to asst prof Ger, Brown Univ, 64-71; asst prof, 68-71, ASSOC PROF GER, CLARK UNIV, 74- *Mem:* AAUP; MLA; Am Asn Teachers Ger; Hoffmann Soc. *Res:* Literature of the Goethe period; relation of literature and music. *Publ:* Auth, Klingers Geschichte Raphaels de Aquillas, In: Festschrift Für Detlev W Schumann, Delp, Munich, 70; Zur Struktur von Klingers Faust, Jahrbuch Freien Deut Hochstifts, 70; Mozarts Don Giovanni und ETA Hoffmanns Don Juan, Mitteilungen der ETA Hoffmann-Gesellschaft, 75; Zu Mörikes Mozart-Novelle, Jahrbuch des Freien Deut Hochstifts, 77. *Mailing Add:* Dept of Foreign Lang & Lit Clark Univ Worcester MA 01610

KAISER, LEO MAX, b St Louis, Mo, Dec 5, 18; m 45; c 6. CLASSICAL PHILOLOGY. *Educ:* St Louis Univ, AB, 40; Univ Ill, AM, 41, PhD(Greek hagiography), 43. *Prof Exp:* Res asst, Univ Ill, 43-44, 45-46, instr classics, 44-45; from instr to asst prof, St Louis Univ, 46-52; asst prof Ger & chmn dept classics, St Joseph's Col, Pa, 52-54; asst prof classics, 54-59, assoc prof class philol, 59-65, PROF CLASS PHILOL, LOYOLA UNIV, 65- *Mem:* Am Philol Asn; Medieval Acad Am; MLA; Am Class League; Int Soc for Promoting Neo-Latin Studies. *Res:* Literary aspects of classical literature; classical Americana; 18th century American journalism. *Publ:* Auth, Thoreau's Translation of Aeschylus' Seven Against Thebes, Emerson Soc, 60; Selections from Tibullus, Loyola Univ Bookstore, 64; coauth, Index Verborum in Ciceronis Thetorica, Univ Ill, 64; John Quincy Adams and his Translation of Juvenal 13, Proc Am Philos Soc, 70; The earliest verse of the New World, Renaissance Quart, 1/72; Tercentenary of an oration, Harvard Libr Bull, 73; auth, Thirteen early American Latin elgies, Early Am Lit, 74; Carmen gratitudinis, Humanistica Lovaniensia, 77. *Mailing Add:* Dept of Class Studies Loyola Univ Chicago IL 60626

KALBFLEISCH, HERBERT KARL, b Zurich, Ont, May 26, 02; m 28; c 2. GERMAN LANGUAGE & LITERATURE. *Educ:* Univ Western Ont, BA, 28; NY Univ, MA, 30; Univ Mich, MA, 50, PhD, 53. *Prof Exp:* From instr to assoc prof, 31-50, PROF GER, UNIV WESTERN ONT, 50- *Mem:* MLA; Asn Can Univ Teachers Ger (pres, 68-69); fel Int Inst Arts & Lett; Nat Carl Schurz Asn. *Res:* History of the Germans in Canada; German literature, especially the classical period and Romanticism. *Publ:* Auth, German Grammar for Science Students, Copp, Clark, Can, 57; The History of the Pioneer German Language Press of Ontario, Canada, 1835-1918, C J Fahle, Münster & Univ Toronto, 68. *Mailing Add:* Dept of Ger Univ Col Univ Western Ont London ON N6A 3K7 Can

KALBOUSS, GEORGE, b New York, NY, June 21, 39; m 62; c 2. RUSSIAN LANGUAGE & LITERATURE, DRAMA. *Educ:* Columbia Univ, AB, 60, AM, 61; NY Univ, PhD(Slavic lang), 68. *Prof Exp:* Vis instr Russ, Dartmouth Col, 66; instr, Purdue Univ, 66-67; asst prof, Dartmouth Col, 67-73, asst dean, 68-73; ASSOC PROF SLAVIC LANG & LIT, OHIO STATE UNIV, 73- *Honors & Awards:* Distinguished Teaching Award, Ohio State Univ, 77. *Mem:* Am Asn Teachers Slavic & E Europ Lang; Am Asn Advan Slavic Studies. *Res:* Works of Fiodor Sologub; poetry and prose of Russian symbolism; computer-assisted instruction. *Publ:* Auth, Stylistics in the curriculum of second-year Russian, spring 71 & The plays of Nikolai Evreinov, fall 72, Russ Lang J; Computer assisted instruction in the study of Russian, Slavic & E Europ J, spring 74; Armenian riddles and their offspring, Radio Erevan, Slavic & E Europ J, fall 77; contribr, Birth of modern Russian drama, In: Banff '74 Proceedings, Slavica, 77; Russian Culture: An Outline, OSU Libr Publ Comt, 82. *Mailing Add:* Dept of Slavic Lang & Lit Ohio State Univ Columbus OH 43210

KALIDOVA, THEODORE B, b Erie, Pa, July 10, 30; m 52; c 5. ROMANCE LANGUAGES, EDUCATION. *Educ:* Wheaton Col, Ill, BA, 53; La State Univ, MA, 56; Okla State Univ, EdD, 67. *Prof Exp:* Instr English, Col Libertad, Trujillo, Peru, 53-54; adminr, La State Univ Armed Forces Prog, CZ, 56-57, dir div Latin Am rels, 57-62; asst prof Span & advan foreign studies, Okla State Univ, 62-67; ASSOC PROF SPAN, UNIV GA, 67- *Concurrent Pos:* US Dept State & Nat Asn Foreign Studies Affairs study grant, SEAsia & Europe, 65. *Mem:* Nat Asn Foreign Studies Affairs; Am Asn Teachers Span & Port; Am Coun Teaching Foreign Lang. *Publ:* Auth, The importance and use of oral language in modern foreign language departments, Mod Lang J, 12/67; coauth, The audio-motor unit: A listening comprehension strategy that works, 5/71 & Teaching culture through the audio-motor unit, 10/72, Foreign Lang Ann; auth, Foreign Language Education: A Reappraisal, Nat Textbook Co, 72. *Mailing Add:* 625 Forest Rd Athens GA 30601

KALLY, KONSTANTIN MICHAEL, b Russia, July 27, 14; US citizen; m 44; c 2. RUSSIAN LANGUAGE. *Educ:* Pedag Inst, Russia, dipl Russ lang & lit, 41; Ind Univ, MAT, 61. *Prof Exp:* Teaching assoc Russ, Air Force Lang Prog, Ind Univ, 59-60; asst prof, 61-71, assoc prof, 71-80, EMER PROF RUSS, FRANKLIN & MARSHALL COL, 80- *Concurrent Pos:* Vis lectr Russ, summer Slavic workshop, Ind Univ, 60-70; co-ed, Vedomosti, 66-76; mem bd dir, Congr Russ Am, 73-79; ed, Russian-American, Congr Russ Am, New York, 73-; adj prof Russ, Franklin & Marshall Col, 80-81. *Mem:* AAUP; Am Asn Teachers Slavic & EEurop Lang. *Res:* Russian writers who are little known or unknown to the West. *Publ:* Auth numerous articles on general topics in Russian newspapers and magazines. *Mailing Add:* Dept of Russ Franklin & Marshall Col Lancaster PA 17604

KALTENBACH, PHILIP EDWARD, b Baltimore, Md, Feb 19, 21; m 47; c 3. LATIN, ANCIENT HISTORY. *Educ:* Loyola Col, AB, 42; Johns Hopkins Univ, PhD, 48. *Prof Exp:* From asst prof to assoc prof, 48-55, actg dean students Day Div, 69-70, dean students Eve & Grad Div, 70-73, PROF CLASSICS, LOYOLA COL, MD, 55-, DEAN FRESHMEN, 73- *Concurrent Pos:* Consult, US Dept Health, Educ & Welfare, 67. *Mem:* Am Philol Asn. *Res:* Ancient history; philology; Latin literature. *Mailing Add:* 4501 N Charles St Baltimore MD 21210

KALWIES, HOWARD H, b Wanne-Eickel, Ger, Mar 21, 36; US citizen; m 64; c 5. FRENCH RENAISSANCE LITERATURE & CIVILIZATION. *Educ:* Brigham Young Univ, BA, 63, MA, 64; Univ Ky, PhD(French lit), 69. *Prof Exp:* Assoc prof, 67-80, PROF FRENCH RENAISSANCE LIT, WESTERN ILL UNIV, 80- *Honors & Awards:* Ludwig Vogelstein Found Award, 78. *Mem:* Am Asn Teachers Fr; Renaissance Soc Am; Asn Humanisme et Renaissance. *Res:* French Renaissance poetry; medieval and Renaissance civilization of France; music and poetry in medieval and Renaissance France. *Publ:* Hugues Salel and Francois Rabelais, 72 & Hugues Salel and Pierre de Ronsard, 73-74, Romance Notes; Marot's De la Ville de Lyon: the problem of authenticity, Bibliot Humanisme et Renaissance, 73-74; Poetry and music in fifteenth and sixteenth-century France, Centerpoint, 76; The first verse translation of the Iliad in Renaissance France, bibliotheque d'Humanisme et Renaissance, 78; Clement Marot and Hugues Salel, Romance Notes, 78; Hugues Salel: A Study of His Life and Works, 79. *Mailing Add:* Dept of Foreign Lang Western Ill Univ Macomb IL 61455

KAMINSKA, ALEXANDRA BARBARA, b Brzezany, Poland; US citizen. FRENCH, COMPARATIVE LITERATURE. *Educ:* Ecole d'interpretes, Geneva, Switzerland, Translator's degree, 56; Univ Lwow, Poland, MA, 38; Univ Maryland, PhD(comp lit), 72. *Prof Exp:* Prof foreign lang, Univ Lwow, US, 45-46, Gdansk Higher Sch Visual Arts and Sopot, Highers Sch of Music, 54-55 & Poznan Higher Inst Econ, 55-56; instr foreign lang, Monmouth Col, 60-63; assoc prof French & comp lit, Univ Wis, Stevens Point, 63-79; RETIRED. *Mem:* MLA; Am Comp Lit Asn; Independent Journalists, Lett to Polish People; Wis Asn Foreign Lang Teachers; Wis Acad Sci, Arts and Lett. *Res:* Literature and the other arts, classical and anti-classical trends; French writers in search of truth v/s acceptance of the world as it is; the history of comedy in world literature. *Publ:* Auth, La Valeur des pronoms personnels en et y dans Aucassin et Nicolette, Cantefable du Moyen Age, Revue de Linguistique Romane I-VI tome XXIX; translr, Philippe Quinault's Comedy The Indiscreet Lover, or The Master Blunderer, Exposition Press; contribr, Dictionary of Literary Themes and Motifs, Greenwood Press. *Mailing Add:* 1527 N Second Drive Stevens Point WI 54481

KAMINSKI, EDMUND JOSEPH, b Minersville, Pa, Aug 19, 25. FOREIGN LANGUAGES. *Educ:* Temple Univ, BA, 48; Yale Univ, MA, 49; Princeton Univ, MA, 54. *Prof Exp:* Instr Ger, Lawrence Col, 49-51; part-time instr, Princeton Univ, 52-54; instr, Pa State Univ, 55-56; instr, Rice Univ, 56-61; from asst prof to assoc prof, 61-60, PROF MOD LANG, MARIETTA COL, 70-, CHMN DEPT, 73- *Mem:* Am Asn Teachers Ger; Nat Asn Lang Lab Dirs. *Res:* Seventeenth century literature. *Mailing Add:* Dept of Mod Lang Marietta Col Marietta OH 45750

KAMINSKY, AMY KATZ, b New York, NY, Apr 13, 47; m 69; c 2. LATIN AMERICAN LITERATURE. *Educ:* Queens Col, City Univ NY, BA, 67; Rutgers Univ, MA, 69; Pa State Univ, PhD(Spanish), 75. *Prof Exp:* ASST PROF SPANISH, STATE UNIV NY, COL AT OSWEGO, 76- *Mem:* MLA; Am Asn Teachers Span & Port; Nat Women's Studies Asn; Women's Caucus for Mod Lang. *Res:* Contemporary Spanish American fiction; women writers of Spanish America. *Publ:* Auth, El Calendario y los Cartones de Madrid de Alfonso Reyes, Nueva Revista de Filologia Hispanica, 73; The Real Circle of Iron Mothers and Children, Children and Mothers, Four Argentine Novels, Lat Am Lit Rev, 76. *Mailing Add:* Dept of Span State Univ of NY Oswego NY 13126

KAMM, LEWIS ROBERT, b New York, NY, Nov 14, 44; m 74; c 2. FRENCH LITERATURE & LANGUAGE. *Educ:* Rutgers Univ, BA, 66; Brown Univ, AM, 67, PhD(French), 71. *Prof Exp:* Teaching asst French, Brown Univ, 68-71; asst prof French, 71-76, assoc prof, 76-82, PROF FRENCH, SOUTHEASTERN MASS UNIV, 82- *Concurrent Pos:* Res grant French, Southeastern Mass Univ, 73-74; Nat Endowment for Humanities, summer sem, 80; consult, 19th Century Fr Studies, Fr Rev, Univ Calif Press, 82-83. *Mem:* Am Asn Teachers Fr. *Res:* Nineteenth-century novel; 20th century novel and theatre; 17th-century moralists. *Publ:* Auth, Time and Zola's characters in the Rougon-Macquart, Romance Notes, 74; People and things in Zola's Rougon-Macquart: Reification re-humanized, Philol Quart, 74; Zola's conception of time in Les Rougon-Macquart, French Rev, 74; The structural and functional manifestation of space in Zola's Rougon-Macquart, 19th Century French Studies, 75; auth, Pascal and nineteenth-century Ennui, Romance Notes, 76; The Object in Zola's Rougon-Macquart, Porrua-Turanzas, 78; Zola's object and the surrealist, 19th Century Fr Studies (in press). *Mailing Add:* 38 Church St Tiverton RI 02878

KAMPF, LOUIS, Comparative Literature, History. See Vol II

KAMUF, PEGGY, b Cleveland, Ohio, Apr 12, 47; m 75. FRENCH LITERATURE & CRITICISM. *Educ:* Bucknell Univ, AB, 69; Cornell Univ, PhD(Romance studies), 75. *Prof Exp:* Asst prof, 75-80, ASSOC PROF FRENCH, MIAMI UNIV, 80- *Concurrent Pos:* Am Coun Learned Socs fel French lit, 78-79. *Mem:* Soc Critical Exchange; MLA; Midwest Mod Lang Asn. *Res:* Eighteenth-century French literature and philosophy; Modern literary criticism and theory. *Publ:* Auth, Rousseau's politics of visibility, Diacritics, winter 75; Inside Julie's Closet, Romanic Rev, 11/78; Abraham's Wake, Diacritics, spring 79; Fictions of Feminine Desire: Disclosures of Heloise, Univ Nebr, 82. *Mailing Add:* Dept of French & Ital Miami Univ Oxford OH 45056

KANE, JOHN ROBERT, b Newport, Great Britain, Dec 16, 33; m 64; c 2. MEDIEVAL FRENCH LITERATURE. *Educ:* Oxford Univ, BA, 57, MA, 61; Univ Colo, PhD(Fr), 69. *Prof Exp:* Asst prof, Kalamazoo Col, 67-71; ASSOC PROF FRENCH, KENT STATE UNIV, 71- *Mem:* MLA; Am Asn Teachers Fr. *Res:* French medieval drama; Mary Magdalen in medieval literature; medieval epic. *Publ:* Coauth, Rossignol: An Edition and Translation, Kent State Univ Press, 78; La Querelle de la Rose: Letters and Documents, Univ NC Press, 78; auth, Mary Magdalen: A la recherche d'une dame perdue, Mid-Hudson Lang Studies, 81. *Mailing Add:* Dept of Romance Lang & Lit Kent State Univ Kent OH 44242

KANES, MARTIN, b Philadelphia, Pa, Sept 21, 27; m 53. ROMANCE LANGUAGES. *Educ:* Univ Paris, Dr(comp lit), 53; Univ Pa, PhD, 59. *Prof Exp:* Instr Romance lang, Univ Pa, 53-59; asst prof French, Univ Calif, Davis, 59-66; assoc prof French lit, Univ Calif, Santa Cruz, 66-71, prof Fr & comp lit, 71-79. *Concurrent Pos:* Fels, Guggenheim & Fulbright, 65-66. *Mem:* MLA. *Res:* French and comparative literature of the 19th century; Zola; Balzac. *Publ:* Auth, Zola's La bete Humaine: A Study in Literary Creation, Univ Calif, 62; L'Atelier de Zola, Geneva, 63; Balzac's Comedy of Words, Princeton Univ, 75. *Mailing Add:* State Univ NY Albany NY 12203

KANTOR, MARVIN, b New York, NY, May 9, 34; m 61; c 2. SLAVIC LINGUISTICS, RUSSIAN LITERATURE. *Educ:* Copenhagen Univ, Cand Art, 61; Fordham Univ, MA, 63; Univ Mich, PhD(Slavic ling), 66. *Prof Exp:* Asst prof Russ, Brooklyn Col, 66-67; asst prof, 67-73, ASSOC PROF SLAVIC LANG & LIT, NORTHWESTERN UNIV EVANSTON, 73- *Concurrent Pos:* Nat Endowment for Humanities grant, 78-79. *Mem:* Am Asn Teachers Slavic & EEurop Lang; Mediaeval Acad Am; Am Soc 18th Century Studies. *Publ:* Auth, Phonological rewrite rules for the derivation of contemporary standard Polish, Scando-Slavica, 67; A note on the verbal prefixes s-, sa-, su- in Serbo-Croation, Slavic & E Europ J, 72; Aspectual Derivation in Contemporary Serbo-Croation, Mouton, The Hague, 72; Dramatic works of D I Fonuizin, Bern, 74; The vita of Constantine and the vita of Methodius, Ann Arbor, 76. *Mailing Add:* Dept of Slavic Lang & Lit Northwestern Univ 633 Clark St Evanston IL 60201

KANYORO, RACHEL ANGOGO, b Nairobi, Kenya, Nov 30, 53; m 77. LINGUISTICS. *Educ:* Univ Nairobi, BA, 75; Univ Tex, Austin, MA, 78, PhD(ling), 80. *Prof Exp:* Teacher lang, High Sch, Kenya, 70-71; res fel ling & Swahili, Univ Nairobi, 72-76; lectr Bantu struct, Toronto Inst Ling, summer 77; teaching asst Swahili, Univ Tex, 78-79; CONSULT LANG RES, UNITED BIBLE SOC, 80- *Concurrent Pos:* Transl consult, Africa Regional Ctr, United Bible Soc, 80-; vis scholar Hebrew & Greek, Harvard Univ, 81. *Mem:* Ling Soc Am; Kenya Lang Asn; African Lit Asn. *Res:* Linguistics and languages; Bible translation. *Publ:* Auth, Language and politics in South Africa, Studies African Ling, 78; English in Africa, English Worldwide, 80; East African English, E Schmidt Verlag, Berlin, 81; Issues in the use of standard Swahili, Tex Ling Forum, Univ Tex, Austin, 81; An inventory of Kiswahili related pidgins and creoles, Bashiru, Vol 10, No 2; Dialect problems and Bible translation: A case study of Union version, Bible Transl, 1/82; Swahili Today, Oxford Univ Press (in prep); Language and Society in East Africa, Muttton, The Hague (in prep). *Mailing Add:* PO Box 42726 Nairobi Kenya

KAO, SHUHSI MARIE-LOUISE, US citizen. MODERN FRENCH LITERATURE. *Educ:* Univ Ill, Urbana, MA, 69; Yale Univ, MPhil, 74, PhD(Fr), 79. *Prof Exp:* Instr French, Univ Wis-La Crosse, 69-71 & Univ Tex, San Antonio, 76-78; ASST PROF FRENCH, UNIV CALIF, LOS ANGELES, 78- *Concurrent Pos:* Ed, Blaise Cendrars Inst Soc Bull, 82- *Mem:* MLA; Blaise Cendrars Int Soc; Northest Mod Lang Asn; Am Asn Teachers French; Philol Asn Pac Coast. *Res:* Modern French poetry; contemporary literary criticism and theory; twentieth century American and German poetry. *Publ:* Auth, Les Colchiques d'Apollinaire et la Modernite, Essays Fr Lit, 11/80; Structures et signification dans les nouvelles de Yu Dafu, In: La litterature Chinoise au temps de la guerre de resistance coutre le Japon (de 1937 a 1945), Ed Fondation Singer-Polignac, Paris, 82. *Mailing Add:* French Dept Univ of Calif Los Angeles CA 90024

KAPETANOPOULOS, ELIAS, b Pentalophos, Kozane, Greece, May 25, 29; m 57; c 2. CLASSICS, GREEK & ROMAN HISTORY. *Educ:* Wayne State Univ, BA, 57; Yale Univ, MA, 59, PhD(Classics), 64. *Prof Exp:* From instr to asst prof classics, Univ Nebr, 63-68; from asst prof to assoc prof, 68-77, PROF GREECE & ROME, CENT CONN STATE COL, 77- *Mem:* Am Philol Asn; Am Soc Papyrologists; Asn Etudes Grecques; Hellenike Archaiologike Hetaireia; Hetaireia Makedonikon Spoudon. *Res:* Attic epigraphy and prosopography and Roman civitas in Attica. *Publ:* Auth, Leonides VII of Melite and his family, Bull de Correspondance Hellenique, 68; Attic inscriptions: Notes, 68 & The family of Dexippos I Hermeios, 72, Archaiologike Ephemeris; A Phalerian family and its relations, Archaiologikon Deltion, 71; Gaius Julius Nikanor, Neos Homeros kai Neos Themistokles Rivista di Filologia, 76; Three Athenian Archons, ΕΛΛΗΝΙΚΑ, 76; Some remarks on the Athenian Prytaneis, Ancient World, 81; Hadrianis and the boule of five hundred, Balkan Studies, 81. *Mailing Add:* Dept of Hist Cent Conn State Col New Britain CT 06050

KAPLAN, ARTHUR, b Oudtshoorn, SAfrica, Aug 11, 08; US citizen; m 40. GREEK & LATIN CLASSICS. *Educ:* Brown Univ, AB, 29, MA, 40; Univ Va, PhD(Latin), 44. *Prof Exp:* Asst Greek & Latin classics, Brown Univ, 39-40; part-time instr Latin, Univ Va, 40-43; from asst prof to assoc prof classics, Univ Ga, 47-54; asst prof hist, Grad Sch Educ, Yeshiva Univ, 59-62; asst prof classics, Stern Col Women, 62-64; from asst prof to assoc prof class lang, St Francis Col, NY, 64-73; RETIRED. *Concurrent Pos:* Lectr classics, Ohio State Univ, 55; Jewish historian, NShore Jewish Ctr, Miami Beach, Fla, 57-59. *Mem:* Am Class League; Int Platform Asn. *Publ:* Auth, Catiline: The man and his role in the Roman Revolution, Exposition, 68; The just argument shall prevail, 2/72 & Women's suffrage and the right of appeal in Rome, 6/73, Class Outlook; Religious dictators of the Roman Republic, Class World, 73-74; contribr, Sulla's watergate, 5/76, Pompey's influence on Orthodox Judaism, 5/77 & Was Cato right after all, 6/77, Class Outlook; auth, Dictatorships and Untimate Degrees in the Early Roman Republic, 501-202 BC, Revisionist Press, 77. *Mailing Add:* 2803 Wayland Dr Raleigh NC 27608

KAPLAN, EDWARD KIVIE, b Boston, Mass, Mar 4, 42; m 68; c 1. FRENCH LITERATURE. *Educ:* Brown Univ, BA, 64; Columbia Univ, MA, 66, PhD(French), 70. *Prof Exp:* Instr French, Barnard Col, Columbia Univ, 67-71; asst prof, Amherst Col, 71-78; ASST PROF FRENCH, BRANDEIS UNIV, 78- *Mem:* MLA; Am Asn Teachers Fr; Soc Etud Romantiques; Soc Values Higher Educ. *Res:* Nineteenth century French literature; Jules Michelet; religious experience and language. *Publ:* Auth, Gaston Bachelard's Philosophy of Imagination, Philos & Phenomenol Res, 9/72; Language and reality in A J Heschel's Philosophy of Religion, J Am Acad Relig, 3/73; Les Deux sexes de l'esprit: Michelet phenomenologue de l'imagination . . ., Europe, 12/73; Michelet's Poetic Vision: A Romantic Philosophy of Nature, Man, and Woman, Univ Mass, 77; Mysticism and despair in Abraham J Heschel's religious thought, J Relig, 1/77; Michelet's revolutionary symbolism: From Hermeneutics in politics, 4/77 & The courage of Baudelaire and Rimbuad: The anxiety of faith, 12/78, Fr Rev. *Mailing Add:* Dept of Romance & Comp Lit Brandeis Univ Waltham MA 02154

KAPLAN, JAMES MAURICE, b Worcester, Mass, Mar 16, 43. FRENCH LITERATURE. *Educ:* Univ Mass, Amherst, BA, 64; Univ Calif, Berkeley, PhD(French), 71. *Prof Exp:* Teaching asst French, Univ Calif, Berkeley, 65-66, 67-69; asst English, Lycee Bellevue, Toulouse, France, 66-67; escort-interpreter French & Swed, US Dept State, 72-76; asst prof, 76-80, ASSOC PROF FRENCH, MOOREHEAD STATE COL, 80- *Concurrent Pos:* Fulbright fel, 66-67; Swed Govt fel, 69-70; Nat Endowment for Humanities grants, 78 & 81; resident dir, St Cloud State Univ prog in France, 81. *Mem:* MLA. *Res:* French 18th century poetry; French 18th century opera; Jungian literary analysis. *Publ:* Auth, Une demarmontelisation de Marmontel, Studies Voltaire & 18th Century, 73; Notes on Le Neveu de Rameau, Romance Notes, 79; Polymnie, Studies on Voltaire (in press). *Mailing Add:* Dept of Foreign Lang Moorehead State Col Moorhead MN 56560

KAPLAN, JANE PAYNE, b Richmond, Va, Oct 3, 37; m 64; c 2. FRENCH LANGUAGE & LITERATURE, LINGUISTICS. *Educ:* Univ NC, Chapel Hill, BA, 59; La State Univ, Baton Rouge, PhD(Romance philol), 70. *Prof Exp:* Lectr French, Yale Univ, 64-65; instr, Southern Conn State Col, 65-67; asst prof, Quinnipiac Col, 69-70; asst prof French & ling, 71-74, ASSOC PROF FRENCH, ITHACA COL, 74- *Honors & Awards:* Danforth Associate. *Mem:* Am Soc 18th Century Studies; Soc Etudes XVIIe Siecle. *Res:* Eighteenth century literature; seventeenth century theater; semiotics. *Publ:* Auth, Complexity of character and the overlapping of a single personality in Cocteau's Les Enfants Terribles, Australian J Fr Studies, XII: 89-104; A visual and temporal decoding of the pragmatic structure of Jaques le fataliste, Semiotica, 36: 1-25; Diderot, In: Encyclopedic Dictionary of Semiotics (in press). *Mailing Add:* Dept of Foreign Lang Ithaca Col Ithaca NY 14850

KAPLAN, ROBERT B, b New York, NY, Sept 20, 29; m 51; c 3. LINGUISTICS, ENGLISH AS SECOND LANGUAGE. *Educ:* Willamette Univ, AB, 52; Univ Southern Calif, MA, 57, PhD(English), 63. *Prof Exp:* Instr English, Univ Ore, 57-60; instr English as second lang, 60-61, coordr English commun prog foreign studies, 61-63, dir, 63-73, asst prof English, 63-65, assoc prof English & ling, 65-73 & 77-78, chmn, Dept Ling, 67-69, PROF APPLIED LING, UNIV SOUTHERN CALIF, 73- *Concurrent Pos:* Consult field serv prog, Nat Asn Foreign Studies Affairs, 66, chmn Southern Calif dist bd, 66 & 67; vchmn, Am Asn Teachers English as Second Lang, 67, chmn, 68; consult, English Lang Serv Inc, 68; Bd Foreign Scholar-Fulbright Comn sr fel, 78; consult, Selct Comt Immigration & Refugee Policy, 80. *Mem:* Nat Asn Foreign Studies Affairs (2nd vpres, 72-73, pres-elect, 82-83); Teachers English to Speakers Other Lang; Ling Soc Am; fel Royal Anthrop Inst Gt Brit & Ireland; Am Asn Applied Ling (interim secy, 77-78). *Res:* Applied linguistics; bilingualism; language policy. *Publ:* Auth, Cultural thought patterns in inter-cultural education, Lang Learning, 66; coauth, Teachers guide to transformational grammar, 68 & Learning English thought typewriting, 69, English Lang Serv; The anatomy of rhetoric, Ctr Curric

Develp, 72; auth, On the scope of applied linguistics, Newbury House, 80; The language needs of migrant workers, NZ Coun Ed Res, 80; Annual Review of Applied Linguistics, Vol I, 81, Vol II, 82, Newbury House. *Mailing Add:* Dept of Ling Univ of Southern Calif Los Angeles CA 90007

KAPLOWITT, STEPHEN JOSEPH, b Newark, NJ, May 28, 30; m 53; c 2. GERMANIC LANGUAGES & LITERATURE. *Educ:* Hamilton Col, BA, 51; Univ Pa, MA, 54, PhD(Ger), 62. *Prof Exp:* Instr Ger, Columbia Univ, 58-62; from asst prof to assoc prof Ger & Slavic lang, 62-76, actg head dept Ger & Slavic Lang, 66-69, prof, 76-80. *Res:* Medieval German literature. *Publ:* Auth, The historical basis of the Bechelaren episode of Nibelungenlied, Ger Rev, 1/64; Reflections of the crusades in the Kaiserchronik, Neophilologus, 5/65; The non-literary sources of Graf Rudolf: A reevaluation, Studies Philol, 7/69. *Mailing Add:* 58 Birchwood Heights Rd Storrs CT 06268

KAPPLER, RICHARD G, b New York, NY, Apr 6, 28; m 55; c 3. RUSSIAN, ITALIAN. *Educ:* Cornell Univ, BA, 46; Columbia Univ, MA, 49, PhD(Russ, French), 60; Oxford Univ, dipl Slavonic studies, 69; Charles Univ, Prague, cert Czech lang, 71. *Prof Exp:* Asst prof foreign lang, Univ Idaho, 52-60; asst prof Russ, Univ Victoria, 60-62; assoc prof foreign lang & lit, 62-72, PROF FOREIGN LANG & LIT, WASH STATE UNIV, 72- *Mem:* Am Asn Advan Slavic Studies. *Res:* Franco-Russian literary relations; Old Russian literature; Slavic civilization. *Publ:* Auth, Pushkin and Benjamin Constant, Proc Pac Northwest Conf Foreign Lang, 4/67; Turgenev as critic of French literature, Comp Lit, spring 68; transl, A P Chekhov, The lady with a dog, In: Studies in Short Fiction, Holt, 71. *Mailing Add:* Dept of Foreign Lang & Lit Wash State Univ Pullman WA 99163

KARANIKAS, ALEXANDER, American Literature. See Vol II

KARATEEW, NICHOLAS J, b Russia, Aug 2, 17; m 55; c 1. RUSSIAN, SLAVIC LINGUISTICS. *Educ:* Univ Alta, BA, 49; Cornell Univ, AM, 50, PhD(Slavic ling, cult anthrop), 53. *Prof Exp:* Teaching fel, Cornell Univ, 50-53, asst prof Russ & actg head dept, 53-54; asst prof Russ & Air Force Inst Tech Russ Training Prog, 54-73, ASSOC PROF SLAVIC LANG & LIT, SYRACUSE UNIV, 73- *Mem:* Ling Soc Am; Am Asn Teachers Slavic & EEurop Lang. *Res:* Russian military terminology; machine translation linguistics, especially Russian-English and English-Russian; the problems of teaching Russian to speakers of American English. *Publ:* Auth, Russian pattern drills. *Mailing Add:* 104 Dover Rd Fayetteville NY 13066

KARCH, DIETER, b Ludwigshafen/Rhine, Ger, Nov 29, 27; US citizen; m 59. GERMANIC LINGUISTICS, GENERAL LINGUISTICS. *Educ:* Univ of Washington, MA, 64, PhD(Ger Philol), 67. *Prof Exp:* From instr to assoc prof Ger, 66-76, PROF MOD LANG, UNIV NEBR, 76- *Concurrent Pos:* Woods-fac fel, Univ Marburg, 71-72; sr fac res, IDS Mannheim, 77. *Mem:* MLA; Am Asn Teachers Ger. *Res:* (Settlement) Dialectology; Standard German; Colloquial German. *Publ:* Auth, Gimmeldingen Krs Neustadt an der Weinstrasse/Mutterstadt Krs Ludwigshafen am Rhein Phonai 13, 73, Mannheim-Umgangssprache Phonai 16, 75 & Zur Morphologie vorderpfälzischer Dialekte Phonai Beiheft 3, 75, Niemeyer, Tübingen; Siedlungspfälzisch im Kreis Waterloo, Ontario Kanada Phonai 18, 77 & Braunschweig-Veltenhof Pfälzische Sprachinsel in Ostfälischen Phonai 20, 78, Niemeyer, Tübingen; Neuburg am Rhein Eine alemannische Sprachinsel in der südlichen Vorderpfalz, Univ Nebr, 78; Jockgrim Krs Germersheim/ Niederhorbach Krs Landau-Bad Berrgzabern Niemeyer Tübingen Phonai 22, 80; Phonemidistribution Dargestellt an rheinhessischen Ortsmundarten DDG 107 I/II Elwert, Marburg. *Mailing Add:* Dept of Mod Lang & Lit Univ of Nebr Lincoln NE 68588

KARGLEDER, CHARLES LEONARD, b Milbank, SDak, July 19, 39. SPANISH & LATIN-AMERICAN LITERATURE. *Educ:* SDak, BA, 60; Univ Ala, MA, 62, PhD(Romance lang), 68. *Prof Exp:* From instr to asst prof, 63-71, assoc prof & chmn dept lang, 71-80, PROF SPAN, SPRING HILL COL, 80- *Mem:* Am Asn Teachers Span & Port; AAUP; Am Transl Asn; Am Coun Teaching For Lang; Southeastern Conf Latin Am Studies. *Res:* Contemporary Latin American literature; contemporary Spanish literature. *Publ:* Auth, A Translation of Jorge Guillen's Muchas gracias, adios, Motley, spring, 65; Alvaro Obregon as characterized by writers of the revolution, Southeastern Latin Americanist, 6/76; Una bibliografia selectira de la literatura costarricense, San Jose, Costa Rica, Ed Costa Rica, 78. *Mailing Add:* Dept of Lang Spring Hill Col Mobile AL 36608

KARLINSKY, SIMON, b Harbin, Manchuria, Sept 22, 24; US citizen. SLAVIC LANGUAGES & LITERATURES. *Educ:* Univ Calif, Berkeley, BA, 60, PhD(Slavic), 64; Harvard Univ, MA, 61. *Prof Exp:* Acting asst prof, 63-64, from asst prof to assoc prof, 64-67, chmn dept, 67-69, PROF SLAVIC LANG & LIT, UNIV CALIF, BERKELEY, 67- *Concurrent Pos:* Vis assoc prof, Harvard Univ, 66; Guggenheim Mem Found fel, 69-70 & 77-78. *Mem:* MLA; Am Asn Advan Slavic Studies; Am Asn Teachers Slavic & East Europ Lang; Philol Asn Pac Coast. *Res:* Modern Russian literature; comparative literature. *Publ:* Auth, Marina Cvetaeva: Her Life and Art, Univ Calif, 65; ed, Letters of Anton Chekhov, Harper, 73; auth, The Sexual Labyrinth of Nikolai Gogol, Harvard Univ, 76; Anton Chekhov's Life and Thought, rev ed, 77 & co-ed, The Bitter Air of Exile: Russian Literature in the West, 1922-1972, 77, Univ Calif; ed, The Nabokov-Wilson Letters, Harper, 79; A Difficult Soul: Znaida Gippius, Univ Calif, 80. *Mailing Add:* Dept of Slavic Lang & Lit 5416 Dwinelle Hall Univ of Calif Berkeley CA 94720

KARSEN, SONJA PETRA, b Berlin, Ger, Apr 11, 19; nat US. SPANISH. *Educ:* Carleton Col, BA, 39; Bryn Mawr Col, MA, 41; Columbia Univ, PhD, 50. *Prof Exp:* Instr Span, Lake Erie Col, 43-45; instr mod lang, Univ PR, 45-46; instr Span, Syracuse Univ, 47-50; instr, Brooklyn Col, 50-51; personal asst to dept dir-gen, UNESCO, Paris, France, 51-52, Latin Am desk, prog div tech assistance dept, 52-54, mem tech assistance mission, Costa Rica, 54; asst prof mod lang, Sweet Briar Col, 55-57; assoc prof Span, 57-61, chmn dept Romance lang, 57-65, fac res lectr 63, chmn dept mod lang, 65-79, PROF SPAN, SKIDMORE COL, 61- *Concurrent Pos:* Contribr ed, Bks Abroad, 65-67; Fulbright lectr, Free Univ Berlin, 68; mem, Fulbright North-East Regional Screening Comt, 70-71, chmn 71 & 74. *Honors & Awards:* Chevalier, Palmes Academiques, 63; Foreign Language Leader Award, New York State Asn Foreign Lang Teachers, 73; Nat Distinguished Lectr Award, NY State Asn Lang Teachers, 79; Spanish Heritage Award, 81. *Mem:* MLA; Am Asn Teachers Span & Port; Nat Asn Self-Instr Lang Prog (treas, 73-77, vpres, 81-82); Am Asn Univ Women; Asn Int Hispanistas. *Res:* Spanish American literature; Latin American literature and culture; translation. *Publ:* Auth, Jaime Torres Bodet, Twayne, 71; contribr & auth, La corrupcion del gobierno de Venezuela segun Blanco-Fombona en el Hombre de oro, In: La Literatura Iberoamericana del siglo XIX, Univ Ariz, 74; auth, Friedrich Gerstäcker in South America, Mod Lang Studies, 75; contribr & auth, Jaime Torres Bodet, cornista de su vida, In: Ensayos contemporaneos sobre Jaime Torres Bodet, Univ Nacional Autonoma, Mex, 76; auth, Latin America through German eyes, Tex Quart, winter 77; Guillermo Valencia, Poeta Modernista, Bol del Inst Caro y Cuervo, Gojota, XXXV: 1-8; La Poesia de Nicanor Parra, In: Actas Del Sexto Congreso Internacional De Hispanistas, Univ Toronto, 80; Dona Barbara: Cinconenta Anos De Critica, In: Relectura De Ronuto Gallegos, Caracas: Ediciones del Centro de Estudios Idtiuoduioiucauos Roueolo Gallegos, 80. *Mailing Add:* Dept of Mod Lang & Lit Skidmore Col Saratoga Springs NY 12866

KASCHUBE, DOROTHEA VEDRAL, b Chicago, Ill, Nov 6, 27; US citizen; m 50; c 2. ANTHROPOLOGICAL LINGUISTICS. *Educ:* Indiana Univ, BA, 51, MA, 53, PhD(anthrop), 60. *Prof Exp:* PROF ANTHROP, UNIV COLO, 55- *Mem:* Am Anthrop Asn; Ling Soc Am; Am Asn Advan Sci. *Res:* Language and culture; American Indian languages; biolinguistics. *Publ:* Auth, Tone in Crow, Int J Am Ling, 1/54; Dyslexia: A language disorder, Anthrop Ling, 12/72; coauth, Word Prosodic Systems, Working Papers on Lang Universals, 76. *Mailing Add:* Dept of Anthrop Univ of Colo Boulder CO 80309

KASELL, WALTER, b Brooklyn, NY. COMPARATIVE & FRENCH LITERATURE. *Educ:* Amherst Col, BA, 66; Cornell Univ, MA, 70, PhD(comp lit). *Prof Exp:* From instr to asst prof French, Princeton Univ, 72-78; ASST PROF FRENCH & COMP LIT, BRANDEIS UNIV, 78- *Concurrent Pos:* Alexander von Humboldt Found fel, 75-76. *Mem:* MLA. *Res:* Proust; modern criticism; 19th and 20th century novel. *Publ:* Auth, Proust the pilgrim: His idolatrous reading of Ruskin, Revue Litt Comparee, 10-12/75; Gerard de Nerval: The possibility of biography, Studies in Romanticism, 1/76; Proust as a reader of Nerval, Romanic Rev, 5/77; Nerval's innocent double, Stanford Fr Rev. *Mailing Add:* Dept of Romance & Comp Lit Brandeis Univ Waltham MA 02154

KASHUBA, IRMA MERCEDES, b Philadelphia, Pa, June 4, 33. FRENCH & RUSSIAN LANGUAGE & LITERATURE. *Educ:* Chestnut Hill Col, AB, 61; Fordham Univ, MA, 64; Middlebury Col, DML (French), 71. *Prof Exp:* Elem teacher, Philadelphia & Harrisburg Parochial Schs, 55-60; teacher French & Latin, Bishop McDevitt High Sch, Wyncote, Pa, 60-62; chmn foreign lang & lit, 76-81, PROF FRENCH & RUSS, CHESTNUT HILL COL, 63- *Concurrent Pos:* Int Res & Exchanges Bd fel, Moscow State Univ, 73. *Honors & Awards:* Lindbak Award, 75. *Mem:* MLA; Am Asn Teachers Fr; Am Coun Teaching Foreign Lang; Am Asn Teachers Slavic & EEurop Lang. *Res:* Nineteenth century French literature; nineteenth & twentieth centuries Russian literature. *Publ:* Auth, Charles Peguy et le Monde Moderne, Feuillets de l'Amities Peguy, 4/76; Charles Peguy, un classique quis' ignore, USF Lang Quart, fall 78; contribr, Encyclopedic Dictionary of Religion, Corpus, 79; auth, La Russie vue des Cahiers, Feuillets de l'Amitie Peguy, 79; The Fullness of Creation as envisioned by Berdiaev, Am Benedictine Rev, 81. *Mailing Add:* Dept Foreign Lang & Lit Chestnut Hill Col Philadelphia PA 19118

KASKE, ROBERT EARL, English, Comparative Linguistics. See Vol II

KASPAREK, JERRY LEWIS, b Sulfur, Okla, Mar 18, 39; m 61; c 2. CLASSICS, COMPARATIVE LITERATURE. *Educ:* Univ Okla, BA, 61; Vanderbilt Univ, PhD(comp lit), 71. *Prof Exp:* Asst prof class, 64-71, ASSOC PROF CLASS & COMP LIT, BALL STATE UNIV, 71-, CHMN DEPT FOREIGN LANG, 73-, PROF FOREIGN LANG, 80- *Mem:* Am Philol Asn; MLA; Am Class League. *Res:* Moliere; satire; comedy. *Publ:* Auth, Moliere's Tartuffle and the Traditions of Roman Satire, Univ NC (in press). *Mailing Add:* Dept of Foreign Lang Ball State Univ Muncie IN 47306

KASSATKIN, SERGE, b Omsk, Siberia, Oct 5, 17; nat US; m 47; c 2. ORIENTAL LANGUAGES, RUSSIAN LANGUAGE. *Educ:* Univ Calif, BA, 50, MA, 52. *Prof Exp:* Transl, interpreter & teacher, Japanese, Chinese & Russian, various firms, Harbin, Manchuria & Shanghai, China, 36-45; lang officer Major, Brit Army, Singapore, Hong Kong, Java & Japan, 46-48; instr Russ, Army Lang Sch, Presidio of Monterey, Calif, 48-49; teacher Russ & head teacher, Far East & Russ Lang Sch, exten div, 49-53, asst res linguist, Mongolian Dictionary Proj, Inst East Asiatic Studies, 50-59, lectr Russ, 59-73, SR LECTR RUSS, UNIV CALIF, BERKELEY, 73-, DEPT ADV, 59- *Publ:* Coauth, Mongolian-English Dict, Univ Calif, 60; The category of aspect in Japanese, Phi Theta Annual, Univ Calif; Studies in Synonyms (articles in Russian), A Guide to Teachers of the Russian Language in America, 71-72: 62-70, 73: 3-11. *Mailing Add:* 741 The Alameda Berkeley CA 94707

KASSIER, THEODORE LAURENCE, b New York, NY, Jan 12, 46; m 70. MEDIEVAL & GOLDEN AGE SPANISH LITERATURE. *Educ:* Columbia Univ, AB, 66; Princeton Univ, MA, 68, PhD(Romance lang & lit), 72. *Prof Exp:* Asst prof Hisp studies, Vassar Col, 70-76, dir Vassar-Wesleyan sem in Madrid, 72-73; ASSOC PROF FOREIGN LANG, UNIV TEX, 76- *Concurrent Pos:* Escort-interpreter off, US Dept State, 65- *Mem:* MLA; AAUP. *Res:* Spanish Golden Age prose and poetry; Renaissance and Baroque literature. *Publ:* Auth, The rhetorical devices of the Spanish Vida de Santa Maria Egipciaca, Anuario Estudios Medievales; Cancionero poetry and the Celestina: From metaphor to reality, Hispanofila. *Mailing Add:* Dept of Foreign Lang Univ of Tex San Antonio TX 78215

KASTEN, LLOYD (AUGUST WILLIAM), b Watertown, Wis, Apr 14, 05. SPANISH. *Educ:* Univ Wis, AB, 26, AM, 27, PhD, 31. *Hon Degrees:* LittD, Univ of South. *Prof Exp:* Instr Span, Univ Fla, 27-28; instr, 29-37, from asst prof to prof, 37-68, Antonio G Solalinde distinguished prof, 68-75, EMER PROF SPAN & PORT, UNIV WIS, MADISON, 75-, SEM MEDIEVAL SPAN STUDIES, 37- *Concurrent Pos:* Markham traveling fel, 32-33; Guggenheim fel, 56-57; ed, Luso-Brazilian Rev, 65-78; Nat Found Humanities grant, 67-68; Nat Endowment for Humanities grant, 73- *Mem:* MLA; Mediaeval Acad Am; Ling Soc Am; Am Orient Soc; Hisp Soc Am. *Res:* Computer-aided concordance, frequency count, and morphological analysis of the works of Alfonso X of Castile as represented by MSS of the Royal Scriptorum; medieval Spanish lexicon to 1500; contemporary Brazilian novel. *Publ:* Coauth, Tentative Dictionary of Medieval Spanish, Univ NC, 46; ed, Seudo Aristoteles: Poridat de las pordidades, Madrid, 57; Alfonso X: General estoria, 57-61 & Alfonso X: Libro de las cruzes, 61, Consejo Super Invest Cient; Concordance to the Celestina (1499), Hisp Sem Medieval Studies, 76; coauth, Concordances and texts of the Royal Scriptorium Manuscripts of Alfonso X, el Sabio, 78 & Complete concordances and texts of the fourteenth-century Aragonese Manuscripts of Juan Fernandez de Heredia, 82, Hisp Sem Medieval Studies. *Mailing Add:* Dept of Span & Port Univ of Wis Madison WI 53706

KASTER, ROBERT ANDREW, b New York, NY, Feb 6, 48; m 69; c 2. CLASSICAL LANGUAGES AND LITERATURES. *Educ:* Dartmouth Col, BA, 69; Harvard Univ, MA, 71, PhD(classics), 75. *Prof Exp:* Instr classics, Colby Col, 73-74; asst prof, 72-82, ASSOC PROF CLASSICS, UNIV CHICAGO, 82- *Concurrent Pos:* Ed, Class Philol, 81- *Honors & Awards:* Nat Endowment for the Humanities fel independent study & res, 80-81. *Mem:* Am Philol Asn; Vergilian Soc. *Res:* Ancient education and scholarship; Latin poetry; textual history and criticsm. *Publ:* Auth, A note on Catullus, c.71.4, Philologus, 78; Servius and idonei auctores, Am J Philol, 78; Macrobius and Servius, Harvard Studies Class Philol, 80; The grammarism's authority, Class Philol, 80. *Mailing Add:* 1050 E 59th St Chicago IL 60637

KASTNER, GEORGE RONALD, b Woodbury, NJ, Jan 21, 49; m 74. COMPARATIVE LITERATURE. *Educ:* Colgate Univ, BA, 71; Univ Iowa, MA, 74, PhD(comp lit), 78. *Prof Exp:* RES & WRITING, 78- *Mem:* Am Philol Asn; Am Theol Soc. *Res:* Early Byzantine literature. *Publ:* Coauth, A Lost Tradition: Women Writers of the Early Church, Univ Pres Am, 81. *Mailing Add:* 175 9th Ave New York NY 10011

KATES, CAROL A, Philosophy. See Vol IV

KATO, HIROKI, b Hiroshima, Japan, Jan 28, 42; m 68; c 2. SOCIOLINGUISTICS, POLITICAL SCIENCE. *Educ:* Int Christian Univ, Tokyo, BA, 66; Wash Univ, MA, 68; Univ Chicago, PhD(polit sci), 74. *Prof Exp:* Asst prof, Japanese/polit sci, Earlham Col, 71-76; asst prof, 76-80, ASSOC PROF JAPANESE, UNIV HAWAII, 80- *Concurrent Pos:* Vis prof E Asian lang & civilization, Harvard Univ, 81. *Mem:* Am Polit Sci Asn; Asn Asian Studies; MLA; Asn Teachers Japanese. *Res:* Sociolinguistics; language teaching; comparative politics. *Publ:* Auth, The Red Guard Movement: Its origin, Asian Forum, 4/73; Some thoughts on oral examinations, System, 10/77; Asita Yakyun o Asobimasyoo, Proc Conf Japanese Ling & Lang Teaching, fall 77; Advantages of Japanese orthography, Gengo, 1/79; Japanese for Business People, Level I, II & III, 82. *Mailing Add:* Dept of E Asian Lang Univ of Hawaii Honolulu HI 96822

KATO, KAZUMITSU WAKO, b Nagoya, Japan, Jan 7, 30; m 55; c 2. FOREIGN LANGUAGES, COMPARATIVE RELIGIONS. *Educ:* San Francisco State Col, BA, 55; Univ Pac, MA, 57, PhD, 59. *Prof Exp:* Instr comp relig & Japanese lit, Col Pac, 56-59; asst prof philos, San Jose State Col, 60-62; lectr Orient lang, Univ Calif, Berkeley, 62-63; assoc prof Japanese, 63-72, PROF JAPANESE, CALIF STATE UNIV, LOS ANGELES, 72- *Concurrent Pos:* Lectr, San Francisco Soto Zen Beddhist Church, 52-63; lectr, Downtown Ctr, San Francisco State Col, 60-61, asst prof, 61-63. *Mem:* Am Orient Soc; Asn Asian Studies; Int Soc Gen Semantics; Japanese Asn Indian & Buddhist Studies. *Res:* Life and teaching of Dogen; influence of the Sanskrit words in the Japanese language. *Publ:* Ed, introd, Chinese symbolism and art motives, Julian, 61; auth, Some notes on Mono no aware, J Am Orient Soc, 63; ed, Japan's Religion: Shinto and Buddhism, Univ Bks, 64. *Mailing Add:* Dept of Foreign Lang Calif State Univ Los Angeles CA 90032

KATSH, ABRAHAM ISSAC, b Poland, Aug 10, 08; nat US; m 43; c 3. HEBREW & ISLAMIC STUDIES. *Educ:* NY Univ, BA, 31, MA, 32, JD, 36; Dropsie Col, PhD, 44. *Hon Degrees:* DHL, Hebrew Union Col, 64, Villanova Univ, 77; LittD, Col Jewish Studies, 68; DD, Christian Theol Sem, 70, Univ Dubuque, 71; LLD, Lebanon Valley Col, 71, Dropsie Univ, 76. *Prof Exp:* Head teacher, Talmudical Sch Brooklyn, 27-33; prin, Inst Jewish Studies Adults, 33-36; first instr modern Hebrew, NY Univ, 34-37, prof Hebrew culture & educ & chmn dept, 37-59, prof Hebrew & Near Eastern studies, Grad Sch Arts & Sci, 59-62, Abraham Katsch prof Hebrew culture & educ & dir & prof, Inst Hebrew Studies, 62-67, distinguished res prof, 67-68, pres, 67-76, EMER PRES & DISTINGUISHED RES PROF, DROPSIE UNIV, 76-; EMER PROF HEBREW CULTURE & EDUC, NY UNIV, 76- *Honors & Awards:* B'rith Abraham Medal, 52; Abraham I Katsh Endowed Chair of Hebrew, 57, Ernest O Melby Award, 62 & Pres Citation, 65, NY Univ; Schneiderman Prize, 65; Brotherhood Award, Chapel of the Four Chaplains, 67. *Mem:* Nat Asn Prof Hebrew (hon pres, 50-); Jewish Acad Arts & Sci (pres); Am Orient Soc; Soc Bibl Lit; Am Acad Relig. *Publ:* Auth, The Antonin Geniza Collection in Leningrad, 63; Midrash David Hanagid, Mosad Harav Kook, Jerusalem, 63; Scroll of Agony, 65, English & Fr ed, 66, Swiss & Ger ed, 67; Megilat Yesurin, 65; The Antonin Mishanah Geniza, 71; The Antonin Talmudic Geniza, 73; ed & transl, The Warsaw Diary of Chaim A Kaplan, Collier, 73; auth, Biblical Heritage of American Democracy, 77. *Mailing Add:* Dropsie Univ Philadelphia PA 19132

KATTAN, OLGA, b San Pedro Sula, Honduras, May 18, 28; US citizen. ROMANCE LANGUAGES. *Educ:* Rider Col, AB, 55; Univ Pa, BA, 58, MA, 61; Univ Madrid, Licenciatura, 62, PhD(Span), 63. *Prof Exp:* Lectr English, Dame de Sion, Jerusalem, 47-48; lectr, Am Cult Inst, Honduras, 49-53; asst instr Span, Univ Pa, 58-61; asst prof, Wells Col, 63-66; asst prof, 66-72, ASSOC PROF SPAN, BROOKLYN COL, 72- *Concurrent Pos:* Lectr, Rosemont Col, 58-61; Fulbright grant, Spain, 61-63; dir prog abroad, Univ Seville, 69-73. *Mem:* MLA. *Res:* Twentieth century novel; Arabic influence in Spanish literature. *Publ:* Auth, Theatre of Valle-Inclan, Univ Madrid, 63; La guerrilla de Azorin, Cuadernos Homenaje, 68; La gallarda Toledana de Lope de Vega, 69 & Cartas de Nueva York, 69, Estafeta Literaria, Madrid; Gines de Pasamonte, 69, Notas sobre Tirano Banderas, 69 & Madrid en fortunata y Jacinta y en La lucha por la vida, 70-71, Cuadernos Hispanoam, Madrid. *Mailing Add:* Dept of Mod Lang Brooklyn Col Brooklyn NY 11210

KATZ, ELI, b Brooklyn, NY, Aug 10, 28; m 46; c 3. GERMANIC LINGUISTICS. *Educ:* City Col New York, BSS, 49; Univ Calif, Los Angeles, MA, 59, PhD(Ger lang), 63. *Prof Exp:* Asst prof foreign lang, San Diego State Col, 61-62; asst prof, Los Angeles State Col, 62-63; asst prof Ger, Univ Calif, Berkeley, 63-72; asst prof Am ethnic studies, 70-72, assoc prof, 72-75, PROF LING, SONOMA STATE UNIV, 75- *Mem:* MLA; Ling Soc Am. *Res:* Linguistics; Yiddish language and literature; folklore. *Publ:* Auth, Isaac Bashevis Singer and the classical Yiddish tradition, In: The Achievement of Isaac Bashevis Singer, Southern Ill Univ, 69; coauth, Tradition and adaptation in American Jewish humor, J Am Folklore, 4-6/71; auth, Morris Rosenfeld, Jewish Currents, 11/73; Bashevis Zinger in Yidish un in iberzetsung, Khezhbm, 4-6/79; The legacy of Sholem Asch, Jewish Currents, 11/80. *Mailing Add:* Dept of Linguistics Sonoma State Univ Rohnert Park CA 94929

KATZ, MICHAEL RAY, b New York, NY, Dec 9, 44. RUSSIAN LANGUAGE & LITERATURE. *Educ:* Williams Col, BA, 66; Oxford Univ, BA, MA & DPhil(Russ), 72. *Prof Exp:* Asst prof, 72-78, chmn prog comp lit, 77-78, ASSOC PROF RUSS, WILLIAMS COL, 78-, CHMN DEPT GER & RUSS, 80- *Concurrent Pos:* Vis scholar, Univ Calif, Berkeley, 75-76. *Mem:* Am Asn Advan Slavic Studies; Am Asn Teachers Slavic & EEurop Lang. *Res:* Russian romantic poetry; dreams in Russian fiction; Russian intellectual history. *Publ:* Auth, The Literary Ballad in Early Nineteenth Century Russian Literature, Oxford Univ, 76. *Mailing Add:* Dept of Russ Williams Col Williamstown MA 01267

KAUF, ROBERT, b Vienna, Austria, Feb 12, 22; US citizen; m 50; c 2. GERMAN LANGUAGE & LITERATURE. *Educ:* Univ Tex, BA, 44; Univ Chicago, MA, 50, PhD(Ger), 55. *Prof Exp:* From instr to assoc prof Ger, 53-66, foreign lang fel, 58 & 64, grad col res grants, 59-60, 66-67, 73, PROF GER, UNIV ILL, CHICAGO CIRCLE, 66- *Concurrent Pos:* Rev ed, Ger Quart, 68-70; Am Philos Soc res grant, 70; Danforth assoc, 70- *Honors & Awards:* Silver Circle Award for Excellence in Teaching, Univ Ill, 76; Award, Osterreichische Bundesministerium Wissenschaft und Forschung, 78 & Osterreichische Gesellschaft Lit, 78. *Mem:* MLA; Am Asn Teachers Ger; Am Coun Studies Austrian Lit; Midwest Mod Lang Asn. *Res:* Twentieth century German literature; Austrian literature; ethical and religious problems in literature. *Publ:* Coauth, George Kaiser's Social Tetralogu and the Social Ideas of Walter Ratheanau, PMLA, 62; Lady Montagus Brief Uber Die Hanswurst-Komodie, Maske U Kothurn, 67; Proben Deutscher Prosa: Ein Literaturlesbuch Mit Hor- und Sprechubugen, Norton, 70; Verantwortung: The Theme of Kafka's Landarzt Cycle, Mod Lang Quart, 72; Ernst Waldinger in Exile, Lit S Krihk, 76; Auch Hier Geshieht, Was Langst Geschah, Faust, v 11286, Jahrbuch Freien Deutschen Hochshifts, 77; Divine and Human Justice in the Works of Kafka, Col Germanica, 78. *Mailing Add:* Dept Ger Univ Ill Chicago Circle Chicago IL 60680

KAUFKE, PIERRE H G, b Mulhouse, France, Jan 8, 44; wid; c 1. ENGLISH, FOREIGN LANGUAGES. *Educ:* Univ Strasbourg, BA, 66; Stetson Univ, MA, 67; Univ SC, PhD(comp lit), 72. *Prof Exp:* ASST PROF FOREIGN LANG & ENGLISH, UNIV W FLA, 70- *Concurrent Pos:* Consult, Panhandle Area Educ Coop, 72- *Res:* Baroque age; novel. *Mailing Add:* Dept of Foreign Lang Alpha Col Univ of WFla Pensacola FL 32504

KAUFMAN, STEPHEN ALLAN, Ancient Near Eastern Languages, Old Testament. See Vol IV

KAUFMAN, TERRENCE SCOTT, b Portland, Ore, June 12, 37; m 64. LINGUISTICS. *Educ:* Univ Chicago, AB, 59; Univ Calif, Berkeley, PhD(ling), 63. *Prof Exp:* Asst prof ling, Ohio State Univ, 63-64; asst prof, Univ Calif, Berkeley, 64-70; ASSOC PROF ANTHROP, UNIV PITTSBURGH, 71- *Concurrent Pos:* Tech dir ling, Francisco Marroquin ling proj, Antigua, Guatemala, 71- *Mem:* Ling Soc Am. *Res:* Mayan synchronic and diachronic linguistics; comparative and historical linguistic method and theory; Romani linguistics. *Publ:* Auth, Teco: A new Mayan language, Int J Am Ling, 69; Tzeltal Phonology and Morphology, Univ Calif, 69; El proto Tzeltal-Tzotzil, Nat Univ Mex, 72; Areal linguistics and Middle America, In: Current Trends in Linguistics, Mouton, The Hague, 73. *Mailing Add:* Dept of Anthrop Univ of Pittsburgh 234 Atwood St Pittsburgh PA 15260

KAY, RICHARD L, Medieval History. See Vol I

KAYE, ALAN STEWART, b Los Angeles, Calif, Mar 2, 44; m 72; c 2. LINGUISTICS, NEAR EASTERN STUDIES. *Educ:* Univ Calif, Los Angeles, BA, 65; Univ Calif, Berkeley, MA, 68, PhD(ling), 71. *Prof Exp:* Asst prof, Univ Colo, 68-71; asst prof, 71-74, assoc prof & chmn ling, 74-78, PROF & DIR, LAB PHONETIC RES, CALIF STATE UNIV, FULLERTON, 78- *Concurrent Pos:* Nat Endowment Humanities grant, 73-74; Am Philos Soc grant, 73-74 & 75-76; Fulbright res grant, 78-79; instr, Pepperdine Univ, 74-76; consult, Rockwell Int, 76-; instr, Univ Calif, Irvine, 77- *Mem:* Philos Asn Pac Coast; Am Orient Soc; Ling Soc Am; Can Ling Asn; Mid East Studies Asn NAm. *Res:* Arabic dialectology; Semitic linguistics; field linguistics (Africa, S Asia). *Publ:* Auth, Modern standard Arabic and the colloquials, Lingua, 71; Arabic/ziim/: A synchronic and diachronic study, Ling, 72;

Towards a generative phonology of Arabic, Int J Mid-East Studies, 74; More on diglossia in Arabic, Int J Mid-East Studies, 75; Nigerian Arabic and diachronic linguistics, In: From Meaning to Sound, Univ Nebr, 75; Chadian and Sudanese Arabic, Mouton, 76; The Hebrew grammarians and the history of linguistics, In: Festschrift for Robert A Hall Jr, 77; More on Moolah, Am Speech, 81; Spinoza as linguistic, Hebrew Ann Rev, 81; A Dict of Nigerian Arabic, Undena, 82. *Mailing Add:* Dept of Ling Calif State Univ 800 N State College Blvd Fullerton CA 92634

KAYE, ELDON FENTON, b Wellington, NZ, Aug 13, 27; m 57; c 3. FRENCH. *Educ:* Univ Canterbury, NZ, MA, 50; Univ Dijon, Lic es Lett, 52, dipl, 54; Univ Besancon, DUniv, 58. *Prof Exp:* Asst prof French, Mem Univ Nfld, 58-60; asst prof col, Univ Toronto, 60-63; from asst prof to assoc prof, 63-69, PROF FRENCH, CARLETON UNIV, 69- *Mem:* Acad Sci et Beaux-arts of Besancon. *Res:* French romanticism; Second empire; correspondents of Charles Weiss. *Publ:* Auth, Charles Lassailly, 1809-1843, 62, Journal de Xavier Marmeir, 1848-1890 (2 vols), 68, Xavier Forneret, 71 & Marie Mattei, lettres a Theophile Gautier, 72, Droz, Geneva. *Mailing Add:* Dept of French Carleton Univ Colonel By Dr Ottawa ON K1S 5B6 Can

KAYSER, H CHRISTOPH, b Bielefeld, Ger, June 15, 35; m 66; c 2. GERMAN LANGUAGE & LITERATURE. *Educ:* Univ Kiel, Staatsexamen, 61; St Louis Univ, MA, 66; Wash Univ, PhD(Ger), 69. *Prof Exp:* Lectr Ger, Folkuniversitetet Stockholm, 61-62; lectr, Studienseminar Kiel, 62-64; teaching asst, St Louis Univ, 64-65; instr, 65-68; asst prof, Univ Wis, Whitewater, 68-70; asst prof, 70-79, ASSOC PROF GER, STATE UNIV NY COL BROCKPORT, 80-- *Concurrent Pos:* Asst prof, Alternate Col, 73- *Mem:* Northeast Mod Lang Asn; Am Asn Teachers Ger; AAUP. *Res:* Nineteenth and 20th century German literature; popular culture; literary onomastics. *Publ:* Auth, Rilke: Das Rosen-Innere, Werner Neuse Festschrift, 69; Rilke Die Turnstunde, Mod Lang Studies, summer 72; The sadist and the clown, J Popular Cult, spring 77. *Mailing Add:* Dept of Foreign Lang & Lit State Univ of NY Col Brockport NY 14420

KAZAZIS, KOSTAS, b Athens, Greece, July 15, 34; m 58; c 2. BALKAN LINGUISTICS. *Educ:* Univ Lausanne, Lic es Sci Polit, 57; Univ Kans, MA, 59; Ind Univ, PhD(ling), 65. *Prof Exp:* Instr ling, Univ Ill, Urbana, 64-65; from asst prof to assoc prof, 65-77, PROF LING, UNIV CHICAGO, 77- *Concurrent Pos:* NDEA grant, 67-68. *Mem:* Ling Soc Am; Mod Greek Studies Asn; Soc Romanian Studies; Soc Albanian LStudies; Am Asn Southeast Europ Studies. *Res:* Languages in contact; bilingualism; sociolinguistics. *Publ:* coauth, Reference Grammar of Literary Dhimotiki, Mouton, The Hague, 64; auth, On a Generative Grammar of the Balkan Languages, Found Lang, 67; Sunday Greek, Papers 4th Regional Meeting Chicago Ling Soc, 68; The status of turkisms in the present day Balkan languages, Aspects of Balkans, 72; On some aspects of linguistic hellenocentrism, Proc 11th Int Cong Ling, 75; coauth, Reduplication of indefinite direct objects in Albanian and modern Greek, Lang, 76; Learnedisms in Costas Taktsis's Third Wedding, Byzantine & Mod Greek Studies, 79; On Modern Greek poi-, Who?, In: Papers from the Parasession on Pronouns and Anaphora, Chicago Ling Soc, 80. *Mailing Add:* Dept of Ling Univ of Chicago Chicago IL 60637

KEANEY, JOHN JOSEPH, b Boston, Mass, May 8, 32; m 57; c 3. CLASSICS. *Educ:* Boston Col, AB, 53; Harvard Univ, AM, 55, PhD, 59. *Prof Exp:* From instr to assoc prof, 59-78, PROF CLASSICS, PRINCETON UNIV, 78- *Mem:* Am Philol Asn. *Res:* Greek political theory, paleography and lexicography. *Publ:* Auth, The structure of Aristotle's Athenaion Politeia, Harvard Studies Class Philol, 63; The text of Androtion F 6 and the origin of ostracism, Historia, 70; Moschopulea, Byzantinische Zeitschrift, 71; Alphabetization in Harpocration, Greek, Roman & Byzantine Studies, 73; Theophrastus on Greek judicial procedure, Trans Am Philol Asn, 74. *Mailing Add:* 103 E Pyne Princeton Univ Princeton NJ 08540

KEARLEY, F FURMAN, b Montgomery County, Ala, Nov 7, 32; m 51; c 2. CLASSICAL HEBREW & GREEK. *Educ:* Ala Christian Col, BA, 54; Harding Grad Sch of Reglig, MA, 56, MRE, 65, MDiv, 65; Auburn Univ, MEd, 60; Hebrew Union Col, PhD(Hebrew & ancient Near East hist), 71. *Prof Exp:* Asst prof relig & Greek, Ala Christian Col, 56-60, chmn, Bible Dept, 60-67; dean, Ala Christian Sch of Relig, 67-69; chmn, Bible Dept, Lubbock Christian Col, 70-75; prof, 75-79, DIR GRAD STUDIES, ABILENE CHRISTIAN UNIV, 79- *Concurrent Pos:* Lectr, Churches of Christ, 70-82; staff writer, The World Envagelist, Power for Today, Sound Doctrine 20th Century Christian, Firm Found, 70-82; adj prof, Ala Christian Sch of Relig, 74-82; consult, Sweet Publ Co, 75-82. *Mem:* Soc Bibl Lit; Evangel Theol Soc; Am Soc for Oriental Res. *Res:* Biblical languages; Ancient Near East history and archaeology; Christian apologetics. *Publ:* Auth, God's Indwelling Spirit, Parchment Press, 74; Problems and dangers in the use of the Dead Sea Scrolls, Restoration Quart, 74; The tongues of I Corinthians 14, Abilene Christian Col Lectures, 75; What about the alleged discrepancies in the Bible?, Upreach Mag, 78; Exegesis of Matthew 24, Abilene Christian Col Lectures, 80; The conditional nature of prophecy, Sound Doctrine, 81. *Mailing Add:* Dept of Relig & Bibl Lang Abilene Christian Col Abilene TX 79699

KEATING, LOUIS CLARK, b Philadelphia, Pa, Aug 20, 07; m 36; c 3. FRENCH LITERATURE, SPANISH TRANSLATION. *Educ:* Colgate Univ, AB, 28; Harvard Univ, AM, 30, PhD(Romance lang), 34. *Prof Exp:* Instr French, Colgate Univ, 28-29; asst prof Span, Macalester Col, 34-36; asst prof French & Span, Monticello Col, 36-37; assoc, Univ Ill, 37-39; from asst prof to prof Romance lang, George Washington Univ, 39-57, chmn dept, 46-57; prof, Univ Cincinnati, 57-60; prof, 63-74, chmn dept mod foreign lang, 63-66, EMER PROF FRENCH, UNIV KY, 74- *Concurrent Pos:* Vis prof, Univ Ky, 62-63; vis prof French, Univ Calgary, 69-70. *Mem:* MLA; Am Asn Teachers Fr. *Res:* Sixteenth and 20th century French literature. *Publ:* Auth, Studies on the Literary Salon in France, 1615, Harvard Univ, 41; Critic of Civilization: George Duhamel, Univ Ky, 65; Andre Maurois, Twayne, 69; transl, J L Borges, Introduction to American Literature, Univ Ky, 71; auth, Joachim du Bellay, 71 & Etienne Pasquier, 72, Twayne; transl, J L Borges: Introduction to English Literature, 74 & co-transl, The Book of Count Lucanor, 77, Univ Ky. *Mailing Add:* 608 Raintree Rd Lexington KY 40502

KECK, CHRISTIANE ELISABETH, b Jena, Ger, July 19, 40; US citizen. GERMANIC LANGUAGE & LITERATURES. *Educ:* Col New Rochelle, AB, 61; Columbia Univ, MA, 62; Univ Tex, Austin, PhD(Ger), 66. *Prof Exp:* PROF GER, PURDUE UNIV, WEST LAFAYETTE, 64-, CHMN GER & CLASSICS, 73- *Concurrent Pos:* Dir honors, Purdue Univ, West Lafayette, 79-, asst dean grad sch, 80- *Mem:* MLA; Am Asn Teachers Ger; Am Comp Lit Asn. *Res:* Italian Renaissance as an influence on German literature; 19th century German drama and novelle; the European historical novel. *Publ:* Auth, Renaissance and Romanticism: Tieck's Conception of Cultural Decline as Portrayed in his Vittoria Accorombona, In: Ser, German Studies in America, Vol 20, 76. *Mailing Add:* Dept of Foreign Lang & Lit Purdue Univ West Lafayette IN 47907

KEELE, ALAN FRANK, b Provo, Utah, Nov 17, 42; m 66; c 6. GERMAN LANGUAGE & LITERATURE. *Educ:* Brigham Young Univ, AB, 67; Princeton Univ, PhD(Ger), 71. *Prof Exp:* Asst prof, 71-77, ASSOC PROF GER, BRIGHAM YOUNG UNIV, 77- *Res:* Contemporary German literature; 1890-1945; Romanticism. *Publ:* Auth, Die atom-tiger von Manhatten, 12/74 & Who's Afraid of Hogan's Heroes?, 9/75, Dokumente, Cologne; Ethics in embryo: Abortion and the problem of morality in post-war German literature, Ger Rev, 5/76; Paul Schallueck and the Post-War German Don Quixote, Lang, Bern, 76; The Führer's new clothes: Helmuth Hübener and the case of the Mormons in the Third Reich, 11-12/80 & Trailing clouds of glory? Artistic treatments (and mistreatments) of the preexistence, 7-8/81, Sunstone; Through a (dark) glass clearly. . .: Magic spectacles and the motif of the mimetic mantic in postwar German literature, Ger Rev, 8/82; The terrible toys: A view from German literature at the process of play-time psychological pre-conditioning for dictatorship, war and Holocaust, Soundings, 7/82. *Mailing Add:* Dept of Ger Brigham Young Univ Provo UT 84602

KEENE, DONALD LAWRENCE, b New York, NY, June 18, 22. JAPANESE LITERATURE. *Educ:* Columbia Univ, AB, 42, PhD, 49; Cambridge Univ, MA,49. *Hon Degrees:* D Litt, Cambridge Univ, 78. *Prof Exp:* Lectr Japanese, Cambridge Univ, 49-53; from asst prof to assoc prof, 54-60, PROF JAPANESE, COLUMBIA UNIV, 60- *Concurrent Pos:* Guggenheim fel, 61-62 & 71-72; vis prof, Univ Pa, 72. *Honors & Awards:* Order of the Rising Sun, Japanese Govt, 76. *Mem:* Am Acad Arts & Sci; Japan Soc; Am Orient Soc. *Res:* A history of Japanese literature. *Publ:* Auth, Major Plays of Chikamatsu, Columbia Univ, 61; Bunraku, The Art of the Japanese Puppet Theatre, 65 & No, The Classical Theatre of Japan, 66, Kodansha; transl, Essays in Idleness, 67, ed, Twenty Plays of the No Theatre, 70 & auth, Chushingura: The Treasure of Loyal Retainers, 71, Columbia Univ; Landscapes and Portraits, Kodansha, 71; World Within Walls, Holt, 76. *Mailing Add:* 407 Kent Hall Columbia Univ New York NY 10027

KEENER, FREDERICK M, English, Comparative Literature. See Vol II

KEETON, KENNETH E, b Owensboro, Ky, June 6, 27; m; c 2. GERMANIC LANGUAGES & LITERATURE. *Educ:* Georgetown Col, BA, 50; Univ Ky, MA, 52; Univ NC, PhD(Ger), 56. *Prof Exp:* Instr Ger & Span, Wake Forest Col, 52-54; asst prof Ger, 56-60; actg chmn div mod lang, 72-73, PROF GER, ECKERD COL, 60-, CHMN COLLEGIUM COMP CULT, 73- *Concurrent Pos:* Instr, Univ NC, 54-56, teaching fel, 55-56; ed, Newslett, SAtlantic Teachers Ger, 57-65; consult foreign lang, Gibbs Jr Col, 62-64. *Mem:* Am Asn Teachers Ger; SAtlantic Mod Lang Asn (vpres, 68-69). *Res:* Franz Kafka; Hermann Hesse; comparative cultures of Western Europe. *Publ:* Auth, The Berliner Montags Klub; ed, Programmed German for classroom on independent study, Ed Pro Schola, 65; Scherz und Ernst, Appleton, 67; auth, The husband of Charlotte von Stien. *Mailing Add:* 1141 Third Ave S Tierra Verde FL 33715

KEFFER, LOWELL WILLIAM, b Newmarket, Ont, Dec 24, 32. FRENCH-CANADIAN LITERATURE. *Educ:* Univ Toronto, BA, 54, Hons, 58; Ont Col Educ, Dipl, 55; Laval Univ, MA, 60. *Prof Exp:* Sec sch teacher, Barrie Dist Col Inst, 55-57; exchange teacher, Staatliches Ludwigsgymnasium, Saarbrücken, Ger, 58-59; asst prof mod lang, 60-67, assoc prof French, 67-72, chmn dept French & Que studies, 73-76, assoc prof, 72-79, PROF FRENCH-CAN LIT, BISHOP'S UNIV, 80-- *Concurrent Pos:* Can Coun fels, 64-65 & 70-72. *Mem:* MLA; Asn Can Univ Teachers Fr; Can Inst Int Affairs; Asn des litt canadiennes et quebecoise; Asn canadienne-francaise l'avancement des sci. *Res:* French-Canadian literature, especially contemporary novel; Quebec novel of the 19th century; Quebec civilization. *Publ:* Auth, Andre Langevin, Yves Theriault & Bertrand Vac, In: Suppl, Oxford Companion to Canadian History and Literature, 1967-1972, 73; contrib, Frustration, conflict and revolt: Aspects of the theme in selected Quebec novels (bilingual text), ABQ-QLA Bull, 7-9/77. *Mailing Add:* Etudes francaises et quebecoises Bishop's Univ Lennoxville PQ J1M 1Z7 Can

KEILSTRUP, DUANE VICTOR, b Wayne, Nebr, Aug 21, 35; c 3. GERMAN, OLD NORSE. *Educ:* Univ Nebr, BA, 57, MA, 59, PhD(Ger), 73. *Prof Exp:* Instr Ger, Univ Tex, Arlington, 60-61 & NTex State Univ, 61-62; asst prof, Univ Tulsa, 62-63; ASSOC PROF GER, UNIV TEX, ARLINGTON, 63- *Concurrent Pos:* Co-ed, Schatzkammer, 75- *Mem:* Am Coun Teaching Foreign Lang; Soc Advan Scand Studies; Am Asn Teachers Ger; Southern Conf Lang Teaching; SCent Mod Lang Asn. *Res:* Pedagogy: Old Norse; German language. *Publ:* Auth, The Texas experiment in closing the gap between high school and college learning programs: a positive alternative to the college placement dilemma, ADFL Bull, 11/74; coauth, A source list for teachers of German, Schatzkammer, spring 75, additions, spring 76, spring 77 & spring 78; The Texas Novemberfest, Die Unterrichtspraxis, fall 75; An algorithm for choosing the imperative forms, Schatzkammer, spring 77; auth, Building Enrollment Through the Total Act, 79 & Guidelines for Directing a Foreign Language Play, 79, Tex AATG Presentations; Using the Situation-Oriented Miniplay and the Videotape Recorder in Teaching Advanced Converstation, Foreign Lang Annals, 80; An Advanced Intensive Language Program: Practical Guidelines and Techniques, Mod Lang J, 81. *Mailing Add:* Dept of Ger Univ of Tex Arlington TX 76019

KELLER, ABRAHAM CHARLES, b Cleveland, Ohio, Feb 21, 16; m 41; c 2. FRENCH. *Educ:* Ohio State Univ, AB, 36, AM, 37; Univ Calif, PhD, 46. *Prof Exp:* Instr, Stockton Jr Col, 45-46; instr, Harvard Univ, 46-48; from asst prof to assoc prof, 48-63, PROF FRENCH, UNIV WASH, 63- *Mem:* MLA; Renaissance Soc Am; Am Asn Teachers French. *Res:* French literature and intellectual history, especially Renaissance. *Publ:* Auth, The Telling of Tales in Rebelais: Relativity in the Essays of Montaigne. *Mailing Add:* Dept of Romance Lang Univ of Wash Seattle WA 98105

KELLER, DANIEL SCHNECK, b Lancaster, Pa, Nov 21, 21; m 49; c 3. SPANISH-AMERICAN LITERATURE. *Educ:* Univ Calif, AB, 47, MA, 49, PhD(Romance lit), 53. *Prof Exp:* Lectr, 52-53, from instr to asst prof, 53-60, ASSOC PROF SPAN, UNIV CALIF, DAVIS, 60- *Mem:* Am Asn Teachers Span & Port. *Res:* Spanish American drama; literary translation. *Mailing Add:* Dept of Span & Classics Univ of Calif Davis CA 95616

KELLER, GARY D, b San Diego, Calif, Jan 1, 43; m 67; c 1. SPANISH-ENGLISH BILINGUALISM, CHICANO LITERATURE. *Educ:* Univ of the Americas, BA, 63; Columbia Univ, MA, 67, PhD(Span), 71; New Sch Social Res, MA, 72. *Prof Exp:* Instr Span, Pace Col, 67-69; instr, Columbia Col, Columbia Univ, 69-70; asst prof, City Col New York, 70-74; assoc prof, Dept Foreign Lang & Humanities, York Col, City Univ New York, 74-78, chmn dept, 74-76; prof, William Paterson Col NJ, 78-79; DEAN, GRAD SCH, EASTERN MICH UNIV, 79- *Concurrent Pos:* Vis asst prof, NY Univ, 73 & 77; adj prof, Teachers Col, Columbia Univ, 77-79. *Mem:* MLA; Ling Soc Am; Int Ling Asn. *Res:* Spanish-English bilingualism; higher education administration. *Publ:* Auth, The Significance and Impact of Gregorio Maranon, Univ NC, 74, Bilingual Press, 76; coauth, Espana en el siglo veinte (anthology of Spanish literature), Harcourt, 74; Spanish Here and Now, 77, Student Manual/Programmed Instruction/Self-Testing for Spanish Here and Now, 78, Viva la lengua!, Harcourt Brace Jovanovich, 79; Hispanics in the US, Bilingual Press, Vol I, 80, Vol II, 82; Leo y Entiendo, 82 & Bilingual Education in ghe United States for Hispanic Students, 82, Teachers Col Press. *Mailing Add:* Grad Dean Eastern Mich Univ Ypsilanti MI 48197

KELLER, HANS-ERICH, b Balsthal, Switz, Aug 8, 22; nat US citizen; m; c 2. MEDIEVAL FRENCH LITERATURE, HISTORY OF ROMANCE LANGUAGES. *Educ:* Univ Basel, Mittellehrerexamen, 47, Oberlehrerexamen, 50, Doktorexamen(French, Ital), 52, Privatdozent, 58. *Prof Exp:* Privatdozent French medieval lit, Univ Basel, 58-59 & French ling, 60-61; substitute prof, Univ Innsbruck, 59-60; vis prof French & Romance ling, Univ Mich, Ann Arbor, 61-63; prof French & Occitan ling & dir inst, Univ Utrecht, 63-69; PROF FRENCH LANG & MEDIEVAL LIT, OHIO STATE UNIV, 69- *Mem:* Soc Ling Romane; MLA; Soc Rencesvals Etude Epopees Romanes (pres, Dutch Nat Br, 64-69); Int Arthurian Soc; Int Courtly Lit Soc. *Res:* French and Occitan dialectology; Rolandian matter; Arthuriana. *Publ:* Coauth, Bibliographie des Dictionnaires Patois Supplement, Droz, Geneva, 54; auth, Etudes Linguistiques sur les Parlers Valdotains, Francke, Bern, 58; ed, Französisches Etymologisches Wörterbuch, Vol VI, I Zbinden, Basel, 68; auth, Bibliographie des Dictionnaires Patois Galloromans (1550-1967), Librairie Droz, Geneva, 69; La version dionysienne de la Chanson de Roland, Philologica Romanica, 75; La Chanson de Roland: poeme de propagande pour le royaume capetien du milieu du XIIe siecle, Travaux de Linguistique et de Litterature, 76; Changes in Old French Epic Poetry and Changes in the Taste of its Audience, In: The Epic in Medieval Society, 77; The Song of Roland and its audience, Olifant, 79. *Mailing Add:* 1594 Essex Rd Columbus OH 43221

KELLER, HOWARD HUGHES, b Brooklyn, NY, Sept 5, 41; m 69. THEORETICAL LINGUISTICS, RUSSIAN LITERATURE. *Educ:* Fordham Univ, AB, 63; Georgetown Univ, PhD(Russ), 67. *Prof Exp:* Asst prof ling, Southern Ill Univ, Carbondale, 66-67; Fulbright lectr, Univ Sofia, 67-68; assoc prof, 70-80, PROF RUSS, MURRAY STATE UNIV, 80- *Concurrent Pos:* Bk rev ed, Slavic & East Europ J, 78-; Nat Endowment for Humananities fel, 78; Presidential res fel, Murray State Univ, 79; ed, Slavic & East Europ J, 80-; Nat Endowment for Humanities fel, 81. *Mem:* Am Asn Teachers Slavic & East Europ Lang; Ling Soc Am; Am Asn Advan Slavic Studies; Am Asn Teachers Ger; Ling Soc Am. *Res:* Slavic and Germanic word formation; language teaching methodology; language and the brain. *Publ:* Auth, German Root Lexicon, Univ Miami, 73; Polysemy and homonymy: Word form and concept representation, Proc SECOL 13, 3/75; The need for a topical vocabulary checklist, Lang Today, 1/76; FLA-101: A cultural introduction to languages, Foreign Lang Ann, 1/76; Sourcebooks in Russian culture, Slavic & East Europ J, fall 77; Studying languages without learning one, Change Mag, 1/78; Vocabulary Presentation and Review: Some Alternatives (monogr), Ctr Applied Ling, 78; German Word Family Dictionary, Univ Calif, 78; Memory: Poetic and neurophysical descriptions, Slavic & East Europ J, spring 82; Vocabulary flashcards on the microcomputer, Russ Lang J, winter 82. *Mailing Add:* Dept of Foreign Lang Murray State Univ Murray KY 42071

KELLER, JEAN PAUL, b Cleveland, Ohio, July 21, 12; m 44; c 3. SPANISH. *Educ:* Heidelberg Col, AB, 33; Ohio State Univ, MA, 40; Univ Wash, PhD(Romance lang & lit), 49. *Prof Exp:* Instr Span, Univ Wash, 48-53; asst prof French & Span, Cent Wash Col Educ, 53-55; asst prof, 55-79, EMER ASST PROF SPAN, ALBION COL, 80-, CHMN DEPT MOD LANG, 64- *Mem:* Mediaeval Acad Am; MLA; Am Asn Teachers Span & Port. *Res:* Columbian folk poetry; Spanish mediaeval literature. *Publ:* Auth, The hunt and prophecy episode in Poema de Fernan Gonzalez & The structure of the Poema de Fernan Gonzales, Hisp Rev; The mysterious origin of Fernan Gonzalez, Nueva Rev Filol Hisp. *Mailing Add:* Dept of Mod Lang Albion Col Albion MI 49224

KELLER, JOHN ESTEN, b Lexington, Ky, Sept 27, 17. ROMANCE LANGUAGES. *Educ:* Univ Ky, AB, 40, AM, 42; Univ NC, PhD, 46. *Prof Exp:* Instr, Univ NC, 43-46; asst prof, Univ Ky, 46-47; from asst prof to assoc prof, Univ Tenn, 47-50; from asst prof to prof Romance lang, Univ NC, Chapel Hill, 50-67, exec secy curric in folklore, 63-67; assoc dean, Col Arts & Sci, 67-72, PROF SPAN & CHMN DEPT SPAN & ITAL, UNIV KY, 67- *Honors & Awards:* UK Sang Award Outstanding Contribr to Grad Educ, 73. *Mem:* MLA; Mediaeval Acad Am; Am Asn Teachers Span & Port; SAtlantic Mod Lang Asn (pres, 67-68); corresp mem Hisp Soc Am. *Res:* Roman philology; Old Spanish literature; iconography of brief medieval Spanish narrative. *Publ:* Auth, Motif-index of Mediaeval Spanish Exempla, Univ Tenn; ed, El libro de los gatos, 58, El libro de los Exemplos por a b c, 61 & Calila et Digna, 67, Consejo Super Invest Cient, Madrid, 67; auth, Alfonso X, el sabio, 67 & Gon alo de Berceo, 72, Twayne; The Book of Count Lucanor and Patronio, Univ Ky, 77. *Mailing Add:* Dept of Span & Ital Univ of Ky Lexington KY 40506

KELLER, THOMAS LAWRENCE, b Pasadena, Calif, Mar 22, 42; m 71; c 2. GERMANIC LINGUISTICS & LITERATURE. *Educ:* Univ Idaho, BA, 66; Univ Colo, MA, 70, PhD(Ger), 75. *Prof Exp:* Resident dir, Univ Colo, Regensburg, 71-72; asst prof, 75-80, ASSOC PROF GER, SOUTHERN ILL UNIV, 81- & DIR, AUSTRIA/ILL EXCHG PROG, 82- *Mem:* MLA; Am Asn Teachers Ger; Pedagog Sem Ger Philol . *Res:* Modern German dialects, especially Bavarian; middle high German language; middle high German literature. *Publ:* Auth, The City Dialect of Regensburg, Hamburger Phonetische Beiträge, 76; The modern history of E Kranzmayer's Bairische Kennwörter in Regensburg, Germany, 78 & Some orthographic problems in the Vorau manuscript, 79, Orbis; MF205,1 Sit ich den sumer truoc as Microcosm of Iwein and Hartmann von Aue, Germanic Notes, Vol 11; Iwein and the lion, Amsterdamer Beiträge zur älteren Germanistick, Vol 15; German dialects in the classroom, USF Lang Quart, Vol 18; Establishing a basis of articulation--ann important step in the teaching of German pronunciation, J Ling Assoc Southwest, Vol 3; The dragon in Beowulf Revisited, Aevum, Vol 55. *Mailing Add:* Dept of Foreign Lang Southern Ill Univ Carbondale IL 62901

KELLER, WERNER OSWIN, b Auerbach, Ger, Nov 25, 20; US citizen; m 43; c 5. GERMAN. *Educ:* Univ Leipzig, State Exam, 48. *Prof Exp:* Teacher high sch, Ger, 44-52 & pvt sch, 52-56; asst prof Ger, 60-65, assoc prof, 65-79, PROF GER, LENOIR RHYNE COL, 80- *Mem:* SAtlantic Mod Lang Asn; Am Asn Teachers Ger. *Mailing Add:* Box 290 Lenoir Rhyne Sta Hickory NC 28601

KELLEY, EMILIA NAVARRO, b Madrid, Spain, Jan 3, 40; c 1. SPANISH POETRY & NOVEL. *Educ:* Bowling Green State Univ, BA, 61; Tulane Univ, MA, 65, PhD(Span), 70. *Prof Exp:* From instr to asst prof, 68-74, ASSOC PROF SPAN, EMORY UNIV, 74-, CHMN DEPT ROMANCE LANG, 76-, CHMN DEPT MOD LANG & CLASSICS, 78- *Mem:* MLA; AAUP. *Res:* Sixteenth and 17th century Spanish poetry; 16th and 17th century Spanish novel; 16th and 17th century comparative poetry. *Publ:* Ed, Victor Hugo's Los Miserables, NAUTA, Barcelona, 72; auth, El concepto metafisica en la poesia de Quevedo, Cuadernos Hispanoamericanos, 72; La poesia metafisica de Quevedo, Guadarrama, Madrid, 73; Sobre la estetica de Gongora, Revista de la Universidad de Mexico, 9/75; ed, introd & notes, In: Beatus Vir: Carne de Hoguera C Ponce de La Fuente y Fr Jeronimo Gracian de la Madre de Dios, In: Nacional, Biblioteca de Visionarios, Marginados y Heterodoxos, 78. *Mailing Add:* Dept of Mod Lang & Classics Emory Univ Atlanta GA 30322

KELLEY, KATHLEEN ANN, b Ames, Iowa, Dec 6, 47. CLASSICS. *Educ:* Loyola Univ Chicago, BA, 70; Univ Wis-Madison, MA, 72, PhD(classics), 75. *Prof Exp:* ASST PROF CLASSICS, EMORY UNIV, 75- *Concurrent Pos:* Woodrow Wilson fel, 70. *Mem:* Am Philol Asn; Archaeol Inst Am; Class Asn Mid West & South. *Res:* Greek tragedy. *Mailing Add:* Dept of Classics Emory Univ Atlanta GA 30322

KELLEY, LINDA MURPHY, b St Louis, Mo, Aug 6, 50; m 74; c 81. SPANISH AMERICAN LITERATURE, BRAZILIAN LITERATURE. *Educ:* Univ Denver, BA, 72; St Louis Univ, MA, 74, PhD(Port & Span), 78. *Prof Exp:* Translr Span, Port, French, US Govt, Defense Mapping Agency, Aerospace Ctr, 78-81. *Res:* Feminine image in literature; Brazilian literature; Spanish American literature. *Mailing Add:* 194 Horseshoe Dr St Louis MO 63122

KELLING, HANS-WILHELM L, b Schwerin, Ger, Aug 15, 32; US citizen; m 58; c 2. GERMAN LANGUAGE & LITERATURE. *Educ:* Brigham Young Univ, BA, 58; Stanford Univ, MA, 60, PhD(Ger), 67. *Prof Exp:* Teaching asst Ger, Brigham Young Univ, 57-58; asst, Stanford Univ, 58-61; from asst prof to assoc prof, 62-72, chmn, Dept Germanic Lang, 77-82, PROF GER, BRIGHAM YOUNG UNIV, 72-, CHMN DEPT GERMANIC & SLAVIC LANG, 82- *Mem:* MLA; Rocky Mountain Mod Lang Asn; Am Asn Teachers Ger. *Res:* German literature of the classical period; cultural history. *Publ:* Coauth, Deutsche Aufsatzhilfe, Brigham Young Univ, 67 & 68; auth, Bettina von Arnim--a study in Goethe idolatry, Bull Rocky Mountain Mod Lang Asn, 6/69; The idolatry of poetic genius, Yearbk English Goethe Soc, 70; The Idolatry of Poetic Genius in German Goethe Criticism, Herbert Lang, Berne, 70; coauth, Deutscwhie Man's Sagt und Schreibt, 72 & auth, Deutsche Kulturgeschichte, 73; Holt; Goethe the Dichterprophet, Ger Life & Lett, 73. *Mailing Add:* 270 Maeser Bldg Brigham Young Univ Provo UT 84602

KELLINGER, JOSEF MICHAEL, b Ambridge, Pa, Oct 7, 16; m 61; c 2. GERMAN. *Educ:* Capital Univ, AB, 41; Ohio State Univ, MA, 42; Syracuse Univ, PhD(Ger), 52. *Prof Exp:* Instr Ger, Syracuse Univ, 48-51; asst prof, Univ Rochester, 52-57; assoc prof & chmn dept, Wilson Col, 57-59, prof, 59-79; prof, Dickinson Col, 79-81; EMER PROF GER, WILSON COL, 81- *Concurrent Pos:* Vis prof Ger, Ford Found grant, Univ Göttingen, 70-71. *Honors & Awards:* Christian R & Mary F Lindback Found Distinguished Teaching Award, 65. *Mem:* Am Asn Teachers Ger; MLA. *Res:* History of words and semantics; comparative philology and linguistics; 18th, 19th and 20th century comparative and German literature. *Publ:* Auth, Über den Einfluss der Franzosischen Revolution auf die Deutsche Sprache; Passport to German, Columbia Rec, 62. *Mailing Add:* Dept of Ger Wilson Col Chambersburg PA 17201

KELLOGG, ROBERT LELAND, English. See Vol II

KELLY, DAVID H, b Philadelphia, Pa, Sept 23, 29. CLASSICAL LINGUISTICS. *Educ:* Cath Univ Am, BA, 52; Univ Pa, MA, 54, PhD, 58. *Prof Exp:* From asst prof to assoc prof classics & ling, La Salle Col, 61-70, chmn dept foreign lang, 67-69, dean arts & sci, 69-70; PROF CLASSICS, MONTCLAIR STATE COL, 70- *Mem:* Ling Soc Am; Am Philol Asn; Class Asn Atlantic States (pres, 77-78). *Res:* Language teaching methodology; classical humanities; syntax of Greek and Latin. *Publ:* Auth, Distinctive feature analysis in Latin phonology, Am J Philol, 67; Transformations in the Latin nominal phrase, Class Philol, 68; Tense in the Latin independent operative, Glotta, 72; Latin the tool subject, Class Outlook, 73; Revolution in classical studies, Class J, 73. *Mailing Add:* Dept of Classics Montclair State Col Upper Montclair NJ 07043

KELLY, DOROTHY JEAN, b Akron, Ohio, Aug 27, 52; m 79. FRENCH LITERATURE, LITERARY CRITICISM. *Educ:* Smith Col, BA, 74; Yale Univ, MA, 75, PhD(Fr), 80. *Prof Exp:* Instr French, Yale Univ, 77-78; lectr, 80, vis asst prof, 81, ASST PROF FRENCH, BOSTON UNIV, 81- *Mem:* MLA. *Res:* Nineteenth century French literature; literary criticism and critical theory. *Publ:* Auth, Language as knowledge or language as power, Ling in Lit, Vol V, 80; Review of Balzac et les Parent Pauvres, Romanic rev, 3/82; Balzac's L'Auberge Rouge: On reading an ambiguous text, Symposium, spring 82; The ghost of meaning: Language in the fantastic, Substance, fall 82; What is the message in Le Message, 19th Cent Fr Studies (in press). *Mailing Add:* Dept of Mod Foreign Lang Boston Univ Boston MA 02215

KELLY, FREDERICK DOUGLAS, b Los Angeles, Calif, July 17, 34; c 2. FRENCH. *Educ:* Univ Southern Calif, BA, 56; Univ Wis, Madison, MA, 59, PhD(French), 62. *Prof Exp:* From instr to assoc prof, 62-70, PROF FRENCH, UNIV WIS, MADISON, 70- *Concurrent Pos:* Vis prof, Inst Res in Humanities, 67-68; asst ed, Fr Rev, 67-71; Am Coun Learned Soc fel, 74-75; fel, Romnes Fac, Univ Wis, 76-80. *Mem:* Int Arthurian Soc (vpres, 81-84); MLA; Mediaeval Acad Am; Int Courtly Lit Soc; Int Soc Hist Rhet. *Res:* Medieval French literature; Provencal language and literature; Medieval Latin literature. *Publ:* Auth, Sens and Conjointure in the Chevalieer de la Charrette, Mouton, The Hague & Paris, 66; The scope of the treatment of composition in the twelfth and thirteenth century arts of poetry, Speculum, 66; The source and meaning of conjointure in Chretien's Erec 14, Viator, 70; Chretien de Troyes: An Analytic Bibliography, Grant & Cutler, London, 76e; Medieval Imagination: Rhetoric and the Poetry of Courtly Love, Univ Wis, 78; Topical invention in medieval French literature, In: Medieval Eloquence: Studies in the Theory and Practice of Medieval Rhetoric, Univ Calif Press, 78; Translatio studii: Translation, adaptation, and allegory in medieval French literature, Philol Quart, 78; Les Inventions ovidiennes de Froissart: Reflexions intertextuelles comme imagination, Litterature, 81. *Mailing Add:* Dept of French & Ital Univ of Wis Madison WI 53706

KELLY, JAMES MICHAEL, b Detroit, Mich, Nov 6, 36; m 60; c 1. TURKIC LINGUISTICS, ARABIC STUDIES. *Educ:* Wayne State Univ, BA, 60; Univ Wash, MA, 64; Harvard Univ, PhD(Turcology), 70. *Prof Exp:* ASSOC PROF TURKISH & ARABIC, UNIV UTAH, 68- *Concurrent Pos:* Fel, Am Res Inst Turkey, 73. *Mem:* Mediaeval Acad Am; Am Orient Soc; MidE Studies Asn NAm; Turkish Studies Asn. *Res:* Islamic history; Central Asian history. *Publ:* Auth, On defining Dhu a th-Thalathah and Dhu al-Arba'ah, J Am Orient Soc, 71; Remarks on Kasyari's Phonology I, linguistic terminology, 72 & Remarks on Kasyari's Phonology II, orthography, 73, Ural-Altaische Jahrbucher. *Mailing Add:* MidE Ctr Univ of Utah Salt Lake City UT 84112

KELLY, JOHN RIVARD, b Chicago, Ill, Dec 7, 39; m 65. SPANISH, PORTUGUESE. *Educ:* Mexico City Col, AB, 61; Univ Southern Calif, MA, 64, PhD, 67. *Prof Exp:* Asst prof Span & Port, Univ Calif, Santa Barbara, 65-74; ASSOC PROF SPAN & PORT, NC STATE UNIV, 74- *Mem:* Am Asn Teachers Span & Port; Philol Asn Pac Coast; Pac Coast Coun Latin Am Studies; SAtlantic Mod Lang Asn. *Res:* Chilean literature; Brazilian literature; Latin American culture. *Publ:* Auth, Name symbolism in Eduardo Barrios' El hermano asno, Romance Notes, fall 71; An annotated bibliography of the early writings of Jose Luis do Rego, Luso-Brazilian Rev, summer 72; La ensenanza de la literatura hispano-americana entraduccion inglesa, Hispania, 12/73; Pedro Prado, Twayen, 73. *Mailing Add:* Dept of Foreign Lang & Lit NC State Univ Raleigh NC 27607

KELLY, LOUIS GERARD, b Helensville, NZ, Nov 17, 35; Can & NZ citizen; m 61; c 4. LINGUISTICS. *Educ:* Univ NZ, BA, 58, MA, 59, dipl Latin, 61; Laval Univ, PhD(ling), 67. *Prof Exp:* Asst master lang, NZ Educ Dept, 61-63; lectr ling, Laval Univ, 63-65; res assoc, Royal Comn Bilingualism & Biculturalism, Can Govt, 65-67; from asst prof to assoc prof, 67-78, PROF LING, UNIV OTTAWA, 78- *Concurrent Pos:* Consult, Int Comt English in Liturgy, 69-71; mem, Humanities Res Coun Can, 69-77; consult, Ont Dept Educ, 70-; vis scholar, Cambridge Univ, 73-74 & 80-81. *Mem:* Can Asn Ling; NZ Ling Soc; MLA; Int Phonetic Asn. *Res:* History of linguistics; bilingualism; history of translation. *Publ:* Auth, De modis generandi; points of contact between Noam Chomsky and Thomas of Erfurt, Folia Ling, V:225-252; Punning and the linguistic sign, Linguistics, 66:5-11; English as a second language: An historical sketch, English Lang Teaching, XXV: 120-132; Twenty Five Centuries of Language Teaching, Newbury House, 69; Description and Measurement of Bilingualism, Univ Toronto, 69; Quaestiones Alberti de Modis Significandi, Benjamins, Amsterdam, 77; The True Interpreter, Blackwells, Oxford, 79. *Mailing Add:* Dept of Ling & Mod Lang Univ of Ottawa Ottawa ON K1N 6N5 Can

KELLY, MARIE-THERESE, b Ireland, Nov 4, 13; US citizen. FRENCH. *Educ:* Marymount Col, NY, BA, 38; Univ Calif, Los Angeles, MA, 49; Laval Univ, PhD(French), 54. *Prof Exp:* Prof French, 38-78, PROF FRENCH LIT, LOYOLA MARYMOUNT UNIV, 68- *Mem:* AM Asn Teachers Fr; MLA. *Res:* French; life and physical sciences; philosophy. *Publ:* Auth, Culte Marial chez Charles Peguy, Can Publ, 54; Charles Peguy rassembleur des siecles du Christianisme, Romance Notes, 60; L'Influence de Charles Peguy aux Etats-Unis, L'Amitie Charles Peguy, Paris, 9/71. *Mailing Add:* Dept of French Loyola Marymount Univ Los Angeles CA 90045

KELLY, THOMAS EDWARD, b Pittston, Pa, Dec 19, 32; m 64; c 3. ROMANCE LANGUAGES. *Educ:* Wilkes Col, BA, 54; Inst de Phonetique, Paris, cert, 56; Univ Iowa, MA, 57; Univ Calif, Berkeley, PhD(romance lit), 68. *Prof Exp:* Instr French, Dartmouth Col, 62-67; from instr to asst prof, 67-73, ASSOC PROF FRENCH, PURDUE UNIV, WEST LAFAYETTE, 73- *Concurrent Pos:* Lilly Endowment fel, 82. *Mem:* MLA; Int Arthurian Soc; Medieval Acad Am; Am Asn Teachers Fr. *Res:* Medieval French literature; Arthurian romance; interdisciplinary studies. *Publ:* Auth, Interdisciplinary studies, In: Annual Review of Modern Foreign Language Education, Am Coun Teaching Foreign Lang, 73; Le haut Livre du Graal: Perlesvaus--A Structural Study, Droz, Geneva, 74; Chartres Cathedral as a visual focus for interdisciplinary study, Fr Rev, 12/74; Love in the Perlesvaus: Sinful passion or redemptive force?, Romanic Rev, 1/75. *Mailing Add:* Dept of Foreign Lang & Lit Purdue Univ West Lafayette IN 47907

KENDALL, CALVIN B, English. See Vol II

KENKEL, KONRAD O, b Tilsit, Ger, July 1, 38; m 68; c 1. GERMAN LITERATURE & HISTORY. *Educ:* Ind Univ, PhD(Ger lit), 75. *Prof Exp:* Lectr Ger, Ind Univ, 68-72; instr, St Olaf Col, 72-74; instr, 74-75, asst prof, 75-81, ASSOC PROF GER, DARTMOUTH COL, 81- *Concurrent Pos:* Am Coun Learned Soc grant in aid Kandinsky, 78. *Mem:* MLA; Am Asn Teachers Ger. *Res:* Mythology and literature; German expressionism; European modern drama. *Publ:* Auth, Die Funktion der Sprache bei Hofmannsthal, In: Texte und Kontexte, Francke Verlag, Bern, 73; Medeadramen: Entymythisierung und Remythisierung, Bouvier Verlag, Bonn, 79; Was liefert dir die Welt?, Rauch, Nebel und Gedichte; Die Lyrik des Andreas Gryphius, In: Text und Kritik, 7/8, Munchen ed, 80. *Mailing Add:* Dept of Ger Dartmouth Col Hanover NH 03755

KENNEDY, GEORGE ALEXANDER, b Hartford, Conn, Nov 26, 28; m 55; c 1. CLASSICS. *Educ:* Princeton Univ, AB, 50; Harvard Univ, AM, 52, PhD(classics), 54. *Prof Exp:* Instr classics, Harvard Univ, 55-58; from asst prof to assoc prof, Haverford Col, 58-65; prof & chmn dept, Univ Pittsburgh, 65-66; prof, 66-72, chmn dept, 66-76, PADDISON PROF CLASSICS, UNIV NC, CHAPEL HILL, 72- *Concurrent Pos:* Mem managing comt, Am Sch Class Studies, Athens, 58-; Guggenheim fel, 64-65; Fulbright fel, Italy, 64-65; dir Am off, L'Annee Philol, 68-74; chmn bd gov, Univ NC Press, 72-; trustee, Am Acad Rome, 77-80; Am Acad LArts & Sci fel, 78-; Dumbarton Oaks Ctr for Byzantine Studies fel, 79-80; Nat Coun for Humanities, 80-; Southeast Regional chmn, Mellon Fellowships, 82- *Honors & Awards:* Golden Anniversary Award, Speech Commun Asn, 73; Goodwin Award of Merit, Am Philol Asn, 75. *Mem:* Am Philol Asn (vpres, 77-78, pres, 79); Archaeol Inst Am; Speech Commun Asn; Inst Early Am Hist & Cult; Int Soc Hist Rhetoric (vpres, 81-84). *Res:* History of rhetoric; classics in America. *Publ:* Auth, The Art of Persuasion in Greece, Princeton Univ, 63; Quintilian, Twayne, 69; The Art of Rhetoric in the Roman World, Princeton Univ, 72; Classical rhetoric and its Christian and secular tradition, Univ NC, 80; Greek rhetoric under Christian emperors, Princeton Univ, 82. *Mailing Add:* Dept of Classics Univ of NC Chapel Hill NC 27514

KENNEDY, RUTH LEE, b Centerville, Tex, Oct 15, 94. SPANISH LITERATURE. *Educ:* Univ Tex, AB, 16, AM, 17; Univ Pa, PhD, 31. *Prof Exp:* Instr, Okla Col Women, 19-20; instr, Univ PR, 20-21; prof Span, Southwest Tex State Teachers Col, 22-23, 25-26; prof Span, lang & lit, San Antonio Jr Col, Tex, 27-28, 29-30; from asst prof to prof, Smith Col, 30-61; vis prof, 50-51, prof, 61-71, EMER PROF SPAN, UNIV ARIZ, 71-; EMER PROF SPAN, SMITH COL, 61- *Concurrent Pos:* Am Asn Univ Women Palmer fel, 37-38, Justin fel, 45-56; lectr, Oxford Univ & Cambridge Univ, 46; Guggenheim fel, 51-52; consult, new master's degree in Romance lang, Univ NC, Greensboro, 67. *Honors & Awards:* Athena Award for Prof Women, Pan-Hellenic Soc, Tucson, Ariz, 78. *Mem:* Hist Soc Am; MLA. *Res:* Tirso de Molina and his competitors; Tirso and the New Regime of Philip IV and Olivares; Tirso and various literary movements of 1617-1626. *Publ:* Auth, La prudencia en la mujer and the ambient that brought it forth, Pac Mod Lang Asn, 12/48; A reappraisal of Tirso's relations to Lope and his theater, Bull The Comediantes, fall 65 & spring 66; coauth, Tirso's No hay peor sordo: Its date and place of composition, In: Homenaje a Rodriguez Monino, Castalia, Madrid, 66; auth, Studies in Tirso, Vol I, In: The Dramatist and His Competitors, Univ NC Studies in Romance Languages & Literatures, 74; El condenado por desconfiado: Its ambient and its date of composition, In: Homenaje a Guillermo Guastavino, 74; Tirso's El mayor desengano: Its date of composition, its ambient, and its interpretation, Revista de archivos, biblioteras y muscos, 76; El condenado por desconfiado: Various reasons for questioning its authenticity in Tirso's theatre, 76 & El condenado por desconfiado: Yet further reasons for questioning its authority in Tirso's theatre, 77, Ky Quart. *Mailing Add:* 1201 E Helen Tucson AZ 85719

KENNEDY, SIGHLE AILEEN, Modern Literature. See Vol II

KENNY, LORNE MILFORD, Modern Arab History, Arabic Language. See Vol I

KENSTOWICZ, MICHAEL JOHN, b Chicago, Ill, Aug 18, 45. LINGUISTICS, PHONOLOGY. *Educ:* San Jose State Col, BA, 66; Univ Ill, Urbana, PhD(ling), 71. *Prof Exp:* Asst prof, 71-74, assoc prof, 74-80, PROF LING & SLAVIC LANG, UNIV ILL, URBANA-CHAMPAIGN, 81- *Mem:* Ling Soc Am. *Res:* Slavic linguistics; Baltic linguistics; Semitic linguistics. *Publ:* Coauth, Multiple application problem in phonology, Studies Generative Phonology Ling Res, 73; co-ed, Issues in Phonological Theory, 73 & auth, Rule application in pregenerative phonology, In: The Application and Ordering of Grammatical Rules, 76, Mouton, The Hague; coauth, Topics in Phonological Theory, 77 & Generative Phonology, 79, Academic; Functional explanations in generative phonology, In: Phonology in the 1980's, 81; Phonology of Chukchee consonants, In: Studies in the Languages of the USSR, Ling Res Inc, 82; Vowel harmony in Palestinian Arabic, Linguistics, 19: 5. *Mailing Add:* Dept of Ling Univ of Ill Urbana IL 61801

KERN, EDITH, French & Comparative Literature. See Vol II

KERN, GARY WOOWARD, b Washington, DC, Oct 4, 38; m 60; c 2. RUSSIAN LITERATURE. *Educ:* George Washington Univ, BA, 63; Univ Manchester, MA, 65; Princeton Univ, PhD(Russ lit), 69. *Prof Exp:* Asst prof Russ lit, Univ Rochester, 69-76; lectr Russ, Univ Calif, Riverside, 76-77; LECTR RUSS LIT, UNIV SOUTHERN CALIF, 81- *Res:* Soviet Russian literature. *Publ:* Ed, Lev Lunts i Serapionovy bratya, Novyi Zhurnal, 66; auth, The Serapion Brothers: A dialectics of fellow traveling, Russ Lit Triquart, 72; ed & transl, The Young Tolstoi, by B Eikhenbaum, 72 & Before Sunrise, by M Zoshchenko, 74, Ardis; auth, Solzhenitsyn's Portrait of Stalin, Slavic Rev, 74; ed & translr, Snake Train: Poetry and Prose by Velimir Khlebnikov, Ardis, 76; auth, Trotsky's Autobiography, Russ Rev, 77; Ivan the Worker, Mod Fiction Studies, 77; transl, The Education of a True Believer by Lev Kopelev, 80; auth, In Search of Fantasy, Bridges to Fantasy, 82. *Mailing Add:* 545 Highlander Dr Riverside CA 92507

KERR, JOHN AUSTIN, JR, b Bahia, Brazil, Apr 9, 34; US citizen; c 2. PORTUGUESE, HISTORY. *Educ:* Cornell Univ, BA, 55, M Ed, 61; Univ Wis-Madison, MA, 65, PhD(Port), 70. *Prof Exp:* Transl/interpreter Span & Port, Kelly-Springfield Tire Co, Md, 58-60; teacher Span, McDonogh Sch, Md, 61-64; instr Port, Ohio State Univ, 69-70; asst prof Span & Port, Stanford Univ, 70-72; asst prof, 72-78, ASSOC PROF SPAN & PORT, NORTHERN ILL UNIV, 78- *Concurrent Pos:* Prog reviewer Span & Port, Nat Endowment Humanities, 77- *Mem:* Am Asn Teachers Span & Port; Int Conf Group on Mod Portugal; Mod Lang Asn Am; Midwest Mod Lang Asn; Pac Northwest Coun For Lang. *Res:* Contemporary Portuguese literature; contemporary Brazilian literature; colonization in Brazil. *Publ:* Auth, The quotidian element in Cecilia Meireles' Poemsas Escritos na India, Proc of Pac NW Coun Foreign Lang, 75; Cattle-raising in Brazil: an overview, Revista Geografica, 12/75; An overview of Migueis' prose fiction, 1923-1968: questions of time, place, selected thematic content and the author's view of the world, Estudos Ibero-Am, 7/76; Noite de Festa as an example of Migueis' early thematic interests, Romanische Forschungen, 76; Some considerations on Rodrigues Migueis' Leah, World Lit Today, spring 77; Colonization in Parana: lessons from the south, Luso-Brazilian Rev, summer 77; Migueis--To the Seventh Decade, Romance Monographs, Univ Miss, 77; Jorge de Sena on Rodrigues Migueis: A personal perspective, Studies on Jorge de Sena, 81. *Mailing Add:* Dept of Foreign Lang & Lit Northern Ill Univ De Kalb IL 60115

KERR, RICHARD A, b Glasgow, Scotland, June 13, 15; m 48; c 2. ROMANCE LANGUAGES. *Educ:* Univ Glasgow, MA, 37. *Prof Exp:* Lectr Span, Univ Southampton, 49-67; vis lectr Romance lang, 67-76, ASSOC PROF ROMANCE LANG, STATE UNIV NY BINGHAMTON, 76- *Concurrent Pos:* Vis prof, Univ Ore, 63-64. *Mem:* Am Asn Teachers Span & Port. *Res:* Spanish literature of 16th century. *Publ:* Auth, El problema Villalon y un manscrito desconocido del Scholastico, Clavileno, Madrid, 55; Prolegomena to an edition of Villalon's Scholastico, Bull Hisp Studies, 55; Cristobal de Villalon, El scholastico, Vol I, Consejo Super Invest Cient, Madrid, 67. *Mailing Add:* 4000 Franklin Pl Binghamton NY 13903

KERSLAKE, LAWRENCE CARL, b Toronto, Ont, Aug 25, 39; m 62; c 3. FRENCH LITERATURE. *Educ:* Univ Toronto, BA, 61; Univ Chicago, AM, 62, PhD(French), 72. *Prof Exp:* From lectr to asst prof, 66-75, assoc chmn dept, 75-77, actg chmn, 78, ASSOC PROF FRENCH, UNIV TORONTO, 75- *Mem:* Am Soc 18th Century Studies; Societe Francaise d'Etude du XVIIIe Siecle. *Res:* Seventeenth century French theater; 18th century French literature; correspondence of Madeame De Graffigny. *Publ:* Johann Georg Sulzer and the supplement to the Encycl Studies on Voltaire and the Eighteenth Century, 148: 225-247; Silvain's Traite Du Sublime: Authorship and reception, Romance Notes, 19: 38-43; An Early Eighteenth Century Theory of the Sublime, Revue De L'Universite D'Ottawa, 50: 262-279. *Mailing Add:* Dept of Fr Trinity Col Univ of Toronto Hoskin Ave Toronto ON M5S 1H8 Can

KERSON, ARNOLD LEWIS, b New Haven, Conn, Aug 9, 31; m 60. SPANISH & SPANISH AMERICAN LITERATURE. *Educ:* Yale Univ, BA, 53, PhD(Span), 63. *Prof Exp:* Instr Span, Wesleyan Univ, 56-58; instr, Yale Univ, 58-60; from instr to asst prof, 60-69, ASSOC PROF SPAN, TRINITY COL, CONN, 69- *Mem:* MLA; Am Asn Teachers Span & Port; New England Coun Latin Am Studies; Northeast Mod Lang Asn; Int Asn Neo-Latin Studies. *Res:* Spanish cassical drama; Spanish American literature, especially the Colonial Period. *Publ:* Auth, Francisco Javier Alegre: Humanista Mexicana del siglo XVIII, Cuadernos Am, Mex, 9-10/68; El concepto de utopia de Rafael Landivar en la Rusticatio Mexicana, Rev Ibero-Am, 6-12/76; Francisco Javier Alegre's translation of Boileau's Art Poetique, Mod Lang Quart, 6/81. *Mailing Add:* Dept of Mod Lang Trinity Col Hartford CT 06106

KESS, JOSEPH FRANCIS, b Cleveland, Ohio, Feb 27, 42; m 66. LINGUISTICS. *Educ:* Georgetown Univ, BS, 62; Univ Hawaii, MA, 65, PhD(ling), 67. *Prof Exp:* From asst prof to assoc prof, 67-80, PROF LING, UNIV VICTORIA, 80- *Concurrent Pos:* Am Philos Soc Phillips Fund award, 67-68; Can Coun grant, 73-74; res grant, Immigration Hist Res Ctr, Univ Minn, 76; ling rep, Publ Comt, Humanities Res Coun Can, 77. *Mem:* Ling Soc Am; Int Ling Asn; Can Ling Asn. *Res:* Slovenian, Tagalog and Haida; languages in contact; psycholinguistic investigation of ambiguity. *Publ:* Auth, English influences in Japanese as spoken in Hawaii, Te Reo, 69; A bibliography of the Haida language, Can J Ling, 69; Ribence tales among the American Slovenians, J Ohio Folklore, 69; The semantics of focus, Anthrop Ling, 75; On redefining the notion of focus in Tagalog, Pac Ling, 75; On linguistic insecurity, English Quart, 75; Reversing directions in psycholinguistics, Lang Sci, 76; Psycholinguistics, Academic, 76; Ambiguity in Psycholinguistics, John Bensamins, 82. *Mailing Add:* Dept of Ling Univ of Victoria Victoria BC V8W 2Y2 Can

KETCHIAN, SONIA, b Lowell, Mass. RUSSIAN LITERATURE & LANGUAGE. *Educ:* Harvard Univ, MA, 68, PhD(Slavic lang & lit), 75. *Prof Exp:* From instr to asst prof Russ lang & lit, Dartmouth Col, 73-76; preceptor Russ lang, Harvard Univ, 76-77, fel Russ lit, Russ Res Ctr, 77-81; ASST PROF RUSS LIT & LANG, SMITH COL, 78- *Concurrent Pos:* Vis scholar, Russ Res Ctr, 81-82; Int Res & Exchanges Bd sr scholar/Soviet Ministry of Educ Exchange, 81-82; Fulbright-Hays fac res grant, 81-82. *Mem:* Am Asn Teachers Slavic & E Europ Lang; Semiotics Soc Am Res, Am Asn Advan Slavic Studies. *Res:* Russian poetry and drama, Dostoevsky. *Publ:* Auth, Linguostylistic devices in the temporal structure of Lev Tolstoy's Childhood, Boyhood and youth, Die Welt Slaven, 78; Vehicles for duality in Pushkin's The Bronze Horseman: Similes and period lexicon, Semiotica, 79; Perplexities in the semantic structure of Leonid Andreev's He Who Gets Slapped, Russ Lang J, 79; Imitation as poetic mode in Achmatova's Imitation from I F Annenskii, Scando-Slavica, 79; The Psychological Undertow in Dostoevsky's The Landlady, Die Welt Slaven, 80; Metempsychosis in the verse of Anna Axmatova, Slavic & E Europ J, 81; The Genre of Imitation and Anna Axmatova, Russ Lit (in prep). *Mailing Add:* Russ Res Ctr Harvard Univ Cambridge MA 02138

KETCHUM, ANNE, b Paris, France; c 2. ROMANCE LANGUAGES. *Educ:* Univ Paris, Lic es Lett, 50, Dr lit, 64. *Prof Exp:* Mem fac, Harvard Univ, 58-60; instr, Wellesley Col, 60-62; instr French, Boston Univ, 63-65, grad sch grant, 68, asst prof, 65-79; ASSOC PROF FRENCH, UNIV COLO, BOULDER, 80- *Concurrent Pos:* Transl, French Libr, Boston, 64- *Mem:* MLA; Soc Fr Prof Am; Am Asn Teachers Fr; Int Fed Teachers Fr. *Res:* Contemporary French novel, poetry, and civilization; women writers in France today. *Publ:* Auth, Colette et La naissance du jour, Minard, Paris, 68. *Mailing Add:* Dept of French Univ of Colo Boulder CO 80309

KEUL, CARL, b Ellwood City, Pa, Dec 4, 18; m 47; c 4. GERMAN. *Educ:* Westminster Col, Pa, AB, 47; Cornell Univ, AM, 48, PhD(Ger lit & Ger ling), 55. *Prof Exp:* Instr Ger, Colgate Univ, 48-49; from instr to asst prof, Fla State Univ, 49-60; prof Ger & head dept mod lang, Stephen F Austin State Univ, 60-79; RETIRED. *Mem:* Am Asn Teachers Ger. *Res:* German literature of naturalism. *Mailing Add:* Dept of Mod Lang Stephen F Austin State Univ Nacogdoches TX 75962

KEULS, EVA CLARA, b Amsterdam, Holland; US citizen; div; c 2. CLASSICAL PHILOLOGY. *Educ:* Hunter Col, BA, 61; Columbia Univ, MA, 62, PhD(Greek), 65. *Prof Exp:* Instr classics, Brooklyn Col, 65-66; asst prof, Emory Univ, 66-67; assoc prof, Howard Univ, 67-73; assoc prof, 73-78, PROF CLASSICS, UNIV MINN, MINNEAPOLIS, 78- *Concurrent Pos:* Lectr, Ecole Hautes Etudes, Univ Paris, 65; Southern Fel Found fel, 69; Guggenheim fel, 73; Neth Inst Advan Study fel, 76-77; mem, Inst for Advan Study, 80-81. *Mem:* Am Philol Asn; Archaeol Inst Am; Int Soc Papyrologists. *Res:* The history of aesthetics in antiquity; relations between Greek and Roman literature and the fine arts; mystery symbolism in classical literature. *Publ:* Auth, Greece, Methuen, 66, Follett, 68; The samia of Menander, Zeitschrift fur Papyrologie und Epigraphik, 73; The Water Carriers in Hades, A Study of Catharis Through Toil in Classical Antiquity, Hakkert, Amsterdam, 74; Une cible de la satire: le locus amoenus, Les Etudes Classiques, 74; Skiagraphia once again, Am J Archaeol, 75; Plato and Greek Painting, E J Brill, Leiden, Holland, 78; The Reign of the Phallas: Sex and Aggression in Classical Athens, McGraw-Hill (in prep). *Mailing Add:* Dept of Classics Univ of Minn Minneapolis MN 55455

KEVELSON, ROBERTA, Philosophy. See Vol IV

KEY, MARY RITCHIE (MRS AUDLEY E PATTON), b San Diego, Calif, Mar 19, 24; m; c 3. LINGUISTICS. *Educ:* Univ Tex, MA, 60, PhD(ling), 63. *Prof Exp:* Asst prof ling, Chapman Col, 63-66; from asst prof to assoc prof, 66-78, chmn prog ling, 69-71, 75-77, PROF LING, UNIV CALIF, IRVINE, 78- *Concurrent Pos:* Foreign student adv, Chapman Col, 64-66; consult English textbks, Calif State Curric Comn, 66 & 74-75; Bur Indian Affairs consult, Ctr Applied Ling, Washington, DC, 67 & 69; Univ Calif regent's grant, 74; Am Dialect Soc regional secy, 74-; Fulbright-Hays grant, 75; vchancellor acad affairs grant, 75; deleg to Senate Rep Assembly, 75-77 & 81-83. *Honors & Awards:* Friends Libr Bk Award, Univ Calif, 76. *Mem:* Ling Soc Am; Am Dialect Soc; Ling Asn Can & US; Soc Int Ling Fonctionnelle; Soc Ling Europaea. *Res:* Comparative linguistics; nonverbal communication; sociolinguistics. *Publ:* Auth, Comparative Tacanan Phonology, Mouton, 68; Male/Female Language, 75, Paralanguage and Kinesics, 75 & Nonverbal Communication, 77, Scarecrow; The Grouping of South American Indian Languages, Gunter Narr, Tubingen, 79; Catherine the Great's Linguistic Contribution, Ling Res, Edmonton, 80; ed, The Relationship of Verbal and Nonverbal Communication, 80 & Nonverbal Communication Today, 82, Mouton. *Mailing Add:* Dept of Ling Univ of Calif Irvine CA 92717

KEYES, GORDON LINCOLN, b Kearney, Ont, Mar 5, 20; m 45; c 2. HISTORY, CLASSICS. *Educ:* Univ Toronto, BA, 41, MA, 42; Princeton Univ, PhD, 44. *Prof Exp:* Asst prof Latin & Greek, Birmingham-Southern Col, 45-47; from lectr to assoc prof classics, 47-63, chmn dept classics, 71-74, prin Victoria Col, 76-81, PROF ANCIENT HIST, VICTORIA COL, UNIV TORONTO, 63- *Concurrent Pos:* Can Coun sr res fel, 59-60; vis prof, Univ Victoria, 70. *Mem:* Soc Promotion Roman Studies; Class Asn Can; Am Philol Asn; Mediaeval Acad Am. *Res:* St Augustine's philosophy of history; religious life of the Roman Empire. *Publ:* Auth, Christian Faith and the Interpretation of History: A Study of St Augustine's Philosophy of History, Univ Nebr, 66. *Mailing Add:* Victoria Col Queens Park Toronto ON M5S 1K7 Can

KEYT, DAVID, Philosophy. See Vol IV

KHOURI, MOUNAH, b Lebanon, Nov 26, 18; m 56; c 2. ARABIC LITERATURE. *Educ:* Am Unin Beirut, BA, 52, MA, 56; Harvard Univ, PhD(Arabic studies), 64. *Prof Exp:* Instr Arabic, Int Col, Lebanon, 50-56; instr, Georgetown Univ, 59-60; assoc prof Arabic lit, Univ Calif, Berkeley, 60-72, prof & chmn, Dept Near Eastern Studies, 72-75. *Concurrent Pos:* Fel, Humanities Inst, Univ Calif & Soc Sci Res Coun fel, 68-69; dir, US Ctr Arabic Studies Abroad, 70-74. *Mem:* Am Orient Soc; Am Asn Teachers Arabic; Mid EStudies Asn NAm. *Res:* Classical and modern Arabic literature. *Publ:* Auth,

Toynbee's View of Islamic Hisotyr (Arabic), Dar Al-Ilm, Beirut, 60; coauth, Advanced Arabic Readers, Univ Calif, Berkeley, Vols I & II, 61 & 62; auth, Mutran's contribution, Ling Studies, 66; Three Critics: Eliot, Richards and MacLeish (Arabic), Dar al-Thaqafa, 66; Poetry and the Making of Modern Egypt (1882-1922), Brill, Leiden, 69; coauth, Elementary Modern Standard Arabic, Univ Mich Press, 70; auth, An Anthology of Modern Arabic Poetry, Univ Calif, Berkeley, 74. *Mailing Add:* Dept of Near Eastern Studies Univ of Calif Berkeley CA 94720

KIBBEE, DOUGLAS ALAN, b Chicago, Ill, Aug 18, 49; m 70; c 1. FRENCH & ROMANCE LINGUISTICS. *Educ:* Colgate Univ, BA, 71; Ind Univ, Bloomington, MA, 75, PhD(French ling), 79. *Prof Exp:* ASST PROF FRENCH, WESTERN KY UNIV, 79- *Mem:* MLA; Ling Soc Am; SAtlantic Mod Lang Asn; Southeast Conf Ling; Mediaeval Acad Am. *Res:* History of the French language; history of grammatical thought; French syntax. *Publ:* Auth, Ico/co: The i-forms of the demonstratives in the Chanson de Roland, Southeast Conf Ling Rev, summer 82. *Mailing Add:* Dept of Mod Lang Western Ky Univ Bowling Green KY 42101

KIBLER, LOUIS WAYNE, b Clifton Forge, Va, July 23, 39; m 60; c 3. ITALIAN, FRENCH. *Educ:* Ind Univ, BA, 61, PhD(French), 65. *Prof Exp:* Asst prof Ital & French, Ind Univ, Bloomington, 65-72; assoc prof mod lang, Sweet Brair Col, 72-74; ASSOC PROF ITAL, WAYNE STATE UNIV, 74- *Mem:* MLA; Am Asn Teachers Ital; AAUP. *Res:* Twentieth century Italian and French novel; medieval Italian theater. *Publ:* Coauth, Giorno per Giorno, Macmillian, 71; auth, Imagery as expression; Moravia's Indifferenti, Italica, fall 72; Reality and realism of Moravia, Ital Quart, summer 73; Imagery in Georges Bataille's Le Bleuduciel, Fr Rev, spring 74; Patterns of time, In: Pavese's La luna e ifalo, Forum Italicum, fall 78; Moravia and Guttuso: A la recherche de la realite perdue, Italica, summer 79. *Mailing Add:* Dept of Romance & Ger Lang Wayne State Univ Detroit MI 48202

KIBLER, WILLIAM W, b Rochester, NY, Jan 22, 42; m 68; c 2. MEDIEVAL FRENCH, ROMANCE PHILOLOGY. *Educ:* Univ Notre Dame, AB, 63; Univ NC, MA, 66, PhD(Romance philol), 68. *Prof Exp:* Asst prof French, Univ Ark, 67-69; asst prof, 69-73, assoc prof, 73-82, PROF FRENCH, UNIV TEX, AUSTIN, 82- *Mem:* MLA; Am Asn Teachers French; Int Arthurian Soc; Soc Rencesvals; Mediaeval Acad Am. *Res:* Medieval French epic; Middle French poetry. *Publ:* Auth, The unity of Baudouin de Sebourc, Studies Philol, 70; Roland's pride, Symposium, 72; Bertrand de Bar-sur-Aube, author of Aymeri de Narbonne?, Speculum, 73; Self-delusion in Froissart's Espinette Amoureuse, Romania, 76; ed, Eleanor of Aquitaine, Patron and Politician, Univ Tex, 76; auth, Poet and patron: Froissart's Prison Amoureuse, Esprit Createur, 78; ed, Lion de Bourges, poeme epique du XIVe siecle, Droz, Geneva, 80; ed & transl, Chretien de Troyes, Lancelot, Garland, 81. *Mailing Add:* Dept of Fr & Ital Univ of Tex Austin TX 78712

KIDDLE, LAWRENCE BAYARD, b Cleveland, Ohio, Aug, 20, 07; m 32; c 2. ROMANCE LANGUAGES & LITERATURES. *Educ:* Oberlin Col, AB, 29; Univ Wis, AM, 30, PhD, 35. *Prof Exp:* Asst Span & French, Univ Wis, 30-35; from instr to asst prof Romance lang, Univ NMex, 35-38; instr Span, Princeton Univ, 38-40; from asst prof to assoc prof Romance lang, Tulane Univ, 40-43; from asst prof to assoc prof Span, 47-54, prof, 54-78, EMER PROF ROMANCE LING, UNIV MICH, ANN ARBOR, 78- *Concurrent Pos:* Fulbright lectr ling, Inst Caro y Cuervo, Colombia, 63-64. *Honors & Awards:* Order of Ayacucho, Peru, 47. *Mem:* Nat Fed Mod Lang Teachers Asn (vpres, 56); Am Asn Teachers Span & Port (pres, 52); Ling Soc Am; MLA; corresp mem, Hisp Soc Am. *Res:* Medieval Spanish language and literature; Spanish dialectology. *Publ:* Co-ed, Mariano Azuela, Los de abajo, 39 & Veinte cuentos hispanoamericanos, 56, Appleton; Alfonso X, El libro de las Cruces, Consejo Super Invest Cient, Madrid, 61; Veinte cuentos espanoles, Appleton-Century-Crofts, 61; Blasco Ibanez, La barraca, Holt, 61; Cuentos americanos, Norton, 70. *Mailing Add:* Dept of Romance Lang Univ of Mich Ann Arbor MI 48109

KIEFFER, BRUCE, b Akron, Ohio, Aug 27, 51; m 71. GERMAN LITERATURE. *Educ:* Columbia Col, BA, 73; Princeton Univ, PhD(Ger), 79. *Prof Exp:* ASST PROF GERMAN, WILLIAM COL, 78- *Mem:* MLA; Lessing Soc; Am Nietzsche Soc. *Res:* German literature and thought of 18th and 19th centuries. *Publ:* Auth, Herder's treatment of Suessmilch's theory of origin of language, Germanic Rev, 78; Wieland and Lessing: Musarion and Minna, Lessing Yearbook, 82; Tragedy in the logocentric world: Schiller's Kabal und Liebe, Ger Studies Rev, 82. *Mailing Add:* Weston Lang Ctr Williams Col Williamstown MA 01267

KIESER, ROLF, b Zurich, Switz, May 14, 36. GERMAN LITERATURE & HISTORY. *Educ:* Univ Zurich, PhD(hist, Ger lit), 63. *Prof Exp:* Instr Ger lit, City Col New York, 64-65; asst prof Queens Col, NY, 65-73; chmn dept Ger & Scand, 73-76 & 80-81; resident dir, prog studies abroad in Ger, 67-68; fac res award, 72-73, 75-77, assoc prof, 73-76, PROF GER, GRAD SCH, CITY UNIV NEW YORK & QUEENS COL, NY, 76- *Concurrent Pos:* Lectr Am cult & hist, Univ Kiel, 67-68; mem Fulbright screening comt scholar Cent & East Europe, 70-71, chmn, 71; PSC-BHE fac res awards, 72 & 75-77. *Mem:* MLA; Swiss Am Hist Soc (lst vpres, 72-81); Northeast Mod Lang Asn. *Res:* Contemporary German literature; Switzerland as a literary exile (1933-1950); contemporary narrative prose. *Publ:* Georg Kaiser im Schweizer Exil, Schweizer Monatashefte, 76; Das Tagebuch als Idee und Struktur, Frisch, Prosawerk, 78; Faustische Elemente in Max Frischs Don Juan, Buhnenwerk, 79; Jakob Schaffner, Amsterdamer Beitrage, 79; An Interview with Adolf Muschg, Basis, 79; Frisch und Brecht, Revue d' Allemagne, 79; Between Sils-Maria and Golgatha, Klett, 80; Beyond Brecht and Aristotle, Theatrum Mundi, 80. *Mailing Add:* 82 Irving Pl New York NY 10003

KIFFER, THEODORE EDWIN, b Edneavor, Pa, July 28, 25; m 46; c 3. ENGLISH, LINGUISTICS. *Educ:* Roberts Wesleyan Col, BA, 51; Pa State Univ, University Park, MA, 61, PhD(English), 65. *Prof Exp:* Clergyman, Free Methodist Church, 51-60; instr English, Pa State Univ, 60-65; assoc prof ling, Kutztown State Col, 65-67; assoc prof English, Univ Liberia, 67-68; asst dir, Berks Ctr, 68-70, res assoc 70-71, ASSOC PROF ENGLISH & LING, PA STATE UNIV, UNIVERSITY PARK, 68-, DIR GEN EDUC, 71-, ASSOC HEAD DEPT, 76- *Concurrent Pos:* Fulbright Sr Lectr, 67-68. *Mem:* Asn Gen & Lib Studies; Ling Soc Am; MLA. *Res:* English phrasal verbs and modals; administrative models. *Publ:* Coauth, Human service occupations: A handbook, Ctr Studies Higher Educ, 6/72; auth, Preface to the Urbanization of Man, 72 & ed, Urbanization of Man, rev ed, 76, McCutchan. *Mailing Add:* 119 Sparks Bldg Pa State Univ University Park PA 16802

KILCHENMANN, RUTH JOHANNA, b Langnau, Switz, Jan 1, 17; US citizen; wid; c 2. GERMAN & COMPARATIVE LITERATURE. *Educ:* Univ Southern Calif, PhD, 56. *Prof Exp:* Lectr Ger, Univ Southern Calif, 55-56; instr, Cent Col, Iowa, 56-57; asst prof Ger & Span, Lycoming Col, 57-58; assoc prof Ger, Southwestern Campus, Southern Ill Univ, 58-61; vis assoc prof, Mich State Univ, 61-63; foreign lang consult, Minn State Dept Educ, 63-64; assoc prof Ger, State Univ NY Albany, 64-65; assoc prof Ger & comp lit, Queens Col, NY, 65-68; prof Ger & chmn dept foreign lang, Shippensburg State Col, 68-69; chmn foreign lang, Am Col Switz, 69-73; ed & educ consult, Hoffmann-La Roche Inc, Basel, Switz, 73-74; RES & WRITING, 74- *Concurrent Pos:* Coordr, foreign lang in elem schs, workshop, Southern Ill Univ, 61; instr methods & demonstration teaching, NDEA, 62; consult, US dependent schs Europ area, 62, 64, 67. *Mem:* MLA; Am Comp Lit Asn; Am Asn Teachers Ger; Int Comp Lit Asn; Am Coun Teaching Foreign Lang. *Res:* Comparative literature; teaching methods. *Publ:* Auth, Ein amerikanischer Beitrag zur Hesseforschung, Bund, Berne, 8/58; Teaching lyric poetry in first year German, Ger Quart, 5/62; Die deutsche und die amerikanische Kurzgeschichte: Beziehungen und Einflüsse, Proc Comp Lit Asn, 66; Die Kurzgeschichte, Formen und Entwicklung, Kohlhammer, Stuttgart, 67, 68, 71, 75 & 78; Bilder aus Deutschlands Gegenwart und Vergangenheit, Ed Atlantic Forum, 67; ed, Rezept für die bösen Weiber-Kalendergeschichten, Peter Hammer, 70; auth, Schlauekisten machen Geschichten: Anthology about Robots and Computers in Literature, IBM-Europe, Stuttgart, 77. *Mailing Add:* Haus Vasudeva CH 1531 Gletterens Switzerland

KILEY, CORNELIUS JOSEPH, East Asian History. See Vol I

KILKER, JAMES ANTHONY, b Chicago, Ill, Oct 24, 25; m 63; c 2. FRENCH LITERATURE & HISTORY. *Educ:* Univ Mo, AB, 49, PhD(French & Span lit), 61; Univ Md, MFS, 56. *Prof Exp:* Instr French lang, Univ Mo, 56-59; from asst prof to assoc prof French lit & lang, Univ Scranton, 59-64; assoc prof French lit, Duquesne Univ, 64-65 & Western Ill Univ, 65-67; ASSOC PROF FRENCH LIT, SOUTHERN ILL UNIV, CARBONDALE, 67- *Mem:* Am Asn Teachers Fr; MLA; Am Asn Teachers Span & Port; Soc Fr Hist Studies. *Res:* Maupassant; Emmanuel Robles and North African writers of French expression; French historical studies in 18th century North America, especially Medwestern. *Publ:* Auth, Maupassant, pacifist and patriot, Can Mod Lang J, spring 68; coauth, Internsely French: A new program, Fr Rev, 3/72; translr, Emmanuel Robles, Gorgone, Contemp Lit Translr, spring 73; coauth, The Druon Affair: A documentary, Educ Theatre J, 10/74; Georges Michel promotes a Utopian proposal, Drama & Theatre, fall 75; translr, Oeillets Carnations, Pembroke Mag, spring 77; Three Plays by Emmanuel Robles, Southern Ill Univ, 77. *Mailing Add:* Dept of Foreign Lang & Lit Southern Ill Univ Carbondale IL 62901

KILLEAN, CAROLYN GARVER, b Columbus, Ohio, Jan 24, 36; div; c 2. ARABIC LINGUISTICS. *Educ:* Univ Mich, BA, 57, MA, 62, MA, 63, PhD(ling), 66. *Prof Exp:* Asst prof, 67-72, ASSOC PROF ARABIC & LING, UNIV CHICAGO, 72- *Concurrent Pos:* Fel, Am Res-Ctr Egypt, 66-67; Fulbright-Hays fel, Cairo, 73-74; mem, Am Coun Learned Soc-Soc Sci Res Count Joint Comt on Near & MidE, 76; Mid East Adv Comt, Fulbright Coun Int Exchange Scholars, 78-82. *Mem:* Ling Soc Am; Am Asn Teachers Arabic (exec secy-treas, 76-); MidE Studies Asn NAm. *Res:* Linguistic study of Egyptian colloquial and modern literary Arabic; sociolinguistics in the Arab world. *Publ:* Auth, Classical Arabic, Current Trends Ling, Vol VI. *Mailing Add:* Dept of Near Eastern Lang & Civilizations Univ of Chicago 1155 E 58th St Chicago IL 60637

KILMER, ANNE DRAFFKORN, b Chicago, Ill, June 1, 31; div; c 1. ANCIENT NEAR EASTERN HISTORY & LITERATURE. *Educ:* State Univ Iowa, BA, 53; Univ Pa, PhD(Assyriol), 59. *Prof Exp:* Res asst assyriol, Orient Inst, Chicago, 57-63; vis lectr, 63-64, from asst prof to assoc prof, 65-72, chmn, Dept Near Eastern Studies, 70-72, dean humanities, Col Lett & Sci, 72-76 & 80-82, PROF NEAR EASTERN STUDIES, UNIV CALIF, BERKELEY, 72- *Concurrent Pos:* Guggenheim fel, 61-63; Am Asn Univ Women res fel, 64-65; Humanities Inst res grant & fel, Univ Calif, Berkeley, 67, 69, 70, 76, 79 & 82; Nat Endowment for Humanities res grant studies in Ancient music, Univ Calif, Berekeley, 76-77. *Mem:* Am Schs Orient Res; Am Orient Soc. *Res:* Ancient Mesopotamian music, games and entertainment; Sumero-Akkadian lexical texts; Sumero-Akkadian literature and mythology. *Publ:* Coauth, Materialien zum sumerischen Lexikon, Vol VIII/1, 60 & Vol VIII/2, 63, Pontif Bibl Inst; auth, The Mesopotamian concept of overpopulation and its solution as reflected in the mythology, Orientalia, 72; Symbolic gestures, J Am Orientsl Soc, 74; Akkadian contracts from Alalakh and Ugarit: Another interpretation, Rev Assyriologie, 74; coauth, Sounds from Silence: Recent Discoveries in Ancient Near Eastern Music (bk and 12 inch stereo rec), Bit Enki Pulb, 76; Note on overlooked word play in Akkadian Gilgamesh, In: Zikir Shumim, Leiden, 82. *Mailing Add:* Dept of Near Eastern Studies Univ of Calif 1229 Dwinelle Hall Berkeley CA 94720

KILPATRICK, ROSS STUART, b Toronto, Ont, Oct 3, 34; m 60; c 3. CLASSICS. *Educ:* Univ Toronto, BA, 57, MA, 64; Yale Univ, MA, 65, PhD(classics), 67. *Prof Exp:* Teacher classics & English, EYork Col Inst, Toronto, 57-64; from instr to asst prof classics, Yale Univ, 67-70; ASSOC PROF CLASSICS, QUEEN'S UNIV, ONT, 70- *Concurrent Pos:* Can Coun leave fel, 77-78. *Mem:* Am Philol Asn; Class Asn Can (secy, 73-75). *Res:* Epistles and Arts Poetica of Horace; Roman satire; classical influences. *Publ:* Auth, Fact and fable in Horace, Epistle 1.7, Class Philol, 73; Juvenal's Patchwork satires: 4 and 7, Yale Class Studies, 73; Remember us, Galatea:

Horace, Carmina 3.27, Grazer Beiträge, 75; Horace and his critics: Epistle 1. 19, Phoenix, 75; A note on The Room by Harold Pinter, Theatre Ann, 75; Apocolocyntosis and the vision of Claudius, Class J, 79; Hamlet the scholar, Melanges Gareau, 82. *Mailing Add:* Dept of Classics Queen's Univ Kingston ON K7L 3N6 Can

KIM, CHIN-WU, b Chungju, Korea, Mar 22, 36; m 64; c 2. LINGUISTICS, PHONETICS. *Educ:* Yonsei Univ, Korea, BA, 58; Wash State Univ, BA, 62; Univ Calif, Los Angeles, MA, 64, PhD(ling), 66. *Prof Exp:* From asst prof to assoc prof, 67-72, dir, Tehran Res Univ, 74-76, PROF LING, UNIV ILL, URBANA, 72-, CHMN DEPT, 79- *Concurrent Pos:* Fel, Res Lab Electronics, Mass Inst Technol, 66-67; vis prof ling, Univ Hawaii, Manoa, 72-73, assoc dir, Ling Inst, 77. *Mem:* Ling Soc Am; Ling Asn Gt Brit; Ling Soc Korea. *Res:* Experimental phonetics; generative phonology; African and Altaic linguistics. *Publ:* Auth, The vowel system of Korean, Lang, 9/68; A theory of aspiration, Phonetica, 70; Experimental phonetics, In: A Survey of Linguistic Science, 71; co-ed, Papers in African Linguistics, Ling Res, Inc, 71; auth, Rule ordering in Korean phonology, 77 & Linguistics and language, 78, Korean Studies, Ctr Korean Studies, Univ Hawaii; ed, Papers in Korean Linguistics, Hornbeam Press, 78; auth, The Korean language and linguistics, In: Korean Studies Guide, Univ Hawaii Press, 80; The rhythmic structure of Sijo, Hangul, 81. *Mailing Add:* Dept of Ling Univ of Ill Urbana IL 61801

KIM, HACK CHIN, b Po-un, Chung Chong Pokto, Korea, Mar 7, 26; US citizen, m 62; c 8. CLASSICAL PHILOLOGY, COMPARATIVE LITERATURE. *Educ:* Simpson Col, BA, 54; Univ Wash, MA, 57, PhD(comp lit), 64. *Prof Exp:* Instr Greek, Latin & French, Univ Ore, 60-64, asst prof classics, 64-66; from asst prof to assoc prof, 66-77, PROF CLASSICS & HUMANITIES, WASH STATE UNIV, 77- *Concurrent Pos:* Vis scholar, Cambridge Univ, 72-73. *Mem:* Hellenic Soc; Cambridge Philol Soc; Int Arthurian Soc. *Res:* Writing, especially syllabic scripts; medieval Latin manuscripts; Mycenaean and Homeric Greek. *Publ:* Contrib & transl, Euripides, Orestes, In: Ritual, Realism, and Revolt, Scribner, 72; ed, The Gospel of Nicodemus (Tornonto Medieval Latin texts), Pontif Inst Mediaeval Studies, Toronto, 73. *Mailing Add:* Dept of Foreign Lang & Lit Wash State Univ Pullman WA 99164

KIMBALL, ANNE SPOFFORD, b Bangor, Maine, July 2, 37. FRENCH LANGUAGE & LITERATURE. *Educ:* Mount Holyoke Col, AB, 59; Harvard Univ, MAT, 60; Middlebury Sch French, France, MA, 61; Univ Wis-Madison, PhD(French), 69. *Prof Exp:* Lectr English, Univ Lille, France, 61-62; teacher French, Winsor Sch, Boston, 62-63; instr, Mount Holyoke Col, 63-65 & 67-69, asst prof, 69-74, assoc dean studies, 74-75; ASSOC PROF FRENCH & DEAN, RANDOLPH-MACON WOMAN'S COL, 75- *Concurrent Pos:* Nat Endowment Humanities fel, 71-72. *Mem:* Am Asn Teachers Fr; MLA; Alliance Fr. *Res:* Max Jaco; modern novel; film. *Publ:* Auth, Slides on the French Revolution (French version), J Weston Walch, 73; Women authors of the twentieth century: A course outline and commentary, Femaile Studies, 75; ed, Lettres de Max Jacob a Marcel Jouhandeau, Droz, Geneva (in press); auth, French Civilization Through Pictures and Photographs, J Weston Walch (in prep). *Mailing Add:* Randolph-Macon Women's Col Lynchburg VA 24503

KIMBALL, MERL DOUGLAS, JR, b Salt Lake City, Utah, Oct 13, 28; m 57; c 2. FRENCH LITERATURE & LANGUAGE. *Educ:* Univ Utah, BA, 53, MA, 64; Brigham Young Univ, PhD(French lang & lit), 70. *Prof Exp:* From instr to asst prof, 67-74, assoc prof, 74-80, PROF FRENCH, BRIGHAM YOUNG UNIV, 80- *Mem:* Am Asn Teachers Fr; Rocky Mountain Mod Lang Asn; Pac Northwest Conf Foreign Lang. *Res:* French literature of the 19th and 20th centuries. *Publ:* Auth, Emile Zola and French impressionism, Bull Rocky Mountain Mod Lang Asn, 6/69; Zola's Une Page d'Amour: Pictures at an exhibition, Proc Pac Northwest Conf Foreign Lang, 4/72; The Phoenix flies on swiftly, Sport Flying, 6/73. *Mailing Add:* Dept of French & Ital Brigham Young Univ Provo UT 84602

KIMBER, RITA HAUSAMMANN, b Switz, Jan 6, 34; US citizen. GERMAN & COMPARATIVE LITERATURE. *Educ:* Univ Mass, BA, 59; Harvard Univ, PhD(comp lit), 67. *Prof Exp:* Cataloguer rare bks, Harvard Libr, 67-68; assoc prof Ger, Wellesley Col, 68-70; FREE-LANCE TRANSLR HIST & LIT, 70- *Publ:* Cotranslr, Unschlecht, Little, 75; Revolutionary Patience, Orbis, 77; First American Constitutions, Inst Early Am Hist & Cult, Univ NC, 79; Art in the Third Reich, Pantheon, 79; Laws of the Game, 81, The Thirty Years Peace, 81 & Mars, 82, Knopf. *Mailing Add:* RFD Temple ME 04984

KIMBROUGH, MARY ALICE, b Detroit, Mich, June 10, 32; m 54; c 2. FRENCH. *Educ:* Univ Mich, Ann Arbor, AB, 54; Univ Ill, Urbana, MA, 61, PhD(French). 66. *Prof Exp:* Asst prof, 66-73, assoc prof, 73-77, PROF FRENCH, TEX SOUTHERN UNIV, 77- *Mem:* Am Asn Teachers Fr; SCent Mod Lang Asn; Am Soc 18th Century Studies; South Cent Soc 18th Century Studies. *Res:* Eighteenth century French political literature; medieval French studies. *Mailing Add:* Dept of Foreign Lang Tex Southern Univ Houston TX 77004

KIMMEL, ARTHUR S, b Brooklyn, NY, Sept 1, 30; m 55; c 2. ROMANCE LANGUAGES. *Educ:* Univ Miami, AB, 53, MA, 54; Univ Calif, Berkeley, PhD(Romance lang & lit), 66. *Prof Exp:* Asst French, Univ Calif, Berkeley, 55-59; instr, Sacramento State Col, 59-62; asst prof, Univ SC, 62-65; asst prof hist western cult & dir audio lab, Calif State Col Hayward, 65-68; assoc prof French, Salem State Col, 68-72; ASSOC PROF FRENCH, WESTERN WASH UNIV, 72- *Concurrent Pos:* Fel, Camargo Found, Cassis, France, 78; dir For Study Off & mem bd dirs, Counc Int Educ Exchange, 78-80. *Mem:* MLA; Am Asn Teachers Fr; Philol Asn Pack Coast; Soc Rencesvals. *Res:* Middle Ages, especially Provencal; 17th century. *Mailing Add:* Dept of French Western Wash Univ Bellingham WA 98225

KIMMICH, FLORA GRAHAM HORNE, b Raleigh, NC, Feb 3, 39; m 65. GERMAN LITERATURE. *Educ:* Duke Univ, BA, 59; Yale Univ, MA, 61, PhD(Ger lit), 69. *Prof Exp:* Lectr Ger, Queens Col, 67-70, asst prof, 70-72; ASST PROF GER, PRINCETON UNIV, 72- *Concurrent Pos:* Alexander von Humboldt-Stiftung fel & Am Coun Learned Socs fel, 71-72. *Mem:* AAUP; MLA; Am Asn Teachers Ger; Int Arbeitskreis deutsche Barockliteratur; Am Soc Ger Lit 16th & 17th Centuries. *Res:* Seventeenth century; nineteenth century; lyric poetry. *Publ:* Auth, The end of requirements: A new era for foreign language departments, 69 & If we must retrench . . . , 72, Asn Depts Foreing Lang Bull; Nochmals zur Umarbeitung der Sonette von Andreas Gryphius, Euphorion, 74; Sonnets of Catharina von Greiffenberg: Methods of Composition, Univ NC, 75; Sonnets before Opitz: The evolution of a form, Ger Quart, 76; Weckherlin, Petrarchism, and the renewal of Vernacular poetry, Dahpnis, 78; Opitz's Five Sonnets to Landmarks, Argenis, 78. *Mailing Add:* Dept of Ger Lang & Lit Princeton Univ Princeton NJ 08540

KIM-RENAUD, YOUNG-KEY, b Pusa, Korea, Feb 24, 41; US citizen; m 67; c 1. LINGUISTICS. *Educ:* Ewha Womans Univ, Seoul, Korea, BA, 63; Univ Calif, Berkeley, MA, 65; Univ Paris, Sorbonne, France, cert, 66; Univ Hawaii, Honolulu, PhD(ling), 74. *Prof Exp:* Instr Korean, Asia Training Ctr, Univ Hawaii, Honolulu, 68-69; lectr English & French, Sogang Univ, Seoul, Korea, 71; consult, Asian Am Studies, Asian Forum Inc, 76; adj asst prof, Dept Commun Arts & Sci, Howard Univ, Washington, DC, 77 & 79; RESEACHER APPL LING, UNIV DE PARIS VIII, 80- *Concurrent Pos:* Res grant, Ctr Korean Studies, Univ Hawaii, Honolulu, 75; Joint Comt Korean Studies of Am Coun Learned Socs & Soc Sci Res Coun res award, 75; prin lang & cult of Korea, Korean Sch Va, Arlington, 77-; guest lectr, Asian educ & Asian women, Univ Va, 77-78; asst prog dir ling, Nat Sci Found, 78-79; prin, Korean Sch Va, Arlington, 77-79; guest lect multicultural educ, George Mason Univ, 82. *Mem:* Ling Soc Am; Ling Soc Korea; Int Circle Korean Ling; Korean Lang Res Soc; English Lang & Lit Soc Korea. *Res:* Theoretical and applied linguistics; foreign language training; bilingual/multicultural education. *Publ:* Auth, Syllable boundary phenomena in Korean, Korean Studies, 1:243-273; Semantic features in phonology: Evidence from vowel harmony in Korean, Korean Ling, 1:1-18; The Syllable in Korean Phonology, Papers in Korean Ling, Hornbeam Press, 78; Probing into generative grammar: An interview with Noam Chomsky (in Korean), Lit & Thought, 6:44-70; transl, Noam Chomsky, Language and Unconscious Knowledge (into Korean), In: Psychiatry and the Humanities, 3:3-44; coauth (with Harold S Chu & Kumi Kang), Minimal Objectives for Reading Essentials in Korean: Grade 1-3, 79 & (with Harold S Chu), Oral Proficiency Test in Korean: Grade K-6, 79, Arlington Co Pub Schs; auth, Vers la competence de communication en seconde langue, Cours et Etudes de Ling Contrastive et Appliquee de Vincennes, Univ Paris VIII, No 26, 81. *Mailing Add:* 1340 Merrie Ridge Rd McLean VA 22101

KINDRICK, ROBERT LEROY, Medieval Literature, Linguistics. See Vol II

KING, CHARLES LESTER, b Gosford, Calif, Feb 15, 22; m 49; c 3. SPANISH. *Educ:* Univ NMex, AB, 48; Univ Southern Calif, MA, 50, PhD, 53. *Prof Exp:* Instr Span, La State Univ, 53-54; grant, Binat Crts, Bolivia, Uruguay, Colombia & Iran, 54-60; consult, lang inst, US Off Educ, 60-61, specialist, 61-64; from asst prof to assoc prof, 64-74, PROF SPAN, UNIV COLO, 74- *Concurrent Pos:* Consult, US Off Educ, 64-67; ed, Mod Lang J, 71-79. *Mem:* MLA; Am Asn Teachers Span & Port. *Res:* Contemporary Spanish literature. *Publ:* Auth, Sender's spherical philosophy, PMLA, 12/54; Surrealism in two novels by Sender, Hispania, 5/68; Ramon J Sender, Twayne, 74; Ramon J Sender: An Annotated Bibliography, 1928-1974, Scarecrow, 76. *Mailing Add:* 2870 Duke Circle Boulder CO 80303

KING, DONALD BERNARD, b Bristol, Conn, Sept 3, 13; m 38; c 6. CLASSICAL PHILOLOGY. *Educ:* Dartmouth Col, AB, 35; Princeton Univ, PhD, 40. *Prof Exp:* Instr classics, Dartmouth Col, 38-39; jr fel, Harvard Univ, 39-41; asst prof English, Pa State Col, 41-46; assoc prof classics & hist & head dept classics, Beloit Col, 46-51; from assoc prof to prof classics & English, Col Mt St Joseph, 51-67; dean, St Norbert Col, 67-79. *Concurrent Pos:* Evaluator and consult, NCent Asn Cols & Schs, 60-, mem comn cols & univs, 68-72. *Mem:* AAUP; Am Asn Higher Educ; Class Asn Mid W & S; Conf Acad Deans. *Res:* Ancient and medieval rhetoric and poetic; history of ideas; Greek colonies. *Publ:* Coauth, Erasmus De Copia, Marquette Univ,63. *Mailing Add:* Rte 1--Box 98 Perkinsville VT 05151

KING, EDMUND LUDWIG, b St Louis, Mo, Jan 10, 14; m 51. SPANISH LITERATURE. *Educ:* Univ Tex, AB, 33, AM, 34, PhD, 49. *Prof Exp:* Asst prof, Miss State Col, 36-41; instr, Univ Tex, 46; from instr to assoc prof Span, 46-66, chmn dept Romance lang & lit, 66-72, PROF SPAN, PRINCETON UNIV, 66- *Concurrent Pos:* Vpres, Int Inst, Madrid, 69- *Mem:* MLA. *Res:* Spanish literature. *Publ:* Auth, Becquer: From Painter to Poet, Porrua Hermanos; translr, The Structure of Spanish History, Princeton Univ; auth, What is Spanish Romanticism, Studies Romanticism, autumn 62; ed, El humo dormido, Dell 67. *Mailing Add:* Dept of Romance Lang & Lit Princeton Univ Princeton NJ 08540

KING, HAROLD VOSBURGH, b Hartford, Conn, Mar 19, 17; m 38; c 2. LINGUISTICS. *Educ:* Univ Mich, AB, 38, MA, 39, PhD(ling), 50. *Prof Exp:* Asst prof ling & Span, Foreign Serv Inst, US Dept State, 50-52; dir courses, Binat Ctr, Bogota, Colombia, 52-54, San Jose, Costa Rica, 54-56; vis prof, Caracas, Venezuela, 56; vis prof, Cornell Univ, 56-58; from asst prof to assoc prof, 58-70, prof, 70-79, EMER PROF ENGLISH, UNIV MICH, ANN ARBOR, 79- *Res:* English syntax and semantics. *Publ:* Auth, Verb Forms of English, 57 & Modern American English, 63, Longmans; Guide and Workbook in the Structure of English, Prentice-Hall, 67; English Sentence Structure Review, Univ Mich, 77. *Mailing Add:* 921 Robin Rd Ann Arbor MI 48103

KING, HARRY LEE, JR, b Aug 1, 16. ROMANCE LANGUAGES. *Educ:* Univ Richmond, BA, 36; Univ NC, MA, 53, PhD, 61. *Prof Exp:* Instr Span, Hampden-Sydney Col, 46-47; part time instr, Univ NC, 47-52; instr, Univ Richmond, 53-60; instr Span, 60-61, asst prof Romance lang, 61-67, assoc prof, 67-69, PROF SPAN, WAKE FOREST UNIV, 69- *Mem:* MLA; Am Asn Teachers Span & Port. *Res:* Historical novels of Manuel Galvez; Argentine historical novel. *Mailing Add:* Dept of Romance Lang Wake Forest Univ Winston-Salem NC 27109

KING, JAMES CECIL, b Uniontown, Pa, Sept 14, 24; m 52; c 2. GERMAN. *Educ:* George Washington Univ, BA, 49, MA, 50, PhD(Ger philol), 54. *Prof Exp:* Master French, Ger & Latin, St Albans Sch, Washington, DC, 52-55; from asst prof to assoc prof, 55-65, PROF GER, GEORGE WASHINGTON UNIV, 65- *Concurrent Pos:* Ger Acad Exchange Serv grant, 63. *Mem:* Am Asn Teachers Ger; Am Goethe Soc; Ling Soc Am; Mediaeval Acad Am; MLA. *Res:* German language from beginnings to present day; Old High German literature; general, Indo-European and Germanic linguistics. *Publ:* Ed, Peter hat Pech, Holt, 61; co-compiler, sect on Germanic linguistics, German linguistics, German literature before 1500, In: Modern Language Association International Bibliography, NY Univ, 63-66; co-ed & contribr, Germanic Studies in Honor of Edward Henry Sehrt, Univ Miami, 68; ed, Notker der Deutsche, Boethius' Bearbeitung der Categoriae des Aristoteles, 72, Notker der Deutsche, Boethius' Bearbeitung von Aristoteles' Schrift De Interpretatione, 75 & Notker der Deutsche, Martianus Capella, De Nuptiis Philologiae et Mercurii, 79, Max Niemeyer. *Mailing Add:* Dept Germanic Lang & Lit George Washington Univ Washington DC 20052

KING, JESSE FANNIN, b Tremonton, Utah, Dec 26, 14. ROMANCE LANGUAGES & LITERATURES. *Educ:* Pomona Col, AB, 36; Harvard Univ, AM, 37. *Prof Exp:* Tutor, Eliot House, Harvard 43, Dunster House, 43-44, Lowell House, 44-45 & sr tutor, Dunster House, 45-46; asst prof, 46-55, dormitory dir, 46-53, acting chmn dept Romance lang, 70-71, ASSOC PROF ROMANCE LANG, CLARK UNIV, 55-, FOREIGN STUDENT ADV, 54- *Mem:* Am Asn Teachers Span & Port. *Res:* Seventeenth century French drama; 19th century French poetry; medieval romances. *Mailing Add:* Dept of Mod Lang & Lit Clark Univ Worcester MA 01610

KING, NORMA R, b Roanoke, Va, Jan 1, 37; m 74. SPANISH. *Educ:* Asbury Col, AB, 58; Ind Univ, Bloomington, AM, 65; Inter-Am Univ Mex, PhD(Span), 66; ECarolina Univ, MLS, 74. *Prof Exp:* Teacher, High Sch, Va, 58-59; teacher, Col Am, Rosario, Argentina, 59-60; dir relig educ & teacher English, San Carlos de Bariloche, Arg, 60-63; instr Span, Ferrum Jr Col, 63-64; teaching asst, Ind Univ, Bloomington, 64-65; from asst prof to assoc prof Span, ECarolina Univ, 66-74, coordr Latin Am Studies Comt, 73-74; LIBRN, NEWPORT NEWS PUB SCHS, 74- *Mem:* Peninsula Area Librarians (pres elect, 81-82, pres, 82-83). *Res:* Latin American literature, Argentine literature and Chicano literature; foreign language books and audio-visuals in public school media centers. *Mailing Add:* Newport News Pub Sch 12465 Warwick Blvd Newport News VA 23606

KING, ROBERT DESMOND, b Hattiesburg, Miss, Nov 25, 36; m 73; c 3. LINGUISTICS. *Educ:* Ga Inst Technol, BS & MS, 59; Univ Wis, MA, 62, PhD(Ger), 65. *Prof Exp:* Asst prof Ger, 65-68, from asst prof to assoc prof, 68-73, dean col social & behav sci, 76-79, PROF LING, UNIV TEX, AUSTIN, 73-, DEAN COL LIB ARTS, 79- *Mem:* Ling Soc Am; MLA. *Res:* Historical and Germanic linguistics; phonological theory. *Publ:* Auth, Klopstock as spelling refromer, J English & Ger Philol, 4/67; Functional load and sound change, Language, 7/68; Root vs suffix accent in the Germanic present, J Ling, 9/68; Historical Linguistics and Generative Grammar, Prentice-Hall, 69. *Mailing Add:* Calhoun 501 Univ of Tex Austin TX 78712

KING, ROBERT GENE, Communication, Rhetoric. See Vol II

KING, WILLARD FAHRENKAMP, b Roswell, NMex, July 13, 24; m 51. SPANISH LITERATURE. *Educ:* Univ Tex, BA, 43, MA, 46; Brown Univ, PhD, 57. *Prof Exp:* Instr Span, Univ Tex, 45-47; from asst prof to assoc prof, 58-69, prof Span, 69-79, DORTHY NEPPER MARSHALL PROF HISP-AM STUDIES, BRYN MAWR COL, 80-, CHMN DEPT, 62- *Mem:* MLA; Renaissance Soc Am. *Res:* Spanish novel and drama of the Golden Age; literary academies in 17th century Spain. *Publ:* Auth, Prosa novelistica y academias literarias en el siglo XVII, Real Acad Espanola, 63; La ascendencia paterna de Juan Ruiz de Alarcon y Mendoza, Nueva Rev Filol Hisp, 70; ed, Lope de Vega, The Knight of Olmedo, Univ Nebr, 72. *Mailing Add:* Dept of Span Bryn Mawr Col Bryn Mawr PA 19010

KINGSBURY, EDWIN C, b Santa Monica, Calif, Aug 19, 31; m 59; c 2. OLD TESTAMENT, SEMITIC LANGUAGES. *Educ:* Univ Calif, Los Angeles, BA, 53; Louisville Presby Theol Sem, BD, 56; Hebrew Union Col, PhD(Semitic lang), 62. *Prof Exp:* Asst prof Span & hist, Pikeville Col, 62-63; prof Bibl studies, Payne Theol Sem, 63-70; TEACHER SPAN, FRENCH & HEBREW, GREENEVIEW HIGH SCH, JAMESTOWN, OHIO, 70- *Mem:* Am Orient Soc; Soc Bibl Lit. *Res:* Babylonian cuneiform. *Publ:* Auth, A Seven Day Ritual in the Old Babylonian Cult at Larsa, Hebrew Union Col Annual, 63; The prophets and the council of Yahweh, 65 & The theophany Topos and the mountain of God, 67, J Bibl Lit; La Dixieme annee de Sumuel, Rev d'Assyriologie, 77; coauth, Early Old Babylonian Documents (YOS XIV), Yale Univ, 78. *Mailing Add:* 1695 Lower Bellbrook Rd Xenia OH 45385

KINKADE, MARVIN DALE, b Hartline, Wash, July 18, 33. ANTHROPOLOGICAL LINGUISTICS. *Educ:* Univ Wash, BA, 55, MA, 57; Ind Univ, PhD, 63. *Prof Exp:* Mem fac Ger, Univ Wash, 57; instr, Cent Wash State Col, 61-62, asst prof, 62-64; from asst prof to prof ling & anthrop, Univ Kans, 64-73, chmn dept anthrop, 68-71; PROF LING, UNIV BC, 73- *Concurrent Pos:* Nat Sci Found grant, 67-74. *Mem:* Ling Soc Am; Am Antrhop Asn; Can Ling Asn; Soc Study Indigenous Lang Am. *Res:* Language of the Upper Chehalis and Columbian Indians; comparative Salish. *Publ:* Auth, Phonology and morphology of Upper Chehalis, 7/63, Uvularpharyngeal resonants in Interior Salish, 7/67, coauth, Proto-Eastern interior Salish vowels, 1/72 & auth, The copula and negatives in Inland Olympic Salish, 76, Int J Am Ling; The source of the Upper Chehalis reflexive, Int J Am, Ling, Vol 47: 336-339; Interior Salishan particles, Anthrop Ling, Vol 23: 327-343; Dictionary of the Moses-Columbia Language, Colville Confederated Tribes, 81. *Mailing Add:* Dept of Ling Univ of BC Vancouver BC V6T 1W5 Can

KINKADE, RICHARD PAISLEY, b Los Angeles, Calif, Jan 7, 39; m 62; c 3. ROMANCE LANGUAGES. *Educ:* Yale Univ, BA, 60, PhD(Span), 65. *Prof Exp:* Instr Span, Yale Univ, 60-62, 63-65; from asst prof to assoc prof Romance lang, Univ Ariz, 65-71; prof Romance lang & chmn dept, Emory Univ, 71-74; prof Romance lang & head dept Romance & class lang, Univ Conn, 77-82; PROF SPAN & DEAN, FAC OF HUMANITIES, UNIV ARIZ, 82- *Concurrent Pos:* Bus mgr, La Coronica, 72-76; consult, div educ, Nat Endowment for Humanities, 76-77, res grant, 78-79. *Mem:* MLA; Mediaeval Acad Am; SAtlantic Mod Lang Asn; Asn Int Hispanistas; Am Asn Teachers Span & Port. *Res:* Medieval Spanish language and literature. *Publ:* Auth, The historical date of the coplas and the death of Jorge Manrique, Speculum, 3/70; A new Latin source for Berceo's Milagros: MS 110 of Madrid's Biblioteca Nacional, Romance Philol, 11/71; Sancho IV: puente literario entre Alfonso el Sabio y Juan Manual, PMLA, 10/72; Arabic mysticism and the Libro de buen amor, In: Estudios literarios de hispanistas norteamericanos dedicados a H Hatzfeld, 74; La evidencia para el influjo de los antiguos immrama irlandeses en la literatura espanola medieval, Actas del V Cong Int de Hispanistas, 78; Mito y realidad en el mundo medieval espanol, In: John Esten Keller Festschrift, 80; Iconography and literature: King Alfonso's most personal appearance in the Cantigas de Santa Maria, Miracle 209, Hispania (in prep); coauth (with John E Keller), Iconography and Narrative Art in Medieval Spanish Fiction, Univ Press Ky (in prep). *Mailing Add:* Fac of Humanities Univ Ariz Tucson AZ 85721

KINLAW, DENNIS F, b Lumberton, NC, June 26, 22; m 43; c 5. LINGUISTICS, PHILOLOGY. *Educ:* Asbury Col, AB, 43; Asbury Theol Sem, BD, 46; Brandeis Univ, MA, 61, PhD(Mediter studies), 67. *Hon Degrees:* LLD, Houghton Col, 71. *Prof Exp:* Pastor, Ind, Vt, NC & NY, 46-63; assoc prof Old Testament, Asbury Theol Sem, 63-67, prof Old Testament lang & lit, 67-68; PRES, ASBURY COL, 68- *Concurrent Pos:* Vis prof theol, Seoul Theol Col, Korea, 58. *Mem:* Soc Bibl Lit; Am Sch Orient Res; Evangel Theol Soc. *Res:* Personal names in Akkadian material from Ras Shamra; Coptic; Near Eastern languages. *Publ:* Auth, Song of Songs & Ecclesiates, In: Wesleyan Bible Commentary, Eerdmans, 68; Leviticus, In: Beacon Bible Commentary, Beacon Hill, 69. *Mailing Add:* Office of the Pres Asbury Col Wilmore KY 40390

KINLOCH, A MURRAY, b Greenock, Scotland, Apr 18, 23; m 50. ENGLISH. *Educ:* St Andres, MA, 44, MA, 50, PhD(English), 56. *Prof Exp:* Asst English, Univ Hull, 52-54; asst, Univ Col Wales, 54-55, lectr, 55-59; assoc prof, 59-72, PROF ENGLISH, UNIV NB, FREDERICTON, 72- *Concurrent Pos:* Assoc ed, Am Speech, 71- *Mem:* Asn Can Univ Teachers English; Am Name Soc; Can Ling Asn; Ling Soc Am; MLA. *Res:* Anglo-Saxon; dialects of English in New Brunswick; Canadian English. *Publ:* Auth, The Anglo Saxon period, Our Lit Heritage, 66; Survey of Canadian English: Possible evidence for pronunciation, 71 & Survey of Canadian English: A first look at New Brunswick results, 72-73, English Quart. *Mailing Add:* Dept of English Univ of NB Fredericton NB E3B 5A3 Can

KINSER, SAMUEL, Modern History. See Vol I

KINTGEN, EUGENE ROBERT, JR, English Literature & Language. See Vol II

KINZL, KONRAD HEINRICH, b Vienna, Austria, July 18, 40; Can citizen; m 68. CLASSICS. *Educ:* Univ Vienna, DrPhil(ancient hist), 67. *Prof Exp:* Asst prof classics, Univ Ottawa, 69-71; asst prof, 71-75, ASSOC PROF CLASSICS, TRENT UNIV, 75- *Mem:* Class Asn Can; Am Philol Asn; Asn Ancient Historians; Soc Promotion Hellenic Studies; Soc Promotion Roman Studies. *Res:* Greek history; Greek historiography; Late Roman Empire. *Publ:* Auth, Miltiades-Forschungen, Notring, Vienna, 68; coauth, Der Kleine Pauly, Druckenmüller, Stuttgart, Vols 3-5, 69-75; auth, Miltiades' Parosexpedition . . ., Hermes, 76; ed, Greece and the Eastern Mediterranean, 77 & contribr, Athens: Between Tyranny and Democracy, 77, De Gruyter, Berlin & New York; auth, Demokratia Studie . . ., Gymnasium 78; contrib, Betrachtungen zur älteren Tyrannis, 78 & ed, Die ältere Tyrannis, 78, Wiss Buchgesellschaft, Darmstadt. *Mailing Add:* 512 Homewood Ave Peterborough ON K9H 2N3 Can

KIPA, ALBERT ALEXANDER, b Kiev, Ukraine, Sept 10, 39; US citizen; m 66; c 2. GERMAN & SLAVIC LITERATURE. *Educ:* City Col NY, BA, 62; Univ Pa, AM, 64, PhD(Ger), 72. *Prof Exp:* Vis lectr English, Univ Freiburg, 64-65; from instr to asst prof, 66-73, assoc prof Ger & Russ, 73-79, PROF GER, RUSS & HUMANITIES, MUHLENBERG COL, 79- *Concurrent Pos:* Mem Nat Adv Coun, Ethnic Heritage Studies, US Dept Educ, 80-82; sr Fulbright fel, Germany, 81. *Honors & Awards:* Lindback Found Award for Distinquished Teaching, 80. *Mem:* MLA; AAUP; Am Asn Teachers Ger; Am Asn Teachers Slavic & EEurop Lang. *Res:* Germano-Slavic literary relations; translation theory and practise. *Publ:* Auth, Gerhart Hauptmann in Russia: First notices, Mod Lang Notes, 10/73; Gerhart Hauptmann in Russia: 1880-1917, Helmut Buske, 74; K D Bal'mont and Gerhart Hauptmann, In: Views and Reviews of Modern German Literature, Delp, 74; Ivan Franko's view of Gerhart Hauptmann, In: Probleme der Komparatistik und Interpretation, 77 & co-ed, Probleme der Komparatistik und Interpretation, 77, Bouvier; Aufnahme--Weitergabe: Literarische Impulse um Lessing und Goethe, Helmut Buske, 82. *Mailing Add:* Dept of Foreign Lang Muhlenberg Col Allentown PA 18104

KIRBY, CAROL LYNN BINGHAM, b Akron, Ohio, Oct 12, 46; m 69. SPANISH GOLDEN AGE LITERATURE. *Educ:* Univ Akron, BA, 67; Univ Wis-Madison, MA, 69; Univ Ky, PhD(Span), 77. *Prof Exp:* Teacher Span, Riverview Mid Sch, Plymouth, Wis, 69-70; teacher English, Briam Inst, Madrid, Spain, 70-71; instr, 75-76, ASST PROF SPAN, PURDUE UNIV, 77- *Mem:* MLA; Asn Teachers Span & Port; Midwest Mod Lang Asn; Asn Int de Hispanistas. *Res:* Seventeenth-century Spanish drama; 16th and 17th century Spanish literature. *Publ:* Observaciones preliminares sobre el teatro historico de Lope de Vega, In: Lope de Vega y los origenes del teatro espanol, Actas del I Congreso Internacional sobre Lobp de Vega, Madrid, 81; Theater and the quest for anointment in El rey don Pedro en Madrid y el infanzon de Illescas, Bull Comediantes, 81; Theater and history in Calderon's El medico de su honra, J Hisp Philol, 81. *Mailing Add:* Dept of Foreign Lang & Lit Purdue Univ West Lafayette IN 47907

KIRBY, HARRY LEE, JR, b Cleveland, Ohio, Oct 23, 31. NINETEENTH CENTURY SPANISH LITERATURE. *Educ:* Univ Ill, BA, 54, MA, 58, PhD, 63. *Prof Exp:* From instr to asst prof Span, Rutgers Univ, 63-65; ASSOC PROF SPAN, LA STATE UNIV, BATON ROUGE, 65-, HEAD SECT SPAN & PORT, 72- *Mem:* Am Asn Teachers Span & Port; SCent Mod Lang Asn. *Res:* Spanish realistic and naturalistic novel. *Publ:* Auth, Pardo Bazan, Darwinism, and La madre naturaleza, Hispania, 12/64; Emilia Pardo Bazan, Obras completas: Cuentos y critica literaria, Vol III, Aguilar, 73; Pardo Bazan's Use of the Cantar de los Cantares in La Madre Naturaleza, Hispania, 12/78. *Mailing Add:* Dept of Foreign Lang La State Univ Baton Rouge LA 70803

KIRBY, PAUL FRANCIS, b Pittsburgh, Pa, Jan 14, 26. CLASSICS. *Educ:* Mt Carmel Col, PhB, 47; Duquesne Univ, MA, 50; Univ Pittsburgh, PhD(classics), 62. *Prof Exp:* Teacher Latin & hist, Harmony Twp Jr High Sch, 54-56; teacher & counsel Latin & English, Westinghouse High Sch, 56-64; assoc prof Latin, 64-69, acting dean, Col Arts & Sci, 77-78, actg chmn dept geog/geol, 78-80, PROF LATIN CLASSICS, EASTERN ILL UNIV, 69-, ASST DEAN, COL ARTS & SCI, 75- *Concurrent Pos:* Mem, Bicentennial bd lectrs on classic humanities in Am Repub, Am Philol Asn & Nat Endowment for Humanities, 75- *Mem:* Am Class League; Am Philol Asn; Class Asn Mid W&S; Brit Class Asn; Vergilian Soc. *Res:* Classical influences in Latin writers of the Italian Renaissance; classical influences in the formation of the United States; Hercules in classical literature. *Publ:* Auth, Classical references in the pre-1455 AD letters of Aeneas Silvius Piccolomini, Pius II, Diss Abstr, 62; Behavioral objectives in teaching the Iliad, Class J, 4-5/74. *Mailing Add:* 615 Warren Ave Charleston IL 61920

KIRBY, STEVEN DARRELL, b Waukegan, Ill, Feb 21, 45; m 69. SPANISH MEDIEVAL LITERATURE. *Educ:* Univ Va, Charlottesville, BA, 67, MA, 68; Univ Ky, Lexington, PhD(Span), 76. *Prof Exp:* Asst teacher English, Briam Inst, Madrid, 70-71; instr Span, Purdue Univ, 74-76, asst prof, 76-81. *Concurrent Pos:* Managing ed, La Coronica, 76-78. *Mem:* Asoc Int Hispanistas; Am Asn Teachers Span & Port; MLA; Midwest Mod Lang Asn. *Res:* Juan Ruiz and his Libro de buen amor; medieval Spanish narrative poetry; Old Spanish language and linguistics. *Publ:* Auth, Escripto con estoria (Libro de buen amor, st 1571c), Romance Notes, 73; Berceo's Descanto, Hisp Rev, 75; contribr, Juan Ruiz, Don Ximio and the law, In: Studies in Language and Literature, Eastern Ky Univ, 76; auth, Concordances to Old Spanish texts: Present status and proposed future, 77 & Facsimile editions of Old Spanish literary manuscripts: Present status, 78, La Coronica; Juan Ruiz and Don Ximio: The Archpriest's art of declamation, Bull Hisp Studies, 78; Microfiche Research Tools for the Study of Old Spanish Literary Manuscripst, La Coronica, 81. *Mailing Add:* Dept of Foreign Lang & Lit Purdue Univ Stanley Coulter Hall West Lafayette IN 47907

KIRCH, MAX SAMUEL, b Philadelphia, Pa, Mar 28, 15; m 39. MODERN LANGUAGES. *Educ:* Univ Pa, BA, 34, MA, 49, PhD(Ger), 51. *Prof Exp:* Instr Ger, Univ Pa, 46-53; from instr to assoc prof, 53-64, chmn dept lang & lit, 63-71, PROF MOD LANG, UNIV DEL, 64- *Concurrent Pos:* Mem exam comt Ger, Col Entrance Exam Bd, 63-67. *Honors & Awards:* Officier de l'ordre des palmes academiques, Govt France, 70. *Mem:* MLA; Am Asn Teachers Ger; Ling Soc Am; Mid States Asn Mod Lang Teachers (pres, 71-72, 77-78 & 79-81); Nat Fed Mod Lang Teachers Asn (vpres, 77-78). *Res:* Germanic philology; linguistics; methods of teaching foreign languages. *Publ:* Coauth, Functional German, Am Bk Co, 59, rev ed, 67; The island dwellers of Pliny and Tacitus, Z deut Altertum; Scandinavian influence on English syntax, PMLA, 12/59. *Mailing Add:* Dept of Lang & Lit Univ of Del Newark DE 19711

KIREMIDJIAN, GARABED DAVID, b New York, NY, Nov 29, 36; m 60; c 2. COMPARATIVE LITERATURE. *Educ:* Yale Univ, BA, 58, PhD(comp lit), 64. *Prof Exp:* Instr humanities, New Haven Col, 62-64; asst prof English, Adelphi Univ, 64-66; asst prof, 66-80, ASSOC PROF COMP LIT, BROOKLYN COL, 80- *Mem:* MLA; Am Comp Lit Asn. *Res:* Psychology; anthropology; aesthetics. *Publ:* Auth, The aesthetics of parody, JAAC, winter 69; Dostoevsky and matricide, J Orgonomy, spring 75; Dostoevskij e il problema del matricidio, Gradwa, summer 76; Crime and Punishment: Matricide and the woman question, American Imago, winter 76. *Mailing Add:* Dept of Comp Lit Brooklyn Col Brooklyn NY 11210

KIRKHAM, VICTORIA EULALIA, b Jersey City, NJ, May 17, 42. ITALIAN LITERATURE. *Educ:* Wellesley Col, BA, 64; Univ Ill, Urbana, MA, 67; Johns Hopkins Univ, MA, 69, PhD(Romance lang), 72. *Prof Exp:* Asst prof Ital, State Univ NY Buffalo, 70-72; asst prof, 72-78, ASSOC PROF ITAL, UNIV PA, 78- *Concurrent Pos:* Fulbright teaching asst English, Italy, 64-65; I Tatti fel, Harvard Univ Ctr Ital Renaissance Studies, Florence, 77-78. *Mem:* MLA; Dante Soc Am; Am Asn Teachers Ital; Renaissance Soc Am; Am Boccaccio Asn (secy, 76-78). *Res:* Medieval Italian literature; Boccaccio; numerology. *Publ:* Auth, Reckoning with Boccaccio's Questioni d'amore, Mod Lang Notes, 1/74; coauth, Amore e virtu: Two salvers depicting Boccaccio's Comedia delle ninfe fioentine in the Metropolitan Museum, Metrop Mus J, 75; auth, Numerololgy and allegory in Boccaccio's Caccia de Diana, Traditio, 78; Love's Labors Rewarded and Paradise Lost (Decameron III, 10), Romanic Rev, 1/81. *Mailing Add:* Dept of Romance Lang Williams Hall Univ of Pa Philadelphia PA 19104

KIRKNESS, WILLIAM JOHN, b Wellington, NZ, Nov 17, 38. FRENCH LANGUAGE & LITERATURE. *Educ:* Univ Auckland, BA, 60, MA, 61; Besancon, DUniv, 63. *Prof Exp:* Lectr French, Univ Auckland, 64-68; asst prof, 68-70, ASSOC PROF HUMANITIES, SCARBOROUGH COL, UNIV TORONTO, 70- *Concurrent Pos:* Dir, Off Educ Develop, Univ Toronto, 76- *Mem:* Can Soc Studies Higher Educ; Am Asn Higher Educ; Am Educ Res Asn. *Res:* Seventeenth century French theatre; French language in the Americas; Educational development in higher education. *Publ:* Auth, Datations et documents lexicographiques, In: Les Belles Lettres, Didier, Paris, 63-70; Le Francais du Theatre Italien, Droz, Geneva, 71; Aspects of Corneille's Use of Vocabulary in Attila, Ling Res Inc, 72. *Mailing Add:* Div of Humanities Scarborough Col Univ of Toronto Toronto ON M5S 1V4 Can

KIRKWOOD, GORDON MACDONALD, b Toronto, Ont, May 7, 16; m 40; c 2. CLASSICAL PHILOLOGY. *Educ:* Univ Toronto, AB, 38; Cornell Univ, AM, 39; Johns Hopkins Univ, PhD(Greek), 42. *Prof Exp:* Latin master, Lower Can Col, 45-46; from instr to prof, 46-73, chmn dept, 63-72, FREDERIC J WHITON PROF CLASSICS, CORNELL UNIV, 73- *Concurrent Pos:* Ford fel, 53-54; Guggenheim fel, 56-57; Am Coun Learned Soc fel, 62-63; co-ed, Cornell Studies in Class Philol; Nat Endowment for Humanities fel, 77. *Mem:* Am Philol Asn; Class Asn Atlantic States; AAUP. *Res:* Greek literature. *Publ:* Auth, A Study of Sophoclean Drama, Cornell Univ, 58; A Short Guide to Classical Mythology, Holt, 60; Early Greek Monody, 74 & ed, Poetry and Poetics, Studies in Honor of James Hutton, 75, Cornell Univ; Selections from Pindar, Am Philol Asn, 82. *Mailing Add:* Dept of Classics Cornell Univ Ithaca NY 14850

KIRRMANN, ERNEST NESTOR, b Strasbourg, France, Feb 28, 05; US citizen; m 34, 68. GERMAN & FRENCH LITERATURE. *Educ:* City Col NY, BSc, 30; Univ Strasbourg, cert, 32; Columbia Univ, MA, 33; Northwestern Univ, PhD, 46. *Prof Exp:* Instr & sr master French & Ger, Mt Hermon Sch Boys & Northfield Sch Girls, 31-59; assoc prof Ger & French, 59-64, chmn dept mod lang, 61-64, prof, 64-70, EMER PROF GER, SWEET BRIAR COL, 70-; TRANSL SCI MAT, 78- *Concurrent Pos:* Fulbright exchange teacher English & French, Schadow Sch, Berlin, Ger, 53-54; vis lectr Ger, Sweet Briar Col, 58-59; vis prof French, Randolph-Macon Woman's Col, 59; indust lang consult, Lynchburg firms, 72- *Mem:* MLA; Am Asn Teachers Ger; Am Asn Teachers Fr; Am Transl Asn. *Res:* Franco-German literary relations, especially Erckmann-Chatrian; German romanticism and theories of allegory; Faust. *Publ:* Transl, Johann von Saaz, Death and the Plowman, Univ NC, 57. *Mailing Add:* PO Box 3 Sweet Briar Col Sweet Briar VA 24595

KIRSNER, ROBERT, b Lithuania, July 9, 21; nat US; m 47; c 5. ROMANCE LANGUAGES. *Educ:* Univ Cincinnati, AB, 43, AM, 45; Princeton Univ, AM, 47, PhD, 49. *Prof Exp:* Asst, Univ Cincinnati, 42-43, 44-45; instr, Princeton Univ, 45-49; from asst prof to prof Romance lang, Univ Cincinnati, 49-64; chmn dept foreign lang, 65-73, PROF SPAN, UNIV MIAMI, 64- *Concurrent Pos:* Dir, Rollins Col semester in Colombia, Univ Andes, 64; co-ed, Caribe, 75-; reader, Educ Testing Serv, Princeton, 78- *Mem:* AAUP; MLA; Am Asn Teachers Span & Port; SAtlantic Mod Lang Asn (pres, 78). *Res:* Perez Galdos; Romulo Gallegos; Camilo Jose Cela. *Publ:* Auth, Buero's Historia de una escalera: A Play in Search of Characters Ed Castalia, Madrid, 66; Four Colombian novels of La violencia, Hispania, 3/66; La ironia del bien en misericordia, Col Mex, 12/70; La tesis de Nancy de Ramon Sender: Una leccion para exilados, Papeles de Son Armadans, 10/73; La suspension de mitos en algunas obras representativas de la nueva novela hispanoamericana, Revista de estudios hispanicos, 75; De dona Barbara a Luisiana: Feminismo refinado, Caribe, 76; Camilo Jose Cela: La conciencia literaria de su sociedad, Cuadernos Hispanoamericanos, 78; Veinte Anos de matrimonio en la novela de galdos, Torres Libr Lit Studies, 82. *Mailing Add:* Dept of Foreign Lang Univ of Miami Coral Gables FL 33124

KIRSNER, ROBERT SHNEIDER, b Chicago, Ill, Oct 18, 41; m 68; c 2. NETHERLANDIC LINGUISTICS. *Educ:* Oberlin Col, BA, 62; Columbia Univ, MA, 68, PhD(ling), 72. *Prof Exp:* Staff mem dept ling, Univ Amsterdam, 69; preceptor ling, Columbia Univ, 70-71, lectr, 71-72; asst prof, 72-79, ASSOC PROF DUTCH, AFRIKAANS LANG & LIT, UNIV CALIF, LOS ANGELES, 79- *Concurrent Pos:* Fel, Netherlands Inst Advan Study, 79-80. *Mem:* Ling Asn Am; Algem Ver voor Taalwetensch; MLA; Int Ver voor Neerlandistiek Asn Comput Ling. *Res:* The semantics of grammatical systems: the semantics of the lexicon; English, Dutch, Afrikaans and German grammar in the light of modern liguistics. *Publ:* Auth, The role of zullen in the grammar of modern standard Dutch, Lingua, 69; De onechte lijdende vorm, Spektator: tijdschrift voor neerlandistiek, 76; coauth, The role of pragmatic inference in semantics: A study of sensory verb complements in English, Glosa, 76; auth, On the subjectless pseudo-passive in standard Dutch and the semantic of background agents, In: Subject and Topic, Academic, 76; Deixis in discourse: An exploratory quantitative study of the modern Dutch demonstrative adjectives, In: Discourse and Syntax, Academic, 79; The Problem of Presentative Sentences in Modern Dutch, NHolland, Amsterdam, 79; coauth, On the inference of inalienable possesion in Swahili, J African Lang and Ling, 80; On the opposition between deze (dit) and die (dat) in written Dutch: A discriminant analysis, In: Linguistics in the Netherlands 1980, NHolland, Amsterdam, 80. *Mailing Add:* Dept of Germanic Lang 310 Royce Hall Univ of Calif Los Angeles CA 90024

KIRTLAND, LYNN, b Exeter, NH, May 17, 13. CLASSICAL LANGUAGES. *Educ:* Williams Col, AB, 35; Princeton Univ, AM, 37, PhD, 38. *Prof Exp:* Master Latin & Greek, St Paul's Sch, Concord, NH, 38-40; instr Latin & hist, Phillips Exeter Acad, 40-49; asst prof class lang, Univ Tex, 49-53; from asst prof to prof classics, 53-73, asst to pres acad affairs, 67-69, Koch prof humanities, 73-81, EMER PROF GREEK & LATIN, WELLS COL, 78- *Mem:* Am Philol Asn; Am Inst Archit. *Mailing Add:* PO Box 25 Aurora NY 13026

KISH, KATHLEEN VERA, b Trenton, NJ, June 21, 42. SPANISH LITERATURE. *Educ:* Univ Calif, Berkeley, AB, 64; Univ Wis-Madison, MA, 65, PhD(Span), 71. *Prof Exp:* From lectr to asst prof, 69-76, ASSOC PROF SPAN, UNIV NC, GREENSBORO, 76- *Concurrent Pos:* Res grant, Grad Sch, Univ NC, Greensboro, 72-73, 80-81 & 81-82, res assignment, 73-74. *Mem:* MLA; Renaissance Soc Am; Am Soc 18th Century Studies; Asn Int de Hisp; Int Courtly Lit Soc. *Res:* Spanish balladry; the Celestina; 18th century Spanish literature. *Publ:* Ed, An Edition of the First Italian Translation of the Celestina, Univ NC, 73; auth, The wages of sin is life for a sixteenth-century best seller, Theoria, 76; coauth, The Celestina phenomenon in sixteenth century Germany: Christof Wirsung's translations of 1520 and 1534, Celestinesca, 11/80; contribr, Actas del sexto congreso internacional de hispanistas, Asn Int de Hispanistas, 80; auth, The Spanish ballad in the eighteenth century: A reconsideration, Hispanic Rev, summer 81; contribr, La Chispa 81, Selected Proceedings, 2nd La Conf on Hispanic Lang & Lit, Tulane Univ, 81; coauth, On translating juevos asados: Clues from Christ of Wirsung, Celestinesca, fall 81; contribr, Women in Hispanic Literature: Icons and Fallen Idols, Univ Calif, 82. *Mailing Add:* Dept of Romance Lang Univ of NC Greensboro NC 27412

KISTLER, MARK OLIVER, b New Tripoli, Pa, Apr 21, 18; m 48; c 2. GERMAN. *Educ:* Dickinson Col, AB, 38; Columbia Univ, AM, 41; Univ Ill, PhD(Ger), 48. *Prof Exp:* Instr Ger, Dickinson Col, 43-46; asst, Univ Ill, 46-48; instr, Temple Univ, 48-49; from asst prof to assoc prof, 49-68, PROF GER, MICH STATE UNIV, 68- *Mem:* MLA; Am Asn Teachers Ger. *Res:* Eighteenth century German literature; modern German literature. *Publ:* Auth, The source of the Goethe-Tobler Fragment, Die Natur, Monatschefte; Dionysian elements in Wieland, Ger Rev, 4/60; Drama of the Storm and Stress, Twayne, 69. *Mailing Add:* Dept of Ger & Russ Mich State Univ East Lansing MI 48824

KITAGAWA, CHISATO, b Tokyo, Japan, July 29, 32; US citizen; m 61; c 2. LINGUISTICS. *Educ:* Rikkyo Univ, Japan, BA, 58; Univ Mich, Ann Arbor, MA, 61; Episcopal Theol Sch, Cambridge, Mass, BD, 64; Univ Mich, PhD(ling), 72. *Prof Exp:* Lectr Japanese, Univ Mich, 70-72; asst prof, Univ Mass, Amherst, 72-76; ASSOC PROF JAPANESE LING, UNIV ARIZ, 76- *Mem:* Ling Soc Am; Asn Teachers Japanese. *Res:* Japanese linguistics; language teaching. *Publ:* Auth, Purpose expressions in English, Lingua, 74; Case marking and causativization, Papers Japanese Ling, 74; Nakute to naide, Nihongo Kyoiku, 76; coauth, The deep structure binding and anaphoric bleeding, Lang, 76; Semantics of Japanese purpose expressions, 77 & A source of feminity in Japanese, 77, Linguistics; Saying yes in Japanese, J Pragmatics, 80; coauth, Prenominal modification in Chinese and Japanese, Linguistic Analysis, 82. *Mailing Add:* Oriental Studies Univ of Ariz Tucson AZ 85721

KITCHING, LAURENCE PATRICK ANTHONY, b Sussex, England, 1937; m; c 4. MODERN LANGUAGE & LITERATURE. *Educ:* Univ BC, BA, 61, MA, 67; Ind Univ, PhD, 73. *Prof Exp:* From instr to asst prof Ger & French, Ore State Univ, 63-66; asst prof Ger, Univ Kans, 70-73; asst prof, 73-75, chmn, Dept Mod Lang, 75-77, ASSOC PROF GER, LAURENTIAN UNIV, 75- *Concurrent Pos:* Can Coun res grant, 75. *Mem:* Am Asn Teachers Ger; Can Asn Univ Teachers Ger; Int Brecht Soc. *Res:* German literature since 1750; Bertolt Brecht; comparative literature. *Publ:* Auth, Der Hofmeister: A Critical Analysis of Bertolt Brecht's Adaptation of J M R Lenz's Drama, Fink, Munich, 76. *Mailing Add:* Dept of Ger Laurentian Univ Sudbury ON P3E 2C6 Can

KITE, RALPH BEVERLY, b DeQueen, Ark, Nov 9, 38; m 78; c 4. LATIN AMERICAN LITERATURE. *Educ:* Univ Ariz, BA, 59; Univ NMex, PhD(Iberoam studies), 67. *Prof Exp:* Instr Span, Univ NMex, Peace Corps Ctr, 63-64; instr Span & Port, Univ Wis-Milwaukee, 64-68, ling dir, Peace Corps Ctr, 64-67; asst prof Span & Port, 68-77, chmn, 74-81, ASSOC PROF SPAN & PORT, UNIV COLO, BOULDER, 77- *Concurrent Pos:* Consult, Kalamazoo Col, 64-67. *Mem:* AATSP; Inst Int de Lit Iberoam. *Res:* Spanish American novel; Brazilian literature; Portuguese language teaching. *Publ:* Coauth, Oral Brazilian Portuguese, Univ Wis-Milwaukee, rev, ed, 68; auth, Socialist realism in the Puerto Rican Nationalist novel, Rev Interamericana, fall 74; coauth, Intermediate Spanish, Holt, Rinehart & Winston, 77; Telemundo, 80 & Puertas a la lengua espanola, 82, Random House. *Mailing Add:* Dept Span & Port Univ Colo Boulder CO 80302

KITTAY, EVA FEDER, Philosophy. See Vol IV

KLAUSENBURGER, JURGEN, b Reghin, Romania, July 22, 42; US citizen; m 67; c 3. ROMANCE LINGUISTICS. *Educ:* Univ Mich, Ann Arbor, BA, 64, MA, 66, PhD(Romance ling), 69. *Prof Exp:* Asst prof, 69-75, assoc prof, 75-81, PROF FRENCH & ROMANCE LING, UNIV WASH, 81- *Mem:* Ling Soc Am. *Res:* Historical Romance linguistics; French phonology; phonological theory. *Publ:* Auth, French Prosodics and Phonotactics: An Historical Typology, 70 & Historische Franzosische Phonologie aus Generativer Sicht, 74, Max Niemeyer, Tübingen, Ger; Rule inversion, opacity, conspiracies: French liaison and elision, Lingua 34, 74; Latin vocalic quantity to quality: A pseudo-problem?, In: Diachronic Studies in Romance Linguistics, Mouton, The Hague, 75; (De)-morphologization in Latin, Lingua 40, 76; French linking phenomena: A natural generative analysis, Lang, 78; Morphologization: Studies in Latin and Romance Morphophonology, Max Niemeyer, Tübingen Ger, 79; Romance Phonological Studies in the 70's, In: Proceedings of the Tenth Anniversary Symposium on Romance Linguistics, Univ Wash, 81. *Mailing Add:* Dept of Romance Lang Univ of Wash Seattle WA 98195

KLAWITER, RANDOLPH JEROME, b Grand Rapids, Mich, Oct 14, 30; m 54; c 7. GERMAN LANGUAGE & LITERATURE. *Educ:* Aquinas Col, BA, 53; Univ Mich, MA, 54, PhD(Ger), 61. *Prof Exp:* Teaching asst Ger, Univ Mich, 56-59; instr, Aquinas Col, 59-61; from asst prof to assoc prof, 61-73, PROF GER, UNIV NOTRE DAME, 73- *Mem:* Int Stefan Zweig Soc; Int Arthur Schnitzler Soc; Soc Amici Thomae Mori. *Res:* European Renaissance, Reformation, and humanism; 20th century Austrian literature, especially the Viennese school. *Publ:* Auth, Stefan Zweig--A Bibliography, Univ NC, 65; translr & ed, Idealism and Naturalism in Gothic Art, Univ Notre Dame, 66; auth, Peter Altenberg, J Arthur Schnitzler Soc, 69; Ulrich von Hutten--A Discussion, Moreana, 72; The artist and society, In: Festschrift for Prof Fr Coenen, Univ NC, 73; translr & ed, The Polemics of Erasmus and Ulrich von Hutten, Univ Notre Dame, 77. *Mailing Add:* Dept of Mod & Class Lang Univ of Notre Dame Notre Dame IN 46556

KLEIN, DENNIS ALLAN, b New York, NY, Oct 19, 43. SPANISH. *Educ:* Univ Kans, BSEd, 65, MA, 67; Univ Mass, PhD(Span), 73. *Prof Exp:* Asst prof, Southwest Mo State Univ, 73-75; vis instr, Univ Mo-Rolla, 75-76; asst prof, 76-78, ASSOC PROF SPAN, UNIV S DAK, 78- *Concurrent Pos:* Bibliog, MLA; Nat Endowment for Humanities summer fel, 79; Exxon Foreign Lang Workshop, 81. *Mem:* MLA; Am Asn Teachers Span & Port. *Res:* Spanish drama; bibliography; comparative drama. *Publ:* Auth, Asi que pasen cinco anos: A search for sexual identity, J Span Studies: 20th Century, 75; The old women in the theatre of Garcia Lorca, 75 & Christological imagery in Lorca's Yerma, 78, Garcia Lorca Rev; coauth, Garcia Lorca: A Selectively Annotated Bibliography of Criticism, Vol I, 79 & Vol II (in press), Garland; auth, Peter Shaffer, Twayne, 79; Literary onomastics in Peter Shaffer's Shrivings and Equus, Lit Onomastic Studies, 80; Peter and Anthony Shaffer: A Reference Guide, G K Hall, 82; Amadeus: The Third Part of Peter Shaffer's Dramatic Trilogy, Mod Lang Studies (in prep). *Mailing Add:* Dept of Mod Lang Univ of S Dak Vermillion SD 57069

KLEIN, HARRIET ESTHER MANELIS, b New York, NY, Sept 8, 36; m 56; c 3. LINGUISTICS, ANTHROPOLOGY. *Educ:* Univ Chicago, AB, 58; Columbia Univ, PhD(anthrop), 73. *Prof Exp:* Asst prof anthrop, Montclair State Col, 72-74; vis asst prof, Univ Toronto, 74-75; asst prof, 75-80, ASSOC PROF ANTHROP, MONTCLAIR STATE COL, 80- *Mem:* Fel Am Anthrop Asn; Ling Soc Am. *Res:* Semantics of Toba (an Amerindian language spoken primarily in Argentina); Gran Chaco Indian languages; ethnohistory. *Publ:* Auth, Tense and aspect in the Damara verbal system, African Studies, 76; coauth, Indian languages of the Paraguayan Chaco, Anthrop Ling, 77; The Russian collection of Amerindian languages in Spanish archives, Int J Am Ling, 78; auth, Noun classifiers in Toba, In: Ethnolinguistics: Boas, Sapir and Whorf Revisited, Mouton, The Hague, 79; Location and direction in Toba: Verbal morphology, Int J Am Ling, Vol 47, No 3, 227-235. *Mailing Add:* Montclair State Col Russ Hall 205 Upper Montclair NJ 07043

KLEIN, JARED STEPHEN, b Cleveland Ohio, Aug 5, 46; m 74; c 2. LINGUISTICS, INDO-EUROPEAN PHILOLOGY. *Educ:* Case Western Reserve Univ, BA, 68; Yale Univ, MA, 71, MPhil, 72, PhD(ling), 74. *Prof Exp:* Asst prof, 72-79, ASSOC PROF CLASSICS, UNIV GA, 79- *Concurrent Pos:* Fel ling, Yale Univ, 74-75; Andrew W Mellon fac fel ling, Harvard Univ, 78-79. *Mem:* Ling Soc Am; Am Orient Soc; Ling Soc Paris; Philol Soc England; Lodogermaische Ges. *Res:* Vedic Sanskrit; Indo-European linguistics. *Publ:* Auth, The Particle u in the Rigveda: A Synchronic and Diachronic Study, Vandenhoeck & Ruprecht, 78; The system of coordinate conjunctions in the Rigveda, Indo-Iranian J, 78; The Indo-Iranian prehistory of the Sanskrit Asau/Amum pronoun, J Indo-Europ Studies, 78; The diachronic syntax of the particle u in the RIGVEDA, J Am Orient Soc, 78; Atha, Adha and a typology of Rigvedic conjunction, Indo-Iranian J, 80; The origin of the Rigvedic vayav indras ca construction, Miinchener Studien zur Sprachivissenschaft, 81; Review of T Burrow, the problem of shwa in sanskrit, Language, 81; Riguedic tu and su, Die Sprache, 82. *Mailing Add:* Dept of Classics Park Hall Univ of Ga Athens GA 30602

KLEIN, KURT A, b Taganrog, Russia, July 9, 12; US citizen; m 46, 61; c 2. RUSSIAN LANGUAGE. *Educ:* Univ Saratov, MA, 37; Graz Univ, PhD(Russ lang & lit), 49. *Prof Exp:* Lectr Ger lang, Inst Foreign Lang, Dnepropetrovsk, USSR, 37-43; lectr Russ lang, Graz Univ, 45-50; instr, Univ Kans, 50-58; from asst prof to assoc prof, 58-72, PROF RUSS LANG, UNIV ILL, URBANA, 72- *Mem:* Am Asn Teachers Slavic & EEurop Lang. *Res:* Soviet Russian language policy; problems of standardization; Russian lexicology. *Publ:* Coauth, Na Dne, Bradda, 66. *Mailing Add:* 1098 David Dr Champaign IL 61820

KLEIN, RUDOLF MANFRED, b Bensen, Ger, Mar 26, 33; US citizen; m 63; c 2. GERMAN LITERATURE & LINGUISTICS. *Educ:* Univ Wis-Milwaukee, BS, 62; Rice Univ, PhD(Ger), 69. *Prof Exp:* Instr, Berlitz Sch Lang, Munich, Ger, 62-63; teacher Ger, French & Span, G W Sr High Sch, Guam, Mariana Islands, 63-65; from instr to asst prof Ger, 68-70, resident dir, Foreign Studies Prog at Univ Regensburg, Ger, 70-72, chmn dept foreign lang, 73-79, ASSOC PROF GER & SPAN, MIDWESTERN STATE UNIV, 72-, CHMN DEPT FOREIGN LANG, 73- *Mem:* MLA; Am Asn Teachers Ger. *Res:* German medieval epics, especially Nibelungenlied; dramatic art of German classicism, especially Schiller; the German novelle of the 19th century. *Publ:* Methodology and Motivation in Modern Language Instruction, Prisma, winter 78. *Mailing Add:* Dept of Foreign Lang Midwestern State Univ Wichita Falls TX 76308

KLEIN, THEODORE MICHAEL, b Johannesburg, SAfrica, Aug 12, 47; m 74. ANCIENT LITERATURE, COMPARATIVE LITERATURE. *Educ:* Univ of Witwatersrand, BA, 68; State Univ NY, Buffalo, PhD(classics), 73. *Prof Exp:* Instr classics, State Univ NY, Buffalo, 73-74; asst prof, 74-77, ASSOC PROF CLASSICS, TEXAS TECH UNIV, 77- *Concurrent Pos:* Ed, Helios, J Class Asn of Southwestern US, 74-; Nat Endowment for Humanities fel, Instr for Post-Biblical Found, 78. *Mem:* Am Philol Asn; Class Asn Midwest & South; Class Asn of Southwestern US. *Res:* Classics; philosophy. *Publ:* Auth, The Role of Calimachus on the Development of the Concept of the Counter-Genre, Latomus, 74; Callimachus, Apollonius Rhodius and the Concept of the Big Book, Eranos, 75; Callimachus' Two Aetia Prologues, Zivaantika, 76; Classical Myth and Symbolism in Camus and Beckett, Comp Lit, 76; The Greek Shepherd in Virgil, Gide, Geret and Barthes, Hilios, 78. *Mailing Add:* Dept Classical & Romance Lang Texas Tech Univ Lubbock TX 79409

KLEINHARDT, WERNER BERNHARD, b Parchin, Ger, Apr 29, 30; m 55; c 1. ROMANCE LANGUAGES, GERMAN. *Educ:* Univ Hamburg, Dr Phil(comp lit), 62. *Prof Exp:* Lectr Ger, Sorbonne, 62-65; asst prof Ger & comp lit, 65-70, ASSOC PROF GER & COMP LIT, DARTMOUTH COL, 70- *Mem:* MLA. *Res:* European drama; fable literature; political philosophy. *Publ:* Auth, Medea, Originalitat und Variation einer Rache, Univ Hamburg, 63; transl, George Arnaud, Gefahrliche Kurven, Rowohlt, Hamburg, 63. *Mailing Add:* Dept Ger Dartmouth Col Hanover NH 03755

KLEINHENZ, CHRISTOPHER, b Indianapolis, Ind, Dec 29, 41; m 64; c 2. ITALIAN LITERATURE, PHILOLOGY. *Educ:* Ind Univ, Bloomington, AB, 64, MA, 66, PhD(Ital), 69. *Prof Exp:* From instr to asst prof Ital, Univ Wis-Madison, 68-70; vis asst prof Ital, Ind Univ, Bloomington & resident dir foreign studies prog, Bologna, Italy, 70-71; asst prof, 71-75, assoc prof, 75-80, PROF ITAL & CHMN MEDIEVAL STUDIES, UNIV WIS-MADISON, 80- *Concurrent Pos:* Fel, Inst Res in Humancities, 74-75; counillor, Medieval Asn MidW, 77-80; coun assoc, Dante Soc Am, 80-85. *Mem:* MLA; Medieval Acad Am; Dante Soc Am; Int Arthurian Soc; Am Asn Teachers Ital. *Res:* Medieval Italian literature; Romance philology; textual criticism. *Publ:* Auth, Dante's towering giants: Inferno XXXI, Romance Philol, 2/74; Stylistic gravity: Language and prose rhythms in Decameron I, 4, Humanities Asn Rev, 4/75; Infernal guardians revisited: Cerbero, il gran vermo (Inf VI, 22), Dante Studies, 75; contribr, Petrarch and the art of the sonnet, In: Francis Petrarch, Six Centuries Later: A Symposium, 75 & auth & ed, Medieval Manuscripts and Textual Criticism, 76, Univ NC; contribr, Boccacciana: Bibliografia delle Edizioni e Degli Scritti Critici (1939-1974), Longo Ed, 76; auth, Giacomo da Lentini and Dante: The early Italian sonnet tradition in perspectives, J Medieval & Renaissance Studies, 8/78; auth & co-ed, Medieval Studies in North America, Medieval Inst, 82. *Mailing Add:* Dept of Fr & Ital Unif of Wis Madison WI 53706

KLEINJANS, EVERETT, b Zeeland, Mich, Sept 6, 19; m 46; c 5. LINGUISTICS, EDUCATIONAL ADMINISTRATION. *Educ:* Hope Col, AB, 43; Univ Mich, Ann Arbor, MA, 48, PhD(ling, educ), 58. *Hon Degrees:* LHD, George Williams Col, 69; LLD, Hawaii Loa Col, 74; LittD, Chung-Ang Univ, Korea, 76. *Prof Exp:* Instr English, Univ Mich, Ann Arbor, 48; instr, Talmadge Col, China, 48-50; prin, Am Sch Japan, 52; prof English, Meiji Gakuin Univ, 52-56; prof English lang & ling, Int Christian Univ, Japan, 58-67, chmn div lang, dean col lib arts & vpres acad affairs, 65-67; from dep chancellor to chancellor, East West Ctr, Univ Hawaii, 67-75, pres, 75-80. *Concurrent Pos:* Dir, Inter-Univ Ctr Japanese Studies, Japan, 65-67; mem vis comt ling, Ind Univ; vchmn, Comt Coop English in Japan; mem, Comn Advan Christian Higher Educ in Asia. *Mem:* Ctr Appl Ling; Inst Relig & Social Change; Asn Asian Studies; Ling Soc Am. *Publ:* Auth, The Comparison of Japanese and English and English Education, 59, coauth, New Approach to English, Vol 1, 60, A Short Course in Oral English (2 vols), 61 & Teacher's Guide for New Approach in English, 62, Taishukan; auth, Cross-cultural linguistic communication, On culture learning, On learning a second language & Linguistic methods and the teaching of grammar, East-West Ctr Cult Learning Inst, 8/71; Cross roads in communication, Asian Mass Commun Res & Info Ctr, 72. *Mailing Add:* 5112 Maunalani Circle Honolulu HI 96816

KLEINSCHMIDT, JOHN ROCHESTER, b Logan, Ohio, July 21, 15; m 42. FRENCH. *Educ:* Oberlin Col, AB, 37; Brown Univ, AM, 40; Univ Geneva, Dr es Let, 48. *Prof Exp:* Asst, Brown Univ, 38-41; from asst prof to assoc prof mod foreign lang, 48-60, prof French, 60-77, EMER PROF FRENCH, GRINNELL COL, 77- *Concurrent Pos:* Fund Advan Educ fel, 51-52. *Res:* Seventeenth and 18th century French literature; French language printing of the 18th century; Voltaire. *Publ:* Auth, Les Imprimeurs et Libraires de la Republique de Geneve, 1700-1798, A Jullien, Geneva, 48. *Mailing Add:* Dept of French Grinnell Col Grinnell IA 50112

KLEIS, CHARLOTTE COSTA, b Detroit, Mich. FRENCH RENAISSANCE LITERATURE. *Educ:* Univ Mich, BA, 58, MA, 59, PhD(romance lang), 67. *Prof Exp:* ASSOC PROF FRENCH, TEMPLE UNIV, 63- *Mem:* Soc Francaise des Seiziemistes; Inst Renaissance Interdisciplinary Studies; MLA; Am Asn Teachers French. *Res:* Rabelais; Montaigne. *Publ:* Auth, Structural parallels and thematic unity in Rabelais, Mod Lang Quart, 12/70; Diversity, integration, and the universal Chacun: The evolution of the perceptual experience, Five Col Int Colloquium on the Occasion of the 400th Anniversary of the Essays, 80. *Mailing Add:* 550 Spring Ln Philadelphia PA 19118

KLEMM, FREDERICK ALVIN, b Harrisburg, Pa, Dec 19, 12; m 40; c 3. GERMANICS. *Educ:* Dickinson Col, AB, 33; Duke Univ, AM, 35; Univ Pa, PhD, 39. *Prof Exp:* Instr Ger, Univ Pa, 35-47; from asst prof to assoc prof, 47-55, chmn dept mod lang, 59-76, chmn div humanities, 61-64, PROF GER UNION COL, NY, 55- *Mem:* MLA; Am Asn Teachers Ger; Royal Inst Gt Brit. *Res:* Modern German literature; German-American relations. *Publ:* Auth, The death problem in the life and works of Gerhart Hauptmann; Genesis-Thanatos in Gerhart Hauptmann, Ger Rev; Frederick the Great and the German language, Mod Lang Quart. *Mailing Add:* Dept of Mod Lang Union Col Schenectady NY 12308

KLIBBE, HELENE FOUSTANOS, b Lyon, France; US citizen; c 2. FRENCH LITERATURE. *Educ:* Sorbonne, Lic es Lett; Syracuse Univ, PhD(French lit), 64. *Prof Exp:* Lectr, Hunter Col, 60-61 & Queens Col, NY, 61-64; PROF FRENCH & CHMN DEPT, MONTCLAIR STATE COL, 64- *Concurrent Pos:* Fulbright & Smith Mundt grants. *Mem:* MLA; Am Asn Teachers Fr; Soc Fr Prof Am; Soc Amis Univ Paris; Int Cult Ctr Cerisy-la-Salle. *Res:* Contemporary French literatuare. *Mailing Add:* Dept of Fr Sch of Humanities Montclair State Col Upper Montclair NJ 07043

KLIBBE, LAWRENCE H, b Utica, NY, Oct 7, 23; m 52; c 2. ROMANCE LANGUAGES. *Educ:* Syracuse Univ, AB, 49, MA, 51, PhD, 54. *Prof Exp:* From instr to assoc prof mod lang, Le Moyne Col, 53-59; assoc prof, St John's Univ, NY, 59-65, dept rep, Brooklyn Ctr, 60-65; ASSOC PROF SPAN, NY UNIV, 65- *Mem:* Am Asn Teachers Span & Port. *Res:* Spanish 19th and 20th century literature; United State-Spanish literary relations. *Mailing Add:* Dept of Span NY Univ 19 University Pl New York NY 10003

KLIMA, EDWARD STEPHEN, b Cleveland, Ohio, June 21, 31; m 68. LINGUISTICS, THEORY OF LANGUAGE. *Educ:* Dartmouth Col, BA, 53; Harvard Univ, MA, 55, PhD(ling), 65. *Prof Exp:* From instr to assoc prof ling, Mass Inst Technol, 57-67; PROF LING, UNIV CALIF, SAN DIEGO, 67- *Concurrent Pos:* Consult, Bolt, Beranek & Newman, 65-66 & lang acquisition proj, Harvard Univ, 65-67; Nat Sci Found fel, 66-67; partic, Edinburgh Conf Psycholing, 66 & Ciba Found Conf, London, Eng, 68. *Mem:* Ling Soc Am; Int Ling Asn. *Res:* Linguistics; psycholinguistics; historical linguistics. *Publ:* Auth, Grimm's law, phonetic law, phonology, In: Funk and Wagnall's New Int Encycl, 58; Negation in English, In: Readings in the Philosophy of Language, Prentice-Hall, 64; coauth, Syntactic regularities in the speech of children, Proc Edinburgh Conf Edinburgh Univ, 66; auth, Knowing language and getting to know it, Proc Univ Mich Conf Lang & Lang Behav, Appleton, 68; Relatedness between grammatical systems, In: Modern Studies in English, Prentice-Hall, 69. *Mailing Add:* Dept of Ling Univ of Calif San Diego PO Box 109 La Jolla CA 92093

KLIMAS, ANTANAS, b Lithuania, Apr 17, 24; US citizen; m 54; c 4. LINGUISTICS. *Educ:* Univ Pa, MA, 50, PhD, 56. *Prof Exp:* Asst instr Ger, Univ Pa, 50-56, instr, 56-57; asst prof, 57-62, assoc prof foreign lang, 62-71, PROF GER & LING, UNIV ROCHESTER, 71- *Concurrent Pos:* Mem sci comt, 1st Int Cong Gen Dialectol, Louvain-Brussels, 60; ed, Lituanus, 69- *Mem:* Lithuanian Cath Acad Sci; Inst Lithuanian Studies; Am Asn Teachers Ger; Ling Soc Am; MLA. *Res:* General and historical linguistics; Baltic linguistics; Germanic and Indo-European linguistics. *Publ:* Auth, Lithuanian and the Germanic languages, 6/58 & Lithuanian and the Slavic languages, 3/59, Lituanus; Primitive Germanic Kunigaz in non-Germanic languages, Annali Inst Univ Napoli, Sezione Ling, Rome, 11/59; coauth, Introduction to Modern Lithuanian, 66, 2nd ed, 72, Lithuanian Reader for Self-Instruction, 67, Franciscan Fathers & Lithuanian-English Glossary of Linguistic Terminology, 71, Pa State Univ. *Mailing Add:* Dept of Lang & Ling Univ of Rochester Rochester NY 14627

KLIMENKO, MICHAEL, b Vladimir, Russia, Aug 20, 24; m 59; c 4. RUSSIAN LITERATURE & CHURCH. *Educ:* Theol Sem, BD, 55; Univ Erlangen, PhD(Slavic philol), 57. *Prof Exp:* Assoc res Russ church, Univ Erlangen, 57-60; instr Russ, Wittenberg Univ, 60-61; asst prof, Univ Kans, 61-68; assoc prof, 68-75, PROF RUSS, UNIV HAWAII, MANOA, 75- *Concurrent Pos:* Elizabeth Watkins fel, 64; Ford Found grant, 64-65; Am Philos Soc grant, 70. *Mem:* Am Asn Advan Slavic Studies; Am Asn Slavic & EEurop Lang; AAUP. *Res:* Russian church and religion; Russian literatuare. *Publ:* Auth, Stefan von Perm, 66 & Die religiöse Welt von Terz-Sinjavskij, 68, Kyrios, Kiel-Berlin; Ausbreitung des Christentums in Russland, Luther, 68; Andrei Boznesenskii, In: Encyclopedia of World Literature, Vol III, Ungar, 71; The World of Young Sholokhov, Vision of Violence, Christopher, 72; Das Neueste über Rublëv, In: Glaube in der 2 Welt, Vol IV, 76, Zürich-Küsnacht; Sergeii of Radnonezh, Nordland, 80; The East-West Dialogue: Thoughts, Diakonia, Vol XVI, No 2. *Mailing Add:* Dept of Europ Lang Univ of Hawaii Manoa Honolulu HI 96822

KLIMOV, ALLA, b Kiev, Russia, Dec 25, 35; US citizen; m 58. RUSSIAN LITERATURE. *Educ:* City Col NY, BBA, 58; Hunter Col, MA, 66; NY Univ, PhD(Russ lit), 73. *Prof Exp:* Lectr Russ, Hunter Col, 63-66; grad asst, NY Univ, 66-69; LECTR RUSS, COLUMBIA UNIV, 69- *Concurrent Pos:* Consult, Revlon Int Corp, 73. *Mem:* Am Asn Teachers Slavic & EEurop Lang. *Res:* Early 20th century Russian poetry. *Publ:* Auth, Alfavit i krylatye slova, Novoye Russkoye Slovo, 7/73; Vyrazhenia, osnovannye na naimenovaniakh tserkovnoslavianskikh bukv, Russ Word in Can, 7/73. *Mailing Add:* Dept of Slavic Columbia Univ Lewisohn Hall New York NY 10027

KLINE, GALEN RICHARD, b Youngstown, Ohio, May 7, 35. ROMANCE LANGUAGES. *Educ:* Sorbonne, dipl, 55; Oberlin Col, BA, 59; Western Reserve Univ, MA, 61, PhD(French), 66. *Prof Exp:* Teaching fel French, Western Reserve Univ, 59-63; from instr to asst prof, Lafayette Col, 63-67; asst prof, Va Polytech Inst, 67-68; assoc prof, Windham Col, 68-72; ASSOC PROF FRENCH, VA POLYTECH INST & STATE UNIV, 72- *Mem:* MLA; Medieval Acad Am; Int Arthurian Soc. *Res:* Medieval French literature--humor; Russian-French and French Russian literature influences. *Mailing Add:* Dept of French Va Polytech Inst & State Univ Blacksburg VA 24060

KLINE, THOMAS JEFFERSON, b Washington, DC, July 16, 42; c 2. FRENCH LITERATURE. *Educ:* Oberlin Col, BA, 64; Columbia Univ, MA, 66, PhD(French), 69. *Prof Exp:* Instr French, Columbia Univ, 68-69, asst prof, 70; asst prof, 70-72, assoc provost, Fac Arts & Lett, 76-79, mem prof comp lit, 78-79, assoc prof, State Univ NY, Buffalo, 72-79; PROF FRENCH & CHMN MOD LANG & LIT, BOSTON UNIV, 79- *Concurrent Pos:* Adj prof, Univ Grenoble, 72-73. *Mem:* Malraux Soc; Northeast Mod Lang Asn; AATF. *Res:* Modern French novel; contemporary European drama and film. *Publ:* Auth, Andre Malraux and the Metamorphosis of Death, Columbia Univ, 73; Le temps (du Mepris) retrouve, In: Andre Malraux: Visages duRomancier, Minard, Paris, 11/73; Giraudoux's crisis of language, Romanic Rev, fall 74; Orpheus transcending: Bertolucci's Last Tango, Int Rev Psychoanal, 76; Deconstructing death: Malraux's Lapsus Lazari, Twentieth Century Lit, fall 78 ; The birth of an authentic language in Claudel's Announce, Structuralist Rev, spring 79; The Unconforming Conformist in European Filmmakkers and the Art of Adaptation, Ungar, 80; Endymion's wake, the dream in Bertolucci's Luna, Dreamworks, fall, 81. *Mailing Add:* Dept Mod For Lang & Lit Boston Univ Boston MA 02215

KLINE, WALTER DUANE, b Valparaiso, Ind, Feb 26, 23; m 48; c 2. ROMANCE LANGUAGES. *Educ:* Ind State Teachers Col, AB, 44; Univ Wis, MA, 47; Univ Mich, PhD(Romance lang), 57. *Prof Exp:* Teaching fel Span, Univ Wis, 45-47; instr French & Span, Emory Univ, 47-60; prof mod lang & head dept, Parsons Col, 60-63; assoc prof Span, 63-66, chmn dept foreign lang & lit, 66-72, PROF SPAN, CALIF STATE UNIV, FULLERTON, 66- *Res:* Colonial Latin American literature; 16th and 17th century Spanish literature. *Publ:* Transl, Concolorcorvo: El Lazarillo, Ind

Univ, 65; coauth, Spanish: Contemporary Methodology, 67, German: Contemporary Methodology, 67 & French: Contemporary Methodology, 67, Colo State Dept Educ. *Mailing Add:* 2200 Victoria Dr Fullerton CA 92631

KLOESEL, CHRISTIAN JOHANNES WILHELM, English, Semiotics. See Vol II

KLOPP, CHARLES, b Palatine, Ill, Apr 14, 37; m 62; c 3. ITALIAN LITERATURE. *Educ:* Princeton Univ, AB, 59; Harvard Univ, MA, 65, PhD(Ital lit), 70. *Prof Exp:* Instr English, Robert Col, Istanbul, 59-64; teaching fel humanities, Harvard Univ, 65-67; lectr Ital, Stanford Univ, 68-69; asst prof Ital, Princeton Univ, 69-76; asst prof, 76-80, ASSOC PROF ITAL, OHIO STATE UNIV, 80- *Mem:* Am Asn Teachers Ital; Midwest Mod Lang Asn; MLA; Am Asn Univ Prof Ital. *Res:* Modern Italian literature. *Publ:* Auth, Cassola's Orfano, Italica, winter 74; Nature and human nature in Vigano, Ital Quart, summer-fall, 75; Ariosto and Machiavelli's Prince, In: Ariosto in America, 76; Alliterazione e rima nel Petrarca, Lingua e stile, 77; Peregrino and Errante in the Gerusalemme liberata, Mod Lang Notes, 79; coauth, Coupling and Uncoupling in Rebora, Italica, 79; auth, Beasts and Bestiality in Tozzi, Ital Quart, 80; contribr, Columbia Dictionary of Modern European Literature, 80. *Mailing Add:* Dept of Romance Lang & Lit Ohio State Univ Columbus OH 43210

KLUCAS, JOSEPH ARTHUR, b Ames, Iowa, Feb 1, 48; m 72. SPANISH & PORTUGUESE LANGUAGES. *Educ:* Univ Iowa, BA, 70, MA, 72, PhD(Span & Port), 78. *Prof Exp:* Vis asst prof Span, Cornell Col, 79-80; LECTR SPAN & PORT, CALIF STATE UNIV, SACRAMENTO, 81- *Res:* Renaissance history; Renaissance literature; Christian humanism. *Publ:* Auth, Erasmus and Erasmians on the Jews in Sixteenth-Century Portugal, Luso-Brazilian Rev, winter 80; Erasmus and Erasmians on education in sixteenth-century Portugal, Erasmus Rotterdam Soc Yearbk, 81. *Mailing Add:* 8004 La Riviera Dr No 37 Sacramento CA 95826

KNAPP, ARTHUR BERNARD, Archeology & Ancient History. See Vol I

KNAPP, BETTINA, b New York, NY, m 49; c 2. FRENCH LITERATURE. *Educ:* Columbia Univ, BA, 47, MA, 49, PhD, 55. *Prof Exp:* Lectr French lit, Columbia Univ, 52-59; assoc prof, Hunter Col, 60-73; PROF ROMANCE LANG, HUNTER COL & GRAD CTR CITY, UNIV NY, 73- *Concurrent Pos:* Guggenheim fel, Am Philos Soc grant; ed adv, Drama & Theatre, Nineteenth Century Fr Studies & 20th Century. *Honors & Awards:* Shuster Award; Palmes Academiques, French Govt; Alliance Francaise medal. *Res:* French theatre, poetry, novel; comparative mythology and literature. *Publ:* Auth, Louis Jouvet Man of the Theatre, Columbia Univ Press, 57; coauth, That was Yvette: A biography of Yvette Guilbert, Holt, Rinehart & Winston, 64; auth, Jean Racine, Mythos and Renewal in Modern Theatre, 71 &; Celine Man of Hate, 74, Univ Ala Press; Antonin Artaud, Man of Vision, Avon Bks, 71 & Ohio Univ Press, 80; Jean Genet: A Critical Study, St Martin's Press, 74; Dream and Image: Troy, 77 & The Prometheus Syndrome, 79, Whitston Press. *Mailing Add:* Dept of Fr Hunter Col 68th St & Park Ave New York NY 10021

KNAPP, GERHARD PETER, b Bad Kreuznach, Ger. LITERARY CRITICISM, LINGUISTICS. *Educ:* Tech Univ, Berlin, MA, 68, Dr Phil(Ger, philos), 70. *Prof Exp:* Asst prof Ger, Tech Univ, Berlin, 68-70; asst prof, Lakehead Univ, 70-72; asst prof, 72-74, assoc prof, 74-79, PROF GER & COMP LIT, UNIV UTAH, 79- *Concurrent Pos:* Corresp ed, Utah Studies Lit & Ling, 74-; vis prof Ger, Univ Amsterdam, 77-78. *Mem:* MLA; Am Asn Teachers Ger; Can Asn Univ Teachers Ger; Int Brecht Soc. *Res:* Late medieval studies; 19th and 20th century literature; theory of literary criticism. *Publ:* Auth & coauth of 13 books, auth of 40 articles & ed & co-ed of 26 books on German & comp lit. *Mailing Add:* Dept of Lang Univ of Utah Salt Lake City UT 84112

KNAPP, MONA LINDA, b Salt Lake City, Utah, Sept 8, 52; m 75; c 2. GERMAN & MODERN BRITISH LITERATURE. *Educ:* Univ Utah, BA, 73, MA, 74, PhD(Germanics), 79. *Prof Exp:* RES & WRITING, 77- *Mem:* Am Lit Transl Asn; Doris Lessing Soc; Women in Ger. *Res:* Post-war German and Swiss literature; contemporary British novel; 20th century feminist literature. *Publ:* Auth, Die Verjüngung der alten Dame Dürrenmatt in den US, Text & Kritik, 77; Der Techniker Walter Faber: Zu einem kritischen Missverständnis, Germanic Notes, 77; co-auth, Samuel Beckett: Warten auf Godot, 78 & Max Frisch: Andorra, Diesterweg, 80; auth, Ein Kind nimmt Abschied: Deutungsperspektiven zu G Wohmann, Neophilologus, 80; Zwischen den Fronten: Frauengestalten bei Gabriele Wohmann, Amsterdamer Beiträge, 80; Antifeminism in Friedrich Dürrenmatt's Die Frist, Germanic Notes, 80; coauth, Gabriele Wohmann, Athenäum, 81. *Mailing Add:* 4135 Shanna St Salt Lake City UT 84117

KNAPP, RICHARD GILBERT, b Litchfield, Conn, Nov 24, 40. FRENCH LITERATURE & LANGUAGE. *Educ:* Wesleyan Univ, BA, 62; Columbia Univ, MA, 64, PhD(Fr), 69. *Prof Exp:* From inst to asst prof French, Lafayette Col, 67-71; asst prof, 71-74, ASSOC PROF FRENCH, MARS HILL COL, 74- *Mem:* AAUP; MLA; Am Coun Teaching Foreign Lang; Am Soc 18th Century Studies; Am Asn Teachers Fr. *Res:* Voltaire; Diderot; history of ideas. *Publ:* Auth, The fortunes of Poe's Essay on Man in 18th century France, Vol 82, In: Studies on Voltaire and the Eighteenth Century, Inst et Musee Voltaire, Geneva, 71. *Mailing Add:* Dept of Mod Foreign Lang Mars Hill Col Mars Hill NC 28754

KNAPP, ROBERT CARLYLE, b Lansing, Mich, Feb 12, 46; m 74; c 1. ANCIENT HISTORY, CLASSICS. *Educ:* Cent Mich Univ, BA, 68; Univ Pa, PhD(ancient hist), 73. *Prof Exp:* Vis asst prof classics, Colby Col, 73; asst prof hist, Univ Utah, 73-74; asst prof, 74-80, ASSOC PROF CLASSICS, UNIV CALIF, BERKELEY, 80- *Mem:* Asn Ancient Historians; Am Philol Asn; AHA. *Res:* Roman Spain; Latin historians. *Publ:* Auth, Aspects of the Roman Experience in Iberia, 206-100 BC, Anejos IX Hisp Antiqua, 77; The date and purpose of the Iberian denarii, Numis Chronicle, 77; The origins of provincial prosopography in the West, Ancient Soc, 78; Cato in Spain, 195-194 BC, In: Studies in Latin Literature and Roman History II, C Deroux, Brussells, 80; La epigrafia y la historia de la Cordoba romana, Annario de Filologia, 80; Festus 262L and Praefecturae in Italy, Athenaeum, 80; L Axius Naso and Pro legato, Phoenix, 81. *Mailing Add:* Dept of Classics Dwinelle Hall Univ of Calif Berkeley CA 94720

KNAUER, GEORG NICOLAUS, b Hamburg, Ger, Feb 26, 26; m 51; c 1. CLASSICAL STUDIES. *Educ:* Univ Hamburg, Ger, Dr Phil, 52; Freie Univ, Berlin, Habilitation, 61. *Prof Exp:* Res asst Latin lexicography, Thesaurus Linguae Latinae, Munich, 52-54; asst classics, Sem für Klassische Philol, Freie Univ, Berlinü, 54-61; from lectr to full prof, 61-74, chmn dept, 78-82, PROF CLASS STUDIES, UNIV PA, 75- *Concurrent Pos:* Vis prof, Yale Univ, 65; Columbia Univ, 76; mem, Inst Advan Study, Princeton, NJ, 73-74; Guggenheim fel, 79-80. *Honors & Awards:* Nellie Wallace Lectr, Oxford Univ, England, 69. *Mem:* Am Philol Asn; Renaissance Soc Am. *Res:* Homer in Vergil; Vergilian commentaries; Homer, especially Latin translations and commentaries. *Publ:* Auth, Psalmzitate in Augustins Confessionen, Vandenhoeck und Ruprecht, Göttingen, 55; Die Aeneis und Homer, Hypomnemata 7, Göttingen, 64. *Mailing Add:* Dept of Class Studies Univ of Pa 720 Williams Hall CU Philadelphia PA 19174

KNECHT, LORING D, b Wimbledon, NDak, Sept 19, 21; m 50; c 2. FRENCH LANGUAGE & LITERATURE. *Educ:* St Olaf Col, BA, 47; Univ Wis, MA, 49, PhD, 57. *Prof Exp:* From asst prof to assoc prof, 51-64, chmn dept romance lang, 57-80, chmn div lang & lit, 70-73, PROF FRENCH, ST OLAF COL, 64- *Mem:* MLA; Am Asn Teachers Fr. *Res:* The French novel. *Publ:* Auth, Language studies, In: Christian Faith and the Liberal Arts, Augsburg, 60; A new reading of Andre Gide's La Porte Etroite, PMLA, 12/67; Echos de Notre Monde, Holt. *Mailing Add:* Dept of Romance Lang St Olfa Col Northfield MN 55057

KNELLER, JOHN WILLIAM, b Oldham, Eng, Oct 15, 16; nat US; m 43; c 1. FRENCH LITERATURE. *Educ:* Clark Univ, BA, 38; Yale Univ, MA, 48, PhD, 50. *Hon Degrees:* LittD, Clark Univ, 70. *Prof Exp:* From instr to prof French, Oberlin Col, 50-69, chmn dept Romance lang, 58-65, provost, 65-69; prof mod lang & pres, 69-79, EMER PRES, BROOKLYN COL, 79-; PROF HUMANITIES & ARTS, HUNTER COL & GRAD CTR, CITY UNIV NEW YORK, 79- *Concurrent Pos:* Managing ed, Fr Rev, 62-65, ed, 65-68; trustee, Clark Univ, 68-74 & Brooklyn Inst Arts & Sci, 71-79; chmn, subcomt enrollment goals & projections, NY State Educ Comn Adv Coun on Higher Educ & mem adv coun. *Honors & Awards:* Chevalier, Ordre Palmes Academiques, 72. *Mem:* MLA; Am Asn Teachers Fr. *Res:* J J Rousseau; 19th century French literature; music and literature. *Publ:* Coauth, The poet and his Moira, El Disdichado, PMLA, 60; Introduction a la Poesie Francaise, Ginn, 62; Initiation au Francais, Macmillan, 63; auth, The changing college, Oberling Alumni Mag, 66; Translation and transformation: New roles for research, Proc MLA Conf, 72; Newer clothes for emperors, Centerpoint, fall 74; The terrifying pips of reality, Fr Rev, 3/78. *Mailing Add:* PhD Prog Fr Grad Ctr City Univ New York 33 W 42nd St New York NY 10036

KNIGHT, ADELE IRENE, b Cleveland, Ohio, June 28, 10. CLASSICAL LANGUAGES. *Educ:* Western Reserve Univ, BA, 32, MA, 48. *Prof Exp:* Teacher Latin, Willoughby-Eastlake N High Sch, 33-72; teacher Latin & supvr student teachers, Notre Dame Col, Ohio, 72-82. *Honors & Awards:* Martha Holden Jennings Master Teacher Award, 65; Freedoms Found Valley Forge Teacher's Medal, 65. *Mem:* Vergilian Soc (secy, 75-77); Am Class League (secy, 68-75); Am Coun Teaching Foreign Lang; NEA; Archaeol Inst Am. *Res:* Virgil; Cicero; Greek and Roman mythology. *Publ:* Auth, Armilustrium, Class J, 10/66. *Mailing Add:* 37946 Barber Ave Willoughby OH 44094

KNIGHT, ALAN EDGAR, b Plant City, Fla, Sept 7, 31; c 2. FRENCH & COMPARATIVE LITERATURE. *Educ:* Fla State Univ, BA, 58; Fordham Univ, MA, 60; Yale Univ, PhD(French), 65. *Prof Exp:* Acting instr French lang & lit, Yale Univ, 63-64; asst prof French lit, 64-70, ASSOC PROF FRENCH & COMP LIT, PA STATE UNIV, UNIVERSITY PARK, 70- *Concurrent Pos:* Assoc ed, Treteaux. *Mem:* MLA; Mediaeval Acad Am; Soc Int l'Etude Drama. *Res:* Medieval drama; literary theory; literature and society. *Publ:* Auth, A previously unknown prose Joseph d'Arimathie, Romance Philol, 11/67; The medieval theater of the absurd, PMLA, 71; The farce wife, In: A Medieval French Miscellany, Univ Kans, 72; Fragments de trois farces du Recueil de Florence, Romania, 73; The farce lover, L'Esprit Createur, 76; Bilingualism in medieval French drama, In: Jean Misrahi Memorial Volume, Fr Lit Publ Co, 77; From the Sacred to the Profane, Treteaux, 78; Drama and society in late medieval Flanders and Picardy, Chaucer Rev, 80. *Mailing Add:* Dept of French 316 Burrowes Pa State Univ University Park PA 16802

KNIGHT, ELIZABETH C, b New Haven, Conn, Apr 5, 14; m 40; c 4. GERMAN LANGUAGE & LITERATURE. *Educ:* Vassar Col, BA, 35; Yale Univ, PhD(German lit), 38. *Prof Exp:* Instr German, Wheaton Col, Mass, 39-40; teacher hist & math, Day Sch, New Haven, 57-60; teacher hist & German, Day Prospect Hill Sch, 60-62; from instr to assoc prof mod foreign lang, 67-69, PROF GERMAN LIT & CHMN DEPT FINE ARTS, LANG & PHILOS, QUINNIPIAC COL, 69- *Mem:* MLA; Am Asn Teachers Ger. *Publ:* Co-ed & translr, Selected Writing of E T A Hoffmann, Univ Chicago, 69. *Mailing Add:* Quinnipiac Col Mt Carmel Ave Hamden CT 06518

KNOERLE, JEANNE, b Cleveland, Ohio, Feb 24, 28. COMPARATIVE & ASIAN LITERATURE. *Educ:* St Mary-at-the-Woods Col, BA, 49; Ind Univ, MA, 61, PhD(comp lit), 66. *Hon Degrees:* LittD, Rose-Hulman Inst Technol, 71; LLD, Ind State Univ, 72; DD, Ind Cent Univ, 78. *Prof Exp:* Teacher, St Columbkille High Sch & Providence High Sch, Chicago, Ill, 52; teacher, Cent Cath High Sch, Ft Wayne, Ind, 53 & Immaculata High Sch, Washington, DC, 53-54; chmn dept jour, St Mary-of-the-Woods Col, 54-63; vis prof English, Providence Col, Taichung, Taiwan, 66-67; asst to pres, 67-68, PRES, ST MARY-OF-THE-WOODS COL, 68- *Concurrent Pos:* Educ couns, Purdue Univ Old Masters Prog, 70; comnr, Gov Comn on Status of Women in India, 73-75. *Mem:* Nat Cath Educ Asn; Asn Am Col; Asn Asian Studies; Am Soc Aesthet; Asn Cath Cols & Univs. *Res:* Chinese fiction and poetry; critical work on 18th century novel; censorship and the press. *Publ:* Auth, The poetic theories of Lu Chi, with a brief comparison with Horace's Ars Poetica, J Aesthet & Art Criticism, winter 66; The Dream of the Red Chamber, A Critical Study, Ind Univ, 72; Ezra Pound and the literature of China, Tamkang Rev, Taipei, 73. *Mailing Add:* St Mary-of-the-Woods Col St Mary-of-the-Woods IN 47876

KNOLL, SAMSON BENJAMIN, History. See Vol I

KNOP, CONSTANCE KAY PETERSEN, b Kenosha, Wis, Sept 15, 37; m 59; c 3. FRENCH, EDUCATION. *Educ:* Univ Wis-Madison, BS, 58, MA, 61, PhD(educ, French), 69. *Prof Exp:* Teacher English & French, Cleveland Pub Schs, 58-59; teacher French, Madison Pub Schs, 61-62; teacher, Lab Sch, Univ Wis, 62-63; from instr to asst prof, 63-70, ASSOC PROF FRENCH & EDUC, UNIV WIS-MADISON, 70- *Mem:* Am Asn Teachers Fr; Am Coun Teaching Fr; Cent States Conf Teaching Foreign Lang. *Res:* Training and supervision of French teachers; in-service training of French teachers. *Publ:* Auth, Alternatives in student teacher supervision and evaluation, 12/72 & On using culture capsules and culture assimilators, 10/77, Fr Rev; Developing a model for student teacher supervision, Foreign Lang Ann, 12/77; Directions for change in an audio-lingual approach, Can Mod Lang Rev, 5/81; Notional-functional syllabus: From theory to classroom applications, In: A Global Approach to Foreign Language Teaching, Nat Textbk Co, 81; Teaching a Second Language a Guide for the Student Teacher, Ctr Appl Ling, 80; A program for training & supervising the teaching assistants in french, In: The Teaching Apprentice Program in Language & Literature, MLA, 81. *Mailing Add:* 225 N Mills Univ of Wis Madison WI 53706

KNORRE, MARTHA LEE, b Dayton, Ohio, June 14, 45. SPANISH. *Educ:* Ohio Univ, AB, 67; Ohio State Univ, MA, 69, PhD(foreign lang educ), 75. *Prof Exp:* ASST PROF SPAN, UNIV CINCINNATI, 75- *Concurrent Pos:* Contrib bibliogr, Am Coun Teaching Foreign Lang, 74- *Mem:* Am Asn Teachers Span & Port; MLA; Am Coun Teaching Foreign Lang; Ling Soc Am; Am Asn Teachers Fr. *Res:* Psycholinguistics; theory of second-language learning; teacher education. *Publ:* Coauth, Cara a Cara, 77 & Reflejos, 78, Holt; auth, A contemporary rationale for foreign language study, In: Nat Textbk Am Coun Teaching Foreign Lang Educ Ser, Vol 10, 78. *Mailing Add:* Dept of Romance Lang Univ of Cincinnati Cincinnati OH 45221

KNOWLES, DONALD ROLAND JOHN, b Eleuthera, Bahamas, Oct 26, 35; Brit citizen; m 59; c 3. GENERAL LINGUISTICS, SPANISH. *Educ:* Cambridge Univ, BA, 58, MA, 66; Univ London, PhD(ling), 70. *Prof Exp:* Lectr Span, Kilburn Polytech, 63-66; instr, 66-70, ASST PROF LING & SPAN, SIMON FRASER UNIV, 70- *Mem:* Ling Soc Am; Can Ling Asn. *Res:* Transformational syntax; applications to description of Spanish and English. *Publ:* Auth, Analisis transformacional de uma excepcion en el sistema de los adverbios de/mo do, Actas IV Cong Int Hispanists, 71. *Mailing Add:* 2793 Sunny Bridge Burnaby BC V5A 3T9 Can

KNOWLTON, EDGAR COLBY, JR, b Delaware, Ohio, Sept 14, 21. ROMANCE LANGUAGES. *Educ:* Harvard Univ, AB, 41, AM, 42; Stanford Univ, PhD(Span), 59. *Prof Exp:* Censorship clerk & translr Port, Off Censorship, NYC, 42; commun clerk, US Dept Navy, Washington, DC, 42-44; teacher, High Sch, Mass, 46; instr Span, 48-50, instr Span & French, 50-51, 52-53, from asst prof to assoc prof, 54-65, PROF EUROP LANG, UNIV HAWAII, MANOA, 65- *Concurrent Pos:* Smith-Mundt vis prof ling,Univ Malaya, 62-64; mem bibliog comt, MLA, 69-; Fulbright vis prof ling, Univ Cent de Venezuela, 75. *Honors & Awards:* Transl Prize, Sec of State Info & Tourism, Port, 71. *Mem:* Ling Soc Am; Am Asn Teachers Span & Port; MLA. *Res:* Contacts between speakers and writers of Spanish and Portuguese and those of Asian and Pacific languages; history of literatures and languages of Spanish and Portuguese speaking countries. *Publ:* Transl, Sa de Meneses, The Conquest of Malacca, Univ Malaya, 71; coauth, V Blasco Ibanez, Twayne, 72; translr, Machado de Assis, You, love, and love alone, Bol Inst Luis de Camoes, Macao, fall-winter 72; contribr, Languages, In: Atlas of Hawaii, Univ Hawaii, 73; auth, Echeverria, traductor de un fragmento del Fausto de Goethe,, Bol Acad Argentina de Letras, 75; Carajo and Hispanic Congeners in Borrow, Byron, Ford and Scott, Maledicta, 80; Mickiewicz and Brazil's Machado de Assis, Polish Rev, 81; Un problema textual de La Respuesta a Sov Filotea de la Cruz, Anuario de Letras, 81. *Mailing Add:* 1026 Kalo Pl Apt 403 Honolulu HI 96826

KNOX, BERNARD MACGREGOR WALKER, b Bradford, Eng, Nov 24, 14; nat US; m ; c 1. CLASSICAL PHILOLOGY. *Educ:* Cambridge Univ, BA, 36; Yale Univ, PhD, 48. *Hon Degrees:* MA, Harvard Univ, 61; LittD, Princeton Univ, 64; DHL, George Washington Univ, 77. *Prof Exp:* Instr Classics, Yale Univ, 47-48; asst prof & fel, Branford Col,48-54, from assoc prof to prof, 54-60; DIR, CTR HELLENIC STUDIES, WASHINGTON DC, 61- *Concurrent Pos:* Guggenheim fel, 56-57; Sather lectr, Univ Calif, Berkeley, 63; chmn, Soc Preserv Greek Heritage, 77-; Martin lectr, Oberlin Col, 81. *Honors & Awards:* Award for Lit, Nat Inst Arts & Lett, 67; George Jean Nathan Award for Dramatic Criticism, Mfrs Hanover Trust, 78. *Mem:* Am Philol Soc; Am Archaeol Inst; AAAS; Am Philol Asn (pres 80). *Res:* Greek tragedy; Latin and Greek literature. *Publ:* Auth, Oedipus at Thebes, Yale Univ, 57; The Heroic Temper, Univ Calif, 64; Word and action: Essays on the ancient theater, Johns Hopkins Press, 79; asst ed & contribr, Cambridge History of Classical Literature, Vol I (in press); coauth (with Robert Foyles), The Theban plays of Sophocles, Viking Press (in prep). *Mailing Add:* 3100 Whitehaven St Washington DC 20008

KNOX, EDWARD CHAPMAN, b Meriden, Conn, Oct 5, 39; m 65. ROMANCE LANGUAGES. *Educ:* Wesleyan Univ, BA, 61; Yale Univ, PhD(French), 66. *Prof Exp:* Asst prof Romance lang, Case Western Reserve Univ, 66-69; asst prof French, 69-74, dean French sch, 73, assoc prof, 74-79, PROF FRENCH, MIDDLEBURY COL, 80-, DEAN FRENCH SCH, 76- *Mem:* MLA; Am Asn Teachers Fr; Am Coun Teaching Foreign Lang. *Res:* Literary style. *Publ:* Ed, Rencontres, Harcourt, 72; auth, La bruyere, Twayne, 74. *Mailing Add:* Dept of French Middlebury Col Middlebury VT 05753

KNOX, ROBERT BAKER, b Prineville, Ore, Nov 22, 17; m 40. SPANISH. *Educ:* Univ Ore, BA, 40, MA, 42; Univ Mich, PhD(Romance lang), 52. *Prof Exp:* From instr to asst prof Span, 48-57, assoc prof foreign lang, 57-62, actg chmn dept, 55-56, PROF FOREIGN LANG, WASH STATE UNIV, 62-, CHMN PROJ LIT STUDIES, 76- *Mem:* MLA; Am Asn Teachers Span & Port; Philol Asn Pac Coast; Am Comp Lit Asn. *Res:* Contemporary Hispanic novel; Pio Baroja. *Publ:* Auth, The structure of El Mayorazgo de Labraz, Hispania; Notes on the identity of Pedro Gutierrez de Santa Clara and some members of his family, Rev Hist Am; La mariposa negra and the raven, Symposium. *Mailing Add:* Dept of Foreign Lang Wash State Univ Pullman WA 99163

KNUST, HERBERT, b Cologne, Ger, May 9, 35. GERMAN, COMPARATIVE LITERATURE. *Educ:* Tulane Univ, MA, 58; Pa State Univ, PhD, 61. *Prof Exp:* Asst prof Ger & comp lit, Pa State Univ, 63-65; asst prof Ger, 65-67, assoc prof, 67-73, chmn dept comp lit, 70-72, 73-74, PROF GER & COMP LIT, UNIV ILL, URBANA, 73-, HEAD DEPT GER LANG & LIT, 82- *Concurrent Pos:* Am Philos Soc grant, 71-72; dir, Illinois-Austria Exchange Prog, Baden & Vienna, 79-80; actg dir, Prog in Comp Lit, 81-82. *Mem:* Am Asn Teachers Ger; Am Comp Lit Asn; MLA; Int Brecht Soc. *Res:* Modern literature; drama; criticism. *Publ:* Auth, Wagner, The King, and The Waste Land, Pa State Univ, 67; Moderne Variationen des Jedermann-Spiels, In: Helen Adolf Festschrift, Ungar, 68; Camus' Le Malentendu and Doderer's Zwei Lügen, Archiv, 71; Brechts braver Schweyk, PMLA, 73; ed & contribr, Materialien zu Schweyk im Zweiten Weltkrieg, Suhrkamp, 73; co-ed, Essays on Brecht: Theater and Politics, Univ NC, 74; ed & contribr, Montage, Satire and Cultism: Germany Between the Wars, Univ Ill, 75; ed, George Grosz, Briefe 1913-1959, Rowohlt, 79. *Mailing Add:* Dept of Ger Lang & Lit Univ of Ill Urbana IL 61801

KNUTSON, HAROLD CHRISTIAN, b Minneapolis, Minn, Dec 18, 28; m 67. FRENCH. *Educ:* Univ Minn, AB, 49, MA, 52; Univ Calif, Berkeley, PhD(Romance lit), 62. *Prof Exp:* Teaching asst, Univ Minn, 51-52 & Univ Calif, Berkeley, 55-59; from instr to assoc prof, 60-75, asst dean, fac arts, 69-72 & assoc dean, 77-82, PROF FRENCH, UNIV BC, 75- *Concurrent Pos:* Can Coun Leave fel, 72-73; Social Sci & Humanities Res Coun Can leave fel, 79-80. *Mem:* Asn Can Univ Teachers Fr; MLA; NAm Soc 17th Century Fr Lit; Can Comparative Lit Asn. *Res:* French drama of the 17th century; comedy; criticism. *Publ:* Auth, The Ironic Game: A Study of Rotrou's Comic Theater, Univ Calif, 66; Le Denouement heureux dan la tragedie francaise du dix-septieme siecle, Zeitschrift Franzöisische Sprache u Literatur, 67; Le Cid deCorneille: Un heros se fait, Studies Francesi, 73; Moliere: An Archetypal Approach, Univ Toronto, 76; Moliere, Mauron and myth, Esprit Createur, 76; Yet another last word on Moliere's raisonneur, Theatre Survey, 81; Corneille's early comedies: Variations in comic form, Papers in Seventeenth century French Lit, 82. *Mailing Add:* Dept of French Univ of BC Vancouver BC V6T 1W5 Can

KOBLER, JASPER FRED, English, American Literature. See Vol II

KOCH, ERNST, b Berlin, Ger, Sept 20, 06; US citizen; m 46; c 2. GERMANIC LANGUAGES & LITERATURES. *Educ:* Pa State Univ, AB, 28, AM, 31; NY Univ, PhD(Ger), 34. *Prof Exp:* Teacher, Jr High Sch, NJ, 28-29; instr Ger, Pa State Univ,29-31; from instr to asst prof, NY Univ, 33-46; from asst prof to prof, 46-73, chmn dept, 52-56, assoc dean students, 67-68, asst dean acad adjustments, 68-73, EMER PROF GER, BROOKLYN COL, 73- *Concurrent Pos:* Consult, Ger, col text dept, Am Bk Col, 47-52. *Mem:* MLA. *Res:* Eighteenth century German literature, especially Schiller and Lessing; Scandinavian literature, especially Ibsen; problems of administration in higher education. *Publ:* Auth, The key to Sudermann, PMLA, 9/36; Dauer im Wechsel, 37 & Elementary German Reader with Grammar Review, 39, Prentice-Hall; Exemption examination practices in higher education, Sch & Soc, 2/50; A foreign language approach to critical evaluation in general literature, Ger Quart, 5/50;coauth, Essentials of German, Oxford Univ, 57; The Counseling of College Students, Free Press, 68; coauth (with Clarence J Schein) of several articles on Theodore Billrath, 78-80. *Mailing Add:* 780 E 32nd St Brooklyn NY 11210

KOCH, PHILIP, b New York, NY, Dec 31, 27; m 52; c 2. ROMANCE LANGUAGES. *Educ:* Harvard Univ, AB, 49, AM, 51, PhD(French & Ital), 55. *Prof Exp:* Instr French lang, Phillips Exeter Acad, 49; instr French lang, Northwestern Univ, 55-56; from instr to asst prof French, Bryn Mawr Col, 56-61; from asst prof to assoc prof, 61-66, chmn dept French & Ital, 66-72, PROF FRENCH, UNIV PITTSBURGH, 66- *Concurrent Pos:* Reader advan placement French, Educ Testing Serv, 60-65; consult French, Regents Doc Eval Proj, NY State, 75-76 & Masters Rev Proj, City Univ New York, 82. *Mem:* Am Asn Teachers Fr; NAm Soc 17th Century Fr Lit; Am Soc 18th Century Studies; Societe Francaise d'Etude du XVIIIe Siecle. *Res:* French literature of the 17th and 18th centuries; modern Italian literature; influence of the Commedia dell'arte on French comedy. *Publ:* Auth, On Marivaux's expression, Se donner la comedie, Romanic Rev, 2/65; Reflections on Racine's Oreste, Ky Romance Quart, Vol XV, No 4; ed, F Galiani's Dialogues entre M Marquis de Roquemaure et M le Chevalier Zanobi, Vittorio Klostermann, 68; auth, Innocent Hippolyte, Fr Rev, 4/70; Les veritables dialogues de Galiani, Problemi Attuali de Scienza e di Cultura, 75; Regnard and Collin d'Harleville, Studies 18th Century Cult, Vol VIII; Les Dernieres Annees de Mezzetin, XVIIIe Siecle, 79; L'Histoire de l'Ancien Theatre-Italien, Studies Voltaire & 18th Century, Vol CXCIX. *Mailing Add:* Dept of Fr & Ital Univ of Pittsburgh Pittsburgh PA 15260

KOCH, REGINA MARIE, b Longbranch, NJ, Sept 23, 26. GERMANIC LANGUAGES & LITERATURE. *Educ:* Boston Col, MA, 56; Harvard Univ, PhD(Ger), 64. *Prof Exp:* From instr to asst prof Ger, Regis Col, Mass, 64-73, acad dean, 70-73; prof Ger lang & dean, Univ Maine, Presque Isle, 73-76; HEAD DEPT FOREIGN LANG & LIT, PURDUE UNIV, CALUMET CAMPUS, 76- *Concurrent Pos:* Mem accreditation comt, New England Asn Schs & Cols. *Mem:* MLA; Am Coun Teaching Foreign Lang; Am Asn Teachers Ger; AAUP; Medieval Acad Am. *Res:* Mechthild of Magdeburg; the Ritter in German literature from 1250; German-American studies. *Mailing Add:* Schereville IN 46375

KOCHER, MYRON LOW, b Bloomsburg, Pa, Dec 29, 21. FRENCH. *Educ:* Wake Forest Col, BA, 48; Middlebury Col, AM, 49; Univ NC, PhD(Romance lang), 65. *Prof Exp:* Instr French, Wake Forest Col, 46-47; instr, Univ NC, 49-54, 58-59; instr mod foreign lang, Univ Ga, 55-58; asst prof, 59-67, assoc prof, 67-81, PROF MOD FOR LANGS, FURMAN UNIV, 81- *Mem:* MLA; Am Asn Teachers Fr; SAtlantic Mod Lang Asn. *Res:* French literature of the 17th century. *Publ:* Auth, Le Misanthrope revisited, Furman Rev, 70; Charles Sorel and the drama, Furman Studies, 74. *Mailing Add:* Dept of Mod Foreign Lang Furman Univ Greenville SC 29613

KOCHMAN, THOMAS MICHAEL, b Berlin, Ger, May 19, 36; US citizen; m 61; c 2. ANTHROPOLOGICAL LINGUISTICS. *Educ:* City Col NY, BA, 58; NY Univ, MA, 62, PhD(ling), 66. *Prof Exp:* Teacher, Jr High Sch, NY, 61-66; from asst prof to assoc prof ling, Northeastern Ill State Col, 66-70; assoc prof speech, 70-74, PROF COMMUN, UNIV ILL, CHICAGO CIRCLE, 74- *Mem:* MLA; Ling Soc Am; Am Name Soc; Am Anthrop Asn; Soc Applied Anthrop. *Res:* Sociolinguistics; Afro-American speech behavior; cross-cultural communication. *Publ:* Auth, Rapping in the Black Ghetto, Transaction, 69; Cross-cultural communication: Contrastive perspectives, conflicting sensibilities, Fla Foreign Lang Reporter, spring-fall, 71; Black American speech events and a language program for the classroom, In: The Functions of Language in the Classroom, Teachers Col, Columbia Univ, 72; ed, Rappin and Styling' Out: Communication in Urban Black American, Univ Ill, 72; Orality and literacy as factors of Black and White communicative behavior, Int J Sociol Lang, 9/74; Perceptions along the power axis: A cognitive residue of inter-racial encounters, Anthrop Ling, 9/76; Black and White Styles in Conflict, Univ Chicago Press, 81. *Mailing Add:* Dept of Commun & Theatre Univ of Ill Chicago IL 60680

KOCKS, GÜNTER HERMANN, b Mönchengladbach, Ger, Dec 19, 35; m 66; c 2. GERMAN LANGUAGE & LITERATURE. *Educ:* Univ Cologne, Philosophikum, 60, DPhil(Ger lit), 65. *Prof Exp:* Lectr Ger lang, Ger Ctr, Stockholm, Sweden, 63-64; lectr Ger lit, Ger Acad Exchange Serv, Japan, 66-68; asst prof Ger lang & lit, Nanzan Univ,Nagoya, Japan, 68-70; ASSOC PROF GER LANG & LIT, UNIV REGINA, 70-, CHMN DEPT, 71- *Concurrent Pos:* Consult, Dept Cult & Youth, Sask & chmn Ger curric comt, Sask Dept Educ, 73- *Mem:* Japanese Soc Ger Studies; Humanities Asn Can; Can Asn Teachers Ger. *Res:* Baroque literature; German expressionism; modern drama. *Publ:* Auth, Das Bürgertum in Johann Fischarts Werk, Rudolf Stehle, Düsseldorf, 65; Gestallungsmerkmale der expressionistische Lyrik, 67 & Das moderne deutschen Dramader Gegenwart, 68, Academia; Strukturen und Substanzen in der moderne duetsche Lyrik, Doitsu Bungaku, Tokyo, 69. *Mailing Add:* 3534 Argyle Rd Regina SK S4S 2B8 Can

KOCOUREK, ROSTISLAV, b Prague, Czech, Sept 4, 29; Can citizen. TERMINOLOGY & LEXICOLOGY, LINGUISTICS. *Educ:* Charles Univ, BA & MA, 52, PhD(English ling & lit), 53, CSc, 62; Czech Fed Ministry of Educ, docent, 65. *Prof Exp:* Lectr foreign lang, Agr Univ Prague, 53-55, asst prof, 56-64, assoc prof, 65-70; asst prof, 70-75, assoc prof, 75-81, PROF FRENCH, DALHOUSIE UNIV, 81- *Concurrent Pos:* Dir, Ctr for Doc & Terminol, Tunis, 67-68; head, Ctr Terminol & Ling Questions, Frankfurt, 69-70. *Mem:* Int Asn Terminol; Can Asn Appl Ling; Ling Soc Am; Can Ling Asn; Soc de Ling et Philol Romanes. *Res:* Specialized vocabularies and terminology; linguistic aspects of the language of science and technology. *Publ:* Auth, Synonymy and semantic structure of terminology, Travaux Ling de Prague, 68; A semantic study of terminology and its application in teaching technical language, The Prague Sch Ling & Lang Teaching, Oxford Univ Press, 72; Terminological remarks on deep structure, Proc of the 9th Int Congr of Ling, 74; Comprehension et semantique linguistique, Proc of the XIVth Congr of Romance Ling & Philol, 77; La nature du francais technique et scientifique, Wörterbuch d industriellen Technik, 80; Prerequisites for an applicable linguistic theory of terminology, Proc of the 5th Congr of Int Asn Appl Ling, 81; Technical language and function, Form and Functions, 81; La Langue Francaise de la Technique et de la Science, 82. *Mailing Add:* Dept of French Dalhousie Univ Halifax NS B3H 3J5 Can

KODJAK, ANDREJ, b Prague, Czech, Nov 16, 26; c 3. RUSSIAN LITERATURE. *Educ:* Univ Montreal, MA, 57; St Vladimir's Theol Acad, BD, 59; Univ Pa, PhD(Slavic philol), 63. *Prof Exp:* Asst prof Slavic lang & lit, Univ Pa, 63-64; vis assoc prof, Vanderbilt Univ, 64-65, assoc prof, 65-68; vis assoc prof, 68-69, ASSOC PROF & CHMN DEPT SLAVIC, NY UNIV, 69- *Concurrent Pos:* Consult Russ lang, Educ Testing Serv, 69-; mem adv comt soviet studies lit, Int Arts & Sci Press, 73- *Mem:* Am Asn Teachers Slavic & E Europ Lang; Am Asn Advan Slavic Studies; MLA. *Res:* Pushkin and his epoch; structuralism in literary studies; East Christian theology. *Publ:* Auth, Shifr Pushkina, New Rev, 70; Ustnaja rec Puskina v zapisi Titova, In: American Contributions to VIIth International Congress of Slavists, Mouton, The Hague, 73; Queen of Spades in context of the Faust legend, In: Alexander Puskin--Symposium on 175th Anniversary of His Birth, 76 & co-ed, Alexander Puskin--A Symposium on the 175th Anniversary of His Birth, 76, NY Univ; auth, Political conversion in Solzhenitsyn's fiction, Mod Fiction Studies, 77; Puskin's last fairytale The Golden Cockerel, In: American Contributions to VIIIth International Congress of Slavists, Slavica, 78; Alexander Solzhenitsyn, Twayne, 78; coauth, Pushkin's Kirdzali: An informational model, Russ Lit, 78. *Mailing Add:* Dept of Slavic NY Univ 19 University Pl New York NY 10003

KOEHLER, LUDMILA, b Troitzk, Russia, Mar 30, 17; US citizen. RUSSIAN LITERATURE. *Educ:* Univ Munich, MA, 47; Univ Wash, PhD(Slavic lang & lit), 63. *Prof Exp:* Asst prof Russ & Ger, Pac Univ, 63-64; asst prof Russ lit, Univ Iowa, 64-66; asst prof, Mich State Univ, 66-67; asst prof, 67-70, assoc prof, 70-81, PROF RUSS LIT, UNIV PITTSBURGH, 81- *Concurrent Pos:* Int Res & Exchange Bd exchange prof, Univ Moscow, 73. *Mem:* Am Asn Advan Slavic Studies; Am Asn Teachers Slavic Lang. *Res:* Russian literature and intellectual life. *Publ:* Auth, A A Delvig--A Classicist in the Time of Romanticism, Mouton, The Hague, 70; The grotesque poetry of Dostoevsky, Slavic & East Europ J, spring 70; The identity of Pushkin's Sublime Gaul, Slavonic & East Europ Rev, 10/71; NF Fedorov, In: Friedrich Ueberwegs Grundriss der Geschichte der Philosophie, Reihe VII, Philosophie des 19 Jahnrhunderts; N F Fedorov, The Philosophy of Action, 81. *Mailing Add:* Dept of Slavic Lang & Lit Univ of Pittsburgh Pittsburgh PA 15260

KOEKKOEK, BYRON J, b Mich, May 19, 24; m 55; c 2. GERMANIC & GERMAN LINGUISTICS. *Educ:* Olivet Col, BA, 49; Univ Mich, MA, 50; Univ Vienna, PhD, 53. *Prof Exp:* From instr to assoc prof, 53-65, chmn dept Germanic & Slavic, 71-76, PROF GER, STATE UNIV NY, BUFFALO, 65- *Concurrent Pos:* Corresp overseas mem, Inst fur deutsche Sprache, Mannheim, Ger, 69- *Mem:* MLA; Ling Soc Am; Ling Asn Can & US; Am Asn Teachers Ger. *Res:* Germanic and German linguistics. *Publ:* Auth, Zur Phonologie der Wiener Mundart, Giessen, Ger, 55; Amerikanische Arbeiten zur Phonologie des Deutschen, Z Mundartforsch, 2/58; On the status of umlaut in standard German morphology, J English & Ger Philol, 10/65; Transformational grammar, Studia grammatica, and the description of German, Ger Quart, 1/70; What does German Spelling Spell, Monatshefte, 4/77. *Mailing Add:* Dept of Mod Lang & Lit State Univ NY Buffalo NY 14260

KOENEN, LUDWIG, b Cologne, Ger, Apr 5, 31; m 55; c 4. CLASSICAL PHILOLOGY, PAPYROLOGY. *Educ:* Univ Cologne, Dr(class philol), 57, Drhabil(class philol), 69. *Prof Exp:* From asst prof to assoc prof & from cur to chief cur class philol & papyrology, Univ Cologne, 56-75; PROF PAPYROLOGY, UNIV MICH, ANN ARBOR, 75- *Concurrent Pos:* Res study papyri Cairo, Univ Cologne, 62-65; field dir papyri, Photog Arch Egyptian Mus, Cairo Int Asn Papyrologists, 69, 71, 73 & 76; corresp mem, Ger Archaeol Inst, 75. *Mem:* Am Philol Asn; Am Soc Papyrologists (vpres, 78-80, pres, 81-); Int Asn Papyrologists. *Res:* Classical philology; papyrology; patristics. *Publ:* Auth, Eine Ptolemäische Königsurkunde, Harrassowitz, Wiesbaden, 57; coauth, Didymos der Blinde, Kommentar zu Hiob, II & Three Rolls of the Early Scptuag, Habelt, Bonn, 68 & 80; auth, Die Leichenrede des Augustus auf Agrippa, 70-71 & coauth, Ein griechischer Mani-Codex, 70, 75, 79, 81 & 82, Zeitschrift Papyrologie & Epigraphik; auth, Eine agonistische Inschrift aus Ägypten und Frühptolemäische Königsfeste, Hain Meisenheim am Glan, 77; Augustine and Manichaeism in Light of the Cologne Mani Codex, III Class Studies, 78; From Baptism to the Snosis of Manichaeism, In: The Rediscovery of Gnosticism, Brill Leiden, 81. *Mailing Add:* 1312 Culver Ann Arbor MI 48103

KOENIG, JEAN-PAUL FRANCOIS XAVIER, b Tananarive, Madagascar, Mar 12, 33; French citizen; m 61; c 3. FRENCH, AFRICAN LITERATURE. *Educ:* Univ NC, Chapel Hill, MA, 67; Universite de Toulouse, France, Doctorat (compt lit), 73. *Prof Exp:* Instr, 67-73, ASST PROF FRENCH, UNIV NC, GREENSBORO, 74- *Mem:* SAtlantic Mod Lang Asn. *Res:* Malagasy literature. *Publ:* Auth, L'influence de la Litterature Francaise dans l'oeuvre de Jacques Rabemananjara, 12/77 & L'histoire Malgache dans l'oeuvre de Jacques Rabemananjara, 5/78, Univ Sherbrooke. *Mailing Add:* Dept of Romance Lang Univ of NC Greensboro NC 27412

KOENIG, VIRGINIA CHARLOTTE, b Cleveland, Ohio, Oct 24, 09. FRENCH. *Educ:* John Carroll Univ, AB, 31; McGill Univ, MA, 42; Univ Paris, dipl, 64. *Prof Exp:* Teacher sec schs, 38-48; from instr to assoc prof French, Rosary Col, 48-66; dir French & Span, NDEA Lang Inst, 60-64; asst prof, 66-69, ASSOC PROF FOREIGN LANG, UNIV SOUTHWESTERN LA, 69- *Concurrent Pos:* Dir French, NDEA Inst, Univ Southwestern La, 68; consult, La State Foreign Lang Curric, 70-73. *Mem:* Am Asn Teachers Fr; MLA; SCent Mod Land Asn; Nat Asn Foreign Student Adv; Teachers English as Second Lang. *Res:* Twentieth century French literature; English as a second language and second language learning and teaching; applied linguistics. *Publ:* Auth, Imitation of Mary, Newman, 40; ed, Loup de Gubbio, Seraphic, 50; auth, Cours de Conversation, 54 & Basic French Vocabularies, 58, Edwards Bros; A Basic French Vocabulary, co-transl, Historical Journal of the Establishment of the French in Louisiana, 71, ed & transl, Meutre de Martin Begnaud, 74 & auth, Mastery of French Verbs, 75, Univ Southwestern La. *Mailing Add:* PO Box 4-0250 Univ of Southwestern La Lafayette LA 70504

KOEPKE, WULF, b Luebeck, Ger, Sept 24, 28; m 53; c 4. GERMAN LANGUAGE & LITERATURE. *Educ:* Univ Freiburg, PhD(Ger lit), 55. *Prof Exp:* Lectr Ger, Univ Malaya, 55-59; head div, Goethe-Inst, Munich, 59-65; assoc prof Ger, Unin Ill, Chicago, 65-68; assoc prof, Rice Univ, 68-71; assoc prof, 71-73, PROF GER, TEX A&M UNIV, 73- *Mem:* MLA; Jean-Paul-Ges; Lessing Soc; Am Soc 18th Century Studies; Western Asn Ger Studies. *Res:* Eighteenth century and 20th century German literature; the structure of the German language; German culture and civilization. *Publ:* Coauth, Kultarkune und Textlektuere, Die Unterrichtspraxis, 71; Die Deutschen Vergangenheit und Gegenwart, Holt, 71, 2nd ed, 80; Die Exilschriftsteller und der amerikanische Buchmarkt, In: Deutsche Exilliteratur Seit 1933, Vol 1, Francke, Bern, 76; Max Frischs Stiller als Zauberberg-Parodie, Wirkendes Wort, 77; Erfolglosigkeit zum Fruehwerk Jean Pauls, W Fink München, 77; Thomas Mann und Ludwig Lewisohn, Col Cserm, 79; Die emanzipierte Frau der Goethezeit und ihre Darstellung in der Literature, In: Die Frauals Heldinun Autorin, Francke, Bern, 79; Innovator Through the Ages, Bouvier, Bonn, 82. *Mailing Add:* Dept of Mod Lang Tex A&M College Station TX 77843

KOERNER, CHARLOTTE WITTKOWSKI, b Dessau, Ger, June 12, 29; US citizen. GERMAN LITERATURE & LANGUAGE. *Educ:* NY Univ, BA, 59; Univ Mich, Ann Arbor, MA, 64, PhD(Ger), 70. *Prof Exp:* From instr to asst prof, 66-72, ASSOC PROF GER LIT & LANG, CLEVELAND STATE UNIV, 72- *Concurrent Pos:* Vis assoc prof, State Univ NY, Albany, 80 & Skidmore Col, 80-81. *Mem:* Am Asn Teachers Ger; AAUP; MLA. *Res:* Bertolt Brecht; contemporary German literature; language pedagogy. *Publ:* Auth, Das Verfahren der Verfremdung in Brechts frueher Lyrik, In: Brecht Heute-Brecht Today, Vol III, Athenaeum, 73; Professional management in higher eduction?, Asn Depts Foreign Lang Bull, 11/73; William Vaughn Moody: The Great Divide, In: Drama und Theater in Amerika, Erich Schmidt, Berlin, 78; Er: Kommentar: Humor and self-irony in Kafka's style, In: Perspectives on Contemporary Literature, Univ Louisville, 78; V Brauns Unvollendete Geschichte: Erinnerung an Buechners Lenz, In: Basis, 79. *Mailing Add:* Dept of Mod Lang Cleveland State Univ 22nd & Euclid Cleveland OH 44115

KOERNER, E F KONRAD, b Hofleben near Thorn, Ger, Feb 5, 39. GENERAL LINGUISTICS. *Educ:* Free Univ Berlin, BPhilos, 65; Justus-Liebig Univ, Giessen, MA & dipl Ger & English philol, 68; Simon Fraser Univ, PhD(gen ling), 71. *Prof Exp:* Social scientist res assoc, Univ Tex, Austin, 72; vis res assoc, Res Ctr Lang Sci, Ind Univ, Bloomington, 72-73; res assoc & lectr, Univ Regensburg, Ger, 73-76; ASSOC PROF LING, UNIV OTTAWA, 76- *Concurrent Pos:* Overseas rep, Linguistische Berichte, 71-73; ed-in-chief, Historiographia Linguistica, Amsterdam, 73-; gen ed, Amsterdam Studies Theory & Hist Ling Sci, 73-; vis prof ling & phonetics, Univ Trier, Ger, summer, 76 & 78; vis prof philos & ling, Univ NMex, 80. *Honors & Awards:* Bronze Medal & Diplome d'Honneur, City of Lille, France, 81. *Mem:* Ling Soc Am; Societas Ling Europaea; Can Ling Asn; Ling Asn Can & US; Int Soc Hist Ling (vpres, 81-). *Res:* Saussure and post-Saussurean European structuralism, including semiotics; general linguistic theory and historical linguistics; history of linguistics and history and philosophy of science. *Publ:* Auth, Contribution au debat post-asussuriem dur le signe linguistique, Mouton, The Hague, 72; Bibliographia Suassureana, 1870-1970, Scarecrow Press, 72; Ferdinand de Saussure: Origin and Development of his Linguistic Theory, F Viewag, Braunschweig, 73 & 74, Span transl, Gredos, Madrid, 82, Japanese transl, Taishukan, Tokyo, 82; The Importance of Techmer's Internationale Zeitschrift für Allgemeine Sprachwissenshaft in the Development of General Linguistics, 73, ed, The Transformational-Generative Pardigm and Modern Linguistic Theory, 75, auth, Toward a Historiography of Linguistics, 78, ed, Progress in Linguistic Historiography, 80 & co-ed, Studies in Medieval Linguistic Thought: Festschrift for G L Bursill-Hall, 80, J Benjamins, Amsterdam. *Mailing Add:* Dept of Ling Univ of Ottawa Ottawa ON K1N 6N5 Can

KOESTER, RUDOLF ALFRED, b Mar 16, 36; m 73. GERMANIC LANGUAGES & LITERATURES. *Educ:* Univ Calif, Los Angeles, BA, 58, MA, 59; Harvard Univ, PhD (Ger lang & lit), 64. *Prof Exp:* Acting instr Ger, Univ Calif, Los Angeles, 62-64, asst prof, 64-69; assoc prof, 69-76, PROF GER, UNIV NEV, LAS VEGAS, 76- *Mem:* MLA; Philol Asn Pac Coast; Rocky Mountain Mod Lang Asn; Int Ver Ger Sprach-u Literaturwiss; Am Asn Teachers Ger. *Res:* Nineteenth and 20th century German literature. *Publ:* Auth of numerous studies on Kleist, Fontane, Thomas Mann, Hesse, Georg Kaiser, Hofmannsthal, Dürrenmatt and others in Maonatshefte, Ger Rev, Ger Life & Lett, Rev Langues Vivantes, Orbis Litterarum, Ger Quart & Librarium; Hermann Hesse, Metzler, Stuttgart, 75; Die Hesse-Rezeption in den USA, In: Hermann Hesses Weltweite Wirkung-Internationale Rezeptionsgeschichte, Suhrkamp, Frankfurt/Main, 77; Joseph Roth, Colloquium Verlag, Berlin, 82. *Mailing Add:* Dept of Foreign Lang Univ of Nev Las Vegas NV 89154

KOGAN, VIVIAN, b Cairo, Egypt; US citizen; m 69. ROMANCE LANGUAGES. *Educ:* Grinnell Col, AB, 62; Brown Univ, AM, 66, PhD(French), 72. *Prof Exp:* Instr, 69-71, ASST PROF FRENCH, DARTMOUTH COL, 71- *Mem:* MLA. *Res:* The contemporary French novel; 19th century fiction. *Publ:* Auth, Signs and signals in La Chartreuse de Parme, 19th Century Fr Studies, 11/73; Le jeue de la regle et du hasard, Fr Rev, 12/75; L'emploi du temps, l'emploi des temps, Teaching Lang Through Lit, 4/76; Raymond Queneau: A critical bibliography, In: A Critical Bibliography of French Literature (in prep). *Mailing Add:* Dept of French Dartmouth Col Hanover NH 03755

KOHL, STEPHEN WILLIAM, b Grand Island, Nebr, Apr 23, 44; m 67; c 1. JAPANESE LANGUAGE & LITERATURE. *Educ:* Univ Wash, BA, 67, PhD(Japanese), 74. *Prof Exp:* Instr, 72-74, asst prof, 74-79, ASSOC PROF JAPANESE LANG & LIT, UNIV ORE, 79- *Concurrent Pos:* Dir, Ore Japan Study Ctr, Waseda Univ, 74-75; chmn, Asian Studies Prog, Univ Ore, 78-80, dept chmn, East Asian Lang, 81- *Mem:* Asn Asian Studies; Asn Teachers Japanese; Am Orient Soc; Japan Soc; Philol Asn Pac Coast. *Res:* Contemporary Japanese literature; Japanese-Americans in the Northwest; translation. *Publ:* Coauth, The White Birch School of Japanese Literature, Asian Studies Prog, Univ Ore, 75; auth, Shiga Naoya and the literature of experience, Monumenta Nipponica, Vol 32, No 2; coauth, The three crabs, Japan Quart, Vol XXV, No 3; auth, I for the Mysterious, Dread Japan: The quest of Ronald McDonald, The East, 78; An early account of Japanese life in the Pacific Northwest, Pac Northwest Quart, 79; The Cliff's Edge, 80 & Withered Fields, 82, Midwest Publ Int; Strangers in a strange land: Japanese castaways and the opening of Japan, Pac Northwest Quart, 82. *Mailing Add:* Dept of East Asian Lang Univ of Ore Eugene OR 97403

KOHLER, LOTTE E, b Rostock, Ger, Dec 15, 19; US citizen; wid. GERMAN LANGUAGE & LITERATURE. *Educ:* Univ Münster, PhD, 48. *Prof Exp:* Asst lectr Ger, Royal Holloway Col, Univ London, 50-51; teacher French & Ger, Ft Lee High Sch, NJ, 56-60; asst prof, 60-71, ASSOC PROF GER, CITY COL NEW YORK, 71- *Mem:* MLA; Am Asn Teachers Ger. *Res:* Nineteenth and 20th century German literature. *Mailing Add:* Dept of Ger City Col of New York New York NY 10031

KOHN, INGEBORG MARGARET, b Lienz, Austria, Apr 5, 38; US citizen; m 61; c 2. FRENCH LITERATURE. *Educ:* Univ Ariz, BS & BA, 62, MS, 68, PhD(French), 69. *Prof Exp:* Asst prof, 69-76, ASSOC PROF FRENCH, UNIV ARIZ, 76- *Res:* French literature of La Belle Epoque; African-French literature. *Publ:* Auth, Comment enseigner Proust dans les annees 70, Proust Res Asn News, fall 73; La voyage de Montaige, 74 & Montaigne et Edward Gibbon: le perlerinage a Rome, 75, B Societe des Amis de Montaigne, Paris; The Proustian universe: Worlds in motion, Winthrop Symp-Proust, fall 78. *Mailing Add:* Dept of French Univ of Ariz Tucson AZ 85715

KOLB, PHILIP, b Chicago, Ill, Aug 29, 07; m 41; c 3. ROMANCE LANGUAGES. *Educ:* Univ Chicago, PhB, 31, AM, 32; Harvard Univ, PhD, 38. *Prof Exp:* Instr Span & French, Williams Col, 38-39; res asst Span, Harvard Univ, 39-40; prof Span & French, Cumberland Univ, 40-41; dep chief allied censorship group, Supreme Hq Allied Expeditionary Forces, Belgium, 44-45; instr Span & French, 45-47, from asst prof to prof, 47-75, univ grant, France, 48, 55, assoc mem, Ctr Advan Studies, 60-61, 62-63, EMER PROF FRENCH, UNIV ILL, URBANA, 75- *Concurrent Pos:* Univ Ill res grants, France, 48 & 55; Fulbright res fel, 51-52, sr res fel, France, 65-66; Am Philos Soc grants, 53, 55, 58; assoc mem, Ctr Advan Studies, 60-61 & 62-63; deleg, Int Fedn Mod Lang & Lit, 60; co-dir, Symp on Proust, Cerisy-la-Salle, France, 62; Am Coun Learned Soc fel, 65-66; consult, Comp Lit Studies, 68-77; dir Proust Centennial Prog, Univ Ill, 71; Nat Endowment for Humanities sr fel, 72-73; Guggenheim fel, 75-76; Nat Endowment for Humanities grants, 79 & 80. *Honors & Awards:* Chevalier, Order of Leopold, Belgium; Prix, 51 & Grand Prix, 76, Acad Francaise. *Mem:* AAUP; Asn Amis Pontigny-Cerisy; MLA; Am Asn Teachers French; Asn Int Etudes Fr. *Res:* Modern French literature; life, work and period of Marcel Proust. *Publ:* Ed, Marcel Proust, Le Carnet de 1908 Cahiers Marcel Proust, 76 & Marcel Proust-Jacques Riviere: Correspondance 1914-1922, rev ed, 76, Gallimard, Paris; Marcel Proust: Correspondance Texte etabli, presente et annote, Tome I, rev ed, 76, Tome II, 1896-1901, 76, Tome III, 1902-1903, 77, Tome IV, 1904, 78, Tome V, 1905, 79, Tome VI, 1906, 80, Tome VII, 1907, 81, Tome VIII, 1908, 81 & Tome IX, 1909 (in press), Plon, Paris. *Mailing Add:* 711 W Nevada St Urbana IL 61801

KOLBERT, JACK, b Perth Amboy, NJ, Apr 25, 27; m 49; c 2. ROMANCE LANGUAGES. *Educ:* Univ Southern Calif, AB, 48, AM, 49; Columbia Univ, PhD(French lit), 57. *Prof Exp:* Lectr French, Columbia Univ, 53; Ford Found instr French & Span, Wesleyan Univ, 54-55; from asst prof to prof Romance lang, Univ Pittsburgh, 55-65, chmn dept Romance lang & lit, 59-65; prof French lit, Univ NMex, 65-77; pres higher educ, Monterey Inst Foreign Studies, 77-80; DIR DEVELOP, CALIF ACAD SCI, 80- *Concurrent Pos:* Fulbright res fel, 63-64; mem bibliog & res comt, MLA, 65-; mem Comn Foreign Lang, State NMex, 66-77; Hidalgo de Nobleza, Sec of State, NMex, 67-77; vis prof Romance lang, Pomona Col, 70-71; hon consult, French Repub, NMex, 70-77; pres city coun, City of Albuquerque, 74-77; hon French consult, Cent Calif, 78-; adj prof, Univ San Francisco & World Col West, 80- *Honors & Awards:* Officier, Palmes Academiques, 65. *Mem:* MLA; Am Asn Teachers Fr. *Res:* Andre Maurois; modern French literature; French literary criticism. *Publ:* Coauth, A First French Handbook, 58, rev ed, 62 & A Second French Handbook, 60, rev ed, 62, Univ Pittsburgh; auth, Edmond Jaloux, Critique Litteraire, Minard & Droz, Paris, 62; L'art de Michel Butor, Oxford Univ, 70; L'annee litteraire 1972, 9/73 & Andre Maurois et L'amerique, 5/76, Fr Rev. *Mailing Add:* Develop & Membership Calif Acad of Sci San Francisco CA 94118

KOLDEWYN, PHILLIP, b Loma Linda, Calif, Mar 2, 31; m 65; c 2. LATIN AMERICAN LITERATURE & INTELLECTUAL HISTORY. *Educ:* Brigham Young Univ, BA, 58; Univ Calif, Berkeley, MA, 60, PhD(Romance lang & lit), 65. *Prof Exp:* Asst prof Span, Claremont Men's Col, 64-70, asst prof, Claremont Grad Sch, 65-70, ASSOC PROF LATIN AM LIT & HIST, CLAREMONT GRAD SCH, CLAREMONT MEN'S COL, 70- *Concurrent Pos:* Fulbright-Hays res fel, Mex, 70-71; evaluation consult, Bicult/Biling Proj, Univ Calif, Riverside, 71- *Mem:* Philol Asn Pac Coast; Int Inst Iberoam Lit. *Res:* Latin American essay, novel and intellectual history. *Publ:* Auth, Alfonso Reyes y la critica esencial, La Palabra Hombre, Mex, 1/67; Alfonso Reyes y los estudios gongorinos, In: Presencia de Alfonso Reyes, Fondo de Cult Econ, Mex, 69; Dos libros filosoficos de A Reyes, Bol Capilla Alfonsina, 71. *Mailing Add:* Dept of Lit & Lang Claremont Men's Col Claremont CA 91711

KOLONOSKY, WALTER F, b Danville, Pa, Jan 16, 38; m 63; c 2. RUSSIAN LANGUAGE & LITERATURE. *Educ:* Lycoming Col, BA, 63; Univ Pa, MA, 65; Univ Kans, PhD(Russian), 72. *Prof Exp:* Instr Russ & French, Kans State Col, 65-67; asst prof Russ lang & lit, Pa State Univ, 70-73; ASSOC PROF RUSS LANG & LIT, KANS STATE UNIV, 73- *Concurrent Pos:* Assoc ed, Studies in 20th century lit, 76-; dir, Off Study Abroad, Kans State Univ, 77-; exchange prof, Int Res & Exchanges Bd, summer 78; Fulbright adv, Kans State Univ, 78- *Mem:* AM Asn Teachers Slavic & East Europ Lang; Nat Asn For Student Affairs. *Res:* Twentieth century Russian literature; comparative literature; Russian folklore. *Publ:* Auth, Andrey Sinyavsky: The chorus and the critic, Can-Am Slavic Studies, 75; Thirteen years after Ivan Denisovich: A new Kontinent, Bks Abroad, 76; The semiotics of the train in Doctor Zhivago, Archit Reading, 76; Perception and perspective: The function of windows in Doctor Zhivago, Mod Fiction Studies, 81; Inherent and ulterior design in Sinjavsky's Pxenc, Slavic & E Europ J, 82; Pasternak and Proust: Towards a comparison, Russ Lit Triquart (in prep). *Mailing Add:* 514 Wickham Rd Manhattan KS 66502

KOLSTI, JOHN SOTTER, b Boston, Mass, Sept 30, 35; m 66; c 2. SLAVIC LANGUAGES & LITERATURE. *Educ:* Harvard Univ, BA, 57, MA, 62, PhD(Slavic), 68. *Prof Exp:* Asst prof, 66-73, ASSOC PROF SLAVIC, UNIV TEX, AUSTIN, 73- *Concurrent Pos:* Am Coun Learned Socs & Soc Sci Res Coun fel, Albanian Heroic Epic Poetry, 68. *Mem:* Am Folklore Soc; Am Asn Advan Slavic Studies; Am Asn Teachers Slavic & East Europ Lang. *Res:* Balkan studies; Slavic folklore; Old Russian literature and history. *Publ:* Auth, Serbo-Croatian: First Course, 74 & Readings in Russian, 75, Slavic Dept,

Univ Tex; A song about the Noli Government in Albania, Folklore, Nationalism & Politics, Slavica Publ, 78; Albanianism: From the Humanists to Hoxha (in press). *Mailing Add:* Dept of Slavic Lang Box 7217 Univ of Tex Austin TX 78712

KOM, AMBROISE, b Bayangam, Cameroon, Dec 15, 46; m 69; c 2. BLACK COMPARATIVE LITERATURE. *Educ:* Univ Fed Cameroon, lic es lett, 70, DES, 71; Univ Pau, France, Dr III Cycle (NAm studies), 75; Univ Sorbornne, Nouvelle, Paris, Dr d'Etat es lettres, 81. *Prof Exp:* Instr French lang & African lit, Brown Univ, 72-75; asst prof French lang & African civilization, Dalhousie Univ, 75-77; asst prof African lit, Celef, Univ Sherbrooke, 78-82; ASSOC PROF LIT, UNIV MOHAMMED V, 82- *Mem:* Asn Can Lit Comp; Asn Can Etudes Africaines; African Lit Asn. *Res:* Francophone and Anglophone African Literature; Black American literature; Anglophone Caribbean literature. *Publ:* Auth, Chester Himes et Sembene Ousmane: Un meme message aux peuples noirs, L'Afrique Litt & Art, 4th Quart, 76; Pour une litterature comparee du monde noir, Presence Francophone, spring 78; Le Harlem de Chester Himes, Ed Naaman, 78; La langue francaise en Afrique noire postcoloniale, Peuples Noirs-Peuples Africains, 11, 12/79; In the Castle of My Skin: George Lamming and the colonial Caribbean, World Lit Written in English, 11/79; Projet de pays: George Lamming et le mythe de San Cristobal, Etudes Creoles, Vol III: 56-74; Londres des Negres dans The Emigrants et dans Water With Berries de George Lamming, Etudes Anglaises, XXXIV: 44-60; Dictionnaire des oeuvres litteraires negro-africaines de langue francaise: Des origines a 1978, Naaman, Sherbrooke (in press); Ambroise Kom, George Lamming et le destin des Caribes, Didier (in press). *Mailing Add:* 1212 Cherbourg St Sherbrooke PQ J1K 2R1 Can

KOMAI, AKIRA, b Tokyo, Japan, Nov 3, 31; m 61. JAPANESE LINGUISTICS, CLASSICAL JAPANESE. *Educ:* Kyoto Univ Educ, BA, 55; Univ Mich, MA, 58, PhD(ling), 63. *Prof Exp:* From instr to asst prof Japanese, Princeton Univ, 61-65; lectr English, Kyoto Univ, 65-67; from asst prof to assoc prof Japanese, Univ Wis-Madison, 67-75; PROF JAPANESE, UNIV CHICAGO, 75- *Mem:* Ling Soc Am; Asn Asian Studies; Asn Teachers Japanese (pres, 75-78). *Res:* History of Japanese language; grammar of Heian prose; morphology of Kyoto dialect. *Publ:* Auth, A Transformational Model for Japanese, Georgetown Univ, 63; Aural Comprehension and Pronunciation Exercises for the Teachers of English, 67 & Pronunciation Exercises for the Teachers of English, 67, Kyoto City Bd Educ; Some problems in learning Japanese as a foreign language, Bull Inst Res Lang Teaching, 72; A Grammar of Classical Japanese, Culver Publ, 79. *Mailing Add:* Dept of Far Eastern Lang & Civilization Univ of Chicago Chicago IL 60637

KOMAR, KATHLEEN LENORE, b Joliet, Ill, Oct 11, 49. MODERN GERMAN & ENGLISH LITERATURE. *Educ:* Univ Chicago, BA, 71; Princeton Univ, MA, 75, PhD(comp lit), 77. *Prof Exp:* ASST PROF GER LANG & COMP LIT, UNIV CALIF, LOS ANGELES, 77- *Concurrent Pos:* Am Coun Learned Soc grant, 78. *Mem:* MLA; Am Comp Lit Asn; Philol Asn Pac Coast; Western Asn Ger Studies. *Res:* Fragmented, multilinear narratives in the early 20th century: German and American; the poetry of Rainer Maria Rilke and Wallace Stevens; the works of Hermann Broch. *Publ:* Auth, Fichte and the structure of Novalis' Hymnen an die Nacht, Ger Rev, fall 79; A structural study of Faulkner's As I Lay Dying, Faulkner Studies, 1/80; Structure and meaning in Döblin's Berlin Alexanderplatz, Ger Quart, 5/81; The structure of Heine's Harzreise: Should we take the narrator at his word, Ger Rev, fall 81; Fact, fiction and focus: Their structural embodiment in CF Meyer's Der Heilige, Colloquia Ger, No 4, 81; Pattern and Chaos: The Multilinear Novels of Dos Passos, Döblin, Faulkner and Koeppen, Camden House (in press). *Mailing Add:* Dept of Ger Lang Univ of Calif Los Angeles CA 90024

KOMENAKA-PURCELL, APRIL R, b Hilo, Hawaii, Apr 22, 40; m 64; c 2. SOCIOLINGUISTICS, WRITING. *Educ:* Univ Hawaii-Manoa, BA, 61, MA, 75, PhD(ling), 79; Univ Calif, Berkeley, MA, 63. *Prof Exp:* Instr, Univ Hawaii-Manoa, 63-64; prof, Sophia Univ, Toyko, 64-66; asst prof, Western Col for Women, 67-70; ASST PROF ENGLISH, UNIV HAWAII-HILO, 73- *Concurrent Pos:* Materials developer, Calif State Univ, Hayward, 66-67. *Mem:* Ling Soc Am; NCTE; MLA. *Res:* Discourse analysis; writing strategies of academics and young people. *Publ:* Auth, Code-shifting and accommodation Hawaiian style, Int J of the Sociol of Lang (in prep). *Mailing Add:* Dept of English Univ of Hawaii Hilo HI 96720

KONISHI, HARUO, b Tokyo, Japan, Dec 20, 32; Can citizen. CLASSICS. *Educ:* Int Christian Univ, Tokyo, BA, 57; Univ Pa, MA, 60; Univ Liverpool, PhD(ancient hist), 66. *Prof Exp:* Asst prof, 67-73, assoc prof, 73-79, PROF CLASSICS, UNIV NB, FREDERICTON, 80- *Mem:* Am Philol Asn. *Res:* Greek historiography; Greek dramaturgy; Greek oral epics. *Mailing Add:* Dept of Classics Univ of NB Fredericton NB E3B 5A3 Can

KONRAD, ALEXANDER N, b Galati, Romania, Nov 24, 20; US citizen; m 56. RUSSIAN & GERMAN LANGUAGE, LITERATURE. *Educ:* Univ Pa, PhD, 60. *Prof Exp:* Instr Ger & French, Hershey Col, 58-60; asst prof Russ & Ger, Univ NH, 60-61; asst prof, 61-66, chmn, Dept Slavic & East Europ Lang, 63-72, ASSOC PROF RUSS, CASE WESTERN RESERVE UNIV, 66-, CHMN RUSS PROG, 72- *Concurrent Pos:* Lectr, Foreign Lang Inst, Univ Linz, Austria, 67- *Mem:* Am Asn Teachers Slavic & E Europ Lang; MLA; Sudost & Osteuropa-Forschung. *Res:* Russian literary criticism; the 1880s in Russian literature. *Publ:* Auth, Travel to the USSR, Patriot, 60; The Chord Resounds Still, Case Western Reserve Univ, 63; coauth, Russkoje Literaturnoje Proiznosenije, Iklody, Linz, 67; Biyad Halashon, EMC Corp, 72; auth, Russian Literature-Oriental and Byzantine Origins of Russian Culture, Univ Vienna, 74; Russian-Jewish Intelligentia (in prep). *Mailing Add:* Dept of Slavic & E Europ Lang Case Western Reserve Univ Cleveland OH 44106

KONRAD, LINN BRATTETEIG, b Naerbo, Norway, May 17, 42; m 68. FRENCH LITERATURE. *Educ:* Univ Oslo, BA, 68; Univ Wis, MA, 72; Univ Minn, PhD(French), 78. *Prof Exp:* Asst prof French, Univ Tex, Austin, 78-80; ASST PROF FRENCH, RICE UNIV, 80- *Mem:* MLA; SCent Mod Lang Asn; Am Coun Teaching Foreign Lang; Am Comp Lit Asn. *Res:* Ninteenth century French literature; French symbolist drama; Scandanavian symbolist drama. *Publ:* Auth, Comment comprendre le tragique quotidien de Maurice Maeterlinck?, Ann Fondation Maurice Maeterlinck, fall 79; Modern hieratic ideas on theatre: Maurice Maeterlinck and Antonin Artaud, Mod Drama, fall 79; Symbolic action in modern drama: Maurice Maeterlinck, Themes Drama 4: Drama & Symbolism, 82; Maurice Maeterlinck in the Pharmaceutical Tradition, Romanic Rev, spring 82. *Mailing Add:* Dept of French & Ital Rice Univ Houston TX 77001

KONSTAN, JAY DAVID, b New York, NY, Nov 1, 40; m 81; c 2. GREEK, LATIN. *Educ:* Columbia Univ, BA, 61, MA, 63, PhD(Greek, Latin), 67 . *Hon Degrees:* MA, Wesleyan Univ, 77. *Prof Exp:* Lectr Classics, Hunter Col, 64-65 & Brooklyn Col, 65-67; from asst prof to assoc prof, 67-77, PROF CLASSICS, WESLEYAN UNIV, 77- *Mem:* Am Philol Asn; Int Soc Comp Study of Civilizations. *Res:* Classical literature; ancient philosophy; comedy. *Publ:* Auth, Some Aspects of Epicurean Psychology, E J Brill, 73; Marxism and Roman slavery, Arethusa, 75; Catullus' Indictment of Rome: The Meaning of Catullus 64, Hakkert, 77; Roman Comedy, Cornell, 82. *Mailing Add:* Dept of Classics Wesleyan Univ Middletown CT 06457

KOOREMAN, THOMAS EDWARD, b St Louis, Mo, Feb 7, 36; m 67; c 2. SPANISH, SPANISH AMERICAN LITERATURE. *Educ:* Northeast Mo State Univ, BS, 59; Univ Mo, Columbia, MAT, 66, PhD(Span), 70. *Prof Exp:* Asst prof, 70-74, assoc prof, 74-82, PROF SPAN, BUTLER UNIV, 82- *Mem:* Am Asn Teachers Span & Port; Inst Int Lit Iberoam; Am Coun Teaching Foreign Lang; AAUP. *Res:* Spanish American literature; Nineteenth century Spanish literature; foreign-language methodology. *Publ:* Auth, Teoria y estilo en la primera rima de Becquer, Explicacion de textos literarios, 74; Las novelas de Clemente Airo, evolucion hacia una realidad completa, Thesaurus, 75; Los guantes negros, simbolo del confilcto en Lopez Velarde, Nivel, 81; Reader interest in Aura: A search for confirmation, In: In Honor of Boyd G Carter, Univ Wyo, 81. *Mailing Add:* Dept of Mod Foreign Lang Butler Univ Indianapolis IN 46208

KOPACZYNSKI, GERMAIN, Philosophy, Theology. See Vol IV

KOPFF, EDWARD CHRISTIAN, b Brooklyn, NY, Nov 22, 46. GREEK, LATIN. *Educ:* Haverford Col, BA, 68; Univ NC, Chapel Hill, PhD(classics), 74. *Prof Exp:* Asst dir classics, Intercol Ctr Class Studies, Rome, Italy 72-73; asst prof, 73-76, ASSOC PROF CLASSICS, UNIV COLO, BOULDER, 76- *Concurrent Pos:* Bk rev ed, Class J, 77-; Nat Endowment for the Humanities fel, Am Acad Rome, 78-79; Am ed, Quaderai di storis, 82- *Mem:* Am Philol Asn; Asn Ancient Historians; Class Asn Midwest & South. *Res:* Transmission of ancient literature; Greek palaeography; ancient drama. *Publ:* Auth, Thucydides 7.42.3: An unrecognized fragment of Philistus, Greek, Roman & Byzantine Studies, 76; Thomas Magister and the text tradition of Sophocles' Antigone, Trans Am Philol Asn, 76; coauth, Sappho 31.9: A defense of the Hiatus, Glotta, 76; coauth, Aeneas: False dream or messenger of the manes? (Aeneid 6.893 ff.), Philologus, 76; auth, Was Socrates murdered? (Aristophanes, Nubes 1493 ff.), Greek, Roman & Byzantine Studies, 77; Virgil and the Cyclic Epics, Aufstieg & Miedergang der Römischen Welt, Berlin, 81; ed, Euripides, Bacchae, Teubner Verlag, Leipzig, 82. *Mailing Add:* Dept of Classics Univ of Colo Boulder CO 80309

KOPP, RICHARD L, b New York, NY, June 23, 34; m 58; c 2. ROMANCE LANGUAGES. *Educ:* Queens Col, BA, 55; State Univ Iowa, MA, 57; NY Univ, PhD(French), 67. *Prof Exp:* From instr to asst prof French, Col of the Holy Cross, 59-69; asst prof, 69-74, chmn dept, 73, assoc prof, 74-78, PROF MOD LANG, FAIRLEIGH DICKINSON UNIV, 78- *Concurrent Pos:* Ford Found grant, 69; fac res grant, Fairleigh Dickinson Univ, 72-73. *Honors & Awards:* Founders Day Award, NY Univ, 68. *Mem:* MLA; Soc Amis Marcel Proust; Asn Study Higher Educ; Am Asn Higher Educ. *Res:* Proust; Gide; Svevo. *Publ:* Auth, Proust's Elstir and the meaning of social success, Laurel Rev, fall 70; Marcel Proust as a Social Critic, Fairleigh Dickinson Univ, 71; The presentation of the artist in Proust and Svevo, Univ SFla Lang Quart, winter 76; contribr, Critical Bibliography of French Literature, 79; The Moralist Tradition in France, Asn Fac Press, 82. *Mailing Add:* Dept of Mod Lang Fairleigh Dickinson Univ Madison NJ 07940

KOPP, W LAMARR, b Ephrata, Pa, May 6, 30; m 58; c 3. GERMAN. *Educ:* Goshen Col, BA, 52; Univ Minn, MA, 54; Pa State Univ, PhD(Ger), 65. *Prof Exp:* Asst prof Ger, Goshen Col, 57-59; from asst prof to assoc prof, 65-75; res dir jr year in Marburg, Ger, 66-67, asst dean resident instr, 69-73, PROF GER, PA STATE UNIV, UNIVERSITY PARK, 75-, ASSOC DEAN UNDERGRAD STUDIES, 73- *Concurrent Pos:* Consult, Dept Pub Instr, Pa, 67; advert mgr, German Quart, 67-76 & Die Unterrichtspraxis, 69-76; mem bed dirs & chmn acad prog adv coun, Nat Carl Schurz Asn, 76- *Mem:* MLA; Am Asn Teachers Ger (treas, 69-76); Coun Cols Arts & Sci (secy-treas, 75-77); Nat Carl Schurz Asn. *Res:* Contemporary German literature; Heine; foreign language teaching methodology. *Publ:* Auth, German Literature in the United States: 1945-1960, Univ NC, 67; Das klassische drama auf den New York Bühnen, Z Kulturaustausch, 70; Goethe's Faust on the New York stage since 1945, Faust-Blätter, 70; German drama on the New York stage 1945-1965, Mod Lang J, 12/71. *Mailing Add:* 136 Sparks Bldg Pa State Univ University Park PA 16802

KOPPENHAVER, JOHN HOLLEY, b Newton, Kans, Oct 31, 41; m 60; c 4. CONTEMPORARY SPANISH LITERATURE. *Educ:* Univ Wichita, BA, 64; Univ Iowa, MA, 66, PhD(Span), 74. *Prof Exp:* ASST PROF SPAN, WICHITA STATE UNIV, 72-, CHAIRPERSON, DEPT ROMANCE LANG, 79- *Mem:* Am Asn Teachers Span & Port; MLA. *Res:* Contemporary Spanish theatre; Spanish grammar. *Publ:* Auth, Estudio estilistico sobre el Romance de Gerineldo, Hipanofila, 5/80; coauth & transl, Kindergarten (play), Mod Int Drama, fall, 82; Essential Spanish Grammar in Review, Scott, Foresman & Co, 12/82. *Mailing Add:* Dept of Romance Lang Wichita State Univ Wichita KS 67208

KOPPISCH, MICHAEL SEIBERT, b Baltimore, Md, July 12, 42; m 73. FRENCH. *Educ:* Johns Hopkins Univ, BA, 64, MA, 67, PhD(French), 70. *Prof Exp:* Instr French, Northwestern Univ, 67-70; asst prof, 70-76, assoc prof, 76-81, PROF FRENCH, MICH STATE UNIV, 81- *Mem:* MLA; Am Asn Teachers Fr; North Am Soc 17th Century Fr Lit. *Res:* Seventeenth century French literature; European novel. *Publ:* Auth, La Bruyere's Changing Perspective on the Monarchy: From Aesthetics to Politics, French Lit Ser, 73; The faux devot from Moliere to Marivaux, In: Moliere and the Commonwealth of Letters, Univ Miss, 75; The ambiguity of social status in La Bruyere's Caracteres, Esprit Createur, 75; The dynamics of jealousy in the works of Madame de Lafayette, Mod Lang Notes, 79; The Dissolution of Character: Changing Perspectives in La Bruyere's Caracteres, Fr Forum Publ, Inc, 81. *Mailing Add:* Dept of Romance Lang Mich State Univ East Lansing MI 48823

KORINKO, STEPHEN JOHN, English, Linguistics. See Vol II

KORN, DAVID, b Poland, Apr 27, 34; US citizen; m 61; c 2. LANGUAGES, LINGUISTICS. *Educ:* Georgetown Univ, BS, 58, MS, 60, PhD(Russ ling), 64. *Prof Exp:* Res assoc, machine translation, Georgetown Univ, 57-63; asst prof, Col William & Mary, 59-61; prof & chmn dept Ger & Russ studies, Howard Univ, 61-78, dir, Lang Lab, 68; sr researcher, Nat Inst Educ, Dept Health, Educ & Welfare, 73-74; GRAD PROF RUSSIAN STUDIES, HOWARD UNIVERSITY, 68- *Concurrent Pos:* Assoc dir, Peace Corps Training Prog for Guyana, 66; assoc resident dir, Coun Int Educ Exchange, Leningrad, USSR, 68; sr consult, Off Asst Sec Educ, Dept Health, Educ & Welfare, 73; spec asst to Secy State, Dept State, Washington DC & coordr, External Educ, 81- *Mem:* Ling Soc Am; Am Asn Teachers Slavic & EEurop Lang; MLA; Am Soc Cybernetics. *Res:* Slavic linguistics; literature and Russian language; minorities in the USSR. *Publ:* Auth, Russian Sentence Separators, Georgetown Univ, 59; The Russian Verb, V Kamkin, 66; Genitive or accusative after negation, Slavic & EEurop J, 67; The Turkic words structure, Studies Ling, 68; Turgenev in 19th century America, Russian Rev, 68. *Mailing Add:* Dept of Ger & Russ Howard Univ Washington DC 20001

KOROL, MADELEINE F, b Paris, France, July 22, 31; US citizen. FRENCH. *Educ:* Adelphi Col, BA, 52; Columbia Univ, MA, 53, PhD, 60. *Prof Exp:* From instr to asst prof French, St John's Univ, NY, 58-60; assoc, 60-62, LECTR FRENCH, UNIV CALIF, LOS ANGELES, 62- *Concurrent Pos:* French Govt scholar, 55. *Mem:* MLA; Am Asn Teachers Fr. *Res:* Stylistics; contemporary French theater. *Mailing Add:* Dept of French Univ of Calif Los Angeles CA 90024

KOSSOFF, ARON DAVID, b Hartford, Conn, Nov 9, 18; m 48. SPANISH. *Educ:* Amherst Col, AB, 45; Brown Univ, AM, 47, PhD, 54. *Prof Exp:* From instr to assoc prof, 51-68, PROF SPAN, BROWN UNIV, 68- *Concurrent Pos:* Fulbright res fel, Spain, 60-61. *Mem:* MLA; Am Asn Teachers Span & Port; Renaissance Soc Am; New Eng Mod Lang Asn (pres, 71-72). *Res:* Fernando de Herrera; Cervantes; Erasmist influences. *Publ:* Auth, El Medico de su honra and la amiga de Bernal Frances, Hisp Rev, 56; Sobre largo, luengo en Herrera, Rev Filol, Espanola, 57; Algunas variantes de Herrera, Nueva Rev Filol Hisp, 58; auth, Vocabulario de la Obra poetica de Fernando de Herrera, Read Acad Espanola, 66; ed, Lope de Vega's El perro del hortelano y El castigo sin venganza, 70 & co-ed, Homenaje a William L Fichter, estudios sobre el teatro antiguo hispanico y otros ensayos, 71, Castalia, Madrid. *Mailing Add:* Dept of Hisp & Ital Studies Brown Univ Providence RI 02912

KOSSOFF, RUTH HORNE, b Worcester, Mass, Apr 7, 13; m 48. SPANISH LITERATURE. *Educ:* My Holyoke Col, BA, 34; Brown Univ, MA, 35, PhD(lang & lit), 47. *Prof Exp:* Teaching asst Span, Brown Univ, 39; instr, Wheaton Col, 41; teacher French & Span, Wareham High Sch, Mass, 41-43 & 44-46; instr Span, Brown Univ, 43-44, 46-48, asst prof, 48-50; lectr, Brown Univ, Conn Col & Univ RI, 51-64; from asst prof to assoc prof, 64-73, chmn dept lang, 70-73, prof, 73-78, EMER PROF SPAN, UNIV RI, 78- *Mem:* MLA; Renaissance Soc Am; Am Asn Teachers Span & Port; Asoc Int Hispanistas. *Res:* Prose of Spanish Golden Age. *Publ:* Ed, Delibes: El Camino, Holt, 60. *Mailing Add:* Old Carr Landing Rd PO Box F Wareham MA 02571

KOSTIS, NICHOLAS, b Sanford, Maine. CONTEMPORARY FRENCH LITERATURE. *Educ:* Bowdoin Col, BA, Columbia Univ, MA, 63, PhD(French), 65. *Prof Exp:* Instr French, Brown Univ, 63-65; ASSOC PROF FRENCH, BOSTON UNIV, 65- *Mem:* MLA. *Res:* Celine; contemporary French theater and novel. *Publ:* Auth, Albertine: Characterization through image and symbol, PMLA, 1/69; The Exorcism of Sex and Death in Julien Green's Novels, Mouton, The Hague, 73. *Mailing Add:* Dept of French Boston Univ Boston MA 02215

KOSTKA, EDMUND K, b Ger, Oct 1, 15; m 46; c 2. MODERN LANGUAGES, COMPARATIVE LITERATURE. *Educ:* Columbia Univ, MA, 51, PhD, 61. *Prof Exp:* Teacher Ger & hist, Adelphi Acad, 48-51; from asst prof to assoc prof, Col St Elizabeth, 51-68, chmn dept, 68-77, prof mod lang, 68-81; PROF GER, JUILLIARD SCH, 79- *Mem:* Am Asn Teachers Ger; MLA; Am Asn Teachers Slavic & East Europ Lang; Am Asn Teachers Ital. *Res:* Schiller; Pushkin; Croce. *Publ:* Auth, Grillparzer and the East, Monatshefte, 55; At the roots of Russian Westernism, Slavic & East Europ Studies, 61; Russo-German cross currents, Rev Lit Comp, 63; Schiller in Russian Literature, Univ Pa, 65; Glimpses of Germanic-Slavic Relations, Bucknell Univ, 75; Schiller in Poland, In: Probleme der Komparatistik, Bouvier Verlag, Bonn, 78. *Mailing Add:* Acad Dept Juilliard Sch Lincoln Ctr Plaza New York NY 10023

KOSTOROSKI-KADISH, EMILIE PAULINE, b Oswego, NY, Nov 9, 34; m 73. FRENCH LANGUAGE & LITERATURE. *Educ:* Nazareth Col, AB, 57; Middlebury Col, AM, 61; Case Western Reserve Univ, PhD(French), 70. *Prof Exp:* Teacher French, Nazareth Acad, Rochester, NY, 60-62; instr, Nazareth Col, 63-65; asst prof, Kent State Univ, 69-70 & Case Western Reserve Univ, 71-77. *Concurrent Pos:* Am Coun Learned Soc fel, 75-76. *Mem:* Am Asn Teachers Fr. *Res:* Medieval French and Italian literature; French theater. *Publ:* Auth, Further echoes from Roland's horn, Romance Notes, 72; Quest and query in the Chastelaine de Vergi, Medievalia & Humanistica, 72; Two ballads of Villon reconsidered, Fr Rev, 73; Moliere and Voltaire, In: Moliere and the Commonwealth of Letters, Univ Mo, 75; Feminism in the Jeu d'Adam, Ky Romance Quart, 75; The proem of Griselda and Petrarch's image of nature, Mediaevalia, 76; Petrarch's Griselda: An English translation, Mediaevalia, 77; Comedy after Moliere: An interpretive essay, Degre Second, 78. *Mailing Add:* 13906 Larchmere Blvd Cleveland OH 44120

KOTT, JAN K, Drama, Comparative Literature. See Vol II

KOUBOURLIS, DEMETRIUS JOHN, b Rion-Patras, Greece, June 18, 38; m 62; c 4. SLAVIC LINGUISTICS. *Educ:* Calif State Univ, Sacramento, BA, 63; Univ Wash, PhD(Slavic), 67. *Prof Exp:* Asst prof Slavic ling, Tulane Univ, 67-68; asst prof, Univ NC, Chapel Hill, 68-71; asst prof, 71-73, assoc prof, 73-75, PROF RUSS LANG & LIT, UNIV IDAHO, 75- *Concurrent Pos:* Ed, Lang Ser, Idaho Res Found, Moscow, 72- *Mem:* Am Asn Teachers Slavic & E Europ Lang; Asn Comput Machinery; Western Slavic Asn; Asn Comput Ling; Asn Lit & Ling Comput. *Res:* Computational linguistics; Slavic linguistics. *Publ:* Auth, Soviet Academy Grammar: Phonology and Morphology, A Computer-Aided Index, Lang Ser, Idaho Res Found, 72; ed, Topics in Slavic Phonology, Slavica, 74; ed, A Concordance to the Poems of O Mandelstam, Cornell Univ, 74; auth, Computer sequencing and non-alphabetic interference in language date processing, Comput & Humanities, Vol 7, No 3; Phoneme non-randomness and the mechanical morpheme segmentation of Russian, In: Topics in Slavic Phonology, Slavica, 74; From a wordform concordance to a dictionary-form concordance, In: Computers in the Humanities, Univ Edinburgh, 74. *Mailing Add:* Dept of Foreign Lang & lit Univ of Idaho Moscow ID 83843

KOUTSOUDAS, ANDREAS, b Alexandria, Egypt, Feb 6, 30; US citizen; m 59. LINGUISTICS. *Educ:* Univ Mich, BA, 54, MS, 58, PhD(ling), 61. *Prof Exp:* Dir machine transl proj, Willow Run Lab, Univ Mich, 55-60, instr ling univ, 60-62; from asst prof to assoc prof, Ind Univ, Bloomington, 62-67, from assoc prof to prof ling & Near Eastern lang & lit, 67-76, consult, Ctr Appl Ling, 66-75; prof ling & chmn dept, Univ Wis-Milwaukee, 75-76; PROF LING, UNIV IOWA, 76- *Concurrent Pos:* Consult, Rand Corp, 57-59; Ind Univ Ford Found study grant, 65-66. *Mem:* Ling Soc Am; Int Ling Asn; Asn Comput Ling; Ling Asn Gt Brit. *Res:* Linguistic theory; psycholinguistics; English as a second language. *Publ:* Auth, Writing Transformational Grammars: An Introduction, 66 & Workbook in Syntax, 69, McGraw; Gapping, conjunction reduction and coordination deletion, Found Lang, 71; The strict order fallacy, Language, 72; ed, On the Application and Ordering of Grammatical Rules, Mouton, The Hague, 76; auth, The morphophonemic-allophonic distiction, Phonologia, 77. *Mailing Add:* Dept of Ling Univ of Iowa Iowa City IA 52242

KOUVEL, AUDREY LUMSDEN, b Liverpool, Eng, Mar 28, 19; US citizen; m 53; c 2. ROMANCE LITERATURES. *Educ:* Univ Liverpool, BA, 41, MA, 43; Harvard Univ, PhD(Romance lang), 65. *Prof Exp:* Asst lectr Span, Univ Glasgow, 41-43; lectr, Univ Liverpool, 43-48; lectr, Univ Leeds, 48-53; from asst prof to assoc prof mod lang, State Univ NY, Albany, 59-64, prof Romance lang & comp lit, 64-69; PROF SPAN, UNIV ILL, CHICAGO CIRCLE, 69- *Concurrent Pos:* Mem regional comt, Woodrow Wilson Nat Fel Found, 62-66; Am Coun Learned Soc fel, 67-68; Nat Endowment for Humanities & Newberry fel, 80; joint Span-US Comn Educ & Cult Affairs fel, 81. *Mem:* MLA; Asoc Int Hispanistas; Am Asn Teachers Span & Port. *Res:* Spanish Golden Age literature; literary theory and criticism. *Publ:* Auth, Aspectos de la tecnica poetica de Pedro Espinosa, Univ Seville, 53; Frayluis de Leon's haven: A study in structural analysis, Mod Lang Notes, 74; Garcilaso de la Vega, poeta latino, In: La poesia de Garcilaso, Ariel, 74; coauth, The enchantress Almone revealed: A note on Sor Juana Ines de la Cruz' use of a classical source, Rev Canadiense de Estudios Hispanicos, 77. *Mailing Add:* Dept of Span Ital & Port Univ of Ill Chicago Circle Chicago IL 60680

KOVACH, EDITH M A, b New York, Mar 29, 21. CLASSICAL LANGUAGES. *Educ:* Wayne State Univ, AB, 42, MEd, 42; Univ Mich, MA, 45, PhD(class studies), 50. *Prof Exp:* Teacher foreign lang & head dept, Pub Schs, Detroit, 42-65; from assoc prof to prof class lang, 65-76, chmn dept, 66-71, PROF CLASSICS & EDUC, UNIV DETROIT, 76-, COORDR CLASSICS, 71- *Concurrent Pos:* Assoc ed, Class Outlook, 72- *Honors & Awards:* Ovatio, Class Asn Mid W & S, 70. *Mem:* Am Class League; Archaeol Inst Am; Class Asn Mid W & S; Am Philol Asn; Nat Ed Asn. *Res:* Foreign language education especially uses and development of audio-visual materials; classical civilization; Latin literature. *Publ:* Coauth, Progress Tests, First Year Latin, 56- & First and Second Year Latin (tape prog), 62 & 65, Macmillan; contribr, Britannica Review of Foreign Language Education, Vol I, Encycl Britannica, 69. *Mailing Add:* Dept of Lang & Ling Univ of Detroit Detroit MI 48221

KOVACS, PAUL DAVID, b Kenosha, Wis, Nov 12, 45; m 69; c 2. CLASSICAL LANGUAGE & LITERATURE. *Educ:* Col Wooster, BA, 67; Harvard Univ, AM, 69, PhD(class philol), 76. *Prof Exp:* Asst prof, 76-82, ASSOC PROF CLASS, UNIV VA, 82- *Concurrent Pos:* Jr fel, Ctr for Hellenic Studies, DC, 81-82. *Mem:* Am Philol Asn; Class Asn Middle West & South. *Res:* Greek tragedy; Greek textual criticism. *Publ:* Auth, Three passages from the Andromache, Harvard Studies in Class Philol, 77; Andromache 1009-1018, Am J of Philol, 78; Four passages from Euripidesion, Trans of the Am Philol Asn, 79; Shame, pleasure and honor in Phaedra's great speech, Am J of Philol, 80; Euripides Hippolytus 100 and the meaning of the prologue, Class Philol, 80; The Andromache of Euripides, Scholars Press, 81; Tyrants and Demagogues in tragic interpolation, Greek, Roman, and Byzantine Studies, 82. *Mailing Add:* Dept of Class Univ of Va Charlottesville VA 22903

KOVARY, TOM TIBOR, b Bratislava, Czech, June 23, 20; nat US; m 50; c 2. SPANISH, GERMAN. *Educ:* Ohio State Univ, BS, 52, MA, 53. *Prof Exp:* Teacher English to foreign students, Columbus Adult Educ Prog, 49-50; teaching fel Spanish, Cornell Univ, 53-58, instr ling, 58-59; actg chmn dept foreign lang, 62-63, ASST PROF MOD LANG, STATE UNIV NY COL CORTLAND, 59- *Concurrent Pos:* Lectr Ger & Span, Ithaca Col, 56-58. *Mem:* MLA; Ling Soc Am; Am Coun Teachers Foreign Lang. *Res:* Spanish linguistics; Romance linguistics, especially Sardinian, Hungarian, and Esperanto. *Mailing Add:* Dept of Int Commun & Cult State Univ of NY Col Cortland NY 13045

KOZAUER, NIKOLAUS J, Social Science, Foreign Languages. See Vol I

KOZMA, JANICE M, b Wyandotte, Mich, Dec 20, 45. ITALIAN LANGUAGE & LITERATURE. *Educ:* Univ Florence, dipl/cert Ital, 65; Univ Mich, Ann Arbor, BA, 68, MA, 70, PhD(Romance lang & lit), 73. *Prof Exp:* Vis asst prof Ital, Univ Ky, Lexington, 73-74; adj prof, Fla Int Univ, 74-75; asst prof, 77-80, ASSOC PROF ITAL, UNIV KANS, 80- *Concurrent Pos:* Teaching fels, Univ Mich, 68-73. *Honors & Awards:* Cavaliere dello Stato: Knight of the Order of Merit of the Italian Republic. *Mem:* MLA; Am Asn Teachers Ital; Am Asn Univ Profs Ital; Midwest Mod Lang Asn. *Res:* Italy's post-war neo-realistic novels; narrative techniques. *Publ:* Auth, Carosello: A Cultural Reader, Holt, Rinehart & Winston, 78, 2nd ed, 82; Vasco Pratolini, In: Columbia Dictionary of Modern European Literature, Columbia Univ Press, 2nd ed, 80; Pratolini's Il Quartiere: The metaphor, Ky Romance Quart, XXIX: 37-45; Metaphor in Pratolini's novels: Il Quartiere and Cronache Di Poveri Amanti, Romance Notes, XX: 1-6; Scholl, Bianco, V, 60--Glod, A Quattr'Occhi, Italica, 57: 215; Functions of Metaphor in Pratolini's Cronache Di Pover Amanti: Maciste and the Signora, Ital Cult (in press). *Mailing Add:* Dept of French & Ital Univ of Kans Lawrence KS 66045

KRA, PAULINE, b Lodz, Poland, July 30, 34; US citizen; m 55; c 2. FRENCH LITERATURE. *Educ:* Barnard Col, BA, 55, Columbia Univ, MA, 63, PhD(French), 68. *Prof Exp:* Lectr French, Queens Col, 64-65; asst prof, 68-74, assoc prof, 74-82, PROF FRENCH, YESHIVA UNIV, 82- *Mem:* Am Soc for 18th Century Studies; Northeast Am Soc for 18th Century Studies; Am Asn Teachers French; MLA. *Res:* Montesquieu; 18th century French fiction; La Bruyere. *Publ:* Auth, The invisbile chain of the Lettres persanes, Studies on Voltaire and the 18th Century, 63; Religion in Montesquieu's Lettres persanes, Institut et Musee Voltaire, 70; Note on the derivation of names in Voltaire's Zadig, Romance Notes, 75; The Role of the Harem, In: Imitations of Montesquieu's Lettres persanes, Studies on Voltaire and the Eighteenth Century, 79. *Mailing Add:* Dept of French Yeshiva Univ 500 W 185th St New York NY 10033

KRABBE, JUDITH, b Michigan City, Ind, Feb 5, 31. CLASSICAL LANGUAGES. *Educ:* St Mary's Col, Ind, BA, 55; Cath Univ Am, MA, 61, PhD, 65. *Prof Exp:* Asst prof Latin, St Mary's Col, Ind, 63-69; ASSOC PROF ENGLISH, JACKSON STATE COL, 69- *Mem:* Am Philol Asn; NCTE; Conf Col Compos & Commun. *Res:* Patristic Latin; Prosper of Aquitaine; classical literature. *Publ:* Auth, The epistula ad Demetriadem de vera Humilitate, Cath Univ Am, 65; Demetrias, In: New Cath Encycl, McGraw. *Mailing Add:* Dept of English Jackson State Col Jackson MS 39217

KRAFT, CHARLES H, Anthropology, Communication. See Vol IV

KRAFT, WALTER CARL, b Washington, DC, Jan 14, 17; m 42. GERMAN, SPANISH. *Educ:* Univ Ore, BA, 38, MA, 41; Univ Calif, PhD(Ger ling), 50. *Prof Exp:* From asst prof to prof Ger, 50-64, head dept foreign lang, 56-73, PROF GER & LING, ORE STATE UNIV, 64- *Concurrent Pos:* Fulbright exchange award, Vienna, Austria, 53-54; resident dir, Ore Studies Ctr in Ger, Univs Stuttgart & Univ Tübingen, 68-69, 74-75; ed, Proc Pac Northwest Conf Foreign Lang, 70-74. *Mem:* MLA; Am Asn Teachers Span & Port; Pac Northwest Conf Foreign Lang (pres, 71-72); Ling Soc Am; Am Asn Teachers Ger. *Res:* Linguistics; early German literature; paleography. *Publ:* Auth, Codices Vindobonenses Hispanici: A Catalog of the Spanish, Portuguese, and Catalan Manuscripts in the Austrian National Library in Vienna, Ore State Univ, 57. *Mailing Add:* Dept of Foreign Lang & Lit Ore State Univ Corvallis OR 97331

KRAGNESS, SHEILA IONE, b Excelsior, Minn, July 14, 16. FRENCH LANGUAGE & LITERATURE. *Educ:* Univ Minn, BS, 38, MA, 39, PhD, 48. *Prof Exp:* Teaching asst, Univ Minn, 39-41; instr French, Knox Col, 46-50; from instr to asst prof, 50-63, assoc prof, 63-79, PROF FRENCH, ALBION COL, 80- *Mem:* MLA; Am Asn Teachers Fr. *Res:* Seventeenth century French literature; Moliere; contemporary French literature. *Mailing Add:* 312 N Mingo Albion MI 49224

KRAHMALKOV, CHARLES R, b New York, NY, June 6, 36; m 68; c 2. ANCIENT NEAR EAST HISTORY. *Educ:* Univ Calif, Berkeley, AB, 57; Harvard Univ, PhD(Hebrew & Northwest Semitic philol), 65. *Prof Exp:* Asst prof Near E lang & lit, Univ Mich, 65-66; asst prof, Univ Calif, Los Angeles, 66-68; asst prof, 68-71, assoc prof, 71-79, PROF NEAR EAST LANG & LIT, UNIV MICH, ANN ARBOR, 80- *Res:* Early Northwest Semitic philology; Egyptology; Biblical exegesis. *Mailing Add:* 1905 Dunmore Ann Arbor MI 48103

KRAMARAE, CHERIS, Speech Communication. See Vol II

KRAMER, FRANK RAYMOND, b Baraboo, Wis, Jan 2, 08; m 35; c 2. CLASSICAL HISTORY. *Educ:* Univ Wis, BHum, 29, AM, 31, PhD, 36. *Prof Exp:* Prof class lang, Heidelberg Col, 38-78; prof class lang, Ohio State Univ, 78-79. *Concurrent Pos:* Assoc res, Univ Wis & Ford Found, Univ Wis Comt Studies Am Civilization grants, 48-49 & 51-52; Soc Sci Res Coun grant, 51. *Mem:* Class Asn Midwest & South; Am Philol Asn. *Res:* Greek and Roman history; American folk belief; ancient and modern studies. *Publ:* Auth, Voices in the Valley: Mythmaking and Folk Belief in the Shaping of the Middle West, Univ Wis, 64; The implications of the Delian Confederacy for Union Now movements, 4/43, The altar of right: Reality and power in Aeschylus, 10/60 & Institutes on ancient and modern studies, 2-3/74, Class J; A medium for discovery, Class Outlook, 10/76; New light from old lamps, Liberal Educ, 3/77. *Mailing Add:* 25 Lincoln Rd Tiffin OH 44883

KRAMER, KARL D, b Seattle, Wash, Jan 19, 34; m 55; c 1. RUSSIAN LANGUAGE & LITERATURE. *Educ:* Univ Wash, AB, 55, MA, 57, PhD(comp lit), 64. *Prof Exp:* From instr to asst prof Russ, Northwestern Univ, 61-65; asst prof Slavic lang & lit, Univ Mich, Ann Arbor, 65-70; ASSOC PROF SLAVIC LANG & LIT, UNIV WASH, 70- *Mem:* MLA; Am Asn Advan Slavic Studies; Am Asn Teachers Slavic & EEurop Lang. *Res:* Nineteenth century Russian literature; Soviet literature. *Publ:* Auth, Chekhov at the end of the eighties: The question of identity, Slavic & EEurop Studies, spring 66; Jurij Kazakov: The pleasures of isolation, spring 66 & Satiric form in Saltykov's Gospoda Golovlevy, winter 70, Slavic & EEurop J; The Chameleon and the Dream: The Image of Reality of Cexov's Stories, Mouton, The Hague, 70. *Mailing Add:* Dept of Slavic Lang & Lit Univ of Wash Seattle WA 98105

KRAMER, STEVEN PHILIP, Contemporary European History. See Vol I

KRANCE, CHARLES ANDREW, b Paris, France, Oct 7, 37; US citizen; m 61; c 1. FRENCH LANGUAGE & LITERATURE. *Educ:* Univ Wis-Madison, BS, 61, PhD(French), 70; Middlebury Col, MA, 62. *Prof Exp:* Instr French, Ripon Col, 62-63; instr, Lawrence Univ, 66-69; asst prof, 69-75, ASSOC PROF FRENCH, UNIV CHICAGO, 75- *Mem:* Am Asn Teachers Fr; Midwest Mod Lang Asn; MLA; Soc Etudes Celiniennes; Samuel Beckett Soc. *Res:* Sixteenth and 20th century novel. *Publ:* Auth, L'ouvre-boite et la conscience narrative dans Comment C'est, Saggi Ricerche Lett Francese, 75; Alienation and form in Beckett's How It Is, Perspectives Contemp Lit, 11/75; Semmelweis, oi l'accouchement de la biographie celinienne, Rev Let Mod, 76; Le Recit comme provignement: Mort a Credit, 76; Giraudoux's Suzanne et le Pacifique, Australian J Fr Studies, 8/77; Montaigne's last Krapp, NY Lit Forum, autumn 78; contribr, Cabeen Bibliography of French Literature, Syracuse Univ, 79; auth, Guignol's Band et la rhetorique de geste celinien, Fr Forum, 5/79. *Mailing Add:* Dept Romance Lang & Lit Univ of Chicago Chicago IL 60637

KRASNOV, VLADISLAV G, b Perm, USSR, Feb 24, 37; Nat US; m 70; c 2. RUSSIAN LITERATURE, SOVIET STUDIES. *Educ:* Moscow Univ, USSR, dipl hist & anthrop, 60; Univ Wash, MA, 68, PhD(Russ lit), 74. *Prof Exp:* Fel slavic area, Univ Chicago, 66; lectr Russ lang & lit, Univ Lund, Sweden, 63-65; instr Russ lang, Univ Tex, Austin, 71-74; asst prof Russ lang & lit, Southern Methodist Univ, 74-78; asst prof Russ studies, 78-80, ASSOC PROF RUSSIAN STUDIES, MONTEREY INST INT STUDIES, 80- *Concurrent Pos:* Vis prof, Hokkaido Univ, Sapporo, Japan, 80-81; vis scholar, Hoover Inst, Stanford Univ, 81- *Mem:* Am Asn Advan Slavic Studies; Am Asn Teachers Slavic & East Europ Lang; Asn Russ-Am Scholars. *Res:* Aleksandr Solzhenitsyn; samizdat; East-West cultural interaction. *Publ:* Auth, Polyphonic arrangement of characters in Solzhenitsyn's First Circle, Russ Lang J, fall 75; Soviet literature in Soviet schools, In: The Soviet Union: The Seventies and Beyond, Heath, 75; Karl Marx as Frankenstein, Mod Age, winter 78; Richard Pipe's foreign strategy, Russ Rev, 4/79 & Encounter, London, 4/80; Solzhenitsyn and Dostoevsky, Univ Ga Press, 80. *Mailing Add:* Dept of Russian Studies Monterey Inst Int Studies Monterey CA 93940

KRATINS, OJARS, English. See Vol II

KRATZ, BERND, b Saarbruecken, Ger, Jan 25, 35. GERMANIC LINGUISTICS, MEDIEVAL GERMAN LITERATURE. *Educ:* Univ Marburg, Staatsexamen, 62, PhD(Ger, French, Span), 63. *Prof Exp:* Wiss asst Ger, Univ Marburg, 63-66; assoc prof, 67-74, PROF GER, UNIV KY, 74- *Concurrent Pos:* Ed, Colloquia Germanica, Francke, Bern, 76- *Mem:* MLA. *Res:* Germanic linguistics; Medieval German literature. *Publ:* Auth, Gawein und Wolfdietrich, Euphorion, 72; Die Crone Heinrichs von dem Türlin, Germanisch-Romanische Monatsschrift, 72; Zur Kompositionstechnik Heinrichs, Amsterdamer Beiträge, 73; Von Werwölfen, Glückshauben, Herrigs Archiv, 74; Zur Biographie Heinrichs, Amsterdamer Beiträge, 77; Die Ambraser Mantel-Erzählung, Euphorion, 77; Die Geschichte vom Maultier, Arcadia, 78. *Mailing Add:* Dept of Ger Lang & Lit Univ of Ky Lexington KY 40506

KRATZ, DENNIS MERLE, b Baltimore, Md, June 22, 41; m 64; c 1. MEDIEVAL LATIN LITERATURE. *Educ:* Dartmouth Col, AB, 63; Harvard Univ, AM, 64, PhD(medieval Latin), 70. *Prof Exp:* Instr Latin & Greek, Roxbury Latin Sch, 64-72; asst prof, Ohio State Univ, 72-77, assoc prof classics, 77-78; ASSOC PROF HUMANITIES, UNIV TEX, DALLAS, 78- *Concurrent Pos:* Fel, Grad Sch Educ, Harvard Univ, 70-71; consult, Lang Res Found, 70-72; Nat Humanities Fac, 71-73; ed, Translation Rev, 79- *Mem:* Am Philol Asn; Mediaeval Acad Am; Am Lit Translators Asn. *Res:* Classical tradition; translation. *Publ:* Auth, Ruodlieb: Christian epic hero, 12/73 & Fictus Lupus: The werewolf in Christian thought, 76, Class Folia; Aeneas or Christ? An epic parody by Sedulius Scotius, Class World, 76; Quid Waltharius Ruodliebque cum Christo, In: The Epic in Medieval Society, Niemeyer, Tübingen, Ger, 77; Mocking Epic, Jose Porrua Turanoas, Madrid, 80; Waltharius and Ruodlieb, Garland Press (in press). *Mailing Add:* Univ of Tex Box 688 Richardson TX 75080

KRATZ, HENRY, b Albany, NY, Mar 23, 22; m 51; c 1. GERMANIC LANGUAGES. *Educ:* NY State Col Teachers, BA, 42; Ohio State Univ, MA, 46, PhD, 49. *Prof Exp:* Asst Ger, Ohio State Univ, 45-48, instr, 48-49; instr, Univ Mich, 49-53; instr, Univ Mass, 53-55; asst ed, G & C Merriam Co, 55-60; from asst prof to assoc prof Ger, Univ Ore, 60-65; PROF GER, UNIV TENN, KNOXVILLE, 65-, HEAD DEPT GER & SLAVIC LANG, 72- *Mem:* Soc Advan Scand Studies; Am Name Soc. *Res:* Middle High and Old High German; Old Norse. *Publ:* Asst ed, Webster's New International Dict, Merriam, 61; auth, Frühes Mittelalter, Vor- und Frühgeschichte des Deutschen Schrifttums, 70 & Wolfram von Eschenbach's Parzival, An

Attempt at a Total Evaluation, 73, Francke, Bern; A reading of Wolfram's lyrics, Semasia, 75; The Parcevals Saga and Li Contes del Graal, Scand Studies, 77. *Mailing Add:* Dept of Ger & Slavic Lang Univ of Tenn Knoxville TN 37916

KRAUSE, MAUREEN THERESE, b Evanston, Ill. GERMAN. *Educ:* Northwestern Univ, BA, 69; Ohio State Univ, MA, 70, PhD(Ger), 80. *Prof Exp:* Instr Ger, Ohio State Univ, 80-81; ASST PROF GER, ROSE-HULMAN INST TECHNOL, 81- *Mem:* MLA; Am Asn Teachers Ger; E T A Hoffmann Ges; Am Coun Teaching Foreign Lang. *Res:* German romanticism, novel theory, pedagogy. *Publ:* Auth, Practicing sehen, hören, lassen and helfen with dependant infinitives, Die Unterrichtspraxis, spring 82. *Mailing Add:* Div of Humanities Rose-Hulman Inst of Technol Terre Haute IN 47803

KRAUSS, MICHAEL E, b Cleveland, Ohio, Aug 15, 34; m 62; c 2. LINGUISTICS. *Educ:* Univ Chicago, BA, 53; Western Reserve Univ, BA, 54; Columbia Univ, MA, 55; Univ Paris, cert, 56; Harvard Univ, PhD, 59; Univ Iceland, Bacc Philol Isl, 60. *Prof Exp:* From asst prof to assoc prof, 60-68, head dept ling & foreign lang, 61-63, PROF LING & DIR ALASKA NATIVE LANG CTR & CHMN PROG, UNIV ALASKA, 73- *Concurrent Pos:* French Govt scholar, 55-56; prin investigator res prog, Nat Sci Found, 61-; Nat Endowment for Humanities, 69-; vis prof, Mass Inst Technol, 69-70; ed, Alaska Native Lang Res Papers, 79- *Mem:* Ling Soc Am; MLA. *Res:* Celtic, Scandinavian and American Indian linguistics; native languages of Alaska. *Publ:* Auth, Eyak: A preliminary report, Can J Ling, 65; Eyak Texts, 70 & Eyak Dictionary, 70, Boston; Na-Dene, 73 & Eskimo-Aleut, 73, Current Trends Ling. *Mailing Add:* Alaska Native Lang Ctr Univ of Alaska Fairbanks AK 99708

KRAUSSE, HELMUT K, b Chemnitz, Ger, May 7, 26; Can citizen; m 52; c 4. GERMANIC LANGUAGES & LITERATURE. *Educ:* Univ Ore, BA, 57, MA, 59; Univ Wash, PhD(Ger), 64. *Prof Exp:* Instr Ger, Univ Ore, 58-59; instr, Univ Wash, 62-64; from asst prof to assoc prof, 64-74, PROF GER LANG & LIT, QUEEN'S UNIV, ONT, 74-, HEAD DEPT, 76- *Mem:* Am Asn Teachers Ger; Asn Can Univ Teachers Ger; MLA; Int Arbeitskreis für deutsche Barockliteratur; Deutsche Schillergesellschaft. *Res:* Middle high German literature; Baroque literature; 17th century novel. *Publ:* Auth, Zur Sprache des Simplicissimus, Neuphilolog, Mitteilungen, 69; Junger mensch und alter got - Walthers Religiositat . . . Ger Quart, 69; Die Darstellung von Siegfrieds Tod und die Entwicklung des Hagenbildes in der Nibelungendichtung, Ger-Romanische Monatsschrift, 71; ed, W C Printz, Werke I: Die Musikerromane, 74 & W C Printz, Werke II: Satirische Schriften und Historische Beschreibung der edelen Singund Klingkunst, de Gruyter, Berlin, 79; auth, Herz und Mund und Tat und Leben: Some thoughts on J S Bach's Church Cantatas, Mosaic, 79; Die unverbotne Lust, Erdmann Neumeister und die galante Poesie, Daphnis, 80; Die Circe-Episode in Rollenhagens Froschmeuseler, Arcadia, 80. *Mailing Add:* Dept of Ger Lang & Lit Queen's Univ Kingston ON K7L 3N6 Can

KRAWCZENIUK, JOSEPH V, b Tarnopol, Ukraine, Oct 7, 24; US citizen; m 57; c 4. GERMAN, RUSSIAN. *Educ:* Univ Munich, PhD(Ger), 51; Columbia Univ, MSLS, 60. *Prof Exp:* Cataloguer, Butler Libr, Columbia Univ, 60-62; from asst prof to assoc prof mod lang, 62-72, PROF GER, KING'S COL, PA, 72- *Mem:* MLA; Shevchenko Sci Soc. *Res:* Comparative literature; bibliography; problems of ecumenism. *Publ:* Auth, The giant from St George's Hill: Metropolitan Andrew Sheptytzky, Redeemer's Voice, Can, 63; The cult of Sts Cyril and Methodius in Ukraine, Lohos, Can, 64; Ucrainica in foreign languages, Asn Ukrainian Writers Almanach, 65; Ivan Franko and his foreign friends, 68 & Gerhart Hauptmann's works in Ukrainian: A bibliographic review, 78, Shevchenko Sci Soc Proc; transl, Taras Schevchenko's works, America, 79; auth, Reverend John Volansky, First Ukrainian Priest in the US, Lohos, Can, 81; Henrik Ibsen and Ukrainian literature, Ukrainian Nat Asn Almanach, 81. *Mailing Add:* Box 1513 King's Col Wilkes-Barre PA 18711

KREIDLER, CHARLES WILLIAM, b Frankfort, Ky, Aug 5, 24; m 59; c 2. LINGUISTICS. *Educ:* Univ Cincinnati, AB, 48; Univ Mich, MA, 51, PhD (ling), 58. *Prof Exp:* From instr to asst prof mod lang, St Peter's Col, 54-58; Fulbright lectr ling, Cent Univ Ecuador, 58-59; from lectr to asst prof, Univ Mich, 59-63; from asst prof to assoc prof, 63-72, PROF LING, GEORGETOWN UNIV, 72-, HEAD PROG APPLIED LING, 63-, CHMN DEPT, 81- *Concurrent Pos:* Consult, Am Coun Educ, US Dept State & Defense, 67; consult, Tex Educ Agency, 73; consult, US Civil Serv Comn, 77; vis prof, Univ Regensburg, 75. *Mem:* Ling Soc Am: Teachers English to Speakers Other Lang; MLA; Am Dialect Soc. *Res:* English phonology; applied linguistics; history of the English language and the methodology of language teaching and testing. *Publ:* Auth, The alternative question as a teaching device, Lang Learning, 63; Reading as skill, structure, and communication, Proc 2nd Ann TESOL Conf, 64; The influence of linguistics in school grammar, Ling Reporter, 66; coauth, The Dynamics of Language (6 vols), Heath, 71; auth, Diacritics in English phonology, Georgetown Univ Working Papers in Lang & Ling, 71; Teaching English pronunciation and spelling, TESOL Quart, 72; English orthography: A generative approach, In: Studies in Honor of Albert H Marckwardt, TESOL, 72; Case grammar and language teaching, Proc 3rd Cong Asn Int de Linguistique Appliquee, Copenhagen, 72; Creating new words by shortening, J English Ling, 79. *Mailing Add:* 4512 Verplanck Pl NW Washington DC 20016

KREISS, PAUL THEODORE, b Riedisheim, France, May 11, 26; US citizen; m 42; c 10. FRENCH, GERMAN. *Educ:* Concordia Teachers Col, Ill, BSEd, 52; Boston Univ, MEd, 57; Northwestern Univ, PhD(French), 68. *Prof Exp:* Teacher-prin elem sch, Mass, 52-56; teacher elem sch, Mo, 56-60; from instr to asst prof French & Ger, 60-73, ASSOC PROF FRENCH, CONCORDIA TEACHERS COL, ILL, 73- *Concurrent Pos:* Ed foreign lang sect, Instruct Mat Guide for Lutheran Elem Schs, 68-; mem, Lutheran Curric Resource Comt, 68- *Mem:* Am Asn Teachers Fr; Am Coun Teaching Foreign Lang. *Res:* French literature of the 17th and 18th centuries; teaching foreign language in the elementary schools. *Publ:* Auth, Foreign languages in elementary schools, Lutheran Educ, 6/61; Fleshpots or Angels Food, Motif, fall 62. *Mailing Add:* Dept of Foreign Lang Concordia Teachers Col River Forest IL 60305

KREITZ, HELMUT, b Düsseldorf, Ger, Feb 20, 20; m 52; c 3. GERMAN. *Educ:* Univ Saarland, Dr Phil, 58. *Prof Exp:* Viola player, Städtisches Theater Saarbrücken, 53-59; prin viola sect, Städtisches Theatre Duisburg, 59-61; asst prof Ger, Fla Presby Col, 61-64; assoc prof foreign lang, 64-73, chmn dept, 64-76, PROF GER, NORTHERN MICH UNIV, 73- *Concurrent Pos:* Chmn rep, Städtisches Orchester Saarbrücken, 54-56; mem city comn munic theatre, Saarbrücken, 57-58; consult, Scott, Foresman & Co, 66-68. *Mem:* Am Asn Teachers Ger; MLA. *Res:* The classical period in German literature; philosophy; existentialism. *Publ:* Auth, Die Zeit und die Zukunft, Gewerkschaftsblatt, 1/54; Nachwuchsprobleme der deutschen Kultur orchester, Das Orchester, 60; Wir Lernen Deutsch, Scott, 74. *Mailing Add:* Dept of Foreign Lang Northern Mich Univ Marquette MI 49855

KRELL, DAVID FARRELL, Philosophy, Comparative Literature. See Vol IV

KRESIC, STEPHEN, b Donje Hrasno, Croatia, Feb 22, 15; Can citizen; m 60; c 4. CLASSICS. *Educ:* Class Col Jesuits, Yugoslavia, BA, 36; Univ Zagreb, DES(class philol), 41. *Prof Exp:* News transl, Croatia, 42-45; lit ed & lit translr, pub houses, Zagreb, 45-59; prof classics, Brussels, 59-60; assoc prof, 61-70, prof, 70-80, EMER PROF CLASS LANG & LIT, UNIV OTTAWA, 81- *Concurrent Pos:* Can Coun & Fed Swiss Govt grant, 64-66. *Mem:* Class Asn Can: Soc Latin Studies, France; Am Philol Asn; Croatian Acad Am; Soc Can Lit Translators. *Res:* Theory and practice of translation; exile in Latin literature; Croatioan language in macrolinguistics. *Publ:* Auth, Theocritus' Pharmakeutriai, 43 & Idyllic Poetry in Ancient Literatures, 44, Prof Soc; Handbook of English Pronunciation, 47; L'enseignement des classiques en traduction, Rev Univ Ottawa, 64; L'image de Virgile au XXe siecle, 68 & Le Rameau d'or chez Virgile, 68, Class News & Views; Contemporary Literary Hermeneutics and Interpretation of Classical Texts, Univ Ottawa Press, 81. *Mailing Add:* 1973 Camborne Crescent Ottawa ON K1H 7B6 Can

KREUSLER, ABRAHAM ARTHUR, b Western Ukraine, Oct 1, 97; nat US; m 27; c 1. RUSSIAN STUDIES. *Educ:* Yaghellonian Univ, Cracow, MA, 28, PhD, 29, MA, 32. *Prof Exp:* Teacher mod lang, Gym, Wloclawek, 24-36, prin, Lyceum, 36-39; asst prof mod lang, Teachers Col, Stanislav, 39-41; assoc prof, Teachers Col, Frunze, 44-46; prof, 48-71, EMER PROF RUSS STUDIES, RANDOLPH-MACON WOMAN'S COL, 71- *Mem:* Am Asn Advan Slavic Studies; Am Asn Teachers Slavic & East Europ Lang. *Res:* Russian education. *Publ:* Auth, A P Chekhov, The Three Sisters; The Teaching of Modern Languages in the USSR & A Teacher's Experiences in the Soviet Union, 65, E J Brill, Leiden; coauth, Perspectives on World Education, W C Brown, 70; auth, A P Chekhov, The Cherry Orchard, The Proposal, Va Chap Am Asn Teachers Slavic & East Europ Lang, 73. *Mailing Add:* 210 Cleveland Ave Lynchburg VA 24503

KREUTER, KATHERINE ELIZABETH, b Rockford, Ill. FRENCH LITERATURE. *Educ:* Northern Ill Univ, BA, 54; Univ Paris, Magistere, 73; Univ Calif, Los Angeles, PhD(Fr), 79. *Prof Exp:* Instr, Calif State Univ, Northridge, 80-81; ASST PROF FRENCH, SCRIPPS COL, 82- *Concurrent Pos:* Instr French, Univ Calif, Los Angeles Extension, 79-; dir, MA Prog in French, Int Col, Los Angeles, 81- *Mem:* MLA. *Res:* Philosophical, psychological and theological implications of the work of Samuel Beckett in 20th century French literature; Gerard de Nerval in 19th century French literature. *Publ:* Transl, The Muzzle, (transl George Matore, La Muselliere), La Presse Universelle Paris, 75. *Mailing Add:* 71-301 Sahara Rd Rancho Mirage CA 92270

KRIEG, MARTHA FESSLER, b Canton, Ohio, May 31, 48; m 68; c 2. ROMANCE LINGUISTICS, OLD & MIDDLE ENGLISH. *Educ:* Col Wooster, BA, 70; Univ Mich, MA, 71, AMLS, 72, PhD(Romance ling), 76. *Prof Exp:* Res asst, Middle English Dict, 75-81; RES & WRITING, 81- *Concurrent Pos:* Co-managing ed, Mythprint, 73-74. *Mem:* Mediaeval Acad Am; Medieval Asn Midwest. *Res:* Color words in Mediaeval languages; Mediaeval studies; the Oxford Christians. *Publ:* Auth, A history of English pronimal and verbal forms, Parma Eldalamberon, 72; Color terms in medieval French, proc PMR conf 3, 78; The influence of French color vocabulary on Middle English, Mich Academician II, 79; Latinate color terminology in Middle English medical and herbal treatises, Fifteenth Century Studies, 79; illusr, Traditional Music in Modern Java, Univ Hawaii, 80; auth, A computerized edition of a Middle-English Primer, Fifteenth Century Studies, 81. *Mailing Add:* 3362 Williamsburg Ann Arbor MI 48104

KRISPYN, EGBERT, b Haarlem, Neth, June 14, 30. GERMAN & COMPARATIVE LITERATURE. *Educ:* Univ Melbourne, BA, 57, MA, 58; Univ Pa, PhD(Ger), 63. *Prof Exp:* Lectr Ger & Netherlandic, Univ Pa, 61-63; asst prof Ger, Univ Fla, 63-64; from asst prof to assoc prof, Univ Pa, 64-68; prof Ger & chmn dept Ger & Russ, Univ Fla, 68-72; PROF GER LIT, UNIV GA, 72- *Concurrent Pos:* Alexander von Humboldt Found res grant, 65; ed, Neth sect, Twayne World Auth Ser, Twayne Publ, Inc, 65-; ed, Libr Netherlandic Lit, 69-; Am Philos Soc grant, 68. *Mem:* MLA; Mod Humnities Res Asn; Int Ver Ger Sprach-u Literaturwiss; SAtlantic Mod Lang Asn; Southern Comp Lit Asn. *Res:* Radio play; contemporary literature and exile literature; baroque liberature. *Publ:* Auth, Georg Heym: A Reluctant Rebel, Univ Fla, 68; Günter Eich, Twayne, 71; The fiasco of Weh dem, der lügt, Ger Life & Lett, 72; Exil als Lebensform, In: Exil und Innere Emigration II, Athenäum, 73; Mary and Mariken, J English & Ger Philol, 76; contribr, William S Schlamm und der politische Coriolis-Effekt, In: Osterreicher im Exil 1934 bis 1945, Österreichischer Bundesverlag, 77; auth, Anti-Nazi Writers in Exile, Univ Ga, 78; Koningklyke Herderin Aspasia und ihre Bearbeiter, De Nieuwe Taalgids, 81. *Mailing Add:* Dept of Ger & Slavic Lang Univ of Ga Athens GA 30602

KROHN, ROBERT KARL, b Detroit, Mich, July 1, 37; m 62. LINGUISTICS, ENGLISH AS A SECOND LANGUAGE. *Educ:* Univ Mich, Ann Arbor, BA, 61, MA, 64, PhD(ling), 69. *Prof Exp:* Instr ling & English as a second lang, Univ Mich, Ann Arbor, 69-70; asst prof, 70-79, ASSOC PROF ENGLISH AS SECOND LANG, UNIV HAWAII, MANOA, 80- *Mem:*

Ling Soc Am; Teachers English to Speakers Other Lang. *Res:* English phonology; English syntax; Germanic linguistics. *Publ:* Auth, The role of linguistics in TEFL methodology, Lang Learning, 70; coauth, English Sentence Structure, Univ Mich, 71; auth, On the sequencing of tautosegmental features, Papers Ling, 72; Underlying vowels in modern English, Glossa, 72. *Mailing Add:* Dept of English as a Second Lang Univ of Hawaii at Manoa Honolulu HI 96822

KROLL, PAUL WILLIAM, b Detroit, Mich, Apr 24, 48. CHINESE MEDIEVAL LITERATURE. *Educ:* Univ Mich, BA, 70, MA, 73, PhD(Chinese lit), 76. *Prof Exp:* Lectr Chinese, Univ Mich, 75-76; asst prof, Univ Va, 76-79; asst prof, 79-82, ASSOC PROF CHINESE, UNIV COLO, BOULDER, 82- *Concurrent Pos:* Rev ed, Chinese Lit: Essays, Articles & Rev, 79-; assoc ed, Soc Study Chinese Relig Bull, 79-; vis asst prof Chinese, Univ Calif, Berkeley, fall, 81. *Mem:* Am Orient Soc; Medieval Acad Am; Asn Asian Studies; T'ang Studies Soc; Soc Study Chinese Relig. *Res:* Medieval Chinese literature and religion, especially of the T'ang dynasty. *Publ:* Auth, The quatrains of Meng Hao-jan, Monumenta Serica, 74-75; Szu-ma Ch'eng-chen in T'ang verse, Soc Study Chinese Relig Bull, 78; The egret in medieval Chinese literature, Chinese Lit: Essays, Articles & Rev, 79; Meng Hao-jan, G K Hall & Co, 81; Notes on three Taoist figures of the T'ang dynasty, Soc Study Chinese Relig Bull, 81; The dancing horses of T'ang, T'oung Pao, 81; Wang Shih-yuan's preface to the poems of Meng Hao-jan, Monumenta Serica, 81; coauth, A Concordance to the Poems of Meng Hao-jan, Chinese Materials Ctr Inc, 82. *Mailing Add:* Dept of Orient Langs & Lits Univ of Colo Boulder CO 80309

KROMER, GRETCHEN, b Boston, Mass, June 11, 46. GREEK & LATIN LITERATURE. *Educ:* Goucher Col, AB, 68; Johns Hopkins Univ, PhD(classics), 73. *Prof Exp:* Jr instr Latin, Johns Hopkins Univ, 69-70; asst prof classics, Mt Holyoke Col, 73-77; VIS ASST PROF CLASSICS, IND UNIV, BLOOMINGTON, 77- *Mem:* Am Philol Asn. *Res:* Greek lyric poetry; Greek and Latin didactic poetry; 19th century French literature. *Publ:* Auth, The redoubtable PTYX, Mod Lang Notes, 5/71; Homer and Odysseus in Nemean 7.20-27, Class World, 75; The value of time in Pindar's Olympian 10, Hermes, 76. *Mailing Add:* 932 Ballantine Rd Bloomington IN 47405

KRONEGGER, MARIA ELISABETH, b Graz, Austria, Sept 23, 32. MODERN LANGUAGES. *Educ:* Sorbonne, dipl, 54; Univ Kans, ME, 57; Fla State Univ, PhD, 60; Univ Graz, MA, 60. *Prof Exp:* Asst prof French, Ger, English lit, Rosenberg Col, Switz, 61-62; asst prof French lit & humanities, Hollins Col, 62-64; PROF FRENCH & COMP LIT, MICH STATE UNIV, 64- *Concurrent Pos:* Chmn & adv, Nat Screening Comt for Grants Grad Study Abroad, Inst Int Educ, Fulbright Hays & other progs, 71-77. *Honors & Awards:* Certificate Distinguished Serv, Int Inst Educ, 77. *Mem:* MLA; Int Comp Lit Asn; Soc Fr Prof Am; AAUP; Chinese Comp Lit Asn. *Res:* Baroque literature and the other arts; impressionist literature and the other arts; phenomenology and structuralism. *Publ:* Auth, Impressionist Literature, Col & Univ, 73; Authors and impressionist reality, Fr Lit Conf, Univ SC, 3/73; A problem of periodization: Literary impressionism, Proc VII Cong Comp Lit, 8/73; Tragic justice based on myth: Phedre and Hippolyte viewed as Baroque protagonists, Fr Lit Ser, Univ SC, 3/76; Litterature impressionniste et le reel, Proc Int Comp Lit Asn, Budapest, 78; L'ecrivain dans une societe en mutation: Le cas d'Hermann Bahr (1863-1934), Aix-en Provence, 78 & Impressionist stylistic devices, Sydney, Australia, Proc Fedn Int des Langues et Litteratures Mo-ernes; From the Impressionist to the Phenomenological Novel, Bilingual, 78. *Mailing Add:* Dept of Romance Lang Mich State Univ Wells Hall 502 East Lansing MI 48823

KRONER, PETER ALBERT, b Bucharest, Rumania, Nov 6, 11; m 38; c 2. FOREIGN LANGUAGES. *Educ:* Univ Bucharest, BA, 35, MA, 38; Univ Erlangen, PhD(Ger), 41. *Prof Exp:* Chmn dept foreign lang, Am High Sch, US Army Dependents, Nurnberg, Ger, 42-54; prof Ger, 54-76, chmn dept foreign lang, 54-72, PROF FOREIGN LANG & COMP LIT, UNIV WIS-STEVENS POINT, 76- *Concurrent Pos:* Asst Ger dept, Univ Erlangen & chmn dept foreign lang, Ger High Sch, Forcheim, Ger, 42-45; interpreter, Am Mil Govt, Ger, 45-46. *Mem:* MLA; Am Asn Teachers Ger. *Res:* Comparative literature; Romanticism; Scandinavian literature, especially Danish. *Publ:* Auth, Adelbert von Chamisso, Univ Erlangen, 41; Friedrich Schiller: Der Geisterseher, 44 & Eduard Mörike: Maler Nolten, 44, Brüsseler Zeitung. *Mailing Add:* Dept of Foreign Lang Univ of Wis Stevens Point WI 54481

KRONIK, JOHN WILLIAM, b Vienna, Austria, May 18, 31; nat US; m 55; c 2. SPANISH LANGUAGE & LITERATURE. *Educ:* Queens Col, NY, BA, 52; Univ Wis, MA, 53, PhD(Span), 60. *Hon Degrees:* DHL, Ill Col, 79. *Prof Exp:* Asst prof Romance lang, Hamilton Col, 58-63; from asst prof to assoc prof Span, Univ Ill, 63-66; assoc prof, 66-71, dir grad studies, 70-73, PROF ROMANCE STUDIES, CORNELL UNIV, 71- *Concurrent Pos:* Fulbright fel, Madrid, 60-61; mem, nat screening comt for Spain & Portugal, Inst Int Educ, 62-64, chmn, 63-64; adv ed Span, Appleton-Century-Crofts, 62-75; vis lectr, Columbia Univ, 68; assoc ed, Hispania, 70-81; Am Philos Soc res grant, 70; mem Grad Rec Exam Comt Examiners 72, chmn, 78-; vis prof, Syracuse Univ, 72; consult, Nat Endowment for Humanities, 73-; ed assoc, Ky Romance Quart, 74-; mem adv comt, PMLA, 77-81; vis prof Span, Bryn Mawr Col, Madrid, 73, Purdue Univ, 78, Middlebury Col Grad Sch Span, 79, 80 & Brigham Young Univ, 82; assoc ed, Monogr Romance Lang, Purdue Univ, 78-; Rockefeller res residency, Italy, 75. *Mem:* MLA; Am Asn Teachers Span & Port; Int Asoc Hispanists; Acad Lit Studies; Int Galdos Assoc (pres, 81-). *Res:* Spanish literature of the 19th and 20th centuries; Franco-Spanish literary relationships; critical theory. *Publ:* Co-ed, La familia de Pascual Duarte, Appleton, 61; La modernidad de Leopoldo Alas, Papeles de Son Armadans, 5/66; La farsa (1927-1936) y el teatro espanol de preguerra, Estudis Hispanofila-Castalia, 71; Buero Vallejo's El tragaluz and man's existence in history, Hisp Rev, spring 73; Usigili's El gesticulador and the fiction of truth, Latin Am Theatre Rev, fall 77; Galdos and the grotesque, Anejo, Anales Galdosianos, 78; Galdosian reflections: Feijoo and the fabrication of Fortunata, Mod Lang Notes, spring 82. *Mailing Add:* Dept of Romance Studies Cornell Univ Ithaca NY 14853

KROTKOFF, GEORG, b Vienna, Austria, May 21, 25; m 52. ARABIC PHILOLOGY. *Educ:* Univ Vienna, PhD, 50. *Prof Exp:* Lectr Ger, Ain Shams Univ, Cairo, 51-55; from lectr to asst prof, Univ Baghdad, 55-59; asst prof Arabic, Orient Sem, 60-66, ASSOC PROF ARABIC, JOHNS HOPKINS UNIV, 66- *Mem:* Am Orient Soc; Am Asn Teachers Arabic; MidE Studies Asn NAm. *Res:* Arabic philology and linguistics; dialects of Arabic and modern Aramaic. *Publ:* Auth, Taschenbuch der Russischen Grammatik, Globus, 50, 54, 56; Lehrbuch der Deutschen Sprache mit Arabischer Anleitung, Cairo, 54, 55, Baghdad, 58; Beduinenrecht und gesatztes Recht, Wiener Zeitschrift Kunde Morgenlandes, 60; A possible Arabic ingredient in the history of Spanish usted, Romance Philol, 63; Bagdader Studien II, Ein Einakter im Bagdader Dialekt, Zeitschrift Deutschen Morgenländischen Gesellschaft, 64; Langenscheidts Taschenwörterbuch Arabisch-Deutsch, Langenscheidt, 76; The Neo-Aramaic Dialect of Araden (in prep). *Mailing Add:* Dept of Near Eastern Studies Johns Hopkins Univ Baltimore MD 21218

KRUEGER, JOHN RICHARD, b Fremont, Nebr, Mar 14, 27; m 57; c 2. LINGUISTICS. *Educ:* George Washington Univ, BA, 48; Univ Wash, PhD, 60. *Prof Exp:* Res analyst, Soviet & EEurop affairs, US Dept Army, 48-52; instr Ger, Univ Wash, 56-57; instr Ger & ling, Reed Col, 58-60; lectr Orient lang, Univ Calif, Berkeley, 61; from asst prof to assoc prof, 61-69, PROF URALIC & ALTAIC STUDIES, IND UNIV, BLOOMINGTON, 69- *Concurrent Pos:* Am Coun Learned Soc res grants Uralic & Altaic studies, 61, 62; Fulbright fel, Univ Copenhagen, 68. *Mem:* Mongolia Soc; Am Orient Soc. *Res:* Turco-Mongolian and central Asian linguistics and folk-literature; general linguistics; American Indian linguistics, especially Salishan. *Publ:* Coauth, Introduction to Classical Mongolian, Harrasowitz, Ger, 55; auth, Poetical Passages in the Erdeni-yin Tobci, Mouton, The Hague, 61; Chuvash Manual, 61 & Yakut Manual, 62, Ind Univ; Kalmyk-Mongolian Vocabulary in Stralenberg's Geography, Stockholm, 75; ed, Tuvan Manual, Ind Univ, 77. *Mailing Add:* 142 Goodbody Hall Ind Univ Bloomington IN 47405

KRUG, CLARA ELIZABETH, b Baltimore, Md, Aug 21, 46. FRENCH LANGUAGE & LITERATURE. *Educ:* James Madison Univ, BA, 68; Mich State Univ, MA, 70, PhD(French), 78. *Prof Exp:* Instr French, Western Mich Univ, 70-71 & Western Ill Univ, 71-74; lectr, Univ Wis-La Crosse, 77-78; ASST PROF FRENCH, GA SOUTHERN COL, 78- *Mem:* MLA; SAtlantic Mod Lang Asn; Am Coun Teaching Foreign Lang. *Res:* Seventeenth century; literature and the arts; error analysis in French composition. *Publ:* Contribr, Le Soleil couchant, In: Baroque Poetry in France, Tropos, spring 75; Promoting a positive attitude toward writing, Notes on Teaching English, Vol IX, No 1, 10-12. *Mailing Add:* Dept of Foreign Lang Ga Southern Col Statesboro GA 30458

KRUGOVOY, GEORGE G, b Kharkov, USSR, Jan 15, 24; US citizen; m; c 2. RUSSIAN PHILOSOPHY & LITERATURE. *Educ:* Philos Inst, Salzburg, Austria, BA & LPh, 51, PhD, 53. *Prof Exp:* Instr Russ, Air Force Inst Tech Lang Prog, Syracuse Univ, 59-60; instr Russ & Russ philos, Princeton Univ, 60-63; asst prof Russ lit & hist Russ civilization, NY Univ, 63-64; asst prof Russ lit & Russ philos, Princeton Univ, 64-68; assoc prof, 68-74, PROF RUSS LANG & LIT, SWARTHMORE COL, 74- *Concurrent Pos:* Oliver Ellsworth Bicentennial Preceptor, Princeton Univ, 64-68; Old Dominion grant, Swarthmore Col, 72; vis lectr Russ philos, Bryn Mawr Col, 78-79. *Mem:* NAm Dostoevsky Soc; Asn Russ-Am Scholars in USA. *Res:* Russian folklore; Russian literature; medieval studies. *Publ:* Auth, La lotta col drago nell'epos eroico russo, Ctr Studies Russia Cristiana, Seriate-Bergamo, 67; A Norman legal formula in Russian chronicles and Slovo o polku Igoreve, 69; Evolution of a metaphor in Old Russian literature, 72, A motif from Old Russian Vita Sanctorum in Arthurian romance, 73 & The Tristan and Isolt theme in the tale of Peter and Fevronia of Murom, Can Slavonic Papers, 76; Gnostic Novel of M Bulgakov, Novy Zhurnal, 79; Numerology in The master and Margarita, GRANI, 82. *Mailing Add:* Dept of Mod Lang & Lit Swarthmore Col Swarthmore PA 19081

KRYNSKI, MAGNUS JAN, b Warsaw, Poland, May 15, 22; US citizen; m 52. SLAVIC LANGUAGES. *Educ:* Univ Cincinnati, BA, 52; Brown Univ, MA, 55; Columbia Univ, MA & cert, Russ Inst, 56, PhD, 62. *Prof Exp:* Asst prof Russ lang & lit & Polish lang, Univ Pittsburgh, 61-63; assoc prof Russ lang & lit, Kenyon Col,64-66; assoc prof Russ & Polish lit, 66-75, PROF SLAVIC LIT, DUKE UNIV, 75-, CHMN DEPT SLAVIC LANG & LIT, 66- *Concurrent Pos:* Vis assoc prof, Ohio State Univ, 66; trustee, Polish Inst Arts & Sci, NYC, 78- *Honors & Awards:* Warsaw Authors Soc Award, 81. *Mem:* PEN Club; MLA; Am Asn Teachers Slavic & E Europ Lang; Am Asn Advan Slavic Studies; Polish Inst Arts & Sci Am. *Res:* Polish and Russian literature of the 20th century; Pushkin and his era; 18th century Russian literature. *Publ:* Auth, Poland's literary thaw: Dialectical phase or genuine freedom?, fall 56, The metamorphoses of Jerzy Hlasko--the lyrical naturalist, fall 61 & Politics and poetry: The case of Julian Tuwim, 73, Polish Rev; co-transl & coauth introd, Rozewicz Tadeusz, The Survivor and Other Poems, Princeton Univ, 76; auth, Poland 1977: The emergence of uncensored literature, Polish Rev, spring 78; co-transl & coauth intro, Swirszczynska Anna, Building the barricade, Wyd Literackie, Krakow, 79; Szymborska Wislawa, Sounds, Feelings, Thoughts: Seventy Poems, Princeton Univ, 81. *Mailing Add:* Dept of Slavic Lang & Lit Duke Univ Durham NC 27706

KRYSINSKI, WLADIMIR ROMUALD, b Warsaw, Poland, Aug 28, 35; div. SLAVIC & COMPARATIVE LITERATURE. *Educ:* Univ Lodz, MA, 57; Univ Strasbourg, PhD(French & comp lit), 66. *Prof Exp:* Lectr Polish lit, Univ Lodz, 58-59; lectr Polish lang, Univ Strasbourg, 59-66; from asst prof to assoc prof French & comp lit, Carleton Univ, 66-76; MEM FAC FRENCH, UNIV MONTREAL, 76- *Mem:* Asn Can Univ Teachers Fr; Can Comp Lit Asn; MLA. *Res:* Polish poetry of XXth century; studies of Pirandello's influence on French theater; semiotics of the modern theatre. *Publ:* Auth, L'acte gratuit ou l'experience de l'authenticite chez Dostoïevski et Gide, In: Les problemes des genres litteraires, Lodz, 71; Pirandello et Gombrowicz, deux visions de l'homme inauthentique, Rev Lett Mod Comparate, Fizeuze, 9/73; Formotropic (poetry & criticism), Galerie Curzi, Montreal, 77; Semiotic modalities of the body in modern theatre, Poetics Today, Tel Aviv, 81; Ponge et les idiolectes de la poesie moderne, Etudes Francaises, Montreal, 81; Carrefours de signes, Essais sur le roman modern, Mouton, The Hague, 81; Sartre et la metamorphose du cercle pirandellien, Esprit Createur, 82. *Mailing Add:* Dept of French Univ of Montreal Montreal PQ H3C 3J7 Can

KRYZYTSKI, SERGE, b Russia, Aug 26, 17; US citizen; m 43; c 2. RUSSIAN LITERATURE & LANGUAGE. *Educ:* Univ Bridgeport, BS, 59; Yale Univ, MA, 60, PhD(Slavic lang & lit), 65. *Prof Exp:* Instr Russ lang, Yale Univ, 59-60; asst prof Russ lang & lit, Univ Vt, 60-61; from asst prof to assoc prof, 63-74, PROF RUSS LANG & LIT, OBERLIN COL, 75- *Concurrent Pos:* Mem selection comt, Coun Int Educ Exchange, 67- *Mem:* Am Asn Teachers Slavic & EEurop Lang. *Res:* I A Bunin; Russian emigre literature. *Publ:* Auth, The Works of Ivan Bunin, Mouton, The Hague, 71; Vas Grossman: Vsë techet, Vozrozhdenie, 5/71; Zhizn' i tvorchestvo I A Bunina v emigratsii, In: Russian Emigre Literature, Univ Pittsburgh, 72; Anatoli Kuznetsov, New Rev, 3/73; ed, I A Bunin, Okayannye dni, 73 & I A Bunin, Pod Serpom i Molotom, 77, Zariai, London, Ont. *Mailing Add:* Dept of Ger & Russ Oberlin Col Oberlin OH 44074

KRZYZANOWSKI, JERZY ROMAN, b Lublin, Poland, Dec 10, 22; US citizen; m 48; c 3. SLAVIC LANGUAGES & LITERATURE. *Educ:* Univ Warsaw, Phil Mag, 59; Univ Mich, PhD(comp lit), 65. *Prof Exp:* Vis lectr Polish, Univ Calif, 59-60; lectr, Univ Mich, 60-63; asst prof Slavic, Univ Colo, 63-64; assoc prof, Univ Kans, 64-67; assoc prof, 67-70, PROF SLAVIC, OHIO STATE UNIV, 70- *Mem:* Am Asn Advan Slavic Studies; Asn Advan Polish Studies (pres, 77-79); Polish Inst Arts & Sci Am; North Am Study Ctr Polish Affairs. *Res:* Polish literature; Russian literature; comparative literature. *Publ:* Auth, Ernest Hemingway, Wiedza Powazechna, Warsaw, 63; H Sienkiewicz to J Curtin: Some unpublished letters, Polish Rev, 65; coauth, A Modern Polish Reader, Pa State Univ, 70; auth, On the history of ashes and diamond, Slavic & EEurop J, 71; Wladyslaw Stanislaw Reymont, Twayne, 72; General Leopold Okulicki, Odnowa, 81; ed, Janta-Czlowiek l Pisarz, PFK, 82. *Mailing Add:* Dept of Slavic Lang & Lit Ohio State Univ Columbus OH 43210

KUCERA, HENRY, b Czech, Feb 15, 25; nat US; m 51; c 2. SLAVIC LANGUAGES & LINGUISTICS. *Educ:* Charles Univ, Prague, MA, Harvard Univ, PhD(Slavic lang), 52; Brown Univ, MA, 58. *Prof Exp:* Asst prof foreign lang, Univ Fla, 52-55; asst prof mod lang, 55-58, assoc prof, 58-63, PROF SLAVIC LANG, LING & COGNITIVE SCI, BROWN UNIV, 63- *Concurrent Pos:* Ford fel, 60-61; Guggenheim Found fel, 60-61; Howard Found fel, 60-61, mem admin bd, 78-; Int Bus Machines Corp res assoc, Mass Inst Technol, 60-63; mem, Am Comt Slavists, 65-68; vis prof, Univ Mich, 67; consult, ling panel, Am Heritage Dictionary, 67-69; Nat Endowment for Humanities sr fel, 68-69; vis prof, Univ Calif, Berkeley, 69; Am Coun Learned Soc fel, 69-70; res assoc, Harvard Univ, 77- *Mem:* Ling Soc Am; MLA; Asn for Comput Ling; Am Asn Teachers Slavic & East Europ Lang; Cognitive Sci Soc. *Res:* General and Slavic linguistics; computers in linguistic research; language and cognition. *Publ:* Auth, The Phonology of Czech, Mouton, The Hague, 61; coauth, Computational Analysis of Present-Day American English, Brown Univ, 67; A Comparative Quantitative Phonology of Russian, Czech, and German, Am Elsevier, 68; ed, American Contributions to the 6th International Congress of Slavists, Mouton, The Hague, 68; auth, Computers in Linguistics and in Literary Studies, Brown Univ, 69; coauth, Time in Language, Univ Mich, 75; Frequency Analysis of English Usage, Houghton Mifflin Co, 82. *Mailing Add:* Dept of Slavic Lang PO Box E Brown Univ Providence RI 02912

KUCHAR, ROMAN VOLODYMYR, b Lviv, Ukraine, Feb 21, 20; US citizen; m 53; c 3. GERMAN, RUSSIAN & LATIN. *Educ:* Univ Heidelberg, MA, 48; Univ Colo, BM, 52; Pratt Inst, MLS, 59; Ukrainian Free Univ, Ger, PhD, 62. *Prof Exp:* Lectr, Jr Displaced Persons Cols, Ger, 47-50; emigration off, Int Refugee Orgn, Munich & Frankfurt, 50-51; lectr, civic orgns, Denver & Boulder, Colo, 52; opera & concert singer, Munich, Ger, 53; lectr & free lance writer, Newburgh, NY, 54-56; librn, humanities, Brooklyn Pub Libr, NY, 57-59; librn, humanities & music, State Univ NY Col Potsdam, 59-62; from asst prof to assoc prof Ger & Russ, 62-75, dir interlibr loans, 74-75, PROF LANG, FT HAYS STATE UNIV, 75- *Concurrent Pos:* Inst res grants, 65-66, 67-68; co-ed, Original Works, 66-; co-ed, The Dawn, 67-; Slavic res, Europe, 68, 72. *Honors & Awards:* Manifold Award, London, 69. *Mem:* Am Asn Teachers Slavic & EEurop Lang (pres, 72-73); Shevchenko Sci Soc; Am Asn Teachers Ger. *Res:* Slavic philology and linguistics and Soviet civilization; German literature; clandestine literature in the USSR. *Publ:* Auth, Hearts Aflame (poetry collection), Ukrainian Publ Co, London, 64; Life Aloft, Original Works, Chicago, 70; Banners of Thought, Svitannia, Toronto, 70; Poetry in Translation, Original Works, Belgium, 71; Space and Freedom, Original Works, Victoria, BC, 72; A Contemporary Miniature Theater, 73 & Dawning of the Nation, 73, Cicero, Munich; Farewell, Days of York, Svitannia, NY, 78; Dawning of the Nation, Vol 2, 78; First Ukrainian Academic School in Lviv, Alumni Asn, London, 81. *Mailing Add:* Dept of Foreign Lang Ft Hays State Univ Hays KS 67601

KUDLATY, JOHN MICHAEL, b Cleveland, Ohio, July 29, 36; m 63; c 2. SPANISH LANGUAGE & LITERATURE. *Educ:* Wabash Col, BA, 59; Univ Iowa, MA, 61, PhD(Span), 71. *Prof Exp:* Instr Span, Wabash Col, 61-63; res-resident, Univ Iowa, 63-65; asst prof, 65-71, ASSOC PROF SPAN, WABASH COL, 71-, CHMN DEPT ROMANCE LANG, 70-, CHMN DEPT MOD LANG, 80- *Mem:* MLA; Am Asn Teachers Span & Port; Cervantes Soc Am. *Res:* Cervantes; Spanish Golden Age literature; literary theory and stylistics. *Mailing Add:* Dept of Romance Lang Wabash Col Crawfordsville IN 47933

KUDSZUS, WINFRIED, b Dillingen, Ger, Sept 10, 41. GERMAN LITERATURE. *Educ:* Univ Calif, Berkeley, MA, 66, PhD(Ger), 68. *Prof Exp:* From actg asst prof to asst prof Ger, Stanford Univ, 67-68; asst prof, Univ Calif, Berkeley, 68-70; res fel humanities, Soc Humanities, Cornell Univ, 69-70; assoc prof Ger, Univ Calif, Berkeley, 70-74; vis prof, Univ Tübingen, Ger, 71-72; PROF GER, UNIV CALIF, BERKELEY, 74- *Concurrent Pos:* Vis res prof lit theory & psychiat, Univ Mainz, Ger, 75-76; spec appt lit theory & psychoanal, Univ Frankfurt, Ger, 76. *Mem:* Int Soc Lit Studies & Psychiat; MLA; Hölderlin-Gesellschaft. *Res:* German literature 18th-20th centuries; literary and cultural theory; literature and psychology. *Publ:* Auth, Erzählhaltung und Zeitverschiebung in Kafkas Prozess und Schloss, Deut Vierteljahrsschrift fur Literaturwissenschaft & Geistesgeschichte, 64; Sprachverlust und Sinnwandel: Zur Späten und spätesten Lyrik Hölderlins, Metzler-Verlag, 69; Geschichtsverlust und Sprachproblematik in den Hymnen an die Nacht, Euphorion, 71; Understanding media: Zur Kritik dualistischer Humanität im Zauberberg, In: Besichtigung des Zauberbergs, 74; Nach der Vor-schrift: Zur Lyrik Paul Celans, In: co-ed, Austriaca: Beitrage zur Österreichischen Literatur (Festschrift for Heinz Politzer), 75; ed, Literatur und Schizophrenie: Theorie und Interpretation eines Grenzgebiets, dtv/Niemeyer, 77; auth, Reflections on the double bind of literature and psychopathology, Sub-Stance, 78; co-ed, Psychoanalytische und psychopathologische literaturinterpretation, Wissenschaftliche Buchgesellschaft, 81. *Mailing Add:* Dept of Ger Univ of Calif Berkeley CA 94720

KUEPPER, KARL JOSEF, b Cologne, Ger, Aug 8, 35; m 63; c 2. GERMAN LINGUISTICS. *Educ:* Univ Cologne, MA, 62, MEd, 64; Univ Muenster, DPhil, 70. *Prof Exp:* From asst prof to assoc prof, Univ NB, 65-78, prof, 78-79, actg assoc dean arts, 75-76 & 77-78; DEAN OF FAC, BISHOP'S UNIV, 80- *Mem:* Can Asn Univ Teachers Ger; Can Ling Asn; Can Asn Advan Netherlandic Studies; Can Asn Applied Ling. *Res:* Historical German linguistics; contrastive and applied linguistics. *Publ:* Auth, Gesture and postuer as elemental symbolism in Kafka's The Trial, In: Mosaic III, Univ Man, 70; Studien zur Verbstellung in den Kölner Jahrbüchern des 14/15 Jahrhunderts, Ludwig Röhrscheid, Bonn, 71; Vergessenes Material zum historischen Kölner Sprachschatz: Bartholomäus Joseph Blasius Alfter: Alt Franckisch und Deutsches Diplomatisches Worterbuch, Rheinische Vierteljahrsblätter, 75; Die Situation des Indianers im Spiegel der nordamerikanischen literatur, In: Beiträge zur Fachdidaktik: Texte für den politischen unterricht, A Henn Verlag, 76; coauth, Strangers in Their Own Land: The North-American Indian in the Modern Short Story, Klett, Stuttgart, 76; Anleitung zum freien Gespräch, Zielsprache Deutsch, 76; auth, Der Grosse Brockhaus, Wiesbaden, 77 . *Mailing Add:* Office of the Dean Bishop's Univ Lennoxville PQ J1M 1Z7 Can

KUFNER, HERBERT LEOPOLD, b Freutsmoos, Ger, Nov 10, 27. GERMANIC LINGUISTICS. *Educ:* Emory Univ, BA, 49; Cornell Univ, PhD, 56. *Prof Exp:* Teaching asst Ger, Russ & Ukrainian, Cornell Univ, 52-54, instr Czech, Russ & Ger, 55-56; instr Ger, Harvard Univ, 56-58; from asst prof to assoc prof, 58-65, PROF LING, CORNELL UNIV, 65- *Concurrent Pos:* Lectr, Ithaca Col, 55-56; Am Coun Learned Soc grant, Vienna, 59-60; proj linguist contrastive English-Ger studies, Ctr Appl Ling, 59-62; John S Guggenheim fel, 65-66; mem adv res coun, Inst Deut Sprache, 68-; prof ling, Univ Heidelberg, 70-71; prof ling, Bogazici Univ, Istanbul, 74-75. *Mem:* Ling Soc Am; Am Asn Teachers Ger; MLA. *Res:* Structural linguistics; dialect geography; language pedagogy. *Publ:* Auth, Strukturelle Grammatik der Münchner Stadmundart, Oldenbourg, 61; The Grammatical Structures of English and German, Univ Chicago, 62; Kontrastive phonologie: Deutsch-Englisch, Klett, Stuttgart, 71; coauth & co-ed, Toward a Grammar of Proto-Germanic, Niemeyer, Tübingen, 72. *Mailing Add:* Dept of Mod Lang & Ling Cornell Univ Morrill Hall Ithaca NY 14850

KUHN, ANNA KATHARINA, b New York, NY, Apr 26, 44. GERMAN LITERATURE. *Educ:* Queens Col, NY, BA, 66; Middlebury Col, MA, 67; Stanford Univ, PhD(Ger studies), 77. *Prof Exp:* Instr Ger, Bates Col, 73-76; preceptor, Harvard Univ, 77-79; ASST PROF GER, UNIV PA, 79- *Mem:* MLA; Am Asn Teachers Ger. *Res:* Christa Wolf; German film; epic elements in drama. *Publ:* Auth, Der Dialog bei Frank Wedekind, Carl Winter Universitätsverlag, Heidelberg, 81; Schlöndorffs Die verlorene Ehre der Katharina Blum: Melodrama und Tendenz, 13th Amherst Colloquium: Lit & Film (in press); Rainer Werner Fassbinder, In: New German Filmmakers, Ungar Press (in press); Peter Hacks' Ein Gesprach im Hause Stein über den abwessenden Herrn Von Goethe: A feminist reinterpretation of the Genibegriff?, Proc Hofstra Col Colloquium Goethe in 20th Century (in press); The romanticization of Arthur Schnitzler: Max Ophuls' adaptations of Liebelei and Reigen, In: Festschrift for Walter Sokel, Niemeyer Verlag (in press). *Mailing Add:* Dept of Ger Univ of Pa Philadelphia PA 19104

KUHN, BRIGITTA JOHANNA, b Leipzig, Ger, Sept 22, 20; US Citizen. FRENCH. *Educ:* Eastern Ill Univ, BEd, 42; Univ Laval, MA, 48; Paris, DUniv(French), 53. *Prof Exp:* Teacher high sch, Ill, 42-43; transl French & Ger, T-2 Civil Serv, Ohio, 45-47; teacher French, Hockaday Sch, Tex, 48-51; asst prof French, Ger & Span, Morningside Col, 53-55; asst prof French & Ger, Univ Wichita, 55-61; assoc prof French, 61-65, PROF FRENCH, ILL STATE UNIV, 65- *Concurrent Pos:* Secy, chmn, French I, Midwest Mod Lang Asn, 63-65; consult, Title III NDEA, Dept Pub Instr, Ill, 68-71. *Mem:* Am Coun Teachers Foreign Lang; MLA; Am Asn Teachers Fr. *Res:* French literature of the 17th century, especially Moliere and LaFontaine; French-German comparative literature of the 19th century; French-English comparative literature of the 19th century. *Mailing Add:* Dept of French Ill State Univ Normal IL 61761

KUHN, IRA ASTRIDE, b Riga, Latvia, Mar 17, 37; US citizen; m 63; c 2. FRENCH & COMPARATIVE LITERATURE. *Educ:* Douglass Col, New Brunswick, BA, 59; Univ Kans, MA, 61, PhD(Ger), 70. *Prof Exp:* Instr Ger, State Univ NY, Buffalo, 63-64; from instr to asst prof, 67-77, ASSOC PROF FRENCH, UNIV RI, 77-, COORDR COMP LIT STUDIES, 81- *Concurrent Pos:* Howard Found res grant, 72-73; Camargo fel, 78-79. *Mem:* MLA; AAUP; Kafka Soc Am; Am Asn Teachers Fr; Am Comp Lit Asn. *Res:* French-German literary relationships; Kafka. *Publ:* Auth, The metamorphosis of The Trial, Symposium, fall 72; Speculations about games and reality: Robbe-Grillet and Uwe Johnson, In: Fiction, Form, Experience: The French Novel from Naturalism to the Present, Ed France-Que, Montreal, 76. *Mailing Add:* Dept of Lang Univ of RI Kingston RI 02881

KUHN, SHERMAN MCALLISTER, English. See Vol II

KUHN, STEVEN THOMAS, Philosophy. See Vol IV

KUHN, THOMAS SAMUEL, b Cincinnati, Ohio, July 18, 22; m 48; c 3. HISTORY & PHILOSOPHY OF SCIENCE. *Educ:* Harvard Univ, BS, 43, MA, 46, PhD(physics), 49. *Hon Degrees:* LLD, Univ Notre Dame, 73; DHL, Rider Col, 78; Doctorate, Linköping Univ, Sweden, 80. *Prof Exp:* Civilian employee, Off Sci Res & Develop, Harvard Univ, 43-45, instr gen educ, 51-52, asst prof gen educ & hist of sci, 52-56; from asst prof to prof hist of sci, Univ Calif, Berkeley, 56-74; prof, Princeton Univ, 64-68, M Taylor Pyne Prof, 69-79; PROF PHILOS & HIST SCI, MASS INST TECHNOL, 79- *Concurrent Pos:* Lowell lectr, 51; Guggenheim fel, 54-55; fel, Ctr Advan Studies Behav Sci, 58-59; dir, Sources Hist of Quantum Physics Proj, 61-64; bd dirs, Soc Sci Res Coun, 64-67; assoc ed physics, Dict Sci Biog, 64-; dir prog hist & philos of sci, Princeton Univ, 67-72; mem, Inst Advan Study, 72-79 & Assembly Behav & Soc Sci, 80- *Honors & Awards:* Howard T Behrman Award, Princeton Univ, 77. *Mem:* Nat Acad Sci; Am Philos Soc; Am Acad Arts & Sci; Hist Sci Soc (pres, 68-70); Am Philos Asn. *Res:* Reconstruction of out-of-date scientific ideas; description and abstract analysis of the way languag an ideas change in scientific development. *Publ:* Auth, The Copernican Revolution: Planetary Astronomy in the Development of Western Thought, Harvard Univ, 57 & Vintage, 59; The Structure of Scientific Revolutions, Univ Chicago, 62 & 70; coauth, Sources for history of quantum physics, Memoirs, Am Philos Soc, 67; The Essential Tension: Selected Studies in Scientific Tradition and Change, Univ Chicago, 77; The Black-body Problem and the Quantum Discontinuity, 1894-1912, Oxford Univ, 78. *Mailing Add:* Dept of Ling & Philos Mass Inst of Technol Cambridge MA 02139

KUITUNEN, MADDALENA TERESA, b Crespiatica, Italy, Jan 30, 32; Can citizen; m 57; c 2. ITALIAN LANGUAGE, LITERATURE. *Educ:* Univ Cattolica, Milan, D Lett Straniere, 56; Univ Toronto, M Phil, 67. *Prof Exp:* Teacher Latin, St Joseph Convent, Toronto, 57-58; instr, 63-65, lectr, 65-67, asst prof, 67-70, assoc prof, 70-82, PROF ITAL, UNIV TORONTO, 82- *Mem:* MLA; Ont Mod Lang teachers Asn; Am Asn Teachers Ital; Can Soc Ital Studies (vpres, 74-76). *Res:* Modern Italian literature-pedagogy. *Publ:* Auth, Metodi per l'insegnamento dell'italiano, Can Mod Lang Rev, 65; motivo dell'eta adolescente in Moravia, Forum Italicum, 69; The dilemma of Moravia's intellectuals, Laurentian Rev, 69; co-ed, L'avventura e altri racconti, La Tribuna, 70; contribr, Petrarch to Pirandello, Univ Toronto, 73; auth, Il Commento del Cantu alla monaca di Monza, Romanische Forschungen, 75; Sviluppi tematici nei primi romanzi di Silone, Esperienze Letterarie, 77; La narrativa di Guiseppe Antonio Borgese, 82. *Mailing Add:* Dept of Ital Studies Univ of Toronto Toronto ON M5S 1A1 Can

KUIZENGA, DONNA, b Princeton, NJ, Jan 30, 47. FRENCH LANGUAGE & LITERATURE. *Educ:* Adelphi Univ, AB, 68; City Univ New York, PhD(French), 74. *Prof Exp:* Instr French, Adelphi Univ, 69-71; asst prof, 74-79, ASSOC PROF FRENCH, UNIV MO-COLUMBIA, 79- *Concurrent Pos:* Vis assoc prof Fr, Univ Wis-Madison, 79-80. *Mem:* MLA; Am Asn Teachers French; NAm Soc Study Seventeenth Century French Lit; Asn Int Etudes Fr; AAUP. *Res:* Seventeenth-century French literature; women's studies. *Publ:* Auth, Narrative Strategies in La Princesse de Cleves, Fr Forum Publ, 76; La Fontaine's Le Faucon: A lesson of experience, Fr Forum, 77; Mithridate: A reconsideration, Fr Rev, 78; Yvan Goll's Hemispheres: A forgotten French-American review of the '40's, Fr-Am Rev, 78; The language of love: La Fontaine's Elegies pour Clymene, Papers French 17th century Lit, 80. *Mailing Add:* Dept of Romance Lang Univ of Mo Columbia MO 65211

KUK, ZENON M, b Ortynychi, Ukraine, Nov 21, 22; m 63; c 1. SLAVIC LANGUAGES & LITERATURES. *Educ:* Univ Chicago, MA, 64; Ohio State Univ, PhD, 73. *Prof Exp:* Lectr Russ, Univ Chicago, 65; instr, Roosevelt Univ, 67; from instr to asst prof mod lang, Ohio Univ, 68-75; asst prof Russ, 75-80, PROF RUSS, UNIV TOLEDO, 80- *Mem:* Am Asn Teachers Slavic & East Europ Lang; AAUP; Asn Advan Polish Studies. *Res:* Comparative Slavic literature; Zeromski and Tolstoy; Zeromski and Russian literature. *Publ:* Auth, An approach to the formation of diminutives of personal proper names in Ukrainian and Russian, Occasional Papers in Lang, Lit & Ling, 9/73; Premonition or vanity?, Mich Academician, winter 79; Depiction of fictional characters in Tolstoy's War and Peace and Zeromski's Ashes, Polish Rev, Vol XXV, No 2; The Napoleonic Era in Tolstoy's War and Peace and Zeromski's Ashes, Univ Hartford Studies in Lit, Vol 11, No 2;. *Mailing Add:* 2451 Orchard Rd Toledo OH 43606

KUNO, SUSUMU, b Tokyo, Japan, Aug 11, 33; m 67; c 2. LINGUISTICS. *Educ:* Univ Tokyo, AB, 56, AM, 58; Harvard Univ, PhD(ling), 64. *Prof Exp:* From instr to assoc prof, 64-69, PROF LING, HARVARD UNIV, 69-, CHMN DEPT, 72- *Concurrent Pos:* Trustee, Lang Res Found, Cambridge, Mass, 69-; Guggenheim fel, 77-78. *Mem:* Asn Comput Mach; Asn Comput Ling (pres, 67); Ling Soc Am. *Res:* Generative grammar; Japanese and English syntax; computational linguistics. *Publ:* Auth, Computer analysis of natural languages, Proc Symp Applied Math, 67; Locatives in existential sentences, 72 & Functional sentence perspective, 72, Ling Inquiry; The Structure of the Japanese Language, Mass Inst Technol, 73. *Mailing Add:* Dept of Ling Harvard Univ Cambridge MA 02138

KUNST, ARTHUR EGON, b Oak Park, Ill, Nov 21, 34. COMPARATIVE LITERATURE. *Educ:* Univ Toledo, BA, 56; Ind Univ, PhD(comp lit), 61. *Prof Exp:* Instr English, Univ NDak, 59-61; instr, Ind Univ, 61-62; form asst prof to assoc prof comp lit, 62-71, chmn dept, 68-69, PROF COMP LIT, UNIV WIS-MADISON, 71- *Concurrent Pos:* Lectr comp lit, Ind Univ, 61; Fulbright lectr, Kyushu Univ, 67-68. *Mem:* MLA; Asn Asian Studies; Midwest Mod Lang Asn. *Res:* Problems in the translation of fiction; comparative studies in Oriental-Western literatures. *Publ:* Auth, Annual Index of translations, Yearbk Comp Lit, 61-66; L Hearn vis a vis French literature, Comp Lit Studies, 67; Ying I: Feng qiao ye po Ping Shi, Tsing Hua J, 68. *Mailing Add:* Dept of Comp Lit Univ of Wis Madison WI 53706

KUNSTMANN, PIERRE MARIE FRANCOIS, b Marseilles, France, May 29, 44; Can citizen. MEDIEVAL LITERATURE, FRENCH PHILOLOGY. *Educ:* Univ Aix-en-Provence, Lic es Lett, 65, dipl classics, 66, Agrege, 67; Sorbonne Univ, DUniv(French philol), 71. *Prof Exp:* Asst teacher French & classics, Col Provence, France, 66-67; asst prof classics, 67-68, asst prof, 68-71, assoc prof, 71-82, PROF FRENCH, UNIV OTTAWA, 82- *Mem:* Mediaeval Acad Am; Anglo-Normand Texts Soc; Asn de Semiotique du Can; Societe de Ling Romane. *Res:* Linguistique Francaise. *Publ:* Ed, Livre des Miracles de Notre-Dame de Chartres, Chartres and Ottawa, 73; auth, Vierge et Mereille, Paris, 10-18/81; Treize miracles de Notre-Dame tires dums, Paris BNfr2094, Ottawa, 81; Concordance analytique de la Mort Artu, Univ Ottawa Mediaeval Texts and Studies, 82; Adgar, Gracial, Ottawa, 82. *Mailing Add:* 14-240 Stewart Ottawa ON K1N 6K2 Can

KUNTZ, MARION LEATHERS DANIELS, b Atlanta, Ga; m 73; c 2. CLASSICS, RENAISSANCE STUDIES. *Educ:* Agnes Scott Col, AB, 45; Emory Univ, MA, 62, PhD(Latin Renaissance studies), 69. *Prof Exp:* Lectr Latin, Lovett Sch, Atlanta, Ga, 63-66; from asst prof to prof Latin & Greek, 66-75, REGENTS PROF CLASSICS & CHMN DEPT FOREIGN LANG, GA STATE UNIV, 75- *Concurrent Pos:* Am Class League consult, 66-70; Am Coun Learned Soc grant, 70-81. *Honors & Awards:* Latin Teacher of the Year, State of Ga, 65; Semple Award, Class Asn Mid W & S, 65. *Mem:* Am Philol Asn; Renaissance Soc Am; Int Soc Neo-Latin Studies; Class Asn Mid W & S; Class Soc Am Acad Rome (secy-treas, 71-). *Res:* Renaissance literature; history; philosophy. *Publ:* Pythagorean Cosmology and Its Identification, In: Bodin's Colloquium Heptaplomeres, Acta Conventus Neo-Latini Touronensis, Troisieme Cong Int d'Etude Neo-Latins, II: 685-696; Journey as Restitutio in the Thought of Guillaume Postel, J Hist Europ Ideas, Vol 1, No 4; Guillaume Postel e la Vergine Veneziana Appunti Storici sulla Vita Spirituale dell'ospedaletto nel cinquecento, Quarderni, Publicazione di Centro Tedesco di Studi Veneziani, 81; A recently discovered epistolary fragment of Postel: An Hypothesis Concerning the Addresse, In: Guillaume Postel, Prophet of the Restitution of All Things: His Life and Thought, 81 & Postel on the Highest Grade of Nourishment, In: Guillaume Postel, Prophet of the Restitution of All Things: His Life and Thought, 81, Archives Int d'Histoire des Idees, Neth; Guillaume Postel: Prophet of the Restitution of All Things: His Life and Thought, Nijhoff, 81; Guillaume Postel and the Universal Monarchy: The State as a Work of Art, 82 & Guillaume Postel and the Idea of a One-World State, 82, J Hist Europ Ideas. *Mailing Add:* 1655 Ponce de Leon Atlanta GA 30307

KUNZ, DON, English Literature. See Vol II

KUNZE, WOLFGANG P F, b Stettin, Ger, Oct 6, 38; c 2. GERMAN & GERMAN-AMERICAN LITERATURE. *Educ:* Sem Marienhöhe, Ger, dipl theol, 62; Atlantic Union Col, BA, 64; Middlebury Col, MA, 68, Univ Calif, Los Angeles, PhD(Ger lang), 77. *Prof Exp:* ASSOC PROF GER LANG & LIT, ANDREWS UNIV, 67-, CHMN DEPT MOD LANG, 80- *Mem:* Am Asn Teachers Ger; Am Folklore Asn; Adventist Lang Teachers Asn; Soc Ger-Am Studies. *Res:* Eighteenth and 20th century German literature; German-American culture; Germanic folklore and mythology. *Publ:* Auth, A national videotheque as a means of information and communication in the field of German-American literature and culture, In: Germanica Americana, Univ Kans, 77; Krankheitsdamonen: Demons and Demonic Agents of Disease of Germanic Oral Literature, Custom, and Belief, Ann Arbor, 77; The use of videotape in teaching advanced conversational German, Adventist Lang Teachers Asn, fall 78; German-American Studies, fall 79; Changes of the Christ Image in Folk Art, Pittsburg, 80. *Mailing Add:* Dept of Mod Lang Andrews Univ Berrien Springs MI 49104

KUNZER, RUTH GOLDSCHMIDT, b Prague, Czech; US citizen; m 56. GERMANIC LANGUAGES, JEWISH STUDIES. *Educ:* Calif State Univ, Northridge, BA, 66; Univ Calif, Los Angeles, MA, 67, PhD(Ger lang & folklore), 70. *Prof Exp:* Actg asst prof Ger, 70-72, LECTR JEWISH LIT, JEWISH STUDIES PROG, UNIV CALIF, LOS ANGELES, 72-; PROF JEWISH LIT & HIST, HEBREW UNION COL, CALIF, 72- *Mem:* Am Asn Teachers Ger; Jewish Studies Asn Am. *Res:* German literature and criticism; Jewish literature and history; Jewish folklore. *Publ:* Coauth, Georg Lukacs: A Biographical Study, Ungar, 72; auth, The Tristan of Gottfried von Strassburg--An Ironic Perspective, Univ Calif, 73; coauth, Culinary Marxism, Diacritic, 73; auth, Exile authors and artists at California universities, In: Exile Authors, Francke, Berne, Switz, 74. *Mailing Add:* 14017 Burton St Van Nuys CA 91402

KUPCEK, JOSEPH R, b Chicago, Ill, Mar 12, 14. SLAVIC LANGUAGES & LITERATURES. *Educ:* Comenius Univ, Bratislava, PhD(Slavic & Romance philol), 43. *Prof Exp:* Instr French & Russ, Univ Ill, 46-49; asst prof, Univ Denver, 50-54, Creighton Univ, 54-60 & Univ Northern Iowa, 60-62; assoc prof Russ lang & lit, 62-70, PROF RUSS LANG & LIT, SOUTHERN ILL UNIV, 70-, HEAD RUSS SECT, 67- *Concurrent Pos:* Consult Russ textbks, US Armed Forces Inst, Madison, Wis. *Mem:* MLA; Am Asn Teachers Slavic & East Europ Lang. *Publ:* Auth, Aspects of Russian Culture, 69 & Comparative Conversational Slavic Languages, 72, Stipes. *Mailing Add:* Dept of Foreign Lang Southern Ill Univ Carbondale IL 62901

KUPSH, LINZEY, b Menominee, Mich, Oct 21, 32; m 58; c 4. LINGUISTICS, ENGLISH. *Educ:* St Norbert Col, BA, 56; Laval Univ, MA, 58; Univ Wis, PhD, 62. *Prof Exp:* Instr English, Col St Jean Eudes, Que, 57-59; instr, Laval Univ, 58-59; asst prof English & ling, Fresno State Col, 62-65; ASSOC PROF ENGLISH & LING, UNIV MONTREAL, 66- *Concurrent Pos:* Fulbright lectr, Univ Rome, 64-66. *Mem:* Ling Soc Am; Can Ling Asn. *Res:* Second language teaching. *Mailing Add:* Dept of English Univ of Montreal Montreal PQ H3C 3J7 Can

KURATH, HANS, b Austria, Dec 13, 91. LINGUISTICS. *Educ:* Univ Tex, AB, 14; Univ Chicago, PhD, 20. *Hon Degrees:* LHD, Univ Chicago, 60, Univ Wis-Milwaukee, 68. *Prof Exp:* Instr Ger, Univ Tex, 14-16, 17-19; from instr to asst prof, Northwestern Univ, 20-27; prof Ger & ling, Ohio State Univ, 27-

32; prof Ger lang & gen ling & chmn dept Ger lang, Brown Univ, 32-46, chmn div mod lang, 42-46; prof English & ed, 46-61, EMER PROF ENGLISH LANG & LIT & EMER ED, MIDDLE ENGLISH DICTIONARY, UNIV MICH, ANN ARBOR, 61- *Concurrent Pos:* Dir, Ling Atlas US, 30-63; vis prof, Yale Univ, 38-40, dir Ling Inst, 47-50; ed, Ling Atlas New Eng, 39-43. *Mem:* Ling Soc Am (pres, 41); MLA; Am Acad Arts & Sci. *Res:* American English; speech, settlement and culture areas in the United States; middle English. *Publ:* Coauth, Middle English Dictionary, 52-63, The Pronunication of English in the Atlantic States, 61 & auth, A Phonology and Prosody of Modern English, 64, Univ Mich; Studies in Area Linguistics, Ind Univ, 72. *Mailing Add:* 1125 Spring St Ann Arbor MI 48103

KURCZABA, ALEX, b Watenstedt, Ger, Sept 14, 47; US citizen; m 70; c 1. SLAVIC LANGUAGES & LITERATURES. *Educ:* Canisius Col, BA, 69; State Univ NY, Buffalo, MA, 71; Univ Ill, PhD(comp lit), 78. *Prof Exp:* Teaching asst Ger, Univ Ill, Urbana-Champaign, 71-73, teaching asst English, 75-76, res asst comp lit, 76-77; ASST PROF POLISH LANG & LIT, UNIV ILL, CHICAGO CIRCLE, 79- *Concurrent Pos:* Jr fac fel, Univ Ill, Chicago Circle, summer, 80. *Mem:* MLA; Am Comp Lit Asn; Am Asn Advan Slavic Studies; Polish Inst Arts & Sci Am. *Res:* Polish-German literary relations; old Polish literature; autobiography. *Publ:* Transl, Krzysztof Kamil Bacynski's White Magic, A Melody, Erotic & The Glimpse (poems), Modern Poetry in Translation, 75; auth, German-Polish literary relations, Germano-Slavica, 76; The impact of Latin American exile on Polish and German literature, Polish Rev, 79; Gombrowicz and Frisch: Aspects of the Literary Diary, Bouvier, 80. *Mailing Add:* Dept of Slavic Lang & Lit Univ Ill Chicago Circle Chicago IL 60680

KURLAND, JORDAN EMIL, History. See Vol I

KURMAN, GEORGE, b Tallinn, Estonia, June 10, 42; US citizen; m 65; c 4. COMPARATIVE & ESTONIAN LITERATURE. *Educ:* Cornell Univ, BA, 62; Columbia Univ, MA, 66; Ind Univ, PhD(comp lit), 69. *Prof Exp:* Transl Estonian epic poetry, UNESCO, 69-70; from asst prof to assoc prof, 70-80, PROF ENGLISH & COMP LIT, WESTERN ILL UNIV, 80- *Concurrent Pos:* Int Res & Exchanges Bd fel, Estonian lit, 72-73. *Mem:* Asn Advan Baltic Studies; corresp mem Inst Estonian Lang & Lit. *Publ:* Auth, The Development of Written Estonian, Uralic & Altaic Ser, Ind Univ, 68; Negative comparison in literary epic narrative, Comp Lit, 69; Literatures in contact: Finland and Estonia, Estonian Learned Soc Am, 72; Ecphrasis in epic poetry, Comp Lit, 73; Entropy and the death of tragedy: Notes for a theory of drama, Comp Drama, 75; Literary censorship in general and in Soviet Estonia, J Baltic Studies, 77; A methodology of thematics: The literature of the palgue, Comp Lit Studies, 82; Kaleripreg, Symposia Press, 82. *Mailing Add:* Dept of English Western Ill Univ Macomb IL 61455

KURODA, SIGE-YUKI, b Tokyo, Japan, Aug 18, 34. LINGUISTICS. *Educ:* Univ Tokyo, BA, 59; Nagoya Univ, MA, 61; Mass Inst Technol, PhD(ling), 65. *Prof Exp:* Instr ling, Mass Inst Technol, 65-66; asst prof, 66-69, PROF LING, UNIV CALIF, SAN DIEGO, 69- *Concurrent Pos:* Am Coun Learned Soc fel, 68-69. *Mem:* Ling Soc Am. *Res:* Linguistic theory. *Publ:* Auth, Classes of languages and linear bounded automata, Info & Control, 64; Causative forms in Japanese, Found Lang, 65; Yawelmani Phonology, Mass Inst Technol, 67; English relativization and certain related problems, Lang, 68; Edmund Husserl, grammaire generale et raisonnee and Anton Marty, Found Lang, 73; Reflections on the foundations of narrative theory, In: Pragmatics of Language & Literature, 76; A topological study of phrase-structure languages, Info & Control, 76; Description of presuppositional phenomena . . ., Linguisticae Investigationes, 77. *Mailing Add:* Dept of Ling Univ of Calif San Diego PO Box 109 La Jolla CA 92037

KURRIK, MAIRE JAANUS, English & German Literature. See Vol II

KURTH, ARTHUR LINCOLN, b New York, NY, 16; m 46; c 2. FRENCH. *Educ:* Yale Univ, AB, 37, PhD, 42; Univ Dijon, cert, 38. *Prof Exp:* Asst instr, Yale Univ, 38-42, instr, 45-47; from asst prof to assoc prof French & Ital, Univ Fla, 47-62; assoc prof, 62-63, chmn dept, 63-73, PROF ROMANCE LANG, GETTYSBURG COL, 63- *Mem:* Am Asn Teachers Fr. *Res:* French 17th century. *Publ:* Auth, A Critical Bibliography of French Literature. *Mailing Add:* Dept of Romance Lang Gettysburg Col Gettysburg PA 17325

KURTH, LIESELOTTE E, b Wuppertal, Ger. GERMAN LITERATURE. *Educ:* Johns Hopkins Univ, MA, 60, PhD(Ger), 63. *Prof Exp:* From asst prof to assoc prof, 64-73, PROF GER, JOHNS HOPKINS UNIV, 73- *Mem:* MLA; Am Asn Teachers Ger; Deutsche Gesellschaft für die Erforschung des 18 Jahrhunderts; SAtlantic Mod Lang Asn. *Res:* C M Wieland; the German novel in European context; German literature of the 18th century. *Publ:* Auth, Historiographie und historischer Roman: Kritik und Theorie, Mod Lang Notes, 64; Rahmerzählung und Rahmenroman im achtzehnten Jahrhundert, In: Jahrbuch der Deutschen Schillerges, 69; Die Zweite Wirklichkeit, Studien zum Roman des 18 Jahrhunderts, Univ NC, 69; ed, Perspectives and Points of View: The Early Works of Wieland, Johns Hopkins Univ, 74; auth, The reception of C M Wieland in America, In: Studies in Honor of K J R Arndt, Univ Pr New Eng, 76; auth & ed, Briefe Theodor Fontanes an Ludwig Pietsch, Jahrbuch der deutschen Schillergesellschaft, 77; auth, Wieland and the French Revolution, In: Studies in 18th Century Culture, Univ Wis, 78; Die Tabula Cebetis und Agathon--Wielands Beziehungen zur Emblematik, Jahrbuch der dt Schillergesellschaft, 79. *Mailing Add:* Dept of Ger Johns Hopkins Univ 34th & Charles Baltimore MD 21218

KURTH, WILLIAM CHARLES, b Waterloo, Iowa, Oct 23, 32; m 58; c 3. LATIN, GREEK. *Educ:* Univ Northern Iowa, AB, 53; Univ Tex, MA, 59; Univ NC, PhD(classics), 65. *Prof Exp:* Teacher, High Sch, Wis, 55-56; instr Latin, Baylor Univ, 57-59; from instr to asst prof classics, Univ Ill, 62-67; assoc prof, 67-73, chmn dept, 67-76, PROF CLASSICS, LUTHER COL, IOWA, 73- *Concurrent Pos:* Consult programmed Latin, Macalester Col, 67; Nat Endowment for Humanities fel, Univ Tex, 77-78. *Mem:* Am Philol Asn; Am Class League; Class Asn Mid W & S. *Res:* Aulus Gellius: the minor Latin rhetoricians. *Publ:* Coauth, Epic and etiquette in Tacitus' Annals, Studies Philol, 10/61; The De Rhetorica of Aurelius Augustinus, Speech Monogr, 3/68. *Mailing Add:* Dept of Classics Luther Col Decorah IA 52101

KURTZ, JOHN WILLIAM, b Earlville, Ill, Nov 17, 06; m 32; c 4. GERMAN LITERATURE. *Educ:* Wartburg Col, AB, 27; Univ Ill, PhD, 32. *Prof Exp:* From instr to prof, 32-73, head dept Ger & Russ, 56-73, EMER PROF GER, OBERLIN COL, 73- *Concurrent Pos:* Analyst, US Strategic Bombing Surv, Ger, 45; univ adv, Off High Comnr for Ger 48-50. *Honors & Awards:* Officer's Cross, Order of Merit, Ger Fed Repub, 66. *Mem:* Am Civil Liberties Union. *Publ:* Auth, John Frederic Oberlin, Westview, 76; Johann Friedrich Oberlin, Ernst Franz/Sternberg, Metzingen, 82. *Mailing Add:* 67 S Cedar St Oberlin OH 44074

KURZ, EDMUND PAUL, b Hamburg, Ger, Nov 14, 11. GERMAN LITERATURE. *Educ:* City Col New York, AB, 33; NY Univ, AM, 39, PhD, 47. *Prof Exp:* Tutor ger, 40-46, from instr to asst prof, 46-61, assoc prof Ger lang, 61-66, actg chmn dept, 62-64, prof Ger & comp lit, 66-76, chmn dept, 64-76, EMER PROF GER & COMP LIT, QUEENS COL, NY, 76- *Concurrent Pos:* Lectr, Brooklyn Col, 46; mem final selection comt for grants by WGer univs, Inst Int Educ, 64-67. *Mem:* MLA; Am Asn Teachers Ger. *Res:* Marxist interpretations of Goeth's Faust; Marxist aesthetic criticism; regional novel. *Publ:* Co-tansl, Schiller's Love and Intrigue, Barron's, 62; coauth, Advanced Expository Prose Reader, Heath, 63; auth, The regional novel of Gorch Fock, 1/65 & Mahler's Symphony No 8 and the final scene of Goethe's Faust, 2/66, Rev Langues Vivantes; Probleme unsere Zeit, Appleton, 71. *Mailing Add:* 1009 A Heritage Village Southbury CT 06488

KUSCH, MANFRED, b Ger, Sept 11, 41. FRENCH LITERATURE, COMPARATIVE LITERATURE. *Educ:* Univ Göttingen, Ger, MA, 66; Univ Calif, Berkeley, PhD(comp lit), 73. *Prof Exp:* Asst prof, 71-80, ASSOC PROF FRENCH, UNIV CLAIF, DAVIS, 80- *Mem:* MLA; Am Soc 18th Century Studies; Philol Asn Pac Coast. *Res:* French novel of the 18th century; theory of the novel; comparative literature. *Publ:* Auth, Manon Lescaut, or voyage du chevalier des Grieux dans la basse Romancie, Studies Voltaire & 18th Century, 75; Narrative technique and cognitive modes in La Princesse de Cleves, Symposium, 76; Landscape and literary form: Structural parallels in La Nouvelle Heloïse, L'Esprit Createur, 77; The river and the garden: Basic spatial models in Candide and La Nouvelle Heloïse, Eighteenth Century Studies, 78. *Mailing Add:* Dept of French & Ital Univ of Calif Davis CA 95616

KUSHNER, EVA M, b Prague, Czech, June 18, 29; Can citizen; m 49; c 3. FRENCH LITERATURE. *Educ:* McGill Univ, BA, 48, MA, 50, PhD, 56. *Prof Exp:* Sessional lectr French, McGill Univ, 52-55; sessional lectr, Carleton Univ, 61-62, lectr, 62-63, from asst prof to prof, 63-76; PROF FRENCH & CHMN DEPT, McGILL UNIV, 76- *Concurrent Pos:* Sessional lectr philos, Sir George Williams Univ, 52-53; lectr French & philos, Sault Ste Marie Exten, Univ Western Ont, 57-58 & 60-61; Can Coun leave fel, 69-70; chmn, Humanities Res Coun Can, 70-72; mem ed comt, Can Comp Lit Rev, 73-, mem adv bd, Comp Lit studies, 73-; mem, Can Coun, 75-, mem exec comt, 78- *Mem:* MLA; Can Comp Lit Asn (vpres, 70-72); fel Royal Soc Can; Int Comp Lit Asn (vpres, 73-79); Can Soc Renaissance Studies. *Res:* Sixteenth century French poetry, especially Pontus de Tyard; the Renaissance dialogue, its history and poetics; theory of literary history. *Publ:* Auth, Saint-Denys-Garneau, Seghers, Paris, 67; Sartre et Baudelaire, Annales Fac Lett & Sci Humaines, Nice, 68; Rina Lasnier, Seghers, Paris, 69; Orphee et l'orphisme chez Victor Segalen, Cahiers Asn Int Etudes Fr, 70; Mauriac, Desclee de Brower, Paris, 72, Japanese transl, Jordan, Tokyo, 76; Reflexions sur le dialogue en France du 16e siecle, Revue des Sci Humaines, 72; The role of platonic symbols in the poetry of Pontus de Tyard, Yale Fr Studies, 73; Le dialogue en France e la Renaissance: quelques criteres genologiques, Can Comp Lit Rev, 78. *Mailing Add:* Dept of French McGill Univ 3460 McTavish St Montreal PQ H3A 1X9 Can

KUSHNIR, SLAVA MARIA, b Lviv, Ukraine; Can citizen. FRENCH. *Educ:* McGill Univ, BA, 60, MA, 62; Univ Bordeaux, DUniv, 64. *Prof Exp:* From instr to assoc prof French, Univ Victoria, 64-67; ASSOC PROF FRENCH, QUEEN'S UNIV, ONT, 67- *Mem:* Asn Can Univ Teachers Fr (secy-treas, 67-69); MLA; Societe des Amis de F Mauriac; Asn Gabriel Marcel. *Res:* The novel, its history, techniques and esthetic problems; the Ukraine--history and literature; 20th century French literature, history and philosophy. *Publ:* Auth, Valery Larbaud, Precurseur de Butor?, Rev Sci Humaines, summer 73; The Function of Torcy in the Journal d'un Cure de Campagne (Bermanos), Degre Second, 7/77; Mauriac journaliste, Minard, Paris, 79; Mauriac journaliste devant l'Eglise, In: No 3, Lettres Modernes, Serie Francois Mauriac, 80; Le journalisme de Mauriac: Lyrisme et polemique, In: Cahiers Francois Mauriac, Gasset, No 8, 81. *Mailing Add:* Dept French Queen's Univ Kingston ON K7L 3N6 Can

KUXDORF, MANFRED, b Cologne, Ger, July 4, 33; Can citizen; m 63; c 2. GERMAN LITERATURE. *Educ:* Univ Waterloo, BA, 63, MA, 65; Univ Alta, PhD(Ger), 69. *Prof Exp:* Assoc chmn dept Ger lang, 74-75, ASSOC PROF GER, UNIV WATERLOO, 74- *Concurrent Pos:* Humanities Res Coun Can publ grant, 71; Can Coun res grants, 71, 72 & leave fel, 75-76; vis prof, Univ Mannheim, 72-73; Ger Acad Exchange Serv stipend, 72-73; assoc ed, German-Slavica, 73- *Mem:* Can Asn Univ Teachers Ger; Int Arthur Schnitzler Res Asn; MLA; Int Vereinigung fur Germanistische Sprach - u Literaturwissenschaft. *Res:* Modern German literature, especially expressionism. *Publ:* Auth, Das Schicksal im Werk Authur Schnitzlers, J Int Arthur Schnitzler Res Asn, 66; Die Suche Nach Dem Menschen Im Drama Georg Kaisers, Herbert Lang & Cie, Bern, 71; Russian Elements in Georg Kaiser's Die Sorina, Germano-Slavica, Waterloo, spring 76; Salomo Friedlaender/Mynona: Forschungsbericht, Zeitgeschichte, Salzburg, 12/77. *Mailing Add:* Dept Ger & Slavic Lang & Lit Univ Waterloo Waterloo ON N2L 3G1 Can

KYES, ROBERT LANGE, b Allegan, Mich, July 8, 33; m 56; c 2. GERMAN, LINGUISTICS. *Educ:* Univ, Mich, BA, 58, PhD(Ger ling), 64; Brown Univ, MA, 59. *Prof Exp:* From instr to assoc prof, 62-74, PROF GER, UNIV MICH, ANN ARBOR, 74- *Concurrent Pos:* Vis assoc prof Ger ling, Univ Colo, 68-69; Rackham fac grant, Univ Mich, 72; local ed, Mich Ger Studies,

75- *Honors & Awards:* Univ Mich Distinguished serv Award, 66. *Mem:* Ling Soc Am; Am Asn teachers ger; Ling Asn Can & US. *Res:* Comparative Germanic linguistics; history and structure of Dutch; foreign language teaching methods. *Publ:* Auth, Old Low Franconian Phonology, Univ Mich, 64; coauth, German in review, Macmillan, 66; auth, The evidence for iumlaut in Old Low Franconian, Lang, 9/67; ed, The Old Low Franconian Psalms and glosses, Univ Mich, 69; coauth, Contemporary German, McGraw, 2nd ed, 71; auth, The medieval Dutch fricatives, Lingua, 71; coauth, Germanic and its Dialects: A Grammar of Proto-Germanic, Benjamins, 77. *Mailing Add:* Dept of Ger Univ of Mich Ann Arbor MI 48109

KYGER, M ELLSWORTH, b Port Republic, Va, Sept 6, 20. COMPARATIVE LINGUISTICS. *Educ:* Bridgewater Col, BA, 41, BS, 42; Univ Md, MA, 50; Cath Univ Am, PhD, 55. *Prof Exp:* Teacher, High Sch, Va, 47-48, 50-51 & Md, 53-55; asst prof Span & Ger, 55-62, prof Ger, 62-68, PROF GER & LING, BRIDGEWATER COL, 68- *Mem:* Ling Soc Am; Am Asn Teachers Ger. *Res:* Comparative Indo-European linguistics; lexicogology of Pennsylvania German. *Publ:* Coauth, The Pennsylvania Germans in the Shenandoah Valley, Pa Ger Soc, 64; auth, Indo-European words and locations, Danger. *Mailing Add:* Dept of Lang Bridgewater Col Bridgewater VA 22812

KYRITZ, HEINZ GEORG, b Ger, Mar 1, 26; Can citizen; m 50; c 2. GERMAN. *Educ:* McGill Univ, MA, 56, PhD, 61. *Prof Exp:* Teaching asst, Univ Toronto, 57-58; sessional lectr Ger, McMaster Univ, 58-59; from instr to asst prof, Univ Sask, 60-64; asst prof, Univ Toronto, 64-67; assoc prof, 67-79, PROF GER, STATE UNIV NY COL PLATTSBURGH, 80- *Concurrent Pos:* State Univ NY grant-in-aid, 68-70. *Mem:* Am Asn Teachers Ger; Can Asn Univ Teachers Ger. *Res:* Rainer Maria Rilke; Agnes Miegel. *Publ:* Auth, Das Unbewusste im Dichtungserlebnis Agnes Miegels, Ger Quart, 1/71; Jahresgabe 1972, 3/72 & Jahresgabe 1977, 3/77, Agnes-Miegel-Gesellschaft. *Mailing Add:* Dept of Mod Lang State Univ of NY Col Plattsburgh NY 12901

KYTE, ELINOR CLEMONS, b Garrett, Ind, Nov 2, 22; m 68; c 2. LINGUISTICS, ENGLISH. *Educ:* Miami Univ, BA, 50; Univ Tex, Austin, MA, 57, PhD(English ling), 61. *Prof Exp:* From asst prof to assoc prof, 61-67, PROF ENGLISH & ENGLISH LING, NORTHERN ARIZ UNIV, 68- *Mem:* Ling Soc Am; MLA; Teachers English to Speakers Other Lang. *Res:* Old English, especially language and netrics; English as a second language. *Publ:* Coauth, Bliss' light verses in Beowulf, J English & Ger Philol, 4/67; auth, For cars who think young, Word Studies, 2/68; On the composition of hypermetric verses in Old English, Mod Philol, fall 73. *Mailing Add:* Box 5598 Northern Ariz Univ Flagstaff AZ 86001

L

LABBAN, GEORGE, JR, b Houston, Tex, Oct 15, 21; m 46; c 2. CLASSICAL LANGUAGES & LITERATURE. *Educ:* Univ Tex, BA, 46, MA, 48, PhD(classics), 52. *Prof Exp:* Asst prof Greek & Latin, Baylor Univ, 50-51; from asst prof to assoc prof classics, 52-60, PROF CLASSICS, DAVIDSON COL, 60- *Mem:* Am Philol Asn. *Res:* Alexander romance. *Mailing Add:* Dept of Classics Davidson Col Davidson NC 28036

LABRADOR, JOSE JULIAN, b Castejon, Cuenca, Spain, Apr 8, 41; US citizen; m 66; c 1. SPANISH LANGUAGE & LITERATURE. *Educ:* Univ Madrid, BA, 60; Case Western Reserve Univ, MA, 68, PhD(Romance lang), 72. *Prof Exp:* From instr to asst prof, 69-74, ASSOC PROF SPAN, CLEVELAND STATE UNIV, 74- *Mem:* Mediaeval Soc Am; Midwest Mod Lang Asn. *Res:* Spanish medieval literature and history; European literature and history; Medieval philosophy. *Publ:* Auth, La poesia dialogada, Estudio y antologia, Ed Maisal, SAm, 74; Las preocupaciones doctrinales de los poetas del Cancionero, Boletin Inst Fernan Gonzalez, 74; El mito de venus: Un descubrimiento de los poetas castellanos medievales, Eastern Ky Univ Studies Lang & Lit, 76; coauth, Teaching Spanish through video tape, In: Personalizing Foreign Language Instruction, Nat Txtbk Co, 77; auth, Dios es fortuna: Una polemica medieval, 15th Century Studies, 78. *Mailing Add:* Dept of Span Cleveland State Univ Cleveland OH 44115

LACASA, JAIME, b Alcira, Spain, Oct 16, 29; m 69; c 2. SPANISH LANGUAGE & LITERATURE. *Educ:* Univ Catolica del Ecuador, Lic Phil, 56; Pontificia Facultas Sancti Gregorii, Ecuador, Lic Phil, 58; Iowa State Univ, PhD(sociol & anthrop), 70 . *Prof Exp:* Inst Spanish, 66-74, asst prof foreign lang, 74-79, ASSOC PROF SPANISH, IOWA STATE UNIV, 79- *Concurrent Pos:* Vis lectr sociol & anthrop, Drake Univ, 71-79. *Mem:* Am Coun Teaching Foreign Lang; Am Asn Teachers Span & Port. *Res:* Spanish grammar; computer translation of language; colonial Spanish American literature. *Publ:* Contribr, Arbol, Encycl de la Biblia, 63; coauth, Spanish: A Basic Course, 71 & Spanish: An Intermediate Course, 75, Holt, Rinehart and Winston; Handbook of Spanish Verbs, Iowa State Univ Press, 80. *Mailing Add:* Dept Foreign Lang & Lit Iowa State Univ Ames IA 50011

LACASA, JUDITH NOBLE, b Blue Island, Ill, Aug 10, 36; m 69; c 2. SPANISH LANGUAGE & LITERATURE. *Educ:* La State Univ, BS, 58, PhD(Span lang & lit), 68. *Prof Exp:* Instr French & Span, 63-66, from asst prof to assoc prof, 66-75, PROF SPAN, IOWA STATE UNIV, 75- *Mem:* Am Asn Teachers Span & Port; Am Coun Teaching Foreign Lang. *Res:* Nineteenth century Spanish drama; Spanish grammar; Romance philology, primarily Spanish philology. *Publ:* Coauth, Spanish: A Basic Course, 71, rev ed, 77 & Spanish: An Intermediate Course, 75, Holt; Handbook of Spanish Verbs, Iowa State Univ Press, 80. *Mailing Add:* Dept of Foreign Lang Iowa State Univ Ames IA 50010

LACASSE, RODOLPHE ROMEO, b Sherbrooke, PQ, June 6, 26; m 69. CONTEMPORARY FRENCH & COMPARATIVE LITERATURE. *Educ:* Sem Sherbrooke, BA, 48; Univ Montreal, Lic-es-Lett, 59, MA, 60; Univ Fribourg, D-es-Lett (comp lit), 68. *Prof Exp:* Asst prof French lit, Sem Sherbrooke, 52-66; PROF FRENCH & COMP LIT, UNIV SHERBROOKE, 68- *Concurrent Pos:* Lectr, Univ Quebec, Three Rivers, 72-73; dir, Centre d'Etudes des Lit d'Expression Francaise, 77- *Mem:* MLA; Comp Lit Asn; Can Comp Lit Asn. *Res:* French Baroque literature; the picaresque novel. *Publ:* Auth, Hemingway/Malraux: Destins de l'homme, Cosmos, 72; coauth, Les Equipements et les Besoins Culturels dans l'estrie, 72 & Communications en estrie, 75, Univ Sherbrooke. *Mailing Add:* Faculty of Arts Univ of Sherbrooke Sherbrooke PQ J1K 2R1 Can

LA CHARITE, RAYMOND CAMILLE, b Winnipeg, Man, Dec 20, 37; US citizen; m 64; c 2. ROMANCE LANGUAGES. *Educ:* Wayne State Univ, BA, 62; Univ Pa, MA, 65, PhD(French), 66. *Prof Exp:* Asst prof French, Univ NC, Chapel Hill, 66-69; assoc prof, 69-76, chmn dept, 72-75, dir grad studies French, 69-73 & 75, PROF FRENCH, UNIV KY, 76- *Concurrent Pos:* Univ NC res grant, 67-69; Univ Ky res grant, 70-75; assoc ed, Ky Romance Quart, 70-73; Nat Endowment for Humanities fel, 73; co-founder & co-ed, Fr Forum & Fr Forum Monographs, 76- *Mem:* MLA; Renaissance Soc Am; Am Asn Teachers Fr; Mod Humanities Res Asn; Soc Fr Hist Studies. *Res:* Renaissance. *Publ:* Auth, Montaigne's Concept of Judgement, Martinus Nijhoff, 68; co-ed & transl, Bonaventure des Periers's Novel Pastimes and Merry Tales, 72 & ed, From Marot to Montaigne: Essays on French Renaissance Literature, 72, Univ Ky; auth, The unity of Rabelais's Pantagruel, Fr Studies, 72; Mundus inversus: The fictional world of Pantagruel, Stanford Fr Rev, 77; ed, O Un amy! Essays on Montaigne in Honor of Donald M Frame, 77 & auth, Recreation, Reflection, and Re-Creation: Perspectives on Rabelais's Pantagruel, 80, Fr Forum; ed, The Sixteenth Century, Vol II, In: A Critical Bibliography of French Literature, Syracuse Univ, rev ed (in prep). *Mailing Add:* 1830 Cantrill Dr Lexington KY 40505

LA CHARITE, VIRGINIA ANDING, b Philadelphia, Pa, Jan 18, 37; m 64; c 2. ROMANCE LANGUAGES. *Educ:* Col William & Mary, AB, 57, AM, 62; Univ Pa, MA, 65, PhD(French), 66. *Prof Exp:* Instr French, Col William & Mary, 59-62; lectr, Univ NC, Chapel Hill, 66-69; assoc prof, 69-78, chmn comp lit curriculum, 70-74, PROF FRENCH, UNIV KY, 78- *Concurrent Pos:* Univ NC res grant, 68-69; Univ Ky res grant, 70-72; assoc ed, Ky Studies in Romance Lang & Lit, 70-72; co-founder & co-ed, Fr Forum & Fr Forum Monographs, 76- *Mem:* MLA; Am Asn Teachers Fr; Asn Studies Dada & Surrealism. *Res:* Contemporary and late 19th century French poetry. *Publ:* Auth, The Poetics and the Poetry of Rene Char, Univ NC, 68; co-ed & transl, Bonaventure des Periers's Novel Pastimes and Merry Tales, Univ Ky, 72; auth, The Role of Rimbaud in Char's Poetry, PMLA, 74; Beyond the poem: Rene Char's La Nuit talismanique, Symposium, 76; Henri Michaux, Twayne, 77; Dis-order and unity in the work of Henri Michaux, Mod Lang Rev, 78; Mallarme's Livre: The Graphomatics of the Text, Symposium, 80; Mallarme and the Plastic Circumstances of the Text, Nineteenth Century French Studies, 80. *Mailing Add:* 1830 Cantrill Dr Lexington KY 40505

LACOMBE, ANNE, b Issoudun, France, June 6, 44. FRENCH LANGUAGE & LITERATURE. *Educ:* Sorbonne, Lic de Lett, 65, Dipl class lang, 66, Agregee de Grammaire, 67. *Prof Exp:* Prof de lett French, Latin & Greek, Lycee de Jeunes Filles de Chartres, France, 67-69; vis asst prof French, Univ Kans, 69-70 & Univ NC, Chapel Hill, 70-71; asst prof, Douglass Col, Rutgers Univ, 71-72; from asst prof to assoc prof, Univ Kans, 72-77; assoc prof French, Univ Notre Dame, 77-80. *Mem:* MLA; Am Soc 18th Century Studies; Soc Fr Etudes XVIIIe Siecle; AAUP. *Res:* Eighteenth century French literature; stylistics and textual analysis; new criticism and literature. *Publ:* Auth, Decouverte du Cure Meslier, Romance Notes, winter 71; Les Contes de Voltaire: Tentative de bibliographie critique, Chimeres, fall, 72; La lettre sur la petite verole et les lettres philosophiques, 74 & Du theatre au roman: Sade, 75, Studies Voltaire; Les Infortunes de la Vertu: le Conte et la Philosophie, L'Esprit Createur, winter 75; French for business and journalism, Fr Rev, 10/77; Invention et mise en application du systeme metrique, Fr Rev, 12/79. *Mailing Add:* Dept of Mod & Class Lang Univ of Notre Dame Notre Dame IN 46556

LACOSTA, FRANK, b Spain, Apr 14, 22; US citizen; m 68. SPANISH, FRENCH. *Educ:* Brigham Young Univ, BA, 58, MA, 59; Univ Mo, PhD(Span), 61. *Prof Exp:* Asst prof Span, Temple Univ, 61-65; asst prof, 65-76, ASSOC PROF MOD LANG, BROOKLYN COL, 76- *Mem:* MLA. *Publ:* Auth, El humor en Enrique Jardiel Poncela, Hispania, 64; El infinito mundo de las proverbios: Don Quijote, Univ Buenos Aires, 65; Galdos y Balzac, Cuadernos Hispanoam, Madrid, 68; Una noche de primavera sin sueno, Appleton, 68. *Mailing Add:* Dept of Mod Lang Brooklyn Col Bedford Ave & Ave H Brooklyn NY 11210

LACY, GREGG FARNSWORTH, b New Castle, Ind, Dec 21, 43; m 70. FRENCH. *Educ:* Col Wooster, BA, 65; Univ Kans, MA, 67, PhD(French), 72. *Prof Exp:* Asst prof French, 72-76, chmn mod lang, 72-78, actg dean, Col Humanities & Soc Sci, 76-77, assoc prof, 76-81, asst vpres acad affairs, 77-81, PROF FRENCH, NDAK STATE UNIV, 81- *Concurrent Pos:* Fel, Acad Admin, Am Coun Educ, 78-79; hon fel, Inst Res Humanities, Univ Wis, 81-82. *Mem:* MLA; Am Asn Teachers French; Soc Renscesvales; Arthurian Soc. *Res:* Old French Fabliaux; curriculum planning. *Publ:* Auth, Le Mouvement: Une conception de l'unite dans le Tristan de Beroul, Chimeres, winter 70; The scholastic Milieu and Fabliaux stylistic humor, Proc Ling Circle, 10/74; Augustinian imagery and fabliaux obscenity: Studies on the seven sages of Rome and other essays in medieval literature, Educ Res Asn, Honolulu, 78; Fabliaux stylistic humor, Ky Romance Quart, 3/79; Changing the non-major curriculum: Reflection on process, ERIC, George Washington Univ, 80; Form, context, and disjunction in the Fabliaux World, Essays on Early French Literature Presented to Barbara Craig, French Lit Publ Co, 82. *Mailing Add:* Dept of Mod Lang N Dak State Univ Fargo ND 58105

LACY, KLUENTER WESLEY, JR, b Winston-Salem, NC, Apr 8, 43. FRENCH LANGUAGE AND LITERATURE. *Educ:* Wake Forest Univ, BA, 65; Univ Wis, MA, 66, PhD(French), 72. *Prof Exp:* Asst prof French, Marquette Univ, 69-78. *Concurrent Pos:* Organist & choirmaster, All Saints' Cathedral, Episcopal, 75-; comn church music, Diocese of Milwaukee, 77- *Mem:* MLA. *Res:* French novel, 1761-1820; feminism and feminist literature of the 18th century; narrative techniques, 18th and 19th century French novel. *Publ:* Auth, An enlightenment feminist: Madame Riccoboni, Revue de Louisiane, summer 73; A forgotten bestseller: Madame de Krudenor's Valerie, Romance Notes, spring 78. *Mailing Add:* 1827 E Wood Place Shorewood WI 53211

LACY, MARGRIET BRUYN, b Amsterdam, Holland, Apr 4, 43; Dutch citizen; m 70. FRENCH, GERMAN. *Educ:* Univ Amsterdam, Drs, 69; Univ Kans, PhD(French), 72. *Prof Exp:* High sch teacher French, Almere Col, Kampen, Holland, 69; instr Ger, Concordia Col, Moorhead, Minn, 72-74; lectr French, 73-74, asst prof French & Ger, 74-78, ASSOC PROF FRENCH & GER, N DAK STATE UNIV, 78-, CHMN DEPT MOD LANG, 81- *Concurrent Pos:* Mem teaching fac, Humanities Forum, Tri-Col Univ, 75-76. *Mem:* Am Asn Teachers French; MLA; Rocky Mt Mod Lang Asn; Am Soc 18th-Century Studies. *Res:* Belle van Zuylen (alias Madame de Charriere); novels of Marivaux; 17th and 18th century French novels. *Publ:* Contribr, Translation of Paul Zumthor, classes and genres in Medieval literature, Medieval French Miscellany, 72; auth, Ideas by Marivaux on a natural style, Pro Ling Circle, 75; Madame de Charriere and the constant family, Romance Notes (in prep). *Mailing Add:* Dept of Mod Lang N Dak State Univ Fargo ND 58105

LACY, NORRIS JOINER, b Hopkinsville, Ky, Mar 8, 40. MEDIEVAL FRENCH LITERATURE. *Educ:* Murray State Univ, AB, 62; Ind Univ, Bloomington, MA, 63, PhD(French), 67. *Prof Exp:* Lectr French, Ind Univ, Bloomington, 65-66; from asst prof to assoc prof, 66-75, PROF FRENCH, UNIV KANS, 75-, CHMN FRENCH & ITALIAN, 78- *Concurrent Pos:* Am Coun Learned Soc study fel, 73; vis assoc prof French, Univ Calif, Los Angeles, 75-76; ed-in-chief, Fr Lit Publ Co, 81- *Mem:* Mediaeval Acad Am; Int Arthurian Soc; MLA; Am Asn Teachers Fr; Soc Rencesvals. *Res:* Arthurian literature; medieval romance; medieval lyric poetry. *Publ:* Ed & contribr, A Medieval French Miscellany, 72 & ed, From Camelot to Joyous Guard, 74, Univ Kans; ed, 26 Chansons de la Renaissance, Klincksieck, Paris, 75; ed & coauth, The Comic Spirit in Medieval France, Soler, Valencia (Spain), 76; auth, Vilon in his work: The Testament and the problem of personal poetry, L'Esprit Createur, 78; The Craft of Chretien de Troyes: An Essay on Narrative Technique, Davis Medieval Texts & Studies, 80; co-ed & contribr, Essays in Early French Literature, 82 & ed, L'Istoyre de Jehan Couault, 82, Fr Lit Publ Co. *Mailing Add:* Dept of French & Ital Univ of Kans Lawrence KS 66045

LADEFOGED, PETER, b Sutton, England, Sept 17, 25; m 53; c 3. LINGUISTICS, ENGLISH. *Educ:* Univ Edinburgh, MA, 51, PhD, 59. *Prof Exp:* Lectr phonetics, Univ Edinburgh, 53-61; WAfrican Lang Surv fel, 61-62; from asst prof to assoc prof English, 62-65, PROF LING, UNIV CALIF, LOS ANGELES, 65- *Concurrent Pos:* Team leader, Uganda Lang Surv, 68. *Mem:* Acoust Soc Am; Int Phonetic Asn; Int Asn Voice Identification; Am Speech & Hearing Asn; Ling Soc Am (pres). *Res:* Experimental phonetics; African languages; phonology. *Publ:* Auth, Elements of Acoustic Phonetics, Univ Chicago, 62; A Phonetic Study of West African Languages, Cambridge Univ, 64, 2nd ed, 68; Three Areas of Experimental Phonetics, Oxford Univ, 67; Preliminaries to Linguistic Phonetics, Univ Chicago, 71; A Course in Phonetics, Harcourt, 75, 2nd ed, 82. *Mailing Add:* Dept of Ling Univ of Calif Los Angeles CA 90024

LADUSAW, WILLIAM ALLEN, b Louisville, Ky, Apr 6, 52. LINGUISTICS. *Educ:* Univ Ky, BA, 74; Univ Tex Austin, MA, 77, PhD(ling), 79. *Prof Exp:* Instr semantics, Univ Conn, 78; ASST PROF SYNTAX & SEMANTICS, UNIV IOWA, 79- *Concurrent Pos:* Vis asst prof, Ling Dept, Univ Calif, Los Angeles, 81-82. *Mem:* Ling Soc Am; Asn Comput Ling. *Res:* syntactic theory; natural language semantics. *Publ:* Coauth (with PK Halvorsen), Montague's Universal Grammar: An introduction for the linguist, Ling & Philos, Vol 3, No 2; auth, Affective or, factive verbs, and negative-polarity items, In: Papers from the 16th Regional Meeting of the Chicago Linguistic Society, 80; On the notion affective in the analysis of negative-polarity items, J Ling Res, Vol 1, No 2; Semantic constraints on the English partitive construction, Proc First W Coast Conf Formal Ling, Stanford Univ (in prep). *Mailing Add:* Dept of Ling Univ of Iowa Iowa City IA 52242

LAFARGE, CATHERINE, b Paris, France, May 22, 35. ROMANCE LANGUAGES. *Educ:* Mt Holyoke Col, AB, 57; Yale Univ, PhD(French), 66. *Prof Exp:* Actg instr French, Yale Univ, 64-66; from instr to asst prof, 66-74, assoc prof, 74-80, PROF FRENCH, BRYN MAWR COL, 80-, CHMN DEPT, 79- *Mem:* Int Soc 18th Century Studies; Am Soc 18th Century Studies; Soc Francaise d'Etude 18th Siecle; Am Asn Teachers Fr; Asn Int Etudes Francaises. *Publ:* Auth, The emergence of the Bourgeoisie, Yale Fr Studies, 64; Reverie et realite dans les Nuits de Paris de Restif de la Bretonne, La Ville au XVIIIe siecle, 75; Paris and myth: One vision of horror, In: Studies in Eighteenth Century Culture, Vol V, 76; Les Delices de l'Amour de Restif de la Bretonne: Attaque efficace contre Sade?, Studies Voltaire & 18th Century, 76; L'Anti-Fete dans le Nouveau Paris de L S Mercier, La Fete Revolutionnaire, 77; coauth (with J P Bouler), Les emprunts de mme Dupin a la Bibliothque du Roi dans les annees, 1748-1750, Vol CLXXII, 79 & L'Infortuna litteraire des Dupin: Essai de bibliographie critique, Vol, CLXXXII, 79, Studies on Voltaire & 18th Century; Catalogue topographique partiel des papiers Dupin-Rousseau disperses de 1951 a 1958, Annales de la Societe Jean-Jacques Rousseau, Vol XXXIX, 80. *Mailing Add:* Dept of Fr Bryn Mawr Col Bryn Mawr PA 19010

LAFLEUR, RICHARD ALLEN, b Newburyport, Mass, Sept 22, 45; m 67; c 3. CLASSICAL STUDIES. *Educ:* Univ Va, BA, 68, MA, 70; Duke Univ, PhD (class studies), 73. *Prof Exp:* Asst prof, 72-77, ASSOC PROF CLASSICS, UNIV GA, 77-, ACTG HEAD DEPT, 80- *Concurrent Pos:* Ed, Class Outlook, 79-; chmn, comt Prom Latin, 79-81, exec comt, 79-83, S sect secy-treas, 78-; Class Asn Midwest & South. *Mem:* Am Class League; Am Philol Asn; Archaeol Inst Am; Class Asn Mid W & S; Vergilian Soc. *Res:* Juvenal; Roman satire; Roman law of libel and treason. *Publ:* Auth, A note on Juvenal, Am J Philol, 72; Juvenal's Friendly Fingernails, Wiener Studien, 75; coauth, Vanni Fucci and Laocoon, Traditio, 76; auth, Umbricius and Juvenal Three, Ziva Antika, 76; Juvenal 1.80: Cluvianus?, Rev Philol, 76; Amicitia and the unity of Juvenal's first book, Ill Class Studies, 79; A re-examination of the Mallia insect pendant, Am J Archaeol, 79; Horace and onomast: Komodein: The law of satire, Aufstieg und Niedergang Röm Welt, 81. *Mailing Add:* Dept Classics Univ of Ga Athens GA 30602

LA FOLLETTE, JAMES E, b Jacksonville, Fla, Apr 3, 23; m 50. FRENCH. *Educ:* Xavier Univ, BA, 47; Laval Univ, MA, 49, PhD, 52; Inst de Phonetique, Univ Paris, Dipl, 53. *Prof Exp:* Asst prof French & chmn Romance lang, Bellarmine Col, Ky, 53-54; instr French, 54-59, asst prof, 59-64, chmn dept, 63-79, assoc prof, 64-70, PROF FRENCH, GEORGETOWN UNIV, 70- *Concurrent Pos:* Pres, Alliance Francaise de Wash Inc, June 63-; mem bd trustees, French Int Sch Wash, 66-70. *Honors & Awards:* Palmes Academiques; Legion d'honneur. *Mem:* Can Ling Asn; MLA; Am Asn Teachers Fr; Ling Soc Am; AAUP. *Res:* French linguistics; Canadian French. *Publ:* Auth, Etude Linguistique de Quatre Contes Folkloriques du Canada francais, Presses Univ Laval, 69; Observations sur le comportement du schwa en canadien-francais, 61 & coauth, Un Curieux Emploi de la negation en francais canadien, 62, Can J Ling. *Mailing Add:* 4620 N Park Ave 507 E Chevy Chase MD 20015

LAGERWEY, WALTER, b Grand Rapids, Mich, June 11, 18; m 42; c 5. GERMANIC LANGUAGES. *Educ:* Calvin Col, AB, 49; Columbia Univ, AM, 51; Univ Mich, PhD, 58. *Prof Exp:* From instr to assoc prof, 53-63, PROF DUTCH & GER, CALVIN COL, 63- *Concurrent Pos:* US Off Educ res grants, 60-61, 63-65, & 66-68; Fulbright res grant, Free Univ, Amsterdam, 67-68; consult, Ctr Appl Ling, 75- *Mem:* Soc Neth Lit; Int Asn Netherlandics; Int Asn Studies & Prom AV & Structuro-Global Methods; MLA; Nat Asn Self-Instruct Lang Prog (vpres, 75, pres, 76). *Res:* Comparative study of Dutch-German literature of the 18th century; history of Calvinism in the Netherlands; Dutch grammar and syntax; structure of Dutch and English. *Publ:* Auth, The history of Calvinism in the Netherlands, In: The Rise and Development of Calvinism, Eerdmans, 59; Guide to Dutch Studies, 61 & rev exp ed, 64 & Guide to Netherlandic Studies, 64, Calvin Col; Speak Dutch, an Audio-Lingual Course, Meulenhoff, Amsterdam, 68 & 4th ed, 72; Workbook for Speak Dutch (2 vols), Calvin Col, 73; The Netherlandic muse in the forests, on the plains, in the cities of America from 1850 to 1975, Proc Comp Lit Symp, 5/78; Neen Nederland, 'k vergeet u niet, Een beeld van het immigrantenleven in Amerika tussen 1846 en 1945 in verhalen, schetsen en gedichten, Bosch & Keuning, Neth, 82. *Mailing Add:* Dept of Lang Calvin Col 3201 Burton St SE Grand Rapids MI 49506

LAGGINI, JOSEPH ENRICO, b Plainfield, NJ, June 3, 23; m 48; c 5. ITALIAN LANGUAGE & LITERATURE. *Educ:* Rutgers Univ, BS, 53, MEd, 57; Middlebury Col, DML, 62. *Prof Exp:* From instr to assoc prof, 57-70, from asst dean to assoc dean, 67-80, actg dean instr, 73-74, PROF ITAL, RUTGERS COL, RUTGERS UNIV, NEW BRUNSWICK, 70- *Concurrent Pos:* Am Coun Educ fel, 66-67; educ consult, Am Inst Banking, 69-74. *Mem:* Am Asn Teachers Ital (secy-treas, 67-76, pres, 76-80); MLA; Am Coun Teaching Foreign Lang. *Publ:* Auth, La poesia di Lionello Fiumi, Ghidini & Fiorini, Verona, Italy, 64; Elemire Zolla and the industrial novel, Italica, 6/66; coauth, articles, In: Encycl World Lit in 20th Century, Ungar, 67. *Mailing Add:* Dept of Ital Rutgers Col New Brunswick NJ 08903

LAGOS, RAMIRO, b Sept 24, 22; m 57; c 2. SPANISH & SPANISH AMERICAN LITERATURE. *Educ:* Off Sch Jour, Madrid, dipl, 52; Univ Salamanca, dipl philol, 55; Pontif Univ Javeriana, MA, 59, PhD(philos & lit), 60. *Prof Exp:* Asst prof Span & Span Am lit, Univ Notre Dame, 61-65; assoc prof, 65-79, PROF SPAN & SPAN AM LIT, UNIV NC, GREENSBORO, 80- *Concurrent Pos:* Mem examining comt master degree cand in Span lang & lit, Univ Notre Dame, 61-65. *Mem:* Am Asn Teachers Span & Port. *Res:* Poetry of protest in the Latin American Republics. *Publ:* Auth, Sinfonia del corazon distante (poetry), Ed ABC, Colombia, 58; Vision del mundo eslavo (essay), El Voto Nac, Colombia, 60; Testimonio de las horas grises (poetry), Studium, Madrid, 64; Ritmos de vida cotidiana (poetry), Ed Dos Mundos, Madrid, 67; contribr poems, Letras Nac, 68 & Vanguard Poetry Rev, 68. *Mailing Add:* Dept of Romance Lang Univ of NC Greensboro NC 27412

LAGUNA-DIAZ, ELPIDIO, b Puerto Rico, Feb 15, 45; US citizen. SPANISH LITERATURE AND CIVILIZATION. *Educ:* Univ of Puerto Rico, BA, 66; St John's Univ, MA, 68; City Univ of NY, PhD(Hispanic studies), 74. *Prof Exp:* From instr to asst prof, 72-77, ASSOC PROF HISPANIC LIT & CIVILIZATION, RUTGERS UNIV, 77- *Mem:* MLA; Asociacion de Escritores Puertorriquenos. *Res:* Hispanic literature and civilization; philosophy and literature; history of ideas. *Publ:* Auth, El Tratamiento del Tiempo Subjetivo en Miro, Ed Espiritualidad, Madrid, 68; Dos Instantes de Julia de Burgos, Asomante, 1-3/69; Las Biografias y Retratos de Gomez de la Serna, San Juan, PR, 70; The phenomenology of nothingness in the poetry of Julia de Burgos, In: Latin American Women Writers, Pittsburgh, 77; Pablo, Ed Espiritualidad, Madrid, 68. *Mailing Add:* Dept of Spanish Rutgers Univ 175 University Ave Newark NJ 07102

LAIDLAW, LAURA ANNE, b New York, NY, Apr 16, 31. CLASSICS, ANCIENT ART. *Educ:* Bryn Mawr Col, AB, 52; Yale Univ, MA, 57, PhD(classics), 63. *Prof Exp:* Intern teacher Latin, Westtown Sch, Pa, 52-53; teacher Latin & English, George Sch, Bucks Co, Pa, 53-56; instr classics & actg chmn dept class lang, 61-63, asst prof Greek & Latin & chmn dept, 63-68, assoc prof, 68-74, PROF CLASSICAL STUDIES, HOLLINS COL, 74-

Concurrent Pos: Mem staff, Am Acad Excavations at Cosa, 65-; Nat Endowment for Humanities fel, 68-69; dir, Excavations in the House of Sallust, Pompeii, 69-; classicist-in-residence, Am Acad Rome, 75-76; consult, Pompeii AD 79, Am Mus Natural Hist, 78. *Honors & Awards:* Tatiana Warscher Award, 65. *Mem:* Archaeol Inst Am. *Res:* Ancient art and archaeology; Pompeian studies; Roman painting. *Publ:* Auth, The tomb of Montefiore: A new Roman tomb painted in the second style, Archaeology, spring 64; A reconstruction of the first style decoration in the Alexander Exedra in the House of the Faun, Neue Forschungen in Pompeii, 75; Reconstructions of the first style decorations in the House of Sallust in Pompeii, In: In Memoriam, Otto J Brendel: Essays in Archaeology and the Humanities, 76. *Mailing Add:* Dept of Class Studies Hollins College VA 24020

LAILLOU-SAVONA, JEANNETTE, b Bordeaux, France, July 31, 29. FRENCH, ENGLISH. *Educ:* Univ Bordeaux, Lic es Lett, 51, DES, 54, Dr Univ(English), 68. *Prof Exp:* Fulbright instr French & English, Stephens Col, Columbia, Mo, 61-63; from instr to asst prof French, 63-73, ASSOC PROF FRENCH, TRINITY COL, UNIV TORONTO, 73- *Concurrent Pos:* Can Coun res fel, 76-77. *Mem:* MLA; Can Asn Univ Teachers. *Res:* Twentieth century French drama; theory of drama; 20th century American novel. *Publ:* Auth, The Blacks by Jean Genet: A dimensional approach, Australian J French Studies, 73; Le Juif Dans le Roman Americain Contemporain, Didier-Can, Montreal, 74; contribr, La piece a l'interieur de la piece ou la notion d'art dans Caligula de Camus, In: Camus 7, Rev Lett Mod, Minard, Paris, 75; Narration et actes de parole dans le texte dramtique, Vol 13, No 3, 80 & ed, Theatre et theatralite, 12/80, Etudes litteraires; Jean Genet fifteen years later: An interview with Roger Blin, Mod Drama, 6/81; co-ed, Theory of drama and performance, Mod Drama, 3/82. *Mailing Add:* Dept of French Trinity Col Univ of Toronto Hoskin Ave Toronto ON M5S 1H8 Can

LAING, DONALD RANKIN, JR, b Richeyville, Pa, Oct 5, 31; m 51; c 4. CLASSICS, ANCIENT HISTORY. *Educ:* Washington & Jefferson Col, BA, 53; Univ Cincinnati, MA, 60, PhD(classics), 65. *Prof Exp:* Instr Greek & relig, Washington & Jefferson Col, 55-59; actg instr ancient hist, Univ Cincinnati, 60-61; asst prof classics, 62-68, ASSOC PROF CLASSICS, CASE WESTERN RESERVE UNIV, 69-, CHMN DEPT, 79- *Concurrent Pos:* Danforth grant, 59-60; Olivia James traveling fel, Archaeol Inst Am, 67-68; mem managing comt, Am Sch Class Studies, Athens, 68-; Am Coun Learned Soc fel, 74-75. *Mem:* Archaeol Inst Am; Am Philol Asn. *Res:* History of the Athenian fleet, 5th and 4th centuries BC, especially epigraphical records; Greek historiography and orators. *Publ:* Auth, A reconstruction of I G II2, 1628, Hesperia, 37:244-254. *Mailing Add:* Dept of Classics Case Western Reserve Univ Cleveland OH 44106

LAIRET, DOLORES PERSON, b Cleveland, Ohio; wid; c 2. FRENCH LANGUAGE & LITERATURE. *Educ:* Wheaton Col, Mass, AB, 57; Middlebury Col, AM, 58; Case Western Reserve Univ, PhD(French lang & lit), 72. *Prof Exp:* Teacher French, The Fox Lane Sch, Bedford, NY, 60-62 & John Marshall High Sch, Cleveland, 63-65; sr personnel asst, City of Cleveland, 69-71; from instr to asst prof, 71-77, ASSOC PROF MOD LANG, CLEVELAND STATE UNIV, 77- *Mem:* Am Asn Teachers Fr; AAUP; Am Coun Teaching Foreign Lang; Music Critics Asn; African Lit Asn. *Res:* Francophone African novel as written extention of African oral literature; jazz as extension of African oral literary forms; literature and mental health therapy. *Publ:* Coauth, L'Afrique Noire Equatoriale, Les litteratures de la francophonie: Actes de l'atelier francophone de l'ACTFL, 11/73; auth, Weather report: The more shorter the better, 5/76, Trumpeting the virtues of a South African, 6/76 & Not all crusaders teams break up, 7/76, Cleveland Press/Showtime; The Francophone African Novel: Perspectives for Critical Evaluation, Presence Africaine (in press). *Mailing Add:* Dept of Mod Lang Cleveland State Univ 1983 E 24th St Cleveland OH 44115

LAJOHN, LAWRENCE ANTHONY, b Jamestown, NY, Nov 21, 30; m 61; c 4. SPANISH. *Educ:* NY State Col Teachers, Albany, AB, 52; Univ Chicago, MA, 53; Ind Univ, PhD(Span), 57. *Prof Exp:* Teaching fel, Univ Chicago, 52-53; teaching asst, Univ Iowa, 53-54; teaching assoc, Ind Univ, 54-56; asst prof Span, Boston Col, 56-59; assoc prof, Northeast Mo State Col, 59-61; assoc prof, Ind State Col, 61-64; assoc prof mod lang, Ohio Univ, 64-68, prof, 68-80, chmn dept, 71-80. *Concurrent Pos:* Dir Bowling Green-Ohio Univ Year Abroad Prog, Madrid, 68-69. *Mem:* Am Asn Teachers Span & Port; Cent States Mod Lang Teachers Asn; MLA; Midwest Mod Lang Asn (secy, 67); Am Coun Teaching Foreign Lang. *Res:* Generation of 1898 in Spanish literature; Spanish drama of the 19th and 20th centuries; Spanish literature of the Golden Age. *Publ:* Auth, Azorin and the Spanish Stage, Columbia Univ Hisp Inst US, 61; Surrealism in Azorin's Theatre, Ky Foreign Lang Quart, 3/63; Azorin's Criticism of Jose Echegaray, Occasional Papers Lang & Lit, Ohio Univ, 3/68. *Mailing Add:* 169 G Pinegrove Heights Athens OH 45701

LAKICH, JOHN J, b Vrsac, Yugoslavia, Dec 26, 25; US citizen; m 56; c 2. MODERN LANGUAGES. *Educ:* Wayne State Univ, BA, 55, MA, 57, PhD(mod lang), 64. *Prof Exp:* Instr French, Wayne State Univ, 58-59 & 60-63; from instr to asst prof, 63-71, ASSOC PROF FRENCH, STATE UNIV NY, BINGHAMTON, 71- *Mem:* Am Asn Teachers Fr; MLA; AAUP. *Res:* Albert Camus; French literature of commitment of commitment; French theater. *Publ:* Auth, Metaphysical, ethical, and political quest in expressionism and the literature of commitment, Ky Romance Quart, 1/68; The ideal and reality in the French theater of the 1920s, Mod Lang Quart, 3/70; Tragedy and Satanism in Camus's La Chute, Symposium, fall 70; Gide and Camus: The Modern French Novel, In: Studies in Romance Languages and Literatures, Coronado Press, 79. *Mailing Add:* Dept of Romance Lang & Lit State Univ of New York Binghamton NY 13901

LAKOFF, ROBIN TOLMACH, b Brooklyn, NY, Nov 27, 42; m 63; c 1. LINGUISTICS. *Educ:* Radcliffe Col, BA, 64; Ind Univ, Bloomington, MA, 65; Harvard Univ, PhD(ling), 67. *Prof Exp:* Textbk ed, Lang Res Found, Cambridge, Mass, 68-69; asst prof ling, Univ Mich, Ann Arbor, 69-71; fel, Ctr Advan Studies Behav Sci, Stanford Univ, 71-72; assoc prof, 72-76, PROF LING, UNIV CALIF, BERKELEY, 76- *Concurrent Pos:* NIMH trainee, Mass Inst Technol, 67-68; co-prin investr, Nat Sci Found grant on pragmatics of nat lang, 73- *Mem:* Ling Soc Am. *Res:* Languages and society; syntax and semantics; syntactic change. *Publ:* Auth, Abstract Syntax and Latin Transformational Grammar, MIT, 68; Syntactic argument for negative transportation, Papers Fifth Regional Meeting Chicago Ling Soc, 5/69; Language in context, Language, 12/72; Language and women's place, Lang in Soc, 4/73. *Mailing Add:* Dept of Ling Univ of Calif Berkeley CA 94720

LALLY, TIM DOUGLAS PATRICK, Old & Middle English Language & Literature. See Vol II

LALONDE, GERALD VINCENT, b Bellingham, Wash, May 18, 38; m 69; c 2. CLASSICS, ANCIENT HISTORY. *Educ:* Univ Wash, BA, 62, MA, 64, PhD(classics), 71. *Prof Exp:* Instr classics, Univ Wash, 68-69; from instr to asst prof, 69-74, assoc prof, 74-79, PROF CLASS, GRINNELL COL, 80- *Mem:* Archaeol Inst Am; Am Philol Asn; Brit Class Asn. *Res:* Greek epigraphy, history and archaeology. *Publ:* Auth, A fifth century Hieron southwest of the Athenian Agora, 68 & A Boiotien decree in Athens, 77, Hisperia. *Mailing Add:* Dept of Classics Grinnell Col Grinnell IA 50112

LAMB, ANTHONY JOSEPH, b Somerville, Mass, Mar 21, 30; m 59; c 4. SPANISH LANGUAGE & LITERATURE. *Educ:* Suffolk Univ, AB, 59, Univ Kans, PhD(Span), 68. *Prof Exp:* Instr Span, Univ Vt, 61-63; asst prof, Western Ill Univ, 65-69; assoc prof & chmn dept foreign lang, 69-75, ASSOC PROF FOREIGN LANG, PURDUE UNIV, CALUMET CAMPUS, 75-, CHMN DEPT, 79- *Mem:* MLA; Am Asn Teachers Span & Port; Ling Soc Am; Am Coun Foreign Lang Teachers; Am Dialect Soc. *Res:* Dialectology; comparative linguistics; semiotics; South American dialectology; Spanish stylistics. *Publ:* Auth, La estilistica aplicada/Applied Spanish Stylistics, Scott, 70. *Mailing Add:* Dept of Foreign Lang Purdue Univ Calumet Campus 2233 171st St Hammond IN 46323

LAMB, EVA K, b Köln, Ger, Jan 31, 26; US citizen; m 48; c 2. FOREIGN LANGUAGE, FINE ARTS. *Educ:* NMex State Univ, BFA, 62, MA, 68. *Prof Exp:* Teacher, Holy Cross Parochial Elem Sch, 59-61, instr fine arts, 61-62; from instr to asst prof, 62-71, assoc prof, 71-79, EMER ASSOC PROF GER, NMEX STATE UNIV, 80- *Mem:* MLA; Am Asn Teachers Ger; AAUP; Goethe Inst, Ger. *Res:* Germanic mythology; art of the Maya civilization; comparative culture. *Publ:* Auth, Heimat oder Ausland, Macmillan (in prep). *Mailing Add:* 1855 Evans Pl Las Cruces NM 88001

LAMB, RUTH STANTON, US citizen. SPANISH LITERATURE. *Educ:* Pomona Col, AB, 36; Claremont Grad Sch, AM, 37; Univ Southern Calif, PhD, 43. *Prof Exp:* Instr, Northwestern Univ, 42-44; from asst prof to assoc prof, 44-56, PROF SPANISH & LATIN AM LIT, SCRIPPS COL & CLAREMONT GRAD SCH, 56- *Concurrent Pos:* Fulbright lectr, Brazil, 63; Fulbright vis prof Am lit, Nat Univ Cuyo, 67-68; Fulbright res scholar, Romania, 73; vis prof Latin Am studies, Grad Inst Int Studies, Japan, 77. *Mem:* MLA; Am Asn Teachers Span & Port; Inst Int Lit Iberoam; Western Hist Asn; Asoc Int Hispanists. *Res:* Argentine literature; Latin American literature; women in literature, United States and Latin American. *Publ:* Auth, Latin America: Sites and Insights, Creative Press, 63; Mexican Americans: Sons of the Southwest, Ocelot, 70; Three Contemporary Latin American Plays, Xerox, 71; America Latina: Contrastes e Confrontos, Grafica Panam, 73; Mexican Theatre of the Twentieth Century, 75 & The World of Romanian Theatre, 76, Ocelot; Role of the theatre in the preservation of minority languages and cultures in Romania, In: Languages and Literatures in the Formation of National and Cultural Communities, Australian Univ Lang & Lit Asn, 76; Papel de la mujer en la obra teatral de seis escritoras mexicanas, In: Actas, VI Congr, Asoc Int Hispanistas, 78. *Mailing Add:* Dept of Span Scripps Col Claremont CA 91711

LAMBASA, FRANK SLAVKO, b Sibenik-Dalmatia, Yugoslavia, Aug 10, 21; nat US; m 46. COMPARATIVE LITERATURE. *Educ:* State Univ Iowa, BA, 51, MA, 52 PhD(Ger), 54. *Prof Exp:* Instr Ger, Univ Mich, 54-59; from asst prof to assoc prof, 59-68, dir NDEA summer insts Ger, 64 & 65, chmn dept comp lit & lang, 68, PROF COMP LIT & LANG, HOFSTRA UNIV, 68-, DEPT REP FOR GER, 59- *Concurrent Pos:* Horace Rackham fel, 59; mem, NY Univ Sem to India, 67-68. *Mem:* MLA; Am Asn Teachers Ger; Cent States Mod Lang Teachers Asn. *Res:* Contemporary political drama in Germany. *Publ:* Auth, Franz Werfel, Univ Pittsburgh, 61; contribr, Encycl Europ Auth, Wilson, 67; George Sand Papers, AMS Press, 80. *Mailing Add:* Dept of Comp Lit & Lang Hofstra Univ Hempstead NY 11550

LAMBERT, L GARY, b Ogden, Utah, Nov 9, 37; m 61; c 5. FRENCH LANGUAGE & LITERATURE. *Educ:* Univ Calif, Berkeley, BA, 63; Univ Calif, Santa Barbara, MA, 65; Rice Univ, PhD(French lit), 69. *Prof Exp:* Asst prof, 69-73, ASSOC PROF FRENCH, BRIGHAM YOUNG UNIV, 73- *Mem:* Rocky Mountain Mod Lang Asn. *Res:* Eighteenth century French novel; French poetry; Jean-Jacques Rousseau. *Publ:* Auth, Richard Wagner vu par Baudelaire, Pac Northwest Conf Foreign Lang Proc, 4/71. *Mailing Add:* Dept of French & Ital 361 MCKB Brigham Young Univ Provo UT 84601

LAMBERT, ROY EUGENE, b Tacoma, Wash, Nov 16, 18; m 45; c 4. LINGUISTICS, CYBERNETICS. *Educ:* Univ Wash, BA, 49, MA, 50; Univ Ill, Urbana, PhD(philol), 57. *Prof Exp:* Asst prof English lit & ling, Tex Technol Col, 57-59; ASSOC PROF ENGLISH LIT & LING, UNIV FLA, 60-, CHMN DEPT CYBERNET, 72- *Mem:* MLA; NCTE. *Res:* Humanities. *Publ:* Coauth & ed, Twentieth Century Values, 70 & auth, Machines and Man in the 21st Century, 74, Mss Info. *Mailing Add:* 1403 NW 9th Ave Gainesville FL 32605

LAMBERTS, JACOB J, b Rochester, NY, July 3, 10; m 42; c 1. ENGLISH, LINGUISTICS. *Educ:* Calvin Col, BA, 31; Univ Mich, MA, 49, PhD, 54. *Prof Exp:* Teaching fel English, Univ Mich, 49-53; from instr to asst prof, Northwestern Univ, 53-60; assoc prof, 60-63, PROF ENGLISH, ARIZ

STATE UNIV, 63- *Concurrent Pos:* Vis lectr, Univ Minn, 58-59. *Mem:* MLA; Ling Soc Am; NCTE. *Res:* English grammar and usage; history of English language. *Publ:* Auth, A Short Introduction to English Usage, McGraw, 72. *Mailing Add:* 237 Broadmor Dr Tempe AZ 85282

LAMONT, ROSETTE C, b Paris, France; US citizen. FRENCH & COMPARATIVE LITERATURE. *Educ:* Hunter Col, BA, 47; Yale Univ, MA, 48, PhD, 54. *Prof Exp:* From tutor to assoc prof, 50-65, PROF FRENCH & COMP LIT, QUEENS COL, NY 65-, PROF PhD PROG FRENCH, GRAD CTR, CITY UNIV NEW YORK, 69-, PROF COMP LIT, 72- *Concurrent Pos:* Guggenheim fel, 73-74. *Honors & Awards:* Chevalier, Palmes Academiques, 72, Officier, 78. *Mem:* Am Asn Teachers Fr; MLA; Am Comp Lit Asn; Am Soc Theatre Res; PEN Club. *Res:* Symbolist poetry; modern drama; Proust. *Publ:* Auth, Death and tragi-comedy, Mass Rev, winter-spring 65; coauth, La farce pathaphysique, In: Saul Bellow, Gassett, Paris, 67; ed & auth, Ionesco, Prentice-Hall, 73; auth, Baudelaire's Reve Parisien: A space/time/dream poem, Centerpoint, fall 77; Yuri Zhivago's Fairy Tale: A dream poem, World Lit Today, autumn 77; An interview with Patrice Chereau, Educ Theatre J, 12/77; ed & auth, The Two Faces of Ionesco, Whitston, 78. *Mailing Add:* Dept of Comt Lit Grad Ctr City Univ of New York New York NY 10023

LAMSE, MARY JANE, b Grand Rapids, Mich. GERMAN LANGUAGE & LITERATURE. *Educ:* Calvin Col, BA, 62; Univ Mich, MA, 63, PhD(Ger), 69. *Prof Exp:* Lectr, 69-77 & 78-79, ASSOC PROF GER LANG, CALVIN COL, 80- *Concurrent Pos:* Fulbright fel Ger, 78-; vis asst prof Ger, Hope Col, 78. *Mem:* Am Soc 18th Century Studies; Am Asn Teachers Ger. *Res:* Hugo von Hofmannsthal; Heinrich Böll. *Mailing Add:* Dept of Ger Lang Calvin Col Grand Rapids MI 49506

LANCASTER, ALBERT LAKE, b Union, SC, Sept 17, 16; m 47; c 1. GERMAN PHILOLOGY. *Educ:* Wofford Col, AB, 37; Univ NC, AM, 40, PhD, 49. *Prof Exp:* Instr Ger & French, 40-42, asst prof mod lang, 46-47, assoc prof Ger, 49-55, PROF MOD LANG, VA MIL INST, 55-, HEAD DEPT, 61- *Mem:* MLA; Am Asn Teachers Ger. *Res:* Early new High German; German linguistics. *Mailing Add:* Dept of Mod Lang Va Mil Inst Lexington VA 24450

LANCASTER, PATRICIA ANNE, b Spartanburg, SC, May 12, 42; m 75. FRENCH, MODERN FRENCH THEATER. *Educ:* Coker Col, BA, 63; Emory Univ, MA, 70, PhD(French), 71. *Prof Exp:* Instr French, Clemson Univ, 66-67; asst prof, 70-75, co-dir summer studies prog in France, 72 & dir, 73, assoc prof, 75-80, PROF FRENCH, ROLLINS COL, 80- *Concurrent Pos:* Consult & translr, Martin-Marietta Aerospace, Orlando, Fla, 74-76; Arthur Vining Davis fel, 82. *Mem:* Southern Comp Lit Asn; MLA; AAUP; SAtlantic Mod Lang Asn. *Res:* French avant-garde theater, 20th century; French culture since 1850 (interdisciplinary). *Mailing Add:* Box 2700 Rollins Col Winter Park FL 32789

LANCE, BETTY RITA GOMEZ, b San Jose, Costa Rica, Aug 28, 23; US citizen. ROMANCE LANGUAGE & LITERATURE. *Educ:* Cent Mo State Col, BS, 44; Univ Mo, MA, 47; Wash Univ, PhD, 59. *Prof Exp:* Prof elem pub schs, Costa Rica, 41-42; instr Span, Univ Mo, 48-49; asst, Wash Univ, 55-59; instr Span, Univ Mo, 48-49; asst, Wash Univ, 55-59; instr Span, Univ Ill, 59-61; PROF SPAN LANG & LIT, KALMAZOO COL, 61- *Concurrent Pos:* Dir, Puerta de Oportunidad, 72-76. *Mem:* Am Asn Teachers Span & Port; Latin Am Studies Asn; Asn Lit Femenina Hispanica. *Res:* Agricultural chemistry research; 20th century Spanish; peninsular and Spanish American literatures. *Publ:* Auth, El indio y la naturaleza en los cuentos de Lopez-Albujar, Rev Iberoam, 60; Picarismo en las novelas de Juan Antonio Zunzunegui, Asomante, 63; Existe una promocion del cuarenta en el cuento puertorriqueno? Rev Iberoam, 64; Los cuentos de Rene Marques, La Universidad, 65; La actitud picaresca en la novela espanola del siglo XX, Ed B Costa-Amic, Mexico, DF, 69; Vivencias, Trejos Hnos, Costa Rica, 81. *Mailing Add:* Dept of Span Kalamazoo Col Kalamazoo MI 49001

LANCE, DONALD MAX, b Gainesville, Tex, July 10, 31. ENGLISH LINGUISTICS. *Educ:* Tex A&M Col, BA, 52; Univ Tex, Austin, MA, 62, PhD(English), 68. *Prof Exp:* Teacher English & Span, McCamey Pub Schs, Tex, 57-59 & Corpus Christi Pub Schs, Tex, 56-64; asst prof English, Tex A&M Univ, 67-69; from asst prof to assoc prof, 69-78, PROF ENGLISH LING, UNIV MO-COLUMBIA, 78- *Mem:* MLA; Ling Soc Am; Am Dialect Soc; Teachers English to Speakers Other Lang; NCTE. *Res:* Dialectology; applied linguistics; bilingualism. *Publ:* Co-ed, From Soundstream to Discourse, Ling Prog, Univ Mo, 71; auth, Whoever and Whomever, Lang Sci, 73; Dialectal and Nonstandard Forms in Texas Spanish & Spanish-English Code Swtiching, In: El Lenguaje de los Chicanos, Ctr Appl Ling, 74; coauth, The Use of the Computer in Plotting Dialect Boundaries, Comput & Humanities, 76. *Mailing Add:* Dept English Univ Mo Columbia MO 65201

LANDAR, HERBERT (JAY), b New York, NY, Dec 7, 27. LINGUISTICS. *Educ:* Queens Col, NY, BA, 49; Yale Univ, MA, 55, PhD(ling), 60. *Prof Exp:* Instr humanities, Reed Col, 57-58, instr humanities & ling, 58-59; from asst prof to assoc prof, 60-66, PROF ENGLISH, CALIF STATE UNIV, LOS ANGELES, 66- *Concurrent Pos:* Guggenheim fel, Eng Spain & France, 67-68; vis prof anthrop, Ind Univ, Bloomington, 76; Indonesia res, Univ Northern Sumatra, 79. *Mem:* Ling Soc Am; Am Anthrop Asn; Am Folklore Soc; Asn Comput Ling; Royal Anthrop Inst Gt Brit & Ireland. *Res:* Grammatical theory; language and culture; linguistic bibliography. *Publ:* Auth, Language and Culture, Oxford Univ, 66; The language of pain in Navaho culture, In: Studies in Southwestern Ethnolinguistics, 67 & Theme of incest in Navaja folklore, In: Man, Language and Society, 72, Mouton, The Hague; Kotoba-to Bunka, Taishukan, Tokyo, 77. *Mailing Add:* Dept of English Calif State Univ 5151 State University Dr Los Angeles CA 90032

LANDEIRA, RICARDO, b El Ferrol, Spain, Feb 25, 44; US citizen. SPANISH LITERATURE. *Educ:* Ariz State Univ, BA, 66, MA, 67; Ind Univ, PhD(Span & comp lit), 70. *Prof Exp:* Asst prof Span, Duke Univ, 70-72; Fulbright lectr English philol, Univ Santiago, 72-73; asst prof Span lit, Duke Univ, 73-76; assoc prof, 76-80, FULL PROF SPAN, UNIV WYO, 80- *Mem:* MLA; Am Asn Teachers Span & Port; Asoc Int Hispanistas. *Res:* Peninsular Spanish literature of the 19th and 20th century. *Publ:* Auth, Espronceda: Tres poemas narrativos, Rev Hisp Mod, 10/69; Machado en su poema, Mod Lang Notes, 3/71; Gabriel Miro: Trilogia de Siguenza, Ed Hispanofila, 72; Los encantadores de don Quijote, Anales Cervantinos, 1/74; Aura, the Aspern papers, a rose for Emily, JSSTC, 75; La desilusion poetica de Espronceda, BRAE, 75; auth, Ramiro de Maetzu, 78 & Jose de Espronceda, 82, Twayne. *Mailing Add:* Dept of Mod Class Lang Univ of Wyo Laramie WY 82071

LANE, EUGENE NUMA, b Washington, DC, Aug 13, 36; m 64; c 2. CLASSICS. *Educ:* Princeton Univ, AB, 58; Yale Univ, MA, 60, PhD(classics), 62. *Prof Exp:* Asst prof(classics), Univ Va, 62-66; assoc prof, 66-79, PROF CLASS LANG, UNIV MO-COLUMBIA, 80-- *Mem:* Am Philol Asn; Archaeol Inst Am. *Res:* Religious history of the Roman Empire. *Publ:* Auth, An unpublished inscription from Lakonia, Hesperia, 62; A restudy of the God Men, part I, Berytus, 15, parts II-III, Berytus, 17; A group of Steles from Byzantium, 3 & Two votive hands in Missouri, 4, Muse; Corpus monumentorum religionis dei menis, I, In: The Monuments and Inscriptions, Brill, Leiden, 71. *Mailing Add:* Dept of Class Studies 411 Gen Classroom Bldg Univ of Mo Columbia MO 65201

LANE, NANCY E, b Pittsburgh, Pa, Nov 12, 47. FRENCH LITERATURE, CONTEMPORARY DRAMA. *Educ:* Wittenberg Univ, BA, 69; Ind Univ, MA, 71, PhD(French), 76. *Prof Exp:* ASST PROF FRENCH, UNIV SC, 77- *Mem:* MLA; S Atlantic Mod Lang Asn; Am Asn Teachers French. *Res:* Modern French theatre; 17th century French literature. *Publ:* Auth, Homogenization of human and non-human elements in 20th Century French theatre, West Va Univ Philol Papers, fall 78. *Mailing Add:* Dept of Foreign Lang & Lit Univ of SC Columbia SC 29208

LANG, FREDERICK FRANK, b Brooklyn, NY, Mar 22, 30; m 59; c 8. GERMANIC LANGUAGE & LITERATURE. *Educ:* St John's Col, NY, BA, 51; Univ Wis, MA, 55. *Prof Exp:* Instr Ger, Manhattan Col, 58-61; ASST PROF GER, ST JOHN'S UNIV, NY, 61- *Concurrent Pos:* Instr Ger, NY Univ, 60-61. *Mem:* Am Asn Teachers Ger. *Res:* Gothic; Germanic linguistics. *Mailing Add:* Dept of Mod Foreign Lang St John's Univ Jamaica NY 11439

LANG, FREDERICK RICHARD, b Randolph, Ohio, July 13, 28. CLASSICAL STUDIES. *Educ:* Univ Mich, Ann Arbor, MA, 62; Pontif Inst Higher Latin Studies, Rome, BA, 66, MA, 67, PhD, 69. *Prof Exp:* Instr Latin, St Joseph's Col, Ind, 60-61, asst prof Latin & Greek, 62-63, assoc prof class studies, 64-76; assoc prof cult hist, Cardinal Newman Col, 77-78, acad dean, 78-81; LECTR CLASS LANG, ST JOSEPH'S COL, IND, 82- *Mem:* Class Asn Midwest & S. *Res:* Latin philosophical and psychological terminology; Greek derivatives in English. *Publ:* Auth, Greek-English Derivatives, Pamphlet-privately publ, 65; Psychological terminology in the Tusculans, J Hist Behav Sci, 72. *Mailing Add:* St Joseph's Col Rensselaer IN 47979

LANG, MABEL LOUISE, b Utica, NY, Nov 12, 17. CLASSICAL PHILOLOGY. *Educ:* Cornell Univ, AB, 39, Bryn Mawr Col, AM, 40, PhD, 43. *Hon Degrees:* LittD, Holy Cross Col, 75, Colgate Univ, 78. *Prof Exp:* From instr to assoc prof class philol, 43-59, actg dean, 58-59 & 60-61, PROF GREEK, BRYN MAWR COL, 59- *Concurrent Pos:* Fulbright res grant, Greece, 59-60; chmn comt admis & fels, Am Sch Class Studies, Athens, 67-72, chmn managing comt, 75-80; Blegen Distinguished Vis Res prof, Vassar Col, 76-77; Martin lectr, Oberlin Col, 82. *Mem:* Archaeol Inst Am; Am Philol Asn; Am Philos Soc. *Res:* Greek history, literature and epigraphy. *Publ:* Auth, Pylos tablets, 1957-1962, Am J Archaeol, 58-63; The Athenian Citizen, 60 & Weights and Measures of the Athenian Agora, 64, Am Sch Class Studies, Athens; The palace of Nestor, Vol II, In: The Frescoes, Princeton Univ, 68; The Athenian Agora, XXI, Graffiti and Dipinti, 76 & Socrates in the Agora, 78, Am Sch Class Studies, Athens. *Mailing Add:* Dept of Greek Bryn Mawr Col Bryn Mawr PA 19010

LANGACKER, RONALD WAYNE, b Fond du Lac, Wis, Dec 27, 42; m 66. LINGUISTICS. *Educ:* Univ Ill, AB, 63, AM, 64, PhD(ling), 66. *Prof Exp:* From asst prof to assoc prof, 66-76, PROF LING, UNIV CALIF, SAN DIEGO, 76- *Concurrent Pos:* Assoc ed, Language 71-77; Nat Endowment for Humanities sr fel, 73-74; Guggenheim fel, 78-79. *Mem:* Ling Soc Am; AAUP. *Res:* Linguistic theory; Uto-Aztecan languages. *Publ:* Auth, Language and Its Structure, Harcourt, 68; On pronominalization and the chain of command, In: Modern Studies in English, Prentice-Hall, 69; The vowels of proto Uto-Aztecan, Int J Am Ling, 70; ed, Introduction to the Luiseno Language, Malki Mus, 71; auth, Fundamentals of Linguistic Analysis, Harcourt, 72; Non-distinct arguments in Uto-Aztecan, Univ Calif Press, 76; An overview of Uto-Aztecan grammar, Summer Inst Ling & Univ Tex, Arlington, 77; Space grammar, analysability, and the English passive, Language, 82. *Mailing Add:* Dept of Ling Univ of Calif San Diego La Jolla CA 92037

LANGDON, DAVID JEFFREY, b Newport, Eng. FRENCH LITERATURE, PHILOSOPHY. *Educ:* Oxford Univ, BA, 56; Univ BC, PhD(French lit), 70. *Prof Exp:* ASST PROF FRENCH, UNIV ALTA, 70- *Mem:* Soc Fr Etude XVIIIe Siecle. *Res:* The moral and social thought of Diderot; the French philosophers of the 18th century. *Publ:* Auth, Interpolations in the Encyclopedie article Liberte, Studies Voltaire & 18th Century, 77. *Mailing Add:* 1155 73 Ave Edmonton AB T6G 0C5 Can

LANGDON, MARGARET HOFFMANN, b Louvain, Belg, Apr 24, 26; US citizen; m 64; c 1. LINGUISTICS, AMERICAN INDIAN LANGUAGES. *Educ:* Univ Calif, Berkeley, AB, 62, PhD(ling), 66. *Prof Exp:* Actg asst prof, 65-66, asst prof, 66-72, assoc prof, 72-79, PROF LING, UNIV CALIF, SAN DIEGO, 80- *Concurrent Pos:* Fel ed bd, Romance Philol, 65-67; Am Philos Soc Phillips Found grant, 67-68. *Mem:* Ling Soc Am; Am Anthrop Asn; Ling

Asn Gt Brit; Ling Soc Europe. *Res:* Yuman languages; language and culture; historical linguistics. *Publ:* Auth, A general linguist's view of word formation in Middle French, Romance Philol, 8/64. *Mailing Add:* Dept of Ling Univ of Calif San Diego La Jolla CA 92037

LANGE, VICTOR, b Leipzig, Ger, July 13, 08; m 45; c 2. GERMAN LITERATURE. *Educ:* Univ Toronto, MA, 31; Univ Leipzig, PhD, 34. *Hon Degrees:* DHL, Monterey Inst Foreign Studies, 78. *Prof Exp:* Dir Akad Auslandsstelle, Leipzig, 31-32; lectr Ger, Univ Col, Univ Toronto, 32-38; from asst prof to prof Ger & chmn Ger Studies, Cornell Univ, 38-57; prof, 57-77, John N Woodhull prof mod lang, 68-77, EMER PROF GER LIT & CHMN GER STUDIES, PRINCETON UNIV, 77- *Concurrent Pos:* Examr in chief Ger, Col Entrance Exam Bd, 42-50, advan placement prog, 57-66; vis prof, Smith Col, Univ Chicago, Univ Calif, Univ Cologne, Univ Heidelberg, Columbia Univ, Yale Univ, Melbourne Univ & Univ Mich; vis prof, Free Univ Berlin, 60 & 62, hon prof Ger lit, 63-; Guggenheim fels, 50-51 & 67-68; mem, Deut Akad Sprache u Dichtung, Darmstadt, Ger, 55; trustee, Goethe House, NY; co-ed, Comp Lit & Germanistik; McCosh fel, 67-68. *Honors & Awards:* Bundesverdienst-kreuz, 58. *Mem:* MLA (1st vpres, 56); Nat Carl Schurz Asn; Int Germanic Studies (pres, 65-70); Am Soc Eighteenth Century (pres, 76); Goethe Soc NAm (pres, 78-83). *Res:* Comparative literature; history of criticism. *Publ:* Ed, Goethe: Twentieth Century Views, McGraw, 69; Humanistic Scholarship in America, Princeton Univ Press, 69; auth, Language as the Topic of Fiction, In: Festschrift E Stahl, Clarendon, 70; ed, J C Wezel: Tobias Knaut, Metzler, 72; auth, Goethe: Weltiteratur und Nationalliteratur, In: Goethe Jahrbuch, Boehlau, 72; Thomas Mann: Tradition and Experiment, Univ Calif, Davis, 77; contribr, Introduction to Contemporary German Criticism, 79 & co-ed (with R Amacher) & introd to New Perspectives in German Literary Criticism, 79, Princeton Univ Press; The Classical Age of German Literature, Arnold, London, 82. *Mailing Add:* 343 Jefferson Rd Princeton NJ 08540

LANGEBARTEL, WILLIAM WINTER, b Quincy, Ill, Feb 17, 16; m 46. GERMANIC PHILOLOGY. *Educ:* Univ Ill, AB, 37; Univ Wis, AM, 38; Univ Pa, PhD, 48. *Prof Exp:* Teaching asst Ger, Univ Ill, 38-39; asst instr, Univ Pa, 45-46; instr mod lang, Carnegie Inst Technol, 46-47; from instr to asst prof Ger & Russ, 47-73, assoc prof, 73-79, PROF GER & RUSS, TEMPLE UNIV, 80-, CHMN DEPT, 72- *Concurrent Pos:* Instr, Res Lab, Westinghouse Elec Corp, 47; ed, Bull, Am Asn Teachers Slavic & East Europ Lang, 48-53. *Mem:* Ling Soc Am; MLA; Am Asn Teachers Slavic & East Europ Lang (secy-treas, 49-53); Am Asn Teachers Ger; Soc Advan Scand Studies. *Res:* Alamannic dialects; Old Icelandic; Russian language and literature. *Publ:* Auth, Rudolf von Tavel, Swiss Rec. *Mailing Add:* Dept Ger & Russ Temple Univ Philadelphia PA 19122

LANGENDOEN, DONALD TERENCE, b Paterson, NJ, June 7, 39. LINGUISTICS, ENGLISH. *Educ:* Mass Inst Technol, SB, 61, PhD(ling), 64. *Prof Exp:* From asst prof to assoc prof ling, Ohio State Univ, 64-69; PROF ENGLISH, BROOKLYN COL, CITY UNIV NEW YORK, 69-, PROF LING, GRAD CTR, 71- *Concurrent Pos:* Vis assoc prof, Rockefeller Univ, 68-69; sr Fulbright lectr, Rijksuniv Utrecht, The Neth, 77; co-ed, Lang & Thought Ser, Harvard Univ Press, 78- *Mem:* Fel NY Acad Sci; Ling Soc Am; Asn Comput Ling. *Res:* English syntax; linguistic theory; psycholinguistics. *Publ:* Auth, The Study of Syntax, 69, Essentials of English Grammar, 70 & coed, Studies in Linguistic Semantics, 71, Holt; coed, An Integrated Theory of Linguistic Ability, Crowell, 76. *Mailing Add:* PhD Prog Ling Grad Sch City Univ New York New York NY 10036

LANGER, LAWRENCE L, Literature. See Vol II

LANGER, ULLRICH GERT, b Kennewick, Wash, Mar 10, 54. FRENCH LITERATURE. *Educ:* Univ Wash, BA, 73, MA, 75; Princeton Univ, 80. *Prof Exp:* ASST PROF FRENCH, BRYN MAWR COL, 80- *Mem:* Renaissance Soc Am; MLA. *Res:* Renaissance lyric poetry, Ronsard to Malherbe; psychoanalytic approaches to literary history; rhetoric and literature. *Publ:* Auth, La poudre a canon et la transgression poetique: L'Elegie du verre de Ronsard, Romanic Rev, 3/82; Rhetorique et intersubjectivite: Les Tragiques d'Agrippa d'Aubigne, Papers Fr 17th Century Lit, 10/82. *Mailing Add:* Dept of French Bryn Mawr Col Bryn Mawr PA 19010

LANGLOIS, WALTER G, b Springfield, Mass, May 27, 25; m 59; c 2. ROMANCE LANGUAGES. *Educ:* Yale Univ, BA, 50, MA, 52, PhD(17th century theatre), 55; Ecole Prof Francais a l'Etranger, Univ Paris, Dipl, 49. *Prof Exp:* Instr French & Ital, Univ Wis, 54-56; prof, Lycee Sisowath, Phnom Penh, Cambodia, 56-57; asst prof French & Asian studies, Boston Col, 57-64; from assoc prof to prof French, Univ Ky, 64-74, dir grad studies French, 65-67, interim chmn dept, 69; head dept, 74-77, PROF FRENCH MOD & CLASS LANG, UNIV WYO, 74- *Concurrent Pos:* Smith-Mundt grant, Cambodia, 56-57; fel Asian studies, Harvard Univ, 60-61; Guggenheim fel, 67-68; Am Coun Learned Soc fel, 72; ed, Malraux Miscellany; Nat Endowment for Humanities sr fel, 80-81. *Mem:* Am Asn Teachers Fr; MLA; Manuscript Soc (vpres); Malraux Soc; Am Comp Lit Asn. *Res:* Andre Malraux; 20th century French novel; Asian literature in translation. *Publ:* Auth, Andre Malraux: L'aventure Indochinoise, Mercure de France, Paris, 67; ed, The Persistent Voice: Hellinism in French Literature Since the 18th Century, NY Univ, 71; auth, Malraux Criticism in English, 1924-1970, 72, ed, Malraux: du farfelu aux Antimemoires, 72, Malraux: visages du romancier, 73 & Malraux: influences et affinites, 75, Minard, Paris; auth, Andre Malraux: Biographical Essays, Hofstra Univ Press, 78; ed, Malraux et l'art, 78 & Malraux et l'histoire, 82, Minard, Paris. *Mailing Add:* Dept of Mod & Class Lang Box 3603 Univ of Wyo Laramie WY 82071

LANHAM, CAROL DANA, b Englewood, NJ, Jan 18, 36; m 57. CLASSICS. *Educ:* Conn Col, AB, 57; Univ Calif, Los Angeles, MA, 68, PhD(classics), 73. *Prof Exp:* Asst classics, Univ Calif, Los Angeles, 69, assoc, 71-72; asst prof, Brown Univ, 73-74; SR ED, CTR MEDIEVAL & RENAISSANCE STUDIES, UNIV CALIF, LOS ANGELES, 75- *Mem:* Am Philol Asn; Philol Asn Pac Coast; Medieval Asn of Pac. *Res:* Latin language and literature; medieval Latin. *Publ:* Auth, Enjambement in the Annales of Ennius, Mnemosyne, 70; The bastard at the family reunion: Classics and medieval Latin, Class J, 75; Salutatio Formulas in Latin Letters to 1200: Syntax, Style, and Theory, Arbeo-Gesellschaft, 75; coauth, Zu den neugefundenen Salzburger Formelbuchern und Briefen, Eranos, 75; More on teaching medieval Latin, Class J, 80; (with Carol D Larham), Renaissance and Renewal in the Twelth Century, Harvard Univ Press (in prep). *Mailing Add:* Ctr Medieval & Renaissance Studies Univ of Calif Los Angeles CA 90024

LANIUS, EDWARD W, b York, Pa, Nov 11, 35. ROMANCE LANGUAGES. *Educ:* Dickinson Col, AB, 57; Middlebury Col, AM, 58; Univ Pa, PhD(Romance lang), 64. *Prof Exp:* Instr French, Trinity Col, Conn, 62-64; asst prof, Univ Va, 64-67; asst prof, 67-79, ASSOC PROF FRENCH, UNIV MIAMI, 80- *Mem:* MLA. *Res:* Spanish literature; French literature of the 17th century; 16th century literature, especially Jean Lemaire de Belges and the grands Rhetoriqueurs. *Publ:* Auth, Cyrano de Bergerac and the Universe of the Imagination, Droz, Geneva, 67; Sense of group and accommodation in Rabelais's Comic universe, Zeitschrift für Romanische Philol 73; Lemaire de Belges' use of history is Les illustrations de Gaule et singularitez de Troye, Romanische Forsch, 73. *Mailing Add:* Dept of Foreign Lang Univ of Miami Coral Gables FL 33124

LANSING, RICHARD HEWSON, b Rochester, NY, May 14, 43; m 72. ITALIAN & COMPARATIVE LITERATURE. *Educ:* Columbia Col, NY, AB, 65; Univ Calif, Berkeley, MA, 67, PhD(comp lit), 72. *Prof Exp:* Teaching asst Ital, Univ Calif, Berkeley, 67-69, assoc, 69-70, actg instr comp lit, 70-71; asst prof, 72-78, ASSOC PROF ITAL & COMP LIT & CHMN DEPT COMP LIT, BRANDEIS UNIV, 78- *Concurrent Pos:* Mabelle McLeod Lewis mem fund grant, 72. *Mem:* MLA; Dante Soc Am; Mediaeval Acad Am; Am Asn Univ Prof Ital; Am Asn Teachers Ital. *Res:* Dante; comparative medieval literature; epic and romance. *Publ:* Auth, Two similes: The shipwrecked swimmer and Elijah's ascent, Romance Philol, 74; Submerged meanings in Dante's similes, Dante Studies, 76; Stylistic and structural duality in Manzoni's I Promessi Sposi, Italica, 75; From Image to Idea: A Study of the Simile in Dante's Commedia, Longo, Ravenna, 77; The structure of meaning in Lampedusa's Il Gattopardo, PMLA, 5/78; Dante's unfolding vision, approaches to teaching Dante's divine comedy, MLA, 82. *Mailing Add:* Dept of Romance & Comp Lit Brandeis Univ Waltham MA 02154

LANTOLF, JAMES PAUL, b Scranton, Pa, Nov 24, 47; m 71; c 2. LINGUISTICS, SPANISH. *Educ:* Univ Scranton, BS, 69; Pa State Univ, MA, 71, PhD(ling), 74. *Prof Exp:* Asst prof Span & ling, State Univ NY Col Geneseo, 74-77 & Univ Tex, San Antonio, 77-80; ASSOC PROF LING, UNIV DEL, 80- *Concurrent Pos:* Chmn exec comt applied ling, MLA. *Mem:* Am Asn Applied Ling; Teachers English to Speakers Others Lang; Ling Asn Can & US; MLA; Am Asn Teachers Span & Port. *Res:* Second language learning and teaching; Spanish language in the United States. *Publ:* Auth, On Teaching Intonation, Mod Lang J, 76; Aspects of Change in Foreign Language Study, Mod Lang J, 77; Evolution Change in Syntax: Speculations on Interrogative Word Order in Puerto Rican Spanish, In: Proc of the Eighth Annual Linguistic Symmposium on the Romance Languages, Newbury House, 78; co-ed, Colloqium on Hispanic and Luso-Brazilian Linguistics, Georgetown Univ, 79; auth, Explaining Linguistic Change: The Loss of Voicing in the Old Spanish Sibilants, Orbis, 79; Information Structure and Pragmatics in Spanish Discourse, In: The Sixth LACUS Forum 1979, Hornbeam Press, 80; co-ed, Current Research in Romance Languages, IULC, 82. *Mailing Add:* Dept Lang & Lit Univ of Del Newark DE 19711

LANZINGER, KLAUS, b Woergl, Austria, Feb 16, 28; nat US; m 54; c 2. AMERICAN & GERMAN LITERATURE. *Educ:* Bowdoin Col, BA, 51; Univ Innsbruck, PhD(English, Am lit & hist), 52. *Prof Exp:* Asoc prof, 67-77, PROF GERMAN, UNIV NOTRE DAME, 77- *Concurrent Pos:* Fulbright res fel, Univ Pa & Huntington Libr, San Marino, Calif, 61; res dir, Study Prog Innsbruck, Univ Notre Dame, 69-71, 76-78 & 82-84. *Mem:* MLA; Deutsche Gesellschaft fur Amerikastudien; Thomas Wolfe Soc. *Res:* Herman Melville and Thomas Wolfe; 19th century and early 20th century American novel; American European literary relations--comparative approach. *Publ:* Auth, Primitivismus und Naturalismus im Prosaschaffen Herman Melvilles, Wagner, Innsbruck, 59; Unterschiede im Gebrauch von slave, seiner Wortfamilie und Sinnverwandten, In: Jahrbuch fur Amerikastudien, Vol 7, 92-105; Die Epik im amerikanischen Roman: Eine Studie zu James F Cooper, Herman Melville, Frank Norris und Thomas Wolfe, Moritz Diesterweg, Frankfurt, 65; Die Entstehung des grossen amerikanischen Romans bei Thomas Wolfe, Studium Generale, Vol 21, 36-48; ed, Americana-Austriaca, Am Studies Series (5 vols), 66-80. *Mailing Add:* 52703 Helvie Dr South Bend IN 46635

LAO, YAN-SHUAN, b Peking, China, Jan 14, 34; m 62; c 2. CHINESE LANGUAGE, LITERATURE & HISTORY. *Educ:* Taiwan Univ, BA, 55; Harvard Univ, PhD, 62. *Prof Exp:* Asst prof Chinese, Univ Wash, 63-68; ASSOC PROF CHINESE LANG & LIT, OHIO STATE UNIV, 68- *Mem:* Am Orient Soc. *Res:* Chinese institutional history, traditional period; Chinese prose and bibliography. *Publ:* Auth, Korean slaves and other comparable groups during the Yüan Dynasty, In: Symposium in Honor of Dr Li Chi, 67 & Notes on non-Chinese terms in the Yüan dietary compendium Yin-shan cheng-yao, In: Symposium in Honor of Dr Li Fnag-kuei, 69, Acad Sinica. *Mailing Add:* 1341 Langston Dr Columbus OH 43220

LAPIERRE, ANDRE, Can citizen. FRENCH & FRENCH-CANADIAN LINGUISTICS. *Educ:* Univ Ottawa, BA, 64, MA, 68; Univ Strasbourg, PhD(ling), 72. *Prof Exp:* Lectr French, 66-69, asst prof ling, 72-82, ASSOC PROF LING, UNIV OTTAWA, 82- *Concurrent Pos:* Book rev ed, Onomastica, 81- *Mem:* Can Soc Study Names (pres, 82-); Am Name Soc; Can Ling Asn. *Res:* North American French place-names; French and French Canadian lexicology and dialectology. *Publ:* Auth, Quelques aspects quantitatifs de la conjugaison en francais contemporain, Le francais moderne, 74; Situation du francais ontarien, Protee, 79; L'orthographe de la langue maternelle: le cas des Franco-Ontariens, Can Mod Lang J, 79; Le Manuel de l'abbe Thomas Maguire et la langue quebecoise au XIXe siecle, Rev hist Am francaise, 81; Toponymie francaise en Ontario, Etudes vivantes, Montreal, 81; ed, L'Ontario francais du sud-ouest: temoignages oraux, Univ Ottawa Press, 82. *Mailing Add:* Dept of Ling Univ of Ottawa Ottawa ON K1N 6N5 Can

LAPPERT, STEPHEN FREDERICK, Old & Middle English, Philology. See Vol II

LAPPIN, JOHN EUGENE, b New York, NY, Sept 27, 35. FRENCH, ENGLISH. *Educ:* Cath Univ Am, BA, 58, MA, 61; Harvard Univ, PhD(Romance lang), 75. *Prof Exp:* Asst headmaster, Col Notre Dame, Ethiopia, 67-70; teaching fel French, Dept Romance Lang, Harvard Univ, 71-75; asst prof French & English, Pa State Univ, Scranton Campus, 75-76; DEPT CHMN LANG, NEWPORT COL-SALVE REGINA, 76- *Concurrent Pos:* Fac consult French, Pa State Univ, 75-76. *Mem:* MLA; Am Asn Teachers Fr. *Res:* French Romanticism's origins; comparative literature and cultures; Middle Eastern literature and culture. *Publ:* Auth, The Anabase of Saint-John Perse, Cath Univ, 61; Notes on language and literature, 62 & Academic interest diagnostic profile, 64, privately publ, Ethiopia; The Queen of Sheba in Literature, Harvard Univ, 75; ed, Handbook of Standard American English, Franklin/SRC, 77; auth, Writing skills for administration personnel, 78 & ed, Missions, goals, and objectives, 78, Newport Col-Salve Regina; auth, Educating for the eighties, Newport Mag, spring 78. *Mailing Add:* Newport Col-Salve Regina Ochre Point Ave Newport RI 02840

LAPRADE, JOHN HARRY, b Ft Worth, Tex, Aug 26, 32; m 53; c 2. SPANISH. *Educ:* Southern Methodist Univ, BA, 53; Univ NC, Chapel Hill, MA, 59, PhD(Romance lang), 63. *Prof Exp:* From instr to asst prof, 60-68, ASSOC PROF SPAN, SOUTHERN METHODIST UNIV, 68- *Mem:* Am Asn Teachers Span & Port; SCent Mod Lang Asn; SAtlantic Mod Lang Asn; MLA; AAUP. *Res:* Cervantes; Spanish drama; Spanish syntax. *Mailing Add:* Dept of Foreign Lang & Lit Southern Methodist Univ Dallas TX 75275

LAPUENTE, FELIPE ANTONIO, ROMANCE LANGUAGES, PHILOSOPHY. *Educ:* Univ Madrid, MA, 59; St Louis Univ, PhD(Span & philos), 68. *Prof Exp:* Asst prof Romance lang, Univ Mo-Columbia, 66-70; assoc prof, 70-79, PROF SPAN & CLASS, MEMPHIS STATE UNIV, 80-- *Mem:* MLA; Am Asn Teachers Span & Port. *Res:* Spanish thinkers; relationship of literature and philosophy; 20th century peninsular Spanish poetry and essay. *Publ:* Auth, Estudios hispanicos en Mo, 68 & La critica norteamerica frente e Cela, 71, Bol de filol esp; coauth, Diccionario de seud onimos literarios espanoles, Gredos, Madrid, 77. *Mailing Add:* Dept of Foreign Lang Memphis State Univ Memphis TN 38152

LAREW, LEONOR A, b New York, NY, May 29, 25; m 51; c 1. FOREIGN LANGUAGES. *Educ:* NY Univ, BSJ, 46, MA, 50; Univ Mo, PhD, 60. *Prof Exp:* Instr Span, Univ Tenn, 50-51; teacher English, Knoxville Eve High Sch, 51-53; teacher, Spring Gel Sch, 54-55; teacher Span, Hamden High Sch, 55-56; PROF SPAN, STATE UNIV NY COL GENESEO, 60- *Concurrent Pos:* Prof English, St George's Col, Santiago, Chile, 68; Delta Kappa Gamma res grant, 72; assoc ed, Hispania. *Mem:* Am Asn Teachers Span & Port. *Res:* Methods of teaching foreign languages. *Publ:* Auth, Foreign languages in the elementary school, Elem Sch J, 3/61; Optimum age for the initiation of foreign language, Mod Lang J, 5/61; Teach poetry to your high school students, Hispania, 12/62. *Mailing Add:* Dept of Foreign Lang State Univ of NY Col Geneseo NY 14454

LARIVIERE, RICHARD WILFRED, b Chicago, Ill, Jan 27, 50; m 71. SANSKRIT, INDOLOGY. *Educ:* Univ Iowa, BA, 72; Univ Pa, PhD(Sanskrit), 78. *Prof Exp:* Vis lectr Sanskrit, Univ Pa, 78-79; vis asst prof, Univ Iowa, 80-81; ASST PROF SANSKRIT, UNIV TEX, AUSTIN, 82- *Concurrent Pos:* Fel, Fulbright-Hays, 76-77, Am Inst Indian Studies, 76-77 & 80, Soc Sci Res Coun, 79 & Nat Endowment for Humanities, 79-83; panelist, National Endowment for Humanities, 80. *Mem:* Am Orient Soc; Asn Asian Studies; Royal Asiatic Soc; Bhandarkar Orient Res Inst; Asiatic Soc Bengel. *Res:* Classical Indian culture and philosophy; classical and modern Hindu law; history of religions. *Publ:* Auth, The Indian Supreme Court and the freedom of religion, J Const & Parliamentary Studies, 75; A note on the kosadivya, Adyar Libr Bull, 76; Madhyamamimamsa--The Sankarsakanda, Wiener fur die Kunde Sudasiens, 81; Ordeals in India and Europe, J Am Orient Soc, 81; The Divy tattva of Raghunandana Bhattacarya: Ordeals in Hindu Law, Manohar, New Delhi, 81; The judicial wager in Hindu law, Ann Bhandarkar Orient Res Inst (in press); Asedha and akrosa--Arrest in the Sarasvativilasa, Festschrift J D M Derret (in press); A compilation of Pitamaha verses found in two manuscripts from Nepal, Studien zur Indologie & Iranistik (in press). *Mailing Add:* Dept of Orient & African Lang & Lit Univ of Tex Austin TX 78712

LARKIN, JAMES BRIAN, b Milwaukee, Wis, June 17, 29; m 56; c 3. SPANISH. *Educ:* Univ Wis-Madison, BSEd, 52, MA, 53; Stanford Univ, PhD(Span), 66. *Prof Exp:* From instr to asst prof foreign lang, Pac Univ, 58-61; asst prof 61-67, assoc prof, 67-80, PROF SPAN, COE COL, 80- *Concurrent Pos:* Consult, Nat Endowment for Humanities, 77- *Mem:* Mid-West Mod Lang Asn; AAUP; MLA; Am Asn Teachers Span & Port. *Res:* Spanish language, medieval through 15th century; Spanish literature, especially medieval; the Golden Age. *Publ:* Auth, How credible is the credibility gap?, Hispania, 5/74; Avellaneda versus Cervantes: Rival or unwitting accomplice?, Papers Lang & Lit, summer 76; ed, Alfonso Martinez de Toledo's Atalaya de las Coronicas, Hispanic Sem Medieval Studies, Univ Wis-Madison (in press). *Mailing Add:* Box 7 Hickok Coe Col Cedar Rapids IA 52402

LARKIN, NEIL MATTHEW, b Milwaukee, Wis, Dec 19, 36. ROMANCE LANGUAGES & LITERATURES. *Educ:* Trinity Col, Conn, BA, 58; Johns Hopkins Univ, MA, 62, PhD(Romance philol), 69. *Prof Exp:* Instr French lit, Univ Rochester, 63-65, asst prof French, 65-70, ASSOC PROF FRENCH, UNIV RICHMOND, 70- *Mem:* MLA; Dante Soc Am; AAUP; Mediaeval Acad Am; Renaissance Soc Am. *Res:* French literature of 16th and 17th centuries; autobiography; aesthetics. *Publ:* Auth, Another look at Dante's Frog and Mouse, 62 & Inferno XXIII, 4-9 again, 66, Mod Lang Notes; Montaibne's Last Words, L'Esprit Createur, 75. *Mailing Add:* Dept of Mod Foreign Lang Univ of Richmond Richmond VA 23173

LARKINS, JAMES EDWARD, b Findlay, Ohio, Mar 19, 33; m 55; c 2. SPANISH. *Educ:* Miami Univ, AB, 55; Ohio State Univ, MA, 61, PhD(Span), 66. *Prof Exp:* Asst Span, Ohio State Univ, 59-61, instr, 62-64; instr Span & French, Miami Univ, Dayton Campus, 64-66; asst prof, 66-71, ASSOC PROF SPAN, WRIGHT STATE UNIV, 71- *Mem:* Am Asn Teachers Span & Port. *Res:* Twentieth century Spanish novel; Spanish culture; second language learning. *Publ:* Coauth, Non-semantic auditory discrimination: Foundation for second language learning, Mod Lang J, 4/72; Improving auditory discrimination for beginning Spanish students, Hispania, 12/75; Children in the early fiction of Juan Goytisolo, Memorias del Cuarto Congreso de Literatureas Hispanicas, Ind Univ, 78; The mythical aspect of death in the world of the Romancero Gitano, In: The world of nature in the works of Federico Garcia Lorca, Winthrop Col, 80; Myth upon myth: Five animals of the Romancero Gitano, Hispania, 3/81. *Mailing Add:* 550 Rising Hill Dr Fairborn OH 45324

LAROCHE, ROLAND ARTHUR, b Berlin, NH, Mar 4, 43; m 65; c 3. CLASSICS. *Educ:* Boston Col, BA, 65; Tufts Univ, MA, 66, PhD(classics), 72. *Prof Exp:* Teacher French, Latin & Greek, Pingree Sch, S Hamilton, Mass, 66-70; asst prof classics, State Univ NY, Potsdam, 70-77; teacher Latin & French, Cheshire Acad, Conn, 77-81; TEACHER LATIN & GREEK & CHMN, FOREIGN LANG DEPT, ALBANY ACAD, 81- *Mem:* Am Class League; Class Asn Atlantic States. *Res:* Greek and Roman numerical practices; Livy; early Roman historiography. *Publ:* Auth, Numerical inconsistencies at Livy: XXXIII, 10, 7-10: A possible explanation, Classica et Mediaevalia, 77; Valerius Antias and his numerical totals: A reappraisal, Historia, 77; The Albany King-list in Dionysius I, 70-71: A numerical analysis, Historia, 82; Early Roman history: Its schematic nature, Studies Latin Lit & Roman Hist, 82. *Mailing Add:* Albany Acad Albany NY 12210

LARSEN, ANNE RICKIE, b Lahore, Pakistan, Feb 28, 50; US citizen; m 73. FRENCH. *Educ:* Hope Col, BA, 70; Columbia Univ, MA, 71, PhD, 75. *Prof Exp:* Instr, 74-75, ASST PROF FRENCH, COLGATE UNIV, 75- *Mem:* Am Asn Teachers Fr; MLA. *Res:* Sixteenth century French literature; 18th century French literature. *Publ:* Auth, Ethical mutability in four of Diderot's tales, Studies Voltaire & 18th Century, 73; Ronsard's treatment of death in Sur Lamor de Marie and Les Derniers Sers, Univ SFla Lang Quart (in press). *Mailing Add:* Dept of French Colgate Univ Hamilton NY 13346

LARSON, CHARLES RAYMOND, Literature, Creative Writing. See Vol II

LARSON, DONALD NORMAN, b Chicago, Ill, Nov 1, 25; m 49; c 3. LINGUISTICS, ANTHROPOLOGY. *Educ:* Wheaton Col, BA, 49; Univ Chicago, MA, 57, PhD(ling), 65. *Prof Exp:* Assoc prof Greek & ling, Trinity Col, 49-61; dir ling, Interchurch Lang Sch, 61-63; spec secy-transl ling, Am Bible Soc, 63-66; PROF LING & ANTHROP, BETHEL COL, MINN, 66- *Concurrent Pos:* Dir studies, Toronto Inst Ling, 57-; consult, Foreign Mission Bd, Southern Baptist Convention, 67- & Union Lang Sch, Bangkok, 72-73; assoc missiology, Gospel in Context, 78. *Mem:* Ling Soc Am; fel Am Anthrop Asn. *Res:* Applied linguistics; cross-cultural communication; second language learning. *Publ:* Auth, Structural Approach to Greek, Lincoln Col, 58; Philippine Lang Scene, Interchurch Lang Sch, 63; coauth, Becoming Bilingual, William Carey, 72. *Mailing Add:* 3570 N Rice St St Paul MN 55112

LARSON, DONALD ROY, b International Falls, Minn, May 20, 35. SPANISH LITERATURE. *Educ:* Harvard Univ, AB, 57, AM, 62, PhD(Romance lang & lit), 67. *Prof Exp:* Instr Span, Princeton Univ, 62-65; from actg asst prof to asst prof, Univ Calif, Berkeley, 65-73; ASSOC PROF ROMANCE LANGS, OHIO STATE UNIV, 73-, CHMN DEPT, 78- *Concurrent Pos:* Vis assoc prof Hisp lang, State Univ NY, Stony Brook, 77-78. *Mem:* MLA. *Res:* Spanish theater of the Golden Age; modern Spanish poetry. *Publ:* Contribr, Lope de Vega Studies: 1937-1962, Univ Toronto, 64; auth, Los Comendadores de Cordoba: An early honor play, In: Homenaje a William L Fichter, Castalia, 71; La Dama Boba and the comic sense of life, Romanische Forschungen, 73; The Honor Plays of Lope de Vega, Harvard Univ, 77. *Mailing Add:* Dept of Romance Lang Ohio State Univ Columbus OH 43210

LARSON, ROSS, b Gravenhurst, Ont, Apr 12, 35. LATIN AMERICAN LITERATURE. *Educ:* Univ Toronto, BA, 59, MA, 62, PhD(Span-Am lit), 73. *Prof Exp:* Asst prof, 68-73, ASSOC PROF SPAN-AM LIT, CARLETON UNIV, 74-, CHMN DEPT, 76- *Concurrent Pos:* Can Coun leave fel, 75-76. *Mem:* Inst Int Lit Iberoam; Am Asn Teachers Span & Port; MLA; Can Asn Hispanists; Can Asn Latin Am Studies. *Res:* Modern and contemporary Latin American novel; short fiction. *Publ:* Auth, La literaturea hispanoamericana en las tesis doctorales de los Estados Unidos, Anales de la Univ de Chile, 1-3/65; La evolucion textual de Huasipungo de Jorge Icaza, Rev Iberoam, 7-12/65; La vision realista de Juan Jose Arreola, Cuadernos Am, 7-8/70; La literatura de ciencia-ficcion en Mexico, Cuadernos Hispanoam, 2/74; Fantasy and Imagination in the Mexican Narrative, Ctr Latin Am Studies, Ariz State Univ, 77. *Mailing Add:* Dept of Span Carleton Univ Ottawa ON K1S 5B6 Can

LASLEY, MARION MURRAY, b Lewisburg, Ky, June 5, 23; m 47; c 2. SPANISH. *Educ:* Univ Fla, AB, 44; Columbia Univ, AM, 49, PhD(Span philol), 53. *Prof Exp:* From instr to asst prof Span, Columbia Univ, 50-56; ASSOC PROF SPAN, UNIV FLA, 56- *Mem:* MLA; Am Asn Teachers Span & Port. *Res:* Spanish philology; Old Spanish literature; Romance philology. *Mailing Add:* Dept of Romance Lang & Lit Univ of Fla Gainesville FL 32601

LASRY, ANITA BENAIM, b Gibraltar, Gt Brit, Aug 21, 49; m 66; c 5. MEDIEVAL SPANISH LITERATURE. *Educ:* Hunter Col, BA, 72; Columbia Univ, MA, 74, PhD(Span), 79. *Prof Exp:* Adj asst prof, Stern Col, 80; asst prof, Vassar Col, 80-81 & Columbia Univ, 81-82. *Mem:* MLA; Int Asn

Hispanists. *Res:* The medieval romance, French and Spanish; the role of the heroine in medieval romance; history of the Spanish language. *Publ:* Auth, Two Romances: Carlos Maynes and La enperatris de Roma, Juan de La Cuesta Hispanic Monogr, 82; A comparison of courtly love in the sentimental fiction of medieval Spain and of Muslim Spain, Al-Qantara, Vol 11, 82. *Mailing Add:* 135 Central Park W New York NY 10023

LASS, ROGER, b Brooklyn, NY, Jan 1, 37; m 57. LINGUISTICS. *Educ:* New Sch Social Res, AB, 61; Yale Univ, PhD(English), 65. *Prof Exp:* From lectr to assoc prof English, Ind Univ, Bloomington, 64-73; LECTR LING, UNIV EDINBURGH, 73-, READER, 78- *Mem:* Ling Soc Am; Ling Asn Gt Brit; Ling Soc Europe. *Res:* Old and Middle English language; historical linguistics; linguistic theory. *Publ:* Ed, Approaches to English Historical Linguistics, Holt, 69; coauth, Old Enlgish Phonology, 75 & auth, English Phonology and Phonological Theory, 76, Cambridge Univ; Variation studies and historical linguistics, Lang in Soc, 76; Internal reconstruction and generative phonology, Trans Philol Soc, 77; Centers of gravity in language evolution, Die Sprache, 77; On Explaining Language Change, Cambridge Univ, 80. *Mailing Add:* Dept of Ling Univ of Edinburgh Edinburgh EH8 9LL Scotland United Kingdom

LASSALETTA, MANUEL CLAUDIO, b Alicante, Spain, Dec 18, 29; US citizen; m 62; c 4. SPANISH LITERATURE, LINGUISTICS. *Educ:* Univ Murcia, Spain, BA, 49; Middlebury Col, MA, 63, DML, 69. *Prof Exp:* Instr mod & class lang, pub & pvt schs, 53-64; instr Span, Hollins Col, 64-67; assoc prof, Univ Va, 68-76 & Inter-Am Univ PR, 76-78; assoc prof, Heritage Univ, 78-79; RES & WRITING, 79- *Honors & Awards:* Rivadeneyra Prize, Real Acad Lengua Espanola, Madrid, 73; Hispania Award, Am Asn Teachers Span & Port, 76. *Mem:* MLA; Am Asn Teachers Span & Port. *Res:* Religious renovation in the 60's and 70's; religion: American and European ecumenical tendencies. *Publ:* Auth, Un estudio del verbo hablar en Fortunata y Jacinta, 12/71 & Un drama nuevo y el realismo literario, 12/74, Hispania; Stylistic analysis of Epitalamio & Stylistic analysis of Bostezo de Luz, In: Antologia Comentada del Modernismo, Calif State Univ, 74; Aportaciones al Estudio del Lenguaje Coloquial Galdosiano, Insula, 74; Nuevas Aportaciones al Estudio del Lenguaje Coloquial Galdosiano (in press). *Mailing Add:* 2301 Starbrook Dr Charlotte NC 28210

LATEINER, DONALD, b New Rochelle, NY, June 1, 44. CLASSICAL STUDIES, ANCIENT HISTORY. *Educ:* Univ Chicago, BA, 65; Cornell Univ, MA, 67; Stanford Univ, MA, 70, PhD(classics), 72. *Prof Exp:* Lectr hist, San Francisco State Col, 68-69; actg asst prof classics, Stanford Univ, 71-72; asst prof class studies, Univ Pa, 72-79; asst prof, 79-82, ASSOC PROF HUMANITIES-CLASSICS, OHIO WESLEYAN UNIV, 82- *Mem:* Am Philol Asn; Am Asn Ancient Historians; Archaeol Inst Am; Friends Ancient Hist. *Res:* Greek historiography; Latin elegy; Greek oratory. *Publ:* Auth, The speech of Teutiaplus, Greek, Roman & Byzantine Studies, 75; Tissaphernes and the Phoenician fleet, Trans Am Philol Asn, 76; Heralds and corpses in Thucydides, Class World, 77; Obscenity in Catullus, Ramus, 77; Pathos in Thucydides, Antichthon, 77; No laughing matter: A literary tactic in Herodotus, Trans Am Philol Asn, 77; An analysis of Lysias' Defense Speeches, Rivista Storica dell'Antichita, 81; The failure of the Ionian Revolt, Historia, 82. *Mailing Add:* Dept of Humanities-Classics Ohio Wesleyan Univ Delaware OH 43015

LATIMER, JOHN FRANCIS, b Clinton, Miss, May 16, 03; m 46. CLASSICAL LANGUGAGES & LITERATURES. *Educ:* Miss Col, AB, 22; Univ Chicago, AM, 26; Yale Univ, PhD(classics), 29. *Hon Degrees:* DLitt, Miss Col, 64. *Prof Exp:* Instr classics, Vanderbilt Univ, 26-27; master, Taft Sch, Watertown, Conn, 29-31; asst prof, Knox Col, Ill, 31-33; assoc prof, Drury Col, 33-36; from asst prof to assoc prof, 36-54, chmn dept, 36-71, asst dean col gen studies, 51-56, univ marshal, 53-69, prof class lang, 54-73, from asst dean to assoc dean fac, 56-64, dir foreign student affairs, 64-66, EMER PROF CLASSICS, GEORGE WASHINGTON UNIV, 73- *Concurrent Pos:* Mem managing comt, Am Sch Class Studies, Athens, 50-72; mem comt, Fulbright Int Exchange of Persons, 59-71; Am Philol Asn deleg, Am Coun Learned Soc, 63-67. *Mem:* Am Philol Asn; Class Asn Atlantic States (pres, 55-57); Am Class League (pres, 60-66). *Res:* Classical education in antiquity and today; history of curriculum in secondary schools. *Publ:* Auth, What's happened to our high schools?, Pub Affairs, 58; ed, Airlie House Conference on Classical Studies in American Education, George Washington Univ, 65; The Oxford Conference and Related Activities, French-Bray, 68; auth introd, A Life of George Washington, in Latin Prose, 76, ed & auth foreword, A Grammatical and Historical Supplement to A Life of George Washington, 76 & ed & contribr, A Composite Translation of A Life of George Washington, 76, George Washington Univ. *Mailing Add:* 3601 Connecticut Ave NW Washington DC 20008

LATTA, ALAN DENNIS, b Wichita, Kans, June 28, 40; m 62; c 1. GERMAN LANGUAGE & LITERATURE. *Educ:* Univ Kans, AB, 62; Yale Univ, MA, 65, PhD(Ger), 69. *Prof Exp:* From lectr to asst prof, 67-76, ASSOC PROF GER, TRINITY COL, UNIV TORONTO, 76- *Mem:* MLA; Can Asn Univ Teachers Ger. *Res:* Thomas Mann; German literature since 1945; novel. *Publ:* Auth, The mystery of life: A theme in Der Zauberberg, Monatshefte, 74; Lessing and the drug scene: Notes on the bunte Blumen-metaphor in Nathan der Weise, Lessing Yrbk, 74; Symbolic structure: Toward an understanding of Thomas Mann's Zauberberg, Ger Rev, 1/75; Walter Faber and the allegorization of life: A reading of Max Frisch's Novel, Homo faber, Germanic Rev, 4/79. *Mailing Add:* Dept of Ger Univ of Toronto 97 St George St Toronto ON M5S 1A1 Can

LATTEY, ELSA MARIA, b Brooklyn, NY, Nov 28, 41; c 1. LINGUISTICS, ENGLISH AS A SECOND LANGUAGE. *Educ:* Brooklyn Col, BA, 62; Hunter Col, MA, 74; City Univ New York, PhD(ling), 80. *Prof Exp:* Transl Ger & English, Standard Oil Co, 63-65 & Carl Zeiss, Inc, 65; proofreader & copy-ed, Am Heritage Dict, Time, World, New Am Libr, Random House, 65-72; adj lectr ling, Queens Col, 72-73; ASST PROF LING, ENGLISH DEPT, UNIV TÜBINGEN, 74- *Concurrent Pos:* Workshop coordr, Ger-Am Inst, Tüingen, 82; lectr English, Univ Maryland European Div. *Mem:* Ling Soc Am; Am Asn Applied Ling; Deutsche Gesellschaft für Sprachwissenschaft; Gesellschaft für angewandte Ling; Soc Caribbean Ling. *Res:* Bilingualism and language variation; second language acquistion and language pedagogy; translation studies. *Publ:* Coauth, Temporary language acquisition: Migrant workers' speech in Germany, Proc 4th Int Cong Applied Ling, Hoshschulverlag, 76; contribr, Second-Language Acquisition: Environments & Strategies, In: German in Contact with Other Languages, Scriptor Verlag, 77; auth, Utterance potential, code switching & speech errors, Langage et L'Homme, 79; Beyond variable rules, Pac Ling A 57, 79; contribr, Individual and Social Aspects of Bilingualism, Elements of Biling Theory Study Series, Univ Brussels, 81; What is the same thing in interlinguistic comparison?, Contrastive Grammar, Karoma Publ, 82; coauth, Using Idioms: Situationsbezogene Redewendungen, Max Niemeyer Verlag (in prep). *Mailing Add:* Seminar für englishe Philol Univ Tübingen 7400 Tübingen Germany, Federal Republic of

LATTIMORE, STEVEN, b Bryn Mawr, Pa, May 25, 38. CLASSICS, CLASSICAL ARCHEOLOGY. *Educ:* Dartmouth Col, AB, 60; Princeton Univ, MA, 64, PhD(class archaeol), 68. *Prof Exp:* Instr class archaeol, Dartmouth Col, 64; instr Greek, Haverford Col, 65-66; asst prof classics & class archaeol, Intercol Ctr Class Studies, Rome, 66-67; asst prof, 67-74, ASSOC PROF CLASSICS, UNIV CALIF, LOS ANGELES, 74- *Concurrent Pos:* Guggenheim Found fel, 75-76. *Mem:* Archaeol Inst Am; Am Philol Asn. *Res:* Classical sculpture; Greek literature; mythology. *Publ:* Auth, The bronze apoxyomenos from Ephesos, Am J Archaeol, 72; Battus in Theocritus' fourth Idyll, Greek, Roman & Byzantine Studies, 73; A Greek pediment on a Roman temple, Am J Archaeol, 74; The Marine Thiasos in Greek Sculpture, Archaeol Inst Am, 76. *Mailing Add:* Dept of Classics Univ of Calif Los Angeles CA 90024

LAU, JOSEPH SHIU-MING, b Hong Kong, July 9, 34; US citizen; m 68; c 2. CHINESE, COMPARATIVE LITERATURE. *Educ:* Nat Taiwan Univ, BA, 60; Ind Univ, MA, 64, PhD(comp lit), 66. *Prof Exp:* Lectr Chinese, Miami Univ, 64-65; actg asst prof, Univ Hawaii, 65-66; asst prof Chinese & comp lit, Univ Wis-Madison, 66-68; lectr English, Chung Chi Col, Chinese Univ Hong Kong, 68-71; sr lectr, Univ Singapore, 71-72; assoc prof Chinese, Univ Hawaii, Manoa, 72-73; assoc prof, 73-76, PROF CHINESE, UNIV WIS-MADISON, 77- *Concurrent Pos:* Am Coun Learned Soc res fel, 75-76; co-ed, Chinese Transl Ser, Ind Univ Press, 77-; Soc Sci Res Coun fel, 79-80; Rockefeller Found fel, 81-82. *Mem:* Asn Asian Studies. *Res:* Chinese fiction; modern Chinese literature in general. *Publ:* Auth, The Peking man and Ivanov. . ., Contemp Lit, winter 69; Ts'ao Yu: A Study in Literary Influence, Univ Hong Kong, 70; translr, Bernard Malamud's The Magic Barrel, 70, The Assistant, 71 & Saul Bellow's Herzog, 71, World Today, Hong Kong; ed, Chinese Stories from Taiwan: 1960-1970, 76, co-ed, Traditional Chinese Stories: Themes & Variations, 78 & Modern Chinese Stories & Novellas: 1919-1949, 81, Columbia Univ Press. *Mailing Add:* Dept of East Asian Lang & Lit Univ of Wis Madison WI 53706

LAUNAY, JEAN EUGENE LOUIS, b Bourges, France, Feb 19, 13; m 36; c 2. FRENCH & COMPARATIVE LITERATURE. *Educ:* Univ Paris, Lic-es-Let, 32, dipl, 33, Agrege, 37. *Prof Exp:* Prof, Lycee de Garcons de Rennes, France, 36-39, prof-in-charge, 38-39; prof fac lett, Univ Rennes, 45-46; dir transl courses, 46, chmn dept Romance lang, 46-64, dir French summer sch, 47-63, chmn humanities group, 57-64, chmn dept French lang & lit, 64-66, PROF FRENCH, MCGILL UNIV, 46- *Concurrent Pos:* Mem adv coun, Dept Romance Lang, Princeton Univ, 60-69. *Honors & Awards:* Knight, Order of Leopold, Belg; Officer, Acad Francaise, 54; Chevalier, Legion d'honneur, 62; Officer, Palmes Academiques, 69. *Mem:* MLA; Soc Fr Prof Am (vpres, 49-); Asn Can Univ Teachers Fr. *Res:* Nineteenth century French literature; Stendhal; problems in translation. *Publ:* Transl, Jean-Paul des Laurentides, 53; Precis de litterature francaise, 59. *Mailing Add:* Dept of French McGill Univ Montreal PQ H3A 2T6 Can

LAURENTI, JOSEPH L, b Hesperange, Luxembourg, Dec 10, 31; US citizen. FOREIGN LANGUAGES. *Educ:* Univ Ill, AB, 58, MA, 59; Univ Mo, PhD(Span), 62. *Prof Exp:* Instr Span, Univ Mo, 59-62; asst prof Span, Ital & Ger, 62-66, PROF SPAN & ITAL, ILL STATE UNIV, 66- *Concurrent Pos:* US corresp, Quad Ibero-Am; consult, PMLA. *Mem:* Am Asn Teachers Span & Port. *Res:* Modern Italian literature; Spanish Golden Age. *Publ:* Auth, Ensayo de una Bibliografia de la Novela Picaresca Espanola (2 vols), AMS Press, 81; Estudios sobre la novela picaresca espanola, 70 & coauth, Ensayo bibliografico del prologo en la literatura, 71, Consejo Super Invest Cient, Madrid; auth, Los prologos en las novelas picarescas espanolas, Castalia, Madrid, 71; coauth, Literary Relations Between Spain and Italy, GK Hall, 72; auth, A Bibliography of Picaresque Literature from its Origins to the Present, 73 & coauth, The World of Federico Garcia Lorca, 74, Scarecrow; auth, The Spanish Golden Age (1472-1700), A Catalog of Rare Books in the Library of the University of Illinois and in Selected North American Libraries, G K Hall & Co, 79; Juan de Luna: Segunda parte de la vida de Lazarillo de Tormes, Edicion, Prologo y notas de Joseph L Laurenti, Madrid, Espasa-Calpe, SA, 79. *Mailing Add:* Dept of Span Ill State Univ Normal IL 61761

LAURETTE, PIERRE, b Fourmies, France, May 1, 34. FRENCH. *Educ:* Univ Nancy, Lice es Lett, 56; Univ Saarlandes, dipl, 59, Dr Phil, 61, Dr es Litt, 65. *Prof Exp:* Asst comp lit, Univ Saarlands, 59-63; asst prof Romance lang, 65-67, ASSOC PROF ROMANCE LANG, CARLETON UNIV, 67- *Res:* Stylistics, linguistics; semiotics. *Publ:* Auth, Le theme de l'Arbre chez Valery, C Klincksieck, 67; La notion d'influence chez Valery, Actes, Mouton, 67; Paul Valery et Teilhard de Chardin, Rev Sci Humaines, 68; Proces metaphorique et proces metonymique, Ling Rev, Mouton, 71; contribr, Les critiques de notre temps et Valery, Ed Gernier, Paris, 71. *Mailing Add:* Dept of French Carleton Univ Ottawa ON K1S 5B6 Can

LAURION, GASTON, b White Plains, NY, Jan 25, 27; Can citizen; m. MEDIEVAL FRENCH LANGUAGE & LITERATURE. *Educ:* Univ Paris, BA, 46, dipl d'Etudes Super, 49, DUniv, 63; Univ Montreal, Lic es Let, 48. *Prof Exp:* Res asst Greek philol, Nat Ctr Sci Res, Paris, 52-53; lectr classics, Univ Ottawa, 57-59; lectr French, McMaster Univ, 59-62, from asst prof to assoc prof, 62-68; assoc prof, 68-73, chmn dept French studies, 69-73, PROF FRENCH, CONCORDIA UNIV, 73- *Concurrent Pos:* Can Coun res grant, France, 68. *Mem:* Asn Can Univ Teachers Fr; Fr-Can Asn Advan Sci. *Res:* History of the Greek texts; medieval hymns of the Holy Cross; written accounts of French travelers to the Holy Land. *Publ:* Auth, Les principales bibliotheques de manuscrits grecs, Phoenix, Toronto, 61; Essai de groupement des hymnes medievales a la Croix, Cahiers de Civilisation Medievale, 64; L'Avalee des Avales et le refus d'etre adulte, Rev Univ Ottawa, 7-9/68; L'Orchidee-soeur (poems), Ed Aquilaltee, 72. *Mailing Add:* Dept of French Studies Concordia Univ Montreal PQ H3G 1M8 Can

LAUZIERE, ARSENE ERNEST, b Assiniboia, Sask, May 1, 16; m 42; c 2. FRENCH LITERATURE & LANGUAGE. *Educ:* Univ Ottawa, BA, 39; Univ Montreal, MA, 49; Univ Paris, DUniv, 51. *Prof Exp:* Asst prof French, Royal Roads Mil Col, 51-52; from asst prof to assoc prof, Royal Mil Col, Ont, 52-64; chmn dept French studies, 65-68, dept mod lang, 66-68, PROF FRENCH LANG & LIT & QUEBEC LIT, CONCORDIA UNIV, 64- *Concurrent Pos:* Can Arts Coun fel, 69-70. *Mem:* Ling Soc Can; Can Humanities Asn; Soc Romantic Studies; Asn Prof Fr Univ Can; Fr-Can Asn Advan Sci. *Res:* French 19th century; Quebec novel; Romanticism. *Publ:* Auth, Coups de sonde dans le roman canadien contemporain; A la recherche du visage romantique canadien; Primeveres du roman canadien francais: probleme de filiation; Le romantisme de Francois-Xavier Garneau; Francois-Xavier Garneau; Histoire de la litterature-francaise du Quebec. *Mailing Add:* Dept of French Studies Concordia Univ Loyola Montreal PQ H4B 1R6 Can

LAVALLEE-WILLIAMS, MARTHE, b New York, NY; div. FRENCH LITERATURE & LANGUAGE. *Educ:* Col Mt St Vincent, AB, 46; Columbia Univ, MA, 48, PhD(French), 55. *Prof Exp:* Instr French, Edgewood Park Jr Col, 47-48 & Skidmore Col, 48-52; from instr to asst prof, Mt Holyoke Col, 53-57; asst prof, Columbus Sch, Ohio, 57-59, State Univ NY Buffalo, 60-63 & Ursinus Col, 63-64; adj asst prof, Temple Univ, 64-67; asst prof, Univ Puget Sound, 68-69; asst prof, 69-80, chmn, Dept French & Ital, 75-80, ASSOC PROF FRENCH, TEMPLE UNIV, 80- *Concurrent Pos:* Consult reader, MLA, 78- & J Hist of Ideas. *Mem:* AAUP; MLA; Am Asn Teachers French; Claudel Soc. *Res:* Camus; Claudel; new novel and experimental theatre. *Publ:* Coauth, Advanced placement bulletin, Northeast Conf Foreign Lang Teachers, 55; auth, Biblical allusions in La Chute, Agora, fall 73; Staging Claudel, Renascence, Vol VIII, No 1; Demystitying verbal structure and forms in second language teaching, Leshonenu La'am, Japan & LLD, fall, 81. *Mailing Add:* Dept of French & Ital Temple Univ Philadelphia PA 19122

LAVERY, GERARD B, b Brooklyn, NY, Feb 3, 33. CLASSICAL LANGUAGES. *Educ:* Fordham Univ, AB, 55, MA, 56, PhD(classics), 65. *Prof Exp:* Asst prof, 61-72, ASSOC PROF CLASS LANG, COL OF THE HOLY CROSS, 72- *Concurrent Pos:* Batchelor Ford fac fel, 69. *Mem:* Am Philol Asn; AAUP. *Res:* Plutarch; Roman history and politics; Lucretius. *Publ:* Auth, Cicero's Philarchia and Marius, Greece & Rome, 10/71; O Romule Arpinas, Class Bull, 4/73. *Mailing Add:* Box 89 A Col of the Holy Cross Worcester MA 01610

LAW, DAVID ANDREW, b Blackfoot, Idaho, Feb 2, 25; m 45; c 3. RUSSIAN LANGUAGE & CIVILIZATION. *Educ:* Brigham Young Univ, BA, 49, MA, 51; Univ Utah, PhD(educ admin), 66. *Prof Exp:* Instr Russ, Mesa Col, 59-60; teacher high sch, Utah, 60-66; ASSOC PROF RUSS, UNIV MO-ROLLA, 66- *Concurrent Pos:* Docent, Volgograd Pedag Inst, 72 & 79. *Mem:* Am Asn Teachers Slavic & E Europ Lang. *Res:* A comparative study of the concepts of truth, freedom and democracy in American and Soviet education systems. *Publ:* Auth, Russian Civilization, MSS Inform Corp, 75. *Mailing Add:* Dept of Humanities Univ of Mo Rolla MO 65401

LAW, HOWARD W, b Long Beach, Calif, June 22, 19; m 44; c 2. LINGUISTICS, ANTHROPOLOGY. *Educ:* Seattle Pac Col, BA, 51; Univ Tex, MA, 60, PhD(ling), 62. *Prof Exp:* Instr ling, Summer Inst Ling, 46-63; vis lectr, Univ Calif, Los Angeles, 63-65; asst prof, Hartford Sem Found, 65-67; assoc prof, Univ Minn, Minneapolis, 67-72 ; acad dean, 72-81, PROF ANTHROP, SIMPSON COL, 72-, PROF MISSIONS, 81- *Concurrent Pos:* Res assoc, Univ Tex, 62-63, lectr anthrop, 63; Univ Minn Grad Sch res grant, Nahuatl Concordance Proj, Mex, 67-68. *Mem:* Ling Soc Am; fel Am Anthrop Asn. *Res:* Anthropological linguistics; applied anthropology; translation theory and practice. *Publ:* Translr, The Letters of Peter, James and Jude, Am Bible Soc, 60; auth, Obligatory Constructions of Isthmus Nahuat Grammar, Mouton, The Hague, 66; Winning a Hearing, Eerdmans, 67. *Mailing Add:* Office of Acad Dean Simpson Col San Francisco CA 94134

LAWALL, GILBERT WESTCOTT, b Detroit, Mich, Sept 22, 36; m 57; c 2. CLASSICS. *Educ:* Oberlin Col, AB, 57; Yale Univ, PhD(classics), 61. *Prof Exp:* Instr classics, Yale Univ, 61-63 & 64-65, jr fel, Ctr Hellenic Studies, 63-64; asst prof classics, Amherst Col, 65-67; from asst prof to assoc prof, 67-72, PROF CLASSICS, UNIV MASS, AMHERST, 72- *Honors & Awards:* Barlow-Beach Award Distinguished Serv, Class Asn New England, 79; Oustanding contrib For Lang Educ, Class Asn Empire State, 79. *Mem:* Am Philol Asn; Class Asn New Eng (vpres, 72-73, secy-treas, 80-); Vergilian Soc; Archaeol Inst Am; Am Class League (pres, 76-80). *Res:* Hellenistic Greek poetry; Senecan tragedy; classics pedagogy. *Publ:* Auth, Theocritus' Coan Pastorals: A Poetry Book, Ctr Hellenic Studies, 67; The green cabinet and the pastoral design: Theocritus, Euripides, and Tibullus, Ramus: Critical Studies Greek & Roman Lit, 75 & In: Ancient Pastoral: Ramus Essays on Greek and Roman Pastoral Poetry, Aureal, Melbourne, 75; Herodas 6 and 7 reconsidered, Class Philol, 76; The college classics department as a catalyst for new Latin programs in public schools, Class World, 78; Teaching the classics in England and America today and some thoughts for the future, Class Outlook, 78; The Phaedra of Seneca: Latin Text and Study Materials, Bolchazy-Carducci Publ, 81; Death and perspective in Seneca's Troades, Class J, No 77, 82. *Mailing Add:* Dept of Classics Univ of Mass Amherst MA 01003

LAWALL, SARAH NESBIT, b Wellesley, Mass; m 57; c 2. COMPARATIVE LITERATURE, FRENCH. *Educ:* Oberlin Col, AB, 56; Yale Univ, PhD(comp lit), 61. *Prof Exp:* From asst prof to assoc prof French, 66-74, actg chmn dept comp lit, 69, chmn dept, 74-78, PROF COMP LIT, UNIV MASS, AMHERST, 74-, ADJ PROF FRENCH, 78- *Concurrent Pos:* Ed mod sect, World Masterpieces & Continental Masterpieces, Norton & Co Inc, 77- *Mem:* Am Comp Lit Asn; MLA; AAUP; Am Asn Teachers Fr; Int Soc Comp Study Civilizations. *Res:* Modern poetry and poetics, especially French; phenomenological literary theory; practical criticism. *Publ:* Auth, Critics of Consciousness: The Existential Structures of Literature, Harvard Univ, 68; Ponge and the poetry of self-knowledge, Contemp Lit, 70; Yves Bonnefoy and Denis Roche: Art and the art of poetry, In: About French Poetry from Dada to Tel Quel, Wayne State Univ, 74; coauth, Decouverte de l'essai, Harcourt, 74; auth, A style of silence: Two readings of Yves Bonnefoy's poetry, Contemp Lit, 75; The poem as utopia, Fr Forum, 76; Poetry taking place, World Lit Today, 79; The time and space of translation, Pac Quart, 80. *Mailing Add:* Dept of Comp Lit Univ of Mass Amherst MA 01003

LAWLER, JAMES RONALD, b Melbourne, Australia, Aug 15, 29; m 54; c 2. FRENCH LITERATURE. *Educ:* Univ Melbourne, BA, 50, MA, 52; Univ Paris, DUniv, 54. *Prof Exp:* Lectr French, Univ Queensland, 55-56; sr lectr, Univ Melbourne, 57-62; prof & head dept, Univ Western Australia, 63-71; prof & chmn dept, Univ Calif, Los Angeles, 71-74; McCulloch prof, Dalhousie Univ, 74-79; PROF FRENCH, UNIV CHICAGO, 79- *Concurrent Pos:* Brit Coun interchange scholar, 67; Australian Acad Humanities fel, 70-; Guggenheim Found fel, 74; asst ed, Fr Rev, 74-; ed, Dalhousie French Studies, 79; vis fel, Australian Nat Univ, 81. *Honors & Awards:* Officier, Palmes Academiques, 70. *Mem:* MLA; Am Asn Teachers Fr; Asn Can Univ Prof Fr; Int Asn Fr Studies (vpres, 74-). *Res:* Modern French poetry; poetics; 20th century novel. *Publ:* Auth, Form and Meaning in Valery's Le Cimetiere Marin, Melbourne Univ, 59; Lecture de Valery: Une etude de Charmes, Presses Univs France, 63; ed, Essays in French Literature, Univ Western Australia, 64-74; auth, The Language of French Symbolism, 69, coauth, Paul Valery: Poems, 71 & Paul Valery: Leonardo, Poe, Mallarme, 72, Princeton Univ; auth, The Poet as Analyst, Univ Calif, 74; ed, Paul Valery: An Anthology, 77 & auth, Rene Char: The Myth and the Poem, 78, Princeton Univ. *Mailing Add:* Dept of French Dalhousie Univ Halifax NS B3H 4J5 Can

LAWLER, JOHN MICHAEL, b De Kalb, Ill, Feb 12, 42; m 67; c 1. LINGUISTICS. *Educ:* St Benedict's Col, Kans, AB, 64; Univ Wash, MA, 67; Univ Mich, Ann Arbor, PhD(ling), 73. *Prof Exp:* Asst prof ling & English as foreign lang, Utah State Univ, 67-72; asst prof, 72-79, ASSOC PROF LING, UNIV MICH, ANN ARBOR, 80- *Res:* Generative semantics; structure of English; applied linguistics. *Publ:* Auth, Generic to a fault, Papers 8th Meeting Chicago Ling Soc, 72; The eclectic company, or, Explanatory power to the people, Georgetown Univ Round Table, 73; Studies in English generics, Vol I, In: Univ Mich Papers in Linguistics, 73. *Mailing Add:* 1201 Granger Ave Ann Arbor MI 48104

LAWLER, TRAUGOTT, English. See Vol II

LAWRENCE, DEREK WILLIAM, b Croyden, England, June 10, 31; m 57; c 2. MODERN FRENCH LITERATURE. *Educ:* Univ London, BA, 63, MA, 64, PhD(French), 67. *Prof Exp:* Asst prof French, Univ Sask, 64-68; asst prof, 68-73, assoc prof, 73-82, PROF FRENCH, DALHOUSIE UNIV, 82- *Concurrent Pos:* Can Coun res grants, 68, 69 & 73-74. *Mem:* Am Asn Teachers Fr. *Res:* Twentieth century French novel. *Publ:* Auth, The transitional works of Jean Giono, 1937-1946, winter 70 & The ideological writings of Jean Giono, 2/72, Fr Rev; translr, L'Administration municipale au Nouveau-Brunswick, 78; contribr, Cabeen: Critical Bibliography of French Literature, 20th Century, Syracuse Univ (in press). *Mailing Add:* Dept of French Dalhousie Univ Halifax NS B3H 4J5 Can

LAWRENCE, FRANCIS LEO, b Woonsocket, RI, Aug 25, 37; m 58; c 4. FRENCH & ITALIAN. *Educ:* St Louis Univ, BS, 59; Tulane Univ, PhD(French & Ital), 62. *Prof Exp:* Frenchom instr to assoc prof, 62-71, chmn, Dept Fr & Ital, 69-76, actg dean col, 76-78, dep provost univ, 78-81, actg provost & grad dean, 81-82, PROF FRENCH, NEWCOMB COL, TULANE UNIV, 71-, ACAD VPRES & PROVOST, 82- *Honors & Awards:* Chevalier, Palmes Academiques, 77. *Mem:* Am Asn Teachers Fr; NAm Soc 17th Century Fr Lit; MLA. *Res:* Moliere, Saint-Amant, La Ceppede. *Publ:* Auth, Jean de La Ceppede and Ignatian meditation, Comp Lit, 65; Moliere: The comedy of unreason, Tulane Studies in Romance Lang & Lit, 68; Peotry as painting, In: Jean de La Ceppede: An appeal to the senses or to the understanding, Symposium, 73; L'Hiver des Alpes: A structural analysis, Romanic Rev, 78; Dom Juan and the Manifest God: Moliere's Anti-Tragic Hero, PMLA, 78; A post-structuralist critique of Saint-Amant's four season sonnets, L'Esprit Createur, 80; ed, Visages de Moliere, Oeuvres et Critiques, Jean-Michel Place, 81; Actes de New Orleans, Biblio 17, Papers on French Seventeenth Century Lit, 82. *Mailing Add:* Dept of French & Ital Newcomb Col Tulane Univ New Orleans LA 70118

LAWRENCE, IRENE, Theology, Language Theory. See Vol IV

LAWSON, RICHARD HENRY, b San Francisco, Calif, Jan 11, 19; m 49. GERMAN. *Educ:* Univ Ore, BA, 41, MA, 48; Univ Calif, Los Angeles, PhD(Ger ling), 56. *Prof Exp:* Instr Ger, Wash State Univ, 53-57; from asst prof to prof, 57-76, chmn dept Ger & Russ, 65-68 & div humanities, 68-69, actg assoc dean, 72-73, asst dean grad studies, 73-74, chmn dept Germanic lang, 76-79, PROF GER, UNIV NC, CHAPEL HILL, 76- *Concurrent Pos:* Consult etymologies, Websters New Int Dictionary, 3rd ed, G & C Merriam Co, 55-57; bibliog ed, Twentieth Century Lit, 67-81; ed, Univ NC Studies in the Germanic Langs and Lits, 80- *Mem:* MLA; Am Asn Teachers Ger; Int

Arthur Schnitzler Res Asn; Am Comp Lit Asn; Int Vereinigung für germanische Sprach- und Literaturwissenschaft. *Res:* Old High German linguistics; comparative literature; modern German literature. *Publ:* Auth, Edith Wharton and German Literature, Bouvier Verlag, 74; Edith Wharton, Frederick Ungar Publ, 77; Linguistic transmission on the Frankish Alemannic Ostrogothic Frontier in the sixth century, Rev Belge de Philol et d'Hist, 78; Poets and physicians in Arthur Schnitzler's The Bachelor's Death and An Author's Last Letter, Med & Lit, 80; Pathologische Geisteszustände an der Grenze des Übernatürlichen in Schnitzlers Werken, Akten des VI Int Germanisten Kongresses, 80; Paratactic tho in Old High German Tatian, Neuphilologische Mitteilungen, 80; Latin and the infinitive form of the Old High German weak verb, J English & Ger Philol, 80; The Rule of St Benedict in Thirteenth and Fourteenth Century Germany: Conceptual Implications of Lexical Variation, Amsterdamer Beiträge zur Älteren Germanistik, 81. *Mailing Add:* Dept of Ger Univ of NC Chapel Hill NC 27514

LAWSON, URSULA D, b Frankfurt, Ger, July 9, 21; US citizen; m 47; c 2. GERMAN LITERATURE & PHILOSOPHY. *Educ:* Western Ky State Univ, BS, 58; Univ Ky, MA, 60; Vanderbilt Univ, PhD(Ger lit), 66. *Prof Exp:* Instr Ger lit, Univ Ky, 60-61; asst Ger Lang, Vanderbilt Univ, 61-63, instr, 63-64; from instr to asst prof Ger lit, Univ NH, 64-67; from instr to assoc prof, 67-76, PROF MOD LANG, OHIO UNIV, 76- *Mem:* Am Asn Teachers Ger; MLA. *Res:* Eighteenth and nineteenth century German literature. *Publ:* Auth, Pathological time in E T A Hoffmann's Der Sandmann, Monatsh, 4/68; Musical structure in E T A Hoffmann's fiction, 4/68 & Subjective time in E T A Hoffmann's Der Goldne Topf, 5/68, Occasional Papers Lang Lit & Ling. *Mailing Add:* Dept of Mod Lang Ohio Univ Athens OH 45701

LAWTON, DAVID LLOYD, b Manhattan, NY, Mar 20, 24; m 49; c 2. ENGLISH, CREOLIZED LANGUAGES. *Educ:* Hiram Col, BA, 50; Western Reserve Univ, MA, 50; Mich State Univ, dipl, 60, PhD(English, ling), 63. *Prof Exp:* Chmn dept English & Span, Windham High Sch, 51-54; instr English, Alpena Community Col, 54-57; chmn English & ling, Inter-Am Univ PR, 64-65, dean col arts & sci, 65-66, prof English & ling & dean fac, 66-67; PROF ENGLISH & LING, CENT MICH UNIV, 68-, DIR LING, 71- *Concurrent Pos:* Smith-Mundt vis prof, Univ Guadalajara, 60-62; Peace Corps consult, Jamaica Prog, 63; consult, Col Bd PR, 65-67; Fulbright lectr, Univ Quito, Ecuador, 71. *Mem:* Linc Soc Am; Teachers English to Speakers Other Lang; Am Dialect Soc; Soc Caribbean Ling. *Res:* English and Hispanic Creolized languages; bilingualism; social dialectology. *Publ:* Auth, The teaching of a Creolized language to Peace Corps volunteers, Lang Learning, 12/63; The implications of tone for Jamaican Creole, Anthrop Ling, 6/68; The question of Creolization in Puerto Rican Spanish, In: Pidginization and Creolization of Languages, Cambridge Univ, 71; Chicano Spanish: Some sociolinguistic considerations, Bilingual Rev, 75; White man, black man, coolie man: Pejorative terms in a Creole society, Mich Ling Soc Papers, 76; Language attitude, discreteness and code shifting in Jamaican Creole, In: English World-Wide, Julius Groos Verlag, 80; Paradox and paradigm: Language planning and language teaching in Jamaica, In: Zeitschrift für Dialektologie und Linguistik Beihefte, Franz Steiner Verlag, 32: 167-171. *Mailing Add:* Dept of English Cent Mich Univ Mt Pleasant MI 48859

LAYCHUK, JULIAN LOUIS, b High Prairie, Alta, July 23, 33; m 60; c 2. RUSSIAN & SOVIET LITERATURE. *Educ:* Univ Alta, BA, 59, MA, 60; Charles Univ, Prague, PhD(Russian lit), 68. *Prof Exp:* Asst prof Russian, Univ Alta, 62-69; ASSOC PROF RUSSIAN, UNIV OF CALGARY, 69- *Concurrent Pos:* Res fel, Slavonic and Asian Res Inst Univ of BC, 73-74. *Mem:* Rocky Mountain Mod Lang Asn; Am Asn Teachers of Slavic & East Europ Lang; Am Asn for Advan of Slavic Studies; Can Soc for Asian Studies; Can Asn of Slavists. *Res:* I G Ehrenburg, Soviet literature; Russian romanticism; Chinese language. *Publ:* Auth, The evolution of I G Ehrenburg's Weltanschauung, Canadian Slavonic Papers, 70; Poslednie issledovaniia po rusistike v Kanade, Ceskoslovenska Rusistika, 71; The ebb and flow of Sino-Soviet literary relations, Survey, 75; Ilya Ehrenburg: Early apostle of pacifism, Soviet Jewish Affairs, 75; The lyric verse of I G Ehrenburg, Canadian Slavonic Papers, 77. *Mailing Add:* Dept of Germanic & Slavic Studies Univ of Calgary 2920 24 Ave NW Calgary AB T2N 1N4 Can

LAYMAN, BEVERLY JOSEPH, English. See Vol II

LAZENBY, FRANCIS D, b Hopewell, Va, Oct 21, 16. CLASSICAL ARCHEOLOGY, PHILOLOGY. *Educ:* Univ Va, AB, 37, AM, 39, PhD, 41; Univ Mich, AMLS, 55. *Prof Exp:* Instr, Col William & Mary, 46; from instr to asst prof classics, Univ Ill, 46-54; asst prof, 55-64, librn, Medieval Inst, 55-61, asst dir libr, div humanities, 61-71, assoc prof, 64-79, EMER ASSOC PROF CLASS, UNIV NOTRE DAME, 80-- *Mem:* Am Philol Asn. *Publ:* Contribr, New Cath Encycl, 66 & Encycl Dict of Religions, 77, McGraw. *Mailing Add:* Dept of Classics Univ of Notre Dame Notre Dame IN 46556

LAZZARINO, GRAZIANA, b Genoa, Italy, Nov 6, 30. ITALIAN & FRENCH. *Educ:* Cambridge Univ, Cert English, 51; Univ Genoa, Dr Lett, 53. *Prof Exp:* Asst Ital, Col Mod Jeunes Filles, Clermont-Ferrand, France, 54-55 & Lycee St Just, Lyon, 55-56; instr Ital & French, Univ Nebr, 56-57 & Northampton Sch Girls, 57-58; instr Ital, Wellesley Col, 58-60 & Ist Villa Mercede, Florence, 60-62; asst prof Ital & French, Univ Nebr, 62-64; asst prof, 64-68, assoc prof, 68-80, PROF ITAL, UNIV COLO, 80- *Concurrent Pos:* Fulbright travel grant, 56-57; asst prof, NDEA Inst, Cent Conn State Col, 64, 65, assoc prof, 66; consult evaluating USAFI courses beginning Ital, Comn Accreditation Serv Experiences, Am Coun Educ, 68; mem, exam comt Ital listening comprehension test, Col Entrance Exam Bd, 68-69; consult lang exam testing, Educ Testing Serv, Princeton, NJ, 69-72; assoc ed, Il Giornalino, 80- *Mem:* Am Asn Teachers Ital (vpres, 80-); Am Coun Teaching Foreign Lang; Joint Nat Comt Lang. *Res:* Language teaching methods; translation techniques. *Publ:* Auth, Individual report, In: The MLA Foreign Language Proficiency Tests for Teachers and Advanced Students: A Professional Evaluation and Recommendations for Test Development, MLA, 66; Workbook for Basic Italian, 4th ed, 77 & Da Capo: A Review Grammar, 79, Holt; Prego: An Invitation to Italian, 80 & Per Tutti I Gusti, 81, Random House. *Mailing Add:* Dept of French & Italian Univ of Colo Boulder CO 80302

LEACH, ELEANOR WINSOR, b Providence, RI, Aug 16, 37; m 62. ENGLISH, LATIN. *Educ:* Bryn Mawr Col, AB, 59; Yale Univ, MA, 60, PhD, 63. *Prof Exp:* Instr English, Bryn Mawr Col, 62-65; asst prof class ling, Villanova Univ, 65-71; vis assoc prof classics, Univ Tex, Austin, 72-74 & Wesleyan Univ, 74-76; assoc prof, 76-80, PROF CLASS STUDIES, IND UNIV, BLOOMINGTON, 80- *Concurrent Pos:* Am Philos Soc grant-in-aid, 71; Am Coun Learned Soc grant-in-aid, 72; fel, ctr humanities, Wesleyan Univ, 74; Guggenheim Mem Found fel, 76-77; vis prof classics, Barnard Col, Columbia Univ, 81-82. *Mem:* Am Philol Asn; Archaeol Inst Am; Class Asn Mid W & S; Vergilian Soc. *Res:* Latin literature; Roman art. *Publ:* Auth, Vergil's Eclogues: Landscapes of Experience, Cornell Univ, 74; Ekphrasis and the problem of artistic failure in Ovid's Metamorphoses, 74 & Neronian pastoral and the world of power, 75, Ramus; Parthenian caverns: Remapping of an imaginative territory, J Hist Ideas, 78; Georgics and the poem Arethusa, 81; Metamorphoses of the Acteon Myth in Campanian Painting, Roemische Mitteilungen, 81; Painters, patrons and pattern books: The anonymity y romano: Campanian painting and the transition from the second to the third style, In: Studies in Roman Literary and Artistic Patronage, Univ Tex Press, 82. *Mailing Add:* Dept of Class Studies 547 Ballantine Hall Ind Univ Bloomington IN 47401

LEAKE, ROY EMMETT, JR, b Danbury, NC, Sept 6, 23; m 54; c 2. FRENCH. *Educ:* Guilford Col, AB, 43; Bryn Mawr Col, MA, 59, PhD(French), 64. *Prof Exp:* Br off cashier, Jefferson Standard Life Ins Co, NC, 50-54; asst finance secy, Am Friends Serv Comt, Phila, 54-57; from lectr to asst prof, 61-68, ASSOC PROF FRENCH, IND UNIV, BLOOMINGTON, 68- *Concurrent Pos:* Dir, Ind-Purdue Foreign Studies Prog, Strasbourg, France, 67-68; dir, Ind Univ Hon Prog French, St Brieuc, France, summers, 70-74. *Mem:* MLA; AAUP; Soc des Amis de Montaigne; Int Asn Fr Studies; Am Asn Teachers Fr. *Res:* Montaigne; French 16th century rhetoric and poetry. *Publ:* Auth, Jean-Baptiste Chassignet and Montaigne, 61, More coches of Montaigne, 67 & Relationship of two Ramist rhetorics, 68, Bibliot Humanisme et Renaissance; Montaigne's Gascon proverb again, Neophilologus, 68; Antoine Fouquelin and the Pleiade, Bibliot Humanisme et Renaissance, 70; Concordance des Essais de Montaigne, Librairie Droz, 81. *Mailing Add:* Dept of French & Ital Ind Univ Bloomington IN 47401

LEAL, LUIS, b Linares, Mex, Sept 17, 07; nat US; m 36; c 2. SPANISH. *Educ:* Northwestern Univ, BA, 40; Univ Chicago, AM, 41, PhD, 50. *Prof Exp:* Instr Span, Univ Chicago, 42-43, 46-48, asst prof, 48-52; assoc prof mod lang, Univ Miss, 52-56; assoc prof, Emory Univ, 56-59; assoc prof, 59-62, prof, 62-76, EMER PROF SPAN, UNIV ILL, URBANA, 76- *Concurrent Pos:* Vis prof, Univ Ariz, 55-56, Univ Calif, Santa Barbara, 76-77 & Univ Calif, Los Angeles, 77-78; actg dir, Ctr for Chicano Studies, Univ Calif, Santa Barbara, 80- *Mem:* Am Asn Teachers Span & Port; MLA. *Res:* Spanish American literature, especially the short story; Mexican literature; Chicano literature. *Publ:* Auth, Historia del Cuento Hispanoamericano, Studium, 66; Panorama de la Literatura Mexicana Actual, Pan Am Union, 68; Mariano Azuela, Twayne, 71; Breve Historia de la Literatura Hispanoamericana, Knopf, 71; ed, Cuentistas Hispanoamericanos del Siglo XX, Random, 72; Mariano Azuela: Paginas Escogidas, 73 & Cuentos de la Revolucion, 77, Nat Univ Mex, 77; coauth, A decade of Chicano literature, 1970-1979, La Causa, 82. *Mailing Add:* 542 Wessex Ct Goleta CA 93017

LEAMON, MAX PHILLIP, b Greenfield, Ind, Oct 24, 24; m 47; c 2. FRENCH. *Educ:* US Army Univ France, Cert Etudes French, 45; Butler Univ, AB, 49; Ind Univ, MA, 50, PhD(French), 62. *Prof Exp:* Asst prof French English, Murray State Univ, 50-51; vprin high sch, Ind, 51-57, teacher, 51-59; coordr foreign lang, Ind Univ, Bloomington, 59-67; prof lang educ, 68-78, PROF INSTRUCT DESIGN & PERSONNEL DEVELOP, FLA STATE UNIV, 78- *Concurrent Pos:* Lectr French, Butler Univ, 51-58; mem steering comt, Nat Carl Schurz Asn, 66-; dir hons prog foreign studies, Ind Univ. *Mem:* Am Coun Teaching Foreign Lang; Nat Educ Asn; Am Asn Teachers Fr. *Res:* Foreign language cirriculum development and teacher preparation. *Publ:* Coauth, Foreign language teaching, World Topics Yearbook, 60 & Good teaching practices, Reports Surv & Studies, 11/61; auth, The Indiana language program, Ling Reporter, 3/63; coauth, Effective Foreign Language Instruction, Prentice-Hall, 69. *Mailing Add:* Col of Educ Fla State Univ Tallahassee FL 32306

LEASKA, MITCHELL A, English Literary Criticism. See Vol II

LEBANO, EDOARDO ANTONIO, b Palmanova, Italy, Jan 17, 34; US citizen; m 57; c 2. ITALIAN. *Educ:* Cath Univ Am, MA, 61, PhD(Romance lang, Ital & French), 66. *Prof Exp:* Instr Ital lang, Sch Lang, Foreign Serv Inst, US Dept State, 59-61; lectr Ital lang & lit, Univ Va, 61-66; from asst prof to assoc prof Ital, Univ Wis-Milwaukee, 66-71; assoc prof Ital & assoc chmn dept, 71-73, dir, Ctr Ital Studies, Ind Univ, Bloomington, 74-77. *Concurrent Pos:* Ed, Wis Asn Foreign Lang Teachers Bull, 67-70; resident dir, Ind Univ-Univ Wis Centro di Studi, Bologna, Italy, 73-74, 78-79; ed, Am Asn Teachers Ital Newslett, 77- *Honors & Awards:* Uhrig Award, Univ Wis-Milwaukee, 68. *Mem:* MLA; Renaissance Soc Am; AAUP; Boccaccio Soc Am; Pirandello Soc Am; Am Asn Teachers Ital (secy-treas, 80-84); Dante Soc Am. *Publ:* Ed, Luigi Pirandello, Pensaci, Giacomino!, Ginn, 71; auth, Note sulla religiosita di Luigi Pulci, Forum Italicum, Vol IV, No 4; Vittorio Alfieri and the United States of America, Comp Lit Studies, Vol VIII, No 4; Luigi Pulci and late Fifteenth-Century humanism in Florence, Renaissance Quart, 74; coauth, A Look at Italy: Italia antica e moderna, Firenze, Sandron, 76; auth, Where to earn a degree in Italian: A 1975 survey of Italian undergraduate and graduate programs in the United States and Canada, Am Asn Teachers Ital Handbook for Teachers of Italian, 76; coauth, Il Trattato del prete colle monache, Interpres, Roma, Vol II, 79; Inediti di Ada Negri e Ugo Oietti, conferenzieri alla Dante Alighieri di Bologna, Can J Italian Studies, summer 81. *Mailing Add:* Ctr for Ital Studies Ind Univ Bloomington IN 47401

LEBEAU, BERNARD PIERRE, b Metz, France, Aug 3, 32; US citizen; m; c 2. FRENCH LANGUAGE & LITERATURE. *Educ:* Ohio Univ, BA, 55; Ohio State Univ, MA, 57. *Prof Exp:* Instr French, Antioch Col, 56; from instr to asst prof, Washington Col, 58-61; asst prof, US Naval Acad, 61-66; assoc prof, 66-81, chmn foreign lang, 76-81, PROF FRENCH & CHMN, LANG & LIT DIV, N CENT COL, 81- *Concurrent Pos:* Lang consult, Kent Co bd educ, Chestertown, Md, 59-61; prog dir FLES, Chestertown sch syst, 59-61; consult, ctr continuing educ & grad dept psychol, George Williams Col, 72-78; consult, Ill Dept Conserv Hist Div, 80- *Mem:* MLA; Am Asn Teachers Fr; Am Coun Teaching Foreign Lang; AAUP. *Res:* Modern French novel; French poetry, 1850-1914; literature in culture. *Publ:* Contribr, Naval Documents of the American Revolution, US Govt Printing Off, Vols I & II, 65 & 66; auth, Precis de Grammaire Francaise, NCent Col, 67. *Mailing Add:* Dept of Foreign Lang NCent Col Naperville IL 60540

LEBLANC, HERVE A, b St Joseph, NB, Oct 15, 16; US citizen. MODERN LANGUAGES. *Educ:* Univ Notre Dame, AB, 41, MA, 51. *Prof Exp:* Teacher, Holy Cross Sem, 45-51; asst prof, 51-62, head dept mod lang, 54-62, acad dean, 62-64, ASSOC PROF FRENCH, KING'S COL, PA, 64- *Concurrent Pos:* Mem, Nat Fedn Mod Lang Teachers Asn. *Mem:* Am Asn Teachers Fr; MLA. *Mailing Add:* Dept of French King's Col Wilkes-Barre PA 18710

LEBLANC, WILMER JAMES, b Abbeville, La, Nov 1, 28; m 61; c 3. LINGUISTICS. *Educ:* Univ Southwestern La, BA, 52; State Univ Iowa, MA, 54. *Prof Exp:* From instr to assoc prof Span, Loras Col, 54-67, chmn dept mod foreign lang, 64-67; jr instr Span, Univ Va, 68-70; asst prof, Madison Col Va, 70-71; instr, Univ Va, 71-72; asst prof French & English, 72-75, ASSOC PROF MOD LANG, PAUL D CAMP COMMUNITY COL, 75- *Mem:* Am Asn Teachers Span & Port; Am Asn Teachers Fr. *Res:* History of the Spanish language; Golden Age, Spanish American and contemporary Spanish drama. *Mailing Add:* Div of Commun Paul D Camp Community Col Franklin VA 23851

LEBLON, JEAN MARCEL JULES, b St Remy, Belgium, June 7, 28; US citizen; m 52; c 2. FRENCH LITERATURE, ROMANCE LANGUAGES. *Educ:* Emporia State Univ, BSEd, 51; Yale Univ, PhD(French), 60. *Prof Exp:* Instr French, Conn Col, 53-59; instr French & Span, City Col New York, 59-62; assoc prof mod lang & chmn dept, Hollins Col, 62-65; assoc prof, 66-74, dir, Vanderbilt-in-France, Aix-en-Provence, 69-71 & summers, 73-78, chmn, Dept French & Ital, 71-80, PROF FRENCH, VANDERBILT UNIV, 74- *Concurrent Pos:* Chmn writing comt French, MLA & Educ Testing Serv Coop Testing Prog, 60-63; vis prof NDEA insts, Univ Maine, Kans State Teachers Col & Fairfield Univ, 62-67; chmn French achievement test comt of examrs, Col Entrance Exam Bd, 71-74 & 81- & French lang develop comt, 76-81. *Mem:* Col Entrance Exam Bd; Am Asn Teachers Fr; SAtlantic Mod Lang Asn; Soc French Professors Am; SAtlantic Asn Depts Foreign Lang. *Res:* French theatre since 1890; the novel since 1672, particularly 18th and 20th centuries; French culture and civilization. *Publ:* Transl, Zola, Grove, 60; auth, Laboratory Manual, Le francais courant, Allyn & Bacon, 63; coauth, Precis de civilisation francaise, 66 & ed, Les Choses, 70, Appleton; coauth, La Condition humaine de Malraux, roman historique, Rev d'Hist Litteraire France, 5-7/75. *Mailing Add:* Dept of French & Ital Vanderbilt Univ Nashville TN 37235

LEBOFSKY, DENNIS STANLEY, b Philadelphia, Pa, Oct 28, 40; m 65; c 5. LINGUISTICS, HISTORY & STRUCTURE OF ENGLISH. *Educ:* Temple Univ, BA, 61; Princeton Univ, MA, 65, PhD(ling), 70. *Prof Exp:* Instr, 65-72, ASST PROF ENGLISH, TEMPLE UNIV, 72- *Res:* Philadelphia English. *Mailing Add:* Dept of English Temple Univ Philadelphia PA 19122

LECLERC, PAUL OMER, b Lebanon, NH, May 28, 41; m 80. FRENCH. *Educ:* Col of the Holy Cross, BS, 63; Columbia Univ, MA, 66, PhD(French), 69. *Prof Exp:* From instr to asst prof French, Union Col NY, 66-71, assoc prof, 71-78, chmn dept mod lang & lit, 72-78; UNIV ASSOC DEAN ACAD AFFAIRS & CHMN HUMANITIES DIV, CITY UNIV NEW YORK, 79- *Concurrent Pos:* Am Coun Learned Soc grant-in-aid, 73. *Mem:* Am Soc 18th Century Studies; Int Soc Studies 18th Century; Fr Soc Studies 18th Century. *Res:* The French Enlightenment; Voltaire; the abbe Andre Morellet. *Publ:* Auth, Deux inedits relatifs a la correspondance de Voltaire, Rev Hist Lit France, 3-4/72; Voltaire and Crebillon Pere: history of an enmity, Vol CXV & Unpublished letters from Morellet to Voltaire, Vol CVI, In: Studies on Voltaire and the Eighteenth Century, 73. *Mailing Add:* Off Acad Affairs City Univ New York New York NY 10021

LECOMPTE, NOLAN P, JR, b Houma, La, Aug 21, 35. LINGUISTICS, ENGLISH. *Educ:* Nicholls State Col, BA, 60; La State Univ, MA, 62, PhD(ling), 67. *Prof Exp:* Asst English, La State Univ, 60-61, teaching asst, 61-63, instr, 63-64; asst prof, 64-67, head dept, 71-72, assoc prof, 67-80, PROF ENGLISH, NICHOLLS STATE UNIV, 80-, DEAN COL LIB ARTS, 72- *Mem:* S Cent Mod Lang Asn; Am Dialect Soc. *Res:* Louisiana dialects; medieval literature, especially the works of the Gawain poet. *Publ:* Auth, Certain points of dialectical usage in South Louisiana, La Studies, summer 68. *Mailing Add:* PO Box 2020 Thibodaux LA 70301

LECROY, ANNE KINGSBURY, b Summit, NJ, Jan 21, 30; m 56; c 3. CLASSICS, ENGLISH. *Educ:* Bryn Mawr Col, AB, 47, MA, 48; Univ Cincinnati PhD, 52. *Prof Exp:* Teacher Latin & hist, Girls Latin Sch, Baltimore, Md, 50-51; instr classics, Western Reserve Univ, 52-55; asst prof, Univ NMex, 55-56; asst dean, Endicott Jr Col, 56-57; asst prof English, 59-63, assoc prof English & Greek, 63-67, PROF ENGLISH, E TENN STATE UNIV, 67- *Concurrent Pos:* Consult, Standing Liturgical Comn of Episcopal Church, 70- & mem, 76-; secy, Bishop's Comt for Revision of Eucharist, 72-; fel in res, Univ of the South, 78; consult & jurist papers Carolina Symposium on British Studies, 82. *Mem:* Am Fedn Teachers; Am Philol Asn; Archaeol Inst Am; NEA; S Atlantic Mod Lang Asn. *Res:* Semantics, modern generative grammar and comparative linguistics; literature, especially liturgical history; women's regional literature. *Publ:* Auth, Eucharistic change and the Tennessee layman, 72, Semantic problems in liturgical change--a sampling, 73 & No women to speak in the churches--a Pauline fallacy, 73, Tenn Churchman; contribr, Proposed Book of Common Prayer, 76 & Lesser Feasts & Fasts, 78, Church Hymnal Corp; ed, Commentary on the American Prayer Book, Seabury, 81; consult & contribr, Episcopalian Hymnal, 82; The comic stripped American woman, Cartonaggio, 81. *Mailing Add:* Dept of English E Tenn State Univ Johnson City TN 37601

LECUMBERRI-CILVETI, ANGEL, b Pamplona, Spain, Nov 26, 33; US citizen; m 67; c 2. SPANISH LITERATURE & PHILOSOPHY. *Educ:* Univ Barcelona, Phil Lic, 60, PhD, 64. *Prof Exp:* Asst prof, 70-74, assoc prof, 74-80, PROF SPANISH LIT, UNIV ROCHESTER, 80- *Mem:* MLA; Asn Int Hispanistas; Spanish Intellectual Hist; Spanish Golden Age. *Publ:* Ed, La vida es sueno, 70; auth, El significado de la vida es sueno, Albatros-Castalia, 71; La funcion de la metafora en La vida es sueno, Nueva Rev, de Fil Hispanica, 73; Introduccion a la mistica espanola, Catedra, 74; El demonio en el teatro de Calderon, Albatros, 77; Thomas Merton y San Juan de la Cruz, Rev de Espiritualidad, 77; Roland Barthes y San Ignacio de Loyola: La definicion semiologica de los Ejercicios espirituales, Letras de Deusto, 81; Dramatizacion de la alegoria biblica en Primero y segundo Isaac, Critical Perspectives on Calderon, Spanish American Studies, 81. *Mailing Add:* Dept of Foreign Lang, Lit & Ling Univ Rochester Rochester NY 14627

LECUYER, MAURICE ANTOINE FRANCOIS, b Beaune, France, May 25, 18; m 73. FRENCH. *Educ:* Univ Paris, Lic es Let, 43, Dipl, 44; Yale Univ, PhD(French), 54. *Prof Exp:* Instr French, Mt Allison Univ, 46-48 & Yale Univ, 48-52; instr Romance lang, Queens Col NY, 52-55; asst prof, Univ Ore, 55-59; asst prof French, Univ Chicago, 59-62; assoc prof, 62-69, prof, 69-79, EMER PROF FRENCH, RICE UNIV, 80- *Concurrent Pos:* Guggenheim fel, 68-69. *Mem:* MLA; Am Asn Teachers Fr; Soc Prof Fr Am. *Res:* Linguistics; modern French literature and criticism, especially 20th century. *Publ:* Auth, Balzac et Rabelais, Belles-Lett, Paris, 54; Etude de la prose de Paul Valery dans La soiree avec Monsieur Teste, Minard, Paris, 64; Robbe-Grillet's La jalousie and a parallel in the graphic arts, Hartford Studies Lit, 5/71; Les Propos et anecdotes de Jean Giono, ou un heureux art de vivre, Rice Univ Studies, spring 71; Les negres et au-dela, Obliques, 10/72. *Mailing Add:* Dept of French & Ital Rice Univ Houston TX 77001

LEDDY, JOHN FRANCIS, b Ottawa, Ont, Apr 16, 11; m 38. CLASSICS. *Educ:* Univ Sask, BA, 30, MA, 31; Oxford Univ, BLitt, 35, DPhil, 38, MLitt, 80. *Hon Degrees:* DLitt, St Francis Xavier Univ, 53 & Univ Ottawa, 57; LLD, Assumption Univ, 56, Univ Sask, 65, Univ Toronto, 66, Hanyang Univ, Korea, 71, Notre Dame Univ, Nelson, 71, Waterloo Lutheran Univ, 72 & Univ Western Ont, 75; D es L, Laval Univ, 56; DCL, St Mary's Univ, Can, 60. *Prof Exp:* From instr to prof classics, Univ Sask, 36-64, head dept, 46-64, dean col arts & sci, 49-64, acad vpres, 61-64; pres, Univ Windsor, 64-78. *Concurrent Pos:* Chmn, Humanities Res Coun, Can, 49-50 & 54-55; secy-treas, Nat Conf Can Univs, 53-56; mem, Can Coun, 57-60; vchmn, 64-69, pres, Can Nat Comn, UNESCO, 60-62; chmn, World Univ Serv, Can, 61-65 & Can Univ Serv Overseas, 62-65. *Honors & Awards:* Officer, Order Can, 72. *Mem:* Fel Royal Hist Soc; Class Asn Can (pres, 56-58); Humanities Asn Can (pres, 50-52); Can Cath Hist Asn (pres gen, 60-61). *Res:* History of the Roman Empire; history of the early Christian Church; Paulinus of Nola. *Publ:* Auth, The Humanities in an Age of Science, St Dunstan's Univ, 61; The Humanities in Modern Education, Gage, 65. *Mailing Add:* Univ of Windsor Windsor ON N9B 3P4 Can

LEDERER, HERBERT, b Vienna, Austria, June 9, 21; US citizen; m 48; c 2. GERMAN. *Educ:* Brooklyn Col, BA, 48; Univ Chicago, MA, 49, PhD(Ger), 53. *Prof Exp:* Instr Ger, Univ Chicago, 49-52; asst prof, Wabash Col, 52-53, assoc prof & chmn dept, 53-57; assoc prof, Ohio Univ, 57-61 & Queens Col NY, 61-69; head, Dept Ger & Slavic Lang, 69-79, PROF GER, UNIV CONN, 69- *Concurrent Pos:* Mem staff, Ger Summer Sch, Middlebury Col, 53-69; chief reader Ger Advan Placement, Educ Testing Serv, 64-67; chmn Ger comt, Col Entrance Exam Bd, 67-; Leo Baeck Soc Am Coun Learned Soc res grant, 68-69; vpres, Nat Fed Mod Lang Teachers Asn, 71, pres, 72; pres, Am Coun Study Austrian Lit, 72-80, Asn Depts Foreign Lang, 78. *Honors & Awards:* Austrian Cross of Honor for Arts & Letters, First Class, 76. *Mem:* Am Asn Teachers Ger; MLA; Int Arthur Schnitzler Res Asn; AAUP; Am Coun Studies Austrian Lit. *Res:* Modern German literature, especially Schnitzler and the young Vienna school; contemporary theater; linguistics and teaching methodology. *Publ:* Auth, Arthur Schnitzler's typology, PMLA, 63; Basic German: An Introduction, Scribner, 66; coauth, Fides: A Festschrift for Werner Neuse, Diagonale, Berlin, 68; coauth, A Reference Grammar of the German Language, Scribner, 69; ed, Frühe Gedichte von Arthur Schnitzler, Ullstein, Berlin, 69; Theater in the German Democratic Republic in Perspectives & Personalities, Heidelberg, Carl Winter, 78; coauth, Fortschritt Deutsch, Holt, 76; Glossary of Grammatical Terminology, 2nd ed, Am Asn Teachers Ger, 81. *Mailing Add:* Dept of Ger & Slavic Lang Univ of Conn Storrs CT 06268

LEDERER, RICHARD HENRY, Linguistics, Morphology. See Vol II

LEDUC, ALBERT LOUIS, b Vincennes, Ind, June 18, 11; m 33; c 3. MODERN LANGUAGES, FRENCH. *Educ:* Ind Univ, AB, 31, AM, 35; Univ Wis, PhD, 52. *Prof Exp:* Mem fac, Earlham Col, 31-33, Ind Univ, 33-36, Huntingdon Col, 36-40, Univ Wis, 40-41 & US Mil Acad, 42-47; from asst prof to assoc prof mod lang, Fla State Univ, 47-62; prof, 62-72, EMER PROF MOD LANG, HAMPDEN-SYDNEY COL, 72- *Concurrent Pos:* Vis prof, Stephen F Austin State Univ, summer 61 & Appalacchian state Univ, summers, 65 & 68. *Mem:* MLA; Am Asn Teachers Fr; S Atlantic Mod Lang Asn. *Res:* French theater; French 17th century. *Publ:* Co-ed, Selected speeches of Robert M Strozier, Fla State Univ Studies, 60; coauth, American Traveler's Companion, Fielding, 66. *Mailing Add:* 2035 Doomar Dr Tallahassee FL 32308

LEDYARD, GARI KEITH, b Syracuse, NY, Apr 28, 32; m 61; c 3. EAST ASIAN LANGUAGES, HISTORY. *Educ:* Univ Calif, Berkeley, BA, 58, MA, 63, PhD(Chinese lang & lit), 66. *Prof Exp:* From asst prof to assoc prof, 64-75, PROF KOREAN, COLUMBIA UNIV, 75- *Concurrent Pos:* Mem joint comt Korean studies, Am Coun Learned Soc-Soc Sci Res Coun, 67-, chmn, 69 & 77-; govt consult, Nat Defense Foreign Lang Fels, 67-71; mem Columbia Univ Sem on Korea, 71-, chmn, 72-75; mem, Comt Korean Studies, Asn Asian Studies, 66-68 & 77-, chmn, 77-78; consult, Nat Endowment for Humanities, 75- *Mem:* Am Orient Soc; Asn Asian Studies. *Res:* Chinese historical linguistics; Korean language and history; early Japanese history. *Publ:* Auth, Two Mongol documents from the Koryo sa, J Am Orient Soc, 63; The Mongol campaigns in Korea and the dating of the Secret history of the Mongols, Cent Asiatic J, 64; Cultural and political aspects of traditional Korean Buddhism, Asia, 68; The Dutch Come to Korea, Royal Asiatic Soc, Seoul, 71; Korean travellers in China over 400 years, Occassional Papers Korea, 74; Galloping along with the horseriders, looking for the founders of Japan, J Japanese Studies, 75. *Mailing Add:* 406 Kent Hall Columbia Univ New York NY 10027

LEE, CHARLES NICHOLAS, b Washington, DC, July 27, 33; m 56; c 4. RUSSIAN LITERATURE. *Educ:* Univ Md, BA, 55, MA, 58; Harvard Univ, PhD(Russ), 64. *Prof Exp:* Instr French, Ger & Russ, Univ Md, 56-60; asst prof Ger & Russ, Bucknell Univ, 63-65; from asst prof to assoc prof, 65-74, chmn, Dept Slavic Lang & Lit, 67-69, PROF RUSS, UNIV COLO, BOULDER, 74-, CHMN, DEPT SLAVIC LANG & LIT, 80- *Concurrent Pos:* NDEA summer fel, 65; Am Coun Learned Soc humanities fel, 75-76. *Mem:* Am Asn Advan Slavic Studies; Am Asn Teachers Slavic & E Europ Lang. *Res:* Russian prose of the 20th century emigration; Tolstoy in Russian & Western literature; A I Solzhenitsyn. *Publ:* Auth, The philosophical tales of M A Aldanov, Slavic & East Europ J, 71; Mark Aleksandrovic Aldanov: Zizn'i tvorcestvo, Russkaja lit v emigracii, 72; Dreams and daydreams in the early fiction of L N Tolstoy, Am Contrib Seventh Int Congr Slavists, 73; The short stories of M A Aldanov, In: Mnemozina; studia litteraria in honorem Vsevolod Setchkarev, 74; Man and the land in the fiction of Solzhenitsyn, Rocky Mountain Soc Sci J, 74; Mark Aldanov, In: Mod Encycl Russ & Soviet Lit, 77; Ecological ethics in the fiction of L N Tolstoj, Am Contrib Eighth Int Congr Slavists, 78; Mark Aldanov: Russian, Jewry and the World, Midstream, 81. *Mailing Add:* Dept of Orient & Slavic Lang & Lit Univ of Colo Boulder CO 80309

LEE, DAVID ELWOOD, b Trenton, NJ, Dec 16, 40; m 66. GERMAN LANGUAGE & LITERATURES. *Educ:* Princeton Univ, BA, 62; Stanford Univ, MA, 64, PhD, 68. *Prof Exp:* From instr to assoc prof Ger, Fisk Univ, 66-70, chmn dept foreign lang, 67-70; ASSOC PROF GER, UNIV TENN, KNOXVILLE, 70- *Concurrent Pos:* Am Coun Learned Soc study fel, 71-72. *Mem:* Am Asn Teachers Ger; Am Coun Teaching Foreign Lang. *Res:* German 18th century literature; language pedagogy. *Publ:* Auth, A new source for Goethe's Im Gegenwartigen Vergangnes, Monatshefte, 66; Die Rolle der Musik bei der Entstehung von Goethes, West-ostlichem Divan, In: Interpretationen zum West-ostlichen Divan Goethes, Wiss Buchgesellschaft, Darmstadt, 73; Objektivitat oder dichterische Eigenart? Goethes Verhaltnis zu seinen Quellen im Noten-Kapitel Blumen und Zeichenwechsel, Goethe Jahrbuch, 77; Two pages in Goethe's Deutscher Divan of 1814, Mod Lang Notes, 4/78. *Mailing Add:* Dept of Ger Univ of Tenn Knoxville TN 37916

LEE, GREGORY, b Hamilton, Ohio, Mar 2, 42; m 68. LINGUISTICS. *Educ:* Harvard Univ, AB, 64; Ohio State Univ, MA, 67, PhD(ling), 71. *Prof Exp:* Vis asst prof ling, Ohio State Univ, 70-71; ASST PROF LING, UNIV HAWAII, 71- *Mem:* Ling Soc Am. *Res:* Phonology; semantics. *Publ:* Auth, Notes in defense of case grammar, 69 & coauth, Another mouthful of divinity fudge, 74, Chicago Ling Soc; auth, English word and phrase stress, In: Essays on the Sound Pattern of English, Story-Scientia, 75; Presuppositions of conjoined sentences, 75, Natural phonological descriptions, Part I & II, 75 & 76, Interpretive phonological rules, 76 & There are no quantifiers (Ex), (x), 76, UHM Working Papers Ling. *Mailing Add:* Dept of Ling Moore 569 Univ of Hawaii 1890 East-West Road Honolulu HI 96822

LEE, HUGH MING, b Honolulu, Hawaii, Feb 10, 45. CLASSICS. *Educ:* St Mary's Col, Calif, BA, 66; Stanford Univ, MA, 71, PhD(classics), 72. *Prof Exp:* Instr classics, Ind Univ, Bloomington, 71-72, asst prof, 72-78; asst prof, Miami Univ, Ohio, 78-79; ASST PROF CLASSICS, UNIV MD, COLLEGE PARK, 79- *Concurrent Pos:* Nat Endowment for Humanities fel, 79-80. *Mem:* Am Philol Asn; Archaeol Inst Am; Vergilian Soc; Classical Asn Atlantic States. *Res:* Pindar; Greek and Roman athletics; Greek Literature. *Publ:* Auth, The Terma and the javelin in Pindar: Nemean 7.70-3, and Greek athletics, JHS, 96: 70-79; Purcell's Dido and Aeneas: Aeneas as romantic hero, Vergilius, 77; Slander (Diabole) in Herodotus 7.10 and Pindar 2.76, Hermes, 78; The historical Bundy and encomiastic relevance in Pindar, CW, 72: 65-72; Pindar, Bach, and Beethoven, Humanitas, 3: 16-18; Can a Christian be an athlete, can an athlete be a Christian?: Athletics and Christianity in western civilization, In: Publ Proc of US Olympic Acad V, 81; Pindar and the Art of His Time, Studies in Honor of T B L Webster (in press). *Mailing Add:* Dept of Classics Univ of Md College Park MD 20742

LEE, JOSEPH PATRICK, b Leitchfield, Ky, Nov 30, 42; m 72. FRENCH LANGUAGE & LITERATURE. *Educ:* Brescia Col, BA, 63; Fordham Univ, PhD(French), 71. *Prof Exp:* Asst prof French, Brescia Col, 67-71 & Univ Ga, 71-78; acad dean, Belmont Abbey Col, 78-81; VPRES ACAD AFFAIRS & PROF FRENCH, BARRY UNIV, 81- *Concurrent Pos:* Am Philos Soc res grant, 74. *Mem:* MLA; Am Asn Teachers Fr; Am Soc 18th Century Studies; Soc Fr Etude XVIIIe Siecle; SAtlantic Mod Lang Asn. *Res:* Eighteenth century French literature; Voltaire; Anglo-French literary relations. *Publ:* Contribr, The Complete Works of Voltaire, Voltaire Found, 68-; Dictionnaire des journalistes de langue francaise (1600-1789), Univ Grenoble, 76; auth, Voltaire and Cesar de Missy, Studies Voltaire & 18th Century, 76; Le Sermon philosophique: A Voltairean creation, Studies Lang & Lit, Eastern Ky Univ, 76; Voltaire and Massillon: Affinities of the heart, Fr Rev, 77. *Mailing Add:* VPres for Acad Affairs Barry Univ Miami Shores FL 33161

LEE, LEO OU-FAN, b Honan, China, Apr 9, 39. MODERN CHINESE LITERATURE & HISTORY. *Educ:* Nat Taiwan Univ, BA, 61; Harvard Univ, MA, 64, PhD(hist & Far Eastern lang), 70. *Prof Exp:* Instr hist, Dartmouth Col, 69-70; lectr, Chinese Univ Hong Kong, 70-71; asst prof, Princeton Univ, 72-76; assoc prof, Chinese lit, Ind Univ, Bloomington, 76-82; PROF CHINESE LIT, UNIV CHICAGO, 82- *Res:* Modern Chinese intellectual history; modern Chinese literature. *Publ:* Auth, The Romantic Generation of Modern Chinese Writers, Harvard Univ, 73. *Mailing Add:* Dept of EAsian Lang Univ of Chicago Chicago IL 60605

LEE, M OWEN, b Detroit, Mich, May 28, 30. CLASSICS. *Educ:* Univ Toronto, BA, 53, MA, 57; St Michael's Col, Univ Toronto, STB, 57; Univ BC, PhD, 60. *Prof Exp:* From lectr to asst prof classics, St Michael's Col, Univ Toronto, 60-68; from assoc prof to prof, Univ St Thomas, Tex, 68-72; assoc prof, Loyola Univ Chicago, 72-75; assoc prof, 75-79, PROF CLASSICS, UNIV TORONTO, 79- *Mem:* Am Philol Asn. *Res:* Myth of Orpheus; Roman poets; Wagner. *Publ:* Auth, Word, Sound, and Image in The Odes of Horace, Univ Mich, 69; Baptism of song, Bayreuther Festspiele, 70; Fathers and sons in Virgil's Aeneid, SUNY Press, 79. *Mailing Add:* St Michael's Col 81 St Mary St Toronto ON M5S 1J4 Can

LEE, MEREDITH ANN, b St Louis, Mo, July 11, 45; m 78. GERMAN LITERATURE, GERMAN LANGUAGE. *Educ:* St Olaf Col, BA, 68; Yale Univ, MPhil, 71, PhD(Ger), 76. *Prof Exp:* Actg instr, Yale Univ, 73-74; asst prof, 74-81, ASSOC PROF GER, UNIV CALIF, IRVINE, 81-, ASSOC DEAN HUMANITIES & UNDERGRAD STUDIES, 82- *Mem:* MLA; Am Asn Teachers Ger; Soc Values Higher Educ; Eighteenth Century Soc; Goethe Gesellschaft. *Res:* Age of Goethe; German poetry; German-Scandinavian literary relations. *Publ:* Auth, Goethe's Lyric Cycles, Univ NC, 78; The imperiled poet: Images of shipwreck and drowning in three Klopstock odes, No 12, 80 & Klopstock's temple imagery, No 13, 81, Lessing Yearbook; A question of influence: Goethe, Klopstock and Wanderers Sturmlied, Ger Quart, No 55, 82. *Mailing Add:* Dept of Ger Univ of Calif Irvine CA 92717

LEE, PETER HACKSOO, b Seoul, Korea, Jan 24, 29; m 62; c 2. LANGUAGES. *Educ:* Col St Thomas, BA, 51; Yale Univ, MA, 53; Univ Munich, PhD, 58. *Prof Exp:* Asst prof Korean & Japanese, Columbia Univ, 60-62; assoc prof East Asian comp lit, 62-70, chmn, Dept East Asian Lit, 73-76, PROF EAST ASIAN COMP LIT, UNIV HAWAII, MANOA, 70- *Concurrent Pos:* Bollingen Found, 62-63 & Guggenheim Found, 75; vis prof Orient lang, Univ Calif, Berkeley, 69-70; bk rev ed, J Asian Studies, 72-75; mem Int Coun Acad Sci Transl Ctr, Sch Arts, Columbia Univ, 75-; ed, Korean Studies, 80- *Mem:* Asn Asian Studies; Am Orient Soc; Am Comp Lit Asn; Chindan Soc, Korea. *Res:* Korean literary and intellectual history; East Asian comparative literature. *Publ:* Auth, Kranich am Meer: Koreanische Gedichte, Carl Hanser, Munich, 59; Anthology of Korean Poetry, Day, 64; Lives of Eminent Korean Monks, Harvard Univ, 69; ed & contribr, Flowers of Fire, Univ Hawaii, 74; auth, Songs of Flying Dragons: A Critical Reading, 75 & Celebration of Continuity: Themes in Classic East Asian Poetry, 79, Harvard Univ; ed & contribr, The Silence of Love: Twentieth-Century Korean Poetry, 80 & Anthology of Korean Literature: From Early Times to the Nineteenth Century, 81, Univ Hawaii. *Mailing Add:* Dept of East Asian Lit Univ of Hawaii at Manoa Honolulu HI 96822

LEE, SONIA M, b Paris, France, Jan 25, 38; m 58; c 3. FRENCH LITERATURE. *Educ:* Univ Wis, BS, 64, MA, 66; Univ Mass, PhD(French lit), 74. *Prof Exp:* Instr French, Univ Mass, 67-72 & Univ PR, 72-73; asst prof, 73-80, ASSOC PROF FRENCH, TRINITY COL, 81- *Mem:* MLA; Am Asn Teachers Fr; Soc Study Multi-Ethnic Lit US. *Res:* Women writers of French speaking world. *Publ:* Auth, The awakening of the self in the heroines of Sembene Ousmane, Critique, 12/75; The image of the woman in the African folk-tale from the sub-Saharan Francophone area, Yale Fr Studies, 76; French Literature of New England: Two Significant Writers, Soc Study Multi-Ethnic Lit US, 78; A selective bibliography of three prominent African authors, In: Critical Bibliography of French Literature of the 20th Century, Syracuse Univ, 79; A Critical Essay on Camara Laye, Twayne (in prep). *Mailing Add:* Trinity Col Box 1355 Hartford CT 06106

LEE, VERA G, b New Haven, Conn; c 1. ROMANCE LANGUAGES. *Educ:* Russell Sage Col, BA, 46; Yale Univ, MA, 49; Boston Univ, PhD(Romance lang), 62. *Prof Exp:* From asst prof to assoc prof mod lang, 64-77, PROF ROMANCE LANG, BOSTON COL, 77-, CHMN DEPT, 80- *Concurrent Pos:* Carnegie Gilman fel, 74; Am Philos Soc grant, 77. *Mem:* MLA; Am Asn Teachers Fr; Am Soc 18th Century Studies; Northeast Mod Lang Asn; Palmes Academiques. *Res:* French 20th century theater; 18th century French literature. *Publ:* Auth, Quest for a Public: French Popular Theater Since 1945, Schenkman, 70; ed, Through the looking glass with Eugene Ionesco, Drama & Theatre, winter 71-72; The Sade machine, Studies Voltaire & 18th Century, 72; Eugene Ionesco's Victims du devoir, Houghton, 72; auth, Key to Literary Criticism in French, 73 & The Reign of Women in 18th-Century France, 75, Schenkman; Cocteau, after a fashion, Am Soc Legion Hon Mag, 76. *Mailing Add:* 15 Claremont St Newton MA 02158

LEEBER, VICTOR F, b Elkins, WVa, Feb 18, 22. ROMANCE LANGUAGES. *Educ:* Boston Col, AB, 46, MA, 47; Weston Col, STL, 54; Univ Madrid, PhD(Span), 57. *Prof Exp:* From instr to assoc prof, 47-66, PROF MOD LANG, FAIRFIELD UNIV, 66-, CHMN DEPT, 57- *Mem:* MLA; Am Asn Cols Teacher Educ; Am Asn Teachers Span & Port. *Res:* Golden Age Spanish literature; neoclassical Mexican literature; Romance philology. *Publ:* Auth, Perfiles Literarios, Holt, 63; El P Abad y su obra Poetica, Porrua, Spain, 65. *Mailing Add:* Dept of Mod Lang Canisius Hall Fairfield Univ Fairfield CT 06430

LEED, RICHARD LEAMAN, b Lititz, Pa, Jan 31, 29; m 56; c 3. SLAVIC LINGUISTICS. *Educ:* Oberlin Col, BA, 54; Cornell Univ, PhD(Slavic ling), 58. *Prof Exp:* From asst prof to assoc prof, 58-68, PROF LING, CORNELL UNIV, 68- *Concurrent Pos:* Consult, US-USSR Acad Exchange Prog, 63-64. *Mem:* Ling Soc Am; Int Ling Asn; Am Asn Teachers Slavic & East Europ

Lang. *Res:* Russian-English contrastive linguistics; Russian intonation and dialectology. *Publ:* Coauth, Basic Conversational Russian, Holt, 64; auth, Russian and English intonation contours, Slavic & East Europ J, spring 65; A phonemic interpretation of the g-isogloss in Great Russian, Rev Can Ling, 66; Distinctive features and analogy, Lingua, 70; transl, Nominal Accentuation in Baltie and Slavic, Mass Inst Technol Press, 79; coauth, Advanced Russian, 80, Beginning Russian, Vol I, 81 & Beginning Russian, Vol II, 82, Slavica Publ. *Mailing Add:* Dept of Mod Lang & Ling Morrill Hall Cornell Univ Ithaca NY 14853

LEEDER, ELLEN LISMORE, b Havana, Cuba, July 8, 31; US citizen; m 57; c 1. SPANISH & SPANISH AMERICAN LANGUAGE & LITERATURE. *Educ:* Univ Havana, DrEduc, 55; Univ Miami, MA, 66, PhD(Span), 73. *Prof Exp:* From instr to prof Span, 60-75, chmn dept foreign lang, 75-76, PROF SPAN LANG & LIT, BARRY UNIV, 75-, COORDR FOREIGN LANG PROG, 76- *Concurrent Pos:* Consult, Dale County Pub Sch, Fla, 75- & Fla Nat Endowment for Humanities, 81-; vis prof, Valdosta State Col, 82. *Mem:* Am Asn Teachers Span & Port; MLA; SAtlantic Mod Lang Asn; Am Coun Teachers Foreign Lang; AAUP. *Res:* Spanish contemporary novel; Latin American literature. *Publ:* Auth, El Tema del Desarraigo en las Novelas de Angel Maria de Lera, Universal Ed, Fla, 78; Justo Sierra y el Mar, Univ educ, 79. *Mailing Add:* Dept of English & Foreign Lang Barry Univ Miami FL 33161

LEEMING, DAVID ADAMS, English, Comparative Literature. See Vol II

LEES, ROBERT B, b Chicago, Ill, July 9, 22; m 42; c 4. LINGUISTICS. *Educ:* Univ Chicago, AM, 50; Mass Inst Technol, PhD(elec eng), 59. *Prof Exp:* Jr chemist, Argonne Nat Lab, 46-50; ling ed, Univ Chicago, 50-52; ling group leader English as foreign lang, Georgetown Univ, Ankara, 54-55; linguist res mach transl, Mass Inst Technol, 56-57; res ling, Int Bus Mach Res Ctr, 59-61; assoc prof English & ling, Univ Ill, Urbana, 61-64, prof ling & head dept, 64-69; PROF LING & HEAD DEPT, TEL-AVIV UNIV, 69- *Mem:* Ling Soc Am. *Res:* English grammar; Turkish. *Publ:* Auth, Konusulan Ingilizce, Am Coun Learned Soc, 54; The Grammar of English Nominalizations, Res Ctr Anthrop, Folklore & Ling, Ind Univ, Bloomington, 60; The Phonology of Modern Standard Turkish, Vol IV, In: Uralic and Altaic Series, Ind Univ, 61; Analysis of the cleft sentence in English, Phonetik, 63; Turkish harmony and the phonological description of assimilation, Türk Dili Arastirmalari Yilligi Belleten, 67. *Mailing Add:* Dept of Ling Tel-Aviv Univ Ramat Aviv Israel

LEFKOWITZ, MARY ROSENTHAL, b New York, NY, Apr 30, 35; m 56, 82; c 2. CLASSICS. *Educ:* Wellesley Col, BA, 57; Radcliffe Col, MA, 59, PhD, 61. *Prof Exp:* Instr Greek, 59-63, from asst prof to assoc prof Greek & Latin, 63-75, chmn dept, 70-72 & 75-78, PROF GREEK & LATIN, WELLESLEY COL, 75-, ANDREW W MELLON PROF HUMANITIES, 79- *Concurrent Pos:* Fel, Radcliffe Inst, 66-67, 72-73, Am Coun Learned Soc fel, 72-73; mem managing comt, Am Sch Class Studies, Athens, 71-; consult, Nat Endowment for Humanities, 75-; vis prof, Univ Calif, Berkeley, 78; vis fel, St Hilda's Col, Oxford, 79-80; Nat Endowment for Humanities fel, 79-81. *Mem:* Am Philol Asn; Archaeol Inst Am. *Res:* Greek poetry; classical mythology; ancient biography. *Publ:* Auth, The first person in Pindar, 63 & Autobiographical fiction in Pindar, 80, Harvard Studies Class Philol; The influential fictions in the scholia to Pindar's Pythian 8, Class Philol, 75; The Victory Ode, Noyes, 76; co-ed, Women in Greece and Rome, Samuel Stevens, 77; Heroines and Hysterics, St Martin's, 81; The Lives of the Greek Poets, 81, & Women's Life in Greece and Rome, 82, Johns Hopkins. *Mailing Add:* Dept of Greek & Latin Wellesley Col Wellesley MA 02181

LEGARE, CLEMENT, b Quebec, Que, Feb 21, 23. SEMANTICS, SEMIOTICS. *Educ:* Bathurst Col, baccalaureat, 46; Univ Laval, Lic es Lett, 57; Ecole Hautes Etudes, Paris, dipl, 70; Sorbonne, PhD(ling), 72. *Prof Exp:* ASST PROF LING, UNIV QUE, TROIS-RIVIERES, 72- *Mem:* Can Ling Asn; Fr Can Asn Advan Sci; Asn Can Rech Semiotique (vpres). *Publ:* Auth, La Structure Semantique, Univ Quebec, Montreal, 76; coauth, Les Contes Populaires En Mauricie, Fides, Montreal, 78. *Mailing Add:* 4250 Savard Apt 514 Trois-Rivieres PQ G8Y 2G6 Can

LEGASSICK, TREVOR JOHN, b Kent, England, Aug 19, 35; m 63. ARABIC. *Educ:* Univ London, BA, 58, PhD(Arabic), 60. *Prof Exp:* Vis lectr Arabic, Univ Wis, 62-63; asst prof Asian Studies, Ind Univ, Bloominton, 63-66; asst prof, 66-69, assoc prof, 70-79, PROF ARABIC, UNIV MICH, ANN ARBOR, 79- *Concurrent Pos:* Fel, Am Res Ctr, Egypt, 64-65. *Mem:* Fel Am Orient Soc; fel MidE Studies Asn. *Res:* Contemporary Arabic literature and thought. *Publ:* Transl, Midaq Alley by Naguib Mahfuz, Khayats, Beirut, 67 & Heinemann, London, 74; Halim Barakat, Days of Dust, Medina Press, 74; Yusut Idris, Flip Flop and his Master, In: Arabic Writing Today, Cairo, 77; Ehsan Abdel Kuddous, I Am Free and Other Stories, Gen Egyptian Bk Orgn, Cairo, 78; auth, Major Themes in Modern Arabic Thought, Univ Mich, 78; transl, The Secret Life of Saeed, Vantage Press, 82; The Defense Statement of Ahmad 'Urabi, Am Univ Cairo, 82. *Mailing Add:* 3701 Riverside Dr Ann Arbor MI 48104

LEHISTE, ILSE, b Tallinn, Estonia, Jan 31, 22. LINGUISTICS. *Educ:* Univ Hamburg, PhD, 48; Univ Mich, PhD(ling), 59. *Hon Degrees:* DU, Univ Essex, Eng, 77, Univ Lund, Sweden, 82. *Prof Exp:* Mem fac, Univ Hamburg, 48-49; assoc prof Ger philol, Kans Wesleyan Univ, 50-51; assoc prof mod lang, Detroit Inst Technol, 51-56; res assoc acoustic phonetics, Commun Sci Lab, Univ Mich, 57-63; assoc prof ling & Slavic lang & lit, 63-65, chmn dept, 65-71, PROF LING, OHIO STATE UNIV, 65- *Concurrent Pos:* Nat Sci Found res grants, 61-63 & 63-65; guest prof, Univ Cologne, 65; Guggenheim fel, 69 & 75-76; guest prof ling, Univ Vienna, Austria, 74; Ctr Advan Study Behav Sci fel, 75-76; guest prof, Univ Tokyo, 80. *Honors & Awards:* Distinguished Res Award, Ohio State Univ, 80. *Mem:* Fel Acoust Soc Am; Ling Soc Am; Ling Soc Europe; Int Soc Phonetic Sci. *Res:* Acoustic phonetics; perception of spoken language; historical phonology. *Publ:* Auth, An acoustic-phonetic study of internal open juncture, Phonetica Suppl, 60; coauth, Accent in Serbocroatian: An Experimental Study, 63; auth, Acoustical Characteristics of Selected English Consonants, Ind Univ & Mouton, 64; Some Acoustic Characteristics of Dysarthric Speech, Karger, 65; Consonant Quantity and Phonological Units in Estonian, Ind Univ & Mouton, 66; ed, Readings in Acoustic Phonetics, 67 & auth, Suprasegmentals, 70, MIT, Isochrony reconsidered, J Phonetics, 77; coauth, Principles and Methods for Historical Linguistics, MIT, 79. *Mailing Add:* Dept of Ling Ohio State Univ 1841 Millikin Rd Columbus OH 43210

LEHMANN, WINFRED PHILIPP, b Surprise, Nebr, June 23, 16; m 40; c 2. LINGUISTICS & GERMANTIC PHILOLOGY. *Educ:* Northwestern Col, AB, 36; Univ Wis, AM, 38, PhD(Ger philol), 41. *Prof Exp:* From instr to asst prof, Wash Univ, 46-49; from assoc prof to prof Ger, 49-63, ASHBEL SMITH PROF LING & GER LANG, UNIV TEX, AUSTIN, 63- *Concurrent Pos:* Fulbright fel, Norway, 50-51; dir Georgetown Univ English Lang Prog, Ankara, Turkey, 55-56; Guggenheim fel, 72-73; mem bd dirs, Am Coun Learned Soc, 72- & Inst Deut Sprache, 73-; chmn, Ling Deleg to Peoples Repub China, 74. *Honors & Awards:* Brothers Grimm Prize, Philipps-Univ, Marburg, Ger, 75; Nehru Mem Lectr, 81. *Mem:* Ling Soc Am (pres, 73); MLA; Ling Soc Paris; Indogermanische Gesellschaft; foreign mem, Royal Acad Sci, Denmark. *Res:* Indo-European linguistics; general linguistics. *Publ:* Auth, The Development of Germanic Verse Form, Univ Tex, 56, Gordian, 71; Descriptive Linguistics: An Introduction, Random, 72, 2nd ed, 76; Historical Linguistics: An Introduction, Holt, 73; Proto-Indo-European Syntax, Univ Tex, 74; coauth, Introduction to Old Irish, MLA, 75; ed, Language and Linguistics in the PRC, 75 & Syntactic Typology, 78,; Linguistische Theorien der Moderne, Peter Lang, 81. *Mailing Add:* Univ Tex 3800 Eck Lane Austin TX 78734

LEHMEYER, FREDERICK ROBERT, b Baltimore, Md, June 10, 33; m 65. GERMAN LITERATURE. *Educ:* Johns Hopkins Univ, BA, 61; Univ Calif, Berkeley, MA, 65, PhD(Ger), 71. *Prof Exp:* Asst prof Ger, Univ Ba, 67-73; ASSOC PROF GER & CHMN DEPT MOD FOREIGN LANG, UNIV ALA, BIRMINGHAM, 73- *Mem:* MLA; Am Asn Univ Adminr; Am Asn Teachers Ger. *Res:* German baroque literature; Austrian literature; medieval literature. *Publ:* Auth, Anton Ulrichs Andromeda und seine Quellen, In: Europäische Tradition und Deutscher Literatur Barock: Uberlieferund und Umgestaltung, Francke, Bern, 73. *Mailing Add:* Univ of Ala Univ State Birmingham AL 35294

LEHN, WALTER, b Herschel, Sask, Mar 22, 26; m 51; c 2. LINGUISTICS, HISTORY. *Educ:* Tabor Col, BA, 51; Cornell Univ, PhD(gen ling), 57. *Prof Exp:* Asst prof ling & dir English Lang Inst, Am Univ Cairo, 57-60; assoc prof gen & Arabic ling, Univ Tex, Austin, 60-66, from assoc dir to dir Mid East Ctr, 60-66; prof ling & chmn dept, Univ Minn, Minneapolis, 66-74; prof ling & Mid East studies, Birzeit Univ, West Bank, Palestine, 77-78; dir study Palestinian people, UN, Beirut, Lebanon, 78-80; PROF & CHMN, ENGLISH DEPT, NAJAH UNIV, NABLUS, WEST BANK, PALESTINE, 81- *Concurrent Pos:* Hon mem Inst Peruano de Altos Estudios Islamicos. *Mem:* Ling Soc Am; Asn Arab-Am Univ Grads. *Res:* Modern Arabic dialects; phonology; modern Arab history. *Publ:* Auth, Vowel contrasts in a Saskatchewan English dialect, J Can Ling Asn, 59; coauth, Learning English, a Review Grammar for Speakers of Arabic, Am Univ Cairo, 61; Beginning Cairo Arabic, Hemphill's, 65; auth, The Palestinians: Refugees to guerrillas, Mid East Forum, 72; The Jewish national fund, J Palestine Studies, 74; The Development of Palestinian Resistance, Asn Arab-Am Univ Grads, 74; Determination of Israel's land policies, J Palestine Studies, 78. *Mailing Add:* c/o J Hildebrand 8 W Hampton Rd St Catharines ON L2T 3E5 Can

LEHNERT, HERBERT HERMANN, b Luebeck, Ger, Jan 19, 25; m 52; c 2. GERMAN. *Educ:* Univ Kiel, PhD, 52. *Prof Exp:* Studienrat Ger & hist, State of Schleswig-Holstein, Ger, 52-57; lectr Ger, Univ Western Ont, 57-58; lectr, Rice Univ, 58-59, from asst prof to prof, 59-67; prof, Univ Kans, 68-69; PROF GER, UNIV CALIF, IRVINE, 69- *Concurrent Pos:* Vis prof, Harvard Univ, 70; fels, Nat Endowment for Humanities, 73, 78 & Guggenheim, 78-79. *Mem:* MLA; Am Asn Teachers Ger; Hugo von Hofmannsthal Ges; Thomas Mann Ges; Int Ver Ger Sprach-u Literaturwiss. *Res:* German literature from 1750 to the present. *Publ:* Auth, Thomas Mann: Fiktion, Mythos, Religion, 65 & Struktur und Sprachmagie, 66, Kohlhammer, Stuttgart; Thomas Mann Forschung: Ein Bericht, Metzler, Stuttgart, 69; Fiktionale Struktur und physikalische Realität in Dürrenmatt die Physiker, Sprachkunst, 70; Die Gruppe 47, In: Die deutsche Gegenwartsliteratur, 71 & 81; Fictional orientations in Thomas Mann's biography, PMLA, 10/73; Bert Brecht und Thomas Mann im Streit über Deutschland, In: Deutsche Exilliteratur seit 1833, Kalifornien, 76; Geschichte der deutschen Literatur vom Jugendstil zum Expressionismus, Reclam, Stuttgart, 78. *Mailing Add:* Dept of Ger Univ of Calif Irvine CA 92717

LEHOUCK, EMILE, b Brussels, Belgium, June 25, 35; m 62; c 1. ROMANCE LANGUAGES, FRENCH LITERATURE. *Educ:* Free Univ Brussels, Lic en philol romane & Agrege, 57, PhD, 65. *Prof Exp:* Aspirant, Belgian Nat Found Sci Res, 61-66; asst prof, Univ Congo, 66-67; asst prof, 67-72, assoc prof, 72-79, PROF FRENCH, UNIV COL, UNIV TORONTO, 80- *Res:* Charles Fourier and the French literature; the romantic theatre. *Publ:* Auth, Le talent litteraire de Flora Tristan, 64 & Baudelaire fut-il fourieriste?, 66, Rev Univ Brussels; L'Education sentimentale et la critique en 1869, Rev Belge Philol et Hist, 66; Fourier Aujourd'hui, Denoel, 66. *Mailing Add:* Dept of French Univ Col Univ of Toronto Toronto ON M5S 1A1 Can

LEHRER, ADRIENNE JOYCE, b Minneapolis, Minn, Jan 16, 37; m 57; c 2. LINGUISTICS. *Educ:* Univ Minn, BS, 57; Brown Univ, MAT, 60; Univ Rochester, 68. *Prof Exp:* From instr to asst prof ling, Univ Rochester, 67-74; assoc prof, 74-79, chmn col comt ling, 74-79, PROF LING, UNIV ARIZ, 79- *Concurrent Pos:* Fel, Ctr Adv Studies Behav Sci, 73-74; Ariz Found res grant, 77. *Mem:* Ling Soc Am. *Res:* Structural semantics; psycholinguistics. *Publ:* Auth, Semantic cuisine, J Ling, 69; co-ed, The Theory of Meaning, Prentice-Hall, 70; auth, Semantic Fields and Lexical Structure, North Holland, 74; Talking about wine, Lang, 75; coauth, Nounlike quantifiers and the problem of determining the head, Ling Analysis, 76; auth, We talked, we drank wine, and a good time was had by all, Semiotica, 78; coauth, Semantic fields and the structure of metaphor, Studies in Lang, 81; Wine and Conversation, Ind Univ (in press). *Mailing Add:* Dept of Ling Univ of Ariz Tucson AZ 85721

LEHRMAN, EDGAR HAROLD, b New York, NY, Apr 13, 26; m 63; c 3. RUSSIAN LITERATURE. *Educ:* Cornell Univ, BA, 48; Columbia Univ, MA, 50, PhD(Slavic lang), 54 Cert, Russ Inst, 56. *Prof Exp:* Instr Russ, Duke Univ, 51-52 & Dartmouth Col, 54-55; admin asst to dir, Russ Inst, Columbia Univ, 55-56; asst prof Russ, Pa State Univ, 56-59; assoc prof & chmn dept, Emory Univ, 59-67; PROF RUSS & CHMN DEPT, WASH UNIV, 67- *Concurrent Pos:* Inter-Univ Comt Travel grants fac exchange, Moscow State Univ, 62-63. *Mem:* Am Asn Advan Slavic Studies; Am Asn Teachers Slavic & East Europ Lang; AAUP. *Res:* Russian literature since 1800, especially 19th century Russian and Soviet Russian prose; annotating great Russian prose for use by Americans. *Publ:* Transl, The Theatre in Soviet Russia, Columbia Univ, 57; ed, Turgenev's Letters: A Selection, Knopf, 61; auth, Akimov stages Hamlet, In: Essays on Shakespeare, Pa State Univ, 65; Konstantin Georgievich Paustovsky, In: Soviet Leaders, Crowell, 67; Needed: American handbooks for masterpieces in Russian, Slavic & E Europ J; A Handbook to the Russian Text of Crime and Punishment, Mouton & de Gruyter, 77; A Guide to the Russian Texts of Tolstoy's War and Peace, Ardis, 80. *Mailing Add:* Dept of Russ Wash Univ St Louis MO 63130

LE HUENEN, ROLAND JEAN, b St Pierre et Miquelon, Can, Apr 10, 45; m 66; c 2. FRENCH LITERATURE, SEMIOTICS. *Educ:* Univ Caen, Lic es Lett, 65, dipl ES, 66; Univ Strasbourg, PhD(philos), 68. *Prof Exp:* Asst prof, 68-73, assoc prof, 73-81, PROF FRENCH LIT, VICTORIA COL, UNIV TORONTO, 81- *Concurrent Pos:* Consult French, Humanities Res Coun Can, 75- & Quebec Ministry Educ, 78-; dir, Serie 3L Series, Didier, Can, 78- *Mem:* Groupe Int de Recherches Balzaciennes. *Res:* Nineteenth and twentieth century French literature; semiotics of the literary text; literature and psychoanalysis. *Publ:* Contribr, La Lecture Sociocritique du Texte Romanesque, Hakkert, 75; auth, Structure actantielle et inversion dans La Peste, Albert Camus 8, 77; Psychanalyse et Langages Litteraires, Nathan, Paris, 77; Balzac et La Peau de chagrin, Sedes, Paris, 79; coauth, Balzac Semiotique du personnage romanes que, l'exemple d'Eugenie Grandet, Didier & Presses de l'Univ de Montreal, 80; co-ed & contribr, Le roman de Balzac, Didier, Montreal, 80; contribr, Balzac et Les Parents pauvres, Sedes, Paris, 81. *Mailing Add:* Dept of French Victoria Col Univ of Toronto Toronto ON M5S 1K7 Can

LEIBER, JUSTIN FRITZ, Philosophy, Psycholinguistics. See Vol IV

LEICHTY, ERLE VERDUN, b Alpena, Mich, Aug 7, 33; m 63. ASSYRIOLOGY. *Educ:* Univ Mich, BA, 55, MA, 57; Univ Chicago, PhD(Assyriol), 60. *Prof Exp:* From res asst to res assoc Assyriol, Orient Inst, Univ Chicago, 60-63; from asst prof to assoc prof ancient hist, Univ Minn, 63-68; assoc prof Assyriol, 68-71, PROF ASSYRIOL, UNIV PA, 71-, CUR AKKADIAN LANG & LIT, UNIV MUS, 68- *Concurrent Pos:* Guggenheim fel, 64-65; ed, Expedition, 70-73 & J Cuneiform Studies, 72- *Mem:* Am Orient Soc; Archaeol Inst Am; Am Schs Orient Res. *Res:* Ancient Near Eastern history. *Publ:* Auth, A Bibliography of the Kuyunjik Collection of the British Museum, Trustees Brit Mus, 64; The Omen Series Shumma Izbu, J J Augustin, 69; A Remarkable Forger, 70 & Demons and Population Control, 71, Expedition; Two Late Commentaries, Arch fur Orientforsch, 73. *Mailing Add:* Dept Orient Studies Univ Pa Philadelphia PA 19104

LEIGH, JAMES ANTHONY, b Nashua, NH, May 5, 46; m 71; c 1. FRENCH LITERATURE, COMPARATIVE LITERATURE. *Educ:* Coe Col, BA, 69; Univ Maine, Orono, MA, 74; State Univ NY, Buffalo, PhD(French), 76. *Prof Exp:* ASST PROF FRENCH, MIAMI UNIV, 76- *Mem:* MLA. *Res:* Contemporary French literature; comparative innovative fiction; contemporary literary criticism and theory. *Publ:* Auth, Reading Compact, Mod Fiction Studies, autumn 74; A Reader's Guide to Circus and Code, Substance: 17, fall 77; coed, Nietzsche's Return, Semiotext(e):7, spring 78; auth, Michel Leiris: The Figure of Autobiography, Mod Lang Notes, 5/78; contribr, Another Beckett, 4th York College Colloquium on Contemporary Critical Methods, Bilingual, 78. *Mailing Add:* 805 S College Oxford OH 45056

LEIGHTON, CHARLES HENRY, b Boston, Mass, Nov 25, 24; m 55; c 2. SPANISH. *Educ:* Harvard Univ, AB, 51, AM, 53, PhD, 61. *Prof Exp:* Teacher French & Span, Beverly High Sch, Mass, 55-56; from instr to assoc prof, 56-73, chmn dept foreign lang & lit, 64-65 & dept Span & classics, 65-69, prof span, 73-79, PROF SPAN & HUMANITIES, UNIV NH, 79- *Mem:* Am Asn Teachers Span & Port; MLA; Renaissance Soc Am; Mod Humanities Res Asn. *Res:* Spanish literature of the 15th, 16th and 17th centuries; contemporary Spanish literature. *Publ:* Auth, Alejandro Casona's Pirandellism, Symposium, 63; Alejandro Casona as essayist: The message finds its medium, Rev Estud Hisp, 72; Alejandro Casona and suicide, Hispania, 72. *Mailing Add:* Dept Mod Lang & Lit Murkland Hall Univ of NH Durham NH 03824

LEIGHTON, LAUREN GRAY, b Virginia, Minn, June 21, 34; m 60; c 2. RUSSIAN LITERATURE, ROMANTICISM. *Educ:* Univ Wis-Madison, BA, 60; Ind Univ, MA, 62; Univ Wis-Madison, PhD(Slavic lang), 68. *Prof Exp:* Instr Russian, Mercer Univ, 62-63; instr, Grinnell Col, 63-64; asst prof Slavic, Univ Va, 67-72; assoc prof, Northern Ill Univ, 72-78; PROF SLAVIC, UNIV ILL, CHICAGO CIRCLE, 78- *Concurrent Pos:* US-USSR Acad Exchange, IREX-USSR Ministry Higher Educ, 70 & IREX-USSR Acad Sci, 77; ed, Slavic and East Europ J, 75-78. *Mem:* MLA; Asn Advan Slavic Studies; Am Asn Univ Prof; Am Asn Teachers Slavic & East Europ Lang. *Res:* Russian romanticism; Pushkin; modern Russian fiction. *Publ:* Auth, Bestuzhev-Marlinsky's lyric poetry, Slavonic Rev, 67; A romantic idealist notion in Russian romantic criticism, Can Slavic Studies, 71; Alexander Bestuzhev-Marlinsky, Twayne, 75; Russian Romanticism: Two Essays, Mouton, 75; Marlinizm: Istorija odnoj stilistiki, Russian Lit, 75; Numbers and numerology in Pushkin's The Queen of Spades, Can Slavonic Papers, 77; Gematria in The Queen of Spades: A decembrist puzzle, Slavic & E Europ J, 77; On translating One Day in the Life of Ivan Denisovich, Russian Lang J, 78. *Mailing Add:* Dept of Slavic Lang & Lit Univ of Ill Chicago Circle Chicago IL 60680

LEINER, JACQUELINE, b Caen, France. FRENCH & COMPARATIVE LITERATURE. *Educ:* Sch Orient Lang, Paris, dipl, 45; Sorbonne, Lic es Lett, 45, Dipl Inst Art, 45 & Dipl Advan Studies, 48; Univ Strasbourg, Dr es Lett(French lit), 69. *Prof Exp:* Cur, Nat Libr, Paris, 52-57; asst prof French lit & civilization, French Inst Sarrebrüch, 57-59; cur, Libr Univ Paris, 59-62; lectr French lit & civilization, 67-71, from asst prof to assoc prof, 71-77, PROF FRENCH LIT, DEPT ROMANCE LANG & DEPT, COMP LIT, UNIV WASH, 77- *Concurrent Pos:* Dir, Oeuvres et Critiques, 76-79; head conf Francophone lit, Int Ctr Francophones Studies, Univ Paris-Sorbonne, 77-78. *Mem:* Am Asn Teachers Fr; MLA; African Lit Asn; Soc Lit Generale & Comparee; Centre Rech sur l'Imaginaire. *Res:* Commitment in modern French literature; surrealism; Francophone literature, Africa, North Africa, West Indies and Quebec. *Publ:* Auth, Le probleme du langage chez F Fanon, M Haddad et A Memmi, 74 & Des problemes de la creation litteraire chez un ecrivain africain: entretien avec le romancier guineen, Camara Laye, 75, Presence Francophone; Preface-Bifur, re-ed, 76 & Preface-La Surrealisme au Service de la Revolution, re-ed, 76, Jean-Michel Place, Paris; Rene Depestre ou du surrealisme comme moyen d'acces a l'identite, Romanische Forschungen, 77; Marcel Duchamp devant la critique francaise d'Apollinaire a Michel Leiris, Oeuvres et Critiques, 77; Entretien avec Aime Cesaire, Jean-Michel Place, Paris, 77; Aime Cesaire: poesie et engagement, Esprit Createur, 77. *Mailing Add:* 4905 NE 40th St Seattle WA 98105

LEINER, WOLFGANG, b Ottenhausen, Ger, Oct 21, 25; m; c 1. ROMANCE LANGUAGES, COMPARATIVE LITERATURE. *Educ:* Univ Toulouse, dipl, 48, cert, 49; Univ Saarbrucken, DrPhil, 55, Habilitation, 63. *Prof Exp:* Asst Romance Lang, Univ Saarbrucken, 55-63, privatdocent, 63-65; vis lectr, 64-65, assoc prof, 65-67, PROF ROMANCE LANG, UNIV WASH, 67- *Concurrent Pos:* Ed, Papers on French Seventeenth Century Lit, 73- & Oeuvres et Critiques, 76; prof, Univ Tübingen, 75. *Mem:* MLA; Am Asn Teachers Fr; Int Asn Fr Studies; Soc Etudes XXeme Siecle. *Res:* French and Italian 16th and 17th centuries literature; history and aspects of theatre; criticism and rhetoric. *Publ:* Auth, Der Widmungsbrief in der Französischen Litteratur, Carl Winter Univ, Heidelberg, 65; Etudes sur les Lettres portugaises, Romanische Forsch, 65 & 66 & Oeuvres et Critiques, 76; L'uomo solo di Pavese, Neueren Spachen, 66; Deux sonnets de Chassignet et de Ronsard, Z Franzose Sprache und Lit, 74 & Ky Romance Quart, 75; Le Reve de Francion, Coherence Interieure, 77; Ionesco Rhinoceros, Franzose Theater; coauth, Cinna ou le pardon d'Emilie, Etudes Lit Fr, 78. *Mailing Add:* Dept of Romance Lang Univ of Wash Seattle WA 98195

LEINIEKS, VALDIS, b Liepaja, Latvia, Apr 15, 32; US citizen. CLASSICS. *Educ:* Cornell Univ, BA, 55, MA, 56; Princeton Univ, PhD, 62. *Prof Exp:* From instr to asst prof classics, Cornell Col, 59-64; assoc prof, Ohio State Univ, 64-66; assoc prof, 66-71, PROF CLASSICS, UNIV NEBR, LINCOLN, 71-, CHMN DEPT, 67-, CHMN COMP LIT PROG, 70- *Mem:* Am Orient Soc; Am Philol Asn; Ling Soc Am; Archaeol Inst Am; Am Comp Lit Asn. *Res:* Greek and Latin literature and linguistics; linguistic theory; comparative literature. *Publ:* Auth, Morphosyntax of the Homeric Greek Verb, Mouton, The Hague, 64; The Structure of Latin: An Introductory Text Based on Caesar and Cicero, MSS Educ Publ, 75; Index Nepotianus, Univ Nebr, 76; The plays of Sophokles, Amsterdam: Gru6ner, 82. *Mailing Add:* Dept of Classics Univ of Nebr Lincoln NE 68588

LEITCH, VINCENT BARRY, English & American Literature. See Vol II

LEITER, SHARON L, b Brooklyn, NY, Aug 12, 42; m 62; c 1. RUSSIAN LITERATURE, RUSSIAN LANGUAGE. *Educ:* Brandeis Univ, BA, 63; Boston Col, MSW, 67; Univ Mich, PhD(Russian Lang & Lit), 77. *Prof Exp:* ASST PROF RUSSIAN LANG & LIT, UNIV VA, 77- *Concurrent Pos:* Sesquicentennial associateship, Univ Va, 81. *Mem:* Am Asn Teachers Slavic & E Europ Lang. *Res:* Nineteenth and 20th century Russian literature; Osip Mandelstam; Anna Akhmatova. *Publ:* Auth, The Lady and the Bailiff of Time, Ardis, 74; Mandelstam's Petersburg: early poems of the city dweller, Slavic & E Europ J, Vol 22, No 4, 78; Mandelstam's Moscow: Eclipse of the Holy City, Russ Lit, Vol VII, 3/80; Peredonov's World: Aspects of the hero-narrator relationship in Sologub's The Petty Demon, Russ Lang J, No 122, winter 82; Osip Mandelstam, In: The Encycl of World Literature in the 20th Century, Frederick Ungar Publ Co, 82; Akhmatova's Petersburg, Univ Pa Press (in prep). *Mailing Add:* Dept of Slavic Lang & Lit Univ Va Charlottesville VA 22903

LEKI, ILONA, b Dieburg, Ger, Dec 24, 47; nat US. FRENCH LITERATURE, ENGLISH AS A SECOND LANGUAGE. *Educ:* Univ Ill, AB, 68, AM, 70, PhD(French), 75. *Prof Exp:* Instr English, Knox County Adult Educ, 74-76; instr, 76-80, ASST PROF ENGLISH, UNIV TENN, 80- *Concurrent Pos:* Translr French, US Govt Joint Publ Res, 74-; sr ed fac publ, Univ Tenn, 75-77; asst prof French, Knoxville Col, 75-77. *Mem:* MLA; SAtlantic Mod Lang Asn; Am Asn Teachers Fr; Southern Comp Lit Asn; Alliance Francaise (treas, 77-78). *Res:* French New Novel, particularly novels of Alain Robbe-Grillet; prose works of Henri Michaux; second language acquisition. *Publ:* Auth, Confrontations with reality: The travels of Henri Hichaux, Exploration, summer 78; Alain Robbe-Grillet, Twayne (in press). *Mailing Add:* 502 Longview Rd Apt E Knoxville TN 37919

LELAND, CHARLES WALLACE, English Literature, Scandinavian Drama. See Vol II

LEMKE, VICTOR JACOB, b LaCrosse, Wis, July 18, 11; m 35; c 1. MODERN GERMAN LITERATURE. *Educ:* Univ Wis, AB, 33, AM, 34, PhD, 38. *Prof Exp:* Instr Ger, Univ Minn, 37-38 & Univ Wis, 38-39; from instr to prof, 39-77, head dept, 49-62, EMER PROF GER, WVA UNIV, 77- *Concurrent Pos:* Assoc ed, WVa Univ Philol Papers, 49-; ed, WVa Foreign Lang Bull, 55-69; found travel fel, WVa Univ, 61. *Mem:* MLA; Am Asn Teachers Ger; SAtlantic Mod Lang Asn; Int Ver Ger Sprach-u Literaturwiss; Am Coun Teaching Foreign Lang. *Res:* Goethe; lyric poetry; Gottfried Keller. *Publ:* Auth, Hans Heinrich Ehrler, 38, The Idea of das Ganze in Goethe, 1766-1775, 39 & The Deification of Gottfried Keller, 56, Monatschefte. *Mailing Add:* Dept of Foreign Lang WVa Univ Morgantown WV 26506

LEMOINE, FANNIE JOHN, b Langdale, Ala, Dec 26, 40; m 70; c 1. CLASSICS, COMPARATIVE LITERATURE. *Educ:* Univ Iowa, BA, 61, MA, 62; Bryn Mawr Col, PhD(Latin), 68. *Prof Exp:* From instr to assoc prof, 66-78, PROF CLASSICS & COMP LIT, UNIV WIS-MADISON, 78- *Concurrent Pos:* Inst Res Humanities fel classics, 76-77. *Mem:* Mediaeval Acad Am; Am Philol Asn; MLA; Soc Bibl Lit; Renaissance Soc Am. *Res:* Late Latin and early Medieval literature. *Publ:* Auth, Martianus Capella: A Literary Evaluation, Arbeogesellschaft, Munich, 72; Judging the beauty of diversity: A critical approach to Martianus Capella, Class J, 72. *Mailing Add:* Dept of Classics Univ of Wis 908 Van Hise Hall Madison WI 53706

LEMUS, GEORGE, b Del Rio, Tex, Apr 14, 28; m 57; c 5. SPANISH, LATIN AMERICAN STUDIES. *Educ:* Univ Tex, BA, 52, MA, 56, PhD(Latin Am studies), 63. *Prof Exp:* Teacher, Aberdeen High Sch, Idaho, 52-53; teaching fel, Univ Tex, 55-57; instr, US Air Force Lang Sch, Lackland Air Force Base, Tex, 57-58; instr Span, Loyola Univ Los Angeles, 58-60; from asst prof to assoc prof, 60-68; chmn Latin Am studies comt, 63-66, grad adv Latin Am studies & Span prog, 66-70, PROF SPAN, SAN DIEGO STATE UNIV, 68- *Concurrent Pos:* Del Amo Found fel, Spain, 70-71. *Mem:* Am Asn Teachers Span & Port; Asn Latin Am Studies; Pac Coast Coun Latin Am Studies (secy-treas, 64); Real Soc Bascongada Amigos del Pais, Bilboa, Spain; Philol Asn Pac Coast. *Res:* Mexican historical literature; Latin American political literature and government; the Basques in the United States. *Publ:* Auth, Pedagogia mexicana y norteamericana comparada, Hispania, 9/62; Francisco Bulnes: su vida y sus obras, Ed Andrea, Mexico City, 65. *Mailing Add:* Dept of Span & Port Lang & Lit San Diego State Univ San Diego CA 92182

LENARD, YVONE V, b France; US citizen. FRENCH. *Educ:* Col Cherbourg, Baccalaureat, 38; Col Perpignan, Baccalaureat, 39; Faculte de droit, Univ Bordeaux, Certificat de licence en droit, 42; Univ Calif, Los Angeles, BA, 55, MA, 56. *Prof Exp:* Lectr French, Univ Calif, Los Angeles, 55-67; assoc prof, 68-72, chmn dept, 72-79, PROF FRENCH, CALIF STATE UNIV, DOMINGUEZ HILLS, 72- *Honors & Awards:* Chevalier des Palmes Acad, 70; Knight, French Order of Sci, Art & Lett; French Order Merite et Devouement. *Mem:* Am Asn Teachers Fr; MLA. *Res:* Methodology; culture; civilization. *Publ:* Auth, Parole et pensee, 65, 71 & 77, L'Art de la conversation, 67, ed, Le matin des magiciens, 67, auth, Jeunes voix, jeunes vistages, 69, Fenetres sur la France, 70 & Tresors du temps, 72, Harper. *Mailing Add:* 567 N Beverly Glen Los Angeles CA 90024

LENARDON, ROBERT JOSEPH, b Ft William, Ont, Sept 8, 28. CLASSICS. *Educ:* Univ BC, BA, 49; Univ Cincinnati, MA, 50, PhD(classics), 54. *Prof Exp:* Instr Greek & Latin, Columbia, Univ, 54-57; asst prof classics, Univ Wash, 57-59; asst prof class lang, 59-64, assoc prof classics, 64-70, dir grad studies, 68-77, PROF CLASSICS, OHIO STATE UNIV, 70- *Concurrent Pos:* Bk rev ed, Class J, 61-68; vis fel, Corpus Christi Col, Cambridge, 71. *Mem:* Am Philol Asn; Archaeol Inst Am; Class Asn Midwest & S. *Res:* Greek history and literature. *Publ:* Auth, The archonship of Themistokles, 56 & The chronology of Themistokles' ostracism and exile, 59, Historia; Charon, Thucydides, and Themistokles, Phoenix, 61; coauth, Classical Mythology, Longman, 2nd ed, 77; auth, The Saga of Themistocles, Thames & Hudson, 78. *Mailing Add:* Dept Classics Ohio State Univ Columbus OH 43210

LENCEK, RADO L, b Mirna, Yugoslavia, Oct 3, 21; US citizen; m 46; c 2. SLAVIC PHILOLOGY & CIVILIZATIONS. *Educ:* Univ Chicago, MA, 59; Harvard Univ, PhD(Slavic lang & lit), 62. *Prof Exp:* Prof Slavic lang, Ist Tech Commerciale, Ist Magistrale Statale Sloveno, Trieste, 44-55; asst prof Slavic ling, Univ Ill, Urbana, 62-65; from asst prof to assoc prof, 65-74, PROF SLAVIC LANG, COLUMBIA UNIV, 74- *Concurrent Pos:* Participant exchange scholars with Acad Sci USSR, Am Coun Learned Soc grant, 69-72; vis prof, NY Univ, 69-72 & Yale Univ, 74. *Mem:* Ling Soc Am; Am Asn Teachers Slavic & East Europ Lang; Czech Soc Arts & Sci in US; Am Asn Southeastern Europ Studies; Soc Slovene Studies (pres, 74-). *Res:* Slavic linguistics; Slovene; Slavic cultures and their history. *Publ:* Auth, An Outline of the Course on Slavic Civilizations, Columbia Univ, 70, 73; On the morphophonemic patterning of Slavic imperative, In: American Contributions to VII International Congress of Slavists, 73 & co-ed, Xenia Slavica: Papers Presented to Gojko Ruzicic, 75, Mouton; ed, Papers in Slovene Studies, 1975 & 1976, 75-77; co-ed, The Dilemma of the Melting Pot: The Case of the South Slavic Languages, Pa State Univ, 76; auth, Jan Baudouin de Courtenay on the Dialects Spoken in Ven Slovenia and Rezija, Soc Slovene Studies, 77; The Structure and History of the Slovene Language, Slavica Publ, 82; co-ed, To Honor Jernej Kopitar, 1780-1980, Mich Slavic Publ, 82. *Mailing Add:* Columbia Univ 420 West 228th St New York NY 10027

LENNOX, JOHN WATT, Comparative Canadian Literature. See Vol II

LENOWITZ, HARRIS, b San Antonio, Tex, Jan 24, 45; m 66; c 2. LINGUISTICS, JEWISH STUDIES. *Educ:* Univ Tex, Austin, BA, 66, PhD(ling), 71. *Prof Exp:* Instr English as second lang, Dept English & instr Hebrew lit, Dept Orient & African Lang & Lit, Univ Tex, 70-71; asst prof lang & ling, 72-76, ASSOC PROF LANG, LING & COMP LIT, MID EAST CTR, DEPT LANG, UNIV UTAH, 76- *Concurrent Pos:* Dean's award Frank studies, Univ Utah, 76-77; vis prof, Mid East Studies Ctr, Portland State Univ, 78 & 80. *Honors & Awards:* Transl Award, PEN Am Ctr, 75. *Mem:* Am Acad Relig; Soc Biblical Lit; Am Schs Orient Res; Asn Jewish Studies; Nat Asn Prof Hebrew. *Res:* Jacob Frank, Messianism-Jewish; biblical literature, Psalms; Jewish poetry and poetics, mystic and modern. *Publ:* Coauth, An introduction to Mediterranean cosmogony, Alcheringa: Ethnopoetics, 74; auth, Din and Razel, Margins, 75; Rothenberg: The Blood, Vort, 76; co-ed, Origins, Doubleday/Anchor & AMS, 76 & 77; A Big Jewish Book, Doubleday/Anchor, 78; auth, The Sayings of the Lord Jacob Frank, Tree/Tzadikim, 78; An introduction and the first fifty sayings of the Lord Jacob Frank, Alcheringa: Ethnopoetrics, 78; Introduction to the Sayings of Jacob Frank, Proc Eighth World Cong Jewish Studies, Jerusalem, 81. *Mailing Add:* Mid East Ctr Univ Utah Salt Lake City UT 84112

LENSKI, BRANKO ALAN, b Zagreb, Yugoslavia, Dec 4, 28; US citizen; m 56; c 1. MODERN FRENCH & YUGOSLAV LITERATURE. *Educ:* NY Univ, PhD(French), 66. *Prof Exp:* Instr French, Tufts Univ, 62-66; asst prof, Univ Wash, 66-70, ASSOC PROF FRENCH, GETTYSBURG COL, 70- *Mem:* MLA; Am Asn Teachers Fr; Am Coun Teaching Foreign Lang; Am Asn SSlavic Studies. *Res:* The theatre in 20th century French literature; the metaphysical novel in 20th century French literature; the novel in 20th century Yugoslav literature. *Publ:* Ed, Death of a Simple Giant and Other Modern Yugoslav Stories, Vanguard, 65; Andre Gide: les nourritures terrestres, Peter Pauper, 69; Krleza, Vanguard, 72; Yuboslav literature and politics, Suvr Mag, 72; Jean Anouilh: Stages in Rebellion, Humanities, 73. *Mailing Add:* Dept of Romance Lang Gettysburg Col Gettysburg PA 17325

LENSON, DAVID ROLLAR, Comparative Literature. See Vol II

LENZ, HAROLD F H, b Milwaukee, Wis, Sept 11, 08; m 34; c 3. GERMAN LANGUAGE & LITERATURE. *Educ:* NY Univ, BS, 28, MA, 30, PhD(Ger), 34. *Prof Exp:* From grad asst to instr Ger, Univ Col, NY Univ, 28-38; from instr to prof & dean students, Queens Col, 38-68; prof, 68-78, EMER PROF GER, UNIV HOUSTON, 78-; EMER PROF QUEENS COL, 68- *Concurrent Pos:* Radio instr comp lit, WNYC, New York, 58-59; TV instr Ger, Queens Col, Ford Found, 61-63. *Mem:* MLA; Am Asn Teachers Ger. *Res:* German drama; European drama. *Publ:* Auth, Dramatics in the German Club, Ger Quart, 5/37; Franz Grillparzer's political ideas, J English Ger Philol, 4/38; coauth, Goethe's Urfaust (text ed), Harper, 38; auth, Der Deutschlehrer u Lessing's Nathan, Ger Quart, 41; Scientific German for Intermediate Students (text book), Norton, 41; coauth, Practical American English, Book I, Longmans Green, 56; auth, Study Guide for Contemporary European Drama, Queens Col, 58; Germany, In: Reader's Encycl of World Drama, Crowell, 69. *Mailing Add:* Dept of Ger Univ of Houston Cullen Blvd Houston TX 77004

LEO, ERNEST JOHN, b New York, NY, July 20, 29. GERMAN. *Educ:* Columbia Col, BA, 50; Northwestern Univ, MA, 51. *Prof Exp:* Instr Ger, Columbia Univ, 56-61; instr, Univ Pittsburgh, 62-64; lectr, City Col New York, 64-68; instr, 69-79, LECTR GER, BROOKLYN COL, 80- *Concurrent Pos:* Fel Harvard, 51-62, 54-56; Fulbright grant, Univ Munich, 61-62. *Mem:* MLA; Am Asn Teachers Ger. *Res:* Heinrich von Kleist; German Romanticism; 19 century European novella and short story. *Publ:* Ed, German Ballads, Prentice-Hall, 66. *Mailing Add:* 910 W End Ave Apt 14F New York NY 10025

LEON, PEDRO, b Ligre, France, Mar 12, 26; m 49; c 1. PHONETICS, LINGUISTICS. *Educ:* Univ Paris, Lic es Lett, 51; Univ Besancon, DUniv, 60; Sorbonne, Dr es Lett, 72. *Hon Degrees:* Dr, Univ de Nancy, 82. *Prof Exp:* Asst prof, Inst Phonetics, Sorbonne, 50-58; asst prof French, Ohio State Univ, 58-60, dir lang lab, Ctr Appl Ling & maitre asst, Fac Lett, Univ Besancon, 60-63, assoc prof French, 63-64; assoc prof, 64-65, PROF FRENCH & DIR EXP PHONETICS LAB, UNIV TORONTO, 65- *Concurrent Pos:* Can Coun res grants, 65-66, 69-71 & 73-74. *Honors & Awards:* Palmes academiques, 77. *Mem:* MLA; Inst Soc Phonetic Sci; Speech Commun Asn; Fr-Can Asn Advan Sci; Can Ling Asn. *Res:* Canadian French; phonostylistics; prosody. *Publ:* Co-ed, Prosodic Feature Analysis/Analyse des Faits Prosodiques, Studia Phontica III, 70, auth, Essais de Phonostylistique, Studia Phonetica IV, 71 & co-ed, Problem of Textual Analysis/Problemes de l'Analyse Textuelle, 71, Didier, Paris; Ou en sont les etudes sur l'intonation, Proc Seventh Int Congr Phonetic Sci, 73; auth, De l'analyse psychologique a la categorisation des emotions dans la parole, J Psychologie, 7-12/76; La Phonologie, Klincksieck, Paris, 77; coauth, Toronto English, Studies in Phonetics, Studia Phonetica XIV, 79; Problemes de prosodie, Studia Phonetica XVII et XVIII, 82. *Mailing Add:* Exp Phonetics Lab Univ of Toronto 39 Queen's Park Crescent E Toronto ON M5S 1A1 Can

LEON, PIERRE R, b Ligre, France, Mar 12, 26; m 49; c 1. PHONETICS, LINGUISTICS. *Educ:* Univ Paris, Lic es Lett, 51; Univ Besancon, DUniv, 60; Sorbonne, Dr es Lett, 72. *Hon Degrees:* Dr, Universite de Nancy, 82. *Prof Exp:* Asst prof, Inst Phonetics, Sorbonne, 50-58; asst prof French, Ohio State Univ, 58-60, dir lang lab, Ctr Apple Ling & maitre asst, Fac Lett, Univ Besancon, 60-63, assoc prof French, 63-64; assoc prof, 64-65, PROF FRENCH & DIR EXP PHONETICS LAB, UNIV TORONTO, 65- *Concurrent Pos:* Can Coun res grants, 65-66, 69-71 & 73-74. *Mem:* MLA; Inst Soc Phonetic Sci; Speech Commun Asn; Fr-Can Asn Advan Sci; Can Ling Asn. *Res:* Canadian French; phonostylistics; prosody. *Publ:* Coauth, Prolegomenes a l'Etude des Structures Intonatives, Studia Phonetica II, 70, coed, Prosodic Feature Analysis/Analyse des Faits Prosodiques, Studia Phontica III, 70, auth, Essais de Phonostylistique, Studia Phonetica IV, 71 & coed, Problem of Textual Analysis/Problemes de l'Analyse Textulle, 71, Didier, Paris; Ou en Sont les Etudes sur l'Intonation, Proc Seventh Int Congr Phoetic Sci, 73; auth, De l'Analyse Psychologique a La Categorisation des Emotions Dans La Parole, J Psychologie, 7-12/76; La Phonologie, Klincksieck, Paris, 77; coauth, Toronto English, Studies in Phonetics, Studia Phonetica XIV, 79; Problemes de prosodie, Studia Phonetica XVII et XVIII, 82. *Mailing Add:* Exp Phonetics Lab Univ Toronto Toronto ON M5S 1A1 Can

LEONARD, CLIFFORD SHATTUCK, JR, b New Haven, Conn, Apr 22, 28; m 56; c 2. ROMANCE LINGUISTICS. *Educ:* Yale Univ, BA, 50; Middlebury Col Grad Sch French, France, MA, 53; Cornell Univ, PhD(Romance ling), 60. *Prof Exp:* Teacher French & Latin, Barnard Sch Boys, 63-64; instr French, Cornell Univ, 59-60, asst prof, 60-66; assoc prof French & Ital, Univ Wis-Madison, 67-69; ASSOC PROF ROMANCE LING, UNIV MICH, ANN ARBOR, 69- *Concurrent Pos:* Asst dir develop proj, Cornell-ETS lang exams, 61-64; res grant, Cornell Univ, 66-67. *Mem:* Ling Soc Am. *Res:* Comparative Romance dialectology. *Publ:* Auth, A Reconstruction of Proto-Lucanian, Orbis, 69; The Romance stammbaum in the west, Romance Philol, 70; The Vocalism of Proto-Rhaeto-Romance, Orbis, 72. *Mailing Add:* Dept of Romance Lang Univ of Mich Mod Lang Bld Ann Arbor MI 48104

LEONARD, ETTA LOUISE, b Bangor, Main, Oct 21, 99. FRENCH. *Educ:* Smith Col, AB, 21, MA, 22. *Prof Exp:* Teacher high sch, Bangor, Maine, 22-24; from instr to assoc prof, 26-70, EMER ASSOC PROF MOD LANG, HOOD COL, 70- *Honors & Awards:* Chevalier, Palmes Acad, 71. *Mem:* MLA; Am Asn Teachers Fr; AAUP. *Res:* French literature of the 19th and 20th centuries; French phonetics. *Publ:* Ed, Premier de Cordee. *Mailing Add:* Parkview Apt 10-C Frederick MD 21701

LEPINIS, ASTA HELENA, b Daugavpils, Latvia. GERMAN & SCANDINAVIAN LITERATURE. *Educ:* Queen's Univ, Ont, BA, 59, MA, 61; Yale Univ, PhD(Ger), 70. *Prof Exp:* From instr to asst prof, 63-70, chmn dept, 68-76, ASSOC PROF GER, WHEATON COL, MASS, 70- *Mem:* Am Asn Teachers Ger; AAUP; MLA; Am Asn Prof Yiddish. *Res:* Literary theory; Yiddish literature; Robert Musil. *Mailing Add:* Dept of Ger Wheaton Col Norton MA 02766

LEPKE, ARNO KARL, b Zuhlsdorf, Ger, Feb 28, 22. GERMAN, FRENCH. *Educ:* Univ Marburg, PhD, 47. *Prof Exp:* Instr, Woodstock Prep Sch, 48-49; asst prof lang, Univ NH, 49-54, assoc prof, 54-60, prof mod lang, 60-61; actg head dept lang, 61-62, head, 62-68, chmn div humanities, 68-79, dir int studies, 70-79, PROF MOD LANG, UNIV AKRON, 61-, MASTER UNIV HONS PROG, 76- *Concurrent Pos:* chmn NDEA Ger Inst foreign Elem Sch Teachers, Univ NH, 60. *Mem:* MLA; Am ASn Teachers Ger. *Res:* Comparative literature; humanities. *Publ:* Auth, Do we meet our responsibilities, 1/53 & Emphases in the teaching of comparative literature, 4/57, Mod Lang J; Who is Doctor Stockman?, Scand Studies, 5/60. *Mailing Add:* Div of Humanities Univ of Akron Akron OH 44325

LEPPMANN, WOLFGANG A, b Berlin, Ger, July 9, 22; m 46; c 3. GERMAN. *Educ:* McGill Univ, BA, 48, MA, 49; Princeton Univ, PhD, 52. *Prof Exp:* Instr Ger, Brown Univ, 51-54; from asst prof to assoc prof, 54-64; chmn dept, 64-66 & 67-68, PROF GER, UNIV ORE, 64- *Concurrent Pos:* Alexander von Humboldt fel, 58-59, 62-63 & 73; Guggenheim fels, 62 & 71-72; vis prof Ger, Vassar Col, 66-67, Univ Toronto, 68-69, Yale Univ, 75 & Univ Va, 79. *Mem:* MLA; Am Asn Teachers Ger; Goethe Soc; Auth League. *Res:* Goethe; modern German literature. *Publ:* Auth, The German Image of Goethe, Oxford Univ, 62; Goethe und die Deutschen, Stuttgart, 63; Pompeji-eine Stadt in Literatur und Leben, Nymphenburger, 66; Pompeii in Fact and Fiction, Elek Bks, 68; Winckelmann, Knopf, New York, 70, Gollancz, London, 71 & Propyläen, Berlin, 72; Rilke, Scherz, Munich, 81. *Mailing Add:* Dept of Ger Univ of Ore Eugene OR 97403

LERNER, ISAIAS, b Buenos Aires, Arg, Mar 13, 32; m 67; c 1. SPANISH LITERATURE. *Educ:* Univ Buenos Aires, professor, 59; Univ Ill, Urbana-Champaign, PhD(Span), 69. *Prof Exp:* Instr Latin & Span, Univ Buenos Aires, 60-66; asst prof Span lit, Univ Ill, Urbanna-Champaign, 69-71; assoc prof, 71-79, PROF SPAN LIT & CHMN DEPT, HERBERT H LEHMAN COL, CITY UNIV NEW YORK, 79-, PROF LETTERS, 80- *Concurrent Pos:* Guggenheim fel Span lit, 77-78; fel, Herbert H Lehman Col, 77-78. *Honors & Awards:* Premio Extraordinario Augusto Malaret, Real Acad Espanola, 73. *Mem:* MLA; Am Asn Teachers Span & Port. *Res:* Spanish literature of the XVI and XVII century; history of the Spanish language; XVIII century Spanish lexicography. *Publ:* Co-ed, El Ingenioso Hidalgo Don Quijote de la Mancha, Ed Univ Buenos Aires, 69; contribr, The Ibero-American Enlightenment, Univ Ill, 71; auth, Arcaismos lexicos del Espanol de America, 74 & contribr, Estudios de Literatura Espanola Ofrecidos a Marcos A Morinigo, 74, Insula; auth, El texto de La Araucana: la edicion de Medina, Revista Iberoam, 74; Para una nueva lectura de Dona Perfecta de Galdos, Lexis; Nota lexica cervantina: Las Algarrovillas, Revista Filol Espanola, 77; A proposito del lenguaje coloquial galdosiano, Anuario Letras, 77. *Mailing Add:* Herbert H Lehman Col Bedford Park Blvd W Bronx NY 10468

LERNER, LIA SCHWARTZ, b Corrientes, Arg. SPANISH & COMPARATIVE LITERATURE. *Educ:* Univ Buenos Aires, Prof en Let, 65; Univ Ill, PhD(Span lit), 71. *Prof Exp:* Instr Latin & Greek, Univ Buenos Aires, 62-65; instr Span, Univ Ill, 70-71; asst prof, 71-80, ASSOC PROF SPAN & COMP LIT, FORDHAM UNIV, 80- *Mem:* MLA; Asn Int Hispanistas; Am Comp Lit Asn; Cervantes Soc Am. *Res:* Spanish literature of the Golden Age; comparative literature: relations; classical satirists-writers of the Renaissance and Baroque. *Publ:* Auth, Tradicion literaria y heroinas indias en La Araucana de Ercilla, Revista Iberoam, 72; El juego de palabras en las prosa satirica de Quevedo, Anuario Letras, Mex, 73; Notas sobre el retrato literario en la obra satirica de Quevedo, Revista del IN del Profesorado, Buenos Aires, 74; Martial and Quevedo: Re-creation of satirical patterns, Antike und Abendland, Berlin, 77. *Mailing Add:* Fordham Univ Lincoln Ctr Campus New York NY 10023

LESKO, LEONARD HENRY, b Chicago, Ill, Aug 14, 38; m 66. EGYPTOLOGY. *Educ:* Loyola Univ Chicago, AB, 61, MA, 64; Univ Chicago, PhD(Egyptol), 69. *Prof Exp:* Instr Latin & Greek, Quigley Prep Sem S, Chicago, 61-64; res asst, Orient Inst, Univ Chicago, 64-65; actg instr Egyptology, Univ Calif, Berkeley, 66-67, actg asst prof, 67-69, from asst prof to assoc prof, 69-77, dir, Near Eastern Studies Ctr, 73-75, chmn dept Near Eastern studies, 75-77 & 79-81, prof, 77-82, chmn prog ancient hist & archaeol, 78-79; WILBUR PROF EGYPTOLOGY & CHMN DEPT, BROWN UNIV, 82- *Concurrent Pos:* Nat Endowment for Humanities younger humanist fel, 70-71; collab ed Coffin texts, Orient Inst, Univ Chicago, 71-; Am Coun Learned Soc award, 73-74; Nat Endowment for Humanities proj grant, 75-79. *Mem:* Egypt Explor Soc; Am Orient Soc; Am Res Ctr Egypt; Fondation Egyptol Reine Elisabeth, Brussels; Int Asn Egyptologists. *Res:* Ancient Egyptian religious literature; Egyptian history and language. *Publ:* Auth, Some observations on the composition of the Book of Two Ways, J of Am Orient Soc, 71; The field of Hetep in Egyptian Coffin texts, J of Am Res Ctr Egypt, 71-72; The Ancient Egyptian Book of Two Ways, Univ Calif, 72; Glossary of the Late Ramesside Letters, privately printed, 75; King Tut's Wine Cellar, B C Scribe, 77; The shortest book of Amduat?, In: Studies in Honor of George R Hughes, Univ Chicago, 77; The Berkeley late Egyptian dictionary, Comput & Humanities, 77; Index of the spells on Egyptian Middle Kingdom coffins and related documents, B C Scribe, 79. *Mailing Add:* Dept of Egyptology Brown Univ Providence RI 02912

LESLEY, ARTHUR MICHAEL, JR, b Newark, NJ, Mar 15, 43. COMPARATIVE LITERATURE, HEBREW LITERATURE. *Educ:* Univ Calif, Berkeley, BA, 65, MA, 66, PhD(comp lit), 76. *Prof Exp:* Vis instr Hebrew, Ohio State Univ, 72-74; asst prof, Hebrew Union Col, New York, 74-77; ASST PROF HEBREW, UNIV TORONTO, 77- *Mem:* Asn Jewish Studies; MLA; Renaissance Soc Am. *Res:* Modern Hebrew literature; Hebrew literature in Renaissance Italy. *Mailing Add:* 324 Cormaught Toronto ON M2R 2L9 Can

LETTAU, REINHARD, b Erfurt, Ger, Sept 10, 29; US citizen. GERMANIC LITERATURES. *Educ:* Harvard Univ, PhD, 60. *Prof Exp:* From instr to assoc prof Ger lang & lit, Smith Col, 57-67; PROF GER LIT & CREATIVE WRITING, UNIV CALIF, SAN DIEGO, 67- *Concurrent Pos:* Lectr, Mt Holyoke Col, 59-60 & Univ Mass, 60-61; fel, Arts Inst, Univ Calif, 70-71. *Mem:* MLA; PEN Club. *Res:* Postwar German literature; 18th century drama and prose. *Publ:* Auth, Feinde, 68 & Täglicher Faschismus, 71, Hanser, Munich, Rowohlt, Hamburg, 73 & Reclam, Leipzig, 74; Enemies, Calder & Boyars, London, 73; Immer kürzer werdende Geschicten, 73 & Frühstücksgespräche in Miami, 77, Hanser, Munich; co-ed, Karl Marx Love Poems, City Lights, San Francisco, 77; ed, Franz Kafka, Aeroplane von Brescia, S Fischer, Frankfurt, 77; Zerstreutes Hinausschaun (essays), Hanser, Munich, 80. *Mailing Add:* Dept of Lit Univ of Calif La Jolla CA 92037

LETTS, JANET TAYLOR, b Ho-Ho-Kus, NJ, Sept 19, 30. FRENCH LITERATURE. *Educ:* Swarthmore Col, BA, 52; Univ Strasbourg, dipl, 55; Yale Univ, PhD, 62. *Prof Exp:* Instr French, Wellesley Col, 59-60; from instr to assoc prof, 67-76, PROF FRENCH, WHEATON COL MASS, 76-, CHMN DEPT, 66- *Concurrent Pos:* Mem adv comt, Jr Year in France, Sweet Briar Col. *Mem:* MLA; Int Asn Fr Studies; Soc Fr Hist Studies. *Res:* Seventeenth century French literature. *Publ:* Auth, Le Cardinal de Retz, Historien et Moraliste du Possible, Nizet, Paris, 66. *Mailing Add:* Dept of French Wheaton Col Norton MA 02766

LEUNG, KAI-CHEONG, b Hong Kong, June 19, 36; US citizen; m 68; c 2. CHINESE LANGUAGE & CULTURE. *Educ:* Hong Kong Univ, BA & MA, 63; Leeds Univ, Dipl, 66; Int Phonetic Asn, Cert, 66; Univ Calif, Berkeley, PhD(Orient lang), 74. *Prof Exp:* Lectr English & educ, Grantham Col Educ, 64-69; lectr, English & extra-mural studies, Chinese Univ Hong Kong, 67-69; asst prof Chinese, 73-79, ASSOC PROF CHINESE, SAN JOSE STATE UNIV, 79- *Concurrent Pos:* Consult, Asian-Am Bilingual Ctr, Berkeley, 80-81. *Mem:* Int Phonetic Asn; Asn Asian Studies; Philol Asn Pac Coast; Chinese Lang Teachers Asn. *Res:* Chinese drama; East-West literary relations; pedagogy. *Publ:* Auth, The Cantonese Student in the mandarin class: Some special problems, J Chinese Lang Teachers Asn, 2/78; The dramatic quality of three Yüeh-fu Poems, Chinese Cult, Vol XIV, 73; Visions of Cathay: China in English literature of the Romantic Period, Tsing Hua J Chinese Studies, 12/79; Literature in the service of politics: The Chinese literary scene since 1949, World Lit Today, winter 81. *Mailing Add:* Dept of Foreign Lang San Jose State Univ San Jose CA 95008

LEVI, JUDITYH NAOMI, b New York, NY, March 19, 44. LINGUISTICS. *Educ:* Antioch Col, BA, 64; Univ Chicago, MA, 72, PhD(ling), 75. *Prof Exp:* Lectr mod Hebrew, 72-73, instr ling, 73-75, asst prof, 75-79, ASSOC PROF LING, NORTHWESTERN UNIV, 79- *Mem:* Ling Soc Am. *Res:* Syntax and semantics; word formation; language and the law. *Publ:* Auth, A semantic analysis of Hebrew compound nominals, In: Studies in Modern Hebrew Syntax & Semantics, North Holland, 76; The constituent structure of complex nominals, In: Chicago Ling Soc XIII, 77; The Syntax and Semantics of Complex Nominals, Acad Press, 78; Linguistics, language & the law: A topical bibliography, Ind Univ Ling Club, 82. *Mailing Add:* Dept of Ling 2016 Sheridan Rd Evanston IL 60201

LEVIN, DONALD NORMAN, b Rochester, NY, Feb 1, 27; m 49; c 2. CLASSICS. *Educ:* Cornell Univ, BA, 49, MA, 52; Harvard Univ, MA, 54, PhD(class), 57. *Prof Exp:* Asst class, Tufts Col, 53-54; Ford Found intern class & humanities, Reed Col, 54-55; from instr to asst prof class, Wash Univ, 56-59; asst prof, Mt Holyoke Col, 59-63; assoc prof, 63-68, PROF CLASS, RICE UNIV, 68- *Concurrent Pos:* Wash Univ res grants, 57-59. *Mem:* Am Philol Asn; Archaeol Inst Am; Asn Int Papyrologues; Class Asn Midwest & South; Soc Ancient Greek Philos. *Res:* Greek drama and early Greek philosophy; Hellenistic literature; Latin poetry, especially elegy and lyric. *Publ:* Auth, Quaestiones Erinneanae, Harvard Studies Class Philol, 62; An epithet for Argos in Appollonius, Greek, Roman & Byzantine Studies, 63; Horace's preoccupation with death, Class J, 67-68; Apollonius' Argonautica reexamed, In: The Neglected First and Second Books, E J Brill, 71. *Mailing Add:* Dept of Classics Rice Univ Houston TX 77001

LEVIN, JULES FRED, b Chicago, Ill, Jan 25, 40; m 67; c 1. LINGUISTICS. *Educ:* Univ Calif, Los Angeles, BA, 61, MA, 64; PhD(Balto-Slavic ling), 71. *Prof Exp:* Vis lectr Russ, Univ Calif, Santa Barbara, 68-69; acting asst prof Russ & ling, 69-71, asst prof, 71-77, ASSOC PROF RUSS & LING, UNIV CALIF, RIVERSIDE, 77- *Mem:* Ling Soc Am; Am Asn Teachers Slavic & EEurop Lang; Asn Advan Baltic Studies. *Res:* Linguistics: historical and dialectology; Balto-Slavic linguistics: historical, dialectology, phonology. *Publ:* Auth, -ja stems and -e stems in the Elbing vocabulary, In: Baltic Literature and Linguistics, Asn Advan Baltic Studies-Ohio State Univ, 73; The Slavic Element in the Old Prussian Elbing Vocabulary, Univ Calif, 74; Slavic borrowings in the Elbing vocabulary and their implication for Prussian phonology, Gen Ling, Vol XII, No 3. *Mailing Add:* Dept of Lit & Lang Univ of Cal Riverside CA 92521

LEVIN, MAURICE IRWIN, b Boston, Mass, Feb 13, 31; m 53; c 2. SLAVIC LINGUISTICS. *Educ:* Boston Univ, BA, 53; Harvard Univ, MA, 58, PhD(Slavic), 64. *Prof Exp:* Instr mod lang, Mass Inst Technol, 61-63; asst prof Russ, Bowdoin Col, 63-65; asst prof Slavic, Ind Univ, Bloomington, 65-68; assoc prof, 68-72, PROF SLAVIC, UNIV MASS, AMHERST, 72- *Mem:* Am Asn Teachers Slavic & EEurop Lang; Am Coun Teachers Russ. *Res:* Russian language; structure of Russian; pedagogy of Russian. *Publ:* The Stress Patterns of the Russian Verb, Russ lang J, 71; Variant Forms in Russian Conjugation, Slavic & EEurop J, 72; Some Uses of the Accusative Case in Time Expressions, 73 & Stress Notation in the Russian adjective, 75, Russian Lang J, 75; Irregularities in Imperfective Derivation, Slavic & EEurop J, 77; Russian Declension and Conjugation: A Structural Description with Exercises, Slavica Publ, 78; Stress Notation in Russian Declension, Folia Slavica, 78; On Predicting the Genitive Case of Pluralia Tantum Nouns, Russ Lang J, 80. *Mailing Add:* Dept of Slavic Lang & Lit Univ of Mass Amherst MA 01003

LEVIN, SAMUEL R, Linguistics. See Vol II

LEVIN, SAUL, b Chicago, Ill, July 13, 21; m 51; c 6. CLASSICS. *Educ:* Univ Chicago, AB, 42, PhD(Greek), 49. *Prof Exp:* Instr hist, Univ Chicago, 49-51; from asst prof to assoc prof classics, Wash Univ, 51-61; prof, 61-65, PROF ANCIENT LANG, STATE UNIV NY BINGHAMTON, 65- *Concurrent Pos:* Fund Advan Educ fac fel, 53-54. *Mem:* Am Philol Asn; Soc Bibl Lit; Nat Asn Prof Hebrew; Am Orient Soc; Ling Asn Can & US (pres, 80-81). *Res:* Comparison of Semitic and Indo-European languages; classical Greek, especially the Homeric dialect; Hebrew scriptures. *Publ:* Translr, Aelius Aristides, To Rome, Free Press, 50; auth, The Linear B Decipherment Controversy Re-Examined, State Univ NY, 64; Hebrew Grammar: An Objective Introduction to the Biblical Language, State Univ NY Binghamton, 66; The Indo-European and Semitic Languages, State Univ NY, 71; Know thyself: Inner compulsions uncovered by oracles, In: Fons Perennis: Saggi Critici di Filologia Classica Raccolti in Onore del Prof Vittorio D'Agostino, Baccola & Gili, 71; The Father of Joshua/Jesus, State Univ NY Binghamton, 78; The etymology of nektar: Exotic scents in early Greece, Studi Micenei ed Egeo-anatolici, XIII: 31-50; The significance of dialect words, Greek Lit; Homeric word for goddess, Gen Ling, XXI: 236-247. *Mailing Add:* Dept of Classics State Univ of NY Binghamton NY 13901

LEVINE, DANIEL BLANK, b Cincinnati, Ohio, Sept 22, 53. CLASSICAL LANGUAGE & LITERATURE. *Educ:* Univ Minn, BA, 75; Univ Cincinnati, PhD(classics), 80. *Prof Exp:* ASST PROF CLASSICS, UNIV ARK, 80- *Concurrent Pos:* Ed, Ark Class Newslett, 80- *Mem:* Class Asn Mid West & South; Am Philol Asn. *Res:* Epic poetry; archaic Greek history. *Publ:* Auth, Odyssey 18: Iros as paradigm for the suitors, Class J, 82; Counterfeit man, Festschrift (in prep). *Mailing Add:* Dept of Foreign Lang Univ of Ark Fayetteville AR 72701

LEVINE, EDWIN BURTON, b Chicago, Ill, Nov 11, 20; m 44; c 2. GREEK & LATIN. *Educ:* Univ Chicago, PhD(class lang & lit), 53. *Prof Exp:* Instr classics, Univ Nebr, 51-52; instr Greek, Univ Chicago, 54-55; from instr to asst prof ancient lang, Wayne State Univ, 55-61; high sch teacher, Mich, 61-62 & Ill, 62-64; vis lectr English, Univ Ill, Chicago Circle, 64-65, asst prof classics, 65-66, assoc prof classics, 66-68, prof, 68-69, in-chg prog, 65-69, head dept, 69-74. *Concurrent Pos:* Vis lectr, Recanati Sch, Ben Gurion Univ of Negev; vis lectr cont educ prog, Kupat Holim, Tel Aviv, spring 82. *Mem:* Am Philol Asn; Class Asn Midwest & South; Archaeol Inst Am; Soc Hist Med; fel AAAS. *Res:* History of medicine, philosophy and rhetoric; Greek and Latin lexicography; Greek tragic drama. *Publ:* Coauth, Hippocrates father of nursing too?, Am J Nursing, 12/65; compiler Latin-to-English sect, World Latin Dict, Follett, 67; auth, Introduction to Classical Greek, Stipes, 67; translr, Latin poems of Walter Savage Landor, Bull John Rylands Libr, fall 68; auth, Hippocrates, Twayne, 71. *Mailing Add:* 550 Sheridan Sq Evanston IL 60202

LEVINE, PHILIP, b Lawrence, Mass, Sept 8, 22; m 55; c 2. CLASSICAL PHILOLOGY. *Educ:* Harvard Univ, AB, 44, AM, 48, PhD(class philol), 52. *Prof Exp:* From instr to asst prof classics, Harvard Univ, 52-59; assoc prof, Univ Tex, 59-61; assoc prof, 61-63, acting dir, Ctr Medieval & Renaissance Studies, 65-66, PROF CLASSICS, UNIV CALIF, LOS ANGELES, 63-, DEAN DIV HUMANITIES, 65- *Concurrent Pos:* Guggenheim fel, 57-58; Fulbright res scholar, Italy, 57-58; Bromberg Award, 60; chief reader Latin advan placement prog, Col Entrance Exam Bd, 61-65, mem exam comt Latin, 63-67 & 73-77, chief examr, 77-80; mem adv coun, Sch Class Studies, Am Acad Rome, 62-; mem rev comt sr fel prog, Nat Endowment for Humanities, 66 & 67. *Honors & Awards:* Knight Order Merit of Repub Italy, Ital Govt, 73. *Mem:* Am Philol Asn; Philol Asn Pac Coast; Mediaeval Acad Am; Renaissance Soc Am. *Res:* Latin palaeography and textual criticism; early Christian Latin authors; Latin poetry. *Publ:* Auth, Early Latin Versions of Gregory of Nyssa's De Opficio Hominis, Harvard Studies Class Philol, 58; Augustine, City of God, Books 12-15, Vol IV, Loeb Class Libr, Harvard, 66; The Continuity and Preservation of the Latin Tradition, In: The Transformation of the Roman World, Univ Calif, 66; Catullus c 1: A Prayerful Dedication, 69 & Catullus c 68: A New Perspective, 9/76, Calif Studies Class Antiq. *Mailing Add:* Dept Classics Univ Calif Los Angeles CA 90024

LEVISI, MARGARITA, b Turin, Italy, Feb 22, 31. ROMANCE LANGUAGES. *Educ:* Univ Buenos Aires, Lic lit, 55; Ohio State Univ, PhD(Span), 64. *Prof Exp:* Instr Span & Ital, 62-64, from asst prof to assoc prof Span lit, 66-73, PROF SPAN LIT, OHIO STATE UNIV, 73- *Mem:* MLA; Renaissance Soc Am. *Res:* Spanish baroque and Renaissance literature. *Publ:* Auth, Las figuras compuestas en Arcimboldo y Quevedo, Comp Lit, 68; La pintura en la narrativa de Cervantes, Bol Bibliot Menendez y Pelayo, 73; La funcion de lo visual en La Fuerza de la Sangre, Hispanofila, 73; La expresion de la interioridad en la poesia de Quevedo, Mod Lang Notes, 73; La crueldad en los Deseganos amorosos de Maria de Zayas, Estud Homenaje Prof Helmuth Hatzfeld, 75; Los elementos visuales en la Egloga II de Garcilaso, Bol Bibliot Menendez Pelayo, 77; Los monstruos en el Criticon de Gracian, Actas del VI Congreso Internacional de Hispanistas, 80; La interioridad visualizable en Garcilaso, Hispanofila, No 73, 81. *Mailing Add:* Dept of Romance Lang Ohio State Univ Columbus OH 43210

LEVITINE, EDA MEZER, b Russia, Feb 16, 27; US citizen; m 44; c 3. FRENCH LITERATURE. *Educ:* Boston Univ, AB, 50, MA, 52. *Prof Exp:* From instr to asst prof French, Lesley Col, 57-64; asst prof, 64-69, ASSOC PROF FRENCH, TRINITY COL, 69-, CHMN DEPT, 70- *Mem:* Am Asn Teachers Fr. *Res:* French 19th century literature; Baudelaire, Flaubert; relationship between French literature and French art. *Publ:* Auth, Baudelaire: Fashion and modernity, In: Hommage a Baudelaire, Univ Md, 68; transl, Flaconet, Reflexions sur la peinture, In: George Levitine, The Sculpture of Falconet, NY Graphic, 72; transl, Twentieth century masterpieces from the Musee de Grenoble, Univ Md, 11/73; transl, Couffignal, Apollinaire, Ala Univ, 75. *Mailing Add:* Dept of French Trinity Col Washington DC 20017

LEVITSKY, IHOR ALEXANDER, b Freistadt, Austria, Sept 3, 15; US citizen; m 52; c 1. SLAVIC LANGUAGES & LITERATURE. *Educ:* Univ Rochester, AB, 36; Univ Buffalo, MA, 38, BS, 40; Duke Univ, PhD, 48. *Prof Exp:* Asst prof philos, Univ Vt, 47-51; cur spec collections, Univ Mo Libr, 52-54; sr cataloger, Princeton Univ Libr, 54-56; head catalog div, Univ Ga Libr, 56-58; asst prof Ger & Russ, Univ Ga, 58-62; from asst prof to assoc prof, 62-68, PROF GER & RUSS, UNIV WATERLOO, 68- *Mem:* MLA; Am Asn Advan Slavic Studies; Am Asn Teachers Slavic & East Europ Lang; Can Asn Slavists. *Res:* Nineteenth and 20th century Russian literature; Russian cultural history; comparative literature. *Mailing Add:* Dept of Ger & Russ Univ of Waterloo Waterloo ON N2L 3G1 Can

LEVITT, JESSE, b New York, NY, June 15, 19; m 58; c 2. ROMANCE LANGUAGES & LINGUISTICS. *Educ:* City Col New York, BA, 38; Columbia Univ, MA, 40, PhD(Romance philol), 63. *Prof Exp:* Translr & later info specialist, Fed Commun Comm & US War Dept, 41-54; teacher high schs, Md, 55-56; teacher, Jr High Sch, NY, 56: teacher high sch, NY, 57-59; from instr to asst prof French & Span, Wash State Univ, 60-65; assoc prof French & Romance ling, 65-70, chmn dept foreign lang, 75-81, PROF FRENCH & ROMANCE LING, UNIV BRIDGEPORT, 70- *Concurrent Pos:* Ed, Geolinguistics, Am Soc Geoling, 73- *Mem:* Am Soc Geoling (2nd vpres, 71-72, 1st vpres, 72-73, pres, 73-74, secy, 80-); Int Ling Asn; MLA; Am Asn Teachers Fr; Am Name Soc. *Res:* French linguistics, 17th to 20th centuries; French literature of the 20th century; Spanish linguistics. *Publ:* Auth, The Grammaire des Grammaires of Girault-Duvivier: A Study of Nineteenth-Century French, Mouton, The Hague, 68; The concept of euphony in traditional French grammar, In: Studies in Honor of Mario A Pei, Univ NC, 72; The agreement of the past participle in Modern French, Linguistics, 10/73; The influence of English on Spanish, English Around World, 11/75 & 11/77; Names in Beckett's theater: irony and mystification, 77 & Irony and allusiveness in Gide's onomastics, 76, Lit Onomastics; The influence of orthography on phonology: A comparative study (English, French, Spanish, Italian, German), Linguistics, 78; From literature to the lexicon: Names of authors, books and literary characters as vocabulary in the romance languages, Papers in Onomastics, Univ Mo-Rolla, 11/81 . *Mailing Add:* 485 Brooklawn Ave Fairfield CT 06432

LEVY, CLAUDE M L, b May 5, 35; Can citizen. FRENCH MEDIEVAL LITERATURE, OLD FRENCH. *Educ:* Sir George Williams Univ, BA, 65; McGill Univ, MA, 67, PhD(French), 74. *Prof Exp:* Sessional lectr French, 67-69, asst prof, 69-74, ASSOC PROF FRENCH, CONCORDIA UNIV, SIR GEORGE WILLIAMS CAMPUS, 74- *Mem:* MLA. *Res:* Prose versions of Floriant et Florete rimed medieval romances (1400) critical edition. *Publ:* Auth, Jean Renart est-il l'auteur de Floriant et Floriete, Bulletin de l'Apfuc, 2/75. *Mailing Add:* Dept of French Concordia Univ Sir George Williams Campus Montreal PQ H3G 1M8 Can

LEVY, DIANE WOLFE, b Washington, DC, June 6, 44; m 66; c 1. FRENCH LITERATURE, COMPARATIVE LITERATURE. *Educ:* Barnard Col, BA, 66; Columbia Univ, MA, 69, PhD(French & Romance philol), 73. *Prof Exp:* Asst prof French, Columbia Univ, 73-74; asst prof French, State Univ NY, Albany, 74-80. *Mem:* MLA; Nat Asn Teachers Fr; Northeast Mod Lang Asn. *Res:* Urban literature; narrative structure. *Publ:* Auth, History as art: Ironic parody in Anatole France's Les Sept Femmes de la Barbe-Bleue, Nineteenth-Century Fr Studies, spring 76; coauth, How to Use French Verbs, Barron's Educ Ser, 77; auth, Cityscapes: Towards a definition of urban literature, Mod Fiction Studies, spring 78; Ironic Techniques in the Short Stories of Anatole France, NC Ser Romance Lang & Lit (in press). *Mailing Add:* 9317 Ocala St Silver Spring MD 20901

LEVY, HOWARD S, b Brooklyn, NY, Apr 5, 23; m 61; c 5. ORIENTAL LANGUAGES & LITERATURES. *Educ:* Brooklyn Col, BA, 43; Univ Mich, MA, 47; Univ Calif, PhD(Chinese lang & lit), 51. *Prof Exp:* Teaching asst Orient lang, Univ Calif, 50-51; instr, Univ Denver, 52-53; Denver exten, Univ Colo, 53-57; dir Chinese lang sch, US Dept State, Taiwan, 57-61, dir Japanese lang sch, Tokyo, Japan, 61-69, chmn lang div, Vietnamese Training Ctr, 69-72, dir Japanese, Japanese Lang Sch, Yokohama, 74-78, dir linguist Asian lang, Foreign Serv Inst, 74-78, linguist, US Dept State, Washington, DC, 69-79. *Concurrent Pos:* Inter-Univ fel lang studies, Taiwan, 56-57; mem Int Conf Asian Hist, Univ Hong Kong, 63- *Honors & Awards:* Merit Award, US Dept of State, 75. *Mem:* Asn Asian Studies; Am Orient Soc; Conf Asian Affairs (secy-treas, 55); Asn Teachers Chinese; Asn Teachers Japanese. *Res:* Chinese folklore; East Asian erotic humor; Chinese literature in translation; East Asian sexology; East Asian folklore; Sino-Japanese literature in translation. *Publ:* Auth, Chinese Footbinding, History of an Erotic Custom, Twayne, 66, Langstaff Bks, 77; coauth, The Tao of Sex Manners, Shibundo, 68 & 70; auth, Oriental Sex Manners, New England Libr, 71, Langstaff Bks, 78; Japanese Sex Jokes in Traditional Times, 73 & China's Dirtiest Trickster, 74, Warm-Soft Village Press; Japan's Best-Loved Poetry Classic: Hyakuninshu, Langstaff Bks, 77; Translations from Po Chu-i's Poetry, Chinese Materials Ctr, Vols III-IV, 77-78; Japan's Dirty Old Man, Langstaff Bks, 78. *Mailing Add:* 6645 Seneca Dr Columbia MD 21046

LEVY, ISAAC JACK, b Rhodes, Italy, Dec 21, 28; US citizen; m 61 c 2. ROMANCE LANGUAGES. *Educ:* Emory Univ, BA, 57; Univ Iowa, MA, 59; Univ Mich, PhD(Romance lang, Span), 66. *Prof Exp:* From asst prof to assoc prof foreign lang, 63-73, chmn div Span & Port, 72-74, head dept, 75-77, PROF SPAN, UNIV SC, 73- *Concurrent Pos:* Univ SC study grants, 65-68 & 81; Lucius N Littauer Found study grant, 68 & 82; ed, Sephardic Scholar, Am Soc Sephardic Studies, 68-; dir & co-ed, Hisp Studies, 74-; Atlanta Jewish Fedn grant, 82. *Mem:* Am Asn Teachers Span & Port; SAtlantic Mod Lang Asn; MLA; Southeastern Conf Latin Am Studies; Am Soc Sephardic Studies (1st vpres, 68). *Res:* Sephardic culture; Medieval Spanish civilization and literature; Latin American colonial period. *Publ:* Auth, Sephardic Ballads and Songs in the United States, privately publ, 59; En torno a la interpretacion del termino gabba, Romance Notes, 67; Cancion mosquita ? traduccion de Ruben Dario?, Rev Iberoam, spring 68; Prolegomena to the Study of the Refranero Sefardi, Las Americas, 68; Folklore and reality: The key to a people, 72-73, A look at socio-politico connotations in Judeo-Spanish poetry from Dreyfus to the present, 73 & Holocaust poetry: The forgotten sephardim, 73, Sephardic Scholar; The Proverbs and Popular Sayings of the Spanish Jews & The Sephardim: End of an Odyssey, In: Sephardim and a History of Congregation or Veshalom, 81. *Mailing Add:* Dept of Foreign Lang Univ of SC Columbia SC 29208

LEVY, KURT LEOPOLD, b Berlin, Ger, July 10, 17; Can citizen; m 47; c 5. SPANISH. *Educ:* Univ Toronto, BA, 45, MA, 46, PhD(Span), 54. *Prof Exp:* Instr Span lang & lit, 45-50, lectr Span & Span Am lit, 50-55, from asst prof to assoc prof, 55-65, dir Latin Am studies & assoc chmn dept Hisp studies, 65-70, PROF HISP STUDIES, UNIV TORONTO, 65-, CHMN DEPT SPAN & PORT, 78- *Concurrent Pos:* Govt Columbia lectr, SAm, 55; Can Coun sr res fel, Columbia & Latin Am Univs, 65; external examr Span, Univ West Indies, 69-71; Rockefeller vis prof lit, Univ Valle, Columbia, 71-73; treas, Int Fedn Insts Teaching Span, 72- *Mem:* Can Asn Latin Am Studies (pres, 69-71); MLA; Am Asn Teachers Span & Port; Inst Int Lit Iberoam (pres, 67-69); Am Coun Teaching Foreign Lang. *Res:* Spanish American prose fiction, specifically Colombian. *Publ:* Auth, Vida y obras de Tomas Carrasquilla, Ed Bedout, Medellin, 58; Releyendo a Maria, In: La Novela Iberoamericana Contemporanea, Caracas, 68; ed, Book List on Latin America for Canadians, Can Comn for UNESCO, Ottawa, 69; El ensayo y la critica literaria en Iberoamerica, Univ Toronto, 70; auth, Las alas en Pedro Prado, Actas, Tercer Congreso Int Hispanistas, Mex, 70; La luciernaga: Title, leitmotif, and structural unity, Philol Quart, 1/72; ed, La Marquesa de Yolombo, Inst Caro y Cuervo, 74; auth, The contemporary Hispanic American novel: Its relevance to society, Latin Am Lit Rev, fall-winter 74. *Mailing Add:* 11 Rathnelly Ave Toronto ON M4V 2M2 Can

LEWALD, HERALD ERNEST, b Königsberg, Ger, Oct 31, 22; US citizen; m 49; c 2. SPANISH. *Educ:* Univ Minn, BA, 51, MA, 55, PhD, 61. *Prof Exp:* Instr Span & Ger, Ga Inst Technol, 54-57; asst prof Span, Carleton Col, 58-62 & 63-66; assoc prof, Orange State Col, 62-63; head dept Romance lang, 68-70, PROF SPAN, UNIV TENN, KNOXVILLE, 66- *Concurrent Pos:* Orgn Am States res grants, 65, 68, 74; assoc ed, Hispania, 68-; Am Coun Learned Soc grant, 72. *Mem:* MLA; Am Asn Techers Span & Port; Latin Am Studies Asn. *Res:* Argentine and Mexican literature; literature as a cultural interpreter; River Plate Women writers. *Publ:* Auth, Buenos Aires: retrato de una sociedad hispanica a traves de su literatura, Houghton, 68; Diez cuentistas argentinas, Riomar, 68; Argentina: analisis y autoanalisis, Sudamericana, 69; co-ed, Escritores Platenses, Houghton, 71; auth, The Cry of Home: Cultural Nationalism and the Modern Writer, Univ Tenn, 72; Latinoamerica: sus culturas y sociedades, McGraw, 73; Eduardo Mallea, Twayne, 77. *Mailing Add:* Dept of Romance Lang 617 McClung Univ of Tenn Knoxville TN 37916

LEWES, ULLE ERIKA, Medieval & Comparative Literature. See Vol II

LEWIS, BARTIE LEE, JR, b Dallas, Tex, June 29, 46. LATIN AMERICAN & PENINSULAR SPANISH LITERATURE. *Educ:* Southern Methodist Univ, BA, 67; Univ NMex, MA, 69, PhD(Romance lang), 73. *Prof Exp:* From instr to asst prof Span, Sam Houston State Univ, 71-74; ASST PROF SPAN, TEX A&M UNIV, 74- *Mem:* Asn Teachers Span & Port; MLA; Southwestern Coun Latin Am Studies (pres, 77-78); Southeastern Conf Latin Am Studies. *Res:* Nineteenth century Latin American prose fiction; twentieth century Latin American novel and drama. *Publ:* Auth, Myth in Federico Gamboa's Santa, Mester, fall 76. *Mailing Add:* Dept of Mod Lang Tex A&M Univ College Station TX 77843

LEWIS, BRIAN ARTHUR, b Cardiff, Wales, Sept 24, 40; Brit citizen; m 68. GERMAN LINGUISTICS. *Educ:* Univ London, BA, 62; Univ Wis, PhD(Ger), 68. *Prof Exp:* ASST PROF GER, UNIV COLO, 69- *Concurrent Pos:* Fel, Univ Wis, 68-69. *Mem:* Am Asn Teachers Ger; Ling Soc Am. *Res:* Language contact; bilingualism; applied linguistics. *Publ:* Auth, Uber die Glarner Mundart von New Glarus, einer schweizerdeutschen Sprachinsel im amerikanischen Mittelwesten, In: Bericht des Schweizerdeutschen Wörsterbuchs über das Jhr 1969. *Mailing Add:* Dept of Ger Lang & Lit Univ of Colo Boulder CO 80302

LEWIS, DAVID WILFRID PAUL, b Clacton-on-Sea, Eng, Jan 24, 32; m 59; c 4. MODERN LANGUAGES. *Educ:* Oxford Univ, BA, Hons, 53, MA, 68; Col Europe, dipl int relat, 57; Univ Paris, Dr, 73. *Prof Exp:* Dean students, Col Europe, 57-58; Coun of Europe, Strasbourg, info off, 58-62, adminr educ prog, 62-65; secy, Europ Comt Conserv Nature & Natural Resources, 65-68; assoc prof mod lang, Lakehead Univ, 68-77, chmn dept, 68-70; PROF MOD LANG & CHMN DEPT MOD FOREIGN LANG, LEHIGH UNIV, 77- *Concurrent Pos:* Vis prof, Univ Ottawa, 71, Univ Prince Edward Island, 74 & Univ Ottawa, 77; campus dir admin, Champlain Regional Col, St Lambert, Quebec, 75-76; transl consult, secy state, Govt Can, 76-77. *Honors & Awards:* French Govt Award of Merit for Contrib to Europ Coop in Educ, 63; ODK Nat Honor Soc, 80. *Mem:* Int Arthurian Soc; Asn Int Etud Fr; Am Asn Teachers Fr; Asn Int Docteurs Univ Paris. *Res:* Modern languages, especially 19th century French poetry and French for business and international affairs; international relations, especially European integration. *Publ:* Coauth, Higher Civil Servants, Col Europe, 58; Youth and Development Aid, Coun of Europe, 66; auth, Albert Glatigny et la Tradition Boheme, Can Asn Univ Teachers Fr, 72; Dans le Sillon des Voyageurs: Experiment in French (educational) television, Can Rev Mod Lang, 74. *Mailing Add:* Dept of Mod Foreign Lang Lehigh Univ Bethlehem PA 18015

LEWIS, EARL NICHOLAS, JR, b Houston, Tex, Oct 28, 24. GERMAN. *Educ:* Univ Tex, BA, 49, MA, 50, PhD, 55. *Prof Exp:* Instr, NTex State Col, 50-51; instr, Univ Houston, 54-55; instr, Reed Col, 55-56; from instr to asst prof Ger, La State Univ, Baton Rouge, 56-64, prof Ger lang & lit, 64-80. *Concurrent Pos:* Consult, Nat Educ Act, 60-61. *Mem:* MLA; Am Asn Teachers Ger; AAUP. *Res:* Germanic languages and literature; etymology; the art of translation. *Publ:* Auth, Deutsch Eins, La State Univ, 57, 60 & 66; Qidhush, the Son and Others, Vantage, 63; auth-translr, Wolfgang Wyrauch: Ich bin einer, ich bin keiner (radio play), 1/68, Wolfgang Weyrauch: Etwas geschieht (novel), 2/69, Wolfgang Weyrauch: Zeichensprache (story), 5/72, Wolfgang Weyrauch: Alexanderschlacht (radio play), 5/72 & Wolfgang Weyrauch: Kein nachtwächter, ein Tagwächter (poem), 7/74, Dimension. *Mailing Add:* 2925 Alaska Baton Rouge LA 70802

LEWIS, GERTRUD JARON, b Frankfurt-Main, Ger, Oct 27, 31; Can citizen; m 60; c 3. MEDIEVAL GERMAN LITERATURE. *Educ:* Univ Alta, MA, 67, PhD(Ger), 71. *Prof Exp:* Instr Ger & French, Univ Redlands, 59-62; asst prof Ger, 72-78, ASSOC PROF GER, LAURENTIAN UNIV, 78- *Concurrent Pos:* Can Coun publ grant, 73; Laurentian Univ publ grant, 74; Soc Sci & Humanities Res Coun Can fel, 80; Soc Sci & Humanities grant, 82. *Mem:* MLA; Can Asn Univ Teachers Ger; Can Comp Lit Asn; Mediaeval Acad Am; Int Arthurian Soc. *Res:* Middle high German epic; German women mystics of the Middle Ages. *Publ:* Auth, Daz häzliche spil in Iwein: Ein Beispiel der Erzählkunst Hartmanns von Aue, Seminar, 73; Das Tier und seine dichterische Funktion in Eric, Iwein, Parzival und Tristan, Lang, 74; Die unheilige Herzeloyde: Ein ikonoklastischer Versuch, J English & Ger Philol, 75; contribr, Kommunikative Metaphorik, Bouvier, 76; auth, Vitzliputzli revisited, Can Lit, 78; daz vil edel wip, In: Die Frau als Heldin und Autorin, 79; Blechtrommel--Tin Drum, Lebende Sprachen, 79. *Mailing Add:* Dept of Mod Lang Laurentian Univ Ramsey Lake Rd Sudbury ON P3E 2C6 Can

LEWIS, HANNA B. b Berlin, Ger, Aug 20, 31; US citizen; m 50; c 4. GERMANICS, COMPARATIVE LITERATURE. *Educ:* Rice Univ, BA, 52, MA, 61, PhD(Ger), 64. *Prof Exp:* Instr Ger, Rice Univ, 62-65; from asst prof to assoc prof, Stephen F Austin State Univ, 67-74; ASSOC PROF GER, SAM HOUSTON STATE UNIV, 74- *Mem:* Hugo von Hofmannsthal Ges; Southern Mod Lang Asn; MLA; Am Asn Univ Prof; Am Asn Teachers Ger. *Res:* Hugo von Hofmannsthal; German Judaica; German-Americana. *Publ:* Auth, Hofmannsthal and America, Rice Univ Studies, summer 69; Hofmannsthal and Milton, Mod Lang Notes, 10/72; Hofmannsthal and Moliere, Moliere and the commonwealth of letters, 73; Hofmannsthal, Shelley and Keats, Ger Life & Lett, 74; Salome and Elektra: sisters of strangers, Orbis Litterarum, 76; Kafka's Elf Sohne: A further dimension, Orbis Litterarum, 78. *Mailing Add:* 165 Circle Dr Cleveland TX 77327

LEWIS, MARTHA HOFFMAN, b Newton, Mass, Nov 8, 22; m 54; c 2. CLASSICS. *Educ:* Univ Calif, Berkeley, AB, 43; Bryn Mawr Col, MA, 49, PhD, 51. *Prof Exp:* Teacher Latin & English, Red Bluff High Sch, Calif, 44-45, Piedmont High Sch, 45-48; Fulbright scholar & fel, Am Acad Rome, 51-53; asst prof classics & educ, Univ Ill, 53-56; asst prof Latin, 63-66, ASSOC PROF LATIN & ENGLISH, ROCKHURST COL, 66- *Mem:* Am Philol Asn; Am Asn Ancient Historians. *Res:* Roman history, especially late republic and early empire; modern poetry. *Publ:* Auth, The official priests of Rome under the Julio-Claudians, Am Acad Rome, 55. *Mailing Add:* 716 W 109th Terr Kansas City MO 64114

LEWIS, PHILIP EUGENE, b Kingsport, Tenn, Sept 8, 42; m 66; c 2. FRENCH LITERATURE. *Educ:* Davidson Col, BA, 64; Yale Univ, PhD(French), 69. *Prof Exp:* Asst prof, 68-74, chairperson dept, 73-76, assoc prof, 74-79, ed, Diacritics, 76-81, chmn dept, 78-80, PROF ROMANCE STUDIES, CORNELL UNIV, 79- *Res:* Seventeenth century French literature; Semiotics. *Publ:* Auth, La Rochefoucauld: The Art of Abstraction, Cornell Univ, 76. *Mailing Add:* Dept of Lang Cornell Univ Ithaca NY 14853

LEWIS, ROBERT ENZER, English Language & Literature. See Vol II

LEWIS, WARD BEVINS, JR, b Minneapolis, Minn, May 8, 38; m 61; c 3. MODERN GERMAN LITERATURE. *Educ:* Amherst Col, BA, 60; Univ Minn, Minneapolis, MA, 65; Univ Pa, PhD(Ger), 68. *Prof Exp:* Asst prof, Univ Iowa, 68-71; asst prof, 71-73, ASSOC PROF GER, UNIV GA, 73- *Concurrent Pos:* Alexander von Humboldt res fel, 79-80. *Mem:* MLA; AAUP. *Res:* Modern German drama; American-German literary relations. *Publ:* Auth, The early dramas of Reinhold Johannes Sorge, Mod Drama, 72; Walt Whitman: Johannes Schlaf's Neuer Mensch, Rev Litt Comparee, 74; Poetry and Exile: An Annotated Bibliography of Paul Zech, Lang, 75; Message from America: The verse of Walt Whitman as interpreted by German authors in exile, Ger Life & Lett, 76; Activism and the Argentinean exile theatre, Jahrbuch für Internationale Germanistik, 77; Starting anew: The exile years of Kurt Pinthus, Ger Life & Lett, 80; Kasimire Edschmid's image of America and her relation to Germany, Mod Lang Studies, 80; Bret Harte and Germany, Rev Litt Comparee, 80. *Mailing Add:* Dept of Ger & Slavic Ling Univ of Ga Athens GA 30602

LEY, RALPH JOHN, b New York, NY, June 17, 29; m 66; c 2. GERMAN. *Educ:* St Joseph's Sem & Col, BA, 51; Rutgers Univ, MA, 58, PhD(Ger), 63. *Prof Exp:* Instr, 59-63, asst prof, 63-68, assoc prof, 68-79, PROF GER, RUTGERS UNIV, 79-, CHAIRPERSON, DEPT GERMANIC LANG & LIT, FAC ARTS & SCI, 81- *Concurrent Pos:* Mem, Nat Screening Comt for Fulbright travel grants to Ger, Austria, Scandinavia, 74-76; assoc ed, Ill Lang & Cult Ser, Appl Lit Press, 77- *Mem:* MLA; AAUP; Am Asn Teachers Ger; Brecht Soc. *Res:* German expressionism; modern German drama; literature and ideology. *Publ:* Coauth, The Drama of German Expressionism: A German-English Bibliography, Univ NC, 60; Brecht: Science and cosmic futility, Ger Rev, 5/65; contribr, In: Studies in German Literature of the 19th and 20th Centuries, Univ NC, 70; ed, Böll für Zeitgenossen, Harper, 70; contribr, Essays on Brecht: Theater and Politics, Univ NC, 74; auth, Heinrich Bölls other Rhineland, Univ Dayton Rev, 76; co-ed, Perspectives and Personalities: Studies in Modern German Literature, Carl Winter Univ, Heidelberg, 78; auth, Brecht as Thinker: Studies in Literary Marxism and Existentialism, Appl Lit Press, 79. *Mailing Add:* Dept of Ger Lang & Lit Rutgers Univ New Brunswick NJ 08903

LI, CHARLES N, b Shanghai, China, Feb 6, 40. LINGUISTICS. *Educ:* Bowdoin Col, BA, 63; Univ Calif, Berkeley, PhD(ling), 71. *Prof Exp:* Asst prof, 70-80, PROF LING, UNIV CALIF, SANTA BARBARA, 80- *Concurrent Pos:* Am Coun Learned Soc fel, 74-75. *Mem:* Ling Soc Am. *Res:* Linguistics theory. *Publ:* Coauth, Explanation of word order change, Found Lang, 74; The meaning and structure of complex sentences with -ZHE in Mandarin Chinese, J Am Orient Soc, 74; ed, Word Order and Word Order Change, Univ Ind, 75; Subject & Topic, Acad Press, 76; Mechanisms of Syntactic Change, Univ Tex, 77; coauth, The causative in Wappo: a special case of doubling, Proc Third Ann Meeting Berkeley Ling Soc, 77; The acquisition of tone in Mandarin-speaking children, J Child Lang, 77; Mandarin Chinese: A Functional Reference Grammar, Univ Calif, 81. *Mailing Add:* Dept of Ling Univ of Calif Santa Barbara CA 93106

LI, CHI, b Changsha, Hunan, China, June 6, 03; US citizen. CHINESE & ENGLISH LITERATURE. *Educ:* Ginling Col, Nanking, BA, 31; Oxford Univ, BLitt, 36. *Prof Exp:* Prof English, Nat Hunan Univ, China, 37-42; prof English lit, Nat Norm Univ, 42-44, Nat Chekiang Univ, 44-48, Lingnan Univ, 48-49, & Nat Taiwan Univ, 49-50; res linguist, Univ Calif, Berkeley, 55-60; vis lectr Chinese lit, Univ Mich, 60-63; assoc prof, 64-66, prof, 66-68, EMER PROF CHINESE LIT, UNIV BC, 71- *Concurrent Pos:* Adj res scientist, Ctr Chinese Studies, Univ Mich, 72- *Res:* Chu Hsi's literary criticism; tz'u of the Ching period. *Publ:* Auth, Wordsworth and his Prelude, Commercial, Shanghai, 47; Studies in Chinese Communist Terminology (nine studies), Univ Calif, 56-62; The changing concept of the recluse in Chinese literature, Harvard J Asiatic Studies, 62-63; transl, The Love of Nature: Hsü Hsia-k'o and his Early Travels, Western Wash State Col, 71; auth, Chu Hsi the poet, Toung Pao, 72; transl, The Travel Diaries of Hsü Hsia-k'o, 74 & auth, Collected Poems (Chinese), 76, Chinese Univ, Hong Kong. *Mailing Add:* Two Tiger Book Hut 1012 E University Ann Arbor MI 48104

LI, FANG KUEI, Canton, China, Aug 20, 02; US citizen; c 3. LINGUISTICS. *Educ:* Univ Mich, AB, 26; Univ Chicago, MA, 27, PhD(ling), 28. *Hon Degrees:* DLit, Univ Mich, 72; LLD, Chinese Univ of Hong Kong, 76. *Prof Exp:* Fel res, Acad Sinica, 29-46; lectr Asian lang, Harvard Univ, 46-48; vis prof Orient lang, Yale Univ, 48-49; vis prof Asian lang, 49-50, prof Chinese ling, 59-69, EMER PROF CHINESE LING, UNIV WASH, 69-; EMER PROF ASIAN LING, UNIV HAWAII, MANOA, 73- *Concurrent Pos:* Vis prof Orient studies, Yale Univ, 37-39; vis prof East Asian studies, Princeton Univ, 73; prof Asian ling, Univ Hawaii, Manoa, 69-73. *Mem:* Ling Soc Am; Asn Asian Studies; Am Orient Soc. *Res:* Chinese linguistics; Tai linguistics; American Indian linguistics. *Publ:* Auth, Mattole, an Athabaskan Language, Univ Chicago, 30; The Tai Dialect of Wu ming, Acad Sinica, 56; The Tibetan Inscription of the Sino-Tibetan Treaty of 821-122, T'oung Pao, 55; A tentative classification of Tai dialects, In: Culture in History, Columbia Univ, 60; Studies on archaic Chinese phonology, Tsing Hua J Chinese Studies, 71; A Handbook of Comparative Tai, Univ Hawaii, 77. *Mailing Add:* Dept of Ling Univ of Hawaii at Manoa Honolulu HI 96822

LIBERMAN, ANATOLY, b Leningrad, USSR, Mar 10, 37; US citizen; m 69; c 1. LINGUISTICS, OLD GERMANTIC LITERATURE. *Educ:* Hertsen Teacher Training Col, Leningrad, USSR, BA, 59, Univ Leingrad, USSR, PhD(English philol), 65; Acad Sci, Leningrad, USSR, PhD(Scand philol), 72. *Prof Exp:* Teacher English, Nazia Boarding Sch, Zhikharevo, USSR, 59-62; instr English, Polytech Inst, Leningrad, USSR, 62-65; res fels Scand, Inst Ling, Acad Sci, Leningrad, USSR, 65-75; Hill vis prof, 75-76, assoc prof, 76-78, PROF GER PHILOL, UNIV MINN, 78- *Concurrent Pos:* Guggenheim fel, 81. *Mem:* MLA; Ling Soc Am; Soc Advan Scad Study; Int Asn Phonetic Sci. *Res:* Germanic phology; general phonology. *Publ:* Auth, Some notes on the history of Middle English e and o in open syllables, In: Zeitschrift fur Anglistik und Amerikanistik, 65; Problems of Germanic accentology, Acta Ling Hafniensia, 69; Izuchenie Islandskoj Fonetiki Bibliograficheskij Obzor, I-II, Skand Sbornik, Tallinn, 69 & 72; Islandskaja Prosodika, Nauka, Leningrad, USSR, 71; The order of rules in phonology and the reality of distinctive features, Linguistics, 74; Scandinavian circumflexes, Norweg J Ling, 75; Scandinavian accents in their relation to one another, Studia Ling, 75; The origin of Scandinavian accentuation, Arkiv Nordisk Filol, 76; Germanic Accentology I, Univ Minn Press, 82. *Mailing Add:* Dept of Ger Univ of Minn 9 Pleasant St Se Minneapolis MN 55455

LIBERTSON, JOSEPH, b Rochester, NY, Apr 22, 46; m 69; c 1. FRENCH LITERATURE, CRITICAL THEORY. *Educ:* Northwestern Univ, BA, 68; Univ Maine, MA, 71; Johns Hopkins Univ, PhD(French), 74. *Prof Exp:* Asst prof French, Yale Univ, 76-79; VIS ASST PROF FRENCH, NORTHWESTERN UNIV, 79- *Mem:* MLA. *Res:* Difference; proximity; communication. *Publ:* Auth, Bataille and communication, Mod Lang Notes French Issue, 5/74; Savoir, non-savoir, glissement, rire, 74 & Proximity and the word, 76, Substance; Excess and imminence, Mod Lang Notes Comp Lit Issue, 12/77. *Mailing Add:* Dept of French Northwestern Univ Evanston IL 60201

LIBHART, BYRON R, b Marietta, Pa, Dec 8, 28. ROMANCE LANGUAGES. *Educ:* Franklin & Marshall Col, BA, 50; Pa State Univ, MA, 55; Northwestern Univ, PhD(Romance lang), 64. *Prof Exp:* Asst prof French, Northwestern Univ, 64-65; asst prof, Univ Ill, Chicago, 65-70; assoc prof, French & Ger, 70-80, PROF FRENCH & GER, WILBUR WRIGHT COL, CITY COLS CHICAGO, 80- *Mem:* MLA; Am Asn Teachers Fr. *Res:* Madame de Staël; Franco-German literary relations, especially of the 19th century; Julien Green. *Publ:* Auth, A neglected challenge: The aural comprehension of unfamiliar material, Fr Rev, 4/70; Madame de Staël, Charles de Villers and the death of God in Jean Paul's Songe, Comp Lit Studies, 6/72; Julien Green's Troubled American: A fictionalized self-portrait, PMLA, 3/74. *Mailing Add:* Dept of Foreign Lang Wilbur Wright Col Chicago IL 60634

LIBRIE, GILLES RAPHEL, b Springfield, Mass, Sept 10, 39; m 65; c 1. CONTEMPORARY FRENCH & QUEBEC LITERATURE. *Educ:* Univ Montreal, BA, 60; Univ Mass, MA, 66, PhD(French lit), 71. *Prof Exp:* Instr French, Easthampton High Sch, Mass, 62-64 & Northhampton Sch for Girls, Mass, 65-66; from instr to asst prof, 70-77, ASSOC PROF FRENCH, CENT MICH UNIV, 77- *Mem:* Am Asn Teachers French . *Res:* Contemporary French literature; Quebec literature and culture. *Mailing Add:* Dept of Foreign Lang Cent Mich Univ 310 Pearce Hall Mt Pleasant MI 48859

LICH, GLEN ERNST, American Civilization, Rhetoric & Composition. See Vol I

LICHTBLAU, MYRON I, b New York, NY, Oct 10, 25; m 56; c 2. SPANISH. *Educ:* City Col New York, BA, 47; Nat Univ Mex, MA, 48; Columbia Univ, PhD, 57. *Prof Exp:* Teacher Span sec schs, NY, 48-57; instr, Ind Univ, 57-59; from asst prof to assoc prof Romance lang, 59-68, acting chmn dept , 67-68, chmn dept, 68-74, PROF ROMANCE LANG, SYRACUSE UNIV, 68-, ASSOC CHMN SPAN & PORT, DEPT FOR LANG LIT, 81- *Concurrent Pos:* Rev ed, Symposium, 66- & Hispania, 74- *Mem:* MLA; Am Asn Teachers Span & Port; Inst Int Lit Iberoam; AAUP. *Res:* Latin American literature; modern Argentine novel; 19th century fiction. *Publ:* Auth, Ironic devices in Manuel Rojas' Hijo de ladron, Symposium, fall 65; El arte estilistico de Eduardo Mallea, Goyanarte, Buenos Aires, 67; Manuel Galvez, Twayne, 72; The dictator theme as irony in Lafourcade's La fiesta del Rey Acab, Latin Am Lit Rev, fall 73; A Practical Reference Guide to Reading Spanish, Las Americas, 77; Eduardo Caballero Calderon's Manuel Pacho, Editorial Kelly, Bogota, 80; Voces Narrativas en Pronombres pesrsonales de E Lafourcade, Narradores Latinoamericanos, 81; Recent Spanish-American Fiction: Trial and Success, Syracuse Scholar, fall 81. *Mailing Add:* Dept of Foreign Lang & Lit Syracuse Univ Syracuse NY 13210

LICHTENSTADTER, ILSE, b Hamburg, Ger, Sept 10, 07; US citizen. ISLAM, ARABIC LITERATURE. *Educ:* Univ Frankfurt, PhD, 31; Oxford Univ, DPhil, 37. *Prof Exp:* Cataloguer, Judaica & Orient, Jewish Theol Sem Am, 38-45; prof Arabic & Islam, Asia Inst, 42-52; lectr Islam, NY Univ, 52-60; lectr Arabic & Islam, 60-74, EMER LECTR ARABIC & ISLAM, HARVARD UNIV, 74- *Concurrent Pos:* Fel, Notgemeinschaft Deut Wiss, 32; Soc Sci Res Coun travel grant-in-aid, 50 & 55; lectr Near East hist, Rutgers Univ, 59-60; Fulbright res scholar, 63. *Mem:* Am Orient Soc. *Res:* Arabic literature; mediaeval and modern Islam. *Publ:* Auth, Women in the Aiyam al-'Arab, Royal Asiatic Soc, Eng, 35; ed, Kitab al-Muhabbar, Da'irat al-Ma'arif, Hyderabad, India, 42; auth, Islam and the Modern Age, Bookman Assoc, 58; ed, Library of Classical Arabic Literature, 72- & auth, Introduction to Classical Arabic Literature, 74, Twayne; Omelyan Pritsak, 81. *Mailing Add:* Ctr for Mid Eastern Studies Harvard Univ Cambridge MA 02138

LICHTENSTEIN, AARON, b Milan, Italy; US Citizen. SEMITIC STUDIES. *Educ:* Brooklyn Col, BA, 58; NY Univ, MA, 63, PhD(Hebrew cult), 67. *Prof Exp:* Staff ed, Encycl Judaica, 69-71; lectr Bible & ancient hist, Yeshiva Col, Yeshiva Univ, 65-71; B Z Immanuel lectr hist, Jews Col, London Univ, 72-74; grants officer scholarly proj, Mem Found Jewish Cult, 75-76; assoc prof relig, Univ Denver, 76-79; ADJ PROF FOREIGN LANG, BERNARD BARUCH COL, CITY UNIV NEW YORK, 81-, ADJ PROF GERMANIC, HEBRAIC & ORIENTAL LIT, 82- *Concurrent Pos:* Prin, Tallman Acad, Suffern, NY, 65-66; lectr & guide, Yeshiva Univ tours, 67; dir, Jewish Cult Found, NY Univ, 67-68; lectr, Free Univ-Hillel, London, 73-74; Nat Endowment for Humanities fel, Ohio State Univ, Columbus, 76 & 79; lectr YMHA & YWHA, New York, 80-81; adj prof Jewish lang & lit, Bramson Ort Tech Inst, 82- *Mem:* fel Jewish Acad Arts & Sci; Nat Asn Prof Hebrew; Asn Jewish Studies; Coun Jewish Educ; Asn Prof Yiddish. *Res:* Matriarchal aspects of patriarchial society; wisdom literature; interpreting ancient texts and literatures. *Publ:* Co-ed, Encycl Judaica (16 vols) & auth, 19 articles in Encyl Judaica, Macmillan & Keter, Jerusalem, 72; auth, History of the Jews of Portugal, In: Encycl Hebraica, Vol XXVII, Jerusalem & NY, 75; Holocaust homily and response, Hebrew Studies, winter 78; ed, The Un-Chosen People, 1939-1945, Univ Denver, 78; auth, Toward a literary understanding of the Book of Job, Hebrew Studies, spring 79; Torah & Jewish Calendar, in: Abingdon Dict of Living Religions, Abingdon Press, 81; The Seven Laws of Noah, Z Berman Bks, 81; Genesis according to Michalangelo, J Evolutionary Psychol, 82. *Mailing Add:* Dept of Hebraic & Orient Lang & Lit Baruch Col City Univ of New York New York NY 11210

LICHTMAN, CELIA S, b Brooklyn, NY, May 9, 32; m 65; c 2. ROMANCE LANGUAGES. *Educ:* Brooklyn Col, BA, 52; NY Univ, MA, 55, PhD(Romance lang), 65. *Prof Exp:* Instr mod lang, Rutgers Univ, 60-65; assoc prof, 65-80, PROF MOD LANG, LONG ISLAND UNIV, BROOKLYN CTR, 80- *Concurrent Pos:* Lectr sch gen studies, Hunter Col, 60-67. *Mem:* MLA. *Res:* Garcia Lorca; 20th century Spanish literature; la generacion del 27. *Publ:* co-ed, Hojas literarias, Vols I, II & III, Van Nostrand, 72. *Mailing Add:* Dept of Mod Lang Long Island Univ Brooklyn Ctr Brooklyn NY 11201

LICKLIDER, PATRICIA MINICHINO, Comparative Renaissance Literature. See Vol II

LIDA, DENAH LEVY, b New York, NY, Sept 9, 23; m 55. SPANISH. *Educ:* Hunter Col, BA, 43; Columbia Univ, MA, 44; Nat Univ Mex, DrLet(Span), 52. *Prof Exp:* From instr to asst prof Span, Smith Col, 45-53; asst prof mod lang, Sweet Briar Col, 54-55; from instr to assoc prof Span, 55-67, chmn dept Romance & comp lit, 64-66 & 74-77, PROF SPAN, BRANDEIS UNIV, 67- *Concurrent Pos:* Assoc scholar, Radcliffe Inst Independent Study, 61-62, chmn, Joint Prog Lit Studies, 78-81, chmn, Humanities Coun, 81-82. *Mem:* MLA; Renaissance Soc Am; Asoc Int Hispanistas; Asoc Int Galdositas. *Res:* Comparative literature, the Don Juan theme; Sephardic Spanish; 19th century Spanish literature. *Publ:* Ed, Pronunciation of Smyrnian Judeo-Spanish 52 & On Almudena and his speech, Nueva Rev Filol Hispanica, 61; El amigo manso, Oxford Univ, 63; Sobre el Krausismo de Galdos, Anales Galdosianos, 68; El crimen de la calle de Fuencarral, Homenaje a Casalduero, 72; Galdos entre cronica y novela, 73 & Galdos y sus santas modernas, 75, Anales Galdosianos; The Catalogues of Don Giovanni and Don Juan Tenorio, Hispano-Italic Studies, 79. *Mailing Add:* Dept of Romance & Comp Lit Brandes Univ Waltham MA 02154

LIEBERMAN, PHILIP, b Brooklyn, NY, Oct 25, 34; m 57; c 2. LINGUISTICS. *Educ:* Mass Inst Technol, BSEE & MSEE, 58, PhD(ling), 66. *Prof Exp:* Res asst elec eng, Mass Inst Technol, 56-58; phys scientist speech, Air Force Comn Res Labs, 58-67; assoc prof ling & elec eng, Univ Conn, 67-69, prof ling, 69-74; PROF LING, BROWN UNIV, 74- *Concurrent Pos:* Guest, inst ling, Mass Inst Technol, 67-70; mem staff ling, Haskins Lab, New York, 67-74. *Mem:* Acoust Soc Am; Ling Soc Am; MLA; fel Am Anthrop Asn; fel Am Asn Phys Anthrop. *Res:* Speech production and perception; innate mechanisms and linguistic ability; evolution of linguistic ability. *Publ:* Auth, Intonation, Perception and Language, Mass Inst Technol, 67; Speech of Primates, Mouton, The Hague, 72; Phonetic ability and related anatomy of the newborn and adult human, Neanderthal man & the chimpanzee, Am Anthrop, 6/72; On the Origins of Language, Macmillan, 75; Speech Physiology & Oronstis Phonetics, Macmillan, 76. *Mailing Add:* Dept of Ling Brown Univ Providence RI 02912

LIEBERMAN, STEPHEN JACOB, b Minneapolis, Minn, Mar 21, 43. ASSYRIOLOGY, LINGUISTICS. *Educ:* Univ Minn, BA, 63; Harvard Univ, PhD(Near Eastern lang), 72. *Prof Exp:* From asst prof to assoc prof Near Eastern studies, New York Univ, 71-75; res specialist, Sumerian Dict, Univ Mus, Univ Pa, 76-79; ASSOC PROF ASSYRIOL & SEMITIC LING, DROPSIE UNIV, 82- *Concurrent Pos:* Fel Mesopotamian civilization, Baghdad Ctr Comt, Am Schs Orient Res, 70-71; Nat Endowment for Humanities fel, 75-76; Guggenheim fel, 79-80; Inaugural fel, Found for Mesopotamian Studies, 80- *Mem:* Am Orient Soc; AHA; Archaeol Inst Am; Ling Soc Am; NAm Conf Afro-Asiatic Ling. *Res:* Sumerian and Akkadian languages and cultures; Semitic linguistics; Mesopotamian history. *Publ:* Auth, The Aramaic Argillary script in the seventh century, Bull Am Schs Orient Res, 68; An Ur III text from Drehem recording Booty from the Land of Mardu, J Cuneiform Studies, 68-69; ed, Sumerological Studies in Honor of Thorkild Jacobsen (Assyriological Studies 20), Univ Chicago, 76; auth, The Sumerian Loanwords in Old-Babylonian Akkadian (Harvard Semitic Studies 22), Scholars Press, 77; The names of the cuneiform graphemes in Old Babylonian Akkadian, Memoirs Conn Acad Arts & Sci, 77; On the historical periods of the Hebrew language, Jewish Lang Asn Jewish Studies, 78; The Phoneme /o/ in Sumerian, Studies in Honor of Tom B Jones, Neukirchener, 79; Of clay pebbles, hollow clay balls and writing: A Sumerian view, Am J Archaeol, 80. *Mailing Add:* Dept Assyriol & Semitic Ling Dropsie Univ Philadelphia PA 19132

LIEDLOFF, HELMUT, b Bremen, Ger, Jan 5, 30. GERMAN. *Educ:* Univ Marburg, PhD, 56; Southern Ill Univ, MA, 62. *Prof Exp:* Instr Ger, Milwaukee-Downer Col, 58-59; from asst prof to assoc prof, 59-75, PROF GER, SOUTHERN ILL UNIV, 75-, CHAIR LANG & LIT, 81- *Concurrent Pos:* Reader in Ger advanced placement exam, Educ Testing Serv, Princeton, NJ, 66-72. *Mem:* Am Asn Teachers Ger; MLA. *Res:* Translation; puppets in folklore and language teaching. *Publ:* Auth, Steinbeck in German Translation: A Study of Translational Practices, Southern Ill Univ, 65; coauth, Literature and Society, 1961-1965, a Selective Bibliography, Univ Miami, 67; auth, Two war novels, a critical comparison, Rev Lit Comp, 68; coauth, Deutsch heute: Grundstufe, Houghton, 74, 2nd ed, 79; auth, Kulturthemen im Anfaengerunterricht am College, Unterrichtspraxis, fall 75; coauth, German Today (2 vols), 76, 3rd ed, 82 & Ohne Mühe, 80, Houghton. *Mailing Add:* Dept of Foreign Lang Southern Ill Univ Carbondale IL 62901

LIEDTKE, KURT ERNST HEINRICH, b Elbing, Ger, Sept 14, 19; US citizen; m 59; c 3. GERMAN. *Educ:* Univ Erlangen, PhD, 54; Mich State Univ, MA, 52. *Prof Exp:* Instr Ger, English & French, Gymnasium, Erlangen, 50-51; asst master, Gymnasium, Nürnberg, 52-54; instr Ger, US Army Lang Sch, Monterey, Calif, 55; instr Ger & French, Monterey Peninsula Col, 56; asst prof, Southeastern La Col, 56-57; PROF GER & HUMANITIES, SAN FRANCISCO STATE UNIV, 57-, COORDR GER PROG, 67- *Concurrent Pos:* Instr Ger, US Naval Grad Sch, Monterey, 56. *Mem:* MLA; Am Asn Teachers Ger; Philol Asn Pac Coast; Am Coun Teaching For Lang. *Res:* Teaching of beginning German; German culture and civilization, especially its contributions to California; 19th century German literature. *Publ:* Coauth, A Solid Foundation in German, Ginn, 65; auth, It can be done-introducing German in the elementary schools, 1/68 & A common concern: Future teachers of German, 68, Unterrichtspraxis; Start German earlier-where do we begin?, Ger Quart, 1/69. *Mailing Add:* 2475 Trenton Dr San Bruno CA 94066

LIEM, NGUYEN DANG, b Cho-Long, SVietnam, Feb 06, 36; m 68; c 1. LINGUISTICS, FOREIGN LANGUAGES. *Educ:* Univ Mich, MA(English) & MA(ling), 61; Univ Saigon, Lic es Lett, 62; Australian Nat Univ, PhD(ling), 67. *Prof Exp:* Lectr English & ling, & chief bur univ affairs, Univ Saigon, 62-64; linguist, Asia Training Ctr, 67-68, from asst prof to assoc prof Southeast Asian lang, 68-76, PROF SOUTHEAST ASIAN LANG & LIT, UNIV HAWAII, MANOA, 76- *Concurrent Pos:* Mem res staff, Southeast Asian regional English prog, Univ Mich-US Oper Missions, Saigon, 62-64; vis res fel, Res Sch Pac Studies, Australian Nat Univ, 74-75; pres, Asian & Pac Prof Lang & Educ Serv, 77- *Mem:* Ling Soc Am; Ling Soc Australia; Am Coun Teaching Foreign Lang; Asn Asian Studies. *Res:* Theoretical linguistics; linguistics of English, French and Southeast Asian languages; bilingual education and cross-cultural studies. *Publ:* Auth, English Grammar, a Combined Tagmemic and Transformational Approach, 66, A Contrastive Grammatical Analysis of English and Vietnamese, 67 & Vietnamese Grammar, a Combined Tagmemic and Transformational Approach, 69, Australian Nat Univ; Four-Syllable Idiomatic Expressions in Vietnamese, East-West Ctr, Honolulu, 69 & Australian Nat Univ, 72; A Contrastive Phonological Analysis of English and Vietnamese, Australian Nat Univ, 70; Vietnamese Pronunciation, Univ Hawaii, 70; Intermediate Vietnamese (2 vols), Seton Hall Univ, 71; Cases, Clauses and Sentences in Vietnamese, Australian Nat Univ, 75. *Mailing Add:* Dept of Indo-Pac Lang Univ of Hawaii 2528 The Mall Honolulu HI 96822

LIGHT, TIMOTHY, b Kalamazoo, Mich, Nov, 5, 38; m 64; c 2. EAST ASIAN LANGUAGES & LITERATURE. *Educ:* Yale Univ, BA, 60; Union Theol Sem, MDiv, 65; Columbia Univ, MA, 66, PhD(ling), 74. *Prof Exp:* Tutor English, Near Asia Col, Chinese Univ Hong Kong, 60-62, lectr, 66-70, chmn, 68-69; sr rep, Yale in China Asn, 70-71; asst prof Orient studies, Univ Ariz, 74-79, assoc prof, 79-80; PROF & CHMN EAST ASIAN LANG, OHIO STATE UNIV, 80- *Concurrent Pos:* Consult, New Asia, Yale-in-China Chines Ctr, 76 & 79; mem, Nat China Coun, 77-81; ed, J Chinese Lang Teachers Asn, 78-82. *Mem:* Chinese Lang Teachers Asn; Ling Soc Am; Assoc Asian Studies; Am Orient Soc. *Res:* Chinese syntax and phonology; language pedology. *Publ:* Coauth (with M Wei), A Newspapers Vocabulary, Chinese Univ Hong Kong, 73; The Chinese phonological final, Cornell Univ East Asia Papers, 76; auth, Some potential for the resultative, J Chinese Lang Teachers Asn, Vol XII, 77; Word order and word order change in Mandarin Chinese, J Chinese Ling, Vol 7, No 2; Tonogenesis: Analysis and implications, Lingua, 78; Foreign language teaching in the Peoples Republic of China, In: TESOL 78: EFL Policies, Programs and Practices, 79; Conceptual contrastive analyses, In: Foreign Language Teaching, Foreign Lang Inst, China, 80; Bilingualism and standard language in the PRC, Georgetown Roundtable Proc, 80. *Mailing Add:* Dept of Orient Studies Ohio State Univ Columbus OH 43210

LIGHTFOOT, DAVID WILLIAM, b Looe, England, Feb 10, 45; c 2. LINGUISTICS. *Educ:* Univ London, BA, 66; Univ Mich, Ann Arbor, MA, 68, PhD(ling), 71. *Prof Exp:* Asst prof ling, McGill Univ, 70-75, assoc prof, 75-78; PROF ENGLISH LING, UNIV UTRECHT, 78- *Mem:* Ling Soc Am; Can Ling Asn; Ling Asn Gt Brit. *Res:* Syntax; semantics; historical linguistics. *Publ:* Auth, Natural Logic and the Greek Moods, Mouton, 74; Principles of Diachrome Syntax, Cambridge Univ Press, 79; coauth (with N Hornstern) Explanation in Linguistics, Longman, 81; The Language Lottery, Mass Inst Technol Press, 82. *Mailing Add:* Univ Utrecht Kromme Nieuwegracht 29 Utrecht Netherlands

LIGHTNER, THEODORE M, b New York, NY, Sept 5, 34. LINGUISTICS, SLAVIC LANGUAGES. *Educ:* Mass Inst Technol, PhD(ling), 65. *Prof Exp:* Asst prof ling & Slavic lang & lit, Univ Ill, Champaign, 65-70; assoc prof ling, Univ Tex, Austin, 70-73; PROF LING, UNIV PARIS, VINCENNES, 73- *Mem:* Ling Soc Am; Int Ling Asn. *Res:* Phonology; semantics; derivational morphology. *Publ:* Auth, Problems in the Theory of Phonology, Ling Res, Inc, 72; Remarks on universals in phonology, In: The Formal Analysis of Natural Languages, 73 & A problem in the analysis of some vowel-zero alternations in Russian, In: Slavic Forum: Essays in Linguistics and Literature, 74, Mouton, The Hague; Role of derivational morphology in generative grammar, Language, 75; Note on McCawley's review of SPE, Int J Am Ling, 76; Introduction to English derivational morphology, Amsterdam J, 82. *Mailing Add:* Univ de Paris VII LADL Tour Centrale 9e etage 2 Place Jussiue Paris 05 France

LIHANI, JOHN, b Czech, Mar 24, 27; nat citizen; m 50; c 3. SPANISH LANGUAGE & LITERATURE. *Educ:* Case Western Reserve Univ, BS, 48; Ohio State Univ, MA, 50; Univ Tex, PhD(Romance lang), 54. *Prof Exp:* Asst Span, Tulane Univ, 50-51; instr, Univ Tex, 53-54; from instr to asst prof, Yale Univ, 54-62; assoc prof Romance lang, Univ Pittsburgh, 62-69; PROF SPAN LING & LIT, UNIV KY, 69- *Concurrent Pos:* Morse fel, 60-61; Fulbright prof, Inst Caro y Cuervo, Colombia, 65-66; ed, La Coronica, 72-73; assoc ed, Bull Comediantes, 73-; Int Res & Exchanges Bd res award, 74; Am Philos Soc res award, 77; Am Coun Learned Soc grant, 80. *Mem:* MLA; Am Asn Teachers Span & Port; SAtlantic Mod Lang Asn. *Res:* Romance linguistics; Spanish medieval and classical literature; general linguistics. *Publ:* Auth, La pronunciacion del ingles de los EEUU, Univ Javeriana, 66; Lucas Fernandez, Farsas y eglogas, Las Americas, 69; Observations on the Spanish of South America, Ky Romance Quart, summer 69; New biographical ideas on B de Torres Naharro, Hispania, 12/71; El lenguaje de Lucas Fernandez, Inst Caro y Cuervo, Bogota, 73; Lucas Fernandez, 73 & Bartolome de Torres Naharro, 79, Twayne; La tecnicaa de recapitulacion autentica en el teatro del siglo XVI, Actas del Primer Congreso sobre Lope de Vega, 81. *Mailing Add:* Dept Span & Ital Univ of Ky Lexington KY 40506

LIJERON, HUGO, b Trinidad, Bolivia, May 6, 30; US citizen; m 61; c 2. ROMANCE LANGUAGES, SPANISH-ROMANIC PHILOLOGY. *Educ:* San Francisco Xavier de Chuquisaca, Bolivia, LLB & LLD, 54; Middlebury Col, MA, 62; Univ Madrid, PhD(Romanic philol), 65. *Prof Exp:* Instr Span, Williams Col, 60-62; from asst prof to assoc prof, 63-74, PROF SPAN, UNIV AKRON, 74-, DIR LATIN AM STUDIES, 73- *Honors & Awards:* Honorary consul Bolivia, 68- *Mem:* MLA; Am Coun Teaching Foreign Lang; Am Asn Teachers Span & Port; Bolivian Inst Sociol. *Res:* Unamuno and existentialism; Bolivia novel; Bolivian short story. *Publ:* Auth, The Bolivian novel, 49 & Tin in the Bolivian economy, 50, San Francisco Univ Mag; Raza de Bronce, Hispania, 9/63; Unamuno y la novela existencialista, Amigos del Libro, La Paz, Bolivia, 70; coauth, Cuentos Bolivianos Contemporáneos, Populares Camarlinghi, 75. *Mailing Add:* Dept of Mod Lang Univ of Akron Akron OH 44304

LILLYMAN, WILLIAM J, b Sydney, Australia, Apr 17, 37; m 62. GERMAN COMPARATIVE LITERATURE. *Educ:* Sydney Univ, BA, 59; Stanford Univ, PhD(Ger), 64. *Prof Exp:* Asst prof Ger lit, Stanford Univ, 64-67; from asst prof to assoc prof, Univ Calif, Santa Cruz, 67-72; assoc prof & chmn dept, 72-73, prot Ger & dean humanities, 73-82, VICE CHANCELLOR, UNIV CALIF, IRVINE, 82- *Concurrent Pos:* Humanities res fel, Univ Calif, Irvine,

73; dir, Goethe Res Prog, 81- *Mem:* MLA; Am Asn Teachers Ger. *Res:* Nineteenth century German and comparative literature. *Publ:* Auth, Otto Ludwig's Zwischen Himmel und Erde: A Study of Its Artistic Structure, Mouton, The Hague, 67; The interior monologue in James Joyce and Otto Ludwig, Comp Lit, 71; ed, Ludwig Tieck: Vittoria accorombona, Reclam, 73; Otto Ludwig Romane und Romanstudien, Carl Hanser, 77; auth, Reality's Dark Dream: The Narrative Fiction of Ludwig Tieck, DeGruyter, Berlin, 79. *Mailing Add:* Office of Vice Chancellor Univ of Calif Irvine CA 92717

LIMA, EBION DE, b Frutal, Brazil, Oct 13, 24; m 67; c 2. ROMANCE LANGUAGES, RELIGION. *Educ:* Fac Lorena, Brazil, MA, 48; Pontif Ateneo, Turin, MA, 55; Cath Univ Sao Paulo, PhD(theol), 67. *Prof Exp:* Prof Brazilian lit, Fac Lorena, Brazil, 52-60, prof ethics, 56-58, prof philos, 57-58; prof dogmatics, Pio Xi, Theol Inst, Sao Paulo, 60-64, mystical theol, 62-64; ASSOC PROF PORT, UNIV MO-COLUMBIA, 65- *Concurrent Pos:* Mem comt found, Fac Lorena, Brazil, 51; comt Brazilian folklore, UNESCO, 55; prof morals, Cath Univ Sao Paulo, 62-64; Univ Mo asst prof res grant, 68- *Mem:* Am Asn Teachers Span & Port; Am Port Cult Soc. *Res:* Brazilian literature; education; Portuguese literature of the barroque period. *Publ:* Auth, Rui Barbosa, Edicoes Salesianas, 49; Licoes de literatura Brasileira, Linografica, Sao Paulo, 55, 64, 66 & 67; Educacoa moral e civica, Atualidades Pedagogicas, 55; Pas des omelettes . . ., 56 & Diletantismo e educacao, 56, Vozes, Brazil; Rodolfo Komorek, Edicoes D Bosco, 57; M Bernardes, vida, obra, doutrina espiritual,, Ed Moraes, Port; A Congregacao do Oratorio no Brasil, Vozes, Brazil, 81. *Mailing Add:* Dept of Romance Lang Univ of Mo Columbia MO 65201

LIMA, ROBERT F, JR, b Havana, Cuba, Nov 7, 35; US citizen; m 64; c 4. SPANISH & COMPARATIVE LITERATURES. *Educ:* Villanova Univ, BA, 57, MA, 61; NY Univ, PhD(Romance lit), 68. *Prof Exp:* Lectr Romance lit, Hunter Col, 62-65; asst prof Span & humanities, 65-69, assoc prof Span & comp lit, 69-73, PROF SPAN & COMP LIT, PA STATE UNIV, UNIVERSITY PARK, 73- *Concurrent Pos:* Ed assoc, Mod Int Drama, Max Reinhart Arch, State Univ NY, 67-81; fel poetry, Cintas Found, 71-72; sr fel, Fulbright-Hays, 76-77; vis prof comp lit, Pontif Univ Catolica Peru, 76-77; poet-in-residence, Univ Nac Mayor San Marcos, Peru, 76-77. *Mem:* MLA; Am Asn Teachers Span & Port; Int Comp Lit Asn; Am Comp Lit Asn; Archeol Inst Am. *Res:* World drama, generation of 1898, Spain; occultism in literature. *Publ:* Auth, The Theatre of Garcia Lorca, Las Americas, 63; ed & transl, Barrenechea's Borges the Layrinth Maker, NY Univ Press, 65; auth, Ramon del Valle-Inclan, Columbia Univ Press, 72; An Annotated Bibliography of Ramon del Valle-Inclan, Pa State Univ Libr, 72; ed, Surrealism, a celebration, J Gen Educ, 75; auth, Poems of Exile and Alienation, Anvil Press, 76; ed & contribr, Literature and the Occult, Univ Tex Press, 77; auth, Fathoms, Carnation Press, 81. *Mailing Add:* Dept of Span Pa State Univ University Park PA 16802

LIN, CHAOTE, b Peikang, Formosa, Dec 9, 30; m 62. JAPANESE. *Educ:* Nat Taiwan Univ, BA, 53; Univ Ore, BA, 56; MA, 58; Univ Mich, PhD(comp lit), 66. *Prof Exp:* Teaching fel French, Univ Mich, 60-61, asst prof Japanese, 64-66; instr, Univ Minn, 60-62; asst prof, Univ Calif, Berkeley, 62-64; from asst prof to assoc prof Japanese & French, 66-76, PROF JAPANESE & FRENCH, SAN JOSE STATE UNIV, 76- *Mem:* MLA; Asn Asian Studies; NEA. *Res:* Oriental and Romance languages and literature; comparative linguistics and literature; French stylistics. *Publ:* Coauth, Bibliographical Series of Japanese Reference and Research Materials, Univ Mich, 60. *Mailing Add:* Dept of Foreign Lang San Jose State Univ San Jose CA 95192

LIN, HELEN T, b Mar 29, 29; US citizen; m. CHINESE LANGUAGE. *Educ:* Nat Taiwan Univ, Taipei, BS, 50. *Prof Exp:* Teaching asst, Dept Agr Econ, Nat Taiwan Univ, Taipei, Taiwan, 50-54; instr Chinese, USFSI Chinese Lang & Area Training Ctr, Taichung, Taiwan, Repub China, 57-62; instr, Far Eastern Lang Inst, Yale Univ, 62-66; lectr Chinese & dir, Chinese Prog, 66-70, from asst prof to assoc prof, 70-78, PROF CHINESE, WELLESLEY COL, 78-, CO-DIR, EAST PROG, 72-, CHMN DEPT, 72- *Concurrent Pos:* Supvr Mandarin Dept, Taipei Lang Inst, Taiwan, 64-65; curric consult, Newton Chinese Lang Sch. *Honors & Awards:* Notable American Award, Am Biog Inst, Hist Preserv Am, 76-77. *Publ:* Auth, On co-operative farms in Taiwan, Taiwan Co-op Monthly, 10/50; An outline in Chinese agricultural economics, USFSI Lang Sch, Taiwan, 57; A Teacher's Guide on Taipei Language Institute Teaching Materials, Taipei Lang Inst, Taiwan, 65; coauth, Speak Mandarin Student's Workbook, Yale Ling Ser, 67, co-ed, Speak Mandarin, (in press), Yale Univ; Survey of Commonly Used Expressions in Chinese and an Analysis of Its Possible Implication on Language Teaching on the College Level, Educ Resources Info Ctr, Ctr Appl Ling, 74; Essentials of Modern Chinese Grammar, Cheng & Tsui Co, 6/81; Survey of Common Expressions Used in Daily Life in the People's Republic of China, Educ Resources Info Ctr, Ctr Appl Ling, 6/82. *Mailing Add:* Dept of Chinese Lang Wellesley Col Wellesley MA 02181

LIN, PAAUL PUO-YAUN, b China, Oct 6, 28; US citizen; m 61; c 1. CHINESE LINGUISTICS & LITERATURE. *Educ:* Taiwan Normal Univ, cert lang, 50; Univ Tex Austin, MA, 67, PhD(ling), 79. *Prof Exp:* High Sch Teacher English, Taiwan Educ Syst, 50-60; instr English grammar, Taiwan Normal Unvi, 62-65; res consult, Chinese affairs, Int Off Univ Tex Austin, 65-66; instr Chinese & Japanese, Univ Iowa, 68-69; actg asst prof, Univ Hawaii Manoa, 69-72; instr, 73-80, asst prof, 80-82, ASSOC PROF CHINESE & JAPANESE, OKLA STATE UNIV, 82- *Concurrent Pos:* Admin asst, Univ Tex Adv Team, Taiwan Normal Univ, 62-65. *Mem:* MLA; Semoitic Soc Am; Soc Teaching Japanese For Lang; Chinese Lang Teachers Asn; Southwest Conf Asian Studies. *Res:* Linguistic approaches to Chinese and Japanese literature; Semiotic perspectives on linguistics; Japanese linguistics. *Publ:* Coauth transl, A A Hill, Linguistic Approach to Teaching English as a Second Language, Univ Tex Team, Taiwan Normal Univ, 65; auth, Semiotic perspectives on Chinese: A picturesque language, Semiotic, 80 & Plenum Press, 81; Japanese and Chinese scripts as visual aids for teaching humanities, 81 Proc Southwest Conf Asian Studies, 82; contribr, The Beijing Language Institute: An inside view, J Chinese Lang Teachers Asn, Vol XVI, No 1. *Mailing Add:* 2818 W 17th Ave Stillwater OK 74074

LIND, LEVI ROBERT, b Trenton, NJ, July 29, 06; m 29; c 1. CLASSICAL PHILOLOGY. *Educ:* Univ Ill, AB, 29, AM, 32, PhD, 36. *Prof Exp:* Instr classics, Wabash Col, 29-32, from asst prof to assoc prof, 32-40; asst prof Latin & Greek, 40-52, prof, 52-64, chmn dept, 45-64, UNIV DISTINGUISHED PROF CLASSICS, UNIV KANS, 64- *Concurrent Pos:* Am Coun Learned Soc grant-in-aid fel, Univ Chicago, 40; Fulbright res grant, Rome, Italy, 54-55; US Pub Health Serv grant, 60-63. *Mem:* Am Philol Asn; Mediaeval Acad Am; Class Asn Mid W&S; Vergilian Soc. *Res:* Medieval Latin rhymed saints' lives; Roman ideas; Renaissance Latin anatomy. *Publ:* Auth, Vergil's Aeneid, Translated into Verse, Ind Univ; Epitome of Andreas Vesalius, Macmillan; Ecclesiale by Alexander of Villa Dei, 58 & Goethe, Roman Elegies and Venetian Epigrams, 74, Univ Kans; Twentieth Century Italian Poetry: A Bilingual Anthology, Bobbs-Merrill, 74; Studies in Pre-Vesalian Anatomy, Am Philos Soc, 75; translr, Ovid, Tristia, Univ Ga, 75; Andre Chenier, Elegies and Camille, Univ Am, 78. *Mailing Add:* 1714 Indiana St Lawrence KS 66044

LINDAHL, ROY ELWIN, JR, b Owosso, Mich, Apr 15, 32; m 55; c 3. CLASSICAL PHILOLOGY. *Educ:* Monmouth Col, Ill, BA, 54; Pittsburgh Theol Sem, MDiv, 57; Univ Mich, Ann Arbor, AM, 59; Tulane Univ, PhD(class lang), 71. *Prof Exp:* From instr to asst prof class lang & Bible, Maryville Col, 60-66; teaching asst class lang, Tulane Univ, 66-68; asst prof, 68-73, assoc prof & chmn dept, 73-78, PROF CLASS LANG, FURMAN UNIV, 79- *Mem:* Am Class League; Class Asn Midwest & S; Am Philol Asn; North Am Patristics Soc; AAUP. *Mailing Add:* Dept of Class Lang Furman Univ Greenville SC 29613

LINDBERG, JOHN D, b Vienna, Austria, Feb 22, 22. GERMAN LITERATURE. *Educ:* Univ Calif, Los Angeles, BA, 58, MA, 59, PhD(Ger), 64. *Prof Exp:* Teaching asst Ger, Univ Calif, Los Angeles, 58-60; instr, Pomona Col, 60-63; asst prof, 63-65; asst prof, Univ Calif, Irvine, 65-67; assoc prof, 67-69, PROF GER, UNIV NEV, LAS VEGAS, 69- *Concurrent Pos:* Ed, Daphnis, 72-76 & Argenis, 77- *Mem:* Philol Asn Pac Coast; Rocky Mountain Mod Lang Asn; MLA; Am Soc Ger Lit 16th & 17th Centuries. *Res:* German Baroque drama; German Baroque novel. *Publ:* Auth, Gottsched gegen die Oper, Ger Quart, 11/67; Algarotti, Calsabigi und Wieland, Seminar, spring 68; The German Baroque opera libretto: A forgotten genre, Univ Tex Ger Symp Monogr, 69; ed, Words of Christian Weise, De Gruyter, Berlin, 25 vols, 69-; ed-in-chief, Nachdrucke deutscher Literatur des 17 Jahrhunderts, 50 vols, Peter Lang, Bern, 69-; co-ed, Grimmelshausin-Zum Gedenkjahr 1976, Western Univ, 77. *Mailing Add:* 4505 Maryland Parkway Las Vegas NV 89154

LINDENBERGER, HERBERT (SAMUEL), Comparative Literature. See Vol II

LINDENFELD, JACQUELINE, b Rouen, France, Feb 17, 34; US citizen. LINGUISTICS, ANTHROPOLOGY. *Educ:* Univ Caen, France, Lic Anglais, 56; Univ Calif, Los Angeles, PhD(ling), 69. *Prof Exp:* Asst prof, 71-75, assoc prof, 75-80, PROF ANTHROP, CALIF STATE UNIV, NORTHRIDGE, 80- *Concurrent Pos:* NIMH fel, 69-71. *Mem:* Am Anthrop Asn; Ling Soc Am; MLA; Semiotic Soc Am; Southwestern Anthrop Asn. *Res:* Sociolinguistics and ethnography of communication; syntax and semantics. *Publ:* Auth, The social conditioning of syntactic variation in French, Am Anthropologist, 69; Verbal and non-verbal elements in discourse, Semiotica, 71; Yaqui Syntax, Univ Calif, 73; Affective states and the syntactic structure of speech, 73, Syntactic structure and kinesic phenomena in communicative events, 74 & Communicative patterns at French marketplaces, 78, Semiotica; Correlational sociolinguistics and the ethnography of communication, In: Language and Society, Mouton, 80. *Mailing Add:* Dept of Anthrop Calif State Univ Northridge CA 91330

LINDERSKI, JERZY, b Lwow, Poland, Aug 21, 34; US citizen. CLASSICAL LANGUAGES, ANCIENT HISTORY. *Educ:* Univ Cracow, MA, 55, PhD(hist), 60. *Prof Exp:* Sr asst ancient hist, Univ Cracow, 56-62, adj prof, 62-68; prof, Univ Ore, 71-79; PADDISON PROF LATIN, DEPT CLASSICS, UNIV NC, CHAPEL HILL, 79- *Concurrent Pos:* mem, Inst Advan Study, Princeton, 70-71 & 77-78; fel, Guggenheim Found, 77-78. *Mem:* Am Philol Asn; Asn Ancient Historians; Soc Promotion Roman Studies; Am Numismatic Soc. *Res:* Roman constitutional history; Roman religion; Latin language. *Publ:* Auth, Ciceros Rede pro Caelio und die Ambitus- und Vereinsgesetzgebung, Hermes, 61; Roman State and the Collegia, Sci Publ, Cracow, 61; Constitutional aspects of the Consular elections in 59 BC, Historia, 65; Roman Electoral Assemblies from Caesar to Sulla, Ossolineum, Wroclaw, 66; Der Senat und die Vereine, Gesellschaft und Recht im Griechisch-Römischen Altertum, 68; The Aedileship of Favonius, Curio the Younger and Cicero's election to the Augurate, Harvard Studies in Class Philol, 72; The Mother of Livia Augusta and the Aufidii Lurcones of the Republic, Historia, 74; Two cruces in Seneca, Am J Philol, 82. *Mailing Add:* Dept Classics Univ NC Chapel Hill NC 27514

LINDOW, JOHN FREDERICK, b Washington, DC, July 23, 46; m 68; c 2. GERMANIC & SCANDINAVIAN LINGUISTICS. *Educ:* Harvard Univ, AB, 68, PhD(Ger lang), 72. *Prof Exp:* Acting asst prof, 72-74, asst prof, 74-77, ASSOC PROF SCAND, UNIV CALIF, BERKELEY, 77- *Mem:* Am Folklore Soc; Mediaeval Acad Am; Soc Advan Scand Studies. *Res:* Germanic philology; Scandinavian folklore and mythology; Old Norse language and literature. *Publ:* Auth, Personification and narrative structure in Scandinavian plague legends, Arv, 73-74; A note on the sources of redundancy in oral epic, J Am Folklore, 74; Riddles, Kennings, and the complexity of Skaldic poetry, Scand Studies, 75; Comitatus, Individual and Honor, Univ Calif, 76; A mythic model in Bandamanna saga and its significance, Mich Ger Studies, 77; The two Skaldic stanzas in Gylfaginning, Arkiv för Nordisk Filologi, 77. *Mailing Add:* Dept of Scand Univ of Calif Berkeley CA 94720

LINDSAY, FRANK WHITEMAN, b Philadelphia, Pa, Oct 14, 09; m 42; c 3. FRENCH. *Educ:* Haverford Col, BA, 30; Columbia Univ, MA, 32, PhD, 46. *Prof Exp:* Instr Romance lang, Haverford Col, 37-38; teacher, Bentley Sch, 38-41, Blair Acad, 41-42 & Brooklyn Friends Sch, 42-46; asst prof Romance lang, NY State Maritime Col, 46-47; instr French, Princeton Univ, 47-50; assoc prof, 50-64, prof, 64-75, chmn dept, 50-71, EMER PROF FRENCH, RUSSELL SAGE COL. 75- *Res:* Seventeenth and 18th century French drama. *Publ:* Co-ed, Trois Nouvelles de Georges Simenon, Appleton, 66; Realite et Fantaisie: Neuf Nouvelles Modernes, Xerox, 71; Choix de Siminon, Appleton, 72; auth, Neron and Narcisse: A duality resolved, Mod Lang Quart; Alceste and the sonnet, Fr Rev. *Mailing Add:* 1139 Morningside Ave Schenectady NY 12309

LINDSAY, MARSHALL, b Milwaukee, Wis, Mar 22, 29; m 73. FOREIGN LANGUAGES. *Educ:* Univ Wis, BA, 51, MA, 54; Columbia Univ, PhD, 59. *Prof Exp:* Actg instr French, 57-59, from instr to assoc prof, 60-71, PROF FRENCH, UNIV CALIF, DAVIS, 71- *Concurrent Pos:* Fulbright res grant, Paris, 64-65. *Mem:* MLA. *Res:* Contemporary French novel; symbolist poetry; renaissance and baroque French poetry. *Publ:* Auth, Notes pour une edition critique des Amour jaunes, Rev Lang Vivantes, 62; The versification, Symposium, 72; Le Temps Jaune: Essais Sur Corbiere, Univ Calif, 72. *Mailing Add:* Dept of French Univ of Calif Davis CA 95616

LINDSEY, BYRON TRENT, b El Paso, Tex, Sept 8, 35; m 73. RUSSIAN LANGUAGE & LITERATURE. *Educ:* Univ Tex, Austin, BA, 57; Univ Ill, Urbana, MA, 65; Cornell Univ, PhD(Russ lit), 74. *Prof Exp:* Instr Russ, St Louis Univ, 69-71; ASST PROF RUSS, UNIV NMEX, 71- *Mem:* Am Asn Advan Slavic Studies; Am Asn Teachers Slavic & East Europ Lang Asn. *Res:* Chekhov's stories; Tolstoy's later works; Soviet painting. *Mailing Add:* Dept of Mod & Classical Lang Univ of NMex Albuquerque NM 87131

LINDSTROM, NAOMI E, b Chicago, Ill, Nov 21, 50. LATIN AMERICAN LITERATURE. *Educ:* Univ Chicago, AB, 71; Ariz State Univ, MA, 72, PhD(Span), 74. *Prof Exp:* Instr Span, Ariz State Univ, 74-75; asst prof, 75-82, ASSOC PROF SPAN & LATIN AM STUDIES, UNIV TEX, 82- *Concurrent Pos:* Consult, Women & World Issues Study Group, Washington, DC, 80-; lit ed, Rocky Mountain Rev Lang & Lit, 80- *Mem:* Inst Int Lit Iberoam; Rocky Mountain Mod Lang Asn; Studies Latin Am Popular Cult; MLA; Am Asn Teachers Span & Port. *Res:* Argentine vanguard literature 1920-1940; contemporary Argentine literature; ethnic studies. *Publ:* Auth, Literary Expression in Argentina, Ariz State Univ, 77; Macedonio Fernandez and Jacques Serrida: Co-Visionaries, Rev Ctr Inter Am Rels, 78; Narrative Garble in Arlt: A study in the conventions of expressionism, Ky Romance Quart, 79; La elaboracion de un discurso contracultural en las Aguafertes de Arlt, Hisp J, 80; Feminist criticism of Latin American literature, Latin Am Res Rev, 80; Macedonio Fernandez, Studies in Span & Span-Am Authors, 81; Echeverria to Quiroga, In: The Latin American Short Story, Twayne Publ, 82; Woman's Voice in Latin American Literature, Three Continents Press (in prep). *Mailing Add:* Dept of Span & Port Univ of Tex Austin TX 78712

LINDSTROM, THAIS S, b Petrograd, Russia, Sept 1, 16; US citizen. RUSSIAN LANGUAGE & LITERATURE. *Educ:* Hunter Col, BA, 34; Univ Calif, MA, 48; Sorbonne, PhD (comp lit), 51. *Prof Exp:* Instr Russ, Manhattanville Col, 52-54; vis lectr French, Queens Col, 54-55; asst prof foreign lang, Mont State Univ, 55-57 & comp lit, Western Reserve Univ, 57-60; prof Russ lang & lit, Sarah Lawrence Col, 60-71; prof, 71-80, EMER PROF COMP LIT, SCRIPPS COL, 80- *Concurrent Pos:* Am Asn Univ Women res grant, 57-58; Am Philos Soc res grants, 57-58, 68; mem, Coop Undergrad Prog Critical Lang, 57-; Inst Etudes Slaves. *Mem:* Northeastern Asn Am Scholars Slavic Studies; MLA; Am Asn Teachers Slavic & E Europ Lang; PEN Club. *Publ:* Auth, Tolstoi en France, Inst Etudes Slaves, 52; From chapbooks to classics, Am Slavic & E Europ Rev, 57; Manual of Beginning Russian, Am Bk Co, 59; Rubakin: Architect of popular enlightenment, Slavic & EEurop J, 59; Pirandellian masks in the Gorky Theatre, Theatre Ann, 61; A Concise History of Russian Literature, Vol I, From the Beginnings to Chekhov, 66 & Vol II, From 1900 to the Present, 75, NY Univ; Nikolai Gogol, His Life and Works, Twayne, 72. *Mailing Add:* Dept of Comp Lit Scripps Col Claremont CA 91711

LINN, MICHAEL D, b Aberdeen, SDak, Mar 7, 36; m 62; c 1. LINGUISTICS, AMERICAN ENGLISH. *Educ:* Univ Mont, BA, 60, MA, 62; Univ Minn, MA, 70, PhD(commun), 74. *Prof Exp:* Instr English, Lamara State Col of Tech, 63-65; res asst ling, Univ Minn, 68-71 & Cent Midwest Regional Educ Lab, 71-72; from instr to asst prof English, Va Commonwealth Univ, 72-77; asst prof, 77-80, ASSOC PROF ENGLISH & ANTHROP, UNIV MINN, DULUTH, 80- *Concurrent Pos:* Consult, Cent Midwest Regional Educ Lab, 72-73, Richmond Pub Sch, 74-75 & Va State Dept of Educ, 74-75; tape collector, US Dialect Tape Depository, 75-78; reader & consult, Choice, 75-; lectr, Arrowhead Speaker Serv, 78-81; manuscript reader, Halcyon, 78-; res fel, Mass Inst of Technol, 78; manuscript referee, J of Teacher Educ, 79-81. *Mem:* NCTE; Am Dialect Soc; MLA; Ling Soc Am; Asn Appl Ling. *Res:* American dialects; language variation; the teaching of writing. *Publ:* Coauth, Learing a Standard English, Cemrel, 72; auth, Black rhetoric and the teaching of composition, Col Compos and Commun, 75; Yes Virginia, there is Black ethnic pride, Sociol Res Symposium IV, 76; contribr, MLA Bibliography, MLA, 81 & 82; auth, Language change as reflected in Pidgins and Creoles, Alfred Knopf, 82; coauth, Black and white adolescent and pre-adolescent attitudes toward Black English, In: Research in the Teaching of English, 82; co-ed, Readings in Applied Linguistics, Alfred Knopf, 82. *Mailing Add:* English Dept Univ of Minn Duluth MN 55812

LINN, ROLF NORBERT, b Herne, Ger, June 20, 13; US citizen; m 60; c 2. GERMAN. *Educ:* Tex Col Mines, BA, 41; Univ Calif, Los Angeles, MA, 42, PhD, 49. *Prof Exp:* From lectr to assoc prof, 48-68, prof, 68-80, EMER PROF GER, UNIV CALIF, SANTA BARBARA, 80- *Mem:* Ger Shiller Ges. *Res:* Modern German literature. *Publ:* Auth, Heinrich Mann, Twayne, 67; Schillers junge Idealisten, Mod Philol ser, Univ Calif, 73; Uber Komodien von Expressionisten, St Michael, J G Blaschke Verlag, 78. *Mailing Add:* 1460 Crestline Dr Santa Barbara CA 93105

LINT, ROBERT GLEN, b Howard City, Mich, Dec 13, 22; m 46; c 4. ENGLISH LINGUISTICS, STYLISTICS. *Educ:* Univ Mich, Ann Arbor, BA, 48, MA, 48, MA, 50; Ohio Univ, PhD(English lang & ling), 67. *Prof Exp:* Teacher English, math & Latin, Howell High School, Mich, 50-54; instr English & Latin, R A Long High Sch & Lower Columbia Col, Wash, 54-64; from instr to asst prof English, Ohio Univ, 64-67; assoc prof, 67-75, PROF LING & ENGLISH, CALIF POLYTECH STATE UNIV, SAN LUIS OPISPO, 75- *Concurrent Pos:* NDEA Proj asst dir, Ohio Univ, 67; consult, Teacher Corps, San Diego, 76; consult-ed ling data, Inst for Cult Pluralism, 76-77. *Mem:* Am Dialect Soc; Am Class League; Int Reading Asn; Western Am Lit Asn; MLA. *Res:* English punctuation in relation to structural choices; computer processing of linguistic data; linguistic field work and language description. *Publ:* Auth, Structural art in Williams' The Red Wheelbarrow, Lang & Style, 72; Academia invents a new brand of Chicano migrant, La Luz, 72; Language as original sin, Cafe Solo, 72; Syntactic imagery in Williams' Young Sycamore, Lang & Style, 75; The total linguistic art in Jose Montoya's Resonant Valley, La Luz, 75; English Punctuation - English Grammar, El Corral, 76; The Barrio endowment to American literature, Eric, NCTE, 77; First Steps in Stylistics, El Corral, 78. *Mailing Add:* Dept of English Calif Polytech State Univ San Luis Obispo CA 93407

LIPOVSKY, JAMES PETER, b Washington, DC, June 13, 50; m 73; c 4. CLASSICAL LANGUAGES & LITERATURE. *Educ:* Univ Cincinnati, BA, 72; Princeton Univ, MA, 75, PhD(classics), 79. *Prof Exp:* Taylor lectr classics, Colby Col, 76-77; asst prof, Univ SC, 77-81; TEACHER CLASSICS, THE HEIGHTS SCH, MD, 81- *Mem:* Am Philol Asn. *Res:* Classical historians. *Publ:* Auth, A Historiographical Study of Livy, Books VI-X, Arno Press, 81; contribr, Livy, In: Ancient Writers: Greece and Rome, Scribner's, 82. *Mailing Add:* 4412 Oliver St Hyattsville MD 20781

LIPP, SOLOMON, b New York, NY, Oct 15, 13; m 44; c 2. SPANISH LITERATURE & HISTORY. *Educ:* City Col New York, BS, 34, MS, 35; Harvard Univ, PhD, 49. *Prof Exp:* Teacher & supvr foreign lang, sec schs, NY, 35-40; consult, US Army-Navy Span Proj, 40-41; from asst prof to prof Romance lang, Col Lib Arts, Boston Univ, 47-70; prof & chmn dept, 70-80, EMER PROF HISPANIC STUDIES, MCGILL UNIV, 70- *Concurrent Pos:* Vis prof, San Carlos Univ, Guatemale, 56 & Univ Costa Rica, 58; Fulbright vis prof, Nat Univ, Cordoba, 63; Soc Sci Res Coun & Am Philos Soc fels, res Santiago, Chile, 70; consult, humanities res div, Can Coun, 71- *Mem:* Latin Am Studies Asn; MLA; Am Asn Teachers Span & Port; Can Asn Hispanists; Int Inst Ibero Am Lit. *Res:* Spanish and Hispanic American literature and philosophy; philosophic thought in Argentina, Chile and Mexico. *Publ:* Auth, Three Argentine Thinkers, Philos Libr, 69; coauth, Hispanoamerica vista por sus ensayistas, Scribner's, 69; Spanish Cultural Reader, Heath, 70; auth, Fernando Alegria: Guerrero optimista, In: Homenaje a Fernando Alegria, Las Americas, 72; Three Chilean Thinkers, Wilfrid Laurier Univ, 75; Leopoldo Zea: From Mexicanidad to a Philosophy of History, Wilfrid Laurier Univ Press, 80. *Mailing Add:* Dept of Hispanic Studies McGill Univ 1001 Sherbrooke St West Montreal PQ H3A 1B1 Can

LIPPERT, ANNE, Comparative & African Literature. See Vol II

LIPPMANN, JANE N, b New York, NY, Mar 17, 38; M 69. FRENCH. *Educ:* Univ Miami, AB, 59; Univ Ill, AM, 60, PhD(French), 65; Univ Paris, cert lang pratique, 62. *Prof Exp:* Asst prof, 64-69, asst dean col arts & sci, 69-73, asst dean col humanities, 73-78, ASSOC PROF FRENCH, UNIV TEX, AUSTIN, 69-, ASST DEAN COL LIBERAL ARTS, 79- *Mem:* SCent Mod Lang Asn; Am Asn Teachers Fr; Am Coun Teaching Foreign Lang; Acad Affairs Administrators. *Res:* Seventeenth century French drama, especially Racine; foreign language methodology; educational administration. *Publ:* Auth, Foreign languages in the age of Aquarius, Dialog, Ind Foreign Lang Proj, 4/71; To each his own, Newslett Tex Foreign Lang Asn, 9/73; Rationale for langugage learning, In: The Challenge of Communication, Vol 6, Am Coun Teachers Foreign Lang, Lang Educ ser, Nat Textbk Co, 74. *Mailing Add:* Dept of French & Ital Univ of Tex Sutton Hall 121 Austin TX 78712

LIPSCHUTZ, ILSE HEMPEL, b Bönnigheim, Ger, Aug 19, 23; US citizen; m 52, c 4. FRENCH. *Educ:* Inst Prof Francais a l'Etranger, dipl, 43, Sorbonne, Lic es Let, 43, dipl Etudes Super, 44; Univ Madrid, dipl Estud Hisp, 45; Harvard Univ, MA, 49, PhD, 58. *Prof Exp:* Teaching fel French & Span, Harvard Univ & Radcliffe Col, 47-51; instr, 51-58, asst prof, 58-63, assoc prof, 63-72, prof French, 72-81, ANDREW W MELLON PROF HUMANITIES, VASSAR COL, 81-, CHMN DEPT, 75- *Concurrent Pos:* Am Asn Univ Women fel, 50-51; Anne Radcliffe fel, 50-51; Vassar Col fac fel, 60-61 & 66-67; US-Spain Treatise of Friendship res fel, 79-80 & 81. *Mem:* MLA; AAUP; Am Asn Univ Women; Int Soc Fr Studies; Soc Etudes Romantiques; Soc Theophile Gautier. *Res:* Nineteenth century Hispano-French relations; Theophile Gautier's art criticism; painting and literature. *Publ:* Auth, El despojo de obras de arte durante la Guerra de Independencia, 61 & El pintor y las poetas, Goya y los romanticos franceses, summer 68, Arte Espanol; Spanish Painting and the French Romantics, Harvard Univ, 72; Victor Hugo, Louis Boulanger, Francisco de Goya: Amities, affinites, influences, Nineteenth-Century Fr Studies, fall-winter 75-76; Theophile Gautier, su Espana legendaria y los Caprichos de Giya, Revista de Occidente, 12/76; Theophile Gautier et son Espagne retrouvee dans l'oeuvre grave de Goya, Bull Soc Theophile Gautier, 80; Imagenes y palabras, los franceses ante la pintura espanola, In: La Imagen Romantica de Espana, Madrid, 81. *Mailing Add:* Dept of French Vassar Col Poughkeepsie NY 12601

LIPTON, WALLACE S, b Brooklyn, NY, May 24, 30. ROMANCE LINGUISTICS. *Educ:* Brooklyn Col, BA, 51; Yale Univ, MA, 53, PhD(Romance philol), 57; NY Univ, MA, 57. *Prof Exp:* Substitute mod lang, Brooklyn Col, 55-57; instr French, Yale Univ, 57-59; adj asst prof, Long Island Univ, 59: instr, 59-64, from asst prof to assoc prof, 65-73, PROF MOD LANG, BROOKLYN COL, 74- *Res:* Old French language; Old Provencal language; Middle High German language. *Publ:* Auth, Anti-iconic preliminaries to the Biblia de Alba, Romance Philol, 69; Clues for readers of Wolfram von Eschenbach's Willehalm, Mod Lang Notes, 72; Identifying the speaker in Wolfram von Eschenbach's Willehalm, 228-18-19, Papers Lang & Lit, 72. *Mailing Add:* Dept of Mod Lang Brooklyn Col Brooklyn NY 11210

LISKER, LEIGH, b Philadelphia, Pa, Dec 7, 18; m 47; c 3. LINGUISTICS. *Educ:* Univ Pa, BA, 41, MA, 46, PhD(ling), 49. *Prof Exp:* Asst instr Ger, 47-48; from instr to assoc prof ling & Dravidian ling, 48-64, chmn dept, 76-80, PROF LING, UNIV PA, 64- *Concurrent Pos:* Am Coun Learned Soc fel, 47-48; Fulbright grant, India, 51-52, 59-60; res consult, Haskins Labs, NY, 53-; vis lectr, Deccan Col Post-Grad & Res Inst Poona, India, 59-60. *Mem:* Acoust Soc Am. *Res:* Structural and Dravidian linguistics; acoustic and physiological phonetics. *Publ:* Auth Introduction to Spoken Telugu, Am Coun Learned Soc, 63. *Mailing Add:* Dept of Ling Univ of Pa Philadelphia PA 19174

LISKO, BONNIE D, b Zanesville, Ohio, Dec 15, 24; m 53; c 3. FOREIGN LANGUAGES. *Educ:* Capital Univ, AB, 46; Middlebury Col, MA, 52. *Prof Exp:* Instr Romance lang, Concordia Jr Col, NY, 47-51; instr, Berea Col, 52-53; from instr to assoc prof, 54-73, PROF MOD LANG, CAPITAL UNIV, 73- *Mem:* MLA; Am Asn Teachers Fr. *Res:* Francophone literature and culture; the French media. *Publ:* Auth, Programming the computer, Fr Rev, 4/71. *Mailing Add:* Dept of Mod Lang Capital Univ Columbus OH 43209

LISLE, ROBERT, b Reno, Nev, Sept 20, 25; m 68; c 2. CLASSICS. *Educ:* Harvard Univ, AB, 50; Johns Hopkins Univ, PhD(classics), 55. *Prof Exp:* Asst prof English, Morgan State Col, 55-57; head dept English, St Timothy's Sch for Girls, Md, 57-65; dean col lib arts, Univ Baltimore, 65-68; prof English, Catonsville Community Col, 68-69; PROF CLASSICS, JAMES MADISON UNIV, 69- *Mem:* Am Philol Asn; Class Asn Mid W & S; AAUP. *Res:* Greek and Roman historiography. *Publ:* Auth, The court-martial of Adam Stephen, major-general, Continental Army, 72 & Power, self-interest, justice, and honor: some comments on Thucydides, 73, Madison Col Studies & Res Bull; Ancient and modern education, Class J, fall 73; Power, self-interest, liberty, honor: some comments on Tacitus, 75 & The classical content of political thought in 18th-century America, 76, Madison Col Studies & Res Bull; Thucydides, 1.22.4, Class J, 5/77; Tacitean utilitas, Class Outlook, 10/78. *Mailing Add:* Dept of Foreign Lang James Madison Univ Harrisonburg VA 22807

LISTERMAN, RANDALL WAYNE, b Denver, Colo, Nov 10, 38; m 65; c 1. MODERN LANGUAGES. *Educ:* Miami Univ, BA, 60; Middlebury Col, MA, 61; Univ Mo-Columbia, PhD(Span), 71. *Prof Exp:* Instr Span & Ger, DePauw Univ, 62-65; instr Ger, 66-68, asst prof, 71-78, ASSOC PROF SPAN, MIAMI UNIV, 78- *Mem:* MLA; Am Asn Teachers Ger; Am Asn Teachers Span & Port; Am Coun Teaching Foreign Lang. *Res:* Sixteenth century European drama; innovative approaches to language instruction. *Publ:* Auth, Innovative invitation to foreign language study, Foreign Lang Ann, 12/73; An interpretation of Günter Grass's The Tin Drum via Ortega's concept of art, East Ky Univ Rev, spring 74; The film experiment at Miami University, Accent on Am Coun Teaching Foreign Lang, spring 74. *Mailing Add:* Dept of Span Miami Univ Oxford OH 45056

LITMAN, THEODORE ARMAND, b Liege, Belgium, Aug 13, 39; US citizen; m 71. FRENCH LITERATURE. *Educ:* City Col New York, BA, 61; Middlebury Col, MA, 62; Harvard Univ, PhD(French lit), 67. *Prof Exp:* Instr French lit, Northeastern Univ, 66-67; asst, Boston Col, 67-68; asst prof, 68-76, ASSOC PROF FRENCH, CITY COL NEW YORK, 76- *Mem:* MLA; AAUP; 17th Century Fr Lit Soc; Mid-Hudson Mod Lang Asn. *Res:* French literature of the 17th century; the theatre; Corneille, Moliere and Racine. *Publ:* Auth, Le Sublime en France 1660-1714, 71 & Les comedies de Corneille, 81, Nizet. *Mailing Add:* Dept of Romance Lang City Col New York NY 10031

LITSAS, FOTIOS-FRANK K, Greek History and Culture. See Vol I

LITTERAL, ROBERT LEE, b Wheelersburg, Ohio, May 8, 38; m 63; c 2. LINGUISTICS, SOCIOLINGUISTICS. *Educ:* Wheaton Col, BA, 60, MA, 64; Univ Mich, MA, 61; Univ Pa(ling), 80. *Prof Exp:* Instr ling, Summer Inst Ling, Univ Okla, 62-63; instr phonology, Summer Inst Ling, Gordon Col, summer 70; prin, NZ Summer Inst Ling, 72-74; vis lectr transl, Univ Papua, New Guinea, summers, 74-75 & 77-79; INT LING CONSULT, PAC SUMMER INST LING, 76- *Concurrent Pos:* Ling consult, Summer Inst Ling, 68-73, sr ling consult, 73-75. *Mem:* Ling Soc Am; Ling Soc New Guinea. *Res:* Discourse analysis; language planning; multilingualism. *Publ:* Auth, A Programmed Course in New Guinea Pidgin, Jacarenda Press, 69, rev ed, 71; Rhetorical predicates and time topology, Found Lang, 72; Language planning activity in Papua, New Guinea, Workpapers in Papua New Guinea Lang, 77; Sociolinguistic Apects of Language Learning and Teaching, Oxford Univ Press, 80; Factors in Papua New Guinea multilingualism, In: Patterns of Bilingualisms, Univ Singapore Press, 80; Anggor referential prominence, In: Syntax and Semantics in Papua New Guinea Languages, 81; Papua New Guinea, In: Lang Planning & Lang Problems in the Pacific, Ling Soc Papua New Guinea, 82. *Mailing Add:* PO Box 59 Ukarumpa via Lae Papua New Guinea

LITTLE, GRETA D, b Asheville, NC, Dec 3, 43. LINGUISTICS, ENGLISH AS A FOREIGN LANGUAGE. *Educ:* Carleton Col, BA, 65; Univ NC, MA, 69, PhD(ling), 74. *Prof Exp:* Peace Corps teacher English, Haile Selassie 1st Sch, Ethiopia, 65-67; teaching asst Swahili, Univ NC & Duke Univ, 72; inst ling, Univ NC, 72-73; Fulbright lectr English, Cyril & Methodius Univ, Skopje, 73-74; dir English for Foreign Students, 77-79, ASST PROF ENGLISH & LING, UNIV SC, 74- *Concurrent Pos:* assoc ed, Southeastern Conf Ling Rev, 77- *Mem:* Ling Soc Am; Ling Asn Can & US; Southeastern Conf Ling; Southern Asn Africanists; Teachers English to Speakers Other Lang. *Res:* Syntactic change; African languages. *Publ:* Contribr, Syntactic evidence of language contact, In: Towards Tomorrow's Linguistics, Sch Lang & Ling, Georgetown Univ, 74; auth, Does word order in noun compounds reflect sentential syntax?, In: The Second Lacus Forum, Hornbeam, 76; Internal grammar in Amharic place-names, Names, 3/78; Word order function typology: The Amharic connection, Studies African Ling, 78; Subject Deletion in English, In: The Fifth LACUS Forum, Hornbeam, 79; Toward describing punctuation, In: SECOL Bull, spring 80; Politeness in the courtroom, In: The Eighth LACUS forum, Hornbeam, 82. *Mailing Add:* English Dept Univ of SC Columbia SC 29208

LITTLE, W A, b Boston, Mass, July 28, 29. GERMAN LITERATURE. *Educ:* Tufts Univ, AB, 51; Trinity Col, London, LTCL, 52; Harvard Univ, MA, 53; Univ Mich, PhD(Ger), 61. *Prof Exp:* Asst prof Ger, Williams Col, 57-63; assoc prof, Tufts Univ, 63-66; chmn, 66-72, PROF GER, UNIV VA, 66- *Concurrent Pos:* Sequicential fel, Univ Va, 72-73 & 78-79; ed, Ger Quar, Am Asn Teachers Ger, 70-77. *Mem:* MLA; Am Asn Teachers Ger; S Atlantic Mod Lang Asn; Lessing Soc; Nat Soc Lit & Arts. *Res:* Eighteenth century German (Lessing, Burger, et al); nineteenth century Austrian (Grillparzer, Anzengruber, et al); German American literary relations. *Publ:* Auth, Grillparzer's Excursions into Autobiography, Ky Foreign Lang Quar, 64; Some Early Translations of Shakespeare, Prologue, 64; Walt Whitman & the Nibelungenlied, PMLA, 65; Lessing and Schonaich, Lessing Yrbk (I), 69; Grillparzer and Gurney, Ger Quar, 72; Gottfried August Burger, Twayne, 74; Grillparzer's Esther: A Fragment for Good Reason, Mich Ger Studies, 75; ed, Organ Works of Felix Mendelssohn Bartholdy, Vol 1, 77, Vols 2 & 3 (in prep), DVFM, Leipzig. *Mailing Add:* Dept Ger Lang & Lit Univ Va Charlottesville VA 22903

LITTLEJOHN, JOSEPH EDWARD, Linguistics, English. See Vol II

LITZINGER, ELIZABETH, b Baltimore, Md, Oct 10, 20. FRENCH. *Educ:* Col Notre Dame Md, AB, 42; Johns Hopkins Univ, MA, 47. *Prof Exp:* Asst prof French & Span, Western Md Col, 46-49; teacher French, Span & Latin, Baltimore County, Md, 49-62; teacher French, Latin, & German, Western High Sch, Baltimore, 62-81, head dept foreign lang, 63-81; RETIRED. *Mem:* Am Asn Teachers Fr; Am Asn Teachers Ger (secy-treas); Mid States Asn Mod Lang Teachers (1st vpres, secy-treas). *Mailing Add:* 901 West 38th St Baltimore MD 21211

LIU, JAMES JO-YU, b Peking, China, Apr 14, 26; US citizen; div; c 1. CHINESE & COMPARATIVE LITERATURE. *Educ:* Cath Univ, Peking, BA, 48; Bristol Univ, MA, 52. *Prof Exp:* Lectr Chinese, Sch Orient & African Studies, Univ London, 51-56, Univ Hong Kong, 56-59; assoc prof, New Asia Col, Hong Kong, 59-61; asst prof Chinese, Univ Hawaii, 61-64; vis assoc prof, Univ Pittsburgh, 64-65; assoc prof Chinese lit, Univ Chicago, 65-67; chmn dept Asian lang, 69-75, PROF CHINESE, STANFORD UNIV, 67-, COURTESY PROF COMP LIT, 77- *Concurrent Pos:* External examr, Bristol Univ, 53; Univ London, 58, Chinese Univ Hong Kong, 68; Guggenheim Found fel, 71; Am Coun Learned Soc grant, 71-72 & 82; Nat Endowment for Humanities fel, 78-79. *Mem:* Am Orient Soc; Chinese Lang Teachers Asn; Asn Asian Studies; Am Comp Lit Asn. *Res:* Classical Chinese literature and literary criticism; comparative literary theory; interlingual hermeneutics. *Publ:* Auth, The Art of Chinese Poetry, 62, The Chinese Knight-errant, 67 & The Poetry of Li Shang-yin, 69, Univ Chicago; Major Lyricists of the Northern Sung, Princeton Univ, 74; Chinese Theories of Literature, Univ Chicago, 75; Essentials of Chinese Literary Art, Wadsworth Publ Co, 79; The Interlingual Critic, Ind Univ, 82. *Mailing Add:* Dept of Asian Lang Stanford Univ Stanford CA 94305

LIU, WU-CHI, b China, July 27, 07; m 32; c 1. CHINESE LANGUAGE & LITERATURE. *Educ:* Lawrence Col, BA, 28; Yale Univ, PhD(English), 31. *Prof Exp:* Prof English & chmn dept, Nankai Univ, Tientsin, 32-41; prof foreign lang, Nat Cent Univ, 41-46; vis prof English & Chinese cult, Rollins Col, 46-48; Bollingen Found fel, 48-51; vis prof Chinese lang & lit, Yale Univ, 51-53; prof Chinese studies & chmn dept, Hartwick Col, 53-55; sr ed, human rels area files, Yale Univ, 55-60; prof Chinese lang & lit, Univ Pittsburgh, 60-61; prof, 61-76, chmn dept EAsian lang & lit, 62-67, EMER PROF CHINESE LANG & LIT, IND UNIV, BLOOMINGTON, 76- *Concurrent Pos:* Nat Found Arts & Humanities sr fel, 67-68; panelist, Nat Endowment for Humanities, 69-71; Dewar prof hist, Hartwick Col, spring 75; vis prof Chinese lit, Univ Calif, Berkeley, spring, 81. *Honors & Awards:* Distinguished Alumni Award, Lawrence Univ, 78. *Mem:* Am Orient Soc; Asn Asian Studies. *Res:* Chinese and English literature; history of Chinese drama. *Publ:* Auth, A Short History of Confucian Philosophy, Penguin, 55; Confucius, His Life and Time, Philos Libr, 55; An Introduction to Chinese Literature, Ind Univ, 66; Literature, of the twentieth century, In: A Supplement in History of Chinese Literature, Ungar, 67; coauth, Readings in Contemporary Chinese Literature (3 vols), Far East Publ, 67-68; auth, Su Man-shu, Chinese Authors ser, Twayne, 72; coauth, Sunflower Splendors, An Anthology of Chinese Poetry, Doubleday, 75. *Mailing Add:* 2140 Santa Cruz Ave E305 Menlo Park CA 94025

LIVINGSTONE, LEON, b Boston, Mass, Aug 23, 12; m 48; c 3. SPANISH LITERATURE. *Educ:* Univ Toronto, BA, 34; Brown Univ, AM, 39, PhD, 47. *Prof Exp:* Asst, Brown Univ, 38-42, from instr to asst prof, 46-50; from asst prof to assoc prof Span lit, Wayne State Univ, 50-61; chmn dept Span, Ital & Port & Coun Mod Lang, 67-69, prof, 61-80, EMER PROF SPAN, STATE UNIV NY, BUFFALO, 80- *Concurrent Pos:* Ford fac fel, Spain, 54-55; vis prof Span, Univ Calif, Los Angeles, 64-65; Guggenheim fel, 74-75; res dir, State Univ NY Stage a Grenoble, France, 77-79. *Mem:* MLA; Am Asn Teachers Span & Port. *Res:* Modern-contemporary Spanish literature; aesthetics of the novel. *Publ:* Auth, Interior duplication and the problem of form in the modern Spanish novel, PMLA, 58; The novel as self-creation, In: Unamuno: Creator and Creation, Univ Calif, 66; Tema y forma en las novelas de Azorin, Gredos, Madrid, 70; On significant reality, In: Galdos Studies II, Tamesis, London, 74. *Mailing Add:* Dept of Mod Lang State Univ of NY Buffalo NY 14260

LIVOSKY, ISABEL C, b Dominguez, Argentina, Feb 15, 35; US citizen. SPANISH LANGUAGE & LITERATURES. *Educ:* Columbia Univ, BA, 70; NY Univ, PhD(Span), 77. *Prof Exp:* Instr Span, York Col, City Univ New York, 74-76; ASST PROF MOD LANG, KNOX COL, 77- *Concurrent Pos:* Managing ed, Bilingual Press, 75-77; res dir, Knox Col Prog in Barcelona, Spain, 79-81; mem exec comt, Asn Am Prog Madrid, Spain, 80-81. *Mem:* MLA; Am Asn Teachers Span & Port. *Res:* Spanish Golden Age and contemporary literature; contemporary Latin American literature; literary criticism. *Publ:* Co-ed, Bibliographical Index for Spanish & Spanish-American Studies in the United States, Anaya-Las Americas, 74; transl, Ronald G

Woods, Introduccion a las ciencias de la educacion, Ediciones Anaya, Salamanca, 76; collaborator (with Jose A Hernandez), Interview Juan Goytisolo--1975, Mod Lang Notes, Hisp Issue, 76 & Destino, Barcelona, 76; auth, Sobre la estructura narrativa de El Criticon de Gracian, In: The Analysis of Hispanic Texts, York Col, City Univ New York, 76; co-ed (with Mary A Beck et al), The Analysis of Hispanic Texts: Current Trends in Methodology, 1st York Col Colloquium, 76 & (with Lisa E Davis), The Analysis of Hispanic Texts: Current Trends in Methodology, 2nd York Col Colloquium, 77, Bilingual Press; auth, Critical Introduction to Baltasar Gracian's El Heroe, El Discreto, El Criticon, Porrua, Mex, 77. *Mailing Add:* Dept Mod Lang Knox Col Galesburg IL 61401

LIZE, EMILE JEAN-CLAUDE, b Guemene-Penfao, France, July 25, 43; Can citizen; m 72; c 1. FRENCH LITERATURE. *Educ:* Univ Ottawa, MA, 71; Sorbonne, PhD(French lit), 74. *Prof Exp:* Asst prof, 74-78, ASSOC PROF FRENCH LIT, UNIV OTTAWA, 78- *Concurrent Pos:* Can Coun Acad Sci, USSR, res award, 77. *Mem:* Soc Hist Lit France; Soc Fr Etudes 18th Siecle; Soc Can Etudes 18th Siecle. *Res:* History of the press in the 18th century; biography of Voltaire. *Publ:* Auth, Une curieuse affaire de pommes a Ferney: Adam vs Bigex, Studies Voltaire, 75; Voltaire, Collaborateur de la CL, Klincksieck, Paris, 76; Deux faceties du baron d'Holbach, 78 & Memoires inedits de Diderot, 78, Dix-Huitieme Siecle; Dear Teacher, Potlatch Publ, 79; L'Homme de lettres et le faquin: Voltaire et Jean Neaulme, Romanische Forschungen, 92: 126-131; De deux motifs recurrents chez Diderot: La pierre et le couteau, Transactions of the Fifth Congress on the Enlightment, Studies on Volitaire and the Eighteenth Century, Voltaire Found, 193: 1629-1636. *Mailing Add:* L'Ashdale Ave Box 653 Ottawa ON K2C 3H1 Can

LLOYD, ALBERT L, b Evanston, Ill, Aug 10, 30; m 59; c 1. GERMANIC LANGUAGES & LITERATURES. *Educ:* George Washington Univ, AB, 51, MA, 54, PhD, 57. *Prof Exp:* Assoc Ger, George Washington Univ, 54-57; from instr to assoc prof, 57-70, chmn dept, 72-80, PROF GER, UNIV PA, 70- *Concurrent Pos:* Mem nat adv bd, Jr Year in Munich & Freilburg prog, 62-80; Am Philos Soc res grant, 66; mem, Inst Deut Sprache, 69-; res grant, Nat Endowment for Humanities, 78- & panelist evaluation applications, 79-80. *Mem:* MLA; Ling Soc Am; Am Asn Teachers Ger; Mediaeval Acad Am. *Res:* Germanic philology; medieval German literature; Indo-European linguistics. *Publ:* Auth, The MSS and Fragments of Notker's Psalter, Schmitz, Giessen, Ger, 58; coauth, Germanic sect, PMLA Ann Bibliog, 59-63; auth, Is there a an a-umlaut of i in Germanic?, Language, 66; coauth, Deutsch und Deutschland heute, Am Bk Co, 67, 2nd ed, D Van Nostrand, 81; auth, Vowel plus h in Notker's Alemannic, In: Germanic Studies in Honor of E H Sehrt, Univ Miami, 68; ed, Der Münchener Psalter des 14 Jahrhunderts, Erich Schmidt, Berlin, 69; Prolegomena to a Theory of Gothic Verbal Aspect, In: Linguistic Method: Herbert Penzl Festschrift, The Hague, 79; Anatomy of the Verb, J Benjamins, Amsterdam, 79. *Mailing Add:* 745 Williams Hall Univ of Pa Philadelphia PA 19104

LLOYD, DANUTA SWIECICKA, b Wilno, Poland, Mar 27, 33; US citizen; m 59; c 1. GERMAN LITERATURE. *Educ:* Temple Univ, BA, 54; Univ Pa, MA, 57, PhD(Germanics), 69. *Prof Exp:* Instr, Temple Univ, 56-57; lectr, Bryn Mawr Col, 67-68 & Drexel Univ, 68-73; ASST PROF GERMAN, URSINUS COL, 75- *Concurrent Pos:* Reader, Mod Austrian Lit, 77-78 & 81-82. *Mem:* Am Asn Teachers Ger; MLA; Polish Inst Arts & Sci. *Res:* Nineteenth and 20th century German literature; German-Slavic literary relations. *Publ:* Auth, Waifs and strays: The youth in Marie von Ebner-Eschenbach's village tales, Views & Rev Mod Ger Lit: Festchrift for Adolf D Klarmann, Munich, 74; German-Polish literary relations in the nineteenth century, Probleme der Komparatistik und Interpretatin: Festschrift für A V Gronicka, Bonn, 78; Dorf and Schloss: The socio-political image of Austria as reflected in Marie von Ebner-Eschenbach's works, Mod Austrian Lit, Vol 12, No 3 & 4; coauth, Deutsch und Deutschland heute, D Van Nostrand Co, 81. *Mailing Add:* German Dept Ursinus Col Collegeville PA 19246

LLOYD, PAUL M, b Rochester, NY, Sept 15, 29; m 52; c 2. ROMANCE PHILOLOGY. *Educ:* Oberlin Col, AB, 52; Brown Univ, AM, 54; Univ Calif, Berkeley, PhD, 60. *Prof Exp:* Teaching asst Span, Brown Univ, 52-54 & Univ Calif, 54-58; instr, Dartmouth Col, 58-60 & ling sci Romance lang, Sch Lang, Foreign Serv Inst, 60-61; from asst prof to assoc prof, 61-70, PROF ROMANCE LANG, UNIV PA, 70- *Concurrent Pos:* Assoc ed, Hisp Rev, 65-; Fulbright lectr English, Univ Deusto, Spain, 66-67. *Mem:* Ling Soc Am; Am Asn Teachers Span & Port; Soc Ling Romane; Ling Asn Can & US; Sci Fiction Res Asn. *Res:* Romance philology; general and Spanish linguistics. *Publ:* Auth, Verb-complement Compounds in Spanish, Max Niemeyer, Tübingen, 68; L'action du substrat et la structure linguistique, In: Actele celui de-al XII-lea Congres International de Linguistica si Filologie Romanica, 1968, 71; Contribucion al estudio del tema de Don Juan en las comedias de Tirso de Molina, In: Homenaje al Prof William L Fichter, 71; coauth, A Graded Spanish Review Grammar with Composition, Prentice-Hall, 73; auth, La metafonia vocalica y el sistema verbal romanico, In: Proceedings of the 14th International Congress of Romance Linguistics and Philology, Amsterdam, Benjamins, 77; On the definition of Vulgar Latin, Neuphilogische Mitteilungen, 79. *Mailing Add:* Dept of Romance Lang Univ of Pa Philadelphia PA 19104

LLOYD, ROBERT BRUCE, b Toledo, Ohio, July 10, 26; m 51; c 4. CLASSICAL PHILOLOGY. *Educ:* Oberlin Col, AB, 48; Johns Hopkins Univ, MA, 49, PhD(classics), 52. *Prof Exp:* Instr Classics, Oberlin Col, 52-56; asst prof, Cornell Col, 56-58; from asst prof to assoc prof, 58-64, prof & chmn dept, 64-73, Charles A Dana prof classics, 73-81, MARY FRANCES WILLIAMS CHAIR HUMANITIES, RANDOLPH-MACON WOMAN'S COL, 82- *Concurrent Pos:* Mem managing comt, Am Sch Class Studies, Athens, 65-69; Fulbright res fel, Rome, 66-67; ed, Verjiliuis, 80-; dir, Summer Sch Verjiliair Soc Am, Cermal, Italy, 83. *Mem:* Am Philol Asn; Archaeol Inst Am; Vergilian Soc Am (vpres, 78-80); Class Asn Midwest & South. *Res:* Servius and the other Vergilian commentators; Vergil; topography of ancient Rome. *Publ:* Auth, Aeneid III: A new approach, 57 & Superbus in the Aeneid, 72, Am J Philol; Republican authors in Servius and the Scholia Danielis, Harvard Studies Class Philol; articles on Roman mythology in Encycl Britannica; auth, Humor in the Aeneid, Class J, 77; The Aqua Virgo Eiuripus and Pous Agrippae, Am J Archaeol, 79. *Mailing Add:* Dept of Classics Randolph-Macon Woman's Col Lynchburg VA 24503

LO, CHIN-TANG, b Lungsi, Kansu, China, July 27, 29; m 59; c 1. CHINESE. *Educ:* Nat Taiwan Univ, BA, 52, MA, 56, LittD, 61. *Prof Exp:* Assoc prof, New Asian Col, Chinese Univ Hong Kong, 60-61; lectr, Univ Hong Kong, 61-66; assoc prof, 66-70, PROF CHINESE, UNIV HAWAII, MANOA, 71- *Concurrent Pos:* Vis prof, Univ Hamburg, 72-73, Nat Taiwan Univ, 79-80. *Publ:* Auth, An introduction to the literary value of Confucian classics, 67; The development of Chinese fiction, 68; translr, Early Chinese Literature, B Watson, 69; Clues leading to the discovery of Hsi Yu Chi Ping-hua, 69; Popular stories of Wei and Chin period, 71; Goethe and the novels of Ming Dynasty, 73; Chinese point of view to drama, 73; On Classical Chinese drama, 77; Chinese Study and Sinology, 79; The Development of Chinese Drama, 80. *Mailing Add:* Dept of East Asian Lit Univ of Hawaii at Manoa Honolulu HI 96822

LO, IRVING YUCHENG, b Foochow, China, Sept 19, 22; US citizen; m 45. COMPARATIVE LITERATURE, CHINESE. *Educ:* St John's Univ, China, BA, 45; Harvard Univ, MA, 49; Univ Wis, PhD(English), 54. *Prof Exp:* Prof English, Stillman Col, 52-57; from asst prof to assoc prof, Western Mich Univ, 57-64; assoc prof Chinese, Univ Iowa, 64-66; Fulbright-Hays fel, 66-67; assoc prof East Asian lit, 67-71, PROF EAST ASIAN LANG & LIT, IND UNIV, BLOOMINGTON, 71- *Concurrent Pos:* Ed, Lit East & West, 63-; vis prof Asian lang, Stanford Univ, 71-72. *Mem:* MLA: Asn Asian Studies; Am Orient Soc. *Publ:* Auth, Wen T'ing-yun, In: Encycl Britannica, 67; Style and vision in Chinese poetry, Tsing Hua J Chinese Studies, 6/68; Hsin Ch'i-Chi (Twayne world auth ser), Twayne, 71; co-ed & contribr, Sunflower Splendor: Three Thousand Years of Chinese Poetry, Ind Univ, Doubleday & Anchor Bks, 75; K'uei Yeh Chi, Ind Univ, 76; ed, Chinese Literature in Translation Series, Ind Univ Press, 76. *Mailing Add:* 248 Goodbody Hall Ind Univ Bloomington IN 47401

LOBO FILHO, BLANCA, b Vienna, Austria, Apr 2, 07; m 26; c 2. ROMANCE LANGUAGES. *Educ:* Columbia Univ, BS, 60, MA, 62; NY Univ, PhD(Port), 65. *Prof Exp:* Assoc prof, 65-72, EMER ASSOC PROF PORT, PORTLAND STATE UNIV, 72- *Mem:* Am Asn Teachers Span & Port. *Publ:* Auth, Interpretation of the Lirica of Henriqueta Lisboa, 65, The Poetry of Henriqueta Lisboa, 66 & The Poetry of Emily Dickinson and Henriqueta Lisboa, 73, Imprensa Nac, Belo Horizonte, Brazil; Selected Poems by Henriqueta Lisboa, 78 & The Poetry or Emily Dickinson and Henriqueta Lisboa, 78, Norwood Editions. *Mailing Add:* Dept of Foreign Lang Portland State Univ PO Box 751 Portland OR 97207

LOCHER, KASPAR THEODORE, b St Gallen, Switz, Dec 15, 20; m; c 2. COMPARATIVE LITERATURE, GERMAN. *Educ:* Univ Chicago, PhD, 49. *Prof Exp:* Asst instr Ger, Univ Chicago, 46-47; instr, Vanderbilt Univ, 48-50; instr, 50-51, asst prof, 51-55, assoc prof, 56-58, PROF GER & HUMANITIES, REED COL, 58- *Concurrent Pos:* Fund Advan Educ fel, 55-56; vis prof Ger, Univ Wash, 63; Am Coun Learned Soc fel, 72-73; vis prof Ger, Univ Ore, 78. *Mem:* MLA: Am Asn Teachers Ger; Philol Asn Pac Coast. *Res:* Nineteenth and 20th century German literature; Gottfried Keller. *Publ:* Auth, G Keller and the fate of the Epigone, Ger Rev, 60; About Truth and Reality in Keller's Early Lyrics, DVjs; Gottfried Keller: Der Weg zur Reife, Francke, Berne, 69; Gottfried Keller's Der Apotheker von Chamounix, Jahrbuch der deutschen Schillergesellschaft, XVI, 72; Das Schiller-Bild Gottfried Kellers, Ger Quart, 5/75. *Mailing Add:* Div of Lit & Lang Reed Col Portland OR 97202

LOCK, PETER WILLIAM, b Desborough, England, May 12, 31; m 59; c 2. FRENCH LITERATURE. *Educ:* Oxford Univ, MA, 55; Univ Calif, Berkeley, PhD(Romance lang & lit), 63. *Prof Exp:* Asst prof French, Dartmouth Col, 63-66; assoc prof, 66-72, PROF FRENCH, UNIV MINN, MINNEAPOLIS, 72- *Mem:* Am Asn Teachers Fr. *Res:* Nineteenth century French literature, especially the novel. *Publ:* Auth, Hoarders and spendthrifts in the Comedie humaine, Mod Lang Rev, 1/66; Pattern and meaning in Maupassant's Amour, Fr Rev, 10/67; Balzac's Le Pere Goriot, Arnold, London, 67; ed, Le Pere Goriot, Macmillian, London, 68. *Mailing Add:* Dept of French & Ital Univ of Minn Minneapolis MN 55455

LOCKARD, THADDEUS (CONSTANTINE), JR, b Meridian, Miss, Mar 12, 13. MODERN LANGUAGES. *Educ:* Univ Miss, AB, 34; Harvard Univ, AM, 38. *Prof Exp:* Instr English & French, Univ Miss, 34-35, 36-37; teaching fel & tutor English, Harvard, 38-42; mem staff, UNRRA, Austria, 45-48; asst prof Ger, Univ of the South, 50-51; instr English, Univ Va, 53-56; supvr lang courses, overseas prog, Univ Md, 57-58; asst prof Ger & French, 58-71, asst prof, 71-80, EMER PROF GER & ITAL, UNIV OF THE SOUTH, 80- *Concurrent Pos:* Fulbright scholar, Oxford, 49-50. *Res:* English Literature. *Publ:* Co-translr, The Lost Letters of Jenny Lind, Gollancz, London, 66. *Mailing Add:* Dept of Ger Univ of the South Sewanee TN 37375

LOCKE, FREDERICK WILLIAM, b Boston, Mass, June 16, 18; m 42; c 4. CLASSICS, COMPARATIVE LITERATURE. *Educ:* Harvard Univ, AB, MA, PhD(comp lit), 53. *Prof Exp:* Instr French, Cath Univ Am, 51-54; from asst prof to assoc prof, Stanford Univ, 55-60; prof, State Univ NY, Binghamton, 60-67; PROF MEDIEVAL LIT, UNIV ROCHESTER, 67- *Mem:* Dante Soc Am; Mediaeval Acad Am; MLA. *Res:* Grail legend; medieval vision literature. *Publ:* Auth, Dante and T S Eliot's Prufrock, Mod Lang Notes. *Mailing Add:* Dept of Classics and Comparative Lit Univ of Rochester River Campus Rochester NY 14627

LOCKE, JOHN ROBERT, Comparative Literature, Linguistics. See Vol II

LOCKE, WILLIAM NASH, b Watertown, Mass, June 28, 09; m 38; c 3. MODERN LANGUAGES. *Educ:* Bowdoin Col, BS, 30; Harvard Univ, AM, 37, PhD, 41; Sch Prep Prof Fr Abroad, Paris, cert, 36; Inst de Phonetique, Univ Paris, dipl, 36. *Prof Exp:* Asst French, Shady Hill Sch, Cambridge, Mass, 37-38; instr, Harvard Univ, 38-43; prof mod lang, 45-72, head dept mod lang, 45-64, dir libr, 56-72, dir foreign studies adv, 72-74, EMER PROF MOD LANG, MASS INST TECHNOL, 74- *Concurrent Pos:* Prof French exten courses, Harvard Univ, 46-74; dir, Coun Pub Schs, 62-70; mem, Int Fedn Doc Ling doc comt, 63-67, chmn 67-72; vpres, Nat Fedn Mod Lang Teachers Asn, 67-71. *Honors & Awards:* Officier, Palmes Academiques, 49; chevalier, Legion d'honneur. *Mem:* Asn Res Libr; MLA; Ling Soc Am; Am Asn Teachers Fr (vpres, 48); Am Dialect Soc. *Res:* Machine processing of information; speech analysis; French phonetics and dialectology. *Publ:* Auth, Prounciation of the French Spoken at Brunswick, Maine, Publ Am Dialect Soc, 49; co-ed, Machine Translation of Languages, 55 & auth, Scientific French 57, Wiley. *Mailing Add:* South Harpswell ME 04079

LOCKETT, LANDON JOHNSON, b Ft Benning, Ga, May 22, 29. LINGUISTICS, PORTUGUESE. *Educ:* Univ Tex, Austin, BA, 54, LLB, 57, PhD(ling), 68; Southern Methodist Univ, MCL, 59. *Prof Exp:* Instr Port, Univ Tex, Austin, 65-67, asst prof Port & ling, 68-75; VIS PROF LING, UNIV FED RIO GRANDE NORTE, NATAL, BRAZIL, 78- *Concurrent Pos:* Vis prof ling, Cath Univ, Rio Grande do Sul, Porto Alegre, Brazil, 70; vis prof ling, Univ Autonoma, Guadalajara, Mex, 76-77. *Mem:* Ling Soc Am; MLA; Am Asn Teachers Span & Port. *Res:* Brazilian Portuguese linguistics; linguistics applied to foreign language teaching; sociolinguistics. *Publ:* Auth, O uso do infinitivo num Corpus de Portugues coloquial Brasileiro, Alfa, 69; The role of reading at the intermediate level, Mod Lang J, 11/72. *Mailing Add:* Dept of Ling Univ Fed do Rio Grande do Norte 59000 Natal, RN Brazil

LOCKHART, DONALD M, b Cambridge, Mass, Mar 14, 23; m 60; c 3. ROMANCE LANGUAGES & LITERATURES. *Educ:* Bowdoin Col, AB, 48; Harvard Univ, AM, 49, PhD, 59. *Prof Exp:* Instr French & Span, Manlius Sch, 51-53; instr French & Latin, Cambridge Sch Weston, 57-58; asst prof Romance lang, Ripon Col, 58-63; assoc prof, 63-71, PROF MOD LANG, NORWICH UNIV, 71-, CHMN DEPT, 72- *Mem:* MLA; Soc His Discoveries; Hakluyt Soc. *Res:* Seventeenth and 18th century French literature; Portuguese literature of exploration. *Publ:* Auth, The fourth son of the mighty emperor: The Ethiopian background of Johnson's Rasselas, PMLA, 12/63; The Palmella manuscript of Dom Joao de Castro's Red Sea Rutter, In: Proceedings of the Third International Conference of Ethiopian Studies, Addis Ababa, 69; co-ed, Jeronimo Lobo's Itinerario e outros escritos ineditos, Livraria Civilizacao, Oporto, Port, 71. *Mailing Add:* Dept of Mod Lang Norwich Univ Northfield VT 05663

LOCKHART, PHILIP N, b Smicksburg, Pa, May 3, 28; m 59; c 2. CLASSICAL STUDIES. *Educ:* Univ Pa, BA, 50; Univ NC, MA, 51; Yale Univ, PhD(classical lang), 59. *Prof Exp:* Teacher, Ezel Mission Sch, Ky, 51-52; instr class lang, Univ Mo, 54-56; instr class studies, Univ Pa, 57-61, asst prof, 61-63; assoc prof class lang & chmn dept, 63-68, prof, 68-71, ASBURY J CLARKE PROF LATIN & CHMN DEPT, DICKINSON COL, 71- *Concurrent Pos:* Vis prof, Ohio State Univ, 69-70. *Honors & Awards:* Ganoe Award Teaching, Dickinson Col, 69, 73. *Mem:* Am Philol Asn; Archaeol Inst Am; Am Class League; Vergilian Soc Am. *Res:* Latin poetry; fourth century AD; Homeric background. *Publ:* Auth, The Laodice inscription from Didyma, Am J Philol, 61; Phronein in Homer, Class Philol, 66. *Mailing Add:* Dept of Class Lang Dickinson Col Carlisle PA 17013

LOCKWOOD, DAVID G, b Chicago Heights, Ill, June 27, 40. GENERAL & SLAVIC LINGUISTICS. *Educ:* Univ Mich, BA, 62, MA, 63, PhD(ling), 66. *Prof Exp:* From asst prof to assoc prof ling & Russ, 66-72, assoc prof, 72-75, PROF LING, MICH STATE UNIV, 75- *Mem:* Ling Soc Am; Ling Asn Can & US; Am Asn Teachers Slavic & East Europ Lang. *Res:* Stratificational theory; structure of Slavic languages; historical linguistics. *Publ:* Auth, Markedness in stratificational phonology, Language, 69; contribr, Phonological Theory: Evolution and Current Practice, Holt, 72; auth, Introduction to Stratificational Linguistics, Harcourt, 72; co-ed, Readings in Stratificational Linguistics, Univ Ala, 73; The First LACUS Forum, 1974, Hornbeam, 75; contribr, Linguistics at the Crossroads, Liviana Editrice & Jupiter, 77; auth, Grammatical conditioning in stratificational phonology, Forum Linguisticum, 78; contribr, Papers in Cognitive-Stratificational Linguistics, Rice Univ Studies, 80. *Mailing Add:* Dept of Ling Wells Hall Mich State Univ East Lansing MI 48824

LOCOCO, VERONICA GONZALEZ-MENA, b Puebla, Mexico, Dec 16, 34; US citizen; m 59; c 2. SECOND LANGUAGE LEARNING, PSYCHOLINGUISTICS. *Educ:* Univ Femenina, Mexico City, MS, 56; Univ Santa Clara, MAT, 70; Stanford Univ, PhD(second lang, biling educ), 75. *Prof Exp:* Instr Span, Skyline Col, 69-70; LECTR SPAN & GER, UNIV SANTA CLARA, 70- *Concurrent Pos:* Consult, San Mateo County, Calif Sch Dist, 76-77 & Monterey County, Calif Sch Dist, 77-78; reader, Lang Learning, 80-81; consult, Houghton Mifflin & Scott Foresman, summer 81. *Res:* Error analysis; second language learner comprehension and production strategies; code switching. *Publ:* Auth, The salient differences between Chicano Spanish and standard Spanish, Bilingual Rev, 74; A look at Spanish irregular verbs, Hispania, 75; An analysis of Spanish and German learner's errors, 75, A comparison of three methods for the collection of L2 data..., 76 & A cross sectional study on L3 acquisition, 76, Working Papers on Bilingualism; A semantic analysis of Spanish se constructions, Hispania, 76; Writing skills of grade 3 compound and coordinate bilinguals in a bilingual program, Indian J Applied Ling, 77; El camion, Pepin, La navidad de Miguelito, In: El Mosaico de la Vida, Antologia de Cuentos, Harcourt, Brace, Jovanovich, 81. *Mailing Add:* 1708 Pine Knoll Dr Belmont CA 94002

LODING, DARLENE MARILYN, b Minneapolis, Minn, Jan 25, 42. ASSYRIOLOGY, ANCIENT HISTORY. *Educ:* Univ Minn, BA, 63, MA, 67; Univ Pa, PhD(assyriol), 74. *Prof Exp:* RES ASSOC, UNIV PA MUS, 73-, RES SPECIALIST & ASSOC ED, SUMERIAN DICT PROJ, 76- *Concurrent Pos:* Am Philos Soc fel Sumerian, 76; lectr, Dept Orient Studies, Univ Pa, 77- *Mem:* Am Orient Soc; Archaeol Inst Am. *Res:* Study of the Sumerican economic documents dating to the period of the Third Dynasty of Ur with special emphasis on the material culture of the period. *Publ:* Auth, A new chronological source for the Isin-Larsa Period, Archiv Orientforschung, 73; Old Babylonian Fund, 76; Royal epithets in economic texts from Ur, Alter Orient Altes Testament, 78; Review of S T Kang, Sumerian economic texts from the Umma Archive, J Cuneiform Studies, 78. *Mailing Add:* Univ of Pa Mus 33rd & Spruce Sts Philadelphia PA 19104

LOEB, ERNST, b Andernach, Ger, Dec 8, 14; Can citizen; m 44; c 2. GERMAN LANGUAGE & LITERATURE. *Educ:* Univ Pa, BA, 54, MA, 56; Wash Univ, PhD, 61. *Prof Exp:* Instr Ger, Park Col, 56-57; instr, Wash Univ, 57-58; instr, Univ BC, 59-60; acting asst prof, Univ Wash, 60-61, from asst prof to prof, 61-70; assoc prof, Univ BC, 64-65; prof, 70-80, EMER PROF GER, QUEEN'S UNIV, ONT, 80- *Mem:* Am Asn Teachers Ger; Can Asn Univ Teachers Ger; Goethe-Gesellschaft; Heine-Gesellschaft. *Res:* Classical and modern period of German literature. *Publ:* Auth, Die Symbolik des Wasserzyklus bei Goethe, Ferdinand Schoeningh, Paderborn, Ger, 67; Heinrich Heine, Weltbild und geistige Gestalt, Bouvier, Bonn, Ger, 76; co-ed (with Walter Dietze), Johann Gottried Herder, Briefe und Aufzeichnungen uber eine Reise nach Italien, 1788-1789: Blob für Dich Geschrieben, Rutten und Loeing, Berlin, GDR, 80. *Mailing Add:* Dept of Ger Queen's Univ Kingston ON K7L 3N6 Can

LOEWEN, HARRY, b Ukraine, Dec 8, 30; Can citizen; m 53; c 3. GERMAN LITERATURE, REFORMATION HISTORY. *Educ:* Univ Western Ont, BA, 59; Univ Man, MA, 61; Univ Waterloo, PhD(Ger), 70. *Prof Exp:* Teacher Ger, hist & English, Mennonite Brethren Col Inst, 61-65; lectr Ger & hist, Mennonite Brethren Col Arts, 64-68; asst prof, 68-74, chmn dept, 72-78, ASSOC PROF GER, WILFRID LAURIER UNIV, 74- *Mem:* Can Asn Univ Teachers Ger; Am Kafka Soc; Mennonitischer Geschichtsverein. *Res:* German classicism and romanticism; 20th century German literature; renaissance and reformation history. *Publ:* Auth, Goethe's Response to Protestantism, Lang, Berne, 72; Goethe and the Anabaptists, Mennonite Life, 6/73; Goethe's pietism as seen in his early letters and Dichtung und Wahrheit, In: Deutung und Bedeutung, Mouton, The Hague, 73; Luther and the Radicals: Another Look at Some Aspects of the Struggle Between Luther and the Radical Reformers, Waterloo Lutheran Univ, 74; Human involvement in Turgenev's and Kafka's country doctors, Ger-Slav, spring 74; Luther and Muentzer: Unity of opposites, In: Unity in Diversity, Waterloo Lutheran Univ, 77; co-ed & translr, The Mennonite Brotherhood in Russia 1789-1910, Bd Christian Lit, Fresno, 78; auth, Solzhenitsyn's Kafkaesque narrative art in The Gulag Archipelago, Ger-Slav, fall 78. *Mailing Add:* Dept of Ger Wilfrid Laurier Univ 75 University Ave W Waterloo ON N2L 3C5 Can

LOEWEN, JACOB ABRAM, b Romanovka, Russia, Sept 1, 22; Can citizen; m 45; c 4. LINGUISTICS, MODERN LANGUAGES. *Educ:* Tabor Col, AB, 47; Univ Wash, MA, 54, PhD, 58. *Prof Exp:* Missionary linguist, Bd Foreign Missions, Mennonite Brethren Church, Colombia, SAm & Panama, 45-53, 55-57; instr Ger, Univ Wash, 57-58; prof ling, mod lang & anthrop, Tabor Col, 58-64; transl consult SAm, 64-70, TRANSL CONSULT EAST CENT AFRICA, UNITED BIBLE SOC, 70- *Mem:* Can Ling Asn; Am Anthrop Asn; Mennonite Col Cult Conf (pres, 61-); Soc Appl Anthrop. *Res:* Communications in Christian missions; experimentation in literacy with Aboriginal groups; research on Indian settlement in Chaco, Paraguay. *Publ:* Coauth, Studies in Chaco language, Int J Am Ling, 60-63; M a c'awa q'uirea b a, 7 primers for Sambu, Bd Missions, 61; auth, Applied anthropology in mission, Practical Anthrop, 68; Culture & Human Values: Christian Intervention in Anthropological Perspective, 75. *Mailing Add:* 32238 Peardonville Rd Abbotsford BC V2T 1M5 Can

LOFLIN, MARVIN D, b Calexico, Calif, Oct 13, 35; c 6. LINGUISTICS, ANTHROPOLOGY. *Educ:* Brigham Young Univ, BA, 60, MA, 62; Ind Univ, PhD(ling), 65. *Prof Exp:* Asst assoc prof anthrop & ling, Univ Mo, Columbia, 67-71; chmn dept ling, Univ Wis, Milwaukee, 71-72, assoc acad dean, lett & sci, 72-75; dean arts & lett, Univ Nev, Las Vegas, 75-77; PROF ANTHROP & DEAN ACAD AFFAIRS, UNIV ALASKA, ANCHORAGE, 77- *Mem:* Ling Soc Am; Am Anthrop Asn; Asn Computational Ling. *Res:* Linguistics; beliefs; Black English. *Publ:* Auth, A note on the deep structure of non standard English in Washington, Glossa, 67; A teaching problem in non standard English, English J, 67; On the passive in non standard Negro English, J English as Sec Lang, 69; Negro nonstandard and standard: Same or different deep structure, Orbis, 69; coauth, Black American English and syntactic dialectology, Perspective Black English, 75; Black English deep structure, Assessing Ling Arguments, 76; auth, A culture as a set of beliefs, Current Anthrop, 76; co-ed, Discourse and Inference in Cognitive Anthropology, Chicago Adlin Publ, 78. *Mailing Add:* Univ of Alaska Col Arts & Sci 3221 Providence Dr Anchorage AK 99504

LOFSTEDT, BENGT, b Lund, Sweden, Nov 14, 31; m 61; c 4. LATIN. *Educ:* Univ Uppsala, MA, 54, Phil lic, 57, PhD(Latin), 61. *Prof Exp:* Asst prof Latin, Univ Uppsala, 62-67; assoc prof, 67-68, PROF MEDIEVAL LATIN, UNIV CALIF, LOS ANGELES, 68- *Concurrent Pos:* Alexander von Humbolt-Stiftung fel, 61-62; Univ Calif fel, Humanities Inst, 68 & 72; Am Coun Learned Soc grant, 72. *Mem:* Am Philol Asn; Soc Etudes Latines; Indoger Ges. *Res:* History of the Latin language, with emphasis on the later periods; medieval Latin grammarians; patristics. *Publ:* Auth, Studien über die Sprache der langobardischen Gesetze, 61 & Der hibernolateinische Grammatiker Malsachanus, 65, Univ Uppsala; ed, Zenonis Veronensis tractatus, In: Corpus Christianorum, Vol XXII, 71; Die Konstruktion c'est lui qui l'a fait im Lateinischen, 66, Bemerkungen zum Adverb im Lateinischen, 67 & Spätes VulGärlatein--ein abgegrastes Feld?, 70, Indoger Forsch; Ars Laureshamensis, XL A, 77, Sedulius Scottus, In: Donati artem maiorem, XL B, 77, Sedlius Scottus, In: Donati artem minorem; In Priscianum; In Eutychem, XL C, 77, Corpus Christianorum, Continuatio Mediaevalis. *Mailing Add:* Dept of Classics Univ of Calif Los Angeles CA 90024

LOGAN, MARIE-ROSE VAN STIJNVOORT, b Brussels, Belg, May 26, 45; m 68; c 1. FRENCH LITERATURE & THOUGHT. *Educ:* Univ Brussels, Lic en Philol Class, 66, Agrege, 67; Yale Univ, MA, 70, MPhil, 72, PhD(Romance lang), 74. *Prof Exp:* Instr philos, Univ Brussels, 64-66; instr Romance lang & lit, Yale Univ, 72-74; ASST PROF FRENCH & ROMANCE PHILOL, COLUMBIA UNIV, 74- *Concurrent Pos:* Harvard Univ fel, Villa I Tatti, Florence, Italy, 75-76; Columbia Soc fel humanities, 76-78. *Mem:* Int Comp Lit Asn; Int Neo-Latin Studies Asn; MLA; Renaissance Soc Am. *Res:* Renaissance studies (including Neo-Latin literature); the theory of literature; contemporary French thought. *Publ:* Contribr, Actualite d'erasme, Syntheses, 69; ed, Graphesis: Perspectives in literature and philosophy, spec issue, Yale Fr Studies, 76; contribr, La portee theorique du debat de Folie et d'amour de Louise Labe, Saggi e Ricerche di Lett Fr, 77; Rhetorical analysis: Towards a tropology of reading, New Lit Hist, 78; Bovillus on language, Acts 2nd Neo Latin Studies Cong, 78; assoc ed, Columbia Dictionary of Modern European Literature, rev ed; contribr, Histoire Comparee des Langues et des Litteratures Europeennes, Paris, 79. *Mailing Add:* Columbia Univ 504 Philos Hall New York NY 10027

LOGAN, PAUL ELLIS, b Washington, DC, Oct 5, 45. GERMAN LANGUAGE & LITERATURE. *Educ:* Howard Univ, BA, 66; Univ Md, MA, 70, PhD(Ger), 74. *Prof Exp:* Instr German, Univ Md, 69-73; assoc prof, Morgan State Univ, 73-77; CHMN DEPT GER/RUSSIAN, HOWARD UNIV, 77- *Concurrent Pos:* Faculty res grant, Morgan State Univ, 76; Fulbright scholar, 76 & 82; German Acad Exchange Serv fel, 79 & 81. *Mem:* Col Lang Asn; Mod Lang Asn; Frobenius-Gesellschaft; Am Asn Teachers Ger; Afrika-Gesellschaft. *Res:* German Africa travelogs of the 16th and 17th century; American Slavery as a theme in German literature of the 18th and 19th century. *Publ:* Auth, Gottfried Finckelthaus rediscovered, CLA J, 75; Leo Frobenius and Negritude, Negro Hist Bull, 78; Leo Frobenius: The demonic child, CLA J, 78; transl, The Sign and the Sense(Le signe et le sens-Der Sinn und das Mittel), CLA J, 78; Leo Frobenius, Negritude and the escape of Caliban, In: Festschrift for Leon-Gontran Damas, 79; The image of the Black in J LE Kolb's Erzählungen von den Sitten und Schicksalen der Negersklaven, Monatshefte, 81; J E Kolb's Der Neger Makandal, Negro Hist Bull, 81. *Mailing Add:* Dept of Ger & Russ Col of Liberal Arts Howard Univ Washington DC 20059

LOGRASSO, ANGELINE HELEN, b Buffalo, NY. ROMANCE PHILOLOGY, HISTORY. *Educ:* Univ Rochester, AB & AM; Harvard Univ, PhD, 27. *Prof Exp:* Instr Romance lang, Univ Rochester, 17-25, asst prof French & Ital, 28-30; from assoc prof to prof Ital & chmn dept, 30-65, EMER PROF ITAL, BRYN MAWR COL, 65-; LECTR & WRITER, 65- *Concurrent Pos:* Dir lang, Army Specialized Training Prog, Haverford Col, 43-44; vol lang work, Off Strategid Serv, 43-44; Fulbright res fel, Italy, 54-55; mem, Fulbright screening comt on Italy & Greece, 60-61; dir, Luigi Sturzo Found Sociol Study, Inc. *Honors & Awards:* Lindback Prize, Bryn Mawr Col, 65; Caveja d'Oro Award, City of Forli, Italy. *Mem:* MLA; Am Asn Teachers Ital (vpres; pres, 53); Renaissance Soc Am; Medieval Acad Am; AHA. *Res:* The philosophical, social, political and religious thought of Don Luigi Sturzo; the Italian Risorgimento; Dante studies in progress. *Publ:* Auth, Dante e la madonna, Marietti, Rome, 55; Piero Marconcelli, Ed Ateneo, Rome, 58; Byron traduttore del Pellico, Olschki, Firenzo, 59; From the Ballata of the Vita nuova to the carols of the Paradiso: A study in hidden harmonies and balance, Ann Report Dante Soc Am, 65; Dante e Mister Justice Holmes, Atti del Congresso Int Studies Danteschi, Vol II, 66; Jacopone da Todi & Giuseppe Giusti, In: New Cath Encycl, McGraw, 67. *Mailing Add:* Bryn Mawr Col Libr Bryn Mawr PA 19010

LOHNES, WALTER F W, b Frankfurt, Ger, Feb 8, 25; US citizen; m 50; c 3. GERMAN. *Educ:* Harvard Univ, PhD, 56. *Prof Exp:* Instr Ger, Univ Mo, 49-50; head dept, Phillips Acad, Andover, Mass, 51-61; from asst prof to assoc prof, 61-69, chmn dept, 73-80, PROF GER, STANFORD UNIV, 69- *Concurrent Pos:* Asst Ger folklore, Univ Frankfurt & instr Ger, US Army Troop Info & Educ, Ger, 47-48; mem Ger comt, Advan Placement Prog, Col Entrance Exam Bd, 55-62, chmn, 62-68; mem test develop comt, MLA, 58-62; mem staff, Stanford Univ NDEA Advan Inst, Ger, 61-62, assoc dir, 62, dir, 63-69; chmn comt examr, Grad Record Exam Bd, Ger, 70-; ed, Unterrichtspraxis, 72-74. *Mem:* Am Asn Teachers Ger (vpres, 61-62, 1st vpres, 69-70); MLA. *Res:* German language and linguistics. *Publ:* Coauth, German: A Structural Approach, Norton, 67; German Studies in the United States, Univ Wis. *Mailing Add:* Dept of Ger Studies Stanford Univ Stanford CA 94305

LOKKE, KARI ELISE, b Iowa City, Iowa, Apr 5, 49. COMPARATIVE LITERATURE, EUROPEAN ROMANTICISM. *Educ:* Ind Univ, BA, 71; Washington Univ, MA, 74, PhD(comp lit), 79. *Prof Exp:* ASST PROF COMP LIT, UNIV WIS-MADISON, 79- *Concurrent Pos:* Res Asst, Dept Romance Lang, Univ Konstanz, 75; lectr, Fachhochschule Konstanz, 76. *Mem:* MLA. *Res:* Romantic literature and aesthetics; myth and folklore; 18th century and romantic socialist utopian and chiliastic movements as reflected in the writings of Heine, Nerval, Michelet and Sand. *Publ:* Auth, The role of sublimity in the development of modernist aesthetics, J Aesthet & Art Criticism, summer 82. *Mailing Add:* Comp Lit Univ Wis Madison WI 53706

LOMBARDI, RONALD PAUL, b Philadelphia, Pa, Aug 21, 35. SPANISH, ITALIAN. *Educ:* Univ Pa, BSEd, 57, MA, 61, PhD(Romance lang), 71. *Prof Exp:* Teacher, Philadelphia Pub Sch Syst, 57-61; instr Span, Rider Col, 61-62; from asst prof to assoc prof Span & Ital, 62-72, PROF ROMANCE LANG, WEST CHESTER STATE COL, 72- *Concurrent Pos:* Asst prof Span, eve div, Rutgers Univ, 63-66; vis lectr Span & Ital, eve div, Univ Pa, 66-68. *Honors & Awards:* Anne & Frank Baccari Award, Am Asn Teachers Ital. *Mem:* Am Asn Teachers Ital; Am Asn Teachers Span & Port. *Res:* Modern Italian drama; Spanish and Italian linguistics. *Publ:* Adapter & translr, Lights and shadows in Dante's Vita nuova, In: Highpoints in the History of Italian Literature, McKay, 58; coauth (with A Boero de Peters), Modern Spoken Spanish: An Interdisciplinary Perspective, Univ Press Am, 81. *Mailing Add:* Dept of Foreign Lang West Chester State Col West Chester PA 19380

LOMBARDI, STEPHANIE ORTH, b Nuremberg, Ger, June 22, 12; nat US. GERMAN LITERATURE. *Educ:* Univ Kans City AB, 36; Univ Calif, Los Angeles, AM, 37; Univ Calif, PhD, 46. *Prof Exp:* Teaching fel, Univ Calif, Los Angeles, 38 & Univ Calif, 38-41, 43 & 46; instr, Stanford Univ, 46-49; from instr to asst prof Ger lit, Univ NMex, 49-53; teacher high sch, Calif, 53-55; LECTR GER, UNIV CALIF, LOS ANGELES, 55- *Mailing Add:* Dept of Ger Univ of Calif Los Angeles CA 90024

LONCHYNA, BOHDAN IVAN, b Lviv, Ukraine, Jan 2, 17; US citizen; m 44; c 5. ROMANCE PHILOLOGY. *Educ:* Univ Dijon, dipl French, 37; Univ Vienna, PhD(Romance philol), 42. *Prof Exp:* Lectr French lit, Ukrainian Free Univ, Munich, 46-48; from instr to prof French, Span & Ger, Col Steubenville, 49-59; assoc prof French lang & lit & Ital lang, Univ Detroit, 59-75; RETIRED. *Mem:* Am Asn Teachers Fr; Ukrainian Am Asn Univ Prof; Shevchenko Sci Soc. *Res:* Medieval French and Spanish epic poems; Dante's Divine Comedy. *Publ:* Auth, Estudiamos el espanol, Ukrainian Am Comt, Munich, 48; Ukrainian culture (in Ukrainian), Educ Coun, 71; translr, Poem of the Cid, Ukrainian Cath Univ, Rome, 72; The Song of Roland, Ukrainian Cath Univ, Rome 77. *Mailing Add:* 41837 Langley Dr Sterling Heights MI 48078

LONDON, J DALTON GEORGE, b Woodstock, NB, Feb 22, 42; m 66; c 2. SECOND LANGUAGE DIDACTICS, FRENCH LITERATURE. *Educ:* Acadia Univ, BA, 64, MA, 66; Univ Grenoble, France, Dd'U, 68. *Prof Exp:* Asst prof French lang & lit, 68-75, assoc prof, 75-77, assoc prof French & English didactics, 77-81, PROF SECOND LANG DIDACTICS, DEPT ROMANCE LANG, UNIV NEW BRUNSWICK, 81- *Concurrent Pos:* Second lang consult, Dept Educ, NB govt, 77-82. *Mem:* Can Asn Second Lang Teachers. *Res:* Second language curriculum development; communicative approach in second language didactics. *Publ:* Auth, Curriculum Guide for French as a Second Language, NB Dept Educ, 79; From manipulation to exploitation: Defining our objectives, Can Mod Lang Rev, 5/81. *Mailing Add:* Fac Educ Univ NB Fredericton NB E3B 4L3 Can

LONG, HERBERT STRAINGE, b Dexter, NY, Mar 23, 19; m 52; c 3. CLASSICS, HISTORY OF ANCIENT PHILOSOPHY. *Educ:* Hamilton Col, AB, 39; Princeton Univ, AM, 41, PhD(classics), 42. *Hon Degrees:* LittD, Hamilton Col, 72. *Prof Exp:* Instr math, Hamilton Col, 43-44; asst prof, Colgate Univ, 44-46 & classics, Yale Univ, 46-51; Edward North prof Greek, Hamilton Col, 52-58; PROF CLASSICS, CASE WESTERN RESERVE UNIV, 68- *Concurrent Pos:* Annual mem, Inst Advan Study, Princeton Univ, 51-52, 65-66; spec res fel & vis prof, Am Sch Class Studies, Athens, 58-59; ed, Ultimate Reality & Meaning, 78- *Honors & Awards:* Award of Merit, Am Philol Asn, 65. *Mem:* Am Philol Asn. *Res:* Greek literature; history of Greek philosophy; Greek textual criticism. *Publ:* Auth, Diogenis Laertii Vitae Philosophorum (2 vols), Clarendon, 64. *Mailing Add:* 2820 Chadbourne Rd Cleveland OH 44120

LONG, MICHAEL J, b Bethlehem, Pa, June 6, 29. CLASSICAL STUDIES, BIBLICAL LANGUAGES. *Educ:* St Charles Sem, MA, 57; Univ Pa, MA, 67. *Prof Exp:* Instr relig, La Salle Col, 57-64; PROF GREEK & LATIN & CHMN DEPT, ST CHARLES BORROMEO SEM, 65- *Mem:* Class Asn Atlantic States; Vergilian Soc. *Res:* The environment of early Christianity; religion in the Roman empire; Greek and Roman philosophy. *Publ:* Auth, New Testament Greek: A Basic Course, St Charles Sem, 76. *Mailing Add:* Dept of Greek & Latin St Charles Borromeo Sem Philadelphia PA 19151

LONG, TIMOTHY, b Cincinnati, Ohio, Jan 31, 43. CLASSICS. *Educ:* Xavier Univ, Ohio, BA, 65; Princeton Univ, MA, 67, PhD(classics), 71. *Prof Exp:* From lectr to asst prof, 69-74, ASSOC PROF CLASSICS, IND UNIV, BLOOMINGTON, 74- *Mem:* Am Philol Asn; AAUP. *Res:* Greek comedy. *Publ:* Auth, P Hibeh 154: Export of wine, Bull Am Soc Papyrologists, 7/69; Two questions of attribution in Aristophanes' Vespae, Am J Philol, 7/72; Persuasion and the Aristophanic agon, Trans Am Philol Asn, 72. *Mailing Add:* Dept of Class Studies 547 Ballantine Hall Ind Univ Bloomington IN 47401

LONGACRE, ROBERT EDMONDSON, b Akron, Ohio, Aug 13, 22; m 46; c 4. LINGUISTICS. *Educ:* Houghton Col, AB, 43; Faith Theol Sem, BD, 46; Univ Pa, MA, 54, PhD(ling), 55. *Hon Degrees:* LLD, Houghton Col, 79. *Prof Exp:* Prof grammar, Summmer Inst Ling, Okla, 60-67, chief ling consult, Mex Br, 60-67, int ling consult, 67-, PROF LING, UNIV TEX, ARLINGTON, 75- *Concurrent Pos:* Lectr ling, Univ Mich, 60-61; vis assoc prof, State Univ NY, Buffalo, 66-67; prin investr, Off Educ grant Phillipine Lang, 67-68 & proj dir grant New Guinea lang, 70; adj prof, Univ Tex, Arlington, 72-75; joint grant, Nat Sci Found, Nat Endowment for Humanities, 74-75. *Mem:* Ling Soc Am; Ling Soc Can & US; Ling Asn Southwest. *Res:* Comparative reconstruction of Mesoamerican languages; theory of grammar; structure of discourse. *Publ:* Auth, Grammar Discovery Procedures, Mouton, 64; Prolegomena to lexical structure, Linguistics, 64; Some fundamental insights of tagmemics, Language, 65; Comparative reconstruction of indigenous languages, Current Trend Ling, 68; coauth, Totonac: From Clause to Discourse, 68 & auth, Discourse, Paragraph, and Sentence Structure in Selected Philippine Languages, 69, Summer Inst Ling; auth, Hierarchy and Universality of Discourse Constituents in New Guinea Languages (2 vols), Georgetown Univ, 72; An Anatomy of Speech Notions, Peter de Pidder, 76; Discourse structure of the flood narrative, J Am Acad Relig, 79; The grammar of discourse, Plenum (in press). *Mailing Add:* Dept of Foreign Lang & Ling Univ of Tex Arlington TX 75236

LONIGAN, PAUL RAYMOND, b New York, NY, May 27, 35; m 65; c 4. ROMANCE LANGUAGES. *Educ:* Queens COl, NY, BA, 60; Johns Hopkins Univ, PhD (Romance lang), 67. *Prof Exp:* Instr French, Russell Sage Col, 63-65; assoc prof Romance philol, State Univ NY, Col Oswego, 65-67; from lectr to asst prof, 67-72, ASSOC PROF ROMANCE LANG, QUEENS COL, NY, 68- *Concurrent Pos:* Dep exec off, PhD Prog in French, Queens Col, NY, 69-72; City Univ New York res grant, 69-70. *Mem:* Circulo de Cult Panam; Mediaeval Acad Am; Irish Am Cult Inst; Irish Texts Soc. *Res:* Middle

Ages; philology; Renaissance & Irish Studies. *Publ:* Auth, Does the Gormont el Isembart contain lyric elements?, Neophilologus, 4/70; Ganelon before Marsile--Laisses XXXII-LII of the Chanson de Roland, 70 & The authorship of the Guillaume d'Angleterre: A new approach, 72, Studies Francesi; An Unexplored question: Celtic church influence on Old French hagiography, Eire-Ireland, IX, 73-79; The Cliges and the Tristan legend, 53, 201-212, & Calogrenant's Journey and the Mood of the Yvain, 58, 1-20, Studi Francesi; Gormont et Isembart: Problems and Interpretation of an Old French Epic, Univ Microfilms Int, City Univ Univ New York Grad Ctr, 76. *Mailing Add:* Dept Romance Lang Queens Col Flushing NY 11367

LOPEZ, MARIANO, b Segovia, Spain, Sept 11, 31; US citizen; m 69; c 2. SPANISH LANGUAGE & LITERATURE. *Educ:* Univ Salamanca, Spain, lic, 56; State Univ NY, Buffalo, MA, 69, PhD(Span), 74. *Prof Exp:* Instr Span, Bishop Turner High Sch, 66-67 & State Col Plattsburgh, NY, 70-71; asst, State Univ NY, Buffalo, 71-74; asst prof, 74-78, ASSOC PROF SPAN, MISS STATE UNIV, 78- *Mem:* AAUP; MLA; Am Asn Teachers Span & Port. *Res:* Nineteenth and 20th century Spanish and Spanish-American literature. *Publ:* Auth, Puntualizaciones en torno la naturalismo literario espanol, Cuadernos Americanos, 78; Antinaturalismo y humanismo en Galdos: Angel Guerra, Nazarin y Halma, Hispania, 78; El fin de siglo y los escritores de la Restauracion, Nueva Revista Filol Hisp, 78; En torno a la segunda manera de Pardo Bazan: Una Cristiana y La Prueba, Hispanofila, 78; Naturalismo y espiritualismo en Los Pazos de Ulloa, Revista Estudios Hisp, 78; El perfil humano de La Charca de Zeno Gandia, Sin Nombre, 79; Aspecto y fondo del naturalismo galdosiano, Cuadernos Hispanoamericanos, 79; Naturalismo y humanismo en Misericordia, Sin Nombre, 80. *Mailing Add:* Dept of Foreign Lang Miss State Univ Mississippi State MS 39762

LOPEZ-GASTON, JOSE ROMON, b Havana, Cuba, Nov 14, 28; US citizen; m 62; c 5. FOREIGN LANGUAGES, SPANISH LITERATURE. *Educ:* Univ Villanueva, Dr Filos y Let(Span lit), 55; Univ Fla, MA, 67, PhD(Romance lang), 68. *Prof Exp:* Instr hist & Span, Col Champagnat, Cuba, 51-61; instr Span & French, Inst Patria, Mexico, DF, 61-62 & Span & Latin, La Salle High Sch, Cincinnati, Ohio, Joseph Col, Md, 69-72; asst prof Span & French, 72-76, ASSOC PROF SPAN & FRENCH & CHMN DEPT, NMEX HIGHLANDS UNIV, 76- *Mem:* Am Asn Span & Port Teachers. *Res:* Spanish medieval literature. *Publ:* Auth, Los recursos literarios de la poesia de D Pedro Lopez de Ayala, Ed Universal, Miami, Fla: El fuego en las cenizas, Ed Circulo, Saragosa, Spain. *Mailing Add:* Dept of Span & French NMex Highlands Univ Las Vegas NM 87701

LOPEZ-GRIGERA, LUISA, b La Coruna, Spain, Sept 21, 26. SPANISH PHILOLOGY. *Educ:* Univ Nac Buenos Aires, Prof lett, 54; Univ Cent Madrid, lic, 64, PhD(Romance philol), 65. *Prof Exp:* Prof adj ling, Univ Catolica Argentia, Buenos Aires, 59-61; asst prof Span, Univ Tex, Austin, 66-68; from assoc prof to prof Span stylistics, Univ Deusto, Bilbao, Spain, 68-75; PROF SPAN, UNIV MICH, ANN ARBOR, 75- *Mem:* MLA; Am Asn Teachers Span & Port; Renaissance Soc Am. *Res:* Spanish Golden Age: textual criticism; diacronic stylistic of the prose of Spanish Golden Age: textual criticism; diacronic stylistic of the prose of Spanish Golden Age. *Publ:* Auth, Un problema bibliografico en Quevedo: La primera edicion de La Cuna y la Sepultura, Filologia, 64; Quevedo, La Cuna y la Sepultura Edicion Critica, Prology Notas, Real Acad Espanola, Madrid, 69; Releccionde La Hora de Todos de Quevedo, Univ Deusto, Bilbao, Spain, 71; En torno al arte de escribir de E Wilde en La Lluvia, Anales Lit Hispanoam, 73-74; Algunas precisiones sobre el estilo de Antonio de Guevara, In: Studia Hispanica in Honor of R Lapesa, Madrid, 75; La silva El Pincel de Quevedo, Homenaje Inst Filol Hisp, 75; Quevedo, La Hora de Todos Edicion, Estudio y Notas, Ed Castalia, Madrid, 75; Un nuevo codice de los Proverbios Morales de Sem Tob, Boletin Real Acad Espanola, 76. *Mailing Add:* Dept of Romance Lang Univ of Mich Ann Arbor MI 48104

LOPEZ-MORILLAS, CONSUELO, b Iowa City, Iowa, July 7, 44; m 71; c 1. ROMANCE & HISPANO-ARABIC LITERATURE. *Educ:* Bryn Mawr Col, BA, 65; Univ Calif, Berkeley, PhD(Romance philol), 74. *Prof Exp:* Asst prof, Ohio State Univ, 74-77; asst prof, 77-82, ASSOC PROF SPANISH, IND UNIV, 82- *Concurrent Pos:* Vis asst prof Arabic, Ohio State Univ, 79. *Mem:* MLA; Am Oriental Soc; Asociacion Internacional de Hispanistas. *Res:* Hispano-Arabic language and literature; Romance linguistics; Hispanic linguistics (historical). *Publ:* Auth, Aljamiado akosegir and its old provencal counterparts, Romance Philol, 75; Los bereberes Zanata en la historia y la leyenda, Al-Andalus, 77; Trilingual Marginal notes in a Morisco manuscript from Toledo, J of the Am Oriental Soc, 82; La oracion como dialogo en un comentario morisco sobre la Fatiha, Nueva Revista de Filologia Hisp, 82; The Quran in 16th Century Spain: Six Morisco Versions of Sura 79, Tamesis Books, London, 82. *Mailing Add:* Dept of Spanish & Portuguese Ind Univ Bloomington IN 47405

LOPEZ-MORILLAS, JUAN, b Jaen, Spain, Aug 11, 13; US citizen; m 37; c 3. SPANISH, COMPARATIVE LITERATURE. *Educ:* Univ Madrid, BLitt, 29; State Univ Iowa, PhD(Romance lang), 40. *Hon Degrees:* DHL, Brown Univ, 79. *Prof Exp:* Instr Romance lang, State Univ Iowa, 39-41, asst prof, 41-43; from asst prof to prof, Brown Univ, 43-65, alumni Univ prof Hisp Studies & comp lit, 65-73, William R Kenan, Jr Univ prof, 73-78; prof Span, 78-79, ASHBEL SMITH PROF SPAN, UNIV TEX, AUSTIN, 79- *Concurrent Pos:* Vis lectr, Harvard Univ, 47 & 59; Guggenheim fels, 50-51 & 57-58; Am Philos Soc grant, 54; chmn, Dept Span & Ital, Brown Univ, 60-67, Dept Comp Lit, 67-71; Phi Beta Kappa vis scholar, 66-67; vis fel, Trinity Col, Oxford Univ, 72; vis Andrew W Mellon prof, Univ Pittsburgh, 74; Am Coun Learned Soc grant, 74; vis scholar, Univ Ctr Va, 76-77. *Mem:* MLA; Hisp Soc Am; Asoc Int Hispanistas (vpres, 65-71, pres, 80-83); Am Comp Lit Asn. *Res:* Modern Spanish literature; 19th century intellectual history; 19th century European novel. *Publ:* Ed, Krausismo: Estetica y literatura, Ed Labor, Barcelona, 73; auth, Utopia y antiutopia, Sistema, 5, Madrid, 74; Unamuno y Costa, In: La crisis de fin de siglo, Ed Ariel, Barcelona, 75; transl, F M Dostoyevski: Tres novelas cortas, Ed Laia, Barcelona, 76; transl, F M Dostoyevski: El jugador, Alianza Educ, Madrid, 80; auth, The Kraulist Movement and Ideological Change in Spain, Cambridge, 81; transl, F M Dostoyevski, Un episodio vergonoso y otros relatos, Alianza Educ, Madrid, 82; ed, Textos del Krausismo espanol, Almar Salamanco, 82. *Mailing Add:* 2200 Hartford Rd Austin TX 78703

LORAINE, MICHAEL B, b Cairo, Egypt, June 7, 35; m 72. ISLAMIC STUDIES, PERSIAN. *Educ:* Cambridge Univ, BA, 58, MA, 62, PhD(poet Bahar), 68. *Prof Exp:* Asst prof, 67-74, ASSOC PROF NEAR EASTERN LANG & LIT & COMP LIT, UNIV WASH, 74- *Mem:* Royal Asiatic Soc; Asn Brit Orient; Royal Cent Asian Soc; Am Orient Soc; MidE Studies Asn. *Res:* Persian literatuare. *Publ:* Auth, A memoire on the life and poetical works of Maliku'l-shu'ara' Bahar, Int J Mid E Studies, 72; Bahar in the context of the Persian Constitutional Revolution, Iranian Studies, 72. *Mailing Add:* Dept of Near Eastern Lang & Lit Univ of Wash Seattle WA 98195

LORAM, IAN CRAIG, b SAfrica, Feb 26, 17; nat US; m 41; c 2. GERMAN LITERATURE. *Educ:* Yale Univ, BA, 39, PhD(Ger), 49; Columbia Univ, MA, 41. *Prof Exp:* From instr to asst prof Ger, Northwestern Univ, 49-54; instr, Cornell Univ, 54-58; from assoc prof to prof, Univ Kans, 58-64; prof, 64-80, chmn dept, 66-76, assoc dean grad sch, 68-80, EMER PROF GER, UNIV WIS-MADISON, 80- *Concurrent Pos:* Am Philos Soc grant, 63. *Mem:* MLA; Am Asn Teachers Ger; Midwest Mod Lang Asn. *Res:* Modern drama; 19th century literature; Goethe. *Publ:* Auth, Goethe and His Publishers, Univ Kans, 63; Fritz Hochwälder, 66 & Odön von Horvath, 67, Monatshefte. *Mailing Add:* Dept of Ger Univ of Wis Madison WI 53706

LORBE, RUTH ELISABETH, b Nuremberg, Ger, May 2, 25. MODERN GERMAN LITERATURE. *Educ:* Univ Erlangen, PhD, 52. *Prof Exp:* Student Raetin Ger, hist & English, intermediate sch, Nuremberg, 52-54, 55-60 & 62-64; lectr Ger, Univ Col North Staffordshire, 54-55; from instr to assoc prof, 60-72, PROF GER, UNIV ILL, URBANA, 72- *Mem:* MLA; Am Asn Teachers Ger; Am Comp Lit Asn; Hofmannsthal-Gesellschaft; Int Brecht Soc. *Res:* Children's songs, especially nursery rhymes; modern German poetry; German literataure after 1850. *Publ:* Auth, Spuren Elemente der Lyrik im Kinderreim, Akzente, 54; Wechselseitige Erhellung der Kuenste im Deutschunterricht, Deutschunterricht, 55; Die deutsche kurzgeschichte im Unterricht, Deutschunterricht, 57, excerpts Reclam, 77; German lyric poetry, 1950-1960, Mod Lang J, 62; Lyrische Standpunkte, Bayerischer Schulbuch, 68; Die Welt des Kinderliedes, Julius Beltz, Weinheim/Berlin/Basel, 71; contribr, Kinderlyrik, In: Kinder-und Jugendliteratur, Reclam, Stuttgart, 74; Poetry on two levels, Dimension, 79. *Mailing Add:* Dept of Ger Lang & Lit Univ of Ill Urbana IL 61801

LORCH, MARISTELLA DE PANIZZA, b Bolzano, Italy, Dec 8, 19; nat US; m 45, 56; c 3. ITALIAN. *Educ:* Liceo Classico Giosue Carducci, Merano, Italy, 37; Univ Rome, DLet, 41. *Prof Exp:* Prof classics, Liceo Virgilio, Rome, 41-44; assoc prof, Col St Elizabeth, 47-51; from asst prof to assoc prof, 51-65, PROF ITAL, BARNARD COL, COLUMBIA UNIV, 66-, CHMN MEDIEVAL & RENAISSANCE PROG, 74-, CHMN ITAL ETUDIES PROG, 76- *Concurrent Pos:* Mem staff, Dictionary of Medieval Latin, 41-42; vis assoc prof, Univ Calif, Berkeley, 63; assoc coordr, Eighth Cong, Int Cong Ital Lit, 72-73; dir, Casa Ital, Columbia Univ, 72-76; ed, Romanic Rev, 72-; dir, Ctr Int Scholarly Exchange, 80-; vis prof, Univ of Rome, 82. *Honors & Awards:* Cert of Merit, Ital Govt, 73; Woman of the Year Ital Literature, 73. *Mem:* MLA; Renaissance Soc Am; Am Asn Teachers Ital; Pirandello Soc (pres, 73-78); Int Asn Studies Ital Lang & Lit. *Res:* Latin literature of the Renaissance; Latin humanistic comedy; Italian theatre, especially Renaissance. *Publ:* Ed, Critical edition, De Vero Bono; ed introd & notes & coauth, Michaelida, Ziliolo Zilioli, Finck, Munich; transl & coauth, De Vero Bono, Abaris Books; auth, The Attribution Janus Sacerdos to Panormita, Quad Cult Classica, Urbino, Italy, 68. *Mailing Add:* 206 Milbank Hall Barnard Col Columbia Univ New York NY 10027

LORD, ELIZABETH GRUNBAUM SANDS, b Heidelberg, Ger, Apr 23, 21; US citizen; m 61; c 8. GERMAN LANGUAGE & LITERATURE. *Educ:* Rice Univ, BA, 50; Univ Ill, Urbana, MA, 52, PhD(Ger), 56. *Prof Exp:* From instr to assoc prof, 56-73, PROF FOREIGN LANG, WASH STATE UNIV, 73- *Mem:* MLA; Am Asn Teachers Ger. *Res:* Twentieth century German literature; modern German syntax. *Publ:* Coauth, Not small talk, but something solid to talk about, Unterrichtspraxis, fall, 69; auth, Borcherts Ballade von den Bergrabenen, In: Festschrift für Detlev W Schumann, Delp, Munich, 70; Vergen um die Wette--grammatical blockhead, Forum, 1/74; translr, Günter Grass, The Ballad of the Black Cloud, Lit Rev XVII: 4. *Mailing Add:* Dept of Foreign Lang & Lit Thompson Hall Wash State Univ Pullman WA 99164

LORD, JOHN BIGELOW, SR, English. See Vol II

LORD, MARY LOUISE, b Buffalo, NY, June 11, 16; m 50; c 2. CLASSICS. *Educ:* Univ Buffalo, BA, 38; Cornell Univ, AM, 39, PhD(classics), 41. *Prof Exp:* Instr classics, Elmira Col, 41-42; asst prof, Bates Col, 42-47; lectr Latin & ancient hist, Wellesley Col, 47-50; asst prof humanities, Boston Univ, 50-54; assoc prof, 61-69, prof, 69-81, EMER PROF CLASSICS, CONN COL, 81- *Mem:* Am Philol Asn; Class Asn New Eng (pres, 77-78). *Res:* Homer; classical rhetoric in the Latin patristic literature; Vergilian commentaries, 1200-1400. *Publ:* Auth, Roman examples of fortitude in the Latin Christian apologists, Class Philol, 4/48; Withdrawal and return: An epic story pattern in the Homeric hymn to Demeter and in the Homeric poems, Class J, 3/67; Dido as an example of chastity: The influence of example literature in two parts, Harvard Libr Bull, 1 & 4/69; Petrarch and Vergil's First Eclogue: The Codex Ambrosianus, Harvard Studies in Class Philol, 86: 253-276. *Mailing Add:* 23 Francis Ave Cambridge MA 02138

LORE, ANTHONY GEORGE, b Cleveland, Ohio, Feb 21, 22; m; c 1. ROMANCE LANGUAGES. *Educ:* La State Univ, BA, 48, MA, 49; Univ NC, PhD(Romance lang), 65. *Prof Exp:* ASSOC PROF SPAN & METHODOLOGY & DIR LANG LAB, UNIV NC, CHAPEL HILL, 60- *Mem:* Am Asn Teachers Span & Port; MLA; Nat Asn Lang Lab Dir, NEA; Nat Soc Prog Instr. *Mailing Add:* 105 Dey Hall Univ of NC Chapel Hill NC 27514

LORENZO-RIVERO, LUIS, b La Bola, Spain, Dec 13, 34; m 63. SPANISH LANGUAGE & LITERATUARE. *Educ:* Univ Salamanca, MA, 61; Ind Univ, PhD(Span), 67. *Prof Exp:* Instr Span, Univ Houston, 66-67; asst prof, Carleton Univ, 67-69; assoc prof Span & Port, 69-73, PROF LANGUAGES, UNIV UTAH, 73- *Concurrent Pos:* Can Coun res grant, 68; participant Gullen Conf, Univ Okla, 68; Univ Utah res grants, 71 & 73; ed, Utah Studies, 72-; ed adv, Estudos Ibero-Americanos, 75-; vis prof Span, Univ Catolica Rio Grande Sul Brazil, 76. *Mem:* Nat Soc Lit & Arts; Am Asn Teachers Span & Port; MLA; Latin Am Studies Asn. *Res:* Nineteenth and 20th century essay and poetry; Larra, Sarmiento, Unamuno and Alberti. *Publ:* Auth, Larra y Sarmiento; parlelismos historicos y literarios, Ed Guadarrama, 68; Neruda y Alberti: amistad y poesia, Cuadernos Am, 72; Becquer: vinculo literario entre Larra y el 98, Cuadernos Hispanoam, 72; El suicido: una obsesion de Unamuno, Cuadernos Am, 73; Larra: Fantasia y realidad, Boletin Real Acad Espanola, 74; Estudios de literatura espanola moderna: De Mariano J de Larra R Alberti, PUC-EMMA, 76; Larra: lengua y estilo, Ed Playor, 77; La corrida en Pany Toros, Cuandernos Americanos, 81. *Mailing Add:* Dept of Lang Univ of Utah Salt Lake City UT 84112

LORRAH, JEAN, Medieval Literature, Linguistics. See Vol II

LOSADA, LUIS ANTONIO, b New York, NY, Jan 7, 39; m 66. CLASSICS, ANCIENT HISTORY. *Educ:* Hunter Col, AB, 60; Columbia Univ, MA, 62, PhD(Greek & Latin), 70. *Prof Exp:* From lectr to asst prof classics, 68-74, ASSOC PROF CLASSICS, LEHMAN COL, 74-, CHMN DEPT CLASS & ORIENT LANG, 73- *Concurrent Pos:* Assoc mem, Univ Sem Class Civilization, Columbia Univ, 72- *Mem:* Am Philol Asn; Petronian Soc; Am Inst Archaeol. *Res:* Greek history and numismatics; the teaching of classical languages. *Publ:* Auth, The Aetolian indemnity of 189 and the Agrinion hoard, Phoenix, 65; coauth, The time of the shield signal at Marathon, Am J Archaeol, 70; auth, Fifth columns in the Peloponnesian War: How they worked and the defense against them, Klio, 72; The Fifth Column in the Peloponnesian War, E J Brill, 72. *Mailing Add:* 15 W 72nd St #27B New York NY 10023

LOSEFF, LEV LIFSCHUTZ, b Leningrad, USSR, June 15, 37; US citizen; m 59; c 2. RUSSIAN LITERATURE. *Educ:* Leningrad State Univ, MA, 59; Univ Mich, PhD(Russ lit), 80. *Prof Exp:* Free-lance writer, Leningrad, 61-62; mem ed staff, Kostyor, Leningrad, 62-75; instr Russ, Grand Valley State Col, 76; teaching asst, Univ Mich, 77-78; asst prof Russ lang & lit, Mich State Univ, 78-79; instr, 79-81, ASST PROF RUSS LANG & LIT, DARTMOUTH COL, 81- *Concurrent Pos:* Writer radio prog, Voice of America, 79- *Mem:* Am Asn Advan Slavic Studies; Am Asn Teachers Slavic & East Europ Lang. *Res:* Russian poetry; censorship and culture; literature for children (Russian). *Publ:* Auth, Unwritten reportages, 76 & 77 & From nowhere with love: Notes on Joseph brodsky's poetry, 77, Kontinent, Paris; What it means to be censored, 78, Books as Vodka, 79, NY Rev Bks, 79; Between Shelomian and Solomon, Russ Lang J, 79; Russian children's literature, Modern Encycl of Russian Soviet Literature, 80; ed, M Bulgakov The Notes on the Cuff, Silver Age Publ, 82. *Mailing Add:* Russ Dept Dartmouth Col Hanover NH 03755

LOSSE, DEBORAH NICHOLS, b Boston, Mass, May 6, 44; m 66; c 1. FRENCH LITERATURE. *Educ:* Conn Col, BA, 66; Univ NC, Chapel Hill, MA, 70, PhD(French), 73. *Prof Exp:* Asst prof, 73-80, ASSOC PROF FRENCH, ARIZ STATE UNIV, 80- *Mem:* Renaissance Soc Am; Am Asn Teachers Fr; MLA; African Lit Asn; Am Coun Teachers Foreign Lang. *Res:* Literature of the French Renaissance: Rabelais, Marguerite de Navarre, Montaigne; African literature of French expression. *Publ:* Auth, Multiple masks in L'Ecole des Maris, 70 & Thematic and structural unity in the symposium of Rabelais's Tiers Livre, 75, Romance Notes; Frivolous charm and serious bagatelle: Lyrical and burlesque paradox in the works of Francois Robelais, Sixteenth Century J, 79; Rhetoric at Play, Rabelais and Satirical Eulogy, Peter Lang, 80; The beggar as folk character in African literature of French expression, Ba Shiru, J African Langs and Lit, 80; Distortion as a means of reassessment, Marguerite de Navarre's Heptameron and the querelle des femmes, J Rocky Mountain Medieval & Renaissance Asn, 82. *Mailing Add:* Dept of Foreign Lang Ariz State Univ Tempe AZ 83287

LOTT, ROBERT EUGENE, b Miami, Fla, Nov 30, 26; m 54. SPANISH, ROMANCE STYLISTICS. *Educ:* Athens Col, AB, 51; Univ Ala, MA, 52; Cath Univ Am, PhD, 58. *Prof Exp:* Teaching asst, Univ Ala, 51-52; instr, Cath Univ Am, 52-56, teaching asst, 56-58; from asst prof to assoc prof Span, Univ Ga, 58-66; assoc prof mod Span, 66-68, assoc mem ctr advan studies, 72, PROF MOD SPAN LIT, UNIV ILL, URBANA, 68- *Mem:* MLA; Am Asn Teachers Span & Port; Midwest Mod Lang Asn. *Res:* Modern and Contemporary Spanish literature; Romance stylistics; the modern novel. *Publ:* Auth, Siglo de oro Tradition and Modern Adolescent Psychology in Pepita Jimenez: A Stylistic Study, Cath Univ Am, 58; The Structure and Style of Azorin's El caballero inactual, Univ Ga, 63; Azorin's experimental period and surrealism, PMLA, 64; Functional flexibility in Buero Vallejo's plays, Symposium, summer 66; Sobre el metodo narrativo y el estilo en las novelas de azorin, CHA, 68; Language and Psychology in Pepita Jimenez, Univ Ill, 70. *Mailing Add:* Dept Foreign Lang Univ of Ill Urbana IL 61801

LOTT, THOMAS WESLEY, b Hattiesburg, Miss, May 8, 37; m 60. SPANISH. *Educ:* William Carey Col, BA, 59; Monterrey Inst Technol & Higher Educ, MA, 65; Int Univ, Mex, Dr en Filos, 70. *Prof Exp:* Teacher English, Collins High Sch, Miss, 59-60; teacher Span, Marcus Whitman Jr High Sch, Port Orchard, Wash, 60-65 & Orme Ranch Sch, Mayer, Ariz, 65-67; asst prof, St Andrews Presby Col, 67-71; assoc prof Span & chmn dept foreign lang, Pembroke State Univ, 71-73; PROF SPAN & CHMN DEPT FOREIGN LANG, WILLIAM CAREY COL, 73- *Mem:* Am Coun Teaching Foreign Lang; Am Asn Teachers Span & Port; SAtlantic Mod Lang Asn. *Res:* Mexican death theme. *Mailing Add:* Dept of Foreign Lang William Carey Col Hattiesburg MS 39401

LOTZE, DIETER PAUL, b Hannover, Ger, Dec 12, 33; US citizen; m 58. GERMAN LANGUAGE & LITERATURE. *Educ:* Innsbruck Univ, PhD(Ger & English), 61. *Prof Exp:* From instr to assoc prof, 67-72, PROF MOD LANG, ALLEGHENY COL, 72- *Concurrent Pos:* Vis prof, Colorado Col, summers 66, 68 & 69; chmn, Nat Endowment for Humanities, 82- *Honors & Awards:* Best Scholarly Work, Südosteuropa-Gesellschaft, Munich, 61. *Mem:* Am Hungarian Educator's Asn; AAUP; MLA; Am Asn Teachers Ger; Am Coun Teaching For Lang. *Res:* German-Hungarian literary relations; 19th Century German literature; modern German literature. *Publ:* Auth, Deutsche Lyrikarbeitsgemeinschaft als Erganzung zum Anfängerunterricht, Deutschunterricht Ausländer, Munich, 63; Zu Celans Todesfuge im Mittelstufenunterricht, Unterrichtspraxis, spring 69; Buschs Jacke aus Heines Frack?, Wilhelm Busch Jahrbuch, 75; Struktur von Kafkas Prozess, Kafka-Symp, Berlin: Agora, 78; Victor Hugo and Imre Madach, Neo-Helicon, Budapest, 78; Wilhelm Busch, Twayne, 78; Imre Madach, Twayne, 81; Wilhelm Busch Leben und Werk, Belser Verlag, Stuttgart/Zürich. *Mailing Add:* Dept of Mod Lang Allegheny Col Meadville PA 16335

LOUD, MARY BETH, b Merrill, Wis, Feb 26, 42. SPANISH LITERATURE & LANGUAGE. *Educ:* Univ Wis-Madison, BA, 64; Univ NC, Chapel Hill, MA, 67; Univ Ky, PhD(Span), 70. *Prof Exp:* Lectr Span, State Univ NY, Buffalo, 68-69, asst prof, 69-70; asst prof, 70-78, ASSOC PROF SPAN & CHAIR FOREIGN LANG, YOUNGSTOWN STATE UNIV, 78- *Mem:* AAUP; Am Asn Teachers Span & Port; MLA; Am Coun Teachers Foreign Lang. *Res:* Spanish drama, particularly of the 17th century; comedy; Spanish prose, especially of Middle Ages-Golden Age. *Publ:* Auth, Tirso's Comic masterpiece: Marta la Piadosa, Hispanofila, spring 74; Pride & Prejudice: some thoughts on Lope de Vega's El Villanoensurincon, Hispania, 12/75; Individualized instruction in Spanish, Proc First Nat Conf Individualized Instruction Foreign Lang, Ohio State Univ, 79. *Mailing Add:* Dept of Foreign Lang Youngstown State Univ Youngstown OH 44503

LOUNSBURY, RICHARD CECIL, b Yorkton, Sask, Jan 3, 49. CLASSICAL LANGUAGES, AMERICAN INTELLECTUAL HISTORY. *Educ:* Univ Calgary, BA, 70; Univ Tex, Austin, MA, 72, PhD(classics), 79. *Prof Exp:* Lectr classics, Univ Witwatersrand, 79-81; asst prof, Univ Victoria, 81-82; ASST PROF CLASSICS & COMP LIT, BRIGHAM YOUNG UNIV, 82- *Mem:* Am Philol Asn; Class Asn Can; Am Comp Lit Asn; Int Soc Hist Rhetoric. *Res:* Roman literature of the early Empire; classical rhetoric; intellectual history of the American South. *Publ:* Auth, The death of Domitius in the Pharsalia, Trans Am Philol Asn, 75; History and motive in book seven of Lucan's Pharsalia, Hermes, 76; Restoring the generous past: Recent books of rhetoric and criticism, Mich Quart Rev, 79; contribr, Intellectual Life in Antebellum Charleston, Johns Hopkins Univ Press (in press). *Mailing Add:* Dept of Humanities Classics & Comp Lit Brigham Young Univ Provo UT 84602

LOURIA, YVETTE, b St Petersburg, Russia; US citizen; m 37. ROMANCE & SLAVIC LANGUAGES. *Educ:* Columbia Univ, MA, 51, PhD(French), 56. *Prof Exp:* Lectr French, Columbia Univ, 51-54; teacher, Brearley Sch, 55-56; instr Ger, Hunter Col, 56-57; asst prof French & Russ, C W Post Col, 58-59; from instr to assoc prof, Queens Col NY, 59-70, prof, 70-81; prof, 68-81, EMER PROF FRENCH & COMP LIT, PHD PROG, CITY UNIV NEW YORK, 81- *Concurrent Pos:* Adj prof Russ, Yeshiva Univ & Polytech Inst NY, 81- *Mem:* MLA; Am Asn Teachers Fr; Am Comp Lit Asn; Am Asn Teachers Slavic & E Europ Lang. *Res:* French 20th century literature, especially Marcel Proust; Russian 19th century literature; comparative literature, mainly French, Russian & German. *Publ:* Coauth, Ivan Goncharov's Oblomov: the anti-Faust as Christian hero, Can Slavic Studies, spring 69; auth, La convergence stylistique chez Proust, Nizet, Paris, 71; Proust and Lunacharskii, Romanic Rev, 4/71; An analysis of Dostoevskii's Nastasia Filippovna, Newsletter MLA Conf, 12/71; Nabokov and Proust: The Challenge of Time, Bks Abroad, summer 74; Moliere and Griboiedor, In: Moliere and the Commonwealth of Letters: Patrimony and Posterity, Univ Press Miss, 75; Germani: Mekhaber Hamakhazeh Harussi Harishon, Keshet, fall 75; As tecnicas estelisticas da convergencia , In: Teoria da Literatura em Suas Fontes, Livr Francisco Alves, Rio de Janeiro, 75. *Mailing Add:* 10E 85th St New York NY 10028

LOURIE, MARGARET ANN, English, Linguistics. See Vol II

LOVE, FREDERICK RUTAN, b Brooklyn, NY, Feb 20, 27. GERMAN LANGUAGE & LITERATURE. *Educ:* Yale Univ, AB, 49, PhD, 58; Univ Calif, Berkeley, MA, 51. *Prof Exp:* From instr to asst prof, 56-64, assoc prof, 64-80, PROF GER, BROWN UNIV, 80- *Mem:* MLA; Am Asn Teachers Ger. *Res:* Nineteenth and 20th century German literature, especially the drama; Nietzsche. *Publ:* Auth, Young Nietzsche and the Wagnerian Experience, Univ NC, 63; Nietzsche and Peter Gast in Basel, 72 & Nietzsche's quest for a new aesthetic of music, 77, Nietzsche-Studien; Nietzsche, music & madness, Music & Lett, 79; Nietzsche's St Peter, de Gruyter, 81. *Mailing Add:* Dept of Ger Box E Brown Univ Providence RI 02912

LOVELESS, OWEN ROBERT, b Junction City, Kans, Dec 30, 13; div; c 2. LINGUISTICS, JAPANESE. *Educ:* Kans Univ, BA, 35; Sorbonne, cert ling, 36; Univ Colo, cert Japanese lang, 44; Columbia Univ, MIA, 49; Univ Mich, PhD(ling), 63. *Prof Exp:* Linguist Amharic textbks, Ministry Educ, Addis Ababa, 55-57, lectr English lang teacher training, Laos, 58-61, sr scholar Okinawan lexicography, East-West Ctr, 63-64; assoc linguist, Soc Sci Res Inst, Univ Hawaii, 64-66; asst prof, Univ Minn, Minneapolis, 66-67, assoc prof Japanese Ling, 67-79, asst chmn dept EAsian lang, 69-73, RETIRED. *Concurrent Pos:* Consult design English lang radio teaching prog, Voice of Am, Southeast Asia, 62; mem, Peace Corps Study Comt, 68-69. *Mem:* Ling Soc Am. *Res:* Okinawan, Japanese and Amharic languages. *Publ:* Auth, The Okinawan Languages, Univ Mich, 63. *Mailing Add:* Dept of EAsian Lang Univ of Minn Minneapolis MN 55455

LO VERSO, ROSABIANCA, b Italy, May 17, 27; US citizen; c 2. FRENCH & ITALIAN LIETERATURE. *Educ:* Sacramento State Univ, BA, 63; Univ Calif, Davis, MA, 65, PhD(French lit), 67. *Prof Exp:* Teacher foreign lang, Bellavista High Sch, Sacramento, 61-63; chmn dept, Del Campo High Sch, Sacramento, 63-64; assoc French & Ital, Univ Calif, Davis, 64-67; chmn, dept Fr & Ital, 67-80, PROF FRENCH & ITAL & CHMN DEPT FOR LANG, 80- *Res:* Nineteenth century French and Italian literature; 20th century criticism. *Publ:* Auth, Nouvelles Remarques sur le Structuralisme, Univ Ky, 68; Fate in Zola, in Verga, Univ Wis, 69; Spazio e tempo nei Malavoglia, 72; Peche et divinite dans La Faute de l'Abbe Mourte, Univ Ky, 73; La mitologia della roba nell mastro Don Gesuald, Proc Pac Northwest Conf Foreign Lang, 74. *Mailing Add:* 1582 Response Rd Sacramento CA 95015

LOVETT, GABRIEL H, b Berlin, Ger, Aug 11, 21; US citizen; m 52; c 4. ROMANCE LANGUAGES. *Educ:* NY Univ, BA, 42, MA, 46, PhD(Romance lang), 51. *Prof Exp:* Instr Span, Wash Sq Col, NY Univ, 44-52, asst prof, 52-57; instr Span, French & Ger, Monmouth Col, NJ, 57-60; vis assoc prof Span, Wash Sq Col, NY Univ, 60-61; assoc prof, 61-65, prof, 66-69; PROF SPAN, WELLESLEY COL, 69- *Concurrent Pos:* Resident dir, NY Univ in Spain, 60-65; NY Univ res grant, 67-68. *Honors & Awards:* NJ Asn Teachers English Author Award, 66. *Mem:* MLA; Am Asn Teachers Span & Port. *Res:* Spanish drama before Lope de Vega; 18th and 19th century Spanish literature; 19th century Spanish history. *Publ:* Coauth, An Encyclopedia of Latin-American History, Abelard & Schuman, 56, Bobbs, 2nd ed, 68; Al buen hablador, Norton, 58; A Concept Approach to Spanish, Harper, 59, 2nd ed, 65; auth, Vision de la Espana y el Madrid de comienzos del siglo XIX, Hispania, 7-9/62; Napoleon and the Birth of Modern Spain, Vols I & II, NY Univ, 65; Patriotism and other themes in Becquer's El beso, Mod Lang Quart, 9/68; The Semantic evolution of Spanish guerrilla, Romance Notes, fall 68; The Duke of Rivas, Twayne, 77. *Mailing Add:* 15 Regis Rd Wellesley MA 02181

LOWE, DAVID ALLAN, b Carlinville, Ill, Jan 15, 48. RUSSIAN LITERATURE & LANGUAGE. *Educ:* Macalester Col, BA, 69; Ind Univ, MA, 72, PhD(Russian), 77. *Prof Exp:* Assoc instr Russ, Ind Univ, 71-74; instr, Macalester Col, 75-77; vis lectr, Ind Univ, 77-78; asst prof, Macalester Col, 78-79; ASST PROF RUSS, VANDERBILT UNIV, 79- *Concurrent Pos:* Instr, Summer Slavic Workshop, Ind Univ, 72- *Mem:* Am Asn Teachers Slavic & East Europ Lang; Am Asn Advan Slavic Studies. *Publ:* Auth, Bulgakov and Dostoevsky, Russ Lit Triquart, 77; Comedy and tragedy in Turgenev's Fathers and Sons, Can-Am Slavic Studies, 79; contribr, Columbia Encycl of Modern European Literature, 80; auth, Turgenev and Besy, Russ Lang J, 81; Odoevsky as opera critic, Slavic Rev, 82; A generic approach to Babel's Red Calvary, Mod Fiction Studies, 82; ed, Turgenev's Letters (in prep) & auth, Turgenev's Fathers and Sons (in prep), Ardis. *Mailing Add:* Dept Russ Box 75-B Vanderbilt Univ Nashville TN 37235

LOWE, PARDEE, JR, b Oakland, Calif, Mar 16, 36; m 63; c 4. GERMANIC LANGUAGES & LINGUISTICS. *Educ:* Univ Calif, Berkeley, BA, 58, MA, 61, PhD(Ger Ling), 65. *Prof Exp:* Asst prof Ger & Ling, Rice Univ, 65-66; asst prof Ger & Icelandic, Cornell Univ, 66-74; CHIEF TESTING, CENT INTEL AGENCY LANG SCH, 74- *Concurrent Pos:* Vis lectr Ger & Icelandic, Harvard Univ, 68-69; ed, Language Testing Newslett, Interagency Lang Roundtable. *Mem:* Ling Soc Am; MLA; Soc Advan Scand Studies. *Res:* Linguistics; modern standard German; old and modern Icelandic. *Publ:* Auth, An Introduction to Tape Lesson Materials, Parts I & II, Univ Calif, 63; Discourse analysis and the thattr: Speaker tagging, In: Studies for Einar Haugen, 72; Germanic word formation, In: Toward a Grammar of Proto-Germanic, 72; Information retrieval and the old Norse dict, Studies Ling; The Oral Language Proficiency Test, Interagency Lang Roundtable, 76; King Harald and the Icelanders: Five Icelandic Stories, Penmaen Press, 79. *Mailing Add:* 2831 Brook Dr Falls Church VA 22042

LOWENSTAM, STEVEN, b Springfield, Ill, Dec 14, 45. CLASSICAL LANGUAGES. *Educ:* Univ Chicago, BA, 67; Harvard Univ, MA, 69, PhD(classics), 75. *Prof Exp:* Asst prof, 75-81, ASSOC PROF CLASSICS, UNIV ORE, 81- *Mem:* Am Philol Asn; Archaeol Inst Am; Philol Asn Pac Coast. *Res:* Archaic epic; literary criticism; glyptics. *Publ:* Auth, Patroclus death in the Iliad and the inheritance of an Indo-European Myth, Archaeol News, 77; The meaning of IE dhal-, Trans Am Philol Asn, 79; The Death of Patroklos: A Study in Typology, Anton Hain, 81; Irus Queenly Mother and the problem of the irrational use of Homeric epithets, Pac Coast Philol, 81. *Mailing Add:* Dept of Classics Univ of Ore Eugene OR 97403

LOWIN, JOSEPH GERALD, b New York, NY, Apr 10, 41; m 68; c 2. FRENCH LANGUAGE & LITERATURE. *Educ:* City Col New York, BA, 62; Yale Univ, PhD(French), 68. *Prof Exp:* Instr French, Yale Univ, 68-70; asst prof, Univ Miami, 70-73; chmn dept lang & lit, 73-78, actg asst dean acad affairs, 74-75, ASSOC PROF FRENCH, TOURO COL, 73- *Concurrent Pos:* Recipient & chmn, Moore Fund grant for improv undergrad teaching, Yale Univ, 68-69. *Mem:* MLA; Am Asn Teachers Fr; Northeast Mod Lang Asn; Asn Jewish Studies. *Res:* Nineteenth century French Literature; literary framing; philosemitism in French literature. *Publ:* Auth, Apollinaire and his Jews, Australian J Fr Studies, 1-4/72; Theophile Gautier et ses Juifs, Rev Etudes Juives, 7/72; Two inedits of Theophile Gautier: letters to Carlotta Grisi a propos of Spirite, Romance Notes, 74; On classifying Gautier's short stories, In: The French Short Story, Univ SC, 75; La vision peripherique dans L'Hereslouque et Cie d'Apollinaire, Rev Lett Mod, 78; The dream frame in Gautier's Contes Fantastiques, Nineteenth Century Fr Studies, 80. *Mailing Add:* Dept of Lang & Lit Touro Col New York NY 10036

LOWRIE, JOYCE OLIVER, b Curitiba, Brazil, Dec 16, 36; US citizen; m 59; c 1. ROMANCE LANGUAGES. *Educ:* Baylor Univ, BA, 57; Yale Univ, PhD, 66. *Prof Exp:* Asst prof, 66-71, assoc prof, 71-77, PROF FRENCH, WESLEYAN UNIV, 77- *Mem:* Am Asn Teachers Fr. *Publ:* Auth, Motifs of kingdom and exile in Atala, Fr Rev, 4/70; The structural significance of sensual imagery in Paul et Virginie, Romance Notes, spring 71; The structural and ideological significance of Vigny's man of destiny in Stello, PMLA, spring 71; The Violent Mystique: Thematics of Retribution and Expiation in Balzac, Barbey d'Aurevilly, Bloy and Huysmans, Droz, Geneva, 74; The function of repetition in Pinget's Lettre Morte, Fr Rev, 4/76; The question of Mimesis in Gautier's Contes Fantastiques, Nineteenth-Century Fr Studies, fall-winter 79-80; The Rota Fortunae, In: Pieyre de Mandiargues's La Motocyclette, 2/80 & Entretien avec Andre Pieyre de Mandiargues, 12/81, Fr Rev. *Mailing Add:* Dept of Romance Lang Wesleyan Univ Middletown CT 06457

LOY, JOHN ROBERT, b Harrisburg, Pa, July 15, 18. FRENCH LANGUAGE & LITERATURE. *Educ:* Univ Paris, Dipl, 39; Columbia Univ, AB, 40, PhD, 49. *Prof Exp:* Instr, Columbia Univ, 46-50; instr French, Univ Calif, 50-55; asst prof, Univ Vt, 56; prof French & chmn dept mod lang, Hobart & William Smith Cols, 56-59; chmn dept, 68-76, PROF MOD LANG, BROOKLYN COL, 59-, MEM EXEC COMT DOCTORAL PROG, CITY UNIV NEW YORK, 68- *Concurrent Pos:* Fulbright lectr, France, 62-63. *Mem:* MLA. *Res:* French literature and thought of the 18th century; French literature of the 20th century; comparative literature. *Publ:* Auth, Diderot's Determined Fatalist, King's Crown; Things in Modern French Literature, PMLA, 56; transl, Introd & Notes, Jacques le Fatalist, NY Univ, 59; auth, Diderot's Claude et Neron, Cahiers Asn Int, Etudes Francaises, 60; transl, Persian Letters, Meridian, 61; auth, Nature, Reason and Enlightenment, Studies Voltaire, 63; Montesquieu, Twayne, 68. *Mailing Add:* Dept Mod Lang Brooklyn Col Brooklyn NY 11210

LOYA, ARIEH R, b Baghdad, Iraq, Feb 25, 26; US citizen; m 61; c 2. MIDDLE EASTERN LANGUAGES & LITERATURES. *Educ:* Hebrew Univ, Jerusalem, Israel, BA, 56; Univ Pa, MA, 65, PhD(Arabic lit & Mid East hist), 68. *Prof Exp:* Lectr Arabic lang & lit, Univ Pa, 64-68; ASSOC PROF & COORDR HEBREW, BOSTON UNIV, 79- *Concurrent Pos:* Mem, United Nat Armistice Comn, UN, 50-53; Israel Ambassador to Chad, 62-64; assoc prof Arabic & Hebrew, Stanford Univ, 66-69 & Temple Univ, 68-72; res grant, Univ Pa, 70 & 71 & Van Leer Found, Israel, 74; assoc prof Hebrew, Univ Tex, Austin, 72-74; chmn & prof, Defense Lang Inst, 74-76; B'nai Brith Hillel Found grant, Stanford Univ, 77-78. *Mem:* Mid East Studies Asn; Am Acad Polit & Soc Sci; Asn Jewish Studies; Am Polit Sci Asn; AAUP. *Res:* Arabic poetry; Middle Eastern politics; Middle Eastern religions. *Publ:* Auth, Arabic Legal & Diplomatic Terminology and Cases, Govt Press, Jerusalem, 57; coauth, Modern Near East: Literature & Society, Ctr Int Studies, 71; auth, The social position of women as reflected in Arabic Poetry, Muslim World, 71; Contemporary Arabic Literature, Al-Sharq Press, Jerusalem, 72; The detribalisation of Arabic poetry, 74 & Poetry as a social document, 74, J Mid East Studies; Israeli Hebrew (2 vols), 76 & Modern Arabic (3 vols), 81, Int Commun Syst. *Mailing Add:* 7535 Fern Ct Carmel CA 93923

LOZADA, ALFREDO RUIZ, b Guayaquil, Ecuador, Sept 19, 22; US citizen; m 58; c 2. ROMANCE LITERATURE. *Educ:* Univ Calif, Berkeley, BA, 52, MA, 54, PhD, 62. *Prof Exp:* Instr Span, Northwestern Univ, 58-62; from asst prof to assoc prof, 62-72, PROF SPAN, LA STATE UNIV, BATON ROUGE, 72- *Concurrent Pos:* Soc Sci Res Coun res grant, 62. *Mem:* Am Asn Teachers Span & Port. *Res:* Latin American poetry. *Publ:* Auth, Sequedad, Ed Univ Santiago, Chili, 59. *Mailing Add:* Dept of Foreign Lang La State Univ Baton Rouge LA 70803

LOZANO, CARLOS, b Zamora, Mex, Jan 12, 13; US citizen. ROMANCE LITERATURES. *Educ:* Univ Calif, Berkeley, AB, 41, PhD, 62. *Prof Exp:* Asst prof Ital & Span, George Washington Univ, 59-63; assoc prof Span, St Louis Univ, 63-64 & Univ Ore, 64-66; prof, St Mary's Col, Calif, 66-70; PROF SPAN, CALIF STATE COL, BAKERSFIELD, 70- *Concurrent Pos:* Assoc ed, Hispanic Press, Calif State Col & Univ Syst, 78- *Mem:* MLA; Am Asn Teachers Span & Port; Philol Asn Pac Coast. *Res:* Hispanic American novel; contemporary Hispanic American poetry; Golden Age of Spanish literature. *Publ:* Coauth, Novelistas contemporaneos hispanoam, Heath, 64; auth, Ruben Dario y el modernismo en Espana, Las Americas, 68; Ruben Dario y los intelectuales Franceses, Homenaje a Ruben Dario, 70; Autodefinicion, compromiso e identificacion en la obra de Fernando Alegria & El epiteto como elogio, In: Homenaje a Fernando Alegria, Las Americas, 70; Rosas y lirios, Antologia Comentada Mod, 74; La influencia de Ruben Dario en Espana, Univ Nicaragua, Leon, 78; The other fire, David Valjalo, (trans, Carlos Lozano, Illustrated by Mario Toral), DeLuxe Bilingual Edition, fall 82. *Mailing Add:* Dept of Foreign Lang Calif State Col Bakersfield CA 93309

LU, JOHN H-T, b China, Aug 13, 23; US citizen; m 53; c 4. THEORETICAL LINGUISTICS. *Educ:* Taiwan Norm Univ, BA, 52; Univ Mich, Ann Arbor, MA, 56; Ohio State Univ, PhD(ling), 72. *Prof Exp:* Instr English, Taiwan Norm Univ, 56-60, prof, 60-64; asst prof Ling & Chinese, George Washington Univ, 65-67; asst prof, 67-72, assoc prof, 72-77, PROF LING & CHINESE, FLA STATE UNIV, 78- *Mem:* Am Ling Soc; MLA; Chinese Lang Teachers Asn; Southeast Conf Ling. *Res:* Relationship between syntax and semantics; language in context; Chinese syntax. *Publ:* Auth, Form and agreement vs function words, 77 & An investigation of case in Chinese Grammar by Li Yin-che, 77, Chinese Lang Teachers Asn; Resultative verb compounds vs directional verb compounds in Mandarin, J Chinese Lang, 77; A Functional Analysis on the Extent Construction in Mandarin, Proc Symposium on Chinese Ling, 77 & Ling Inst Ling Soc Am, Student Book Co, Taiwan; A study of quantifiers in Mandarin Chinese, J Chinese Lang Teachers Am, Vol XV, No 3; Topic and Presupposition, Selections in Chinese Linguistics, Student Book Co, Taiwan, 82; A response to the questions with regard to Re Re de He Yi Wan Cha by C P Sobelman, J Chinese Ling, Vol X, No 1; The Development of Linguistic Theories: A Series of Ten Lectures Given at Hua-Tung Normal University, Shanghai, China, Shanghai Educ Press, 82. *Mailing Add:* Dept of Mod Lang Fla State Univ Tallahassee FL 32306

LUBETSKI, MEIR, b Mar 21, 38; US citizen; m 68; c 3. JUDAICA. *Educ:* Hebrew Univ Jerusalem, BA, 64, MA, 66; Brooklyn Col, City Univ New York, MS, 72; NY Univ, PhD(Hebrew educ & cult), 76. *Prof Exp:* Instr Hebrew lang & lit, Ferkauf Grad Sch Educ, Yeshiva Univ, 69-76; asst prof,

72-80, ASSOC PROF HEBREW LANG & LIT, BARUCH COL, CITY UNIV NEW YORK, 80- *Concurrent Pos:* Am Coun Learned Soc grant-in-aid, 78; scholar assistance award, Baruch Col, 78, 79 & 80. *Mem:* Nat Asn Professors Hebrew; Jewish Studies Asn; MLA; World Union Jewish Studies; Soc Bibl Lit. *Res:* East Mediterranean studies; Bible and ancient literature; marine studies of the Ancient Near East. *Publ:* Coauth, Current acquisitions in the Jewish field, Libr Res & Tech Serv, fall 74; Writings on Jewish History, Am Jewish Comt, 74; auth, New light on old seas, Jewish Quart Rev, 10/77; Oceanos, Kovetz Massad, 78; Limen, Jewish Quart Rev, 79; And I Shall Place His Hand in the Sea, Bitzaron, 80. *Mailing Add:* Dept of Mod Lang Baruch Col New York NY 10010

LUCE, STANFORD LEONARD, b Boston, Mass, May 19, 23; m 47; c 4. FRENCH LANGUAGE & LITERATURE. *Educ:* Dartmouth Col, BA, 47; Yale Univ, MA, 48, PhD, 53; Univ Montpellier, dipl, 49. *Prof Exp:* Asst instr, Yale Univ, 49-51; instr French & Span, Clark Univ, 51-52; asst prof, 52-62, assoc prof, 62-79, PROF FRENCH, MIAMI UNIV, 79- *Mem:* Am Asn Teachers Fr; MLA. *Res:* French slang in contemporary literature; contemporary French theater, since 1890; Celine. *Publ:* Auth, The whimsical and the sordid in Jean Anouilh, Ky Foreign Lang J, Vol XII, No II; A family year in France, Fr Rev, 5/66; contribr, A Gentle Revolution (pamphlet), Willow Press, 69; auth, Report on intensive French course, Bull Asn Foreign Lang Dept, 74; The languishing art, Verbatim, 75; Increment & excrement, Celine & Lang of hate, Maledicta, 77; Glossary of Celine's Fiction, Univ Microfilms, 79; Learning French genders with 'e's', Fr Rev, 4/79. *Mailing Add:* Dept of French & Ital Miami Univ Oxford OH 45056

LUCE, TORRY JAMES, JR, b Elmira, NY, Aug 28, 32. CLASSICS, ANCIENT HISTORY. *Educ:* Hamilton Col, AB, 54; Princeton Univ, PhD(classics), 58. *Prof Exp:* From asst prof to assoc prof, 58-74, asst dean col, 65-70, PROF CLASSICS, PRINCETON UNIV, 74-, CHMN DEPT, 77- *Concurrent Pos:* Procter & Gamble fac fel, 59-60; deleg, Am Coun Learned Soc, 72- *Mem:* Am Philol Asn; Am Numis Soc; Vergilian Soc. *Res:* Roman historiography; Roman history; Greek history. *Publ:* Auth, Political propaganda on Roman republican coins: Circa 92-82 BC, Am J Archaeol, 68; Marius and the Mithridatic command, Historia, 70; Design and structure in Livy: 5.32-55, Trans Am Philol Asn, 71; Livy: The composition of his History, Princeton Univ, 77. *Mailing Add:* Dept of Classics 111 E Pyne Princeton Univ Princeton NJ 08540

LUCENTE, GREGORY L, b Evanston, Ill, Apr 10, 48. ITALIAN & COMPARATIVE LITERATURE. *Educ:* Yale Col, BA, 70; Univ di Firenze, MA, 73; Univ Wis-Madison, PhD(comp lit), 79. *Prof Exp:* Instr Ital, Loyola Univ Chicago, 78-79; ASST PROF ITAL, JOHNS HOPKINS UNIV, 79- *Concurrent Pos:* Ed, Mod Lang Notes, 79- *Mem:* MLA; Am Soc Teachers Ital; Am Asn Univ Professors Ital; Am Comp Lit Asn. *Res:* Modern Italian narrative; medieval and Renaissance lyric; literary theory. *Publ:* Auth, The fortunate fall of Andreuccio da Perugia, Forum Italicum, 12/76; Lampedusa's Il gattopardo: Figure and temporality in an historical novel, 1/78 & The ideology of form in Verga's La Lupa: Realism, myth, and the passion of control, 1/80, Mod Lang Notes; D'Annuio's Il fuoco and Joyce's Portrait of the Artist: From allegory to irony, Italica, 9/80; The creation of myth's rhetoric: Views of the mythic sign, Comp Lit Studies, 3/81; The Narrative of Realism and Myth: Verga, Lawrence, Faulkner, Parese, Johns Hopkins Univ Press, 81; Vico's notion of divine providence and the limits of human knowledge, freedom and will, Mod Lang Notes, 1/82; Lyric tradition and the desire of absence: Rudel, Dante, Michelangelo Vorreinoler, Can Rev Comp Lit (in prep). *Mailing Add:* Dept of Romance Lang Johns Hopkins Univ Baltimore MD 21218

LUCHTING, WOLFGANG ALEXANDER, b Muenchen, Ger, Sept 29, 27. GERMAN, SPANISH. *Educ:* Univ Munich, Dr phil(Am studies), 56. *Prof Exp:* Lectr mod Ger lit, San Marcos Univ & Cath Univ, Lima, Peru, 61-62; asst prof Ger, Antioch Col, 62-64, Goethe-Inst, Radolfszell & Berlin, Ger, 64-65, asst prof Ger & Span, Univ Mo, St Louis, 65-66; assoc prof, 66-70, PROF SPAN & GER, WASH STATE UNIV, 70- *Concurrent Pos:* Lectr, Inst Raul Porras Barrenechea, Lima, Peru, 65-, San Marcos Univ, Lima, 66, Oficina Difusion Cult Pres Chile, Santiago, 67, Galeria Cult y Libertad, Lima, 67, Univ Educ, Peru, 67, 68, Agrarian Univ, Peru, 68 & Inst Cult Las Condes, Santiago, Chile, 68; Soc Sci Res Coun grant, 70-71. *Mem:* Am Asn Teachers Span & Port; Inst Int lit Latino-am; MLA. *Res:* American literature, especially North; modern Latin American literature; modern German literature. *Publ:* Auth, TR Ribeyro y sus dobles, Inst Nat Cult, Lima, 70; Pasos a desnivel, Mont Avila, Caracas, 72; A Bryce: Humores y malhumores, Milla Batres, Lima, Peru, 75; Liberacion de las mujeres o revolucion, Ecoma, Lima, Peru, 76; Apuntes para una lectura de Dabeiba, In: Aproximaciones a Gustavo Alvarez Gardeazabal, Plaza & Janes, 78; Escritores peruanos: Que piensan/que dicen, Ecoma, Lima, Peru, 78; Desarticulador de Realidades: Introduccion a Mario Vargas Llosa, Plaza & Janes, Bogota, Col, 78. *Mailing Add:* Dept of Foreign Lang & Lit Wash State Univ Pullman WA 99164

LUCK, GEORG H, b Bern, Switz, Feb 17, 26; m 58; c 3. CLASSICS. *Educ:* Harvard Univ, AM, 52; Univ Bern, PhD(classics), 53. *Prof Exp:* Instr classics, Yale Univ, 52-53, Brown Univ, 53-55 & Harvard Univ, 55-58; lectr, Univ Mainz, 58-62; prof, Univ Bonn, 62-71; PROF CLASSICS, JOHNS HOPKINS UNIV, 71- *Concurrent Pos:* Guggenheim Found fel, 59-60; Swiss Nat Res Coun grant; vis prof, Brown Univ, 69, Johns Hopkins Univ, 70-71 & Univ Calif, Los Angeles, 74; ed, Am J Philol, 71-81. *Mem:* Am Philol Asn; Archaeol Inst Am. *Res:* Latin poetry; Greek philosophy. *Publ:* Auth, Der Akademiker Antiochos, Paul Haupt, Bern, 53; The Latin love elegy, Methuen, London, 59, 2nd ed, 69; Über einige Inerjektionen, 64 & ed, Ovid, Tristia, Vol 1, 67, vol II, 78, Winter, Heidelberg; Eine Schweizer Reise, Haupt, Bern, 81. *Mailing Add:* Dept of Classics Johns Hopkins Univ Baltimore MD 21218

LUCKYJ, GEORGE STEPHEN NESTOR, b Janchyn, June 11, 19; Can Citizen; m 44; c 3. SLAVIC LANGUAGES & LITERATURE. *Educ:* Univ Birmingham, BA, 42, MA, 43; Columbia Univ, PhD, 53. *Prof Exp:* Lectr, Univ Sask, 47-49; chmn dept, 55-60, PROF SLAVIC STUDIES, UNIV TORONTO, 52- *Concurrent Pos:* Consult, res prog, USSR; ed, Can Slavonic Papers; assoc dir, Can Inst Ukrainian Studies, Univ Alberta, Edmonton, 76. *Honors & Awards:* Governor General's Silver Jubilee Medal, 78. *Mem:* Can Asn Slavists. *Res:* Russian and Soviet literature; Ukrainian literature and history. *Publ:* Auth, English for Ukrainians, Thomas Allen, Toronto, 50; Literary Politics in the Soviet Ukraine, 1917-1934, Columbia Univ, 56; Between Gogol and Shevchenko, Harvard Univ, 71; ed, Modern Ukrainian Short Stories, Ukrainian Acad Press, 73; ed, Discordant Voices; the Non-Russian Soviet Literatures, Mosaic, 75; D Cyzevs'kyj, A History of Ukrainian Literature, Ukrainian Acad Press, 75; The VAPLITE Collection, Mosaic, 77; Shevchenles and the Critics, Univ Toronto Press, 80. *Mailing Add:* 5Kendall Ave Toronto ON M5R 1L5 Can

LUDWIG, JEANNETTE MARIE, b Denver, Colo, Sept 29, 49; m 81; c 4. APPLIED LINGUISTICS. *Educ:* Drake Univ, BA, 71; Univ Mich, MA, 73, PhD(Romance Ling), 77. *Prof Exp:* ASST PROF FRENCH, STATE UNIV NY, BUFFALO, 77- *Honors & Awards:* Chancellor Award for Excellence in Teaching, 80. *Mem:* MLA: Am Coun Teaching For Lang. *Res:* Error analysis; verbal memory; history of French. *Publ:* Auth, Error analysis & the cognitive approach: A new horizon, Am Coun Teaching For Lang, FLA 12: 209-12; Factors affecting vocabulary acquisition, Methodology Workshop, Ind Univ Pa (in press); Defining the need for a pedagogical grammar: Relative usage in French Proceedings of the Language Studies Symposium, Univ Del Press (in press); Native speaker judgements of second language learners' errors: A survey, Mod Lang J (in press). *Mailing Add:* Dept of Mod Lang & Lit State Univ of NY Buffalo NY 14260

LUEKER, ERWIN LOUIS, US citizen. FOREIGN LANGUAGES. *Educ:* Concordia Sem, BD, 39; Wash Univ, MA, 40, PhD, 42. *Prof Exp:* Assoc prof lang & humanities, St Paul's Col, Mo, 46-55; prof syst theol & philos, Concordia Sem, 55-74, dir correspondence sch, 57-74, acting dir grad sch, 65-66; prof syst theol, Christ Sem-Seminex, 74-80. *Concurrent Pos:* John W Behnken Fel, 70; vis fel, Princeton Theol Sem, 82. *Mem:* Am Philol Asn; Lutheran Acad Scholarship. *Res:* Scandinavian theology; New Testament Manuscripts; religion and poetry. *Publ:* Auth, Concordia Bible Dictionary, 63 & coauth, Church and Ministry in Transition, 64, Concordia; Structured musings of EL, privately publ, 68, 69, 73 & 80; auth, Change and the Church, Concordia, 69; Theology-philosophy-poetry: Toward a synopsis, 7-8/71 & Doctrinal emphasis in the Missouri Synod, 4/72, Concordial Theol Monthly; Lutheran Cyclopedia, revised ed, 75; Development-Tension-Crisis, privately publ, 80. *Mailing Add:* 7201 Waterman St Louis MO 63130

LUENOW, PAUL FERDINAND, JR, b Spokane, Wash, Aug 20, 17. FOREIGN LANGUAGES. *Educ:* Univ Wash, MA, 48; Univ NMex, PhD(Span), 55. *Prof Exp:* From instr to assoc prof Span, Lewis & Clark Col, 47-58; asst prof, 58-66, ASSOC PROF SPAN, ARIZ STATE UNIV, 66- *Mem:* Am Asn Teachers Span & Port; Rocky Mountain Coun Latin Am Studies. *Res:* Spanish American Literature. *Mailing Add:* Dept of Foreign Lang Ariz State Univ Tempe AZ 85287

LUG, SIEGLINDE, b Ger; US citizen. COMPARATIVE MEDIEVAL & FEMINIST LITERATURE. *Educ:* Munich Univ, BA, 66; Univ Calif, San Diego, PhD(comp lit), 74. *Prof Exp:* Asst prof Ger, Univ Colo, Denver, 76-78; ASST PROF GER & COMP LIT, UNIV DENVER, 78- *Concurrent Pos:* Guest ed, Denver Quart, 82. *Mem:* MLA; Am Comp Lit Asn; Rocky Mountain Mod Lang Asn; Women Ger. *Res:* Feminist perspectives in medieval German literature; feminist perspectives in 20th century German women writers; classical Arabic literature. *Publ:* Auth, Towards a definition of excellence in classical Arabic poetry, J Am Orient Soc, 81; Poetic Techniques and Conceptual Elements in Ibn Zaydun's Poetry, Univ Press Am, 82. *Mailing Add:* Dept Foreign Lang & Lit Univ Denver Denver CO 80208

LUIS, WILLIAM, b New York, NY, July 12, 48. SPANISH AMERICAN LITERATURE. *Educ:* State Univ NY, Binghamton, BA, 71; Univ Wis-Madison, MA, 73; Cornell Univ, PhD(Span Am lit), 80. *Prof Exp:* Instr, 79-80, ASST PROF SPAN, DARTMOUTH COL, 80- *Concurrent Pos:* Consult ed, Ediciones del Norte, 80-81; consult & contrib ed, Handbook of Latin Am Studies, 81- *Mem:* MLA; Asn Caribbean Studies. *Res:* Contemporary Spanish American literature; black narratie in Latin America; literary criticism. *Publ:* Auth, Juan el gallo (short story), Rev Chicano-Riquena, Vol 3, No 3; Con Cesar Leante (interview), Bohemia, Vol 70, No 48; Myth and reality in Cesar Leante's Muelle de Caballeria, Latin Am Lit Rev, Vol 8, No 16; co-ed, Los Dispositivos en la flor, Ediciones del Norte, 81; auth, The antislavery novel and the concept of modernity, Cuban Studies, Vol 11, No 1; La novela antiesclavista: Texto, contexto y escritura, Cuadernos Am, Vol 236, No 3; Autopsia de Lunes de Revolucion: Entrevista a Pablo Armando Fernandez (interview), Plural, Vol 17, No 126. *Mailing Add:* Dept of Span & Port Dartmouth Col Hanover NH 03755

LUJAN, MARTA ELIDA, b Buenos Aires, Arg. SPANISH LINGUISTICS. *Educ:* Univ Tex, Austin, PhD(ling), 72. *Prof Exp:* Asst prof, 72-77, ASSOC PROF SPAN & LING, UNIV TEX, AUSTIN, 78- *Mem:* Ling Soc Am. *Res:* Syntax and semantics of modern Spanish. *Publ:* Auth, Sintaxix y semantica del adjetivo, Ed Catedra, 78; Direct object nouns and the preposition a in Spanish, 78 & Adverbial adjectives in Spanish, 79, Tex Ling Forum; La enclisis y el modo en los complementos verbales: Un analisis transformacional, Revista de Linguistica Teorica y Aplicada, 19-47, 79; Critic promotion and mood in Spanish verbal complements, Linguistics, 381-484, 80; The Spanish copulas as aspectual indicators, Lingua 54, 165-210, 81; The specified subject condition, trace theory and clitic movement in Spanish, Tex Ling Forum, 63-87, 81; El principio de consistencia universal ed el habla de los ninos bilingues, Lexis, 82. *Mailing Add:* 2301 Townes Lane Austin TX 78703

LULL, DAVID JOHN, Religion, New Testament. See Vol IV

LUNA, NORMAN JOSEPH, b Denver, Colo, Sept 7, 36. SPANISH. *Educ:* St Thomas Sem, BA, 59; Univ Colo, Boulder, MA, 67, PhD(Span), 69. *Prof Exp:* Asst prof Span, Univ Nebr, 69-74, assoc prof, 74-80. *Mem:* Am Asn Teachers Span & Port; Int Inst Lit Iberoam. *Res:* Chicano literature; Latin American literature. *Publ:* Auth Ulysses and Al filo del agua, Int Studies, Univ Nebr, 75; Experimental Fiction of A Yanez, Foreign Lang Dimensions, Nebr Foreign Lang Asn, 76; J Rulfo's World of Special Intemporality, Foreign Lang, Nebr, 76; J S Brushwood, The Spanish American Novel, Revista Iberoamericana, 76; J O Jimenez, Estudios criticos . . ., J Span Studies 20th century, 77; Three Experimental Novels by Carlos Fuentes, 77 & The Chicano Novel, 78, Foreign Lang Dimension, Nebr Foreign Lang Asn; H J Becco et al, Trayectoria de la Poesia . . ., Hispania, 78. *Mailing Add:* 5828 Erskine Omaha NE 68104

LUNDELL, TORBORG LOVISA, b Stockholm, Sweden, US citizen. COMPARATIVE LITERATURE, FOLKTALE. *Educ:* Univ Calif, Berkeley, PhD(comp Lit), 73. *Prof Exp:* Actg asst prof, 69-72, lectr, 72-73, asst prof, 73-77, ASSOC PROF SWED, UNIV CALIF, SANTA BARBARA, 77- *Mem:* Soc Advan Scand Studies; MLA; Philol Asn Pac Coast; Am Comp Lit Asn; C G Jung Found Anal Psychol. *Res:* Modern Swedish Novel; film. *Publ:* Auth, Lars Ahlin's concept of the writer as identificator and förbedjare, Scandinavica, 75; Lars Ahlin's concept of equality, Scand Studies, 75; Lars Ahlin, Twayne, 77; Kommentar til Lars Ahlin's definition av författaren 'som en opersonlig älskare', Samlaren; Whisperings (poem), Bitterroot, 79; coauth (with Anthony Mulac), Husbands and wives in Bergman films: A close analysis based on empirical data, J Univ Film Asn, 81; The creative night and other aspects of creativity in Isak Dinesen's life and work, Am J Social Psychiat, 81; Lots of Souvenirs But No Roses, Pac Rim, 82. *Mailing Add:* Dept of Ger & Slavic Lang Univ of Calif Santa Barbara CA 93106

LUNSFORD, RONALD FRANKLIN, English Composition, Linguistics. See Vol II

LUNT, HORACE GRAY, b Colorado Springs, Colo, Sept 12, 18. SLAVIC LINGUISTICS. *Educ:* Harvard Univ, AB, 41; Univ Calif, AM, 42; Columbia Univ, PhD, 50. *Prof Exp:* Teaching asst Slavic langs, Univ Calif, 46; lectr Serbocroatian, Columbia Univ, 48-49; from asst prof to assoc prof, 49-59; PROF SLAVIC LANG & LIT, HARVARD UNIV, 59- *Concurrent Pos:* Guggenheim fel, 60-61. *Mem:* Ling Soc Am; Am Asn Advan Slavic Studies; MLA; Am Asn Teachers Slavic & East Europ Lang. *Res:* Church Slavonic; comparative Slavic linguistics. *Publ:* Auth, Grammar of the Macedonian Literary Language, Skopje, 52; Fundamentals of Russian, Norton, 2nd ed, 68; Old Church Slavonic Grammer, Mouton, The Hague, 6th ed, 74; Progressive Palatalization of Common Slavic, Skopje, 81. *Mailing Add:* Dept of Slavic Lang Harvard Univ Cambridge MA 02138

LUPLOW, CAROL ANN, b Prineville, Ore, Oct 20, 42; m 68. RUSSIAN LANGUAGE & LITERATURE. *Educ:* Stanford Univ, BA, 64; Univ Mich, Ann Arbor, MA, 66, PhD(Slavic lang & lit), 73. *Prof Exp:* Lectr Russ Lang & Lit, Univ Mich, 68-73; asst prof, 73-80, ASSOC PROF RUSS LANG & LIT, DARTMOUTH COL, 80- *Res:* Soviet literature; Russian prose and poetry, 1880-1917. *Publ:* Translr, Jurij Tynjanov, on literary evolution, In: Readings in Russian Poetics: Formalist and Structuralist Views, Mass Inst Technol, 71; coauth & contribr, Issac Babel, In: The Mod Encyclopedia of Russian & Soviet Literature, 78. *Mailing Add:* Dept of Russ Dartmouth Col Hanover NH 03755

LURIA, MAXWELL SIDNEY, English, Medieval Studies. See Vol II

LUSETTI, WALTER ITALO, b Jeannette, Pa, June 5, 23; m 46; c 2. SPANISH EDUCATION. *Educ:* Univ Pittsburgh, BA, 49, MLit, 50; Univ Ore, PhD(educ), 67. *Prof Exp:* Teacher Multnomah Co Schs, Ore, 50-52, prin, 57-63; teacher Span pub schs, Portland, Ore, 52-57; asst prof Lewis & Clark Col, 63-64; ASSOC PROF SPAN & EDUC, ORE STATE UNIV, 67-, CHMN, DEPT MOD LANG, 73- *Concurrent Pos:* Dir Ital studies ctr, Ore State Syst Higher Educ, Pavia, Italy, 70-72. *Mem:* Am Asn Teachers Span & Port; Am Coun Teachers Foreign Lang. *Res:* Linguistics; second language acquisition. *Mailing Add:* Dept of Mod Lang Ore State Univ Corvallis OR 97331

LUSHER, HAROLD EDWARD, b Hazeleton, Pa, Apr 18, 27. GERMAN LANGUAGE & LITERATURE. *Educ:* Bowdoin Col, BA, 48; Johns Hopkins Univ, MA, 53, PhD(German lit), 58. *Prof Exp:* From asst prof to assoc prof, 56-72, PROF GERMAN, UNIV NB, FREDERICTON, 72-, PROF RUSS, 80- *Res:* Modern German literature especially, Thomas Mann; Austrian literature; Austrian drama, Volkstheatre. *Mailing Add:* Dept of Ger Univ of NB Fredericton NB E3B 5A3 Can

LUTCAVAGE, CHARLES PATRICK, b Frankfurt, Ger, Jan 13, 48; US citizen. GERMAN LANGUAGE & LITERATURE. *Educ:* LaSalle Col, BA, 70; Harvard Univ, MA, 74, PhD(German), 76. *Prof Exp:* Asst prof, Univ NH, 76-77; PRECEPTOR GERMAN, HARVARD UNIV, 77- *Mem:* Am Asn Teachers German; Am Coun Teaching Foreign Lang; Goethe Soc New England. *Res:* Language pedagogy; Austrian history and literature. *Publ:* Auth, Geographical grammar: The Dative-Acussative prepositions, 80, Drilling the indirect objecct, 81 & Short-wave radio: An aid to language learning, 82, Die Unterrichtspraxis. *Mailing Add:* 1070 Beacon St Apt 3B Brookline MA 02146

LUTES, PHILIP HAYNES, b Chicago, Ill, Oct 20, 34; m 60; c 3. FRENCH LITERATURE. *Educ:* Brown Univ, AB, 56; Univ Mich, Ann Arbor, MA, 60, PhD(French), 69. *Prof Exp:* Instr French, Lafayette Col, 63-68, asst prof, 70; asst prof, 70-80, ASSOC PROF FRENCH, UNIV MONT, 80-, HEAD FRENCH SECT, DEPT FOREIGN LANG & CO-CHMN COMP LIT, 73- *Concurrent Pos:* Dir, Univ Mont Study Abroad Prog in Burgundy, 76, 78. *Mem:* Am Asn Teachers Fr Amis Jean Giono. *Res:* The works of Jean Giono; psychology of literature; comparative mythology. *Mailing Add:* Dept of Foreign Lang Univ of Mont Missoula MT 59812

LUTHER, GISELA, b Eisenach, Ger, July 14, 23; US citizen. GERMAN LITERATURE & LANGUAGE. *Educ:* Univ Heidelberg, MA, 47; Stanford Univ, PhD(Ger), 68. *Prof Exp:* From instr to asst prof Ger, Stanford Univ, 59-70; head dept, 72-79, ASSOC PROF GER, CASE WESTERN RESERVE UNIV, 70- *Mem:* MLA; AAUP; Am Asn Teachers Ger; Int Asn Germanists. *Res:* Seventeenth & 18th century German literature. *Publ:* Auth, Barocker Expressionismus? Zur Problematic der Beziehungen zwischen der Bildlichkeit expressionistischer und barocker Lyrik, Mouton, The Hague, Paris, 69; contribr, Interpretationen zum West-Oestlichen Divan Goethes, Wiss Buchgesellschaft, Darmstadt, 73. *Mailing Add:* Dept of Ger Case Western Reserve Univ Cleveland OH 44106

LUTHY, MELVIN JOSEPH, b Logan, Utah, Nov 15, 36; m 65; c 4. LINGUISTICS, ENGLISH LANGUAGE. *Educ:* Utah State Univ, BS, 62; Ind Univ, PhD(ling), 67. *Prof Exp:* Asst prof English & ling, Univ Wis-Oshkosh, 69-71; assoc prof, 71-80, PROF ENGLISH & LING, BRIGHAM YOUNG UNIV, 80- *Mem:* Ling Soc Am; Teachers of English Speakers Other Lang; Rocky Mountain Mod Lang Asn. *Res:* Modern grammars; language pedagogy; Finnish language and literature. *Publ:* Auth, Study in English Grammars, Brigham Young Univ Homestudy, 73; Phonological and Lexical Aspects of Colloquial Finnish, Ind Univ, 73; coauth, TICCIT Composition and Grammar Course, 74 & auth, Finnish Noun/Adjective/Verb Wheels, 76, Brigham Young Univ; Why transformational grammar fails in the classroom, Col Compos & Commun, 77; The case of Prufrock's grammar, Col English, 78; A comparative generative junction approach to Finnish morphosyntax, J Uralic & Altaic Studies, 82. *Mailing Add:* Dept of English Brigham Young Univ Provo UT 84602

LUTZ, CORA ELIZABETH, b Rockville, Conn, Oct 23, 06. CLASSICAL PHILOLOGY. *Educ:* Conn Col, AB, 27; Yale Univ, AM, 31, PhD(classics), 33. *Prof Exp:* Teacher Latin & French, Killingly High Sch, 27-29; asst classics, Judson Col, 33-35; from asst prof to prof, 35-69, EMER PROF CLASSICS, WILSON COL, 69- *Concurrent Pos:* Kellogg res fel, Yale Univ, 43-44; Guggenheim fel, 49-50, 54-55; Bollingen Found fel, 66-67; cataloguer Mediaeval manuscripts, Beinecke Libr, Yale Univ, 69-77. *Honors & Awards:* Distinguished Alumni Award, Conn Col, 70. *Mem:* Am Philol Asn; Mediaeval Acad Am; Class Asn New Eng; Renaissance Soc Am. *Res:* Early mediaeval commentaries; Renaissance commentaries; Mediaeval manuscripts. *Publ:* Ed, Iohannis Scotti: Annotationes in Marcianum, Mediaeval Acad Am, 39; Dunchad: Glossae in Martianum, Am Philol Asn, 44; Musonius Rufus, Yale Class Studies, 47; Remigius Autissiodorensis: Commentum in Martianum Capellam, E J Brill, Leyden, Vols I & II, 62 & 65; auth, Essays on Manuscripts and Rare Books, 75 & Schoolmasters of the Tenth Century, 77, Archon; The Oldest Library Motto and Other Library Essays, Archon, 79. *Mailing Add:* 24 Charlton Hill Mt Carmel CT 06518

LÜTZELER, PAUL MICHAEL, b Doveren, W Ger, Nov 4, 43; m 72; c 2. GERMAN & COMPARATIVE LITERATURE. *Educ:* Ind Univ, Bloomington, MA, 70: PhD(Ger), 72. *Prof Exp:* Asst prof, 73-77, assoc prof, 77-81, PROF GER, WASH UNIV, 81- *Concurrent Pos:* Vis prof Ger, Ind Univ, Bloomington, 72-73 & Tubingen Univ, 81; res fel Ger lit, Am Coun Learned Soc, 78; ed, complete works of Hermann Broch, 17 vols, 74-81; Guggenheim fel, 81 & Humboldt fel, 82. *Mem:* MLA; Am Asn Teachers Ger; Lessing Soc; Soc Study 18th Century. *Res:* European Romanticism; German Enlightenment; 20th century. *Publ:* Auth, Hermann Broch, Ethik und Politik, Munich, 73; co-ed, Nobility in German Literature, Stuttgart, 79; West German Literature since 1965, Konigstein, 80; ed, Novels of German Romanticism: New Essays, Stuttgart, 81; Europ--Visions of the European Romantics, Frankfurt, 82. *Mailing Add:* Dept of Ger Wash Univ St Louis MO 63130

LUXENBURG, NORMAN, b Cleveland, Ohio, Apr 15, 27; m 65; c 2. HISTORY, RUSSIAN. *Educ:* Univ Mich, BA, 49, 51, PhD, 56; Univ Md, MA, 50. *Prof Exp:* Assoc prof mod lang, Detroit Inst Technol, 56-59, Russ, Ill State Univ, 59-65 & hist, Purdue Univ, 65-67; PROF RUSS, UNIV IOWA, 67- *Mem:* AHA; Am Asn Teachers Slavic & E Europ Lang. *Publ:* Ed, Siege and Survival, 71 & auth, Europe since 1939, 73, Southern Ill Univ; Current Trends in Soviet Literature, Bks Abroad; Soviet agriculture since Khrushchev, Russ Rev; England and the Caucasus during Crimean War, In: Jahrbuecher Geschichte Osteuropas, Wiesbaden. *Mailing Add:* Dept of Russ Univ of Iowa Iowa City IA 52240

LUZAY, JOSEPH YUSUPH, b Kanina Valona, Albania, Feb 21, 14; m 36; c 6. CLASSICAL & MODERN LANGUAGES. *Educ:* Jesuit Fathers Col, Albania, BA, 30; Sorbonne, MA, 33, MS, 35, PhD(philos), 37. *Hon Degrees:* LittD, Sorbonne, 39; LLD, Univ Albania, 44. *Prof Exp:* Asst prof lang, Ecole Normale Superieure, Albania, 36-37 & high sch, Albania, 37-38; assoc prof, bus col, Valona, Albania, 38-44, Sem Cath, Brescia, Italy, 44-45 & State Univ, Buenos Aires, Arg, 45-65; teacher, Colebrook Acad, NJ, 67-68; prof & chmn foreign lang, Barat Col Sacred Heart, 68-69; assoc prof, 69-80, EMER PROF LANG, ST JOSEPH'S COL, IND, 80- *Concurrent Pos:* Vis prof lang, Univ St Marco's, Peru, 50, Univ Rio de Janeiro, 51 & Nat Univ Mex, 53; prof, Univ France, Buenos Aires, 50-67. *Mem:* AAUP; Am Coun Teaching Foreign Lang; Am Asn Teachers Span & Port; Am Asn Res Romance Lang (pres, 49-75); Pan-Albanian-Am Cult Asn Vatra (pres, 65-72). *Res:* Epistemology; origins of Romance languages; techniques of the revolutions. *Publ:* Auth, Historic Materialism: A Danger of the Western Civilization, Laterza Bari, Italy, 44; Los rios bajan rojos, 54, Problemas fundamentales de la philosophia, 57, Manual de psicologia, 60, Albanian-French and French-Albanian vocabulary, 62, Teoria de conocimiento: theory of knowledge, 63, Albania-Italian-Albanian vocabulary, 63 & Albanian-Spanish and Spanish-Albanian, 65, Ultramar, Buenos Aires. *Mailing Add:* Dept of Lang St Joseph's Col Rensselaer IN 47978

LUZBETAK, LOUIS JOSEPH, b Joliet, Ill, Sept 19, 18. LINGUISTIC ANALYSIS, CULTURAL ANTHROPOLOGY. *Educ:* Divine Word Sem, BA, 42; Pontif Gregorian Univ, STL, 46, JCB, 47; Univ Fribourg, PhD(anthrop), 51. *Prof Exp:* Prof anthrop, ling & missiology, Divine Word

Sem, Ill, 51-52, 56-58; lectr & summer asst prof appl anthrop, Cath Univ Am, 60-65; exec dir, Ctr Appl Res in Apostolate, Washington, DC, 65-73; pres, Divine Word Col, Iowa, 73-78; ED, ANTHROPOS, INT REV ETHNOLOGY & LING, 79- *Concurrent Pos:* Dir, Anthropos Inst, St Augustin bei Sieberg, WGer, 51-; Ford Found fel, 52-54; cult anthrop & ling field work, New Guinea, 52-56; lectr appl anthrop, Ctr Intercult Formation, Cuernavaca, Mex, 60-65; Ctr for Intercult Commun, Cath Univ PR, 60-65; rector, Divine Word Col, DC, 68-73; Walsh-Price fel, Ctr Mission Studies, Maryknoll, NY, 78-79. *Honors & Awards:* Pierre Charles Award, Fordham Univ, 64. *Mem:* Fel Am Anthrop Asn; Cath Anthrop Asn (vpres, 61-62, pres, 62-69); Ling Soc Am; Soc Appl Anthrop; Am Soc Missiology (pres, 75-76). *Publ:* Auth, Marriage and the Family in Caucasia, Studies Inst Anthrop, Moedling bei Wein, Austria, 51; Middle Wahgi Phonology, Oceania, Sydney, Australia, 56; The Church and Cultures: An Applied Anthropology for the Religious Worker, 63, 70, 76, 77 & ed, The Church in the Changing City, 66, Divine Word Publ; auth, Unity in diversity: Ethnotheological sensitivity in cross-cultural evangelism, 4/76 & Two centuries of cultural adaptation in American church action: Praise, censure or challenge?, 1/77, Missiology. *Mailing Add:* Anthropos Arnold-Janssen-Str 22 5205 Sankt Augustin 1 52045 Germany, Federal Republic of

LUZURIAGA, GERARDO, b Loja, Ecuador, July 20, 39; m 66; c 3. SPANISH AMERICAN LITERATURE. *Educ:* Cath Univ Quito, BA, 61; Cent Univ, Quito, dipl, 65; Univ Iowa, MA, 67, PhD(Span), 69. *Prof Exp:* Asst prof, 69-75, assoc prof, 75-81, PROF SPAN, UNIV CALIF, LOS ANGELES, 81- *Mem:* Inst Int Lit Iberoam; Int Asn Hispanists. *Res:* Spanish American theatre and drama; Spanish American poetry and prose fiction. *Publ:* Auth, Del Realismo Al Expresionismo: El Teatro de Aguilera-Malta, Plaza Mayor, Madrid, 71; co-ed & co-transl, The Orgy: Modern One-Act Plays from Latin America, Univ Calif, Latin Am Ctr, Los Angeles, 74; co-ed, Los Clasicos del Teatro Hispano-Americano, Fondo de Cult Economica, Mex, 75; ed, Popular Theater for Social Change in Latin America, Univ Calif, Latin Am Ctr, Los Angeles, 78; auth, Sigüenza y Gongora Y Sor Juana: Disidentes de la Cultural Oficial, Cuadernos Americanos, 82. *Mailing Add:* Dept Span & Port Univ Calif Los Angeles CA 90024

LYDAY, LEON FAIDHERBEE, III, b Danville, Va, Sept 24, 39; m 62; c 3. ROMANCE LANGUAGES. *Educ:* Univ NC, AB, 61, MA, 64, PhD(Romance lang), 66. *Prof Exp:* From asst prof to assoc prof, 66-76, PROF SPAN, PA STATE UNIV, UNIVERSITY PARK, 70- *Concurrent Pos:* Fulbright fel, Colombia, 61-62; ed assoc, Mod Int Drama, 67-; Am Philos Soc grant, 69; assoc ed, Hispania, 72-74. *Mem:* MLA; Am Asn Teachers Span & Port; Inst Int Lit Iberoam; Asn Int Hispanists. *Res:* Colombian literature; Latin American theatre; Spanish American poetry. *Publ:* Auth, Satire in the Comedies of Martin Pena, Luso-Brazilian Rev, 68; History and legend in El virrey Solis of Antonio Alvarez Lleras, Hispania, 69; The Colombian theatre before 1800, Latin Am Theatre Rev, 70; co-ed, Ancha es Castilla, Van Nostrand, 71; auth, Egon Wolff's Los invasores: A play within a dream, Latin Am Theatre Rev, 72; co-ed, En un acto: Nueve piezas Hispanoamericanas, Van Nostrand, 74; coauth, Dramatists in Revolt: The New Latin American Theatre, Univ Tex, 75; Bibliography of Latin American Theatre Criticism, Univ Tex, 76. *Mailing Add:* Dept of Span Pa State Univ University Park PA 16802

LYNCH, JOHN PATRICK, b Great Barrington, Mass, Aug 30, 43; m 73; C 2. CLASSICS. *Educ:* Harvard Col, BA, 65; Yale Univ, MA, 68, MPhil, 69, PhD(class philol), 70. *Prof Exp:* Asst prof, 70-73, ASSOC PROF CLASSICS, COWELL COL, UNIV CALIF, SANTA CRUZ, 74- *Concurrent Pos:* Jr fel, Harvard Univ, Ctr Hellenic Studies, Washington DC, 76-77; assoc dir, Univ Calif Study Ctr, London, 79-81. *Mem:* Am Philol Asn; Hellenic Soc; Vergilian Soc. *Res:* History of education; Greek philosophy; Greek and Roman poetry. *Publ:* Auth, Aristotle's School: A Study of a Greek Educational Institution, Univ Calif, 72. *Mailing Add:* Cowell Col Univ of Calif Santa Cruz CA 95064

LYNCH, THEOPHILUS S, b Philadelphia, Pa, Jan 2, 23. MODERN LANGUAGES. *Educ:* Williams Col, AB, 47; Univ Pa, AM, 51, PhD, 59. *Prof Exp:* Instr French & Span, Williams Col, 47-48; asst instr, Univ Pa, 48-53, 54-55; teacher Span, Bryn Mawr Col, 52-53; instr French & Span, Denison Univ, 53-54 & mod lang, Princeton Univ, 55-57; asst prof Romance lang, Rutgers Univ, 59-61 & Span, Ohio Univ, 62-65; asosc prof, 66-72, PROF SPAN & COMP LIT, UNIV MICH-FLINT, 72- *Concurrent Pos:* Rev ed, J Afro-Am Affairs, 77-80. *Mem:* MLA; Am Asn Teachers Span & Port. *Res:* Spanish literature of the Renaissance; modern Brazilian novel; psychic phenomena in Latin-American literature. *Publ:* Auth, El segundo libro de las eneydas of Francisco de las Natas, 10/67 & More on Francisco de las Natas and a note on Sonces, 1/72, Hisp Rev; The psychic sciences, Flint J, 6/80. *Mailing Add:* Dept of Foreign Lang Univ of Mich Flint MI 48503

LYNES, CARLOS, JR, b Atlanta, Ga, Feb 20, 10. FRENCH LITERATURE. *Educ:* Emory Univ, AB, 32, AM, 34; Princeton Univ, AM & PhD, 39. *Prof Exp:* Teacher prep schs, 34-36 & 42-45; instr French, Loyola Univ, La, 38-39 & Princeton Univ, 39-42; from instr to prof, 45-75, EMER PROF FRENCH, UNIV PA, 75- *Concurrent Pos:* Fulbright res grant, France, 55-56; vis prof Romance lang, Johns Hopkins Univ, 66-67. *Mem:* MLA; Int Asn Fr Studies; Asn Int Etude Dada & Surrealisme. *Res:* Crevel; surrealism; 20th century French poetry. *Publ:* Auth, Chateaubriand as a Critic of French Literature, Johns Hopkins Univ, 46; coauth, Camus's L'Etranger, Appleton, 55; auth, Rene Crevel Vivant, Ed Subervie, 56; Solitude de Rene Crevel, Fr Studies, 4/58; Jean Cayrol, In: The Novelist as Philosopher, Oxford Univ, 62; Surrealism and the novel: Breton's Nadja, Fr Studies, 10/66; Production et theorie romanesques chez Philippe Sollers: Lecture du Parc, Ky Romance Quart, 73; Ecrire/mecrire (poetique et antipoetique chez Denis Roche), Fr Forum, 1/77. *Mailing Add:* 52 Quai de Jemmapes 75010 Paris France

LYON, JAMES KARL, b Rotterdam, Holland, Feb 17, 34; US citizen; m 59. GERMANIC LANGUAGES & LITERATURES. *Educ:* Univ Utah, BA, 58, MA, 59; Harvard Univ, PhD, 63. *Prof Exp:* Instr Ger, Harvard Univ, 62-63, asst prof, 66-71; from assoc prof to prof, Univ Fla, 71-74; PROF GER, UNIV

CALIF, SAN DIEGO, 74-, ASSOC DEAN GRAD SCH, 77- *Concurrent Pos:* Nat Endowment for Humanities younger humanist fel, 70-71; Guggenheim Found fel, 74-75. *Mem:* MLA; Am Asn Teachers Ger; Brecht Soc. *Res:* Twentieth century German literature; German exile literature; German lyric poetry. *Publ:* Auth, Paul Celan and Martin Buber: poetry as dialogue, PMLA, 1/71; coauth, Konkordanz zur Lyrik Gottfried Benns, Georg Olms, 71; auth, Bertolt Brecht's Hollywood years: The dramatist as film writer, Oxford Ger Studies, 71-72; Paul Celan's language of stone: The geology of the poetic landscape, Colloquia Germanica, 74; Brecht und die New Yorker Theatre Union Briefwechsel, 1935, Brecht-Jahrbuch, 75; Bertolt Brecht and Rudyard Kipling: A Marxist's Imperialist Mentor, Mouton, The Hague, 75; Lyrik am Rande der Sprache: Von den Konkretisten zu Paul Celan, Leistungen Moderner Lyrik, 77; Bertolt Brecht's American Cicerone, Bouvier, 78. *Mailing Add:* Dept of Lit B-001 Univ of Calif San Diego La Jolla CA 92093

LYON, THOMAS EDGAR, JR, b Salt Lake City, Utah, May 13, 39; m 62; c 5. ROMANCE LANGUAGES, LATIN AMERICAN LITERATURE. *Educ:* Univ Utah, BA, 63; Univ Salamanca, dipl, 63; Univ Calif, Los Angeles, PhD(Latin Am lit), 67. *Prof Exp:* Asst prof, Univ Okla, 67-69; asst prof, Univ Wis-Madison, 69-72; dir Latin Am Studies, 75-79, PROF SPAN, BRIGHAM YOUNG UNIV, 72- *Concurrent Pos:* Founder of jour Chasqui, Wis, 72; Nat Endowment for Humanities fel, 68. *Mem:* MLA; Am Asn Teachers Span & Port. *Res:* Chicano literature and culture; 20th century Latin American prose and religion in Latin American literature; Golden Age Spanish literature. *Publ:* Auth, Miguel Angel Asturias: Timeless fantasy, Bks Abroad, spring 68; Orderly objections to symbolic imaging: The Latin American novel from 1920-1960, Hispania, 9/71; Martin Fierro y la narracion fluctuante como clave de interpre, Palabra Hernandista 9/72; Borges and the (somewhat) personal narrator, Mod Fiction Studies, autumn 73; Ontological motifs in the short stories of J Rulfo, J Span Studies: 20th Century, winter 73; Heresy as motif in the short stories of Borges, Latin Am Lit Rev, fall 74; El engano de la razon: Quiroga, Borges, Cortazar, Vinas, Texto Critico, 5-8/76; Loss of innocence in Chicano prose, Critical Approaches to Chicano Lit, 3/78. *Mailing Add:* 3008 North 175 East Provo UT 84601

LYONS, JOHN DAVID, b Springfield, Mass, Oct 14, 46; m 71. ROMANCE LANGUAGES & LITERATURES. *Educ:* Brown Univ, AB, 67; Yale Univ, MA, 68, PhD(French), 72. *Prof Exp:* ASST PROF FRENCH & ITALIAN, DARTMOUTH COL, 72- *Mem:* MLA; Am Asn Teachers Fr; NAm Soc 17th Century Fr Lit. *Res:* Seventeenth century French literature; literary theory; French and Italian cinema. *Publ:* Auth, Saint-Amant's La Solitude, OL, 78; Temporality in the Lyrics of Theophile de Viau, Australian J Fr Studies, 79; L'Economie des marques dan La Princesse de Cleves, NM, 80; The Cartesian Reader and the Methodic Subject, Essays in Criticism, 81; Being and Meaning: The Example of the Honnete Text, PFSCL, 82; Narrative, Interpretation and Paradox, RR, 81; Truth and Authority: Corneille's Le Menteur, PFSCL, 82; Subjectivity and Imitation in the Discours de la Methode, Neophil, 82. *Mailing Add:* Dept of French & Italian Dartmouth Col Hanover NH 03755

LYOVIN, ANATOLE VLADIMIROVICH, b Leskovats, Yugoslavia, Nov 13, 38; US citizen; m 63; c 2. CHINESE LINGUISTICS, PHONOLOGY. *Educ:* Princeton Univ, AB, 64; Univ Calif, Berkeley, PhD(ling), 72. *Prof Exp:* Asst prof, 68-73, ASSOC PROF LING, UNIV HAWAII, MANOA, 73- *Concurrent Pos:* Co-prin investr, Northwest Lang Relationships Proj, Pac & Asian Ling Inst, 72-73. *Mem:* Ling Soc Am. *Res:* Phonological change; historical phonology of Chinese; northwest Amerindian languages. *Publ:* Auth, Notes on the addition of final stops in Maru, 6/68; A Chinese dialect dictionary on computer: Progress report, Proj Ling Anal Reports, 6/68; co-ed, CLIBOC: Chinese Linguistics Bibliography on Computers, Cambridge Univ, 70; auth, Sound change, homophony and lexical diffusion, Proj Ling Analy Reports, 11/71. *Mailing Add:* Dept of Ling Univ of Hawaii at Manoa Honolulu HI 96822

LYTLE, ELDON GREY, b Cedar City, Utah, June 6, 36; m 59; c 7. LINGUISTICS. *Educ:* Brigham Young Univ, BA, 61, MA, 62; Univ Ill, Urbana-Champaign, PhD(Slavic ling), 71. *Prof Exp:* From instr to asst prof ling, Brigham Young Univ, 68-73, assoc prof, 74-80. *Concurrent Pos:* Dir automatic lang processing res & develop proj, Brigham Young Univ, 70- *Mem:* Asn Comput Ling. *Res:* Theoretical, computational and contrastive linguistics. *Publ:* Auth, A Grammar of Subordinate Structures in English, Mouton, The Hague, 74; Remarks on the structure of discourse, 72 & An analysis of non-verbal participles, 73, Proc Brigham Young Univ Ling Symp. *Mailing Add:* 1258 Jordon Ave Provo UT 84601

LYTLE, EVELYN POMROY, b Indiana, Pa, Dec 5, 20. SPANISH & PORTUGUESE LITERATURE & LANGUAGE. *Educ:* Ind Univ Pa, BS, 43; Princeton Theol Sem, MA, 47; Tulane Univ, PhD(Span & Port), 67. *Prof Exp:* Instr Span & Port, Univ New Orleans, 58-65; asst prof Span, Randolph-Macon Woman's Col, 65-67; asst prof, 67-71, assoc prof, 71-78, PROF SPAN & PORT, UNIV NEW ORLEANS, 78- *Concurrent Pos:* Vis prof English, Pontif Univ Sao Paulo, 50-51; ed & transl, IIAA Washington Notes, US Dept of State, 52-53; Brazilian Ministry of Foreign Affairs scholar, 53-54; Fulbright scholar, 62; Ford Venture Fund grant, 75; off of educ, Nat Adv Coun on Biling Educ, 74-77 & chmn, 76-77; consult, Judicial Conf, US Bicentennial Comt, 77. *Mem:* MLA; Dante Soc Am; Renaissance Soc Am. *Res:* Spanish and Portuguese literature of the Renaissance and Baroque periods. *Publ:* Auth, Os Novissimos do homen: um poema biblico da epica portuguesa, Univ Sao Paulo, 70; The Coimbra Ms 362 of Quevedo's Manzanares, Manzanares, 77 & Three manuscripts of Quevedo's Manzanares, Manzanares: Unpublished Ajuda Codex, 51-VI-2; Evora Codex CXIV/1-3; and Ajuda Codex 52-IX-27, 82, Romance Notes, Univ NC. *Mailing Add:* 6169 Paris Ave #100 New Orleans LA 70122

M

MA, SEN, b Jinan, China, Sept 4, 32; m 63; c 2. CHINESE LANGUAGE & LITERATURE. *Educ:* Taiwan Norm Univ, BA, 55, MA, 59; Univ BC, PhD(sociol), 77. *Prof Exp:* Teacher Chinese lit, Dajia High Sch, Taichung, Taiwan, 55-56; lectr Chinese lang, Mandarin Training Ctr, Taiwan Norm Univ, 57-60, asst prof Chinese lit, Dept Chinese, 59-60; prof Chinese lang, Ctr Studies & Res Ling, Paris, 63-66; prof Chinese lang & lit, Ctr Orient Studies, Col Mex, 67-73; asst prof Chinese, Univ Alberta, 77-78; asst prof, Univ Victoria, 78-79. *Mem:* Asn Asian Studies; Am Acad Polit & Soc Sci; Can Soc Asian Studies. *Res:* Chinese short story, novel, modern drama and fiction; people's communes in China. *Publ:* Auth, Bibliography of Chuang-tse, J Chinese Lit Res Inst, Taiwan, 58; On Lao She's novels, Ming Pao Monthly, Hong Kong, 71; Sketches of the French Society, Col Life, Hong Kong, 72; coauth, La casa de los liu y otros cuentos, Col Mex, 73; auth, A Collection of Plays, Lien-ching, Taipei, 78; Living in a Vase, Four Seasons, Taipei, 78; Mao Tse-tung y la literatura: teoria y practica, Estudios Orientales, Vol VI, No 1. *Mailing Add:* 349 E 55th Ave Vancouver BC V5X 1N2 Can

MA, YAU-WOON, b Hong Kong, Sept 7, 40; Brit citizen; m 68; c 2. CHINESE LITERATURE, BIBLIOGRAPHY. *Educ:* Univ Hong Kong, BA, 65; Yale Univ, PhD(Chinese lit), 71. *Prof Exp:* Actg asst prof Chinese lit, 70-71, asst prof, 71-76, ASSOC PROF CHINESE LIT, UNIV HAWAII, MANOA, 76- *Mem:* MLA; Am Orient Soc; Asn Asian Studies; Chinese Lang Teachers Asn. *Res:* Traditional Chinese fiction; traditional Chinese prose. *Publ:* Coauth, On the dates of the stories in the Ching-pen t'ung-su hsiao-shuo and the authenticity of the collection, Tsing-hua J Chinese Studies, 7/65; auth, Prose writings of Han Yu and Ch'uan-ch'i literature, J Orient Studies, 7/69; Themes and characterization in the Lung-t'u kung-an, T'oung Pao, 73. *Mailing Add:* Dept of E Asian Lit Univ of Hawaii at Manoa Honolulu HI 96822

MACADAM, ALFRED JOHN, b Nov 2, 41; US citizen; m 68; c 2. LATIN AMERICAN LITERATURE, COMPARATIVE LITERATURE. *Educ:* Rutgers Univ, BA, 63; Princeton Univ, MA, 65, PhD(Latin Am lit), 69. *Prof Exp:* From instr to asst prof Span, Princeton Univ, 66-70; from asst prof to assoc prof, Yale Univ, 70-77; ASSOC PROF SPAN, UNIV VA, 77- *Concurrent Pos:* Contrib ed, Handbk Latin Am Studies, Libr Cong, 76- *Mem:* Inst Int Lit Iberoam; MLA. *Res:* Literary theory. *Publ:* Auth, Modern Latin American Narratives: The Dreams of Reason, Univ Chicago, 77. *Mailing Add:* 1710 King Mountain Rd Charlottesville VA 22901

MACADOO, THOMAS OZRO, b Pulaski, Va, Oct 28, 22. CLASSICAL LANGUAGES, GERMAN. *Educ:* Roanoke Col, BA, 43; Univ Ill, Urbana, MA, 47, PhD(class philol), 52. *Prof Exp:* Instr classics, Univ Ill, 54-56; vis lectr, Univ NMex, 56-57; from instr to asst prof English & Ger, 58-68, assoc prof Ger, 68-77, ASSOC PROF LATIN & GREEK, VA POLYTECH INST & STATE UNIV, 77-, DIR LANG LAB, 63- *Concurrent Pos:* Consult, Va State Bd Educ, 67- *Mem:* Am Philol Asn; Am Asn Teachers Ger. *Res:* Grammatical terminology. *Mailing Add:* Dept of Foreign Lang Va Polytech Inst & State Univ Blacksburg VA 24601

MACARY, JEAN LOUIS, b Paris, France, Jan 26, 31; m 59; c 3. FRENCH LITERATURE. *Educ:* Sorbonne, Lic Lett & dipl etudes super, 54, Agregation Lett, 62. *Prof Exp:* Asst French lit, Sorbonne, 65-68; lectr, Princeton Univ, 69-70, asst prof, 70-76; assoc prof, 76-80, PROF FRENCH LIT & CHMN DEPT FORDHAM UNIV, 80- *Mem:* Am Soc 18th Century Studies; Int Soc Studies 18th Century; MLA. *Res:* Seventeenth & 18th century French literature; history of ideas. *Publ:* Ed, Voltaire, Faceties, Presses Univ, France, 73; auth, Mas que et lumieres au XVIIIe: A-F2 des landes, citoyen et philosophe, 1689-1757, Nijhoff, The Hague, 75; ed, Essays on the Age of Enlightenment, In Honor of Ira O Wade, Droz, Geneva, 77. *Mailing Add:* Dept of Mod Lang Fordham Univ Bronx NY 10458

MACBAIN, WILLIAM, b Murthly, Scotland, May 21, 30; m; c 1. MEDIEVAL FRENCH LANGUAGE & LITERATURE. *Educ:* Univ St Andrews, MA, 52, PhD(medieval French), 55. *Prof Exp:* Actg asst lectr French & Ger, Univ Otago, NZ, 55-56, lectr, 56-60; sr lectr French, Univ Melbourne, 60-64; assoc prof, Univ Wis-Milwaukee, 64-67; chmn dept French & Ital, 68-76, PROF FRENCH, UNIV MD, COLLEGE PARK, 67- *Concurrent Pos:* Univ NZ Res Found travel grant, 57-58. *Mem:* Anglo-Norman Text Soc; Soc Anciens Textes Francais; MLA. *Res:* Medieval French; Anglo-Norman; 17th century French literature. *Publ:* Auth, Literary apprenticeship of Clemence Barking, J Australasian Univ Lang & Lit Asn, 58; Life of St Catherine, Oxford Univ, 64. *Mailing Add:* Dept of French & Ital Univ of Md College Park MD 20742

MCCALL, MARSH HOWARD, JR, b New York, NY, Mar 11, 39; m 60; c 3. CLASSICS. *Educ:* Harvard Univ, BA, 60, PhD(class philol), 65. *Prof Exp:* Instr classics, Harvard Univ, 65-68, jr fel, Ctr Hellenic Studies, 68-69; from asst prof to assoc prof classics, Johns Hopkins Univ, 69-75, chmn dept, 71-73 & 77-80; assoc prof, 76-81, assoc dean undergrad studies, 78-80, PROF CLASSICS & CHMN DEPT, STANFORD UNIV, 81- . *Concurrent Pos:* Assoc ed, Am J Philol, 70-75; Am Coun Learned Soc fel, 73-74; vis prof Greek, Univ Col, Univ London, 73-74; vis assoc prof classics, Univ Calif, Berkeley, 75-76; Fulbright sr scholar, Univ Melbourne, 80. *Mem:* Am Philol Asn; Archaeol Inst Am; Hellenic Soc. *Res:* Greek literature; Greek tragedy; ancient rhetoric and literary criticism. *Publ:* Auth, Ancient Rhetorical Theories of Simile and Comparisn, Harvard Univ, 69; ed & contribr, Aeschylus, a Collection of Critical Essays, Prentice-Hall, 72; auth, Divine and human action in Sophocles: The two burials of the Antigone, Yale Class Studies, 72; Sophocles' Trachiniae: Structure, focus and Heracles, Am J Philol, 72; The principal source of Robortello's Edition of Scholia to Aeschylus' Supplices, Bull Inst Class Studies, 75; The secondary choruses in Aeschylus' Supplices, Calif Studies Class Antiquity, 76; The sources of Robortello's Edition of Aeschylus' Supplices, Bull Inst Class Studies, 81. *Mailing Add:* Dept of Classics Stanford Univ Stanford CA 94305

MCCANN, DAVID RICHARD, b Lewiston, Maine, July 1, 44; m 68; c 2. KOREAN & JAPANESE LITERATURE. *Educ:* Amherst Col, BA, 66; Harvard Univ, MA, 71, PhD(Korean lit), 76. *Prof Exp:* Asst prof, Cornell Univ, 76-77, asst prof Japanese lit, 78-79; staff writer, 79-80, ASST DIR FEDN RELS, UNIV DEVELOP, 80- *Honors & Awards:* Pushcart Prize, Pushcart Prize Anthology III, 78. *Mem:* Asn for Asian Studies; Asn Teachers of Japanese (secy, 78-); Poetry Soc of Am; Poets & Writers, Inc. *Res:* Japanese and Korean verse literature; modern poetry. *Publ:* Ed & contribr, Black Crane: An Anthology of Korean Literature, Cornell Univ EAsian Papers, 11/77; auth, Arirang: The national folksong of Korea & co-ed & contribr, Studies on Korea in Transition, Univ of Hawaii, (in press); The Middle Hour: Selected Poems of Kim Chi Ha, Stanfordville, 80; Keeping Time, Troubadour Press, 81; Winter sky: The selected poems of So Chongju, Quart Rev Lit, New Poetry Series III, 81. *Mailing Add:* 726 University Ave Univ Develop Ithaca NY 14850

MCCARREN, VINCENT PAUL, b New York, NY, Mar 22, 39; m 68. CLASSICAL STUDIES, MEDIEVAL LITERATURE. *Educ:* Fordham Univ, AB, 60; Columbia Univ, AM, 67; Univ Mich, PhD(class studies), 75. *Prof Exp:* Lectr Greek & Latin, Brooklyn Col, 63-68; instr, Hunter Col, 68-69, class lang & lit, Herbert H Lehman Col, 69-70; lectr Greek & Latin, 75-76, acad coun gen acad areas, 77-78, RESEARCHER, MIDDLE ENGLISH DICT, UNIV MICH, 79- *Mem:* Am Soc Papyrologists; Am Philol Soc. *Res:* Documentary papyrology; Greek and Latin etymological studies. *Publ:* Ed (cum aliis), Auctoris Incerti de Physiognomonia Libellus, Paris, 81; auth, A Critical Concordance to Catullus, Leiden, 77; Michigan Papyrl XIV, Scholars Press, Chico, Calif, 81; ed, Notated readings in Berichtigungsliste der Griechischen Papyrusurkunden aus Ägypten, Leiden (in press); coauth, Ergänzende Bemerkungen zu P Mich XIV 675, ZPE (in prep). *Mailing Add:* Middle English Dict 555 S Forest Ann Arbor MI 48104

MCCARTHY, JOHN ALOYSIUS, b St Clair, Mich, Jan 9, 42; m 65; c 2. GERMAN. *Educ:* Oakland Univ, BA, 64; State Univ NY Buffalo, MA, 67, PhD(Ger), 72. *Hon Degrees:* AM, Univ Pa. 79. *Prof Exp:* Instr Ger, Oakland Univ, 69-72; asst prof, 72-78, ASSOC PROF GER, UNIV PA, 79- *Concurrent Pos:* Ed, Ger Sect, ECCB, 77-80; undergrad chmn, Univ Pa, 73-75; Am Philos Soc grant, 77, Pa res found fel, 82. *Mem:* Am Lessing Soc; Am Asn 18th Century Studies; Am Asn Teachers Ger; MLA; Deutsche Schiller Gesellschaft. *Res:* Eighteenth century German and European literature; Christoph Martin Wieland; eighteenth century reading habits. *Publ:* Auth, Fantasy and Reality: An Epistemological Approach to Wieland, Herbert Lang, Bern, 74; Wielands metamorphose?, Deutsche Vierteljahresschrift Litgesch, 75; Some aspects of imagery in Büchners Woyzeck, Mod Lang Notes, 76; Wieland as essayist, Lessing Yearbk, 76; Shaftesbury and Wieland: The question of enthusiasm, SECC, 77; Die republikanische Freiheit des Lesers Zum Lesepublikum von Schillers, In: Der Verbrecher aus verlorener Ehre, Wirkendes Wort, 78; C M Wieland, Twayne, 79; The poet as journalist and essayist, Vol XII, No 1 & Vol XIII, No 1, JIG. *Mailing Add:* Dept of Ger Lang Univ of Pa 745 Williams Hall Philadelphia PA 19174

MCCARTHY, KEVIN MICHAEL, Linguistics, American Literature. See Vol II

MCCARTHY, MARY FRANCES, b Springfield, Mass, July 25, 16. FOREIGN LANGUAGES & LITERATURE. *Educ:* Trinity Col, DC, AB, 37; Cath Univ Am, AM, 38; Johns Hopkins Univ, PhD, 61. *Prof Exp:* Teachers Latin & English, Archdiocesan High Schs, Phila, Pa, 41-56; instr English, Trinity Col, DC, 57-59, from asst prof to prof Ger & Russ, 60-75; pres, Emmanuel Col, Mass, 75-78; dir found res, 78-80, SECY COL, TRINITY COL, DC, 81- *Concurrent Pos:* Chmn southern sect, Nat Screening Comt for Fulbright fels to Ger, 73, NCent sect, 73; Nat Endowment for Humanities sr fel, 72-73. *Res:* Mediaeval German literature; Nibelungenlied. *Publ:* Contribr, New Cath Encycl, McGraw, 67; translr, Paul Konrad Kurz, On Modern German Literature, Univ Ala, Vol I, 70, Vol II, 71, Vol III, 73, Vol IV, 77; Siegmund, Buddhism and Christianity, The Christian State of Life, Balthasar (in press). *Mailing Add:* Trinity Col Washington DC 20017

MCCARTHY, MARY SUSAN, b Cleveland, Ohio, July 24, 49. FRENCH LITERATURE & LANGUAGE. *Educ:* Marygrove Col, BA, 71; Univ Wis-Madison, MA, 72, PhD(French lit), 77. *Prof Exp:* ASST PROF FRENCH, HOPE COL, 77- *Concurrent Pos:* Mellon Found grant res, Hope Col, 78; dir, ALM/GLCA prog in Humanities, Newberry Libr, 80-81. *Mem:* MLA; Am Asn Teachers French. *Res:* Nineteenth century French novel, especially Balzac's Comedie Humaine; reader-oriented criticism; historical writing in the literary mode. *Publ:* Auth, Balzac and his reader: A study of the creation of meaning in La Comedie Humaine, Univ Mo Press (in press). *Mailing Add:* Dept of Foreign Lang & Lit Hope Col Holland MI 49423

MCCARTHY, MARY THERESA, b Plainfield, NJ, Aug 13, 27. FRENCH LANGUAGE & LITERATURE. *Educ:* Georgian Court Col, BA, 57; Laval Univ, MA, 65; Inst Cath Paris, dipl d'Etudes Francaises, 67; Sorbonne, dipl cult Francaise contemp, 67; Rutgers Univ, PhD(French), 73. *Prof Exp:* Teacher Latin, Mt St Mary Acad, North Plainfield, NJ, 45-46; teacher social studies, St Mary Sch, South Amboy, NJ, 47-49; teacher prim grades, Cathedral Grammar Sch, Trenton, 49-56; teacher mid grades, St Matthew Sch, Edison, 56-57; teacher Latin & French, Holy Spirit High Sch, Atlantic City, 57-59; instr French, 59-75, PROF FRENCH, GEORGIAN COURT COL, 75- *Concurrent Pos:* Fulbright Scholar French, Univ Paris, 66-67; Nat Endowment Humanities fel comp lit, Univ Chicago, 75; reader, advan placement tests French lang, Educ Testing Serv, 76-; Exxon Educ Found grant lang model workshop, Dartmouth Col, 77; assoc Danforth Found, 78-84; Nat Endowment for Humanities fel French lit, Princeton Univ, 79; sr lang consult, Rassias Found, 79-; writer, Col Bd French Achievement Test, 80; consult, NJ Comt for Humanities, 80-81. *Mem:* MLA; Am Asn Teachers French; Am Translr Asn; Asn Amis Fonds Documentation Henri-Bosco. *Res:* Modern French literature, especially the modern French novel, most especially Henri Bosco's dream novels. *Publ:* Contribr, The Adventures of

Pascalet, Oxford Univ, 76; Historic Houses of New Jersey, William H Wise & Co, 77; Culotte the Donkey, Oxford Univ, 78; auth, Winter Idyl (poem), Poet Lore, spring 78; Today Never Came (poem), Revue de Louisiane/La Rev, fall 78; Autumn Passion (poem), NJ Poetry Monthly, 10/78; Faith on Easter Morn (poem), 4/81 & Autumn Air (poem), 10/81, Villager. *Mailing Add:* Georgian Court Col Lakewood NJ 08701

MCCARUS, ERNEST NASSEPH, b Charleston, WVa, Sept 10, 22; m 55; c 2. LINGUISTICS. *Educ:* Univ Mich, BA, 45, MA, 49, PhD(ling), 56. *Prof Exp:* From instr to assoc prof, 52-67, chmn dept, 69-77, PROF NEAR EASTERN STUDIES, UNIV MICH, ANN ARBOR, 67-, DIR, CTR ARABIC STUDY ABROAD, 74- *Concurrent Pos:* Ed, Newslett, Am Asn Teachers Arabic, 67-70; mem, MLA Task Force on Uncommonly Taught Lang, 77-78. *Mem:* Ling Soc Am; Am Orient Soc; MidE Studies Asn NAm; Am Asn Teachers Arabic (pres, 73). *Res:* Arabic linguistics; Kurdish linguistics. *Publ:* Auth, Kurdish Grammar, Am Coun Learned Soc, 58; ed, Contemporary Arabic Readers, 60-64; auth, A Kurdish-English Dict, 67, coauth, Kurdish Basic Course, 67 & Newspaper Kurdish, Vol I, Kurdish essays, Vol II & Kurdish short stories, Vol III, In: Kurdish Readers, 67, Univ Mich; Elementary Modern Standard Arabic, Univ Mich, 68; co-ed, Word Count of Elementary Modern Literary Arabic Textbooks, 69, Modern Standard Arabic, Intermediate Level, 72 & auth, A semantic analysis of Arabic verbs, In: Michigan Oriental Studies in Honor of George G Cameron, 76, Univ Mich. *Mailing Add:* Dept of Near Eastern Studies Univ of Mich 3085 Frieze Bldg Ann Arbor MI 48109

MCCASH, JUNE HALL, b Newberry, SC, June 8, 38; m 74; c 2. MEDIEVAL FRENCH & COMPARATIVE LITERATURE. *Educ:* Anges Scott Col, AB, 60; Emory Univ, MA, 63, PhD(comp lit), 67. *Prof Exp:* Instr French & humanities, Emory Univ, 64-67; from asst prof to assoc prof French, 67-75, dir hon prog, 73-80, PROF FRENCH, MID TENN STATE UNIV, 75-, CHAIRPERSON, DEPT FOREIGN LANG, 80- *Concurrent Pos:* Nat Endowment for Humanities younger humanist fel, 75, sem, 78. *Mem:* MLA; SAtlantic Mod Lang Asn; Societe Rencesvals; Medieval Acad Am; Int Courtly Lit Soc. *Res:* Medieval literature; epic, courtly romance. *Publ:* Auth, The divisions of the Chanson de Roland, Romance Notes, spring 65; Order, morality, and justice as traditional epic themes: a comparison of the Cantar de Mio Cid with the Odyssey and the Chanson de Roland, Southern Humanities Rev, fall 67; Love's Fools: Aucassin, Troilus, Calisto and the Parody of the Courtly Lover, Tamesis, London, 72; Eleanor of Aquitaine and Marie de Champagne: A Relationship Reexamined, Speculum, 79; Scientia and Sapientia in the Chansonde Roland, Medievalia et Humanistica, 82. *Mailing Add:* Box 79 Mid Tenn State Univ Murfreesboro TN 37132

MCCAWLEY, JAMES D, b Glasgow, Scotland, Mar 30, 38; US citizen. LINGUISTICS. *Educ:* Univ Chicago, MS, 58; Mass Inst Technol, PhD(ling), 65. *Prof Exp:* Asst prof ling, 64-70, PROF LING, UNIV CHICAGO, 70- *Mem:* Ling Soc Am; Soc Exact Philos; Asn Teachers of Japanese. *Res:* Semantics; structure of English and Japanese. *Publ:* Auth, The Phonological Component of a Grammar of Japanese, Mouton, The Hauge, 68; Conversational implicature and the lexicon, In: Pragmatics, Academic Press, 78; Adverbs, Vowels, and Other Objects of Wonder, Univ Chicago Press, 79; Everything that Linguistics have Always Wanted to Know About Logic, Univ Chicago Press, 82; An un-syntax, In Current Approaches to Syntax, Academic Press, 82; The syntax and semantics of English relative clauses, Lingua, Vol 53, 81; Thirty Million Theories of Grammar, Croom Helm, 82. *Mailing Add:* Dept of Ling Univ of Chicago Chicago IL 60637

MCCAWLEY, NORIKO AKATSUKA, b Kyoto, Japan, Mar 17, 37; m 72. LINGUISTICS. *Educ:* Doshisha Univ, BA, 59; Univ Ill, MA, 69, PhD(ling), 72. *Prof Exp:* Instr Japanese & ling, Ohio State Univ, 71-72; asst prof, 72-78, ASSOC PROF LING, UNIV CHICAGO, 78- *Mem:* Ling Soc Am; Asn for Asian Studies; Mod Lang & Lit Asn; Asn Teachers Japanese. *Res:* Epistenese and English. *Publ:* Auth, Boy! Is syntax easy!, Papers from Nineth Chicago Ling Soc, 4/73; A Study of Japanese Reflexivization & On experiencer causatives, Academic, 76; Review of Kuno's The Structure of the Japanese Language, Lang, 76; From OE/ME impersonal to modern English personal constructions: What is a subject-less sentence?, Papers from 12th Chicago Ling Soc Parasession Diachronic Syntax, 76; What is the emphatic root transformation phenomenon?, Papers from 13th Chicago Ling Soc, 77; Another look at No, Koto and To: Epistemology and complementizer choice in Japanese, Kaitakusha, Tokyo, 78. *Mailing Add:* 1010 E 59th St Goodspeed Hall 105 Univ Chicago Chicago IL 60637

MCCLAIN, M PATRICK, b Wilmerding, Pa, Nov 30, 11. ROMANCE LANGUAGES. *Educ:* Mt Mercy Col, BA, 38; Cath Univ Am, MA, 42; Univ Laval, cert, 51; Fordham Univ, PhD(French), 57. *Prof Exp:* High sch teacher Latin & Span, Our Lady of Mercy Acad, Pa, 36-43; instr French & Span, Carlow Col, 46-49, assoc prof French, 51-74, chmn dept Romance lang, 51-56, dir studies, Carlow Col & St Mary's, 57-63, prof mod Lang, 74-78, acad vpres & dean instr, 63-74. *Concurrent Pos:* Dir personnel, Congregation Sisters of Mercy, 75-78; med librn, Holy Cross Hosp, 78-82. *Honors & Awards:* Pres Award for Distinguished Serv, Carlow Col, 74. *Mem:* Am Asn Teachers Fr; Asn High Educ. *Res:* Modern French theatre; the theatre of Francois Mauriac. *Mailing Add:* Carlow Col 3333 Fifth Ave Pittsburgh PA 15213

MCCLAIN, WILLIAM H, b Cleveland, Ohio, July 22, 17. GERMAN LITERATURE. *Educ:* Western Reserve Univ, AB, 39; Univ Wis, AM, 40, PhD, 43. *Prof Exp:* Instr Ger, Univ Wis, 43-44 & French, 44-45; Am vconsul, foreign serv, US Dept State, 45-46; from instr to asst prof Ger, Harvard Univ, 46-53; assoc prof, 53-63, chmn humanities group, 68-70, chmn dept, 73-80, PROF GER, JOHNS HOPKINS UNIV, 63- *Concurrent Pos:* Ed, Mod Lang Notes, 54-81. *Honors & Awards:* Lindback Distinguished Teaching Award, Johns Hopkins Univ, 62. *Mem:* Am Asn Teachers Ger; MLA; Goethe Soc (pres, 54-56); SAtlantic Mod Lang Asn. *Res:* Nineteenth and 20th century German literature; history of publication; Rezeptionsgeschichte. *Publ:* Co-auth, Deutsch, Holt, 57; auth, Between Real and Ideal, 63 & Immermann's protrait of a folk-hero, In: Festschrift for F E Coenen, 70, Univ NC; coauth, Karl Gutzkows Briefe an Hermann Costenoble, In: Archiv für Geschichtes des Buchwesens, Frankfut/Main, 71; co-ed, Festschrift for H Jantz, Delp, Munich, 72; auth, Stefan George's Hyperion, In: Festschrift for G Loose, Bern, Francke, 74; coauth, Friedrich Gerstäckers Briefe an Hermann Costenoble, In: Archiv für Geschichte des Buchwesens, 74 & Friedrich von Bodenstedts Briefe an Hermann Costenoble, In: Arch für Geschichte des Buchwesens, 77, Frankfurt/Main. *Mailing Add:* Dept of Ger Johns Hopkins Univ Baltimore MD 21218

MCCLAIN, YOKO MATSUOKA, b Tokyo, Japan; US citizen; m 56; c 1. JAPANESE LANGUAGE & LITERATURE. *Educ:* Univ Ore, BA, 56, MA, 67. *Prof Exp:* ASSOC PROF JAPANESE LANG & LIT, UNIV ORE, 69- *Mem:* Asn Asian Studies; Asn Teachers Japanese. *Res:* Modern Japanese grammar; contemporary Japanese women authors; writers of early 20th century. *Publ:* Auth, Intermediate Japanese Reading Aids: Vol I Verbs and Verb-following Expressions, Hokuseido Press, 71; coauth, The White Birch School (Shirakabaha) of Japanese Literature: Some Sketches and Commentary, Univ Ore Asian Studies Comt, 74; Thirty-six Portrait Prints by Sekino Jun'ichiro, Univ Ore Asian Studies Comt, 77; auth, Ariyoshi Sawako: Creative social critic, J Asn Teachers Japanese, 78; Soseki: A tragic father, Monumenta Nipponica, 78; Handbook of Modern Japanese Grammar, Hokuseido Press, 81; Eroticism and the writings of Enchi Fumiko, J Asn Teachers Japanese, 81. *Mailing Add:* Dept of East Asian Lang & Lit Univ Ore Eugene OR 97403

MCCLELLAN, EDWIN, b Kobe, Japan, Oct 25; m 55; c 2. JAPANESE LANGUAGE & LITERATURE. *Educ:* Univ St Andrews, MA, 52; Univ Chicago, PhD(Japanese lit), 57; Yale Univ, MA, 73. *Prof Exp:* Instr English, The Col, Univ Chicago, 57-59, from asst prof to prof Japanese lang & lit, 59-70, Carl Darling Buck prof, 70-72, Willett fac fel, 62, chmn comt Far East civilizations, 63-66, chmn dept Far Eastern lang & civilizations, 66-72; prof Japanese lit, 72-, chmn dept EAsian lang & lit, 73-, chmn, coun EAsian studies, 79-82, SUMITOMO PROF JAPANESE STUDIES, 79- *Concurrent Pos:* Mem adv coun, dept EAsian studies, Princeton Univ, 66-71; chmn coun on humanities, Yale Univ, 75-77. *Mem:* Orient Soc; fel Am Acad Arts & Sci. *Publ:* Transl, Kokoro, Regnery, 57; Grass on the Wayside, 69 & auth, Two Japanese Novelists: Soseki and Toson, 69, Univ Chicago; transl, A Dark Night's Passing, Kodansha Int, 76. *Mailing Add:* Dept Japanese Yale Univ New Haven CT 06520

MCCLELLAND, BENJAMIN WRIGHT, English. See Vol II

MCCLELLAND, JOHN A, b Toronto, Ont, May 19, 34. FRENCH. *Educ:* Univ Toronto, BA, 56, MA, 58; Univ Chicago, PhD(French), 65. *Prof Exp:* Instr French & Span, Mt Allison Univ, 58-59 & Univ Western Ont, 59-61; asst prof French, 64-72, ASSOC PROF FRENCH, VICTORIA COL, UNIV TORONTO, 72- *Mem:* MLA; Renaissance Soc Am; Asn Can Univ Teachers Fr. *Res:* French Renaissance poetry; comparative Renaissance literature; French novel of the 18th and 19th centuries. *Publ:* Ed, Pontus de Tyard's Erreurs Amoureuses, Droz, Geneva, 67. *Mailing Add:* 256 Forest Hill Toronto ON M5P 2N5 Can

MCCLENDON, CARMEN CHAVES, b Porto Alegre, Brazil, July 6, 48; US citizen; m 68; c 2. SPANISH LANGUAGE & LITERATURE. *Educ:* Miss State Univ, BA, 68, MA, 69, PhD(hist & Span), 76. *Prof Exp:* Instr, 70-76, asst prof, 76-80, ASSOC PROF FOREIGN LANG, MISS STATE UNIV, 81- *Concurrent Pos:* Develop Found grant, Miss State Univ, 76; Nat Endowment for Humanities summer fel, 77 & 80; vis prof Port, Univ of Pittsburgh, 80-81; dir honors, Miss State Univ, 81-; proj dir, Nat Endowment for Humanities grant, 81-82. *Mem:* MLA; Am Soc 18th Century Studies; Am Asn Teachers Span & Port. *Res:* Eighteenth century Spanish literature; women in 18th century Spain. *Publ:* Coauth, Dissertations in Medieval Hispanic Languages and Literatures Accepted in the United States and Canada, 1967-1976, La Coronica, 78; auth, Josefa Amar y Borbon y la Educacion Femenina, Letras Femeninas, 78; Do's and Dont's: A Set of Rules for the Enlightened Spanish Female, Estudos Ibero-Americanos, 78; Satan and the Stars: Zamora's treatment of fatalism in Judas Iscariot, Critica Hisp. *Mailing Add:* Drawer FL Miss State Univ Mississippi State MS 39762

MCCLUNEY, DANIEL C, JR, b Chicago, Ill, Feb 13, 16; m 38; c 1. GERMAN LITERATURE. *Educ:* Wash Univ, AB, 37, AM, 38; Stanford Univ, PhD, 49. *Prof Exp:* Teacher, Taylor Sch, 38-42 & Country Day Sch, St Louis, Mo, 42-45; asst, Wash Univ, 45-46; actg instr Ger, Stanford Univ, 46-49, from asst prof to assoc prof, 50-64; prof, 64-66, head dept, 64-66, actg dean col lib arts & sci, 66-67, dean fac, 67-72, vchancellor, 68-72, prof, 72-79, EMER PROF GER, UNIV ILL, CHICAGO CIRCLE, 80- *Mem:* MLA. *Res:* Eighteenth and 19th century German literature. *Publ:* Auth, Im Geist der Gegenwart, Oxford, 59; Lesen und Horen, 63 & co-ed, Proben Deutscher Prosa, 70, Norton. *Mailing Add:* Dept of Ger Univ of Ill at Chicago Chicago IL 60680

MCCONNELL, WINDER, b Belfast, Ireland, Nov 19, 45; m 73; c 1. GERMAN MEDIEVAL LITERATURE. *Educ:* McGill Univ, BA, 67; Univ Kans, MA, 69, PhD(Ger), 73. *Prof Exp:* Instr Ger, Univ Western Ont, 72-73; Ordinarius English, hist & gemeinschaftskunde, Gym Münden, West Ger, 73-74; res & teaching fel Ger, Stanford Univ, 74-76; asst prof, Johns Hopkins Univ, 76-78; asst prof, 78-82, ASSOC PROF GERMAN, UNIV CALIF, DAVIS, 82- *Mem:* MLA; Am Asn Teachers Ger; Philol Soc Pac Coast. *Res:* Medieval German heroic epic; Germanic mythology; spielmannsepik. *Publ:* Auth, Wate and Wada, MLN, 77; The Wate Figure in Medieval Tradition, Peter Lang Verlag, 78; Ritual and literary tradition: The brobdingnagian element in Dukus Horant, Mediaevalia, 81; Hagen and the otherworld in Kudrun, Res Publ Litterarum, 82; Kriemhild and Gerlind, Houston Ger Studies, 82; Marriage in the Nibelungenlied and Kudrun: A contrastive analysis, Festschrift for George F Jones, 83; The Nibelungenlied, Twayne's World Authors Series (in prep). *Mailing Add:* Dept of Ger Univ of Calif Davis CA 95616

MCCORMACK, WILLIAM CHARLES, b Sutherland, Iowa, Mar 31, 29; Can citizen; m 62. ANTHROPOLOGY, LINGUISTICS. *Educ:* Univ Chicago, BA, 48; Stanford Univ, BA, 49, MA, 50; Univ Chicago, PhD(anthrop), 56. *Prof Exp:* Assoc res anthrop Hindu law, mod India proj, Univ Calif, Berkeley, 58-59; asst prof anthrop, Univ London, 59-60; vis lectr Indian anthrop, ling & Indian studies, Univ Wis-Madison, 60-64; assoc prof anthrop, Duke Univ, 64-69; head dept ling, 72-73, PROF ANTHROP & LING, UNIV CALGARY, 69- *Concurrent Pos:* Jr ling fel, Rockefeller Found, 56-58; Am Coun Learned Soc grant-in-aid, 62-63; prin contractor, Kannada lang, US Off Educ & Univ Wis-Madison, 62-64; res coun grant, Duke Univ, 64-66, comt for comp studies social syst & inst grant, 67-68; Fulbright-Hays award, US Off Educ, 66; Duke Endowment Found res grants, 65-67, 67-68; mem nat selection comt anthrop, US NIH, 67; res grant, Univ Calgary, 69-71; mem nat selection comt humanities & soc sci, Shastri Indo-Can Inst, 70, 71 & 77 & 78, chmn, 79 & 80; The Linguist, IX Int Cong Anthrop & Ethnol Sci, 73; Univ Calgary res grant, 76-77 & 81; Soc Sci & Humanities Res Coun Can conf grant, 79. *Mem:* Fel Am Anthrop Asn; fel Royal Anthrop Inst Gt Brit & Ireland; Ling Soc Am; Semiotic Soc Am; Am Acad Relig. *Res:* Linguistic semiotic, and cognitive anthropology; Khasi and Lingayat culture and social organization; varieties of modernization in Asia. *Publ:* Auth, Forms of communication in Virasaiva religion, In: Traditional India: structure and change, J Am Folklore, 7-9/58; Lingayats as a sect, J Royal Anthrop Inst, 63; Kannada: A Cultural Introduction to the Spoken Styles of the Language, Univ Wis Press, 66; Language identity, In: Chapters in Indian Civilization, Vol II, British and Modern Period, Kendall-Hunt, 2nd ed, 70; ed, Language and Man, 76, Language and Thought, 77, Approaches to Language, 78 & Language and Society, 79, Mouton, The Hague & Paris. *Mailing Add:* Dept of Anthrop Univ of Calgary Calgary AB T2N 1N4 Can

MCCORMICK, EDWARD ALLEN, b Fairfax Co, Va, July 1, 25; m 52; c 3. GERMAN, COMPARATIVE LITERATURE. *Educ:* Randolph-Macon Col, AB, 48; Univ Berne, PhD, 51. *Hon Degrees:* MA, Dartmouth Col, 65. *Prof Exp:* From instr to asst prof Ger, Princeton Univ, 51-58; instr, Univ Mich, 52-53; instr, Harvard Univ, 53-54; asst prof, Brown Univ, 58-59; from asst prof to assoc prof, Dartmouth Col, 59-63, prof & chmn dept, 63-66, fac fel, 62-63; prof Ger & comp lit & dir, Dept Comp Lit, Queen's Col, NY, 66-70; chmn, Dept Comp Lit, 71-74, PROF GER & COMP LIT, GRAD SCH & UNIV CTR, CITY UNIV NEW YORK, 70-, EXEC OFFICER GERMANIC LANG, 80- *Concurrent Pos:* Bicentennial preceptor, Princeton Univ, 54-57. *Mem:* Am Asn Teachers Ger; MLA; Am Comp Lit Asn; Am Soc Aesthetics. *Res:* Nineteenth century and modern German literature; criticism and theory; nineteenth and twentieth century comparative literature. *Publ:* Coauth, Lebendige Literatur, Houghton, 60, 74; auth, Lessing: Laocoön, Bobbs, 62; Theodor Storms Novellen, Univ NC, 64; Poema pictura loquens, Compt Lit Studies, 9/76; Decadence and Heimatdichtung, Mod Austrian Lit, 77. *Mailing Add:* Grad Sch & Univ Ctr City Univ New York New York NY 10036

MCCORMICK, JOHN OWEN, b Thief River Falls, Minn, Sept 20, 18; m 42, 54; c 4. COMPARATIVE LITERATURE. *Educ:* Univ Minn, BA, 41; Harvard Univ, MA, 47, PhD, 51. *Prof Exp:* Teaching fel English, Harvard Univ, 47-51, sr tutor, Adams House, 49-51; dean & lectr, Salzburg Sem in Am studies, Austria, 51-52; lectr Am studies, Free Univ Berlin, 52-53, prof, 54-59; prof Am studies, 59-61, chmn dept comp lit, 61-72, prog dir comp lit, 76-79, PROF COMP LIT, RUTGERS UNIV, NEW BRUNSWICK, 61- *Concurrent Pos:* DeWitt Jennings Payne award, Univ Minn, 41; Bell traveling fel, Harvard Univ, 50; vis prof, Bennington Col & Rockefeller res grant, 56-57; Smith-Mundt prof, Nat Univ Mex, 61-62; Guggenheim fel, 64-65; vis prof English & Bruern fel, Univ Leeds, England, 75-76; vis lectr, Tokyo, 79. *Mem:* Brit Asn Am Studies; MLA; Am Comp Lit Asn. *Res:* History and the novel; G Santayana. *Publ:* Auth, Catastrophe and Imagination, Longmans, London, 57; Der Moderne Amerikanische Roman, Vandenhoek & Ruprecht, Goettingen, 60; coauth, Versions of Censorship, Doubleday, 62; auth, The Complete Aficionado, World, New York & Weidenfeld, Nicolson, London, 67; The Middle Distance, Free, 71; ed, Syllabus of Comparative Literature, Scarecrow, 72; Fiction as Knowledge, Rutgers Univ, 75. *Mailing Add:* Dept of Comp Lit Rutgers Univ New Brunswick NJ 08903

MCCORT, DENNIS PETER, b Hoboken, NJ, Sept 26, 41; m 73; c 2. GERMAN LANGUAGE & LITERATURE. *Educ:* St Peter's Col, AB, 63; Johns Hopkins Univ, MA, 64, PhD(Ger), 70. *Prof Exp:* Asst prof, 68-78, ASSOC PROF GER, SYRACUSE UNIV, 78- *Mem:* MLA; NE Mod Lang Asn; Am Asn Teachers Ger. *Res:* German romanticism; German realistic fiction; literature and psychology. *Publ:* Auth, Perspectives on Music in German Fiction, Lang, 74; Johann Conrad Beissel, colonial mystic poet, Ger-Am Studies, fall 74; Goethe and the Threnody, Univ Dayton Rev, winter 74; Historical consciousness versus action in C F Meyer's Das Amulett, Symposium, summer 78; The method in Ritter Gluck's madness: An existential view, J Altered States Consciousness, fall 78; The dreadful weight of days: The hilarious heroism of old age in Kingsley Amis's Ending Up, The Sphinz: A Mag Lit & Soc, spring 82; R D Laing and the German romantic quest for transcendence, WVa Univ Philol Papers, summer 82. *Mailing Add:* Foreign Lang & Lit/Ger Syracuse Univ Syracuse NY 13210

MACCOULL, LESLIE SHAW BAILEY, b New London, Conn, Aug 7, 45. CLASSICS, PAPYROLOGY. *Educ:* Vassar Col, AB, 65; Yale Univ, MA, 66; Cath Univ Am, PhD(Semitics), 73. *Prof Exp:* Res fel Coptic, Inst Christian Orient Res, Cath Univ Am, 73-74, curator, 74-77; fel Coptic, Am Res Ctr in Egypt, 78-79; DIR STUDIES, SOC COPTIC ARCHAEOL, 79- *Concurrent Pos:* Consult, Coptic Encyclopaedia. *Mem:* Am Soc Papyrologists; Inst Asn Coptic Studies. *Res:* Byzantine papyrology; Coptic papyrology; the later Roman Empire. *Publ:* Auth, Greek and Coptic Papyri in the Freer Gallery of Art, Diss Cath Univ, 73; Coptic Documentary Papyri in the Pierpont Morgan Library, BSAC 24, 82; ed, Coptic Studies presented to Mirrit Boutros Ghali, Cairo, 79; transl, Ignazio Guidi's Elements of Coptic, Cairo, 80; auth, The Coptic Archive of Dioscorus of Aphrodito, Chron d'Eg 56, 81; Coptic Documentary Papyri in the Beinecke Library, Texte et Doc, Soc d'Archeol Copte, Cairo (in press). *Mailing Add:* Soc Coptic Archaeology 222 Ramses St Cairo Egypt

MCCOY, JOHN, JR, b Valeda, Kans, July 30, 24; div; c 2. CHINESE & JAPANESE LINGUISTICS. *Educ:* Univ Chicago, MA, 48; Cornell Univ, PhD(ling), 66. *Prof Exp:* Asst prof ling & Asian studies, 66-68, assoc prof ling & Chinese lit, 68-76, PROF LING & CHINESE LIT, CORNELL UNIV, 76- *Concurrent Pos:* Examr Chinese lang, NY State Neglected Lang Prog, 66-; consult Chinese lang & lit, Comt Int Exchange Persons, 67-; Fulbright-Hays res fel, 69-70; secy, Comt Chinese Oral & Performing Lit, 69- *Mem:* Ling Soc Am; Hong Kong Br Royal Asiatic Soc; Ling Soc Japan; Chinese Lang Teachers Asn. *Res:* Chinese linguistics; Chinese folk literature. *Publ:* Auth, The dialects of Hong Kong boat people, J Hong Kong Br Royal Asiatic Soc, 65; The phonology of Toishan City, Orbis, 69; The linguistic and literary value of the Ming Dynasty mountain songs, J Hong Kong Br Royal Asiatic Soc 69; Chinese kinterms of reference and address, In: Family and Kinship in Chinese Society, Stanford Univ, 70. *Mailing Add:* Dept of Mod Lang & Ling Cornell Univ Ithaca NY 14853

MCCRARY, WILLIAM CARLTON, b Portsmouth, Va, Jan 19, 32; m 56. SPANISH. *Educ:* Univ Fla, BA, 51; Univ Wis, MA, 52, PhD, 58. *Prof Exp:* From instr to asst prof Span, Univ Mich, 58-63; from asst prof to assoc prof, Univ NC, Chapel Hill, 63-67; assoc prof, 67-70, PROF SPAN, UNIV KY, 70- *Concurrent Pos:* Am Coun Learned Soc grant-in-aid, 63; Am Philos Soc grant, 63; asst ed, Ky Romance Quart, 67- *Mem:* MLA; Am Asn Teachers Span & Port; Renaissance Soc Am. *Res:* Spanish Golden Age drama. *Publ:* Auth, Fuenteovejuna: Its platonic conception and execution, Studies Philol, 4/61; La elaboracion de una escena simbologica de Tirso de Molina, 61 & coauth, La balanza sujetiva-objetiva en el teatro de Tirso de Molina, 58, Hispanofila; The Goldfinch and the Hawk: A Study of Lope de Vega's Tragedy, El cabellero de Olmedo, Univ NC, 66. *Mailing Add:* Dept of Span & Ital Univ of Ky Lexington KY 40505

MCCREADY, WARREN THOMAS, b New York, NY, Feb 8, 15. ROMANCE LANGUAGES. *Educ:* Univ Chicago, MA, 49, PhD(Romance lang), 61. *Prof Exp:* Lectr Span, Queen's Univ, Ont, 55-56; lectr, 56-60, from asst prof to assoc prof, 60-69, PROF SPAN, UNIV TORONTO, 69- *Mem:* Mod Humanities Res Asn; Am Asn Teachers Span & Port; Asoc Int Hispanistas; Can Asn Hispanists. *Res:* Spanish Golden Age drama; bibliography. *Publ:* Co-ed, Angelica y Medoro, Quad Ibero-Americani, Torino, 58; auth, Lope de Vega's birth date and horoscope, Hisp Rev, 10/60; La heraldica en las obras de Lope de Vega y sus contemporanees, privately publ, 62; Bibliografia tematica de estudios sobre el teatro espanol antiguo, Univ Toronto, 66; ed, Lope de Vega, El mejor mozo de Espana, Anaya, Salamance, 67; auth, Bibliographical supplement, In: Spanish Drama Before Lope de Vega, Univ Pa, 67; Las comedias sueltas de la casa de Orga, In: Homenaje a William L Fichter, Ed Castalia, Madrid, 71. *Mailing Add:* Dept of Hisp Studies Univ of Toronto Toronto ON M5S 1A1 Can

MCCULLOCH, DONALD F, b New York, NY, Aug 29, 21; m 63. LINGUISTICS. *Educ:* NY Univ, PhD, 59. *Prof Exp:* Instr French, Brooklyn Prep Sch, NY, 44-47; instr mod lang, Seton Hall Univ, 47-52; instr & chmn dept, St John's Prep Sch, 52-60; instr French, Good Counsel Col, 61-62; assoc prof, 62-76, PROF MOD LANG, BRONX COMMUNITY COL, 76- *Mem:* Am Asn Teachers Fr. *Res:* Linguistics for teaching modern languages; structural linguistics of Old French. *Publ:* Auth, Old French verb forms, Revised Dating, Orbis, 1/61. *Mailing Add:* Dept of Mod Lang Bronx Community Col Bronx NY 10453

MCCULLOCH, FLORENCE, b Washington, DC, June 23, 23. FRENCH. *Educ:* Vassar Col, AB, 44; Univ NC, MA, 49, PhD, 56. *Prof Exp:* From instr to asst prof French, Sweet Briar Col, 54-60; from asst prof to assoc prof, 60-72, PROF FRENCH, WELLESLEY COL, 72- *Mem:* Mediaeval Acad Am; MLA. *Res:* Mediaeval literature; illuminated manuscripts; Old French saints' lives. *Publ:* Medieval Latin and French Bestiaries, Univ NC, rev ed, 62. *Mailing Add:* Dept of French Wellesley Col Wellesley MA 02181

MCCULLOCH, JAMES A, b Braddock, Pa, July 11, 22; m 46; c 5. CLASSICS. *Educ:* Duquesne Univ, BA, 47; Univ Pittsburgh, MLitt, 48, PhD(Latin, Greek), 51. *Prof Exp:* Lectr Greek, Univ Pittsburgh, 49-50; indust eng, Jones & Laughlin Steel Corp, 51-55; from instr to assoc prof Latin & Greek, 55-63, PROF LATIN & GREEK, DUQUESNE UNIV, 63-, DEAN COL LIB ARTS & SCI, 68- *Concurrent Pos:* Lawrence fel, Univ Pittsburgh, 56; instr Greek, Chatham Col, 59-61; Danforth Assoc, 66- *Mem:* Am Conf Acad Deans; Am Asn Higher Educ; Am Asn Cols Teacher Educ. *Res:* Etymology; epigraphy. *Publ:* Auth, Selections from the Metamorphoses of Ovid, Duquesne Univ, 58, 65; Medical Greek and Latin Workbook, C C Thomas, 62, 70 & 77. *Mailing Add:* Col of Lib Arts & Sci Duquesne Univ Pittsburgh PA 15219

MCCULLOH, WILLIAM EZRA, b McPherson, Kans, Sept 8, 31; m 56; c 2. CLASSICAL LANGUAGES & LITERATURES. *Educ:* Ohio Wesleyan Univ, AB, 53; Oxford Univ, BA, 56; Yale Univ, PhD, 62. *Prof Exp:* Instr classics, Wesleyan Univ, 56-61; from instr to assoc prof, 61-68, PROF CLASSICS, KENYON COL, 68- *Mem:* Am Philol Asn; Class Asn Mid W & S; Soc Ancient Greek Philos; NAm Patristics Soc. *Res:* Greek poetry and philosophy; the ancient novel; Greek patristics. *Publ:* Auth, Introduction to Greek Lyric Poetry, Bantam, 62; Metaphysical solace in Greek tragedy, Class J, 12/63; Aristophanes seen whole, Sewanee Rev, fall 65; Longus, Twayne, 70. *Mailing Add:* Dept of Classics Kenyon Col Gambier OH 43022

MCCULLOUGH, WILLIAM H, b Dallas, Tex, Dec 15, 28; m 52; c 1. JAPANESE LITERATURE. *Educ:* Univ Calif, Berkeley, BA, 52, MA, 54, PhD, 62. *Prof Exp:* Actg asst prof Japanese, Stanford Univ, 60-62, from asst prof to assoc prof, 62-71, asst dir, lang prog, Stanford Ctr Japanese Studies, Tokyo, 61-63; PROF ORIENT LANG, UNIV CALIF, BERKELEY, 71- *Concurrent Pos:* Charles F Kofoid fel Orient lang, Univ Calif, 56-58; Ford Overseas Area Training fel, 59-60; Fulbright-Hays fel, 67-68; mem joint comt Japanese studies, Soc Sci Res Coun-Am Coun Learned Soc, 68-69. *Mem:* Am ient Soc; Asn Asian Studies; Asn Teachers Japanese; Am Coun Teaching Foreign Lang. *Res:* Medieval Japanese literature and history. *Publ:* Auth, Japanese marriage institutions in the Heian Period, Harvard J Asiatic Studies, 67. *Mailing Add:* Dept of Orient Lang Univ of Calif Berkeley CA 94720

MACCURDY, RAYMOND RALPH, b Oklahoma City, Okla, May 12, 16; m 39; c 2. SPANISH LITERATURE. *Educ:* La State Univ, AB, 39, AM, 41; Univ NC, PhD, 48. *Prof Exp:* Asst to dean jr div, La State Univ, 39-40; instr Span, Univ NC, 46-48; assoc prof mod lang, Univ GA, 48-49; assoc prof, 49-53, actg head dept mod & class lang, 50-51, chmn dept, 63-69, PROF SPAN, UNIV N MEX, 54- *Concurrent Pos:* Ford fac fel, 54-55; Fulbright res scholar, Spain, 60-61; consult, Nat Found for Humanities, 69-74. *Mem:* MLA; Rocky Mt Mod Lang Asn (pres, 56); mem Hisp Soc Am. *Res:* Spanish literature of the Renaissance and Golden Age; Spanish folklores and dialectology; Spanish heritage of Louisiana. *Publ:* Auth, Francisco de Rojas Zorilla and the tragedy, Univ NMex, 58; ed, Morir pensando matar, Clasicos Castellanos, Madrid, 61; Lucrecia y Tarquino, Univ N Mex, 63; Tirso de Molina, El burlador de Sevilla and La prudencia en la mujer, Dell, 65; auth, Francisco de Rojas Zorrilla, Twayne, 69; ed, Spanish drama of the Golden Age: Twelve Plays, Appleton, 71; auth, The Tragic Fall: Don Alvaro de Luna and Other Favorites in Spanish Golden Age Drama, NC Studies Romance Lang & Lit, 78. *Mailing Add:* Dept of Mod & Class Lang Univ of N Mex Albuquerque NM 87131

MCDANIEL, GORDON LAWRENCE, b Sumas, Wash, Dec 31, 43. SLAVIC PHILOLOGY, MEDIEVAL LITERATURE. *Educ:* Ft Lewis Col, BA, 64; Univ Wash, Seattle, PhD(Slavic lang), 80. *Prof Exp:* Lectr Russ, Bellevue Community Col, 79; LECTR SERBO-CROATIAN, UNIV WASH, SEATTLE, 81- *Mem:* Am Asn Advan Slavic Studies; Am Asn Teachers Slavic & East Europ Lang; Am Asn Southeast Europ Studies; NAm Soc Serbian Studies; Bulgarian Studies Group. *Res:* Medieval Balkan history; medieval Slavic literature; textology. *Publ:* Auth, Prilozi k Proucavanju istorije teksta Zivota kraljeva i arhepiepiskopa srpskih od Danila II, Arheografski prilozi, Narodna Biblioteka, Beograd, Vol III, 82; The house of Anjou and Serbia, Festschrift for King Louis (in press). *Mailing Add:* 5024 1/2 22nd Ave NE Seattle WA 98105

MCDANIEL, SUSAN LEAS, Medieval Literature, Linguistics. See Vol II

MCDANIEL, THOMAS FRANCIS, Near Eastern Studies, Archeology. See Vol IV

MCDAVID, RAVEN IOOR, JR, b Greenville, SC, Oct 16, 11; m 50; c 5. LINGUISTICS, DIALECTOLOGY. *Educ:* Furman Univ, BA, 31; Duke Univ, MA, 33, PhD(English), 35. *Hon Degrees:* LittD, Furman Univ, 66 & Duke Univ, 72. *Prof Exp:* Instr English, The Citadel, 35-38 & Mich State Univ, 38-39; asst prof, Southwestern La Univ, 40-42 & Univ Ill, 49-50; asst prof mod lang, Cornell Univ, 50-51; asst prof English, Case Western Reserve Univ, 52-57; assoc prof, 57-64, prof English, ling anthrop & educ, 64-77, EMER PROF, UNIV CHICAGO, 77- *Concurrent Pos:* Rosenwald fel, 41-42; Am Coun Learned Socs grants, Yale Univ, 42-43; linguist, Army Lang Sect, 42-45 & US Bd Geog Names, 47; assoc ed, Ling Atlas of NCent States, 54-75, ed-in-chief, 75-; US Off Educ grant, 63-66, linguist, 66-69; ed-in-chief, Ling Atlas of Mid & SAtlantic States, 64-; Fulbright lectr, Mainz, 65, Odense, 80 & Trondheim, 81; Nat Endowment for Humanities sr fel, 75. *Honors & Awards:* David Russell Award, NCTE, 69. *Mem:* AAAS, Am Anthrop Asn; Ling Soc Am; MLA; Am Name Soc. *Publ:* Auth, Dialect geography and social science problems, Social Forces, 46; coauth, Relationship of the speech of American Negroes to the speech of whites, Am Speech, 51; The Pronunciation of English in the Atlantic States, Univ Mich, 61; ed, The American Language, Knopf, 63; coauth, Communication Barriers to the Culturally Deprived, US Off Educ, 66; auth, Dialects in Culture, Univ Ala, 79; Varieties of American English, Stanford Univ, 80; Linguistic Atlas of the Middle and South Atlantic States, Univ Chicago, 80- *Mailing Add:* Dept of English Univ of Chicago 1050 E 59th St Chicago IL 60637

MCDERMOTT, MADELEINE GUENSER, b France; m 65. FRENCH LITERATURE & CIVILIZATION. *Educ:* Sorbonne, Lic es Lett, 53; Johns Hopkins Univ, MA, 65, PhD(Romance lang), 68. *Prof Exp:* Asst prof French, Mt St Agnes Col. 62-68; lectr eve col, Johns Hopkins Univ, 63-66; lectr, Univ Md, Baltimore County, 68; ASSOC PROF FRENCH, TOWSON STATE UNIV, 69- *Mem:* MLA; AAUP; Am Asn Teachers Fr. *Res:* Television communications; women's studies. *Mailing Add:* Dept of Mod Lang Towson State Univ Baltimore MD 21204

MCDERMOTT, WILLIAM COFFMAN, b Connellsville, Pa, Aug 31, 07; m 32, 63; c 1. CLASSICAL STUDIES. *Educ:* Dickinson Col, AB, 28; Johns Hopkins Univ, AM, 30, PhD, 34. *Hon Degrees:* LittD, Dickinson Col, 78. *Prof Exp:* Instr Latin, Allegheny Col, 30-33; from instr to asst prof, Lehigh Univ, 35-39; asst prof, 39-48, from assoc prof to prof class studies, 48-75, EMER PROF CLASS STUDIES, UNIV PA, 75- *Concurrent Pos:* Assoc ed, Class Weekly, 45-49; mem Latin comt, Col Entrance Exam Bd, 52-56; Morgan prof classics & class archaeol, Univ Kans, 67. *Mem:* Am Philos Asn; Class Asn Atlantic States. *Res:* Roman history; the Ciceronian period; Merovingian history. *Publ:* Auth, The Ape in Antiquity, Johns Hopkins, 38; Gregory of Tours, Univ Pa, 48; coauth, Readings in the History of the Ancient World, 2nd ed, Holt, 70; auth, Fabricius Veiento, Am J Philol, 70; In ligarianam, Transactions Am Philol ASn, 72; Cicero's Consular Orations, Philologus, 72; Felix of Nantes, Traditio, 75; The Verrine jury, Rheinisches Mus, 77. *Mailing Add:* Dept of Class Studies Williams Hall 720 CU Univ of Pa Philadelphia PA 19104

MCDIARMID, JOHN BRODIE, b Toronto, Ont, June 6, 13; US citizen; m 42; c 3. CLASSICS. *Educ:* Univ Toronto, BA, 36; Johns Hopkins Univ, PhD(Greek), 40. *Prof Exp:* From instr to asst prof classics, Johns Hopkins Univ, 45-49; assoc prof, 49-56, PROF CLASSICS, UNIV WASH, 56- *Concurrent Pos:* Mem, Inst Advan Studies, Princeton, NJ, 52-53, 57-58; Guggenheim fel, 57-58. *Mem:* Am Philol Asn; Soc Ancient Greek Philos; Archaeol Inst Am; Class Asn Pac States. *Res:* Greek philosophy and literature. *Publ:* Auth, Theophrastus on the Presocratic causes, Harvard Studies Class Philol, 53. *Mailing Add:* Dept of Classics Univ of Wash Seattle WA 98105

MACDONALD, ANTONINA HANSELL, b Oxford, England, Mar 2, 50; US citizen; m 76. COMPUTATIONAL LINGUISTICS. *Educ:* Univ Mich, AB, 71, AM, 74, PhD(ling), 79. *Prof Exp:* TECH STAFF, BELL LAB, 79- *Mem:* Ling Soc Am; Asn Comput Ling. *Res:* Computational analysis of writing. *Publ:* Auth, The writer's workbench: Computer aids for text analysis, Inst Elec & Electronics Engrs Trans Commun, 1/82. *Mailing Add:* Six Corporate Pl Room IM-206 Bell Lab Piscataway NJ 08854

MACDONALD, GERALD JOHN, b New York, NY, Sept 25, 34; m 61; c 2. SPANISH PHILOLOGY & MEDIEVAL LITERATURE. *Educ:* Queens Col, NY, BA, 55; Univ Iowa, MA, 57; Univ Pa, PhD(Romance philol), 67; Drexel Univ, MS, 79. *Prof Exp:* From instr to asst prof Span, Ohio Univ, 65-68; asst prof Temple Univ, 69-75, co-chmn dept Span & prof Span, Ohio Univ, 65-68; asst prof Temple Univ, 69-75, co-chmn dept Span & Port, 71-75; Mellon fac fel humanities, Harvard Univ, 76-77; ASST PROF SPAN, BARUCH COL, 79- *Concurrent Pos:* Vis prof Span, Univ Pa, 74. *Mem:* MLA; AAUP; Am Librn Asn; Dict Soc NAm. *Res:* Spanish lexicography. *Publ:* Auth, Hamihala, a hapax in the Auto de los reyes magos, Romance Philol, 64; Antonio de Nebrija, the lexicographer, Ky Romance Quart, 73; ed, Antonio de Nebrija: Vocabulario de Romance in Latin, Temple Univ & Ed Castalia, Madrid, 73; auth, Spanish textile and clothing nomenclature in -an, -i, and -in, Hisp Rev, 74; The evolution of the dictionary: Glossography to lexicography, Lektos (spec issue), 76; Lexicography in Spain before the 18th century, J Dict Soc Am, 78; assoc ed, Nomenclator Litterarius, Francke, Munich, 80. *Mailing Add:* 204 Brion Lane Chalfont PA 18914

MCDONALD, JOHN PAUL, b Fall River, Mass, Nov 30, 41. FRENCH LITERATURE & HISTORY. *Educ:* Manhattan Col, BA, 63; Brown Univ, MA, 65; Univ Paris, PhD(lett), 82. *Prof Exp:* Teacher hist & lang, Portsmouth Abbey Sch, 66-76; INSTR FRENCH, GERMANTOWN ACAD, 82- *Mem:* MLA; Am Asn Teachers Fr. *Res:* Erudition in 17th century France; Maurists and the publications; relations between the court of Louis XIV and Italy. *Publ:* Auth, Mabillon's Iter Germanicum of 1683, Downside Rev, England, 73; Mabillon and the birth of diplomatics, Studies in Relig/Sci Relig, 79; The Maurist edition of Saint Augustine, Am Benedictine Rev, 80. *Mailing Add:* Germantown Acad Ft Washington PA 19034

MCDONALD, MARIANNE, b Chicago, Ill, Jan 2, 37; c 6. CLASSICS. *Educ:* Bryn Mawr Col, BA, 58; Univ Chicago, MA, 60; Univ Calif, Irvine, PhD(classics), 75. *Prof Exp:* Asst classics, Univ Calif, Irvine, 72-74, instr, 75-79; WRITING & RES, 79- *Mem:* Philol Asn Pac Coast; Am Class League; Mod & Class Lang Asn; Am Philol Asn. *Res:* Euripides' vocabulary; Homeric vocabulary; Virgilian vocabulary. *Publ:* Auth, Aeneas and Turnus: Labor vs Amor, Pac Coast Philol, 72; Sunt Lacrimae Rerum, Class J, 72-73; Acies: Virgil Georgics 1.395, Class Philol, 73; auth, Semilemmatized Concordances to Euripides' Alcestis, 77 Andromache, 78, Medea, 78, Heraclidae, 79, Hippolytus, 79, Hecubai, 82; Terms for Happiness in Euripides, Vandenhoeck u Ruprecht, 78; Does Euripides call the Gods Makarioi?, Ill Class Studies, 79; Euripides in Cinema: The Heart Made Visible, Centrum, 82; Terms for life in Homer: An examination of early concepts in psychology, J Col Physicians Philadelphia, 82. *Mailing Add:* Dept of Classics Univ of Calif Irvine CA 92717

MACDONALD, ROBERT ALAN, b Salamanca, NY, Mar 25, 27. SPANISH. *Educ:* Univ Buffalo, BA, 48; Univ Wis, MA, 49, PhD(Span), 58. *Prof Exp:* From asst prof to assoc prof Span, 55-67, chmn dept mod foreign lang, 64-69, PROF SPAN, UNIV RICHMOND, 67- *Concurrent Pos:* Res asst, Old Span Dictionary proj Mod Lang Asn, Univ Wis, 48-51, 53-55, Markham Traveling fel, Spain & Europe, 58-59; ed, Bull Mod Foreign Lang Asn Va, 62-67, 72-; prof reviewer, Nat Endowment for Humanities, 77- *Honors & Awards:* Laureate Va, Va Cult Laureate Ctr, 77. *Mem:* MLA; Medieval Acad Am; Am Asn Teachers Span & Port; Am Coun Teaching Foreign Lang; Renaissance Soc Am. *Res:* Alfonso X of Castile; Hispanic languages, literatures and history. *Publ:* Auth, Progress and problems in editing Alfonsine juridical texts, La Coronica, spring 78; Politics and law in Alfonsine Castile, 1252-1284 (in press); Alfonsine Law, the Cantigas, and justice (in press); ed, El texto juridico llamado Especulo atribuido al Rey de Castilla don Alfonso X, el Sabio (in press). *Mailing Add:* Box 278 Univ of Richmond Richmond VA 23173

MCDONALD, WILLIAM CECIL, b Mt Clemens, Mich, Jan 26, 41; m 68; c 1. MEDIEVAL GERMAN LITERATURE & LANGUAGE. *Educ:* Wayne State Univ, BE, 62, MA, 63; Ohio State Univ, PhD(Ger medieval studies), 72. *Prof Exp:* Instr, Wayne State Univ, 62-64; teaching asst, Ohio State Univ, 65-68, instr, 68-71; asst prof, Va Polytech Inst, 71-75; asst prof, 75-80, ASSOC PROF GER, UNIV VA, 80- *Concurrent Pos:* Assoc ed, Semasia, 74-76 & Ger Quart, 76-77; exec coun, Southeastern Medieval Asn, 77-; vis prof, Ger Acad Exchange Serv, 77; bd rev ed, Tristania, 82- *Mem:* Int Courtly Lit Soc (Am pres, 80-82); South Atlantic Mod Lang Asn; MLA; Medieval Acad; Southeastern Medieval Asn. *Res:* Medieval rhetoric; development of literary motifs; late medieval studies. *Publ:* Coauth, German Medieval Literary Patronage from Charlemagne to Maximilian I: A Critical Commentary with Special Emphasis on Imperial Promotion of Literature, Amsterdam, Rodopi, 73; auth, Michel Beheim reconsidered: On imagery in his Erzgräberbispel, Ger Quart, 75; ed, Semasia: Essays in Honor of Wolfgang Fleischhauer, Amsterdam, 75; Auth, Maximilian I of Habsburg and the veneration of Hercules: On the revival of myth and the German Renaissance, J Medieval & Renaissance Studies, 76; King Mark: Gottfried's version of the Ovidian husband-figure?, Forum Mod Lang Studies, 78; Concerning ambiguity as the poetic principle in Kürenberg's Falcon Song, Euphorion, 78; The maiden in Hartmann's Armen Heinrich: Enite redux?, Deut Vierteljahrs-schrift Lit-wiss u Geistesge, 79; Whose Bread I Eat: The Song-Poetry of Michel Beheim, Göppingen, 81. *Mailing Add:* Dept of Ger Lang Univ of Va Charlottesville VA 22903

MCDONOUGH, JAMES THOMAS, JR, b Boston, Mass, Mar 8, 34. ANCIENT GREEK. *Educ:* Boston Col, AB, 55; Columbia Univ, (Greek), 66. *Prof Exp:* From instr to asst prof classics, 60-72, ASSOC PROF CLASSICS, ST JOSEPH'S COL, PA, 72- *Concurrent Pos:* Dir, Off Humantistic Res, 66-;

ed, Hephaistos, 68- *Mem:* Am Philol Asn; Class Asn Can. *Res:* The Homeric hexameter; the use of computers in humanistic research. *Publ:* Auth, Computers and classics, 11/59 & Bibliography of The New Menander, 6/60, Class World; Computers and the classics, Computers & Humanities, 9/67. *Mailing Add:* Dept of Class Lang St Joseph's Col Philadelphia PA 19131

MACDONOUGH, RICHARD BRIAN, b Bangor, Maine, Feb 26, 35. FRENCH LANGUAGE & LITERATURE. *Educ:* Assumption Col, Mass, BA, 56; St Mary's Univ, Md, STB, 58, STL, 60; Univ Laval, MA, 62; Univ Ky, France, PhD(French), 71. *Prof Exp:* Instr French, St Edward's Sem, Wash, 60-62; from asst prof to assoc prof, St Thomas Ctr, Bellarmine Col, Ky, 63-71, acad dean, 68-70; from assoc prof to prof French & humanities, St Mary's Sem & Univ, Md, 71-78, acad dean, 74-77; acad dean, 78-80, PROF HUMANITIES, ST PATRICK'S COL, MOUNTAIN VIEW, CALIF, 78- *Concurrent Pos:* Exchange teacher French, Catonsville Community Col, 73-74. *Mem:* Am Asn Teachers Fr; MLA. *Res:* Pierre Charron; 17th century French literature and thought; French Catholic authors. *Publ:* Auth, New directions: Biblical revival in France, Voice St Mary's Sem 2/59; transl, Y B Tremel, Servants of the word, In: The Word: Readings in Theology, Kenedy, 64; auth, The age of Aquarius: A new age of Erasmus, Delta Epsilon Sigma Bull, 5/70; A thematic study of Peguy's Tapisseries, Claudel Studies, Vol I, No 4. *Mailing Add:* Dept of Humanities St Patrick's Col Mountain View CA 94042

MCDOWELL, CHARLES TAYLOR, b Twin Falls, Idaho, Nov 23, 21; m 49; c 2. FOREIGN LANGUAGES & LINGUISTICS. *Educ:* Tex A&M Univ, BS, 43, PhB, 56; Columbia Univ, MA, 53; FAST, Detachment R, US Dept Army, 55. *Prof Exp:* From instr to assoc prof hist & Russ, Univ Md, 58-60; prof mil & int rels & chmn dept, Arlington State Col, 60-64; asst to pres, 66-68, dean students & asst provost, 68-70, from asst prof to assoc prof, 66-78, PROF USSR & E EUROP AREA STUDIES, UNIV TEX ARLINGTON, 78-, DIR SOVIET & E EUROP CTR, 70- *Concurrent Pos:* Consult Russ translr, Cent Intel Agency, 66-76; rep, Int Res & Educ Bd, 74-; consult Russ Tex Instruments, 76- *Honors & Awards:* Amoco Outstanding Teacher Award, Univ Tex Arlington, 74; Outstanding Dean Award, Am Inst Foreign Study (for USSR Tours), 76. *Mem:* Southwest Asn Advan Slavic Studies (pres, 75-76); Rocky Mountain Mod Lang Asn (pres, 77-78); Am Translr Asn (pres, 74); Int Res & Educ Bd. *Res:* Translation teaching techniques (Russian to English); area studies concerning the USSR and Eastern Europe; linguistic computer research. *Publ:* Auth, Military document translation (Russian), 54 & The role of the Komsomol in the USSR, 55, Detachment R, Dept Army; coauth, Glossary of Soviet military terminology (TM), US Dept Defense, 57; auth, Me Translate Russian, Multilingual, 76; Comparison of the USA and USSR, Tex Instruments, 77. *Mailing Add:* Univ of Tex Soviet & EEurop Ctr Arlington TX 76019

MCDUFFIE, KEITH A, b Feb 12, 32; US citizen; c 2. LATIN AMERICAN LITERATURE. *Educ:* Gonzaga Univ, BA, 54; Middlebury Col, MA, 60; Univ Pittsburgh, PhD(Hisp lang & lit), 69. *Prof Exp:* Instr Span, Univ Pittsburgh, 64-65; from asst prof to prof, Univ Mont, 67-75; PROF LATIN AM LIT & CHMN DEPT HISP LANG & LIT, UNIV PITTSBURGH, 75- *Concurrent Pos:* Mellon fel, Univ Pittsburgh, 74-75. *Mem:* MLA; Int Inst Iberoam Lit (pres, 77-79); Latin Am Studies Asn; Asn Teachers Span & Port; Asoc Int de Hispanistas. *Res:* Twentieth century Latin American poetry and novel. *Publ:* Auth, Trilce I y la function de la palabra en la poetica de Cesar Vellejo, Rev Iberoam, 5-6/70; Cesar Vallejo, In: Encycl World Lit, Ungar, 71; Lo babilonico en Trilce, In: Approximaciones a Cesar Vallejo, Vol II, Las Americas, 72; El zorro de arriba y el zorro de abajo de Jose Maria Arguedas, Latin Am Indian Lit, 77; El logos vallejiano entre lo dialectico y lo trilcico, Rev Iberoam, 1-2/78; Cesar Vallejo y el humanismo socialista vs el surrealismo, In: Memoria, XVII Congreso del Insto Internacional de Literatura Ibero-Americana, Univ Pa, 78; co-ed (with Alfredo Roggiano), Texto/Contexto en la Literatura Iberoamericana, Memoria del XIX Cong del Inst Int de Lit Iberoamericana, Madrid, 80. *Mailing Add:* Dept of Hisp Lang & Lit Univ of Pittsburgh Pittsburgh PA 15260

MACE, CARROLL E, b Neosho, Mo, Dec 5, 26. SPANISH. *Educ:* Drury Col, BA, 49; Tulane Univ, MA, 52, PhD(Span), 66. *Prof Exp:* Asst prof, Univ SC, 60-63; instr Span, Tulane Univ, 63-65; asst prof, 65-67, assoc prof, 67-70, PROF SPAN, XAVIER UNIV LA, 71-, CHMN DEPT MOD LANG, 72- *Mem:* Am Asn Teachers Span & Port; SCent Mod Lang Asn. *Res:* Cervantes and the generation of 1898; folk literature of Guatemala. *Publ:* Auth, The Patzca dance of Rabinal, El Palacio, fall 61; transl, The day of the dead of 1836: Figaro in the cemetery by Larra, Shenandoah, winter 65; auth, New information about dance-dramas of Rabinal and the Rabinal-Achi, Xavier Univ Studies, 2/67; Two Spanish-Quiche Dance-Dramas of Rabinal, Tulane Studies Romance Lang & Lit, 70; Charles Etienne Brasseur de Bourbourg, Handbk Mid Am Indians, 73; Los Negritos: A Maya Christmas comedy, Xavier Rev, 1/81; Algunos apuntes sobre los bailes de Guatemala y de Rabinal, Mesoamerica, 2/81. *Mailing Add:* Dept of Mod Lang Xavier Univ New Orleans LA 70125

MCELRATH, MILES KENNETH, JR, b New Haven, Conn, Dec 3, 26. JAPANESE LANGUAGE & LITERATURE, LINGUISTICS. *Educ:* Univ Calif, Berkeley, BA, 51; Yale Univ, MA, 53; Univ Mich, Ann Arbor, MA, 55, PhD(far Eastern lang & lit), 71. *Prof Exp:* Asia Found vis leetr English & ling, Kanazawa Univ, Japan, 55-57 & Nagasaki Univ, 57-58; asst prof Japanese, Univ Hawaii, 59-64; vis asst prof, Univ Mich, Ann Arbor, 64-65, asst prof, 65-70; asst prof EAsian lang & lit, 70-71, ASSOC PROF E ASIAN LANG & LIT, OHIO STATE UNIV, 71-, CHMN DEPT, 75- *Mem:* Asn Asian Studies; Asn Teachers Japanese; Am Orient Soc. *Res:* Wit and humor in premodern Japanese literature; medieval and Edo period prose genres; minor classical monogatari. *Publ:* Auth, Osaragi Jiro no Kikyo ni tsuite no shohyoron, Kaishaku, kokugo-kokubun, 7/55; coauth, Japanese on a Higher Level, an Intermediate-Advanced Course in the Standard Spoken Language, Univ Hawaii, 64; auth, The three primary colors (transl, Mishima Yukio's Sangenshoku), Occasional Papers No 11, Ctr Japanese Studies, Univ Mich, 69. *Mailing Add:* Dept of EAsian Lang & Lit Ohio State Univ Columbus OH 43210

MCELWEE, JUDSON RENE, b Brownington, Mo, Feb 10, 21; m 51; c 4. FOREIGN LANGUAGES. *Educ:* Rockhurst Col, BS, 51; Univ Paris, cert, 52; Middlebury Col, AM, 53; Univ Kans, PhD, 63. *Prof Exp:* Instr French & Span, Rockhurst Col, 51-54, from asst prof to assoc prof French & Span, 64-76, PROF MOD LANG, CENT MO STATE COL, 76-, HEAD DEPT, 80- *Concurrent Pos:* Asst, Univ Kans, 54-56. *Mem:* Am Asn Teachers Fr. *Res:* Nineteenth century French Literature; English as a second language. *Mailing Add:* Int House Dept of Foreign Lang Cent Mo State Col Warrensburg MO 64093

MCENERNEY, JOHN IGNATIUS, b Philadelphia, Pa, Step 23, 13; m 42; c 8. CLASSICS. *Educ:* Georgetown Univ, AB, 37; Woodstock Col, Md, PhL, 38; Univ Pa, AM, 46, PhD, 50. *Prof Exp:* Teacher Latin, Germantown Acad, 42-47; from asst prof to assoc prof class lang, 47-57, asst to vpres acad affairs, 57-73, PROF CLASS LANG & CHMN DEPT, VILLANOVA UNIV, 57- *Mem:* Am Philol Asn; NAm Patristic Soc. *Res:* Greek and Latin literature; Greek Patristics. *Mailing Add:* Dept of Classic Lang Villanova Univ Villanova PA 19085

MACFARLANE, KEITH H, b Hibbing, Minn, May 13, 34; m 67. ROMANCE LANGUAGES. *Educ:* Carleton Col, BA, 56; Yale Univ, PhD(French), 65. *Prof Exp:* Instr French, Smith Col, 60-63; assoc prof Romance lang, Wesleyan Univ, 64-68; ASSOC PROF FRENCH, UNIV CALIF, RIVERSIDE, 68- *Mem:* MLA;. *Res:* Seventeenth and 19th century French literature; late 19th century French poetry; 17th century French theater. *Publ:* Auth, Tristan Corbiere dans les amours jaunes, Minard, 74; LeCygne de Baudelaire, Info Litteraire, 75; Baudelaire's revaluation of the classical allusion, Studies Romanticism, 76. *Mailing Add:* Dept of Lit & Lang Univ of Calif Riverside CA 92521

MCGAHA, MICHAEL DENNIS, b Dallas, Tex, Dec 31, 41; m 64; c 2. SPANISH LANGUAGE & PENNINSULAR LITERATURE. *Educ:* Univ Dallas, BA, 65; Univ Tex, Austin, PhD(Span), 70. *Prof Exp:* Instr Span, Univ Tex, Austin, 69-70; asst prof, 70-77, ASSOC PROF SPAN, POMONA COL & CLAREMONT GRAD SCH, 77- *Concurrent Pos:* Nat Endowment for Humanities fel, 80-81. *Mem:* Am Asn Teachers Span & Port; MLA. *Res:* Cervantes; Spanish theatre of Golden Age; history and literature of Jews in Spain. *Publ:* Auth, In defense of Tan largo me lo fiais, Bull Comediantes, 77; The structure of El cabellero de Olmedo, Hispania, 77; Cervantes and Virgil: A new look at an old problem, Comp Lit Studies; The sources and meaning of the Grisostomo-Marcela Episode in the 1605 Quijote, Anales Cervantinos; The Theater in Madrid during the Second Republic, Grant & Cutler, 79; ed, Cervantes and the Renaissance, Juan de la Cuesta, 80; auth, Approaches to the Theatre of Calderon, Univ Press Am, 82. *Mailing Add:* Mason Hall 201 Pomona Col Claremont CA 91711

MCGALLIARD, JOHN CALVIN, English. See Vol II

MCGANN, JEROME JOHN, English. See Vol II

MCGAW, JESSIE BREWER, b Montgomery Co, Tenn, Oct 17, 13; div; c 2. ENGLISH. *Educ:* Duke Univ, AB, 35; George Peabody Col, MA, 40. *Prof Exp:* Mem fac Latin & English, Clarksville High Sch, 36-38; mem fac Latin, Ward Belmont Sch, Nashville, 38-40; mem fac hist, Lausanne Sch, Memphis, 41-42; asst prof, 52-62, ASSOC PROF ENGLISH & LATIN, UNIV HOUSTON, 62- *Concurrent Pos:* Delta Kappa Gamma study grant in Greece, 72. *Honors & Awards:* Cokesbury Juv Award, 57; Theta Sigma Phi Lit Award, 59. *Mem:* SCent Mod Lang Asn; Am Class League; Class Soc Am Acad Rome; Vergilian Soc. *Res:* Graphic languages, especially pictographs of the American Plains Indians and the petroglyphs of the Aztecs; literary translations from the Latin. *Publ:* Auth, How Medicine Man Cured Paleface Woman, W R Scott, 56; Painted Pony Runs Away, 58 & Little Elk Hunts Buffalo, 61, Nelson; Heptaplus, Translation from Latin of Philosophical Treatise by Pico della Mirandola, Philos Libr, 77; Chief Red Horse Tells About Custer, Elsenir/Nelson, 81. *Mailing Add:* 2405 Dickey Place Houston TX 77019

MCGHEE, DOROTHY MADELEINE, b Grand Rapids, Minn, May 4, 01. COMPARATIVE LITERATURE. *Educ:* Univ Minn, AB, 22, AM, 23; Univ Paris, Dipl, 26; Ohio State Univ, PhD, 30. *Prof Exp:* From instr to assoc prof Romance lang, 24-25 & 26-28, prof & head dept, 30-68, EMER PROF MOD LANG & HEAD DEPT, HAMLINE UNIV, 68- *Concurrent Pos:* Mem, US Planning Bd Spec Personnel; midwest translr comp lit & lang; mem midwest comt, Student Proj for Amity Among Nations. *Mem:* MLA; Am Asn Teachers Fr; Am Asn Teachers Span & Port (secy, 60); Am Comp Lit Asn; 18th Century Studies. *Res:* French and Spanish phonology for drama; Le Conte Moral; Duclos. *Publ:* Auth, Valtarian Narrative Devices, Banta, 33 & Russell, 73; contribr, A Critical Bibliography of French Literature, Eighteenth Century, Syracuse Univ, 51; auth, Conparative phonology for Drama, Ypsilanti, 52; Fortunes of a Tale, 54; The Cult of the Conte Moral, Banta, 60; Encyclopedism and its conscience: Evolutin and revolution, In: Honoris Volume to Professor Havens, Ohio State Univ, 75. *Mailing Add:* 1617 Sherburne Ave St Paul MN 55104

MCGILLIVRAY, RUSSELL GEORGE, b Montreal, Que, Sept 21, 28. FRENCH. *Educ:* McGill Univ, BA, 51; Yale Univ, PhD, 59. *Prof Exp:* Instr French Harvard Univ, 59-62; asst prof, 62-64, ASSOC PROF FRENCH, MCGILL UNIV, 64- *Mem:* MLA; Asn Can Univ Teachers Fr; Am Asn Teachers Fr. *Res:* Late Middle Ages; the 17th century. *Publ:* Auth, La preciosite: essai de mise au point, Rev Sci Humaines, 62. *Mailing Add:* 162 Sommer Hill DDO Roxboro PQ H9A 1X1 Can

MCGLATHERY, JAMES MELVILLE, b New Orleans, La, Nov 22, 36; m 63; c 3. GERMANIC LANGUAGES. *Educ:* Princeton Univ, AB, 58; Yale Univ, AM, 59, PhD(Ger), 64. *Prof Exp:* Instr Ger, Phillips Andover Acad, 59-60; instr, Harvard Univ, 63-65; asst prof, 65-71, ASSOC PROF GER, UNIV ILL, URBANA-CHAMPAIGN,71- *Concurrent Pos:* Managing ed, J English & Ger Philol, 72- *Mem:* MLA; Am Asn Teachers Ger. *Res:*

Romanticism and the 19th century literature. *Publ:* Auth, The suicide motif in E T A Hoffmann's Der goldne Topf, Monatshefte, 6/66; Kleist's Über das Marionetten-Theater, Ger Life & Lett, 7/67; Fear of perdition in Droste-Hülshoff's Judenbuche, In: Lebendige Form: Festschrift für Heinrich E K Henel, Wilhelm Fink, Munich, 70; Kleist's version of Moliere's Amphitryon: olympian cuckolding and unio mystica, In: Moliere and the Commonwealth of Letters, Univ Miss, 75; Der Himmel hängt ihm voller Geigen: E T A Hoffmann's Rat Krespel, Die Fermate, and Der Baron von B, Ger Quart, 3/78; Bald dein Fall ins-Ehebett?: A new reading of E T A Hoffman's Goldner Topf, Ger Rev, No 3, 78; Demon love: E T A Hoffmann's Elixiere des Teufels, Colloquia Germanica, Nos 1/2, 79; Mysticism and Sexuality: E T A Hoffmann Part One: Hoffmann and His Sources, Peter Lang, Berne, 81. *Mailing Add:* Dept of Ger Lang & Lit Univ of Ill Urbana IL 61801

MCGOLDRICK, JOHN MALCOLM, b Heswall, England, June 24, 42; m 68; c 2. FRENCH, FRENCH LITERATURE. *Educ:* Univ Hull, BA, 64, PhD(French), 67. *Prof Exp:* Lectr French, Univ Liverpool, 67-70; asst prof, 70-73, ASSOC PROF FRENCH, UNIV REGINA, 73- *Mem:* Can Asn Univ Teachers; Asn Can Univ Prof Fr; Humanities Asn Can; Soc Fr Studies; Am Asn Teachers Fr. *Res:* French Romanticism and the Bible; French Romanticism; Vigny. *Publ:* Auth, Vigny's unorthodox Christ, Mod Lang Notes, 5/70; Surrender and revolt in Vigny's writings, Romanische Forsch, 72. *Mailing Add:* 73 Motherwell Cres Regina SK S4S 3Z3 Can

MCGRADY, DONALD LEE, b Greenhurst, Md, Jan 17, 35; m 58; c 4. SPANISH. *Educ:* Swarthmore Col, AB, 57; Harvard Univ, MA, 58; Ind Univ, PhD(Span & Latin Am lit), 61. *Prof Exp:* From instr to asst prof Romance lang, Univ Tex, Austin, 61-64; from asst prof to assoc prof Span, Univ Calif, Santa Barbara, 64-69; assoc prof, 69-71, PROF SPAN, UNIV VA, 71- *Concurrent Pos:* Teaching asst, Ind Univ, 58-60; Univ Calif Humanities Inst fel, 68-69; vis assoc prof Span, Univ Calif, Berkeley, 69; Univ Va fac fels, 70, 71, 72; John Simon Guggenheim Mem Found, 72-73; Nat Endowment for Humanities sr fel, 76-77. *Res:* Spanish Golden Age literature; Spanish Medieval literature; comparative literature. *Publ:* Auth, Mateo Aleman, Twayne, 68; Romeo and Juliet has no Spanish source, Shakespeare Studies, 69; Jorge Isaacs, Twayne, 72; The comic treatment of conjugal honor in Lope's Las ferias de Madrid, Hisp Rev, 73; ed, Cristobal de Tamariz, Novelas en verso, Bibliot Siglo Oro, 74; auth, Chaucer and the Decameron reconsidered, Chaucer Rev, 77; The story of the painter and his little lamb, Thesaurus, 80; ed, Lope de Vega's La Francesilla, Bibliot Siglo Oro, 81. *Mailing Add:* Dept of Span, Ital & Port Univ of Va Charlottesville VA 22903

MACGREGOR, ALEXANDER PAUL, JR, US citizen. CLASSICS, PALAEOGRAPHY. *Educ:* Xavier Univ, Ohio, AB, 63; Univ Chicago, MA, 64, PhD(classics), 69. *Prof Exp:* Instr classics, William & Mary Col, 66-71; asst prof, Ind Univ, 71-72; asst prof, 72-80, ASSOC PROF CLASSICS, UNIV ILL, 80- *Mem:* Am Philol Asn. *Res:* Seneca's Tragedies; numerical taxonomy; Alciatus' Emblems. *Publ:* Auth, Ante renatas in Italia litteras: The mss of Seneca's tragedies, Trans Am Philol Asn, 71; coauth, The enchantress Almone revealed, Rev Can Estudios Hisp, 77; The Emblems of Alciatus, Coronado (in press); auth, Par 8031; a new delta-MS of Seneca's Tragedies, Philologus (in press). *Mailing Add:* Dept of Classics Univ of Ill 601 S Morgan Rm 1600 Chicago IL 60680

MCGREGOR, MALCOLM FRANCIS, b London, Eng, May 19, 10; m 38; c 2. CLASSICAL PHILOLOGY, ANCIENT HISTORY. *Educ:* Univ BC, BA, 30, MA, 31; Univ Cincinnati, PhD, 37. *Hon Degrees:* DCL, Bishop's Univ, 70; DLitt, Acadia Univ, 71 & Mem Univ, 82. *Prof Exp:* Acting instr classics, Univ Cincinnati, 36-37, from instr to prof classics & ancient hist, 37-54, acting dean grad sch arts & sch, 41-42; prof classics & head dept, 54-77, asst to dean fac arts & sci, 57-63, mem senate, 63-66, 72-77, dir ceremonies, 68-77, EMER PROF CLASSICS, UNIV BC, 77- *Concurrent Pos:* Mem Inst Advan Studies, 37-38, 48; fels, Guggenheim, 48; Can Coun, 67-68; vis prof, Am Sch Class Studies, Athens, 67-68; instr hist, Vancouver Community Col, Langara Campus, 77-; hon prof humanities, Univ Calgary, 78- *Honors & Awards:* Award, Am Philol Asn, 54. *Mem:* Fel Royal Soc Can; Class Asn Pac Northwest (pres, 72-73); Am Philol Asn (vpres, 68, pres, 70); Archaeol Inst Am; Class Asn Can (pres, 68-70, hon pres, 77-). *Res:* History and documents of sixth and fifth century BC Athens; Attic epigraphy; Athenian politics. *Publ:* Coauth, The Athenian Tribute Lists, Vol I, Harvard, 39, Vols II-IV, Am Sch Class Studies, Princeton Univ, 49-53; Studies in Fifth-Century Attic Epigraphy, Univ Okla, 74. *Mailing Add:* 4495 W Seventh Ave Vancouver BC V6R 1X1 Can

MCGREGOR, ROB ROY, JR, b Vernonia, Ore, Jan 15, 29; m 60; c 1. FRENCH LANGUAGE & LITERATURE, LATIN. *Educ:* Erskine Col, BA, 52; Columbia Theol Sem, BD, 57; Univ SC, MA, 65; Univ Ga, PhD(Romance lang), 69. *Prof Exp:* Teacher French, English, Latin & Ger, Sch Dist Five, Anderson, SC, 54-56, 57-63; asst prof French, 67-73, assoc prof, 73-80, PROF FRENCH, CLEMSON UNIV, 80- *Mem:* Am Asn Teachers Fr; MLA; Mediaeval Acad Am; Am Class League. *Res:* Fourteenth, eighteenth and nineteenth century French literature. *Publ:* Auth, An error in a letter of Flaubert to Baudelaire, 68 & The misunderstanding over the Sabbath in Candide, 71, Romance Notes; ed, The Lyric Poems of Jehan Froissart, NC Studies Romance Lang & Lit, 75; auth, Heraldic quarterings and Voltaire's Candide, Studies on Voltaire and the Eighteenth Century, 80; Pangloss' final observation, an ironic flaw in Voltaire's Candide, Roman Notes, 80. *Mailing Add:* Dept of Lang Clemson Univ Clemson SC 29631

MACHE, ULRICH, b Märkisch-Friedland, Ger, Nov 24, 28; US citizen; m 63; c 1. GERMAN LITERATURE. *Educ:* Univ BC, BA, 59, MA, 61; Princeton Univ, PhD(Ger), 63. *Prof Exp:* Instr Ger, Harvard Univ, 63-64; asst prof, Princeton Univ, 64-67; assoc prof, 67-70, PROF GER, STATE UNIV NY ALBANY, 70- *Concurrent Pos:* Res Found State Univ NY fac fel, 68, 70, 74, 78, grant-in-aid, 68-70; Am Coun Learned Soc grant-in-aid, 68; mem res awards comt, Res Found, State Univ NY, 71-73. *Mem:* MLA; Am Asn Teachers Ger; Inter Arbeitskreis deutsche Barockliteratur; Goethe Soc Am. *Res:* Seventeenth and eighteenth century German literature. *Publ:* Auth, Uberwindung des Amadisromans, Zeitschr Philol, 66; Zesen als Poetiker, Deut Vierteljschr, 67; Zu Goethes Faust: Studierzimmer I, Euphorion, 71 & Wege der Forschung, Vol 145; Critical Edition of Philipp von Zesen, Poetologische Schriften (3 vols), De Gruyter, Berlin, 71, 73, 77; Three essays, In: Philipp von Zesen Beiträge zu seinem Leben und Werk, Steiner, Wiesbaden, 72; A H Bucholtz, Teutscher Herkules, reprint, 73-78 & Bucholtz, Herkuliskus and Herkuladisla, reprint, 82, Peter Lang, Bern. *Mailing Add:* Dept of Ger State Univ of NY Albany NY 12222

MCHUGH, MICHAEL P, b Lackawanna, NY, June 7, 33; m 61; c 4. CLASSICAL PHILOLOGY, PATRISTIC STUDIES. *Educ:* Cath Univ Am, AB, 55, MA, 56, PhD(classics), 65. *Prof Exp:* From instr to asst prof classics & humanities, Howard Univ, 58-68; from asst prof to assoc prof, 68-77, PROF CLASSICS, UNIV CONN, STORRS, 77- *Mem:* NAm Patristic Soc; Am Philol Asn; Vergilian Soc; Am Class League; Medieval Acad Am. *Res:* St Ambrose; Prosper of Aquitaine; textual studies. *Publ:* Auth, Observations on the text of the Carmen de Providentia Dei, 68 & Observations on the text of the Carmen de Ingratis, 71, Manuscripta; Satan and Saint Ambrose, Class Folia, 72; translr, St Ambrose, Seven Exegetical Works, Fathers of Church ser, Cath Univ Am, 72; auth, Linen, wool, and colour, their appearance in Saint Ambrose, Bull Inst Class Studies, 76; The Demonology of Saint Ambrose in Light of the Tradition, Wiener Studien, 78. *Mailing Add:* Box U-57 Univ of Conn Storrs CT 06268

MACIAS, MANUEL JATO, b Portland, Ore, Mar 25, 29. SPANISH. *Educ:* Univ Portland, AB, 51, AM, 52; Univ Madrid, DrPhil & Let, 56; Northwestern Univ, PhD, 63; Univ Coimbra, dipl, 70; Univ Portland, MA, 77. *Prof Exp:* Instr mod lang, Marquette Univ, 55-57, asst prof Span, 57-58; from asst prof to assoc prof, 58-69, admin dir prog in Spain, Univ Navarre, 70-72, PROF SPAN, UNIV PORTLAND, 69-, CHMN DEPT FOREIGN LANG, 72- *Concurrent Pos:* Lectr, Portland State Col, 59; Fulbright exchange prof, Gt Brit, 59-60; vis assoc prof Span, Lewis & Clark Col, 68-69; lectr Span, Portland State Univ, 76-78. *Mem:* Am Asn Teachers Span & Port; Philol Asn Pac Coast; AAUP; Pac Northwest Foreign Lang Conf (pres, 68-69); Am Coun Foreign Lang Teaching. *Res:* Nineteenth and twentieth century Spanish drama; modern Galician literature. *Publ:* Auth, La ensenanza del espanol en los EEUU de American, Ed Cult Hisp, 61. *Mailing Add:* Dept of English & Mod Lang Univ of Portland 5000 N Willamette Blvd Portland OR 97203

MCINNIS, JUDY BREDESON, b Roseau, Minn, Sept 22, 43; m 67; c 2. COMPARATIVE LITERATURE, SPANISH. *Educ:* Bemidji State Col, BS, 64; Univ NC, Chapel Hell, PhD(compt lit), 74. *Prof Exp:* Peace Corps vol English, US Govt, Santiago, Chile, 64-66; instr, 71-75, asst prof, 75-82, ASSOC PROF SPAN, UNIV DEL, 82- *Mem:* Am Comp Lit Asn; MLA; Am Asn Teachers Span & Port; Southern Comp Lit Asn. *Res:* Spanish literary criticism 1400-1700; Spanish poetry 1400-1700; Federico Garcia Lorea. *Publ:* Auth, Allegory, mimesis and the Italian critical tradition in Alonso Lopez Pinciano's Philosophia Antigua, Hispano-Italic Studies, fall 76; The moral and formal dimensions of Fernando de Herrera's purist aesthetics, Proc IXth Cong Int Comp Lit Asn, Vol 1, Class Models in Lit, AMOC, Innsbruck, 81; Irene de Borbon Parma: The noble voice of Spanish feminism, Letras femeninas, Vol 7, No 1, spring 81; coauth (with Elizabeth Bohning, The child, the daemon and death, In: Romance de la luna, luna, Garcia Lorca Rev, Vol 9, No 2, fall 81; auth, A computer-assisted study of Spanish-English transfer, The first Delaware Symposium on Language Studies, Univ Del Press, 82. *Mailing Add:* Dept of Lang & Lit Univ of Del Newark DE 19711

MCINTOSH, RUSTIN CAREY, English. See Vol II

MACK, GERHARD GEORG, b Stuttgart, Ger, May 12, 39; m 67. GERMAN LITERATURE. *Educ:* Calif State Univ, Los Angeles, AB, 65; Univ Southern Calif, AM, 67, PhD(Ger), 71. *Prof Exp:* Instr Ger, Calif State Univ, 66-69 & Univ Mont, 69-70; asst prof, 70-76, assoc prof, 76-79, PROF GER, CALIF STATE COL, STANISLAUS, 80- *Concurrent Pos:* Asst Ger, Univ Southern Calif, 66-68. *Mem:* Am Asn Teachers Ger. *Res:* German exile literature; 20th century German literature; 18th century German literature. *Publ:* Contribr, Deutsche Exilliteratur nach 1933 in Kalifornien, Franke Verlag, 73; The Writer in Exile, Univ Southern Calif, 73; Deutsche Exilliteratur nach 1933 in Oster, Franke Verlag, 74. *Mailing Add:* Dept of Foreign Lang Calif State Col Stanislaus Turlock CA 95380

MACK, SARA, b New Haven, Conn, May 1, 39; div; c 2. CLASSICAL PHILOLOGY. *Educ:* Smith Col, BA, 61; Harvard Univ, AM, 64, PhD(class philol), 74. *Prof Exp:* asst prof, 76-81, ASSOC PROF CLASSICS, UNIV NC, CHAPEL HILL, 81-, ASST DEAN HONS, 81- *Concurrent Pos:* Fel, Nat Humanities Ctr, 80-81. *Mem:* Am Philol Asn; Class Asn Midwest & South; Vergilian Soc; AAUP. *Res:* Greek and Roman epic; Latin lyric and elegiac. *Publ:* Auth, Patterns of Time in Vergil, Archon Bks, 78; Ruit oceano nox, Class Quart, 5/80; The single supply, Ramus, spring 81. *Mailing Add:* Dept of Classics Univ of NC Chapel Hill NC 27514

MCKAUGHAN, HOWARD PAUL, b Canoga Park, Calif, July 5, 22; m 43; c 5. LINGUISTICS. *Educ:* Univ Calif, Los Angeles, AB, 45; Dallas Theol Sem, MTh, 46; Cornell Univ, MA, 52, PhD, 57. *Prof Exp:* Mem ling res, Summer Inst Ling, Philippines, 46-61, from assoc dir to dir, 53-61; from res asst prof to res assoc prof anthrop, Univ Wash, 61-63; assoc prof ling, 63, dir Pac & Asian ling inst, 66-69, assoc dean grad div, 66-72, dean grad div & dir res, 72-79, actg chancellor, 79, PROF LING, UNIV HAWAII, MANOA, 64-, INTERIM VCHANCELLOR, 81- *Concurrent Pos:* Prin investr, Nat Sci Found grants, grammatical analysis Jeh lang of SVietnam, 69-70 & Maranao ling studies, 70-72; prin investr, lang materials develop ctr, Defense Supply Serv, 69-70; dir, develop lang training materials in seven Philippine lang, Peace Corps, 69-71; Fulbright prof ling, Philippines, 77. *Mem:* Ling Soc Am; Int Ling Asn; Ling Soc Philippines; Western Asn Grad Sch (pres, 78-79). *Res:* Descriptive linguistics of the Philippines and New Guinea; lexicography. *Publ:* Auth, The Inflection and Syntax of Maranao Verbs, Inst Nat Lang, Manila, 58; ed & contribr, Sequences of clauses in Tairora, Oceanic Ling, summer 66; coauth, A Maranao Dictionary, Univ Hawaii, 67; ed & contribr, Topicalization in Maranao, an addendum, In: Pacific Linguistic Studies in Honour of Arthur Capell, Australian Nat Univ, 70; ed, Pali Language Texts: Philippines (21 vols), Univ Hawaii, 71; ed & contribr, Minor languages of the Philippines, In: Current Trends in Linguistics, Linguistics in Oceania, Mouton, The Hague, 71; The Languages of the Eastern Family of the East New Guinea Highlands Stock, Univ Wash, 73. *Mailing Add:* Off of Chancelllor Univ of Hawaii at Manoa Honolulu HI 96822

MCKAY, ALEXANDER GORDON, b Toronto, Ont, Dec 24, 24; m 64; c 2. CLASSICAL ART & ARCHITECTURE. *Educ:* Univ Toronto, BA, 46; Yale Univ, AM, 47; Princeton Univ, AM, 48, PhD(classics), 50. *Prof Exp:* Instr classics, Princeton Univ, 47-49, Wells Col, 49-50 & Univ Pa, 50-51; lectr, Univ Man, 51-52 & Mt Allison Univ, 52-53; from asst prof to assoc prof, Waterloo Univ Col, 53-55; asst prof, Univ Man, 55-57; from asst prof to assoc prof, 57-61, chmn dept, 62-68 & 76-78, dean humanities, 68-73, PROF CLASSICS, McMASTER UNIV, 61- *Concurrent Pos:* Dir, Class Summer Sch, Cumae, Italy, 57-82; vpres, Archit Conservancy Ont, 63-66; vis prof Univ Colo Athens, 65; contrib ed, Vergilius & Class World; pres, Hamilton Philharmonic Orchestra, 67-69; Can Coun leave fel, 73-74; mem, adv bd, Nat Libr Can, 77-79; deleg, Can Fedn for Humanities & dir, Union academique int, 78-80 & 81-83; Killiam sr res fel, Can Coun, 79-80. *Honors & Awards:* Silver Jubilee Medal, 77. *Mem:* Fel Royal Soc Can; Vergilian Soc Am(pres, 72-74); Am Philol Asn; Archaeol Inst Am; Class Asn Mid W & S (pres, 72-73); Class Asn Can(vpres, 71-73, pres, 78-80). *Res:* Vergilian studies; Roman art and architecture; Aeschylus. *Publ:* Auth, Ancient Rome, the City and the Monuments: Ancient Latium and Etruria, Vergilian Soc Am, 62; coauth, Roman Lyric Poetry: Catullus and Horace, MacMillan, 69; auth, Vergil's Italy, NY Graphic Soc, 70; Cumae and the Phlegraean Fields, Naples and Coastal Campania, Cromlech Press, Ont, 72; Piranesi's Impression of Rome, Hakkert, Toronto, 73; Houses, Villas, and Palaces in the Roman World, Thames & Hudson & Cornell Univ Press, 75; coauth, Roman Satire: Horace, Juvenal, Persius, Petronuis, and Seneca, Macmillan, 76; coauth, Roman Satire: Horace, Juvenal, Persius, Petronius, and Seneca, Macmillan, 76; auth, Vitruvius: Architect and Engineer, Macmillan, 78; Vitruvius, Architect and Engineer: Buildings and Building Techniques in Augustan Rome, Macmillan, 78; transl & rev, Römische Hauser, Villen und Paläste, Atlantis Verlag, 80. *Mailing Add:* 1 Turner Ave Hamilton ON L8P 3K4 Can

MACKAY, ALISTAIR R, b Vancouver, BC, Nov 14, 31. ROMANCE LANGUAGES & LITERATURES. *Educ:* Univ BC, BA, 53; Univ Calif, Los Angeles, MA, 55; Univ Calif, Berkeley, PhD(Romance lang & lit), 64. *Prof Exp:* From instr to asst prof, 62-69, ASSOC PROF FRENCH, UNIV BC, 69- *Concurrent Pos:* Can Coun fel, 67-68 & study leave fel, 76-77. *Res:* Sixteenth century French literature. *Publ:* Auth, Olivier de Magny: Les gayetez, Droz, Geneva, 68. *Mailing Add:* Dept of French Univ of BC Vancouver BC V6T 1W5 Can

MACKAY, CAROL HANBERY, English Literature, Rhetoric & Composition. See Vol II

MCKAY, DOUGLAS RICH, b Salt Lake City, Utah, Nov 12, 36. SPANISH. *Educ:* Univ Utah, BA, 62; Univ Ore, MA, 64; Mich State Univ, PhD(Span), 68. *Prof Exp:* Instr Span, Mich State Univ, 65-67; asst prof, Univ Hawaii, 67-68; from asst prof to assoc prof, 68-76, chmn foreign lang dept, 68-76, PROF SPAN, UNIV COLO, COLORADO SPRINGS, 76- *Concurrent Pos:* Vis prof, Univ Hawaii, 78-79; summer fel, Nat Endowment for Humanities, Univ Calif, Berkeley, 78 & 81. *Honors & Awards:* Distinguished Res & Publ Award, Univ Colo, Colorado Springs, 76. *Mem:* Am Asn Teachers Span & Port; Rocky Mt Mod Lang Asn. *Res:* Modern and contemporary Spanish peninsular literature, principally drama; local Colorado history; humor in literature. *Publ:* Auth, Carlos Arniches, 72 & Enrique Jardiel Poncela, 74, Twayne; Misterio y pavor: trece cuentos, Holt, 74; Understanding the Spanish Subjunctive, Centennial Ed, 76; Miguel Mihura, Twayne, 77; History of the Cragmor Sanatorium, (in prep); Asylum of the Gilded Pill, Colo Hist Soc, 82. *Mailing Add:* Dept of Foreign Lang Univ of Colo Cragmor Rd Colorado Springs CO 80907

MCKAY, JANET HOLMGREN, English, Linguistics. See Vol II

MACKAY, PIERRE A, b Toronto, Ont, Feb 19, 33; US citizen; m 63. CLASSICS, NEAR EASTERN STUDIES. *Educ:* Yale Univ, AB, 54; Univ Calif, Berkeley, MA, 59, PhD(classics), 64. *Prof Exp:* Instr classics, Univ Ore, 57-58; lectr Greek, Bryn Mawr Col, 63-64; Archaeol Inst Am Olivia James traveling fel, 65-66; asst prof classics & comp lit, 66-69, assoc prof classics, comp lit & Near Eastern lang & lit, 69-76, PROF CLASSICS, COMP LIT & NEAR EASTERN LANG & LIT, UNIV WASH, 76- *Concurrent Pos:* Vis mem, Inst Advan Study, Princeton, NJ, 73-74. *Mem:* Archaeol Inst Am; Am Numismatic Soc; MidE Studies Asn; Am Orient Soc. *Res:* Classical Byzantine and Islamic studies; computer processing of Arabic script texts. *Publ:* Auth, Acrocorinth in 1668, a Turkish account, Hesperia, 68; Macedonian tetradrachms of 148-147 BC, Am Numismatic Soc, 68; Certificates of Transmission on a Manuscript of the Maqamat of Hariri, Trans Am Philos Soc, 71; The manuscripts of the Seyahatname of Evliya Celebi, Der Islam, 75; coauth, Mendes II, Aris & Phillips, Warminster, 76; auth, Setting Arabic with a computer, Scholarly Publ, 77. *Mailing Add:* Dept of Classics Univ of Wash Seattle WA 98195

MCKEEN, DON HAYES, b Julesburg, Colo, Dec 3, 28. ROMANCE LANGUAGES & LITERATURES. *Educ:* Harvard Univ, MA, 57, PhD(Romance lang & lit), 67. *Prof Exp:* Instr French, Colby Col, 57-59, spec instr, 60-63, from instr to assoc prof, 63-78, PROF FRENCH, SIMMONS COL, 78- *Mem:* MLA; Am Asn Teahers Fr;. *Res:* Symbolist poetry; Rimbaud. *Mailing Add:* Dept of Mod Foreign Lang & Lit Simmons Col 300 Fenway Boston MA 02115

MACKENDRICK, PAUL LACHLAN, b Taunton, Mass, Feb 11, 14; m 45; c 2. CLASSICAL PHILOLOGY. *Educ:* Harvard Univ, AB, 34, AM, 37, PhD, 38. *Prof Exp:* Asst classics & tutor ancient lang, Harvard Univ, 37-38; instr Latin, Phillips Acad, 38-41; instr English, Harvard Univ, 46; asst prof classics, 46-48, from assoc prof to prof, classics & integrated lib studies, 48-75, LILY ROSS TAYLOR PROF CLASSICS, UNIV WIS-MADISON, 75- *Concurrent Pos:* Trustee, Am Acad Rome, 64-72; Guggenheim fel, 57-58; vis prof, Univ Ibadan, 65-66; Martin class lectr, Oberlin Col, 66; Phi Beta Kappa nat lectr, 70; prof-in-charge, Inter-col Ctr Class Studies, Rome, 73-74; overseas fel, Churchill Col, Cambridge, 77-78. *Mem:* Am Philol Asn (secy-treas, 54-56); Archaeol Inst Am; Am Coun Learned Soc (secy, 56-63); Class Asn Midwest & South (pres, 72). *Res:* Athenian aristocracy and political history; Roman colonization and archaeology. *Publ:* Auth, The Roman Mind at Work, Van Nostrand, 58; The Mute Stones Speak, 60 & The Greek Stones Speak, 62, St Martin's, new ed, Norton, 82; The Athenian Aristocracy, 399-31 BC, Harvard Univ, 69; The Iberian Stones speak, 67 & Romans on the Rhine, 70, Funk; Roman France, St Martin's, 72; The Dacian Stones Speak, 75 & The North African Stones Speak, 80, Univ NC. *Mailing Add:* 914 Van Hise Hall Univ of Wis Madison WI 53706

MCKENNA, ANDREW JOSEPH, b Massapequa, NY, Nov 29, 42; m 64; c 1. FRENCH LITERATURE. *Educ:* Col Holy Cross, AB, 64; Johns Hopkins Univ, MA, 66, PhD(Romance lang), 70. *Prof Exp:* Instr French, Northwestern Univ, 67-70; asst prof, 71-80, ASSOC PROF FRENCH, LOYOLA UNIV, CHICAGO, 80- *Res:* Nineteenth century French literature; 20th century French literature; critical theory. *Publ:* Auth, History of the ear: Ideology and poetic deconstruction, Centrum, spring 76; Mass media: Flaubert and the art of nihilism, Enclitic, spring 77; Biblioclasm: Joycing Jesus and Borges, Diacritics, fall 78; Lex Icon: Freud and Rimbaud, Visible Lang, No. 3, 80; Writing in the novel: Remarks on Bouvard et Pecuchet, Lang & Style, spring 81; Alphabestiary: On names in Flaubert, Cream City Rev, winter 81; Allodidacticism: Flaubert 100 years after, Yale Fr Studies (in press). *Mailing Add:* Loyola Univ of Chicago 6525 N Sheridan Rd Chicago IL 60626

MCKENNA, JAMES BRIAN, b Jersey City, NJ, Jan 23, 36. ROMANCE LANGUAGES. *Educ:* Princeton Univ, AB, 56; Harvard Univ, MA, 62, PhD(Romance lang), 65. *Prof Exp:* Lectr Span, Ind Univ, 64-65, asst prof, 65-66; asst prof, 66-69, actg vpres lib studies, 71-73, ASSOC PROF SPAN, STATE UNIV NY, STONY BROOK, 69-, DIR ACAD PLANNING, 73- *Mem:* MLA. *Res:* Spanish and Portugese literature and history. *Publ:* Auth, A Spaniard in the Portuguese Indies, Harvard Univ, 67. *Mailing Add:* Off of Acad VPres State Univ NY Stony Brook NY 17790

MCKENNA, JOHN FRANCIS, b New York, NY, Apr 2, 23. FRENCH. *Educ:* Fordham Univ, AB, 43, MA, 49, PhD, 57. *Prof Exp:* From instr to asst prof French, Univ Scranton, 49-59; from asst prof to assoc prof, 59-75 chmn dept mod lang & lit, 66-69, PROF FRENCH, COL HOLY CROSS, 75- *Mem:* Am Asn Teachers French. *Publ:* Auth, The noble savage in the Voyage of La Perouse 1785-1788, Ky Foreign Lang Quart, Vol XII, No 1; Ageirotics: In aid of the Socratic method in intermediate college French, 4/71 & The proverb in humanistic Studies: Language, literature and culture theory and classroom practice, 12/74, French Rev. *Mailing Add:* Dept of Mod Lang Col of the Holy Cross Worcester MA 01610

MCKENZIE, MARGARET, b Great Falls, Mont, Feb 25, 18. GERMAN. *Educ:* Scripps Col, BA, 40; Radcliffe Col, MA, 44; Univ Chicago, PhD, 58. *Prof Exp:* From asst prof to assoc prof Ger & French, Adams State Col Colo, 51-56; from asst prof to assoc prof Ger, Colo Col, 56-60; vis lectr, Univ Colo, 60-61; assoc prof, 61-76, chmn dept, 61-66 & 74-77, PROF GER, VASSAR COL, 76- *Concurrent Pos:* Mem bd trustees, Scripps Col, 75-; vis scholar, Dept Germanic Lang & Lit, Univ Chicago, 81- *Mem:* MLA; Am Asn Teachers Ger (pres, 72, 73); AAUP; Mod Humanities Res Asn; Am Asn Adv Humanities. *Res:* Hofmannsthal; classical period of German literature. *Publ:* Auth, Hofmannsthals Operntext Die aegyptische Helena, In: Atlantische Begegnungen: eine Freundesgabe für Arnold Bergstraesser, Rombach, Freiburg, 64; Hofmannsthals Semiramis-Entwürfe auf Grund der Quellen interpretiert, Deut Beiträge zur geistigen Ueberlieferung, 70. *Mailing Add:* Dept of Ger Vassar Col Poughkeepsie NY 12601

MACKEY, CHARLES RUYLE, b Oxnard, Calif, Aug 27, 33; m 64; c 2. ROMANCE LANGUAGES. *Educ:* Occidental Col, AB, 55; Yale Univ, PhD(French), 65. *Prof Exp:* Instr French, Occidental Col, 58-59; instr, Yale Univ, 63-65; from asst prof to assoc prof, 65-77, chmn dept foreign lang, 68-74, PROF FRENCH, SIMMONS COL, 77-, DEAN HUMANITIES, 77- *Mem:* Am Conf Acad Deans; Am Asn Teachers Fr; Am Coun Teaching Foreign Lang. *Res:* Seventeenth century French literature; Romantic poetry and theater. *Publ:* The French Press, The Fr Rev, 2/82. *Mailing Add:* Dept of Humanities Simmons Col 300 The Fenway Boston MA 02115

MACKEY, WILLIAM FRANCIS, b Winnipeg, Man, Jan 26, 18; m 49; c 2. LINGUISTICS, BILINGUALISM. *Educ:* Univ Man, BA, 40; Laval Univ, MA, 42; Harvard Univ, MA, 47; Univ Geneva, DLitt, 65. *Prof Exp:* Sr lectr ling method, Univ London, 48-50; assoc prof English philol, 50-54, prof English philol & ling, 54-61, dir lang lab, 57-69, dir div lang didactics, 61-69, prof lang didactics, 61-71, exec dir, Int Ctr Res Bilingualism, 67-70, RES PROF, LAVAL UNIV, 71- *Concurrent Pos:* Consult, Comt Educ of Poles, English, 48; Commonwealth Off Educ, Australia, 49; Intergovt Comt Europ Migration, Geneva, 55-56; Dept Citizenship & Immigration, Can, 57-69; mem Humanities Res Coun Can, 60-70; US Dept Health, Educ & Welfare, 66-70; Royal Comn Bilingualism & Biculturalism, 66, consult, 66-68; mem acad senate, Can Coun, 67; mem Lang Attitudes Res Comt, Irish Govt, 71-; ed, Studies Bilingual Educ, 71-; fed comnr, Bilingual Districts Adv Bd, Can Govt, 72-; comnr, Kommission für sprachpolitische Integrationsfragan europäischen Gemeinschaft, 75-; chmn, lang policy, Can Coun Develop Comt on Individual, Lang & Soc, 75-77, comnr, Fed Govt Comn Lang Training in Pub Serv Can, 75-77. *Honors & Awards:* 1974 Jubilee Medal, Inst Ling, London, England, 75. *Mem:* Ling Soc Am; Can Ling Asn; Ling Soc Paris; Int

Phonetic Asn; fel Royal Soc Can. *Res:* Bilingualism; geolinguistics; lexicometrics. *Publ:* Auth, International Bibliography on Bilingualism, Laval Univ, 72; co-ed, The Multinational Society, Newbury House, 75; auth, Bilinguisme et contact des langues, Klincksieck, Paris, 76; coauth, Bilingual Schools for a Bicultural Community, 77 & co-ed, Bilingualism in Early Childhood, 77, Newbury House; The Bilingual Education Movement: Essays on Its Progress, Tex Western Col, 77; Gengo Kyoku Buseki, Taishukan, Tokyo, 79; co-ed, Sociolinguistic Studies in Language Contact: Methods and Cases, Mouton, The Hague, 80. *Mailing Add:* Int Ctr Res Bilingualism Laval Univ Quebec PQ G1K 7P4 Can

MCKIBBEN, WILLIAM TORREY, b Seattle, Wash, Sept 30, 16; m 44; c 2. CLASSICS. *Educ:* Stanford Univ, AB, 37, MA, 38; Univ Chicago, PhD(Latin lang & lit), 42. *Prof Exp:* Lectr classics, Univ Utah, 46-47, asst prof, 47-50; from assoc prof to prof class lang, 52-61, BENEDICT PROF CLASS LANG, GRINNELL COL, 61- *Concurrent Pos:* Am acad Rome fel, 49-50; Fulbright grant, Italy, 50-51. *Mem:* Am Philol Asn; Class Asn Mid W & S; Archaeol Inst Am; Class Soc Am; Am Coun Teaching Foreign Lang. *Res:* Homer; Lucretius; Augustan poetry. *Publ:* Auth, In Bovem Mugire, Class Philol. *Mailing Add:* Dept of Classics Grinnell Col Grinnell IA 50112

MCKINLEY, MARY B, b Pittsburgh, Pa, May 15, 43. FRENCH RENAISSANCE LITERATURE. *Educ:* Seton Hill Col, BA, 65; Univ Wis, MA, 66; Rutgers Univ, PhD(French), 74. *Prof Exp:* Instr French, Albertus Magnus Col, 67-69; acad dir Ital, Exp Int Living, 72-73; asst prof, 74-80, ASSOC PROF FRENCH, UNIV VA, 80- *Concurrent Pos:* Mem Cent Exec Comt, Folger Inst Renaissance & 18th Century Studies, 76- *Mem:* MLA: Renaissance Soc Am; Am Asn Teachers Fr. *Res:* Montaigne; history of rhetoric and language theory. *Publ:* Auth, The City of God and the city of man: Limits of language in Montaigne's Apologie, Romanic Rev (in press); Words in a corner: Studies in Montaigne's Latin Quotations, 81 & co-ed, Columbia Montaigne conference papers, 81, Fr Forum Publ. *Mailing Add:* Dept of French 302 Cabell Hall Univ of Va Charlottesville VA 22903

MCKINNEY, JAMES E, b Emory, Tex, Feb 28, 27; m 51; c 3. MODERN LANGUAGE. *Educ:* ETex State Col, BA, 48; Middlebury Col, MA, 53; Purdue Univ, PhD, 60. *Prof Exp:* Instr Span, Western Mil acad, 48-54; instr pub sch, Baytown, Tex, 54-56; from instr to asst prof mod lang, Purdue Univ, 56-63, assoc prof mod lang & educ, 63-66; PROF FOREIGN LANG & CHMN DEPT, WESTERN ILL UNIV, 66- *Concurrent Pos:* Assoc & reviewer Span courses, Midwest Proj Airborne TV Instr, 59-66; foreign lang consult, McGraw-Hill Bk Co, Inc, 61-71; consult, Mod Lang Asn Am, 65-, Educ Testing Serv, 66-; ed, Bull Ill Foreign Lang Teachers Asn, 70-81. *Mem:* Am Asn Teachers Span & Port; MLA; Am Coun Teaching Foreign Lang; AAUP. *Publ:* Coauth, The modern language class, NEA J, 3/58; Learning Spanish in Modern Way, McGraw, Vols I, II & III, 62, 2nd ed, Vols I & II, 67; auth, Inservice training: Ways and means, 12/64 & The new key in a large school system, 11/65, Mod Lang J; coauth, Paginas de un diario, McGraw, 66. *Mailing Add:* Dept of Foreign Lang Western Ill Univ Macomb IL 61455

MCKIRAHAN, RICHARD DUNCAN, JR, b Berkeley, Calif, July 27, 45; m 79. CLASSICS, PHILOSOPHY. *Educ:* Univ Calif, Berkeley, AB, 66; Oxford Univ, BA, 69; Harvard Univ, PhD(class philos), 73. *Prof Exp:* Asst prof, 73-79, ASSOC PROF CLASSICS & PHILOS, POMONA COL, 79-, CHMN, CLASSICS DEPT, 81- *Concurrent Pos:* Vis assoc prof classics, Univ Calif, Berkeley, 80. *Mem:* Am Philol Asn; Soc Ancient Greek Philos. *Res:* Greek philosophy; history of science. *Publ:* Auth, Plato & Socrates: A Comprehensive Bibliography, 1958- 1973, Garland, 78; Aristotle's Subordinate Sciences, Brit J Hist Sci, 78; Diodorus and Prior and the master argument, Synthese, 79; Aristotelian epagoge in Prior Analytics 2.21 and Posterior Analytics 1.1, J Hist of Philos (in prep). *Mailing Add:* Dept of Classics Pomona Col Claremont CA 91711

MACKIW, THEODORE, b Strutyn, Ukraine, May 30, 18; US citizen; m 58; c 1. EAST EUROPEAN HISTORY, RUSSIAN. *Educ:* Univ Frankfurt, PhD, 50. *Prof Exp:* Instr Latin, Cushing Acad, 55-56; vis prof hist, Schwyz Col, Switz, 56-57; prof, Lane Col, 57-58; instr Latin & Russ, Hamden Hall Country Day Sch, 58-60; asst prof Russ, Univ RI, 60-62; assoc prof Slavic lang, 62-73, res grant, 62, PROF MOD LANG & DIR SOVIET STUDIES, UNIV AKRON, 73- *Concurrent Pos:* Scholar, Inst World Affairs, 52 & Seton Hall Univ, 53-54; res fel Yale Univ, 59-62; Univ RI res grant, 60-61. *Mem:* Am Asn Advan Slavic Studies; Am Asn Teachers Slavic & EEurop Lang; AHA; Shevchenko Sci Soc; Ukrainian Acad Arts & Sci US. *Res:* Eastern European history of the 17th century; revolution in the Ukraine in the English press of 1648-1657. *Publ:* Auth, Prince Mazepa, Hetman of Ukraine, in Contemporary English Publications, 1687-1709, Ukrainian Res Inst, Chicago, 67; Mazepas Fürstentitel im Lichte seines Briefes an Kaiser, Arch, Kulturgeschichte, Vol XLIV, Nov 3; Nove u pidsovetskij literaturi, Novyj Shlakh, Vol XXXVI, No 21; Washington-Peking-Moscow, Ukrainian Rev, Vol XIII, No 3; Imperial envoy to Hetman Khmelnytsky in 1657, Ann Ukrainian Acad, 69-72; Ukraina v raportakh anglijskoho posla do Moskvy, 1705-1710, Ukrainskyj Istoryk, Munich-NY, 73; Rückversicherungsvertrag--Bismarckscher Wegweiser zur deutschen Ostpolitik, Naukovi Zapysky . . ., 74-75; The rise of the Ukrainian Military Republic (The Metmanstate), 1649-1764, Ukrainian Rev, 76. *Mailing Add:* Dept of Mod Lang Univ of Akron Akron OH 44325

MCKNIGHT, CHRISTINA SODERHJELM, b Uppsala, Sweden, Apr 27, 43; m 61; c 4. SCANDINAVIAN LITERATURE. *Educ:* Univ Calif, Berkeley, BA, 66, MA, 67, PhD(Scand), 78. *Prof Exp:* Actg asst prof, 76-78, LECTR SWED, DEPT SCAND, UNIV CALIF, BERKELEY, 78- *Mem:* Soc Advan Scand Studies. *Res:* Development in modern Scandinavia; women's roles in Scandinavia especially in literature; immigrants' position in Scandinavian societies. *Publ:* Auth, Lars Forssell: The jester as conscience, World Lit Today, winter 81. *Mailing Add:* Dept of Scand Univ of Calif Berkeley CA 94720

MACKSEY, RICHARD ALAN, b Glen Ridge, NJ, July 25, 31; m 56; c 1. COMPARATIVE LITERATURE, ENGLISH. *Educ:* Johns Hopkins Univ, MA, 53, PhD, 57. *Prof Exp:* Jr instr English, Johns Hopkins Univ, 53-55; from instr to asst prof, Loyola Col, 56-58; asst prof writing sem, 58-63, assoc prof humanistic studies, 64-73, Carnegie lectr sem hist ideas, 62-64, chmn sect lang, lit & cult, 66-72, actg dir humanities ctr, 68-69, PROF HUMANISTIC STUDIES & CHMN HUMANITIES CTR, JOHNS HOPKINS UNIV, 73- *Concurrent Pos:* Chmn comt internal evidence, Bibliog Conf, 62; lectr, Baltimore Mus Art, 64-65; dir, Bollingen Poetry Festival, Turnbull lect, Theatre Hopkins, Center Stage, Tantamount Films, Carroll House & Levering Hall; moderator, Dialogue of the Arts, CBS; ed comp lit, Mod Lang Notes & Structure. *Mem:* MLA; Am Soc Aesthet; Renaissance Soc Am; Mediaeval Acad Am; Col English Asn. *Res:* European and English novel; poetics, rhetoric, and theory of literature; interrelation of arts, comparative methodology and intellectual history. *Publ:* Auth, Poems from the Hungarian Revolution, Cornell Univ, 66; Forerunners of Darwin, 2nd ed, 68, The Languages of Criticism and the Sciences of Man, 69 & Interpretation: Theory and Practice, Johns Hopkins, 69; coauth, Negative metaphor and Proust's rhetoric of absence, Mod Lang Notes, 70; co-ed, The Structuralist Controversy, 72 & auth, Velocities of Change, Johns Hopkins; Gloria Victis, Nemzetör, Munich, 66. *Mailing Add:* Ctr for Humanities Johns Hopkins Univ Baltimore MD 21218

MCLAIN, RICHARD LEE, English Literature, Linguistics. See Vol II

MCLAREN, JAMES CLARK, b Halifax, NS, June 19, 25. FRENCH. *Educ:* Dalhousie Univ, BA, 45, MA, 46; Columbia Univ, PhD, 51. *Prof Exp:* Tutor French, Dalhousie Univ, 45-46; instr sch gen studies, Columbia Univ, 47-48; from instr to asst prof, Johns Hopkins Univ, 48-56; from assoc prof to prof, Chatham Col, 56-65, chmn mod lang, 57-65; PROF FRENCH, UNIV DEL, 65- *Concurrent Pos:* Vis lectr, Goucher Col, 54-55 & Univ Pittsburgh, 57-63. *Honors & Awards:* French Govt Medal, Dalhousie Univ, 45. *Mem:* MLA; Am Asn Teachers Fr. *Res:* The works of Andre Gide; contemporary French theatre; Baudelaire and the French symbolists. *Publ:* Auth, The Theatre of Andre Gide: Evolution of a Moral Philosopher, Johns Hopkins, 53; Criticism and creativity; poetic themes in Mallarme and Valery, winter 64 & Diderot and the paradox of versatility, spring 68, L'Esprit Createur; Identical contexts: Greek myth, modern French drama, Renascence, fall 68; Qu'est-ce que le Romantisme?, Romance Notes, Vol XVI, 75; The imagery of light and darkness, In: Les Fleurs du mal', Nineteenth Century Fr Studies, fall-winter, 78-79. *Mailing Add:* Dept of Lang & Lit Univ of Del Newark DE 19711

MCLAUGHLIN, BLANDINE LAFLAMME, b Fairfield, Maine, Dec 4, 29; wid. ROMANCE LANGUAGES. *Educ:* Colby Col, AB, 60; Middlebury Col, AM, 61; Univ Paris, DUniv(French), 66. *Prof Exp:* Instr French, Mary Washington Col, 63-64; asst prof, Smith Col, 66-72; assoc prof, 72-80, PROF FRENCH, UNIV ALA, BIRMINGHAM, 80- *Mem:* MLA; Soc Int Etude du XVIIIe Siecle; Am Soc 18th Century Studies; Southeastern Am Soc 18th Century Studies (secy-treas, 78-82); SAtlantic Mod Lang Asn. *Publ:* Auth, Answer to despair, Int J Parapsychol, 65; A new look at Diderot's Fils naturel, Diderot Studies, 68; Diderot et l'Amitie, Studies Voltaire & 18th Century, 73, Gabriel Marcel: A personal tribute, Parapsychol Rev, 74; Les Liaisons Dangereuses-a quest for freedom, ADAM Int Rev, 79. *Mailing Add:* Dept of For Lang Univ of Ala Birmingham AL 35233

MCLAUGHLIN, JOHN DENNIS, b Dorchester, Mass, Mar 15, 47. CLASSICAL STUDIES. *Educ:* Boston Col, BA, 69; Univ Mich, MA, 71, PhD(class studies), 75. *Prof Exp:* Asst prof classics, Fordham Univ, 75-82. *Mem:* Am Philol Asn. *Res:* Latin poetry, especially comedy and erotic elegy; ancient religion and mythology; Roman law. *Publ:* Auth, Vengeance with a Twist: Another look at the Proemium to Ovid's Ars Amortoria (fascicule 3), 31: 269-271 &; Who is Hesiod's Pandora (fascicule 1), 33: 17-18, Mara. *Mailing Add:* Dept of Classics Fordham Univ Bronx NY 10458

MCLEAN, EDWARD F, b Willow Springs, NC, Jan 18, 27; m 50; c 5. SPANISH. *Educ:* Unin Oriente, BA, 56; Duke Univ, MA, 58, PhD(Span), 61. *Prof Exp:* Asst prof Span, Fla Southern Col, 59-60; assoc prof, 60-71, PROF MOD LANG, UNIV S FLA, TAMPA, 71- *Res:* Naturalism in the novel of 19th century Spain; 19th and 20th century literature. *Mailing Add:* Dept of Mod Lang Univ of SFla Tampa FL 33620

MCLEAN, HUGH, b Denver, Colo, Feb 5, 25; m 57; c 3. SLAVIC LANGUAGES & LITERATURES. *Educ:* Yale Univ, AB, 47; Columbia Univ, AM, 49; Harvard Univ, PhD(Slavic lang & lit), 56. *Prof Exp:* From instr to asst prof Slavic lang & lit, Harvard Univ, 53-59; from assoc prof to prof Russ lit, Univ Chicago, 59-68, chmn dept Slavic lang & lit, 61-67; chmn dept, 70-72, 74-76, dean div humanities, Col Lett & Sci, 76-81, actg provost & dean, 80-81, PROF SLAVIC LANG & LIT, UNIV CALIF, BERKELEY, 68- *Concurrent Pos:* Fulbright award, UK, 58-59; Am Coun Learned Soc fel humanities, 58-59; Guggenheim fel, 65-66. *Mem:* Am Asn Teachers Slavic & East Europ Lang; Am Asn Advan Slavic Studies. *Res:* Russian literature of the 19th and 20th centuries. *Publ:* Auth, The development of modern Russian literature, Slavic Rev, 9/62; Nikolai Leskov: The Man and his Art, Harvard Univ, 77. *Mailing Add:* Dept of Slavic Lang & Lit Univ of Calif Berkeley CA 94720

MACLEAN, HUGH ARNOLD, b St Thomas, Ont, Sept 22, 29; m 55. CLASSICS. *Educ:* McMaster Univ, BA, 51; Univ Wis, MA, 52, PhD(classics), 54. *Prof Exp:* Asst prof classics, Mt Allison Univ, 54-65; ASSOC PROF CLASSICS, WILFRID LAURIER UNIV, 65-, CHMN DEPT, 67- *Mem:* Class Asn Can (secy, 67-69); Archaeol Inst Am. *Res:* Roman colonization; Tacitus; topography of Campus Martius. *Mailing Add:* Dept of Class Wilfrid Laurier Univ Waterloo ON N2L 3C5 Can

MCLEAN, MALCOLM DALLAS, b Rogers, Tex, Mar 10, 13; m 39; c 1. HISTORY, FOREIGN LANGUAGE. *Educ:* Univ Tex, BA, 36, PhD, 51; Nat Univ Mex, MA, 38. *Prof Exp:* Field ed in charge Span transl, Tex Hist Record Surv, 38-39; asst dir & archivist, San Jacinto Mus Hist, Houston, Tex,

39-41; res analyst, US War Dept, 41-46; Span transl libr, Univ Tex, Austin, 46-47, instr Romance lang, Univ Tex, Austin, 47-51; from asst prof to assoc prof, Univ Ark, 51-56; dir, Bi-Nat Ctr, US Info Agency, Tegucigalpa, Honduras, 56-59, Guayaquil, Ecuador, 59-61; from assoc prof to prof Span, 61-76, assoc dean arts & sci, 64-74, EMER PROF SPAN, TEX CHRISTIAN UNIV, 77-; PROF HIST & SPAN, UNIV TEX, ARLINGTON, 76- *Concurrent Pos:* Consult Span, Britannica World Lang Dict, 55; J M West Tex Corp res grant, 67; Dr Malcolm D McLean Scholar, Tex Christian Univ, 72; hon dir Span Tex microfilm ctr, Sons Repub Tex, Goliad, 73-74; Tex State Geneal Soc fel, 76. *Honors & Awards:* Distinguished Serv Award, Sons Repub Tex, 71; Knight of the Order of San Jacinto, Sons Rep Tex, 73; Coral Horton Tullis Mem Prize, 74; Summerfield G Roberts Award, 74; Award of Merit, Am Asn for State & Local Hist, 76; res award, Tex Hist Found, 81; Medalla Merito, Soc Nuevoleonesa de Hist, Geog y Estadistica, 82. *Mem:* Am Asn State & Local Hist; Orgn Am Historians; Western Hist Asn. *Res:* Robertson's colony in Texas. *Publ:* Auth, Vida y obra de Guillermo Prieto, Fondo Cult Econ, Mex, 60; co-ed, Descripcion del nuevo reino de Leon 1735-1740, Inst Tecnol y Estud Super Monterrey, 63, English ed, 64; auth, Contenido literario de El Siglo Diez y Nueve, Secretaria Hacienda y Credito Publico, 65; Fine Texas Horses: Their Pedigrees and Performance, 1830-1845, Tex Christian Univ, 66; Notas para una bibliografia sobre Guillermo Prieto, Secretaria Hacienda y Credito Publico, 68; ed, Papers Concerning Robertson's Colony in Texas, Tex Christian Univ, Vol I-III, 74-76 & Univ Tex, Arlington, Vol IV-VIII, 77-81. *Mailing Add:* UTA Box 19959 Tex Christian Univ Arlington TX 76019

MCLEAN, SAMMY KAY, b Eldorado, Kans, Sept 29, 29; div. COMPARATIVE LITERATURE, GERMANICS. *Educ:* Univ Okla, BA,52; Univ Mich, MA, 57, PhD, 63. *Prof Exp:* From instr to asst prof Ger lang & lit, Dartmouth Col, 61-65; lectr, Univ Md Overseas Prog, London, England, 65-67; asst prof, 67-73, ASSOC PROF COMP LIT & GERMANICS, UNIV WASH, 73- *Mem:* Int Brecht Soc; MLA; Am Lit Transl Asn. *Res:* Twentieth century German, French and American poetry; Bertolt Brecht and non-Aristotillian drama; Franz Kafka. *Publ:* Auth, Bertolt, Brecht: A poetic credo, Marab, spring-summer 66; The Bäukelsang and the Work of Bertolt Brecht, Mouton, The Hague & Paris, 72; Messianism in Bertolf Brecht's Der gute Mensch von Sezuan and Der Kaukasische Kreidekleis, Seminar, 11/78; Doubling and sexual identity in stories by Franz Kafka, Hartford Studies in Lit, Vol 12, No 1; Wife as mother and double: The origin and importance of bipolar personality and erotic ambivalence in the work of Gerhart Hauptmann, In: Fearful Symmetry: Doubles and Doubling in Literature and Film, Univ Presses of Fla, 81. *Mailing Add:* Dept of Comparative Lit Univ of Wash Seattle WA 98195

MACLEISH, ANDREW, b Philadelphia, Pa, Aug 30, 23; m 50; c 3. LINGUISTICS, PHILOLOGY. *Educ:* Roosevelt Univ, AB, 50; Univ Chicago, MA, 51; Univ Wis, PhD(English philol), 61. *Prof Exp:* Instr English, Valparaiso Univ, 51-53 & Rockford Col, 56-58; from asst prof to assoc prof, Northern Ill Univ, 58-67; assoc prof English, Univ Minn, Minneapolis, 67-68, assoc prof English & ling, 68-71, prof English & Ling, 71-80. *Concurrent Pos:* Dir, US Off Educ English Proj, Curric Ctr Ling, 64-67; Peace Corps res grant, 65-67; consult, Hilo Lang Develop Proj, Hawaii, 65-68. *Mem:* Nat Coun Teachers English; Ling Soc Am; Midwest Mod Lang Asn. *Res:* English in Southeast Asia; descriptive historical English linguistics; materials for teaching standard English in Hawaii. *Publ:* Coauth, The American Revolution through the British Eyes, Harper & Row, 62; auth, The Pronunciation of English in Sabah, Peace Corps, DC, 67; Writing pattern practice drills, Teachers English Speakers Other Lang, Ser III, 67; The vowels of Hawaiian Island dialect, Pac Speech, 68; The Dictionary and Usage: A Book of Readings, Holt, 68; The Middle English Subject-Verb Cluster, Mouton, 68; coauth, Oedipus: Myth and Drama, Odyssey, 68; auth, Some remarks on Old English syntax, Proc Mid Am Ling Conf, 74. *Mailing Add:* 3709 Upton Ave S Minneapolis MN 55410

MCLENDON, WILL LOVING, b Center, Tex, Aug 26, 25. FRENCH. *Educ:* Univ Tex, BS, 45; Middlebury Col, MA, 47; Univ Paris, DUniv, 52. *Prof Exp:* Instr French, Tex Technol Col, 47-48; instr, Southern Methodist Univ, 50; from asst prof to assoc prof, 53-68, PROF FRENCH, UNIV HOUSTON, 68-, CHMN DEPT, 77- *Honors & Awards:* Chevalier, Palmes Academiques, 65. *Res:* The 20th century novel; the works of Jean Giraudoux; modern poetry. *Publ:* Co-transl, Charles Mauron, Introduction to the Psychoanalysis of Mallarme, Univ Calif, 63; auth, Giraudoux and the impossible couple, PMLA, 5/67; Themes wagneriens dans les romans de Julien Gracq, Fr Rev, 2/68; Lettre inedite de Marcel Proust a Leon Bailby, Soc Amis Marcel Proust, 71; Proust: la presentation differee, Revue Pacifique, 77; The Grotesque in Jean Lorrain's New Byzantium, in pre-text, text, context, Ohio State Univ, 80; Une Tenebreuse Carriere: Le Comte de Courchamps, Minard, Paris, 81. *Mailing Add:* Dept of French Univ of Houston Houston TX 77004

MCLEOD, WALLACE EDMOND, b East York, Ont, May 30, 31; m 57; c 4. CLASSICS. *Educ:* Univ Toronto, BA, 53; Harvard Univ, AM, 54, PhD(class philol), 66. *Prof Exp:* Instr class lang, Trinity Col, Conn, 55-56; instr classics, Univ BC, 59-61; lectr, Univ Western Ont, 61-62; from asst prof to assoc prof, Victoria Col, 62-74, assoc chmn dept, 75-78, actg chmn dept classics, Univ Toronto, 78-79, PROF, VICTORIA COL, 74- *Concurrent Pos:* Assoc ed, Phoenix, Class Asn Can, 65-70, actg ed, 73 & actg rev ed, 76-77; Can Coun leave fel, Am Sch Class Studies, Athens, 70-71. *Mem:* Am Philol Asn; Class Asn Can (secy, 63-65); Soc Archer-Antiq; A Archaeol Inst Am. *Res:* Homer; Greek topography and pre-history; history of freemasonry. *Publ:* Auth, Composite bows from the Tomb of Tut'ankhamun, Griffith Inst, Oxford, 70; ed & contribr, The Sufferings of John Coustos, Masonic Bk Club, 79; Whence Come We? Freemasonry in Ontario, Grand Lodge AF & Am, 80; auth, Self Bows and Other Archery Tackle from the Tomb of Tut'ankhamun, Griffith Inst, Oxford, 82. *Mailing Add:* Dept of Classics Victoria Col 38A Univ of Toronto Toronto ON M5S 1K7 Can

MCMAHON, DOROTHY, b Troy, NY, Dec 2, 12. SPANISH. *Educ:* Univ Ariz, AB, 35, AM, 38; Univ Southern Calif, PhD, 47. *Prof Exp:* From instr to assoc prof Spanish, 44-60, head dept, 59-71, prof, 60-80, EMER PROF SPANISH, UNIV SOUTHERN CALIF, 80- *Concurrent Pos:* Del Amo res scholar, Spain, 48-49. *Mem:* Am Asn Teachers Span & Port (vpres, 67, pres, 68); MLA; AAUP. *Res:* Literature of the Spanish conquest in America; modernism; contemporary Spanish literature. *Publ:* Auth, Leopoldo Lugones, Mod Philol, 54; Spanish and foreign editions of Zarate, Papers Bibliog Soc Am, 55; Changing trends in the Spanish novel, Bks Abroad, 60; coauth, Iberoamerica, Scribner, 65; auth, Edicion del libro V, con estudio preliminar, de Zarate, Historia de la conquista del Peru, Univ Buenos Aires, 65. *Mailing Add:* Dept of Span & Portugues Univ of Southern Calif Los Angeles CA 90007

MCMAHON, JAMES VINCENT, b Buffalo, NY, Oct 10, 37; m 63; c 3. GERMAN LITERATURE & LANGUAGE. *Educ:* St Bonaventure Univ, BA, 60; Univ Tex, PhD(Ger), 67. *Prof Exp:* From instr to asst prof, 64-71, ASSOC PROF GER, EMORY UNIV, 71-, CHMN DEPT, 72- *Mem:* MLA; Am Asn Teachers Ger; Mediaeval Acad Am; AAUP; Am Translators Asn. *Res:* Medieval German textual criticism; Middle High German language and literature; music of minnesang. *Publ:* Auth, Enite's relatives: The girl in the garden, Mod Lang Notes, 4/70. *Mailing Add:* Dept of Ger Emory Univ Atlanta GA 30322

MCMAHON, JOHN FREDERICK, b Philadelphia, Pa, Mar 3, 11; m 43; c 1. GERMAN. *Educ:* Haverford Col, AB, 33; Univ Pa, AM, 35; Columbia Univ, PhD, 62. *Prof Exp:* Teacher Ger & Latin, Harrisburg Acad, Pa, 39-42; asst prof Ger, Beloit Col, 46-47; from assoc prof to prof, 47-76, EMER PROF GER, LAWRENCE UNIV, 76- *Mem:* Am Asn Teachers Ger; MLA; Deutsche Schillergesellschaft. *Mailing Add:* 1024 W Fourth St Appleton WI 54911

MCMAHON, JOSEPH H, b New York, NY, Oct 21, 30. FRENCH. *Educ:* Manhattan Col, AB, 52; Stanford Univ, MA, 59, PhD, 60. *Hon Degrees:* MA, Wesleyan Univ, 74. *Prof Exp:* From asst prof to assoc prof French, Yale Univ, 60-68, dean, Pierson Col, 63-66; assoc prof Romance lang & lit, 68-74, chmn dept, 72-78, dean univ, 68-69, PROF ROMANCE LANG & LIT, WESLEYAN UNIV, 74- *Concurrent Pos:* Fels, Pierson Col, Yale Univ, 62- & Guggenheim, 72; ed, Yale Fr Studies; asst ed, Fr Rev, 77- *Mem:* Am Asn Teachers Fr; AAUP. *Res:* Twentieth century French literature. *Publ:* Auth, The Imagination of Jean Genet, Yale Univ, 63; From things to themes: Jean Santeuil, 65, Where does real life begin: Sade and Durrell, 65 & More perfect souls, 67, Yale Fr Studies; Humans Being: The World of Jean-Paul Sartre, Univ Chicago, 71; Marxist fictions: The novels of John Berger, Contemporary Lit, 82. *Mailing Add:* Dept of Romance Lang & Lit Wesleyan Univ Middletown CT 06457

MCMAHON, KATHRYN KRISTINE, b Bryn Mawr, Pa, Aug 21, 46; m 73. FRENCH. *Educ:* Beloit Col, BA, 68; Cornell Univ, PhD(French), 76. *Prof Exp:* Instr French, Rice Univ, 72-73; asst prof, Ill Wesleyan Univ, 73-75; lectr, 77-80, ASST PROF FRENCH, UNIV PA, 80- *Mem:* MLA; Am Asn Teachers Fr; Soc Rencesvals; Mediaeval Acad Am; Int Arthurian Soc. *Res:* Old French language and literature; applied linguistics. *Publ:* Coauth, Lecturas periodisticas, Heath, 78. *Mailing Add:* Dept of Romance Lang Univ of Pa Philadelphia PA 19174

MCMANAMON, JAMES EDWARD, b Chicago, Ill, Jan 26, 11; m 42; c 1. MODERN LANGUAGES. *Educ:* Univ Notre Dame, BA, 34; Univ Wash, MA, 39; Univ Ill, PhD, 55. *Prof Exp:* Assoc prof mod lang, Knox Col, 48-62; assoc prof Span, State Univ NY Col Fredonia, 62-65; chmn dept foreign lang, 65-70, PROF SPAN, CENT MICH UNIV, 65- *Concurrent Pos:* Instr French, Seattle Univ, 40-41; Smith-Mundt vis prof English, Monterrey Inst Technol, Mex, 58-59. *Mem:* Am Asn Teachers Span & Port; Am Asn Teachers Fr; MLA; People to People Orgn; Nat Fed Mod Lang Teachers Asn. *Res:* Spanish Renaissance epic; Medieval Spanish and French literature; Spanish American literature. *Mailing Add:* 309 W Grand Ave Mt Pleasant MI 48858

MACMASTER, ROBERT ELLSWORTH, History, Literature. See Vol I

MCMULLEN, EDWIN WALLACE, JR, b Quincy, Fla, Dec 8, 15; m 46; c 2. LINGUISTICS, ENGLISH. *Educ:* Univ Fla, BA, 36; Columbia Univ, MA, 39, PhD(English), 50. *Prof Exp:* Instr English, Hazleton Undergrad Ctr, Pa State Univ, 46-48 & State Univ Iowa, 50-52; spec instr & sr reporter, US Dept Defense, DC, 52-57; asst ed, Merriam Webster Dict Co, Mass, 57; asst prof English, Lehigh Univ, 57-61; from asst prof to assoc prof, 61-72, PROF ENGLISH, FAIRLEIGH DICKINSON UNIV, 73- *Concurrent Pos:* Ed, Am Name Soc, 62-65; dir, Names Inst, Fairleigh Dickinson Univ, 62-; Am Civilization Inst, NJ, res grant, 67-69. *Mem:* Am Name Soc (pres, 76); NCTE; MLA; Int Cong Onomastic Soc; Am Dialect Soc. *Res:* New Jersey place-names; Morris County family names 1953; topographic terms. *Publ:* Auth, English Topographic Terms in Florida, 1563-1874, Univ Fla, 53; The origin of the term Everglades, Am Speech, 2/53; The term Prairie in the United States, Names, 3/57; ed, Pubs, Place-Names, and Patronymics: Selected Papers of the Names Institute, Fairleigh Dickinson Univ, 80. *Mailing Add:* Fairleigh Dickinson Univ Madison NJ 07940

MCMURRAY, GEORGE RAY, b Grinnell, Iowa, Oct 14, 25; m 50. ROMANCE LANGUAGE. *Educ:* Mex City Col, BA, 49; Univ Nebr, MA, 51, PhD(Romance lang), 55. *Prof Exp:* Instr Span, Wash State Univ, 55-56; from instr to asst prof Romance lang, Univ Nev, 56-60; assoc prof, 60-66, PROF ROMANCE LANG, COLO STATE UNIV, 66- *Mem:* MLA; Am Asn Teachers Span & Port. *Res:* Mexican short story, twentieth century French novel and Latin American novel. *Publ:* Auth, Salvador Elizondo's Farebeuf, 9/67 & Form and content relationships in La cuidad y los perros, 9/73, Hispania; Santelices de Jose Donoso, In: El cuento hispanoamericano ante la critica, Ed Castalia, Madrid, 73. *Mailing Add:* Dept of Foreign Lang Colo State Univ Ft Collins CO 80521

MCNAMARA, ALEXANDER, b Portsmouth, Va, Apr 29, 42. GERMAN LANGUAGE & LITERATURE. *Educ:* Kenyon Col, BA, 64; Ind Univ, Bloomington, MA, 67, PhD(Ger), 71. *Prof Exp:* Instr Ger, C W Post Col, LI Univ, 69-71; asst prof Ger, Va Commonwealth Univ, 71-79; ASST DEAN ACAD ADVISING, ST LOUIS UNIV, 80- *Mem:* Am Asn Teachers Ger; MLA; Int Brecht Soc. *Res:* German drama of the 1920's; Bertolt Brecht; post-was German literature. *Publ:* Auth, Translation of Woyzeck by Büchner, Stage Ctr Theatre, 3/76; The Transfer Student: A Dual Approach, NACADA J, 3/82. *Mailing Add:* Off Acad Advising St Louis Univ St Louis MO 63103

MCNAUGHTON, WILLIAM F, b Westboro, Mo, May 21, 33; div; c 2. CHINESE LANGUAGE & LITERATURE. *Educ:* Brooklyn Col, BA, 61; Yale Univ, PhD(Chinese lang & lit), 65. *Prof Exp:* Asst prof Chinese, Oberlin Col, 65-70; vis lectr classics & mod lang, Denison Univ, 72-78; TEACHER, US NAVY PACE PROG, 78- *Concurrent Pos:* Great Lakes Cols Asn non-western studies fel, 66, humanities fel, 67-68; Oberlin Col Powers travel fel, 67; Nat Transl Ctr fel, 67; Fulbright-Hays fac fel, 68-69; vis lectr Chinese, Bowling Green State Univ, 73-74; trustee arts & Lett, Ctr Class Studies, 75-77. *Mem:* Am Orient Soc; Asn Asian Studies. *Res:* The book of songs; Chinese poetics. *Publ:* Auth, The Book of Songs, Twayne, 71; The Taoist Vision, Univ Mich, 71; coauth, A Gold Orchid, 72 & ed, Chinese Literature: An Anthology, 73, Charles E Tuttle; auth, The Confucian Vision, Univ Mich, 74; coauth, As Though Dreaming, Mushinsha, 77; ed, Light from the East, Dell, 78; auth, Reading & Writing Chinese, Charles E Tuttle, 78. *Mailing Add:* 172 Shipherd Circle Oberlin OH 44074

MCNEELY, JAMES A, b Vancouver, BC, July 16, 21; m 55; c 3. GERMAN. *Educ:* Univ BC, BA, 49; Univ Calif, Berkeley, MA, 51; PhD, 58. *Prof Exp:* Teaching asst, Univ Calif, Berkeley, 49-51, 52-53; instr Ger, 51-52, 53-59, asst prof, 59-62, ASSOC PROF GER, UNIV BC, 62- *Mem:* Can Asn Univ Teachers Ger. *Res:* Drama of the Goethe period; C M Wieland; Enlightenment politcal though. *Publ:* Auth, Historical relativism in Wieland's concept of the ideal state, Mod Lang Quart, 9/61. *Mailing Add:* 2160 W 53rd Ave Vancouver BC V6P 1L7 Can

MCNEILL, DAVID, b Santa Rosa, Calif, Dec 21, 33; m 57; c 2. PSYCHOLINGUISTICS. *Educ:* Univ Calif, Berkeley, AB, 53, PhD(psychol), 62. *Prof Exp:* Res fel, Ctr Cognitive Studies, Harvard Univ, 63-65; from asst prof to assoc prof psychol, Univ Mich, 65-68; PROF BEHAV SCI & LING, UNIV CHICAGO, 69- *Concurrent Pos:* Guggenheim Found fel, 73-74; mem, Inst Advan Studies, 73-75. *Mem:* Ling Soc Am; Am Asn Advan Sci. *Res:* Psychological processes involved in the use of language; comparison of gestures for language; development of gesture in children. *Publ:* Contribr, Developmental psycholinguistics, In: The Genesis of Language, MIT Press, 66; auth, The Acquisition of Language, Harper, 70; The Conceptual Basis of Language, Erlbaum Assocs, 79. *Mailing Add:* Dept of Behav Sci Univ of Chicago Chicago IL 60637

MACOY, KATHERINE WALLIS, b Oshkosh, Wis, May 25, 26; m 47; c 2. SPANISH & LATIN AMERICAN LITERATURE. *Educ:* Shippensburg State Col, BS, 65; Villanova Univ, MA, 68; Emory Univ, PhD(Span & Latin Am lit), 70. *Prof Exp:* Instr Span, Penn Hall Jr Col, 65-67; teaching asst, Emory Univ, 68-69; ASSOC PROF SPAN, MARS HILL COL, 70- *Concurrent Pos:* Piedmont Univ grant, 73. *Mem:* AAUP; Am Asn Univ Women; MLA. *Res:* Hispanic literature; Latin American affairs; contemporary mysticism. *Mailing Add:* Dept of Mod Lang Mars Hill Col Mars Hill NC 28754

MCPHEETERS, DEAN WILLIAM, b Milton, Iowa, Jan 6, 17; m 48; c 2. ROMANCE LANGUAGES. *Educ:* Univ Ill, BS, 40; Univ Fla, MA, 41; Columbia Univ, PhD, 52. *Prof Exp:* Instr Span, La State Univ, 47-49; from asst prof to prof Romance lang, Syracuse Univ, 51-64; PROF SPAN, NEWCOMB COL, TULANE UNIV, 64- *Concurrent Pos:* Ed, Symposium, 54-64, assoc ed, 64-; ed, Tulane Studies Romance Lang & Lit, 65-77. *Mem:* MLA; Am Asn Teachers Span & Port; Hisp Soc Am; Int Asn Hispanists. *Res:* Spanish literature of the Golden Age and the Renaissance; Spanish writings of Alonso de Madrigal. *Publ:* Auth, El humanista espanol Alonso de Proaza, Ed Castalia, Valencia, 61; Una traduccion hebrea de La Celestina en el siglo XVI, In: Homenaje al profesor Rodriguez-Monino, Ed Castalia, Madrid, 66; Camilo Jose Cela, Twayne Span Ser, 69; ed, Guia de nuevos temas de literatura espanola por Homero Seris, Hisp Soc Am & Castalia, 73; Bartolome de Torres Naharro's Comedias: Soldadesca, Tinelaria, Himenea, Clasicos Castalia, 73; auth, Melibea and the new learning, in: Volume in Honor of A D Menut, Coronado, 73; Ovid and the jealous old man of Cervantes, In: Volume in Honor of Helmut Hatzfeld, Cath Univ, 73; La Celestina en Portugal en el siglo XVI, In: La Celestina y su contorno social, Hispam, Barcelona, 77. *Mailing Add:* Dept of Span & Port Tulane Univ New Orleans LA 70118

MCQUOWN, NORMAN ANTHONY, b Peoria, Ill, Jan 30, 14; m 42; c 2. ANTHROPOLOGICAL LINGUISTICS. *Educ:* Univ Ill, AB, 35, AM, 36; Yale Univ, PhD(Indo-Europ & gen ling), 40. *Prof Exp:* Lectr ling, Nat Sch Anthrop, Mex, 39-42; lectr Turkish, Ind Univ, 42-43; lang technician, lang sect, Army Serv Forces, 43-45; lectr Russ, Hunter Col, 45-46; from asst prof to assoc prof anthrop, 46-58, PROF ANTHROP, UNIV CHICAGO, 58- *Concurrent Pos:* Res assoc Totonac, Dept Indian Affairs, Mex, 39-40, Turkish, Am Coun Learned Soc, 41-43 & Maya, Carnegie Inst Wash, 46-47; US deleg Int Sem Teaching Mod Lang, UNESCO, Ceylon, 53; vis prof, Univ Seville, 62-63; mem Inter-Am Prog Ling & Lang Teaching, 63-, pres, 65-71; vis prof, Univ Uruguay, 66, Univ Mex, 67-68, Univ Hamburg, 71-72 & Univ Mex, 82-83. *Mem:* Ling Soc Am (vpres, 68); Am Anthrop Asn; AAAS. *Res:* Linguistic analysis of Totonac, Nahuatl, Huastec, Mam, Yucatec Maya, Quiche Maya, Turkish, linguistic analysis of psychiatric interview materials. *Publ:* Coauth, Spoken Turkish, Holt, 45-46; co-ed & contribr, Latin American indigenous languages, Am Anthrop, 55; Linguistic transcription and specification of psychiatric interview materials, Psychiatry, 57; Los origenes y la diferenciacion de los mayas segun se infiere del estudio comparativo de las lenguas mayanas, In: Desarrollo cultural de los Mayas, Univ Nac Autonoma de Mex, 64; ed & contribr, Linguistics, Vol V, In: Handbook of Middle American Indians, Univ Tex, 67; co-ed & contribr, Ensayos de antropologia en la zona central de Chiapas, Inst Nac Indigenista, Mex, 70; auth, American Indian Linguistics in New Spain, Peter de Ridder, Lisse, Netherlands, 76; Language, culture, and education, Stanford, 82. *Mailing Add:* Dept of Anthrop Univ of Chicago Chicago IL 60637

MACRIS, JAMES, b Hoboken, NJ, Apr 25, 19; m 45; c 2. LINGUISTICS, ENGLISH. *Educ:* St Johns Univ NY, BBA, 41; Columbia Univ, MA, 50, PhD(ling), 55. *Prof Exp:* Instr English as second lang, Queens Col, NY, 46-48; lectr speech, Hunter Col, 53-54; asst prof, Rutgers Univ, 56-57; vis assoc prof English, Univ Calif, Los Angeles, 57-58; assoc prof, Rutgers Univ, 59-61 & Hunter Col, 61-68; PROF ENGLISH & LING, CLARK UNIV & COL OF THE HOLY CROSS, 68- *Mem:* Nat Asn Foreign Studies Affairs; MLA; Col English Asn; AAUP; Int Ling Asn (pres, 60-63 & 66-69, vpres, 64-66). *Res:* Systems analysis; general linguistic theory; language and culture contact. *Publ:* Auth, Changes in the lexicon of New York City Greek, Am Speech, 5/57; coauth, The English Verb System, 62 & Parametric Linguistics, 67, Mouton, The Hauge; Perspectives in functionalism, In: Linguistic Studies Presented to Andre Martinet, 67 & Towards a nonsubjective evaluative system for literature: Some linguistic analogues, Lang & Style, spring 68. *Mailing Add:* Dept of English Clark Univ Worcester MA 01610

MACRIS, PETER JOHN, b Buffalo, NY, Oct 6, 31; m 63; c 3. GERMAN LANGUAGE & LITERATURE. *Educ:* State Univ NY, Buffalo, BS, 56; Middlebury Col, MA, 63; NY Univ, PhD(Ger lang & lit), 68. *Prof Exp:* From asst prof to assoc prof, 64-70, PROF GER LANG & LIT, STATE UNIV NY, COL ONEONTA, 70- *Mem:* AAUP; Am Asn Teachers Ger; Int Brecht Soc. *Res:* Modern drama; Bertolt Brecht; literary texts used in music. *Publ:* Stephen Zweig as dramatist, State Univ NY (in prep). *Mailing Add:* Dept of Foreign Lang State Univ of New York Col Oneonta NY 13820

MACRO, ANTHONY DAVID, b London, England, July 10, 38; m 67; c 2. CLASSICAL PHILOLOGY, ANCIENT HISTORY. *Educ:* Oxford Univ, BA, 61, MA, 64; Johns Hopkins Univ, PhD(classics), 69. *Prof Exp:* Teaching assoc classics, Ind Univ, Bloomington, 61-62; instr, Univ Md, College Park, 65-67; jr instr, Johns Hopkins Univ, 67-69; asst prof, 69-75, ASSOC PROF CLASSICS, TRINITY COL, CONN, 75- *Concurrent Pos:* Leverhulme Commonwealth fel, Univ Wales, 75-76. *Mem:* Am Philol Asn; Soc Prom Hellenic Studies; Soc Prom Roman Studies. *Res:* Greek epigraphy; Roman imperial history; comparative linguistics. *Publ:* Auth, Sophocles, Trachiniai, 112-21, Am J Philol, spring 73; Imperial provisions for Pergamum: OGIS 484, Greek, Roman & Byzantine Studies, summer 76; A confirmed Asiarch, Am J Philol, 79; The Cities of Asia Minor under the Roman imperium, Aufstieg und Niedergang der romischen Welt, Vol II, No 7, Berlin, 80; Applied classics: Using Latin and Greek in the modern world, Class Outlook, 81. *Mailing Add:* Dept of Classics Trinity Col Hartford CT 06106

MCSORLEY, BONNIE SHANNON, b Chicago, Ill, May 19, 45; m 69. SPANISH, ITALIAN. *Educ:* Univ Colo, BA, 66; Northwestern Univ, MA, 67; PhD(Span), 72. *Prof Exp:* From teaching asst to instr, 66-72, asst prof, 73-79, ASSOC PROF SPAN, NORTHEASTERN UNIV, 79- *Mem:* MLA; Asn Teachers Span & Port; Northeast Mod Lang Asn. *Res:* Contemporary Spanish theater. *Publ:* Auth Historia de una escalera and El tragaluz: Twenty years and one reality, Mod Lang Studies, winter, 79-80; Ditirambo en USA, Estreno, fall 79; Nature's sensual and sexual aspects in three Gypsy ballads by Garcia Torca, In: The World of Nature in the Works of Federico Garcia Torca, Winthrop Studies, 80. *Mailing Add:* 17 Liberty St Natick MA 01760

MCSPADDEN, GEORGE ELBERT, b Albuquerque, NMex; m; c 4. SPANISH LANGUAGE & LITERATURE. *Educ:* Univ NMex, AB, 33, AM, 35; Univ Chile, cert, 39; Stanford Univ, PhD, 47. *Prof Exp:* Teacher pub schs, NMex, 33-34 & high sch, 34-35; teaching asst Romance lang, Stanford Univ, 35-39, instr, 40-41; instr Span & Latin, Univ Idaho, 39-40; officer instr Span & Ital, US Naval Acad, 43-46; assoc prof Span lang & lit, Univ BC, 46-54; assoc prof Span, Univ Chicago, 54-57; prof Romance lang, George Washington Univ, 57-67; head dept, 67-75, prof, 67-80, dir Latin Am studies, 75-80, EMER PROF ROMANCE LANG, UNIV NC, GREENSBORO, 80- *Concurrent Pos:* Vis prof, Univ Chicago, 53-54; lectr ling & lang learning, Gordon Col, 66. *Mem:* MLA; Am Asn Teachers Span & Port (vpres, 63-66); Inst Int Lit Iberoam; Pac Northwest Conf Foreign Lang Teachers (pres, 51). *Res:* Spanish and English lexicology; phonetics; methods of teaching. *Publ:* Auth, Some Semantic and Philological Facts of the Spanish Spoken in Chilili, New Mexico, Univ NMex, 35; The Spanish prologue before 1700, In: Abstracts of Dissertations, Stanford Univ & Univ Microfilms, 47 & 76; An Introduction to Spanish Usage, Oxford Univ, 56; New light on speech rhythms from Jorge Guillen's reading of his poem Gra silencio (based on measurements of sound spectrograms), Hisp Rev, 7/62; Phonetics, intonation, metrics and stylistics, In: Patterns of Literary Style, Yearbook of Comparative Criticism, Vol III, Pa State Univ, 71. *Mailing Add:* 3004 W Market St Greensboro NC 27403

MCVICKER, CECIL D, b Hartford City, Ind, Mar 27, 23; m 42; c 3. ROMANCE LANGUAGES. *Educ:* Univ Nebr, BSc & MA, 48; Univ Mo, PhD(French), 53. *Prof Exp:* Assoc prof French & Span, Cottey Col, 48-52; PROF FRENCH & SPAN, IOWA STATE UNIV, 53- *Mem:* Am Asn Teachers Fr; Am Asn Teachers Span & Port. *Res:* Contemporary Spanish novel; 19th century French novel; Spanish Renaissance. *Publ:* Auth, Balzac and Otway, Romance Notes; Reading technical French, 55-57 & Selections From Technical French, 57, Burgess; coauth, Temas de Arciniegas, 67 & Latino-America: El Continente de Siete Colores, 67, Harcourt; auth, Poe and Anacreon, Poe Newslett, 68; Narcotics and excitants in the Comedie humaine, Romance Notes, 69. *Mailing Add:* Dept of Foreign Lang Iowa State Univ Ames IA 50010

MCWILLIAMS, JAMES ROBERT, b Chicago, Ill, Jan 17, 25; m 54; c 2. GERMAN. *Educ:* Univ Calif, BA, 51, MA, 57, PhD(Ger), 63. *Prof Exp:* From instr to asst prof, 60-72, ASSOC PROF GER, UNIV ORE, 72- *Concurrent Pos:* Am Philos Soc res grant, 67-68; resident dir overseas studies, Stuttgart Ctr, Ore State Syst Higher Educ, Ger, 72-74. *Res:* Modern German literature. *Publ:* Auth, Conflict and compromise--Tonio Kroger's paradox, Rev Langues Vivantes, 66; Thomas Mann's Die Betrogene--a study in ambivalence, CLA J, 9/66; The failure of a repression: Thomas Mann's Tod in Venedig, Ger Life & Lett, 4/67; coauth, Unterwegs, 68 & Meisterwerke der Deutschen Literatur, 69, Random. *Mailing Add:* Dept of Foreign Languages Univ of Oregon Eugene OR 97403

MADDOX, DONALD, b Billings, Mont, Apr 2, 44; m; c 3. FRENCH, MEDIEVAL STUDIES. *Educ:* Univ Kans, BA, 66; Duke Univ, MA, 69, PhD(Fr), 70. *Prof Exp:* Asst prof French, Univ Okla, 70-71; asst prof, Univ Calif, Santa Barbara, 71-76; Mellon asst prof medieval studies, Brandeis Univ, 76-79; asst prof, 80-81, ASSOC PROF, UNIV CONN, 81- *Concurrent Pos:* Nat Endowment for Humanities fel, 74-75; Mellon fel, 76-79; vis assoc prof, Boston Col, 81-82. *Honors & Awards:* Award for Achievement in Old French Studies, New Orleans Ctr Medieval & Renaissance Studies, 75. *Mem:* MLA; Medieval Acad Am; Int Arthurian Soc; Int Courtly Lit Soc; Soc Rencesvals. *Res:* Old French literature; medieval Arthurian romance; structuralist poetics. *Publ:* Auth, Pilgrimage narrative and meaning in MSS L and A of the Vie de Saint Alexis, Romance Philol, 11/73; Greimas in the realm of Arthur: Toward an analytical model of medieval romance, Esprit Createur, 1-7/77; The hunting scenes in L'Estoire de Griseldis, In: Voice of Conscience, Temple Univ, 77; Chrestien de Troyes, In: Les Grands Ecrivains du Monde, Nathan, Vol II, 77; The prologue to Chretien's Erec and the problem of meaning, In: Misrahi Memorial Volume, 77; Structure and Sacring: The Systematic Kingdom in Crhetien's Erec, Fr Forum Mongr, 78; co-ed, Medieval Poetics and Semiotic Theory, Esprit Createur, 78; Semiotics of Deceit: The Pathlin Era, Bucknell Univ (in press). *Mailing Add:* Dept of Romance & Class Lang Univ of Conn Storrs CT 06268

MADES, LEONARD, b Brooklyn, NY, div. SPANISH LITERATURE. *Educ:* Brooklyn Col, BA, 40; Columbia Univ, MA, 47, PhD(English & comp lit), 65. *Prof Exp:* Lectr, Brooklyn Col, 46-47; instr, Rutgers Univ, 60-61; asst prof, Columbia Univ, 47-65; PROF SPAN, STATE UNIV NY, HUNTER COL, 66- *Honors & Awards:* PEN Translation Award, PEN Club, 73. *Mem:* MLA; Hisp Inst; Span Inst; PEN Club; Am Asn Teachers Span & Port. *Res:* Cervantes, Sapnish drama of the golden age. *Publ:* Auth, The Armor and the Brocade: A Study of Don Quixote and The Courtier, Las Americas, 68; co-ed, Diez Comedias del Siglo de Oro, Harper, 68. *Mailing Add:* Dept of Span State Univ NY Hunter Col New York NY 10021

MADLAND, HELGA STIPA, b Klodnitz, Upper Silesai, 1939. GERMAN LITERATURE & LANGUAGE. *Educ:* Idaho State Univ, BA, 74; Univ Wash, MA, 79, PhD(German & Span), 81. *Prof Exp:* ASST PROF GERMAN, UNIV OKLA, 81- *Mem:* MLA; SCent Mod Lang Asn; Lessing Soc; Am Asn Teachers German. *Res:* Eighteenth century German literature; dramatic theory. *Publ:* Auth, Communication through visual symbols, Proc PNCFL, 79; Revolution and Conservation im Eichendorff: Das Schloss Dürande and Der Adel und die Revolution, Neue Germanistik, 80; Time in Pepita Jimenez, Romance Notes, 80; J M R Lenz's Soldaten: The language of realism--a collision of codes, Selecta, 82. *Mailing Add:* Dept Mod Lang & Lit Univ Okla Norman OK 73069

MADSEN, BØRGE GEDSØ, b Fjerritslev, Denmark, Mar 16, 20; US citizen; m 49; c 3. FOREIGN LANGUAGES. *Educ:* Aarhus Univ, BA, 43; Univ Copenhagen, MA, 48; Univ Minn, PhD(comp lit, Scand, Fr & Eng), 57. *Prof Exp:* Instr mod lang, Univ Utah, 48-51; res asst Scand, Univ Minn, 51-56; instr French, Univ Ill, 56-57; asst prof Scand, 57-62, ASSOC PROF SCAND, UNIV CALIF, BERKELEY, 62- *Mem:* Soc Advan Scand Studies; Am-Scand Found. *Res:* Scandinavian languages and literatures, especially Danish; comparative literature, especially French and English. *Publ:* Auth, Strindberg's Naturalistic Theatre, Univ Wash & Munksgaard, 62. *Mailing Add:* Dept Scand Univ Calif Berkeley CA 94720

MAGGS, BARBARA WIDENOR, b Scranton, Pa, Apr 5, 36; m 60; c 4. COMPARATIVE LITERATURE, SLAVIC LITERATURE. *Educ:* Middlebury Col, AB, 58; Harvard Univ, AM, 60; Univ Ill, PhD(comp lit), 73. *Prof Exp:* INSTR ENGLISH AS A SECOND LANG, PARKLAND COL, 80- *Concurrent Pos:* Assoc, Russian & East Europ Ctr, Univ Ill, Urbana-Champaign, 73- *Mem:* Am Asn for the Advan of Slavic Studies; Am Asn East Europ Studies; Am Soc Eighteenth Century Studies. *Res:* Eighteenth century Russian and South Slavic literature; Western European influences in the Russian enlightenment; China in eighteenth century Russian literature. *Publ:* Auth, Answers from eighteenth century China to certain questions on Voltaire's Sinology, Studies on Voltaire and the Eighteenth Century, 74; The Jesuits in China: Views of an eighteenth century Russian observer, Eighteenth Century Studies, 74-75; Eighteenth Century Russian reflections on the Lisbon earthquake, Voltaire and Optimism, Studies on Voltaire and the Eighteenth Century, 75; The poetry of eighteenth century fireworks displays, Eighteenth Century Life, 75; Firework art and literature: Eighteenth century pyrotechnical tradition in Russia and Western Europe, Slavonic and East Europ Rev, 76; Reljkovic, Satyrs and the enlightenment in eighteenth century Croatia, Slavic and East Europ J, 76; Reljkovic's Satyr and the Georgic tradition: Didactic poetry in 18th century Croatia, Zagadnienia Rodzajow literackich, 78; Voltaire and the Balkans: Aspects of the enlightenment in 18th century Croatia and Serbia, Studies on Voltaire and the Eighteenth Century, 80. *Mailing Add:* 2011 Silver Ct E Urbana IL 61801

MAGILL, ROBERT A, b Tsingtao, China, Aug 15, 25; US citizen. FRENCH. *Educ:* Univ Va, BA, 47, MA, 49; Columbia Univ, PhD(French), 64. *Prof Exp:* Instr French, Univ Va, 47-49; master French & Span, Va Episcopal Sch, 50-54; instr French, Columbia Univ, 55-56; prof French & Span, Ferrum Jr Col, 56-60; asst prof, Centre Col Ky, 60-62; from asst prof to assoc prof French, 62-68, chmn dept mod lang, 64-73, PROF FRENCH, TOWSON STATE UNIV, 68- *Mem:* MLA; AAUP. *Res:* Politcal significance of La Bruyere's Les Caracteres; part one of Voeux du Paon by Jacques de Longuyon: an edition of manuscripts S, S1, S2, S3, S4, S5 and S6. *Mailing Add:* Abbeyville Boyce VA 22620

MAGNARELLI, SHARON DISHAW, US citizen. HISPANIC LITERATURE. *Educ:* State Univ NY, Oswego, BA, 68; Cornell Univ, PhD(Romance studies), 75. *Prof Exp:* Asst prof, 76-80, ASSOC PROF SPAN, ALBERTUS MAGNUS COL, 80- *Mem:* MLA; Inst Int Lit Iberoam; Am Asn Teachers Span & Port. *Res:* Spanish-American literature; contemporary novel; women. *Publ:* Auth, The Writerly in Tres Tristes Tigres, In: Analysis of Hispanic Texts, 76; El Obsceno Pajaro De La Noche: Fiction, Monsters and Packages, Hisp Rev, fall 77; Amidst the Illusory Depths of the First Person Pronoun and El Obsceno Pajaro de la Noche, Mod Lang Notes, 3/78; La ciudad y los perros: Women and Language, Hispania, 5/81; Gatos, lenguaje y mujeres en El gato eficaz de Luisa Valenzuela, Rev Iberoam, 79; Maria and History, Hisp Rev, spring 81; The Baroque, the picaresque and el obsceno pajaro de la noche by Jose Donoso, Hisp J, spring 81; El gato eficaz de Luisa Valenzuela: Juego/Fuego, Cuadernos Americanos. *Mailing Add:* Dept Span Albertus Magnus Col New Haven CT 06472

MAGNER, THOMAS FREEMAN, b Buffalo, NY, Oct 8, 18; m 44; c 3. SLAVIC LINGUISTICS. *Educ:* Niagara Univ, BA, 40; Fordham Univ, MA, 42; Yale Univ, PhD, 50. *Prof Exp:* Asst prof ling & Russ, Univ Minn, 50-56, assoc prof Slavic ling, 56-59, chmn dept Slavic & Orient lang, 57-59; chmn dept Slavic lang, 60-66, PROF SLAVIC LANG, PA STATE UNIV UNIVERSITY PARK, 59-, ASSOC DEAN RES, 66- *Concurrent Pos:* Off observer, Am Teachers Exchange, Moscow State Univ, 63; Fulbright fel & Am Coun Learned Soc res grant, Yugoslavia, 65-66; ed, Gen Ling, 67-70; Fulbright fel, Yugoslavia, 82-83. *Mem:* Ling Soc Am; Am Asn Teachers Slavic & EEurop Lang (vpres,54, pres, 67-68); Am Asn Advan Slavic Studies; Am Asn Southeast Europ Studies. *Res:* Russian; Serbo-Croatian; sociolinguistics. *Publ:* Auth, Manual of Scientific Russian, Prentice-Hall, 58; Applied Linguistics: Russian, Heath, 61; A Zagreb Kajkavian Dialect, 66; co-ed, Baltic Linguistics, 70 & coauth, Word Accent in Modern Serbo-Croatian, 71, Pa State Univ; auth, Introduction to the Croatian and Serbian Language, Singidunum, 72; co-ed, The Dilemma of the Melting Pot: The Case of the South Slavic Languages, Gen Ling, Vol 16, 76; ed, Slavic Linguistics and Language Teaching, Slavic Publ, 76. *Mailing Add:* Lib Arts Res Off 116 Sparks Bldg Pa State Univ University Park PA 16802

MAGNOTTA, MICHAEL, b Guardia Lombardi, Italy, Apr 16, 40; US citizen; m 68; c 1. FOREIGN LANGUAGES & LITERATURE. *Educ:* Geneva Col, BA, 65; Case Western Reserve Univ, MA, 67, PhD(Span lit), 69. *Prof Exp:* Asst prof, 69-75, ASSOC PROF SPAN LANG & LIT, YORK UNIV, 75- *Concurrent Pos:* Humanities Res Coun Can publ grant, 73. *Res:* Medieval Spanish literature; 16th and 17th century Spanish literature; 19th century Spanish literature. *Publ:* Auth, Sobre la critica del CMC: problemas en torno al autor, 1750-1970, Anuario Letras, Mex, 71; Per abat y la tradicion oral y escrita en el PMC, Hisp Rev, 75; Historia y bibliografia de la critica sobre el Poema de Mio Cid, 1750-1971, NCSRLL, 76. *Mailing Add:* 110 Castle Rock Dr Richmond Hill ON L4C 5K4 Can

MAGUIRE, JOSEPH PATRICK, b Meriden, Conn, Jan 2, 08; m 41. CLASSICS, PHILOSOPHY. *Educ:* Col Holy Cross, AB, 29; Yale Univ, MA, 31, PhD(classics), 36. *Prof Exp:* Mem staff classics, Boston Col, 36-44; educ assoc, Conn State Comn Against Discrimination, 44-46; assoc prof classics, Univ Hawaii, 46-49; prof, 49-73, EMER PROF CLASSICS, BOSTON COL, 73- *Concurrent Pos:* Fund Advan Educ fac fel, 52-53; vis prof, Univ Hawaii, 63-64; lectr philos, Boston Col, 73-78. *Mem:* Am Philol Asn; Soc Ancient Greek Philos. *Res:* Greek literature and philosophy. *Publ:* Auth, Plato's theory of natural law, Yale Class Studies, 47; Thrasymachus-- or Plato?, 71 & Protagoras--or Plato?, Vols I & II, 74 & 77, Phronesis. *Mailing Add:* 45 Clinton Pl Newton Centre MA 02159

MAGUIRE, ROBERT A, b Canton, Mass, June 21, 30. LANGUAGE, LITERATURE. *Educ:* Dartmouth Col, AB, 51; Russ Inst, cert, 53; Columbia Univ, MA, 53, PhD, 61. *Prof Exp:* Instr Russ lang & lit, Duke Univ, 58-60; asst prof, Dartmouth Col, 60-62; from asst prof to assoc prof, 62-70, chmn dept Slavic lang, 77-80, PROF RUSS LIT, COLUMBIA UNIV, 70- *Concurrent Pos:* Am Coun Learned Soc post-doctoral exchange with Soviet Acad Sci, 67; Guggenheim fel, 69-70; mem adv comt, Int Res & Exchanges Bd, 71-74; Nat Endowment for Humanities, 71-; sr Fulbright-Hays Prog, 71-; mem bd, Am Asn Advan Slavic Studies, 77-79. *Mem:* MLA; Am Asn Teachers Slavic & East Europ Lang; Am Asn Advan Slavic Studies; Polish Inst Arts & Sci in Am; Kosciuszko Found. *Res:* Twentieth century Russian literature; history of criticism; prose fiction. *Publ:* Coauth, Russian Short Stories, Random, 65; auth, Red Virgin Soil: Soviet Literature in the 1920's, Princeton Univ, 68; Literary conflicts in the 1920's, Survey, 72; Macrocosm or microcosm?, The symbolists on Russia, Rev Nat Lit, Vol III, No 1; The pioneers: Pilnyak and Ivanov, In: Major Soviet Authors, Oxford Univ, 73; Gogol From the Twentieth Century: Eleven Essays, Princeton Univ, 74, rev ed, 76; co-ed & transl, Tadeusz Rozewicz, The Survivor and Other Poems, Princeton Univ, 76; Andrei Bely, Petersburg, Ind Univ, 78. *Mailing Add:* Dept of Slavic Lang Columbia Univ New York NY 10027

MAH, KAI-HO, b Canton, China, Nov 11, 28; US citizen; m 63. FRENCH & CHINESE LITERATURE & LANGUAGE. *Educ:* Calif Col Arts & Crafts, BAA, 51; Univ Calif, Los Angeles, BA, 60; Univ Ill, Champaign, MA, 62; Univ Wash, PhD(comp lit), 67. *Prof Exp:* Instr French, Millikin Univ, 63; ASST PROF FRENCH, COLO STATE UNIV, 67- *Mem:* Am Asn Teachers Fr. *Res:* Modern French drama; symbolist and post-symbolist French poetry; Chinese poetry. *Publ:* Transl, By a hair (transl, Jean Giraudoux, D'un cheveu), 3/70 & A propos of Conan Doyle, by Maurice LeBlanc, 6/71, Baker St J; auth, The lamps of China allusion in Who's Afraid of Virginia Woolf?, Explicator, summer 77; Themes and techniques in Chinese visual propaganda, Selected Papers Asian Studies, autumn 78. *Mailing Add:* Dept of Foreign Lang Colo State Univ Ft Collins CO 80523

MAHAN, MARY JUAN, b Brookline, Mass, Mar 14, 16. FRENCH. *Educ:* Regis Col, AB, 44; Boston Col, MA, 49; Fordham Univ, PhD(French), 60. *Prof Exp:* From asst prof to assoc prof, 60-69, PROF FRENCH, REGIS COL, MASS, 69-, CHMN DEPT, 63- *Concurrent Pos:* Res scholar medieval French Archit, Harvard, 71-72. *Mem:* MLA; Am Asn Teachers Fr. *Res:* The Age of Enlightenment; 19th century poetry. *Mailing Add:* Dept of French Regis Col Weston MA 02193

MAHARG, JAMES, b Glasgow, Scotland, May 12, 40; m 67; c 2. SPANISH AMERICAN & BRAZILIAN LITERATURES. *Educ:* Univ Glasgow, MA, 67; Univ Ill, Urbana, PhD(Span-Am lit), 70. *Prof Exp:* Asst prof, Univ Mich, Ann Arbor, 70-76; ASSOC PROF SPAN & PORT, UNIV ILL, CHICAGO CIRCLE, 76- *Concurrent Pos:* Nat Endowment for Humanities res grant, 73; reader Span, Col Entrance Bd, 77. *Res:* Reputation of Jose Ortega y Gasset in Latin America; modern Brazilian and Spanish American literatures; realism and naturalism in Brazil. *Publ:* Auth, Reflexiones en torno a la ideologia de Ezequiel Martinez Estrada, Cuadernos Hispanoam, 11/72; Meditaciones americanas sobre Ortega y Gasset, Rev Occidente, Madrid, 1/73; The paradises of Walter Beneke, Latin Am Theatre Rev, spring 75; From romanticism to modernism: The peomaspiadas of Oswald de Andrade as parodies, Luso-Brazilian Rev, winter 76; Fructiferous exile: Martinez Estrada and the encounter with Marti, Estudos Ibero-Am, 12/76; A Call to Authenticity: The Essays of Ezequiel Martinez Estrada, Romance Monogr, Miss, 77. *Mailing Add:* Dept Span Ital & Port Univ of Ill, Chicago Circle Chicago IL 60680

MAHDI, MUHSIN SAYYID, b Karbala, Iraq, June 21, 26; m 59; c 1. ARABIC, ISLAMIC PHILOSPHY & RELIGION. *Educ:* Am Univ Beirut, BBA, 47; Univ Chicago, PhD, 54. *Prof Exp:* Instr hist, Univ Baghdad, Iraq, 55-57; from asst prof to assoc prof Arabic, Univ Chicago, 57-75, prof Arabic & Islamic studies, 65-70, chmn dept Near Eastern lang & civilizations, 68-70; J R JEWETT PROF ARABIC & DIR CTR MID EASTERN STUDIES, HARVARD UNIV, 70- *Concurrent Pos:* Univ Chicago/Univ Paris exchange fel, 54-55; lectr Near Eastern studies, Univ Freiburg, 55-59, vis prof, 60; Rockefeller Found res fel, 60-61; consult ed, J Near Eastern Studies; 63-; vis prof, Univ Calif, Los Angeles, 68-; pres, Am Res Ctr Egypt, 78- *Mem:* Soc Study Islamic Philos & Sci (pres, 68-); Am Orient Soc; Int Soc Study Mediaeval Philos; Mid East Study Asn NAm. *Res:* Arabic philology; politcal philosophy; literary criticism. *Publ:* Auth, Ibn Khaldun's Philosophy of History, Allen & Unwin, 57; Alfarabi's Philosphy of Plato and Aristotle, 62 & coauth, Medieval Political Philosophy, 63, Free Press; auth, Alfarabi, In: History of Political Philosophy, Rand McNally, 63; Averroes on divine law and human wisdom, In: Ancients and Moderns, Basic Bks, 64; Alfarabi against Philoponus, J Near Eastern Studies, 10/67. *Mailing Add:* Ctr for Mid Eastern Studies Harvard Univ Cambridge MA 02138

MAHER, JOHN PETER, b Johnson City, NY, July 31, 33; m 61; c 2. GENERAL & HISTORICAL LINGUISTICS. *Educ:* Harpur Col, BA, 55; Cath Univ Am, MA, 58; Ind Univ, PhD(ling), 65. *Prof Exp:* Teacher high schs, NY, 56-57, 61-63; from instr to prof ling, Northeastern Ill Univ, 64-75; mem staff ling & philol, Sem English Speech & Cult, Univ Hamburg, 75-78. *Res:* Language and perception in the contexts of society, culture and history; history of linguistics; general linguistics. *Publ:* Auth, More on the history of the comparative method: The tradition of Darwinism in August Schleicher's work, Anthrop Ling, 3/66; The paradox of creation and tradition in grammar: Sound pattern of a palimpsest, Lang Sci, 10/69; The situational motivation of syntax and the syntactic motivation of polysemy and semantic change: Spanish-Italian bravo, etc, In: Studies in Diachronic Romance and Linguistics, Mouton, The Hague, 73; Papers on Language Theory and History I, Benjamins, Amsterdam. *Mailing Add:* 6215 N Drake Ave Chicago IL 60659

MAHLENDORF, URSULA R, b Strehlen, Silesia, Oct 24, 29; US citizen. GERMAN LITERATURE. *Educ:* Brown Univ, PhD, 58. *Prof Exp:* Asst Ger, Brown Univ, 54-57; from instr to assoc prof, 57-77, PROF GER, UNIV CALIF, SANTA BARBARA, 77-, CHMN DEPT GER & SLAVIC LANG, 80- *Concurrent Pos:* Assoc dir, Educ Abroad Prog, 68-71. *Mem:* MLA; Int Asn of Social Psychol; Am Asn of Social Psychiat; Asn Applied Psychoanal. *Res:* Nineteenth and 20th century literature; psychology. *Publ:* Auth, E T A Hoffmann's The Sandman: The fictional psychobiography of a romantic poet, 75, Mörike's Mozrt on the Way to Prague: Sources, stages, and outcomes of the creative process, 76 & Arthur Schniztler's The Last Letter of a Litterateur: The artist as destroyer, 77, Am Imago; Güther Grass' The Tin Drum: Sculptures and mother figures, Psychoanal Rev, 79; Creativity of Women, Dynamic Psychiatry, 81. *Mailing Add:* 399 Loma Media Santa Barbara CA 93103

MAHLER, ANNEMARIE ETTINGER, b Vienna, Austria, Apr 8, 26; US citizen; m 48; c 3. COMPARATIVE LITERATURE, HISTORY OF ART. *Educ:* Univ Calif, Berkeley, BA, 48; Ind Univ, Bloomington, MA, 62, PhD(comp lit), 70. *Prof Exp:* Instr art hist, Ind Univ, Bloomington, 70-71, asst prof comp lit, 71-72; ASST PROF COMP LIT, UNIV CINCINNATI, 72- *Concurrent Pos:* Am Coun Learned Soc grant-in-aid, 76-77. *Mem:* AAUP; MLA; Am Comp Lit Asn; Medieval Acad Am. *Res:* Relationships between literature and the visual arts; medieval literature and art; images of architecture in Medieval literature and art. *Publ:* Auth, Art and visual imagery: A methodology for the study of medieval styles, Yearbk Comp & Gen Lit, 72; The representation of visual reality in Perceval and Parzival, PMLA, 5/74; Lignum Domini in The Dream of the Rood, Speculum, 78; Medieval image style and Saint Augustine's theory of threefold vision, Mediaevalia, 78. *Mailing Add:* Dept of Comp Lit Univ Cincinnati Cincinnati OH 45221

MAHMOUD, PARVINE, b Tehran, Iran, Mar 21, 13; US citizen; div. FRENCH & PERSIAN LITERATURE. *Educ:* Ind Univ, MA, 50, PhD(French), 57. *Prof Exp:* From instr to asst prof French, Rutgers Univ, 55-65; assoc prof, 65-71, PROF FRENCH, NORTHERN ILL UNIV, 71- *Mem:* MLA. *Res:* Seventeenth and eighteenth century French literature. *Publ:* Auth, Les Persans de Montesquieu, Fr Rev, 60; Omar Khayyam, the Rubaiyat (a literal trans with introd & notes), Kashani, Tehran, 69; L'Explication du nom Gour employe par Victor Hugo, 72 & Le songe d'un habitant du Mogol et l'historiette du Gulistan, 73, Romance Notes; Plaidoyer pour OEnone, Rev Langues Vivantes, 74; Whose murderous hand?--La main de Phedre, comme l'indique le texte de Racine, Romance Notes, 76. *Mailing Add:* 229 Joanne Lane De Kalb IL 60115

MAHONEY, ELIZABETH VERONICA, b Cambridge, Mass, Mar 14, 24. SPANISH. *Educ:* Emmanuel Col, AB, 45; Boston Univ, AM, 46. *Prof Exp:* Teacher jr high sch, 46-47; asst prof Span, Emmanuel Col, 47-59; assoc prof, 59-80, PROF SPAN, STONEHILL COL, 80-, CHMN DEPT MOD LANG, 62- *Mem:* Am Asn Teachers Span & Port; MLA. *Res:* Drama of Golden Age; Romance philology. *Mailing Add:* 8 Edwards St Canton MA 02021

MAHONEY, JOHN FRANCIS, English, Classics. See Vol II

MAIER, CAROL SMITH, b Pittsburgh, Pa, June 10, 43; m 62; c 2. HISPANIC LITERATURE. *Educ:* Douglass Col, BA, 68; Rutgers Univ, MA, 72, PhD(Span), 75. *Prof Exp:* Asst prof, 76-80, ASSOC PROF SPAN, BRADLEY UNIV, 80- *Mem:* MLA; Am Asn Teachers Span & Port; Am Lit Translr Asn; Women's Caucus Mod Lang; Asoc Int de Hispanistas. *Res:* Ramon del Valle-Inclan; literary translation; women's studies. *Publ:* Auth, La aportacion cerrvantina a Yo soy aquel que ayer no mas decia, Mester, 5/66; Symbolist Aesthetics in Spanish: The concept of language in Valle-Inclan's La lampara maravillosa, Waiting for Pegasus, Studies of the Presence of Symbolism and Decadence in Hispanic Letters, Essays in Lit, 79; The poetry of Ana Castillo: A dialogue between poet and critic, Letras Femeninas, spring 80; Notas sobre melancolia y creacion en dos narradores valleinclanescos: El Marques de Brandomin y el poetta de La lampara marvillosa, Revista de Estudios Hispanicos, 1/81; Notas hacia una definicion del concepto de la historia en La lampara maravillosa, Explicacion de Textos Literarios, Vol IX, No 2; Xose Conde Corbal e a estetica do grabado: Una reforma do ollo por medio da deformacion da lina, Grial, Vol 70, 80; Transl, Imagination and (Un) academic Activity, Transl Rev, winter 80; Por tierras de Portugal y de Espana e Galicia: Unha rectificacion da perspectiva castiza, planteada por Valle-Inclan, Grial, Vol 75, 82. *Mailing Add:* Dept of English & Foreign Lang Bradley Univ Peoria IL 61625

MAIER, JOHN, English. See Vol II

MAILLOUX, STEVEN JOHN, Critical Theory, American Literature. See Vol II

MAINOUS, BRUCE HALE, b Appalachia, Va, Aug 2, 14; m 41; c 2. FRENCH. *Educ:* Col William & Mary, AB, 35; Univ Ill, MA, 39, PhD(Romance lang & Ger), 48. *Prof Exp:* Asst d'anglais, Lycee de Garcons, Nimes, France, 35-36; prin grade sch, Va, 36-37; from instr to assoc prof French, 48-64, asst dean col lib art & sci, 56-57, head dept French, 65-73, dir unit foreign lang studies & res, 72-76, actg dir div English as second lang, 76-77, PROF FRENCH, UNIV ILL, URBANA, 64-, DIR LANG LEARNING LAB, 76- *Honors & Awards:* Chevalier & Officier, Palmes Academiques, 63. *Mem:* MLA; Am Asn Teachers Fr; Am Coun Teaching Foreign Lang. *Res:* Sainte- Beuve; foreign language pedagogy. *Publ:* Auth, Basic French: An Oral Approach, 61, 2nd ed, 68 & coauth, Basic French: An Oral Approach, Workbook and Laboratory Manual, 68, Scribner; A Sainte-Beuve Bibliography, 1938-1952, Univ Rochester; auth, Recent Sainte-Beuve publishing and research, Ky Foreign Lang Quart. *Mailing Add:* Dept of French Univ of Ill at Urbana 2090 Foreign Lang Urbana IL 61801

MAIO, EUGENE ANTHONY, b Trinidad, Colo, Nov 23, 29; m 70. HISPANIC LANGUAGE & LITERATURE. *Educ:* St Louis Univ, BA, 53, PhL, 54, MA, 57, STL, 61; Univ Calif, Los Angeles, PhD(Span), 67. *Prof Exp:* Asst prof Span, St Louis Univ, 67-70; ASSOC PROF SPAN, UNIV AKRON, 70- *Concurrent Pos:* Libr consult, Univ Southern Ill, Edwardsville, 70. *Mem:* Am Asn Teachers Span & Port: MLA; AAUP. *Res:* Comparative mysticism; the occult; witchcraft. *Publ:* Auth, The synoptic problem and the Vaganay hypothesis, Irish Theol Quart, 59; Ignatian contemplation, Rev for Relig, 64; St John of the Cross: The Imagery of Eros, Playor, Madrid, 73. *Mailing Add:* Dept of Mod Lang Univ of Akron Akron OH 44325

MAIONE, MICHAEL, b Syracuse, NY, Dec 3, 45. FRENCH LANGUAGE & LITERATURE. *Educ:* St Lawrence Univ, BA, 68; Univ Conn, MA, 72, PhD(French), 74. *Prof Exp:* Asst prof, 74-80, PROF FRENCH, GUSTAVUS ADOLPHUS COL, 80- *Mem:* Am Asn Teachers Fr; Nineteenth Century Fr Studies; African Lit Asn. *Res:* Nineteenth century French literature; African literature. *Publ:* Auth, Critique architectuale dans Les Rougon-Macquart, Nineteenth Century Fr Studies, fall 81. *Mailing Add:* Gustavus Adolphus Col St Peter MN 56082

MAISSEN (DELLA CASACRAP), AUGUSTIN, b Glion-Ilanz, Switz, Jan 18, 21; US citizen. ROMANCE LANGUAGES, MINOR ROMANCE PHILOLOGY. *Educ:* Col Claustra Muster, Switz, BA, 71; Univ Berne, BS, 44; Univ Fribourg, PhD, 49; Univ Michoacan, MA, 57. *Prof Exp:* Instr French, Ger & Span, El Camino High Sch, Sacramento, Calif, 53-57; vis prof English, Inst Mex-NAm, Mex, 57; instr Span, Col William & Mary, 59-61; asst prof Span & French civilization, Christopher Newport Col, 61-63; assoc prof Romance lang, Utica Col, 63-67; ASSOC PROF ROMANCE LANG & MINOR ROMANCE PHILOL, UNIV NC, CHAPEL HILL, 67- *Concurrent Pos:* Va Univ Ctr grant, 60; asst prof Ital, Col William & Mary Exten, NASA Res Ctr, Langley AFB, Va, 62-63; ed, Rev Reto-Romontscha, 63-; Fulbright res grant, Romania, 72-73. *Mem:* MLA; Int Soc Ethnol & Folklore; Am Name Soc; Romansh-Am Found (secy, 54-); Swiss-Am Hist Soc (pres, 66-). *Res:* Romance philology, especially Rumanian, Catalan and Raeto-Romance; onomastics; history of Swiss-American relations. *Publ:* Auth, Il Stats Univ dell'America, Radioscola, Cuera, Vol 18, No 4; ed, Studia Raetoromanica, Vols I-X, 65-74 & auth, Ei dat Biars Songtgaclaus (novel), 69, Ed RRR, Cuera; Art mural sursilvan, Igl Ischi, Cuera, 73; Romania Literara, Bucharest, 73. *Mailing Add:* Dept of Romance Lang Univ of NC Chapel Hill NC 27514

MAJOR, JEAN-LOUIS, b Cornwall, Ont, July 16, 37; m 60; c 1. FRENCH & FRENCH CANADIAN LITERATURE. *Educ:* Univ Ottawa, BA & BPh, 59, LPh, 60, MA, 61, PhD, 65. *Prof Exp:* Lectr philos, 61-64, asst prof lit, 65-67, assoc prof French lit, 67-71, PROF FRENCH LIT, UNIV OTTAWA, 71- *Concurrent Pos:* Can Coun leave fel, 68-69 & 75-76; vis prof French-Can lit, Univ Toronto, 70-71; coord, Corpus d'editions critiques, 81- *Mem:* Fel Royal Soc Can; Can Semiotic Assoc. *Res:* Twentieth century French and French Canadian literature; semiotics; critical editions. *Publ:* Auth, Saint-Exupry, l'ecriture et la pensee, Univ Ottawa, 68; Leone de Jean Cocteau, Univ Ottawa, 75; Anne Hebert et le miracle de la parole, Univ Montreal, 76; Radiquet, Cocteau, Les Joues en feu & La litterature francaise par les Textes theoriques: 19e siecle, Univ Ottawa, 77; Paul-Marie Lapointe: la nuit incendiee, Univ Montreal, 78; Le jeu en etoile, Univ Ottawa, 78. *Mailing Add:* Dept of Lettres Fr Univ of Ottawa Ottawa ON K1N 6N5 Can

MAKINO, SEIICHI, b Jan 20, 35; Japanese citizen; m; c 1. LINGUISTICS. *Educ:* Waseda Univ, Japan, BA, 48, MA, 60; Univ Tokyo, BA, 62, MA, 64; Univ Ill, Urbana-Champaign, PhD(ling), 68. *Prof Exp:* Res asst English, Inst Lang Teaching, Waseda Univ, 62-64; asst prof, 68-71, ASSOC PROF JAPANESE & LING, UNIV ILL, URBANA-CHAMPAIGN, 71- *Concurrent Pos:* Dir, Japanese Sch, Middlebury Col. *Mem:* Ling Soc Am; Ling Soc Japan; Asn Teachers Japanese. *Res:* Generative transformational analysis of semantic and discourse structures of Japanese. *Publ:* Auth, Adverbial scope and the passive construction in Japanese, Papers in Ling, 72; An analysis of Japanese verb understand, Papers in Japanese Ling, 73; The passive construction in Japanese, In: Issues in Linguistics, Univ Ill, 73; Is there psych movement in Japanese, In: Gengo Kenkyu, Ling Soc Japan, 74; Nominal compounds, In: Japanese Generative Grammar, Acad Press, 76; Can a single sentence have more than one empathy focus?, Chicago Ling Soc Papers, 76; On the nature of the Japanese potential constructions, Papers in Japanese Ling, 76; Kurikaeshi no Bunpoo, Taishukan, Japan, 80. *Mailing Add:* Ctr for Asian Studies Univ Ill Urbana-Champaign Urbana IL 61801

MAKKAI, ADAM, b Budapest, Hungary, Dec 16, 35; nat US; m 66; c 2. LINGUISTICS. *Educ:* Harvard Univ, BA, 58; Yale Univ, MA, 62, PhD(gen ling), 65. *Prof Exp:* Asst prof English, Calif State Univ, Long Beach, 66-67; from asst prof to assoc prof ling, 67-74, PROF LING, UNIV ILL CHICAGO CIRCLE, 74-, EXEC DIR & DIR PUBL, LING ASN CAN & US, 74- *Concurrent Pos:* Paderewski Found grant ling, Univ Malaya, Kuala Lumpur, 63-64; Am Coun Learned Soc, Yale Univ, 64-65; NSF grant comput ling, Rand Corp, Santa Monica, Calif, 65-66; asst prof Russ, Occidental Col, 66-67; managing ed jour, Word, Int Ling Asn, 73-74; exec dir & dir publ & ed jour, Forum Ling, Ling Asn Can & US. *Mem:* Ling Soc Am; MLA; Int Ling Asn; Ling Asn Can & US. *Res:* Idomaticity and English semantics; English lexicography, poetry and translation; stratificational grammar. *Publ:* Auth, Szomj es ecet (Collected Poems), Amerikai Magyar Irok, 66; Idiom Structure in English, Mouton, 72; co-ed, Readings in Stratificational Linguistics, Univ Ala, 73; ed, A Dict of Space English, Consolidated Bk Publ, 73; co-ed, The First LACUS Forum, Hornbeam, 74; A Dict of American Idioms, Barron's Educ Ser, 74; ed & transl, Toward a Theory of Context in Linguistics and Literature, Mouton, 76; co-ed, The Poetry of Hungary, Jupiter (in press). *Mailing Add:* Dept of Ling Univ of Ill, Chicago Circle Chicago IL 60680

MAKKAI, VALERIE JUNE BECKER, b Vinton, Iowa, July 29, 36; m 66; c 2. LINGUISTICS. *Educ:* Mo Valley Col, BA, 57; Yale Univ, MA, 62, PhD(ling), 64. *Prof Exp:* Instr French & Span, MacMurray Col, 58-60; asst prof ling, Purdue Univ, West Lafayette, 65-66; asst prof, 67-70, ASSOC PROF LING, UNIV ILL, CHICAGO CIRCLE, 70- *Concurrent Pos:* Nat Sci Found res fel, comput ling, Rand Corp, Santa Monica, Calif, 66-67; ed consult, Studies Lang Learning, 74-; coord ed, publ of Ling Asn Can & US, 74-; pres, Jupiter Press, 76-; managing ed, Forum Linguisticum, 76- *Mem:* Ling Soc Am; MLA; Ling Asn Can & US (secy-treas, 74-). *Res:* Phonological theory; field methods in linguistics; descriptive methodology. *Publ:* Ed & contribr, Phonological Theory: Evolution and Current Practice, Jupiter Press, 72; auth, On the correlation of morphemes and lexemes in the Romance languages, In: Readings in Stratificational Linguistics, Univ Ala, 73; co-ed & contribr, The First LACUS Forum, Hornbeam, 75; The competence-performance dichotomy as manifested in the phonology of Bilinguals, Studies Lang Learning, 76; coauth, The nature of linguistic change and modern linguistic theories, Proc 2nd Int Conf Hist Ling, North Holland, Amsterdam, 77; co-ed & contribr, Linguistics at the Crossroads, Jupiter, Lake Bluff, Ill, 77; auth, Maternal diglossia: the adult use of baby talk as an instructional device, Hornbeam, 78. *Mailing Add:* Dept of Ling Univ of Ill at Chicago Circle Chicago IL 60680

MAKWARD, CHRISTIANE PERRIN, b Hyeres, France, Jan 6, 41; m 60; c 2. FRENCH LITERATURE, WOMEN'S STUDIES. *Educ:* Sorbonne, Lic es Lett, 63, DLit(French), 74; Univ Dakar, DES, 65. *Prof Exp:* From asst lectr to lectr French lang & lit, Univ Ibadan, Nigeria, 62-67; lectr French lit, Univ Wis, 68-69 & 74-75; lectr, Univ Que-Rimouski, 76-77; asst prof, 77-80, ASSOC PROF FRENCH, PA STATE UNIV, 80- *Concurrent Pos:* Ed, BREFF, Pa State Univ, 76- *Mem:* MLA; Am Asn Teachers Fr; Women's Caucus Mod Lang; Asn Int Femmes Ecrivians; Asn Amis Cerisy-la-Salle. *Res:* Contemporary French literature; psychoanalysis; stylistics. *Publ:* Auth, Mallarme and Ricardou: Echoes, 73, Claude Simon: Earth, Eros and death, 74 & Interview with Helene Cixous, 76, Sub-Stance; La critique feministe: Elements d'une problematique, Revue Sci Humanies, Lille, 12/77; auth, Aspects of bisexuality in Claude Simon's works, In: Blinded Orion, Bucknell Univ (in press); Structures du silence/du delire: Marguerite Duras/Helene Cixous, Poetique, Paris (in press); Nouveau regard sur la crituque feministe, Revue de l'Univ d'Ottawa, Vol 50, No 1; Colette and signs, In: Colette, The Woman, The Writer, Pa State Univ Press, 81. *Mailing Add:* Dept of French Pa State Univ University Park PA 16802

MALBY, MARIA BOZICEVIC, b Zagreb, Yugoslavia, May 16, 37; div; c 1. RUSSIAN & SERBO-CROATIAN LANGUAGES & LITERATURES. *Educ:* Fla State Univ, BA, 62; Harvard Univ, AM, 63, PhD(Slavic lang & lit), 70. *Prof Exp:* Asst prof, Frostburg State Col, 66-70; assoc prof, 70-80, PROF GER & RUSS, EAST CAROLINA UNIV, 80- *Mem:* AAUP; MLA; SAtlantic Mod Lang Asn; Am Asn Teachers Slavic & East Europ Lang; Am Asn Slavic Scholars. *Res:* Comparative Russian and Serbo-Croatian literature; German. *Publ:* Transl mod Yugoslav lit in anthologies & jour, Fairleigh Dickinson Univ Lit Rev, 68 & Nin, Zagreb, 72; auth, Yugoslav literature, Twayne, 73. *Mailing Add:* Dept of Foreign Lang & Lit East Carolina Univ Greenville NC 27834

MALECOT, ANDRE, b Paris, France, May 5, 20; US citizen; m 42; c 3. LINGUISTICS. *Educ:* Univ Del, BA, 42; Middlebury Col, MA, 47; Univ Pa, PhD, 52. *Prof Exp:* Instr Romance lang, Haverford Col, 49-52; from asst prof to assoc prof French, Univ Calif, Riverside, 53-62; prof Romance Lang, Univ Pa, 62-69; PROF FRENCH & DIR PHONETICS RES FACILITY, UNIV CALIF, SANTA BARBARA, 69- *Concurrent Pos:* Researcher, Haskins Labs, New York, 53-57; head French phonetics, Ecole Francaise, Middlebury Col, 58-71; NDEA consult foreign lang teaching, Univ Southern Calif, 59-60; guest investr, Centre Audio-Visuel, Ecole Norm Super St Cloud, France, 60-61; NSF res grant phonetics, 63-73; Fulbright fel, 67-68; sr sci fel, NATO, 73; dir, Univ Calif, Santa Barbara Inst French Lang & Cult, 77- *Honors & Awards:* Palmes Academiques, French Govt, 78. *Mem:* Am Asn Teachers Fr; Am Asn Phonetic Sci; Int Asn Phonetic Sci. *Res:* Phonetics; descriptive linguistics; Paris project, a computerized analysis of standard French pronunciation. *Publ:* Auth, Luiseno, a structural analysis, Int J Am Ling, 63; The Lenis-Fortis opposition: Its physiological parameters, J Acoust Soc Am, 6/70; New procedures in descriptive phonetics, In: Papers in Linguistics and Phonetics to the Memory of Pierre Delattre, Mouton, 72. *Mailing Add:* Phonetics Res Facil Univ of Calif Santa Barbara CA 93106

MALEY, CATHERINE ANNE, b St Paul, Minn. ROMANCE LINGUISTICS. *Educ:* Univ Minn, Minneapolis, BS, Univ Mich, Ann Arbor, AM, 66, PhD(Romance ling), 70. *Prof Exp:* Teacher English, Span & French, Edina Sr High Sch, Minneapolis, Minn; asst dir NDEA/EPDA French Inst, Univ Mich, Ann Arbor, 66-69; dir French & Span, 70-72, asst prof French ling & phonetics methods, 70-76, ASSOC PROF ROMANCE LANG, UNIV NC, CHAPEL HILL, 76-, DIR LOWER UNDERGRAD FRENCH, 72- *Mem:* Ling Soc Am; Am Asn Teachers Fr; Am Asn Teachers Span & Port; Am Coun Teaching Foreign Lang; Southern Mod Lang Asn. *Res:* Language learning and teaching; sociolinguistics; applied linguistics. *Publ:* Auth, Historically speaking, tu or vous?, Fr Rev, 4/72; The French pronouns of direct address, In: Current Issues in Teaching French, Chilton-Didier, 72; The evolution of the French plural of respect, Romance Notes, 73. *Mailing Add:* Dept of Romance Lang Univ of NC Chapel Hill NC 27514

MALIK, JOE, JR, b Christopher, Ill, Sept 2, 19; m 45; c 3. SLAVONIC LANGUAGES. *Educ:* Univ Tex, BS, 45, MEd, 47; Univ Pa, PhD, 55. *Prof Exp:* From instr to asst prof Slavonic lang, Univ Tex, 49-60; assoc prof Russ, 60-63, PROF RUSS, UNIV ARIZ, 63-, CHMN DEPT, 72- *Concurrent Pos:* Mem, Inter-Univ Comt travel grant, 62- *Mem:* Am Asn Teachers Slavic & East Europ Lang (exec secy-treas, 68-); Czech Soc Arts & Sci in US; Am Coun Teaching Foreign Lang. *Res:* Slavic languages and literatures; methods of teaching language. *Mailing Add:* Dept of Russian Univ of Arizona Tucson AZ 85721

MALIN, JANE WOFFORD, b Lawrence, Kans, Jan 30, 26. FRENCH LITERATURE. *Educ:* Univ Kans, BA, 45, MA, 47; Univ Tex, PhD, 61. *Prof Exp:* Instr French, Span & Ger, Univ Okla, 47-49; instr, 56-60, asst prof French, 60-67, ASSOC PROF FRENCH, UNIV HOUSTON, CENT CAMPUS, 67- *Honors & Awards:* Knight, Palmes Acad, 72. *Mem:* SCent Mod Lang Asn; MLA; Am Asn Teachers Fr. *Res:* Twentieth century French drama; history of French drama and theatre; surrealism. *Publ:* Auth, Theatre-going in Paris, Inst Int Educ Bull, 5/55; Georges Neveux, dramaturge surrealiste?, Bayou, autumn 59; Surrealism in the French Theatre Between Two Wars, Univ Tex, 61. *Mailing Add:* Dept of French Univ of Houston Houston TX 77004

MALINAK, EDWARD MICHAEL, b Centerline, Mich, Jan 22, 43; m 69; c 2. SPANISH LITERATURE. *Educ:* Univ Mex, dipl, 64; Univ Mich, BA, 65; Mich State Univ, MA, 67; Univ Ky, PhD(Span), 77; Estudio Int Sampere, Madrid, cert & dipl, 79. *Prof Exp:* Teaching asst Span, Mich State Univ, 65-67 & Univ Ky, 69-71 & 72-74; instr, Univ of the South, 71-72; asst prof, 74-80, ASSOC PROF SPAN, NAZARETH COL, ROCHESTER, 81- *Concurrent Pos:* Res asst, Dept Span & Port, Univ Ill, 67-68; lectr Span, Dept Romance Lang, Mich State Univ, 68-69; res grants, Nazareth Col, Rochester, 76 & 79; instr Span, Puerto Rican Arts & Cult Ctr, Rochester, 80 & Evening Col, Univ Rochester, 81. *Mem:* Am Asn Teachers Span & Port; MLA. *Res:* Golden age Spanish literature, Renaissance and Baroque; medieval Spanish literature; comparative literature. *Publ:* Auth, Intermediate Spanish, Univ Ky Press, 74; The honor code in El Poema de Mio Cid, Ariel Publ, 74. *Mailing Add:* 35 Summit St Fairport NY 14450

MALKIEL, YAKOV, b Kiev, Russia, July 22, 14; nat US; wid. ROMANCE PHILOLOGY. *Educ:* Univ Berlin, PhD, 38. *Hon Degrees:* DHL, Univ Chicago, 69; LittD, Univ Ill, Urbana-Champaign, 76. *Prof Exp:* Instr, Univ Wyo, 42; from lectr to asst prof Span & Port, 42-48, from assoc prof to prof Romance philol, 48-66, assoc dean, grad div, 63-66, PROF LING & ROMANCE PHILOL, UNIV CALIF, BERKELEY, 66- *Concurrent Pos:* Ed in chief, Romance Philol, 47-; Guggenheim fels, 48-49, 59, 67; Intramural res fel humanities, 68-69; consult, Can Coun, 70 & Nat Endowment for Humanities, 77. *Mem:* MLA; Ling Soc Am (vpres, 55, pres, 65); Am Orient Soc; Philol Asn Pac Coast (vpres, 63, pres, 65); Soc Ling Romane. *Res:* General and Romance linguistics; theory of etymology; Hispanic lexicology. *Publ:* Auth, The Hispanic Suffix (i)ego, 51 & Studies in the Reconstruction of Hispano-Latin Word Families, 54, Univ Calif; Essays on Linguistic Themes, Balckwell, 68; coauth, Directions for Historical Linguistics, Tex, 68; auth, Linguistics and Philology in Spanish America, Mouton, The Hague, 72; Etymological Dictionaries: A Tentative Typology, Univ Chicago, 76. *Mailing Add:* Dept of Ling 2321 Dwinelle Hall Univ of Calif Berkeley CA 94720

MALL, RITA SPARROW, b New York, NY. FRENCH LITERATURE. *Educ:* Brooklyn Col, BA, 57; NY Univ, MA, 60; Univ Ill, Urbana, PhD (French), 69. *Prof Exp:* Instr French, Univ Mass, Amherst, 60-62; asst prof, 68-76, ASSOC PROF FRENCH & ASST DEAN ARTS & SCI, LA SALLE COL, 76- *Concurrent Pos:* Asst French, NY Univ, 58-59 & Univ Ill, Urbana, 64-65 & 67-68. *Mem:* Am Asn Teachers Fr; AAUP. *Res:* Nineteenth and twentieth century French novel. *Mailing Add:* Dept of Foreign Lang La Salle Col Philadelphia PA 19141

MALLIA, NORMA, b New York, NY. FRENCH LITERATURE. *Educ:* Columbia Univ, AM; Sorbonne, dipl. *Prof Exp:* From asst prof to assoc prof, 45-60, prof, 60-80, chmn dept, 60-80, EMER PROF FRENCH LIT, ST JOSEPH'S COL, NY, 80- *Mem:* MLA; Am Asn Teachers Fr; AAUP. *Mailing Add:* Dept of French St Joseph's Col Brooklyn NY 11205

MALONE, DAVID HENRY, Comparative Literature. See Vol II

MALONE, JOSEPH LAWRENCE, b New York, NY, July 2, 37; m 64; c 2. LINGUISTICS. *Educ:* Univ Calif, Berkeley, BA, 63, PhD(ling), 67. *Prof Exp:* From instr to assoc prof, 67-75, PROF LING, BARNARD COL, COLUMBIA UNIV, 75-, CHMN DEPT, 67- *Concurrent Pos:* Contrib consult ling, Arete Publ Co, NJ, 77- *Mem:* Ling Soc Am; Am Orient Soc; Int Ling Asn. *Res:* Linguistic theory; Semitic linguistics; translation. *Publ:* Auth, Wave theory, rule ordering, and Hebrew-Aranaic segolation, J Am Oriental Soc, 91: 44-66; The free lunch lives!, NY News Mag, 10/73; Heavy segments vs the paradoxes of segment length: The evidence of Tiberian Hebrew, Linguistics, (spec issue), 78; Source language polysemy and problems of translation, Babel, 25: 207-209; Irish na, a disambiguation of perceptually equivocal surface structures, Studies in Lang, 4: 25-63; Linguistics, Academic American Encycl, Anete Publ Co, Vol 12, 80; Desertion, translation from Irish of a short story by Siobhan Ni Shuilleabhain, Webster Rev, 5: 19-31; Roaring the streets of Henry Miller, then and now, The Brooklyn Col Alumni Lit Rev, fall-winter/81-82. *Mailing Add:* Dept of Ling Barnard Col Columbia Univ New York NY 10027

MALONEY, ELLIOTT CHARLES, New Testament Studies, Biblical Languages. See Vol IV

MALONEY, JAMES CHARLES, b Fairmont, Minn, Apr 10, 38; m 64; c 2. HISPANIC LITERATURE. *Educ:* Mankato State Col, BS, 61; Univ Ariz, MA, 71, PhD(Span), 73. *Prof Exp:* Teacher English & Span, Franklin Jr High Sch, Fargo, NDak, 61-63; cult ctr dir, US info agency, Popayan, Colombia, 63-64; instr English & vchmn dept mod lang, Univ of the Andes, Colombia, 64-65; teacher Span, Oak Park & River Forest High Schs, Ill, 65-68; from instr to asst prof, Tulane Univ, 71-77; ASSOC PROF SPAN & HEAD DEPT FOREIGN LANG, PAN AM UNIV, 77- *Concurrent Pos:* Dir, Rulane Sem Abroad Prog, Colombia, 76-77; ed, Modern Lang Studies, Edinburg, Texas, 77- *Mem:* MLA. *Res:* Seventeenth century Spanish drama; Spanish Golden Age poetry. *Publ:* Auth, A Critical Edition of Mira de Amescua's La Fe de Hungria and El Monte de la Piedad, Tulane Studies in Romance Lang & Lit, 75. *Mailing Add:* Dept of Foreign Lang Pan Am Univ Edinburg TX 78539

MALTI-DOUOGLAS, FEDWA, b Beirut, Lebanon, Jan 12, 46; US citizen. ARABIC LITERATURE, ISLAMIC CIVILIZATION. *Educ:* Cornell Univ, AB, 70; Univ Calif, Los Angeles, MA, 73, PhD(Near East lang), 77. *Prof Exp:* Chercheur Associe Arabic, Centre Nat de la Recherche Scientifique, 76; lectr, San Diego State Univ, 76-77; asst prof Arabic, Univ Va, 77-80; ASST PROF ARABIC, UNIV TEX, AUSTIN, 80- *Concurrent Pos:* Consult Arabic onomastics, Von Grunebaum Ctr UCLA, 76-77; fel, Am Res Ctr in Egypt, 77-78, Soc Sci Res Coun & Am Philos Soc, 80, Can Coun Learned Soc, 81 & Am Res Inst, Turkey, 82. *Mem:* Am Oriental Soc; Middle East Studies Asn; Societe Asiatique; Am Asn Teachers Arabic; Mediaeval Acad Am. *Res:* Arabic literature; Islamic civilization. *Publ:* Coauth, The Treatment by Computer of Medieval Arabic Biographical Data . . ., Ctr Nat Recherche Scientifique, 76; Controversy and its effects in the biographical tradition of al-Khatib at Baghdadi, Studia Islamica, 77; Pour une rhetorique onomastique: les noms des aveugles chez as-Safadi, Cahiers d'Onomastique Arabe, 78; Yusuf ibn Abd al-Hadi and his autography of the Wuquc al-Bala bil-Bukhl wal-Bukhala, Bull d'Etudes Orientales, 79; Dreams, the blind, and the semiotics of the biographical notice, Studia Islamica, 80; Structure and organization in a monographic Adab work: al-Tatfil of al-Khatib al-Baghdadi, J Near Eastern Studies, 81; Traditional Elements in Modern Arabic Literature: Dreams in Three Short Stories (in Arabic), Fusul, 82; Structures of Avarice: The Bukhala' in Medieval Arabic Literature, E J Brill (in press). *Mailing Add:* Univ of Tex 2601 Univ Ave Austin TX 78712

MALUEG, SARA ELLEN, b Kittanning, Pa, May 11, 32; m 64; c 2. ROMANCE LANGUAGE, COMPARATIVE LITERATURE. *Educ:* Muskingum Col, BA, 54; Univ Wis-Madison, MA, 57, PhD(French), 65. *Prof Exp:* Teaching asst French, Univ Wis-Madison, 54-58; instr French & Span, Juniata Col, 58-60; teaching asst French, Univ Wis-Madison, 61-62, proj asst, exten div, 60-62; instr, Lawrence Univ, 62-64; from instr to asst prof, Univ Wis-Madison, 64-66; from asst prof to assoc prof, 66-77, gen res fund grant, 67-77, PROF FRENCH & CHMN DEPT FOREIGN LANG & LIT, ORE STATE UNIV, 77- *Mem:* Am Asn Teachers Fr; Am Coun Teaching Foreign Lang; Pac Northwest Conf Foreign Lang (secy-treas, 70-74, vpres, 75-76 & pres, 76-78); AAUP; Am Soc 18th Century Studies. *Res:* Denis Diderot; the Encyclopedie; French and American literary interaction in eighteenth century. *Publ:* Auth, La Promenade du Sceptique, The Earliest Expression of Diderot's Interest in External Nature, Proc Pac Northwest Conf Foreign Lang, fall 68; Diderot's Descriptions of Nature, 1759-1762, Studies Voltaire & 18th Century, 72; A Frenchman's Response to a Colonist's Plea: Diderot's Review of John Dickinson's Farmer's Letters, Enlightenment Essays, 74; America in the Encyclopedie, Studies Voltaire & 18th Century, 76. *Mailing Add:* Dept of Foreign Lang Ore State Univ Corvallis OR 97331

MALYSHEV, ALEXEY N, Russian History & Language. See Vol I

MAMAN, ANDRE, b Oran, Algeria, June 9, 27; m 57; c 4. FRENCH. *Educ:* Univ Toulouse, Lic en Droit & Lic-es-Lett, 48, Dipl Sci polit, 50, Dr en Droit(sci economiques), 56; Sorbonne, Lic-es-Lett, 60; Paris Univ, CAPES, 76. *Prof Exp:* Asst prof French, Mt Allison Univ, 55-58; from instr to assoc prof, 58-76, asst dean col, 68-72, PROF FRENCH, PRINCETON UNIV, 76- *Concurrent Pos:* Procter fel, 60-61; mem, Higher Coun Frenchmen Living Abroad, 72-81. *Honors & Awards:* Palmes Acad, French Govt, 74 & Legion Hon, 76. *Mem:* Am Asn Teachers Fr; Soc Fr Prof Am (pres, 66-74); MLA; Int Fedn Prof Fr; Fedn Fr Prof Living Abroad (hon vpres, 72-). *Res:* French civilization; methodology of language teaching; French political history. *Publ:* Auth, Les instituts de langues NDEA, Bull Soc Fr Prof Am, 63; coauth, La France: Une Tapisserie, Le Francais, 65 & 72; Langue Ecrite et Langue Parlee, 67 & La France: Ses Grandes Heures Litteraires, 68, McGraw; Grammaire et Style, Appleton, 67; auth, Ombres et lumieres dans l'enseignement americain, 68 & Avantages et limites des tests objectifs dans l'apprentissage du francais, 73, Bull Fedn Int Prof; L'enseigivement du Francais Daws le Monde, Counceil Superieur des Francais de L'entranger, 80. *Mailing Add:* Dept of Romance Lang Princeton Univ Princeton NJ 08544

MANALICH, RAMIRO, b Havana, Cuba, Oct 20, 17; US citizen; m 56; c 1. LANGUAGE, LAW. *Educ:* Univ Havana, DLaw, 49, DLett, 51. *Prof Exp:* Instr Span, Concordia Col, Moorhead, Minn, 63-66; assoc prof Span, 66-81, EMER FAC, UNIV WIS-LA CROSSE, 81- *Concurrent Pos:* Instr Span, NDak State Univ, 64-66. *Mem:* Am Asn Teachers Span & Port. *Res:* Spanish and Latin American literature, civilization and culture; consititutional and civil law; communism, especially in Latin American countries. *Publ:* Auth, La Celestina (brochure), Purdue Univ, 69; Hispanoamerica: Enfoque historico, cultural, politico, economico, social y literario, Albon Int, 70. *Mailing Add:* 5240 N Lovers Lane Apt 4 Milwaukee WI 53225

MANCING, HOWARD, b Beaver Falls, Pa, July 11, 41; m 65; c 2. SPANISH LITERATURE. *Educ:* Geneva Col, AB, 63; Univ Fla, PhD(Span), 70. *Prof Exp:* Asst prof Span, Lycoming Col, 66-70; asst prof, 70-74, chmn, Dept Romance Lang, 77-80, acad assoc to vpres acad affairs, 80-81, ASSOC PROF SPAN, UNIV MO-COLUMBIA, 74- *Mem:* MLA; Am Asn Teachers Span & Port; AAUP; Am Asn Advan Humanities; Asn Int Hispanistas. *Res:* Cervantes; Picaresque novel; novel in general. *Publ:* Auth, Dulcinea's ass: A note on Don Quijote, part II, chap 10, Hisp Rev, 72; The comic function of chivalric names in Don Quijote, Names, 73; The deceptiveness of Lazarillo de Tormes, PMLA, 75; Cervantes y Saul Bellow, Anales Cervantinos, 77; El pesimismo radical del Lazarillo de Tormes, Actas del I Cong Int sobre la Picaresca, 79; The picaresque novel: A protean form, Col Lit, 79; El Dialogo del Capon y la tradicion picaresca, Actas del VI Cong de la Asoc Int de Hispanistas, 80; The Chivalric World of Don Quijote, Univ Mo Press, 82. *Mailing Add:* Dept of Romance Lang Univ of Mo Columbia MO 65201

MANCINI, ALBERT NICHOLAS, b Trenton, NJ, Sept 15, 29; m 68; c 2. LITERARY HISTORY. *Educ:* Univ Naples, DLett, 57; Univ Calif, Berkeley, PhD(Romance lit), 64. *Prof Exp:* Teaching asst Ital lang, Univ Calif, Berkeley, 57-61; instr Ital lang & lit & comp lit, Princeton Univ, 62-64; from asst prof to assoc prof, 64-72, consult, Sch Educ, 65-66, PROF ITAL LANG & LIT, OHIO STATE UNIV, 72- *Concurrent Pos:* Assoc ed, Forum Italicum, 78-; consult, Univ Toronto Press, Univ Calif Press, Princeton Univ Press & Ohio State Univ Press; evaluator, Nat Endowment for Humanities; vis prof, Ital Sch Middlebury Col, 78 & 82. *Mem:* MLA; Am Asn Teachers Ital; Dante Soc Am; Renaissance Soc Am; Am Boccaccio Asn. *Res:* Italian literature of the 15th, 16th and 17th centuries; cross-influences in Romance literatures in the same periods; bibliography. *Publ:* Auth, Il Romanzo nel Seicento: Saggio di Bibliografia, Studi Secenteschi, XI-XII, Olschki, Florence, 70-71; ed & contribr, Seicento revisited, spec issue, 6/73 & Settecento revisited, spec issue, 76, Forum Italicum; Il Romanzo nel Seicento: Saggio di Bibliografia delle traduzioni in lingua straniera, Studi Secenteschi, Olschki, Florence, 76; Romanzi Italiani del Seicento: Retrospettiva e prospettive, In: Letteratura e Critica, Vol IV, Bulzoni, Rome, 77; I Capitoli Inediti di Francesco Bolognetti, Forum Ital, Vol XIII, No 1; Motivi e Schemi Picareschi ne Il Don Antonio o Il Birba Finto Principe, In: La Piu Stupenda e Gloriosa Macchina, 81 & Romanzi e Romanzieri del Seicento, 81, Societa Editrice Npoletana, Naples. *Mailing Add:* Dept of Romance Lang Ohio State Univ 1841 Millikin Rd Columbus OH 43210

MANDEL, ADRIENNE S, b Italy, Oct 10, 33; US citizen; m 60. ROMANCE LANGUAGES. *Educ:* Hunter Col, BA, 54; Columbia Univ, MA, 55. *Prof Exp:* Lectr French, Calif Inst Technol, 64-65; asst prof, 65-68, assoc prof, 68-80, PROF FOREIGN LANG, CALIF STATE UNIV, NORTHRIDGE, 80- *Concurrent Pos:* Escort interpreter, Dept State, Washington, DC, 66- *Mem:* MLA. *Res:* Theatre. *Publ:* Coauth, The Theatre of Don Juan, Univ Nebr, 63; Seven Comedies by Marivaux, Cornell Univ, 68; auth, La Celestina studies, Scarecrow, 71. *Mailing Add:* Dept of Romance Lang Calif State Univ Northridge CA 91324

MANDEL, OSCAR, English, Comparative Literature. See Vol II

MANDEL, SIEGFRIED, English, Comparative Literature. See Vol II

MANIER, MARTHA JANE, b Dayton, Ohio, Sept 24, 46. SPANISH. *Educ:* Miami Univ, BA, 67; Univ Wis, MA, 69; Univ Colo, PhD(Span), 76. *Prof Exp:* Lectr, Univ Wis-Marathon County, 69-71; spec lectr, Regis Col, 77-78; instr, 76-80, ASST PROF SPAN, UNIV COLO, DENVER, 80- *Mem:* Am Asn Teachers Span & Port. *Res:* Medieval Spanish short narrative; rise of the novel; contemporary Latin American short story. *Mailing Add:* 5379 Estes Apt 4 Arvada CO 80002

MANKIN, PAUL A, b Berlin, Ger, July 11, 24; US citizen; div; c 2. ROMANCE LANGUAGE & LITERATURE. *Educ:* Univ Calif, Los Angeles, BA, 48, MA, 53; Yale Univ, PhD, 59. *Prof Exp:* Instr French, Yale Univ, 54-59; asst prof, Univ Ill, 60-63; assoc prof, 63-74, PROF FRENCH & LIT, UNIV MASS, AMHERST, 74-, CHMN WESTERN EUROP AREA STUDIES, 77- *Concurrent Pos:* Ital Govt grant, 59-60; guest prof comp lit,

Univ Freiburg, 69-70; Fulbright travel grant, 72-73; vis prof Am lit, Centre Univ, Avignon, 72-73. *Mem:* MLA; Am Asn Teachers Fr; Am Comp Lit Asn. *Res:* Contemporary French and Italian theatre; contemporary European novel; parody and satire in European novel. *Publ:* Co-ed, Anthologie d'Humour Francais, Scott, 71; auth, Precious Irony: The Theatre of J Giraudoux, Mouton, The Hague, 71; ed, 19th, 20th Century French Black Poetry Readings (3 rec), Folkways Rec, 77. *Mailing Add:* Dept of French & Ital Univ of Mass Amherst MA 01003

MANLEY, TIMOTHY MCLEMORE, b Washington DC, Nov 13, 25; m 66; c 2. LINGUISTICS. *Educ:* Harvard Univ, BA, 48; Am Embassy Lang Sch, dipl Japanese, 58, dipl Chinese, 64; Univ Hawaii, Manoa, MA, 68, PhD(ling), 71. *Hon Degrees:* JD, Cleveland State Univ, 77. *Prof Exp:* Vconsult, US Dept State Foreign Serv, Japan, 51-55, third secy, Tokyo, 56-58, consult, Nagoya, 59-60, foreign affairs officer, Washington, DC, 60-62, foreign serv officer, Formosa, 62-64, second secy, Indonesia, 64-65, Formosa, 65-67; DIR FAR EASTERN LANG, KENT STATE UNIV, 71-, DIR CRITICAL LANG PROG, 78- *Mem:* Ling Soc Am. *Res:* Linguistic description of Southeast Asian languages of the Austroasiatic group; applied linguistics; teaching English to foreigners. *Publ:* Auth, Outline of Sre Structures, Univ Hawaii, 72. *Mailing Add:* Critical Lang Prog Kent State Univ Kent OH 44242

MANNING, ALAN, b London, England, Nov 12, 45; m 71; c 2. FRENCH MEDIEVAL LITERATURE & LANGUAGE. *Educ:* Univ Wales, BA Hons, 69; Univ Wis-Milwaukee, MA, 72; Pa State Univ, PhD(French), 76. *Prof Exp:* Asst prof transl, Laurentian Univ, 76-80; ASST PROF TRANSL, UNIV LAVAL, 80- *Concurrent Pos:* Can Coun res grant, Res Coun Can, 78. *Res:* French Medieval treatises on heraldry; Medieval French literature and language. *Publ:* Auth, Heraldry: Modern and Medieval, Heraldry in Can, 9/77; Relationship Between Medieval Treatises and Rolls of Arms, Coat of Arms, autumn 78; The Argentaye Tract: A Critical Edition, Univ of Toronto Press (in prep). *Mailing Add:* Dept of Transl Univ of Laval Quebec PQ G1K 7P4 Can

MANSOOR, MENAHEM, b Port Said, Egypt, Aug 4, 11; US citizen; m 51; c 2. BIBLICAL & SEMITIC STUDIES. *Educ:* Univ London, BA, 39; Trinity Col, Dublin, BA, 42, PhD(Samaritan lang), 44. *Prof Exp:* Reader Arabic & Hebrew, Ministry Info, Brit Govt, 44-45; sr educ off, Dept Educ, 46-48; chief-interpreter & asst press attache, Brit Embassy, Israel, 49-54; lectr mod & class Arabic & res assoc, Johns Hopkins Univ, 54-55; prof & chmn dept, 55-77, JOSEPH L BARON PROF HEBREW & SEMITIC STUDIES, UNIV WIS, MADISON, 77- *Concurrent Pos:* Grants, Nat Asn Educ Broadcasters, Fulbright, 54 & Kohut, Yale Univ, 55; res fel, Harvard Univ, 61-62 & 66-67; mem Col Entrance Exam Bd, Hebrew, 62-64, chmn, 64-; mem educ testing serv, Arabic exam for Nat Defense Inst, 62-63 & 64-65. *Honors & Awards:* Hadassah Myrtle Award, 79; Wisconsin Society for Jewish Learning Award, 81. *Mem:* Soc Bibl Lit; Am Orient Soc; MLA; Am Jewish Hist Soc; Mid East Studies Asn NAm. *Res:* Translation and critical study of the Dead Sea Scrolls; Samaritan language and literature; Arabic dialects and mediaeval manuscripts. *Publ:* Auth, Newspaper Hebrew Reader, 71 & Advanced Modern Hebrew Literature Reading (2 vols), 71, KTAV; Linguaphone Hebrew Course, London, 73; Ibn Pakuda, Duties of the Heart, 73; Contemporary Hebrew-I, Behrman House, 76; Biblical Hebrew, Step By Step, Baker Bks, 78; coauth, Linguaphone Arabic Course, London, 78; auth, Political and Diplomatic History of the Arab World: 1900-1967 (16 vols), NCT Microcard, 78. *Mailing Add:* Dept of Hebrew & Semitic Studies Univ of Wis Madison WI 53706

MANSOUR, GEORGE PHILLIP, b Huntington, WVa, Sept 4, 39; m 61; c 2. SPANISH LITERATURE. *Educ:* Marshall Univ, AB, 61; Mich State Univ, MA, 62, PhD(Span lit), 65. *Prof Exp:* From instr to asst prof, 64-68, assoc prof, 68-77, assoc chairperson romance & class lang, 72-82, PROF SPAN, MICH STATE UNIV, 77- *Mem:* Am Asn Teachers Span & Port; MLA. *Res:* Nineteenth century Spanish literature; Don Juan theme; Spanish Romanticism. *Publ:* Auth, El convidado de piedra: A zarzuela by Rafael de Castillo, Hispania, 12/65; Time in the prose of J Echegaray, Ky Foreign Lang Quart, 68; Algunos Don Juanes olvidados del siglo XIX, Rev Estudios Hisp, 11/69; Concerning Rivas unexplained localization of Don Alvaro, Romance Notes, winter 78; Parallelism in Don Juan Tenorio, Hispania, 5/78; The poetization of experience, Hisp J, 81. *Mailing Add:* Dept of Romance Lang Mich State Univ East Lansing MI 48824

MANTEIGA, ROBERT CHARLES, b Brooklyn, NY, June 8, 47; m 70. SPANISH LETTERS. *Educ:* Univ Va, BA, 69, PhD(Span), 77; NY Univ, MA, 71. *Prof Exp:* Instr Span, Univ Va, 72-73; instr, Univ RI, 73-75; lectr, Rutgers Univ, 75-76; asst prof, 76-80, ASSOC PROF SPAN, UNIV RI, 81- *Mem:* MLA; Am Asn Teachers Span & Port; AAUP. *Res:* Medieval lyric poetry; 20th century peninsular literature. *Publ:* Auth, Rafael Alberti,s Poetry: A visual Approach, Tamesis, London, 78. *Mailing Add:* Dept of Lang Univ RI Kingston RI 02881

MANTERO, MANUEL, b Sevilla, Spain, July 29, 30; m 63; c 5. MODERN HISPANIC POETRY. *Educ:* Univ Seville, lic Derecho, 53; Univ Salamanca, Dr Derecho, 57. *Prof Exp:* Prof, Univ Madrid, 60-69; from vis prof to prof, Western Mich Univ, 69-73; PROF SPAN, UNIV GA, 73- *Concurrent Pos:* Fels, Ital Govt & Coun Sci Res, Spain; mem, Coun Sci Res, Spain. *Honors & Awards:* March Found Award, Spain; Nat Prize Lit, Spain, 60; Fastenrath Prize, Royal Span Acad Lang, 66. *Mem:* Am Asn Teachers & Span & Port; SAtlantic Mod Lang Asn. *Res:* Twentieth century Spanish and Spanish-American poetry; modern Spanish literature. *Publ:* Auth, Misa Solemne, Ed Nacional, 66; Poesia Espanola Contemporanea, 66 & Poesia, 1958-71, 72, Plaza y Janes; La Poesia Del Yo Al Nosotros, Guadarrama, 72; Los Derechos Humanos en la Poesia Hispanica Contemporanea, Gredos, 73; Ya Quiere Amanecer, Dulcinea, 75; ed, Jorge Guillen Antologia, Plaza y Janes, 75 & 77; Memorias de Deucalion, Plazay Jane's, 82. *Mailing Add:* Dept Romance Lang Univ Ga Athens GA 30601

MAPA, MARINA VARGAS, b Iloilo, Philippines, Sept 4, 25. SPANISH LANGUAGES & LITERATURE. *Educ:* San Francisco Col Women, BA, 52, MA, 55; Stanford Univ, PhD(Span), 60. *Prof Exp:* Instr Span & Latin, San Francisco Col Women, 56-61, from asst prof to assoc prof Span, 61-69, chmn dept, 63-69, lang lab dir, 65-69, registr, 66-68; ASSOC PROF SPAN & LANG LAB DIR, UNIV SAN DIEGO, 69- *Mem:* Nat Asn Lang Lab Dirs; Am Asn Teachers Span & Port; AAUP; Am Coun Teaching Foreign Lang. *Res:* Methods of teaching Spanish. *Mailing Add:* Dept of Foreign Lang Univ of San Diego San Diego CA 92110

MAPLES, ROBERT JOHN BARRIE, b Rochester, NY, May 1, 34; m 61. ROMANCE LANGUAGES, FRENCH LITERATURE. *Educ:* Univ Rochester, AB, 56; Yale Univ, PhD(French), 65. *Prof Exp:* Instr French, Univ Rochester, 62-65; asst prof, Univ Mich, Ann Arbor, 65-69; ASSOC PROF FRENCH, LYCOMING COL, 69-, CHMN DEPT FOREIGN LANG & LIT, 75- *Mem:* MLA; Am Asn Teachers Fr. *Res:* French Romantic literature. *Publ:* Auth, Individuation in Nodier's La fee aux miettes, Studies Romanticism, fall 68. *Mailing Add:* Dept of Foreign Lang & Lit Lycoming Col Williamsport PA 17701

MARAHRENS, GERWIN, b Breslau, Ger, Dec 12, 29; m 62; c 1. GERMAN LANGUAGE & LITERATURE. *Educ:* Univ Freiburg, PhD, 58. *Prof Exp:* Asst lectr Ger lang & lit, Univ Edinburgh, 58-61; from asst prof to assoc prof, 62-72, actg chmn dept, 70, PROF GER LANG, UNIV ALTA, 72-, CHMN DEPT, 71- *Mem:* Can Asn Univ Teachers Ger; Am Asn Teachers Ger; MLA; Am Soc 18th Century Studies. *Res:* Eighteenth to 20th century literature; Goethe. *Publ:* Auth, Narrator and narrative in Goethe's Die Wahlverwandtschaften, In: Essays in Honor of G Joyce Hallamore, Univ Toronto, 68; Druckmanuskripte oder Erstdrucke? Kritische Betrachtungen zu zwei Nietzsche-Monographien, Z Philos Forsch, 69; Friedrich Dürrenmatt: Studien zum Werk, Lothar Stiehm, Heidelberg, 76; Die organisch-vegetative metaphorik in Goethes klassischen dramen Iphigenie auf Tauris, Torquato Tasso und Die Naturliche Tochter, In: Kommunikative Metaphorik: Die Funktion des Literarischen Bildes in der Deutschen Literatur von Ihren Anfängen bis zur Gegenwart, Bouvier, Bonn, 76. *Mailing Add:* Dept of Ger Lang Univ of Alta Edmonton AB T6G 2E6 Can

MARANTZ, ENID GOLDSTINE, b Winnipeg, Man, Dec 25, 23; m 61. FRENCH. *Educ:* Univ Man, BA, 46; Univ Paris, DUniv, 49. *Prof Exp:* Lectr, 51-52, 53-58, asst prof, 58-68, dep registr, 66-67, registr, Univ Col, 68-71, ASSOC PROF FRENCH, UNIV MAN, 68- *Concurrent Pos:* Vpres, Alliance Francaise de Winnipeg, 64-70; mem, Second Lang Curric Coun, Prov Man, 69-73; pres, Alliance Francaise, Man, 70-73; adv, Fed Alliances Francaises du Can, 71-; mem bd teacher educ & certification, Prov Man, 77-78; mem senate, Univ Man, 76-81, senate exec, 79-81. *Mem:* Asn Can Univ Teachers Fr; Can Comp Lit Asn; Soc des Amis de Marcel; Praust et des Amis de Cornbray; MLA. *Res:* Comparative literature; Marcel Proust; 20th century novel and drama. *Publ:* Auth, Six Authors in Search of A Character: Les Soirees de Medan, Man Arts Rev, 56-57; The Theme Of Alienation in the Literary Works of Jean-Paul Sartre, fall 68 & The Proust Centenary: An Accounting, summer 72, Mosaic; Pinget's Fable, recit: An Allegory in the Style of the New, New Novel, 20th Century Lit, 77; The Topography of Cornbray or the Inversion of the Sacred and the Profane, Praust et le Texte Producteur, 80; Proust et ses traduchteurs et adapteurs auglais, Bull de la Societe des Amis de Marcel Praust et des Amis de Cornbray, Vol 31, 81; Les romans champetres de George Sand dans La Reserche: Urtertextes, Avant textes et texte, Bull d'Informations Proustiennes, 3/82. *Mailing Add:* 467 Univ Col Univ Man Winnipeg MB R3T 2N2 Can

MARCEAU, WILLIAM CHARLES, b Rochester, NY, Feb 23, 27. FRENCH LITERATURE. *Educ:* Univ Western Ont, BA, 52; Univ Laval, M-es-A, 64, PhD(French lit), 68; Sorbonne, dipl French lit, 69. *Hon Degrees:* MA, Univ Laval, 75. *Prof Exp:* Prof English, Sec Inst Sacre-Coeur, Annonay, France, 60-62; head dept lang, Aquinas Inst Rochester, 63-65; chmn dept lang, 68-72, ASSOC PROF FRENCH LIT, ST JOHN FISHER COL, 68-, COORDR FOREIGN STUDIES PROG, 80- *Concurrent Pos:* Fulbrigt prog adv, St John Fisher Col. *Mem:* AAUP; Am Asn Teachers Fr; Acad Salesienne; Am Coun Teaching Foreign Lang; NAm Soc 17th Century Fr Lit. *Res:* History of modern French philosophy; history of French literature; French spirituality of the 17th century. *Publ:* Auth, St Francis de Sales, spiritual director, Salesian Studies, 69; La theorie de la bonte naturelle dans l'Emile de J-J Rousseau, Mod Lang Studies, 71; Overseas studies as incentive for American college students, Midwest Educ Rev, 9/73; L'Optimisme dans les Oeuvres de Saint Francois de Sales, Dessain et Tolra, Paris, 73; Stoicism and St Francis de Sales, Salesian, 73; Le renouveau par l'indifference, Les annales salesiennes, 1/77. *Mailing Add:* Dept of Mod Lang St John Fisher Col Rochester NY 14618

MARCHAND, JAMES WOODROW, b Birmingham, Ala, Nov 11, 26; m; c 3. GERMANIC LANGUAGES. *Educ:* George Peabody Col, BA, 50; Vanderbilt Univ, MA, 51; Univ Mich, PhD(Germanic lang), 55. *Prof Exp:* Asst prof mod lang, Cumberland Univ, 50-51; asst prof, Howard Col, 51-52; instr Ger, Wayne Univ, 53-54; instr, Univ Mich, 54-55; asst prof, Wash Univ, 55-58; assoc prof, Univ Calif, 58-60; prof, Vanderbilt Univ, 60-67; prof, Cornell Univ, 67-69; prof, univ, 69-71, PROF GER, CTR ADVAN STUDY, UNIV ILL, URBANA, 71- *Concurrent Pos:* Vis lectr, Harvard Univ, 57; Guggenheim fel, 58; researcher, Nat Endowment for Humanities, 76-77. *Mem:* MLA; Ling Soc Am; Soc Advan Scand Studies. *Res:* Mediaeval literature; Germanic linguistics; general linguistics. *Publ:* Auth, Applied Linguistics: German, Heath, 61; Internal reconstruction of phonemic split, Lang; The Sounds and Phonemes of Wulfila's Gothic, Mouton, The Hague, 75. *Mailing Add:* Ctr for Advan Study Univ of Ill Urbana IL 61801

MARCHIONE, MARGHERITA FRANCES, b Little Ferry, NJ, Feb 19, 22. ROMANCE LANGUAGES; AMERICAN HISTORY. *Educ:* Georgian Court Col, AB, 43; Columbia Univ, AM, 49, PhD(Ital), 60. *Prof Exp:* Teacher parochial & private high schs, 43-54; instr lang, Villa Walsh Col, 54-67; assoc prof, 67-77, chmn dept lang, 67-68, PROF ITAL, FAIRLEIGH

DICKINSON UNIV, FLORHAM-MADISON CAMPUS, 77- *Concurrent Pos:* Res grants, Fairleigh Dickinson Univ, 68-69, 71-82; NDEA grant Ital inst undergrad, US Off Educ, 68; consult & rep, Gallery Mod Art, 68, 69; dir Ital Inst, Univ Salerno, 72, Tivoli, 73, Rome, 74; mem exec coun, Am Ital Hist Asn, 77-79; mem adv bd, NJ Cath Hist Rec Comn, 77-; NJ Hist Comn, 78-; Nat Hist Publ & Records Comn, 78, 79, 80 & 81; Nat Endowment for Humanities grant, 80-83. *Honors & Awards:* Am-Ital Achievement Award in Educ, 71; UNICO Nat Rizzuto Award, 77; Star of Solidarity of Ital Repub, Pres Italy, 77. *Mem:* Am Asn Teachers Ital; MLA; Am Coun Teaching Foreign Lang; Am Inst Ital Studies (pres, 77-80); Am Ital Hist Asn. *Res:* Contemporary Italian culture and literature; Dante; the papers of Philip Mazzei. *Publ:* Transl & ed, Philip Mazzei: Jefferson's Zelous Whig, Am Inst Ital Studies, 75; ed, Lettere di Clemente Rebora, Ed di Storia e Letteratura, Rome, vol I, 76, vol II, 82; auth, Clemente Rebora, G K Hall, 78; ed, Philip Mazzei: My life and wanderings, Am Inst Ital Studies, 80; Philip Mazzei: The comprehensive microfilm edition of his papers, Kraus-Thomson Orgn Ltd, 82; Guiseppe Prezzolini: Un secodo di attivita, Ruscovi Books, Milan, 82; Philip Mazzei: Selected Writings and Correspondence, 1730-1816, Ed di Storia a Letteratura, Rome, vol I, 82. *Mailing Add:* Col of Arts & Sci Fairleigh Dickinson Univ Florham-Madison Campus Madison NJ 07940

MARCONE, ROSE MARIE, b White Plains, NY, Nov 5, 38. SPANISH. *Educ:* Mary Washington Col, BA, 60; Johns Hopkins Univ, PhD(Span), 64. *Prof Exp:* Asst prof, 64-67, assoc prof, 67-74, PROF SPAN & ITAL, UNIV RICHMOND, 74-, CHMN DEPT MOD FOREIGN LANG, 72- *Mem:* MLA; AAUP; Am Asn Teachers Span & Port. *Res:* Contemporary Spanish literature; Golden Age drama. *Mailing Add:* Dept of Mod Foreign Lang Univ of Richmond Richmond VA 23173

MARGITIC, MILORAD R, b Kragujevac, Yugoslavia, June 6, 34; US citizen; m 69; c 2. FRENCH LITERATURE. *Educ:* Univ Leiden, Neth, Cand, 63; Wayne State Univ, PhD(mod lang), 71. *Prof Exp:* From instr to asst prof French, Wayne State Univ, 65-72; asst prof, Univ Chicago, 72-78; asst prof, 78-80, PROF FRENCH, WAKE FOREST UNIV, 80- *Mem:* MLA; Am Asn Teachers Fr; NAm Soc 17th Century Fr Lit; AAUP. *Res:* Seventeenth century French drama. *Publ:* Auth, Essai Sur la Mythologie du Cid, Romance Monogr, 76; Paysages et sexualite chez laforgue, Romantisme, 77; ed, Pierre Corneille La Suivante, Droz, Geneva, 78; Androuaque ou la lecture des signes: Etude de l'ironie tragique, Papers on French 17th Century Lit, 79; Pierre Corneille La Galerie du Palais, Droz, Geneva, 81; Corneille courique: Nine studies of Pierre Corneille's comedy with an introduction and a bibliography, Bibliog 17, Paris-Seattle-Buebingea, 82. *Mailing Add:* Dept of Romance Lang Wake Forest Univ 7566 Reynolda Sta Winston-Salem NC 27109

MARGOLIN, URI, b Tel Aviv, Israel, Dec 22, 42; Can citizen; m 68; c 1. COMPARATIVE LITERATURE, POETICS. *Educ:* Hebrew Univ, Jerusalem, BA, 64; Cornell Univ, MA, 70, PhD(comp lit), 72. *Prof Exp:* ASSOC PROF COMP LIT, UNIV ALTA, 72- *Concurrent Pos:* Alexander von Humboldt postdoctoral comp lit, W Ger, 76-77; Can Coun fel comp lit, Ottawa, 77. *Mem:* Int Comp Lit Asn; Can Comp Lit Asn. *Res:* Poetics; theory of genres; literary methodology. *Publ:* Auth, Historical literary genre: The concept & its uses, Comp Lit Studies, 73; On three deductive models in genre theory, Zagadnienia Rodzajow Literackich, 74; On the object of study in literary history, Neohelicon, 75; Ju Lotman on creation of meaning in literature, Can Rev Comp, Lit, 75; The demarcation of literature & the contemporary reader, Orbis Litterarum, 76; The independence of poetics, PTL, 80; On the vagueness of critical concepts, Poetics, 81. *Mailing Add:* Dept of Comp Lit Univ of Alta Edmonton AB T6G 2E6 Can

MARGOLIS, NADIA, b Neuilly-sur-Seine, France, Apr 27, 49; US citizen. MEDIEVAL LITERATURE, FRENCH POETRY. *Educ:* Univ NH, AB, 71; Stanford Univ, PhD (French), 77. *Prof Exp:* Ed asst, Speculum, Mediaeval Acad Am, 77-78; ASST PROF FRENCH, AMHERST COL, 78- *Concurrent Pos:* Attache res humanisme francais, Ctr Nat Res Sci, 73-; Nat Endowment for Humanities independent res fel, 81-82. *Mem:* MLA; Mediaeval Acad Am; Soc Rencesvals; Int Courtly Lit Soc. *Res:* Fifteenth century France; French poetic theory; comparative Medieval literature. *Publ:* Auth, The prison motif in Christine de Pizan, Charles d'Orleans, and Francois Villon, 15th Century Studies, 78. *Mailing Add:* Dept of Romance Lang Amherst Col Amherst MA 01002

MARIANI, UMBERTO CARLO, b Lissone, Italy, Nov 6, 27; m 56. ITALIAN. *Educ:* Univ Pavia, Doctorate(mod Ital lit), 55; NY Univ, MA, 59. *Prof Exp:* Prof Ital & Latin, Col Ghelfi, Pavia, 53-54; prof Ital, Latin, Greek, hist & geog, Col Ballerini, Italy, 54-56; teacher Latin, hist & geog, UN Int Sch, New York, 59; from instr to assoc prof, 59-68, PROF ITAL, RUTGERS UNIV, NEW BRUNSWICK, 68- *Concurrent Pos:* Fac res grant, Italy, 63-64. *Mem:* MLA; Am Asn Univ Professors Italian; Am Asn Teachers Ital. *Res:* Italian and American literature; comparative literature. *Publ:* Auth, L'esperienza italiana di Henry James, 60 & Il relismo di John W DeForest, 61, Studi Am; Vico nella poetica pavesiana, Forum Ital, 12/68; L'aventura di Celestino V in Silone e in Dante, La Fusta, spring 78; Enrico IV o della logica potente e profonda, Rivista di studi pirandelliani, 80. *Mailing Add:* Dept of Ital Rutgers Univ Box 3001 New Brunswick NJ 08903

MARICHAL, JUAN, b Teneriffe, Spain, Feb 2, 22; m 47; c 2. SPANISH. *Educ:* Univ Algiers, bachelier, 41; Princeton Univ, MA, 48, PhD(Romance lang), 49. *Prof Exp:* Instr Span, Princeton Univ, 46-48 & Johns Hopkins Univ, 48-49; asst prof Romance lang, Harvard Univ, 49-53; assoc prof Span, Bryn Mawr Col, 53-58; assoc prof Romance lang, 58-61, prof, 61-80, SMITH PROF ROMANCE LANG & LIT, HARVARD UNIV, 80- *Concurrent Pos:* Guggenheim fel, 59 & 71-72; syndicator, Univ Press, Harvard Univ, 65-69; mem educ adv bd, Guggenheim Found, 67- *Honors & Awards:* Hon chair, San Marcos Univ, Lima, 65. *Mem:* Corresp mem Hisp Soc Am; MLA; Am Asn Teachers Span & Port. *Res:* Spanish history, 1898-1936; Latin American intellectual history, 1810-1960. *Publ:* Auth, El nuevo pensamiento politico espanol, Finisterre, Mex, 66; La vocacion de Manuel Azana, Oasis, Mex, 66; ed, Manuel Azana, obras completas (4 vols), Oasis, Mex, 66-68; auth, Edicusa, Madrid, 68; co-ed, Luminous Reality: The Poetry of Jorge Guillen, Univ Okla, 68; auth, Selecta, Rev Occidente, Madrid, 72; Tres voces de Pedro Salinas, Taller Ed, Madrid, 76; Cuatro fases de la historia intelectual latinoamericana, March Found, Madrid, 78. *Mailing Add:* Widener Libr 708 Harvard Univ Cambridge MA 02138

MARICHAL, SOLITA SALINAS, b Seville, Spain, Jan 18, 20; US citizen; m 47; c 2. FOREIGN LANGUAGES & LITERATURES. *Educ:* Wellesley Col, AB, 42; Univ PR, MA, 45; Bryn Mawr Col, PhD(Span), 66. *Prof Exp:* Instr Span, Vassar Col, 45-47; from instr to prof Span, Simmons Col, 58-76; RES & WRITING, 76- *Concurrent Pos:* Lectr Harvard Univ Extension. *Res:* Spanish lyrical poetry; the poetry of Rafael Alberti; edition of Pedro Salinas' works. *Publ:* Auth, On Rafael Alberti, In: The Poem Itself, Holt, 60; El mundo poetico de Rafael Alberti, Gredos, Madrid, 68; ed, Pedro Salinas, Poesias Completas, 75, 2nd ed, 81 & Pedro Salinas, Narrativa Completa, 76, Barral, Barcelona. *Mailing Add:* 29 Lancaster St Cambridge MA 02140

MARIGOLD, W GORDON, b Toronto, Ont, May 24, 26; m 53. GERMAN LITERATURE. *Educ:* Univ Toronto, BA, 48, PhD, 53; Ohio State Univ, MA, 49. *Prof Exp:* Instr Ger, Univ Western Ont, 49-50; master French, Latin & Ger, Trinity Col Schs, Port Hope, Ont, 52-53; asst prof Ger, Univ Va, 53-56; assoc prof, 56-57, PROF MOD LANG, UNION COL, KY, 57-, CHMN DIV LANG, 59- *Concurrent Pos:* Vis prof Ger, Univ Ill, Urbana-Champaign, 77. *Honors & Awards:* Grawemeyer Award for Fac, Univ Louisville, 74 & 81. *Mem:* Am Asn Ger Lit 16th & 17th Centuries; MLA; SAtlantic Mod Lang Asn; Am Asn Teachers Ger; AAUP. *Res:* German drama of the 17th century; patronage of art and literature in Germany in the 17th century; German organs of the Baroque period. *Publ:* Ed, Johann Philipp v Schönborn, Die Psalmen des Königlichen Propheten Davids, Johnson Reprint, 72; auth, De Leone Schönbornico: Huldigungsgedichte an Johann Philipp u Lothar Franz v Schönborn, Archiv f mittelrhein Kirchengesch, 74; Die schöne Brunnenquell Zu einigen Huldigungen f Damian Hugo v Schönborn, Zeitschrift f d Gesch d Oberrheins, 76; Gelehrsamkeit u Spielerei: Huldigungen f Fürstbischof Friedrich Karl v Schönborn, Mainfränk Jahrbuch f Gesch u Kunst, 79; ed, Johann Philipp v Schönborn, Catholische Sonn- vnd Feyertägliche Evangelia, APA-Holland Univ Press, 81; auth, Die Bekehrungswelle im 17 u 18 Jahrhundert u die Familie Schönborn, Jahrbuch f fränk Landesforschung, 81; Damian Hugo v Schönborn in Hamburg: Norddeutsche Künstler ehren einen katholischen Staatsmann, Zeitschrift f d Gesch d Oberrheins, 81; Protestanten ehren den katholischen Landesvater: Schönborn-Huldigungen aus Kitzingen, Mainfränk Jahrbuch f Gesch u Kunst, 81. *Mailing Add:* 416 N Main Barbourville KY 40906

MARIN, DIEGO, b Ciudad Real, Spain, Mar 23, 14; m 41; c 3. SPANISH. *Educ:* Univ London, BA, 43; Univ Toronto, MA, 53, PhD, 56. *Prof Exp:* Asst lectr Span, Univ Birmingham, 41-48; instr, Univ Western Ont, 49-51; from lectr to assoc prof, 51-64, PROF SPAN, UNIV TORONTO, 64- *Concurrent Pos:* Can Coun sr fel, 65-66. *Mem:* Am Asn Teachers Span & Port; corresp mem Hisp Soc Am; Asoc Can di Hispanistas (vpres, 74). *Res:* Golden Age Spanish drama and poetry; modern Spanish poetry. *Publ:* Auth, La intriga secundaria en el teatro de Lope de Vega, Univ Toronto, 58; La civilizacion espanola, Holt, 61; Uso y funcion de la versificacion en Lope de Vega, Castalia, 62; coauth, Lope de Vega: El galan de la Membrilla, R Acad Espanola, 62; Breve historia de la literatura espanola, 66 & auth, Literatura espanola, seleccion, 68, Holt; ed, Lope de Vega, La dama boba, Catedra, 76; Poesia paisajistica espanola 1940-70, Estudio y Antologia, Tamesis, 76. *Mailing Add:* Dept of Hisp Studies Univ of Toronto Toronto ON M5S 1A1 Can

MARING, JOEL MARVYL, b Waterloo, Iowa, Jan 17, 35; m 59; c 6. ANTHROPOLOGY, LINGUISTICS. *Educ:* Wartburg Col, BA, 56; Ind Univ, PhD(anthrop), 67. *Prof Exp:* Asst prof, 63-70, chmn Asian studies prog, 65-72, ASSOC PROF ANTHROP & LING, SOUTHERN ILL UNIV, CARBONDALE, 70- *Concurrent Pos:* Consult, Bur Indian Affairs, 72- *Mem:* Fel Am Anthrop Asn; Am Asian Studies. *Res:* Linguistics and ethnology of American Southwest Indians, especially the Keresan Pueblos; linguistics and ethnology of Papua and New Guinea; Indo-Chinese immigrant assimilation. *Publ:* Auth, Anthropological Considerations of Evaluators, Innovators and Implementers in American Education, Eureka Col Studies Ctr, 69; coauth, Historical and Cultural Dict of the Philippines, 73 & Historical and Cultural Dict of Burma, 73, Scarecrow. *Mailing Add:* Dept of Anthrop Southern Ill Univ Carbondale IL 62901

MARINO, NANCY FRANCES, b New York, NY, June 17, 51; m 81. SPANISH MEDIEVAL LITERATURE. *Educ:* State Univ NY, New Paltz, BA, 71; Univ Mass, PhD(Hisp lang & lit), 74. *Prof Exp:* Vis asst prof Span, Ind Univ, 74-76; ASSOC PROF SPAN, UNIV HOUSTON, 76- *Mem:* MLA. *Res:* Spanish cancionero poetry; the Serranilla. *Publ:* Auth, Una parte del cancionero perdido de Martinez de Burgos, Revista de Archivos, Biblioecas y Museos, 76; Hugo de Urries: Embajador, traductor, poeta, Boletin de la Biblioteca Menendez y Pelayo, 77; Dezir que fizo Juan Alfonso de Baena, Albatros-Hispanofila, 78; Juan Agraz: Poeta elegiaco y amoroso del Siglo XV, Boletin de la Biblioteca Menendez y Pelayo, 80; The Serranillas of the Cancionero de Stuniga, Revista de Estudios Hispanicos, 81. *Mailing Add:* Span Dept Univ of Houston Houston TX 77004

MARINO, NICHOLAS JOSEPH, b Brooklyn, NY, June 28, 29; m 53; c 1. ROMANCE LANGUAGES. *Educ:* Queens Col, NY, BA, 51; Hofstra Univ, MA, 64. *Prof Exp:* Teacher, Bellport Cent Sch Dist 4, 59-62; from instr to assoc prof Romance lang, 62-68, chmn dept Romance lang, 64-68, asst dean instr, 68-80, PROF FOREIGN LANG, SUFFOLK COUNTY COMMUNITY COL, 80- *Concurrent Pos:* Vis lectr continental Span lit, Hofstra Univ, 64-66; vis lectr Span lit, lang & hist, Adelphi Suffolk Col, 66-67. *Mem:* MLA; Am Asn Teachers Span & Port; Am Asn Teachers Ital; Nat Asn Foreign Lang Teachers. *Res:* Romanticism--continental Spanish; Siglo de Oro drama and poetry. *Mailing Add:* 46 Indianhead Dr Sayville NY 11782

MARKER, FREDERICK J, English Literature, Comparative Drama. See Vol II

MARKEY, CONSTANCE, b Waukesha, Wis, Sept 12, 45; m 73; c 3. ITALIAN LITERATURE & FILM. *Educ:* Rosary Col, BA, 65; Univ Chicago, MA, 70; Univ Ill, Urbana, PhD(Ital), 80. *Prof Exp:* Teaching fel Ital, Univ Ill, Urbana, 75-76; lectr, Univ Ill, Chicago, 76-77; INSTR ITAL & FILM, NEW TRIER EXTEN, WILMETTE, 77-; INSTR ITAL, LOYOLA UNIV, CHICAGO, 79- *Concurrent Pos:* Coordr study abroad prog Ital, New Trier Exten, Wilmette, 78-; res grant, Loyola Univ, 81-82 & 82-83. *Mem:* Am Asn Univ Professors Ital; MLA; Soc Cinema Studies; Screen Educator's Soc; Midwest Mod Lang Asn. *Res:* Italian and American film; modern Italian literature; baroque drama. *Publ:* Coauth, Federico Fellini: A Guide to References & Resources, G K Hall, 78; auth, Portrait of a film producer, Camden Courier Post, 12/18/81; Dante and All That Jazz, Mise en Scene, fall 81; The tarot cards as a subversive tool in Calvino, In: Scope of the Fantastic II, Greenwood Press, 82; Calvino and the existential dilemma, Italica (in press); Italo Calvino, the contemporary fabulist: An interview, Italian Quart (in press). *Mailing Add:* 326 Oxford Rd Kenilworth IL 60043

MARKEY, THOMAS LLOYD, b Dayton, Ohio, May 29, 40; m 74. LINGUISTICS, GERMANIC PHILOLOGY. *Educ:* Hamilton Col, BA, 62; Univ Chicago, MA, 65; Univ Uppsala, PhD (Scand), 69. *Prof Exp:* Res student Scand, Peterhouse Col, 67-68; res assoc, Harvard Univ, 68-69, asst prof, 69-73; vis asst prof, 73-74, from asst prof to assoc prof, 74-78, PROF GER/LING, UNIV MICH, 78- *Concurrent Pos:* Am-Scand Found Travel fel, 77; ed, Mich Ger Studies, 77- *Mem:* Mediaeval Acad Am; Ling Soc Am; Am Name Soc; Soc Ling Europ; Ling Asn Can & US. *Res:* Onomastics, dialectology, comparative grammar--all in Germanic and Indo-European. *Mailing Add:* Dept of Ger Univ of Mich Ann Arbor MI 48109

MARKOV, VLADIMIR, b Leningrad, Russia, Feb 24, 20; US citizen; m 47. HISTORY OF LITERATURE. *Educ:* Univ Calif, Berkeley, PhD, 58. *Prof Exp:* From acting asst prof to assoc prof, 57-63, PROF RUSS LIT, UNIV CALIF, LOS ANGELES, 63- *Concurrent Pos:* Guggenheim fel, 63-64; Nat Endowment for Humanities sr fel, 67-68. *Honors & Awards:* Annual transl award, PEN Club, 67. *Mem:* Am Asn Teachers Slavic Lang; Am Asn Advan Slavic Studies. *Res:* Russian poetry, especially of the 20th century; Russian futurism. *Publ:* Auth, The Longer Poems by V Khlebnikov, Univ Calif, 62; co-ed, Modern Russian Poetry, Macgibbon & Kee, England, 66, Bobbs, 67; ed, Die Manifeste und Programmschriften der Russischen Futuristen, 67 & ed, V Khlebnikov, Works, 68-71, Vols I-IV, Wilhelm Fink, Munich; auth, Russian Futurism: A History, Univ Calif, Los Angeles, 68, Ital transl, Einaudi, Torino, 73; Georgy Ivanov: Nihilist as light bearer, Tri-quart, spring 73; ed, K Balmont, Selected Poetry, 75 & co-ed, M Kuzmin, Collected Poetry, Vols 1-3, 77, Fink, Munich; auth, Russian Imagism 1919-1927 (2 vols), Schmitz, Giessen, 80. *Mailing Add:* Dept of Slavic Lang Univ of Calif Los Angeles CA 90024

MARKS, ELAINE, b New York, NY, Nov 13, 30. FRENCH LITERATURE, WOMEN'S STUDIES. *Educ:* Bryn Mawr Col, BA, 52; Univ Pa, MA, 53; NY Univ, PhD(French), 58. *Prof Exp:* From instr to asst prof French, NY Univ, 58-63; assoc prof, Univ Wis, Milwaukee, 63-65; prof, Univ Mass, 65-66, 72-73; from assoc prof to prof, 66-68, PROF FRENCH, UNIV WIS-MADISON, 80-, DIR WOMEN'S STUDIES RES CTR, 77- *Concurrent Pos:* Johnson fel, Inst Res in Humanities, Univ Wis, 62-63. *Mem:* MLA; Am Asn Teachers Fr; Midwest Mod Lang Asn; Nat Women's Study Asn. *Res:* Biography and autobiography; feminist theory; 20th century literature. *Publ:* Auth, Colette, Rutgers Univ, 60; French Poetry From Baudelaire to the Present, Dell, 62; The relevance of literary biography, Mass Rev, fall 66; Simone de Beauvoir: Encounters with Death, 73 & The dream of love study of three autobiographies, In: Twentieth Century French Fiction, 75, Rutgers Univ; I am my own heroine: On women and autobiographies in France, Female Studies, Feminist Pr, 75; co-ed (with George Stambolion), Homosexualities and French Literature, 79; (with Isabelle de Courtivron), New French Feminisms, 80. *Mailing Add:* 2202 Martin St Madison WI 53713

MARLOW, ELISABETH A, b Colombes, France, Nov 15, 30; m 56. ROMANCE LANGUAGES. *Educ:* Sch Advan Com Studies, France, dipl econ, 53; Univ Ore, MA, 58, PhD(Romance lang), 66. *Prof Exp:* Instr mod lang, 58-60, from instr to ASST PROF ROMANCE LANG, UNIV ORE, 62- *Concurrent Pos:* TV instr, Col of the Air, Univ Ore, 60-62. *Mem:* Philol Asn Pac Coast; MLA; Am Asn Teachers French. *Res:* Modern French literature, especially theatre; 17th century French literature, especially Corneille, Racine and Moliere. *Mailing Add:* Dept of Romance Lang Univ of Ore Eugene OR 97403

MARQUARDT, PATRICIA ANN, b Milwaukee, Wis, Dec 21, 44; m 67. CLASSICAL LANGUAGES & PHILOLOGY. *Educ:* Ripon Col, BA, 66; Univ Chicago, MA, 67; Univ Wis-Madison, PhD(class lang), 76. *Prof Exp:* Instr English, Rufus King High Sch, Milwaukee, 67-68; instr Latin & Greek, Mt Mary Col, Milwaukee, 68-69; instr, Univ Wis-Milwaukee, 69-71, lectr, 71-77; ASST PROF LATIN & GREEK, MARQUETTE UNIV, 78- *Mem:* Class Asn Midwest & S; Am Philol Asn. *Res:* Hesiod; classical and Near-Eastern mythology; ancient religions and mythology. *Publ:* Auth, Portrait of Hecate, Am J Philol, Vol 102, 81; The two faces of Hesiod's muse, Ill Classic Studies, Vol 7, 82; Hesiod's ambivalent view of woman, Classic Philol, Vol 78 (in press). *Mailing Add:* 5330 N Shoreland Ave Milwaukee WI 53217

MARQUES, SARAH, b Colon, Cuba; US citizen. FOREIGN LANGUAGE. *Educ:* Univ Havana, DPedagogy(educ), 52; City Univ New York, MA, 65; New York Univ, PhD(Span & Latin Am lit), 76. *Prof Exp:* Teacher, elem & sec schs, Cuba, 52-59; bilingual teacher, Bd Educ, NY, 65-67; instr Span grammar, Columbia Univ, 67; ASSOC PROF GRAMMAR & LIT, MARYMOUNT COL TARRYTOWN, 67- *Concurrent Pos:* Instr grammar, St John's Univ, 79. *Mem:* AAUP; Am Asn Teachers Spanish & Port. *Res:* Latin American literature. *Publ:* Auth, Arte y sociedad en las novelas de Carlos Loveira, Ed Universal, 76. *Mailing Add:* 142-01 41st Ave Flushing NY 11355

MARQUESS, HARLAN EARL, b Sheridan, Wyo, Jan 23, 31; m 58; c 3. SLAVIC LINGUISTICS, RUSSIAN LANGUAGE. *Educ:* Univ Calif, Berkeley, AB, 58, MA, 60, PhD(Slavic lang & lit), 66. *Prof Exp:* From instr to asst prof, 64-71, ASSOC PROF SLAVIC LANG, UNIV WIS, MADISON, 71- *Mem:* Ling Soc Am; Int Ling Asn; Am Asn Teachers Slavic & E Europ Lang; Am Asn Advan Slavic Studies. *Res:* Structure of Russian; nonstandard Russian speech; morphology of Czech. *Publ:* Coauth, Soviet Prison Camp Speech, Univ Wis, 72. *Mailing Add:* Dept of Slavic Lang Univ of Wis Madison WI 53706

MARQUEZ, FRANCISCO, b Seville, Spain, Mar 21, 31; m 60; c 3. SPANISH LANGUAGE & LITERATURE. *Educ:* Univ Seville, Spain, PhD(lit), 58. *Prof Exp:* Prof adj Span lit, Univ Seville, Spain, 55-59; instr Romance lang, Harvard Univ, 59-62; asst prof, Univ BC, 62-65 & Harvard Univ, 65-67; prof, Rutgers Univ, 67-68 & Grad Ctr, City Univ New York, 68-78; PROF SPAN, HARVARD UNIV, 78- *Mem:* MLA; Int Asn Hispanists; Soc Span & Port Hist Studies. *Res:* Mediaeval and Golden Age Spanish literature; intellectual and religious history; comparative literature. *Publ:* Auth, Investigaciones Sobre Juan Alvarez Gato, Span Acad, 60; coauth, H de Talavera, Catolica Impugnacion, Flors, 61; auth, Espiritualidad y Literatura en el Siglo XVI, Alfaguara, 68; Fuentes Literarias Cervantinas, Gredos, 73; Personajes y Temas del Quijote, Taurus, 75; Relecciones de Literatura Medieval, Univ Sevilla, Spain, 77. *Mailing Add:* Dept of Romance Lang Harvard Univ Cambridge MA 02138

MARROCCO, MARY ANNE WILKINSON, b Corpus Christi, Tex, Nov 15, 42; c 1. SPANISH LINGUISTICS. *Educ:* Northwestern Univ, BA, 64; Univ Ill, AM, 69, PhD(Span lit), 72; Corpus Christi State Univ, MS, 80. *Prof Exp:* Teacher Span, Corpus Christi Pub Schs, Tex, 65-67; teaching asst, Univ Ill, 67-71; asst prof Span ling & dir undergrad studies, Vanderbilt Univ, 71-73; asst prof Span, Tex A&I Univ, Corpus Christi, 73-75; consult, Educ Serv Ctr, II, Corpus Christi, 75-79; FOREIGN LANG/LANG DEVELOP CONSULT, CORPUS CHRISTI INDEPENDENT SCH DIST, 79- *Res:* English as a second language; foreign language methodology. *Publ:* Auth, The Spanish of Corpus Christi, Texas, Univ Ill, 73; Handbook for English for speakers of other languages, CCISD, 79. *Mailing Add:* 526 Peerman Pl Corpus Christi TX 78411

MARRONE, NILA GUTIERREZ, b La Paz, Bolivia, US citizen. SPANISH LINGUISTICS, SPANISH AMERICAN LITERATURE. *Educ:* Columbia Univ, BA, 70, NY Univ, MA, 72, PhD(Span & ling), 75. *Prof Exp:* Lectr Span, New York Univ, 72-73; assoc, Columbia Univ, 73-74; ASST PROF SPAN, UNIV CONN, 75- *Mem:* Am Asn Teachers Span & Port; MLA. *Res:* Descriptive Spanish linguistics; applied and sociolinguistics. *Publ:* Auth, Investigacion sobre variaciones lexicas en el mundo hispano, Rev Bilingue, 74; contribr, The Analysis of Hispanic Texts: Current Trends in Methodology, Bilingual, 76; auth, Guide to the Cultural Resources of the Spanish & Portuguese Communities in Conn, Univ Conn, 77-78; El estilo de Juan Rulfo: Estudio linguistico, Bilingual, 78. *Mailing Add:* Dept of Span Univ of Conn Storrs CT 06268

MARSH, JOHN OSBORN, b Rahway, NJ, Sept 28, 17; m 42; c 4. ROMANCE LANGUAGES. *Educ:* Rutgers Univ, BA, 39, MA, 41; Univ Wis, PhD(Span), 51. *Prof Exp:* From instr to assoc prof Span, Univ Ill, Chicago, 48-67; chmn dept mod lang, 70-79, PROF SPAN & FRENCH, CALIFORNIA STATE COL, PA, 67- *Mailing Add:* Dept of Mod Lang Calif State Col California PA 15419

MARSHALL, ANTHONY JOHN, b Cardiff, Eng, May 22, 37. CLASSICS, ROMAN HISTORY. *Educ:* Oxford Univ, BA, 59, MA, 62, MLitt, 63. *Prof Exp:* Instr classics, Amherst Col, 61-62 & Bryn Mawr Col, 62-63; asst prof, 63-69, assoc prof, 69-79, PROF CLASSICS, QUEEN'S UNIV, 79- *Mem:* Soc Prom Roman Studies; Class Asn Can; Class Asn Atlantic States; Am Philol Asn; Asn Ancient Historians. *Res:* Roman law; Roman provincial administration. *Publ:* Auth, Pompey's organization of Bithynia-Pontus, J Roman Studies, 68; Romans under Chian law, Greek, Roman & Byzantine Studies, 69; contribr, Aufstieg und Niedergang der Romischen Welt, De Gruyter, Berlin, 72 & 80; Roman women and the provinces, Ancient Soc, 75; Flaccus and the Jews of Asia, 75 & Library resources and creative writing at Rome, 76, Phoenix; Livius Drusus and the Italian question, Can Hist Asn Papers, 76. *Mailing Add:* Dept of Classics New Humanities Bldg Queen's Univ Kingston ON K7L 3N6 Can

MARSHALL, DAVID FRANKLIN, b Perry, Okla, Jan 6, 38; m 66; c 2. ENGLISH LINGUISTICS. *Educ:* Tex Christian Univ, BA, 60; Union Theol Sem, MDiv, 64; NY Univ, PhD(ling), 75. *Prof Exp:* Art ed, United Church Herald, New York, 64-69; dir bk publ, Pilgrim Press & United Church Press, Philadelphia, 69-72; instr English, Villanova Univ, 72; asst prof English, Atlantic Christian Col, 72-76, assoc prof, 76-80; ASSOC PROF ENGLISH, UNIV NDAK, 80- *Concurrent Pos:* Ed, Quadrant, C G Jung Found Analytical Psychol, 67-71; Lilly vis scholar humanities, Duke Univ, 76-77; vis scholar, Nat Endowment for Humanities, Stanford Univ, 79. *Mem:* AAUP; Ling Soc Am; MLA; New Chaucer Soc. *Res:* Transformational grammar; Chaucer studies. *Publ:* Ed, Creative Ministries, Pilgrim, 68 & United Church, 68; auth, A conversation with Noam Chomsky, Colloquy, 3/71; This is a poet: Poetry of Francis Warner, spring 73 & The linguistic foundations of poetry, fall 73, Crucible; A note on Chaucer's Manciple's Tale 105-10, Chaucer Newsletter 1: 1; Implications of a witch switching transformation, SECOL Bull, 5:2, 81; Unmasking the last pilgrim: How and why Chaucer uses the retraction, Christianity & Lit (in prep). *Mailing Add:* Dept English Univ of NDak Grand Forks ND 58202

MARSHALL, GROVER EDWIN, b Portland, Maine, Mar 28, 30; m 66; c 1. FRENCH, ITALIAN. *Educ:* Bowdoin Col, BA, 51; Princeton Univ, MA, 54, PhD(French), 71. *Prof Exp:* Instr French & Ital, Princeton Univ, 54-58; instr, Williams Col, 58-60, asst prof Romanic lang, 60-64, lectr, 64-65; ASST PROF FRENCH & ITAL, UNIV NH, 65-, CHMN DEPT, 73- *Mem:* Am Asn Teachers Fr; Am Asn Teachers Ital. *Res:* French Romanticism. *Mailing Add:* Dept French Murkland Hall Univ of NH Durham NH 03824

MARSHALL, JAMES F, b Indianapolis, Ind, Aug 15, 12; m 43. MODERN LANGUAGES. *Educ:* Ind Univ, AB, 37; Univ Ill, MA, 39, PhD(Fr), 48. *Prof Exp:* Asst prof French, Univ Ariz, 48-49; assoc prof & head dept mod lang, Whittier Col, 49-58; prof, 58-74, EMER PROF FRENCH & ITAL, UNIV WIS-MILWAUKEE, 74- *Concurrent Pos:* Am Coun Learned Soc res grant, 51; Fund Adv Educ fac fel, Europe, 55. *Mem:* Am Asn Teachers Fr. *Res:* Nineteenth century French literature; Stendhal. *Publ:* Critical ed, Henri III, Univ Ill, 52; auth, Alfred de Vigny and Wm Charles Macready, PMLA, 3/59; V Jacquemont, Letters to A Chaper, Am Philos Soc, 60; Quelques personnages des Souvenirs d'egotisme racontes par une touriste americaine, Stendhal Club, 10/60; Mme de Staël et Mme de Tesse, Rev Hist Litt France, 1/67; De Staël-de Pont Correspondence, Univ Wis, 68. *Mailing Add:* 4746 N Oakland Ave Milwaukee WI 53211

MARSHALL, PETER K, b Cardiff, Wales, July 2, 34; div; c 2. CLASSICAL LANGUAGES, MEDIEVAL LITERATURE. *Educ:* Univ SWales, BA, 54; Oxford Univ BA, 56, MA, 60. *Hon Degrees:* MA, Amherst Col, 73. *Prof Exp:* Instr classics, 59-61, asst prof, 62-68, assoc prof, 68-73, PROF CLASSICS, AMHERST COL, 73- *Concurrent Pos:* Asst lectr Latin & Greek, Univ Liverpool, England, 61-62; ACLS fel, 76-77; Guggenheim fel, 80-81. *Mem:* Class Asn Gt Brit; Am Philol Asn; Medieval Acad Am; Int Soc Hist Rhetoric. *Res:* The textual transmission of classical Latin authors; the Commentarii of Servius; the De Proprietatibus Rerum of Bartholomaeus Anglicus. *Publ:* Auth, Utopia, Sir Thomas More, Washington Sq Press, 65; ed, A Gellii Noctes Atticae, 2 vols, Oxford Univ Press, 68; auth, The Manuscript Tradition of Cornelius Nepos, Univ London, 77; ed, Cornelii Nepotis Vitae cum Fragmentis, Teubner, Leipzig, 77; Isidore, Etymologies Book II, Les Belles Lett, Paris, 82. *Mailing Add:* Dept of Classics Amherst Col Amherst MA 01002

MARSHALL, ROBERT G, b Houston, Tex, Feb 19, 19; m 49; c 3. ROMANCE LANGUAGES. *Educ:* Rice Univ, AB, 41, AM, 46; Yale Univ, PhD, 50. *Prof Exp:* Asst instr French, Yale Univ, 47-49; asst prof, Tex State Col Women, 49-51; from asst prof to prof Romance lang, Wells Col, 51-72, chmn dept Romance lang, 55-72, coordr summer prog, 63-67; PROF FRENCH & DIR JR YEAR IN FRANCE, SWEET BRIAR COL, 72- *Concurrent Pos:* Am Coun Learned Soc ling studies grant, 53; Fulbright res scholar, Rome, Italy, 59-60; mem readers comt, Advan Placement French, Educ Testing Serv, 62-67; dir NDEA Summer Inst, Wells Col, 63-67; dir Paris off, Sweet Briar jr year in France, 67-68; mem adv comt, Romance lang, Conf Bd Assoc Res Coun, Int Exchange of Persons, 68-71, chmn, 70-71. *Honors & Awards:* Chevalier Dans L'Ordre Des Palmes Academiques, 80. *Mem:* MLA; Am Asn Teachers Fr; Nat Asn Foreign Student Affairs; Am Soc 18th Century Studies; Soc Profs Francais en Amerique. *Res:* French literature of the 18th century. *Publ:* Auth, The importance of Solaria, Cesare Barbiere Courier, fall 69; co-ed, T S Eliot et le Baudelaire de Swinburne, Le Bayou; ed, Short Title Catalogue of Italian Books Printed in the 16th Century (3 vols), G K Hall 70; co-ed, Trois Pieces Surrealistes, Appleton, 70; auth, Winter theatre in Paris, 10/70 & ed, Study programs in France, 74, Fr Rev; contribr, Secussa Handbook, Nat Asn Foreign Student Affairs, 75; New Guide to Study Abroad, Harper, 78; Columbia Dictionary of Modern European Literature, Columbia Univ, 80. *Mailing Add:* PO Box 54 Sweet Briar Col Sweet Briar VA 24595

MARSHALL, ROBERT T, b Johnstown, Pa, Sept 22, 19; m 43; c 10. FOREIGN LANGUAGES, LINGUISTICS. *Educ:* St Vincent Col, AB, 41; Cath Univ Am, MA, 48, PhD(Latin), 51. *Prof Exp:* Prof foreign lang & chmn dept, 49-77, PROF CLASSICS, MT ST MARY'S COL, 77- *Mem:* Am Class League; Am Coun Teaching Foreign Lang. *Res:* Classical languages; St Augustine and Patristic Latin. *Publ:* Auth, The Socio-Political Terminology of the City of God, Cath Univ Am, 51. *Mailing Add:* Dept of Lang & Ling Mt St Mary's Col Emmitsburg MD 21727

MARSHALL, THOMAS EDWARD, b San Francisco, Calif, May 20, 24; m 49; c 3. ROMANCE LANGUAGES. *Educ:* Univ Calif, AB, 45, MA, 46, PhD(Romance lit), 59. *Prof Exp:* Teaching asst French, Univ Calif, 45-47, lectr, 51-53; instr French & Ger, Univ San Francisco, 47-50; from instr to assoc prof Romance lang, Univ Ore, 53-69; PROF FRENCH, STATE UNIV NY COL OSWEGO, 69- *Concurrent Pos:* Europ dir, City Univ NY prog study abroad, Reims, France, 66-68. *Mem:* Am Asn Teachers Fr; MLA. *Res:* Poetry of Guillaume Apollinaire; theory and practice of poetry in the works of Paul Valery; new French criticism. *Mailing Add:* Dept of French State Univ of NY Col Oswego NY 13126

MARTEL, J LUKE, SR, b Montreal, Que, Sept 23, 21; US citizen; m 45; c 3. FRENCH LITERATURE. *Educ:* Univ Ariz, AB, 50; Univ Montpellier, Lic es Let, 52; Univ Aix Marseille, DUniv(French), 57. *Prof Exp:* Lectr Am studies, Univ Montpellier, 51-52; instr French, State Univ NY Col Potsdam, 53-54; lectr English, Lycee Toulon, France, 54-55, Col Brignoles, 55-56 & Col Fabre, 56-57; instr French, Univ Ill, Urbana, 57-58; asst prof, Georgetown Univ, 58-63; assoc prof, 63-75, PROF FRENCH, COL WILLIAM & MARY, 75- *Concurrent Pos:* Lectr English, Col Michelet, France, 51-52; pres, Alliance Francaise, Williamsburg, 65- *Honors & Awards:* Officier des Palmes Academiques, Fr Govt, 73. *Mem:* Am Asn Teachers Fr. *Res:* The Felibrige movement in Provence, France; regionalism in French literature with emphasis on Provencal literature. *Mailing Add:* Dept of Mod Lang Col of William & Mary Williamsburg VA 23185

MARTI, ANTONIO M, b Alcover, Spain, Sept 21, 31; m 66. SPANISH. *Educ:* Univ Barcelona, MA, 54, MA, 57, PhD(Span lit), 65; Orient Lang Inst, Tokyo, dipl, 60; Sophia Univ, Japan, BSc, 62; Escuela Cent Idiomas de Madrid, dipl English, 62. *Prof Exp:* Lectr Span, Sophia Univ, 61-62 & Col Penafort, Barcelona, 63-64; lectr English, Inst Cervantes, Madrid, 64-65; asst prof Span lit, Ohio State Univ, 65-66; assoc prof, 66-80, PROF SPAN, UNIV WESTERN ONT, 80- *Concurrent Pos:* Can Coun res grant, 68- *Honors & Awards:* Tarragona Prov Bk Award, 68. *Mem:* MLA. *Res:* Spanish literature in the Golden Age; the philosophical tendencies of Golden Age Spanish literature. *Publ:* Auth, Sallustius, Folia, 59; Japon, guia, Japan Travel Bur, 62. *Mailing Add:* Dept of Span Univ of Western Ont London ON N6A 5B8 Can

MARTI, BERTHE MARIE, b Vevey, Switz. CLASSICAL PHILOLOGY. *Educ:* Univ Lausanne, Lic es Let, 25; Bryn Mawr Col, AM, 26, PhD, 33. *Prof Exp:* From instr to prof Latin, Bryn Mawr Col, 30-64; prof, 64-76, EMER PROF LATIN, UNIV NC, CHAPEL HILL, 76- *Concurrent Pos:* Guggenheim fel, 54-55; Fulbright fel & res fel, Am Acad Rome, 60-61, vis prof, 62-63; mem exec comt, Catalogus Translationum et Commentariorum. *Mem:* Am Philol Asn; fel Mediaeval Acad Am. *Res:* Literature and the Roman Stoics; survival of the classics during the Middle Ages; classical and mediaeval Latin literature. *Mailing Add:* Dept of Classics Univ of NC Chapel Hill NC 27514

MARTI, JORGE LUIS, b Santa Clara, Cuba, Sept 9, 11; m 37. SPANISH. *Educ:* Escuelas Pias, Havana, Cuba, BA, 30; Univ Havana, Dr Law, 37, Dr Soc Sci, 39; State Univ NY Buffalo, MA, 66, PhD(Span), 70. *Prof Exp:* From instr to assoc prof hist soc ideas, Univ Havana, 51-60; instr lang & lit, Chadron State Col, 62-63; asst prof Span & French, 63-64; asst prof, 64-65, assoc prof, 65-71, prof, 71-81, EMER PROF SPAN, STATE UNIV NY COL BROCKPORT, 82- *Concurrent Pos:* Chief ed dept, El Mundo, 39-54, asst ed, 55-60; Dept State studies grant, sch jour, Univ Minn, 45; dean, Cuban Prof Col Soc Sci, 56-58; ed, Folio, number on 20th century Cuban lit. *Honors & Awards:* Cuban Nat Jour Award Juan G Gomez, 51, Justo de Lara, 54; Inter-Am Press Asn Mergenthaler Prize, 54. *Mem:* Caribbean Studies Asn; Am Asn Teachers Span & Port; MLA; Circulo Cult Pan-Am (pres, 72). *Res:* Social, ideological and literary evolution of 20th century Cuba; Spanish American contemporary novel and essay; Cuba in Jorge Manach's works. *Publ:* Auth, Perspectivas de la politica mundial, Ed Selecta, Havana, 41; Una utopia para la democracia, 59 & Cuba: Conciencia y existencia, 59, Lib Marti, Havana; Consideraciones sobre la novela indianista, La Torre, Univ PR, 67; ed, Papers on French, Spanish, Luzo, Brazilian, Spanish, American literary relations, State Univ NY Brockport, 70; auth, Class attitudes in Cuban society on the eve of the revolution, Specialia, 71; The Cuban society as reflected in its literature (1900-1930), Ann Southeastern Conf Latin Am Studies, 73; El periodismo literario de Jorge Manach, Univ PR, 77. *Mailing Add:* Apt 60 71 West Ave Brockport NY 14420

MARTI DE CID, DOLORES, b Madrid, Spain, Sept 6, 16; m 39; c 1. ROMANCE PHILOLOGY & LINGUISTICS. *Educ:* Inst Segunda Ensenanza, Cuba, BSA, 33; Univ Havana, MA, 40, PhD, 43. *Prof Exp:* Mem fac, Univ Havana, 42-60; vis prof, Univ Kans, 61, assoc prof, 61-63; assoc prof mod lang, 63-66, PROF MOD LANG, PURDUE UNIV, WEST LAFAYETTE, 66- *Concurrent Pos:* Arg Nat Comn Cult fel, 46; vis prof Cuban lit, Univ Cuyo, 48-49; gen secy, Cong Int Inst Span Am Lit, 49; Ital govt fel, 56; vis prof hisp Am lit, Univ Rome, 56-57; consult, Encycl Britannica, 62; lectr hisp lit, univs in Latin Am, Spain & Italy. *Mem:* MLA; Am Asn Teachers Span & Port; Mod Humanities Res Asn, England; Soc Colombista Panam, Cuba; Acad Nac Artes y Let, Cuba. *Res:* Latin American culture and literature; pre-Columbian, colonial and modern Spanish American theater; history, linguisitics and stylistics of the Spanish language; Romance philology and drama. *Publ:* Coauth, Gramatica y redaccion del espanol, Ed Cult, Cuba, 56-58, 60; auth, Teatro cubano contemporaneo, 59, 2nd ed, 62 & coauth, Teatro indio precolumbino, 64, Aguilar, Madrid; Paginas de un diario, McGraw, 66; Teatro indoamericano colonial, Aguilar, Madrid, 73. *Mailing Add:* Dept of Modern Lang Purdue Univ West Lafayette IN 47906

MARTIN, CATHERINE-RITA, US citizen. FRENCH. *Educ:* Fordham Univ, BSEd & MA; Columbia Univ, PhD, 56. *Prof Exp:* ASSOC PROF MOD LANG, LIB ARTS COL, FORDHAM UNIV, LINCOLN CTR, 46- *Res:* Works of Paul Claudel and Petrus Borel; oral approach to study of modern language on college level; foreign languages in the elementary school. *Publ:* Auth, La Signification de L'ordere dans la Vision Claudelienne, Nouvelle Rev Luxembourgeoise, 73. *Mailing Add:* Dept of Humanities, Lib Arts Col Fordham Univ, Lincoln Ctr New York NY 10023

MARTIN, CHARLES EDWARD, b Mantee, Miss, Sept 3, 30; m 53; c 3. MODERN LANGUAGES. *Educ:* Miss Col, BA, 51; US Army Lang Sch, dipl, 52; Tulane Univ, MA, 58, PhD(Span), 65. *Prof Exp:* Asst prof mod lang, 57-62, assoc prof, 62-67, head, Dept Foreign Lang, 66-69, PROF SPAN, MISS COL, 67-, VPRES ACAD AFFAIRS, 69- *Concurrent Pos:* Chmn, Southern Baptist Col Deans, 80 & Nat Deans' Conf, 81. *Mem:* Am Asn Teachers Span & Port. *Res:* The generation of 1898 in Spain. *Mailing Add:* Dept of Foreign Lang Miss Col Clinton MS 39056

MARTIN, DANIEL, b Madrid, Spain, Dec 7, 32; US citizen; m 60; c 1. FRENCH RENAISSANCE LITERATURE. *Educ:* Univ Ill, Chicago Circle, BA, 69; Yale Univ, MPhil, 72, PhD(Romance lang, French), 73. *Prof Exp:* asst prof, 73-80, ASSOC PROF FRENCH, UNIV MASS, AMHERST, 80- *Mem:* Soc Amis Montaigne Paris; MLA; Renaissance Soc Am. *Res:* Montaigne; structural criticism; the philosophy of chance. *Publ:* Ed, Michel de Montaigne, Essais 1580 avec une introduction et des notes sur les variantes, Libr Slatkine, Geneva, 76; auth, Montaigne et la Fortune Essai sur le hasard et le language, Libr Champion, Paris, 77. *Mailing Add:* Dept of French & Ital Univ of Mass Amherst MA 01003

MARTIN, DELLITA LILLIAN, b New Orleans, La, Oct 27, 46; m; c 2. SPANISH LITERATURE, COMPARATIVE LITERATURE. *Educ:* La State Univ, BA, 68; Ohio State Univ, MA, 71, PhD(Romance lang & lit), 75. *Prof Exp:* Instr Span & French, St Matthias Cath Sch, 76; asst prof, 76-82, ASSOC PROF SPAN & AM LIT, UNIV ALA, BIRMINGHAM, 82- *Concurrent Pos:* Univ Col fac res grant, Univ Ala, Birmingham, 78-79; secy, Comt Humanities Ala, 78-81. *Mem:* African Lit Asn; AAUP; Asn of Caribbean Studies; Col Lang Asn; MLA. *Res:* Contemporary Latin American prose fiction and poetry; the Francophone writers of West Africa and the Caribbean; Afro-American and Afro-Hispanic literatures. *Publ:* Auth, Langston Hughes's use of the blues, Col Lang Asn J, 12/78; West African and Hispanic Elements in Nicolas Guillen's La cancion del bongo, SAtlantic Bull, 1/80; In our own Black images: Afro-American literature in the 1980's, MELUS, summer 81; The Madam poems as dramatic monologue, Black Am Lit Forum, fall 81; Oral traditions and Biografia de un Cimarron, J Caribbean Studies, summer 82. *Mailing Add:* Dept of Foreign Lang Univ of Ala Univ Sta Birmingham AL 35294

MARTIN, GREGORIO CERVANTES, b Salamanca, Spain, Oct 30, 38. SPANISH LITERATURE. *Educ:* Univ Salamanca, BA, 58; Univ Pittsburgh, MA, 71, PhD(Span lit), 74. *Prof Exp:* Vis prof Span, Cath Univ Rio Grande do Sul, Brazil, 74-75; asst prof Span, 76-79, ASSOC PROF SPAN, WAKE FOREST UNIV, 79- *Concurrent Pos:* Ed, Estudos Ibero-Americanos, 76-; Nat Enowment for Humanities summer grant, summer, 77; Am Coun Learned Soc travel grant, 78-; res grant, Wake Forest Univ, 78; consult ed, Critica Hispanica, 79- *Mem:* MLA; Smithsonian Inst; AAUP. *Res:* Eighteenth Century Spanish literature; Nineteenth Century Spanish theatre; Nineteenth Century Spanish Romanticism. *Publ:* Auth, Nuevos datos sobre el padre de Figaro (Sobre el ambiente familiar de Larra), Papeles de Son Armadans, 74; Juventud y vejez en El Jarama, Papeles de Son Armadans, 75; Larra: periodista urugayo, 76, Personajes en Los bravos: el buen samaritano, 76 & Cartas familiaress de Fernando VII, 77, Estudos Ibero-Am; Un auto inedito de Lope: Las hanzanas del sugundo David, Critica Hispanica, 79; El parnasillo: Origen y circunstancias, La Chispa 81 Selected Proc, 81; El origen catalan de Larra, Critica Hispanica, 81. *Mailing Add:* Dept of Romance Lang Wake Forest Univ Winston-Salem NC 27109

MARTIN, HUBERT M, JR, b Chattanooga, Tenn, May 7, 32; m 52; c 2. CLASSICS. *Educ:* Univ Chattanooga, AB, 54; Johns Hopkins Univ, MA, 55, PhD, 58. *Prof Exp:* Assoc prof Greek, Randolph-Macon Col, 58-59, prof, 59-60; from asst prof to assoc prof Classics, Univ NC, Chapel Hill, 60-69; assoc prof, 69-74, PROF CLASSICS, UNIV KY, 74-, CHMN DEPT CLASS LANG, 76- *Concurrent Pos:* Fel, Ctr Hellenic Studies, 62-63; mem managing comt, Am Sch Class Studies, Athens, 70- *Mem:* Am Philol Asn; Archaeol Inst Am; Class Asn Midwest & S; Am Class League; AAUP. *Res:* Plutarch's Vitae and Moralia; Greek lyric poetry; early Christian literature and thought. *Publ:* Auth, The concept of Philanthropia in Plutarch's Lives, Am J Philol, 61; The character of Plutarch's Themistocles, Trans Am Philol Asn, 61; Plutarch's Themistocles, 2 and Nicias, 2, 6, Am J Philol, 64; Amatorius, 756 E-F: Plutarch's citation of Parmenides and Hesiod, Am J Philol, 69; Plutarch's citation of Empedocles at Amatorius 756 D, Greek, Roman & Byzantine Studies, 69; Alcaeus, Twayne, 72; Plutarch's De Facie: The recapitulations and the lost beginning, Greek, Roman & Byzantine Studies, 74; Commentary on Plutarch's Amatorius, In: Plutarch's Ethical Writings and Early Christian Literature, Brill, 78. *Mailing Add:* Dept of Class Lang Univ of Ky Lexington KY 40506

MARTIN, JACQUELINE, b Luneville, France, Apr 19, 22; nat US. ROMANCE LANGUAGES & LITERATURE. *Educ:* Boston Univ, AM, 52; Univ Ore, PhD(comp lit), 67. *Prof Exp:* Instr French & Span, Cent Wash Col Educ, 47-48; instr, Univ Puget Sound, 48-51, from instr to assoc prof, 54-65; asst prof Romance lang, Pitzer Col, 65-67, assoc prof, 68-69; chmn dept foreign lang & dir comp lit prog, 70-76, PROF COMP LIT & ROMANCE LANG, UNIV PUGET SOUND, 69- *Mem:* MLA; Am Asn Teachers Fr; Am Coun Teaching For Lang; Am Comp Lit Asn; African Lit Asn. *Res:* Twentieth century French, Spanish and Hispanoamerican literature; existentialism in literature and philosophy. *Mailing Add:* Dept of For Lang Univ of Puget Sound Tacoma WA 98416

MARTIN, JANET MARION, b Bogalusa, La, Oct 24, 38. CLASSICS. *Educ:* Radcliffe Col, AB, 61; Univ Mich, MA, 63; Harvard Univ, PhD(Medieval Latin), 68. *Prof Exp:* From instr to asst prof classics, Harvard Univ, 68-72; asst prof, 73-76, ASSOC PROF CLASSICS, PRINCETON UNIV, 76- *Concurrent Pos:* Fel Post-classical & humanistic studies, Am Acad Rome, 71-73. *Mem:* Am Philol Asn; Mediaeval Acad Am. *Res:* Medieval Latin literature; ancient and medieval rhetoric and poetics; the classical tradition. *Publ:* Ed, Peter the Venerable: Selected Letters, Pontifical Inst Mediaeval Studies, 74; auth, John of Salisbury's manuscripts of Frontinus and of Gellius, J Warburg & Courtauld Insts, 77; Uses of tradition: Gellius, Petronius, and John of Salisbury, Viator, 79; contribr, chap, In: The Renaissance of the Twelfth Century, Harvard Univ, 82. *Mailing Add:* Dept of Classics Princeton Univ Princeton NJ 08544

MARTIN, JOAN MARY, b New York, NY, Nov 26, 42. GERMANIC LANGUAGES & LINGUISTICS. *Educ:* Hunter Col, BA, 64; Univ Mich, Ann Arbor, MA, 66, PhD(Ger lang & lit), 70. *Prof Exp:* Asst prof Ger, Univ Ariz, 70-80. *Mem:* MLA; Am Translr Asn; Am Asn Univ Women; Pedag Sem Ger Philol. *Res:* Germanic languages, especially Gothic, Old High German and Old Saxon; applied linguistics in the field of German. *Mailing Add:* 922 Shirley Manor Rd Reisterstown MD 21136

MARTIN, JOHN WATSON, b Winnipeg, Man, Can, June 20, 22; US citizen. SPANISH LANGUAGE & LITERATURE, PORTUGUESE LANGUAGE. *Educ:* Univ Wash, BA, 49, MA, 56, PhD(Romance lang & ling), 56. *Prof Exp:* Asst prof Span, Wash State Univ, 56-57; asst prof Span & Latin, Fresno State Col, 57-60; sr lectr ling, Fulbright Comn, Ecuador, 60-61; vis assoc prof English & ling, Univ Calif, Los Angeles in Bogota, Columbia & founding dir, Inst Ling Colombo-Am, 61-65; prof ling, Antioch Col, dir Centro de Estud Univ Colombo-Am, 65-68; sr lectr Univ Chile, Valparaiso, Fulbright Comn, Santiago, 68-69; prof-in-charge postgrad prog lings, Cath Univ Sao Paulo & Fundacao de Amparo a Pesquisa do Estado de Sao Paulo, 69-70; prog specialist Port ling, Ford Found, Rio de Janeiro, 70-72; specialist for design advan ling progs, Cath Univ Rio de Janeiro, 72; prof, Univ Estadual de Campinas, Sao Paulo, 72; prof ling, coordr & chmn grad studies, Cath Univ Campinas, Sao Paulo, 73-74; coordr grad studies & prof Port ling, Faculdades Integradas do Inst Educ Piracicabano, Piracicaba, Sao Paulo, 74-75; vis prof ling, Univ Fed do Parana, Curitiba, Parana, 75-76; PROF SPAN & PORT LING, UNIV ARIZ, 77- *Concurrent Pos:* Vis prof ling, Unified Post-Grad Prog Ling, Nat Mus & Fed Univ Rio de Janeiro. *Mem:* MLA; Inst Int Lit Iberoam. *Res:* Syntactic theory; diachronic syntax; structure of Spanish and Portuguese. *Publ:* Auth, Some uses of the old Spanish past subjunctive, Romance Philol, 58; Remarks on the origin of the Portuguese inflected infinitive, Word, 60; Distinctive-Feature Systems of English and Spanish Sounds, 65 & coauth, The Grammatical Systems of English and Spanish, 65, Univ Chicago; auth, Observations on the linguistic design of materials for the teaching of English to speakers of Spanish, In: Actas del Segundo Simposiodiod; Tense, mood and the inflected infinitive in Portuguese, Readings Port Ling, 76. *Mailing Add:* Dept of Romance Lang Univ of Ariz Tucson AZ 85721

MARTIN, JOSE LUIS, b Vega Baja, PR, July 11, 21; US citizen; m 47; c 5. ROMANCE LANGUAGES. *Educ:* Univ PR, BA, 42, MA, 53; Columbia Univ, PhD(Span & Span Am Lit), 65. *Prof Exp:* From instr to asst prof Span & humanities, Univ PR, 52-58; from lectr to instr Span & Span Am lit, Columbia Univ, 58-60; instr Span Am lit, Queens Col, NY & Hunter Col, 60-65; assoc prof stylistics & Span Am lit, Inter-Am Univ PR, 65-68; assoc prof Span Am lit, Ill State Univ, 68-71; assoc prof, PR lit & stylistics, City Col New York, 71-76; ASST PROF SPAN, INTER-AM UNIV, 76- *Concurrent Pos:* Mem bd dirs, Inst PR, NY City, 72- *Mem:* MLA; Inst Int Lit Iberoam. *Res:* Spanish stylistics; Spanish-American literature; psychical research. *Publ:* Auth, La Poesia De Jose Eusebio Caro, Inst Caro, Inst Cary Y Cuervo, 66; Hostos Escritor, Rev Inst Cult Puertorriquena, 71; La Critica Metodica De Anderson Imbert, Cuadernos Hispanoam, 72; La Yuxtaposicion Tiempo-Espacial En El Francotirador De P J Soto, Nueva Narrativa Hispanoam, 72; El Retorno, Ed Latinoam, Mex, 72; Critica Estillistica, Ed Gredos, Madrid, 73; Literatura Hispano-Americana Contemporanea, Ed Edil, San Juan, 73; La Narritiva De Vargas Llosa, Ed Gredos, Madrid, 74. *Mailing Add:* Dept Span Int Am Univ San German PR 00753

MARTIN, LYNN SIMPSON, b Haddon Heights, NJ, July 26, 33. ENGLISH PHILOLOGY. *Educ:* Yale Univ, BS, 55; Univ Pa, MA, 60, PhD(English philol), 66. *Prof Exp:* Instr English, Univ NC, Chapel Hill, 62-66; asst prof, 66-69, supvr student teachers, 66-71, ASSOC PROF ENGLISH, ST JOHN'S UNIV, 69- *Concurrent Pos:* Co-ed, Humanitas of St John's Univ, 70-71, assoc ed, 71; gen ed, Erasmus Rev: J of Humanities, 71. *Mem:* Early English Text Soc; Int Arthurian Soc; Ling Soc Am; Mediaeval Acad Am; MLA. *Res:* Sir Thomas Malory; Middle English language and literature; applications of linguistics to the teaching of English languages and literature. *Publ:* Auth, Arthur as Pendragon in Geoffrey of Monmouth, Wace and Lawman, Bibliog Bull Int Arthurian Soc, 24: 184-185; Richard Beauchamp, Earl of Warwick and Sir Gareth, Studies Medieval Cult; Renaissance for the university, Humanitas of St John's Univ, summer 70. *Mailing Add:* Dept of English St John's Univ Jamaica NY 11432

MARTIN, NICHOLAS O, b Budapest, Hungary, June 29, 31; US citizen; m 57. FRENCH. *Educ:* Eötvös Lorand, BA, 56; Univ Southern Calif, BA, 59; Princeton Univ, MA, 61, PhD(French), 63. *Prof Exp:* Instr French, Princeton Univ, 62-63; asst prof, Univ Southern Calif, 63-67; asst prof, 67-80, ASSOC PROF FRENCH & MEN'S PHYS EDUC, PASADENA CITY COL, 80- *Concurrent Pos:* Part-time asst prof, Univ Southern Calif, 67- *Mem:* MLA; Philol Asn Pac Coast. *Res:* The French novel between the two world wars; 17th century French literature; Montherlant and Hemingway: a comparison. *Mailing Add:* Dept of Foreign Lang Pasadena City Col Pasadena CA 91106

MARTIN, NORMAN FRANCIS, Latin American History. See Vol I

MARTIN, PHILIPPE JEAN, b Brussels, Belgium, Jan 4, 44. LINGUISTICS, ACOUSTICS. *Educ:* Free Univ Brussels, Ingenieur civil, 67, Dr(sci), 73; Univ Nancy, Dr 3rd cycle, 72. *Prof Exp:* Res engr acoustics, 68-70, lectr phonetics, 70-72, asst prof, 72-75, assoc prof, 75-77, PROF PHONETICS, UNIV TORONTO, 81- *Concurrent Pos:* Res assoc, Royal Mus Cent Africa, Brussels, 71-; sr researcher, Inst Phonetics, Univ Bruxelles, 74-77; lectr phonetics, Univ Provence, 78-81. *Res:* Syntax; intonation. *Publ:* Coauth, Prolegomenes a l'Etude des Structures Intonatives, Didier, Paris, 70; Classification Formelle Automatique et Industries Lithiques, Mus Tervuren, 72; auth, Analyse phonologique de la phrase Francaise, Linguistics, 75; Questions de phonosyntaxe et de phonosemantique en Francais, Linqustica Investigationes, 78; coauth, Toronto English, Didier; auth, Vers une theorie syntaxique de l'intonation, In: Intonation: de l'acoustique a la semantique, Klincksieck, Paus, 81; Pitch Analysis by Spectral Combination Method, Proc ICASSP, 82. *Mailing Add:* Exp Phonetics Lab 39 Queen's Park Crescent E Toronto ON M5S 1A1 Can

MARTIN, SAMUEL ELMO, b Pittsburg, Kans, Jan 29, 24. LINGUISTICS. *Educ:* Univ Calif, AB, 47, AM, 49; Yale Univ, PhD, 50. *Prof Exp:* From instr to asst prof Japanese & Korean, 50-58, assoc prof Far Eastern ling, 58-62, chmn dept East & South Asian lang, 63-65, chmn dept ling, 66-80, PROF FAR EASTERN LING, YALE UNIV, 62- *Concurrent Pos:* Vis prof, Georgetown Univ, 55, Univ Mich, 56, Univ Alta, 59 & Univ Wash, 62-63; secy, Comt Uralic & Altaic Studies, Am Coun Learned Soc, 58-64; vis prof ling & dir Pac & Asian ling inst, Univ Hawaii, 65-66. *Mem:* Ling Soc Am; Am Orient Soc; Asn Asian Studies. *Res:* Phonemics, morphophonemics and historical phonology of Japanese, Korean and Chinese. *Publ:* Auth, Morphophonemics of standard colloquial Japanese, Ling Soc Am, 52; The phonemes of ancient Chinese, Am Orient Soc, 53; Korean-English Dict, Yale Univ, 68. *Mailing Add:* Dept of Ling, Grad Sch Yale Univ New Haven CT 06520

MARTINEZ, H SALVADOR, b Leon, Spain, Mar 31, 36. MEDIEVAL SPANISH LITERATURE, PHILOSOPHY OF HISTORY. *Educ:* Univ Rome, Dr Laurea, 60; Gregoriana Univ, Rome, Laurea(philos), 68; Univ Toronto, PhD(medieval studies), 72. *Prof Exp:* Prof Span lit & philos, Angelo State Univ, 72-76; PROF MEDIEVAL SPAN LIT, NY UNIV, 76- *Mem:* Soc Rencesvals; Asoc Int Hispanistas; Mediaeval Acad Am; MLA; Am Acad Res Historians Medieval Spain. *Mailing Add:* Dept of Span & Port NY Univ 19 Univ Pl New York NY 10003

MARTINEZ, JOSE RAMON, b Matanzas, Cuba, Nov 15, 24; US citizen; m 57; c 3. SPANISH, COMPARATIVE LITERATURES. *Educ:* Univ Havana, Dr Pedag, 54; Middlebury Col, MA, 64; Fla State Univ, PhD(Span), 71. *Prof Exp:* Teacher, Elem Schs, Cuba, 46-58 & Adult Educ Schs, 54-60; teacher Span, Winter Park High Sch, Fla, 62-65; asst prof, 65-75, ASSOC PROF SPAN & FRENCH, FLA SOUTHERN COL, 75-, CHMN DEPT MOD LANG, 77- *Concurrent Pos:* Instr, Candler Col, Havana, 54-56 & Havana Bus Univ, 55-58. *Mem:* Am Asn Teachers Span & Port. *Res:* Golden Age Spanish theatre; Lope de Vega; Spanish-American short story. *Mailing Add:* Dept of Mod Foreign Lang Fla Southern Col Lakeland FL 33802

MARTINEZ, MIGUEL ANGEL, b Santiago, Cuba, July 5, 30; US citizen; m 53; c 3. SPANISH & SPANISH AMERICAN LITERATURE. *Educ:* Univ Oriente, Cuba, lic Educ, 52; Loyola Univ, Chicago, MA, 65; Northwestern Univ, Evanston, PhD(Span lit), 69. *Prof Exp:* Instr Span, St Xavier Col, 64-65; from instr to asst prof, 65-72, vchmn dept, 68-72, dir grad prog dept mod lang, 72-73, ASSOC PROF SPAN, LOYOLA UNIV CHICAGO, 72- *Mem:* MLA; Am Asn Teachers Span & Port. *Res:* Spanish American novel; contemporary Spanish literature; Caribbean studies. *Publ:* Auth, Causa, tesis y tema en la novela de Carlos Loveira, 71 & Los personajes secundarios en las novelas de Carlos Loveira, 73, Hispania; The multiple meaning of Liborio in the novels of Carlos Loveira, Caribbean Studies, 73; Criollismo y humorismo en la obra de regino E Boti, Revista de estudio hispanicos, 77. *Mailing Add:* Dept of Mod Lang Loyola Univ Chicago IL 60611

MARTINEZ-BONATI, FELIX, b Santiago, Chile, Mary 7, 29; m 57; c 2. SPANISH LITERATURE, AESTHETICS. *Educ:* Univ Goettingen, DrPhil, 57; Univ Chile, dipl Span, 58. *Prof Exp:* Prof Span, Univ Chile, 57-62; pres, Univ Southern Chile, Valdivia, 62-68; Alexander von Humboldt fel, 69-70; prof Span & comp lit, Univ Iowa, 71-77; prof Span, Univ Ill, Chicago Circle, 77-78; PROF SPAN, COLUMBIA UNIV, 78- *Concurrent Pos:* Vis prof philos, Univ Goettingen, 64-66; co-ed, Dispositio, Univ Mich, Ann Arbor, 77- *Mem:* MLA; Am Asn Teachers Span & Port. *Res:* Theory of literature; Cervantes; contemporary literature. *Publ:* Auth, La concepcion del lenguaje en la filosofia de Husserl, 60 & Las ideas esteticas de Schiller, 60, Univ Chile; Ueber Aesthetische Urteile, Archeol Philos, 60; ed, Seix-Barral, Barcelona, 72; auth, Die Logische Struktur der Dichtung, Deut Vierteljahresschrift fur Literaturwiss und Geistesgeschichte, 73; Cervantes y las regiones de la imaginacion, 4/77 & La unidad del Quijote, 5-6/77, Dispositio; Fictive Discourse and the Structures of Literature, Cornell Univ Press, 81. *Mailing Add:* Dept of Span Box 4348 Columbia Univ New York NY 10027

MARTINEZ GANDARA, JULIO ANTONIO, Philosophy, Chicano Studies. See Vol IV

MARTINEZ-LOPEZ, ENRIQUE, b Granada, Spain, Aug 18, 28; US citizen; m 54; c 3. SPANISH. *Educ:* Univ Granada, BA, 47; Univ Madrid, MA, 52, PhD, 64. *Prof Exp:* Mem fac Span, Univ Paraiba, Brazil, 54-56 & Univ Recife, 56-59; asst prof, Univ Houston, 59-63; from asst prof to assoc prof, 63-72, chmn dept Span & Port, 70-74, PROF SPAN, UNIV CALIF, SANTA BARBARA, 72- *Concurrent Pos:* Fel, Consejo Super Invest Cient, Madrid, 52-54; Univ Calif, Inst Humanities grant, 66, 74; Am Philos Soc Span & Port; MLA; Inst Int Lit Iberoam; Am Soc Sephardic Studies; vis lectr, Univ Wis-Madison, summers, 66, 67; Am Philos Soc Span & Port grant, 71. *Mem:* Inst Brasileiro Cult Hisp (pres, 56-58); Am Asn Teachers Span & Port; MLA; Inst Int Lit Iberoamericana; Asoc Int Hisp. *Res:* Golden Age and Modern Spanish Literature; Brazilian colonial literature. *Publ:* Auth, Poesia religiosa de Manuel Botelho de Oliveira, Rev Iberoamericana, 69; ed, Federico Garcia Lorca, Granada paraiso cerrado y otras paginas granadinas, M Sanchez, Granada, 71; auth, Sobre aquella bestialidad de Garcilaso, Pac Mod Lang Asn, 72; La cuartana de amor del caballero de Olmedo, In: Estudios sobre literatura y arte dedicados al professor Emilio Orozco Diaz, Univ Granada, 79; La variacion en el corrido mexicano, In: El Romancero hoy: Poetica, Madrid, 79; El rival de Garcilaso, Bol Real Acad Espanola, 81. *Mailing Add:* Dept of Span & Port Univ of Calif Santa Barbara CA 93106

MARTINEZ-TOLENTINO, JAIME, b Salinas, PR, Jan 10, 43; US citizen; m 67; c 2. FRENCH. *Educ:* NY Univ, BA, 65, MA, 66; Univ Madrid, PhD(French), 70. *Prof Exp:* Assoc prof, 66-80, PROF FRENCH, UNIV PR, MAYAGUEZ, 80- *Concurrent Pos:* Lectr English, Catholic Univ PR, Mayaquez, 78; lectr Span lit, Interamerican Univ PR, San German, 81. *Res:* French literature; French language; Puerto Rican literature. *Publ:* Auth, Las ciencias biologicas en La Comedie Humaine, Filol Mod, Spain, 11/70; De la cognomologia en la literatura, La Torre, PR, 4-6/72; Cuentos Modernos, Ed Edil, PR, 75; El Enfermo Imaginario, Plus Ultra Educ, 77; Normas Ortograficas del Frances, Florentia Publ, 77; Le Verbe Francais, Univ PR, 79; La Imagen del Otro, Inst PR Culture, 80; Cuentos Fantasticos, Univ PR (in press). *Mailing Add:* Dept Humanities Univ PR Mayaguez PR 00708

MARTINS, HEITOR MIRANDA, b Belo Horizonte, Brazil, July 22, 33; m 58; c 2. PORTUGUESE. *Educ:* Univ Minas Gerais, BA, 59, PhD, 62. *Prof Exp:* Instr Port, Univ NMex, 60-62; from asst prof to assoc prof, Tulane Univ, 62-68; chmn dept Span & Port, 73-80, PROF PORT, IND UNIV, BLOOMINGTON, 68- *Mem:* MLA; Am Comp Lit Asn; Am Asn Teachers Span & Port. *Res:* Portuguese and Brazilian literature; Brazilian dialectology. *Publ:* Auth, Das Emocoes Necessarias, Complemento, Brazil, 55; Sirgo Nos Cabelos, Livraria Portugal, 61; Manuel de Galhegos, Anadia, Portugal, 63; Bocage E Minas, Imprensa Oficial, Belo Horizonte, 65; Jacinto Cordiro E La Estrella De Sevilla, Actas V Coloquio Estud Luso-Brasileiro, 66; No Urubuquaqua, Em Colonia, Rev Hisp Mod, 69; O Inico Do Conservatismo Ideologico De Olavo Bilac, Occidente, 70; ed, M Botelho De Oliveira's Lyre Sacra, Conselho Estadual Cult, Sao Paulo, 71. *Mailing Add:* Dept Spanish & Portuguese Indiana Univ Bloomington IN 47401

MARTINS, WILSON, b Sao Paulo, Brazil, Mar 3, 21; m 43. ROMANCE LANGUAGES. *Educ:* Univ Parana, BLaw, 44, PhD, 52. *Prof Exp:* Prof French lit, Univ Parana, 52-62; prof Brazilian lit, Univ Kans, 62-63; prof, Univ Wis, 63-65; PROF BRAZILIAN LIT, NY UNIV, 65- *Concurrent Pos:* Fulbright fel, 62-63; Guggenheim fel, 67-68; reviewer lit, Nat Endowment for Humanities, 77- *Honors & Awards:* Literary Prize, PEN Club Brazil, 77; Jabuti, Camara Brasileira do Livro, Brazil, 77. *Mem:* Am Asn Teachers Span & Port. *Res:* Brazilian literature; Brazilian intellectual history. *Publ:* Auth, A critica literaria no Brasil, Dept di Cultura, 52; Um Brasil diferente, 55 & A palavra escrita, 57, Anhembi; O modernismo, Cultrix, 65; The Modernist Idea, NY Univ, 70; Historia da inteligencia Brasileira (7 vols), Cultrix, 79. *Mailing Add:* Dept of Span & Port NY Univ New York NY 10003

MARTINSON, STEVEN DELAMAR, b Puyallup, Wash, Aug 10, 49; m 75; c 3. GERMAN LITERATURE. *Educ:* Seattle Pac Univ, BA, 71; Univ Wash, MA, 73, PhD(Ger),77. *Prof Exp:* Asst prof, Ger lang & lit, Northwestern Univ, 77-80; ASST PROF GER LIT, UNIV CALIF, LOS ANGELES, 80- *Mem:* Am Asn Teachers Ger; Lessing Soc; Goethe Soc NAm; Western Soc 18th Century Studies; West Asn Ger Studies. *Res:* German literature of the 18th century: Lessing, Goethe, Schiller, poetics and drama; German literature of the 20th century: Gunter Eich, Georg Lukacs, drama. *Publ:* Auth, On Imitation, Imagination and Beauty, Bouvier Verlag, Bonn, 77; Wo die Wege sich scheiden: Georg Lukacs' criticism of modernism, Forum Mod Lang Studies, 79; German poetry in transition: Canitz, Besser, and the early Aufklarer, Mich Ger Studies, 80; Authority and criticism: Lessing's critical and dramatic procedure, In: Humanitat und Dialog Supplement to the Lessing Yearbook, Wayne State Univ Press, 82; ed, Johann Elias Schlegel: Vergleichung Shakespears un Andreas Gryphs und andere dramentheoretische Schriften, Reclam Verlag, Stuttgart, 82. *Mailing Add:* Dept of Ger Lang Univ of Calif Los Angeles CA 90024

MARTY, FERNAND LUCIEN, b Paris, France, Mar 30, 20; nat US. FRENCH. *Educ:* Middlebury Col, MA, 50. *Prof Exp:* Prof mod lang, Hollins Col, 60-72; PROF FRENCH, UNIV ILL, URBANA, 72- *Concurrent Pos:* Hon prof French, Fac Grad Studies, Dalhousie Univ, 72-80. *Honors & Awards:* Palmes Academiques, Fr Govt, 67. *Mem:* MLA; Am Asn Teachers Fr. *Res:* Methods of foreign language teaching; computer-based education. *Mailing Add:* Dept of French Univ of Ill Urbana IL 61801

MARZI, ALFEO HUGO, b New Britain, Conn, July 21, 27; m 51; c 3. ITALIAN, FRENCH. *Educ:* Univ Lille, PhD(French), 56. *Prof Exp:* From instr to asst prof French, Fordham Univ, 52-67, assoc prof French & Ital, 67-80. *Mem:* Am Asn Teachers Fr; MLA; Poetry Soc Am. *Res:* Contemporary French literature; 16th century France. *Publ:* Auth, Underpass, 64 & The Park of Jonas, 65, Fordham Univ; Bronx Crossing, 66, Dilexi, 67 & Urban Poetry, 68, Branden; Chiaroscuro, Fordham Univ, 68. *Mailing Add:* 16 Ft Charles Pl Bronx NY 10463

MASCIANDARO, FRANCO, b Taranto, Italy, May 7, 38; US citizen; m 64; c 2. ITALIAN LITERATURE. *Educ:* Brooklyn Col, BA, 63; Tulane Univ, MA, 66; Harvard Univ, PhD(Romance lang & lit), 70. *Prof Exp:* Actg asst prof Ital lit, Univ Wash, 69-70; asst prof Ital lit, 70-77, ASSOC PROF ITAL, UNIV CALIF, LOS ANGELES, 77- *Mem:* Dante Soc Am; Am Asn Teachers Ital; Medieval Acad Am; Pac Northwest Coun Foreign Lang; Philol Asn Pac Coast. *Res:* The Middle Ages; Dante. *Publ:* Auth, I'castellucci e i 'ghiribizzi' del Machiavelli epistolografo, Italica, 69; Inferno I-II: Il dramma della conversione e il tempo, Studi Danteschi, 72; La Problematica del Tempo nella Commedia, Long, 76; Notes on the image of the point in the Divine Comedy, Italica, 77. *Mailing Add:* Dept of Ital Univ of Calif Los Angeles CA 90024

MAS-LOPEZ, EDITA, b Havana, Cuba, US citizen. TWENTIETH-CENTURY ART & LITERATURE, SPANISH LITERATURE & CIVILIZATION. *Educ:* Inst de la Habana no 1, Bachelor's degree; Univ Havana, PhD(Span & Ital lit). *Prof Exp:* Instr Span, Fla State Col Women & Hunter Col; asst prof, Col Mt St Vincent; ASSOC PROF SPAN, QUEENS COL, 60- *Mem:* Am Asn Span & Port; MLA; AAUP. *Res:* Fordes in modern Spanish literature; Spanish and Catalonian poetry of the 19th century; Clarin's essays. *Publ:* Auth, The last Poems of Migues De unamuno, Farleigh Dickinson Univ Press, 74; En El Primer Aniversario De La Muerte De Salvardor De Madariaga, Cuadernos Americanos, 1/80; Apeles Mestres: Poetic lyricist, The Opera J, 80; Apeles Mestres, poeta lirico catalan, Cuadernos Americanos, 81. *Mailing Add:* Apt 10-J 185 E 85th St New York NY 10028

MASON, HERBERT WARREN, Islamic History and Religion. See Vol IV

MASON, HUGH JOHN, b Norwich, England, July 29, 43; Can citizen; m 70; c 3. CLASSICS. *Educ:* McGill Univ, BA, 64; Harvard Univ, AM, 65, PhD (classics), 68. *Prof Exp:* Asst prof, 68-72, ASSOC PROF CLASSICS, UNIV TORONTO, 72-, REGISTR, NEW COL, 77- *Mem:* Archaeol Inst Am; Am Philol Asn; Am Soc Papyrologists; Class Asn Can; Mod Greek Studies Asn. *Res:* Ancient novels; linguistics of Greek and Latin; Greek world under Roman rule. *Publ:* Auth, Lucius at Corinth, Phoenix, 71; coauth, Appius Claudius Pulcher and the hollows of Euboia, Hesperia, 72; auth, Glabrio, Archon of Asia, Class Philol, 73; Greek Terms for Roman Institutions: A Lexicon and Analysis, Am Studies Papyrology, 74; Favorinus' disorder, Janus, 79; Longus and the topography of Lesbos, Transactions Am Philol Asn, 79. *Mailing Add:* New Col Univ of Toronto Toronto ON M5S 1A1 Can

MASSON, JEFFERY LLOYD, b Chicago, Ill, Mar 28, 41; m 71. SANSKRIT. *Educ:* Harvard Univ, BA, 64, PhD(Sanskrit), 71. *Prof Exp:* Assoc prof, 70-80, PROF SANSKRIT, UNIV TORONTO, 80- *Mem:* Am Orient Soc; Asn Asian Studies. *Res:* Sanskrit aesthetics; application of psychoanalysis to Indian literature mythology; psychoanalysis of the childhood of Krsna. *Publ:* Coauth, Santarasa and Abhinavagupta's philosophy of aesthetics, Bhandarkar Orient Res Inst, 69; Avimaraka--love's enchanted world, Motilal Banarsidass, 70; Aesthetic Rapture, 2 vols, Deccan Col Res Inst. *Mailing Add:* Dept of Sanskrit & Indian Studies Univ of Toronto Toronto ON M5S 1V4 Can

MASTERS, GEORGE MALLARY, b Savannah, Ga, June 19, 36. ROMANCE LANGUAGES. *Educ:* Columbia Univ, BS, 60; Johns Hopkins Univ, MA, 62, PhD(Romance lang), 64. *Prof Exp:* Asst prof French, Univ Mo, 64-66; asst prof Romance lang, State Univ NY, Binghamton, 66-69, assoc prof, 69-70; assoc prof, 70-78, PROF ROMANCE LANGS & LITS, UNIV NC, CHAPEL HILL, 78- *Concurrent Pos:* Univ Mo Res Coun Grants-in-aid, 64-66; State Univ NY Res Found grant-in-aid, 67-69, grant-in-aid & fel, 69-70; Am Coun Learned Soc fel, 76-77. *Mem:* SAtlantic Mod Lang Asn; Am Asn Teachers Fr; Renaissance Soc Am. *Res:* French Renaissance; Rabelais; Jehan Thenaud. *Publ:* Auth, The hermetic and platonic traditions in Rabelais's Dive Bouteille, Studi Francesi, 66; Rabelais and Renaissance figure poems, Etudes Rabelaisiennes, 68; Rabelaisian Dialectic and the Platonic-Hermetic Tradition, State Univ NY Albany, 69; La Lignee de Saturne de Jehan Thenaud, Geneve, Droz, 73; Structured prisons, imprisoned structures: The prisons of Marguerite de Navarre, Renaissance Papers, 73; Panurge at the crossroads: A mythopetic study of the Pythagorean Y in Rabelais's satirical romance (CL/33-34), 73 & On Learned Ignorance or how to read Rabelais, 78, Romance Notes; Panurge's quest: Psyche, self, wholeness: A Rabelais symposium, Esprit Createur, 81. *Mailing Add:* PO Box 778 Chapel Hill NC 27514

MASTERSON, ALLENE H, b Clintonville, Pa, June 14, 14; m 42. ROMANCE LANGUAGES. *Educ:* Geneva Col, AB, 35; Univ Pittsburgh, MLitt, 44, PhD(educ), 70. *Prof Exp:* Teacher, Elem Sch, Pa, 36-37; high sch, 37-58, counr, 58-62; assoc prof French & Span, Clarion State Col, 62-80; RETIRED. *Mem:* Am Asn Teachers Fr; Am Asn Teachers Span & Port; MLA; NEA; Am Transl Asn. *Publ:* Auth, A History of the George Junior Republic in Pennsylvania, Knox Printing, 70. *Mailing Add:* PO Box 832 Oil City PA 16301

MASTRONARDE, DONALD JOHN, b Hartford, Conn, Nov 13, 48; m 71;. CLASSICAL PHILOLOGY. *Educ:* Amherst Col, BA, 69; Oxford Univ, BA, 71; Univ Toronto, PhD(classical studies), 74. *Prof Exp:* Asst prof, 73-79, ASSOC PROF CLASSICS, UNIV CALIF, BERKELEY, 79- *Concurrent Pos:* Am Coun Learned Soc, fel, 78-79. *Mem:* Am Philol Asn. *Res:* Greek tragedy; Greek and Latin poetry. *Publ:* Auth, Theocritus' Idyll 13: love and the hero, Trans Am Philol Asn, 99, 68; Seneca's Oedipus: the drama in the word, Trans Am Philol Asn 101, 70; Iconography and imagery in Euripides' Ion, Calif Studies in Class Antiquity 8, 75; Introduction to Attic Greek, privately publ, 76; Are Euripides' Phoinissai 1104-1140 interpolated?, Phoenix, Vol 32; Contact and Discontinuity: Some conventions of speech and action on the Greek tragic stage, Univ Calif Publ Class Studies, Vol 21, 79; P Strasbourg WG 307 re-examined (Eur Phoin 1499-1581, 1710-1736), Zeitschrift fuer Papyrologie und Epigraphik 38, 1; coauth, The Textual Tradition of Euripides' Phoinissai, Univ Calif Publ Class Studies, Vol 27, 82. *Mailing Add:* Dept of Class Dwinelle Hall Univ Calif Berkeley CA 94720

MATAS, JULIO, b Havana, Cuba, May 12, 31; US citizen. HISPANIC LANGUAGES & LITERATURES. *Educ:* Inst No 3, Havana, BA, 48; Univ Havana, LLD, 55; Harvard Univ, MA, 58, PhD, 70. *Prof Exp:* Stage dir & prof drama, Nat Theatre Cuba, 60-65; from instr to asst prof, 65-71, undergrad Span adv, 66-71, assoc prof, 71-80, PROF SPAN, UNIV PITTSBURGH, 80- *Mem:* Inst Int Lit Iberoam (secy-treas, 66-75); MLA; Am Asn Teacher Span & Port; Latin Am Studies Asn. *Res:* Nineteenth and 20th centuries Hispanic literatures; 20th century Latin American drama; comparative literature in 20th century fiction and drama. *Publ:* Auth, Becquer en el teatro, Univ Havana, 1-2/63; Theater and cinematography, In: Revolutionary Change in Cuba, 71 & coed, Selected Latin American One Act Plays, 73, Univ Pittsburgh; auth, El contexto moral en algunos cuentos de Julio Cortazar, 6-12/73 & Orden y vision de Tres tristes tigres, 1-6/74, Rev Iberoam; Contra el honor, Las novelas normativas de Ramon Perez de Ayala, Sem y Ediciones, Madrid, 74; Adolfo Bioy Casares o la aventura de narrar, Nueva Revista de Filologia Hispanica, 6-12/77; La cuestion del genero literario Casos de las letras hispanicas, Gredos, Madrid, 78. *Mailing Add:* 1309 Cathedral of Learning Univ of Pittsburgh Pittsburgh PA 15260

MATEJIC, MATEJA, b Smederevo, Yugoslavia, Feb 19, 24; US citizen; m 49; c 5. SLAVIC LANGUAGES & LITERATURES. *Educ:* Theol Acad, Eboli, Italy, degree theol, 46; Wayne State Univ, BA, 63; Univ Mich, PhD(Slavic lang & lit), 67. *Prof Exp:* Asst prof Slavic lang & lit, Case Western Reserve Univ, 67-68; PROF SLAVIC LANG & LIT, OHIO STATE UNIV, 68- *Concurrent Pos:* Priest, Monroe, Mich, 56-67 & Columbus, Ohio, 67-; ed, Path of Orthodoxy, 68-; dir, Hilandar Microfilming Proj, 70- *Mem:* Am Asn Teachers Slavic & E Europ Lang; Am Asn Advan Slavic Studies. *Res:* Medieval Slavic manuscripts; medieval Russian and Serbian literature; theology. *Publ:* Coauth, Phrase Book: Serbian-English, YMCA, WGer, 49; auth, Njegoseva Luca Mikrokozma . . . , Avala, Windsor, Ont, 64; Pesme (poems), privately publ, 64; coauth, Na stazama izbeglickim . . . , Thought, Melbourne, 68; auth, The Eastern Orthodox Church, Mid East in Transition, 70; On contemporary Yugoslav novel, Can Slavic Studies, 71; Hilandar Slavic Codices, Ohio State Univ, 76; Biography of St Sava, 76. *Mailing Add:* Dept Slavic Lang & Lit Ohio State Univ Columbus OH 43210

MATEJKA, LADISLAV, b Suche Vrbne, Czech, May 30, 19. SLAVIC LANGUAGES & LITERATURES. *Educ:* Charles Univ, Prague, PhD, 48; Harvard Univ, PhD, 61. *Prof Exp:* Lectr Slavic lang & lit, Univ Lund, 48-54 & Harvard Univ, 55-59; assoc prof, 59-69, PROF SLAVIC LANG & LIT, UNIV MICH, ANN ARBOR, 69- *Concurrent Pos:* Fulbright-Hays fel, Yugoslavia, 65-66. *Publ:* Auth, On translating from Latin into Church Slavonic, In: American Contributions to the Sixth International Congress of Slavists, Mouton, The Hague, 68; coauth, Word Accent in Standard Serbocroatian, Pa State Univ, 71; ed, Readings in Russian Poetics, Mass Inst Technol, 71; American Contributions to the Seventh International Congress of Slavists, Mouton, The Hague, 73; Cross Roads of Sound and Meaning, Ridder, 75; Semiotics of Art, Mass Inst Technol, 76; Sound, Sign and Meaning, 76 & Reading in Soviet Semiotics, 77, Mich Slavic Publ. *Mailing Add:* Dept of Slavic Lang & Lit Univ of Mich Ann Arbor MI 48104

MATENKO, PERCY, b Ekaterinoslav, Russia, June 30, 01; nat US; m 39; c 1. YIDDISH, GERMAN ROMANTICISM. *Educ:* Univ Toronto, BA, 24, MA, 25; Columbia Univ, PhD, 33. *Prof Exp:* Instr Ger, exten div, Columbia Univ, 25-26, 27-29; instr, Hunter Col, 29-30; from instr to prof mod lang, 30-65, adj prof Yiddish, Sch Gen Studies, 66-74, EMER PROF MOD LANG, BROOKLYN COL, 65- *Mem:* Am Asn Prof Yiddish (pres, 73-); Yivo Inst Jewish Res; MLA; Am Asn Teachers Ger. *Res:* German American literary relations; Yiddish. *Publ:* Auth, Tieck and Solger, B Westermann Co, 33; co-ed, Letters of Ludwig Tieck Hitherto Unpublished, 1792-1853, MLA & Oxford Univ, 37; auth, Ludwig Tieck and America, 54 & co-ed, Letters to and from Ludwig Tieck and His Circle, 67, Univ NC; coauth, The Aqedath Jishaq, Part I & auth, Job and Faust, Part II, In: Two Studies in Yiddish Culture, E J Brill, Leiden, 68; ed & translr, Yitskhok Rudashevski's The Diary of the Vilna Ghetto, June 1941-April 1943, Beit Lohamei Haghetaot, Ghetto Fighters' House, Israel & Hakibbutz Hameuchad, 73. *Mailing Add:* 2601 Glenwood Rd Apt 3J Brooklyn NY 11210

MATHENEY, M PIERCE, JR, Old Testament, Hebrew. See Vol IV

MATHENY, WILLIAM EDWARD, European History, Latin American Studies. See Vol I

MATHER, RICHARD B, b Paoting, China, Nov 11, 13; US citizen; m 39; c 1. CHINESE LANGUAGE & LITERATURE. *Educ:* Princeton Univ, BA, 35, Princeton Theol Sem, BTh, 39; Univ Calif, Berkeley, PhD, 49. *Prof Exp:* Pastor, Belle Haven Presby Church, Va, 39-41; from asst prof to assoc prof, 49-64, PROF CHINESE, UNIV MINN, MINNEAPOLIS, 64- *Concurrent Pos:* Fulbright res grant & Guggenheim fel, Kyoto Univ, 56-57; Fulbright res grant & Am Coun Learned Soc res Grant, Kyoto Univ, 63-64. *Mem:* Am Orient Soc (pres, 79-80); Am Asian Studies; Soc Study Chinese Relig. *Res:* Chinese literature of the Six Dynasties; Chinese Buddhism; Taoism. *Publ:* Auth, Biography of Lü Kuang, Univ Calif, 59; The controversy over conformity and naturalness during the Six Dynasties, Hist Relig, 69-70; Shih-shuo Hsin-yü, A New Account of Tales of the World, Univ Minn, 76. *Mailing Add:* Dept of EAsian Lang Univ of Minn Minneapolis MN 55455

MATHESON, LISTER MALCOLM, English, Philology. See Vol II

MATHESON, WILLIAM HOWARD, b Flint, Mich, July 21, 29. ROMANCE LANGUAGES. *Educ:* Univ Mich, BA, 51, MA, 52, PhD, 62. *Prof Exp:* Instr French, Yale Univ, 53-58; instr, Univ Mich, 58-59; from instr to asst prof, Tufts Univ, 59-64; from asst prof to assoc prof, Brandeis Univ, 64-72; chmn dept, 72-81, PROF COMP LIT, WASHINGTON UNIV, 72- *Mem:* MLA; Northeast Mod Lang Asn; Claudel Soc; Am Comp Lit Asn. *Res:* Heian Japanese poetry; contemporary French poetry; contemporary and modern Japanese literature. *Publ:* Auth, Claudel and Aeschylus, 65 & coauth, Selected Odes of Pindar, 68, Univ Mich; Toward a modern Japanese poetry, Lit East & West. *Mailing Add:* Dept Comp Lit Washington Univ St Louis MO 63130

MATHIAS, GERALD BARTON, b Berkeley, Calif, July 9, 35; m 59; c 2. JAPANESE LANGUAGE & LITERATURE, LINGUISTICS. *Educ:* Univ Calif, Berkeley, AB, 61, MA, 65, PhD(orient lang), 68. *Prof Exp:* From lectr to asst prof East Asian lang & lit, Ind Univ, 67-75; ASSOC PROF JAPANESE, UNIV HAWAII, MANOA, 75- *Mem:* Asn Asian Studies; Asn Teachers Japanese; Ling Soc Am; Asn Computational Ling. *Res:* Prehistory of Japanese language; semantic structure of language; mechanical parsing. *Publ:* Auth, Toward the semantics of -te-i- attachment, J Newslett Asn Teachers Japanese, 69; On the modification of certain reconstructions of proto- Korean-Japanese, 73 & Some problems with word meaning, 73, Papers Japanese Ling; Seven tales of Yamato, In: K'uei Hsing, Ind Univ, 74; Subject and topic in Korean, Japanese, and English, Korean Ling, 78. *Mailing Add:* Dept of East Asian Lang Univ of Hawaii Honolulu HI 96822

MATHIEU, GUSTAVE BORDING, b Mannheim, Ger, Mar 1, 21; nat US; m 54; c 1. GERMAN LITERATURE. *Educ:* Columbia Univ, BS, 49, MA, 51, PhD, 57. *Prof Exp:* Instr Ger, Columbia Col, 49-57; asst prof, Pomona Col, 57-60; FOUNDING CHMN DEPT FOREIGN LANG & LIT & PROF GER, CALIF STATE UNIV, FULLERTON, 60- *Concurrent Pos:* Assoc ed, Ger Quart, 61-63; consult, US Off Educ, 62-66; founder & ed, Mod Lang Abstr, 62-66; resident dir, Calif State Int Prog, Ger, 66-68, France, 70-72. *Mem:* Am Asn Teacher Ger (pres, 76-78). *Res:* H V Kleist; propaganda and literature; Klaus Staeck culture and social criticism. *Publ:* Auth, A modern view of Kleist's Prinz von Homburg, Ger Life ' Lett, 4/60; co-auth, Technik und Arbeitsformen des Sprach Labors, Cornelsen, Berlin, 65; In Briefen Erzählt, Huebner, Munich, 66; auth, Brechts Kreide kreis, Montatshefte, 9/71; Teaching German through relevant literature, 9/71 & A solution to boredom with literature, spring 74, Unterrichtspraxis; Kleist asas propaganda tool, Komparatistik & Rezeption Bouvier, Bonn, 78; coauth, Perspektiven zu Aktuellen Fragen, Holt, 78; Deutsch für alle, Wiley, 80; Fortschritt Deutsch, Holt, 79; K Staeck, Boom to Landes Kunde, Unterrichts Praxis, 81. *Mailing Add:* 315 High Dr Laguna Beach CA 92651

MATHIEU-HIGGINBOTHAM, CORINA SARA, b Buenos Aires, Arg; US citizen; m 74; c 1. LATIN AMERICAN LITERATURE. *Educ:* Portland State Univ, BA, 63; Univ Wash, MA, 66; Stanford Univ, PhD(Span & Port), 73. *Prof Exp:* Lectr Span, Lone Mountain Col, San Francisco, 70-71; ASSOC PROF SPAN, UNIV NEV, LAS VEGAS, 72-, CHMN DEPT FOREIGN LANG, 81- *Concurrent Pos:* Collab scholar, Handbk Latin Am Studies, Hisp Found & Libr Cong, 76-78. *Mem:* MLA; Philol Asn Pac Coast; Rocky Mountain Mod Lang Asn; Asn Lit Femenina; Rocky Mountain Coun Latin Am Studies. *Res:* River Plate narrative XIX and XX centuries. *Publ:* Auth, Aspectos del mundo burgues de Mario Benedetti, 74 & La ambigüedad racial en Los Rios Profundos, 74, Proc Pac Northwest Conf Foreign Lang; coauth, The contemporary Uruguayan novel: Reflections of a society in crisis, Latin Am Lit Rev, 76; auth, La mujer argentina en la novelistica de Silvina Bullrich, In: Latin American Women Writers: Yesterday and Today, Carnegie-Mellon Univ, 77; Faulkner y Onetti: una vision de la realidad a traves de Jefferson y Sta Maria, Hispanofila, 77. *Mailing Add:* Univ of Nev 4505 Maryland Pkwy Las Vegas NV 89154

MATHIOT, MADELEINE, b Saulxures-sur-Moselotte, France, June 11, 27; US citizen; m 60; c 1. LINGUISTICS, ANTHROPOLOGY. *Educ:* Georgetown Univ, BS, 54, MS, 55; Cath Univ Am, PhD(anthrop), 66. *Prof Exp:* Asst prof anthrop, Univ Calif, Los Angeles, 67-69; assoc prof ling, 69-74, PROF LING & ANTHROP, STATE UNIV NY BUFFALO, 74-, DIR, CTR STUDIES CULT TRANSMISSION, 74- *Mem:* Am Anthrop Asn; Ling Soc Am; Semiotic Soc Am. *Res:* Lexicology; ethnosemantics; face-to-face interaction. *Publ:* Auth, An Approach to the Cognitive Study of Language,

68 & A Papago Dictionary of Usage, Vol I, 73, Vol 2, 78, Ind Univ; ed, Approaches to the Analysis of Face-to-Face Interaction, Semiotica, 78; Ethnolinguistics: Boas, Sapir, Whorf Revisited, Mouton, 79; A meaning based theory of face to face interaction, Int J Soc Ling (in prep). *Mailing Add:* Dept Ling State Univ NY Buffalo NY 14261

MATHISEN, RALPH WHITNEY, Ancient History, Classics. See Vol I

MATISOFF, JAMES ALAN, b Boston, Mass, July 14, 37; m 62; c 2. LINGUISTICS, SOUTHEAST ASIAN STUDIES. *Educ:* Harvard Univ, AB, 58, AM, 59; Univ Calif, Berkeley, PhD(ling), 67. *Prof Exp:* From instr to asst prof, Columbia Univ, 66-70; assoc prof, 70-80, PROF LING, UNIV CALIF, BERKELEY, 80- *Concurrent Pos:* Am Coun Leanred Soc grant for res in Asia, 70; vis scholar, Summer Inst Ling Soc Am, Ann Arbor, Mich, 73. *Mem:* Ling Soc Am; Northern Thai Soc. *Res:* Psycho-semantics. *Publ:* Auth, Verb concatentation in Lahu, Acta Ling, 69; Glottal dissimulation and the Lahu high-rising tone, J Am Orient Soc, 70; The Loloish Tonal Split Revisited, Ctr S & Southeast Asian Studies, Univ Calif, 72; The Grammar of Lahu, Univ Calif, 73; Psycho-ostensive expressions in Yiddish, Ha-sifrut, Jerusalem, 73. *Mailing Add:* Dept of Ling Univ of Calif Berkeley CA 94720

MATLACK, CHARLES W, b Moorestown, NJ, Oct 7, 23; m 48; c 3. SPANISH. *Educ:* Haverford Col, AB, 47; Middlebury Col, MA, 49; Univ NMex, PhD(Span), 54. *Prof Exp:* Instr Span, Ursinus Col, 47-50; asst prof, NMex Highlands Univ, 53-54; from asst prof to assoc prof, 54-72, PROF SPAN, EARLHAM COL, 72- *Honors & Awards:* Honor Award, Nat Soccer Coaches Asn, 82. *Mem:* Am Asn Teachers Span & Port; Cent States Mod Lang Asn. *Res:* Naturalism in the Spanish novel, 1880-1890; programing instructional materials for elementary Spanish. *Mailing Add:* 660 SW 21st St Richmond IN 47374

MATLAW, RALPH E, b Berlin, Ger, Feb, 4, 27; US citizen; m 49; c 2. RUSSIAN & COMPARATIVE LITERATURE. *Educ:* Univ Mich, AB, 49; Harvard Univ, AM, 52, PhD, 54. *Prof Exp:* Teaching fel gen educ, Harvard Univ, 51-52 & 53-54, instr Slavic & gen educ, 54-57, lectr, 57-58; asst prof Russ, Princeton Univ, 58-60; assoc prof & head dept, Univ Ill, 60-63; PROF RUSS LIT, UNIV CHICAGO, 63- *Mem:* MLA; Am Asn Teachers Slavic & East Europ Lang; Am Comp Lit Asn. *Res:* Modern Russian literature. *Publ:* Auth, The Brothers Karamazov: Novelistic Technique, Mouton, The Hague, 57; Apollon Grigoryev, Dutton, 62; ed, Fathers and Sons, Norton, 64; Tolstoy, Prentice-Hall, 67. *Mailing Add:* Dept of Russ Lit Univ of Chicago Chicago IL 60637

MATLUCK, JOSEPH H, b Brooklyn, NY, Nov 25, 17; m 47. ROMANCE LANGUAGES. *Educ:* Brooklyn Col, BA, 40; Mex City Col, MA, 48; Nat Univ Mex, PhD(Hisp studies), 51. *Prof Exp:* Instr Romance lang, Northwestern Univ, 51-55; asst prof, 55-61, assoc prof, 61-80, PROF ROMANCE LANG, UNIV TEX, AUSTIN, 80- *Concurrent Pos:* Vis prof English & AV consult educ, TV & radio, Univ PR, 58-59; vis assoc prof appl ling, Univ NMex, 60-61; Fulbright advan res scholar, Rome, Italy, 63-64. *Mem:* MLA; Ling Soc Am; Am Asn Teachers Span & Port; Am Libr Recorded Dialect Studies. *Res:* Linguistics; dialectology; phonetics. *Publ:* Auth, La Pronunciacion en El Espanol del Valle de Mexico, A Morales, Mexico City, 51; The presentation of Spanish pronunciation in American Textbooks, Mod Lang J, 5/57; Fonemas finales en el consonantismo puertorriqueno, Nueva Rev Filol, 61; Entonacion hispanica, Anuario Letras, Nat Univ Mex, 65. *Mailing Add:* Dept of Romance Lang Univ of Tex Austin TX 78712

MATSEN, PATRICIA PADEN, b Atlanta, Ga, June 27, 33. CLASSICAL LANGUAGES & LITERATURES. *Educ:* Anges Scott Col, BA, 55; Univ Miss, MA, 57; Bryn Mawr Col, PhD(Greek & Latin), 68. *Prof Exp:* Asst prof, 69-74, ASSOC PROF GREEK, UNIV SC, 74- *Mem:* Am Philol Asn; Archaeol Inst Am; Mediaeval Acad Am; Class Asn Midwest & S. *Res:* Classical mythology; Greek poetry and prose. *Publ:* Auth, Social status in Callinus 1, Class J, 10-11/73; Jesus and Socrates: A Beginner's Reader in New Testament and Classic Greek, privately publ, 74; Appendix II: From Spengel, Rhetores Graeci, Vol 3, 81. *Mailing Add:* Dept of Foreign Lang & Lit Univ of SC Columbia SC 29208

MATSUDA, SHIZUE, b Honolulu, Hawaii, May 14, 21. CHINESE LITERATURE, JAPANESE BIBLIOGRAPHY. *Educ:* Columbia Univ, BS & MS, 66, MA, 68, PhD(Chinese lit), 78. *Prof Exp:* LIBRN, EAST ASIAN COLLECTION, MAIN LIBR, IND UNIV, 72- *Concurrent Pos:* Consult, East Asian Studies Prog, Ohio State Univ, 77, East Asian Collection, Ohio State Univ Libr, 81 & Coun Japanese Studies & Coun Chinese Studies, Univ Wis, 82. *Mem:* Asn Asian Studies; Int Asn Orientalist Librns; Mita Soc Libr & Info Sci; Am Libr Asn; Am Asn Univ Professors. *Publ:* Auth, The beauty and the scholar in Li Yu's short stories, Studies in Short Fiction, summer 73; Rain on the Wu T'ung tree, Renditions, autumn 74; Resource sharing: A view from a smaller collection, In: Workshop for Japanese Collection Librarians in American Research Libraries, 78; ed, Current Japanese Serials in the Humanities and Social Sciences Received in American Libraries, Ind Univ, 80. *Mailing Add:* East Asian Collection Rm E860 Ind Univ Libr Bloomington IN 47401

MATTE, EDWARD JOSEPH FRANCIS, b Leoville, Sask, Aug 27, 33; m 59; c 4. FRENCH LITERATURE & LINGUISTICS. *Educ:* Univ BC, BA, 60; Univ Calif, Santa Barbara, MA, 66, PhD(French), 68. *Prof Exp:* Teacher elem French, Prince Rupert Sch Dist, BC, 51-52; teacher sec French, Prince George, 58-59 & Vancouver, 59-60; from teaching asst to assoc of French, Univ Calif, Santa Barbara, 64-68; ASST PROF FRENCH, UNIV BC, 68- *Mem:* Can Asn Univ Teachers. *Res:* French philology; French phonetics and phono-stylistics; French Canadian linguistics. *Publ:* Coauth, La desinence -ons: manifestation de l'influence analogique de habere, Rev Langues Romanes, 70; auth, Le Substrat Celtique et la Syllabation Fermee en Gall-Roman, Actes du XIIIe Cong Int Ling et Philol Romanes, 73. *Mailing Add:* 2314 Rosedale Vancouver BC V5P 2R1 Can

MATTESON, MARIANNA MERRITT, b Kalispell, Mont, Mar 25, 32; m 71. SPANISH LANGUAGE & LITERATURE. *Educ:* Univ Mont, BA, 54; Wash State Univ, MA, 56; Univ Wash, PhD(Romance lang), 68. *Prof Exp:* Instr Span, Univ Idaho, 57-62 & 63-65; asst prof, 65-72, ASSOC PROF SPAN, WASH STATE UNIV, 73- *Mem:* Am Asn Teachers Span & Port; MLA; Pac Northwest Coun Teaching Foreign Lang. *Res:* Modernism in Latin America; contemporary Latin American literature; applied linguistics. *Publ:* Auth, Imagery in Diaz Rodriguez' Sangre Patricia, Hispania, 12/73; Motivos sintacticos en Sangre Patricia, 74 & Quijotismo en una novela de Rufino Blanco Fombona, 79, Explicacion de Textos Lit; On the function of the imposter in the plays of Rodolfo Usigli, Selecta, Vol 2: 120-123. *Mailing Add:* Dept of Foreign Lang & Lit Wash State Univ Pullman WA 99164

MATTEUCIG, GIACINTO, b Udine, Italy, June 11, 15. CLASSICAL ARCHEOLOGY. *Educ:* Univ Calif, AB, 36, AM, 38; Harvard Univ, PhD, 42. *Prof Exp:* Res assoc class archaeol, Univ Calif, 42-43; instr, Army Specialized Training Prog, Stanford Univ, 43-44; instr Latin, St Mary's Col, Calif, 45-46; from asst prof to assoc prof classics, Univ San Francisco, 46-63, prof, 63-80; PROF CLASSICS, FROMM INST, 80- *Concurrent Pos:* Fulbright res fel, Am Acad Rome, 64-65. *Mem:* Am Philol Asn; Archaeol Inst Am. *Res:* Etruscology. *Publ:* Auth, Poggio Buco: The Necropolis of Statonia, Greenwood Press, 72. *Mailing Add:* 55 Aerial Way San Francisco CA 94116

MATTHEWS, HESTER POOLE, b Bennettsville, SC, Nov 18, 16. SPANISH & FRENCH LITERATURE. *Educ:* Winthrop Col, AB, 38; Duke Univ, MA, 47; Univ NC, PhD, 57; Univ Madrid, dipl Span cult, 64. *Prof Exp:* Teacher Span, French & English, High Schs, SC, 38-43; teacher French, Span & hist, Newton-Conover High Sch, NC, 43-44; price & specifications clerk, US Govt Printing Off, 44-46; instr French & Span, Sullins Col, 47-51; instr Span, Agnes Scott Col, 51-54; asst, Univ NC, 54-56; instr Span, ETex State Col, 57-58; assoc prof, Austin Col, 58-62; prof, Delta State Col, 62-66; assoc prof, Winthrop Col, 66-69; assoc prof Span & chmn Span teachers, Edinboro State Col, 69-71; head foreign lang dept, Bennettsville High Sch, SC, 71-82, RETIRED. *Mem:* Am Asn Teachers Span & Port; NEA; Daughters Am Revolution; Am Asn Teachers Fr. *Res:* Spanish ballads; historical drama of Spain. *Mailing Add:* 108 Moore Bennettsville SC 29512

MATTHEWS, JOHN H, b Swansea, Wales, Sept 11, 30; m 55; c 3. FRENCH. *Educ:* Univ Wales, BA, 49, BA, 51; Univ Montpellier, DUniv, 55; Univ Wales, DLitt, 77. *Prof Exp:* Tutor French, Univ Col Swansea, Wales, 55-56; asst lectr, Univ Exeter, 56-57; from asst lectr to lectr, Univ Leicester, 57-63; from asst prof to assoc prof Romance lang, Univ Minn, 62-65; PROF ROMANCE LANG, SYRACUSE UNIV, 65- *Concurrent Pos:* Fulbright travel grant, Gt Brit-US, 60-61; vis lectr Romanic lang, Williams Col, 60-61; ed, Symposium, 65- *Res:* Surrealism; 19th & 20th century French novel. *Publ:* Ed, The Custom-House of Desire, Univ Calif, 75; auth, Benjamin Peret, Twayne, 75; Toward the Poetics of Surrealism, 76 & The Imagery of Surrealism, 77, Syracuse Univ; Le Theatre de Raymond Roussel, Minard, 77; The Inner Dream: Celine as Novelist, Syracuse Univ, 79; Surrealism and American Feature Films, Twayne, 79; Surrealism, Insanity and Poetry, 82 & Eight Painters: The Surrealist Context, 82, Syracuse Univ. *Mailing Add:* 210 H B Crouse Hall Syracuse Univ Syracuse NY 13210

MATTHEWS, ROBERT JOSEPH, Philosophy. See Vol IV

MATTHEWS, VICTOR JOHN, b Londonderry, Northern Ireland, Jan 29, 41; m 67; c 1. CLASSICS. *Educ:* Queen's Univ, Belfast, BA, 63, dipl educ, 64, PhD(Greek), 68; McMaster Univ, MA, 65. *Prof Exp:* From lectr to asst prof, 65-74, ASSOC PROF CLASSICS, UNIV GUELPH, 74- *Mem:* Am Philol Asn; Class Asn Can Hellenic Soc. *Res:* Greek epic poetry; Roman history and historiography; ancient athletics. *Publ:* Auth, The libri punici of King Hiempsal, Am J Philol, 4/72; On planning a year-round distance program, Track Tech, 9/72; Some puns on Roman cognomina, Greece & Rome, 4/73; Panyassis of Halikarnassos: Text and Commentary, E J Brill, Leiden, 74; The Hemerodromoi; ultra long-distance running in antiquity, Class World, 11/74; Swift-footed Achilles, Class News & Views, 4/75; Naupaktia and Argonautika, Phoenix, fall 77; Atlas, Aietes, and Minos oloophron, Class Philol, 7/78. *Mailing Add:* Classics Sect, Dept of Lang Col of Arts, Univ of Guelph Guelph ON N1G 2W1 Can

MATTINGLY, IGNATIUS G, b Detroit, Mich, Nov 22, 27; m 51; c 2. LINGUISTICS. *Educ:* Yale Univ, BA, 47, PhD, 68; Harvard Univ, AM, 59; Cambridge Univ, MA, 71. *Prof Exp:* Instr English, Groton Sch, 47-48; instr, Yale Univ, 50-51; analyst, US Dept Defense, 51-66; lectr, 66-67, 67-68, assoc prof, 68-72, PROF LING, UNIV CONN, 72- *Concurrent Pos:* Guest researcher, Joint Speech Res Unit, Eastcote, 63-64; mem res staff, Haskins Lab, New Haven, 66-; mem tech comt speech speech commun, Acoust Soc Am, 66-69; Fulbright sr res grant, Cambridge Univ, 70-71, fel, King's Col, Cambridge Univ, 70-71. *Mem:* Acoust Soc Am; Ling Soc Am; Int Ling Asn. *Res:* Speech synthesis; speech perception; reading. *Publ:* Coauth, Speech synthesis by rule, 7/64 & auth, Synthesis by rule of prosodic features, 1/66, Lang & Speech; Speech cues and sign stimuli, Am Scientist, 5/72; co-ed, Language by Ear and by Eye, Mass Inst Technol, 72. *Mailing Add:* Dept of Ling Univ of Conn Storrs CT 06268

MATTLINGLY, JOHN ROBERT, b Celina, Ohio, Nov 17, 02; m 34; c 1. CLASSICAL PHILOLOGY. *Educ:* Univ Chicago, AB, 26; Yale Univ, PhD, 31. *Prof Exp:* Instr, Yale Univ, 29-31; from asst prof to assoc prof Greek & Latin, 31-47, from prof to Benjamin-Bates prof, 47-73, EMER PROF LATIN, HAMILTON COL, 73- *Concurrent Pos:* Lectr, Kirkland Col, 74. *Mem:* Am Philol Asn; Renaissance Soc Am; Furniture Hist Soc. *Res:* History of ancient philosophy; iconology of Renaissance painting. *Publ:* Auth, When Men Were Animals and Animals Were Men: A Study of the Graphic Work of David Itchkawich, Angelica, 76. *Mailing Add:* 118 Utica Rd Clinton NY 13323

MATUAL, DAVID MICHAEL, b LaSalle, Ill, Mar 19, 44. RUSSIAN. *Educ:* Ill State Univ, BA, 66; Univ Wis, MA, 68, PhD(Russ), 71. *Prof Exp:* Asst prof, 72-77, ASSOC PROF RUSS, WRIGHT STATE UNIV, 77- *Mem:* Am Asn Teachers Slavic & EEurop Lang. *Res:* The religious writings of Leo Tolstoy; Russian literature in the 19th century. *Publ:* Auth, On the poetics of Tolstoj's Confession, Slavic & EEurop J, fall 75; Fate in Crime and Punishment, Int Fiction Rev, 7/76; O prepodavanii predikativnykh konstruktsii--predikativy neobkhodimosti, winter 77 & Vlast' t'my L N Tolstogo-- Tolkovanie dvukh nazvanii, spring 77, Russ Lang J; Chekhov's Black Monk and Byron's Black Friar, Int Fiction Rev, 1/78. *Mailing Add:* Dept of Mod Lang Wright State Univ Dayton OH 45435

MATULA, ANNE ELIZABETH, b Middletown, Pa, July 8, 13. FRENCH, SPANISH. *Educ:* Lebanon Valley Col, AB, 34; Pa State Univ, MA, 40. *Prof Exp:* Teacher, high schs, Pa, 35-61; asst prof French & Span, 61-66, assoc prof, 66-80, EMER ASSOC PROF FRENCH & SPAN, KUTZTOWN STATE COL, 80- *Honors & Awards:* Super Teaching award, Kutztown State Col, 67. *Mem:* Am Asn Teachers Fr; Am Asn Univ Women. *Mailing Add:* 305 Fairview Dr Kutztown PA 19530

MATURE, ALBERT P, b New York, NY, May 26, 30; m 52; c 4. ROMANCE LANGUAGES. *Educ:* Univ SC, AB, 56, MEd, 57; Univ Ill, PhD(Span), 67. *Prof Exp:* Instr Span, Univ SC, 56-57; asst prof, Newberry Col, 58-64; instr, Univ Ill, 66-67; dir int studies, 71-75, PROF SPAN & HEAD DEPT MOD LANG, NEWBERRY COL, 67- *Mem:* MLA; Am Asn Teachers Span & Port; SAtlantic Mod Lang Asn; Nat Asn Foreign Student Affairs; Mountain Interstate Mod Lang Asn. *Res:* Contemporary and modern Spanish literature. *Publ:* Auth, Wenceslao Fernandez Florez y su novela, In: Coleccion studium, Ed Andrea, Mexico City, 68; El ente de ficcion liberado en el teatro de Unamuno, Hispanofile, 73; Humor y fantasia de Wenceslao Fernandez Florez, 73. *Mailing Add:* Dept of Foreign Lang Newberry Col Newberry SC 29108

MAUBREY, PIERRE REMI, b France, July 14, 23; US citizen; m 50; c 3. FRENCH, LINGUISTICS. *Educ:* Univ Poitiers, Lic es Let, 44; Cath Univ Am, PhD(French lit), 59. *Prof Exp:* Instr English, Col St Julien, 43-44; instr English, Col Charles de Foucauld, Casablance, 45; instr English, Col Mariste, Lagny, 46-47; instr English, sec schs, Brighton, 47-48; instr English, Col Albert de Mun, Nogent, 48-50; from instr to assoc prof, 51-69, PROF LANG & LING, GEORGETOWN UNIV, 69- *Concurrent Pos:* Dir, French Int Sch, Washington, DC, 63-65; consult, Md, Va & DC, Pub schs systs; mem, bd adv, Franco Am Comt Educ Travel & Studies, 71- *Honors & Awards:* Teacher of the Year Award, 69 & Gold Medal, 71, Georgetown Univ; Chevalier, Palmes Academiques, 73. *Mem:* MLA; Am Asn Teachers Fr; Soc Fr Prof Am; Soc Amis Georges Bernanos. *Res:* Descriptive study of the French structure, linguistics and methodology; French contemporary language. *Publ:* Auth, Introductory French, Georgetown Univ, 52; L'expression de la passion interieure dans le style de Bernanos Romancier, Cath Univ Am, 59, AMS Press, 68; Enseigner, C6est choisir, Fr Dans Monde, 6/65; coauth, New foundation course in French, Raytheon, Heath, 68; auth, Language familiarization course in French, Raytheon, Heath, 68; auth, Language familiarization course, World Publ, 69; First Textbook of Connaissance du Francais, Scott, 73. *Mailing Add:* Dept of Lang & Lit Georgetown Univ Washington DC 20007

MAURACH, BERNHARD, b Berlin, Ger, May 21, 27; Can citizen; m 60; c 2. GERMAN LITERATURE & LANGUAGE. *Educ:* Univ BC, BA, 64, MA, 68; Univ Wash, PhD(Ger), 71. *Prof Exp:* Asst prof, Univ Kans, 70-71; ASSOC PROF GER, UNIV OTTAWA, 71- *Concurrent Pos:* Founder, Can Summer Sch, Ger. *Res:* The age of Goethe; background to the age of Goethe; A v Kotzebue, G Merkel & K A Boettiger & contemporaries. *Publ:* Auth, J G Seume über einen Besuch von J I Baggesen in Weimar, Danske Studier, 77; Die Affäre um Goethese inszenierung des schlegelschen ion, Neophilogus, 77; Zeitgenosse Goethe, J Freien Deut Hochstifts, 78. *Mailing Add:* Dept of Mod Lang & Lit Univ of Ottawa Ottawa ON K1N 6N5 Can

MAURER, WALTER HARDING, b New York, NY, July 13, 21; m 61. SANSKRIT. *Educ:* Univ Vt, BA, 43; Univ Pa, PhD(Sanskrit), 62. *Prof Exp:* Instr Greek & Ger, Univ Vt, 46-47; ref librn S Asia sect, Libr Cong, 50-62; asst prof Sanskrit, 62-64, cur S Asia collection, East-West Ctr, 62-63, assoc prof Sanskrit & hist, 64-68, assoc chmn dept Asian & Pac lang, 70-71, chmn dept Indo-Pac lang, 71-80, PROF SANSKRIT, UNIV HAWAII, MANOA, 68- *Concurrent Pos:* Lang consult, Philos E & W, 67-; Am Coun Learned Soc area study grant, Tübingen, Ger & London, England, 68-69; vis honorary fel, Inst Advan Studies Humanities, Univ Edinburgh, Scotland, summer 78. *Mem:* Am Orient Soc; Tibet Soc; Royal Asiatic Soc; Int Cong Orientalists. *Res:* Sanskrit language and literature, especially as related to Indian philosophy and religion; Indo-European philology. *Publ:* Auth, Pancatantrakathasamcarah, Sarada, 60; Aspects of Jaina Sanskrit, Adyar Libr Bull, 62; Sugamanvaya Vrtti (2 vols), Deccan Col, Poona, India, 65; The rainbow in Sanskrit literature, Adyar Libr Bull, 67-68; A re-examination of Rgveda X.129, the Nasadiya Hymn, J Indo-European Studies, 75; On the name Devanagari, J Am Orient Soc, 76. *Mailing Add:* 2333 Kapiolani Blvd Apt 813 Honolulu HI 96826

MAURIN, MARIO, b France, Dec 22, 28; nat US. FRENCH. *Educ:* Yale Univ, BA, 48, MA, 49, PhD(French), 51. *Prof Exp:* From asst prof to assoc prof, 53-65, chmn dept, 59-67, PROF FRENCH, BRYN MAWR COL, 65- *Concurrent Pos:* Guggenheim fel, 59; columnist in Span, Agencia Latino Am, 75- *Honors & Awards:* Prix de la Langue Francaise, Academie Francaise, 73. *Mem:* Am Asn Teachers Fr; Soc Fr Prof Am. *Res:* Modern poetry and its background; French literature from 1880-1920. *Publ:* Auth, Leopardi, Seghers, 61; Henri de Regnier: Le Labyrinthe et le Double, Univ Montreal, 72. *Mailing Add:* Dept of French Bryn Mawr Col Bryn Mawr PA 19010

MAURINO, FERDINANDO D, b Italy, Nov 12, 15; m; c 2. COMPARATIVE ROMANCE LITERATURE. *Educ:* City Col NY, AB, 39; Columbia Univ, AM, 41, PhD, 49. *Prof Exp:* Instr Romance lang, Army Specialized Training Prog, State Univ Iowa & Atlanta Army Training Sch, 43-45; asst prof Romance lang, Syracuse Univ, 46-48; assoc prof, Dickinson Col, 48-56, prof Romance lang & lit, 56-65; prof, Tex Tech Univ, 65-68; prof, 68-81, EMER PROF ROMANCE LANG & COMP LIT, UNIV TENN, KNOXVILLE, 81- *Concurrent Pos:* Chmn Renaissance lit sect, Mod Lang Meeting, 55; vis prof, Fordham Univ, 56-57; Dickinson Col Coun res awards, Italy & Spain, 58, 60, 63-64; Univ Tenn res grant, 77 & 79; vis prof, Univ Southern Fla, Tampa, 82. *Honors & Awards:* Knight for Meritorious Academic Serv, Repub of Italy, 82. *Mem:* MLA; Dante Soc; SAtlantic Mod Lang Asn. *Res:* Medieval literature; Renaissance and 20th century Italian and Spanish literature; Italian, Spanish and comparative Romance literature. *Publ:* Auth, Di Giacomo's Uocchie, PMLA, 5/67; Pirandello, Folklore Ital, 12/67; Theme of Yesteryear . . ., Filos e Lett, 68; Dal Cavo delle Mani; Pellegrini, Italy, 68; Poliziano and Cetina . . ., Hisp Rev, 7/69; Modern Spanish Dictionary, Simon & Schuster, 75; Petrarca and Fray Luis, Italianistica, summer 78; The spirit of travel in Italian literature, In: Travel, Quest and Pilgrimage as a Literary Theme, Ann Arbor Soc Span & Other Studies, 78. *Mailing Add:* 1283 Madelena Ave Casselberry FL 32708

MAUTNER, FRANZ H, b Vienna, Austria, June 8, 02. GERMAN, COMPARATIVE LITERATURE. *Educ:* Univ Heidelberg & Univ Vienna, PhD, 26. *Prof Exp:* Teacher, Gym, Vienna, 27-29, 30-32, prof, 33-38; lectr & charge de cours, Univ Besancon, 29-30; dozent, People's Univ, Vienna, 36-38; asst prof Ger, Ind Univ, 39-40; asst prof, Hobart Col, 41-44; asst prof lang & lit, Ohio Wesleyan Univ, 44, 46-48; prof writer Ger, US Dept State, 45; assoc prof Ger & comp lit, Kenyon Col, 48-52; lectr Ger, Sarah Lawrence Col & Queens Col, NY, 53-55; from assoc prof to prof, 55-72, EMER PROF GER, SWARTHMORE COL, 72- *Concurrent Pos:* Vis lectr, Johns Hopkins Univ, 39; Am Coun Learned Soc scholar, 54-55; vis prof Ger, Princeton Univ, 62 & Univ Pa, 64; Guggenheim fel, 64-65, 68-69; vis prof, Bryn Mawr Col, 71 & Cornell Univ, 75. *Honors & Awards:* Austrian Cross of Honor, First Class; Friedrich Gundolf Preis, Deutsche Akademie f Sprache u Dichtung, 77. *Mem:* Mod Humanities Res Asn; Int Arthur Schnitzler Res Asn; Am Comp Lit Asn; Int Ver Ger Sprach-u Literaturwiss; Deutsche Akademie f Sprache und Dichtung. *Res:* German and comparative literature from 1750; Lichtenberg, Nestroy, and Moerike; history and esthetics of literary and stylistic forms. *Publ:* Auth, Wortgewebe, Sinngefüge und Idee in Büchners Woyzeck, In: Georg Büchner, Wis Buchgesellschaft, Darmstadt, 65; ed, Lichtenberg, Gedankenbücher, rev ed, 67 & auth, Randbemerkungen zu Brigitta, In: Adalbert Stifter, Studien und Interpretation, 68, Stiehm, Heidelberg; Lichtenberg, Geschichte seines Geistes, de Gruyter, Berlin, 68; Nestroy, Komödien (3 vols), 70 & Wort und Wesen, 74, Insel, Frankfurt; Nestroy, Stiehm, Heidelberg, 74; contribr, Georg Christoph Lichtenberg, In: Deutsche Dichter des 18 Jahrhunderts, Erich Schmidt, Berlin, 77; Die Wiener Volkskomödie, Raimund und Nestroy, In: Handbuch des deutschen Dramas Bagel, Düsseldorf, 80. *Mailing Add:* 408 Walnut Lane Swarthmore PA 19081

MAX, STEFAN LEOPOLD, b Sofia, Bulgaria, Nov 24, 29; Can citizen. FRENCH LANGUAGE & LITERATURE. *Educ:* Sir George Williams Univ, BA, 59; McGill Univ, MA, 61; Univ Calif, Los Angeles, PhD(French), 64. *Prof Exp:* Teaching asst French, Univ Calif, Los Angeles, 60-62; instr, Pomona Col, 62-64; PROF FRENCH, SAN DIEGO STATE UNIV, 64- *Concurrent Pos:* Creative writing ed, French Rev, 72- *Mem:* Am Asn Teachers Fr. *Res:* Nineteenth and 20th century French literature; literary criticism. *Publ:* Auth, Les metamorphoses de la Grande Ville dans les Rougon-Macquart, Nizet, Paris, 66; Dialogues et situations, Heath, 70, 2nd ed, 80; Crescendo Satanique (a play), La Pensee Univ, 75. *Mailing Add:* Dept of French & Ital San Diego State Univ San Diego CA 92115

MAXFIELD-MILLER, ELIZABETH, b Philadelphia, Pa, July 20, 10; div; c 1. ROMANCE, MOLIERE. *Educ:* Swarthmore Col, AB, 31; Radcliffe Col, AM, 36, PhD, 38. *Prof Exp:* Secy to dir foreign study group in France, Univ Del, 32-33; registr & teacher French, George Sch, Pa, 33-35; instr French, Milwaukee-Downer Col, 38-40; from instr to asst prof, Wheaton Col, Mass, 40-45, asst prof, 48-52, 54-55; part-time mem staff libr, Harvard Univ, 45-46; instr, Cambridge Jr Col, 46-47; secy libr, Swarthmore Col, 47-48; asst dir foreign study group in France, Sweet Briar Col, 52-54; teacher French, Concord Acad, 55-75; RETIRED. *Concurrent Pos:* Travel grants, Concord Acad, 69 & 71. *Honors & Awards:* Chevalier, Palmes Academiques, 66 & Ordre Arts et Lett, 68; Radcliffe Grad Soc Medal for Res & Teaching, 74. *Mem:* New England Hist Geneal Soc; Thoreau Soc. *Res:* Life and friends of Moliere; Concord authors; genealogical research. *Publ:* Auth, Studies in Modern Romansh Poetry in the Engadine . . ., Cambridge Univ, 38; coauth, Cent ans de recherches sur Moliere, sur sa famille et sur les comediens de sa troupe, Arch France, Paris, 63; auth, Elizabeth Hoar of Concord and Thoreau, Thoreau Soc Bull, No 106: 1-3; Emerson and Elizabeth of Concord, Harvard Libr Bull, XIX: 290-306; Moliere and the court painters, especially Pierre Mignard, In: A Festschrift Moliere 1973: Moliere and the Commonwealth of Letters, Univ Southern Miss, 73. *Mailing Add:* 159 Elsinore St Apt 8 Concord MA 01742

MAXWELL, DANIEL NEWHALL, b Worcester, Mass, Nov 7, 47. LINGUISTICS. *Educ:* Trinity Col, Hartford, BA, 70; Ind Univ, MA, 77, PhD(gen ling), 79. *Prof Exp:* Lektor English lang, Wilhelms Westfülische Universität Münster, 79-81; WISSENSCHAFTLICHER ASST LING, TECH UNIVERSITÄT, BERLIN, 82- *Mem:* Ling Soc Am; Universala Esperanto Asocio. *Res:* Syntactic typology; historical syntax; interlinguistics. *Publ:* Auth, Noun phrase accessibility and strategies of relativization, Lang, 79; coauth, Sprache beschreiben und erklaeren Akten des 16, Linguistischen Kolloquiums, Max Niemeyer Verlag, 82; auth, Implications of noun phrase accessibility for diachronic syntax, Folia Ling Hist, 82; The functor content hierarchy and universals of word order, Technische Universitaet Berlin, 82. *Mailing Add:* Institut fuer Linguistik Techische Univeritaet Berlin 1 Berlin 10 Germany, Federal Republic of

MAXWELL, DAVID EVANS, b New York, NY, Dec 2, 44; m 68; c 2. SLAVIC LANGUAGES & LITERATURES. *Educ:* Grinnell Col, BA, 66; Brown Univ, MA, 68, PhD(Slavic lang & lit), 74. *Prof Exp:* From instr to asst prof, 71-77, assoc prof & dir prog, 77-81, DEAN, UNDERGRADUATE & ACAD AFFAIRS, 81- *Concurrent Pos:* Assoc, Russ Res Ctr, Harvard Univ, 73-77, visitor, 77-80; Int Res & Exchanges Bd travel grants, 76 & 77; co-ed & coordr Am contrib, Problemy Izucenija Cexova v SSSR i SSA, Nauka, Moscow, 82. *Mem:* Am Asn Teachers Slavic & E Europ Lang; MLA; Am Asn Advan Slavic Studies; Am Coun Teachers Russ; Northeast Mod Lang Asn. *Res:* Nineteenth century Russian prose; Chekhov; literary theory and criticism. *Publ:* Auth, A system of symbolic gesture in Cexov's Step, Slavic & E Europ J, 73; Cechov's Nevesta: A structural approach to the role of setting, Russ Lit, 74; The structural unit of Cexov's Malen'kaja Trilogija, In: The Art duality in two Chekhov stories, Problemy Izucenija Cexova v SSSR i SSA, Moscow, 82. *Mailing Add:* Dept of Ger & Russ Tufts Univ Medford MA 02155

MAXWELL, HARRY J, b Los Angeles, Calif, Dec 2, 25; c 4. GERMANIC LANGUAGES, LATIN AMERICAN STUDIES. *Educ:* Univ Calif, Riverside, BA, 57; Stanford Univ, MA, 63, PhD(Ger), 64. *Prof Exp:* Teacher elem schs, Calif, 55-56 & Bear Valley Unified Sch Dist, 56-60; vprin, Big Bear Lake Elem Sch, 58-60; instr Ger, Menlo Col, 62-63; asst prof, Univ Wis-Milwaukee, 64-66; chmn dept mod lang, Adrian Col, 66-67; dean, Univ Wis, Wash County Campus, 67-72; dean acad affairs, 72-77, actg pres, 77-78, PROF LATIN AM STUDIES, RICKS COL, 81- *Concurrent Pos:* Univ Wis-Milwaukee grant, 65, grad sch grant, 65-66. *Publ:* Auth, Aspects of futurity in modern uses of sollen, Ger Quart, 5/68. *Mailing Add:* Dept Latin Am Studies Ricks Col Rexburg ID 83440

MAY, BARBARA DALE, b Denver, Colo, Mar 10, 50; m 72. SPANISH LITERATURE, LITERARY CRITICISM. *Educ:* Univ Utah, BA, 72, MA, 73, PhD(Span lit), 75. *Prof Exp:* Assoc instr Span, Univ Utah, 75-76; asst prof, 76-80, PROF ROMANCE LANG, UNIV ORE, 80- *Concurrent Pos:* Grad res fel, Univ Utah, 75-76; fac res award, Univ Ore, 77-78. *Mem:* Am Asn Teachers Span & Port; MLA. *Res:* Nineteenth and 20th century Spanish poetry; Black American poetry; Spanish feminist literature. *Publ:* Auth, Progresion ciclica y tragica del yo unamuniano, Cuadernos Hispanoam, 8-9/76; Tres poetas en busca de America: Albert, Guillen y Hughes, Estudos Ibero-Am, 12/76; El Dilema de la Nostalgia en la Poesia de Alberti, Utah Studies Lit & Ling, 78; The Search for America in Alberti, Guillen and Hughes, McMaster Univ, 79; Poetry and Political Commitment: Alberti, Guillen and Hughes, City Univ New York, 79; Byron, Espronceda, and the critics, Selecta, Vol I, 80; The endurance of dreams deferred, In: Black Flags, Red Flags, Cath Univ Am Press, 82. *Mailing Add:* Dept of Romance Lang Univ of Ore Eugene OR 97403

MAY, GEORGES (CLAUDE), b Paris, France, Oct 7, 20; m 49; c 2. FRENCH LITERATURE. *Educ:* Univ Paris, Lic es Lett, 41; Univ Montpellier, dipl, 41; Univ Ill, PhD, 47. *Prof Exp:* Instr, 45-46, 47-48, from asst prof to prof, 48-71, dean, Yale Col, 63-71, chmn dept, 78-80, provost, 79-81, STERLING PROF FRENCH, YALE UNIV, 71- . *Concurrent Pos:* Guggenheim fel, 50-51; secy, 4th Int Cong on Enlightenment, 71-75. *Honors & Awards:* Chevalier, Legion d'honneur, France, 71. *Mem:* MLA; Am Asn Teachers Fr; Soc Hist Lit France; Am Soc 18th Century Studies (vpres, 72-74); Am Acad Arts & Sci. *Res:* Various parts of French literature. *Publ:* Auth, J J Rousseau par Lui-Meme, Ed Seuil, France, 61; Le Dilemme du Roman au XVIIIe Siecle, Presses Univs, France & Yale Univ, 63; L'unite de sang chez Racine, Rev Hist Litteraire, France, 72; co-ed, Diderot's La Religieuse and Preface, In: Diderot's Oeuvres Completes, Hermann, Paris, 75; auth, Autobiography and the eighteenth century, In: The Author in His Work, Yale Univ, 78; L'Autobiographie, Presses Univs France, Paris, 79; Biography, autobiography and the novel in 18th century France, In: Bibliography in the 18th Century, Garland Publ Co, 80; co-ed, Diderot's Sur Terence, In: Diderot's Oeuvres Completes, Paris: Hermann, 80. *Mailing Add:* 7 W L Harkness Hall Yale Univ New Haven CT 06520

MAY, GITA, b Brussels, Belgium, Sept 16, 29; nat US; m 47. FRENCH. *Educ:* Hunter Col, BA, 53; Columbia Univ, MA, 54, PhD, 57. *Prof Exp:* From lectr to instr, 53-58, from asst prof to assoc prof, 58-68, PROF FRENCH LIT & DEPT REP FRENCH, COLUMBIA UNIV, 68- *Concurrent Pos:* Coun Res Humanities grants, 60, 67 & 69; Am Coun Learned Soc grant, 61; Guggenheim fel & Fulbright grant, 64-65; US Educ Comn lectr, Gt Brit, 65; Nat Endowment for Humanities sr fel, 71-72. *Honors & Awards:* Hunter Col Award for Outstanding achievement, 63; Chevalier, Palmes Academiques, 68; Van Amringe Distinguished Bk Award, 71 . *Mem:* Am Asn Teachers Fr; MLA; Northeast Am Soc 18th Century Studies (vpres, 80-81, pres, 81-82); Fr Soc Studies 18th Century; Am Soc Fr Acad Palms. *Res:* Aesthetics and history of ideas in the Age of Enlightenment; Diderot and Rousseau; Stendhal. *Publ:* Auth, Diderot and Baudelaire, Art Critics, de Jean-Jacques Rousseau a Madame Roland; Les pensees detachees sur la pointure de Diderot, Rev d'Hist Lit France, 1/70; Diderot et Roger de Piles, PMLA, 5/70; Madame Roland and the Age of Revolution, 70 & Stendhal and the Age of Revolution, 77, Columbia Univ; Les Confessions, Roman picaresque, Fritz Schalk Festschrift, 82. *Mailing Add:* 404 W 116th St New York NY 10027

MAY, JAMES MICHAEL, b Youngstown, Ohio, Sept 2, 51; m 74. CLASSICAL PHILOLOGY. *Educ:* Kent State Univ, BS Ed, 73; Univ NC, PhD(class philol), 77. *Prof Exp:* ASST PROF CLASSICS, ST OLAF COL, 77- *Mem:* Am Philol Asn; Class Asn Mid-West & South; Am Class League; Mediaeval Acad Am; Friends Am Acad at Rome. *Res:* Classical rhetoric and oratory; Roman Golden Age and Augustan poetry; rhetoric in the middle ages. *Publ:* Auth, The Ethica Digresio and Cicero's Pro Milone: A progression of intensity from Logos to Ethos to Pathos, The Class J, 74: 240-246; The image of the ship of State in Cicero's Pro Sestio, Maia: Revista di letterature classiche, fascicolo III, 9/80; A syllabus for intermediate Latin, The Class J, 77: 65-67; The rhetoric of advocacy and patron-client identification: Variation on a theme, The Am J of Philol, 102: 308-315. *Mailing Add:* St Olaf Col Northfield MN 55057

MAY, JANET GRACE, b Flushing, NY, June 16, 49; m 78. LINGUISTICS, SPEECH SCIENCES. *Educ:* State Univ NY Col, Oneonta, BA, 71; Univ Pa, MA, 73; Univ Conn, PhD(ling), 79. *Prof Exp:* LINGUIST, GEN INSTRUMENT CORP, 81- *Concurrent Pos:* Adj asst prof, NY Univ, 79; guest researcher, Haskins Labs, New Haven, 79-81; lectr, Wagner Col, Staten Island, 81. *Mem:* Ling Soc Am; Acoust Soc Am. *Res:* Speech synthesis; speech perception; speech production. *Publ:* Auth, Article, J Acoust Soc Am, Vol 65, Suppl 1, spring 76; Article, speech Commun Papers, 6/79; Acoustic factors that may contribute to categorical perception, In: Language and Speech, Vol 24, Part 3, 81; Speech synthesis using allophones, Speech Technol, 4/82. *Mailing Add:* 600 West John St Hicksville NY 11802

MAYBERRY, NANCY KENNINGTON, b St Thomas, Ont; m 67; c 2. SPANISH DRAMA & LITERATURE. *Educ:* Univ Western Ont, BA, 61; Univ NC Chapel Hill, MA, 63, PhD(Span), 66. *Prof Exp:* Asst prof Span & French, Univ NC, Greensboro, 65-66; asst prof Span, Univ Western Ont, 66-67; assoc prof Span & French, 67-75, assoc prof, 75-82, PROF SPAN & FRENCH, EAST CAROLINA UNIV, 82- *Res:* Spanish Golden Age drama; 19th century Spanish romanticism. *Publ:* Auth, The fate of Aldonza in part III of Tirso's Santa Juana, Hispanofila, 75; Tirso's use of myths & symbols in part I of the Pazarro trilogy, Ky Romance Quart, 75; On the structure of Tirso's Santa Juana trilogy, South Atlantic Bull, 76; The role of the warrior women in Amazonas en las Indias, Bull Comediantes, 77; Tirso's La Venganza de Tamar: Second part of a trilogy?, Bull Hisp Studies, 78; More on the role of David in Calderon's Los cabellos de Absalon, Revista de Estudios Hispanicos, 80; Sobre la autenticidad de El milagro por los celos, Actas del primer congreso internacional sobre Lope de Vega y los Origines del teatro, 81. *Mailing Add:* Dept of Foreign Lang East Carolina Univ Greenville NC 27834

MAYER, EDGAR NATHAN, b New York, NY, Sept 24, 24; m 50; c 1. LINGUISTICS. *Educ:* Cornell Univ, AB, 44; Harvard Univ, MA, 48, PhD(ling), 52. *Prof Exp:* Instr French & Russ, Williams Col, 48-50; instr French, Princeton Univ, 50-51; instr French & Russ, Wash Univ, 51-52; instr, Lafayette Col, 53-56; asst prof English as foreign lang & dir dept, Wayne State Univ, 56-59; assoc prof French & Russ, Univ Buffalo, 59-70; PROF FRENCH, UNIV COLO, BOULDER, 70- *Concurrent Pos:* Fulbright lectr ling, Tokyo Univ Educ, 65-66. *Mem:* Ling Soc Am; Am Asn Teachers Fr. *Res:* Linguistic structure of French, Russian and English. *Publ:* Coauth, Handbook of French Structure, Harcourt, 68; auth, Structure of French, New Century, 69; Stems in the French verb, Fr Rev, 3/69. *Mailing Add:* Dept of French Univ of Colo Boulder CO 80302

MAYER, SIGRID, b Göttingen, Ger, US citizen; c 3. GERMAN LANGUAGE & LITERATURE. *Educ:* Univ NMex, BA, 68; Univ Utah, MA, 69, PhD(Ger), 73. *Prof Exp:* Asst prof, 73-78, ASSOC PROF GER, UNIV WYOMING, 78- *Mem:* MLA; Rocky Mountain MLA; Am Asn Teachers Ger; Pac NW Coun Foreign Lang; Am Lit Translrs Asn. *Res:* German literature 19th & 20th centuries; comparative literature; comparative arts. *Publ:* Auth, Der Golem-Stoff in den Vereinigten Staaten: Ein Querschnitt durch die zeitgenossische Rezeption, In: Elemente der Literatur, Beitrage zur Stoff- Motiv- und Themenforschung, Elisabeth Frenzel zum 65, Geburtstag, Kroner Themata, Stuttgart, 80; Kreuzwege deutscher Geschichte und Literaturgeschichte: Das Treffen in Telgte von Gunter Grass, Selecta, Vol 1, 80/81; Der Butt: Lyrische und graphische Quellen, In: Gunter Grass' Der Butt: Critical Essays, Houston Ger Studies, Vol III, 80/81; Gabriele Wohmann: Eine Einfuhrung, Selecta, Vol 2, 81; Besuch Der Alten Dame, Diesterweg, Frankfurt, 81; contribr, The Electronic Language Translator: Teaching Tool or Teacher Substitute?, In: Sprache und Literatur, Festschrift fur Arval L Streadbeck zum 65, Geburtstag, Lang, Bern, 81; The Critical Reception of The Flounder in the United States: Epic and Graphic Aspects, In: Gunter Grass's The Flounder in Critical Perspective, AMS Press, 82; Gunter Grass: Zeichnungen und Texte, 1954-1977, In: Zeichnen & Schreiben, Luchterhand, Berlin, 8/82. *Mailing Add:* Dept of Mod & Class Lang Univ of Wyoming Laramie WY 82071

MAYERS, MARVIN KEENE, b Canton, Ohio, Oct 25, 27; m 52; c 2. ANTHROPOLOGY, LINGUISTICS. *Educ:* Wheaton Col, BA, 49; Fuller Theol Sem, MDiv, 52; Univ Chicago, MA, 58, PhD(anthrop), 60. *Prof Exp:* Field tech transl, Summer Inst Ling, 52-65; prof anthrop, Wheaton Col, 65-74; prof ling, Univ Tex, Arlington, 74-82; prof, Tex Sch Int Ling, Dallas, 74-82, dir, 76-82; PROF INTERCULT STUDIES, BIOLA COL, 82- *Mem:* Am Anthrop Asn. *Res:* Cross cultural communication, social anthropology; cross cultural education. *Publ:* Ed, Pocomchi Texts, Summer Inst Ling & Univ Okla, 58; auth, The phonemes of Pocomchi, Anthrop Ling, 60; The Pocomchi: A Sociolinguistic Study, Univ Chicago, 61; ed, Languages of Guatemala, Mouton, 65; co-auth, Reshaping Evangelical Higher Education, Zondervan, 72; auth, Christianity Confronts Culture, Zondervan, 74; A Look at Latin American Lifestyles, Summer Inst Ling, 76; co-auth, Cultural Anthropology, A Christian Perspective, Zondervan, 78; auth, A look at Filipino lifestyles, Summer Inst Ling, 80. *Mailing Add:* Dept of Anthrop Biola Col La Mirada CA 90638

MAYERSON, PHILIP, Classics. See Vol I

MAYES, JANIS ALENE, b Houston, Tex, July 7, 49. AFRICAN LITERATURE, FRENCH LITERATURE. *Educ:* Fisk Univ, BA, 71; Brown Univ, MA, 73, PhD(French), 75. *Prof Exp:* ASST PROF COMP LIT, UNIV TEX-DALLAS, 75- *Mem:* African Lit Asn; MLA. *Res:* Modern African fiction; Modern Ivorian literature; uses of irony in African, Caribbean and African-American literature. *Publ:* Ed, Mundus Artium: Selection of African Writers and Artists, Mundus Artium, 76; auth, Bernard Dadie and the aesthetics of the chronique, Presence Africaine, 77; Uses of irony in Modern African fiction, In: History of African Literature in European Languages, Int Comp Lit Asn, (in press). *Mailing Add:* Fac of Comp Lit Univ of Tex Dallas Box 688 Richardson TX 75080

MAYFIELD, MILTON RAY, b Cullman Co, Ala, Jan 14, 36; m 56; c 1. SPANISH, LATIN-AMERICAN HISTORY. *Educ:* Birmingham-Southern Col, BA, 60; Univ Ala, Tuscaloosa, MA, 63, PhD(admin higher educ), 77. *Prof Exp:* From instr to asst prof, 63-69, ASSOC PROF SPAN & CHMN DEPT FOREIGN LANG, UNIV MONTEVALLO, 69- *Mem:* SAtlantic Mod Lang Asn; Am Asn Teachers Span & Port. *Mailing Add:* Dept of Foreign Lang Col of Arts & Sci Univ of Montevallo Montevallo AL 35115

MAYNE, JUDITH, b Grove City, Pa, Feb 26, 48. FRENCH, FILM. *Educ:* Indiana Univ Pa, BA, 70; State Univ NY Buffalo, MA, 72, PhD(French), 75. *Prof Exp:* Lectr comp lit, Univ Wis-Milwaukee, 74-76; asst prof comp lit, 76-77, ASST PROF ROMANCE LANG, OHIO STATE UNIV, 77- *Concurrent Pos:* Fel film study, Ctr 20th Century Studies, Univ Wis-Milwaukee, 76-77. *Mem:* MLA; Soc Cinema Studies. *Res:* Film and literature; women in literature and film; French cinema. *Publ:* Auth, King Kong and the ideology of spectacle, Quart Rev Film Studies, fall 76; S/Z and film criticism, Jump Cut, fall 76; Kino-truth and Kino-praxis: Vertov's Man with a Movie Camera, Cine-tracts, 8/77; Fassbinder and spectatorship, New Ger Critique, fall, 77; Hiroshima Mon Amour: Ways of seeing, ways of telling, Purdue Film Studies Annual, 78; Mediation, the novelistic, and film narrative, Narrative Strategies, 81; The woman at the keyhole: Women's cinema and feminist criticism, 81 & Female narration, women's cinema, 82, New German Critique. *Mailing Add:* Dept of Romance Lang 248 Dieter Cunz Hall Ohio State Univ 1841 Millikin Rd Columbus OH 43201

MAZEIKA, EDWARD JOHN, b Shenandoah, Pa, May 28, 26; m 53; c 3. DEVELOPMENTAL PSYCHOLINGUISTICS. *Educ:* Pa State Col, BA, 51; Univ Houston, MA, 58; Univ Rochester, PhD(ling), 71. *Prof Exp:* Instr psychol, Rochester Inst Technol, 65-67; res assoc ling, Univ Houston, 68-73; asst prof, 75-80, ASSOC PROF ENGLISH & LING, MORNINGSIDE COL, 80- *Concurrent Pos:* Vis prof psychol, Univ Houston, 67-68; vis prof ling, Tex Southern Univ, 71; partic, J J Rousseau Inst, Univ Geneva, 74. *Mem:* Soc Res Child Develop; Ling Soc Am. *Res:* Linguistic ontogenesis; bilingualism; genetic epistemology. *Publ:* Auth, Language loyalty in the Barrios of Houston, Texas, J Ling Asn Southwest, 1/76; The description of an instrment to assess the receptive language of monolingual or bilingual (Spanish/English) children 12 to 36 months of age, Proc 1st Int Conf Frontiers in Lang Proficiency & Dominance Testing, 77; The Houston Parent-Child Development Orthopsychiat. *Mailing Add:* Dept of English Morningside Col Sioux City IA 51106

MAZUR, OLEH, b Ukraine; US citizen; m 62; c 1. ROMANCE LANGUAGES. *Educ:* Univ Pa, BA, 60, MA, 63, PhD(Span), 66. *Prof Exp:* Asst prof, 65-71, assoc prof, 71-82, PROF SPAN, VILLANOVA UNIV, 82- *Concurrent Pos:* Res grant, Villanova Univ, 78 & Am Philos Soc, Penrose Fund, 78. *Mem:* MLA; Int Fed Mod Lang & Lit; Ukrainian Am Asn Univ Prof; Shevchenko Sci Soc; Northeast Mod Lang Asn. *Res:* Spanish Golden Age and 16th century drama; Spanish 20th century prose and theater; Ukrainian 20th century prose. *Publ:* Auth, Various folkloric impacts upon the salvaje in the Spanish comedia, Hisp Rev, 68; Lope de Vega's salvajes, indios and barbaros, Iberoromania, 70; Different aspects of love in Lope de Vega's salvajes, indios and barbaros, Northeast Mod Lang Asn Newslett, 70; El teatro de Sebastian de Horozco con una breve historia del teatro espanol anterior a Lope de Vega: Tipos, modos y temas, Rocana, 77; Los campesinos de Sebastian de Horozco y sus contrafiguras en algunos teatros europeos, In: Studies in Honor of Raymond R MacCurdy, 82. *Mailing Add:* Dept of Mod Lang & Lit Villanova Univ Villanova PA 19085

MAZZA, ROSARIO RAPHAEL, b Trinidad, Colo, July 2, 15. FOREIGN LANGUAGES & LITERATURES. *Educ:* St Louis Univ, AB, 39, MA, 41; Univ NMex, PhD(Span & Luso-Brazilian studies), 56. *Prof Exp:* From asst prof to assoc prof Span lit, 57-72, actg chmn dept mod lang, 59-61, chmn, 61-69, PROF SPAN LIT, ST LOUIS UNIV, 72- *Concurrent Pos:* Lang consult, Peace Corps for Hunduras, 61. *Mem:* MLA; Am Asn Teachers Span & Port. *Res:* Neo-Platonism in Spanish literature--a Christian heritage; methods of teaching college poetry--evolution of form and ideas; 16 and 17th century Spanish literature, especially prose. *Publ:* Auth, Juan Ruiz: libro den buen amor, 68 & Garcilaso de la Vega: Spanish poet, 68, In: Catholic Encyclopedia, Holt. *Mailing Add:* Dept of Modern Languages St Louis Univ 221 N Grand Blvd St Louis MO 63103

MAZZARA, RICHARD ALFRED, b Trinidad, Colo, July 2, 15. FOREIGN LANGUAGES & LITERATURES. *Educ:* St Louis Univ, AB, 39, MA, 41; Univ NMex, PhD(Span & PhD(Span & Luso-Brazilian studies), 56. *Prof Exp:* From asst prof to assoc prof Span lit, 57-72, actg chmn dept mod lang, 59-61, chmn, 61-69, PROF SPAN LIT, ST LOUIS UNIV, 72- *Concurrent Pos:* Lang consult, Peace Corps for Hunduras, 61. *Mem:* MLA; Am Asn Teachers Span & Port; Am Asn Teachers French. *Res:* Modern Brazilian drama; translations of Latin American works; 17th century French literature. *Publ:* Auth, Structure and verisimilitude in the novels of Erico Verissimo, PMLA, Vol 80, No 4, The hope of God's kingdom of earth in 17th century French tragedy, Forum, Vol 7, No 3; The Phaedo and Theophile de Viau's Traicte de l'immortalite de l'am, Fr Rev, Vol 40, No 3. *Mailing Add:* Dept of Modern Languages & Literatures St Louis Univ St Louis MO 63103

MAZZEO, GUIDO ETTORE, b New York, NY, Aug 14, 14; m 41; c 1. SPANISH LANGUAGE & LITERATURE. *Educ:* City Col New York, BA, 36; Columbia Univ, MA, 38, PhD, 61. *Prof Exp:* Instr Span, Fordham Univ, 38-46; asst prof, US Navy Intel Sch, Washington, DC, 46-50; conf doc specialist, Inter-Am Defense Bd, Washington, DC, 50-58; assoc prof, 58-68, PROF SPAN, GEORGE WASHINGTON UNIV, 68-, CHMN DEPT ROMANCE LANG, 77- *Concurrent Pos:* Instr, City Col New York, 39-40 & Columbia Univ, 40-46. *Mem:* MLA; Am Asn Teachers Span & Port; Am Soc 18th Century Studies. *Res:* Spanish Jesuit exiles of XVIII century; Spanish literature of XVIII and XIX centuries. *Publ:* Auth, The Abate of Juan Andres: Literary Historian of the XVIII Century, Hisp Inst US, 65; Contrastes entre el teatro neoclasico y romantico, Hispania, 66; Spanish literature: Neoclassic and Romantic period, In: New Catholic Encyclopedia, McGraw, 67; Los jesuitas espanoles del siglo XVIII en el destierro, Rev Hisp Mod, 68; ed, Ensayos espanoles, Prentice-Hall, 73; auth, Los jesuitas espanoles y la cultura hispanoitaliana del siglo XVIII, Centro Asoc Tortosa, 77; Poligrafia y enciclopedismo en el Abate Juan Andres, jesuita expulso dieciochista, Bull 18th Century Studies, 77; The noticias literarias of the Abate Juan Andres, Hisp Ital Studies, 78. *Mailing Add:* Dept of Romance Lang George Washington Univ Washington DC 20052

MAZZOCCO, ANGELO, b Isernia, Italy, May 13, 36; nat US. ROMANCE LANGUAGES & LITERATURES. *Educ:* Ohio State Univ, BA & BSc, 59, MA, 63; Univ Calif, Berkeley, PhD(Romance lang & lit), 73. *Prof Exp:* Instr Span, John Carroll Univ, 62-65; teaching asst Ital, Univ Calif, Berkeley, 66-69; asst prof Ital, Northern Ill Univ, 70-75; asst prof Ital & Span, 75-76, ASSOC PROF ITAL & SPAN, MT HOLYOKE COL, 76-, CHMN DEPT, 81- *Concurrent Pos:* Univ Calif Italian-Am traveling fel, 69-70; fel, Nat Endowment for Humanities, 81. *Mem:* MLA; Am Asn Teachers Ital; Dante Soc Am; Renaissance Soc Am; Am Asn Teachers Span & Port. *Res:* Latin humanism; medieval and Renaissance Italian and Spanish literature. *Publ:* Auth, Il senso della caducita nella poesia del Petrarca, Lingua Bella, 74; Petrarch, Poggio, and Biondo: Humanism's Foremost Interpreters of Roman Ruins, In: Francis Petrarch, Six Centuries Later: A Symposium, NCSRLL & Newberry Libr, 75; The Antiquarianism of Francesco Petrarca, J Medieval & Renaissance Studies, 77; Strains of Castiglione's Il Cortegiano in the Squire of Lazarillo de Tormes, In: The Two Hesperias, Literary Studies in Honor of Joseph Fucilla, Jose Porrua, Turanzas, SA, 78; Some philological aspects of Biondo Flavio's Roma Truimphans, Humanistica Lovaniensia, J Neo-Latin Studies, 79. *Mailing Add:* Dept of Span & Ital Mt Holyoke Col South Hadley MA 01075

MAZZOLA, MICHAEL LEE, b Frankfort, NY, Jan 19, 41. ROMANCE LINGUISTICS. *Educ:* Le Moyne Col, NY, AB, 62; Middlebury Col, MA, 64; Cornell Univ, PhD(Romance ling), 67. *Prof Exp:* Lectr French, Cornell Univ, 65-66, asst prof ling, 66-68; asst prof French & Ital, Ind Univ, Bloomington, 68-75; asst prof, 75-79, ASSOC PROF FRENCH & ITAL, NORTHERN ILL UNIV, 79- *Mem:* Ling Soc Am; MLA. *Res:* French and Italian dialectology; French phonology and syntax; general linguistics. *Publ:* Auth, La position du Sicilien dans la reconstruction du proto-Roman, Actes du XII eme Congres International de Linguistique et Philologie Romanes, 69; Proto-Romance and Sicilian, Peter de Ridder, Lisse, Neth, 76; The Rome-Ancona isoglosses and the Norman kingdom, In: Ensayos linguisticos: homenaje a R A Hall, Ed Playor, Madrid, 77; The Romance Stammbaum in the South, Semasia, Vol V, 78. *Mailing Add:* Dept of Foreign Lang & Lit Northern Ill Univ De Kalb IL 60115

MAZZOTTA, GIUSEPPE F, b Curinga, Italy, Jan 1, 42; Can citizen; m 72; c 3. ITALIAN LANGUAGE, LITERATURE. *Educ:* Univ Toronto, BA, 65, MA, 66; Cornell Univ, PhD(Ital), 69. *Prof Exp:* Asst prof Italian, Cornell Univ, 69-70 & Yale Univ, 70-72; assoc prof, Medieval Italian, Univ Toronto, 72-73; assoc prof 73-78, PROF ITALIAN & ESTHETICS, CORNELL UNIV, 78- *Concurrent Pos:* Vis prof, Grad Ctr, City Univ NY, 77-78 & Yale Univ, fall 79. *Res:* Dante; esthetics; Medieval and Renaissance literature. *Publ:* Auth, The Decameron: The marginality of literature, Univ Toronto Quart, fall 72; Dante's literary typology, Modern Lang Notes, 1/72; contribr, Enciclopedia Dasntesca, Vol V, Rome, 74; auth, Petrarch and the language of self, Studies Philos, 7/78; Dante, Poet of the Desert, Princeton Univ Press, 79. *Mailing Add:* Dept Romance Studies Cornell Univ Ithaca NY 14853

MEAD, ROBERT G, JR, b Cleveland, Ohio, Dec 30, 13; m 45. SPANISH. *Educ:* Univ Calif, Los Angeles, AB, 41, MA, 42; Univ Mich, PhD(Romance lang & Span), 49. *Prof Exp:* Instr English, Acad Anness, Mex, 36-37; res analyst, Off Strategic Serv, 42-45 & US Dept State, 45-47; from instr to assoc prof, 49-60, PROF FOREIGN LANG, UNIV CONN, 60- *Concurrent Pos:* Assoc ed, Hispania, 52-56, ed, 57-62, adv ed, 63-; int adv ed, Hisp Am Report, 58-; consult, Latin Am studies, US Off Educ, 60-; mem bd dir, Northeast Conf Teaching Foreign Lang, 65-, chmn, 68; assoc ed, Latin Am Res Rev Bd, 65-; mem int jury, Rodo Centennial, Orgn Am States, Montevideo, 73; mem adv bd, Calif Inst Foreign Studies, 70-; adv ed, Revista de estudios hispanicos, 76- *Honors & Awards:* Distinguished Leadership Award, Northeast Conf Teaching Foreign Lang, 71. *Mem:* MLA; Am Asn Teachers Span & Port (pres, 65); Am Coun Teaching Foreign Lang; Int Inst Iberoam Lit; Latin Am Studies Asn. *Res:* Spanish American literature, especially the essay; history of ideas in Spanish America; Mexican literature. *Publ:* Auth, Gonzales Prada: prosista y pensador, Hisp Inst US, 55; Breve historia de ensayo hispanoamericano, 56, Temas hispanoamericanos, 59 & ed, Iberoamerica: sus lenguas y literatuas vistas desde los Estados Unidos, 62, Ed De Andrea, Mex; auth, Perspectivas interamericanas: literatura y libertad, Las Americas, 67; coauth, Historia del ensayo hispano-americano, Ed De Andrea, 73; auth, Sarmiento, Marti y los Estados Unidos, Cuadernos Americanos, 76. *Mailing Add:* Dept of Romance Lang Univ of Conn Storrs CT 06268

MEAD, WILLIAM CURTIS, b Cortland, NY, July 30, 25; m 52; c 2. FRENCH, COMPARATIVE LITERATURE. *Educ:* Univ Md, BA, 47; Yale Univ, PhD(French lit), 58. *Prof Exp:* From instr to asst prof French, Smith Col, 53-64; assoc prof, Purdue Univ, 64-66; ASSOC PROF FRENCH, UNIV CALIF, RIVERSIDE, 66- *Mem:* MLA. *Res:* Eighteenth century French; Rousseau; Romanticism. *Publ:* Auth, Jean Jacques Rousseau ou Le romancier enchaine, Presses Universitaires de France, 66; Manon Lescaut, c'est moi, L'Esprit Createur, summer 66; Gautier and Romantic fiction, Univ Calif Studies Comp Lit, 67; The puzzle of Prevost, L'Esprit Createur, summer 72. *Mailing Add:* Dept of Lang & Lit Humanities 3333 Univ of Calif Riverside CA 92502

MEADOWS, GAIL KEITH, b Galesburg, Ill, July 17, 14. PHILOLOGY, MEDIEVAL LITERATURE. *Educ:* Knox Col, AB, 34; Harvard Univ, AM, 38, PhD, 44; Univ Perugia, dipl, 39. *Prof Exp:* Tutor, Queens Col, NY, 40-42; instr, Harvard Univ, 44-46; asst prof, Amherst Col, 46-48; assoc prof Romance lang, Stanford Univ, 48-61; chmn dept foreign lang, 61-66, dir div humanities, 62-69, EMER PROF, C W POST COL, LONG ISLAND UNIV,

80- *Mem:* Mediaeval Acad Am. *Res:* Old French and Italian; Romanian; classical philology. *Publ:* Auth, The Development of Vulgar Latin Hiatus Groups in the Romance Languages. *Mailing Add:* 95 Summit Ave Jersey City NJ 07304

MEANS, JOHN BARKLEY, b Cincinnati, Ohio, Jan 2, 39. PORTUGUESE & BRAZILIAN LITERATURE. *Educ:* Univ Ill, Urbana, BA, 60, MA, 63, PhD(ling), 68. *Prof Exp:* Latin Am res analyst, US Govt, Washington, DC, 62-64; asst prof, 68-72, co-chmn dept, 71-75, assoc prof, 72-82, PROF SPAN & PORT, TEMPLE UNIV, 82-, DIR, CTR CRITICAL LANG, 75- *Concurrent Pos:* Exec dir, Nat Asn Self-Instruct Lang Prog. *Mem:* Am Asn Teachers Span & Port; Am Coun Teaching Foreign Lang; Nat Asn Self-Instr Lang Progs; Asn Asian Studies; Latin Am Studies Asn. *Res:* Self-instructional foreign language learning and language teaching methods; modern Brazilian prose fiction; Luso-Brazilian civilization and culture. *Publ:* Auth, Political kidnappings and terrorism, 70 & Anti-Americanism in the neighborhood, 71, NAm Rev; Essays on Brazilian Literature, Simon & Schuster, 71; Brazil: The hemisphere's lost empire, NAm Rev, 72. *Mailing Add:* Ctr for Critical Lang Temple Univ Philadelphia PA 19122

MECKE, GUNTER ADOLF, b Oberhausen, Rheinland, Ger, Apr 26, 28; m 65; c 2. GERMANIC & CLASSICAL PHILOLOGY. *Educ:* Ludwig-Maximilians Univ, Munich, PhD(medieval Ger), 64. *Prof Exp:* Asst prof Ger, Goethe Inst, Munich, 59- 65; prof Ger cult, Western Ill Univ, 65-66; asst clin psychol, Duke Univ, 67-68; ASSOC PROF LATIN, GER & HUMAN DEVELOP, CALIF STATE UNIV, HAYWARD, 68- *Res:* Psychology of language and literature; narcissism, especially homosexuality; early infantile autism. *Publ:* Auth, Zwischenrede, Erzählerfigur und Erzählhaltung in Hartmanns von Aue Erec, Uni-Druck, Munich, 65; Hair or, the Ligurinus Shock: On a Narcissistic Crisis in Puberty and its Recurrence in the Man of Fifty, Libra, 75, transl in Ger, Psyche, 4-5/75; Die Trompeten der Nacht: Franz Kafkas offenbares geheimnis: Eine Psychopathographie, Psyche, 78. *Mailing Add:* Dept of Foreign Lang & Lit Calif State Univ Carlos Bee Blvd Hayward CA 94542

MECUM, KENT BRUCE, b Chicago, Ill, June 22, 30; m 55; c 3. SPANISH AMERICAN LITERATURE & INTELLECTUAL HISTORY. *Educ:* Butler Univ, BS, 52; Ind Univ, Bloomington, MA, 63, PhD(Hisp lit), 71. *Prof Exp:* Lectr Span & Port, Ind Univ, Bloomington, 67-68; from instr to asst prof Romance lang, 68-78, ASSOC PROF ROMANCE LANG, DEPAUW UNIV, 78- *Mem:* Am Asn Teachers Span & Port; Conf Latin Hist; Latin Am Studies Asn; Midwest Asn Latin Am Studies (pres, 75-76). *Res:* Enlightenment; Ecuador; Mexico. *Publ:* Auth, Vicente Rocafuerte, humanista ecuatoriano, Congreso Latinoam Sociol, San Jose, Costa Rica, 74; El idealismo practico de Vicente Rocafuerte, un verdadero americano independiente y libre, Cajica, Puebla, Mex, 76. *Mailing Add:* Dept of Romance Lang DePauw Univ Greencastle IN 46135

MEDINA, JEREMY TYLER, b Orange, NJ, Aug 1, 42; m 66; c 3. SPANISH, SPANISH LITERATURE. *Educ:* Princeton Univ, AB, 64; Middlebury Span Sch, Spain, MA, 66; Univ Pa, PhD(Span), 70. *Prof Exp:* Instr Span, Phillips Acad, Andover, Mass, 64-65; from instr to asst prof, 68-75, dir in residence, acad year in Spain, 74-75, 79-80, assoc prof, 75-82, PROF SPAN, HAMILTON COL, 82-, GEN DIR ACAD YEAR IN SPAIN, 74- *Mem:* MLA; AAUP; Am Asn Teachers Span & Port. *Res:* Nineteenth century Spanish realism; generations of 1898 and 1927 in Spain. *Publ:* Auth, Theme and structure in Herrera's Cancion de Lepanto, 72 & Theme and structure of Alarcon's El sombrero de tres picos, 73, Romance Notes; Introduction to Spanish Literature: An Analytical Approach, Harper 74, Krieger, 82; The artistry of Blasco Ibanez' Canas y barro, Hispania, 77; Spanish Realism: The Theory and Practice of a Concept in the Nineteenth Century, Jose Porrua, 78; The artistry of Blaco Ibanez' Flor de Mayo, Hispania, 82; Leopoldo Alas (Clarin), Vicente Blasco Ibanex & Benito Perez Galdos, In: Critical Survey of Long Fiction, Salem Press (in press). *Mailing Add:* Dept of Romance Lang Hamilton Col Clinton NY 13323

MEDISH, VADIM, Russian & East European Area Studies. See Vol I

MEDLIN, DOROTHY MOSER, b Monroe, NC, Sept 21, 31. FRENCH. *Educ:* Winthrop Col, AB, 53; Tulane Univ, PhD(French), 66. *Prof Exp:* Teacher, High Schs, NC, 53-59; instr, 63-64, from asst prof to assoc prof, 65-72, PROF FRENCH, WINTHROP COL, 72- *Concurrent Pos:* Nat Endowment for Humantities summer sem, 76. *Mem:* Am Asn Teachers Fr; MLA; Am Coun Teaching Foreign Lang; AAUP. *Res:* Eighteenth century French literature. *Publ:* Auth, The Verbal Art of Jean-Francois Regnard, Tulane Univ, 66; Benjamin Franklin and the French language, Fr-Am Rev, fall 77; Voltaire, Morellet, and LeFranc de Pompignan, Studies Voltaire & 18th Century, 77; Thomas Jefferson, Andre Morellet, and the French version of Notes on the State of Virginia, William & Mary Quart, 1/78; Andre Morellet, translator of liberal thought, 78 & Andre Morellet and the idea of progress, 80, Studies Voltaire & 18th Century; Benjamin Franklin's Ragatelles for Madame Helvetius, Early Am Lit, 80. *Mailing Add:* Dept of Mod Lang Winthrop Col Rock Hill SC 29730

MEEHAN, THOMAS CLARKE, b Detroit, Mich, Nov 22, 31; m 57; c 2. ROMANCE LANGUAGES. *Educ:* Wayne State Univ, BA, 53; Univ Mich, MA, 57, PhD(Span), 65. *Prof Exp:* Instr Span, Dartmouth Col, 61-64; from instr to asst prof, Brown Univ, 64-67; asst prof Span Am lit, 67-71, ASSOC PROF SPAN AM LIT, UNIV ILL, URBANA, 71- *Mem:* MLA; Inst Int Lit Iberam; Am Asn Teachers Span & Port; Asoc Int Hispanistas. *Res:* Spanish American literature especially modern fiction and drama; contemporary Argentine fiction; modern Spanish novel. *Publ:* Auth, Ernesto Sabato's sexual metaphysics: Theme and form in El Tunel, Mod Lang Notes, 3/68; El desdoblamiento interior en Dona Ines de Azorin, Cuadernos Hispanoamericanos, 69; Estructura y tema de El sueno de los heroes por Adolfo Bioy Casares, Ky Romance Quart, 73; Jenaro Prieto: The man and his work, Tradition and Renewal: Essays 20th Century Latin Am Lit & Cult, 75; Bibliografia de y sobre la literature fantastica, Revista Iberoamericana, 46: 243-256; Essays on Argentine Narrators, Valencia, Spain, 82. *Mailing Add:* Dept of Spanish Italian & Portuguese Univ Illinois Urbana IL 61801

MEGENNEY, WILLIAM WILBER, b Langley AFB, Va, Apr 13, 40; m 63; c 3. LATIN AMERICAN LINGUISTICS. *Educ:* Rutgers Univ, BA, 62; Univ NMex, MA, 67, PhD(Latin Am studies), 69. *Prof Exp:* ASSOC PROF SPAN & PORT, UNIV CALIF, RIVERSIDE, 69- *Mem:* Am Asn Teachers Span & Port; Ling Soc Am; Caribbean Studies Asn. *Res:* Latin American literature. *Publ:* Auth, Problemas raciales y culturales en dos piezas de Demetrio Aguilera Malta, Cuadernos Am, 5/71; co-ed, Research Guide to the Godoi-Diaz-Perez Collection in the Library of the University of California, Riverside, Univ Calif, Riverside, 73; auth, Apuntes sobre el lexico de la costa colombiana, Hispania, 12/73; The Black Puerto Rican: An analysis of racial attitudes, Phylon, 3/74; The Black in Hispanic-Caribbean and Brazilian poetry: A comparative perspective, Revista/Rev Interamericana, 75; The world and beyond: Mario de Sa-Carneiro's struggle for perfection, Hispania, 76; El elemento subsaharico en el lexico costeno de Colombia, Revista espanola de lingüistica, 7-12/76. *Mailing Add:* Dept of Lit & Lang Univ of Calif Riverside CA 92521

MEGOW, GERHARD F, b Markirch, France, Sept 15, 13; US citizen; m 42; c 2. FOREIGN LANGUAGES. *Educ:* Ind Univ, BA, 51, MA, 52, PhD, 59. *Prof Exp:* Asst prof Ger, Murray State Col, 54-59; from asst prof to prof, 59-76, EMER PROF GER, HOPE COL, 76- *Mem:* MLA; Am Asn Teachers Ger. *Res:* German literature 18th and 19th century; modern literature. *Publ:* Contribr, Encyclopedia of World Literature, Ungar, 67. *Mailing Add:* Dept of Foreign Languages Hope College Holland MI 49423

MEHL, JANE RIMA, b Philadelphia, Pa, Oct 17, 45; m 67; c 2. GERMANIC LANGUAGE & LITERATURE. *Educ:* Douglass Col, BA, 67; Middlebury Col, MA, 68; State Univ NY Binghamton, PhD(Ger), 74. *Prof Exp:* Teacher Ger, Bridgewater-Raritan High Sch, 67-68; teaching asst, State Univ NY Binghamton, 68-70; part-time lectr, Catonsville Community Col, 72; instr, 73-74 & 76, ASST PROF GER, UNIV MD, COLLEGE PARK, 77- *Concurrent Pos:* Am Philos Soc fel, 78; spec training consult to US small bus admin, 81- *Mem:* MLA; Am Asn Teachers Ger; Am Goethe Soc; SAtlantic Mod Lang Asn; Soc Ger Lit 16th & 17th Centuries. *Res:* Baroque lyric; Emblemata; Romantic lyric. *Publ:* Auth, Catharina Regina von Greiffenberg: Modern traits in a baroque poet, SAB (in prep); Lexical Functions in Building German Vocabulary, Unterrichtspraxis. *Mailing Add:* Dept of Ger & Slavic Lang & Lit Univ of Md College Park MD 20742

MEI, TSU-LIN, b Peking, China, Feb 14, 33; m 61; c 3. CHINESE LINGUISTICS, PHILOSOPHY. *Educ:* Oberlin Col, BA, 54; Harvard Univ, MA, 55; Yale Univ, PhD(philos), 62. *Prof Exp:* Instr Chinese, Univ Pittsburgh, 60-61; instr philos, Yale Univ, 62-64; from asst prof to assoc prof Chinese, Harvard Univ, 64-71; assoc prof, 71-78, dir China-Japan prog, 77-80, PROF CHINESE LIT & PHILOS, CORNELL UNIV, 78- *Concurrent Pos:* Mem bd dir, Asn Asian Studies, 74-77, mem China & Inner Asia Coun, 74-77. *Mem:* Am Philos Asn; Ling Soc Am. *Res:* Chinese historical linguistics; Chinese philosophy; Chinese poetry. *Publ:* Auth, Chinese Grammar and the Linguistic Movement in Philosophy, Rev Metaphys, 61; Tones and prosody in Middle Chinese and the origin of the rising tone, 70 & coauth, Syntax, diction and imagery in T'ang poetry, 71, Harvard J Asiatic Studies; auth, Tones and tone sandhi in 16th century Mandarin, J Chinese Ling, 77; coauth, Meaning, metaphor and allusion in T'ang poetry, Harvard J Asiatic Studies, 78; auth, Chronological strata in derivation by tone-change, Zhongguo Yuwen, 80. *Mailing Add:* Dept of Asian Studies Cornell Univ Ithaca NY 14853

MEID, VOLKER, b Darmstadt, Ger, May 8, 40. GERMAN LITERATURE. *Educ:* Univ Frankfurt, PhD(Ger lit), 65. *Prof Exp:* Asst prof Ger lit & folklore, Univ Frankfurt, 66-69; asst prof Ger lit, Univ NC, Chapel Hill, 69-70; assoc prof, 70-75, PROF GER LIT, UNIV MASS, AMHERST, 75- *Mem:* MLA; Am Asn Teachers Ger. *Res:* Seventeenth century studies; history of the novel. *Publ:* Ed, Philipp von Zesen, Assenat, 1670, Niemeyer, Tübingen, 67; auth, Barocknovellen? Zu Harsdörffers moralischen Geschichten, Euphorion, 68; ed, Philipp von Zesen, Werke, de Gruyter, Berlin & NY, Vols V, VI & VII, 70, 72 & 77; auth, Heilige und weltliche Geschichten: Zesens biblische Romane, In: Philipp von Zesen 1619-1969, Steiner, 72; Vergils Aeneis als Barockroman, In: Rezeption und Produktion Zwischen 1570 und 1730, Francke, 72; ed, Der Deutsche Barockroman, Metzler, Stuttgart, 74; auth, Abolutismus und Barockroman, In: Der Deutsche Roman und seine Historischen und Politischen Bedingungen, Francke, Bern & München, 77. *Mailing Add:* Dept of Ger Lang & Lit Univ of Mass Amherst MA 01003

MEIDEN, WALTER, b Grand Haven, Mich, July 12, 07. ROMANCE LANGUAGES. *Educ:* Univ Mich, AB, 31; Ohio State Univ, MA, 33, PhD, 45. *Prof Exp:* From asst to prof, 31-74, EMER PROF ROMANCE LANG, OHIO STATE UNIV, 74- *Mem:* MLA. *Res:* Visio Pauli; methods of modern language teaching; Old French philology. *Publ:* Coauth, Onze Contes: An Introduction to Reading French, 56 & auth, Contes de Michelle Maurois, 66, Houghton; Anouilh, Le Voyageur sans Bagage, Holt, sch ed, 73; French for Oral and Written Review, Holt, 3rd ed (in prep); Beginning French, 5th ed, 78 & Beginning Spanish, 4th ed, 79, Houghton; Spanish for Oral and Written Review, Holt, 81. *Mailing Add:* Dept of Romance Lang Ohio State Univ Columbus OH 43210

MEIER, MARGA, b Bad Kissingen, Ger, Apr 22, 22. LANGUAGES. *Educ:* Univ Wurzburg, PhD, 44. *Prof Exp:* Court interpreter, Nürnberg War Crimes Trials, 46-49 & US Court Appeals, Frankfurt, 49-52; Assoc prof Ger, 55-76, PROF LANG, IND CENT UNIV, 76- *Mem:* Am Asn Teachers Ger; Foreign Lang Teachers Asn. *Mailing Add:* Dept of Foreign Lang Indiana Cent Univ Indianapolis IN 46227

MEINHARDT, WARREN LEE, b Lennox, Calif, Mar 30, 31; m 53; c 4. LATIN AMERICAN LITERATURE. *Educ:* Pomona Col, BA, 53; Stanford Univ, MA, 55: Univ Calif Berkeley, PhD(Romance lang & lit), 65. *Prof Exp:* Asst instr Span, Univ Ill, Urbana, 60-64; from instr to asst prof, 64-69; asst prof foreign lang, 69-73, ASSOC PROF FOREIGN LANG & LIT, SOUTHERN ILL UNIV, CARBONDALE, 73- *Concurrent Pos:* Fac fel,

Univ Ill, Urbana, 66; Univ Ill fac fel, 66 & 73; Nat Endowment for Humanities fels, summer 78 & 81. *Mem:* Am Asn Teachers Span & Port. *Res:* Latin American prose fiction; the new Latin American novel; Chicano literature. *Publ:* Auth, Entrando a El tunel de Ernesto Sabato, Rev Iberoam, 72; coauth, Hacia una bibliografia de la novela contemporanea en Latinoamerica, Nueva Narativa Hispanoam, 72; auth, Cabrera Infante: Asi en el cuento como en la novela?, Chasqui, 72; Juan Zorrilla de San Martin, JAPOS, 4/81. *Mailing Add:* Dept of Foreign Lang & Lit Southern Ill Univ Carbondale IL 62901

MEININGER, ROBERT ALAN, b Torrington, Wyo, Mar 29, 38; m 62; c 1. ROMANCE LANGUAGES. *Educ:* Univ Wyo, BA, 61; Univ Nebr, MA, 64, PhD(Romance lang), 70. *Prof Exp:* Instr French, Univ Nebr, 68-70; asst prof, 70-72, assoc prof, 72-80, PROF FRENCH, NEBR WESLEYAN UNIV, 80-, CHMN DEPT, 72-, CHMN, HUMANITIES DIV, 78- *Mem:* MLA; Am Asn Teachers Fr. *Res:* Twentieth century French novel; Belgium cultural history. *Publ:* Auth, Belgian culture, In: Encycl Am, Grolier, 68 & 74. *Mailing Add:* Dept of Foreign Lang Nebr Wesleyan Univ Lincoln NE 68504

MELCUK, IGOR A, b Odessa, USSR, Oct 19, 32; Can citizen; m 60; c 3. LINGUISTICS, ARTIFICIAL INTELLIGENCE. *Educ:* Univ Moscow, MA, 56; Acad Sci, USSR, PhD(syntax), 62. *Hon Degrees:* Dr, Univ Besancon, France, 77. *Prof Exp:* From jr res fel to sr res fel, Inst Ling, Acad Sci, USSR, 56-76; vis prof ling, 77-78, PROF LING, UNIV MONTREAL, 78- *Mem:* Soc Ling Paris; Am Ling Soc; Asn Ling Can & Etats Unis. *Res:* General linguistics, with emphasis on semantics, syntax, and morphology; French lexicography; Russian studies. *Publ:* Auth, Towards a Theory of Meaning-Text Linguistic Models, Nauka Publ, Moscow, 74; Das Wort, Fink Verlag, Munich, 76; Studies in Dependency Syntax, Karoma Publ, 79; Animacy in Russian cardinal numerals and adjectives, Language, 56: 4; Meaning-text models: A recent trend in Soviet linguistics, Annual Rev Anthrop, 81; coauth, Un nouveau type de dictionnaire: Le dictionnaire explicatif et combinatoire du francais moderne, Cahiers de lexicologie, 38: 1; auth, Types de dependance syntagmatique entre les mots-formes d'une phrase, Bull S de lin de Paris, 76: 1; Towards a language of linguistics, Fink Verlag, Munich, 82; 160 scientific publ. *Mailing Add:* Ling Dept Univ Montreal Montreal PQ H3C 3J7 Can

MELE, JOSEPH CHARLES, Communication Arts. See Vol II

MELIA, DANIEL FREDERICK, b Fall River, Mass, Mar 2, 44. CELTIC LANGUAGES & LITERATURE. *Educ:* Harvard Col, BA, 66, Harvard Univ, MA, 70, PhD(Celtic lang & lit), 72. *Prof Exp:* Asst prof, 72-78, ASSOC PROF RHETORIC, UNIV CALIF, BERKELEY, 78-, ASSOC DEAN, COL LETT & SCI, 81- *Concurrent Pos:* Vis asst prof English, Univ Calif, Los Angeles, 73-74; Nat Endowment for Humanities jr res fel Celtic & Regents fac fel humanities, Univ Calif, 75. *Mem:* Celtic Studies Asn (secy-treas, 77-79); fel Medieval Acad Ireland; MLA; Medieval Acad Am; Am Folklore Soc. *Res:* Medieval Celtic literature; folklore and mythology; rhetoric and poetics. *Publ:* Auth, The Lughnasa musician in Ireland and Scotland, J Am Folklore, 68; auth, Parallel versions of the Boyhood Deeds of Cuchulainn, Forum Mod Lang Studies, 74; A note on translation, Z Celtische Philol, 76; The Grande Tromenie at Locronan: A major Breton Lughnasa celebration J Am Folkore, 78; Empty Figures in Irish syllabic poetry, Philol Quart, 78; Remarks on the structure and composition of the Ulster Death Tales, Studia Hibernica, 78; Some remarks on the affinities of Medieval Irish Saga, Acta Antiqua, 80; The Irish church in the Irish laws, Brit Archaeol Reports, 82. *Mailing Add:* Dept of Rhetoric Univ of Calif Berkeley CA 94720

MELLEN, PHILIP ALLAN, b Gardner, Mass, Dec 3, 42; m 63; c 1. GERMAN LITERATURE, GERMAN LANGUAGE. *Educ:* Portland State Univ, BA, 69, MA, 71; Univ Calif, Davis, PhD(Ger), 75. *Prof Exp:* ASST PROF GER, KENT STATE UNIV, 76- *Mem:* Am Asn Teachers Ger; Int Ver fur ger Sprachund Lit-wiss. *Res:* Nineteenth century literature; Gerhart Hauptmann; comparative literature. *Publ:* Gerhart Hauptmann and Utopia, Stuttgarter Arbeiten zur Germanistik, 76; Gerhart Hauptmann's Other Reality, Ger Notes, 76; Ambiguity and Intent in Die Judenbuche, Ger Notes, 78. *Mailing Add:* Dept of Ger Lang Kent State Univ Kent OH 44242

MELLIZO-CUADRADO, CARLOS, b Madrid, Spain, Oct 2, 42; m 70; c 2. CONTEMPORARY SPANISH LITERATURE. *Educ:* Univ Madrid, BA, 65, MA, 66, PhD(philos), 70. *Prof Exp:* From instr to assoc prof, 68-77, res grant, 73-74, PROF SPAN, UNIV WYO, 77- *Honors & Awards:* Iberoam Poets & Writers Guild Literary Award, 74; Good Teaching Award, Amoco Found, 75; Hucha de Plata Literary Award, Confederacion Espanola de Cajas de Ahorros, 77. *Mem:* Col Drs Philos & Lett, Spain. *Res:* British philosophy of the 18th century; 20th century Spanish thought. *Publ:* Auth, Los cocdrilos, Indice Editorial, 70; ed transl, Hume's Resumen del tratado de la naturaleza humana, 73 & Hume's Dialogos sobre la religion natural, 74, Aguilar, SA; ed, Homenaje a Azorin, Univ Wyo, 74; auth, Romero, La Encina Ed, 75; David Hume Hoy, Cuadernos Salmantinos, 76; co-ed, Ignacio Aldecoa: A collection of critical essays, 77 & ed, Aleixandre: Portrait of a novel prize, 77, Univ Wyo. *Mailing Add:* Dept of Mod Langs Univ of Wyo Laramie WY 82071

MELLOR, CHAUNCEY JEFFRIES, b Pittsburgh, Pa, Nov 10, 42; m 77. GERMANIC PHILOLOGY. *Educ:* Univ Chicago, BA, 65, MA, 67, PhD(Ger), 72. *Prof Exp:* Instr, 70-72, ASST PROF GER, UNIV TENN, KNOXVILLE, 72- *Concurrent Pos:* Ed, Der Spottvogel, Am Asn Teachers Ger, 72- *Mem:* Am Asn Teachers Ger; Ling Soc Am; MLA. *Res:* German lexicography. *Publ:* Auth, Jacob Grimm's use of the term Fremdwort, 72 & Theodor Mommsen, Daniel Sanders and the establishment of the term Lehnwort in German, 72, Mod Lang Notes; Contirbr, Selected Proceedings of MIFLC: Kriemhild and Hagen in MSS B and C of the Nibelungenlied, ETenn State Univ, 78; auth, Jacob Grimm's inclusion of loanwords and compounds in the Deutsches Wörterbuch, J English & Ger Philos, (in press). *Mailing Add:* Dept of Ger & Slavic Univ of Tenn Knoxville TN 37916

MELLOR, RONALD JOHN, b Brooklyn, NY, Sept, 30, 40; m 69; c 1. ANCIENT HISTORY, CLASSICS. *Educ:* Fordham Univ, AB, 62; Princeton Univ, AM, 65, PhD(classics), 67. *Prof Exp:* Asst prof classics, Stanford Univ, 65-75; res assoc Greek, Univ Col, London, 69-70, res fel Latin, 72-73; assoc prof, 76-82, PROF HIST, UNIV CALIF, LOS ANGELES, 82- *Concurrent Pos:* Fels, Nat Endowment for Humanities, 69 & Am Counc Learned Soc, 75; lectr, San Francisco Art Inst, 80. *Mem:* Am Philol Asn; Asn of Ancient Historians; Soc for Prom Roman Studies. *Res:* Roman history; Roman law; Hellenistic history. *Publ:* Auth, The Worship of the Goddess Roma in the Greek World, Vandenhoeck & Ruprecht, 75; The dedications on the Capitoline Hill, Chiron, 78; A new Roman military diploma, Bull of J Paul Getty Mus, 78; The historian and civil disobedience, Humanities Soc, 79; The Goddes Roma, Ajfstieg und Niedergang der Römischen Welt, 81. *Mailing Add:* Dept of Hist Univ of Calif 405 Hilgard Ave Los Angeles CA 90024

MELTZER, FRANCOISE CLAIRE, b Paris, France, July 1, 47; US & Fr citizen. COMPARATIVE LITERATURE, FRENCH LITERATURE. *Educ:* Ohio Univ, BA, 69; Univ Calif, Berkeley, MA, 70, PhD(comp lit), 75. *Prof Exp:* Asst prof, 75-80, ASSOC PROF COMP LIT & FRENCH, UNIV CHICAGO, 80- *Mem:* MLA. *Res:* Nineteenth and twentieth century French, German and English; psychoanalysis and literature; critical theory. *Publ:* Auth, Preliminary excavations of Robbe-Grillet's Phantom City, Chicago Rev, fall 76; transl, Robbe-Grillet's Topologie d'une cite Fantome, Chicago Rev, fall 76; Christian Metz Trucage and Cinema, Critical Inquiry, fall 77; auth, Color as cognition in French symbolist verse, Critical Inquiry, winter 78; Rimbaud's Voyelles, Mod Philol, 5/79; Laclos' purloined letters, Critical Inquiry, 82; The Uncanny Rendered Canny: Freud's Blindspot in Reading Hofmann's Sandman, In: Psychoanalysis and Literature, Brunner/Mazel (in prep); transl, La Poesie Eclatee, Univ Chicago (in press). *Mailing Add:* Comp Studies Lit & Romance Lang & Lit Univ of Chicago 1050 E 59th St Chicago IL 60637

MELZI, ROBERT C, b Milano, Italy, Mar 12, 15; US citizen; m 48; c 3. ROMANCE LANGUAGES. *Educ:* Univ Padua, D in L, 38; Univ Pa, MA, 53, PhD, 62. *Prof Exp:* Asst instr Romance lang, Univ Pa, 50-53; interpreter French & Ital, US Dept Justice, 53-56; teacher French & Span, Plymouth Whitemarsh High Sch, 58-61; assoc prof, Millersville State Col, 62-63; assoc prof, 63-67, prof French & chmn dept mod lang, 67-80, PROF ROMANCE LANG, WIDENER COL, 67- *Concurrent Pos:* Vis lectr, Univ Pa, 68-69. *Mem:* MLA; Dante Soc Am; Renaissance Soc Am; Am Asn Teachers Ital. *Res:* Italian Renaissance; Lodovico Castelvetro; bilingual lexicography. *Publ:* Auth, Castelvetro's Annotations to the Inferno, Mouton, 66; coauth, Renaissance Drama 1966, Northwestern Univ, 67; auth, The principle of separate entries for homographs in Italian lexicography, Ling, 70; The Bantam New College Italian and English Dictionary, Bantam, 76; The New College Italian and English Dictionary, Amsco, 76. *Mailing Add:* Dept of Mod Lang Widener Col Chester PA 19013

MEMMO, PAUL EUGENE, JR, b May 25, 18. ENGLISH & COMPARATIVE STUDIES. *Educ:* Fordham Univ, AB, 39; Columbia Univ, MS, 40, MA, 47, PhD, 59. *Prof Exp:* Secy prom dept, New York Daily News, 40-42; from instr to asst prof English & comp lit, 48-65, chmn grad curric comt, English Dept, 75-78, ASSOC PROF ENGLISH & COMP STUDIES & DIR DEPT, FORDHAM UNIV, 65- *Concurrent Pos:* Lectr, Conf on Humanities, Marymount Col, 60. *Honors & Awards:* Bene Merenti Medal, Fordham Univ, 68. *Mem:* Renaissance Soc Am; MLA; NCTE; Shakespeare Asn Am. *Res:* Philosophical and religious traditions in Italian, French and English Renaissance literature; philosophical and theological symbolism in Michelangelo's poetry; Shakespeare's use of Greek and Roman mythologems for the dramatic evolution of King Lear. *Publ:* Auth, Three sonnets of Michalangelo, NMex Quart, summer 61; Giordano Bruno's Gli eroici furori and the emblematic tradition, Romanic Rev, 2/64; translr & introd, Giordano Bruno's The Heroic Frenzies, Univ NC, 64; auth, The poetry of the Stilnovisti and Shakespeare's Love's labour's lost, Comp Lit, winter 66. *Mailing Add:* Dept of English & Comp Studies Fordham Univ Rose Hill Campus Bronx NY 10458

MENDELOFF, HENRY, b New York, NY, Jan 1, 17. FOREIGN LANGUAGES. *Educ:* City Col NY, BSS, 36, MS in Ed, 39; Cath Univ Am PhD, 60. *Prof Exp:* Teacher foreign lang, Sec Sch, NY, 37-42 & Washington, DC, 45-60; asst prof foreign lang educ, 60-64, assoc prof, 64-68, gen res bd grants, 63, 66, chmn medieval panel, 70-73, prof, 68-79, chmn dept span & port, 74-79, EMER PROF FOREIGN LANG, UNIV MD, COLLEGE PARK, 79- *Concurrent Pos:* Dir, teaching foreign lang high sch sem, Cath Univ Am, 60, consult prog affil, 62-66. *Mem:* Am Asn Teachers Span & Port; MLA. *Res:* Old Spanish; comparative Romance linguistics; medieval Spanish literature. *Publ:* Auth, The Evolution of Conditional Sentence Contrary to Fact in Old Spanish, Cath Univ Am, 60; The passive voice in Old Spanish, Romanistisches Jahrbuch, 64; A note on the affirmative commands in Old Spanish, Philol Quart, 1/65; A Manual of Comparative Romance Linguistics: Phonology and Morphology, Cath Univ Am, 69; The epithet in La Celestina, In: Studi di filologia romanza, Liviana, Padova, 71; contribr, Hierarchy, democracy, and charisma in medieval Spanish literature, In: Studies in Honor of Tatiana Fotitch, Cath Univ Am, 72; The conditional sentence contrary to fact in the Quijote, In: Hispanic Studies in Honor of Helmut A Hatzfeld, Ed Hispam, Barcelona, 73; auth, El epiteto peyorativo en Berceo, Ky Romance Quart, 74. *Mailing Add:* Dept of Span & Port Univ of Md College Park MD 20742

MENDELS, JUDICA (IGNATIA HENDRIKA), b Zaandam, Apr 15, 06. GERMAN, DUTCH. *Educ:* Univ Amsterdam, MA; Johns Hopkins Univ, MA, 50, PhD(philol), 53. *Prof Exp:* Teacher Dutch lang & lit, City Col Girls, Amsterdam, 28-31; res asst philol, Leeuwenhoeck-Comt Royal Dutch Acad Sci, 34-47; librn, York Jr Col, Pa, 52-53; asst prof Ger, Cedar Crest Col, 53-56; assoc prof, Lewis Col, 56-61, chmn dept mod lang, 56-61; prof, 61-71, EMER PROF GER, CANISIUS COL, 71- *Concurrent Pos:* Guest prof, McMaster Univ, 71-72. *Mem:* Swiss-Am Hist Soc; MLA; Int Soc Ger Philol & Lit; Am Asn Teachers Ger; Asn Acad Women. *Res:* German philology; older German and Dutch literature; mining and oresmelters language. *Publ:* Auth, German Mining Language, Muttersprache; German oresmelters language in the Middle Ages, In: Festschrift Gerhard Eis, Metzler, Stuttgart, 68; Mittelalterliche Elemente in G A Brederos Lyrik, Ger Notes, 72. *Mailing Add:* Wüzzenbachstrasse 61 CH 6006 Lucerne Switzerland

MENDELSOHN, RICHARD LLOYD, Philosophy, Linguistics. See Vol IV

MENOCAL, MARIA ROSA, b Havana, Cuba, Apr 9, 53; US citizen. ROMANCE PHILOLOGY, ITALIAN LITERATURE. *Educ:* Univ Pa, AB, 73, MA, 75, PhD(romance philol), 79. *Prof Exp:* Mellon fel comp lit, Bryn Mawr Col, 79-80; ASST PROF ROMANCE LANG, UNIV PA, 80- *Mem:* MLA; Ling Soc Am; Am Asn Teachers Ital. *Res:* Origins and structure of lyric poetry in medieval Europe; linguistic thought in Renaissance Italy. *Publ:* Auth, Close encounters in medieval provence: A new synthesis of courtly love, Hisp Rev, 49: 43-64; coauth, Primavera: An Introduction to Italian, Holt, Rinehart, Winston (in press). *Mailing Add:* Dept of Romance Lang Univ Pa Philadelphia PA 19104

MENTON, SEYMOUR, b New York, NY, Mar 6, 27. SPANISH AMERICAN LITERATURE. *Educ:* City Col NY, BA, 48; Nat Univ Mex, MA, 49; NY Univ, PhD(Span Am lit), 52. *Prof Exp:* Teacher English & hist of Span lang, Inst Recapacitation, Mex, 48-49; teacher, Pub Schs, NY, 49-52; instr Span & Span Am lit, Dartmouth Col, 52-54; from asst prof to prof, Univ Kans, 54-65; chmn dept foreign lang, 65-70, PROF SPAN & PORT, UNIV CALIF, IRVINE, 65- *Concurrent Pos:* Ed, Hispania, 63-65. *Mem:* Int Inst Span Am Lit; Am Asn Teachers Span & Port; MLA. *Res:* Cuban prose fiction; Mexican novel; Spanish American short story. *Publ:* Auth, El cuento costarricense, Studium, Mex, 64; coauth, Teatro Brasileiro contemporaneo, Appleton, 66; auth, La estructura epica de Los de Abajo y un prologo especulativo, Hispania, 12/67; El cuento hispanoamericano, Fondo Cult Economica, 70; ed, Frutos de mi tierra, Inst Caro y Cuervo, Bogota, 72; auth, Prose Fiction of the Cuban Revolution, Univ Tex, 75; La novela Colombiana: Planetas y satelites, Plaza y Janes, Bogota, 78; Magic realism rediscovered, 1918-1981, Philadelphia Art Alliance Press, 82. *Mailing Add:* 2641 Basswood St Newport Beach CA 92660

MENZEL, PETER, b Vienna, Austria, Nov 13, 31; Can citizen; m 60; c 2. LINGUISTICS. *Educ:* Univ Calif, PhD. *Prof Exp:* Res ling, Univ Calif, Los Angeles, 66-69; asst prof English, Fla State Univ, 69-76, assoc prof, 76-80; PROF ENGLISH & LING, J W GOETHE-UNIVERSITÄT, FRANKFURT, GER, 80- *Concurrent Pos:* Res ling, Southwest Regional Lab Educ Res & Develop, Los Angeles, 66-69; consult, Readability Proj, Univ Chicago, 67-71. *Mem:* Ling Soc Am; Am Dialect Soc; Southeast Conf Ling. *Res:* Linguistic theory; psycholinguistics; dialectology. *Publ:* Auth, Why gerundive phrases cannot be extraposed, Vol 2, No 2, & A constraint on the deletion of embedded subjects, Vol 6, No 2, Papers Ling; coauth, On the Theory of Achievement Test Items, Univ Chicago, 70; auth, Semantics and Syntax in Complementation, Mouton, The Hague, 73; Sentence types and semantic information, Proc 11th Int Con Ling, 74. *Mailing Add:* J W Goethe-Universitat Frankfurt Senckenberganlage 31 6000 Frankfurt Am Main Postfach 111932 32306 Germany, Federal Republic of

MERCHANT, FRANK ELDREDGE, English, Linguistics. See Vol II

MERCIE, JEAN LUC, b Le Mans, France, Mar 27, 39; m 63; c 2. FRENCH LITERATURE. *Educ:* Univ Grenoble, BA, 59, MA(French) & MA(English), 62, DES, 63, PhD(French), 65. *Prof Exp:* Asst prof French, Lycee Champollion, Grenoble, 63-64; asst prof, Univ Grenoble, 64-65; asst prof, Mil Hq, Grenoble, 66-67; assoc prof, 67-73, PROF FRENCH, UNIV OTTAWA, 73- *Concurrent Pos:* Nat Art Coun Can grants, 67-69; lectr radio & TV, Can, 67-69; Can Coun res grants, 69-73; dir art, Art Vif Can, 73- *Mem:* MLA. *Res:* Modern European art; shaped and concrete poetry; 20th century French literature. *Publ:* Auth, Victor Hugo et Clara Duchastel, 66 & Victor Hugo et Julie Chenay, 67, Minard, Paris; Anacreon le Jeune, 71, Le Regne Vegetal, 72 & Manuscrits des XIX et XXe Siecles, 72, Univ Ottawa; Antoni Clave, Musee de Poche, Paris, 74; Picabia, Belfond, Paris, 75; Flaubert, Gallimard, France, 78. *Mailing Add:* Dept of Foreign Lang Univ of Ottawa Ottawa ON K1N 6N5 Can

MEREDITH, HUGH EDWIN, b Muskogee, Okla, Oct 7, 30; m 55; c 4. GERMANIC LANGUAGES & LITERATURE. *Educ:* Okla Baptist Univ, BA, 52; Int Baptist Theol Sem Ruschlikon, Zurich, Switz, cert, 53; Southwestern Baptist Theol Sem, BD, 55; Univ Tex, MA, 60, PhD, 63. *Prof Exp:* Prof Ger & vpres acad afairs, Angelo State Univ, 67-74; pres, Sul Ross State Univ, 74-76; PROF MOD LANG, SAM HOUSTON STATE UNIV, 76- *Mem:* MLA; Am Asn Teachers Ger; Ling Soc Am. *Res:* Eighteenth and 19th century German literature; Karl Philipp Moritz; Jeremias Gotthelf. *Mailing Add:* Dept of Foreign Langs Sam Houston Univ Huntsville TX 77341

MERIVALE, PATRICIA, English, Comparative Literature. See Vol II

MERIZ, DIANA TERESA, b San Francisco, Calif, Sept 13, 40; m 73. FRENCH & PROVENCAL LINGUISTICS. *Educ:* Stanford Univ, AB, 61; Harvard Univ, MA, 63, PhD(Romance lang), 69. *Prof Exp:* Asst prof French, Rutgers Univ, 69-70; asst prof, 70-76, ASSOC PROF FRENCH, UNIV PITTSBURGH, 76- *Mem:* AAUP; MLA; Mediaeval Acad Am; Am Asn Teachers Fr; Ling Soc Am. *Res:* Old French syntax; old Provencal syntax. *Publ:* Auth, O F Imp ET/OU Imp: Two problems, In: Essays in Honor of Louis Francis Solano, Univ NC, 70; Encore une fois pleine sa hanste, 73 & A propos du classement d'ancien francais ez (ecce), 74, Romania; contribr, O F dites me tost/dites moi tost, In: Voices of Conscience: Essays on Medieval and Modern French Literature in Memory of James D Powell and Rosemary Hodgins, Temple Univ, 77. *Mailing Add:* Dept of French & Ital Univ of Pittsburgh Pittsburgh PA 15260

MERKEL, GOTTFRIED FELIX, b Jan 16, 05; US citizen; m 35; c 6. GERMAN. *Educ:* Univ Leipzig, PhD(Ger lang & lit), 29. *Prof Exp:* Prof Ger lang & lit, Univ Athens, 30-39; mem fac, Univ Conn, 39-40, Upsala Col, 40-42 & State Univ NY Col Teachers, Albany, 44-46; Charles Phelps Taft prof Ger & fel grad sch, 46-76, EMER PROF GER, UNIV CINCINNATI, 76- *Concurrent Pos:* Am Coun Learned Soc fel, 62-63; Fulbright travel grant, 68; Am Philos Soc res grant, 68. *Mem:* Am Asn Teachers Ger; MLA; Am Lessing Soc (pres, 69-71); Lessing Akad, Ger. *Res:* German literature of the Middle Ages; Reformation; German baroque. *Publ:* Auth, Das Aufkommen der duetschen Sprache in den stadtischen Kanzleien des ausgenhenden Mittelalters; Die Epochen der detuschen Schriftsprache; ed, On Romanticism and the art of translation: Predigt/Rede, In: Literatur Lexikon, Fischer, 65, 2nd ed, 68; Vom Fortleben der Lutherischen Bibelsprache im 16/17 Jahrhundert, Zeitschrift fur Deut Sprache, 67; Deutsche Erbauungsliteratur, Jahrbuch fur Internat Germanistik, 71. *Mailing Add:* 5825 Glenview Ave Cincinnati OH 45224

MERLER, GRAZIA, b Trento, Italy, June 16, 38; Can citizen. FRENCH & FRENCH CANADIAN LITERATURE. *Educ:* Univ BC, BA, 59; Laval Univ, MA, 61, PhD(French), 67. *Prof Exp:* Instr French & Ital, Univ Tex, 63-65; lectr Ital, Univ BC, 65-66; prof French, Col Ste-Foy, 67-69; asst prof, 69-76, chmn French, 75-77, ASSOC PROF FRENCH, DEPT MOD LANG, SIMON FRASER UNIV, 76- *Concurrent Pos:* Can Coun leave fel, 77-78. *Mem:* MLA; Can Semiotics Res Asn; Asn Can Studies; Asn Can Univ Teachers Fr. *Res:* Literary theory; Canadian short story. *Publ:* Auth, La realite dans la prose d'A Hebert, Ecrits du Can Francais, 71; Connaissance et communication chez Stendhal, Stendhal Club, 73; Translation and the creation of cultural myths in Canada, West Coast Rev, 10/76; Rapports associatifs dans le discours litteraire, Francia, 77; Mavis Crallant, Narrative Patterns and Devices, Tecumseh Press, 78; Recit et description chez Stendhal, 80, & Description et espace dons la Chartiense de Perme, 80, Stendhal Club. *Mailing Add:* Dept of Lang Lit & Ling Simon Fraser Univ Burnaby BC V5A 1S6 Can

MERMALL, THOMAS, b Czech, Sept 20, 37; US citizen; m 77. ROMANCE LANGUAGES. *Educ:* Ill Wesleyan Univ, BA, 61; Univ Conn, MA, 65, PhD(Span), 68. *Prof Exp:* Asst prof Span, State Univ NY, Stony Brook, 68-72; asst prof, 73-75, assoc prof, 75-80, PROF SPAN, BROOKLYN COL, 80- *Mem:* MLA. *Res:* Contemporary Spanish essay; history of ideas. *Publ:* Auth, Esthetics and politics in Falangist culture, Bull Hisp Studies, 4/73; Unamuno's mystical rhetoric, In: Analysis of Hispanic Texts-First York College Colloquium, 76 & The Rhetoric of Humanism, 76, Bilingual; Sentido del bufon en F Ayala, Insula, Madrid, 10/76; El texto iconico, Hispanic Rev (in press). *Mailing Add:* Dept of Mod Lang Brooklyn Col Brooklyn NY 11210

MERMIER, GUY R, b Grenoble, France, Oct 20, 31; m 54; c 2. ROMANCE LANGUAGES & LITERATURE. *Educ:* Univ Grenoble, Lic es-let & DES, 53; Univ Pa, PhD, 61. *Prof Exp:* Instr French, Amherst Col, 52-53; instr Romance lang, Univ Mass, 54-55; asst instr, Univ Pa, 55-56; instr foreign lang, Temple Univ, 56-61; from instr to asst prof Romance lang, 61-67, Rackham grant, 62, ASSOC PROF ROMANCE LANG, UNIV MICH, ANN ARBOR, 67- *Concurrent Pos:* Fulbright grant, Amherst Col, 52-53; Smith-Mundt fel, 52; NDEA consult, Temple Univ, 56; prof, Laval Univ, 57; dir, Mich-Wis Jr Year in France, 67-68; pres, Alliance Francaise, Ann Arbor, 68- *Mem:* MLA; Am Asn Teachers French; Int Arthurian Soc; Mod Humanities Res Asn; Am Asn Teachers Ital. *Res:* Medieval; Renaissance; 19th century literature and existentialist 20th century literature. *Publ:* Auth, De Pierre de Beauvais, Romanische Forsch, 66; coauth, Le roman de Tristan et D'Iseult, Honore Champion, Paris, 67; auth, L'essai Du repentir de Montaigne, Fr Rev, 2/68; The bestiaire of Gervaise, Mich Acad Sci, Arts & Lett, 68. *Mailing Add:* Dept of Romance Lang Univ of Michigan Ann Arbor MI 48104

MERRIFIELD, DORIS FULDA, b Hamburg, Ger, May 17, 34; US citizen; m 65; c 2. GERMANIC LANGUAGES. *Educ:* Univ Tex, Austin, MA, 62, PhD(Ger), 64. *Prof Exp:* Asst prof Ger & Latin, Sam Houston State Teachers Col, 63-65; from asst prof to assoc prof, 65-72, PROF GER, CALIF STATE UNIV, FULLERTON, 72- *Mem:* MLA; Am Asn Teachers Ger. *Res:* 18th century German literature; contemporary German-Swiss literature; literary forms. *Publ:* Auth, Senecas Moralische Schriften im Spiegel der deutschen Literatur des 18 Jhdts, Deutsche Vierteljahresschrift fur Literaturwissenschaft und Geistesgeschichte, 67; Max Frischs Mein Name sei Gantenbein Versuch einer Strukturanalyse, Monatshefte, 7/68; Gottfried Kellers Dietegen, eine Interpretation, Ger Quart, 3/69; Das Bild der Frau bei Max Frisch, Universitätsverlag Eckhard Becksmann, Freiburg, 71; Julika: An enigmatic figure in Max Frisch's Stiller, Vis a Vis: An Interdisciplinary J, Div Libr Sci, Calif State Univ, Fullerton, 10/73. *Mailing Add:* Dept of Foreign Lang & Lit Calif State Univ Fullerton CA 92634

MERRIFIELD, WILLIAM R, b Chicago, Ill, Sept 28, 32; m 52; c 4. LINGUISTICS, ANTHROPOLOGY. *Educ:* Wheaton Col, Ill BA, 54; Cornell Univ, MA, 63, PhD(cult anthrop), 65. *Prof Exp:* Ling consult in Mex, 62-74, coordr anthrop res in Mex, 65-69, coordr ling res in Mex, 65-59, 72-74, dir sch, Univ Okla, 74-77, INT COORDR ANTHROP & COMMUN DEVELOP, SUMMER INST LING, 72-, DIR, MUS ANTHROP, TEX, 74- *Concurrent Pos:* Vis asst prof ling,Univ Wash, 65-72; vis prof anthrop, Wheaton Col, 71-72; adj prof ling, Univ Tex, Arlington, 74-; adj prof anthrop, Univ Okla, 75-77, adj prof ling, 77. *Mem:* Am Anthrop Asn; Ling Soc Am; Am Sci Affiliation; Am Asn Mus; Ling Asn Can & US. *Res:* Cultural and applied anthropology; social organization; theory of grammar. *Publ:* Coauth, Laboratory Manual for Morphology and Syntax, Summer Inst Ling, Santa Ana, 60, 5th rev ed, 74; auth, On the form or rules in a generative grammar, In: Georgetown Univ Monogr Ser on Lang & Ling, 67; coauth, The verb phrase in Huixtec Tzotzil, Lang, 68; auth, Palantla Chinantec Grammar, Museo Nacional de Antropologia, Mex, 68; coauth, Two Studies on the Lacandones of Mexico: Recent History of the Southern Lacandones and Lacandone Subsistence, Summer Inst Ling of Univ Okla, 71; Los Lacandones de Mexico: Dos Estudios, Instituto Nacional Indigenista, Mex, 72; auth, Meso-American Indian cultures, Encycl Britannica, 74; ed, Studies in Otomanguean Phonology, Summer Inst Ling & Univ Tex, Arlington 77. *Mailing Add:* Summer Inst of Ling 7500 Camp Wisdom Rd Dallas TX 75236

MERRILL, JUDITH SENIOR, b Brooklyn, NY, July 3, 31; m 57; c 1. ROMANCE PHILOLOGY. *Educ:* Oberlin Col, BA, 52; Radcliffe Col, MA, 53, PhD(Romance philol), 56. *Prof Exp:* From instr to asst prof Span, Univ Calif, Los Angeles, 56-59; asst prof mod lang, Western Col Women, 59-60; assoc prof, 60-65, PROF MOD LANG, HOBART & WILLIAM SMITH COLS, 65- *Mem:* Am Asn Teachers Span & Port; MLA; Ling Soc Am. *Res:* Old Spanish language; Spanish grammar. *Publ:* Auth, Notas sobre Nebrija, Nueva Rev Filol Hisp, 60; The presentation of case and declension in early Spanish grammars, Z Romanische Philol, 62; ed, Esta noche es la vispera, Odyssey, 69. *Mailing Add:* Dept of Mod Lang Hobart & William Smith Cols Geneva NY 14456

MERRIM, STEPHANIE, US citizen. LATIN AMERICAN & BRAZILIAN LITERATURE. *Educ:* Princeton Univ, AB, 73; Yale Univ, PhD(Span & Port), 78. *Prof Exp:* Instr Span, Univ Tex, Austin, 78-81; ASST PROF SPAN, BROWN UNIV, 81- *Res:* Modern Latin American novel; Colonial Latin American writings; Brazilian literature. *Publ:* Auth, The Motivation of Language: Cratylus Kingdom, Diacritics, 81; A Secret Idiom: The Rule and Grammaral Language, In: Trites Tigres, Latin Am Literary Rev, 81; The Castle of Discourse: Ferinandez de Oviedos Claribalte 1519, Mod Lang Notes, 82. *Mailing Add:* 6807 Lexington Rd Austin TX 78731

MERSEREAU, JOHN, JR, b San Jose, Calif, Apr 16, 25; m 53. SLAVIC LANGUAGES & LITERATURES. *Educ:* Univ Calif, MA, 50, PhD(Slavic lang & lit), 57. *Prof Exp:* Res asst Slavic inst, Univ Calif, 52-54; instr Slavic lang & lit, 56-61, chmn dept, 61-71, PROF SLAVIC LANG & LIT, UNIV MICH, ANN ARBOR, 61- *Concurrent Pos:* Am Coun Learned Soc grant, 62; mem exec comt, Am Comt Slavists, 63; fel, Guggenheim Found, 72-73; chmn joint comt Eastern Europe, Am Coun Learned Soc, 72- *Mem:* Am Asn Advan Slavic Studies; Am Asn Teachers Slavic & East Europ Lang; MLA. *Res:* Russian and Polish literature. *Publ:* Coauth, Reading and Translating Contemporary Russian, Pitman, 63; auth, Mikhail Lermontov, 61 & Baron Anton Delvig's Northern Flowers: Literary Almanac of the Pushkin Pleiad, 68, Southern Ill Univ. *Mailing Add:* 6776 Marshall Rd Dexter MI 48130

MESCALL, ELOISE THERESE, b Los Angeles, Calif, Dec 20, 19. ROMANCE LANGUAGES. *Educ:* Univ Calif, Los Angeles, AB, 46, MA, 48, PhD, 59. *Hon Degrees:* Dipl, Univ Madrid, 52. *Prof Exp:* Assoc prof, 48-61, chmn dept, 48-60, dir downtown campus, 59-64, dir develop, 61-67, PROF ROMANCE LANG, MT ST MARY'S COL, CALIF, 61-, CHMN DEPT, 78- *Concurrent Pos:* Mem, Alliance Francaise; vis prof, Fontbonne Col, 67-68; vis prof Romance lang, Cath Univ, Louvain, 72-73. *Honors & Awards:* Palmes Academiques, French Govt, 60, Officier, 75; Distinguished Serv Award, Mod & Class Lang Asn Southern Calif, 69. *Mem:* Am Asn Teachers Fr; Mediaeval Acad Am; MLA; Am Asn Teachers Span & Port. *Res:* Mediaeval French lives of the saints; contemporary French novel; trends in contemporary Spain. *Mailing Add:* 12001 Chalon Rd Los Angeles CA 90049

MESSENGER, WILLIAM EDMUND, English. See Vol II

MESSIER, LEONARD NORBERT, b Chambly, Can, Jan 24, 12; US citizen; m39; c 2. FRENCH. *Educ:* San Diego State Col, AB, 35; Univ Calif, MA, 36, PhD(Romance lit), 46. *Prof Exp:* Instr French, Mills, Col, 37-40; asst, Univ CAlif, 404-2; transl, US Off Censorship, 42-43; chmn mod lang dept, Napa Jr Col, 43-46; dir campus abroad, Rouen, France, 62, chmn dept Ital & French, 66-76, prof, 46-80, EMER PROF FRENCH, SAN DIEGO STATE UNIV, 80- *Concurrent Pos:* Resident dir, Calif State Int Prog, Aix-en-Provence, France, 65-66; mem, Alliance Francaise. *Honors & Awards:* Chevalier, Palmes Academiques, 57, Officer, 70. *Mem:* AAUP; Am Asn Teachers French. *Res:* French literature of the 16th and 18th centuries; French Canadian literature. *Publ:* Auth, Adapting a foreign language porogram to a changing curriculum, Femmes de Lett du Can Francais. *Mailing Add:* Dept of French & Italian San Diego State Univ 5402 College Ave San Diego CA 92115

MESSING, GORDON MYRON, b Toledo, Ohio, Mar 4, 17; m 46; c 4. INDO-EUROPEAN LINGUISTICS. *Educ:* Harvard Univ, AB, 38, AM, 40, PhD(classics, ling), 42. *Prof Exp:* Asst prof classics & ling, Univ Wis, 46-47; vconsul, Am Embassy, Foreign Serv, US Dept State, Vienna, 48-53, attache, Athens, 55-60 & Reykjavik, 62-65; assoc prof classics, 67-70, assoc prof, 70-71, PROF CLASSICS & LING, CORNELL UNIV, 71- *Concurrent Pos:* Nat Endowment for Humanities sr fel, 73-74; Am Philos Soc & NSF fels, 78. *Mem:* Ling Soc Am; Am Philol Asn. *Res:* Latin and Greek historical grammar; Indo-European and Romance philology; Balkan studies. *Publ:* Ed, Greek Grammar, Harvard Univ, 56. *Mailing Add:* Dept of Classics Cornell Univ Ithaca NY 14850

MESSNER, CHARLES A, JR, b Boston, Mass, Oct 18, 25; m 54. FRENCH. *Educ:* Univ Chicago, PhB, 45. *Prof Exp:* Asst instr French, Yale Univ, 49-50; from instr to assoc prof, 53-76, PROF FRENCH, CARLETON COL, 76- *Mem:* MLA; Am Asn Teachers Fr; Nat Asn Lang Lab Dir. *Res:* Twentieth century French literature; Language laboratories. *Mailing Add:* Dept of French Carleton Col Northfield MN 55057

METCALF, GEORGE J(OSEPH), b Kewanee, Ill, Apr 15, 08; wid; c 2. GERMANIC PHILOLOGY. *Educ:* Wabash Col, AB, 28; Harvard Univ, MA, 31, PhD(Ger philol), 35. *Hon Degrees:* LHD, MacMurray Col, 65. *Prof Exp:* Instr Ger & Latin, Wabash Col, 28-29; instr Ger, Harvard Col, 31-35; instr, Univ Ala, 35-37; asst prof, Univ Kans, 37-38; asst prof, Washington Univ, 38-42; from asst prof to prof Ger philol, 42-73, dir lang inst, 55, chmn dept Ger lang & lit, 56-69, Colvin res prof, 63, EMER PROF GER PHILOL, UNIV CHICAGO, 73- *Concurrent Pos:* US Dept State grant, Munich, 52; vis prof, Univ Mich, 58. *Mem:* MLA; Ling Soc Am; Am Asn Teachers Ger(pres, 68-69). *Res:* Linguistic theories of the 16th, 17th, and 18th centuries; lexicography; history of sounds in German. *Publ:* Auth, Forms of address in German: 1500-1800, Wash Univ Studies Lang & Lit, 38; assoc ed, Langenscheidt's Encyclopaedic Dictionary of the English and German Languages, Langenscheidt, Berlin (2 vols), 62-63; Philipp Clüver and his Lingva Celtica, In: Deut Beiträge zur Geistigen Überlieferung, 74; The Indo-European hypothesis in the 16th and 17th centuries, In: Studies in the History of Linguistics, Ind Univ, 74; The Copyright Patent in Schottelius' Ausführliche Arbeit (1663), In: Wege der Worte: Festschrift für Wolfgang Fleischhauer, Vienna, 78; Theodor Bibliander (1504-1564) and the Languages of Japhet's Progeny, Historiographia Linguistica, Vol 7: 323-333. *Mailing Add:* 1211 Delaware Ave Santa Cruz CA 95060

METCALF, WILLIAM EDWARDS, Roman Numismatics, Ancient History. See Vol I

METZGER, BRUCE MANNING, New Testament Language & Literature. See Vol IV

METZGER, ERIKA ALMA, b Berlin, Ger, Apr 8, 33; US citizen; m 58. GERMAN LANGUAGE & LITERATURE. *Educ:* Teachers' Training Col, Göttingen, dipl, 54; Free Univ Berlin, dipl, 58; Cornell Univ, MA, 61; State Univ NY Buffalo, PhD(Ger), 67. *Prof Exp:* Teaching asst Ger, Cornell Univ, 58-61; instr, Univ Ill, 61-63; instr, Millard Fillmore Col, 63-67; asst prof, 67-72, assoc prof, 72-79, PROF GER, STATE UNIV NY, BUFFALO, 79. *Mem:* MLA; Am Asn Teachers Ger, Int Ver Ger Sprach-u Literaturwiss. *Res:* Development of German lyric poetry; Baroque; 20th century. *Publ:* Coauth, Paul Klee, 67 & Clara and Robert Schumann, 67, Houghton; ed, H A von Abschatz, Werke, Herbert Lang, Bern, 70; co-ed, Neukirch-Anthologie, Vol III, IV & V, Niemeyer, Tübingen, 70; coauth, Stefan George, Twayne, 72; ed, H A von Abschatz, Gedichte, Herbert Lang, Bern, 73; auth, Marc-Antoine de Saint-Amant und Hans ABmann von Abschatz, In: Europäische Tradition, Francke, Bern, 73; Diatonisch-Doppelt-Erfahrenes, Blaeschke, Darmstadt, 77; co-ed, A Albertinus: Hofschul, Lang, Bern, 78. *Mailing Add:* Dept of Mod Lang 910 Clemens Hall State Univ of NY Buffalo NY 14260

METZGER, MICHAEL MOSES, b Frankfurt, Ger, June 2, 35; US citizen; m 58. GERMAN LANGUAGE & LITERATURE. *Educ:* Columbia Univ, BA, 56; Cornell Univ, PhD(Ger lit), 62. *Prof Exp:* Instr Ger, Univ Ill, Urbana, 61-63; from asst prof to assoc prof, 63-71, PROF GER, STATE UNIV NY, BUFFALO, 71- *Concurrent Pos:* Guest prof Ger lit, Univ Va, Charlottesville, 77. *Mem:* MLA; Am Asn Teachers Ger; Internationale Vereinigung für Germanische; Sprach-und Literaturwissenschaft. *Res:* German literature of the Enlightenment and 20th century; Lessing; the early 18th century. *Publ:* Auth, Lessing and the Language of Comedy, Mouton, The Hague, 66; coauth, Paul Klee, 67 & Clara und Robert Schumann, 67, Houghton; Der Hofmeister und die Gouvernante, de Gruyter, 69; Stefan George, Twayne, 72; co-ed, Aegidius Albertinus Hof-Schul, Lang, Bern, 78; Neukirch-Anthologie, Vol V, Niemeyer, Tübingen, 81; Fairy Tales as Ways of Knowing, Lang, Bern, 81. *Mailing Add:* Dept of Mod Lang & LIt 910 Clemens Hall State Univ of NY Buffalo NY 14260

METZIDAKIS, PHILIP, b Springfield, Mass, Sept 11, 31; m 55; c 2. FOREIGN LANGUAGES. *Educ:* Dartmouth Col, BA, 53; Univ Salamanca, dipl, 55; Yale Univ, PhD, 60. *Prof Exp:* Instr Span, Yale Univ, 57-60; from asst prof to assoc prof, Mills Col, 60-68; assoc prof, 68-76, PROF SPAN, SWARTHMORE COL, 76- *Concurrent Pos:* Res grant, Mills Col, 61-63; Danforth fel, 62-; mem, Woodrow Wilson Nat Scholar Comt, 62-; Nat Endowment for Humanities younger humanist fel, 71-72. *Mem:* Am Asn Teachers Span & Port; MLA. *Res:* The writings of Miguel de Unamuno; 20th century Spanish literature; modern Greek literatur. *Publ:* Auth, Unamuno frente a la poesia de Ruben Dario, Rev Iberoam, 1/61; El poeta nacional griego Kostis Palamas y Unamuno, In: Cuadernos de la catedra Miguel de Unamuno, 62; Unamuno: sus mejores paginas, Prentice-Hall, 66; La hispanidad, segun don Miguel de Unamuno, Comunidad, Mex, 4/68. *Mailing Add:* Dept of Mod Lang Swarthmore Col Swarthmore PA 19081

MEWS, SIEGFRIED, b Berlin, Ger, Sept 28, 33. GERMAN, COMPARATIVE LITERATURE. *Educ:* Univ Hamburg, Staatsexamen, 61; Southern Ill Univ, MA, 63; Univ Ill, Urbanna, PhD(comp lit), 67. *Prof Exp:* Instr Ger, Centre Col, 62-63; instr, Univ Ill, 66-67; from asst prof to assoc prof Ger, 67-77, ed, Studies Germanic Lang & Lit, 68-80, PROF GER, UNIV NC, CHAPEL HILL, 77- *Mem:* MLA; Am Asn Teachers Ger; AAUP; Am Comp Lit Asn; Int Brecht Soc. *Res:* German and comparative literature of the 19th and 20th centuries. *Publ:* Ed, Studies in German Literature of the Nineteenth and Twentieth Centuries, Univ NC, 70, 2nd ed, 72; Carl Zuckmayer: Der Hauptmann von Döpenick, 72, 3rd ed, 82 & Zuckmayer: Des Teufels General, 73, 2nd ed, 79, Diesterweg; co-ed, Essays on Brecht: Theater and Politics, Univ NC, 74 & 79; ed, Bertolt Brecht: Herr Puntila und sein Knecht Matti, 75 & Brecht: Der Kaukasische, Kreidedreis, 80, Diesterweg; auth, Carl Zuckmayer, 81, Twayne; ed, The Fisherman and His Wife: Gunter Grass's The Flounder in Critical Perspective, AMS Press, 82. *Mailing Add:* Dept of Ger Lang Univ of NC Chapel Hill NC 27514

MEYER, DORIS L, b Summit, NJ, Jan 2, 42. ROMANCE LANGUAGES. *Educ:* Radcliffe Col, BA, 63; Univ Va, MA, 64, PhD(Span), 67. *Prof Exp:* Asst prof Span, Wilmington Col, NC, 67-69; asst prof, 69-77, assoc prof, 77-79, PROF SPAN, BROOKLYN COL, 80- *Concurrent Pos:* City Univ NY fac res award, 73-74, 76-77 & 77-78; Am Philos Soc award, 76-77; Nat Endowment for Humanities fel, 77-78. *Mem:* MLA; Am Asn Teachers Span & Port; Latin Am Studies Asn; PEN Am Ctr; Nat Women's Studies Asn. *Res:* Latin American literature; women's studies; Mexican-American literature. *Publ:* Auth, Traditionalism in the Work of Francisco de Quevedo, Univ NC, 70; Quevedo and Diego Lopez: A curious case of prologue duplication, Hisp Rev, spring 75; Anonymous poetry in Spanish-language New Mexico newspapers, 1880-1900, Bilingual Rev, 9-12/75; Banditry and poetry: Verses by two outlaws of Old Las Vegas, NMex Hist Rev, 10/75; Felipe Maximiliano Chacon: A forgotten Mexican-American poet, New Scholar, 77; Early Mexican-American responses to negative stereotyping, NMex Hist Rev, 1/78; Victoria Ocampo: Against the Wind and the Tide, Braziller, 79; Victoria Ocampo: 1890-1979 (a memorial note), Rev 24, 5/79. *Mailing Add:* Dept of Mod Lang & Lit Brooklyn Col Brooklyn NY 11210

MEYER, MARTINE DARMON, b Casablanca, Morocco, Apr 15, 29; nat US; c 1. FRENCH. *Educ:* Smith Col, BA, 49; Univ Wis, MA, 51, PhD(French), 64. *Prof Exp:* Teaching asst French, Univ Wis, 49-53; instr, Smith Col, 53-54; acting instr, Univ Wis, 54-55; instr French & Ital, 56-64, from asst prof to assoc prof, 64-73, chmn dept French & Ital, 70-78, PROF FRENCH, UNIV WIS, MILWAUKEE, 73- *Honors & Awards:* Chevalier, Palmes Academiques, 67. *Mem:* Am Asn Teachers Fr; Am Asn Univ Women; AAUP. *Res:* Eighteenth century literature, especially Diderot; critical edition of Voltaire's complete works; contemporary French society. *Publ:* Auth, Lettres et Reponses de Diderot a Sophie Volland, Minard, 67; coauth, Le Francais: Langue et Culture, Van Nostrand, 74 & 79. *Mailing Add:* Dept of French & Ital Univ of Wis Milwaukee WI 53201

MEYER, MARVIN WAYNE, New Testament Studies, Hellenistic Religions. See Vol IV

MEYER, PAUL HUGO, b Berlin, Ger, Dec 5, 20; nat US; m 46; c 3. FRENCH. *Educ:* McGill Univ, BA, 43, MA, 45; Columbia Univ, PhD(French), 54. *Prof Exp:* Lectr French, Columbia Univ, 51-52; instr, Bryn Mawr Col, 52-54; instr, 54-57, asst prof, 57-62, assoc prof, 62-66, PROF FRENCH, UNIV CONN, 66- *Concurrent Pos:* Am Coun Learned Soc res grant-in-aid, 58; Fulbright res scholar in France, 61-62; mem nat selection comt, Inst Int Educ, 71-73. *Mem:* MLA; Am Asn Teachers Fr; Am Soc 18th Century Studies; Int Asn Fr Studies; Soc Fr Etud XVIIIe Siecle. *Res:* French philosophers; 18th century French and comparative literature; history of ideas. *Publ:* Auth, The attitude of the enlightenment towards the Jew, Inst Voltaire, 63; ed, Lettre sur les Sourds et Muets, Droz, 65; auth, Politics and morals in the thought of Montesquieu, Studies Voltaire, 67; contribr, Diderot, Oeuvres Completes, Club Francais du Livre, 69-71; auth, Diderot's Prince: The principes de politique des souverains, In: Essays on Diderot & the Enlightenment, Droz, 74; contribr, Diderot, Oeuvres Completes, Hermann (in press); Complete Works of Voltaire, Univ Toronto, (in press); auth, Le Rayonnement de Moise Mendelssohn hors d'Allemagne, Dix-huitieme Siecle, 81. *Mailing Add:* Dept of Romance Lang Univ of Conn Storrs CT 06268

MEYER, ROBERT T, b Cleveland, Ohio, Aug 6, 11; m 37; c 4. CELTIC & COMPARATIVE PHILOLOGY. *Educ:* John Carroll Univ, AB, 33, AM, 34; Univ Mich, PhD, 43, AMLS, 59. *Prof Exp:* Instr English philol, St Louis Univ, 46-47; from instr to asst prof Sanskrit & comp philol, 47-53, assoc prof, 53-57, prof, 57-80, EMER PROF CELTIC & COMP PHILOL, CATH UNIV AM, 80-, ASST CHAPLAIN, 71- *Concurrent Pos:* Fel, Johns Hopkins Univ, 47-50, instr, 48-49; fel, Dublin Inst Advan Study, 53-55; lectr, Oxford Univ, 61, 65, 68, 70 & 72; consult Celtic, Libr of Congr, 71- *Mem:* Ling Soc Am; MLA; Medieval Acad Am; Am Philol Asn; Irish Texts Soc. *Res:* Armenian and Georgian translations of Greek patristic writers; early Celtic law; mediaeval lexicography. *Publ:* Translr, Athanasius, Vita Antoni, Newman, 50; ed, Merugud Uilix meic Leirtis, Dublin Inst Advan Studies, 58; translr, Palladius, Historia Lausiaca, Newman, 64; auth, Middle Cornish miracle play Beunans für Johannes Quasten, 70; Note on Wachter Glossairum germanicum, In: Studies in Honor Tatiana Fotitch, 72; Old Irish rhetorical terms in the Milan glosses, Word: Celtic Lang, 1976, 77; translr, St Bernard Vita S Malachiae with Notes, Indices, Cistercian, 78. *Mailing Add:* Div of Celtic Studies Cath Univ of Am Washington DC 20017

MEZZACAPPA, CARMINE ANTHONY, b Monacilioni, Campobasso, Italy, Apr 29, 27; US citizen; m 53; c 4. ITALIAN LANGUAGE & LITERATURE. *Educ:* NY Univ, BA, 58, MA, 61, PhD(Ital & comp lit), 68. *Prof Exp:* Instr Ital, Washington Sq Col & Div Adult Educ, NY Univ, 59-63; instr, 63-67, lectr, 67-68, asst prof, 68-70, ASSOC PROF ITAL, NEWARK COL ARTS & SCI, RUTGERS UNIV, 70-, CHMN, DEPT FOREIGN LANG & LIT, 78- *Concurrent Pos:* Dir, Rutgers Jr Year in Italy, 78-79. *Mem:* Am Asn Teachers Ital; Asn Int Studi Ling Lit Ital; AAUP. *Res:* Nineteenth century Italian literature particularly the poetry of Giacomo Leopardi and Salvatore Di Giacomo; 20th century Italian literature particularly the poetry of Giuseppe Ungaretti and Eugenio Montale; comparative literature. *Publ:* Auth, Caino, o del sentimento ungarettiano di noia e inquietudine, Studium, Vol LXV, No 6-7; Noia e inquietudine nella Vita d'un uomo di Giuseppe Ungaretti, Rebellato, Padova, Italy, 70; La realta poetica, morale e umana nella Vita d'un uomo di G Ungaretti, Studium, Vol LXVIII, No 6; Il Michelangelo in Ungaretti, Lettere, Vol V, No l; Di Giacomo, Salvatore, In: Columbia Dict of Moderne European Literature, Columbia Univ Press, 80. *Mailing Add:* 71 De Kay St Staten Island NY 10310

MIAO, RONALD CLENDINEN, b Shanghai, China, Oct, 25, 36; US citizen; m 58; c 2. CHINESE LANGUAGE & LITERATURE. *Educ:* Univ Calif, Berkeley, BA(English) & BA(Orient lang), 63, MA, 67, PhD(Chinese), 69. *Prof Exp:* Asst prof Chinese, Univ Mich, 69-73; ASSOC PROF CHINESE LANG & LIT, UNIV ARIZ, 73- *Concurrent Pos:* Mem EAsian comp lit comt, Asn Asian Studies, 69- *Mem:* Asn Asian Studies; Am Orient Soc. *Res:* Chinese classical poetry; Chinese literary criticism; comparative literature, particularly Chinese and English. *Publ:* Auth, The Ch'i ai shih of the Late Han and Chin Periods (I), Harvard J Asiatic Studies, 73; T'ang frontier poetry: An exercise in archetypal criticism, Tsing Hua J Chinese Studies, 74; ed, Studies in Chinese Poetry and Poetics (2 vols), Chinese Materials Ctr, Inc, 78; Early Medieval Chinese Poetry: The Life and Verse of Wang Ts'an, Franz Steiner Verlag, 82. *Mailing Add:* Dept of Orient Studies Univ of Ariz Tucson AZ 85721

MICHAEL, WOLFGANG FRIEDRICH, b Freiburg, Ger, Feb 23, 09; nat US; m 52; c 3. GERMAN. *Educ:* Univ Munich, Phd, 34. *Prof Exp:* Instr Ger, Bryn Mawr Col, 39; asst prof, Chestnut Hill Col, 39-46; from asst prof to assoc prof, 46-61, PROF GER, UNIV TEX, AUSTIN, 61- *Honors & Awards:* Verdienstkreuz der Bundesrepublik, Goethemedaille. *Mem:* MLA. *Res:* Renaissance and Reformation; Thomas Mann. *Publ:* Auth, The staging of the Bozen Passion Play, Ger Rev; Das deutsche Drama und Theater vor der Reformation: ein Forschungsbericht, 57 & Stoff und Idee im Tod in Venedit, 59, Deut Viertel-jahrs-schrift fur Literaturwissenschaft und Geistesgeschichte; Die Anfaenge des Theaters zu Freiburg im Breisgau; Die Geistlichen Prozessionsspiele in Deutschland; Frühformen der Deutschen Bühne, Selbstverlag der Ges für Theatergeschichte, Berlin, 63 Das Deutsche Drama des Mittelalters, de Gruyter, Berlin, 71. *Mailing Add:* Dept of Ger Univ of Tex Austin TX 78712

MICHAELS, DAVID, b New York, NY, Apr 20, 36; m 62; c 2. LINGUISTICS. *Educ:* Univ Minn, Minneapolis, BA, 56; Columbia Univ, MA, 65; Univ Mich, Ann Arbor, PhD(ling), 69. *Prof Exp:* Lectr English, Yala Col, Thailand, 62-63; lectr, Chulalongkorn Univ, Bangkok, 63; asst prof, 68-74, assoc prof, 74-81, PROF LING & HEAD DEPT, UNIV CONN, 81- *Mem:* Ling Soc Am; Int Ling Asn. *Res:* Phonology; syntax; language contact. *Publ:* Auth, Notational devices and elsewhere rules, Papers in Ling, 71; A note on some exceptions in Zuni phonology, Int J Am Ling, 71; Sinhalese sound replacements and feature hierarchies, 73 & Sound replacements and phonological systems, 74, Ling; Linguistic relativity and color terminology, Lang & Speech, 77; co-auth (with H Lasnik), A reanalysis of English vowel alternations, Proc XIIth Int Congr of Linguists, Vienna, 78; auth, Spelling and the phonology of tense vowels, Lang & Speech, 80; Allomorphy, phonetic rules and derivational phonology, Phonologica, 80 & 82; Upside-down rules, via-rules and derivational phonology, In: Phonology in the 1980's, Storia-Scienta, Ghent, 81. *Mailing Add:* Dept of Ling U-145 Univ of Conn Storrs CT 06268

MICHAELS, JENNIFER ELIZABETH, b England, May 19, 45; US citizen; m 70. GERMAN & COMPARATIVE LITERATURE. *Educ:* Edinburgh Univ, MA Hons, 67; McGill Univ, MA,71, PhD(Ger & comp lit), 74. *Prof Exp:* Teaching asst Ger, Wesleyan Univ, Conn, 67-68; instr, Bucknell Univ, 68-69; asst prof, 75-80, ASSOC PROF GER & COMP LIT, GRINNELL COL, 80- *Mem:* MLA; Midwest Mod Lang Asn; Am Asn Teachers Ger; Western Asn Ger Studies; D H Lawrence Soc. *Res:* German expressionism; modern German drama; D H Lawrence. *Publ:* Auth, The Polarity of North and South, Bouvier, 76; The horse as a life-symbol in the works of D H Lawrence, Int Fiction Rev, 78; Chaplin and Brecht: The gold rush & The rise and fall of the city of Mahagonny, Lit/Film Quart, 80; The fiction of Leonhard Frank, Int Fiction Rev, 81; Anarchy and Eros: Otto Gross and German Expressionism, Peter Lang, 82. *Mailing Add:* Dept of Ger Grinnell Col Grinnell IA 50112

MICHALCZYK, JOHN JOSEPH, b Scranton, Pa, June 26, 41. FRENCH LITERATURE, CINEMA. *Educ:* Boston Col, BA, 66, MA, 67; Harvard Univ, PhD(French lit & cinema), 72; Weston Col, MDiv, 74. *Prof Exp:* Instr & chmn French & cinema, Loyola High Sch, Towson, Md, 67-69; asst prof French & cinema, 74-80, ASSOC PROF FINE ARTS DEPT, BOSTON COL, 80- *Mem:* Am Asn Teachers Fr; Malraux Soc; MLA. *Res:* French novelists and filmmakers; Andre Malraux and Spanish Civil War; political film. *Publ:* Auth, Malraux, le cinema, et La Condition humaine, 1/74 & Le cinema polonais en '73, 4/74, Cinema '74; Camus/Malraux: A staged version of Le Temps du mepris, 10/76 & Robbe-Grillet, Michelet and Barthes: From La Sorciere to Glissements progressifs du plaisir, 12/77, Fr Rev; Andre Malraux's Film Espoir: The Propaganda/Art Film and the Spanish Civil War, Romance Monogr, 77; Ingmar Bergman: La Passion d'etre homme aujourd'hue, Beauchesne, Paris, 77; Recurrent imagery of the Labyrinth in Robbe-Grillet's Films, Stanford Fr Rev, spring 78; The French Literary Filmmakers, Asn Univ Press, 80. *Mailing Add:* Fine Arts Dept Boston Col Chestnut Chestnut Hill MA 02167

MICHALSKI, ANDRE STANISLAW, b Lodz, Poland, July 17, 32; Can citizen. SPANISH LITERATURE. *Educ:* McGill Univ, BA, 56; Princeton Univ, MA, 58, PhD (Span), 64. *Prof Exp:* Asst prof Span, La Salle Col, 59-61; asst prof mod lang, Loyola Col, Que, 61-65, chmn dept, 63-65; asst prof Span, Yale Univ, 65-67; asst prof Romance lang, Univ NC, Chapel Hill, 67-70; ASSOC PROF SPAN, MCGILL UNIV, 70-, CHMN HISP STUDIES, 80- *Concurrent Pos:* Assoc mem, Patronato Arcipreste de Hita, Spain, 76. *Mem:* MLA; Am Asn Teachers Span & Port; Inst Int Lit Iberoam; Can Asn Hispanistas; Asn Can-Francaise pour l'Avancement des Sci. *Res:* Mediaeval Spanish literature; Golden Age literature; Spanish-American literature. *Publ:* Auth, Juan Ruiz's troba cazurra: Cruz cruzada panadera, 69 & coauth, El soneto Otono de Julio Herrera y Reissig, 79, Romance Notes; auth, Dona Barbara: un cuento de hadas, PMLA, 70; La parodia hagiografica y el dualismo Eros-Thanatos en el Libro de Buen Amor, In: El Arcipreste de Hita: Actas del I Congreso Int sobre el Arcipreste de Hita, Seresa, Barcelona, 73. *Mailing Add:* Dept of Hisp Studies McGill Univ Montreal PQ H3A 1G5 Can

MICHALSKI, JOHN, b Czernowitz, Rumania, Oct 13, 34; US citizen. COMPARATIVE LITERATURE & LINGUISTICS. *Educ:* Univ Toledo, BA, 53; Inst World Affairs, cert; Northwestern Univ, MA, 54. *Prof Exp:* Asst Ger, Northwestern Univ, 53-55; lectr mod lang, Roosevelt Univ, 56-57; instr, Marquette Univ, 57-61; asst prof Europ lang, Univ Hawaii, 61-68; asst to dean educ serv, 70-71, chmn First Hawaiian Innovations Inst, 72-73, INSTR GER, SPEECH -COMMUN, LING & CHMN DIV LANG ARTS, LEEWARD COMMUNITY COL, 68- *Concurrent Pos:* Consult export & import policies, 54-; co-dir int serv ctr, Chicago Machine Tool Expos, 55; ed, Hawaii Lang Teacher. *Mem:* MLA; Am Asn Teachers Ger; Am Anthrop Asn; Am Comp Lit Asn; Am Coun Teaching Foreign Lang. *Res:* Language teaching; communications; creative writing. *Publ:* Contribr, Am Peoples Encycl, 56-57 & Encycl World Lit, 63-64; auth, Stefan Andres: Wir sind Utopia, Heath, 63; Deutsche Dichter und Denker, Blaisdall, 67; Ferdinant Raimund, Twayne, 68. *Mailing Add:* Div of Lang Arts Leeward Community Col Pearl City HI 96782

MICHEL, JOSEPH, b Mex, Mar 29, 22; US citizen; m 59. FOREIGN LANGUAGE EDUCATION, SPANISH. *Educ:* De LaSalle Col, BA, 44; Nat Univ Mex, MA, 47; Univ NMex, PhD(Span lit), 61. *Prof Exp:* Teacher, Bernalillo Elem, NMex, 42-43, Inst Regiomontano, Mex, 44-49, Cathedral High Sch, Tex, 49 & St Paul's, La, 50-52; prof foreign lang & chmn dept, Col Santa Fe, 52-59; dir foreign lang instr, State Dept Educ, NMex, 59-61; assoc prof curric & instr & Romance lang, Col Educ & Col Arts & Sci, Univ Tex,

Austin, 62-67, prof foreign lang educ, curric & instr, Col Educ & Humanities, 67-73, dir, Foreign Lang Educ Ctr, 63-73, prof humanities, 71-73; DEAN COL MULTIDISCIPLINARY STUDIES, UNIV TEX, SAN ANTONIO, 73- *Concurrent Pos:* Consult bilingual educ, Serv Ctr XIII, 70; univ res inst grant, Univ Tex, San Antonio, 73. *Mem:* Am Asn Teachers Span & Port; Am Coun Teaching Foreign Lang; MLA; Southern Conf Lang Teaching; Nat Fed Mod Lang Teachers Asn. *Res:* A recorded survey of the language of the five year old Texas bilingual; teaching reading to the Spanish-English bilingual; reading content for the Spanish-English bilingual. *Publ:* Ed, Foreign Language Teaching, An Anthology, Macmillan, 67; coauth, Tesoro Hispanico, McGraw, 68; ed, Valle-Inclan Paginas selectas, Prentice Hall, 69; coauth, Galeria Hispanica, McGraw, 71. *Mailing Add:* Off Multidisciplinary Studies Univ of Tex San Antonio TX 78285

MICHELS, AGNES KIRSOPP LAKE, b Leiden, Neth, July 31, 09; nat US; m 41; c 1. CLASSICS. *Educ:* Bryn Mawr Col, BA, 30, AM, 31, PhD(Latin), 34. *Prof Exp:* From instr to prof Latin, 34-75, Mellon prof humanities, 70-75, EMER PROF LATIN, BRYN MAWR COL, 75- *Concurrent Pos:* Ford fac fel, 53-54; Guggenheim fel, 60-61; Martin lectr, Oberlin Col, 69; vis Paddison prof Latin, Univ NC, Chapel Hill, 77-79; vis prof Latin, Duke Univ, 81- *Honors & Awards:* Goodwin Award of Merit, Am Philol Asn, 70; Lindback Award, Bryn Mawr Col, 74. *Mem:* Vergilian Soc; Am Philol Asn (pres, 71-72). *Res:* Latin literature; Roman religion. *Publ:* Auth, The topography and interpretation of the Lupercalia, 53 & Death and two poets, 55 Trans & Proc Am Philol Asn; Early Roman religion, 1945-1952, Class Weekly, 55; The Calendar of the Roman Republic, Princeton Univ, 67; The versatility of Religio, In: The Mediterranean World, Trent Univ, 76; The Insomium of Aeneas, Class Quart, 81. *Mailing Add:* 143 Carol Woods Chapel Hill NC 27514

MICHON, JACQUES, b Montreal, Que, May 12, 45; Can citizen. FRENCH, FRENCH CANADIAN LITERATURE. *Educ:* Univ Montreal, BA, 66; McGill Univ, MA, 69; Univ Paris, Dr(French), 73. *Prof Exp:* Sessional lectr French, McGill Univ, 74-75; PROF FRENCH, UNIV SHERBROOKE, 75- *Concurrent Pos:* Humanities Res Coun Can fel, 74 & 81. *Mem:* Can Semiotics Res Asn. *Res:* French and Quebec literatures; semiotics; literary criticism. *Publ:* Auth, Mallarme et les Mots anglais, Univ Montreal, 78; Nelligan, Rev Sci Humaines, Lille, 79; Les Grands-peres de V-L Beaulieu, Voix et Images, 80; Aspects du roman quebecois des annees soixante, Fr Rev, 5/80; Semiotique et histoire litteraire, Etudes Litteraires, 81. *Mailing Add:* Dept of French Studies Univ of Sherbrooke Sherbrooke PQ J1K 2R1 Can

MICKEL, EMANUEL JOHN, JR, b Joliet, Ill, Oct 11, 37; m 59; c 3. ROMANCE LANGUAGES. *Educ:* La State Univ, AB, 59; Univ NC, AM, 61, PhD(Romance lang), 65. *Prof Exp:* Instr French, Univ NC, 64-65; from asst prof to assoc prof French & Span, Univ Nebr, Lincoln, 65-68; assoc prof, 68-73, assoc dean grad sch, 77-79, PROF FRENCH, IND UNIV, BLOOMINGTON, 73-, DIR MEDIEVAL STUDIES INST, 76- *Concurrent Pos:* Nat Endowment for Humanities grants, 80-82 & 82-83; Lilly Open fel, 81-82. *Mem:* MLA; Mediaeval Acad Am; Soc Rencesvals. *Res:* Mediaeval French & Spanish literature; 19th century French literature. *Publ:* Auth, The Artifical Paradises in French Literature, Vol I, Univ NC, 69; A reconsideration of Chretien's Erec, Romanische Forschungen, 72; Marie de France's use of irony as a stylistic and narrative device, Studies Philol, 74; Marie de France, Twayne, 74; The theme of honor in Chretien's Lancelot, Zeitschrift für romanische Philol, 75; co-ed, The Old French Crusade Cycle, Vol I: La Naissance du Chevalier au Cygne, Univ Ala, 77; Vol V: Les Chetifs, Univ Ala, 81; Eugene Froment, Twayne, 82. *Mailing Add:* Dept of French & Ital Ind Univ Bloomington IN 47401

MICKLESEN, LEW R, b Red Wing, Minn, Jan 9, 21; m 50; c 3. SLAVIC LINGUISTICS. *Educ:* Univ Minn, BS, 42; Harvard Univ, PhD, 51. *Prof Exp:* Instr Russ & Span, US Navel Acad, 45-46; sr instr Russ, Air Force Russ Prog, Syracuse Univ, 51-52; asst prof, Univ Ore, 52-53; asst prof Slavic ling, Univ Wash, 53-59; group mgr mech transl, Int Bus Machines Res Ctr, 59-63; assoc prof Slavic ling, Univ Colo, 63-64; prof, Univ Ill, 64-66; PROF SLAVIC LING, UNIV WASH, 66- *Mem:* Am Asn Teachers Slavic & EEurop Lang; Ling Soc Am; Int Ling Asn. *Res:* Balto-Slavic accentology; Russian morphology; Russian syntax. *Publ:* Coauth, Linguistic and Engineering Studies in Automatic Language Translation of Scientific Russian into English, 58 & Linguistic and Engineering Studies in Automatic Language Translation of Scientific Russian into English, Phase II, 60, Univ Wash; auth, Source-language specification with table lookup and high-capacity dictionary, Proc 1st Int Conf Machine Transl Lang, 61; Impersonal sentences in Russian, Am Contributions 6th Int Cong Slavists, Prague, 68; The structure of the Russian verb stems, Slavic World, 72; The common Slavic verbal system, Am Contributions 7th Int Cong Slavists, 73; The Slavic comparative, Topics Slavic Phonology, 74; Practical aspects of West Slavic verbal morphology, Slavic Ling & Lang Teaching, 76. *Mailing Add:* Dept of Slavic Lang & LIt Univ of Wash Seattle WA 98195

MIDDENDORF, MARVIN LUTHER, b Larson, NDak, Dec 29, 27; m 53; c 4. FOREIGN LANGUAGES, COMPARATIVE RELIGION. *Educ:* Concordia Theol Sem, MST, 54; Wash Univ, MA, 56; Concordia Sem, ThD, 69. *Prof Exp:* Instr Greek, Latin & relig, St Paul's Col, Mo, 55-57; asst prof, 57-67, ASSOC PROF GREEK & LATIN, CONCORDIA COL, MINN, 67- *Mem:* Soc Bibl Lit; Am Philol Asn; Lutheran Acad Scholar. *Res:* Classical and Biblical studies; history. *Mailing Add:* Concordia Col St Paul MN 55104

MIDDLETON, JOHN CHRISTOPHER, b Truro, Eng, June 10, 26; m 53; c 3. GERMANIC LANGUAGES. *Educ:* Oxford Univ, BA, 51, MA & PhD(Ger), 54. *Prof Exp:* English lektor, Univ Zurich, 52-55; from asst lectr to sr lectr Ger, King's Col, Univ London, 55-66; vis assoc prof, 61-62, PROF GER, UNIV TEX, AUSTIN, 66- *Concurrent Pos:* Guggenheim poetry fel, 74-75; Nat Endowment for Humanities poetry fel, 80. *Honors & Awards:* Faber Poetry Prize, 64; Univ Tex Bromberg Award, 66; Nat Transl Ctr awards, 66 & 67. *Res:* Twentieth century German literature; Dada and expressionism; mountain symbolism since the Sumerians. *Publ:* Auth, Our Flowers & Nice Bones, Fulcrum, 69; Wie wir Grossmutter zum Markt Bringen, Eremiten, WGer, 70; Selected Poems of Friedrich Hölderlin and Eduard Mörike, Univ Chicago, 72; The Lonely Suppers of W V Balloon, Carcanet & Godine, 75; Pataxanadu & Other Prose, 77, Bolshevism in Art: Expository Writings, 78, & Carminalenia, 80, Carcanet; Wooden Dog, Burning Deck, 82. *Mailing Add:* Dept of Ger Lang Batts Hall Univ of Tex Austin TX 78712

MIEL, JAN, b Wayne, Pa, Oct 10, 30; m 60; c 2. FRENCH LITERATURE, HISTORY OF IDEAS. *Educ:* Harvard Univ, AB, 52; Princeton Univ, AM, 59, PhD(French), 64. *Prof Exp:* Instr French, Goucher Col, Md, 60-62; asst prof, Mass Inst Technol, 62-64; from asst prof to assoc prof French & lett, 64-76, PROF FRENCH & LETT, WESLEYAN UNIV, 76- *Concurrent Pos:* Fels humanities, Johns Hopkins Univ, 67-68, Nat Endowment for Humanities, 75 & Guggenheim Mem Found, 76. *Mem:* MLA; NAm Soc 17th Century Fr Lit. *Res:* Blaise Pascal; French classical drama; structuralism. *Publ:* Auth, Jacques Lacan and the structure of the unconscious, Yale Fr Studies, 10/66; Pascal, Port-Royal, and Cartesian linguistics, J Hist Ideas, 6/69; Temporal form in the novel, Mod Lang Notes, 12/69; Pascal and Theology, Johns Hopkins Univ, 70; Ideas or epistemes: Hazard versus Foucault, Yale Fr Studies, spring 75. *Mailing Add:* Col of Lett Wesleyan Univ Middletown CT 06457

MIERENDORFF, MARTA, b Berlin, Ger, Oct 9, 11. SOCIOLOGY & PHILOSOPHY. *Educ:* Friedrich Wilhelm Univ, Berlin, Dr Phil(sociol & philos), 49. *Prof Exp:* Asst prof sociol, Univ Berlin, 49-60; asst prof Ger, 71-74, ASSOC PROF GER, UNIV SOUTHERN CALIF, 74- *Concurrent Pos:* Dir, Inst Sociol of Arts, 53- *Mem:* Soc sociol, Ger; MLA; Int Schutzverband deut Schriftsteller, Switz. *Res:* Sociology of the arts; the refugee artist in exile from 1933 to the present; cultural patterns of various nations. *Publ:* Contribr, Soziologen- Lexikon, Enke, Stuttgart, 55; coauth, Einfuehrung in die Kunstsoziologie, Westdeutscher, Koeln, 57; auth, Lebt das Theater? Der Wicclair Test, Inst Kunstsoziologie, Bad Ems, 60; Anpassungsverweigerung, Das Exilwerk Leonhard Franks & Spekulierende Einbildungskraft und historische Analyse, Franz Werfel . . ., In: Die Deutsche Exilliteratur 1933-45, Reclam, Stuttgart, 73. *Mailing Add:* Dept of Ger Univ of Southern Calif Los Angeles CA 90007

MIESS, MARTIN MICHAEL, b Siebenbürgen, Oct 16, 26; US citizen. GERMAN LITERATURE & PHILOLOGY. *Educ:* Univ Innsbruck, PhD(Ger), 52. *Prof Exp:* Instr Ger, US Army Lang Sch, 55-56; from asst prof to assoc prof, 56-64, head foreign lang dept, 62-76, PROF GER, EASTERN ILL UNIV, 64- *Mem:* MLA; Am Asn Teachers Ger. *Res:* Methodology; literature; dialectology. *Publ:* Auth, Im Regenbogen, Wilhelm Ennsthaler Verlag, Steyr, 75. *Mailing Add:* Dept of Foreign Lang Eastern Ill Univ Charleston IL 61920

MIGNANI, RIGO, b Florence, Italy, June 11, 21; nat US; m 51. ROMANCE PHILOLOGY. *Educ:* Univ Florence, DLett, 45; Univ Wash, PhD, 57. *Prof Exp:* Instr Ital, Harvard Univ, 48-51; from asst prof to assoc prof Romance lang, 55-72, PROF ROMANCE PHILOL, STATE UNIV NY, BINGHAMTON, 72- *Mem:* MLA; Mod Humanities Res Asn; Dante Soc Am; Mediaeval Acad Am. *Res:* Mediaeval Spanish literature; historical linguistics; Spanish-American dialectology. *Publ:* Co-auth, Ritratto dell' Italia, Heath, 67; The Book of Good Love by Juan Ruiz, State Univ NY, 70; auth, Un canzoniere italiano inedito del XIV secolo, Sansoni Licosa, 73; coauth, A Concordance to Juan Ruiz, 77 & Ruiziana, 77, State Univ NY; co-ed, A Concordance to George Herbert, Cornell Univ, 77; ed, Don Jaun Manuel, El Conde Lucanor, Sansoni Licosa, 79. *Mailing Add:* Dept of Romance Lang State Univ of NY Binghamton NY 13901

MIGNOLO, WALTER D, b Cordoba, Arg, Jan 4, 41; m 71; c 1. LATIN AMERICAN LITERATURE, SEMIOTICS. *Educ:* Univ Cordoba, MA, 69; Ecole Pratique des Hautes Etudes, Paris, Dr III Cycle, 74. *Prof Exp:* Lectr Latin Am lit, Toulouse Univ, France, 70-72; vis lectr, Ind Univ, 73-74; asst prof, 74-80, ASSOC PROF LATIN AM LIT & SEMIOTICS, UNIV MICH, 80- *Mem:* Inst Lit Iberoam; Semiotic Soc Am; Int Asn Semiotic Studies. *Res:* Text theory; literary texts. *Publ:* Auth, Elementos Para Una Teoria del Texto Literario, Critica-Grijalbo, 78; What is wrong with the theory of literature, The Sign: Semiotics around the World, Slavic Publ, 78; Paradiso: Derivacion y red, Texto Critico, 79; Semantizacion de la ficcion literaria, Dispositio, 80-81; El metatexto historiografico y la historiografia indiana, MLN, No 96, 81; Textos, modelos y metaforas, Universidad Veracruzana, 82; Teoria del texto e interpretacion de textos, UNAM, 82; Que clase de textos son generos, Acta Poetica, No 4, 82. *Mailing Add:* 800 Pauline Blvd Ann Arbor MI 48103

MIHAILOVICH, VASA D, b Prokuplje, Yugoslavia, Aug 12, 26; US citizen; m 57; c 2. SLAVIC LANGUAGES & LITERATURES. *Educ:* Wayne State Univ, BA, 56, MA, 57; Univ Calif, Berkeley, PhD(Ger), 66. *Prof Exp:* Teaching asst Ger, Univ Calif, Berkeley, 57-61; instr Russ, 61-63, from asst prof to assoc prof, 63-75, PROF SLAVIC LANG & LIT, UNIV NC, CHAPEL HILL, 75- *Mem:* MLA; Am Asn Teachers Slavic & EEurop Lang; Am Asn Advan Slavic Studies; Am Asn SSlavic Studies; NAm Soc Serbian Studies. *Res:* Russian literature; Yugoslav literatures; comparative study of Russian and Yugoslav literature and German. *Publ:* Auth, Herman Hesse as a Critic of Russian Literature, Arcadia, 67; ed, Modern Slavic Literatures, Vol I, 72 & coed, Vol II, 76, Ungar; Introduction to Yugoslav Literature, An Anthology of Fiction and Poetry, Twayne, 73; Yugoslav Literature in English: A Bibliography of Translations and Criticism (1821-1975), Slavica, 76; ed, White Stones and Fir-Trees: An Anthology of Contemporary Slavic Literature, Fairleigh Dickinson Univ, 77; Contemporary Yugoslav Poetry, Univ Iowa, 77. *Mailing Add:* Dept Slavic Lang & Lit Univ NC Chapel Hill NC 27514

MIHALCHENKO, IGOR S, b Penza, Russia, Sept 26, 13; US citizen; m 50; c 1. RUSSIAN LANGUAGE & LITERATURE. *Educ:* Univ Lvov, Poland, MLaw, 35, MDipl, 36; Yale Univ, MA, 58; NY Univ, PhD(Slavic lang & lit), 71. *Prof Exp:* Lectr Russ, Yale Univ, 58-69; asst prof, 69-77, chmn dept, 73-

80, assoc prof, 77-80, EMER ASSOC PROF RUSS, MT HOLYOKE COL, 80- *Concurrent Pos:* Asst prof Russ, eve classes, Danbury State Col, 60-66; consult, Harcourt, Brace & World Publ Corp, 62-66 & Pitman Publ Corp, 66-70; vis prof, Int Russ Sem-Unterweissenbach, Austria, 67 & 71. *Mem:* AAUP; Am Asn Teachers Slavic & EEurop Lang. *Res:* Soviet Russian literature and Russian village in Soviet Russian literature; methods of teaching Russian in West European universities; why Russian is neglected as an important language in the United States. *Publ:* Ed, Russian Intermediate Reader, Pitman, 67. *Mailing Add:* Dept of Russ Mt Holyoke Col South Hadley MA 01075

MIKALSON, JON DENNIS, b Milwaukee, Wis, Aug 1, 43; m 66. GREEK RELIGION & LITERATURE. *Educ:* Univ Wis-Madison, BA, 65; Harvard Univ, PhD(class philol), 70. *Prof Exp:* Asst prof, 70-76, ASSOC PROF CLASSICS, UNIV VA, 76-, CHMN DEPT, 78- *Concurrent Pos:* Nat Endowment for Humanities fel, 77-78. *Mem:* Am Philol Asn; Archaeol Inst Am; Class Asn of Midwest & S. *Publ:* Auth, Noumenia and Epimenia in Athens, Harvard Theol Rev, 72; Prothyma, Am J Philol, 72; The Sacred and Civil Calendar of the Athenian Year, Princeton Univ, 75; Ennius' usage of Is Ea Id, Harvard Studies Class Philol, 76; Religion in the attic Demes, 77 & Erechtheus and the Panathenaia, 76, Am J Philol; Athenian Popular Religion, NC Univ (in prep). *Mailing Add:* Dept of Classics Univ Va Charlottesville VA 22903

MIKKELSON, GERALD, b Antigo, Wis, May 16, 37; m 63; c 3. SLAVIC LANGUAGES. *Educ:* Univ Wis-Madison, BS, 59, MA, 63, PhD(Slavic lang), 71. *Prof Exp:* Asst prof Slavic lang, 67-74, ASSOC PROF SLAVIC LANG, UNIV KANS, 74- *Concurrent Pos:* Resident prog dir, Coun Int Educ Exchange, 74-75. *Mem:* MLA; Am Asn Teachers Slavic & EEurop Lang; Am Asn Advan Slavic Studies; Cent Slavic Conf (secy-treas, 70); Rocky Mountain Asn Slavic Studies. *Res:* Pushkin and Russian poetry of 19th century; contemporary Russian prose and poetry; Russian historical fiction. *Publ:* Auth, The tales of Boris Vasil'ev: A quiet dawn in Soviet Russian prose, Bks Abroad, spring 73; The mythopoetic element in Pushkin's historical novel The Captain's Daughter, Can Am Slavic Studies, summer 73. *Mailing Add:* Dept of Slavic Lang & Lit Univ of Kansas Lawrence KS 66044

MILECK, JOSEPH, b St Martin, Rumania, May 28, 22; US citizen; m 51; c 3. GERMAN. *Educ:* McMaster Univ, BA, 45; Harvard Univ, MA, 46, PhD, 50. *Prof Exp:* From instr to assoc prof, 50-74, PROF GER, UNIV CALIF, BERKELEY, 74- *Concurrent Pos:* Am Philos Soc grant, 54, 75 & 81; assoc ed, Ger Quart, 58-62; Am Coun Learned Soc grant-in-aid, 60; Fulbright travel grant, 60. *Mem:* MLA; Am Asn Teachers Ger. *Res:* Nineteenth and 20th century German prose and drama. *Publ:* Auth, Wolfgang Borchert, 59 & Names and the creative process, 61, Monatshefte; Das Glasperlenspiel: Genesis, manuscripts, and history of publication, Ger Quart, 70; contribr, Hermann Hesse as an editor, In: Studies in German Literature of the Nineteenth and Twentieth Centuries, Univ NC, 70; auth, Hermann Hesse: Biography and Bibliography, 77 & Hermann Hesse: Life and Art, 78, Univ Calif; Freud and Jung, psychoanalysis and literature, art and disease, Seminar, 78; Herman Hesse: Dichter, Sucher, Bekenner, Bertelsmann, 79. *Mailing Add:* 1050 Sterling Ave Berkeley CA 94708

MILEHAM, JAMES WARREN, b Aruba, WIndies, Mar 31, 43; US citizen. FRENCH LITERATURE. *Educ:* Lafayette Col, AB, 65; Univ Ala, MA, 69; Univ Wis- Madison, PhD(French), 75. *Prof Exp:* Asst prof, 75-81, ASSOC PROF FRENCH, UNIV WIS-MILWAUKEE, 81- *Mem:* MLA. *Res:* French novel. *Publ:* Auth, A web of conspiracy: Structure and metaphor in Balzac's novels, Ky Romance Quart, 79; Blazac's Seven of Probation, winter 80 & Numbers in the Comedic humaine, Vol XXII, No 1, Romance Notes; The Conspiracy Novel: Structure and Metaphor in Balzac's Comedic humaine, Fr Forum Publ, 82. *Mailing Add:* Dept of French & Ital Univ of Wis Milwaukee WI 53201

MILES, DAVID HOLMES, b Bangor, Maine, May 25, 40. GERMAN. *Educ:* Univ Maine, Orono, BA, 62; Princeton Univ, PhD, 68. *Prof Exp:* Asst prof Ger, Univ Mass, Boston, 67-72; assoc prof, Ohio State Univ, 72-75; chmn dept, 78-80, ASSOC PROF GER, UNIV VA, 75- *Concurrent Pos:* Alexander von Humboldt fel, Freiburg, Ger, 70-71; Guggenheim fel, 76-77; mem, Ctr Advan Study, Univ Va, 77-78. *Honors & Awards:* PMLA Parker Prize, 79. *Mem:* MLA; Am Asn Teachers Ger. *Res:* Modern German literature; comparative literature; literary theory and the visual arts. *Publ:* Auth, The past as future: Pfad and Bahn as images of temporal conflict in Hölderlin, Ger Rev, 3/71; Hofmannsthal's Novel Andreas: Memory and Self, Princeton Univ, 72; The picaro's journey to the confessional: The changing image of the hero in the German Bildungsroman, PMLA, 10/74; Literary sociology; some introductory notes, Ger Quart, 1/75; Portrait of the Marxist as a Young Hegelian: Georg Lukacs' Theory of the Novel, PMLA, 1/79. *Mailing Add:* Dept of Ger Univ of Va Charlottesville VA 22903

MILETICH, JOHN STEVEN, b Toronto, Canada, Mar 29, 35. SPANISH MEDIEVAL LITERATURE. *Educ:* Catholic Univ Am, BA, 61; Middlebury Col, MA, 66; Univ Chicago, PhD(for lit), 73. *Prof Exp:* Lectr Serbo-Croatian, Univ Chicago, 71-74; asst prof Span, Ind State Univ, 74-75; asst prof, 75-80, ASSOC PROF SPAN, UNIV UTAH, 81- *Concurrent Pos:* Lectr Span, Loyola Univ, Chicago, 72-73; grant, res, Ind State Univ, 74-75, Fulbright-Hays & Int Res & Exchange Bd, 76-77 & 81 & David P Gardner, Univ Utah, 77; res assoc, Russ & East Europ Ctr, Univ Ill, Urbana, 75; ed, La Coronica, 81-83. *Mem:* Assoc Int Hispanistas; Am-Can Soc Rencesvals; MLA; Rocky Mountain Mod Lang Asn; Am Asn Teachers Slavic & East Europ Lang & Lit. *Res:* Comparative Hispanic and Slavic folk literature; theory of literature. *Publ:* Auth, The Lute and the Lattice: Croatian Poetry of the 15(th) and 16(th) Centuries, The Bridge, Asn Croatian Writers, Vol 25, 71; Priguveni i jarki tonovi u simbolistivkim i ekspresionistivkim pjesmama, Umjetnost rijevi, 71; Narrative style in Spanish and Slavic traditional narrative poetry: Implications for the study of the romance epic, Olifant, 74; The south Slavic bugarvtica and the Spanish romance: A new approach to typology, Int J Slavic Ling & Poetics, 75; The quest for the Formula: A comparative reappraisal, Mod Philol, 76; The poetics of variation in oral-traditional narrative, Forum Iowa Russ Lit, 76; Oral literature and Pucka Knjivevnost: Toward a generic description of medieval Spanish and other narrative traditions, In: Folklore and Oral Communication, Zavod za istravivanje folklora, 81; Repetition and aesthetic function in the Poema de mio Cid and south-Slavic oral and literary epic, Bull Hisp Studies, 81. *Mailing Add:* Dept of Lang Univ of Utah Salt Lake City UT 84112

MILHAM, MARY ELLA, b Waukesha, Wis, Mar 22, 22. CLASSICS. *Educ:* Carroll Col, BA, 43; Univ Wis, MA, 44, PhD(classics, ling), 50. *Prof Exp:* Instr classics & integrated lib studies, Univ Wis, 50-54; from asst prof to assoc prof, 54-68, PROF CLASSICS, UNIV NB, 68- *Concurrent Pos:* Can Coun sr res fel, 61-62, leave fel, 68-69; Soc Sci Human Res Coun leave fel, 81-82. *Mem:* Am Philol Asn; Ling Soc Am; Class Asn Can (vpres, 76-78); Humanities Asn Can (secy-treas, 66-68); Renaissance Soc Am. *Res:* Late Latin; Renaissance Latin; textual criticism. *Publ:* Auth, A Glossarial Index to de re Coquinaria of Apicius, Univ Wis, 52; coauth, Study Guide for English Composition, Part I, 52 & auth, Part II, 52, US Armed Forces Inst; Case and prepositional usage in Apicius, Glotta, 61; Toward a stemma and fortuna of Apicius, Italia Mediovale et Humanistica, 67; Apicii Decem Libri Etexcerpta Apici, B G Teubner, 69; The Latin editions of Platina's De Honesta Voluptate, Gutenberg Jahrbuch, 77; The Vernacular editions of De Honesta Voiuptate, Gutenberg Jahrbuch, 79; Pomponius Mela and C Julius Solinus, Catalogus Commentariorum et Translationum (in press). *Mailing Add:* 20900 W Cleveland Ave New Berlin WI 53151

MILIC, LOUIS TONKO, English, Stylistics. See Vol II

MILICIC, VLADIMIR, b V Vukovie, Yugoslavia, Dec 21, 29; US citizen; m 57; c 1. SLAVIC LANGUAGES, LINGUISTICS. *Educ:* Univ Chicago, MA, 65. *Prof Exp:* Instr Russ, 62-65, asst prof Russ lang & lit, 65-79, PROF RUSS & LING, WESTERN WASH UNIV, 79- *Mem:* Am Asn Teachers Slavic & East Europ Lang; Semiotic Soc Am; Ling Soc Am; Int Asn Semiotic Studies; Western Slavic Asn. *Res:* Slavic poetics; general linguistics; semiotics. *Publ:* Auth Reverse Index of the Macedonian Language, Univ Skopje, 67; ed, Papers of Symposium on Structuralism, Western Wash State Col, 73; auth, Rhymes of Milan Rakic, Savremenik, Belgrade, 1/73; Subliminal signifiers and signifieds in R Frost's The Road Not Taken, Semiotica, 3-4/80; Conventions of poetry a iconic signs, Semiolic Soc Am, 82; Subliminal structures in folklore: Anagrammatized answers to riddles, Slavic & East Europ J, spring 82; A contribution to discussions on Serbo-Croaian metrics, Int J Slavic Ling & Poetics, XXII/2, 82. *Mailing Add:* Dept of Foreign Languages Western Washington Univ Bellingham WA 98225

MILLER, ARNOLD, b New York, NY, Aug 24, 31; m 63; c 2. FRENCH. *Educ:* Columbia Col, AB, 52; Harvard Univ, AM, 54; Univ Paris, cert mod French lit & French phonetics, 57; Columbia Univ, PhD(French), 68. *Prof Exp:* Instr French, Columbia Univ, 59-66; from instr to assoc prof, 66-77, PROF FRENCH, UNIV WIS, MADISON, 77- *Concurrent Pos:* Sr exchange scholar, Int Res & Exchanges Bd, 76; fels, Am Coun Learned Soc & Camargo Found, 79-80. *Mem:* MLA; Am Asn Teachers Fr; Am Soc 18th Century Studies. *Res:* French 18th century literature; influence of French Englightenment on 19th century Russia; Rousseau and Russia. *Publ:* Auth, Pisarev and Diderot, Diderot Studies, 64; The Annexation of a Philosophe: Diderot in Soviet Criticism, 1917-1960, Droz, Geneva, 71; Vera Zasulich's Jean-Jacques Rousseau, Studies Voltaire & 18th Century, 75; Rousseau and Russia: Some uses of the Contrat Social, Essay Lit, 78; Rousseau's Confessions in Russian criticism, Oeuvres et Critiques, 78; Rousseau and the Authoritarian Impulse, Essay Lit, 79; Louis Moreri's Grand Dictionnaire Historique, In: Predecessors of the Encyclopedie, 81. *Mailing Add:* Dept of French & Ital Univ of Wis Madison WI 53706

MILLER, BETH, b Chicago, Ill, Jan 13, 41. LATIN AMERICAN STUDIES, COMPARATIVE LITERATURE. *Educ:* Northwestern Univ, BS, 62; Univ Calif, Berkeley, MA, 65, PhD(Romance lang), 73. *Prof Exp:* Teaching asst Span, Univ Calif, Berkeley, 63-67; instr, San Francisco State Col, 67-68; asst prof Span & French, State Univ Col NY New Paltz, 68-69; instr & asst prof Span, Rutgers Univ, 69-76; ASSOC PROF SPAN, UNIV SOUTHERN CALIF, 76- *Concurrent Pos:* Fulbright fel, Peru, 81. *Mem:* Am Asn Teachers Span & Port; Pac Coast Coun Latin Am Studies; MLA; Latin Am Studies Asn; Inst Interamericano Lit Iberoamericana. *Res:* Mexican literature; modern poetry; women writers. *Publ:* Auth, Avellaneda, nineteenth century feminist, Interamerican Rev, 74; La Tristana feminista de Bunuel, Dialogos, 74; Imagen e ideologia en la Tristant de Galdos, Revista Mexicana Cult, 76; ed, Ensayos Contemporaneos sobre Jaime Torres Bodet, 76 & Siete Poetas Norteamericanas Contemporaneas, 77, Univ Nacional Autonoma Mexico; auth, Mujeres en la Literatura, Fleischer Ed, Mexico City, 78; Women and feminism in the works of Rosario Castellanos, In: Feminist Criticism: Essays on Theory, Poetry and Prose, Scarecrow, 78; ed, Women in Hispanic literature: Icons and fallen idos, Univ Calif Press, 82. *Mailing Add:* Dept of Span & Port Univ of Southern Calif University Park Los Angeles CA 90007

MILLER, CHARLES ANTHONY, b Tacoma, Wash, June 23, 37. GERMAN. *Educ:* Stanford Univ, BA, 64, MA, 66, PhD(Ger), 68. *Prof Exp:* Instr Ger, Wesleyan Univ, 67-68, asst prof, 68-73. *Publ:* Auth, Nietzche's Discovery of Dostoevsky, 73 & Nietzsche's Daughters of the Desert: a Reconsideration, 73, In: Vol II, Nietzsche- Studien, de Gruyter, Berlin; The Nihilist as tempter-redeemer: Dostoevsky's Man-God in Nietzsche's Notebooks, Vol IV, Nietzsche-Studien, de Gruyter, Berlin, 75; Nietzsches Soteriopsychologie im Spiegel von Dostoevskijs Auseinandersetzung mit dem Europäischen Nihilismus, Aneignung und Umwandlung, de Gruyter, Berlin, 78. *Mailing Add:* Yacht Haven Friday Harbor San Juan Island WA 98250

MILLER, D GARY, b Allentown, Pa, Dec 12, 42; m 67; c 2. LINGUISTICS, CLASSICS. *Educ:* Moravian Col, AB, 64; Harvard Univ, PhD(ling), 69. *Prof Exp:* Instr ling, Southern Ill Univ, 68-69; asst prof, Univ Ill, Urbana, 69-71 & McGill Univ, 71-72; asst prof ling & classics, 72-76, ASSOC PROF LING & CLASSICS, UNIV FLA, 76- *Concurrent Pos:* Pres, Academics Plus, Inc.

Mem: Ling Soc Am; Philol Soc. *Res:* Indo-European studies; linguistic theory. *Publ:* Auth, On the motivation of phonological change, In: Issues in Linguistics: Papers in Honor of Henry and Renee Kahane, Univ Ill, 73; Indo-European: VSO, SOV, SVO, or all three?, Lingua, 75; Liquids plus s in ancient Greek, Glotta, 76; Language change and poetic options, Language, 77; Was Grassmann's Law reordered in Greek?, Zeitschrift fur Vergleichende Sprachforschung, 77; Tripartism, sexism, and the rise of the femine gender in Indo-European, Fla J Anthrop, 77; Bratholamae's law and an Indo-European root structure constraint, In: Studies in Descriptive and Historical Linguistics: Festschrift for Winfred P Lehmann, 77; Some theoretical and typological implications of an Indo-European root structure constraint, In: Proceedings from the conference on Indo-European and typology, J Indo-European Studies, 78. *Mailing Add:* Dept of Classics Univ of Fla Gainesville FL 32611

MILLER, ELINOR SMITH, b Chicago, Ill, Jan 25, 31; m 53; c 4. FRENCH LANGUAGE & LITERATURE. *Educ:* Wesleyan Col, Ga, AB, 51; Univ Chicago, MA, 54, PhD(French), 66. *Prof Exp:* Asst instr English compos, Ohio State Univ, 57-58; instr French & humanities, Shimer Col, 58-67, actg chmn humanities, 65-66; assoc prof French, Temple Buell Col, 67-68; assoc prof, Rollins Col, 68-73, prof & dir, Fr Overseas Prog, 73-81; PROF FRENCH LANG & LIT, ST MARY'S COL, 81- *Concurrent Pos:* Mem women's caucus mod lang, SAtlantic Mod Lang Asn, 70-, ed, Newslett, 70-72, chmn sect women's studies, 74; Nat Endowment for Humanities fel, 71-72; Camargo Found fel, 77. *Mem:* MLA; Am Coun Teachers Foreign Lang; SAtlantic Mod Lang Asn; AAUP. *Res:* Ronsard as satirist; Catholic literary propaganda during the Reformation; Francophone literature of Africa and the West Indies. *Publ:* Transl, Virginia des Rieux's La Satyre, World, 66; Michel Butor's Niagara, Regnery, 68; auth, Cleaver and Jumirer: Black man and White woman, Black Am Lit Forum, spring 77; Approaches to the Cataract: Butor's Niagara, Studies 20th Century Lit, spring 78; The identity of the narrator in Edward Glissant's La Lezarde, SAtlantic Mod Lang Asn Bull, 5/78. *Mailing Add:* Dept of French St Mary's Col St Mary's City MD 20686

MILLER, EUGENE WESLEY, b Apollo, Pa, Dec 3, 00; m 38; c 1. CLASSICAL LANGUAGE & LITERATURE. *Educ:* Thiel Col, AB, 22; Univ Pittsburgh, PhD, 32. *Prof Exp:* Teacher, High Sch, Pa, 22-23, prin, 23-30; instr, Thiel Col, 33-35; from instr to assoc prof classics, Univ Pittsburgh, 38-60; prof, 60-71, EMER PROF CLASS LANG, THIEL COL, 71- *Mem:* Am Philol Asn; Class Asn Atlantic States (secy-treas, 49-54, pres, 58-60). *Res:* Index verborum of Pliny the Younger; introduction to Latin. *Publ:* Ed, Amphitruo, privately publ, 65. *Mailing Add:* 13 Ruth St Greenville PA 16125

MILLER, HERBERT CLEO, b Indianapolis, Ind, Jan 5, 30; m 56. SLAVIC LINGUISTICS. *Educ:* Butler Univ, BA, 52; Cornell Univ, cert, 53; Ind Univ, MA, 58, PhD(Russ intonation), 67; Moscow State Univ, cert, 63, 69. *Prof Exp:* From resident lectr to asst prof Russ & Ger, 60-72, assoc prof, 72-78, PROF SLAVIC LANG, IND UNIV, KOKOMO, 78- *Concurrent Pos:* Grant, Inter-Univ Comt Travel Grants, 68-69; group leader in USSR, Int Res & Exchanges Bd, 69; consult, Am Friends Serv Comt, 69. *Mem:* Am Asn Advan Slavic Studies; Am Asn Teachers Slavic & EEurope Lang. *Res:* Russian intonation patterns. *Mailing Add:* Off of the Dean of Faculties Ind Univ 2300 S Washington St Kokomo IN 46901

MILLER, JAMES IVAN, JR, English. See Vol II

MILLER, JAMES WHIPPLE, b Evanston, Ill, May 7, 45; m 66; c 3. COMPARATIVE & CHINESE LITERATURE. *Educ:* Yale Univ, BA, 67; Princeton Univ, PhD(comp lit), 73. *Prof Exp:* Asst prof chinese, Univ Calif, Berkeley, 72-77; PRES, BERKELEY RES PUBL, INC, 76-; GEN ED, ASIAN HUMANITIES SER, 76- *Mem:* Am Comp Lit Asn; Asn Asian Studies; Chinese Lang Teachers Asn. *Publ:* Auth, English romanticism and Chinese nature poetry, Comp Lit, summer 72; ed, Essays in Chinese Poetry, 78 & co-ed, Comparative Essays in Chinese Literature, 78, Berkeley Res Publ. *Mailing Add:* 162 Panoramic Way Berkeley CA 94704

MILLER, JIM WAYNE, b Buncombe Co, NC, Oct 21, 36; m 58; c 3. GERMAN LANGUAGE & LITERATURE, AMERICAN LITERATURE. *Educ:* Berea Col, AB, 58; Vanderbilt Univ, PhD(Ger), 65. *Prof Exp:* Asst prof, 63-65, assoc prof, 66-70, PROF GER, WESTERN KY UNIV, 70-, DEPT GRAD ADV, 71- *Concurrent Pos:* Dir Appalachian Studies Worshop, Berea Col, 73-74 & 76-77. *Honors & Awards:* Univ Award for Res & Creativity, Western Ky Univ, 76. *Mem:* Am Asn Teachers Ger; MLA; AAUP. *Res:* Nineteenth century German literature; 20th century American Southern literature; Appalachian studies. *Publ:* Translr, The Figure of Fulfillment poems, Green River, 75; auth, A mirror for Appalachia, In: Voices From the Hills, Ungar & Appalachian Consortium, 75; Jesse Stuart's Gift Outright: W-Hollow, In: Jesse Stuart: Essays on His Work, Univ Ky, 77; Appalachian education: A critique and suggestions for reform & Appalachina literature, Appalachian J, autumn 77; two poems, In: A Geography of Poets, Bantam, 78; The Mountains Have Come Closer (poems), Appalachian Consortium Press, 80; I Have a Place, Alice Lloyd Col, 81; The Salzach Sibyl (poems), trans from Emil Lerperger, Green River Press, 82. *Mailing Add:* Dept of Foreign Lang Western Ky Univ Bowling Green KY 42101

MILLER, JOHN FRANCIS, b Washington, DC, Feb 4, 50; m 72. CLASSICAL LANGUAGES. *Educ:* Xavier Univ, Ohio, BA, 68; Univ NC, Chapel Hill, MA, 74, PhD(classics), 78. *Prof Exp:* Vis asst prof, NC State Univ, Raleigh, 77-78; ASST PROF CLASSICS, UNIV MINN, 78- *Res:* Latin poetry; hellenistic poetry. *Publ:* Auth, Ritual directions in Ovid's Fasti: Dramatic hymns and didactic poetry, 80 & Propertius' tirade against Isis (2. 33a), 81-82, Class J; Callimachus and the Augustan aetiological elegy, Aufstieg u Niedergang der römischen Welt, Vol II, No 30. *Mailing Add:* Dept of Classics Univ of Minn Minneapolis MN 55455

MILLER, JOHN LOUIS, b Longview, Tex, Sept 30, 35; m 58; c 1. GERMAN, MUSIC. *Educ:* Northwestern State Univ, BM, 57; Eastman Sch, Univ Rochester, MM, 61; Univ Ore, MA, 70, PhD(Ger), 72. *Prof Exp:* Asst prof music, Linfield Col, 59-68; instr, Portland State Univ, 68-69; teaching asst Ger, Univ Ore, 69-72; assoc prof, 72-80, PROF GER, SOUTHERN ORE STATE COL, 80-, CHMN DIV HUMANITIES, 76- *Mem:* Am Asn Teachers Ger; MLA. *Res:* Interrelationship between German literature and the other arts, in particular music; E T A Hoffmann and visual arts. *Publ:* Auth, Five Fragments (musical composition), Pyraminx, 61; Goethe and music, Seminar, spring 72; Musical structures in Der Goldene Topf, Germanistische Dissertationen Kurzfassung, Reihe B, Band 3, 76. *Mailing Add:* Dept of Foreign Lang Southern Ore State Col Ashland OR 97520

MILLER, LEONARD HAVEN, b Los Angeles, Calif, Mar 30, 13; m 39; c 3. MODERN LANGUAGES. *Educ:* George Peabody Col, BS, 38, AM, 43. *Prof Exp:* Instr high sch, Tenn, 39-43; prof, David Lipscomb Col, 43-46, dean of men, 44-46; asst prof Span, 46-51, assoc prof mod lang, 51-80, EMER ASSOC PROF FOREIGN LANG, ABILENE CHRISTIAN COL, 80- *Mem:* SCent Mod Lang Asn. *Res:* Spanish-American and Mexican literature. *Mailing Add:* Dept of Foreign Languages Abilene Christian College Abilene TX 79601

MILLER, MARY RITA, b Williamsburg, Iowa, Mar 4, 20; m 47; c 1. LINGUISTICS. *Educ:* Univ Iowa, BA, 41; Univ Denver, MA, 59; Georgetown Univ, PHD(ling), 69. *Prof Exp:* From instr to asst prof Span & French, Regis Col, 62-65; asst prof, 68-71, ASSOC PROF LING, UNIV MD, COLLEGE PARK, 71- *Concurrent Pos:* Am Philos Soc grant, 70; Univ Md Gen Res Bd grant, 71 & 82. *Mem:* Ling Soc Am; MLA; Am Dialect Soc; Am Name Soc; Southeastern Conf Ling. *Res:* Place names; language acquisition; language and education problems of bilinguals and ethnic minorities. *Publ:* Auth, Bilingualism in Northern New England, Publ Am Dialect Soc, 69; The language and language beliefs of Indian children, Anthrop Ling, 70; Teaching place names in the elementary and secondary school, Md English J, 72; Competence in English language learning by American Indian monolinguals and bilinguals, In: Language and Man: Anthropological Issues, Mouton, 76; Place names of the Northern neck of Virginia, Names, 76; Children of the Salt River, Ind Univ, 77; Linguistic theory and the study of literary style, Proc XIIth Int Cong of Linguists, 78; Place-names of the northern neck of Virginia, Va State Libr, 82. *Mailing Add:* Dept of English Univ of Md College Park MD 20742

MILLER, OWEN JAMES, b Auckland, NZ, May 13, 36; m 67; c 1. FRENCH, COMPARATIVE LITERATURE. *Educ:* Univ Auckland, MA, 58; Univ Strasbourg, dipl, 61, DUniv(comp lit), 66. *Prof Exp:* From lectr to asst prof, 66-72, acting chmn comp lit, 76-78, ASSOC PROF FRENCH, UNIV TORONTO, 72- *Mem:* MLA; Midwest Mod Lang Asn; Can Comp Lit Assoc. *Res:* Twentieth century French and comparative literature. *Publ:* Co-ed (with M Valdes), Interpretation of Narrative, Univ Toronto Press, 81. *Mailing Add:* Grad Prog in Comp Lit Univ of Toronto Toronto ON M5S 1V4 Can

MILLER, ROBERT L, b Kansas City, Mo, Dec 21, 28; m 52. LINGUISTICS. *Educ:* Wayne State Univ, BA, 52; Univ Mich, MA, 54, PhD(ling), 63. *Prof Exp:* Instr Ger, Wayne State Univ, 56-61; instr, Brooklyn Col, 62-64; asst prof ling, Univ Md, 64-67; assoc prof, McGill Univ, 67-69; teaching English as second lang, Am Univ Cairo, 69-71; PROF LING, MONTCLAIR STATE COL, 71- *Mem:* Ling Soc Am; Teaching English to Speakers Other Lang; Int Ling Asn. *Res:* General linguistics; English linguistics. *Publ:* Auth, The word and its meaning, Ling, 12/66; The Linguistic Relativity Principle and Humboldtian Ethnolinguistics, Mouton, The Hague, 68. *Mailing Add:* Dept of Ling Montclair State Col Upper Montclair NJ 07043

MILLER, ROBIN FEUER, b Poughkeepsie, NJ, May 23, 47; m 71; c 2. RUSSIAN & COMPARATIVE LITERATURE. *Educ:* Swarthmore Col, BA, 69; Columbia Univ, MA, 74, PhD(Russ & comp lit), 77. *Prof Exp:* Instr Russ, Hobart & William Smith Col, 75-76; lectr Russ lit, Harvard Univ, 79-80; vis asst prof, Columbia Univ, 81; jr fel & asst prof comp lit, Cornell Univ, 81-82; FEL, RUSS RES CTR, HARVARD UNIV, 82- *Concurrent Pos:* Fel, Russ Res Ctr, Harvard Univ, 79-81; tutor, Leverett House, Harvard Univ, 79-81 & 82- *Mem:* Am Asn Advan Slavic Studies; Am Asn Teachers Slavic & East Europ Lang. *Res:* The gothic novel--its development and influence on major writers of the 19th century; the influence of Rousseau on Dostoevsky, Chernyshevsky, Tolstoy; Dostoevsky's narrative techniques. *Publ:* Auth, The role of the reader in The Idiot, Slavic & East Europ J, Vol 23, No 2; Rousseau and Dostoevsky: The morality of confession reconsidered, In: Western Philosophical Systems in Russian Literature, Southern Calif Press, 79; Notions of narratives in the notebooks for The Idiot, Ulbandus Rev, No 2, 80; Dostoesky and The Idiot: Author, Narrator and Reader, Harvard Univ Press, 81; Dostoevsky and the tale of terror, In: The Russian Novel from Pushkin to Pasternak, Yale Univ Press (in prep). *Mailing Add:* Russ Res Ctr Harvard Univ Cambridge MA 02138

MILLER, ROY ANDREW, b Winona, Minn, Dec 5, 24. LINGUISTICS. *Educ:* Gustavus Adolphus Col, BA, 46; Columbia Univ, MA, 50, PhD, 53. *Hon Degrees:* MA, Yale Univ, 64. *Prof Exp:* Lectr Japanese, Univ Calif, Berkeley, 55; from asst prof to prof ling, Int Christian Univ, Japan, 55-62; from assoc prof to prof Far Eastern lang, Yale Univ, 62-71, chmn dept E & SAsian lang & lit, 65-71, dir, Inst Far Eastern Lang, 62-71; chmn dept, 72-77, PROF ASIAN LANG & LIT, UNIV WASH, 71- *Concurrent Pos:* Dir, Inter-Univ Ctr Japanese Studies, Tokyo, 64-65; ed, Jour-Newslett, Asn Teachers Japanese, 66-71; vis prof Asian lang & lit, Univ Wash, 70-71; Japan Found sr fel, 77, mem Am adv comt, 78-90; Guggenheim fel, 78. *Mem:* Am Orient Soc; Ling Soc Am; Asn Teachers Japanese; Soc Uralo-Altaica. *Res:* Japanese language and linguistics; Altaic comparative linguistics. *Publ:* Auth, The Japanese Language, Univ Chicago, 67; ed, Bernard Bloch on Japanese, Yale Univ, 70; Japanese and the Other Altaic Languages, Univ Chicago, 71; The Footprints of the Buddha, Am Orient Soc, 75; Studies in the History of the Grammatical Tradition in Tibet, John Benjamins, Amsterdam, 76; The Japanese Language in Contemporary Japan, Some Sociolinguistic Observations, Stanford Univ Hoover Inst, 77; Origins of the Japanese Language, Univ Washington Press, 80; Japan's Modern Myth, The Language and Beyond, Weatherhill, 82. *Mailing Add:* Dept of Asian Lang & Lit Univ of Wash Seattle WA 98195

MILLER, ROYCE W, b Liberty, Maine, Dec 26, 27; m 58; c 2. ROMANCE LANGUAGES, LINGUISTICS. *Educ:* Bates Col, 48; Middlebury Col, MA, 53; George Washington Univ, PhD(Span ling), 67. *Prof Exp:* Asst prof mod lang, 56-62, assoc prof foreign lang, 62-68, PROF FOREIGN LANG, GORDON COL, 68-, CHMN DEPT LANG, 63- *Mem:* MLA; Am Asn Teachers Span & Port; Nat Asn Lang Lab Dir; Am Soc Sephardic Studies. *Res:* Sephardic ballads; Spanish literature. *Publ:* Auth, The Biblical Ballads of the Sephardic Jews, 69; The classical ballads of the Sephardic Jews, Hispania, 72; The Carolingian ballads of the Sephardic Jews, Rev Etudes Juives, 72; Explicaciones de Texto, Univ Microfilms Int, 77. *Mailing Add:* Dept of Languages Gordon College Wenham MA 01984

MILLER, STEPHEN GAYLORD, b Goshen, Ind, June 22, 42; m 71. CLASSICS, CLASSICAL ARCHEOLOGY. *Educ:* Wabash Col, AB, 64; Princeton Univ, Am, 67, PhD(class archaeol), 70. *Prof Exp:* Agora fel class archaeol, Am Sch Class Studies, Athens, 69-72; res asst, Inst Advan Studies, NJ, 72-73; asst prof, 73-75, assoc prof, 75-80, PROF CLASS ARCHAEOL, UNIV CALIF BERKELEY, 80-, FIELD DIR, NEMEA EXCAVATIONS, 73- *Concurrent Pos:* Fulbright fel, Greece, 68-69; Am Coun Learned Soc grant-in-aid, 72; dir, Am Sch Class Studies, Athens, 82- *Mem:* Archaeol Inst Am; Hellenic Soc; corresp mem Deut Archaeol Inst; Am Philol Asn. *Res:* Greek and Roman architecture, topography, epigraphy. *Publ:* The Prytaneion at Olympia, Athenische Mitteilungen, 71; A Roman Monument in the Athenian Agora, Hesperia, 72; The date of the west building at the Argive Heraion, Am J Archaeol, 73; The date of Olympic festivals, Athenische Mitteilungen, 75; Excavations at Nemea 1980, Hesperia, 77 & 81; The Prytaneion, Univ of Calif, 78; The date of the first Pythiad, Calif Studies Class Antiq, 78; Turns and lanes in the Ancient Stadium, Am J Archaeol, 80. *Mailing Add:* Dept of Classics Univ of Calif Berkeley CA 94720

MILLER, TIMOTHY SINGLEY, History, Classics. See Vol I

MILLER, WILLIAM HENRY, JR, b Feb 8, 19. FRENCH. *Educ:* Furman Univ, AB, 41; Univ Va, AM, 43; Columbia Univ, PhD, 55. *Prof Exp:* Asst, Univ Va, 42-43; lectr French, Columbia Univ, 44-47; assoc prof, 47-59, PROF FRENCH, COL CHARLESTON, 59- *Res:* Twentieth century French literature. *Publ:* Auth, Proust's Irony. *Mailing Add:* Dept of French Col of Charleston Charleston SC 29401

MILLER, WILLIAM IRVIN, b Cincinnati, Ohio, Nov 14, 42; m 70; c 1. SPANISH LANGUAGE & LITERATURE. *Educ:* Wittenberg Univ, BA, 65; Univ Fla, PhD(Romance lang), 70. *Prof Exp:* ASST PROF SPAN, UNIV AKRON, 70- *Mem:* Am Asn Teachers Span & Port; Nat Asn Learning Lab Dir; Am Coun Teachers Foreign Lang. *Res:* Hispanic and Romance Linguistics; foreign language pedagogy. *Mailing Add:* Dept of Mod Lang Univ of Akron Akron OH 44325

MILLER, YVETTE ESPINOSA, b Lota, Chile; US citizen; c 6. SPANISH & SPANISH AMERICAN LITERATURE. *Educ:* Univ Concepcion, BA; Univ Pittsburgh, MA, PhD(Span lit), 70. *Prof Exp:* Lectr Span lang, Univ Pittsburgh, 66; asst prof Span lang & lit, Chatham Col, 69-71; ASSOC PROF SPAN LANG & LIT, CARNEGIE-MELLON UNIV, 67- *Concurrent Pos:* Founder & ed-in-chief, Latin Am Lit Rev, 72-; Falk grantee, Carnegie-Mellon Univ, 74, pres, Ctr Inter-Am Women Writers, 75- *Mem:* MLA; Am Asn Teachers Span & Port; Inst Int Lit Iberoam. *Res:* Spanish and Spanish American literature. *Publ:* Auth, La Novelistica de Gabriel Miro, Ed Distrib Codice, Madrid, 75; The Chicanos: Emergence of a Social Identity Through Literary Outcry, 75 & The Social Message in Chicano Fiction: Tomas Rivera's And the Earth Did Not Part and Raymond Barrio's The Plum Plum Pickers, 76, Univ Wis; ed, Latin American Women Writers: Yesterday and Today, 77 & Special issue of Chicano literature, 77, Latin Am Lit Rev; El temario poetico de Roasario Castellanos, Hispamerica, No 29, Agosto, 81; Vargas Llosa: Contexto y estructura de La tia Julia y el escribidor, Texto-Contexto en la literatura Iberoamericana, Revista Iberoamericana, 80. *Mailing Add:* Dept of Mod Lang Carnegie-Mellon Univ Schenley Park Pittsburgh PA 15213

MILLS, CARL RHETT, b Hillsboro, Ore, May 5, 42; m 68; c 1. LINGUISTICS, ENGLISH LITERACY. *Educ:* Cent Wash State Col, BA, 69; Univ Ore, MA, 72, PhD(English & ling), 75. *Prof Exp:* Instr English, Ore State Correctional Inst, 71-73; teacher, Univ Ore, 74-75; instr ling, 75-76, chmn English lang & ling comt, 75-82, asst prof ling, 76-81, ASSOC PROF LING, UNIV CINCINNATI, 81- *Concurrent Pos:* Vpres, Grad Student Coun, Univ Ore, 70-72; Fulbright lectr, Univ Tromsø, Norway, 77-78 & Cairo Univ, Egypt, 82-83. *Res:* Psycholinguistics; sociolinguistics; computer approaches to literacy research. *Publ:* Auth, Stylistic application of ethnosemantics, Lang & Style, 76; Perceptual economy and sound change, Lang Today, 76-77; contribr, Papers for the Fourth Scandinavian Conference of Linguistics, Odense Univ Press, 78; Language Use and the Uses of Language, Georgetown Univ Press, 80; auth, The sociolinguistics of the merger in Pacific Northwest English, Papers Ling, 80; Speech samples in analysis of language attitudes, J Psycholing Res, 81; contribr, Proceedings of the Conference on Phonolgical Distinctive Features, Ling Prog, State Univ NY Stony Brook (in prep). *Mailing Add:* Dept of English Univ of Cincinnati Cincinnati OH 45221

MILLS, DAVID OTIS, b Chicago, Ill, May 6, 36; m 63; c 2. JAPANESE LANGUAGE & LITERATURE, LINGUISTICS & LANGUAGE. *Educ:* Univ Tex, Austin, BA, 58; Univ Mich, Ann Arbor, MA, 66, PhD(Japanese Lang & Lit), 74. *Prof Exp:* Instr, 70-74, asst prof, 74-77, ASSOC PROF JAPANESE & CHMN DEPT E ASIAN LANG & LIT, UNIV PITTSBURGH, 77- *Concurrent Pos:* Fulbright fel & ed adv & sr translr The Japan Interpreter, 75-76; co-ed, J Asn Teachers Japanese, 77- *Mem:* Asn Teachers Japanese; Soc Study Japanese Lang; Soc Teaching Japanese as Foreign Lang; Asn Asian Studies. *Res:* History of the Japanese language; teaching Japanese as a second language; Japanese literature. *Publ:* Auth, The Japanese Copular expression in the Nara Period, Descriptive & Applied Ling 10, 77; Teaching the Japanese Copula, J Asn Teachers Japanese, 77; Romaji in the elementary Japanese classroom, In: Proceedings of Symposium on Japanese Language Teaching, Summer Inst Ling Soc Am, 78. *Mailing Add:* Dept Foreign Lang & Lit Univ of Pittsburgh Pittsburgh PA 15260

MILLS, DOROTHY HURST, b Huntington Beach, Calif, Jan 8, 28; m 51; c 1. LINGUISTICS, SPANISH. *Educ:* Univ Southern Calif, BA, 49, MA, 50, PhD(Span & ling), 55; Univ Madrid, cert Span, 50. *Prof Exp:* Teacher Span & ling, Pac Christian Col, 50-53; teacher Span high schs, Calif, 53-56; asst prof Span, English, Latin & educ, Calif State Col, Long Beach, 56-61; Smith Mundt prof English as second lang, Univ Veracruz, 61-62; PROF SPAN, LING & ENGLISH AS SECOND LANG, CHAPMAN COL, 65- *Concurrent Pos:* Consult, NDEA Inst Instr Syst Technol, 66-68; Span teacher, Disneyland, 76- *Mem:* Am Asn Univ Women. *Res:* Contrastive linguistics; English. *Publ:* Auth, Spanish case, 2/51 & Why learn contrasing intonation contours, 5/69, Hispania. *Mailing Add:* Humanities Off Chapman Col Orange CA 92666

MILLS, EDGAR, b Buczacz, Poland, June 15, 15; US citizen; m 37; c 2. GERMAN. *Educ:* Conserv Music, Vienna, BA, 35; Rutgers Univ, MA, 58; NY Univ, PhD(Ger), 64. *Prof Exp:* Instr Ger, Rutgers Univ, 60-61 & NY Univ, 62-64; from instr to asst prof mod lang, Seton Hall Univ, 64-72, assoc prof, 72-80. *Res:* German literature. *Publ:* Auth, Die Geschichte der Einsiedlergestalt, 68 & Luther and the Jews, 69, Europäischer, Vienna; A Chassidic Friday eve service, 70 & A Saturday morning service, 72, Transcontinental Music. *Mailing Add:* 84 W Williamson Ave Hillside NJ 07205

MILLS, HARRIET CORNELIA, b Tokyo, Japan, Apr 2, 20; US citizen. CHINESE. *Educ:* Wellesley Col, BA, 41; Columbia Univ, MA, 46, PhD, 63. *Prof Exp:* Lectr Chinese, Columbia Univ, 59-60; asst prof, Cornell Univ, 60-66; assoc prof, 66-74, PROF CHINESE, UNIV MICH, ANN ARBOR, 74- *Mem:* Asn Asian Studies; MLA. *Res:* Chinese literature; teaching of Chinese language. *Publ:* Coauth, Intermediate Reader in Modern Chinese, Cornell Univ, 67. *Mailing Add:* Dept of Far Eastern Lang Univ of Mich Ann Arbor MI 48104

MILLS, JUDITH OLOSKEY, b Boston, Mass, July 31, 40; m 70; c 1. RUSSIAN LITERATURE & LANGUAGE. *Educ:* Regis Col, Mass, BA, 61; Univ Pa, MA, 63, PhD(Russ lang & lit), 66. *Prof Exp:* From instr to asst prof Russ, Univ NH, 65-67; asst prof, 67-75, asst dean, Thomas More Col, 73-74, ASSOC PROF RUSS LIT, FORDHAM UNIV, 75- *Mem:* MLA; Am Asn Teachers Slavic & EEurop Lang. *Res:* Russian short story, especially prose narrative techniques; 20th century Russian literature; the grotesque in Russian literature. *Publ:* Auth, Translr, K Paustovksy, Momentary meetings (from Russian), Poet Lore, Vol LIX, No 3; co-translr, V Kreve, Lion's last days (from Lithuanian), Lituanus, Vol XI, No 3; auth, Theme and symbol in First Love, Slavic & EEurop J, 71; Gogol's Overcoat: The pathetic passages reconsidered, PMLA, 74; Narrative technique in Pil'nyak's Mother Earth, J Russ Studies, 74; coauth, Solzhenitsyn's cry to the Soviet leaders, Commonweal, 74. *Mailing Add:* Fordham Univ Bronx NY 10458

MILLS, LEONARD RUSSELL, b Pawtucket, RI, July 31, 17. ROMANCE LANGUAGES. *Educ:* Brown Univ, BA, 39; Columbia Univ, PhD(French & Romance philol), 63. *Hon Degrees:* LittD, Univ Rome, 44. *Prof Exp:* From instr to asst prof, 62-65, ASSOC PROF FRENCH & ITAL, STATE UNIV NY COL, STONY BROOK, 65- *Concurrent Pos:* State Univ NY grants, 65, 67 & 68. *Mem:* Mediaeval Acad Am. *Publ:* Ed, Le mystere de St Sebastien, Droz, 65; auth, Une vie inedite de St Sebastien, Bibliot Humanisme Renaissance, 66; ed, L'Histoire de Barlaam et Josaphat, Droz, 73. *Mailing Add:* Dept of French State Univ NY Col Stony Brook NY 11790

MILLS, WILLIAM D, b Long Beach, Calif, Feb 17, 25; m 49; c 4. SPANISH, LINGUISTICS. *Educ:* Univ Calif, Berkeley, BA, 49; Univ Southern Calif, MA, 50; Univ Madrid, PhD (Span ling), 64. *Prof Exp:* Teacher, High Sch, 50-52; prof French, English, Span, & English as a second lang, 52-66, PROF SPAN & ENGLISH AS A SECOND LANG & HEAD DEPT, LONG BEACH CITY COL, 67- *Mem:* MLA; Teachers of English to Speakers of Other Lang. *Res:* Spanish and French literature; application of linguistics to language teaching. *Publ:* Coauth, Los toros: Bullfighting, Indice, 65; auth, Developing Sentence Habits, Am Bk Co, 66; Generating the Paragraph and the Short Essay, Appleton, 70. *Mailing Add:* Dept of Span Long Beach Col Long Beach CA 90808

MILLWARD, CELIA MCCULLOUGH, b Endicott, NY, July 27, 35; m 54; c 1. LINGUISTICS, ENGLISH. *Educ:* Syracuse Univ, AB, 55; Brown Univ, AM, 63, PhD(ling), 66. *Prof Exp:* From instr to assoc prof, 66-77, PROF ENGLISH, BOSTON UNIV, 77-, DIR FRESHMAN-SOPHOMORE ENGLISH, 71- *Concurrent Pos:* Nat Endowment for Humanities jr fel, 72-73. *Honors & Awards:* Metcalf Award, Boston Univ, 77. *Mem:* Ling Soc Am; Int Ling Asn; Am Name Soc. *Res:* Old English language and literature; Middle English grammar; modern English grammar. *Publ:* Auth, Pronominal case in Shakespearean imperatives, Language, 1-3/66; Place-name generics in Providence, RI, 1636-1736, Names, 9/71; Imperative Constructions in Old English, Mouton, The Hague, 72; coauth, Whatever happened to Hiawatha?, Genre, 9/73. *Mailing Add:* 53 Forest St Providence RI 02906

MILOSZ, CESLAW, b Szetejnie, Lithuania, June 30, 11; m 44; c 2. POLISH LITERATURE. *Educ:* Univ Wilno, mag jur, 34. *Hon Degrees:* LLD, Univ Mich, 77. *Prof Exp:* Nat Cult Fund grant lit, Poland, 34-35; lectr, 60-61, prof, 61-79, EMER PROF SLAVIC LIT, UNIV CALIF, BERKELEY, 80- *Concurrent Pos:* Creative Arts Inst, Univ Calif, fel, 67- *Honors & Awards:* Prix Litteraire Europeen, Geneva, 53; Neustadt Int Lit Prize, Univ Okla, 78. *Mem:* Am Asn Advan Slavic Studies; PEN Club. *Publ:* Auth, The Captive Mind, Knopf, 53; Postwar Polish Poetry, An Anthology, 65 & Native Realm, 68, Doubleday; The History of Polish Literature, MacMillan, 69; Selected Poems, Seabury, 73. *Mailing Add:* Dept Slavic & Lit Univ Calif Berkeley CA 94720

MILOVSOROFF, BASIL, b Siberia, Russian, Dec 31, 06; US citizen; m; c 2. LANGUAGE & LITERATURE. *Educ:* Oberlin Col, BA, 32, MA, 34. *Prof Exp:* Instr Russ lang, Cornell Univ, 43-44; asst, 57-58, from instr to prof, 58-72, dir NDEA Russ Lang Inst, summers, 60-67, chmn dept Russ lang & lit,

63-67, EMER PROF RUSS LANG, DARTMOUTH COL, 72- *Concurrent Pos:* Sculptor, designer & producer puppet plays, The Little Humpbacked Horse, 36 & Tsar Saltan, 37; designer & producer animated films, Muzzleshy, 56 & Poison in the House, 57; Darmouth fac fel, Oxford Univ, 61-62. *Mem:* AAUP. *Res:* Theatre and films; sound, color, form, non-anthropomorphic motion, color shadow dimensional changes related to puppet theatre art; use of legitimate stage technology in puppet theatre. *Publ:* Auth, Puppets and Robots, Puppetry J, 5-6/51; Reality with Strings Attached, Theatre Arts Mag, 7/53; Among My Souvenirs, 7-8/74 & Random Reflections of Puppets and Art, 11-12/76, Puppetry J. *Mailing Add:* Hopson Rd Norwich VT 05055

MILOWICKI, EDWARD JOHN, English. See Vol II

MILSTEIN, BARNEY M, b Orange, NJ, May 13, 36. GERMAN LANGUAGES & LITERATURE. *Educ:* NY Univ, BA, 62; Middlebury Col, Ger, MA, 63; Princeton Univ, PhD (Ger), 68; Rutgers Univ, MLS, 79. *Prof Exp:* Instr Ger, Wellesley Col, 67-68; asst prof, Princeton Univ, 68-71; assoc prof lit, 71-78, assoc prof info & systems sci, Stockton State Col, 78-80; SR SYST REP, RADIO CORP AM COMPUTER SERV, 81- *Mem:* Asn Develop Computer Based Instr. *Res:* Computer assisted instruction in languages; language teaching; data processing, information science. *Publ:* Contribr, 16 articles, The Reader's Encycl World Drama, Crowell, 69; auth, Eight Eighteenth Century Reading Societies, Lang & Cie, 72; Language pattern drills with coursewriter II, NJ Educ Computer Network, 74; Word order drills with coursewriter, Asn Develop Computer Based Instr, 74; A universal word game in basic, Creative Computing, 75; coauth, Instructional Strategies Utalizing a Computer Based Instructional Language, Int Bus Machines, 76; Computer assistance in foreign language instruction, Educ Resources Info Ctr, 77; auth, Plural: A program for testing and drilling English plural formation, NJ Educ Computer Networ, 3/78. *Mailing Add:* Sr System Representative Radio Corp America Cherry Hill NJ 08358

MINADEO, RICHARD WILLIAM, b Milton, NY, Nov 16, 29; m 64; c 2. CLASSICS. *Educ:* Syracuse Univ, AB, 51; Univ Wis, MS, 56, PhD(classics), 65. *Prof Exp:* From instr to assoc prof, 61-74, PROF CLASSICS, WAYNE STATE UNIV, 74- *Mem:* Am Philol Asn; Class Asn Mid W & S. *Res:* Latin poetry; Greek tragedy. *Publ:* Auth, The formal design of De Rerum Natura, Arion, 65; Three textual problems in Lucretius, Class J, 68; Theme plot and menaing in Sophocles' Electra, Classica et Mediaevalia, 69; The Lyre of Science, Wayne State Univ, 69; Sexual symbolism in Horace's Love Odes, Latomus, 75. *Mailing Add:* Dept of Greek & Latin Wayne State Univ Detroit MI 48202

MINAR, EDWIN LEROY, JR, b Portland, Ore, Apr 17, 15; div; c 3. CLASSICAL PHILOLOGY. *Educ:* Reed Col, BA, 36; Univ Wis, PhD(classics), 40. *Prof Exp:* Asst prof foreign lang, Dakota Wesleyan Univ, 39-40; from asst prof to assoc prof classics, Conn Col, 40-51; assoc prof, 51-54, head dept class studies, 51-80, prof Greek, 54-80, EMER PROF CLASS STUDIES, DEPAUW UNIV, 80- *Concurrent Pos:* Fund Advan Educ fac fel, 54-55; vis prof classics, Ind Univ, 61. *Mem:* Am Philol Asn; Soc Ancient Greek Philos. *Res:* History of ancient philosophy and political thought; Pythagoreanism. *Publ:* Auth Early Pythagorean Politics, Conn Col Monogr, 42; translr, Burkert: Lore and Science in Ancient Pythagoreanism, Harvard Univ, 72. *Mailing Add:* Dept of Class Studies DePauw Univ Greencastle IN 46135

MINC, ROSE S, b Buenos Aires, Argentina; US citizen. LATIN AMERICAN & SPANISH LITERATURE. *Educ:* Douglass Col, BA, 63; Rutgers Univ, MA, 64, PhD(Spanish), 75. *Prof Exp:* ASSOC PROF SPANISH, MONTCLAIR STATE COL, 67- *Mem:* MLA; Rocky Mountain Mod Lang Asn; Northeast Mod Lang Asn; Am Asn Teachers Spanish & Portuguese. *Publ:* Auth, Guadalupe, Duenas: La Obsesiva e Implacable Busqueda de La Realidad, Foro Literario, Uruguay, 77; Lo Fantastico y Lo Real en La Narrativa de J Rulfo y G Duenas, 77 & ed, The contemporary Latin American short story, 79, Senda Nueva De Ediciones; auth, Convergencias Judeo-Cubanas en La Poesia de J Kozer, Cuadernos Americanos, Mex, 80; Revelacion y Consagracion de lo Hebraico en La Poesia de J Kozer, Chasqui, 80; ed, Latin American Fiction Today, 80, co-ed, requiem for the Boom: Premature?, 81 & ed, Literature and Popular Culture, 82, Hispamerica. *Mailing Add:* 11 Crossbrook Pl Livingston NJ 07039

MINKOFF, HARVEY, b New York, NY. LINGUISTICS, ENGLISH. *Educ:* City Col New York, BA, 65, MA, 66, Grad Ctr, PhD(ling), 70. *Prof Exp:* Asst prof English, Iona Col, 67-71; ASSOC PROF ENGLISH & LING, HUNTER COL, 71- *Mem:* Ling Soc Am; MLA. *Res:* Applications of linguistics to language teaching and learning; theory and practice of literary translation. *Publ:* Ed, Teaching English Linguistically: Five Experimental Curricula, 71 & auth, The English Verb System, 72, Iona Col Press; (N)ever write like(?) you talk: Teaching the syntax of reading & composition, English Record, 74; coauth, Mastering Prestige English, Villa Press, 75; auth, Teaching the transition from print to script analytically, Elementary English, 75; Some stylistic consequences of Aelfric's theory of translation, Studies in Philol, 76; coauth, Transitions: A key to mature reading and writing, In: Classroom Practices in Teaching English, NCTE, 77; auth, Theory and practice of Biblical translation, City Univ New York English Forum, 82. *Mailing Add:* Dept of English Hunter Col New York NY 10021

MINTER, ELSIE GREY, b Martinsville, Va, May 4, 25. ROMANCE LANGUAGES, COMPARATIVE LITERATURE. *Educ:* Univ Richmond, BA, 47; Univ NC, MA, 48, PhD(comp lit), 63; Southern Baptist Theol Sem, MRE, 50. *Prof Exp:* From asst prof to assoc prof, 62-72, PROF MOD LANG, STETSON UNIV, 72-, DIR, INT PROGS, 75- *Mem:* MLA; Am Asn Teachers Fr; Nat Asn Foreign Student Affairs. *Res:* Henry James and the French realists; American influences on the French nouveau roman. *Mailing Add:* 815 Liberty Ct De Land FL 32720

MINTON, WILLIAM WARREN, b Hamilton, Ohio, June 30, 17; m 55; c 2. CLASSICS. *Educ:* Harvard Univ, AB, 39, AM, 40; Columbia Univ, PhD, 59. *Prof Exp:* Teacher Latin, St George's Sch, 48-50, St Paul's Sch, Garden City, LI, NY, 50-52 & Irving Sch, 53-55; asst prof classics, Hood Col, 55-57; asst prof, Vassar Col, 59-61; asst prof, 61-66, assoc prof, 67-77, chmn dept class & orient lang, 71-73, PROF CLASSICS, LEHMAN COL, 77- *Concurrent Pos:* Mem nominating comt, Am Philol Asn, 71-74, chmn, 72-73. *Honors & Awards:* City Univ New York Res Award, 78-79. *Mem:* Class Asn Atlantic States; Am Philol Asn (secy-treas, 66-68). *Res:* Hesiod; Homer; Greek drama. *Publ:* Auth, Homer's Invocations of the Muses, 60; Invocation and catalogue in Hesiod and Homer, 62, The fallacy of the structural formula, 65 & The proem-hymn of Hesiod's Theogony, 70, Trans & Proc Am Philol Asn; Hesiod's Theogony, Harvard Studies Class Philol, 75; The frequency and structuring of traditional formulas in Hesiod's Corpus, E J Brill, Leiden, 76. *Mailing Add:* Dept of Class & Orient Lang Lehman Col Bronx NY 10468

MIRABEAU, ROCH LUCIEN, b Port-au-Prince, Haiti, Feb 12, 24; US citizen; m 48; c 5. FRENCH. *Educ:* Univ Haiti, dipl, 44; Johns Hopkins Univ, MAT, 59; Univ Ill, PhD(French), 67. *Prof Exp:* From instr to asst prof French & ceramics, Fla Agr & Mech Univ, 48-61; from assoc prof to prof French, Southern Univ, Baton Rouge, 61-73, dean jr div, 69-73; prof & dir div humanities, 73-75, dean arts & sci, 75-81, PROF FRENCH, MIAMI-DADE COMMUNITY COL, 81- *Concurrent Pos:* Consult, Southern Asn Cols & Schs, 68-74; consult, Nat Humanities Fac, 76-77, mem bd trustees, 77-80; mem, Comn on Humanities, 78-80. *Res:* Creole linguistics and folklore. *Publ:* Auth, Can Haiti be helped?, Nat Mag, 5/63; The Black Scholar, Vol I, 69, Vol II, 70, A New Look at Haiti Under Duvalier, 70, Une revolution, 70 & Cinq poemes, 70, privately publ; Without Tommorrow (poem), In: New Voices in American Poetry, 72; Vautrin et le mythe balzacien, Nineteenth Century Fr Studies, 78. *Mailing Add:* PO Box 161332 Miami FL 33116

MIRANDA, ROCKY, b Mangalore, India, Sept 19, 37; US citizen. LINGUISTICS. *Educ:* Madras Christian Col, India, BA, 57; Banaras Hindu Univ, MA, 60; Cornell Univ, PhD(ling), 71. *Prof Exp:* Lectr Hindi, S B Col, India, 60-62, Dhempe Col, India, 62-64 & Cornell Univ, 69; from instr to asst prof ling, 70-77, ASSOC PROF LING, UNIV MINN, MINNEAPOLIS, 77- *Concurrent Pos:* Adj fac mem, Dept of South Asian Studies, Univ Minn, 72-; fel, Ctr for Res in Human Learning, Univ Minn, 75-76. *Mem:* Ling Soc Am; Am Orient Soc; Ling Soc India. *Res:* Historical linguistics; South Asian linguistics; Indo-European linguistics. *Publ:* Auth, Sound change and other phonological change, Minn Papers Ling & Philos Lang, 74; Internal reconstruction: Scope and limits, Lingua, 75; Indo-European gender: A study in semantic and syntactic change, J Indo-European Ling, 75; Bilingualism and genetic relationship, Studies Lang Learning, 76; Assimilation of Dravidian loans to Konkani phonological and morphological patterns, Indo-Iranian J, 77; Caste, religion and dialect differentiation in the Konkani area, Int J Sociol Lang, 78; Proto-language reconstruction from modern Indo-Aryan evidence, Indian Ling, 78; On reconstructing syntactic change, Proc Twelfth Int Cong Linguists, 78. *Mailing Add:* Dept of Ling Unif of Minn Minneapolis MN 55455

MISH, JOHN L, b Hajduki Wielkie, Poland, Jan 4, 09; US citizen; m 48; c 1. CHINESE PHILOSOPHY. *Educ:* Sem Orient Sprachen, Berlin, Ger, dipl, 32; Univ Berlin, PhD, 34. *Prof Exp:* Prof & dep dir, Sch Orient Studies, Warsaw, Poland, 34-39; prof Ger & English, Markaziyah Col, 40-41 & Chinese off, Govt of India, Bombay, 41-46; chief, Orient Div, Pub Libr, New York, 46-78; RETIRED. *Concurrent Pos:* Instr, Univ Warsaw, 35-37; cult attache, Polish Legation, Vienna, 37; assoc prof orient lang & Far Eastern hist, Asia Inst, 46-51; chief, Slavonic Div, Pub Libr, New York, 55-76; Guggenheim fel, 56; Fulbright res fel, Rome, 59-60; vis prof comp relig, Dropsie Col, 61-63; adj prof Asian studies, Seton Hall Univ, 63-76 & Ben Salem Exp Col, Fordham Univ, 67-69; adj prof, Barnard Col, Columbia Univ, 70-73. *Mem:* Am Orient Soc; PEN Club; Asn Asian Studies. *Res:* Manchu studies; early China history. *Publ:* Auth, Conditional Sentence in Classical Chinese, Augustin, Hamburg, 35; A Catholic catechism in Manchu, Monumenta Serica Nagoya, 58; coauth, Chinese Jade Books in the Chester Beatty Library, Hodges Figgis, Dublin, 63; Creating an image of Europe for China: Aleni's Hsi-Fang Ta-wen, Monumenta Serica, 64; The return of the Turgut J Asian Hist, 70; The world as languages, PEN Am Ctr, 71; The Manchu version of the Heart Sutra, Etudes Mongoles, Paris, 74. *Mailing Add:* 900 Palmer Rd Bronxville NY 10708

MISIEGO-LLAGOSTERA, MICHAELA, b Barcelona, Spain. MODERN LITERATURE, ROMANCE & GERMANIC LINGUISTICS. *Educ:* Univ Barcelona, Lic, 46, dipl English, 55, PhD(Anglosaxon), 68 Cambridge Univ, dipl English, 56; Deut Inst, Spain, dipl Ger, 57; NY Univ, MA, 61. *Prof Exp:* Instr classics & Span, Damas Negras Sch, Barcelona, 46-55; instr Span, Univ Barcelona, 55-60 & St Lawrence Univ, 61-62; instr Span ling, Univ Barcelona, 62-64; from instr to asst prof Span ling & lit, Douglass Col, Rutgers Univ, 64-68; prof Anglosaxon & Germanic ling, Univ Santiago, 68-70; ASSOC PROF SPAN LING, DOUGLASS COL, RUTGERS UNIV, 70- *Mem:* Indo-European tribal beliefs and superstitions. *Publ:* Auth, The Viking Origins of Prince Hamlet (four parts), Grial, Vigo, Spain, 69; The Origins of Anglosaxon civilization, Ariel, Barcelona, 70; Protest and Existentialism in British Contemporary Novel, Eidos, Madrid, 71; Pride and Prejudice of Jane Austen, 70 & The Scarlet Letter of Hawthorne, 72, Bitacora, Madrid; Black Poetry, El Pont, Barcelona, 73. *Mailing Add:* Dept of Romance Languages Douglass Col Rutgers Univ New Brunswick NJ 08903

MISTACCO, VICKI, b Brooklyn, NY, Nov 18, 42. FRENCH LANGUAGE & LITERATURE. *Educ:* NY Univ, BA, 63; Middlebury Col, MA, 64; Yale Univ, M Phil, 68, PhD(French), 72. *Prof Exp:* Instr, 68-72, asst prof, 72-78, chmn dept, 78-81, ASSOC PROF FRENCH, WELLESLEY COL, 78- . *Mem:* MLA; NE Mod Lang Asn. *Res:* Twentieth century French fiction; theories of reading; narratology. *Publ:* Auth, Narcissus and the image: symbol and meaning in L'Immoraliste, Ky Romance Quart, 76; co-auth, Interview: Alain Robbe-Grillet, Diacritics, winter 76; auth, Robbe-Grillet's Topologie d'une cite fantome: The theory and practice of reading Nouveaux Romans, In: The Reader in the Text, Princeton Univ, 80; Reading The Immoralist: The relevance of narrative roles, Bucknell Rev, 81. *Mailing Add:* Dept of French Wellesley Col Wellesley MA 02181

MISTRY, PURUSHOTTAM J, b Bombay, India, Oct 6, 33. LINGUISTICS. *Educ:* Univ Bombay, BA, 54, MA, 57; Univ Pa, MA, 64; Univ Calif, Los Angeles, PhD(ling), 69. *Prof Exp:* Lectr Gujarati lit, M J Col, Gujarat Univ, India, 56-61; asst prof ling, Univ Utah, 67-69; from asst prof to assoc prof, 69-76, PROF LING, CALIF STATE UNIV, FRESNO, 76-, CHMN DEPT, 73- *Mem:* Ling Soc Am; Ling Soc India. *Res:* General linguistics; Indo-Aryan linguistics; Gujarati literature. *Mailing Add:* Dept of Ling Calif State Univ Fresno CA 93740

MITCHELL, BREON, b Salina, Kans, Aug 9, 42; m 65; c 2. COMPARATIVE LITERATURE, GERMAN. *Educ:* Univ Kans, BA, 64; Oxford Univ, DPhil(comp lit), 68. *Prof Exp:* From asst prof to assoc prof, 68-78, PROF GER & COMP LIT, IND UNIV, BLOOMINGTON, 78-, CHMN COMP LIT PROG, 77- *Concurrent Pos:* Alexander von Humboldt Stiftung res fel, Bad Godesberg, Ger, 71. *Mem:* MLA; Am Comp Lit Asn. *Res:* Modern comparative literature; art history; literature and the other arts. *Publ:* Auth, Expressionism and English prose, In: Expressionism as an International Literary Phenomenon, Kiado, Budapest & Didier, Paris, 73; Franz Kafka's Elf Söhne: A new look at the puzzle, Ger Quart, 74; Art in microcosm: The manuscript stages of Beckett's Come and Go, Mod Drama, 76; James Joyce and the German Novel: 1922-1933, Ohio Univ, 76; Beyond Illustration: The Livre d'Artiste in the Twentieth Century, Lilly Libr, Publ, 76; ed, Literature and the other arts, Yr Bk Comp & Gen Lit, Vol 27, 78; Ghosts from the dungeons of the world within: Franz Kafka's Ein Brudermord, Montashefte, 81; The Complete Illustrations from Delacroix's Faust and Manet's The Raven, Dover, 81. *Mailing Add:* Dept of Comp Lit Ind Univ Bloomington IN 47401

MITCHELL, ELEANOR RETTIG, English, Linguistics. See Vol II

MITCHELL, JOHN LAWRENCE, Old & Middle English Language. See Vol II

MITCHELL, KATHERINE BLANC, b Henderson, Ky, July 20, 14; m 45; c 2. ROMANCE LANGUAGES. *Educ:* Centre Col, BA, 36; Univ Ill, MA, 41. *Prof Exp:* Sec teacher pub schs, Ky, 36-42 & 55-56; asst prof French & Span, Ky Wesleyan Col, 42-45; teacher, Ward-Belmont Jr Col, 45-47; asst prof, 57-62, assoc prof, 62-79, EMER ASSOC PROF FRENCH & SPAN, KY WESLEYAN COL, 80- *Mem:* Am Asn Teachers Fr; Am Asn Teachers Span. *Res:* Nineteenth century French literature. *Mailing Add:* 2600 S Griffith Ave Owensboro KY 42301

MITCHELL, M BONNER, b Livingston, Tex, Nov 28, 29. FRENCH, ITALIAN. *Educ:* Univ Tex, BA, 49, MA, 51; Ohio State Univ, PhD(Romance lang), 58. *Prof Exp:* From asst prof to assoc prof, 58-67, chmn dept Romance lang, 72-75, PROF FRENCH & ITAL, UNIV MO, COLUMBIA, 67- *Mem:* MLA; Am Asn Teachers Fr; Am Asn Teachers Ital; Renaissance Soc Am. *Res:* French literary theory in the 19th and 20th centuries; Italian Renaissance literature; Renaissance festivals. *Publ:* Auth, Les Manifestes Litteraires de la Belle Epoque, Seghers, Paris, 66; coauth, A Renaissance Entertainment: The Marriage of Cosimo I, Duke of Florence, Univ Mo, 68; auth, Rome in the High Renaissance: The Age of Leo X, Univ Okla, 73; The attack on Gustave Lanson and literary history, 1908-1914, Univ SC Fr Lit Ser, 77; Italian Civic Pageantry in the High Renaissance: A Descriptive Bibliography, Olschki, Florence, 79; The triumphal entry as a theatrical genre in the Cinquecento, Forum Italicum, 80. *Mailing Add:* Dept of Romance Lang Univ of Mo Columbia MO 65201

MITCHELL, MARGARETE KOCH, b Ger, Feb 8, 23; US citizen; m 57. GERMAN, SPANISH. *Educ:* Univ Heidelberg, dipl, 45; Ind Univ, Bloomington, AM, 53, AM, 61, PhD(Ger lit), 65. *Prof Exp:* Instr Ger & Span, Hiram Col, 53-57; resident lectr, Ind Univ Southeast, 62-65, asst prof Ger & Span, Stratford Col, 65-68; chmn dept Ger, 68-71, assoc prof, 68-80; LECTR GER, HOLLINS COL, 80- *Mem:* MLA; Am Asn Teachers Ger; Am Asn Teachers Span & Port; Hugo von Hofmannsthal Ges. *Res:* Comparative studies of points of contact between the German and Spanish cultures and literatures. *Mailing Add:* Dept of Ger Hollins Col Hollins VA 24020

MITCHELL, P M, b Sept 23, 16; m 41; c 3. GERMANIC LANGUAGES & LITERATURES. *Educ:* Cornell Univ, BA, 38; Univ Ill, PhD, 42. *Prof Exp:* Tutor Ger, Cornell Univ, 45-46; instr, Harvard Univ, 46-49; from asst prof to assoc prof, Univ Kans, 50-58; PROF GER, UNIV ILL, URBANA, 58- *Concurrent Pos:* Managing ed, J English & Ger Philol, 59-81 & Scandinavian Studies, 81- *Res:* Danish literature; bibliography; J C Gottsched. *Mailing Add:* Dept of Ger Lang Univ of Ill Urbana IL 61801

MITCHELL, ROBERT L, b Brooklyn, NY, Nov 6, 44; m 68; c 2. FRENCH POETRY. *Educ:* Williams Col, BA, 66; Columbia Univ, MA, 70; Harvard Univ, PhD(French), 74. *Prof Exp:* Instr French, Purdue Univ, 72-74; asst prof French, Ohio State Univ, 74-81; RES & WRITING, 81- *Concurrent Pos:* Ohio State Grad Sch grant-in-aid, 77-78. *Honors & Awards:* Ohio State Publ Award, French, 76-77. *Mem:* Midwest Mod Lang Asn; MLA; Northeast Mod Lang Asn; Am Asn Teachers French; Nineteenth Century French Studies. *Res:* French lyric poetry; stylistics; poetic theory. *Publ:* Auth, The muted fiddle: Tristan Corbiere's I Sonnet as Ars (Im) Poetica, French Rev, 76; Mint, thyme, tobacco: New possibilities of affinity in the Artes Poeticae of Verlaine and Mallarme, French Forum, 77; Baudelaire's feline: The lady or the tiger?, 19th Century French Studies, 78; Corbiere Helas!: A case of Antirayonnement, French Rev, 78; Malediction et resurrection: l'acceuil critique de Tristan Corbiere depuis 1960, Oeuvres et Critiques, 79; Tristan Corbiere, Twayne, 79; ed, Pre-text/Text/Context: Essays on Nineteenth-Century French Literature, Ohio State Univ Press, 80; Corbiere, Mallarme, Valery: Preservations and Commentary, Anma Libri, 81. *Mailing Add:* 11 Lawrence Farms Crossway Chappaqua NY 10514

MITCHELL, STEPHEN ARTHUR, b Niagara Falls, NY, Apr, 22, 51. SCANDINAVIAN LITERATURE, FOLKLORE & MYTHOLOGY. *Educ:* Univ Calif, Berkeley, AB, 74; Univ Minn, MA, 77, PhD(Scand), 80. *Prof Exp:* ASST PROF SCAND, HARVARD UNIV, 80- *Mem:* Am Folklore Soc; Medieval Acad Am; Soc Advanc Scand Studies. *Res:* Old Norse literature and mythology; Swedish literature; Scandinavian folklore. *Publ:* Auth, Address and decision-making in modern Sweden, Anthrop Ling, 79; Kamaloka and Correspondences: A new look at Spoksonaten, Meddelanden fran Strindbergssallskapet, 79; For Scirnis as mythological model: frio at kaupa, Arkiv for nordisk filologi (in prep); co-ed, A Concordance of Five Legendary Sagas, G K Hall (in prep). *Mailing Add:* Dept Germanic Lang & Lit Harvard Univ Cambridge MA 02138

MITCHELL, THOMAS N, b Castlebar, Ireland, Dec 7, 39; m 65; c 3. ANCIENT CLASSICS. *Educ:* Nat Univ Ireland, BA, 61, MA, 62; Cornell Univ, PhD(ancient classics), 66. *Prof Exp:* Instr classics, Cornell Univ, 65-66; asst prof, Swarthmore Col, 66-67; lectr, Nat Univ Ireland, 67-68; asst prof, 68-73, ASSOC PROF SWARTHMORE COL, 73- *Concurrent Pos:* Am Coun Learned Soc fel, 71-72. *Mem:* Am Philol Asn. *Res:* Cicero; Roman Republican history; Latin literature. *Publ:* Auth, Cicero Before Luca, Trans Am Philol Asn, 69; Cicero and the Senatus Consultum Ultimum, Historia, 71; Cicero, Pompey and the rise of the First Triumvirate, Traditio, 73. *Mailing Add:* Dept of Classics Swarthmore Col Swarthmore PA 19081

MITHUN, MARIANNE, b Bremerton, Wash, Apr 8, 46. LINGUISTICS. *Educ:* Pomona Col, BA, 69; Yale Univ, MA, 72, PhD(ling), 74. *Prof Exp:* Asst prof, 73-80, ASSOC PROF ANTHROP, STATE UNIV NY ALBANY, 80- *Concurrent Pos:* Vis prof ling, Univ Quebec, 73-; Phillips Fund grant, Am Philos Soc, 76. *Mem:* Ling Soc Am; Am Anthrop Asn. *Res:* Amerindian linguistics, especially Iroquoian; syntax, historical linguistics. *Publ:* Auth, Unmarked subordination in Tuscarora, Chicago Ling Soc, 73; A Grammar of Tuscarora, Garland, 76; Kanien'keha' Aokaira', NY State Museum Bull, 76; Mohawk Spelling Dictionary, NY State Museum Bull, 77; co-ed, Native Languages of North American, Univ Tex, 78; Linguistics, Philosophy, and Montague Grammar, Univ Tex, 78; Proto-Iroquoia and the Proto-Iroquoians: Cultural reconstruction from lexical sources, In: Extending the Rafters, Syracuse Univ, 78; Stalking the Susquehannas, Int J Am Ling (in press). *Mailing Add:* Dept of Anthrop State Univ of NY Albany NY 12222

MITROVICH, MIRCO, b Vranje, Yugoslavia, Dec 26, 21; US citizen; m 51; c 1. FOREIGN LANGUAGES. *Educ:* Univ Ill, BA, 55, MA, 57, PhD, 63. *Prof Exp:* Asst Ger, Univ Ill, 55-59; instr Ger & Russ, John Carroll Univ, 59-61; asst prof, 61-63, assoc prof Ger, French & Russ, 63-76, PROF GER, MUSKINGUM COL, 76- *Mem:* MLA; Midwest Mod Lang Asn. *Res:* German Baroque literature; German classic writers; comparative literatures, especially German, French, Serbo-Croatian and Russian. *Mailing Add:* Dept of Modern Languages Muskingum College New Concord OH 43762

MITSCH, RUTHMARIE H, b Saint Paul, Minn, Oct 20, 49. MODERN LANGUAGES. *Educ:* Rosary Col, BA & MA, 71; Univ Fla, PhD(French), 74. *Prof Exp:* Lectr, Lake Forest Col, 75-76 & Northwestern Univ, 76-77; ASST PROF FRENCH, IND UNIV SOUTHEAST, 79- *Mem:* Am Asn Teachers French; MLA; Medieval Acad Am; Am Coun Teaching Foreign Lang. *Res:* Medieval romance literature; Tristan legend. *Publ:* Auth, The monologues of Tristan in Thomas, Tristania, 5/77. *Mailing Add:* Div of Humanities Ind Univ Southeast New Albany IN 47150

MITTELSTADT, MICHAEL CHARLES, b Kansas City, Mo, Feb 15, 33; m. CLASSICS. *Educ:* Rockhurst Col, AB, 59; Stanford Univ, AM, 61, PhD(classics), 64. *Prof Exp:* Asst prof classics, Kalamazoo Col, 62-65; asst prof 65-72, ASSOC PROF CLASSICS, STATE UNIV NY COL, BINGHAMTON, 72- *Mem:* Am Philol Asn. *Publ:* Auth, Longus: Daphnis and Chloe and Roman narrative painting, Latomus, 7-9/67; Tacitus and Plutarch: Some interpretive methods, Rivista Studies Classici, 68. *Mailing Add:* Dept of Classics State Univ of NY Col Binghamton NY 13901

MITTMAN, BARBARA G, b Sidney, Nebr, June 28, 30; m 50; c 2. EIGHTEENTH CENTURY FRENCH THEATRE. *Educ:* Univ Ill, BA, 50; Northwestern Univ, MA, 61, PhD(French), 68. *Prof Exp:* Instr French, Northwestern Univ, 66-68; asst prof, 68-74; asst dean, 72-77, resident dir, Year Abroad in France, 76-77, ASSOC PROF FRENCH, UNIV ILL, CHICAGO CIRCLE, 74- *Res:* Eighteenth century French theatre. *Publ:* Auth, Ambiguity and unresolved conflict in Diderot's Theatre, Eighteenth Century Studies, 12/71; Diderot's First Entretien and Goldoni, Mod Lang Rev, 4/73; Some sources of the Andre scene in Diderot's Fils Naturel, Studies Voltaire & 18th Century, 73; Mystification and the good deed in Diderot's theatre, Australian J Fr Studies, 73. *Mailing Add:* Dept of French Univ of Ill PO Box 4348 Chicago IL 60680

MIX, ERVING R, b Avon, NY, Nov 25, 26; m 57; c 3. CLASSICAL LANGUAGES, ANCIENT HISTORY. *Educ:* Alfred Univ, BA, 52; Univ Pittsburgh, PhD, 61. *Prof Exp:* Instr Latin, ancient hist, Friends Acad, NY, 54-59; asst prof classics, Univ Pittsburgh, 61-64; Merrill fac fel, 62; asst prof, 64-66, assoc prof, 66-77, PROF CLASSICS, ELMIRA COL, 78- *Mem:* Am Philol Asn; Class Asn Atlantic States; Archaeol Inst Am; Class Soc Am Acad Rome (secy-treas, 67-68). *Res:* Greek and Roman historiography; classical tradition; late Roman Empire. *Publ:* Auth, Selected Latin Prose, Univ Pittsburgh, 62; Cicero and Regulus, Class World, 2/65; M Atilius Regulus: Exemplum Historicum, Mouton, The Hague, 70. *Mailing Add:* Elmira Col Elmira NY 14901

MOAYYAD, HESHMAT, b Hamadan, Iran, Nov 28, 27; m 58; c 2. ORIENTAL LANGUAGES. *Educ:* Univ Teheran, LL, 49; Univ Frankfurt, PhD(Persian lit, Ger), 58. *Prof Exp:* Lectr Persian, Univ Frankfurt, 52-59; lectr, Univ Naples, 60-61, assoc prof, 64-65; lectr, Harvard Univ, 62-63; from asst prof to assoc prof, 65-74, PROF PERSIAN LIT, UNIV CHICAGO, 74- *Mem:* Am Orient Soc; MidE Studies Asn NAm. *Res:* Persian literature and philology; German literature. *Publ:* Auth, Die Magamat des Gaznawi, Univ

Frankfurt, 59; Zum Problemkreis und Stand der Perischen Lexikographie, 62, Nachtrag zum Deutsch-Persischen Wörterbuch von Eilers, 62 & Eine Wiedergefundene Schrift über Ahmad-E Gam und Seine Nachkommen, 64, Annali 1st Univ Napoli; Parvin's poems: A cry in wilderness, In: Festschrift for Prof F Meier, Wiesbaden, Steiner, 73; ed, Faraid-I Chianthi (Medieval text), Vol I & II, Bonyad-I Farhang-I, Iran, 77-78. *Mailing Add:* Dept of Near East Lang Univ of Chicago Chicago IL 60637

MOCEGA-GONZALES, ESTHER P, b Las Villas, Cuba; US citizen. SPANISH-AMERICAN LITERATURE. *Educ:* Col Remedios, BA & BS, 39; Univ Havana, Dr Filosofia y Letras; Univ Chicago, PhD(Span lit), 73. *Prof Exp:* Prof, Inst Superior Educ, Cuba, 45-59; prof, Univ Cent de Santa Clara, 59-62; from instr to asst prof, 62-74, assoc prof, 74-80, PROF SPAN, NORTHERN ILL UNIV, 80- *Concurrent Pos:* Prof, Inst Superior Educ, Santa Clara, 59-60 & Havana, 60-62; dir sec educ, Santa Clara, 59-60; gen dir sec educ, Cuba, 60-61. *Honors & Awards:* Excellence in Teaching Award, Northern Ill Univ, 76. *Mem:* MLA; Inst Int Lit Ibero-Am; Latin-Am Studies Asn: Am Asn Teachers Span & Port. *Res:* Alejo Carpentier, Cuban writer; the Latin-American short story; the Spanish-American novel. *Publ:* Coauth, El trasfondo hispanico en la narrativa carpentieriana, Anales de Lit Hispanoamericana, 5: 253-273; El reino de este mundo de Alejo Carpentier, Cuadernos Hispanoamericanos, 4-5/77; Los pasos perdidos, a proposito de la estructura mistica del viaje, Texto critico, Mexico, 9: 71-82; El nuevo hombre en La ultima mujer y el proximo combate de Manuel Cofino Lopez, Memoria, XVIII Congreso del Inst Int de Lit Ibereroam, Madrid, 78; La revolucion y el hombre en el cuento, El llano en llamas, Cuadernos americanos, Mexico, 79; Julio Cartazar: lo de El nuevo hombre desde la ladera revolucionaria, Mexico, 4: 65-76; Alejo Carpentier: Estudios sobre su narrative, Playor, Madrid, 80; Presencia religiosa en La noche que lo dejaron solo, Memoria, XIX Congreso del Instituto Int de Lit Iberoam, Madrid, 80. *Mailing Add:* Northern Ill Univ De Kalb IL 60115

MOCHA, FRANK, b Silesia, Poland, Feb 18, 23; US citizen; m 51 c 3. POLISH LANGUAGE AND LITERATURE. *Educ:* Columbia Univ, USc, 61, MA, 63, PhD(Slavic lit), 66. *Prof Exp:* Asst prof Polish & Russ, Univ Pittsburgh, 66-71; exchange scholar Russ, Int Res & Exchanges Bd, 71-72; asst prof Polish, NY Univ, 74-76; assoc prof Polish, Univ Ill, Chicago Circle, 76-79. *Concurrent Pos:* Res scholar Polish & Russ, Kosciuszko Found, 72-73; assoc ed, Polish Rev, 73-75. *Mem:* Polish Inst Arts & Sci Am; Am Asn Advan Slavic Studies; Am Asn Teachers Slavic & East Europ Lang; Asn Advan Polish Studies; MLA. *Res:* Polish-Russian literary relations; history and culture of American Polonia. *Publ:* Auth, History as literature, Polish Rev, autumn 67; The Karamzin-Lelewel controversy, Slavic Rev, 9/72; Mazeppa in Euopean romanticism, Polish Rev, autumn 74; Tadeusz Bulharyn (F V Bulgarin) 1789-1859: A Study in Literary Maneuver, 74 & Pushkin's Poltava as a Reaction to the Revolutionary Politics and History, 75, Antemurale, Rome & London; Poles in America: A bicentennial view, Rev J Philos & Social Sci, 77; ed, Poles in America: Bicentennial Essays, Worzalla, 78. *Mailing Add:* 411 W 115th St New York NY 10025

MOELLER, HANS-BERNHARD, b Hannover, Ger, June 26, 35; m 62; c 1. GERMAN LITERATURE, EUROPEAN STUDIES. *Educ:* Knox Col, GA, 60; Univ Southern Calif, MA, 62, PhD(Ger), 64. *Prof Exp:* Instr, Northwestern Univ, 62-64; asst prof, Univ Md, College Park, 64-66; lectr, Inst Aleman Cult, Goethe Inst, Barcelona, Spain, 67-68; asst prof, Hofstra Univ, 69-70; asst prof, 70-72, ASSOC PROF GER, UNIV TEX, AUSTIN, 72- *Concurrent Pos:* Andrew Mellon fel, Univ Pittsburgh, 68-69. *Mem:* MLA; Am Asn Teachers Ger; AAUP; Western Asn Ger Studies. *Res:* Exile literature; literature and film; the novel. *Publ:* Auth, Perception, Word-Play and the Printed Page: Arno Schmidt and His Poe Novel, BA, 71; auth, Exilautoren als Drehbuchautoren, In: Die dt Exillit ab 1933 in Kalifornien, Francke, Bern, 73; Feuchtwanger's Rousseau, J Spalek; ed, Latin America and the Literature of Exile: A Comparative View of 20th Century European Refugee Writers in the New World, Heidelberg: Winter Verlag, 82. *Mailing Add:* Dept of Ger Lang Univ of Tex Austin TX 78712

MOELLER, JACK R, b New Bremen, Ohio, July 28, 25; m 49; c 2. GERMAN. *Educ:* Oberlin Col, BA, 49; Princeton Univ, PhD(Ger), 55. *Prof Exp:* Instr Ger, Oberlin Col, 53-56; teacher high sch, Mich, 56-62; from asst prof to assoc prof Ger, 62-69, PROF GER, OAKLAND UNIV, 69- *Concurrent Pos:* Mem exam comt-- Advan Placement Ger, 58-62, mem reading comt, 59-70. *Mem:* Am Asn Teachers Ger; Am Coun Teaching Foreign Lang; AAUP. *Res:* Methodology; German romanticism. *Publ:* Auth, First book in German, Ginn, 63; coauth, German today I & II, 70, III, 82; Blickpunkt Deutschland, 73 & Deutsche Heute, 2nd ed, 79; Ohn Mühe 1980, Noch dazu, 80. *Mailing Add:* Dept of Ger Oakland Univ Rochester MI 48063

MOENKEMEYER, HEINZ, b Hamburg, Ger, Sept 16, 14; US citizen; m 45. LANGUAGES. *Educ:* Univ Pa, MA, 50, PhD, 52. *Prof Exp:* Instr Ger, Univ Pa, 52-55; asst prof, Wilson Col, 55-57; from asst prof to assoc prof, 57-69, PROF GER & GEN LIT, UNIV PA, 69- *Mem:* Am Lessing Soc; MLA; Am Asn Teachers Ger; Deutsche Schillerges; Theodor-Storm-Ges. *Res:* German and comparative literature; philosophy. *Publ:* Auth, Erscheinungsformen der Sorge bei Goethe, Vol II, Beiträge Deut Philol, 54; coauth, Functional German, Am Bk Co, 59; Francois Hemsterhuis, Twayne, 75. *Mailing Add:* Dept of Ger Univ of Pa Philadelphia PA 19104

MOES, PETER CHRISTIAAN, b Bussum, Neth, Sept 9, 28; Can citizen; m 53; c 3. FRENCH LANGUAGE & LITERATURE. *Educ:* McMaster Univ, BA, 52; Univ Toronto, MA, 53, BLS, 54, PhD(French), 63. *Prof Exp:* Librn, Univ Toronto, 54-56; instr French, Univ Sask, 56-58; lectr, 60-63, asst prof, 63-66, ASSOC PROF FRENCH, SCARBOROUGH COL, UNIV TORONTO, 66- *Mem:* MLA; Can Asn Univ Teachers; Can Soc 18th Century Studies. *Res:* Beaumarchais, theatre of the French Revolution. *Mailing Add:* Dept of French Scarborough Col Univ Toronto Toronto ON M5S 1A1 Can

MOEVS, MARIA TERESA, Classical Archeology, Italian Literature. See Vol I

MOHLER, STEPHEN CHARLES, b Washington, DC, Mov 28; 37; m 59; c 3. SPANISH & PORTUGUESE LANGUAGES. *Educ:* George Washington Univ, PhD(Romance lang & lit), 69. *Prof Exp:* Teacher Span, George C Marshall High Sch, 62-70; asst prof Romance lang & lit, Univ NC, Greensboro, 70-76, chmn dept, 74-76; ASSOC PROF MOD FOREIGN LANG, UNIV TENN, MARTIN, 76-, CHMN DEPT, 77- *Mem:* SCent Mod Lang Asn; Am Asn Teachers Span & Port. *Res:* Teaching Spanish and Portuguese; Spanish American literature; language teaching methods. *Publ:* Auth, El Estilo Poetico de Leon de Greiff, Tercer Mundo, 75; coauth, Descubrir y Crear, Harper & Row, 76, 2nd ed, 81. *Mailing Add:* Dept of Mod Foreign Lang Univ of Tenn Martin TN 38238

MOLINARO, JULIUS A, b Toronto, Ont, June 13, 18; m 45; c 2. ROMANCE LANGUAGES. *Educ:* Univ Toronto, BA, 39, MA, 41, PhD, 54. *Prof Exp:* Instr Ital & Span, 46-49, lectr, 49-55, from asst prof to assoc prof, 55-67, PROF ITAL, UNIV TORONTO, 67- *Concurrent Pos:* Ed, Renaissance & Reformation, 69- *Honors & Awards:* Silver Medal, Soc Dante Alighieri, Rome. *Mem:* Am Asn Teachers Ital; Dante Soc Am; Can Soc Ital Studies (pres, 72-74); fel Royal Soc Can. *Res:* Sixteenth century and contemporary Italian poetry; Italian bibliography. *Publ:* Co-ed, The World of Dante: Six Studies in Language and Thought, Univ Toronto, 66; auth, A note on Leopardi's Il passero solitario, Studies Philol, 7/67; Bibliography of Italian studies in America, 12/67-12/72; Ariosto and the seven deadly sins, Forum Italicum, 6/69; auth, A Bibliography of Sixteenth Century Italian Verse Collections in the University of Toronto Library, 69 & ed, Petrarch to Pirandello, 73, Univ Toronto; co-ed, The culture of Italy: Mediaeval to modern, 79. *Mailing Add:* Dept of Ital Studies Univ of Toronto Toronto ON M5S 1A1 Can

MOLINSKY, STEVEN J, b Hartford, Conn, June 9, 41; m 66; c 2. LINGUISTICS, ENGLISH AS A SECOND LANGUAGE. *Educ:* Trinity Col, Conn, AB, 63; Harvard Univ, AM, 66, PhD(ling), 70. *Prof Exp:* Asst prof Russ & ling, 69-75, ASSOC PROF EDUC, BOSTON UNIV, 75- *Mem:* MLA; Teachers English to Speakers Other Lang. *Res:* Methodology of second language teaching. *Publ:* Auth, Patterns of Ellipsis in Russian Compound Noun Formations, Mouton, 73; coauth, A Russian course, Slavica, 77; Side by Side: English Grammar through Guided Conversations, Book One, 80 & Book Two, 81, Prentice Hall. *Mailing Add:* 15 Arnold Rd Wellesley Hills MA 02181

MOLLENAUER, ROBERT RUSSELL, b Denver, Colo, Mar 1, 32; div. LANGUAGES. *Educ:* Dartmouth Col, BA, 54; Ind Univ, MA, 58, PhD, 60. *Prof Exp:* From instr to asst prof, 60-65, ASSOC PROF GER, UNIV TEX, AUSTIN, 66- *Concurrent Pos:* Vis assoc prof Ger, Rice Univ, 71-72. *Mem:* MLA. *Res:* Romanticism and 19th-20th century German literature. *Publ:* Auth, The three periods of E T A Hoffmann's Romanticism: An attempt at a definition, In: Studies in Romanticism, Boston Univ, 63; ed, Introduction to Modernity: A Symposium on Eighteenth-Century Thought, Univ Tex, Austin, 65. *Mailing Add:* Dept of Langs Univ Tex Austin TX 78712

MOLLENHAUER, HANS-JOACHIM GÜNTHER, b Königsberg, Ger, July 13, 28; US citizen; m 61; c 1. MODERN LANGUAGES. *Educ:* Univ Chicago, MA, 63; Middlebury Foreign Lang Schs, PhD(mod lang), 73. *Prof Exp:* From instr to assoc prof, 63-77, PROF GER & CHMN DIV HUMANITIES, N PARK COL & THEOL SEM, 78- *Mem:* AAUP; MLA; Am Asn Teachers Ger; Am Asn Teachers Fr; Am Coun Teaching Foreign Lang. *Res:* West-European Romanticism. *Mailing Add:* Dept of Ger N Park Col & Theol Sem Chicago IL 60625

MOLLOY, SYLVIA, b Buenos Aires, Arg, Aug 29, 38. LATIN AMERICAN & COMPARATIVE LITERATURE. *Educ:* Univ Paris, Lic es Lett, 60, dipl etudes super, 61, Dr Univ, 67. *Prof Exp:* Instr Span, Sarah Lawrence Jr Yr Abroad Prog, Paris, 60-62; instr French, Univ Buenos Aires, 64-65; lectr, Cath Univ Arg, 64-66; asst prof Span, State Univ NY Buffalo, 67-69 & Vassar Col, 69-70; asst prof, 70-73, assoc prof, 73-81, PROF SPAN, PRINCETON UNIV, 81- *Concurrent Pos:* Bicentennial preceptor, Princeton Univ, 70-73; vis lectr, Bryn Mawr Col, 71. *Mem:* MLA; Inst Int Lit Iberam; Associacion Internacional de Hispanistas. *Res:* Spanish American Literature; Nineteenth-twentieth centuries; Literary theory. *Publ:* Auth, Silvina Ocampo: La exageracion como lenguaje, Sur 320, 69; La Diffusion de la litterature hispanoamericaine en France au XXe siecle, Presses Univ France, 72; coauth, La estrella junto a la luna: variantes de la figura materna en Pedro Paramo, Mod Lang Notes, 92, 77; El personaje de Susana San Juan: Clave de enunciados y de enunciacion en Pedro Paramo, Hispamerica 20, 78; auth, Las letras de Borges, Buenos Aires: Sudamericana, 79; Conciencia del publico y conciencia del yo en el primer Dario, kRevista Iberoamericana 108-109, 79; El relato como mercancia: Los adioses de Juan Carlos Onetti, Hispamerica 23-24, 79; Voracidad y solipsismo en la poesia de Dario, Sin nombre XI, 3. *Mailing Add:* Dept of Romance Lang & Lit Princeton Univ Princeton NJ 08540

MOLONEY, RAYMOND L, b San Luis, Colo, July 13, 20; m 41; c 3. SPANISH & PORTUGUESE LANGUAGE & LITERATURE. *Educ:* Univ Colo, AB, 48, MA, 49, PhD, 54. *Prof Exp:* Instr Span, Univ Colo, 47-48, instr mod lang, 48-54; instr Span & Port, Miami Univ, 54-55; from instr to asst prof, Univ Wis, 55-59, from acting asst dean to asst dean, Col Lett & Sci, 57-59; assoc prof, Portland State Col, 59-60; PROF SPAN & CHMN DEPT, MIAMI UNIV, 60- *Concurrent Pos:* Mem, Ohio Parana Partners of the Americas Comt, 65-; hon consul of Brazil, Cleveland, Ohio, 78. *Mem:* MLA; Am Asn Teachers Span & Port. *Res:* Unamuno; contemporary Brazilian literature. *Mailing Add:* Dept of Span & Port Miami Univ Oxford OH 45056

MOMMSEN, KATHARINA, b Berlin, Ger, Sept 18, 25; m 48. GERMAN LITERATURE. *Educ:* Univ Tübingen, DrPhil(Ger philol), 56; Free Univ Berlin, DrHabil(Ger philol), 62. *Prof Exp:* Researcher Ger lit, Ger Acad Sci, Berlin, 49-62; privatdocent, Free Univ Berlin, 62-67, prof, 67-70; prof, Carleton Univ, 70-74; PROF GER LIT, STANFORD UNIV, 74- *Concurrent Pos:* Guggenheim fel, 76-77; Humboldt res grant, 81-82. *Res:* Goethe;

Hofmannsthal; 18th to 20th century. *Publ:* Auth, Goethe und der Islam, Stuttgarter Goethe-Ges, 64; Natur und Fabelreich in Faust II, Gruyter, Berlin, 68; ed, Georg Herwegh: Literatur und Politik, Insel, Frankfurt, 69; Schiller: Anthologie aus dem Jahr 1782, Metzler, Stuttgard, 72; auth, Gesellschaftskritik bei Fontane und Thomas Mann, 73 & Kleists Kampf mit Goethe, 74, Stiehm, Heidelberg; ed, Herder: Journal meiner Reise im Jahr 1769, Reclam, Stuttgart, 75; auth, Hofmannsthal und Fontane, Lang, Bern, 78; Goethe und 1001 Nacht, Suhrkamp, Frankfurt, 81. *Mailing Add:* Dept of Ger Studies Stanford Univ Stanford CA 94305

MONAHAN, PATRICK JOSEPH, JR, b Bayonne, NJ, Jan 3, 42; m 64; c 1. LITERATURE, LINGUISTICS. *Educ:* St Peter's Col, NJ, AB, 63; Univ Mo-Columbia, PhD(French lit), 73; Rutgers Law Sch, JD, 80. *Prof Exp:* Instr French, Gonzaga Univ, 70-73, asst prof French & ling & dir hon prog, 73-76; ASSOC PROF FRENCH & LING, ST PETER'S COL, 77- *Concurrent Pos:* Nat Endowment for Humanities fel in residence comp lit, Yale Univ, 76-77; lectr law, Rutgers Law Sch, 81- *Mem:* AAUP; MLA; Am Bar Asn; Am Soc 18th Century Studies. *Res:* Intellectual currents in French Renaissance and Englightenment; Romance linguistics; law and language. *Publ:* Auth, Aspect in the Latin verb, Proc Pac Northwest Conf Foreign Lang, 71; contribr, A Critical Bibliography of French Literature (20th Century), Syracuse Univ, (in press). *Mailing Add:* 15 Baldwin Ave Morganville NJ 07751

MONAS, SIDNEY, b New York, NY, Sept 15, 24; m 48; c 3. RUSSIAN LANGUAGE & HISTORY. *Educ:* Princeton Univ, AB, 48; Harvard Univ, AM, 51, PhD(hist), 55. *Prof Exp:* Instr hist, Amherst Col, 55-57; from instr to asst prof, Smith Col, 57-62; assoc prof, Univ Rochester, 62-63, prof, 63-65, prof hist & foreign & comp lit, 65-69; chmn dept, 69-75, PROF SLAVIC & HIST, UNIV TEX, AUSTIN, 69- *Concurrent Pos:* Smith Col jr fac fel, 60-61; mem, nat adv bd & exec comt, Nat Transl Ctr, Austin, Tex, 65-66; Fulbright lectr Russ hist, Hebrew Univ, Jerusalem, 66-67; Nat Endowment for Humanities sr res fel, 73-74; Nat Humanities Inst, Univ Chicago, fel, 77-78. *Mem:* AHA; Am Asn Advan Slavic Studies; MLA. *Res:* The Petersburg theme in Russian literature and its relationship to the history of the city; the family theme in Russian literature; modern European history. *Publ:* Auth, The Third Section: Police and Society in Russia under Nicholas I, Harvard Univ, 61; Engineers of martyrs: Dissent and the intelligentsia, In: In Quest of Justice, Praeger, 70; Amalrik's vision of the end, In: Will the Soviet Union Survive until 1984?, Harper, 70; Leontiev: a meditation, J Mod Hist, 9/71; Introd, Essays on Russian Intellectual History, Univ Tex, 71; ed & introd, Selected Works of N S Gumilev, 72 & The Complete Works of Osip Mandelstam, 73, State Univ NY; ed, Osip Mandelstam, Selected Essays, Univ Tex, 77. *Mailing Add:* Dept of Slavic Lang Univ Tex Austin TX 78712

MONGA, LUIGI, b Desio, Milan, Italy, June 19, 41; US citizen; m 69; c 1. FRENCH ITALIAN. *Educ:* State Univ NY, Buffalo, MA, 70, PhD(French), 72. *Prof Exp:* Instr French, Diocese Fort-Archambault, Chad, 64-66; instr Latin & Ital, Sacred Heart Col, Sunningdale, Berks, Eng, 66; asst prof French & Ital, State Univ NY Col, Buffalo, 69-76; ASSOC PROF FRENCH & ITAL, VANDERBILT UNIV, 76- *Mem:* MLA; Renaissance Soc Am; Am Asn Teachers Ital; Northeast Mod Lang Asn; SAtlantic Mod Lang Asn. *Res:* Italian and French Renaissance pastoral poetry; Neo-Latin poetry; Italian 19th century regional literature . *Publ:* Auth, Porta nei ricordi milanesi di Stendhal, Osservatore Politico & Lett, 76; Carlo Porta: Poeta e milanese tra Francesi e Austriaci, Parola Popolo, 77; P G Bertarelli: A Milanese wayfarer to Eldorado, Southern Calif Quart, 77; Il Porta Tascabile: Poesie Scelte, Pan, Milan, 78; Carlo Porta in the light of recent criticism, Northeast Mod Lang Asn Ital Studies, 78; Salel imitateur de Sannazar dans sa bucolique marine, Melanges Franco Simone, 80; Le eclogae piscatoriae de Sannazar et les pescherie de Belleau, Reforme, Humanisme, Renaissance, 81; Un'imitazione del Sannazaro nel Cinquecento francese, Studi francesi, 81. *Mailing Add:* Box 1660 Sta B Vanderbilt Univ Nashville TN 37235

MONGUIO, LUIS, b Tarragona, Spain, June 25, 08; nat US; m 79. SPANISH, SPANISH AMERICAN LITERATURE. *Educ:* Univ Madrid, Lic en Derecho, 28; Univ Calif, AM, 41. *Hon Degrees:* LLD, Mills Col, 61. *Prof Exp:* Consult & secy embassy, Span Diplomatic Serv, 30-39; instr Span, Mills Col, 42-43, from asst prof to prof Romance lang, 46-57; prof, 57-75, EMER PROF SPAN, UNIV CALIF, BERKELEY, 75- *Concurrent Pos:* Guggenheim fel, 51; secy, Span Am lit group, MLA, 54, chmn, 55, chmn contemporary Span Am lit group, 60, secy, Span Am lit to 1900 group, 65, chmn, 66; fac res prof humanities, Univ Calif, Berkeley, 66; joint comt Latin Am studies, Soc Sci Res Coun & Am Coun Learned Soc grant, 60; life hon prof, Nat Univ San Marcos, Lima, 71-; vis prof, Bennington Col, 80-81, State Univ NY, Albany, 81 & 81-82. *Honors & Awards:* Knight's Cross Order of Civilian Merit, Spain, 31. *Mem:* MLA; Mod Humanities Res Asn; Am Asn Teachers Span & Port; Am Soc Aesthet; Inst Int Lit Iberoam (pres, 51-53). *Publ:* Auth, Cesar Vallejo, Columbia Univ, 52; La poesia posmodernista peruana, 54, Sobre un escritor elogiado por Cervantes, 60, Don Jose Joaquin de Mora y el Peru del Ochocientos, 67 & ed, Poesias de Don Felipe Pardo y Aliga, 73, Univ Calif; auth, Notas y estudios de literatura peruana y americana, Loera y Chavez, Bibliot Nuevo Mundo, Mex, 73. *Mailing Add:* Dept of Span & Port Univ of Calif Berkeley CA 94720

MONROE, GEORGE KARL, b Wheeling, WVa, Oct 3, 36; m 59; c 2. LINGUISTICS, GERMAN. *Educ:* Muskingum Col, BS, 58; Brown Univ, MA, 61, PhD(ling), 65. *Prof Exp:* Instr Ger, Lafayette Col, 64-65; asst prof Ger ling, 65-68; assoc prof, 68-71, PROF ENGLISH LING, KUTZTOWN STATE COL, 71- *Mem:* Ling Soc Am; NCTE; Am Dialect Soc. *Res:* German and English phonology; sound/writing correlation; computer applications in linguistics. *Publ:* Coauth, A Comparative Quantitative Phonology of Russian, Czech, and German, Am Elsevier, 68. *Mailing Add:* Dept of English Kutztown State Col Kutztown PA 19530

MONROE, JAMES T, b Dallas, Tex, Dec 21, 36; m 65. ARABIC & COMPARATIVE LITERATURE. *Educ:* Univ Houston, BA, 59; Harvard Univ, MA, 61, PhD(Span), 64. *Prof Exp:* Asst prof Arabic & Span lit, Univ Calif, San Diego, 64-70; assoc prof, 70-76, PROF ARABIC & COMP LIT, UNIV CALIF, BERKELEY, 76- *Concurrent Pos:* Nat Endowment for Art & Humanities res award, Spain & Morocco, 68-69; fel, Guggenheim Found, 71-72. *Mem:* Am Orient Soc; Mideast Studies Asn. *Publ:* Auth, The Shu'ubiyya in Al-Andalus, The Risala of Ibn Garcia and five refutations, 69, Hispano-Arabic poetry: A study anthology, 70 & Risalat at-Tawabi wa-z-zawabi: The treatise of familiar spirits and demons, 71, Univ Calif; A 10th century Hispano-Arabic epic poem: The Arjuza of Ibn Abd Rabbihi of Cordova, J Am Orient Soc, 70; Oral composition in pre-Islamic poetry, J Arabic Lit, 72; Hispano-Arabic poetry during the Caliphate of Cordova: Theory and practice, In: Arabic Poetry: Theory and Development, O Harrassowitz, 73. *Mailing Add:* Dept of Near Eastern Lang Univ of California Berkeley CA 94720

MONSANTO, CARLOS HUGO, b Guatemala City, Guatemala, Apr 16, 35; US citizen; m 57; c 2. SPANISH, FRENCH. *Educ:* Univ Iowa, BA, 58, MA, 59, PhD(Romance lang), 67. *Prof Exp:* Instr Span & French, Harpur Col, State Univ NY, 59-60; instr Span lang lab, Univ Iowa, 62-66; asst prof Span & French, Sam Houston State Col, 66-69; asst prof, 69-73, asst prof, 69-73, ASSOC PROF SPAN, UNIV HOUSTON, 73- *Concurrent Pos:* Hon vconsul of Guatemala in Houston; Am Philos Soc grant, 72-; grants, Inst Hisp Cult & Latin Am Studies & Publ Comt, Univ Houston, 72-; ed, Tex Foreign Lang Asn Bull, 72-74. *Mem:* AAUP; SCent Mod Lang Asn; MLA; Am Coun Teaching Foreign Lang; Int Inst Lit Iberoam. *Res:* Latin American and Spanish literature; Latin American folklore; the origin and development of the Guatemalan Marimba. *Publ:* Transcendencia de Antonio Acevedo Hernandez en la dramaturgia chilena, Contemporary Latin America, Univ Houston Latin Am Studies, 67; Determinacion de la protesta social en la obra dramatica de Antonio Acevedo Hernandez, Contemporary Latin America, Trinity Univ Latin Am Studies, 68; Funcion dramatica de Bolton en El gesticulador, El Imparcial, Guatemala City, 7/71; George Santayana, A Spanish Glory in American Philosophy and Letters, Golden Bk, 78; La marimba, 79, Sobre seis literatos guatemaltecos, 79, Guatemala; El teatro hispanoamericano deprotesta social y la polarizacion politca: El caso de Antonio Acevedo Hernandez (in prep); Manuel Galich: Dramaturgo olvidado guatemalteco,Latin Am Theatre Rev (in prep). *Mailing Add:* Dept of Spanish & Other Lang Univ of Houston Houston TX 77004

MONSON, DON ALFRED, b Brooklyn, NY, Oct 14, 43; m 74. MEDIEVAL FRENCH & PROVENCAL LITERATURE. *Educ:* Univ Utah, BA, 65; Univ Chicago, MA, 68, PhD(Fr), 74. *Prof Exp:* Lectr French, Univ Mich, 70-73; vis asst prof, Univ Utah, 74-75; asst prof, 76-79, ASSOC PROF FRENCH, COL WILLIAM & MARY, 79- *Concurrent Pos:* Mem Comt Accreditation Am Transl Asn, 81-; Mellon fel, Univ Pa, 81-82. *Mem:* MLA; Am Asn Teachers Fr; Medieval Acad Am; Int Arthurian Soc; Int Courtly Lit Soc. *Res:* Courtly love; didactive literature; lyric poetry. *Publ:* Translr, Jacques Robichon, The French Riviera, 77, Gaston Bonheur, To Live in France, 77 & Antoine Blondin, To Live in Paris, 77, Ed SUN, Paris; translr, entries in Rolls of Parliament, In: President's power to pardon: Constitutional history, William & Mary Law Rev, 77; auth, Les Ensenhamens occitans: Essai de definition et de delimitation du genre, Klincksieck, Paris, 81; transl, Chantal Collard, Relations between the Guidar of Northern Cameroon and the Fulbe, Studies in Third World Societies, 11: 107-125; auth, Lyrisme et sincerite: Sur une chanson de Bernart de Ventadorn, Studia occitanica in memoriam Paul Remy, Univ Toronto Press, 82. *Mailing Add:* Dept of Mod Lang Col of William & Mary Williamsburg VA 23185

MONSON, SAMUEL CHRISTIAN, b Logan, Utah, June 7, 19; m 48; c 5. ENGLISH. *Educ:* Utah State Univ, BS, 41; Columbia Univ, MA, 48, PhD(English), 53. *Prof Exp:* Lectr English, Univ Western Ont, 48-49; instr, Ricks Col, 50-52; from asst prof to assoc prof, Brigham Young Univ, 52-61; dir ed,Thorndike-Barnhart Dictionaries, Scott, Foresman & Co, 61-72, exec ed, 72; PROF ENGLISH, BRIGHAM YOUNG UNIV, 72- *Concurrent Pos:* Asst prof, Humboldt State Col, 59-60. *Mem:* Int Asn Univ Prof English. *Res:* Phonetic alphabets; history of the English language; lexicography. *Publ:* Auth, Word Building, Macmillan, 58, 2nd ed, 68. *Mailing Add:* Dept of English Brigham Young Univ Provo UT 84601

MONTANTE, MICHELA, b Caltanissetta, Italy, Aug 20, 38. COMPARATIVE ITALIAN & SPANISH LITERATURE. *Educ:* Magistrale Inst, Mag Ital, 58; State Univ, Palermo, Dr foreign lang & lit, 62; Fla State Univ, PhD(humanities), 74. *Prof Exp:* Prof Ital & English, Camerino Women Col, 62-63 & Perugia Women Col, 63-70; instr Ital, Fla State Univ, 73-74; ASST PROF ITAL & SPAN, MARQUETTE UNIV, 75- *Mem:* Dante Soc; MLA; Midwest Mod Lang Asn; Pirandello Soc. *Res:* G Verga, a social approach; Leonard Sciascia; L Pirandello; Lina Wertmüller. *Publ:* Auth, A Psycho-Social Study of the Sicilian People Based on Selected Characters from Verga's Novels, Sciascia, Italy, 76; El concepto de dios en la Muerte y la Brujula de Borges y en Todo Modo de L Sciascia, Nuevamerica, Arg, 77. *Mailing Add:* Dept of Langs Marquette Univ Milwaukee WI 53233

MONTES, YARA GONZALEZ, b Havana, Cuba; US citizen; m 53; c 2. SPANISH PENINSULAR LITERATURE. *Educ:* Havana Inst, BA, 48; Univ Havana, PhD(philos), 55; Univ Pittsburgh, PhD(Span lit), 78. *Prof Exp:* From instr to asst prof, 65-72, ASSOC PROF SPAN, UNIV HAWAII, 72- *Mem:* MLA; Am Asn Teachers Span & Port. *Res:* Contemporary Spanish poetry; Golden Age theater; women writers. *Publ:* Auth, Formas afiladas en la poesia de Miguel Hernandez, Pac Northwest Conf Foreign Lang, 4/70; Maremagnun: El horror totalitario hecho poesia, Rev Estud Hispanicos, 10/71; Los ojos en Lorca a traves de Santa Lucia y San Lazaro, Hisp Rev, 7/72; coauth, Bibliografia Critica de la Poesia Cubana 1959-61, Plaza Mayor, 72; auth, Los conflictos de Amon en La Venganza de Tamar de tirso, Hispanofila, Spec Golden Age Issue, 75; Mecanica socio-economica en la orba de Federico Garcia Lorca, Garcia Lorca Rev, fall 80; La Lozana Andaluza: Voluntad femenina individual en la picaresca albertiana in La Picaresca: Origenes, textos y estructura, Fundacion Universitaria Espanol, Madrid, 79. *Mailing Add:* Dept of European Lang & Lit Univ Hawaii 1890 East-West Rd Honolulu HI 96822

MONTES-HUIDOBRO, MATIAS, b Sagua, Cuba, Apr 26, 31; m 53; c 2. SPANISH PENINSULAR & CARIBBEAN LITERATURE. *Educ:* Univ Havana, PhD, 52. *Prof Exp:* Prof, Sch Jour, Havana, 25-61; teacher, Meadville Area Sch Dist, Pa, 62-64; from asst prof to asosc prof, 64-72, PROF SPAN, UNIV HAWAII, MANOA, 72- *Concurrent Pos:* Ed, Caribe, 76- *Mem:* MLA; Am Asn Teachers Span & Port. *Res:* Stylistics and creative writing; peninsular literature of the 19th and 20th centuries; Latin American drama and Caribbean literature. *Publ:* Auth, La anunciacion y otros cuentos cubanos, Clemares, 67; XIX: Superficie y fondo en el estilo, Castalia, 71; La sal de los muertos (drama), Escelicer, 71; coauth, Bibliografia critica de la poesia cubana, Plaza Mayor, 72; Persona, vida y mascara en el teatro cubano, Universal, 73; Desterrados al fuego (novel), Fondo de Cult Econ, 75; Segar a los muertos (novel), 80 & Ojos papa no ver (drama), 80, Universal. *Mailing Add:* Dept of Europ Lang Univ of Hawaii at Manoa Honolulu HI 96822

MONTGOMERY, THOMAS (ANDREW), b Seattle, Wash, May 19, 25; m 53; c 3. SPANISH. *Educ:* Wash State Univ, BA, 49; Univ Wis, MA, 50, PhD(Span), 55. *Prof Exp:* Instr Span, Univ Wichita, 54-55; asst prof French & Span, Elmira Col, 55-58; from asst prof to assoc prof, 58-69, PROF SPAN, TULANE UNIV, 69-, CHMN DEPT SPAN & PORT, 78- *Mem:* MLA; Am Asn Teachers Span & Port; Ling Soc Am. *Res:* Old Spanish language and literature; Romance philology. *Publ:* Co-ed, El Nuevo Testamento segun el manuscripto escurialense I.I.6, Real Acad Espanola, 70; auth, El apocope en espanol antiguo y la i final latina, In: Studia hispanica in honorem R Lapese, Gredos, Vol III, 75; Grammatical causality and formulism in the Poema de Mio Cid, In: Studies in Honor of Lloyd A Kasten, Hisp Sem Medieval Studies, 75; Complementarity of stem-vowels in the Spanish second and third conjugations, Romance Philol, 76; Basque models for some syntactic traits of the Poema de Mio Cid, Bull Hisp Studies, 77; The Poema de Mio Cid: oral art in transition, Mio Cid Studies: Tamesis, 78; Iconicity and lexical retention in Spanish, Language, 78; Vocales cerradas y acciones perfectivas, Boletin de la Real Academia Espanola, 80. *Mailing Add:* Dept of Span & Port Tulane Univ New Orleans LA 70118

MONTOYA, EMILIO, b Algeciras, Spain, June 28, 23; Can citizen; m 54; c 4. SPANISH LANGUAGE & LITERATURE. *Educ:* Ottawa Univ, BA, 67; Waterloo Lutheran Univ, MA, 68. *Prof Exp:* Lectr Span, Univ Waterloo, 66-67; lectr, Waterloo Lutheran Univ, 67-71; ASST PROF SPAN, MEM UNIV NFLD, 71- *Mem:* Int Asn Hispanists; Can Asn Hispanists; Can Asn Latinoamerican Studies. *Res:* Problemas escatologicos en las novelas de Antonio Prieto-usos y abusos de anglicismos en el espanol contemporaneo. *Mailing Add:* Dept of French & Span Mem Univ of Nfld St John's NF A1C 5S7 Can

MONTY, JEANNE RUTH, b Holyoke, Mass, July 19, 35. FRENCH LITERATURE. *Educ:* Univ Montreal, BA, 54; Univ Vt, MA, 57; Ohio State Univ, PhD(Romance lang), 60. *Prof Exp:* From instr to asst prof French, Univ Ill, 60-63; from asst prof to assoc prof, 63-71, PROF FRENCH, TULANE UNIV, 71- *Concurrent Pos:* Guggenheim fel, 68-69. *Mem:* Am Asn Teachers Fr; Am Soc 18th Century Studies; Soc Fr Etudes XVIIIeme Siecle. *Res:* Voltaire; 18th century novel. *Publ:* Auth, La Critique Litteraire de Melchior Grimm, Droz, Geneva & Minard, Paris, 61; Etude sur le Style Polemique de Voltaire: Le Dictionnaire Philosophique, Inst et Musee Voltaire, Geneva, 66; contribr, The Complete Works of Voltaire, Voltaire Found, 68-; auth, Les Romans de L'Abbe Prevost: Techniques Romanesques et Pensee Morale, Inst et Musee Voltaire, Geneva, 70; Voltaire's Opinion en Alphabet and the Encyclopedie, In: Literature and History in the Age of Ideas, Ohio State Univ, 75. *Mailing Add:* Dept of French Tulane Univ New Orleans LA 70118

MOODY, MARVIN DALE, b New Harmony, Ind, Mar 13, 38; m 66. FRENCH LANGUAGE & LINGUISTICS. *Educ:* Ind Univ, Bloomington, AB, 62, MAT, 63, PhD(French ling), 72. *Prof Exp:* Teacher French & Span, Evansville-Vanderburg Sch Corp, 63-66; lectr French, Ind Univ, Bloomington, 69-72, asst prof, 72-80. *Mem:* Ling Soc Am; MLA; Am Asn Teachers Fr; Int Ling Asn; Am Classroom Teachers Foreign Lang. *Res:* Modern French syntax; applied French linguistics; modern French morphology. *Publ:* Auth, A Classification and Analysis of Noun plus de plus Noun Construction in French, Mouton, The Hague, 72; coauth, A Workbook to Accompany a Basic Course in French, Macmillan, 74; Faire faire quelque chose al par quelau un: The causative triangle, Mod Lang J, 1-2/78; auth, Stable final consonants in French, Fr Rev, 2/78; Some preliminaries to a theory of morphology, Glossa, 4/78. *Mailing Add:* 508 S Fess Ave Bloomington IN 47401

MOODY, MICHAEL WESTON, b Caldwell, Idaho, Aug 5, 40. SPANISH, LATIN AMERICAN LITERATURE. *Educ:* Univ Wash, BA, 62, MA, 66, PhD(Span), 69. *Prof Exp:* Asst prof Span, Univ Ariz, 69-70; asst prof, 72-76, assoc prof, 76-80, PROF SPAN & CHMN DEPT, UNIV IDAHO, 80- *Concurrent Pos:* Vis prof ling, Univ Cuenca, Ecuador, 74-75; Nat Endowment for Humanities summer seminar fel, 76. *Mem:* Am Asn Teachers Span & Port. *Res:* Contemporary Latin American literature; Chicano literature. *Publ:* Auth, Don Anselmo and the myth of the hero in La casa verde, Int Fiction Rev, 77; A small whirlpool: Narrative structure in La casa verde, Tex Studies Lit & Lang, 77; San Juan del la Cruz: Analisis Textual y Estilistico de Aunque es de noche, Cuadernos del Guayas, 78; A verbal reality: Stylistic method in La casa verde, Symposium, 78; Neruda's Arrables (cancion triste): The poetic transformation of ideology, Romance Notes, 79; George Lukacs, the historical novel, and El siglo de las luces, Rev Estud Hisp, 79; Landscapes of the damned: Natural setting in la casa verde, Ky Romance Quart, 80; Paisaajes de los condenados en la casa verde, Revista Iberoamericana, 81. *Mailing Add:* Dept of For Lang & Lit Univ of Idaho Moscow ID 83843

MOODY, PATRICIA A, English Language & Linguistics. See Vol II

MOODY, RAYMOND ALBERT, b San Diego, Calif, Oct 28, 36; m 57; c 2. HISPANIC LANGUAGES & LITERATURES. *Educ:* Stanford Univ, BA, 58; Univ Calif, Los Angeles, PHD(Span & Port), 67. *Prof Exp:* Lectr Span & Port, Ind Univ, Bloomington, 64-67, asst prof, 67-71; ASSOC PROF SPAN & PORT, UNIV HAWAII, MANOA, 71- *Mem:* Am Asn Teachers Span & Port; MLA; AAUP. *Res:* Applied Portuguese and Spanish linguistics; Brazilian and Spanish-American literatures. *Publ:* Auth, More on teaching Spanish adjective position: Some theoretical and practical considerations, Hispania, 5/71; Teaching Spanish direct object pronouns, Hawaii Lang Teacher, 3/72; Protuguese prepositions: Some semantic categories, Luso-Brazilian Rev, 6/72; coauth, Coordinating the teaching of European languages, 12/73 & Current research on learning and teaching, 12/73, Educ Perspectives; auth, A semantic organization of the Portuguese subjunctive, Hispania, 9/75; Student achievement and student evaluations of teaching in Spanish, PMLA, 12/76. *Mailing Add:* Dept of Foreign Lang Univ of Hawaii at Manoa Honolulu HI 96822

MOON, HAROLD KAY, b Mesa, Ariz, July 24, 32; m 59; c 8. SPANISH, FRENCH. *Educ:* Brigham Young Univ, BA, 57, MA, 59; Syracuse Univ, PhD(Span), 63. *Prof Exp:* Instr Span, Syracuse Univ, 62-63; from asst prof to assoc prof, 63-72, PROF SPAN, BRIGHAM YOUNG UNIV, 72- *Mem:* Am Asn Teachers Span & Port; Rocky Mountain Mod Lang Asn. *Res:* Archetypal symbolism in modern Spanish literature; pedagogical problems in literary analysis; contemporary French literature. *Publ:* Auth, Description: Flaubert's external world in L'Education sentimentale, Fr Rev, 2/66; Alejandro Casona, Playwright, Brigham Young Univ, 70; Spanish Literature: A Critical Approach, Xerox Col Publ, 72; Possible Dreams: A collection of shortstories, Brigham Young Univ, 82. *Mailing Add:* Dept of Span Brigham Young Univ Provo UT 84601

MOORE, CORNELIA NIEKUS, b Amsterdam, Holland, Dec 9, 38; US citizen; m 61; c 3. GERMAN, DUTCH. *Educ:* Univ Colo, BA & MA, 66; Ind Univ, PhD(Ger), 71. *Prof Exp:* Asst Ger & Dutch, Ind Univ, 66-68, lectr, 69-70; asst prof, 71-78, ASSOC PROF GER & DUTCH, UNIV HAWAII, MANOA, 78- *Mem:* MLA; Am Asn Teachers Ger. *Res:* German Reformation and baroque literature; German language teaching; Dutch colonial literature. *Publ:* Auth, The Secularization of Religious Language in the Love Poetry of Christian Hofmann von Hofmannswaldau, Ind Univ, 71; The lover and the beloved in Hofmannswaldau's poetry, Who is glorified?, Daphnis, Vol 1: 150-167; A note on the graduate reading course, Unterrichtspraxis, Vol 6: 107; ed, Insulinde, Selected Translations from Dutch Writers of Three Centuries on the Indonesian Archipelago, Univ Hawaii, 78. *Mailing Add:* Dept of Europ Lang Univ of Hawaii Honolulu HI 96822

MOORE, ERNA MARIE, b Vienna, Austria, Aug 3, 18; US citizen; wid; c 2. GERMAN LITERATURE. *Educ:* Univ Ark, BA, 58; Univ Kans, MA, 61, PhD(Ger), 65. *Prof Exp:* Asst prof Ger, Tex Christian Univ, 63-66; ASSOC PROF GER, STATE UNIV NY ALBANY, 66- *Concurrent Pos:* State Univ NY res grant, 68-70; guest prof, Univ Würzburg, 68-69. *Mem:* MLA; Am Asn Teachers Ger. *Res:* Text revisions of the critical edition of W Heinse's works based on the manuscripts of the Frankfort, Germany public library; newly evolving literary forms, especially the diary and the aphorism. *Publ:* Auth, Die Tagebucher Wilhelm Heinses, Wilhelm Fink, Munich, 67. *Mailing Add:* Dept of Ger State Univ of NY Albany NY 12222

MOORE, FREDERICK WILLARD, b Watertown, NY, June 18, 18; m 39; c 4. FRENCH. *Educ:* Hobart Col, BA, 39; Harvard Univ, MA, 40; Yale Univ, PhD, 56. *Prof Exp:* Instr Span, Seabreeze Private Sch, Daytona Beach, Fla, 40-41; jr admin asst, visa div, US Dept State, 41-43; instr mod lang, Hobart Col, 46-48, 51; asst French, Yale Univ, 48-51; from asst prof to assoc prof mod lang, 54-64, chmn dept Romance lang, 71-72, PROF ROMANCE LANG, STATE UNIV NY, ALBANY, 64- *Mem:* MLA; Am Asn Teachers Fr. *Res:* Theater of Paul Scarron. *Mailing Add:* Dept French State Univ NY Albany NY 12222

MOORE, JOACHIM MICHAEL, b Berlin, Ger, Nov 12, 14; US citizen; m 52; c 3. FOREIGN LANGUAGE EDUCATION. *Educ:* Wagner Col, AB, 42; Columbia Univ, MA, 44; Univ Berne, PhD(philos), 51. *Prof Exp:* Instr Ger, St John's Univ, NY, 43-46; instr, Muhlenberg Col, 47-49; emigration consult & resettlement officer, Lutheran World Fed, Geneva, Switz, 49-51; lectr & asst, Acad de Rennes & Acad d'Aix en Provence, France, 51-53; instr Ger, Manhattan Col & Queens Col, NY, 53-54; instr, Defense Lang Inst, Monterey, Calif, 54-55; instr French & Ger, San Diego City Col, 55-62, chmn div humanities, 57-62; specialist foreign lang educ, San Diego City Schs, 62-66; chmn dept foreign lang, 73-75, prof, 66-80, EMER PROF FRENCH & GER, SAN DIEGO MESA COL, 80- *Concurrent Pos:* Foreign lang consult, Calif State Dept Educ, 62-63; mem, Articulation Conf Calif, 66-80; mem adv bd, Europ studies prog, Cent Col, Iowa, 68-80; US Info Agency lectr, Berlin, Munich, Stuttgart, Vienna, 71. *Mem:* AAUP; MLA; Am Asn Teachers Ger; Am Asn Teachers Fr; Am Coun Teaching For Lang. *Res:* Modern language teaching methods; foreign language education with special emphasis on the use of audiovisual media. *Publ:* Auth, The articulation jungle, Fr Rev, 12/70; filmstrips & cassettes, Focus on German Language, 74, Focus on French Language, 76, Industrie & Technik, 79, Saktuelle Gespräche, 79, Les Loisirs de Dubois, 80, Deux produits soduisnts, 81, Wie regieren sie sich?, 81 & Fondue Herkunft & Zubereitung, 81, Encore Visual Educ, Inc. *Mailing Add:* Dept of Foreign Lang San Diego Mesa Col San Diego CA 92111

MOORE, JOHN AIKEN, b Badin, NC, Oct 27, 20; m 59; c 1. SPANISH LITERATURE. *Educ:* Davidson Col, BS, 42; Univ NC, MA, 48, PhD(Romance lang), 54. *Prof Exp:* From instr to assoc prof, 50-65, PROF SPAN, COL WILLIAM & MARY, 65- *Mem:* Am Asn Teachers Span & Port; SAtlantic Mod Lang Asn. *Res:* Cervantes; La Celestina; Ramon de la Cruz. *Publ:* Auth, The idealism of Sancho Panza, 3/58 & Ambivalence of will in La Celestina, 5/65, Hispania; Ramon de la Cruz, Twayne, 72; Death as a theme in Casona's plays, SAtlantic Bull, 74; Fray Luis de Granada, Twayne, 77. *Mailing Add:* Dept of Mod Lang Col of William & Mary Williamsburg VA 23185

MOORE, JOHN VIRGIL, JR, b Atlanta, Ga, Mar 27, 33. GERMAN LITERATURE, MUSIC. *Educ:* Harvard Univ, AB, 56; Princeton Univ, MA, 62, PhD(Ger), 64. *Prof Exp:* From instr to asst prof Ger, Univ Pa, 62-70; ASSOC PROF GER, MONTCLAIR STATE COL, 70-, CHMN DEPT GER & RUSS, 72- *Mem:* MLA; Am Asn Teachers Ger; AAUP. *Res:* German art song; German romantic poetry; German Baroque literature. *Mailing Add:* Dept of German & Russian Montclair State Col Upper Montclair NJ 07043

MOORE, ROGER, b Gower, Wales, Jan 16, 44. SPANISH. *Educ:* Bristol Univ, BA, 66; Univ Toronto, MA, 67, PhD(Span), 75. *Prof Exp:* Teaching asst Span, Univ Toronto, 66-69; lectr, Univ NB, 71-72; lectr Span-French, 72-75, asst prof span, 75-79, chmn dept Romance Lang, 77-80, ASSOC PROF SPANISH, ST THOMAS UNIV, 79- *Concurrent Pos:* Ed, Boletin de la Asociacion Canadiense de Hispanistas, 81- *Mem:* Atlantic Provinces Hispanists; Am Asn Teachers Span & Port; MLA; Int Asn Hispanists; Can Asn Hispanists; Sociedad Biblioteca de Menedez Pelayo. *Res:* Spanish Golden Age literature; translation-Spanish to English; Spanish poetry. *Publ:* Auth, Towards a chronology of Quevedo's poetry, York, 77; Conceptual unity and associative fields in two of Quevedo's sonnets, Renaissance & Reformation, 7/78; Leonor's Role in El Esclavo del Demonio, Revista Canadiense de Estudios Hispanicos, 79-; Ornamental and Organic Conceits in Moreto's El lego del Carmen, Bull Comediantes, 79; Reality (good) and appearance (evil) as elements of thematic unity in Mira de Amescua's El esclavo del demonio, Perspectivas de la Comedia, 79-; Lisi, Lisa and the caballero de la Tenaza, Boletin de la Biblioteca de Menendez Pelavo, 80-; Introducing translation--The comparative approach, Can Mod Lang Rev, 81; Metatheater and magic in El Magico Prodigioso, Bull Comediantes, 81. *Mailing Add:* Dept of Romance Lang St Thomas Univ Fredericton NB E3B 5G3 Can

MOORE, WOODROW WILSON, b Norfolk, Va, Oct 15, 30, m 64; c 2. SPANISH LANGUAGE & LITERATURE. *Educ:* Southwestern at Memphis, BA, 57; Univ Nac Mex, MA, 61. *Prof Exp:* Teacher English, NY Inst, Mex City, 57-60; teacher Span, Cradock High Sch, 62-63; teacher English, Binational Ctr, US Info Agency, 63-65; ASST PROF SPAN, OLD DOMINION UNIV, 65- *Concurrent Pos:* Mem ed staff, Spanish Today Mag, 71-73. *Res:* Translation of poetry, short stories, philosophy. *Publ:* Ed & transl, Cuba and Her Poets, Ediciones Universal, 74; transl, Matter in Plotinus and Samkara, Neoplatonism and Indian Thought, State Univ NY, Albany, 82. *Mailing Add:* Dept Foreign Lang Old Dominion Univ Norfolk VA 23508

MORA, GABRIELA, b Santiago, Chile; m 69. SPANISH, HISPANIC AMERICAN LITERATURE. *Educ:* Univ Chile, Bachiller, 49, cert prof Span, 54; Smith Col, PhD(hisp lit), 71. *Prof Exp:* Prof Span, Rancagua, 54-57; prof, Santiago Col, Chile, 57-60; instr, Arlington State Col, 61-63; instr, Univ Mass, Amherst, 63-69; asst prof Span lang & Hispanic Am lit, City Col NY, 71-77; asst prof Span, Columbia Univ, 77-80; ASSOC PROF SPAN, RUTGERS UNIV, 80- *Concurrent Pos:* Consult, Bilingual Press, 75-; Columbia Univ Coun for res in humanities fel, 79. *Mem:* MLA; Latin Am Studies Asn. *Res:* Theatre and fiction in Hispanic American literature; women studies. *Publ:* Auth, Notas sobre el teatro chileno actual, Rev Interam Bibliog, 10-12/68; Regreso de trea mundos: Paradigma de lo autobiografico en Hispanoamerica, Anuario de Letras, Univ Mex, 73; Los perros y La mudanza de Elena Garro: Designio social y virtualidad feminista, Latin Am Theatre Rev, 75; Hispanic American fiction and drama written by women: Suggested readings, In: Female Studies IX Teaching About Women in the Foreign Languages, Feminist, 75; La otra cara de Ifigenia: Una revaluacion del personaje de Teresa de la Parra, Sin Nombre, 10-12/76; Hostos Intimista: Introduccion a su Diario, Inst Cult Puertorriquena, Puerto Rico, 76; ; El mito degradado de la familia en El libro demis primos de Cristina Peri Rossi, The Analysis of Literary Texts, 80 & Theory and Practice of Feminist Literary Criticism, 82, Bilingual Press. *Mailing Add:* 560 Riverside Dr New York NY 10027

MORAIN, GENELLE GRANT, b Indianola, Iowa, Mar 3, 28; wid; c 2. FOREIGN LANGUAGE. *Educ:* Simpson Col, BA, 49; Ohio State Univ, PhD(French educ), 68. *Prof Exp:* Teacher English & speech, Cherokee High Sch, Iowa, 49-50; teacher, Indianola High Sch, Iowa, 52-53, teacher French, 61-65; assoc prof French & French educ, 68-80, PROF LANG EDUC & ROMANCE LANG, UNIV GA, 80- *Concurrent Pos:* Dir Fr div, Southeastern Lang Ctr, 69-71; dir, Tri-State Foreign Lang Inst, 77-78. *Honors & Awards:* Co-winner, Stephen Freeman Award, Northeast Conf Teaching Foreign Lang, 71, 74. *Mem:* Am Asn Teachers Fr; Am Coun Teaching Foreign Lang; Am Folklore Soc; Southern Conf Teaching Lang. *Res:* Culture in foreign language teaching; cross-cultural understanding; folklore. *Publ:* Auth, Cultural pluralism, In: Vol III, The Britannica Review of Foreign Language Education, 71; coauth, Fusion of the four skills: a technique for facilitating communicative exchange, Mod Lang J, 72 & The culture cluster, Foreign Lang Ann, 73; A magaplan for cross-cultural instruction, In: Essays on the Teaching of Culture, Advan Pr Am, 74; coauth, Effects of social situation on language use: theory and application, Ctr Applied Ling Ser, 75; auth, Visual literary: signs and designs in the foreign culture, Foreign Lang Ann, 5/76. *Mailing Add:* Dept of Romance Lang Univ of Ga Athens GA 30602

MORAN, WILLIAM LAMBERT, b Chicago, Ill, Aug 11, 21. ASSYRIOLOGY. *Educ:* Loyola Univ (Il), AB, 44; Johns Hopkins Univ, AM, 48, PhD(Semitics), 50; Pontif Bibl Inst, AM, 57. *Hon Degrees:* Am, Harvard Univ, 68. *Prof Exp:* Assoc prof Old Testament exegesis, Pontif Bibl Inst, 58-66; lectr Assyriol, 66-68, PROF ASSYRIOL, HARVARD UNIV, 68- *Publ:* Auth, The use of the Canaanite infinitive absolute as a finite verb in the Amarna Letters from Byblos, J Cuneiform Studies, 50; Early Canaanite Yaqtula, Orientalia, 60; coauth, Chicago Assyrian Dictionary, Vol 7, Orient Inst, Univ Chicago & JJ Augustin, Gluckstadt, 60; auth, The Hebrew language in its northwest Semitic background, In: The Bible and the Ancient Near East, Doubleday, 61. *Mailing Add:* 56 Fairmont St Belmont MA 02178

MORAUD, MARCEL IAN, b Washington, DC, Dec 27, 17; m 45; c 2. FRENCH. *Educ:* Lycee de Limoges, B es L, 36; Univ Tex, AM, 38; Univ Paris, Lic es L, 38, dipl, 39, DUniv, 48. *Prof Exp:* Asst, Brown Univ, 41-42; instr, Biarritz Am Univ, 45-46; from instr to asst prof, Brown Univ, 46-50; assoc prof, 50-55, chmn dept, 50-81, PROF FRENCH, HAMILTON COL, 55- *Concurrent Pos:* Vis asst prof, Yale Univ, 50; asst ed, NY Fed Foreign Langs Bull, 54-56; vis prof, NY Univ, 57; dir, Hamilton Col Jr Year in France, 57-58, 61-62, 66-67, 70-71, 74-75, 78-79 & 82-83; vis prof, Univ Cincinnati, 60. *Mem:* MLA; Am Asn Teachers Fr. *Res:* Comparative literature; Italo-British literary relations, 1815-1830. *Publ:* Auth, Lady Morgan; coauth, Graded Cultural French Readers (7 vols), Am Bk Co, 57-70; Selections de Moliere, Voltaire, Hugo, Van Nostrand, 73. *Mailing Add:* Dept of French Hamilton Col Clinton NY 13323

MORAVCEVICH, JUNE, b Madison, Wis; m 60. FRENCH LITERATURE. *Educ:* Univ Wis-Madison, BS, 59, MA, 61, PhD(French), 70. *Prof Exp:* Asst prof, 70-76, ASSOC PROF FRENCH, UNIV ILL, CHICAGO CIRCLE, 76-, ASST DEAN LIB ARTS & SCIENCES, 78- *Mem:* MLA; Am Asn Teachers Fr. *Res:* French theater; 17th century French literature. *Publ:* Auth, Racine and the classical monologue, Ky Romance Quart, summer 72; Racine and Rotrou, Fr Rev, 72; La Nausee and Les Mots, Studies Philol, 73; Racine's Andromaque and the rhetoric of naming, Papers Lang & Lit, 76; Reason and rhetoric in the fables of La Fontaine, Australian J Fr Studies, 79. *Mailing Add:* 1212 N Lake Shore Dr Chicago IL 60610

MORAVCEVICH, NICHOLAS, b Zagreb, Yugoslavia, Dec 10, 35; US citizen; m 60. COMPARATIVE LITERATURE, SLAVIC STUDIES. *Educ:* Univ Belgrade, BA, 55; Art Inst Chicago, BFA, 59, MFA, 60; Univ Wis-Madison, PhD(comp lit), 64. *Prof Exp:* Asst prof comp lit, Stephens Col, 64-66; asst prof drama, 66-68, assoc prof, 68-71, head dept, 68-81, PROF SLAVIC LANG & LIT, UNIV ILL, CHICAGO CIRCLE, 71-, DIR CAMPUS DEVELOP, 81- *Concurrent Pos:* Adj prof, Goodman Sch Drama, Art Inst Chicago, 71-73; ed, Serbian Studies, 80- *Mem:* Int Comp Lit Asn; MLA; Am Comp Lit Asn; Midwest Mod Lang Asn(secy, Slavic sect, 66-67, 71-72, pres, 67-68, 72-73); Am Asn Advan Slavic Studies. *Res:* Slavic literature; international drama. *Publ:* Auth, Gorky and the Western naturalists: Anatomy of a misalliance, Comp Lit, winter 69; Chekhov and naturalism: From affinity to divergence, Comp Drama, winter 70; Ivo Andric and the quintessence of time, Slavic & East Europ J, fall 72; Romantization of the prostitute in Dostoevskij's fiction, Russ Lit, summer 76; contribr, Chekhov's Art of Writing, Slavica, 77; auth, The peasant in the prose of Petar Kocic, J Slavic & East Europ, winter77; The theme of irreversible fall in Milos Crnjanski's Migrations, Can Slavonic Papers, fall 78; contribr, Chekhov's Great Plays: A Collection of Critical Essays, NY Univ Press, 82. *Mailing Add:* Apt 14B-S 1212 North Lake Shore Drive Chicago IL 60610

MORAVCSIK, EDITH ANDREA, b Budapest, Hungary, May 2, 39; US citizen. LINGUISTICS. *Educ:* Univ Budapest, Hungary, DrDipl(classics), 63; Ind Univ, MA, 68, PhD(ling), 71. *Prof Exp:* Instr classics, Univ Debrecen, Hungary, 63-64 & Vassar Col, 64-66; teaching asst & lectr Hungarian, Ind Univ, 66-68; coordr, Lang Universals Proj, Stanford Univ, 68-72; actg asst prof ling, Univ Calif Los Angeles, 72-74; coordr, Lang Universals Proj, Stanford Univ, 75-76; from asst prof to ASSOC PROF LING, UNIV WIS-MILWAUKEE, 76- *Concurrent Pos:* Ed, Working Papers Lang Universals, 68-76; vis prof ling, Univ Vienna, 74 & 80; consult, Proj Lang Typology & Syntactic Fieldwork, NSF, 76-78; assoc ed, Lang, 81- *Mem:* Ling Soc Am. *Res:* Language universals; language typology; syntax. *Publ:* Auth, Agreement, Working Papers Lang Universals, 71; Borrowed verbs, Wiener Ling Gazette, 75; Necessary and possible universals about temporal constituent relations in language, Ind Ling Club, 77; Universals of language contact, Vol I & On the case-marking of objects, Vol IV, In: Universals of Human Language, Stanford Univ Press, 78; co-ed, Universals of Human Language, Vol I-IV, Stanford Univ Press, 78; auth, On the distribution of ergative and accusative patterns, Lingua, 78; co-ed, Current Approaches to Syntax, Acad Press, 80. *Mailing Add:* Dept of Ling Univ of Wis Milwaukee WI 53201

MORCOS, GAMILA, b Egypt, Jan 8, 28; m 51; c 3. FRENCH LITERATURE. *Educ:* Cairo Univ, Lic es Lett, 50; Ecole Norm Super, St Cloud, France, dipl, 54; Univ Paris, Dr, 54. *Prof Exp:* Lectr French lit, Ain Shams Univ, Cairo, 57-67; asst prof French lit, Laurentian Univ, 67-70, assoc prof, 70-80, dean humanities, 75-80; PROF & DEAN FAC SAINT-JEAN, UNIV ALBERTA, 80- *Mem:* Am Asn Teachers Fr; MLA; Asn Univ Partiellement ou Entierement de Lang Francaise; Asn Can D'Educ. *Res:* Camus; Butor; la nouvelle critique. *Publ:* Coauth, Le Francais par les Textes (3 vols), Imprimerie Gouvernementale & Ed Livres de France, Le Caire, 57 & 59; auth, Instruction et education, Rev Fac Pedag, Le Caire, 59; coauth, Mon Livre de Lecture, Imprimerie Amiria, 67; auth, L'influence du theatre d'Ibsen sur Henry Bataille, 2/68 & La litterature est elle a la hauteur des preoccupations actuelles?, 2/73, Rev Laurentian Univ; Les Contes folkloriques: essai d'interpretation, Fabula, 78; Henry Beyle a travers la Chartreuse de Parme, Stendhal Club, 80; Mobile de Butor: Typographie et justification, Australian J Fr Studies, XVIII: 56-76. *Mailing Add:* Univ of Alberta 8406-91 St Edmonton AB T6G 4G9 Can

MORDAUNT, JERROLD L, b Ogden, Utah, July 3, 31; m 68. SPANISH LANGUAGE & LITERATURE. *Educ:* Univ Utah, BA, 54, MA, 55; Stanford Univ, PhD(Span), 67. *Prof Exp:* ASST PROF SPAN, UNIV VICTORIA, 67- *Mem:* MLA; Pac Northwest Conf Foreign Lang (secy, 68-69, pres, 69-70); Philol Asn Pac Coast; Can Asn Hispanists. *Res:* Medieval Spanish prose; medieval Spanish language and literature. *Publ:* Ed, Proc Pac Northwest Conf Foreign Lang, Vol 19, 68 & Vol 10, 69. *Mailing Add:* 706-777 Blanshard Victoria BC V8W 2G9 Can

MOREAU, GERALD E, b Somerset, Man; m 70; c 1. FRENCH & FRANCO-CANADIAN LITERATURE. *Educ:* Univ Man, BA, 51; Laval Univ, MA, 55, cert AV instr of French, 71; Poitiers Univ, DUniv, 57. *Prof Exp:* ASSOC PROF FRENCH LANG & LIT & COORDR FRENCH LANG DIPL PROG, UNIV VICTORIA, BC, 71- *Honors & Awards:* Centennial Medal,

Fed Govt Can. *Mem:* Asn Can Univ Teachers Fr. *Res:* French literature. *Publ:* Coauth, Le Quebec: Tradition et Evolution (2 vols), Gage, 67; auth, L'homme: son identite, 70, A de Saint-Exupery: son enfance: nostalgie au bouclier?, 72 & Le reve et le realisme dans La belle bete et Marie-Claire Blais, 72, Rev Univ Ottawa; Anthologie du Roman Canadien-Francais, Lidec, 72; Le Commis (novel), Le Pensee Univ, Paris. *Mailing Add:* 3125 Midland Victoria BC V8R 6G1 Can

MORELAND, FLOYD LEONARD, b Passaic, NJ, Oct 18, 42. CLASSICAL LANGUAGES & LITERATURES. *Educ:* Middlebury Col, BA, 64; Univ Calif, Berkeley, PhD(classics), 71. *Prof Exp:* Teaching asst classics, Intercol Ctr Class Studies, Rome, 66-67; asst prof classics & humanities, Reed Col, 69-70; asst prof classics, 71-76, assoc prof, 76-80, PROF CLASSICS, BROOKLYN COL, 80-, DIR SUMMER LATIN INST, 71- *Mem:* AAUP; Am Philol Asn; Petronian Soc. *Res:* Methods of intensive language teaching; Latin Literature. *Publ:* Auth, From amo, amas, amat to Vergil in ten weeks, Northern Calif Foreign Lang Newslett, 5/68; Summer Latin, Class Outlook, 5-73; An experiment in accelerating Language teaching, Foreign Lang Annals, 3/74; coauth, An Intensive Course in Latin, Univ Calif, 74. *Mailing Add:* Dept of Classics Brooklyn College Brooklyn NY 11210

MORENBERG, MAX, b New York, NY, Mar 14, 40; m 62; c 3. LINGUISTICS, COMPOSITION . *Educ:* Fla State Univ, BS, 64, MA, 68, PhD(English, ling), 72. *Prof Exp:* Instr English, Univ SAla, 70-72; asst prof, 72-79, ASSOC PROF ENGLISH & LING, MIAMI UNIV, 79- *Concurrent Pos:* Res in comp grant, Exxon Educ Found, 76-77; Res asst grant, Comprehensive Employ Training Act, 78. *Mem:* Nat Coun Teachers English; Ling Soc Am; SAtlantic Mod Lang Asn; Am Asn Appl Ling. *Res:* Composition; literary style; rhetoric. *Publ:* Coauth, Sentence combining and syntactic maturity, Col Comp & Commun, 2/78; The effects of intensive transform SC, Lang & Style, 9/78; The Writer's Options, Harper, 78, 2nd ed, 82; Sentence Combining and the Teaching of Writing, L & S Books, 79; Sentence Combining and College Compostion, Perceptual & Motor Skills, 80. *Mailing Add:* Dept of English Miami Univ Oxford OH 45056

MORENO, ANTONIO WILLIAM, b Youngstown, Ohio, Dec 20, 12; m 37; c 2. FOREIGN LANGUAGES. *Educ:* Miami Univ, BS, 34; Univ Mich, AM, 45; Univ Pittsburgh, PhD, 54. *Hon Degrees:* LHD, Washington & Jefferson Col, 80. *Prof Exp:* Instr, Abraham Lincoln Sch, Corozal, PR, 37-38; instr & dir lang, schs, Hamilton, Ohio, 38-45; instr Span, Ohio State Univ, 45-46; asst prof foreign lang, 46-56, from assoc prof to prof mod lang, 56-80, dir mod & class lang lab, 69-80, chmn dept, 77-80, EMER PROF, ISABEL MCKENNAN LAUGHLIN FOUND, WASHINGTON & JEFFERSON COL, 80- *Concurrent Pos:* Instr, adult educ prog, YMCA, Hamilton, Ohio, 42-44; consult Latin-Am affairs, Wash Steel Co, 54-; vchmn, Munic Authority, City of Washington, 63-66, 68-76 & chmn, 77-81; teacher Span, YWCA Adult Educ Prog; bus mgr, Topic, 68-, ed, 60-80, adv ed spec issue, Studies Latin Am Lit, 71; translr, Findlay Clay Products. *Mem:* MLA; NEA; Am Asn Teachers Span & Port. *Publ:* Auth, El elemento femenino en el teatro beneaventino, Loteria, Panama, 59; Villaurrutia: El desarrollo de su teatro, Humboldt, Spain, 62; Spanish-American literature: Reflection of repression, Topic, fall 70. *Mailing Add:* Dept of Foreign Lang Washington & Jefferson Col Washington PA 15301

MORENO, ERNESTO ENRIQUE, b Holguin, Cuba, June 20, 15; US citizen; m 57; c 2. SPANISH LANGUAGE & LITERATURE. *Educ:* Univ Havana, Dr in Ped, 45; Univ Minn, MA, 64, PhD(Span), 66. *Prof Exp:* Asst prof Span, Macalester Col, 65-66; assoc prof, 66-80, PROF SPAN, UNIV TOLEDO, 80- *Mem:* Am Asn Teachers Span & Port; MLA. *Res:* Nineteenth and 20th century Spanish literature. *Mailing Add:* Dept of Foreign Lang Univ of Toledo Toledo OH 43606

MORENO, NESTOR A, b Havana, Cuba, Aug 25, 21; US citizen; m 43; c 3. LATIN AMERICAN STUDIES. *Educ:* Inst Vedado, Havana, BA, 39; Univ Havana, Dr Law, 43, Dr Pub Law, 45; Univ SC, MA, 66. *Prof Exp:* Instr, 66-68, from lectr to asst prof, 68-72, coordr Span sect, 69-70, ASSOC PROF SPAN AM NOVEL, CULT & LATIN AM POLITICS, UNIV SC, 73-, CHMN LATIN AM STUDIES, 69- *Res:* Spanish American novel; Spanish American culture; national politics of middle America. *Publ:* Auth, Arcitectura legal y Financiera, Univ Villanova, Cuba, 58; Castroism versus communism in Latin America, 67 & auth & ed, Contrabando, 73, Ed Universal. *Mailing Add:* Dept of Latin Am Studies Univ of SC Columbia SC 29208

MORETTA, EUGENE LAWRENCE, b Staten Island, NY. SPANISH-AMERICAN LITERATURE. *Educ:* Rutgers Col, BA, 64; Harvard Univ, MA, 65, PhD(Romance Lang), 69. *Prof Exp:* Asst prof, Yale Univ, 71-78; ASST PROF SPAN, BROOKLYN COL, 78- *Mem:* MLA; Am Asn Teachers of Span & Portuguese; Inst Int Lit Iberoamericana. *Res:* Twentieth century Mexican poetry; contemporary Spanish-American theater. *Publ:* Auth, La poesia de Xavier Villaurrutia, Fondo de Cult Econ, 76; Villaurrutia y Gorostiza: Hacia una vision amplia . . ., Cuadernos Am, 5-6/79; Spanish-American theatre of the 50's and 60's . . ., Latin Am Theatre Rev, spring 80; Cuesta: La flor su oculta exuberancia ignora, Siempre, 8/20/80; Sergio Magana and Vicente Lenero: Prophets . . ., Hisp J, spring 81. *Mailing Add:* Dept Mod Lang Brooklyn Col Brooklyn NY 11210

MORFORD, MARK PERCY OWEN, b Kotagala, Sri Lanka, Sept 21, 29; m 58; c 3. CLASSICS, ANCIENT HISTORY. *Educ:* Oxford Univ, BA, 52, MA, 55; Univ London, PhD(classics), 63. *Prof Exp:* From instr to assoc prof, 63-69, chmn dept, 68-80, PROF CLASSICS, OHIO STATE UNIV, 69- *Concurrent Pos:* Vis prof classics, Univ BC, 70 & 74; chmn, campus adv serv, Am Philol Asn, 71-72. *Mem:* Soc Prom Roman Studies; Am Philol Asn; Archaeol Inst Am; Joint Asn Class Teachers; Class Asn Midwest & South (pres, 81-82). *Res:* Greek and Roman literature; Roman history; classical tradition in art and literature. *Publ:* Auth, A New Latin Reader, Longmans, 62; The Poet Lucan, Blackwells, 67; The training of three Roman emperors, Phoenix, 4/68; The distortion of the Domus Aurea tradition, Eranos, 68; coauth, Classical Mythology, Longman, 71, 2nd ed, 77; ed, The Endless Fountain, Ohio State Univ, 72; auth, Juvenal's thirteenth satire, 73 & Juvenal's fifth satire, 77, Am J Philol; coauth, Aspects of Roman Civilization, Merrill, 79; Persius, G K Hall, 82. *Mailing Add:* Dept of Classics Ohio State Univ Columbus OH 43210

MORGAN, GARETH, b Port Talbot, Wales, June 18, 28; m 49; c 3. RENAISSANCE GREEK, CLASSICAL LANGUAGES. *Educ:* Oxford Univ, BA, 49, MA, 56, DPhil(mod lang), 57. *Prof Exp:* Asst master classics, Royal Grammar Sch, High Wycombe, 55-57; head dept & acting asst headmaster, Raynes Park Grammar Sch, 57-66; vis assoc prof, 66-68, acting chmn dept classics, 68-72, PROF CLASSICS & EDUC, UNIV TEX, AUSTIN, 68- *Concurrent Pos:* Korais lectr, King's Col, Univ London, 56- *Res:* Renaissance Greek; education in classic languages; oral poetry. *Publ:* Auth, French and Italian elements in Erotocritos, Kretika Chronika, 53; A Greek gunner's manual, Ann Brit Sch Athens, 54; Cretan Poetry, Kalokairinos, Heracleion, 61; Emblems of Erotocritos, Tex Quart, 68; Hagen and Aetius, Classica et Mediaevalia, 73; The laments of Mani, Folklore, 73; The Venetian Claims Commission of 1278, Byzantinische Zeitschrift, 76; Apbrodite Cytherea, TAPA, 79. *Mailing Add:* Dept of Classics Univ of Tex Austin TX 78712

MORGAN, JERRY LEE, b Mt Clemens, Mich, June 4, 39. LINGUISTICS. *Educ:* Ind Univ, AB, 66; Univ Chicago, PhD(ling), 73. *Prof Exp:* From instr to asst prof, 70-76, ASSOC PROF LING, UNIV ILL, 76- *Res:* Linguistic theory; pragmatics; computational linguistics. *Publ:* Co-ed, Speech Acts, In: Vol 3, Syntax and Semantics, Acad Press, 75; auth, Conversational postulate revisited, Language, 77; Two types of convention in indirect speech acts, In: Syntax and Semantics, Vol 9, Acad Press, 78. *Mailing Add:* Dept of Ling Univ Ill Urbana IL 61801

MORGAN, OWEN REES, b Crynant, Wales, Mar 15, 37; m. FRENCH LANGUAGE & LITERATURE. *Educ:* Univ Nottingham, BA, 58, MA, 62. *Prof Exp:* Asst master French, Nottingham High Sch, 61-63; from lectr to asst prof, 63-70, ASSOC PROF FRENCH, MCMASTER UNIV, 70- *Mem:* MLA; Asn Can Univ Teachers Fr; Soc Litterare des Amis di Emile Zola. *Res:* French naturalist novel and theatre; correspondence of Emile Zola. *Publ:* Auth, Leon Hennique and the disintegration of naturalism, Nottingham Fr Studies, 10/62; Leon Hennique et Emile Zola, Les Cahiers Naturalistes, 12/65; The plays of Leon Hennique, Nottingham Fr Studies, 10/66 & 5/67; (with A Pages), Une piece inconnue de Zola en 1879, Cahiers de l' UER Froissart, Automne, 80; Lettres inedires de J-K Huysmans a Leon Hennique, Bull de la Soc J-K Huysmans, 5/81. *Mailing Add:* Dept of Romance Lnag McMaster Univ Hamilton ON L8S 4M4 Can

MORGAN, RALEIGH, JR, b Nashville, Tenn, Nov 12, 16; m 41; c 3. LINGUISTICS. *Educ:* Fisk Univ, AB, 38; Univ Mich, AM, 39, PhD(ling), 52. *Prof Exp:* Dept head French, NC Col, Durham, 46-49, 51-56; dir US Cult Ctr, Cologne, Ger, 56-57; dep chief, Cult Opers, Am Embassy, Bonn, 57-59; assoc dir, MLA Ctr Appl Ling, 59-61; prof Romance lang & head dept, Howard Univ, 61-65; PROF ROMANCE LING, UNIV MICH, ANN ARBOR, 65- *Concurrent Pos:* Carnegie fac res grant, 52, Am Coun Learned Soc grant, ling inst, Ind Univ, 53; Georgetown Univ, 55; US Dept State lectr ling, Nicaragua & Haiti, 56, Francophone Africa, 64; mem adv comn, ctr Applied Ling, 62; consult linguist, A-L M French, second level, Harcourt, Brace & World, 62; consult, US Info Agency English teaching adv panel, 64-67; Univ Mich Rackham fac res grant, 67; French humanities prog, Ann Arbor & Grosse Pointe schs, 69; mem comt on least commonly taught lang, MLA, 71; mem vis comt Germanic lang, bd overseers, Harvard Univ, 72-80; mem assembly of behav & soc sci, Nat Res Coun, 73-; vis prof ling, Cornell Univ, 73; chmn, Mich Coun Humanities, 74-77; Univ Mich Rackham fac res grant, 78. *Mem:* MLA; Int Ling Asn; Soc Ling Romane; Ling Soc Am; Soc Caribbean Ling. *Res:* History of the French language and related dialects; French language of Canada; Occitan. *Publ:* Auth, Old French jogleor and kindred terms, Romance Philol, 5/54; Playing dead thrice: Louisiana Creole animal tale, Rev La, 75; The Regional French of County Beauce, Quebec, Mouton, 75; Lexical correspondences between metropolitan and Canadian French, Ling Approaches to the Romance Lexicon, 78; Les occlusives dans les parlers francais de l'Amerique du Nord: Structuration des aires dialectales, Revue de l'universite de Moncton, 11/78; Occitan verbal substantives in -dor, -doira, Italic and Romance Ling Studies, 80; The penetration of French into the speech of Occitan bilinguals, Cont Studies in Romance Lang, 80; Guadeloupean creole pronouns: A study of expansion in morphoyntactic structure, Historicity & Variation in Creole Studies, 81. *Mailing Add:* 3157 Bluett Dr Ann Arbor MI 48105

MORGAN, ROBERT EARLE, b Rutherfordton, NC, Mar 2, 35. FRENCH, MATHEMATICS. *Educ:* Lenoir Rhyne Col, AB, 56; Univ NC, Chapel Hill, MEd, 61, PhD(higher educ & French), 71. *Prof Exp:* Teacher French & math, Wadesboro High Sch, NC, 56-59; teacher, Wingate Col, 59-67; assoc prof, 67-76, PROF FRENCH & MATH, GARDNER WEBB COL, 76- *Mem:* Am Asn Teachers Fr; SAtlantic Mod Lang Asn; Math Asn Am. *Publ:* Auth, Portrait of myself, Observer, 65. *Mailing Add:* PO Box 903 Boiling Springs NC 28017

MORGAN, WILLIAM INGRAHAM, b Burlington, Iowa, Oct 26, 22. GERMAN. *Educ:* State Univ Iowa, BA, 48, PhD(Ger), 51. *Prof Exp:* Asst prof Ger, Mankato State Col, 51-53; from asst prof to assoc prof, 53-74, chmn dept mod & class lang, 63-66, PROF GER, UNIV NDAK, 74- *Res:* Eighteenth century German literature. *Publ:* Translr, Gerhart Hauptmann and Silesia, Univ NDak, 62. *Mailing Add:* Dept of Mod & Class Lang Univ of NDak Grand Forks ND 58202

MORITA, JAMES R, b Salem, Ore, June 13, 31; c 2. JAPANESE LITERATURE. *Educ:* Univ Mich, MA, 59, MA, 60; Univ Chicago, PhD(Far Eastern lang & civilizations), 68. *Prof Exp:* Instr Japanese, Univ Chicago, 66-68, asst prof Japanese lit, 68-69, Japanese librn, Far Eastern libr, 67-69; asst prof Japanese lit, Univ Ore, 69-72; ASSOC PROF E ASIAN LANG & LIT,

OHIO STATE UNIV, 72- *Concurrent Pos:* Am Coun Learned Soc & Soc Sci Res Coun fel, 70; Japan Found prof fel, 77-78. *Mem:* Asn Teachers Japanese; MLA; Asn Asian Studies. *Res:* Modern Japanese literature, especially poetry. *Publ:* Auth, Shigarami-zoshi, 69, Garakuta bunko, 69 & Shimazaki Toson's four collections of poems, 70, Monumenta Nipponica; Poems of Kaneko Mitsuharu, Lit E & W, 73; The Jojoshi, J Asn Teachers Japanese, 75; Haru to shura, In: Miyazawa Kenji Kenkyu Sosho, Vol 4, Gakuge Shorin, 75; Soseki no eishi-shiyakn shiron, 10/77-1/78, Hon'yaku no Sekai; Kaneko Mitsuharu, Twayne Publ, 80. *Mailing Add:* Dept of EAsian Lang & Lit Ohio State Univ Columbus OH 43210

MORNEAU, KENNETH ARMAND, b New Britain, Conn. FRENCH & SPANISH LANGUAGE & LITERATURE. *Educ:* Harvard Univ, BA, 50; Univ Pa, MBA, 55; Middlebury Col, MA, 66; Univ Pa, PhD(French), 75. *Prof Exp:* Teacher, Peddie Sch, 57-66; PROF FRENCH & SPAN, BUCKS COUNTY COMMUNITY COL, 66- *Res:* Medieva; French epic poetry. *Mailing Add:* Bucks County Community Col Swamp Rd Newtown PA 18940

MORNIN, EDWARD, b Greenock, Scotland, Nov 27, 38; Can citizen; m 63; c 2. MODERN GERMAN LITERATURE. *Educ:* Univ Glasgow, MA, 61, PhD(Ger), 69. *Prof Exp:* Lectr English, Univ Cologne, Ger, 63-64; instr Ger, 65-68, asst prof, 68-77, ASSOC PROF GER, UNIV BC, 77- *Mem:* Can Asn Univ Teachers Ger; Can Comp Lit Asn; MacKay-Gesellschaft. *Res:* German Romanticism/19th century; J H Mackay. *Publ:* Ed, Die Schöne Magelone, Reclam, 75; translr, Outpourings of an Art-Loving Friar, 75 & contribr, Three Eerie Tales From 19th Century German, 75, Ungar; auth, Some patriotic novels and tales by La Motte Fouque, Seminar, 75; Taking games seriously: observations on the German sports-novel, Ger Rev, 76; Art and alienation, In: Franz Sternbald, Mod Lang Notes, 79; Tieck's revision of Franz Sternbald, Seminar, 79; Drinking in Joseph Roth's novels and tales, Int Fiction Rev, 79. *Mailing Add:* Dept of Ger Studies Univ of BC Vancouver BC V6T 1W5 Can

MORON-ARROYO, CIRIACO, b Pastrana, Spain, Aug 8, 35; m 62; c 7. SPANISH LITERATURE, PHILOSOPHY. *Educ:* Pontif Univ Salamanca, Lic Phil, 57; Univ Munich, PhD(philos), 62. *Prof Exp:* Lectr Span, Univ Giessen, 62-63; from asst prof to prof Romance lang, Univ Pa, 63-71; EMERSON HINCHLIFF PROF SPAN LIT, CORNELL UNIV, 71- *Concurrent Pos:* Assoc ed, Hisp Rev, 63-71; Guggenheim Mem Found fel, 72-73. *Mem:* MLA; Mod Humanities Res Asn; Am Asn Teachers Span & Port; Asn Int Hispanistas. *Res:* Spanish intellectual history; history of German philosophy; Hispano-German cultural relations. *Publ:* Auth, Abstraktion und Illumination: Probleme der Metaphysik Bonaventuras, Gahmig, Giessen, 63; El sistema de Ortega y Gasset, 68 & La mistica espanola (2 vols), 71-73, Ed Alcala, Madrid; Sentido y forma de La Celestina, 74 & Nuevas meditaciones del Quijote, 76, Ed Catedra, Madrid; Calderon: Pensamiento y teatro, Santander Biblioteca de Menendez Pelayo, 82; The Spanish source of Hamlet, Hisp J (in prep). *Mailing Add:* Dept of Romance Studies Cornell Univ Ithaca NY 14853

MOROT-SIR, EDOUARD B, b Autun, France, Apr 1, 10; m 35; c 2. HISTORY OF IDEAS, LITERARY CRITICISM. *Educ:* Sorbonne, BA, 31, Agrege, 34, DUniv, 47. *Hon Degrees:* 11 from Am Univs. *Prof Exp:* Prof philos, Univ Bordeaux, 47-50, Univ Cairo, 50-52 & Univ Lille, 52-57; rep French univs in US, 57-69; prof French, Univ Ariz, 69-72; WILLIAM RAND KENAN JR PROF FRENCH, UNIV NC, CHAPEL HILL, 72- *Concurrent Pos:* Dir, Fulbright Comn for France, Paris, 52-57. *Mem:* Am Asn Teacher Fr (vpres, 70-); MLA; Century Asn. *Res:* Theory of language and literary criticism; 17th century French literature; 20th century French literature. *Publ:* Auth, La Pensee Negative, 47 & Philosophie et Mystique, 47, Ed Montaigne; coed & contribr, Litterature Francaise, I & II, Larousse, 69 & 70; auth, La Pensee Francaise d'Aujourdhui, 70, La Metaphysique de Pascal, 73 & Pascal, 73, Presses Univ France; Les Mots de Jean-Paul Sartre, Hachette, 75; coauth, Samuel Beckett: The Art of Rhetoric, NCSRLL, 76. *Mailing Add:* Dept Romance Lang Univ NC Chapel Hill NC 27514

MORPHOS, PANOS PAUL, b Erythrae, Greece, Sept 20, 04; nat US; m 48; c 2. ROMANCE LANGUAGES. *Educ:* Univ Paris, Lic en Droit, 25; Univ Calif, AM, 29; Johns Hopkins Univ, PhD, 36. *Prof Exp:* Res asst, Johns Hopkins Univ, 31-37, instr Romance lang, 37-42; war correspondent, Newsweek, 42-47; assoc prof, 47-53, chmn dept, 60-71, prof, 53-80, EMER PROF ROMANCE LANG, GRAD SCH, TULANE UNIV, 80- *Mem:* MLA; Mediaeval Acad Am; Renaissance Soc Am; Acad Polit Sci; Soc Byzantine & Mod Greek Studies. *Res:* Humanism in French literature; mythological imagery in French Renaissance poetry; French Renaissance bibliography. *Publ:* Auth, Digenis Akritas: The Byzantine Epic in History and Poetry, Nat Herald, 42; L'Image de la Grece chez les Voyageurs Francais, Furst, 47; Renaissance tradition in Rousseau's Second Discours, Mod Lang Quart, 3/52; The Dialogues of Guy de Brues, With a Study on Renaissance Scepticism and Relativism, Johns Hopkins Univ, 53; ed, Freud and Literature, Proc Tulane Humanities Soc, Symbolism, 57; auth, The Composition of Le Temple d'Honneur et de Vertus of Lemaire de Belges, Studies Philol, 7/62; The pictorialism of Lemaire de Belges in Le Temple d'Honneur et de Vertus, Ann Ist Univ Napoli, 1/63; The legacy of Montaigne, Exploration in Renaissance Lit, 74. *Mailing Add:* PO Box 5003 Tulane Univ New Orleans LA 70118

MORRIS, J VINCENT, b Denver, Colo, June 28, 24; m 48; c 4. GREEK. *Educ:* Westmont Col, BA, 51; Dallas Theol Sem, ThM, 55; Ariz State Univ, MA, 67, EdD(higher educ), 72. *Prof Exp:* Mem Fac, Ariz Bible Col, 64-71, acad dean, 66-68, exec dir, 68-71; admin asst, 71-72, ASSOC PROF GREEK, BIOLA UNIV, 71-, DEAN STUDENTS, 72- *Mem:* Nat Asn Students Personnel Adminr. *Res:* Motivation among college students; motivation among college faculty. *Mailing Add:* Dept of Greek Biola Col 13800 Biola Ave La Mirada CA 90639

MORRIS, MADELEINE P FIELDS, b France, Feb 5, 23; nat citizen; c 2. FRENCH. *Educ:* Univ Dijon, Lic es Let, 44; Columbia Univ, PhD, 59. *Prof Exp:* From instr to asst prof French, Brown Univ, 56-63; assoc prof Romance lang, 63-71, PROF ROMANCE LANG, QUEENS COL, CITY UNIV NEW YORK, 71-, PHD PROG FRENCH, GRAD CTR, 80- *Mem:* Am Asn Teachers Fr; MLA; Am Soc Eighteenth Century Studies. *Publ:* Auth, Le Chevalier de Jaucourt, Un Ami de la terre, 1704-1780, Geneve, Droz, 79; Nouveaux regards sur Manon Lescaut, Fr Rev, 10/70; Faust a' Bouville, Rev de Lit Comparee, 10-12/68; coauth, A Critical Bibliography of French Literature, Vol IV, Syracuse Univ Press, 68; auth, La derniere escarmouche entre Voltaire et Freron, Fr Rev, 2/63; Voltaire et Rameau, J Aesthet & Art Criticism, summer 63; De la Critique de la raison dealectique aux Sequestres d'Altona, PMLA, 12/63; Voltaire et le Mercure de France, Studies on Voltaire Eighteenth Century, XX:175-215. *Mailing Add:* Dept of Romance Languages Queens College Flushing NY 11367

MORRIS, MARSHALL, b Altus, Okla, Apr 8, 42. TRANSLATION, SOCIAL ANTHROPOLOGY. *Educ:* Univ Tex, Austin, BA, 65, MA, 70; Oxford Univ, dipl(social anthrop), 74. *Prof Exp:* Assoc dir honors prog, 72-73, ASST PROF TRANSL, UNIV PR, RIO PIEDRAS, 70- *Concurrent Pos:* Asst ed, Rev Interam, 76- *Mem:* Fel, Royal Anthrop Inst; MLA; Am Translr Asn. *Res:* Sociology of language. *Publ:* Translr, Jorge Enjoto's On Translation in Three Lectures on Translation, Univ PR, Rio Piedras, 72; Maria de los Angeles Castro de Davila's The Place of San Juan de Puerto Rico Among Hispanic American Cities, Rev Interam, summer 76, San Juan Star, 10/9/77; Amador Cobas' Commentary on Dr Wigner's Article, Rev Interam, winter 76-77; Ismael Rodriquez Bou's Education and Social Change in Puerto Rico: The Role of Education in Puerto Rico, or The Path to Equality of Educational Opportunity, Proc 18th Int Conf Social Welfare, Columbia Univ, 77; Alfonso Garcia Martinez's Prologue, In: The CommonLaw Zone in Panama: A Case Study in Reception, Inter-Am Univ, 77; Eduardo Forastieri's Garcilaso: Translation and tradition (on some Vergilian texts in the Ecolgue I), in Problems in Translation, 78 & Valentin Garca Yebra's Three Spanish Translations of Voyelles in Problems in Translation, 78, Unv PR, Rio Piedras. *Mailing Add:* MA Prof in Translation Univ of PR Box 22613 San Juan PR 00931

MORRIS, ROBERT JEFFRY, b Jackson Heights, NY, Aug 12, 40; m 66; c 3. SPANISH & PORTUGUESE LANGUAGE & LITERATURE. *Educ:* Univ NC, Chapel Hill, AB, 62, MA, 66; Univ Ky, PhD(Span), 68. *Prof Exp:* Asst prof Span, Univ Cincinnati, 68-71; from asst prof to assoc prof, 71-78, PROF SPAN, TEX TECH UNIV, 78- *Mem:* Am Asn Teachers Span & Port; South Western Coun Latin Am Studies (pres, 76-77); South Cent Mod Lang Asn. *Res:* Contemporary Peruvian theatre; contemporary Peruvian prose fiction; Colonial Hispanic American literature. *Publ:* Auth, The theatre of Sebastian Salazar Bondy, Latin Am Theatre Rev, fall 70; The dramatic perspective in contemporary Peru, Rev Estud Hisp, 1/71; The theatre of Julio Ortega, Latin Am Theatre Rev, fall 72; The Black in the Hispanic American theatre, Am Hispanist, 3/76; The Contemporary Peruvian Theatre, Tex Tech Univ, 77. *Mailing Add:* Dept of Class & Romance Lang Tex Tech Univ Lubbock TX 79409

MORRIS, WALTER D, b Austin, Tex, June 24, 29; m 56; c 4. GERMANIC LANGUAGES & LITERATURES. *Educ:* Univ Calif, Los Angeles, BA, 49; Univ Tex, Austin, MA, 55, PhD(Ger), 59. *Prof Exp:* Assoc prof Ger, Birmingham-Southern Col, 58-62; assoc prof, Bowling Green State Univ, 62-70; PROF GER, IOWA STATE UNIV, 70- *Mem:* MLA; Am Asn Teachers Ger. *Res:* German literature of the 19th century, especially Conrad Ferdinand Meyer; Norwegian literaure, especially Ibsen and post World War II. *Publ:* Auth, The image of America in modern Norwegian literature, Am Scand Rev, fall 68; A forum for the new Norwegian writing, Bks Abroad, fall 68; Tarjei Vesaas, In: Encycl of World Lit, Vol III, 71; Ibsen and ethics of self-realization, Ger Notes, summer 74; Thomas Mann and teachers, Univ Dayton Rev, spring 76; Jens Bjorneboe & Solveig Christov, In: Encycl of World Lit, Vol 1, 2nd ed, 81; coauth (with A T David), Chance, In: Encycl of Statist Sci, Vol 1, 82. *Mailing Add:* Dept of Foreign Lang Iowa State Univ Ames IA 50010

MORRISON, ROBERT REID, b Gainesville, Fla, Aug 1, 29; m 51; c 2. SPANISH, FRENCH. *Educ:* George Washington Univ, AB, 50; Middlebury Col, MA, 54; Univ Fla, PhD, 63. *Prof Exp:* From asst prof to assoc prof Span, ECarolina Univ, 58-67; prof mod lang & chmn dept, 67-82, CHMN, DIV ARTS & LETTS, SOUTHERN MISSIONARY COL, 82- *Concurrent Pos:* Ed, ALTA Vox, Adventist Lang Teachers Asn, 68-69. *Mem:* MLA; Am Asn Teachers Span & Port; Am Coun Teaching Foreign Lang; Nat Asn Learning Lab Dir; Adventist Lang Teachers Asn (pres, 70-72). *Res:* Spanish Golden Age drama, especially religious drama; French. *Publ:* Auth, Zarzuelas on Records, Hispania, 3/59; Articulation In Foreign Language Study, ALTA Vox, 10/69. *Mailing Add:* PO Box 475 Collegedale TN 37315

MORRISSETTE, BRUCE ARCHER, b Richmond, Va, Apr 26, 11; m 40; c 1. FRENCH LITERATURE. *Educ:* Univ Richmond, BA, 31; Univ Clermont-Ferrand, DUniv, 33; Johns Hopkins Univ, PhD, 38. *Hon Degrees:* LittD, Univ Richmond, 75. *Prof Exp:* Jr instr French, Johns Hopkins Univ, 34-38; from asst prof to prof Romance lang, Wash Univ, 38-62; chmn dept Romance lang & lit, 67-70, PROF FRENCH, UNIV CHICAGO, 62-, CHMN DEPT ROMANCE LANG & LIT, 73- *Concurrent Pos:* Guggenheim res fel, France, 59; vis prof, Univ Ill, Urbana, 67-68 & Univ Calif, Los Angeles, 69; Fulbright lectr, Univ Western Australia, 69; Bernard E & Ellen C Sunny distinguished serv prof, Univ Chicago, 74. *Honors & Awards:* Chevalier, Palmes Academiques, 62; Chevalier, Ordre du Merite Nat, 80. *Mem:* MLA; Am Asn Teachers Fr; Int Asn Fr Studies; Am Comp Lit Asn. *Res:* Seventeenth century French fiction and baroque literature; French symbolism and Rimbaud; contemporary French novel and film. *Publ:* Auth, Life and Works of Mlle Desjardins, Wash Univ, 47; La Bataille Rimbaud, Nizet, Paris, 59; Les Romans de Robbe-Grillet, Minuit, Paris, 63; translr, The novels of Robbe-Grillet, Cornell Univ, 75; Intertextual Assemblage in Robbe-Grillet from Topology to the Golden Triangle, York Press, 81. *Mailing Add:* Dept of Romance Lang & Lit Univ of Chicago 1050 E 59th St Chicago IL 60637

MORROW, JOHN HOWARD, b Hackensack, NJ, Feb 5, 10; m 36; c 2. FRENCH LITERATURE. *Educ:* Rutgers Univ, AB, 31; Univ Pa, AM, 42, PhD, 52; Univ Paris, cert avance, 47. *Hon Degrees:* LHD, Rutgers Univ, 63. *Prof Exp:* Teacher, New Lincoln Jr High Sch, Trenton, NJ, 31-35; acad div, Bordentown Inst, 35-45; prof French, Span & head dept mod lang, Talladega Col, 45-54; prof, Clark Col, 54-56; prof French & chmn dept, NC Col Durham, 56-59; US Ambassador Extraordinary & Plenipotentiary to Repub of Guinea, WAfrica, 59-61; mem US deleg, 15th UN Gen Assembly, 61; US permanent rep, UNESCO, Paris, 61-63; chmn Am grantee & Foreign serv officer univ training prog, Sch Foreign Affairs, Foreign Serv Inst, US Dept State, 63-64; prof, 64-78, EMER PROF FOREIGN LANG & CHMN DEPT, UNIV COL, RUTGERS UNIV, NEW BRUNSWICK, 78- *Concurrent Pos:* Pres, Alliance Francaise de New Brunswick, 69-71; mem deleg assembly, MLA, 71-74, mem resolutions comt, 73. *Mem:* MLA; Am Asn Teachers Fr. *Res:* The comic element in the work of Marcel Proust; French politics and the colonial problem; 20th century French literature. *Publ:* Auth, First American Ambassador to Guinea, Rutgers Univ, 68; The comic element in A la Recherche du Temps Perdu, Fr Rev; Unrest in North Africa, Phylon; Gaston Monnerville, president of the Council of the Republic, Motive. *Mailing Add:* Dept of For Lang Rutgers Univ New Brunswick NJ 08903

MORTIMER, ARMINE KOTIN, b Detroit, Mich, May 13, 43. FRENCH LITERATURE & CRITICISM. *Educ:* Radcliffe Col, BA, 64; Univ Calif, Los Angeles, MA, 70; Yale Univ, MPhil & PhD(Romance lang & lit), 74. *Prof Exp:* Asst prof, 74-80, ASSOC PROF FRENCH, UNIV ILL, URBANA-CHAMPAIGN, 80- *Concurrent Pos:* Fel French lit, Ctr Advan Study, Univ Ill, 77. *Mem:* MLA; Asn Int des Etudes Fr; Soc Values Higher Educ; Midwest Mod Lang Asn. *Res:* Study of narrative, in particular techniques of narrative closure and finality in French mimetic fictions. *Publ:* Auth, Le Titre des nouvelles de Philippe de Vigneulles: Un eclaircissement, Bibliot d'Humanisme et Renaissance, 77; Pantagruel: language vs communication, Mod Lang Notes, 77; Jean Arp, poet and artist, Dada/Surrealism, 77; The Narrative Imagination: Comic Tales by Philippe de Vigneulles, Univ Ky, 77; La Maison Nucingen, ou le recit financier, Romanic Rev, 1/78; On the subject of reading, J Practical Structuralism, 79; La lecture de la mort: Le Scarabee d'or d'Edgar Allen Poe, Litterature, 80; Narrative Finality, Studies in Twentieth Century Lit, 82. *Mailing Add:* Dept of French 2090 Foreign Lang Bldg Univ of Ill Urbana IL 61801

MORTON, BRIAN NEVILLE, b London, England, July 25, 30; US citizen; c 2. FRENCH LITERATURE, FRENCH AMERICAN RELATIONS. *Educ:* Columbia Univ, BS, 57, MA, 63, PhD(French lit), 67. *Prof Exp:* Instr French lit, Williams Col, 64-67; asst prof, 69-72, ASSOC PROF FRENCH LIT, UNIV MICH, ANN ARBOR, 72- *Concurrent Pos:* Fulbright & Schepp Found res fel, 67-69; Nat Endowment for Humanities res fel, 72-73. *Honors & Awards:* Gilbert Chinard Prize, Inst Francais de Washington, 77. *Res:* Beaumarchais; French aid to the American Revolution, 1774-1783. *Publ:* Ed, Beaumarchais: Correspondance, Nizet, Paris, Vols I, II & III, 69, 70 & 72; auth, La derniere aventure de Beaumarchais, l'affaire des fusils de Hollande, Arch Lettres Mod, Paris, 70; Beaumarchais, In: Dizionario Critico della Letteratura Francese, 73; Beaumarchais et Vergennes, 4/73 & Le reputation de Beaumarchais en Amerique au XVIIIe siecle, 4/74, Rev Europe. *Mailing Add:* Dept of Romance Lang Univ of Mich Ann Arbor MI 48104

MORTON, JACQUELINE, b Paris, France, Oct 21, 34; US citizen; c 3. TWENTIETH CENTURY FRENCH LITERATURE. *Educ:* Hunter Col, BA, 54; Columbia Univ, MA, 65, PhD(French), 69. *Prof Exp:* Instr, Smith Col, 66-67; asst prof, 75-79, PROF FRENCH, WAYNE STATE UNIV, 80- *Mem:* Asn des Amis d'Andre Gide; Am Asn Teachers French; MLA. *Res:* Andre Gide; Francois Mauriac; Andre Gide translator. *Publ:* Ed, La Correspondance d'Andre Gide et de Francois Mauriac, Gallimard, Paris, 71; coauth, La Presse Contemporary Issues in French Newspapers, Heath, 72; auth, Andre Gide and his American translator Justin O'Brien, Mich Aca, 77; coauth, La Presse II, Heath, 77; Mosaique, Van Nostrand, 77; English Grammar for Students of French, 79 & ed, English Grammar Series, 79, Olivia & Hill Press. *Mailing Add:* 905 Olivia Ann Arbor MI 48104

MOSE, KENRICK EWART, b Trinidad, WIndies, Nov 19, 35; m 60; c 3. SPANISH LANGUAGE & LITERATURE. *Educ:* Univ London, BA, 58; Univ WIndies, dipl educ, 59; Univ Toronto, MA, 62, PhD(Span), 69. *Prof Exp:* Instr French & Span, St George's Col, Trinidad, West Indies, 59-61; lectr Span, Univ West Indies, 64-67; lectr, Acadia Univ, 69-70; asst prof, 70-77, acting chmn dept lang, 78-79, coordr Span, 77-79, ASSOC PROF SPAN, UNIV GUELPH, 77- *Concurrent Pos:* Instr Span, Polytech Inst, Trinidad, 59-61; mem exec comt, Ont Coop Prog Latin Am & Caribbean, 72-74, chmn 76-78; Can Coun Arts res grant, 73-74, 76-77; Humanities Res Coun Can leave fel, 80-81. *Mem:* Can Asn Latin Am Studies; Am Asn Teachers Span & Port. *Res:* Uruguayan prose fiction; Colombian prose fiction; social problems in Spanish American literature. *Publ:* Auth, Enrique Amorim: The Passion of a Uruguayan, Plaza Mayor Ed, Madrid, 72; Academic involvement in Canada in the languages & literatures of Latin American, Ocplacs Reports, 75; A donde va Alvarex Gardeazabal, Arco, Colombia, 76; The fire next time? Three visions of violence in Uruguayan literature, Can J Latin Am Studies, 76; contribr, Aproximaciones a Gustavo Alvarez Gardeazabal, Plaza y Janes, Colombia, 77. *Mailing Add:* Dept of Lang Univ of Guelph Guelph ON N1G 2W1 Can

MOSELEY, WILLIAM WHATLEY, b Columbus, Ga, Oct 31, 27; m 50. SPANISH. *Educ:* Univ Miami, AB, 48; Univ NMex, MA, 50, PhD(Span), 54. *Prof Exp:* From asst prof to assoc prof Span, La Col, 54-58; from asst prof to assoc prof, La State Univ, New Orleans, 58-67, chmn dept foreign lang, 60-61, dean jr div, 61-67; PROF SPAN, COLO STATE UNIV, 67-, CHMN DEPT FOR LANG & LIT, 79- *Mem:* Am Asn Teachers Span & Port; Am Coun Teaching Foreign Lang; MLA. *Res:* Spanish philology; Gil Vicente. *Publ:* Auth, Students and university life in the Spanish Golden Age, Origins of the Chilean historical novel & An introduction to the Chilean historical novel, Hispania; coauth, A Concordance to the Libro de Buen Amor of Juan Ruiz (2 vols) 76 & auth, A Concordance to the Spanish in the Works of Gil Vicente (2 vols), 77, Xerox Monogr Ser. *Mailing Add:* Dept of Foreign Lang Colo State Univ Ft Collins CO 80523

MOSER, CHARLES A, b Knozville, Tenn, Jan 6, 35. SLAVIC LANGUAGE & LITERATURE. *Educ:* Yale Univ, BA, 56; Russian Inst, Columbia Univ, MA, 58, PhD, 62. *Prof Exp:* Instr Russ, Yale Univ, 60-63, asst prof Slavic lang, 63-67; assoc prof, 67-77, chmn dept Slavic lang, 69-74, PROF SLAVIC, GEORGE WASHINGTON UNIV, 77-, CHMN DEPT, 80- *Mem:* Am Asn Teachers Slavic & East Europ Lang; Am Asn Advan Slavic Studies; Bulgarian Studies Asn (pres, 73-78). *Res:* Russian literature of the 18th century; Russian literature of the 1860's; modern Bulgarian literature. *Publ:* Auth, The journal Zlatorog and modern Bulgarian letters, Slavic & East Europ J, 63; Antinihilism in the Russian Novel of the 1860's, Mouton, The Hague, 64; Pisemsky: A Provincial Realist, Harvard Univ, 69; Ivan Turgenev, Columbia Univ, 72; A History of Bulgarian Literature, 865-1944, Mouton, The Hague, 72; The problem of the Igor tale, Can-Am Slavic Studies, summer 73; Denis Fonvizin, Twayne, 79; Dimitrov of Bulgaria, Caroline House, 79. *Mailing Add:* Dept of Slavic Lang George Washington Univ Washington DC 20006

MOSER, GERALD MAX JOSEPH, b Leipzig, Ger, 15. ROMANCE LANGUAGES. *Educ:* Univ Paris, Lic es Let, 35, dipl, 37, DUniv, 39. *Prof Exp:* Instr, Bridgewater Col, 39-41; res asst, Am Coun Leanred Soc, 42; instr, Cornell Univ, 43-44; instr, Univ Wis, 44-45; asst prof, Univ Ill, 45-49; from asst prof to prof Span & Port, Pa State Univ, University Park, 49-78; RETIRED. *Concurrent Pos:* Surv ed, Mod Lang J, 46-54; assoc ed, Hispania, 54-75; Fulbright res scholar, Univ Lisbon, 62-63; adv ed, Studies Romanticism; Am Philos Soc res grant, Spain & Port, 66; adv ed, Luso-Brazilian Rev, 73- *Mem:* MLA; Am Asn Teachers Span & Port; African Lit Asn. *Res:* Portuguese, Spanish and Brazilian literature. *Publ:* Auth, Les Romantiques Portugais et L'Allemagne, Jouve, Paris, 39; coauth, Ruben Dario y El cojo ilustrado, Hisp Inst, 64; auth, Essays in Portuguese-African Literature, Pa State Univ, 69; A Tentative Portuguese-African Bibliography, Pa State Univ Libr, 70. *Mailing Add:* Dept of Span Ital & Port Pa State Univ University Park PA 16802

MOSER, WALTER KARL, b Baden, Switz, May 26, 42; m 68; c 2. COMPARATIVE LITERATURE, GERMAN LITERATURE. *Educ:* Univ Zurich, PhD(18th Century French lit), 68. *Prof Exp:* Vis asst prof French, Yale Univ, 69-71; asst prof, Univ Zurich, 71-74; asst prof, 74-76, actg chmn comp lit prog, 77-78, ASSOC PROF COMP LIT & GER, UNIV MONTREAL, 77- *Mem:* Am Soc 18th Century Studies; Am Semiotic Soc; MLA; Can Semiotics Res Asn; Can Compt Lit Asn. *Res:* Eighteenth century; discourse analysis; interdisciplinary research on parts and wholes. *Publ:* Auth, Jean-Georges Sulzer, Mod Lang Notes, 71; De la signification d'une poesie insignifiante: La poesie fugitive au XVIIIe siecle, 72 & Pour et contre la Bible, 76, Studies Voltaire; Les discours dans le Discours Preliminaire, Romanic Rev, 76; D'Alembert: L'ordre philosophique de ce discourse, Mod Lang Notes, 76; Herder et la toupie des origines, Rev Sci Humaines, 77; Lorenzaccio: Le Carnaval et la Cardinal, Romantisme, 78. *Mailing Add:* Prog de Litt Comp Univ Montreal Montreal PQ H3T 1J4 Can

MOSES, GAVRIEL, b Haifa, Israel. ITALIAN & COMPARATIVE LITERATURE. *Educ:* London Sch Film Tech, dipl, 64; Univ Fribourg, lic, 69; Brown Univ, PhD(comp lit), 74. *Prof Exp:* Asst prof, 73-80, ASSOC PROF ITAL & FILM, UNIV CALIF, BERKELEY, 80- *Concurrent Pos:* Mellon fel comp lit, Ctr for Humanities, Wesleyan Univ, 77-78. *Mem:* MLA; Am Asn Teachers Ital; Renaissance Soc; Am Comp Lit Asn; Am Musicol Soc. *Res:* Renaissance; literature and other arts; film studies. *Publ:* Auth, Antonioni's Eclipse: Opening Sequence, Macmillan Films, 75; Gubbio in Gabbia: Pirandello's cameraman and the entrapments of film vision, Mod Lang Notes, 1/79; Tasso to Monteverdi: Renaissance musical setting and the poetics of Genera Mixta, Yale Ital Studies, 79. *Mailing Add:* Dept of Ital Univ Calif Berkeley CA 94720

MOSES, RAE ARLENE, b Oakland, Calif, May 30, 35; m 67; c 1. LINGUISTICS, AFRICAN LANGUAGES. *Educ:* San Francisco State Col, BA, 60; Univ Tex, PhD(ling), 65. *Prof Exp:* Lang coordr Swahili, Univ Wis, 64-65; asst prof ling, 65-80, asst dean col arts & sci, 69-76, ASSOC PROF LING, NORTHWESTERN UNIV, 80- *Concurrent Pos:* Peace Corps lang training consult, 64-66, instr, Psychoanal Inst, 79- *Mem:* Ling Soc Am. *Res:* Child language; linguistics and education. *Publ:* Auth, The Literary Crisis: The Search for Remedy, The Chicago Tribune Perspective, 12/76; coauth (with Harvey Daniels & R Gundlach), What teachers believe: An historical investigation of language attitudes and the implication for bidialectalism in the schools, Ariz English Bull, 2/77; (with Harvey Daniels & R Gundlach), Children's Language and the Multicultural Classroom, In: Ch 6, Teaching in a Multicultural Society, Free Press, 77; (with Harvey A Daniels & R Gundlach), Teachers' language attitudes and bidialectalism, Int J Sociol Lang, Mouton, 77; co-ed (with R Gundlach & B Litowitz), The Ontogenesis of the Writer's Sense of Audience: Rhetorical Theory and Children's Written Discourse, Rhetoric 78, Univ Minn Press, 79; auth, What is rug time?, Proc of the Parasession CLS, Univ Chicago Press, 81. *Mailing Add:* 2016 Sheridan Rd Evanston IL 60201

MOSHER, HAROLD FREDERICK, JR, English, Comparative Literature. See Vol II

MOSKOS, GEORGE, b Charleston, SC, Oct 16, 48; div. FRENCH LITERATURE. *Educ:* Davidson Col, BA, 70; Univ Wis-Madison, MA, 73, PhD(French), 75. *Prof Exp:* Teaching asst, Univ Wis, 73-75; ASST PROF FRENCH, SWARTHMORE COL, 75- *Res:* Flaubert; Stendhal; romanticism. *Publ:* Auth, Mythe, ecriture et revolution, In: Espagne erivains: Guerre civile, Pantheon Press, Paris, France, 75; coauth, Saint Oedipus: Psychocritical Approaches to Flaubert's Art, Cornell Univ Press, 82. *Mailing Add:* Dept Mod Lang & Lit Swarthmore Col Swarthmore PA 19081

MOSSHAMMER, ALDEN ADAMS, Ancient History, Classics. See Vol I

MOST, GLENN WARREN, b Miami, Fla, June 12, 52. COMPARATIVE LITERATURE, CLASSICAL LANGUAGES. *Educ:* Harvard Univ, AB, 72; Yale Univ, MPhil, 78, PhD(comp lit), 80; Tübingen, WGer, DPhil, 80. *Prof Exp:* Teaching asst philos, Yale Univ, 75, teaching asst lit, 76; teaching asst Latin, Univ Tübingen, 77-78; vis lectr lit theory, Yale Univ, 78-79; teaching asst classics, Univ Heidelberg, 79-80; MELLON ASST PROF CLASSICS, PRINCETON UNIV, 80- *Concurrent Pos:* Mellon fel, Am Acad Rome, 82-83. *Res:* Literature; literary theory; philosophy. *Publ:* Auth, Principled reading, Diacritics, 79; Sappho Fr 16 6-7 LP, Class Quart, 81; Callimachus and Herophilus, Hermes, 81; On the arrangement of Catullus' Carmina Maiora, 81 & Neues Zur Geschichte des Terminus Epyllion, 82, Philologus; contribr, Geschichtsbewusstsein und Rationalität: Zum Problem der Geschichtlichkeit in der Theoriebildung, Klett-Cotta Verlag, West Ger, 82; Ancient Writers: Greece and Rome, Charles Scribner's Sons, 82; co-ed, G W Leibniz, Specimen Dynamicum, Felix Meiner Verlag, Hamburg, West Ger, 82. *Mailing Add:* Dept of Classics Princeton Univ Princeton NJ 08544

MOST, WILLIAM G, Latin & Greek. See Vol IV

MOST, WOODROW LLOYD, b Mt Clemens, Mich, Apr 11, 17; m 47; c 1. FRENCH FOLKLORE. *Educ:* Univ Mich, AB, 39, AM, 40; Laval Univ, PhD, 53. *Prof Exp:* Head foreign lang dept, Kemper Mil Sch, 42-46; asst prof Romance lang, DePauw Univ, 46-53, from assoc prof to prof Romance lang & dir lang lab, 53-64; prof, 64-80, EMER PROF FOREIGN LANG & CHMN DEPT, UNIV NEBR, OMAHA, 80- *Mem:* Nat Fed Mod Lang Teachers Asn; Am Asn Teachers Fr; MLA; Am Coun Teaching Foreign Lang; AAUP. *Res:* Seventeenth century French theater. *Mailing Add:* Dept of Foreign Lang Univ of Nebr Omaha NE 68101

MOTLEY, MICHAEL TILDEN, b Salt Lake City, Utah, Jan 4, 45. SPEECH COMMUNICATION, LINGUISTICS. *Educ:* Univ Tex, Austin, BA, 65, MS, 67; Pa State Univ, PhD(speech commun), 70. *Prof Exp:* Instr speech commun, Pa State Univ, 67-70; asst prof commun disorders, Fresno State Col, 70-71; asst prof speech commun, Calif State Univ, Los Angeles, 71-77; asst prof, Ohio State Univ, 77-82; ASSOC PROF COMMUN (RHET), UNIV CALIF, DAVIS, 82- *Concurrent Pos:* Vis prof, Ohio State Univ, 77. *Mem:* Western Speech Commun Asn; Speech Commun Asn; Int Commun Asn. *Res:* Communication theory; psycholinguistics. *Publ:* Auth, Verbal conditioning-generalization in encoding, Speech Monogr, 74; Semantic bias effects on verbal slips, Cognition, 76; Laboratory induced Freudian slips, J Speech & Hearing Res, 79; Personality and situational influences upon verbal slips, Human Commun Res, 79; Syntactic criteria in prearticulatory editing, J Psycholing Res, 81; Verifying assumptions of laboratory-induced slips of the tongue, Human Commun Res, 81; Linguistic analysis of glossolalia, Commun Quart, 81; Formulation and editing of anomalies in speech production, J Verbal Learning Verbal Beh, 82. *Mailing Add:* Dept of Rhet Univ Calif Davis CA 95616

MOTTE, WARREN FRANCIS, JR, b Boston, Mass, Oct 5, 51; m 77; c 1. FRENCH. *Educ:* Univ Pa, AB, 74, AM, 79, PhD(Fr), 81; Univ Bordeaux III, Maitrise, 76. *Prof Exp:* Lectr English, Univ Bordeaux III, 75-77; lectr French, Univ Pa, 81-82; ASST PROF FRENCH, UNIV NEBR, 82- *Mem:* MLA; Northeast Mod Lang Asn; Am Asn Teachers Fr. *Res:* Twentieth century French literature; theory of literature; comparative literature. *Publ:* Auth, Introduction to San-Antonio: Du Grand Dard, Fr Forum, Vol 4, 79; Procedes anthroponymiques chez Rabelais, Neophilologus, Vol 64, 80. *Mailing Add:* Dept of Mod Lang & Lit Univ of Nebr Lincoln NE 68588

MOTTO, ANNA LYDIA, b New York, NY; m 59; c 2. CLASSICS. *Educ:* Queen's Col, NY, BA, 46; NY Univ, MA, 48; Univ NC, PhD, 53. *Prof Exp:* Asst, Univ NC, 49-50, part-time instr, 51-52; asst prof Latin, Greek & Span, Washington Col, 53-57; teacher Latin & French, Northport High Sch, NY, 57-58; asst prof Latin & Greek & chmn dept classics, Alfred Univ, 58-65; assoc prof Latin & Greek & chmn dept, Muhlenberg Col, 65-66; assoc prof, St John's Univ, NY, 66-68; from assoc prof to prof, Drew Univ, 68-73; chmn dept for lang, 74-78, PROF CLASSICS, UNIV SOUTH FLA, 73- *Concurrent Pos:* Fulbright grant, Am Acad Rome & Vergilian Soc, Cumae, 56; vis prof, Univ Mich, 69. *Mem:* Classic Asn Atlantic States (vpres, 72-73); Am Philol Asn; Am Classic League; MLA; SAtlantic Mod Lang Asn. *Res:* Seneca the philosopher; Roman Stoicism; Roman satire. *Publ:* Auth, Seneca Sourcebook: Guide to the Thought of Lucius Annaeus Seneca, Adolf Hakkert, Amsterdam, 70; Seneca's ironic art, Classic Philol, 4/70; Seneca's prose writings: A decade of scholarship, 1958-1968, Classic World, 1-2/71; Et terris iactatus et alto: The art of Seneca's Epistle 53, Am J Philol, 4/71; Seneca, Twayne, 73; co-ed, Satire: That Blasted Art (anthology), Putnam, 73; Philosophy and poetry: Seneca and Vergil, Classic Outlook, 9-10/78; Art and ethic in the drama: Senecan pseudotragedy reconsidered, Ill Classic Studies, 82. *Mailing Add:* Dept of Classics Univ of SFla Tampa FL 33620

MOTTOLA, ANTHONY C, b Nashville, Tenn, Aug 12, 15; m 46; c 1. FOREIGN LANGUAGE. *Educ:* Cath Univ Am, BA, 37, MA, 45; Manhattan Col, MA, 44; Fordham Univ, PhD, 61. *Prof Exp:* Teacher French, Loughlin High Sch, Brooklyn, NY, 38-42; instr Span, De La Salle Col, Washington DC, 42-45; from instr to asst prof French & Span, St Francis Col, NY, 46-54; from instr to assoc prof mod lang, 54-73, asst dean, 66-69, assoc dean col lib arts, 69-72, assoc dean & dir grad studies, 72-76, prof, 73-81, actg dean, Sch Educ, 77, dean, Sch Educ, 77-81, EMER PROF EDUC, FORDHAM UNIV, LINCOLN CTR, 81- *Mem:* Am Asn Teachers Span & Port; MLA; Am Coun Teaching Foreign Lang; Am Asn Cols Teacher Educ. *Res:* Seventeenth century Spanish literature; urban education; development of career opportunities programs for auxiliary school personnel. *Publ:* Coauth, The spiritual exercise of St Ignatius, Image, 63; auth, Innovation in education--the Fordham program, Sci News, 68. *Mailing Add:* Sch of Educ Fordham Univ at Lincoln Ctr New York NY 10023

MOULD, WILLIAM ANDERSON, b Utica, NY, Aug 16, 37; m 66; c 2. FRENCH LANGUAGE & LITERATURE. *Educ:* Hamilton Col, AB, 59; Middlebury Col, AM, 60; Univ Kans, PhD(French), 68. *Prof Exp:* Instr French Hamilton Col, 62-63; from instr to asst prof, 67-76, ASSOC PROF FRENCH, UNIV SC, 76-, DIR UNIV HONORS PROG, 73- *Mem:* MLA; Am Asn Teachers Fr; SAtlantic Mod Lang Asn; Nat Col Honors Coun. *Res:* French theater; 17th century; Racine. *Publ:* Auth, Jocaste: Mother of evil, L'Esprit Createur, summer 68; Illusion and reality: A new resolution of an old paradox, In: Moliere and the Commonwealth of Letters, Univ Southern Miss, 74; The innocent strategeme of Racine's Andromaque, Fr Rev, 2/75. *Mailing Add:* Dept of Foreign Languages Univ of South Carolina Columbia SC 29208

MOULTON, THORA MARY, b Springfield, Mass, May 19, 21. GERMAN CIVILIZATION & LANGUAGE. *Educ:* Mt Holyoke Col, BA, 42; Univ Chicago, MA, 44; Univ Tubingen, PhD, 58. *Prof Exp:* From instr to assoc prof, 44-58, PROF GER, VALPARAISO UNIV, 58- *Mem:* Am Asn Teachers Ger; MLA. *Res:* Modern German literature. *Mailing Add:* Dept of German Valparaiso Univ Valparaiso IN 46383

MOULTON, WILLIAM GAMWELL, b Providence, RI, Feb 5, 14; m 38; c 2. LINGUISTICS. *Educ:* Princeton Univ, AB, 35; Yale Univ, PhD, 41. *Hon Degrees:* DLitt, Middlebury Col, 74. *Prof Exp:* From instr to asst prof Ger, Yale Univ, 37-47; from assoc prof to prof ling, Cornell Univ, 47-60; prof ling & chmn prog ling, Princeton Univ, 60-79; RETIRED. *Concurrent Pos:* Fulbright res award, Netherlands, 53-54; Am Coun Learned Soc fel, Switz, 58-59; Guggenheim fel, Switz, 64-65; pres, Permanent Int Comt Linguists, 72-77; vis prof, Univ Calif, Davis, fall 79, Univ Calif, Berkeley, winter 81 & Univ Munich, summers 80, 81 & 82. *Mem:* Ling Soc Am (pres, 67); MLA; Am Asn Teachers Ger; Soc Netherlands Lit; Am Acad Arts & Sci; Royal Acad Netherlandic Lang & Lit, Belgium. *Res:* General linguistics; German and Dutch dialects; older Germanic. *Publ:* Auth, Swiss German Dialect and Romance Patois, Kraus, 41; The Sound of English and German, Univ Chicago, 62; A Linguistic Guide to Language Learning, MLA, 66, 2nd ed, 70. *Mailing Add:* 318 E Pyne Bldg Princeton Univ Princeton NJ 08540

MOURELATOS, ALEXANDER PHOEBUS DIONYSIOU, Philosophy, Classical Philology. See Vol IV

MOUTSOS, DEMETRIUS GEORGE, b Nov 6, 34; Greek citizen. LINGUISTICS. *Educ:* Univ Athens, dipl classics, 56; Univ Chicago, AM, 60, PhD(ling), 63. *Prof Exp:* From instr to assoc prof, 63-77, PROF LING, UNIV ROCHESTER, 77- *Mem:* Ling Soc Am; Am Name Soc. *Publ:* Auth, The origin of a Balkanism, Z Balkanologie, 69; Romanisn stapin and OChCl stopans, Z Vergleichende Sprachforsch, 70; The origin of a Balkan pastoral term, Sprache, 72; Byzantion, Zietschrift für Balkanologie, Z Vergleichende Sprachforschung Akten des internationalen Kolloquicuims, Innsbruck, 72. *Mailing Add:* Dept of Foreign Lang Lit & Ling Univ of Rochester Rochester NY 14627

MOYLAN, PAUL A, b Cambridge, Mass, Dec 28, 18; m 62. FRENCH & ITALIAN LITERATURES. *Educ:* Harvard Univ, AB, 40, AM, 42; Univ Mich, PhD(Romance lang), 57. *Prof Exp:* Instr French, La State Univ, 47-49; instr, Bradford Jr Col, 51-52; instr French & Span, Flint Community Jr Col, 55-61; prof, State Univ NY Col Potsdam, 61-65; PROF FRENCH & SPAN & CHMN DEPT, EMERSON COL, 65- *Concurrent Pos:* Vis prof French lang & lit, Univ Honduras at Tegucipalga, 72. *Mem:* Am Asn Teachers Fr; MLA. *Res:* Nineteenth century Neo-Romantic literature, especially fiction--French. *Publ:* Auth, Jerome and Jean Tharaud's romantic representation of Judaism, Fr Rev, 10/65; Ernest Psichari's mystic heroism, Renascence, (in press); Jerome and Jean Tharaud and Afro-Western relations, Presence Africaine, 70; contribr, Columbia Dict of Modern European Literature, 80. *Mailing Add:* Dept of French & Span Emerson Col 148 Beacon St Boston MA 02116

MOYLE, NATALIE KONONENKO, b Kornberg, Ger, Feb 23, 46; US citizen. FOLKLORE, SLAVIC STUDIES. *Educ:* Radcliffe Col, BA, 67; Harvard Univ, MA, 70, PhD(folklore), 76. *Prof Exp:* Teaching fel Russ & folklore, Harvard Univ, 70-74; asst prof, 74-80, asst dean, 75-79, ASSOC PROF SLAVIC, UNIV VA, 80- *Concurrent Pos:* Social Sci Res Coun fel, 78. *Honors & Awards:* Teacher of Year, WVA, 78-79. *Mem:* Am Folklore Soc; Am Asn Advan Slavic Studies; Am Asn Teachers Slavic Lang; MLA; Mid Atlantic Folklore Soc. *Res:* Folklore theory; applied psychology; Turkology. *Publ:* Auth, Techniques of Turkish minstrelsy, Uluslararasi Turk Folklor Kongresi Bildirleri, 76; Yunus Emre ve oral theory, Uc eminer Bildirleri, 77; contribr, The Ukrainian Dumy, Mosaic, 79; auth, Changing concepts of minstrelsy, Edebiyat; Russian concepts of space, NY Folklore, 82. *Mailing Add:* Dept of Slavic Lang Univ of Va Charlottesville VA 22903

MOYSEY, ROBERT ALLEN, b Richmond, Ind, June 27, 49. CLASSICAL LANGUAGES, ANCIENT HISTORY. *Educ:* Univ Cincinnati, BA, 71; Princeton Univ, MA, 73, PhD(class), 75. *Prof Exp:* Teaching asst class, Princeton Univ, 73-75; vis asst prof, Hamilton Col, 77-78; vis asst prof hist, Univ Del, 79-80; ASST PROF CLASS, UNIV MISS, 80- *Mem:* Archaeol Inst Am; Am Philol Asn; Asn Ancient Historians; Am Numis Soc. *Res:* Greek history, 4th century BC; Greek epigraphy; Greek numismatics. *Publ:* Auth, The date of the Strato of Sidon Decree, Am J of Ancient Hist, 76; The thirty and the Pnyx, Am J of Archaeol, 81. *Mailing Add:* Dept of Class Univ of Miss University MS 38677

MOZEJKO, EDWARD, b Czemierniki, Poland, July 15, 32; m 68; c 1. COMPARATIVE LITERATURE. *Educ:* Jagiellonian Univ, MA, 56, PhD(Slavic lit), 64. *Prof Exp:* Asst prof Slavic lit, Jagiellonian Univ, 57-65; lectr, Polish lang & lit, 69-71, assoc prof Russ & comp lit, 71-76, PROF SLAVIC LANG, UNIV ALTA, 76- *Concurrent Pos:* Alexander von Humboldt fel, Univ Munich, 71-72. *Mem:* Can Asn Slavists; Int Comp Lit Asn. *Res:* Avant-garde trends; theory of literature; eastern-western literary relations in Europe. *Publ:* Auth, Sztuka pisarska Jordana Jovkova, Polish Acad Sci, 64; Ivan Vazov, Wiedza Pawszech, Warsaw, 67. *Mailing Add:* Dept of Comp Lit Univ of Alberta Edmonton AB T6G 2G2 Can

MUCKLEY, ROBERT L, b Johnstown, Pa, Apr 21, 28; m 54; c 4. ENGLISH AS A SECOND LANGUAGE. *Educ:* Univ Colo, Boulder, BA, 49; Teachers Col, Columbia Univ, MA, 52, dipl(teaching English as a second lang), 68. *Prof Exp:* Teacher English as foreign lang, Col Americano, Bogota, Colombia, 53-55; teacher English, Orgn Am States, Pan Am Union, Int Ctr Rural Educ, Rubio, Venezuela, 56-58; asst prof English as second lang, Inst Latin Am Studies, Miss Southern Col, 58-60; asst prof, Park Col, 60-61; actg chmn dept, 66-67, coordr basic English prof for Span speakers & chmn dept, 71-75, ASSOC PROF ENGLISH AS SECOND LANG, INTER-AM UNIV PR, SAN GERMAN, 61- *Mem:* PR Teachers English to Speakers Other Lang; Am Coun Teaching Foreign Lang. *Res:* Development of materials and procedures for ethnic language retention among minority groups in the United States; curriculum development; English as a second language. *Publ:* Auth, Relatives in review, Lang Learning, 62; A Manual of English Structure, Inter-Am Univ PR, San German, 63; El discrimen en Puerto Rico, El Mundo, 7/67; On the co-occurence of do and be in English, J English as Second Lang, 69; co-ed, Cuentos Puertorriquenos, 74 & coauth, Leyendas de Puerto Rico, 76, Nat Textbk. *Mailing Add:* Dept of English Univ of PR San German PR 00753

MUELLER, DENNIS MELVIN, b St Louis, Mo, Dec 30, 35; m 65; c 3. GERMAN & COMPARATIVE LITERATURE. *Educ:* St John's Univ, Minn, BA, 57; Washington Univ, MA, 61, PhD(Ger), 64. *Prof Exp:* Asst prof Ger, Univ Pittsburgh, 64-68; asst prof, 68-70, assoc prof, 70-81, PROF GER, UNIV MO-COLUMBIA, 81- *Concurrent Pos:* Fulbright exchange teacher English, Gottfried Keller Gym, Berlin, Ger, 70-71. *Mem:* AAUP; Am Asn Teachers Ger. *Res:* 18th century German literature; influence of English literature on German literature; German detective stories. *Publ:* Coauth, Lab Drill Manual for German Review Grammar, DC Heath, 2nd ed, 70; auth, Wieland's Hamlet translation and Wilhelm Meister, Shakespeare-Jahrbuch, 71; Characterization of types in Feuchtwanger's novels, In: Lion Feuchtwanger, The Man, his Ideas, and his Works, Hennessey & Ingalls, 72; Kurze Krimis, Holt, Rinehart & Winston, 81. *Mailing Add:* Dept of Ger & Slavic Univ of Mo Columbia MO 65201

MUELLER, HUGO JOHANNES, b Hamburg, Ger, July 4, 09; m 36. GERMAN LANGUAGE & LITERATURE. *Educ:* Univ Hamburg, PhD, 33. *Prof Exp:* Prof, 59-74, chmn dept lang & ling, 59-68, EMER PROF GER & LING, AM UNIV, 74- *Mem:* Ling Soc Am; MLA. *Res:* Germanic structure; methology of language teaching. *Publ:* Auth, Deutsch Erstes Buch, 58; Deutsch Zweites Buch, 59, & Deutsch Drittes Buch, 62, Bruce; Gelenkte Schritte, Scribner, 73. *Mailing Add:* 5309 Westpath Way Bethesda MD 20816

MUELLER, KLAUS ANDREW, b Leipzig, Ger, June 17, 21; US citizen; m 44; c 4. FOREIGN LANGUAGES, LINGUISTICS. *Educ:* Columbia Univ, BA, 48, MA, 49. *Prof Exp:* Instr & lectr foreign lang, Columbia Univ, 46-49; instr, Princeton Univ, 49-51; chmn dept Ger lang, US Army Lang Sch, 51-57; dir Romance & Germanic lang depts, 57-60; coordr lang instr prog, Assoc Cols Midwest, 60-65; SR LECTR GER, UNIV CALIF, BERKELEY, 65- *Concurrent Pos:* Vis prof or vis lectr, Ind Univ, Univ Wash, Univ Colo, Univ Hawaii, Stanford Univ, Northwestern Univ, Purdue Univ; res scholar, Ger Acad Exchange Serv, 76. *Mem:* Asn Higher Educ; Am Coun Teaching Foreign Lang; Am Asn Teachers Ger. *Publ:* Coauth, Spanish for Secondary Schools, 62, Cultura Conversacion y Repaso, 67, Heath; Moderne Deutsche Sprachlehre, 67-80 & Individualized Instruction Program in Basic German, 71 & 80, Random; auth, Die Presse, Heath, 76. *Mailing Add:* Dept Ger Univ Calif Berkeley CA 94720

MUELLER, PAUL EUGENE, b Brooklyn, NY, Apr 29, 09. GERMAN. *Educ:* Columbia Univ, BS, 35, MA, 36, PhD(Ger), 56. *Prof Exp:* Instr English foreign students, Queens Col, NY, 46-47; instr Ger, St John's Univ, NY, 47; assoc prof, Moravian Col, 47-65; prof Ger & chmn dept mod foreign lang, Geneva Col, 65-67; prof & chmn dept Ger & Class Lang, 67-75, EMER PROF GER LANG & LIT, THIEL COL, 75- *Mem:* Moravian Hist Soc; MLA; Am Coun Teaching Foreign Lang; Am Asn Teachers Ger; Am Asn Teachers Fr. *Publ:* Auth, David Zeisberger's Official Diary, Fairfield, 1791-1795. *Mailing Add:* Dept of Ger & Class Lang Thiel Col Greenville PA 16125

MUELLER, THEODORE HENRY, b Mulhouse, France, Aug 18, 24; nat US; m 50; c 5. FRENCH. *Educ:* Northwestern Univ, PhD(classics), 53. *Prof Exp:* Instr French, Wayne State Univ, 54-57; asst prof, Univ Fla, 57-63; assoc prof, Univ Akron, 63-66; prof French, 66-69, prof, 69-80, EMER PROF EDUC, UNIV KY, 80- *Concurrent Pos:* US Off Educ res grants, 61, 62-64. *Mem:* Am Coun Teaching Foreign Lang. *Res:* Linguistics; Foreign language teaching and programmed language instruction; application of case grammar. *Publ:* Auth, Basic French--A Programmed Course, Appleton, 68; Handbook of French Structure, Harcourt, 68; Intermediate French, Intermedia, Hull, Que, 72; coauth, Programmed Instruction and Educational Technology, Ctr Curric Develop, 72; Vocalic communication in second language learning, Fr Rev, 75; auth, New Testament Greek: A Case Grammar Approach, Concordia Theol Sem, 78. *Mailing Add:* Dept of French Univ of Ky Lexington KY 40506

MUELLER-VOLLMER, KURT, b Hamburg, Ger, June 28, 28; m 58. GERMAN, HUMANITIES. *Educ:* Univ Cologne, dipl, 53; Brown Univ, MA, 55; Stanford Univ, PhD, 62. *Prof Exp:* From instr to acting asst prof Ger, 58-62, asst prof Ger & humanities, 62-64, assoc prof, 64-67, PROF GER, STANFORD UNIV, 67- *Concurrent Pos:* Am Philos Soc res grant, 65-66; Nat Endowment for Arts & Humanities fel, 68, sr fel, 72-73; consult & ed, Urizen Press, Inc, NY, 76- *Mem:* MLA; Am Soc Aesthet; Soc d'Etudes Staëleinnes. *Res:* Literary theory; literature of the 18th, 19th and 20th centuries; structuralism in the humanities. *Publ:* Auth, Toward a Phenomenological Theory of Literature: A Study of W Dilthey's Poetik, Mouton, The Hague, 63; Poesie und Einbildungskraft: Zur Dichtungstheorie Wilhelm von Humboldts, Metzler, Stuttgart, 67; ed, W von Humboldt: Studienausgabe, Fischer, Frankfurt, Vols I & II, 70 & 71; auth, W von Humboldt and der Beginn der Amerikanischen, Sprachvissenschaft, Die Briefe an John Pickering, A E Klostermann, Frankfurt, 76. *Mailing Add:* Dept of Ger Studies Stanford Univ Palo Alto CA 94305

MUJICA, BARBARA LOUISE, b Altoona, Pa, Dec 35, 43; m 66; c 3. SPANISH LITERATURE. *Educ:* Univ Calif, Los Angeles, AB, 64; Middlebury Col, France, MA, 65; NY Univ, PhD(Span), 74. *Prof Exp:* Teacher French, Univ Calif, Los Angeles, 63-64; assoc ed Span, Harcourt, 66-73; instr, Baruch Col, City Univ New York, 73-74; asst prof, 74-78, ASSOC PROF SPAN, GEORGETOWN UNIV, 78- *Concurrent Pos:* Ed, Verbena; fac, Nat Endowment for Humanities, Inst Span & Contemp Affairs, 80. *Mem:* MLA; Am Asn Teachers Span & Port; SAtlantic Mod Lang Asn; Am Coun Teaching Foreign Lang; Northeast Mod Lang Asn. *Res:* Counter-Reformation origins of existentialism; development of the European pastoral novel; methods of teaching Spanish. *Publ:* Auth, Violence in the pastoral novel: From Sannazaro to Cervantes, Hisp-Ital Studies, fall 76; The rapist and his victim: Calderon's No Hay Cosa Como Callar, Hispania, 79; Antiutopian elements in the Spanish Pastoral novel, Ky Romance Quart, 79; Aqui y Ahora, Holt, 79; coauth, Pasaporte, Wiley, 80; Calderon's Characters: An Existential Point of View, Puvill, 81; auth, Entrevista, Holt, 82; Lope's Arcadia: A step toward the modern novel, Hispanic J. *Mailing Add:* Sch of Lang & Ling Georgetown Univ Washington DC 20057

MULLEN, EDWARD J, b Hackensack, NJ, July 12, 42;. ROMANCE LANGUAGES. *Educ:* WVa Wesleyan Col, BA, 64; Northwestern Univ, MA, 65, PhD(Romance lang), 68. *Prof Exp:* Instr Span, Purdue Univ, West Lafayette, 67, asst prof, 68-71; assoc prof, 71-77, PROF SPAN, UNIV MO, COLUMBIA, 78- *Mem:* MLA; Am Asn Teachers Span & Port; Col Lang Asn. *Res:* Contemporary Spanish American literature, particularly poetry and the essay; Afro-Caribbean literature. *Publ:* Auth, Poetic Revision in Jaime Torres Bodet's Cancion de Cuna, Papers Lang & Lit, spring 70; ed, La Revista Contemporaneos: Seleccion y Prologo, Anaya, 72; auth, Encuentro: Ensayos De La Actualidad, 74 & ed, Lecturas Basicas, 76, Holt; Carlos Pellicer, Twayne, 77; Langston Hughes in the Hispanic World and Haiti, Archon, 77; El Cuento Hispanico, Random House, 80; auth, The Life and Poems of a Cuban Slave: Juan Francisco Manzano 1797-1854, Archon Bks, 81. *Mailing Add:* Dept of Span Univ Mo Columbia MO 65201

MULLEN, KAREN A, b July 5, 41; US citizen. ENGLISH, LINGUISTICS. *Educ:* Grinnell Col, BA, 63; Univ Iowa, MA, 66, PhD(English), 73. *Prof Exp:* Asst rhet, 66-70, asst ling, 70-73, from instr to asst prof ling, 74-75, coord English as foreign lang prog, 75-77, assoc dir, Intensive English Prog, Univ Iowa, 76-78; ASSOC PROF & DIR INTENSIVE ENGLISH, UNIV LOUISVILLE, 78- *Concurrent Pos:* Ed, News lett for spec interest group lang anal & studies humanities, Asn Comput Mach, 71-75; consult ed, Comput & Humanities, 72-75. *Mem:* Asn Teachers English to Speakers Other Lang; Ling Soc Am; MLA; Nat Asn Foreign Student Affairs; Asn Comput Mach. *Res:* Cloze-passage test; relationship between second-language proficiency and intelligence. *Publ:* Auth, In-core PL/I sort and search procedures for lexical data, Siglash Newslett, 73; The Wanderer: Considered again, Neophilologus, 74; Rater reliability and oral proficiency evaluations, Occas Papers Ling, 77; Using rater judgments in the evaluation of writing proficiency for non-native speakers of English, Teaching & Learning English as 2nd Lang: Trends Res & Pract, 77; Direct evaluation of second language proficiency, Lang Learning, 79; More on Cloze tests, Concepts Lang Testing 79; An alternative to the Cloze test, TESOL, 79; Evaluating writing in ESL, chap 15 & Rater reliability and oral proficiency evaluations, chap 8, In: Research in Language Testing, Newbury House, 80. *Mailing Add:* Dept of English Univ of Louisville Louisville KY 40208

MULLER, LIGUORI, b Philadelphia, Pa, June 24, 17. GREEK, LATIN. *Educ:* St Bonaventure Univ, BA, 40, MA, 43; Cath Univ Am, PhD(Greek, Latin), 56. *Prof Exp:* Instr Greek & Latin, Siena Col NY, 44-50; prof, St Joseph's Seraphic Sem, 54-67, vrector, 54-61, rector & relig super, 61-67; PROF GREEK & LATIN & VICAR RELIG COMMUNITY, SIENA COL, NY, 67- *Mem:* Am Philol Asn. *Res:* Latin patristics, especially St Augustine. *Publ:* Auth, Introd, transl & commentary, The De Haeresibus of St Augustine, Cath Univ Am, 56; articles on early Heresies, In: Corpus Dictionary of Religion, Corpus Instrumentorum. *Mailing Add:* Siena Col Loudonville NY 12211

MULLER, MARCEL, b Forty Fort, Pa, June 2, 26. FRENCH. *Educ:* Athenee Royal de Charleroi, Belgium, BA, 44; Univ Liege, MA, 51; Univ Wis, MA, 54, PhD(French), 65. *Prof Exp:* Instr French & Latin, Ill Col, 54-56; teaching asst, Univ Wis, 57-58; instr French & Ger, Lawrence Univ, 58-59; from instr to asst prof French, 61-66; assoc prof, 66-76, PROF FRENCH, UNIV MICH, ANN ARBOR, 76- *Concurrent Pos:* mem fac, French School, Middlebury, 72; Nat Endowment for Humanities summer grant, 79; mem, Inst Res in Humanities, Wis, 79-80. *Mem:* Am Asn Teachers French; MLA; Soc Amis Marcel Proust; Int Asn Fr Studies. *Res:* Proust; Valery; structuralism. *Publ:* Auth, Paul Valery lecteur de Leon Bloy, Romanic Rev, 10/59; Romananfang und Romanschluss bei Marcel Proust, In: Romananfänge: Versuch zu einer Poetik des Romans, Literarisches Colloquium, Berlin, 65; Les voix narratives dans La Recherche du temps perdu, Droz, 65; La naturalisation de Charlus, Poetique, fall 71; Charlus dans le metro, Etudes proustiennes, 78; Ancien Testament et Noveau Testament dans 'A la Recherche du Temps Perdu, French Forum Monogr, 79; La Dialectique De L'ouvert Et Du Ferme Chez Paul Valery, Mich Romance Studies, 80. *Mailing Add:* Dept of Romance Lang Univ of Mich Ann Arbor MI 48109

MÜLLER-BERGH, KLAUS, b Gütersloh, Ger, Nov 28, 36; US citizen; m 63; c 2. LATIN AMERICAN & COMPARATIVE LITERATURE. *Educ:* Univ Notre Dame, BA, 59; Yale Univ, MA, 60, PhD(Latin Am & Span lit), 66. *Prof Exp:* Asst Span & Port, Yale Univ, 61-64, instr, 65-66, asst prof Span & Port & Latin Am lit, 66-71; joint head grad studies, 72-74, acting head dept Span, Ital & Port, 75-76, assoc prof, 71-79, PROF LATIN AM LIT, UNIV ILL, CHICAGO CIRCLE, 80- *Concurrent Pos:* Univ Ill, Chicago Circle res grant, spring 73; Am Coun Learned Soc, Social Sci Res Coun grant, 74-75; sr Fulbright res grant, 82-83. *Mem:* MLA; Am Coun Teaching Foreign Lang; Hisp Soc Am; Inst Int Lit Iberoamericana; Am Asn Teachers Span & Port. *Res:* Cuban literature; 20th century Latin American novel; 20th century Latin American poetry. *Publ:* Auth, Unamuno y Cuba, Cuadernos Am, 9-10/69; La poesia de Octavio Paz en los anos treinta, Rev Iberoam, 71; Alejo Carpentier: estudio biografico critico, Anaya-Las Am, Madrid, 72; ed & coauth, Asedios a Carpentier, Ed Univ, Santiago de Chile, 73; Sentido y color de Concierto barroco, Rev Iberoam, No 92-93: 445-464; Feijoada, coke & the urbanoid: Brazilian poetry since 1945, World Lit Today, winter 79; Poesia hispanoamericana de vanguardia, La Muralla, Madrid, 82. *Mailing Add:* Dept of Span, Ital & Port Univ of Ill Chicago Circle Chicago IL 60680

MULLETT, FRED MAURICE, b Greencastle, Ind, May 10, 25; m 53; c 4. FOREIGN LANGUAGES. *Educ:* Univ Mo, AB, 48, PhD, 59; Univ Md, MA, 50. *Prof Exp:* Instr French & Ger, William Woods Col, 53-55; from instr to asst prof, Monmouth Col, Ill, 55-60; prof, Nat Col, 60-64; assoc prof, 64-82, PROF FRENCH & GER, HANOVER COL, 82- *Mem:* MLA; Am Asn Teachers Fr. *Res:* Contemporary French literature; French drama of the past century. *Mailing Add:* Dept of Foreign Lang Hanover Col Hanover IN 47243

MULLICAN, JAMES STANLEY, Rhetoric, English. See Vol II

MULLIGAN, JOHN J, b Boston, Mass, July 30, 18; m 48; c 4. FOREIGN LANGUAGES. *Educ:* Boston Col, AB, 40; Rutgers Univ, AM, 42; Boston Univ, PhD(Ger lang & lit), 57. *Prof Exp:* From instr to asst prof Ger lang & lit, Boston Col, 48-58; asst prof Ger lang & lit & Latin, Long Beach State Col, 58-61; assoc prof, 61-66, PROF GER LANG & LIT, VILLANOVA UNIV, 66- *Concurrent Pos:* Mem adj fac, US Marine Corps Develop & Educ Command, Quantico, Va, 69-73. *Mem:* Col Am Asn Teachers Ger; MLA; Lessing Soc. *Res:* Nineteenth century and post-World War II Germany and German literature; methodology in foreign language teaching; eighteenth century. *Publ:* Auth, The foundations of humor in Karl Heinrich Waggerl, Ger Quart, 11/61; Jetzt Lesen Wir, Scott, 65, rev ed, 70; The physical disposition of teachers and students and the learning process in the classroom, A-zimuth, spring 66; ed, Gestern, Heute und Morgen, Scribner's, 68; auth, Von Stufe zu Stufe, Harper, 69; coauth, Modern College German, Harper, 71; coauth & co-ed, Junge Deutsche Autoren, Van Nostrand, 73. *Mailing Add:* Dept of Mod Lang Villanova Univ Villanova PA 19085

MULVIHILL, EDWARD ROBERT, b Boulder, Colo, May 20, 17; m 39; c 3. SPANISH. *Educ:* Univ Colo, AB, 38; Univ Wis, AM, 39, PhD, 42. *Prof Exp:* Spec agent, Fed Bur Invest, 42-46; from asst prof to assoc prof, 46-55, chmn dept Span & Port, 52-72, chmn dept comp lit, 78-80, PROF SPAN, UNIV WIS-MADISON, 55-, ASSOC DEAN COL LETT & SCI, 60- *Concurrent Pos:* Ford fac fel, 53-54. *Honors & Awards:* Order of Vasco Nunez de Balboa, Panama, 46; Order of Isabel the Catholic, Spain, 59. *Mem:* MLA; Am Asn Teachers Span & Port; Cent States Mod Lang Asn. *Res:* Contemporary Spanish literature, especially the novel; Jacinto Benavente and modern Spanish stage craft. *Publ:* Ed, Laforet, Nada, 58, Marias, Modos de vivir, 64 & Galdos, Miau, 70, Oxford Univ. *Mailing Add:* 5619 Lake Mendota Dr Madison WI 53705

MUNOZ, WILLY OSCAR, b Cochabamba, Bolivia, Apr 6, 49. LATIN-AMERICAN & SPANISH LITERATURE. *Educ:* Loras Col, BA, 72; Univ Iowa, MA, 74, PhD(Span), 79. *Prof Exp:* Teaching asst Span, Univ Iowa, 72-76; instr, St Ambrose Col, 76-77; instr English, Centro Boliviano Am, 77; instr Span, Clarke Col, 78-79; lectr Latin Am lit, Inst Idiomas Maryknoll, 79-80; secy, Univ Coun, San Simon, 80; ASST PROF SPAN, CENTRE COL KY, 81- *Concurrent Pos:* Nat Endowment for Humanities fel, 82. *Mem:* Union Nac Poetas Escritores, Bolivia. *Res:* Disintegration in Latin-American fiction: Alejo Carpentier, Julio Cortazar, Jose Donoso; concept of modernity in Latin-American literature; critical studies of Bolivian plays. *Publ:* Auth, Tecnica narrativa de Hijo de opa, Los Tiempos, 1/78; Medio siglo de milagros, Letras Bolivianas, 12/79; Los invasores o el resurgimiento de los espectros del hambre, Los Tiempos, 3/80; Precursores del teatro boliviano, Presencia, 5/80; El monje de Potosi de Guillermo Francovich, 5/80 & Redescubrimiento de Sergio Suarez Figueroa, 5/80, Facetas, Los Tiempos; La autopista del sur o la epica de la humanidad, Los Tiempos, 9/80; Teatro boliviano contemporaneo, Casa Municipal Cult Franz Tamayo, 81. *Mailing Add:* Centre Col Box 735 Danville KY 40422

MUNRO, PAMELA LANG, b Ithaca, NY, May 23, 47; m 68; c 1. LINGUISTICS. *Educ:* Stanford Univ, AB, 69; Univ Calif, San Diego, AM, 71, PhD(ling), 74. *Prof Exp:* Actg asst prof, 74-75, adj asst prof, 75-77, ASST PROF LING, UNIV CALIF, LOS ANGELES, 77- *Concurrent Pos:* Jr fac fel, Univ Calif, Los Angeles, 77. *Mem:* Ling Soc Am; Am Anthrop Asn; Malki Mus Asn; Polynesian Soc. *Res:* American Indian languages; historical linguistics; descriptive and theoretical syntax. *Publ:* Coauth, Reduplication and rule ordering in Luiseno, Int J Am Ling, 73; Passives and their meaning, Language, 75; auth, Mojave Syntax, Garland, 76; Subject copying, predicate raising, and auxiliarization: The Mojave evidence, Int J Am Ling, 76; On the form of negative sentences in Kawaiisu, Proc 2nd Berkeley Ling Soc, 76; coauth, A Mojave Dictionary, privately publ, 76; auth, Copular sentences in Pima, Proc 3rd Berkeley Ling Soc, 77. *Mailing Add:* Dept of Ling Univ of Calif Los Angeles CA 90024

MUNSELL, PAUL EDWIN, b Philadelphia, Pa, Oct 2, 39; m 61; c 4. ENGLISH AS A SECOND LANGUAGE. *Educ:* Wheaton Col, AB, 61; Univ Mich, MA, 63, PhD(educ), 70. *Prof Exp:* Teaching fel English, Univ Mich, 62-66; asst prof, Univ Ryukyus, 66-68; asst prof, 68-76, ASSOC PROF ENGLISH, MICH STATE UNIV, 76- *Mem:* Nat Asn Foreign Student Affairs; Teachers English to Speakers Other Lang. *Res:* Relationship of aural discrimination and oral production; cognitive processes in language learning; teaching of reading and writing. *Mailing Add:* English Language Center CIP Michigan State Univ East Lansing MI 48824

MURAD, TIMOTHY, b Los Angeles, Calif, Feb 1, 44; m 68; c 2. SPANISH & LATIN AMERICAN LITERATURE. *Educ:* Rutgers Univ, BA, 66, PhD(Span), 75. *Prof Exp:* From instr to asst prof Span, Univ Vt, 71-78, dir, Latin Am studies prog, 73-77; asst prof, Univ Ark, 78-79; asst prof, 79-81, ASSOC PROF SPAN, UNIV VT, 81- *Mem:* Am Asn Teachers Span & Port; MLA; Inst Int Lit Iberoam; Latin Am Studies Asn. *Res:* Mexican novel; poetry of Jorge Luis Borges; Mariano Azuela. *Publ:* Auth, Before the storm: Jose Revueltas and the beginnings en Dios en la tierra, Texto Critico, 78; Animal imagery and structural unity in Azuela's Los De Abajo, J Span Studies: Twentieth Century, 79; Jorge Luis Borges' poetic biography of Juan Facundo Quiroga, Rev Estudios Hisp, 80; Foreshadowing, duplication, and structural unity in Azuela's Los De Abajo, Hispania, 81. *Mailing Add:* Dept of Romance Lang Univ of Vt Burlington VT 05405

MURATORE, MARY JO, b Ravenna, Ohio, Aug 16, 50. FRENCH CLASSICAL LITERATURE. *Educ:* Kent State Univ, BA, 72, MA, 74; Univ Calif-Davis, PhD(Fr), 79. *Prof Exp:* Vis asst prof, Va Polytech Inst & State Univ, 79-80; ASST PROF FRENCH, PURDUE UNIV, 80- *Mem:* MLA; Am Asn Teachers Fr; South Atlantic Mod Lang Asn. *Res:* French drama of 17th century; narrative strategies. *Publ:* Auth, Narration and correlation in La Fontaine's Psyche, Romance Notes, 79; The evolution of the Cornelian heroine, Studia Humanitatis, 82; Aphorism as discursive weaponry: Corneille's language of ammunition, L'Esprit Createur, 82. *Mailing Add:* 7480 Knoll Rd Kent OH 44240

MURGIA, CHARLES EDWARD, b Boston, Mass, Feb 18, 35. CLASSICS. *Educ:* Boston Col, AB, 56; Harvard Univ, MA, 60, PhD(class philol), 66. *Prof Exp:* Instr classics, Franklin & Marshall Col, 60-61; vis instr, Dartmouth Col, 64-65; asst prof, 66-72, assoc prof, 72-78, PROF CLASSICS, UNIV CALIF, BERKELEY, 78-, CHMN, 80- *Concurrent Pos:* Am Coun Learned Soc grant-in-aid, 68; appointed to edit Vol V of Editio Harvardiana of Servius; Univ Calif Humanities Res Comt res fels, fall 70; Am Coun Learned Soc fel, 74-75; Nat Endowment for Humanities fel, 78-79. *Mem:* Am Philol Asn; Philol Asn Pac Coast. *Res:* Latin textual criticism; Latin paleography; classical literature. *Publ:* Auth, Critical notes on the text of Servius' commentary on Aeneid III-V, Harvard Studies Class Philol, 67; Avienus' supposed iambic version of Livy, 70 & More on the Helen episode, 71, The Donatian life of Virgil, DS, and D, 74, Calif Studies Class Antiq; Prolegomena to Servius V--the manuscripts, Vol 11, Class Studies Ser, Univ Calif, 75; The minor works of Tacitus--a study in textual criticism, Class Philol, 77; The length of the lacuna in Tacitus' Dialogus, Calif Studies Class Antiq, 79; The date of Tacitus' Dialogus, Harvard Studies Class Philol, 80. *Mailing Add:* Dept of Classics Univ of Calif Berkeley CA 94720

MURILLO, LOUIS ANDREW, b Pasadena, Calif, Dec 13, 22. SPANISH LITERATURE. *Educ:* Univ Southern Calif, BA, 47, MA, 49; Harvard Univ, PhD(Span lit), 53. *Prof Exp:* Instr Span, Harvard Univ, 53-57; from instr to assoc prof, 58-71, PROF SPAN, UNIV CALIF, BERKELEY, 71- *Mem:* Renaissance Soc Am. *Res:* Sixteenth century Spanish prose; Cervantes' Don Quijote. *Publ:* Auth, The Cyclical Night: Irony in James Joyce and Jorge Luis Borges, Harvard Univ, 68; The Golden Dial, Temporal Configuration in Don Quijote, Dolphin, Oxford, 75; Lanzarote and Don Quijote, Folio, State Univ NY Brockport, Vol 10, No 77; Don Quijote, texto, introd, notas, bibliografia, Castalia, Madrid, 78. *Mailing Add:* Dept of Span & Port Univ of Calif Berkeley CA 94720

MURPHY, ALLEN FORREST, b Maysville, Ky, Nov 17, 31; m 53; c 4. FOREIGN LANGUAGES, SPANISH. *Educ:* Kenyon Col, AB, 53; Ohio State Univ, MA, 61, PhD(Romance lang), 72. *Prof Exp:* Instr Span, Mt Union Col, 61-63; instr comp lit, Ohio State Univ, 64-65; instr Span, Wright State Univ, 65-69; asst prof, Franklin Col, 69-72; assoc prof, 72-75, chmn dept, 75-81, PROF FOREIGN LANG, BLOOMSBURG COL, 75- *Mem:* Am Asn Teachers Span & Port; Am Coun Teaching Foreign Lang; Nat Asn Bilingual Educ. *Res:* Contemporary Spanish American literature; Chicano literature; teaching of foreign languages. *Mailing Add:* Dept of Lang & Cult Bloomsburg State Col Bloomsburg PA 17815

MURPHY, JOSEPH ANTHONY, b Philadelphia, Pa, Mar 27, 37. FOREIGN LANGUAGE EDUCATION, ROMANCE LANGUAGES. *Educ:* LaSalle Col, BA, 58; Ohio State Univ, PhD(foreign lang educ), 68. *Prof Exp:* asst prof French, Mich State Univ, 68-70; assoc prof, Lycoming Col, 70-72; ASSOC PROF FRENCH & LANG EDUC, WVA UNIV, 72- *Mem:* Am Asn Teachers Fr; Am Coun Teaching Foreign Lang; Teachers English to Speakers Other Lang. *Res:* Foreign culture and English as second language library reference materials; language teaching methodology; French and English as second language culture reader production. *Publ:* coauth, The use of the language laboratory to teach the reading lesson, Mod Lang J, 1/68; auth, MLA cooperative FL proficiency tests, 7th Mental Measurements Yearbk, 72; A mini-course in problem solving, Foreign Lang Annals, 12/73; contribr, How to do library research on a foreign culture, Eric Doc, 11/75; auth, Advanced placement in French literature & national teacher examinations: French, 8th Mental Measurements Yearbk, 78; French Review index of non-literary articles: 1960-79, Fr Rev, 3/80; ed, Proc Conf Southern Grad Schs, 80-82; auth, Cadres Culturels, Heinle & Heinle (in prep). *Mailing Add:* Dept of Foreign Lang WVa Univ Morgantown WV 26506

MURPHY, MICHAEL ANTHONY, Medieval English. See Vol II

MURPHY, PATRICIA, b Brooklyn, NY, Oct 22, 35. FRENCH. *Educ:* Univ Rochester, BA, 57; Univ Wis, MA, 61, PhD(French), 68. *Prof Exp:* Lectrice Am, Univ Rennes, 57-58; instr French, Univ Fla, 61-62; from lectr to asst prof, 66-73, ASSOC PROF FRENCH, UNIV NMEX, 73-, CHMN COMP LIT PROG, 77- *Mem:* MLA; Am Soc 18th Century Studies; AAUP; Am Asn Teachers Fr. *Res:* Sixteenth and 18th century French literature. *Publ:* Auth, Est-il bon? Est-il mechant--theory vs practice, 12/71 & Fantasy and satire in Rousseau's La Reine Fantasque, 3/74, Fr Rev; Ballet reform in mid-eighteenth century France: The Philosphoes and Noverre, Symposium, spring 76; Rabelais and Jarry, Fr Rev, 10/77. *Mailing Add:* 8428C Chambers Court NE Albuquerque NM 87111

MURPHY, PAUL ROBERT, b Dexter, Iowa, Feb 4, 13; m 36; c 3. LATIN. *Educ:* State Univ Iowa, AB, 33, AM, 34; Harvard Univ, PhD(classic philol), 42. *Prof Exp:* From asst prof to assoc prof Latin, Mt Union Col, 38-47; from asst prof to assoc prof, 47-57, PROF CLASS LANG, OHIO UNIV, 57- *Mem:* Am Philol Asn; AAUP; Am Class League. *Res:* Latin literature, lexicography and syntax. *Mailing Add:* 15 Roosevelt Dr Athens OH 45701

MURRAY, FREDERIC WILLIAM, b Vancouver, BC, Jan 24, 33; US citizen; m 59; c 3. IBERO AMERICAN STUDIES. *Educ:* Univ NMex, BA, 59, PhD(Ibero-Am studies), 68. *Prof Exp:* From instr to asst prof Span, Univ Maine, 62-69; ASSOC PROF SPAN AM LIT, NORTHERN ILL UNIV, 69- *Mem:* Am Asn Teachers Span & Port; Midwest Mod Lang Asn; Inst Int Lit Iberoam; Latin Am Studies Asn. *Res:* Spanish American poetry; archetype criticism; Spanish American civilization. *Publ:* Auth, La imagen arquetipica en la poesia de Ramon Lopez Velarde, Estudios de Hispanofila, Castalia, 72; Trends in departmental structure in the field of Hispanic studies, Hispania, 9/72; Huizinga's Fall, Spengler's Decline: the poetry of Jaime Augusto Shelly, Chasqui, 11/74. *Mailing Add:* Dept of Foreign Lang Northern Ill Univ De Kalb IL 60115

MURRAY, JACK, b Atlantic City, NJ, Oct 25, 30. FRENCH. *Educ:* Wesleyan Univ, BA, 52; Yale Univ, MA, 55, PhD, 57. *Prof Exp:* From instr to asst prof, 57-64, assoc prof, 64-79, PROF FRENCH, UNIV CALIF, SANTA BARBARA, 80- *Mem:* Am Asn Teachers Fr; MLA. *Res:* Contemporary French poetry, theatre and novel. *Publ:* Auth, Mind and Reality in Robbe-Grillet and Proust, Wis Studies Contemp Lit, summer 67; Proust's Views on Perception as a Metaphoric Framework, Fr Rev, 2/69; Proust, Montesquiou, and Balzac, Tex Studies Lit & Lang, spring 73. *Mailing Add:* 21 W Quinto St Santa Barbara CA 93105

MURRAY, JAMES CHRISTOPHER, b Wilkes-Barre, Pa, Dec 4, 39. MEDIEVAL SPANISH LANGUAGE & LITERATURE. *Educ:* King's Col, Pa, AB, 64; Cornell Univ, PhD(Span), 69. *Prof Exp:* Asst prof Span, Duke Univ, 67-73; ASST PROF SPAN, GA STATE UNIV 73-, DIR GRAD STUDIES, 81- *Mem:* MLA; Southeastern Mod Lang Asn; Medieval Acad Am; Am Asn Teachers Span & Port. *Res:* Spanish humanism; 16th century Spanish language and literature; Juan Luis Vives. *Publ:* Auth, Nature: A measure of conduct in the Libro de buen amor, Ky Romance Quart, 74; coauth, A New Shorter Spanish Review Grammar, Scribner's 75. *Mailing Add:* Dept of Foreign Langs Ga State Univ Atlanta GA 30303

MURRAY, ROBERT J, b Cleveland, Ohio, July 14, 32; m 56; c 4. CLASSICAL LANGUAGES. *Educ:* Xavier Univ, Ohio, AB, 54, MA, 57; Ohio State Univ, PhD(classics), 60. *Prof Exp:* Asst prof, 60-67, assoc prof, 67-70, chmn dept, 70-77, PROF CLASS LANG, XAVIER UNIV, OHIO, 70- *Mem:* Am Philol Asn; Class Asn Mid W&S. *Res:* Roman Republic; Greek literature. *Publ:* Auth, Attitude of the Augustan poets toward Rex and related words, Class J, 3/65; Cicero and the Gracchi, Trans & Proc Am Philol Asn, 66. *Mailing Add:* Dept of Classics Xavier Univ Cincinnati OH 45207

MURRAY, TIMOTHY C, Comparative Drama. See Vol II

MURSTEIN, NELLY KASHY, b Bagdad, Iraq, Apr 13, 32; US citizen; m 54; c 2. FRENCH. *Educ:* Univ Paris, BA, 49; Univ Tex, BA, 53; Rice Univ, MA, 53, PhD, 60. *Prof Exp:* Lectr French, Univ Portland, 59-60; instr, Reed Col, 61-62; from instr to assoc prof, 62-76, chmn dept French & Ital, 70-74 & 80-82, PROF FRENCH, CONN COL, 76- *Mem:* MLA; Am Asn Teachers French; Am Asn Dept Foreign Lang. *Res:* Contemporary theatre and poetry. *Publ:* Auth, Jean Giraudoux: A passing fad?, New Theater Mag, summer 69; Une entrevue avec Eugene Ionesco, French Rev, 2/72; L'Etrange Electra de J Giraudoux, Rice Univ Studies, summer 73. *Mailing Add:* Dept of French & Ital Box 1503 Connecticut College New London CT 06320

MURTAUGH, KRISTEN OLSON, b La Crosse, Wis, May 23, 43; m 68; c 2. ITALIAN RENAISSANCE LITERATURE. *Educ:* Univ Toronto, BA, 66; Harvard Univ, MA, 71, PhD(Romance lang & lit), 78. *Prof Exp:* Instr French, Dana Hall Sch, 67-69; lectr, 77-78, ASST PROF ITALIAN, MANHATTAN COL, 78- *Concurrent Pos:* Dir coop educ, Manhattan Col, 81- *Mem:* MLA; Dante Soc Am; Renaissance Soc Am; Coop Educ Asn. *Res:* Italian romance epic; Spenser; concept of Imitatio in the Renaissance. *Publ:* Auth, Ariosto and the Classical Simile, Harvard Univ Press, 81. *Mailing Add:* 179 E Mosholu Pkwy Bronx NY 10467

MUSA, MARK, b Parma, Italy, May 27, 34; US citizen; m 61; c 3. ITALIAN. *Educ:* Rutgers Univ, BA, 56; Johns Hopkins Univ, MA, 59, PhD, 61. *Prof Exp:* From asst prof to assoc prof, 61-65, PROF ITAL & FRENCH, IND UNIV, BLOOMINGTON, 65- *Concurrent Pos:* Guggenheim Found res fel, 71-72. *Mem:* MLA; Dante Soc Am; AAUP (pres, 80-). *Res:* Early Italian literature; Dante; Provencal literature. *Publ:* Auth, Machiavelli's Prince, St Martin's Press, 64; Dante's Inferno, 71, Dante's Vita nuova: An essay, 73 & Advent at the Gates, 74, Ind Univ; The Portable Machiavelli, Viking Press, 79; Dante's Purgatory, Ind Univ, 81; The DeCameron, Mentor Books, 82; transl & contribr, Dante's Divine Comedy (3 vols), Penguin Bks (in press). *Mailing Add:* Dept of French & Ital Ind Univ Bloomington IN 47401

MUSCARELLA, GRACE FREED, b Philadelphia, Pa, Feb 17, 29; m 57; c 2. LATIN, CLASSICAL PHILOLOGY. *Educ:* Univ Pa, BA, 50, MA, 51, PhD, 58. *Prof Exp:* Instr Latin, Swarthmore Col, 53-55; docent, Univ Mus, Univ Pa, 55-57; archaeol exped artist, Gordion, Turkey, 57 & Am Sch Class Studies, Athens, 58-59; vis lectr, Univ Pa, 60; instr class lang & Hebrew, City Col New York, 62-68; asst prof classics & Hebrew, 68-75. *Mem:* Am Philol Asn. *Res:* Archaeological drawing; Renaissance translations of Aristotle, especially the translator Giovanni Argyropoulos. *Publ:* Auth, A Latin Translation of the Pseudo-Aristotle De Mundo by Argyropoulos: Text and Analysis; illusr, Aesop Without Morals, Yoseloff, 61; auth, Aristoteles Latinus, Bruges, Paris, 65. *Mailing Add:* 70 La Salle St 18F New York NY 10027

MUSSER, FREDERIC OMAR, b Philadelphia, Pa, Jan 31, 30. FRENCH. *Educ:* Haverford Col, AB, 51; Yale Univ, PhD(French), 55. *Prof Exp:* Asst prof Romance lang, Wesleyan Univ, 57-64; assoc prof, 64-70, chmn dept mod lang, 71-75, PROF FRENCH, GOUCHER COL, 70- *Mem:* MLA; Am Asn Teachers Fr. *Res:* Seventeenth century French literature; 19th century French poetry. *Publ:* Auth, Strange Clamor: A Guide to the Critical Reading of French Poetry, Wayne State Univ, 65; The French classical vision, Class World, 2/68. *Mailing Add:* Dept of Mod Lang Goucher Col Baltimore MD 21204

MUST, GUSTAV, b Estonia, Feb 2, 08; nat US; m 39. GERMANIC PHILOLOGY, COMPARATIVE LINGUISTICS. *Educ:* Tartu State Univ, PhM, 38; Univ Göttingen, PhD, 49. *Prof Exp:* Teacher Ger & Estonia, col, Estonia, 34-44; asst prof Ger philol, Baltic Univ, Ger, 46-49; res assoc mod lang, Cornell Univ, 52; asst prof Ger, Baldwin-Wallace Col, 56-57; from asst prof to assoc prof, Augustana Col, Ill, 57-60, head dept, 57-60; assoc prof, Univ Conn, 60-62; assoc prof, 62-68, res prof, 67-70, prof, 68-78, EMER PROF GER, VALPARAISO UNIV, 78- *Concurrent Pos:* Am Coun Learned Soc fel, 50-51. *Mem:* MLA; Ling Soc Am. *Res:* Germanic and other Indo-European languages; West Finnic languages; comparative philology. *Publ:* Auth, The origin of the Germanic dental preterit, Language, 51, 52; The problem of the inscription on helmet B of Negau, Harvard Studies Class Philol, 57; The origin of the German word Ehre, PMLA, 61; The spelling or Proto-Germanic /f/ in Old High German, Language, Vol 43; Das St Galler Paternoster, Akten des V Int Germanisten-Kongresses Cambridge 1975, 76; Das ST Galler Credo, Frühmittelalterliche Studien 15, 81. *Mailing Add:* 1953 Lawndale Dr Valparaiso IN 46383

MUST, HILDEGARD, b Estonia; US citizen; m 39. LINGUISTICS. *Educ:* Univ Tartu, PhM, 40; Univ Hamburg, PhD, 47. *Prof Exp:* Asst prof English philol, Baltic Univ, Ger, 46-49; asst prof, 62-64, ASST PROF FOREIGN LANG, VALPARAISO UNIV, 66- *Mem:* MLA; Am Name Soc. *Res:* Onomastics; Finno-Ugric and Indo-European linguistics. *Publ:* Auth, Duration of speech sounds in Estonia, Orbis, 59; Trends in Estonian namegiving from 1900-1945, 64 & Scandinavian Kalf and Estonian Kalev, 69, Names. *Mailing Add:* Dept of Foreign Lang Valparasiso Univ Valparaiso IN 46383

MUSUMECI, ANTONINO, b Bolzano, Italy, Mar 26, 38; m 77. ITALIAN, FRENCH. *Educ:* Col d'Adda, Maturita Classica, 64; Catholic Univ, STL, 64; Duquesne Univ, BS, 67; Cornell Univ, PhD(Ital), 73. *Prof Exp:* Instr philos & theol, Carlow Col, 66-68; instr math & physics, Educ Instr Pittsburgh, 68-69; asst prof Ital, Lake Erie Col, 73-75; ASSOC PROF ITAL, UNIV ILL, URBANA-CHAMPAIGN, 75- *Concurrent Pos:* Res grants, Univ Ill, 75-78; travel grant, Am Coun Learned Soc, 77. *Mem:* Am Asn Teachers Ital; MLA; Midwest Mod Lang Asn. *Res:* Modern Italian literature--novel & poetry; Avantgarde literature. *Publ:* Auth, Silenzi montaliani: Note sull'enjambement nella poesia di Montale, Forum Italicum 72; Vocativi dannunziani, Nuova Antologia, 74; Pavese e la gratuita del movimento, Studi Piemontesi, 76; Tasso, Zola and the vicissitudes of Pastoralism, 19th Century French studies, 76; Le parentesi nel Canzoniere petrarchesco, Lingua e Stile, 76; Poliziano e la disposizione avverativa, Atti Dell'istituto Veneto, 76-77; Verga and the changing metaphor, Mod Lang Notes, 78; Sanguineti: The revolutionary dimension of the word, Perspectives on Contemp Lit, 78. *Mailing Add:* 4028 Foreign Lang Bldg Univ of Ill Urbana IL 61801

MUYSKENS, JUDITH ANN, b Holland, Mich, June 5, 48. FOREIGN LANGUAGE EDUCATION, FRENCH CIVILIZATION. *Educ:* Cent Col, BA, 70; Ohio State Univ, MA, 73, PhD(lang educ), 77. *Prof Exp:* Instr French & educ, Va Polytech Inst & State Univ, 76-77; asst prof, 77-78; ASST PROF FRENCH, UNIV CINCINNATI, 78- *Mem:* MLA; Am Asn Teachers Fr; Am Coun Teaching For Lang; Am Asn Univ Supervisors & Coordrs Foreign Lang Prog. *Publ:* Coauth, French women in language textbooks: The fiction and the reality, Contemp Fr Civilization, fall 77; A personalized approach to the teaching of literature at the elementary and intermediate levels of instruction, For Lang Ann, 2/80; Rendez-vous: An Invitation to French, 81 & Rendez-vous: Anthologie Litteraire, 82, Random House; University and secondary school articulation: Four steps for creating a resource network, In: ESL and the Foreign Language Teacher, Nat Textbook Co, 82. *Mailing Add:* Dept of Romance Lang & Lit Univ of Cincinnati Cincinnati OH 45221

MUZYCHKA, STEPHAN, b Ukraine, Dec 3, 26; m 60; c 2. FOREIGN LANGUAGES. *Educ:* Univ Madrid, Spain, MA, 58. *Prof Exp:* Asst prof, 60-72, ASSOC PROF SPAN LANG & LIT, MEM UNIV NFLD, 72- *Res:* Unamuno; Baroja; Azorin. *Mailing Add:* Dept of Spanish Memorial Univ Newfoundland St John's NF A1C 5S7 Can

MYERS, EUNICE DOMAN, b Lexington, NC, Dec 1, 48; m 69; c 1. SPANISH LITERATURE & LANGUAGE. *Educ:* Univ NC, Chapel Hill, BA, 71, MA, 73, PhD(Romance lang), 77. *Prof Exp:* Teaching asst Span, Univ NC, Chapel Hill, 71-76; vis instr, NC State Univ, 76-77; asst prof, 77-81; ASST PROF SPAN, WICHITA STATE UNIV, 81- *Concurrent Pos:* Consult & reviewer, Eirik Borve Inc, 77- & Scott Foresman, 78- *Mem:* Am Asn Teachers Span & Port; MLA; Asoc Pensamiento Hisp. *Res:* Modern Spanish novel; modern women authors from Spain especially Rosa Chacel; Ramon Perez de Ayala's essays. *Publ:* Auth, Tradition and modernity in Perez de Ayalas literary theories, Critica Hisp, Vol II, No 1; contribr, Sentimental Club: Un cuento filos ofico de Ramon Perez de Ayala, In: Simposio Int Ramon Perez de Ayala, Imprenta Flores, Gijon, 81. *Mailing Add:* Dept of Romance Lang Wichita State Univ Wichita KS 67208

MYERS, GAIL ELDRIDGE, Speech. See Vol II

MYERS, M KEITH, b 1922; US citizen; c 4. ROMANCE LANGUAGES. *Educ:* Univ Chicago, BA, 42; Univ Ill, MA, 47, PhD(French lit), 55. *Prof Exp:* Assoc prof French & Russ, Ohio Northern Univ, 56-57; assoc prof French, Span & Russ & dir AV dept, Earlham Col, 57-65; ASSOC PROF FRENCH & DIR LANG LAB, UNIV ILL, URBANA, 65- *Concurrent Pos:* Consult, Wilmington Col Lang Lab, 63. *Mem:* Am Asn Teachers Slavic & EEurop Lang. *Res:* Computer education; language laboratories. *Mailing Add:* 1009 Westlawn Ave Champaign IL 61820

MYERS, OLIVER TOMLINSON, b Newark, NJ, Apr 25, 29; m 58; c 5. SPANISH. *Educ:* Drew Univ, AB, 49; Columbia Univ, MA, 51, PhD(Span), 61. *Prof Exp:* Instr Span, Columbia Univ, 56-61; from instr to asst prof, Univ Calif, Davis, 61-66; assoc prof, 66-70, asst to vchancellor, 75-81, PROF SPAN, UNIV WIS, MILWAUKEE, 70-, CHMN DEPT SPAN & PORT, 81- *Mem:* MLA; Am Asn Teachers Span & Port; Ling Soc Am. *Res:* History of

Spanish language; medieval and Renaissance literature of Spain. *Publ:* Auth, A decade of progress in generative phonology as applied to Spanish, Romance Philol, 72; Symmetry of form in the Libro de buen amor, Philol Quart, 72; Multiple authorship of the Poema de Mio Cid: A final word?, Mio Cid Studies 77. *Mailing Add:* Dept of Span & Port Univ of Wis Milwaukee WI 53201

MYERS, ROBERT LANCELOT, b Stratford, Ont, Dec 3, 25; m 55; c 3. FRENCH LITERATURE. *Educ:* Univ Western Ont, BA, 48; Johns Hopkins Univ, MA, 49, PhD (French), 51. *Prof Exp:* Instr French & Span, Rich Univ, 52-53, from asst prof to assoc prof, 53-66, PROF OF FRENCH, UNIV WATERLOO, 66-, CHMN DEPT CLASSICS & ROMANCE LANG, 67- *Mem:* MLA. *Res:* Early influence of Shaftesbury in France; 18th century French dramatic theory; Remond de Saint-Mard, neglected literary amateur of 18th century France. *Publ:* Auth, The Dramatic Theories of Elie-Catherine Freron, Droz, 62; Voltaire's Mahomet the Prophet, Ungar, 64; Lectures en Prose et en Vers, Odyssey, Vols I & II, 65; The aesthetics of Remond de Saint-Mard, Rev Univ Ottawa, 66; Remond dialogues, 68 & Remond de Saint-Mard, a study of his major works, 70, Studies Voltaire & 18th Century. *Mailing Add:* BSMT 376 Albert Waterloo ON N2L 3V1 Can

MYKYTA, LARYSA ANN, b Regensgurg, Ger, June 10, 48; US citizen. FRENCH LITERATURE. *Educ:* Ohio State Univ, BA, 70, MA, 72; State Univ NY, Buffalo, PhD(Fr lit), 80. *Prof Exp:* ASST PROF FRENCH LANG & LIT, MIAMI UNIV, OHIO, 79- *Concurrent Pos:* Co-ed, Soc Critical Exchange Reports, 81- *Mem:* MLA; Midwest Mod Lang Asn; Soc Critical Exchange; Int Philos & Lit Asn. *Res:* Twentieth century literary theory and criticism; feminism and psychoanalysis; 19th and 20th century French literature. *Publ:* Women as the obstacle & the way, Mod Lang Notes, Vol 95, 80; Blanchot, In: Encycl of World Literature in the 20th Century, Frederick Ungar, 81; Blanchot's Au moment voulu: Women as the eternally recurring figure of writing, Boundarys, fall 82; Thomas L'obscur: a tangled web of sexuality & textuality, Enclitic, fall 82; The obscuring clarity of reason: Foucault's History of Sexuality, Soc Critical Exchange Reports, fall 82; Lacan, literature & the look: Women in the eye of psychoanalysis, Sub-stance (in press). *Mailing Add:* 4810 Krueger Parma OH 44134

MYRSIADES, KOSTAS J, Comparative Literature, Classical & Modern Greek Literature. See Vol II

N

NAAMAN, ANTOINE, b Port-Said, Egypt, June 30, 20; Can citizen; m 54; c 5. FRENCH LITERATURE. *Educ:* Cairo Univ, Lic es Lett, 42- MA, 48; Sorbonne, dipl etudes super, 50, DUniv, 51, Dr es Lett, 62; ENS, Saint-Cloud, dipl educ & civilization, 51. *Prof Exp:* Teacher French in sec schs, 42-49; head dept, Higher Tech Inst, Chebine-el-Kom, Egypt, 51-52; assoc prof & head dept, Ain-Chams Univ, Egypt, 62-65; prof mod lang & head dept, Univ Ghana, 65-66; PROF FRENCH & DIR CTR STUDIES LIT FRENCH EXPRESSION, UNIV SHERBROOKE, 66- *Concurrent Pos:* Mem comn French scholarly works, Ministry Educ, Egypt, 56-58 & comn French prog & baccalaureat exam, 64-65; mem search comt, Univ Sherbrooke, 68-72, pres comt rights of auth, 70-71; dir Presence Francophone, 69-; pres, Ed Cosmos, 69- & Ed Nasman, 73- *Honors & Awards:* Officer de l'Ordre du merite du Grand-Duche de Lunenbourg, 81. *Mem:* Asn Prof Egyptiens de Francais (secy, 46-56); Can Asn Comp Lit; Asn Can Univ Teachers French; Can-Fr Asn Advan Sci; Soc Etudes Romantiques. *Res:* Francophonie internationale; French comparative literature. *Publ:* Auth, Les debuts de Gustave Flaubert, 62; Les lettres d'Egypte de Gustave Flaubert, d'apres les manuscrits autographes, 65 & Mateo Falcone de Merimee, 67, Nizet, Paris; Guide bibliographique des theses litteraires canadiennes de 1921 a 1969, Cosmos, Sherbrooke, 70; coauth, Repertoire des theses litteraires canadiennes, de janvier 1969 a septembre 1971, Univ Sherbrooke, 71; Repertoire des theses litteraires canadiennes, de 1921 a 1976, Edit Naaman, 79. *Mailing Add:* Marcil 1695 Sherbrooke PQ J1J 2H7 Can

NABERS, NED PARKER, Classical Archeology & Philology. See Vol I

NABROTZKY, RONALD HEINZ DIETER, b Breslau, Ger. GERMAN LANGUAGE & LITERATURE. *Educ:* Univ Utah, BA, 65; Northwestern Univ, MA, 66, PhD(Ger lit), 73. *Prof Exp:* From instr to asst prof, 70-77, ASSOC PROF GER, IOWA STATE UNIV, 77- *Concurrent Pos:* Iowa State Univ fac improv leave, 78. *Mem:* Rocky Mountain Mod Lang Asn; MLA; Am Asn Teachers Ger. *Res:* Political Heine interpretations. *Publ:* Auth, Die DDR-Heinrich Heines verwirklichter Lebenstraum, 4/77 & Heines Prophezeiung vom Sieg des Kommunismus, 4/78, Mod Lang Notes; Karl Marx als Heinrich Heines politischer und poetischer Mentor: Die Legende von Marx' Mitarbeit an Heines Wintermärchen, In: Sparache und Literatur: Festschrift für Arval L Streadbeck zum 65, Geburtstag, Verlag Peter Lang, Bern & Frankfurt am Main, 81. *Mailing Add:* Dept of Foreign Lang & Lit Iowa State Univ Ames IA 50011

NACCI, CHRIS NATALE, b Abruzzi, Italy, Dec 24, 09. MODERN LANGUAGES. *Educ:* Ohio State Univ, BS, 32, BEd, 33, AM, 47; Nat Univ Mex, PhD, 51. *Prof Exp:* Mem bus staff, Bellaire Daily Leader, Ohio, 32-33; ed staff, Martins Ferry Daily Times, 33-34; chmn dept Romance lang, high sch, Ohio, 34-43; head dept pub rel, Standard Products Co, 43-45; instr of French & Span, Ohio State Univ, 45-47; prof Romance lang & chmn dept, Capital Univ, 47-63; prof mod lang & mem grad fac, Univ Akron, 63-68; PROF MOD LANG & CHMN DEPT, CAPITAL UNIV, 68- *Concurrent Pos:* Consult, Encycl Britannica World Dict, 54; Span Govt indust translr, Battelle Mem Inst, 55; vis prof, consult & lectr, Arg, Uruguay & Paraguay,

55-57; consult teacher testing, MLA, 60; prof 26-unit ser Span lang progs, TV, 63; mem working comt on lit, Northeast Conf, 66-67; eminent Hispanist, Ministerio de Asuntos Exteriores, Madrid, Spain, 72- *Honors & Awards:* Silver Award, Inst Cult Arg-Norte Am, 57; Award for Outstanding Contributions, Am Asn Teachers Span & Port, 68. *Mem:* Cent States Mod Lang Teachers Asn; MLA; Am Coun Teaching Foreign Lang; Am Asn Teachers Span & Port (secy-treas, 47-50, pres, 53-54 & 73-75, vpres, 65-73. *Res:* Ideological content of the Mexican theatre of the 20th century; development of reading and conversational performance. *Publ:* Auth, El teatro mexicano ante la Revolucion Social, Ky, Foreign Lang Quart, 54; Veinticuatro enfoques de la actual filosofia de la educacion en los Estados Unidos, US Embassy, Buenos Aires, 56 & 57; La ternura en Abrojos de Ruben Dario, Ministry Educ, Nicaragua, 62; El enderezamiento del caracter varonil, Ky Foreign Lang Quart, 63; Altamirano, Twayne, 670. *Mailing Add:* 2630 Sonata Dr Columbus OH 43209

NACHTSHEIM, MARY HENRY, b St Paul, Minn, Feb 21, 16. FRENCH, GERMAN. *Educ:* Col St Catherine, BA, 37; Laval Univ, MA, 52, DUniv, 61. *Prof Exp:* Teacher French, Arcadia Col, 39-40; instr Ger, 40-41, instr, 43-51, from asst prof to assoc prof, 52-66, PROF FRENCH, COL ST CATHERINE, 66-, COORDR INT STUDIES, 77- *Concurrent Pos:* Lectr, Macalester Col, 66-68; vis prof, Univ Minn, 72. *Honors & Awards:* Chevalier, Ministere de l'Education, France, 75. *Mem:* Am Asn Teachers Fr; MLA; Am Coun Teaching Foreign Lang; Alliance Francaise; Amite Charles Peguy. *Res:* Contemporary French and African literature. *Publ:* Contribr, Two Ends of a Log, Univ Minn, 58; auth, La Charite: Peguy et Pascal, Rev Univ Laval, 5/62; Peguy's Debt to Pascal, L'Esprit Createur, summer 62. *Mailing Add:* Dept of French Col of St Catherine St Paul MN 55105

NADAR, THOMAS RAYMOND, b Chicago, Ill, Jan 26, 46. TWENTIETH CENTURY GERMAN DRAMA & CINEMA. *Educ:* Univ Notre Dame, BA, 67; Univ Mich, Ann Arbor, MA, 68, PhD(Ger lang & lit), 74. *Prof Exp:* Asst prof, State Univ NY Albany, 74-79; ASST PROF GER, UNIV ORE, 80- *Concurrent Pos:* Prog head, Ctr Foreign Study, 71-78. *Mem:* MLA; Northeast Mod Lang Asn; Int Brecht Soc; Midwest Mod Lang Asn. *Res:* Twentieth century drama; film; music and literature. *Publ:* Auth, Hermann Hesse: Ein Märchen, Juggler, fall 67; Wolfgang Borchert: Lesebuchgeschichten, Generation, spring 68; Hermann Hesse: Ein Flötentraum, Overflow, winter 68; Bertolt Brecht and Kurt Weill in New York: Their Collaboration in America 1942-1944, Mod Lang Studies, 5/76; The eternal road--Max Reinhardt, Franz Werfel and Kurt Weill in American Exile, Mod Lang J, 4/77; Georg Heym's Jonathan, Omega, fall 78; Moderne Dichter Dramen, Monatshefte, spring 82. *Mailing Add:* Dept of Germanic Lang & Lit Univ of Ore Eugene OR 97403

NADEAU, ROBERT, b Montreal, Can, Nov 5, 44; m 67; c 1. EPISTEMOLOGY, PHILOSOPHY OF SCIENCE. *Educ:* Univ Montreal, BPh, 66, MAPh, 67; Univ Paris, PhD, 73. *Prof Exp:* PROF EPISTEMOLOGY, UNIV QUEBEC, MONTREAL, 71- *Concurrent Pos:* Consult, Soc Sci & Humanities Res Coun Can, 76; referee, Philosophiques, 76, Philos Archives, 77 & Philos of Sci, 82. *Mem:* Can Philos Asn; Can Soc Hist & Philos Sci; Philos Sci Asn. *Res:* Comparative epistemology and philosophy of science; philosophy of language. *Publ:* Co-ed, Genese de la pensee linguistique, Librairie Armand Colin, Paris, 73; auth, Bibliographie des textes sur Ernst Cassirer, Int Philos Rev, 74; co-ed, La philosophie et les savoirs, Bellarmin, 75; auth, Les elements kantiens de la philosophie du langage de E Cassirer, In: Actes du Congres d'Ottawa sur Kant, Univ Ottawa Press, 76; ed, Philosophie et Psychologie, Vol 4, 77, Vol 5, 78 & auth, Problematique de la preuve en epistemologie contemporaine, Vol 7, 80, Philosophiques. *Mailing Add:* 5535 Cote St-Antoine Montreal PQ H4A 1R3 Can

NADEL, BENJAMIN IRVING, History, Classics. See Vol I

NADIN, MIHAI, Aesthetics, Semiotics. See Vol IV

NAESS, HARALD S, b Oddernes, Norway, Dec 27, 25; m 50; c 3. SCANDINAVIAN STUDIES. *Educ:* Univ Oslo, Cand Phil, 52. *Prof Exp:* Lector Norweg, King's Col, Univ Durham, 53-58, lectr, 58-59; vis lectr, 59-61, assoc prof, 61-67, TORGER THOMPSON PROF SCAND STUDIES, UNIV WIS-MADISON, 67- *Concurrent Pos:* Fulbright scholar, 59-61; mem ed comt, Nordic Trans Serv, Univ Wis, 64-; ed, Scand Studies, 73-77. *Mem:* Soc Advan Scand Studies; Norweg-Am Hist Soc. *Res:* Scandinavian, particularly Norwegian, eighteenth and nineteenth century literature; American-Norwegian Immigration history. *Publ:* Auth, Knut Hamsuns brevveksling med postmester Frydenlund (1862-1947), 59 & Forsøk over Vesaas' prosastil, 62, Edda; Knut Hamsun og Amerika, Gyldendal, 69; ed, Norway number, Lit Rev, 69; co-ed, Americana-Norvegica III, 71 & auth, Norsk litteraturhistorisk bibliografi, 75, Universitetsforlaget; Norwegian Influence on the Upper Midwest, Univ Minn, 76. *Mailing Add:* Dept of Scand Studies Univ Wis Madison WI 53706

NAFF, WILLIAM E, b Wenatchee, Wash, Feb 14, 29; m 57. JAPANESE. *Educ:* Univ Wash, MA, PhD(Japanese lang), 66. *Prof Exp:* Asst Japanese, Univ Calif, Los Angeles, 58-59; lectr, Stanford Univ, 59-60; from asst prof to assoc prof, Univ Ore, 62-69; assoc prof, 69-80, PROF ASIAN STUDIES & CHMN PROG, UNIV MASS, AMHERST, 80- *Concurrent Pos:* Dir ctr Japanese studies, Univ Ore, 65-66 & 67-68. *Mem:* Asn Asian Studies; Asn Teachers Japanese. *Res:* Japanese language; history of Japanese literature; modern Japanese literature. *Publ:* Auth, Shimazaki Toson, an introduction, Univ Wash. *Mailing Add:* Asian Studies Prog Univ of Massachusetts Amherst MA 01002

NAGARA, SUSUMU, b Hiroshima, Japan, Aug 21, 32; m 63; c 2. LINGUISTICS, JAPANESE LANGUAGE. *Educ:* Hiroshima Univ, BA, 55, MA, 59; Univ Wis, PhD(ling), 69. *Prof Exp:* Instr English, Hiroshima Univ High Sch, 55-57; instr Kyoto Women's Univ, 59-61; lectr, 66-69, asst prof, 69-72, ASSOC PROF JAPANESE, UNIV MICH, ANN ARBOR, 72-

Concurrent Pos: Evaluator, Neglected Lang Prog, Kalamazoo Col, 66-; res grant, Soc Sci Res Coun, 72-73. *Mem:* Ling Soc Am; Asn Asian Studies; Asn Teachers Japanese (secy, 71-73); Am Coun Teaching Foreign Lang; Soc Teaching Japanese as Foreign Lang. *Res:* Problems of bilingualism and language contact; teaching Japanese as a second language; history of the Japanese language. *Publ:* Auth, A study on the classification of function words, Eng Lit Rev, Kyoto, 59; coauth, Computer experiment in transformational grammar, Japanese, In: Working Paper, DCCS, Univ Mich, 70; auth, Japanese Pidgin English in Hawaii, Univ Hawaii, 72; Teaching basic sentence construction in Japanese, 75 & A suggestion for teaching the Japanese Keigo system, 76, J Assoc Teachers Japanese; coauth, Handbook to Action English, I, II & III, 76, 77, 78, World Times of Japan. *Mailing Add:* Dept of Far Eastern Lang & Lit 3070 Frieze Bldg Univ of Mich Ann Arbor MI 48104

NAGEL, ALAN FREDERICK, Comparative Literature, English. See Vol II

NAGEL, BERT, b Ger, Aug 27, 07; m 35; c 2. GERMAN. *Educ:* Univ Heidelberg, PhD(Ger lit), 29. *Prof Exp:* Privatdozent Ger lit, Univ Heidelberg, 49-56, prof, 56-67; prof Ger, 68-76, EMER PROF GER, UNIV CALIF, IRVINE, 76- *Concurrent Pos:* Ger Forschungsgemeinschaft fel, 32-34, vis prof, Univ Saarlandes, 64, NY Univ, 66 & 67 & Univ Mannheim, 67. *Honors & Awards:* Grand Cross of Merit, Fed Repub Ger, 72. *Mem:* MLA; Deut Germanisten Verband. *Res:* German medieval literature; Kafka and the world literature; medieval and modern art of drama. *Publ:* Auth, Das Nibelungenlied, Hirschgraben, Frankfurt, 2nd ed, 70; Nene Deutsche Bibliographie, Munchen, 72; Iud Suss und Strafkolonie (Feuchtwanger/Kafka), In: Festschrift f H Eggers, 72; Die Sprachkrise eines Dichters (Hofmannsthal), Gedenkband f H Guntert, Innsbruck, 73; Unerreichbares Muster, In: Heidelberger Jahrbuch, 73; Ego, Clamor Validus Gandeshemensis (Hrotsvit), Ger-Roman Monatsschr, 73; Franz Kafka, Aspekte zur Interpretation und Wertung, Erich Schmidt, Berlin, 74; Stanfische Klassik, Deutsche Dichtung um 1200, Lothar Stiehmn, Heidelberg, 74. *Mailing Add:* Dept of German Sch of Humanities Univ of Calif Irvine CA 92664

NAGELE, RAINER, b Triesen, Liechtenstein, Aug 2, 43; m 71. GERMAN LITERATURE, LITERARY THEORY. *Educ:* Univ Calif, Santa Barbara, PhD, 71. *Prof Exp:* Asst prof Ger, Univ Iowa, 71-74; assoc prof Ger lit, Ohio State Univ, 75-77; ASSOC PROF GER LIT, JOHNS HOPKINS UNIV, 77- *Mem:* MLA; Am Asn Teachers Ger. *Res:* German literature of the 20th century; German literature from 1700 to present; literary theory and aesthetics. *Publ:* Auth, Zwischen Erinnerung und Erwartung: Gesellschaftskritik u Utopie bei M Walser, Basis, 72; Theater und keqn Gutes: Theatersymbolik u Rollenpsychologie in Heinrich Mann, Colloquia Germanica, 73; Die Vermittelte Welt Fiktion u Wirklichkeit, J Deutschen Schillergesellsch, 75; Hermetik u Öffentlichkeit, Hölderlix J 19/20, 75-77; Heinrich Böll Einführung in das Werk u Forschung, Fischer-Athenäum, Frankfurt, 76; Literatur u Utopie Versuche zu Hölderlin, Lothar Stiehm, Heidelberg, 78; Peter Handke, Beck, München, 78; Freud und die Topologie des Testes, Mod Lang Notes, 78. *Mailing Add:* Dept of Ger Johns Hopkins Univ Baltimore MD 21218

NAGLE, BETTY ROSE, b Washington, DC, Nov 6, 49. CLASSICAL STUDIES. *Educ:* Univ Pa, BA, 70; Ind Univ, MA, 73, PhD(classics), 75. *Prof Exp:* Instr, Smith Col, 75-76; vis asst prof, 76-78, ASST PROF CLASSICS, IND UNIV, 78- *Mem:* Am Philol Asn; Class Asn Middle West & South. *Res:* Ovid; Latin literature; theory and practice of literary criticism. *Publ:* Auth, Tristia: Poet's autobiography and poetic autobiography, Trans Am Philol Asn, 76; Divine wit vs divine folly: Mercury and Apollo in Metamorphoses, Class J, 2-3/77; Francis Cairns' Theory of Genre and Generic Composition, Helios, spring 77; The Poetics of Exile: Program and Polemic in the Tristia and Epistulae ex Ponto of Ovid, Collection Latomus 170, Brussels, 80. *Mailing Add:* Dept Class Studies Ind Univ Bloomington IN 47401

NAGLE, D BRENDAN, Ancient History. See Vol I

NAGLER, MICHAEL NICHOLAS, b New York, NY, Jan 20, 37; m 59; c 2. CLASSICAL LITERATURE AND SOCIETY. *Educ:* NY Univ, BA, 60; Univ Calif, Berkeley, MA, 62, PhD(comp lit), 66. *Prof Exp:* Instr foreign lang, San Francisco State Col, 63-65; asst prof, 65-73, humanities res fel, 68-69, ASSOC PROF CLASSICS & COMP LIT, UNIV CALIF, BERKELEY, 73- *Concurrent Pos:* Am Coun Learned Soc study grant, Sanskrit lang & lit, 71-72. *Mem:* Am Philol Asn; Int Comp Lit Asn. *Res:* Oral poetry, chiefly Homer, Old English and Sanskirt; myth and religion; peace and conflict studies. *Publ:* Auth, Towards a generative view of the Homeric formula, Trans Am Philol Asn, 67; Oral poetry and the question of originality in literature, Proc Vth Cong Int Comp Lit Asn, 67; Spontaneity and Tradition: A Study of Homer's Oral Art, Univ Calif, 74; Dread goddess endowed with speech, Archaeol News, 77; Mysticism: A hardheaded definition for a romantic age, Study Mystica, 78; Peace as a paradigm shift, Bull Atom Scientists, 81; America Without Violence, Island Press, 82. *Mailing Add:* Dept of Classics Univ of Calif Berkeley CA 94720

NAGY, EDWARD, b Yugoslavia, Sept 27, 21; US citizen; m. ROMANCE LANGUAGES. *Educ:* Univ Zagreb, Can Zwv, 45; Univ Madrid, Lic, 50, PhD, 52. *Prof Exp:* Instr Span & Ital, 56-60, from asst prof to assoc prof Span, 60-67, dir Span grad prog, 67-81, PROF SPAN, RUTGERS UNIV, NEW BRUNSWICK, 67- *Mem:* MLA; Am Asn Teachers Span & Port; Cervantes Soc Am. *Res:* Picaresque novel and drama of the Spanish Golden Age. *Publ:* Auth, Rodrigo Fernandez de Ribera, El meson de mundo, 63, Miguel de Cervantes, Pedro de Urdemalas, 65, Las Americas; Lope de Vega y la Celestina, Univ Veracruzana, Mex, 68; El anhelo del Guzman de Aleman de conocer su sangre, Ky Romance Quart, 69; La parodia y la satira en El alcaide de si mismo de Pedro Calderon de la Barca, Romanische Forschungen, 71; El Prodigo ye el Picaro, Ed Sever-Cuesta, Valladolid, 74; El galeote de Lepanto de Luis Velez de Guevara: la diversion en vez del escarmiento, Bull of Comediantes, 77; ed, Miguel de Cervantes, El Rufian Dichoso, Ediciones Catedra, Madrid, 77; La picardia castrense en Flandes y su utilizacion por Lope de Vega, Lope de Vega y los origenes del Teatro Espanol, Actas del I Congreso Internacional sobre Lope de Vega, Patronato Archipreste de Hita, Madrid, 81. *Mailing Add:* Dept of Span & Port Rutgers Univ New Brunswick NJ 08903

NAGY, ELEMER JOSEPH, b Oros, Czech, Sept 19, 16; US citizen; m 42; c 1. FOREIGN LANGUAGES. *Educ:* Univ Budapest, MA, 40, PhD(Latin), 43. *Prof Exp:* Instr Latin, Hungarian, Slovak & Ger, State High Sch, Ipolysag, Hungary, 40-44; instr Hungarian, US Army Lang Sch, Monterey, Calif, 51-59; asst prof Latin & Ger, Fresno State Col, 60-61; teacher, Theodore Roosevelt High Sch, Fresno, Calif, 61-62; asst prof Latin, Ger & Russ, 62-66, assoc prof Latin & Ger, 66-69, PROF CLASSICS, CALIF STATE UNIV, FRESNO, 69- *Mem:* Class Asn Pac States (pres, 65-66). *Res:* Classics; linguistics; mythology. *Publ:* Auth, Francisci Faludi Omniarium, Univ Pecs, 43. *Mailing Add:* Dept Foreign Lang Calif State Univ Fresno CA 93710

NAGY, GREGORY JOHN, b Budapest, Hungary, Oct 22, 42; US citizen. CLASSICS, LINGUISTICS. *Educ:* Ind Univ, AB, 62; Harvard Univ, PhD(classics), 66. *Prof Exp:* Instr classics & ling, Harvard Univ, 66-69, asst prof classics, 69-73; from assoc prof to prof, Johns Hopkins Univ, 73-75; PROF CLASSICS, HARVARD UNIV, 75- *Mem:* Am Philol Asn; Ling Soc Am. *Res:* Greek literature; Indo-European linguistics; poetics. *Publ:* Auth, Observations on the sign-grouping and vocabulary of linear A, Am J Archaeol, 65; On dialectal anomalies in Pylian texts, Atti Memorie 1st Cong Int Micenologia, 68; Greek Dialects and the Transformation of an Indo-European Process, Harvard Univ, 70; coauth, Greek: A Survey of Recent Work, Mouton, The Hague: 73; auth, Phaethon, Sappho's Phaon, and the White Rock of Leukas, Harvard Studies Class Philol, 73; Comparative Studies in Greek and Indic Meter, Harvard Univ, 74. *Mailing Add:* Dept of Classics Harvard Univ Cambridge MA 02138

NAGY, MOSES MELCHIOR, b Hadikfalva, Rumania, Jan 5, 27; US citizen. ROMANCE LANGUAGES. *Educ:* Marquette Univ, MA, 56; Laval Univ, PhD(French), 60; Sorbonne, dipl French lang & lit, 66. *Prof Exp:* Chmn dept, 65-76, PROF FRENCH, UNIV DALLAS, 65- *Concurrent Pos:* Pres, Cercle Francais, Dallas, 70; vpres, Alliance Francaise, Dallas, 72; ed-in-chief, Claudel Studies, 72- *Mem:* MLA; Am Asn Teachers French; SCent Mod Lang Asn; Paul Claudel Soc Am. *Res:* French Catholicism and literature; surrealism; La Joie dans l'oeuvre de Claudel. *Publ:* Auth, Claudel's Immortal Heroes, Am Benedictine Rev, 6/72; Report on rencontres internationales Claudeliennes de Branques, Claudel Studies, spring 73; Claudel: From the Absurd of Death to the Joy of Life, Rev Nat Lit, fall 73. *Mailing Add:* Dept of Languages PO Box 1330 Univ of Dallas Irving TX 75060

NAHRGANG, WILBUR LEE, b Iowa Park, Tex, June 6, 39; m 64. MODERN GERMAN LITERATURE. *Educ:* Texas Christian Univ, BA, 60; Univ Kans, MA, 63, PhD(Ger), 66. *Prof Exp:* From instr to assoc prof, 65-69, ASSOC PROF GER, NORTH TEX STATE UNIV, 69- *Concurrent Pos:* Co-ed, Schatzkammer, 77- *Mem:* Am Asn Teachers Ger; Am Coun Teaching Foreign Lang; MLA Western Asn Ger Studies. *Res:* Heinrich Böll and his works; German novels of World War II. *Publ:* Heinrich Böll's war books: A study in changing literary purpose, Mod Lang Notes, 10/73. *Mailing Add:* Dept of Foreign Lang & Lit Tex State Univ Denton TX 76203

NAIM, CHOUDHRI MOHAMMED, b Bara Banki, India, June 3, 36. URDU LANGUAGE & LITERATURE. *Educ:* Univ Lucknow, BA, 54, MA, 55; Univ Calif, Berkeley, MA, 61. *Prof Exp:* From instr to asst prof, 63-71, ASSOC PROF URDU, UNIV CHICAGO, 71- *Concurrent Pos:* Co-ed, J South Asian Lit, 63-; reader Urdu, Aligarh Muslim Univ, India, 71-72. *Mem:* Asn Asian Studies. *Res:* Cultural history of Muslim South Asia; Muslim society in India, Pakistan and Bangladesh. *Publ:* Ed, Readings in Urdu: Prose and Poetry, East-West, Honolulu, 65; auth, The consequences of Indo-Pakistani war for Urdu language and literature, J Asian Studies, 69; Arabic orthography and some non-Semitic languages, In: Islam and Its Cultural Divergence, Univ Ill, 71; Yes, the poem itself, Lit East & West, 72; Muslim contribution to literature in India: The Medieval period, Encycl Brittanica, 15th ed, 74; Muslim press in India and the Bangladesh crisis, Quest, 75; Introductory Urdu (2 vols), Cosas, 75. *Mailing Add:* Dept of SAsian Lang Foster Hall 1130 E 59th St Univ of Chicago Chicago IL 60637

NAJAM, EDWARD WILLIAM, b Danbury, Conn, 28, 16; m 46; c 1. FRENCH LANGUAGE & LITERATURE. *Educ:* Bowdoin Col, AB, 38, Duke Univ, MA, 51; Univ NC, PhD, 53. *Prof Exp:* Risk analyst, Dept Crime, Liberty Mutual Ins Co, Boston, Mass, 38-42; instr mod lang, Tabor Acad, 42-47; instr French, Duke Univ, 47-50; instr French & Span, Univ NC, 50-54; from asst prof to assoc prof French, 55-70, asst dean col arts & sci, 58-63, PROF FRENCH, IND UNIV, BLOOMINGTON, 70- *Concurrent Pos:* US Off Educ Experienced Teacher Fel grant, for retraining high sch teachers of French & Span, 66-69. *Honors & Awards:* Chevalier, Palmes Academiques. *Res:* Teaching of language; international affairs; 17th and 19th century literature. *Publ:* Ed, Materials and techniques for the language laboratory, 1/62 & co-ed, Language learning: The individual and the process, 1/66, Int J Am Ling. *Mailing Add:* 1301 Longwood Dr Bloomington IN 47401

NAJITA, TETSUO, b Honokaa, Hawaii, Mar 30, 36; m 58; c 2. MODERN & JAPANESE HISTORY. *Educ:* Grinnell Col, BA, 58; Harvard Univ, MA, 60, PhD(hist), 65. *Prof Exp:* Asst prof hist, Carleton Col, 64-66; asst prof, Wash Univ, 66-68; assoc prof, Univ Wis-Madison, 68-69; assoc prof, 69-74, PROF HIST & FAR EASTERN LANG & CIVILIZATIONS, UNIV CHICAGO, 74- *Concurrent Pos:* Fulbright res grant, Japan, 68-69; Nat Endowment for Humanities sr fel, 73-74 & 80-81; Guggenheim fel, 81-82; dir, Ctr for Far Eastern Studies, 74-80. *Honors & Awards:* John K Fairbank Priza, AHA, 69. *Mem:* Asn Asian Studies (bd dirs, 77-80); AHA. *Res:* Tokugawa political thought; 20th century politics and political thought. *Publ:* Auth, Hara Kei in the Politics of Compromise, Harvard Univ, 67; Oshio Heihachiro (1793-1837), In: Personality in Japanese History, Univ Calif, 70; Nakano Seigo and the spirit of the Meiji Restoration in twentieth century Japan, In: Dilemmas of Growth in Prewar Japan, Princeton Univ, 71; Political economism in the thought of Dazai Shundai (1680-1747), J Asian Studies, 8/72; Japan, The Intellectual Foundations of Japanese Politics, 74 & 80 & ed, Japanese Thought in the Tokugawa Period (1600-1868): Methods and Metaphors, 78, Univ Chicago; ed, Conflict in Modern Japanese History: The Neglected Tradition, Princeton (in press). *Mailing Add:* Dept of Hist Univ of Chicago Chicago IL 60637

NANTELL, JUDITH ANN, b Cleveland, Ohio, Mar 1, 49. MODERN LANGUAGE & LITERATURE. *Educ:* Cleveland State Univ, BA, 71; Ind Univ, MA, 74, PhD(Span lit), 78. *Prof Exp:* Asst prof, Univ Wis-Madison, 78-80; ASST PROF SPAN, FLA STATE UNIV, 80- *Mem:* MLA; SAtlantic Mod Lang Asn. *Res:* Modern Spanish; 20th century Hispanic poetry, especially from the generation of 1927 and contemporary Spain. *Publ:* Auth, Death and resurrection in Rafael Alberti's Capital de la Gloria, Essays Lit, fall 79; Alberti's Yo Era un Tonto close-up: The Keatonesque fool, Anales Lit Espanola Contemp, fall 81; Poetry for politics' sake: Rafael Alberti's Consignas, Critica Hisp (in prep); Francisco Brines's Aun No: Poetry as Knowledge, Ky Romance Quart (in prep). *Mailing Add:* Dept of Mod Lang & Ling Fla State Univ Tallahassee FL 32306

NARDOCCHIO, ELAINE F, b Sydney, NS. FRENCH-CANADIAN. *Educ:* St Francis Xavier Univ, BA, 65; Middlebury Col, MA, 66; Laval Univ, PhD(French), 78. *Prof Exp:* Lectr French lang & lit, Mem Univ, 66-67 & Brock Univ, 67-68; lectr Can lit & civilization, Guelph Univ, 70 & Univ Western Ont, 70-71; ASST PROF FRENCH, McMASTERS UNIV, 71- *Concurrent Pos:* Soc Sci & Humanities Res Coun Can leave fel, 80-81. *Mem:* Can Asn Prof Fr; MLA; Am Asn Teachers French. *Res:* Quebec theatre; semiotics; computers. *Publ:* Auth, Les Belles-Soeurs et la reevolution tranquille, Liaction Nationale, 12/80; Dimensions socio-politiques dans Les Grands Soleils de Jacques ferron, Presence Fiancophone, spring 81; Semiotics and Quebec Theatre: The case of Marcel Dube's Pauvre Amour, Koditias/Code, 82; An Introduction to the History of Theatre in Quebec (in press). *Mailing Add:* Dept of Romance Lang McMaster Univ Hamilton ON L8S 4M2 Can

NARO, ANTHONY JULIUS, b Nashville, Tenn, Nov 12, 42; m 66; c 2. LINGUISTICS. *Educ:* Polytech Inst NY, BSc, 63; Mass Inst Technol, PhD(ling), 68. *Prof Exp:* Asst prof ling & philol, Univ Chicago, 68-74; prof ling, Fed Univ & prof lett, Pontif Cath Univ, Rio de Janeiro, 74-79; RES PROF LING, NAT COUN RES & SCI DEVELOP, BRAZIL, 79- *Concurrent Pos:* Researcher, Univ Coimbra, 68; Angola Sci Res Inst, 70-72; vis prof, Fed Univ Rio de Janeiro, 72; researcher, Ctr Philol Res, Lisbon, 73; res dir, Brazilian Literacy Found & Brazilian Found Res. *Mem:* Ling Soc Am; Asn Brasileira Ling; Asn Lit & Ling Comput; Asn Comput Ling. *Res:* Historical linguistics; Pidgins and Creoles; romance linguistics. *Publ:* Auth, Da metrica medieval galaico-portuguesa, Ocidente, Lisbon, 402: 227-236; On f h in Castilian and western Romance, Z romanische Philol, 88: 435-447; ed, Tendencias Atuais da Linguistica e da Filologia no Brasil, Livraria Francisco Alves, Rio de Janeiro, 76; auth, The Genesis of the Reflexive Impersonal in Portuguese, 76 & A Study on the Origins of Pidginiation, 78, Language, coauth, Competencias Basicas do Portugues, Fundacao Mobral, 78; Portuguese in Brazil, In: Trends in Romance Linguistics and Philology, Mouton Publ, 82; The social and structural dimensions of a syntactic change, Language, 57: 63-98. *Mailing Add:* 191 Waverly Pl New York NY 10014

NARVAEZ, RICARDO AUGUSTO, b Jayuya, PR, Dec 24, 21; m 44; c 4. SPANISH, LINGUISTICS. *Educ:* Concordia Teachers Col, BS, 43; Univ Minn, Minneapolis, MA, 48, PhD(Span ling), 59. *Prof Exp:* Instr Span, Univ Minn, Minneapolis, 47-51; assoc prof Greek & ling, Northwestern Col, 51-52; asst prof English, Univ PR, 52-58; asst prof, 61-65, assoc prof, 65-71, PROF SPAN, UNIV MINN, MINNEAPOLIS, 71- *Concurrent Pos:* Vis lectr & Smith-Mundt grant, Univ Guadalajara, 59-60; vis lectr & Fulbright grant, Inst Caro y Cuervo, Colombia, 62-63; vis lectr & Fulbright grant, Univ Navarre, 65-66; ed, Lutheran Lit Comt, 68- *Mem:* Ling Soc Am; MLA; Int Ling Asn. *Res:* Hispanic gestures; Spanish morphology; English as a second language. *Publ:* Auth, Acronyms in Spanish, Lang Learning, 62; Algunos comentarios sobre la pronunciacion del castellano en Puerto Rico, Cultura, Colombia, 9/63; From San Juan to Guadalajara, Hispania, 12/63; Instruction in Spanish Pronunciation, Vols I & II, 67 & 70 & An Outline Spanish Morphology, 70, EMC Corp. *Mailing Add:* Dept of Span & Port Univ of Minn Minneapolis MN 55455

NASH, JERRY CARROLL, b Longview, Tex, May 5, 46. FRENCH LANGUAGE & LITERATURE. *Educ:* Tex Tech Univ, BA, 68; Kans Univ, M Phil, 70, PhD(French), 72. *Prof Exp:* Asst prof, 72-76, assoc prof, 76-81, PROF FRENCH, UNIV NEW ORLEANS, 81- & CHMN FOREIGN LANG, 77- *Concurrent Pos:* Res grant, La State Univ Found, 75; Nat Endowment for Humanities grant, 78. *Mem:* MLA; S Cent Mod Lang Asn; Renaissance Soc Am; S Cent Renaissance Conf; Am Asn Teachers French. *Res:* French Renaissance literature; Francois Rabelais; Maurice Sceve. *Publ:* Auth, Rabelais and stoic portrayal, Studies in Renaissance, 74; ed, Maurice Sceve: Concordance de la Delie, In: NC Studies in Romance Lang (2 vols), 76; auth, Stoicism and the stoic theme of Honestum in early French Ren Lit, Studies in Philol, 79; The notion and meaning of art in Delie, Romanic Rev, 80; Louise Labe and learned levity, Romance Notes, 80; ed, A rabelais symposium, In: L'Espirit Createur, Vol 21, 81; co-ed, Essays in Early French Ranaissance Literature presented to Barbara M Craig, Fr Lit Publ Co, 82; ed, Pre-Pleiade Poetry, Fr Forum Publ, 83. *Mailing Add:* Dept of Foreign Lang Univ of New Orleans New Orleans LA 70122

NASH, LAURA L, b Madison, Wis, Oct 20, 48; m 74. CLASSICAL PHILOLOGY. *Educ:* Conn Col, AB, 70; Harvard Univ, MA, 72, PhD(classics), 76. *Prof Exp:* Teaching fel classics, Harvard Univ, 72-75; asst prof classics, Brown Univ, 77-80. *Mem:* Am Philol Asn; Soc Values in Higher Educ; Class Asn New Eng. *Res:* Greek literature and mythology. *Publ:* Auth, Olympian 6: Alibaton and Iamos emergence into light, Am J Philol, fall 75; Concepts of existence: Greek origins of generational thought, Daedalus, fall 78. *Mailing Add:* 11 Buckingham St Cambridge MA 02138

NASH, ROSE, b Chicago, Ill, c 1. LINGUISTICS, ENGLISH AS SECOND LANGUAGE. *Educ:* Northwestern Univ, BMus, 46; Middlebury Col, MA, 60; Ind Univ, PhD (ling), 67. *Prof Exp:* Lectr ling, Ind Univ, 60-62; vis prof English, Hebrew Univ Jerusalem, 70; researcher phonetics, Univ Edinburgh, 70; vis prof ling, Univ PR, 72; researcher phonetics, Haskins Labs, New Haven, 74; prof ling, Ling Inst, Tampa, 75; PROF LING, INTER AM UNIV, 67- *Concurrent Pos:* Researcher, Am Coun Learned Soc, 68-69; sr scholar exchange, USSR, 70; researcher, Nat Endowment Humanities, 73-74; researcher, Nat Inst Mental Health, 76-78. *Honors & Awards:* Best Acad Book of Yr, Choice mag, 70. *Mem:* Ling Soc Am; Am Soc Phonetic Sci; Ling Asn Can & US; Teachers English to Speakers of Other Lang; Int Ling Asn. *Res:* Spanish-English bilingualism and language contact; experimental phonetics; computerized lexicography. *Publ:* Auth, A Multilingual Lexicon of Linguistics and Philology, Univ Miami, 68; ed, Readings in Spanish-English Contrastive Linguistics, Inter Am Univ, Vol I, 74, Vol II, 80, Vol III, 82; contribr, Spanglish: Language contact in Puerto Rico, Am Speech, 74; Englanol: More language contact in Puerto Rico, Am Speech, 74; Phantom cognates in Puerto Rican Englanol, La Monda Lingvo-Problemo, 76; auth, Comparing Spanish and English: Patterns in Phonology and Orthography, Regents Publ Co, 77; The intonation of verifiability, In: The Melody of Language, Univ Park Press, 80; Pringlish: Still more language contact in Puerto Rico, In: The Other Tongue, English Across Cultures, Univ Ill Press, 82. *Mailing Add:* Inter Am Univ Hato Rey PR 00919

NASH, SUZANNE JULIE CRELLY, b Cleveland, Ohio; m; c 2. FRENCH LITERATURE. *Educ:* Wells Col, BA; Cornell Univ, MA; Princeton Univ, PhD, 72. *Prof Exp:* Instr, 72-73, asst prof, 73-80, ASSOC PROF FRENCH, PRINCETON UNIV, 80- *Concurrent Pos:* Jonathan Dickinson Bicentennial Preceptorship, Princeton Univ, 77-79. *Mem:* MLA; Northeast Mod Lang Asn. *Res:* Nineteenth and 20th century French poetry, Victor Hugo and Paul Valery in particular. *Publ:* Auth, Les Contemplations' of Victor Hugo: An Allegory of the Creative Process, 76 & Paul Valery's Album de Vers Amiens: A Past Transfigured, 82, Princeton Univ Press. *Mailing Add:* Dept of Romance Lang & Lit Princeton Univ Princeton NJ 08540

NASON, MARSHALL RUTHERFORD, b Deloraine, Man, Sept 23, 17; nat US; m 49; c 1. ROMANCE LANGUAGES. *Educ:* La State Univ, BA, 39; MA, 47; Univ Chicago, PhD, 58. *Prof Exp:* Exec secy, div Latin Am relat, La State Univ, 39-46, instr romance lang, 46-47; instr, 47-48, from asst prof to assoc prof, 49-64, PROF MOD LANG, UNIV NMEX, 64-, DIR IBERO-AM STUDIES & LATIN AM CTR, 65- *Concurrent Pos:* Dir, div foreign studies, Univ Peace Corps Chile, Argentina, Uruguay, 61-62; dir, Univ Peace Corps Training Ctr for Latin Am, 63; Consult higher educ, Fulbright, Comn, Buenos Aires, 69; dir, XIII Sem Higher Educ in the Americas, 72. *Mem:* Am Asn Teachers Span & Port; MLA; Inst Int Lit Iberoam (exec secy-treas, 49-60); Latin Am Studies Asn. *Res:* Latin American literature; Spanish language and literature. *Publ:* Coauth, Charlar Repasando; co-ed, Radiografia de la Universidad en las Americas, 73 & contribr, The Caciques: Oligarchial Politics & the System of Caciquismo in the Luso-Hispanic World, 73, Univ NMex. *Mailing Add:* Latin Am Ctr 229 Ortega Hall Univ of NMex Albuquerque NM 87131

NATALICIO, DIANA, b St Louis, Mo, Aug 25, 39; m 66. LINGUISTICS, ENGLISH AS SECOND LANGUAGE. *Educ:* St Louis Univ, BS, 61; Univ Tex, Austin, MA, 64, PhD (ling), 69. *Prof Exp:* Res assoc eval res, Ctr Commun Res, 70-71; asst prof ling & mod lang, 71-73, chmn mod lang & assoc prof, 73-77, assoc dean lib arts, 77-79, PROF LING & MOD LANG, UNIV TEX, EL PASO, 77- & DEAN LIB ARTS, 79- *Concurrent Pos:* Res grant, US Office Educ, 72. *Mem:* Ling Soc Am; Am Asn Teachers Span & Port; Teachers English to Speakers of Other Lang; Nat Coun Res English; Int Reading Asn. *Res:* Language acquisition; bilingualism; language testing. *Publ:* Coauth, A comparative study of English pluralization by native and non-native English speakers, Child Develop, 71; auth, Sentence repetition as a language assessment technique: Some issues and applications, Bilingual Rev/La Rev Bilingue, 77; coauth, The Sounds of Children, Prentice-Hall, 77 & 81; contribr, Theory & Practice or Early Reading, Lawrence Earlbaum Assoc, 79; auth, Repetition and dictation as language testing techniques, Mod Lang J, 79; contribr, Festschrift in Honor of Jacob Ornstein: Studies in General and Sociolinguistics, Newbury House, 80; coauth, Some characteristics of word classification in a second language, Mod Lang J, 82. *Mailing Add:* Col of Liberal Arts Univ of Tex El Paso TX 79968

NATELLA, ARTHUR A, JR, b Yonkers, NY, Nov 8, 41. SPANISH & LATIN AMERICAN LANGUAGE & LITERATURE. *Educ:* Columbia Univ, BA, 63; Syracuse Univ, MA, 65, PhD(Span), 70. *Prof Exp:* Asst Span, Columbia Univ, 62-63; Romance lang, Syracuse Univ, 63-66, instr, 66-69; asst prof Span & Port, Univ MD, College Park, 69-80; ASSOC PROF SPAN, FORDHAM UNIV, BRONX, NY, 80- *Mem:* AAUP; MLA; Am Asn Teachers Span & Port. *Res:* Latin American drama and fiction; comparative literature; modern Spanish literature. *Publ:* Auth, Enrique Solari Swayne and Collacocha, Latin Am Theatre Rev, 4/71; Anacronismo de la nueva novela latinoamericana, Probs Lit, 9/72; Ernesto Sabato y el hombre superfluo, Rev Iberoam, 12/72; The Hispanic Heritage in America, 74, The Spanish in America, 1513-1979, 80, Oceana Bks; The new theatre of Peru, Senda Nueva de Ediciones, 82. *Mailing Add:* Dept of Modern Lang Fordham Univ Bronx NY 10458

NATHAN, GEOFFREY STEVEN, b Hove, England, Oct 18, 49. LINGUISTICS. *Educ:* Univ Toronto, BA, 71; Univ Hawaii, MA, 72, PhD(ling), 78. *Prof Exp:* Vis asst prof, Univ Mont, 77-78 & Univ Hawaii, 78-80; vis asst prof, 80-82, ASST PROF LING, SOUTHERN ILL UNIV, 82- *Mem:* Ling Soc Am; Teachers English Speakers Other Lang; Acoustic Soc Am. *Res:* English as a second language; phonology; syntax. *Publ:* Auth, Nauruan in the Austronesian language family, Oceanic Ling, Vol XII, No 1-2; Towards a literate level of language, Elements: Chicago Ling Soc Parasession, 78; What's these facts about?, Ling Inquiry, Vol 12, No 1; Nauruan: A small language with an uncertain future, Lang Policy & Planning (in press); coauth, Negative polarity and romance syntax, Ling Symp Romance Lang, Vol XII, Benjamin (in press). *Mailing Add:* Dept of Ling Southern Ill Univ Carbondale IL 62901

NATHAN, LEONARD E, Rhetoric. See Vol II

NATIONS, ELISABETH S, b Berlin, Ger, May 4, 21; US citizen; m 54; c 1. GERMAN. *Educ:* Univ Calif, Berkeley, BA, 59, MA, 61; Univ Iowa, PhD(Ger), 73. *Prof Exp:* Instr Ger & French, 61-62, asst prof, 63-73, ASSOC PROF GER, AUGUSTANA COL, ILL, 73- *Mem:* Am Asn Teachers Ger; MLA AAUP. *Res:* Fontane; 19th century. *Mailing Add:* Dept of Lang Augustana Col Rock Island IL 61201

NAUDEAU, OLIVIER LEONCE, b Nantes, France, May 8, 33; m 64; c 2. ROMANCE PHILOLOGY, MEDIEVAL & RENAISSANCE LITERATURE. *Educ:* Univ Mass, AB, 59; Univ Cincinnati, PhD(French), 70. *Prof Exp:* From instr to asst prof French, Univ Cincinnati, 63-71; asst prof, Emory Univ, 71-74; assoc prof, 74-80, PROF FRENCH, TEX A&M UNIV, 80- *Mem:* Soc Fr Prof Am; MLA; Mediaeval Acad Am; Renaissance Soc Am. *Res:* Dialectology; Montaigne. *Publ:* Auth, Autour de L'Anagramme Nature Quite, Etudes Rabelaisiennes, 71; La Pensee de Montaigne et la Composition des Essais, In: Travaux d'Humanisme et Renaissance, Droz, Geneva, 72; La Portee Philosophique du Vocabulaire de Montaigne, Bibliot d'Humanisme & Renaissance, 73; L'adverbe joi en afr Vient-il de Gaudium ou de Jam Hodie?, Zeitschrift fur Romanische Philol, 75; Remarques sur Ostra Ultra Dans Thebes et les Traitements Dans L'ouest du Groupe-ULT, Romance Philol, 75; L'expression des Modes Philosophiques Chez Montaigue: Le mot Forme, J Medieval & Renaissance Studies, 76; Za, sa, cha, ca, articles occitans et le latin IPSA(M), Romance Philol, 79; La Passion de Sainte Catherine d'Alexandrie per Aumeric, In: Beihefte zur Zeitschrift fùr romanische Philologie, Niemeyer, Tübingen, 82. *Mailing Add:* 2401 Briar Oaks Dr Bryan TX 77801

NAUDIN, MARIE, b Auxerre, France, June 18, 26; div; c 1. ROMANCE LANGUAGES. *Educ:* Sorbonne, BA, 46; Univ Pittsburgh, MA, 62, PhD, 66. *Prof Exp:* From instr to asst prof French, Univ Mich, 64-67; asst prof, 67-71, ASSOC PROF FRENCH, UNIV CONN, 71- *Mem:* Am Asn Teachers Fr; MLA; Soc Fr Prof Am. *Res:* Relation between music and French poetry; 19th century French literature. *Publ:* Auth, La chanson francaise contemporaine, Fr Rev, 5/67; Evolution Parallele de la Poesie et de la Musique en France, Nizet, Paris, 68. *Mailing Add:* Dept of Romance & Class Lang Univ of Conn Storrs CT 06268

NAUGHTON, HELEN THOMAS, b New York, NY, Feb 11, 12; m 38; c 4. FRENCH LANGUAGE & LITERATURE. *Educ:* Stanford Univ, BA, 32, MA, 34, PhD, 61. *Prof Exp:* Asst, Stanford Univ, 34-37; instr French & Span, 56-59, from asst prof to assoc prof, 59-67, prof French & chmn dept foreign lang, 67-77, EMER PROF FRENCH, COL NOTRE DAME, CALIF, 77- *Concurrent Pos:* Speaker-colloquia, Cerisy-la-Salle, France, 72, 74. *Mem:* MLA; Am Asn Teachers Fr (vpres, 73-75, exec coun, 75-77). *Res:* French literature, 1900-1940; French criticism, 1900-1940; modern French theater. *Publ:* Auth, Temperament and Creed--a Note on Jacques Riviereee, Fr Rev, 4/63; The Realism of Jacques Rivier, Mod Lang Quart, 64; A Comtemporary Views Proust, L'Esprit Createur, spring 65; Jacques Rivier: The Development of a Man and a Creed, Mouton, 66; The Critics Cure: Riviere's Aimee, Renascence, fall 66; coauth, Essai D'une Bibliographie de Jacques Riviere, Cahiers 20e Siecle 3, 75. *Mailing Add:* Dept of Foreign Lang Col of Notre Dame Belmont CA 94002

NAUMANN, MARINA TURKEVICH, b Princeton, NJ, July 15, 38; m 61; c 2. RUSSIAN LITERATURE AND LANGUAGE, COMPARATIVE LITERATURE. *Educ:* Wellesley Col, BA, 60; Univ Pa, MA, 62, PhD(Slavic lang & lit), 73. *Prof Exp:* ASST PROF RUSS LIT & LANG, DOUGLASS COL, RUTGERS UNIV, 74- *Concurrent Pos:* Res Coun fel, Rutgers Univ, 76, fac acad study prog, 78. *Mem:* Am Asn Teachers Slavic & E Europ Lang; Am Asn Advan Slavic Studies; MLA; NAm Dostoevsky Soc; Vladimir Nabokov Soc. *Res:* Russian literature of 19th century; Russian Emigre literature; comparative literature. *Publ:* Auth, Raskol'nikov's shadow: Porfirij Petrovic, Slavic & E Europ J, 72; Nabokov as viewed by fellow Emigres, winter 74 & The colored handkerchief and magic rope of Nabokov, fall 77, Russ Lang J; Grin's Grinlandia and Nabokov's Zoorlandia, Ger-Slavica, fall 77; Blue Evenings in Berlin: Nabokov's Short Stories of the 1920's, NY Univ, 78; Tolstoyan reflections in Hemingway: War and Peace and For Whom the Bell Tolls, In: American Contributions to the 8th International Congress of Slavists, Slavica Publ, 78. *Mailing Add:* Dept of Foreign Lang Douglass Col New Brunswick NJ 08903

NAUSS, JANINE ROSSARD, b Toulouse, France. FRENCH, ENGLISH. *Educ:* Sorbonne, Lic en Lett, 46, dipl, 51, CAPES, 55; Bowling Green State Univ, MA, 49; Univ Iowa, PhD(French stylistics), 53. *Prof Exp:* From instr to asst prof French, Woman's Col NC, 56-62; asst prof, Duquesne Univ, 62-64; asst prof, 64-68, ASSOC PROF FRENCH, ST JOHN'S UNIV, NY, 68- *Concurrent Pos:* MLA; Am Asn Teachers Fr. *Res:* Eighteenth and 19th century French literature. *Publ:* Auth, La Mort Mysterieuse de Virginie, 69 & La Pudeur de Joubert--Romantique ou Classique?, 71, Fr Rev; Le Desir de Mort Romantique dans Caliste, PMLA, 72; Le Peuplier, Arbre Romantique, Romance Notes, 72; Pudeur et Amour Romantique, 19th Century Fr Studies, 74; Une Clef du Romantisme: La Pudeur, 74 & Pudeur et Romantisme (in press), Nizet, Paris. *Mailing Add:* Dept of French St John's Univ Jamaica NY 11439

NAVARRO, JOAQUINA, b Madrid, Spain, Sept 1, 16; US citizen. FOREIGN LANGUAGES & LITERATURE. *Educ:* Inst Escuela, Madrid, BA, 34; Columbia Univ, MA, 43, PhD, 54. *Prof Exp:* From instr to assoc prof, 43-66, prof, 66-81, EMER PROF SPAN, SMITH COL, 81- *Concurrent Pos:* Soc Sci Res Coun-Am Coun Learned Soc grant, 60-61. *Mem:* MLA; Am Asn Teachers Span & Port. *Res:* Spanish literature of the 19th century; Latin American literature, especially the novel; phonetics. *Publ:* Auth, La Novela Realista Mexicana, Compania Gen Ed, Mex, 55; Jorge Luis Borges: Taumaturgo de la Metafora, 65 & La Obra Hispanista de Federico de Onis, 68, Rev Hisp Mod; Ritmo y Sentido en Cancion de Otono en Primavera, Thesaurus, 69. *Mailing Add:* 24 Hastings Heights Florence MA 01060

NAVASCUES, MICHAEL, b Madrid, Spain, Aug 19, 36; US citizen; m 66; c 1. HISPANIC STUDIES. *Educ:* Franklin & Marshall Col, BA, 59; Univ Montpellier, cert French, 60; Univ Madrid, Lic en Filos y Let, 61; Rutgers Univ, New Brunswick, MA, 67, PhD(Span), 71. *Prof Exp:* Instr English, Acad Estud Super, 60-62; instr Span, Am Sch Madrid, 62; instr French & Span, Hollins Col, 62-63; teaching asst Span, Rutgers Univ, 63-65; asst prof, Kutztown State Col, 66-67; lectr Span & French, Upsala Col, 68; from instr to asst prof Span, 68-75, ASSOC PROF HISP STUDIES, UNIV RI, 75- *Mem:* Am Asn Teachers Span & Port. *Res:* Modern theater; lyric poetry; modern Hispanic literature. *Publ:* Auth, El Teatro de Jacinto Grau, Ed Playor, 75; Fantasy and the view of destiny in the theater of Jacinto Grau, Rev Estudios Hisp, 5/77; ed, Lecturas Modernas de Hispanoamerica, Prentice-Hall, 80. *Mailing Add:* Dept of Lang Univ of RI Kingston RI 02881

NAVAS-RUIZ, RICARDO, b Briones, Spain, Nov 6, 32; m 60; c 1. ROMANCE LANGUAGES. *Educ:* Univ Salamanca, MA, 57, PhD(lang), 60. *Prof Exp:* Asst Romance lang, Univ Salamanca, 57-60; prof Span, Univ Sao Paulo, 60-64; asst prof Romance lang, Northwestern Univ, 64-65, assoc prof, 65-67; prof Span, Univ Geneva, 67-68; prof, Univ Calif, Davis, 68-70; PROF SPAN, UNIV MASS, BOSTON, 70- *Concurrent Pos:* Lit adv, Almar Publ, 77. *Mem:* Am Asn Teachers Span & Port; Iberoam Lit Inst. *Res:* Spanish and Spanish American literature; Spanish languages. *Publ:* Auth, El Romanticismo Espanol, Anaya, 70, 2nd ed, 72, 3rd ed, 82; coauth, Literatura de la America Hispanica, Dodd, Vols 1, 2 & 3, 71-75; Hartzenbusch Fabulas, 73 & Rivas' Don Alvaro, 75, Espaso-Calpe; Larra's Articulos Politicos, Almar, 77; Asturias El Senor Presidente, Klienksieck, 78; Imagenes liberales, 79 & Oscura region poemas, 80, Almar. *Mailing Add:* Dept of Span Univ of Mass Boston MA 02125

NAYLOR, ERIC WOODFIN, b Union City, Tenn, Dec 6, 36. ROMANCE LANGUAGES. *Educ:* Univ of the South, BA, 58; Univ Wis, MA, 59, PhD(Span), 63. *Prof Exp:* From instr to assoc prof, 62-76, PROF SPAN, UNIV OF THE SOUTH, 76- *Concurrent Pos:* Fulbright res grant, 64-65; lectr, Escuela de Investigacion Lingüistica, Madrid, 70. *Mem:* Mediaeval Acad Am; Am Asn Teachers Span & Port; MLA; SAm Mod Lang Asn. *Res:* Medieval Spanish literature; Golden Age literature. *Publ:* Coauth, Libro de Buen Amor, Consejo Super Invest Cientificas, 65; auth, La encomienda del Capitan Conreras, Rev Span Philol, 70; coauth, Glosario del Libro de Buen Amor, Soc Espanola de Reimpresiones y Edicones, SA, Barcelona, 73; Libro de buen amor: Edicion critica y artistica, Ed Aguilar, 76; Libro de Buen Amor, Facsimil, Introduccion y Transcripcion del Codice de Toledo (2 vols), Espasa Calpe, Madrid, 77. *Mailing Add:* Dept of Span Univ of the South Sewanee TN 37375

NAYLOR, KENNETH EDWIN, b Philadelphia, Pa, Feb 27, 37. SLAVIC LANGUAGES, LINGUISTICS. *Educ:* Cornell Univ, AB, 58; Ind Univ, AM, 60; Univ Chicago, PhD(Slavic ling), 66. *Prof Exp:* Res asst lang of world, Ind Univ, 58-59; res asst Slavic ling, Univ Chicago, 61-62; asst prof ling, Univ Pittsburgh, 64-66; from asst prof to assoc prof, 66-75, PROF SLAVIC LING, OHIO STATE UNIV, 75- *Concurrent Pos:* Univ develop fund fac fels, Ohio State Univ, 67 & 71; ed, Am Bibliog Slavic & E Europ Studies, 68-73; Fulbright-Hays fac res grant, 70-71; Am Philos Soc grant, 69 & 73; res grants, Joint Comt Eastern Europe, Am Coun Learned Socs, 74-75; 77; ed, Balkanistica, 74-; ed, Folia Slavica, 76-; consult, Nat Ednowment for Humanities, 77- *Mem:* Am Asn Advan Slavic Studies; Am Asn Southeast Europ Studies (vpres, 72, pres, 73); Am Asn Teachers Slavic & E Europ Lang; MLA; Ling Soc Am. *Res:* Russian and South Slavic linguistics, especially dialectology and accentology; comparative Slavic morphology and morphophonemics; Yugoslav history. *Publ:* Auth, Bulgarian dialects in the South Slavic framework, Zbornik za filologiju i lingvistiku, 73; ed, The American Bibliography of Slavic and East European Studies for 1968 and 1969, Am Asn Advan Slavic Studies, 74; Odziv na Vukove reforme srpskohrvatskog jezika kod Hrvata u drugoj polovini XIX veka, Naucni sastanak Slavista u Vukove dana: Referati i saopstenja, Medjunarodni slavisticki centar, 74; The search for a Croatian literary language in the 19th century: Some observations, In: Xenia Slavica, Mouton, 75; Morphophonemics of the Serbocroatian conjugation, Int J Slavic Ling & Poetics, 75; A note on the quanitification form in Russian, Folia Slavica, 77; Some observations on the grammatical categories of Slavic declensions, In: American Contributions to the 8th Int Congr Slavicists, Vol I, Ling & Poetics, Slavica Publ, 78; The literary language of the Serbs and Croats, In: Formation of Slavic Literary and National Languages, Yale Univ, 78. *Mailing Add:* Dept of Slavic Lang & Lit Ohio State Univ Columbus OH 43210

NAZZARO, ANTHONY M, b Dover, NJ, June 8, 27; m 55; c 4. FRENCH. *Educ:* Princeton Univ, BA, 49; Yale Univ, MA, 51, PhD, 58. *Prof Exp:* Instr, Oberlin Col, 55-56; instr, Russell Sage Col, 57-62; from asst prof to assoc prof, 62-72, PROF FRENCH, SKIDMORE COL, 72- *Mem:* Am Asn Teachers Fr. *Res:* Nineteenth and twentieth century French literature. *Publ:* Co-auth, Trois Nouvelles de George Simenon, Appleton, 66; Realite et Fantaisie Neuf Nouvelles Modernes, Xerox Col Publ, 71; Choix de Simenon, Appleton, 72. *Mailing Add:* Dept of Mod Lang Skidmore Col Saratoga Springs NY 12866

NEAT, (SISTER) CHARLES MARIE, b Albany, NY, July 12, 13. GERMAN. *Educ:* Col St Rose, AB, 35; Cath Univ Am, AM, 46, PhD, 54. *Prof Exp:* Assoc prof Ger & Ital, 39-56, chmn dept foreign lang, 69-74, PROF GER, 56-, COL ARCHIVIST, 75- *Concurrent Pos:* Fulbright grant, Munich, Ger, 56. *Mem:* Am Asn Teachers Ger; Soc Am Archivists. *Publ:* Auth, Guide to Catholic German authors of the seventeenth century; German literature and literary criticism as reflected in the German Catholic magazine, Literarischer Handweiser; The role of the college chairmen: What it is and what it might be, NY State Asn Foreign Lang Teachers Asn Bull, 1/72. *Mailing Add:* Humanities Div Col of St Rose Albany NY 12203

NEATROUR, ELIZABETH BAYLOR, b Buffalo, NY, June 21, 34; m 56; c 1. RUSSIAN LANGUAGE & LITERATURE. *Educ:* Mary Washington Col, BA, 54; Univ Paris, cert French studies, 55; Madison Col, Va, MAEduc, 60; Ind Univ, Bloomington, MA, 66, PhD(Russ lang & lit), 73. *Prof Exp:* Teacher

English & French, Robert E Lee High Sch, Staunton, Va, 58-61; asst prof French & Russ, 61-64, 68-72, assoc prof Russ, 73-77, PROF RUSS & FRENCH, JAMES MADISON UNIV, 77-, HEAD DEPT FOREIGN LANG & LIT, 74- *Mem:* Am Asn Advan Slavic Studies; Am Asn Teachers Slavic & E Europ Lang. *Res:* Russian literature of the 19th and 20th centuries. *Publ:* Auth, The role of Platon Karataev in War and Peace, 3/70 & The role of the children in The Brothers Karamazov, 3/74, Madison Col Studies & Res. *Mailing Add:* Dept of Foreign Lang & Lit James Madison Univ Harrisonburg VA 22801

NEBEL, HENRY MARTIN, JR, b New York, NY, Sept 29, 21; m 68; c 4. RUSSIAN LITERATURE & AESTHETICS. *Educ:* Columbia Col, BA, 43; Columbia Univ, MA, 50, PhD(Russian lit), 61. *Prof Exp:* Asst prof Russian, US Merchant Marine Acad, 55-56; asst prof Russian lit, Duke Univ, 56-57; PROF RUSSIAN LIT, NORTHWESTERN UNIV, 57- *Concurrent Pos:* Dir, Nat Defense Educ Act Inst, 62-64; book rev ed, Mod Lang J, 63-70; ed, Publ of Eighteenth Century Russian LIt, Northwestern Univ, 68-71. *Mem:* AAUP; Soc for Eighteenth-Century Lit. *Res:* Eighteenth century Russian literature; Russian Preromanticism and Romanticism. *Publ:* Ed, St Sophia in Kiev, Suoboda Press, 55; coauth, Russian: An Elementary Course, Norton and Co, 66; auth, N M Karamzin: A Russian Sentimentalist, Mouton & Co, 66; ed, Selected Tragedies of A P Sumarokov, Northwestern Univ Press, 70; auth, Selected Aesthetic Works of Sumarokov and Karamzin, Univ Press of Am, 81. *Mailing Add:* Slavic Dept Northwestern Univ Evanston IL 60201

NEBEL, SYLVIA SUE, b Grand Rapids, Mich, Mar 20, 40; m 67; c 2. GERMAN LITERATURE. *Educ:* Albion Col, BA, 61; Univ Colo, Boulder, MA, 63; Northwestern Univ, Evanston, PhD(Ger), 69. *Prof Exp:* From instr to asst prof, 66-76, ASSOC PROF MOD LANG, LOYOLA UNIV, CHICAGO, 76-, HUMANITIES DEAN, COL ARTS & SCI, 77- *Mem:* Am Asn Teachers Ger; Am Soc 18th Century Studies. *Res:* Eighteenth century German literature; Freud. *Publ:* Auth, Hamann's view of human reason, Studies in 18th Century Cult, 75. *Mailing Add:* Dept of Mod Lang Loyola Univ 6525 N Sheridan Chicago IL 60626

NEEDLER, HOWARD, b Manchester, England, July 22, 37; US citizen; m 63; c 2. ITALIAN LITERATURE. *Educ:* Yale Univ, BS, 58; Oxford Univ, BA, 60, MA, 65; Columbia Univ, PhD, 65. *Prof Exp:* Instr Ital, Barnard Col, Columbia Univ, 63-64; lectr, Yale Univ, 64-65; asst prod, Univ Colo, 67-69; asst prof, 69-72, ASSOC PROF LETT, WESLEYAN UNIV, 72- *Mem:* Dante Soc Am. *Res:* Medieval literature, especially Dante; modern poetry; Jewish history, especially in medieval Italy. *Mailing Add:* Col of Lett Wesleyan Univ Middletown CT 06457

NEEL, GEORGE WASHINGTON, IV, b Mansfield, Pa, May 4, 30; m 53. GERMAN & ROMANCE LANGUAGES. *Educ:* Glassboro State Col, BS, 51; Univ Heidelberg, dipl Ger lang & lit, 56; Univ Aix Marseille, dipl French lang & lit, 59; Rutgers Univ, New Brunswick, AM, 73. *Prof Exp:* Teacher, High Sch, Del, 59-63; ASSOC PROF GER & FRENCH, BLOOMSBURG STATE COL, 64- *Mem:* Am Asn Teachers Ger; Am Asn Teachers Fr; MLA. *Res:* German and French literature; modern German literature. *Mailing Add:* Dept of Foreign Lang Bloomsburg State Col Bloomsburg PA 17815

NEGLIA, ERMINIO, SPANISH AMERICAN LITERATURE, ITALIAN & SPANISH THEATRE. *Educ:* Roosevelt Univ, BA, 63; Univ Ill, MA, 65; Wash Univ, PhD(Span), 69. *Prof Exp:* Instr Span, Wash Univ, 65-69; asst prof, 69-74, assoc prof, 74-79, PROF SPAN, UNIV TORONTO, 79- *Mem:* Am Asn Teachers Span & Port, Assoc Intern de Hisp; Inst Int de Lit Iberoam. *Res:* Spanish-American literature and theatre; Spanish theatre; Italian theatre and Luigi Pirandello. *Publ:* Auth, Pirandello y la Dramatica Rioplatense, Valmartina, 70; Aspectos del Teatro Moderno Hispanoamericano, Editorial Stella, 75; coauth, Repertorio Selecto del Teatro Contemporaneo Hispanoamericano, Ariz State Univ, 78. *Mailing Add:* 3622 Credit Woodlands Mississauga ON L5C 2K9 Can

NEGUS, KENNETH GEORGE, b Council Bluffs, Iowa, Dec 23, 27; m; c 3. GERMAN. *Educ:* Princeton Univ, BA, 52, MA, 54, PhD, 57. *Prof Exp:* Asst instr Ger, Princeton Univ, 53-54; instr, Northwestern Univ, 55-57; instr, Harvard Univ, 57-59; asst prof, Princeton Univ, 59-61; from asst prof to assoc prof, 61-66, PROF GER, RUTGERS UNIV, 66- *Mem:* MLA; Am Asn Teachers Ger; ETA Hoffmann Ger; Am Soc Ger Lit of 16th & 17th Cent. *Res:* Symbolism of the occult; German Romanticism; German Baroque literature. *Publ:* Auth, ETA Hoffmann's Other World, Univ Pa, 65; Paul Heyse's Novellentheorie: A Revaluation, Ger Rev, 65; Grimmelshausen, World Authors Series, Twayne, 74. *Mailing Add:* 175 Harrison St Princeton NJ 08540

NEHRING, WOLFGANG, b Oppeln, Ger, Nov 15, 38; m 64. GERMAN LITERATURE. *Educ:* Univ Bonn, PhD, 65. *Prof Exp:* Sci asst Ger Lit, Univ Bonn, 65-66; asst prof, Boston Col, 66-67; from asst prof to assoc prof, 67-78, PROF GER LIT, UNIV CALIF, LOS ANGELES, 78- *Concurrent Pos:* Co-ed, Kritische Hofmannsthal-Ausgabe, Arbeitsstelle Basel, 71-73; adv bd, Hugo von Hofmannsthal Ges, 76- *Mem:* Am Asn Teachers Ger; Int Arthur Schnitzler Res Asn; Hugo von Hofmannsthal Ges (secy, 71-74); Int Asn Ger Studies; Schiller Ges. *Res:* German Romanticism; Jahrhundertwende/Moderne; Austrian literature, especially Hofmannsthal and Schnitzler. *Publ:* Ed, E T A Hoffmann, Prinzessin Brambilla, 71 & Wackenroder/Tieck, Phantasien über die Kunst, 73, Reclam, Stuttgart; auth, Hofmannsthal und der Wiener Impressionismus, 75 & E T A Hoffmanns Erzählwerk, Ein Modell und seine Variationen, 76, Z Deut Philol; Eichendorff und der Leser, Aurora, 77; Die Bühne als Tribunal Der zweite Weltkrieg im dokumentarischen Theater, In: Gegenwartslit/Drittes Reich, Reclam, Stuttgart, 77; Der Beginn der Moderne, In: Handbuch der deutschen Erzählung, Bagel, Düusseldorf, 81; E T A Hoffmann: Die Elixiere des Teufels, In: Romane und Erzählungen der deutschen Romantik, Reclam, Stuttgart, 81. *Mailing Add:* Dept of Ger Lang Univ Calif Los Angeles CA 90024

NELSON, CHARLES L, b Greenville, NC, Jan 29, 22; m 47; c 3. SPANISH. *Educ:* Univ NC, AB, 48, MA, 64, PhD(Romance lang), 66. *Prof Exp:* Instr Span, Univ NC, 63-65; asst prof, Univ Colo, 65-67; PROF SPAN & CHMN DEPT FOREIGN LANG, EASTERN KY UNIV, 67- *Mem:* Am Asn Teachers Span & Port; Mediaeval Acad Am; MLA; SAtlantic Mod Lang Asn. *Res:* Medieval Spanish literature; Spanish philology. *Publ:* Auth, The Book of the Knight Zifar, Ky Univ (in press). *Mailing Add:* Dept of Foreign Lang Eastern Ky Univ Richmond KY 40475

NELSON, DANA A, b Erie, Pa, Aug 20, 26; m 60; c 2. SPANISH LANGUAGE & LITERATURE. *Educ:* Allegheny Col, AB, 49; Univ Iowa, MA, 51; Am Inst Foreign Trade, BFT, 52; Stanford Univ, PhD(Span), 65. *Prof Exp:* Asst prof Span, Univ Wis, 64-68; assoc prof, 68-74, PROF SPAN, UNIV ARIZ, 74- *Concurrent Pos:* Am Coun of Learned Socs fel, 74-75; publ grant, Ludwig Vogelstein Found, 77. *Res:* Medieval language and literature, especially Peninsular Alexander lore and traditions of chivalry. *Publ:* Coauth, Lengua Hispanica Modrna, Holt, 67; auth, Syncopation in El libro de Alexandre, Publ Mod Lang Asn Am, 10/72; The domain of Old Spanish -er and -ir verbs: A clue to the provenience of the Alexandre, Romance Philol, 11/72; A Reexamination of synonymy in Berceo and the Alex, Hisp Rev, 6/75; In Quest of the select lexical base of Berceo, Ky Romance Quart, 3/75; Generic vs individual style, Romance Philol, 11/75; Clave de la creatividad de Berceo, Bol Real Acad Espanola, 1/76; ed, Gonzalo de Berceo, El Libro de Aliandre, Gredos, Madrid, 79. *Mailing Add:* Dept of Span & Port Univ of Ariz Tucson AZ 85721

NELSON, DEBORAH HUBBARD, b Springfield, Ohio, July 19, 40; m 63; c 2. MEDIEVAL FRENCH & PROVENCAL LANGUAGE & LITERATURE. *Educ:* Wittenberg Univ, BS, 60; Univ Grenoble, Certificat d'Etudes Francaises, 61; Ohio State Univ, MA, 64, PhD(Romance lang), 70. *Prof Exp:* Asst Prof, Western Col, 70-74; asst prof, 74-81, ASSOC PROF FRENCH, RICH UNIV, 81- *Concurrent Pos:* Res grant, Rice Univ, 75. *Mem:* MLA; S Cent Mod Lang Asn; Int Courtly Lit Soc; Soc Rencesvals. *Res:* Twelfth and thirteenth century French and Provencal poetry; teaching of modern French language. *Publ:* Auth, Animal imagery in Marcabru's poetry, Studies in Medieval Culture XI, 77; Bird imagery in Marcabru's poetry, Round Table, 10/77; Yonec: A religious and chivalric fantasy, Univ S Fla Lang Quart, spring 78; The implications of love and sacrifice in Fresne and Eliduc, S Cent Bull, winter 78; Eliduc's saluation, Fr Rev, 10/81; The public & private images of chiges, Fenice Reading Medieval Studies, Vol VII, 81. *Mailing Add:* Dept Fr & Ital Rice Univ Houston TX

NELSON, DONALD FREDERICK, b Minneapolis, Minn, July 17, 29; m 56; c 1. GERMAN LITERATURE & LINGUISTICS. *Educ:* Univ Minn, BA, 53, MA, 63, PhD(German), 66. *Prof Exp:* Teaching asst Ger, Univ Minn, 60-62, instr, 62-66; ASST PROF GER, OHIO STATE UNIV, 66- *Res:* The 20th century novel; style in prose fiction; transformational grammar and language theory. *Publ:* Auth, Portrait of the Artist as Hermes . . ., Univ NC, 71. *Mailing Add:* 94 E Como Ave Columbus OH 43202

NELSON, ESTHER WHITT, b San Antonio, Tex, Sept 28, 36. SPANISH LANGUAGE, HISPANIC LITERATURES. *Educ:* Univ NMex, BA, 66, MA, 68; Univ Tex, PhD(Span), 74. *Prof Exp:* Asst prof romance lang, Gallaudet Col, 74-78; ASST PROF SPAN, UNIV SOUTHERN CALIF, 78- *Mem:* MLA; Am Asn Teachers Span & Port; Cued Speech Asn; Philol Asn Pac Coast. *Res:* Literary criticism and theory; 20th century Hispanic narrative; 20th century Hispanic poetry. *Publ:* Auth, The space of longing: La ultima niebla, Am Hisp, Vol 3, 77; Basic Conversational Spanish (videotape), Gallaudet Col, 76; Relaciones entre transmisores y receptors en la familia de Pascual Duarte, In: Estructura y Expacio en la Novela y en la Poesia, Hispanic Press, 80; Is there any justification for teaching literature?, Vientos del Sur, Vol 2, 80; Narrative perspective in Juan Benet's Volveras a Region, The Am Hispanist, Vol 4, 79; The self-creating narrator of Juan Goytisolo's Juan sin Tierra, Symposium 35, 81. *Mailing Add:* Dept of Span & Port Univ Southern Calif Los Angeles CA 90007

NELSON, JAN ALAN, b Pensacola, Fla, Mar 25, 35; m 61; c 2. ROMANCE LANGUAGES. *Educ:* Univ of the South, BA, 60; Univ NC, Chapel Hill, MA, 62, PhD(Romance lang), 64. *Prof Exp:* Asst prof French, Univ Iowa, 64-67; assoc prof, 67-72, chmn dept romance lang & classics, 76-80, PROF FRENCH, UNIV ALA, 73- *Mem:* SAtlantic Mod Lang Asn; Soc Rencesvals (ed, Bibliogr Note, 67-78, co-ed, Olifant, 73-78). *Res:* Medieval French; Provencal; Spanish. *Publ:* Co-ed, Yvain ou le Chevalier au Lion, Appleton, 68; ed, The Old French Crusade Cycle, Vol I, La Naissance du Chevalier au Cygne, Part II, Beatrix, Univ Ala, 78. *Mailing Add:* PO Box 1963 University AL 35486

NELSON, JOHN CHARLES, b Rome, Italy, Oct 9, 25; US citizen; m 48; c 1. ITALIAN. *Educ:* Columbia Univ, BA, 44, MA, 50, PhD(Ital), 54. *Prof Exp:* Instr Ital, Columbia Univ, 53 & Ital & English, Univ Rochester, 53-56; lectr Ital, Columbia Univ, 56-57; instr Ital lang & lit, Harvard Univ, 57-58, asst prof, 58-62; assoc prof Ital lit, 62-66, chmn dept, 66-70, PROF ITAL, COLUMBIA UNIV, 66- *Concurrent Pos:* Guggenheim fel, 60-61. *Mem:* Renaissance Soc Am; MLA; Am Asn Teachers Ital; Dante Soc Am. *Res:* Renaissance literature and philosophy; Italian literature. *Publ:* Co-ed, A Renaissance Treasury, Doubleday, 53; auth, Renaissance Theory of Love, Columbia Univ, 58; ed, Francesco Patrizi, L'amorosa filosofia, Sansoni, Florence, 63. *Mailing Add:* 502 Casa Italiana Columbia Univ New York NY 10027

NELSON, LOWRY, JR, b Provo, Utah, May 1, 26. COMPARATIVE LITERATURE. *Educ:* Harvard Univ, AB, 47; Yale Univ, PhD(comp lit), 51. *Prof Exp:* Instr Romance lang, lit & humanities, Harvard Univ, 54-56; from asst prof to assoc prof English, Univ Calif, Los Angeles, 56-64; assoc prof, 64-71, PROF COMP LIT, YALE UNIV, 71- *Concurrent Pos:* Jr fel, Soc Fels, Harvard Univ, 51-54; co-ed, Ital Quart, 56-; Guggenheim fel, 61; mem nat screening comt, Foreign Area Fel Prog, 64-66; panelist, Nat Endowment for Humanities, 78-82. *Mem:* MLA; Am Comp Lit Asn; Dante Soc Am;

Medieval Acad Am; Renaissance Soc Am. *Res:* Medieval Latin and vernacular literature; Italian 19th and 20th century literature; literary criticism and aesthetics. *Publ:* Auth, Baroque Lyric Poetry, Yale Univ, 61, 2nd ed, Octagon Books, 79; Night thoughts on the Gothic novel, Yale Rev, 63; The fictive reader and literary self-reflexiveness, In: The Disciplines of Criticism, Yale Univ, 68; ed & Contribr, Cervantes: A Collection of Critical Essays, Prentice, 69; Spanish, In: Versification, MLA & NY Univ, 72; Leopardi first and last, Ital Lit, Yale Univ, 76; Erich Auerbach, Yale Rev, 80. *Mailing Add:* Dept of Comp Lit Yale Univ New Haven CT 06520

NELSON, RICHARD JOHN ANDREW, b Chicago, Ill, Mar 25, 33. ROMANCE LINGUISTICS & LITERATURES. *Educ:* Northwestern Univ, Evanston, BA, 55, MA, 60, PhD(Span & Ital), 75. *Prof Exp:* Chmn lang dept, King Sch, Stamford, Conn, 69-70 & Jacksonville Espiscopal High Sch, Fla, 70-73; instr Span & French, Lake Erie Col, 73-74; asst prof Span, Ohio Dominican Col, 74-75; training instr English, Defense Lang Inst, 75-77; asst prof Span & French, Lycoming Col, 78-79; TEACHER ITAL & FRENCH, POMPANO BEACH HIGH SCH, FLA, 81- *Concurrent Pos:* Compiler & ed bilingual dict, Follett Publ Co, 62-69; researcher, Medieval & Renaissance Ctr, Ohio State Univ, 77-78. *Mem:* MLA; Ling Asn Great Brit; Dict Soc NAm; Am Asn Teachers Span & Port; Am ASn Teachers Fr. *Res:* Influences of Italian vocabulary on the creation of Spanish forms, as well as semantic loans, and the contrary influence of Spanish on Italian, especially in the Middle Ages and the Renaissance; the Questione della Lingua in Spain in the Renaissance and the Siglos de Oro; bilingual dictionaries: ordering of entries and accurate concept transfer across language boundaries. *Publ:* Coauth, The World-Wide Spanish Dictionary, New Cent Publ, 66; transl, The Ultimate Tennis Book, Follett Publ Co, 75; auth, Problems in bilingual lexicography: Romance and English, Hispania, 75; English At Your Fingertips: Ingles al dedillo, New Cent Publ, Inc, 78; Translation and translating dictionaries, Incorp Ling, J Inst Ling, 78; The problem of meaning across the boundary between Spanish and English: An expanding role for the bilingual dictionary, Dict, 80-81; Tense substitution as an aid to fluency in oral and written Spanish mastery, Incorp Ling, 81; Linguistica quinientista: las obras de Pedro Bembo, Sperone Speroni y Juan de Valdes, Thesaurus, Bol del Inst Caro y Cuervo, Bogota, Colombia, 81. *Mailing Add:* 3216 NE 15th St Pompano Beach FL 33062

NELSON, ROBERT JAMES, b Woodside, NY, Mar 29, 25; m 47; c 2. FRENCH. *Educ:* Columbia Univ, BA, 49, MA, 50, PhD, 55. *Prof Exp:* Instr French, Columbia Col, 53-55; instr, Yale Univ, 55-58; asst prof, Univ Mich, 58-59; from assoc prof to prof Romance lang, Univ Pa, 59-69; PROF FRENCH & COMP LIT, UNIV ILL, URBANA, 69, HEAD DEPT, 73- *Concurrent Pos:* Morse fel, Yale Univ, 57-58; grant-in-aid fels, Am Coun Learned Soc, 60 & 65; Am Philos Soc, 63; dir Northeast Conf Teaching Foreign Lang, 64-68; Guggenheim fel, 66-67; assoc, Ctr for Adv Study, Univ Ill, 76. *Honors & Awards:* Chevalier, Palmes Academiques, 72. *Mem:* MLA; Am Asn Teachers Fr. *Res:* Pascal; world theater; French civilization. *Publ:* Auth, Play Within a Play: The Dramatist's Conception of His Art--Shakespeare to Anouilh, Yale Univ, 58; Corneille: His Heroes and Their Worlds, Univ Pa, 63; Immanence and Transcendence: The Theater of Jean Rotrou (1609-1650), Ohio Univ, 69; Bipolarity of French classicism, Essays Fr Lit, 71; Classicism: The Crises of the Baroque, Esprit Createur, 71; The fiction of John Williams, Denver Quart, 73. *Mailing Add:* Dept of French Univ of Ill Urbana IL 61822

NELSON, ROY JAY, b Pittsburgh, Pa, July 27, 29; m 54; c 2. FRENCH LITERATURE. *Educ:* Univ Pittsburgh, AB, 51; Middlebury Col, MA, 52; Univ Ill, PhD, 58. *Prof Exp:* From instr to assoc prof, 57-72, actg chmn, Dept Romance lang, 77, PROF FRENCH, UNIV MICH, ANN ARBOR, 72- *Concurrent Pos:* Fulbright scholar, 51-52; non-resident fel, Univ Ill, 55-56; correspondent, French VII Bibliogr, 61-67; Rackham Found res grant, 67-68; dir, Mich-Wis Jr Year in France, 71-72. *Mem:* MLA; Am Asn Teachers Fr; Amitie Charles Peguy. *Res:* Twentieth century French literature; French poetics. *Publ:* Peguy, Poete du Sacre, Amitie Charles Peguy, 60; Alain Robbe-Grillet: Vers une esthetique de l'absurde, 2/64 & L'analyse visuelle de l'harmonie vocalique dans le vers francais, 12/66, Fr Rev; Malraux and Camus: The myth of the beleaguered city, Ky Foreign Lang Quart, 66; Gidean causality: L'Immoraliste and La Porte Etroite, Symposium, spring 77. *Mailing Add:* Dept of Romance Lang Univ of Mich Ann Arbor MI 48109

NEMES, GRACIELA PALAU DE, b Cuba, Mar 24, 19; US citizen; m 43; c 1. SPANISH. *Educ:* Trinity Col, Vt, AB, 42; Univ Md, MA, 49, PhD(Span & Span Am lit), 52. *Prof Exp:* Instr Span, 46-57, from asst prof to assoc prof, 57-65, PROF SPAN & SPAN AM LIT, UNIV MD, COLLEGE PARK, 65- *Concurrent Pos:* Am Philos Soc grants, Univ PR, 56, Spain, 60; vis assoc prof Romance lang, Johns Hopkins Univ, 64-65; vis lectr, Foreign Serv Inst, Dept of State, 66-; vis prof Span-Am lit, Univ Wis, spring 69; mem, Inst Int Educ Nat Screening Comt, 72-73, chmn 74-; Nat Endowment for Humanities proj grant, fall 81. *Honors & Awards:* Order of Merit, Spain, 73; Juanramoniana de Honor Medal, Spain, 81. *Mem:* Am Asn Teachers Span & Port; MLA; Asoc Int Hispanistas; Inst Int Lit Iberoam; Latin Am Studies Asn. *Res:* Life and works of Juan Ramon Jimenez; modernism; contemporary Hispanic literature. *Publ:* Auth, Rafael Landivar and Poetic Echoes of the Enlightenment, In: The Ibero American Enlightenment, Univ Ill, 71; Octavio Paz: Invention and Tradition or the Metaphor of the Void, In: The Perpetual Present: The Poetry and Prose of Octavio Paz, Univ Okla, 73; Vida y obra de Juan Ramon Jimenez: La Poesia Desnuda, Vols 1 & II, Gredos, Madrid, 74; La poesia en movimiento de Oscar Hahn, Insula, 1/77; La Dofia Barbara de Gallegos: Transparencia onomastica y opacidad historica, In: Nine essays on Romulo Gallegos, Univ Calif, 12/79; Entre el espacio y el vacio en la poesia de Damaso Alonso, Cuadernos para investigacion, Cult Hisp, 2-3/80. *Mailing Add:* Dept of Span & Port Univ of Md College Park MD 20740

NEMOIANU, VIRGIL PETRE, b Bucharest, Romania, Mar 12, 40; stateless; m 69; c 1. COMPARATIVE LITERATURE, ENGLISH. *Educ:* Univ Bucharest, Lic filologie, 61; Univ Calif, PhD(comp lit), 71. *Prof Exp:* Asst prof English, Univ Bucharest, 64-73; lectr Romanian, Univ London, Romanian & comp lit, Univ Calif, Berkeley, 75-78; asst prof English & comp lit, Univ Cincinnati, 78-79; ASSOC PROF & DIR COMP LIT, CATH UNIV AM, 79- *Concurrent Pos:* Res fel, Alexander Von Humboldt Soc, 75; Nat Endowment Humanities fel, 79. *Mem:* Am Comp Lit Asn; MLA; Am Soc 18th Century Studies; Goethe Soc. *Res:* European romanticism; critical theory; intellectual history. *Publ:* Auth, Structuralismul, Univ Bucharest, 67; Simptome, EPL, Bucharest, 69; Calmul Valorilor, Dacia, Cluj, 71; Utilul si Placutul, Eminescu, Bucharest, 73; Micro-Harmony the Growth and Uses of the Idyllic Model in Literature, Peter Lang, Bern, 77; The dialectics of movement in Keat's Autumn, PMLA, 78; Is there an English Biedermeier, Can Rev Comp Lit, 79. *Mailing Add:* Dept of English Cath Univ Am Washington DC 20064

NEMOY, LEON, b Balta, Russia, Dec 29, 01; m 30. ARABIC PHILOLOGY, BIBLIOGRAPHY. *Educ:* Yale Univ, AM, 26, PhD, 29. *Hon Degrees:* LHD, Hebrew Union Col, Jewish Inst Relig, Cincinnati, New York, 76. *Prof Exp:* Cataloguer, libr, Soc Propagation Knowledge, Odessa, 14-21; asst librn, Acad Libr, 19-21; cataloguer, libr, Univ Lemberg, Poland, 22-23; cur Hebrew & Arabic lit & res assoc bibliog, libr, 23-66, ED, YALE JUDAICA SER, YALE UNIV, 56-; RES PROF KARAITIC AND ARABIC LIT, DROPSIE UNIV, 67- *Mem:* AM Acad Jewish Res; Am Libr Asn. *Res:* Arabic literature and manuscripts; Oriental bibliography and medicine. *Publ:* Auth, Catalog of the Asch Collection at Yale; Karaite anthology; Arabic manuscripts at Yale; Al-Qirgisani's Kitab al-anwar (5 vols). *Mailing Add:* Dropsie Univ Broad at York St Philadelphia PA 19132

NEPAULSINGH, COLBERT IVOR, b Sangre Grande, Trinidad, West Indies, May 10, 43; m 66. SPANISH LANGUAGE & LITERATURE. *Educ:* Univ BC, BA, 66, MA, 67; Univ Toronto, PhD(Span lang & lit), 73. *Prof Exp:* Lectr Span, Acadia Univ, 68-70; lectr, 72-73, ASSOC PROF SPAN, STATE UNIV NY ALBANY, 73- *Concurrent Pos:* Res Found State Univ NY res fel, 74; Guggenheim fel, 81. *Mem:* MLA; Medieval Acad Am; Int Asn Hispanists. *Res:* Medieval Spanish literature; Spanish literature of the Golden Age. *Publ:* Auth, La poesia de Micer Francisco Imperial, Clasicos Castellanos; Sobre Juan Ruiz y las duenas chicas, Cuadernos Hispanoam, spring 74; The rhetorical structure of the prologues to the Libro de buen amor and the Celestina, Bull Hisp Studies, 74; Talavera's Prologue, Romance Notes, 75; The structure of the Libro de buen amor, Neophilologus, 77; Cervantes, Don Quijote: The unity of the action, Rev Can Estud Hispan, 78. *Mailing Add:* Dept of Hisp & Ital Studies State Univ of NY Albany NY 12222

NERJES, HERBERT GUENTHER, b Ludwigsburg, Ger, May 7, 21; US citizen; m 51. GERMAN. *Educ:* Brown Univ, AB, 57; Yale Univ, AM, 58, PhD, 63. *Prof Exp:* Asst prof Ger, Clark Univ, 61-63; asst prof, 63-67, ASSOC PROF GER, UNIV CALIF, DAVIS, 67- *Mem:* MLA; Am Asn Teachers Ger; Schiller Ges; Philol Asn Pac Coast. *Res:* German literature; classical period. *Publ:* Auth, Schiller und Karl August von Weimar, Monatshefte, 11/64; Ein Unbekannter Schiller, Erich Schmidt, Berlin, 65; Symbolik und Groteske in Achim von Arnims Majoratsherren, Seminar, fall 67. *Mailing Add:* Dept of German Univ of Calif Davis CA 95616

NESSELROTH, PETER WILLIAM, b Berlin, Ger, Mar 1, 35; Us citizen; m 66; c 2. FRENCH, COMPARATIVE LITERATURE. *Educ:* City Univ New York, BA, 57; Columbia Univ, MA, 58, PhD(French), 68. *Prof Exp:* Lectr French, City Univ New York, 58-68, asst prof, 68-69; asst prof, 69-70, ASSOC PROF FRENCH, UNIV TORONTO, 70- *Concurrent Pos:* Can Coun res fel French, 75-76. *Mem:* MLA; Northeast Mod Lang Asn; Asn Study Dada & Surrealism; Can Asn Res Semiotics; Am Semiotics Asn. *Res:* Theory of literature; literary semiotics; 19th and 20th century French literature. *Publ:* Auth, Lautreamont's Imagery, Droz, 69; co-ed, Problems of Textual Analysis, Didier, 71; contribr, Psychanalyse et Langages Litteraires, Nathan, 77. *Mailing Add:* Dept of French Univ Col Univ of Toronto Toronto ON M5S 1A1 Can

NETHERCUT, WILLIAM ROBERT, b Rockford, Ill, Jan 11, 36. CLASSICS. *Educ:* Harvard Univ, AB, 58; Columbia Univ, MA, 60, PhD(classics), 63. *Prof Exp:* From instr to asst prof Greek & Latin, Columbia Univ, 61-67; from assoc prof to prof Classics, Univ Ga, 67-75; PROF CLASSICS, UNIV TEX, AUSTIN, 75- *Concurrent Pos:* Lawrence Chamberlain fel, Columbia Univ, 67; lectr, First Int Conf on Ovid, Constanta, Romania, 72, Int Soc Homeric Studies, Athens, 73, 74, Int Congr Cypriot Studies, 74 & Int Congr SE Europ Studies, 74. *Mem:* Am Philol Asn; Class Asn Mid W & S; Archaeol Inst Am; Vergilian Soc Am; Petronian Soc. *Res:* Propertius; Vergil; Greek poetry. *Publ:* Auth, The conclusion of Lucretius' fifth book, Class J, 12/67; Notes on the structure of Propertius, book IV, Am J Philol, 10/68; Apuleius' literary art, Class J, 69; The ironic priest: Propertius' Roman elegies, Am J Philol, 10/70; Propertius, 3/11, Trans Am Philol Asn, 71; The imagery of the Aeneid, Class J, 71-72; Vergil's De Rerum Natura, 73 & The epic journey of Achilles, 76, Ramus. *Mailing Add:* Dept of Classics 123 Waggener Hall Univ of Tex Austin TX 78712

NEUBAUER, JOHN, b Budapest, Hungary, Nov 2, 33; US citizen; m 64; c 2. GERMANIC & COMPARATIVE LITERATURE. *Educ:* Amherst Col, BA, 60; Northwestern Univ, MS & MA, 62, PhD, 65. *Prof Exp:* From instr to asst prof Ger, Princeton Univ, 64-69; assoc prof, Case Western Reserve Univ, 69-73; assoc prof, 73-76, chmn dept Ger lang & lit, 73-78, PROF GER, UNIV PITTSBURGH, 76-, DIR WEST EUROP STUDIES, 81- *Concurrent Pos:* Vis prof, Univ Valle, Colombia, 67-68; Fulbright res grant, 72-73; vis prof, Harvard Univ, fall 79. *Honors & Awards:* Guggenheim fel, 80-81. *Mem:* MLA; Am Asn Teachers Ger; Am Soc 18th Century Studies; Am Comp Lit Asn. *Res:* Romanticism; intellectual history. *Publ:* Auth, The Sick Rose as an Aesthetic Idea: Kant, Blake, and the symbol in literature, In: Studies in Eighteenth Century Culture, Vol II, 72; The Idea of History in Schiller's Wallenstein, Neophilologus, 72; The artist as citizen: On Georg Lukacs' view of Thomas Mann, Ger Life & Lett, 73; Scientific law and poetic form: A dialogue on literature and science, Yearbk Comp & Gen Lit, 75; Die Abstraktion vor der wir uns fürchten: Goethes auffassung der Mathematik, Festschrift Erich Heller, 76; Symbolismus und Symbolische Logik Die Idee der ars Combinatoria in der Entwicklung der Modernen Dichtung, Fink, 78; Novalis, K G Hall, 80; The Mines of Falun: Temporal Fortunes of a Romantic Myth of Time, Studies in Romance, 80. *Mailing Add:* Dept of Ger Lang & Lit Univ Pittsburgh Pittsburgh PA 15260

NEUFELD, GERALD G, b Glasgow, Mont, July 6, 40; m 64; c 3. PSYCHOLINGUISTICS. *Educ:* Univ Calif, Santa Barbara, BA, 62; Univ Calif, Berkeley, MA, 67, PhD(psychol & ling), 69. *Prof Exp:* Asst prof, 69-74, ASSOC PROF PSYCHOLING, GEN LING & FOREIGN LANG ACQUISITION, UNIV OTTAWA, 74- *Concurrent Pos:* Grants, Univ Ottawa, 71-72 & Secy State Can, 73, 78. *Mem:* Can Asn Appl Ling; Can Asn Univ Prof. *Res:* Psychology of bilingualism; linguistics applied to study of foreign language acquisition; speech perception. *Publ:* Auth, Psycholinguistic Studies in Bilingualism, Univ Ottawa; The influence of second language learning upon the intellectual development of the child, Proc Second Can Symp Appl Ling, 70 & Foreign language aptitude: An enduring problem, In: Some Aspects of Canadian Applied Linguistics, Centre Educ & Cult Montreal; Personality and foreign language learning, Proc Can Asn Appl Ling, Laval Univ, 72; The bilingual's lexical store, Int Rev Appl Ling Lang Teaching, 76; The case for case studies, Individual Lang & Soc Can, 77; On the acquisition of prosodic and articulatory features in adult language learning, Can Mod Lang Rev, 78; A theoretical perspective on the nature of linguistic, Int Rev Appl Ling Lang Teaching, spring 78. *Mailing Add:* Dept of Ling Univ Ottawa Ottawa ON K1N 6N5 Can

NEUGAARD, EDWARD JOSEPH, b Jamestown, NDak, Mar 1, 33; m 57; c 3. ROMANCE LANGUAGES. *Educ:* Jamestown Col, BA, 55; Univ Wis, MA, 57; Univ NC, PhD(Romance lang), 64. *Prof Exp:* Instr Span & Ger, Col William & Mary, 59-64; from asst prof to assoc prof, 64-73, PROF SPAN, PORT & ROMANCE PHILOL, UNIV SOUTH FLA, 73- *Concurrent Pos:* Mem: Interam Prog Ling & Lang Teaching. *Mem:* MLA; Am Asn Teachers Span & Port; Am Folklore Soc; Ling & Philol Asn Latin Am; Int Asn Lengua & Lit Catalanes. *Res:* Old Catalan philology; Old Spanish and Catalan folk tales; Romanian linguistics. *Publ:* Auth, The Curioso Impertinente and its relationship to the Quijote, Lang Quart, spring-summer 66; The Sources of the Folk Tales in Ramon Llull's Libre de les Besties, J Am Folklore, 71; Una Edicion Valenciana mal Identificada del Flor de Virtuts, Bull Soc Castellonense Cult, 71; A motif index study of the Faules of Francesc Eiximenis, In: Catalan Studies: In Memory of Josephine de Boer, Hispam, Barcelona, 77; co-ed, Vides de Sants Rosselloneses (3 vols), Fundacio Salvador Vives Casajuana, Barcelona, 77. *Mailing Add:* Dept of Foreign Lang Univ SFla Tampa FL 33620

NEUMANN, ALFRED ROBERT, b Frankfurt-am-Main, Ger, Jan 26, 21; nat US; m 44; c 2. GERMAN. *Educ:* Marshall Univ, AB, 40; Univ Ky, MA, 41; Harvard Univ, AM, 48; Univ Mich, PhD, 51. *Hon Degrees:* LLD, Marshall Univ, 64. *Prof Exp:* Teacher, High Sch, Md, 41-42; instr Ger & French, Tulane Univ, 46; teaching fel Ger, Harvard Univ, 46-48 & Univ Mich, 48; instr, 48-52, asst prof, 53-56, assoc prof, 56-61, asst to vpres acad affairs, 56-57, asst to pres, 57-58, actg dean, 58-59, dean col arts & sci, 59-72, prof Ger, 61-72, PROF LIT & CHANCELLOR, UNIV HOUSTON, CLEAR LAKE CITY, 72- *Concurrent Pos:* Am Coun Learned Soc scholar, 52-53; prog annotator Houston Symphony Soc, 58-75; exam Ger listening comprehension comt, Col Entrance Exam Bd, 62-65; Southern Conf Acad Deans, 66-67; chmn, MLA, 68-70; consult accredition, Southern Conf Cols & Schs, 70-; chmn comt Int Prog, Am Asn State Cols & Univs, 78-79. *Honors & Awards:* Commander's Cross, Bundesverdienstkreuz, WGer, 73. *Mem:* MLA; SCent Mod Lang Asn (pres, 65-66); Am Asn Teachers Ger; Southern Humanities Conf (chmn, 69-70). *Res:* The interrelation of literature and the other arts; relation of music and German literature; history of opera as it affects and is affected by literature. *Publ:* Coauth, Literature and the Other Arts: A Select Bibliography, 1952-1958, NY Public Libr, 59. *Mailing Add:* 906 Forest Lake Dr Seabrook TX 77586

NEUMANN, DWIGHT KEITH, b Wichita, Kans, Mar 18, 44; c 1. SPANISH LITERATURE & LANGUAGE. *Educ:* Calif State Univ, Long Beach, BA, 66, MA, 74; Univ Calif, Los Angeles, PhD(Hisp lang & lit), 80. *Prof Exp:* Teaching assoc, Univ Calif, Los Angeles, 75-76; lectr Span lang & lit, Calif State Univ, Long Beach, 77-78; LECTR SPAN, CALIF STATE POLYTECH UNIV, POMONA, 79-; lectr Span & Hisp Pastoral Inst, Loyola Marymount Univ, 82; LECTR SPAN, UNIV SOUTHERN CALIF, 82- *Concurrent Pos:* Lectr Span, Univ Southern Calif, 79-82, Univ Calif, Los Angeles Ext, 82 & Loyola Marymount Univ, 82. *Mem:* Nat Asn Psychoanal Criticism. *Res:* Spanish Golden Age theater and prose; Spanish medieval literature; 19th century Spanish novel. *Publ:* Auth, La Regenta and Madame Bovary: Don Juan Tenorio and Lucia de Lammermoor, El Alba, 4/78; Excremental fantasies and shame in Quevedo's Buscon, Lit & Psychol, Vol XXVIII, No 3-4, 78; En torno a la critica de La Regenta and Madame Bovary, El Alba, 5/79; La introversion, la timidez, y los sentimientos de inferioridad de unos personajes galdosianos: Maximo Manso, Amparo Sanchez Emperador, y Maxi Rubin, Neophilol, 1/80; Guzman de Alfarache, Gracia, y la gracia divina, Kanina, Rev Artes & Letras Univ Costa Rica, 1/80; La defensa temprànera del Libro de buen amor, Romanische Forschungen, Vol 92, No 4. *Mailing Add:* 10039 Palms Blvd Los Angeles CA 90034

NEUMANN, EDITHA SCHLANSTEDT, b Burg, Ger, Jan 6, 24; US citizen; m 55. GERMAN LANGUAGE & LITERATURE. *Educ:* Col Music, Berlin, Ger, MMus, 47; Univ Pittsburgh, MSW, 57; Tulane Univ, PhD(Ger), 69. *Prof Exp:* Docent music educ & social work, Children's Hosp, Pestalozzi-Fröbel-Haus, Berlin, 48-55; field instr social work, Children's Hosp, Pittsburgh, Pa, 57-61; instr music, Univ Pittsburgh, 58-61; assoc prof Ger, 62-77, PROF FOREIGN LANG & CHMN DEPT, UNIV SOUTHERN MISS, 77- *Mem:* MLA; SCent MLA; Am Asn Teachers Ger; Nat Asn Social Workers; Viola da Gamba Soc Am. *Res:* Modern German literature; comparative literature. *Publ:* Auth, Musik in Frank Wedekind's Buhnenwerken, 1/71 & Die Lieder in Goethe's Goetz von Berlichingen, 5/73, Ger Quart, coauth, Five Wedekind poems, Southern Quart, 10/73; auth, The Artist-World Conflict in Frank Wedekind's Drama (in press) & co-ed, Moliere and the Commonwealth of Letters (in press), Univ & Col Press Miss. *Mailing Add:* Dept of Foreign Lang Univ of Southern Miss Hattiesburg MS 39401

NEUMARKT, PAUL, b Berlin, Ger, Oct 2, 13; US citizen; m 70; c 2. GERMAN LANGUAGE & LITERATURE. *Educ:* Brooklyn Col, BA, 43; NY Univ, MA, 53, PhD(Ger), 58; Duquesne Univ, MS, 78. *Prof Exp:* Instr Ger, Brooklyn Col, 43-44; lectr English, Hebrew Univ, Jerusalem, 60-70; assoc prof, 70-75, PROF GERMAN, DUQUESNE UNIV, 75- *Concurrent Pos:* Mem staff, Kultur und Leben, 66-; ed newslett, Asn Appl Psychoanalysis, 77-; ed-in-chief, J Evolutionary Psycol, 79- *Mem:* Assoc Asn Appl Psychoanal. *Res:* Literary criticism from a psychoanalytical aspect; world literature. *Publ:* Auth, Pan and Christ: An Analysis of the Hieros Gamos Concept in D H Lawrence's Short Story The Overtone, Dos Continentes, Madrid, Spain, 71-72; Modern man in search of a self: an analysis of the technique and personality of Henry Miller, J Human Relat, Cent State Univ, Ohio, 72; The Soviet collective in the works of Alexander Solzhenitsyn, Kesheth, Tel-Aviv, Israel, 73. *Mailing Add:* 5117 Forbes Ave Pittsburgh PA 15213

NEUSE, ERNA KRITSCH, b Austria, Aug 7, 23; US citizen. GERMAN LANGUAGE & LITERATURE. *Educ:* Univ Vienna, Austria, PhD, 47. *Prof Exp:* PROF GERMAN, RUTGERS UNIV, NEW BRUNSWICK, 54- *Concurrent Pos:* Dir, Grad Prog, Rutgers Univ, New Brunswick. *Mem:* MLA; Am Asn Teachers Ger. *Res:* Modern German literature; methods of teaching German. *Publ:* Auth, Modernes Deutsch, 60, Moderne Erzählungen, 64, Neue deutsche Prosa, 68 & Modern German, 70, Prentice-Hall; Büchners Lenz-zur Struktur der Novelle, Ger Quart, 3/70; Deutsch für Anfänger, Prentice-Hall, 71; Die Funktion von Motiven und Stereotypen Wendungen in Schnitzlers Reigen, Monatshefte, winter 72; Das Rhetorische in Dürrenmatts Der Besuch der alten Dame, Zur Funktion des Dialogs im Drama, Seminar, 2/75; Die deutsche Kurzgeschichte, Bouvier, Bonn, 80. *Mailing Add:* 7 Cobb Rd New Brunswick NJ 08901

NEWBERRY, WILMA J, b Covington, Ky, Jan 1, 27. SPANISH. *Educ:* Western Reserve Univ, BA, 56; Univ Wash, MA, 59, PhD, 60. *Prof Exp:* Teaching asst, Univ Wash, 56-59; asst prof Span, Carthage Col, 59-60; asst prof, Univ Ore, 61-63; from asst prof to assoc prof, 63-73, PROF SPAN, STATE UNIV NY BUFFALO, 73- *Mem:* Am Asn Teachers Span & Port; MLA; Am Asn Teachers Ital; Northeast Modern Lang Asn. *Res:* Twentieth century Spanish literature; twentieth century Spanish theatre; Pirandello and Spain. *Publ:* Auth, Pirandello and Azorin, Italica, 3/67; Cubism and pre-Pirandellianism in Gomez de la Serna, Comp Lit, winter 69; Aesthetic distance in Garcia Lorca's El Publico; Pirandello and Ortega, Hisp Rev, 4/69; The Pirandellian Mode in Spanish Literature, State Univ Ny, 73; Three examples of the midsummer theme in modern Spanish literature, Ky Romance Quart, 74; The Baptist betrayed: Juan Goytisolo's La Resaca and Fin de Fiesta, Rev Estud Hisp, 75; Patterns of negation in La Casa de Bernarda Alba, Hispania, 12/76; Perez de Ayala's concept of the doppelganger, In: Belarmino y Apolonio, Symposium, 80. *Mailing Add:* Dept of Mod Lang & Lit State Univ of NY Buffalo NY 14260

NEWELL, SANFORD, b Jackson, Miss, Nov 2, 29; m 50; c 4. ROMANCE LANGUAGES. *Educ:* Millsaps Col, BA, 50; Univ NC, MA, 52, PhD(Romance lang), 55. *Prof Exp:* PROF MOD LANG, CONVERSE COL, 55-, CHMN DEPT, 80- *Mem:* SAtlantic MLA; Southern Conf Lang Teaching. *Res:* Eighteenth century French literature; linguistics and language teaching. *Publ:* Ed, Dimension: Languages 66-68, Southern Conf Lang Teaching, 68 & 69. *Mailing Add:* 229 Maxine Dr Spartanburg SC 29302

NEWMAN, FRANCES STICKNEY, b Sexsmith, Alta, Can, Mar 27, 41; m 70; c 3. CLASSICAL PHILOLOGY. *Educ:* Univ Alta, BA, 64, MA, 67; Univ Ill, Urbana-Champaign, PhD(class philol), 72. *Prof Exp:* Vis asst prof classics, Wabash Col, 73; asst prof classics, Ohio State Univ, 77-79. *Concurrent Pos:* Can Coun res fel Pindar, 72-73. *Mem:* Am Philol Asn. *Res:* Pindar. *Publ:* Auth, Unity in Pindar's Fourteenth Olympian Ode, Revue belge de philologie et d'hist, 74; coauth, L'unite musicale dans les odes de Pindare: La deuxieme Nemeenne, Les Etudes Classiques, 74; auth, The Relevance of the Myth in Pindar's Eleventh Pythian, Hellenika, 79; coauth, Chromius and Heracles: Komic Elements in Pindar's First Nemean, EOS, 82. *Mailing Add:* 703 W Delaware Ave Urbana IL 61801

NEWMAN, JOHN KEVIN, b Bradford, England, Aug 17, 28; m 70; c 3. CLASSICAL PHILOLOGY, COMPARATIVE LITERATURE. *Educ:* Oxford Univ, BA(lit humaniores), 50, BA(Russ), 52, MA, 53; Bristol Univ, PhD(classics), 67. *Prof Exp:* Master classics, Downside Sch, Bath, England, 55-69; assoc prof, 70-80, PROF CLASSICS, UNIV ILL, URBANA, 80-, CHMN DEPT, 81- *Concurrent Pos:* Ed, Ill Class Studies, 81- *Honors & Awards:* Awards, Vatican Int Latin Poetry Competition, 60, 63, & 66; Certamen Capitolinum, 68 & 80. *Res:* Greek and Latin poetic traditions. *Publ:* Auth, Augustus and the new poetry, 67 & The concept of Vates in Augustan poetry, 67, Collection Latomus; Pushkin's Bronze horseman and the epic tradition, Comp Lit Studies, 72; co-ed, Serta Turyniana, 74; Univ Ill; Latin Compositions, 76, Golden Violence, 76 & Dislocated: An American Carnival, 77, Ex Aedibus, Urbana, Ill; De Novo Galli Fragmento in Nubia Eruto, Latinitas, 80. *Mailing Add:* 703 West Delaware Ave Urbana IL 61801

NEWMAN, KAREN ALISON, Renaissance Literature, Shakespeare. See Vol II

NEWMAN, LAWRENCE W, JR, b New York, NY, July 23, 35; m 63; c 3. SLAVIC LANGUAGES & LITERATURE. *Educ:* Yale Univ, BA, 57; Harvard Univ, MA, 61, PhD(Slavic), 67. *Prof Exp:* Asst prof Slavic lang & lit, Ind Univ, Bloomington, 67-74; asst prof, Ohio State Univ, 74-76; ASSOC PROF, OHIO WESLEYAN UNIV, 77- *Concurrent Pos:* Bibliogr, MLA, 71. *Res:* Russian and Czech; Slavic linguistics. *Publ:* Coauth, Towards a new classification of Czech verbs, Seej, 72; auth, The unpublished grammar of A H Barsov 1783-88, 75 & The notion of verbal aspect in 18th century Russian, 76, Russ Ling; Remarks on the category of person in Russian, Russ Lang J, 76; Towards a Prague school theory of semantics, Semiotica, 77; The Russian Case system reconsidered, Am Contrib VIII Int Congr Slavicists, 78; Prepositive modification in Russian and English: Subset or compound?, Russ Lang, 80; The Comprehensive Grammar of Russian by A A Barsov, Slavica, 80. *Mailing Add:* 331 E Torrence Rd Columbus OH 43214

NEWMAN, LEA BERTANI VOZAR, b Chicago Ill, Aug 3, 26; m 47, 76; c 5. AMERICAN LITERATURE. *Educ:* Chicago Teachers Col, BA, 47; Wayne State Univ, Detroit, MA, 66; Univ Mass, Amherst, PhD(English), 79. *Prof Exp:* Instr compos, Macomb Community Col, 65-66; instr compos & lit, Pa State Univ, Schuylkill, 66-68; instr, 68-73, asst prof, 73-79, assoc prof, 79-81, PROF COMPOS & LIT, NORTH ADAMS STATE COL, 81- *Concurrent Pos:* Dir, Nat Endowment for Humanities pilot grant, 81-82. *Mem:* Nathaniel Hawthorne Soc; MLA; NE Mod Lang Asn; Col English Asn. *Res:* Nathaniel Hawthorne's fiction; interdisciplinary approaches to teaching literature; nineteenth century American short stories. *Publ:* Auth, Yeats, Swift, Irish Patriotism and rationalistic anti-intellectualism, Mass Studies English, III: 108-16; A Reader's Guide to the Short Stories of Nathaniel Hawthorne, G K Hall, 79. *Mailing Add:* 120 Imperial ave Bennington VT 05201

NEWMAN, PAUL, US citizen. AFRICAN LINGUISTICS. *Educ:* Univ Pa, BA, 58, MA, 61; Univ Calif, Los Angeles, PhD(ling), 67. *Prof Exp:* From lectr to assoc prof anthrop, Yale Univ, 66-73; prof Nigerian lang, Ahmadu Bello Univ, Nigeria, 72-75; Wet Hoofdmedewerker, 75-79, PROF AFRICAN LING, RIJKSUNIVERSITEIT TE LEIDEN, 79- *Concurrent Pos:* Ed, J of African Lang & Ling, 78- *Mem:* Ling Soc Am. *Publ:* Auth, Tera Folktale Texts (2 vols), Human Relations Area Files, 68; A Grammar of Tera, Univ Calif, 70; coauth, West African Travels and Adventures, Yale Univ, 71; auth, The Kanakuru Language, Univ Leeds, 74; ed, Special Chadic issue, J African Lang, 71; coauth, Modern Hausa-English Dictionary, Oxford Univ, 77; Chadic classification and reconstructions, Afroasiatic Ling, 77; The Classification of Chadic within Afroasiatic, Univ Pers Leiden. *Mailing Add:* Afrikaanse Taalkunde Postbus 9507 2300 RA Leiden Netherlands

NEWMAN, RICHARD WILLIAM, b Boston, Mass, Sept 10, 13; m 46; c 2. ROMANCE LANGUAGES. *Educ:* Boston Univ, AB, 35, PhD(romance lang), 56; Boston State Col, MEd, 36. *Prof Exp:* Teacher, Boston Pub Schs, 37-55, asst prin, 55-57; prof French & Span, Boston State Col, 57-82, chmn dept foreign lang, 63-82, dir prog bilingual multicult studies, 72-82; PROF ENGLISH, UNIV MASS, BOSTON, 82- *Concurrent Pos:* Educ consult, Army Security Agency Sch, 57; Fulbright scholar, France, 64; mem working comt III, Northeast Conf, 73-74. *Honors & Awards:* Distinguished Serv Award, Mass Foreign Lang Asn, 77. *Mem:* MLA; Am Coun Teaching Foreign Lang; Am Asn Teachers Fr; Am Asn Teachers Span & Port; Teacher English Speakers Other Lang. *Res:* Psycholinguistics; sociolinguistics; Spanish linguistics. *Mailing Add:* Dept of Foreign Lang & Lit Boston State Col Boston MA 02115

NEWMAN, STANLEY STEWART, b Chicago, Ill, July 18, 05; m 30; c 1. ANTHROPOLOGY, LINGUISTICS. *Educ:* Univ Chicago, PhB, 27, AM, 28; Yale Univ, PhD(anthrop), 32. *Prof Exp:* Instr English, Univ Tex, 28-29; res fel ling, Inst Human Relations, Yale Univ, 32-37; res fel ling/psychol, Gen Educ Bd, 37-39; res fel ling, Intensive Lang Prog, Am Coun Learned Soc, 41-43; lang tech, ling, War Dept, Inform & Educ Div, New York, 43-45; anthropologist, ling, Inst Social Anthrop, Smithsonian Inst, 45-49; from assoc prof to prof, 49-71, EMER PROF ANTHROP, UNIV NMEX, 71- *Concurrent Pos:* Instr anthrop, Brooklyn Col, 43-43; co-ed, Southwestern J Anthrop, 61-73; ed, Univ N Mex Publ Anthrop, 62-68. *Honors & Awards:* Annual Res Lectr, Univ N Mex, 67. *Mem:* AAAS; Am Anthrop Asn; Ling Soc Am. *Res:* American Indian language; comparative linguistics; sociolinguistics. *Publ:* Auth, Further experiments in phonetic symbolism, Am J Psychol, 33; coauth, Language in General Education, D Appleton-Century, 40; auth, Yokuts Language of California, Viking Fund Publ in Anthrop, Vol 2, 47; Zuni Dictionary, Ind Univ Res Ctr Anthrop, Publ 6, 58; Zuni Grammar, Univ NMex Publ Anthrop, No 14, 65; Classical Nahuatl, Handbook of Mid Am Indians, Ling, Vol 5, 68; The Salish independent pronoun system, Int J Am Ling, 77; Zuni, Handbook NAm Indians, Lang, Vol 17 (in press). *Mailing Add:* Anthrop 158 Univ NMex Albuquerque NM 87131

NEWMAN-GORDON, PAULINE, b New York, NY, Aug 5, 25. FRENCH LITERATURE. *Educ:* Hunter Col, BA, 47; Columbia Univ, MA, 48; Univ Paris, DUniv, 51. *Prof Exp:* Instr French, Wellesley Col, 52-53; from instr to assoc prof, 53-68, PROF FRENCH LIT, STANFORD UNIV, 58- *Concurrent Pos:* Stanford comt fac res award, 56-57; Am Asn Univ Women res fel, 62-63; Am Philos Asn res grant, 70-71. *Honors & Awards:* Hunter Col Award, 57; Cert Distinguished Serv, Inst Int Educ, 81. *Mem:* MLA; Am Asn Teachers of Fr; Soc Friends of Marcel Proust. *Res:* Late 19th and early 20th century French literature. *Publ:* Auth, Marcel Proust et l'Existentialisme, 53; Corbiere Laforgue et Apollinaire ou le Rire en Pleurs, Debresse, 64; Dictionnaire des Idees dan l'Oeuvre de Marcel Proust, Mouton, 68; Helene de Sparte: La Fortune du Mythe en France, Nouvelles Ed Debresse, 68; Andre Spire: Influences humanitaires dans Et vous riez! (documents inedits), Australian J Fr Studies, spring 75; L'image du jardin chez Proust, Stanford Fr Rev, spring 77; Sartre, lecteur de Proust ou le paradoxe de La Nausee, BSAMP, Nos 19 & 21, 79-81; Bijoux et Pierres Precieuses chez Proust, Stanford Fr Rev, winter 80. *Mailing Add:* Dept of French & Ital Stanford Univ Stanford CA 94305

NEWMARK, LEONARD, b Attica, Ind, Apr 8, 29; m 51; c 2. LINGUISTICS. *Educ:* Univ Chicago, AB, 47; Ind Uiv, MA, 51, PhD, 55. *Prof Exp:* From instr to asst prof English, 54-61, assoc prof ling, 61-62; assoc prof, Ind Univ, 62-63; dir Ctr Res Lang Acquistion, 72-75, actg chmn dept music, 77-78, PROF LING, UNIV CALIF, SAN DIEGO, 63- *Concurrent Pos:* Grants, Soc Sci Res Coun, 51, 53; Am Philos Soc, 57; Nat Sci Found 63 & Am Coun Learned Soc, 71-72. *Mem:* Ling Soc Am; Am Asn Appl Ling. *Res:* Language acquisition; Albanian grammar; language teaching. *Publ:* Auth, Structural Grammar of Albanian, Ind Univ Res Ctr, 57; coauth, A Linguistic Introduction to the History of English, Knopf, 63; Using American English, Harper, 64; Necessity and sufficiency in language learning, Int Rev Appl Ling Lang Teaching, 68; coauth, Spoken Albanian, Spoken Lang Services, 80; Standard Albanian: A Reference Grammar for Students, Stanford Univ Press, 82. *Mailing Add:* Dept of Ling Univ Calif San Diego La Jolla CA 92037

NEWMYER, STEPHEN THOMAS, b Pittsburgh, Pa, July 10, 48; m 78. CLASSICS. *Educ:* Duquesne Univ, BA, 70; Univ NC, Chapel Hill, PhD(classics), 76. *Prof Exp:* asst prof, 76-80, ASSOC PROF CLASSICS, DUQUESNE UNIV, 80- *Concurrent Pos:* Fel, Inst Teaching Post-Bibl Found Western Civilization, Jewish Theol Sem Am, 78. *Mem:* Am Philol Asn; Vergilian Soc; Class Asn Middle West & South; Class Asn Atlantic States. *Res:* Roman epic poetry; classical influence on later literature; medicine. *Publ:* Auth, Pessimistic Prometheus: A Comparison of Aeschylus and Robert Lowell, Helios, fall-winter 78-79, The Silvae of Statius: Structure and Theme, Brill, Leiden, 79; Ancient and Talmudic Medicine: A Course Description, Helios, winter-spring 79-80; Talmudic medicine: A Classicist's perspective, Judaism, 29: 360-367; Robert Lowell and the weeping philosopher, Class and Mod Lit, winter 80; Talmudic medicine, Jewish Digest, 2/81; Charles Anthon: Knickerbocker scholar, Class Outlook, 12-1/81-82. *Mailing Add:* 119 S 21st St Pittsburgh PA 15203

NEWTON, BRIAN ELLIOTT, b Wigan, England, July 24, 28; m 55; c 2. LINGUISTICS, MODERN GREEK. *Educ:* Oxford Univ, BA, 50, MA, 53. *Prof Exp:* Lectr classics, Univ Cape Town, 57-64; sr lectr ling, Univ Witwatersrand, 64-65; from asst prof to assoc prof, 65-71, PROF FRENCH & LING, SIMON FRASER UNIV, 71- *Concurrent Pos:* SAfrican Nat Coun Soc & Indust Res sr bursars, 63; Can Coun leave fel, 68-69; Guggenheim Found fel, 74. *Mem:* Ling Soc Am. *Res:* Modern Greek dialectology; historical linguistics. *Publ:* Auth, Grammatical Integration of Italian and Turkish Substantives into Modern Greek, Word, 63; Phonology of Cypriot Greek, 67 & Spontaneous Gemination in Cypriot Greek, 68, Lingua; Cypriot Greek, Mouton, The Hague, 72; The Generative Interpretation of Dialect, Cambridge Univ, 72. *Mailing Add:* Dept of Mod Lang Simon Fraser Univ Burnaby BC V5A 1S6 Can

NEWTON, CANDELAS MARIA, b Santander, Spain, Nov 13, 48; m 74; c 2. FOREIGN LANGUAGES. *Educ:* Univ Salamanca, Spain, BA, 72; Univ Pittsburgh, MA, 76, PhD(Hisp lang & lit), 80. *Prof Exp:* Lectr Span, St Ursula's Grammar Sch, London, 72-73 & Carlow Col, 73-74; teaching asst, Univ Pittsburgh, 75-76; instr, 78-80, vis asst prof, 80-82, ASST PROF SPAN, WAKE FOREST UNIV, 82- *Mem:* Garcia Lorca Soc; MLA; Am Asn Teachers Span & Port; Northeast Mod Lang Asn. *Res:* Garcia Lorca's poetry; poetry: generation of 1927 in Spain; 20th century Spanish poetry. *Publ:* Auth, Two aspects of nature in Libro de poemas: Nature as the lost paradise and nature as teacher, In: The World of Nature, 80; Nostalgia del paraiso infantil en Libro de poemas: El poeta sobre su Pegaso, Garcia Lorca Rev, Vol VIII, No 1 & 2; Emilio Carrere en la formacion poetica de Federico Garcia Lorca, Cirtica Hisp, fall 82; Trasfondo popular y folklore infantie en Libro de Poemas de Garcia Lorca, Revista de Estudios Hisp (in press). *Mailing Add:* Dept of Romance Lang Wake Forest Univ Winston-Salem NC 27019

NEWTON, FRANCIS LANNEAU, b Winston-Salem, NC, Feb 28, 28; m 51; c 4. LATIN. *Educ:* Wake Forest Col, BA, 47, MA, 48; Univ NC, PhD, 54. *Prof Exp:* Instr Latin, Wake Forest Col, 50-51; instr classics, Univ NC, 52-53; asst prof class lang, Vanderbilt Univ, 53-58, assoc prof, 58-66, prof, 66-67; chmn dept class studies, 69-71, PROF LATIN, DUKE UNIV, 67-, CHMN DEPT CLASS STUDIES, 80- *Concurrent Pos:* Am Coun Learned Soc fel, 71-72; Nat Endowment for Humanities Fel, 78. *Mem:* Am Philol Asn; Class Asn Mid W & S (pres, 67-68); Mediaeval Acad Am. *Res:* Virgil; Roman elegy and lyric; paleography. *Publ:* Auth, Recurrent imagery in Aeneid IV, 57 & Tibullus in two grammatical florilegia of the Middle Ages, 62, Trans Am Philol Asn; ed, Laurentii Monachi Casinensis Archiepiscopi Amalfitani Opera, Monumenta Germaniae Hist, 73; auth, The Desiderian Scriptorium at Monte Cassino: The chronicle and some surviving manuscripts, Dumbarton Oaks Papers, 30: 35-54. *Mailing Add:* Dept Class Studies Duke Univ Durham NC 27706

NEWTON, ROBERT PARR, b San Antonio, Tex, July 31, 29; m 59; c 2. MODERN GERMAN LITERATURE, STYLISTICS. *Educ:* Rice Univ, BA, 50, MA, 58; Johns Hopkins Univ, PhD(Ger), 64. *Prof Exp:* From instr to asst prof Ger, Univ Pa, 62-70; assoc prof, 70-76, PROF GER, UNIV NC, GREENSBORO, 76- *Concurrent Pos:* Vis Lectr Ger, Swarthmore Col, 65-70. *Mem:* MLA; SAtlantic Mod Lang Asn; Am Asn Teachers Ger; AAUP. *Res:* Linguistic metrics, German poetry, modern German drama. *Publ:* Auth, Dada, expressionism and some modern modes, Rice Univ Studies, summer 69; The first voice: Vowel configuration in the German lyric, J English & Ger Philol, 10/69; Vokallänge und Vokalgleichklang als rhythmische Antriebs- und Gestaltungsmomente, LiLi: Z Ling und Lit, 9/71; Form in the Menschheitsdämmerung, The Hague, 71; Ditonic rhythmemes: Formal elements of rhythmic patterning, Poetics: Int Rev Theory Lit, 74; Trochaic and iambic, Lang & Style, Int J, spring 75; Vowel Undersong: Studies of Vocalic Timbre and Chroneme Patterning in German Lyric Poetry, The Hague, 81; Eye Imagery in Else Lasker-Schüer, Mod Lang Notes, 3/82. *Mailing Add:* Univ NC Greensboro NC 27412

NEY, JAMES WALTER, b Nakuru, Kenya, July 28, 32; US citizen; m 54; c 3. ENGLISH, LINGUISTICS. *Educ:* Wheaton Col, Ill, AB, 55, AM, 58; Univ Mich, EdD(English), 63. *Prof Exp:* English specialist, Dade County Pub Schs, Fla, 61-62 & Univ Ryukyus, 62-64; asst prof, Mich State Univ, 65-69; assoc prof, 69-75, PROF ENGLISH, ARIZ STATE UNIV, 75- *Concurrent Pos:* Res grant, NCTE, 76, chmn comt to evaluate ling, 77-80. *Mem:* Can Ling Soc; Nat Asn Foreign Student Affairs; Teaching English to Speakers Other Lang; Ling Soc Am; MLA. *Res:* Teaching English as a second language; teaching of written composition to native speakers of English. *Publ:* Coauth, Readings on American Society, 69, Readings from Samuel Clemens, 69, Blaisdell; Adventures in English, Laidlaw Bros, 72; Marckwardt, 72; Two apparent fallacies in current grammatical thought, Gen Ling, 74; Linguistics, Language Teaching and Composition in the Grades, Mouton, The Hague, 75; The modals in English: A floating Semantic feature analysis, J English Ling, 76; Sexism in the English language: A biased view in a biased society, ETC, 76; Semantic Structures, Mouton, The Hague, 81. *Mailing Add:* Dept of English 504 Ariz State Univ Tempe AZ 85281

NGATE, JONATHAN, b Crampel, Centrafrica, Jan 28, 48. AFRICAN LITERATURES. *Educ:* State Univ NY Buffalo, BA, 72; Brown Univ, MA, 74; Univ Wash, PhD(comp lit), 79. *Prof Exp:* Asst prof French, Mich State Univ, 80; ASST PROF FRENCH, UNIV MICH, 80- *Mem:* African Lit Asn; African Studies Asn; Am Comp Lit Asn; MLA; Am Asn Teachers French. *Res:* Afro-occidental literary relations; the aesthetics of difference. *Publ:* Auth, Mauvais Sang de Rimbaud et Cahier d'un retour au pays natal de Cesaire: La poesie au service de la revolution, Cahiers cesairiens, No 3, 77. *Mailing Add:* Dept of Romance Lang Univ of Mich Ann Arbor MI 48109

NGUYEN, DINH-HOA, b Hanoi, Vietnam, Jan 17, 24; m 52; c 4. LINGUISTICS, LITERATURE. *Educ:* Union Col, BA, 50; NY Univ, MA, 52, PhD(English educ), 56. *Prof Exp:* Lectr Vietnamese, Columbia Univ, 53-57; from asst prof to prof English & ling, Univ Saigon, 57-65, dean fac lett, 57-58, chmn dept, 57-65; PROF LING & FOREIGN LANG, SOUTHERN ILL UNIV, CARBONDALE & DIR CTR VIETNAMESE STUDIES, 69- *Concurrent Pos:* Dir cult affairs, Ministry of Educ, Saigon, Vietnam, 62-65; secy-gen, Vietnam Nat Comn, UNESCO, 62-65; vis prof, Univ Wash, 65-66; cult counr, Embassy of Vietnam, Washington, DC, 66-69; Fulbright prof ling & English, Rabat, Morocco, 81-82; two res grants, Nat Endowment for Humanities, 77-82; Fulbright grant ling, Morocco, 81-82. *Mem:* Ling Soc Am; Am Orient Soc; Asn Asian Studies; Dict Soc NAm; Am Coun Teachers Uncommonly-Taught Asian Lang (pres, 76-77 & 77-78). *Res:* Students' review grammar of Vietnamese; English-Vietnamese dictionary; outline of Vietnamese culture. *Publ:* Auth, Read Vietnamese, 66 & Hoa's Vietnamese-English Dictionary, 66 Tuttle; Vietnamese-English Student Dictionary, 71 & Colloquial Vietnamese, 74, Southern Ill Univ; Beginning English for Vietnamese Speakers & Intermediate English for Vietnamese Speakers, Tuttle, 76; 201 Vietnamese Verbs, Barron's 79; Language in Vietnamese Society, 80 & Essential English- Vietnamese Dictionary, 80, Asia Bks. *Mailing Add:* Dept of Ling Southern Ill Univ Carbondale IL 62901

NICHOLAS, ROBERT LEON, b Lebanon, Ore, Dec 10, 37; m 67; c 2. MODERN SPANISH LITERATURE. *Educ:* Univ Ore, BA, 59, MA, 63, PhD(romance lang), 67. *Prof Exp:* From instr to assoc prof, 65-76, chmn dept Span & Port, 79-82, PROF SPAN, UNIV WIS-MADISON, 76- *Concurrent Pos:* Dir study prog, Madrid, 72-73. *Mem:* Am Asn Teachers Span & Port; MLA. *Res:* Modern Spanish theatre; modern Spanish novel; generation of 1898. *Publ:* Contribr, The history plays: Buero Vallejo's experiment in dramatic expression, Rev Estud Hispanicos, 11/69; auth, El Mundo de Hoy, Scott, 71; The Tragic Stages of Antonio Buero Vallejo, Estud Hispanofila, Univ NC, 72; coauth, En Camino!, Adelante! & Churros y Chocolate!, Scott, 77; La historia de historia de una escalera, Estreno, spring 79; En Camino! Adelante! Scott, 2nd ed, 81; El proceso de creacion en Abel Sanchez, Homenaje a Antonio Sanchez-Barbudo: Ensayos de literatura espanola moderna, Univ Wis-Madison, 81; La camisa, entre el sainete y el melodrama, Primer Acto, 82; coauth, En camino: motivos de conversacion, Scott (in prep). *Mailing Add:* Dept of Span & Port Room 1038 Van Hise Hall Univ Wis Madison WI 53706

NICHOLLS, JAMES CHASE, b Madison, Wis, Jan 23, 30; m 55; c 2. ROMANCE LANGUAGES. *Educ:* Univ Wis, BA, 51, MA, 52, PhD, 62. *Prof Exp:* Instr French, Univ Tex, 60-62; from asst prof to assoc prof, 62-66, PROF FRENCH, COLGATE UNIV, 74- *Mem:* MLA; Am Asn Teacher Fr; Am Soc 18th Century Studies. *Res:* Eighteenth century French literature. *Publ:* Ed, Mme Riccoboni's letters to David Hume, David Garrick and Sir Robert Liston: 1764-1783, Voltaire Found, Oxford, Eng, 76. *Mailing Add:* Dept of Romance Lang Colgate Univ Hamilton NY 13346

NICHOLLS, ROGER ARCHIBALD, b London, Eng, May 24, 22; m 55. GERMAN. *Educ:* Oxford Univ, BA, 49; Univ Calif, PhD, 53. *Prof Exp:* Instr Ger, Univ Toronto, 52-54; asst prof, Univ Chicago, 54-61; assoc prof, Reed Col, 61-63; asst prof, 63-65, PROF GER, UNIV ORE, 65- *Mem:* MLA; Am Asn Teachers Ger; Philol Asn Pac Coast (pres, 67-68). *Res:* Nineteenth century drama; literary movements at the end of the nineteenth century; Thomas Mann. *Publ:* Auth, Nietzsche in the Early Work of Thomas Mann, Univ Calif, 55; The Dramas of CD Grabbe, Mouton, 68. *Mailing Add:* 2840 Elinor St Eugene OR 97403

NICHOLS, JAMES MANSFIELD, b Alpine, Tex, Aug 5, 46. SPANISH & ARABIC LANGUAGES, APPLIED LINGUISTICS. *Educ:* Trinity Univ, BA, 67; Univ NC, Chapel Hill, MA, 70, Phd(Romance lang), 75. *Prof Exp:* Asst prof Span, Pan Am Univ, 76; ASST PROF SPAN, UNIV MICH, DEARBORN, 76- *Mem:* MLA; Mediaeval Acad. *Res:* Medieval Spanish literature; Hispano-Arabic literature; history of rhetoric and language pedagogy. *Mailing Add:* Univ of Mich 4901 Evergreen Rd Dearborn MI 48128

NICHOLS, PATRICIA CAUSEY, b Conway, SC, Dec 29, 38; m 59; c 2. ENGLISH, LINGUISTICS. *Educ:* Winthrop Col, BA, 58; Univ Minn, MA, 66; San Jose State Univ, MA, 72; Stanford Univ, PhD(ling), 76. *Prof Exp:* Teacher, Hampton Pub Schs, Va, 58-60; LECTR ENGLISH, LING & EDUC, SAN JOSE STATE UNIV, 76- *Concurrent Pos:* Co-ed, Women & Lang News, 76; vis asst prof English, Univ SC, 80-81; vis instr, Univ Calif, Santa Barbara, 82. *Mem:* MLA; Ling Soc Am; Am Dialect Soc. *Res:* Gullah; gender and sex differences in speech; American dialects. *Publ:* Auth, A sociolinguistic perspective on reading and black children, Lang Arts, 54: 150-157; Ethnic consciousness in the British Isles, Lang Problems & Lang Planning, 1: 10-31; Black women in the rural south: Conservative and innovative, Int J Sociol Lang , Vol 17, 78; Planning for language change, San Jose Studies, 6: 18-25; Variation among Gullah speakers in rural South Carolina, In: Language Use and the Uses of Language, Georgetown Univ Press, 80; Women in their speech communities, In: Women and Language In Literature and Society, Praeger Publ, 80; Creoles in the USA, In: Language in the USA, Cambridge Univ Press, 81; Linguistic options and choices for black women in the rural South, In: Language, Gender and Society, Newbury House Publ (in press). *Mailing Add:* 1430 Westmont Ave Campbell CA 95008

NICHOLS, STEPHEN G, JR, b Cambridge, Mass, Oct 24, 36; m 57, 72; c 4. ROMANCE LANGUAGES, COMPARATIVE LITERATURE. *Educ:* Dartmouth Col, AB, 58; Yale Univ, PhD(comp lit), 63. *Prof Exp:* Asst prof French, Univ Calif, Los Angeles, 63-65; assoc prof comp lit, Univ Wis-Madison, 65-68; chairperson comp lit, 69-71, 74 & 79-82, chairperson Romance lang, 75-77, PROF ROMANCE LANG & COMP LIT, DARTMOUTH COL, 68-, CHAIRPERSON FRENCH & ITAL, 82- *Concurrent Pos:* Adv, Inst Etudes Fr Avignon, Bryn Mawr, 66-; fel, Inst Res Humanities, Univ Wis, 66-67; adv ed, Fr Rev, 68-; vis prof, Tel-Aviv Univ, 77 & Exeter Univ, 80; Nat Endowment for Humanities fel, 78-79; mem adv coun comp lit dept, Princeton Univ, 82- *Mem:* MLA; Mediaeval Acad Am; Soc Rencesvals (treas, 64-68); Am Comp Lit Asn; Acad Lit Studies (secy-treas, 78-). *Res:* Medieval literature, especially Old French, Provencal and Icelandic; literary criticism. *Publ:* Co-ed, The Meaning of Mannerism, Univ Press New England, 72; auth, Toward an aesthetic of the Provencal Lyric II: Marcabru, In: Italian Literature: Foundations and Development, 74; Signs of royal beauty bright: Word and image in the Legend of Charlemange, Olifant, 76; CansoConso: Structure of parodic humor in Three Songs of Guilhem IX, L'Esprit Createur, 76; A poetics of historicism? Recent trends in medieval literary criticism, Medievalia & Humanistica, 77; Sign as (hi)story in the Couronnement de Louis, Romanic Rev, 80; Mimesis: From Mirror to Method, Univ Press New England, 82; Romanesque Signs, Yale Univ (in prep). *Mailing Add:* Dept of Romance Lang Dartmouth Col Hanover NH 03755

NICHOLSON, JOHN GREER, b Peacehave, England, May 8, 29; Can citizen; m 52; c 3. LINGUISTICS, PHILOLOGY. *Educ:* Cambridge Univ, BA, 52, MA, 58; Univ Montreal, PhD, 63. *Prof Exp:* Lectr Russ, Univ London, 52-54; ed Russ, Inst Study USSR, Munich, Ger, 54-56, dep head Soviet studies, 56-57; res ed current Soviet policies, policy coordr dept, Int Serv, Can Broadcasting Corp, 57-60, head Russ radio prog, Russ sect, 60-61; charge de cours Russ, Univ Montreal, 57-61; asst prof, McMaster Univ, 61-62; assoc prof, McGill Univ, 62-65, chmn dept, 62-77, chmn dept French, 73-74, prof Russ, 65-79. *Concurrent Pos:* Can Coun short-term res fel, USSR, 66; mem, Can Inter-Univ comt on exchanges with USSR & EEurope, 66-, chmn, 76-; vis prof Russ, Oxford Univ, 72; mem nat publ comt, Humanities Res Coun Can, 72- *Mem:* Can Inst Int Affairs; Can Asn Slavists; Am Asn Advan Slavic Studies; Am Asn Teachers Slavic & E Europ Lang; Mod Humanities Res Asn. *Res:* Russian phonetics and grammatical structure; the language of Lenin; international political communication. *Publ:* Auth, Modern Russian word stress patterns, 62, Anomalies dans l'accentuation des noms de famille russes, 65 & Russian verbal aspect and Aktionsart, 67, Slavic & EEurop Studies; Russian Normative Stress Notation, McGill Univ, 68; Problems of Accent in the Eastern Slavic Langugage, Proceed Int Prosodic Conf, Didier, 70; Suppletion and semantic distance, 73 & Suppletion, spatial correlatives and the boundary concept, 76, Slavic & EEurop Studies. *Mailing Add:* 364 Stewart St Ottawa ON K1P 6G4 Can

NICOLAI, RALF ROCHUS, b Brandenburg, Ger, May 4, 35; m 59; c 2. GERMAN LITERATURE & PHILOSOPHY. *Educ:* Tex Western Col, BA, 64; Univ Tex, El Paso, MA, 66; Univ Kans, MPhil & PhD(Ger), 69. *Prof Exp:* Instr Span & Ger, Univ Tex, El Paso, 64-66; instr foreign lang educ, Univ Kans, 66-68; asst prof, 69-74, assoc prof, 75-78, PROF GER, UNIV GA, 78- *Concurrent Pos:* Prof-in-charge grad studies Ger, Syst Studies Austria, Univ Ga, 69-70; prof-in-charge & resident dir Ger, Syst Studies Abroad Erlangen Univ, Ger, Univ Ga, 70-72; vis prof, Univ Houston, 80. *Honors & Awards:* Univ Ga Res Award, 82. *Mem:* MLA; Am Asn Teachers Ger; Kafka Soc; SAtlantic Mod Lang Asn; SCent Mod Lang Asn. *Res:* German prose of the 19th and early 20th century; modern Austrian literature; comparative literature. *Publ:* Auth, Kafkas Stellung zu Kleist und der Romantik, 73 & Kafkas Affassung von Freiheit, 74, Studia Neophilologica; Zum historischen Gehalt in Bölls Erzählung Steh auf, steh doch auf, Lit Wissenschaft Unterricht, 75; Konflikt zweier Welten: Kafkas Triadik und Der Bau, Jahrbuch Freien Deutschen Hochstifts, 75; Die Marionette als Interpretationsansatz zu Bölls Ansichten eines Clowns, Univ Dayton Rev, spring 76; Ende oder Anfang: Zur Einheit der Gegensaetze in Kafkas Schloss, Fink Verlag, Munich, 77; Purzelchen im Lichte der spaeten Romane Sudermanns, Hermann Sudermann; Wahrheit und Luege bei Kafka und Nietzsche, Literaturwissenschaftliches Jahrubuch, 81; Kafkas Amerika-Roman Der Verschollene--Motive und Gestalten, Koenigshausen & Neumann, Wuerzburg, 81. *Mailing Add:* 218 Cavalier Rd Athens GA 30606

NICOLICH, ROBERT NICHOLAS, b New York, NY, July 1, 40. FRENCH LITERATURE. *Educ:* Fordham Univ, BA, 61; Mich State Univ, PhD(French), 65. *Prof Exp:* Asst prof, 65-73, head sect, 70-73, ASSOC PROF FRENCH, CATH UNIV AM, 73- *Concurrent Pos:* Vis asst prof, George Washington Univ, fall 66, 67. *Mem:* Am Asn Teachers Fr; AAUP; MLA; SAtlantic Mod Lang Asn; 17th Century Fr Lit (secy, 73-). *Res:* French 17th century literature; literature and art interrelationships. *Publ:* Contribr ed, French 3 bibliography for French Seventeenth Century Literature, 69-; The language of vision in La Princesse de Cleves, Lang & Style, fall 71; Classicisme and baroque in the Bourgeois Gentilhomme, Fr Rev, summer 72; Maynard and some sonnets on death: Speculations on the concepts of mannerism and Baroque, Cahiers Asn Amis Maynard, 12/75; The Baroque dilemma: Some recent French mannerist and Baroque criticism, Oeuvres & Critiques, summer 76; Les decors des pompes funebres de Louis XIV a Saint Denis et les services a Notre-Dame et a La Sainte-Chapelle, Bull Soc Hist Art Francais, 76; Restraint-release patterns in Mme de la Fayette's Comtesse de Tende, Princesse de Montpensier and Princesse de Cleves, Papers Fr 17th Century Lit, summer 76; coauth, The seventeenth century, In: Years Work in Modern Language Studies, 76 & auth, 77. *Mailing Add:* Dept of Mod Lang Cath Univ Am Washington DC 20064

NICOLS, JOHN, Ancient History, Classics. See Vol I

NIDA, EUGENE ALBERT, b Oklahoma City, Okla, Nov 11, 14; m 43. LINGUISTICS, ANTHROPOLOGY. *Educ:* Univ Calif, Los Angeles, AB, 36; Univ Southern Calif, MA, 39; Univ Mich, PhD(ling), 43. *Hon Degrees:* DD, Eastern Baptist Theol Sem, 56; DD, Southern Calif Baptist Sem, 59; ThD, Univ Münster, 66; LittD, Heriot-Watt Univ, Scotland, 74. *Prof Exp:* SECY TRANSL, AM BIBLE SOC, 43- *Concurrent Pos:* Transl res coordr, United Bible Socs, New York, 72-80. *Honors & Awards:* Gutenberg Award, Chicago Bible Soc, 57; Alexander Gode Medal, Am Translr Asn, 77. *Mem:* Ling Soc Am (pres, 68); Am Anthrop Asn; Soc New Testament Studies; Soc Bibl Lit; Soc Ling Europaea. *Res:* Linguistic structure of aboriginal languages; acculuration; semantics. *Publ:* Coauth (with Paul Ellingworth), A Translators Handbook on Paul's Letters to the Thessalonians, Vol 17, 75, (with Daniel Arichea), A Translators Handbook on Paul's Letter to the Glatians, Vol 18, 76 & (with I-Jin Loh), A Translators Handbook on Paul's Letter to the Philippians, Vol 19, 77, United Bible Soc, Stuttgart, Ger; Good News for Everyone, Word Bks, 77; (with Barclay M Newman), A Translator's Handbook on the Gospel of John, 80 & (with Daniel C Arichea), A Translator's Handbook on the First Letter from Peter, 80, United Bible Soc; (with William D Reyburn), Meaning Across Cultures, Orbis Bks, 81; (with Robert G Bratcher), A Translator's Handbook on Paul's Letter to the Ephesians, United Bible Soc, 82. *Mailing Add:* Am Bible Soc 1865 Broadway New York NY 10023

NIEDERAUER, DAVID JOHN, b San Francisco, Calif, Sept 6, 24; m 47; c 4. FRENCH. *Educ:* SAN Jose State Col, BA, 47; Univ Calif, Berkeley, MA, 51, PhD(French lit), 62. *Prof Exp:* Instr French, Univ BC, 55-60; dir lang lab, San Francisco State Col, 60-61; asst prof, 61-68, assoc prof, 68-81, PROF FRENCH, UNIV BC, 81- *Concurrent Pos:* Can Coun res grant, 63; Can Coun sr fel, 67-68; Can Coun leave fel, 75-76. *Mem:* Asn Can Univ Teachers Fr. *Res:* French symbolist period. *Publ:* Ed, Henri de Regnier: Lettres a Andre Gide, Droz, Geneva, 72; Pierre Louys, his life and art, Can Fedn for Humanities, 81. *Mailing Add:* Dept of French Univ of BC Vancouver BC V6T 1W5 Can

NIEDZIELSKI, HENRI, b Troyes, France, Mar 30, 31; US citizen; m 57; c 4. ENGLISH & FRENCH LINGUISTICS. *Educ:* Univ Dijon, Propedeutique Russ-Ger, 54; Univ Conn, BA, 59, MA, 63, PhD(romance philol), 64. *Prof Exp:* Instr French, Univ Conn, 62 & Univ Mass, 62-64; asst prof Medieval French lit, Laval Univ, 64-65; asst prof French, Univ Mass, 65-66; assoc prof, 66-72, PROF FRENCH, UNIV HAWAII, MANOA, 72- *Concurrent Pos:* Univ Mass res coun grants, 65-66; Univ Hawaii res grants, 66-67, 69 & 82; consult, Univ Ky Res Grants, 67-68 & 69; Fulbright-Hays sr lect grant, 72-74 & 80-81; lectr teaching English as a foreign lang & ling, Univ Lodz, Poland, 73 & Jagiellonian Univ, 72-74 & 75-76. *Mem:* Int Asn Teachers English as Second Lang; Int Sociol Asn; Am Asn Teachers Fr; MLA; Int Asn Appl Ling. *Res:* Sociolinguistics; applied linguistics; programmed instruction in modern and Old French language and culture. *Publ:* Coauth, Handbook of French Structure: A Sytematic Review, Harcourt, 68; auth, Semantics and relative pronouns . . ., Int Rev Appl Ling, 75; Contrastive sound visuals: English-French, Educ Res Assoc, 76; Some performance objectives for the teaching of English composition, Glottodidactica, 76; co-ed, Studies on the Seven Sages of Rome, Fr Lit, 77 & 78; auth, The influence of society and environment on first language usage, La Monda Linguoproblemo, 77; Le Corteete, le raisonnement et l'intuition dans l'apprentissage individualise de la lecture, The Fr Rev, 79; Teaching English in Francophore, Africa, World Lang English, 82. *Mailing Add:* Dept of Europ Lang Univ of Hawaii Honolulu HI 96822

NIELSON, ROSEMARY MULLIN, b Hamilton, Ohio, Oct 4, 40; m 67. LATIN & GREEK LANGUAGES & LITERATURE. *Educ:* Mt Mercy Col, BA, 62; Univ Wash, MA, 64, PhD, 67. *Prof Exp:* Teaching asst, Univ Wash, 63-65; asst prof, 66-73, ASSOC PROF CLASSICS, UNIV ALTA, 73- *Concurrent Pos:* Can Coun fel, 69-70. *Mem:* Am Philol Asn Can Class Asn. *Res:* Greek and Latin poetry and drama. *Publ:* Auth, Horace: Ode I.23 innocence, Arion, winter 70; Virgil: Eclogue I, latomus, 3/72; Alcestis: A paradox in dying, Ramus, 76. *Mailing Add:* Dept of Classics Univ Alberta Edmonton AB T6G 2E6 Can

NIEMAN, NANCY DALE, b St Paul, Minn, May 10, 39. ROMANCE LANGUAGES. *Educ:* Beloit Col, BA, 61; Middlebury Col, Vt, MA, 62; Inst Phonetique, Univ Paris, dipl, 65; Univ Madrid, Dr Philos & Lett(Span), 66; Inst Brasil-Estados Unidos, cert, 74. *Prof Exp:* Instr Span, Wayne State Col, 62-64; from instr to asst prof, Beloit Col, 64-71, assoc prof mod lang, 71-79; sr lectr, Univ Southern Calif, 79-81; PROF MOD LANG, SANTA MONICA COL, 81- *Mem:* Am Asn Teachers Span & Port; MLA; AAUP; Am Asn Advan Humanities. *Res:* Contemporary Spanish literature, especially theater and novel. *Publ:* Auth, El mundo poetico de Alejandro Casona, Rev Univ Madrid, 10/66; The festival of the dove, Beloit Daily News, 3/23/73. *Mailing Add:* Dept Spanish Santa Monica Col Santa Monica CA 90405

NIENHAUSER, WILLIAM H, JR, b St Louis, Mo, Dec 10, 43; m 61; c 2. CHINESE LITERATURE. *Educ:* Ind Univ, AB, 66, AM, 68, PhD(Chinese lang & lit), 72. *Prof Exp:* Vis asst prof Ger, Ind Univ, 72-73; asst prof, 73-79, assoc prof, 79-82, PROF CHINESE LANG & LIT, UNIV WIS, 82- *Mem:* Chinese Lang Teachers Asn; Am Orient Soc; Asn Asian Studies; MLA; Am Comp Lit Asn. *Res:* Classical language Chinese fiction; companion to traditional Chinese literature. *Publ:* Coauth, Liu Tsungyüan, Twayne, 73; ed, Critical Essays on Chinese Literature, Chinese Univ Hong Kong, 76; auth, An allegorical reading of Han Yü's Mao Ying Chuan, Oriens Extremus, 12/76; A structural reading of Chuan in the Wen-Yüan ying-hua, J Asian Studies, 5/77; Once again, the authorship of the Hsi-ching tsa-chi, J Amer Orient Soc, 78; Diction, dictionaries and the translation of classical Chinese Poetry, T'oung pao, 78; co-ed, Chinese Literature: Essays, Articles and Reviews, Coda, 1/79; auth, P'i Jih-hsiu, Twayne, 79. *Mailing Add:* Dept of E Asian Lang & Lit Univ of Wis Van Hise Hall 1216 Madison WI 53706

NIKOULIN, DILARA, b Yalta, USSR, Apr 20, 21; Can citizen; m 45; c 1. RUSSIAN LITERATURE & HISTORY. *Educ:* Univ Leningrad, BA, 37, MA, 41; Univ Montreal, MA, 62. *Prof Exp:* With Inst Med Technol, Yalta, USSR, 41-42; prof Latin & Greek, Ger & French prep schs, 43-49; lectr Russ & lit, Univ Ill, Urbana, 62-63; prof Ger & Russ lang & lit, Miami Univ, 63-69; ASSOC PROF RUSS LANG & LIT, CLARION STATE COL, 69- *Mem:* AAUP; Asn Can Univs & Cols; Am Asn Advan Slavic Studies. *Res:* New ideas in Soviet literature; Russian affricates; Dostoevsky and contemporary psychology. *Publ:* Auth, Several Articles in the Field of Medicine. *Mailing Add:* Dept of Russ Clarion State Col Clarion PA 16214

NILSEN, ALLEEN PACE, Linguistics. See Vol II

NILSEN, DON LEE FRED, Spanish Fork, Utah, Oct 19, 34; m 58; c 3. ENGLISH LINGUISTICS. *Educ:* Brigham Young Univ, BA, 58; Am Univ, MA, 61; Univ Mich, Ann Arbor, PhD(ling), 71. *Prof Exp:* Asst prof English ling, State Univ NY Oswego, 64-66; specialist compos, Teachers Col, Columbia Univ, 67-69; dir sect ling & teaching English as foreign lang, Univ Northern Iowa, 71-73; assoc prof, 73-77, PROF ENGLISH LING, ARIZ STATE UNIV, 78- *Mem:* Ling Soc Am; MLA; NCTE; Am Dialect Soc; Workshop Libr World Humour. *Res:* Componential analysis; language deviation; linguistic humor. *Publ:* Coauth, English Conversational Practices, Univ Mich, 68; auth, Toward a Semantic Specification of Deep Case, 72, English Adverbials, 72 & The Instrumental Case in English, 73, Mouton, The Hague; Pronunciation Contrasts in English, Regents, 2nd ed, 73; coauth, Semantic Theory: A Linguistic Perspective, 75 & Language Play: A Intro to Linguistics, 78, Newbury House. *Mailing Add:* 1884 E Alameda Dr Tempe AZ 85282

NILSSON, KIM G, b Helsinki, Finland, Feb 28, 39; m 62. LINGUISTICS, SCANDINAVIAN LANGUAGES. *Educ:* Ind Univ, BA, 63; Univ Wis, PhD(ling), 66. *Prof Exp:* From instr to asst prof, 65-71, assoc prof, 71-80, PROF SCAND STUDIES, UNIV WIS-MADISON, 80- *Mem:* Ling Soc Am; Soc Advan Scand Studies. *Publ:* Auth, The Development of Sibilants in Swedish, Phonetica, 65; Noun and Article in Swedish, Studia Ling, 68. *Mailing Add:* Dept of Scand Studies Univ of Wis Madison WI 53706

NILSSON, USHA SAKSENA, b Kanpur, India, Dec 24, 30; m 62. INDIAN LANGUAGE & LITERATURE, ENGLISH. *Educ:* Univ Allahabad, BA, 51, MA, 53, PhD, 56. *Prof Exp:* Lectr English, Univ Delhi, 56-59, Univ Allahabad, 59-61; comp lit, Ind Univ, Bloomington, 62-63; from asst prof to assoc prof Indian studies, 64-76, fac res fel, Am Inst Indian Studies, 65-66, PROF S ASIAN STUDIES, UNIV WIS-MADISON, 76- *Concurrent Pos:* Fulbright exchange grant, Ind Univ, Bloomington, 61-62. *Mem:* MLA; AAUP; Asn Asian Studies. *Res:* Sur Das--translations from Braj dialect of Hindu; modern Hindu fiction: a dual language reader; women in Hindu literature. *Publ:* Auth, Ek Koi Dusra (short stories), Fifty-five Columns, 61 & Radhika (novel), 67, Akshar Prakashan, New Delhi; Readings in Hindu literature, 67 & Intermediate Hindu, 67, Col Printing & Typing; Mira Bai: Life and Works and Translations, Sahilya Akademi, New Delhi, 69; Kitana Baraa Jhooth (short stories), Rajamad, New Delhi, 72. *Mailing Add:* Dept of SAsian Studies Univ of Wis Madison WI 53706

NIMETZ, MICHAEL GERSON, b New York, NY, Apr 16, 38. ROMANCE LANGUAGES. *Educ:* Oberlin Col, BA, 58; Middlbury Col, MA, 59; Yale Univ, PhD(Span), 66. *Prof Exp:* From instr to asst prof Span, Yale Univ, 62-71; asst prof, 71-76, assoc prof, 76-79, PROF SPAN, HUNTER COL, 79- *Mem:* MLA; Am Asn Teachers Span & Port. *Res:* Spanish novel of the 19th century; Spanish literature of the 20th century. *Publ:* Coauth, Novel Prize symposium: Spain & Spanish America, Bks Abroad, winter 67; auth, Humor in Galdos, Yale Univ, 68; auth, Eros and Ecclesia in Clarin's Vetusta, Mod Lang Notes, 3/71. *Mailing Add:* Dept of Romance Lang Hunter Col 695 Park Ave New York NY 10021

NIMS, CHARLES FRANCIS, b Norwalk, Ohio, Oct 19, 06; m 31. EGYPTIAN ARCHEOLOGY & PHILOLOGY. *Educ:* Alma Col, AB, 28; McCormick Theol Sem BD, 31; Univ Chicago, PhD, 37. *Prof Exp:* Res asst, Orient Inst, Chicago, 34-40; minister, First Presby Church, Eldorado, Ill, 40-43; Egyptologist, 46-48, res assoc, 48-67, from assoc prof to prof, 67-72, EMER PROF ORIENT INST, UNIV CHICAGO, 72- *Concurrent Pos:* Mem staff, McCormick Theol Sem/Am Sch Orient Res Archaeol Exped, Bethzur, Palestine, 31; mem staff, Sakkarah Exped, 34-36; mem staff epigraphic surv, Luxor, Egypt, 37-39 & 46-72, field dir, 64-72; mem staff, Univ Chicago Archaeol Exped, Tolmeita, Libya, 54, 56, 57 & 58; consult, Doc Ctr, Abu Simbel, Egypt, 56; mem, Fond Egyptol Reine Elisabeth, Ger Archaeol Inst & Am Res Ctr, Egypt. *Mem:* Asn Int l'Etude du Droit Pharaonique (hon pres); Am Orient Soc; Am Sch Orient Res; Soc Bibl Lit; Egypt Explor Soc. *Publ:* Coauth, Mastaba of Mereruka (2 vols), 38, Medinet Habu, Vols IV-VII, 40-60 & Reliefs and Inscriptions in Karnak, Vol III, 54, Univ Chicago; auth, Thebes of the Pharoahs, Stein & Day, 65; coauth, Medinet Habu, Vol VIII, Univ Chicago, 68; The Tomb of Kheruef, 80 & The Temple of Khonsul, Vol I, 79 & Vol II, 81, Orient Inst. *Mailing Add:* Orient Inst Univ of Chicago 1155 E 58th St Chicago IL 60637

NIMS, JOHN FREDERICK, English Literature. See Vol II

NISETICH, FRANK JOSEPH, b Sacramento, Calif, May 29, 42. CLASSICAL PHILOLOGY, POETRY. *Educ:* Univ Calif, Berkeley, BA, 65, MA, 67; Harvard Univ, PhD(class philol), 73. *Prof Exp:* From instr to asst prof, 71-78, fac growth grant, 77, ASSOC PROF CLASSICS, UNIV MASS, BOSTON, 78- *Concurrent Pos:* Vis asst classics, Yale Univ, 73-74. *Honors & Awards:* Translation Award, 78; Chancellor's Distinguished Scholar Award, 81. *Mem:* Am Philol Asn; Vergilian Soc. *Res:* Classical philology; ancient Greek lyric poetry. *Publ:* Auth, Olympian 1.8-11: An epinician metaphor, Harvard Studies Class Philol, 75; The leaves of triumph and mortality, Trans Am Philol Asn, 77; Convention and occasion in Isthm.2, Calif Studies in Class Antiquity, 77; Pindar's Victory Songs, Johns Hopkins Univ, 80. *Mailing Add:* Dept of Classics Harbor Campus Univ of Mass Boston MA 02125

NITTI, JOHN JOSEPH, b Yonkers, NY, Oct 28, 43; m 66; c 2. SPANISH & PORTUGUESE LANGUAGE & LITERATURE. *Educ:* Univ Va, BA, 65, MA, 67; Univ Wis, PhD(Span & Port), 72. *Prof Exp:* PROJ ASSOC, SEM MEDIEVAL SPAN STUDIES, UNIV WIS-MADISON, 72-, ASST PROF SPAN, 74- *Concurrent Pos:* Managing ed, Luso-Brazilian Rev, 72-; mem comput adv comt, Nat Endowment for Humanities, grant. *Mem:* Am Asn Teachers Span & Port; MLA; Medieval Acad Am. *Res:* Medieval Spanish language and literature; Romance philology; dictionary of Old Spanish language. *Publ:* Auth, 201 Portuguese Verbs, Barron's Educ Ser, 68; coauth, Bibliography of Old Spanish Texts, 77, Concordances and Text of Alfonso X, The Wise (in press), Edition and study of the Aragonese Version of the Book of Marco Polo (in press), Hispanic Sem Medieval Studies, Ltd. *Mailing Add:* Sem Medieval Span Studies Univ of Wis Madison WI 53706

NITZSCHE, JANE CHANCE, English, Medieval Literature. See Vol II

NIWA, TAMAKO, b Berkeley, Calif, Nov 6, 22. JAPANESE LANGUAGE. *Educ:* Radcliffe Col, BS, 44, MA, 46, PhD(Japanese lit & hist), 56. *Prof Exp:* Prog staff, Int House Japan, Tokyo, 55-56; sci linguist Japanese lang, Am Embassy, Tokyo, 56-62; from asst prof to assoc prof, 62-77, PROF JAPANESE LANG, UNIV WASH, 77- *Concurrent Pos:* US Dept Health, Educ & Welfare studies grant, 65-66. *Res:* Asn Teachers Japanese. *Publ:* Coauth, Basic Japanese for College Students, Univ Wash, 64; auth, Adaptation of Kanjincho and The Zen Substitute, French, 66; First Course in Japanese, Univ Wash, 71. *Mailing Add:* 3363 W Commodore Way Seattle WA 98199

NIXON, RUTH A, Ft Dodge, Iowa, Aug 27, 15; m 50. ROMANCE LANGUAGES, EDUCATION. *Educ:* Univ Minn, BS, 37; Univ Iowa, MA, 44; Fla State Univ, PhD(foreign lang educ), 68. *Prof Exp:* Teacher High Schs, Iowa, 37-43; teacher jr high sch, Mich, 43-45; instr French & Span, Wis State Teachers Col, La Crosse, 45-46; instr, Albion Col, 46-47; assoc prof, 47-68, PROF SPAN, UNIV WIS, LA CROSSE, 68-, CHMN DEPT FOREIGN LANG, 66- *Concurrent Pos:* Area rep & mem adv coun, Am Coun Teaching Foreign Lang, 69- *Mem:* Am Asn Teachers Span & Port. *Res:* Foreign language education. *Mailing Add:* Dept of Foreign Lang Univ Wis La Crosse WI 54601

NIYEKAWA, AGNES MITSUE, b Tokyo, Japan, May 9, 24; US citizen; m 54, 66; c 2. PSYCHOLINGUISTICS, JAPANESE LINGUISTICS. *Educ:* Tokyo Woman's Col, BA, 45; Univ Hawaii, BA, 52; Bryn Mawr Col, MA, 54; NY Univ, PhD(social psychol), 60. *Prof Exp:* Res assoc social psychol, res ctr human relat, NY Univ, 59-61; US Pub Health Serv fel psycholing, NY State Psychiat Inst, 61-63; asst prof educ psychol, Univ Hawaii, 64-67; assoc prof psychol in educ, Northeastern Univ, 68-69; sr specialist, Inst Advan Proj, East-West Ctr, 69-70; researcher & coordr, East-West Cult Learning Inst, 70-71; prof human develop, 71-73, chmn dept E Asian Lang, 73-81, PROF JAPANESE, UNIV HAWAII, MANOA, 73- *Concurrent Pos:* Vis scholar ling, Columbia Univ, 61-63; US Off Educ res grant on second lang learning, 65-67; consult, int English comt, Int Eval Educ Achievement Proj, Stockholm, 66-; Am Coun Learned Soc fac res grant, Mass Inst Technol, 67-68; Nat Inst Ment Health res grant on lang & thought, 68-70; consult, dept of educ, Am Samoa, 72; Fulbright res grant, Japan, 81-82. *Mem:* Am Psychol Asn; Asn Asian Studies; Ling Soc Am; Japanese Psychol Asn; Am Asn Teachers Japanese. *Res:* Language and cognitive processes; second language and culture learning: methodology in cross-cultural and language research. *Publ:* Auth, Authoritarianism in an authoritarian culture, Int J Social Psychiat, 66; A Study of Second Language Learning, US Off Educ, 68; Biculturality and cognitive growth: theoretical foundations for basic and applied research, East-West Ctr, 70; coauth, Passivization, In: Syntax and Semantics, V: Japanese Generative Grammar, Academic, 76; Cross-Cultural Learning and Self-Growth: Getting to Know Ourselves and Others, Inst Asn Schs Social Work, 77. *Mailing Add:* Dept of E Asian Lang Univ Hawaii Manoa Honolulu HI 96822

NOAKES, SUSAN JEANNE, b 1945; US citizen. MEDIEVAL & RENAISSANCE LITERATURE. *Educ:* Univ Chicago, AB, 67; Yale Univ, MPhil, 72, PhD(comp lit), 75. *Prof Exp:* Actg instr Italian & comp lit, Yale Univ, 73-74; asst prof romance & comp lit, Univ Chicago, 74-81; ASST PROF FRENCH & ITALIAN, UNIV KANS, 81- *Mem:* MLA; Medieval Acad Am; Dante Soc Am; Am Boccaccio Asn; Am Asn Univ Professors of Italian. *Res:* Dante; history of reading and reading education; hermeneutic theory. *Publ:* Auth, Dino Compagni and the vow in San Giovanni: Inferno XIX, Dante Studies, 68; The fifteen Oes, the Disticha Catonis, Marculfius and Dick, Jane and Sally, Univ Chicago Libr Soc Bull, 77; Self-reading and temporal irony in Aurelia, Studies in Romanticism, 77; The development of the book market in late Quattrocento Italy, J Medieval and Renaissance Studies, 81; An English translation of Emilio Betti's Teoria Generale Della Interpretazione, Mod Lang Studies, 82; Hermeneutics and semiotics: Betti's Debt to Peirce, Proc Semiotic Soc of Am, 83; The double misreading of Paolo and Francesca, Philol Quart, 83; Dante's Vista Nova: Paradiso XXXIII, Quaderni d'Italianistico, 83. *Mailing Add:* 1412 E 54th Pl Chicago IL 60615

NOAKES, WARREN DAVID, b Hunter Twp, Nebr, July 31, 25. FRENCH LANGUAGE & LITERATURE. *Educ:* Harvard Col, AB, 49; NY Univ, MA, 56, PhD(French), 63. *Prof Exp:* Tutor French, Queens Col, NY, 56-58; lectr English, Univ Paris, 58-59; instr, Ecole de Guerre, 59-60; instr French, Smith Col, 60-62; instr, Columbia Col, Columbia Univ, 62-67; ASSOC PROF FRENCH & DIR LA MAISON FRANCAISE, NY UNIV, 67- *Concurrent Pos:* Fulbright student grant, France, 50-51. *Honors & Awards:* Officier dans l'Ordre des Palmes Academiques, French Govt, 78. *Mem:* Am Asn Teachers Fr; PEN club. *Res:* History of Racine criticism; exchanges between writers and composers in France between 1913 and 1939; trends in French literature since the Second World War. *Publ:* Translr, Jazz: Its Evolution and Essence, Grove, 56; Sweet confessions, Evergreen Rev, 57; The Brain, Grove, 62; auth, Boris Vian, Ed Univ, Paris, 64; coauth, Prevert Vous Parle, Prentice-Hall, 68; Raymond Radiguet, Seghers, Paris, 68. *Mailing Add:* 100 Bleecker St 16-E New York NY 10012

NOBLE, BETH WILSON, b New Haven, Conn, Aug 27, 18. MODERN FOREIGN LANGUAGES. *Educ:* Albertus Magnus Col, BA, 39; Yale Univ, MA, 41, PhD(Romance lang), 48; Ind Univ, cert Russ, 60. *Prof Exp:* Instr Span & Port, Mary Washington Col, 42-43; sr translr, cent translating div, US Dept State, 43-45; instr Span, Smith Col, 45-47; instr, Univ Kans, 47-49; from asst prof to assoc prof mod foreign lang, 49-58; dir Russ prog, 61-67, chmn dept Span, 62-64, 66-67, 68-72, 74-75, 76-77, PROF SPAN, GRINNELL COL, 58- *Concurrent Pos:* Danforth Found studies & travel grant, USSR, 60; Ford Found studies & travel grant, Spain, 73. *Mem:* MLA (regional del, assembly, 71-75). *Res:* Literature in translation, Russian, Spanish; 19th and 20th century drama and novel of Spain; 20th century novel of Latin America. *Publ:* Co-ed, Una Vuida Dificil, Norton; auth, The descriptive genius of Perez de Ayala in La caida de los Limones & Sound in the plays of Buero Vallejo, 58, Hispania; After the storm, Asn Dept Foreign Lang Bull, 9/71. *Mailing Add:* 1527 Summer St Grinnell IA 50112

NOBLE, FRANCES E, b Chicago, Ill, Sept 3, 03. FOREIGN LANGUAGES. *Educ:* Northwestern Univ, BA, 24, MA, 26, PhD, 45. *Prof Exp:* From assoc prof to prof, 31-73, EMER PROF FRENCH, WESTERN MICH UNIV, 73- *Honors & Awards:* Palmes Academiques, 56. *Mem:* Am Asn Teachers Fr. *Res:* Nineteenth century French literature. *Publ:* Auth, Les Idees politiques d'Alfred de Musset, Northwestern Press, 45; Destiny's Daughter, Tower Publ, 80. *Mailing Add:* Dept of Lang Western Mich Univ Kalamazoo MI 49008

NOBLE, GLADWYN KINGSLEY, JR, b New York, NY, Nov 10, 23; m 69; c 1. ANTHROPOLOGY, LINGUISTICS. *Educ:* Washington & Lee Univ, BA, 48; Northwestern Univ, MA, 53; Columbia Univ, PhD(anthrop), 61. *Prof Exp:* Asst prof, 63-67, ASSOC PROF ANTHROP, SAN JOSE STATE UNIV, 67- *Mem:* AAAS; fel Am Anthrop Asn. *Res:* South American Indian language history. *Publ:* Auth, Proto-Arawaken and Its Descendants, Mouton, The Hague, 65. *Mailing Add:* Dept of Anthrop San Jose State Univ San Jose CA 95192

NOBLE, SHLOMO, b Sanok, Poland, July 5, 05; m 27; c 1. GERMANIC & YIDDISH PHILOLOGY. *Educ:* St Thomas Col, AB, 29; Ohio State Univ, PhD, 39. *Prof Exp:* Asst to dir res, Yiddish Sci Inst, 44-49; vis prof Jewish lit & hist, Univ Judaism, 49-50; SECY COMN RES, YIVO INST JEWISH RES, 50-, VCHMN COMN RES & TRAINING, 80- *Concurrent Pos:* Prof hist, Jewish Teachers Sem, 64- *Res:* Mediaeval Hebrew literature. *Publ:* Auth, The Image of the American Jew in Hebrew and Yiddish Literature in America, 1870-1900, Yivo Ann of Jewish Soc Sci, 55; Hebraisms in the Yiddish of 17th Century Central Ashkenaz, For Max Weinreich on his 70th Birthday, 64; The Jewish Woman in Medieval Martyrology, Studies in Jewish Bibliography, History and Literature in Honor of I Edward Kiev, 71; coauth (with Joshua Fishman), History of the Yiddish Language (2 vols), Univ Chicago Press, 80. *Mailing Add:* 3415 Corlear Ave Bronx NY 10463

NOBLITT, JAMES STARKEY, b Baltimore, Md, Aug 13, 35; c 2. ROMANCE LANGUAGES. *Educ:* Univ Va, BA, 57, MA, 63; Harvard Univ, PhD(French ling), 68. *Prof Exp:* Linguist French, Ctr Appl Ling, Washington, DC, 65-67; asst prof, 67-72, assoc prof, 72-79, PROF LING, CORNELL UNIV, 79- *Concurrent Pos:* Vis assoc prof Romance lang & lit, Harvard Univ, 73-74; Nat Adv Bd, ERIC Clearinghouse Lang & Lit, 77-80; rev ed appl ling, Mod Lang J, 78-79. *Mem:* Ling Soc Am; Am Asn Appl Ling. *Res:* Medieval French; second language acquisition. *Publ:* Auth, Pedagogical grammar, Int Rev Appl Ling, 72; Pacing and systemization, Mod Lang J, 75; Nouveau Point de Vue, Heath, 78. *Mailing Add:* Dept Mod Lang & Ling Cornell Univ Ithaca NY 14853

NOCE, HANNIBAL SERGIO, b Italy, Dec 11, 15; US citizen. ITALIAN LANGUAGE & LITERATURE. *Educ:* Univ Calif, Berkeley, AB, 40, MA, 41, PhD, 51. *Prof Exp:* Lectr Ital, Univ Calif, Berkeley, 51-52; instr, Univ Chicago, 52-54; from asst prof to assoc prof, 55-66, PROF ITAL, UNIV TORONTO, 66- *Mem:* Am Asn Teachers Ital; Dante Soc Am; Renaissance Soc Am; MLA. *Res:* Italian literature of the 17th and 18th century. *Publ:* Auth, Lettere di PJ Martello a La Muratori, Aedes Muratoriana, Modena, Italy, 55; Scritti Critici e Satirici di PJ Martello, Bari, Laterza, Italy, 63; P J Martello: Teatro (3 vols), Bari, Laterza, 80-82. *Mailing Add:* Dept of Ital Studies Univ Toronto Toronto ON M5S 1A1 Can

NOETHER, ROGER E, Chinese History & Literature. See Vol I

NOLAN, BARBARA, English. See Vol II

NOLAN, PHILIP JEROME, b Kennedy, NY, Dec 20, 16; m 45. CLASSICS, COMPARATIVE LITERATURE. *Educ:* Cornell Univ, AB, 38, MA, 39, PhD, 53. *Prof Exp:* Instr English, Cornell Univ, 42-43; instr, Marquette Univ, 44-50; asst prof class lang & lit & English, 53-54, from asst prof to assoc prof, 55-64, chmn dept, 59-77, PROF CLASSICS, UNIV OKLA, 64-, DIR LETT, 55-, CUR CLASS ART & ARCHAEOL, 67- *Concurrent Pos:* Mem adv coun, Am Sch Class Studies, Athens & Am Acad Rome, 58- *Mem:* Am Philol Asn; Class Asn Am; Renaissance Soc Am; Class Asn Mid W & S; Am Class League. *Res:* Classical tradition in European literature; ancient criticism and rhetoric; Platonism in the French Renaissance. *Mailing Add:* Dept of Classics Univ Okla Norman OK 73019

NOLAN, WILLIAM JOSEPH, b Philadelphia, Pa, Mar 12, 23; m 50; c 1. ROMANCE LANGUAGES. *Educ:* Univ Kans, BS, 58, MA, 61, PhD(educ), 68. *Prof Exp:* Teacher jr high sch, Kans, 59-62; teacher, Col Bolivar, Colombia, 62-63; teacher jr high sch, Kans, 63-65; instr Span & educ, Univ Kans, 65-68; from asst prof to assoc prof, 68-75, PROF SPAN & EDUC, WESTERN KY UNIV, 75-, DIR INT EXCHANGE & STUDENT AFFAIRS, 78- *Concurrent Pos:* Chmn, Latin Am Studies Comt, 70-74; consult, Univ Indust de Santander, Colombia, 74. *Mem:* Am Asn Teachers Span & Port; Am Coun Teaching Foreign Lang. *Res:* Romance languages; Latin American education. *Publ:* Coauth, Teaching Foreign Languages in the Elementary Schools, Univ Kans, 67; Castellanizacion in Guatemala, Lang Today, 5/74; Test as a Teaching Device, Foreign Lang Ann, 9/77. *Mailing Add:* Dept of Foreign Lang Western Ky Univ Bowling Green KY 42101

NOLLENDORFS, VALTERS, b Riga, Latvia, Mar 22, 31; US citizen; m 55, 67; c 6. GERMAN & LATVIAN LITERATURE. *Educ:* Univ Nebr, BSc in Ed, 54, MA, 55; Univ Mich, PhD, 62. *Prof Exp:* Teaching asst, Univ Nebr, 54-55; instr Ger, Univ Mich 59-61; from instr to assoc prof, 61-74, PROF GER, UNIV WIS, MADISON, 74-, CHMN DEPT, 75- *Concurrent Pos:* Ed, Monatshefte, 72-; mem exec bd, Asn Advan Baltic Studies, 74, pres, 76-78; mem exec comt, div 18th & early 19th century Ger Lit, MLA. *Mem:* MLA; Am Asn Teachers Ger; Asn Advan Baltic Studies. *Res:* Age of Goethe; Goethe's Faust; contemporary Latvian literature. *Publ:* Auth, Der Steit um den Urfaust, Mouton, The Hague, 67; The rite of life: A theme and its variations in the poetry of Soviet Latvia, Mosaic, 73; Time and experience in Goethe's Trilogie der Leidenschaft, In: Husbanding the Golden Grain, Studies in Honor of Henry Nordmeyer, Ann Arbor, 73; The demythologization of Latvian literature, Books Abroad, 73; Partial rhyme in contemporary Latvian poetry, Baltic Lit & Ling, 73; The voices of one calling: The mastering of the Latvian legacy in Bels and Rungis, J Baltic Studies, 75; co-ed, Ger Studies in the United States: Assessment and Outlook, Univ Wis, 76; auth, Latvian literature, In: Reader's Adviser, Bowker, 77. *Mailing Add:* Dept of Ger Univ of Wis Madison WI 53706

NORBU, THUBTEN JIGME, b Tsongon, Tibet, Aug 16, 22, US citizen; m 60; c 3. TIBETAN LANGUAGE & CULTURE. *Educ:* Kumbum Monastery, Tibet, Dutra, 40; Drepung Monastery, Tibet, Pharchin, 44. *Prof Exp:* Abbot, Kumbum Monastery, 48-50; instr, Univ Wash, 59-60; cur Tibetan collection, Mus Natural Hist, New York, 61-65; ASSOC PROF URALIC & ALTAIC STUDIES, IND UNIV, BLOOMINGTON, 65- *Mem:* Hon mem Explorers Club; Mongolian Soc; Tibet Soc. *Publ:* Coauth, Tibet is My Country, Dutton, 59; Tibet, Simon & Schuster, 68, The Younger Brother Don Yod, 69 & translr, Tibetan Buddhist Chant, W Kaufmann, 75, Ind Univ, Bloomington. *Mailing Add:* Dept of Uralic & Altaic Studies Ind Univ Bloomington IN 47401

NORDEN, ERNEST ELWOOD, b Chicago, Ill, July 11, 38; m 63; c 2. ROMANCE LANGUAGES. *Educ:* Purdue Univ, BS, 61; Univ Ore, MA, 63; Univ Calif, Berkeley, PhD(Romance lang), 74. *Prof Exp:* Teacher Span, John F Kennedy High Sch, Calif, 67-69; asst prof Span, Univ Colo, 69-71; asst prof Romance lang, Northeast La Univ, 71-75; chmn, 80-82, PROF SPAN, BAYLOR UNIV, 75-, DIR, 77- *Concurrent Pos:* Fulbright lectr Am Studies, Univ Seville, Spain, 72-73. *Mem:* Am Asn Teachers Span & Port; MLA; SCent Mod Lang Asn. *Res:* Nineteenth-century peninsular Spanish literature; twentieth-century peninsular Spanish literature; literary stylistics. *Publ:* Auth, Elementos estilisticos del Corpus de Gabriel Miro, Explicacion de Textos Literarios, 9/77; The father figure in the romances of Chretien de Troyes, South Central Bull, 38: 155-157; Celestial imagery in Gabriel Miro's Dentro del cercado, J Span Studies: Twentieth Century, 7: 73-86; Trends in Gabriel Miro's style revealed by his revision of La Senora, los suyos y los otros, Soc Span and Span-Am Studies, 79; An individualized course on the generation of 1898, In: Directory of Teaching Innovations in Foreign Lanuages, Studies in Higher Educ, 81. *Mailing Add:* Div Span & Port Baylor Univ Waco TX 76798

NORDMEYER, GEORGE, b Burgoerner, Ger, Jan 11, 12; nat US; m 35; c 2. GERMANIC LINGUISTICS. *Educ:* Yale Univ, PhD, 34. *Prof Exp:* Res asst, Yale Univ, 32-34, Sterling res fel, 34-35; from instr to asst prof Ger, WVA Univ, 35-39; from instr to assoc prof, Yale Univ, 39-62; prof, 62-77, chmn dept, 65-77, EMER PROF GER, HUNTER COL, 77- *Concurrent Pos:* Vis prof, NY Univ, 66. *Mem:* MLA; Ling Soc Am; Am Asn Teachers Ger. *Res:* German philology; Old High and Middle High German. *Publ:* Auth, Martin Luther's Jugendjahre, 37 & Werden und Wesen der Deutschen Sprache, 39, Farrar & Rhinehart; coauth, Deutsche Kulturepochen, Prentice, 49. *Mailing Add:* 501 Forest Ave #710 Palo Alto CA 94301

NORIEGA, TEOBALDO ALBERTO, b Colombia, Dec 29, 44; Can citizen. SPANISH AMERICAN & LATIN AMERICAN LITERATURE. *Educ:* Univ Pedagogica de Colombia, Licenciado, 67; Univ Alta, MA, 72, PhD(Hisp lit), 79. *Prof Exp:* ASST PROF SPAN AM LIT, TRENT UNIV, 77- *Mem:* Asoc Can Hisp; Can Asn Latin Am & Caribbean Studies; Am Asn Teachers Span & Port. *Res:* Latin American contemporary fiction; emphasis in the areas of Brazil and Spanish Caribbean. *Publ:* Auth, Musicalizacion narrativa en El compadre, de Carlos Droguett, Cuadernos Hispanoam, 82; Literatura y realidad: El compromiso latinoamericano, Cadernos de Lit, 82; Narrador, tiempo y realidad en Patas de perro de C Droguett, Rev Can Estudios Hisp, 82; La muerte como tema en la novela mexicana contemproanea, Mayurqa, 82. *Mailing Add:* Hisp Studies Trent Univ Peterborough ON K9J 7B8 Can

NORKELIUNAS, CASIMIR JOHN, b Kybartai, Lithuania, Mar 2, 37; m 63; c 3. SLAVIC LITERATURES. *Educ:* Univ Bridgeport, BA, 60; Fordham Univ, MA, 62; NY Univ, PhD(slavic lang & lit), 78. *Prof Exp:* Chmn, Dept Foreign Lang, 72-81, ASST PROF RUSS & GER, DEPT MOD LANG, MARIST COL, 63- *Mem:* Am Asn Teachers Slavic & Eastern Europ Lang. *Res:* Russian symbolism; 20th century Lithuanian poetry; Jurgis Baltrusaitis, Lithuanian-Russian poet symbolist. *Publ:* Auth, Silence and the inexpressible in the poetry of Jurgis Baltrusaitis, 79 & Baltrusaitis as rescuer of fellow artists from Lenin's and Stalin's terror, 82, Proc Inst Lithuanian Studies. *Mailing Add:* 63 Fuller Lane Hyde Park NY 12538

NORLAND, HOWARD BERNETT, English. See Vol II

NORMAN, GEORGE BUFORD, JR, b Columbus, Miss, July 26, 45. FRENCH LITERATURE, MUSICOLOGY. *Educ:* Davidson Col, AB, 67; Yale Univ, MPhil, 70, PhD(French), 71. *Prof Exp:* Asst prof foreign lang, Iowa State Univ, 71-75, assoc prof French, 75-80; ASSOC PROF FRENCH, UNIV SC, 80- *Mem:* MLA; Am Asn Teachers Fr; NAm Soc 17th Century Fr Lit. *Res:* Seventeenth century French literature; 17th and 18th century French music. *Publ:* Auth, Thought and language in Pascal, Yale Fr Studies, 73; Logic and anti-rhetoric in Pascal's Pensees, Fr Forum 2, 77; Cyrano and Pascal: A similarity of method, L'Esprit Createur, Vol 18, 79; L'Idee de regle chez Pascal, In: Methods chez Pascal, PUF, 79; The theme of names and its relationship to Racinian Tragedy, Vol 12, 79 & 80 & Knowledge, meaning and style in variants of La Rochefoucauld's Maximes, Vol 4, No 1, 81, PFSCL; Nicole's Essais de Morale: Logic and Persuasion, In: French Literature Series, Univ SC, 82; Editing and Interpreting Fragmentary Texts: A Justification of Pascal's Text, MSL 527-Br 40, Soc Textual Scholar, 82. *Mailing Add:* Dept Foreign Lang & Lit Iowa State Univ Columbia SC 29208

NORMAN, ISABEL H, b Carolina, PR; m 54. SPANISH, PORTUGUESE. *Educ:* Hunter Col, BA, 58; Columbia Univ, MA, 60; Yale Univ, PhD(Span), 66. *Prof Exp:* Lectr Span, Yale Univ, 61-63, Columbia Univ, 63-65 & Hunter Col, 65-66; asst prof, St John's Univ, NY, 66-68; assoc prof, 68-77, PROF SPAN, QUEENSBOROUGH COMMUNITY COL, 77- *Mem:* Hisp Inst US; MLA. *Res:* Anthropology; photography. *Publ:* Auth, Miguel Antonio Caro: vida y obra, Inst Caro y Cuervo, Columbia, 68; La novela romantica en la Antillas, Ateneo Puertorriqueno NY, 69. *Mailing Add:* 56 Seventh Ave New York NY 10011

NORMAN, JERRY, b Watsonville, Calif, July 16, 36; m 68. CHINESE LINGUISTICS. *Educ:* Univ Calif, Berkeley, BA, 61, MA, 65, PhD(Orient lang), 69. *Prof Exp:* Lectr ling, Nat Taiwan Univ, 66-67; lectr Chinese & staff linguist, Chinese ling proj, Princeton Univ, 67-69, asst prof & assoc dir, 69-71; asst prof, 71-74, assoc prof, 74-80, PROF CHINESE, UNIV WASH, 80- *Concurrent Pos:* Nat Endowment for Humanities jr fel, 71-72; Guggenheim fel, 81. *Mem:* Am Orient Soc. *Res:* Chinese and Altaic linguistics. *Publ:* Auth, Tonal Development in Min, J Chinese Ling, 1: 222-238; A Sketch of Sibe Morphology, Cent Asiatic J, 18: 159-174; coauth (with T L Mei), The Austroasiatics in Ancient South China: Some Lexical Evidence, Monumenta Serica, 32: 274-301; auth, A Concise Manchu-English Lexicon, Univ Washington Press, 78; Chronological Strata in the Min Dialects, Fangyan, 4: 268-273. *Mailing Add:* Dept of Asian Lang & Lit Gowen Hall DO-21 Univ Wash Seattle WA 98195

NORMAND, GUESSLER, b Feb 24, 37; US citizen. FRENCH LITERATURE, FOREIGN LANGUAGE EDUCATION. *Educ:* Southern Univ, BA, 61; Univ Aix-Marseille, dipl Fr, 63; Univ Ky, MA, 67, PhD(French), 70. *Prof Exp:* Instr French, Southern Univ, 61-62 & 63-64, Univ Akron, 68-70; ASST PROF FRENCH, UNIV TOLEDO, 70- *Concurrent Pos:* Fac res fel, Univ Toldeo, summer, 79. *Mem:* An Asn Teachers Fr; AAUP; Am Coun Teaching Foreign Lang. *Res:* Twentieth century French literature; the literature of commitment. *Publ:* Henri Barbusse and his Monde (1928-1935): Progeny of the Clarte Movement and the Rev Clarte, J Contemp Hist, 7/76; Henri Barbusse and his Monde (1928-1935): Precursors to the Litterature Engagee Movement, Ky Romance Quart, Vol XXIV, No 4, 449-460; Meeting individual needs in the college foreign language classroom, Foreign Lang Ann, 2/79; Toward better articulation between high school and college foreign language teachers, ADFL Bull, 3/80; Motivating with media: The use of video in the foreign language classroom, Can Mod Lang Rev, 10/80. *Mailing Add:* 3414 Drummond Rd Toledo OH 43606

NORRIS, FRANK PELLETIER, b Sioux City, Iowa, May 11, 38; m 61. MEDIEVAL ROMANCE LITERATURE. *Educ:* Davidson Col, BA, 60; Univ Calif, Los Angeles, PhD(Romance lang & lit), 65. *Prof Exp:* Asst prof, 65-68, ASSOC PROF ROMANCE LANG, UNIV MIAMI, 68- *Mem:* MLA; Mediaeval Acad Am; Soc Rencesvals; Int Courtly Lit Soc; Southeastern Medieval Asn. *Res:* Medieval Romance literature; the legend of Troy. *Publ:* Auth, La Coronica Troyana: A Medieval Spanish Translation of Guido de Colonna's Historia Destructionis Troiae, Univ NC, 70; Notes on the first Castilian translation of Guido de Colonna's Historia Destructionis Troiae, Vol XIV, No 1 & Mariana and the classical tradition of statecraft, Vol XXIV, No 4, Ky Romance Quart. *Mailing Add:* Dept of Foreign Lang Univ Miami Coral Gables FL 33124

NORRIS, WILLIAM EDWARD, b Oak Park, Ill, Dec 24, 26; m 66; c 3. APPLIED LINGUISTICS, ENGLISH AS A FOREIGN LANGUAGE. *Educ:* Northwestern Univ, Evanston, BS, 50; Univ Mich, Ann Arbor, AM, 57. *Prof Exp:* Instr English, Int Col, Am Univ Beirut, 51-54; Fulbright teacher ling & English lang, Tokyo Univ Educ, 57-58; lectr English as foreign lang, Univ Mich, Ann Arbor, 58-66; asst prof ling, Univ Pittsburgh, 66-73; ASST PROF ENGLISH AS FOREIGN LANG & HEAD DEPT, GEORGETOWN UNIV, 73- *Concurrent Pos:* Mem exec comt, Teachers English to Speakers Other Lang, 69-70 & 77-80; Am specialist grant, Dept State, 76. *Mem:* Teachers English to Speakers Other Lang (vpres, 68-69); Am Coun Teaching Foreign Lang; Asn Teachers English as Second Lang; Nat Asn Foreign Student Affairs. *Res:* Applied linguistics in language teaching. *Publ:* Coauth, Teaching second language reading at the advanced level: Goals, techniques and procedures, TESOL Quart, 70; co-ed, Guidelines for certification and preparation of teachers of ESOL, 72 & On TESOL 74, 75, Teachers English Speakers Other Lang; coauth, English for Today (bks 4 & 5), McGraw, 75 & 76; Language Teaching Methodology: A Return to the Social Context, RELC, 82; Techniques in Teaching Reading, Oxford Univ Press, 82. *Mailing Add:* Div of English as Foreign Lang Sch of Lang & Ling, Georgetown Univ Washington DC 20057

NORTH, HELEN FLORENCE, b Utica, NY, Jan 31, 21. CLASSICAL LITERATURE, RHETORIC. *Educ:* Cornell Univ, AB, 42, AM, 43, PhD(classics), 45. *Prof Exp:* Sibley fel, 45-46; instr class lang, Rosary Col, 46-48; asst prof Greek & Latin, 48-53, assoc prof, 53-62, William J Kenan prof, 73-78, PROF CLASSICS, SWARTHMORE COL, 62-, CHMN DEPT, 59-, CENTENNIAL PROF, 78- *Concurrent Pos:* Ford & Fulbright fels, Rome, 53-54; vis assoc prof, Barnard Col, Columbia Univ, 54-55; Guggenheim fel, Rome, 58-59; secy adv coun, Sch Class Studies, Am Acad Rome, 60-62 & 64, mem bd trustees, 72-75 & 77-79; Asn Univ Women res fel, Rome, 62-63; Nat Endowment for Humanities sr fel, Rome, 67-68; chmn, Cath Comn on Intellectual & Cult Affairs, 68-69; mem bd dir, King's Col, Pa, 69-71 & 73-75; Am Coun Learned Soc fel, Rome, 71-72; Martin class lectr, Oberlin Col, 72; mem bd trustees, La Salle Col, 73-; Guggenheim fel, 75-76. *Honors & Awards:* Harbison Teaching Prize, Danforth Found, 69; Charles A Goodwin Award for Sophrosyne, Am Philol Asn, 69. *Mem:* Am Philol Asn (2nd vpres, 74, pres, 76); Class Asn Atlantic States; Class Soc Am Acad Rome (pres, 60-61); AAAS. *Res:* Concept of Sophrosyne in Greek literature; Plato's rhetoric; Roman rhetoric. *Publ:* Auth, Milton's second defence of the English people, In: Vol IV, Complete Prose Works of John Milton, Yale Univ, 66; Sophrosyne: Self-Knowledge and Self-Restraint in Greek Literature, 66 & co-ed, Of Eloquence; Studies in Ancient and Mediaeval Rhetoric, 70, Cornell Univ; ed, Interpretations of Plato: A Swarthmore Symposium, Brill, 77; auth, The yoke of necessity: Aulis and beyond, Class World, 77; From Myth to Icon, Cornell Univ, 79. *Mailing Add:* 604 Ogden Ave Swarthmore PA 19081

NORTH, ROBERT, Biblical Archeology. See Vol IV

NORTHCOTT, KENNETH J, b London, England, Nov 25, 22; m 50, 80; c 4. OLDER GERMAN LITERATURE. *Educ:* Univ London, BAG 50, MA,53. *Prof Exp:* Tutorial asst Ger, King's Col, Univ London, 50-52; asst, Univ Glasgow, 52-53; lectr, Univ Sheffield, 53-61; assoc prof older Ger lang & lit, 61-65, prof, 65-73, dean students div humanities, 66-68, chmn dept Ger lang & lit, 69-78, actg chmn dept comp studies lit, 77-78, PROF COMP LIT, UNIV CHICAGO, 73- *Concurrent Pos:* Sir Ernest Cassell res fel, 57; vis asst prof, Univ Chicago, 58-59; mem, Conf Teachers Ger, Univ Gt Brit & Ireland; chmn bd gov, Inst Europ Studies, 67-; vis prof, Univ Toronto, 80 & Univ Freiburg, 79. *Mem:* Midwestern Mod Lang Asn (pres, 71-73); MLA; Am Asn Teachers Ger; Medieval Acad Am; Brit Asn Univ Teachers. *Res:* Medieval German epic and lyric poetry; mediaeval and early Renaissance rhetoric; early German drama. *Publ:* Ed, German Literary Classics in Translation, 72- & translr, Minna von Barnhelm (Lessing), 73, Univ Chicago; auth, Verhalten und Ansehen im Nibelunglied, In: Wege und Forschung, Nibelungenlied und Kudrun, Darmstadt, 73; ed, A Literary History of Germany, Croom Helm, 75-; transl, The Prologue to Wolfram's Parzival: Again, Festschrift 0 Springer, 79; Watther von der Vogehreide, Scribner's, 82; The Sociology of Art, A Hauser, 82. *Mailing Add:* Dept of Ger Lang Univ Chicago 1050 E 59th St Chicago IL 60637

NORTHEY, ANTHONY DROSTE, b Washington, DC, Oct 29, 42; m 64; c 2. GERMAN. *Educ:* McGill Univ, BA Hons, 65, PhD(Ger), 74; Queen's Univ, MA, 69. *Prof Exp:* Lectr, 70-75, asst prof, 75-80, ASSOC PROF GER, ACADIA UNIV, 80- *Concurrent Pos:* Can Coun res grant Ger, 76-77 & 77-78. *Mem:* Can Asn Univ Teachers Ger; MLA; Kafka Soc Am. *Res:* Biography of Franz Kafka; methods of teaching German as a foreign language. *Publ:* coauth, Fremdsprache in Handlungszusammenhängen gelernt, Zielsprache Deutsch, 77; auth, The American cousins and the Prager Asbestwerke, In: The Kafka Debate, 77; Franz Kafkas Verbindung zu Amerika, In: Franz Kafka Symposium, 78; Dr Kafka in Gablonz, Mod Lang Notes, 78; Unbefugte Kafka-Nachdrucke, Mod Lang Notes, 79; Berufliche Schriften, In: Kafka-Handbuch, Vol II, 80; Irma Kafka, Germanic Notes, 80; Robert Kafka, Newsletter of the Kafka-Society of America, 80. *Mailing Add:* Acadia Univ Box 272 Wolfville NS B0P 1X0 Can

NORTON, GLYN PETER, b Exeter, Eng, May 22, 41; US citizen; m 66. ROMANCE LANGUAGES, FRENCH RENAISSANCE. *Educ:* Univ Mich, BA, 63, MA, 65 PhD(French lit), 68. *Prof Exp:* Asst prof French & comp lit Renaissance, Dartmouth Col, 68-71; asst prof 16th century French lit, 71-73, fac fel, Inst Arts & Humanistic Studies, fall 73, ASSOC PROF 16TH CENTURY FRENCH LIT, PA STATE UNIV, 73- *Concurrent Pos:* Nat Endowment for Humanities fel, 73-74; Camargo Found fel, 79-80; Am Counc Learned Soc grant, 79-80. *Mem:* MLA; Renaissance Soc Am; Am Asn Teachers Fr. *Res:* Franco-Italian literary relations of the Renaissance; 16th century French literature; French Renaissance translation. *Publ:* Auth, De trois commerces and Montaigne's Populous solitude, Fr Rev, 71; Laurent de Premierfait and the fifteenth-century French assimilation of the Decameron: a study in tonal transformation, Comp Lit Studies, 72; Image and introspective imagination in Montaigne's Essais, PMLA, 73; Montaigne and the Introspective Mind, 75; Rabelais and the epic of palpability: Enargeia and History, Cinquiesme Livre: 38-40, Symposium, Vol 33, 171-85; Humanist foundations of translation theory (1400-1450): a study in the dynamics of word, Canadian Rev of Comparative Lit, Vol 8, 173-203; Narrative function in the Heptameron frame-story, In la nouvelle francaise a la Renaissance, Paris and Geneva: Slatkine, 81; French Renaissance translators and the dialectic of myth and history, Renaissance and Reformation, Vol 17, 189-202. *Mailing Add:* Dept of French S404 Burrowes Pa State Univ University Park PA 16802

NORTON, MARY ELIZABETH, b Ann Arbor, Mich, Sept 14, 13; m 40; c 2. CLASSICAL LANGUAGES. *Educ:* Univ Mich, Ab, 35, MA, 38. *Prof Exp:* Instr Latin, DePauw Univ, 58-64; asst prof, 64-73, ASSOC PROF LECTR CLASSICS, GEORGE WASHINGTON UNIV, 73- *Concurrent Pos:* Vergilian Soc study tour, Greece, 72, Cyprus, Turkey, 74 & Roman Africa, 78. *Mem:* Am Class League; Am Philol Asn; Class Asn Atlantic States; Vergilian Soc. *Res:* Vergil; classics in translation; classics in Colonial America. *Publ:* Auth, Let them read, 1/69 & Roman Britain today, 4-5/70, Class Outlook; A Selective Bibliography on the Teaching of Latin and Greek, 1920-1969, MLA/ERIC Clearinghouse Teaching Foreign Lang, 71; Pedagogical literature in the classics: 1920-1970, Class World, 2/71; Classical Sicily today, 3/74, The classics as humanities, 5/75, Vergil and the bicentennial, 10/76 & The Greek Woman in Art, 3-4/78, Class Outlook. *Mailing Add:* 3614 Melfa Lane Bowie MD 20715

NORTON, ROGER C, b Rochester, Mich, May 11, 21; m 48; c 2. GERMAN LANGUAGE & LITERATURE. *Educ:* Univ Mich, BM, 43, MA, 47, PhD, 51. *Prof Exp:* Instr Ger, Univ Mich, 49-51; instr, Clark Univ, 51-52; instr, Univ Ill, 53-58; from asst prof to assoc prof, Cedar Crest Col, 58-66, assoc prof, 66-68, chmn dept, 68-70, PROF GER, HARPUR COL, STATE UNIV NY, BINGHAMTON, 68- *Concurrent Pos:* Fulbright res award, Univ Vienna, 52-53. *Mem:* MLA; Am Asn Teachers Ger. *Res:* German literature of the 19th and 20th centuries; Hugo von Hofmannsthal; Hermann Hesse. *Publ:* Auth, Hofmannsthal's Magische Werkstatte, Ger Rev, 61; The inception of Hofmannsthal's Der Schwierige, PMLA, 64; Variant endings of Hesse's Glasperlenspiel, Monatshefte, 68; Hermann Hesse's Futuristic Idealism, Herbert Lang, Bern, 73; transl, Voices East and West: German Short Stories Since 1945, Ungar, 82. *Mailing Add:* Dept of Ger State Univ NY Binghamton NY 13901

NORTWICK, THOMAS VAN, b Geneva, Ill, Oct 10, 46; m 69. CLASSICAL LANGUAGES & LITERATURE. *Educ:* Stanford Univ, BA, 69; Yale Univ, MA, 72; Stanford Univ, PhD(classics), 75. *Prof Exp:* Instr, 74-75, asst prof, 75-81, ASSOC PROF CLASSICS, OBERLIN COL, 81- *Concurrent Pos:* Am Coun Learned Soc res fel, 81. *Mem:* Am Philol Asn; Archeol Inst Am; Am Sch Class Studies at Athens. *Res:* Early Greek poetry; Augustan Latin poetry. *Publ:* Coauth, Enjambment in Greek Hexameter Poetry, Trans Am Philos Asn, 77; Apollonos Apate: Associative imagery in the Homeric Hymn to Hermes, Class World, 74:1-5; Penelope and Nausicaa, 109:296-76 & Aeneas, Turnus and Achilles, 110:303-314, Trans Am Philos Asn. *Mailing Add:* Dept Classics Oberlin Col Oberlin OH 44074

NORWOOD, EUGENE L, b Hudson, Mass, Jan 19, 26; m 56; c 1. GERMAN. *Educ:* Boston Univ, BA, 49; Univ Wis, MA, 50, PhD, 58. *Prof Exp:* Instr Ger, Bryn Mawr Col, 54-56; from instr to asst prof, Univ Kans, 56-60; from asst prof to assoc prof, Univ Wis-Milwaukee, 60-66, chmn dept, 62-66, prof & assoc dean humanities, 66-67; prof Ger & chmn dept, Univ Kans, 67-69; prof Ger & assoc dean, grad sch, Univ Wis-Milwaukee, 69-71; dean, Col Sci & Soc, 71-76, assoc dean fac, 76-77, chmn, Humanities Div, 79-82, PROF GERMAN, UNIV WIS-PARKSIDE, 71- *Mem:* Am Asn Teachers Ger; MLA. *Res:* Lessing; 19th century drama. *Mailing Add:* Col of Sci & Soc Univ of Wis-Parkside Kenosha WI 53141

NOSCO, PETER ERLING, Japanese & Chinese Intellectual History. See Vol I

NOSTRAND, HOWARD LEE, b New York, NY, Nov 16, 10; m 33, 67; c 3. FRENCH CULTURE. *Educ:* Amherst Col, AB, 32; Harvard Univ, AM, 33; Univ Paris, DUniv, 34. *Prof Exp:* Instr, Univ Buffalo, 34-36 & US Naval Acad, 36-38; asst prof French, Brown Univ, 38-39; chmn dept, 39-64, prof, 39-80, EMER PROF ROMANCE LANG, UNIV WASH, 80- *Concurrent Pos:* Romance ed, Mod Lang Quart, 40-45; cult relat attache, US Embassy, Peru, 44-47; El sol del Peru, 47; Guggenheim fel, 53-54; mem adv comt, New Media Prog, US Off Educ, 58-61; dir NDEA Inst Lang Teachers, Univ Wash, 59-60, proj, dir, res in culturography, 62-63; mem Nat Comn Teacher Educ & Prof Standards, Nat Educ Asn, 63-67, chmn, 66-67; mem ERIC adv Bd, MLA, 66-71; Nat comn Ethnography, Am Asn Teachers French, 74-; vis prof Col France, 75; Stepladder prog, Am Coun Teaching Foreign Lang, 81-; vis prof, Simon Fraser Univ, 82. *Honors & Awards:* Palmes Academiques, 50; Chevalier, Legion d'honneur, 62; Leadership Award, Northeast Conf Teaching Foreign Lang, 78; Northeast Conf Award, 78; Officier dans l'Ordre des Arts et des Letters, 79. *Mem:* Am Asn Teachers Fr(vpres, 56-58, pres, 60-62); MLA. *Res:* Modern French literature; history of ideas; description of literate cultures. *Publ:* Auth, Ortega y Gasset's Mission of the University, Princeton Univ; The Cultural Attache, The Hazen Found; coauth, Research on Language Teaching: An Annotated International Bibliography for 1945-64, 65; Background Data for Teaching French, 67; Honored by Festschrift, Essays on the Teaching of Culture, Advancement Press, Am, 74. *Mailing Add:* Dept of Romance Lang GN-60 Univ of Wash Seattle WA 98195

NOTHNAGLE, JOHN THOMAS, b Rochester, NY, Jan 23, 26; m 54; c 4. FRENCH LANGUAGE & LITERATURE. *Educ:* Univ Rochester, BA, 49; Univ Wis, MA, 52, PhD(French), 59. *Prof Exp:* Instr French, Montana State Univ, 54-57; asst prof, Cornell Col, 57-59; from asst prof to assoc prof, 59-73, PROF & CHMN DEPT FRENCH, UNIV IOWA, 73- *Concurrent Pos:* Vis prof Am studies, Univ Poitiers, 70-71. *Mem:* MLA; Renaissance Soc Am; Soc Rencesvals; Am Asn Teachers Fr. *Res:* French Renaissance literature; mythopoetics; literature of travel. *Publ:* Auth, Myth in the Poetic Creation of Agrippa d'Aubigne, Univ Nebr, 63; Hierophant or poet: another view of the poetic fury, Cretien de Troves and the rise of realism, 65 & Les discours of Ronsard, 70, Esprit Createur. *Mailing Add:* Dept of French & Ital Univ Iowa Iowa City IA 52240

NOVAK, RICHEY ASBURY, b Palestine, Tex, Dec 2, 27; m 53; c 2. FOREIGN LANGUAGES. *Educ:* Columbia Col, AB, 55, Columbia Univ, MA, 56; Johns Hopkins Univ, PhD(Ger), 69. *Prof Exp:* Instr French & Ger, Wilson Col, 58-59, instr Ger, 59-60, asst prof, 60-66; jr instr, Johns Hopkins Univ, 66-69; from asst prof to assoc prof, Duke Univ, 69-75; head dept English & humanities, Abadan Inst Technol, Abadan, Iran, 75-79; PROF HUMANITIES & DEAN COL LIBERAL ARTS, MCNEESE STATE UNIV, 80- *Concurrent Pos:* WGerman Govt Dankstipendium, 56-57. *Mem:* MLA; Am Asn Teachers Ger. *Res:* Modern German literature; philosophy of language; English as the World language. *Publ:* Auth, Wilhelm von Humboldt as a Literary Critic, Herbert Lang & Cie Bern, 72; Essentials of German Vocabulary, 72; coauth, A Handbook of English-German Idioms, Harcourt, 73. *Mailing Add:* Col Liberal Arts McNeese State Univ Lake Charles LA 70605

NOVAK, SIGRID SCHOLTZ, b Reichenbach, Ger, Oct 4, 31; US citizen; m 53; c 2. EUROPEAN LITERATURE, TEACHING ENGLISH AS A SECOND LANGUAGE. *Educ:* Sorbonne, dipl Fr civilization, 53; Johns Hopkins Univ, MA, 62, PhD(Ger lit), 71. *Prof Exp:* Instr, Wilson Col, 62-64; asst prof Ger, Mary Baldwin Col, 72-75; assoc prof teaching English second lang & lit, Abadan Inst Technol, 75-79; ASSOC PROF MOD LANG, McNEESE STATE UNIV, 80- *Mem:* AAUP; MLA; Asn Prof English in Iean. *Res:* Teaching English to speakers of other languages multimedia program planning; modern European literature; women writers. *Publ:* Auth, The invisible woman: The case of the female playwright in German literature, J Social Issues, 72; Intensive English language institutes, Forum, 78; A Tribute to Hanna Reitsch, Inst Women Pilots' Asn, 1/81. *Mailing Add:* Mod Lang Dept McNeese State Univ Lake Charles LA 70609

NOZICK, MARTIN, b June 28, 17. ROMANCE LANGUAGES & LITERATURES. *Educ:* Brooklyn Col, AB, 36; Columbia Univ, AM, 41, PhD, 53. *Prof Exp:* Instr, Brooklyn Col, 43-46, Colgate Univ, 46-47, Oberlin Col, 47-49; instr, 49-66, PROF ROMANCE LANG & LIT & COMP LIT, QUEENS COL, NY, 66- *Concurrent Pos:* Co-ed, Selected works of Unamuno, Bollingen ser, 66-; prof PhD prog Span, grad ctr, City Univ NY,

69- *Mem:* MLA; Am Asn Teachers Span & Port. *Res:* Jose Ortega y Gasset; the Spanish Enlightenment. *Publ:* Coauth, The Generation of 1898 and After, Dodd, 60; Funcionario Publico, Oxford Univ, 63; Spanish Literature 1700-1900, Dodd, 65; auth, Unamuno and the Second Spanish Republic, In: Spanish Thought and Letters in the Twentieth Century, Vanderbilt Univ, 66; Miguel de Unamuno, Twayne, 71; coauth, Spanish Literature Since the Civil War, Dodd, 73. *Mailing Add:* Dept of Romance Lang Queens Col Kissena Blvd Flushing NY 11367

NUESSEL, FRANK HENRY, b Evergreen Park, Ill, Jan 22, 43. SPANISH & APPLIED LINGUISITICS. *Educ:* Ind Univ, AB, 65; Mich State Univ, MA, 67; Univ Ill, Urbana-Champaign, PhD(Span), 73. *Prof Exp:* Instr Span, Northern Ill Univ, 67-60; teaching asst, Univ Ill, 70-73; asst prof, Ind State Univ, 73-75; asst prof, 75-78, assoc prof, 78-82, PROF SPAN LING, UNIV LOUISVILLE, 82- *Concurrent Pos:* Ed, Comp Romance Ling Newsletter, Univ Louisville, 75-77. *Mem:* Ling Soc Am; MLA; Am Asn Teachers Span & Port. *Res:* Applied linguistics, general linguistics, foreign language pedagogy. *Publ:* Ed, Linguistic Approaches to the Romance Lexicon, Georgetown Univ, 78; auth, An annotated, critical bibliography of generative-based grammatical analyses of Spanish: Phonology and morphology, 78 & An annotated, critical bibliography of generative-based gramatical analyses of Spanish: Syntax and semantics, 79, Bilingual Rev; Contemporary Studies in Romance Languages, Indiana Univ Ling Club, 80. *Mailing Add:* Dept of Mod Lang Univ of Louisville Louisville KY 40208

NUGENT, GREGORY, b Troy, NY, Oct 17, 11. GERMAN. *Educ:* Cath Univ Am, AB, 34; NY Univ, AM, 39, PhD(Ger), 45. *Hon Degrees:* LLD, Manhattanville Col, 63 & Iona Col, 63; DRE, Providence Col, 71; LHD, Pace Univ, 73; LittD, Col Mt St Vincent, 75. *Prof Exp:* Instr lang, De La Salle Inst, 34-46; instr Ger exten div, Manhattan Col, 39-43, from asst prof to prof, 46-75, head dept Ger, 47-54, asst dean lib arts, 51-52, dean sch arts & sci, 52-59, acad vpres coll, 59-62, pres, 62-75, spec asst to pres, 75-78, EXEC ASST TO PRES & SECY OF UNIV, CATH UNIV AM, 78- *Concurrent Pos:* Trustee, Col Entrance Exam Bd, 62-65; mem comn fed rels, Am Coun Educ, 68-72. *Mem:* Relig Educ Asn; Nat Cath Educ Asn. *Res:* German literature, drama and philology; Catholicism in German literature. *Publ:* Auth, Catholicism in Schiller's Dramas, NY Univ, 49. *Mailing Add:* 104 Exec Offices Cath Univ of Am Washington DC 20064

NUGENT, ROBERT L, b Tacoma, Wash, Sept 12, 20. FRENCH. *Educ:* Univ Calif, Los Angeles, AB, 42; Yale Univ, PhD, 50; Univ Calif, Berkeley, BLS, 54. *Prof Exp:* Teaching asst French, Yale Univ, 46-48; instr, Univ Calif, Santa Barbara, 50-53; res asst librarianship, Berkeley, 53-54; ref librn, Assoc Cols Claremont, 54-56; from asst prof to assoc prof, 56-67, PROF MOD LANG, LAKE ERIE COL, 67- *Concurrent Pos:* Librn, Lake Erie Col, 60- *Mem:* Am Asn Libr Asn. *Res:* Contemporary and Baroque poetry. *Publ:* Auth, Paul Eluard, Twayne, 74; Vigny's Stello and Existential Freedom, Nineteenth-Century French Studies, fall-winter, 79-80; transl & ed (with E Lunardi), Pascoli's Convivial (poems), Lake Erie Col Studies, 79-81. *Mailing Add:* Dept of Mod Lang Lake Erie Col Painesville OH 44077

NUNEZ, BENJAMIN, b Salta, Argenian, July 13, 12; US citizen; m 70. LINGUISTICS, LATIN AMERICAN CIVILIZATION. *Educ:* Northern Sem, Catamarca, BPh, 36; Nat Univ Buenos Aires, Prof en Let, 44; Columbia Univ, MA, 52, PhD(Span ling), 57. *Prof Exp:* Asst prof Span, Salta Inst Lib Arts, Argentina, 48-51; lectr, Columbia Univ, 52-54; asst prof ling, Georgetown Univ, 57-67; assoc prof Span, West Chester State Col, 67-70, prof Span & ling, 70-78; RETIRED. *Concurrent Pos:* Fulbright scholar, Argentina, 64-65. *Mem:* AAUP; Name Soc; Dict Soc NAm. *Res:* Lexicographer; Afro-Latin America; Portuguese Africa. *Publ:* Auth, Applied Anthropology and Fundamental Education, Georgetown Univ Monog Ser, 60; Terminos Topograficos en la Argentian Colonial, Pan Am Union, 65; Marriage and family in Atamisqui, a Northwest Argentina community, In: XXXVIII International Congress of Americanists, Stuttgart, Munich, 68; Dict of Afro-Latin American Civilization, Greenwood Press, 80. *Mailing Add:* 315 Seventh St NW Washington DC 20002

NUNN, ROBERT RAYMOND, b East Orange, NJ, Oct 21, 29; m 59; c 3. ROMANCE LANGUAGES. *Educ:* Rutgers Univ, AB, 51; Middlebury Col, MA, 55; Columbia Univ, PhD(French), 66. *Prof Exp:* Lectr French, Columbia Univ, 58-59; from instr to asst prof, 59-68, ASSOC PROF ROMANCE LANG, BOWDOIN COL, 68- *Mem:* MLA. *Res:* French 17th century novel; Canadian French. *Mailing Add:* Dept of Romance Lang Bowdoin Col Brunswick ME 04011

NUTE, DONALD ELMER, Philosophy, Linguistics. See Vol IV

NYABONGO, VIRGINIA SIMMONS, b Baltimore, Md, Mar 20, 13. FRENCH LITERATURE. *Educ:* Bennett Col, AB, 34; Univ Wis, AM, 37, PhD, 44; Univ Grenoble, cert & dipl, 39; Columbia Univ, AM, 48. *Prof Exp:* Teacher English & educ, Bennett Col, 34-36, secy & actg registr, 34-35; asst prof French, Wilberforce Univ, 37-41; dean students, Bennett Col, 41-42; prof French & dir student personnel & res, Tenn State Univ, 44-78; RETIRED. *Concurrent Pos:* Fulbright res fel, Inst Pedag, Paris, 52-53; assoc Japanese studies prog, Syracuse Univ, 56; travel grants, Am Soc African Cult, 59, 65; African Studies Asn, 61 & Tenn State Univ; mem; Writer's Inst Honors. *Honors & Awards:* Cert Merit, Nat Asn Personnel Workers, 62; Chevalier, Palmes Academiques, 63, officier, 68. *Mem:* Fel AAAS; fel African Studies Asn; fel Soc Values Higher Educ; fel Int Inst Arts & Lett; Nat Asn Women Deans, Admin & Counsel. *Res:* French literature of the 17th century; student personnel; African studies. *Publ:* Auth, Whitecaps (poems), Antioch, 42; Meditations (2 vols & Leaflet), Hemphill, 50, 51, 52; Les Palmiers (poems), Ed Lex, Havana, 51; The Homeland (poem), Observer, 3/65; Higher education in Africa, 11/66 & A visit to the Chateau de Coppett-home of Madame de Staël, 11/67, Fac J, Tenn State Univ. *Mailing Add:* Dept of Mod Lang Tenn State Univ 35th Ave & Centennial Blvd Nashville TN 37203

NYE, JEAN C, b New Sewickley Twp, Pa, Mar 16, 32; m 55. ROMANCE LANGUAGES. *Educ:* Geneva Col, BA, 53; Univ Pittsburgh, MLitt, 57; Univ Toledo, PhD, 72. *Prof Exp:* Teacher English & French, Zelienople High Sch, 53-59; from asst prof to assoc prof, 59-72, PROF SPAN & FRENCH, FINDLAY COL, 72- *Concurrent Pos:* Spanish transl, Centrex Corp; mem bd dirs, Cent States Conf Teaching Foreign Lang. *Mem:* Teachers English to Speakers Other Lang; MLA; Am Asn Teachers Span & Port. *Res:* Teaching of English in the junior high schools in Puerto Rico; bilingual, bicultural education. *Publ:* Auth, Christmas as portrayed in Spanish art, 12/66 & Easter as protrayed in Spanish art, 3/70, Church Advocate. *Mailing Add:* Dept of Mod Lang Findlay Col Findlay OH 45840

NYENHUIS, JACOB EUGENE, b Mille Lacs Co, Minn, Mar 25, 35; m 56; c 4. CLASSICS. *Educ:* Calvin Col, AB, 56; Stanford Univ, AM, 61, PhD, 63. *Prof Exp:* Asst class lang, Calvin Col, 57-59; from asst prof to prof Greek & Latin, Wayne State Univ, 62-75, actg chmn dept, 65-67, chmn dept, 67-75, actg chmn dept Near Eastern lang & lit, 68-69, fac res award, 70, grants-in-aid, 71-72; dean humanities, 75-78, PROF CLASSICS, HOPE COL, 75-, DEAN ARTS & HUMANITIES, 78- *Concurrent Pos:* Mem managing comt, Am Sch Class Studies at Athens, 65-75, 77-, vis prof, 73-74; Danforth assoc, 66-; vis assoc prof classics, Univ Calif, Santa Barbara, 67-68; gen ed, Wayne State Univ Class Texts Ser, 68-75; dir, US Off Educ Dept Grant Teacher Trainers Proj, Wayne State Univ & Detroit Pub Schs, 70-71; mem, Danforth Assoc Regional Selection Comt, 71-73; consult, Mich Dept Educ, 71-72; proj dir, Nat Endowment for Humanities grants, 75-78; mem bd dirs, Mich Coun for Humanities, 76, mem exec comt, 77-78, vchmn, 78-80. *Honors & Awards:* Probus Award, 66. *Mem:* Am Philol Asn; Class Asn Midwest & S; Am Class League; MLA; Nat Col Honors Coun. *Res:* Greek mythology; Greek drama, especially Euripides; the role of myth in the creative process. *Publ:* Coauth, Introductory Latin for College Students, privately publ, 64, rev ed, 69 & 73; Coining new terms for polymer science, J Chem Doc, 5/65; auth, Daedalus and Icarus: Symbol for our time?, Grad Comment, 12/67; Mich classical spring: 1967-the growth and success of an idea, Class World, 5/68; coauth, Plautus: Amphitruo, 70, Petronius: Cena Trimalchionis, 70 & Latin via Ovid, 77, Wayne State Univ, auth, Michael Ayrton: Sculpture, Drawings, Paintings, and Etchings (exhibition catalogue), Hope Col, 78; Michael Ayrton's world of mazes and minotaurs, Labrys, A Mag of the Arts, summer 78; Journey Through a Labyrinth: A Study of the Work of Michael Ayrton, Secker & Warburg, London, 79. *Mailing Add:* Div of Arts & Humanities Hope Col Holland MI 49423

NYGARD, HOLGER OLOF, English, Folklore. See Vol II

O

OATES, JOHN FRANCIS, Ancient History. See Vol I

OATES, MICHAEL DAVID, b Derby, Conn, Sept 23, 39; m 63; c 2. FRENCH LINGUISTICS & METHODOLOGY. *Educ:* Fairfield Univ, AB, 61; Assumption Col, MAT, 63; Georgetown Univ, PhD(French ling), 70. *Prof Exp:* Intern French, Framingham High Sch, Mass, 61-62; teacher, Malden High Sch, 62-65; assoc prof, 67-75, PROF FRENCH, UNIV NORTHERN IOWA, 75- *Concurrent Pos:* Pres, Study Ed Asn Conn, 60-61; honors intern, Assumption Col, 61-62; Univ Northern Iowa study grant, Univ Besancon, 72. *Mem:* Am Coun Teachers Foreign Lang; Am Asn Teachers Fr. *Res:* French linguistics; language teaching research. *Publ:* Auth, A Syntactic Classification of French Verbs as a Basis for a Monostructural Presentation at the Beginning Level, Current Issues in Teaching French, 4/72; Principles and Techniques for Stimulating Foreign-Language Conversation, Foreign Lang Annals, 1/-72; Grass Roots Efforts to Encourage the Study of French, 4/76 & Commentetre francais, 11/78, AATF Nat Bull; A Non-Intensive FLES Program in French, Fr Rev, 3/80; Oral Translation: An Old Horse for the New Frontier, In: The Report of the 1980 Central States Conference on the Teaching of Foreign Languages, New Frontiers in Foreign Lang Educ, 80; Cooperative Grouping in French Conversation and Composition, In: Proceedings of the Second National Conference on Individualized Instruction in Foreign Languages, Ohio State Univ, 81; Keys to Study Abroad Programs, Alberta Mod Lang J, spring 81. *Mailing Add:* Dept of Foreign Lang Unif of Northern Iowa Cedar Falls IA 50613

OBAID, ANTONIO HADAD, b Rancagua, Chile, May 22, 17; nat US; m 48; c 1. SPANISH LITERATURE. *Educ:* Carleton Col, AB, 41; Univ Nebr, AM, 42; Univ Minn, PhD(Span & French), 53. *Prof Exp:* Teacher English, Polytech Inst, Santiago, 38 & Col San Ignacio, Santiago, 38-39; teaching fel Span, Univ Nebr, 41-42; instr, 42-44, asst prof Span & Russ, 46-47, from asst prof to prof Span, 47-61, PROF SPAN & RUSS, CARLETON COL, 61- *Concurrent Pos:* Ford Fund Advan Educ study fel, Spain, 53-54; Louis W & Maud Hill Family Found res & study grants, Latin Am, 58 & 64; prof Russ, St Olaf Col, 60-62; Fulbright res study grant, Spain, 68. *Mem:* MLA; Am Asn Teachers Span & Port; Latin Am Studies Asn. *Res:* Nineteenth and 20th century literature. *Publ:* Coauth, An Allinace for Progress: The Challenge and the Problem, Denison, 64; auth, The other shore, (transl, Jose Lopez-Rubio, La otra orilla), The Voice, 5/66; A sequence of tenses?--What sequence of tenses?, 12/66 & The vagaries of the Spanish 's', 3/73, Hispania. *Mailing Add:* Dept of Span Carleton Col Northfield MN 55057

OBER, JOSIAH, Ancient History, Greek. See Vol I

OBER, KENNETH HARLAN, b Ark, Feb 9, 30; m 58; c 1. COMPARATIVE LITERATURE, FOREIGN LANGUAGES. *Educ:* Univ Ark, BA, 52; Ind Univ, AM, 55; Univ Ill, PhD(comp lit), 74. *Prof Exp:* Instr Russ, Kans State Col Pittsburg, 60-62; asst prof Russ, Ill State Univ, 62-69; SESSIONAL LECTR COMP LIT, UNIV ALTA, 77- *Concurrent Pos:* Killam Mem scholar, Dept Comp Lit, Univ Alta, 77. *Mem:* MLA; Can Comp Lit Asn; Soc Advan Scand Study. *Res:* Scandinavian-Russian literary relations; 19th-century Danish literature; early 19th-century Russian poetry. *Publ:* Auth, O I Senkovskij, Russia's first Icelandic scholar, Scand Studies, 68; coauth, Zukovskij's translation of The Prisoner of Chillon, Slavic & E Europ J, 73; Zukovskij and Southey's ballads: The translator as rival, Wordsworth Circle, 74; auth, Meir Goldschmidt as a writer of English, Orbis Litterarum, 74; coauth, Bibliography of Modern Icelandic Literature in Translation, Cornell Univ, 75; auth, Meir Goldschmidt, Twayne, 76; P Em Hansen and P Ganzen: A Danish literary missionary in Russia, Svantevit, 77; co-ed, The Royal Guest and Other Classical Danish Narrative, Univ Chicago, 77. *Mailing Add:* Dept of Comp Lit Univ of Alta Edmonton AB T6G 2E6 Can

OBERGFELL, SANDRA CHESHIRE, b Feb 24, 47; US citizen; m 68; c 1. MEDIEVAL FRENCH LITERATURE. *Educ:* Butler Univ, BA, 68; Ind Univ, Bloomington, MA, 70, PhD(Fr lit), 74. *Prof Exp:* Vis prof 17th century French lit, Purdue Univ, 74-76; asst prof French lang, lit & civilization, Wabash Col, 76-79; ASST PROF FRENCH LANG, LIT & CIVILIZATION, MARS HILL COL, 79- *Res:* Children's literature in France; foreign language pedagogy: language and thought relationships. *Publ:* Auth, The problem of didacticism in the romance epic: Aiol, Olifant, 78; Patterns of behavior in French children's literature, Contemp Fr Civilization, 79; The father-son combat motif as didactic theme in Old French literature, Ky Romance Quart, 79; Popular American arthuriana: A cultural context, WVa Univ Philol Papers, 81; The use of the fairy tale as a cultural context int eh foreign language classroom, French Rev (in press). *Mailing Add:* Dept Mod For Lang Mars Hill Col Mars Hill NC 28754

OBERHELMAN, HARLEY DEAN, b Clay Center, Kans, June 30, 28; m 54; c 2. SPANISH LANGUAGE & LITERATURE. *Educ:* Univ Kans, BSEd, 50, MA, 52, PhD(romance lang), 58. *Prof Exp:* Teaching asst Span, Univ Kans, 50-56; dir foreign lang, Lawrence Pub Schs, Kans, 56-58; from asst prof to assoc prof foreign lang, 58-64, chmn dept, 63-70, PROF CLASS & ROMANCE LANG, TEX TECH UNIV, 64- *Concurrent Pos:* Lectr Span methodology, Univ Wis, 55, Univ NMex, 56, Eastern Mont Col, 59 & Univ Kans, 60; Fulbright lectr, Nat Univ Tucuman, 61; State of Tex res study grant, Uruguay, 61 & Colombia, 77; assoc ed, Hispania, 62-66; chmn Latin Am area studies, Tex Tech Univ, 69-77. *Mem:* Am Asn Teachers Span & Port. *Res:* Spanish American literature; methodology of second language teaching; River Plate literature. *Publ:* Auth, Sobre la vida y las ficciones de Ernesto Sabato, In: Obras de Ficcion, Losada, Buenos Aires, 67; Ernesto Sabato, Twayne, 70; coauth, Espanol Moderno, Merrill, 70; auth, Jose Donoso and the Nueva Narrativa, Revista de Estudios Hispanicos, 1/75; Garcia Marquez and the American South, Chasqui, 11/75; Education and history of knowledge, In: Cien Anos de Soledad, Studies by SCMLA, 4/75; Myth and structure in Sabato's Abaddon, Am Hispanist, 3/76; The Presence of Faulkner in the Writings of Garcia Marquez, Tex Tech Press, 80. *Mailing Add:* Dept of Class & Romance Lang Tex Tech Univ Lubbock TX 79409

OBERHELMAN, STEVEN MICHAEL, b Leavenworth, Kans, July 23, 50; m 81. CLASSICAL LANGUAGES, BYZANTINE LITERATURE. *Educ:* Univ Minn, BS, 74, MA, 76, PhD(classics), 81. *Prof Exp:* MELLON FEL CLASSICS, CASE WESTERN RESERVE UNIV, 81- *Concurrent Pos:* Asst prof classics, St Bonaventure Univ, 81. *Mem:* Am Inst Archaeol; Am Philol Asn; Soc Ancient Med. *Res:* Accentual prose rhythms in Empire Latin prose; dreams in classical and medieval literature; Greek history. *Publ:* Auth, Popular dream interpretation in ancient Greece and Freudian psychoanalysis, J Popular Cult, 77; A survey of dreams in ancient Greece, Class Bull, 79; Greek and Roman witches: Literary conventions or agrarian fertility priestesses, In: 5000 Years of Popular Cult, Bowling Green Univ Press, 80; Prolegomena to the Byzantine Oneirokritika, Byzantion, 80; Two marginal notes from Achmet in the cod Laurent plut, 87, 8, Byzantinische Zeitschrift, 81; The interpretation of prescriptive dreams in ancient Greek medicine, 81 & Galen, On diagnosis from dreams, 83, J Hist Med; coauth, Milton's use of classical meters in the sylvarum liber, Mod Philol (in press). *Mailing Add:* Dept Classics Case Western Reserve Univ Cleveland OH 44106

OBERLANDER, BARBARA JOYCE, b Springfield, Mo, May 5, 33. ROMANCE LANGUAGES. *Educ:* Southwest Mo State Univ, BS, 54; La State Univ, PhD(romance lang & philol), 69. *Prof Exp:* Teacher high sch, Mo, 54-57; teacher sr high sch, Wash, 57-60; asst Span, La State Univ, 60-64; instr, Southeastern La State Univ, 64-66; assoc prof, 66-69, PROF SPAN LANG & LIT, EAST STROUDSBURG STATE COL, 69- *Mem:* Am Asn Teachers Span & Port; Am Asn Univ Prof; Latin Am Studies Asn. *Res:* Spain's religious drama; Golden Age drama; MesoAmerican anthropology-Maya. *Mailing Add:* Dept of Foreign Lang PO Box 74 East Stroudsburg State Col East Stroudsburg PA 18301

O'BRIEN, JOAN V, b Meriden, Conn. CLASSICAL LANGUAGES & LITERATURE. *Educ:* Albertus Magnus Col, BA, 46; Fordham Univ, MA, 55, PhD(classics), 60. *Prof Exp:* From asst prof classics to assoc prof, Albertus Magnus Col, 55-66; res asst & fel, Sch Relig, Univ Iowa, 67-69; ASSOC PROF CLASSICS, SOUTHERN ILL UNIV CARBONDALE, 69- *Concurrent Pos:* Fulbright fel, Am Acad Rome, 63; vis fel classics & relig, Yale Univ, 76. *Mem:* Am Acad Relig; Cath Theol Asn Am; Am Philol Asn. *Res:* Sophocles Antigone; classical and comparative mythology; women's studies. *Publ:* Auth, Bilingual Selections from Sophocles: An Introduction to the Text for the Greekless Reader, 77 & Guide to Sophocles Antigone, 78, Southern Ill Univ; In the Beginning: Creation myths from ancient Mesopotamia, Israel and Greece, Scholars Press, 82. *Mailing Add:* Dept of Foreign Lang & Lit Southern Ill Univ Carbondale IL 62901

O'BRIEN, MACGREGOR, b Arequipa, Peru, June 20, 49; US & Peru citizen; m 73. MODERN LANGUAGES & LITERATURES. *Educ:* Univ Wis-Superior, BA, 72; Univ Wis-Milwaukee, MA, 74; Univ Mo, PhD(Romance lang), 79. *Prof Exp:* ASST PROF SPAN LANG, CULT & LIT, FROSTBURG STATE COL, 78- *Mem:* MLA; Asn Teachers Span & Port. *Res:* The essay as a literary genre; Latin American literary periodicals; Ramon Perez de Ayala. *Publ:* Auth, Ramon Perez de Ayala y el ensayo, In: Los Ensayistas, 81; El odeal clasico de Ramon perez de Ayala en sus ensayos en La Prensa, Inst Estudios Asturianos, 81; ed, El Lazarillo de Tormes, Acqueron Press, 82. *Mailing Add:* Dept Mod For Lang Frostburg State Col Frostburg MD 21532

O'BRIEN, MICHAEL JOHN, b New York, NY, Apr 27, 30; m 59. CLASSICS. *Educ:* Fordham Univ, BA, 51; Princeton Univ, MA, 53, PhD, 56. *Prof Exp:* Instr classics, Wesleyan Univ, 55-56; from instr to assoc prof, Yale Univ, 56-66; assoc prof, 66-69, chmn dept, 73-81, PROF CLASSICS, UNIV TORONTO, 69- *Concurrent Pos:* Morse res fel, 63-64; Guggenheim res fel, 72-73. *Mem:* Class Asn Can; Am Philol Asn; Brit Class Asn. *Res:* Greek philosophy and drama. *Publ:* Auth, The unity of the Laches, Yale Class Studies, 63; Orestes and the Gorgon: Euripides' Electra, Am J Philol, 1/64; The Socratic Paradoxes and the Greek Mind, Univ NC, 67; ed, Twentieth Century Interpretations of Oedipus Rex, Prentice-Hall, 68; auth, Protagoras, In: The Older Sophists, Univ SC, 72. *Mailing Add:* Dept of Classics Univ of Toronto Toronto ON M5S 1A1 Can

OBUCHOWSKI, CHESTER W, b Manchester, Conn, Aug 2, 19; m 46; c 3. FOREIGN LANGUAGES. *Educ:* Fordham Univ, BA, 41, MA, 43; Yale Univ, PhD(French), 50. *Prof Exp:* Teaching fel French, Yale Univ, 46-49; instr foreign lang, Univ Conn, Hartford, 49-55, from instr to assoc prof, 55-69, PROF FOREIGN LANG, UNIV CONN, STORRS, 69- *Concurrent Pos:* Mem, Conn State Adv Comt Foreign Lang Instr, 55-71; consult foreign lang instr, Engelhardt, Engelhardt & Leggett, Educ Consult, Westchester County, NY; vis examr, Bates Col Honors Prog Fr, 72-73 & 74. *Mem:* Am Asn Teachers Fr; MLA; Am Coun Teaching Foreign Lang. *Res:* French war literature; foreign language methodology. *Publ:* Auth, The concentrationary world of Pierre Gascar, 2/61, French writers look at the dirty war, 5/67 & Algeria: The tortured conscience, 10/68, Fr Rev; Mars on Trial: War As Seen by French Writers of the Twentieth Century, Jose Porrua Turanzas, Madrid, Spain, 78. *Mailing Add:* Dept Foreign Lang Univ of Conn Storrs CT 06268

OCHRYMOWYCZ, OREST ROBERT, b Lvov, Poland, July 7, 35; US citizen; m 62; c 2. SPANISH, RUSSIAN. *Educ:* St Mary's Col, Minn, BA, 57; Univ Iowa, MA, 59, PhD(Span), 68. *Prof Exp:* From asst prof to assoc prof, 62-72, PROF SPAN & RUSS, ST MARY'S COL, MINN, 72-, CHMN DIV HUMANITIES, 69- *Mem:* Am Asn Teachers Span & Port. *Res:* Spanish epic and ballad; Spanish drama of the Golden Age; Cervantes. *Publ:* Auth, Aspects of oral style in the Romances juglarescon of the Carolingian cycle, Studies Romance Lang & Lit, Univ Iowa. *Mailing Add:* Dept of Mod Lang St Mary's Col Winona MN 55987

OCHSENSCHLAGER, EDWARD LLOYD, b Aurora, Ill, Apr 5, 32. CLASSICAL LANGUAGES, ARCHEOLOGY. *Educ:* Columbia Univ, BS, 54; NY Univ, MA, 61. *Prof Exp:* From asst prof to assoc prof, 67-73, chmn dept archaeol, 73-79, PROF CLASSICS, DIR ARCHAEOL RES INST, BROOKLYN COL, 73-, CHMN DEPT ANTHROP & ARCHAEOL, 79- *Concurrent Pos:* Dir, Classical excavations at Thmuis, Egypt, 64-67; field dir, Excavations at Sirmium, Yugoslavia, 68-77; asst field dir, Exped to al'Hiba, Iraq, 69-; participant, Am Res Ctr in Egypt; co-dir, Mendes Exped, 77-80. *Mem:* Archaeol Inst Am; Am Sch Orient Studies. *Res:* Classical archaeology; Greek and Roman religion; pottery technology. *Publ:* Auth, Excavations at Thmuis, J Am Res Ctr Egypt, 69; The cosmic significance of the Plemochoe, Hist Relgion, 70; coauth & co-ed, Sirmium Archaeological Investigations in Syrmian Pannonia, Vol I & II, Sirmium Excavations, 71-73; coauth, Excavations at Sirmium, 73 & Ancient and modern sun-dried mud objects from al-Hiba, 74, Archaeology; Potters at al Hiba, In: Ethnoarchaeology, Univ Calif, 75; Der spätkaiserzeittiche Hippodrom in Sirmium, Germania, 76; Taposiris Magna Acts First International Congress of Egyptology, 79; Tell-Timai-Ancient Thmois, In: Mendes II, Aris & Phillips, Warminster, England, 81. *Mailing Add:* Dept of Classics Brooklyn Col Brooklyn NY 10021

O'CONNELL, DAVID JOSEPH, b New York, NY, Nov 27, 40; m 67 & 80; c 3. FRENCH LITERATURE. *Educ:* St Peter's Col, NJ, AB, 62; Princeton Univ, AM, 64, PhD(French), 66. *Prof Exp:* Instr French, Fordham Univ, 68; from asst prof to assoc prof, Univ Mass, Amherst, 68-77; PROF & HEAD DEPT FRENCH, UNIV ILL, CHICAGO CIRCLE, 77- *Concurrent Pos:* Am Philos Soc res grants, 72 & 80; Am Coun Learned Soc res award, 74, travel award, 76; assoc bibliogr, MLA Bibliog, 75-; ed, French Monographs, Twayne. *Mem:* MLA; AM Asn Teachers Fr; Am Transl Asn; Am Coun Teachers Foreign Lang. *Res:* 20th century French novel; 13th-century France. *Publ:* Auth, The Teachings of Saint Louis, Univ NC, 72; Les Propos de Saint Louis, Gallimard, Paris, 74; Louis Ferdinand Celine, Twayne, 76; The Instructions of Saint Louis, Univ NC, 80. *Mailing Add:* Dept of French Univ of Ill Chicago IL 60680

O'CONNELL, JOSEPH THOMAS, Comparative Religion. See Vol IV

O'CONNELL, RICHARD B, b St James, Minn, Jan 30, 19; m 67; c 2. GERMAN. *Educ:* Univ Minn, MA, 49, PhD(Ger), 51. *Prof Exp:* From instr to asst prof Ger, Univ SDak, 49-52; Fulbright exchange teacher sec schs, Vienna, Austria, 52-53; from assoc prof to prof Ger & Span, Univ SDak, 53-59; assoc prof, Wis State Univ, Superior, 59-61; prof, Slippery Rock State Col, 61-67; chmn Dept Lang, 79-82, PROF GER, MEMPHIS STATE UNIV, 67- *Mem:* Am Asn Teachers Ger; SCent Mod Lang Asn. *Res:* Goethe's Faust; contempory German literature. *Publ:* Auth, English in Austrian secondary schools, Mod Lang J, 3/55; Gorostiza's Contigo, pan y cebolla and Sheridan's The Rivals, Hispanis, 9/60; Rivas' El desengano en un sueno and Grillparzer's Der Traum ein Leben, Philol Quart, 10/61; ed & transl, Report about and from America, J G Häcker, Miss Valley Collection Bull, Vol 3 & 4, 70-71. *Mailing Add:* Dept Foreign Lang Memphis State Univ Memphis TN 38152

O'CONNELL, RICHARD JAMES, English & American Literature. See Vol II

O'CONNOR, BASILIDES ANDREW, b New York, NY, July 9, 13. FRENCH LITERATURE. *Educ:* Cath Univ Am, AB, 33, AM, 34, PhD, 43. *Prof Exp:* Instr French lang & lit, De La Salle Col, 33-34, 36-43; from asst prof to assoc prof, 46-70, head dept mod foreign lang, 46-72, prof, 70-80, EMER PROF FRENCH, MANHATTAN COL, 80- *Mem:* Int Arthurian Soc. *Res:* Medieval French literature; Henri D'Arci's Vitas Patrum; 13th century Anglo-Norman rimed translation of the Berba Seniorum. *Mailing Add:* Dept of French Manhattan Col Riverdale NY 10471

O'CONNOR, DAVID, b Cork, Ireland, July 2, 49; m 71; c 3. ANALYTIC PHILOSOPHY, PHILOSOPHY OF RELIGION. *Educ:* Nat Univ Ireland, BA, 71, MA, 73; Marquette Univ, PhD(philos), 79. *Prof Exp:* Asst philos, Villanova Univ, 79-80; PROF PHILOS, SETON HALL UNIV, NJ, 80- *Mem:* Am Philos Asn. *Res:* Metaphysics; philosophy of mind; the logic of theistic beliefs. *Publ:* Auth, On the viability of Macquarrie's God-talk, Philos Studies Vol 23, 75; Remarks of Macquarrie's philosophy of death, Expository Times, Vol 88, 77; Identification and description in Ayer's sense-datum theory, Mod Schoolman, Vol 57, 80; Moore and the Paradox of analysis, Philosophy, Vol 57, 82; The Metaphysics of G F Moore, D Reidel, Dordrecht, Boston, 82; contribr, Etienne Gilson, Nelson Goodman, Charles Morris, In: Twentieth Century Thinkers, Macmillan & Gale Res (in prep). *Mailing Add:* Dept of Philos Seton Hall Univ South Orange NJ 07079

O'CONNOR, JOHN JOSEPH, b New York, NY, Jan 16, 24; div; c 1. COMPUTATIONAL LINGUISTICS. *Educ:* Columbia Univ, BA, 45, PhD(philos), 52; Cornell Univ, MA, 47. *Prof Exp:* Instr philos, Brooklyn Col, 48-49; from instr to asst prof, Pa State Univ, 49-57; mem staff res & develop, Remington-Rand Univac, 57-59, Inst Coop Res, Univ Pa, 59-63, Inst Sci Info, 63-66 & Inst Advan Med Commun, 66-67; PROF INFO SCI, LEHIGH UNIV, 67- *Concurrent Pos:* Grants, US Off Naval Res, 59-70, US Air Force Off Sci Res, 61-65, NSF, 71-73 & 75-77 & NIH, 72-74 & 76-78. *Mem:* Asn Comput Mach; Asn Comput Ling; Am Soc Info Sci. *Res:* Computer retrieval of answer-passages; document retrieval; computer processing of natural language text. *Publ:* Auth, The Scan Column Index, Am Documentation, 62; Automatic subject recognition in scientific papers, J Asn Comput Mach, 65; Text searching retrieval of answer-sentences and other answer-passages, J Am Soc Info Sci, 73; Data retrieval by text searching, J Chem Info & Comput Sci, 77. *Mailing Add:* Ctr for Info Sci Mart 8 Lehigh Univ Bethlehem PA 18015

O'CONNOR, MARY LUCILDA, b Chicago, Ill, June 7, 16. FOREIGN LANGUAGES. *Educ:* Clarke Col, BA, 40; Loyola Univ, Ill, MA, 48; Univ Minn, PhD, 61. *Prof Exp:* From instr to assoc prof, 43-63, PROF SPAN, CLARKE COL, IOWA, 63-, CHMN DEPT, 78- *Mem:* Am Asn Teachers Span & Port; MLA. *Res:* Novels of the 19th and 20th centuries. *Mailing Add:* Dept of Span Clarke Col Dubuque IA 52001

O'CONNOR, PATRICIA W, b Memphis, Tenn, Apr 26, 31; m 53, 67; c 2. ROMANCE LANGUAGES. *Educ:* Univ Fla, BAE, 53, MA, 54, PhD(Span & French), 62. *Prof Exp:* From instr to assoc prof Span, 62-72, PROF SPAN LANG & LIT, UNIV CINCINNATI, 72- *Concurrent Pos:* Taft res grant, Spain, 65, 72, 75, 79 & 81; Am Philos Soc, 71. *Honors & Awards:* Rieveschl Award for creative & scholarly works, 82. *Mem:* Am Asn Teachers Span & Port; MLA; Midwest Mod Lang Asn; AAUP. *Res:* Contemporary Spanish theater; post-war Spanish novel; sexism in literature. *Publ:* Auth, Government censorship in the contemporary Spanish theater, Educ Theater Rev, 12/66; Women in the Theater of Gregorio Martinez Sierra, American, 67; Censorship in the plays of Antonio Buero Vallejo, Hispania, spring 69; Francisco Garcia Pavon's sexual politics in the Plinio novels, J 20th Century Span Studies, spring 73; Gregorio and Maria Martinez Sierra, Twayne, 77; Contemporary Spanish Theater, Scribner's, 80; transl & ed, Plays of Protest from the Franco Era, Madrid, 81. *Mailing Add:* Dept of Romance Lang & Lit Univ of Cincinnati Cincinnati OH 45221

O'CONNOR, THOMAS AUSTIN, b New York, NY, Aug 19, 43; m 69; c 2. SPANISH. *Educ:* Iona Col, BA, 65; State Univ NY Albany, MA, 68; PhD(Span), 71. *Prof Exp:* Teacher Span, Bishop Gibbons high sch, 65-67; from asst prof to assoc prof, State Univ NY Col Cortland, 71-76; from assoc prof to prof, Tex A&M Univ, 76-80; PROF SPAN & HEAD MOD LANG, KANS STATE UNIV, 80- *Concurrent Pos:* Am Coun Learned Soc fel, 75. *Mem:* MLA; AM Asn Teachers Span & Port; Asoc Int Hispanistas; Cervantes Soc Am; Comediantes. *Res:* Spanish drama of the Golden Age; Spanish literature of the Golden Age; history of European drama. *Publ:* Auth, The interplay of Prudence and Imprudence in El medico de su honra, Romanistisches J, 73; Is the Spanish Comedia a metatheater?, Hisp Rev, 75; Language, Irony and Death: The Poetry of Salazar y Torres' El encanto es la hermosura, Romanische Forschungen, 78; coauth, Estupro y politica en El mejor alcalde, el rey, Actas VI Cong Asoc Int Hispanistas, Toronto, 80; auth, The Knight of Olmedo and Oedipus: Perspectives on a Spanish tragedy, Hisp Rev, 80; El medico de su honra y la victimizacion de la mujer: La critica social de Calderon de la Barca, Actas VII Cong Asoc Int Hispanistas, Venice, 81; Violacion, amor y entereza en Fortunas de Andromeda y Perseo de Calderon de la Barca, Homenaje a Gonzalo Torente ballester, Salamanca, 81; Calderon and Reason's Impasse: The Case of La estatua de Prometeo, LA CHISPA 81, New Orleans, 81. *Mailing Add:* Dept of Mod Lang Kans State Univ Manhattan KS 66506

ODENKIRCHEN, CARL JOSEF, b Uerdingen, West Ger, Jan 28, 21; nat US; m 48. ROMANCE LANGUAGES & LITERATURE. *Educ:* Col Charleston, AB, 42; Univ Chicago, MA, 47; Univ NC, PhD, 51. *Prof Exp:* Instr mod lang, State Univ NY, , Col Teachers, Albany, 50-53; asst prof mod lang & Latin, Lake Forest Col, 56-58; assoc prof mod lang & comp lit, 58-62, prof romance langs & lit, 62-76 & chmn dept comp lit, 62-71, PROF ROMANCE LANG, STATE UNIV NY, ALBANY, 76- *Mem:* MLA; Am Asn Teachers Fr; Am Asn Teachers Ital; Am Comp Lit Asn. *Res:* Romance linguistics; comparative romance literatures; humanistic studies. *Publ:* Auth, The play of Adam (Ordo representacionis Ade), In: Classical Folia Editions, Vol V, 76 & The life of St Alexius, In: Clasical Folia Editions, Vol IX, 78. *Mailing Add:* 47 Brookview Ave Delmar NY 12054

ODOM, WILLIAM LEE, b Richmond, Va, Dec 28, 34; m 56; c 2. GREEK LANGUAGES & LITERATURE. *Educ:* Hampden-Sydney Col, BA, 57; Univ Va, MA, 59, PhD(Greek), 61. *Prof Exp:* From assoc prof to prof Greek, Randolph-Macon Col, 61-65; prof Greek & chmn freshman humanities prog, Hampden-Sydney Col, 65-69; dean, Keuka Col, 69-75, vpres, 70-75; PRES, BETHEL COL, 75- *Concurrent Pos:* Lectr, Richmond Pub Schs Humanities Inst, 65-69; ed, Nuntius, 68-69. *Mem:* Am Philol Asn; Am Asn Higher Educ; Archaeol Inst Am. *Res:* Social position of Greek women. *Mailing Add:* Off of the Pres Bethel Col McKenzie TN 38201

O'DONNELL, JAMES JOSEPH, b Giessen, Ger, Feb 26, 50; US citizen. CLASSICS, PATRISTICS. *Educ:* Princeton Univ, AB, 72; Yale Univ, PhD(Medieval studies), 75. *Hon Degrees:* MA, Univ Pa, 82. *Prof Exp:* Lectr Latin, Bryn Mawr Col, 75-76; asst prof Greek & Latin, Cath Univ Am, 76-77; dir medieval studies, 79-81, asst prof classics, Cornell Univ, 77-81; ASSOC PROF CLASS STUDIES & GRAD CHAIR, UNIV PA, 81- *Mem:* Am Philol Asn; NAm Patristics Soc. *Res:* Late Latin language and literature; patristics; Late Roman history. *Publ:* Auth, The career of Virius Nicomachus Flavianus, Phoenix, 78; The demise of paganism, Traditio, 79; Cassiodorus, Univ Calif, 79; Augustine's classical readings, Recherches Augustiniennes, 80; Libenus the Patrician, Traditio, 81; The Aims of Jordanes, 82. *Mailing Add:* Dept of Class Studies Univ Pa Philadelphia PA 19104

O'DONNELL, JOHN FRANCIS, English. See Vol II

O'FLAHERTY, JAMES CARNEAL, b Henrico Co, Va, Apr 28, 14; m 36; c 1. GERMAN. *Educ:* Georgetown Col, BA, 39; Univ Ky, MA, 41; Univ Chicago, PhD, 50. *Prof Exp:* Instr hist & relig, Georgetown Col, 39-41; from instr to assoc prof, 47-58, chmn dept, 61-69, PROF GER, WAKE FOREST UNIV, 58- *Concurrent Pos:* Am Philos Soc res grant, Ger, 58; Beecher lectr, Amherst Col, 58; Fulbright res fel, Ger, 60-61; lectr Kulterelles Wort Ser, Südwestfunk, Baden-Baden, Ger, 61; mem adv comt, Fulbright Awards, 62, chmn, 63; lectr, 4th Int Cong Germanists, Princeton Univ, 70; lectr, 1st Int Hamann-Colloquium, Lüneburg, Ger, 76. *Mem:* SAtlantic Mod Lang Asn; Am Asn Teachers Ger; NAm Nietzsche Soc. *Res:* Johann Georg Hamann; Nietzsche; philosophy of language. *Publ:* Auth, Unity and Language: A Study in the philosophy of Johann Georg Hamann, Univ NC, Chapel Hill, 52, AMS Press, 66; Max Planck and Adolf Hitler, AAUP Bull, 56; Hamann's Socratic Memorabilia, Johns Hopkins Univ, 67; East and West in the thought of Hamann, Ger Rev, 68; Eros and creativity in Nietzsche's Birth of Tragedy, In: Studies in German Literature of the Nineteenth and Twentieth Centuries, Univ NC, 70; The Concept of knowledge in Hamann's Sokratische Denkwürdigkeiten and Nietzsche's Geburt der Gragödie, Monatshefte, 4/72; co-ed & contribr, Studies in Nietzsche and the Classical Tradition, Univ NC, Chapel Hill, 76; auth, Johann Georg Hamann, G K Hall, 79. *Mailing Add:* 2164 Faculty Drive Winston-Salem NC 27106

O'GORMAN, RICHARD F, b St Louis, Mo, July 22, 28; m 59; c 2. FRENCH. *Educ:* Wash Univ, AB, 55, AM, 57; Univ Pa, PhD, 62. *Prof Exp:* From asst prof to assoc prof French, Ind Univ, Bloomington, 62-67; chmn dept French & Ital, 67-72, PROF FRENCH, UNIV IOWA, 67- *Concurrent Pos:* Am Philos Soc grants, 70, 73 & 77; Nat Endowment for Humanities sr fel, 72-73. *Mem:* Mediaeval Acad Am; MLA; Int Arthurian Soc; Am Asn Teachers Fr. *Res:* Medieval French; old French philology; textual criticism. *Publ:* Auth, Ecclesiastical tradition and the holy grail, Australian J Fr Studies, 69; The prose version of Robert de Boron's Joseph D'Arimathie, Romance Philol, 70; La tradition manuscrite du Joseph en prose de Robert de Boron, Rev L'Hist Textes, 71; An unknown leaf of the Vulgate Old Testament: Jeremiah 46: 13, Manuscripta, 72; The Middle French redaction of Robert de Boron's Joseph D'Arimathie, Am Philos Soc Proc, 78; coauth, Un manuscrit inconnu de Bartolomeo Visconti: Les dialogi de Gregoire le Grand, Scriptorium, 78; A Note on the Orthodoxy of Robert de Boron, Neuphilologische Mitteilungen, 79; l'Article Seignor Schwiegervater dans l'Altfranzösisches Wörterbuch, Studia Neophilologica, 82. *Mailing Add:* Dept of French Univ of Iowa Iowa City IA 52242

OHALA, JOHN JEROME, b Chicago, Ill, July 19, 41; m 69. LINGUISTICS. *Educ:* Univ Notre Dame, BA, 63; Univ Calif, Los Angeles, MA, 66, PhD(ling), 69. *Prof Exp:* Nat Sci Found fel, Res Inst Logopedics & Phoniatrics, Fac Med, Univ Tokyo, 69-70; asst prof, 70-72, assoc prof, 72-77, PROF LING, UNIV CALIF, BERKELEY, 77- *Concurrent Pos:* Vis lector, Inst Fonetik, Copenhagen Univ, 73. *Mem:* Ling Soc Am; AAAS; Acoust Soc Am. *Res:* Physiology of speech; sound change; phonology. *Publ:* Auth, Aspects of the Control and Production of Speech, Univ Calif, 70; Physical Models in Phonology, Proc Cong Phonetic Sci, 72; contribr, Experimental historical phonology, In: Historical Linguistics II, North Holland, 74; Production of tone, In: Tone: A Linguistic Survey, Acad Press, 78. *Mailing Add:* Dept of Ling Univ of Calif Berkeley CA 94720

O'HARE, THOMAS JOSEPH, b Sioux Fall, SDak, Oct 22, 37; m 59; c 4. LINGUISTICS, GERMANIC LANGUAGES. *Educ:* Marquette Univ, BS, 59; Univ SDak, MA, 62; Univ Tex, Austin, PhD(ling), 64. *Prof Exp:* Dir Saudi Arabia Training Proj English as Foreign Lang, Univ Tex, Austin, 62-64; prof ling, Indonesia Proj, State Univ NY, 64-65; consult ministry educ, United Arab Repub, Univ Tex, Brown Univ & Cornell Univ, 65-66; asst prof ling & Ger lang, 66-68, asst prof, 68-72, ASSOC PROF GER LANG & EDUC, UNIV TEX, AUSTIN, 72- *Concurrent Pos:* Dir lang lab, Univ Tex, 66-74, int officer Peace Corps training, 66-68; consult, Southwest Educ Develop Lab, Austin, 67-68. *Mem:* Ling Soc Am; Am Asn Teachers Ger. *Res:* Elementary language pedagogy; experimental phonetics; English as foreign language teacher training. *Publ:* Coauth, Teaching English: A Collection of Readings, Am Bk Co, 68; Laboratory Handbook for Active German, rev ed, 68 & German: Language and Culture, 72, Holt. *Mailing Add:* Dept of Ger Lang Univ of Tex Austin TX 78712

O'HEALY, ANNE-MARIE, b Galway, Ireland, Feb 2, 48. ITALIAN, FRENCH. *Educ:* Univ Col, Galway, BA, 69, MA, 71; Univ Wis, PhD(Ital), 76. *Prof Exp:* Lectr Ital, Univ Col, Galway, 73-74; asst prof Ital, Univ Ga, 76-82; ASST PROF ITAL, UNIV NOTRE DAME, 82- *Mem:* MLA; Soc Ital Studies, Gr Brit. *Res:* Modern Italian poetry and prose. *Publ:* Auth, Cesare Pavese, Twayne, 79. *Mailing Add:* Dept of Romance Lang Univ of Notre Dame Notre Dame TN 46556

OHLENDORF, HARALD HANS, b Soest, Ger; Can citizen. GERMAN LITERATURE. *Educ:* Queen's Univ, Ont, BA, 63; Stanford Univ, MA, 65, PhD(Ger), 73. *Prof Exp:* Instr Ger, Univ Mass, Amherst, 67-68; asst prof, 68-78, ASSOC PROF GER, SCARBOROUGH COL, UNIV TORONTO, 68- *Mem:* Can Asn Univ Teachers Ger. *Res:* German literature of the 18th to 20th centuries; German-English literary relations; comparative literature. *Publ:* Auth, The poet and his masks: some remarks on implicit structures in Goethe's Westöstlicher Divan, Mod Lang Rev, 7/74. *Mailing Add:* 230 Albany Drive Toronto ON M5R 3C6 Can

OHLGREN, THOMAS HAROLD, Medieval English Literature. See Vol II

OINAS, FELIX JOHANNES, b Estonia, Mar 6, 11; nat US; m 37; c 2. SLAVIC & FINNO-UGRIC LINGUISTICS. *Educ:* Tartu Univ, MA, 37; Ind Univ, PhD(ling), 52. *Prof Exp:* Lectr Finno-Ugric, Pazmany Peter Univ, Budapest, 38-40; vis lectr Estonian, Baltic Univ, Ger, 46-48; lectr Slavic lang & lit, 51-52, from instr to assoc prof, 52-65, actg chmn Uralic & Altaic prog, 60-61, PROF SLAVIC LANG & LIT & URALIC & ALTAIC STUDIES, IND UNIV, BLOOMINGTON, 65- *Concurrent Pos:* Fulbright scholar, Finland, 61-62; Guggenheim scholar, Finland, 61-62 & 66-67; Fulbright-Hays grant, Yugoslavia, 64-65; Nat Endowment for Humanities grant, 74; fel, Folklore Inst, Ind Univ Commemorative Medal, Finnish Govt, 68; vis prof folklore, Univ Calif, Berkeley, 76. *Honors & Awards:* Cultural Award, Found Estonian Arts & Lett, 78; First Prize, Arthur Puksow Found, 80. *Mem:* MLA; corresp mem Finnish Lit Soc; Asn Advan Baltic Studies (vpres, 72-73); fel Am Folklore Soc; Finnish Acad Sci. *Res:* Slavic and Finno-Ugric linguistics and folklore. *Publ:* Auth, Estonian General Reader, 63 & Basic Course in Estonian, 66, Mouton; Studies in Finnic-Slavic Folklore Relations, Finnish Acad Sci, 69; co-ed, The Study of Russian Folklore, Mouton, 75; ed, Folklore, Nationalism, and Politics, Slavica, 78; Heroic Epic and Saga: An Introduction to the World's Great Folk Epics, Ind Univ, 78; Kalevipoeg kütkeis, Mana, 79; ed, European Folklore, Trickster Press, 81. *Mailing Add:* 2513 E Eighth St Bloomington IN 47401

OKSENHOLT, SVEIN, b Larvik, Norway, Jan 12, 25; US citizen; m 61. GERMAN. *Educ:* Pac Union Col, BA, 50; Univ Nebr, MA, 53; Univ Southern Calif, PhD, 59. *Prof Exp:* Teaching asst Ger, Univ Nebr, 51-53; teacher Ger & prin, Abercrombie High Sch, 53-55; teaching asst & lectr Ger, Univ Southern Calif, 55-58; teacher, Great Falls High Sch, 58-61; asst prof Ger & educ, Univ Kans, 61-62; asst prof Ger, San Diego State Col, 62-63; assoc prof Ger & chmn dept foreign lang, Doane Col, 63-64; from asst prof to prof Ger, Col Great Falls, 64-67, admin asst, 64-65, chmn dept mod & class lang, 65-67; head dept foreign lang, 67-73, PROF GER, EASTERN MONT COL, 67-, PROF NORWEGIAN, 77- *Honors & Awards:* St Olav's Medal, 79. *Mem:* Am Asn Teachers Ger; Soc Advan Scandinavian Studies. *Res:* Scandinavian studies; German 18th century literature; Kierkegaard. *Publ:* Auth, Thoughts Concerning Education in the Works of Georg Christoph Lichtenberg, Martinus Nijhoff, The Hague, 63; Deutsch der Gegenwart, Prentice, 71; Lichtenberg and Kierkegaard; a Reconsideration, 4/65, Undervisnings Metodik i Tyska, Malmo, Sweden, 5/73; Put a Shortwave Radio in your Foreign Language Classroom, Audiovisual Instruction, 5/77, In: Learning Via Tele-Communication: Readings From Audiovisual Instruction, 78 & In: Nonprint in the Secondary Curriculum: Readings for Reference, 82; Norsk Idag, 2nd year Norwegian Text, Eastern Mont Col, 82. *Mailing Add:* 3014 Laredo Pl Billings MT 59101

OLCHYK, MARTA, b Havana, Cuba, Oct 19, 38; US citizen; m 59; c 2. SPANISH, LATIN AMERICAN HISTORY. *Educ:* Univ Havana, BA, 60; Tex Woman's Univ, MA, 62; Tex Christian Univ, PhD(Latin Am hist), 72. *Prof Exp:* Instr Span, Isrealite Ctr Cuba, Havana, 58-60; grad asst, Tex Woman's Univ, 61-62; teacher, Irving High Sch, Tex, 62-63; assoc, 65-69, ASSOC PROF SPAN & LATIN AM HIST, UNIV PLANO, 72- *Concurrent Pos:* Equal opportunity specialist, Dept Health, Educ & Welfare Off Civil Rights, High Educ, 76-78. *Res:* Latin American and Spanish culture and civilization; cultural discrimination and its effect on delivery of social services to minorities. *Publ:* Auth, Research on Cultural Discrimination, US Dept Health, Educ & Welfare, 77. *Mailing Add:* 10323 Boedeker Dallas TX 75230

OLDCORN, ANTHONY, b Longridge, Eng, June 20, 35; m 60; c 2. ITALIAN LANGUAGE AND LITERATURE. *Educ:* Oxford Univ, BA, 58; Univ Virginia, MA, 61; Harvard Univ, PhD(Romance land & lit), 70. *Hon Degrees:* MA, Brown Univ, 77. *Prof Exp:* Instr French & Ital, Boston Col, 60-62; teaching fel, Harvard Univ, 62-65; from instr to asst prof Ital, Wellesley Col, 66-71, acting chmn dept, 69-70; asst prof, 71-76; assoc prof, 76-80, PROF ITAL STUDIES, BROWN UNIV, 80- *Concurrent Pos:* Nat Endowment for Humanities fel, 78-79; vis prof Ital, Vassar Col, 80-81, Dante Autolini chair, 81-; Ital field ed, Twayne World Authors Series, 81- *Mem:* Am Asn Teachers Ital; Am Comt Hist 2nd World War; Dante Soc Am; MLA. *Res:* Medieval, Renaissance, baroque and modern Italian literature; textual criticism; rhetoric and literary stylistics. *Publ:* Auth, A Recensio of the Sources of the Gerusalemme Conquistata: Notes for a New Edition, Forum Italicum, 75; Virgilio Giotti (poems) (Transl), Copper Beech Press, 75; Pirandello o del candore?, Mod Lang Notes, 76; The Textual Problems of Tasso's Gerusalemme Conquistata, Longo, 76; Tasso's Epic Theory, Italica, 77. *Mailing Add:* Dept of Hisp & Ital Studies Brown Univ Providence RI 02912

OLESON, JOHN PETER, Classical Archeology & Philology. See Vol I

OLIPHANT, ROBERT T, b Tulsa, Okla, Oct 25, 24; m 57; c 2. LINGUISTICS. *Educ:* Washington & Jefferson Col, AB, 48; Stanford Univ, MA, 58, PhD, 62. *Prof Exp:* Actg instr English, Stanford Univ, 55-59; from asst prof to assoc prof, 59-67, PROF ENGLISH, CALIF STATE UNIV, NORTHRIDGE, 67- *Concurrent Pos:* Calif State Univ, Northridge grant, 63; vis assoc prof English, Stanford Univ, 65-66. *Mem:* Ling Soc Am; Col English Asn. *Res:* Old English lexicography; playwriting; musical composition. *Publ:* Auth, Harley Latin-Old English Glossary, Mouton, 66; Lost Boy: A Musical Play, 71; The Importance of Being Earnest: A Comic Opera Based on the Play by Oscar Wilde, 73; A Piano for Mrs Cimino (novel), 80 & A Trumpet for Jackie Crowell, 82, Prentice-Hall. *Mailing Add:* Dept of English Calif State Univ Northridge CA 91324

OLIVA, JOSEPH, b Buffalo, NY, June 10, 22; m 61; c 3. LINGUISTICS, SEMIOTICS. *Educ:* Roosevelt Univ, BM, 51; State Univ Col Buffalo, MS, 61; State Univ NY Buffalo, PhD(ling), 77. *Prof Exp:* Asst prof, 70-80, ASSOC PROF ENGLISH, STATE UNIV COL BUFFALO, 80- *Mem:* Ling Soc Am; Semiotic Soc Am; Deutche Gesellshaft Semiotik. *Res:* Semiotics of music; semiotic theory. *Publ:* Coauth, The relationship between intonation and syntax in normal and abnormal speakers, ERIC, 75; Structural regularities in the intonation of an abnormal speaker: Psycholinguistic implications, Second LACUS Forum, 75; Three levels of temporal structuring in spoken language, Fourth LACUS Forum, Ling Asn US & Can, 78; Intonation, nonverbal and semantic aspects of the two word utterances of a one and one-half year old normal child, In: Language Acquisition and Developmental Kinesics, Bunka Hyoron, Japan, 78; auth, Structure of Music and Structure of Language, Peter de Ridder, Lisse/The Neth (in press). *Mailing Add:* Dept of Arts & Humanities State Univ Col 1300 Elmwood Ave Buffalo NY 14222

OLIVER, REVILO PENDLETON, b Corpus Christi, Tex, July 7, 10; m 30. CLASSICS, SPANISH & ITALIAN. *Educ:* Univ Ill, AM, 33, PhD(class philol), 40. *Prof Exp:* From instr to assoc prof, 40-53, prof, 53-78, EMER PROF CLASSICS, SPAN & ITAL, UNIV ILL, URBANA, 78- *Concurrent Pos:* From res analyst to dir res, US War Dept, 42-45; Guggenheim fel, 46-47; Fulbright fel, 53-54. *Mem:* Am Philol Asn; Mediaeval Acad Am; Renaissance Soc Am; Brit Class Asn; Soc Prom Roman Studies. *Res:* Humanism and scholarship of the Renaissance; Latin epigraphy; Graeco-Roman philosophy. *Publ:* Ed, Niccolo Perotti's Version of the Enchiridion of Epictetus, Univ Ill, Urbana, 54; Apex and Sicilicus, Am J Philol, 4/66; auth, Lucan's naval battle, In: Homenaje a Antonio Tovar, Madrid, Gredos, 72; Interpolated lines in Ovid, In: Gesellschaft, Kultur: Literatur, Stuttgart, Heirsemann, 75; The second Medicean MS and the Test of Tacitus, 76 & Did Tacitus finish the Annales?, 77, Ill Class Studies; Christianity and the Survival of the West, 2nd ed, Cape Canaveral, Howard Allen, 78; America's Decline, the Education of a Conservative, Londinium Press, London, 82. *Mailing Add:* 701 Ohio St Urbana IL 61801

OLIVER, WILLIAM ANDREW, b Loughborough, England, Oct 16, 41. FRENCH LANGUAGE & LITERATURE. *Educ:* Cambridge Univ, BA, 63, MA, 66; Laval Univ, PhD(French), 67. *Prof Exp:* From asst prof to assoc prof, 66-77, PROF FRENCH, TRINITY COL, UNIV TORONTO, 77- *Concurrent Pos:* Can Coun leave fel, 72-73 & 78-79. *Mem:* Asn Can Univ Teachers Fr; Asn Amis D'Andre Gide; MLA; Soc Fr Studies. *Res:* French literature 19th century, especially Benjamin Constant; French literature 20th century, especially Raymond Radiguet and Andre Gide; aesthetics of the novel. *Publ:* Ed, Constant, Benjamin: Adolphe, Macmillan, 68; auth, Benjamin Constant: ecriture et conquete du moi, Lett Mod M J Minard, 70; Cocteau Radiguet et la genese du Bal du Comte D'Orgel, Cahiers Jean Cocteau, 73; Le Bal du comte d'Orgel: Structure, mythe, signification, La Revue des Langues Romanes, 75, 76; Michel, Job, Pierre, Paul: Intertextualite de la lecture dans L'Immoraliste, 79 & ed, Andre Gide: Perspectives contemporaines, 79, Lett Mod M J Minard. *Mailing Add:* Dept of French Trinity Col Univ of Toronto Toronto ON M5S 1H8 Can

OLIVERA, OTTO HUGO, b Pedro Betancourt, Cuba, Apr 20, 19; m 50; c 3. SPANISH. *Educ:* Univ Havana, Dr, 45; La State Univ, MA, 47; Tulane Univ, PhD, 53. *Prof Exp:* Instr, Tulane Univ, 50-54; from asst prof to prof Romance lang, Syracuse Univ, 54-65; PROF SPAN, TULANE UNIV, 65- *Mem:* MLA; Am Asn Teachers Span & Port; Inst Int Lit Iberoam; AAUP. *Res:* Literature of the Spanish Antilles and the Caribbean; national characteristics of Spanish American literatures; Spanish American modernism. *Publ:* Auth, Breve historia de la literatura Antillana, 57 & Cuba en su poesia, 65, Andrea, Mex; El romanticismo de Jose Eustasio Rivera, No 35, 52 & El Correo de la Tarde, de Ruben Dario, No 64, 67, Rev Iberoam; La literatura en la Gaceta de Puerto Rico, Rev Interamericana Bibliog, Vol 21, 71; coauth, La prosa modernista en Hispanoamerica, Mex, 71; auth, La literatura en publicaciones periodicas de Guatemala, New Orleans, 74; Las relaciones entre los iniciadores del modernismo, No 107-110, 80. *Mailing Add:* Dept of Span Tulane Univ of La New Orleans LA 70118

OLIVIER, LOUIS ANTOINE, b Brooklyn, NY, Oct 30, 35. FRENCH LITERATURE, LITERARY TRANSLATION. *Educ:* Univ Utah, BA, 62, MA, 63; Johns Hopkins Univ, PhD(romance lang), 76. *Prof Exp:* Lectr French, Goucher Col, 65-66; instr, Univ Ore, 66-73; dir, Ore Study Ctr in France, 73-75; instr French, Univ Ore, 75-76, asst prof, 76-78, assoc prof & chair, Dept Romance Lang, 78-80; PROF & CHAIR FOREIGN LANG, ILL STATE UNIV, 80- *Mem:* MLA; Am Soc Eighteenth Century Studies; Am Lit Transl Asn; Western Soc French Hist; Am Asn Teachers of French. *Res:* Laymen, critics, connoiseurs, amateurs and the fine arts in 17th & 18th century France; pre-revolutionary French clandestine journalism; the early 19th century French novel. *Publ:* Auth, Bachaumont the chronicler: A questionable renown, 75 & Theother Bachaumont: Citizen and connoiseur, 76, Studies Voltaire & Eighteenth Century; Felix Grandet--un homme nouveau?, Proc Pac Northwest Conf Foreign Lang, 76; transl, Vim Kardine, Oasis-New York, 76 & Claude Herviant, Le Soleil des taupes, 77, Chambelland; auth, The case for the fine arts in seventeenth century France, Australian J French Studies, 5-8/79; The idea of the connoisseur in France: Roger de Piles and Jonathan Richardson, Annali Sexione Romanza, Inst Univ

Orient, 1/82; Artists, amateurs and bureaucrats: A study of the role of amateurs honoraires in the Royal Academy of Painting and Sculpture, 1648-1777, Proceedings Western Soc French Hist, 82. *Mailing Add:* Dept of Foreign Lang Ill State Univ Normal IL 61761

OLLER, JOHN WILLIAM, JR, b Las Vegas, NMex, Oct 22, 43; m 63; c 2. LINGUISTICS, PSYCHOLOGY. *Educ:* Fresno State Col, BA, 65; Univ Rochester, MA, 68, PhD(ling), 69. *Prof Exp:* From asst prof to assoc prof psycholing, Univ Calif, Los Angeles, 69-73; assoc prof educ found & ling & chmn dept ling, Univ NMex, 72-76; vis prof ling, Southern Ill Univ, 76-77; assoc prof, 77-80, PROF LING, UNIV NMEX, 80- *Concurrent Pos:* Mem comt exam English as foreign lang, Educ Testing Serv, 72-75. *Mem:* Ling Soc Am; MLA; Teachers English to Speakers Other Lang. *Res:* Linguistics and psycholinguistics; psychology and language acquisition; education and the applications of linguistics. *Publ:* Auth, Transformational theory and pragmatics, Mod Lang J, 70; Coding Information in Natural Languages, Mouton, The Hague, 71; On the relation between syntax, semantics, and pragmatics, Linguistics, 72; Cloze tests of second language proficiency and what they measure, Lang Learning, 73; coauth, Focus on the Learner, 73 & Language in Education: Testing the Tests, 78, Newbury House; auth, Language Tests at School, Longman, 79; Research in Language Testing, 80 & Issues in Language Testing Research, 82, Newbury House. *Mailing Add:* Dept of Ling Univ of NMex Albuquerque NM 87131

OLORUNTO, SAMUEL BOLAJI, Afro-American & African Studies. See Vol II

OLSEN, MARILYN ADA, b San Francisco, Calif, May 15, 39. MEDIEVAL LITERATURE. *Educ:* Univ Calif, Berkeley, BA, 63; Univ Am, MA, 65; Univ Wis-Madison, PhD(Span), 75. *Prof Exp:* Instr, Univ Wis Ctr-Waukesha, 72-74; lectr, Univ Wis Ctrs-Janesville & Baraboo, 76-78; ASST PROF SPAN, UNIV NEBR-LINCOLN, 78- *Mem:* MLA; Asoc Int Hisp; Am-Can Br Soc Rencesvals; Int Courtly Lit Soc; Medieval Acad Am. *Res:* Medieval Spanish romance, particularly the Libro del Cauallero Zifar; editing old Spanish texts; the transmission of medieval literature, especially written texts. *Publ:* Auth, Three observations on the Zifar, La Coronica, 80; A reppraisal of methodology in medieval editions: The extant material of the Libro del Cavallero Zifar, Romance Philol, 82; A tentaive bibliography of the Libro del Cavallero Zifar, La Coronica (in prep). *Mailing Add:* Dept of Mod Lang Univ of Nebr Lincoln NE 68588

OLSEN, SOLVEIG, b Hamburg, Ger, Aug 23, 40; US citizen. GERMAN LANGUAGE & LITERATURE. *Educ:* Univ Oslo, Cand Mag, 63, Cand Phil, 64; Pedag Sem, Oslo, Norway, teaching cert, 65; Rice Univ, Phd(Ger), 68. *Prof Exp:* Adj Ger, English & Norweg, Manglerud Komb Sk, Oslo, Norway, 60-64, lector, 64-65; asst prof, 68-74, ASSOC PROF GER & CHAIRPERSON DEPT FOREIGN LANG & LIT, NTEX STATE UNIV, 74- *Concurrent Pos:* Res grant NTex State Univ, 76; Danforth fel, Danforth Found, 77- *Mem:* MLA; AAUP; Am Asn Teachers Ger; Int Arbeitskreis für Barockliteratur; Am Coun Teaching Foreign Lang. *Res:* German baroque literature; comparative literature; language pedagogy. *Publ:* Auth, Der Anfang der Weltlichen Kantate in Deutschland, Lang Quart, Univ SFla, 72; Chr Hch Postels Beitrag zur Deutschen Literatur: Versuch einer Darstellung, Rodopi, Amsterdam, 73. *Mailing Add:* Dept of Foreign Lang & Lit NTex State Univ Denton TX 76203

OLSON, PAUL RICHARD, b Rockford, Ill, Nov 2, 25; m 53; c 4. ROMANCE LANGUAGES. *Educ:* Univ Ill, AB, 48, AM, 50; Harvard Univ, PhD, 59. *Prof Exp:* From instr to asst prof Span, Dartmouth Col, 56-61; from asst prof to assoc prof, 61-68, PROF SPAN, JOHNS HOPKINS UNIV, 68- *Concurrent Pos:* Guggenheim fel, 64-65; Fulbright Award, Spain, 64-65. *Mem:* MLA; Asoc Int Hispanistas. *Res:* Spanish literature. *Publ:* Auth, Circle of Paradox: Time and Essence in the Poetry of Juan Ramon Jimenez, Johns Hopkins Press, 67; Galdos and history, MLN, 70; Unamuno's lacquered boxes, RHM, 74; Unamuno's Niebla, Ga Rev, 75; ed, Miguel de Unamuno: Como se nace una novela, Ediciones Guadarrama, Madrid, 77; contribr, Dos metafisicas del texto poetico, Asn Int Hisp, Toronto, 78. *Mailing Add:* 806 W University Pkwy Baltimore MD 21210

OMAGGIO, ALICE CATHERINE, b Philadelphia, Pa, Nov 24, 47. FOREIGN LANGUAGES. *Educ:* Pa State Univ, BS, 69; Ohio State Univ, MA, 73, PhD(foreign lang educ), 77. *Prof Exp:* Assoc dir, ERIC Clearinghouse Lang & Ling, Washington, DC, 77-79; asst prof, Univ NMex, 79-80; ASST PROF FRENCH, UNIV ILL URBANA-CHAMPAIGN, 80- *Concurrent Pos:* Co-ed, Am Coun Teaching Foreign Lang, Cent State Conf Reports, 76-77; vis asst prof methods, Purdue Univ, 78 & Univ Tex Arlington, 80; consult, Sch Lang, Defense Lang Inst, Monterey, 81 & 82. *Honors & Awards:* Stephen A Freeman Award, Northeast Conf Teaching Foreign Lang, 79; Paul Pimsleur Award Res, Am Coun Teaching Foreign Lang, 80. *Mem:* Am Coun Teaching Foreign Lang; Am Asn Univ Supvr & Coordr. *Res:* Teaching and testing second language skills in context; cognitive styles and learner strategies for second language learning and acquisition; the effects of pictorial and other organizers on language processing and comprehension. *Publ:* Auth, Pictures and second language comprehension: Do they help?, Foreign Lang Ann, Vol 12, No 2; Games and Simulations in the Foreign Language Classroom, 79 & Helping Learners Succeed: Activities for the Foreign Language Classroom, 81, Ctr Applied Ling; coauth, Diagnosing and responding to individual learner needs, Mod lang J, Vol 62, No 7 & 81; auth, Priorities in classroom testing in the 1980s, Nat Priorities Conf, 81; coauth, Rendez-vous, Random House, 82; auth, Games and interaction activities for the development of functional language skills, Can Mod Lang Rev, spring 82; Testing Language Skills in Context, Ctr Appl Ling (in press). *Mailing Add:* 2510 Sheridan Dr Champaign IL 61820

O'MARA, PATRICK F, European History, Egyptology. See Vol I

O'MEARA, MAUREEN FRANCES, b Peabody, Mass, Aug 4, 49. FRENCH. *Educ:* Trinity Col, DC, BA, 71; Cornell Univ, PhD(French), 76. *Prof Exp:* ASST PROF FRENCH, UNIV MICH, ANN ARBOR, 77- *Mem:* Am Soc 18th Century Studies; MLA. *Res:* Eighteenth century narrative prose; historical discourse; critical theory. *Publ:* Auth, Le Taureau Blanc and the activity of language, Studies Voltaire, 76; From linguistics to literature: The un-time-liness of tense, Diacritics, summer 76; Towards a typology of historical discourse: The case of Voltaire, Mod Lang Notes (in prep). *Mailing Add:* Dept of Romance Lang Univ of Mich Ann Arbor MI 48109

O'NAN, MARTHA (BIRCHETTE), b Shelbyville, Ky, June 28, 21. SPANISH, FRENCH. *Educ:* Agnes Scott Col, BA, 41; Univ Ky, MA, 42; Northwestern Univ, PhD, 52; Univ Paris, cert, 53; Univ Wis-Madison, cert univ admin, 77. *Prof Exp:* Instr Span, Pikeville Col, 42-44; instr Span & French, Jacksonville State Col, 44-46; asst prof, Centre Col, 46-48; prof & chmn dept French, Elmhurst Col, 51-54; from assoc prof to prof mod lang, Millikin Univ, 56-63, chmn dept, 58-63; from assoc prof to prof, Ohio Univ, 64-69; chmn dept, 69-77, PROF FOREIGN LANG & LIT, STATE UNIV NY COL BROCKPORT, 69- *Concurrent Pos:* Fr govt fel, 52-53; State Univ NY grant improv undergrad educ, 76; col evaluator, Comn Higher Educ, Mid States Asn Col & Schs, 77-; grants, State Univ NY, 80, 81. *Mem:* Am Asn Teachers Span & Port; MLA; Soc Study Multi-Ethnic Lit US; Am Asn Univ Prof. *Res:* Contemporary French literature; comparative literature; 20th century foreign women writers. *Publ:* Co-ed, Studies in Honor of Harvey L Johnson, Porrua, Madrid, 79; Letter of introduction to Mouloud Feraoun's Family, Celfan, 82; Bouzareah, Celfan, 82; Names in Rene de Obaldia's Du Vent dans les branches de sassafras, Names, 82; Women, would-be-overthrowers of men, Novels of Michele Perrein, Literary Onomastics Studies, 82; Roger Martin du Gard aux Etats-Unis, Rev d'Histoire Litteraire de la France, 82; Une lettre de Roger Martin du Gard, Cahiers Roger Martin du Gard, 82. *Mailing Add:* Dept of Foreign Lang & Lit State Univ of NY Col Brockport NY 14420

O'NEAL, JOHN COFFEE, b Birmingham, Ala, Nov 8, 50; m 76; c 2. FRENCH LITERATURE. *Educ:* Washington & Lee Univ, BA, 72; Middlebury Col, MA, 75; Univ Calif, Los Angeles, PhD(French), 80. *Prof Exp:* Teacher French & Humanities, Red Mountain Sch, Birmingham, Ala, 73-74; teaching asst French, Univ Calif, Los Angeles, 76-77, teaching assoc, 78-79, teaching fel, 79-80; ASST PROF FRENCH, ST MARY'S COL, IND, 80- *Mem:* MLA; Am Soc 18th Century Studies; Soc Jean-Jacques Rousseau; Soc Rousseau Studies; Am Asn Teachers Fr. *Res:* Jean-Jacques Rousseau; 18th century French literature; theories of perception. *Publ:* Auth, Morality in Rousseau's public and private society at Clarens, Rev Metaphysique & Morale (in prep); Jean-Jacques Rousseau, In: Critical Survey of Long Fiction, Salem Press (in prep). *Mailing Add:* Dept of Mod Lang St Mary's Col Notre Dame IN 46556

O'NEIL, EDWARD NOON, b Memphis, Tenn, Oct 19, 22; m 43; c 3. CLASSICS. *Educ:* Univ Calif, PhD(classics), 54. *Prof Exp:* Instr class lang, DePauw Univ, 54-55; asst prof, Univ Ore, 55-57; from asst prof to assoc prof classics, 57-64, chmn dept, 58-72, PROF CLASSICS, UNIV SOUTHERN CALIF, 64- *Concurrent Pos:* Nat Found Arts & Humanities fel, 67-68. *Mem:* Am Philol Asn; Philol Asn Pac Coast; Class Asn Pac States (pres, 57 & 61). *Res:* Latin poetry; mythology; Plutarch. *Publ:* Coauth, Plutarch's Quotations, Am Philol Asn, 59; auth, Cynthia and the Moon, Class Philol; A Critical Concordance of the Tibullan Corpus, Am Philol Asn, 63; coauth, Tibullus 2.6: A new interpretation, Class Philol, 7/67. *Mailing Add:* Dept of Classics Univ of Southern Calif Univ Park Los Angeles CA 90007

O'NEILL, ELMER WESLEY, JR, b Philadelpha, Pa, Aug 17, 13; m 39; c 2. ROMANCE LANGUAGES, METHODOLOGY. *Educ:* Princeton Univ, AB, 35, MA, 40, PhD(French lit), 52. *Prof Exp:* Head dept mod lang, William Penn Charter Sch, 42-58, French, Roxbury Latin Sch, 58-63; assoc prof French, Colo State Univ, 63-65; prof, 65-76, dir summer prog, France, 69, EMER PROF FRENCH, UNIV MAINE, 76- *Concurrent Pos:* Fulbright exchange teacher, Brussels, Belgium, 56-57; dir NDEA Inst French, Univ Maine, 66-68. *Honors & Awards:* Bronze Star Medal; Croix de Guerre, Belgium. *Mem:* MLA; Am Asn Teachers Fr; Am Philatelic Soc. *Res:* Chateaubriand: life and works; French numismatics: references in history and literature; foreign language teaching methodology. *Publ:* Auth, A trend in fable literature, 4/54 & French coinage in history and literature, 10/65, Fr Rev; ed, La France d'Aujourd'hui, Univ Maine, 68; auth, A little known collection of the coins of Bearn, Numis Rev, 12/70; J'ai gagne, Six Games in French Culture, J W Walch, 81. *Mailing Add:* Ten Roundabout Lane Cape Elizabeth ME 04107

O'NEILL, JAMES CALVIN, b Canandaigua, NY, Dec 12, 09; m 45; c 4. FRENCH. *Educ:* Univ Mich, AB, 30, AM, 32, PhD, 42. *Prof Exp:* From instr to assoc prof French, 32-60, chmn dept Romance lang, 60-73, prof, 60-69, EMER PROF FRENCH, UNIV MICH, ANN ARBOR, 70- *Honors & Awards:* Chevalier, Palmes Academiques, 63. *Mem:* MLA; Am Asn Teachers Fr; Cent State Mod Lang Teachers Asn. *Res:* Modern French literature and criticism; French language pedagogy. *Publ:* Philosophy and criticism: Bergson and Thibaudet; An intellectual affinity: Bergson and Valery. *Mailing Add:* Dept of Fr Univ of Mich Ann Arbor MI 48104

O'NEILL, PATRICK JAMES, b Wicklow, Ireland, Aug 9, 45; m 68; c 4. GERMAN, COMPARATIVE LITERATURE. *Educ:* Nat Univ Ireland, BA, 66, MA, 68; Queen's Univ, PhD(Ger), 72. *Prof Exp:* Asst Ger, Univ Col, Dublin, 67-68; asst prof, 70-78, ASSOC PROF GER, UNIV BC, 78- *Mem:* MLA; Can Asn Univ Teachers Ger; Can Comp Lit Asn; Int Asn Study Anglo-Irish Lit; Can Asn Irish Studies. *Res:* Twentieth century fiction and narrative theory; literature and humor. *Publ:* Auth, Alfred Döblin's Babylonische Wandrung: a Study, Herbert Lang, Bern, 74; Günter Grass: A Bibliography, 1955-75, Univ Toronto, 76; German Literature in English Translation: A Select Bibliography, Univ Toronto, 81. *Mailing Add:* Dept of Ger Studies Univ of BC Vancouver BC V6T 1W5 Can

O'NEILL, SAMUEL J, b Lowell, Mass, Apr 7, 32; m 56; c 3. ROMANCE LANGUAGES. *Educ:* Boston Col, AB, 53; Fordham Univ, AM, 55; Univ Md, PhD(Span Am lit), 65. *Prof Exp:* Asst prof Span & French, US Naval Acad, 61-66, assoc prof, 66-67; chmn div humanities, 67-77, dean acad affairs, 77-79, PROF SPAN, FRENCH & SPEECH, MT WACHUSETT COMMUNITY COL, 67- *Mem:* MLA; Am Asn Teachers Span & Port; Am Coun Teaching Foreign Lang; Asn Depts English. *Res:* Contemporary novel. *Publ:* Auth, Interior monologue in Al Filo de Agua, Hispania, 9/68. *Mailing Add:* Mt Wachusett Community Col Gardner MA 01440

ONEY, EARNEST RALPH, b Wellington, Ohio, May 31, 20; m 46; c 2. INDO-EUROPEAN LINGUISTICS, MIDDLE EAST POLITICS. *Educ:* Ashland Col, AB, 42, BS, 46; Univ Chicago, PhD(ling), 50. *Prof Exp:* Teacher pub schs, Ill, 47-49; bibliog asst ed libr, Univ Chicago, 49-51; area analyst Mid East, US Govt, 51-57 & 60-62; res officer, US Army, Iran, 57-59, plans officer, 62-65; area analyst Mid East, US Govt, 65-79; CONSULT, 79- *Mem:* Ling Soc Am; Am Philol Asn; Am Orient Soc. *Res:* Anatolian languages; modern Iranian languages; history of the Middle East. *Publ:* Laryngeals 3 and 4 in hieroglyphic Hittite, 57 & Note on present dialect studies in Iran, 59, Gen Ling; Revolution in Iran: Religion & Politics in a Traditional Society, 80. *Mailing Add:* 7602 Marian Ct Falls Church VA 22042

ONYSHKEVYCH, LARISSA M L, b Stryi, Ukraine; US citizen; m 61; c 3. SLAVIC LITERATURES & LANGUAGES. *Educ:* Univ Toronto, BA, 63; Univ Pa, MA, 69, PhD(Slavic lang & lit), 73. *Prof Exp:* Vis asst prof Ukrainian lit, civilization, lang & drama, Rutgers Univ, 74-78; freelance ed & researcher, 78-81; ACAD RES, INST ADVAN STUDY, 81- *Concurrent Pos:* Dir, Sch Ukrainian Studies, 73-81; researcher, G W Ball Inst, 79-81; Shevchenko Sci Soc grant, 80. *Mem:* MLA; Am Asn Advan Slavic Studies; Am Asn Teachers Slavic & E Europ Lang; Asn Study Nationalities; Ukrainian Free Acad Arts & Sci. *Res:* Twentieth century Slavic drama; modern Ukrainian drama & literature; Ukrainian onomastics. *Publ:* Ed, Kontrasty, Plast, 70; coauth, Introd article In: Dictionary of Ukrainian Family Names in Canada, 74; auth, Introd article, In: Vohon Kupala, Smoloskyp, 75; Ukrainian dramaturgy in the USA, Nash Teatr, Shevchenko Sci Soc, 75; F Kolessa's works on folklore, In: The Jubillee Colection of UFAcSc, 76; A matter of choice in Richard's existentialist quest, In: Ukrainka's In the Wilderness, Lesia Ukrainka, 1871-1971, Harvard Ukrainian Res Inst, 80; The Modern Encycl of Russian and Soviet Literatures, Acad Int Press, 81; coauth, Ukrainian theater, Ethnic Theater in the US, Greenwood Press, 82. *Mailing Add:* 9 Dogwood Dr Lawrenceville NJ 08648

OONK, GERRIT JOHAN, b Diepenveen, Neth, Jan 30, 39; US citizen; m 65; c 1. MEDIEVAL GERMAN LITERATURE, LINGUISTICS. *Educ:* Sch Lang & Lit, The Hague, BA, 62, MA, 65; Univ Wash, PhD(Ger), 70. *Prof Exp:* Asst prof Ger & English, Southern Ore Col, 70-72; asst prof Ger, Univ Ariz, 72-76; ASST PROF GER, NORTH TEX STATE UNIV, DENTON, 77- *Mem:* MLA. *Res:* Medieval German literature, especially courtly Romance and Minnesong; Dutch. *Publ:* Auth, Recht minne in Heinrich von Veldekes Eneide, Neophilologus, 7/73; Eneas, Tristan, Parzival und die Minne, Zeitschrift für deutsche Philologie, 1/76. *Mailing Add:* 1902 Whippoorwill Denton TX 76201

OPPENHEIMER, FRED E, b Berlin, Ger, Feb 22, 29; US citizen; div; c 2. GERMAN LANGUAGE & LITERATURE. *Educ:* Cent Mich Col, BA, 51; Univ Wis, MA, 57, PhD(Ger), 61. *Prof Exp:* From instr to asst prof Ger, Purdue Univ, 61-65; asst prof, Colo Col, 65-71; ASSOC PROF GER, MILLERSVILLE STATE COL, 71-, DIR JR YEAR ABROAD, 72- *Mem:* Am Asn Teachers Ger; MLA. *Res:* Literature of German Classicism; the German novelle; literary allusion in the novels of Theodor Fontane. *Mailing Add:* Dept of Foreign Lang Millersville State Col Millersville PA 17551

OPPENHEIMER, MAX, JR, b New York, NY, July 27, 17; m 42; c 2. MODERN LANGUAGES & LITERATURE. *Educ:* Univ Paris, BLitt, 35; NY Univ, AB, 41; Univ Calif, Los Angeles, AM, 42; Univ Southern Calif, PhD, 47. *Prof Exp:* Instr, San Diego State Col, 47-49; asst prof romance lang, Wash Univ, 49-51; mil intel officer, US Dept Army, 56-58; assoc prof mod lang, Fla State Univ, 58-61; prof Russ & chmn dept, Univ Iowa, 61-67; chmn dept, 67-73, prof, 67-76, EMER PROF MOD LANG, STATE UNIV NY COL FREDONIA, 76- *Concurrent Pos:* State Univ NY fac res fel, 73. *Mem:* MLA; Am Soc Geoling (pres, 75-76). *Res:* French, German, Russian and Spanish language and literature; comparative literature; translation. *Publ:* Auth, A Basic Outline of Russian Grammar, Lucas Bros, 62; translr, A S Davydov, Theory of Molecular Excitons, McGraw, 62; A A Kostyukov, Theory of Ship Waves and Wave Resistance, Effective Commun, 68; auth, The German adaptations of Calderon de la Barca's El Astrologo Fingido, In: Geprägte Form - Festschrift für Robert Rie, Europäischer Verlag Wien, 75; ed & translr, The Lady Simpleton, (Lope de Vega, La Dama Boba), Don Juan The Beguiler from Seville and the Stone Guest, (Tirso de Molina, El Burlador de Sevilla y Convidado de Piedra) & Pedro Calderon de la Barca, The Fake Astrologer, Coronado, 76; auth, Problems of translation, Geolinguistics, 77. *Mailing Add:* PO Box 5529 Santa Fe NM 87502

OPPENHEIMER, PAUL, Medieval Literature, Writing. See Vol II

ORCHARENKO, MARIA M, b Ukraine, June 19, 09; US citizen; wid. SLAVIC PHILOLOGY. *Educ:* Jagiellonian Univ, Poland, MA, 34; Charles Univ, Prague, PhD, 45. *Prof Exp:* Instr ling, State Col, Lvov, USSR, 39-41; asst prof foreign lang, Western State Col Colo, 61-62; vis assoc prof Russ, Tulane Univ, 62-64; assoc prof, 64-68, prof, 68-80, EMER PROF FOREIGN LANG, EASTERN ILL UNIV, 80- *Concurrent Pos:* Res worker, Acad Arts & Sci Ukraine, USSR, 39-41. *Honors & Awards:* Distinguished Fac Award, Eastern Ill Univ, 77. *Mem:* Shevchenko Sci Soc; Am Asn Advan Slavic Studies. *Res:* Slavic languages and literatures; 20th century Ukrainian poetry. *Publ:* Auth, The Dialects on the Boundaries of Sian Dialect, Shevchenko Scie Soc, 54; Accent in Ivan Franko's poetry, 61; Serhij Yefremov, Shevchenko Sci Soc, 62; Gogol and Osmachka, 69; Symbolism in T Osmachka's novel The Best Man, In: Symbolae in Honorem Georgii Y Shevelov, 71; Lina Kostenko-the poet of the freedom of spirit and of the truth of the word, The Ukrainian Rev, spring 76. *Mailing Add:* Dept of Foreign Lang Eastern Ill Univ Charleston IL 61920

ORDON, EDMUND, b Detroit, Mich, Jan 2, 18. POLISH, ENGLISH. *Educ:* Wayne Univ, BA, 40, MA, 41; Univ Ottawa, PhD(Slavic studies), 53. *Prof Exp:* Instr English, 41-43, 45-49, from asst prof to assoc prof, 49-71, acting chmn dept English, 49-71, prof Slavic & Eastern lang & lit, 49-76, vchmn dept, 71-76, PROF POLISH, WAYNE STATE UNIV, 76- *Mem:* Am Asn Teachers Slavic & EEurop Lang; Polish Am Hist Asn; Cent States Mod Lang Teachers Asn. *Res:* Anglo-Polish cultural relations; European romanticism; Polish and Western European literary relations. *Publ:* Auth, Michiewicz and Emerson; translr, The Forgotten Battlefield; A tentative bibliography of the Polish short story in English translation, Polish Rev. *Mailing Add:* Dept of Slavic & Eastern Lang & Lit Wayne State Univ Detroit MI 48202

ORDONEZ, ELIZABETH JANE, b Los Angeles, Calif, July 27, 45. SPANISH LITERATURE. *Educ:* Univ Calif, Los Angeles, BA, 66, MA, 69; Univ Calif, Irvine, PhD(Span lit), 76. *Prof Exp:* Asst prof Span, Ripon Col, 74-79; ASSOC PROF SPAN, UNIV TEX, ARLINGTON, 79- *Concurrent Pos:* Span Govt grant, Ministerio de Asuntos Exteriores, 77. *Mem:* MLA; Am Asn Teachers Span & Port; Asoc Lit Femenina Hisp; Sch Latin Am; Am Asoc Advan Humanities. *Res:* Spanish feminist literary theory and practice; film; Chicana literature. *Publ:* Auth, Forms of alienation in Matute's La Trampa, J Span Studies: 20th Century, winter 76; Symbolic vision in Clarice Lispector's The Applie in the Dark, Letras Femeninas, spring 76; Nada: initiation into bourgeois patriarchy, In: The Analysis of Hispanic Texts: Current Trends in Methodology, Bilingual Press, 77; Mitificacion e imagen de la mujer en La Enferma de Elena Quiroga, Letras Femeninas, fall 77; The decoding and encoding of sex roles in Carmen Martin Gaite's Retahilas, Ky Romance Quart, 80; The female quest pattern in Concha Alos Os habla Electra, Revista de estudios hispanicos, 1/80. *Mailing Add:* Dept Foreign Lang & Ling Univ of Tex Arlington TX 76019

ORDOUBADIAN, REZA, b Tabriz, Iran, Apr 18, 32; US citizen; m 57; c 4. LINGUISTICS. *Educ:* Univ Teheran, BA, 54; Auburn Univ, MA, 65, PhD(ling, English), 67. *Prof Exp:* Translr English, French & Persian, Teheran, Iran, 52-54; chmn dept English, Webb Sch, Bell Buckle, Tenn, 58-62; PROF ENGLISH & LING, MID TENN STATE UNIV, 62- *Concurrent Pos:* Ed-in-chief, The SECOL Bull, Southeastern Conf Ling. *Mem:* Am Ling Soc; Southeastern Conf Ling (secy-treas, 75-81); SAtlantic Mod Lang Asn. *Res:* Syntax; Azarbayjani language; Persian language. *Publ:* Auth, Views on Language, Inter-Univ, 75; contribr, Azarbayjani: A perspective, In: Languages and Literatures of the Non-Russian Peoples of the Soviet Union, MacMaster Univ, Can, 77; Rutherfords County: A bicentennial perspective, onomastics, In: Third Lacus Forum, 77 & Language and politics, In: Fourth Lacus Forum, 78, Hornbeam. *Mailing Add:* 1911 Greenland Dr Murfreesboro TN 37130

O'REILLY, ROBERT FRANCIS, b Watertown, NY. FRENCH & COMPARATIVE LITERATURE. *Educ:* Syracuse Univ, BA, 61; Univ Wis, MA, 63, PhD(French), 67. *Prof Exp:* Asst prof, 67-75, chmn dept, 76-80, ASSOC PROF FRENCH, SYRACUSE UNIV, 76- *Mem:* MLA. *Res:* Eighteenth and 20th century French literature. *Publ:* Auth, Form and meaning in the Lettres Persanes, Studies Voltaire & 18th Century, 69; Psyche, myth and symbol in Gide's L'Immoraliste, 74 & Cazotte's Le Diable Amoureux and the structure of romance, 77, Symposium. *Mailing Add:* Dept of French Syracuse Univ Syracuse NY 13210

ORIA, TOMAS G, b Moron City, Cuba, May 22, 26; US citizen; m 52; c 1. SPANISH AMERICAN LITERATURE. *Educ:* Inst Ciego de Avila, Cuba, BA, 49; Univ Havana, DL, 54; Assumption Col, MA, 71; Univ Mass, PhD(Span), 80. *Prof Exp:* Teacher Span, New Hampton Sch, NH, 66-67; chair, Lang Dept, Kingsley Hall Sch, Conn, 67-68; asst prof, Hawthorne Col, 68-72; teaching assoc, Univ Mass, 72-75, vis instr, 77-78; vis instr, Rivier Col, NH, 80-81; ASST PROF SPAN, CENT MICH UNIV, 81- *Concurrent Pos:* Legal Coun Cuba RR, 54-59, judge, 59-60. *Mem:* MLA; Am Asn Teachers Span & Port; Circulo de Cultura Panamericano. *Res:* The work of Jose Marti; the Krausism thought; Hispanic American modernism. *Publ:* Auth, El derecho aduanal cubano, Gutenberg Press, 56; Aduana y arancelles, Cultural, 57; articles, Cuban Democratic Judiciary Bull in Exile, 63-65; Marti, el moralista del Krausismo, Ediciones Universal (in prep); El krausismo en el ideal martiano de la liberacion cubana, Boletin de la Biblioteca Menendez Pelayo (in prep); Marti: su concepcion krausista del arte, Circulo: Revista de Cultura (in prep). *Mailing Add:* Cent Mich Univ Mt Pleasant MI

ORJUELA, HECTOR HUGO, b Bogota, Colombia, July 6, 30; m 65; c 5. SPANISH AMERICAN LITERATURE, HISPANIC POETRY. *Educ:* NTex State Univ, BA & MA, 52; Univ Kans, PhD(Span), 60. *Prof Exp:* From instr to asst prof Span, Va Mil Inst, 56-60; from asst prof to assoc prof, Univ Southern Calif, 60-60; PROF SPAN AM LIT, UNIV CALIF, IRVINE, 70- *Concurrent Pos:* Dir educ abroad prog, Univ Calif, Mex, 78-80; consult, Inst Caro y Cuervo. *Honors & Awards:* Int Lit Prize, Laureano Carus Pando, Mex, 78. *Mem:* MLA; Am Asn Teachers Span & Port; Inst Int Lit Iberoam; Acad Colombiana de la Lengua; Inst Caro y Cuervo. *Res:* Colombian literature. *Publ:* Auth, Poemas de Encrucijada, 72 & Relatos y Ficciones, 75, Ed Cosmos, Bogota; La Obra Poetica de Rafael Pombo, 75 & De Sobremesa y Otros Estudios Sobre Jose Asuncion Silva, 77, Inst Caro y Cuervo, Bogota; El primer Silva, Bol Acad Colombiana de la Lengua, 78; La imagen de los Estados Unidos en la poesia de Hispano America, UNAM, Mex, 80; Poesia de la America indigena, Ed Cosmos, Bogota, 80; Literatura hispana americana: Ensayos de interpretacion y de critica, Inst Caro y Cuervo, Bogota, 80. *Mailing Add:* Dept of Span & Port Univ of Calif Irvine CA 92717

ORLANDI, MARY-KAY GAMEL, b Springfield, Mass, Sept 15, 42; m 69. CLASSICS, COMPARATIVE LITERATURE. *Educ:* Smith Col, BA, 63; Harvard Univ, MA, 64; Univ Calif, Berkeley, PhD(comp lit), 72. *Prof Exp:* Instr classics & world lit, San Francisco State Col, 65-66; asst prof classics, Boston Univ, 69-73; asst prof classics & comp lit, Univ Calif, Santa Cruz, 73-80. *Mem:* Am Philol Asn. *Res:* Ovid; medieval and Renaissance literature; Italian literature. *Publ:* Auth, Comparative literature and the classics, Am Philol Asn, 77; Ovid true and false in Renaissance poetry, Pac Coast Philol, 78. *Mailing Add:* 2519 Empire Grade Rd Santa Cruz CA 95060

ORLINSKY, HARRY MEYER, b Owen Sound, Ont, Mar 14, 08; nat US; m 34; c 2. BIBLICAL PHILOLOGY & HISTORY. *Educ:* Univ Toronto, BA, 31; Dropsie Col, PhD, 35. *Hon Degrees:* DHL, Baltimore Hebrew Col, 72 & Spertus Col, 79. *Prof Exp:* Nies scholar, Am Sch Orient Res, Jerusalem, 35-36; prof Bibl lit & Jewish hist, Baltimore Hebrew Col, 36-44; vis instr, 43-44, asst prof, 44-45, PROF BIBLE, HEBREW UNION COL-JEWISH INST RELIG, NY, 45- *Concurrent Pos:* Fel, Johns Hopkins Univ, 36-41; lectr, New Sch Social Res, 47-49; assoc trustee, Am Schs Orient Res, 48-, ed ann, 49-51; chmn, Am Friends Israel Explor, 54-; ed, Libr Bibl Studies, 67; Guggenheim Found fel, 68-69; vis prof, Grad Theol Union, 69; ed, Int Orgn Septuagint & Cognate Studies, 73-; Grinfield lectr, Oxford, 73-75; Albright Mem lectr, Johns Hopkins Univ, 77. *Honors & Awards:* Frank L Weil Award, Nat Jewish Welfare Bd, 59; Horace Kallen Lectr, Merzlia-Jew Teachers Sem, 76; Soc Bibl Lit Centennial Award for Bibl Scholar, 79. *Mem:* Soc Bibl Lit (vpres, 69, pres, 70); fel Acad Jewish Res (secy, 53-55, treas, 56-); Brit Soc Old Testament Studies; Int Orgn Septuagint & Cognate Studies; Int Orgn Masoretic Studies (pres, 72-). *Res:* Biblical history and Biblical exegesis; present state of Proto-Septuagint studies; Rashi's commentary on the Pentateuch. *Publ:* Auth, Ancient Israel, Cornell Univ, 54; ed, New Translation of the Holy Scriptures: The Torah, Jewish Publ Soc Am, 62; auth, The So-Called Servant of the Lord and Suffering Servant in Second Isaiah, Brill, Leiden, 67 & 77; ed, Notes on the New Translation of the Torah, 69 & coauth, The Five Megilloth and Jonah, 69, Jewish Publ Soc Am; auth, Understanding the Bible through history and archaeology, 72 & Essays in Biblical culture and Bible translation, 74, KTAV; auth, The Prophets, Jewish Publ Soc Am, 78; The prophets, 78 & The writings, 82, Jewish Publ Soc Am. *Mailing Add:* Hebrew Union Col-Jewish Inst of Relig 1 W Fourth St New York NY 10012

ORRINGER, NELSON ROBERT, b Pittsburgh, Pa, Nov 9, 40; m 65; c 3. HISPANIC PHILOSOPHY & LITERATURE. *Educ:* Dartmouth Col, AB, 62; Brown Univ, AM, 65, PhD(Hisp lett), 69. *Prof Exp:* Lectr Span, Williams Col, 69-70, asst prof Romanic lang, 70-74; assoc prof, 74-81, PROF SPAN, UNIV CONN, 81- *Concurrent Pos:* Res grant, Coun Int Exchange Scholars, 81; vis prof Span, Univ Mich, Ann Arbor, 81; Brown Univ Alumni scholar, 81; Univ Granada Inaugural speaker philos, 81. *Mem:* MLA;; Asoc Int de Hispanistas; Asoc de Pensamiento Hispanico. *Res:* Twentieth century Spanish literature; history of philosophy; comparative literature. *Publ:* Auth, Responsabilidad y evasion en La cabeza del cordero de Francisco Ayala, Hispanofila, 1/74; Nobles in La rebelion de las masas: Ortega's Source, Am Hispan, 1/76; Depth perception in Ortega and Jaensch, Comp Lit Studies, Muertes de perro de Ayala: Critica del Estado, Hispania, 9/77; Ortega y sus fuentes germanicas, Gredos, Madrid, 79; Ser y no-ser en Platon, Hartmann y Ortega, Nueva Revista de Filologia Hispanica, 80; Foreword, The Artist & the City by Eugenio Trias, Columbia Univ Press, 82; Sobre la teologia protestante liberal en Del sentimiento tragico de la vida, Cuadernos Salmantinos de Filosofia, 82. *Mailing Add:* Dept of Romance and Class Univ of Conn Storrs CT 06268

ORSTEN, ELISABETH M, b Vienna, Austria, Nov 8, 27; Can citizen. ANGLO SAXON & MIDDLE ENGLISH. *Educ:* Oxford Univ, BA, 55, MA, 60; Univ Toronto, PhD, 66. *Prof Exp:* Instr English, Niagara Univ, 56-57; asst prof, Mem Univ Nfld, 62-66; vis asst prof mediaeval lit, Brandeis Univ, 66-67; from asst prof to assoc prof, 67-77, PROF ENGLISH, TRENT UNIV, 77- *Concurrent Pos:* Can Coun res fel, 68-69. *Mem:* Mediaeval Acad Am; Int Asn Univ Prof Eng. *Res:* Patristics; Middle English, especially Langland; Piers Plowman. *Publ:* Auth, The ambiguities in Langland's Rat Parliament, 61 & Patientia in the B text of Piers Plowman, 69, Mediaeval Studies; Heaven on earth--Langland's vision of life within the cloister, Am Benedictine Rev, 12/70. *Mailing Add:* Dept of English Trent Univ Peterborough ON K9J 7B8 Can

ORTAL, AMERICA YOLANDA, b Encrucijada, Las Villas, Cuba; US citizen; div. SPANISH LANGUAGE & LITERATURE. *Educ:* Univ Havana, DPhil & DLit, 60. *Prof Exp:* Teacher Span, Clarence Cent High Sch, 62-64; PROF SPAN LIT & LANG, COL ST ROSE64- . *Res:* Iberian and Latinamerican literature. *Publ:* Auth, Poemas de Angustia, Torre Tavira (spec ed), Spain, 65; La Muerte en Julian del Casal, Papeles de Son Armandans, Spain, 69; Selection of four poems in anthology: . . . Y Era; Cuba; Fugas & Y Voy Quebrandome la Garganta al Viento, Norte (spec ed), Amsterdam, 71; El Cadaver, In: Voces de Manana, Harper; Madrugada, In: 20 Cuentistas Cubanos, Ed Universal, Miami, 78; Four Poems, Antologia de Poetas Hispanoam, Argentina, Panorama Poetica Hispanoamericano I, 78. *Mailing Add:* 21 Knauf Lane Loudonville NY 12211

ORTALI, RAYMOND, b Thoirette, France, Feb 22, 28. ROMANCE LANGUAGES. *Educ:* Univ Dijon, Law degree, 49; Ecole Sci Polit, Paris, dipl, 52; Univ Mich, PhD(French lit), 67. *Prof Exp:* Instr French, Army Lang Sch, Monterey, 60-63; asst prof, Am Inst Foreign Trade, Phoenix, 63-64; teaching fel, Univ Mich, 64-67; asst prof, Yale Univ, 67-70; assoc prof, 70-78, PROF FRENCH, STATE UNIV NY ALBANY, 78- *Honors & Awards:* Prix Lagrange, Acad Inscriptions et Belles-Lett, 77. *Mem:* Am Asn Teachers Fr; MLA. *Res:* French 16th century literature. *Publ:* Auth, Un Poete de la Mort: J B Chassignet, Droz, 68; Entre Nous, Macmillan, 72; Aujourd'hui, Harcourt Brace, 76; Cl Malleville: Oeuvres Poetiques (2 vols), Didier, critical ed, 76. *Mailing Add:* Dept of French State Univ NY Albany NY 12203

ORTEGA, JOSE, b Granada, Spain, Nov 11, 33; US citizen; m 59; c 3. ROMANCE LANGUAGES. *Educ:* Univ Granada, Lic filos y let, 58, Dr, 81; Ohio State Univ, PhD, 63. *Prof Exp:* Teacher Span, Maristas High Sch, 58-59; instr Span lit, Inst Ensenanza Media, 59-60; asst instr Span lang, Ohio State Univ, 60-62; instr Span & French, Mercer Univ, 62-63; from instr to asst prof Span lang & lit, Smith Col, 63-69, dir jr year Madrid, 65-67; assoc prof Span, Case Western Reserve Univ, 69-70; assoc prof, 70-73, PROF SPAN, UNIV WIS-PARKSIDE, 73- *Concurrent Pos:* Asst to prof, Granada Univ, 58-59; instr, Ohio Wesleyan Univ, 61; Am Philol Soc grant, 68. *Mem:* Am Asn Teachers Span & Port; MLA; Latin Am Studies Asn; Soc Span & Port Hist Studies; Asoc Int Hispanistas. *Res:* Modern Spanish literature; Latin America literature. *Publ:* Ed, Temas Sobre la Moderna Narrativa Boliviana, Los Amigos del Libro, Bolivia, 73; Letras Bolivianas de Hoy: Renato Prada y Pedro Shimose, F Garcia Cambeiro, Buenos Aires, 73; Antonio Ferres y Martinez Menchen: Novelistas de la Soledad, Cath Univ Andres Bello, 73; auth, Ensayos de la Novela Espanola Moderna, 74, Letras Hispanoamericanas de Nuestro Tiempo, 76 & coauth, Diccionario de Terminos Literarios, 77, Porrua Turanzas, Madrid; contribr, Diccionario de Literatura Boliviana, Guttentag, Bolivia, 77; contribr, Columbia Dict of Modern European Literature, 80. *Mailing Add:* Dept of Span Univ Wis-Parkside Kenosha WI 53140

ORTEGA, JULIO, b Peru, 42; m 64; c 3. LATIN AMERICAN LITERATURE. *Educ:* Univ Catolica, Peru, Lic es Let, 63, DLit, 67. *Prof Exp:* Vis asst prof Latin Am lit, Univ Pittsburgh, 69-70; lectr, Yale Univ, 70-71; vis lectr, Univ Tex, Austin, 73-74; PROF LATIN AM LIT, UNIV TEX, AUSTIN, 78- *Concurrent Pos:* Guggenheim Memorial Found fel, 74; dir Nat Press, Inst Nac Cult, Lima, 74-75; asst ed jour, Correo, Lima, 74-76. *Mem:* MLA; Latin Am Studies Asn. *Res:* New Latin American experimental writing; Latin American avant-garde; semiotics of culture. *Publ:* Auth, La Contemplacion y la Fiesta, Monte Avial, Caracas, 69; Figuracion de la Persona, Edhasa, Barceloan, 71; Relato de la Tuopia, Gaya Ciencia, Barcelona, 73; ed, Julio Cortazar: La Casilla de los Morelli, Tusguets, Barcelona, 73; auth, Ceremonia y Otros octos, Posdata, Lima, 74; Tierra en el Dia, Villanueva, Lima, 75; Rituales (poetry), Mosca Azul, Liam, 76; ed, Cesar Moro: La Tortuga Escuestre, Monte Avila, Caracas, 76. *Mailing Add:* Dept of Span Univ of Tex Austin TX 78712

ORTEGA, NOEL GUILHERME, b Tras-os-Montes, Portugal; nat US. PORTUGUESE. *Educ:* Harvard Univ, BA, 69, MA, 70, PhD(Port philol & lit), 74. *Prof Exp:* Instr Span & Port, Tamkang Col Arts & Sci, China, 68-69; instr Span, Col Chinese Cult, Taiwan, 69; instr Port lang & Brazilian lit, Harvard Univ, 73-74, asst prof, 74-79; PROF, DEPT ROMANCE LANG, TUFTS UNIV, 79- *Mem:* Amigos de Braganca; MLA; Am Asn Teachers Span & Port. *Res:* Portuguese dialectology; overseas Portuguese literature; Brazilian and Portuguese literature of the 16th, 19th and 20th centuries. *Publ:* Contribr, Portugal: macau e timor, In: Falando Portugues, Rio, 75; auth, Spaniards in North America, Balch Inst, 12/76; Capitaes e fidalgos bragancanos mencionados na Peregrinacao de Fernao Mendes Pinto, Bol Grupo Amigos de Braganca, 12/76; As cores na Peregrinacao de Fernao Mendes Pinto, 78 & A musica e o teatro na Peregrinacao de Fernao Mendes Pinto, 78, Bol Inst Luis de Camoes. *Mailing Add:* Dept of Romance Lang Tufts Univ Medford MA 02155

ORTISI, DOMENICO, b Augusta, Italy, Mar 26, 21; US citizen; m 49; c 2. LANGUAGES. *Educ:* Univ Catania, Dr Jurisp, 43; Univ Calif, Berkeley, PhD(Romance lang & lit), 56. *Prof Exp:* Acting instr & instr Ital, Univ Calif, Los Angeles, 55-57; from asst prof to assoc prof foreign lang, Mont State Univ, 57-64; assoc prof Ital, Univ Wis, Madison, 64-65; assoc prof, 65-67, PROF ITAL, UNIV MONT, 67- *Mem:* Am Asn Teachers Ital; MLA. *Res:* Seventeenth century Italian literature; Renaissance literature. *Publ:* Auth, La Filli di Sciro di G Bonarelli, Ausonia, 66; La Poesia del Pastor Fido del Guarini, Convivium, 67; Fulvio Testi: Lettere, A Cura de M L Doglio, Italica, 68. *Mailing Add:* Dept of Foreign Lang Univ of Mont Missoula MT 59801

ORTUNO, MANUEL JOSEPH, b West Palm Beach, Fla, Jan 29, 42; m 72; c 3. SPANISH LITERATURE. *Educ:* Ohio State Univ, BA, 63, MA, 67; Univ Mich, PhD(Romance lang & lit; Span), 73. *Prof Exp:* Instr Span, Lafayette Col, 72-73, asst prof, 73-75; asst prof, 75-78, ASSOC PROF SPAN, BAYLOR UNIV, 78- *Mem:* MLA; Am Asn Teachers Span & Port. *Res:* Golden Age Spanish literature; Francisco de Quevedo. *Publ:* Auth, Religious Ritual in the Poetry of Francisco de Quevedo, Revista de Estudios Hispanicos, 15; 251-264; Revisions and their significance in Quevedo's Poema heroico a Cristo resucitado, Hispanofila (in press). *Mailing Add:* Dept of Mod Foreign Lang Baylor Univ Waco TX 76703

ORTUNO, MARIAN MIKAYLO, b Brooklyn, NY, Jan 31, 47; m 72; c 3. SPANISH LITERATURE. *Educ:* Queens Col, BA, 67; Univ Mich, MA, 69, PhD(Span), 73. *Prof Exp:* Lectr Span, State Univ NY Albany, 72-73; asst prof, Northampton Community Col, 73-74; RES & WRITING, 74- *Mem:* MLA. *Res:* Seventeenth century Spanish literature; Spanish religious drama; Spanish language teaching. *Publ:* Auth, Pagan myth and African legend in Tirso's auto El Laberinto de Creta, Romanische Forschungen, No 88, 76; From theology to drama: The artistic evolution of Tirso's auto Los hermanos parecidos, Neophilologus, No 62, 78; Apicultural allegory in Tirso's auto El colmenero divino, Ky Romance Quart, No 29, 82. *Mailing Add:* 414 Oreintal Rd Waco TX 76710

ORVIETO, ENZO UMBERTO, b Florence, Italy; US citizen; m 52. ITALIAN LANGUAGE & LITERATURE. *Educ:* Univ Pa, MA, 62, PhD(Romance lang), 67. *Prof Exp:* Instr Ital, Univ Pa, 62-67; from asst prof to assoc prof, 67-75 PROF ITAL LANG & LIT, UNIV CINCINNATI, 75- *Mem:* Mediaeval Acad Am; Dante Soc Am; Am Asn Teachers Ital; Renaissance Soc Am; Am Asn Univ Prof. *Res:* Italian literature of the Middle Ages and Renaissance. *Publ:* Auth, Guido da Pisa e il Commento Inedito all'Inferno Dantesco, Italica, 69; Castel della Pieve e l'esilio di Dante, Dante Studies, 69; Due Sonetti Inediti di A Tassoni, Forum Italicum, 69; Il Primo Romanzo Epistolare del Rinasmento da un Autografo Inedito di Giannozzo Salviati, Giornale de Bordo, 71, 72; San Francesco e il Diavolo: Contrasto Inedito Cinquecentesco, Forum Italicum, 73-74; La Datazione del Commento all'Inferno Dantesco di Guido da Pisa, Ky Romance Quart, 76; Un Poemetto Inedito di Bernardo Giambullari, 77 & La Burla di Lorenzo de'Medici a fra Mariano, 81, Bibliot d'Humanisme et Renaissance; La Burla di Lorenzo de'Medici a fra Mariano, Bibliot d'Humanisme et Renaissance, 81. *Mailing Add:* Dept of Romance Lang Univ of Cincinnati Cincinnati OH 45221

ORWEN, GIFFORD PHILLIPS, b Rochester, NY, m 47; c 1. ROMANCE LANGUAGES. *Educ:* Cornell Univ, PhD(romance lang), 37. *Prof Exp:* Instr French & Ital, Cornell Univ, 34-38, Univ Buffalo, 38-41, US Army Intel, 41-45, Strategic Bombing Surv, 45-46, US Dept State, 46-48, Libr Cong, 48-51

& US Dept Defense, 51-60; prof French & Ital, Bethany Col, 60-62; prof English lang & chmn dept, State Univ NY Col Geneseo, 62-80; RES & WRITING, 80- *Concurrent Pos:* Res Found State Univ NY grant-in-aid, 66-68. *Mem:* MLA; Am Asn Teachers Fr; Am Asn Teachers Ital. *Res:* French literature of 17th and 19th centuries; Italian; linguistics. *Publ:* Coauth, Italian Reference Grammar, Kings Crown, 43; auth, Introduction to Italian, 66 & Upgrade Your Italian, 70, Vanni; Cecco Angiolieri, A Study, Univ NC, 79; Jean-Francois Regnard, Twayne, 82. *Mailing Add:* Dept Foreign Lang State Univ NY Geneseo NY 11454

OSBORNE, ROBERT EDWARD, b Indianapolis, Ind, Dec 17, 14. MODERN SPANISH LITERATURE. *Educ:* Univ Ala, AB & AM, 38; Brown Univ, PhD, 48. *Prof Exp:* Instr French & Span, Whitman Col, 42-43; instr Span, Brown Univ, 46-48; from asst prof to prof, Univ Conn, 48-76; RETIRED. *Concurrent Pos:* Am Philos Soc grant, 63. *Mem:* Am Asn Teachers Span & Port; MLA. *Res:* Angel Ganivet. *Publ:* Auth, Cuentos del Mundo Hispanico, Am Bk Co, 57; Emilia Pardo Bazan, su vida y sus obras, Andrea, Mex, 64; Observations on Ganivet's La Conquista de Maya, In: Homenaje a Rodriguez-Monigo, Castalia, Madrid, 66; Bibliografia Selecta de Estudios Suecos Sobre las Lenguas y Literaturas Francesa, Espanola e Hispanoamericana, Bol Filol Espanola, Madrid, 1-5/67; Voces y Vistas: Active Spanish for Beginners, Harper & Row, 78. *Mailing Add:* RR 2 Anagance NB E0E 1A0 Can

OSBURN, CARROLL DUANE, Biblical Studies, Descriptive Linguistics. See Vol IV

OSGOOD, CHARLES EGERTON, b Somerville, Mass, Nov 20, 16; m 39; c 2. PSYCHOLINGUISTICS, INTERNATIONAL RELATIONS. *Educ:* Dartmouth Col, AB, 39; Yale Univ, PhD(psychol, anthrop), 45. *Hon Degrees:* ScD, Dartmouth Col, 62. *Prof Exp:* Instr psychol, Yale Univ, 45-46; asst prof, Univ Conn, 46-49; from assoc prof to prof, Univ Ill, Urbana, 49-65, dir, Inst Commun Mes, 57-65, PROF PSYCHOL, CTR ADVAN STUDIES, UNIV ILL, URBANA, 65-, DIR, CTR COMP PSYCHOLING, 63- *Concurrent Pos:* Soc Sci Res Coun fac fel, 50-52; Guggenheim fels, 55-56 & 72-73; Ctr Advan Study Behav Sci Fel, 58-59. *Honors & Awards:* Distinguished Scientific Contribution Award, Am Psychol Asn, 60; Kurt Lewin Mem Award, Soc Psychol Study Social Issues, 71; Interam Psychol Award, 76. *Mem:* Nat Acad Sci; AAAS; Am Psychol Asn (pres, 62-63); hon men NY Acad Sci; Int Peace Sci Soc (pres, 76-77). *Res:* Cross-cultural research. *Publ:* Coauth, The Measurement of Meaning, Free Press & Univ Ill, 57; auth, Alternative to War or Surrender, Univ Ill, 62; coauth, From Ying and Yang to and or but, Lang, 73; Cross-cultural Universals of Effective Meaning, Univ Ill, 74; auth, Focus on Meaning: Psycholinguistic Papers, Mouton, The Hague, 74; Probing subjective culture, J Commun, 74; coauth, Salience and sentencing: Real direct object in bitransitive sentences please stand up? In: Linguistic Studies Offered to Joseph Greenberg, Anna Libr, 77. *Mailing Add:* Inst of Commun Res Univ of Ill Urbana IL 61801

OSIEK, BETTY TYREE, b Lennox, Ky, Apr 2, 31; m 58. ROMANCE LANGUAGES. *Educ:* Lindenwood Col, AB, 62; Wash Univ, PhD, 66. *Prof Exp:* Asst prof Latin Am lit & French & Span lang, Univ Mo, St Louis, 66-68; asst prof, 68-72, assoc prof, 72-78, PROF SPAN, SOUTHERN ILL UNIV, EDWARDSVILLE, 78- *Mem:* Am Asn Teachers Span & Port; Inst Int Lit Iberoam; Midwest Asn Latin Am Studies (vpres, 77-78); Latin Am Studies Asn; Am Transl Asn. *Res:* New narrative of Spanish America; revolutionary writers of Latin America, especially poets and prose writers; research on dictatorship in the fiction of Spanish America. *Publ:* Auth, Jose Asuncion Silva: estudio estilistico de su poesia, Ed Andrea, Mex, 68; co-ed & contribr poetry sect, Handbook of Latin American Studies, Vols, 32, 34, 36, 38, 40, 42, Libr Cong, 70, 72, 74, 76, 78, 80; Jose Asuncion Silva, Twayne World Author Ser, 78. *Mailing Add:* Southern Ill Univ Edwardsville IL 62025

OSMUN, GEORGE FEIT, b Easton, Pa, Aug 20, 21. GREEK, LATIN. *Educ:* Lafayette Col, AB, 43; Columbia Univ, MA, 47; Univ Mich, PhD(Greek & Latin), 52. *Prof Exp:* Teacher high sch, Pa, 47-48; instr, State Univ Iowa, 52-54; teacher high sch, Iowa, 54-55; instr classics, Univ Tex, 55-58; asst prof, Univ Southern Calif, 58-60 & St Mary's Col, Calif, 60-64; PROF CLASSICS, WESTERN MICH UNIV, 64- *Mem:* Am Philol Asn; Archaeol Inst Am; Vergilian Soc Am; Class Asn Mid West & South; Class Asn Am Acad Rome. *Res:* Greek new comedy; mythology; Greek and Roman elagiac poetry. *Publ:* Auth, Pindar, Olympian XIV, Class World, 9/67; Roses of antiquity, 6/75 & Night in Propertius, 5/77, Class Outlook; Dialogue in the Menandrean monologue, Trans Am Philol Asn; Palaephatus--pragmatic mythographer, Class J; Intralinear change of speaker in Menander, Class Philol; Changes of Sex in Greek and Roman Mythology, Class Bull, 3/78. *Mailing Add:* Dept of Lang Western Mich Univ Kalamazoo MI 49008

OSSAR, MICHAEL LEE, b Bryn Mawr, Pa, Mar 31, 38; m 63; c 2. GERMAN LITERATURE. *Educ:* Cornell Univ, AB, 61; Univ Pa, MS, 63, MA, 67, PhD(Ger lit), 73. *Prof Exp:* Res fel physics, Univ Pa, 61-61, teaching fel Ger, 63-67; lektor English, Univ Freiburg, Ger, 67-68; instr Ger, Sweet Briar Col, 68-71; asst prof, 71-77, ASSOC PROF GER, KANS STATE UNIV, 78- *Concurrent Pos:* Vis lectr, Swarthmore Col, 66; Nat Endowment for Humanities grant, 76, 77 & 81; ed, Studies in Twentieth Century Lit, 78- *Mem:* MLA; Am Asn Teachers Ger. *Res:* Expressionism; post-war German literature; politics and literature. *Publ:* Auth, Das Erdbeben in Chili und Die Marquise von O--, Revue des Langues Vivantes, 68; Die Kunstlergestalt in Goethes Tasso und Grillparzers Sappho, Ger Quart, 72; Note on relativity theory in Der Zauberberg, PMLA, 73; Ernst Toller's Masse-Mensch, Germanic Rev, 76; Anarchism in the Dramas of Ernst Toller, Suny Press, 80; Der eigebildete Kranke bei Adolf Muschg, Neophilogus, 82. *Mailing Add:* Dept of Mod Lang Kans State Univ Manhattan KS 66506

OSTERLE, HEINZ D, b Ulm, Ger, Aug 29, 32; m 60; c 3. GERMAN LITERATURE. *Educ:* Univ Freiburg, MA, 57; Brown Univ, PhD(Ger), 64. *Prof Exp:* From asst prof to assoc prof Ger, George Washington Univ, 60-65; asst prof, NY Univ, 65-67 & Yale Univ, 67-72; dir div Ger & classics, 73-74, assoc prof, 72-82, PROF GER, NORTHERN ILL UNIV, 82- *Concurrent Pos:* Mem screening comt Ger lit, Int Educ & Cult Exchange Prog, 69-72, chmn comt, 71-72. *Honors & Awards:* Am Asn Teachers Ger Award for Best Article in Unterrichts praxis, 81. *Mem:* MLA; Am Asn Teachers Ger. *Res:* Twentieth-Century German literature; German literature in exile 1933-45; American-German literary relations. *Publ:* Auth, The other Germany: Resistance to the Third Reich in German literature, Ger Quart, 1/68; Alfred Döblin's Revolutionstrilogie November 1918, Monatshefte, spring 70; Hermann Broch, Die Schlafwandler: Kritik der Zentralen Metapher, Deutsche Vierteljahrsschrift Literaturwissenschaft und Geistesgeschichte, summer 70; Hermann Broch, Die Schlafwandler: Revolution and Apocalypse, PMLA, 10/71; Uwe Johnson, Jahrestage: Das Bild der USA, Ger Quart, 11/75; Denkbilder über die USA: Gunter Kunerts Reisebuch Der andere Plante, In: Basis: Jahrbuch für deutsche Literatur der Gegenwart, Frankfurt Suhrkamp, 77; Alfred Döblins Revolutionsroman, postscript to Alfred Döblin, November 1918, (4 vols), Munich, 78; coauth, German studies in America, In: German Studies Notes Ser, Inst Ger Studies, Ind Univ, Bloomington, 78; The lost utopia: New images of America in German literature, Ger Quart, 12/81. *Mailing Add:* Dept of Foreign Lang Northern Ill Univ De Kalb IL 60115

OSTWALD, MARTIN, b Dortmund, Ger, Jan 15, 22; nat US; m 48; c 2. CLASSICAL PHILOLOGY. *Educ:* Univ Toronto, BA 46; Univ Chicago, AM, 48; Columbia Univ, PhD, 52. *Prof Exp:* Instr class philol, Wesleyan Univ, 50-51; lectr & assoc Greek & Latin, Columbia Univ, 51-54, asst prof, 54-58; assoc prof, 58-66, PROF CLASSICS, SWARTHMORE COL, 66-; PROF CLASS STUDIES, UNIV PA, 68- *Concurrent Pos:* Fulbright res fel, Greece, 61-62; Am Coun Learned Soc res fel, 65-66; Nat Endowment for Humanities sr fel, 70-71; vis fel, Balliol Col Oxford Univ, 70-71; mem, Inst Adv Study, Princeton Univ, 74-75 & 81-82; dir, Nat Endowment for Humanities fel-in-residence in classics, 76-77; Guggenheim fel, 77-78. *Mem:* Soc Prom Hellenic Studies; Am Philol Asn; Class Asn Can; Archaeol Inst Am. *Res:* Greek social and political thought and institutions; Greek history, philosophy and literature. *Publ:* Auth, The Athenian legislation against tyranny and subversion, Trans Am Philol Asn, 55; co-ed, Plato: Protagoras, 56, Plato: The Statesman, 57, ed, Aristotle: The Nicomachean Ethics, 62 & coauth, The Meters of Greek and Latin Poetry, 63, Bobbs; auth, Nomos and the Beginnings of the Athenian Democracy, Clarendon, Oxford, 69; Pindar, Nomos, and Heracles, Harvard Studies Class Philol, 109-138; Autonomia: Its Genesis and Early History, Scholars, 82. *Mailing Add:* 2 Whittier Pl Swarthmore PA 19081

OSUNA, RAFAEL, b Cordoba, Spain, Jan 6, 33; m 62; c 2. ROMANCE LANGUAGES. *Educ:* Santa Maria de la Rabida Univ, Dipl Latin Am studies, 53; Univ Madrid, MAG 56; Brown Univ, PhD(Span), 66. *Prof Exp:* Lectr Span, Univ Southampton, 60-61 & Queens Col, 63-64; from instr to asst prof, Middlebury Col, 64-68, chmn dept Span & Ital, 67-68; assoc prof, Univ NC, Greensboro, 68-73; prof, State Univ NY Albany, 73-77; PROF SPAN, DUKE UNIV, 77- *Concurrent Pos:* Dir, Middlebury Col Grad Sch Spain, 66-67. *Res:* Golden Age; 20th century Spanish literature; hemerography. *Publ:* Auth, Una imitacion de Lope de la Fabula de Polifemo ovidiana, Bull Hisp, 68; Las fechas del Persiles, Thesaurus, 70; La Arcadia de Lope de Vega, Real Acad Espanola, 72; Cuestiones de Onomatologia Americana en los Cronistas de Indias, Inst Caro y Cuervo, 73; Los Sonetos de Calderon en sus Obras Dramaticas, Univ MC, 74; Celos y tibiezas de la hemerografia espanola, Cuadernos Bibliog, 75; Sin Orden ni Concierto, Uguina, 76; Un espanol Olvidado: Don Jose Marchena, Papeles de Sons Armadans, 77. *Mailing Add:* Dept of Romance Lang Duke Univ Durham NC 27706

OSWALT, JOHN NEWELL, Old Testament, Semitic Languages. See Vol IV

OSWALT, ROBERT L, b Ft Huachuca, Ariz, Mar 6, 23; m 52; c 2. LINGUISTICS. *Educ:* Univ Calif, Berkeley, BS, 44, MS, 47, PhD(ling), 61. *Prof Exp:* Chemist, Donner Lab, Univ Calif, Berkeley, 48 & Radiation Lab, 48-55, lectr speech, univ, 59-61, assoc, 60-61, asst prof, 61-66, head English prog foreign studies, 63-64, prin investr, Pomo Lang Proj, 65-68, RES ASSOC LING, UNIV CALIF, BERKELEY, 72-; PRES, CALIF INDIAN LANGUAGE CTR, 77- *Concurrent Pos:* Consult, Machine Transl Russ Chem Lit, 58-59; NSF grants, 64-68; vis assoc prof ling, Univ Calif, San Diego, 71-72; Smithsonian Res Found grant, 76. *Mem:* Ling Soc Am; Int Ling Asn; fel Am Anthrop Asn; assoc Current Anthrop. *Res:* American Indian languages; lexicostatistics; use of computers in linguistics. *Publ:* Auth, Kashaya Texts, Univ Calif, 64; The internal relationships of the Pomo family of languages, Acts of 35th Int Cong Americanists, 64; The detection of remote linguistic relationships, Comput Studies in Humanities & Verbal Behav, 10/70; Comparative verb morphology of Pomo, In: Januarum Linguarum, series practica 181, Mouton, The Hague, 76. *Mailing Add:* 99 Purdue Ave Kensington CA 94708

OTERO, CARLOS PEREGRIN, b Lorenzana, Spain, May 18, 30; US citizen. SPANISH LINGUISTICS & LITERATURE. *Educ:* Univ Madrid, LLM, 52; Univ Calif, Berkeley, PhD, 59. *Prof Exp:* In charge Span studies, Monterey Inst Foreign Studies, 57-58; from instr to assoc prof Span & Port, 59-69, chmn Romance ling & lit, 69-76, PROF SPAN & ROMANCE LING, UNIV CALIF, LOS ANGELES, 69-, DIR LANG LAB SPAN & PORT, 64- *Concurrent Pos:* Res grant, Italy, 63, 66; assoc dir, Univ Calif Madrid Studies Ctr, 65-67; assoc, Current Anthrop. *Mem:* Ling Soc Am; Int Ling Asn; MLA; Am Acad Polit & Soc Sci; Ling Asn Gt Brit. *Res:* Linguistics and literature; Romance linguistics, especially Spanish; culture history, especially Hispanic. *Publ:* Auth, Letras I, Tamesis Bks, London, 66 & 2nd ed, enlarged, Barcelona, 72; Gramaticalidad y Normativismo, 8/66 & Problemas del diccionario historico, 8/67, Romance Philol; Spanish transl & notes, Aspectos de la Teoria de la Sintaxis, Madrid, 70; Introduccion a la Linguistica Transformactional, Mex, 70 & 73; Evolucion y Revolucion en Romance, Barcelona, 71, 2nd ed, enlarged, 74; Spanish transl & notes, Conocimiento y Libertad, Barcelona, 72 & Estructuras Sintacticas, Mex, 74. *Mailing Add:* Dept of Span & Port Univ of Calif Los Angeles CA 90024

OTERO, JOSE, b Ecuador, July 18, 32; m 57; c 2. HISPANIC AMERICAN LITERATURE. *Educ:* Univ NMex, BA, 62, MA; 64, PhD(Span), 69. *Prof Exp:* Teaching asst Span, Univ NMex, 64-68; asst prof, 68-73, ASSOC PROF SPAN, COLO STATE UNIV, 73- *Mem:* Rocky Mountain Mod Lang Asn; Am Asn Teachers Span & Port; Casa Cult Am, Filial de Guayaquil. *Res:* Hispanish American poetry and novel. *Publ:* Auth, Los Pajaros en la Poesia de Jorge Carrera Andrade, El Comercio, Quito, 67; El tiempo en la poesia de Jose Asuncion Silva, Bull Rocky Mountain Mod Lang Asn, 70; Nuevas voces del reino de Strossner, Nueva Narrativa Hispanoam, 71; La estetica del doble en Aura de Carlos Fuentes, Explicacion de Textos Lit, 76; Hispanic Colorado, Centenial, 76; H G Wells y E Anderson Imbert: The Truth About Pyecraft y El leve Pedro, Hispanofila, 79; El misticismo poetico de Pablo, Explicacion de Textos Literarios, 80-81; Delmira Agustini: Erotismo poetico o misticismo erotico?, In: In Honor of Boyd G Carter, Univ Wyo, 81. *Mailing Add:* Dept of Foreign Lang Colo State Univ Ft Collins CO 80523

OTT, FRIEDRICH PETER, b Duisburg, Ger, Jan 1, 31; m 65; c 1. COMPARATIVE LITERATURE, GERMAN. *Educ:* Univ Mainz, MA, 58; Marquette Univ, MA, 60; Harvard Univ, PhD(comp lit), 68. *Prof Exp:* Instr Ger, Marquette Univ, 60-61; instr Ger & French, Northeastern Univ, 62-65; from instr to asst prof, 65-72, chmn dept, 74-77, ASSOC PROF GER, UNIV MASS, BOSTON, 72- *Mem:* MLA; Am Asn Teachers Ger. *Res:* Arno Schmidt; prose theory; East German literature. *Publ:* Auth, Tradition and innovation: An introduction to the prose theory and practice of Arno Schmidt, Ger Quart, 1/78; Arcadia-1939: Momentos de la vida de un fauno, Camp de l'arpa, Vol 58, 78; El servidor de lo banal: Una introduccion a la obra de Arno Schmidt, Esprial, 5/79; El caso de Arno Schmidt, Quimera, 4/81; Arno Schmidt: 1914-1979, Partisan Rev, 1/82; Gedankenspiel als (Selbst-)Porträt: Arno Schmidts KAFF auch Mare Crisium, Protokolle, 1/82. *Mailing Add:* Dept of Ger Univ of Mass Boston MA 02125

OTTEN, ANNA VON KUTSCHIG, b Nestemice, Czech; m 58. FRENCH & GERMAN LANGUAGE & LITERATURE. *Educ:* Univ Waterloo, BA, 53; Univ Western Ont, MA, 54, PhD(French), 58. *Prof Exp:* From asst prof to assoc prof French & German, 56-70, chmn dept foreign lang, 68-70, PROF FRENCH & GER LANG & LIT, ANTIOCH COL, 70- *Concurrent Pos:* Danforth Found study grant, Univ Barcelona, 60; Nat Endowment for Humanities res grant, Harvard Univ, 78. *Mem:* MLA. *Res:* German and French radio drama; modern French and German prose; modern Continental European literature. *Publ:* Auth, Mensch und Zeit, 66 & Handbook and Tapes for Mensch und Zeit, 66, Appleton; ed, Hirche, Nähe des Todes, 66, H Böll, Die Spurlosen, 67 & L Ahlsen, Philemon und Baukis, 67, Odyssey; auth, Voix et Silences, Appleton, 67; Hesse Companion, Suhrkamp, Frankfurt, 70; ed, Wolfgang Borchert Readings, Holt, 73. *Mailing Add:* Dept of Foreign Lang Antioch Col Yellow Springs OH 45387

OTTEN, ARTHUR JAMES, US citizen. FRENCH LANGUAGE & LITERATURE. *Educ:* Calvin Col, AB, 49; Laval Univ, MA, 52, DUniv(French lit), 69. *Prof Exp:* From instr to assoc prof, 52-69, PROF FRENCH, CALVIN COL, 69-, CHMN DEPT, 80- *Mem:* Am Asn Teachers Fr. *Res:* Recent French poetry. *Mailing Add:* Dept of Romance Lang Calvin Col Grand Rapids MI 49506

OTTEN, ROBERT THEODORE, b Sheboygan, Wis, Oct 4, 22; m 48; c 2. CLASSICS. *Educ:* Calvin Col, AB, 49; Univ Mich, MA, 51, PhD(class studies), 57. *Prof Exp:* From instr to asst prof, 52-62, PROF CLASS LANG, CALVIN COL, 62-, CHMN DEPT, 68- *Concurrent Pos:* Fulbright res scholar, 59-60. *Res:* Late ancient and early Christian language and thought. *Mailing Add:* Dept of Classics Calvin Col Grand Rapids MI 49506

OTTO, KARL FREDERICK, JR, b Saginaw, Mich, Sept 3, 40. GERMAN LITERATURE. *Educ:* Aquinas Col, BA, 62; Northwestern Univ, MA, 63, PhD(Ger), 67. *Prof Exp:* From asst prof to assoc prof, 67-75, PROF GER, UNIV ILL, CHICAGO, 75- *Concurrent Pos:* Alexander von Humboldt Found res fel, 73-74. *Mem:* MLA; Am Coun Teaching Foreign Lang; Int Arbeitskreis Deutsche Barocklit; Am Asn Study Ger Lit 16th & 17th Centuries; Lessing Soc. *Res:* Philipp von Zesen; Sprachgesellschaften; Baroque Literature. *Publ:* Auth, Philipp von Zesen: A Bibliographical Catalogue, Francke, Berne & Munich, 72; Die Sprachgesellschaften des 17 Jahrhunderts, Metzler, Stuttgart, 72; ed, Martin Opitz: Schafferey von der Nimfen Hercinie, Lang, Berne & Frankfort, 76. *Mailing Add:* Univ Ill Chicago Circle Box 4348 Chicago IL 60680

OTTO, VIRGINIA, b Baltimore, Md, Apr 15, 17; m 48. FOREIGN LANGUAGES. *Educ:* Col Notre Dame, Md, AB, 40; Cath Univ Am, PhD, 48. *Prof Exp:* Instr French & Span, Dunbarton Col Holy Cross, 42-45, Col Notre Dame Md, 47-52; asst prof, Hood Col, 52-55; assoc prof, 57-69, PROF FRENCH & SPAN & CHMN DEPT FOREIGN LANG, NAZARETH COL ROCHESTER, 69-, DIR CTR ITAL STUDIES, 77- *Concurrent Pos:* Fulbright res grant, 65. *Honors & Awards:* Chevalier, Ordre Palmes Academiques, France. *Mem:* MLA; Am Asn Teachers Fr. *Res:* Contemporary French novel, especially works of Marcel Proust. *Publ:* Auth, Landscape in the Works of Marcel Proust, Cath Univ Am, 48. *Mailing Add:* 141 Wyatt Dr Rochester NY 14610

OUIMETTE, VICTOR, b Calgary, Alta, Apr 21, 44; m 67. SPANISH LITERATURE. *Educ:* McGill Univ, BA, 65; Yale Univ, PhD(Span), 68. *Prof Exp:* Asst prof, 68-73, ASSOC PROF SPAN, McGILL UNIV, 73- *Mem:* MLA; Am Asn Teachers Span & Port; Can Asn Hispanists; Northeast Mod Lang Asn; Asoc Pensamiento Hisp. *Res:* The generation of 1898; the realist novel in Spain and France; modern Spanish currents of ideas. *Publ:* Auth, Reason aflame: Unamuno and the Heroic Will, Yale Univ, 74; Unamuno, Blasco Ibanez and Espana con Honra, Bull Hisp Studies, 10/76; The liberalism of Baroja and the second Republic, Hispia, 3/77; Unamuno and Le Quotidien, Rev Can Estudios Hispan, 10/77; Jose Ortega y Gasset, G K Hall, 82. *Mailing Add:* Dept of Hisp Studies McGill Univ Montreal PQ H3A 1G5 Can

OULANOFF, HONGOR, b Prague, Czech, Aug 1, 29; US citizen; m 62; c 2. RUSSIAN LITERATURE & LANGUAGE. *Educ:* Sch Orient Lang, Paris, Dipl Arabic, 52; Univ Paris, Lic es lett, 53; Harvard Univ, PhD(Slavic), 61. *Prof Exp:* Lectr Russ, Harvard Univ, 60-61; asst prof, Vanderbilt Univ, 61-63; from asst prof to assoc prof, 63-70, PROF SLAVIC LANG & LIT, OHIO STATE UNIV, 70-, ACTG CHMN DEPT, 78- *Concurrent Pos:* Res dir foreign lang, Pushkin Inst, Moscow, USSR, autumn, 79. *Mem:* Am Asn Advan Slavic Studies; Am Asn Teachers Slavic & East Europ Lang. *Res:* Modern Russian prose; Soviet Science fiction. *Publ:* Auth, The Serapion Brothers, Mouton, 66; Kaverin--the Soviet novelist of adventure and development, Slavic & East Europ J, winter 68; Erenburg, the Janus of Soviet literature, Can Slavonic Papers, summer 69; The party congress and the art of rhetoric, Can-Am Slavic Studies, spring 72; The Prose Fiction of Veniamin A Kaverin, Slavica, 76. *Mailing Add:* Dept of Slavic Lang & Lit Ohio State Univ Columbus OH 43210

OVERBECK, JOHN CLARENCE, b Tulsa, Okla, Nov 4, 33; m 72; c 1. CLASSICAL ARCHEOLOGY, ANCIENT GREEK. *Educ:* Univ Okla, AB, 55; Univ Cincinnati, PhD(classics), 63. *Prof Exp:* Asst prof, 63-66, ASSOC PROF CLASSICS, STATE UNIV NY ALBANY, 66- *Concurrent Pos:* Mem managing comt, Am Sch Class Studies, Athens, 66-75; dir archaeol surv, Dept of Antiquities, Repub of Cyprus, 70. *Mem:* Archaeol Inst Am; Soc Prom Hellenic Studies; Asn Field Archaeol; Mod Greek Studies Asn. *Res:* Cycladic Bronze Age; early Greek literature. *Publ:* Auth, Tacitus and Dio on Boudicca's rebellion, Am J Philol, 4/69; Greek towns of the Early Bronze Age, Class J, 10/69; Some notes on the interior of the Erechtheum, Athens Ann Archaeol, 4/72; coauth, Two Cypriot Bronze Age Sites at Kafkallia, Paul Aström, Göteborg, Sweden, 72; The date of the last palace at Knossos, Am J Archaeol, spring 76; auth, Pioneers of Attic Vase Painting, In: The Greek Vase, Hudson-Mohawk Asn Cols & Univs, 81; The hub of commerce: Keos and Middle Helladic Greece, In: Temple University Aegean Symposium, Betancourt, 82; coauth, Consistency and diversity in the Middle Cycladic Era, In: Papers in Cycladic Prehistory, Univ Calif, Los Angeles, 79. *Mailing Add:* Dept of Classics State Univ of NY Albany NY 12222

OVIEDO, JOSE MIGUEL, b Lima, Peru, Aug 8, 34; m; c 2. SPANISH AMERICAN LITERATURE. *Educ:* Facultad de Letras, Univ Cath, BA, 58, Doctorate(lit), 62. *Prof Exp:* Vis prof Span Am lit, State Univ NY, Albany, 74; vis prof, Ind Univ, 75-76, prof, 76-80; PROF SPAN AM LIT, UNIV CALIF, LOS ANGELES, 81- *Concurrent Pos:* Fel, Study Cesar Vallejo, Guggenheim Found, 72-73; contrib ed, Handbook Latin Am Studies, Libr Cong, 76- *Mem:* MLA. *Res:* Spanish American literature. *Publ:* Auth, Genio y figura de Ricardo Palma, Eudeba, 65; ed, Narradores peruanos, Monte Avila, 68 & 76; auth, Mario Vargas Llosa: La invencion de una realidad, Barral Editores, 70 & 77; co-ed, Homenaje a Mario Vargas Llosa, Las Americas, Publ, 71; ed, Estos trece, Mosca Azul, 73; Cien tradiciones peruanas de R Palma, Bibliot Ayacucho, 77; auth, La doble exposicion de Manuel Puig, Eco, Bogota, 10/77; Tema del traidor y del heroe: Los militares y los intelectuales en la obra de Vargas Llosa, World Lit Today, 78. *Mailing Add:* Univ of Calif Los Angeles CA

OWECHKO, IWAN, b Melitopol, Ukraine, May 20, 20; US citizen; m; c 2. RUSSIAN LANGUAGE & LITERATURE. *Educ:* Ukrainian Free Univ, PhD(Slavic philol & philos), 71. *Prof Exp:* Teacher Russ lang & lit, Sneshnoje Jr & Sr High Sch, Donbass, USSR, 38-41; teacher Russ lang for Ger, Eichstatt, WGer, 46-48; spec corres, Nash Klych, Buenos Aires, 49-58; columnist, Svoboda, Jersey City, NJ, 61-66; instr Russ & Ger, Ft Hays Kans State Col, 68-69; asst prof, 69-74, assoc prof, 72-80, PROF RUSS, UNIV NORTHERN COLO, 80- *Concurrent Pos:* Co-ed, Free World, 68-73. *Mem:* AAUP; Shevchenko Sci Soc; Ukrainian Asn Univ Prof; Ukrainian Journalists Asn. *Res:* A P Chekhov's ancestry, his relationship to Ukraine and the Ukrainian elements in his life and works; the philosophy of work as seen by various nations, their philosophy and thinking. *Publ:* Auth, You Were a Stranger, Faria & Leite, o Paulo, 57; Don't Grieve, Ukraine! (poems), M Kudanovicz, 65; Selections, Group of Readers, 70; Chekhov and Ukraine, Ukrainian Free Univ, Munich, 73; ed, The Songs of My Heart (poems), 76; Ukrainians in Texas, 76; The Sorrowful Seagull Song, 77; Ukrainian Place Names in USA, 77. *Mailing Add:* Dept of Foreign Lang Univ of Northern Colo Greeley CO 80639

OWEN, CLAUDE RUDOLPH, b Frankfurt, Ger, July 10, 26; Can citizen. GERMANIC LANGUAGES & LITERATURE. *Educ:* Univ Alta, BA, 60, MA, 61; Univ Kans, PhD, 64. *Prof Exp:* Lectr Ger, Univ Alta, exten 59-61, univ, 60-61; asst lectr, Univ Kans, 61-64; asst prof, Univ Mo-Columbia, 64-65; vis asst prof, Univ Nebr, 65-66; asst prof, Univ NB, 66-67; from asst prof to assoc prof Ger, 67-75, chmn dept Ger & Slavic studies, 69-72, PROF GER, BROCK UNIV, 75- *Mem:* Ont Mod Lang Teachers Asn; Can Asn Univ Teachers Ger; Am Asn Teachers Ger; MLA. *Res:* German 20th century literature; 19th century German- Spanish comparative literature; German exile literature, 1933-1945, in Canada. *Publ:* Auth, Heine im Spanischen Sprachgebiet, Goerres Ges, 68, suppl, 73; auth, Dario und Heine, Susquehanna Univ Studies, 6/70; coauth, Deutsch für Kanadier, Brock Univ, Vol I & II, 71 & 73; auth, Ezequiel Martinez Estrada: Heine und die Freiheit, Heine Jahrbuch, 71; Zur Erotik in Stifters Brigitta, Oesterreich in Geschichte u Lit, Graz, 2/71; coauth (with L Abbicht), The Sword, The Pen and the Swastika, Brock Univ, 81. *Mailing Add:* Dept of Ger Brock Univ St Catharines ON L2S 3A1 Can

OWOMOYELA, OYEKAN, b Ifon, Nigeria, Apr 22, 38; US citizen; m 75. AFRICAN LITERATURE. *Educ:* Univ London, BA, 63; Univ Calif, Los Angeles, MFA, 66, PhD(theater hist), 70. *Prof Exp:* Lectr audio visuals, Univ Ibadan, Nigeria, 68-71; asst prof, 72-75, assoc prof, 75-81, PROF LIT & DRAMA, UNIV NEBR-LINCOLN, 81- *Concurrent Pos:* Sr consult, Ctr Mgt Develop, Nigerian, 75. *Mem:* African Studies Asn; African Lit Asn; Am Folklore Soc. *Res:* Sociology of African literature; Yoruba folklore and society. *Publ:* Auth, Folklore and Yoruba theater, Res in African Lit, fall 71; The Sociology of sex and crudity in Yorbua Proverbs, Proverbium: Bull d'information sur les recherches paremiologiques, 20: 751-758; coauth (with

Bernth Lindfors), Yoruba Proverbs: Translations and Annotations, Ohio Univ Ctr Int Studies, 73; auth, Western humanism and African usage: A critical survey of non-African responses to African literature, Issue: A Quart J Opinion IV, winter 74; African Literatures: An Introduction, Crossroads Press, 79; Obotunde Ijimere, the phantom of Nigerian theater, 4/79 & Dissidence and the African writer: Commitment or dependency, 3/81, Studies Rev; The pragmatic humanism of Yoruba culture, J African Studies, fall 81. *Mailing Add:* Dept of English Univ Nebr Lincoln NE 68588

OXENHANDLER, NEAL, b St Louis, Mo, Feb 3, 26; c 3. FRENCH. *Educ:* Univ Chicago, AB, 48; Columbia Univ, MA, 50; Yale Univ, PhD(French), 55. *Prof Exp:* Instr French, Yale Univ, 53-57; from asst prof to assoc prof, Univ Calif, Los Angeles, 57-66; prof French lit, Cowell Col, Univ Calif, Santa Cruz, 66-69; PROF FRENCH LIT, DARTMOUTH COL, 69- *Concurrent Pos:* Fulbright fel, 53; Guggenheim fel, 61-62; cross disciplinary fel, 66 & 67; dir, Nat Endowment for Humanities sem, 81. *Mem:* MLA; Am Asn Teachers Fr; Am Comp Lit Asn. *Res:* French literature of the 19th and 20th centuries; psychoanalysis and literature; French cinema. *Publ:* Auth, Scandal and Parade, Rutgers Univ, 57; coauth, Aspects of French Literature, Appleton, 61; auth, A Change of Gods, Harcourt, 62; Max Jacob and Les Feux de Paris, Univ Calif, 64; French Literary Criticism, Prentice-Hall, 66; Quest for pure consciousness in Husserl and Mallarme, In: Quest for Imagination, Case-Western Reserve, 71; Literature as perception in the work of Merleau-Ponty, In: Modern French Criticism, Univ Chicago Press, 72; Intimacy and Distance in the Cinema of Jean-Luc Godard, Symp, 73. *Mailing Add:* Dept of French & Ital Dartmouth Col Hanover NH 03755

OYLER, JOHN EDWARD, b Innisfail, Alta, Jan 28, 19; m 42; c 4. MODERN FOREIGN LANGUAGES. *Educ:* Univ Alta, BA, 49, MA, 50; Northwestern Univ, PhD, 57. *Prof Exp:* Instr Ger & French, SDak State Univ, 52-56, asst prof mod lang, 56-58; asst prof Ger, Univ NB, 58-60; from asst prof to assoc prof mod lang, 60-70, head dept Ger, 63-71, prof Slavic studies, 68-70, PROF GER, UNIV CALGARY, 68- *Concurrent Pos:* Can Coun res fel, 67-68. *Mem:* Asn Can Univ Teachers Ger (vpres, 67-69); Am Asn Teachers Ger; Can Ling Asn; MLA; Can Asn Univ Teachers Ger (pres, 69-71). *Res:* Literature of the Barock; German language of the 17th century; linguistics. *Publ:* Auth, A Few Changes in Grammar Presentation, Unterrichtspraxis, 69; Noun and Adjective in German, In: Teaching of German, Problems & Methods, 70; Andreas Gryphius, Catharina von Georgien, Sprachlich Modernisierter Text der Erstfassung von 1657, Herausgegeben von J E Oyler und A H Schulze, Peter Lang, Bern, 78; Schottel or Schottelius, Ger Notes, Vol I, No 5. *Mailing Add:* Dept of Ger & Slavic Studies Univ of Calgary Calgary AB T2N 1N4 Can

P

PACE, ANTONIO, b July 7, 14; US citizen. ROMANCE LANGUAGES & LITERATURES. *Educ:* Syracuse Univ, AB, 35; Princeton Univ, PhD, 43. *Prof Exp:* Instr Romance lang, Syracuse Univ, 39-42 & 44-45, instr physics, 43-44, from asst prof to prof, 45-67; PROF ITAL, UNIV WASH, 67- *Concurrent Pos:* Guggenheim fel, 48-49 & 60-61; gen ed, Symposium, 52-58; res assoc, Am Philos Soc. *Honors & Awards:* Knight, Order of Merit, Italy, 63. *Mem:* MLA; Am Asn Teachers Ital (pres, 58-60). *Mailing Add:* Dept of Romance Lang & Lit Univ of Wash Seattle WA 98105

PACHECO, MANUEL TRINIDAD, b Rocky Ford, Colo, May 30, 41; m 66; c 3. LINGUISTICS. *Educ:* NMex Highlands Univ, AB, 62; Ohio State Univ, MA, 67, PhD(lang acquisition, ling), 69. *Prof Exp:* Lectr Span, Western NMex Univ, 64-65; asst prof foreign lang educ, Fla State Univ, 68-71; asst prof Span, Univ Colo, 71-72; prof educ & dean univ, Tex A&I Univ, Laredo, 72-77; coordr multicult educ prof, 77-80, ASSOC PROF EDUC, SAN DIEGO STATE UNIV, 80- *Concurrent Pos:* Vis prof Span, Middlebury Col, 72; consult, Inst Cult Pluralism, Univ NMex, 72-73; mem comn multicult educ, Am Asn Col Teacher Educ, 78-81. *Mem:* Am Asn Teachers Span & Port; Am Coun Teaching Foreign Lang; MLA; Teachers English to Speakers of Other Lang. *Res:* Second language acquisition; bilingual education; sociolinguistics. *Publ:* Auth, Approaches to bilingualism: Recognition of a multi-lingual society, In: The Britannica Review of Foreign Language Education, Vol III, Encycl Britannica, 71; Some Implications of Individualized Instruction for Bilingual Education, 71, English As a Second Language, 71, English As a Second Dialect, 71, Training to teach the non-English home language, In: Designs for Teacher Education, 73 & co-ed, Problems in Applied Educational Sociolinguistics: Readings on Language and Cultural Problems of US Ethnic Groups, 74, Newbury. *Mailing Add:* Sch of Educ San Diego State Univ San Diego CA 92182

PACHECO-RANSANZ, ARSENIO, b Barcelona, Spain, Feb 8, 32; m 56; c 2. SPANISH LITERATURE. *Educ:* Univ Barcelona, BA & MA, 54, DPhil(romance philol), 58. *Prof Exp:* Instr Span lit, Univ Barcelona, 56-57; asst lectr, Univ Glasgow, 57-90; lectr, Univ St Andrews, 59-70; assoc prof, 70-79, PROF SPAN LIT, UNIV BC, 80- *Concurrent Pos:* Asst dir, Col Mayor Hispanoam Fray Junipero Serra, 54-56, hon fel, 56; res fel Catalan lit, Consejo superior Investigaciones Cientificas, Spain, 55-57; vis prof, Univ Pittburgh, 66 & Univ BC, 68-69. *Mem:* MLA; Int Asn Hispanists; Can Asn Hispanists (pres, 78-80); NAm Catalan Soc; Can Fedn for Humanities. *Res:* Medieval Catalan literature; Medieval Spanish literature; the Spanish novel in the 17th century. *Publ:* Ed, Francesc de la Via, Obres (2 vols), Biblio Catalana Obres Antigues, Barcelona, 63 & 68; Histoira de Xacob Xalabin, Ed Barcino, Barcelona, 64; Testament de Bernat Serradella de Vic, Ed Barcino, Barcelona, 71; Viatges a L'Altre Mon, Ed 62, Barcelona, 73; auth, Razon de Amor o Denvestos del Agua y Elvino?, Bull Hisp Studies, 74; Los caballos de Romancero Gitano, Univ BC Hisp Studies, 74; ed, G de Cespedes y Meneses, Varia Fortuna del Soldado Pindaro, Espasa-Calpe, Madrid, 75; auth, El Blandin de Cornualha, In: Catalan Studies in Memory of Josephine de Boer, Hispana Borras Edicions, Barcelona, 77. *Mailing Add:* Dept of Hisp & Ital Studies Univ BC Vancouver BC V6T 1W5 Can

PACHMUSS, TEMIRA, b Skamja, Estonia, Dec 24, 27. RUSSIAN LITERATURE & LANGUAGE. *Educ:* Univ Melbourne, BA, 54, MA, 55; Univ Wash, PhD(Slavic lang & lit), 59. *Prof Exp:* Court interpreter, US Mil Govt Court, Ger, 45-49; instr Russ, Univ Melbourne, 52-54, teacher, Univ High Sch, 54-55; teaching assoc Russ, Univ Wash, 55-58; instr, Russ lang, Univ Mich, 58-59; instr Russ lang & lit, Univ Colo, 59-60; from instr to assoc prof, 60-68, PROF RUSS LIT, UNIV ILL, URBANA, 68- *Mem:* Estonian Learned Soc Am. *Res:* Works of Dostoevsky and Zinaida Hippius; women writers in Russian modernism; Russian literature in exile 1921-1939. *Publ:* Contribr, Lev Tolstoy, In: Encyclopedia of World Literature of the Twentieth Century, Ungar, 71; The theme of love and death in Tolstoy's The Death of Ivan Ilyich, In: Classic Short Fiction: An International Collection, Bobbs-Merrill, 72; ed, Zinaida Hippius: Collected Poetical Works (2 vols), 72 & auth, Intellect and Ideas in Action: Selected Correspondence of Zinaida Hippius, 72, Wilhelm Fink; Selected Works of Zinaida Hippius, 72, Between Paris and St Petersburg: Selected Diaries of Zinaida Hippius, 75 & Women Writers in Russian Modernism, 78, Univ Ill; A Russian Cultural Revival, Univ Tenn, 81. *Mailing Add:* Dept of Slavic Lang & Lit Univ of Ill Urbana IL 61801

PACIFICI, SERGIO, b Leghorn, Italy, Jan 12, 25; US citizen; m 48; c 2. LANGUAGES. *Educ:* Univ Calif, Los Angeles, BA, 49; Univ Wash, MA, 50; Harvard Univ, MA, 51, PhD(Romance lang), 53. *Prof Exp:* Instr Ital, Univ Minn, 53-54; instr, Yale Univ, 54-57, asst prof, 57-63; assoc prof Romance lang, City Col NY, 63-65; PROF ROMANCE LANG, QUEEN'S COL, NY, 65- *Concurrent Pos:* Morse fel, 58-59, fac grants, 59-63; Am Philos Soc grants, 58-59; Guggenheim fel, 61-62; City Univ New York Res Found grant, 77-78 & 79-80; Fulbright travel fel, 72. *Mem:* MLA; Am Asn Teachers Ital; Dante Soc. *Res:* Modern and contemporary literature. *Publ:* Auth, A Guide to Contemporary Italian Literature: From Futurism to Neorealism, Meridian, 62, Southern Ill Univ, reprint, 72; From Verismo to Experimentalism: Essays on the Modern Italian Novel, Ind Univ, 69; Vita e Cultura (textbook), Random, 69; Italian literature, In: Encycl Americana, Grolier, 69; The Modern Italian Novel: From Capuana to Tozzi, Southern Ill Univ, Vol 2, 72; contribr, World Book Encycl, Field; auth, The Modern Italian Novel From Pea to Moravia, Southern Ill Univ, 78; Natalia Ginzburg, Primo Levi, In: Columbia Dictionary of Modern Literature. *Mailing Add:* Dept of Romance Lang Queen's Col Flushing NY 11367

PADEN, WILLIAM DOREMUS, JR, b Lawrence, Kans, June 20, 41; m 73; c 2. MEDIEVAL LITERATURE, ROMANCE PHILOLOGY. *Educ:* Yale Univ, BA, 63, PhD(comp lit), 71; Univ Ill, Urbana, MA, 66. *Prof Exp:* From instr to asst prof, 68-74, assoc prof, 74-81, PROF FRENCH & ITAL, NORTHWESTERN UNIV, EVANSTON, 81- *Concurrent Pos:* Nat Endowment for Humanities fel, 76-77. *Mem:* Int Courtly Lit Soc; Mediaeval Acad Am; MLA. *Res:* Troubadours; medieval lyric. *Publ:* Coauth, The troubadour's lady: Her marital status and social rank, Studies in Philol, 75; auth, Bertran de Born in Italy, In: Italian Literature: Roots and Branches, Yale Univ, 76; L'emploi vicaire du present verbal dans les plus anciens textes narratifs romans, XIV Cong Int di, Ling e Filologia Romanza, 77; De l'identite historique de Bertran de Born, Romania, 80; De monachis rithmos facientibus: Helinant de Froidmont, Bertran de Born, and the Cistercian general chapter of 1199, Speculum, 80; Pound's Use of Troubadour manuscripts, Comp Lit, 80; co-ed, Poems of the Trobairitz na Castelloza, Romance Philol, 81; Poems of the Troubadour Bertran de Born, Univ Calif Press (in press). *Mailing Add:* Dept of French & Ital Northwestern Univ Evanston IL 60201

PAINE, STEPHEN W, b Grand Rapids, Mich, Oct 28, 08; m 34; c 5. CLASSICS. *Educ:* Wheaton Col, Ill, AB, 30, LLD, 39; Univ Ill, AM, 31, PhD(classics), 33. *Hon Degrees:* LHD, Houghton Col, 76. *Prof Exp:* Instr Greek, 33-34, prof, 34-72, dean, 34-37, pres, 37-72, EMER PROF GREEK & EMER PRES, HOUGHTON COL, 72- *Concurrent Pos:* Mem comt Bible transl, New Int Version of the Bible, 67- *Mem:* Class Asn Atlantic States; Evangel Theol Soc (vpres, 66, pres, 67). *Res:* Classical Greek nomenclature; basic authority and Christian faith; Biblical translation into English. *Publ:* Auth, Toward the Mark--Studies in Philippians, 53 & Studies in the Book of James, 55, Revell; Beginning Greek--a Functional Approach, Oxford Univ, 61; I and II Peter, In: Wycliffe Commentary, Moody, 61; Maintaining the witness to inerrancy, winter 66 & The Christian man and the Bible, winter 68, Bull Evangel Theol Soc. *Mailing Add:* 7 Circle Dr Houghton NY 14744

PALANDRI, ANGELA CHIH-YING JUNG, b Peking, China, Aug 6, 26; US citizen; m 56; c 2. CHINESE LANGUAGE & LITERATURE. *Educ:* Fu Jen Univ, Peking, BA, 46; Univ Wash, MA, 49, MLA, 54, PhD(English), 55. *Prof Exp:* Librn, Univ Ore, 54-56, instr Chinese, 55-56; instr English, Ore State Syst Higher Educ, 60-62; from asst prof to assoc prof, 62-74, chmn dept Chinese & Japanese, 74-77, 78-79, PROF CHINESE, UNIV ORE, 74- *Concurrent Pos:* Fulbright fac res grant abroad, US Dept Educ, 77-78. *Mem:* Asn Asian Studies; Philol Studies Pac Coast; Chinese Teachers Asn. *Res:* Comparative literature; women writers in contemporary China; Italian images of Ezra Pound. *Publ:* Auth, La pietra mi e viva nella mano, le traduzioni dal cinese di E Pound, Il Verri, Revista Lett, Milan, summer 68; ed, Modern Verse From Taiwan, Univ Calif, 72; auth, Yuan Chenas a poet engage, Tamkang Rev, 76; Yüan Chen, Twayne, 77; ed & transl, Italian Images of Ezra Pound, Mei-Ya Publ, Taipei, 79; ed, Women Writers of 20th Century China, Univ Ore, 82. *Mailing Add:* Dept of EAsian Lang Univ of Ore Eugene OR 97403

PALENCIA-ROTH, MICHAEL, b Girardot, Colombia, June 26, 46; US citizen; m 68; c 2. COMPARATIVE LITERATURE. *Educ:* Vanderbilt Univ, BA, 68; Harvard Univ, MA, 71, PhD(comp lit), 76. *Prof Exp:* Tutor comp lit, Harvard Univ, 71-73; from instr to asst prof, Univ Mich, Dearborn, 74-77;

ASST PROF COMP LIT, UNIV ILL, 77- *Concurrent Pos:* Assoc ed, Philos & Lit, 75-77; asst ed, Comp Lit Studies, 77-; Nat Endowment for Humanities fel, 80-81. *Mem:* MLA; Am Comp Lit Asn; Int Soc Comp Study Civilizations; Inst Int de Lit Iberoamericana. *Res:* The Faustiansensibility; philosophical and psychoanalytic approaches to literature. *Publ:* Auth, Thomas Mann's non relationship to James Joyce, Mod Lang Notes, 76; The anti-faustian ethos of Die Blechtrommel, J Europ Studies, 79; Faust and the cultural stages of Wagner's Ring, The Opera J, 79; The Contexts of Busoni's Doktor Faust, Science/Technology and the Humanities, 79; Mothers, fathers and the life of reason in Mill's Autobiography, Comp Civilizations Rev, 80; Albrecht Dürer's Melecolia I and Thomas Mann's Doktor Faustus, Ger Studies Rev, 80; La imagen del Urboros: el incesto en Cien anos de soledad, Caudernos Americanos, 81; Los pergaminos de Aureliano Babilonia, Revista Iberoamericana (in press). *Mailing Add:* 2070 Foreign Lang Bldg Univ of Ill Urbana IL 61801

PALERMO, JOSEPH, b Trenton, NJ, Sept 9, 17; m 43; c 3. ROMANCE PHILOLOGY. *Educ:* Temple Univ, AB, 40; Princeton Univ, AM, 48, PhD(Romance lang & lit), 50; Univ Poitiers cert, 60. *Prof Exp:* Asst ed Merriam-Webster Dictionaries, 40-45; instr romance lang, Temple Univ, 45-51; from instr to assoc prof, 51-61, prof, 61-72, EMER PROF ROMANCE LANG, UNIV CONN, 72-; PROF ROMANCE LANG, VA POLYTECH INST & STATE UNIV, 74- *Concurrent Pos:* Instr div univ exten, State Dept Educ, Mass, 41-45; Am Philos Soc grants, 54, 60, 65, 82; Belgian-Am Educ Found fel, 58; lectr, Ecole Libres des Hautes Etudes, NY, 61-62 & Alliance Francaise, 67-; vis prof, Univ Palermo, 73-; Am Coun Learned Soc grants, 62, 63, 65, 67; Univ Conn Res Coun grants, 68-69, 70-72; mem nat screening comt, Inst Int Educ, 72-; head dept foreign lang, Va Polytech Inst & State Univ, 74-75; Va Tech Educ Found grant, 82. *Mem:* Mediaeval Acad Am; MLA; Am Asn Teachers Ital; Soc Ling Romance; Soc Prof Fr Am. *Res:* Medieval French language and literatuare; Provencal language and literature; romance philology. *Publ:* Auth, La Poesie provencale a la cour de Frederic II de Sicile, Rev Ling Romane, 67; L'Oxytonisme: Clef de la structure francaise, Actes Int Cong Ling, Bucharest, 70; Rythme occitan et rythme oxyton: Cle de la scission gallo-romane, Rev Ling Romane, 71; ed, Le Roman d'Hector et Hercule: Chant Epique en Octosyllables Italo-Francais, Librairie Droz, Geneva, 72; L'oeuvre francaise d'um proscrit sicilien: Michel Palmieri de Micciche, Studi Francesi, 71: 243-250; Vivien de Montbranc: personnage epique ambivalent, Actes du Congres, Pamplona, 81; L'Historicite de l'oeuvre dramatique de Michel Palmiere de Micciche, South Atlantic Mod Lang Asn, 11/80; ed, Le Nouveau Gargantua, Cantania (in press). *Mailing Add:* Dept of Foreign Lang & Lit Va Polytech Inst & State Univ Blacksburg VA 24061

PALEY, NICHOLAS MIROSLAV, b Bohdanivka, Ukraine, Dec 7, 11; US citizen; m 44; c 2. ROMANCE & SLAVIC LANGUAGES. *Educ:* Ohio State Univ, BA, 43, MA, 74; Univ Interam, Mex, PhD, 68. *Prof Exp:* Asst Romance lang, Ohio State Univ, 44-50; from instr to assoc prof, 50-68, prof, 69-77, EMER PROF MOD LANG, BELOIT COL, 77- *Mem:* Am Asn Teachers Span & Port; Ukrainian Acad Sci. *Res:* Spanish-Ukrainian literary influences; translations from Spanish into Ukrainian. *Publ:* Auth, Nadiyni Dni, Academia, Muenchen, 47; Tesis Profesionales, Ediciones Univ, Mex, 69; Etcetera (poetry), Arcadia, Mex, 70; auth & ed, La viada de Lazarillo de Tormes(transl into Ukrainian), 70 Tamayo y Baus, The New Drama (transl into Ukrainian), 72 Sentimental Ukraine, 74 & With Ardent Blood, 78, J Serediak, Buenos Aires; Romantic Ukraine, 80 & Dudyo and I, 80, J Serediak, Buenos Aires. *Mailing Add:* Dept of Mod Lang & Lit Beloit Col Beloit WI 53511

PALLESKE, SIEGWALT ODO, b Staten Island, NY, Apr 9, 07; m 38. MODERN LANGUAGES & LITERATURE. *Educ:* Wagner Col, AB, 28; Columbia Univ, AM, 31; Univ Strasbourg, Dr Univ, 38. *Prof Exp:* Asst prof, Miami Univ, 39-45; from assoc prof to prof, 45-76, EMER PROF MOD LANG, UNIV DENVER, 76- *Concurrent Pos:* Lectr, Inst Lit, 50. *Honors & Awards:* Distinguished Serv Award, Col Cong of Foreign Lang Teachers, 78. *Mem:* Am Asn Teachers Fr; Am Asn Teachers Ger. *Res:* Comparative literature; comparative culture. *Publ:* Translr, Legaut: Meditations of a believer; Avril: Sunday radio sermons; Maurice Maeterlinck en Allemagne. *Mailing Add:* 900 Race St Denver CO 80206

PALLEY, JULIAN, b Atlantic City, NJ, Sept 16, 25; m 50; c 4. ROMANCE LANGUAGES. *Educ:* Mexico City Col, BA, 50; Univ Ariz, MA, 52; Univ NMex, PhD, 58. *Prof Exp:* Asst Romance lang, Univ NMex, 52-55; instr, Rutgers Univ, 56-59; asst prof Span, Ariz State Univ, 59-62; assoc prof, Univ Ore, 62-66; assoc prof Span, 66-73, chmn dept Span & Port, 70-73, PROF SPAN & PORT, UNIV CALIF, IRVINE, 73- *Mem:* MLA; Am Asn Teachers Span & Port. *Res:* Contemporary Spanish literature; Pedro Salinas; modern Spanish novel. *Publ:* Auth, La Luz no Usada: La Poesia de Pedro Salinas, Studium, Mex, 66; ed, Jorge Guillen: Affirmation, A Bilingual Anthology, 1919-1966, Univ Okla, 68; auth, Spinoza's Stone and Other Poems, JNR Publ, 76; El Laberinto y la Esfera: Cien Anos de la novela Espanola, Insula, Madrid, 78. *Mailing Add:* Dept of Span & Port Univ of Calif Irvine CA 92717

PALLISTER, JANIS LOUISE, b Rochester, Minn, Jan 12, 26. ROMANCE LANGUAGES. *Educ:* Univ Minn, BA, 46, MA, 48, PhD(French), 64. *Prof Exp:* Instr French, Span & English, Black Hills Teachers Col, 48-50; teaching asst French, Univ Wis, 51-52; teaching asst, Univ Minn, 54-59; instr, Colby Col, 59-61; from instr to assoc prof, 61-71, prof French, 71-79, UNIV PROF, BOWLING GREEN STATE UNIV, 79- *Honors & Awards:* OEA Human Rels Comn Award, 79. *Mem:* Am Asn Teachers Fr; MLA; AAUP; Renaissance Soc Am; Mediaeval Acad Am. *Res:* French medieval language and literature; French Renaissance and baroque literature; lyric poetry. *Publ:* Auth, Beroalde de Verville's Stances de la Mort and Soupirs Amoureux, Nottingham French Studies, 70; Presentation motifs in the prologue of Claudel's L'Annonce Faite a Marie, Romance Notes, 72; coauth, En attendant Godot, tragedy or comedy?, Esprit Createur, fall 71; auth, The World View of Beroalde de Verville, Vrin, Paris, 71; translr, Bolamba's Esanzo, 77; coauth, Waiting for Death: The Philosophical Significance of Beckett's En Attendant Godot, Univ Ala, 79; The Bruised Reed, Naaman, 78; On Monsters and Marvels, Univ Chicago, 82. *Mailing Add:* Dept of Romance Lang Bowling Green State Univ Bowling Green OH 43402

PALLOTTA, AUGUSTUS G, b Benevento, Italy, May 4, 38; US citizen; m 69; c 1. ITALIAN LITERATURE. *Educ:* Boston Univ, BA, 62; Ind Univ, Bloomington, MA, 64; Columbia Univ, PhD(Ital), 72. *Prof Exp:* Asst prof, 72-74, ASSOC PROF SPAN & ITAL, SYRACUSE UNIV, 76- *Concurrent Pos:* Dir, Syracuse Univ Semester in Italy, 77-78. *Mem:* Am Asn Teachers Ital; Asn Int Studio Lingua Ital; Am Asn Univ Professors Ital; Nat Ital Hon Soc (treas, 77-82). *Res:* Modern Italian literature; 19th century Spanish literature. *Publ:* Auth, Il Manzoni in Catalogna, Riv Lett Mod e Comparate, 3/73; The Spanish Translations of Manzoni's Il Cinque Maggio, Forum Ital, winter 73; British and American Translations of I Promessi Sposi, winter 73, Some Reflections on a New Anthology of Italian Poetry, spring 76, Italica; contribr, The Romantic Movement: A Selective & Critical Bibliography; Manzoni's Relationship with Spain, Italica, summer 80; A Spanish poet on the unification of Italy, Ital Quart, summer 80; Characterization through Understatement: A Study of Manzoni's Don Rodrigo, Italica, spring 81. *Mailing Add:* Fac of Foreign Lang Ital Syracuse Univ Syracuse NY 13210

PALMATIER, ROBERT ALLEN, b Kalamazoo, Mich, July 22, 26; m 46; c 2. LINGUISTICS, ENGLISH. *Educ:* Western Mich Univ, BA, 50, MA, 55; Univ Mich, PhD(ling), 65. *Prof Exp:* From instr to prof English, 55-68; prof ling & chmn dept, 68-81, CHMN DEPT LANGS, WESTERN MICH UNIV, 81- *Concurrent Pos:* Ed, The Informant. *Mem:* Ling Soc Am; MLA. *Res:* Generative grammar; English grammar; critical languages. *Publ:* Auth, A Descriptive Syntax of the Ormulum, Mouton, 69; A Glossary for English Transformational Grammar, Appleton, 72; Metrical-e in the ormulum, J English Ling, 3/72. *Mailing Add:* Dept of Lang & Ling Western Mich Univ Kalamazoo MI 49008

PALMER, JOE DARWIN, b Decker, Ind, Nov 16, 34; m 54; c 4. LINGUISTICS, ENGLISH AS A SECOND LANGUAGE. *Educ:* Ind State Univ, BA, 56; Univ Mich, Ann Arbor, MA, 62, PhD(English), 68. *Prof Exp:* Teacher English & French, Romeo High Sch, Mich, 57-61; fel instr English, English Lang Inst, Univ Mich, 61-68, lectr ling, 68-69; asst prof educ, Nat Teacher Educ Ctr, Afgoi, Somali Republic, 66-68; asst prof Univ Pittsburgh in Thailand, 69-71; assoc prof, Am Univ Cairo, 71-72; asst prof humanities, Univ Mich, Dearborn, 72-73; ASSOC PROF LING, CONCORDIA UNIV, SIR GEORGE WILLIAMS CAMPUS, 73- *Concurrent Pos:* Consult, UNESCO in Somali Republic, 66-68; Regional English Lang Ctr, Singapore, 69-71; Brit Coun lectr, Salonika & Fulbright lectr, Athens, 72. *Mem:* NCTE; Teachers English Speakers Other Lang; Int Asn Teachers English Foreign Lang. *Res:* Contrastive analysis of languages; language policy; language learning. *Publ:* Auth, Advanced English: Lessons in Transformational Grammar, USAID-Somalia, 67; co-ed, A contrastive analysis of English and Arabic, 73 & ed, A contrastive analysis of English and Arabic, 73 & ed, A contrastive analysis of English and Thai, 73, Defense Lang Inst, Tex. *Mailing Add:* Dept of Ling Concordia Univ Montreal PQ H3G 1M8 Can

PALMER, JOE LERNER, b Wichita Falls, Tex, July 3, 37; m 66. SPANISH LITERATURE. *Educ:* NTex State Univ, BA, 60, MA, 64; Univ Colo, Boulder, PhD(Span), 69. *Prof Exp:* Asst prof Span, Univ Ga, 68-74; ASSOC PROF SPAN, NORTHERN ILL UNIV, 74- *Mem:* Am Soc 18th Century Studies; Am Asn Teachers Span & Port; Centro Estudios Siglo XVIII. *Res:* Spanish 18th century literature; Padre Jose Francisco de Isla; prose of Spanish 18th century. *Publ:* Auth, Elements of Social Satire in Padre Issla's Fray Gerundio de Campazas, Ky Romance Quart, 72; La Juventud Triunfante and the Origin of Padre Isla's Satire, Hispania, 73; Dia grande de Navarra and the Evolution of Padre Isla's Satire, Univ S Fla Lang Quart; Spanish for health care personnel, Hispania. *Mailing Add:* Dept of Foreign Lang & Lit Northern Ill Univ De Kalb IL 60115

PALMER, MELVIN DELMAR, b Mitchell County, Ga, July 14, 30; m 62; c 4. COMPARATIVE LITERATURE, SPORTS FICTION. *Educ:* Univ Md, College Park, BA, 57, MA, 59, PhD(comp lit), 69. *Prof Exp:* Asst prof English, Western Ky State Univ, 59-62; instr, Univ Md, 62-65; assoc prof, 65-80, PROF COMP LIT & CHMN DEPT, WESTERN MD COL, 80- *Mem:* Am Comp Lit Asn; Int Comp Lit Asn. *Res:* Development of long narrative fiction; sports novel; the creative process. *Publ:* The History of Adolphus..., Philol Quart, 10/70; Madame D'Aulnoy's Pseudoautobiographical Works on Spain, Romanische Forsch, 71; The Sports Novel: Mythic Heroes and Natural Men, Quest, 1/73; Madam d'Aulnoy in England, Comp Lit, summer 75; co-ed, Drum Major for a Dream: Poetic Tributes to Martin Luther King, Jr, Writers Workshop, Calcutta, 77; Tagore's Poetry in English, In: Rabindranath Tagore: American Interpretations, Writers Workshop, Calcutta, 81; The heyday of the football novel, J Popular Cult, 82. *Mailing Add:* Dept of Comp Lit Western Maryland Col Westminster MD 21157

PALMER, RICHARD E, b Phoenix, Ariz, Nov 6, 33; m 56; c 3. COMPARATIVE EUROPEAN LITERATURE & PHILOSOPHY. *Educ:* Univ Redlands, BA, 55, MA, 56, PhD (comp lit), 59. *Prof Exp:* Asst prof humanities, 59-64, assoc prof humanities & world lit, 64-69, dir humanities core lit prog, 65-76, prof humanities & world lit, 69-71, prof philos & lit, 72-80, CHMN DEPT PHILOS & LIT, MACMURRAY COL, 80- *Concurrent Pos:* Am Coun Learned Soc fel, 64-65; Nat Endowment for Humanities younger humanist fel philos, Univ Heidelberg, 71-72, grant, 78. *Mem:* Am Philos Asn; MLA; Am Comp Lit Asn; Soc Phenomenol & Existential Philos; Heidegger Conf Scholars. *Res:* Existentialism and phenomenology; Romantic literature and philosophy; hermeneutics. *Publ:* Auth, Hermeneutics: Interpretation theory, In: Schleiermacher, Dilthey, Heidegger, and Gadamer, Northwestern Univ, 69; Husserl's Brittanica article: A retranslation, J Brit Soc Phenomenol, 5/71; Toward a postmodern interpretive self-awareness, J Relig, 7/75; The postmodernity of Heidegger, winter 76 & Postmodernity and hermeneutics, winter 77, Boundary 2; contribr, Toward a postmodern hermeneutics of performance, In: Performance in Postmodern Culture, Coda, 78; Allegorical, philological, and philosophical hermeneutics, Univ Ottawa Quart, 5/81; contribr, Hermeneutics 1966-78--Review of research, In: Vol 2, Contemporary Philosophy: A New Survey, Nijhoff, 82. *Mailing Add:* Dept of Philos & Lit MacMurray Col Jacksonville IL 62650

PALMER, ROBERT EVERETT ALLEN, b Boise, Idaho, Aug 15, 32; m 59; c 1. CLASSICAL STUDIES. *Educ:* Johns Hopkins Univ, AB, 53, AM, 54, PhD, 56. *Prof Exp:* From instr to asst prof classics, Univ Ill, 58-61; from asst prof to assoc prof classics & ancient hist, 61-70, chmn dept ancient hist, 66-67, Lare fel, 67-68, grad chmn class studies, 68-72, chmn dept class studies, 73-78, 79-80, PROF CLASS STUDIES & ANCIENT HIST, UNIV PA, 70- *Concurrent Pos:* Am Coun Learned Soc grant-in-aid, 68; vis prof classics, Princeton Univ, 75-76; Nat Endowment for Humanities res fel, 78. *Mem:* Am Philol Asn; Class Asn Atlantic States. *Res:* Classical philology; ancient history; epigraphy. *Publ:* Auth, The King and the Comitium, Steiner, 69; The Archaic Community of the Romans, Cambridge Univ, 70; Roman Religion and Roman Empire: Five Essays, Univ Pa, 74; Severan Ruler-Cult and the Moon in the City of Rome, Aufstieg und Niedergang der roemischen Welt, 78; Octavian's First Attempt to Restore the Constitution, Athenaeum, 78; The Vici Lucceii in the Forum Boarium and some Lucceii in Rome, Bullettino della Commissione Archeologica Comunale di Rome, 76-77, 80; Customs on Marke & Goods Imported into the City of Rome, Memoirss Am Acad in Rome, 80; The Topography and Social History of Rome's Trastevere, Proc Am Philos Soc, 81. *Mailing Add:* Dept of Class Studies Univ pf Pa Philadelphia PA 19104

PALMER, RUPERT ELMER, JR, English Language & Literature. See Vol II

PANE, REMIGIO UGO, b Italy, Feb 5, 12; nat US; m 41, 64; c 2. ROMANCE LANGUAGES. *Educ:* Rutgers Univ, AB, 38, AM, 39. *Prof Exp:* From instr to prof, 39-57, in charge Ital sect, army specialized training prog, 43-44, chmn dept romance lang, 52-71, dir Jr Yr Prog, Italy, 71-73, prof, 57-81, assoc dean, 77-80, EMER PROF ROMANCE LANG, RUTGERS UNIV, 81- *Concurrent Pos:* Mem Int Bibliog Comt, MLA, 60-70; chmn, Northeast Conf Teaching Foreign Lang, 60; chmn, Col Entrance Exam Bd Exam Comt Ital Achievement Test, 64-71; mem, Nat Scholarship Comt ILGWU, 64-; asst managing ed Ital, Mod Lang J, 65-71; vpres, Nat Fedn Mod Lang Teachers Asn, 69, pres, 70. *Honors & Awards:* Croce del Laterano, 54; Commander, Star of Solidarity, Italy, 55, Grand Off, 70; Sovereign Order St John of Jerusalem, Knights of Malta, 76. *Mem:* MLA; Am Asn Teachers Ital (pres, 68-70); Am Asn Teachers Span & Port; AAUP; Am Coun Teaching Foreign Lang. *Res:* Italian language and literatuare; Spanish and Latin American literatuare; bibliography. *Publ:* Auth, English Translations From the Spanish: 1484-1943, A Bibliography, Rutgers Univ, 44; Annual bibliography of Italian language and literature, PMLA, 61-70; Spanish literature, In: The Literatures of the World in Translation, Vol III, Part I, Ungar, 70; Present status of Italian studies in the United States and Canada, Mod Lang J, 11/70. *Mailing Add:* 69 Lincoln Ave Highland Park NJ 08904

PANICO, MARIE J, b New York, NY, Jan 31, 36. SPANISH. *Educ:* Queens Col, NY, BA, 58; Univ Md, MA, 60, PhD(Span Am lit), 66. *Prof Exp:* Asst, Univ Md, 58-60, from instr to asst prof, 60-69; assoc prof Span, 69-76, PROF MOD LANG, FAIRFIELD UNIV, 76- *Concurrent Pos:* Consult Hisp lit, Libr Congr, 64-65; Gen Res Bd grant, 68. *Mem:* Am Asn Teachers Span & Port; Asn Int Hispanistas; New Eng Coun Latin Am Studies; Int Inst Ibero-Am Lit. *Res:* Spanish American literature and civilization. *Publ:* Auth, Unamuno: Doubt or denial?, Hispania, 9/63. *Mailing Add:* Dept of Mod Lang Fairfield Univ Fairfield CT 06430

PANTHEL, HANS WALTER, b 1935; Can Citizen; m; c 2. MODERN GERMAN LITERATURE. *Educ:* Univ Waterloo, BA, 62, PhD(Ger & Fr lit), 70; Univ Cincinnati, MA, 64. *Prof Exp:* Asst & lectr Ger, Univ Cincinnati, 62-64; lectr, 66-70, asst prof, 70-74, ASSOC PROF GER LIT, UNIV WATERLOO, 74- *Concurrent Pos:* Can Coun grants, 71-73; Univ Waterloo res grant, 72. *Mem:* Asn Can Univ Teachers Ger; Rilke-Ges; Ger Ethnic Cult Asn (pres, 73-). *Res:* German literature form 1890- 1930; French-German literary relations; German literature of the 18th century. *Publ:* Ed, M Maeterlinck's Pelleas und Melisande, Reclam, Stuttgart, 72; auth, R M Rilke und Maurice Maeterlinck, E Schmidt, Berlin, 73; Zu Rilkes Gedichtzyklus Les Fenetres, Etudis Germaniques, Vol 24, No 1; J Stillings Weltendzeit und Zar Alexander I, Germano-Slavica, 74; Rilke's Lettres a une Amie Venitienne, Studi Germanici, 77; J H J-Stilling, Briefe an Freunde, Verwandte u Fremde von 1787-1816, H A Gerstenberg, Hildesheim, 78. *Mailing Add:* Dept of Ger & Slavic Lang Univ of Waterloo Waterloo ON N2L 3G1 Can

PANUNZIO, WESLEY CONSTANTINE. b North Cohassett, Mass, Jan 12, 13; m 42, 58, 67; c 5. ROMANCE LANGUAGE & LINGUISTICS. *Educ:* Harvard Univ, AB, 35, AM, 40, PhD(Romance ling), 57. *Prof Exp:* Asst prof French & Span, Univ Maine, 46-52; asst prof French, Tufts Univ, 53-54; asst prof French & Span, Univ RI, 57-59; assoc prof English as second lang & asst dir English Lang Inst, Park Col, 61-62; ling researcher, English Lang Serv, 62-64; asst prof French & Span, 64-73, ASSOC PROF ROMANCE LANG & LING, SOUTHEASTERN MASS UNIV, 73- *Mem:* Nat Soc Prof Instr; Am Coun Teaching Foreign Lang; Ling Soc Am; Int Ling Asn. *Res:* Academy of human relations; psychology of language learning; sensitivity training. *Mailing Add:* Dept of Mod Lang Southeastern Mass Univ North Dartmouth MA 02747

PAO, KUO-YI, b Inner Mongolia, China, Jan 26, 16; m 41; c 3. ORIENTAL LANGUAGES. *Educ:* Cath Univ, Peking, BA, 42; Univ Wash, MA, 61, MA, 66. *Prof Exp:* Res assoc Mongolian, Univ Wash, 62-65, lectr, 64-65; LECTR MONGOLIAN & CHINESE, UNIV CALIF, LOS ANGELES, 65- *Mem:* Chinese Lang Teachers Asn. *Res:* Mongolian language, literature and history; study of a Mongolian village. *Publ:* Auth, Family and kinship structure of the Khorchin Mongols, 64 & Marriage customs of the Khorchin Mongols, 64, Cent Asiatic J; Studies on the Secret History of the Mongols, Ind Univ, Bloomington, 65; Childbirth and child training in a Khorchin Mongol village, 66 & The lama temple and Lamaism in Bayin Mang, 70-71, Monumenta Serica, J Orient Studies. *Mailing Add:* Dept of Orient Lang Univ of Calif Los Angeles CA 90024

PAOLINI, GILBERTO, b L'Aquila, Italy, Dec 22, 28; US citizen; m 60; c 2. ROMANCE LANGUAGES & LITERATURE. *Educ:* Univ Buffalo, BA, 57, MA, 59; Univ Minn, PhD(Span), 65. *Prof Exp:* Instr Ital & Latin lit, Univ Mass, 58-60; from instr to asst prof Span & Ital, Syracuse Univ, 62-67; assoc prof, 67-76, PROF SPAN LIT, TULANE UNIV, 76- *Concurrent Pos:* Reader, Educ Testing Serv, Princeton, 79; exec bd, Southeastern Am Soc 18th Cent Studies, 79-82. *Honors & Awards:* Distinguished Service Award, Soc Espanola, 79. *Mem:* MLA; Am Asn Teachers Span & Port; Asn Int Hispanistas; Am Soc 18th Century Study; AAUP. *Res:* Nineteenth century Spanish and Italian novel; naturalism; Galdos. *Publ:* Auth, Bartolome Soler, novelista: Procedimientos estilisticos, Ed Juventud, 63; An aspect of spiritualistic naturalism in the novels of B P Galdos: Charity, Las Americas, 69; Galdos and Verga: A rapprochement, Rev Letras, 9/70; Voluntad y el ideario galdosiano, Estudios Escenicos, 74; La psicopatologia en la literatura italo-espanola: D'Annunzio y Palacio Valdes, The Two Hesperias, 78; Tipos Psicopaticos en Declaracion de un vencido de Alejandro Sawa, Critica Hispanica, 1/79; ed, La Chispa '81: Selected Proceedings, New Orleans, 81; auth, The Confluence of the Mythic, Artistic and Psychic Creation in Valera's Dona Luz, Rev Estudios Hispanicos, 82. *Mailing Add:* Dept of Span & Port Tulane Univ New Orleans LA 70118

PAP, LEO, b Zurich, Switz, Nov 4, 15; nat US;. HISPANICS, LINGUISTICS. *Educ:* Columbia Univ, AM, 40, PhD(Hisp), 48. *Prof Exp:* Instr Hisp, Brown Univ, 41-43; foreign lang specialist, Off War Info, 43-45, UN, 46-47; asst prof mod lang, US Foreign Serv Inst & Naval Intel Sch, 49-51; res assoc sociol, 52-53; lectr ling & semantics, New Sch Social Res & Span, Columbia Univ, 55-57; PROF LING, STATE UNIV NY COL NEW PALTZ, 57- *Concurrent Pos:* Res grants, Inst de Alta Cult, Portugal, 53-54, Am Coun Leanred Soc, 59 & State Univ NY Res Found, 58-60, 63; vis assoc prof ling, City Univ New York, 64, 66-67. *Mem:* Ling Soc Am; Int Soc Gen Semantics; Int Ling Asn; Immigration Hist Soc. *Res:* Semantics; ethnolinguistics; acculturation of Portuguese immigrants in United States. *Publ:* Auth, What do we mean by applied linguistics?, Studies Lang & Lit, 72; On the scope of semiotics, Proc 1st Congr Int Asn Semiotics Soc, 74; Linguistic terminology as a source of verbal fictions, Lang Sci, 2/76; On the scope of linguistics, Word, 4/78; Tipping behavior as a semiotic process, Semiotics, 80; The Portuguese-Americans, Twayne, 81. *Mailing Add:* 1 Rita St New Paltz NY 12561

PAPAY, TWILA YATES, Writing, British Literature. See Vol II

PAPER, HERBERT HARRY, b Baltimore, Md, Jan 11, 25; m 49; c 2. LINGUISTICS. *Educ:* Univ Colo, BA, 43; Univ Chicago, MA, 48, PhD(Assyriology), 51. *Prof Exp:* Res asst, Orient Inst, Univ Chicago, 49-51; res assoc, Div Mod Lang, Cornell Univ, 52-53; from asst prof to assoc prof Near Eastern lang & ling, Univ Mich, Ann Arbor, 53-62, prof ling, 62-76, chmn Dept, 63-68; PROF LING & DEAN GRAD STUDIES, HEBREW UNION COL, 77- *Concurrent Pos:* Fulbright fel, Iran, 51-52; Am Coun Learned Soc fel, Cambridge, 59-60; mem comt lang prog, Am Coun Learned Soc, 59-, chmn, 61-63; mem comt, Near & Mid East Studies, Am Coun Learned Soc-Social Sci Res Coun, 62-63; Nat Sci Found res grant, 68-70; res prof, Ben-Zvi Inst, Hebrew Univ, Jerusalem, 68-69; trustee, Ctr Appl Ling, 73-75; NEH fel, 75-76; vis prof Hebrew Univ, Jerusalem, 75-76. *Mem:* Ling Soc Am; Am Orient Soc; Am Asn Jewish Studies. *Res:* Indo-Iranian linguistics; modern Persian including Judeo-Persian; Elamite. *Publ:* Coauth, English for Iranians, 55 & The Writing System of Modern Persian, 55, Am Coun Learned Soc; auth, The Phonology and Morphology of Royal Achaemenid Elamite, Univ Mich, 55; ed, Jewish Languages: Theme & Variations, Am Asn Jewish Studies, 70; auth, A Judeo-Persian Pentateuch, Ben-Zvi Inst, Hebrew Univ Jerusalem, 72; Biblia Judaeo-Persica: Editio Variorum, Univ Microfilms, 73; ed, Language and Texts, Univ Mich, 75; coauth, The Song of Songs in Judeo-Persian, Royal Danish Acad, 77. *Mailing Add:* Sch of Grad Studies Hebrew Union Col Cincinnati OH 45220

PAPMEHL, KASIMIR A, Russian Literature & History. See Vol I

PAPPANASTOS, GEORGIA, b Montgomery, Ala, Apr 26, 31. SPANISH LANGUAGE & LITERATURE. *Educ:* Univ Ala, AB, 65; Univ NC, Chapel Hill, MA, 67; Univ Ky, PhD(Span), 69. *Prof Exp:* Asst prof, 69-76, asst chmn, 72-78, chmn, 78-81, ASSOC PROF SPAN, MARQUETTE UNIV, 76- *Mem:* MLA; Am Asn Teachers Span & Port; Am Coun Teaching Foreign Lang. *Res:* Spanish Golden Age drama. *Publ:* Auth, Verbal subtlety in Castro's El amor constante, Bull Comediantes, spring 76; The heroic ideal in Guillen de Castro's First Play, Ky Romance Quart, 76. *Mailing Add:* Span Dept Marquette Univ Milwaukee WI 53233

PAPPAS, JOHN NICHOLAS, b Brackenridge, Pa, July 11, 21; m 49. FRENCH. *Educ:* Columbia Univ, AB, 48, MA, 49, PhD(French lit), 55. *Prof Exp:* Lectr, Univ Lille, 51-52; from lectr to instr French, Columbia Col, Columbia Univ, 52-56; from asst prof to prof, Ind Univ, Bloomington, 56-65; prof, Univ Pa, 65-67; PROF FRENCH, FORDHAM UNIV, 67- *Concurrent Pos:* Fulbright res grant, 60-61. *Mem:* MLA; Am Asn Teachers Fr; Soc Fr Prof Am; Int Asn Fr Studies. *Res:* French literature and thought of the 18th century. *Publ:* Auth, Berthier's journal de Trevoux and the philosophes, Vol III, In: Studies on Voltaire and the 18th Century, Inst Musee Voltaire, Geneva, 57; Rousseau and d'Alembert, PMLA, 3/60; Voltaire et la guerre civile philiosophique, Rev Hist Lit Fr, 10-12/61; Voltiare and d'Alembert, Ind Univ, 62; Diderot, d'Alembert et l'Encyclopedie, Diderot Studies IV, Geneva, 63; Le moralisme des Liaisons dangereuses, Dix-Juitieme Siecle, 70; ed, Essays on Diderot and the Enlightenment, Droz, 74. *Mailing Add:* Dept of Romance Lang Fordham Univ Bronx NY 10458

PAPPAS, LUKE THEODORE, b Rhodes, Greece, Feb, 2, 22; US citizen; m 53; c 3. MODERN LANGUAGES. *Educ:* Morris Harvey Col, BA, 52; La State Univ, Baton Rouge, MA, 53; Univ Seville, PhD(Span), 69. *Prof Exp:* Teacher Span, Orange County Pub Schs, Fla, 53-56; from asst prof to assoc prof, 56-69, PROF SPAN, THE CITADEL, 69- *Mem:* Am Asn Teachers Span & Port. *Res:* The modernist movement in Spain; Salvador Rueda, precursor of modernism in Spain. *Publ:* Auth, Breve Biografia de Salvador Rueda, Citadel Monog Ser, 70. *Mailing Add:* Dept of Mod Lang The Citadel Charleston SC 29409

PARAM, CHARLES, US citizen. SPANISH AMERICAN & BRAZILIAN LITERATURE. *Educ:* Okla State Univ, BA, 46; Univ Ariz, MA, 67, Phd(Span, Port & Russ), 68. *Prof Exp:* Asst prof Span lit & lang, Tex A&I Col, 64-65, Span & Russ lit & lang, Okla State Univ, 65-68, Span lit & lang & Port lang, Idaho State Univ, 68-69; assoc prof Span & Brazilian lit & Lang & Ital, 69-76, PROF SPAN, WESTERN WASH UNIV, 76- *Mem:* Am Asn Teachers Span & Port; Inst Int Lit Iberoam; Pac Northwest Conf Foreign Lang. *Res:* Spanish American short story and novel; Brazilian short story and novel; Russian 19th century short story and novel. *Publ:* Auth, Soledad de la sangre: A study in symmetry, 5/68, Horacio Quiroga and his exceptional protagonists, 9/72 & Politics in the novels of Machado de Assis, 9/73, Hispania. *Mailing Add:* Dept of Span Western Wash Univ Bellingham WA 98225

PARDEE, DENNIS GRAHAM, b Portland, Ore, Aug 14, 42; m 66; c 2. SEMITIC PHILOLOGY. *Educ:* La Sierra Col, BA, 64; Sem Adventiste Saleve, Teol Lic, 68; Univ Chicago, PhD(Northwest semitic philol), 74. *Prof Exp:* Asst prof, 74-80, ASSOC PROF NORTHWEST SEMITIC PHILOL, UNIV CHICAGO, 80- *Concurrent Pos:* Fulbright sr lectr, Syria, 80-81. *Mem:* Am Oriental Soc; Am Schs Oriental Res; Soc Bibl Lit. *Res:* Ugaritic philology; Hebrew philology; Hebrew epistolography. *Publ:* Auth, The preposition in Ugaritic, Ugarit-Forschungen, 75, 76 & 77; The Ugaritic Text 2106: 10-18: A bottomry loan?, J Am Oriental Soc, 75; An emendation in the Ugaritic Aqht text, J Near Eastern Studies, 77; A new Ugaritic letter, Bibliotheca Orientalis, 77; yph witness in Hebrew and Ugaritic, Vetus Testamentum, 78; An overview of ancient Hebrew letters, J Bibl Lit, 78; Handbook of Ancient Hebrew Letters, Scholars Press, 82. *Mailing Add:* Oriental Inst 1155 E 58th St Chicago IL 60637

PARENT, DAVID J, b Hamlin, Maine, May 31, 31; m 71; c 2. GERMAN LANGUAGE & LITERATURE. *Educ:* Marist Col, BA, 53; Univ Heidelberg, cert, 57; Univ Cincinnati, MA, 65, PhD(Ger), 67. *Prof Exp:* Instr Ger & Russ, Col Mt St Joseph, 63-66; from instr to asst prof Ger, Boston Col, 66-68; ASSOC PROF GER, ILL STATE UNIV, 68- *Concurrent Pos:* Ed, Appl Lit Press, 76-; ed assoc, TELOS, 78- *Mem:* MLA; Am Asn Teachers Ger. *Res:* Modern German literature. *Publ:* Transl, Michael Landmann's Reform of the Hebrew Alphabet, 76; Juan Garcia Ponce's Modern Literature and Reality, 76; Jorge Millas' The Intellectual and Moral Challenge of Mass Society, 77; Michael Landmann's Philosophy: Its Mission and its Disciplines, 77; Alienatory Reason, 78; Gustav Landauer's For Socialism, 78; Michael Landmann's De Homine: Man in the Mirror of his Thought, 79; auth, Franz Kafka, and ETA Hoffmann, In: Critical Survey of Short Fiction, 81. *Mailing Add:* Dept of Foreign Lang Ill State Univ Normal IL 61761

PARENTE, JAMES ANDREW, JR, b Bryn Mawr, Pa, Mar 27, 53; m 74. GERMAN LITERATURE. *Educ:* Haverford Col, BA, 74; Yale Univ, MA, 76, PhD(Ger), 79. *Prof Exp:* Instr Ger, Yale Univ, 77-79; ASST PROF GER, PRINCETON UNIV, 79- *Mem:* MLA; Renaissance Soc Am; Am Soc 16th & 17th Century Ger Lit; 16th Century Studies Conf; Soc Advan Scandinavian Studies. *Res:* Sixteenth and 17th century German & Netherlandic literature; neo-Latin literature; 18th and 19th century Danish and Norwegian literature. *Publ:* Auth, Counter reformation polemic and Senecan tragedy: The dramas of Gregorius Holonius, Humanistica Lovaniensia, No 30, 81. *Mailing Add:* Dept of Ger Lang & Ling Princeton Univ Princeton NJ 08544

PARISH, CHARLES, b Shreveport, La, May 11, 27; m 65; c 3. LINGUISTICS, ENGLISH AS FOREIGN LANGUAGE. *Educ:* Brooklyn Col, BA, 52; Univ NMex, MA, 55, PhD(English, ling), 58. *Prof Exp:* Instr English, Univ Wichita, 56-57, asst prof, 58-59; asst prof English & ling, Southern Ill Univ, Alton, 59-63; assoc prof, 65-71, PROF LING, SOUTHERN ILL UNIV, CARBONDALE, 71- *Concurrent Pos:* Fulbright lectr, Univ Mandalay, 61-62 & Univ Rome, 62-64, 68-69; Coun Am Study Rome, 63-65; consult, Univ Rome, 79. *Mem:* Ling Soc Am; MLA; Teachers English to Speakers Other Lang. *Res:* English as a foreign language teacher-training; second-language acquisition. *Publ:* Ed, Corso d'Inglese Parlato, Vol 3, 65 & coauth, Vol 4, 68, Harcourt; auth, Some phonetic problems for Burmese speakers of English, Lang Learning, 64; Tristram Shandy Notes, Cliff's Notes, 68; Agenbite of Agendath Netaim, James Joyce Quart, spring 69; The Shandy Bull vindicated, Mod Lang Quart, 3/70; ESL practice-teaching utilizing videotape, 76 & A practical philosophy of pronunciation, 77, TESOL Quart. *Mailing Add:* Dept of Ling Southern Ill Univ Carbondale IL 62901

PARKER, CAROLYN ANN, b Houston, Tex, Nov 16, 46. SWAHILI, FOLKLORE. *Educ:* Univ Houston, BA, 67; Univ Wash, MA, 70, PhD(anthrop), 74. *Prof Exp:* Asst prof, 73-80, PROF SWAHILI, UNIV TEX, AUSTIN, 80- *Concurrent Pos:* Mem exec comt, African Lit Asn, 78- *Mem:* African Lit Asn; African Studies Asn; Am Folklore Soc. *Res:* Swahili literature and folklore; proverbs. *Publ:* Auth, How to be/treat a lady in Swahili culture: An expression of ideal, Ba Shiru, 77; Swahili proverbs: The nature and value of painful experience, Gar, 78. *Mailing Add:* Dept of Orient & African Lang & Lit Univ of Texas Austin TX 78712

PARKER, CHARLES HALDOR, b Manitou, Man, May 25, 21; m 50; c 3. LINGUISTICS, RELIGION. *Educ:* United Col, Man, BA, 49, dipl, 52, BD, 58; Columbia Univ, PhD(relig), 70. *Prof Exp:* PROF HEBREW & OLD TESTAMENT, QUEEN'S THEOL COL & PROF HEBREW & RELIG, QUEEN'S UNIV, ONT, 61- *Concurrent Pos:* Registr, Queen's Theol Col, 69-73, actg prin, 72-74. *Mem:* Can Soc Bibl Studies (pres, 73-74); Soc Bibl Lit. *Res:* Ezekiel studies; Phoenicia. *Mailing Add:* Dept of Hebrew & Old Testament Queen's Theol Col Kingston ON K7L 3N6 Can

PARKER, FRANK PEYTON, b Ft Worth, Tex, Nov 28, 46; m 69. LINGUISTICS. *Educ:* Univ Houston, BA, 71; Purdue Univ, MA, 73, PhD(English, ling), 76. *Prof Exp:* Asst prof English, 77-79; ASSOC PROF LING & ENGLISH, LA STATE UNIV, 79- *Mem:* Am Dialect Soc; MLA; Ling Soc Am; Acoust Soc Am; Am Speech-Lang-Hearing Asn. *Res:* Language change; distinctive features; typology. *Publ:* Auth, Distinctive features in speech pathology: Phonology or phonemics?, J Speech & Hearing Disorders, 76; Language change and the passive voice, Lang, 76; Perceptual cues and phonological change, J Phonetics, 77; Distinctive features and acoustic cues, J Acoust Soc Am, 77; A comment on Baran and Seymour's The influence of three phonological rules, J Speech & Hearing Res, 79; Typology and word order change, Linguistics, 80; Resyllabification and phonological change, J Phonetics, 81; Walker Percy's theory of language, Delta, 81. *Mailing Add:* Interdept Ling Prog La State Univ Baton Rouge LA 70803

PARKER, JACK HORACE, b Parkersville, Ont, Apr 4, 14; m 46; c 2. SPANISH & PORTUGUESE. *Educ:* Univ Toronto, BA, 35, MA, 36, PhD(Romance lang), 41. *Prof Exp:* Instr Ital & Span, Univ Toronto, 36-41; instr Span, Columbia Univ, 41-42; instr, Ind Univ, 42-43; instr Port & Span, Carleton Col, 44-45; asst prof Span, Univ BC, 45-46; from asst prof to assoc prof Ital, Span & Port, 46-57, chmn dept, 66-69, assoc dean humanities, Sch Grad Studies, 69-73, PROF ITAL & HISP STUDIES, UNIV TORONTO, 66- *Concurrent Pos:* Am Coun Learned Soc fel, Univ Vt, 42; res off, Nat Res Coun, 43-45; assoc ed, Can Mod Lang Rev, 53-73; vis prof Span & Port, Univ Ill, spring 62 & State Univ NY Buffalo, fall 62. *Honors & Awards:* Cross of Knight of the Order of Civil Merit, King Juan Carlos I of Spain, 77. *Mem:* Fel Royal Soc Can; MLA; Am Asn Teachers Span & Port(pres, 75); Inst Int Lit Iberoam (vpres, 67-69); Can Asn Hispanists (pres, 68-70). *Res:* Literature of the Spanish Renaissance and Golden Age; bibliography; Portuguese literature. *Publ:* Auth, Breve Historia del Teatro Espanol, Ed Andrea, Me, 57; coauth, A Bibliography of Comedias Sueltas, 59 & Lope de Vega Studies, 1937-1962, 64, Univ Toronto; auth, Gil Vicente, Twayne, 67; ed, Moreto's El Desden Con el Desden, Anaya, Salmanca, Spain, 70; coauth, Calderon de la Barca Studies, 1951-68, Univ Toronto, 71; auth, Some aspects of Moreto's Teatro menor, Philol Quart, 72; Juan Perez de Montalvan, Twayne, 75. *Mailing Add:* Dept of Span & Port Univ of Toronto Toronto ON M5S 1A1 Can

PARKER, JOHN ERNEST, JR, b Emporia, Va, Mar 22, 20; m 42; c 2. ROMANCE LANGUAGES. *Educ:* Wake Forest Col, AB, 40; Syracuse Univ, MA, 42, PhD(Romance lang), 52. *Prof Exp:* Instr French, Syracuse Univ 46-50; from instr to prof mod lang, 50-76, PROF EDUC & ROMANCE LANG, WAKE FOREST UNIV, 76- *Concurrent Pos:* Mem bd adv, MAT prog, Sch Int Training, Exp in Int Living, Brattleboro, Vt, 69- *Mem:* MLA; Am Asn Teachers Fr. *Res:* Medieval French scientific literature; 18th century French literature; language methodology. *Mailing Add:* Dept of Educ Wake Forest Univ Box 7266 Winston-Salem NC 27109

PARKER, KELVIN MICHAEL, b Panama City, Panama, Mar 11, 19, US citizen. ROMANCE LINGUISTICS. *Educ:* Univ Chicago, MA, 48, PhD(Span), 53. *Prof Exp:* Instr Span, Marquette Univ, 51-54; teacher, Chicago Pub Sch Syst, 54-67; assoc prof, 67-76, chmn Span sect, Dept Foreign Lang, 73-78, res grants, 69-70 & 71-73, prof, 76-80, EMER PROF SPAN, ILL STATE UNIV, 80- *Mem:* MLA; Am Asn Teachers Span & Port; AAUP. *Res:* Old Galician language and Medieval Galician language; Romance lexicography. *Publ:* Auth, Spanish- American literature in 1951, In: American Peoples Encyclopedia Yearkbook, Grolier, 52; Vocabulario de la Cronica Troyana, Univ Salamanca, 58; Historia troyana, Consejo Super de Invest Cient, 75; Vocabulario clasificado de los folios gallegos de la Historia troyana, 77 & La version de Alfonso XI del Roman de Troie, 77, Appl Lit Press. *Mailing Add:* Dept of Foreign Lang Ill State Univ Normal IL 61761

PARKER, MARGARET, b Lubbock, Tex, Nov 10, 41; m 65. SPANISH. *Educ:* Tex Tech Univ, BA, 63, MA, 64; Ind Univ, PhD(Span), 69. *Prof Exp:* Instr Span, Odessa Col, 64-65; instr, 68-69, asst prof, 69-78; ASSOC PROF SPAN, LA STATE UNIV, BATON ROUGE, 79- *Mem:* MLA; Am Asn Teachers Span & Port; Am Coun Teaching Foreign Lang; SCent Mod Lang Asn. *Res:* Spanish medieval literature; Hispano-Arabic studies. *Publ:* Auth, The Didactic Structure and Content of El libro de Calila e Digna, Ed Universal, 78. *Mailing Add:* Dept of Foreign Lang La State Univ Baton Rouge LA 70803

PARKER, SAMUEL EMMETT, b Birmingham, Ala, Dec 8, 29; m 59; c 2. FRENCH LANGUAGE & LITERATURE. *Educ:* Howard Col, AB, 52; Univ Ala, MA, 56; Univ Wis, PhD(French), 63. *Prof Exp:* Asst prof French, Temple Univ, 62-64; from asst prof to assoc prof, 64-72, chmn dept Romance lang, 72-76, PROF FRENCH, UNIV ALA, 72- *Mem:* Am Asn Teachers Fr; MLA. *Res:* Twentieth century French literature especially the Engagement Movement in the French novel. *Publ:* Auth, Albert Camus: The Artist in the Arena, Univ Wis, 65. *Mailing Add:* Dept of Romance Lang Univ of Ala University AL 35486

PARKER, STEPHEN JAN, b Brooklyn, NY, Aug 5, 39; m 65; c 2. RUSSIAN & COMPARATIVE LITERATURE. *Educ:* Cornell Univ, BA, 60, MA, 62, PhD(Russ & comp lit), 69. *Prof Exp:* Asst prof Russ, Univ Okla, 66-67; asst prof, 67-73, ASSOC PROF RUSS, UNIV KANS, 73-, ASSOC CHMN & DIR GRAD STUDIES, 78- *Concurrent Pos:* Nat Endowment for Humanities younger humanist fel, 70-71; reviewer, World Lit Today, 75-; mem nat selection comt, Coun Int Educ Exchange, Russ Lang Prof, 77; ed, Vladimir Nabokov Soc Res Newslett, 78- *Mem:* MLA; Am Asn Advan Slavic Lang; Am Asn Teachers Slavic & East Europ Lang; Vladimir Nabokov Soc. *Res:* Russian prose fiction of the 19th and 20th centuries; Europan and American modern novel; writings of Vladimir Nabokov. *Publ:* Auth, Hemingway's revival in the Soviet Union: 1955-1962, Am Lit, 1/64; contribr, Vladimir Nabokov: A Bibliography, McGraw, 73; coauth, Russia on Canvas: Ily a Repin, Pa State Univ Press, 81; Vladimir Nabokov: Dict Literary Biography: Yearbk, 80, Gale Res Co, 81; Annual Nabokov bibliographies, Valdimir Nabokov Res Newsletter, Univ Kans, 78-; Valdimir Nabokov, Dict Literary Biography: Documentary Series, Bruccol, Clark, 82. *Mailing Add:* Dept of Slavic Lang & Lit Univ of Kans Lawrence KS 66045

PARKES, FORD BRITON, b Cleveland, Ohio, Jan 10, 37; m 66; c 2. GERMAN MEDIEVAL LITERATURE. *Educ:* Kent State Univ, BA, 64, MA, 66; Mich State Univ, PhD(Ger lit), 71. *Prof Exp:* Instr Ger lang & lit, Cleveland State Univ, 65-66; asst prof, 69-76, ASSOC PROF GERMAN,

UNIV IOWA, 76- *Mem:* Am Asn Teachers Ger. *Res:* German and Latin medieval literature. *Publ:* Auth, Epische Elemente in Jakob Michael Reinhold Lenzens Drama Der Hofmeister, Alfred Kümmerle, Goppingen, 73; Irony in Waltharius, Mod Lang Notes, 74; Shifting narrative perspectives in Kleist's Findling, J English & Ger Philol, 12/77. *Mailing Add:* Dept of Ger Univ of Iowa Iowa City IA 52242

PARKS, ALGER FRANKLIN, II, Neoclassical Literature. See Vol II

PARKS, JOHN H, b Pittsburgh, Pa, July 27, 15; m 47; c 4. LATIN, GREEK. *Educ:* La Salle Col, AB, 36; Johns Hopkins Univ, PhD, 45. *Prof Exp:* Prof Latin, La Salle Col, 46-47; PROF LATIN & GREEK, KENT STATE UNIV, 48-, CHAIRPERSON CLASS STUDIES, 76- *Mem:* Int Mark Twain Soc. *Res:* Classical literature; ancient rhetoric. *Publ:* Auth, Roman rhetorical schools as a preparation for the courts under the early empire. *Mailing Add:* Dept of Romance Lang & Classics Kent State Univ Kent OH 44240

PARLE, DENNIS JEROME, b Pontiac, Mich, June 7, 42; m 69; c 3. SPANISH LANGUAGE, LATIN AMERICAN LITERATURE. *Educ:* Oakland Univ, BA, 64; Univ Wis, MA, 68; Univ Kans, PhD(Span), 76. *Prof Exp:* Foreign student adv, DePaul Univ, 66-68; instr, Grinnell Col, 74-76; ASSOC PROF SPAN, UNIV HOUSTON, 76- *Concurrent Pos:* Span lang consult, Rio Grande Assoc, 80- *Mem:* Am Asn Teachers Span & Port; Southwest Coun Latin Am Studies; Nat Asn Foreign Student Affairs. *Res:* Mexican literature; 20th century Latin American literature. *Publ:* Auth, El papel de la caracterizacion en la estructura de La creacion de Agustin Yanez, Symp, winter 78; Las funciones del tiempo en la estructura de El resplandor de Magdaleno, Hispania, 3/80; El punto de vista y la vision poetica en Flor de juegos antiguos de Agustin Yanez, La semana de Bellas Artes, Mex, 2/80; Narrative style and technique in Nellie Campobello's Cartucho, Ky Romance Quart (in prep). *Mailing Add:* Span Dept Univ of Houston Houston TX 77004

PARNELL, CHARLES EPHRAIM, b Seneca, Kans, Oct 31, 17; m 46; c 3. MODERN FRENCH LITERATURE. *Educ:* Nebr State Teachers Col, AB, 38; Univ Nebr, AM, 40; Yale Univ, PhD, 48. *Prof Exp:* From asst prof to assoc prof, 48-66, PROF FRENCH, UNIV NOTRE DAME, 66-, DIR FOREIGN STUDY PROG, 75- *Concurrent Pos:* Dir NDEA Summer Lang Insts, Univ Notre Dame, 62, 64, Can, 63 & Angers, France, 66, 67; dir Univ Notre Dame sophomore yr in France, Angers, France, 66-68 & 72-74. *Honors & Awards:* Medaille d'Honneur, Univ Cath Angers, 74. *Mem:* Am Asn Teachers Fr; MLA. *Res:* Contemporary French literature; Andre Gide. *Publ:* Auth, Les structures de l'enseignement superieureaux Etats-Univ, Impacts, 1/67. *Mailing Add:* Dept of Mod Lang Univ of Notre Dame Notre Dame IN 46556

PARR, JAMES ALLAN, b Ritchie, Co, WVa, Oct 7, 36; m 57, 68; c 1. ROMANCE LANGUAGES. *Educ:* Ohio Univ, AB, 59, MA, 61; Univ Pittsburgh, PhD(Span), 67. *Prof Exp:* Instr Span, Ohio Univ, 60-61; instr, Univ Toledo, 63-64; prof Span & chmn dept mod for lang, Murray State Univ, 64-70; ASSOC PROF SPAN, UNIV SOUTHERN CALIF, 70-, CHMN DEPT SPAN & PORT, 78- *Concurrent Pos:* Dir, NDEA Inst Advan Studies Span, 66, 67, 69; Southeastern Inst Medieval & Renaissance Studies fel, Duke Univ, 68; res scholar Spain, Del Amo Found, 77; ed, Bull Comediantes, 73-; assoc ed, Hispania, 74- *Mem:* MLA; Am Asn Teachers Span & Port; AAUP; Am Comp Lit Asn; Asn Int de Hispanistas. *Res:* Spanish Golden Age literature; Spanish intellectual history to 1700; literary criticism. *Publ:* Ed, Critical Essays on the Life and Work of Juan Ruiz de Alarcon, Dos Continentes, Madrid, 72; auth, Todo es ventura? Alarcon's Fortune Plays, Bull Comediantes, 72; An essay on critical method, applied to the comedia, Hisp, 74; On fate, suicide and free will in El dueno de las estrellas, Hisp Rev, 74; La estructura satirica del Lazarillo, Actas del I Congreso sobre la Picaresca, 78; Aesthetic distance in Don Quijote, In: Homage to Gerald E Wade, 79; Don Quijote: Texto y contextos, Actas Del I Congreso sobre Cervantes, 81. *Mailing Add:* Dept of Span & Port Univ of Southern Calif Los Angeles CA 90007

PARRIS, JEAN JACOB, b Huron, SDak, July 27, 22; m 45; c 2. ROMANCE LANGUAGES & LITERATURE. *Educ:* Univ Ill, BA, 42; Radcliffe Col, MA, 50, PhD(Romance lang & lit),61. *Prof Exp:* From instr to asst prof Romance lit, Cornell Univ, 61-66, assoc prof French lit & chmn dept Romance studies, 66-70; prof comp lit, 72-77, chmn dept, 72-74, chmn dept lang & lit, 74-77, ASSOC PROVOST, RUTGERS UNIV, NEW BRUNSWICK, 77- *Mem:* MLA. *Publ:* Auth, La religieuse: Edition critique avec notes et variantes, Studies Voltaire, 5/63; Conception, evolution et forme fina le de la religieuse, Romanische Forsch, winter 63; Illusion et realite dans les romans de Marivaux, Fr issue, Mod Lang Notes, 64; coauth, La Religieuse, Hermann, Parisa, 74. *Mailing Add:* 88 Mountain Ave Princeton NJ 08540

PARROTT, RAY JENNINGS, JR, b Elmhurst, Ill, Feb 11, 37; m 63; c 2. RUSSIAN LANGUAGE & LITERATURE. *Educ:* Cornell Col, BA, 63; Univ Mich, MA, 67, PhD(Slavic), 74. *Prof Exp:* Instr Russ, Univ Mich, 69-71; instr, 71-74, asst prof, 74-77, ASSOC PROF RUSS, UNIV IOWA, 77- & CHMN, 75- *Concurrent Pos:* Assoc ed lang, Iowa Foreign Lang Bull, 75-; assoc ed lit, Forum Iowa on Russ Lit, 74-78; assoc ed lang, Russ Lang J, 79- *Mem:* Am Asn Advan Slavic Studies; Am Asn Teachers Slavic & E Eur Lang. *Res:* 19th and 20th centuries Russian literature; literary theory and criticism; literary parody. *Publ:* Auth, Mythological allusions in Kochanowski's Laments, Polish Rev, winter 69; co-translr, V M Zhirmunsky, on classical and romantic poetry, Russ Lit Triquart, fall 74; auth, That reference shelf for teachers of Russian: An up-date, Iowa Foreign Lang Bull, 10/75; Linguostylistic analysis and the language classroom, Russ Lang J, spring 76; On Babel, Gladkov, etc., Parodies, Univ Iowa, 76; Aesopian language, Mod Encycl Russ & Soviet Lit, 77; Questions of art, fact and genre in Mikhail Prishvin, Slavic Rev, 9/77; Evolution of a critical response: Mikhail Prishvin, Russ Lang J, winter, 78. *Mailing Add:* Dept of Russ Univ of Iowa Gilmore Hall 420 Iowa City IA 52242

PARSELL, DAVID BEATTY, b Charleston, SC, Dec 4, 41; m 67; c 2. FRENCH LANGUAGE & LITERATURE. *Educ:* Hamilton Col, AB, 63; Vanderbilt Univ, MA, 68, PhD(French), 70. *Prof Exp:* Instr French, Grinnell Col, 67-69; from instr to asst prof, 69-77, ASSOC PROF MOD FOREIGN LANG, FURMAN UNIV, 77- *Mem:* Am Asn Teachers Fr; Southern Comp Lit Asn. *Res:* Georges Neveux; French theatre 1930-1960; surrealism. *Publ:* Auth, Le Voyageur Sans Bagage and the case against tragedy, Fr Rev, 3/77; Sign and Image in Peret and Magritte, Univ SC Fr Lit Ser, Vol 5, 78. *Mailing Add:* Dept of Mod Foreign Lang Furman Univ Greenville SC 29613

PARSHALL, LINDA BRYANT, b Chicago, Ill, June 8, 44; m 67. MEDIEVAL GERMAN LITERATURE. *Educ:* Northwestern Univ, BA, 66; Ind Univ, MA, 68; Queen Mary Col, Univ London, PhD(medieval Ger), 74. *Prof Exp:* ASST PROF GER, PORTLAND STATE UNIV, 75- *Concurrent Pos:* Am Asn Univ Women fel, 78-79. *Mem:* Am Asn Teachers Ger; Medieval Asn Pac; MLA; Pac Northwest Renaissance Conf; Philol Asn Pac Coast. *Res:* Medieval German literature; translation; Renaissance studies. *Publ:* Auth, Walther von der Vogelweide, Portland Rev, 77; translr, Picture Gallery, Berline: Catalogue of Paintings, Staatliche Museen, Berlin, 78; auth, Narrative Technique in the German Middle Ages: Wolfram's Parzival and Albrecht's Jüngerer Titurel, Cambridge Univ, 79. *Mailing Add:* Dept of Foreign Lang Portland State Univ PO Box 751 Portland OR 97207

PARSLOW, MORRIS, b Williamston, Mich, Mar 24, 22; m 51; c 4. FRENCH. *Educ:* St John's Col, Md, BA, 48; Princeton Univ, MA, 52, PhD(French), 55. *Prof Exp:* From instr to asst prof French, Univ Chicago, 53-59; assoc prof, State Univ NY Long Island Ctr, 59-62; assoc prof, 62-67, chmn dept, 65-68 & 72-74, chmn, div humanities, 76-79, chmn fac, 80-82, PROF FRENCH, GRINNELL COL, 67- *Mem:* MLA; AAUP. *Res:* Montaigne; linguistics; Alain. *Publ:* Auth, Montaignes' Fat Man and the meaning of Des Coches, Renaissance News, spring 58. *Mailing Add:* Dept of French Grinnel Col Grinnell IA 50112

PARSLOW, ROBERT LAVERNE, b Williamston, Mich, Jan 24, 24; m 47; c 3. LINGUISTICS, LIBERAL ARTS. *Educ:* St John's Col, Md, BA, 51; Univ Mich, Ann Arbor, MA, 52, PhD(ling), 67; Univ Pittsburgh, MLS, 76; Univ London, MA, 76. *Prof Exp:* Lectr English as foreign lang, Univ Mich, 52-56; lectr, Boston Univ, 56-62; lectr English, Emerson Col, 62-63; mathematician traffic surv, Wilber Smith Assoc, 63-64; ASSOC PROF LING, UNIV PITTSBURGH, 64- *Concurrent Pos:* Ed, Lang Learning, 53-55; mem Comt Intensive English Prog, 67-70; dir Pittsburgh Dialect Proj, Univ Pittsburgh, 70- *Mem:* Am Dialect Soc; Am Libr Asn; Libr Asn, UK. *Res:* Regional dialects; forensic linguistics; humanities education. *Publ:* Contribr, A Various Language, Holt, 71; articles in American reference books annual, Librairies Unlimited. *Mailing Add:* Dept of Gen Ling Univ of Pittsburgh Pittsburgh PA 15260

PARSONS, ADELAIDE HEYDE, b Cape Girardeau, Mo, Dec 3, 47; m 80. PSYCHOLINGUISTICS. *Educ:* Northwestern Univ, BS, 69; Univ Mich, MA, 71, PhD(ling), 79. *Prof Exp:* Lectr & teaching asst, English Lang Inst, Univ Mich, 73-79; ASST PROF LING, OHIO UNIV, 79-, DIR ENGLISH, OHIO PROG INTENSIVE ENGLISH, 80- *Concurrent Pos:* Dir, English Prog, Inst Estudios Superiores, 71; fac, Lower Brule High Sch, 71-73 & Manchester Pub Sch & Ann Arbor Basic Educ Prog, 73-76; consult, Mid-Am Inst, Ashland Col, 75, Manchester Sch, 76, Athnes East Elem Sch, 80-83, Int Prog, Ohio Univ, 81-82. *Mem:* Nat Asn For Student Affairs; Teachers English Speakers Other Languages. *Res:* Self-concept and language acquisition; bilingualism; acquisition of speaking and listening skills. *Publ:* Auth, Curriculum materials, Supv & Curric Develop, 69; The relationship between self esteem and the oral production of a second language, Teacher English Speakers Other Lang, 77; The structure of magic in teacher-student interactional patterns, Gulf Teachers English Speakers Other Lang, 82; The LEA and self-concept in a biliteracy program, New Directions for Teachers English Speakers Other Lang (in prep); The use of role play to overcome cultural fatigue, Teachers English Speakers Other Lang Quart (in prep). *Mailing Add:* Box 66 Rte 6 Athens OH 45701

PARTEE, BARBARA HALL, b Englewood, NJ, June 23, 40; m 73; c 3. LINGUISTICS. *Educ:* Swarthmore Col, BA, 61; Mass Inst Technol, PhD(ling), 65. *Prof Exp:* From asst prof to assoc prof ling, Univ Calif, Los Angeles, 65-72; PROF LING & PHILOS, UNIV MASS, AMHERST, 72- *Concurrent Pos:* Consult, Syst Develop Corp, 66-69; assoc ed, Language, 67-73; co-ed, Squibs Sect, Ling Inquiry, 71-73; Ctr for Advan Study in Behav Sci fel, 76-77. *Honors & Awards:* Chancellor's Medal, Univ Mass, 77. *Mem:* Asn for Comput Ling; Ling Soc Am; Am Philos Asn. *Res:* Transformational grammar; Montague semantics; English syntax and semantics. *Publ:* Coauth, A mathematical model of transformational grammar, Info & Control, 69; auth, Opacity, coreference and pronouns, Synthese, 70; On the requirement that transformations preserve meaning, In: Studies in Linguistic Semantics, Holt, 71; coauth, The Major Syntactic Structures of English, Holt, 72; auth, Some transformational extensions of Montague grammar, J Philos Logic, 73 & In: Contemporary Research in Philosophical Logic and Linguistic Semantics, Riedel; Montague grammar and transformational grammar, Ling Inquiry, 75; ed, Montague Grammar, Academic, 76; auth, John is easy to please, In: Linguistic Structures Processing, North-Holland, Amsterdam, 77. *Mailing Add:* Dept of Ling Univ of Mass Amherst MA 01003

PASCAL, CECIL BENNETT, b Chicago, Ill, May 4, 26; m 59; c 1. CLASSICAL PHILOLOGY. *Educ:* Univ Calif, Los Angeles, AB, 48, MA, 50; Harvard Univ, MA, 53, PhD, 56. *Prof Exp:* Instr classics, Univ Ill, 55-56; instr, Cornell Univ, 57-60; asst prof classic lang, 60-65, head dept classics, Chinese & Japanese, 65-67 & 72-73, assoc prof, 65-76, PROF CLASSICS, UNIV ORE, 76-, HEAD DEPT CLASSICS, 78- *Concurrent Pos:* William Amory Gardner traveling fel, Harvard Univ, 56-57; Fulbright-Hays res fel, Univ Rome, 67-68. *Mem:* Am Philol Asn; Philol Asn Pac Coast; Classic Asn Pac Northwest; Archaeol Inst Am; AAUP. *Res:* Latin and Greek literature; Roman religion. *Publ:* Auth, Horatian Chiaroscuro, In: Hommages a Marcel Renard, Latomus, 69; Rex Nemorensis, Numen, 76; October Horse, Harvard State Col Philol, 81. *Mailing Add:* Dept of Classics Univ of Ore Eugene OR 97403

PASCAL, PAUL, b New York, NY, Mar 26, 25; m 48; c 2. CLASSICS, MEDIEVAL LATIN. *Educ:* Univ Vt, BA, 48; Univ NC, PHD(classics), 53. *Prof Exp:* PROF CLASSICS, UNIV WASH, 53- *Mem:* Am Philol Asn. *Res:* Mediaeval Latin literature. *Publ:* Coauth, The Institutionum Disciplinae of Isidore of Seville, Traditio, 57; Notes on Minus Sum in Vineam of Walter of Chatillon, Studies in Honor of B L Ullman, Rome, 64; The Conclusion of the Pervigilium Veneris, Neophilologus, 65; The Julius Exclusus of Erasmus, Ind Univ, 68. *Mailing Add:* Dept of Classics Univ of Wash Seattle WA 98105

PASCHAL, MARY, b Wake Forest, NC, Feb 18, 23. ROMANCE LANGUAGES. *Educ:* Wake Forest Univ, BA, 43; Univ NC, Chapel Hill, MA, 53, PhD, 58. *Prof Exp:* Instr French, Wake Forest Univ, 44-56; asst prof Romance lang, Ohio Northern Univ, 59; assoc prof, Catawba Col, 59-62, E Carolina Univ, 62-66; asst head dept mod lang, 73-76, ASSOC PROF FRENCH, NC STATE UNIV, 66- *Concurrent Pos:* Fel, Southeastern Inst Medieval & Renaissance Studies, 65. *Mem:* Am Asn Teachers Fr; SAtlantic MLA; Mountain Interstate Foreign Lang Conf; Southeastern Renaissance Conf. *Res:* Renaissance and contemporary French literature. *Publ:* Auth, A sixteenth century French lecturer: Bernard Palissy, Renaissance Papers 1961, 62; The new world in Les Sepmaines of Du Bartas, Romance Notes, 69; Disappearance in the novels of Mauriac, SAtlantic Bull, 71. *Mailing Add:* Dept of Mod Lang NC State Univ Box 5156 Raleigh NC 27607

PASCO, ALLAN HUMPHREY, b Nashville, Tenn, Aug 29, 37; m 60; c 4. ROMANCE LANGUAGES. *Educ:* Whitman Col, BA, 60; Northwestern Univ, MA, 61; Univ Mich, PhD(Romance lang), 68. *Prof Exp:* Asst prof French, Univ Chicago, 67-73; assoc prof, 73-79, PROF FRENCH, PURDUE UNIV, WEST LAFAYETTE, 79- *Concurrent Pos:* Lilly Libr res fel, Ind Univ, 76; ed for French, Purdue Univ Monogr in Romance Lang, 77-; vis prof French, Univ Calif, Los Angeles, fall, 79. *Mem:* MLA; Am Asn Teachers Fr. *Res:* French novel of the 19th and 20th centuries; criticism. *Publ:* Auth, Marcel, Albertine and Balbec in Proust's Allusive complex, Romanic Rev, 4/71; Myth, metaphor and meaning in Germinal, Fr Rev, 3/73; A study of allusion: Barbey's Stendhal In Le Rideau cramoisi, PMLA, 5/73; Irony and art in Gide's L'Immoraliste, Romancic Rev, 73; The Color-Keys to A La Recherche, Droz, 76; Proust's reader and the voyage of self-discovery, Comtemp Lit, 77 ; Love a la Michelet in Zola's La Faute de l'abbe Mouret, 19th Century Fr Studies, 79; Descriptive narration in Balzac's Gobseck, Va Quart Rev, 80. *Mailing Add:* Dept of Foreign Lang & Lit Purdue Univ West Lafayette IN 47907

PASLICK, ROBERT H, b Denver, Colo, Feb 11, 30; m 58; c 3. GERMAN LITERATURE. *Educ:* Univ Louisville, AB, 52; Ind Univ, MA, 58, PhD(Ger), 62. *Prof Exp:* From instr to asst prof, 61-74, ASSOC PROF GER, UNIV MICH, ANN ARBOR, 74- *Honors & Awards:* Sinclair Counseling Award, 68. *Res:* European 20th century prose. *Publ:* Auth, Dialectic and non-attachment: The structure of Hermann Hesse's Siddhartha, Symp, 3/73; The tempter: Bergengruen's Grande Prince and the Hermetic tradition, Neophilologus, 3/73; Narrowing the distance: Siegfried Lenz's Deutschstunde, Ger Quart, 3/73. *Mailing Add:* Dept of Ger Lang & Lit Univ Mich Ann Arbor MI 48104

PASQUARIELLO, ANTHONY MICHAEL, b New York, NY, Sept 3, 14; m 44, 78; c 1. ROMANCE LANGUAGES. *Educ:* Brooklyn Col, BA, 37; Columbia Univ, MA, 40; Univ Mich, PhD(Romance lang), 50. *Prof Exp:* From instr to asst prof Span & Ital, Univ Mich, 49-58; assoc prof Span, Univ Colo, 58-64; prof Span, Ital & Port & chmn dept, Pa State Univ, 64-69; chmn dept, 69-76, PROF SPAN, ITAL & PORT, UNIV ILL, URBANA, 69- *Concurrent Pos:* Fund Advan Educ fel, 55-56. *Mem:* Am Asn Teachers Span & Port (vpres, 71, pres, 72); AAUP; MLA. *Res:* Contemporary literature in Spain; Colonial theater in Spanish America. *Publ:* Coauth, Alfonso Sastre y Escuadra hacia la muerte, Hispanofila, 62; The evolution of the Loa in Spanish America, Latin Am Theatre Rev, 70; Miguel Mihura's Tres sombreros de copa: A farce to make you sad, Symposium, 72; Una causa en busca de comprension y direccion: La educacion bilingüe y bicultural, Hispania, 73; co-ed, Antonio Buero Vallejo, El Tragaluz, Scribner's Sons, 77; contribr, The seventeenth-century interlude in the new-world secular theater, In: Homage to Irving A Leonard, 77; coauth, Buero Vallejo: El hombre y la obra, Estreno, 79; co-ed, Contemporary Spanish Theater: Seven One-Act Plays, Scribner's, 80. *Mailing Add:* Dept of Span, Ital & Port Univ of Ill Urbana IL 61801

PASSAGE, CHARLES EDWARD, b Dansville, NY, Dec 13, 13. COMPARATIVE LITERATURE. *Educ:* Univ Rochester, BA, 35; Harvard Univ, MA, 38, PhD(comp lit), 42. *Prof Exp:* Instr Ger & Slavic, Harvard Univ, 46-49; asst prof Ger, Northwestern Univ, 49-50 & Columbia Univ, 50-53; asst prof, 54-56, from asst prof to prof comp lit, 56-71, EMER PROF COMP LIT, BROOKLYN COL, 71- *Res:* German-Russian literary relations in the romantic period; Wolfram von Eschenbach. *Publ:* Auth, Dostoevski the Adapter, Univ NC, 54; transl & introd, Goethe's Faust, Bobbs, 65; Three Marchen of ETA Hoffmann, Univ SC, 71; coauth, Amphitryon: The Legend and Three Plays (Plautus, Moliere, Kleist), Univ NC, 74; transl & introd, Wolfram's Willehalm, Ungar, 77; Goethe's Plays, Ungar, 77; auth, Character Names in Dostoevski's Fiction, Ardis, 82; transl, Complete Works of Horace (original meters), Ungar, 82. *Mailing Add:* 8 Lincoln Ave Danville NY 14437

PASTOR, BEATRIZ, b Seo de Urgel, Spain, July 25, 48; m 78; c 2. LATIN AMERICAN & SPANISH LITERATURE. *Educ:* Univ Barcelona, BA, 68; Univ Minn, Minneapolis, MA, 71, PhD(Latin Am lit), 77. *Prof Exp:* ASST PROF LATIN AM, SPAN & COMP LIT, DARTMOUTH COL, 76- *Mem:* Latin Am Studies Asn; MLA. *Res:* Contemporary Latin American literature; colonial Latin American literature. *Publ:* Auth, Rupture y Limiles and la narrative de Roberto Arlt, Revista de Critica Lit Latinam, 80; Los 7 Locos y Los Lanfallamas: De le rebelion al Jascismo, Hisp Rev, spring 81; Roberto Arlt y la Rebelion Alienada, Hispamerica, 81; El Mib en la Historie: Camino de Santiago de A Carpenter, Cuadernos Hispanoam, 82. *Mailing Add:* Dept of Span & Port Dartmouth Col Hanover NH 03755

PASTOR, LESLIE P, b May 8, 25; US citizen; c 2. EUROPEAN HISTORY, GERMAN. *Educ:* Seton Hall Univ, AB, 56; Columbia Univ, MA, 59, PhD(hist), 67; Inst ECent Europe, cert, 60. *Prof Exp:* Instr Seton Hall Prep Sch, 56-60; from instr to asst prof, 60-68, ASSOC PROF GER, SETON HALL UNIV, 68- *Mem:* Am Asn Advan Slavic Studies; Am Asn Teachers Ger; Am Asn for Study Hungarian History. *Res:* German language and literature; 18th and 19th century Hungarian history; history of East Central Europe; modern East European history. *Mailing Add:* Dept of Mod Lang Seton Hall Univ South Orange NJ 07079

PATERNOST, JOSEPH, b Yugoslavia, Mar 17, 31; US citizen; m 60. LANGUAGES. *Educ:* Ohio Univ, BA, 55; Ind Univ, MA, 56, PhD(Slavic ling), 63. *Prof Exp:* From instr to asst prof Russ, 60-68, assoc prof Slavic lang, 68-77, PROF SALVIC LANG, PA STATE UNIV, UNIVERSITY PARK, 77- *Concurrent Pos:* Nat Defense Foreign Lang fel, 59-60. *Mem:* Am Asn Teachers Slavic & EEurop Lang; Am Asn Advan Slavic Studies; MLA; Am Asn Southeast Europ Studies; Soc Slovene Studies. *Res:* Slovenian; Russian; theory and practice of translation. *Publ:* Auth, Russian-English Glossary of Linguistic Terms, 65 & Slovenian-English Glossary of Linguistic Terms, 66, Pa State Univ; From English to Slovenian: Problems in Translation Equivalence, Pa State Univ, 70; The Adequacy of Translations from English into Slovenian from the Point of View of Formal and Dynamic Equivalence & Three-Level Theory of Translation (both written in Slovenian), Prostor in cas, Ljubljana, Yugoslavia, 72; Slovenian lanugage on Minnesota's iron range: Some sociolinguistic aspects of language maintenance and language shift, Gen Ling, summer/fall 76. *Mailing Add:* N-438 Burrowes Pa State Univ University Park PA 16802

PATKOWSKI, MARK S, b Mt Kisco, NY, June 3, 53. APPLIED LINGUISTICS. *Educ:* Columbia Col, BA, 74; New York Univ, MA, 77, PhD, 80. *Prof Exp:* Asst prof English as a second lang, Hostos Community Col, NY, 79-81; DIR ENGLISH LANG PROG, HOFSTRA UNIV, NY, 81- *Concurrent Pos:* Adj prof psycholing, Grad Sch William Paterson Col, 81- *Mem:* Teachers English to Speakers Other Lang. *Res:* Second language acquisition; applied linguistics. *Publ:* Auth, The sensitive period for the acquisition of syntax in a second langage, Lang Learning, Vol 30, No 2; A Test of Linguistic Intuitions, Proc of the 1980 Southern Ill Lang Testing Conf, Southern Ill Univ, 80; coauth, English as a second language, an interdisciplinary approach, Kendall-Hunt, Vol 4, 81; auth, The sensitive period for the acquisition of syntax in a second language, In: Child Adult Differences in Second Language Acquisition, Newbury House (in prep). *Mailing Add:* 2572 Seminole Ave Seaford NY 11783

PATT, BEATRICE PENELOPE, b New York, NY, June 27, 19; m 40; c 2. SPANISH LITERATURE. *Educ:* Hunter Col, BA, 40; Bryn Mawr Col, MA, 41, PhD, 45. *Prof Exp:* Teaching asst, Univ Calif, Berkeley, 41-42; instr Span, Bryn Mawr Col, 43-45, Smith Col, 45-47; from instr to assoc prof, 49-67, prof, 67-80, EMER PROF ROMANCE LANG, QUEENS COL, NY, 80- *Mem:* MLA; Am Asn Teachers Span & Port; Am Comp Lit Asn. *Res:* Medieval Spanish religious drama; modern novel. *Publ:* Coauth, The Generation of 1898 and After, Dodd, 60; Retratos de Hispano-America, Holt, 62; Funcionario Publico, Oxford, 63; Spanish Literature: 1700-1900, Dodd, 65; auth, Pio Baroja, Twayne, 71; Spanish Literature Since the Civil War, Dodd, 72. *Mailing Add:* Dept of Romance Lang Queens Col Flushing NY 11367

PATTERSON, CHANNING FORD, b Honobia, Okla, May 24, 25. LANGUAGES, MEXICAN STUDIES. *Educ:* Cent State Col, Okla, AB, 53; Inter-Am Univ, Mex, MA, 62, PhD(span), 64. *Prof Exp:* Primary teacher, Shawnee, Okla, 47-48; teacher oral English, Govt Schs Ethiopia, 53-55; head teacher elem, Pahrump Sch, Pahrump, Nev, 55-60; teacher Span, Ysleta Pub Schs, El Paso, Tex, 60-63; instr, Cottey Col, 63; asst prof, Albion Col, 64-66; asst prof, 66-74, ASSOC PROF SPAN, UNIV NDAK, 74- *Concurrent Pos:* State of Nuevo Leon Congressional Aide, Nat Cong, Mexico City. *Mem:* Am Asn Teachers Span & Port. *Res:* Mexican culture. *Mailing Add:* Dept of Lang Univ of NDak Grand Forks ND 58201

PATTERSON, WILLIAM TAYLOR, b Hattiesburg, Miss, Oct 25, 31. FRENCH, ROMANCE LINGUISTICS. *Educ:* Univ Kans, BA, 54; Univ Montpellier, cert, 55; Pa State Univ, University Park, MEd, 61; Stanford Univ, PhD(ling), 67. *Prof Exp:* Asst prof French, 61-64, assoc prof French & Romance ling, 68-74, PROF FRENCH & ROMANCE LING, TEX TECH UNIV, 74- *Concurrent Pos:* Vis prof, Univ Nebr, 62, Stillman Col, 64, Colo State Univ, 65 & Emory Univ, 66; mem, Nat Fulbright Selection Comt for France, 79-80. *Honors & Awards:* Distinguished Teaching Award, Standard Oil, 71. *Mem:* Am Asn Teachers Fr; Am Asn Teachers Span & Port; MLA; SCent Mod Lang Asn. *Res:* Romance lexicology; Old French; Occitan. *Publ:* Auth, On the genealogical structure of the Spanish vocabulary, Festschrift Martinet, 4/68; The Spanish lexicon: a genealogical and functional correlation, Hisp, 4/73; A genealogical classification of Spanish words, Ling, 10/73; The Spanish lexicon: a genealogical and physical correlation, Revista de Estudios Hisp, 74; The lexical Structure of Spanish, Mouton, The Hague, 75; A genealogical classification of French words, Can Mod Lang Rev, winter 82; The Spanish Lexicon: A Correlation of Basic Word Properties, Univ Press Am, 82. *Mailing Add:* Dept of Classical & Romance Lang Tex Tech Univ Lubbock TX 79409

PATTY, JAMES SINGLETON, b Florence, Ala, July 17, 25. FRENCH. *Educ:* Univ NC, AB, 45, MA, 47, PhD(Romance lang), 53. *Prof Exp:* Instr French, Univ NC, 46-53; instr French & Span, Univ Colo, 53-54; from asst prof to assoc prof French, Univ Tenn, 54-60; assoc prof, Washington & Lee Univ, 60-64; assoc prof, 64-69, PROF FRENCH, VANDERBILT UNIV, 69- *Concurrent Pos:* Co-ed, Bull Baudelairien; foreign corresp, Soc Hist Lit France. *Mem:* Am Asn Teachers Fr; MLA; Am Comp Lit Asn; Soc Etudes Romantiques. *Res:* Nineteenth century French literature; Baudelaire; Romanticism. *Publ:* Auth, Baudelaire's knowledge and use of Dante, Studies Philol, 10/56; Baudelaire and Bossuet on laughter, Publ Mod Lang Asn Am, 9/65; ed, Jean Giraudoux's Electre, Appleton, 65; auth, Baudelaire et Hippolyte Babou, Rev Hist Lit France, 4-6/67; co-ed, Hommage a W T Bandy, La Baconniere, 73. *Mailing Add:* Box 1630 Station B Vanderbilt Univ Nashville TN 37235

PAUCK, CHARLES E, b St Marys, Ohio, Mar 11, 05; m 34; c 3. GERMAN LITERATURE. *Educ:* Ohio State Univ, AB, 27, AM, 28, PhD, 37. *Prof Exp:* Prof, 29-72, EMER PROF GER, BEREA COL, 72- *Concurrent Pos:* Chmn Ky Div, Nat Ger Contest for High Sch Students, 63-; pres, Mt Inter State Foreign Lang Asn, 65-66. *Mem:* MLA; Am Asn Teachers Ger. *Res:* A concentrated language course; the merchant in literature; the Duden moves to Switzerland. *Mailing Add:* 1208 Berea Col PO Berea KY 40403

PAUL, GEORGE MACKAY, b Glasgow, Scotland, July 16, 27; m 56; c 3. CLASSICS, ANCIENT HISTORY. *Educ:* Oxford Univ, BA & MA, 54; Univ London, PHD(classics), 63. *Prof Exp:* From asst lectr to lectr classics, Univ WIndies, 55-64; from asst prof to assoc prof, 64-70, chmn dept, 73-76, PROF CLASSICS, McMASTER UNIV, 70- *Concurrent Pos:* Mem, Comt Coord Acad Libr Serv Ont Univs, 66-67; Can Coun leave fel, 71-72. *Mem:* Class Asn Can (treas, 67-69); Am Philol Asn; Soc Prom Roman Studies; Asn Ancient Historians; Soc Prom Hellenic Studies. *Res:* Greek and Roman historiography; Roman history. *Publ:* Auth, Sallust, In: Latin Historians, Routledge & Kegan Paul, 66; Oxford Classical Dictionary, Oxford Univ, 70 & Encycl Britannica, 74. *Mailing Add:* Dept of Classics McMaster Univ Hamilton ON L8S 4M2 Can

PAUL, NORMAN HENRY, b Holyoke, Mass, June 6, 22. ROMANCE LANGUAGES. *Educ:* Syracuse Univ, BA, 49, MA, 56; NY Univ, PhD, 61. *Prof Exp:* Asst French, Syracuse Univ, 54-56; asst, NY Univ, 56-58; tutor, 58-61, instr, 61-65, asst prof, 66-70, resident dir study abroad, Reims, 65-66, Nice, 66-67, spec asst study abroad prog, 67-68, protocol off & spec asst to dean fac, 68-69, ASSOC PROF FRENCH, QUEENS COL, NY, 70- *Concurrent Pos:* Asst dir, Maison Fr, NY Univ, 57-58; dir, study abroad int sem, Ajaccio, summers 70, 71 & French Prog, Paris, summer 72; assoc ed, Registres III du Vieux Colombier, Par Jacques Copeau, Gallimard Paris, 79, Registres IV, 82. *Honors & Awards:* PSC-BHE Award, City Univ NY, 78-81. *Mem:* Am Asn Teachers Fr; Soc Hist Theatre; Les Amis de Jacques Copeau. *Res:* Contemporary French theatre; French romanticism; complete edition of works of Jacques Copeau. *Publ:* Auth, France: society and cultural life, In: Collier's Encycl, Collier-Macmillan, 61, 64; L'Apport de Jacques Copeau, In: Actes du Colloque de London, Minard, Paris, 74; contribr, Registres I Appels, par Jacques Copeau, Gallimard, Paris, 74; auth, Jacques Copeau looks at the American state, 1917-1919, Educ Theatre J, 3/77; Jacques Copeau, drama critic, Theatre Res Int, 5/77. *Mailing Add:* Dept of Romance Lang Queens Col Flushing NY 11367

PAULIN, HARRY WALTER, b Chicago, Ill, June 17, 28; m 54; c 2. GERMAN LITERATURE. *Educ:* NCent Col, BA, 50; Univ Ill, AM, 55, PhD, 59. *Prof Exp:* Teacher Ger & English, Downers Grove Community High Sch, Ill, 55-57; instr Ger, Northwestern Univ, 59-62; from asst prof to assoc prof, 62-70, PROF GER, SAN DIEGO STATE UNIV, 70- *Concurrent Pos:* Fulbright Exchange teachership, Munich, 66-67. *Mem:* MLA; Am Asn Teachers Ger; AAUP. *Res:* Nineteenth century German literature. *Publ:* Ed, Hier spukt es, Holt, 71; auth, Kohlhaas and family, Ger Rev, 5/77; Through a brass darkly, behold a knight, Christian Sci Monitor, 4/77. *Mailing Add:* Dept of Ger & Slavic Lang & Lit San Diego State Univ San Diego CA 92182

PAULS, JOHN P, b Pavlopol, Russia, Apr 28, 16; US citizen; m 52; c 1. RUSSIAN LANGUAGE & LITERATURE. *Educ:* Warsaw Univ, MA, 39; Univ Munich, PhD(Slavic), 47. *Prof Exp:* Instr Russian lang, Ten Yr Sch, Gorodok, Russia, 39-40; instr Russ & Polish, City Bus Sch, Warsaw, Poland, 40-43; asst prof comp Slavic philol, Univ Munich, 47-50; asst prof Russ lang, Wright Col, Chicago, 58-59; assoc prof, 59-65, PROF RUSS LANG & LIT, UNIV CINCINNATI, 65- *Mem:* Am Asn Teachers Slavic & East Europ Lang; Am Name Soc; Shevchenko Sci Soc. *Res:* Eastern Slavic dialects; Russian literature, especially of the Pushkin epoch and contemporary Soviet; etymology of Slavic names. *Publ:* Auth, The Problem of the Byelorussian and Ukrainian Lingual Boundary, 48 & Ideology of Cyrillo-Methodians and its Origin, 54, Ukrainian Acad Sci; Pushkin's Poltava, Shevchenko Sci Soc, 62; Names for characters in Russian literature, Am Name Soc, 63; Change of e to o in the dialect of Polissye, Abstr Tenth Cong Ling, 67; Ukrainian themes in Ryleev's works, Wiener Slavist J, 72; O kontaktach jezykowych w dialekcie Zach Polesia, Slavic Orientalis, 73; Names in Chekhov's writing, Am Name Soc, 74; On literary onomastics, Onomastica, 77; Maria in Pushkin's Poltava, N R Pribic, 82. *Mailing Add:* 3422 Lyleburn Pl Cincinnati OH 45220

PAULSEN, WOLFGANG, b Düsseldorf, Ger, Sept 21, 10; nat US; m 38; c 1. GERMAN LITERATURE. *Educ:* Univ Berne, PhD, 34. *Prof Exp:* Asst lectr Ger, Univ Durham, 35-37; asst lectr, Univ Reading & asst, Westfield Col, London, 37-38; asst prof mod lang, Southwestern Col, 38-43; asst prof Ger, State Univ Iowa, 43-47; assoc prof, Smith Col, 47-53; assoc prof, NY State Col for Teachers, Albany, 53-54; asst prof, Univ Conn, 54-61, prof, 61-66; chmn dept, 66-71, PROF GER, UNIV MASS, AMHERST, 66- *Mem:* MLA; Schiller Ges. *Res:* Eighteenth to twentieth century German literature; modern German drama. *Publ:* Auth, Georg Kaiser, Die Perspektiven seines Werkes, 60 & Die Ahnfrau, Zu Grillparzers früher Dramatik, 62, Niemeyer, Tübingen; Versuch über Rolf Bongs, Bläschke, Darmstadt, 74; Chr M Wieland, Der Mensch und sein Werk, 75, Eichendorff und sein Taugenichts, 76 & Johann Elias Schlegel und die Komödie, 77, Francke, Bern; Der Expressionismus in der deutschen Literatur, Peter Lang, Bern, 82. *Mailing Add:* Dept of Ger Lang & Lit Univ of Mass Amherst MA 01002

PAULSON, MICHAEL GEORGE, JR, b Pittsburgh, Pa, Sept 27, 45; m 72. FRENCH & SPANISH LANGUAGE & LITERATURE. *Educ:* Kutztown State Col, BS, 67; Fla State Univ, MA, 68, PhD, 73. *Prof Exp:* Asst prof foreign lang, SDak State Univ, 73-76; MEM FAC FRENCH & SPAN, UNIV CENT ARK, 76- *Mem:* Am Asn Teachers Fr; SCent Mod Lang Asn; Am Asn Teachers Span & Port. *Res:* Sixteenth and seventeenth century French literature. *Publ:* Auth, The Ame Faible of Descartes and Racine, 68; The concept of passions in Descartes and Montaigne, 73; The Fallen Crown: Three French Mary Stuart Plays of the Seventeenth Century, Washington Univ Press Am, 80; The death of Mary Stuart: An attempt at order, NDak Quart, 81; La corona tragica de Lope de Vega: Una edicion critica, Span Lit Publ Co, 82; The Gambling Mania On and Off Stage in Pre-Revolutionary France, Washington Univ Press Am, 82. *Mailing Add:* 140 Oaklawn Dr Conway AR 72032

PAULSTON, CHRISTINA BRATT, b Stockholm, Sweden; US citizen; m 63 c 2. LINGUISTICS, LANGUAGE TEACHING. *Educ:* Carleton Col, BA, 53; Univ Minn, Minneapolis, MA, 55; Columbia Univ, EdD(ling), 66. *Prof Exp:* Teacher English, Pub High Schs, Clara City & Pine Island, Minn, 55-60; teacher English & French, Am Sch Tangier, 60-62; teacher, Katrineholm Hogre Allmanna Laroverk, Sweden, 62-63; instr, Teachers Col, Columbia Univ, 64-66; AID spec, Punjab Univ, India, 66 & Cath Univ Peru, 66-67; consult lang teaching, Inst Ling Verano, Peru, 67-68; from asst prof to assoc prof, 69-76, asst dir English Lang Inst, 69-70, PROF LING, UNIV PITTSBURGH, 76-, DIR, ENGLISH LANG INST, 70- *Concurrent Pos:* NDEA & Nat Endowment for Humanities grant & prog dir, Quechua-Aymara Inst, 72. *Mem:* Teachers English to Speakers Other Lang (2nd vpres, 71-72, pres, 75-76); Ling Soc Am; Int Asn Teachers English as Foreign Lang; Am Coun Teaching Foreign Lang; MLA. *Res:* Sociolinguistics; language policy. *Publ:* Coauth, Controlled Composition, Regents, 73; From Substitution to Substance: A Handbook of Structural Pattern Drills, Newbury House, 73; auth, Implications of language learning theory for language planning, Ctr Appl Ling, 75; coauth, Developing Communicative Competence: Roleplays in English as a Second Language, Univ Pittsburgh, 75; Procedures & Techniques in Teaching English as a Second Language, Winthrop, 76; Individualizing the Language Classroom: Learning & Teaching in a Communicative Context, Jacaranda, 76; auth, Bilingual Education: Issues and Theories, Newbury House, 80; English as a Second Language, Nat Educ Asn, 80. *Mailing Add:* Dept of Gen Ling Univ of Pittsburgh Pittsburgh PA 15213

PAUSCH, HOLGER ARTHUR, b Neustadt, Sachsen, Ger, Aug 25, 40. MODERN GERMAN LITERATURE, METHODOLOGY. *Educ:* Freie Univ Berlin, MA, 68; McGill Univ, PhD(Ger philol), 71. *Prof Exp:* Asst prof, 71-74, assoc prof, 74-80, PROF GER LANG & LIT, UNIV ALTA, 80- *Concurrent Pos:* Vis prof Ger lang & lit, Univ Kiel, Ger, 76-77; Can Coun res grant, Univ Alta. *Mem:* Can Asn Univ Teachers Ger. *Res:* Methodology; modern literature; linguistics. *Publ:* Auth, Ammerkungen zu problemen und strukturen der wissenschaftessprache in der modernen physik, Wirkendes Wort, 71; Zur widersprüchlichkeit in der lenzschen dramaturgie: Eine untersuchung der 'Anmerkungen übers theater, Maske & Kothurn, 71; Die metapher, forschungsbericht, Wirkendes Wort, 74; Die substruktur des denkens im mittelhochdeutschen, Seminar II, 75; Ingeborg Bachmann, Colloquium Verlag, Berlin, 75; Literaturwissenschaft Anmerkungen zur deutschsprachigen methodologischen diskussion, Can Rev Comp Lit, 75; ed, Kommunikative Metaphorik Studien über Funktionen des Literarischen Bildes von ihren Anfängen bis zur Gegenwart, Bouvier, Bonn, 76; co-ed (with E Reinhold), Georg Kaiser, Symposium, Agora, Berlin, 80; Paul Celan, Colloquium Verlag, Berlin, 81. *Mailing Add:* 11508-31 Ave Edmonton AB T6J 3T1 Can

PAUSON, MARIAN LAGARDE, Philosophy, Aesthetics. See Vol IV

PAVES-YASHINSKY, PALOMBA, b Bucharest, Rumania, June 23, 29; US citizen; m 48; c 1. FRENCH LITERATURE & LANGUAGE. *Educ:* Wayne State Univ, BA, 49, MA, 62, PhD(mod lang), 69. *Prof Exp:* Instr French, Wayne State Univ, 64-66; instr, Univ Calif, Santa Barbara, 66-68; lectr, 68-69, ASST PROF FRENCH, YORK UNIV, 69- *Mem:* MLA; AAUP; Can Asn Univ Teachers; Am Asn Teachers Fr. *Res:* Nineteenth century French literature; French theater; French art criticism. *Publ:* Auth, Notes sur le type Juif dans la comedie de moeurs de l'epoque 1900, Rev Hist Theatre; Le realisme en litterature et en peinture dans la deuxieme moitie du dixneuvieme siecle en France, Fr Rev, 2/74; Castagnary, lenaturalisme et courbet, 19th Century Fr Studies, spring 76. *Mailing Add:* 6 Bernard Ave Toronto ON M5R 1R2 Can

PAVLANTOS, RUTH ESTHER, b Canton, Ohio, Jan 3, 22; m 55; c 1. CLASSICS. *Educ:* Wooster Col, BA, 44; Univ Cincinnati, MA, 47, PhD(classics), 51. *Prof Exp:* Asst prof classics, Univ Hawaii, 53-62; from asst prof to assoc prof, 63-67, PROF CLASSICS & CHMN DEPT, GETTYSBURG COL, 67- *Concurrent Pos:* Fulbright scholar, Am Sch Class Studies, Athens, 51-52. *Mem:* Am Philol Asn; Am Inst Archaeol. *Res:* Greek history; Greek War of Independence. *Mailing Add:* Dept of Classics Gettysburg Col Gettysburg PA 17325

PAVLOVSKIS, ZOJA, b Daugavpils, Latvia, Apr 30, 36; US citizen. CLASSICS. *Educ:* Bryn Mawr Col, AB, 58; Cornell Univ, MA, 59, PhD, 62. *Prof Exp:* From asst prof to assoc prof classics, 62-73, ASSOC PROF CLASSICS & COMP LIT, STATE UNIV NY BINGHAMTON, 73- *Mem:* Am Philol Asn. *Res:* Latin poetry; Greek drama; irony. *Publ:* Auth, Man in An Artificial Landscape, Suppl 25 to Mnemosyne, Brill, 73; Aristotle, Horace, and the ironic man, 63: 22-41 & Man in a poetic landscape, 56: 151-168, Classic Philol; Vir fortis sine manibus and the handless maiden, Classica et Mediaevalia, 28: 86-113. *Mailing Add:* Dept of Classics State Univ of NY Binghamton NY 13901

PAYNE, ANCIL NEWTON, JR, b Gainesville, Fla, Dec 31, 35; m 74; c 1. CLASSICAL PHILOLOGY. *Educ:* Cornell Univ, AB, 58, AM, 66, PhD(classics), 68; LLM, NY Univ, 81. *Hon Degrees:* LLB, Harvard Univ, 61. *Prof Exp:* Legal asst to reporter, Adv Comt Fed Rules of Civil Procedure, Admin Off US Courts, 61-62; asst prof classics, NY Univ, 68-70; ASST PROF CLASSICS, UNIV OKLA, 70- *Concurrent Pos:* Res fel law, Yale Univ, 81- *Mem:* Am Philol Asn. *Res:* History of later Roman Republic; Cicero's proconsulate; Roman law. *Mailing Add:* Dept of Classics Univ of Okla Norman OK 73019

PAYNE, DAVID LAWRENCE, b Tyler, Tex, Aug 17, 52; m 78; c 3. LINGUISTICS. *Educ:* Trinity Col, BA, 73; Univ Tex, Arlington, MA, 74; Univ Tex, Austin, PhD(ling), 78. *Prof Exp:* MEM FAC LING, SUMMER INST LING, 75-, INT LING CONSULT, 82- *Concurrent Pos:* Vis prof ling, Univ Catolica, Lima, Peru, 79. *Mem:* Ling Soc Am. *Res:* Morphophonemics; orthography; experimental phonology. *Publ:* Auth, Nasalidad en aguaruna, Serie Ling Peruana, No 15, 76; Diccionario asheninca-castellano, Documento Trabajo, No 18, 80; Phonology and morphology of Axininca Campa, Summer Inst Ling Publ in Ling, No 66, 81. *Mailing Add:* Rte 22 Box 396 Tyler TX 75704

PAZ, FRANCIS XAVIER, b Chicago, Ill, Nov 5, 31; m 73; c 1. COMPARATIVE LITERATURE, ORIENTAL STUDIES. *Educ:* Univ Chicago, BA, 52, MA, 57; Columbia Univ, PhD(Orient studies), 72. *Prof Exp:* Lectr humanities, Bishop Col, 56-57; lectr Orient humanities, Columbia Univ, 63-65; PROF ENGLISH & COMP LIT, STATE UNIV NY, NEW PALTZ, 66- *Concurrent Pos:* Univ fel Arabic lit, Columbia Univ, 77- *Mem:* MLA; Am Orient Soc; Mideast Studies Asn. *Res:* Modern American and Arabic fiction. *Publ:* Translr, The Assemblies of Al-Hamadhani, State Univ NY, (in press). *Mailing Add:* Dept Lit State Univ Col New Paltz NY 12562

PAZIK, RONALD STANLEY, b Detroit, Mich, Sept 8, 26; Can citizen. ROMANCE LANGUAGES, RELIGION. *Educ:* Univ Western Ont, BA, 49; Univ Toronto, MA, 55; Univ Madrid, cert Span, 65-66. *Prof Exp:* lectr Span, St Michael's Col, Univ Toronto, 51-55; from lectr to asst prof, 55-68, acting head Hisp & Ital studies & chmn comt Latin Am studies, 68-72, ASSOC PROF SPAN, UNIV WINDSOR, 69- *Mem:* Am Asn Teachers Span & Port; MLA; Latin Am Studies Asn. *Res:* Golden Age drama, especially Calderon de la Barca; contemporary Spanish novel; Mexican novel of the Revolution. *Mailing Add:* Dept of Hisp & Ital Studies Univ of Windsor Windsor ON N90 3P4 Can

PEACHY, FREDERIC, b Seattle, Wash, Dec 29, 15; m 42; c 4. CLASSICS. *Educ:* Univ Paris, Lic es Let, 35, dipl, 36; Harvard Univ, AM, 38, PhD(classics), 48. *Prof Exp:* Instr French, Brown Univ, 45-47; asst prof classics & French, Univ Maine, 48-50; asst prof classics, Univ Calif, 50-56; assoc prof, 56-61, PROF CLASSICS, REED COL, 61- *Concurrent Pos:* Consult, curric study, Portland High Sch, 59. *Mem:* Am Philol Asn; Philol Asn Pac Coast (secy-treas, 57-61, vpres, 74-75, pres, 76); Classical Asn Pac Northwest (vpres, 78, pres, 79); Classical Asn Can; Asn Ancient Historians. *Res:* Poetry; drama; folklore. *Publ:* Auth, Clareti Enigmata, Univ Calif Publ Folklore, 57. *Mailing Add:* Dept of Classics Reed Col Portland OR 97202

PEAK, JOHN HUNTER, b Louisville, Ky, Feb 9, 19; m 62; c 1. NINETEENTH CENTURY SPANISH DRAMA. *Educ:* Hampden-Sydney Col, 41; Univ NC, Chapel Hill, MA, 50, PhD(Span), 55. *Prof Exp:* Instr Span & Latin, Ky Mil IXst, 41-46, Univ NC, Chapel Hill, 46-47, 49-52, Graham-Eckes Sch, Fla, 48-49; asst prof Span, Davidson Col, 52-55; dir binational ctrs, US Inform Agency, Peru & Arg, 55-58; teacher, high sch, Ill, 58-61; asst prof Span, Univ Ky, 61-64; prof & chmn dept, Eastern Ky, Univ, 64-67; chmn dept, 67-77, PROF SPAN, AUBURN UNIV, 67- *Concurrent Pos:* Instr, Univ Louisville, 47-48; sales agent, Reynolds Metals Co, Louisville, 47-48; ed, Univ Ky Mod Foreign Lang Newslett, 62-64. *Mem:* MLA; SAtlantic MLA; NEA. *Res:* Spanish poetry and drama. *Publ:* Auth, Recent publications in field of Romance languages and literature, Univ Ky Foreign Lang Quart, 10/62; Social Drama in Nineteenth Century Span, Univ NC, 64. *Mailing Add:* Dept of Span Auburn University AL 36849

PEARCE, RUTH LILIENTHAL, b Philadelphia, Pa, Oct 3, 18; m 42; c 5. COMPARATIVE LINGUISTICS. *Educ:* Bryn Mawr Col, AB, 40; Univ Pa, MA, 42, PhD, 49. *Prof Exp:* From instr to asst prof, 58-70, ASSOC PROF RUSS, BRYN MAWR COL, 70-, CHMN DEPT, 72- *Concurrent Pos:* Asst Ger, Univ Pa, 57-59. *Mem:* MLA; Am Asn Teachers Slavic & EErop Lang; Am Asn Advan Slavic Studies; Int Langues Lit Slaves; Am Name Soc. *Res:* Russian grammar; Slavic linguistics. *Publ:* Auth, Welsh Place-Names in Southeastern Pennsylvania, Names, 63. *Mailing Add:* Dept of Russ Bryn Mawr Col Bryn Mawr PA 19010

PEARCY, LEE THERON, JR, b Little Rock, Ark, Aug 20, 47; m 70; c 2. CLASSICS. *Educ:* Columbia Univ, BA, 69, MA, 71; Bryn Mawr Col, PhD(Latin), 74. *Prof Exp:* Teacher Latin, English, Englewood Sch for Boys, 69-71; asst prof class, St Olaf Col, 73-77; ASST PROF CLASS, UNIV TEX, AUSTIN, 77- *Concurrent Pos:* Am Coun Learned Soc fel, 79. *Mem:* Am Philol Asn; Soc Promotion of Roman Studies (England); Soc Ancient Med. *Res:* Roman and Greek literature; translation; ancient science. *Publ:* Contrib, The Greek Anthology, Oxford Univ, 73; auth, The structure of Bacchylides' Dithyrambs, Quaderni Urbinati di Cultura Classica, 76; Horace's architectural imagery, Latomus, 77; Achilles Tatius, Leucippe and Clitophon 1.14-15: An unnoticed Lacuna?, Class Philol, 78; Catullus 2B--or not 2B?, Mnemosyne, 79; Marlowe, Dominicus Niger, and Ovid's Amores, Notes & Queries, 80; coauth, The Homeric Hymn to Apollo, Bryn Mawr, 80. *Mailing Add:* Dept of Class Univ Tex Austin TX 78712

PEARL, ORSAMUS MERRILL, b St Johns, Mich, May 15, 08; m 31; c 3. GREEK, LATIN. *Educ:* Univ Mich, PhD(Greek), 38. *Prof Exp:* Instr Latin, Sweet Briar Col, 36-37; from instr to assoc prof Greek, 39-65, PROF GREEK, UNIV MICH, ANN ARBOR, 65- *Concurrent Pos:* Dir, Am Soc Papyrologists, 71-75. *Honors & Awards:* Honorary Volume, Bull Am Soc Papyrologists, 79. *Mem:* Am Philol Asn; Int Asn Papyrologists; Am Soc Papyrologists. *Res:* Papyrology; mythology. *Publ:* Coauth, Tax Rolls from Karanis, Vol I, 36, Vol II, 39 & Papyri and Ostraca from Karanis, 44, Univ Mich; auth, Census documents from Karanis, Chronique d'Egypte, 53; Short texts from Karanis, Aegyptus, 53; coauth, The Michigan musical papyrus, J Egyptian Archaeol, 66; auth, The 94 Klerouchies at Karanis, Akten d XII Int Papyrologenkongresses, 71; Rules for musical contests, Univ Ill Class Studies, 77; Official Correspondence, P Turner, 81. *Mailing Add:* Dept Class Lang Univ Mich Ann Arbor MI 48109

PEARSON, BIRGER ALBERT, History of Religion. See Vol IV

PEARSON, BRUCE L, b Indianapolis, Ind, Apr 30, 32; m 61; c 2. ANTHROPOLOGICAL LINGUISTICS. *Educ:* Earlham Col, BA, 53; Ind Univ, MA, 63; Univ Calif, Berkeley, PhD(ling), 72. *Prof Exp:* Instr English, Friends Sch, Tokyo, 54-55, Tezukayama Col, 55-58, Shortridge High Sch, Indianapolis, 58-63 & Earlham Col, 63-67; asst prof English & anthrop, Calif State Univ, Los Angeles, 69-72; ASST PROF ENGLISH & ANTHROP, UNIV SC, COLUMBIA, 72- *Mem:* Ling Soc Am; Am Anthrop Asn. *Res:* Semantic structure of language; general and historical linguistics; Algonkian languages. *Publ:* Auth, Crazy rules and natural rules in Japanese phonology, Papers in Japanese Ling, 72; Introduction to Linguistic Concepts, Knopf, 77. *Mailing Add:* Dept of English Univ of SC Columbia SC 29208

PEARSON, JUSTUS RICHARD, JR, English & American Literature. See Vol II

PEARSON, LIONEL (IGNATIUS CUSACK), b London, Eng, Jan 30, 08; m 46. CLASSICAL STUDIES. *Educ:* Oxford Univ, BA, 30; Yale Univ, PhD, 39. *Prof Exp:* Lectr Greek, Univ Glasgow, 30-31; lectr classics, Dalhousie Univ, 32-35, asst prof, 36-38; instr, Yale Univ, 35-36; instr Latin, NY State Col Teachers, 39-40; from asst prof to assoc prof, 40-52, prof, 52-73, EMER PROF CLASSICS, STANFORD UNIV, 73- *Concurrent Pos:* Guggenheim fel, 57-58; vis prof classics, Univ Sydney, 68 & Yale Univ, 74-75. *Mem:* Am Philol Asn; Archaeol Inst Am; AHA; Classical Asn, Gt Brit. *Res:* Greek history and literature; Greek historiography. *Publ:* Auth, Early Ionian Historians, Oxford Univ, 39; The lost histories of Alexander the Great, Am Philol Asn, 60; Popular Ethics in Ancient Greece, Stanford Univ, 62; ed, Plutarch, On the Malice of Herodotus, Loeb Classic Libr, 65; ed, Demosthenes, Six Private Orations, Text and Commentary, Okla Univ, 72; auth, The Art of Demosthenes, Anton Hain, Meisenheim, 76, Scholar Press, 81. *Mailing Add:* 12123 Foothill Lane Los Altos Hills CA 94022

PEARSON, LON, b Murray, Utah, Feb 13, 39; m 61; c 5. HISPANIC LANGUAGES & LITERATURES, COMPARATIVE LITERATURE. *Educ:* Univ Utah, AB, 66; Univ Calif, Los Angeles, MA, 68, PhD(Hispanic lang & lit), 73. *Prof Exp:* Assoc instr Span, Univ Calif, Los Angeles, 69-70; instr Span, 70-73, asst prof, 73-77, ASSOC PROF & HEAD LANG, UNIV MO, ROLLA, 77- *Concurrent Pos:* Consult foreign lang, Mo State Dept Educ, 73-; co-ed, Mo Foreign Lang J, 73-76, ed, 76-78; Nat Endowment Humanities Resident fel, Span, Johns Hopkins Univ, 75-76. *Mem:* Int Inst Iberoamerican Lit; Am Asn Teachers Span & Port; MLA. *Res:* Contemporary Chilean novel; William Faulkner's influence on Latin American fiction. *Publ:* Auth, Nicomedes Guzman y el espejo doble del conventillo, Revista de los Sabados, Chile, 71; La novela pastoril-burlesca de Nicomedes Guzman, Revista de Lit Chilena, no 5, 73; Nicomedes Guzman, Univ Mo, 76. *Mailing Add:* Dept of Humanities Univ of Mo Rolla MO 65401

PEAVLER, TERRY J, b Seminole, Okla, Oct 25, 42; c 2. LATIN AMERICAN & COMPARATIVE LITERATURE. *Educ:* Univ Colo, Boulder, BA, 65, MA, 67; Univ Calif, Berkeley, PhD(comp lit), 73. *Prof Exp:* Asst prof, 71-79, ASSOC PROF SPAN & COMP LIT, PA STATE UNIV, UNIVERSITY PARK, 79- *Concurrent Pos:* Nat Sci Found Inst grant, 73-74. *Mem:* MLA; Am Asn Teachers Span & Port. *Res:* Latin American novel; Inter-American literary relations; Cuban literature. *Publ:* Auth, The source for the archetype in Los Pasos Perdidos, Romance Notes, 74; A new novel by Alejo Carpentier, Latin Am Lit Rev, 76; Prose fiction criticism and theory in Cuban journals, Cuban Studies, 77; Edmundo Desnoes and Cuba's lost generation, Latin Am Res Rev, 77; Guillermo Cabrera Infante's Debt to Ernest Hemingway, Hispania, 79; Blow-Up: A reconsideration of Antonioni's Infidelity to Cortazar, PLMA, 79; Teaching film and literature: A few principles, J Gen Educ, 80; Alejo Carpentier and the humanization of Spanish American fiction, Hispanofila, 82. *Mailing Add:* Dept of Span Ital & Port Pa State Univ 352 N Burrowes Bldg University Park PA 16802

PECK, JEFFREY MARC, b Pittsburgh, Pa, Jan 5, 50. GERMAN & COMPARATIVE LITERATURE. *Educ:* Mich State Univ, BA, 72; Univ Chicago, MA, 74; Univ Calif, Berkeley, PhD(comp lit & Ger), 79. *Prof Exp:* Actg instr world lit & comp, Univ Calif, Berkeley, 78; ASST PROF GERMANICS & COMP LIT, UNIV WASHINGTON, 79- *Mem:* MLA; Am Comp Lit Asn; Int Verein Germanistik; Am Asn Teachers Ger; Philol Asn Pac Coast. *Res:* Literary criticism and theory, especially hermeneutics; 19th and 20th century German literature; academic institutionalization of literature and criticism. *Publ:* Auth, Comparative historiography: Canonization and perrodization in German, French and English literary histories, Proc Int Ger Studies Conf, Peter Lang, 80; The politics of reading and the poetics of reading: The Hermeneutic Text--Heinrich von Kleist's Die Marquise von O, Cahiers roumains etudes litteraires, 82; Hermes Disguised: Literary Hermeneutics and the Interpretation of Literature, Kleist, Grillparzer, Fontane, Peter Lang (in press). *Mailing Add:* Dept of Germanics Univ of Wash Denny Hall DH-30 Seattle WA 98195

PEDEN, MARGARET SAYERS, b West Plains, Mo, May 10, 27; m 65; c 4. ROMANCE LANGUAGES. *Educ:* Univ Mo, AB, 48, MA, 63, PhD(Span), 66. *Prof Exp:* Teaching asst French & Span, 63-65, asst prof Latin Am & Span lit, 66-70, assoc prof Span, 70-75, chmn dept of Romance lang, 75-77, Catherine Paine Middlebush prof of Romance lang, 79-82, PROF SPAN, UNIV MO-COLUMBIA, 75- *Concurrent Pos:* Am Asn Univ Women fel, 78; NEA fel, 81. *Honors & Awards:* Byler Distinguished Prof Award, Univ Mo-Columbia, 77; Distinguished Fac Award, Univ Mo-Columbia, 81. *Mem:* PEN; Am Asn Teachers Span & Port; Am Transl Asn; Am Lit Transl Asn. *Res:* Spanish American theater; Spanish American novel; translation. *Publ:* Auth, Chaps on Egon Wolff and Luis Alberto Heiremans, In: Voices of Protest, 76 & transl, The Decapitated Chicken and Other Stories, 76, Univ Tex Press; Terra Nostra, 76 & The Hydra Head, 78, Farrar, Straus & Giroux; auth, Emilio Carballido, G K Hall, 80; transl, Burnt Water, 80 & Distant Relations, 82, Farrar, Straus & Giroux; transl & introd to A Woman of Genius, the Intellectual Autobiography of Sor Juana Ines de la Cruz, Lime Rock Press, 82. *Mailing Add:* 11 Arts & Sci Univ of Mo Columbia MO 65201

PEDERSON, LEE A, b St Louis, Mo, Sept 17, 30; m; c 1. ENGLISH LINGUISTICS & PHILOLOGY. *Educ:* Northern Ill Univ, BS, 54, MS, 57; Univ Chicago, PhD(English), 64. *Prof Exp:* Teacher English, Morgan Park Mil Acad, 54-56, Proviso Township High Sch, 56-58; instr, Wright Jr Col, 59-63; asst prof English ling, Univ Minn, 63-66; assoc prof, 66-71, PROF ENGLISH LING, EMORY UNIV, 71- *Concurrent Pos:* Ling consult, Ling Res & Demonstration Ctr, Rome, Ga, 66; Southeastern Educ Lab in Atlanta, 67; trustee, NCTE Res Found, 68-70; mem ed bd, Am Speech, 70-71; Nat Endowment for Humanities grant & dir, Ling Atlas Gulf States, 73- *Mem:* MLA; Ling Soc Am; Am Dialect Soc. *Res:* Resional and social dialectology; lexicography. *Publ:* Auth, Americanisms in Thoreau's Journal, Am Lit, 5/65; Terms of abuse for Chicago social groups, Publ Am Dialect Soc, 65;

Pronunciation of English in Metropolitan Chicago, Univ Ala, 65; co-ed, A Manual for Dialect Research, Ga State Univ, 72; auth, Practical phonology, Ann NY Acad Sci, 73. *Mailing Add:* Dept of English Emory Univ Atlanta GA 30322

PEDROTTI, LOUIS A, b Los Angeles, Calif, Feb 23, 24. SLAVIC LANGUAGES & LITERATURES. *Educ:* Occidental Col, BA, 48; Univ Calif, Berkeley, MA, 54, PhD(Slavic lang & lit), 59. *Prof Exp:* Instr Russ, Univ Ill, Urbana, 58-59; ASSOC PROF, UNIV CALIF, RIVERSIDE, 59- *Concurrent Pos:* Vis assoc prof Slavic lang, Univ Wash, 70. *Honors & Awards:* Distinguished Teaching Award, Univ Calif, Riverside, 77. *Mem:* Am Asn Teachers Slavic & East Europ Lang; Am Asn Advan Slavic Studies. *Res:* Nineteenth century Russian literature; Russian language instruction; Russian culture. *Publ:* Auth, Genesis of a Literary Alien-Jozef-Julian Sekowski, Univ Calif, 65; Sekowski's defense of Pushkin's prose, Slavic & East Europ J, Vol VII, No 1; The architecture of love in Gogol's Rome, Calif Slavic Studies, 71; Death in Italy: Bunin and Pirandello, Italian Quart, summer-fall 76; Chekhov's Major Plays: A Doctor in the House, In: Chekhov's Great Plays: A Critical Anthology, NY Univ Press, 81. *Mailing Add:* Dept Lit & Lang Univ of Calif Riverside CA 92521

PEER, LARRY HOWARD, b Ogden, Utah, Jan 2, 42; m 67; c 5. COMPARATIVE LITERATURE. *Educ:* Brigham Young Univ, BA, 63, MA, 65; Univ Md, PhD(comp lit), 69. *Prof Exp:* Instr Ger, Univ Md, 67-68; from asst prof to assoc prof comp lit, Univ Ga, 68-75, acting head dept, 73-74; assoc prof, 75-78, dir hon prog, 77-78, chmn dept 78-81, PROF COMP LIT, BRIGHAM YOUNG UNIV, 78- *Concurrent Pos:* Pres, Western Regional Hon Coun, 78-80. *Mem:* Int Comp Lit Asn; Am Comp Lit Asn; MLA; Am Soc Aesthet. *Res:* Literary theory; Romanticism. *Publ:* Auth, Pushkin and Goethe again: Lensky's character, Papers on Lang & Lit, summer 69; Schlegel, Christianity and history: Manzoni's theory of the novel, Comp Lit Studies, fall 62; Friedrich Schelegel's Theory of the Novel, Colloquia Germanica, 76. *Mailing Add:* Dept of Comp Lit Brighan Young Univ Provo UT 84602

PEISCHL, MARGARET THERESA, b Pottsville, Pa, Feb 5, 33. GERMAN LANGUAGE AND LITERATURE. *Educ:* Pa State Univ, BA, 55; Univ Southern Calif, MA, 74, PhD(Ger), 81. *Prof Exp:* Head, English Dept, John Burroughs Jr High Sch, 67-71; instr Ger, El Camino Col, 72-80; asst prof, Old Dominion Univ, 80-81; ASST PROF GER, VA COMMONWEALTH UNIV, 81- *Mem:* MLA; Am Asn Teacher Ger; Theodor-Storm Soc. *Res:* Theodor Storm; 19th century Novella German literature. *Publ:* Auth, Das Damonische im Werk Theodor Storms, Peter Lang, Verlag, Ger, 82. *Mailing Add:* 666 Elgin Terrace Richmond VA 23225

PELL, CARROLL LEE, b Wesson, Miss, Feb 15, 06; m 35; c 2. MODERN LANGUAGES. *Educ:* Miss Col, AB, 27; Peabody Col, AM, 33; Univ Wis, PhD, 49. *Prof Exp:* Prin sec schs, Miss, 27-32; instr mod lang, Western Ky Univ, 32-33; head dept, Oak Ridge Mil Inst, 33-37; acting head dept Span, La Col, 37-38; prof French & Ger, Ouachita Baptist Univ, 38-39; prof foreign lang & head dept, Union Univ, Tenn, 39-46; asst prof mod lang, Miss State Univ, 46-49; prof, Univ Southern Miss, 49-51; assoc prof & acting chmn dept foreign lang, Tex A&I Univ, 51-52; prof mod lang & chmn dept, Southern Ark Univ, 52-56; prof, Furman Univ, 56-59; prof mod lang, La Col, 59-61; prof, 61-73, EMER PROF MOD LANG, MEMPHIS STATE UNIV, 73- *Mem:* MLA; Am Asn Teachers Fr; SCent Mod Lang Asn. *Res:* Classical French literature; modern French and Spanish literature. *Publ:* Auth, The Literary Ideas of Friedrich-Melchior Grimm, Univ Wis, 51; Grimm and the Drame of Diderot, 54 & The hegemony of French culture in the eighteenth century, 64, SCent Mod Lang J; Rousseau's religious ideas in la Profession de Foi du Vicaire Savoyard, Tenn Philol Asn, 66; coauth, Bilingual text: French after Spanish and/or Spanish after French, 80. *Mailing Add:* 3567 Oakley Ave Memphis TN 38111

PELLEGRINI, ANTHONY LOUIS, b July 20, 21; m 50; c 4. ROMANCE LANGUAGES & LITERATURE. *Educ:* Harvard Univ, AB, 43, MA, 47, PhD(Romance lang & lit), 52. *Prof Exp:* Instr French, Ital & Ital lit, Harvard Univ, 52-55; asst prof, Tufts Univ, 55-56; asst prof, Ital lang & lit, Vassar Col, 56-62; assoc prof, 62-66, chmn dept, 64-67, PROF ROMANCE LANG & LIT, STATE UNIV NY, BINGHAMTON, 66-, CHMN DEPT, 81- *Concurrent Pos:* Ed, Dante Studies, 66-; State Univ NY grant-in-aid, 68-70, 73-74. *Mem:* MLA; Am Asn Teachers Ital; Renaissance Soc Am; Dante Soc Am; Mediaeval Acad Am. *Res:* Italian literature. *Publ:* Coauth, Critical Study Guide to Dante's Divine Comedy, Littlefield, 68; auth, American Dante bibliographies, Dante Studies, 54-; The commiato of Dante's Sestina, Mod Lang Notes; co-ed, Dante, Petrarch and Others: Studies in the Italian Trecento Dedicated to Charles S Singleton, MRTS, State Univ NY, 82. *Mailing Add:* Dept of Romance Lang & Lit State Univ of NY Binghamton NY 13901

PELLETIER, FRANCIS JEFFRY, Philosophy, Linguistics. See Vol IV

PELLI, MOSHE, b Haifa, Israel, May 19, 36; m 61; c 2. HEBREW LITERATURE & LANGUAGE. *Educ:* NY Univ, BS, 61; Dropsie Univ, PhD(Hebrew lit), 67. *Prof Exp:* Ed, Niv, Hebrew Lang & Cult Asn, 57-66; asst prof Hebrew lit, Univ Tex, Austin, 67-71, coordr Hebrew study prog, 69; sr lectr Hebrew lit, Univ of the Negev, Israel, 71-74; assoc prof hebrew lit, Cornell Univ, 74-78, Hebrew Lang prog, 75-77, grad field rep, 75-77; ASSOC PROF MOD HEBREW LIT, YESHIVA UNIV, NY, 78- *Concurrent Pos:* Ed, Lamishpaha, 64-66; vis lectr Jewish studies, Rice Univ, spring 70 & 71; vis sr lectr Hebrew lit, Hebrew Univ Jerusalem, 71-72; vis prof Middle Eastern studies, Melbourne Univ, Australia, summer, 77 & 78; Am Coun Learned Soc travel grant, 77; Oxford Ctr for Postgrad Hebrew Studies res fel, 79; vis prof Hebrew lang & lit, Brooklyn Col, 79 & 80. *Honors & Awards:* Short Story Prize, Haboker, Daily, Tel Aviv, 55. *Mem:* Asn Jewish Studies; World Union Jewish Studies; Nat Asn Professors Hebrew; Am Acad Jewish Res; Am Soc 18th Century Studies. *Res:* The Hebrew Enlightenment: literature and religious, social and cultural thought; contemporary Hebrew literature; Holocaust literature. *Publ:* Auth, Moses Mendelssohn: Bonds of Tradition, Alef, Tel Aviv, 72; Introduction to Modern Hebrew Literature in 18th and 19th Centuries, Hebrew Univ, Akademon, Jersualem, 72; Isaac Euchel: Tradition and change in the first generation Haskalah, J Jewish Studies, 75 & 76; Saul Berlin's Ktav Yosher: The beginning of satire in modern Hebrew literature, 75 & 77 & The beginning of the epistolary genre in Hebrew Enlightenment literature in Germany: The affinity between lettres persanes and Igrot Meshulam, 79, Leo Baeck Inst Yearbook; The Age of Haskalah-Studies in Hebrew Literature of the Englightenment in Germany, E J Brill, Leiden, 79. *Mailing Add:* 134 Graham Rd 1-B4 Ithaca NY 14850

PELTERS, WILM ALBERT, b Bersenbrück, Ger, Feb 7, 37. GERMAN LANGUAGE & LITERATURE. *Educ:* Syracuse Univ, MA, 63, PhD(Ger), 65. *Prof Exp:* Assoc Ger, Syracuse Univ, 62-65; asst prof, Univ Calif, Irvine, 65-70; chmn dept & grad coordr, 71-74, PROF GER, CALIF STATE UNIV, LONG BEACH, 72- *Concurrent Pos:* Resident dir, Calif State Univ Int Prog, Heidelberg Univ, 77-78. *Mem:* Am Asn Teachers Ger; MLA; AAUP; Lessing Soc Am. *Res:* Eighteenth century literature and philosophy; poetry; German culture and civilization. *Publ:* Auth, Lessings Standort; Sinndeutung der Geschichte als Kern seines Denkens, Stiehm Verlag, Heidelberg, 72; co-ed, Wahrheit und Sprache: Festschrift für Bert Nagel, Göppingen, 72; auth, Zu Lessings Liedern, In: Wahrheit und Sprache, Göppingen, 72; Anti-candide oder die Apotheose der Vorsehung, In: Lessing in Neutiger Sicht, Jacobi-Verlag, 76. *Mailing Add:* Dept of Ger Russ & Classics Calif State Univ Long Beach CA 90840

PENA, ERVIE, b Estancia, NMex, Mar 22, 34. SPANISH LITERATURE & LINGUISTICS. *Educ:* Univ of the Americas, Mexico City, BA, 59; Univ Southern Calif, MA, 63, PhD(Span), 69. *Prof Exp:* Teaching asst Span, Univ Southern Calif, 59-63; assoc prof, 63-80, PROF SPAN, CALIF STATE UNIV, FULLERTON, 80- *Concurrent Pos:* Comt mem, Comn of Calif, 64-78; Fulbright scholar Span, 65-66; curric writer Span-English, Bilingual Prog, Sweetwater High Sch, Chula Vista, 74-75. *Mem:* Am Asn Teachers Span & Port; MLA. *Res:* Spanish Golden Age literature: the theater; children's literature of the Hispanic world; linguistics: Spanish-English bilingual/biculturalism. *Publ:* Coauth, Five Third Grade Supplementary Readers, Pro Frontier, Title VII Sweetwater High Sch, Chula Vista, Calif, 75; auth, El Periquito Tisu: Literatura infantil, Prof Frontier, Title VII Bilingual Educ Proj, 75; Miguel de Barrois' El Espanol de Oran: A critical edition of the play, Casa Ed: El Dorado, Bogota, Colombia, 78. *Mailing Add:* Dept of Foreign Lang & Lit Calif State Univ Fullerton CA 92634

PENCE, ELLSWORTH DEAN, b Carbon Hill, Ohio, Mar 18, 38. FRENCH LANGUAGE & LITERATURE, LATIN. *Educ:* Ohio Univ, BA, 59; Univ Wis, MA, 64, PhD(French), 71. *Prof Exp:* Teacher French & English, Bettsville High Sch, Ohio, 59-60; instr French, Univ Wis, Ctr-Manitowoc, 67-68; asst prof, Univ Wis, Manitowoc & Green Bay, 68-73; ASSOC PROF FRENCH, HUMBOLDT STATE UNIV, 73- *Concurrent Pos:* Resident dir, Int Prog, Aix-en-Provence, France, 82-83. *Mem:* Am Asn Teachers French. *Res:* French romantic fiction; French prose poem; 19th century French novel. *Mailing Add:* Dept of Foreign Lang Humboldt State Univ Arcata CA 95521

PENCHOEN, THOMAS G, b Auburn, NY, Aug 20, 34; m 63; c 2. LINGUISTICS, BERBER LANGUAGE. *Educ:* Darthmouth Col, BA, 56; Univ Paris, Lic, 63, PhD(ling, Berber), 67. *Prof Exp:* ASSOC PROF BERBER, UNIV CALIF, LOS ANGELES, 67- *Concurrent Pos:* Univ Calif, Los Angeles, Near Eastern Ctr fel, 66-67. *Res:* Berber syntax. *Publ:* Auth, Tamazight of the Ayt Ndhir, Undena, 73; Etude syntaxique d'un parler berbere, Studi Magrebini V, 73. *Mailing Add:* Dept of Near Eastern Lang Univ of Calif Los Angeles CA 90024

PENDERGAST, JOSEPH S, b Chicago, Ill, Nov 26, 23. CLASSICAL PHILOLOGY. *Educ:* St Louis Univ, AB, 46, PhL, 48, AM, 50; West Baden Col, STL, 55; Univ Ill, PhD, 60. *Prof Exp:* Asst prof class lang, Loyla Univ, Ill, 59-64; from asst dean to dean col arts & sci, 60-64; assoc prof class lang, Milford Col, Xavier Univ, Ohio, 64-69, dean Milford Col, 56-69; chmn dept, PROF CLASS STUDIES, LOYOLA UNIV CHICAGO, 69- *Concurrent Pos:* Examiner & consult, NCent Asn Cols & Sec Schs, 61- *Mem:* Am Philol Asn; Archaeol Inst Am. *Res:* Philosophy of history; Tacitus; Pompeius Trogus. *Mailing Add:* Dept of Class Studies Loyola Univ Chicago IL 60626

PENELLA, ROBERT JOSEPH, b Boston, Mass, Feb 16, 47; m 68; c 1. CLASSICS, ROMAN HISTORY. *Educ:* Boston Col, AB, 67; Harvard Univ, MA, 69, PhD(classics), 71. *Prof Exp:* Asst prof, 71-78, chmn dept, 77-83, ASSOC PROF CLASSICS, FORDHAM UNIV, 78- *Mem:* Am Philol Asn; Asn Ancient Historians. *Res:* Imperial Greek prose; Imperial Roman history; Roman historiography. *Publ:* Auth, The Letters of Apollonius of Tyana, Mnemosyne Supplements, 56, E J Brill, 79; A Lowly Born Historian of the Late Roman Empire: Some Observations on Aurelius Victor and His De caesaribus, Thought, 80; Caracalla and his Mother in the Historia Augusta, Historia, 80; An Overlooked Vicar of Asia of the Fourth Century, Byzantion, 81. *Mailing Add:* Dept of Classics Fordham Univ Bronx NY 10458

PENELOPE, JULIA, b Miami, Fla, June 19, 41. ENGLISH, LINGUISTICS. *Educ:* City Col New York, BA, 66; Univ Tex, Austin, PhD(English ling), 71. *Prof Exp:* Res asst English lang, Ling Res Ctr, Univ Tex, Austin, 66-67, teaching asst English compos, 67-68; from instr to asst prof English & ling, Univ Ga, 68-74; asst prof English, Univ SDak, 76; asst prof, 76-77, ASSOC PROF ENGLISH, UNIV NEBR-LINCOLN, 77- *Concurrent Pos:* Nat Endowment for Humanities sr summer res fel, 80; Maude Hammond Fling res fel, 81. *Mem:* NCTE; MLA; Ling Asn Can & US. *Res:* Stylistics; social dialects; semantics. *Publ:* auth, Passive motivation, Found Lang, 75; Stylistics of belief, Teaching about Doublespeak, 76; co-ed, Sexism and Language, NCTE, 77; auth, Sexist grammar, Col English, 78; coauth, Forced inference: uses & abuses of the passive, Papers Ling, 78; Target structures and rule conspiracies: Syntactic exploitation, Forum Linguisticum, 79; Correctness, appropriateness, and the uses of English, Col English, 79; Linguistic problems with patriarchal reconstructions of Indo-European Cultures: A little more than kin, A little less than kind, Women's Studies Int Quart, 80. *Mailing Add:* Dept of English Univ of Nebr Lincoln NE 68588

PENOT, ANDREE, b St Nazaire, France, Mar 6, 23; US citizen. ROMANCE LANGUAGES. *Educ:* Hunter Col, BA, 43; Fordham Univ, MA, 44; Columbia Univ, PhD(French), 53. *Prof Exp:* Instr French, Col New Rochelle, 44-46; from instr to asst prof, Mt St Vincent Col, 46-55; instr, City Col NY, 55-56; instr, Hunter Col High Sch, 56-65; ASSOC PROF FRENCH, STATE UNIV NY COL FREDONIA, 65- *Mem:* MLA; Soc Fr Prof Am; Am Asn Teachers Fr. *Res:* Contemporary French literature; 18th century, especially Voltaire. *Mailing Add:* Dept of Mod Foreign Lang State Univ of NY Col Fredonia NY 14063

PENOT, DOMINIQUE MARIE, b Ales, France, Jan 26, 25; m 47; c 4. ROMANCE PHILOLOGY, FRENCH LITERATURE. *Educ:* Univ Aix Marseille, Lic Ger, 53; Yale Univ, PhD(Romance philol), 64. *Prof Exp:* Lectr French, McGill Univ, 55-56; instr, Yale Univ, 57-62; from instr to asst prof, Univ Okla, 62-68; assoc prof mod lang & chmn dept, Wright State Univ, 68-71; chmn dept mod lang, 71-76, PROF ROMANCE LANG, UNIV ALA, HUNTSVILLE, 71- *Mem:* Am Asn Teachers Fr; MLA. *Res:* French medieval literature. *Publ:* Auth, Psychology of characters in Robbe-Grillet's Jalousie, Bks Abroad, winter 66. *Mailing Add:* Dept of Mod Lang Univ of Ala Huntsville AL 35802

PENUEL, ARNOLD MCCOY, b Old Hickory, Tenn, Feb 9, 36; m 65; c 3. SPANISH LANGUAGE & LITERATURE. *Educ:* Univ Tenn, Knoxville, BA, 58; Am Univ, MA, 63; Univ Ill, Urbana, PhD(Span), 68. *Prof Exp:* Asst prof Span, Univ Ga, 68-72; assoc prof, 72-82, PROF SPAN, CENTENARY COL, LA, 82-, CHMN, DEPT FOREIGN LANG, 78- *Concurrent Pos:* Centenary Col Alumni Asn res grant, 74. *Mem:* Am Asn Teachers Span & Port; MLA; SCent Mod Lang Asn. *Res:* Nineteenth century Spanish novel; 20th century Spanish novel; 20th century Spanish poetry. *Publ:* Auth, The ambiguity of Orozco's virtue in Galdos' La incognita and Realidad, 9/70 & Galdos, Freud, and humanistic psychology, 72, Hisp; Charity in the Novels of Galdos, Univ Ga, 72; The influence of Galdos' El amigo Manso on Dolores Medio's El diario de una maestra, Rev Estudios Hisp, 7/73; Some esthetic implications of Galdos' El Amigo Manso, 74 & The problem of ambiguity in Galdos' Dona Perfecta, 76, Anales Galdosianos; Yet another view of Galdos's Miau, Rev Estudios Hisp, 12/78; Narcissism in Galdos's Dona Perfecton, Hispania, 79. *Mailing Add:* Dept of Foreign Lang Centenary Col of La Shreveport LA 71104

PENUELAS, MARCELINO C, b Spain, Apr 20, 16; US citizen; m 50; c 1. SPANISH. *Educ:* Inst Valencia, Spain, BA, 34; Univ Valencia, ME, 40, MA, 45; Univ Madrid, PhD, 49. *Prof Exp:* From asst prof to assoc prof Span, Univ Denver, 48-63; PROF ROMANCE LANG, UNIV WASH, 63-, CHMN DEPT, 72- *Concurrent Pos:* Vis prof, Stanford Univ, 58-59 & Univ Wash, 63-64; mem comt, Advan Placement Exam in Span, Col Entrance Exam Bd, 72. *Mem:* Am Asn Teachers Span & Port; MLA. *Res:* History and culture of the American Southwest; literature of the 18th century in Spain; contemporary Spanish literature. *Publ:* Auth, Mr Clark no toma Coca-Cola, Gior, Valencia, Spain, 60; Lo espanol en el Suroeste de Estados Unidos, Cult Hisp, Madrid, Spain, 63; Mito Literatura y Realidad, Gredos, Madrid, 65; Jacinto Benavente, Twayne, 68; Introduccion Literatura Espanola, McGraw-Hill, 69; Conversaciones con Ramon Sender, M Espanol, Madrid, 70; La obra narrativa de R J Sender, 71 & Ramon Sender Paginas escogidas, 72, Gredos, Madrid. *Mailing Add:* Dept of Romance Lang Univ of Wash Seattle WA 98105

PENZL, HERBERT, b Neufelden, Austria, Sept 2, 10; m 50. LINGUISTICS. *Educ:* Univ Vienna, PhD, 35. *Prof Exp:* Ed asst, Ling Atlas of US, Brown Univ, 32-34; asst prof Ger, Rockford Col, 36-38; assoc, Univ Ill, 38-39, asst prof, 39-49; assoc prof, Univ Mich, 50-53, prof, 53-63; PROF GER PHILOL, UNIV CALIF, BERKELEY, 63- *Concurrent Pos:* Smith-Mundt vis prof, Kabul Univ, Afghanistan, 58-59; John S Guggenheim Mem Found fel, 67; vis prof, Univ Vienna, Austria, 80 & Univ Regensburg, 81. *Honors & Awards:* Austrian Cross of Honour Sci & Arts, 80; Berkeley Citation, 80. *Mem:* Am Asn Teachers Ger; MLA; Ling Soc Am; Am Dialect Soc; Am Name Soc. *Res:* German, Germanic and general linguistics. *Publ:* Auth, A Grammar of Pashto: A Descriptive Study of the Dialect of Kandahar, Afghanistan, Am Coun Learned Soc, 55; A Reader of Pashto, Univ Mich, 65; Geschichtliche deutsche Lautlehre, 69 & Lautsystem und Lautwandel in den althochdeutschen Dialekten, 71, Max Hueber, Munich; Methoden der germanischen Linguistik, 72 & contribr, Toward a Grammar of Proto-Germanic, 72, Max Niemeyer, Tübingen; coauth, Probleme der historischen Phonologie, Wiesbaden, Steiner Verlag, 74; auth, Vom Urgermanischen zum Neuhochdeutscheneine historische Phonologie, Erich Schmidt Verlag, Berlin, 75; Johann Christian Gottscheds Deutsche Sprachkunst, de Gruyter, Berlin, 80; Frühneuhochdeutsch: Eine Einführung in die Sprache, P Lang Verlag, Bern, 82. *Mailing Add:* Dept of Ger Univ of Calif Berkeley CA 94720

PEPPARD, VICTOR EDWIN, b Orange, NJ, Nov 4, 44; m 68; c 1. RUSSIAN LANGUAGE & LITERATURE. *Educ:* Brown Univ, BA, 66, MA, 68; Univ Mich, PhD(Slavic), 74. *Prof Exp:* Lectr Russ, Univ New SWales, 73-74; asst prof, 75-80, ASSOC PROF RUSS, UNIV S FLA, 80- *Mem:* Am Asn Teachers Slavic & EEurop Lang; Am Coun Teachers Russ. *Res:* Russian literature of the 1920's; Russian childrens literature; 19th and 20th century Russian literature. *Publ:* Auth, Brzenowski and surrealism, Polish Rev, autumn 71; Nikolaj N Nikitin and ornamental prose, Melbourne Slavonic Studies, 73; Russian children's literature and the classroom, Russ Lang J, fall 77; ed & translr, Night and Other Stories, Strathcona, 78. *Mailing Add:* 319 Sleepy Hollow Ave Temple Terrace FL 33617

PERADOTTO, JOHN JOSEPH, b Ottawa, Ill, May 11, 33; m 59; c 4. GREEK & LATIN LANGUAGES & LITERATURE. *Educ:* St Louis Univ, AB, 57, MA, 58; Northwestern Univ, PhD(Greek & Latin), 63. *Prof Exp:* Instr Greek, Latin & English, Western Wash State Col, 60-61; from instr to asst prof Greek & Latin, Georgetown Univ, 61-66; from asst prof to assoc prof classics, State Univ NY Buffalo, 66-73; prof & chmn dept, Univ Tex, Austin, 73-74; chmn dept, 74-77, PROF CLASSICS, STATE UNIV NY BUFFALO, 74-, DEAN, 78- *Concurrent Pos:* Nat Endowment for Humanities fel, Ctr Hellenic Studies, 72-73; ed-in-chief, Arethusa, 75- *Honors & Awards:* Chancellor's Award for Excellence in Teaching, State Univ NY, 75. *Mem:* Am Philol Asn; Class Asn Atlantic States. *Res:* Greek literature; Greek mythology and religion; narrative analysis. *Publ:* Auth, The omen of the eagles and the ethos of Agamemnon, Phoenix, 69; Classical Mythology, Am Philol Asn, 73; Odyssey 8 564-671: Verisimilitude, narrative analysis, and bricolage, Tex Studies Lit & Lang, 74; co-ed, Population Policy in Plato and Aristotle, 75; ed, Classical Literature and Contemporary Literary Theory, 77, Women in the Ancient World, 78, co-ed, Virgil 2000 Years, 81 & Semiotics and Classical Studies, 83, Arethusa. *Mailing Add:* Dept of Classics State Univ of NY Buffalo NY 14260

PERCAS DE PONSETI, HELENA, b Valencia, Spain, Jan 17, 21; nat US; m 61. MODERN FOREIGN LANGUAGES & LITERATURES. *Educ:* Inst Maintenon, Paris, BA, 39; Barnard Col, BA, 42; Inst World Affairs, dipl, 42; Columbia Univ, MA, 43, PhD, 51. *Prof Exp:* Teacher, hist lang & cult, Barnard Col, 42-43; instr, Russell Sage Col, 43-45; instr, Queen's Col, NY, 46-48; from asst prof to assoc prof, 48-51, prof, 51-56, chmn dept mod foreign lang, 56-60, James Morton Roberts prof, 61-62, RICHARDS PROF LANG, GRINNELL COL, 63- *Concurrent Pos:* Mem, Hisp Int US; mem, Inst Hisp Cult; ed staff, Rev Iberoam, 59-; assoc ed, Cervantes, 78- *Honors & Awards:* Int Scholarship Award, Grinnell Col. *Mem:* Am Asn Teachers Span & Port; MLA; Inst Int Lit Iberoamericana; Cervantes Soc Am. *Res:* Latin American literature; Spanish and Golden Age literature; Hispanic culture. *Publ:* Auth, La poesia femenina argentina, 1810-1950, Inst Cult Hisp, Madrid, 58; La cueva de Montesinos, Rev Hisp Mod, 2/68; El concepto artistico de Cervantes, Gredos, Madrid, 75. *Mailing Add:* Dept of Span Grinnell Col Grinnell IA 50112

PERCIVAL, WALTER KEITH, b Leeds, Eng, Feb 24, 30; m 68. LINGUISTICS. *Educ:* Leeds Univ, BA, 51; Yale Univ, MA, 59, PhD(ling), 64. *Prof Exp:* Lectr ling, Brandeis Univ, 62-63; from asst prof to assoc prof, Univ Wis-Milwaukee, 64-69, chmn dept, 64-69; assoc prof, 69-74, PROF LING, UNIV KANS, 74- *Concurrent Pos:* Am Philos Soc res grant, 72- *Mem:* Ling Soc Am; Renaissance Soc Am; Mediaeval Acad Am; Soc Ling Europaea; Int Soc Hist Rhetoric. *Res:* History of linguistics; Austronesian languages; Medieval and Renaissance grammar, rhetoric and logic. *Publ:* Auth, On the Non-Existence of Cartesian Linguistics, In: Cartesian Studies, 72; contribr, The Grammatical Tradition and the Rise of the Vernaculars, In: Current Trends in Linguistics, 75; Deep and Surface Structure Concepts in Syntactic Theory, In: History of Linguistic Thought and Contemporary Linguistics, 76; auth, The Applicability of Kuhn's Paradigms to the History of Linguistics, Language, 76; The Artis Grammaticae Opusculum of Bartolomeo Sulmonese, Renaissance Quart, 78; Ferdinand de Saussure and the History of Semiotics, In: Semiotic Themes, 81; A Grammar of the Urbanised Toba-Batak of Medan, Canberra, The Australian Nat Univ, 81; The Saussurean Paradigm: Fact or Fantasy? Semiotica, 81. *Mailing Add:* Dept of Ling Univ of Kans Lawrence KS 66045

PERELLA, NICOLAS J, b Boston, Mass, Sept 7, 27; m 57. ROMANCE LANGUAGES & LITERATURE, COMPARATIVE LITERATURE. *Educ:* Suffolk Univ, BA, 52; Harvard Univ, PhD, 57. *Prof Exp:* From instr to assoc prof, 57-68, chmn dept, 69-73, PROF ITAL, UNIV CALIF, BERKELEY, 68- *Concurrent Pos:* Guggenheim fel, 64. *Honors & Awards:* Howard R Marraro Prize, MLA, 78 & 80. *Mem:* MLA; Am Asn Teachers Ital; Dante Soc. *Res:* Italian; comparative literature; history of ideas. *Publ:* Auth, Fate, blindness and illusion in the Pastor Fido, Romanic Rev, 12/58; The world of Boccaccio's Filocolo, PMLA, 9/61; The Kiss-Sacred and Profane, 69 & Night and the Sublime in Giacomo Leopardi, 70, Univ Calif; The Critical Fortune of Battista Guarini's Pastor Fido, Leo S Olschki, Florence, 73; Heroic virtue and love in the Pastor Fido, Att del-l'Instituto Veneto 1973-1974, 74; Midday in Italian Literature, Princeton Univ, 79. *Mailing Add:* Dept of Ital Univ of Calif Berkeley CA 94720

PEREYRA-SUAREZ, ESTHER, b Montevideo, Uruguay, Sept 19, 25; US citizen. ROMANCE LANGUAGES. *Educ:* Col Adventista, Chile, BA, 52; Northwestern Univ, MA, 59; Stanford Univ, PhD(Span), 65. *Prof Exp:* Instr French, Alliance Fr Paysandu & Liceo Departamental Paysandu, 47-48; instr Span & French, Col Adventista Chile, 49-53; instr, Broadview Acad, 54-58; PROF FOREIGN LANG, SAN JOSE STATE UNIV, 59- *Concurrent Pos:* Orgn Am States res grant, Buenos Aires, 68-69; asst prof Span-Am lit, Hunter Col, 70-72; contribr ed poetry, Handbook of Latin Am Studies, Vol 40, 77- *Mem:* Am Asn Teachers Span & Port. *Res:* Contemporary Latin-American theatre; contemporary Latin American novel, short story and essay. *Publ:* Auth, La literatura Hispano Americana en 1972, In: Libro del ano 1973, W M Jackson, Mex, 73; Jose Enrique Rodo y la selecion en la democracia, Hisp, 5/75; La dificil convivencia: Modernismo y democracia en la america latina a principios delsiglo XX, Los Ensayistas, 10/77. *Mailing Add:* Dept of Foreign Lang San Jose State Univ San Jose CA 95192

PEREZ, AQUILINO, b Canton, Ohio, May 22, 23; m 51; c 4. SPANISH. *Educ:* Akron Univ, BA, 49; Kent State Univ, ME, 58, MA, 64; Univ Madrid, PhD(Span), 65. *Prof Exp:* From instr to asst prof, 65-71, ASSOC PROF SPAN, KENT STATE UNIV, 71- *Mem:* Am Asn Teachers Span & Port. *Res:* Modernism; medieval literature. *Mailing Add:* Dept of Romance Lang & Classics Kent State Univ Kent OH 44242

PEREZ, CARLOS ALBERTO, b Bolivar, Arg, Jan 2, 29; US citizen. ROMANCE LANGUAGES. *Educ:* Univ Buenos Aires, Profesor en Letras, 55; Ohio State Univ, PhD(Romance lang), 61. *Prof Exp:* Asst prof Span, Univ Conn, 61-65; assoc prof, Western Reserve Univ, 65-66; assoc prof, Univ Conn, 66-80. *Mem:* MLA: Am Asn Teachers Span & Port. *Res:* Golden Age poetry and drama; modern poetry. *Publ:* Auth, Juegos de palabras y formas de engano en la poesia de D Luis de Gongora, 1/64, 5/64 & Verosimilitud psicologica de El condenado por desconfiado, 5/66; Hispanofila; Rafael Albert: So Alberti: Sobre los tontos, Rev Hisp Mod, 7-10/66. *Mailing Add:* 74-D Baxter Rd Mansfield CT 06250

PEREZ, LOUIS CELESTINO, b De Pue, Ill, Feb 7, 23; m 50; c 3. ROMANCE LANGUAGES. *Educ:* Brooklyn Col, BA, 50; Univ Mich, MA, 51, PhD(Span), 57. *Prof Exp:* From instr to assoc prof, Williams Col, 55-67, PROF SPAN, PA STATE UNIV, 67- *Mem:* MLA; Am Asn Teachers Span & Port; Cervantes Soc Am. *Res:* Spanish Siglo de Oro, especially Comedia, Cervantes, Picaresca. *Publ:* Coauth, Afirmaciones de Lope de Vega sobre preceptiva dramatica a base de cien comedias, Consejo Super Invest Cient, Madrid, 61; ed, El tunel, Macmillan, 65; auth, Preceptiva dramatica en El gran teatro del mundo, Hispanofila, 5/67; auth, El telar de Cervantes, In: Filologia y critica hispanica, Homenaje al Prof Federico Sanchez Escribano, Ed Alcala, Madrid, 69; co-ed, Ancha es Castilla, Van Nostrand Reinhold, 71; auth, La fabula de Icaro y El perro del hortelano, In: Estudios literarios de hispanistas norteamericanos dedicados a Helmut Hatzfeld con motivo de su 80 anniversario, Ed Hispam, Barcelona, 74; auth & ed, La Apologia en defensa de las comedias que se representan en Espana de Francisco Ortiz, Estudios de Hispanofila, Chapel Hill, NC, 77; coauth & ed, Juan de la Cueva's Los Inventores de las Cosas: A critical edition and study, Pa State Univ Press, 80. *Mailing Add:* Dept of Span Ital & Port Pa State Univ University Park PA 16802

PEREZ, LUIS A, b Santa Rosa de Osos, Colombia, Sept 28, 22; m 58; c 2. SPANISH. *Educ:* Pontif Univ Javeriana, Colombia, DLett(philos & lett), 54. *Prof Exp:* Instr Span lit, Bolivariana Univ, Colombia, 60-62, hist, Univ Antioquia, 60-64 & 65-66, Span, San Jose State Col, 66-67; asst prof, 67-75, PROF SPAN, UNIV SASK, 75- *Mem:* MLA; Can Asn Hispanist; Semiotic Soc Am; Can Ling Asn; Soc Espanola Ling. *Res:* Lucio Marineo Siculo; Grammatices Institutionibus Critical edition. *Publ:* Auth, Notas Sobre la Filosofia de Miguel Antonio Caro, Ed Minerva, Bogota, 54; Tres Antioquenos alumnos de la Javeriana de 1749 a 1755, Filos y Letras Univ Bolivariana, 3/60; Actualidad de el Quijote, Arco, 11/62; Bases filosoficas y sociologicas de el Memorial de Agravios, Univ Antioquia, 8/67; La educacion del hombre americano, Inter-Am Reb Bibliog, 10-12/74; Ulises en Sabanilla, Magisterio Espanol, Madrid, 78; Terminologia demonologica de Miguel Angel Asturias, Presses Univ de Laval, 76. *Mailing Add:* 2401 York Ave Saskatoon SK S7J 1J4 Can

PEREZ, ROSA PERELMUTER, b Havana, Cuba, Feb 17, 48; US citizen; m 73; c 1. COLONIAL SPANISH AMERICAN LITERATURE. *Educ:* Univ Mass, Boston, BA, 70; Univ Miami, MA, 72; Univ Mich, PhD(Span), 80. *Prof Exp:* Teaching asst Span, Univ Miami, 70-72; instr, Miami-Dade Community Col, 72-73; teaching asst, Univ Mich, 73-78; vis instr, 78-79, instr, 79, ASST PROF SPAN, UNIV NC, CHAPEL HILL, 80- *Mem:* MLA; Am Asn Teachers Span & Port; SAtlantic Mod Lang Asn. *Res:* Colonial Spanish American literature; Golden Age poetry; contemporary Spanish American narrative. *Publ:* Auth, The Rogue as trickster in Guzman de Alfarache, Hispania, 76; El Diablo Mundo y Calderon, Revista de Estudios Hispanicos, 78; Hermetismo y expansion en dos novelas de Gabriel Miro, Hispanofila, 80; Los cultismos herrerianos en el Primero Sueno de Sor Juana Ines de la Cruz, Bull Hispanique, 82; Noche intelectual: La oscuridad idiomatica en el Primero sueno, Universidad Nacional Autonoma de Mexico, 82; Los cultismos no-gongorinos en el Primero sueno, Nueva Revista de Filologia Hispanica, 82; La estructura retorica de la Respuesta a Sor Filotea, Hisp Rev (in press); La hiperbasis en el Primero sueno, Revista Iberoamericana (in press). *Mailing Add:* 103 Cynthia Dr Chapel Hill NC 27514

PEREZ-FIRMAT, GUSTAVO, b Habana, Cuba, Mar 7, 49; US citizen; m 73; c 1. MODERN HISPANIC LITERATURE. *Educ:* Univ Miami, BA, 72, MA, 73; Univ Mich, PhD(comp lit), 79. *Prof Exp:* Teaching asst Span, Univ Mich, 73-77; instr, 78-79, ASST PROF ROMANCE LANG, DUKE UNIV, 79- *Concurrent Pos:* Am Coun Learned Soc fel, 81; Mellon Post-Doctoral fel, 81-82. *Mem:* MLA; Am Asn Teachers Span & Port; SAtlantic Mod Lang Asn. *Res:* Modern Spanish and Spanish American literature; theory of criticism. *Publ:* Auth, Relectura de Trilce 5, Dispositio, 77; The structure of El fulgor y la sangre, 77 & Cosmology and the poem: Damaso Alonso's Sueno de las dos ciervas, 78, Hisp Rev; Apuntes para un modelo de la intertextualidad en literatura, Romanic Rev, 78; The novel as genres, Genre, 79; Locura y muerte de Nadie: Two Novels by Jarnes, Romanic Rev, 81; Repetition and excess in Tiempo de silencio, Publ Mod Lang Asn, 81; Idle Fictions, The Vanguard Novel in Spain and Spanish America, Duke Univ Press, 82. *Mailing Add:* Dept Romance Lang Duke Univ Durham NC 27706

PEREZ-SOLER, VINCENTE, b Valencia, Spain, Apr 21, 24; m 51; c 1. LITERATURE OF THE MIDDLE AGE. *Educ:* Univ Valencia, Lic hist & lit, 55, PhD, 58. *Prof Exp:* Titular prof lit, Real Col Escuelas Pias, Valencia, 55-64; vis prof, Univ San Francisco, 64-65, asst prof, 65-66; asst prof, 66-68, ASSOC PROF LIT, UNIV WINDSOR, 68- *Publ:* Auth, Construcciones con verbos de modo en Espanol, Hispania, 5/66. *Mailing Add:* Dept of Hisp & Ital Studies Univ of Windsor Windsor ON N9B 3P4 Can

PEREZ-STANSFIELD, MARIA PILAR, b Valencia, Spain, Feb 26, 45; US citizen; m 67; c 1. SPANISH LITERATURE. *Educ:* Fla State Univ, BA, 71; Univ Colo, Boulder, MA, 73, PhD(Span lit), 79. *Prof Exp:* Instr Span, Univ Colo, Boulder, 71-77 & lectr Chicano studies, 78-81; LECTR SPAN, RUTGERS UNIV, 81- *Concurrent Pos:* Co-dir, Univ Colo Study Abroad Prog, Xalapa, Veracruz, Mex, 74-75; adj asst prof Span, Drew Univ, 81; asst examiner, Col Bd Test Develop, Educ Testing Serv, 81- *Mem:* Asoc Nac Grupos Folkloricos; Rocky Mountain Mod Lang Asn. *Res:* Contemporary Spanish literature; contemporary theater; hispanic culture. *Publ:* Auth, Tres promotores del teatro espanol de vanguardia, Vida Univ, 6/79; El folklore mestizo veracruzano, Latin-Am Studies Inst, Univ Tex, 80; coauth, Tape Script for Habla espanol? & Language Laboratory Manual for Habla espanol?, Holt, Rinehart & Winston, 81; auth, El teatro espanol de posguerra: evolucion y desafia, Ed Porrua, Madrid, 82. *Mailing Add:* Dept Span & Port Rutgers Univ New Brunswick NJ 08903

PERFECKY, GEORGE A, b Piotrkow, Poland, May 27, 40; US citizen; m 64; c 2. RUSSIAN, SLAVIC PHILOLOGY. *Educ:* Univ Pa, BA, 63; Columbia Univ, MA, 66, PhD(Russ & Slavic philol), 70. *Prof Exp:* Instr, 65-68, asst prof, 68-73, ASSOC PROF RUSS, LA SALLE COL, 73- *Concurrent Pos:* Lectr Ger, Temple Univ, 66-67; teacher advan Russ, Marple Newton Sr High Sch, 73-74. *Mem:* Am Asn Teachers Slavic & East Europ Lang; Am Asn Advan Slavic Studies; MLA; Shevchenko Sci Study Am. *Res:* Eastern Slavic chronicles; literature of Old Rus'; linguistic russification in Soviet Ukraine. *Publ:* Studies on the Galician-Volynian Chronicle, The Ann Ukrainian Acad Arts & Sci in US, Vol XII, No 33-34; The Galician-Volynian Chronicle as a source of medieval German studies, Mediaeval Studies, Toronto, Vol XXXV, 324-332; The Hypatian Codex II: The Galician-Volynian Chronicle, Harvard Univ Series in Ukrainian Studies, Munich, 73; Movne vzajemozbahacennja cy rusyfikacija ukrainskoji movy, 9/76 & Termin Rus--pryklad omansjisxovosty, 4/77, Sucasnist, Munich; A note on the relationship of the Byxovec Chronicle to the Galician-Volynian Chronicle, Harvard Ukrainian Studies, 9/81; We stand today between two abysses, J Ukrainian Studies, fall 81. *Mailing Add:* 621 Garden Rd Glenside PA 19038

PERFLER, OLAF KARL, b Vienna, Austria, Nov 30, 40; m; c 2. GERMAN & AUSTRIAN LITERATURE. *Educ:* Univ Vienna, PhD(Ger lit & Philol), 67. *Prof Exp:* Instr Ger, Am Int Sch, Vienna, Austria, 65-66; asst prof, 67-70, assoc prof, 70-76, PROF GER, CALIF STATE UNIV, SACRAMENTO, 76- *Concurrent Pos:* Chmn dept Ger, classics & Russ, Calif State Univ, Sacramento, 76-79; vis prof, State Univ NY, 79-80. *Mem:* Philol Asn Pac Coast; Am Asn Teachers Ger. *Res:* German literature. *Publ:* Auth, Die Entwicklung der Lyrischen Sprachkunst bei Josef Weinheber, Selbst, Vienna, 67; Josef Weinheber, Dizionario Critico della Lett Tedesca, Torino, Italy, 72; contribr, series of articles, Ring Rund, Vienna, 70-72. *Mailing Add:* 5226 Mississippi Bar Dr Orangevale CA 95662

PERISSINOTTO, GIORGIO, b Trieste, Italy, June 13, 42; US citizen; m 68. HISPANIC LINGUISTICS. *Educ:* Syracuse Univ, BA, 65; Columbia Univ, MA, 66, PhD(Span), 71. *Prof Exp:* Instr Span, State Univ NY Stony Brook, 68-72, asst prof, 72-75; asst prof, Univ Tex, San Antonio, 75-76; ASSOC PROF SPAN, UNIV CALIF, SANTA BARBARA, 76- *Concurrent Pos:* Vis prof ling, Inst Invest Integracion Social Estado Oaxaca, 72-73. *Res:* Hispanic linguistics. *Publ:* Auth, Education reform and government intervention in Mexico, Current Hist, Vol 66, 74; Fonologia del espanol hablado en la ciudad de Mexico, Colegio Mex, 75; La Reconquista en el Poema del Cid: Una nueva lectura, Hispanofila, Vol 65, 79; A proposito de los versos 793 y 794 de las Mocedades de Rodrigo, Cult Neolatina, Vol 39, 79. *Mailing Add:* 5220 Calle Cristobal Santa Barbara CA 93111

PERKELL, CHRISTINE GODFREY, b San Francisco, Calif, Nov 23, 45; m 68; c 1. CLASSICAL PHILOLOGY. *Educ:* Wellesley Col, BA, 67; Harvard Univ, MA, 75, PhD(classics), 77. *Prof Exp:* Instr, 75-77, ASST PROF CLASSICS, DARTMOUTH COL, 77- *Mem:* Am Philol Asn; Class Asn New Eng. *Res:* Virgil; Greek comedy; Greek tragedy. *Publ:* Auth, A reading of Virgil: Georgics 4, Phoenix (in press); On Creusa, Dido, & the quality of victory in Virgil's Aeneid, Women's Studies, 8: 201-223; On the Corycian gardener of Vergil's Fourth Georgic, Trans Am Philos Asn, 111: 167-177. *Mailing Add:* Dartmouth Col Dartmouth Hall Hanover NH 03755

PERKINS, ALLAN KYLE, b Corbin, Ky, Nov 14, 47; m 78; c 1. APPLIED & THEORETICAL LINGUISTICS. *Educ:* Union Col, Ky, BA, 69; Southern Ill Univ, MA, 71; Univ Mich, PhD(ling), 76. *Prof Exp:* Instr, 75-76, asst prof, 76-80, ASSOC PROF LING, SOUTHERN ILL UNIV, 80- *Concurrent Pos:* Vis assoc prof, English Lang Inst, Am Univ Cairo, 82-83. *Mem:* Teachers English Speakers Other Lang; Midwest Mod Lang Asn. *Res:* Language testing; second language testing methodology; theoretical syntax. *Publ:* Coauth, Language in Education: Testing the Tests, 78 & Research in Language Testing, 80, Newbury House Publ Inc; co-ed, On TESOL 79: The Learner in Focus, Teachers English Other Langs, 79; auth, Using objective methods of attained writing proficiency, Teacher English Speaker Other Langs Quart, 80; Determining coreferentiality by sight and sound, Regional English Lang Ctr J, 81; On predicate complements, Int Rev Appl Ling, 81; coauth, Discourse analysis and the art of coherence, Col English, 82; Test of ability to subordinate: Predictive and concurrent validity, Proc Fourth Int Lang Testing Symp, 82. *Mailing Add:* Dept of Ling Southern Ill Univ Carbondale IL 62901

PERKINS, GEORGE W, b July 11, 37; US citizen; m 61; c 6. JAPANESE LITERATURE & LANGUAGE. *Educ:* Brigham Young Univ, BA, 62; Stanford Univ, MA, 67, PhD(Japanese), 77. *Prof Exp:* Lectr Japanese, Stanford Univ, 69-70; lectr, Auckland Univ, 71-74; ASST PROF JAPANESE, BRIGHAM YOUNG UNIV, 75- *Mem:* Asn Asian Studies; Asn Teachers Japanese. *Res:* Pre-modern Japanese literature; the modern Japanese novel. *Mailing Add:* Dept of Asian & Slavic Lang Brigham Young Univ Provo UT 84602

PERKINS, JEAN ASHMEAD, b Bombay, India, Mar 18, 28; US citizen; m 49; c 2. FRENCH. *Educ:* Swarthmore Col, BA, 49; Columbia Univ, MA, 51, PhD, 57. *Prof Exp:* Instr French, Bryn Mawr Col, 54-56; from asst prof to assoc prof, 61-72, prof, 72-76, SUSAN W LIPPINCOTT PROF FRENCH, SWARTHMORE COL, 76- *Concurrent Pos:* Am Coun Learned Soc fel, 79. *Mem:* MLA (1st vpres, 78, pres, 79); Am Soc 18th Century Studies; Soc Fr Etude XIIIeme Siecle; Am Asn Teachers Fr. *Res:* Eighteenth century French literature; history of ideas. *Publ:* Coauth, Supple to Vol IV, Critical Bibliography of French Literature, Syracuse Univ, 68; auth, The Concept of the Self in the French Enlightenment, Droz, Geneva, 69; co-ed, Oeuvres Completes de Voltaire, Voltaire Found; auth, The Physiocrats and the Encyclopedists, Studies in 18th Century Cult, 79; coauth, Working Paper of the Commission on the Future of the Professionn, PMLA, 81. *Mailing Add:* Dept of Mod Lang Swarthmore Col Swarthmore PA 19081

PERKINS, JUDITH B, b Hartford, Conn, June 13, 44; m 68; c 2. CLASSICAL LANGUAGES. *Educ:* My Holyoke Col, BA, 66; Univ Toronto, MA, 67, PhD(class studies), 72. *Prof Exp:* Lectr English, St Alphonsus Col, 73-75; lectr English & classics, ASST PROF CLASSIC LANG, ST JOSEPH COL, 80- *Mem:* Am Philol Asn; Class Asn Can. *Res:* Silver epic; literacy theory. *Publ:* Auth, An aspect of Latin comparison construction, Trans Am Philol Asn, 74; An aspect of the style of Valerius Flaccus' Argonaulicon, Phoenix, 74; Latin poetry and literary criticism, Axion, 76. *Mailing Add:* St Joseph Col Asylum Ave West Hartford CT 06119

PERKINS, MERLE LESTER, b West Lebanon, NH, Apr 16, 19; m 51; c 2. FRENCH, SPANISH. *Educ:* Dartmouth Col, AB, 41; Brown Univ, AM, 42, PhD(French), 50. *Prof Exp:* Instr French, Brown Univ, 48-50; instr, Univ Chicago, 50-53; from asst prof to prof, Univ Calif, Davis, 53-67, chmn dept foreign lang, 62-65, chmn dept French & Ital, 65-67; PROF FRENCH, UNIV WIS-MADISON, 67- *Concurrent Pos:* Penrose Fund res grant, Am Philos Soc, 56-57 & 74; MLA res grant, 56-57; Fulbright res grants, France, 60-61, 67-68; dir, Mich-Wis year abroad, Univs Mich & Wis, 76-77; chmn admis, 77- *Mem:* Am Asn Teachers Fr; MLA; Philol Asn Pac Coast. *Res:* Seventeenth and eighteenth century French literature, intellectual currents antecedent to the American and French Revolutions; novel, theatre, and esthetics. *Publ:* Auth, The Moral and Political Philosophy of the Abbe de Sainte-Pierre, Droz, Minard, 59; Voltaire's Concept of International Order, 65 & Destiny, sentiment and time, In: The Confessions of J J Rousseau, 69, Inst et Musee Voltaire; Jean-Jacques Rousseau on the Individual and Society, Univ Ky, 75; Motivation and behavior in Diderot's Nevew de Rameau, Studies Voltaire & 18th Century, 75; The psychoanalytic Merveilleux in Sade's Florville et Courval, Substance, 76; Diderot and the time-space continuum, Hist Philos, Esthetics & Politics, Oxford Univ (in press). *Mailing Add:* Dept of French & Ital Univ of Wis Madison WI 53706

PERKOWSKI, JAN LOUIS, b Perth Amboy, NJ, Dec 29, 36; m 61; c 3. SLAVIC LANGUAGES. *Educ:* Harvard Univ, AB, 59, AM, 60, PhD(Slavic lang & lit), 65. *Prof Exp:* Asst prof Russ, Univ Calif, Santa Barbara, 64-65; from asst prof to assoc prof slavic lang, Univ Tex, Austin, 65-74, chmn dept, 66-68 & 73-74; PROF SLAVIC LANG, UNIV VA, 74-, CHMN DEPT SLAVIC LANG & LIT, 76- *Mem:* Am Asn Advan Slavic Studies; Am Comt Slavists; Am Asn Southeast European Studies. *Res:* Slavic immigrant languages in English speaking countries. *Publ:* Auth, A Kashubian Idiolect in the United States, Lang Sci Monogr, Ind Univ, 69; Vampires, Dwarves and Witches Among the Ontario Kashubs, Mercury Set 1, Nat Mus of Man, Ottwa, 72; Vampires of the Slavs, Slavica, 76; Linguistic change in Texas Czech, Studies in Czechoslovak Hist, 76; Gusle and Ganga among the Hercegovinians of Toronto, Ann Arbor, 78; The reign of Peter the Great: A catalogue of medals in the Smithsonian collection, Numismatist, 5/82. *Mailing Add:* Dept of Slavic Lang & Lit Univ of Va B-22 Cocke Hall Charlottesville VA 22903

PERRI, DENIS ROY, b Kenosha, Wis, Sept 2, 42; m 70; c 1. SPANISH. *Educ:* Dominican Col, Wis, BA, 64; Univ Iowa, MA, 66, PhD(Span), 72. *Prof Exp:* Instr Span, Univ Wis-Platteville, 66-67; asst prof, 67-74, assoc prof, 74-80, PROF SPAN, GRINNELL COL, 80- *Mem:* MLA; Am Asn Teachers Span & Port. *Res:* Latin American drama; Spanish contemporary poetry. *Publ:* Auth, A note on the origins of El Alcazar de Sevilla, Romance Notes, Vol 15, No 3; The Costa Rican stage: An update, spring 75 & La colina and the theatre of Daniel Gallegos, fall 76, Latin Am Theatre Rev; The grotesque in Rivas' Romances historicos, Hisp, 12/76; Tension, speaker, and experience in Poema del Cante Jondo, Revista Hisp Mod, No 1-2, 76-77. *Mailing Add:* Dept of Span Grinnell Col Grinnell IA 50112

PERRY, KENNETH I, b Salt Lake City, Utah, Mar 2, 29. ROMANCE LANGUAGES & LITERATURES. *Educ:* Brigham Young Univ, BA, 54; Univ Mich, MA, 59, PhD(French), 66; Auburn Univ, MA, 74. *Prof Exp:* Instr French, Eastern Mich Univ, 60-61; instr French lang & lit, Duke Univ, 62-65; instr, 65, asst prof, 66-70, ASSOC PROF FRENCH LIT & LING, UNIV ILL, CHICAGO CIRCLE, 70- *Concurrent Pos:* Res asst, Lang Commun Lab, Univ Mich, 61-62; lang consult, US Air Force Hq Command, Washington, DC, 63- *Mem:* Am Asn Teachers Fr; MLA; Cent States Foreign Lang Teachers Asn; Am Coun Teachers Foreign Lang. *Res:* French 20th and 19th century novel; general French poetry. *Publ:* Coauth, Six sent south, Deseret, 59; auth, Francoise Sagan--unexpressed morality, Chicago Circle Studies, 6/67; The Religious Symbolism of Andre Gide, Mouton, 5/69; ed, Francoise Sagan, La Chamade, Prentice-Hall, 69; auth, Individual mobilization augmentee, 2/74, Michel Butur: A concept of United States unity, 4/74, Air Univ Prof Studies; Une moralite: Deux pieces de Francoise Sagan, Ky Romance Quart, Vol 22, No 3. *Mailing Add:* Dept of French Univ of Ill Chicago Circle Chicago IL 60680

PERRY, THEODORE ANTHONY, b Waterville, Maine, Dec 24, 38; m 66; c 2. ROMANCE LANGUAGES. *Educ:* Bowdoin Col, BA, 60; Yale Univ, PhD(Romance lang), 66. *Prof Exp:* Instr French, Williams Col, 64-65; instr, Smith Col, 65-67; asst prof French & Span, 67-74, assoc prof, 74-80, PROF FRENCH & SPAN, UNIV CONN, 80- *Concurrent Pos:* Nat Found Humanities fel, 69-70; Soc Relig Higher Educ fel, 70-71. *Mem:* MLA; Soc Relig Higher Educ. *Res:* Medieval Romance literatures; Renaissance Romance literatures; Sephardic literature. *Publ:* Auth, Art and Meaning in Berceo's Vida de Santa Orai, Yale Univ, 68; Ideal love and human reality in Montemayor's La Diana, 69 & Dialogue and doctrine in Leone Ebreo's Dialoghi d'amore, 73, PMLA; ed, Leon Hebreu, Dialogues d'amour, Univ NC Press, 74; Erotic Spirituality: The Integrative Tradition from Leone Ebreo to John Donne, Univ Ala Press, 80. *Mailing Add:* Dept of Romance Lang Univ of Conn Storrs CT 06268

PERVUSHIN, NICOLAS, b Kazan, Russia, May 16, 99; US citizen; m 23; c 1. LINGUISTICS, LITERATURE. *Educ:* Univ Kazan, Russia, 21. *Hon Degrees:* Dr of Humanities, Norwich Univ, 77. *Prof Exp:* Instr econ & sociol, Univ Kazan, 19-21, lectr hist of econ, 22-23; prof, Univ Samara, 21-22; prof, Russ lang, UN Lang Courses, NY, 47-53; vis prof Russ lang, lit & drama, McGill Univ, 62-63, assoc prof Russ lit & civilization, 63-71; DIR, RUSS SCH, NORWICH UNIV, 69- *Concurrent Pos:* Prof Russ civilization & lit, Univ Montreal, 62-70; lectr, Univ Ottawa, 67-77, Univ Montreal, 79-; emer dir, Russ Norwich Univ, 81- *Mem:* Am Asn Teachers Slavic & East Europ Lang; Can Asn Slavists; MLA; Am Asn Advan Slavic Studies; Int Dostoevsky Soc. *Res:* Sociology; economics; Russian language and philology and classical and contemporary literature. *Publ:* Auth, Influences occidentales dans oeuvre de Dostevsky, 72, Slavic & East Europ Studies; Dostoevsky's Foma Opiskin and Gogol, Can Slavonic Papers, 72; Rehabilitation of Dostoevsky, Slavic & East Europ Studies, 72; Catharsis as a literary device, Russ Lang J, 74; Epilogues in Tolstay's works, 79; L Tolstoi and his wife, 80 & Dostoevsky's illness and his works, 80, New Rev; Endings in Dostoevsky's works, 81 & Closures in A Blok's poems, 82, Russ Lang J. *Mailing Add:* 5647 Durocher Ave Montreal PQ H2V 3Y3 Can

PETER, KLAUS, b Hanau, Ger, July 2, 37; m 68. GERMAN LITERATURE. *Educ:* Univ Frankfurt, DrPhil(Ger lit), 65. *Prof Exp:* Asst prof Ger lit, Univ Kans, 66-68; asst prof, 68-72, ASSOC PROF GER LIT, UNIV MASS, AMHERST, 72- *Concurrent Pos:* Vis prof, Univ Freiburg, 71-72. *Mem:* MLA; Am Asn Teachers Ger. *Res:* German literature since 1700; literary theory. *Publ:* Auth, Wohldurchdachter Radikalismus, In: Der Dichter und seine zeit, Steihm, Heidelberg, 70; Die Stummheit des Propheten zu Joseph Roths nachgelassenem Roman, Basis I, 70; contribr, Ideologiekritische Studien zur Literatur, Essays I, Athenaum, Frankfurt/M, 72; auth, Idealismus als Kritik, die Philosophie Friedrich Schlegels, Kohlhammer, Stuttgart, 73; Friedrich Schlegel, Metzler, Stuttgart, 78. *Mailing Add:* Dept of Ger Lang Univ of Mass Amherst MA 01003

PETERFREUND, STUART SAMUEL, English Literature. See Vol II

PETERS, ANN MARIE, b Pasadena, Calif, July 31, 38. LINGUISTICS. *Educ:* Bryn Mawr Col, BA, 59; Univ Wis-Madison, MA, 61, PhD(ling), 66. *Prof Exp:* ASSOC RESEARCHER LING, UNIV HAWAII, MANOA, 71- *Mem:* Ling Soc Am. *Res:* Child language acquisition; phonological rule testing; African tone languages. *Publ:* Auth, Algorithms for processing phonological rule schemata, Prof Fourth Int Conf Syst Sci, 1/71; A new formalization of downdrift, Studies African Ling, 7/73; Language learning strategies, Lang, 9/77. *Mailing Add:* Dept of Ling Univ of Hawaii at Manoa Honolulu HI 96822

PETERS, FREDERICK GEORGE, b Philadelphia, Pa, May 9, 35; m 65; c 1. GERMAN HUMANITIES, COMPARATIVE LITERATURE. *Educ:* Univ Pa, BA, 57; Columbia Univ, MA, 59 & 62; Oxford Univ, BLitt, 65; Cambridge Univ, PhD(Ger), 72. *Prof Exp:* Tutor Ger, Christ's & Jesus Cols, Cambridge, 68-69; asst prof Ger, Barnard Col, Columbia Univ, 70-78; Harvard Mellon fac fel in humanities, Harvard Univ, 78-79. *Concurrent Pos:* Fac mem humanities, New Sch Social Res, 74-; adj asst prof humanities, NY Univ, 75-; Harvard-Mellon fac fel in humanities, Harvard Univ, 78-79. *Mem:* MLA; Germanics Inst London; Kafka Soc Am; Int Musil Soc. *Res:* Contemporary German literature; German intellectual history; literature and psychoanalysis. *Publ:* Auth, Kafka and Kleist: A literary relationship, In: Oxford German Studies, Vol 1, Oxford Univ, 66; Robert Musil: Master of the Hovering Life, 78 & Brecht Kafka Musil (3 arts), In: Columbia Encycl of Modern European Writers, 78, Columbia Univ Press; translr, Kleist: Prince Friedrich of Homburg, New Direction, 78; Kafka and Freud, Kafka Soc Am. *Mailing Add:* Dept Humanitites Univ Mich Ann Arbor MI 48109

PETERS, GEORGE FREDERICK, b Portland, Ore, June 3, 44; m 67; c 1. GERMAN LITERATURE & LANGUAGE. *Educ:* Stanford Univ, BA, 66, MA, 67, PhD(Ger), 70. *Prof Exp:* Asst prof, 70-76, ASSOC PROF GER, UNIV NMEX, 76- *Mem:* Am Asn Teachers Ger; MLA. *Res:* Poetry of Goethe; German poetry; literature and music. *Publ:* Auth, Some problems in translating the modals, spring 70 & Why introduction to literature?, spring 74, Unterrichtspraxis; The Trennungsmotive and structural unity in the Buch Suleika of Goethe's Divan, Ger Quart, 1/74; Neue Gedichte: Heine's Buch des Unmuts, Monatshefte, Vol 68, No 3; Air and spirit in Goethe's Divan, Rocky Mountain Rev, Vol 30, No 4; coauth, Culture through experience: The German weekend in New Mexico, Unterrichtspraxis, Vol 9, No 2; auth, The Death of Virgil: Ein englisches Gedicht?, Mod Austrian Lit, Vol 10, No 1. *Mailing Add:* Dept of Mod & Classical Lang Univ of NMex Albuquerque NM 87131

PETERS, H FREDERICK, b Dresden, Ger, Jan 18, 10; US citizen; m 70; c 2. GERMAN & COMPARATIVE LITERATURE. *Educ:* Univ Munich, PhD, 33. *Prof Exp:* Ger master, Marlborough Col, 33-35; foreign lang master, Tonbridge Sch, Kent, Eng, 35-39; instr & asst prof Ger, Reed Col, 40-47, assoc prof, 48-49, prof, 51-59; dir Am studies, Am Inst, Univ Munich, 49-51; prof Ger & comp lit, 59-75, head dept foreign lang, 63-75, dir Cent Europ Studies Ctr, 65-75, EMER PROF GER & COMP LIT, PORTLAND STATE UNIV, 75- *Concurrent Pos:* With Off Strategic Serv, Washington, DC & Overseas, 44-45; consult, Adj Gen Off, Ft Getty Proj, 45; res grant, Am Coun Learned Soc, 58; dir, Deut Sommerschule Pazifik, 58-; consult, Ore Arts Comn, 71-; dir, Deut Festspiele am Pazifik, 71- *Honors & Awards:* Order of Merit, Fed Repub Ger, 61 & Commander's Cross Order of Merit, 75; Goethe Medal, Geothe Inst, 62. *Mem:* MLA; Am Asn Teachers Ger. *Res:* Rainer Maria Rilke; Friedrich Nietzsche; Edgar Allan Poe. *Publ:* Auth, R M Rilke: Masks and the Man, Univ Wash, 60; My Sister, my Spouse, Norton, 62, Fr transl, Ma soeur, mon Epouse, Gallimard, 67; LOU: Das Leben der Lou Andreas-Salome, Kindler, 64; ed, Notes in brief, Ger Quart, 64-67; Nietzsche und seine Schwester: Eine Fussnote, Rice Univ Studies, fall 71; auth, Zarathustra's Sister: The Case of Elisabeth and Friedrich Nietzsche, Crown, 77. *Mailing Add:* Dept of Foreign Lang Portland State Univ Portland OR 97207

PETERS, HOWARD NEVIN, b Hazleton, Pa, June 29, 38; m 63. SPANISH, COMPARATIVE LITERATURE. *Educ:* Gettysburg Col, BA, 60; Univ Colo, PhD(Span & comp lit), 66. *Prof Exp:* Instr humanities & Span, Univ Colo, 64-65; from asst prof to assoc prof Span, 65-76, dir grad div, 68-76 &

78-80, assoc dean col arts & sci, 72-76, dean, 74-81, PROF FOREIGN LANG, VALPARAISO UNIV, 75- . *Mem:* Midwest Mod Foreign Lang Asn. *Res:* Sixteenth and seventeenth century European drama. *Mailing Add:* Dept of Foreign Lang Valparaiso Univ Valparaiso IN 41383

PETERS, ISSA, b Mishtaya, Syria, Mar 15, 35; nat US; m 65; c 1. ARABIC, MIDDLE EAST HISTORY. *Educ:* Univ Damascus, BA, 58; Mich State Univ, MA, 60; Columbia Univ, PhD(Arabic), 74. *Prof Exp:* Teacher English, Midway Jr Col, 64-65; instr English, Northern Ill Univ, 65-68; assoc prof Arabic, Defense Lang Inst, 71-76; assoc prof, 76-80, PROF ARABIC & MIDDLE EAST STUDIES, AM GRAD SCH INT MGT, 80- *Mem:* Am Asn Teachers Arabic; Am Orient Soc; Middle E Studies Asn. *Res:* Contemporary Arabic literature and thought; Middle East history. *Mailing Add:* Dept of Int Studies Am Grad Sch Int Mgt Glendale AZ 85306

PETERS, PAUL STANLEY, JR, b Houston, Tex, Dec 7, 41. THEORETICAL LINGUISTICS. *Educ:* Mass Inst Technol, SB, 63. *Prof Exp:* From asst prof to assoc prof, 66-75, PROF LING, UNIV TEX, AUSTIN, 75-, CHMN DEPT, 77-, CO-DIR CTR FOR COGNITIVE SCI, 80- *Concurrent Pos:* Mem sch soc sci, Inst Advan Studies, Princeton Univ, 72, 73-75; vis researcher, Res Group Quantitative Ling, Stockholm, 72; mem, Math Soc Sci Bd, 72-76. *Mem:* Ling Soc Am. *Res:* Formal properties of transformational grammars; semantics of natural languages; structure of English. *Publ:* Auth, Why there are many universal bases, Papers Ling, 70; coauth, On restricting the base component of transformational grammars, Inform & Control, 71; ed, Goals of Linguistic Theory, Prentice-Hall, 72; coauth, On the generative power of transformational grammars, Inform Sci, 73; What indirect questions conventionally implicate, Papers from 12th Regional Meeting, Chicago Ling Soc, 76; contribr, Basic Problems in Methodology and Linguistics, D Reidel, 77. *Mailing Add:* Dept of Ling Univ of Tex Austin TX 78712

PETERSEN, CAROL OTTO, b Bucarest, Romania, Feb 23, 14; Ger citizen; c 1. GERMAN, FRENCH. *Educ:* Berlin, MA, 46. *Prof Exp:* Prof French, French Inst Berlin, 49-67; assoc prof, 68-81, EMER PROF FOREIGN LANG, VALPARAISO UNIV, 81- *Concurrent Pos:* Teacher Ger & French, Gottfried Keller Gym, 49-68; prof French, Inst Francais, Berlin, 49-67; translr & interpreter Ger-French, Mayor WBerlin & Europa Union, 54-64. *Honors & Awards:* Chevalier Des Palmes Academiques, 65. *Mem:* MLA; John Steinbeck Soc Am; Hölderlin Gesellschaft. *Res:* German and French literature; European and American drama. *Publ:* Auth, Albert Camus, Colloquium, Berlin, 61 & Ungar, New York, 69; Max Frisch, Colloquium, Berlin, 66 & Ungar, New York, 71; Andre Gide, 69, John Steinbeck, 72, Tennessee Williams, 74, Eugene Ionesco, 76 & Stefan George, 80, Colloquium, Berlin. *Mailing Add:* 1904 Valparaiso IN 46383

PETERSEN, GERALD WEGENER, b Castle Dale, Utah, July 2, 35; m 61; c 4. SPANISH AMERICAN LITERATURE. *Educ:* Brigham Young Univ, BA, 61; Univ Ill, Urbana, MA, 63, PhD(Span Am lit), 67. *Prof Exp:* Asst prof Span, Univ Fla, 66-70; asst prof, 70-71, ASSOC PROF SPAN, UNIV NEV, RENO, 71- *Mem:* Am Asn Teachers Span & Port; Am Coun Teaching Foreign Lang; Nat Asn Lang Lab Dir; Int Inst Ibero-Am Lit. *Res:* Contemporary Spanish American novel and short story; prose fiction of Carlos Fuentes and Pedro Prado. *Publ:* Auth, Desnudo en el tejado by Antonio Skarmeta, Hispania, 5/70; Two literary parallels: La cena by Alfonso Reyes and Aura by Carlos Fuentes, Romance Notes, fall 70; Punto de vista y tiempo en La muerte de Artemio Cruz, Rev Estudios Hisp, 1/72. *Mailing Add:* Dept of Foreign Lang Univ of Nev Reno NV 89507

PETERSEN, HANS, b Ger, July 2, 25; US citizen. CLASSICAL PHILOLOGY. *Educ:* Haverford Col, BA, 46; Harvard Univ, MA, 47, PhD, 53. *Prof Exp:* Instr classics, Univ Chicago, 53-55; asst prof, Washington Univ, 55-59; asst prof classics & mem staff Mideast Ctr, Univ Tex, 59-63; asst prof classics, 63-67, assoc prof class lang, 67-80, PROF MOD LANG, UNIV LOUISVILLE, 80- *Mem:* Am Philol Asn; Archaeol Inst Am; Asn Int Papyrologues; Am Soc Papyrologists; Class Asn Midwest & S. *Res:* Epigraphy; onomatology; Coptic. *Mailing Add:* Humanities 328A Univ of Louisville Louisville KY 40208

PETERSEN, KLAUS, b Hamburg, Ger, Oct 13, 37; Can citizen. GERMAN LITERATURE. *Educ:* Univ Hamburg, Staatsexamen, 63; Univ BC, PhD(Ger), 74. *Prof Exp:* Asst prof Ger, Univ Winnipeg, 74-76; asst prof, 76-80, ASSOC PROF GER, UNIV BC, 80- *Mem:* Asn Can Univ Teachers Ger; West Asn Ger Studies. *Res:* Expressionism; literature of the nineteen-twenties; literary theory. *Publ:* Auth, Georg Kaiser: Künstlerbild und Künstlerfigur, Herbert Lang, 76; Ludwig Rubiner: Eine Einführung mit Textauswahl und Bibliographie, Bouvier Verlag, 80; Die Gruppe 1925: Geschichte und Soziologie einer Schriftstellervereinigung, Carl Winter, 81. *Mailing Add:* Dept of Ger Studies Univ of BC Vancouver BC V6T 1W5 Can

PETERSEN, PHILLIP BURNS, b Oxnard, Calif, Aug 28, 21; m 49; c 3. FOREIGN LANGUAGES. *Educ:* Univ Calif, Los Angeles, BA, 42, MA, 47; Univ Calif, Berkeley, PhD, 55. *Prof Exp:* Asst prof foreign lang, St Mary's Col, Calif, 55-62; from asst prof to assoc prof, Calif State Col Hayward, 62-65; SR LECTR SPAN & DIR LANG LAB, STANFORD UNIV, 66- *Concurrent Pos:* Foreign lang consult, Calif State Dept Educ, 62-65. *Mem:* MLA; Am Asn Teachers Span & Port. *Res:* Spanish phonetics; foreign languages and the phonograph; historical performance of opera. *Publ:* Coauth, Espanol para maestros, Fairchild, 63; auth, The elusive phonograph, J Am Phonograph Soc, 10/73; Early versions of the Edison tin foil phonograph, Talking Machine Rev, 2/74; The Rosenthal cylinders, J City London Gramophone & Phonograph Soc, 2/74. *Mailing Add:* 1853 Channing Ave Palo Alto CA 94303

PETERSON, ELMER ROBERT, b Albert Lea, Minn, Sept 2, 30; m 54; c 2. FRENCH. *Educ:* Carleton Col, BA, 52; Middlebury Col, MA, 57; Univ Colo, PhD, 62. *Prof Exp:* Instr French, Beloit Col, 58-60; from asst prof to assoc prof, 60-73, dir develop, 77-79, PROF FRENCH, COLO COL, 73-, CHMN DEPT ROMANCE LANG, 67- *Concurrent Pos:* Resident dir, Colo-Kans Studies Ctr, Bordeaux, 65-66; correspondent, French VII; acting dir, Colo Opera Festival, 76-77; dean summer session, Colo Col, 82- *Mem:* Am Asn Teachers Fr; MLA. *Res:* Surrealism and its affinities; French 20th century poetry. *Publ:* Auth, Tristan Tzara, Rutgers Univ, 70; Salt Seller (the Writings of Marcel Duchamp), Oxford Univ, 73; coauth, The Essential Writings of Marcel Duchamp, Thames & Hudson, London, 75; Duchamp du Signe, Flammarion, Paris, 76. *Mailing Add:* Dept of Romance Lang Colo Col Colorado Springs CO 80903

PETERSON, PAUL W, b Erie, Pa, Aug 5, 20; m 46; c 3. LINGUISTICS. *Educ:* Univ Pittsburgh, BA, 42; NY Univ, MA, 47, PhD, 51. *Prof Exp:* Instr classics, Gannon Col, 46-47; instr, NY Univ, 47-50; from instr to assoc prof, 50-57, PROF CLASSICS & DIR DEPT FOREIGN LANG, GANNON COL, 57-, VPRES, ACAD AFFAIRS, 77- *Concurrent Pos:* Deleg, Joint Nat Comt Lang, 72- *Honors & Awards:* Lang Teacher of Year, Pa State Mod Lang Asn, 76. *Mem:* Nat Fed Mod Lang Teachers (pres, 72-73, secy-treas, 78-); MLA; Ling Soc Am; Int Ling Asn; Am Translators Asn. *Res:* Early mediaeval historical sources; history and structure of English. *Mailing Add:* Dept of Foreign Lang Gannon Col Erie PA 16501

PETERSON, RICHARD GUSTAF, English Literature. See Vol II

PETERSON, RUSSELL WARREN, b St Paul, Minn, Feb 26, 16; m 62; c 2. SPANISH, FRENCH. *Educ:* Univ Minn, BA, 40; Univ Nebr, MA, 49; Middlebury Col, MA, 53; Univ Okla, PhD(Span), 67. *Prof Exp:* Instr French & Span, Cameron Col, 50-57; asst Span, Univ Okla, 57-58; instr, French & Span, Northern Okla Jr Col, 58-59; PROF FRENCH & SPAN, TARLETON STATE UNIV, 59- *Mem:* Am Asn Teachers Span & Port; SCent Mod Lang Asn. *Res:* Spanish historical linguistics; Spanish paleography. *Mailing Add:* Dept of Foreign Lang Tarleton State Univ Stephenville TX 76402

PETREY, DONALD SANDY, b Alexander City, Ala, Aug 29, 41. FRENCH & ITALIAN. *Educ:* Emory Univ, BA, 62; Yale Univ, PhD, 66. *Prof Exp:* Asst prof Romance lang, 66-74, ASSOC PROF FRENCH & COMP LIT, STATE UNIV NY STONY BROOK, 74-, DEAN HUMANITIES & FINE ARTS, 77- *Concurrent Pos:* Nat Endowment for Humanities fel, 72-73. *Mem:* MLA; Am Asn Teachers Fr. *Res:* French 19th century literature; critical theory; linguistic criticism. *Publ:* Auth, Christian imagery in la Chute, Tex Studies, winter 70; Poetry of Louise Labe, Fr Rev, 3/70; Sociocriticism & les Rougen-Marquest, L'Esprit Createur, fall 74; Gonjet as God & worker, Fr Forum, 9/76; Discours social et litterature, Litterature, 5/76; Word associations & lexical memory, Cognition, spring 77; Language of false consciousness, Novel, winter 77; History in the Text, Benjamins, 80. *Mailing Add:* Dept of French State Univ of NY Stony Brook NY 11794

PETRIZZI, DANIEL JOSEPH, b Italy, May 18, 20; US citizen; m 54. ROMANCE LANGUAGE & LITERATURE. *Educ:* Middlebury Col, AB & MA, 48, DML, 63; Sorbonne, dipl, 51. *Prof Exp:* From instr to assoc prof mod lang, Hobart & William Smith Cols, 48-68; PROF MOD LANG, EISENHOWER COL, 68- *Mem:* Am Asn Teachers Fr; MLA. *Res:* Nineteenth and 20th century French literature. *Mailing Add:* Dept of Modern Lang Eisenhower Col Seneca Falls NY 13148

PETROVIC, NJEGOS M, b Vucitrn, Yugoslavia, May 20, 33; m 60; c 3. SERBO-CROATIAN & FRENCH LANGUAGE & LITERATURE. *Educ:* Univ Belgrade, BA, 53, super dipl, 57; Univ Montreal, MA, 62, PhD(comp lit), 67. *Prof Exp:* Instr mod lang, Class Col, Belgrade, 56-57; instr, Univ Paris, 58-61; asst prof French, Class Col St Jean, 61-64, Royal Mil Col, Que, 64-65 & Nebr Wesleyan Univ, 65-67; assoc prof, 67-74, PROF FRENCH, UNIV SCRANTON, 74- *Concurrent Pos:* Chmn, Concert & Theater Ser, 69-; art adv, Pa Coun Arts, 73-76. *Mem:* Humanities Asn Can; MLA; AAUP. *Res:* French, Serbo-Croatian and Russian language and literature of 19th and 20th centuries. *Publ:* Auth, Tisina Kamenja (poems), Prosveta, Belgrade, 54; Reve de bonheur, J Provinces, Paris, 12/59; Carillon, 5/65 & Les Faubourgs, 6/65, Can Fr, St Jean; Ivo Andric, l'homme et l'oeuvre, Les Ed Lemeac, Montreal, 69; ed, Everhart Museum Catalog, Art Print Co, Scranton, Pa, 74. *Mailing Add:* 1010 Monroe Ave Scranton PA 18510

PETROVSKA, MARIJA, b Zagreb, Yugoslavia; US citizen. FRENCH LANGUAGE AND LITERATURE, COMPARATIVE LITERATURE. *Educ:* Inst Advan Study Interpretership, Milano, dipl, 54; Univ Tenn, Knoxville, MA, 65; Univ Ky, PhD(French), 72. *Prof Exp:* Instr Ital & French, 63-72, asst prof French, 72-76, assoc prof French & Czech, 76-80, PROF FRENCH & COMP LIT, UNIV TENN, 80- *Mem:* SAtlantic MLA; Czech Soc Arts & Sci Am; Am Asn Teachers Fr. *Res:* Comparative French-Czech literature; French and comparative theatre; French 19th century literature. *Publ:* Auth, Les sons et le silence dans les romans de Zola, Romance Notes, 72; A Czech admirer of Giosue Carducci, Comp Lit Studies, 74; Manon Lescaut: Prevost et Nezval, Rev Litt Comp, 75; The discovery of Charles Baudelaire in Bohemia, Romance Notes, 75; Un Figaro deguise, Rev Hist Theatre, 76; Victor Hugo: L'Ecrivain Engage en Boheme, Ed A G Nizet, Paris, 77; Un frire spiritual slave de leconte de lisle, Rev Lit Comp, 79; Vigny et baudelaire: Adoraleurs de l'esprit, Romance Notes, 79-80; Prague Diptych, Maryland Bks, 80. *Mailing Add:* Dept of Romance Lang Univ Tenn Knoxville TN 37916

PEYSER, JOSEPH LEONARD, French & American History. See Vol I

PEYTON, MYRON ALVIN, b Louisiana, Mo, Apr 5, 09. HISPANIC LITERATURE. *Educ:* Univ Kans, AB, 30, AM, 31; Northwestern Univ, PhD, 42. *Prof Exp:* Mem fac, Clifton col, 32-33; teacher pub schs, Kans, 34-37; teaching asst, Northwestern Univ, 37-40; from instr to asst prof, Princeton Univ, 40-44; prof Span & head dept, 44-75, EMER PROF SPAN, COL WOOSTER, 75- *Mem:* MLA. *Res:* Seventeenth century Spanish drama and novel. *Publ:* Auth, Some Baroque aspects of Tirso de Molina, Romanic Rev, 2/45; Sa as Barbadillo's Don Diego de Noche, PMLA, 6/49; Lope de Vega and his styles, Romanic Rev, 10/57; Lope de Vega's El Peregrino en su Patria Critical edition and study, Univ NC, 71; Salas Barbadillo, Twayne, 73. *Mailing Add:* 726 Kieffer St Wooster OH 44691

PEZZILLO, SAMUEL JOSEPH, b Mt Pleasant, Pa, Apr 29, 42; m 76; c 2. CLASSICAL LANGUAGES & LITERATURES. *Educ:* Duquesne Univ, BA, 64; Ohio State Univ, PhD(classics), 71. *Prof Exp:* Instr classics, Univ Nebr, 68-70; ASSOC PROF CLASSICS, BIRMINGHAM-SOUTHERN COL, 70- *Concurrent Pos:* Nat Endowment for Humanities grant, Inst for Ancient & Mod Studies, 73, summer sem, Berkeley Univ, 76, Am Acad, 79. *Res:* Textual criticism of Seneca the philosopher; Latin literature; classical tradition. *Mailing Add:* Dept of English & Classics Birmingham-Southern Col Birmingham AL 35204

PFANNER, HELMUT FRANZ, b Hohenweiler, Austria, Nov 8, 33; m 66; c 4. GERMAN LANGUAGE & LITERATURE. *Educ:* Stanford Univ, MA, 61, PhD(Ger), 65. *Prof Exp:* Teacher English, Hauptschule Bregenz, Vorarlberg, Austria, 58-59; instr Ger, Univ Wash, 64-67; asst prof, Univ Va, 67-69; assoc prof, Univ NH, 69-79; PROF GER, PURDUE UNIV, 79- *Concurrent Pos:* Alexander von Humboldt Found fel, 72-73 & 77-78; Am Coun Learned Soc fel, 76-77. *Mem:* Int Asn Germanic Studies; Am Asn Teachers Ger; AAUP; MLA; Int PEN Club. *Res:* Modern German literature; German exile literature; contemporary literature. *Publ:* Auth, Hanns Johst: Vom Expressionismus zum Nationalsozialismus, Mouton, The Hague, 70; co-ed, Oskar Maria Graf: Beschreibung eines Volksschriftstellers, Annedore Leber, Munich, 74; auth, Die Provinzliteratur der zwanziger Jahre, In: Die deutsche Literatur in der Weimarer Republik, Reclam, Stuttgart, 74; Stiller und das Faustische bei Max Frisch, Orbia Litterarum, Vol XXIV, No 3; Deutungsprobleme in Gerhart Hauptmanns Michael Kramer, Monatschefte, Vol LXII, No 1; Oskar Maria Graf: Eine kritische Bibliographie, Francke, Bern, 76; Zur Psychologie des Exils: Eine Deutung der Gestalt Dantes bei C F Meyer, Schweizer Monatshefte, 12/76; Friedrich Sally Grosshut: Nachlassbericht, In: Literaturwissenschaftliches Jahrbuch, Vol XVII, 77. *Mailing Add:* Dept of Ger Purdue Univ West Lafayette IN 47907

PFISTER, GUENTER GEORG, b Duisburg, WGer, Apr 1, 38; US citizen; m 68; c 2. GERMAN. *Educ:* Univ Kans, PhD(Ger methodology), 70. *Prof Exp:* ASSOC PROF GER EDUC, UNIV MD, COLLEGE PARK, 74-, DIR, UNDERGRAD STUDIES, 76- *Mem:* Am Coun Teaching Foreign Lang. *Res:* German methodology; improving instructions in the foreign language classroom. *Publ:* Auth, One man's opinion--is it audio-lingual?, Am Foreign Lang Teacher, winter 72; To make the second year count--a plea for continuity, Mod Lang J, 11/72; The dialogue reinforcement schedule is a workable alternative to dialogue memorization, Foreign Lang Ann, 5/73; Die Deutschen: Ihre Sprache und ihre Kultur, Stipes, 74; Andere Länder, Andere Sitten I and II, 78 & Creativity in L2 Acquisition: Theory and Practice, 82, Stripes. *Mailing Add:* 5716 40th Ave Hyattsville MD 20781

PHAM, HAI VAN (PHAM-VAN-HAI), b Bacninh, Vietnam, May 2, 39; US citizen; m 68; c 2. VIETNAMESE & CHINESE LINGUISTICS. *Educ:* Univ Saigon, Licentiate, 64, MA, 66; Georgetown Univ, PhD(lang & ling), 80. *Prof Exp:* Teacher Vietnamese lit, math & fine arts, Nguyen-Ba-Tong High Sch, 62-71 & teacher Vietnamese lit, Cong-Hoa High Sch, 66-67; lectr Sino-Vietnamese, Da-lat Univ, 67-71; CONSULT, VIETNAMESE CATH STUDENTS & PROFESSIONALS ASN AM, 80- *Concurrent Pos:* Lectr ling, Univ Saigon, 70-71; consult, Arlington County Pub Schs, 80. *Res:* Vietnamese linguistics, literature and culture; Chinese linguistics and literature; theoretical and applied linguistics (bilingualism). *Publ:* Auth, Vietnamese Literature, 64 & A Study of Vietnamese Tones, 73, pvt publ; A Glimpse of the influence of Chinese on the Vietnamese language, 76 & Vietnamese writing system for beginners, 77, Vietnamese Cath Students Asn Am; coauth, Read and Write Vietnamese in 20 Hours: Methodology and Techniques, 79 & Vietnamese Oral Language Proficiency Test I and Test II, 80, pvt publ. *Mailing Add:* 7417 Allan Ave Falls Church VA 22046

PHELPA, LELAND RICHTER, b Flint, Mich, Mar 31, 18; c 3. GERMAN. *Educ:* Ohio State Univ, PhD(Ger), 50. *Prof Exp:* From instr to asst prof Ger lang & lit, Northwestern Univ, 50-61; assoc prof, 61-65, PROF GER LANG & LIT, DUKE UNIV, 65-, CHMN DEPT, 70- *Mem:* MLA. *Res:* German literature of the 18th century; German-American literary relations. *Mailing Add:* 2255 Cranford Rd Durham NC 27706

PHILIP, MICHEL HENRI, b Prades, France, June 24, 32. FRENCH LITERATURE, CREATIVE WRITING. *Educ:* Sorbonne, Lic es Lett, 55, Minister Educ Nat, Agregation, 57. *Prof Exp:* Prof French, Ecole Normale Inst, Orleans, 58-61; from instr to asst prof, Yale Univ, 61-67; assoc prof, 67-71, PROF FRENCH, UNIV MASS, BOSTON, 72- *Mem:* MLA; Soc Prof Francais en Am; anciens eleves de l'Ecole Normale Superieure. *Res:* French poets and novelists 1860-1920. *Publ:* Auth, L'idee d'infini dans les Pensees de Pascal, Rev Sci Humaines, 9/63; Balzac's Heaven and Hell, 10/64 & The hidden onlooker (Proust), 6/65, Yale Fr Studies; Le coeur de Rousseau, Etudes Francaises, 11/68; Lectures de Lautreamont, Armand Colin, 71; Deus ex Machina (short story), Minuit, 11/74; Le paladin du Moude Accidentel (short story), 10/78 & Dandysme et androgynie dans les Diaboliques, 7-8/81, Nouvelle Revue Francaise. *Mailing Add:* Dept of French Univ of Mass Boston MA 02125

PHILIPPIDES, DIA MARY LAURETTE, b New Haven, Conn, May 21, 49. MODERN & ANCIENT GREEK PHILOLOGY. *Educ:* Radcliffe Col, BA, 70; Boston Col, MA, 72, MA, 73; Princeton Univ, PhD(classics), 78. *Prof Exp:* Fulbright fel ancient Greek, Greece, 77-78; LECTR & COORDR MOD GREEK STUDIES, HARVARD UNIV, 78- *Mem:* Am Philol Asn; Mod Greek Studies Asn; Asn Lit & Ling Comput; MLA. *Res:* Form and language of Ancient Greek tragedy; form and language of Modern Greek poetry (17th to 20th century); application of computational and mathematical methods to literary and linguistic analysis. *Publ:* Auth, Computers and Modern Greek, Mantatophoros, 6/81; The Iambic Trimeter of Euripedes: Selected Plays, Arno Press, 81; Euripides: Meter and dramatic effect, Perspectives Comput, 3/82; Survey of the teaching of Modern Greek in American Universities, Mod Greek Studies Asn Bull, spring 82; Concordance to the Sacrifice of Abraham, Hermes Press, Athens, Greece (in prep). *Mailing Add:* Classics Dept Harvard Univ Cambridge MA 02138

PHILIPPIDES, MARIOS, b Athens, Greece, Aug 5, 50; m 73. GREEK, LATIN. *Educ:* Queens Col, BA, 73; State Univ NY Buffalo, MA, 76, PhD(classics), 78. *Prof Exp:* asst prof, Union Col, 77-78; ASST PROF CLASSICS, UNIV MASS, AMHERST, 78- *Mem:* Am Philol Asn; Class Asn New England; Modern Greek Studies Asn; Am Inst Archaeol; Am Class League. *Res:* the palaeologan period of the Byzantine empire; ancient Greek religion and Mediterranean ritual and myth; the ancient novel. *Publ:* Auth, A note on Longus' Lesbiaka, The Class World, 78; The foundation of Taras and the Spartan partheniai, The Ancient World, 79; The Fall of the Byzantine Empire, Univ Mass Press, 80; The digressive aitia in Longus, The Class World, 80; The characters in Freedom or Death, The Charioteer, 80; The pronunciation of Greek, Phone, 81; The fall of Constantinople 1453, Greek, Roman & Byzantine Studies, 81; the prooemium in Longus, The Class Bull, 82. *Mailing Add:* Dept of Classics Univ Mass Amherst MA 01003

PHILIPPSON, ERNST ALFRED, b Muenchen-Gladbach, Ger, Apr 6, 00; m 27; c 2. GERMANIC PHILOLOGY. *Educ:* Univ Cologne, PhD, 22. *Prof Exp:* Asst, Deut Sem, Univ Cologne, 23-28 & 29-31, privat-docent English philol, 28-37; asst prof Ger, Univ Mich, 35-47; assoc prof, 47-51, prof 51-68, EMER PROF GER, UNIV ILL, URBANA, 68- *Concurrent Pos:* Lectr, Univ Wis, 28-29 & Ohio State Univ, 31-33; co-ed, Texte des spaeten Mittelalters, 56- & J English & Ger Philol, 57-71. *Mem:* MLA; Ling Soc Am; Am Asn Teachers Ger. *Res:* Germanic linguistics and literature to 1700; folklore; Germanic religion. *Publ:* Auth, Der Märchentypus von König Drosselbart, Folklore Fels Commun, 50, Helsinki, 23; Germanisches Heidentum beiden Angelsachsen, Koelner Anglist Arbeiten, Tauchnitz, Leipzig, 29; Der germanische Mütter and Matronen Kult am Niederrhein, Ger Rev, 4/44; Die Genealogie der Götter in germanischer Religion, Mythologie und Theologie, Ill Studies Lang & Lit, 53; coauth, B Neukirchs Anthologie Herrn von Hoffmannswaldau und anderer Deutschen Gedichte, Niemeyer, Tübingen, 61 & 65; Phänomenologie, vergleichende Mythologie und germanische Religionsgeshichte, PMLA, 7/62. *Mailing Add:* 114 W Florida Ave Urbana IL 61801

PHILIPS, FRANK CARTER, b New York City, NY, Apr 18, 43; m 65; c 1. CLASSICAL STUDIES. *Educ:* Vanderbilt Univ, BA, 65; Univ Pa, AM, 66, PhD(class studies), 69. *Prof Exp:* Asst prof classics, Vanderbilt Univ, 69-74; hon res asst, Dept of Greek, Univ Col, London, 73; ASSOC PROF CLASSICS, VANDERBILT UNIV, 73-, CHMN DEPT CLASS STUDIES, 80- *Concurrent Pos:* Mem Nat Adv Bd, Project Athena, Nat Endowment Humanities, 78. *Mem:* Am Philol Asn; Calss Asn Mid West & South; Am Soc Papyrologists; Egypt Explor Soc. *Res:* Preclassical Greek literature; Greek religion and mythology; Greek papyrology. *Publ:* Auth, Vocabulary to Iliad 1.4-18, Bull Am Soc Papyrologists, 71; The myths of Prometheus in Hesiod, Class J, 73; Heracles, Class World, 78. *Mailing Add:* Dept of Class Studies Vanderbilt Univ Nashville TN 37235

PHILLIPS, ALLEN WHITMARSH, b Providence, RI, June 17, 22; m 45; c 3. SPANISH, SPANISH AMERICAN LITERATURE. *Educ:* Dartmouth Col, BA, 42; Nat Univ Mex, MA, 47; Univ Mich, PhD(Span), 53. *Prof Exp:* Instr Span, Hamilton Col, 47-48 & Univ Mich, 50-54; from asst prof to prof, Univ Chicago, 54-65; prof, Ind Univ, Bloomington, 66-68 & Univ Tex, Austin, 68-77; PROF SPAN, UNIV CALIF, SANTA BARBARA, 77- *Concurrent Pos:* Guggenheim fels, 60-61 & 73-74. *Honors & Awards:* Comendador, Orden de Alfonso el Sabio, Spain, 77. *Mem:* Corresp mem, Acad Mexicana; MLA; Inst Int Lit Iberoam (vpres, 63-65). *Res:* Modern Spanish and Spanish American literature. *Publ:* Auth, Ramon Lopez Velarde, el poeta y el prosista, 62, Francisco Gonzalez Leon el poeta de Lagos, 64 & Estudios y notas sobre literatura hispanoamericana, 65, Mex; co-ed, Antonio Machado, El escritor y la critica, Taurus, Madrid, 73; auth, Cinco estudios sobre literatura mexicana moderna, Mex, 74; Temas del modernismo hispanico y otros estudios, Ed Gredos, Madrid, 74; Alejandro Sawa, mito y realidad, Turner, Madrid, 76. *Mailing Add:* Dept of Span & Port Phelps Hall Univ of Calif Santa Barbara CA 93106

PHILLIPS, BETTY STEEDLEY, b McRae, Ga, June 16, 49. ENGLISH LINGUISTICS. *Educ:* Duke Univ, BA, 71; Univ Ga, MA, 74, PhD(ling), 78. *Prof Exp:* Lectr writing, Univ Ga, 78-79; vis asst prof ling, State Univ NY, Geneseo, 79-80; adj asst prof, LeMoyne Col, 80-81; RES & WRITING, 81- *Mem:* Ling Soc Am; MLA; Am Dialect Soc; Teachers English to Speakers of Other Lang; Am Name Soc. *Res:* English historical linguistics; lexical diffusion of linguistic change; actuation of linguistic change. *Publ:* Auth, Old English an n on: A new appraisal, J English Ling, 80; coauth, The acquistion of German plurals in native children & non-native adults, Int Rev Applied Ling, 80; auth, Two approaches to a phonological problem, Word, 80; Lexical diffusion and Southern tune, duke and news, Am Speech, 81; The phonetic basis of a late Old English sound change, Phonologica, 80. *Mailing Add:* 3553 N Hills Rd Murrysville PA 15668

PHILLIPS, EWART E, b Miami, Fla, Sept 4, 27; m 50; c 1. ROMANCE LANGUAGES. *Educ:* Baylor Univ, AB, 51, MA, 54. *Prof Exp:* Teacher elem sch, Tex, 51-53; high sch, 53-55; asst prof Span, Arlington State Col, 55-56; teacher high sch, Tex, 56-58; instr Span, Univ Tex, 58-61; asst prof Span & French, Southwest Tex State Col, 61-64; chmn div humanities, 64-72, ASSOC PROF SPAN & FRENCH, HEAD DEPT MOD LANG, HOWARD PAYNE COL, 64- *Mem:* Rocky Mountain Coun Latin Am Studies; SCent MLA; Am Asn Teachers Span & Port; MLA. *Res:* Mexican novel of the Revolution; Spanish novel; Spanish Golden Age drama. *Publ:* Auth, The Genesis of Pito Perez, Hispania, 12/64. *Mailing Add:* Dept of Mod Lang Howard Payne Col Brownwood TX 76801

PHILLIPS, JANE ELLEN, b Philadelphia, Pa, Sept 27, 43. CLASSICS. *Educ:* Millersville State Col, BA, 65; Univ NC, Chapel Hill, PhD(classics), 69. *Prof Exp:* Asst prof classics, Univ NC, Chapel Hill, 69-71; adj instr, Dickinson Col, 71-72; adj instr, Franklin & Marshall Col, 71-72, vis asst prof, 72-73; asst prof, 73-80, ASSOC PROF CLASSICS, UNIV KY, 80- *Concurrent Pos:* Fel in residence for col teachers, Nat Endowment for Humanities, 75-76. *Mem:* Am Philol Asn; Class Asn Midwest & South;

Archaeol Inst Am; Am Class League; Vergilian Soc. *Res:* Latin historiography; age of Augustus; Latin poetry. *Publ:* Auth, Verbs compounded with trans in Livy's triumph reports, 74 & Form and language in Livy's triumph notices, 74, Class Philol; The pattern of images in Catullus, Am J Philol, 76; Juno in Aeneid, Vergilius, 77; Roman mothers and the lives of their adult daughters, Helios, 78; Livy and the beginning of a new society, Class Bull, 79; Lucretian echoes in Shelley's Mont Blanc, Class & Mod Lit, 82. *Mailing Add:* Dept of Classics Univ of Ky Lexington KY 40506

PHILLIPS, JOANNE HIGGINS, b Boston, Mass, Aug 26, 46. CLASSICAL PHILOLOGY. *Educ:* Boston Univ, AB, 68; Harvard Univ, MA, 71, PhD(class philol), 77. *Prof Exp:* ASST PROF CLASSICS, TUFTS UNIV, 77- *Mem:* Am Philol Asn; Class Asn New England; Am Asn Hist Med. *Res:* Greek poetry and prose, 8th through 5th century BC; Latin poetry and prose, Republic and Early Empire; history of Greek and Roman science and medicine. *Publ:* Classics and the undergraduate science major, Class Outlook, 79; The boneless one in Hesiod, Philogus, 80; Early Greek medicine and poetry of Solon, Clio Medica, 80; The emergence of the Greek medical profession in the Roman Republic, Trans and Studies of Col of Physicians Philadelphia, 80; Juxtaposed medical traditions: Pliny NH 27 106 131, 81 & Lucretius on the inefficacy of the medical art: 6 1179 and 6 1226-1238, 82, Class Philol; The hippocratic physician and astronomy, Proc of the IVth Int Colloquium on Hippocratic Med, Lausanne, Switz, 81, 82. *Mailing Add:* Dept of Classics Tufts Univ Medford MA 02155

PHILLIPS, JOHN FREDERICK, b Portsmouth, Ohio. CLASSICAL LANGUAGE, PHILOSOPHY. *Educ:* Ohio Univ, BGS, 72, MA, 74; Univ Wis, PhD(classics), 80. *Prof Exp:* ASST PROF CLASSICS, PHILOS & RELIG, UNIV TENN, CHATTANOOGA, 80- *Mem:* Am Philol Asn; Class Asn Midwest & South. *Res:* Plotinus and Neoplatonism; Plato. *Publ:* Auth, The Universe as prophet: A soteriological formula in Plotinus, Greek, Roman & Byzantine Studies, fall 81; Enneads V 1 2: Plotinus' Hymn to the World Soul and its relation to mystical knowledge, Symoblae Osloenses (in prep). *Mailing Add:* Dept of Philos & Relig Univ of Tenn Chattanooga TN 37402

PHILLIPS, KLAUS PETER, b Munich, Ger. July 30, 47; US citizen; m 71. GERMANIC LANGUAGES AND LITERATURES. *Educ:* Univ Ark, BA, 70, MA, 71; Univ Tex, PhD(Ge), 74. *Prof Exp:* Asst prof Ger & Cinema Studies, Univ Ill, 75-81; ASSOC PROF GER, VA MIL INST, 81- *Concurrent Pos:* Radio personality, ethnic music (Ger), WPCD-FM, Urbana, Ill, 77-81, WLUR-FM, Lexington, Va, 81- *Mem:* MLA; Am Asn Teachers Ger; Soc Cinema Studies; Am Soc Study Ger Lit 16th and 17th Century. *Res:* German and comparative cinema; media culture; 16th and 17th century German literature. *Publ:* Coauth, Fastnachtspiel--Purimshpil: A formal identity?, Yiddish, 73; auth, Exotism in the German cinema of the fifties, Film Studies Ann, 76; Teaching a course the German cinema, Mod Lang J, 78; History reevaluated: Volker Schlöndorff's Plötzlicher Reichtum, Film Studies Ann, 78; Maria Rilke: Nine Plays, Ungar, 79. *Mailing Add:* Dept of Mod Lang Va Mil Inst Lexington VA 24450

PHILLIPS, OLIVER CLYDE, JR, b Kansas City, Mo, Oct 23, 29; m 54; c 2. GREEK, LATIN LANGUAGE & LITERATURE. *Educ:* Univ Kans, BS in Ed, 50; Univ Mo, MA, 54; Univ Chicago, PhD(latin), 62. *Prof Exp:* Teacher jr & sr high schs, Mo, 50-55; assoc prof Latin, William Jewell Col, 55-58, prof Latin & Greek, 60-64; teaching asst Latin, Univ Chicago, 59-60; prof Latin & Greek, 64-76, chmn dept classics, 68--81, assoc prof, 76-80, PROF CLASSICS, UNIV KANS, 81- *Concurrent Pos:* Assoc, Danforth Found, 78- *Honors & Awards:* Oliver Award, Univ Kans, 49; Bray Award, Southern Methodist Univ, 54. *Mem:* Am Philol Asn; Class Asn Midwest & S; Vergilian Soc; Am Class League. *Res:* Latin poetry; mythology; ancient religions. *Publ:* Auth, Lucan Bellum civile 3.682, 4/64 & Lucan's Grove, 4/68, Class Philol; Aeole, Namque Tibi, Vergilius, 80; Francesco Patrizi: Two epigrams on the epigram, Res Public Litterarum, 80; Beginnings: Creation and reproduction, Relig J Kans, 4/81; Scientific creationism, evolution, United Methodist Reporter, 10/81. *Mailing Add:* Dept of Classics Univ of Kans Lawrence KS 66045

PHILLIPS, ROBERT N, JR, b Los Angeles, Calif, May 21, 36. PHONETICS, PHONOLOGY. *Educ:* Univ Redlands, AB, 58; Univ Wis-Madison, MA, 60, PhD(Span), 67. *Prof Exp:* From instr to assoc prof, 63-78, PROF SPAN, MIAMI UNIV, 78- *Mem:* Am Asn Teachers Span & Port; MLA; Ling Soc Am. *Res:* Spanish phonetics and genetics; Spanish dialectology; computer assisted language instruction. *Publ:* Auth, Variations in Los Angeles Spanish, In: Lenguaje de Los Chicanos, Ctr Appl Ling, 75; coauth, Visiones de Latin-America, Harper, 72, 2nd ed, 81; auth, Practicando Espanol Con La Manzana II, Univ Iowa, 81. *Mailing Add:* Dept of Span Miami Univ Oxford OH 45056

PHINNEY, EDWARD STERL, JR, b Bryan, Tex, Dec 15, 35; m 59; c 1. CLASSICS. *Educ:* Univ Ore, BA, 57, MA, 59; Univ Calif, Berkeley, PhD(classic), 63. *Prof Exp:* Instr classics, Univ Ore, 58-59; assoc, Univ Calif, Berkeley, 61-62; from instr to assoc prof, Univ Southern Calif, 62-69; assoc prof, 69-73, PROF CLASSICS, UNIV MASS, AMHERST, 73-, ACTG CHMN DEPT, 80- *Concurrent Pos:* Chmn, Greek comt, Am Class League, 76- *Mem:* Mod Greek Studies Asn; Archaeol Inst Am; Am Philol Asn; Class Asn New England; Teachers Classics New England. *Res:* Hellenistic literature; classical mythology; modern Greek literature. *Publ:* Auth, Hellenistic painting and the poetic style of Apollonius, Class J, 1/67; Narrative unity in the Argonautica, 67 & Perseus' battle with the Gorgons, 71, Trans Am Philol Asn. *Mailing Add:* Dept of Classics Univ of Mass Amherst MA 01003

PIA, JOHN JOSEPH, b Los Angeles, Calif, Jan 6, 33; m 55, 72; c 3. LINGUISTICS. *Educ:* Whittier Col, BA, 54; Univ Mich, MA, 58; Ind Univ, PhD(ling), 65. *Prof Exp:* Prin investr Somali lang, Univ Calif, Los Angeles; res assoc African studies, Mich State Univ, 63; form lectr to asst prof ling, Ind Univ, 63-65; asst prof anthrop, 65-70, chmn dept, 70-75, ASSOC PROF LING, SYRACUSE UNIV, 70- *Concurrent Pos:* Publ contracts, US Off Educ, 61-62 & 67-68 & Peace Corps, 66; pres, LAS Found Inc, 70-; founder, Ctr Acad Serv, 73-; consult res linguist, Develop & Eval Assocs Inc, Syracuse, NY, 77-; convener, NAm Conf Afroasiatic Ling, 78-79. *Mem:* Ling Soc Am; Ling Asn Can & US; Am Anthrop Asn; Soc Gen Systs Res; Int Asn Somali Studies. *Res:* Phonological theory; Afroasiatic linguistics; phonology and general system theory. *Publ:* Sr auth, Beginning in Somali, 66 & Reading in Somali, an Elementary Cultural Reader (2 vols), 69, Syracuse Univ; auth, Two principles of phonology and a Somali Sandhi rule, J African Lang, 70; Grammar and learner as system: Some proposed new directions for research in L2 acquistion, In: Working Papers in Linguistics, City Univ New York Forum, spring 78; Diaversity from within, In: Documents pour servir a l'histoire de la civilisation ethiopienne, 78; The Afroasiatic hypothesis: A prerequisite for further investigation, In: Proceedings of XXX International Congress of the Human Sciences in Asia and North Africa (in press); Multiply tiered vocalic systems, an Afroasiatic trait, In: Proceedings of III International Hamito-Semitic Congress (in press); Multiply tiered vocalic systems in Ethiopian languages, In: Proceedings of V International Congress of Ethiopian Studies, Part A (in press). *Mailing Add:* Dept of Ling/HBC Syracuse Univ Syracuse NY 13210

PIANCA, ALICIA MARGARITA, b Hanover, NH, July 2, 36. ROMANCE LANGUAGES. *Educ:* Brown Univ, AB, 58; Radcliffe Col, MA, 59. *Prof Exp:* From instr to asst prof, 63-66, chmn dept for lang, 72-80, ASSOC PROF SPAN & FRENCH, FRANKLIN COL, 66- *Mem:* MLA; Am Asn Teachers Span; Am Asn Teachers Fr. *Res:* Golden Age Spanish; 20th century Spanish; 17th century French. *Publ:* Auth, La Afrenta de Corpes, Estudios Mercedarios, Madrid, 4-6/66; Los celos de Cervantes, Palabra y Hombr, Mex, spring 69; Lope de Vega, Sannazaro and Montemayor and the Spanish pastoral novel, Horizontes, 4/69. *Mailing Add:* Dept of Foreign Lang Franklin Col Franklin IN 46131

PIANO, FRANK ANTONIO, b Leominster, Mass, Feb 23, 21; m 50; c 2. ROMANCE LANGUAGES. *Educ:* Harvard Univ, AB, 42, AM, 47; Columbia Univ, PhD, 69. *Prof Exp:* Instr Romance lang, Williams Col, 48-49; from instr to asst prof, Hamilton Col, 49-62; asst prof French & Ital, 62-65, assoc prof Span & French, 65-69, dir year abroad prog, 65-66, PROF ROMANCE LANG, ELMIRA COL, 69- *Mem:* Am Asn Teachers Fr; Mod Humanities Res Asn; MLA. *Res:* Sensibility, sensualism and sensuality in JJ Rousseau; French Renaissance and 18th century; contemporary Italian literature. *Mailing Add:* Dept of Foreign Lang Elmira Col Elmira NY 14901

PICCHIO, RICCARDO P, b Alessandria, Italy, Sept 7, 23. SLAVIC LITERATURES. *Educ:* Univ Rome, Dr Humanities, 46, Libera Docenza, 53. *Prof Exp:* Lectr Ital, Univ Warsaw, 47-49; prof extrordinary Russ lit, Univ Florence, 54-61; prof Slavic philol, Univ Rome, 61-68; PROF SLAVIC LIT, YALE UNIV, 68- *Concurrent Pos:* Ed, Ricerche Slavistiche, 52-; vis prof, Univ Pisa, 59-61; dir, Inst Slavic Philol, Rome, 61-68; Ital rep, Int Comt Slavists, 61-68; vis prof, Columbia Univ, 65-66. *Mem:* Ital Asn Slavists (secy, 57-62). *Res:* Comparative Slavic literatures; Old Russian; Polish literature. *Publ:* Auth, Storia della letteratura russa antica, Nuova Accad, 59 & 2nd ed, 68; I racconti di Cechov, Eri, 61; L'Europa orientale dal Rinascimento all' Ita illuministica, Vallardi, 70; ed, La questione della lingua presso gli Slavi, Ateneo, Rome, 72; Etudes Litteraries Slavo-romances, Licosa-Sansoni, 78; plus many articles, Ricerche Slavistiche, 52-58. *Mailing Add:* 168 Westwood Rd New Haven CT 06515

PICCIOTTO, ROBERT S, b Buenos Aries, Arg, Sept 18, 39; US citizen; m 61; c 1. ROMANCE LANGUAGES, COMPARATIVE LITERATURE. *Educ:* Ind Univ, AB, 61, PhD(comp lit), 64. *Prof Exp:* Lectr Spanish, Ind Univ, 63-64; from instr to asst prof, 64-76, ASSOC PROF ROMANCE LANG, QUEENS COL, NY, 76- *Mem:* MLA; Am Asn Teachers Span & Port. *Res:* Literary theory; contemporary Spanish poetry; Mediaeval Spanish literature. *Publ:* Auth, Meditaciones rurales de una mentalidad urbana, La Torre, 65; La zapatera prodigiosa and Lorca's poetic credo, Hispania, 66; Marsile's right hand, Romance Notes, 67. *Mailing Add:* Dept of Romance Lang Queens Col Flushing NY 11367

PICHERIT, JEAN-LOUIS GEORGES, b Bayonne, France, Apr 13, 43; m 70. FRENCH MEDIEVAL LITERATURE, ROMANCE PHILOLOGY. *Educ:* Ecole Suepr Commerce et Admin Entreprises, Lyon, France, dipl, 65; Univ Nebr-Lincoln, MA, 67; Univ NC, Chapel Hill, PhD(French medieval lit & Romance philol), 71. *Prof Exp:* Asst prof Romance lang, Va Commonwealth Univ, 69-76; ASST PROF MOD & CLASS LANG, UNIV WYO, 76- *Mem:* Am Asn Teachers Fr; Amis de la Romania; Mediaeval Acad Am. *Res:* French medieval literature. *Mailing Add:* Dept of Mod & Class Lang Univ of Wyo Laramie WY 82071

PICHOIS, CLAUDE, b Paris, France, July 21, 25; m 61. FRENCH LITERATURE, COMPARATIVE LITERATURE. *Educ:* Hautes Etudes Commerciales, Paris, Dipl, 48; Sorbonne, Doctorat d'Etat, 63. *Prof Exp:* Assoc prof French lit, Faculte des Lettres d'Aix-en-Provence, France, 56, assoc prof comp lit, 58-61; prof French lit, Faculte d'Hist et de Philos, Basel, Switz, 61-70; prof, 70-73, DISTINGUISHED PROF FRENCH LIT, VANDERBILT UNIV, 73- *Concurrent Pos:* C0-ed, Revue d'Hist litteraire de la France, Armand Colin, Paris, 50-, Etudes baudelairiennes, La Baconniere, Switz, 69- & Bull baudelairien, Vanderbilt Univ, 70-; gen ed, Litterature francaise, Arthaud, Paris, 68-80; vis res prof, Inst Res Humanities, Madison, Wis, 68; John Simon Guggenheim Mem Found fel, 78. *Mem:* MLA; Soc d'Hist litteraire France. *Res:* Baudelaire; Nerval; western literary relations. *Publ:* AUth, L'Image de Jean-Paul Richter dans les lettres francasies, 63 & Philarete Chasles et la vie litteraire au temps du romantisme, 65, Jose Corti, Paris; Litterature et Progres: Vitesse et vision du monde, La Baconniere, 73; ed, Baudelaire's Correspondence, 2 vols, 73 & Baudelaire's Complete Works, 2 vols, 75-76, Bibliot de la Pleiade, Paris. *Mailing Add:* Box 6203 Sta B Vanderbilt Univ Nashville TN 37235

PICK, ERNEST, b Prague, Czech, Sept 24, 36; US citizen; m 59; c 1. ROMANCE LANGUAGES. *Educ:* Univ Pa, BA, 58; Univ Bordeaux, MA, 59; Univ Nancy, PhD(Fr), 61. *Prof Exp:* Asst prof French, 61-69, ASSOC PROF MOD FOREIGN LANG & COORDR, LAKE ERIE COL, 69- *Mem:* MLA; Am Asn Teachers Fr. *Res:* Language methodology. *Publ:* Transl, Sociology of literature, Lake Erie Col Studies, 63. *Mailing Add:* Dept of French Lake Erie Col Painesville OH 44077

PICK, MARY MARITZA, b Santa Monica, Calif, Mar 6, 51. COMPARATIVE LITERATURE. *Educ:* Univ Calif, Los Angeles, BA, 72; Brandeis Univ, PhD(comp lit), 80. *Prof Exp:* RES ASSOC LIT, MOD STUDIES GROUP, 78- *Res:* Development of the detective novel since Dostoevsky; 19th century French and German theater; twentieth century Austrian playwrights. *Publ:* Auth, Aspects of Multiplicity: A Comparative Study of the Works of Hermann Hesse and Andre Gide, 80 & ed, Affirmist Manifesto, 82, Mod Studies Group. *Mailing Add:* Mod Studies Group PO Box 5121 Stanford CA 94305

PICKEL, FRANK GIVENS, b Bloomsbury, NJ, Feb 19, 20. CLASSICAL PHILOLOGY. *Educ:* Oberlin Col, AB, 41; Univ Chicago, PhD(Latin lang & lit), 49. *Prof Exp:* Ryerson traveling fel, Univ Chicago, 49-50; instr classics, Washington Univ, 50-54; actg asst prof, Univ Wash, 54-55; asst prof, Univ Vt, 55-57; asst ed etymology, G & C Merriam Co, Springfield, Mass, 57-59; ed & copywriter Latin, advert dept, 60-61, asst ed, Latin ed dept, 61-65, ed-in-charge, 66-71, ed, 71-79, SR ED, DICTIONARY DEPT, SCOTT FORESMAN & CO, GLENVIEW, ILL, 79- *Mem:* Am Philol Asn; Archaeol Inst Am; Class Asn Mid West & South; Brit Class Asn. *Res:* Greek and Latin language and literature; Livy; lexicography. *Mailing Add:* 1311 Chicago Ave Evanston IL 60201

PICKEN, ROBERT A, b Los Angeles, Calif, Aug 5, 34; wid. ROMANCE LANGUAGES, INTERNATIONAL EDUCATION. *Educ:* Dartmouth Col, BA, 56; Oxford Univ, BA, 58, MA, 61, DPhil(Fr), 64. *Prof Exp:* Instr mod lang, Union Col, NY, 60-61; asst prof French, Swarthmore Col, 61-64; asst prof Romance lang, 64-68, dean fac int educ, 68-71, ASSOC PROF ROMANCE LANG, QUEENS COL, NY, 68- *Concurrent Pos:* Res dir, City Univ New York Prog Study Abroad, Nancy, 65-68. *Mem:* MLA; Am Asn Teachers Fr; Mod Greek Studies Asn. *Res:* French literature of the 17th century; international education; modern Greek language and literature. *Mailing Add:* Dept of Romance & Slavic Lang Col Lib Arts Queens Col Flushing NY 11367

PICKENS, RUPERT TARPLEY, b High Point, NC, Feb 20, 40; m 63; c 2. ROMANCE PHILOLOGY, MEDIEVAL FRENCH. *Educ:* Univ NC, Chapel Hill, AB, 61, MA, 64, PhD(Romance philol), 66. *Prof Exp:* Asst prof French, Univ NC, Chapel Hill, 66-69; from asst prof to assoc prof, 69-78, PROF FRENCH, UNIV KY, 78- *Concurrent Pos:* Managing ed, Fr Forum, 75- *Mem:* MLA; Soc Rencesvals; Am Asn Teachers Fr.. *Res:* The Bestiaire and Cumpot of Philippe de Thaün; Old French courtly literature; medieval lyric poetry. *Publ:* Auth, The concept of the feminine ideal in Villon's Testament: Huitain 89, Studies Philol, 73; Thematic Structure of Marie de France's Guigemar, Romania, 74; Somnium and Interpretation in Guillaume de Lorris, Symposium, 74; Estoire, Lai and romance: Chretien's Erec et Enide and Cliges, Romanic Rev, 75; The Welsh Knight: Paradoxicality in Chretien's Conte del Graal, FS Forum, 77; Jafure Rudel et la poetique de la mouvance, Cahiers Civilisation Medievale, 77; The Songs of Jaufre Rudel, Pontif Inst Mediaeval Studies, 78; La Poetique de Marie de France d'apres les prologues des Lais, Les Lett Romanes, 78. *Mailing Add:* Dept of French Univ of Ky Lexington KY 40506

PICKETT, TERRY H, b Washington, Ga, Apr 19, 41; m 61; c 2. GERMAN LITERATURE & HISTORY. *Educ:* Univ Ga, AB, 66; Vanderbilt Univ, PhD(Ger lit), 70. *Prof Exp:* Asst prof, 70-79, PROF GER, UNIV ALA, 80-, CHMN DEPT GER & RUSS, 78- *Concurrent Pos:* Fulbright-Exchange Teacher, Hans-Sachs-Gym & Univ of Erlangen-Nurnberg, 72-73. *Mem:* MLA; Southeastern Mod Lang Asn; Am Asn Teachers Ger. *Res:* Nineteenth century German literature; Tendacious literature 1800-1850; Varnhagen von Ense. *Publ:* Auth, Varnhagen's mistaken identity in two recent works, Germanic Notes, 71; Heinrich Boll's plea for civilization, Southern Humanities Rev, 73; Varnhagen von Ense & his mistaken identity, Ger Life & Lett, 4/74; coauth, Varnhagen von Ense and the reception of Russian literature in Germany, Germano-Slavica, fall 74. *Mailing Add:* Dept of Ger Univ of Ala University AL 35486

PIEDMONT, FERDINAND, b Trier, Ger, Nov 19, 26. GERMAN. *Educ:* Univ Bonn, MA, 53, PhD, 54. *Prof Exp:* Studienrat Ger & English, Schiller Gym, Cologne, 58-63; from asst to assoc prof, 63-76, PROF GER, IND UNIV, BLOOMINTON, 76- *Concurrent Pos:* Fulbright vis lectr, 60-61. *Mem:* MLA; Am Asn Teachers Ger; Am Lessing Soc. *Res:* Late 18th and early 19th century literature; drama and theatre; teaching methodology. *Publ:* Auth, Textsammlung Moderner Kurzgeschichten, Diesterweg, Ger, 59; Coauth, Kurz belichtet (German Literature Reader), Rinehart, 73; auth, Zur Rolle des Erzählers in der Kurzgeschichte, Z Deut Philol, 11/73; Tendenzen moderner Schiller-Auffuehrungen 1965-1975, Jb Deut Schillerges, 77. *Mailing Add:* Dept of Ger Ind Univ Bloomington IN 47401

PIEL, SARA ELIZABETH, b Sharpsburg, Pa. MODERN LANGUAGES. *Educ:* Pa Col Women, AB, 28; Univ Pittsburgh, AM, 29, PhD, 38. *Prof Exp:* Instr mod lang, Erie Ctr, Univ Pittsburgh, 30-33; instr French & Ger, Pa Col Women, 33-38, asst prof Ger & chmn dept, 38-47; from asst prof to assoc prof mod lang, Carnegie Inst Technol, 47-60; prof & chmn dept, 60-75, EMER PROF FOREIGN LANG, LEBANON VALLEY COL, 75- *Mem:* AAUP; MLA; Am Asn Teachers Ger. *Res:* Faust philology; present day requirements and qualifying examinations in modern languages. *Mailing Add:* Dept of Foreign Lang Lebanon Valley Col Annville PA 17003

PIERCE, VAUDAU, b Indian Gap, Tex, Feb 24, 13; m 40; c 3. FOREIGN LANGUAGES. *Educ:* Univ Wichita, BA, 34; Univ Iowa, MA, 39; Univ Kans, PhD, 60; Inst Phonetics, Univ Paris, dipl, 38. *Prof Exp:* Asst, Univ Iowa, 37-39; instr foreign lang, Iola Jr Col, 39-41; asst, Univ Colo, 47-49; asst prof foreign lang, Kans State Col Pittsburg, 49-60, assoc prof, 60-64; dir dept, 64-72, PROF SPANISH, SAM HOUSTON STATE UNIV, 64- *Mem:* Am Asn Teachers Span & Port; Am Asn Teachers Fr. *Res:* Portuguese Philology and semantics; Galician lyric poetry. *Publ:* Auth, US Fifth Army language program, Mod Lang J, 12/59. *Mailing Add:* Dept of Foreign Lang Sam Houston State Univ Huntsville TX 77340

PIERSSENS, MICHEL J, b France, 1945; French citizen. FRENCH LITERATURE, PHILOSOPHY. *Educ:* Univ Tours, Lic es Lett, 66; Univ Tours, Univ Montreal, DES, 67; Univ Aix-en-Provence, Doctorat de 3eme C(French lit), 72. *Prof Exp:* Teacher mod lit, Univ Aix-en-Provence, 68-70; vis lectr French lit, Univ Wis-Madison, 70-72; vis asst prof, 72-75, asst prof, 75-82, ASSOC PROF FRENCH LIT, UNIV MICH, ANN ARBOR, 82- *Concurrent Pos:* Publ & ed jour, Sub-Stance, 71-; prog dir, Univ Mich Sch Paris. *Res:* Literary theory; modern French literature; comparative literature. *Publ:* Auth, La Tour de Babil, Ed Minuit, Paris, 76; plus var art in, Critique Litterature, Diogene, Dada/Surrealism, MLN. *Mailing Add:* Dept of Romance Lang Univ of Mich Ann Arbor MI 48109

PIFER, ELLEN, English, Comparative Literature. See Vol II

PIFFARD, GUERARD, b Fellsmere, Fla, Mar 22, 19. FRENCH PHILOLOGY, ROMANCE LANGUAGES. *Educ:* Colo Col, AB, 41; AM, 48; Stanford Univ, PhD(Fr), 57. *Prof Exp:* Acting instr French, Stanford Univ, 54-55, French & German, 55-56; asst prof, French & German, 56-60, assoc prof, 60-67, PROF FRENCH, SAN DIEGO STATE UNIV, 67- *Mem:* Am Asn Teachers Fr; MLA; Philol Asn Pac Coast. *Res:* Romance philology; Germanic philology; stylo-statistiques. *Publ:* Auth, A Manual of Foreign Language Pronunciation, 60; A Bibliography of Dictionaries and Grammars, 60 & 61, privately publ; coauth, La Chancun de Willame, Univ NC, 61; auth, L'Aspect, Bull Jeunes Romanists, Strasbourg, 65. *Mailing Add:* Dept of French & Ital San Diego State Univ San Diego CA 92115

PIGEON, GERARD GEORGES, b Dakar, Senegal, July 2 38; nat US; m 67; c 1. LITERATURE, LINGUISTICS. *Educ:* Acad Paris, Baccalaureat, 58; Univ Calif, Santa Barbara, MA, 69, PhD(French lit & ling), 73. *Prof Exp:* Teaching asst, French Dept & res asst, Lab Speech & Synthesis Res, 67-70, ASSOC PROF BLACK STUDIES, UNIV CALIF, SANTA BARBARA, 70-, CHMN DEPT, 73- *Concurrent Pos:* Translr & consult for Gen Elec Co, TEMPO Ctr Advan Studies, Santa Barbara, 68-70; ed adv res in African lit, Univ Tex, Austin, 70-71. *Mem:* MLA; African Studies Asn. *Res:* French African and West-Indian literature; French language and phonetics; oral tradition in Afro-American culture and Black studies. *Publ:* Auth, Ombre et Lumiere, Sun Press Publ, 69; Le Theme de la Fatalite dans Un Piege sans fin, Presence Francophone, Sherbrooke, Can, 74; Frontieres, Oswald, Paris, 76; Particularites lexicales du francais des ecrivains Negro-Africains, Sherbrooke, 76; Dynamics of alienation in French Black literature, J Black Studies, 12/77; The teaching of French African literature in American universities, colleges and high schools, Univ Tex, 3/77; Autopsie Du Cahier, Desormeaux, Martinique, 78; Favelas, Edition St Germains-des-Pres, 81. *Mailing Add:* Dept of Black Studies Univ of Calif Santa Barbara CA 93106

PIGMAN, GEORGE WOOD, III, Renaissance Studies, Classics. See Vol II

PIKE, BURTON E, b Boston, Mass, June 12, 30. COMPARATIVE LITERATURE, GERMAN. *Educ:* Haverford Col, BA, 52; Harvard Univ, MA, 55, PhD(comp lit), 58. *Prof Exp:* Lectr English, Univ Hamburg, 57-59; from instr to assoc prof Ger lit, Cornell Univ, 59-69, chmn dept comp lit, 64-68; chmn dept Ger & comp lit, 67-72, PROF COMP LIT, QUEENS COL, NY, 69-; PROF COMP LIT & GER, GRAD SCH, CITY UNIV NEW YORK, 77- *Concurrent Pos:* Guggenheim fel, 66-67; Colloquium fel, NY Univ, 67- *Mem:* MLA; Am Comp Lit Asn (secy, 67-71). *Res:* Twentieth century German and comparative literature, especially novel; autobiography; city in literature. *Publ:* Co-ed, Mark Twain: Die besten Geschichten, Schünemann, Bremen, 60; auth, Robert Musil; An Introduction to his Work, Cornell Univ, 61; Time in autobiography, Comp Lit, fall 76. *Mailing Add:* Dept of Comp Lit Queens Col Flushing NY 11367

PIKE, KENNETH LEE, b Woodstock, Conn, June 9, 12; m 38; c 3. LINGUISTICS. *Educ:* Gordon Col, ThB, 33; Univ Mich, PhD, 42. *Hon Degrees:* LHD, Univ Chicago, 73; Dr, L'Universite Rene Descartes, 78. *Prof Exp:* Res assoc, English Lang Inst, Univ Mich, Ann Arbor, 42-43, lectr phonetics, Ling Inst, 45, Lloyd fel, 45-46, assoc prof, 48-55, prof ling, 55-79. *Concurrent Pos:* Ling researcher, Wycliffe Bible Transl, 35-; ling investr, Summer Inst Ling, 35-, instr phonetics, 36-41, co-dir courses, 42-50, prof, 42-; Am Coun Learned Soc grant-in-aid, 37; ling consult, field trips, Ecuador, Peru, Bolivia, Mex, Philippines, New Guinea, Ghana & Nigeria. *Mem:* Ling Soc Am (pres, 61); liaison fel Am Anthrop Asn; Int Phonetic Asn; Ling Asn Can & US (pres, 77-78). *Res:* Theory of languages, especially Mixtec. *Publ:* Auth, Language in Relation to a Unified Theory of the Structure of Human Behavior, Humanities, rev ed, 67; co-ed, Tone systems of Tibeto-Burman languages of Nepal, Parts I-IV, In: Occasional Papers of the Wolfendon Society on Tibeto-Burman Linguistics, Mouton, The Hague, 70; coauth, Rhetoric: Discovery and Change, Harcourt, 70; Mark My Words, Eerdmans, 71; contribr, Kenneth L Pike: Selected Writings, Mouton, The Hague, 72; Grammatical Analysis, Summer Inst Ling, Dallas, 2nd ed, 82; Tagmemics, Discourse, and Verbal Art, Mich Studies Humanities, 81; Linguistic Concept: An Introduction to Tagmemics, Lincoln, 82. *Mailing Add:* Dept of Ling Univ of Mich Ann Arbor MI 48104

PILLET, ROGER A, b Lyons, France, Dec 21, 17; US citizen; m 39; c 3. ROMANCE LANGUAGES, EDUCATION. *Educ:* Univ Mo, Columbia, AB, 39, MA, 40; Northwestern Univ, PhD(French), 55. *Prof Exp:* Instr French, Univ Mo, 39-41 & Wash Univ, 47-49; lectr, Northwestern Univ, 49-

55; from instr to asst prof, 55-64, assoc prof French & educ, 64-72, ASSOC DIR MAT PROG, UNIV CHICAGO, 68-, PROF EDUC & SECY DEPT & PROF FRENCH, 72- *Concurrent Pos:* Chmn, nat FLES comt, 66-67; consult, Bell & Howell Co, 66-68 & US Off Educ, 68. *Mem:* MLA; Am Asn Teachers Fr; Am Confed Teachers Foreign Lang. *Publ:* Coauth, French in the Elementary School, Univ Chicago, 62; auth, Mon premier dictionnaire, World, 63; French with slides and tapes: A reappraisal, Elem Sch J, 11/64; Demands of new dimensions, Sch Rev, summer 65; French word list for the New key, Fr Rev, 12/65; ed, FLES and the Elementary School Curriculum, Chilton, 67; coauth, Foreign Language Study, 74 & auth, Foreign Languages Perspective and Prospect, 74, Univ Chicago. *Mailing Add:* Dept of Romance Lang & Lit Univ of Chicago Chicago IL 60637

PILLSBURY, PAUL WHIPPLE, b Danbury, NH, Dec 14, 22; m 49; c 2. ENGLISH. *Educ:* Dartmouth Col, AB, 48; Univ Mich, MA, 49, MA, 51, PhD, 61. *Prof Exp:* Instr English, Cornell Univ, 54-58, asst prof, Westminster Col, 58-60; instr, 60-61, from asst prof to assoc prof, 61-67, PROF ENGLISH LANG & LIT, EASTERN MICH UNIV, 67- *Concurrent Pos:* Vis scholar Summer Ling Soc Am Inst, 65; Off Educ res grant, 67-68; Am Philos Soc grant, 67-68. *Mem:* Ling Soc Am; Ling Asn Gt Brit; Early English Text Soc. *Res:* Old English and modern English grammar; linguistic science; computer-aided concordance making. *Publ:* Coauth, English Language Achievement Series, with Teachers' Manual, English Lang Inst, Univ Mich, 63; auth, Descriptive Analysis of Discourse in Late West Saxon Texts, Mouton, 67. *Mailing Add:* Dept of English Lang & Lit Eastern Mich Univ Ypsilanti MI 48197

PILLWEIN, RUDOLF, b Brünn, Czech, Sept 10, 13; US citizen; m 35; c 1. MODERN LANGUAGES, PHILOLOGY. *Educ:* German Univ, Prague, JUDr, 39. *Prof Exp:* Chief admin sect bus admin, Waffenwerke Brünn, Werk Gurein, 39-45; tech transl, US Army & Air Force, Nurnberg, Ger, 47-56; case worker, Dept Pub Welfare, Baltimore, Md, 57; instr mod lang, Villanova Univ, 57-60; from asst prof to prof, 60-80, EMER PROF MOD LANG, ST JOSEPH'S UNIV. *Mem:* Am Asn Teacher Ger. *Res:* Modern Languages; philology. *Mailing Add:* Dept of Mod Lang St Joseph's Col Philadelphia PA 19131

PILUSO, ROBERT VINCENT, b Yonkers, NY, Apr 5, 37; m 67; c 3. ROMANCE LANGUAGES. *Educ:* Fordham Univ, AB, 58, AM, 60; NY Univ, PhD(Romance lang), 65. *Prof Exp:* Instr Span & French, St Peter's Col, 59-60; teacher Span & Latin, Tuckahoe High Sch, 60-63; instr Span & French, Manhattan Col, 63-65; instr Span, Hunter Col, 65-67; assoc prof, 67-72, PROF ROMANCE LANG, STATE UNIV NY COL NEW PALTZ, 72- *Mem:* Am Asn Teachers Span & Port; MLA; Asoc Int Hispanistas. *Res:* Cervantes and Golden Age prose; Golden Age drama; contemporary theater, especially Spanish. *Publ:* Auth, La fuerza de la sangre: Un analisis estructural, Hispania, 64; Amor, matrimonio y honra en Cervantes, Las Americas, 67; Analisis de El infamador, Duquesne Hisp Rev, 68; Honor in Valdivielso and Cervantes, Ky Romance Quart, 70. *Mailing Add:* Dept of Span State Univ of New York Col New Paltz NY 12561

PIMENTEL, RAUL (RAY), b Los Angeles, Calif, July 6, 27; m 64; c 1. GERMAN. *Educ:* Univ Calif, Berkeley, BA, 50, MA, 56, PhD(Ger), 67. *Prof Exp:* Instr Ger, Univ Houston, 59-61 & Univ Calif, Davis, 61-65; asst prof, 65-72, assoc prof, 72-80, PROF GER, SAN JOSE STATE UNIV, 80- *Concurrent Pos:* Resident dir, Calif State Cols & Univ Int Prog, Ger, 69-70. *Mem:* Am Asn Teachers Ger. *Res:* German medieval political lyric. *Mailing Add:* Dept For Lang San Jose State Univ San Jose CA 95192

PINCUS, MICHAEL STERN, b Atlanta, Ga, Jan 18, 36; m 56; c 2. SPANISH, ROMANCE PHILOLOGY. *Educ:* Union Col, NY, BA, 57; Univ NC, MA, 58, PhD(Romance lang), 61. *Prof Exp:* Instr Romance lang, Rutgers Univ, 61-62, asst prof, 62-67; assoc prof foreign lang, State Univ NY Col New Paltz, 67-69; assoc prof Span & classics & chmn dept, Univ NH, 69-72; prof Span & dean sch arts & sci, Mansfield State Col, 72-80; dean of col, Mary Baldwin Col, 80-82; DEAN, COL OF ARTS & SCI, FAIRLEIGH DICKINSON UNIV, 82- *Concurrent Pos:* Part-time instr, Univ NC, 57-59 & 60-61; ed, Comp Romance Ling, 65-66; consult, Rutgers Univ Press, 66-67. *Mem:* Mediaeval Acad Am; MLA; Am Asn Teachers Span & Port; AAUP; Am Asn Univ Adminr. *Res:* Spanish philology; medieval Spanish literature; educational innovation. *Publ:* Auth, Linguistic Dadaism in Sursilvan, 59 & Dona Endrina revisited, 66, Romance Notes; Foreign Languages in the service of liberal arts, Bull Asn Depts Foreign Lang, 71. *Mailing Add:* Dean, Col Arts & Sci Fairleigh Dickinson Univ Rutherford NJ 07070

PINET, CHRISTOPHER PAUL, b Chelsea, Mass, May 6, 44; m 69; c 2. FRENCH LANGUAGE & LITERATURE. *Educ:* Univ Kans, AB, 66; Brown Univ, MA, 68, PhD(French), 71. *Prof Exp:* Asst prof French, Ind State Univ, 71-73; ASST PROF FRENCH, MARQUETTE UNIV, 73- *Mem:* MLA; Am Asn Teachers Fr; Soc Values Higher Educ; Soc Int Du/Theatre Medieval. *Res:* French farce and popular literature of the sixteenth century; contemporary French civilization. *Publ:* Auth, The cobbler in French farce of the Renaissance, Fr Rev, 12/74; Myths and stereotypes in Asterix Le Gaulois, Contemp French Civilization, spring 77, Can Mod Lang Rev, 1/78; French farce: Printing, dissemination and readership from 1500-1560, Renaissance & Reformation/Renaissance et Reforme (in press). *Mailing Add:* Dept of Foreign Lang & Lit Marquette Univ Milwaukee WI 53233

PINKERTON, SANDRA, b Butte, Mont, Sept 10, 42. LINGUISTICS, ANTHROPOLOGY. *Educ:* Univ Tex, Austin, BA, 71, MA, 74, PhD(ling), 76. *Prof Exp:* Coordr English second lang prog, Univ Carabobo, Venezuela, 66-68; acting asst prof ling, Univ Calif, Los Angeles, 76-77; Pub Health Serv Res fel, Nat Inst Neurological & Commun Disorders & Stroke, Univ Calif, Berkeley, 77-79; MEM FAC, DEPT SPAN & PORT, UNIV MINN, 80- *Concurrent Pos:* Consult dialectology, Los Angeles Pub Sch Syst, 77. *Mem:* Ling Soc Am; Acoustical Soc Am; MLA; Am Anthrop Asn; Ling Asn Southwest. *Res:* Mayan linguistics; bilingualism in Mexican-American communities in the Southwest; Spanish vowel Sandhi. *Publ:* Auth,Spanish vowel Sandhi, In: Papers From the Parasession of Natural Phonology, Conf Lit Studies, 74; Word order and the antipassive in K'ekchi, In: Papers From the Mayan Symposium, Am Anthrop Asn, 76; Coauth, Li k'aklek, li a:wk ut li q'olok Native American Text Ser, Int J Ling, 76; ed, Studies in K'ekchi, Univ Tex, 76. *Mailing Add:* Dept of Span & Port Univ of Minn Minneapolis MN 55455

PINO, FRANK, JR, b El Paso, Tex, Nov 11, 42; m. SPANISH, HISTORY. *Educ:* Ariz State Univ, BA, 63, MA, 64; Northwestern Univ, PhD(Span), 71. *Prof Exp:* Instr Span, Northwestern Univ, 66-68; from instr to asst prof, Mich State Univ, 68-73; ASSOC PROF SPAN, UNIV TEX, SAN ANTONIO, 73-, ASST VPRES ACAD AFFAIRS, 76- *Concurrent Pos:* Ed consult classical studies, Argonaut Publ, Inc, 65-68; grants in aid, Mich State Univ, 71, 72 & 73; field consult bilingual educ, Ctr Commun Res, Univ Tex, Austin, 72-73. *Mem:* MLA; Latin Am Studies Asn; Am Asn Teachers Span & Port; Popular Cult Asn. *Res:* Hispanic literatures and cultures; Mexican American literature; popular culture. *Publ:* Transl, Tovar, Antonio, An Introduction to Plato, Argonaut Publ, 69; auth, Chicano poetry: A popular manifesto, J Popular Cult, spring 73; Mexican Americans: A Research Bibliography, Mich State Univ, 74; The Outsider and El otro in Tomas Rivera's . . . y no se lo trago la tierra, Books Abroad, summer 75; La literatura chicana como micro-cosmo del pueblo, Proc 17th Cong Inst Lit Iberoam, 75; El simbolismo en la Poesia de Antonio Machado, Univ NC, Chapel Hill, 76; Love, sex and religion in Tomas Rivera's . . . y no se lo trago la tierra, In: EROS in Film & Literature: Reflections on Contemporary Literature, Coronaco (in press). *Mailing Add:* Dept of Foreign Lang Univ of Tex San Antonio TX 78016

PINTO, PAUL ARTHUR MADDOX, b Belo Horizonte, Brazil, Feb 15, 37; US citizen; m 68. PORTUGUESE LANGUAGE. *Educ:* Univ NC Chapel Hill, BA, 59, PhD(Port), 79; NMex State Univ, MA, 73. *Prof Exp:* Asst prof Span, French & Latin, Calif Baptist Col, 80-82; INSTR PORT, DEFENSE LANG INST, 82- *Concurrent Pos:* Material aid adv, Church World Serv, Africa, 65-71. *Mem:* MLA; Am Asn Teachers Span & Port. *Res:* Contemporary Brazilian drama; metaphysics; Romanian language and literature. *Publ:* Auth, Rivas' operatic characters: The personages of Guiseppe Verdi's La Forza del Destino, Romance Notes, 80; Music as a dramatic and thematic device in Jorge Andrade's Marta, A Arvore e o Relogio, Taller Lit, 82; Jorge Andrade's three enigmas, Hisp, 84. *Mailing Add:* 1705 David Ave Monterey CA 93940

PIPA, ARSHI, b Scutari, Albania, July 28, 20. LANGUAGES. *Educ:* Univ Florence, PhD, 42. *Prof Exp:* Instr humanities, State Lyceum, Scutari & Tirana, Albania, 42-46; vis asst prof Ital, Georgetown Univ, 60-61; lectr, Columbia Univ, 61-62; asst prof, Adelphi Univ, 62-63; asst prof, Univ Calif, Berkeley, 63-66; assoc prof, 66-70, PROF ITAL, UNIV MINN, MINNEAPOLIS, 70- *Mem:* Am Philos Asn; Am Soc Aesthet; Am Asn Teachers Ital; MLA; Dante Soc Am. *Res:* Aesthetics; literary criticism; poetry. *Publ:* Auth, Lundertarë, 44; Libri i burgut, 59 & Rusha, 68, Authorial; Montale and Dante, Univ Minn, 68; Meridiana, Authorial, 69; Le mythe de l'Occident dans la poesie de Migjeni, Südost-Forsch, 71; La Riduzione teatrale di un romanzo di Moravia, Belfagor, 5/72; Storia, dottrina e arte nei Promessi Sposi, Ragioni Critiche, 5/72. *Mailing Add:* Dept of French & Ital Univ of Minn Minneapolis MN 55455

PIPER, ANSON CONANT, b Newton, Mass, Aug 14, 18; m 45; c 3. ROMANCE LANGUAGES. *Educ:* Williams Col, Mass, BA, 40; Univ Wis, MA, 47, PhD(Span), 53. *Prof Exp:* From instr to prof Romanic lang, 49-68, chmn dept, 61-71, WILLIAM DWIGHT WHITNEY PROF ROMANIC LANG, WILLIAMS COL, 68- *Mem:* Am Asn Teachers Span & Port. *Res:* Portuguese literature; Spanish literature, especially 19th century novel; Romance linguisitics. *Publ:* Auth, Asi es la vida, Norton, 58; coauth, Fundamental Portuguese Vocabulary, Univ Louvain, 68. *Mailing Add:* Dept of Romance Lang Williams Col Williamstown MA 01267

PIQUER, MARIANO JULIO, b Zaragoza, Spain, Apr 29, 31. SPANISH LANGUAGE, HISTORY OF SPANISH CIVILIZATION. *Educ:* Univ Zaragoza, Lic en Filos y Let, 61, Dr Filos y Let(Span hist & civilization), 70. *Prof Exp:* Instr Span lang, Hobart & William Smith Cols, 62-63; lectr, 63-65, asst prof, 65-70, ASSOC PROF SPAN LANG & CIVILIZATION, UNIV NB, FREDERICTON, 70- *Mem:* MLA; Am Asn Teachers Span & Port. *Res:* Latin American civilization, colonial period; Spanish linguisitcs. *Mailing Add:* 233 Aberdeen Fredericton NB E3B 1R6 Can

PIRIOU, JEAN-PIERRE JOSEPH, b Paris, France, Apr 10, 43; m 68; c 3. FRENCH LITERATURE. *Educ:* Univ Paris, Lic es Lett, 64, Dipl etudes super English lit, 65; Univ Va, PhD(French lit), 73. *Prof Exp:* Instr English, Col Jean-Jaures, Paris, 62-65; instr French, Univ Va, 68-69; consult French & English, Dept Educ, Que, 69-70; instr French, Univ Va, 70-73, asst prof French lit, 73-74; asst prof, 74-78, assoc prof, 78-82, PROF FRENCH LIT, UNIV GA, 82-, HEAD DEPT ROMANCE LANG, 81- *Concurrent Pos:* Corresp, French XX Bibliog, 71; mem, Am Coun Teaching Fr Social & Cult Studies, 81. *Mem:* Am Asn Teachers Fr; MLA; SAtlantic Mod Lang Asn. *Res:* Twentieth century French literature; comparative literature. *Publ:* Coauth, Genese et critique d'une autobiographie: Les mots de Jean-Paul Sartre, Lett Mod, Minard, Paris, 73; ed & auth introd, Julien Green Memories of Evil Days, Univ Va, 76; auth, Sexualite, Religion et Art chez Julien Green, Nizet, Paris, 76; Julien Green et l'Amerique, S Atlantic Bull, 11/77; Une Grande amitie: Correspondance, Julien Green-Jacques Maritain, 1926-1972, Plon, Paris, 79. *Mailing Add:* Dept of Romance Lang Univ of Ga Athens GA 30602

PIROG, GERALD, b NJ, Jan 12, 48. SLAVIC LANGUAGES AND LITERATURES. *Educ:* Rutgers Univ, AB, 69; Yale Univ, MPhil, 72, PhD(Slavic), 75. *Prof Exp:* Instr Russ, William Patterson Col NJ, 73-75; asst prof, 75-80, PROF RUSS & POLISH, RUTGERS UNIV, 80- *Mem:* Am Asn Advan Slavic Studies; Am Asn Teachers Slavic & E Europ Lang & Lit; MLA. *Res:* Russian symbolist poetry, particularly Aleksandr Blok; early period of Soviet Cinema; Slavic literary theory. *Publ:* Auth, The city, the woman, the

Madonna: Metaphorical inference in Blok's Ital janskie stixi, Forum Iowa Russ Lit, 12/77; Blok's Blagovescenie: A study in iconological transformation, Vol VII, 79 & Blok's Ravenna: The city as sign, Vol VII, 80, Russ Lit; Iconicity & narrative: The Eisenstein-Vertor contraversy, Semiotica (in press); Aleksandr Blok's Italjanski Stikhi: Confrontations and disillusionment, Slavica Publ (in press). *Mailing Add:* Dept of Slavic Rutgers Univ New Brunswick NJ 08903

PIRSCENOK, ANNA (MRS JULIUS M HERZ), b Bethlehem, Pa, Mar 15, 22. SLAVIC & BALTIC STUDIES. *Educ:* Univ Pa, BS, 49, MA, 50, PhD(Slavic & Baltic studies), 56; Columbia Univ, MA, 51. *Prof Exp:* Night supvr, Hahnemann Hosp, Phila, 43-45; instr & supvr surg nursing, Episcopal Hosp, Phila, 48-50; dir sch nursing & nursing serv, Montgomery Hosp, Norristown, Pa, 51-53; res linguist, Inst Coop Res, Univ Pa, 53-58, asst prof Slavic lang & lit, 59-66, lectr Russ, Col, 57-59; assoc prof, 66-70, chmn dept Mod Foreign Lang & Lit, 72-75, PROF RUSS, LEHIGH UNIV, 70- *Concurrent Pos:* Supvr Russ adult educ, Philadelphia Bd Educ, 57-60; broadcaster Russ, WHYY-TV, Philadelphia, 57-60; consult sci & tech Russ, Am Chem Soc, 58-60 & 63-64 & Sun Oil Co, 62-63; Fulbright-Hays fac travel grant, 60 & 64; consult Slavic lang, St Tikhon's Eastern Orthodox Sem, 70-75; dir, Palisades Sch Dist Bd Educ, 79- *Mem:* Am Asn Teachers Slavic & EEurop Lang; MLA; Comp & Int Educ Soc. *Res:* Slavic Languages and literatures; bibliography; Russian 19th and 20th century literature. *Publ:* Auth, Recent Russian books in psychology, Contemp Psychol, 68- *Mailing Add:* Dept of Mod Foreign Lang & Lit Lamberton Hall Lehigh Univ Bethlehem PA 18015

PISTORIUS, GEORGE, b Prague, Czech, Mar 19, 22; m 45; c 1. FRENCH. *Educ:* Univ Strasbourg, Certs, 51; Univ Pa, PhD, 63. *Prof Exp:* Instr Ger, Nat Conserv Music & Dramatic Art, Prague, 43-45; asst comp lit, Charles Univ, Prague, 46-48; from instr to asst prof French, Lafayette Col, 58-63; assoc prof, 63-68, chmn dept romantic lang, 71-82, PROF FRENCH, WILLIAMS COL, MASS, 68- *Mem:* MLA; Am Asn Teachers Fr; Int Asn Fr Studies. *Res:* French literature of the 20th century; comparative literature; Franco-German literary relations. *Publ:* Auth, A Critical Bibliography of the Works of F X Salda, Melantrich, Prague, 48; Destin de la culture Francaise dans une democratie populaire, Les Iles d'Or, Paris, 57; L'image de l'Allemagne dans le roman francais entre les deux guerres, 1918-1939, Debresse, Paris, 64; Structure des comparaisons dans Madame Bovary, Cahiers Asn Int Etudes Fr, 5/71; Proust en Allemagne, Bull Soc des Amis Marcel Proust, 65, 66 & 76; Marcel Proust und Deutschland, Carl Winter, Heidelberg, 81. *Mailing Add:* Dept of Romanic Lang Williams Col Williamstown MA 01267

PITKIN, HARVEY, b New York, NY, Apr 22, 28; m 63; c 2. LINGUISTICS, ANTHROPOLOGY. *Educ:* Univ Calif, Berkeley, BA, 55, PhD(ling), 63. *Prof Exp:* Asst prof ling, Univ Calif, Berkeley, 60-64; assoc prof, 64-80, PROF ANTHROP, COLUMBIA UNIV, 80- *Concurrent Pos:* Ling consult criminal justice, System for Electronic Anal & Retrieval of Criminal Histories. *Mem:* Am Anthrop Asn; Ling Soc Am. *Res:* General linguistics; California Indian languages; language and culture. *Publ:* Coauth, A comparative survey of California Penutian, Int J Am Ling, 7/58; auth, A bibliography of the Wintun family of languages, Int J Am Ling, 28: 43-54; coauth, A comparison of Miwok and Wintun, Univ Calif Publ Ling, 34: 19-48; auth, Language and culture, In: Language and Philosophy, 69; Some problems of method in anthropological linguistics, In: Method and Theory in Linguistics, Mouton, 70; Coyote and Bullhead, a Wintu text, In: Native American Text Series, Int J Am Ling, 2: 82-104; Squirrel and Acorn-Woman (Wintu), In: Coyote Stories, Int J Am Ling, 1: 32-34; Two plus two makes two: An analysis of Wintu numerals, In: American Indian and Indoeuropean Studies, Papers in honor of Madison S Beeler, Mouton, 78. *Mailing Add:* Dept of Anthrop Columbia Univ New York NY 10027

PITKIN, WILLIS LLOYD, JR, b El Monte, Calif, Feb 20, 36; c 5. LINGUISTICS, COMPOSITION THEORY. *Educ:* Univ Southern Calif, AB, 58, MA, 66, PhD(English), 73. *Prof Exp:* Instr English, Calif State Polytech Col, Pomona, 61-64; dir Fr English, Whittier Col, 64-67; asst prof, Calif State Univ, Fullerton, 67-69, Utah State Univ, 69-70 & Ore Col Educ, 70-73; PROF ENGLISH, UTAH STATE UNIV, 73- *Concurrent Pos:* Vis lectr, Univ Calif, Davis, 77-78 & 82. *Mem:* Nat Coun Teachers English. *Res:* Processing the code of discourse, including discourse code and memory. *Publ:* Auth, Discourse Blocs, Col Comp & Commun, 5/69; Hierarchies and the discourse hierarchy, 3/77 & X/Y: Some basic strategies of discourse, 3/77, Col English. *Mailing Add:* UMC 32 Utah State Univ Logan UT 84321

PITOU, SPIRE, b Staten Island, NY, May 5, 12; m 39; c 1. ROMANCE LITERATURE. *Educ:* Wesleyan Univ, AB, 33; Johns Hopkins Univ, PhD, 36. *Prof Exp:* Asst prof mod lang, Ga Inst Technol, 36-37; asst prof Romance & class lang, Col of Mt St Vincent, 37-39; assoc prof Romance lang, Col of New Rochelle, 36-46; asst prof French, Champlain Col, 46-48; from assoc prof to prof mod lang, Marquette Univ, 48-67; prof, 67-77, EMER PROF LANG & LIT, UNIV DEL, 77- *Concurrent Pos:* Ed assoc, Renascence, 52-54 & assoc ed, 54-55 & 56- *Mem:* MLA; Am Asn Teachers Fr; Am Lit Asn (vpres, 56-). *Res:* Aspects of 17th century literature in Italy, France, Portugal and England; 17th century French novel; drama. *Publ:* Auth, La Calprenede's Faramond: A Study of its Sources, Style, and Reputation, Johns Hopkins Univ, 42; contribr, A Critical Bibliography of French Literature: The Seventeenth Century, Syracuse Univ, 61; auth, Une Tragedie francaise ignoree: Maxwell, Rev Sci Humaines, 65; Le prologue et l'autre source des Captifs, Dix-Septieme Siecle, 67; Louis de Cahusac's Warvic retrieved, Studi Francesi, 68. *Mailing Add:* Dept of Mod Lang Univ of Del Newark DE 19711

PIZZINI, QUENTIN A, b Massillon, Ohio, Nov 19, 39. LINGUISTIC THEORY, PORTUGUESE LINGUISTICS. *Educ:* Univ Calif, Berkeley, AB, 64, San Diego, MA, 69, PhD(ling), 72. *Prof Exp:* Asst prof, Univ Estadual de Campinas, 74-77; ASST PROF LING, IND UNIV, 78- *Concurrent Pos:* Asst prof ling, Pontificia Univ Catolica de Campinas, 74-76. *Mem:* Ling Soc Am; Am Asn Teachers Spanish & Portuguese. *Res:* Linguistic theory; syntax of Portuguese; syntax of Spanish. *Publ:* Auth, Tres Tipos de Oragoes relativas em Portugues, Anais do Primerio Encantro Nacional de Linguistica, 76; The placement of clitic pronouns in Portuguese, Ling Anal, 81; Verb stress in Portuguese, Hispania (in prep); The positioning of clitic pronouns in Spanish, Lingua (in prep). *Mailing Add:* Dept of Spanish & Portuguese Ind Univ Bloomington IN 47401

PLAKS, ANDREW HENRY, b New York, NY, Feb 25, 45; m 68; c 2. CHINESE & COMPARATIVE LITERATURE. *Educ:* Princeton Univ, BA, 67, PhD(E Asian studies), 73. *Prof Exp:* Assoc prof, 73-80, PROF E ASIAN STUDIES, PRINCETON UNIV, 80- *Concurrent Pos:* Nat Endowment Humanities fel, 76. *Res:* Chinese and Japanese fiction; comparative narrative theory. *Publ:* Auth, Archetype and Allegory in the Dream of the Red Chamber, Princeton Univ, 76; The problem of structure in Chinese narrative, Tamkang Rev, 76; Issues in Chinese narrative theory, PTL, 77; Conceptual models in Chinese narrative theory, J Chinese Philos, 77; ed & contribr, Chinese Narrative: Critical and Theoretical Essays, Princeton Univ, 77. *Mailing Add:* 210 Jones Hall Princeton Univ Princeton NJ 08540

PLANITZ, KARL-HEINZ, b Hannover, Ger, Mar 30, 14; nat US. GERMAN LANGUAGE & LITERATURE. *Educ:* Univ Ill, AB, 34, AM, 35, PhD, 38. *Prof Exp:* Asst Ger, Univ Ill, 34-38, instr, 38-39; instr, Univ Cincinnati, 39-42; asst prof, Temple Univ, 46-56; master, Lake Forest Acad, 56-57; assoc prof, 57-59, prof, 59-79, chmn dept Ger & Russ, 59-79, PROF EMER GER, WABASH COL, 79- *Concurrent Pos:* Vpres, Nat Fed Mod Lang Teachers Asn, 60 & pres, 61. *Honors & Awards:* Order of Merit, Fed Ger Repub, 60. *Mem:* MLA; Am Asn Teachers Ger (secy, 54-63, pres, 64-67); Cent States Mod Lang Teachers Asn (pres, 62-63). *Res:* Sixteenth and 17th century German literature; folksong; classical German literature. *Publ:* Coauth, Selective List of Materials (German), PMLA, 62 & supplement, 64. *Mailing Add:* Dept of Ger & Russ Wabash Col Crawfordsville IN 47933

PLANK, DALE LEWIN, b Denver, Colo, June 29, 31; m 55; c 2. RUSSIAN LITERATURE. *Educ:* Univ Wash, BA, 54, PhD(Russ lang & lit), 62. *Prof Exp:* Instr math, Everett Jr Col, 59-63; from asst prof to assoc prof, 63-72, PROF RUSS LANG & LIT, UNIV COLO, BOULDER, 72- *Concurrent Pos:* Fulbright-Hays Ctr fac fel, 67-68. *Mem:* Am Asn Teachers Slavic & EEurop Lang. *Res:* Modern Russian poetics; semantics; figurative language. *Publ:* Auth, Pasternak's Lyric: A Study of Sound and Imagery, Mouton, The Hague, 66; Unconscious motifs in Leonov's The Badgers, Slavic & EEurop J, spring 72; Readings of My Sister Life, Russ Lit Triquart, spring 72. *Mailing Add:* Dept of Slavic Lang & Lit Univ of Colo Boulder CO 80302

PLANT, HELMUT R, b Munich, Ger, Jan 15, 32; US citizen; M 57; c 1. GERMAN. *Educ:* Fairmont State Col, AB, 57; Univ Cincinnati, MA, 61, PhD(Ger), 64. *Prof Exp:* Instr Ger, Cornell Univ, 63-65, asst prof, 65-66; wiss asst, Aachen Tech, Ger, 66-67; asst prof, 67-71, ASSOC PROF GER, UNIV ORE, 71- *Mem:* Am Asn Teachers Ger; Ling Soc Europe. *Res:* German grammar; audiovisual instruction. *Publ:* Auth Syntaktische Studien zu den Monseer Fragmenten, Mouton, The Hague, 69; Syntactic devices in the teaching of manuscript Middle High German, Folia Ling, Vol II, Nos 1-2; coauth, Guten Tag at Oregon: an audiovisual experiment, Unterrichtspraxis, Vol VI, No 1. *Mailing Add:* Dept of Ger Univ of Ore Eugene OR 97403

PLANT, RICHARD, b Frankfurt, Ger, July 22, 11; nat US. GERMAN PHILOLOGY. *Educ:* Univ Basel, PhD, 36. *Prof Exp:* From instr to prof, 47-73, EMER PROF GER, CITY COL NEW YORK, 73- *Concurrent Pos:* Lectr, New Sch Soc Res. *Mem:* MLA; Am Asn Teachers Ger; PEN Am Ctr. *Res:* Nineteenth and 20th century modern German literature; crosscurrents of American and German literatures. *Publ:* Coauth, Lizzie Borden (opera), Boosie & Hawks, 65; contrib, New Yorker, Nation & Esquire; auth, Interview with Günther Grass, NY Times Bookreview, 12/79. *Mailing Add:* 23 Perry St New York NY 10014

PLANTE, JULIAN GERARD, b St Paul, Minn. CLASSICAL PHILOLOGY, MEDIEVAL LATIN. *Educ:* St John's Univ, Minn, AB, 61; Fordham Univ, AM, 63, PhD(class philol), 72. *Prof Exp:* Instr Latin & Greek lit, City Col New York, 64-66; asst prof class philol, 66-73, RES PROF CLASS PHILOL, ST JOHN'S UNIV, MINN, 73-, DIR & CUR MANUSCRIPT RES CTR, HILL MONASTIC MANUSCRIPT LIBR, 66- *Concurrent Pos:* Consult reorgn libr, Augustinian Hist Inst, New York, 70-72; mem bd adv, Bakken Mus Elec Life, Minneapolis, 78. *Honors & Awards:* Lalibela Cross, Patriarch of the Ethiopian Orthodox Church, 73. *Mem:* Am Philol Asn; Mediaeval Acad Am; Am Soc Papyrologists; Class Asn Atlantic States; Medieval Asn Midwest (vpres, 81-82, pres, 82-83). *Res:* Roman religion; palaeography; medieval Latin literature. *Publ:* Ed, Translatio Studii: Manuscript and Library Studies Honoring Oliver L Kapsner, 73 & auth, The text of the Brevis Cronica Reichersbergensis, In: Translatio Studii, 73, St John's Univ; The Ethiopian Embassy to Cairo of 1443: A Trier manuscript of Gandulph's report, with an English translation, J Ethiopian Studies, 7/75; Catalogue of manuscripts in the bibliothek der philosophy-theology Hochschule der Diözese Linz, Traditio, 76; The auxerre commentary on the Regula s Benedicti: The prologue to the Regula: The commentator's main concerns, Regulae Benedicti Studia, 76; The Medieval Library of the Augustinerchorherrenstift Reichersberg, Austria: Towards its reconstruction from two surviving catalogues, In: Studia Codicologica, Festschrift for Marcel Richard, Berlin, 77; The Hill Monastic Manuscript Library . . ., Res Publica Ltterarum 2, 79; Papyrus fragments on microfilm at the Hill Monastic Manuscript Library, Anagennesis; A Papyrological J, Athens, Vol I, No 1. *Mailing Add:* 111 Park Ave S St Cloud MN 56301

PLASS, PAUL CHRISTIAN, b Milwaukee, Wis, Sept 29, 33; m 56; c 1. CLASSICAL LANGUAGES. *Educ:* Univ Wis, BA, 56, MA, 57, PhD, 59. *Prof Exp:* Instr class lang, Lawrence Col, 59-61; asst prof classics, Univ Mo, Columbia, 62-64, asst prof, 64-67; assoc prof, 67-76, PROF CLASSICS, UNIV WIS-MADISON, 76- *Mem:* Am Philol Asn; Soc Am Archaeol. *Res:* Plato; neo-Platonic; early Christian theology. *Publ:* Auth, Timeless time in Neo Platonism, Mod Schoolman, 77; Transcendent time in Maximus the Confessor, Thomist, 80. *Mailing Add:* Classics Dept Univ of Wis Madison WI 53706

PLATER, EDWARD M V, b Saginaw, Mich. GERMAN. *Educ:* Univ Mich, AB, 60, MA, 62, PhD(Ger), 68. *Prof Exp:* Instr Ger, Univ Mich, 66-67; instr, 67-68, asst prof, 68-80, ASSOC PROF GER, MIAMI UNIV, 68- *Concurrent Pos:* Nat Endowment for Humanities summer sem, 78. *Mem:* Am Asn Teachers Ger. *Res:* Conrad Ferdinand Meyer; 19th century German literature. *Publ:* Auth, The Banquet of Life: Conrad Ferdinand Meyer's Die Versuchung des Pescara, Seminar, 6/72; The figure of Dante in Die Hochzeit des Mönchs, Mod Lang Notes, 75; Der schöne Leib in the prose of C F Meyer, Seminar, spring 79; The symbolism in Ferdinand von Saar's Norelle, Marianne, Sem, spring 82. *Mailing Add:* Dept of Foreign Lang Miami Univ Oxford OH 45056

PLAYE, GEORGE LOUIS, b Pawtucket, RI, Mar 15, 17; m; c 2. FRENCH LANGUAGE & LITERATURE. *Educ:* Brown Univ, AB, 39, AM, 40; Univ Ill, PhD, 49. *Prof Exp:* From instr to assoc prof, 46-68, adv, comt disciplines of humanities, 49-53, chmn French staff, 52-59, dir financial aid, 57-59, dean undergrad studies, 59-72, PROF FRENCH, UNIV CHICAGO, 68-, CHMN COMT DISCIPLINES OF HUMANITIES, 72- *Concurrent Pos:* Lectr, Ind Univ, 56-80; chmn comput comt, Col Scholar Serv, 61-65; consult, Off Educ, Dept Health, Educ & Welfare, 66-72 & Nat Endowment for Humanities, 77. *Mem:* MLA; Am Asn Teachers Ital; Am Asn Teachers Fr; Nat Asn Student Personnel Adminr; Am Col Personnel Asn. *Res:* Eighteenth century French literature, especially Voltaire; 19th century French literature. *Publ:* Coauth, Basic Facts for Reading French, Univ Chicago, 57; auth, Dedicatory Address-Little Hall, Univ Fla, 67. *Mailing Add:* Dept of Romance Lang Univ of Chicago 5811 Ellis Ave Chicago IL 60637

PLEVICH-DARRETTA, MARY, b New York, NY, Mar 23, 27. SPANISH LANGUAGE & LITERATURE. *Educ:* Hunter Col, BA, 47; Columbia Univ, MA, 50, PhD(Latin Am lit), 57. *Prof Exp:* Dir biblio, Hisp Inst, Columbia Univ, 47-50; instr Span lang & lit, Sweet Briar Col, 50-52 & Queens Col, NY, 52-55; from instr to assoc prof Latin Am lit, 55-71, PROF SPAN, RUTGERS UNIV, NEWARK, 71- *Concurrent Pos:* Fulbright res scholar, Spain, 62-63; lctr, Universidad Internacional Menende Pelayo, Santander, Spain; Reviewer & consult Col Texbook Div Random House. *Mem:* AAUP; Am Asn Teachers Span & Port. *Res:* Latin American novel; 20th century Spanish literature. *Publ:* Auth, Martin Luis Guzman: Su vida y su obra, Nacion, Mex, 51; El origen del arguedismo, Rev Univ Antioquia, 58; Unamuno y Arguedas, Cuadernos Hispanoam, 67; coauth, Hojas literarias (3 vols) Van Nostrand-Reinhold, 71. *Mailing Add:* Dept of Foreign Lang & Lit Rutgers Univ 175 University Ave Newark NJ 07102

PLOTTEL, JEANINE PARISIER, b Paris, France, Sept 21, 34; US citizen; m 56; c 3. LANGUAGES. *Educ:* Columbia Univ, BA, 54, MA, 55, PhD, 59. *Prof Exp:* Lectr French, Columbia Univ, 55-59; res assoc, MLA, 59-60; asst prof French, Juilliard Sch Music, 60-65; from asst prof to assoc prof Romance lang, 65-81, PROF FRENCH, HUNTER COL, 82- *Concurrent Pos:* Lectr, City Col New York, 59-60, French Embassy, 59- & Ecole Libre des Hautes Etudes, 59; City Univ New York res grant, 72-73; ed, New York Lit Forum, 77-; Nat Endowment for Humanities fel, 79-80; fac res fel, City Univ New York, 81. *Mem:* Asn Int Etudes Fr; Soc Paul Valery; MLA; Am Asn Teachers Fr; Am Comp Lit Asn. *Res:* Nineteenth and twentieth century French literature; comparative literature. *Publ:* Auth, Les Dialogues de Paul Valery, Presses Univ France, 60; Structures and counter-structures in Raymond Roussel's Impressions of Africa, Dada/Surrealism, 75; Anamorphose d'un coute, Sub-Stance, 76; Rhetoric of chance, Dada/Surrealism, 77; Anamorphosis in painting & literature, Yearbk Gen & Comp Lit, 79; The mathematics of Surrealism, Romantic Rev, 80; The poetics of autobiography in Paul Valery, L'Eprit Createur, Prevost, Laclos & Constant, Scribner's (in press). *Mailing Add:* Grad center Hunter Col City Univ New York New York NY 10036

PLUMMER, JOHN FRANCIS, Medieval Literature. See Vol II

PLUTSCHOW, HERBERT EUGEN, b Zurich, Switz, Sept 8, 39; m 66; c 2. JAPANESE LITERATURE. *Educ:* Univ Paris, BA, 62; Waseda Univ, Japan, MA, 66; Columbia Univ, PhD(Japanese), 73. *Prof Exp:* Instr Japanese, Univ Ill, 71-73; asst prof, 71-80, ASSOC PROF ORIENTAL LANG, UNIV CALIF, LOS ANGELES, 80- *Concurrent Pos:* Japanese Found fel, 74. *Res:* Japanese literature and religion. *Publ:* Coauth, Nihon Kiko Bungaku Binran, Musashino Shoin, Tokyo, 76. *Mailing Add:* 20528 Rhoda St Woodland Hills CA 91367

POAG, JAMES F, b Ill, Aug 7, 34; m60; c 2. GERMAN PHILOLOGY. *Educ:* Univ Ill, BA, 56, MA, 58, PhD, 61. *Prof Exp:* From instr to assoc prof Ger, Ind Univ, Bloomington, 61-76; PROF GER & CHMN DEPT, WASH UNIV, 76- *Concurrent Pos:* Fulbright & Humbold res grants, Univ Göttingen, 63-64. *Mem:* MLA; Am Asn Teachers Ger. *Res:* Mediaeval German literature. *Mailing Add:* Dept of Ger Wash Univ St Louis MO 63130

PODLECKI, ANTHONY JOSEPH, b Buffalo, NY, Jan, 36; m 62. CLASSICS. *Educ:* Col Holy Cross, AB, 57; Oxford Univ, BA, 60, MA, 63; Univ Toronto, MA, 61, PhD, 63. *Prof Exp:* From instr to asst prof classics, Northwestern Univ, 63-66; from assoc prof to prof, Pa State Univ, University Park, 66-75, head dept, 66-75; PROF CLASSICS & HEAD DEPT, UNIV BC, 75- *Concurrent Pos:* Mem managing comt, Am Sch Class Studies, Athens, 70-; chmn, aid to publ comt, Can Fed for Humanities, 76- *Mem:* Class Asn Can West; Class Asn Pac Northwest (pres, 77-78); Joint Asn Class Teachers; Am Philol Asn; Claudel Soc. *Res:* Greek history and literature and their interrelations; Roman historiography. *Publ:* Auth, The Political Background of Aeschylean Tragedy, Univ Mich, 66; The peripatetics as literary critics, Phoenix, 69; Reciprocity in Prometheus Bound, Greek, Roman & Byzantine Studies, 69; transl, Aeschylus' The Persians, Prentice-Hall, 70; auth, Some Odyssean similes, Greece & Rome, 71; The Life of Themistocles, McGill-Queens, 75; Themistocles in Alexandrian and 18th century drama, Restoration & 18th century Theatre Res, 76. *Mailing Add:* 4524 W Seventh Ave Vancouver BC V6R 1X3 Can

PODUSKA, DONALD MILES, b Chicago, Ill, Dec 2, 34; m 58; c 3. CLASSICAL LANGUAGES. *Educ:* Loyola Univ, Ill, AB, 56; Univ Ky, MA, 57; Ohio State Univ, PhD(class lang), 63. *Prof Exp:* From instr to assoc prof, 60-73, PROF CLASS LANG, JOHN CARROLL UNIV, 73- *Concurrent Pos:* Vis assoc prof class lang, Rome Ctr, Loyola Univ, Ill, 70-71. *Mem:* Am Philol Asn; Am Class League; Vergilian Soc; Class Asn Mid W & S. *Res:* Roman comedy; Roman historians; Vergil. *Mailing Add:* Dept of Class Lang John Carroll Univ Cleveland OH 44118

POESSE, WALTER, b Cleveland, Ohio, July 21, 13. SPANISH. *Educ:* Western Reserve Univ, AB, 35; Wash Univ, MA, 36; Univ Calif, PhD(Romance philol), 40. *Prof Exp:* Prof mod lang, Vincennes Univ, 40-41; assoc prof, 41-42, 46-51 & 52-69, prof, 69-75, EMER PROF SPAN, IND UNIV, BLOOMINGTON, 75- *Mem:* MLA. *Res:* Spanish drama of the Golden Age. *Publ:* Auth, The Internal Line Structure of Thirty Autograph Plays of Lope de Vega, Ind Univ, 49; Ensayo de una bibliografia de Juan Ruiz de Alarcon y Mendoza, Castalia, Valencia, 64; Juan Ruiz de Alarcon, Twayne, 72. *Mailing Add:* Dept of Span Ind Univ Bloomington IN 47401

POGGENBURG, RAYMOND PAUL, b May 28, 26; US citizen. FRENCH. *Educ:* Hofstra Col, BA, 49; Univ Grenoble, Cert, 50; Univ Wis, MA, 52, PhD, 55. *Prof Exp:* From instr to asst prof French, Carleton Col, 55-60; proj assoc, Univ Wis, 60-61; asst prof & chmn dept, State Univ NY Col Long Island, 61-62; assoc prof, 62-69, chmn dept French & Ital, 62-71, prof & dir Vanderbilt-in-France, Aix-en-Provence, 71-72 & 76-78, PROF FRENCH, VANDERBILT UNIV, 69-71 & 72- & DIR GRAD STUDIES, 80- *Concurrent Pos:* Chmn region VII, Woodrow Wilson Nat Fel Found, 63-67; dir, Baudelaire Studies Ctr, 80- *Mem:* MLA; Am Asn Teachers Fr; Am Coun Teaching Foreign Lang; Int Asn Fr Studies; AAUP. *Res:* Baudelaire; symbolist poetry; Anglo-French-American interrelationships in modern poetry. *Publ:* Auth, Baudelaire and Laforgue, In: Jules Laforgue, Essays on a Poet's Life and Work, Southern Ill Univ, 69; Quelques reflexions sur Jean-Jacques Celly, Cahiers Franco-Anglais, Geneva, 69; Baudelaire, Grosley et le jansenisme, In: Baudelaire en son temps, Col Etudes Baudelairiennes, Neuchatel, 73; Racine, la loi et le destin tragique, In: Travaux de Linguistique et de Litterature, Vol XII, Strasbourg, 75. *Mailing Add:* Dept of French & Ital Vanderbilt Univ Box 6123 Sta B Nashville TN 37235

POHLSANDER, HANS ACHIM, b Celle, Ger, Oct 10, 27; US citizen; m 56; c 3. CLASSICS. *Educ:* Univ Utah, BA, 54; Univ Calif, Berkeley, MA, 55; Univ Mich, PhD, 61. *Prof Exp:* Teacher Latin & Ger, Carmel High Sch, Calif, 56-58; asst prof Latin & Greek, Wash Univ, 61-62; from asst prof to assoc prof Latin, Greek & ancient hist, 62-71, chmn dept, 72-78, PROF CLASSICS, STATE UNIV NY ALBANY, 71- *Concurrent Pos:* Am Coun Learned Soc grant-in-aid, 62; vis assoc prof classics & cult studies, Am Univ Beirut, 68-69; Ger Acad Exchange Serv study grant, 82. *Mem:* Am Class League; Am Philol Asn; Archaeol Inst Am. *Res:* Ancient history; early Christianity. *Publ:* Auth, Meters and chronology in Sophocles, Am J Philol, 7/63; The dating of Pindaric odes by comparison, Greek, Roman & Byzantine Studies, summer 63; Metrical Studies in the Lyrics of Sophocles, Brill, Leiden, 64; Victory: The story of a statue, Historia, 12/69; Classical scholarship, Class Outlook, 69-70; Teaching ancient history today, ERIC Focus Report, MLA, 71; Philip the Arab and Christianity, Historia, 80. *Mailing Add:* Dept of Classics State Univ of NY Albany NY 12222

POHORYLES, BERNARD MARTIN, b Plauen, Ger, June 5, 12; nat US; m 40. FRENCH, GERMAN. *Educ:* NY Univ, AB, 48, PhD(Old French lit & ling), 65. *Prof Exp:* Instr French & Ger, NY Univ, 48-55; dir lang lab, 61-64, PROF FOREIGN LANG, PACE UNIV, 62- *Concurrent Pos:* Prof, Lycee Francais, New York, 60-62; lectr, Long Island Univ & Brooklyn Polytech Inst, 60-66; adj assoc prof, 66-71; adj prof, 71-; prof ling, Biling Teacher Training Inst, Long Island Univ, 74. *Honors & Awards:* Chevalier, Palmes Academiques. *Mem:* MLA; Am Asn Teachers Fr; Am Asn Teachers Ger; Soc Ling Romance; Am Coun Teaching Foreign Lang. *Res:* French literature and linguistics, especially Medieval French; comparative studies of French and German literatures; applied linguistics. *Publ:* Auth, Linguistic appetizers, Lang Fed Bull, 68; transl, Peter Fingesten: The craft of creation, Antaios, Stuttgart, 11/68; auth, Herman Hesse, In: Fame in a Name, Pace Col, 72; An outsiders view of the German language, Rundschau, 74; Exemples de syntaxe germanique dans Garin le Loheren, In: Actes du XIIIe Congres International de Linguistique & Philologie Romane, Univ Laval, 76; transl, Emil Froeschels: Kindersprache f Aphasia, Perspectives in Neurolinguistics and Psycholinguistics, Acad Press, 80; Peter Fingesten, 20 articles Worterbuch des Symbolismus, Stuttgart: Kroener Verlag. *Mailing Add:* 8 Stuyvesant Oval New York NY 10009

POIRIER, ROGER LUC, b Paris, France, July 3, 36; m 71; c 1. FRENCH LITERATURE, THE NOVEL. *Educ:* Univ Paris, BA, 59; Case Western Reserve Univ, MA, 68; Johns Hopkins Univ, PhD(French lit), 73. *Prof Exp:* ASSOC PROF FRENCH, TOWSON STATE UNIV, 68- *Mem:* MLA; Am Soc 18th Century Studies; Soc francaise d'etudes du XVIIIeme siecle. *Res:* Collections of abridged novels published in France and Spain at the end of the 18th century. *Publ:* Auth, Le Marquis de Paulmy d'Argenson, In: Dictionaire des journalistes, Univ Grenoble, France, 76; La Bibliotheque Universelle des Romans, editeurs, textes, public, Droz, Geneva, 77. *Mailing Add:* Dept of Mod Lang Towson State Univ Baltimore MD 21204

POITZSCH, MANFRED, b Neukirchen, Ger, Aug 16, 30; m 60; c 2. GERMAN, FRENCH. *Educ:* Free Univ Berlin, MA, 59; Senator f Volksbildung, Berlin, ME, 61; Univ Minn, PhD, 68. *Prof Exp:* Asst Ger, Lycee Garcons, Montpellier, 58-59; Referendar Ger & French, div Gym, Berlin, 59-61; instr, Mankato State Col, 61-64; asst prof Ger & French, 64-68, assoc prof, 68-71, PROF FOREIGN LANG, UNIV WIS-EAU CLAIRE, 71- *Mem:* Deut Philol-Verband; Am Asn Teachers Ger. *Res:* German 18th and 19th century literature; French 19th century literature. *Publ:* Auth, Zeitgenössische Persiflagen auf C M Wieland und seine Schriften, Language, Bern, 72; Das Königreich Tatojaba: Eine Persiflage auf Wieland?, Monatshefte, 72. *Mailing Add:* Dept of Foreign Lang Univ of Wis-Eau Claire Eau Claire WI 54701

POLAK, EMIL JOSEPH, Medieval & Ancient History. See Vol I

POLAND, GEORGE WAVERLY, b Richmond, Va, Feb 23, 14. MODERN LANGUAGES. *Educ:* Col William & Mary, AB, 36; Brown Univ, MA, 40; Univ Salamanca, Dipl, 41; Univ NC, PhD(Romance lang), 53. *Prof Exp:* Instr Span & Ital, Col William & Mary, 36-38; from instr to assoc prof Romance lang, 48-55, from assoc prof to prof mod lang, 55-76, head dept, 55-72, dir English, summer inst foreign students, 66-76, EMER PROF MOD LANG, NC STATE UNIV, 76- *Mem:* MLA; Am Asn Teachers Span & Port; S Atlantic Mod Lang Asn. *Res:* English as a second language; medieval Spanish manuscripts; early Italian novelliere. *Mailing Add:* 3929 Arrow Dr Raleigh NC 27612

POLITER, ROBERT LOUIS, Vienna, Austria, Mar 21, 21; nat US; m 46; c 4. ROMANCE LINGUISTICS. *Educ:* Wash Univ, AB, 41, AM, 43; Columbia Univ, PhD, 47; New Sch Soc Res, DSSc, 50. *Prof Exp:* Lectr French, Columbia Univ, 47-49; from instr to asst prof Romance langs, Univ Wash, 49-52; asst prof, Harvard Univ, 52-56; from assoc prof to prof French & Romance ling, Univ Mich, 56-63; PROF EDUC & ROMANCE LING, STANFORD UNIV, 63- *Concurrent Pos:* Guggenheim fel, 56. *Honors & Awards:* Am Coun Teaching Foreign Lang Award, 78. *Mem:* MLA; Ling Soc Am; Am Asn Teachers Ital; Am Asn Teachers Fr; Am Asn Teachers Span & Port. *Res:* Late Latin; applied linguistics; foreign language education. *Publ:* Auth, Language of Eighth Century Lombardic Documents; Teaching French, Ginn, 60 & 2nd ed, Blaisdell, 65; Teaching Spanish, Ginn, 61 & 2nd ed, Blaisdell, 65; Beitrag zur Phonologie der Nonsberger Mundart, Innsbruck Univ, 67; Teaching German, Blaisdell, 68; Linguistics and Applied Linguistics: Methods and Aims, Rand McNally, 72; coauth, Teaching English as a Second Language, Xerox, 72 & Krieger Publ Co, 81; coauth, A Study of Language Acquisition in two Bilingual Schools, Stanford, 75. *Mailing Add:* Sch of Educ Stanford Univ Stanford CA 94305

POLLITT, JERMOME J, b Fair Lawn, NJ, Nov 26, 34. HISTORY OF ART, CLASSICAL PHILOLOGY. *Educ:* Yale Univ, BA, 57; Columbia Univ, PhD(hist of art), 63. *Prof Exp:* Instr classics, 62-65, from asst prof to assoc prof class art & archaeol, 65-73, chmn, Dept Classics, 75-77, PROF CLASS ARCHAEOL & HIST OF ART, YALE UNIV, 73-, CHMN, DEPT HIST OF ART, 81- *Concurrent Pos:* Morse fel, 67-68; ed, Am J Archaeol, 73-77. *Mem:* Archaeol Inst Am. *Res:* Greek art and archaeology; art criticism. *Publ:* Auth, The Art of Greece: 1400-31 BC, 65 & The Art of Rome: c 753 BC-337 AD, 66, Prentice-Hall; Art and Experience in Classical Greece, Cambridge Univ, 72; The Ancient View of Greek Art, Yale Univ, 74; The impact of Greek art on Rome, Trans Am Philol Asn, 78; Kernoi from the Athenian Agora, Hesperia, 79. *Mailing Add:* Dept of Classics Yale Univ 1967 Yale Sta New Haven CT 06520

POLLOCK, JOHN JOSEPH, Seventeenth Century Literature. See Vol II

POLLY, LYLE R, b Cornwall, NY, Feb 13, 40; m 62; c 3. FRENCH LANGUAGE AND LITERATURE. *Educ:* Geneva Col, BA, 61; Univ Wis, MA, 62; State Univ NY Buffalo, PhD(French), 72. *Prof Exp:* Teacher French, Span & Latin, Ardsley High Sch, 62-64; asst prof French & Span, Geneva Col, 64-67; asst prof French, State Univ NY Geneseo, 70-72; ASSOC PROF FRENCH & SPAN, SOUTHWEST MO STATE UNIV, 72- *Mem:* Am Asn Teachers French; Soc Amis Romania; Am Coun Teaching Foreign Lang; Soc Rencesvals; Nat Fedn Mod Lang Teachers Asn. *Res:* Medieval literature; pedagogy. *Publ:* Coauth, Meusault on trial: multi-skills activities for teaching L'Etranger, Can Mod Lang Rev, 10/78; auth, A note on the rhyme Henri/lit and the dating of the Chanson de Toile Bele Siglentine, Orbis, 27: 31-32; Three Fifteen-Minute Activities for Beginning Foreign Language Students: Reading, Writing, and Arithmetic, NALLD J, fall 79; Two Visuals to Accompany Albert Valdman's Langue et Culture, 5/80 & coauth, Communicative Competence and Ancillary Cources in French, 2/81, Foreign Lang Annals; The Chanson de Toile an the Chanson de Geste: Reconsidering some Considerations, Romance Notes, winter 81. *Mailing Add:* Dept of Foreign Lang Southwest Mo State Univ 901 S National Springfield MO 65802

POLOME, EDGAR CHARLES, b Molenbeek, Belgium, July 31, 20; m 48; c 2. LINGUISTICS. *Educ:* Free Univ Brussels, BA, 40, PhD, 49; Cath Univ Louvain, MA, 43. *Prof Exp:* Prof ling, Univ Officielle Congo, 56-60; vis assoc prof, 61-62, dir Ctr Asian Studies, 63-72, chmn dept, 69-76, PROF ORIENT, AFRICAN & GERMANIC LANG, UNIV TEX, AUSTIN, 62- *Concurrent Pos:* Grant, Ctr Appl Ling, 62-63; trustee, Am Inst Indian Studies, 65- & chmn lang comt, 72-78; team dir Tanzania, Ford Found surv lang use & lang teaching in Eastern Africa, 69-70; consult, Nairobi, Kenya, 73; co-ed, J Indo-Europ Studies, 73-; co-ed, Mankind Quart, 80- *Mem:* Int Ling Asn; Ling Soc Am; Am Orient Soc; African Studies Asn; Asian Studies Asn. *Res:* Indo-European and Germanic comparative grammar; Sanskrit and Hittite; Swahili and Bantu languages. *Publ:* Auth, Le vocabulaire proto-bantou et ses implications culturelles, In: Paleontologia Linguistica, Atti del VI, Convego Internazionale di Linguisti, Inst Lombardo-Accad Sci & Lett, Brescia, Paideia, 77; A few thoughts about reconstructing Indo-European culture and religion, J Dept English, Univ Calcutta, 14: 45-62; Creolization Theory and Linguistic Prehistory, In: Festschrift for Oswald Szemerenyi, John Benjamins, Amsterdam, 79; Some Aspects of the Cult of the Mother Goddess in Western Europe', In: Vistas and Vectors: Essays Honoring the Memory of Helmut Rehder, Univ Tex, Austin, 79; Creolization Processes and Diachronic Linguistics, In: Theoretical Orientations in Creole Studies, Acad Press, 80; ed, Man and the Ultimate, Southwestern Br Am Orient Soc; The Indo-Europeans, Fourth and Third Millennia, Karoma, 82; Urban versus rural multilingualism, Int J Soc Lang, fall 82. *Mailing Add:* PO Box 8058 Univ of Tex Austin TX 78712

POLT, JOHN H R, b Usti nad Labem, Czech, Aug 20, 29; US citizen; m 53. FOREIGN LANGUAGES. *Educ:* Princeton Univ, AB, 49; Univ Calif, MA, 50, PhD (Romance lang & lit), 56. *Prof Exp:* From instr to assoc prof, 56-70, PROF SPAN, UNIV CALIF, BERKELEY, 70- *Concurrent Pos:* Am Philos Soc grant, 59-60; assoc dir, Univ Calif Studies Ctr, Madrid, 64-65, dir, 68-70; vis assoc prof, Univ Calif, Santa Barbara, 65-66; Am Coun Learned Soc fel, 73; Guggenheim Mem Found fel, 74. *Mem:* Am Asn Teachers Span & Port; Philol Asn Pac Coast. *Res:* Spanish literature, 18th to 20th century. *Publ:* Auth, The Writings of Eduardo Mallea, Univ Calif, 59; Jovellanos and His English Sources, Am Philos Soc, 64; ed, Forner, Los Gramaticos, Univ Calif & Ed Castalia, 70; auth, Gaspar Melchor de Jovellanos, Twayne, 71; ed, Poesia del siglo XVIII, Ed Castalia, 75; co-ed, Juan Melendez Valdes, Poesias Selectas: La Liba de marfil, Ed Castalia, 81; Melendez Valdes, Obras en verso, Catedra Feijoo, 81. *Mailing Add:* Dept of Span & Port Univ of Calif Berkeley CA 94720

POLTORATZKY, NIKOLAI PETROVICH, b Istanbul, Turkey, Feb 16, 21; US citizen. RUSSIAN LITERATURE & CIVILIZATION. *Educ:* Sorbonne, DUniv, 54. *Prof Exp:* Instr Russ, US Army Lang Sch, Monterey, Calif, 55; res assoc Russ area, Inwood Proj Intercult Commun, Brooklyn Col, 56-58; asst prof Russ lang & lit, Mich State Univ, 58-60, from assoc prof to prof Russ lit & civilization, 60-67, dir Russ prog, 62-64; chmn dept Slavic lang & lit, 67-74, PROF SLAVIC LANG & LIT, UNIV PITTSBURGH, 67- *Concurrent Pos:* Am Philos Soc res grant-in-aid, 60; Int Commun Inst res grant, Mich State Univ, 64-65; Int Prog res grant, Univ Pittsburgh, 67-68, fac res grant, 71-72; mem fac & asst to dir, Inst Soviet Studies, Middlebury Col, summers, 58-65; vis prof, Univ Calif, Berkeley, summer, 66. *Mem:* Am Asn Advan Slavic Studies; Am Asn Teachers Slavic & Eastern Europ Lang (vpres, 67); MLA; Asn Russ-Am Scholars in US; AAUP. *Res:* Studies in modern Russian thought and literature; postrevolutionary Russian emigration. *Publ:* Ed & coauth, On Themes Russian and General, 65 & auth, Berdiaev and Russia, 67, Soc Friends Russ Cult; ed & coauth, Russian Emigre Literature, Dept Slavic Lang & Lit, Univ Pittsburgh, 72; ed, I A Iljin: Russian Writers, Literature, and Art, Victor Kamkin, 73; ed & coauth, Russian Religious-Philosophical Thought of the 20th Century, Dept of Slavic Lang & Lit, Univ Pittsburgh, 75; auth, I A Iljin and the Polemics Concerning His Ideas on Resistance to Evil by Force, Zaria, 75; Monarchy and Republic as Perceived by I A Iljin, Sodruzhestvo, 79; P B Storuve as a Political Thinker, Zaria, 81. *Mailing Add:* Dept of Slavic Lang, Lit & Cultures Univ of Pittsburgh Pittsburgh PA 15260

POMERANTZ, DONALD, b Brooklyn, NY, July 31, 37; m 61. FRENCH LITERATURE. *Educ:* Brooklyn Col, BA, 58; Fla State Univ, MA, 60,. *Prof Exp:* Asst, Fla State Univ, 58-60; asst Tulane Univ, 60-62; asst prof French, Univ Miss, 62-63; ASST PROF FRENCH, CENT CONN STATE COL, 63-, CHMN DEPT, 80- *Concurrent Pos:* Drama critic, Hartford Times, 67- *Mem:* MLA. *Res:* Contemporary French theatre; transition of Jean Giraudoux from novelist to dramatist. *Publ:* Coauth, Paroles du Terroir, Am Bk Co, 67. *Mailing Add:* Dept of Mod Lang Conn State Col 1615 Stanley St New Britain CT 06050

POMEROY, SARAH B PORGES, b New York, NY, Mar 13, 38. CLASSICAL PHILOLOGY. *Educ:* Barnard Col, BA, 57; Columbia Univ, MA, 59, PhD, 61. *Prof Exp:* Instr class lang, Univ Tex, 61-62; lectr classics, 63-68, asst prof, 68-75, ASSOC PROF CLASSICS, HUNTER COL, 75-, COORDR, WOMEN'S STUDIES PROG, 75- *Concurrent Pos:* Lectr classics, Brooklyn Col, 66-67; Am Coun Learned Soc grant-in-aid, 73-74; Nat Endowment for Humanities summer stipend, 73; fel, 81-82; Ford Found fel, 74-75; res grant, Fac Res Award Prog, City Univ New York, 75-79 & 82-83; Danforth assoc, 76- *Mem:* Am Philol Asn; Archaeol Inst Am; Am Soc Papryologists; Friends Ancient Hist; Asn Ancient Historians. *Res:* Greek literature; women in classical antiquity; social history. *Publ:* Coauth, The financial transactions of Aurelia Tetoueis, Am J Philol, 60; auth, A lease of an olive grove, Trans & Proc Am Philol Asn, 61; The revolt of Saturnius, Gazette Numismatique Suisse, 8/69; Optics and the line in Plato's Republic, Class Quart, 11/71; Andromaque: un exemple Meconnu de Matriarcat?, Rev des Etudes Grecques, 75; The relationship of the married woman to her blood relatives in Rome, Ancient Soc, 76; Technikai kai Mousikai: The education of women in the fourth century and in the Hellenistic Period, Am J Ancient Hist, 77; Goddesses, Whores, Wives and Slaves: Women in Classical Antiquity, Schocken, 75, Robert Hale, London, 76, Ital transl, Einaudi, 78 & Greek transl, Dodone; Charities for Greek Women, Mnemosyne, 82. *Mailing Add:* Dept of Classics Box 1264 Hunter Col 695 Park Ave New York NY 10021

POMORSKA, KRYSTYNA, b Lwow, Poland; US citizen; m 63. RUSSIAN. *Educ:* Slowacki Col, BA, 50; Univ Warsaw, MA, 55; Univ Chicago, PhD(Slavic lang & lit), 63. *Prof Exp:* Instr poetics, Univ Warsaw, 56-59; asst prof Russ lit, Univ Chicago, 62-63; from asst prof to assoc prof, 63-70, PROF RUSS LIT, MASS INST TECHNOL, 70. *Concurrent Pos:* Consult Russ lit, Warsaw Publ House, PIW, 53-59; mem bd avd, Ossobow Island Proj, Savannah, Ga, 70- *Mem:* Am Asn Advan Slavic Studies. *Res:* Russian literature of the beginning of the 20th century; problems of poetics and poetic language; literary theories of the beginning of the 20th century in Slavic countries. *Publ:* Auth, On Gogol Studies: Methodological notes, In: To Honor Roman Jakobson, 67 & Russian Formalist Theory and Its Poetic Ambiance, 68, Mouton, The Hague; ed, Fifty Years of Russian Prose: From Paternak to Solzhenitsyn, an Anthology, 71 & co-ed, Readings in Russian Poetics, 71, Mass Inst Technol; auth, On segmentation of narrative prose, In: Proceedings of the VII International Congress of Slavists, Mouton, The Hague, 73; Themes and Variations in Pasternak's Poetics, Peter De Ridder, 75; On modern prose: Cexov, Solzenicyn, PTL, 76; Ukrainian erotic songs, In: Harvard Ukrainian Studies, Vol I, 77. *Mailing Add:* Dept of Foreign Lit & Ling Mass Inst Technol Cambridge MA 02140

PONCE DE LEON, LUIS SIERRA, b Vigo, Spain, Sept 23, 31. SPANISH LANGUAGE & LITERATURE. *Educ:* Univ Santiago, Lic en Derecho, 53; Stanford Univ, MA, 63, PhD(Span), 66. *Prof Exp:* Asst prof, Stanford Univ, 66-72; PROF SPAN LANG & LIT, CALIF STATE UNIV, HAYWARD, 72- *Mem:* MLA; AAUP; Am Asn Teachers Span & Port. *Res:* Spanish contemporary novel; literature of the Spanish Civil War, 1936-59; comparative grammar. *Publ:* Auth, El arte de la conversacion, Harper, 67 & 3rd ed, 81; La novela de la Guerra Civil de Espana y el modelo Tolstoi, 6/70 & La novela espanola de la Guerra Civil (1936-1939), 71, Insula. *Mailing Add:* Dept of Foreign Lang & Lit Calif State Univ Hayward CA 94542

PONDROM, CYRENA NORMAN, English & Comparative Literature. See Vol II

PONOMAREFF, CONSTANTIN VINCENT, b Cannes La Bocca, France; Can citizen. RUSSIAN & COMPARATIVE LITERATURE. *Educ:* Univ Toronto, BA, 58, MA, 59, PhD(Russ lang & lit), 70. *Prof Exp:* Lectr Russ, Univ Toronto, 60-69; from lectr to asst prof, 69-73, ASSOC PROF RUSS, SCARBOROUGH COL, UNIV TORONTO, 73- *Mem:* Can Asn Slavists. *Res:* Humanism and autocracy in Russian literature, 1709-1910; Russian symbolism. *Publ:* Auth, Death and decay: An analysis of S A Esenin's poetic form, Can Slavonic Papers, summer 68; The image seekers: An analysis of imaginist poetic theory, 1919-1924, fall 68 & Configurations of poetic vision: Belinsky as an idealist-critic, summer 70, Slavic & E Europ J; Alekasandr Blok's The Twelve: A new interpretation, Can Slavonic Papers, autumn 72; V G Belinskii's romantic imagination, Can-Am Slavic Studies, fall 73; Woman as nemesis: Card symbolism in Hebel, Esenin and Pushkin, Germano-Slavica, fall 75; Sergey Esenin, Twayne, 78; The Silenced Vision: An Essay in Modern European Fiction, Peter Lang, 79. *Mailing Add:* Div of Humanities Scarborough Col Univ of Toronto West Hill ON M1C 1A4 Can

POOL, JONATHAN ROBERT, b Chicago, Ill, Sept 5, 42. SOCIOLINGUISTICS, LANGUAGE PLANNING. *Educ:* Harvard Univ, BA, 64; Univ Chicago, MA, 68, PhD(polit sci), 71. *Prof Exp:* Asst prof polit sci, State Univ NY, Stony Brook, 71-77; asst prof, 77-81, ASSOC PROF POLIT SCI, UNIV WASH, 81- *Concurrent Pos:* Vis prof polit sci, Inst Soc Sci, Univ Mannheim, 72-73; assoc, Univ Sem Soviet Nationality Probs, Columbia Univ, 73-; Soc Sci Res Coun Res training fel, McGill Univ, 74-75; vis asst prof polit sci & ling, Stanford Univ, 75. *Mem:* Int Sociol Asn; Am Polit Sci Am; Esperanto Studies Asn Am. *Res:* Economics of language; language politics; communication network expermentation. *Publ:* Contribr, Advances in the Sociology of Language, 72 & Advances in Language Planning, 74, Mouton, The Hague; auth, Coalition formation in small groups with incomplete communication networks, J Personality & Social Psychol, 76; Developing the Soviet Turkic tongues: The language of the politics of language, Slavic Rev, 76; contribr, Soviet Nationality Policies and Practices, Praeger, 78; auth, Langugage planning and identity planning, Int J Sociol of Lang, 79; Sprachliche Gleichheit, sprachliche Ungleichheit und Sprachdiskriminierung: Begriffe und Messung, Grundlagenstudien aus Kybernetik und Geisteswissenschaft, 81; contribr, Angewandte Soziolinguistik, Gunter Narr, Tuebingen, 81. *Mailing Add:* Dept of Polit Sci Univ of Wash Seattle WA 98195

POPE, MARVIN HOYLE, b Durham, NC, June 23, 16. SEMITIC PHILOLOGY. *Educ:* Duke Univ, AB, 38, AM, 39; Yale Univ, PhD, 49. *Prof Exp:* Instr, Duke Univ, 47-49; asst prof Hebrew, 49-55, assoc prof, 55-64, PROF NORTHWEST SEMITIC LANG, YALE UNIV, 64- *Concurrent Pos:* Cir Am Sch Orient Res, Jerusalem, 59-60; mem Old Testmant Sect, Standard Bible Comt, 60-; resident dir, Hebrew Union Col Bibl & Archaeol Sch, Jerusalem, 66-67. *Mem:* Soc Bil Lit; Am Orient Soc; Soc Relig Higher Educ. *Publ:* El in the Ugaritic Texts, Brill Leiden, 55; The Book of Job & other articles, In: Interpreter's Dictionary of the Bible, Abingdon, 62; contribr, Die Mythologie der Ugariter und Phönizier, In: Wörterbuch der Mythologie, Ernest Klett, Stuttgart, 62; auth, The Book of Job: Introduction, Translations and Notes, Doubleday, 65, 3rd ed, 73. *Mailing Add:* Dept of Northwest Semitic Lang Yale Univ New Haven CT 06520

POPE, RANDOLPH D, b Vina del Mar, Chile, Oct 31, 46; m 67. SPANISH & LATIN AMERICAN LITERATURE. *Educ:* Univ Catolica Valparaiso, prof de Castellano, 68; Columbia Univ, MA, 69, PhD(Span),73. *Prof Exp:* Instr Span, Barnard Col, 69-73; lectr, Univ Bonn, WGer, 73-76; asst prof, 76-77, assoc prof, Dartmouth Col, 77-82; ASSOC PROF SPAN & CHMN DEPT HIST STUDIES, VASSAR COL, 82- *Concurrent Pos:* Ed, Ediciones del Norte. *Mem:* MLA; Int Asn Hispanists; Cervantes Soc Am. *Res:* Contemporary Spanish novel; contemporary Latin American novel; Cervantes. *Publ:* Auth, La autobiografia espanola hasta Torres Villarroel, Lang Verlag, 74; Dos novelas album: Libro de Manuel de Cortazar y Figuraciones en el mes de Marzo de Diaz Valcarcel, Biling Rev, 74; The Autobiographical Form in the Persiles, Anales Cervantinos, 74-75; La apertura al futuro: Una categoria para el analisis de la novela hispanoamericana contemporanea, Revista Iberoam, 75; Don Quijote y el Caballero del Verde Gaban: El encuentro a la laz de su contexto, Hisp Rev, 79; Reading a Chilean classic: Eduardo Barrios's Gran Senor y Rajadiablos, Int Fiction Rev, 81; ed, The Analysis of Literary Texts: Current Trends in Methodology, Bilingual Press, Vol III, 80; transl, Geoffrey Wolff, Gato Por Liebre, Norte, 82. *Mailing Add:* Dept of Hist Studies Vassar Col Poughkeepsie NY 12601

POPE, RICHARD WARREN FRANK, b Toronto, Ont, Oct 24, 41. MEDIEVAL RUSSIAN & SOVIET LITERATURE. *Educ:* Univ Toronto, BA, 64; Columbia Univ, cert Russ Inst & MA, 66, PhD(Slaic PhD(Slavic lang), 70. *Prof Exp:* Asst prof Russ lit, Ind Univ, 70-73; chmn dept for lit, 73-78, PROF RUSS LIT, YORK UNIV, 73- *Concurrent Pos:* Can Coun leave fel, 78-79; Soc Study Humanities Res Coun res grant, 81-82. *Mem:* Am Asn Advan Slavic Studies; Am Asn Teachers Slavic & East Europ Lang; Can Asn Slavists. *Res:* Medieval South and East Slavic literature. *Publ:* Auth, Bulgaria: The third Christian kingdom in the Razummik-Ukaz, Slavia, 74; co-ed, The Old Church Slavonic Translation of the Androon Hagioon Biblos in the Edition of Mikolaas van Wijk, Mouton, The Hague, 75; auth, A possible South Slavic source of the doctrine: Moscow the third Rome, Slavia, 75; Observations on the literary technique of Epifanij the Wise, In: The Cultural Heritage of Old Russia, Lixacey Festschrift, 76; Ambiguity and meaning in the Master and Margarita: The role of Afranius, Slavic Rev, 3/77; On the comparative literary analysis of the Patericon story (trans & original) in the Pre-Mongol Period, Can Contrib VIII Int Cong Slavists, 78; Hilandar no 485 as a sbornik, Cyrillomethodianum, Vol V, 81; On the question of the fate of Apocryphal Apocalyses about paradise on earth among the South and East Slavs, Can Contrib IX Int Cong Slavists. *Mailing Add:* Dept For Lit York Univ Toronto ON M3J 1P3 Can

POPKIN, DEBRA, b New York, NY, Sept 26, 44; m 68; c 3. FRENCH LANGUAGE & LITERATURE. *Educ:* Univ Paris, dipl French lit, 64; City Col New York, BA, 65; Columbia Univ, MA, 66, PhD(French lit), 72. *Prof Exp:* Res asst French lit, Columbia Univ, 66-67; lectr French, 67-72, asst prof Romance lang, 72-78, ASSOC PROF ROMANCE LANG, BARUCH COL, 78- *Concurrent Pos:* Consult, Ungar Publ Co, 74-; Exxon Educ Found grant, 77-78; Title III Grant, 79-81; sr lang consult, Rassias Found, 80- *Mem:* MLA; Am Translr Asn; Northeast Mod Lang Asn; Am Asn Teachers Fr; Am Coun Teaching Foreign Lang. *Res:* Twentieth century French literature; seventeenth century French literature; Black French literature. *Publ:* Auth, Bernard Dadie, Ferdinand Oyono & Ousmane Sembene, In: Encycl World Lit in 20th Century, 75 & coauth, Modern French literature (2 vols), In: A Library Literary Criticism, 77, Ungar; Critical Bibliography of Jean Cocteau, In: A Critical Bibliography of French Literature, Vol VI, 20th Century, Syracuse Univ Press, 80; Evaluation of the Dartmouth Intensive Language Model at Baruch College, In: The Ram's Horn, Vol 1, No 2; Albert Camus, In: Encycl of World Lit in 20th Century, rev ed, Vol 1 & co-ed, Major Modern Dramatists (in press), Ungar. *Mailing Add:* Dept of Romance Lang Baruch Col 17 Lexington Ave New York NY 10010

POPLACK, SHANA, b Detroit, Mich. LINGUISTICS. *Educ:* Queens Col, BA, 68; NY Univ, MA, 71; Univ Pa, PhD(ling), 79. *Prof Exp:* Res assoc ling, Ctr Puetro Rican Studies, City Univ New York, 77-81; asst prof, 81-82, ASSOC PROF LING, UNIV OTTAWA, 82- *Concurrent Pos:* Vis asst prof, NY Univ, 78-79. *Mem:* Ling Soc Am; Can Ling Asn. *Res:* Sociolinguistics; bilingualism; Hispanic and French dialectology. *Publ:* Auth, Dialect acquisition among Puerto Rican bilinguals, Lang & Soc, 7: 89-103; Deletion and disambiguation in Puerto Rican Spanish, Language, 56.2: 371-385; Sometimes I'll start a sentence in Spanish y termino in Espanol: Toward a typology of code-switching, Linguistics, 18: 7-8; coauth (with D Sankoff), A formal grammar for code-switching, Papers in Ling, 14:2:3-46; auth, Syntactic structure and social function of code-switching, In: Latino Discourse and Communicative Behavior, Ablex Publ Corp, 81; Bilingualism and the vernacular, In: Issues in International Bilingual Education: The role of the Vernacular, Plenum Publ Corp, 82; coauth, Competing influences on gender assignment: Variable process, stable outcome, Lingua, 56: 139-166. *Mailing Add:* Dept of Ling Univ of Ottawa Ottawa ON K1N 6N5 Can

POPP, DANIEL MCVAGH, b Ft Wayne, Ind, Jan 29, 39; m 62; c 2. GERMANIC LANGUAGES & LITERATURES. *Educ:* Yale Col, AB, 60; Univ Chicago, MA, 62, PhD (Ger lang & lit), 71. *Prof Exp:* Actg asst prof Ger & Scand, Univ Kans, 66-67; asst prof Norweg, St Olaf Col, 67-70; asst prof foreign lang & lit, Moorhead State Col, 70-73; asst prof, 73-77, ASSOC PROF GER & SCAND, UNIV FLA, 77-, UNDERGRAD ADV SCAND, 80- *Mem:* Soc Advan Scand Study; Norsk Folkeminnelag; Landslaget for Bygde--Og Byhistorie. *Res:* Norwegian language; folk literature; contemporary Swedish literature. *Publ:* Coauth, Hamsun and Pasternak: The development of Kionysian tragedy, EDDA, 76; The teller with the tale, Fabula, autumn 77; auth, Asbjørnsen's Linguistic Reform: I Orthography, Universitetsforlaget, Oslo, 77. *Mailing Add:* Dept of Ger & Slavic Lang & Lit Univ of Fla Gainesville FL 32601

PORQUERAS-MAYO, ALBERTO, b Lerida, Spain, Jan 13, 30; m 62. SPANISH LITERATURE. *Educ:* Univ Madrid, Lic en Filos y Let, 52, PhD, 54. *Prof Exp:* Instr Span for foreigners & asst prof Span lit, Univ Madrid, 53-54; lectr Span, Univ Hamburg, 55-58; asst prof, Emory Univ, 58-60; from assoc prof to prof, Univ Mo, 60-68; assoc mem, Ctr Advan Studies, 70-71 & 81-82, resident dir, year abroad prog, Barcelona, 71-72, PROF SPAN, UNIV ILL, URBANA, 68- *Concurrent Pos:* Instr Span for foreigners, Univ Santander, 53-57; lectr, univs & insts in Spain, Ger, & US; Am Philos Soc scholar, 66-67 & 76-77. *Honors & Awards:* Menendez y Pelayo Prize, Consejo Super Invest Cient, Spain, 54. *Mem:* Am Asn Teachers Span & Port; Asoc Int Hispanistas; Asoc Int Llengua i Lit Catalanes (pres, 82-); Asoc Int Hispanistas Europ. *Res:* Catalan literature; Spanish literature, especially of the Golden Age; literary criticism. *Publ:* Auth, El prologo en el manierismo y barroco espanoles, Consejo Super Invest Cient, Spain, 68; Homenaje a Sanchez Escribano, Alcala, 69; coauth, Ensayo bibliografico del prologo en la literatura, 71 & auth, El new criticism de Ivor Winters, In: Historia y estructura de la obra literaria, 71, Consejo Super Invest Cient, Spain; Temas y formas de la literatura espanola, 72 & coauth, Preceptiva dramatica espanola del Renacimiento y el barroco, 2nd ed, 72, Gredos, Madrid; ed & auth introd & notes, Calderon's El principe constante, Clasicos Castellanos, Espasa-Calpe, Madrid, 75; coauth, The Spanish Golden Age, 1472-1700: A Catalog of Rare Books Held in the Library of the University of Illinois and in Selected North American Libraries, G K Hall, 79. *Mailing Add:* Dept of Span Ital & Port Univ of Ill Urbana IL 61801

PORRATA, FRANCISCO EDUARDO, b Cuba; US citizen. FOREIGN LANGUAGES. *Educ:* Moron Inst, Cuba, BA, 39; Univ Havana, LLD, 43; Univ Iowa, MA, 66, PhD, 68. *Prof Exp:* Atty at law, 44-61; teacher Span, Nishna Valley High Sch, 54-66; teaching asst, Univ Iowa, 66-68; asst prof, 69-74, assoc prof, 74-80, PROF SPAN, CALIF STATE UNIV, SACRAMENTO, 80- *Mem:* NEA; Philol Asn Pac Coast. *Publ:* Auth, Syllabication and Stressing, 71 & El romancero y la comedia espanola, 72, Plaza Mayor, Spain; El sueno en la vida es sueno, Abside, Mex, 73; ed, Explicacion de textos literarios, 73. *Mailing Add:* Dept of Foreign Lang Calif State Univ Sacramento CA 95819

PORTER, CHARLES ALLEN, b Chicago, Ill, May 31, 32; m 56. FRENCH LANGUAGE & LITERATURE. *Educ:* Northwestern Univ, BS, 53, MA, 54; Yale Univ, PhD, 62. *Prof Exp:* From instr to assoc prof, 60-75, DIR SUMMER LANG INST, YALE UNIV, 71-, PROF FRENCH, 75-, CHMN DEPT, 80- *Concurrent Pos:* Lecteur, Univ Lyons, 55-56. *Mem:* MLA; Am Asn Teachers Fr. *Res:* Restif de la Bretonne; Chateaubriand; French roman personnel. *Publ:* Auth, Restif's Novels, or an Autobiography in Search of an Author, Yale Univ, 67; Chateaubriand: Composition, Imagination, and Poetry, ANMA Libri, 78. *Mailing Add:* 320 W L Harkness Hall Yale Univ New Haven CT 06520

PORTER, DAVID HUGH, b New York, NY, Oct 29, 35; m 58; c 1. CLASSICS, MUSIC. *Educ:* Swarthmore Col, BA, 58; Princeton Univ, PhD, 62. *Prof Exp:* From instr to asst prof classics & music, 62-68, assoc prof classics, 68-73, chmn Dept Classics, 71-79, PROF CLASSICS & MUSIC, CARLETON COL, 73-, WILLIAM H LAIRD PROF LIBERAL ARTS, 74- *Concurrent Pos:* Res fels, Nat Endowment for Humanities, 69-70 & Am Coun Learned Soc, 76-77; concert pianist & lectr throughout country. *Mem:* Am Philol Asn; Class Asn Midwest & South. *Res:* Latin poetry, especially Horace; Greek drama; contemporary music. *Publ:* Auth, Structural parallelism in Greek tragedy, Trans Am Philol Asn, 71; Reflective symmetry in music and literature, Perspectives New Music, 70; Ancient myth and modern play, Class Bull, 71; Horace, Carmina IV, 12, Latomus, 72; The motif of spring in Horace, Carmina, IV, 7 and IV, 12, Class Bull, 73; The recurrent motifs of Horace, Carmina IV, Harvard Studies Class Philol, 75; The structure of Beethoven's Diabelli Variations, op 120, Music Rev, Vol 31, No 4; Violent juxtaposition in the similes of the Iliad, Class J, Vol 68, No 1. *Mailing Add:* Dept of Classics Carleton Col Northfield MN 55057

PORTER, ELLIS GIBSON, b Baltimore, Md, June 12, 21; m 55; c 1. FOREIGN LANGUAGES. *Educ:* Univ Va, BA, 45; Univ Ill, MA, 49; PhD, 57. *Prof Exp:* Ed clerk, US Dept State, Wash, DC, 46-47; instr French, Univ Tenn, 47-48; part-time asst, Univ Ill, 48-49, 50-52, 53-55; instr, La State Univ, 55-60; assoc prof, Heidelberg Col, 60-63; PROF FRENCH, RIDER COL, 63- *Concurrent Pos:* Mem, Nat Fed Mod Lang Teachers Asn, 50- *Mem:* Am Asn Teachers Fr; MLA; Mid States Asn Mod Lang Teachers (pres, 67-68). *Res:* Nineteenth century French literature, especially Flaubert. *Mailing Add:* Dept of Mod Lang Rider Col Trenton NJ 08602

PORTER, HOWARD NEWTON, b New Haven, Conn, June 24, 16. CLASSICAL PHILOLOGY. *Educ:* Yale Univ, AB, 38, PhD, 42. *Prof Exp:* Instr classics, Yale Univ, 46-50, asst prof, 50-56; assoc prof Greek & Latin, Columbia Univ, 56-66, chmn dept, 68-71, prof, 66-80. *Mem:* Am Philol Asn. *Res:* Homer and Pindar; Greek poetry; repetition in the Homeric Hymn to Aphrodite. *Mailing Add:* 158 Whitfield St Guilford CT 06437

PORTER, LAURENCE M, b Ossining, NY, Jan 17, 36; m 60, 80; c 2. FRENCH & COMPARATIVE LITERATURE. *Educ:* Harvard Univ, AB, 57, AM, 59, PhD(French lit), 65. *Prof Exp:* Instr French, 63-65, from asst prof to assoc prof, 65-73, PROF FRENCH & COMP LIT, MICH STATE UNIV, 73- *Concurrent Pos:* Co-dir, Nat Colloquium 19th Century Fr Studies, 78; vis Andrew W Mellon prof comp lit, Univ Pittsburgh, 80. *Mem:* MLA; AAUP; Am Comp Lit Asn; Int Comp Lit Asn. *Res:* Romanticism; French poetry; literature and psychology. *Publ:* The Narrative Art of Nodier's Contes, Romanic Rev, 12/72; Autobiography versus confessional novel: Guide's Immoraliste and Si le Grain ne meurt, Symposium, summer 76; Mourning and melancholia in Nerval's Aurelia, Studies Romanticism, spring 76; The devil as double in Nineteenth Century Literature; Goethe, Dostoevsky, and Flaubert, Comp Lit Studies, fall 78; The Renaissance of the Lyric in French Romanticism: Elegy, Poëme, and Ode, Fr Forum Monographs, 78; The Literary Dream in French Romanticism: A Psychoanalytic Interpretation, Wayne State Univ Press, 79; Artistic Self-Consciousness in Rimbaud's Poetry, In: Pretext, Text, Context, Ohio State Univ Press, 80; From Chronicle to Novel: Artistic Elaboration in Camus' La Peste, Mod Fiction Studies, 82. *Mailing Add:* Dept of Romance & Class Lang Wells Hall Mich State Univ East Lansing MI 48824

PORTER, MARY GRAY, b Tuscaloosa, Ala, Apr 17, 24. GERMAN. *Educ:* Univ Ala, AB, 47; Univ NC, MA, 55, PhD, 60. *Prof Exp:* From instr to assoc prof, 47-77, PROF GER, UNIV ALA, 77- *Mem:* Am Asn Teachers Ger; Mediaeval Acad Am; S Atlantic Mod Lang Asn. *Mailing Add:* Dept of Ger Univ of Ala University AL 35486

PORTER, MICHAEL, b New Haven, Conn, Feb 26, 42. COMPARATIVE & GERMAN LITERATURE. *Educ:* Yale Univ, BA, 65; Cornell Univ, PhD(comp lit), 70. *Prof Exp:* Lectr Ger, Rutgers Univ, 69-70, asst prof, 70-73; asst prof, Tulane Univ, 73-80. *Mem:* MLA; Am Comp Lit Asn; Hugo von Hofmannsthal Ges; Int Arthur Schnitzler Res Asn. *Res:* Post-Romantic lyric poetry; theory of literature; modern German literature. *Publ:* Auth, Hugo von Hofmannsthal's Der Tor und der Tod: The poet as fool, Mod Austrian Lit, 72; LeitchsanLeicht and schwer in the poetry of Hugo von Hofmannsthal, Monatshefte, 73. *Mailing Add:* 2035 Jenn New Orleans LA 70115

PORTER, THADDEUS COY, b Bristow, Okla, Oct 14, 22; m 45; c 3. SPANISH. *Educ:* Harding Col, BA, 44; George Peabody Col, MA, 46; Vanderbilt Univ, PhD(comp lit), 68. *Prof Exp:* Asst prof English, David Lipscomb Col, 50-52; instr Span, Vanderbilt Univ, 58-63; asst prof, 64-69, head dept mod foreign lang, 69-76, PROF SPAN, MID TENN STATE UNIV, 69- *Mem:* Am Asn Teachers Span & Port; SAtlantic Mod Lang Asn; MLA. *Mailing Add:* Dept of Mod Foreign Lang Tenn State Univ Murfreesboro TN 37132

PORTNER, IRVING ALAN, b Chicago, Ill, May 28, 30. ITALIAN, COMPARATIVE LITERATURE. *Educ:* Princeton Univ, BA, 52; Harvard Univ, MA, 56, PhD(comp lit), 70. *Prof Exp:* From instr to asst prof French & Ital, Univ Pittsburgh, 60-64; instr Ital, Univ Chicago, 64-65; lectr, Columbia Univ, 65-70; asst prof, 70-73, chmn dept foreign lang & lit, 73-80, assoc prof, 73-80, PROF ITAL, JOHN JAY COL CRIMINAL JUSTICE, 80- *Mem:* Am Asn Teachers Ital; Am Coun Teaching Foreign Lang; Asn Dept Foreign Lang; Dante Soc Am; MLA. *Res:* Ariosto; Renaissance drama; the novel. *Mailing Add:* Dept of Foreign Lang & Lit 445 W 59th St John Jay Col of Criminal Justice New York NY 10019

PORTUONDO, ALICIA EDELMIRA, b Santiago, Cuba, Jan 19, 29; m 53. SPANISH. *Educ:* Oriente Univ, Cuba, MA, 53, LLM, 60; Rutgers Univ, MA, 67; State Univ NY, PhD(Span), 76. *Prof Exp:* Prof Span, Oriente Univ, 58-60; asst prof, 61-77, ASSOC PROF SPAN, MONMOUTH COL, NJ, 77-, CHMN DEPT, 80- *Mem:* Am Asn Teachers Span & Port; Am Asn Univ Women. *Res:* Spanish language and literature; painting. *Publ:* Auth, Spanish for Social Workers, Portuonds & Singer. *Mailing Add:* 64 Kings Rd Little Silver NJ 07739

POSNIAK, ALEXANDER RICHARD, b Milan, Italy, Sept 16, 20; US citizen; m 45; c 1. FRENCH & ITALIAN. *Educ:* Univ Md, College Park, BA, 52; George Washington Univ, MA, 62. *Prof Exp:* Intel specialist oper & res, US Army, 40-47; intel staff off oper & res & teaching, US Air Force, 48-68; asst prof, 68-73, actg head dept foreign lang, 71-, assoc prof, 73-81, EMER PROF FRENCH & ITAL, AUBURN UNIV, 81- *Concurrent Pos:* Lectr, Europ div, Univ Md, 62-64. *Mem:* AAUP; Am Asn Teachers Fr; S Atlantic Mod Lang Asn; Am Transl Asn. *Res:* Foreign language teaching methods; history of Italian Fascist diplomacy; modern Italian novel. *Publ:* Co-ed, The Great Encyclopaedia of Aeronautics, Mancini, Milan, 36; coauth, The Book of Flight, Casale Monferrato, Italy, 38; International Relations Study Manuals (ser), Air Command & Staff Col, 65-68. *Mailing Add:* 659 Thorp St Auburn AL 36830

POTT, CLARENCE K, b Amsterdam, Netherlands, Oct 31, 06; nat US; n 38; c 5. GERMANIC LITERATURE. *Educ:* Calvin Col, AB, 31; Univ Mich, PhD, 43. *Prof Exp:* Teacher high schs, Mich, 31-38; from instr to assoc prof Ger, Univ Mich, Ann Arbor, 44-60, prof Ger lang & lit, 60-76, chmn dept, 60-71; RETIRED. *Mem:* Am Asn Teachers Ger; Renaissance Soc Am. *Res:* German literature of the 16th & 17th centuries; Holland-German literary relations; Heinrich von Kleist. *Publ:* Auth, Heinrich von Kleist's Amphitryon in the critical literature of the nineteenth and twentieth centuries; Erasmus and the Reformation, In: The Heritage of John Calvin, Heritage Hall Lectures, 1960-1970, Eerdmans, 73. *Mailing Add:* 1144 Ardmore Holland MI 49423

POTTER, EDITH GEYLER, b Berlin, Ger, Apr 24, 20; US citizen; wid. GERMANIC LANGUAGES. *Educ:* Univ Calif, Los Angeles, BA, 56, MA, 59, PhD(Ger), 65. *Prof Exp:* Asst Ger, Univ Calif, Los Angeles, 60-61, assoc, 62-63; asst prof, Sonoma State Col, 65-67; asst prof, 67-70, assoc prof, 70-80, PROF GER & DIR SCRIPPS YR IN HEIDELBERG, SCRIPPS COL, 80- *Mem:* Am Soc 18th Century Studies; Int Asn Ger Studies; MLA; Am Asn Teachers Ger. *Res:* The use of imagery in the works of Goethe; Faust themes and the modern aspects of Faust; Thomas Mann. *Publ:* Auth, Modern aspects in Goethe's Faust, Akten Int Ger-Kong, 75. *Mailing Add:* Dept of Ger Scripps Col Claremont CA 91711

POTTER, EDITHE JEANMONOD, b Treminis, France; US citizen. FOREIGN LANGUAGE & LITERATURE. *Educ:* Oberlin Col, BA, 48; Middlebury Col, MA, 54; Rice Univ, PhD(French lit), 70. *Prof Exp:* Teacher French, Kents Hill Sch, Maine, 55-58; bilingual admin asst aircraft maintenance, Global Air Assoc, 59-63; teacher French, Dana Hall Sch, Mass, 64-66; asst prof, Northwestern Univ, 70-76; ASSOC PROF FRENCH, BAYLOR UNIV, 76- *Mem:* Am Asn Teachers French; MLA. *Res:* The theater of Moliere; the teaching of French. *Publ:* Auth, French conversation for young adults, Mod Lang J, 12/71; Moliere's comic artistry in L'Etourdi, Ky Romance Quart, 73; L'Etourdi of Moliere: A vision of structured chaos, Romance Notes, 73; Levels of knowing in M de Pourceaugnac, Orbis Literarum, 74; Faith and the absurd in Le Medecin malgre lui, Neophilologus, 74; Plot structure in L'Etourdi and G Dandin, Orbis Litterarum, 75: Problems of knowing in M de Pourceaugnac, Romance Notes, 76; Moliere's Amphitryon: Myth in a comic perspective, Orbis Litterarum, 77. *Mailing Add:* Dept of French Baylor Univ Waco TX 76703

POTTER, JOY HAMBUECHEN, b Zurich, Switz, Mar 4, 35; US citizen; div; c 1. ITALIAN & COMPARATIVE LITERATURE. *Educ:* Radcliffe Col, BA, 56; Harvard-Radcliffe Prog Bus Admin, Cert, 57; Rutgers Univ, PhD(Ital), 67. *Prof Exp:* Instr Ital, Rutgers Univ, 65-67; asst prof, Univ Penn, 67-71; assoc prof, 71-81 PROF ITAL, UNIV TEX, AUSTIN, 81- *Concurrent Pos:* Romantic Lang & Lit Adv Comt, Coun Int Exchange Scholars; Nat Endowment for Humanities fel, 77-78. *Mem:* Mod Humanities Res Asn; MLA; Am Asn Teachers Ital. *Res:* Medieval Italian; modern Italian; semiotics. *Publ:* Auth, La struttura del Mare Amoroso, Cult Neolatina, 63; Vittorini's literary apprenticeship, Forum Italicum, 9/69; The poetic and symbolic function of fable in Erica e i suoi fratelli, spring 71 & An ideological substructure in Conversazione in Silica, winter 75, Italica; Patterns of meaning in Conversazione in Italia, Forum Italicum, 3/75; Boccaccio as illusionist, Humanities Asn Rev, fall 75; Elio Vittorini, GK Hall, 79; Five Frames for the Decameron, Princeton Univ Press, 82. *Mailing Add:* Dept of French & Ital Univ of Tex Austin TX 78703

POULAKIDAS, ANDREAS K, English, Comparative Literature. See Vol II

POULIN, NORMAN ANDRE, b Laconia, NH, June 4, 33; m 56; c 6. FRENCH, FOREIGN LANGUAGES EDUCATION. *Educ:* Univ NH, BA, 57: Canisius Col, MS, 62; New York Univ, PhD(French), 72. *Prof Exp:* Instr French, Niagra Falls Pub Sch, NY, 58-61; instr, Clarkstown Sch, NY, 61-64; instr, Long Beach Sch, NY, 64-66; from instr to asst prof, State Univ NY, Stony Brook, 66-72; asst prof, Univ Md, 72-75; ASST PROF FRENCH, UNIV MO, COLUMBIA, 76-, SUPVR FRENCH TEACHING ASSTS, 77- *Concurrent Pos:* Consult French, Harper Row Publ, 70-76; consult, Xerox Col Publ, 71-75; consult, Rand McNally, 71-76. *Honors & Awards:* Founders Day Award, NY Univ, 72. *Mem:* Am Asn Teachers French; Am Dialect Soc; Int Asn Study & Promotion of AV & Structuro-Global Methods; Am Coun Teaching Foreign Lang. *Res:* Phonology of French Canadian speech; foreign language methodology. *Publ:* Auth, Foreign language study: a new rationale, Clearing House, 70; coauth, French Phonology for Teachers, Didier, France, 71; auth, Oral and Nasal Diphthongization of a New England French Dialect, Didier, France, 73; Testing ability to communicate, Lang Asn Bull, 73; contribr, Voix et Visages de la France, Rand McNally, 74; coauth, Sounds of French, Rand McNally, 74. *Mailing Add:* 3966 E Sonora Ct Columbia MO 65201

POULTNEY, JAMES WILSON, b Baltimore Co, Md, Sept 21, 07. CLASSICAL PHILOLOGY. *Educ:* Johns Hopkins Univ, AM, 32, PhD, 34. *Prof Exp:* Instr Greek, Johns Hopkins Univ, 32-37; instr classics, Univ Nebr, 38; prof, Carthage Col, 38-42 & Univ Pa, 46-47; from asst prof to assoc prof, 47-63, prof class philol, 63-73, EMER PROF CLASSICS, JOHN HOPKINS

UNIV, 73- *Honors & Awards:* Award of Merit, Am Philol Asn, 61. *Mem:* Am Philol Asn; Ling Soc Am; Archaeol Inst Am; Am Orient Soc; Class Asn Atlantic States. *Res:* Greek, Latin, and Italic dialects. *Publ:* Auth, The Syntax of the Genitive Case in Aristophanes, Johns Hopkins Univ, 36; The Bronze Tables of Iguvium, Am Philol Asn, 59. *Mailing Add:* Dept of Classics Johns Hopkins Univ Baltimore MD 21218

POUND, GLEN M, b Remer, Minn, Oct 19, 19; m 53. LINGUISTICS, ENGLISH. *Educ:* Milton Col, BA, 41; Ind State Univ, MA, 59; Ind Univ, PhD(ling), 64. *Prof Exp:* Teaching asst English as Foreign lang, Ind Univ, 61-63; asst prof, 64-67, ASSOC PROF LING, IND STATE UNIV, TERRE HAUTE, 67- *Concurrent Pos:* Lectr phonology, NDEA Inst, 65-66. *Mem:* Ling Soc Am; NCTE; Teachers English to Speakers Other Lang. *Res:* Spoken secret languages, especially of school children; problems in English to speakers of other languages; stylistics in literature and speech. *Mailing Add:* 13 Park Lane Terre Haute IN 47803

POVSIC, BOLESLAV SELIC, b Slovenia, Yugoslavia, Apr 7, 21; US citizen; m 63; c 2. CLASSICS. *Educ:* Ginnasio-Liceo Massimo D'Azeglio, Torino, Italy, Maturita Classica, 45; Univ Rome, PhD(classics), 53. *Prof Exp:* Assoc prof philos, St Joseph Col, Md, 57-62; assoc prof classics, St Francis Col, Pa, 62-63; PROF CLASSICS, BOWLING GREEN STATE UNIV, 63- *Concurrent Pos:* Vis prof, St Michael Col, Vt, 63-66; lectr, Univ Louvain, Belgium & Univ Saarlandes, WGer, 81. *Mem:* Am Philol Asn. *Res:* Latin literature; Christian archaeology. *Publ:* Auth, Ovidiana, Palaestra Latina, 73; De pronuntiandis litteris Latinis, Vita Latina, 73; Report from Constanta, Class Outlook, 74; Grammatica Latina, Ciolfi, Cassino, 74; in Quibus Marci T Ciceronis et Martini L King Scripta inter se Conveniant et Discrepent, In: Melanges Offerts a Leopold Sedar Senghor, Nes Nouvelles Ed Africaines, Dakar, 77; De Nonullis Astutiis in Lingua Latina Docenda, Vita Latina, 77 & 78; Vergiliana Concinnitas seu Rythm in Virgil, Humanitas, 78; Locutiones cotidianae, quae in M Tullii Cicernois epistulis reperiuntur, Vita Latina, 80. *Mailing Add:* Dept of Romance Lang Bowling Green State Univ Bowling Green OH 43403

POWELL, HUGH, b Cardiff, Wales. GERMAN LITERATURE. *Educ:* Univ Wales, BA, 33, dipl educ, 34, MA, 36, DLitt, 62; Univ Rostock, PhD(Ger), 38. *Prof Exp:* Lectr English, Univ Bonn, 38-39; lectr Ger, Univ Wales, 39-40; prof Ger & chmn dept, Univ Leicester, 46-69; PROF GER, IND UNIV, BLOOMINGTON, 69- *Concurrent Pos:* Res grants, Cassell Trust, Brit Acad, Leverhulme Trust & Fritz Thyssen Found, 53-68; Ger Acad Exchange Serv, 80; fel, Univ Col Cardiff, 81- *Mem:* AAUP. *Res:* German literature of the 17th century. *Publ:* Ed, Andreas Gryphius: Carolus Stuardus, Univ Leicester, 63; Andreas Gryphius: Dramen (5 vols), Max Niemeyer, 64-72: Andreas Gryphius: Cardenio u Celinde, 67 & Andreas Gryphius: Peter Squentz, 69, Univ Leicester, J G Schoch: Comoedia vom Studentenleben, H Lang, 76. *Mailing Add:* Dept of Ger Lang Ballantine Hall Ind Univ Bloomington IN 47401

POWELL, MARVIN ADELL, JR, Ancient History, Cuneiform Studies. See Vol I

POWELL, WARD HUGHES, b Minden, Nebr, Aug 10, 17. GERMANIC PHILOLOGY & LITERATURE. *Educ:* Univ Nebr, AB, 38, AM, 40; Univ Colo, PhD, 56. *Prof Exp:* Asst prof Ger, Ill Wesleyan Univ, 40-41, 46-47; asst prof, Univ Denver, 47-51; instr, Univ Colo, 51-55; from asst prof to assoc prof, 55-64, chmn dept, 76-80, prof, 64-80, EMER PROF GER, UNIV MONT, 80- *Mem:* Am Asn Teachers Ger; MLA. *Mailing Add:* Dept of Foreign Lang Univ of Mont Missoula MT 59801

POWERS, PERRY JOHN, b Salem, Ore, July 28, 19. SPANISH LITERATURE. *Educ:* Univ Ore, AB, 41; Johns Hopkins Univ, PhD, 47. *Prof Exp:* From asst prof to assoc prof, 46-67, head dept, 69-75, PROF ROMANCE LANG, UNIV ORE, 67- *Concurrent Pos:* Ford fel, 55-56. *Mem:* MLA; Am Asn Teachers Span & Port; Am Comp Lit Asn. *Res:* Lyric poetry of Lope de Vega; theater of the Golden Age. *Mailing Add:* Dept of Romance Lang Univ of Ore Eugene OR 97403

POYATOS, FERNANDO, b Spain. ROMANCE LANGUAGES. *Educ:* Univ Madrid, MA, 57, PhD(philol), 66. *Prof Exp:* Instr Span lang & lit, Denison Univ, 60-62 & Elmira Col, 62-64; PROF ROMANCE LANG, UNIV NEW BRUNSWICK, 65- *Concurrent Pos:* Can Coun fel, 73-74; consult, Univ Nancy, 76 & Res Ctr Lang & Semiotic Studies, Ind Univ, 76-77. *Honors & Awards:* Best Res Article Award, Can Asn Hispanists, 77. *Mem:* Asn Int Hispanistas; Am Anthrop Asn; Semiotic Soc Am; Soc Espanola Ling; Int Asn Semiotic Studies. *Res:* Nonverbal communication; semiotics of culture; literary semiotics. *Publ:* Auth, Cross-cultural study of paralinguistic alternants in face-to-face interaction, In: The Organization of Behavior in Face-to-Face Interaction, 75 & Analysis of a culture through its culturemes: Theory and method, In: The Mutual Interaction of People and Their Built Environment, 76, Mouton, The Hague; Man Beyond Words: Theory and Methodology of Nonverbal Communication, NY State English Coun, 76; Verbal and nonverbal expression in interaction, In: Proceedings Int Cong Appl Ling, Hochschul, Stuttgart, 76; The Morphological and Functional Approach to Kinesics in the Context of Interaction and Culture, 77, Forms and Functions of Nonverbal Communication in the Novel: A New Perspective of the Author-Character-Reader Relationship, 77 & The Integration of Verbal and Nonverbal Communication in Natural Conversation, 78, Semiotica; Toward a typology of somatic signs, In: Semiotik III: Zeighentypologie, Wilhem Fink, Munich/Salzburg, 78. *Mailing Add:* Dept of Romance Lang Univ of NB Fredericton NB E3B 5A3 Can

POYNTER, JOHN DURWARD, b Manhatten, Mont, June 24, 30; c 2. OLDER GERMAN LITERATURE. *Educ:* Univ Calif, Los Angeles, BA, 54, MA, 60, PhD(Ger lit), 65. *Prof Exp:* From instr to asst prof, 62-70, res fels, 67 & 68, ASSOC PROF GER LIT, CLAREMONT MEN'S COL, 70- *Mem:* Am Asn Teachers Ger; Philol Asn Pac Coast. *Res:* Family patterns in German literature of the 18th and 19th centuries; foreign language learning and teaching. *Publ:* Transl, Mario Jacoby, A contribution to the phenomenon of transference, J Analytical Psychol, 7/69 & In: The Analytic Process: Aims, Analysis, Training, Putnam, 71; auth, The creative process in early Meistergesang, Neophilologus, 1/70; transl, Annemarie Sanger, Child psychotherapy based on the analytical psychology of C G Jung, In: The Analytic Process: Aims, Analysis, Training, Putnam, 71; auth, The pearls of Emilia Galotti, Lessing Yrbk, 78. *Mailing Add:* Dept of Ger Claremont Men's Col Claremont CA 91711

POYTHRESS, VERN SHERIDAN, New Testament, General Linguistics. See Vol IV

PRADO, MARCIAL, b Palencia, Spain, April 15, 33; m 59; c 2. SPANISH LINGUISTICS. *Educ:* Univ Villanueva, Cuba, BA, 60; Georgetown Univ, MS, 70, PhD(ling), 74. *Prof Exp:* Instr Span, Columbus High Sch, Miami, 61-64, Molloy High Sch, NY, 64-65, Defense Lang Inst, 65-69, Georgetown Univ, 69-74: asst prof Span & ling, 74-77, ASSOC PROF SPAN & LING, CALIF STATE UNIV, FULLERTON, 77- *Concurrent Pos:* Consult Span, Lockman Bible Found, 77-78; panel consult, Boers Publ Co, 77-78; grant-in-aid, Calif State Univ chancellor, 78-79. *Mem:* MLA; Ling Soc Am; Hispania; Philol Asn Pacific Coast; Asoc Ling Filologia Am Latina. *Res:* Spanish syntax, general linguistics; Latin American modern literature. *Publ:* Contribr, El pronombre se en espanol, in literature, PAPC, 11/78; Spanish dialects and clitic pronouns, Span Ling Symposium Ling Soc Am, 5/78; Markedness and the gender feature in Spanish, Proc 8th WECOL Annual Mgt, 78; Verb tenses and time in the Spanish discourse, Proc 30th Annual Mgt PNCFL, 79; What's wrong with being wrong?, Selecta, J PNCFL, 80; La teoria de la marcadez y el genero en espanol, Hispania, 82; Practical Spanish Grammar: A Self-Teaching Guide, John Wiley & Sons, 82. *Mailing Add:* Dept of Foreign Lang Calif State Univ Fullerton CA 92634

PRAKKEN, DONALD WILSON, b Holland, Mich, Jan 22, 15. CLASSICAL PHILOLOGY. *Educ:* Whitman Col, AB, 35; Johns Hopkins Univ, AM, 37; Columbia Univ, PhD, 43. *Prof Exp:* Instr Latin & English, Dongan Hall-Arden Country Day Sch, Staten Island, NY, 41-42; instr Latin, Lakeside Sch Boys, Seattle, Wash, 42-43; instr Greek & Latin, Ind Univ, 43-45 & Wash Square Col, 45-46; from asst prof to prof classics, Franklin & Marshall Col, 46-63; prof classics, Pa State Univ, 63-66; PROF CLASSICS, STATE UNIV NY ALBANY, 66- *Concurrent Pos:* Fulbright grant, Greece, 54-55; mem, Inst Advan Studies, 60-61. *Mem:* Am Philol Asn. *Publ:* Contrib, Am J Philol; Class World & Class J. *Mailing Add:* 376 Humanities State Univ of NY Albany NY 12222

PRATOR, CLIFFORD HOLMES, JR, b Ft Valley, GA, July 12, 11; m 37; c 2. ENGLISH AS SECOND LANGUAGE, APPLIED LINGUISTICS. *Educ:* Asbury Col, AB, 32: Univ Mich, AM, 34, PhD-, 39. *Prof Exp:* Instr French & Span, Univ Mich, 39-42; vis prof English, Nat Univ Colombia, 42-43; dir, Centro Colombo-Am, 43-44: teaching specialist English, Inter-Am Educ Found, 45-46; instr French, 46-47, asst prof, 47-51, assoc prof, 51-60, asst dean students & foreign student adv, 47-56, prof, 61-79, vchmn dept, 63-74, EMER PROF ENGLISH, UNIV CALIF, LOS ANGELES, 79- *Concurrent Pos:* Vis prof, Haiti, 45; Fulbright lectr, Philippine Norm Col, 48-49; Del Amo Found grant, Spain, 55; supvr Philippine Ctr Lang Studies, Manila, PI, 57-65; mem adv bd, Ctr Appl Ling, Washington, DC, 61-63; supbr, Inst Ling Colombo-Am, Bogota, 61-66; mem, Nat Adv Coun Teaching English as Second Lang, 61-67; fild dir, Surv Lang Use & Lang Teaching in East Africa, Nairobi, 67-68; vis prof Am Univ, Cairo, 71-72; consult; English lang policy surv of Jordan, Ford Found, 72-73. *Honors & Awards:* Philippine Legion of Honor, 64. *Mem:* Ling Soc Am: Teachers English to Speakers Other Lang. *Res:* Teacher training; pronunciation of English; language surveys. *Publ:* Auth, Manual of American English Pronunciation, Holt, 58; Education Problems Involved in the Teaching of English as a Second Languages, Symp Multilingualism, Brazzaville, 62; Phonetics vs phonemics in the ESL classroom: When is allophonic accuracy important, Teachers English Speakers Other Lang Quart, 3/71; contribr, Toward a cognitive approach to second language acquisition, Ctr Curriculum Develop, 71; auth, In search of a method, English Teaching Forum, 74; coauth, English-language policy survey of Jordan, Ctr Applied Ling, 75; auth, The Cornerstones of Method, Teaching English as a Second or Foreign Language, Newbury House, 79. *Mailing Add:* Dept of English Univ of Calif Los Angeles CA 90024

PRATS, JORGE, b Barcelona, Spain, Aug 1, 32; m 61: c 3. SPANISH. *Educ:* Univ Ill, BA, 60, MA, 62, PhD(Span), 68. *Prof Exp:* Instr, 62-64, asst prof, 68-73, ASSOC PROF SPAN, KNOX COL, ILL, 73- *Concurrent Pos:* Dir, Jr Year Abroad, Barcelona, Spain, 71-72. *Mem:* MLA; Am Asn Teachers Span & Port; Am Coun Teaching Foreign Lang. *Publ:* Coauth, Contribucion a una bibliografia de dialectologia espanola y americana, 67 & auth, America poetica--JMG, 68, Real Acad Espanola. *Mailing Add:* Dept of Lang Knox Col Galesburg IL 61401

PRATT, MARY LOUISE, b Listowel, Ont, Oct 21, 48. COMPARATIVE LITERATURE. *Educ:* Univ Toronto, BA, 70; Univ Ill, Urbana-Champaign, MA, 71; Stanford Univ, PhD(comp lit), 75. *Prof Exp:* Asst prof comp lit, Univ Mass, Amherst, 75-76: ASST PROF SPAN, PORT & COMP LIT, STANFORD UNIV, 76- *Mem:* MLA; Latin Am Studies Assoc; Tabloid Collective. *Res:* Linguistics and literature; narrative theory; colonialism and literature. *Publ:* Auth, Tone in some Kikuyu verb forms, Studies in African Ling, 72; Toward a Speech Act Theory of Literary Discourse, Ind Univ, 77; Mapping ideology: Gide, Camus and Algeria, Col Lit, 81; coauth, Linguistics for Students of Literature, Harcourt, 81; The Ideology of Speech Act Theory, Centrum, 81; Conventions of Representation: Where Discourse and Ideology Meet, Georgetown Univ Roundtable, 82. *Mailing Add:* Dept of Span & Port Stanford Univ Stanford CA 94305

PRATT, NORMAN TWOMBLY, JR, b Providence, RI, July 29, 11; m 36; c 3. CLASSICS, COMPARATIVE LITERATURE. *Educ:* Brown Univ, AB, 32; Princeton Univ, AM, 34, PhD, 35. *Prof Exp:* From instr to asst prof classics, Princeton Univ, 35-42; from assoc prof to prof, 46-76, chmn dept, 46-

71, EMER PROF CLASSICS, IND UNIV, BLOOMINGTON, 76- *Concurrent Pos:* Vis assoc prof, Columbia Univ, 49-50; ed-in-chief, Class J, 56-61; vis prof, Am Sch Class Studies, Athens, 62-63, 69-70; Bollingen fel, 62-63. *Mem:* Am Philol Asn; Class Asn Midwest & South (pres, 64-65); Am Class League (pres, 66-68). *Res:* Classical languages and literatures; ancient tragedy. *Publ:* Auth, Dramatic Suspense in Seneca and in his Greek Precursors, Princeton Univ, 39; The stoic base of Senecan drama, Trans Am Philol Asn, 48; From Oedipus to Lear, Class J, 61; Major systems of figurative language in Senecan melodrama, Trans Am Philol Asn, 63; Seneca's Drama, Univ NC (in prep). *Mailing Add:* 772 Marbury Lane Longboat Key FL 33548

PRATT, SARAH CLAFLIN, b Boston, Mass, Mar 10, 50. RUSSIAN LITERATURE & LANGUAGE. *Educ:* Yale Univ, BA, 72; Columbia Univ, MA, 75, PhD(Russian lit), 78. *Prof Exp:* Asst prof Russian & German, Oberlin Col, 77-80; ASST PROF, RUSSIAN LANG PROG COORDR, UNIV SOUTHERN CALIF, LOS ANGELES, 80- *Concurrent Pos:* Head interpreter, Am-Soviet Youth Forum, 73- *Mem:* Am Asn Advan Slavic Studies. *Res:* Russian 19th and 20th century poetry; romanticism; Tolstoy. *Mailing Add:* Dept Slavic Lang & Lit Univ Southern Calif Los Angeles CA 90007

PREDMORE, MICHAEL P, b New Brunswick, NJ, Feb 5, 38. SPANISH LANGUAGE & LITERATURE. *Educ:* Swarthmore Col, BA, 59; Univ Wis, MA, 61, PhD(Span), 65. *Prof Exp:* From asst prof to assoc prof, 65-74, PROF SPAN, UNIV WASH, 74- *Concurrent Pos:* Jr fel, Inst Res Humanities, Univ Wis, 68-69; Guggenheim Mem Found fel, 75-76; Coun Int Exchange Scholars grant, Spain, 82. *Mem:* Am Asn Teachers Span & Port; MLA. *Res:* Nineteenth and 20th century Spanish peninsular literature; aesthetics. *Publ:* Auth, La obra en prosa de J R Jimenez, Gredos, 66; The structure of Platero y Yo, PMLA, 70; A stylistic analysis of Lo fatal, Hisp Rev, 71; The structure of the Dario de un poeta reciencasado, Contemp Lit, 72; La poesia hermetica de Juan Ramon Jimenez, Gredos, 73; Teoria de la Expresion Poetica and Twentieth Century Spanish lyric poetry, Mod Lang Notes, 74; Una Espana joven en la poesia de Antonio Machado, insula, 81; ed, Platero y yo, 6th ed, Catedra, 82. *Mailing Add:* Dept of Romance Lang Univ of Wash Seattle WA 98195

PREDMORE, RICHARD LIONEL, b Tottenville, NY, Dec 21, 11. SPANISH. *Educ:* Rutgers Univ, AB, 33, AM, 35; Middlebury Col, DML, 41. *Prof Exp:* Teacher, high sch, NY, 36-37; from instr to assoc prof, Rutgers Univ, 37-50, chmn dept Romance lang, 47-50; vis asst prof, Duke Univ, 45-46, secy univ, 61-62, dean grad sch arts & sci, 62-69, vprovost, 66-69, prof Romance lang, 50-77; DIR, INT INST SPAIN, MADRID, 80- *Concurrent Pos:* Rockefeller fel, Cent Am, 42-43; dir, Middlebury Col Grad Sch Span in Spain, 56-57; chief acad prog br, div grad prog, Bur High Educ, US Off Educ, 66-67; mem Grad Record Exam Bd, 69-73; Guggenheim Found fel, 70-71. *Mem:* MLA; Am Asn Teachers Span & Port. *Res:* Spanish language and literature; The Spanish language in America; contemporary Spanish literature. *Publ:* Ed, Incidents of Travel in Central America, Chiapas and Yucatan, Rutgers Univ, 49; auth, Topical Spanish Review Grammar, Holt, 54; El mundo del Quixote, Insula, 58; The World of Don Quixote, Harvard Univ, 67; Cervantes, Dodd, 73; Lorca's New York Poetry: Social Injustice, Dark Love, Lost Faith, Duke Univ Press, 80. *Mailing Add:* 7 Glenmore Dr Durham NC 27707

PREISNER, RIO, b Mukacevo, Czech, Nov 13, 25; m 51; c 1. GERMAN LITERATURE. *Educ:* Charles Univ, Prague, PhD(Ger lit, philos), 49. *Prof Exp:* Asst prof Ger lit, Charles Univ, Prague, 49-52; assoc prof, 69-73, PROF GER LIT, PA STATE UNIV, UNIVERSITY PARK, 73- *Mem:* MLA; PEN Club, Austria. *Res:* German literature since the 18th century; history of ideas. *Publ:* Ed, Johan Georg Forster (in Czech), Odeon, Prague, 64; Franz Kafka, Aphorisms (in Czech), Ceskoslovensky spisovatel, Prague, 68; auth, Johann Nepomuk Nestroy: Schöpfer der tragischen Posse, Hanser, Munich, 69; A Critique of Totalitarianism (in Czech), Vol I, Acad Christiana, Rome, 73; Rilke in Böhmen, In: Rilke heute, Suhrkamp, Frankfurth, 75; Aspekte einer provokativen tschechischen Germanistik Bd 1, Jal-Verlag, Würzburg, 77; Aspekte . . . Bol 2, Jal-Verlag, Würzburg, 81; Culture Without End, Arkyr, Munich, 81. *Mailing Add:* Dept of Ger Pa State Univ University Park PA 16802

PRESTON, DENNIS RICHARD, b Harrisburg, Ill, Feb 10, 40; m 74; c 2. LINGUISTICS. *Educ:* Univ Louisville, BA, 62; Univ Wis, PhD(English), 69. *Prof Exp:* Instr ling, Univ Wis-Milwaukee, 65-67; asst prof, Ohio State Univ, 67-71; assoc prof, 71-76, PROF LING, STATE UNIV NY FREDONDIA, 76- *Concurrent Pos:* Assoc lectr ling, Ind Univ Southeast, 70-72; docent ling, Adam Mickiewicz Univ, Poznan, Poland, 72-74. *Mem:* Am Dialect Soc; Am Name Soc; Ling Soc Am; Int Asn Univ Prof English; Am Folklore Soc. *Res:* General linguistics; sociolinguistics; folk speech. *Publ:* Auth, English as a second language in adult basic education programs, TESOL Quart, 71; Social dialectology in America: A critical rejoinder, Fl AFL Reporter, 72; Southern Indiana place name legends as reflections of folk history, Ind Names, 73; Deeper and deeper contrastive analysis, Papers & Studies Contrastive Ling, 73; Bituminous Coal Mining Vocabulary of the Eastern United States, Am Dialect Soc, 73; Variation in language: Its significance in English as a second language, Studia Anglica Posnaniensia, 74; Proverbial comparisons from Southern Indiana, Orbis, 75; co-ed, The Varieties of American English, Int Commun Agency, 78. *Mailing Add:* Dept of Ling State Univ NY Col Central Ave Fredonia NY 14063

PRESTON, FRED LORENZO, b Athens, Ohio, Dec 7, 13; m 41; c 2. FRENCH. *Educ:* Ohio Univ, AB, 34; Harvard Univ, AM, 35; Ohio State Univ, PhD(French), 51. *Prof Exp:* Critic teacher mod lang, Ohio Univ, 35-41; instr French, Ohio State Univ, 46-49; from asst prof to assoc prof, 49-69, chmn dept, 61-64, prof mod lang, 69-79, EMER PROF FRENCH, DENISON UNIV, 79- *Concurrent Pos:* Asst Inst Int Educ, 35-36; teacher high sch, Ohio, 35-41. *Mem:* MLA; Am Asn Teachers Fr; Am Coun Teaching Foreign Lang. *Res:* Teaching techniques of the French language; 18th century French literature; the language laboratory. *Publ:* Auth, Cahier d'exercices for Roger Martin du Gard's Les Thibault, Denison Univ, 67. *Mailing Add:* Dept of Mod Lang Denison Univ Granville OH 43023

PRETE, SESTO, b Montefiore dell'Aso, Italy, Sept 27, 19; m 55; c 4. CLASSICAL LANGUAGES & LITERATURES. *Educ:* Liceo Classico A Caro, BA, 38; Univ Heidelberg, MA, 43; Univ Cologne, PhD, 44; Univ Bologna, PhD, 45. *Prof Exp:* Lettore Latin lit, Univ Bologne, 45-53; res scholar, Vatican Libr, 53; vis prof classics, Univ Calif, 54; from asst prof to prof, Fordham Univ, 56-68; PROF CLASSICS, UNIV KANS, 68- *Concurrent Pos:* Fulbright-Smith-Mundt fel, 54; Guggenheim fel, 62; pres, Int Convention Humanistic Studies, Montepulciano, 72-; ed, Res Publica Litterarum, 78; pres, Instituto Int Studi Piceni, Sassoferrato, 81- *Honors & Awards:* Commendatore, Order St Gregory the Great, 72. *Res:* Critical edition of Ausonius; Columella, de re rustica; Renaissance poetry, especially Pontano. *Publ:* Auth, Zwei Unbekannte Briefe von Friedrich Wilhelm Ritschl, Rheinisches Mus, 72; Note all' Heautontimoroumenos di Terenzio, Studi classici in onore di Q Cataudella, 72; Codex Vat Lat 3226 and the text of Terence's Phormio, Studia Humanitatis, 73; Il codice di Columella di Stefano Guarnieri, Fano, 74; Decimi Magni Ausonii opuscula, Teubner, Leipzig, 78; Latin Poets in the Quattrocento, Kans Univ, 78; L'Umanista Niccolo Perotti, Sassoferrato, 80; I coolici di Terenrio nella biblioteca di Wolfenbüttel, Wolfenbüttel, 82. *Mailing Add:* Dept of Classics Univ of Kans Lawrence KS 66044

PRETO-RODAS, RICHARD A, b Yonkers, NY, May 30, 36. ROMANCE LANGUAGES. *Educ:* Fairfield Univ, AB, 58; Boston Col, MA, 60; Univ Mich, MA, 63, PhD(Port), 66. *Prof Exp:* Instr English, Fairfield Univ, 60-61; instr Span & Port, Univ Mich, 65-66; asst prof, Univ Fla, 66-70, Humanities Coun res grant, 68-69; assoc prof, 70-77, PROF SPAN & PORT, UNIV ILL, URBANA, 77-, CHMN DEPT, 78- *Mem:* Am Asn Teachers Span & Port. *Res:* Contemporary Brazilian literature; irony as a perspective in Portuguese poetry; Iberian Renaissance. *Publ:* Auth, Negritude as a Theme in the Poetry of the Portuguese-Speaking World, Univ Fla, 70; Anchieta and Vieira: drama as sermon and sermon as drama, Luso-Brazilian Rev, 70; Francisco Rodrigues Lobo: Dialogue and Courtly Lore in Renaissance Portugal, Univ NC, 71; co-ed, Cronicas Brasileiras--a Portuguese Reader, Univ Fla & rev ed, 78; auth, Pronominal confusion in Modern peninsular Portuguese, Hispania, 72; Amazonia in literature: themes and changing perspectives, In: Man in the Amazon, Univ Fla, 74; The Black presence and two Brazilian modernists, In: Tradition and Renewal, Univ Ill, 75. *Mailing Add:* Dept of Span Ital & Port Univ of Ill Urbana IL 61801

PRETZER, DIANA GOODRICH, b Chicago, Ill, Nov 5, 30; m 66. ROMANCE LANGUAGES. *Educ:* Knox Col, BA, 52; State Univ Iowa, MA, 54; Ind Univ, PhD(Span), 66. *Prof Exp:* Instr Span, Wilson Col, 54-55; asst prof, Macalester Col, 56-59; resident dir jr year in Peru, Ind Univ, 60-61; from instr to asst prof, 62-69, ASSOC PROF SPAN, BOWLING GREEN STATE UNIV, 69- *Mem:* MLA; Am Coun Teaching Foreign Lang; Am Asn Teachers Span & Port. *Res:* Contemporary Spanish American novel; linguistics applied to foreign language teaching. *Mailing Add:* Dept of Romance Lang Bowling Green State Univ Bowling Green OH 43403

PREVITALI, GIOVANNI, b New York, NY, Jan 19, 11; m 49; c 4. ROMANCE LANGUAGES & LITERATURE. *Educ:* Oxford Univ, BA, 34, MA, 49; Univ Va, JD, 50; Yale Univ, PhD(Span, Port, Fr lit), 57. *Prof Exp:* Instr Span & Ital, Univ Va, 49-52; dir Span lang instr, Yale Univ, 52-57; asst prof Span & Ital, Univ Tex, 57-59; chmn dept foreign lang, San Francisco State Col, 59-60; prof Ital & comp lit, Univ PR, 60-61; prof Span & Ital, Fla Presby Col, 61-63, dean instr, Lang Abroad Inst, 62-63; prof Romance lang & lit, Univ PR, Mayagüez, 63-67; prof mod lang, Ohio Univ, 67-71, coordr, Ohio Univ in Italy, 68-71; PROF SPAN, CALIF STATE COL, SONOMA, 71- *Concurrent Pos:* Yale Univ rep conf audio-visual methods teaching foreign lang, Mod Lang Asn, New York, NY, 56 & Washington, DC, 57. *Mem:* MLA; Dante Soc; Am Asn Teachers Span & Port; Am Asn Teachers Ital. *Res:* Modern Spanish American literature; the Divine Comedy of Dante Alighieri; modern methods of teaching foreign languages. *Publ:* Auth, Lo inefable en la poesia de Juan Romon Jimenez, Atenea, 61; Ricardo Güiraldes and Don Segundo Sombra: Life and orks, Hisp Inst Columbia, 63; El vardadero Don Segundo Sombra, Rev Ibero-am, 63; El coloquio de los Perros, de Cervantes, Atenea, fall 68. *Mailing Add:* Dept of Span Calif State Col Sonoma Rohnert Park CA 94928

PRIBIC, ELIZABETH, b Sternberg, Czech, Oct 1, 16; m 43; c 1. SLAVIC LANGUAGES & LITERATURES, GERMAN PHILOLOGY. *Educ:* Univ Munich, PhD(Slavic Ger), 56. *Prof Exp:* Docent Czech lang & lit, & Old Church Slavonic, Univ Munich, 52-63; lectr Czech Old Church Slavonic & Russ, Univ Tex, Austin, 63-65; lectr Russ, Czech & Slavic ling, Fla State Univ, 65-69, res grant, 69; from assoc prof to prof Russ lang & lit, Univ Ill, Chicago Circle, 69-78, travel grant, 76; PROF MOD LANG, FLA STATE UNIV, 78- *Concurrent Pos:* Partic, sem foreign Slavists, Macedonian Acad Sci, Sarajevo, Yugoslavia, 52; Deutsche Forschungsgemeinschaft, Bad Godesberg, 60; Ger Acad Exchange Serv res grant, 78. *Mem:* Czech Soc Arts & Sci; MAL; Am Asn Advan Slavic Studies; Am Asn Teachers Slavic & E Europ Lang; AAUP. *Res:* Slavic linguistics, especially Old Church Slavonic; history of the Russian and Czech languages; comparative Slavic studies. *Publ:* Coauth, Kleine slavische Biographie, 58 & auth, Die baltoslavischen Akzent-und Intonationsverhältnisse und ihr quantitaver Reflex im Slovakischen, 61, O Harrassowitz, Wiesbaden; coauth, Lexikon der Weltliteratur, A Kroner, Stuttgart, 62 & 2nd ed, 75; auth, Some problems in Czech prosody, Fla State Univ, Slavic Papers, 67; contribr, Kindlers Lexikon der Weltliteratur, Kindler, Zurich & Munich, Vols IV-VII, 69-72; auth, On the use of prepositional phrases in Russian and Czech, In: Serta Slavica in Memoriam Aloisii Schmaus, Munich, 72; Some observations on the phonological system of the language of the Alaska Herald, In: Topics in Slavic Phonology, Slavica Publ, 74; The preterite system in the writing of Dositej Obradovic, In: Xenia Slavica, Mouton, The Hague, 75. *Mailing Add:* Dept of Mod Lang Fla State Univ Tallahassee FL 32303

PRIBIC, NIKOLA R, b Rijeka, Yugoslavia, May 22, 13; m 46; c 1. SLAVIC LITERATURE & PHILOLOGY. *Educ:* Univ Zagreb, MA, 39; Univ Munich, PhD, 48. *Prof Exp:* Asst Ger, Univ Blegrade, 39-41; dozen Slavic, Univ Munich, 49-61; assoc prof, Univ Tex, Austin, 61-65; prof, 65-81, EMER PROF SLAVIC, FLA STATE UNIV, 81- *Concurrent Pos:* Deut Forschungsgemeinschaft fel, Bonn, Ger, 56-58; Am rep folklore comt, Int Slavic Asn, 73-78; mem Südosteuropa-Inst, Munich. *Mem:* Am Asn Advan Slavic Studies; MLA; Am Asn Teachers Slavic & East Europ Lang; Südost-Europa Ges; Am Asn S Slavic Studies, (pres, 72-73). *Res:* South Slavic languages and literatures; Old Russian literature. *Publ:* Auth, Beiträge zum literarischen Spätbarock, Oldenbourg, Munich, 61; Poesie populaire yogoslave dans les pays de la langue latine dans la premiere moitie du XIX siecle, Südostforsch, 61; coauth, Lexikon der Weltliteratur, Kröner, Stuttgart, 63, rev ed, 75; auth, Das Profil des binnenkroatischen literarischen Barocks, Welt Slaven, 65; George Sagic-Fisher: Patriot of two worlds, Fla State Univ, Slavic Papers, 67; Talvj--pioneer in comparative studies of folklore in America, 73 & The motif of death in V Desnica's prose, 78, Am Contrib Int Congr Slavists; Nikola Tesla: The human side of a scientist, Zeitschrift für Balkanologie, 80. *Mailing Add:* 1940 Sageway Dr Tallahassee FL 32303

PRIBIC, RADO, b Dorfen, Ger, Feb 4, 47; US citizen. GERMAN & RUSSIAN LITERATURES. *Educ:* Fla State Univ, BA, 68; Vanderbilt Univ, MA, 70, PhD(Ger), 72. *Prof Exp:* Teacher Ger, Russ, Latin & World lit, Webb Sch, Bell Buckle, Tenn, 69-71; ASSOC PROF GER, RUSS & COMP LIT, LAFAYETTE COL, 71- *Mem:* Am Asn Teachers Ger; SAtlantic Mod Lang Asn; MLA; Int Dostoevsky Soc; Southern Comp Lit Asn. *Res:* Germano-Slavic literary relations; South German regional literature; 19th century European literature. *Publ:* Auth, Bonaventura's Nachtwachen and Dostoevsky's Notes From the Underground: A Comparison in Nihilism, Otto Sagner, Munich, 74; Alienation in Nachtwachen by Bonaventura and Dostoevskij's Notes From the Underground, Germano-Slavica, 75; America's image in Mayakovski and Essenin, Sci Technol & Humanities, 78; Keyserling's Schwüle Tage and Turgenev's First Love, In: Festschrift for Andre von Gronicka, 78; The Importance of German for the Science Student, Die Unterrisfts Praxis, 80; Young people's literature in the Federal Republic of Germany Today, J Reading, 81. *Mailing Add:* Dept of Lang Lafayette Col Easton PA 18042

PRICE, LARKIN BURL, b Mt Erie, Ill, Jan 25, 27. FRENCH LITERATURE. *Educ:* Univ Ill, BA, 50; Middlebury Col, MA, 60; Univ Wis, PhD(French), 65. *Prof Exp:* From instr to asst prof, 64-70, ASSOC PROF FRENCH, UNIV ILL, URBANA, 70- *Concurrent Pos:* Am Philos Soc res grant, 70. *Mem:* Am Asn Teachers Fr. *Res:* Marcel Proust; 20th century French literature; symbolism. *Publ:* Co-ed, Marcel Proust, Textes Retrouves, Univ Ill, 68, contribr, Marcel Proust, Jean Santeuil precede de Les Plaisirs et les jours, Gallimard, Paris, 71; auth, Marcel Proust's dieu deguise: The artist-myth in Jean Santeuil, L'Esprit Createur, spring 71; Bird imagery suroundin Proust's Albertine, Symposium, fall 72; ed, Marcel Proust: A Critical Panorama, Univ Ill, 73; auth, A Check List of the Proust Holdings at the University of Illinois Library, Univ Ill Libr & Grad Sch Libr Sci, 75. *Mailing Add:* Dept of French Univ of Ill Urbana IL 61801

PRICE, ROBERT HAROLD, b New York, NY, Apr 1, 26; m 56; c 1. FRENCH. *Educ:* Hamilton Col, AB, 50; Univ Montpellier, Cert, 51; Univ Paris, Cert, 52; Middlebury Col, MA, 52; Univ Tex, PhD(Romance lang), 58. *Prof Exp:* Asst English, French Govt, 50-51; instr French, Tex Technol Col, 52-53; teaching asst, Univ Tex, 53-55; from instr to asst prof, Univ Colo, 56-62; assoc prof, Southern Methodist Univ, 62-71; prof French & chmn dept foreign lang, 71-81, COORDR FOREIGN LANG, DIV ENGLISH & FOREIGN LANG & JOUR, SAM HOUSTON STATE UNIV, 81- *Concurrent Pos:* Assoc ed for French, S Cent Mod Lang Asn Bull, 74-76. *Honors & Awards:* Chevalier, Palmes Academiques, 66. *Mem:* MLA; S Cent Mod Lang Asn; Am Asn Teachers Fr. *Res:* Sixteenth century French literature; contemporary French philosophy; phonetics. *Publ:* Contrib, Literature and Society, 1961-1965, A selective Bibliography, Univ Miami, 67; auth, Pantagruel and Le Petit Prince, Symposium, fall 67; A consideration of Paul Valery's ideas concerning art and the artist, S Cent Bull, winter 70; translr, Onze Siecles de Litterature Francaise, Educ Filmstrips Press, 72. *Mailing Add:* Dept of Foreign Lang Sam Houston State Univ Huntsville TX 77341

PRIDEAUX, GARY DEAN, b Muskogee, Okla, Apr 21, 39; m 63. LINGUISTICS. *Educ:* Rice Univ, BA, 61; Univ Tex, PhD(ling), 66. *Prof Exp:* Asst prof, 66-71, ASSOC PROF LING, UNIV ALTA, 71-, CHMN DEPT, 75- *Concurrent Pos:* Fulbright-Hays exchange grant, Japan, 67-68; co-ed, Can J Ling; Experimental Ling, 76. *Mem:* Ling Soc Am; Can Ling Asn. *Res:* Psycholinguistics; linguistic theory, syntax and semantics. *Publ:* Auth, The Syntax of Japanese Honorifics, Mouton, The Hague, 70; On the Notion Linguistically Significant Gerneralization, Lingua, 71; coauth, Grammatical properties of sentences as a basis for concept formation, J Psycholing Res,73; auth, A functional analysis of English questions, J Child Lang, 76; Lexical restructuring is rule addition, In: Festschrift W P Lehmann, 77; Les types de contraintes sur les descriptions grammaticales, Psycholing Experimentale et theorique, 77; co-ed, Experimental Linguistics, Scientia, (in press). *Mailing Add:* Dept of Ling Univ of Alta Edmonton AB T6G 2H1 Can

PRIER, RAYMOND ADOLPH, JR, b Santa Monica, Calif, Dec 2, 39. COMPARATIVE & CLASSICAL LITERATURE. *Educ:* Stanford Univ, BA, 61, MA, 63; Yale Univ, MA, 69, PhD(classics), 70. *Prof Exp:* Asst prof classics, Univ Southern Calif, 70-75; lectr English, Calif State Col, San Bernardino, 78-; VIS ASSOC PROF ENGLISH, UNIV HOUSTON, 82- *Concurrent Pos:* Humboldt fel, 75-77. *Mem:* Am Philol Asn; MLA; Am Comp Lit Asn; Am Asn Univ Professors of Ital; Dante Soc. *Res:* Epic and archaic Greek literature and philosphy; cultural history of the West; Italian and French Renaissance. *Publ:* Archaic Logic, Mouton, 76; Some thoughts on the archaic use of metron, Class World, 76; Empedocles 17: 1-13: A suggested reconstruction and interpretation, Platon, 76; Sema and the symbolic nature of archaic Greek, Quadernic Urbinati, 78; The Critics on Light and Parmenides, Platon, 79; That Gaze of the Hound! Odyssey, 19: 228-231, Rheinisches Mus, 80; A Passing Comment on dokeo and Archilochus P Colon, inv 7511, Platon, 80. *Mailing Add:* Univ Hon Prog Univ of Houston Houston TX 77004

PRIEST, NANCY ELIZABETH, b Crawfordsville, Ind, Dec 23, 47. CLASSICAL STUDIES, GREEK PAPYROLOGY. *Educ:* Brown Univ, AB, 70; Univ Mich, MA, 71, PhD(class studies), 75. *Prof Exp:* Instr class, Univ Tex, 74-75; lectr, Univ Mich, 75-76; ASST PROF CLASS, UNIV TEX, 76- *Mem:* Am Philol Asn; Am Soc Papyrologists; Asn Int Papyrologues. *Res:* Greek Papyrology; Ptolemaic and Roman Egypt; classical Greek literature. *Publ:* Auth, A list of Gods, Zeitschrift für Papyrologie und Epigraphik, 77. *Mailing Add:* Dept of Class Univ of Tex Austin TX 78712

PRIESTLEY, JOHN EDWARD, b Toronto, Ont, Mar 4, 36. FRENCH LITERATURE, HUMANITIES. *Educ:* Univ Toronto, BA, 59, MA, 61; Univ Chicago, PhD(French), 67. *Prof Exp:* Instr French, Victoria Col, Univ Toronto, 61-62; lectr, Laurentian Univ, 62-63 & Victoria Col, Univ Toronto, 63-64; from lectr to asst prof French & humanities, 65-71, sr tutor, Founders Col, 68-71, ASSOC PROF FRENCH LIT & HUMANITIES, YORK UNIV, 71- *Mem:* Renaissance Asn Am; Can Asn Renaissance Studies. *Res:* Renaissance French literature, especially Montaigne; the Age of Enlightenment in France; practical and theoretical literary criticism. *Publ:* Auth, Montaigne and history, Renaissance & Reformation, 74. *Mailing Add:* Dept of French Lit Div of Humanities York Univ Downsview ON M3J 1P3 Can

PRIMEAU, MARGUERITE A, b St Paul, Alta. FRENCH LITERATURE & LANGUAGE. *Educ:* Univ Alta, BA, 46, MA, 48. *Prof Exp:* Instr French lang, Univ Alta, 53-54; from lectr to asst prof French lit & lang, Univ BC, 54-67, assoc prof, 67-79; RETIRED. *Concurrent Pos:* Chmn marking comt, Dept Educ, Victoria Can, 66; consult, Humanities Res Coun Can, 72. *Mem:* Am Asn Teachers Fr; Asn Can Univ Teachers Fr. *Res:* Myth and imagery in the historical plays of Montherlant; French Canadian novel and theatre. *Publ:* Auth, Dans le Muskeg, Ed Fides, Montreal,70; coauth, Contes et scenarios, Holt, 70; auth, L'Aour-passion dans L'Exil de Montherlant, Fr Rev, 12/70; Gratien Gelinas et le theatre populaire au Canada Francais, In: Dramatists in Canada: Selected Essays, 72 & Gabrielle Roy et la prairie canadienne, In: Writers of the Prairies, 73, Can Lit Ser; Structure narcissique de La Reine Morte de Montherlant, Bull Asn Prof Fr of Univs Can, 76-77; H de Montherlant, In: A Critical Bibliography of French Literature: The Twentieth Century, Syracuse Univ Press, 80. *Mailing Add:* 3978 W 12th Vancouver BC V6R 2P2 Can

PRINCE, GERALD JOSEPH, b Alexandria, Egypt, Nov 7, 42; US citizen; m 67. FRENCH. *Educ:* Brooklyn Col, BA, 63; Univ Fla, MA, 63; Brown Univ, PhD(French), 68. *Prof Exp:* From instr to asst prof, 67-73, assoc prof, 73-81, PROF ROMANCE LANG, UNIV PA, 81- *Mem:* Am Asn Teachers Fr; AAUP; MLA. *Res:* Twentieth century French literature; poetics; critical theory. *Publ:* Auth, Metaphysique et technique dans l'oeuvre romanesque de Sartre, Droz, 68; Personnages-romanciers dans Les Faux-Monnayeurs, Fr Studies, 1/71; Introduction a l'etude du narrataire, Poetique, 4/73; A Grammar of Stories: An Introduction, Mouton, The Hague, 73; Narrative signs and tangents, Diacritics, fall 74; La fonction metanarrative dans Nadja, Fr Rev, 2/76; Le discours attributif et le recit, Poetique, 9/78; Narratology: The Form and Functioning of Narrative, Mouton, The Hague, 82. *Mailing Add:* Dept of Romance Lang Univ of Pa Philadelphia PA 19104

PRISCO, CARLO, b New York, NY, July 3, 22; m 48; c 2. ROMANCE LANGUAGES. *Educ:* Seton Hall Univ, AB, 48, AM, 50; Fordham Univ, PhD, 60. *Prof Exp:* Instr Ital, Seton Hall Univ, 48-54, asst prof, 54-60, assoc prof, 60-62; assoc prof Romance lang, St John's Univ, NY, 62-65; assoc prof, Adelphis Univ, 66-68; PROF ROMANCE LANG, COUNTY COL, MORRIS, 68-, CHMN DIV HUMANITIES, 70- *Mem:* Am Asn Teachers Ital; MLA; Am Asn Teachers Fr; Am Asn Teachers Span & Port; Am Coun Teaching Foreign Lang. *Res:* Contemporary Italian poetry. *Mailing Add:* Dept of Romance Lang County Col of Morris Dover NJ 07801

PRITCHET, CHRISTOPHER DIXON, b Colombo, Ceylon, Dec 21, 15; m 41; c 2. CLASSICAL LANGUAGES & LITERATURES. *Educ:* Univ London, BA, 36, dipl, 46, MA, 59; Univ Chicago, PhD(classics), 65. *Prof Exp:* Master classics, Westminster City Sch, London, 46-47; head, Hackney Downs Sch, London, 47-50; asst master, Harrow County Grammar Sch, England, 50-56; head, Chiswick Grammar Sch, London, 56-57; vprin high sch, Alta, 57-60; lectr classics, 60-63, from asst prof to assoc prof & head dept, 63-73, PROF GREEK & ROMAN STUDIES, UNIV SASK, 73- *Mem:* Class Asn Can. *Res:* Palaeography; ancient medicine. *Publ:* Auth, Commentaria Johannis Alexandrini in sextum librum Hippocratis epidimiarum, Brill, Leiden, 75. *Mailing Add:* 912 Arts Bldg Univ of Sask Saskatoon SK S7N 0W0 Can

PRITCHETT, WILLIAM KENDRICK, b Atlanta, Ga, Apr 14, 09; m 42; c 1. GREEK PHILOLOGY. *Educ:* Davidson Col, AB, 29; Duke Univ, AM, 30; Johns Hopkins Univ, PhD, 42. *Prof Exp:* Mem staff, Inst Advan Studies, 36-42 & 46-47; prof classics, Muhlenberg Col, 47-48; from assoc prof to prof, 48-76, chmn dept, 66-70, humanities res prof, 67-68, EMER PROF CLASSICS, UNIV CALIF, BERKELEY, 76- *Concurrent Pos:* Lectr, Princeton Univ, 47; Capps fel, Am Sch Class Studies Athens, 41, ann prof, 62-67 & 76-77; Fulbright fel, Greece, 51-52; Guggenheim fel, 51-52 & 55-56; Nat Endowment for Humanities sr fel, 68; ed, Calif, Studies Class Antiq, 68-70. *Mem:* Am Philol Asn; Archaeol Inst Am; AHA; fel Brit Acad; hon mem Royal Irish Acad. *Res:* Greek epigraphy, topography and history. *Publ:* Auth, Studies in Ancient Greek Topography, Univ Calif, Part 1, 65 , Part 2, 69, Part 3, 80 & Part 4, 82; Choiseul Marble, 70; Ancient Greek Military Practices, Part I, 71; Greek State at War (2 vols), 74 & Vol 3, 79; Dionysius of Halicarnassus on Thucydides, 75. *Mailing Add:* Dept of Classics Univ of Calif Berkeley CA 94720

PROBST, GERHARD, b Leipzig, Ger, June 10, 27; m 51; c 2. GERMAN, COMPARATIVE LITERATURE. *Educ:* Free Univ Berlin, 1st Staatsexamen, 51, 2nd Staatsexamen, 54, PhD, 55. *Prof Exp:* Instr Ger, Univ Ky, 55-57; assoc prof Ger, 61-64, PROF GER & CHMN DEPT MOD FOREIGN LANG, TRANSYLVANIA UNIV, 64- *Concurrent Pos:* Vis prof lit theory, Pädago-gische Hochsch Berlin, 71-72; Nat Endowment for Humanities fel, 75-76 & panelist comp lit, 76- *Mem:* MLA; SAtlantic Mod Lang Asn; Int Arthur Schnitzler Res Asn. *Res:* John Ruskin; 18th and 20th century German literature; theory of literature. *Publ:* Auth, Zur Symbolik und Komposition-stechnik bei Ingeborg Bachmann, Mod Austrian Lit, 70; Deutscher Humor, Holt, 72; Conrad Ferdinand Meyers Gerdict Der römische, Brunnen und Goethese Gesang der Geister über den Wassern, Ger Quart, 74; Zu Lowe-Porters Übers v Tonio Dröger, Ger Notes, 4/76; Thematisierg der Alterität, Ger-Romanische-Monatsschr, 4/77; Gattungsbergriff und Rezept-Asthetick, Colloquia Ger, 76-77; Mein name sei Malina, Mod Austrian Lit, 1/78; Hildesheimers Tynset, Archiv Studium Neueren Sprachen & Literaturen, 1/78. *Mailing Add:* Dept of Foreign Lang Transylvania Univ Lexington KY 40508

PROCTOR, ROBERT EMMET, III, b Los Angeles, Calif, Nov 28, 45. ITALIAN LITERATURE, RENAISSANCE HISTORY. *Educ:* Univ San Francisco, BA, 67; Johns Hopkins Univ, MA, 70, PhD(Romance lang), 71. *Prof Exp:* Asst prof, 71-77, ASSOC PROF ITAL, CONN COL, 77-, DIR ITAL STUDIES, 71- *Concurrent Pos:* Fel, Villa I Tatti, Harvard Univ Ctr for Ital Renaissance Studies, Florence, Italy, 74-75; Nat Humanities Inst fel, 77-78; Nat Endowment for Humanities fel for Col Teachers, 81-82. *Mem:* MLA; Renaissance Soc Am; Union Radical Polit Econ; Conf Group Ital Polit. *Res:* Renaissance humanism; petrarch; modern Italian politics and economics. *Publ:* Auth, Emanuele Tesauro: A Theory of the Conceit, Mod Lang Notes, 1/73; coauth, Capitalist Development, Class Struggle, and Crisis in Italy, 1945-1975, Monthly Rev, 1/76; The Dilemma of the Italian Communist Party, Commonweal, 5/76; auth, Political Impasse in Italy, The Nation, 7-8/76; The Italian Elections, Commonweal, 8/76. *Mailing Add:* Dept of French & Ital Conn Col New London CT 06320

PROFFER, CARL RAY, b Buffalo, NY, Sept 3, 38; m 58; c 4. SLAVIC LANGUAGES & LITERATURES. *Educ:* Univ Mich, BA, 60, MA, 61, PhD(Slavic lang & lit), 63. *Prof Exp:* From instr to asst prof Russ, Reed Col, 63-66; from asst prof to assoc prof Slavic lang & lit, Ind Univ, Bloomington, 66-70; PROF SLAVIC LANG, UNIV MICH, ANN ARBOR, 70- *Concurrent Pos:* Fulbright-Hays Ctr fel, 69; ed, Ardis Publ, 71-; co-ed, Russ Lit Triquart, 71- *Mem:* PEN Club. *Res:* Russian 19th and 20th century literature; contemporary Soviet literature. *Publ:* Ed, The Critical Prose of Alexander Pushkin, 70; From Karamzin to Bunin: An Anthology of Russian Short Stories, 70; co-transl, The Major Plays of Mikhail Bulgakov, Ind Univ, 72; ed, Soviet Criticism of American Literature in the Sixties: An Anthology, 72, The Unpublished Dostoevsky: Diaries and Notebooks 1860-81 (3 vols), 73, A Book of Things about Vladimir Nabokov, 73, co-ed, The Silver Age of Russian Culture, 75 & ed, Contemporary Russian Prose: An Anthology, 82, Ardis Publ. *Mailing Add:* Dept of Slavic Lang & Lit Univ of Mich Ann Arbor MI 48105

PROFFER, ELLENDEA CATHERINE, b Philadelphia, Pa, Nov 24, 44; m 67; c 4. RUSSIAN & COMPARATIVE LITERATURE. *Educ:* Univ Md, BA, 66; Ind Univ, Bloomington, MA, 68, PhD(Slavic lit), 70. *Prof Exp:* Assoc instr Russ, Ind Univ, Bloomington, 69-70; instr, Wayne State Univ, 70-71; ED-IN-CHIEF, ARDIS PUBL, 71- *Concurrent Pos:* Vis asst prof English, Univ Mich, Dearborn, 73- *Mem:* PEN Club. *Res:* Russian 20th century literature; Mikhail Bulgakov. *Publ:* Ed, M Bulgakov, Diaboliad and Other Stories, 72 & The Early Plays of Mikhail Bulgakov, 72, Ind Univ; auth, Unpublished Letters of Pasternak, Russ Lit Triquart, spring 73; co-ed, The Ardis Anthology of New American Poetry, Ardis, 77; Regency Miss, 78 & Double Wedding, 82, Fawcett Crest; auth, Mikhail Bulgakov: Life & Works, 82 & co-ed, Contemporary Russian Prose, 82, Ardis. *Mailing Add:* 2901 Heatherway Ann Arbor MI 48104

PROFIT, VERA BARBARA, b Vienna, Austria, Sept 3, 45. FRENCH & GERMAN LITERATURE. *Educ:* Alverno Col, BA, 67; Univ Rochester, MA, 69, PhD(comp lit), 74. *Prof Exp:* Instr Ger, St Olaf Col, 74-75; asst prof, 75-81, ASSOC PROF GER & COMP LIT, UNIV NOTRE DAME, 81- *Concurrent Pos:* Vis scholar, Harvard Univ, 79-80. *Mem:* MLA; Am Asn Teachers Ger. *Res:* Poetry and novel of the German-speaking countries, written after 1945; 20th century French and German prose and poetry. *Publ:* Auth, Interpretations of Iwan Goll's Late Poetry with a Comprehensive and Annotated Bibliography of the Writings by and about Iwan Goll, Peter Lang, Bern, Switz, 77. *Mailing Add:* Dept of Modern & Class Lang Univ of Notre Dame Notre Dame IN 46556

PRONGER, LESTER JAMES, b Dryden, Ont, Apr 30, 17. FRENCH LITERATURE. *Educ:* Univ BC, BA, 40, MA, 48; Univ Paris, Dr, 50; Harvard Univ, PhD(Romance lang), 59. *Prof Exp:* Asst prof French, Univ BC, 53-54; from asst prof to prof, 60-76, chmn dept mod lang, 62-66, EMER PROF FRENCH, YORK UNIV, 76- *Mem:* MLA. *Res:* Theories of literature; modern French poetry; French romanticism. *Publ:* Co-ed, A Husson, La cuisine des Anges, Harper, 54; auth, La poesie de Tristan Klingsor, Minard, Paris, 65. *Mailing Add:* 1351 W King Edward Ave Vancouver BC V6H 2A1 Can

PRONIN, ALEXANDER, b Luck, Poland, Sept 30, 27; US citizen; m 59. RUSSIAN LANGUAGE & LITERATURE. *Educ:* Univ Calif, Berkeley, BA, 55; Georgetown Univ, PhD(Russ), 65. *Prof Exp:* Instr Russ, Army Lang Sch, 49-50; instr, Johns Hopkins Univ, 59-63; asst prof, Univ Akron, 63-65; from asst prof to assoc prof Russ, 65-76, PROF FOREIGN LANG, CALIF STATE UNIV, FRESNO, 76- *Concurrent Pos:* Ed, Nash Student Am Studies Russ Monthly, 66-68. *Mem:* Am Asn Teachers Slavic & EEurop Lang. *Res:* Russian language and literature; Soviet guerrilla warfare, World War II. *Publ:* Coauth, Formation and Usage of Russian Verbs, SAIS, 61; auth, Russian Vocabulary Builder, Lawwrence Publ Co, 67; HIstory of Old Russian Literature, Possev-Verlag, 68. *Mailing Add:* Dept of Foreign Lang Calif State Univ Fresno CA 93726

PRONKO, LEONARD C, Romance Languages, Theatre. See Vol II

PROPERZIO, PAUL JOSEPH, b Keene, NH, May 20, 47; m 70. CLASSICAL LANGUAGES, ANCIENT HISTORY. *Educ:* Univ NH, BA, 69; Loyola Univ, Chicago, MA, 73, PhD(class studies), 82. *Prof Exp:* Chmn, 75-81, ASST PROF CLASSICS, DREW UNIV, 81- *Concurrent Pos:* Linguist, US Army Reserve, 71-79. *Mem:* Class Asn Atlantic States (second vpres, 82-83); Am Philol Asn; Archaeol Inst Am; Am Coun Teaching Foreign Lang. *Res:* Classical literature especially Greek epic, lyric poetry, drama and classical philology; classical archaeology especially Graeco-Roman periods in the Western Mediterranean; classical mythology and religion especially Near Eastern and Greek. *Publ:* Auth, Rhodian colonization in Iberia: The colony Rhode and the townlet Rhodos, Antipolis: A J Mediterranean Archaeol, 75; Five innovative classics programs in the Atlantic states, New England Class Newlett, 9/82; The Cults and Mythology of Marseilles (Ancient Massalia), Ares Publ, 82. *Mailing Add:* Dept of Classics Drew Univ Madison NJ 07940

PROULX, ALFRED CHARLES, b Norwich, Conn, Aug 10, 31. ROMANCE LANGUAGES. *Educ:* Yale Univ, BA, 53, PhD(French), 59. *Prof Exp:* From instr to assoc prof French, Univ Va, 57-68; chmn dept, 71-73, ASSOC PROF FRENCH, UNIV MASS, BOSTON, 68- *Honors & Awards:* Medaille D'Argent, City of Paris, 79. *Mem:* MLA. *Res:* French novel of the 19th and 20th centuries, especially Zola. *Publ:* Auth, Les sonnets de Victor Hugo, Univ Ottawa Rev, 7/60; Aspects epiques des Rougon-Macquart de Zola, Mouton & Cie, 65. *Mailing Add:* Dept of French Univ of Mass 100 Arlington St Boston MA 02116

PROUSSIS, COSTAS MICHAEL, b Cyprus, June 26, 11; nat US. GREEK & LATIN, HISTORY. *Educ:* Univ Athens, Greece, MA, 34; Univ Chicago, PhD(Greek lang & lit), 51. *Prof Exp:* Vprin & teacher, Gymn Kyrenia, Cyprus, 35-36; teacher, Pancyprian Gymn, 36-48; teacher Greek, Koraes Sch, Chicago, Ill, 48-49; head dept, Plato Sch, Chicago, 52-57; asst prof, 57-59, from assoc prof to prof & chmn dept, 59-78, EMER PROF GREEK, HELLENIC COL, HOLY CROSS GREEK ORTHODOX SCH THEOL, 78- *Concurrent Pos:* Ed, Cyprus Letters, 34-56, Cyprus Studies, 38-49, Greek Orthodox Theol Rev, 58- & Neo-Hellenika, 70- *Honors & Awards:* Awards, Acad of Athens, 46 & Ecumenical Patriarchate, 74. *Mem:* Am Philol Asn; Mod Greek Studies Asn; Ctr Neo-Hellenic Studies; MLA; Soc Cyprus Studies. *Res:* Ancient Greek poetry, especially tragedy; modern Greek literature; Greek folklore. *Publ:* Auth, Grammar of Modern Greek, 34; Latin Grammar, 43; The Poet Costis Palamas, 64; coauth, The Educated Man, Wiley, 65; The Voice of Cyprus, Charioteer, 65; auth, The novels of Angelos Terzakis, Daedalus, fall 66; Fiction in Several Languages, Houghton, 68; coauth, Poems of Cyprus, Coun of Europe, 70; auth, Poreia Zois, Zavallis, 75; Little Agony, Chrysopolitissa, 80. *Mailing Add:* 11 Lehigh Rd Wellesley MA 02181

PRUSOK, RUDI, b East Orange, NJ, Dec 26, 34; m 64; c 2. GERMAN LITERATURE & LANGUAGE. *Educ:* Lafayette Col, AB, 57; Univ Iowa, MS, 62; Wash Univ, MA, 65, PhD(Ger), 67. *Prof Exp:* Photogrammetrist, Topog Br, US Geol Surv, 59-62 & geologist, Surface Water Br, 63-64; from asst prof to assoc prof, 67-78, PROF GER, NORTHERN MICH UNIV, 78-, HEAD, DEPT FOREIGN LANG, 75- *Mem:* MLA; Am Asn Teachers Ger. *Res:* German literature of 19th and 20th centuries; history of German-American Schützen Vereine (shooting societies); relationship between science and contemporary literature. *Publ:* Auth, A stereo-photographic field method of rock outcrop description, Photogram English, 3/60; Ice as stream table bedrock, J Geol Educ, 9/7; Science in Thomas Mann's Zauberberg, PMLA, 1/73. *Mailing Add:* 625 Pine St Marquette MI 49855

PUCCIANI, ORESTE F, b Cleveland, Ohio, Apr 7, 16. FRENCH LITERATURE. *Educ:* Western Reserve Univ, AB, 39; Harvard Univ, AM, 40, PhD, 43. *Prof Exp:* Instr French & Ital, Harvard Univ, 43-46 & 47-48, Sheldon traveling fel, France & Italy, 46-47; from asst prof to assoc prof, 48-60, chmn dept French, 61-66, affil prof, Grad Sch Educ, 73-77, prof, 60-79, EMER PROF FRENCH, UNIV CALIF, LOS ANGELES, 79- *Concurrent Pos:* Asst ed, Mod Lang Forum, 49-53, ed, 53-54. *Honors & Awards:* Knight's Cross, Legion of Honor, France, 66. *Mem:* Am Asn Teachers Fr; Am Soc Legion of Honor. *Res:* Comtenporary French literature; existentialism; philosophy of literature. *Publ:* Coauth, Langue et Langage, 67, 74 & 79 & Langue et Langage: Le Manuel du Professeur, 67, 74 & 79, Holt; ed & contribr, Alain Robbe-Guillet's Le Voyeur, Blaisdell-Ginn, 70; coauth, Lengua y cultura: El Manual del Instructor, Holt, 73; transl & contribr, Oskar Panizza's The Council of Love, Viking, 73; auth, Jean-Paul Sartre, In: Histoire de la Philosophie, 74; contribr (with Michel Rybalka & Susan Gruenheck), Interview with Jean-Paul Sartre & auth, Sartre and Flaubert as dialectic, in the philosophy of Jean-Paul Sartre, Libr Living Philos, 81. *Mailing Add:* 2192 Beech Knoll Rd Los Angeles CA 90046

PUGH, ANTHONY ROY, b Liverpool, Eng, Aug 16, 31; m 62; c 3. FRENCH LITERATURE. *Educ:* Cambridge Univ, BA, 53, MA, 56, PhD(French), 59. *Prof Exp:* Asst lectr French, King's Col, Univ London, 56-59; lectr, Queen's Univ Belfast, 59-69; chmn dept Romance lang, 73-75, PROF FRENCH, UNIV NB, FREDERICTON, 69- *Concurrent Pos:* Vis prof, Univ NB, 68. *Mem:* MLA. *Res:* Balzac; Pascal; form and meaning in French literature. *Publ:* Auth, Le Mariage de Figaro, Macmillan, 68; The Genesis of Cesar Birotteau, Fr Studies, 1/68; The Unity of Theophile's La Solitude, Fr Rev, fall 71; coed, Studies in Balzac and Nineteenth Century, Leicester Univ, 72; Balzac's Recurring Characters, Univ Toronto, 74; Butor on Beethoven, Int Fiction Rev, 76; The autonomy of Belzac's Une Fille d'Eve, Romance Rev, 78; The Ambiguity of Cesar Birotteau, 19th Century Fr Studies, 80. *Mailing Add:* Dept of Fr Univ of NB Fredericton NB E3B 5A3 Can

PUGLIESE, OLGA L, b Toronto, Can, Nov 4, 41; m 69. ITALIAN STUDIES. *Educ:* Univ Toronto, BA, 63, MA, 64, PhD(Romance lang), 69. *Prof Exp:* Lectr, 67-69, asst prof, 70-73, ASSOC PROF ITAL, UNIV TORONTO, 73- *Mem:* Can Soc Renaissance Studies (secy-treas, 76-78); Can Soc Ital Studies; Am Asn Teachers Ital; Am Asn Univ Prof Ital; Renaissance Soc Am (Ital rep, 82-84). *Res:* Renaissance Italian literature; humanism; religious thought. *Publ:* Auth, Trascrizione delle note staziane del Poliziano Adulescens erroneamente attribuita a Girolamo Benivieni, 70 & Girolamo Benivieni: Umanista riformatore (dalla corrispondenza inedita), 70, La Bibliofilia; English translations from the Italian humanists: An interpretive survey and bibliography, Italica, 73; Quattrocento views on love and existence, Can J Ital Studies, 74; Two sermons by Giovanni Nesi and the Language of Spirituality in Late Fifteenth-Century Florence, Bibliotheque d'Humanisme et Renaissance, 80; Il Chronicon di Angelo Clareno nel Rinascimento; volgariamento postillato da G Benivieni, Archivum Franciscanum Historicum, 80; A last testimony by Savonarola and his companions, Renaissance Quart, 81. *Mailing Add:* Dept of Ital Studies Univ of Toronto Toronto ON M5S 1A1 Can

PUHVEL, JAAN, b Tallinn, Estonia, Jan 24, 32; nat US; m; c 3. COMPARATIVE LINGUISTICS, CLASSICAL PHILOLOGY. *Educ:* McGill Univ, BA, 51, MA, 52; Harvard Univ, PhD(ling), 59. *Prof Exp:* Lectr, McGill Univ, 55-56; instr class lang, Univ Tex, 57-58; from asst prof to assoc prof, 58-64, chmn dept classics, 68-75, dir ctr res lang & ling, 62-67, PROF CLASSICS & INDO-EUROP STUDIES, UNIV CALIF, LOS ANGELES, 64- *Concurrent Pos:* Am Coun Learned Soc fel, 61-62 & 75-76; Guggenheim fel, 68-69. *Honors & Awards:* Officer first class, Order of the White Rose, Finland, 67. *Mem:* Ling Soc Am; Am Orient Soc; Am Philol Asn; Asn Advan Baltic Studies (pres, 71-72). *Res:* Indo-European comparative linguistics, especially Anatolian and Greek; Indo-European comparative mythology. *Publ:* Auth, Laryngeals and the Indo-European Verb, 60, coauth & co-ed, Ancient Indo-European Dialects, 66, ed, Substance and Structure of Language, 69 & coauth & ed, Myth and Law Among the Indo-Europeans, 70, Unv Calif; coauth & co-ed, Baltic literature and linguistics, Asn Advan Baltic Studies, 73; Myth in Indo-European Antiquity, Univ Calif, 74; auth, Analecta Indoeuropaea, Univ Innsbruck, 81; Hittite Etymological Dict, Vol I & II, Walter de Gruyter, 82. *Mailing Add:* Dept of Classics Univ of Calif Los Angeles CA 90024

PUHVEL, MARTIN, English. See Vol II

PUKNAT, SIEGFRIED BERTHOLD, b Hamburg, Ger, Aug 28, 14; nat US; m 47. GERMAN & COMPARATIVE LITERATURE. *Educ:* Univ Calif, Los Angeles, AB, 35; Univ Calif, Berkeley, AM, 36; Univ Minn, PhD(Ger), 40. *Prof Exp:* Teaching asst, Univ Minn, 36-39, Univ Calif, 39 & Univ Ore, 40; from instr to asst prof mod lang, Beloit Col, 40-46; assoc prof Ger & chmn dept, Carleton Col, 46-48; from asst prof to prof, Univ Calif, Davis, 48-64, chmn dept foreign lang, 56-62, assoc dean col lett & sci, 64; vchancellor humanities, 67-70, prof, 77-82, EMER PROF GER & COMP LIT, UNIV CALIF, 64-, PROVOST, CROWN COL, 82- *Concurrent Pos:* Ford fac fel, 54-55; vis prof, Univ Kent, 70-71. *Mem:* MLA; Am Asn Teachers Ger; AAUP. *Res:* American-German literary relations; German literature of the 19th and 20th centuries. *Publ:* Coauth, An American Critic and a German Vogue, Colonial Soc Mass, Anthoensen, 66; auth, Literature and theology: A comment On Goethe's Faust, Res Studies, 3/68; coauth, Goethe and modern American poets, Ger Quart, 69; Edith Wharton and Gottfried Keller, Comp Lit, 69. *Mailing Add:* Crown Col Univ of Calif Santa Cruz CA 95064

PULGRAM, ERNST, b Vienna, Austria, Sept 18, 15; nat US. ROMANCE & CLASSICAL LINGUISTICS. *Educ:* Univ Vienna, DPhil, 38; Harvard Univ, PhD, 46. *Prof Exp:* Instr, Harvard Univ, 46; asst prof, Union Col, NY, 46-48; asst prof Romance lang, 48-51, assoc prof, 51-56, prof Romance lang & class ling, 56-80, HAYWARD KENISTON DISTINGUISHED PROF, UNIV MICH, ANN ARBOR, 80- *Concurrent Pos:* Am Coun Learned Soc fels, 51-52 & 59-60; Guggenheim fels, 54-55 & 62-63; vis prof, Univ Florence, 56-57, Univ Cologne, 70, Univ Heidelberg, 72, Univ Regensburg, 75 & Univ Vienna, 77. *Mem:* Ling Soc Am; Int Ling Asn; Int Phonetics Asn; Ling Asn Can & US (vpres, 78, pres, 79). *Res:* Italic, Latin and Romance linguistics; onomastics; general linguistics. *Publ:* Auth, Theory of Names, Am Name Soc, 54; Tongues of Italy, Harvard Univ, 58; Introduction to the Spectrography of Speech, 59 & Syllable, Word, Nexus, Cursus, 70, Mouton, The Hague; Latin-Romance Phonology: Prosodics and Metrics, Fink, Munich, 75; Italic, Latin, Italian: Texts 600 BC to AD 1260, and commentary, C Winter, Heidelberg, 78. *Mailing Add:* Dept of Romance Lang Univ of Mich Ann Arbor MI 48104

PULLEYBLANK, EDWIN GEORGE, b Calgary, Alta, Aug 7, 22; m; c 3. CHINESE LANGUAGE & HISTORY. *Educ:* Univ Alta, BA, 42; Univ London, PhD(Chinese), 51; Cambridge Univ, MA, 53. *Prof Exp:* Lectr class Chinese, Univ London, 48-52, lectr Chinese hist, 52-53; prof Chinese, Cambridge Univ, 53-66; head dept Asian studies, 68-75, PROF CHINESE, UNIV BC, 66- *Concurrent Pos:* Fel, Downing Col, Cambridge Univ, 55-66. *Mem:* Asn Asian Studies; Am Orient Soc; Ling Soc Am; Can Soc Asian Studies (pres, 71-74); fel Royal Soc Can. *Res:* Chinese history; historical phonology and grammar of classical Chinese. *Publ:* Auth, The Background of the Rebellion of An Lushan, Oxford Univ, 55; Chinese History and World History, Cambridge Univ, 55; co-ed, Historians of China and Japan, Oxford Univ, 61; auth, The consonantal system of Old Chinese, Asia Major, 62-63; Chinese and Indo-Europenas, J Royal Asiatic Soc, 66; Late Middle Chinese, Asia Major, 70-71; The final consonants of Old Chinese, Monumenta Serica, 77-78; The nature of the Middle Chinese tones, J Chinese Ling, 78. *Mailing Add:* Dept of Asian Studies Univ of BC Vancouver BC V6T 1W5 Can

PULLEYN, JOHN WILLIAM, JR, b New York, NY, Dec 3, 21; m 45; c 3. FRENCH. *Educ:* Univ Minn, BA, 46, MA, 50, PhD(French), 61. *Prof Exp:* Instr French, Univ Minn, 50-57; instr, Univ Akron, 57-62, asst prof, 62-66; assoc prof, 66-73, chmn dept foreign lang, 66-80, PROF FRENCH, UNIV TOLEDO, 73- . *Mem:* MLA; Am Asn Teachers Fr; AAUP; Mod Humanities Res Asn. *Res:* Gustave Flaubert and the realistic novel; the Goncourt brothers and naturalism; 19th century French poetry. *Mailing Add:* Dept of Foreign Lang Univ of Toledo Toledo OH 43606

PULTE, WILLIAM JOHN, b Gainesville, Tex, Jan 13, 41; m 68; c 1. LINGUISTICS. *Educ:* NTex State Univ, BA, 64, MA, 66; Univ Tex, Austin, PhD(ling), 71. *Prof Exp:* Staff linguist, Cherokee Bilingual Educ Prog, Tahlequah, Okla, 71-73; asst prof ling, 73-78, ASSOC PROF ANTHROP, SOUTHERN METHODIST UNIV, 78- *Concurrent Pos:* Native Am lang specialist, bilingual educ, Fedn Bilingual Training Resource Ctr, Tex Woman's Univ, 77- *Mem:* Ling Soc Am; Am Anthrop Asn; Ling Asn Southwest; Nat Asn Bilingual Educ. *Res:* American Indian linguistics; bilingual education. *Publ:* Auth, Gapping and word order in Quechua, In: Papers from the Seventh Regional Meeting, Chicago Linguistic Society, Univ Chicago, 71; German in Virginia and West Virginia, In: The German Language in America, Univ Tex, 71; Some claims regarding gapping: The evidence from Cherokee, In: Mid-America Linguistics Conference Papers, Okla State Univ, 72; The position of Chickasaw in Western Muskogean, In: Studies in Southeastern Indian Languages, Univ Ga, 75; Writing systems and underlying phonological representation: The case of the Cherokee syllabary, In: 1975 Mid-America Linguistics Conference Papers, Univ Kans, 75; The obligatory-optional principle: A counterexample from Cherokee, In: The Third LACUS Forum 1976, Hornbean, 76; ed, Cherokee-English Dictionary, 75 & coauth, An outline of Cherokee grammar, appendix to Cherokee-English Dictionary, 75, Cherokee Nation Okla. *Mailing Add:* Dept of Anthrop Southern Methodist Univ Dallas TX 75275

PUPO-WALKER, C ENRIQUE, b Holguin, Cuba, Feb 3, 33; US Citizen; m 60; c 3. ROMANCE LANGUAGES, LATIN AMERICAN STUDIES. *Educ:* Univ Havana, Bachiller, 56; George Peabody Col, MA, 62; Univ NC, Chapel Hill, PhD(Romance lang), 66. *Prof Exp:* Instr Span, Vanderbilt Univ, 59-62; instr, Univ NC, 62-66; instr Span lit, Yale Univ, 66-67, asst prof, 67-71; assoc prof, 71-76, PROF SPAN LIT, VANDERBILT UNIV, 76-, DIR, CTR LATIN AM & IBERIAN STUDIES, 81- *Concurrent Pos:* Lectr, Univ NC NDEA Span Inst, Univ NC, 66, Spain, 67; vis prof, Univ Int Menendez Pelayo, Santander, Spain, 77 & 79 & Ind Univ, Bloomington, 80; dir, Nat Endowment for Humanities sem, 81 & sr fel, 82. *Mem:* MLA; Am Asn Teachers Span & Port; Inst Int Lit Iberoam; Am Soc Aesthet; Latin Am Studies Asn. *Res:* Spanish and Spanish American literature; history. *Publ:* Co-ed, The contemporary short story in Latin America, Studies in Short Fiction, Vol VIII, 71; auth, El cuento hispanoamericano ante la critica: Antologia de estudios criticos, Ed Castalia, Madrid, 73; co-ed, Estudios en honor a Jose J Arrom, Studies in Romance Lang, Univ NC, Chapel Hill, 74; auth, La vocacion literaria del pensamiento historico en America: Indagaciones sobre el desarrollo de la prosa de ficcion, Siglos XVI-XIX, Ed Gredos, Madrid, 82; Creacion, historia y profecia en los textos del Inca Garcilaso, 82, co-ed, The Conflicts and Achievements of Democracy: Spain, 1975-1980, 82 & Conflictos y logros de la democracia: Espania, 1975-1980, 82, Ed Porrua, Madrid; Las historias que me cuento: A Study and Annotated Edition of Julio Cortazar's Short Fiction, Ed Nuestra Cultura, Madrid, 82. *Mailing Add:* Dept of Span Vanderbilt Univ Nashville TN 37203

PUPPE, HEINZ W, b Düsseldorf, Ger, June 24, 26; US citizen; m 56; c 2. GERMAN LITERATURE. *Educ:* Univ Calif, Los Angeles, BA, 56; Univ Innsbruck, Dr Phil, 59. *Prof Exp:* Instr Ger, Univ Mich, 59-62, asst prof, 62-64; asst prof, Rice Univ, 64-72; asst prof, Bemidji State Col, 72-74; ASSOC PROF GER, TEX A&M UNIV, 74- *Mem:* MLA. *Res:* German literature of the 19th and 20th century; philosophy; sociology. *Publ:* Auth, Psychologie und Mystik in Klein und Wagner von Hermann Hesse, PMLA, 3/63; H E Nossack und der Nihilismus, Ger Quart, 1/64; Heinrich Heine's Tannhäuser, Monatshefte, fall 74. *Mailing Add:* Dept of Foreign Lang Tex A&M Univ College Station TX 77843

PURCELL, EDWARD THOMAS, b New York, NY, Apr 28, 43; m 68; c 2. SLAVIC LANGUAGES, LINGUISTICS. *Educ:* St Mary's Col, Minn, BA, 64; Univ Wis-Madison, MA, 66, PhD(Slavic lang & lit), 70. *Prof Exp:* Asst prof, 70-77, ASSOC PROF SLAVIC LANG, LIT & LING, UNIV SOUTHERN CALIF, 77- *Mem:* Ling Soc Am; Am Asn Teachers Slavic & EEurop Lang; Acoust Soc Am; Am Asn Phonetic Sci. *Res:* Acoustics phonetics of Slavic languages; computer aided language instruction; speech synthesis by rule. *Publ:* Auth, Acoustic differentiation of Serbo-Croatian accents in statements, Phonetica, 71; contribr, Proceedings of the VIIth International Congress of Phonetic Sciences, 72 & Topics in Slavic Phonology, 73, Mouton, The Hague; auth, The Realizations of Serbo-Croatian Accents in Sentence Environments, Helmut Buske, Hamburg, 73; Pitch peak location and the perception of Serbo-Croatian tone, J Phonetics, 76; The phonetic origins of Balto-Slavic tone, In: Proceedings of the International Congress of Historical Linguistics. *Mailing Add:* Dept of Slavic Lang & Lit Univ of Southern Calif Los Angeles CA 90007

PURCELL, JOHN MARSHALL, b Pittsburgh, Pa, Nov 25, 32. FOREIGN LANGUAGE EDUCATION, SPANISH. *Educ:* Univ Cincinnati, BA, 54, BEd, 55; Middlebury Col, MA, 62; Ohio State Univ, PhD(foreign lang educ), 69. *Prof Exp:* Teacher Span & chmn dept, Hughes High Sch, Cincinnati, Ohio, 59-62 & Aiken Sr High Sch, Cincinnati, Ohio, 62-70; asst prof, 70-73, ASSOC PROF SPAN & FOREIGN LANG EDUC, CLEVELAND STATE UNIV, 73- *Concurrent Pos:* Consult, NDEA title III workships, Ohio, 68-70 & Cleveland Pub Schs Biling-Bicult Prog, 75-79. *Mem:* Am Asn Teachers Span & Port; Am Coun Teaching Foreign Lang; Cent States Conf Foreign Lang Teaching. *Res:* Foreign language methodology. *Publ:* Auth, A liberal education in the United States, J Gen Educ, 71; How to help your student teacher, 10/72 & Teaching the short story, winter 74, Am Foreign Lang Teacher; Simulation and success in business Spanish, Aceent Am Coun Teaching Foreign Lang, 1/75; co-ed, Personalizing Foreign Language Instruction, Nat Txtbk Co, 77; auth, Teaching novels and plays, In: Filling and Fulfilling the Advanced Foreign Language Class & co-ed, Filling and Fulfilling the Advanced Foreign Language Class, 81, Heinle & Heinle; auth, The preparation of modern language teachers in Latin America, The Modern Lang J, 81. *Mailing Add:* Dept of Mod Lang Cleveland State Univ Euclid Ave at 24th st Cleveland OH 44115

PURCZINSKY, JULIUS O, b Levi, Tex, Jan 6, 25. MEDIEVAL PHILOLOGY, STRUCTURAL LINGUISTICS. *Educ:* Baylor Univ, BA, 49; Univ Tex, Austin, MA, 53, PhD(Romance philol), 57. *Prof Exp:* Asst prof Span, Baylor Univ, 57-58; Fulbright lectr English, Nat Univ Athens, 58-59; assoc prof Ger, French & Span, Univ Southwestern La, 59-61; asst prof Span,

Kans State Univ, 61-63; assoc prof Span & French, Univ Nev, 63-65; asst prof, 65-72, ASSOC PROF ROMANCE LING, HUNTER COL, 72- *Mem:* MLA; Int Ling Asn; Ling Soc Am; Mediaeval Acad Am. *Publ:* Auth, Additional Frankish superstratum in Old French, 64 & Germanic influence in the Sainte Eulalie, 65, Romance Philol; A neo-Schushardtian theory of general Romance diphthongization, 70. *Mailing Add:* Dept of Romance Lang Hunter Col 695 Park Ave New York NY 10021

PURDY, STROTHER BEESON, b New York, NY, Sept 6, 32; m 56; c 2. COMPARATIVE PHILOLOGY. *Educ:* Yale Univ, BA, 54; Columbia Univ, MA, 55; Univ Wis, PhD(English), 60. *Prof Exp:* Instr English, Univ Wis-Milwaukee, 60-61; asst prof, Am Univ Beirut, 61-64; from asst prof to assoc prof, 65-78, prof, Marquette Univ, 78-81; PROF ENGLISH, NEW SCH FOR SOCIAL RES, 82- *Concurrent Pos:* Mem Bhandarkar Orient Res Inst. *Mem:* MLA; Ling Soc Am; Archaeol Inst Am; Am Orient Soc; Brit Class Asn. *Res:* Stylistics; literary history; ancient Mediterranean. *Publ:* Auth, Sinuhe and the question of literary types, Zeitschrift Ägyptische Sprache u Altertumshande, 77; The hole in the Fabric: Science, Contemporary Literature and Henry James, Univ Pittsburgh, 77; Of time, motion and motor racing, J Am Cult, 81. *Mailing Add:* Keeler Rd Bridgewater CT 06752

PUSEY, WILLIAM WEBB, III, b Wilmington, Del, Nov 10, m 40; c 2. GERMAN. *Educ:* Haverford Col, BS, 32, Harvard Univ, AM, 33; Columbia Univ, PhD, 39. *Prof Exp:* Asst Ger, Columbia Univ, 35-37, instr Ger & humanities, 37-39; asst prof, 39-47, head dept, 39-76, dean col, 60-71, actg pres, 67-68, PROF GER, WASHINGTON & LEE UNIV, 47- *Concurrent Pos:* Am Coun Learned Soc fac study fel, 52-53. *Mem:* MLA; SAtlantic Mod Lang Asn. *Res:* Comparative literature; Russian literature. *Mailing Add:* Dept of Ger Tucker Hall Washington & Lee Univ Lexington VA 24450

PUTNAM, MICHAEL COURTNEY JENKINS, b Springfield, Mass, Sept 20, 33. CLASSICAL PHILOLOGY. *Educ:* Harvard Univ, AB, 54, AM, 56, PhD, 59. *Prof Exp:* Instr Classics, Smith Col, 59-60; from instr to assoc prof, 60-67, actg dir Ctr Hellenic Studies, 61-62, actg chmn dept classics, 68-69 & 77-78, chmn, 70-72, PROF CLASSICS, BROWN UNIV, 67- *Concurrent Pos:* Rome Prize fel, Am Acad Rome, 63-64, scholar-in-residence, 69-70; Guggenheim Mem fel, 66-67; sole trustee, Lowell Observatory, Flagstaff, Ariz, 67-; Ctr Hellenic Studies sr fel, 71-; trustee, Bay Chamber Concerts, 72-; assoc, Univ Sem Class Civilization, Columbia Univ, 73-; Nat Endowment for Humanities sr fel, 73-74, consult, 74- *Honors & Awards:* Charles J Goodwin Award of Merit, Am Philol Asn, 71. *Mem:* Am Philol Asn; Class Asn New England (dir, 72-75, vpres, 80-82, pres, 82-); Vergilian Soc Am (vpres, 74-76); Cath Comn Intellectural & Cult Affairs; Mediaeval Acad Am. *Res:* Latin literature; Latin palaeography. *Publ:* Auth, The Poetry of the Aeneid, Harvard Univ, 65; Virgil's Pastoral Art, Princeton Univ, 70; Tibullus: A Commentary, Univ Okla, 73; Virgil's Poem of the Earth, 79, Essays on Latin Lyric, Elegy and Epic, 82, Princeton Univ. *Mailing Add:* Dept of Classics Brown Univ Providence RI 02912

PUTTER, IRVING, b Dec 3, 17; c 2. FRENCH LITERATURE. *Educ:* Yale Univ, PhD, 49. *Prof Exp:* Instr, State Univ Iowa, 39-43 & Stephens Col, 43-44; teaching asst, Yale Univ, 44-47; from lectr to assoc prof, 47-61, chmn dept, 68-71, humanities res fel, 71-72 & 78-79, PROF FRENCH, UNIV CALIF, BERKELEY, 61- *Concurrent Pos:* Guggenheim fel, 55-56; Fulbright res fel, 55-56. *Honors & Awards:* Tew Prize, Yale Univ, 45. *Mem:* MLA; Philol Asn Pac Coast; Int Asn Fr Studies. *Res:* Nineteenth century French literature. *Publ:* Auth, Leconte de Lisle and his Contemporaries, 51, The Pessimism of Leconte de Lisle, Sources and Evolution, 54, translr & ed, Atala and Rene, Univ Calif, 57; Lamartine and the genesis of Qaïn, Mod Lang Quart, 12/60; auth, The Pessimism of Leconte de Lisle, the Work and the Time, Univ Calif, 61; Leconte de Lisle and the Catechisme Populaire Republicain, Romanic Rev, 4/66; Les idees litteraires de Leconte de Lisle d'apres une correspondance inedite, Rev Hist Lit, France, 7-9/66; La derniere illusion de Leconte de Lisle, lettres inedites a Emilie Leforestier, Droz, 68. *Mailing Add:* Dept of French Univ of Calif Berkeley CA 94720

PUTZAR, EDWARD DAVID, b San Francisco, Calif, Aug 10, 30; m 62. FOREIGN LANGUAGES, JAPANESE. *Educ:* Univ Calif, Berkeley, BA, 52, MA, 60. *Prof Exp:* LECTR ORIENT STUDIES, UNIV ARIZ, 62- *Res:* Mediaeval Japanese literature. *Mailing Add:* Dept of Orient Studies Univ of Arizona Tucson AZ 85721

PUTZEL, MAX J, b Nuremberg, Ger, Feb 5, 25; nat US; m 73. GERMANIC LANGUAGES & LITERATURE. *Educ:* Univ Chicago, AB, 49, MA, 52, PhD(Ger lang & lit), 65. *Prof Exp:* Instr Ger, col & examr, Univ Chicago, 52-56, asst prof, 56-65, adv off dean students, univ, 52-58, resident head univ residence halls, 54-65, asst dean undergrad students, 58-62, assoc dean, 62-65; asst prof Ger & asst dean, 65-69, assoc prof, 70-74, chmn dept, 67-74, PROF GER, IND UNIV NORTHWEST, 74-, DIR HONORS PROG, 67- *Mem:* Am Asn Teachers Ger; MLA; Am Coun Study Austrian Lit. *Res:* Modern German literature; editing the correspondence of Immanuel Bekker; theatre history. *Publ:* Auth, Letters to Immanuel Bekker from Henriette Herz, S Pobeheim and Anna Horkel, Vol VI, In: German Studies in America, Herbert Lang, Bern 72. *Mailing Add:* 5757 Kenwood Chicago IL 60637

Q

QAFISHEH, HAMDI AHMAD, b Jerusalem, Israel, Nov 21, 35; Jordanian citizen; m 60; c 3. LINGUISTICS, LANGUAGE TEACHING. *Educ:* Univ Baghdad, BA, 60; Univ Mich, Ann Arbor, MA, 65, PhD(ling), 68. *Prof Exp:* Instr English, Unrwa Teacher Training Col, Jordan, 60-64; res asst, Univ Mich, Ann Arbor, 65-68; asst prof ling, Al-Hikma Univ, Baghdad, 68-69; training dir, 69-70, asst prof, 70-71, assoc prof Arabic, 73-80, PROF ORIENTAL STUDIES, UNIV ARIZ, 80- *Concurrent Pos:* Prin investr, US Off Educ, 72- *Mem:* Mid E Studies Asn; Am Asn Teachers Asn; Am Coun Teaching Foreign Lang; Teaching English to Speakers Other Lang; Ling Soc Am. *Res:* Dialects of the Arabian Gulf; language textbooks based on contrastive analysis of English and Arabic. *Publ:* Auth, Basic Gulf Arabic, 70 & Beginning English, 71, Univ Ariz Environ Res Lab; A Basic Course in Gulf Arabic, Univ Ariz, 74; Contrastive analysis and the AFL teacher, 74 & From Gulf Arabic into modern standard Arabic, 74, ERIC. *Mailing Add:* Dept of Orient Studies Univ Of Ariz Tucson AZ 85721

QUACKENBUSH, LOUIS HOWARD, b Bellingham, Wash, Nov 28, 39; m 63; c 7. LATIN AMERICAN LITERATURE. *Educ:* Brigham Young Univ, BA, 65, MA, 67; Univ Ill, Urbana, PhD(Span), 70. *Prof Exp:* Teacher, teacher suprv & counr Span lang training, Lang Training Mission, 63-67, ASSOC PROF SPAN, BRIGHAM YOUNG UNIV, 70- *Mem:* MLA; Rocky Mountain Mod Lang Asn; Am Asn Teachers Span & Port. *Res:* Spanish American drama; Brazilian drama; Spanish American poetry. *Publ:* Auth, The other pastorelas of Spanish American drama, Latin Am Theatre Rev, spring 73; The auto in contemporary Mexican drama, Ky Romance Quart, 74; Theatre of the absurd, reality and Carlos Maggi, J Span Studies: 20th Century, spring 75; La desavenencia religiosa: Una clave a El tuerto es rey de Carlos Fuentes, Explicacion de textos literarios, 75/76; The Contemporary Latin American Short Story, 79; The legacy of Albee's Who's Afraid of Virginia Woolf? in the Spanish American Absurdist Theatre, spring 79 & Pablo Nervda: Sus versos finales y ultimos comienzos, summer 80, Revista/Rev Interamericana. *Mailing Add:* Dept of Span Brigham Young Univ Provo UT 84601

QUAIN, ESTELLE ELEANOR, b New York, NY, Oct 11, 47. SPANISH & LATIN AMERICAN LITERATURE. *Educ:* Goucher Col, AB, 69; Harvard Univ, AM, 70, PhD(Romance lang), 76. *Prof Exp:* Asst prof Span, Conn Col, 76-78; ASST PROF SPAN, BOSTON UNIV, 78- *Mem:* MLA; Latin Am Studies Asn; Am Asn Teachers Span & Port; Am Coun Teaching Foreign Lang. *Res:* Contemporary Latin American fiction; medieval Spanish literature; Cervantes and Golden Age fiction. *Publ:* Auth, Lenguaje y realidad oculta en los cuentos de Jose Donoso, Memorias Del IV Congreso de la Nuevo Narrativa HispanoAmericana, 8/74; The image of the house in the works of Jose Donoso, In: Essays in Honors of Jorge Guillen on the occasion of his 85th year, Abedul, 77. *Mailing Add:* Dept of Mod Foreign Lang & Lit Boston Ave Boston MA 02215

QUINN, BERNARD JOHN, b Sherbrooke, Que, June 15, 45; m 65; c 2. FRENCH LITERATURE & CIVILIZATION. *Educ:* Univ SFla, BA, 66; La State Univ, MA, 68, PhD(French), 70. *Prof Exp:* Vist asst prof French, Univ Ga, 70-72; ASSOC PROF FRENCH, MONT STATE UNIV, 72- *Concurrent Pos:* Ed & founder, Contemporary French Civilization, 76- *Mem:* Am Asn Teachers French; MLA; Rocky Mountain Mod Lang Asn; Pac Northwest Conf Foreign Lang; Northeast MLA. *Res:* French literary existentialism; French Canadian literature and civilization; French civilization. *Publ:* Auth, The authentic woman in the theatre of Jean-Paul Sartre, Lang Quart, spring 72; The politics of hope versus the politics of despair: A look at Bariona, Sartre? first piece engagee, French Rev, spring 72; From Nazareth to Bethlehem: Sartre secularizes the Christian myth of angelic intervention in Bariona, French Lit Ser, 76; A critique of Sartre's On a raison de se revolter, Proc PNCFL, spring 76; Sartre today: A roundtable discussion with Michel Rybalka, Roger Federman, Michael Issacharoff, George Bauer, 76 & De Sainte-Justine a Montreal: Une interview avec Roch Carrier, romancier et dramaturge quebecois, 78, Contemp French Civilization. *Mailing Add:* Dept of Mod Lang Mont State Univ Bozeman MT 59715

QUINN, BETTY NYE, b Buffalo, NY, Mar 22, 21; m 50. CLASSICS. *Educ:* Mt Holyoke Col, AB, 41; Bryn Mawr Col, AM, 42, PhD, 44. *Prof Exp:* Analyst, US Army, 44-46; Cent Intel Agency, 47; from instr to asst prof classics, Vassar Col, 48-59, dir pub relat, 52-59; assoc prof, 59-68, PROF CLASSICS, MT HOLYOKE COL, 68- *Concurrent Pos:* Am Philos Soc grant, 52. *Mem:* Am Philol Asn; Mediaeval Acad Am; Class Asn New England (pres, 70-71); Vergilian Soc Am. *Res:* Roman comedy; Vergil's Eclogues; mediaeval text books. *Publ:* Auth, The Bucolics and the mediaeval poetical debate, Trans Am Philol Asn, 44; Chess in the twelfth century, Chess Rev, 1/58; Venus, Chaucer and Peter Bersuire, Speculum, 63; Theodolus, In: Catalogus translationum et commentariorum: Mediaeval and Renaissance Latin Translations and Comentaries, Cath Univ Am, Vol II, 71; ed, Plautus, Menaechmi, Bolchazy Carducci, 81. *Mailing Add:* Dept of Classics Mt Holyoke Col South Hadley MA 01075

QUINN, JOHN JOSEPH, b San Francisco, Calif, Mar 20, 26; m 57; c 3. ENGLISH LANGUAGE, MEDIEVAL LITERATURE. *Educ:* Univ San Francisco, BS, 50; Stanford Univ, PhD(English philol), 56. *Prof Exp:* Asst prof English, Stephen F Austin State Col, 56-57 & Univ Santa Clara, 57-64; assoc prof, 64-66, fac develop grant, 68-69, PROF ENGLISH, STEPHEN F AUSTIN STATE UNIV, 66- *Concurrent Pos:* Fulbright lectr, Spain, 68-69 & Arg, 71. *Mem:* SCent Mod Lang Asn; Teachers of English Speakers Other Lang; Medieval Acad Am; Nat Asn Bilingual Educ. *Res:* Chaucerian studies; English as a second language; transformational grammar. *Publ:* Auth, Ghost words, obscure lemmata and doubtful glosses in a Latin Old English glossary, 4/61 & Some puzzling lemmata and glosses in manuscript Cotton Cleopatra A-III, 4/66, Philol Quart; An additional relative clause transformation, J English Ling, 3/67; coauth, The Houston-Quinn Phonetikon, Scott-Foresman, 70; contrib, Essays in Honour of Herbert D Meritt, Mouton, The Hague, 70; La Idea de Revolucion en Linguistica, Asn Arg de Estudio Am, Buenos Aires, Arg, 71. *Mailing Add:* Dept of English Stephen F Austin State Univ Nacogdoches TX 75962

QUINN, KENNETH FLEMING, b Greymouth, NZ, Dec 25, 20; m 46. LITERARY CRITICISM, CLASSICS. *Educ:* Victoria Univ, Wellington, BA, 42; Cambridge Univ, BA, 47, MA, 52; Univ Melbourne, MA, 61. *Prof Exp:* Lectr classics, Victoria Univ, Wellington, 48-55; sr lectr, Uinv Melbourne, 55-60, reader, 61-65; prof, Univ Otago, 65-69; PROF CLASSICS, UNIV TORONTO, 69- *Concurrent Pos:* Mem, Australian Humanities Res Coun, 63-65 & Am Philol Asn Colloquium on Classics in Educ, 64-65. *Res:* Roman poetry; literary history; literary criticism. *Publ:* Auth, The Catullan Revolution, Cambridge Univ, 59, Univ Mich, 71; Latin Explorations, Humanities, 63 & 69; Virgil's Aeneid: A Critical Description, Univ Mich, 68 & 69; ed, Catullus: The Poems, St Martin's, 70 & 73; Approaches to Catullus, 72 & auth, Catullus: An Interpretation, 72, Barnes & Noble; Die personliche Dichtung der Klassik, In: Neues Handbuch der Literaturwissenschaft, Vol 3, Akademische Verlagsgesellschaft, 73; Tests and Contexts, Routledge & Kegan Paul, 79; ed, Horace, the Odes, Macmillan, 80; auth, How Literature Works, Am Book Co, 82. *Mailing Add:* Univ Col Univ of Toronto Toronto ON M5S 1A1 Can

QUINTAL, CLAIRE, b Central Falls, RI. FRENCH CULTURE & LITERATURE. *Educ:* Anna Maria Col, AB, 52; Univ Montreal, MA, 58; Univ Paris, DUniv, 61. *Prof Exp:* Prof French hist, Am Col in Paris, 65-68; ASSOC PROF FRENCH, ASSUMPTION COL, MASS, 68-, DIR SUMMER SCH & DEAN OF GRAD SCH, 70- *Mem:* Am Asn Univ Women. *Res:* Medieval history. *Publ:* Coauth, The First Biography of Joan of Arc, 64 & The Letters of Joan of Arc, 69, Univ Pittsburgh. *Mailing Add:* Grad Sch Assumption Col Worcester MA 01609

QUINTANA, JUDITH TERRIE, b Sheboygan, Wis, Sept 10, 40. FRENCH LANGUAGE & LITERATURE. *Educ:* Lawrence Univ, BA, 62; Middlebury Col, MA, 64; Univ Wis-Madison, PhD(French & art hist), 70. *Prof Exp:* Asst prof French, Univ Chicago, 69-75; asst prof, 75-82, ASSOC PROF FRENCH, WASHINGTON & JEFFERSON COL, 82-, CHAIRWOMAN, DEPT MOD & CLASS LANG, 82- *Mem:* Am Asn Teachers Fr; Northeast Mod Lang Asn. *Res:* Malraux; symbolist poetry; existentialism. *Publ:* Auth, L'Art ou l'Homme? sur un livre de Pascal Sabourin, In: Andre Malraux 2: Visages du romancier, Lett Modernes, 73; The Voyant as clarion in Barbare, Rivista di Lett Moderne e Comparate, 9/76; Mallarme's Toute l'ame resumee, Explicator, spring 77; Caterpillars and Butterflies: Metamorphosis, Malraux's Early Fiction J Evolutionary Psychol, 12/80; Essay form, La Tentation de l'Occident, Fr Lit Series, Vol IX, 82; Can Baudelaire be serious?, Topic 35, 81 & ed, Topic 35, 81, Fr Cult. *Mailing Add:* Dept of Fr Washington & Jefferson Col Washington PA 15301

QUINTIAN, ANDRES ROGELIO, b Havana, Cuba, Dec 29, 20; US citizen; m 46; c 2. SPANISH LINGUISTICS. *Educ:* Univ Barcelona, ML, 44; Univ Havana, MDCL, 53, MPAL & DSS, 54; Ind State Univ, Terre Haute, BA, 65, MS, 66; Ind Univ Bloomington, PhD(Hisp lit), 69. *Prof Exp:* Consul, Secy of Embassy & Charge d'affaires, Cuban Foreign Serv, 44-61; dir info, Cuban Coun, 61-63; teacher Span, Greensburgh High Sch, 65-66; asst prof, Ind State Univ, 69-71; chmn dept mod lang, 77-78, asst prof, 71-80, PROF SPAN, BARUCH COL, 80- *Res:* Latin American literature; Spanish literature. *Publ:* Auth, Un progreso indiscutible, 11/55 & Observaciones sobre el Servicio Exterior de Cuba 1918-1955, 1/56, Bol Col Nac Doctores en Ciencias Sociales, Havana; Ruben Dario y la Espana catalan, Rev Cuadernos Hispanoam, Madrid, 3/72; Paradiso de Jose Lezama Lima-escritor neobarroco, XVII Congr del Inst Int de Lit Iberoam, Madrid, 78; coauth, Nueva teoria monetaria, Ed Economia, Madrid, 9/78. *Mailing Add:* 200 E 71st St New York NY 10021

QUIRK, RONALD JOSEPH, b Bristol, Conn, Mar 22, 42; m 67; c 4. SPANISH LANGUAGE & LITERATURE. *Educ:* Trinity Col, BA, 64; Brown Univ, MA, 66, PhD(Span), 71. *Prof Exp:* Instr Span, RI Col, 68-69; from instr to asst prof, Trinity Col, 69-72; asst prof, 72-74, assoc prof, 74-80, PROF SPAN, QUINNIPIAC COL, 80- *Mem:* Am Asn Teachers Span & Port; Northeast Mod Lang Asn. *Res:* Nineteenth century Spanish literature; linguistics and literature of Puerto Rico. *Publ:* Auth, Glosario Borinqueno, Trinity Col, 70; On the extent and origin of questions in the formque tu tienes?, Hispania, 5/72; The authorship of La gruta azul: Juan Valera or Serafin Estebanez Calderon, Romance Notes, spring 74; El problema del habla regional en Los Pazos de Ulloa, Inti, 10/75; Nueve cartas de Estebanez Calderon, Rev de Archivos, Bibliot y Museos, 1-3/76; Temporal adverbs in Puerto Rican Spanish, Hispania, 5/76; The Cebre Cycle: Emilia Pardo Bazan and Galician reform, Am Hispanist, 5/77; Basic Spanish for Legal Personnel, Collegium Bks, 79. *Mailing Add:* Dept of Mod Foreign Lang Quinnipiac Col Hamden CT 06518

R

RAAB, MARY RICARDA, b Chicago, Ill, Apr 9, 26. ROMANCE LANGUAGES, LATIN AMERICAN STUDIES. *Educ:* Col St Teresa, Minn, BA, 59; St Louis Univ, PhD(Span, Latin Am studies), 65. *Prof Exp:* Teacher elem & jr high schs, Minn & Ohio, 48-59; asst prof Span, Col St Teresa, Minn, 64-70; curriculum writer bilingual educ, Sweetwater Union High Sch Dist & three elem dist, Chula Vista, Calif, 70-71; assoc prof Span Lang & Lit, Winona State Col, 71-72; ASSOC PROF SPAN LANG & LIT, COL ST TERESA, MINN, 72- *Mem:* Am Teachers Span & Port. *Res:* Spanish and Latin American literature; bilingual education; Mexican American culture. *Mailing Add:* Box 275 Col of St Teresa Winona MN 55987

RAAPHORST, MADELEINE, b Tours, France, Sept 20, 18; US citizen; m 44; c 2. FRENCH. *Educ:* Univ Paris, Lic en Droit, 42; Rice Univ, PhD, 59. *Prof Exp:* Asst prof French, Tex Southern Univ, 58-60 & Ohio Wesleyan Univ, 60-63; from asst prof to assoc prof, 63-71, chmn dept French & Ital, 72-79, PROF FRENCH, RICE UNIV, 71- *Mem:* MLA; Am Asn Teachers Fr; Asn Fr Prof Am. *Res:* Eighteenth century French literature; poetry from Buadelaire to the present; twentieth century novel. *Publ:* Auth, Colette, Sa Vie et Son Art, Nizet, Paris, 64; Voltaire et la queston du luxe, summer 65 & Choderlos de Laclos et l'education des femmes au 18e siecle, winter 67, Rice Univ Studies; Paul Valery et Voltaire, Fr Rev, 2/67. *Mailing Add:* Dept of French Rice Univ Houston TX 77001

RABASSA, CLEMENTINE CHRISTOS, b New York, NY, July 31, 32; m 66; c 1. HISPANIC LANGUAGES & LITERATURE. *Educ:* Hunter Col, BA, 53, MA, 58; Columbia Univ, PhD, 71. *Prof Exp:* Teacher Span, NY City Pub Sch, 54-58; teacher, Lynbrook Pub Sch, 54-62; instr, Columbia Univ, 63-66; assoc prof Span, 73-80, assoc prof, 73-80, PROF HUMANITIES, MEDGAR EVERS COL, 80- *Concurrent Pos:* Nat Endowment Humanities fel, comp lit, 72-73; proj dir Afro-Hispanic lit, City Univ NY Faculty Res Award Prog, 74-75; co-proj dir Span lang, NY State Educ Dept, 77; Rockefeller Found fel, 79-80. *Mem:* Am Asn Teachers Span & Port; Am Comp Lit Asn; Latin Am Studies Asn; MLA. *Res:* Afro-Hispanic literature; modern drama; epic poetry. *Publ:* Auth, Zoomorfosis y la trayectoria epicocristiana en Siete Lunas y Siete Serpientes, El Dia, 5/70; Cynegetics and irony in the thematic unity of the Lusiads, Luso-Brazilian Rev, 12/73; El aire como materia literaria: La epica, la nueva narrativa, y Demetrio Aguilera-Malta, Nueva Narrativa Hispanoamericana, 9/74; Prolegomeno al tema del negro en la obra de Aguilera-Malta, Hojas Volantes de la Comunidad Latinoamericana de Escritores, 9/74; Contribr, Homenaje a Andres Iduarte, Am Hispanist, 76; auth, Camoes and Boccaccio: The vestal contradiction in the Lusiads and the Oitavas IV, J Am Port Soc, summer 77; Demetrio Aquilera-Malta and Social Justice: The Tertiary Phase of Epic Tradition in Latin American Literature, Fairleigh Dickinson Univ Press, 80; En torno a Aquilera-Malta: Temas epicos y negros, Casa de la Cult Ecuatoriana, Nucleo del Guayas, Guayaquil, 81. *Mailing Add:* 36 Red Creek Rd Hampton Bays NY 11946

RABASSA, GREGORY, b Yonkers, NY, Mar 9, 22; m 66. SPANISH, PORTUGUESE. *Educ:* Dartmouth Col, AB, 45; Columbia Univ, MA, 47, PhD(Port), 54. *Hon Degrees:* LittD, Dartmouth Col, 82. *Prof Exp:* Instr Span, columbia Univ, 47-52, assoc, 52-58, asst prof, 58-63, assoc prof Span & Port, 63-68; PROF ROMANCE LANG, QUEENS COL, NY, 68- *Concurrent Pos:* Assoc ed, Odyssey Rev, 61-64; Fulbright-Hays fel, Brazil, 65-66; Nat Endowment for Humanities fel, 79-80. *Honors & Awards:* Nat Bk Award for transl, 67; Transl Prize, PEN Am Ctr, 77; Am Transl Asn Gode Medal, 80; PEN Transl Medal, 82. *Mem:* Renaissance Soc Am; MLA; Am Asn Teachers Span & Port; Latin Am Studies Asn; PEN Club. *Res:* Brazilian literature; Spanish American literature; modern Spanish literature. *Publ:* Auth, O Negro na ficcao Brasileira, Tempo Brasileiro Rio, 65; The Negro in Brazilian literature, African Forum, spring 67; If this be treason: Translation, Am Scholar, winter 74/75. *Mailing Add:* 36 Red Creek Rd Hampton Bays NY 11946

RABEL, ROBERT JOSEPH, b Pittsburgh, Pa, Aug 21, 48. CLASSICAL LANGUAGES. *Educ:* Univ Pittsburgh, BA, 70; Univ Mich, MA, 71, PhD(classics), 75. *Prof Exp:* Asst prof, 75-82, ASSOC PROF CLASSICS, UNIV KY, 82- *Concurrent Pos:* Guest lectr, 2nd Int Inst Semiotic & Structuralist Studies, summer, 81. *Mem:* Am Philol Asn; Class Asn Middlewest & South; Soc Ancient Greek Philos; Vergilian Soc; Archaeol Inst Am. *Res:* Greek tragedy; Hellenistic philosophy; Roman epic. *Publ:* Auth, Pathei Mathos: A dramatic ambiguity in the Oresteia, 79 & Cledonomancy in the Eumenides, 79, Rivista Di Studi Classici; The meaning of Choephoroi 827-830, Hermes, 80; Vergil, tops and the stoic view of fate, Class J, 81; The structure of Aeneid IX, Latomus, 81; Diseases of soul in stoic psychology, Greek, Roman and Byzantine Studies, 81. *Mailing Add:* Dept of Classics Univ of Ky Lexington KY 40506

RABEL-HEYMANN, LILI, b Goettingen, Ger; US citizen. LINGUISTICS. *Educ:* Univ Mich, AB, 45, MA, 46; Univ Calif, Berkeley, PhD, 57. *Prof Exp:* Instr Ger, Univ Wash, 50-51, instr English, 52-54; instr Span & Ital, Univ Md overseas, Munich, Ger, 57-58 & Stanford Univ, Ger, 58-59; asst prof English, La State Univ, 59-63 & Univ Mass, Amherst, 63-67; assoc prof ling, 67-78, EMER PROF LING, UNIV CALGARY, 78- *Concurrent Pos:* Am Coun Learned Soc grants, 45, 49-50, 51 & 56. *Mem:* Ling Soc Am; Am Name Soc; Ling Asn Can & US; Teachers English as Second Lang. *Res:* Khasi language; present-day American English language. *Publ:* Auth, Khasi, a Language of Assam, La State Univ, 61; Redundants in Khasi, Studies Indian Ling, Poona, 68; Analysis of loanwords in Khasi, Oceanic Ling, 76; Sound symbolism and Khasi adverbs, Pac Ling, 76; Gender in Khasi nouns, Mon-Khmer Studies VI, 77; But how does a bilingual feel?, Fourth Ling Asn Can & US Forum, 77. *Mailing Add:* 1124 Bluelake Sq Mountain View CA 94040

RABINOVITZ, RUBIN, English, Comparative Literature. See Vol II

RABINOWITZ, ISAAC, b Brooklyn, NY, July 3, 09; m 46; c 3. SEMITIC LANGUAGES & LITERATURE. *Educ:* Univ Calif, AB, 29; Yale Univ, PhD, 32. *Prof Exp:* Counr Jewish studies, Yale Univ, 33-34; Am Coun Learned Soc res fel, 34-35; dir youth educ, Union Am Hebrew Congregations, 35-38; dir, Hillel Found, B'nai B'rith, 38-46; exec dir, East New York YMHA & YWHA, 46-55; La Med prof & dir Jewish studies, Wayne State Univ, 55-57; prof Bibl & Semitic studies, 57-75, chmn dept Semitic lang & lit, 65-70, EMER PROF NEAR EASTERN LANG & LIT, CORNELL UNIV, 75- *Concurrent Pos:* Guggenheim fel, 61-62; Nat Endowment for Humanities sr fel, 71-72. *Mem:* Am Asn Jewish Studies; World Union Jewish Studies; Am Orient Soc; Soc Bibl Lit; Am Schs Orient Res. *Res:* Semitic philology; the Bible; Jewish literature and thought. *Publ:* Auth, Sequence and dates of the Extra-Biblical Dead Sea Scroll texts, Vetus Testamentum, 53; Damascus and 390 years in the Damascus Fragments, J Bibl lit, 54; Towards a Valid Theory of Biblical Hebrew Literature, Cornell Univ, 66; Word and literature in ancient Israel, New Lit Hist, 73-74; auth & transl, The Book of the Honeycomb's Flow, Cornell Univ Press, 82. *Mailing Add:* 912 E State St Ithaca NY 14850

RABINOWITZ, PETER JACOB, b Brooklyn, NY, Feb 18, 44. COMPARATIVE LITERATURE. *Educ:* Univ Chicago, BA, 65, MA, 67, PhD(comp lit), 72. *Prof Exp:* Asst prof humanities, City Col Chicago, 68-74; asst prof lit, Kirkland Col, 74-78; asst prof comp lit, 78-81, ASSOC PROF COMP LIT, HAMILTON COL, 81-, CHAIR, 79- *Concurrent Pos:* Panelist, Music Prog, NY State Coun on Arts, 82- *Mem:* MLA; Am Comp Lit Asn; Asn Recorded Sound Collections. *Res:* Literary theory; literature and music. *Publ:* Auth, Truth in fiction: A reexamination of audiences, Critical Inquiry, autumn 77; The click of the spring: The detective story as parallel structure in Dostoyevsky and Faulkner, Mod Philol, 5/79; coauth (with Nancy S Rabinowitz), The critical balance: Reader, text and meaning, 4/80; auth, Rats behind the wainscoting: Politics, convention and Chandler's The Big Sleep, Tex Studies Lit & Lang, summer 80; What's Hecuba to us? The audience's experience of literary borrowing, In: The Reader in the Text: Essays in Audience and Interpretation, Princeton Univ Press, 80; Assertion and assumption: Fictional patterns and the external world, Publ MLA, 5/81; Fictional music: Toward a theory of listening, In: Theories of Reading, Looking and Listening, Bucknell Univ Press, 81 & Bucknell Rev, Vol 26, No 1; Pleasure in conflict: Mahler's sixth, tragedy and musical form, Comp Lit Studies, 9/81. *Mailing Add:* Dept of Comp Lit Hamilton Col Clinton NY 13323

RABINOWITZ, WILSON GERSON, b Kans City, Mo, Feb 9, 19; m 46; c 1. GREEK. *Educ:* Univ Calif, AB, 40, PhD(classics), 55. *Prof Exp:* Instr Greek, Univ Wash, 48-51, acting asst prof, 51-54; from acting asst prof to asst prof, 54-58, ASSOC PROF GREEK, UNIV CALIF, BERKELEY, 58- *Concurrent Pos:* Mem, Inst Advan Study, 57-58; Guggenheim Mem Found, fel, 57-58; Am Coun Learned Soc fel, 61-62. *Mem:* Am Philol Asn; Soc Ancient Greek Philos; Philol Asn Pac Coast. *Res:* The history of ancient Greek Philosophy; ancient Greek literature. *Publ:* Auth, Platonic Piety, Phronesis, Vols II & III, 58; Aristotle's Protepticus and the Sources of its Reconstruction, Univ Calif Publ Calss Philol; Ethica Nicomachea II, In: Aristote et les problemes de methode, Publ Univ de Louvain, 61. *Mailing Add:* Dept of Classics Univ of Calif Berkeley CA 94720

RABOTIN, MAURICE, b Ecuelles, France, Nov 16, 25. LINGUISTICS, FRENCH LANGUAGE. *Educ:* Sorbonne, Lic es Lett, 51. *Prof Exp:* Lectr French, Univ Alta, 55-57; from lectr to asst prof, 57-64, ASSOC PROF FRENCH, MCGILL UNIV, 64-, DIR FRENCH, UNIV SUMMER SCH, 64- *Mem:* Can Ling Asn. *Res:* French civilization, terminology of contemporary linguistics. *Mailing Add:* 4231 del Esplanade Montreal PQ H2W 1T1 Can

RABURA, HORST M, b Brieg, Ger, July 6, 26; m 55; c 2. GERMANIC LANGUAGE & LITERATURE. *Educ:* Seattle Univ, BEd, 59; Univ Wash, MA, 66. *Prof Exp:* Teacher high sch, Wash, 57-62; instr methods teaching foreign lang, NDEA Lang Inst, Univ Wash, 61-63; instr Ger, 63-66, asst prof, 66-73; dir Ger as second lang, Inst Film & Pictures, Munich, Ger, 73-76; ASSOC PROF GER, UNIV WASH, 76- *Concurrent Pos:* Dir, NDEA Foreign Lang Inst, 64-65, asst overseas die, 66-67; dir Europ studies, Experienced Teacher Fel Prog, 68. *Mem:* MLA; Am Coun Teaching Foreign Lang. *Res:* Second language learning; bilingual education; foreign language teachers training. *Publ:* Auth, Final Report, National Defense Education Act, Summer Institute, 64 & 65 & Problems of Articulation Between the Public School German Programs in the State of Washington and the University of Washington, 67, Univ Wash; The preparation of foreign language teachers, Proc Pac Nat Conf Foreign Lang, Bull, 71; Deutsch zur selbstbehauptuus, AV Info Deutsch Aurlander, 73; Zum methodischen aufbaueiner lehreinheit, Deutsch, Aulsuderkinder Deutsch, Schulen Klettverlag, 74; Media Package Sprich mixuur, Inst Film & Pictures, Munich, 75-76; A new concept in teaching German through sprachbausteine, Proc, Univ Northern Iowa, 77. *Mailing Add:* Dept of Ger 340 Henny Hall Univ of Wash Seattle WA 98105

RACEVSKIS, KARLIS, b Latvia, July 2, 39; US citizen; m 66; c 3. FRENCH. *Educ:* City Col New York, BA, 61, MA, 66; Columbia Univ, PhD(French), 71. *Prof Exp:* Lectr French, City Col New York, 64-69; asst prof, Antioch Col, 69-72; asst prof, 72-76, assoc prof, 76-80, PROF FRENCH, WRIGHT STATE UNIV, 80- *Concurrent Pos:* Fel, Soc for the Humanities, Cornell Univ, 80-81. *Mem:* MLA; Am Asn Teachers Fr; Soc Fr Etude XVIIIe Siecle; Semiotic Soc Am. *Res:* Eighteenth-century French literature; contemporary criticism; semiotics. *Publ:* Auth, Voltaire and the French Academy, Univ NC, 75; Le Regne des philosophes a l'Academie francaise, Studies Voltaire & Eighteenth Century, CLIV, 76; Irony as a creative and critical force in three novels of Nathalie Sarraute, Fr Rev, 10/77; The French academy as a proponent of Egalitarianism, Studies on Eighteenth Century Cult, 78; A Return to the Heavenly City: Carl Becker's Paradox in a Structuralist Perspective, CLIO, 79; The theoretical violence of a catastrophical strategy, Diacritics, 79; The discourse of Michel Foucault: A case of an absent and forgettable subject, Humanities in Soc, 80; Michel Foucault and the Subversion of Intellect, Cornell Univ Press, 82. *Mailing Add:* Dept of Mod Lang Wright State Univ Dayton OH 45435

RACINE, DANIEL LEANDRE, b Guadeloupe, French WI, Feb 26, 26; French citizen. FRANCOPHONE & COMPARATIVE LITERATURE. *Educ:* Lycee Louis-le-Grand, Paris, Baccalaureat, 52; Univ Paris, Sorbonne, Lic es-L, 58, Doctorat d'Etat, 72. *Prof Exp:* Lectr French, Glasgow Pub Sch Syst, 57-58; teacher, English, Paris Pub Schs, 60-62 & Pedagogical Ctr, Lille, 62-63; instr & lectr French, Howard Univ, 63-72; lectr, Wellesley Col, 72-73 & Yale Univ, 73-75; asst prof, 75-77, assoc prof, 77-80, PROF FRENCH, HOWARD UNIV, 80- *Concurrent Pos:* Transl, UN, JRD Assocs & US Info Agency, 64-; interpreter, State Dept, 67- *Honors & Awards:* Chevalier Ordre Palmes Academiques, French Govt, 75. *Mem:* MLA; Am Asn Teachers French; Am Asn Comp Lit; African Lit Asn; Soc Professors French. *Res:* Saint John Perse and the United States; Leon Gontran Damas: A critical biography; The negritude movement. *Publ:* Auth, French West Indian poetry, a panoramic view, Black Images, winter 73; L'Univers antillais dans l'Oeuvre poetique de St J Perse, In: Identite Culturelle et Francophonic dans les Ameriques, Univ Laval, 76; Dialectique culturelle et politique en Guadeloupe et Martinique, Presence Africaine, Paris, winter 77; The French dialects in the Mississippi Valley, In: The Reader's Encycl of the American West, Harper & Rowe, 78; A profile of L G Damas, Negro Hist Bull, 7/79; Leon Gontran Damas, Founder of Negritude, Univ Press Am, 79; Poesie et tourisme: St John Perse et Leon Gontran Damas, Administration, Paris, fall 80; J P Sartre and Negritude, Plantation Soc, 82. *Mailing Add:* 4302 River Rd NW Washington DC 20016

RACINE, R JOSEPH, b Three Rivers, Mass, Apr 25, 15. HUMANITIES. *Educ:* Assumption Col, AB, 30; Boston Univ, EDM, 37. *Prof Exp:* Asst prof English, Assumption Col, 30-58; asst prof hist & French, Col Our Lady of the Elms, 58-63; asst prof English & French, Univ Mass, 63-65; assoc prof, 65-80, SR LECTR HUMANITIES, WESTERN NEW ENGLAND COL, 80- *Mem:* Acad Hist & Polit Sci; Col Asn Foreign Lang. *Res:* International relations. *Mailing Add:* Dept of Humanities Western New England Col Springfield MA 01119

RADANDT, FRIEDHELM K, b Gross-Jestin, Ger, Oct 23, 32; m 58; c 3. GERMANIC LANGUAGES. *Educ:* Baptist Theol Sem, Ger, Dipl theol, 57; Univ Chicago, AM, 61, PhD(Ger), 67. *Prof Exp:* Instr Ger, Lake Forest Col, 61-64; from instr to asst prof, Univ Chicago, 64-70; assoc prof, Lake Forest Col, 70-77, actg dean fac, 73-74, dean fac, 74-77; PROF HUMANITIES & VPRES ACAD AFFAIRS, NORTHWESTERN COL, IOWA, 77-, PRES, 79- *Mem:* Am Asn Teachers Ger. *Res:* German literary history of the 18th century; German novel and novella in 18th and 29th centuries. *Publ:* Auth, Transitional time in Keller's Zuricher Novellen, PMLA, 74; From Baroque to Storm and Stress, 1720-1775, Croom & Helm, London & Barnes & Nobel, New York, 77. *Mailing Add:* Dept of Humanities Northwestern Col Orange City IA 51041

RADCLIFF-UMSTEAD, DOUGLAS, b Baltimore, Md, Jan 10, 44; wid. ROMANCE LANGUAGES. *Educ:* Johns Hopkins Univ, BA, 60; Univ Calif, Berkeley, PhD(Romance lang), 64. *Prof Exp:* Asst prof Italian, Univ Calif, Santa Barbara, 64-68; vis assoc prof Italian & French, Univ Pittsburgh, 68-77, dir prog Medieval & Renaissance studies, 71-77; PROF & CHMN ROMANCE LANG, KENT STATE UNIV, 77- *Concurrent Pos:* Mem, Nat Comt Prom Ital in Higher Educ, 65-; Guggenheim fel, 74. *Mem:* Am Asn Teachers Ital; Dante Soc Am; Free World Acad; Pirandello Soc. *Res:* Comparative literature; Medieval and Renaissance studies; Jewish Studies. *Publ:* Auth, Italian Grammar Review, Appleton, 70; Death Before Me Today, Free World Acad, 71; ed, Innovation in Medieval Literature, Univ Pittsburgh, 71; Solorzano's tormented puppets, Latin Am Theatre Rev, 71; The University World, a Synoptic View of Higher Education, 73 & Roles and Images of Women in the Middle Ages and Renaissance, 75, Univ Pittsburgh; auth, The Mirror of our Anguish, A Study of Pirandello's Narrative, Fairleigh-Dickinson Univ, 77; Human Sexuality in the Middle Ages and Renaissance, Univ Pittsburgh, 80. *Mailing Add:* Dept of Romance Lang Kent State Univ Kent OH 44242

RADITSA, LEO FERRERO, Roman History. See Vol I

RADKE, WERNER J, b Frankfurt, Ger, Oct 28, 27; m 51; c 3. GERMAN LANGUAGE & LITERATURE. *Educ:* San Jose State Col, BA, 61; Stanford Univ, PhD(Ger), 66. *Prof Exp:* Teacher, elem & jr high schs, Ger, 48-57; instr Ger, US Army Lang Sch, 57-59; from instr to assoc prof, 60-70, PROF GER, SAN JOSE STATE UNIV, 70- *Mem:* Am Asn Teachers Ger; Philol Asn Pac Coast. *Res:* German classicism; modern German literature; astronomy. *Publ:* Auth, The Non-Copernican Solar System, Selbst, 62. *Mailing Add:* 14630 Palomino Dr San Jose CA 95127

RADLEY, PHILIPPE DANIEL, b Paris, France, Mar 14, 35; US citizen;. SLAVIC LANGUAGES & LITERATURES. *Educ:* Harvard Univ, AB, 56, AM, 59, PhD(Slavic), 65. *Prof Exp:* Reader Russ, Harvard Univ, 59-62, tutor, 60-62; asst prof, Amherst Col, 62-68; ASST PROF RUSS, STATE UNIV NY STONY BROOK, 68- *Mem:* Am Asn Teachers Slavic & EEurop Lang. *Res:* Nineteenth century literary crosscurrents between France, England and Russia; 20th century Russian poetry; Russian emigre literature. *Publ:* Auth, Khodasevich: Poet of the grotesque (in Russ), Aerial Ways, 1/65; Russian novel, Mass Rev, spring 67; transl, Italics are Mine, Harcourt, 69. *Mailing Add:* Dept of Ger & Russ State Univ of NY Stony Brook NY 11790

RADOYCE, LUBOMIR, b Belgrade, Yugoslavia, Feb 18, 25; US citizen; m 59; c 3. SLAVIC & COMPARATIVE LITERATURE. *Educ:* Univ WVa, MA, 52. *Prof Exp:* Instr French, Princeton Univ, 55-57; vis assoc prof Slavic lang & lit, Univ Calif, Los Angeles, 65-66; assoc prof, 66-67, PROF RUSS & COMP LIT, UNIV CALIF, RIVERSIDE, 67- *Concurrent Pos:* Inst Humanities fel, Univ Calif, Riverside, 67. *Mem:* Int Dostoevsky Soc. *Res:* Methods of literary study; novel; thematology. *Publ:* Auth, La conception du poete national chez Gogol, In: Langue et Litterature, Fac Lett, Univ Brussels, 61; Ultime Lettere di F M Dostoevski, 61, La Vita Dell'Arciprete Avvakum, 62 & Lev Tolstoj, Scritti Sull'Arte, 64, Boringhieri, Turin; ed, Ecrits sur l'Art (L Tolstoi), Gallimard, Paris, 71; auth, Writer in hell: Notes on Dostoevksi's Letters, Calif Slavic Studies, 76; Le Lettere di L N Tolstoj, Longanesi, Milan, 77-78; La quete de Dieu dans la correspondance de Tolstoi, Inst d'Etudes Slaves, Paris, 80. *Mailing Add:* Dept of Lit & Lang Univ of Calif Riverside CA 92502

RAEL, JUAN BAUTISTA, b Arroyo Hondo, NMex, Aug 14, 00; m 23; c 4. SPANISH. *Educ:* St Mary's Col, Calif, AB, 23; Univ Calif, AM, 27; Stanford Univ, PhD, 37. *Prof Exp:* Instr Span, St Mary's Col, Calif, 23-24; asst, Univ Calif, 26-27; instr, Univ Ore, 27-34; instr, 34-37, from asst prof to prof, 37-65, EMER PROF SPAN, STANFORD UNIV, 65- *Concurrent Pos:* Dir Guadalajara Summer Sch, Univ Ariz, 53-71, adv, 72-; res grants, Univ Ore,

Stanford Univ & Am Philos Soc. *Mem:* MLA; Am Folklore Soc; Pac Coast Philol Asn. *Res:* New Mexican Spanish folklore and language; alternate forms in the speech of the individual; associative interference in Spanish. *Publ:* Ed, Cuentos Orientales: Contados en Espanol, Oxford Univ, 39; auth, The New Mexican Alabado, 51 & Cuentos Espanoles de Colorado y Nuevo Mexico, 57, Stanford Univ, rev ed, Mus NMex, 77; Sources and Diffusion of the Mexican Shepherds' Plays, Guadalajara, Mex, 65. *Mailing Add:* Apt L308 350 Sharon Park Dr Menlo Park CA 94025

RAGLAND, ELOISE, b Greensboro, NC, Sept 16, 41; m 75; c 1. FRENCH LITERATURE & LANGUAGE. *Educ:* Mich State Univ, BA, 63; Univ Mich, Ann Arbor, MA, 66, PhD(French lit), 72. *Prof Exp:* From instr to asst prof, 70-77, ASSOC PROF FRENCH LANG & LIT, UNIV ILL, CHICAGO CIRCLE, 77- *Concurrent Pos:* Adv comt, Job Market to the MLA, 75-78; Nat Endowment for Humanities fel, 81; consult, Soc Sci & Humanities Res Coun Can, 82. *Mem:* MLA; Am Asn Teachers French; SAtlantic Mod Lang Asn; Renaissance Soc Am. *Res:* Psychoanalysis and literature: Jacques Lacan; reader response theory; Renaissance: Rabelais. *Publ:* Auth, Jacques Lacan: Ecrits, Sub-Stance, 78; Explicating Jacques Lacan: An overview, Hartford Studies in Lit, Vol 11, 79; Julien's quest for self: Qui suis-je?, 19th Cent Fr Studies, Vol 8, 79-80; The psychology of Narcissism in Jean Genet's The Maids, Gradiva, Vol 2, 79; Panurge and Frere Jan: Two characters cast from the same mold?, Ky Romance Quart, Vol 28, 81; coauth (with Peter Barglow), Job loss: Psychological response of university faculty, J Higher Educ, Vol 52, 81; auth, Lacan, language and literary criticism, Lit Rev, Vol 24, 81; coauth (with Henry W Sullivan), Calderon's Las tres justicias en una and the question of Christian Catharsis, In: Critical Perspectives on Calderon de la Barca, Univ Nebr Pres, 81. *Mailing Add:* Dept of French Univ Ill Chicago IL 60680

RAGUSA, OLGA, b Italy, Feb 11, 22; nat US. ITALIAN, COMPARATIVE LITERATURE. *Educ:* Hunter Col, BA, 43; Columbia Univ, MA, 47, PhD(French), 54. *Prof Exp:* Tutor Ital, Army Spec Training Prog, Cornell Univ, 43-44; instr French & ger, Newark Cols, Rutgers Univ, 46-47; instr French, Columbia Univ, 47-49; instr Ital, Vassar Col, 49-52; from instr to assoc prof, 52-65, prof, 65-79, DA PONTE PROF ITAL, COLUMBIA UNIV, 79-, CHMN DEPT, 73- *Concurrent Pos:* Fulbright res grant, Milan, Italy, 58-59; ed, Italica, Am Asn Teachers Ital, 68-; distinguished vis prof humanities, Univ Colo, 72; Am Coun Learned Soc fel, 72. *Mem:* MLA; Am Soc 18th Century Studies; Am Asn Teachers Ital; Am Comp Lit Asn; Dante Soc. *Res:* Italian literature of the 18th, 19th and 20th centuries; theory of literature and criticism; cross-influences in European literatures. *Publ:* Auth, Mallarme in Italy: A Study in Literary Influence and Critical Response, 57 & Verga's Milanese Tales, 64, Vanni; Luigi Pirandello, Columbia, 68; contribr, Essays on the Modern Italian Novel, Ind Univ, 69; Romantic and Its Cognates: The European History of a Word, 72 & Petrarch to Pirandello: Essays in Honor of Beatrice Corrigan, 73, Univ Toronto; auth, Narrative and Drama, Mouton, 76; contribr, The Two Hesperias: Literary Essays in Honor of Joseph G Fucilla, Porrua Turanzas, 78; ed, Romance Sect, Ital & contribr, Columbia Dict Modern European Literature, 2nd ed, Columbia, 80; auth, Pirandello: An Approach to His Theatre, Univ Edinburgh, 80. *Mailing Add:* 30 W 12th St New York NY 10011

RAHMAN, MUNIBUR, b Agra, Uttar Pradesh, India, July 18, 24; Brit citizen; m 52; c 4. PERSIAN & URDU LITERATURE. *Educ:* Aligarh Muslim Univ, India, BA, 40, MA, 42 & 44, LLB, 43; Univ London, PhD(Persian), 53. *Prof Exp:* Res fel Islamic studies, Aligarh Muslim Univ, India, 54-58, reader, 58-70, dir inst Islamic studies, 68-70; ASSOC PROF URDU & HINDI, OAKLAND UNIV, 70- *Mem:* Indian Nat Acad Lett. *Res:* Islamic studies. *Publ:* Auth, Post-revolution Persian Verse, 55 & An Anthology of Modern Persian Poetry (2 vols), 58 & 63, Aligarh Muslim Univ, India; Social satire in modern Persian literature, Bull Inst Islamic Studies, Aligarh, 58-59; Nima Yushij, Arch Orient, Prague, 61; Bazdid (collection of original poems in Urdu), Anjuman Taraqqi-yi Urdu, Aligarh, 65; Problems of Westernization in Persia, In: Studies in Asian History, Indian Coun Cult Rels, New Delhi, 69; Political novels in Urdu, In: Contribution to Asian Studies, York Univ, Ont & Brill, Leiden, Vol 6, 74; Antony and Cleopatra, Urdu transl, Delhi, 79. *Mailing Add:* Dept of Mod Lang Oakland Univ Rochester MI 48063

RAHV, BETTY THOMAS, b Charleston, WVa, Mar 30, 31; m 70; c 1. FRENCH LITERATURE. *Educ:* Sweet Briar Col, BA, 53; Middlebury Col, MA, 54; Ind Univ, Bloomington, PhD(French lit), 68. *Prof Exp:* Instr French lit, Brandeis Univ, 61-64; asst prof, Univ Mass, Boston, 65-70; asst prof, 70-80, ASSOC PROF FRENCH LIT, BOSTON COL, 80-, CHMN ROMANCE LANG, 76- *Mem:* Am Asn Teachers Fr; MLA; AAUP. *Res:* Maurice Sceve; 16th and 20th century French literature; contemporary criticism of prose fiction, especially the French new novel. *Publ:* Auth, Robbe-Grillet's uses of the past, Mod Lang Quart, 68; From Sartre to the New Novel, Kennikat, 74; The Kaliedoscope of Montaigne's Inconstance, Aquila, 76; Montaigne's Man of Understanding: Poet, Pedagogue and moralist, Inscape, 78. *Mailing Add:* Dept of Romance Lang Boston Col Chestnut Hill MA 02167

RAIA-COLANERI, ANN ROSE, b New York, NY, Sept 5, 39; m 67. CLASSICAL LANGUAGES & LITERATURES. *Educ:* Queens Col, BA, 61; Fordham Univ, MA, 63, PhD, 65. *Prof Exp:* Asst prof, 64-73, ASSOC PROF CLASSICS, COL NEW ROCHELLE, 73- *Mem:* Vergilian Soc; Am Philol Asn. *Res:* Classical and mediaeval period; humanistic-Renaissance. *Publ:* Co-ed, Galileo's letter about the libration of the moon, John F Fleming, 65; transl, The Jewish people in the divine plan of salvation, spring 66 & co-auth, Michelangelo and the tomb of Pope Julius II, winter 66, Thought. *Mailing Add:* Dept of Classics Col of New Rochelle New Rochelle NY 10805

RAITIERE, ANNA, b Paris, France, US citizen; c 2. FRENCH LANGUAGE & LITERATURE. *Educ:* Columbia Univ, BS, 61, MA, 63, PhD, 68. *Prof Exp:* Preceptor, Col Gen Studies, Columbia Univ, 61-67; ASSOC PROF FRENCH, YORK COL, NY, 68- *Concurrent Pos:* Instr French, Manhattan Community Col, 66-67. *Mem:* MlA; Am Soc 18th Century Studies; Soc Fr Etudes SVIII Siecle; Am Asn Teachers Fr; Soc Fr Prof Am. *Res:* Eighteenth century French literature and theater. *Publ:* Auth, L'art de l'acteur selon Dorat and Samson, Droz, Geneva, 69; La francaise devient majeru, Fr Rev, 10/74; The status of the French women today, In: Female Studies, Know. *Mailing Add:* Dept of French York Col 150-14 Jamaica Ave Jamaica NY 11432

RALEY, HAROLD C, b Hartselle, Ala, Nov 23, 34; m 62; c 3. ROMANCE LANGUAGES. *Educ:* Athens Col, AB, 59; Univ Ala, Tuscaloosa, MA, 61, PhD(Span), 66. *Prof Exp:* Instr French & Span, NTex State Univ, 62-64; from asst prof to prof Span, Okla State Univ, 64-77, head dept, 67-71 & 76-77; PROF & CHMN DEPT SPAN, UNIV HOUSTON, 77- *Concurrent Pos:* Span ed, SCent Mod Lang Asn, 73-74. *Mem:* Am Asn Teachers Span & Port; MLA; SCent Mod Lang Asn Am; Inst Hisp Cult. *Res:* Contemporary Spanish philosophy and literature; language teaching methodology. *Publ:* Auth, Ortega y el problema de la verdad, Rev Estudios Hisp, 68; Julian Marias: Hacia la superacion de Ortega, 68 & Hacia una teoria estetica en Julian Marias, 70, Hispanofila; Jose Ortega y Gasset: Philosopher of European Unity, Univ Ala, 71; La Vision Responsable, Espasa-Calpe, Madrid, 77; La unificacion europea: Malogro de un ideal orteguiano, Cuadernos Hispanoamericanos, 77; Responsible Vision: The Philosophy of Julian Marias, Am Hispanist, 80. *Mailing Add:* 125 St Cloud Friendswood TX 77546

RALSTON, ZACHARY T, b Hartranft, Tenn, Mar 25, 16. ROMANCE LANGUAGES. *Educ:* Univ Western Ont, BA, 37; Laval Univ, MA, 51; Cath Univ Am, PhD, 61. *Prof Exp:* From asst prof to prof French, St Jerome's Col, Univ Waterloo, 60-71, dean men, 61-65, dean students, 65-70; assoc prof, 71-81, PROF FRENCH, THE CITADEL, 81- *Mem:* Am Asn Teachers Fr; MLA; SAtlantic Mod Lang Asn. *Res:* Gabriel Marcel's drama; Paul Claudel's concept of analogy; poetry of Pierre Reverdy. *Publ:* Auth, Gabriel Marcel's Paradoxical Expression of Mystery, Cath Univ Am, 61; Synesthesia in Gide's La Symphonie Pastorale, The Citadel Monograph Ser, 8/76. *Mailing Add:* Dept of Mod Lang The Citadel Charleston SC 29409

RAMAGE, EDWIN STEPHEN, b Vancouver, BC, July 19, 29; m 56; c 2. CLASSICAL LANGUAGES. *Educ:* Univ BC, BA, 51, MA, 52; Univ Cincinnati, PhD(classics), 57. *Prof Exp:* From instr to assoc prof, 57-68, chmn dept, 71-75, PROF CLASSICS, IND UNIV, BLOOMINGTON, 68- *Mem:* Am Philol Asn; Class Asn Can. *Res:* Cicero; urban problems; Roman urbanity. *Publ:* Auth, Cicero on extra-Roman speech, Trans & Proc Am Philol Asn, 61; Urbanitas: Cicero and Quintilian, a contrast in attitudes, Am J Philol, 10/63; City and country in Menander's Dyskolos, Philologus, 66; Urbanitas: Ancient Sophistication and Refinement, Univ Okla, 73; coauth, Roman Satirists and Their Satire, Noyes, 74; translr, U Knoche, Roman Satire, 75 & ed, Atlantis: Fact of Fiction?, 78, Ind Univ; auth, Juvenal 12: on friendship true and false, Ill Class Studies, 78. *Mailing Add:* Dept of Class Studies Ballantine Hall 547 Ind Univ Bloomington IN 47401

RAMANUJAN, ATTIPAT KRISHNASWAMI, b Mysore, India, Mar 16, 29; m 62; c 2. LINGUISTICS, LITERATURE. *Educ:* Univ Mysore, BA, 49, MA, 50; Ind Univ, PhD(ling), 63. *Prof Exp:* Lectr English, S N Col, India, 50-51; Thiagarajar Col, 51-52, Lingaraj Col, 52-57 & Univ Baroda, 57-58; asst prof Dravidian ling, 62-66, assoc prof Dravidian Studies, 66-68, PROF DRAVIDIAN STUDIES, UNIV CHICAGO, 68- *Concurrent Pos:* Fac res fel, Am Inst Indian Studies, 63-64; mem, Comt Soc Thought, Univ Chicago, 72- *Honors & Awards:* Padma Sri, Govt of India, 76; Asn Indians in North America Award, 82. *Mem:* Ling Soc India; Ling Soc Am; Asn Asian Studies. *Res:* Comparative literature; folklore; linguistics. *Publ:* Auth, The Interior Landscape, Ind Univ, 67 & Peter Owen, London, 70; coauth, Modern Kannada Fiction, Univ Wis, 67; Toward a phonological typology of the Indian linguistic area, In: Current Trends in Linguistics-South Asia, Mouton, 68; auth, The structure of variation, In: Social Change and Social Structure in India, Aldine, 68; transl, Speaking of Siva, Penguin, 2nd ed, 73; Samskara, 76 & auth, Selected Poems, 76 & 81, Oxford; transl, Hymns for the Drowning, Princeton, 81. *Mailing Add:* Foster Hall South Asia Lang & Area Ctr Chicago IL 60637

RAMBALDO, ANA M, b Galvez, Arg; US citizen. SPANISH, SPANISH COMMUNITY RELATIONS. *Educ:* Southern Methodist Univ, BA, 50; NY Univ, MA, 67, PhD(Span), 71. *Prof Exp:* Asst prof, 67-80, PROF SPAN, MONTCLAIR STATE COL, 80- *Mem:* MLA. *Res:* Spanish medieval theater; Renaissance. *Publ:* Auth, El Cancionero de Juan del Encina Dentro de su Ambito Historico y Literario, Castellvi, Arg, 72; Obras Completas de Juan del Encina, Clasicos Castellanos (4 vols), Espasa-Calpe, Madrid, 78-82. *Mailing Add:* Dept of Span Montclair State Col Upper Montclair NJ 07043

RAMEH, CLEA ABDON, b Recife, Brazil, Jan 9, 27. LINGUISTICS, PORTUGUESE LANGUAGE. *Educ:* Univ Sao Paulo, BA, 47, Lic Anglo-Ger lang, 48, Especialization Anglo-Ger lang, 55; Georgetown Univ, MS, 62, PhD(ling), 70. *Prof Exp:* Teacher English State Schs Sao Paulo, Brazil, 51-63 & Regional Ctr Educ Res, Univ Sao Paulo, 63-65; linguist, Res Proj Port, US Naval Acad, 68-69; from instr to asst prof, 69-75, ASSOC PROF PORT, GEORGETOWN UNIV, 75-, CHMN DEPT, 79- *Concurrent Pos:* Consult, Port Res Proj, US Naval Inst, 69-72; chmn, Georgetown Univ Round Table Lang & Ling, 76. *Mem:* Ling Soc Am; MLA; Am Coun Teaching Foreign Lang; Am Asn Teachers Span & Port; Asoc Ling y Filol Am Latina. *Res:* Sociolinguistic implications of Portuguese linguistics; use of computer for language research applied to Portuguese; teaching of foreign languages. *Publ:* Coauth, Portugues Contemporaneo, Vol I, 66, 67, 69, 71, 72 & 75 & Vol II, 67, 69, 71, 73 & 77; Toward a computerized syntactic analysis of Portuguese, Comput & Humanities, 9/71; auth, O preparo de material para analise do Portugues em computador, Construtura, 74; ed, GURT 1976 Semantics: Theory and Application, Georgetown Univ, 76; auth, The Portuguese-English language contact in US, In: The Third LACUS Forum, Hornbeam, 76; Cecilia Meireles: Viagem e Solombra--uma analise linguistica, Rev Brasileira Ling, 77; O Vocabulo Portugues e o Computador, In: SENARA-Revista de filoloxia, Vol II, Colexio Univ, Spain, 80; Aspectos da Lingua Portuguesa nos Estados Unidos da America do Norte, In: From Linguistics to Literature: Romance Studies offered to Francis M Rogers, John Benjamins B V, Holland, 81. *Mailing Add:* Dept of Port Georgetown Univ Washington DC 22057

RAMEY, GEORGE GROVER, Old Testament Archeology, Hebrew Language. See Vol IV

RAMIREZ, MANUEL, b Billings, Okla, Mar 26, 23; m 48; c 1. FOREIGN LANGUAGES. *Educ:* Okla Baptist Univ, BS, 49; Okla State Univ, MA, 53; Interam Univ, Mex, PhD(Span lit), 60. *Prof Exp:* Teacher, Cent High Sch, Muskogee, Okla, 49-54; assoc prof, Okla Baptist Univ, 54-64; prof, Ouachita Baptist Univ, 64-68; PROF SPAN, HENDERSON STATE UNIV, 68- *Mem:* Am Asn Teachers Span & Port; MLA; Am Coun Teaching Foreign Lang. *Res:* Picaresque novel in Spanish literature; Mexican history; archaeology. *Mailing Add:* Dept of Mod Lang Henderson State Univ Arkadelphia AR 71923

RAMIREZ, MANUEL D, b Tampa, Fla, Dec 30, 14; m 41; c 2. SPANISH, SPANISH AMERICAN LITERATURE. *Educ:* Univ Fla, BA, 37, MA, 39; Univ NC, PhD, 59. *Prof Exp:* Instr Span & sci, Fla Mil Inst, 37-38; part-time instr Span & exec secy, Inst Inter-Am Affairs, Univ Fla, 39-42; asst prof mod lang, Kans State Univ, 46-60; assoc prof, Univ Ala, 60-63, prof Romance lang, Kans State Univ, 46-60; assoc prof, Univ Ala, 60-63, prof Romance lang, 63-64; prof Span & Port & grad coordr, Univ Ga, 64-80. *Concurrent Pos:* Appalachian State Teachers Col, 62-63; nat chmn comt awards for nat Span contests, Am Asn Teachers Span & Port, 62- *Mem:* Am Asn Teachers Span & Port; MLA; Inst Int Lit Iberoam; SAtlantic Mod Lang Asn; Southeastern Conf Latin Am Studies. *Res:* Contemporary Spanish and Spanish-American drama; Brazilian literature. *Publ:* Auth, Florencio Sanchez and his social consciousness of the River Plata Region, J Inter-Am Studies, 10/66; Somes notes on the prose style of Eduardo Barrios, Romance Notes, autumn 67; Valle-Inclan's self-plagiarism in plot and characterization, Rev Estud Hisp, 1/72. *Mailing Add:* 230 Rivermont Rd Athens GA 30606

RAMIREZ DE ARELLANO, DIANA, b New York, NY, June 3, 19. ROMANCE LANGUAGES. *Educ:* Univ PR, BA, 41; Columbia Univ, MA, 46; Univ Madrid, PhD(philos, lett), 52, Lic Filol Mod, 59. *Prof Exp:* Instr Span, Univ NC, 46-48; from instr to asst prof, Douglass Col, Rutgers Univ, 48-58; asst prof lang & lit, 58-72, PROF CREATIVE WRITING & POETRY, CITY COL NEW YORK, 72- *Concurrent Pos:* Consult, Ford Found PhD Scholar Prog, 72-73; consult, Dept Health, Educ& Welfare, Washington, DC, 76- & Can Coun for Arts, 76- *Honors & Awards:* First Prize in Lit, Inst Lit Puertorriquena, Univ PR, 58; Dipl de Honor & Gold Medal Poetry, Ateneo Puertorriqueno; Best Bk Written by a Woman Award, Club Civico de Damas de PR, 58; Prize in Lit Criticism, Univ PR, 61; Dipl of Honor, Puerto Rican Asn Journalists & Writers, 63; Silver Medal Prize for Lit, Ministry Cult & Educ Bolivia, 63; Gold Medal & Trophy, CSCD River Oeste Seccion Cult, Guayaquil, 66; Dipl of Honor, Inst Ecuatorian Cult, New York, 66. *Mem:* Corresp mem Hisp Soc Am; Am Asn Teachers Span & Port; MLA; AAUP; Pen Club. *Res:* Spanish Golden Age theater, especially Lope de Vega; contemporary, Spanish and Spanish American poetry and literary criticism; 20th century poetry, especially Pedro Salinas. *Publ:* Auth, Poesia Contemporanea en Lengua Espanola, Bibliot Aristarco Erudicion 7 Criticia, Madrid, 61; Privilegio, Ateneo, PR, 63; Tributo a la poesia de Clara Lair, Rev Inst Cult Puertorriquena, 3/67; Del Senalado Oficio de la Muerte (poetry), Ateneo, Madrid-New York, 74; Homenaje a Andres Iduarte, In: Estudio de Majestad Negra de Pales Matos, Am Hisp, 76; Estudio critico de concepcion de Estevarena, Madrid, 79; Arbol en Vispera (poetry) & Relecxiones en torno a la dimension humana de Josefina Romo-Arregui, Ateneo Puertorrigueno (in press). *Mailing Add:* 23 Harbor Circle Centerport NY 11721

RAMMUNY, RAJI M, b Rammun, Jordan, Nov 9, 33; m 67; c 1. APPLIED LINGUISTICS. *Educ:* Univ Baghdad, BA, 59; Univ Mich, MA, 63, PhD(applied ling), 66. *Prof Exp:* Teacher ministry educ, Jordan, 49-55 & 59-62; asst prof & res assoc, 66-71, assoc prof, 71-77, PROF ARABIC, UNIV MICH, ANN ARBOR, 77- *Concurrent Pos:* Consult, Arabic & Islamic Community Schs in US & Can, 75- & Biling-Bicult Educ, Mich, 76-, Arabic Progs for Non-Arabs in several Arab & African Univs, 81- *Mem:* Mid East Studies Asn (pres, 74); Am Asn Teachers Arabic; Am Coun Teaching Foreign Lang. *Res:* Arabic linguistics; preparation of instructional materials for teaching Arabic; syntax of modern literary Arabic. *Publ:* Coauth, Elementary Modern Standard Arabic, 75; auth, Al-Qirazah al-Arabiyyah, Philol & Scripts, 78; Statistical study of errors made by American studients in written Arabic, Al-Arabiyya, 78; Functional and semantic developments in negation as used in Modern Arabic, JNES, 78; Integration of Literary Texts and A & V Materials in Teaching Advanced Arabic Composition, Al-Arabiyya, 79; Advanced Arabic Composition, Texts and Students Guide, 80; Al-Qirazah al-Arabiyyah: Texts and grammar, 82. *Mailing Add:* Dept of Near Eastern Studies Univ of Mich Ann Arbor MI 48104

RAMOS, ALICIA, b Madrid, Spain, Jan 13, 48. CONTEMPORARY SPANISH LITERATURE. *Educ:* Northern Ill Univ, BA, 74; Northwestern Univ, MA, 75, PhD(Span lit), 80. *Prof Exp:* Teaching asst Span, Northwestern Univ, 74-77; INSTR SPAN & LIT, UNIV MO-ST LOUIS, 77- *Res:* Contemporary Spanish-American literature; modernism. *Publ:* Auth, Cinco poetas espanoles en USA, Cuaderno Literario, No 18, 78; Texto y contexto en Reivindicacion del Conde Don Julian, Insula, 11-12/79; Conversacion con Buero Vallejo, Pueblo, 79; Conversacion con Carmen Martin Gaite, Hisp J, Vol I, No 2; Las transformaciones de Don Alvaro, figuron y seneca en Reivindicacion, Cuadernos de Invest Filol, fall 81; Literature y Confesion, Ed Arame, Madrid, 82; Luis Riaza: El dramaturgo y su obra, Estreno, Vol 8, No 1. *Mailing Add:* Dept of Mod Foreign Lang Univ of Mo St Louis MO 63121

RAMOS, TERESITA VILLARICA, b Pampanga, Philippines. LINGUISTICS, SECOND LANGUAGE TEACHING. *Educ:* Univ Philippines, BS, 52; Univ Mich, MA, 58; Univ Calif, Los Angeles, MA, 64; Univ Hawaii, PhD(ling), 73. *Prof Exp:* Teacher English, Bur Pub Schs, Quezon City, Philippines, 52-59, gen educ supvr I, Instruct Div, Manila, 60-61, supvr II, Sec Educ Div, 61-67, supvr III, 67-70, supvr curric coord, 70-73; from instr to asst prof Tagalog, 70-76, ASSOC PROF FILIPINO, UNIV HAWAII, MANOA, 76- *Concurrent Pos:* Instr English, Univ East, Philippines, 58-60; lang coordr & linguist, Peace Corps training ctr, Univ Hawaii, Hilo, 67-68; asst researcher Tagalog, Pac & Asian Ling Inst, Univ Hawaii, Manoa, 68-69; Fulbright-Smith Mundt scholar, 57-58; Philippine Ctr Lang Study Scholar, 63-64; East-West Ctr Scholar, 64-66. *Mem:* Ling Soc Am; Teachers of English to Speakers of Other Lang; Nat Asn Biling Educ; Nat Asn Asian & Pac Am Educ. *Res:* Second language acquisition; Philippine literature and culture. *Publ:* Auth, Makabagong Balarila ng Pilipino, Rex Bkstore, Manila, 71; coauth, Tagalog for Beginners, 71, auth, Tagalog dictionary, 71 & Tagalog Structures, 71, Univ Hawaii, The microwave approach to teaching Pilipino, Philippine J Lang Teaching, 72; The case system of Tagalog verbs, Pac Long, 73; The role of verbal features in the subcategorization of Tagalog verbs, Philippine J Ling, 75; coauth, Bilingualism and Bilingual Education, Cultural Publ, 75; Intermediate Tagalog, Univ Hawaii, 81; auth, A Teachers Guide to the Teaching of Tagalog for Communication, NODAC, 82. *Mailing Add:* Dept of Indo-Pac Lang Univ of Hawaii Manoa Honolulu HI 96822

RAMOS-GASCON, ANTONIO, b Madrid, Spain, Aug 15, 44; m 70; c 1. SPANISH LITERATURE. *Educ:* Univ Madrid, Lic en Derecho, 67; Univ Calif, San Diego, PhD(Span lit), 70. *Prof Exp:* Prof Span Lit, NY Univ, Spain, 70-71; asst prof, Pa State Univ, 71-73; asst prof, 73-76, ASSOC PROF SPAN LIT, UNIV MINN, MINNEAPOLIS, 76- *Mem:* MLA; Am Asn Teachers Span & Port. *Res:* Contemporary Spanish novel and poetry; 19th century Spanish novel; critical theory. *Publ:* Auth, El canuonero de Unamuno, Ed Taurus, Madrid, 67; Textos, 5/72 & Cuatro libros sabre novela espanola, 5/72, Libre, Paris; Clarin y Unamuno, Cuadernos Hispanoam, 6/72; Clarin Olvidado, Ed Jucar, Madrid, 73. *Mailing Add:* Dept of Span & Port Univ of Minn Minneapolis MN 55455

RAMOS-OREA, TOMAS, b Alcala de Henares, Spain, Sept 29, 36. ENGLISH LITERATURE; MATRIMONIAL LAW. *Educ:* Univ Madrid, lic English philol, 59, Dr en Filol, 61; Univ Granada, Spain, lic law, 77, Dr in Law, 80. *Prof Exp:* From instr to asst prof Span lit, Mich State Univ, 61-63; asst prof, Univ Western Ont, 63-65; assoc prof, Queen's Univ, 65-71; PROF ENGLISH LIT, UNIV GRANADA, SPAIN, 72- *Concurrent Pos:* Arts Res Comt award, Queen's Univ, 67; Can Coun grant, 68; vis lectr, Dept Hisp Studies, Univ Bristol, 82. *Res:* Spanish literature; comparative literature. *Publ:* Auth, La nocion de amor en tres poetas neorromanticons ingleses actuales, Filol Mod, Madrid, 10/66-1/67; Investigacion y creacion, Hispania, 5/69; La nocion de Piedad en el romance Angelica y Medoro de Gongora, Rev Lit, Madrid, 7-12/69; Hacia un intento metodologico para la definicion de poesia y la distincion contrastiva de sus supuestos, 10/76 & Tres poemas del laureado Betjeman, Vol 6-7, 79, Estud Filol Inglesa, Granada; La esencia negocial del matrimonio, In: Tesis doctorales de la Universidad de Granada, Facultad Derecho, Granada, 80; Matrimonio y otros contratos: Aspectos comparativos, equiparables y subsumibles mutuamente, Rev Derecho Notarial, 7-12/81. *Mailing Add:* Dept of Ingles Univ of Granada Granada Spain

RAMSEY, JEROME A, b New Orleans, La, June 5, 29; m 57; c 2. ROMANCE LANGUAGES. *Educ:* Univ Tex, El Paso, BA, 51; Northwestern Univ, MA, 53; Univ Chicago, PhD(French), 62. *Prof Exp:* Asst prof French, Univ Mich, 60-65; ASST PROF FRENCH, STATE UNIV NY BINGHAMTON, 65- *Mem:* MLA. *Res:* Seventeenth century French; literary criticism. *Publ:* Auth, Valincour and the critical tradition, Mod Philol, 5/68. *Mailing Add:* Dept of French State Univ of NY Binghamton NY 13901

RAMSEY, JOHN TYLER, b Auburn, NY, July 13, 46; m 76; c 1. LATIN LITERATURE, ROMAN HISTORY. *Educ:* Harvard Univ, AB, 68, PhD(class philol), 75; Balliol Col, BA, 70. *Prof Exp:* Teaching fel Latin, Harvard Univ, 73-75; asst prof, 75-81, ASSOC PROF CLASSICS, UNIV ILL AT CHICAGO CIRCLE, 81- *Concurrent Pos:* Vis assoc prof classics & hist, Univ Chicago, spring, 82. *Mem:* Am Philol Asn; Am Class League; Class Asn Can; Asn Ancient Historians. *Res:* Roman republican history; Latin prose. *Publ:* Auth, Studies in Asconius, Harvard Studies Class Philol, 76; A reconstruction of Q Gallius' trail for Ambitus, Historia, 80; The prosecution of C Manilius in 66 BC and Cicero's pro Manilio, Phoenix, 80; Cicero, pro Sulla 68 and Catiline's candidacy in 66 BC, Harvard Studies Class Philol, 82; ed, Bellum Catilinae, Scholars Press, 82. *Mailing Add:* Dept of Classics Univ Ill Chicago IL 60680

RAND, EARL JAMES, b Bakersfield, Calif, Aug 5, 33; c 2. ENGLISH AS SECOND LANGUAGE. *Educ:* Univ Calif, Los Angeles, BA, 54; Univ Tex MA, 61, PhD(ling), 66. *Prof Exp:* Ling specialist, Univ Tex, 62-65; asst prof, 66-72, ASSOC PROF ENGLISH, UNIV CALIF, LOS ANGELES, 72- *Concurrent Pos:* Adv ministry educ, Repub China, 62-65; consult, Bur Indian Affairs, US Dept Interior, 67 & 68; adv India Inst Technol, Kanpur, India, 68-70; vis prof English, Chinese Univ Hong Kong, 72-73; adv, Univ Zaire, 74; deleg applied ling to People's Repub China, 77; consult, US Trust Territories, 77. *Mem:* Ling Soc Am; Teachers English to Speakers of Other Lang; Nat Coun Measurement Educ; Am Educ Res Asn. *Res:* Teaching English as a second language, especially testing; composition; computer applications to second language instruction and research. *Publ:* Auth, Oral Approach Drills, 64 & coauth, Oral Approach Drill Pictures, 65, TNU, Taipei; auth, The English irregular verb, English Teaching Forum, 65; Alabaman phonology: A structural sketch, Int J Am Ling, 68; Mandarin Chinese Interrogative Structures, Univ Calif, 68; Constructing Dialogs, 68, Constructing Sentences, 70 & Drills on the English Verb Auxiliary, 70, Holt. *Mailing Add:* Dept of English Univ of Calif Los Angeles CA 90024

RANDALL, EARLE STANLEY, b Rockland, Mass, Aug 7, 11; m 39. GERMAN, FRENCH. *Educ:* Harvard Univ, AB, 33, AM, 34, PhD(Romance lang), 40. *Prof Exp:* Instr Spanish, Harvard Univ, 37-38; from instr to asst prof French & Span, Northwestern Univ, 38-43; lectr French & Ger, Rockford Col, Ill, 48; from assoc prof to prof mod lang, Purdue Univ, West Lafayette, 48-77, emer prof, 77-80; RETIRED. *Concurrent Pos:* Dir mod lang proj, Boston, Mass, 59-61. *Honors & Awards:* Palmes Academiques, 62. *Mem:* MLA; Am Asn Teachers Fr; Am Asn Teachers Ger; Ned Ver Leraren in Levende Talen. *Res:* Foreign language in the elementary school; audiovisual aids; language laboratory. *Publ:* Auth, What have we learned about FLES?, AV Instr, 11/62; The Jewish character in the French novel, 1870-1914. *Mailing Add:* 211 Dehart West Lafayette IN 47906

RANDALL, WILLIAM MADISON, b Belleville, Mich, Aug 16, 99; m 24, 54; c 2. LINGUISTICS. *Educ:* Univ Mich, AB, 21, MA, 24; Hartford Sem Found, PHD(Arabic), 29. *Hon Degrees:* LittD, Univ NC, 71. *Prof Exp:* Instr ling, Kennedy Sch, Hartford Sem Found, 25-29; from assoc prof to prof libr sci, Univ Chicago, 29-42, asst dean students, 38-42; dir libr, Univ Ga, 46-47; dean, US Merchant Marine Acad, 48-51; dean, 51-58, pres, 58-68, prof mod lang, 68-78, PROF ARABIC & LING & EMER PRES, UNIV NC, WILMINGTON, 68- *Concurrent Pos:* Consult, Carnegie Corp, 29-32; Gen Educ Bd fel, Mid East, 35; Am Coun Learned Soc fel, Mid East, 38; consult, Small Bus Admin, US Gov, 70- *Res:* Librarianship; college administration; general linguistics. *Publ:* Auth, The College Library, 32, coauth, Administration of College Library, 35 & 38 & Acquisition and Cataloging of Books, 40, Univ Chicago. *Mailing Add:* 4622 Mockingbird Lane Wilmington NC 28403

RANDOLPH, DONALD ALLEN, b Fresno, Calif, Mar 13, 31; m 59; c 1. SPANISH LANGUAGE & LITERATURE. *Educ:* Univ Calif, Berkeley, BA, 53, PhD(romance lang), 63; Middlebury Col, MA, 57. *Prof Exp:* Asst prof, Calif State Univ, Los Angeles, 63-67; assoc prof, 67-71, PROF SPAN, UNIV MIAMI, 71- *Mem:* MLA; SAtlantic Mod Lang Asn; Asoc Int Hispanistas. *Res:* Eighteenth and 19th century Spanish literature; 19th century Spanish literary criticism. *Publ:* Auth, Eugenio de Ochoa y el romanticismo espanol, Univ Calif, 66; Cartas de D Eugenio de Ochoa a sus cunados, D Federico y D Luis de Madrazo, Boletin Bibl Menendez Pelayo, 67; Un caso de arrepentimiento?: Canete ante la muerte de la Avellaneda, La Torre, 68; Pervivencia de algunos temas del siglo XVIII en la literatura espanola, Boletin Bibl Menendez Pelayo, 71; Don Manuel Canete: Cronista literario del romantiscismo y del posromanticismo en Espana, Univ NC, 72; Unos Caines, sus armas, y el Cain mestizo de Caballero Calderon, Boletin Bibliot Menendez Pelayo, 76; La genesis de La espada y la lira de Fernando de Gabriel, Archivo Hispalense, 77; La imprecision estetica en Klail City y sus alrededores, Revista Chicano-yi quena, 81. *Mailing Add:* Dept of Foreign Lang Univ of Miami Coral Gables FL 33124

RANEY, GEORGE WILLIAM, b Haverhill, Mass, May 5, 38; m 68; c 4. LINGUISTICS, ENGLISH AS A SECOND LANGUAGE. *Educ:* Loyola Univ Los Angeles, BA, 61; Univ Southern Calif, MA, 66, PhD(ling), 72. *Prof Exp:* Lang coordr, Tagalog, Peace Corps, Philippines, 66 & Univ Hawaii, Hilo, 66; Fulbright lectr teaching English as foreign lang, Adam Mickiewicz Univ, Poznan, 67-68; lectr English as second lang, Univ Southern Calif, 68-69; asst prof, 69-74, dir English as second lang, 72-77, fac develop fel, 76, ASSOC PROF LING, CALIF STATE UNIV, FRESNO, 74- *Concurrent Pos:* Consult, Bur Indian Affairs, 67; ed, Calif Ling Newslett, 73-76. *Mem:* Teachers English to Speakers Other Lang; Ling Soc Am; AAUP. *Res:* English grammar; applied linguistics. *Publ:* Auth, Using the National Observer in the ESOL classroom, Teachers English to Speakers Other Lang Newslett, 4/76; On using the National Observer as an ESOL teaching device, Calif Asn of Teachers English to Speakers Other Lang, fall, 76. *Mailing Add:* Dept of Ling Calif State Univ Fresno CA 93740

RANGEL-GUERRERO, DANIEL, b Guadalajara, Mex, Dec 22, 35; m 64. ROMANCE LANGUAGES. *Educ:* Stanford Univ, BA, 62; Univ Ore, MA, 64, PhD(Romance lang), 67. *Prof Exp:* From instr to asst prof Span, Univ NC, Chapel Hill, 66-68; asst prof, Eastern NMex Univ, 68-69; asst prof, 69-72, ASSOC PROF SPAN, WESTERN WASH STATE COL, 72- *Mem:* Am Asn Teachers Span & Port; Pac Northwest Conf Foreign Lang. *Res:* Mexican culture and civilization; Chicano literature; Golden Age literature. *Publ:* Auth, Interpretacion de Sabor a vida, Romance Notes, 68; Algun dia llegara la noche, Original Works, Louvain, 71; Color y luz en Azorin, 71, Gil Vicente: Comedia sobre a divisa da cidade de Coimbra: Una interpretacion, 74 & La responsabilidad en la Comedia de Rubena, 75, Proc Pac Northwest Conf Foreign Lang; Bibliographical checklist for historia Verdadera de la Conquista de la Nueva Espana, Studies Hist & Soc, 76; The Labyrinth of Solitude-Revisited, Proc Pac Northwest Conf Foreign Lang, 77; Poemas en espanol, Tejidos, 77. *Mailing Add:* Dept of Foreign Lang Western Wash State Col Bellingham WA 98225

RANWEZ, ALAIN DANIEL, b Paris, France, June 25, 44; US citizen; m 68; c 2. FRENCH LITERATURE. *Educ:* Montclair State Col, BA, 67; Univ Mo, Columbia, PHD(French, Ital), 74. *Prof Exp:* Asst prof French, Northern State Col, 71-72; asst prof, 72-80, ASSOC PROF FRENCH, METROP STATE COL, 80- *Concurrent Pos:* Nat Endowment for Humanities fel comp lit, Univ Chicago, 75; mem bibliog staff foreign lang, Am Coun Teachers Foreign Lang, 78-; Nat Endowment for Humanities fel, Wash Univ, 80. *Mem:* MLA; Am Coun Teachers Foreign Lang; Rocky Mountain Mod Lang Asn; Am Asn Teachers Fr. *Res:* Post World War II French novel; French feminine writing. *Publ:* Auth, Baudelaire's Une Charogne, Explicator, summer 77; Sartre's Les Temps Modernes, Whitston, 79. *Mailing Add:* Dept of French Metrop State Col Denver CO 80204

RAPHAEL, ROBERT, b Los Angeles, Calif, Sept 25, 27. GERMANIC LANGUAGES & LITERATURES. *Educ:* Univ Calif, Los Angeles, PhD(Ger lit), 61. *Prof Exp:* Asst prof Ger & Scand, 62-72, ASSOC PROF SCAND, QUEENS COL, NY, 72- *Concurrent Pos:* Mem, Publ Comt Am-Scand Found, 74-78. *Mem:* Assoc mem Soc Advan Scan Studies; MLA. *Res:* Interpretation of the dramas of Richard Wagner and Henrik Ibsen; book on relation of eroticism to human behavior in Wagner's Tristan and Parsifal; interrelation of these two works. *Publ:* Auth, Illusion and the self in Ibsen's Wild Duck, Rosmersholm & Lady from the sea, 2/63 & From Hedda Gabler to When We Dead Awaken, 2/64, Scan Studies; Richard Wagner, Twayne, 69; Intro to 2nd English ed of J P Jacobsen's Marie Grubbe, Libr scand Lit, 4/75; Hedda Gabler bis Wenn wir Toten erwachen (Ger transl), In: Wege der Forschung, Vol CDLXXXVII, Wis Buchgesell, Darmstadt, 77. *Mailing Add:* Dept of Lang Queens Col New York NY 10023

RAPPAPORT, GILBERT CHARLES, b Philadelphia, Pa, Oct 5, 51; m 80. SLAVIC LANGUAGES, GENERAL LINGUISTICS. *Educ:* Mass Inst Technol, SB, 73; Univ Calif, Los Angeles, MA, 75, PhD(Slavic lang & lit), 79. *Prof Exp:* ASST PROF SLAVIC LANG, UNIV TEX, AUSTIN, 79- *Mem:* Ling Soc Am; Am Asn Teachers of Slavic & East Europ Lang. *Res:* Syntax of Slavic languages; general linguistic theory. *Publ:* Auth, Deixis and detachment in the adverbial participles of Russian, Forms & Meanings: Morphosyntax in Slavic, Slavica Publ, 80; Distinctive and redundant contrasts in Jakobsonian phonology, Slavic & East Europ J, 81. *Mailing Add:* Dept Slavic Lang Univ Tex Austin TX 78712

RASCO, RAFAEL G, b Sagua La Grande, Cuba, Jan 3, 17; m 57; c 3. SPANISH. *Educ:* Univ Havana, Lic, 47, LLD, 49. *Prof Exp:* Instr Span, St Paul's Sch, Garden City, NY 60-62; Adelphi Suffolk Col, 62-63; asst prof to assoc prof, 63-80, PROF SPAN & DIR LANG LAB, C W POST CTR, LONG ISLAND UNIV, 80- *Mem:* MLA. *Res:* Languages and literature; Spanish and Spanish-American literature; history and history of Spanish and Spanish-American cultures. *Publ:* Auth, Nosotros y la Hispanidad, In: Diario de la marina, 46; El caballo marino, 48; cuentos y leyendas de Cuba, 64. *Mailing Add:* Lang Lab C W Post Ctr Long Island Univ Greenvale NY 11548

RASHKIN, ESTHER JOAN, b New York, NY. FRENCH & COMPARATIVE LITERATURE. *Educ:* Queens Col, BA, 73; Yale Univ, MA, 74, PhD(French), 79. *Prof Exp:* ASST PROF FRENCH, DARTMOUTH COL, 79- *Mem:* Am Asn Univ Professors; MLA; Northeast Mod Lang Asn. *Res:* Nineteenth century prose fiction, European and American; 19th century French symbolist poetry; modern psychoanalytic and linguistic theory. *Publ:* Auth, Truth's turn: Rereading the fantastic in Villiers's Vera, Romanic Rev, 11/81; Secret crimes, haunted signs: Villiers's L'Intersigne, Stanford French Rev, 5/82; Signes cryptes, Rimes dorees: Facino Cane de Balzac, Cahiers de Confrontation, 11/82. *Mailing Add:* 67 E Wheelock St Hanover NH 03755

RASI, HUMBERTO MARIO, b Buenos Aires, Argentina, Mar 23, 35; US citizen; m 57; c 2. SPANISH AMERICAN LITERATURE. *Educ:* Inst Superior Prof, Buenos Aires, prof, 60; San Jose State Col, MA, 66; Stanford Univ, PhD(Span), 71. *Prof Exp:* Asst ed, Pac Press, Mountain View, Calif, 62-66; from asst prof to assoc prof, Andrews Univ, 68-76, chmn mod lang dept, 69-75, prof Span & Span-Am lit & dean sch grad studies, 76-78; CHIEF ED INT PUBL, PACIFIC PRESS PUBL ASN, 78- *Concurrent Pos:* Contrib ed, Handbook of Latin Am Studies, Hispanic Found, Libr Cong, 72-; Nat Endowment Humanities fel, Romance langs dept, Johns Hopkins Univ, 75-76. *Mem:* MLA; Am Asn Teachers Span & Port; Inst Int Lit Iberoam. *Res:* Spanish American literature; modern Spanish literature; Latin American history. *Publ:* Auth, The final creole: Borges' view of Argentine history, TriQ, fall 72; Borges frente a la poesia gauchesca, Rev Iberoam, 3/74; David Vinas, novelista y critico comprometido, Rev Iberoam, 4-6/76; Borges en busca de la patria, Cuadernos Am, 6-7/76; Las anforas de Epicuro: Frontera entre dos Darios, Anales Lit Hispanoam, 76; Borges y los Anales de Buenos Aires, Rev Interam Bibliog, 77; Borges ante Lugones: Divergencias y convergencias, Rev Iberoam, 2/77. *Mailing Add:* PO Box 7000 Mountain View CA 94042

RASICO, PHILIP DONALD, b Indianapolis, Ind, Mar 26, 52; m 78; c 1. HISPANIC & ROMANCE LINGUISTICS. *Educ:* Xavier Univ, Ohio, AB, 74; Ind Univ, Bloomington, MA, 75, PhD(Hisp ling), 81. *Prof Exp:* Asst prof Span & Catalan, Ind Univ, Bloomington, 81-82; ASST PROF SPAN LANG & LING, UNIV NH, 82- *Mem:* MLA; Am Asn Teachers Span & Port; North Am Catalan Soc; Associacio Int Llengua Lit Catalanes. *Res:* Catalan language and linguistics. *Publ:* Auth, Alguns problemes cronologics de les sibilants catalanes, In: Actes de Ier Colloqui d'Estudis Catalans a Nord America, Montserrat, Barcelona, 79; Sobre l'evolucio de les consonants L-, -LL-, N-, -NN- en catala antic, Els Marges, 20: 99-106; El desenvolupament dels fonemes /z/ i /s/ en el catala preliterari, In: Homentage a Josep M de Casacuberta, Montserrat, Barcelona, 2: 5-24; El tractament catala dels grups de nasal o liquida mes oclusiva, In: Miscellania Pere Bohigas, Montserrat, Barcelona, 1: 9-25; Old Catalan COR and the phonological evolutions UA> o, O> ua, Papers in Romance, 3: 179-188; Envers una caracteritzacio fonologica del catala preliterari, In: Actes del IIon Colloqui d'Estudis Catalans a Nord-America, Montserrat, Barcelona, 82. *Mailing Add:* Dept of Ancient & Mod Lang & Lit Univ of NH Durham NH 03824

RASMUSSEN, KENNETH, b Murray, Utah, Sept 18, 36; div; c 5. PORTUGUESE. *Educ:* Brigham Young Univ, BA, 60; Univ Wis-Madison, MA, 66, PhD(Port), 71. *Prof Exp:* ASSOC PROF PORT, STATE UNIV NEW YORK, BUFFALO, 66- *Concurrent Pos:* Examr Port, Ctr Critical Lang, 70- *Mem:* Am Asn Teachers Span & Port; New England Coun Latin Am Studies. *Res:* Hispanic and Luso-Brazilian linguistics. *Publ:* Coauth, A comparative study in the teaching of Spanish through team-teaching and supervised independent study, Mod Lang J, 73; auth, Brazilian Portuguese Terms for Sexual Intercourse, Orbis, 73; Portuguese Studies; Language, In: The Year's Work in Modern Language Studies, 76. *Mailing Add:* Dept of Mod Lang & Lit State Univ NY Buffalo NY 14260

RASSNER, RONALD MARK, b Detroit, Mich, Sept 18, 46; m 69; c 2. AFRICAN ORAL & WRITTEN LITERATURE. *Educ:* Univ Houston, Ba, 68; Univ Wis-Madison, MA, 77, PhD(African lang hist), 80. *Prof Exp:* ASST PROF AFRO-AM STUDIES, SPAN & PORT DEPT, YALE UNIV, 79- *Res:* Comparative folklore; bioaesthetics; literary criticism. *Publ:* Auth (as Tomas Jacinto), The art of Luandino Vieira, In: Critical Perspectives in Lusophone African Literatures, Three Continents Press, 81; Abdias do Nascimento's Sortilegio: One perspective on syncretism and deculturation in Brazil, In: Studies in Afro-Hispanic Literature, Medgar Evers Col Press, 82; Luso-African writers, In: Encycl Britannica Micropaedia Project, Michigan State Univ, 82; Palmares and the freed slave in Afro-Brazilian literature, In: Black Narratives in Latin America, Garland Press, 82; The oral narrative from Africa to Brazil, Res African Lit, fall 82; A supprimer le temps: Image in African oral narrative, J African & Comp Lit, 82; Narrative rhythms in Giryama Ngano: Oral patterns and musical structures, In: The Oral

Performance in Africa, Longman Group, Harlow, England & Ibadan Univ Press (in press); A Bibliography of Written Literatures in African Languages, Garland Press (in press). *Mailing Add:* 6892 Yale Station New Haven CT 06520

RASTATTER, PAUL HENRY, b Dubuque, Iowa, Apr 9, 31. ROMANCE LANGUAGES. *Educ:* Loras Col, BA, 53; Univ Louvain, BA, 57; Univ Ore, MA, 62, PhD(Romance lang), 66. *Prof Exp:* Instr Latin & ethics, Loras Col, 59-60, French & Span, 64-66, asst prof French, 66-69; assoc prof, Emporia State Univ, 69-71; assoc prof, Bradley Univ, 71-75, dir foreign lang, 75-80. *Mem:* MLA; Am Coun Teaching Foreign Lang; AAUP; Am Asn Teachers Fr. *Res:* Language career training; phonetics; language practice. *Mailing Add:* 5818 W Orlando Dr Peoria IL 61614

RATHE, CHARLES EDWARD, b Toronto, Ont, Apr 15, 28; m 61; c 3. FRENCH. *Educ:* Univ Toronto, BA, 50, MA, 52; Syracuse Univ, PhD(humanities), 60. *Prof Exp:* Lectr French, Univ Toronto, 55-58, from asst prof to assoc prof, 58-69; chmn dept, 69-76, PROF FRENCH LIT, YORK UNIV, ONT, 69-, MASTER, FOUNDERS COL, YORK UNIV, 76- *Concurrent Pos:* Coordr, Educ & Cult Exchange Prog, Ont Dept Educ, 67-69. *Mem:* Renaissance Soc Am; Asn Can Univ Teachers Fr; Can Soc Renaissance Studies. *Res:* Innocent Gentillet and 16th century French political theory; Michel de Montaigne; African literature in French. *Publ:* Auth, Innocent Gentillet and the first anti-Machiavel, Bibliot Humanisme et Renaissance, 65; ed, Innocent Gentillet: L'antiMachiavel, Droz, 68; auth, La Sagesse gauloise de Montaigne, Bull Sco Amis Montaigne, 4-6/69; The theatricality of Montaigne and the problem of self-knowledge, In: Essay & Studies in Honor of Albert Menut, Coronado, 73. *Mailing Add:* Dept of French Lit York Univ Downsview ON M3J 1P3 Can

RATIU, BASIL, b Aurora, Ill, Sept 2, 21. ROMANCE LANGUAGES. *Educ:* Univ Chicago, AB, 47; Ind Univ, AM, 49; Columbia Univ, PhD(French), 60. *Prof Exp:* Instr Ger, DePaul Univ, 49-50; instr French, Mundelein Col, 51-52; instr French & Ger, Immaculate Heart Col, 55-57; asst prof French & Ger, Lincoln Univ, Mo; asst prof Ger, Univ Mo, 57-58; asst prof French & Span, Univ NDak, 59-60; asst prof French, Memphis State Univ, 60-61, Vanderbilt Univ, 61-62 & Mich State Univ, 62-63; assoc prof, 63-69, PROF FRENCH, MEMPHIS STATE UNIV, 69- *Mem:* Am Asn Teachers Fr; Am Asn Teachers Ger; Am Asn Teachers Span & Port; SCent Mod Lang Asn (pres, 81). *Res:* Contemporary French drama; 17th century French drama; French phonetics. *Publ:* Auth, L'Oeuvre dramatique de Steve Passeur, Marcel Didier, Paris, 64. *Mailing Add:* Dept of Foreign Lang Memphis State Univ Memphis TN 38152

RATYCH, JOANNA MARIA, b Vienna, Austria, June 12, 26; US citizen; m 57; c 1. GERMAN LANGUAGE & LITERATURE. *Educ:* Univ Munich, Staatsexamen, 56, PhD(English & Ger) 57. *Prof Exp:* From instr to asst prof, 60-70, ASSOC PROF GER, RUTGERS UNIV, 70- *Concurrent Pos:* Consult, Harpr & Row, 65- & Rinehart Press, 73-; mem & chmn, Nat Screening Comt for Fulbright travel grants, 77-78; consult & panelist, Eirik Börve, Inc, 78. *Mem:* MLA; Am Asn Teachers Ger; Am Coun Studies Austrian Lit;AAUP. *Res:* German literature of the 20th century; German stylistics. *Publ:* Auth, Zur Frage des Stilunterrichts im Ausland, Z Unterrichtsmethodik, 67; Vom sprechen zum schreiben, Ger Quart, 68; Die Textanalyse im Aufsatzunterricht, Die Unterrichtspraxis, 2/69; Interessantes aus Deutschen Zeitungen, Appleton, 69; Die bausen Weiber: Eine sprachsoziologische Wortstudie, Die Unterrichtspraxis, 1/76; co-ed, Perspectives and Personalities, Studies in Modern German Literature Honoring Claude Hill, Carl Winter Univ-Verlag, Heidelberg, 78. *Mailing Add:* 13 Outcalt Rd Edison NJ 08817

RATZ, ALFRED EGON, b Lodz, Poland, Aug 19, 30; Can citizen, m 60. GERMAN LANGUAGE AND LITERATURE. *Educ:* Univ Adelaide, BA, 61; Massey Univ, NZ, PhD(Ger), 67. *Prof Exp:* Tutor, Univ Adelaide, 63-64; lectr, Massey Univ, NZ, 64-67; from asst prof to assoc prof, 67-75, PROF GER, MEM UNIV, NEWFOUNDLAND, 75- *Concurrent Pos:* Reader, Humanities Res Coun Can, 72-; mem selection comt doctoral fels, Can Coun, 77-79. *Mem:* Can Asn Univ Teachers Ger (pres, 80-82); MLA. *Res:* Christoph Martin Wieland; Heinrich von Kleist; 19th and early 20th century German literature. *Publ:* Auth, Ricarda Huchs Der letzte Sommer: Individualismus und seine Grenze, seminar, spring 68; C M Wieland: Toleranz, Kompromiss und Ikonsequenz-eine kirtische Betrachtung, Deut Vietrelj Litwiss Geistesges, fall 68; Ausgangspunkte und Dialektik der gesellschaftlichen Ansichten C M Wielands, Seminar, spring 71; Freiheit des Individuums und Gesellschafftsordnung bei Christoph Martin Wieland, Herbert Land & Cie, Bern, 74; Fruhe Kulturarbeit deutscher Herrnhuter in Labrador, Ger-Can Yearbk, 75; Künstler und Kunst im Lichte derr Freiheitsproblematik bei C M Wieland, In: Analecta Helvetica et Germanica Eine Festschrift zu Ehren von Hermann Boeschenstein, Bouvier, Bonn, 79; ed, Proc of the Atlantic University Teachers of German Conf, October, 79, Mem Univ Newfoundland Press, 80. *Mailing Add:* Dept of Ger & Russ Mem Univ Nfld St John's NF A1B 3X9 Can

RAUBITSCHEK, ANTONY ERICH, b Vienna, Austria, Dec 4, 12; nat US; m 42; c 4. CLASSICS. *Educ:* Univ Vienna, PhD, 35. *Prof Exp:* Mem, Inst Advan Study, 38-42 & 54-55; instr classics, Yale Univ, 42-44; sr fel, Am Sch Class Studies, Athens at Inst Advan Study, 44-45; asst prof classics, Yale Univ, 45-47; assoc prof, Princeton Univ, 47-63; prof classics, 63-74, SADIE DERNHAM PATEK PROF HUMANITIES, STANFORD UNIV, 74- *Concurrent Pos:* Lectr, Univ Pa, 50-51; Fulbright vis prof, Oxford Univ & fel, Merton Col, 61; vis prof, Univ Bonn, 62; NATO vis prof, Univ Athens, 63-64, Univ Heidelberg, 65, Univ Wash, 67, Univ Köln, 67 & Am Sch Class Studies, Athens, 77. *Mem:* Ger Archaeol Inst; Austrian Archaeol Inst; Archaeol Inst Am; Am Philol Asn; Soc Prom Hellenic Studies. *Res:* Art, history and literature of Athens. *Publ:* Auth, Ostracism; Roman Athens; Historical Attic Inscriptions; Dedications from the Athenian Akropolis, Archaeol Inst Am, 49; Cretan Armorers, von Zabern, 72. *Mailing Add:* 475 Embarcadero Palo Alto CA 94301

RAUCH, IRMENGARD, b Dayton, Ohio, Apr 17, 33; m; c 2. GERMANIC LINGUISTICS. *Educ:* Univ Dayton, BS, 55; Ohio State Univ, MA, 57; Univ Mich, PhD(Ger ling), 62. *Prof Exp:* From instr to asst prof, Univ Wis, 62-66; assoc prof, Univ Pittsburgh, 66-68; assoc prof, 68-72, PROF GER LING, UNIV ILL, URBANA, 72- *Concurrent Pos:* Nat Sci Found & Ling Soc Am travel grant, Int Cong Ling, Bologna, Italy, fall 72; res bd grants, Univ Ill, 75-78 & 80-82; res grant, Eastern Ill Univ, 76 & Univ Calif, Berkeley, 79-80; ed bd, Allegorica, 76-; reader, Nat Sci Found, 77; Guggenheim fel, 82-83. *Mem:* Ling Soc Am; Int Ling Asn; Semiotic Soc Am; MLA; Am Asn Teachers Ger. *Res:* Linguistic methodology; semiotics; Germanic languages. *Publ:* Auth, The Old High German Diphthongization: A Description of a Phonemic Change, Mouton, 67; co-ed, Approaches in Linguistic Methodology, Univ Wis, 67, Span ed, 74; Der Heliand, Wiss Buchgesellschaft, 74; Linguistic Method: Essays in Honor of Herbert Penzz, Mouton, 79; The Signifying Animal: The Grammar of Language and Experience, Ind Univ Press, 80. *Mailing Add:* Dept of Ger Lang & Lit Univ of Ill Urbana IL 61801

RAUCH, MARGARETE WOELFEL, b Leipzig, Ger, Jan 17, 12; US citizen; m 61. LINGUISTICS. *Educ:* Univ Leipzig, PhD, 36. *Prof Exp:* Asst French & Ger, Höhere Sch Frauenberufe, Leipzig, 35-37; prof French, Ger & Span, Shenandoah Col, 38-42; prof, 42-76, head dept foreign lang, 53-76, EMER PROF FOREIGN LANG, JAMES MADISON UNIV, VA , 76- *Mem:* Am Asn Teachers Fr. *Res:* Teaching modern languages with or without electronic equipment; translations of Seume. *Publ:* Auth, Modern foreign language after the war, Madison Quart, 44; Friedrich Seume, William & Mary Quart, 48. *Mailing Add:* Dept of Foreign Lang James Madison Univ Harrisonburg VA 22801

RAUN, ALO, b Tartu, Estonia, May 8, 05; nat US; m 34; c 2. URALIC LINGUISTICS. *Educ:* Univ Tartu, MPh, 31, PhD, 42. *Prof Exp:* Lectr, Univ Tartu, 35-37; sci secy, Acad Soc Estonian Lang, 37-39; lectr, 39, reader, 40-44; assoc prof, Baltic Univ, 46-49; asst prof Romance lang, Pac Lutheran Univ, 49-51; vis asst prof ling, 52-55, from asst prof to prof, 55-75, EMER PROF LING & URALIC & ALTAIC STUDIES, IND UNIV, BLOOMINGTON, 75- *Concurrent Pos:* Lectr, Univ Turku, 38-39; Guggenheim fel, 51-52; Fulbright res fel, Finland, 60-61; fel, Baltic Res Inst, Bonn, Ger. *Mem:* Emer mem Ling Soc Am; hon mem Soc Uralo-Altaica; fel Finno-Ugric Soc; fel Kalevala Soc; fel Finnish Lit Soc. *Res:* Uralic and general linguistics. *Publ:* Auth, The Mordva, Human Rels Area Files, 55; coauth, The First Cheremis Grammar, Newberry, 56; auth, The equivalents of English than in Finno-Ugric, Am Studies Uralic Ling, 60; coauth, Introduction to Estonian Linguistics, Harrassowitz, 65; auth, Basic Course in Uzbek, Ind Univ, 69; Essays in Finno-Ugric and Finnic Linguistics, Ind Univ, 71; The Mordva, Human Rels Area Files; Etümol teatmik, Maarjamaa, 82. *Mailing Add:* 1419 Nancy St Bloomington IN 47401

RAUSCHER, GERHARD, b Stuttgart, Ger, Nov 1, 29; US citizen. GERMAN. *Educ:* Univ Tübingen, PhD(English, Ger & hist), 57. *Prof Exp:* Studienreferendar & Studienassessor, Wagenburg-Gymnasium, Stuttgart, 58-62; from inst to assoc prof, 62-70, chmn dept, 66-71 & 76-79, PROF GER, UNIV WIS-MILWAUKEE, 70- *Concurrent Pos:* Articulated Instructional Media grant, 65-66; chmn dept Slavic lang, Univ Wis-Milwaukee, 67-68. *Honors & Awards:* Edward & Rosa Uhrig Mem Award Excellent Teaching, 66. *Mem:* MLA; Am Asn Teachers Ger; Am Coun Teaching Foreign Lang; AAUP. *Res:* German civilization and culture; German stylistics; German-Americana. *Publ:* Co-ed, Twain, Mark: Old times on the Mississippi, Diesterweg, Frankfurt/Main, Ger 61. *Mailing Add:* Dept of Ger Univ of Wis PO Box 413 Milwaukee WI 53201

RAVA, SUSAN R, b St Louis, Mo, June 6, 39; m 65; c 3. FRENCH LITERATURE. *Educ:* Vassar Col, BA, 61; Washington Univ, MA, 71, PhD(Fr lit), 77. *Prof Exp:* Instr French, Univ Mo, St Louis, 77-78; vis asst prof, 78-80, LECTR FRENCH, WASHINGTON UNIV, ST LOUIS, 80- *Mem:* MLA; Womens Caucus for Mod Lang; Soc des amis de Marcel Proust. *Res:* Language in the work of Marguerite Duras; Marcel Proust; dialogue in the work of Gustave Flaubert. *Publ:* Auth, The narratee in Proust, Essays in Lit, fall 81. *Mailing Add:* Dept of Romance Lang Box 1077 Washington Univ St Louis MO 63130

RAWLINGS, HUNTER RIPLEY, III, b Norfolk, Va, Dec 14, 44; m 67; c 2. CLASSICAL PHILOLOGY, ANCIENT HISTORY. *Educ:* Haverford Col, BA, 66; Princeton Univ, PhD (classics), 70. *Prof Exp:* Asst prof, 70-74, assoc prof, 75-80, PROF CLASSICS, UNIV COLO, 80- *Concurrent Pos:* Jr fel classics, Ctr Hellenic Studies, 75-76; ed-in-chief, Class J, 77- *Mem:* Am Philol Asn; Class Asn Midwest & South; Am Inst Archaeol; Asn Ancient Historians. *Res:* Greek and Roman historiography; Greek and Roman history; classical linguistics. *Publ:* Auth, A Semantic Study of Prophasis to 400 BC, Hermes Einzelschriften, Heft, 33, 75; Antiochus the Great and Rhodes 197-191 BC, Am J Ancient Hist, 76; Thucydides on the purpose of the Delian League, Phoenix, 77; Giving desertion as a pretext: Thucydides 7.13.2, Class Philol, 78; The Structure of Thucydides' History, Princeton Univ Press, 81. *Mailing Add:* Dept of Classics Univ of Colo Boulder CO 80309

RAYMOND, AGNES G (MRS MARSHALL C HOWARD), b York, Pa, Feb 14, 16; m 43, 62; c 1. MODERN LANGUAGES. *Educ:* Wilson Col, BA, 37; Syracuse Univ, MA, 45; Middlebury Col, DML, 56. *Prof Exp:* Instr, Syracuse Univ, 43-45 & Ind Univ, 45-47; asst prof, Wilson Col, 59-60; from asst prof to assoc prof, 60-77, PROF FRENCH, UNIV MASS, 77- *Mem:* MLA; Am Asn Teachers Fr; Am Coun Teaching Foreign Lang; Soc Amis Jean Giraudoux; Am Asn 18th Century Fr Studies. *Res:* Jean Giraudoux; 18th century French literature; computer assisted literary research and language teaching. *Publ:* Auth, Giraudoux devant la victoire et la defaite, Nizet, Paris, 63; co-auth, La Joie de Lire, Macmillan, 66; auth, Jean Giraudoux: The Theater of Victory and Defeat, Univ Mass, 66; Encore quelques reflexions sur la chaine secrete des Lettres persanes, Studies Voltaire & 18th Century, 72; Le Buste d'Etienne-Noël Damilaville par Marie-Ann Collot, Rev Louvre, 73; La Genese de Jacques le fataliste de Diderot, In: Collection Archives des Lettres Modernes, Minard, 77; contribr, Complete Works of Jean Giraudoux, La Pleiade, Gallimard (in press). *Mailing Add:* Dept of French & Ital Univ of Mass Amherst MA 01003

RAYMOND, ALFRED ERNEST, b London, Ont, Mar 3, 15; m 40; c 1. CLASSICAL PHILOLOGY. *Educ:* Univ Western Ont, BA, 35; Univ Toronto, MA, 36; Univ Chicago, PhD, 49. *Prof Exp:* Lectr, Univ Alta, 39-40; Univ Western Ont, 40-41; assoc prof, Waterloo Univ Col, 44-53; from assoc prof to prof, 53-62, W Sherwood Fox prof, 62-76, head dept, 62-69, EMER PROF CLASSICS, UNIV WESTERN ONT, 76- *Mem:* Class Asn Can. *Res:* Attic orators; Roman oratory. *Publ:* Auth, Note on Virgil's Aeneid, Phoenix. *Mailing Add:* Dept of Class Studies Univ of Western Ont London ON N6A 3K7 Can

RAYMOND, JAMES CHARLES, English Literature, Rhetoric. See Vol II

REA, ANNABELLE MARJORIE, b Edmonton, Alta, June 19, 35; US citizen. FRENCH LITERATURE. *Educ:* Univ Calif, Santa Barbara, BA, 57; Middlebury Col, Paris, MA, 61; Stanford Univ, PhD(French lit), 71. *Prof Exp:* Teacher French & English, San Marcos High Sch, Santa Barbara, Calif, 58-60; chairperson dept lang & ling, ASSOC PROF FRENCH, OCCIDENTAL COL, 66- *Mem:* MLA; Am Asn Teachers Fr. *Res:* Women in French literature; Marcel Proust and the novel late 19th and early 20th century poetry. *Mailing Add:* Dept of Lang & Ling Occidental Col 1600 Campus Rd Los Angeles CA 90041

REA, JOANNE EWING, b Glendale, Calif, Oct 18, 42; m 73. COMPARATIVE & FRENCH LITERATURE. *Educ:* Calif State Univ, Long Beach, BA, 65; San Jose State Univ, MA, 70; Univ Ky, PhD(French), 79. *Prof Exp:* Teaching asst Fr, 70-79, INSTR ENGLISH, UNIV KY, 80- *Mem:* Bronte Soc; James Joyce Found; SAtlantic Mod Lang Asn. *Res:* Comparative studies of Joyce and Camus; comparison of the wordcraft of Rabelais and Joyce; various aspects of the short fiction of Henry James. *Publ:* Auth, James Joyce and Master Francois Sombody, James Joyce Quart, 80. *Mailing Add:* Dept of English Univ of Ky Lexington KY 40506

REA, JOHN A, b Bloomington, Ind, May 12, 23; m 45; c 1. LINGUISTICS, ROMANCE PHILOLOGY. *Educ:* Miami Univ, AB, 48. *Prof Exp:* ASST PROF FRENCH, UNIV KY, 52- *Concurrent Pos:* Southern Fels Fund fel, 54; ed, Gen Ling, 56-62; Fulbright fel, Univ Aix-Marseille, 59-60; Am Coun Learned Soc fel, Univ Mich, 59; Fulbright lectr, Univ Rome, 59-60, 67-68; dir, NDEA Lang Insts, 62-65; consult, 65-66; actg chmn Span 1, Univ Ky, 66-67, dept French, 73. *Mem:* Ling Soc Am; MLA; Am Asn Teachers Ital. *Publ:* Auth, Again the Oaths of Strasburg, Lang, 58; Lend and loan in American English, Am Speech, 2/68; The Idea for O Henry's Gift of the Magi, Southern Humanities Rev, Vol 7, No 3; The Romance Data in the Pilot Studies for Glotto-Chronology, Current Trends Ling, 73; The Form of Aucassin and Nicolete, Romance Notes, 74; Linguistics Speculations of Edward Brerewood, Studies A A Hill, 76; A bit of Lewis Carroll in Ulysses, James Joyce Quart, 77. *Mailing Add:* Dept of French Univ of Ky Lexington KY 40506

READ, CHARLES, b Clinton, Iowa, July 10, 40; m 67; c 2. LINGUISTICS, PSYCHOLINGUISTICS. *Educ:* Haverford, Col, AB, 61; Harvard Univ, MAT, 63, PhD (educ & ling), 71. *Prof Exp:* Assoc prof, 70-80, PROF ENGLISH, UNIV WIS-MADISON, 80- *Concurrent Pos:* Ed, Harvard Educ Rev, 65-67; vis scholar sci ling, Mass Inst Technol, 73-74; vis scholar ling, Univ Nijmegen, Netherlands, 78-79; chmn dept ling, Univ Wis-Madison, 79-82; vis scholar ling, Beijing Normal Univ, 82-83. *Mem:* Ling Soc Am. *Res:* Language development in children; phonetics. *Publ:* Auth, Pre-school children's knowledge of English phonology, Harvard Educ Rev, 71; Lessons to be learned from the pre-school orthographer, In: Foundations of language development, Acad Press, 75; Children's Categorization of Speech Sounds in English, Nat Coun Teachers English, 75; Children's awareness of language, with emphasis on sound systems, In: The Child's Conception of Language, Springer, 78; Creative spelling by young children, In: Standards and dialects in English, Winthrop, 80; Why short subjects are harder to find than long ones, In: Language Acquisition: The State of the Art, Cambridge, 82; Spelling, In: Encyclopedia of Educational Research, Free Press, 5th ed, 82. *Mailing Add:* Dept of English Univ of Wis Madison WI 53706

READ, WILLIAM MERRITT, b Dupont, Ind, June 24, 01; m 24; 48; c 4. CLASSICS. *Educ:* DePauw Univ, AB, 23; Univ Mich, AB, 24, PhD, 27. *Prof Exp:* Instr, Western Reserve Univ, 26-27; from asst prof to prof, 27-72, dir Univ Press, 43-63, EMER PROF CLASS LANG, UNIV WASH, 72- *Mem:* Am Philol Asn; Class Asn Pac NW (pres, 28, secy-treas, 72-); Am Class League; Philol Asn Pac Coast; Pac NW Conf Foreing Lang. *Publ:* Auth, Michigan Manuscript 18 of the Gospels, Univ Wash, 43; Spontaneous generation in Lucretious III, 713-741, Class J; Reading Latin, 2/71 & Teaching by the nature method, 1/72, Class Outlook; A guide for Hans H Oerberg's Lingua latina secundum naturae rationem explicaga, Vols I & II, 72 & 73 & A manual for teachers of Hans H Oerberg's Lingua latina . . ., Vols I-II, 73, Nature Method Lang Inst; Aims and objectives of the Latin program, Foreign Lang Annals, 5/75. *Mailing Add:* Dept of Classics Univ of Wash Classics DH-10 Seattle WA 98195

REARDON, BRYAN PETER, b Manchester, Eng, Dec 30, 28; m 60. CLASSICS. *Educ:* Glasgow Univ, MA, 51; Cambridge Univ, BA, 53; Univ Nantes, D Univ(classics), 68. *Prof Exp:* Asst prof Classics, Mem Univ Nfld, 58-64, assoc prof, 66-67; from assoc prof to prof, Trent Univ, 67-74; prof, Univ Col N Wales, 74-78; PROF CLASSICS & CHMN DEPT, UNIV CALIF, IRVINE, 78- *Concurrent Pos:* Treas, Coun Univ Classics Depts, UK, 75-78; organizer, Int Conf on Ancient Novel, Bangor Wales, 76; ed, Erotica Antiqua, Hellenic Soc, 77. *Honors & Awards:* Prix Theodore Reinach, Asn Etudes Grecques, 72. *Mem:* Class Asn Can; Am Philol Asn; Soc Prom Hellenic Studies; Asn Etudes Grecques. *Res:* Greek literature of the imperial period. *Publ:* Auth, Lucian: selected words (translations) Bobbs, 65; The Greek Novel, Phoenix, 69; Courants litteraires grecs des IIe et IIIe siecles apres JC, Les Belles Lettres, 71; The second sophistic and the novel, In: Approaches to the Second Sophistic, Am Philol Asn, 74; Aspects of the Greek novel, Greece & Rome, 76; The Greek novels: etat de la question, Erotica Antiqua, 77; Theme, Structure and Narrative in Chariton, Yale Class Studies, 82. *Mailing Add:* Dept of Classics Univ of Calif Irvine CA 92717

REBAY, LUCIANO, b Milan, Italy, Apr 23, 28; US citizen. ITALIAN LITERATURE. *Educ:* Univ Aix Marseille, Lic es Let, 51; Columbia Univ, PhD(Ital), 60. *Prof Exp:* Lectr Ital, Ecole Norm, Ajaccio, France, 48-49, Ecole Norm, Nice, 49-50; prof, Lycee Francais, London, England, 52-55; Lycee Francais, New York, 55-56; from instr to assoc prof, Columbia Univ, 57-63, prof Ital, 65-72; GIUSEPPE UNGARETTI PROF ITAL LIT, 73- *Concurrent Pos:* Chamberlain fel, 62-63; Guggenheim fel, 66-67; Am Coun Learned Soc fel, 70-71; fel, Ctr Humanities, Wesleyan Univ, 71; vis prof Ital lit, Univ Calif, Berkeley, spring, 74; vis Mellon prof mod lang, Univ Pittsburgh, fall, 74; Nat Endowment for Humanities fel, 80-81. *Mem:* Am Asn Teachers Ital; MLA. *Res:* Contemporary Italian literature; Italian lyric poetry; Franco-Italian comparative literature. *Publ:* Auth, Le origini della poesia di Giuseppe Ungaretti, Ed Storia e Lett, 62; I diaspori di Montale, Italica, 69; Invitation to Italian Poetry, Dover, 69; Alberto Moravia, Columbia Univ, 70; La rete a strascico di Montale, Forum Italicum, 71; co-ed, Giuseppe Ungaretti, Saggi e interventi, Mondadori, Milan, 74; Sull Autobiografismo di Montale, Olschki, Florence 76; Ungaretti: Gli Scritti Egiziani 1909-1912, Forum Italicum, 80. *Mailing Add:* 503 Casa Italiana Columbia Univ New York NY 10017

REBOUSSIN, MARCEL (A), b Chateaurenault, France, Apr 26, 06; m; c 2. FRENCH. *Educ:* Univ Paris, Agrege, 39. *Prof Exp:* Prof, 46-68, EMER PROF FRENCH, COL WILLIAM & MARY, 68- *Mem:* Am Asn Teachers Fr. *Res:* Period 1820-1850 in France. *Publ:* Auth, Les grandes epoques culturelles de la France, Ronald, New York, 51; Balzac et le mythe de Foedora, 66, Le drame spirituel de Flaubert, 73 & Drieu La Rochelle et le mirage de la politique, 80, Ed Nizet, Paris. *Mailing Add:* 203 Tyler Brooks Dr Williamsburg VA 23185

RECHTSCHAFFEN, BERNARD, b Austria, Feb 12, 22; US citizen; m 51; c 2. GERMAN LANGUAGE & COMPARATIVE LITERATURE. *Educ:* NY Univ, BS, 45, MA, 49, PhD(Ger lit), 54. *Prof Exp:* Asst Ger, NY Univ, 45-46, instr, 46-47; from instr to prof, 47-77, chmn dept, 58-77, PROF HUMANITIES, POLYTECH INST NEW YORK, 77- *Concurrent Pos:* Mem admin bd, Ger Quart, 64-67; adv coun, Vienna Study Coun, 64-80; chmn Germanistentag 65; Nat Conf Teaching & Testing Doctoral Cand in Lang Ability, MLA, 66; consult-examr Ger, New York Bd Educ, 69- *Mem:* MLA; Am Asn Teachers Ger; AAUP. *Res:* German literature; pedagogical research. *Publ:* Auth, Literatur für den Deutschunterricht Erste Stufe, 64, Zweite Stufe, 64, Kurze Deutsche Grammatik, 65 & Lit für den Deutschunterricht, Dritte Stufe, 66, Am Bk Co; German-English, English-German Phonetic Dict, New Am Libr, 67; coauth, German for Research: Biological & Physical Sciences, 72 & German for Research: Humanities & Social Sciences, 73, Random House. *Mailing Add:* Dept of Humanities Polytech Inst of NY Brooklyn NY 11201

RECK, RIMA DRELL, b New York, NY, Sept 29, 33; m 56. COMPARATIVE LITERATURE. *Educ:* Brandeis Univ, BA, 54; Yale Univ, PhD(Romance lang), 60. *Prof Exp:* Instr French, Tulane Univ, 58-61; from asst prof to assoc prof French & comp lit, 61-68, res coun grant, 64, PROF COMP LIT, UNIV NEW ORLEANS, 68- *Concurrent Pos:* Am Philos Soc res grants, 62, 64; assoc ed, Southern Rev, 63-; Am Coun Learned Soc res grant, 68; Guggenheim fel, 72-73. *Mem:* MLA; Am Asn Teachers Fr; SCent Mod Lang Asn; Am Comp Lit Asn; Soc Amis Marcel Proust. *Res:* French novel of the 20th century; the novel and its relation to other arts; 19th century Russian literature. *Publ:* Coauth, Studies in Comparative Literature, 62, ed, Explorations of Literatue, 66 & auth, Literature and Responsibility: The French Novelist in the Twentieth Century, 69, La State Univ; Old and new in the French new novel, Southern Rev, 10/65; Celine and the Aural Novel, Bks Abroad, 65; coauth, Bernanos, Confrontations, Minard, Paris, 66 & The New Orleans Cookbook, 74; auth, The crises of French nationalism in the twentieth century, In: The Cry of Home, Univ Tenn, 72. *Mailing Add:* Dept of Foreign Lang Univ of New Orleans New Orleans LA 70122

RECKFORD, KENNETH J, b New York, NY, May 26, 33; m 54; c 5. CLASSICS. *Educ:* Harvard Univ, BA, 54, PhD(class philol), 57,. *Prof Exp:* Instr classics & gen educ, Harvard Univ, 57-60; from asst prof to assoc prof, 60-68, PROF CLASSICS, UNIV NC, CHAPEL HILL, 68- *Concurrent Pos:* Fel, Ctr Hellenic Studies, Washington, DC, 61-62; Am Coun Learned Soc fel, 69-70. *Mem:* Am Philol Asn. *Res:* Greek and Latin literature. *Publ:* Auth, Studies in Persius, Hermes, 62; Heracles and Mr Eliot, Compt Lit, winter, 64; Horace, Twayne, 69; Medeo's first exit, 69, Phaethon, Hippolytus, and Aphrodite, 72, & Phaedra and Pasiphae: The pull backward, 74, Trans Am Philol Asn; Desire with hope: Aristophanes and the comic catharsis, Ramus, 74; contribr, Some trees in Virgil and Tolikien, In: Perspectives of Roman Poetry, Univ Tex, 74. *Mailing Add:* 304 Murphey Hall Univ of NC Chapel Hill NC 27514

REDDEN, JAMES ERSKINE, b Louisville, Ky, Dec 28, 28; m 50; c 4. LINGUISTICS, AFRICAN STUDIES. *Educ:* Univ Louisville, BA, 50; Ind Univ, Bloomington, PhD(ling), 65. *Prof Exp:* Linguist, Foreign Ser Inst, US Dept State, 61-65; assoc prof ling, Am Univ Beirut, 65-67; assoc prof, 67-71, chmn dept, 71-73, PROF LING, SOUTHERN ILL UNIV, CARBONDALE, 71- *Concurrent Pos:* Chmn African Studies Comt, Southern Ill Univ, Carbondale, 68-71; US Off Educ fac study improv res grant NW Bantu hist ling & adj prof, Fed Univ Cameroon, 71; sr res Fulbright prof, Sem African Lang & Cult, Univ Hamburg, 73-74; Wenner-Gren Found grant, Walapai Indian Reservation, Ariz, 81. *Mem:* Ling Soc Am; Int Ling Asn; Can Ling Asn; Ling Asn Gt Brit. *Res:* African and Amerindian linguistics; Northwest Bantu historical linguistics; instrumental phonetics. *Publ:* Auth, Twi Basic Course, 63, Lingala Basic Course, 63 & More Basic Course, 66, US Govt Printing Off; Walapai Phonology, 1/66 & Morphology, 4/66, Int J Am Ling; Proc of Hokan Lang Workshops, 75-82; Proc Int Conf on Frontiers in Lang Proficiency & Dominance Testing, 78-81; Descriptive Grammar of Ewondo, 79; On Analyzing and Teaching the English Passive, SPEAQ, 79; On Expanding the Meaning of Applied Linguistics, Ling Reporter, 5/81. *Mailing Add:* Dept of Ling Southern Ill Univ Carbondale IL 62901

REDDICK, ROBERT JOHN, b Minn, 39; m 67; c 2. LINGUISTICS. *Educ:* Univ Minn, BS, 66, MA, 69, PhD(English ling), 75. *Prof Exp:* Asst prof English ling, Ball State Univ, 73-75; asst prof, 75-81, ASSOC PROF ENGLISH LING & OLD ENGLISH, UNIV TEX, ARLINGTON, 81- *Concurrent Pos:* Assoc ed, Harold Frederic Ed, 78-; asst ed, Allegorica, 78- *Mem:* Ling Soc Am; MLA; Int Soc Anglo-Saxonists. *Res:* Old English; history of English; syntactic change. *Publ:* Auth, Grammar and Rhetoric, Centrum, 73; Reason adverbials and syntactic constraints in early West Saxon, Glossa, 81; On the underlying order of early West Saxon, J Ling, 82. *Mailing Add:* Dept of English Univ of Tex Arlington TX 76019

REDENBARGER, WAYNE JACOB, b Alton, Ill, Nov 27, 45; m 79. ROMANCE LINGUISTICS, PORTUGUESE. *Educ:* Ind Univ, BA, 71; Harvard Univ, MA & PhD(Romance ling), 76. *Prof Exp:* Lectr Port, Boston Univ, 74-76; asst prof, 76-82, ASSOC PROF PORT & ROMANCE LING, OHIO STATE UNIV, 82- *Mem:* Ling Soc Am; MLA; Am Asn Teachers Span & Port. *Res:* Phonetics and phonology of Portuguese; historical phonology of Western Romance. *Publ:* Auth, Vowel lowering and i-epenthesis in Classical Latin, In: Current Studies in Romance Linguistics, Georgetown Univ, 76; Lusitanian Portuguese a is advanced tongue root and constricted pharynx, In: Studies in Romance Linguistics, Newbury House, 77; Portuguese vowel harmony and the elsewhere condition, In: Contemporary Studies in Romance Linguistics, Georgetown Univ, 78; Portuguese evidence for the non-unitary nature of syllable phrasing, Georgetown Univ, 81; Articulator Features and Portuguese Vowel Height, Harvard Univ, 81. *Mailing Add:* Dept Romance Lang Ohio State Univ Columbus OH 43210

REDFIELD, JAMES M, b Chicago, Ill, May 2, 35. ARCHAIC & CLASSICAL LITERATURE & HISTORY. *Educ:* Univ Chicago, BA, 54, PhD(social thought), 61. *Prof Exp:* Instr social thought, 60-62, asst prof, 62-65, actg chmn, Comt Social Thought, 68-69, chmn, 69-70, assoc prof, 65-75, assoc dean, Col & master, New Col Div, 65-70, PROF SOCIAL THOUGHT, NEW COL DIV, UNIV CHICAGO, 76-, PROF, DEPT CLASS LING & LIT, 77- *Concurrent Pos:* mem vis comt, Haverford Col, 68-70; mem planning staff & teaching fac, Danforth Found Workshop in the Lib Arts, 68-70, & 71-73 & Lilly Endowment Workshop in the Lib Arts, 78-79 & 81-82; vis prof classics, Dartmouth Col, summer, 80. *Honors & Awards:* Quantrell Award for Teaching, Univ Chicago, 65. *Mem:* Am Philol Asn. *Res:* Archaic Greek economic and social development; Archaic and Classic Greek literature and historiography; Plato. *Publ:* Auth, The making of the Odyssey, In: Essays in Western Civilization, 67 & In: Parnassus Revisited, Am Libr Asn, 73; Platonic education, In: The Knowledge Most Worth Having, Univ Chicago Press, 67; Nature and Culture in the Iliad: The Tragedy of Hector, Univ Chicago Press, 75; The Womem of Sparta, Class J, 78; coauth (with Paul Friedrich), Language as a personality symbol: The case of Achilles, Language, 78; The proem of the Iliad: Homer's Art, Class Philol, 79; Notes on the Greek wedding, Arethusa (in prep); Odysseus: The economic man, In: Approaches to Homer (in prep). *Mailing Add:* 1126 E 59th St Chicago IL 60637

REDFIELD, ROBERT LOWELL, b Berkeley, Calif, Feb 26, 43; m 67; c 3. MEDIEVAL LITERATURE. *Educ:* Univ Calif, Berkeley, BA, 65 & 70, MA, 72; Univ Calif, Davis, PhD(Span), 80. *Prof Exp:* Lectr Span, Univ Calif, Davis, 78-80; INSTR SPAN, SACRAMENTO CITY COL, 81- *Mem:* MLA; Am Asn Teachers Span & Port. *Res:* Early Germanic contributions to Spanish: contact between Spain and Ango-Saxon England; comparative religion: Islam, Judaism, and Christianity co-exist in medieval Spain; medieval Spanish literary themes and characters in United States literature. *Publ:* Auth, Fugue as a structure in Pynchon's Entropy, Pac Coast Philol, 10/77; coauth, Pynchon's Spanish source for Entropy, Studies Short Fiction, fall 79. *Mailing Add:* 1806 Palm Place Davis CA 95616

REDFORD, DONALD B, Egyptology. See Vol I

REDICK, PATRICIA C, b Connellsville, Pa, Sept 4, 22; m 52; c 1. ROMANCE LANGUAGES. *Educ:* Univ Pittsburgh, MA, 52, PhD, 59. *Prof Exp:* Conversalionalista Span, Univ Pittsburgh, 50-51, instr, 53-54; asst prof, Chatham Col, 54-63; asst prof, State Univ NY Albany, 63-66; assoc prof, 66-73, PROF SPAN, FROSTBURG STATE COL, 73-, HEAD DEPT FOREIGN LANG & LIT, 80- *Mem:* MLA; Am Asn Teachers Span & Port. *Res:* Eighteenth century of Spanish literature. *Publ:* Auth, Espana, Culture & Civilization of Spain, 81. *Mailing Add:* Dept of Mod Foreign Lang Frostburg State Col Frostburg MD 21532

REDMAN, HARRY, JR, b Richmond, Va, June 18, 28. FRENCH. *Educ:* Emory Univ, AB, 49; Univ Wis, MA, 50, PhD(French), 56. *Prof Exp:* From asst prof to assoc prof Romance lang, Univ Ala, 56-63, res comt grants, 58-60; assoc prof, 63-69, PROF FRENCH & ITAL, TULANE UNIV, 69- *Concurrent Pos:* Fulbright fel, Univ Bordeaux, 52; Am Philos Soc grants, 58 & 59. *Mem:* Am Asn Teachers Fr; MLA; SAtlantic Mod Lang Asn; SCent Mod Lang Asn; Soc Chateaubriand. *Res:* Comparative literature; French literature of the 19th century. *Publ:* Auth, Marivaux's reputation among his contemporaries, Studies Voltaire & the 18th Century, 66; Quand Merimee commentait la Guerre de Secession, Rev Deux Mondes, 8/66; La Louisianaise de Chateaubriand devoilee, Rev Paris, 11/67; Chateaubriand and Washington, Chateaubriand and Napoleon: Some New Perspectives, Univ SC Fr Lit Ser, Vol VIII, 81; Aux pieds du maitre: Le jeune Gustave Flaubert admirateur de Chateaubriand, 19th Century Fr Studies, Vol X, 82; A few more nineteenth-century French treatments of the Don Juan theme, WVa Univ Philol Papers, Vol XXVIII, 82. *Mailing Add:* Dept of Fr & Ital Tulane Univ New Orleans LA 70118

REECE, BENNY RAMON, b Asheville, NC, Dec 7, 30; m 60; c 1. CLASSICAL LANGUAGES. *Educ:* Duke Univ, AB, 53; Univ NC, MA, 54, PhD(Greek & Latin), 57. *Prof Exp:* Asst prof Latin, Mercer Univ, 57-60; chmn dept class lang, 60-72, assoc prof, 60-80, PROF LATIN & GREEK, FURMAN UNIV, 80- *Concurrent Pos:* Southern Fels Fund fel, Duke Univ, 59, coop prog in humanities fel, 66-67; Am Philos Soc fel, 66, 70. *Mem:* Am Philol Asn; Class Asn Midwest & South. *Res:* Latin paleography; Silver Age and medieval Latin literature. *Publ:* Auth, Addenda to Ratherius' Sermones, Latomus, 9/67; Documents Illustrating Cicero's Consular Campaign, Furman Univ, 67; Classical quotations in the works of Ratherius, Class Folia, 11/68; Nero's death date, Am J Philol, 1/69; Sermones Ratherii, Holy Cross, 69; Learning in the Tenth Century, 69, 72, The Role of the Centurion in Ancient Society, 75 & A Bibliography of First Appearances of the Writings by A Conan Doyle, 75, Furman Univ. *Mailing Add:* Dept of Class Lang Furman Univ Greenville SC 29613

REED, ANN MURPHY, b Providence, RI, Jan 19, 44. LINGUISTICS. *Educ:* Swarthmore Col, BA, 65; Univ Pa, MsEd, 68; Brandeis Univ, PhD(ling), 75. *Prof Exp:* Teacher ling, 76-80, ASST PROF LING, DEPT ENGLISH, COL WILLIAM & MARY, 80- *Mem:* Southeastern Conf Ling; Ling Soc Am. *Res:* Transformational syntax; semantics. *Publ:* Auth, Picture Noun Reflexives and Promotion, Proc New England Ling Soc, 77; Theme and difinites, Secol Bull, 79. *Mailing Add:* Dept of English Col of William & Mary Williamsburg VA 23185

REED, CARROLL EDWARD, b Portland, Ore, Nov 21, 14; m 38; c 7. GERMANIC LINGUISTICS. *Educ:* Univ Wash, AB, 36, AM, 37; Brown Univ, PhD, 41. *Prof Exp:* Instr Ger, Brown Univ, 41-42; asst prof, Univ Ga, 46; from instr to assoc prof, Univ Wash, 46-59, prof Ger & ling, 59-66, assoc dean grad sch, 65-66; prof Ger & ling & chmn dept, Univ Calif, Riverside, 66-69; head dept, 71-76, prof, 69-82, EMER PROF GER LANG & LIT, UNIV MASS, AMHERST, 82- *Concurrent Pos:* Lectr, Columbia Univ, 50 & Univ Tex, 58; Fulbright res scholar, Ger, 53-54; ed, Mod Lang Quart, 56-61. *Mem:* MLA; Am dialect Soc; Ling Soc Am; Can Ling Asn. *Res:* Pennsylvania German; Germanic dialects; linguistic geography. *Publ:* Auth, Dialects of American English, World Publ, 67 & Univ Mass, rev ed, 77; ed, The Learning of Language, Appleton, 71; auth, A phonological history of Pennsylvania German, In: Studies for Einar Haugen, Mouton, The Hague, 72; Verb conjugation in modern standard German, In: Sprache der Gegenwart, Schwann, Düsseldorf, 73; The syntax of Pennsylvania German, Orbis, 78; The Pennsylvania German dialect spoken in the counties of Lehigh and Berks; A linguistic atlas of Pennsylvania German. *Mailing Add:* Dept of Ger Lang & Lit Univ of Mass Amherst MA 01003

REED, DAVID WOODERSON, b Boliver, Mo, May 7, 21; m 40; c 3. ENGLISH LANGUAGE. *Educ:* Univ Mo, BS, 42; Univ Mich, AM, 43, PhD, 49. *Prof Exp:* Teacher-trainee, English Lang Inst, Mex, 43-44; teacher English, Uniao Cultural, Brasil-Estados Unidos, Sao Paulo, Brazil, 44-45; instr, Univ Mo, 45-46; asst, Univ Mich, 48; from instr to assoc prof English, Univ Calif, Berkeley, 48-61, from prof English to prof ling & chmn dept, 61-70; chmn dept, 71-73, PROF LING, NORTHWESTERN UNIV, 70-, DIR, PROG ORIENT & AFRICAN LANGS, 78- *Concurrent Pos:* Fulbright lectr, Albert Ludwigs Univ, Ger, 56-57. *Mem:* Ling Soc Am; Int Ling Soc; Am Name Soc; Am Dialect Soc. *Res:* American dialects; statistical linguistics; history of the English language. *Publ:* Auth, History of inflectional n in English verbs before 1500, Univ Calif, 50; A statistical approach to quantitative linguistic analysis, Word, 50; Eastern dialect words in California, Publ Am Dialect Soc, 54. *Mailing Add:* Dept of Ling Northwestern Univ Evanston IL 60201

REED, GERVAIS EYER, b Greeley, Colo, Aug 6, 31; m 60; c 2. FRENCH. *Educ:* Princeton Univ, AB, 54; Brown Univ, MA, 62, PhD(French), 64. *Prof Exp:* Asst prof, 64-70, assoc prof, 70-81, PROF FRENCH, LAWRENCE UNIV, 81- *Mem:* MLA; Am Asn Teachers French. *Res:* French 17th century literature and bibliography. *Publ:* Auth, Claude Barbin, libraire de Paris sous le regne de Louis XIV, Droz, Geneva; Moliere's Privilege of 18 March 1671, The Library, 65; Stylistic and thematic parallels in Corneille's Theatre and his imitation de Jesus Christ, Symposium, XXXIII: 263-87. *Mailing Add:* Dept of French Lawrence Univ Appleton WI 54911

REED, HELEN HUTCHINS, b Chicago, Ill, Sept 12, 39; m 60; c 2. LITERARY THEORY. *Educ:* Smith Col, BA, 61; Syracuse Univ, MA, 72, PhD(Spanish), 81. *Prof Exp:* Instr, 78-81, ASST PROF SPANISH, STATE UNIV NY COL AT ONEONTA, 81- *Concurrent Pos:* Assoc ed book rev, Meutalites, New Zealand, 81- *Mem:* MLA; William Morris Soc. *Res:* Cervantes; Picaresque novel; reader orientated criticism. *Publ:* Auth, The Reader in the Spanish Picaresque Novel, Tamesis Press, London (in prep). *Mailing Add:* 142 Hathaway Rd De Witt NY 13214

REED, WALTER LOGAN, English, Comparative Literature. See Vol II

REED, WILLIAM LAFOREST, b Defiance, Ohio, Jan 9, 12; m 35; c 1. NEAR EASTERN LANGUAGES & LITERATURE. *Educ:* Hiram Col, AB, 34; Yale Univ, BD, 37, PhD, 42; Am Sch Orient Res, Jerusalem, cert, 38. *Prof Exp:* Clergyman, Church of Christ, Conn, 39-42; asst prof relig, Tex Christian Univ, 46-47; from assoc prof to prof Old Testament, Brite Col Bible, 48-53, distinguished prof, 53-56, dir admin & curric, 55-56; prof Old Testament, Lexington Theol Sem, 56-68; prof relig & chmn dept, 68-75, Weatherly prof relig, 74-80, EMER PROF RELIG, TEX, 80- *Concurrent Pos:* Lectr, State Conv Disciples of Christ, Tex, 50; dir, Am Sch Orient Res, Jerusalem, Jordan, 51-52, dir excavation at Dibon, Moab, 52; co-dir, Qumran Daves Exped, Dead Sea Scrolls, 52; McFadin lectr, Tex Christian Univ, 53; exec asst to pres, Am Schs Orient Res, 56-66, trustee, 63, treas, 68; lectr, Atlantic Christian Col, 57; Am Asn Theol Schs fac fel, 61-62; Am Philos Soc res grants, 61-62, 67 & 72-73; sr archaeologist, US AID, Amman, Jordan, 64; ed, Lexington Theol Quart, 65-68; Am Coun Learned Soc res grant, 72-73. *Honors & Awards:* Hiram Col Achievement Award, 69. *Mem:* Soc Bibl Lit; Am Schs Orient Res; Southwest Asn Bibl Instr (vpres, 51, pres, 52); Am Orient Soc; Am Acad Relig. *Res:* The Old Testament idea of grace; archaeological explorations in Saudi Arabia, 1962 and 1967; archaeological history of the ancient Minaean Kingdom. *Publ:* Auth, The Old Testament Asherah; The Excavations at Dibon in Moab, Am Schs Orient Res, 64; coauth, Winery Defenses and Soundings at Gibeon, Univ Pa, 64; contribr, Interpreter's Dictionary of the Bible; auth, The history of Elealeh (el'Al) in Moab, Lexington Theol Quart, 1/65; The Bible and North Arabia, Encounter, 65; coauth, Ancient Records from North Arabia, Univ Toronto, 69. *Mailing Add:* Dept of Relig Tex Christian Univ Ft Worth TX 76129

REEDER, CLAUDIA GENE, b Kansas City, Mo, Dec 8, 44; m 76. FRENCH LANGUAGE & LITERATURE. *Educ:* Univ Kans, BA, 66; Univ Wis-Madison, MA, 72, PhD(French), 76. *Prof Exp:* Teacher French, Notre Dame Sion Col Prep Sch, 68-71; asst, Univ Wis-Madison, 71-73; ASST PROF FRENCH, DARTMOUTH COL, 76- *Mem:* MLA; Semiotic Soc Am; AAUP; Nat Women's Studies Asn; Am Asn Teachers Fr. *Res:* French 20th century literature; semiotic and textual theory; sex differentiation in language (womens studies). *Publ:* Auth, Machine a ecrire, Sub-Stance, 77; Maurice Roche: Seeing is (not) believing, Contemp Lit, 78; Roche aux ecritures, In: Maurice Roche par les Autres Paris: Athanor, 78; Nom-identite ou A la recherche du nom perdu, Litterature, 78; transl, Luce Irigaray, When the Goods Get Together and This Sex Which is not One, New Fr Feminisms, 80; Henri Chopin: The French Connection, Aural Lit Crit: Precisely, 81; ed, Feminist Readings: French texts/American contexts, Yale Fr Studies, 81; Jeanne Hyvrard, Ecrits de femmes (in press). *Mailing Add:* Dept of French & Ital Dartmouth Col Hanover NH 03755

REEDS, JAMES A, b Kansas City, Mo, Nov 16, 21; m 46; c 2. LINGUISTICS. *Educ:* Univ Iowa, BA, 48, MA, 49; Univ Mich, AM, 59, PhD(ling), 66. *Prof Exp:* Instr Ger, Pa State Univ, 52-58; instr, Univ Detroit, 62-65; asst prof, Univ Wis-Milwaukee, 66-69; ASSOC PROF ENGLISH, UNIV MO-KANSAS CITY, 69- *Concurrent Pos:* Fulbright teacher English, Leopoldinum II, Detmold, 56-57; deleg,Int Cong Linguists, Oslo, 57 & Bucharest, 67; vpres, Gen Ling Corp, 75- *Mem:* Am Translr Asn; Am Asn Phoentic Sci; MLA. *Res:* Applied linguistics; perceptual and acoustic phonetics; transformational grammar. *Publ:* Coauth, The perception of stops after /s/, Phonetica, 61; Front vowel aperture and diffuseness, Actes Xeme Congres Int Linguistes, Bucharest, 69; Comprehension and Problem Solving as Language Acquisition Strategies, Mouton, 73; Phonetics, A Manual for Listening, Univ Park, 78. *Mailing Add:* Dept of Speech & Hearing Sci Univ of Mo Kansas City MO 64110

REEDY, DANIEL R, b Marshall, Ill, May 21, 35; m 58; c 3. SPANISH. *Educ:* Eastern Ill Univ, BS, 57; Univ Ill, MA, 59, PhD, 62. *Prof Exp:* Asst instr, Span, Univ Ill, 57-58, 60-61; from inst to assoc prof, Univ NC, Chapel Hill, 62-67; assoc prof, 67-71, actg dean undergrad studies, 73-74, PROF SPAN, UNIV KY, 71-, CHMN DEPT SPAN & ITAL, 76- *Concurrent Pos:* Fulbright res fel, Lima, Peru, 66-67; contribr ed, Handbook Latin Am Studies, 66-; Am Coun Educ fel, acad admin, 75-76. *Honors & Awards:* Outstanding Educator of America, 75. *Mem:* MLA; Am Asn Teachers Span & Port; Inst Int Lit Iberoam; SAtlantic Mod Lang Asn; Latin Am Studies Asn. *Res:* Latin American literature, particularly poetry. *Publ:* Auth, Las Tradiciones en Salsa Verde de Ricardo Palma, Rev Iberoam, 1-6/66; coauth, Narraciones ejemplares de Hispanoamerica, Prentice-Hall, 67; auth, The Lima theatre, 1966-67, Latin Am Theatre Rev, fall 67; The symbolic reality of Cortazar's las babas del diablo, Rev Hisp Mod, 74; Aspects of the feminist movement in Peruvian & letters and politics, Southeastern Conf Latin Am Studies, 75; Through the looking-glass: Cortazar's epiphanies of reality, Bull Hisp Studies, 77. *Mailing Add:* Dept of Span & Ital Univ of Ky Lexington KY 50406

REES, THOMAS MATTHEW, b Salt Lake City, Utah, Aug 25, 18; m 47; c 5. FOREIGN LANGUAGES. *Educ:* Univ Utah, BA, 42; Stanford Univ, MA, 51. *Prof Exp:* Exec secy, Inst Brasileiro-Northam, 48; Centro Cult Inter-Am, Curitiba, Brazil, 49; ed asst Hispanis Am Report & ed, Brazilian secy, 51-53; instr Span, Purdue Univ, 53-54; INSTR MOD LANG, ODESSA COL, 54- *Mem:* AM Asn Teachers Span & Port. *Res:* Teaching for the two-year language requirement; the working-knowledge approach language study as a social science. *Mailing Add:* Dept of English & Foreign Lang Odessa Col Odessa TX 79760

REESE, LOWELL GRANT, b Benson, Utah, Dec 2, 26; m 50; c 6. COMPARATIVE LITERATURE. *Educ:* Utah State Univ, BS, 55, MS, 56; Univ Wash, PhD(comp lit), 62. *Prof Exp:* Instr English, Weber State Col, 55; instr, Utah State Univ, 55-58, from asst prof to prof Span, 60-66; prof Span & assoc dean humanities, Univ W Fla, 66-67; prof Span & chmn dept foreign lang, Memphis State Univ, 67-69; chmn dept lang, 69-75, PROF SPAN, UTAH STATE UNIV, 69- *Mem:* MLA; Am Asn Teachers Span & Port. *Res:* Literatures of Elizabethan England and Spain's Siglo de Oro; Spanish literature of the 19th century; pedagogy of Spanish language. *Mailing Add:* Dept of Lang & Philos Utah State Univ Logan UT 84322

REESOR, MARGARET E, b Toronto, Ont. CLASSICS. *Educ:* Univ Toronto, BA, 45, MA, 46; Bryn Mawr Col, PhD(Greek), 51. *Prof Exp:* Instr Classics, Wells Col, 50-53 & Woman's Col, Univ NC, 54-58, Univ NC, 58-60; asst prof, Univ Ky, 60-61, lectr, 61-63; from asst prof to assoc prof, 67-75, PROF CLASSICS, QUEEN'S UNIV, ONT, 75- *Concurrent Pos:* Vis fel classics, Princeton Univ, 73-74 & 80-81. *Mem:* Am Philol Asn; Can Class Asn; Am Philos Asn. *Res:* Early stoic philosophy. *Publ:* Auth, The Political Theory of the Old and Middle Stoa, Augustin, 51; Fate and possibility in early Stoic philosophy, Phoenix, 65; The Stoics, In: Encycl Britannica, 70; Necessity and Fate in Stoic Philosophy, In: Stoics, Univ Calif Press, 78. *Mailing Add:* Dept of Classics Queen's Univ Kingston ON K7L 3N6 Can

REEVE, FRANKLIN DOLIER, Literature. See Vol II

REEVE, HELEN, b Ljubljana, Yugoslavia, Mar 10, 27; US citizen; m; c 3. SLAVIC LANGUAGES. *Educ:* Northwestern Univ, AB, 51; Columbia Univ, MA, 54, PhD(Russ), 76; Russ Inst, cert, 54. *Prof Exp:* Instr Russ, Long Island Univ, 54-55, 57-58; instr, Hunter Col, 58-60, ASST PROF & CHMN DEPT RUSS, CONN COL, 66- *Concurrent Pos:* Mem Conn Humanities Coun, 73- *Publ:* Translr, Chekhov, The wicked boy, In: Seventy-Five Short Masterpieces, Bantam, 61 & Zoshchenko, Pelageya, In: Great Soviet Short Stories, 62, Dell; coauth, Russian Literature, In: Encycl Am, Grolier, 72. *Mailing Add:* Dept of Russ Conn Col New London CT 06320

REEVE, RICHARD MARK, b Provo, Utah, June 20, 35; m 63; c 3. SPANISH. *Educ:* Univ Utah, BA, 60; Univ Ill, MA, 62, PhD(Span), 67. *Prof Exp:* Instr Span, Univ Ill, 65-66; asst prof, Ohio State Univ, 66-68; asst prof, 68-76, ASSOC PROF SPAN, UNIV CALIF, LOS ANGELES, 76- *Concurrent Pos:* Bk rev ed, Nueva Narrativa Hispanoamericana, 70-75; Andrew Mellon fel, Unit Pittsburgh, 71-72. *Mem:* Am Asn Teachers Span & Port; MLA; Inst Int Lit Iberoam. *Res:* Contemporary Spanish American fiction; Mexican literature. *Publ:* Auth, An annotated bibliography on Carlos Fuentes, Hispania, 10/70; coauth, Los clasicos del teatro hispanoamericano, FCE, Mex, 75. *Mailing Add:* Dept of Span & Port Univ of Calif Los Angeles CA 90024

REEVES, CHARLES HOWELL, b Schenectady, NY, Nov 23, 15; m 45; c 6. CLASSICAL PHILOLOGY. *Educ:* Union Col, AB, 37; Univ Cincinnati, PhD, 47. *Prof Exp:* Instr classics, Ind Univ, 46-49; asst prof Greek, Johns Hopkins Univ, 49-52; from assoc prof to prof classics, Univ Okla, 51-66, chmn dept, 56-60, cur class archaeol, Stovall Mus, 58; chmn dept class, 66-74, PROF CLASSICS, CASE WESTERN RESERVE UNIV, 66- *Concurrent Pos:* Fund Advan Educ fac fel, 55-56; Louise Taft Semple vis scholar, Univ Cincinnati, 61-62. *Mem:* Am Philol Asn; Class Asn Midwest & South; Soc Ancient Greek Philos; NAm Patristic Soc; Am Inst Archaeol. *Res:* Greek literary criticism; later Greek philosophy with transition to Patristic period; Greek poetry. *Publ:* Auth, The parodos of the Agamemnon, Class J, 1/60; cotranslr, Johannes Nider, On the Contracts of Merchants, Translated, Univ Okla, 66; auth, The Aristotelian concept of the tragic hero, Am J Philol. *Mailing Add:* Dept of Classics Case Western Reserve Univ Cleveland OH 44106

REEVES, DONA BATTY, b Kansas City, Mo, Mar 9, 32; m 58. GERMANIC LANGUAGE & LITERATURE. *Educ:* Univ Tex, BA, 53, MA, 55, PhD(Ger), 63. *Prof Exp:* From instr to assoc prof Ger, 61-69, chmn dept mod lang, 67-71, PROF GER, SOUTHWEST TEX STATE UNIV, 69- *Concurrent Pos:* Fed Repub Ger study tour, 72; Danforth Assoc, 77- *Honors & Awards:* Cert of Merit, AATG & Goethe House NY, 78; Foreign Lang Teacher Award, TFLA, 81. *Mem:* Am Asn Teachers Ger; MLA; Am Coun Teaching Foreign Lang; S Cent Mod Lang Asn; Western Asn Ger Studies. *Res:* Medieval and Renaissance German literature and philology; language teaching and linguistics; German-Americana. *Publ:* Auth, A translation of Victor Klein's wedding customs of the Germans in the Soviet Union, spring 77 & A translation of Lew Malinowski's passage to Russia: who were the emigrants, winter 77, Am Hist Soc Ger from Russia Work Paper; co-ed, Thomas Brunners Tobias, Peter Lang, Bern, 78; Retrospect and Retrieval: The German Element in Review, UMI, 78; German Culture in Texas: A Free Earth, GK Hall, 80; transl, Georg Dinges, A Linguistic Map of the Volga German Mother Colonies, Am Hist Soc Ger from Russia, 80; co-transl, Davis Weigum, Aus Heimat und Leben: About My Life and Homeland, Hist Soc Ger from Russia, Vol IV, 81. *Mailing Add:* Mod Lang Dept Southwest Tex State Univ San Marcos TX 78666

REEVES, GEORGE M, b Spartanburg, SC, Oct 18, 21; m 64; c 3. ENGLISH & COMPARATIVE LITERATURE. *Educ:* Wofford Col, BS, 42; Univ Ala, MA, 48; Univ Paris, DUniv, 53. *Prof Exp:* Asst, Univ Ala, 47-48; from instr to asst prof English, Presby Col, 48-50; from instr to assoc prof English & Comp lit, 53-65, dir English grad studies, 64-68, chmn comp lit prog, 64-72, assoc dean, grad sch, 68-72, PROF FOREIGN LANG & LIT, UNIV SC, 65- *Mem:* MLA; SAtlantic Mod Lang Asn; Am Comp Lit Asn; Int Comp Lit Asn. *Res:* Symbolism; French and American literature. *Publ:* Auth, Thomas Wolfe et l'Europe, Jouve, Paris, 55; A note on the life and letters of Thomas Wolfe, SAtlantic Quart, 58; Mr Eliot and Thomas Wolfe, SAtlantic Mod Lang Asn Bull, 11/67; ed, Gustave Flaubert: Poesies de jeunesse inedites, 68 & ed & translr, Maurice Coindreau, The Time of William Faulkner, 71, Univ SC; auth, French windows on modern American fiction, Proc Comp Lit Symp, Tex Tech Univ, 72. *Mailing Add:* Dept of Foreign Lang & Lit Univ of SC Columbia SC 29208

REGALADO, ANTONIO, b Dec 2, 32; US citizen; m 60; c 2. SPANISH LITERATURE. *Educ:* Harvard Univ, BA, 54; Yale Univ, PhD(Span), 65. *Prof Exp:* From instr to asst prof Span, Yale Univ, 60-67; assoc prof, NY Univ, 67-69 & Columbia Univ, 69-71; PROF SPAN, NY UNIV, 72-, CHMN DEPT, 80- *Concurrent Pos:* Guggenheim fel, 71. *Res:* Poetry; 17th century theatre; philosophy and religious history of 17th century. *Publ:* Auth, Benito Perez Galdos y la Novela Historica en Espana 1868-1912, Insula, Madrid, 65; El Siervo y el Senor: La Dialectica Angonica de Miguel de Unamuno, Grodos, Madrid, 68; co-ed & coauth, Espana en el Siglo XX, Harcourt, 74. *Mailing Add:* Dept of Span & Port NY Univ 19 University Pl New York NY 10012

REGALADO, NANCY F, b Boston, Mass, June 8, 35; div; c 2. ROMANCE LANGUAGES. *Educ:* Wellesley Col, BA, 57; Yale Univ, PhD(French), 66. *Prof Exp:* Asst instr French, Yale Univ, 58-62, actg instr, 62-65; from instr to asst prof, Wesleyan Univ, 65-67; from asst prof to assoc prof, 68-77, PROF FRENCH, NY UNIV, 77- *Concurrent Pos:* Nat Endowment for Humanities fel, 79-80; Am Coun Learned Soc grant, 79. *Mem:* MLA; Mediaeval Acad Am. *Res:* Medieval French literature. *Publ:* Coauth, RSVP invitation a ecrire, Harcourt, 65; auth, Poetic Patterns in Rutebeuf, a Study in Non Courtly Poetic Modes of the 18th Century, Yale Univ, 70; Tristan & Renart: Two tricksters, L'Esprit Createur, spring 76; Les Fonchons poetique du nom propre dans le Testament de villon, Cahiers de l'Association Internationale des Etudes Francais, 5/80; Des contraires choses: La fonchon poetique de la citation et des exampla dans le Roman de la Rose de Jean de Meun, Litterature, 2/81. *Mailing Add:* Dept of French NY Univ New York NY 10003

REGAN, MARIANN SANDERS, English & Comparative Literature. See Vol II

REGENOS, GRAYDON WENDELL, b Claypool, Ind, Jan 8, 02; m 28; c 2. CLASSICAL PHILOLOGY, MEDIEVAL LATIN. *Educ:* Ind Cent Col, AB, 23; Ind Univ, AM, 25; Univ Chicago, PhD, 36. *Prof Exp:* Instr Latin & math, high sch, Ind, 23-24; from instr to prof class lang, 27-68, chmn dept, 55-68, EMER PROF CLASS LANG, TULANE UNIV, 68- *Concurrent Pos:* Ed, Nuntius, 51-55; vis prof, Ohio State Univ, fall 68, Rockford Col, 70-71 & Monmouth Col, 70-71. *Mem:* Am Philol Asn; Am Class League; Class Asn Mid West & South (1st vpres, 49, pres, 59-60); Archaeol Inst Am; Vergilian Soc Am. *Publ:* Auth, The Latinity of the Epistolae of Lupus of Ferrieres; Rafael Landivar's Rusticatio Mexicana; The Book of Daun Burnel the Ass, Univ Tex, 59; The Letters of Lupus of Ferrieres, Nijhoff, The Hague, 66; co-ed, Historic Fulton county, Fulton County Hist Soc, 73. *Mailing Add:* 2505 Costa Dr Galesburg IL 61401

REGOSIN, RICHARD LLOYD, b Brooklyn, NY, Sept 3, 37; m 61; c 3. ROMANCE LANGUAGES. *Educ:* Dartmouth Col, BA, 59; Johns Hopkins Univ, PhD(Romance lang), 65. *Prof Exp:* From instr to asst prof French, Dartmouth Col, 63-69; assoc prof, 69-74, PROF FRENCH, UNIV CALIF, IRVINE, 78- *Mem:* MLA. *Res:* French Renaissance literature. *Publ:* Auth, D'Aubigne's Les tragiques: The Poetry of Inspiration, Univ NC, 69; The artist and the Abbaye, Study Philol, 71; Language and the dialect of the self in Montaigne's Essais, Ky Romance Quart, 72; Montaigne's Essaie: The book of the self, L'Esprit Createur, 75; The Matter of my Book, Univ Calif, 77; Sources and resources: The pretexts of originality in Montaigne's Essais, Substance, 78. *Mailing Add:* 18241 Yellowwood Irvine CA 92715

REGUEIRO, JOSE MIGUEL, b Cordoba, Arg, Dec 20, 30; US citizen. SPANISH LITERATURE. *Educ:* Univ Pa, PhD(Span), 72. *Prof Exp:* From instr to asst prof, 70-78, ASSOC PROF SPAN, UNIV PA, 78- *Mem:* Renaissance Soc Am; MLA; Am Asn Teachers Span & Port; AAUP. *Res:* Spanish medieval and Renaissance theater; Spanish Golden Age literature. *Publ:* Auth, A catalogue of the Comedia collection at the University of Pennsylvania Libraries, 71; coauth, Dramatic Manuscripts in the Hispanic Society of America, 78; contrib reviews and articles to literary publications. *Mailing Add:* Dept of Romance Lang 521 Williams Hall Univ of Pa Philadelphia PA 19104

REH, ALBERT M, b Günzburg, Ger, Oct 11, 22; US citizen; m 64. GERMAN LANGUAGE & LITERATURE. *Educ:* Univ Munich, PhD, 57. *Prof Exp:* Asst prof Ger lang & lit, Princeton Univ, 61-64 & Smith Col, 64-67; assoc prof, 67-79, PROF GER LANG & LIT, UNIV MASS, AMHERST, 80- *Concurrent Pos:* Vis prof, Univ Conn, 77-78; sr ed, Lessing Yearbk, 81- *Mem:* MLA; Am Asn Teachers Ger; Lessing Soc (pres, 81-82); Lessing Akademie. *Res:* Eighteenth century German literature; literature and psychology; applied linguistics and methodology. *Publ:* Auth, Was leistet das Tonband im Sprachunterricht?, Die Neueren Sprachen, Das Sprach-Labor, 9/65; Continuing German, A Bridge to Literature, McGraw, 69; coauth, Elementary German, Van Nostrand, 69; auth, Psychologische und psychoanalytische Interpretationsmethoden in der Literaturwissenschaft, In: Psychologie in der Literaturwissenschaft, Stiehm, Heidelberg, 71; Zu Lessings Charakterzeichnung, In: Lessing in Heutiger Sicht, Jacobi Verlag Bremen und Wolfenbüttel, 77; Das Motiv der Rettung in Lessings Tragödie und ernster Komödie, In: Lessing Yearbook XI, 79; Der komische Konflikt in dem Lustspiel Der zerbrochne Krug, In: Kleists Dramen: Neue Interpretationen, Reclam Stuttgart, 81; Die Rettung der Menschlichkeit: Lessings Dramen in literaturpsychologischer Sicht, Francke Bern, Munich, 81. *Mailing Add:* 505 Herter Hall Univ of Mass Amherst MA 01003

REHM, MERLIN DALE, Old Testament, Hebrew. See Vol IV

REICHARD, JOSEPH RUCH, b Galesburg, Ill, Nov 20, 13; m 40; c 2. GERMAN. *Educ:* Lafayette Col, AB, 34; Univ Wis, MA, 36, PhD(Ger lit), 41. *Prof Exp:* Teaching fel & asst Ger, Univ Wis, 36-38; instr, Oberlin Col, 38; instr, Ursinus Col, 38-39; instr, 39-43, from asst prof to assoc prof, 46-58, chmn dept, 72-76, PROF GER, OBERLIN COL, 58- *Concurrent Pos:* Mem MLA teacher inst & classroom testing, 60-63. *Mem:* MLA; Am Asn Teachers Ger. *Res:* German advanced placement; language laboratories; Eduard Moerike. *Publ:* Coauth, Shorter College German & German Grammar Workbook, Appleton, 56; The college board and advanced placement in German, Ger Quart. *Mailing Add:* Dept of Ger & Russ Oberlin Col Oberlin OH 44074

REICHART, WALTER ALBERT, b Austria, Nov 15, 03; US citizen; m 29. GERMAN LANGUAGE & LITERATURE. *Educ:* Univ Mich, AB, 25, AM, 27, PhD, 30. *Prof Exp:* From instr to assoc prof, 25-40, prof, 40-73, EMER PROF GER, UNIV MICH, ANN ARBOR, 73- *Concurrent Pos:* Vis prof, Univ Calif, Berkeley, 65. *Mem:* MLA; Am Asn Teachers Ger (1st vpres, 50, pres, 51); Int Ver Ger Sprach--und Literaturwiss; corp mem Thomas Mann Soc; Gerhart Hauptmann Ges. *Res:* Bibliography; Anglo-German literary relations; Gerhart Hauptman. *Publ:* Auth, Washington Irving and Germany, Univ Mich, 57; coauth, Max Pinkus, W G Korn, München, 58; Das Werk Thomas Manns, S Fischer, Frankfurt, 59; auth, Gerhart Hauptmann's dramas on the American stage, Maske u Kothurn, 9-12/62; Washington Irvings Reise durch Oesterreich, Jahrbuch Wiener Goethe Ver, 62; Grundbegriffe im dramatischen Schaffen Gerhart Hauptmanns, PMLA, 3/67; Gerhart-Hauptman-Bibliographie, Gehlen, Bad Homburg, 69; ed, Journals and Notebooks of Washington Irving, Vol III, 1819-1827, Univ Wis, 70, Vol II, 1807-1822, Twayne, 81. *Mailing Add:* 2106 Londonderry Rd Ann Arbor MI 48104

REICHMANN, EBERHARD, b Stuttgart, Ger, Dec 8, 26; US citizen; m 56; c 2. GERMAN. *Educ:* Paedag Inst Schwaeb Gmuend, BA, 49; Univ Cincinnati, MA, 55, PhD, 59. *Prof Exp:* From instr to assoc prof, 59-68, dir freshman & sophomore Ger, 62-65, PROF GER, IND UNIV, BLOOMINGTON, 68-, DIR GER STUDIES, INST GER STUDIES, 76- *Concurrent Pos:* Alexander von Humboldt fel, Univ Erlangen, 65-66; res dir, Teaching Aid Proj, 66-68; founder & ed, Unterrichtspraxis, 68-71; A V Humboldt Found fel, 79. *Honors & Awards:* Humboldt Medal, A V Humboldt Found, 77. *Mem:* Am Asn Teachers Ger; Int Ver Germanistik. *Res:* Baroque period; the Enlightenment; German culture studies. *Publ:* Auth, Begrundung d dt Aufklarungsasthetik . . . , Monatshefte, fall 67; Die Herrschaft der Zahl, Metzler, 68; ed, The Teaching of German: Problems and Methods, Nat Carl Schurz Asn, 70; co-ed, Teaching Postwar Germany in America, Inst Ger Study, 72; Texte und Kontexte, Francke, 73; Das Studium der Deutschen Literatur, Nat Carl Schurz Asn, 74; auth, German culture studies: Pedagogical Considerations, In: Ger Studies in US, 76; Germanistik Oder Deutsche Studien, In: Rezept Gegenu, Lit im Ausland, 76. *Mailing Add:* Inst Ger Studies Ind Univ Bloomington IN 47401

REID, J RICHARD, b Parsons, Kans, May 1, 14; m 36; c 2. GENERAL & ROMANCE LINGUISTICS. *Educ:* Swarthmore Col, AB, 35; Harvard Univ, AM, 36; PhD, 43. *Prof Exp:* Teaching asst French, Syracuse Univ, 38-39; instr, Harvard Univ, 39-44, Span, 43-44; from asst prof to prof, 44-76, chmn dept, 46-69, EMER PROF ROMANCE LANGS, CLARK UNIV, 76- *Concurrent Pos:* Teacher, Worcester Jr Col, 44-46; vis prof, Assumption Col, 73-74. *Mem:* MLA; Ling Soc Am; Am Asn Teachers Span & Port; Am Asn Teachers Fr; Int Ling Asn. *Res:* Applied linguistics; Mexican literature and culture. *Publ:* Auth, An Exploratory Survey of Foreign Language Teaching by Television in the United States, In: Reports of Surveys and Studies in the Teaching of Modern Foreign Languages, MLA, 61. *Mailing Add:* Romance Lang Clark Univ Worcester MA 01610

REID, LAWRENCE ANDREW, b NZ, June 2, 34. LINGUISTICS. *Educ:* Univ Hawaii, MA, 64, PhD(ling), 66. *Prof Exp:* Instr phonetics & grammar, Summer Inst Ling, Australia, 58-59; field researcher Bontok, Summer Inst Ling, Philippines, 59-63; field researcher Ivatan & Austronesian lang, Philippines & Taiwan, 65; instr ling, Univ Hawaii, 66; asst dir, Summer Inst Ling, Univ Auckland, 67; field researcher, Philippines, 68; chief ling consult, Summer Inst Ling, Philippines, 69; from asst linguist to assoc linguist, Pac & Asian Ling Inst, Univ Hawaii, Manoa, 70-77; RESEARCHER LING, SOC SCI RES INST & DEPT LING, UNIV HAWAII, 77- *Concurrent Pos:* Vis prof, Univ Auckland, 78; ed, Filipinas. *Mem:* Ling Soc NZ; Ling Soc Philippines; Ling Soc Am; Polynesian Soc; Asn Asian Studies. *Res:* Philippine and aboriginal Formosan descriptive and comparative linguistics; ethnography of Northern Luzon; discourse analysis. *Publ:* Auth, A Guinag wedding ceremony, Philippine Sociol Rev, 61; An Ivatan Syntax, Univ Hawaii, 66; ed, Philippine Minor Languages: Word Lists and Phonologies, Univ Hawaii, 72; auth, Central Bontoc: Discourse, paragraph and sentence structures, Summer Inst Ling, 72; Diachronic typology of Philippine vowel systems, In: Current Trends in Linguistics, Vol XI, Mouton, The Hague, 73; Bontoc-English dictionary and finder list, Pac Ling Ser C, 74; The problem *R and *l reflexes in Kankanay, In: Festschrift in Honor of Cecilio Lopez, Ling Soc Philippines, 74; The state of the art of Philippine linguistics, 1970-1980, In: Philippine Studies: Political Science, Economics, and Linguistics, Occas Papers Ctr for Southeast Asian Studies, No 8, Northern Ill Univ, 81. *Mailing Add:* Dept of Ling Univ of Hawaii Honolulu HI 96822

REID, PETER LAWRENCE DONALD, b Edinburgh, Scotland, Jan 30, 37; m 68. CLASSICS. *Educ:* Cambridge Univ, BA, 60, MA, 64; Univ Calif, Los Angeles, PhD(classics), 74. *Prof Exp:* Instr classics, Trinity Col (Scotland), 60-63 & Thacher Sch, Calif, 66-70; asst prof, 73-80, ASSOC PROF CLASSICS, TUFTS UNIV, 80- *Mem:* Am Philol Asn. *Res:* Mediaeval Latin; classical epic. *Publ:* Auth, Ratherii Veronensis Opera Maiora, Brepols, Turnhout, 76 & 82; Tenth Century Latinity, Undena Publ, 81. *Mailing Add:* Dept of Classics Tufts Univ Medford MA 02155

REIF, JOSEPH A, b Philadelphia, Pa, July 28, 30; div; c 4. LINGUISTICS. *Educ:* Univ Pa, AB, 51, AM, 53, PhD(ling), 68. *Prof Exp:* Sci linguist Hindi-Urdu & Hebrew, Foreign Serv Inst, 59-66; from lectr to asst prof ling, SAsian lang & Near East lang & lit, Univ Mich, Ann Arbor, 66-69; SR LECTR LING & HEBREW, BAR-ILAN UNIV, ISRAEL, 69- *Concurrent Pos:* Prof lectr, Am Univ, 62-63. *Mem:* Ling Soc Am; Isreal Asn Appl Ling. *Res:* Semitic and South Asian languages. *Publ:* Auth, The loss of consonantal aleph in Ugaritic, J Semitic Studies, 1/59; coauth, Hebrew Basic C ourse, US Govt Printing Off, 65. *Mailing Add:* Dept of English Bar-Ilan Univ Ramat-Gan Israel

REIFF, DONALD GENE, b Chicago, Ill, Oct 20, 34; m 57; c 2. LINGUISTICS. *Educ:* DePauw Univ, BA, 56; Univ Wis, MA, 58; Univ Mich, MA, 62, PhD(ling), 63. *Prof Exp:* Teaching asst Span, Univ Wis, 57-59; asst res linguist, Proj Audio-Lingual Lang Prog, Univ Mich, 60-61; instr ling, Univ Wash, 62-63; asst prof, 63-68, ASSOC PROF LING, UNIV ROCHESTER, 68- *Concurrent Pos:* Consult second-level Span course, Midwest Prog, Airborne TV Instr, 62; mem working comt III, Northeast Conf Lang Teaching, 67-68. *Mem:* Ling Soc Am; Int Ling Asn; Acad Aphasia. *Res:* Linguistic theory; pathologies of language; language teaching and acquisition problems in general. *Publ:* Coauth, Structural Apperception in the Absence of Syntactic Constraints, Lang & Speech, 10-12/70; Aphasia and Linguistic Competence, Proc 10th Int Congr Linguists. *Mailing Add:* Dept of Foreign Lang, Lit & Ling Univ of Rochester Rochester NY 14627

REILLY, JOHN H, b Penn Yan, NY, Oct 31, 34. ROMANCE LANGUAGES. *Educ:* Syracuse Univ, BA, 56; Univ Wis, MA, 58, PhD(French), 64. *Prof Exp:* Instr French, Bowling Green State Univ, 61-63; lectr, 63-64, from instr to asst prof, 64-71, chmn dept Romance lang, 70-79, assoc prof, 71-79, PROF FRENCH, QUEENS COL, NY, 79- *Mem:* Am Asn Teachers Fr; MLA; Soc des Amis de Jean Giraudoux. *Res:* Jean Giraudoux; Arthur Adamov; theater of the absurd. *Publ:* Auth, Giraudoux's Intermezzo: Its elaboration, Fr Rev, 12/65; ed, Intermezzo, Appleton, 67; coauth, A comparison of the modern methods of language teaching, Fr Rev, 3/71; auth, Arthur Adamov, 74 & Jean Giraudoux, 78, Twayne. *Mailing Add:* Dept of Romance Lang Queens Col Flushing NY 11367

REIMERS, THERESIA ELIZABETH, b Sacramento, Calif, Mar 21, 31. GERMAN. *Educ:* Stanford Univ, AB, 52, AM, 53, PhD, 63. *Prof Exp:* Actg instr Ger, Stanford Univ, 57-58; instr, Inst Europ Studies, Univ Vienna, 58-60 & Univ Hawaii, 60-61; asst prof, 62-67, chmn humanities prog, 65-68, assoc prof, 67-80, PROF GER, HOLLINS COL, 80-, CHMN DEPT MOD LANG, 76- *Mem:* MLA; Am Asn Teachers Ger; AAUP; Siegfried-Wagner-Gesellschaft. *Res:* Opera. *Publ:* Auth, Siegfried Wagner as innovator, Opera, 10/72; Siegfried Wagners Bayreuther Regiearbeit, Opernwelt, Yrbk 1974, 74; Kurt Söhnlein, designer and man of the theatre, Opera, 7/75; Kurt Söhnlein, 7/75, Der drachenkampf, 7/76 & Die suche, 7/77, Festspielnachrichten Nordbayerischer Kurier. *Mailing Add:* Dept of Mod Lang Hollins Col Hollins College VA 24020

REINDORP, REGINALD CARL, b Alamogordo, N Mex, June 3, 07; m 31; c 4. SPANISH. *Educ:* Univ N Mex, AB, 31, AM, 33; Univ Tex PhD, 49. *Prof Exp:* Prin, Span-Am Norm Sch, N Mex, 32-33, dean, 35-37; supt, Reserve Union High Sch, 34-35; instr Span, Univ N Mex, 42-43; US Dept State spec rep coop educ prog, Inst Inter-Am Affairs & Repub El Salvador, 43-48; asst prof Span, Univ Ark, 49-51; dir Inst Latin-Am Studies, Miss Souther Col, 51-61; prof Span & chmn div lang lit & speech, Ft Hays Kans State Col, 62-65; prof foreign lang & chmn dept, Wesleyan Col, Ga, 65-73; RETIRED. *Concurrent Pos:* Chief, UNESCO Tech Educ Mission & specialist in higher educ, Quito, Ecuador, 52-53; consult mod foreign lang, State of Miss, 59-61. *Honors & Awards:* Gold Medal, El Salvador, 48. *Publ:* Auth, Spanish American Customs, Culture and Personality, Southern 68; Metodologia de las lenguas vivas, Libreria Int, Lima; Idiomas, cultura y educacion, Casa Cult, Quito; coauth, The Chronicles of Mechoacan, Univ Okla, 69; The Codex Perex and the Book of Chilam Balam of Mani, Univ Okla, 79. *Mailing Add:* Rte 2 Box 75 Columbia MS 39429

REINER, ERICA, b Budapest, Hungary; US citizen. ASSYRIOLOGY. *Educ:* Sorbonne, Dipl Assyriol, 51; Univ Chicago, PhD(Assyriol), 55. *Prof Exp:* From res asst to res assoc Assyriol, 52-56, from asst prof to prof, 56-73, JOHN A WILSON PROF ASSYRIOL, UNIV CHICAGO, 73- *Concurrent Pos:* Assoc ed, Assyrian Dictionary, Orient Inst, Univ Chicago, 57-62, ed, 62-; Guggenheim fel, 74. *Mem:* Am Orient Soc; Ling Soc Am; Am Philos Soc; fel Am Acad Arts & Sci. *Res:* Linguistics; Babylonian literature. *Publ:* Auth, Surpu: A Collection of Sumerian and Akkadian Incantations, Weidner, Graz, 58; A Linguistic Analysis of Akkadian, Mouton, The Hague, 66; Elamite language, In: Handbuch der Orientalistik, Brill, Leiden, 69; Akkadian, In: Current Trends in Linguistics, Mouton, The Hague, 69; Babylonian Planetary Omens: Parts 1 & 2, Undena, 75 & 81. *Mailing Add:* Orient Inst Univ of Chicago Chicago IL 60637

REINHARDT, GEORGE WILLIAM, b Camden, NJ, Feb 10, 34; m 67; c 3. GERMAN & COMPARATIVE LITERATURE. *Educ:* Univ Pa, BA, 55; Columbia Univ, MA, 57, PhD(Ger), 67. *Prof Exp:* Lectr Ger, Columbia Univ, 55-62, from instr to asst prof, 62-70; asst prof, 70-73, ASSOC PROF GER, UNIV CONN, 73- *Mem:* MLA; Am Asn Teachers Ger. *Res:* Nineteenth and twentieth century German literature. *Publ:* Auth, The politics of the young C F Meyer, Ger Quart, 72; The ordeal of art: Hermann Kasack's Falschungen, Studies Short Fiction, 72; A German, an Austrian, and a Swiss admirer of Camoens, Ocidente, 72; A reading of Grillparzer's Sappho, Studies Ger Drama; Silz-Festschrift, 74; The French sources of K Edschmid's Der aussätzige Wald, Monatshefte, 76; Turbulence and enigma in Kleist's Der Findling, Essays Lit, 77; Thematic development in Ingeborg Bachmann's Malina, Symposium, 79; Georg Lukacs on C F Meyer, Colloq Germ, 82. *Mailing Add:* Dept of Ger Univ of Conn Storrs CT 06268

REINHOLD, ERNEST, b Tann, Ger, Aug 8, 22; Can citizen; wid. GERMAN. *Educ:* Univ Alta, BSc, 46, MA, 49; Univ Mich, PhD(Ger), 56. *Prof Exp:* Lectr, 52-54, from asst prof to assoc prof, 54-65, dir summer sch ling, 58-68, head dept Ger lang & lit, 60-69, PROF GER LANG & LIT, UNIV ALTA, 65-, ASST DEAN FAC ARTS, 77- *Mem:* MLA; Am Asn Teachers Ger; Asn Can Univ Teachers Ger. *Res:* Anglo-German literary relations; 20th century drama; German exile literature. *Mailing Add:* Dept of Ger Lang & Lit Univ of Alberta Edmonton AB T6G 2G2 Can

REINHOLD, MEYER, b New York, NY, Sept 1, 09; m 39; c 2. CLASSICAL LANGUAGE, ANCIENT HISTORY. *Educ:* City Col New York, AB, 29; Columbia Univ, MA, 30, PhD(Greek, Latin & ancient hist), 33. *Prof Exp:* From instr to assoc prof class lang, Brooklyn Col, 39-55; vpres, advert agency, New York, 55-65; assoc prof Greek, Latin & ancient hist, Southern Ill Univ, 65-67; prof class lang, 67-76, Byler distinguished prof, 76-80, EMER PROF CLASS LANG, UNIV MO-COLUMBIA, 80- *Concurrent Pos:* Vis univ prof, Boston Univ, 80- *Mem:* Am Philol Asn; Am Soc Papyrologists; Class Asn New England & S; Vergilian Soc; fel Am Acad Rome. *Res:* Classical traditions in early America; Roman history; Latin literature. *Publ:* Auth, Past and Present, the Continuity of Classical Myths, Hakkert, 72; The quest for useful knowledge in 18th century America, Am Philos Soc, 5/75; The Classick Pages: Classical Reading of 18th Century Americans, 75 & The classics and the quest for virtue in 18th century American, 77, Am Philol Asn; The Golden Age of Augustus, Samuels-Stevens, 78; contribr, Classical political theory and its influences on 18th century American thought, In: Classical Influences on Western Education, Philosophy and Social Theory, 1650-1870, Cambridge Univ, 78; Robert Lowell's Uses of Classical Myths, Helios, 7/80; The Jewish Diasporo among Greeks and Romans, Samuels-Stevens, 82. *Mailing Add:* 63 Sparks St Cambridge MA 02138

REINKE, EDGAR CARL, b Chicago, Ill, June 29, 06. GREEK, LATIN. *Educ:* Univ Chicago, AB, 28, PhD(Greek & Latin), 34; Univ Minn, AM, 57. *Prof Exp:* From asst prof to assoc prof, Ala Col, 37-49; from assoc prof to prof, 49-75, res prof, 72, 73, actg head dept, 63-64, head dept, 64-71, EMER PROF CLASS LANG, VALPARAISO UNIV, 75- *Mem:* Am Philol Asn; Am Class League; Class Asn Mid W & S; Vergilian Soc; Renaissance Soc Am. *Res:* Classical tradition; Vergil. *Publ:* Auth, Vergil's Lacrimae rerum, Class Outlook, 9/63; coauth, Nicolaus Marschalk: Oration, Concordia, 67; auth, A classical debate of the Charleston, South Carolina, library society, Papers Bibliog Soc Am, 2nd quart, 67; Oral portrayal in the poetry of Vergil, Class Outlook, 10/69; Quintilian lighted the way, Class Bull, 3/75; The Dialogus of Andreas Meinhardi, Xerox, 76. *Mailing Add:* Lutheran Haven Oviedo FL 32765

REINMUTH, HARRY GILBERT, b St Louis, Mo, Sept 14, 96; m 20. GERMANIC PHILOLOGY. *Educ:* Clinton Sem, AB, 20; Univ Chicago, PhB, 28, AM, 32; Northwestern Univ, PhD, 37. *Prof Exp:* Prof Ger & Greek, Can Jr Col, 21-23 & Broadview Col, 23-33; prof Ger, Southwestern Jr Col, 33-34; prof Ger & French, Walla Walla Col, 34-48; prof mod & Bibl lang & head dept, 38-72, EMER PROF MOD LANG, UNION COL, NEBR, 72- *Concurrent Pos:* Sr specialist higher educ, Off Mil Govt, Berlin, Ger, 46-47. *Mem:* MLA. *Res:* Germanic linguistics; semantic and etymological study of abstract terms in Notker's Boethius. *Mailing Add:* 4501 Calvert St Lincoln NE 68506

REISH, JOSEPH GEORGE, b Sunbury, Pa, Apr 18, 44; m 78; c 1. FRENCH LANGUAGE & LITERATURE. *Educ:* Georgetown Univ, AB, 66; Middlebury Col, MA, 67; Univ Wis-Madison, PhD(French), 72. *Prof Exp:* Asst prof French, Butler Univ, 71-72; ASSOC PROF FRENCH, WESTERN MICH UNIV, 72- *Mem:* Am Soc Eighteenth Century Studies; Am Coun Teaching Foreign Lang; MLA; Am Asn Teachers French. *Publ:* Auth, Revolution: Three changing faces of Figaro, Mich Academician, fall 76; Madame de Genlis and the early American stage, Proc PNCFL, 77; coauth, The preparation and classroom use of a videotaped play, Can Mod Lang Rev, 1/80; auth, Myth in the age of reason: Madame de Genlis and the Pygmalion theme, Papers in Romance, spring 80; Sonnet-Premiere Etude (poem), Chimeres, 81; The Birds, Our Trust (poem), The Chat, fall 82; contribr, Bibliographical Guide to the Study of the Literature of the USA, Duke Univ Press, 82. *Mailing Add:* 3720 Barrington Dr Kalamazoo MI 49007

REISLER, MARSHA LYNN, b NY, June 26, 48; m 70. FRENCH LITERATURE & LANGUAGE. *Educ:* Univ Rochester, BA, 70; Cornell Univ, MA, 73, PhD(French lit), 75. *Prof Exp:* Asst French lit, Cornell Univ, 71-72, 73-74; ASST PROF FRENCH, UNIV RICHMOND, 74- *Concurrent Pos:* Libr/fac partnership course innovation & bibliog instr, Nat Endowment for Humanities & Am Coun Libr Resources, Univ Richmond 77-78. *Mem:* MLA. *Res:* French literature; literary criticism; psychoanalysis. *Publ:* Auth, Persuasion through antithesis: An analysis of the dominant rhetorical structure of Pascal's Lettres Provinciales, Romanic Rev, 5/78; Dialectic and rhetoric in Voltaire's Lettres Philosophiques, L'Esprit Createur, winter 77. *Mailing Add:* Dept of Mod Foreign Lang Univ of Richmond Richmond VA 23173

REISS, TIMOTHY JAMES, b Stanmore, England, May 14, 42; Brit & Can citizen; m 66; c 3. COMPARATIVE LITERATURE, FRENCH. *Educ:* Univ Manchester, Eng, BA, 64; Univ Ill, MA, 65, PhD(French), 68. *Prof Exp:* Instr French, Univ Ill, 67-68; from instr to asst prof French, Dept Romance Lang, Yale Univ, 68-73; assoc prof, 73-79, dir dept, 76-81, PROF COMP LIT, DEPT ENGLISH, UNIV MONTREAL, 79- *Concurrent Pos:* Morse fel French, Yale Univ, 71-72; vis prof comp lit, Univ Toronto, 76-77; Can Coun study fel comp lit, 77-78; vis prof comp lit, Univ BC, 79; vis prof French, NY Univ, 82; co-ed, Europa, 81-82. *Mem:* MLA; Northeastern Mod Lang Asn (secy, 71-73); Can Asn Res Semiotics; Can Comp Lit Asn (vpres, 81-83). *Res:* Relations of science, philosophy, politics and criticism in 17th and 18th century Europe; modern critical theory and discourse analysis; drama. *Publ:* Auth, Toward Dramatic Illusion: Theatrical Technique and Meaning from Hardy to Horace, Yale Univ, 71; ed, Science, language, and the perspective mind, Yale Fr Studies, 73; auth, Tragedy and Truth: Studies in the Development of a Renaissance and Neoclassical Discourse, Yale Univ Press, 80; The Discourse of Modernism, Cornell Univ Press, 82; On opening the disciplines, Europa, 82; coauth (with Pierre Gravel), Tragique et Tragedie dans la tradition occidentale, Determinations, Montreal, 82. *Mailing Add:* Prog of Comp Lit Univ of Montreal Montreal PQ H3C 3J7 Can

REISSNER, ARTHUR J, b Cottbus, Ger, May 17, 14; US citizen; m 51. FOREIGN LANGUAGES. *Educ:* Univ Basel, LLD, 36; Harvard Univ, LLB, 50; Univ Chicago, PhD(class lang & lit), 71. *Prof Exp:* Instr Ger, Army Lang Sch, 51-55; off mgr foreign corp, Vulcanus do Brasil, Sao Paulo, Brazil, 55-58; asst prof foreign lang, Northern Ill Univ, 59-71, assoc prof class lang, 71-75; RETIRED. *Concurrent Pos:* Interpreter Ger, US Dept State, 59. *Res:* World law; language teaching method; origin of language. *Publ:* Auth, Der Irrtum über die Geschäftsgrundlage, Helbing & Lichtenhahn, 39; coauth, German course part III, Army Lang Sch, 51; auth, College German, Direct Method, Northern Ill Univ, 61; Einführung ins Deutsche-A Flexible Approach, Blaisdell, 68; Three easy steps, Class Outlook, 1/74. *Mailing Add:* PO Box 908 Port Hueneme CA 93041

REITZ, RICHARD ALLEN, b Clay Center, Kans, Sept 14, 37; m 66; c 1. SPANISH. *Educ:* Univ Kans, BA, 59, MA, 61; Univ Ky, PhD(Span), 70. *Prof Exp:* Instr Span, Va Mil Inst, 59-60; asst, Univ Kans, 60-61; assoc prof, 63-74, PROF SPAN, CATAWBA COL, 74- *Concurrent Pos:* Asst prof, Univ Ky, 67-68; Nat Endowment for the Humanities Sem fel, Univ Pittsburgh, 75. *Mem:* Am Asn Teachers Span & Port; AAUP; Mountain Interstate Foreign Lang Conf. *Res:* Spanish American literature; Brazilian literature; Faulkerian influences on Gabriel Garcia Marquez, Paper delivered, 1976. *Publ:* Translr, Noticias Secretas, R & D Bks, Salisbury, NC, 78. *Mailing Add:* Dept of Mod Lang Catawba Col Salisbury NC 28144

REJHON, ANNALEE CLAIRE, b Bathhurst, Australia, July 23, 49; m 81. MEDIEVAL LITERATURE, PHILOLOGY. *Educ:* Univ Calif, Berkeley, BA, 71, MA, 73, PhD(Fr), 79. *Prof Exp:* Lectr French, Univ Calif, Berkeley, 79-80 & Calif State Univ, Hayward, 80-81; Am Coun Learned Soc fel, 81; LECTR MID WELSH, UNIV CALIF, BERKELEY, 82- *Mem:* Mediaeval Acad Am; Soc Rencesvals; Celtic Studies Asn Am. *Res:* Edition of medieval texts; Old French language and literature; Middle Welsh language and literature. *Publ:* Auth, La Version galloise de la Chanson de Roland et sa relation avec les autres redactions du poeme, In: VIII Congreso de la Societe Rencesvals: Pamplona--Santiage de Compostela, 15-25 de agosto de 1978, Instucion de Viana, Pamplona, 81; The Roland-Oliver relationship in the Welsh version of the Chanson de Roland, Romance Philol, 35: 234-242; Can Rolant: The Medieval Welsh Version of the Song of Roland, Univ Calif Press (in prep); Hu Gadarn: Folklore and fabrication, Studies Honor William Heist (in prep). *Mailing Add:* 2420 Hilgard Ave Berkeley CA 94709

REKLAITIS, JANINE KONAUKA, b Dec 27, 42; US citizen; m. BALTIC LANGUAGES & LITERATURE. *Educ:* Loyola Univ Chicago, AB, 65; Univ Calif, Berkeley, MA, 66; Stanford Univ, PhD(ling), 72. *Prof Exp:* Asst prof ling, Lithuanian Studies prog, Univ Ill, Chicago Circle, 72-79; RES & WRITING, 80- *Concurrent Pos:* Fulbright sr lectr, 80. *Mem:* Ling Soc Am; Asn Advan Baltic Studies; Am Asn Teachers Slavic & East Europ Lang; Ling Soc Can & US; Int Ling Assoc. *Res:* Linguistic change; Baltic linguistics; comparative Indo-European. *Publ:* Auth, Case study of an analogical change in Lithuanian, Baltic Lit & Ling, 10/73; Evidence from Lithuanian for directed drift, Scando Slavica, 74; Language contact and language change, In: The Third LACUS Forum, Hornbean, 77; Pie word order and word order in Lithuanian, In: Proc 3rd Int Conf Hist Ling, 81 & Reduction of case markers, In: Proc 4th Int Conf Hist Ling, 80, John Benjamins. *Mailing Add:* Inst of Lithuanian Studies Univ of Ill Chicago Circle Chicago IL 60607

RELYEA, SUZANNE LADUE, b Goshen, NY, Aug 6, 45. FRENCH LITERATURE, WOMEN'S STUDIES. *Educ:* NY Univ, BA, 68; Yale Univ, MPhil, 71, PhD(French), 72. *Prof Exp:* ASSOC PROF FRENCH, UNIV MASS, BOSTON, 72- *Honors & Awards:* Chancellor's Award, Univ Mass, 77. *Mem:* MLA; Northeast Mod Lang Asn; NAm Soc 17th Century Fr Lit; Int Asn Philos & Lit. *Res:* Systems of signification in women's prose, particularly in their portrayals (creation) of reality; Madame de Sevigne; Madame de Lafayette. *Publ:* Auth, Signs, Systems and Meanings: A Semiotic Reading of 4 Moliere Plays, Wesleyan Univ, 9/76; The sign's desire: Colette's creation of the real, In: Colette, The Woman, The Writer, Pa State Univ Press, 81; The symbolic in the family factory: Colette's mes apprentissages, Women's Studies, 8: 273-297; Aggression, enclosure and the caress: L'Honnele homme chet ses amies, Papers Fr 17th Century Lit, Paris, Tuebingen, 82; Ell se nomme: La representation et la lette dans la Princess de Cleves, In: Onze Nouvelles Etudes Sur l'Image de la Femme an XVIIe Siecle, Michel-Place, Paris, 82. *Mailing Add:* Dept of French Univ of Mass Boston MA 02125

REMAK, HENRY HEYMANN HERMAN, b Berlin, Ger, July 27, 16; US citizen; m 46; c 4. GERMAN, COMPARATIVE LITERATURE. *Educ:* Univ Montpellier, lic es let, 36; Ind Univ, AM, 37; Univ Chicago, PhD, 47. *Hon Degrees:* Litt D, Univ Lille, 73. *Prof Exp:* Instr Ger & Span, Indianapolis Exten Ctr, Ind Univ, 39-43; from instr to prof Ger, 46-64, chmn W Europ studies, 66-69, vchancellor & dean fac, 69-74, PROF GER & COMP LIT, IND UNIV, 64- *Concurrent Pos:* Dir Ger summer sch, 67-71; assoc ed, Ger Quart, 58-62; assoc ed, Yearbk Compt & Gen Lit, 61-66, ed, 66-78; Fulbright lectr comp & Ger lit, Univ Hamburg, 67; Guggenheim fel, 67-68; Nat Endowment for Humanities fel, 77-78; dir summer & yr-long seminars, Nat Endowmen for Humanities, 77 & 78-79; pres, Coordr Comt Comp Hist Lit in Europ Langs, Int Comp Lit Asn, 77- *Mem:* Corresp mem Acad Sci, Arts & Lett, Marseilles. *Res:* Franco-German literary relations; modern German literature; general comparative literature. *Publ:* Contribr, Comparative Literature: Method and Perspective, Southern Ill Univ, 71; auth, Der Rahmen in der deutschen Novelle, Delp, Munich, 72; Exoticism in Romanticism, Comp Lit Studies, 3/78; Der Weg zur Weltliteratur: Fontanes bret harte-entwurf, 80; The Users of Comparative Literature, Value Judgment, 81; Die novelle in der Klassik uhd, Romanttik, 82. *Mailing Add:* Dept of Lit Ind Univ Bloomington IN 47401

REMATORE, ANDREW IRVING, b New Haven, Conn, Oct 19, 24; m 53; c 2. SPANISH, LINGUISTICS. *Educ:* Univ Colo, BA, 50, MA, 52; Stanford Univ, PhD(Span), 68. *Prof Exp:* Instr Span & English, Fr Hays Kans State Col, 52-55, asst prof Span & dir honors prog, 55-60, chmn dept, 55-65, from assoc prof to prof lang, 60-65; asst prof Romance Lang, 65-69, chmn dept mod lang & lit, 73-80, ASSOC PROF ROMANCE LANG, UNIV SANTA CLARA, 69- *Concurrent Pos:* Mem accreditation comt, Western Asn Schs & Cols, 70- *Mem:* Am Asn Teachers Span & Port; Am Coun Teaching Foreign Lang; Pac Coast Coun Latin Am Studies. *Res:* Linguistics applied to language learning and teaching; Latin American literature and culture. *Publ:* Auth, Argentina, Paraguay & Uruguay, Hisp Am Report, 58-60; coauth, Honduras, In: Collier's Yearbook, Collier-Macmillan, 59 & Argentina, Uruguay & Paraguay, In Encyclopedia of the Nations, Worldmark, 60. *Mailing Add:* Dept of Mod Lang & Lit Univ of Santa Clara Santa Clara CA 95053

RENALDI, THOMAS WAYNE, b Elkhart, Ind, Apr 27, 28; m 67; c 1. SPANISH AMERICAN LITERATURE. *Educ:* Ind Univ, BA, 60; Univ Houston, MA, 67; Univ Chicago, PhD(Span Am lit), 74. *Prof Exp:* Teacher Span, Chicago Pub Schs, 67-68; instr, Barat Col, 69-71; instr, 71-74, ASST PROF SPAN, UNIV NOTRE DAME, 74- *Mem:* Am Asn Teachers Span & Port; MLA; Midwest Mod Lang Asn. *Res:* Novel of the Mexican Revolution; modernist poetry; Spanish American theater. *Publ:* Auth, Notes on the functions of acaso tal vez and quiza(s) in American Spanish, Hispania, 5/77; coauth, The friendship between Jose Juan Tablada and Ramon del Valle-Inclan, Am Hispanist, 11/77; auth, The Two Versions of Mariano Azuela's Los de Abajo, Gordon Press, 80. *Mailing Add:* 1206 E South St South Bend IN 46615

RENART, JUAN GUILLERMO, b Artigas, Uruguay, Sept 4, 42; Can citizen; m 70; c 3. HISPANIC LITERATURE. *Educ:* Inst Jackson, BA, 66; Univ Toronto, MA, 71, PhD(Hisp lit & Span lang), 77. *Prof Exp:* Lectr, Univ Waterloo, 74-76; lectr, 76-77, ASST PROF HISP LIT & SPAN LANG, UNIV OTTAWA, 77- *Mem:* MLA; Am Asn Teachers Span & Port; Int Asn Hispanists; Can Asn Hispanists; Can Asn Latin-Am Studies. *Res:* Spanish-American and Spanish modern poetry and narrative; semiotics and theory of literature; interdisciplinary use of intrinsic literary study. *Publ:* Contribr, Calderonde la Barca Studies 1951-1969: A Critical Survey and Annotated Bibliography, Univ Toronto, 71; auth, Fervor de Buenos Aires de Borges: Intelecto o emociones primarias?, Rev Can Estud Hisp, fall 76; Imagen tropologiea e imagen bisemica en umpoema projetico de Vicente Aleincandre, Ottawa Hisp, 79; Los Tres Sonetos a Cristo crucificado ante el mar?, Comienzo publico del Bergamin poeta, Camp de l'Arpa, Barcelona, 9-10/79; Mitificacion y desmitificacionde animales en la poesia folklorica quechua de contenido social, Ottawa Hisp, 80; Sobre la estructura de El Cristo de Velazquez de Unamuno: El problema de las sectores desmenbrados, In: Actas del Secto Congreso Internacional de Hispanista, Univ Toronto, 80; La estructura libre de El Cristo De Velazquez de Unamuno, Ottawa Hisp, 82; El Cristo de Velazquez de Unamuno: Estudio estructural y estilistico, Anejos de la RCEH & Univ Toronto Press, 82. *Mailing Add:* Dept Mod Lang & Lit Univ Ottawa Ottawa ON K1N 6N5 Can

RENAUD, ARMAND A, b July 27, 18; nat US; m 48. FRENCH & COMPARATIVE LITERATURE. *Educ:* Wayne Univ, BA, 49; Yale Univ, PhD(Romance lang), 54. *Prof Exp:* Asst French, Wayne Univ, 48-49; asst, Yale Univ, 50-53; from instr to asst prof, NorthWestern Univ, 53-57; from asst prof to assoc prof, 57-64, chmn dept Romance lang, 63-68, dept French & Ital, 68-70, dir grad studies French, 63-70, PROF FRENCH, UNIV MINN, MINNEAPOLIS, 64-, PROF COMP LIT, 65- *Concurrent Pos:* Bibliogr French lang & lit, PMLA Annual Bibliog, 59-65; contrib ed, Bibliog French XVIIth Century Studies, 72-77. *Mem:* MLA; Mod Humanities Res Asn; Int Asn Fr Studies; Int Asn Comp Lit; Am Asn Comp Lit. *Res:* Renaissance and baroque literature; myth in drama; influence of the Orient 1450 to 1700. *Publ:* Auth, La litterature et la vie en 1662; Madame de la Fayette; Satiric and burleque poetry; ed, Acta, Proc Fourth Annual Conf XVIIth Century Fr Lit, Univ Minn, Vol 1, 72; auth, articles, In: Dictionnaire international des termes litteraires, Mouton, The Hague, Vol 1, 74. *Mailing Add:* Dept of French & Ital Univ of Minn Minneapolis MN 55455

RENDALL, STEVEN FINLAY, b Geneva, Ill, May 2, 39; m 79; c 1. ROMANCE & COMPARATIVE LITERATURE. *Educ:* Univ Colo, BA, 61; Johns Hopkins Univ, PhD(Romance lang), 67. *Prof Exp:* Asst prof, 67-72, assoc prof, 72-80, PROF ROMANCE LANG, UNIV ORE, 80- *Concurrent Pos:* Asst ed, Comp Lit, 72-79, assoc ed, 79-; vis scholar rhetoric, Univ Calif, 73-74; Nat Endowment Humanities fel, Sch Criticism & Theory, Univ Calif, Irvine, 77; Alexander von Humboldt-Stiftung res fel, Universitat Konstanz, WGer, 80-82. *Mem:* MLA; Philol Asn Pac Coast. *Res:* Sixteenth and 17th century French and Spanish literature; literary theory. *Publ:* Coauth, Imitation, theme and structure in Garcilaso's First elegy, 67 & auth, Fontenelle and his public, 71, MLN; The rhetoric of Montaigne's self-portrait, Studies in Philol, 76; Dialogue, philosophy, and rhetoric, Philos & Rhetoric, 77; coauth, Rhetoric and Persuasion in Marcela's Address to the Shepherds, Hisp Rev, 78; The Critical We, Orbis Litterarum, 80; Mus in Pice: Montaigne and Interpretation, MLN, 79; ed, Montaigne et la critique actuelle, J M Place, Paris, 82. *Mailing Add:* Dept of Romance Lang Univ of Ore Eugene OR 97403

RENDSBURG, GARY A, b Baltimore, Md, Feb 13, 54; m 77; c 1. HEBREW BIBLE, SEMITIC LINGUISTICS. *Educ:* Univ NC, Chapel Hill, BA, 75; NY Univ, MA, 77, PhD(Hebrew), 80. *Prof Exp:* ASST PROF HEBREW BIBLE, CANISIUS COL, 80- *Mem:* Soc Biblical Lit; Am Oriental Soc; Am Sch Oriental Res; Asn Jewish Studies. *Res:* Hebrew philology; Israelite history. *Publ:* Ed, The Bible World: Essays in Honor of Cyrus H Gordon, Ktav Publ House, 80; auth, Late Biblical Hebrew and the date of P, J Ancient Near Eastern Soc, 80; Hebrew 'sdt and Ugaritic isdym, J Northwest Semitic Lang, 80; A reconstruction of Moabite-Israelite history, J Ancient Near Eastern Soc, 81; Laqtil infinitives: Yiph'il or Hiph'il?, Orientalia, 82; Dual personal pronouns and dual verbs in Hebrew, Jewish Quart Rev, 82; A new look at Hebrew HW', Biblica, 82. *Mailing Add:* Dept of Relig Studies Canisius Col Buffalo NY 14208

RENEHAN, ROBERT, b Boston, Mass, Apr 25, 35; m 66; c 5. CLASSICAL PHILOLOGY. *Educ:* Boston Col, AB, 56; Harvard Univ, AM, 58, PhD, 63. *Prof Exp:* Instr classics, Univ Calif, Berkeley, 63-64 & Harvard Univ, 64-65; from assoc prof to prof Greek & Latin, Boston Col, 66-76; PROF GREEK & LATIN, UNIV CALIF, SANTA BARBARA, 76- *Concurrent Pos:* Nat Endowment Humanities sr fel, 73-74; assoc ed, Class Philol, 76-; assoc ed, Class Antiquity, 81- *Mem:* Am Philol Asn. *Res:* Textual criticism; Greek philosophy, medicine and literature. *Publ:* Auth, Greek Textual Criticism, Harvard Univ, 69; Leo Medicus, Berlin Acad, 69; Aristotle's definition of anger, Philologus, 72; Studies in Greek Texts, 75 & Greek Lexicographical Notes, 76, Vandenhoeck & Ruprecht; On the Greek Origins of the Concepts Incorporeality and Immateriality, Greek Roman and Byzantinus Studies, 80; The Greek Anthropocentric View of Man, Harvard Studies Class Philol, 81; Greek Lexicographical Notes II, Vandenhoeck & Ruprecht, 82. *Mailing Add:* Dept of Classics Univ of Calif Santa Barbara CA 93106

RENELLE, M, b St Louis, Mo, Dec 4, 12. FOREIGN LANGUAGES, LINGUISTICS. *Educ:* St Louis Univ, AB, 36, PhD(Latin, Greek, ling), 60; Western Reserve Univ, AM, 43. *Prof Exp:* Instr Latin & French, Cath Cent High Sch, Iowa, 36-40, Acad Notre Dame, Ill, 41-48; instr & registr, Notre Dame Col, Co, 48-60, prof Latin & French, 60-64; prof foreign lang & chmn dpet, Mt Mary Col, Mankato Campus, 64-70; PROF CLASS LANG & CHMN DEPT, NOTRE DAME COL, MO, 70- *Concurrent Pos:* Lectr, Marquette Univ, 67-; consult, Maria Ctr Learning & Live Enrichment, St Louis, 80- *Mem:* Am Asn Teacher Fr; Am Coun Teaching Foreign Lang; Am Translrs Asn. *Res:* Teaching foreign languages; paleography. *Publ:* Auth, Dating Terence Codex B from Codex C, Manuscripta, 7/61; transl, Two Masters, 66 & The New Priets, 66, Herder. *Mailing Add:* 7748 Mackenzie Rd St Louis MO 63123

RENER, FREDERICK M, b Trieste, Italy, Nov 5, 19. GERMAN. *Educ:* Univ Toronto, BA, 52, MA, 54, PhD, 57. *Prof Exp:* Instr, St Michael's Col, Univ Toronto, 54-57; lectr, Univ Alta, 58-59; prof, Marietta Col, 59-61; PROF GER & ITAL, UNIV NC, GREENSBORO, 61- *Concurrent Pos:* Fulbright exchange fel, Univ Göttingen, 64-65. *Mem:* Am Asn Teachers Ger; MLA; SAtlantic Mod Lang Asn. *Res:* Elizabeth Langgasser; baroque. *Publ:* Auth, Sweet imagery in German baroque poetry, SAtlantic Bull, 71; Spee, Herder, and literary criticism, Ger Quart, 71; Friedrich Spee and Virgil's Fourth Georgic, Comp Lit, 72; contribr, Opitz' Sonett an die Bienen, In: Europäische Tradition und deutscher Literaturbarock, Bern: Francke, 73; auth, Spee's Arcadia revisited, PMLA, 74; Zur Übersetzungskunst im 17 jahrhundert, Acta Neophilol, 74. *Mailing Add:* Dept of Ger & Russ Univ of NC Greensboro NC 27412

RENFROE, WALTER JACKSON, JR, b St Augustine, Fla, Aug 20, 13; m 36; c 2. FOREIGN LANGUAGES. *Educ:* US Mil Acad, BS, 34; Sorbonne, cert, 39; Columbia Univ, MA, 54, PhD, 62. *Prof Exp:* Instr French, US Mil Acad, 39-41, instr Ger, 41-43, asst prof, 46-48, prof foreign lang, 49-80, head dept, 63-80; RETIRED. *Mem:* MLA; Am Asn Teachers Ger. *Res:* Teaching methods for modern foreign languages. *Mailing Add:* 17 Inglewood Rd Asheville NC 28804

RENGSTORF, MICHAEL E, b Sept 28, 38; US citizen. FRENCH LANGUAGE & LITERATURE. *Educ:* Calif Lutheran Col, BA, 70; State Univ NY Buffalo, MA, 72, PhD(French), 76. *Prof Exp:* Lectr English, Univ Tours, France, 74-75; lectr French, 75-76, ASST PROF FRENCH, COLUMBIA UNIV, 76- *Mem:* MLA; Can Semiotic Res Asn; Semiotic Soc Am. *Res:* French fiction of the nineteenth century; the structural analysis of narrative; phonetics & general linguistics. *Publ:* Auth, Literary semiotics: A linguistic reading of text, Diacritics, fall 75; Pour une quatrieme modalite narrative, Langages, 9/76; Les Trois contes de Flaubert: Essai de Semiotique Narrative, Paris: Klincksieck, 78. *Mailing Add:* Dept of French Columbia Univ New York NY 10027

RENNERT, HAL H, b Weimar, Germany, Nov 29, 39; US citizen; m 63; c 1. GERMAN & COMPARATIVE LITERATURE. *Educ:* Wichita State Univ, BA, 66, MA, 69; Univ Wash, PhD(comp lit), 75. *Prof Exp:* Instr, Wichita State Univ 73-74; asst prof, Carnegie-Mellon Univ, 76-79; ASST PROF GERMAN, UNIV FLA, 79- *Concurrent Pos:* Pres, Asn Prof Transl, 78-79. *Mem:* MLA; Am Asn Teachers German; Deutsch Schillergesellschaft; Am Comp Lit Asn; Am Transl Asn. *Res:* Contemporary German literature; German area studies; early 19th century German literature. *Publ:* Auth, A comparison of two transcations of Eduard Mörike's poem auf eine lampe, Univ Santa Fe Lang Quat, 72; Transformations: Thoughts regarding film title translations, Post Scripts, 81; Affinities in Romanticism: Kleist and Keats, Heinrich von Kleist Studies, AMS press and E Schmidt Verlag, 82; The treat of the invisible: The portrait of the physicist in modern German drama, Comp Drama Papers, 82; Deutsche Firmen, Deutsche Sprache in Florida, Unterrichtspraxis, 82. *Mailing Add:* Dept Germanic & Slavic Lang & Lit Univ Fla Gainesville FL 32611

RENOIR, ALAIN, English. See Vol II

RENSKY, MIROSLAV, b Prague, Czech, July 5, 27; m 52; c 1. ENGLISH, LINGUISTICS. *Educ:* Charles Univ, Prague, PhD(English), 51; Czech Acad Sci, CSc(Ger philol), 64. *Prof Exp:* Lectr English, Czech Acad Sci, 54-60, res fel, 60-64, sr res fel, 64-68; vis assoc prof, Hunter Col, 68-70; PROF ENGLISH & LING, CITY UNIV NEW YORK, GRAD SCH & BROOKLYN COL, 70- *Concurrent Pos:* Dir ling prog, Brooklyn Col, 74- *Mem:* NY Acad Sci; Ling Soc Am; Int Ling Asn. *Res:* Modern English syntax; phonology; stylistics. *Publ:* Auth, Funkce slabiky v jazykovem systemu, Slovo a slovesnost, 60; The noun-verb quotient in English and Czech, Philol Pragensia, 4/65; The systematics of paralanguage, Travaux Ling Prague, 66; contribr, The Prague School of Linguistics and language teaching, Oxford, 72. *Mailing Add:* PhD Prog in English Grad Ctr, City Univ New York New York NY 10036

RENTSCHLER, ERIC, b Portland, Ore, Apr 8, 49. GERMAN LITERATURE, CINEMA. *Educ:* Ore State Univ, BA, 70; Univ Wash, Seattle, MA, 71, PhD(Ger), 77. *Prof Exp:* Asst prof Ger, Ohio State Univ, 78-82; ASSOC PROF GER, UNIV CALIF, IRVINE, 82- *Mem:* Am Lessing Soc; Am Soc 18th Century Studies; Mod Lang Soc; Am Asn Teachers Ger. *Res:* German cinema, especially post war period; German comedy; 18th century German literature, especially Lessing. *Publ:* Auth, Lessing's fragmented norm: A re-examination of Der Junge Gelehrte, Ger Rev, 5/75; Lisette the laugher, Lessing Yearbk, 78; Lessing's Damon: Gellert oder die wahre freundschaft, Mod Lang Quart, 3/79; ed, West German Film in the 1970s, Redgrave, 80; Reopening the Cabinet of Dr Kracauer: Teaching German Film as Film, Mod Lang J, Autumn 80; Expanding Film Historical Discourse: Reception Theory's Use Value for Cinema Studies, Cine-Tracts, 81; American Friends and the New German Cinema: Patterns of Reception, New German Critique, fall/winter 81-82; West German Film in the Course of Time, Redgrave, 82. *Mailing Add:* Dept of Ger Ohio State Univ Columbus OH 43210

RESCHKE, CLAUS, b Berlin, Ger, Apr 30, 35; US citizen; m 71; c 3. GERMAN LITERATURE, APPLIED LINGUISTICS. *Educ:* Univ Ore, BA, 68, MA, 69; Cornell Univ, PhD(Ger), 73. *Prof Exp:* Asst prof Ger & English, Lane Community Col, Eugene, Ore, 65-70; asst prof Ger, Cornell Univ, 73-75; asst prof Ger Lit, pedagogy & lang, 75-78, ASSOC PROF GER LIT, PEDAGOGY & LING, UNIV HOUSTON, 78- *Mem:* MLA; Am Coun Teaching Foreign Lang; Am Asn Teachers Ger; Asn Int Ling Appliquee. *Res:* Nineteenth century drama; early 20th century prose; stylistic-linguistic patterns in 18th century drama, especially Sturm und Drang. *Publ:* Auth, The problem of reality in Kafka's Auf der Galerie, Ger Rev, 1/76; Career education at the college level: A modest proposal, Am Dept Foreign Lang Bull, 9/77; Foreign language career education: Some programs and perspectives, Die Unterrichtspraxis, 12/77; Measuring foreign language oral proficiency, Glottodidactia, 3/78; Let's increase, not reduce foreign language offerings, Am Dept Foreign Lang Bull, 5/78; Adaptation of the FSI interview scale for secondary schools and colleges, In: Direct Testing of Speaking Proficiency, Educ Testing Serv, 10/78; Stylistic patterns in Sturm und Drang drama: F M Klinger's early plays, In: University of Houston German Studies Series, Vol II, 10/78; Oral proficiency testing in high school and college: Why and how?, Proc Pac Northwest Coun Foreign Lang, Part II, 11/78. *Mailing Add:* Dept of German Univ of Houston Houston TX 77004

RESLER, W MICHAEL, b Arcadia, Fla, July 7, 48. MEDIEVAL GERMAN LANGUAGE & LITERATURE. *Educ:* Col William & Mary, AB, 70; Harvard Univ, AM, 73 PhD(Ger), 76. *Prof Exp:* Asst prof, 76-80, ADJ PROF GER, BOSTON COL, 76- *Concurrent Pos:* Nat Endowment for Humanities grant, 80-81. *Mem:* MLA; Mediaeval Acad Am; Am Asn Teachers Ger; Goethe Soc New England. *Res:* Mediaeval German language and literature; Arthurian romance. *Publ:* Ed, A structural approach to Aichinger's Spiegelgeschichte, Die Unterrichtspraxis, spring 79; Der Stricker: Daniel von dem Blühenden Tal: Altaeutsche Textbibliothek, No 92, Max Niemeyer Verlag, Tübingen, 81. *Mailing Add:* Dept of Ger Carney Hall Boston Col Chestnut Hill MA 02167

RESNICK, MARGERY, b New York, NY, Dec 14, 44; m 73. HISPANIC LITERATURE. *Educ:* Ind Univ, BA, 65; New York Univ, Madrid, MA, 66; Harvard Univ, PhD(Span), 72. *Prof Exp:* Instr Span, State Univ NY, Stony Brook, 66-67; asst prof, Yale Yniv, 71-77; ASSOC PROF SPAN & CHMN FOREIGN LANG & LIT, MASS INST TECHNOL, 77-, DIR MOD LANG, 80- *Mem:* MLA; Am Asn Teachers Span & Port. *Res:* Contemporary Spanish poetry; nineteenth century novel. *Publ:* Ed, De Soledad y Otros Pesares: Garfias, Helios, Madrid, 71; auth, The poetry of Jorge Guillen: Review, Mod Lang Quart, 3/76; Los usos de la biografia: El caso de Pedro Garfias, El Zaguan, summer 76; La poesia espanola y el desafio de la historia, Revista de la Univ Mex, 1/77; La inteligencia audaz: Vida y poesia de Concha Mendez Papeles de Son Armadans, 2/78; El Ritmo Quebrado: Vida y Poesia de Pedro Garfias, Mortiz, Mex, 79. *Mailing Add:* Off of Dir Foreign Lang & Lit Mass Inst Technol Cambridge MA 02139

RESNICK, MELVYN C, b New York, NY, May 1, 41. SPANISH & APPLIED LINGUISTICS. *Educ:* Hunter Col City Univ New York, BA, 62; Univ Rochester, MA, 65, PhD(ling), 68. *Prof Exp:* Teacher Span, Valley Stream N High Sch, NY, 62-63; instr English as second lang & Span, Univ Rochester, 64-67; asst prof lang & ling, 67-71, assoc prof, 71-79, PROF LANG & LING, FLA ATLANTIC UNIV, 79- *Mem:* Am Asn Teachers Span & Port; Asn Ling Filologia Am Latina; Ling Soc Am; Prog Interam Ling Ensenanza Idiomas; Teachers English Speakers Other Languages. *Res:* Latin American dialectology; history of the Spanish language; applied linguistics. *Publ:* Auth, Dialect zones and automatic dialect identification in Latin American Spanish, Hispania, 69; The redundant English phonemes /c,j,s,z/, 72 & coauth, The status of quality and length in Spanish vowels, 75, Linguistics; auth, Phonological variants and Dialect Identification in Latin American Spanish, Mouton, 75; co-ed, 1975 Colloquium on Hispanic Linguistics, Georgetown Univ, 76; auth, Algunos Aspectos Historico-Geograficos de la Dialectologia Hispanoamericana, Orbis, 76; Introduccion a la Historia de la Lengua Espanola, Georgetown Univ, 81; Spanish for Elementary School Teachers, Newbury House (in press). *Mailing Add:* Dept of Lang & Ling Florida Atlantic Univ Boca Raton FL 33431

RESNICK, SEYMOUR, b New York, NY, Jan 15, 20; m 52. ROMANCE LANGUAGES. *Educ:* City Col New York, BA, 40; NY Univ, MA, 43, PhD(Span), 51. *Prof Exp:* Examr-transl, Off of Censorship, 42-44; instr Span, NY Univ, 44-50; lectr Romance lang, City Col New York, 51-52; teacher high sch, 52-53; instr Romance lang, Rutgers Univ, 53-57; teacher high sch, NY, 57-64; lectr, 59-64, assoc prof, 64-66, PROF ROMANCE LANG, QUEENS COL, NY, 67- *Mem:* MLA; Am Asn Teachers Span & Port. *Res:* Medieval Spanish literature. *Publ:* Co-ed, Anthology of Spanish Literature in English Translation, Ungar, 58; auth, Selections from Spanish Poetry, Harvey, 62; co-ed, Highlights of Spanish Literature, Ungar, 63; auth, Spanish American Poetry, Harvey, 64; Essential Spanish Grammar, 64 & Essential French Grammar, 65, Dover; co-ed, The Best of Spanish Literature in English Translation, Ungar, 76; coauth, En Breve: A concise review of Spanish Grammar, Holt, Rinehart & Winston, 82. *Mailing Add:* 57 Tobin Ave Great Neck NY 11021

RESNIK, BRAMY, b Praugue, Czechoslovakia, June 29, 29; US citizen; m 63 c 2. GERMAN. *Educ:* Hunter Col, BA, 60; NY Univ, MA, 67; Univ Southern Calif, PhD(Ger lit), 72. *Prof Exp:* Teacher Ger & French, Oceanside Sr High Sch, NY, 61-63, Floral Park Sr High Sch, NY, 63-65; asst Ger, Univ Southern Calif, 65-68; ASST PROF GER, E CAROLINA UNIV, NC, 68- *Mem:* Am Asn Teachers Ger; MLA. *Publ:* Auth, The Germans are coming! New East, 10/76. *Mailing Add:* Dept of Foreign Lang East Carolina Univ Greenville NC 27834

RETTIG, JOHN WILLIAM, b Cincinnati, Ohio, Feb 19, 31; m 63; c 2. CLASSICAL LANGUAGES, PATROLOGY. *Educ:* Xavier Univ, AB, 53, MA, 54; Ohio State Univ, PhD(class lang), 63. *Prof Exp:* Instr Greek & Latin, Cath Univ Am, 63-66; asst prof classics, Duquesne Univ, 66-68; from asst prof to assoc prof, 68-74, PROF CLASSICS, XAVIER UNIV, OHIO, 74-, CHMN DEPT & DIR HONORS AB PROG, 77- *Concurrent Pos:* Participant & speaker, Conf Educ Innovation & Smaller Classics Dept, Beloit Col, 6/73. *Mem:* Am Philol Asn; Class Asn Mid W & S; NAm Patristic Soc; Vergilian Soc. *Res:* Latin linguistics; Christian Latin. *Publ:* Auth, Dissolve Frigus: Horace Carm 1.9, Class Bull, 12/65; Foreign language study: a proposal, Lib Educ, 10/68; Quo usque tandem, Latin teacher, Class Outlook, 10/71. *Mailing Add:* Dept of Classics Xavier Univ Cincinnati OH 45207

REVELEY, BETTY BROWN, b Plymouth, Ind, Oct 12, 31; c 2. ENGLISH LINGUISTICS. *Educ:* Calif State Univ, San Jose, AB, 52; Stanford Univ, MA, 58; Univ Tex, Austin, PhD(English lang & lit), 70. *Prof Exp:* Instr, Am River Col, 61-64; from instr to assoc prof, 65-74, PROF ENGLISH, CALIF STATE UNIV, SACRAMENTO, 74- *Res:* Stylistics; applied linguistics; language learning. *Publ:* Auth, Linguistics and the teaching of reading, Calif English J, winter 67; Teaching composition, kindergargen through sixth grade, Area III Co Supt & Curriculum Develop Comt, 12/67; Tutoring in English-adding relevance to the English major, Asn Dept English Bull, 11/70. *Mailing Add:* Dept of English Calif State Univ 6000 Jay St Sacramento CA 95819

REX, WALTER EDWIN, b Bryn Mawr, Pa, Jan 31, 27. FRENCH LITERATURE. *Educ:* Harvard Univ, AB, 50, MA, 51, PhD(Romance lang), 56. *Prof Exp:* Teaching fel, French, Harvard Univ, 51-53, 55; instr, Brown Univ, 56-57, Harvard Univ, 57-60; asst prof, 60-66, assoc prof French lit, 66-72, PROF FRENCH LIT, UNIV CALIF, BERKELEY, 72- *Concurrent Pos:* Univ Calif res fel, 66-67 & 74. *Mem:* MLA; Int Asn Fr Studies; Soc 18th

Century Studies. *Res:* French 17th and 18th century literature, especially Pierre Bayle. *Publ:* Auth, Pierre Bayle, Louis Tronchin et la querelle des Donatistes, Bull Soc Hist Protestantisme Fr, 59; Essays on Pierre Bayle and Religious Controversy, Nijhoff, The Hague, 65; coauth, Inventory of Diderot's Encyclopedie (6 vols), Voltaire Found, 71-72; Figaro's games, PMLA, 74; Pascal's Provincial Letters, An Introduction, Hodder & Stoughton, London, 77. *Mailing Add:* Dept of French Univ of Calif Berkeley CA 94720

REXINE, JOHN EFSTRATIOS, b Boston, Mass, June 6, 29; m 57; c 3. CLASSICS. *Educ:* Harvard Univ, AB, 51, AM, 53, PhD, 64. *Hon Degrees:* LittD, Hellenic Col, 81. *Prof Exp:* Res asst, inst class studies, Harvard Univ, 54-55; from actg instr to instr humanities, Brandeis Univ, 55-57; from instr to prof classics, 57-68, chmn dept, 64-73, Asian studies fel, 65-66, dir div univ studies, 69-72, dir, IBM Corp Inst Liberal Arts for Exec, 69-71, assoc dean fac, 73-74, actg dean fac, 77-78, CHARLES A DANA PROF CLASSICS, COLGATE UNIV, 77-, DIR DIV HUMANITIES, 72- *Concurrent Pos:* Contrib ed, Hellenic Chronicle, 52-; bk rev ed, Athene, 57-67 & Orthodox Observer, 57-72; managing ed, Greek Orthodox Theol Rev, 59-60, assoc ed, 60-67; bk rev columnist, Orthodox Observer, 72-; asst ed, Helios: Class J Southwest US, 76-79; ed, Classical Outlook, 77-79; bk rev ed, Classics & Modern Greek, Mod Lang J, 77-79; Fulbright-Hays sr res scholar, Am Sch Classical Studies, Athens, 79-80. *Honors & Awards:* Helicon Phoutrides Gold Medal, 62. *Mem:* Am Class League; Mediaeval Acad Am; Am Philol Asn; Modern Greek Studies Asn; Inst for Byzantine & Mod Greek Studies (vpres, 74-). *Res:* Classical Greek and Roman literature; modern Greek literature; Byzantine civilization and the Greek Orthodox Church. *Publ:* Auth, Solon and His Political Theory, William Frederick, 58; Religion in Plato and Cicero, Philos Libr, 59; contrib, A Pictorial History of Greece, Crown, 67; auth, Religion in Plato and Cicero, Greenwood, reprint, 68; contrib auth 14 articles on ancient Greek authors, McGraw-Hill, Encycl World Biog, 73; auth, The Hellenic Spirit: Byzantine and Post Byzantine, 81; contribr, Modern Greek Literature, In: Encycl of World Literature in the Twentieth Century, 82. *Mailing Add:* Div of the Humanities Colgate Univ Hamilton NY 13346

REY, ARSENIO, b Valle de las Casas, Spain, Mar 12, 38; US citizen; m 74; c 1. HISPANIC LITERATURE, PHILOSOPHY. *Educ:* Escolasticado Pilar, Madrid, Phil Lic, 60; NY Univ, PhD(Hisp lit), 74; Sorbonne, dipl French lang & lit, 76. *Prof Exp:* Assoc fel Span lang, NY Univ, 70-72; asst prof Span lang & lit, City Univ New York, NY, 74-77; ASST PROF HISP LIT, STATE UNIV NY, GENESEO, 77- *Concurrent Pos:* Translr Span, State Bd Elections, NY, 74-77; fac res, Res Found State Univ NY, 77. *Mem:* MLA; Am Asn Teachers Span & Port; Corpus Reformatorum Hisp. *Res:* Spanish heterodox mysticism; baroque prose stylistics; 20th century Spanish grotesque drama. *Publ:* Auth, Molinos: Crepusculo de la mistica, Arbor, 75; Actualidad de la literatura espanola contemporanea, Estafeta Lit, 76; Poesia y actualidad norteamericanos, Cuadernos Hispanoamericanos, 76; contribr, Estudios de Historia, Literatura y Arte Hispanicos, Insula, Madrid, 77; auth, Hispanophone thespians, Hispania, 77. *Mailing Add:* Dept of Mod Lang State Univ NY Geneseo NY 14454

REY, WILLIAM HENRY, b Frankfurt-am-Main, Ger, Apr 7, 11; m 54; c 1. GERMAN LITERATURE. *Educ:* Univ Frankfurt, PhD, 37. *Prof Exp:* Instr, Ohio State Univ, 47-48; asst prof, Grinnell Col, 48-50; from asst prof to assoc prof, 50-59, exec off dept, 60-73, PROF GER, UNIV WASH, 59- *Mem:* MLA. *Res:* Modern German and Austrian literature; contemporary poetry. *Publ:* Auth, Weltentzweiung und Weltversöhnung in Hofmannsthals Griechischen Dramen, Univ Pa, 62; Arthur Schnitzler: Die späte Prosa als Gipfelseines Schaffens, Schmidt, Berlin, 68; Arthur Schnitzler: Professor Bernhardi, Fink, Munche, 71; Poesie der Antipoesie, Moderne Lyrik: Genesis, Theorie, Struktur, Stiehm, Heidelberg, 78; Revolutionstropodie und Mysterienspiel, Peter Lang, Bern. *Mailing Add:* Dept of Ger Lang & Lit Univ of Wash Seattle WA 98195

REYNOLDS, JOHN FRANCIS, b Everett, Mass, Oct, 23, 42. GERMAN LITERATURE. *Educ:* Tufts Univ, BA, 64, MA, 67; Univ Va, PhD(Ger), 70. *Prof Exp:* Teacher English, Kant Gym, Berlin, Ger, 64-65; Kepler Gym, Reutlingen, 65-66; asst prof, Univ Va, 71-78; ASST PROF GER, COLBY COL, 79- *Concurrent Pos:* Res grant, Univ Va, 73-74; Am Coun Learned Soc fel, 74-75; consult, Adv Testing Placement, Educ Testing Serv, Princeton, 74-; Int Res & Exchange Bd fel, 78. *Mem:* AAUP; Am Asn Teachers Ger; Int Soc 18th Century Studies; MLA; Lessing Soc. *Res:* Eighteenth century German literature; particularly Christian Fuerchtegott Gellert; Romanticism. *Publ:* Translr, The Life of Speech, 72 & Concerning Speech Disorders in the Dream, 74, Univ Va; auth, Achtzehn unveroeffentlichte Briefe Gellerts, In: Handbuch des freien deutschen Hochstifts, 77; ed, C F Gellerts Briefwechsel, W DeGruyter, 78. *Mailing Add:* Dept of Ger Lang & Lit Univ Va Charlottesville VA 22903

REYNOLDS, JOHN JOSEPH, b Redwood City, Calif, June 25, 24. SPANISH. *Educ:* Univ Calif, AB, 46, MA, 48, PhD(Romance lit), 56. *Prof Exp:* Teaching asst, Univ Calif, 46-50; from instr to asst prof, Univ Ariz, 50-60; from asst prof to assoc prof, 60-66, PROF SPAN, ST JOHN'S UNIV, NY, 66- *Mem:* MLA; Am Asn Teachers Span & Port; Renaissance Soc Am; Comediantes; Asn Int Hisp. *Res:* Spanish literature of the Golden Age. *Publ:* Auth, Spanish literature: Siglo de oro, In: New Cath Encycl, McGraw, 67; Mira de Amescua's Octavas al Principe de Gales, Renaissance Quart, 69; A directory for Spanish-speaking New York, Quadrangle, 71; auth, Juan Timoneda, In: TWAS, 367, Twayne, 75; Color symbolism in Juan Timoneda's poetry, In: Studies in Honor of Ruth Lee Kennedy, Univ NC, 77; coauth, A guide to the motif-index of Timoneda's prose fiction, Ky Romance Quart, 78; co-compiler, Bibliography of publications on the comedia, Bull Comediantes, 78, 79, 80 & 81; auth, El condenado por desconfiado: Tres siglos y medio de ediciones, In: Homenaje a Tirso, Rev Estudios, 81. *Mailing Add:* Dept of Mod Foreign Langs & Class Studies St John's Univ Jamaica NY 11439

REYNOLDS, WINSTON ALLIN, b Bakersfield, Calif, Jan 13, 22; m 63; c 5. SPANISH. *Educ:* Univ Calif, Los Angeles, BA, 50, MA, 51; Univ Paris, dipl, 53; Univ Southern Calif, Phd(Span), 57. *Prof Exp:* Lectr Span, Univ Southern Calif, 54-55; from actg instr to assoc prof, 55-70, chmn dept Span & Port, 62-65 & 74, PROF SPAN, UNIV CALIF, SANTA BARBARA, 70- *Concurrent Pos:* Del Amo Found fel, Spain, 59; Fulbright-Hays res fel, Spain, 65-67; dir, Centro de Estudios de las Universidades de Calif e Ill, Barcelona, Spain, 80-81. *Mem:* Asn Int Hispanistas. *Res:* Spanish Golden Age literature, emphasis on poetry; Colonial Spanish American literature; literature of the conquest of America. *Publ:* Auth, To burn one's boats or to burn one's bridges?, Am Speech, 5/59; Hernan Cortes y los heroes de la antigüedad, Rev Filol Espanola, 5/63; Espiritualidad de la conquista de Mejico: Su perspectiva religiosa en las letras de la Edad de Oro, Univ Granada, 66; Romancero de Hernan Cortes (estudio y textos de los siglos XVI y SVII), Ed Alcala, Madrid, 67; El corregidor Diego Diaz del Castillo, hijo del conquistador ante la Inquisicion de Mexico, 1568-1571, Porrua, Madrid, 73; Hernan Cortes en la literatura del Siglo de Oro, Centro Iber de Coop y Edit Nac, Madrid, 78; Los caballeros Soberbiosos obel Amadis, Cuad Hispanoamer, 8/79; Faro de navegantes, cristalina maravilla: De Alejandria a Sor Juana, Actas del AIH, 80. *Mailing Add:* Dept of Span & Port Univ of Calif Santa Barbara CA 93106

RHEIN, PHILLIP HENRY, b Belleville, Ill, Aug 10, 23; m 50; c 2. COMPARATIVE LITERATURE, GERMAN. *Educ:* Wash Univ, AB, 50, MA, 52; Univ Mich, PhD(comp lit), 60. *Prof Exp:* From instr to asst prof English, Valparaiso Univ, 54-57, asst prof Ger, 57-60; from asst prof to assoc prof, 60-70, PROF GER & COMP LIT, VANDERBILT UNIV, 70-, CHMN DEPT GER-SLAVIC, 80- *Concurrent Pos:* Prof lit, eminent scholar, Conquest Chair, Va Mil Inst, spring 79. *Mem:* MLA; Am Comp Lit Asn; S Atlantic Mod Lang Asn; Southern Comp Lit Asn (pres, 76, 77); Int Comp Lit Asn. *Res:* French and German literary relationships; relationship among art, literature and philosophy; 20th century European and American novels. *Publ:* Auth, The Urge to Live, A Comparative Analysis of Kafka's Der Prozess and Camus' L'Etranger, Univ NC, 64 & 66; Albert Camus, Twayne, 70; Camus: A comparatist's view, In: Camus 1970, Univ Sherbrooke, Que, 70; Two examples of twentieth century art: Giorgio di Chirico and Franz Kafka, In: Studies in German Literature of the 19th and 20th Centuries, Univ NC, 70; coauth, Comparative Literature: The Early Years, Univ NC, 73; auth, The northern desert: A comparison of Camus' The Fall and Van Eycks' Ghent Altarpiece, In: Camus, Tex Tech Univ, Lubbock, 76; Myth making in the twentieth century, The Comparatist, 5/77; Two fantastic visions: Franz Kafka and Alfred Kubin, SAtlantic Bull, 5/77. *Mailing Add:* Box 1567 Station B Vanderbilt Univ Nashville TN 37235

RICAPITO, JOSEPH V, b Giovinazzo, Italy, Oct 30, 33; US citizen; m 58; c 2. ROMANCE LANGUAGES. *Educ:* Brooklyn Col, BA, 55; State Univ Iowa, MA, 56; Univ Calif, Los Angeles, PhD(Romance lang), 66. *Prof Exp:* Assoc Span, Univ Calif, Los Angeles, 61-62; from instr to asst prof Span & Ital, Pomona Col, 62-70; assoc prof Span, 70-78, prof Span & comp lit, Ind Univ, 78-80; PROF SPAN & CHMN DEPT, LA STATE UNIV, BATON ROUGE, 80- *Concurrent Pos:* Ford Found & Pomona Col fel, 68-69. *Mem:* MLA; Am Comp Lit Asn; Renaissance Soc Am. *Res:* Italian Renaissance; Spanish Golden Age; comparative literature. *Publ:* Auth, Lazarillo de Tormes y Machiavelli & El contorno picaresco del Conde Lucanor, 72, Romanische Forsch; Americo Castro y la novela picaresca, Insula, 73; La vida de Lazarillo de Tormes, Madrid, Catedra, 10th ed, 76; Bibliografia razonada y anotada . . . Madrid, Castalia, 80. *Mailing Add:* Dept of Span & Port La State Univ Baton Rouge LA 70803

RICARD, FRANCOIS, b Shawinigan, Que, June 4, 47; m 67. FRENCH & QUEBEC LITERATURE. *Educ:* Univ Laval, BA, 66, MA, 68; Aixen-Provence, DUniv, 71. *Prof Exp:* Instr, Sem Ste-Marie, Que, 67-68; asst prof, 71-76, ASSOC PROF FRENCH, McGILL UNIV, 76- *Mem:* Asn Can Univ Teachers Fr. *Res:* Twentieth century French literature, especially R Rolland, Valery; Quebec literature 19th and 20th centuries. *Publ:* Auth, L'arte de F A Savard, Fides, Montreal, 72; Le decor romanesque, Etudes Fr, 11/72; Pierre Vadeboncoeur, Lemeac, 74; Gabrielle Roy, Fides, 75; Lionel Grouix, Voix et images du pays, 75; Le recueil, 76 & L'essai quebecois, 77 Etudes Fr. *Mailing Add:* Dept of French Lang & Lit McGill Univ 3460 McTavish Montreal PQ H3A 1B1 Can

RICCARDI, THEODORE, JR, b Philadelphia, Pa, July 10, 37; m 65. MODERN SOUTH ASIAN LANGUAGES, SANSKRIT. *Educ:* Harvard Univ, BA, 59; Univ Pa, MA, 64, PhD(Orient studies), 68. *Prof Exp:* Exec secy, US Educ Found Nepal, 68; asst prof, 68-74, assoc prof Mideast lang & cult, 74-77, chmn, Dept Mideast Lang & Cult, 77-80, dir, Southern Asian Inst, 78-80, PROF INDIC STUDIES, COLUMBIA UNIV, 78- *Concurrent Pos:* Coun Res Humanities fel, Columbia Univ, 70; Am Coun Learned Soc fel, 73; Fulbright-Hays res fel, Nepal & India; co-ed, Kailash, J Himalayan Studies; counr cult affairs, US Embassy, New Delhi, 80-82; chmn, US Educ Found in India, 80-82; mem, Indo-US Subcomn Educ & Cult, 80-82. *Mem:* Am Orient Soc; Asn Asian Studies. *Res:* Modern Indo-Aryan languages; Nepalese history and literature; Sanskrit literature. *Publ:* Auth, A Nepali Version of the Vetalapancavimsati, Am Orient Soc, 71; co-ed, Introductory Hindi Readings, Univ Pa, 71; An Advanced Course in Bengali, New Delhi, 74; auth, Some preliminary remarks on a Newari painting of Svayambhunath, J Am Orient Soc, 73. *Mailing Add:* Dept of Mid E Lang & Cult Columbia Univ New York NY 10027

RICCIARDI, MARY ELIZABETH, b Plymouth, Ind, June 30, 46. ITALIAN LANGUAGE & LITERATURE. *Educ:* Ind Univ, AB, 68, MA, 71, PhD(Ital), 77. *Prof Exp:* Instr Ital, Northern Ill Univ, 72-74; instr, Wayne State Univ, 75-77, lectr, 77-78; ASST PROF ITAL, UNIV MO-COLUMBIA, 78- *Mem:* MLA; Midwest MLA; Am Asn Teachers Ital. *Res:* Italian literature of the middle ages; Dante; Provensal poetry. *Mailing Add:* Dept of Romance Lang Univ of Mo Columbia MO 65201

RICE, ALLAN LAKE, b Philadelphia, Pa, Mar 1, 05; m 43; c 3. LANGUAGES. *Educ:* Univ Pa, BA, 27, PhD, 32. *Prof Exp:* Instr Ger, Princeton Univ, 30-36; asst prof Ger & Swed, Univ Pa, 36-47; prof, 74-75, EMER PROF, URSINUS COL, 75-; FREE LANCE TRANSLR. *Concurrent Pos:* Asst naval attache, US Legation, Stockholm, Sweden, 42-45. *Honors & Awards:* Nordstjärnan, Sweden, 71. *Mem:* Soc Advan Scand Studies. *Res:* Swedish grammar; lexicography; German grammar. *Publ:* Auth, Swedish: A Pratical Grammar, Augustana, 57, 3rd ed, 68; German: A Practical Grammar, Personal, 73. *Mailing Add:* Box 492 Kimberton PA 19442

RICE, ARGYLL PRYOR, US citizen. SPANISH. *Educ:* Smith Col, BA, 52; Yale Univ, MA, 56, PhD, 61. *Prof Exp:* Instr Span, Yale Univ, 59-60 & 61-63; from asst prof to assoc prof, 64-72, chmn dept, 71-74, PROF HISP STUDIES, CONN COL, 72-, CHMN DEPT, 77- *Mem:* Am Asn Teachers Span & Port; AAUP; MLA. *Res:* Twentieth century Hispanic poetry; Spanish poetry and drama of the Golden Age. *Publ:* Auth, Jubilo y fuga de Emilio Ballagas, Rev Iberoam, 7-12/66; Emilio Ballagas: poeta o poesia, Ed Andrea, 67. *Mailing Add:* Dept of Hisp Studies Conn Col New London CT 06320

RICE, ROBERT CHARLES, English Literature. See Vol II

RICH, CARROLL YOUNG, b Arcadia, La, Aug 13, 33; m 58; c 2. LINGUISTICS. *Educ:* La Tech Univ, BA, 55; La State Univ, MS, 57, PhD, 62. *Prof Exp:* From instr to assoc prof, 59-72, PROF ENGLISH, NTEX STATE UNIV, 72- *Concurrent Pos:* Fulbright lectr English as second lang, Univ Valladolid, 64-65. *Mem:* SCent Mod Lang Asn. *Res:* Language laboratories; English as a second language. *Mailing Add:* Dept of English NTex State Univ Denton TX 76203

RICH, JOHN STANLEY, b Birmingham, Ala, Mar 5, 43. DIALECTOLOGY. *Educ:* Univ Ala, BA, 66, PhD(English), 79; Univ Pa, MS, 68. *Prof Exp:* Instr English, Stillman Col, 68-73; teaching asst, Univ Ala, 73-79; ASST PROF ENGLISH, UNIV SC, AIKEN, 79- *Mem:* MLA; Nat Coun Teachers English; An Dialect Soc; Conf Col Compos & Commun; Conf Christianity & Lit. *Res:* American place names; English composition and rhetoric. *Publ:* Auth, Some South Carolina names transferred to West Alabama, Names in SC, 10/82. *Mailing Add:* PO Box 2582 Aiken SC 29801

RICHARDS, DAVID GLEYRE, b Salt Lake City, Utah, July 27, 35; m 59; c 1. GERMAN LANGUAGE & LITERATURE. *Educ:* Univ Utah, BA, 60, MA, 61; Univ Calif, Berkeley, PhD(Ger), 68. *Prof Exp:* ASSOC PROF GER, STATE UNIV NY, BUFFALO, 68-, DIR UNDERGRAD STUDIES, 79- *Concurrent Pos:* Vis prof Univ Cologne, spring 72. *Mem:* MLA; Am Asn Teachers Ger. *Res:* The German drama; interdisciplinary study of culture. *Publ:* Auth, Zur Textgestaltung von Büchners Woyzeck, Euphorion, 71; Georg Büchners Woyzeck: Interpretation und Textgestaltung, Bouvier Verlag Bonn, Ger, 75; Georg Büchner and the Birth of the Modern Drama, State Univ, NY, 77. *Mailing Add:* Dept of Mod Lang & Lit State Univ of NY Buffalo NY 14261

RICHARDS, DONNIE DEAN, b Lubbock, Tex, Aug 12, 42; m 70. SPANISH. *Educ:* Tex Tech Univ, BA, 64, MA, 72; Univ Ky, PhD(Span), 76. *Prof Exp:* Teacher, Monterey High Sch, Tex, 64-69; teacher, Thousand Oaks High Sch, Calif, 69-71; teaching asst, Tex Tech Univ, 71-73; teaching asst, Univ Ky, 73-76; asst prof, Eastern Ky Univ, 76-77; ASST PROF SPAN, SAM HOUSTON STATE UNIV, 77- *Mem:* MLA; Asm Asn Teachers Span & Port; SAtlantic Mod Lang Asn. *Res:* Twentieth century novel in Spain; twentieth century drama in Spain; 19th and 20th century prose in Spain. *Mailing Add:* Dept of Foreign Lang Sam Houston State Univ Huntsville TX 77341

RICHARDS, HENRY JOSEPH, b Trinidad, Trinidad & Tobago, Nov 18, 36; m 64; c 2. SPANISH LITERATURE. *Educ:* Marquette Univ, BS, 59, MA, 61; Univ Minn, PhD(Span), 64. *Prof Exp:* Asst prof Span, Univ Toledo, 64-65 & Queens Col, City Univ New York, 65-67; asst prof, 67, assoc prof, 70, dir Afro-Am studies, 69-70, dean develop studies, 70-71, asst vpres acad affairs & assoc prof, 71-76, assoc prof, 76-80, PROF SPAN, STATE UNIV NY BUFFALO, 80- *Mem:* MLA; Am Asn Teachers Span & Port; Col Lang Asn. *Res:* Spanish American literature; Afro-Hispanic literature. *Publ:* Auth, Trinidadian dialect and standard English: A contrastive study, Word, 70; Some Spanish words in the English-based dialect of Trinidad, Hispania, 70; coauth, La funcion del marco y la armonia simetrica en el Fausto de Estanislao del Campo, Ky Romance Quart, 70; ed, Topics in Afro-American Studies, Black Acad, 71; coauth, Nicomedes Santa Cruz y la poesia de su conciencia de negritud, Cuadernos Americanos, 75; auth, The characterization of the ontologically insecure in El tunel, Ky Romance Quart, 77; On the plot structure of Rip Van Winkle and Rip Rip, Romance Notes, 80; Narrative strategies in Nelson Estupinan Bass's El ultimo rio, Afro-Hisp Rev, 82. *Mailing Add:* Dept of Span State Univ NY at Buffalo Amherst NY 14260

RICHARDS, KATHARINE COLES, b Tuscaloosa, Ala, Apr 4, 40. SPANISH LANGUAGE. *Educ:* Univ Ala, BA, 62; Tulane Univ, MA, 69, PhD(Span), 71. *Prof Exp:* Instr, 70-72, asst prof, 72-80, ASSOC PROF SPAN, TEX A&M UNIV, 80- *Mem:* MLA; Am Asn Teachers Span & Port; S Cent Mod Lang Asn; SW Coun Latin Am Studies; Asoc Lit Femenina Hisp. *Res:* Twentieth century Spanish literature; 20th century Latin American literature; language teaching. *Publ:* Auth, A cultural note to Unamuno's La Tia Tula, Hispania, 75; The Mexican existentialism of Solorzano's Los Fantoches, Latin Am Lit Rev, 76; Unamuno and The Other, Ky Romance Quart, 76; contribr/translr, Avery Island, In: Five Women Writers of Costa Rica, 78; La moral, la realidad y el arte en El Senor Presidente, Ezplicacion de Textos Literarios, 79-80; The burden of tradition upon the Women in Los Frutos Caidos, Letras Femeninas, 79; Hypocrisy in La Casa de Bernarda Alba, 81. *Mailing Add:* Dept of Mod Lang Tex A&M Univ College Station TX 77843

RICHARDS, KENT HAROLD, Old Testament. See Vol IV

RICHARDSON, EMELINE HILL, b Buffalo, NY, June 6, 10; m 52. CLASSICAL ARCHEOLOGY. *Educ:* Radcliffe Col, AB, 32, MA, 35, PhD(class archaeol), 39. *Prof Exp:* From instr to asst prof class archaeol & classics, Wheaton Col, Mass, 42-49; fel, Am Acad Rome, 49-52; prof classics & class archaeol, Stanford Univ, 63; prof class archaeol, Univ NC, Chapel Hill, 68-78; RETIRED. *Concurrent Pos:* Am Philos Soc Penrose Fund grant, 58-59. *Honors & Awards:* Dignitario dell'Ombra della Sera, Volterra, 80. *Mem:* Archaeol Inst Am; Am Philol Asn; Am Acad Arts & Sci. *Res:* Hellenistic temple terracottas in Etruria; Etruscan votive bronzes. *Publ:* Auth, The Etruscan origins of early Roman sculpture, 53, coauth, Cosa II, the temples of the Arx, 60 & auth, The recurrent geometric in the sculpture of central Italy and its bearing on the origins of the Etruscans, 62, Mem Am Acad Rome; The Etruscans, Their Art and Civilization, Univ Chicago, 64; The Ikon of the heroic warrior, In: Studies Presented to George Hanfmann, Philipp von Zabern, Mainz, 71; The Gods arrive, Archaeol News, 76; The wolf in the west, J Walters Art Gallery, 77. *Mailing Add:* 1103 N Gregson St Durham NC 27701

RICHARDSON, FRANK C, b Detroit, Mich, Apr 22, 28. FOREIGN LANGUAGES, COMPARATIVE LITERATURE. *Educ:* Univ Mich, AB, 50, MA, 54, PhD(comp lit), 60. *Prof Exp:* Teaching asst, Ecole Norm Albertville, Savoie, France, 51-52; instr, Univ Mich, 56-57; from instr to assoc prof, 57-69, CHMN DEPT FOREIGN LANG & LIT, PROF FRENCH & GER, UNIV OF MICH-FLINT, 69-, DIR HONORS PROG, 79- *Mem:* MLA; Am Comp Lit Asn. *Res:* French and German drama of the 19th and 20th centuries; Heinrich von Kleist; 19th century French and Russian literature. *Publ:* Auth, Kleist in France, Univ NC, 62. *Mailing Add:* Dept of Foreign Lang Univ Mich Flint MI 48503

RICHARDSON, HORST FUCHS, b Nuremberg, Ger, June 11, 41; US citizen; m 67, c 2. GERMAN LANGUAGE AND LITERATURE. *Educ:* Univ Calif, Riverside, BA, 63, MA, 66; Univ Conn, PhD(Ger), 76. *Prof Exp:* From instr to asst prof Ger, 65-77, ASSOC PROF GER, COLO COL, 77- *Mem:* Am Asn Teachers Ger; MLA; Asn Depts Foreign Lang. *Res:* German drama and theatre. *Publ:* Auth, The teaching of college German under a modular system, Mod Lang J, 73; A playwrite's experiment in third-yeard German, 73 & German play productions in US and Canadian colleges and universities since 1959, 74, Unterrichtspraxis. *Mailing Add:* Dept of Ger & Russ Colo Col Colorado Springs CO 80903

RICHARDSON, LAWRENCE, JR, b Altoona, Pa, Dec 2, 20; m 52. LATIN ARCHEOLOGY. *Educ:* Yale Univ, BA, 42, PhD(classics), 52. *Prof Exp:* Instr classics, Yale Univ, 46-47; field archaeologist, Am Acad Rome, 52-55; from instr to assoc prof, Yale Univ, 55-66; prof, 66-78, JAMES B DUKE PROF LATIN, DUKE UNIV, 78- *Concurrent Pos:* Guggenheim fel, 58-59; mem, Inst Advan Studies, 67-68; Am Coun Learned Soc fels, 67-68 & 72-73; Nat Endowment for Humanities fel, 79-80; Mellon prof Am Acad Rome, 80-81. *Mem:* Corresp mem, Ger Archaeol Inst; Am Philol Asn; Archaeol Inst Am. *Res:* Latin poetry; Roman archaeology. *Publ:* Auth, Pompeii: The House of the Dioscuri, Am Acad Rome, 55; Cosa and Rome: Comitium and curia, Archaeology, 57; coauth, Cosa: The Temples of the Arx, Am Acad Rome, 60; auth, Furi et Aureli, comites Catulli, Class Philol, 63; Catullus 67: Interpretation and form, Am J Philol, 68; The tribunals of the praetors of Rome, Roemische Mitteilungen 80, 73; ed, Propertius, Elegies I-IV, Univ Okla, 77; auth, Curia Julia and Janus Geminus, Roemische Mitteilungen 85, 78. *Mailing Add:* Dept of Class Studies Duke Univ E Campus Durham NC 27708

RICHARDSON, PETER NICHOLS, b State College, Pa, Feb 26, 43; m 65; c 2. GERMANIC PHILOLOGY. *Educ:* Stanford Univ, BA, 64; Ohio State Univ, MA, 66; Yale Univ, PhD(Ger), 70. *Prof Exp:* Teaching asst Ger, Ohio State Univ, 64-66; from instr to asst prof, 70-76, assoc prof, Yale Univ, 76-80; ASSOC PROF GER, LINFIELD COL, 80- *Concurrent Pos:* Nat Endowment Humanities younger humanist fel, 74-75; Nat Endowment for Humanities pilot grant, 81-83. *Mem:* MLA; Ling Soc Am; Am Name Soc. *Res:* History of the German language; onomastics; Swiss German. *Publ:* Coauth, Zum epithetischen -t im Deutschen, Amsterdamer Beiträge älteren Germanistik, 72; auth, German-Romance Contact: Name-Giving in Walser Settlements, Rodopi, 74; Some notes on a Swiss bicultural onomasticon, Names, 74; Wonne der Wehmuth (Joy of grief), Arch für Studium neueren Sprachen Literaturen, 74; On the meaning of Old Icelandic folk, Semasia, 75; contribr, Zur aussagekraft der vornamen für die siedlungsgeschichte graubündens, In: Beiträge zur Schweizer Namenkunde, Bern, 77; auth, Bemerkungen zur anthroponomie und zum kulturkontakt im alpenraum, Beiträge zur Namenforschung, 77; contribr, Erlöse uns von dem übel': Geisterbannen in der Ostschweiz, Wege der Worte, 78. *Mailing Add:* Linfield Col McMinnville OR 97128

RICHARDSON, WILLIAM HARRISON, Russian History. See Vol I

RICHERT, HANS-GEORG, b Danzig, Ger, Nov 29, 33. GERMAN PHILOLOGY & LITERATURE. *Educ:* Univ Hamburg, PhD, 60; Univ Frankfurt, Dr habil, 74. *Prof Exp:* Lectr, Univ Uppsala, 60-63; asst prof, Univ Frankfurt, 63-69; vis prof, 69-70, assoc prof, 71-76, PROF GER, UNIV CINCINNATI, 76- *Concurrent Pos:* Ger Res Soc stipend, 69-71. *Mem:* Ver Niederdeut Sprache & Lit; MLA; Am Lessing Soc. *Res:* Medieval German philology and literature. *Publ:* Ed, Marienlegenden aus dem Alten Passional, 65 & Judith, Aus der Stuttgarter Handschrift, 69 & Wege und Formen der Passionalu4berlieferung, 78, Tübingen. *Mailing Add:* Dept of Ger Univ of Cincinnati Cincinnati OH 45221

RICHMAN, MICHELE HELENE, b Philadelphia, Pa, Feb 22, 47. TWENTIETH CENTURY FRENCH LITERATURE. *Educ:* Univ Pa, BA, 68; Stanford Univ, PhD(French), 74. *Prof Exp:* ASST PROF FRENCH, UNIV PA, 74- *Concurrent Pos:* Am Coun Learned Soc fel, 77-78. *Mem:* MLA. *Res:* Language of contemporary French literary theory; culture and politics in post-war France. *Publ:* Auth, Literature and sovereignty, Sub-Stance, Univ Wis, 73; Eroticism in the patriarchal order, Diacritics, 76;

Georges Bataille, In: Critical Bibliography of French Literature, 76; auth & contribr, Sex and signs: The language of French feminist criticism, In: Women's Language and Style, 78. *Mailing Add:* Dept of Romance Lang Univ of Pa Williams Hall Philadelphia PA 19174

RICHMOND, GARLAND CAMPBELL, b Iowa Park, Tex, Oct 24, 36; m 58; c 3. GERMAN LITERATURE. *Educ:* Univ Tex, BA, 58, PhD, 62. *Prof Exp:* From instr to asst prof Ger, Western Wash State Col, 62-63; asst prof, 63-70, asst dean, 67-72, ASSOC PROF GER, EMORY UNIV, 70-, ASSOC DEAN COL, 72- *Res:* Eighteenth century German literature; German drama; German comedy in the first half of the 18th century. *Publ:* Auth, Auslese, McGraw, 68. *Mailing Add:* 305 Admin Bldg Emory Univ Atlanta GA 30322

RICHMOND, IAN MCKENZIE, b Diddlebury, England, Jan 5, 44; Can citizen; m 71; c 2. FRENCH LITERATURE & LANGUAGE. *Educ:* Univ Western Ontario, BA, 66, MA, 68, PhF(French), 73. *Prof Exp:* Asst prof French, Royal Mil Col Can, 69-74; ASSOC PROF FRENCH, UNIV WESTERN ONT, 74- *Concurrent Pos:* Humanities Res Coun Can publ grant, 76. *Mem:* Am Asn Teachers Fr; MLA; Asn Can Univ Professors Fr. *Res:* Seventeenth century French literature and society; preciosite. *Publ:* Auth, Les deux Corneille et la preciosite, Revue Univ Laurentienne, 71; L'echec de la tragedie heroique: Oedipe et Ostorius, Signum, 74; Deux oeuvres rendues a L'Abbe de Pure, Revue Hist Lit France, 77; L'evolution du pathetique amoureux de Timocrate jusq'au Duc de Nemours, Bull Apfac, 77; Principes de la sentimentalite racinienne, Fr Rev, 77; Heroisme et Galanterie: L'Abbe de Pure Temoin d'une Crise (1953 a 1665), Ed Naaman, 77. *Mailing Add:* Dept of French Univ of Western Ont London ON N6A 3K7 Can

RICHTER, BODO L O, b Leverkusen, Ger, Feb 13, 15; US citizen. ROMANCE LANGUAGES. *Educ:* Harvard Univ, MA, 41; Univ Pa, PhD, 51. *Prof Exp:* Instr French, Span & Ger, army specialized training prog, Lafayette Col, 42-44; instr French & Span, Phillips Exeter Acad, 44-45; instr French, Span & Ital, Brown Univ, 46-49; from instr to assoc prof, 51-55, PROF FRENCH, SPAN & ITAL, STATE UNIV NY, BUFFALO, 65- *Concurrent Pos:* Newberry Libr fel, 59; vis prof, Washington Univ, 62-63. *Mem:* MLA; Dante Soc Am; Renaissance Soc Am; Am Comp Lit Asn; Mod Humanities Res Asn. *Res:* Poetry of the Pleide; literary contacts between France and Italy during the Renaissance; the Venier literary circle. *Publ:* Auth, Ronsard's Italian annotations in the Rime diverse anthology, Italica; Baudelaire, poete de l'evasion, Lett Mod; The thought of Louis Le Roy according to his early pamphlets, Studies Renaissance; La Venexiana in the light of recent criticism, In: The Drama of the Renaissance: Essays for L Bradner, 70; The French Renaissance epithalamia, In: From Marot to Montaigne, 72; Ronsard studies, Neophilogue; Zwischen Renaissance und Barock: Die Italienische Dichterin Veronica Franco, Revue des langes vivantes; Belleforest, the first critic of Ronsard's Franciade?, In: French Renaissance Studies in Honor of I Silver, 74. *Mailing Add:* Dept of Mod Lang & Lit State Univ of NY Buffalo NY 14260

RICHTER, DAVID HENRY, English, Linguisitics. See Vol II

RICHTER, GLENDA ROBERTA, b Vancouver, BC, Nov 25, 31; US citizen; wid. GERMAN. *Educ:* Univ BC, BA, 52; Univ Alta, MA, 53; Univ Calif, Berkeley, PhD, 57. *Prof Exp:* Instr, Wells Col, 55-56; asst prof, 58-65, PROF GER, HUMBOLDT STATE UNIV, 65- *Mem:* MLA; Am Asn Teachers Ger. *Res:* Modern drama; 17th century literature. *Mailing Add:* Dept of Foreign Lang Humboldt State Univ Arcata CA 95521

RICHTMAN, JACK, b New York, NY, Mar 15, 27. FRENCH LANGUAGE & LITERATURE. *Educ:* Brooklyn Col, AB, 59; Columbia Univ, MA, 61, PhD, 69. *Prof Exp:* Asst prof, 62-70, ASSOC PROF FRENCH, STATE UNIV NY ALBANY, 70- *Concurrent Pos:* Lectr, Columbia Univ, 59-61; NY State Regents fel, 59-61; Fulbright fel, Univ Paris, 61-62; mem, Kettering Found-State Univ NY Proj Improvement Col Teaching, 66-67; State Univ NY Res Found grant, 70-71; coordr, Workshop on Gay Studies & Curricula, Mod Lang Asn, 74-; res found grant, State Univ NY, 78-79. *Mem:* MLA; Am Asn Teachers Fr; AAUP; Am Soc 18th Century Studies; Soc Hist Theatre. *Res:* French 18th century theatre; work of Gide and Camus; Gay studies and curricula. *Publ:* Contribr, Thinking: Focus for the College Teacher, State Univ NY Albany, 66; transl, Aureliu Weiss, The Power of Theatrical Illusion, Theatre Ann, 67; auth, Adrienne Lecouvreur: The Actress and the Age, Prentice-Hall, 71; Mademoiselle Clairon: Actress-Philosopher, Studies on Voltaire and the 18th Century, 76. *Mailing Add:* Dept of French State Univ of NY Albany NY 12222

RICKER-ABDERHALDEN, JUDITH, b St Gallen, Switz. GERMAN & FRENCH LITERATURE. *Educ:* Univ Nebr, MA, 74, PhD(Ger & French), 80. *Prof Exp:* ASST PROF GER LANG & LIT, DEPT FOREIGN LANG, UNIV ARK, 80- *Mem:* MLA; Am Asn Teachers Ger; Philol Asn Pac Coast. *Res:* Contemporary German novel; Swiss literature. *Publ:* Auth, Das Motiv des Fremdkörpers im Werk Adolf Muschgs, & Adolf Muschg und die Kritik, In: Über Adolf Muschg, Suhrkamp Verlag, 79; ed, Über Adolf Muschg, Suhrkamp Verlag, 79. *Mailing Add:* Dept of For Lang Commun Ctr 425 Univ Ark Fayetteville AR 72701

RICKETT, ADELE AUSTIN, b Yonkers, NY, July 9, 19; m 44; c 2. CHINESE LANGUAGES & LITERATURE. *Educ:* Univ NC, AB, 39, BS, 41; Univ Pa, MA, 48, PhD(Chinese), 67. *Prof Exp:* Lectr, 67-72, WATKINS ASST PROF CHINESE STUDIES, UNIV PA, 72- *Concurrent Pos:* Ed jour, Chinese Lang Teachers Asn, 64-68, bk rev ed, 69, mem bd, 72-75. *Mem:* Chinese Lang Teachers Asn; MLA; Am Orient Soc. *Res:* Chinese literary criticism; post-1949 Chinese communist literature. *Publ:* Coauth, Prisoners of liberation, Cameron Assocs, 57; auth, Technical terms in Chinese literary criticism, Lit East & West, XII, 2, 3, 4, 12/68; ed Norman Whitney's Spectator Papers, Am Friends Serv Comt, 71; auth, The personality of the Chinese critic, In: The Personality of the Critic, Vol VI, Yearbook of Comparative Criticism, Pa State Univ, 73; A translation exercise in Chinese poetry, J Chinese Lang Teachers Asn, 4/74; Wang Kuo-wei's Jen-chien Tz'u-hua, A Study in Chinese Literary Criticism, Hong Kong Univ, 77; ed, Chinese Approaches to Literature from Confucius to Liang Ch'i-ch'ao, Princeton Univ, 78; auth, Method and intuition: the poetic theories of Huang T'ing-chien, In: Chinese Approaches to Literature from Confucius to Liang Ch'i-ch'ao, Princeton Univ, 78. *Mailing Add:* 3600 Powelton Ave Philadelphia PA 19104

RICKS, THOMAS MILLER, Middle East History. See Vol I

RIDDELL, JAMES ALLEN, English Literature & Lexicography. See Vol II

RIDGELY, BEVERLY SELLMAN, b Baltimore, Md, Dec 16, 20; m 44; c 3. FRENCH LITERATURE. *Educ:* Princeton Univ, AB, 43, AM, 49, PhD, 53. *Hon Degrees:* MA, Brown Univ, 57. *Prof Exp:* From instr to assoc prof, 50-64, prof, 64-80, EMER PROF FRENCH, BROWN UNIV, 80- *Concurrent Pos:* Asst ed, French Rev, 68-71; vis prof French lit, Princeton Univ, 69; Howard Found fel, 59-60. *Mem:* MLA; Am Asn Teachers Fr; Renaissance Soc Am; AAUP. *Res:* Sixteenth and 17th-century French literature; literature and science; America as viewed by the French. *Publ:* Auth, The Cosmic Voyage in French Sixteenth-century Learned Poetry, Studies Renaissance, 63; ed, La Fontaine, Fables choisies, Prentice-Hall, 67; auth, Disciple de Lucrece une seconde fois: A study of La Fontaine's Poeme du Quinquina, L'Esprit Createur, summer 71; Racan and the Old and New Astronomies, Yale Fr Studies, 73; coauth, Birds of the World on Stamps, Am Topical Asn, Milwaukee, Wis, 74; auth, Beavers, bobacks, and owls: Reality and fantasy in three episodes of animal behavior in the Fables of La Fontaine, Papers on Fr Seventeenth-century Lit, summer 76; A Guide to the Birds of the Squam Lakes Region, New Hampshire, Squam Lakes Asn, Plymouth, NH, 77. *Mailing Add:* Dept of French Studies Box E Brown Univ Providence RI 02912

RIDGWAY, RONALD SIDNEY, b Cannock, UK, Apr 17, 23; Can citizen; m 46; c 2. FRENCH. *Educ:* Univ Sheffield, BA, 48, dipl, 49; Univ Man, MA, 53; Univ Aix-Marseille, DUniv, 58. *Prof Exp:* From instr to assoc prof, 53-67, PROF FRENCH, UNIV SASK, 67- *Concurrent Pos:* Mem, Acad Racinienne, 57-; Can Coun fel, 69-70. *Mem:* Asn Can Univ Teachers Fr (secy, 58-60); Am Soc 18th Century Studies; Can Soc 18th Century Studies. *Res:* Chamfort; Voltaire. *Publ:* Auth, Athalie vue par Voltaire, Bull Liaison Racinnienne, 58; La Propagande Philosophique dan les Tragedies de Voltaire, Inst Musee Voltaire, Geneva, 61; Voltaire and tragedy, Humanities Asn Can Bull, 62-63; Voltaire as an actor, Eighteenth Century Studies, 68; Voltaire and Sensibility, McGill-Queen's Univ, 73; Voltaire's operas, 80 & Camus's favourite moralist, 81, Studies on Voltaire. *Mailing Add:* 1032 Colony St Saskatoon SK S7N 0S4 Can

RIECKMANN, JENS, b Lüneburg, WGer, Sept 29, 44. GERMAN LITERATURE. *Educ:* Harvard Univ, PhD(Ger), 75. *Prof Exp:* Asst prof, Univ Va, 75-81; ASST PROF GER, UNIV WASH, 81- *Concurrent Pos:* Teaching fel, Harvard Univ, 71-75 & Mellon fel, 80-81; assoc ed Ger, German Quart, 76-78. *Mem:* Am Asn Teachers German; MLA. *Res:* Thomas Mann; Fin De Siecle; novel. *Publ:* Auth, Erlösung und Beglaubigung: Thomas Manns Betrachtungen Eines Unpolitischen und Ernst Bertrams Nietzsche: Versuch Einer Mythologie, Mod Lang Notes, 75; Der Zauberberg: Eine Geistige Autobiographie Thomas Manns, Stuttgarter Arbeiten Zur Germanistik 77; Zum Problem des Durchbruchs' in Thomas Manns Doktor Faustus, Wirkendes Wort, 79; Zeitblom und Leverkühn: Traditionelles oder avantgardistisches Kunstverstandnis?, 79 & Von der menschlichen Unzulanglichkeit: Zu Hofmannsthals Das Märchen der 672, Nacht, 81, Ger Quart. *Mailing Add:* Dept of Ger DH-30 Univ Washington Seattle WA 98195

RIEDEL, WALTER ERWIN, b Ger, Aug 3, 36; m 63. GERMAN. *Educ:* Univ Alta, BEd, 60, MA, 63; McGill Univ, PhD(Ger), 66. *Prof Exp:* Teacher high sch, Edmonton, 60-61; instr French & Ger, 62-64, asst prof, 66-70, ASSOC PROF GER, UNIV VICTORIA, BC, 70- *Mem:* Can Asn Univ Teachers Ger; Can Comp Lit Asn. *Res:* Expressionism; translation; German and Canadian literary relations. *Publ:* Coauth, Kanadische Erzähler der Gegenwart, Manesse, 67; Modern Canadian Short Stories, Max Hueber, München, 69; Der Neue Mensch Mythos und Wirklichkeit, Bouvier, Bonn, 70; Moderne Erzähler der Welt Kanada, Erdmann, Tübingen, 76; Das Literarische Kamadabild, Bourier, Bonn, 80. *Mailing Add:* Dept of Ger lang & Lit Univ Victoria Victoria BC V8W 2Y2 Can

RIEMSCHNEIDER, ERNST GUNTHER, b Ger, June 7, 21; US citizen; m 63. GERMAN LITERATURE, HISTORY. *Educ:* Tech Univ Berlin, cert, 52; Univ Ky, MA, 61. *Prof Exp:* Instr Ger, US Army Lang Sch, 55-59 & Monterey Peninsula Col, 58-59; asst prof, St Joseph's Col, 60-65; PROF GER, KEUKA COL, 65- *Concurrent Pos:* Res grant, Fed Repub Ger, 62-63 & Col Ctr Finger Lakes, 71-72; executor, Jochen Klepper Lit Estate, 76. *Mem:* Am Asn Teachers Ger; Am Coun Teaching Foreign Lang; Ges Deutsche Sprache; Deutsche Schiller-Ges. *Res:* Language changes in the Federal Republic of Germany and the German Democratic Republic; Jochen Klepper; German literature since 1933. *Publ:* Auth, Die Sprache als Lebendiger Ausdruck des Technischen Zeitalters, VDI-Nachrichten, 3/62; The Socio-Political Concept of the Plan -Terminology in Soviet Germany, Ky Foreign Lang Quart, 62; Veranderungen der Deutschen Sprache in der Sowj Besetzt Zone Seit 1945, Padagog Verlag Schwann, 63; Ist Jargon Schon Sprache, Zur Sprache in der Zone, Mitteldeutsche Vortrage, 63; Uber die Sprache in Mitteldeutschland, Die Mitte, 64; Sprachliche Veranderungen im Bereich der Landwirtschaft, Aueler Protokoll, 64; ed, Jochen Klepper: Briefwechsel, 73 & auth, Der Fall Klepper. Eine Dokumentation, 75, Deutsche Verlags-Anstalt. *Mailing Add:* Dept of Ger Keuka Col Keuka Park NY 14478

RIESE, LAURE, b Neuchatel, Switz, Feb 28, 10; Can citizen. ROMANCE LANGUAGES, FRENCH. *Educ:* Univ Toronto, BA, 33, MA, 35, PhD, 47; Sorbonne, dipl phonetique, 36. *Prof Exp:* Prof, 29-75, EMER PROF FRENCH LIT, VICTORIA COL, UNIV TORONTO, 75- *Concurrent Pos:* Coed, Mod Drama Rev. *Honors & Awards:* Chevalier, Legion d'honneur,

France, 72. *Mem:* Soc Gens Litt; Acad de l'Art de Vivre. *Publ:* Auth, L'ame de la Poesie Canadienne Francaise, Macmillan, Toronto, 55; The French Literary Salons, Queen's Quart, spring 57; Le Canada, Rev Fois Fr Est, 4/58; La Femme du Nouveau Monde, L'Age Nouveau, Paris, 11-1/60; coauth, Un peu de Nouveau, McGraw, Toronto, 61; auth, Les Salons Litteraires Parisiens du 2nd Empire a nos Jours, Privat Toulouse, 62; Plus Articles in L'Herne, Fr Rev & Rev Univ Ottawa. *Mailing Add:* Dept of French Victoria Col Univ of Toronto Toronto ON M5S 1A1 Can

RIFFATERRE, MICHAEL, b France, Nov 20, 24; US citizen; m; c 2. FRENCH. *Educ:* Sorbonne, Lic es Let & dipl, 47, cert, 52; Columbia Univ, PhD, 55. *Prof Exp:* Lectr French, 53-54, from instr to prof, 54-75, chmn dept Span & Port, 70-73, Knopf prof, 75-82, PROF FRENCH LIT, COLUMBIA UNIV, 82- & CHMN DEPT FRENCH, 74- *Concurrent Pos:* Am Coun Learned Sco grant-in-aid, 60; Guggenheim fel, 61-62, 78; vis lectr French lit, Queens Col, 64, Univ Pa , 67, 70, 75 & Middlebury Col, 69; gen ed, Romanic Rev, 71-; vis prof French, Univ Toronto, fall 73, NY Univ, 75, Princeton Univ, 76 & Yale Univ, 78; sr fel, Sch Criticism & Theory, Northwestern Univ, 80-, Univ Toronto Summer Inst for semiotic, 80, Johns Hopkins Univ, spring, 80 & Col de France, Paric, 81. *Honors & Awards:* Ansley Award, Columbia Univ Press, 55; Officier, Palmes Academiques, 77. *Mem:* Am Asn Teachers Fr; Ling Soc Am; MLA; Int Ling Asn; Am Asn Studies Dada & Surrealism (pres, 73-79). *Res:* French literature of the 19th and 20the century; Romance language poetics; semiotics. *Publ:* Auth, Le Style des Pleiades de Gobineau, Columbia Univ, 57; Essais de Stylistique Structurale, Flammarion, Paris, 71; Interpretation and descriptive poetry, New Lit Hist, 73; Semiotics of Poetry, Ind Univ, 78; La Production du Texte, Seuil, Paris, 79; Flaubert's Presuppositions, Diacritics, 81. *Mailing Add:* French Dept Columbia Univ New York NY 10027

RIGAULT, ANDRE ALBERT, b Chambourcy, France, June 6, 22; m 48; c 6. LINGUISTICS. *Educ:* Univ Paris, Baccalaureat, 41, Lic, 47, dipl, 48. *Prof Exp:* Asst prof phonetics, Univ Paris, 48-49; asst prof French, 49-61, assoc prof gen phonetics, 61-65, chmn dept ling, 66-71, PROF GEN PHONETICS, MCGILL UNIV, 65-, DIR PHONETICS RES LAB, 63- *Concurrent Pos:* Mem, Permanent Int Coun Phonetic Sci, 61-; secy-gen, Int Cong Phonetic Sci, 71; Can Coun res fel, 71-72. *Honors & Awards:* Officier, Palmes Academiques, 69, Chevalier, Legion d'Honneur, 76. *Mem:* Ling Soc Am; Ling Soc Paris; Phonetic Soc Japan; Can Ling Asn (pres, 70-72). *Res:* Experimental phonetics; general and applied phonology; speech perception. *Publ:* Auth, Introduction a la Phonetique Francaise, Hachette, Paris, 65; L'accent en francais et en tcheque, Studia Phonetica, 70; La force articulatoire des consonnes, Academia, Prague, 70; ed, La Grammaire du Francais Parle, Hachette, Paris, 71; co-ed, Proceedings of the VIIth International Congress of Phonetic Sciences, Mouton, The Hague, 72; auth, Accent et demarcationen tcheque, Phonetica Pragensia, Acta Universitatis Carolinae, 72; Kanadska francouzstina, Czech Acad Sci, 74; Voiceless Vowels and Whispered Speech in Japanese, Phonetic Soc Japan, 74. *Mailing Add:* Dept of Ling McGill Univ 1001 Sherbrooke St W Montreal PQ H3A 1G5 Can

RIGG, ARTHUR GEORGE, b Wigan, England, Feb 17, 37; m 64. MEDIEVAL ENGLISH & LATIN. *Educ:* Oxford Univ, BA, 59, MA, 62, DPhil. *Prof Exp:* Lectr English, Merton Col, Oxford Univ, 61-63, Merton & Balliol Cols, 63-66 & Oxford Univ, 65-66; vis asst prof, Stanford Univ, 66-68; assoc prof, 68-76, actg dir ctr, 76-78; PROF ENGLISH & MEDIEVAL LATIN, CTR MEDIEVAL STUDIES, UNIV TORONTO, 76- *Mem:* Mediaeval Acad Am. *Publ:* Auth, English Language; A Historical Reader, Appleton, 68; A Glastonbury Miscellany of the Fifteenth Century, Clarendon, Oxford Univ, 68; contribr, Medium Aevum, Anglia, English Lang Notes & Med Studies; ed, Editing Medieval Texts Written in England, Garland, 77; auth, Golias and other pseudonyms, Studi Medievali, 77; Medieval Latin poetic anthologies I, Mediaeval Studies, 77; Poems of Walter of Wimborne, Pontif Inst, Toronto, 78. *Mailing Add:* Ctr for Medieval Studies Univ of Toronto Toronto ON M5S 1A1 Can

RIGOLOT, FRANCOIS PAUL, b Chateau-du-Loir, France, May 21, 39; m 70; c 2. FRENCH LITERATURE. *Educ:* Sch Advan Studies, Paris, dipl, 61; Northwestern Univ, MA, 63; Univ Wis, MA, 66, PhD(French), 69. *Prof Exp:* Instr French, Univ Wis, 68-69; asst prof, Univ Mich, Ann Arbor, 69-74; assoc prof, 74-78, PROF FRENCH, PRINCETON UNIV, 78- *Concurrent Pos:* Horace H Rackham fel, 71-73; Ferris Thompson Found Preceptorship, 74-77; Nat Endowment for Humanities fel, 79-80; Meredith Howland Ryne professorship French lit, 81-; vis prof, Johns Hopkins Univ, 81-82; Guggenheim fel, 82-83. *Mem:* MLA; Am Asn Teachers Fr; Asn Int Etudes Francaises; Renaissance Soc Am; Amis de Montaigne. *Res:* French Renaissance literature; stylistics and poetics; onomastics. *Publ:* Auth, Les Langages de Rabelais, Droz, Geneva, 72; coauth, L'Atelier D'Ecriture, Seghers, auth, Cratylisme et pantagruelisme, Etudes Rabelaisiennes, 76; Rhetorique du nom poetique, Poetique, 76; Poetiques marginales, Rev de Lit Compt, 77; Poetique et Onomastique, Droz, Geneva, 77; coauth, Semantique de la poesie, Sevil, Paris, 80; auth, Le Texte de la Renaissance, Droz, Geneva, 82. *Mailing Add:* Princeton Univ Princeton NJ 08540

RIGSBY, JEANNE BRINK, b Bucharest, Romania, Feb 26, 25; m 68. FRENCH LANGUAGE & LITERATURE. *Educ:* France,Bacc, 43; Univ Montreal, MA, 58; Univ Paris, Sorbonne, Doctorat en lettres(ling), 65. *Prof Exp:* From asst prof to assoc prof, 59-70, PROF FRENCH, UNIV SAN DIEGO, 70- *Honors & Awards:* Chevalier de l'Ordre des Palmes Academiques, France, 75. *Mem:* Am Asn Teachers French; Am Soc French Acad Palms. *Res:* Francophone literature; linguisitics. *Mailing Add:* Dept of French Univ of San Diego Alcala Park San Diego CA 92110

RIGSBY, KENT JEFFERSON, b Tulsa, Okla, Feb 25, 45; m 69; c 2. CLASSICAL LANGUAGES, ANCIENT HISTORY. *Educ:* Yale Univ, BA, 66; Univ Toronto, MA, 68. *Prof Exp:* Asst prof, 71-77, ASSOC PROF CLASSICS, DUKE UNIV, 77- *Concurrent Pos:* Asst ed, Greek, Roman & Byzantine Studies, 72-77, assoc ed, 77-79, Roman ed, 79 & sr ed, 80- *Mem:* Am Philol Asn. *Res:* Greek epigraphy; Hellenistic history; ancient religion. *Publ:* Auth, Cnossus and Capua, Trans Am Philol Asn, 76; Sacred Ephebie games at Oxyrhynchus, Chronique D'Egypte, 77; The era of the Province of Asia, Phoenix, 79; Seleucid Notes, Trans Am Philol Asn, 80. *Mailing Add:* Dept Class Studies Duke Univ Durham NC 27706

RILEY, ANTHONY WILLIAM, b Radcliffe-on-Trent, England, July 23, 29; Can citizen; m 55; c 3. GERMAN LANGUAGE & LITERATURE. *Educ:* Univ Manchester, BA, 52; Univ Tübingen, PhD, 58. *Prof Exp:* Lectr English, Univ Tübingen, 57-59 & 60-62; asst lectr Ger, Queen Mary Col, Univ London, 59-60; from asst prof to assoc prof Ger lang & lit, 62-68, chmn dpet, 67-76, PROF GER LANG & LIT, QUEEN'S UNIV, ONT, 68- *Concurrent Pos:* Can Coun leave fel, 69-70 & 76-77. *Mem:* Can Asn Univ Teachers Ger (vpres, 73-75, pres, 75-76); MLA; Thomas Mann Ges; Humanities Asn Can; Int Ver für ger Sprach-und Literaturwissenschaft. *Res:* The 20th century German novel; Alfred Döblin's narrative and theoretical works. *Publ:* Auth, Three cryptic quotations in Thomas Mann's Felix Krull, J English & Ger Philol, 1/66; Elisabeth Langgässer and Juan Donoso Cortes, PMLA, 5/68; Elisabeth Langgässer Bibliographie mit Nachlassbericht, Duncker & Humblot, Berlin, 70; Zum unstrittenen Schluss von Alfred Döblins Hamlet-Roman, Literaturwiss Jahrbuch, 74; co-ed, F P Grove, The Master Mason's House, Oberon, Ottawa, 76; auth, Jaufre Rudel in Alfred Döblin's last novel, Mosaic, 2/77; Christianity and Revolution in Döblin's November 1918, In: The First World War in German Narrative Prose, Univ Toronto Press, 80; ed, Alfred Döblin, Ausgewählte Werke in Einzelbänden, Walter-Verlag, Olten & Freiburg (4 vols), 78, 80, 81 & 82. *Mailing Add:* Dept of Ger Queen's Univ Kingston ON K7L 3N6 Can

RILEY, WILLIAM KENT, b Chicago, Ill, Sept 11, 37; m 64. LINGUISTICS, SOCIOLINGUISTICS. *Educ:* Univ Louisville, BA, 64; Mich State Univ, MA, 67; Georgetown Univ, PhD(ling), 74. *Prof Exp:* ASST PROF ENGLISH, OLD DOMINION UNIV, 74- *Mem:* Ling Soc Am; Southeast Conf Ling; SAlantic Mod Lang Asn; Lectological Asn. *Res:* Soclal dialects; male and female speech; folk beliefs about language. *Publ:* Auth, Sentence openers in freshman writing, Col English, 12/64; coauth, Field Techniques in an Urban Language Study, Ctr Appl Ling, 68; auth, A generative phonology of Yak-Yak, In: Studies Out in Left Field, Ling Res, 71; How much variation is there?, In: Views on Language, Inter-Univ, 75; Some uses of implicational analysis, Lang Today, 76-77; Misrepresentation of linguistics in the media, Perspectives on Socioling (in press). *Mailing Add:* Dept of English Old Dominion Univ Norfolk VA 23508

RIMBACH, GUENTHER C, b Dortmund, Ger, Dec 4, 25; US citizen; m 57; c 2. GERMAN & COMPARATIVE LITERATURE. *Educ:* Johns Hopkins Univ, MA, 54, PhD, 58. *Prof Exp:* From instr to asst prof, 57-73, ASSOC PROF GER, UNIV CALIF, RIVERSIDE, 73- *Mem:* MLA; Am Asn Teachers Ger. *Res:* Seventeenth and twentieth century German and French literature; aesthetics. *Publ:* Auth, On Bertolt Brecht and the epic theatre, Educ Theatre J, 62; Sense and nonsense in the poetry of Jean Arp, Ger Quart, 63; Illusions perspektiven in der modernen Lyrik, Ger-Romanische Monatsschr, Vol XIV, No 4. *Mailing Add:* Dept of Ger Univ of Calif Riverside CA 92502

RINGEN, CATHERINE OLESON, b Brooklyn, NY, June 3, 43; m 69. LINGUISTICS. *Educ:* Ind Univ, BA, 70, MA, 72, PhD(ling), 75. *Prof Exp:* Vis lectr ling, Univ Minn, 73-74; asst prof, 75-79, ASSOC PROF LING, UNIV IOWA, 79- *Concurrent Pos:* Fulbright prof, Univ Trondheim, Norway, 80. *Mem:* Ling Soc Am. *Res:* Phonological theory; philosophy of linguistics; phonetics. *Publ:* Auth, On arguments for rule ordering, Found Lang, 8, 72; coauth, Rule reordering and the history of High German vowel length, Papers from Ninth Regional Meeting of Chicago Ling Soc, 73, auth, Obligatory-optional precedence, Found Lang, 74; contribr, Rule Order and Obligatory Rules, Proc of Eleventh Int Congress Ling, 75; Vowel Harmony: Implications for the Alternation Condition, Phonologica, 77; auth, Another view of the theoretical implications of Hungarian vowel harmony, Ling Inquiry, 78; Uralic and Altaic vowel harmony: A problem for Natural Generative Phonology, J Ling, 80; contribr, A concrete analysis of Hungarian vowel harmony, Issues in Vowel Harmony, 80. *Mailing Add:* Dept of Ling Univ of Iowa Iowa City IA 52242

RINGEN, JON D, Philosophy of Science. See Vol IV

RINKEVICH, THOMAS EDWARD, b Grand Rapids, Mich, Apr 24, 41; m 71. CLASSICAL LANGUAGES & LITERATURES. *Educ:* Xavier Univ, Ohio, AB, 64; Ohio State Univ, MA, 66, PhD(Latin), 73. *Prof Exp:* Teaching asst Latin, Greek, Ohio State Univ, 64-67; instr, 67-73, ASST PROF LATIN, GREEK & CLASSICS, UNIV NEBR-LINCOLN, 73- *Mem:* Am Philos Asn. *Res:* Theokritos and pastoral poetry; ancient Near Eastern languages and literatures; Greek literature. *Publ:* Auth, Theokritos' Fifth Idyll: The education of Lakon, Arethusca, 10: 295-305. *Mailing Add:* Dept of Foreign Lang Univ Nebr Lincoln NE 68588

RINKUS, JEROME JOSEPH, b Baltimore, Md, Sept 11, 38. RUSSIAN LITERATURE. *Educ:* Middlebury Col, AB, 60; Brown Univ, AM, 62, PhD(Slavic lang & lit), 71. *Prof Exp:* Teaching asst Russ lang, Brown Univ, 62-64 & 67-68; asst linguist, Intensive Lang Training Ctr, Ind Univ, 65-66; asst prof Russ lang & lit, Bucknell Univ, 68-73; asst prof, 73-79, ASSOC PROF RUSS LANG & LIT & COORDR RUSS PROG, POMONA COL, 79- *Concurrent Pos:* Nat Endowment for Humanities fel, 75 & grant, 78; consult, Nat Endowment for Humanities, 77-78. *Mem:* Am Asn Advan Slavic Studies; Am Asn Teachers Slavic & East Europ Lang; MLA; Am Coun Teaching Foreign Lang; AAUP. *Res:* Nineteenth century Russian literature; the novel; methodology of Russian language teaching. *Publ:* Auth, The Russian language curriculum in the liberal arts college, 74 & Mythological and folkloric motifs in Pil'njak's Mat Syra-Zemlja, 75, Russ Lang J; Reflections on Turgenev's Hamlet and Don Quixote, In: Perspectives on Hamlet, Bucknell Univ, 75; Sergey Timofeevich Aksakov, In: Modern Encyclopedia of Russian and Soviet Literature, 77; Developing mature conversational skills in elementary Russian courses, Russ Lang J, XXXIII: 15-20. *Mailing Add:* Dept of Mod Lang & Lit Pomona Col Harvard Ave at Sixth St Claremont CA 91711

RIORDAN, FRANCIS ELLEN, b Solomon, Kans, Oct 24, 15. FRENCH LITERATURE. *Educ:* Cath Univ Am, MA, 45, PhD, 52. *Prof Exp:* Directress, St Mary Acad, NMex, 50-51; prin, Luckey High Sch, Kans, 51-53 & Sacred Heart Cathedral High Sch, 53-57; instr French, 57-63, PROF FRENCH LANG & LIT, MARYMOUNT COL, KANS, 63-, CHMN DEPT FOREIGN LANG, 61-, CHMN DIV HUMANITIES, 80- *Mem:* Am Asn Teachers Fr. *Res:* Parallels of art and French literature; Manessier, Rouault, Bacon. *Publ:* Auth, The Concept of Love in the Catholic Literary Revival, Cath Univ Am, 52. *Mailing Add:* Dept of Foreign Lang Marymount Col Salina KS 67401

RIOUX, ROBERT N, b Plainfield, Conn, July 14, 27; m 63; c 3. LITERATURE. *Educ:* Univ Conn, BA, 49; Okla State Univ, MA, 50; Univ Paris, D Lett, 56. *Prof Exp:* Instr French, Emerson Col, 50-52; instr French & Span, Woodberry Forest Sch, 52-54; French Govt teaching asst English, Lycee Hoche, Versailles, France, 54-55; asst prof French, Mont State Univ, 56-59; from asst prof to assoc prof Romance lang, 59-72, PROF ROMANCE LANG & DIR FRANCO-AM STUDIES, UNIV MAINE, ORONO, 72- *Concurrent Pos:* Dir, NDEA French Inst, Univ Maine, 63-65; Fulbright-Hays lectr-researcher Am lit, Univ Abidjan, 66-68. *Mem:* Am Asn Teachers Fr; Mod Humanities Res Asn. *Res:* Old French language; Canadian-French language and literature. *Publ:* Auth, Sir Thomas Malory; createur verbal, Etudes Anglaises, 59; Dix ans apres, 8/67 & Americanismes, 8/69, Vie et Language. *Mailing Add:* Dept of Foreign Lang Univ of Maine Orono ME 04473

RIPOLL, CARLOS, b Havana, Cuba, Mar 31, 22; US citizen; m 46. LATIN AMERICAN LITERATURE, ROMANCE LANGUAGES. *Educ:* Univ Havana, MS, 45; Univ Miami, MA, 62; NY Univ PhD(Span & Span Am lit), 63. *Prof Exp:* Assoc prof, 63-68, PROF ROMANCE & SLAVIC LANG, QUEENS COL, NY, 68- *Concurrent Pos:* Ed, Rev Cubana, 68-69; proj dir grants, Nat Endowment for Humanities, 69-71 & Res Found, City Univ New York, 71-72. *Mem:* MLA. *Res:* Spanish and Latin American literature; the essay; the cultural and literary history of Cuba. *Publ:* Auth, Conciencia intelectual de America: antologia del ensayo hispano-americano, 66, rev ed, 70, La Generacion del 23 en Cuba y otros apuntes sobre el vanguardismo, 68 & La Celestina a traves del Decalogo, 69, Las Americas; Escritos desconocidos de Jose Marti, 71, Indice universal de la obra de Jose Marti, 71, Eliseo Torres; coauth, Teatro hispanoamericano: antologia critca, Anaya, Vols I & II, 72 & 73; auth, Jose Marti: Letras y Huellas Desconocidas, Elveo Torres & Sons, 76; Jose Marti, Thoughts/Pensamientos: A Bilingual Anthology, Aliseo Torres Las Americas, 80. *Mailing Add:* Dept of Romance Lang Queens Col Flushing NY 11367

RIPPLEY, LA VERN J, b Waumandee, Wis, Mar 2, 35; m 60; c 2. GERMAN ROMANTICISM & IMMIGRATION HISTORY. *Educ:* Col Holy Cross, BA, 56; Univ Wis, BS, 58; Kent State Univ, MA, 61; Ohio State Univ, PhD(Ger), 65. *Prof Exp:* Teacher, River Falls Sr High Sch, 58-60; teaching asst, Ohio State Univ, 61-63; asst prof Ger, Ohio Wesleyan Univ, 64-67; assoc prof, 67-71, chmn dept, 67-74, PROF GER, ST OLAF COL, 71- *Concurrent Pos:* Ed, Newsletter Soc Ger-Am Studies; Fulbright fel, 63-64 & Deutscher Akademischer Austauschdienst Fulbright, 82. *Mem:* Cent States Mod Lang Asn; MLA; Am Asn Teachers Ger; Am Hist Soc Ger from Russia; Norweg Am Hist Asn. *Res:* German-Americana; German Romanticism; modern German literature. *Publ:* Auth, Of German Ways, Dillon, 70; The house as metaphor in E T A Hoffman's Rat Krespel, Papers Lang & Lit, 71; Gift cows for Germany, NDak Hist, 73 & 77; translr, Excursion through America, R R Donnelley, 73; auth, Russian-German Settlements in the United States, Inst Regional Studies, ND, 74; The German-Americans, Twayne, 74; Archbbishop Ireland and the School Language Controversy, US Cath Historian, fall 80; Germans from Russia, In: Harvard Encycl of American Ethnic Groups, Harvard Univ Press, 80. *Mailing Add:* 909 Ivanhoe Dr Northfield MN 55057

RISCO, ANTONIO, b Allariz, Spain, May 30, 26; m 64. SPANISH LITERATURE. *Educ:* Univ Santiago, Spain, BA, 45; Univ Madrid, MA, 61, PhD, 66. *Prof Exp:* Prof, Col San Jose, Orense, 60-61; lectr, Col Enseignement Gen Fabre, Toulouse, France, 61-64; instr, Univ Ore, 64-66; asst, Mt Allison Univ, 66-69; from asst prof to assoc prof, 69-76, PROF SPAN LIT, LAVAL UNIV, 76-, DIR DIV, 76- *Concurrent Pos:* Vis prof, Univ Calif, Irvine, 72 & Carleton Univ, Ottawa, 77. *Mem:* Can Asn Hispanists; Int Asn Hispanists. *Res:* Spanish literature of the 19th and 20th centuries; comparative Spanish and French literatures; the fantastic in literature. *Publ:* Auth, El Caballero de las Botas Azules, de Rosalia, una obra abierta, Papeles de Son Armadaus, Palma Mallorca, 75; La novela de Azorin y el Nouveau Roman Frances, Rev Can Estud Hispanicos, 76; El Demiurgo y su Mundo: Hacia un Nuevo Enfoque de la obra de Valle-Inclan, Gredos, Madrid, 77; La lucha por la vida de Baroja en la evolucion de la novelistica espanola, Rev Can Estud Hispanicos, 78; Azorin y la ruptura con la novela tradicional, Alhambra, Madrid, 80; Literatura y figuracion, Gredos, Madrid, 82; Literatura y fantasia, Taurus, Madrid, 82; El caso (novel), Akal, Madrid, 82. *Mailing Add:* Dept of Lit Laval Univ Quebec PQ G1K 7P4 Can

RISLEY, WILLIAM ROY, b New York, NY, July 18, 42; m 69; c 2. SPANISH LANGUAGE & LITERATURE. *Educ:* Hamilton Col, BA, 65; Middlebury Col, MA, 66; Univ Wis-Madison, PhD(Span), 74. *Prof Exp:* Instr, Univ Wis-Madison, 70-71; asst prof, 71-77, assoc prof, 77-82, PROF SPAN, WESTERN ILL UNIV, 82- *Concurrent Pos:* Mem, ed adv coun, Anales de la literatura espanola contemporanea, 76-; mem, ed bd & bibliogr, Annual Bibliography of Post-Civil War Spanish Fiction, 77- *Mem:* Midwest Mod Lang Asn; Am Asn Teachers Span & Port; Northeast Mod Lang Asn; MLA; Am Fed Teachers. *Res:* Spanish Literature of the 19th and 20th centuries; comparative literature; literary theory. *Publ:* Auth, Setting in the Galdos Novel, 1881-1885, Hispanic Rev, winter 78; co-ed, Waiting for Pegasus: Studies of the Presence of Symbolism and Decadence in Hispanic Letters, Western Ill Univ, 79; auth, Hacia el simbolismo en la prosa de Valle-Inclan, Anales de la narrativa espanola contemporanea, 79; Symbolic place names in Galdos Early Novelas Espanolas Contemporaneas, Revista de Estudios Hispanicos, 10/80. *Mailing Add:* Dept of Foreign Lang & Lit Western Ill Univ Macomb IL 61455

RITCHIE, GISELA F, b Lyck, Ger, US citizen; m 58; c 2. GERMAN & ENGLISH LITERATURE. *Educ:* Free Univ Berlin, MA, 52; Univ Mich, PhD(Ger), 65. *Prof Exp:* Instr Ger, Bob Jones Univ, 53-54; instr, Wayne State Univ, 54-56; lectr Ger & French, 59-60, asst prof, 65-68, ASSOC PROF GER, WICHITA STATE UNIV, 68- *Mem:* MLA; Am Asn Teachers Ger; Lessing Soc. *Res:* Eighteenth, 19th and 20th century German literature; French literature of the 18th and 19th centuries; English/American literature of the 17th, 18th, 19th and 20th centuries. *Publ:* Auth, Caroline Schlegel-Schelling in Wahrheit und Dichtung, Bouvier, Bonn, 68; Zur Entstehung von Goethes Gedicht Die Geheimnisse und zur Einordnung der fehlenden Stanzen, Goethe J, 69; Stifter und Der Steppenwolf, ein Beitrag zu den geistigen Beziehungen grosser Dichter, In: Husbanding the Golden Grain, Univ Mich, 73. *Mailing Add:* 1206 Farmstead Wichita KS 67208

RITCHIE, WILLIAM CRAIG, b Madison, Wis, Apr 30, 38; m 72. LINGUISTICS, ADULT SECOND LANGUAGE ACQUISITION. *Educ:* Univ Mich, BA, 62, MA, 64, PhD(ling), 69. *Prof Exp:* Res asst English as second lang, English Lang Inst, Ann Arbor, 64-65; asst prof, 69-78, ASSOC PROF LING, SYRACUSE UNIV, 78- *Mem:* Ling Soc Am; MLA; AAUP; Teachers English to Speakers Other Lang; Southeastern Conf Ling. *Res:* Syntax; adult-acquired syntax. *Publ:* Auth, Some implications of generative grammar for the construction of courses in English as a foreign language (2 parts), 67 & On the explanation of phonic interference, 68, Lang Learning; Constraints on adult-acquired syntax, Syracuse Orange Papers, 73; The right roof constraint in an adult-acquired language, Sec Lang Acquisition Res, 78; ed, Second Language Acquisition Research: Issues and Implications, Academic, 78. *Mailing Add:* Dept of Ling 327 H B Crouse Hall Syracuse Univ Syracuse NY 13210

RITTER, NAOMI, b Boston, Mass, Nov 8, 37; div, c 1. MODERN GERMAN LITERATURE. *Educ:* Vassar Col, BA, 59; Harvard Univ, PhD(German), 69. *Prof Exp:* Lectr Ger, Univ Va, 66-67; vis lectr, Mary Baldwin Col, 67-69; vis asst prof, Sweet Briar Col, 70-71; asst prof, Ind Univ, 72-75; ASSOC PROF GER, UNIV MO, COLUMBIA, 75- *Mem:* MLA; Int Arthur Schnitzler Res Asn; Int Comp Lit Asn; Southern Comp Lit Asn. *Res:* Comparative thematics; modern Austrian literature; comparative literature. *Publ:* Auth, On the circus-motif in modern German literature, Ger Life & Letters, Vol XXVII, No 4; House and Individual: The House-Motif in German Literature of the Nineteenth Century, Stuttgart, 77; Kafka, Wedekind and the circus, Ger Notes, Vol VI, No 4; Stifter und Kafka: Berührungspunkte, Vierteljahresschrift des Adalbert Stifter-Instituts des Landes Oberösterreich, 3-4/78; Up in the gallery: Kafka and Pervert, Mod Lang Notes, Ger Issue, Vol XCVI, No 3; contribr, Kafka and the circus, In: Austrian Literature in the Classroom, Austrian Inst, NY, 81; Rilke, Picasso and the street circus: Cross-currents of modern art, In: Rilke and the Visual Arts, Coronado Press, 82; Baudelaire and Kafka: The Triangular Circus Scene, The Comparatist, Vol IX, 82. *Mailing Add:* 454 Gen Classroom Bldg Univ Mo Columbia MO 65211

RITTER, WILLIAM WILLIS, JR, b Norfolk, Va, Feb 7, 25. ROMANCE PHILOLOGY. *Educ:* Univ NC, BS, 46, BA, 49, MA, 51, PhD, 56. *Prof Exp:* Instr Span, Univ NC, 47-56; asst prof, Hamilton Col, 56-57; from asst prof to assoc prof Span & Ital, Univ Richmond, 57-63; ASSOC PROF MOD LANG, HOLLINS COL, 63-, chmn dept, 73-76. *Mem:* MLA; Am Asn Teachers Span & Port; Am Asn Teachers Ital. *Res:* Late Latin and early Romance; Italian dialect poetry. *Publ:* Auth, Romance linguistics, Bull Mod Foreign Lang Va, 10/63; Some notes on Italian dialect poetry: G G Belli and C A Salustri, Italamerican, 64. *Mailing Add:* 111 Turner Hall Hollins College VA 24020

RITTERSON, MICHAEL, b Salem, NJ, Dec 4, 40; m 68; c 2. GERMAN LANGUAGE AND LITERATURE. *Educ:* Franklin and Marshall Col, AB, 62; Harvard Univ, PhD(Ger lang & lit), 73. *Prof Exp:* Instr Ger, Northeastern Univ, 66-67; instr, 68-74, ASST PROF GER, GETTYSBURG COL, 74- *Mem:* Am Asn Teachers Ger; MLA; Lessing Soc; Goethe Soc NAm; Raabe-Gesellschaft. *Res:* Wilhelm Raabe; German literature in the Weimar Republic; eighteenth-century studies. *Publ:* Auth, Rückwendung, Vorausdeutung und Erzählablauf in Wilhelm Raabes Das Odfeld und Hastenbeck, Jahrbuch Raabe-Gesellschaft, 76; Waiting for Synthesis: Kurt Tucholsky Views America, 1925-1935, Occasional Papers Soc Ger-Am Studies, 82. *Mailing Add:* Dept of Ger & Russ Gettysburg Col Gettysburg PA 17325

RITZENHOFF, URSULA CHRISTA, b Remscheid, W Ger. GERMAN LANGUAGE & LITERATURE. *Educ:* Univ Conn, MA, 74, PhD(Ger), 76. *Prof Exp:* Lectr Ger lit, Univ Natal, 75-77; asst prof Ger, Colo State Univ, 77-78; ASST PROF GER, UNIV TENN, 78- *Mem:* MLA; Am Asn Teachers Ger. *Res:* German literature from 1500 to the present; teaching methodology; history of art. *Publ:* Auth, Hermann Brochs PASENOW-Roman: Eine Re-Orientierung, Lang, Switzerland, 77; contribr, Festschrift für Professor M Schmidt-Ihms, Univ Natal, 78; Proc Fourth Int Conf Improving Univ Teaching, Univ Md, 78; auth, Erläuterungen und Dokumente zu Goethe: Die Wahlverwandtschaften, Reclam, 82. *Mailing Add:* Dept of Ger & Slavic Lang Univ of Tenn Knoxville TN 37916

RIVA, RAYMOND THEODORE, b Chicago, Ill, May 9, 28; m 56; c 1. FRENCH. *Educ:* Univ Ill, BA, 51, PhD(French), 60; Middlebury Col, AM, 55. *Prof Exp:* From instr to asst prof French, Univ Wis, 60-66; assoc prof, Washington Univ, 66-68; chmn dept foreign lang, 68-72, PROF FRENCH, UNIV MO, KANSAS CITY, 68-, CHMN DEPT FOREIGN LANG, 81- *Concurrent Pos:* Vis asst prof, Vanderbilt Univ, 63-64. *Mem:* MLA; Midwest Mod Lang Asn; Am Asn Teachers Fr. *Res:* Computer-based research on Proust's Correspondance; Anouilh; Moliere. *Publ:* Auth, A probable model for Proust's Elstir, Mod Lang Notes, 5/63; Marcel Proust: A Guide to the Recurrent Themes, Exposition, 65; Notes & introd to Jean Anouilh's Ardele and Pauvre Bitos, Dell, 65; Marcel Proust: An immodest proposal, summer 68 & Beckett and Freud, spring 70, Criticism. *Mailing Add:* Dept of Foreign Lang Univ Mo Kansas City MO 64110

RIVAS, DANIEL EUSEBIO, b Camaguey, Cuba, Dec 11, 45. FRENCH, SPANISH. *Educ:* Cath Inst Paris, dipl French, 68; Marist Col, BA, 69; Univ Ill, AM, 72, PhD(French), 77; Univ Poitiers, dipl French, 74; Chambre de Com de Paris, dipl com French, 80. *Prof Exp:* Asst English, Lycee Hoche, Versailles, France, 73-74; asst French, Univ Ill, 74-77; asst prof, 77-82, ASSOC PROF FRENCH & SPAN, AUBURN UNIV, 82- *Mem:* Am Asn Teachers French; MLA. *Res:* Modern French and Spanish literature; poetry; criticism. *Publ:* Contribr, French XX Bibliography, French Inst, 76-; auth, Jouve's Mnemosyne: An alchemical view, L'Esprit Createur, summer 78; Metapoetic variations, Dada-Surrealism, winter 79; contribr, Critical Bibliography of French Literature (Proust), Syracuse Univ, 79; auth, A Propos du Temps et de la Creation dans le, J d'un Cure de Campagne, Studi Francesi, 5-8/80; Pierre Jean Jouve's Dark Night of the Soul, Comp Lit Studies, 9/80; Eluard's L'Amoureuse: Mimesis and Semiosis, Fr Rev, 3/82. *Mailing Add:* Dept of Foreign Lang Auburn Univ Auburn AL 36830

RIVAS, FERNANDO, b La Paz, Bolivia, May 3, 26; US citizen; m 62; c 1. ROMANCE LANGUAGES. *Educ:* San Marcos Univ, Lima, BA, 52; Loyola Univ, Ill, MA, 61; Univ San Agustin, Peru, PhD(Span), 66. *Prof Exp:* Instr Span Lit, Rosary Col, 62-63; asst prof, Univ of the Pac, 63-65; from asst prof to assoc prof, 65-77, PROF SPAN LIT, ST MARY'S UNIV, TEX, 77- *Mem:* Am Asn Teachers Span & Port; MLA; Southwest Coun Latin Am Studies. *Res:* Mexican American culture and civilization; linguistics; Mexican American dialects. *Mailing Add:* Dept of Lang St Mary's Univ San Antonio TX 78284

RIVERA, TOMAS, b Crystal City, Tex, Dec 22, 35; m 58; c 3. ROMANCE LITERATURES, ENGLISH. *Educ:* Southwest Tex State Univ, BSEd, 58, MEd, 64; Univ Okla, MA, 69, PhD(romance lit), 69. *Prof Exp:* Teacher English, Edgewood independent sch dist, 57-58; teacher Span, Crystal City independent sch dist, 58-60; teacher, Clear Creek independent sch dist, 60-65; instr Span, French & English & chmn dept foreign lang, Southwest Tex Jr Col, 65-66; instr Span, Univ Okla, 66-69, dir lang lab & dir & supvr studies teachers, 68-69; assoc prof Span, Sam Houston State Univ, 69-71; dir div foreign lang, lit & ling, Univ Tex, San Antonio, 71-73, prof Span lit, 71-78, assoc dean Col Multidisciplinary Studies, 73-78, vpres admin, 76-78; CHANCELLOR, UNIV CALIF, RIVERSIDE, 79- *Concurrent Pos:* Mem, Carnegie Comn on the Future of Pub Broadcasting, 77-78; mem bd trustees, Carnegie Found Advan Teaching, 77-81; mem bd foreign scholarships/ Fulbright Hays, Dept of State, Presidential Appointment, 78-81; corp officer, The Times Mirror Co, 80- *Honors & Awards:* Quinto Sol Nat Lit Award, 70; Milestone Award, Nat Asn Supv & Curriculum Dir, 77. *Mem:* Am Asn Teachers Span & Port; SCent Mod Lang Asn; MLA; Am Coun Teaching Foreign Lang; Nat Coun Chicanos Higher Educ. *Res:* Spanish peninsular literature; Latin American literature; Mexican-American literature. *Publ:* Auth, Poeta de barro, Bks Abroad, 69; Y no se lo trago la tierra, The Earth Did Not Part, Quinto Sol, 71; Always and Other Poems, Sisterdale, 73; contribr, The New Breed, Prickley Pear, 73; auth, Teoria poetica de Leon Felipe, Cuadernos Am, 73; The searchers, In: Ethnic Literatures in the United States, Tex Tech Univ Press, 77; Poetry, In: Revista Chicano-Riquena, Ind Univ, 73; A Blas de Otero, In: Alaluz, Primavera, 80. *Mailing Add:* Chancellor Univ Calif Riverside CA 92521

RIVERA DE ALVAREZ, JOSEFINA, b Mayagüez, PR, Aug 29, 23; m 50; c 1. PUERTO RICAN & SPANISH AMERICAN LITERATURE. *Educ:* Polytech Inst PR, BA, 45; Columbia Univ, MA 47; Univ Madrid, Dr Filos y Let, 54. *Prof Exp:* From instr to assoc prof, 47-60, PROF SPAN, UNIV PR, MAYAGUEZ, 60- *Res:* History of Puerto Rican literature. *Publ:* Auth, Dictionario de literatura puertorriquena, Univ, PR, Rio Piedras, 55; Historia de la literatura puertorriquena (2vols), Departamento Instruccion Publica, San Juan, 69; Diccionario de literatura puertorriquena, rev ed, Vol I, Inst Cult Puertorriquena, San Juan, 70. *Mailing Add:* Dept of Span Univ of Puerto Rico PO Box 5304 Mayaguez PR 00708

RIVERO, ELIANA SUAREZ, b Artemisa, Cuba, Nov 7, 42; US citizen; m 67. SPANISH, LATIN AMERICAN LITERATURE. *Educ:* Univ Miami, BA, 64, PhD(Span), 67. *Prof Exp:* From asst prof to assoc prof, 67-78, PROF SPAN & PORT DEPT, UNIV ARIZ, 78- *Mem:* MLA; Am Asn Teachers Span & Port; Inst Int Lit Iberoam; Latin Am Studies Asn. *Res:* Poetry of Pablo Neruda; poetry of the 20th century; Latin American women writers. *Publ:* Auth, El Gran Amor de Pablo Neruda, Plaza Mayor Ed, 71; Simbolismo tematico y titular de Las manos del dia, Mester, spring 74; La estetica esencial en una oda nerudiana, In: Simposio Pablo Neruda, Las Americas, 75; Analisis de perspectivas y significacion en La Rosa Separada, Rev Iberoam, 76; Dialectica de la Persona poetica en la obra de Julia de Burgos, Rev Critica Lit Latinoam, fall 76; Vision social y feminista en la obra lirica de Rosario Castellanos, In: Estudios de Hispanofila, Univ NC, 79; Reflexiones para una Nueva Poetica, Actas Asoc int de Hispanistas, Toronto, 80; Hacia una Lectura Feminista de Tres Tristes Tigres, Feminist Literary Criticism: Theory and Practice, Bilingual Press, 82. *Mailing Add:* Dept of Span & Port Univ of Ariz Tucson AZ 85721

RIVERO, MARIA LUISA, b Madrid, Spain, Feb 1, 43; m 64; c 2. LINGUISTICS. *Educ:* Univ Rochester, MA, 64, PhD(ling), 70. *Prof Exp:* Asst prof, 70-75, assoc prof, 75-82, PROF LING, UNIV OTTAWA, 82- *Concurrent Pos:* Res grant, Can Coun, 71-82. *Mem:* Ling Soc Am; Can Ling Asn; Soc Espanola de Ling; Asn Can de Hispanistas. *Res:* Romance syntax and semantics; generative grammar; history of logic and linguistics. *Publ:* Auth, Referential properties of Spanish noun phrases, 75 & Specificity and existence: A reply, 77, Lang; coauth, Surface structure and the centrality of syntax, Theoretical Ling, 76; auth, William of Sherwood on composition and division, Historiographia Ling, 76; Estudios de gramatica generativa del espanol, Cathedra, Madrid, 77; On left dislocation and topicalization in Spanish, Linguistic Inquiry, 80; Theoretical implications of the syntax of left-branch modifiers in Spanish, Ling Analysis, 80; coauth, Catalan restrictive relatives: Core and periphery, Lang, 81. *Mailing Add:* Dept of Ling Univ of Ottawa Ottawa ON K1N 6N5 Can

RIVERS, ELIAS LYNCH, b Charleston, SC, Sept 19, 24; m 45; c 3. SPANISH. *Educ:* Yale Univ, AB, 48, MA, 50, PhD(Span), 52. *Hon Degrees:* MA, Dartmouth Col, 62. *Prof Exp:* Instr Span, Yale Univ, 51-52; from instr to asst prof, Dartmouth Uol, 52-62; prof, Ohio State Univ, 62-64; prof, Johns Hopkins Univ, 64-78; PROF SPAN & COMP LIT, STATE UNIV NY, 78- *Concurrent Pos:* Howard fel, 56-57; Guggenheim fel, 59-60; Fulbright res grant, Madrid, 64-65; Nat Endowment for Humanities res grant, 67-68, 70-71 & 81-82, sem dir, 75-76. *Mem:* MLA; Am Asn Teachers Span & Port; Asoc Int Hispanistas (secy-gen, 62-80). *Res:* Renaissance poetry in Spain; oral and written styles of composition. *Publ:* Auth, Francisco de Aldana, Poesias, Espasa-Calpe, 57; Thirty-Six Spanish Poems, Houghton, 57; Garcilaso de la Vega, Obras Completas, Ohio State Univ, 64; Nature, art and science in Spanish poetry of the Renaissance, Bull Hisp Studies, 67; ed, Hijos de la Ira, Labor Barcelona, 70 & English translr, Children of Wrath, Johns Hopkins Univ, 70; Spanish Renaissance & Baroque Poetry, Scribners, 72; auth, Talking and writing in Don Quixote, Thought, 76. *Mailing Add:* Dept of Hisp Studies State Univ NY Stony Brook NY 11794

RIVERS, WILGA MARIE, b Melbourne, Australia. FRENCH, FOREIGN LANGUAGE EDUCATION. *Educ:* Univ Melbourne, dipl educ, BA, 40, MA, 48; Univ Lille, dipl French studies, 50; Univs Lille & Montpellier, Lic es Lett, 52; Univ Ill, Urbana-Champaign, PhD(educ & French), 62. *Prof Exp:* Sr teacher French & English, Australian high & prep schs, 40-59; asst prof French, Northern Ill Univ, 62-64; from lectr to assoc prof, Monash Univ, Australia, 64-69; vis prof, Teachers Col, Columbia Univ, 70-71; prof, Univ Ill, Urbana-Champaign, 71-74; PROF ROMANCE LANG & LANG COORDR, HARVARD UNIV, 74- *Concurrent Pos:* Teacher English Lycee Jeune Filles, Douai, & Norm Sch, Montpellier, 49-52; participant, Can UNESCO sem biling, 67; vis scholar, French govt, 68; consult, Rockefeller Found English teaching proj, Bangkok, 71; prof ling, Mid East Ling Inst, Cairo, 74 & Ling Soc Am, Ling Inst, Oswego, NY, 76; consult, Nat Endowment for Humanities, 75-76; JACET sem, Tokyo, 79. *Honors & Awards:* Florence Steiner Award, Am Coun Teachers Foreign Lang, 77. *Mem:* Am Asn Appl Ling (pres, 77-78); Ling Soc Am; Am Coun Teaching Foreign Lang; Am Asn Teachers Fr; Teachers English to Speakers Other Lang. *Res:* Language teaching; psycholinguistics; college curriculum. *Publ:* Auth, The Psychologist and the Foreign Language Teacher, 64 & Teaching Foreign Language Skills, 68 & 81, Univ Chicago; Speaking in Many Tongues, 72, 76 & co-ed, Changing Patterns in Foreign Language Programs, 72, Newbury House; auth, Practical Guide to the Teaching of French, 75, coauth, Practical Guide to the Teaching of German, 75, Practical Guide to the Teaching of Spanish, 76 & Practical Guide to the Teaching of English SL, 78, Oxford Univ. *Mailing Add:* Dept of Romance Lang & Lit 206 Boylston Hall Harvard Univ Cambridge MA 02138

RIVKIN, LAURA MADELAINE, b Detroit, Mich, Oct 3, 51. SPANISH LITERATURE. *Educ:* Univ Mich, BA, 73; Univ Calif, Berkeley, MA, 75, PhD(hisp lang & lit), 80. *Prof Exp:* ASST PROF MOD SPAN LIT, UNIV VA, 79- *Mem:* MLA; NEast Mod Lang Asn; SAtlantic Mod Lang Asn. *Res:* Nineteenth and 20th century Spanish literature. *Publ:* Auth, El cromatismo en Trilce, Letras de San Marcos, 76; El organicismo de Clarin, Boletin Bibl Menendez y Pelayo, 82; Extranatural art in Clarin's Su unico hijo, Mod Lang Notes, 82; coauth & ed, Edition of Los trabajos del infatigable creador Pio Cid, Catedra, 82. *Mailing Add:* Dept Span, Ital & Port Univ Va Charlottesville VA 22903

ROACH, ELEANOR (ANN), b Philadelphia, Pa, Nov 14, 43. FRENCH & LATIN PALEOGRAPHY. *Educ:* Univ Pa, BA, 65; Harvard Univ, AM, 67; Pa State Univ, University Park, PhD(French), 70. *Prof Exp:* Asst prof French, Univ Chicago, 70-72; res assoc paleography, Inst Res & Hist Texts, Paris, 73. *Mem:* Mediaeval Acad Am; Int Arthurian Soc; Soc Anciens Textes Francais; Soc Antiq Ouest. *Res:* Old French Arthurian literature; late medieval French romances. *Publ:* Auth, Les termes roman et gothique: Essai de definition, Lett Romanes, 75; La tradition manuscrite du Roman de Melusine par Coudrette, In: Revue d'Histoire des Textes 7: 185-233; Brusle amis and the Battle of Bouvines In: Zeitschrift fur romanische Philologie, 95: 21-35; Le Roman de MeLusine ou Histoire de Lusignan par Coudrette (in prep). *Mailing Add:* 329 Clearbrook Ave Lansdowne PA 19050

ROACH, WILLIAM (JOSEPH), b South Bend, Ind, June 20, 07; m 35; c 2. OLD FRENCH LITERATURE, TEXTUAL CRITICISM. *Educ:* Univ Chicago, PhB, 29, PhD, 35. *Prof Exp:* Instr Romance lang, Cath Univ Am, 35-39; from asst prof to prof, 39-77, EMER PROF ROMANCE LANG, UNIV PA, 77- *Concurrent Pos:* Guggenheim fel, 49-50, 56-57; Fulbright res fel, France, 49-50; vis prof Old French,Bryn Mawr Col, 51-72. *Honors & Awards:* Prix de LaGrange, Acad des Inscriptions et Belles Lettres, France, 67. *Mem:* Real Acad Buenas Letras, Barcelona; Mod Humanities Res Asn; Int Arthurian Soc; Am Philos Soc. *Res:* Old French Arthurian romances. *Publ:* Auth, The Didot-Perceval According to the Manuscripts of Modena and Paris, Univ Pa, 41; The Continuations of the Old French Perceval of Chretien de Troyes, Am Philos Soc, 49-82; Le Roman de Perceval ou Le Conte du Graal par Chretien de Troyes, edite d'apres le ms 12576 de la Bibliotheque Nationale, Droz, Geneva, 59; Transformations of the Grail theme in the continuations of the Perceval, 110: 160-164 & Francisque Michel: A pioneer in medieval studies, 114: 168-178, Proc Am Philos Soc. *Mailing Add:* Dept of Romance Lang Univ Pa Philadelphia PA 19104

ROBB, JAMES WILLIS, b Jamaica, NY, June 27, 18. ROMANCE LANGUAGES & LITERATURES. *Educ:* Colgate Univ, AB, 39; Middlebury Col, AM, 50; Cath Univ Am, PhD(Romance lang & lit), 58. *Prof Exp:* Instr Romance lang, Norwich Univ, 46-50; from asst prof to assoc prof, 50-66, PROF ROMANCE LANG, GEORGE WASHINGTON UNIV, 66- *Honors & Awards:* Alfonso Reyes Int Lit Prize, Mexico, 78. *Mem:* MLA; Am Asn Teachers Span & Port; Inst Int Lit Iberoam. *Res:* The works of Alfonso Reyes; modern Spanish American literature; Mexican & Colombian literature. *Publ:* Auth, Repertorio Bibliografico de Alfonso Reyes, Bibliot Nac, Mex, 74; ed, Prosa y Poesia de Alfonso Reyes, Ed catedra, Madrid, 75; auth, Estudios Sobre Alfonso Reyes, Ed El Dorado, Bogota, 76; Estilizacion artistica de temas metafisicos en Alfonso Reyes, In: Homenaje a Luis Leal, Insula, Madrid, 78; Por los caminos de Alfonso Reyes, INBA/Univ Valle Mex, 81; Variedades de ensayismo en A Reyes y German Arciniegas, 81 & La cena de A Reyes, cuento onirico: Surrealismo o realismo, magico?, 81, Thesaurus, Bogota; Caminos cruzados en el epistolario de M Toussaint y A Reyes, In: A Reyes: Homenaje de la Facultad de Filosofia y Letras, Univ Nac Autonoma Mex, Mex, 81. *Mailing Add:* Dept of Romance Lang George Washington Univ Washington DC 20052

ROBBINS, KITTYE DELLE, b Memphis, Tenn, Oct 1, 43. FRENCH LANGUAGE & LITERATURE. *Educ:* Memphis State Univ, AB, 65; Univ Ky, MA, 69, PhD(French), 75. *Prof Exp:* Instr in French, 70-76, ASST PROF FRENCH, MISS STATE UNIV, 76- *Concurrent Pos:* Asst rev ed, Tristania, J Tristan Studies, 76- *Mem:* Int Arthurian Soc; MLA; SAtlantic Mod Lang Asn; Soc Rencesvals; Tristan Soc. *Res:* Medieval French literature; creative writing/criticism; women's studies. *Publ:* Auth, Legends of good women: Medieval images in the novels of Andre Malraux, Malraux Miscellany, autumn 73; Woman/poet: Problem and promise in studying the Trobairitz and their friends, Encomia, 77; auth, What Ganelon dropped: Significant symbolic variation in the presentation scenes in the Oxford Roland, Charlemagne et L'Epopee Romane: Actes du Viie Cong Int Soc Rencesvals, 78; The sword between: Erotic division and union in Tristan and Cliges, Tristania (in press). *Mailing Add:* Dept of Foreign Lang Miss State Univ Mississippi State MS 39762

ROBE, STANLEY LINN, b Tangent, Ore, July 26, 15; m 43; c 2. FOREIGN LANGUAGES. *Educ:* Univ Ore, BA, 36, MA, 39; Univ NC, PhD, 49. *Prof Exp:* From instr to assoc prof, 49-63, PROF SPAN, UNIV CALIF, LOS ANGELES, 63- *Honors & Awards:* Fulbright lectr, Inst Caro y Cuervo, Colombia, 61. *Mem:* MLA; Ling Soc Am; Am Folklore Soc; Folklore Americas. *Res:* Dialectology of American Spanish; folklore of Spanish America. *Publ:* Auth, The Spanish of Rural Panama: Major Dialectal Features, 60, Hispanic Middles from Panama, 63, Mexican Tales and Legends from Los Altos, 70, Mexican Tales and Legends from Veracruz, 71, Amapa Storytellers, 72, Index of Mexican Folktales, 73, Hispanic Folktales from New Mexico, 77 & Azuela and the Mexican Underdogs, 79, Univ Calif. *Mailing Add:* Dept of Span & Port Univ Calif 405 Hilgard Ave Los Angeles CA 90024

ROBERGE, PAUL TIMOTHY, b Portland, Maine, Aug 20, 50; m 73. GERMANIC LANGUAGES, GENERAL LINGUISTICS. *Educ:* Univ Dayton, BA, 72; Univ Mich, MA, 73 & 75, PhD(German & ling), 80. *Prof Exp:* ASST PROF GERMAN & LING, PRINCETON UNIV, 80- *Concurrent Pos:* Rockefeller Found humanities fel, 82-83. *Mem:* Ling Soc Am; Am Asn Teachers German. *Res:* Linguistic change; phonological theory; comparative Germanic grammar. *Publ:* Coauth, Germanic and its Dialects: A Grammar of Proto-Germanic, III: Bibliography, John Benjamins, 77; Contemporary linguistic theory and foreign language instruction, Monatshefte, 79; co-ed, On the Origin and Formation of Creoles: A Miscellany of Articles, Karoma, 79. *Mailing Add:* Prog Ling Princeton Univ Princeton NJ 08544

ROBERTS, AARON HOOD, b Jacksonville, Fla, Aug 11, 28; m 50; c 2. LINGUISTICS. *Educ:* Univ Fla, BA, 51, MA, 55; Univ Wis, PhD, 61. *Prof Exp:* Instr English, Centenary Col La, 55-57; from instr to asst prof, Univ SFla, 61-63; asst prof ling & English as second lang, Case Western Reserve Univ, 63-66; dept dir, Ctr Appl Ling, 66-76; ADJ PROF, ENGLISH LANG INST & PROG LING, AM UNIV, 76- *Concurrent Pos:* Rand Sem in Comput Ling, 63; exec secy, Nat Acad Sci Automatic Lang Processing Adv Comt, 64-66; Am secy, Int Comt Comput Ling, 67-; vchmn adv comt, Survey Lang Use & Lang Teaching in Eastern Africa, 67-69; mem, Systran Panel, Air Force Syst Command Adv Bd, Nat Acad Sci, 70-72. *Mem:* Asn Comput Ling (secy-treas, 70-76); Am Soc Inform Sci; Am Dialect Soc (exec secy, 68-76, pres, 78-). *Res:* Computational linguistics; English as a second language; American dialects. *Publ:* Auth, A Statistical Linguistic Analysis of American English, Mouton, 65; co-ed, Information in the Language Sciences, Elsevier, 68. *Mailing Add:* English Lang Inst & Prog Ling Am Univ Washington DC 20016

ROBERTS, ALAN, b Ashburnham, Mass, Mar 14, 17. FRENCH. *Educ:* Haverford Col, BA, 39; Harvard Univ, MA, 40, PhD, 52. *Prof Exp:* Instr French & Span, Univ Vt, 46-47, asst prof, 49-53; asst prof, 53-62, prof, 62-80, EMER PROF FRENCH & SPANISH, UNION COL, NY, 62- *Res:* Andre Chason; foreign student advising. *Publ:* Ed, Histoires de Tabusse, Odyssey, 65. *Mailing Add:* Humanities Bldg Union Col Schenectady NY 12308

ROBERTS, ALFRED D, b Stowe, Pa, Sept 23, 23; m 46; c 7. ROMANCE LANGUAGES. *Educ:* Ursinus Col, BA, 49; Univ Pa, MA, 50, PhD, 58. *Prof Exp:* From instr to asst prof Romance lang, Ursinus Col, 50-59; chmn dept, 62-73, PROF FOREIGN LANG, WEST CHESTER STATE COL, 59- *Concurrent Pos:* Vpres, Chester County Chap, Alliance Francaise, 62-73. *Mem:* Am Asn Teachers Fr; Am Coun Teaching Foreign Lang; AAUP; Am Transl Asn. *Res:* Nineteenth century French literature. *Mailing Add:* Dept of Foreign Lang West Chester State Col West Chester PA 19380

ROBERTS, EDWARD ARTHUR, b Independence, Kans, Jan 22, 36. FOREIGN LANGUAGES, LINGUISTICS. *Educ:* OLS Scholasticate, BA, 57; Ind Univ, MA, 63, PhD(Span), 70. *Prof Exp:* Asst prof English as Second Lang, Universidad de Costa Rica, 66-69, assoc prof, 69-71; asst prof, 71-76, ASSOC PROF SPAN, CENT MICH UNIV, 76- *Res:* Pre-colonial Latin America; 19th century in Latin America; Indo-European origins of Spanish. *Publ:* Auth, Concepto y limites de la literatura ensayistica, Revista de la Univ Costa Rica, 12/70; Brenes Mesen y Garcia Monge: Maestros de juventudes, Editorial Don Quixote, San Jose, Costa Rica, 71; Trascendencia frente a inmanencia en la poesia de Ruben Dario, Revista de la Univ Costa Rica, 12/72. *Mailing Add:* Span Dept Cent Mich Univ Mt Pleasant MI 48859

ROBERTS, GEMMA, b Havana, Cuba, July 2, 29; US citizen. SPANISH LITERATURE. *Educ:* Vedado Inst, Havana, BA, 46; Univ Havana, PhD(philos), 52; Columbia Univ, PhD(Span lit), 71. *Prof Exp:* Instr Span, State Univ NY, Stony Brook, 65-67; from instr to asst prof, Columbia Univ, 69-74; vis lectr Span lit, Univ NC, Greensboro, 74-75; asst prof, Univ Southern Calif, 76-77; ASSOC PROF SPAN, UNIV MIAMI, CORAL GABLES, 79- *Concurrent Pos:* Ed adv, J Span Studies, XXth Century, 79-80; Anales de la Literatura Espanola Contemporanea, 76- *Res:* Contemporary Spanish and Latin American novel; Philosophical approach to literature. *Publ:* Auth, Notas so bre el realismo psicologico de La Regenta, Archivum, Oviedo, Spain, 68; Temas existenciales en la novela espanoal de postguerra, Gredos, Madrid, 73, 2nd ed, 78; La culpa y la busqueda de la autenticidad en San Camilo, 1936, In: Novelistas espanoles de postguerra, Taurus, Madrid, 76; El poder en lucha con la muerte: El otono del patriarca de Gavcia Marquez, Revista de Archivos, Bibliot y Museos, Madrid, 4-6/76; El sentido de lo comico en Cien anos de soledad, Cuadernos Hispanoamericanos, Madrid, 6/76; La recreacion de la realidad: El Don Sandalio de Unamuno y el Holandes de Hesse, Hisp, 12/77; UUn modo de la existencia religiosa en Pa en la Guerra: Una coincidencia con Kierkegaard, J Span Studies: 20th Century, 79; Ausencia y presencia de Dulcinea en El Quijote, Rev de Archivos, Biblioteca y Museos, Madrid, LXXXII, 4. *Mailing Add:* 7745 S W 86 St D-423 Miami FL 33143

ROBERTS, JENNIFER TOLBERT, Ancient History, Classical Languages. See Vol I

ROBERTS, JOHN TAYLOR, b Yokohama, Japan, Oct 20, 33; US citizen; m 57, 71; c 4. INDIC STUDIES, LINGUISTICS. *Educ:* Oberlin Col, BA, 55; Univ Chicago, MA, 64, PhD(Indic), 66. *Prof Exp:* Instr Hindi & Sanskrit, Univ Chicago, 64-66; asst prof Hindi & ling, 66-72, ASSOC PROF HINDI, UNIV VA, 72-, CHMN DEPT ORIENT LANG, 78- *Mem:* Asn Asian Studies. *Res:* Prakrit language and literature; Hindi language; Sanskrit. *Publ:* Auth, Prthviraja Raso: Canto II, In: Studies in Honour of George Bobrinskoy, Univ Chicago, 67; Hindi Pancatantra Reader, rev ed, 69 & Introduction to the Brahmi Script, 71, Univ Va; Poems from the Prakrit Sattasai, Univ Ala; Some Sanskrit poetic motifs in the Prakrit Sattasai, Mahfil, Vol VIII, No 1. *Mailing Add:* 111 Altamont Circle Charlottesville VA 22901

ROBERTS, LOUIS WILLIAM, b Denver, Colo, Apr 13, 30. CLASSICAL LANGUAGES, ANCIENT PHILOSOPHY. *Educ:* St Louis Univ, AB, 55, PhL, 56, MA, 58; Innsbruck Univ, STL, 63; State Univ NY Buffalo, PhD(classics), 70. *Prof Exp:* Lectr relig studies, St Louis Univ, 63-64; asst prof theol, St Bonaventure Univ, 67-68; teaching assoc classics, Univ Calif, Berkeley, 65-67; ASSOC PROF CLASSICS & CHMN DEPT, SYRACUSE UNIV, 70-; EXEC CHMN, FAC FOREIGN LANG & LIT, 75- *Concurrent Pos:* Asst, Religions-soziologisches Sem, Innsbruck Univ, 60-63; Am Coun Learned Soc res grant, 73; ed, Directory of Patristic Scholars, 74-; assoc ed, Classical Outlook, Am Class League; Nat Endowment for the Humanities planning grant, 76. *Mem:* AAUP; Am Philol Asn; Class Asn Atlantic States; NAm Patristics Soc; Am Class League. *Res:* Development of logic; patristics; Latin literature. *Publ:* Auth, Versuch Einer Integration von drei Ansatzen der Familienforschung mit Hilfe Einer Typologischen Methode, Kolner Z Soziologie & Sozialpsychologie, 1/58; The Achievement of Karl Rahner, Herder & Herder, 67; Karl Rahner, sa Pensee, son Oeuvre, sa Methode, Mame, 69; Notes on the Development of Shorthand in Antiquity, Cithara, 5/69; Origen and Stoic Logic, Trans & Proc Am Philol Asn, 70; The Orpheus Mythologem: Virgil and Rilke, Tex Studies in Lit & Lang, 5/74; The Unutterable Symbols of Ge-Themis, Harvard Theol Rev, 2/75; A Concordance of Lucretius, NY Garland, rev ed, 77. *Mailing Add:* Dept of Classics Syracuse Univ Syracuse NY 13210

ROBERTS, SPENCER EUGENE, b Catawissa, Pa, Apr 17, 20. RUSSIAN LANGUAGE & LITERATURE. *Educ:* Bucknell Univ, AB, 42; Columbia Univ, MA, 50, Russ Inst, cert, 53, PhD(Slavic lang & lit), 61. *Prof Exp:* Attache, Am Embassy, Moscow, 48-50 & Vienna, 50-52; chmn Russ area prog, Rutgers Univ, 57-61; assoc prof, 61-71, PROF RUSS LANG & LIT, BROOKLYN COL, 71- *Concurrent Pos:* Consult, Standard Oil NJ, 58-62. *Mem:* MLA; Am Asn Teachers Slavic & E Europ Lang. *Res:* Russian drama; Russian conservative critics; Russian memoirs. *Publ:* Ed, An Irkutsk Story, 63 & auth, A Workbook to Accompany Basic Russian, 64, Pitman; Soviet Historical Drama: Its Role in the Development of National Mythology, Martinus-Nijhoff, The Hague, 65; Essays in Russian Literature: The Conservative View, 68 & co-transl & ed, Dostoevsky, Tolstoy and Nietzsche, 69, Ohio Univ; Political drama, In: The Soviet System and Democratic Society, Herder, Freiburg, 72; transl & ed, Dostoevsky and the Legend of the Grand Inquisitor, Cornell Univ, 72; auth, Four Faces of Rozanov: Christianity, Sex, Jews, and the Russian Revolution, Philos Libr, 78. *Mailing Add:* Dept of Russ Lang & Lit Brooklyn Col Bedford Ave & Ave H Brooklyn NY 11210

ROBERTS, WILLIAM, b Brooklyn, NY, June 27, 23; m 54; c 3. FRENCH LITERATURE. *Educ:* NY Univ, BA, 47; Univ Paris, 3 cert lic, 46-47, Ecole Preparation, dipl, 48; Yale Univ, PhD, 55; Univ Florence, dipl, 57. *Prof Exp:* From instr to asst prof French, Tex Technol Col, 54-57; asst prof, 57-71, ASSOC PROF FRENCH & ITAL, NORTHWESTERN UNIV, 71- *Concurrent Pos:* French Govt fel, 46-48; asst & instr, Yale Univ, 48-53; instr, Albertus Magnus Col, 53-54; contribr, Cabeen Tibliog French Lit 17th Century, 53-79 & Mod Lang Asn Am Fr 17th Century Studies, 68-; bibliogr, NAm Soc 17th Century Fr Lit, 72- *Honors & Awards:* Chevalier, Palmes Academiques, 65, Officier, 76. *Mem:* MLA; Am Asn Teachers Fr; Am Asn Teachers Ital. *Res:* Seventeenth century French literature; French civilization; history of Paris. *Publ:* Auth, Classical Sources of Saint-Amant's L'Arion, Fr Studies, 63; Saint-Amant, Orinda, and Dryden's Miscellany, English Lang Notes, 63 & 64; Berni's Malo Alloggio Motif in Saint-Amant, Studi Francesi, 65; New Light on the authorship of Almahide, Fr Studies, 71; ed, North American Doctoral Theses on Seventeenth Century French Literature, Oeuvres et Critiques, 76-78; auth, Beyond the Frame: Saint-Amant's Mixing of Poetry, Painting and Ballet, Fr Lit Series, Univ SC, 78; Sources and Style of Saint-Amant's L'Hyver des Alpes, L'Esprit Createur, 80; Bossuet's Henriette-Marie--Indebted to Saint-Amant?, Papers Fr 17th Century Lit, 82. *Mailing Add:* 402 Maple Ave Wilmette IL 60091

ROBERTS, WILLIAM HOLLOWAY, b Parkersburg, WVa, Sept 6, 14; m 42; c 3. ROMANCE LANGUAGES. *Educ:* Williams Col, AB, 36; Univ Wis, MA, 39, PhD(Span), 50. *Prof Exp:* Asst English conversation, Ecole Normale, Aix-en-Provence, France, 36-37; vis lectr Span, Ohio Univ, 40-41; instr French & Span, Southwest La Inst, 42; instr Romance lang, Colo Col, 46-47; from instr to assoc prof, Vanderbilt Univ, 47-61, prof Span & Port, 61-68, chmn dept, 62-68, dir NDEA Summer Lang Inst, 61 & Vanderbilt in France, 61-62; chmn dept mod & class lang, 69-73, prof, 69-79, EMER PROF MOD LANG, UNIV NMEX, 79- *Concurrent Pos:* Asst naval attache, Paraguay, 45-46 & Portugal, 51-54; Gulbenkian Found grant, 66; vpres, Sixth Int Luso-Brazilian Colloquium, 66; dir, Nat Conf on High Sch Port, 67. *Honors & Awards:* Order of Merit, Paraguay, 46 & Portugal, 54. *Mem:* AAUP; Am Asn Teachers Span & Port; Inst Int Lit Iberoam. *Res:* Modern Latin American poetry; Luso-Spanish literary relations; Portuguese literature. *Publ:* Translr, Platero y yo, Dolphin Bk Co, Oxford, 56 & New Am Libr, NY, 60; Hacia una tradicion en la poesia paraguaya, Hispanofila, 61; The figure of King Sebastian in Fernando Pessoa, Hisp Rev, 66; King Sebastian in Antonio Nobre Archivum, 72. *Mailing Add:* 808 Wellesley Dr SE Albuquerque NM 87106

ROBERTSON, HOWARD STEPHEN, b Hamilton, Ont, May 11, 31; m 53; c 2. FRENCH MEDIEVAL LITERATURE. *Educ:* McMaster Univ, BA, 53; Ind Univ, AM, 56, PhD(French), 60. *Prof Exp:* Instr French, Univ Richmond, 57-58 & Univ Akron, 59-61; asst prof, Univ Waterloo, 61-63; assoc prof, Univ Alta, 63-66; assoc prof Romance lang, Case Western Reserve Univ, 66-69; chmn dept, 69-73, PROF FRENCH, GLENDON COL, YORK UNIV, ONT, 69- *Concurrent Pos:* Humanities Res Coun Can res grant, 66; gov, York Univ, 74-76; leave fel, Can Coun, 77. *Mem:* MLA; Mediaeval Acad Am; Soc Rencesvals. *Res:* Old French epic and romances; theory of literature. *Publ:* Auth, La Chanson de Williame: A Critical Study, Univ NC, 66; coauth, A closer look at aims and methods, Mod Lang J, 5/66; auth, Structure and comedy in the Jeu de Saint Nicolas, 7/67 & La vie de Saint Alexis: Meaning and ms A, 10/70, Studies Philol; Love and the other world in Marie De France's Elioul, In: Essays in Honour of Louis Francis Solano, 70; The Song of Roland (transl with introd & notes), J M Dent & Sons, London, 72. *Mailing Add:* Dept of French Glendon Col York Univ 2275 Bayview Ave Toronto ON M4N 3M6 Can

ROBERTSON, NOEL D, b Winnipeg, Man, Aug 15, 36; m 64; c 4. CLASSICS. *Educ:* Univ Toronto, BA, 58; Cornell Univ, MA, 59, PhD(classics), 64. *Prof Exp:* From instr to asst prof classics, Cornell Univ, 63-70; assoc prof, 70-76, chmn dept, 73-81, PROF CLASSICS, BROCK UNIV, 76- *Concurrent Pos:* Leverhulme fel & vis lectr, Bristol Univ, 65-66. *Mem:* Am Philol Asn; Archaeol Inst Am; Class Asn Can; Soc Prom Hellenic Studies. *Res:* Greek history and religion. *Publ:* Ed, & introd, The Archaeology of Cyprus: Recent Developments, Noyes NJ, 75; auth, An Inscription Honoring Corinthian Judges, Hesperia, 76; False Documents at Athens, Hist Reflections, 76; The Thessalian Expedition of 480 BC, J Hellenic Studies, 76; The Myth of the First Sacred War, Class Quart, 78; The Dorian migration and Corinthian ritual, Class Philol, 80; Heracles' Catabasis, Hermes, 80; The true nature of the Delian League, Am J Ancient Hist, 80. *Mailing Add:* Dept of Classics Brock Univ St Catharines ON L2S 3A1 Can

ROBIDOUX, REJEAN, b Sorel, Can, June 24, 28; m 70; c 2. FRENCH & FRENCH CANADIAN LITERATURE. *Educ:* Univ Ottawa, Baccalaureat arts, 55; Laval Univ, Quebec, MA, 57; Sorbonne, Dr(French lit), 62. *Prof Exp:* From lectr to assoc prof French, Univ Ottawa, 57-67; from assoc prof to prof, Univ Toronto, 67-74; PROF FRENCH, UNIV OTTAWA, 74- *Concurrent Pos:* Can Coun fel French lit, 72-73; Soc Sci & Human Resources Coun Can fel French lit, 81-82. *Mem:* Asn Professors Fr Univ Can; Asn Lit Can Quebecoise; Asn Univ Partiellement Entierement Lang Fr; Soc Ecrivains Quebecoise; Soc Royal du Can. *Res:* French literature 19th and 20th centuries (novel, poetry); French Canadian literature (novel, poetry). *Publ:* Auth, Roger Martin du Grad et la Religion, Aubier-Montaigne, Paris, 64; coauth, Le Roman Canadien-Francais du XXe Siecle, Univ Ottawa, 66; auth, Claudel, poete de la Connaissance: la muraille interieure de Tokyo, Cahiers Can Claudel, 67; La signification de Nelligan, Arch Lett Can, 69; Le cycle createur de Gerard Bessette ou le fond c'est la forme, Livres & Auteurs Quebecois 1971, 72; Exegche d'Artemis, Revue Univ Ottawa, 7-9/77; Le Traite du Narcisse (Theorie du Symbole) D'Andre Gide, Univ Ottawa, 78; Francois Mauriac et le combat (agonia) des fius deruieres, Cahiers Francois Mauriac 8, Crosset, Paris, 81. *Mailing Add:* Dept of French Univ of Ottawa Ottawa ON K1N 6N5 Can

ROBINETT, BETTY W, b Detroit, Mich, June 23, 19; c 1. LINGUISTICS. *Educ:* Wayne State Univ, AB, 40; Univ Mich, AM, 41, PhD, 51. *Prof Exp:* Res assoc & admin secy, English Lang Inst, Univ Mich, 45-50, lectr English, 51-52 & 55-56; asst prof, Univ PR, 52-53; assoc prof, Inter Am Univ, PR, 57-59; from asst prof to prof, Ball State Univ, 59-68, admin asst to head dept, 61-68; asst vpres acad affairs, 68-79, PROF LING & DIR PROG IN ENGLISH AS SECOND LANG, UNIV MINN, MINNEAPOLIS, 68- *Concurrent Pos:* Consult, Dept Educ, San Juan, PR, 50-51 & 55; mem English teaching adv panel, US Info Agency, 61-64; consult film proj, MLA & Ctr Appl Ling, 62; consult prog testing of English as foreign lang, MLA, 63; US Dept State grant, 62; ed jour, Teachers English to Speakers Other Lang, 66-73; mem adv screeing comt ling- Comt Int Exchange Persons, 72-75; int prog travel grant, Univ Minn, 77. *Mem:* Am Asn Appl Ling; Ling Soc Am; Nat Asn Foreign Student Affairs; Teachers English to Speakers Other Lang (vpres, 72-73, pres, 73-74); Am Asn Appl Ling (pres, 82). *Res:* English linguistics; American sign language; syntax of scientific and technical English. *Publ:* Auth, Pronunciation of American English for Teachers of English as a Foreign Language, George Wahr, 57; coauth, Manual of American English Pronunciation, Holt, 3rd ed, 72; auth, The domains of TESOL, TESOL Quart, 9/72; Teaching English to Speakers of Other Languages: Substance and Technique, Univ Minn, 78. *Mailing Add:* Dept of Ling Univ of Minn Minneapolis MN 55455

ROBINSON, DAVID FRANKLIN, b New York, NY, July 14, 35; m 64; c 2. SLAVIC & BALTIC LINGUISTICS. *Educ:* Swarthmore Col, BA, 57; Defense Lang Inst, W Coast Br, dipl, 59; Univ Pa, AM, 62, PhD(Balto-Slavic philol), 64. *Prof Exp:* Asst prof, 64-69, actg chmn dept, 73-74, chmn dept, 74-78, ASSOC PROF SLAVIC LING, OHIO STATE UNIV, 69- *Concurrent Pos:* Ctr fac Fulbright-Hays res fel, 68; Am Philos Soc res grant, 70; Int Res Exchanges Bd grant, 78 & 80. *Mem:* Am Asn Teachers Slavic & EEurop Lang; Ling Soc Am; Asn Advan Baltic Studies; Am Asn Advan Slavic Studies; Inst Lithuanian Studies. *Res:* Lithuanian phonology; Slavic and Baltic philology; Slavic and Baltic bibliography. *Publ:* Auth, Some acoustic correlates of tone in standard Lithuanian, Slavic & EEurop J, summer 68; Stress placement and accent classes in the Lithuanian noun, Baltic Ling, 70; Lithuanian books in the British Museum, 1587-1937, Gen Ling, 70; The phonology of Slavic loanwords in Lithuanian, J Baltic Studies, 73; The Goettingen (ex-Koenigsberg) collection of Old Lithuanian and Old Prussian books, Gen Ling, 75; ed, General Linguistics Vol 15, Papers from Fourth Conference on Baltic Studies, Pa State Univ, 75; auth, Lithuanian Reverse Dictionary, Slavica, 76; Baltic Languages, Mod Encycl Russ & Slavic Lit, Vol 2, 78. *Mailing Add:* Dept of Slavic Lang Ohio State Univ Columbus OH 43210

ROBINSON, FRED COLSON, English Philology, Medieval Literature. See Vol II

ROBINSON, HENRY SCHRODER, b Brooklyn, NY, June 6, 14; m 53; c 3. CLASSICS & CLASSICAL ARCHEOLOGY. *Educ:* Duke Univ, AB, 36; Princeton Univ, PhD(class archaeol), 41. *Prof Exp:* Prof classics, Univ Okla, 41-58, assoc dean grad col, 55-58, cur class archaeol, Univ Mus, 53-58; dir, Am Sch Class Studies, Athens, Greece, 59-69; prof, Case Western Reserve Univ, 70-78. *Concurrent Pos:* Fulbright res grant, Athens, 51-52; mem, Inst Advan Study, 52-53 & 69-70; Guggenheim fel, 69-70. *Mem:* Am Philol Asn; Archaeol Inst Am; Soc Promotion Hellenic Studies; Ger Archaeol Inst; Int Asn Class Archaeol. *Res:* Classical philology and archaeology. *Publ:* Auth, Pottery of the Roman Period, Chronology, Vol V, In: The Athenian Agora, 59; A Roman Modiolus from Kenchreai, In: Charisterion for A K Orlandos, Vol III, Athens, 65; Chiron in Corinth, Am J Archaeol, 69; A green-glazed Modiolus from Kenchreai, 72, A monument of Roma at Corinth, 74 & Excavations at Corinth: Temple Hill, 1968-1972, 76; Hesperia; Temple Hill, Corinth, In: Neue Forschungen in griechischen Heiligtumern, Wasmuth, Tubingen, 76; A Greekhead--animal or hybrid, Bull Cleveland Mus Art, 9/77. *Mailing Add:* 409 High St Moorestown NJ 08057

ROBINSON, JANE JOHNSON, b Stephenville, Tex, May 28, 18; m 67. LINGUISTICS. *Educ:* Univ Calif, Los Angeles, BA, 38, MA, 40, PhD, 46. *Prof Exp:* Assoc prof English & ling, Calif State Univ, Los Angeles, 60-66; mem res staff math ling, IBM Res Ctr, 66-73; mem res staff inform sci, 73-76, sr res linguist, 76-81, STAFF SCIENTIST, STANFORD RES INST, 81- *Concurrent Pos:* Consult ling, Rand Corp, Calif, 61-66. *Mem:* Ling Soc Am; Asn Comput Ling; Asn Comput Mach. *Res:* Automatic syntactic analysis; performance grammar; discourse. *Publ:* Auth, A Dependency Based Transformational Grammar, Language, 69; Case, Category and Configuration, J Ling, 70; coauth, Multiple WH Questions, Ling Inquiry, 73; contribr, Performance Grammars, Speech Recognition, Academic, 75; DIAGRAM: A Grammar for Dialogues, CACM, 81. *Mailing Add:* Stanford Res Inst 333 Ravenswood Ave Menlo Park CA 94025

ROBINSON, JAY LUKE, English. See Vol II

ROBINSON, MARIAN SCHOULER, Comparative Medieval Literature. See Vol II

ROBINSON, PETER GORDON, b Margate, UK, May 18, 36; m 60; c 3. PSYCHOLINGUISTICS, SOCIOLINGUISTICS. *Educ:* Univ Paris, DECF, 58; Oxford Univ, MA, 59. *Prof Exp:* Foreign serv off, Foreign Off, London, UK, 59-63; lectr French & Span lit & lang, Mem Univ Nfld, 63-65; asst prof ling & head English as a second lang prog, Univ Laval, 65-70; ASST PROF LING & BILINGUALISM, GLENDON COL, YORK UNIV, 70- *Concurrent Pos:* Consult, English as Second Lang Prog, Cent Mortgage & Housing, Quebec, 67-68, Can Armed Forces, 67-69 & IBM, 68-70. *Mem:* Asn Teachers English as Second Lang; Am Coun Teaching Foreign Lang; Int Fedn Prof Mod Lang; Int Asn Teachers English as Foreign Lang; Teachers English to Speakers Other Lang. *Res:* Second language learning; bilingualism; stylistics. *Publ:* Auth, Towards a Basic Procedure in the Composition of Second Language Tests, Int Rev Apel Ling Lang Teaching, Vol 8, No 1; Oral Expression Tests, Vol 25, No 2 & Testing the Second Language Competence of Children and Adults, Vol 27, No 2, English Lang Teacher. *Mailing Add:* Dept of English Glendon Col York Univ Toronto ON M4N 3M6 Can

ROBINSON, PETER HOLBROOK, b Lancaster, Pa, Aug 3, 39; m 66; c 4. FRENCH LITERATURE. *Educ:* Dartmouth Col, BA, 61; Univ Pa, MA, 63, PhD(Romance lang), 70. *Prof Exp:* Lectr, 66-70, asst prof, 70-73, chmn dept French & Ital, 71-74 & 78-81, dir Honors Div, Col Lib Arts, 74-78, ASSOC PROF FRENCH, UNIV MINN, MINNEAPOLIS, 73- *Res:* French poetry of 19th century. *Mailing Add:* 1518 W 26th St Minneapolis MN 55405

ROBINSON, TERENCE REGINALD, b Belfast, Northern Ireland, UK, Apr 13, 37; m 61; c 2. ANCIENT HISTORY, CLASSICS. *Educ:* Queen's Univ Belfast, BA, 59, MA, 60, PhD(classics), 69. *Prof Exp:* From lectr to asst prof, 62-73, ASSOC PROF CLASSICS, CARLETON UNIV, 73- *Mem:* Fel Royal Soc Antiq Ireland. *Res:* Alexander the Great; history of Greek geography; the Roman Revolution. *Publ:* Coauth, The partial acceptance of the Copernican theory by Athanasius Kircher, 1646, J Royal Astron Soc Can, 73. *Mailing Add:* 10 Rock Ave Ottawa ON K1M 1A6 Can

ROBINSON, THOMAS MORE, Philosophy, Classics. See Vol IV

ROBINSON, WALTER L, b Ft Worth, Tex, Jan 5, 30; m 54; c 3. LANGUAGES. *Educ:* Univ Tex, BA, 50, MA, 55, PhD, 59. *Prof Exp:* Asst prof Ger, Davidson Col, 57-60; from asst prof to assoc prof, 60-65, PROF GER & CHMN DEPT FOREIGN LANG, WESTERN WASH COL, 65- *Mem:* Am Asn eachers Ger; MLA. *Res:* Early German drama, particularly the Fastnacht palys, Thomas Mann; Heinrich Böll. *Mailing Add:* Dept of Foreign Lang Western Wash Univ Bellingham WA 98225

ROBLES, HUMBERTO E, b Manta, Ecuador, Aug 18, 38; US citizen; m 63. SPANISH AMERICAN LITERATURE. *Educ:* Queens Col, NY, BA, 61; Northwestern Univ, MA, 62, PhD(Span), 68. *Prof Exp:* Instr Span, Northwestern Univ, 64-66; from instr to asst prof, Univ Chicago, 66-70; asst prof, 70-75 ASSOC PROF SPAN, NORTHWESTERN UNIV, EVANSTON, 75- *Mem:* MLA; Am Asn Teachers Span & Port; Inst Int Lit Iberoam; Am Soc Aesthetics. *Res:* Spanish American narrative; Spanish American drama; critical methods. *Publ:* Auth, Aproximaciones a Los albaniles de Vicente Lenero, 10-12/70 & Perspectivismo, yuxtaposicion y contraste en El Senor Presidente, 4-6/72, Rev Iberoam; El circulo y la cruz en Hijo de hombre, Nueva Narrativa Hispanoam, 74; Testimonio y tendencia mitica en la obra de Jose de la Cuadra, Casa Cult Ecuatoriana, 76; co-ed, Los Poemas mas Representativos de Placido, Ed Critica, Univ NC, 76; Genesis y vigencia de Los Sangurimas, Revista Iberoamericana, 1-6/79; Pablo Palacio: El anhelo insatisfecho, Cahiers du Monde Hispanique et Luso-Bresilien, Caravelle, 80; Variantes en Pedro Paramo, Nueva Revista de Filologia Hispanica (in prep). *Mailing Add:* Dept of Span & Port Northwestern Univ Evanston IL 60201

ROBSON, ARTHUR GEORGE, b Elyrai, Ohio, Aug 26, 39; m 61; c 3. CLASSICS, COMPARATIVE LITERATURE. *Educ:* John Carroll Univ, BA, 60; Ohio State Univ, MA, 61, PhD, 66. *Prof Exp:* From teaching assoc to instr classics & comp lit, Ohio State Univ, 61-65; from instr to assoc prof, 66-72, assoc prof, 72-80, PROF CLASSICS & COMP LIT, BELOIT COL, 80-, CHMN DEPT, 72- *Concurrent Pos:* Ford Found res grants, 68-70, 73-74; dir & consult, campus adv serv, Am Philol Asn, 71-; proj dir, Nat Endowment for Humanities grant, 73-74. *Mem:* Am Philol Asn; Archaeol Inst Am; Mod Greek Studies Asn. *Res:* Greek historical literature; history of drama; literature and cinema. *Publ:* Co-ed, Latin our Living Heritage, C E Merrill, Bk 3, 64; auth, Catullus 68 53; the coherence and force of tradition, Trans Am Philol Asn, 72; The enfolding couplets: A solution to the problems of Propertius 4 9 71-74, Mnemosyne, 73. *Mailing Add:* Dept of Classics Beloit Col Beloit WI 53511

ROBSON, KENT E, Ethics, Philosophy of Language. See Vol IV

ROBSON, ROY ANTHONY, b Huntington, WVa, Dec 29, 36; m 66; c 1. THEORETICAL & APPLIED LINGUISTICS. *Educ:* Univ Tex, Austin, BA, 63, PhD(ling), 72. *Prof Exp:* Jr lectr English, Al-Yammamah Sch, Riyadh, Saudi Arabia, 63-64; teacher English Lang Div, Saudi Arabia Airlines Training Ctr, Jeddah, 64-65 & Am Col Girls, Istanbul, Turkey, 65-68; asst prof English, Univ Wis-Madison, 71-75; sr assoc, Ctr for Appl Ling, 75-78, dir int activities, 76-78; EXEC DIR, LANG & CULT TRAINING SYSTS, 78- *Mem:* Ling Soc Am; Teachers English to Speakers Other Lang. *Res:* Problems in second language learning; language pedagogy; language planning. *Publ:* Coauth, New Patterns, Nebioglu, Istanbul, Vols I-VI, 68; auth, A reexamination of agent deletion, In: From Soundstream to Discourse, Univ Mo, 72. *Mailing Add:* 1651 N Greenbrier Arlington VA 22205

ROCHE, ALPHONSE VICTOR, b Caderousse, France, May 7, 95; m 27; c 1. FRENCH & MODERN PROVENCAL LANGUAGE & LITERATURE. *Educ:* State Col Wash, AB, 28; Univ Ill, AM, 31, PhD, 35. *Prof Exp:* Instr, State Col Wash, 24-29; asst, Univ Ill, 29-35, instr, 35-36, assoc, 36-37; from asst prof to prof, 37-63, EMER PROF ROMANCE LANG, NORTHWESTERN UNIV, 63- *Concurrent Pos:* Prof Romance lang, Univ Ariz, 63-74; vis prof, Univ Hawaii, Manoa, State Univ NY Albany, Univ Wis-Madison, Univ Ill, Urbana, Ill State Univ, Univ Mo-Columbia, Univ Dallas, Univ Minn. *Mem:* MLA; Am Asn Teachers Fr; Soc Prof Fr Am. *Res:* Regionalism in French literature. *Publ:* Auth, Les idees traditionalistes en France de Rivarol a Charles Maurras, Univ Ill; Provencal Regionalism, Northwestern Univ; coauth, Au Pays du Soleil, Heath; auth, Alphonse Daudet, Twayne, 76. *Mailing Add:* 321 N Sawtelle Ave Tucson AZ 85716

ROCHEMONT, MICHAEL SHAUN, b Montreal, Que, Apr 12, 50. LINGUISTICS. *Educ:* McGill Univ, BA, 73; Univ Mass, Amherst, PhD(ling), 78. *Prof Exp:* Asst prof ling, Univ Calif, Los Angeles, 78-81; fel cognitive sci, Univ Calif, Irvine, 81-82; ASST PROF LING, UNIV BC, 82- *Res:* Formal syntax and semantics; language in context discourse analysis; prosodic structure and its role in interpretation. *Publ:* Auth, SAI and autonomy of syntax, Univ Mass Occasional Papers in Ling, Vol 5, 79; contribr, Remarks on the stylistic component in generative grammar, In: Papers Presented to Emmon Bach, Univ Mass, 79; auth, On the empirical motivation of the raising principle, Ling Inquiry, 81; coauth (with Peter Culicover), Stress and Focus in English, Language, 82. *Mailing Add:* Dept of Ling Univ of BC Vancouver BC V6T 1W5 Can

ROCHER, LUDO, b Hemiksem, Belgium, Apr 25, 26; m 61. SANSKRIT, INDIC STUDIES. *Educ:* State Univ Ghent, Dr Law, 50, PhD(Sanskrit), 52, Agrege, 56. *Prof Exp:* Prof Sanskrit, Univ Brussels, 58-67, dir, Ctr South Asian Studies, 61-67; chmn, Dept Orient Studies, 67-75, chmn, Dept South Asia Reg Studies, 75-79, PROF SANSKRIT, UNIV PA, 66-, W NORMAN BROWN PROF SOUTH ASIAN STUDIES, 81- *Concurrent Pos:* Nat Found Sci Res fel, Belgium, 52-59. *Mem:* Royal Acad Overseas Sci, Belgium; Am Orient Soc; Asn Asian Studies. *Res:* Sanskrit; Indic studies; Hindu law. *Publ:* Auth, Vacaspati Misra's Vyavaharacintamani, 56 & Manual of Modern Hindi, 58, Univ Ghent; Premchand's short stories (in Dutch), Nederlandsche Boekhandel, Antwerp, 58; The theory of proof in ancient Hindu law, Recueils Soc Jean Bodin, 63; Le probleme linguistique en Inde, Acad, Brussels, 68; Smrticintamani of Gangaditya, Orient Inst, Baroda, 76; Paulinus S Bartholomaeo: Dissertation on the Sanskrit Language, Benjamins, Amsterdam, 77. *Mailing Add:* Dept of Orient Studies Univ of Pa Philadelphia PA 19104

ROCHER, ROSANE DEBELS, b Mouscron, Belgium, Aug 10, 37; US citizen; m 61. INDOLOGY, LINGUISTICS. *Educ:* Univ Brussels, MA, 59 & 61, PhD(Indian ling), 65. *Prof Exp:* Res fel Indology, Nat Found Sci Res, Belgium, 61-70; vis lectr, Indo-Aryan lang, 70-71, asst prof, 71-74, assoc prof Indo-Aryan lang, 74-80, PROF S ASIAN STUDIES, UNIV PA, 80- *Concurrent Pos:* Mem joint comt S Asia, Am Coun Learned Soc-Soc Sci Res Coun, 72-76. *Mem:* Am Orient Soc; Ling Soc Am; Asn Asian Studies; Am Soc 18th Century Studies. *Res:* Indology; linguistics; history of orientalism. *Publ:* Auth, Agent et objet chez Panini, J Am Orient Soc, 65; transl, J Gonda, Manuel elementaire de la langue sanskrite, Brill, 66; auth, La theorie des voix du verbe dans l'ecole panineenne, Univ Brussels, 68; Alexander Hamilton (1762-1824): A chapter in the early history of Sanskrit philology, Am Orient Soc, 68; India, Current Trends in Ling, Historiography of Ling, 75; ed, India and Indology--Selected Articles by W Norman Brown, Am Inst Indian Studies, 78; auth, Lord Monbodds, Lanskrit, and Comparative Linguistics, J Am Orient Soc, 80; Orientalism, Poetry, and the Millennium: The Checkered Life of Nathaniel Broky Hathed (1751-1830), Motilal Banarsidass, 82. *Mailing Add:* Dept of S Asia Regional Studies 820 Williams Hall Univ of Pa Philadelphia PA 19104

RODD, LAUREL RASPLICA, b Chicago, Ill, Sept 7, 46; m 68; c 2. JAPANESE LANGUAGE & LITERATURE. *Educ:* DePauw Univ, BA, 68; E Tenn State Univ, MAT, 69; Univ Mich, PhD(Japanese), 77. *Prof Exp:* Asst prof, Univ Va, 74-75; asst prof, 75-81, ASSOC PROF JAPANESE, ARIZ STATE UNIV, 81- *Concurrent Pos:* Vis assoc prof Japanese, Univ Chicago, winter 82. *Mem:* MLA; Asn Teachers Japanese; Asn Asian Studies. *Res:* Medieval Japanese literature and religion; Japanese poetry; methodology of language teaching. *Publ:* Transl, Six-Foot World, Voice, 71; auth, Nichiren and Setsuwa, Japanese J Religious Studies, 78; Nichiren, Ctr Asian Studies, 78; Nichiren: Selected Writings, Univ Press Hawaii, 80. *Mailing Add:* Dept of Foreign Lang Ariz State Univ Tempe AZ 85287

RODEN, JOHANNA WAHL, b Kassel, Ger, Dec 3, 28; US citizen; m 62; c 1. GERMAN LITERATURE. *Educ:* Calif State Univ, Long Beach, BA, 61, MA, 62; Univ Southern Calif, MA, 66, PhD(Ger), 70. *Prof Exp:* Assoc prof, 62-76, PROF GER, CALIF STATE UNIV, LONG BEACH, 76-, CHAIRPERSON DEPT GER, RUSS & CLASSICS, 77- *Concurrent Pos:* Consult, Long Beach Unified Sch Dist, 64-65. *Mem:* Am Asn Teachers Ger; Philol Asn Pac Coast; Am Coun Teachers Foreign Lang. *Res:* German literature in exile, 1933-1945 in the United States. *Publ:* Auth, Wilhelm Speyer, Der literarische Nachlass von Wilhelm Speyer & Hans Wilhelm, In: Deutsche Exilliteratur seit 1933. 1. Kalifornien, Francke, Bern, 76; Emil Ludwig's Political Writings During his US Exile 1940-45, In: Jahrbuch für Internationale Germanistik, Reihe A, Band 10, Peter Lang, Bern, 81. *Mailing Add:* Dept of Ger Calif State Univ 1250 Bellflower Blvd Long Beach CA 90840

RODEN, LETHEM SUTCLIFFE, b Evanston, Ill, May 18, 29; Can citizen. ROMANCE LANGUAGES. *Educ:* Univ Toronto, BA, 51, MA, 53, PhD(Romance lang), 56. *Prof Exp:* Instr French, Univ Kans, 56-58; lectr French & Ital, Univ Western Ont, 59-62; asst prof, 62-64, ASSOC PROF FRENCH, ACADIA UNIV, 64- *Mem:* MLA; Asn Can Univ Teachers Fr; Humanities Asn Can; Can Comp Lit Asn; Can Asn Can & Que Lit. *Res:* French-Canadian language and literature; 19th century French literature. *Mailing Add:* Dept of French Acadia Univ Wolfville NS B0P 1X0 Can

RODGERS, GARY BRUCE, b Neenah, Wis, Dec 16, 40. FRENCH LITERATURE. *Educ:* Univ Calif, Los Angeles, BA, 65, MA, 65; Univ Tex, Austin, PhD(French), 71. *Prof Exp:* Asst English, Col Stanislas, Paris, 69-70; asst prof French, La State Univ, Baton Rouge, 71-74, res grant, 72; asst prof French, Harvard Univ, 74-80; FEL FRENCH, YALE UNIV, 80- *Honors & Awards:* Clark fund, Harvard Univ, 75-77. *Mem:* Am Soc 18th Century Studies; MLA; SCent Mod Lang Asn; Soc Fr Etude 18th Century; Am Asn Teachers French. *Res:* Diderot; 18th century French press; Marivaux. *Publ:* Auth, Diderot and the 18th Century French Press, Voltaire Found, 73; Diderot, Dict des J, Grenoble, 76. *Mailing Add:* Dept of French Yale Univ New Haven CT 06511

RODGERS, JOSEPH JAMES, JR, b Hopewell, Va. FRENCH, SPANISH. *Educ:* Morehouse Col, BA, 62; Univ Wis-Madison, MA, 65; Univ Southern Calif, PhD(French), 69. *Prof Exp:* Asst French & Span, Morehouse Col, 60-62; teacher, Classical High Sch, Providence, RI, 63-64; asst French, Univ Wis, 64-65; instr, Los Angeles City Col, 66-67 & Univ Southern Calif, 68-70; asst prof, Occidental Col, 68-70 & 71-73; prof French & chmn foreign lang dept, Va State Col, 70-71; PROF ROMANCE LANG & CHMN DEPT LANG & LING, LINCOLN UNIV, 73- *Honors & Awards:* Lindback Award for Distinguished Teaching, Lincoln Univ, 74. *Mem:* Am Coun Teaching Foreign Lang; MLA; Asn Dept Foreign Lang; Col Lang Asn; Am Asn Teachers Fr. *Res:* Non-verbal communication; Afro-Hispanic literature; Afro-French literature. *Publ:* Co-ed, Chateaubriand's Essay on English Literature, Univ Wis, 65; auth, Crisis on the educational front, Maghred Digest, 8/66; contribr, Afrique: Face a la Modernisation, Hachette, Paris, 68; coauth, Leadership Ideology in Africa, Praeger, 76; Building an International Curriculum for Vocational Education, Lincoln Univ, 76; contribr, To Speak or Not to Speak, 78 & Souriante Haiti et le voudou, 78, Phelps-Stokes Fund. *Mailing Add:* Dept of Lang & Ling Lincoln Univ Lincoln University PA 19352

RODGERS, MARY COLUMBRO, English, Education. See Vol II

RODGERS, ROBERT HOWARD, b Alexandria, La, May 24, 44; m 73. CLASSICAL PHILOLOGY. *Educ:* Harvard Univ, BA, 66, PhD(mediaeval Latin), 70. *Prof Exp:* Asst prof classics, Univ Calif, Berkeley, 70-75, assoc prof, 75-80. *Concurrent Pos:* Am Coun Learned Soc fel, 76-77; vis lectr classics, Harvard Univ, 80; vis prof classics, Univ Vt, 81-82. *Mem:* Am Philol Asn; Mediaeval Acad Am. *Res:* Latin literature; textual criticism; history of agriculture. *Publ:* Ed, Petri Diaconi Ortus et Vita Iustorum Cenobii Casinensis, UniCalif, 72; Palladii Opus Agriculturae, Teubner, 75; auth, An Introduction to Palladius, Univ London, suppl, Bull Inst Class Studies, 75. *Mailing Add:* Ossco Farm New Haven VT 05472

RODGERS, THEODORE STEPHEN, b Orange, NJ, Aug 12, 34; m 58; c 4. ENGLISH LINGUISTICS, EDUCATION. *Educ:* Amherst Col, BA, 56; Georgetown Univ, MS, 62; Stanford Univ, PhD(ling), 68. *Prof Exp:* Sales rep, Am Airlines, Washington, DC, 56-59; tech ed, Radio Corp Am, Va, 59-60, syst engineer, 60; instr English, Inst Mod Lang, DC, 60-61; lectr-writer, English Lang Serv, 61-62; instr speech, Univ Calif, Berkeley, 62-64; res assoc reading, Inst Math Studies Soc Sci, Stanford Univ, 64-68; asst prof fac ling, psychol, info sci, English lang inst & educ psychol, 68-71, ASSOC PROF LING, PSYCHOL, ENGLISH AS SECOND LANG, EDUC & INFO SCI, UNIV HAWAII, 71- *Concurrent Pos:* Consult proj literacy, Cornell Univ, 66; Job Corps, US Dept Labor, 66; chief planner, Hawaii Curric Ctr, 68 & Hawaii English Proj, 68-73; consult, Dept Educ Govt Am Samoa, 70; Ford Found Adv, Ministry Educ, Malaysia, 73-74. *Res:* Language acquisition; language education; gaming. *Publ:* Auth, Computer-based instruction in economics, In: New Developments in the Teaching of Economics, Prentince-Hall, 67; coauth, An exploration of psycholinguistic units in initial reading, In: Psycholinguistic Natuare of Reading Process, Wayne State Univ, 68; auth, Measuring vocabulary difficulty, Int Rev Appl Ling, 4/71. *Mailing Add:* Dept of Educ Univ of Hawaii at Manoa Honolulu HI 96822

RODINI, ROBERT JOSEPH, b Albany, Calif, Aug 2, 36; m 62; c 2. ROMANCE LANGUAGES. *Educ:* Univ Calif, Berkeley, MA, 60, PhD(Romance lang & lit), 67. *Prof Exp:* From instr to assoc prof, 65-76, PROF ITAL, UNIV WIS-MADISON, 76- *Concurrent Pos:* Dir, Ind Univ-Univ Wis jr year, Bologna, Italy, 71-72; Am Coun Learned Soc fel, 76. *Mem:* MLA; Am Asn Teachers Ital; Renaissance Soc Am. *Res:* Renaissance drama, especially Italian, 16th century; the Italian baroque. *Publ:* Auth, Antonfrancesco Grazzini: Poet, Dramatist and Novelliere, Univ Wis-Madison, 70; contribr, A Renaissance Alphabet, Univ Wis, 71; ed, Opere di Dio, Houghton, 76; Medieval and renaissance spectacle and theatre, Vol XIV, No 3, Forum Italium, 80. *Mailing Add:* Dept of French Univ Wis Madison WI 53706

RODRIGUEZ, ALFONSO, b Mex, Jan 2, 43; US citizen; m 68; c 1. FOREIGN LANGUAGE. *Educ:* Tex A&I Univ, BA, 68, MA, 70; Univ Iowa, PhD(Hispanic Am lit & lang), 76. *Prof Exp:* Teacher Span, Raymondville IDS, Tex, 68-69; instr, Tex A&I Univ, 70; teacher, Presbyterian Pan Am Sch, Tex, 70-71; teaching asst, Univ Iowa, 71-75; instr, Northern Ill Univ, 75-76, asst prof, 76-78; ASSOC PROF SPAN, UNIV NORTHERN COLO, 78-, CHMN DEPT, 80- *Mem:* Am Asn Teachers Span & Port; Midwest Mod Lang Asn; MLA. *Res:* Spanish dialects of the United States; Hispanic-American literature and Chicano literature. *Publ:* Auth, Teaching Spanish to Chicanos, Tresholds in Secondary Educ, summer 76; Samuel Ramos: Influencia de Adler Jung en su estudio sobre el caracter del mexicano, Cuadernos Hispanoamericanos, 8-9/77; El motivo del engano en el Popol Vuh, Cuadernos Americanos (in press). *Mailing Add:* Dept of Foreign Lang Univ of Northern Colo Greeley CO 80631

RODRIGUEZ, ALFRED, b New York, NY, May 21, 32; m 53; c 1. ROMANCE LANGUAGES. *Educ:* Brooklyn Col, AB, 56; Brown Univ, MA, 57, PhD(Span), 63. *Prof Exp:* From instr to assoc prof Span, Rutgers Univ, 59-69; prof Span & Port, Univ Wis-Madison, 69-72; PROF MOD & CLASS LANG, UNIV NMEX, 72- *Mem:* MLA. *Res:* Siglo de Oro theater and prose; Benito Perez Galdos and the 19th century novel; Generation of 1898. *Publ:* Auth, Algunos casos de parodia lirica en Galdos, Insula, Madrid, 5/66; coauth, Una nota al San Manuel Bueno, Martir, Hisp Rev, 10/66; auth, Algunos aspectos de la elaboracion literaria de La familia de Leon Roch, PMLA, 3/67; An introduction to the episodios nacionales of Galdos, Las Americas, 67; Aspectos de la novela de Galdos, Estudios Literarios, Spain, 67; The Modern Spanish Essay, Ginn, 69; ed, Castigo sin venganza, La estrella de Sevilla, El burlador de Sevilla, El zapatero y el rey & Traidor, inconfeso y martir, Clasicos Ebro, Zaragoza, Spain; plus numerous articles in Romance Notes, Papers in Lang & Lit, Comp Lit, Cuadernos Hispanoamericanos, Abside Mod Lang Notes. *Mailing Add:* Dept of Mod & Class Lang Univ of NMex Albuquerque NM 87106

RODRIGUEZ, ANTONIO GUILLERMO, b La Salud-Havana, Cuba, Aug 24, 43; m 64; c 2. FOREIGN LANGUAGE LITERATURE & LINGUISTICS. *Educ:* Georgetown Univ, BSL, 66, MSL, 68; Cath Univ Am, PhD(French & Span), 69. *Prof Exp:* Instr French, Marymount Jr Col, 65-66 & Bullis Sch, Md, 66-67; asst, Cath Univ Am, 67-69; instr Span, Xaverian Col, 68-69; asst prof French, George Mason Univ, 69-72; assoc prof, 72-75, chmn dept, 72-80, PROF ROMANCE LANG, MORGAN STATE COL, 75- *Mem:* Asn Ecrivains Lang Francaise; Am Asn Teachers Fr; MLA; Can Asn Univ Prof. *Res:* Literary criticism; stylistics; linguistics. *Publ:* Auth, Le role de Pascal dans l'oeuvre et dans la pensee de Paul Valery, Lang & Lit, 69; Le Coryphee, Le Cercle du Livre de France, 71; Le deus et machina dans Adolphe ou l'originalite de Benjamin Constant & Apropos d'hesitation de A Bosquet, 71, Fr Rev. *Mailing Add:* Dept of Foreign Lang Morgan State Univ Baltimore MD 21239

RODRIGUEZ, RODNEY TAPANES, b Tampa, Fla, Dec 11, 46; m; c 2. SPANISH LITERATURE. *Educ:* Fla State Univ, BA, 68; Northwestern Univ, MA, 68, PhD(Span), 72. *Prof Exp:* ASSOC PROF SPAN, RIDER COL, 72- *Concurrent Pos:* Nat Endowment for Humanities fel, 77. *Mem:* Cong Int Hispanistas; MLA; Northeastern Mod lang Asn; Am Asn Teachers Span & Port. *Res:* Spanish 19th century prose; Spanish 18th century literature. *Publ:* Contribr, Notes and reviews, Hispania, 74; co-ed, La Cornada, Abra, 78; auth, Las dos Espanas: Two approaches in the novel of the 1840's, Estudos Iberoam, 78; Mariquita y Antonio y los limites del realismo, Actas Cong Int Hispanistas, 78. *Mailing Add:* Dept of Spanish Rider Col Lawrenceville NJ 08648

RODRIGUEZ-ALCALA, HUGO, b Asuncion, Paraguay, Nov 25, 17; US citizen; m 60; c 3. SPANISH. *Educ:* Col San Jose, Paraguay, BA, 36; Univ Asuncion, DJur, 43; Wash State Univ, MA, 50; Univ Wis, PhD(Span), 53. *Prof Exp:* Instr Span, Wash State Univ, 47-50; asst prof, Rutgers Univ, 56-58; from assoc prof to prof, Univ Wash, 58-63; chmn dept, 65-67, PROF SPAN, UNIV CALIF, RIVERSIDE, 63- *Concurrent Pos:* Int Inst Educ fel, 43-45; secy to Supreme Court Justice, Paraguay, 43-47; deleg, Conf Int Acad Span Lang, 64-; Nat Found for Arts & Humanities sr fel, 67. *Honors & Awards:* 1st Lit Prize, Ministry Educ, Paraguay, 58. *Mem:* MLA; Int Inst Lit Iberoam; Asoc Int Hispanistas; Rocky Mountain Coun Latin Am Studies. *Res:* Spanish and Latin American literature; philosophy of law; Latin American philosophy. *Publ:* Auth, Ensayos de Norte a sur, Studium, 61; El arte de Juan Rulfo, 65; Sugestion e ilusion, 67; La Dicha Apenas Dicha, 67; Historia de la lit Paraguaya, 71; Narrativa hispanoamericana, 72; El canto del aljibe, 72; Palabra de los dias, 72. *Mailing Add:* Dept of Span Univ Calif Riverside CA 92521

RODRIGUEZ-FLORIDO, JORGE JULIO, b Manzanillo, Cuba, Mar 15, 43; US citizen. LATIN AMERICAN LITERATURE, STYLISTICS. *Educ:* Univ Miami, BA, 66; Univ Wis-Madison, MA, 67, PhD(Span), 75. *Prof Exp:* Teacher math, Inst de Segunda Ensenanza, Cuba, 60-62; instr Span, Univ Wis-Sheboygan, 67-68; instr, Univ Ill, Chicago Circle, 70-74, asst prof, 75-78; asst prof, 78-81, ASSOC PROF SPAN, CHICAGO STATE UNIV, 81- *Mem:* Am Asn Teachers Span & Port; MLA. *Res:* Modern Latin American literature (prose fiction); stylistics; bibliography. *Publ:* Auth, Positivismo en El Senor Presidente, Explicacion de Textos Lit, 9/74; Bibliografia de y sobre Ciro Alegria, Chasqui, 5/75; Ciro Alegria y el Caribe: 1948-1960, Caribe, winter 76; El Lenguaje en la Obra Literaria, Ed Bedout, Colombia, 77; La funcion del doble en Cuentos negros de Cuba, Homenaje a Lydia Cabrera Ed Universal, 77; Doble salto, Tango, Cuaderno Lit Azor Barcelona, 77; Un secreto a voces, Caribe, 77; El fuego, Azor, 81. *Mailing Add:* Dept of Mod Lang Chicago State Univ Chicago IL 60628

RODRIGUEZ-LUIS, JULIO, b Havana, Cuba, Oct 9, 37; US citizen; m 68. SPANISH. *Educ:* Univ PR, BA, 59; Brown Univ, MA, 60; Princeton Univ, PhD(Romance lang), 66. *Prof Exp:* Instr Span, Brown Univ, 62-63 & Colgate Univ, 63-64; instr, Tufts Univ, 64-65; asst prof, State Univ NY, Binghamton, 65-67 & Wesleyan Univ, 67-70; assoc prof Span, 70-79, PROF COMP LIT & LATIN AM STUDIES, STATE UNIV, BINGHAMTON, 80- *Mem:* MLA; Am Comp Lit Asn; Int Asn Hispanistas. *Res:* Cervantes; contemporary Spanish-American literature; sociology of literature. *Publ:* Ed, Fernan Caballero, La Gaviota, Labor, Barcelona, 72; Fernan Caballero, Clemencia, Catedra, Madrid, 75; co-ed (with A de Albornoz), Sensemaya la poesia negra en el mundo hispanohablante, Origenes, Madrid, 79; auth, Fernan Caballero, La familia de Alvareda, Castalia, Madrid, 79; Picaras: The model approach to the Picaresque, CL, 79; La intencion politica en la obra de Borges, CH, 80; Novedad y ejemplo de las Novelas de Cervantes, Porrus, Madrid, 80; Hermeneutica y praxis del indigenismo, FCE, Mex, 80. *Mailing Add:* Dept of Comp Lit State Univ NY Binghamton NY 13901

RODRIGUEZ-PERALTA, PHYLLIS WHITE, b Naperville, Ill, 1923; m 50; c 1. SPANISH AMERICAN LITERATURE. *Educ:* Univ Ill, AB, 43, AM, 45. *Prof Exp:* Instr Span, Univ Ill, 46-50; head, Dept English, Inst Nacional de Varones, Peru, 50-51; lectr, Univ Mich, 57-60; asst prof, 61-77, ASSOC PROF SPAN, TEMPLE UNIV, CHMN DEPT, 78- *Mem:* Am Asn Teachers Span & Port; MLA; AAUP. *Res:* Spanish American modernism; Peruvian literature, 19th and 20th century; Spanish American literature of 19th and 20th century. *Publ:* Auth, Cesar Vallejo, In: Iberoamerica, de Andrea Mexico, 62; Jose Santos Chocano, Twayne, 70; Images of women in Rosario Castellanos' prose, Lat Am Lit Rev, fall-winter 77; Vargas Llosa: Su presentacion de personajes femeninos en el ambiente de Lima, Cuadernos Americanos, Vol 2: 220-234; Counterpart and contrast, Hispania, Vol 62: 619-625; Maria Luisa Bombal's poetic novels of female estrangement, Rev Estudios Hispasnicos, Vol XIV: 139-155; Gonzalez Prada's social and political thought, Rev Interam Bibliografia, Vol XXX, No 2: 148-156; Liberal undercurrents in Tradiciones peruanas, Rev Estudios Hispanicos, Vol XV: 283-297. *Mailing Add:* Dept of Span & Port Temple Univ Philadelphia PA 19122

RODRIUEZ-SEDA DE LAGUNA, ASELA, b San German, PR, Dec 6, 46; m 75; c 2. COMPARATIVE LITERATURE. *Educ:* Univ PR, Mayaguez, BA, 68; Univ Ill, Urbana, MA, 70, PhD(comp lit), 73. *Prof Exp:* Asst prof, 73-79, ASSOC PROF SPAN, RUTGERS UNIV, NEWARK, 79- *Concurrent Pos:* Adj asst prof, Bilingual Prog, City Col, City Univ New York, 73-74. *Mem:* MLA; Latin Am Studies Asn; Asn Teacher Span & Port; Am & Int Comp Lit Asn. *Res:* Reception and influences of European authors in the Hispanic world; drama; Caribbean novel. *Publ:* Auth, Arms and the Man y El Horoe galopante: La demistificacion del heroismo, Latin Am Theater Rev, spring 76; Puerto Rican narrative: Aspects of frustration, Perspectives on Contemp Lit, 5/76; Entorno a Inventario de Diaz Valcarcel, Revista del Inst de Cult Puertorriquena, 7-9/76; G Bernard Shaw y Nemesio R Canales: Relaciones e influencias, In: Sin Nombre, 7-9/77; El Teatro de Jaime Carrero, Revista Chicano-Riquena, Vol V, No 3; Balance novelistico del trienio 1976-78: Conjuncion de signos, Hispamerica, Vol VIII, No 23; George Bernard Shaw en el Mundo Hispanico, Univ PR Press, 81. *Mailing Add:* Dept of Foreign Lang Rutgers Univ Newark NJ 07102

ROE, HAROLD ANTHONY, JR, b Boston, Mass, Aug 17, 33. GERMANIC LANGUAGES & LINGUISTICS. *Educ:* Harvard Univ, AB, 54, MA, 58, PhD(ling), 65. *Prof Exp:* Instr Ger lang & ling, Harvard Univ, 65-68; ASSOC PROF MEDIEVAL STUDIES, UNIV TORONTO, 68- *Concurrent Pos:* Consult Ger lang, English Dict, Am Heritage Publ Co, 68- *Mem:* Ling Soc Am; Medieval Acad Am; MLA. *Res:* Germanic and Celtic languages; linguistics. *Publ:* Auth, A Note on Loanwords From Old Norse, English Studies, 67; The Importance of Old Frisian in the Reconstruction of Proto-Germanic Phonology, Philol Frisica, Anno 1966, 68. *Mailing Add:* 33 Marlborough Toronto ON M5R 1X5 Can

ROEDERER, LOUIS J M, b Adana, Turkey, July 15, 20; US citizen; c 2. LANGUAGES. *Educ:* Int Col, Am Univ Beirut, dipl, 40; Univ Lyon, BL, 43, lic law & econ, 44; NY Univ, PhD(Romance lang & lit), 71. *Prof Exp:* Asst prof hist, Int Col, Am Univ Beirut, 40-45; counr-at-law, Paris, 46-50; legal adv, UN Relief & Works Agency, 50-55; chmn dept lang, Stony Brook Sch, NY, 55-64; chmn dept foreign lang, 64-66, grad adv foreign lang dept, 66-69, chmn dept French, 69-70, ASSOC PROF FRENCH, MONTCLAIR STATE COL, 64- *Concurrent Pos:* Pres, Hope Publ Corp, NJ, 69- *Res:* Contemporary French Theater; religion. *Publ:* Coauth, Modern Language and Modern Living, The Study of Foreign Languages, Philos Libr, 68; auth, Le Divin et le Theatre Contemporain en France, Univ Microfilms, 71. *Mailing Add:* Dept of Foreign Lang Montclair State Col Upper Montclair NJ 07043

ROEDIG, CHARLES FRANCIS, b St Louis, Mo, Apr 29, 21. FRENCH LANGUAGE & LITERATURE. *Educ:* St Louis Univ, BS, 43; Yale Univ, PhD, 56. *Prof Exp:* Lectr Am lit, Univ Bordeaux, 49-50; ASSOC PROF FRENCH, UNIV NOTRE DAME, 50- *Mem:* Am Asn Teachers Fr; MLA. *Res:* French literature of the 19th and 20th centuries. *Mailing Add:* Dept of Mod & Class Lang Univ Notre Dame Notre Dame IN 46556

ROEMING, ROBERT FREDERICK, b Milwaukee, Wis, Dec 12, 11; m 41; c 1. FRENCH & ITALIAN LITERATURE. *Educ:* Univ Wis, AB, 34, AM, 36, PhD, 41. *Prof Exp:* Asst, Univ Wis-Milwaukee, 34-36, instr French & Ital, 37-43; rep, D C Heath & Co, Mass, 43-46; from asst prof to assoc prof French & Ital, 46-56, asst to dir exten div, 47-48, prof, 56-79, assoc dean col lett & sci, 57-62, dir dept lang labs, 64-70, dir English as second lang, 67-70, actg dir ctr, 68-69, dir ctr twentieth century studies, 70-74, EMER PROF FRENCH & ITAL, UNIV WIS-MILWAUKEE, 80- *Concurrent Pos:* Managing ed, Mod Lang J, 63-70; mem exec comt, Nat Fedn Mod Lang Teachers Asn, 63-70; trustee, Jose Greco Found Hisp Dance, NY, 72-; mem, Wis State Bd Nursing, 77-79, vchmn, 78-79, chmn, 79. *Honors & Awards:* Chevalier, Palmes Academiques, 65, Officier, 74, Commandeur, 80. *Mem:* MLA; Verband Deutscher Schriftsteller, West Ger. *Res:* Contemporary French literature; behavioral aspects of language learning; computerized bibliographical system. *Publ:* Coauth, Introduction to French; auth, Camus: A Bibliography, Univ Wis, 68, 2nd ed, 73, 3rd ed, 74, 4th ed, 75, 5th ed, 76, 6th ed, 77 & 7th ed, 82. *Mailing Add:* Dept of French & Ital Univ of Wis Milwaukee WI 53201

ROGAN, RICHARD GEORGE, b Milwaukee, Wis, Oct 29, 44. GERMAN LITERATURE, SCANDINAVIAN STUDIES. *Educ:* Univ Wis-Milwaukee, BS, 66; Univ Calif, Los Angeles, MA, 68, PhD(Ger & Scand studies), 73. *Prof Exp:* Instr Ger & Norweg, Concordia Col, 73-74; ASST PROF GER, NORTHERN ILL UNIV, 74- *Res:* German enlightenment and classicism. *Mailing Add:* Dept of Foreign Lang & Lit Northern Illinois Univ De Kalb IL 60115

ROGERS, ADRIENNE, b Flushing, NY, June 16, 29. FRENCH. *Educ:* Queens Col, NY, BA, 50; Middlebury Col, MA, 54; State Univ NY Albany, PhD(French), 70. *Prof Exp:* Part-time teacher French, Mont Pleasant high sch, Schenectady, NY, 60-61; teacher, Linton high sch, 61-62; from instr to assoc prof, 62-76; PROF FRENCH, RUSSELL SAGE COL, 76-, CHAIRPERSON DEPT MOD LANG & LIT, 70- *Mem:* Am Soc 18th Century Studies; MLA. *Res:* Legal status of minority groups in 18th century France; literary influence of minority groups in France. *Publ:* Co-ed, Selected Literary References in the Manuscript Journal (1750-1769) of Joseph d'Hemery, State Univ NY, Albany, 73. *Mailing Add:* Dept of Mod Lang & Lit Russell Sage Col Troy NY 12180

ROGERS, ANDREW DAYLON, JR, b Statesville, NC, Oct 30, 40; m 78; c 2. LINGUISTICS. *Educ:* Fla State Univ, BA, 63, MA, 67; Univ Calif, Los Angeles, PhD(ling), 74. *Prof Exp:* From instr to asst prof English & ling, Univ Tex, Austin, 73-77. *Concurrent Pos:* Sr Fulbright lectr ling, Kiev State Univ, USSR, 78-79. *Mem:* Ling Soc Am; Am Philos Asn; MLA. *Res:* Semantics; linguistics and literary criticism; English syntax. *Publ:* Auth, Three kinds of physical perception verbs, Papers Seventh Regional Meeting, 71 & A transderivational constraint on Richard?, Papers Tenth Regional Meeting, 74, Chicago Ling Soc; co-ed, Papers from the Texas conf on performatives, presuppositions, and implicatures, Ctr Appl Ling, 77; auth, Remarks on the analysis of assertion and the conversational role of speech acts, Proc Fourth Ann Meeting Berkeley Ling Soc, 78. *Mailing Add:* 3706 Robinson Ave Austin TX 78722

ROGERS, DOUGLASS MARCEL, b Albany, Wis, Aug 12, 25; m 58; c 1. FOREIGN LANGUAGES. *Educ:* Oberlin Col, BA, 51; Univ Wis, MA, 53, PhD, 65. *Prof Exp:* From instr to asst prof, 58-67, ASSOC PROF SPAN LANG & LIT, UNIV TEX, AUSTIN, 67- *Mem:* Am Asn Teachers Span & Port; MLA. *Res:* Modern Spanish literature, 1800 to present; history of Spanish poetry. *Publ:* Auth, El tiempo en la poesia de Jose Hierro, Archivum, 66; Lenguaje y personaje en Galdos, Cuadernos Hispanoam, 2/67; The descriptive simile in Galdos and Blasco Ibanez, Hispania, 12/70; ed, Benito Perez Galdos, Taurus, Madrid, 73; auth, Don Juan, Donjuanismo, and Death in Clarin, Symposium, winter 76; Sem Tob, poeta lirico moderno?, Univ Oviedo, 77; Unamuno's Don Sandalio and Melville's Bartleby: Two Literary Enigmas, Univ Wis, 81. *Mailing Add:* Batts Hall 112 Univ Tex Austin TX 78712

ROGERS, EDITH RANDAM, b Tallinn, Estonia, Mar 16, 24; US citizen; wid. SPANISH & COMPARATIVE LITERATURE. *Educ:* Univ Denver, BA, 61, MA, 62; Univ Colo, Boulder, PhD(Span), 68. *Prof Exp:* From instr to asst prof, 66-72, assoc prof, 72-79, ASSOC PROF SPAN, UNIV COLO, DENVER, 79- *Mem:* Am Asn Teachers Span & Port. *Res:* Spanish peninsular literature; Hispanic Romancero; comparative balladry. *Publ:* Auth, El color en la poesia del Renacimiento y del Barroco, Rev Filologia Espanola, 64; Games of muscle, mind and chance in the Romancero, Hispania, 72; El conde Olinos: Metempsychosis or miracle, Bull Hispanic Studies, 73; The hunt in the romancero and other traditional ballads, Hispanic Rev, 74; Clothing as a multifarious ballad symbol, Western Folklore, 75; Magic Music: A self-centered ballad motif, Ky Romance Quart, 75; The Perilous Hunt: Symbols in Hispanic and European Balladry, Univ Press Ky, 80. *Mailing Add:* Div Arts & Humanities Univ Colo Denver CO 80202

ROGERS, FRANCIS MILLET, b New Bedford, Mass, Nov 26, 14; m 42, 70; c 1. ROMANCE LANGUAGES & LITERATURES. *Educ:* Cornell Univ, AB, 36; Harvard Univ, AM, 37, PhD(comp philol), 40. *Hon Degrees:* LittD, Loyola Univ, Ill, 52; New Bedford Inst Tech, 63; LHD, Duquesne Univ, 53, Assumption Col, 60, Georgetown Univ, 66; LLD, Miami Univ, 53, Stonehill Col, 57 & Providence Col, 60; Dr, Univ Bahia, 59. *Prof Exp:* Instr French, 39-40, jr fel, Soc Fels, 40-41, fac instr Romance lang & lit, 45-46, assoc prof, 46-52, sr tutor, John Winthrop House, 46-50, chmn dept, 47-49, 61-66, dean grad, sch arts & sci, 49-55, prof romance lang & lit, 52-78, Nancy Clark Smith prof, 78-80, NANCY CLARK SMITH EMER PROF PORT LANG & LIT, HARVARD UNIV, 80- *Concurrent Pos:* US Dept State lectr, Brazil, 50; mem admin bd, Int Asn Univs, 50-55; consult comt, Int Bull Luso-Brazilian Bibliog, 59-73; hon prof, San Marcos Univ, Lima, 61; corresp mem, Acad Int Cult Port, 66. *Honors & Awards:* Chevalier, Legion d'honneur, 50. *Mem:* Am Asn Teachers Span & Port; Mediaeval Acad Am; Insts Navigation; Soc Hist Discoveries; Hisp Soc Am. *Res:* Mediaeval and Renaissance Portuguese language and literature; civilization of Portuguese Atlantic islands, including emigration to the United States; celestial navigation and its history. *Publ:* The Obedience of a King of Portugal, 58 & The Quest for Eastern Christians: Travels and Rumor in the Age of Discovery, 62, Univ Minn; The Travels of the Infante Dom Pedro of Portugal, Harvard Univ, 61; Europe Informed: An Exhibition of Early Books Which Acquainted Europe with the East, 66; Precision Astrolabe: Portuguese Navigators and Transoceanic Aviation, Lisbon, 71. *Mailing Add:* 201 Boylston Hall Harvard Univ Cambridge MA 02138

ROGERS, KENNETH HALL, b Needham, Mass, June 1, 39; m 63; c 1. ROMANCE LINGUISTICS, FRENCH. *Educ:* Boston Univ, BA, 61; Columbia Univ, MA, 63, PhD(Romance philol), 70. *Prof Exp:* Instr French, 68-70, ASST PROF FRENCH & ROMANCE LING, UNIV RI, 70- *Mem:* MLA; Ling Soc Am; Int Ling Asn; Am Asn Teachers Fr; Am Soc Geoling (pres, 77-78). *Res:* Romance linguistics-phonology and morphology; sociolinguistics and linguistic nationlism. *Publ:* Auth, Vocalic Alternation in the Surselvan Romansh Verb, In: Studies in Honor of Mario A Pei, 72; Romance Philology and the Sociology of Language: A Pedagogical Perspective, Yearbk 1975 Pedagog Sem Romance Philol, MLA, 75; La Situation Diglossique dan les Grisons, Cahier Groupe Recherches Diglossie, Univ Montpellier, 76; Rheto-Romance: Dialect and Geography in Southeastern Switzerland, Geoling III, 77; Studies on linguistic nationalism in the Romance languages, In: Trends in Romance Philology and Linguistics, Vol 2, Mouton, The Hague, 81; Selected recent studies in linguistic nationalism in the Romance languages, Rev Can Etudes sur Nationalisme VIII, fall 81; Languages and language policies in the USSR, Geolinguistics, VII, 81. *Mailing Add:* Dept of Lang Univ RI Kingston RI 02881

ROGERS, LAWRENCE WILLIAM, b Oakland, Calif. JAPANESE LITERATURE AND LANGUAGE. *Educ:* Univ Cailf, Berkeley, BA, 61, MA, 66, PhD(oriental lang), 75. *Prof Exp:* Actg instr Japanese, Univ Calif, Berkeley, 72-74; actg asst prof, Univ Calif, Los Angeles, 74-75; asst prof, 76-82, ASSOC PROF JAPANESE, UNIV HAWAII, HILO, 82- *Concurrent Pos:* Vis fac, Univ BC, summer 78 & Int Christian Univ, Tokyo, summers 81 & 82. *Mem:* Asn for Asian Studies; Asn Teachers Japanese; Soc Writers, Ed & Transl. *Res:* Modern Japanese poetry and fiction; the haibun essay. *Publ:* Auth, Rags and tatters: The Uzuragoromo of Yokoi Yayu, Monumenta Nipponica, autumn 79; transl, Leaves & Mount Fuji, Int Poetry Rev, spring 81. *Mailing Add:* Dept of Lang Univ of Hawaii Hilo HI 96720

ROGERS, LINDSEY SWANSON, JR, b Birmingham, Ala, Jan 13, 31; m 57. GERMANIC LANGUAGES. *Educ:* Tulane Univ, Dr Philos, 64. *Prof Exp:* Instr Ger, Univ Ga, 61-64, asst prof Ger & Ger lit, 64-68, assoc prof Ger & Slavic lang, 68-80. *Mem:* Am Asn Teachers Ger; MLA. *Res:* German Romanticism; Schiller's classical period. *Publ:* Coauth, Wagner's Siegfried, Univ Stores, Univ Ga, 66; auth, Hart Crane and Stefan George: Cultural pessimism and literary tradition, Arch, 6/68. *Mailing Add:* 595 Forest Rd Athens GA 30606

ROGERS, R MAX, b Morgan, Utah, May 1, 18; m 41; c 6. MODERN GERMAN LITERATURE. *Educ:* Brigham Young Univ, AB, 40, Am, 42; Stanford Univ, PhD, 51. *Prof Exp:* Teaching fel, Brigham Young Univ, 40-42 & Stanford Univ, 42-44; instr mod Ger lit, 45-46, from asst prof to assoc prof, 46-56, dir travel study, 53-58, chmn dept lang, 63-67, chmn dept Ger & Slavic lang, 67-68, asst dean humanities, 68-74, PROF HUMANITIES, BRIGHAM YOUNG UNIV, 56-, ASSOC DEAN, 74- *Mem:* MLA; Rocky Mountain Mod Lang Asn (pres, 68-69); Am Asn Teachers Ger; Am Coun Teaching Foreign Lang. *Res:* German naturalism and expressionism; elements of expressionism in the prose works of Hans Carossa; the anti-Christian elements in the German naturalistic novel. *Publ:* Coauth, German through Conversational Patterns, 65, 2nd ed, 73, 3rd ed, 81 & Reviewing German, 69, Dodd; Scenes from German Drama, Harper & Row, 78. *Mailing Add:* Off Assoc Dean Brigham Young Univ Provo UT 84602

ROGERS, THOMAS FRANKLYN, b Salt Lake City, Utah, Apr 12, 33; m 58; c 4. RUSSIAN LITERATURE. *Educ:* Univ Utah, BA, 55; Yale Univ, MA, 62; Georgetown Univ, PhD, 68. *Prof Exp:* Instr Ger, Russ & humanities, Howard Univ, 62-66; asst prof Russ, Univ Utah, 66-69; assoc prof, 69-76, PROF RUSS, BRIGHAM YOUNG UNIV, 76- *Concurrent Pos:* Dir hon prog, Brigham Young Univ, 74-77. *Mem:* Am Asn Teachers Slavic & East Europ Lang; Rocky Mountain Mod Lang Asn. *Res:* Soviet literature; drama; playwrighting. *Publ:* Auth, Trends in Soviet prose of the thaw period, Rocky Mountain Mod Lang Asn J, winter 69; The ironic mode in Soviet Russian prose, 69 & The implications of Christ's Passion in Doctor Zhivago, Vol XVIII, No 4, 384-391, Slavic & East Europ J; transl, S Panchev, Turbulence and Random Functions, Pergamon Press, 71; Ethical idealism in Post-Stalin fiction, Rocky Mountain Soc Sci J, 4/75; Hedonism and humanitas: The Pushkin Perplex, The need beyond research, and other essays, Brigham Young Univ Press, 76; The sacred in literature, Lit & Belief, 81; The Suffering Christ in Grotowski's Apokalypsis cum Figuris, Relig & Theatre (in press). *Mailing Add:* Dept of Germanic & Slavic Lang Brigham Young Univ Provo UT 84602

ROGGIANO, ALFREDO ANGEL, b Buenos Aires, Arg, Aug 2, 19. SPANISH. *Educ:* Univ Buenos Aires, DL, 45; Univ Madrid, cert, 49. *Prof Exp:* Prof lit, Nat Univ Tucaman, 47; lectr, Univs Madrid & Granada, 49; vis prof, Univ Chile, 51 & Univs NMex & Calif, 55; assoc prof Span, State Univ Iowa, 56-63; PROF SPAN, UNIV PITTSBURGH, 63- *Concurrent Pos:* Dir, Rev Iberoam, 55-; vis prof, Ind Univ, 58, Nat Univ Mex, 60 & Univ Calif, Los Angeles, 62. *Mem:* MLA; Am Asn Teachers Span & Port; Latin Am Studies Asn; Inst Int Iberoam; Int Studies Asn. *Res:* Spanish American literature. *Publ:* Auth, Una obra Desconocida del Teatro Hispano-Americano, 58 & Pedro Henriquez Urena en los Estados Unidos, 61, State Univ Iowa; coauth, Diccionario de la Literatura Latin-Americana Argentian, Pan Am, 61; En Este Aire de America, Mex, 67; Octario Paz, Madrid, 79. *Mailing Add:* Dept of Span Univ Pittsburgh Pittsburgh PA 15260

ROHLFING, MARTHA MAE, b Belleville, Ill, Aug 11, 44. GERMAN LITERATURE. *Educ:* Univ Ill, BA, 65; Ind Univ, MA, 68, PhD(Ger), 76. *Prof Exp:* Instr Ger, SDak State Univ, 73-74; lectr, Univ Chicago, 74-80. *Mem:* MLA; Am Asn Teachers Ger. *Res:* Nineteenth century didactic fiction; the relationship between history and literature. *Publ:* Auth, Stifter's Bzunte Steine as a cyclical work, Mich Acad, fall 77. *Mailing Add:* 5461 S Cornell Chicago IL 60615

ROHLICH, THOMAS HENRY, b Bellefonte, Pa, June 5, 46; m 76; c 2. JAPANESE LITERATURE & LANGUAGE. *Educ:* Univ Wis-Madison, BA, 71, MA, 75, PhD(Japanese lit), 79. *Prof Exp:* Instr Japanese lit, Univ Wis-Madison, 77; lectr, Univ Ill, Chicago Circle, 78-79, asst prof, 79-82; ASST PROF JAPANESE LANG & LIT, UNIV IOWA, 82- *Mem:* Asn Teachers of Japanese; MLA; Asn for Asian Studies. *Res:* Classical Japanese literature; Heian literature; modern Japanese literature. *Publ:* Auth, A Tale of Eleventh Century Japan: Hamamatsu Chunagon Monogatari, Princeton Univ Press, spring 83. *Mailing Add:* Dept of Ling Box 4348 Univ of Ill Chicago Circle Chicago IL 60680

ROJAS, CARLOS, b Barceloan, Spain, Aug 12, 28; m 66; c 2. SPANISH LITERATURE, HISTORY. *Educ:* Barcelona Univ, MA, 51; Univ Cent, Madrid, PhD(Span lit), 55. *Prof Exp:* Asst prof Romance lang, Rollins Col, 57-60; from asst prof to assoc prof, 60-68, prof, 68-80, CHARLES HOWARD CANDLER PROF ROMANCE LANG, EMORY UNIV, 80- *Concurrent Pos:* Ateneo de Sevilla Prize, 77. *Honors & Awards:* Nat Prize for Lit, Govt Spain, 68; Planeta Prize, Ed Planeta, 73; Nadal Prize, 80. *Mem:* MLA; SAtlantic Mod Lang Asn. *Res:* Contemporary Spanish; art history. *Publ:* Auth, Dialogos Para Otra Espana, Ariel, 66; Auto de Fe, Guadarrama, 68; Diez Figuras Ante la Guerra Civil, Nauta, 73; Azana, 73, La Guerra Civil Vista por los Exiliados, 75, Retratos Antifranquistas, 77 & Memorias Ineditas, 78, Planeta; El Ingenioso Hidalgo y Poeta Federico Garcia Lorca Asciende a los Infiernos, 80, La Barcelonade Picasso, 81. *Mailing Add:* Dept of Romance Lang Emory Univ Atlanta GA 30322

ROJAS, GUILLERMO, b Victoria, Tex, Jan 18, 38; m 67. MEXICAN & CHICANO LITERATURE. *Educ:* NTex State Univ, BA, 63, MA, 65; Univ Ill, Urbana, PhD(Span-Am lit), 70. *Prof Exp:* Asst prof Span & Ger, Southern Univ, Baton Rouge, 66-67; ASST PROF SPAN, UNIV CALIF, DAVIS, 70- *Concurrent Pos:* Nat Endowment for Humanities fel, 72-73; assoc ed, Anuario de Letras Chicanas, 77- *Res:* Mexican history and literature; Chicano literature. *Publ:* Auth, Quetzalcoatl: Serpiente emplumada, falo encabellado o dios de la fecundidad, Cuadernos Am, 3-4/72; Toward a Chicano/Raza bibliography: Drama, prose, poetry, El Grito, 73; La prosa chicana . . ., Cuadernos Am, 5-6/75; Chicano/Raza newspapers and periodical serials listing, Hispania, 12/75. *Mailing Add:* Dept of Span Univ Calif Davis CA 95616

ROJAS, VICTOR JULIO, b Esparta, Costa Rica, Jan 4, 41; m 65. SPANISH LANGUAGE AND LITERATURE. *Educ:* Univ NMex, BA, 65; Tex Tech Univ, MA, 67; Ind Univ, PhD(Span), 75. *Prof Exp:* Instr Span, 71-75, ASST PROF SPAN, STATE UNIV NY BROCKPORT, 75-, CHMN DEPT, 80- *Concurrent Pos:* Grant-in-aid Port, State Univ MY, 76-78; Port examr, Nazareth Col, 76- *Res:* Latin American literature; Luso-Brazilian literature; applied linguistics. *Publ:* Auth, Sobre el negro en la poesia de Luis Pales Matos y de Jorge de Lima, Sin Nombre, 72; El sentido de la desnudez en la poesia de Juan Ramon Jimenez, Explicacion Texos Lit, 73; Holocausto de Leopoldo Lugones, Antologia Comentada Mod, 74; Vida y Obra de Violante do Ceu, Univ Microfilms, 75; Federico Garcia Lorca in Portuguese, Garcia Lorca Rev, 76; Onamastics and the prismatic reality in the poetry of Fernando Pessoa, Lit Onomastics Studies, 77. *Mailing Add:* Dept of Foreign Lang State Univ NY Brockport NY 14420

ROLFE, OLIVER WILLIS, b Alamosa, Colo, Jan 20, 38; m 68; c 2. FRENCH LANGUAGE, LINGUISTICS. *Educ:* Washburn Univ, Topeka, AB, 60; Stanford Univ, AM, 64, PhD(ling), 67. *Prof Exp:* Teacher & tutor, Menninger Found, Topeka, Kans, 58-60; teaching asst French, Stanford Univ, 61-63, actg instr ling, 63-65, instr teaching English as a second lang, 65-66; asst prof Romance ling, Univ Wash, 66-70; assoc prof, 70-76, PROF FOREIGN LANG, UNIV MONT, 76- *Concurrent Pos:* Res asst, Stanford Comput Ctr, 61-63; instr French, San Jose State Col, spring 64. *Mem:* Am Asn Teachers Fr; Am Coun Teaching Foreign Lang; AAUP. *Res:* French and Romance linguistics; language teaching methodology. *Publ:* Co-ed, Linguistic Studies Present to Andre Martinet on the Occassion of His 60th Birthday, Ling Circle of NY, 72; auth, Grammatical frequency and language teaching: Verbal categories in French and Spanish, In: Linguistic Studies Presented to Andre Martinet, 72; Morphological Frequency: French & Spanish Verbal Themes, In: Papers on Linguistics & Child Language, Hague, Mouton, 78. *Mailing Add:* Dept of Foreign Lang Univ Mont Missoula MT 59812

ROLFS, DANIEL JAMES, Univ Calif, Berkeley, BA, 66, MA, 67, PhD(lang & lit), 71. ITALIAN LANGUAGE & LITERATURE. *Prof Exp:* Asst prof Italian, Univ Mich, 71-77; ASST PROF ITALIAN, UNIV ILL, CHICAGO, 77- *Mem:* MLA; Midwest Mod Lang Asn; Am Asn Univ Professors Italian. *Res:* Nineteenth century Italian literature; medieval Italian literature; romance languages and literatures. *Publ:* Auth, Dante and the problem of suicide, Mich Academician, Vol 4, 367-375; The portrayal of suicide in Italian literature of the Counter-Reformation era, Forum Italicum, Vol IX, No 1, 37-59; Dante, Petrarch, Boccaccio and the problem of suicide, Romanic Rev, Vol LXVII, No 3, 200-225; Pirandello's theme of madness, Forum Italicum, Vol X, No 4, 377-397; Sleep, dreams and insomnia, In: Orlando Furioso, Italica, Vol LIII, No 4, 453-474; Sound and silence in Ariosto's narrative, In: Series II, No 2, Renaissance and Reformation, Renaissance et Reforme, 151-169; The Last Cross: A History of the Suicide Theme in Italian Literature, Vol 26, Univ NC Press, 81. *Mailing Add:* 402 N Grove Ave Oak Park IL 60302

ROLLER, DUANE WILLIAMSON, b Lafayette, Ind, Oct 7, 46; m 70. CLASSICAL ARCHEOLOGY, ANCIENT HISTORY. *Educ:* Univ Okla, BA, 66, MA, 68; Harvard Univ, PhD(class archaeol), 71. *Prof Exp:* Asst prof classics, Franklin & Marshall Col, 71-74; ASST PROF CLASSICS, WILFRID LAURIER UNIV, 74- *Concurrent Pos:* Inst lectr, Archaeol Inst Am, 72- *Mem:* Am Philol Asn; Archaeol Inst Am; Class Asn of Can. *Res:* Boiotian archaeology; history of sixth century BC Greece; Herodotos. *Publ:* Auth, Gaius Memmius: patron of Lucretius, Class Philol, 10/70; The date of the walls at Tanagra, Hesperia, 4/74; A new map of Tanagra, Am J Archaeol, 74; An imitation of Xenophanes, Liverpool Class Monthly, 7/77. *Mailing Add:* 901-10 Highland Circle Kitchner ON N2M 5C2 Can

ROLLESTON, JAMES LANCELOT, b England, Dec 5, 39; m 62; c 2. GERMANIC LANGUAGES. *Educ:* Cambridge Univ, Ba, 61; Univ Minn, MA, 62; Yale Univ, PhD(Ger), 68. *Prof Exp:* From actg instr to instr Ger, Yale Univ, 66-69, from asst prof to assoc prof, 69-75; ASSOC PROF GER, DUKE UNIV, 75- *Concurrent Pos:* Morse fel, 70-71. *Mem:* MLA;. *Res:* Nietzsche; modern poetry; Kafka. *Publ:* Auth, Rilke in Transition, Yale Univ, 70; Kafka's Narrative Theater, Pa State Univ, 74; ed, Twentieth-Century Interpretations of the Trial, Prentice-Hall, 76; auth, The expressionist moment: Heym, Trakl and the problem of the modern, Studies 20th Century LIt, 77. *Mailing Add:* 3238 Pickett Rd Durham NC 27705

ROLLINS, ERNEST WILLIAM, JR, b Woodruff, SC, July 3, 32. GERMAN. *Educ:* Wake Forest Col, BA, 59; Ind Univ, MA, 61; Vanderbilt Univ, PhD(Ger), 68. *Prof Exp:* Instr Ger & French, Indian River Jr Col, 61-62; asst prof Ger, Stetson Univ, 62-68; asst prof, 68-72, ASSOC PROF GER, NC STATE UNIV, 72- *Concurrent Pos:* Vis assoc prof, Univ New Orleans Int summer school, Innsbruck, 77; exchange prof, Wolfgang Borchert Realschule, Hattingen, German Federal Republic, 82-83. *Mem:* MLA: Am Asn Teachers Ger. *Res:* Modern German literature; interdisciplinary studies in literature, philosophy, and religion; Albrecht Goes and Martin Buber. *Publ:* Coauth, Mem of Dialogue: Martin Buber and Albrecht Goes, Funk, 69. *Mailing Add:* Dept of Foreign Lang & Lit NC State Univ Raleigh NC 27650

ROLLINS, JACK DRAKE, b Ann Arbor, Mich, Feb 9, 43; m 73; c 1. COMPARATIVE LITERATURE. *Educ:* Univ Mich, BA, 64; Univ Iowa, MFA, 69; Ind Univ, MA, 76, PhD(comp lit), 78. *Prof Exp:* ASSOC PROF ENGLISH & COMP LIT, IND STATE UNIV, 69- *Concurrent Pos:* Tutor in English & Swahili, Nairobi Community Ctr, 66-68; lectr comp lit, Ind Univ, 77-78; maitre de conf, Dept d'Anglais, Univ Nat du Gabon, 79-80. *Mem:* MLA; African Lit Asn; African Studies Asn. *Res:* The history of Swahili prose; the linguistic and socio-linguistic aspects of Oriental influence upon Swahili culture, language and literature. *Publ:* Auth, Varieties of Gnomic literature: The Arabian Hikma and the Islamic Ethos of Shaaban Robert's Neno la Hekima, Res in African Lit, 79; A note on the Arabic etymology of Nabokov, The Vladmir Nabokov Res Newsletter, 81; A history of Swahili prose, part one: From earliest times to the end of the nineteenth century, E J Brill, Leiden (in prep). *Mailing Add:* 1025 E First St Bloomington IN 47401

ROLLINS, PETER CUSHING, American & Film Studies. See Vol I

ROLLINS, YVONNE BARGUES, b Clermont-Ferrand, France, Aug 10, 43; c 1. FRENCH LITERATURE. *Educ:* Univ Clermont-Ferrand, License, 65; Brigham Young Univ, MA, 69; Duke Univ, PhD(French lit), 75. *Prof Exp:* Instr French, Brigham Young Univ, 66-70, Duke Univ, 70-73 & NC State Univ, Raleigh, 73-74; asst prof, Mt Holyoke Col, 74-80; ASST PROF FRENCH, NC STATE UNIV, RALEIGH, 80- *Concurrent Pos:* Panelist & res fel, Am Coun Learned Socs, 80- *Mem:* MLA; Am Asn Teachers French; Soc Estudes Romantiques. *Res:* The grotesque in 19th century French literature; Flaubert; Zola. *Publ:* Auth, Montaigne et le language, Romanic Rev, Vol 64, 73; Baudelaire et le grotesque, French Rev, Vol 50, 76; Baudelaire et le grotesque, Univ Press Am, 78; Madame Bovary et Effi Briest: du symbole au mythe, Stanford French Rev, 81; Une dame macabre: L'Assommoir de Zola, Nineteenth Century French Studies, Vol IX, 81. *Mailing Add:* Dept of Foreign Lang & Lit NC State Univ Raleigh NC 27650

ROLLINSON, PHILIP BRUCE, Renaissance Literature, Critical Theory. See Vol II

ROMANOWSKI, SYLVIE, b Paris, France, May 12, 40; Can citizen. FRENCH LITERATURE. *Educ:* Carleton Univ, BA, 62; Harvard Univ, MA, 63; Yale Univ, PhD(French), 70. *Prof Exp:* Lectr French, York Univ, 68-69; asst prof, Univ Wis-Milwaukee, 69-71; ASSOC PROF FRENCH, NORTHWESTERN UNIV, EVANSTON, 71- *Mem:* AAUP; NAm Soc 17th Century Fr Lit; Midwest Mod Lang Asn; Northeast Mod Lang Asn. *Res:* French literature of the 17th century; modern literary criticism; French literature of the 20th century. *Publ:* Auth, L'Unite du Testament de Villon, Lett Romanes, 68; La nuit dans l'oeuvre romanesque d'Andre Malraux, Rev des Sci Humaines, 68; L'illusion chez Descartes: La structure du discours cartesien, Klincksieck, 74; Le role du langage dans le Dom Juan de Moliere, Neophilologus, 75; Malraux' Antimemoirs: Comic and cosmic consciousness, Cross Currents, 76; Un roman feministe du 17 siecle: Heroisme et langage dans la Pretieuse de l'abbe de Pure, Ky Romance Quart, 77; A Typology of Women in Colette's Novels, In: Colette, The Woman, The Writer, Penn State Univ Press, 81. *Mailing Add:* Dept of French & Ital Northwestern Univ Evanston IL 60201

ROMEISER, JOHN BEALS, b Washington, DC, July 12, 48; m 75; c 1. FRENCH LANGUAGE & LITERATURE. *Educ:* Colgate Univ, BA, 70; Vanderbilt Univ, PhD(French), 75. *Prof Exp:* ASST PROF FRENCH, NEWBERRY COL ,74- *Concurrent Pos:* Asst ed, Studies Short Fiction, 77- *Mem:* MLA; S Atlantic Mod Lang Asn; Am Asn Teachers Fr; Malraux Soc. *Res:* The life and works of Andre Malraux; writers of the Spanish Civil War; film theory and criticism. *Publ:* Auth, Le reportage pendant la guerre d'Espagne, Bull Info Foundation d'Etudes Guerre Civile d'Espagne, 3/77; Malraux and Hemingway chronicle the Spanish Civil War, Malraux Miscellany, autumn 78; L'Espoir devant la critique frano-americaine: 1937-1940, Les Cahiers Malraux, 78; A philosophe on crime and punishment: Diderot's response to Beccaria, Fr Lit Ser, Univ SC, 78. *Mailing Add:* Dept of Foreign Lang & Lit Newberry Col Newberry SC 29108

ROMEO, LUIGI, b Tropea, Italy, Sept 20, 26; US citizen. ROMANCE LINGUISTICS. *Educ:* Wash State Univ, BA, 57; Univ Wash, MA, 59, PhD(Romance lang), 60. *Prof Exp:* Instr & actg asst prof Romance ling, Univ Wash, 59-61; asst prof Ital ling, Univ Toronto, 61-65; assoc prof Romance lang, 65-68, chmn dept ling, 68-75, PROF LING, UNIV COLO, 68-, CHMN ADV COMT SEMIOTICS, 75- *Concurrent Pos:* Hon prof, Inst Super Europ Human Sci, Urbino, Italy, 69-; Univ Colo fac fel, Romanisches Inst, Univ Bonn, Ger, 70-71, fac fel, 76-77; mem Nat Humanities Inst Comt, 74-75; mem Nat Fulbright comt, Inst Int Educ, 75; ed, Uolo Res Ling, 75-76; ed-in-chief, Ars Semeiotica Press, 76-; founder & ed, Int J Am Semiotic, 77- *Mem:* Semiotic Soc Am; Ling Asn Am; Am Asn Advan Humanities; AAAS; Am Asn Am Publ. *Res:* Romance linguistics; history of linguistics; general linguistics. *Publ:* Auth, Heraclitus and the foundations of Semiotics, Vs Quaderni di Studi Semiotici, 9-12/76; The Semiotic foundations of linguistics, Semiotic Scene, 77; The derivation of Semiotics through the history of the discipline, Semiosis, 77; The Bivium Sundrome in the history of Semiotics, 77 & From Lambert to Zawadowski: a chronological microreview of excerpts on the relationship between linguistics and Semiotics, 77, Colo Res Ling; Lettre aux semiologues, Int J Am Simotic, 77; Linguistics and Semiotics at the National Science Foundation, Reductio ab absurdum?, 77 & Ultimum Evangelium Americanum, 77, Semiotic Scene. *Mailing Add:* Adv Comt on Semiotics Old Main 1 Univ of Colo Boulder CO 80309

ROMERO, HECTOR R, b Santa Clara, Cuba, Sept 6, 42; US citizen; c 1. SPANISH LITERATURE. *Educ:* Univ Ill, Urbana, BA, 66, PhD(Span), 70; Roosevelt Univ, MA, 68. *Prof Exp:* From asst prof to assoc prof mod lang, Univ Nebr-Lincoln, 70-78; mem fac Romance & Ger lang, 78-79, ASSOC PROF SPANISH, WAYNE STATE UNIV, 79- *Concurrent Pos:* Woods Res fel. *Publ:* Auth, Los mitos de la Espana sagrada en Reivindicacion del conde don Julian, J Span Studies, 12/73; Juan Sin Tierra: Analisis de un texto literario, Vol I, 76. *Mailing Add:* Dept of Romance & Ger Lang Wayne State Univ Detroit MI 48202

ROOD, DAVID STANLEY, b Albany, NY, Sept 14, 40. GENERAL LINGUISTICS. *Educ:* Cornell Univ, BA, 63; Univ Calif, Berkeley, MA, 65, PhD(ling), 69. *Prof Exp:* Instr Ger & ling, 67-69, asst prof ling, 69-77, assoc prof, 77-82, PROF LING, UNIV COLO, BOULDER, 82- *Concurrent Pos:* Univ Colo Coun Res & Creative Activity, 73-74; NSF grant, 77-81; Nat Endowment for Humanities grant, 77-81; ed, Int J Am Ling, 81- *Mem:* Ling Soc Am; Am Anthrop Asn; Teachers of English to Speakers of Other Lang. *Res:* Applied linguistics in second language teaching; American Indian language; linguistic theory and semantic-based grammar. *Publ:* Auth, Agent and Object in Wichita, Lingua, 71; Aspects of subordination in Lakhota and Wichita, In: You Take the High Node and I'll Take the Low Node, Chicago Ling Asn, 73; Implications of Wichita phonology, Language, 75; Wichita Grammar, Garland, 76; coauth, Beginning Lakhota, Univ Colo, Ling Dept, 76; contribr, Siouan, In: The Languages of Native America, Univ Tex, 79; auth, Locative Expressions in Siouan and Caddoan, Colo Res Ling, 79; User's Handbook for the Siouan Languages Archive, Univ Colo, Dept Ling, 81. *Mailing Add:* Dept of Ling Univ of Colo Boulder CO 80309

ROOP, D HAIGH, b Washington, DC. SOUTHEASTERN ASIAN LANGUAGES, LINGUISTICS. *Educ:* Harvard Univ, BA, 54; Yale Univ, MA, 65 PhD(ling), 70. *Prof Exp:* Actg instr Burmese, Yale Univ, 63-65, lectr Burmese & Thai, 68-71; asst prof Burmese & Thai, 71-76, ASSOC PROF S EASTERN ASIAN LANG, UNIV HAWAII, MANOA, 76- *Mem:* Ling Soc Am; Asn Asian Studies. *Res:* Tibeto-Burman languages & linguistics. *Publ:* Coauth, Beginning Burmese, Yale Univ, 68; auth, The problem of linguistic diversity in Thailand, In: Tribesmen and Peasants in Northern Thailand, Tribal in Thailand, In: Tribesmen and Peasants in Northern Thailand, Tribal Research Centre, Chiengmai, Thailand, 69; An introduction to the Burmese writing system, Yale Univ, 72. *Mailing Add:* Dept of Indo Pac Lang Univ of Hawaii at Manoa Honolulu HI 96822

ROOS, KEITH L, b Peoa, Utah, June 1, 37; m 68; c 3. GERMAN RENAISSANCE LITERATURE. *Educ:* Univ Utah, BA, 64; Rice Univ, PhD(Ger lit), 68. *Prof Exp:* Asst prof, 68-80, ASSOC PROF GER, BRIGHAM YOUNG UNIV, 80- *Mem:* MLA. *Res:* Reformation and baroque literature and culture. *Publ:* Auth, Devil in 16th Century Germany: The Teufelbücher, Herbert Lang, Bern, 72. *Mailing Add:* Dept of Lang Brigham Young Univ Provo UT 84602

ROOT, TAMARA GOLDSTEIN, b Cracow, Poland, Feb 10, 40; Can citizen; m 68. FRENCH LITERATURE. *Educ:* Univ Toronto, BA, 63; Univ Ill, Urbana, MA, 66, PhD(French), 70. *Prof Exp:* Instr, 70-71, asst prof, 71-77, ASSOC PROF FRENCH, HAMLINE UNIV, 77- *Res:* Seventeenth century French literature; 18th century French literature; literary criticism and theory. *Publ:* Auth, Epicurean philosophy and the realism of Les Illustres Francoises, spring 74 & La Solitude: Saint-Amant's expression of unrest, 10/76, Fr Rev; The notion of the heroine in Robert Challe's Les Illustres Francoises, Papers Fr Seventeenth Century Lit, winter 77-78. *Mailing Add:* Dept of Mod Lang & Lit Hamline Univ St Paul MN 55101

ROQUE-NUNEZ, HORACIO, b Coronel Pringles, Arg, Aug 5, 19; m 63; c 2. ROMANCE LANGUAGES, PHILOSOPHY. *Educ:* Cordoba Univ, BV, 38, MPh, 43, PhD(philos & lit), 52; Acad Philos, Sci & Lit, Arg, MST, 58. *Prof Exp:* Prof Span lit, Scholae Piae Inst, 44-46; prof Span lang & lit, high norm sch, 47-51; prof philos, Cordoba Univ, 49-65; prof, Univ Chile, 66; teacher, Plainfield High Schs, 66-67; assoc prof Span & Latin Am lit, Wis State Univ, Stevens Point, 67-69; ASSOC PROF SPAN, LAURENTIAN UNIV, 69- *Concurrent Pos:* Lectr psychol, Cordoba, 44-45; mem First Nat Congr Philos, Mendoza, Arg, 49; prof, Nat Univ Tucuman, 52-54; mem First Nat Congr Psychol, Tucuman, Arg, 54; lectr, Alliance French, Rio Cuarto, Arg, 57-58; pres & founder, Nat Pythagorean Soc, Arg, 65-66. *Mem:* Am Asn Teachers Span & Port; Int Pythagorean Philos Soc. *Res:* Spanish American literature; Spanish literature, especially Golden Age, medieval and Cervantes; history of philosophy. *Publ:* Auth, La vocacion cientifica, Cristal, 44; Etapas de la literatura gauchesca, 54, El tema de dios en Bergson, 54, La escuela eleatica, 54 & Los fragmentos de Heraclito, 54, Cordoba Univ; Los brujos hablan, El Mercurio, 66; The School System in Argentina, Plainfield, 67. *Mailing Add:* Dept of Mod Lang Laurentian Univ Sudbury ON P3D 2C6 Can

ROSALDO, RENATO IGNACIO, b Minatitlan, Mex, Apr 16, 12. LATIN AMERICAN LITERATURE. *Educ:* Univ Ill, AB, 36, AM, 37, PhD, 42. *Prof Exp:* Teaching asst, Univ Ill, 36-42, instr, 42-45; from asst prof to assoc prof Latin Am lit & civilization, Univ Wis, 45-55; vis prof Span, 55-56, co-dir, Guadalajara Summer Sch, Mex, 59-71, acad coordr, 72-77, head dept Romance Lang, Univ, 58-73, PROF SPAN, UNIV ARIZ, 56- *Concurrent Pos:* Vis prof Span, Guadalajara Summer Sch, 55-56, 58; coordr Ariz-Mex W Coast Trade Comn, 59-63; mem grad educ adv comt, US Off Educ, 67-68, adv coun grad educ, 68-71; consult, Ford Found, 68- *Honors & Awards:* Dipl for Cult Work Between Ariz & Sonora, Gov Ariz, 64; Dipl for Cult Work, Gov Mex, 64. *Mem:* MLA; Am Asn Teachers Span & Port (pres, 67); Inst Int Lit Iberoam (pres, 69-71, vpres, 71-73); Latin Am Studies Asn; Philol Asn Pac Coast. *Res:* Mexican literature; Latin America. *Publ:* Auth, Flores de Baria Poesia, un cancionero inedito mexicano de 1577, Abside, Mex, 52; A decade of Mexican literature, Ariz Quart, winter 60; coauth, Six Faces of Mexico, Univ Ariz, 66; Chicano: The Evolution of a People, Winston, 73. *Mailing Add:* Dept of Romance Lang Univ of Ariz Tucson AZ 85721

ROSBOTTON, RONALD CARLISLE, b New Orleans, La, July 15, 42; m 64; c 1. FRENCH LITERATURE. *Educ:* Tulane Univ, BA, 64; Princeton Univ, MA, 66, PhD(Fr), 69. *Prof Exp:* From instr to asst prof French, Univ Pa, 67-73; assoc prof, 73-78, PROF FRENCH, OHIO STATE UNIV, 78-, CHMN, DEPT ROMANCE LANG, 82- *Concurrent Pos:* Ed adv, Eighteenth Century, 73-; ed, Studies 18th Century Cult, 74-76; exec secy, Am Soc 18th Century Studies, 78- *Mem:* MLA: Am Asn Teachers Fr; Am Soc 18th Century Studies; Fr Soc Study 18th Century; Am Comp Lit Asn. *Res:* Eighteenth and 19th century French and English novel; rhetoric and literary criticism; theory of narrative. *Publ:* Contribr, The Varied Pattern, Hakkert, Amsterdam, 71; auth, Mme Riccoboni's continuation of Marianne, In: Studies in Voltaire and the 18th Century, 71; Ira Wade's enlightenment, Studies in Burke in His Time, 73; Marivaux's Novels, Fairleigh Dickinson Univ, 74; A matter of competence, Studies in 18th Century Cult, 76; Choderlos de Laclos, G K Hall, 78; Motifs of epistolary fiction, Esprit Createur, 4/78; Roman et secret, Revue d'histoire litteraire de la France, 11/82. *Mailing Add:* Dept of Romance Lang Ohio State Univ Columbus OH 43210

ROSE, CONSTANCE HUBBARD, b Cambridge, Mass, July 20, 34. SPANISH & COMPARATIVE LITERATURE. *Educ:* Rollins Col, BA, 55; Boston Univ, MA, 61; Harvard Univ, PhD(Romance lang & lit), 68. *Prof Exp:* Asst ed, Houghton Mifflin Co, 56-59; instr Span, Lasell Jr Col, 61-64; lectr, Brandeis Univ, 67-69; asst prof Span & comp lit, Univ Pittsburgh, 69-73, res grant, 71; Am Philos Soc Res grant, 74; Am Coun Learning Soc grant-in-aid, 75; asst prof Span & comp lit, 76, ASSOC PROF SPAN & COMP LIT, NORTHEASTERN UNIV, 78- *Concurrent Pos:* Consult ed, Ginn & Co, 61-63; instr Span, Newton Jr Col, 62-63; Nat Endowment for Humanities jr fel, 73; Am Philos Soc res grant, 75; Am Coun Learned Soc travel grant, 80; Treat of Friendship & Coop Between US & Spain fel, 81. *Mem:* Asn Int Hispanistas; MLA; Renaissance Soc Am; Comediantes; AAUP. *Res:* Spanish literature of the Golden Age; comparative literature of the 16th and 17th centuries; literature of exile. *Publ:* Auth, Antonio Enriquez Gomez and the Literature of Exile, Romanische Forsch, 73; Alonso Nunuz de Reinoso: The Lament of a Sixteenth Century Exile, Fairleigh Dickinson Univ, 71; Spanish Renaissance Translators: I The Exile and the Diplomat: Two Versions of a Passage from Ariosto, II Alfonso de Ulloa, Ariosto and the Word Marrano, Rev Lit Comparee, 71; coauth & coed, Antonio Enriquez Gomez: Fernan Mendez Pinto, Comedia Famosa en dos Partes, Harvard Univ, 74; auth, Who Wrote the Segundu Parte of la Hija del aire?, Rev Belge de Philol et d'Hist, 76; coauth, Enriquez Gomez et Fernandes de Villareal: Deux Destins Paralleles, une Vision Politique Commune, Rev des Etudes Juires et Memoires, 77; Raimundo Lida's contribution to Quevedo Studies, Actas del simposium in Boston para el cuatrocentenario de Quevedo, 82; Dos versiones de un texto de Antonio Enriquez Gomez: Un caso de autocensura, Nueva Revista de Filologia Hispanica, 82. *Mailing Add:* Dept of Mod Lang Northeastern Univ Boston MA 02115

ROSE, ERNST (ANDREAS GOTTLIEB), b Sangerhausen, Ger, June 18, 99; nat US; m 29; c 2. LITERATURE. *Educ:* Univ Leipzig, PhD, 22. *Prof Exp:* Instr Ger, Brearley Sch, NY, 24-25; from instr to prof, Ger, 25-66, instr math, Army Specialized Training Prog, 43, chmn dept Ger, 48-65, head all-univ dept Ger lang & lit, 58-65, EMER PROF GER, NY UNIV, 66- *Concurrent Pos:* vis prof Ger, Univ Calif, Davic, 67-68. *Mem:* MLA; Am Asn Teachers Ger. *Res:* German and comparative literature; relations between German and Chinese literature; Goethe. *Publ:* Auth, Charles Follen, Neue deutsche Biog, 61; Faith From the Abyss: Hermann Hesse's Way From Romanticism to Modernity, NY Univ, 65; coauth, Grosse Vergangenheit, Scribner's, 69; auth, Frederick Heuser, Neue deutsche Biog, 72; contribr, Grimmelshausen and other articles, In: Dizionario Critico della Letteratura Tedesca, Unione Tipografico, Italy, 76; auth, Shakespeare auf der deutschen Bühne unserer

Tage, Theatrum Mundi, 80; Camillo von Klenze, Neue deutsche Biog, 80; Blick nach Osten: Studien zum alten Goethe und zum Chinabilde in der deutschen Literatur des 19 Jahrhundert, Language, Bern, 81. *Mailing Add:* 16 Ramapo Terr Fair Lawn NJ 07410

ROSE, GILBERT PAUL, b New York, NY, Aug 6, 39; m 61; c 2. GREEK & LATIN LITERATURE. *Educ:* Univ Calif, Berkeley, Ab, 63, PhD(classics), 69. *Prof Exp:* From instr to assoc prof, 67-81, PROF CLASSICS, SWARTHMORE COL, 81- *Concurrent Pos:* Vis asst prof, Ohio State Univ, 69; Old Dominion Found fel, 70-71; Mellon Found fel, 74-75; vis assoc prof, Univ Calif, Berkeley, 79. *Mem:* Am Philol Asn; AAUP. *Res:* Homer; Greek tragedy; Latin epic poetry. *Publ:* Auth, The Quest of Telemachus, 67, The Unfriendly Phaeacians, 69 & Odyssey 15 143-82: A Narrative Inconsistency?, 71 & Odysseus' Barking Heart, 79, Trans Am Philol Asn; The Swineherd and the Beggar, Phoenix, 80; ed, Plato's Crito, 80 & Plato's Symposium, 81, Bryn Mawr Commentaries. *Mailing Add:* Dept of Classics Swarthmore Col Swarthmore PA 19081

ROSE, MARILYN GADDIS, b Fayette, Mo, Apr 2, 30; m 68; c 1. COMPARATIVE LITERATURE. *Educ:* Cent Methodist Col, BA, 52; Univ SC, MA, 55; Univ Mo, PhD(French), 58. *Prof Exp:* Asst French, Univ SC, 54-55; instr, Univ Mo, 55-58; assoc prof comp lit, Stephens Col, 58-68; assoc prof French & comp lit, 68-73, chmn dept, 71-78, PROF COMP LIT, STATE UNIV NY, BINGHAMTON, 73-, DIR, TRANSL PROG, 73- *Mem:* MLA; Northeast Mod Lang Asn; AAUP; Am Comt Irish Studies; Am Transl Asn. *Res:* Anglo-Irish literature; French-American literary relations; translating; tanslation theory and pedagogy. *Publ:* Transl, Villiers de l'Isle-Adam, Axel, Dolmen, 70; auth, Julian Green, 71 & Jack B Keats, 72, Herbert Lang; Katharine Tyan, Bucknell, 75; Translation Specturm, State Univ NY; transl, Villiers de l'Isle-Adam, Eve of the Future Eden, Coronado. *Mailing Add:* Dept of Comp Lit State Univ of NY Binghamton NY 13901

ROSE, PETER WIRES, b Paterson, NJ, May 13, 36. CLASSICAL PHILOLOGY. *Educ:* Williams Col, BA, 57; Harvard Univ, MA, 58, PhD(classics), 67. *Prof Exp:* Lectr classics, Yale Univ, 63-66, asst prof, 66-71; asst prof, Univ Tex, Austin, 71-77; mem fac classics, 77-80, PROF OF CLASSICS, MIAMI UNIV, 80-, CHMN DEPT, 80- *Mem:* Am Philol Asn; AAUP. *Res:* Homer; Greek tragedy; Pindar and Greek lyric poetry. *Publ:* Auth, The myth of Pindar's First Nemean: Sportsmen, poetry, and Paideia, 74 & Sophocles' Philoctetes and the Teachings of the Sophists, 75, Harvard Studies Class Philol. *Mailing Add:* Dept of Classics Miami Univ Oxford OH 45056

ROSE, STANLEY LUDWIG, b Richmond, Ind, Feb 3, 36; m 58; c 2. LUSO-BRAZILIAN & SPANISH LANGUAGE & LITERATURES. *Educ:* Univ Ariz, BA, 58; Univ Wis-Madison, MA, 60, PhD(Port), 69. *Prof Exp:* Actg asst Span & Port, Univ Ore, 65-69, asst prof, 69-72; asst prof Port, NDEA Inst Port, Vanderbilt Univ, 68; asst prof, 72-75, ASSOC PROF SPAN & PORT, UNIV MONT, 75- *Mem:* Am Asn Teachers Span & Port. *Res:* Medieval Portuguese language and literature; modern Brazilian literature. *Publ:* Auth, Alberto de Oliveira, In: Encycl World Lit 20th Century, Ungar, 70; translr, Carta de Doacoa and Foral of Duarte Coelho, In: A Documentary History of Brazil, Knopf, 71; auth, Ancedotal narrative in Fernao Lopes' Cronica de D Pedro I, Luso-Brazilian Rev, 71; The land and the peasant in the novel of the Brazilian Northeast, J Rocky Mt Coun Latin Am Studies, 12/75. *Mailing Add:* Dept of Foreign Lang & Lit Univ of Mont Missoula MT 59812

ROSE, THEODORE E, b Long Island City, NY, May 11, 31. SPANISH, PORTUGUESE. *Educ:* Queens Col, NY, BM, 52; NY Univ, MA, 55,PhD, 59. *Prof Exp:* Teacher English & Am Lit, Brazil-US Cult Union, Sao Paulo, 53-54 & St Paul's Christian Day Sch, 55-56; teacher Span & French, Forest Hills High Sch, NY, 56-59; PROF SPAN, PORT & EDUC, UNIV WIS-MADISON, 59- *Concurrent Pos:* Fulbright award, Spain, 63 & 73; dir, Experienced Teacher Fel Prog Span-Educ, 66-67; bibliogr teacher educ & qualifications, Am Coun Teaching Foreign Lang, 70-; consult & mem adv bd, Span Today, Cruzada Span Publ, 70-; ed, Wis Span Teacher, Univ Wis; chmn test develop comt, Nat Span Exam, Am Asn Teachers Span & Port, 73- *Honors & Awards:* Emil H Steiger Distinguished Teaching Award, Univ Wis-Madison, 75. *Mem:* Am Asn Teachers Span & Port; Am Coun Teachers Foreign Lang; MLA. *Res:* Methods of teaching foreign languages; improvement of student teaching of foreign languages in the secondary school. *Mailing Add:* Dept of Span & Port Univ of Wis Madison WI 53706

ROSEMONT, HENRY, JR, Philosophy, Linguistics. See Vol IV

ROSEN, HAROLD EARL, b LaGrande, Ore, Mar 31, 29; m 53; c 5. ROMANCE LANGUAGES. *Educ:* Brigham Young Univ, BA, 54, MA, 59; Univ Ore, PhD(Romance lang), 66. *Prof Exp:* Instr Span, Univ Ore, 61-63; form asst prof to assoc prof, 63-75, PROF SPAN, BRIGHAM YOUNG UNIV, 75- *Mem:* Rocky Mountain Mod Lang Asn; Am Asn Teachers Span & Port. *Res:* Golden Age theatre; comparative literature. *Publ:* Auth, From Revolution to a Restoration: Romanticism in Spain and Spanish America, Brigham Young Univ, 78. *Mailing Add:* 167 Fac Off Bldg Brigham Young Univ Provo UT 84602

ROSEN, KARL MELTZER DRESNER, b Boston, Mass, Aug 3, 30. LINGUISTICS, CLASSICAL LANGUAGES. *Educ:* Harvard Univ, AB, 52; Yale Univ, MA, 53, PhD(ling), 60. *Prof Exp:* Instr French, Span & Ger, Bates Col, 58-60; instr Romance lang, Rutgers Univ, 60-61; asst prof, 61-75, ASSOC PROF CLASSICS & LING, UNIV KANS, 75- *Concurrent Pos:* Am Coun Learned Soc foreign travel grant, Montepulciano, Italy, 73; Univ Kans grant, 73-74, gen res grant, 76-77 & 77-78. *Mem:* Ling Soc Am; Am Philol Asn; Am Name Soc; MLA. *Res:* Indo-European linguistics; Emile Zola; Renaissance humanism, Politian. *Publ:* Auth, Latin Uncia, Language, 1/64; Community names from personal names in Kansas: Post offices, Names, 3/73; Classical place-names in Kansas, Heritage Kans, 9/75; On chapter LXXI of Politian's Miscellany, Interrogativi dell Umanesimo, Olschki, 76. *Mailing Add:* Dept of Classics Univ of Kans Lawrence KS 66045

ROSEN, NATHAN, b New York, NY, May 14, 20. RUSSIAN LITERATURE. *Educ:* Brooklyn Col, BA, 41; Columbia Univ, MA, 48, PhD(Russ lit), 61; Russ Inst, cert, 55. *Prof Exp:* Asst prof Russ & English, US Merchant Marine Acad, 58-59; asst prof Russ & Ger, Bowdoin Col, 59-60; lectr Russ, Hunter Col, 61; asst prof, Amherst Col, 62-63; assoc prof, 63-80, PROF RUSS LIT, UNIV ROCHESTER, 80- *Concurrent Pos:* Inter-Univ Comt Travel Grants Study fel, Leningrad State Univ, 61-62; Ford Found grants; Am Coun Learned Soc & Soc Sci Res Coun grant for Slavic & E Europ study, 68. *Mem:* Am Asn Teachers Slavic & East Europ Lang; Am Asn Advan Slavic Studies; Int Dostoevsky Soc. *Res:* Dostoevsky; Chekhov; Gogol. *Publ:* Auth, Style and Structure in The Brothers Karamazov (the Grand Inquisitor and the Russian Monk), Russ Lit Triquart, fall 71; The unconscious in Cexov's Van'ka (with a note on Sleepy), Slavic & East Europ J, winter 71; Why Dmitrii Karamazov did not kill his father, Can-Am Slavic Studies, summer 72; Chekhov's Religion in the Student, Teoria e Critica (Rome), 3-12/73; The magic cards in The Queen of Spades, Slavic and East Europ J, fall 75; The Defective Memory of the Ridiculous Man, Can-Am Slavic Studies, fall 78; The Life Force in Chekhov's The Kiss, Ulbandus Rev, fall 79; Apollon, In: Notes from Underground, Forum Int, fall 80. *Mailing Add:* Dept of Foreign Lang Univ of Rochester Rochester NY 14627

ROSEN, ROBERT SAMUEL, b Vienna, Austria, June 11, 24; m 60; c 2. GERMAN COMPARATIVE LITERATURE. *Educ:* City Col New York, AB, 53; NY Univ, MA, 59, PhD(Ger), 68. *Prof Exp:* Lectr Ger, City Col New York, 64-68, asst prof Ger & Humanities, 68-70; assoc prof Ger & comp lit, Boston Univ, 70-72; assoc prof, 72-78, PROF GER & COMP LIT, BARUCH COL, 78- *Concurrent Pos:* Res grant, City Univ New York, 73-74. *Mem:* MLA; Am Asn Teachers Ger; Asn Professors Yiddish; Asn Jewish Studies. *Res:* Nineteenth century German literature; drama; Yiddish literature. *Publ:* Auth, Emphasis on a way of life, Sat Rev, 12/69; Enslaved by the queen of the night: The relationship of Ingmar Bergmann to E T A Hoffmann, Film Comment, spring 70; E T A Hossmann's Kater Murr: Aufbauformen un Erzaehlsituationen, Bouvier, 70; The fantastic and the real: Selected writings of E T A Hoffmann, Am Scholar, winter 71; introd, Memoirs of Glückel of Hameln, Schocken Bk, 77. *Mailing Add:* Dept of Mod Lang Baruch Col City Univ of New York New York NY 10010

ROSENBERG, AUBREY, b Doncaster, England, Mar 7, 28; Can citizen; m 52; c 1. FRENCH. *Educ:* Univ Toronto, BA, 62, MA, 66, PhD(French), 70. *Prof Exp:* Sr res asst cardio-respiratory physiol, Toronto Gen Hosp, 62-66; lectr, 68-70, asst prof, 70-74, ASSOC PROF FRENCH, VICTORIA COL, UNIV TORONTO, 74- *Concurrent Pos:* Can Coun leave fel, 77-78. *Mem:* Am Soc 18th Century Studies; Can Soc 18th Century Studies; Soc Fr Etude XVIIIe Siecle; North Am Asn Study Jean-Jacques Rousseau. *Res:* Utopias and imaginary voyages; Nicolas Gueudeville and his work (1652-1727); Rousseau. *Publ:* Contribr, The Varied Pattern, Hakkert, 71; Tyssot de Patot and His Work, Nijhoff, The Hague, 72; auth, The temperamental affinities of Rousseau and Levi-Strauss, Queen's Quart, 75; Emile, l'ens ideal, Univ Toronto Quart, 78; Rousseau's Levite d'Ephraim and the Golden Age, Australian J Fr Studies, No 2, 78; A little-known translation of Moriae Encomium, Gueudeville's L'Eloge de la Folie, Erasmus English, 79-80; Rousseau's view of work and leisure in the community, Australian J Fr Studies, No 1, 81; Nicolas Gueudeville and His Work, Nijhoff, The Hague, 82. *Mailing Add:* Victoria Col Univ of Toronto Toronto ON M5S 1K7 Can

ROSENBERG, CHARLES IRA, b Evanston, Ill, Nov 2, 24; m 52; c 1. FRENCH. *Educ:* Stanford Univ, AB, 49; Middlebury Col, MA, 54; Northwestern Univ, PhD, 59. *Prof Exp:* From instr to assoc prof, 56-69, PROF FRENCH, UNIV ARIZ, 69- *Mem:* MLA; Am Asn Teachers Fr; Soc Fr Prof Am. *Res:* Contemporary French literature; literary criticism; phonetics. *Mailing Add:* Dept of Romance Lang Univ of Ariz Tucson AZ 85721

ROSENBERG, DONALD KARL, b Alliance, Ohio, May 3, 42; m 68; c 2. MEDIEVAL GERMAN LANGUAGE & LITERATURE. *Educ:* Princeton Univ, AB, 64; Johns Hopkins Univ, MA, 65; Ohio State Univ, PhD(Ger), 75. *Prof Exp:* Instr English, Hampton Inst, 65-66; Ger master, Episcopal High Sch, Va, 66-67; lectr English, Ohio State Univ, 70-71; ASST PROF GER, DUKE UNIV, 76- *Concurrent Pos:* Prin investr, Nat Endowment for Humanities transl grant, 77-79. *Mem:* MLA; Am Asn Teachers Ger. *Res:* Early autobiography. *Publ:* Auth, German studies for today: Broad boundaries, oblique paths, Die Unterrichtspraxis, 74; Hermann von Sachsenheim's Schleiertüchlein: The Pilgerberch and Ehingen's Reisen nach der Ritterschaft, In: Wege der Wrote: Feschrift für Wolfgang Fleischhauer, Böhlau-Verlag, 78. *Mailing Add:* Dept of Ger Lang & Lit Duke Univ Durham NC 27706

ROSENBERG, JOEL WILLIAM, b Los Angeles, Calif, Apr 13, 43. HEBREW & COMPARATIVE LITERATURE. *Educ:* Univ Calif, Berkeley, BA, 65; Hebrew Union Col, BHL, 68; Univ Calif, Santa Cruz, PhD(hist of consciousness), 78. *Prof Exp:* Vis lectr relig, Univ Calif, Davis, 73-74; vis lectr, Wesleyan Univ, 76-78, vis asst prof, 78-79; ASST PROF HEBREW LANG & LIT, TUFTS UNIV, 80- *Mem:* MLA; Asn Jewish Studies; Soc Bibl Lit; Am Acad Relig. *Res:* Biblical literature; history of biblical interpretation and research; narrative and literary theory. *Publ:* Auth, Jonah and the prophetic vocation, Response 8:2, summer 74; Meanings, morals, and mysteries: Literary approaches to Torah, Response 9:2, summer 75; The garden story forward and backward--the non-narrative dimension of Genesis 2-3, Prooftexts: J Jewish Lit Hist 1:1, 1/81. *Mailing Add:* Dept of Ger & Russian Tufts Univ Medford MA 02155

ROSENBERG, JUSTUS, b Danzig, Poland, Jan 23, 31; US citizen. APPLIED LINGUISTICS. *Educ:* Sorbonne, BA, 46; Univ Calif, Los Angeles, MA, 48; Univ Cincinnati, PhD(comp lit), 50. *Prof Exp:* Assoc prof foreign lang, Univ Dayton, 46-56 & Swarthmore Col, 56-62; PROF FOREIGN LANG, BARD COL, 62- *Concurrent Pos:* Vis prof, Univ Cincinnati, 51-56 & New Sch Social Res, 60-; fel, Columbia Univ, 65-66; vis prof, Nanyang Univ, 66-68; fel lit, Univ Belgrade, 72. *Mem:* AAUP; MLA; Am Acad Polit & Soc Sci. *Res:*

Political commitment in the literature of the 20th century; methodology for teaching of English as a second language. *Publ:* Auth, Constant Factors in Translation, Princeton Univ, 56; Sound and Structure, D Moore, 68. *Mailing Add:* Dept of Foreign Lang Bard Col Annandale-on-Hudson NY 12504

ROSENBERG, SAMUEL NATHAN, b New York, NY, Jan 19, 36. ROMANCE PHILOLOGY, FRENCH LITERATURE. *Educ:* Columbia Univ, AB, 57; Johns Hopkins Univ, PhD(Romance lang), 65. *Prof Exp:* Instr French, Columbia Univ, 61-62; from lectr to asst prof, 62-69, assoc prof, 69-81, dir, Ind-Purdue Foreign Studies Prog, Strasbourg, France, 72-73, PROF FRENCH & ITAL, IND UNIV, BLOOMINGTON, 81, CHMN DEPT, 77- *Mem:* MLA; Mediaeval Acad Am; Am Asn Teachers Fr; Int Courtly Lit Soc; Soc Rencesvals. *Res:* French philology; medieval poetry. *Publ:* Coauth, The onomastics of Pasinetti, Ital Quart, fall 66; transl, Meillet, The Indo-European Dialects, Univ Ala, 68; auth, Modern French ce: The Neuter Pronoun in Adjectival Predication, Mouton, The Hague, 70; co-ed, French Secular Compositions of the Fourteenth Century (3 vols), Am Inst Musicol, 70-73; auth, Observations on the Chanson of Jacques d'Autun, Romania, 75; coauth, Some terms of abuse in Moliere, L'Esprit Createur, 75; co-transl, Ami and Amile, Fr Lit Publ, 80; co-ed, Chanter M'estuet: Songs of the Trouveres, Ind Univ, 81. *Mailing Add:* Dept of French & Ital Ind Univ Bloomington IN 47401

ROSENFELD, SIDNEY, b Philadelphia, Pa, Jan 15, 31; m 59; c 1. GERMAN LITERATURE. *Educ:* Temple Univ, AB, 53; Univ Ill, MA, 58, PhD(Ger), 65. *Prof Exp:* Instr Ger, Univ Ill, 62-63; asst prof, 63-72, ASSOC PROF GER, OBERLIN COL, 72- *Mem:* Am Asn Teachers Ger; MLA. *Res:* Modern German literature; Austrian literature. *Publ:* Auth, Die Magie des Namens in Joseph Roths Beichte Eines Mörders, Ger Quart, 5/67; Joseph Roths Hiob: Glaube and Heimat im Bild des Raumes, J English & Ger Philol, 10/67; Jews in Post-holocause Germany, Europ Judaism, 71. *Mailing Add:* Dept of Ger & Russ Oberlin Col Oberlin OH 44074

ROSENFIELD, LEONORA COHEN, b New York, NY, Feb 14, 09; m 36; c 1. FRENCH LITERATURE. *Educ:* Univ Grenoble, cert French, 28; Sorbonne, dipl French civilization, 29; Smith Col, BA, 30; Columbia Univ, MA, 31, PhD(French), 40. *Prof Exp:* Teacher French, Ethical Cult Schs, New York, NY, 31-33; instr, Smith Col, 34-35; instr, Brooklyn Col, 36-46; from asst prof to assoc prof French, Univ Md, College Park, 47-66, prof, 66-79. *Concurrent Pos:* Asst prof, US Dept Agr Grad Sch, 48-49; Am Coun Learned Soc fac studies fel, 51-52; Univ Md Grad Sch grant, 57; mem bd ed consult, J Hist Philos, 72- *Mem:* Am Soc 18th Century Studies; Soc Fr Etude 18th Century; MLA; Am Asn Teachers Fr; Am Philos Asn. *Res:* French literature; history of ideas in France; history of philosophy. *Publ:* Auth, From Beast-machine to Man-machine, Oxford, 40, 41, rev ed, Octagon, 68; transl, A Koyre, Discovering Plato, Columbia Univ, 45, 60; contribr, Critical bibliography of French literature, Vol 3, Syracuse Univ, 61; auth, Portrait of a Philosopher, Harcourt, 62; Morris R Cohen, In: International Encyclopedia of Social Sciences, 2nd ed, Macmillan, 68; ed with inrod & bibliog, Ignace Gaston Pardies, Discours de la Connoissance des Bestes, Johnson Reprint, 72; contribr, Renaissance Studies in Honor of I Silver, 74; auth, The rights of women in the French Revolution, Studies in 18th Century Cult, 78. *Mailing Add:* 3749 Chesapeake St NW Washington DC 20016

ROSENGARTEN, FRANK, b New York, NY, June 13, 27; m 58; c 2. ITALIAN LANGUAGE & LITERATURE. *Educ:* Adelphi Col, BA, 50; Columbia Univ, MA, 51, PhD, 62. *Prof Exp:* Adelphi Col, 57-59; lectr, Columbia Univ, 59-60; asst prof Ital, Western Reserve Univ, 62-67; lectr, 57-59, assoc prof, 67-76, PROF ROMANCE LANG, QUEENS COL, NY, 76- *Concurrent Pos:* Nat Found for Humanities younger scholars fel, 68. *Mem:* MLA; Am Asn Teachers Ital. *Res:* Contemporary Italian novel; ideological aspects of Italian resistance movement; Italian humanism in the 15th century. *Publ:* Auth, Vasco Pratolini's Una Storia Italiana and the Question of Literary Realism, Italica, 3/63; Vasco Pratolini: The Development of a Social Novelist, Southern Ill Univ, 65; The Italian Anti-Fascist Press (1919-1945), Case Western Reserve Univ, 68; Silvio Trentin dall'interventismo alla Resistenza, Feltrinelli Editore, Milano, 80. *Mailing Add:* Dept of Romance Lang Queens Col Flushing NY 11367

ROSENMEYER, THOMAS GUSTAV, b Hamburg, Ger, Apr 3, 20; nat US; m 51. CLASSICS, COMPARATIVE LITERATURE. *Educ:* McMaster Univ, BA, 44; Univ Toronto, MA, 45; Harvard Univ, PhD, 49. *Prof Exp:* From instr to asst prof classics, State Univ Iowa, 47-52; asst prof, Smith Col, 52-55; from asst prof to prof, Univ Wash, 55-66; PROF GREEK & COMP LIT, UNIV CALIF, BERKELEY, 66- *Concurrent Pos:* Vis prof, Am Sch Class Studies, Athens, 61-62; vis prof, Princeton Univ, fall, 75. *Mem:* Am Philol Asn; Archaeol Inst Am; Class Asn Can; Am Comp Lit Asn; Brit Class Asn. *Res:* Classical Greek literature; Plato; Hellenistic poetry. *Publ:* Translr, Discovery of the Mind, Blackwell, Harvard Univ, 53; auth, The Masks of Tragedy, Univ Tex, 63; coauth, The Meters of Greek and Latin Poetry, Bobbs, 63; auth, The Green Cabinet; Theocritus and the European Pastoral Lyric, Univ Calif, 69; The Art of Aeschylus, Univ Calif, 82; Drama, In: The Legacy of Greece, Oxford, 81. *Mailing Add:* Dept of Classics Univ of Calif Berkeley CA 94720

ROSENTHAL, ALAN STUART, b Baltimore, Md, Dec 22, 38; m 65; c 1. FRENCH, COMPARATIVE LITERATURE. *Educ:* Univ Md, College Park, BA, 59, MA, 61; Rutgers Univ, PhD(French), 70. *Prof Exp:* Teaching asst French, Rutgers Univ, 61-64; instr, Temple Univ, 65-68; from instr to asst prof, 68-78, ASSOC PROF FRENCH, UNIV MD, BALTIMORE COUNTY, 78- *Mem:* MLA; Am Asn Teachers Fr. *Res:* Nineteenth century French literature; French poetry; 19th century Italian literature. *Publ:* Auth, Baudelaire's knowledge of Italian, Romance Notes, 9/72; Merimee and the supernatural: Diversion or obsession?, 19th Century Fr Studies, 5/73; The strategic position of obsession in Les Fleurs de Mal, Romance Notes, 9/74; Foreign literature in the academic supermarket, Foreign Lang Ann, 3/75; Baudelaire's mysterious enemy, 19th Century Fr Studies, 5/76; The theory and poetry of Ennui: Leopardi and Baudelaire, Neophilologus, 7/76; Baudelaire a-t-il/u Leopardi?, Bull Baudelairier, 10/76; Baudelaire and Leopardi: An affinity in anguish, Essays Lit, 11/76. *Mailing Add:* Dept of Mod Lang Univ of Md, Baltimore Co Baltimore MD 21228

ROSENTHAL, CHARLOTTE JOY, b New York, NY, May 16, 43; m 78. RUSSIAN LITERATURE & LANGUAGE. *Educ:* Cornell Univ, BA, 64; Univ Chicago, MA, 67; Stanford Univ, PhD(Russ), 79. *Prof Exp:* Instr, Univ Utah, 76-78 & Guilford Col, 78-80; ASST PROF RUSS, UNIV HAWAII, MANOA, 81- *Mem:* MLA; Am Asn Teachers Slavic & East Europ Lang. *Res:* Russian literature of the Silver Age; Russian folklore; Russian language teaching. *Publ:* Auth, Science versus the imagination: Russia at the turn of the century, Guilford Rev, spring 79; Term projects in Russian language courses, Am Asn Teachers Slavic & East Europ Lang Newslett, 12/80; coauth, Symbolic patterning in Sologub's Melkij bes, Slavic & East Europ J, spring 82; auth, Remizov's Posolon and Limonar: Folklore in modernists prose, Russ Lit Triquart, Vol 18 (in prep). *Mailing Add:* Dept of Europ Lang & Lit Univ of Hawaii Manoa Honolulu HI 96822

ROSENTHAL, FRANZ, b Berlin, Ger, Aug 31, 14; nat US. ARABIC & SEMITIC LANGUAGES. *Educ:* Univ Berlin, PhD, 35. *Prof Exp:* Asst prof Semitics, Hebrew Union Col, 40-48; from assoc prof to prof Arabic, Univ, Pa, 48-56; Rabinowitz prof semitic langs, 56-67, STERLING PROF NEAR EASTERN LANG, YALE UNIV, 67- *Concurrent Pos:* Guggenheim fel, 46-47. *Honors & Awards:* Levi Della Vida Medal, Univ Calif, Los Angeles, 77. *Mem:* Am Philos Soc; Am Acad Arts & Sci; Am Orient Soc. *Res:* Muslim civilization; Arabic languages and literature; Semitic philology. *Publ:* Auth, A History of Muslim Historiography, 52, 68, The Muslim Concept of Freedom, 60, Knowledge Triumphant, 70 & The Herb: Hashish versus Muslim Soc, 71, Leiden; Ibn Khaldun: The Mugaddimah, Bollingen Ser, 58, 67; Gambling in Islam, Leiden, 75. *Mailing Add:* Dept of Near Eastern Lang & Lit Grad Sch Yale Univ New Haven CT 06520

ROSES, LORRAINE ELENA, b New York, NY; m 81; c 4. SPANISH. *Educ:* Mt Holyoke Col, BA, 65; Harvard Univ, MA, 66, PhD(Romance lang & lit), 74. *Prof Exp:* Lectr English & Span, Tel Aviv Univ, 69-71; instr Span, Mt Holyoke Col, 71-74, asst prof, 74-75; asst prof, Boston Univ, 75-77; asst prof, 77-81, ASSOC PROF SPAN, WELLESLEY COL, 81- *Mem:* MLA; Am Asn Teacher Span & Port; North East Mod Lang Asn; Asn Caribbean Studies. *Res:* Spanish American literature. *Publ:* Auth, Lino Novas Calvo: A sense of the preternatural, Symp, fall 75; Myth montage in a contemporary Puerto Rican tragedy, Latin Am Lit Rev, fall-winter 75; El realismo magico en la critica hispanoamericana, J Span Studies: 20th Century, Vol 4, No 3; La epoca espanola de Lino Novas Calvo: 1936-1939, Chasqui, 5/77; Affirmation of black heritage in Arrin's Mascara puertorriquena, Studies Afro-Hisp Lit, Vol I, 77; La expresion de la inconformidad en la dramaturgia femenina, spring 82 & Entrevista con Elena Poniatowska, spring 82, Plaza. *Mailing Add:* Span Dept Wellesley Col Wellesley MA 02181

ROSIER, JAMES LOUIS, English Literature & Philology. See Vol II

ROSIVACH, VINCENT JOHN, b Jersey City, NJ, May 8, 40; m 66; c 2. CLASSICAL PHILOLOGY. *Educ:* Fordham Univ, AB, 61, MA, 64, PhD(classics), 66. *Prof Exp:* Adj instr Latin, Sch Educ, Fordham Univ, 63-64; from instr to assoc prof, 65-76, PROF CLASSICS, FAIRFIELD UNIV, 76- *Mem:* Am Philol Asn; Class Asn New Eng. *Res:* Greek and Roman drama; ancient history. *Publ:* Auth, Plautine stage settings, Trans & Proc Am Philol Soc, 70; Manuscripts of Matthias Corvinus in the Barberini Collection, Manuscripta, 71; Terence, Adelphoe 155-9, Class Quart, 73; Terence, Adelphoe 60-63, Class Philol, 75; The first stasimon of the Hecuba, Am J Philol, 75; Sophocles' Ajax, Class J, 76; Hector in the Rhesus, Hermes, 77; Earthborns and Olympians: The parodos of the Ion, Class Quart, 77. *Mailing Add:* Dept of Classics Fairfield Univ Fairfield CT 06430

ROSOFF, GARY H, b New York, NY, July 3, 43; m 69; c 1. ROMANCE LANGUAGES, LINGUISTICS. *Educ:* City Col New York, BA, 65; Columbia Univ, MA, 67, PhD(Romance ling), 70. *Prof Exp:* Instr French, LI Univ, 67-69; asst prof Romance Lang, Roanoake Col, 70-72; ASST PROF ROMANCE LANG, BERNARD BARUCH COL, 72- *Honors & Awards:* Medal, French Cult Serv, 64. *Mem:* MLA; Am Asn Fr Teachers; Am Asn Span & Port; Pedag Sem Romance Philol; Southeast Conf Ling. *Res:* Romance diachrony; phonology; language methods. *Publ:* Auth, The definite article: The distinctive feature approach to the development of a plural noun marker, 9/73 & The phonetic framework of the universal sound correlates in Romance vowel diachrony (in press), Linguistics; The function of liaison as a correlate of plurality in spoken French, Can Mod Lang Rev, 74. *Mailing Add:* Dept of Romance Lang Bernard Baruch Col New York NY 10011

ROSS, ALAN CHARLES MOFFATT, b Hamilton, Ont, June 4, 13; m 41, 50; c 3. FRENCH. *Educ:* McMaster Univ, BA, 35, MA, 36; Univ Toronto, PhD, 53. *Prof Exp:* From asst prof to prof French, Victoria Col, Univ Toronto, 47-78, registr, 63-78; RETIRED. *Res:* Criticism; French Canadian; 17th century French literature. *Publ:* transl, P Bourdieu, The Algerians, 62 & G Bachelard, The Psychoanalysis of Fire, 63, Beacon; A Raynauld, The Canadian Economic System, Macmillan, Toronto, 67. *Mailing Add:* 3183 Shappard Ave Tronto ON M1S 1T0 Can

ROSS, JAMES FRANCIS, Religion. See Vol IV

ROSS, ROBERT CHRISTOPHER, b Oakland, Calif, Aug 26, 38; m 61; c 2. CLASSICAL PHILOLOGY, ANCIENT HISTORY. *Educ:* Univ Chicago, AB, 60, AM, 61; Univ Calif, Berkeley, PhD(class philol), 71. *Prof Exp:* From instr to asst prof, 67-73, ASSOC PROF CLASSICS & CHMN DEPT, UNIV WIS-MILWAUKEE, 73- *Mem:* Am Philol Asn; Archaeol Inst Am. *Res:* Greek and Latin lexicography; Greek history; Greek and Latin literature. *Publ:* Auth, Thespian Inscriptions, Hesperia, 68; Catullus 63 and the Galliambic meter, Class J, 69; Ambon/ambe, Latin umbo, Glotta, 71. *Mailing Add:* 2959 N Stowell Milwaukee WI 53211

ROSS, WILLIAM BRAXTON, JR, b Denver, Colo, Aug 31, 31; m 54; c 2. MEDIEVAL LATIN, LATIN PALEOGRAPHY. *Educ:* Williams Col, BA, 53; Univ Geneva, cert French, 57; Harvard Univ, MAT, 60; Univ Colo, Boulder, MA, 62, PhD(hist), 64. *Prof Exp:* Res asst Latin palaeography, Inst

Advan Studies, Princeton, NJ, 64-68; asst prof medieval hist, 68-74, ASSOC PROF CLASSICS, UNIV CHICAGO, 74- *Concurrent Pos:* Am Coun Learned Socs fel, 71-72; Fulbright-Hays sr res fel, Italy, 72; Inst Advan Studies, Princeton, 74-75. *Mem:* Medieval Acad Am. *Res:* Latin manuscript books; transmission of ancient texts to circa 1500. *Publ:* Contribr, Codices Latini Antiquiores, Oxford, Vol XI, 66 & Suppl, 71; auth, Giovanni Colonna, historian at Avignon, Speculum, 70; The Latin Manuscript Book, Univ Chicago, 73. *Mailing Add:* Dept of Classics Univ of Chicago 1126 E 59th St Chicago IL 60637

ROSSBACHER, PETER GEORG, b Berlin, Ger, Feb 20, 28; US citizen; m 58; c 3. RUSSIAN LANGUAGE & LITERATURE. *Educ:* Univ Kiel, PhD(Slavic lang & lit), 59. *Prof Exp:* Lectr Russ, Univ Tex, Austin, 60-61; asst prof, Univ Calif, Riverside, 61-64; assoc prof mod lang, Jamestown Col, 64-66; assoc prof Russ, Univ Hawaii, 66-68; assoc prof, 68-76, PROF RUSS, FOREIGN LANG & LIT, ORE STATE UNIV, 76- *Mem:* Philol Asn Pac Coast; MLA. *Publ:* Auth, Nature and the quest for meaning in Chekhov's stories, Russ Rev, 10/65; Solzhenitsyn's Matrena's home, Etudes Slaves et Est-Europeennes, 67; Chekhov's fragment Solomon, Slavic & EEurop J, 68. *Mailing Add:* Dept of Mod Lang Ore State Univ Corvallis OR 97331

ROSSEL, SVEN HAKON, b Bangkok, Thailand, Oct 25, 43; Denmark citizen. SCANDINAVIAN LANGUAGES & LITERATURE. *Educ:* Univ Copenhagen, Denmark, PhD(comp lit), 68. *Prof Exp:* Ed, Artemis Publ Co, Copenhagen, 66-68; asst prof Danish, Univ Hamburg, West Germany, 68-69 & Univ Kiel, West Germany, 69-71; res fel, Univ Copenhagen, Denmark, 71-74; assoc prof Scand lang & lit, 74-80, PROF SCAND & COMP LANG & LIT, UNIV WASH, 80-, CHMN, SCAND DEPT, 81- *Concurrent Pos:* Trustee, Nordic Heritage Mus, Seattle, 80. *Honors & Awards:* Writers' Award, State Wash, Olympia, 81. *Mem:* Soc Advan Scand Studies; Int Asn Scand Studies; Arbeitsgemeinschaft Norden-Deut; Danish Folklore Soc; Medieval Asn Pac. *Res:* Medieval balladry; Modern Scandinavian and European literature; European romanticism. *Publ:* Auth, Den Litterare Vise i Folketraditionen, Akad Forlag, 71; Skandinavische Literatur 1870-1970, Verlag W Kohlhammer, 73; Dansk Litteratur Mellem Holberg og Ewald, Gyldendal, 75; coauth, Danmarks Gamle Folkeviser, Vol 12, Akad Forlag, 76; co-ed, Hans Christian Andersen's Tales and Stories, Univ Wash Press, 80; auth, A History of Scandinavian Literature 1870-1980, Univ Minn Press, 82; ed, Scandinavian Ballads, Dept Scand, Univ Wis, 82; auth, Johannes V Jensen, Twayne (in prep). *Mailing Add:* Scand Dept Univ of Wash Seattle WA 98195

ROSSER, HARRY L ENRIQUE, b Baltimore, Md, July 6, 43; m 67; c 2. LATIN AMERICAN LITERATURE. *Educ:* Col Wooster, BA, 65; Cornell Univ, MA, 67; Univ NC, Chapel Hill, PhD(Latin Am lit & Span), 75. *Prof Exp:* Linguist, Foreign Serv Inst, US Dept State, 67-69; instr, Brandeis Univ, 74-75, asst prof Span, 75-80; ASST PROF SPAN, BOSTON UNIV, 80- *Mem:* MLA; Am Asn Teachers Span & Port; Am Coun Teaching Foreign Lang. *Res:* Latin American novel; Latin American short story; Spanish linguistics. *Publ:* Auth, Las silvas americanas de Andres Bello, Romance Notes, summer 73; Mexican social realism in Mojarro's Bramadero, Hispanofila, fall 77; Form and content in Elena Garro's Los recuerdos del porvenir, Rev Can Estud Hispanicos, spring 78; Testing oral communicative skills, Foreign Lang Ann, fall 78; Social Realism in Novels of Rural Mexico, Crossroads Press, 79. *Mailing Add:* Dept of Span Boston Univ Boston MA 02215

ROSSI, PATRIZIO, b Genoa, Italy, June 16, 30; US citizen; m 64; c 1. ROMANCE LANGUAGES. *Educ:* Northwestern Nazarene Col, BA, 59; Univ Calif, Berkeley, PhD(Romance lang), 66. *Prof Exp:* Instr Romance lang, Northwestern Univ, 63-66; asst prof, 66-74, ASSOC PROF ITAL, UNIV CALIF, SANTA BARBARA, 74- *Concurrent Pos:* Consult ed, Italica, 67-68. *Mem:* MLA; Am Asn Teachers Ital. *Res:* Italian literature from 1700 to the present, particularly 20th century Italian drama; bibliography for film studies. *Mailing Add:* Dept of French & Ital Univ of Calif Santa Barbara CA 93106

ROSSI, VINIO, b Boston, Mass, July 20, 31; m 59. ROMANCE LANGUAGES. *Educ:* City Col New York, BA, 53; Columbia Univ, MA, 58, PhD, 63. *Prof Exp:* Instr French, Columbia Col, Columbia Univ, 58-59; instr French & Ital, 59-67, from assoc prof to prof, 67-78, McCANDLESS PROF FRENCH, OBERLIN COL, 78- *Concurrent Pos:* Vis prof, Case Western Reserve Univ, 66-67 & 68-69. *Mem:* Am Asn Teachers Fr; Am Asn Teachers Ital. *Res:* French 20th century novel; 20th century Italian poetry; the Renaissance in France and Italy. *Publ:* Auth, Andre Gide: The Evolution of an Aesthetic, Rutgers Univ, 67; Andre Gide, Columbia Univ, 68; Beatrice figure in Claudel and Gide, Claudel Studies, spring 77; Intro to Eugennio Montale: The storm and other poems, Field Transl Series, 78. *Mailing Add:* Dept of Romance Lang Oberlin Col Oberlin OH 44074

ROSWELL, MAY M, b Dublin, Ireland, Sept 19, 14; US citizen; m 40; c 6. FOREIGN LANGUAGES. *Educ:* Trinity Col, Dublin, BA, 36; Cambridge Univ, cert, 37; Univ Md, PhD(Ger), 61. *Prof Exp:* Instr foreign lang, Univ Md, College Park, 58-63, asst prof, 63-66, chmn dept, 70-73, ASSOC PROF FOREIGN LANG, UNIV MD, BALTIMORE COUNTY, 66- *Mem:* Am Asn Teachers Fr; Am Asn Teachers Ger; MLA; AAUP. *Res:* French and German literature. *Publ:* Auth, Brecht's first visit to the United States, 67 & Towards fuller use of the language laboratory, 68, Ger Quart; La Gonfle: Martin Du Gard's unstaged farce, Romance Notes, 73. *Mailing Add:* Dept of Foreign Lang Univ of Md, Baltimore County Baltimore MD 21228

ROTH, MARIA, b Munich, Ger; US citizen. GERMAN LANGUAGE & LITERATURE. *Educ:* Wayne State Univ, BA, 59, MA, 62; Univ Mich, Ann Arbor, PhD(Ger lang & lit), 71. *Prof Exp:* Asst prof, 65-78, ASSOC PROF GER, WAYNE STATE UNIV, 79- *Mem:* MLA; Midwest Mod Lang Asn; Am Asn Teachers Ger; Am Soc Ger Lit 16th & 17th Centuries; Int Arbeitskreis Deutsch Barocklit. *Res:* German baroque literature; German literature of late 18th and early 19th century; criticism. *Publ:* Auth, Mynheer Peeperkorn in the light of Schopenhauer's philosophy, Monatschefte, Vol

LVIII, No 4; contribr biographic-bibliographic articles to Deutsches Literatur-Lexikon, Francke, Bern & Munich, Vol VI-, 78-; auth, Der Philotheus des Laurentius von Schnüffis, 1633-1702, Univ Microfilms Int, 79. *Mailing Add:* Dept of Romance & Ger Lang & Lit Wayne State Univ Detroit MI 48207

ROTH, WOOLFGANG MAX WILHELM, Old Testament. See Vol IV

ROTHBERG, IRVING PAUL, b Philadelphia, Pa, June 8, 21; m 52; c 2. ROMANCE LANGUAGES. *Educ:* Temple Univ, BS, 48; Pa State Univ, MA, 51, PhD(Romance lang), 54. *Prof Exp:* Teacher, Pa Schs, 48-49; instr foreign lang, Univ Conn, 54-58; asst prof Romance lang, Temple Univ, 58-62; assoc prof, 62-67, PROF SPAN, UNIV MASS, AMHERST, 67- *Concurrent Pos:* Fulbright lectr, Colombia, 60; rev ed, Hispania, 57-66, ed-in-chief, 66-74; Am Philos Soc grant, 65; mem, Joint Nat Comt Lang, 71-74. *Honors & Awards:* Caballero de la orden del merito civil, Govt Spain, 77. *Mem:* MLA; Am Asn Teachers Span & Port (pres, 83); Comediantes; New England Mod Lang Asn. *Res:* Spanish Renaissance and Golden Age; Spanish literary criticism; classical influence on Spanish literature. *Publ:* Auth, Hurtado de Mendoza and the Greek epigrams, Hisp Rev; El agente comico de Lope de Vega, Hispanofila; Covarrubias, Gracian und die Griechische Anthologie, In: Das Epigramm, Darmstadt, 69; Lope de Vega and the Greek anthology, Romanische Forschungen, 75; The nature of the solution in El perro del hortelano, Bull Comediantes, 77; Neoclassical Wit and Gracian's Theory of Aqudeza: Epigrammatum, In: Span Transl, Romanische Forschungen, 81. *Mailing Add:* Dept of Hispanic Lang Univ of Mass Amherst MA 01003

ROTHERT, ELAYNE LARSEN, b Paris, Tex, June 9, 16; m 64. FOREIGN LANGUAGES. *Educ:* Univ Tex, BA, 37, MA, 40; Univ Wis, PhD, 58. *Prof Exp:* Teacher English & Span, Oenaville High Sch, Tex, 38 & Roxton High Sch, 38-40; teacher English & French, Paris High Sch, 40-47; instr French & Span, Del Mar Col, 47-56; assoc prof French, Winthrop Col, 58-59; asst prof, Tex Woman's Univ, 59-61; assoc prof French & chmn dept, Hanover Col, 61-80; RETIRED. *Concurrent Pos:* Lilly Found foreign study fel, 62. *Mem:* Am Asn Teachers Fr; MLA; AAUP. *Res:* Contemporary and medieval French literature; contemporary drama. *Mailing Add:* Dept of French Hanover Col Hanover IN 47243

ROTHRAUFF, CONRAD M, b Lock 4, Pa, Aug 5, 30; m 54; c 3. CLASSICS, ENGLISH. *Educ:* Heidelberg Col, AB, 52; Ohio State Univ, MA, 57; Univ Cincinnati, PhD(classics), 64. *Prof Exp:* Asst instr classics, Ohio State Univ, 56-57; from instr to asst prof, Juniata Col, 57-61; instr, Univ Ky, 63-64; PROF ENGLISH, STATE UNIV NY COL POTSDAM, 64- *Concurrent Pos:* Assoc ed, Names, 65-68, ed, 69-80; consult, Greek-English Dict Proj, Univ NDak, 70- *Mem:* Am Philol Asn. *Res:* Classical philology; ancient philosophy; 18th century literature. *Publ:* Auth, The name Savior as applied to gods and men among the Greeks, 3/66 & translr, Y E Boeglin, A propos les noms des petites rivieres, 6/67, Names; auth, Epicurus, Lucretius and the nominis expers, Festschrift in Honor of J B Rudnyckyj, 74. *Mailing Add:* Dept of English State Univ of NY Col Potsdam NY 13676

ROTHSCHILD, HARRIET DOROTHY, b Englewood, NJ, Apr 6, 27. FRENCH LITERATURE. *Educ:* Wellesley Col, AB, 48; Univ Md, MFS, 50; Columbia Univ, PhD(French), 59. *Prof Exp:* Vis instr French, Colby Col, 60; instr, Queens Col, 60-62; from asst prof to assoc prof, 62-74, PROF FRENCH, UNIV RI, 74- *Concurrent Pos:* Univ RI res grants, 62, 63, & 65. *Mem:* MLA; Am Soc for 18th Century Studies. *Res:* Benoit de Maillet, 1656-1738; 18th century French literature; Francois Leopold Rakoczy II. *Publ:* Auth, Benoit de Maillet's Leghorn letters, 64, Benoit de Maillet's Marseilles letters, 65, Benoit de Maillet's letters to the Marquis de Caumont, 68 & Benoit de Maillet's Cairo letters, 77, Studies on Voltaire & the 18th Century. *Mailing Add:* Dept of Lang Univ of RI Kingston RI 02881

ROTHSCHILD, SUZANNE ARVEDON, b Cambridge, Mass, Aug 13, 29; m 52; c 3. ROMANCE LANGUAGE & LITERATURE. *Educ:* Radcliffe Col, BA, 51; Harvard Univ, MA, 52, PhD, 59. *Prof Exp:* From lectr to asst prof, 54-68, ASSOC PROF FRENCH, HUNTER COL, 68- *Mem:* MLA. *Res:* French literature of the 19th century. *Publ:* Contribr, Second Year French, Ginn, 59; auth, A Critical and Historical Study of Alfred de Musset's Barberine, Imprimerie Admin Centrale, Paris, 62. *Mailing Add:* Dept of Romance Lang Hunter Col City Univ New York 695 Park Ave New York NY 10021

ROUBEY, LESTER WALTER, b Baltimore, Md, Feb 11, 15; m 47; c 1. FRENCH & ITALIAN LANGUAGES & LITERATURES. *Educ:* Johns Hopkins Univ, MA, 36, PhD(Romance lang), 38; Hebrew Union Col, MHL, 47. *Hon Degrees:* DD, Hebrew Union Col, 47. *Prof Exp:* Jr instr Ital, Johns Hopkins Univ, 37; adj prof relig, Franklin & Marshall Col, 51-53; assoc prof French, Kutztown State Col, 61-64; lectr, 66-70, assoc prof French & Ital, 70-82, ASSOC PROF PHILOS, RELIGIOUS STUDIES, LA STATE UNIV, BATON ROUGE, 82- *Mem:* MLA; Am Asn Teachers Fr; Am Asn Teachers Ital; S Cent Mod Lang Asn; AAUP. *Res:* Italian Renaissance literature; 16 and 17th century French literature; history of religions. *Mailing Add:* Dept of Philos La State Univ Baton Rouge LA 70803

ROUDIEZ, LEON SAMUEL, b Bronxville, NY, Nov 18, 17; m 45; c 2. TWENTIETH CENTURY FRENCH LITERATURE. *Educ:* Col Stanislas, France, BS, 36; Paris Law Sch, LLB, 39; Columbia Univ, AM, 40, PhD, 50. *Prof Exp:* Instr, Columbia Univ, 46-50; from instr to assoc prof, Pa State Univ, 50-59; assoc prof French, 59-62, chmn dept, 68-69 & 71-74, PROF FRENCH, COLUMBIA UNIV, 62- *Concurrent Pos:* Managing ed, French Rev, 53-62, ed, 62-65. *Mem:* MLA; Am Asn Teachers Fr. *Res:* Contemporary French novel; essay criticism. *Publ:* Auth, Maurras jusqu'a l'action francaise, Andre Bonne, Paris, 57; Michel Butor, Columbia Univ, 65; French Fiction Today: A New Direction, Rutgers Univ, 72; Twelve points from Tel Quel, Esprit Createur, winter 74; L'Espoir, quarante ans apres, Tel Quel, fall 77; Absalom, absalom: The significance of contradictions, Minn Rev, fall 81; ed & transl, Julia Kristeva, Desire in Language, 80 & transl, Julia Kristeva, Powers of Horror, 82, Columbia Univ. *Mailing Add:* French Dept Columbia Univ New York NY 10027

ROUMAN, JOHN CHRIST, b Tomahawk, Wis, May 1, 26. CLASSICS, LINGUISTICS. *Educ:* Carleton Col, BA, 50; Columbia Univ, MA, 51; Univ Wis-Madison, PhD(classics), 65. *Prof Exp:* Teacher, Seton Hall Prep Sch, NJ, 54-56 & Malverne High Sch, NY, 57-59; res asst Greek epigraphy, Inst Advan Study, Princeton Univ, 62-63; asst prof, 65-71, chmn dept Span & classics, 72-76, ASSOC PROF CLASSICS, UNIV NH, 71-, COORDR CLASSICS DEPT ANCIENT & MOD LANG & LIT, 76- *Mem:* Am Philol Asn; Archaeol Inst Am; Class Asn Can; Mod Greek Studies Asn; Class Asn New England. *Res:* Classical philology, especially Pindar and Homer; modern Greek studies; Byzantine history. *Publ:* Auth, Nominal-Compound Epithets in Pindar: A Linguistic Analysis, Univ Microfilms, 67; coauth, More still on the Trojan Horse, Class J, 4-5/72. *Mailing Add:* Dept of Ancient & Mod Lang & Lit Univ of NH Durham NH 03824

ROUNTREE, BENJAMIN C, b Moultrie, Ga, Aug 13, 27; m 53; c 2. FRENCH. *Educ:* Uni Univ Ga, AB, 53, MA, 55; Yale Univ, PhD, 60. *Prof Exp:* Instr French & Span, Park Col, 56-57; from asst prof to assoc prof French, Univ Pittsburgh, 60-66; assoc prof, 66-80, PROF FRENCH, UNIV MASS, AMHERST, 80- *Concurrent Pos:* Alumni fel, Univ Ga, 54-55; Fulbright scholar, Austria, 56-57; Bois fel, Yale Univ, 57-60; exchange prof English, Univ Haute Bretagne, Rennes, France, 77-78. *Mem:* MLA. *Res:* Seventeenth century French literature; 19th century French novel. *Publ:* Auth, H James--Mme de La Fayette, Studies in Short Fiction, summer 64: Moliere's Dom Garcie de Navarre, Romanic Rev, 10/65; L'image...C-L Philippe, Les Amis de C-L Philippe, 12/67; Malebranche in Renan's development, J Hist Philos, 1/68; Moliere's Remerciment au roi, Romance Notes, 68; Joe Bousquet a Jean de Boschere, Revue d'Hist Litt Religieuse, 3-4/71; Lettres inedites a J de Boschere, Revue de Synthese Hist, 11-12/71; Edmond Dulac a J de Boschere, Litteratures, Toulouse, 73. *Mailing Add:* Dept of Romance Lang Univ of Mass Amherst MA 01002

ROUSE, RICHARD H, Medieval History. See Vol I

ROVINSKY, ROBERT THOMAS, b Brooklyn, NY, June 23, 40; m 66; c 2. SCANDINAVIAN LANGUAGES & LITERATURE. *Educ:* Queens Col, BA, 68; Univ Wash, MA, 69, PhD(Scand lit), 72. *Prof Exp:* Instr, 71-72, ASST PROF GER LANG, UNIV TEX, AUSTIN, 72- *Mem:* Soc Advan Scand Study; Am-Scand Found; Carl Schurz Found. *Res:* Swedish lit (19th-20th centuries); Danish literature; Jewish cultural life in Scandinavia. *Publ:* Auth, The Path to Self-Realization: An Analysis of Lagerkuist's Livet, 1911, Scand Studies, 73; coauth, Nordic Area Studies in North America, Am-Scand Found, 75; coed, The Hero in Scandinavian Literature, Univ Tex, 75; auth, Ibsen and Lagerkuist Revisited, Scand Studies, 78; The Assimilation Theme in Danish Jewish Literature, Congress Proc, Jerusalem, 78; translr, Lars Gustafsson, Forays into Swedish Poetry, Univ Tex, 78; auth, On the Fantastic in Lars Gustafsson's Poetry, Scand Studies, 78; Danish Holocaust Literature, Encycl Judaica, 79. *Mailing Add:* Dept of Ger Lang Univ Tex Austin TX 78712

ROVIRA, ROSALINA REINALDA, b Havana, Cuba, Feb 19, 21; US citizen; m 38; c 1. SPANISH LITERATURE & LINGUISTICS. *Educ:* Univ Havana, PhD(law), 42; Univ Iowa, MA, 68, PhD(Span), 71. *Prof Exp:* Instr Span, Estherville Community Sch, 64-68 & Northern Ill Univ, 68-70: asst prof, 72-74, ASSOC PROF SPAN & CHMN DEPT MOD LANG, TEX A & I UNIV, 74- *Mem:* MLA; Am Asn Teachers Span & Port: Am Asn Univ Women. *Res:* Linguistic; contemporary Spanish novel. *Publ:* Contribr, Antologia comentada del modernismo, Calif State Univ, 74. *Mailing Add:* Dept of Mod Lang Tex A & I Univ Kingsville TX 78363

ROVNER, PHILIP, b Philadelphia, Pa, Feb 16, 12; m 36. FOREIGN LANGUAGES. *Educ:* George Washington Univ, BA, 48, MA, 49: Univ Md, PhD(Span lit), 58. *Prof Exp:* ASSOC PROF SPAN, UNIV MD, COLLEGE PARK, 50- *Mem:* MLA; Am Asn Teachers Span & Port. *Res:* Spanish and Latin American literature; methods and materials in teaching foreign languages; Golden Age and 18th century Spanish literature. *Publ:* Auth, A syllabic classification of the Moroccan Arabic verb, An Nashra, 6/70. *Mailing Add:* Dept of Span & Port Univ of Md College Park MD 20742

ROWE, GALEN OTTO, b Wenatchee, Wash, June 22, 37; m 62; c 2. CLASSICS, COMPARATIVE LITERATURE. *Educ:* David Lipscomb Col, AB, 59; Vanderbilt Univ, PhD(comp lit), 63. *Prof Exp:* Asst prof classics & comp lit, Univ Southern Calif, 63-65; from asst prof to assoc prof classics, Univ Iowa, 65-77; PROF FOREIGN LANG & CLASSICS & CHMN DEPT, UNIV IDAHO, 77-, ASST VPRES RES & ACAD AFFAIRS, 80- *Mem:* Am Philol Asn; Classics Asn Midwest & S. *Res:* Ancient rhetoric; Greek and Latin prose. *Publ:* Auth, The adynaton as a stylistic device, Am J Philol, 65; The portrait of Aeschines in the Oration on the Crown, Trans Am Philol Asn, 66; coauth, Demosthenes' On the Crown, A Critical Case Study of a Masterpiece of Ancient Oratory, Randon & Knopf, 67. *Mailing Add:* Dept of Foreign Lang & Lit Univ of Idaho Moscow ID 83843

ROWLAND, ROBERT, JR, Classical Languages. See Vol I

ROY, BRUNO, b Quebec, Can, Aug 8, 35. LITERATURE. *Educ:* Univ de Montreal, PhD(sci medievales), 69. *Prof Exp:* Lectr French, Carleton Univ, 66-67, asst prof, 67-68; charge d'enseignement, 68-69, prof adjoint, 69-73, PROF AGREGE LIT MEDIEVALE, INST D'ETUDES MEDIEVALES, MONTREAL, 73- *Mem:* Medieval Acad Am; Int Courtly Lit Soc. *Res:* Medieval French literature; didactic literature; history of sexuality. *Publ:* Auth, L'Art d'amours, E J Brill, 74: Arnulf or Orleans and the Latin comedy, Speculum, 74: Devinettes Francaises du Moyen Age, Montreal, Paris, 77; ed, L'erotisme au Moyen Age, Ed de l'Aurore, Montreal, 77; La devinette du benedicite et les distiques du Pseudo-Caton, Florilegium, Vol 1, 79; The household almanac as magic kit, J Pop Cult, Vol 14, 80; L'initiation sexuelle de Gargantua, Revue quebecoise de sexologie, Vol 1, 80; Maitre Pathelin, avocat portatif, Treteaux, Vol 2, 80. *Mailing Add:* Inst d'etudes medievales 2910 Edouard-Montpetit Montreal PQ H3C 3J7 Can

ROY, DAVID TOD, b Nanking, China, Apr 5, 33; US citizen; m 67. HISTORY, FAR EASTERN LANGUAGES. *Educ:* Harvard Univ, AB, 58, AM, 60, PhD(hist, Far Eastern lang), 65. *Prof Exp:* Asst prof Chinese lit, Princeton Univ, 63-67; assoc prof, 67-73, PROF CHINESE LIT, UNIV CHICAGO, 73- *Concurrent Pos:* NDEA-Fulbright-Hays advan res grant, Japan, 67. *Mem:* Asn Asian Studies; Chinese Lang Teachers Asn, MLA. *Res:* Chinese history and literature. *Publ:* Auth, The Theme of the Neglected Wife in the Poetry of Ts'ao Chih, J Asian Studies, 11/59; Kuo Mo-jo: The Early Years, Harvard Univ, 71. *Mailing Add:* Dept of Far Eastern Lang & Civilizations Univ of Chicago Chicago IL 60637

ROY, GEORGE ROSS, English, Comparative Literature. See Vol II

ROY, GILBERT WILFRID, b Holyoke, Mass, Dec 3, 37; m 59; c 2. LANGUAGE, LINGUISTICS. *Educ:* Univ Calif, Berkeley, BA, 63, MA, 67, PhD(orient lang), 72. *Prof Exp:* Asst prof, 69-74, asst dean Col Arts & Sci, 76-79, dir EAsia Ctr, 80-82, ASSOC PROF CHINESE & LING, UNIV VA, 74-, CHAIRPERSON ORIENT LANG, 79- *Concurrent Pos:* Asst dir res grants, Nat Endowment for Humanities, 75-76. *Mem:* Am Orient Soc; Asn Asian Studies; Am Coun Teaching Foreign Lang; Chinese Lang Teachers Asn (chmn, 81-82). *Res:* Middle Chinese and early Mandarin phonology; Mongolian phonology, classical to modern; Chinese semasiology. *Publ:* Auth, The Importance of Sui and T'ang Canal Systems, 63 & co-ed, A Seminar on the MuTanT'ing, 65, Phi Thete Papers: Teaching the blind to read and write Chinese, J Chinese Lang Teachers Asn, 10/74. *Mailing Add:* Dept of Orient Lang Univ of Va Charlottesville VA 22903

ROY, JOAQUIN, b Barcelona, Spain, July 9, 43; m 71; c 1. LATIN AMERICAN LITERATURE, LINGUISTICS. *Educ:* Georgetown Univ, MS, 70, PhD(Span), 73. *Prof Exp:* Instr Span, Am Sch Barcelona, 65-67, Gilman Sch, Baltimore, Md, 67-68 & Johns Hopkins Univ, 69-71; instr, Emory Univ, 71-73, asst prof & dir Latin Am Studies, 73-76; ASSOC PROF FOREIGN LANG & LATIN AM STUDIES, UNIV MIAMI, 76- *Concurrent Pos:* Orgn Am States res fel, 77-78. *Mem:* Southern Conf Lang Teaching; MLA; Am Asn Teachers Span & Port; Ling Soc Am; Am Conf Teaching Foreign Lang. *Res:* Argentine literature; Latin American essay and fiction. *Publ:* Auth, Claves de Cortazar, Revista Iberoamericana, 73; co-ed, Inteligentzia USA, El Urogallo, 74; auth, Argumento factico, Sin Nombre, 74; Julio Cortazar ante su sociedad, Peninsula, Barcelona, 74; Fantasia y realidad, Ann Lit, 74; ed, Escritores Hispanoamericanos, El Urogallo, Madrid, 75; Narrativa y critica de Nuestra America, Castalia, Madrid, 78; auth, Martinez Estrada y los Estados Unidos, Revista Interamericana, 78. *Mailing Add:* Dept of Foreign Lang Univ of Miami Coral Gables FL 33124

ROY, PAULETTE B, b Orleans, France, Apr 19, 23; US citizen. FRENCH. *Educ:* Univ Paris, lic es let, 43; City Univ New York, PhD(French), 70. *Prof Exp:* Prof English, Lycee Orleans, France, 44-46 & Lycee Berlin, Ger, 46-48; conf interpreter, Int Orgn, Paris, 49-54; tech writer, Westinghouse Elec Int Co, 54-57; conf interpreter, Dept State, 57-60; PROF FRENCH, INST ALLIANCE FRANCAISE, NEW YORK, 60- *Concurrent Pos:* Asst prof Romance lang, Muhlenberg Col, 67-68; lectr French, City Col New York, 68-69. *Mem:* Int Asn Lit Critics; Am Asn Teachers Fr. *Res:* Contemporary French literature; women's studies; linguistics. *Publ:* Coauth, Le Francais pratique, Vol I, 65, rev ed, 72, Vol II, 72, Fr Bk Guild; auth, Pierre Boulle et son Oeuvre, 70 & Jean-Louis Curtis romancier, 71, Juilliard, Paris; coauth, Principes de la methode, 73, auth, Semantics, 76 & Lectures & Devinettes, 77, Fr Bk Guild. *Mailing Add:* 215 W 78th St New York NY 10024

ROYLE, PETER, b Coventry, England, May 16, 34; m 60: c 2. FRENCH. *Educ:* Oxford Univ, BA, 57, MA, 62; Univ Natal, PhD, 68. *Prof Exp:* Lang asst English, Col Pierre-Puget, Marseille, 57-58; master music, Bablake Sch, Coventry, 58; lectr French, Univ Natal, 59-66; from asst prof to assoc prof, Mem Univ Nfld, 66-69, assoc prof, 69-76, PROF FRENCH & CHMN DEPT, CHAMPLAIN COL, TRENT UNIV, 76- *Concurrent Pos:* Can Coun leave fel, 73-74. *Mem:* Mod Humanities Res Asn, Gt Brit; Asn Can Univ Teachers Fr. *Res:* Twentieth century French literature, particularly existentialism. *Publ:* Auth, Historical inevitability and the Sino-Soviet debate, Polit Quart, London, 7/63; Egoism and the prereflexive Volo, Humanities Asn Bull, spring 70; The ontological significance of Les mouches, Fr Studies, 1/72; Sartre: L'enfer et la liberte, Etude de Huis clos et des Mouches, Laval Univ, 73. *Mailing Add:* Champlain Col Trent Univ Peterborough ON K9J 7B8 Can

ROZUMNYJ, JAROSLAV, b Honcharivka, Ukraine, Sept 6, 25; Can citizen; m 62; c 4. UKRAINIAN & RUSSIAN LANGUAGE & LITERATURE. *Educ:* Ukrainian Cath Sem, Holland, BA, 51; Univ Ottawa, MA, 58, PhD(Slavic studies), 68. *Prof Exp:* Lectr Ukrainian & Russ, Laurentian Univ, 60-63; asst prof Russ, Western Mich Univ, 63-64; asst prof Ukrainian, 64-71, ASSOC PROF UKRAINIAN, UNIV MAN, 71-, HEAD DEPT SLAVIC STUDIES, 76- *Concurrent Pos:* Vis prof, Dept Slavic Studies, Univ Ottawa, 72-73; film adv doc, Ukrainians in Quebec, 1890-1945, 76-79; mem, Aid Publ Comt, Can Fedn for Humanities, 79-82; ed, Ukrainian Acad Arts & Sci Can, 81- *Mem:* Can Asn Slavists; Ukrainian Acad Arts & Sci Can (pres, 76-79); Can Inst Ukrainian Studies; Ukrainian Hist Soc. *Res:* Poetry of Leonid Kyselov; Ivan Drach: yesterday and today; Ukrainian reader: advanced and scientific. *Publ:* Contribr, The Style and Language of O Kobylianska, Naukove Tovarystvo im Shevchenka, 72; Conflicting Ideals in L Ukrainka's Stone Host, Slovo Symp, 73; Etymologies of Proper Names in P Berynda's Lexicon of 1627, Ukrainian Free Acad Sci Can, 76; Byzantinism and idealism in the aesthetic views of T Shevchenko, Can Slavonic Papers, 77; Orchard Lamps by Ivan Drach, Sheep Meadow Press, 78; Drach Ivan Fedorovych, Mod Encycl Russ & Soviet Lit, 82; Myths and Antimyths in L Kyselov's Poetry, Studia ucrainica, 82. *Mailing Add:* 801 Cambridge St Winnipeg MB R3M 3G3 Can

RUBENSTEIN, HERBERT, b Philadelphia, Pa, Dec 24, 20; m 43; c 2. PSYCHOLINGUISTICS, LINGUISTICS. *Educ:* Univ Pa, BA, 42, MA, 43; Columbia Univ, PhD(Slavic ling), 49. *Prof Exp:* Instr Moroccan & Arabic, Army Specialized Training Prog, Univ Pa, 42-43, linguist Japanese, 45-46; linguist-in-charge Russ & Polish, Ind Univ, Bloomington, 43-44; UNRRA, Washington, DC, 44-45; from instr to asst prof Russ, Ger & ling, Mich State Univ, 49-55; educ specialist, Air Force Personnel & Training Res Ctr, Maxwell AFB, 55-58; sci linguist, oper appl lab, US Air Force, Washington, DC & Bedford, Mass, 58-60: supvry res psychol, Decision Sci Lab, Hanscom Field, Bedford, Mass, 60-65, chief infor processing div, 60-65; prof ling, 67-77, adj prof psychol, 72-77, PROF HUMAN DEVELOP, LEHIGH UNIV, 77- *Concurrent Pos:* Consult proposals, NIH, 60- & NSF, 64-; res fel, Ctr Cognitive Study, Harvard Univ, 64-67; vis lectr psycholing, Univ Pa, 68 & NY Univ, 70. *Mem:* Ling Soc Am; Am Psychol Asn; Res English Soc Am; Int Ling Asn. *Res:* Structure of the internal lexicon: sentence comprehension. *Publ:* Coauth, Evidence for phonemic recoding in visual word recognition, J Verbal Learning & Verbal Behav, 71: auth, Some problems of meaning in natural languages, In: Handbook of Communication, Rand McNally, 73; Psycholinguistics: an overview, In: Current Trends in Linguistics, Vol XII, Mouton, The Hague, 74. *Mailing Add:* Dept of Human Develop Lehigh Univ Bethlehem PA 18015

RUBIA-BARCIA, JOSE, b Galicia, Spain, July 31, 14; US citizen; m 45; c 2. MODERN SPANISH LITERATURE. *Educ:* Univ Granada, lic en filos y let, 34. *Prof Exp:* Lectr Span lit, Univ Granada, 35-36 & Princeton Univ, 43-44; from lectr to assoc prof, 47-61, PROF SPAN LIT, UNIV CALIF, LOS ANGELES, 61- *Concurrent Pos:* Guggenheim fel, 61. *Honors & Awards:* National Book Award for Translation, with Clayton Eshleman, 79. *Mem:* MLA. *Res:* Spanish civilizaion; Spanish theater. *Publ:* Auth, Tres en Uno, La Veronica, Habana, 40; Umbral de Suenos, Orbe, Los Angeles, 61; Lengua Y Cultura, Holt, 67; Unamuno, Creator and Creation, 67 & ed, Americo Castro and the Meaning of Spanish Civilization, 76, Univ Calif; auth, Prosas de Razon y Hiel, Casuz, Caracas, 76; co-transl, Cesar Vallejo - The Complete Posthumous Poetry, Univ Calif, 78; auth, Cantigas de Bendizer, Castro, Sada, Spain, 81. *Mailing Add:* Dept of Span & Port 5305 Humanities Bldg Univ of Calif Los Angeles CA 90024

RUBIN, DAVID LEE, b Indianapolis, Ind, Sept 30, 39; m 65. FRENCH LITERATURE. *Educ:* Univ Tenn, BA, 62, Univ Paris, cert, 63; Univ Ill, MA, 64, PhD(French), 67. *Prof Exp:* Asst French, Univ Ill, 63-66, instr, 66-67; asst prof, Univ Chicago, 67-69; asst prof, 69-74, assoc, Ctr Advan Studies, 74 & 80-81, assoc prof, 74-82, PROF FRENCH, UNIV VA, 82- *Concurrent Pos:* US ed, Cahiers Maynard, 75-; assoc ed, Purdue Univ Studies Romance Lang, 78-; Guggenheim fel, 80-81. *Mem:* MLA; Am Asn Teachers Fr; Club Francais du Livre; Societe des Textes Francais Modernes. *Res:* Seventeenth century French literature; poetics; the lyric. *Publ:* Auth, Higher, Hidden Order, Univ NC, 72; co-ed & contribr, Papers on French 17th Century Literature, 77-82 & La Coherence interieure, 77, Ed J M Place, Paris; contribr, Critical Bibliography of French literature IIIA, Syracuse Univ, 78; auth, Knot of Artifice, Ohio State Univ, 81; guest ed, Oeuvres et Critiques, 81 & L'Esprit Createur, 82; contribr, Equilibrium of wit, French Forum, 82. *Mailing Add:* Dept of French Lit Cabell Hall 302 Univ of VA Charlottesville VA 22903

RUBIN, MORDECAI S, b Brooklyn, NY, June 20, 30; m 53; c 3. FOREIGN LANGUAGES. *Educ:* Rutgers Univ, AB, 52; Univ Md, PhD, 61. *Prof Exp:* Instr Span, French & Ital, Gannon Col, 56-59: asst prof Spanish & French, Wash Col, 59-62; asst prof Romance lang, Clark Univ, 62-65; assoc prof, 65-69, PROF SPAN, TEACHERS COL, COLUMBIA UNIV, 69- *Concurrent Pos:* Lang educ consult, UN, Peace Corps & Teacher Corps. *Mem:* Am Asn Teachers Span & Port; MLA. *Res:* Bilingual education. *Publ:* Translr, Cargo loss prevention, Int Insurance Monitor, 63; auth, Una poetica moderna, Univ Ala & Nat Univ Mex, 66; The image of the language teacher, J English As Second Lang, 68; Toward a modern methodology for teaching Chinese, J Am Asn Teachers Chinese, 68; Considerations home dialect and English teaching Spanish bilinguals, In: Anthology, Louisville Linguistics Conference 1977, Georgetown Univ, 3/78. *Mailing Add:* Dept of Span Teachers Col Columbia Univ New York NY 10027

RUBIN, NANCY FELSON, b Indianapolis, Ind, Jan 21, 43; m 74; c 4. CLASSICS. *Educ:* Univ Cincinnati, BA, 64; Columbia Univ, MA, 65, PhD(Greek & Latin), 72. *Prof Exp:* Vis lectr, 74-75, asst prof, 75-81, ASSOC PROF CLASSICS, UNIV GA, 81- *Concurrent Pos:* Jr fel, Ctr Hellenic Studies, 81-82. *Mem:* Am Philol Asn; Am Inst Archaeol; Women's Class Caucus. *Res:* Pindar; Greek mythology; literary and myth theory. *Publ:* Eco's Semiotics: A Classicists' Perspective, Helios, 78-79; Olympian 7: The toast and the future prayer, Hermes, 80; coauth (with Harriet M Deal), One formula, many meanings and the myth of the aloades, Semiotica, 80; auth, Pindar's creation of Epinician symbols, Class World, 80; coauth (with Harriet M Deal), Some functions of the demophon episode in the Homeric Hymn to Demeter, Quaderni Urbinati di Cultura Classica, 80 ; Radical semantic change in Archilochus, Class J, 81; Rictional representations of poetic efficacy in Pindar's Epinikia, Poetics Today (in prep); Hunting and maturation tales: Odysseus and Meleager, Arethusa (in prep). *Mailing Add:* Dept of Classics Univ of Ga Athens GA 30602

RUBIN, STEVEN JOEL, Comparative & American Literature. See Vol II

RUBINCAM, CATHERINE ISOBEL REID, b Belfast, UK, Aug 23, 43; Can citizen; m 74. ANCIENT GREEK HISTORY & LITERATURE. *Educ:* Univ Toronto, BA, 64; Oxford Univ, Eng, BA, 66; Harvard Univ, PhD(class philol), 69. *Prof Exp:* asst prof, 69-80, ASSOC PROF CLASSICS, ERINDALE COL, UNIV TORONTO, 80- *Concurrent Pos:* Can Coun leave fel, 76-77. *Mem:* Am Philol Asn; Can Soc Cult & Intellectual Hist; Class Asn Can; Asn Ancient Hist. *Res:* Ancient Greek history and historiography; Diodorus Siculus; history of classical scholarship. *Publ:* Auth, Ephoros, fragment 76, and Diodoros on the Cypriote War, 74 & A note on Oxyrhynchos Papyrus 1610, 76, Phoenix; Thucydidos 1.74.1 and the use of es with numerals, Class Philol, 74: 327-337; Qualification of numerals in the Constitution of Athens, Phoenix, 33: 293-307; Qualification of numerals in Thucydidos, Am J Ancient Hist, 4: 77-95; Horodotus IV: 233.2 and Thucydidos II: 2.1 and 5.8-9: Two versions of the Theban attack on Plataia in 431 BC, Liverpool Class Monthly, 6: 47-49. *Mailing Add:* Dept of Classics Erindale Col Univ of Toronto 3359 Mississauga Rd Mississauga ON L5L 1C6 Can

RUBINO, CARL A, b Syracuse, NY, Jan 1, 42; m 68. CLASSICS, COMPARATIVE LITERATURE. *Educ:* Fordham Univ, AB, 54, MA, 66; Woodstock Col, PhL, 66; State Univ NY Buffalo, PhD(classics), 73. *Prof Exp:* Instr classics, Le Moyne Col, 66-67; asst prof, 71-78, ASSOC PROF CLASSICS, UNIV TEX, AUSTIN, 78- *Concurrent Pos:* Jr fel, Ctr for Hellenic Studies, 74-75. *Mem:* Am Philol Asn; Class Asn Midwest & S. *Res:* Greek and Roman literature; comparative literature; literary criticism and theory. *Publ:* Co-ed, Myth and interpretation, Tex Studies Lit & Lang, spec issue, 74; ed, Essays on prose fiction, Genre, spec issue, 74; auth, Myth & Mediation in the Attis Poem of Catullus, Ramus, 74; Towards a New Dialectic of Language, Sub-Stance, 74; Vis Mea Lex: Social Social Crisis and Political Discourse, Yale Rev, 75; The Erotic World of Catullus, Class World, 75; Lectio difficilior praeferenda est: Some Remarks on Cont French Thought and the Study of Classical literature, Arethusa, 77; Texts and Histories: Classicists, Structuralism, and Jonathan Culler's Structuralist Poetics, Helios, 77. *Mailing Add:* Dept of Classics Univ of Tex Austin TX 78712

RUBIO, NIEVES DEL ROSARIO MARQUEZ, b Cardenas, Matanzas, Cuba, Nov 15; US citizen; m 49; c 3. SPANISH LANGUAGE, LITERATURE. *Educ:* Inst Cardenas, BA, 42, MA, 44; Havana Univ, Dr Pedagogia, 48. *Prof Exp:* Elem teacher, Escuela Premaria #153, Hanava, 49-53; teacher social sci, Escuela Premaria Superior #25, Hanava, 53-60; INSTR SPAN, BAYLOR UNIV, 63- *Concurrent Pos:* Historian, Am Asn Univ Women, Waco Branch, 81-82. *Mem:* SCent Mod Lang Asn; Am Asn Teachers Span & Port; Southwestern Coun Latin Am Studies; Am Asn Univ Women; Asoc Lit Femenina Hisp. *Res:* Spanish writers; Spanish American writers. *Publ:* Auth, Copos de Nieve, J-Tribunal Interbalnearia, 78; Raices y Alas & Una Isla, la Mas Bella, Ediciones Universal, 81; Juego and Busqueda (poems), Asoc Lit Femenina, Letras Femenias, 81; coauth, La Amiga en el Stop (poem), Foro Lit, Montevideo, Uruguay, 81. *Mailing Add:* 3108 Bagby Waco TX 76711

RUBIO, SUSANA GONZALES, b Mallorca, Spain, July 7, 13. SPANISH LANGUAGE & LITERATURE. *Educ:* Inst de San Isidro, Madrid, AB, 31; Univ Madrid, AM, 40, PhD(hist, lit), 44. *Prof Exp:* Asst prof hist, Univ Madrid, 44-50, asst prof hist & lit, 51-52; exchange prof, Stanford Univ, 50-51; asst prof Span lit, Russell Sage Col, 52-56; assoc prof Span, 56-76, prof, 76-80, EMER PROF SPAN, LAKE ERIE COL, 80- *Mem:* MLA; Am Asn Teachers Span & Port. *Res:* Spanish history. *Publ:* Auth, Political aspects of the 19th century in Spain, Hispania, 47. *Mailing Add:* Box 334 Lake Erie Col Painesville OH 44077

RUBULIS, ALEKSIS, b Latvia, Oct 11, 22; US citizen. EAST EUROPEAN LITERATURE. *Educ:* Baltic Univ, MA, 49, PhD, 51. *Prof Exp:* Instr Ger & Russ, Barry Col, 61-62; asst prof, Niagara Univ, 62-65; ASSOC PROF MOD LANG, UNIV NOTRE DAME, 65- *Mem:* MLA. *Res:* East European literature; Russian literature; literature of Soviet republics. *Publ:* Auth, Ar navi uz tu, Skirmants, 54; Via Tua, 56 & Katram says, 56, Kalnajs; Latvia literature, Daugavas Vanags, 64; Baltic literature, Univ Notre Dame, 70. *Mailing Add:* Dept of Mod Lang Univ of Notre Dame Notre Dame IN 46556

RUCH, BARBARA, b Philadelphia, Pa. JAPANESE LANGUAGE & LITERATURE. *Educ:* Earlham Col, BA, 54; Univ Pa, MA, 60; Columbia Univ, PhD(Japanese Studies), 65. *Prof Exp:* From lectr to instr Japanese Lang & Lit, Harvard Univ, 64-66; asst prof, 66-69, ASSOC PROF JAPANESE LANG & LIT, UNIV PA, 69-, DIR INST MEDIEVAL JAPANESE STUDIES, 68- *Concurrent Pos:* Harvard Univ Canaday humanities fund res grant, 66; vis assoc prof, Columbia Univ, 70, 72 & 77; Soc Sci Res Coun grant, 74-; Japan Found grant, 74-75. *Honors & Awards:* Lindback Award, 70. *Mem:* Am Orient Soc; Asn Asian Studies; Asn Teachers Japanese; Chusei Gakkai. *Res:* Medieval Japanese literature and performing arts; medieval Japanese religious and secular picture scrolls; medieval soceity in Japan, 1200-1600. *Publ:* Transl, Origins of the companion library: an anthology of medieval Japanese short stories, J Asian Studies, 5/71; Otogi Zoshi, Dictionary of Orient Lit, Prague, 72; ed, Zaigai Nara ehon--Chusei kinsei emaki ezoshi, Kadokawa Shoten, 81. *Mailing Add:* Dept of Orient Studies Univ of Pa Philadelphia PA 19174

RUCK, CARL ANTON PAUL, b Bridgeport, Conn, Dec 8, 35. GREEK LANGUAGE & LITERATURE. *Educ:* Yale Univ, BA, 58; Univ Mich, Ann Arbor, MA, 59; Harvard Univ, PhD(classics), 65. *Prof Exp:* From instr to assoc prof, 64-76, PROF CLASSICS, BOSTON UNIV, 76- *Mem:* Am Philol Asn. *Res:* Greek tragedy and comedy; Greek mythology; teaching methods for Greek. *Publ:* Auth, IG II1 2323: The List of Victors in Comedy at the Dionysia, Brill, 67; coauth, Pindar: Selected Odes (transl & essays), Univ Mich, 68; auth, Ancient Greek: A New Approach, Mass Inst Technol, 68, 72 & 79; On the sacred names of Iamos and Ion: ethnobotanical referents in the hero's parentage, Class J, 76; Duality and the madness of Herakles, Arethusa, 76; coauth, The Road to Eleusis: Unveiling the Secret of the Mysteries, Harcourt, 78; Mushrooms and Philosophers, 81 & The Wild and the Cultivated: Wine in Euripides' Bacchae, 82, J Ethnopharmacology. *Mailing Add:* Dept of Classics Boston Univ Charles River Campus 745 Commonwealth Ave Boston MA 02215

RUDALL, DAVID NICHOLAS, b Llanelli, SWales, Feb 18, 40; m 65. CLASSICS. *Educ:* Cambridge Univ, BA, 61; Cornell Univ, PhD(classics), 69. *Prof Exp:* Asst prof, 66-73, ASSOC PROF CLASSICS, UNIV CHICAGO, 73-, DIR UNIV THEATRE, 71- *Res:* Aristophanic comedy. *Mailing Add:* Dept of Classics Univ of Chicago Chicago IL 60637

RUDAT, WOLFGANG E H, English & American Literature. See Vol II

RUDAVSKY, TAMAR, b Brooklyn, NY, Sept 10, 51; m 82. MEDIEVAL PHILOSOPHY. *Educ:* Simmons Col, BA, 72; Brandeis Univ, PhD(philos), 76. *Prof Exp:* Asst prof, Trinity Col, Conn, 76-77; ASST PROF PHILOS, OHIO STATE UNIV, 78- *Mem:* Am Philos Asn; Asn Jewish Studies; Soc Medieval & Renaissance Studies; Soc l'Etude Philos Medievale. *Res:* Jewish philosophy; history of philosophy. *Publ:* Auth, Conflicting motifs in Ibn Gabirol's discussion of matter and evil, New Scholasticism, winter 78; The doctrine of individuation in Dons Scotus I, winter 80 & The doctrine of individuation in Dons Scotus II, winter 81, Franzeskanische Studien. *Mailing Add:* Dept Philos Ohio State Univ Columbus OH 43210

RUDD, MARGARET T, b Ponce, PR, Dec 15, 07; US citizen. HISPANIC LITERATURE. *Educ:* Univ Richmond, BA, 29; Columbia Univ, MA, 37. *Prof Exp:* Dean, Blackstone Jr Col, 37-39; teacher Span, Stevens Col, 40-42; asst prof, Westhampton Col, Univ Richmond, 42-45; asst dir, Cult Inst, Concepcion, Chile, 45-46; assoc prof Span, Westhampton Col, Univ Richmond, 58-63, former chmn dept mod foreign lang; Orgn Am States res grant, Chile, 63; RES & WRITING, 63- *Concurrent Pos:* Assoc emer prof, Univ Richmond, Va, 63- *Mem:* Am Asn Teachers Span & Port; World Poetry Soc. *Res:* Spanish and Spanish-American literature. *Publ:* Coauth, Nuestros vecionos mexicanos, Ronald, 45; auth, The Lone Heretic, Univ Tex, 63; contribr, Gabriela Mistral: A voice for America, Soc Educ, 10/70, Neruda-Mistral dialogue, Americas, 5/72 & Augusto iglesias: Ercilla y la Arancana, Bol Acad Chilena, 72; coauth, ... And Three Small Fishes (poems), McClure, 74; auth, The Spanish tragedy of Gabriela Mistral, Romance Notes, 77. *Mailing Add:* 2013 Franklin Ave McLean VA 22101

RUDNYCKYJ, JAROSLAV BOHDAN, b Peremyshl, Galicia, Nov 28, 10; m 43; c 2. SLAVIC PHILOLOGY. *Educ:* Univ Lvov, PhM, 34, PhD, 37; Ukrainian Free Univ Prague, DHabil, 40. *Prof Exp:* Docent, Ukrainian Free Univ Prague, 40-43, extraordinary prof, 43-45; Ukrainian Free Univ Munich, 45-48; from asst prof to prof, 49-77, head dept Slavic studies, 49-76, EMER PROF SLAVIC LANG, UNIV MANITOBA, 77- *Concurrent Pos:* Ed-in-chief, Slavistica, 48-82 & Onomastica, 51-76; consult, Libr Congr, 56 & 77-79; mem, Royal Comn Bilingualism & Biculturalism, Ottawa, 63-71; consult, Nat Libr, Ottawa, 80-81. *Mem:* Am Asn Teachers Slavic & East Europ Lang; Ling Soc Am; Am Name Soc (pres); MLA; Ukrainian Mohylo-Mazepian Acad Sci (pres). *Res:* Comparative Indo-European linguistica; folklore; library science. *Publ:* Auth, Suffixes, -ysce, -ysko, -sko; Geographic names of Bojkovia; Etymological dictionary. *Mailing Add:* #404 5790 Rembrandt Montreal-Cote St Luc PQ H4W 2V2 Can

RUDNYTZKY, LEO DENNIS, b Lviv, Ukraine, Sept 8, 35; US citizen; m 64; c 2. GERMAN & SLAVIC LITERATURES. *Educ:* La Salle Col, BA, 58; Univ Pa, MA, 60; Ukrainian Free Univ, Munich, PhD(Slavic), 65. *Prof Exp:* Prof foreign lang, 63-75, PROF SLAVIC & GER LIT, LA SALLE COL, 75- *Concurrent Pos:* Consult, Cath Renascence Soc, 65-68,; prof, Ukrainian Free Univ, 75; ethic heritage studies grants, 80 & 81; Nat Endowment for Humanities grant, 82. *Mem:* Shevchenko Sci Soc; MLA (secy); Am Asn Teachers Ger; Am Asn Teachers Slavic & EEurop Lang. *Res:* comparative literature; history of Easten churches and Eastern spirituality; the Ukrainian Catholic Church. *Publ:* Coauth, Ukrainian literature, In: New Catholic Encyclopedia, McGraw, 67; auth, Changing aspects of teaching German, In: Study of Foreign Languages, Philos Libr, 68; Ivan Franko and German Literature, Ukrainisches Technisch-Wirtschaftliches Inst, Munich, 74; co-ed, The Ukrainian Catholic Church, 1945-1975, St Sophia, 76; ed, Ukranian Literature, In: Modern Slavik Literatures, Vol II, 76 & contribr, Encyclopedia of World Literature in the 20th Century, 81, Frederick Ungar Publ Co; co-ed, Dictionary of Ukranian Synonyms, Shevchenko Sci Soc, NY, 82. *Mailing Add:* Dept of Foreign Lang & Lit La Salle Col 20th & Olney Ave Philadelphia PA 19141

RUDOLF, OTTOMAR I, b Pforzheim, Ger, Dec 24, 29; US citizen. GERMANIC LANGUAGES, HUMANITIES. *Educ:* Univ Pa, PhD(Ger), 64. *Prof Exp:* From instr to asst prof Ger, Haverford Col, 58-63; from asst prof to assoc prof Ger & Humanities, 63-74, PROF GER & HUMANITIES, REED COL, 74- *Mem:* MLA. *Res:* German theatre; the German Sturm und Drang, J M R Lenz. *Publ:* Coauth, X-mal Deutschland, Harcourt, 68; auth, Jacob Michael Reinhold Lenz: Moralist und Aufklärer, Athenäum, Gehlen, 70. *Mailing Add:* Dept of Ger Reed Col Portland OR 97202

RUDOLPH, CELESTA, b Pittsburgh, Pa, Sept 4, 22. MODERN GERMAN LITERATURE, ENGLISH. *Educ:* Duquesne Univ, BEd, 55; Spalding Col, Ky, MA, 60; Univ Freiburg, WGer, PhD(Ger), 66. *Prof Exp:* Teacher parochial schs, Pittsburgh, Pa, 42-50, teacher Ger, English & hist, pvt high schs, Diocese, 51-61; PROF GER, LA ROCHE COL, 66-, CHAIRPERSON HUMANITIES, 80- *Concurrent Pos:* Nat Endowment for Humanities grant, 75. *Honors & Awards:* Outstanding Educr Am Award, La Roche Col, 72. *Mem:* Am Asn Teachers Ger; Am Coun Teachers Foreign Lang; MLA; Pac State Mod Lang Asn; Am Asn Advan Humanities. *Res:* Faculty development. *Mailing Add:* Dept of German La Roche Col 9000 Babcock Blvd Pittsburgh PA 15237

RUDOLPH, RICHARD CASPER, b San Francisco, Calif, May 21, 09; m 44; c 4. CHINESE CULTURE. *Educ:* Univ Calif, BS, 32, AM, 36, PhD, 42. *Prof Exp:* From res assoc to instr Chinese, Univ Chicago, 37-40; res assoc Orient lang, Univ Calif, 42-43; asst prof Chinese & head Chinese lang sect, US Dept Navy Lang Sch, Univ Colo, 43-45; asst prof Chinese studies, Univ Toronto, 45-46, assoc prof Chinese & actg dir sch Chinese studies, 46-47; assoc prof, 47-52, prof, 52-80, EMER PROF ORIENT LANG, UNIV CALIF, LOS ANGELES, 80- *Concurrent Pos:* Asst keeper Far Eastern Antiq, Royal Ont Mus, 45-47; Fulbright res scholar, China, 48-49 & Formosa, 59-60; Guggenheim fel, Japan, 53 & Formosa, 59-60; Am Philos Soc travel & studies grant, Japan & Korea, 56; consult, Nat Asn Standard Med Vocab, 63-; assoc ed, Monumenta Serica, 63-; Ford fel int & comp studies, Ger, 66; ed, Bibliog Chinese Archaeol, 68-; Am Coun Learned Soc fel, 67-68; Univ Calif Humanities Inst Award, 72; dir, Univ Calif Study Ctr, Chinese Univ Hong Kong, Shatin, 77-79; Ctr Chinese Art & Archaeol fel, 78- *Mem:* Am Orient Soc; Asn Asian Studies; Archaeol Inst Am. *Res:* History of Chinese science, archaeology and printing; classical Chinese; current archaeology in People's Republic of China. *Publ:* Auth, Han Tomb Art of West China, Univ Calif, 51; Chinese Printing Manual, Ritchie, 54; Preliminary notes on Sung archaeology, J Asian Studies, 2/63; Newly discovered painted tombs, Archaeol, autumn 65; Primitive art: Prehistoric Asia, In: Encycl Britannica, 66; The bas-reliefs of Nanyang, Orient Art, summer 78. *Mailing Add:* Univ Calif Study Ctr Chinese Univ Hong Kong Shatin Hong Kong

RUDOWSKI, VICTOR ANTHONY, b Amsterdam, NY, Dec 10, 24. GERMAN LITERATURE, COMPARATIVE LITERATURE. *Educ:* Union Col, BA, 55; Harvard Univ, PhD(Ger), 64. *Prof Exp:* From instr to asst prof Ger, Univ Cincinnati, 62-72; asst prof English, 72-76, ASSOC PROF ENGLISH, CLEMSON UNIV, 76- *Mem:* MLA; Am Coun Teaching Foreign Lang; Am Asn Teachers Ger. *Res:* German literary criticism, especially 18th century aesthetics; Anglo-German literary relations; foreign language teaching methodology. *Publ:* Auth, Action as the essence of poetry: A revaluation of Lessing's argument, PMLA, 10/67; PhD's, Novel prize winners, and the foreign-language requirement, Mod Lang J, 11/68; introd, vocabulary section, The teaching of German: Problems and methods, Nat Carl Schurz Found, 69. *Mailing Add:* Dept of English Clemson Univ Clemson SC 29631

RUDY, PETER, b Buffalo, NY, Apr 9, 22; m 47; c 2. RUSSIAN LANGUAGE & LITERATURE. *Educ:* Univ Buffalo, BA, 43, MA, 48; Columbia Univ, PhD(Slavic), 57. *Prof Exp:* Instr English, Univ Buffalo, 46 & 47; instr English & Russ, Dartmouth Col, 47-48; instr Russ, Northwestern Univ, 51-52; asst prof, Pa State Univ, 52-58; assoc prof, 58-70, chmn dept Slavic lang & lit, 58-73, PROF SLAVIC, NORTHWESTERN UNIV, EVANSTON, 70- *Mem:* Am Asn Teachers Slavic & E Europ Lang; MLA. *Res:* Leo Tolstoy; literary theory; comparative literature. *Publ:* Ed, Darkness and Light: Three Short Works of Leo Tolstoy, Holt, 65; coauth, Russian: A Complete Elementary Course, Norton, 70. *Mailing Add:* Dept of Slavic Lang & Lit Northwestern Univ Evanston IL 60201

RUEBEL, JAMES SHERMAN, Ancient Roman History, Classical Languages. See Vol I

RUEGG, S DOMINIC, b San Francisco, Calif, Aug 31, 18. CLASSICAL PHILOLOGY, ARCHEOLOGY. *Educ:* St Mary's Col, Calif, AB, 41; Cath Univ Am, AM, 47, PhD, 51; Univ Notre Dame, MA, 56. *Prof Exp:* Instr classics, De LaSalle Col, 46-49; assoc prof 49-66, acad vpres admin, 74-78, PROF CLASSICS & THEOL, ST MARY'S COL CALIF, 66- *Concurrent Pos:* Coun Underwater Archaeol grant, 66-67; Archaeol Inst Am lectr, 68-70; Am Philos Soc grants, 69, 71 & 77. *Mem:* Archaeol Inst Am; Am Philol Asn; Cath Bibl Asn Am; Inst Nautical Archaeol. *Res:* Underwater survey of ancient wrecks at Tremiti Islands, Italty and Majorca, Spain; underwater excavation of Garigliano River, Italy. *Publ:* Auth, S Aurelii Augustini De Utilitate Ieiunii, Cath Univ Am, 51; Preliminary report on the Garigliano River, Italy 1967, St Mary's Col, 68; Report on underwater excavation of Garigliano River, Am J Archaeol, 68, 72 & Int J Nautical Archaeol, I: 198, Report on underwater excavation at the Tremiti Islands 1970, Am J Archaeol, 71 & Int J Nautical Archaeol, I: 198-199. *Mailing Add:* St Mary's Col of Calif PO Box 141 Moraga CA 94575

RUGALEVA, ANELYA ELIZABETH, b Moscow, USSR, Apr 8, 38; US citizen; m 58; c 2. SLAVIC LANGUAGES, LINGUISTICS. *Educ:* Moscow Bauman Inst Technol, BA, 61; Moscow Lenin Pedag Inst, BA, 68, PhD(ling), 71; Ohio State Univ, PhD(Russ ling), 76. *Prof Exp:* Asst prof English & ling, Moscow Lenin Pedag Inst, 71-73; lectr Russ, 76-79, ASST PROF RUSS & LING, OHIO STATE UNIV, 79- *Mem:* Ling Asn Am; Ling Asn Can & US; Am Asn Advan Slavic Studies. *Res:* Comparative syntax, lexicology and semantics; text grammar; linguo-stylistics. *Publ:* Auth, Nominalization of possessive sentences, Lang Sci, 47: 1-6; On the localist semantic model in Russian, 108: 49-60 & On semantic agreement in Russian, 113: 7-18, Russ Lang J; Nominalization in the localist framework, 3: 1-23 & The advantages of constraint in a linguistic model, 3: 77-81, Forum Linguisticum; The structure of deictic sign, 117: 25-42 & Semantic differentiation of reflexive and personal possessives in Russian, 118: 51-71, Russ Lang J. *Mailing Add:* Slavic Dept Ohio State Univ Columbus OH 43210

RUGGERIO, MICHAEL JOHN, b Lyons, NJ, May 5, 36. ROMANCE LANGUAGES & LITERATURES. *Educ:* Lafayette Col, AB, 57; Harvard Univ, MA, 59, PhD(Romance lang), 64. *Prof Exp:* Asst prof Span, Univ Calif, Berkeley, 64-71; assoc prof, Wash Univ, 71-76 & State Univ Col NY Brockport, 76-77; assoc prof, 77-81, PROF SPAN & FRENCH, UNIV MIAMI, 81- *Mem:* MLA; Renaissance Soc Am. *Res:* Spanish Golden Age Literature; La celestina; Spanish literature of the 15th century. *Publ:* Auth, The Evolution of the Go-Between in Spanish Literature Through the Sixteenth Century, Univ Calif, 66; Lope and his role as figura del donaire, 66 & The term comedia in Spanish dramaturgy, 72, Romanische Forsch; Some approaches to structure in the Spanish Golden Age comedia, Orbis Litterarum, 73; Dramatic conventions and their relationship to structure in the Spanish Golden Age Comedia, Rev Hisp Mod, 75; The religious message of La Celestina, Folio, 77; ed, Studies in the literature of Spain--sixteenth and seventeenth centuries, 77 & Studies in the sixteenth and seventeenth century theatre of the Iberian Peninsula, 80, Spec No Folio. *Mailing Add:* Dept of Foreign Lang Univ of Miami Coral Gables FL 33124

RUIZ, ROBERTO, b Madrid, Spain, Dec 20, 25; m 56; c 1. SPANISH LANGUAGE & LITERATURE. *Educ:* Nat Univ Mex, MA, 52; Princeton Univ, MA, 56. *Prof Exp:* Instr Span, Mt Holyoke Col, 53-56; lectr, Hunter Col, 56-58 & Middlebury Col, 59-61; asst prof, Dickinson Col, 61-63; from asst prof to assoc prof, 63-73, chmn dept, 66-81, PROF SPAN, WHEATON COL, 73- *Mem:* MLA; Am Asn Teachers Span & Port; Intl Asn Hispanists. *Res:* Spanish novel of the 20th century. *Publ:* Auth, La etica de Saint-Exupery, Presencia, Mex, 52; Esquemas, Bajel, Mex, 54; Plazas sin muros, De Andrea, Mex, 60; El ultimo oasis, 64, Los jueces implacables, 70 & Paraiso cerrado, cielo abierto, 77, Joaquin Mortiz, Mex; Contra la luz que muere, Las Americas, 82. *Mailing Add:* Dept of Span Wheaton Col Norton MA 02766

RUIZ-DE-CONDE, JUSTINA, b Madrid, Spain, Nov 30, 09; m 34. ROMANCE PHILOLOGY. *Educ:* Univ Cent Madrid, lic en derecho, 31; Radcliffe Col, PhD, 45. *Prof Exp:* Prof French, Inst Nat de Segunda Ensenanza de Valdepenas, Spain, 33-34 & Salmeron, Barcelona, 36-38; instr Span, Abbot Acad, Mass, 39-41; chmn dept, 46-52, 54-58 & 61-62, from instr to prof, 41-75, EMER PROF SPAN, WELLESLEY COL, 75- *Mem:* Corresp mem Hisp Soc Am; Am Asn Teachers Span & Port; MLA. *Res:* Romance of chivalry; contemporary Spanish poetry. *Publ:* Auth, El amor y el Matrimonio Secreto en los Libros de Caballerias, Aguilar, Madrid, 48; Antonio Machado y Guiomar, Insula, Madrid, 64; El Cantico Americano de Jorge Guillen, Turner, Madrid, 74; coed, Homenaje a Jorge Guillen, Insula, Madrid, 78. *Mailing Add:* Dept of Span Wellesley Col Wellesley MA 02181

RUIZ-FORNELLS, ENRIQUE, b Madrid, Spain, Dec 6, 25; m 59. FOREIGN LANGUAGES. *Educ:* Univ Madrid, MA, 50, PhD, 58. *Prof Exp:* Lectr Span, McGill Univ, 58-61; asst prof, Univ SC, 61-63; assoc prof Span lit, 63-66, PROF SPAN LIT, UNIV ALA, 66- *Concurrent Pos:* Prof summer courses, Univ Madrid, 55-75; Am Embassy, Madrid, 55-57; ed, Rev Estud Hisp, 66-; vis prof, Wash Univ, 67-68 & Miss State Univ, 68-74. *Honors & Awards:* Medalla al Merito Turistico, Span Govt, 68; Encomienda del Merito Civil, 72; Comendador de Numero de la Orden del Merito Civil, 77. *Mem:* Asoc Cult Hisp-Norteam, Madrid (secy-treas, 56-57); Am Asn Teachers Span & Port (pres, 76); MLA; Asoc Int Hisp; SAtlantic Mod Lang Asn. *Res:* Golden Age literature; 20th century Spanish literature. *Publ:* Auth, La muralla, Classroom Ed, Appleton, 62; The Spanish theatre in the last twenty-five years, Drama Critique, 66; Ensayo de una bibliografia de las publicaciones hispanicas en los Estados Unidos, Espanol Actual, 66-70; Bibliografia de revistas y publicaciones hispanicas en los Estatod Unidos, Cuadernos Hispanoam, 67-; coauth, Dissertations in Hispanic Languages and Literatures, 1876-1966, United States and Canada, Univ Ky, 69; ed, A concordance to the poety of Gustavo Adolfo Becquer, Univ Ala, 70; auth, Las Concordancias del Ingenioso Hidalgo Don Quijote de la Mancha, Ed Cult Hisp, 76; A Concordance to the Poetry of Leopoldo Panero, Univ Ala, 78. *Mailing Add:* Dept of Romance Lang & Classics Univ of Ala University AL 35486

RUIZ-RAMON, FRANCISCO JOSE, b Xativa, Spain, Feb 17, 30; US citizen; m 58; c 3. SPANISH DRAMA & LITERATURE. *Educ:* Univ Madrid, Licenciatura, 53, Doctorado(romance lang & lit), 62. *Prof Exp:* Lectr Span lit, Univ Oslo, Norway, 57-63; from asst prof to assoc prof, Univ PR, 63-68; assoc prof, 68-72, PROF SPAN LIT, PURDUE UNIV, 72- *Concurrent Pos:* Chmn Span & Port dept, Purdue Univ, 76-78. *Mem:* MLA; Asn Teachers Span & Port. *Res:* Spanish drama; Galdos; contemporary poetry. *Publ:* Auth, Tres personajes galdosianos, Madrid Revista de Occidente, 64; ed, Lope de Vega El Duque de Viseo, 66, Calderon de la Barca Tragedias (3 vols), 67-69, auth, Hisotria del teatro espanol, vol 1, 67, 2nd ed, 72 & vol 2, 71, Madrid Alianza Editorial; Historia del teatro espanol, Siglo XX, 75, 2nd ed, 77 & ed, J Martin Recuerda Las salvajes--Las Arreecogias, 77, Madrid, Catedra; auth, Estudios sobre teatro espanol clasico y contemporaneo, Madrid, Fundacion, 3/78. *Mailing Add:* Dept of Foreign Lang & Lit Purdue Univ West Lafayette IN 47907

RUMOLD, RAINER Y, b Elbing, Ger, Oct 29, 41; m; c 1. GERMAN LANGUAGE & LITERATURE. *Educ:* Univ NMex, BA, 68; Stanford Univ, MA, 69, PhD(Ger), 71. *Prof Exp:* Asst, Stanford Univ, 68-71; asst prof Ger lang & lit, Iowa State Univ, 71-76; asst prof, 76-81, ASSOC PROF GER, NORTHWESTERN UNIV, 81- *Concurrent Pos:* Vis asst prof, Stanford Univ, 73-76; Am Coun Learned Soc grant-in-aid, 78; mem, Inst Res in Humanities, Univ Wis, 80-81. *Mem:* MLA; Am Asn Teachers Ger; Pac Coast Philol Asn; Deutsche Schiller Ges. *Res:* German expressionism & European modernism; Gottfried Benn. *Publ:* Auth, Verfremdung und experiment Zur Standortbestimmung der demonstrationen Helmut Heissenbüttels, Sprache im Technischen Zeitalter, 37: 26-44; Sprachliches Experiment und Literarische Tradition Zu den Texten Helmut Heissenbüttels, Lang, Frankfurt, 75; Warnung vor spiegeln - zur kulturpolitischen und sprachlichen problematik des schwarzen lehrgedichts Günter Kunerts, Monatshefte, winter 76; Carl Sternheims komödie Die Hose Sprachkritik, sprachsatire und der verfremdungseffekt vor Brecht, Mich Ger Studies, 6/78; Sprachkrise und gescheitertes experiment absoluter prosa Zur lyrik und romantheorie Carl Einsteins, In: Gedenkschrift für Edgar Lohner, E Schmidt Verlag, 82; Ein kleines Ja, ein grosses Nein: George Grosz im Spiefel seiner Begegnung mit Benn und Brecht, In: Festschrift fuer Walter Sokel, Niemeyer, 82; Gottfried Benn und der Expressionismus: Provokation des Lesers absolute Dichtung, Athenaeum Verlag, 82; Gottfried Benns Kunst als Waffe Saekularisation als sprachbildende Kraft, Neophilologus, Amsterdam (in prep). *Mailing Add:* Dept of Ger Northwestern Univ Evanston IL 60201

RUNDELL, RICHARD JASON, b Chicago, Ill, Dec 15, 39; m 69; c 2. GERMAN LITERATURE & LINGUISTICS. *Educ:* Colo Col, BA, 61; Middlebury Col, MA, 62; Univ Colo, PhD(Ger lit), 72. *Prof Exp:* Instr Ger, St Lawrence Univ, 62-65 & Univ Colo, 69-71; asst prof, Emporia Kans State Col, 71-72; lectr English, Univ Regensburg, W Ger, 72-75; asst prof, 75-80, ASSOC PROF GER, NMEX STATE UNIV, 80- *Mem:* Am Asn Teachers Ger; Int Brecht Soc; MLA; Western Asn Ger Studies. *Res:* Twentieth century German literature; Brecht; East German literature. *Publ:* Auth, Duerer year 1971, Ger Postal Spec, 71; The Brechtian influence and German Dem Repub poetry of political, criticism, Weber & Heinen: Bertolt Brecht, Polit Theory & Lit Pract, 78; Ragtime, bicentennial: Nostalgia, Gulliver, Deutsch-englische Jahrbk, 78; Keller's Kleider machen leute as novelle and film, Unterrichtspraxis 13, 80. *Mailing Add:* Dept of Foreign Lang NMex State Univ Las Cruces NM 88003

RUNGE, RICHARD MARTIN, b Denison, Iowa, Sept 18, 36; m 59; c 1. GERMANIC LINGUISTICS. *Educ:* Univ Iowa, BA, 61, MA, 63, PhD(Ger ling), 67. *Prof Exp:* Instr Ger, 66-67, asst prof, 67-79, ASSOC PROF GER, UNIV IOWA, 79- *Mem:* Ling Soc Am; Am Asn Teachers Ger. *Mailing Add:* Dept of Ger Univ of Iowa Iowa City IA 52240

RUNNING, LEONA GLIDDEN, b Mt Morris, Mich, Aug 24, 16; wid. SEMITIC LANGUAGES. *Educ:* Emmanuel Missionary Col, BA, 37; Seventh-Day Adventist Theol Sem, MA, 55; Johns Hopkins Univ, PhD(Semitic lang), 64. *Prof Exp:* Teacher, Laurelwood Acad, Ore, 37-41; lang secy, Voice of Prophecy Radio Broadcast, 44-48; ed secy, Gen Conf Seventh-Day Adventists, 50-54; from instr to assoc prof, 55-69, prof, 69-81, EMER PROF BIBL LANG, ANDREWS UNIV, 81- *Mem:* Soc Bibl Lit; Nat Asn Prof Hebrew. *Res:* The Syriac manuscripts of Isaiah and of Susanna. *Publ:* Auth, An investigation of the Syriac version of Isaiah, 7/65, 1/66 & 7/66 & Syriac variants in Isaiah 26, 1/67, Andrews Univ Sem Studies; coauth, William Foxwell Albright, A Twentieth-Century Genius, Morgan, 75. *Mailing Add:* Theol Sem Andrews Univ Berrien Springs MI 49104

RUNTE, HANS R, b Brieg, Ger, Oct 15, 43; m 69. FRENCH LITERATURE. *Educ:* Univ Tübingen, cand phil, 66; Univ Kans, MA, 69, MPh, 70, PhD(French), 72. *Prof Exp:* Instr French, Bethany Col, W Va, 70-71; ASST PROF FRENCH, DALHOUSIE UNIV, 71- *Mem:* MLA; Int Comp Lit Asn; Int Courtly Lit Soc; Can Comp Lit Asn; Am Asn Teachers Fr. *Res:* French-Canadian (Acadian) literature; French Medieval literature; French philology. *Publ:* Auth, Li Ystoire de la male marastre--Version M of the Roman des 7 sages, Max Niemeyer, Tübingen, Ger, 74; A forgotten old French version of the old man of the mountain, Speculum, 74; Zur textgeschichte des Roman des Sept sages de Rome, Neuphilol Mitteilungen, 74; co-ed, Jean Misrahi Memorial Volume, French Lit Publ, 77; Identite Culturelle et Francophonie dans les Ameriques, Ind Univ, 76. *Mailing Add:* Dept of French Dalhousie Univ Halifax NS B3H 4H8 Can

RUNTE, ROSEANN, b Kingston, NY, Jan 31, 48; m 69. FRENCH, COMPARATIVE LITERATURE. *Educ:* State Univ NY Col New Paltz, BA, 68; Univ Kans, MA, 69, PhD(French), 74. *Prof Exp:* Asst French, Univ Kans, 69-70; instr French & dir lang lab, Bethany Col, 70-71; instr, Adult Studies, St Mary's Univ, 71-72. *Concurrent Pos:* Mem bd dir, Humanities Res Coun, 77-, vpres, 81-82, pres, 82- *Mem:* Atlantic Soc 18th Century Studies (pres, 72-76); Can Soc 18th Century Studies (pres, 75-76); Int Soc 18th Century Studies; Humanities Res Coun; corresp mem, Soc Francaise d'etude du XVIIIe Siecle. *Res:* Conte; 18th century French fable; comedy. *Publ:* Auth, Actors and authors: The characters in Les Liaisons Dangereuses, In: Laclos, Studia Humanitatis Ser, 78; Lesage's Theatre and his novel, Crocker Festschrift, 79; Irony in La Fontaine, Australian Fr Studies, 79; Vocabulary of death in English & French novels, Can Rev Comp Lit, 80; La Chaumiere indienne, Fr Rev, 80; Paul et Virginie, Mod Lang Rev, 80; Death in comedy, Studi Francesi, 80; Beaumarchais, Ky Romance Quart, 82. *Mailing Add:* Dept of French Dalhousie Univ Halifax NS B3H 3J5 Can

RUNYON, RANDOLPH PAUL, b Maysville, Ky, Feb 13, 47. FRENCH LITERATURE, AMERICAN STUDIES. *Educ:* Johns Hopkins Univ, PhD(French), 73. *Prof Exp:* Asst prof, Case Western Reserve Univ, 74-76; asst prof, 77-80, ASSOC PROF FRENCH, MIAMI UNIV, 80- *Mem:* MLA; Soc des Amis de Montaigne; Midwest Mod Lang Asn; Am Studies Asn. *Res:* Sixteenth century French literature; 20th century French literature; literary criticism. *Publ:* Auth, Deliverance: Souffrir non souffrir, Mod Lang Notes, 5/73; La Parole genee: Genese et palinodie, Change, 11/73; The errors of desire, Diacritics, fall 74; Sceve's Aultre Troye, Mod Lang Notes, 5/75; Fragments of an amorous discourse: Canon in U-bis, Visible Lang, fall 77; Montaigne bis, In: Resnaissance et Nouvelle Critique, State Univ NY, Albany, 78; Fowles, Irving, Barthes: Canonical Variations on an Apocryphal Theme, Ohio State Univ Press, 81. *Mailing Add:* Dept of French & Ital Miami Univ Oxford OH 45056

RUPERTSBERGER-LEINFELLNER, ELISABETH MARIA, b Vienna, Austria; c 1. LINGUISTICS. *Educ:* Univ Vienna, PhD(German), 62. *Prof Exp:* Manuscript ed, 62-66; instr German, Doane Col, 68-69; mem fac, Speech Dept & Centennial Col, Univ Nebr, 75; lektor, German Dept, Univ Vienna, 76; MANAGING ED, SCHRIFTENREIHE DER WITTGENSTEIN GESELLSCHAFT, 77- *Concurrent Pos:* Lektor, German Dept, Univ Wien, 80-81, researcher, Dept Med Cybernetics, 80-81. *Mem:* Inst Arts & Sci, Vienna, Austria; Northeast Mod Lang Asn. *Res:* German language and literature; philosophy of language. *Publ:* Auth, Towards a nominalistic foundation of linguistics and philosophy of language: Fritz Mauthner and Ludwig Wittgenstein (in German), Studium Gen, 69; Euphemism in Political Language (in German), 71 & coauth, Ontologie, Systemtheorie und Semantik, 78, Duncker & Humblot, Berlin; coauth & translr, Adam Mueller's Twelve Lectures on Rhetoric, Univ Nebr & Univ Microfilms Int, 78; co-ed, Proc of the Second International Wittgenstein Symposium, Hoelder-Pichler-Tempsky, Wien, 78; auth, Words, meaning and reality, Proc 12th Int Congr Ling, 78; Kausalität und Sprache, Oesterreichische Studiengesellschaft für Kybernetik, Wien, 80; coauth, Ontology and Semantics in the Computer, In: Proc 6th Int Wittgenstein Symposium, Hoelder-Pichler-Tempsky, Wien, 82. *Mailing Add:* 839 S 15th Lincoln NE 68508

RUPLIN, FERDINAND, b Minneapolis, Minn, July 22, 34; m 59; c 5. GERMAN, LINGUISTICS. *Educ:* Univ Minn, BA, 56, MA, 61, PhD(Ger, ling), 65. *Prof Exp:* Instr Ger, Univ Minn, 61-63; from instr to asst prof, 63-71, ASSOC PROF STATE UNIV NY STONY BROOK, 71-, ASSOC, INSTRUCT RESOURCES IN COMPUTER ASSISTED INSTR, 72- *Concurrent Pos:* Lang coordr, Peace Corps Training Progs Pakistan, Univ Minn, 62-63, consult ling, 63-64; Thomas J Watson Res Ctr, Int Bus Machines Corp, 66-67; consult ling, PDC, 81-82. *Mem:* MLA; Am Asn Teachers Ger; Ling Soc Am; Am Coun Teaching Foreign Lang. *Res:* Comparative Germanic and descriptive linguistics; Indic languages, especially Sindhi; applied linguistics in the teaching of foreign languages. *Publ:* Coauth, A type of computer assisted instruction, Ger Quart, 12/67; A generative-transformational phonology of Sindhi, Acts Xth Int Cong Linguists, 9/68; Basic German, Appleton, 68. *Mailing Add:* Dept of Ger State Univ of NY Stony Brook NY 11790

RUPP, THEODORE HANNA, b Windham, NY, Oct 22, 15; m 40; c 2. ROMANCE LANGUAGES. *Educ:* Franklin & Marshall Col, AB, 35; Pa State Univ, MA, 42; Univ Pa, PhD, 54. *Prof Exp:* Teacher pub schs, Lancaster, Pa, 35-37; teacher French, Span & English, Franklin & Marshall Acad, 37-42; teacher French, Solebury Sch, New Hope, Pa, 43; teacher English, Latin & math, Shady Side Acad Pittsburgh, Pa, 43-44; chmn dept, 54-79, dir, Summer Grad Schs, 67-79, PROF FOREIGN LANG, MILLERSVILLE STATE COL, 46-, DIR FR SCH, 80- *Concurrent Pos:* Teacher, Pa Area Col, 46-48; ed, Bull, Pa State Mod Lang Asn, 70-; consult, Pa State Dept Educ, 76-78. *Honors & Awards:* Educ of the Year, Pa State Mod Lang Asn, 75. *Mem:* MLA; Am Asn Teachers Fr; Am Coun Teaching Foreign Langs; AAUP; Int Arthurian Soc. *Res:* Applied linguistics; medieval French lit; French phonology. *Publ:* Auth, The junior year abroad--some second thoughts, Bull Pa State Mod Lang Asn, 12/65; Evaluating the foreign study program, Fr Rev, 12/66; Articulation of language teaching, In: The Study of Foreign Languages, Philos Libr, 68; Guidelines for the Planning and Conduct of Meetings of the Pennsylvania State Modern Language Association, 3rd ed, Pa State Mod Lang Asn, 77. *Mailing Add:* Dept of Foreign Lang Millersville State Col Millersville PA 17551

RUPPERSBURG, HUGH MICHAEL, b Atlanta, Ga, Mar 1, 50; m 78; c 1. AMERICAN LITERATURE, THE NOVEL. *Educ:* Univ Ga, AB, 72; Univ SC, MA, 74, PhD(Am lit), 78. *Prof Exp:* Instr, 77-79, ASST PROF ENGLISH, UNIV GA, 79- *Mem:* MLA; SAtlantic Mod Lang Asn; Soc Study Southern Lit; NCTE; Philol Asn Carolinas. *Res:* Southern literature; American novelists; William Faulkner. *Publ:* Auth, Byron Bunch and Percy Grimm: Strange twins of Light in August, 77 & The narrative structure of Requiem for a Nun, 78, Miss Quart; George V Higgins, 78, Peter Davison, 80, John Irving, 80 & Keith Laumer, 81, In: Dict of Literary Biography, Gale Res Co; Image as structure in Faulkner's Pylon, SAtlantic Rev, 82; Voice and Eye in Faulkner's Fiction, Univ Ga Press (in press). *Mailing Add:* Dept of English Univ of Ga Athens GA 30602

RUPPRECHT, ARTHUR A, b Saylesville, RI, June 22, 31; m 53; c 1. CLASSICAL LANGUAGES. *Educ:* Houghton Col, AB, 52; Univ Ill, MA, 54; Univ Pa, PhD, 60. *Prof Exp:* Asst prof class lang, Taylor Univ, 57-61; ASST PROF CLASS LANG, WHEATON COL, ILL, 61-, CHMN DEPT, 80- *Mem:* Class Asn Mid W & S; Evangel Theol Soc. *Res:* Early Greece; late Roman Republic. *Mailing Add:* Dept of Class Lang Wheaton Col Wheaton IL 60187

RUSCH, FREDERICK A, b Ft Wayne, Ind, Nov 16, 38; m 61; c 4. CLASSICAL LANGUAGES. *Educ:* Concordia Sr Col, BA, 59; Concordia Sem, Mo, BD, 62; Northwestern Univ, MA, 64, PhD(class lang), 68. *Prof Exp:* From instr to assoc prof class lang, Concordia Sr Col, 65-76, chmn dept, 66-76; ASSOC PROF CLASS LANG, AUGUSTANA COL, 76- *Mem:* Am Philol Asn; Am Asn Papyrologists; Soc Bibl Lit. *Res:* The physiological and philosophical theories of Galen; Plato's philosophy. *Mailing Add:* 2608 S Lincoln Sioux Falls SD 57105

RUSHTON, PETER HALLIDAY, b Doylestown, Pa, Apr 20, 50; m 77; c 3. CHINESE LANGUAGE & LITERATURE. *Educ:* Univ Wis-Madison, BA, 72; Stanford Univ, MA, 74, PhD(Chinese), 79. *Prof Exp:* Lectr Chinese, Univ Calif, Santa Barbara, 78-80; asst prof, Univ Minn, 80-81; asst prof, Univ BC, 81-82; ASST PROF CHINESE, IND UNIV, 82- *Mem:* Asn Asian Studies; Am Orient Soc. *Res:* Chinese narrative (traditional and modern). *Publ:* Contribr, Traditional Chinese Stories: Themes and Variations, Columbia Univ Press, 78; auth, An interpretation of Hsi K'ang's eighteen poems presented to Hsi Hsi, J Am Orient Soc, 79; The novel in seventeenth century China review article, Ming Studies (in prep). *Mailing Add:* Dept of East Asian Lang & Cultures Ind Univ Goodbody Hall 248-250 Bloomington IN 47405

RUSSELL, CHARLES COULTER, b Philadelphia, Pa, May 6, 34; m 62; c 2. ITALIAN LANGUAGE & LITERATURE. *Educ:* Oberlin Col, BA, 56; Bryn Mawr Col, MA, 64; Harvard Univ, PhD(Ital), 70. *Prof Exp:* Instr Ital, Smith Col, 64-65 & Brandeis Univ, 68-70; dir, Ctr Int Studi, Verona, Italy, 70-74; asst prof, 74-78, ASSOC PROF ITAL, UNIV MD, 78- *Mem:* Am Asn Teachers Ital; Am Asn Univ Professors Ital. *Res:* Dante; Italian opera librettos. *Publ:* Auth, Italo Svevo's Trieste, Italica, Vol 51, No 1; Italo Svevo's close friend: Umberto Veruda, Forum Italicum, Vol 9, No 2-3; Italo Svevo, the Writer from Trieste: Reflections on his Background and his Work, A Longo, Italy, 78; Don Giovanni's operatic ancestors, Opera J, 11/79; The first Don Giovanni opera: La pravita castigata by Eustachio Bambini, Mozart-Jahrbuch, 82. *Mailing Add:* Dept of French & Ital Univ of Md College Park MD 20742

RUSSELL, DANIEL, b Ilion, NY, Dec 7, 37; m 66; c 2. ROMANCE LANGUAGES. *Educ:* Hamilton Col, BA, 59; NY Univ, MA, 61, PhD(French), 68. *Prof Exp:* Prof English, Lycee Francais New York, 61-63; instr French, Hamilton Col, 65-68; asst prof, 68-74, dir prog in France, 71 72, ASSOC PROF FRENCH, UNIV PITTSBURGH, 74-, DIR MEDIEVAL & RENAISSANCE STUDIES PROG, 77- *Mem:* MLA; Renaissance Soc Am; AAUP; Am Asn Teachers Fr. *Res:* Literature of the French Renaissance; emblem literature; methods and theory of literary criticism. *Publ:* Transl, The Art of Bertolt Brecht, NY Univ, 63; G Bachelard's The Poetics of Reverie, Orion, 69; auth, Du Bellay's emblematic vision of Rome, Yale Fr Studies, 72; A note on Panurge's 'pusse en l'aureille, 74 & Panurge and his new clothes, 78, Etudes rabelaisiennes; The term 'embleme in sixteenth century France, Neophilologus, 75; On Montaigne's device, Studi francesi, 75; Alciati's Emblems in Renaissance France, Renaissance Quart, 81. *Mailing Add:* 1328 C L Univ of Pittsburgh Pittsburgh PA 15260

RUSSELL, JAMES, b Glasgow, Scotland, Sept 11, 35; m 59; c 4. CLASSICAL ARCHEOLOGY & PHILOLOGY. *Educ:* Univ Edinburgh, MA, 57, dipl, 58; Univ Chicago, PhD(classics), 65. *Prof Exp:* Master classics, Trinity Acad, Edinburgh, 58-59; lectr, Univ Man, 59-63, asst prof, 63-66; asst prof, 66-70, assoc prof, 70-80, PROF CLASSICS, UNIV BC, 80- *Concurrent Pos:* Study fel, Can Coun, 71-72 & 78-79, mem acad adv panel, 76-79; dir, Excavation of Anemurium, Cilicia; vis fel, Dumbarton Oaks Ctr for Byzantine Studies, 78. *Mem:* Asn Field Archaeol; Archaeol Inst Am; Can Class Asn; Am Inst Archaeol; Soc Prom Roman Studies. *Res:* History and archeology of the Roman provinces; ancient city planning. *Publ:* Auth, The origin and development of Republican forums, Phoenix, 68, Ancient lamps in Vancouver, Levant, 73; Calchas Tectus: A note on Vergil, Aeneid II, Latomus, 73; New inscriptions from Anemurium, Phoenix, 73; Mosaic inscriptions from the Palaestra at Anemurium, Anatolian Studies, 74; Anemurium, eine römische Kleinstadt in Kleinasien, Antike Welt, 76; Restoration, conservation and excavation at the Necropolis of Anemurium, Turkey, J Field Archaeol, 77; Julius Caesar's last words: A reinterpretation, Vindex Humanitatis, 80. *Mailing Add:* Dept of Classics Univ of BC Vancouver BC V6T 1W5 Can

RUSSELL, JOHN R, b Nashville, Tenn, Apr 8, 29; m 56; c 3. GERMAN LANGUAGE & LITERATURE. *Educ:* Princeton Univ, AB, 54, AM, 57, PhD(Ger), 66. *Prof Exp:* Asst prof Ger, Wabash Col, 58-64; asst prof, Centenary Col, 64-65; asst prof, 65-71, ASSOC PROF GER, STATE UNIV NY STONY BROOK, 71-, ASSOC, INSTRUCT RESOURCES IN COMPUTER ASSISTED INSTR, 72- *Concurrent Pos:* Fulbright exchange teacher, Ger, 61-62. *Mem:* Am Asn Teachers Ger; Am Coun Teaching Foreign Lang; Int Ver Germanstik. *Publ:* Auth, Why we send students to Germany, Ger Quart, 1/62; coauth, Basic German, Appleton, 69. *Mailing Add:* Dept of Ger State Univ of NY Stony Brook NY 11790

RUSSELL, KRISTINA SANDBERG, b Erfurt, Ger, Sept 17, 42; m 63; c 2. GERMAN LITERATURE. *Educ:* Univ Hartford, BA, 68; Univ Conn, MA, 78, PhD(Ger), 80. *Prof Exp:* Lectr Ger, Cent Conn State Col, 77-78; lectr, Independent Ger Lang Sch Conn, 78-81; LECTR GER, UNIV HARTFORD, 81- *Concurrent Pos:* Lectr Ger, Univ Hartford, 68-81 & Trinity Col, 76-78. *Mem:* Am Asn Teachers Ger. *Res:* Keller and Moritz; 20th century German novellas as a literary genre. *Publ:* Auth, Das Problem der Identität in Gottfried Keller's Prosawerk, Peter Lang, Bern, 81. *Mailing Add:* PO Box 312 Farmington CT 06032

RUSSELL, LOIS ANN, b New Brunswick, NJ. FRENCH LITERATURE & LANGUAGE. *Educ:* Douglass Col, BA, 52, Fordham Univ, MA, 60; Bryn Mawr Col, PhD(French lit), 75. *Prof Exp:* Asst prin, Oak Knoll Sch, Summit, NJ, 56-64; dept chmn, Sch of Holy Child, Rye, NY, 64-68; coordr French, 74-79, chmn fac affairs, 75-77 & 81-82, ASSOC PROF FRENCH, ROSEMONT COL, 68- *Concurrent Pos:* Consult, Choice, 76- *Mem:* Societe Francaise d'Etude du 18e Siecle; MLA; Am Asn Teachers of French; Am Soc 18th Century Studies; Alliance Francaise. *Res:* Eighteenth-century novel; Challe; literary illustration. *Publ:* Auth, Une Etude lexicologique du mot fatal dans La Chartreuse de Parme, 19th Century French Studies, 76; Robert Challe: A Voice for Reform, 18th Century Life, 77; Robert Challe: A Utopian Voice in the Early Enlightenment, Porrua, 78; Challe et Quebec, Revue d'Histoire Litteraire de la France, 79; Challe and Diderot: Tales in Defense of Woman, J Western Soc Fr Hist (in press); Les Jeux de l'ecriture dans la Chartreuse de Parme, Stendhal Club (in press). *Mailing Add:* Dept of French Rosemont College Rosemont PA 19010

RUSSELL, OLGA WESTER, b Conn, June 20, 13; wid; c 1. FOREIGN LANGUAGES. *Educ:* Univ Calif, MA, 39; Harvard Univ, MA, 44, PhD, 57. *Prof Exp:* Instr French, Cambridge Jr Col, 43-44, Wheaton Col, 44-46 & Tufts Univ, 46-48 & 51-52: asst prof, Chatham Col, 56-61 & Univ SFla, 61-63; prof foreign lang & chmn dept, Longwood Col, 63-65; assoc prof French, Eastern Ill Univ, 65-66: prof, 66-78, PROF EMER FRENCH, UNIV MAINE, ORONO, 78- *Concurrent Pos:* TV teaching, WQED, Pittsburgh, Pa, 56-60. *Mem:* MLA. *Res:* Seventeenth century French literature; Hugo. *Publ:* Auth, Etude historique et critique des Burgraves de Victor Hugo, Nizet, Paris, 62; Humor in Pascal, Christopher, 77. *Mailing Add:* 11 Webster Rd Orono ME 04473

RUSSELL, RINALDINA, b Ancona, Italy, US citizen; m 60. ITALIAN LITERATURE. *Educ:* Columbia Univ, PhD(Ital medieval poetry), 71. *Prof Exp:* Instr Ital lang & lit, Barnard Col, Columbia Univ, 69-71; asst prof Romance lang, 71-76, ASSOC PROF ROMANCE LANG, QUEENS COL, NY, 76- *Mem:* MLA; Dante Soc Am; Renaissance Soc Am; Am Asn Teachers Ital; Medieval Soc Am. *Publ:* Auth, Tre versanti della poesia stilnovistica: Guinizzelli, Cavalcanti e Dante, Adriatica Editrice, Bari, 73; Generi poetici medievali, Modelli e funzioni letterarie, Societa Editrice Napoletana, Naples, 82. *Mailing Add:* Dept of Romance Lang Queens Col Flushing NY 11367

RUSSELL, ROBERT HILTON, b Oak Park, Ill, Dec 26, 27; m 56. SPANISH LITERATURE. *Educ:* Knox Col, AB, 49; Harvard Univ, AM, 50, PhD, 63. *Hon Degrees:* AM, Dartmouth Col, 68. *Prof Exp:* Instr Span, 57-61, from asst prof to assoc prof, 61-67, PROF ROMANCE LANG, DARTMOUTH COL, 67- *Concurrent Pos:* Ed consult, Pergamon Press, Oxford, Eng, 63-; corporator, Int Inst Spain, 73; ed consult, Prentice-Hall, 81- *Mem:* MLA; Asn Int Hispanistas; Asn Int Galdosistas. *Res:* Nineteenth century Spanish novel; Perez Galdos; theory of literature. *Publ:* Auth, El amigo manso: Galdos with a mirror, Mod Lang Notes, 63; The Christ figure in Misericordia, Anales Galdosianos, 67; De fortunata y su habla, Actas IV Congr Asoc Int Hispanistas, 73; El licenciado Vidriera: nomenclatura y estructura, Studia Philol Salmanticensia, 78. *Mailing Add:* 344 Dartmouth Hall Dartmouth Col Hanover NH 03755

RUSSO, GLORIA MARION, b Newton, Mass. EIGHTEENTH CENTURY LITERATURE, PEDAGOGY. *Educ:* Regis Col, Mass, BA, 68; Tufts Univ, MA, 70; Univ Ill, Urbana, PhD(French), 76. *Prof Exp:* Teacher French, Secondary Sch System, Mass, 60-70; teacher English, Lycee Mixte de Gisors, France, 71-72: course coordr teaching & res asst French, Univ Ill, 72-76; ASST PROF FRENCH, UNIV VA, 76- *Mem:* Am Asn Teachers French; Am Soc 18th Century Studies; MLA; Northeast Conf Teaching Foreign Lang. *Res:* Voltaire; La Pucelle, histories, role of myth; 18th century novel. *Publ:* Auth, Sexual roles and religious images in Voltaire's La Pucelle, Studies in Voltaire & 18th Century. *Mailing Add:* Dept of French & Gen Ling Univ of Va Charlottesville VA 22903

RUSSO, JOSEPH ANTHONY, b Brooklyn, NY, Apr 14, 37; m 60. CLASSICS. *Educ:* Brooklyn Col, BA, 58; Yale Univ, MA, 60, PhD, 62. *Prof Exp:* From instr to assoc prof Classics, Yale Univ, 62-70; assoc prof, 70-76, PROF CLASSICS, HAVERFORD COL, 76-, CHMN DEPT, 80- *Concurrent Pos:* Fel, Ctr Hellenic Studies, Wash, DC, 65-66; Nat Endowment for Humanities younger humanist fel, 73-74; Am Coun Learned Soc grant-in-aid, 74; vis prof class studies, Univ Mich, 77-78. *Mem:* Class Asn Atlantic States; Am Philol Asn. *Res:* Greek literature and metrics; Homeric poetry; oral literature and folklore. *Publ:* Auth, A Closer Look at Homeric Formulas, Trans Am Philol Asn, 64; The Structural Formula of Homeric Verse, Yale Class Studies, 66; coauth, Homeric Psychology and the Oral Epic Tradition, J Hist Ideas, 68; Homer Against his Tradition, Arion, 68; The Inner Man in Archilochus and the Odyssey, Greek, Roman & Byzantine Studies, 74; Reading the Greek Lyric Poets, Arion, 75; How, and what, does Homer communicate, Class J, 76; contribr, Is Aural or oral composition the cause of Homer's formulaic style?, In: Oral Literature and the Formula, Univ Mich, 76. *Mailing Add:* Dept of Classics Haverford Col Haverford PA 19041

RUSSO, MARY, b New York, NY, Aug 29, 15. CLASSICAL LANGUAGES & LITERATURES. *Educ:* Col New Rochelle, AB, 35; Fordham Univ, AM, 51, PhD(classics), 61. *Prof Exp:* Instr classics, 52-55, dean col, 57-64, assoc prof classics, 64-67, prof, 68-80, EMER PROF CLASSICS, COL NEW ROCHELLE, 80- *Mem:* Am Philol Asn; Mediaeval Acad Am. *Res:* Archaeology of Greece and Rome; 12th century Latin literature; Latin literature of Renaissance, especially Petrarch. *Mailing Add:* Dept of Classics Col of New Rochelle New Rochelle NY 10805

RUTLEDGE, HARRY CARRACI, b Chillicothe, Ohio, Jan 23, 32. CLASSICS. *Educ:* Ohio State Univ, BScEd, 54, MA, 57, PhD, 60. *Prof Exp:* From asst prof to assoc prof classics, Univ Ga, 60-68; assoc prof, head Romance lang, 72-79, PROF CLASSICS, UNIV TENN, KNOXVILLE, 69-, HEAD DEPT, 68- *Concurrent Pos:* Secy adv coun, Am Acad Rome, 71-75. *Mem:* Am Philol Asn; Archaeol Inst Am; Vergilian Soc (pres, 77-79); Southern Comp Lit Asn (pres, 78-79); Class Asn Mid West & South (pres, 79-80). *Res:* Literature of the Augustan Age; Vergil; class tradition in the 20th century. *Publ:* Auth, Propertius' Tarpeia: The poem itself, Class J, 11/64; Eliot and Vergil: Parallels in the Sixth Aeneid and Four Quartets, Vergilius, 66; Classical Latin poetry: An art for our time, In: The Endless Fountain, Ohio State Univ, 72; Contest and possession: Classical imagery in Henry James' The Golden Bowl, Comparatist, 5/77; Vergil's Dido in modern literature, Class & Mod Lit, summer 81. *Mailing Add:* Dept of Classics Univ of Tenn Knoxville TN 37996

RUTTER, JEREMY BENTHAM, Archeology, Classics. See Vol I

RUTTKOWSKI, WOLFGANG, b Hirschberg, Ger, Feb 5, 35. GERMAN, COMPARATIVE LITERATURE. *Educ:* Univ Gottingen, MA, 61; Staatl Studienseminar, Hannover, Ger, Assessor-E, 63; McGill Univ, PhD(Ger), 65. *Prof Exp:* Studienassessor Ger lit & hist, Schiller Gymnasium, Hannover, Ger, 61-63; asst prof Ger, Univ Southern Calif, 65-68; assoc prof Ger & comp lit, NY Univ, 69-72 & Univ Tokyo, 72-74; assoc prof, 74-80, PROF GER & COMP LIT, TEMPLE UNIV, 80-, CHMN DEPT, 79- *Concurrent Pos:* Guest prof, Teaching Aid Proj V, Ger, 68; vis lectr, Univ Calif, Riverside, 69. *Mem:* MLA; Am Asn Teachers Ger; Can Asn Univ Teachers Ger; Japanische Ges Germanistik. *Res:* Poetics of literary genres; cabaret songs; dramatics. *Publ:* Auth, Die literarischen Gattungen, 68, Francke, Bern; Probleme der Gattungspoetik, Pac Coast Philol, 5/68; coauth, Glossary of Literary Terms, Francke, Bern, 69; auth, Bibliographie der Gattungspoetik, Hueber, Munich, 73; ed & contribr, Das Studium der deutschen Literatur, Nat Carl Schurz Asn, Philadelphia, 73; auth, Typologien und Schichtenlehren, Rodopi, Amsterdam, 74; auth, Typen and Schichten, 78 & ed & contribr, Nomenclator Litterarius, 80, Francke, Bern. *Mailing Add:* Dept of Ger Temple Univ Philadelphia PA 19122

RUYTER, HANS C, b Tebing Tinggi, Jan 14, 22; US citizen; m 46; c 3. LANGUAGES. *Educ:* State Univ Leyden, Netherlands, LittDrs, 51. *Prof Exp:* ASSOC PROF HIST & LANG OF SOUTH & SOUTHEAST ASIA, CLAREMONT GRAD SCH, 61- *Mem:* Royal Inst Ling, Geog & Ethnol, Netherlands; Asn Asian Studies. *Res:* Islamic tradition literature; Indonesian languages. *Publ:* Coauth, Concordance de la tradition musulmane, Tome III, Brill, 55. *Mailing Add:* Dept of Hist & Foreign Lang Claremont Grad Sch Claremont CA 91711

RYAN, JUDITH LYNDAL, b Sydney, Australia, Apr 6, 43; m 64; c 2. GERMAN. *Educ:* Univ Sydney, BA, 65; Univ Munster, DPhil(Ger), 70. *Prof Exp:* From instr to asst prof Ger, 67-75, assoc prof, 75-80, prof, 80-82, DORIS SILBERT PROF IN HUMANITIES, SMITH COL, 82- *Concurrent Pos:* Alexander von Humboldt travel grant, 70-71; Nat Endowment for Humanities res fel, 78; vis assoc prof, Brown Univ, 79-80. *Mem:* MLA; Am Asn Teachers Ger; AAUP. *Res:* Twentieth century German literature; German Romantic literature; comparative literature. *Publ:* Auth, Die swei Fassungen der Beschreibung eines Kampfes: Zur Entwicklung von Kafkas Erzähltechnik, 70 & Hypothetisches Erzählen: Zur Funktion von Phantasie und Einbildung in Rilkes Malte Laurids Brigge, 71, Jahrbuch der Deutschen Schiller-Gesellschaft; Umschlag und Verwandlung: Poetische Struktur und Dichtungstheorie in R M Rilkes Lyrik der mittleren Periode, Winkler, Munich, 72; Creative subjectivity in Rilke and Valery, Comp Lit, 74; Some epistemological problems in Franz Kafka, Festschrift Farrell, Lang, 77; Resistance and resignation: A re-interpretation of Grass' Katz und Maus, Ger Rev, 77; The Vanishing Subject: Empirical Psychology and the Modern Novel, PMLA, 80. *Mailing Add:* Dept of Ger Smith Col Northampton MA 01060

RYAN, LAWRENCE, b Sydney, Australia, Dec 20, 32; m 64; c 2. GERMAN. *Educ:* Univ Sydney, BA, 54; Univ Tübingen, Dr Phil(Ger), 58. *Prof Exp:* Lectr Ger, Univ Sydney, 59-61, sr lectr, 62-65, reader, 65-67; PROF GERMAN, UNIV MASS, AMHERST, 67- *Concurrent Pos:* Deut Forschungsgemeinschaft res scholar, 61; vis assoc prof, Rice Univ, 66-67; Guggenheim fel, 74-75. *Mem:* MLA; Am Asn Teachers Ger. *Res:* Literature of German classicism and Romanticism, especially Hölderlin; 20th century literature. *Publ:* Auth, Hölderlins Lehre vom Wechsel der Töne, Kohlhammer, Stuttgart, 60; Friedrich Hölderlin, 62, 2nd ed, 67 & Hölderlins Hyperion: exzentrische Bahn und Dichterberuf, 65, Metzler, Stuttgart; Hebbels Herodes und Mariamne: Tragödie und Geschichte, In: Hebbel in Neuer Sicht, 63 & 69; Die Tragödie des Dichters in Goethes Torquato Tasso, Jahrbuch Deut Schiller-Ges, 65; Die Marionette und das unendliche Bewusstsein bei Heinrich von Kleist, In: Kleists Aufsatz über das Marionettentheater, 67. *Mailing Add:* Dept of Ger Univ of Mass Amherst MA 01002

RYAN, MARLEIGH, b Brooklyn, NY, May 1, 30; m 50; c 1. JAPANESE LITERATURE. *Educ:* NY Univ, BA, 51; Columbia Univ, MA, 56, Cert, E Asian Inst, 56, PhD(Japanese lit), 65. *Prof Exp:* Res assoc Japanese res tech, Columbia Univ, 60-61, from lectr to asos assoc prof Japanese, 61-72; assoc prof, 72-75, CHMN DEPT E ASIAN LANG & LIT, UNIV IOWA, 72-, PROF JAPANESE, 75- *Concurrent Pos:* Consult Japanese lang teaching methods, Inter-Univ Comt, Tokyo Ctr Japanese Studies, 66; ed, Asn Teachers Japanese J, 71-; consult, Soc Sci Res Coun, 72-77; mem screening comt, Foreign Area Fel Prog, 72-74; Japan Found fel, 73; mem bd adv, J Japanese Studies, 74-; consult, Nat Endowment for Humanities & Off Educ, Dept Health, Educ & Welfare, 75- *Honors & Awards:* Van Am Distinguished Book Award, Columbia Col, 68. *Mem:* Asn Teachers Japanese (secy, 62-71); Asn Asian Studies; MLA. *Res:* Modern Japanese literature; Japanese language; Japanese narrative techniques. *Publ:* Auth, Japan's First Modern Novel: Ukigumo of Futabatei Shimei, Columbia Univ, 67; Tsubouchi Shoyo & Fukuzawa Yukichi, In: Dictionary of Oriental Literatures, 73; The Development of Realism in the Fiction of Tsubouchi Shoyo, Univ Wash, 75; Modern Japanese fiction: Accommodated truth, J Japanese Studies, summer 76. *Mailing Add:* Dept of E Asian Lang & Lit Univ of Iowa Iowa City IA 52242

RYBALKA, MICHEL, b Sens, France, Dec 7, 33; m 64; c 3. FRENCH & ENGLISH LITERATURE. *Educ:* Univ Nancy, lic es let, 56; Univ Calif, Los Angeles, MA, 59, PhD(French lit), 66. *Prof Exp:* Instr French, Univ Calif, Santa Barbara, 62-64; asst prof, Reed Col, 64-66; from asst prof to assoc French lit, Univ Rochester, 66-72; PROF FRENCH, WASHINGTON UNIV, 72- *Concurrent Pos:* Guggenheim fel, 70-71; Nat Endowment for Humanities summer sem dir, 80; vis prof, Univ Warwick, 81. *Mem:* MLA; Am Asn Teachers Fr; Midwest Mod Lang Asn Am. *Res:* Contemporary French literature; Sartre and existentialism; literary criticism and bibliography. *Publ:* Auth, Boris Vian, Lettres Mod, Paris, 69; coauth, Les ecrits de Sartre, 70 & co-ed, Sartre: Un theatre de situations, 73, Gallimard, Paris; auth, Bibliographie d' A Robbe-Grillet, Obliques, 78; Camus et les problemes de la biographie, In: Camus, Univ Fla Press, 81; Interview of Sartre and bibliography, In: The Philosophy of J P Sartre, Open Court, 81; coauth, Oeuvres Romanesques de Sartre, Gallimard, Pleiade, Paris, 82. *Mailing Add:* Dept of Romance Lang Washington Univ St Louis MO 63130

RYDELL, MIREILLE GUILLET, b Rabat, Morocco, Dec 2, 27; US citizen; m 53; c 1. FOREIGN LANGUAGE. *Educ:* Univ Bordeaux, France, Lic es Lett, 50; Univ Minn, MA, 58, PhD(French), 68. *Prof Exp:* Lectr French, Univ Md, Japan, 61-62; lectr, Univ Minn, 66-68; assoc prof, 68-73, PROF FRENCH, CALIF STATE COL, SAN BERNARDINO, 73- *Concurrent Pos:* Chmn, Bicentennial Comn, San Bernardino, 75-76; ed, Forum, J for Mod & Clin Lang Asn, Southern Calif, 76. *Mem:* Philol Asn Pac Coast; Medieval Inst; Int Arthurian Soc; Western Folklore Soc; MLA. *Res:* Medieval French literature; epics-Arthurian romances; folklore: British and American. *Publ:* Coauth, Floire and Blancheflore, Univ Miss Monogr, 73; auth, Nature and role of marriage in Breton lays, Romania, France, 74. *Mailing Add:* Dept of French California State Col 5500 Calif State Pkwy San Bernardino CA 92407

RYDER, FRANK GLESSNER, b Minneapolis, Minn, Dec 23, 16; m 48; c 3. GERMANIC LINGUISTICS & LITERATURE. *Educ:* Univ Minn, AB, 37, AM, 38; Univ Mich, PhD, 50. *Prof Exp:* Instr & res assoc, English Lang Inst, Univ Mich, 40; instr Ger, Dartmouth Col, 45-47, asst prof, 47-53, prof, 53-63; prof Ger & chmn dept, Ind Univ, Bloomington, 63-71; Kenan prof, 71-81, EMER KENAN PROF GER, UNIV VA, 82- *Concurrent Pos:* Am Coun Learned Soc fac study fel, 51; Ford fel, 55-56; vis prof, Univ Wis, 67-68, Univ Hamburg, 70 & Monash Univ, Australia, 72; prof in residence, Ripon Col, 68 & Univ Ore, 74; consult, Nat Endowment Humanities, 74-, Fulbright-Hays, 74 & Am Coun Learned Soc, 75. *Honors & Awards:* Goethe Medal, 70. *Mem:* MLA; Am Asn Teachers Ger; Asn Depts Foreign Lang (pres, 71). *Res:* Age of Goethe; language of German poetry. *Publ:* Auth, George Ticknor's Sorrows of Young Werter, Univ NC, 52: coauth, Lebendige Literatur, Houghton, 60; auth, The Songs of the Nibelungs, Wayne State Univ, 62; ed, Gottfried Keller, Stories, 82. *Mailing Add:* Dept of Ger Lit Univ of Va Charlottesville VA 22901

RYDING, WILLIAM WELLINGTON, b Detroit, Mich, May 11, 24; m 49; c 1. FRENCH. *Educ:* Univ Mich, AB, 48, MA, 49; Columbia Univ, PhD(comp lit), 61. *Prof Exp:* Instr English, Western Ill State Col, 54-55; asst prof French, Augustana Col- Ill, 55-56; instr, Wayne State Univ, 56-58; from instr to asst prof, Columbia Univ, 58-67; assoc prof, 67-73, PROF FRENCH, FAIRLEIGH DICKINSON UNIV, 73- *Mem:* MLA; AAUP; Asn Studies Dada & Surrealism; Mediaeval Acad Am. *Res:* Medieval lyric and narrative literature. *Publ:* Auth, Faus semblant, Romanic Rev, 10/69; Structure in Medieval Narrative, Mouton, The Hague, 71; coauth, Au jour le jour, Prentice-Hall, 2nd ed, 74. *Mailing Add:* Dept of French Fairleigh Dickinson Univ Rutherford NJ 07070

RYSAN, JOSEF, b Czech, Apr 6, 14, US citizen; m 41. GERMANIC & SLAVIC LANGUAGES. *Educ:* Univ Chicago, PhD, 48. *Prof Exp:* Asst prof Ger & Russ, Carleton Col, 47-48; from asst prof to assoc prof, Vanderbilt Univ, 48-55, from acting chmn dept to chmn dept, 52-76, prof, 55-80. *Mem:* MLA; Czech Soc Arts & Sci in US; Am Asn Advan Slavic Studies. *Res:* German-Russian literary relations of the 19th century; folklore. *Publ:* Auth,

Wilhelm Meinhold's Bernsteinhexe: A Study in Witchcraft and Cultural History, Univ Chicago, 48; Is our civilization creating a new folklore?, Southern Folklore Quart, 6/52; Theodor Storm and psychic phenomena, Mod Philol, 8/55; Solution of crisis by myth: parallel between Luther's and Nazi German, In: Festschrift for John G Kunstmann, Univ NC, 59. *Mailing Add:* 334 Walnut Dr Nashville TN 37205

RYWKIN, MICHAEL, b Wilno, Poland, Nov 23, 25; US citizen. FOREIGN LANGUAGES, POLITICAL SCIENCE. *Educ:* City Col New York, MA, 55; Columbia Univ, PhD, 60. *Prof Exp:* Spec lectr, US Air Force specialists prog, Russ Inst, Columbia Univ, 54-56; instr Russ, Colgate Univ, 59-60; asst prof Russ & Russ govt, NY Univ, 60-62; res fel Soviet affairs, Russ Res Ctr, Harvard Univ, 62-63; from asst prof to assoc prof Russ, 63-72, PROF RUSS & RUSS AREA STUDIES, CITY COL NEW YORK, 72-, CHMN RUSS AREA STUDIES PROG, 70-, DEPT GER & SLAVIC LANG, 73- *Concurrent Pos:* Vis prof, Univ Okla, Munich Ctr, Ger, 69-70; vis scholar, Columbia Univ, 80-81. *Mem:* Am Asn Advan Slavic Studies. *Res:* Soviet affairs; Russian language and literature; Russian colonization. *Publ:* Auth, Russia in Central Asia, Collier, 63; Moscow's Muslim Challenge, Sharpe, 82. *Mailing Add:* Dept of Ger & Slavic City Col New York Convent Ave 138th St New York NY 10031

S

SABATINI, ARTHUR VINCENT, b Schenectady, NY, Aug 22, 40; m 62; c 2. FRENCH LITERATURE. *Educ:* Union Col, NY, AB, 62; State Univ NY, Buffalo, MA, 65, PhD(French lang & lit), 72. *Prof Exp:* Part-time instr French, State Univ NY, Buffalo, 66-67, instr, 67-69; asst prof, 69-73, ASSOC PROF FRENCH, STATE UNIV NY COL, OSWEGO, 73-, DIR INT EDUC, 76- *Concurrent Pos:* NDEA fel, State Univ NY, Buffalo, 63-66. *Res:* French literature of the 17th century; 19th century novel and short story. *Mailing Add:* Dept of Fr Ital & Classics State Univ of NY Oswego NY 13126

SABAT-RIVERS, GEORGINA, b Santiago, Cuba; US citizen; m 44, 69; c 4. SPANISH LITERATURE, FRENCH. *Educ:* Sorbonne, dipl French, 55; Johns Hopkins Univ, PhD(Span & French), 69. *Prof Exp:* Asst prof French, Univ Oriente, Cuba, 55-61; asst prof, Georgetown Visitation Col, 62-63; asst prof French & Span, Western Md Col, 63-69, from assoc prof Span to prof, 69-78, head dept foreign lang, 74-78; PROF SPAN, STATE UNIV NY, 78-, CHMN DEPT HISP LANG & LIT, 81- *Concurrent Pos:* Fel, Johns Hopkins Univ, 65-66. *Honors & Awards:* Fac Publ Medal, Philos Soc Philadelphia, 76 & 78. *Mem:* MLA; AAUP; Am Asn Teachers Span & Port; Asn Int Hispanistas. *Res:* Sor Juana Ines de la Cruz; Quevedo; Lazarillo de Tormes. *Publ:* Auth, A proposito de Sor Juana Ines de la Cruz: Tradicion poetica del tema Sueno en Espana, Mod Lang Notes, 3/69; Nota bibliografica sobre Sor Juana Ines de la Cruz: Son tres las ediciones de Barcelona, 1693, Nueva Rev Filol Hisp XXXIII, Mexico City, 74; Sor Juana y su Sueno: Antecedentes cientificos en la poesia espanola del Siglo de Oro, Cuadernos Hispanoam, 4/76; coauth, Antologia de Sor Juana Ines de la Cruz, Ed Noguer, Barcelona, 76; auth, El Sueno de Sor Juana Ines de la Cruz: Tradiciones y originalidad, Tamesis, London, 77; auth, Quevedo, Floralba y el Padre Tablares, Mod Lang Notes, 3/78; Sor Juana, In: Historia de la literatura Hispanoamericana, Madrid, 82; ed, Inundacion Castalida, Ed Castalia, Madrid, 82. *Mailing Add:* Dept Hisp Lang & Lit State Univ NY Stony Brook NY 11794

SABISTON, ELIZABETH JEAN, English & American Literature. See Vol II

SABLE, MARTIN HOWARD, b Sept 24, 24; US citizen; m 50; c 2. LATIN AMERICAN STUDIES, LIBRARY SCIENCE. *Educ:* Boston Univ, AB, 46, MA, 52; Nat Univ Mex, Dr en Let(Span), 52; Simmons Col, MS, 59. *Prof Exp:* Bibliogr & ref librn, Northeastern Univ Libr, 59-63; ref librn, Dept Humanities, Calif State Univ, Los Angeles, 63-64; Los Angeles County Pub Libr, 64-65; asst res prof, Latin Am Ctr, Univ Calif, Los Angeles, 65-68; assoc prof, 68-72, PROF LIBR SCI, UNIV WIS-MILWAUKEE, 72- *Concurrent Pos:* Mex-Am Cult Comn fel, Nat Univ Mex, 52; hon consul for Repub Mex, Providence, RI, 55; Mem Found Jewish Cult fel, 71-72; vis prof, Dept Span & Latin Am Studies Hebrew Univ Jerusalem, 72-73. *Mem:* AAUP; Conf Latin Am Hist; Latin Am Studies Asn; Am Libr Asn; Sem Acquisition Latin Am Libr Mat. *Res:* Latin American studies as a field of higher education; Latin American bibliography; reference services. *Publ:* Lat American urbanization: A guide . . ., 71 & International and area studies librarianship: Case studies, 73, Scarecrow; Guerilla movement in Latin America since 1950: An international bibliography, Ctr Latin Am, Univ Wis, 77; Latin American Jewry: A Research Guide, Hebrew Union Col Press, 78; Bibliographic instruction in Latin American studies, Latin Am Res Rev, spring 79; A Guide to Nonprint Materials for Latin American Studies, 79 & The Latin American Studies Directory, 81, Blaine Ethridge-Books; Translation, In: Encycl Libr & Info Sci, Vol 31, 81. *Mailing Add:* 4518 N Larkin St Milwaukee WI 53211

SABOURIN, PASCAL, Can citizen. FRENCH MODERN NOVEL. *Educ:* Univ Sudbury, BA, 60; Univ Ottawa, MA, 63; Univ Strasburg, PhD(French mod novel), 68. *Prof Exp:* Lectr French lit, 62-66, asst prof, 68-70, ASSOC PROF FRENCH NOVEL, LAURENTIAN UNIV, 70- *Concurrent Pos:* Consult transl, Univ Sudbury, 68-74; chmn French dept, Laurentian Univ, 71-74 & 78-80, dean humanities fac, 80- *Mem:* Asn Can Univ Teachers Fr. *Res:* French novel 1930-39; political problems. *Publ:* Auth, Deux conceptions de l'amour chez Andre Malraux, Ottawa, Tel Quel, 4/62; Andre Malraux, ecrivain dadaiste, Bull de L'APFUC, 4/71; Canada: Le pays et ses habitants, traduit et adapte, Gage, Toronto, 79; Geographie G 23, cours par correspondance, traduit et adapte par Pascal Sabourin, Ministere de l'Education, Toronto, 79; Histoire du Canada et des Canadiens, traduit et adapte, Gage, Toronto, 80; Le Centre des Sciences de Sudbury, traduit par Pascal Sabourin, Toronto, 80; Quant il pleut sur ma ville, recit, Sherbrooke, Naaman, 81; Poemes du Nord et d'Ailleurs, recueil de poesie, Cobalt, Highway Book Shop. *Mailing Add:* Dept of Lit Laurentian Univ Sudbury ON P3E 2C6 Can

SACHS, JACQUELINE S, b Chicago, Ill, Apr 8, 39. LINGUISTICS, PSYCHOLOGY OF LANGUAGE. *Educ:* Northwestern Univ, Evanston, BA, 60; Univ Calif, Berkeley, PhD(psychol), 66. *Prof Exp:* Nat Insts Health fel ling, Mass Inst Technol, 66; mem tech staff psychol of lang, Bell Telephone Labs, Murray Hill, NJ, 66-68; res assoc speech, 68-69, asst prof, 69-73, ling, 72-73, assoc prof speech & ling, 73-78, PROF COMMUN SCI, PSYCHOL & LING, UNIV CONN, 78- *Concurrent Pos:* Fulbright fel, Univ Bonn, 60-61; asst prof psychol, Rutgers Univ, Newark, 67. *Mem:* Ling Soc Am; Am Psychol Asn; Soc Res Child Develop. *Res:* Psycholinguistics; language acquisition. *Publ:* Auth, Recognition memory for syntactic and semantic aspects of connected discourse, Perception & Psychophysics, 67; Anatomical and Cultural Determinants of Male and Female Speech, Georgetown Univ, 73; Memory in reading and listening to discourse, Memory & Cognition, 74; coauth, Young children's use of age-appropriate speech, J Child Lang, 76; contribr, The development of speech, Academic Press, 76; The adaptive significance of linguistic input, Cambridge Univ, 77; Of two-word instructions, J Child Lang, 78; Topic selection, Discourse Processes, 79. *Mailing Add:* Dept of Speech Univ of Conn Storrs CT 06268

SACHS, MURRAY, b Toronto, Ont, Apr 10, 24; US citizen; m 61; c 2. FRENCH, COMPARATIVE LITERATURE. *Educ:* Univ Toronto, BA, 46; Columbia Univ, AM, 47, PhD(French), 52. *Prof Exp:* Lectr French, Columbia Univ, 46-48; instr, Univ Calif, 48-50; instr mod lang, Univ Detroit, 51-52; instr Romanic lang, Williams Col, Mass, 54-57, asst prof, 57-60; from asst prof to assoc prof, 60-66, chmn dept Europ lang & lit, 62-63, dept Romance & comp lit, 67-71, chmn joint grad prog lit studies, 75-78, PROF FRENCH LIT, BRANDEIS UNIV, 66-, CHMN, DEPT ROMANCE & COMP LIT, 81- *Concurrent Pos:* Mem fac, adv & consult, Nat Humanities Fac, 78-81. *Honors & Awards:* Chevalier, Palmes Academiques, 71. *Mem:* MLA; Am Asn Teachers Fr; Mod Humanities Res Asn; Am Coun Teaching Foreign Lang. *Res:* The French short story; the novel in 19th-century France; theory of fiction. *Publ:* Auth, The French Short Story in the 19th Century: A Critical Anthology, Oxford Univ, 69; Flaubert's Trois contes: The reconquest of art, L'Esprit Createur, spring 70; Anatole France: The Short Stories, Edward Arnold, London, 74; The emergence of poetics in the French short story, French Lit Series, 75; The present as past: Anatole France's Histoire Contemporaine, Nineteenth-Century French Studies, spring 77; contribr, Columbia Dict of Modern European Literature, 80; Critical Survey of Short Fiction, 81; auth, The legacy of Flaubert, Univ Houston Forum, spring 82. *Mailing Add:* Dept of Romance & Comp Lit Brandeis Univ Waltham MA 02154

SACIUK, BOHDAN, b Dubno, Volhynia, Ukraine, July 12, 41; US citizen; m 63; c 1. GENERAL & IBERO-ROMANCE LINGUISTICS. *Educ:* Univ Ill, Urbana, AB, 64, MA, 65, PhD(ling), 69. *Prof Exp:* From asst prof to assoc prof ling, Span & Port, Univ Fla, 69-76; assoc prof ling, English & Span, 76-82, chmn dept lang & ling, 79-80, PROF LING, ENGLISH & SPAN, INTER-AM UNIV PR, SAN GERMAN, 82-, CHMN DEPT HUMANITIES, 80- *Concurrent Pos:* Mem exec comt, Caribbean Inst and Study Ctr Latin Am, 76- *Mem:* Ling Soc Am; MLA; Am Asn Teachers Span & Port; Southeastern Conf Ling (pres, 75-76); Int Soc Phonetic Sci; Teachers English Speakers Other Lang. *Res:* Spanish and Portuguese phonology and dialectology; Ukrainian linguistics; contrastive Spanish-English linguistics and bilingualism. *Publ:* Auth, The Stratal Division of the Lexicon, Papers Ling, 69; Some basic rules of Portuguese phonology, In: Studies Presented to R B Lees by His Students, Ling Res, 70; co-ed & contribr, Generative Studies in Romance Languages, Newbury House, 72; auth, Spanish stress and language change, In: Linguistic Studies in Romance Languages, Georgetown Univ, 74; co-ed, 1975 Colloquium on Hispanic Linguistics, Georgetown Univ, 76; auth, Las realizaciones multiples o polimorfismo del fonema y en el espanol puertorriqueno, Boletin de la Academia Puertorriquena de la Lengua Expanola, 77; Estudio comparativo de las realizaciones foneticas d y en dos dialectos del Caribe hispanico, In: Dialectologia hispanoamericana: Estudios actuales, Georgetown Univ, 80. *Mailing Add:* Box 3268 Inter-Am Univ San German PR 00753

SACIUK, OLENA HIKAWYJ, Comparative & American Literature. See Vol II

SACKETT, THEODORE ALAN, b Los Angeles, Calif, Mar 24, 40; m 64; c 2. SPANISH. *Educ:* Univ Calif, Riverside, BA, 62; Univ Ariz, MA, 65, PhD(Span), 66. *Prof Exp:* Lectr Romanic lang, Williams Col, 65-67; from asst prof to assoc prof Span, Univ NMex, 67-71, actg chmn dept, summer 69; chmn dept Span & Port, 71-77, ASSOC PROF SPAN, UNIV SOUTHERN CALIF, 71- *Concurrent Pos:* NDEA fel, Univ Ariz, 63-65. *Mem:* MLA; Am Asn Teachers Span & Port; Philol Asn Pac Coast. *Res:* Benito Perez Galdos, novels, theatre; 19th century Spanish novel and theatre; Ecuatorian literature. *Publ:* Auth, Annotated Bibliography of Perez Galdos, Univ NMex, 68; Miau, Perez Galdos, Anales Galdosianos, 69; El arte en la novelistica de Jorge Icaza, Quito, Casa Cult Ecuatoriana, 74; Canas y barro, Blasco Ibanez, Hispanofila, 77; Galdos y las mascaras; historia teatral y bibliografia anotada, Porrua, 78; Tristana, Perez Galdos, Anales Galdosianos, 78. *Mailing Add:* Dept of Span & Port Univ of Southern Calif Los Angeles CA 90007

SACKS, NORMAN PAUL, b Philadelphia, Pa, Feb 11, 14; m 43; c 3. HISPANIC LINGUISTICS & CIVILIZATION. *Educ:* Temple Univ, BS, 35; Univ Pa, AM 37, PhD(Span & Port), 40. *Prof Exp:* Asst instr Romance lang, Univ Pa, 38-40; instr Span & Port, Univ Hawaii, 40-42; instr Span, Temple Univ, 45-46; from instr to prof, Oberlin Col, 46-61; prof Span & Port & dir Ibero-Am Area Studies Ctr, Univ Wis-Madison, 61-75, chmn dept Span & Port, 77-79. *Concurrent Pos:* Vis prof, Univ Calif, Berkeley, Western Reserve

Univ, Univ Southern Calif, Univ NMex, Univ Wis & Harvard Univ; consult, US Office Educ, 60-70; Fulbright-Hays res fel, Chile, 67-68; Am Philos Soc grant, 76. *Honors & Awards:* Best Article Prize, Hispania, 71. *Mem:* Am Asn Teachers Span & Port (pres, 66); MLA; Ling Soc Am; Latin Am Studies Asn; Am Coun Teaching Foreign Lang. *Res:* Hispanic linguistics; Spanish and Spanish American intellectual history; Chilean thinkers. *Publ:* Auth, Latinity of Dated Documents in the Portuguese Territory & co-auth, MLA Project Modern Spanish, Harcourt, 60; auth, Cuentos de hoy y de ayer, rev ed, 65 & Spanish for Beginners, 66, Ronald; The making of the Hispanist 1966, Hispania, 3/67; Los chuetas de Mallorca y Los muertos mandan de Blasco Ibanez: Un capitulo en la historia de los judios en Espana, Davar, Buenos Aires, 70; Jose Victorino Lastarria: Un intelectual comprometido en la America Latina, Rev Chilena Hist y Geog, Santiago, 72; The man who entered through the window: The memoirs of Salvador de Madariaga, Hispania, 76. *Mailing Add:* Dept of Span & Port Univ of Wis Madison WI 53706

SACKS, RICHARD, b Rhinebeck, NY, June 24, 51; m 77. COMPARATIVE LITERATURE, INDO-EUROPEAN LINGUISTICS. *Educ:* Harvard Univ, AB, 74, PhD(comp lit), 78. *Prof Exp:* ASST PROF COMP LIT, COLUMBIA UNIV, 78- *Res:* Greek literature; Old English literature; Old Norse literature. *Publ:* Auth, Old Norse modsefa tjold and Greek deltois phrenon, Indo-Europ Studies II, 75; Germanic seventh class strong verbs, Indo-Europ Studies III, 77. *Mailing Add:* Dept of English & Comp Lit Columbia Univ New York NY 10027

SACOTO, ANTONIO, b Ecuador, Nov 30, 32; US citizen; c 6. SPANISH & LATIN AMERICAN LITERATURE. *Educ:* Univ Cuenca, Bachiller, 52; City Col NY, BA, 63, MA, 64; Columbia Univ, PhD, 67. *Prof Exp:* Lectr Span, Hunter Col, 63-64; from asst prof to assoc prof, 64-76, PROF SPAN & CHMN, DEPT ROMANCE LANG, CITY COL NY, 76-, DIR LATIN AM AREA STUDIES, 73- *Publ:* Auth, The Indian in the Ecuadorian Novel, Las Americas, 67; El pensamiento de Montalvo . . ., 5-6/68; El indio en el ensayo de la America espanola, Las Americas, 71; Sobre autores ecuatorianos, Cuenca: Casa de la Cultura, 72; Juan Montalvo: El escritor y el estilista, Casa de Cultura Ecuatoriana, 73; Cinco novelas claves de la literatura hispanoamericana, New York: Eliseo Torres, 79; La nueva novela ecuatoriana, Cuenca: Universidad de Cuenca, 81; El indio en el ensayo de la America espanola, NY, Las Americas, 70, 2nd ed, Cuenca: Casa de la Cultura, 81. *Mailing Add:* 51 Landscape Ave Yonkers NY 10210

SADOUSKI, JOHN, b Zaluzza, Byelorussa, July 15, 26; Can citizen; m 61; c 2. BYELORUSSIAN LANGUAGE & LITERATURE. *Educ:* Univ Rome, DottL, 64; Univ London, DPhil(Russ), 67. *Prof Exp:* Asst prof, Univ Ill, Chicago Circle, 68-69; ASSOC PROF RUSS, QUEEN'S UNIV, ONT, 69- *Concurrent Pos:* Contractor, Nat Mus of Can, 71 & Secy State Can, 74. *Mem:* Can Asn of Slavists; Byelorussian Inst Arts & Sci, (Can pres, 69-72); MLA; Northeast Mod Lang Asn; Can Inst Onomastic Sci. *Res:* History of Byelorussians in Canada. *Publ:* Auth, Belorussian culture in the sixteenth century, Can Slavonic Papers, Ottawa, 70; Ledsikal 'nyia asablivastsi Knihi Tsartvau Skaryny, Zapisy, 70; Belorussian studies, Vols 33-38, Year's Work Mod Lang Studies, 72-77; Bryl, Yanka, 79, Charot, Mikhas, 81 & Chorny, Kuz'ma, 81, In: The Modern Encycl of Russian and Soviet Literature; Soviet Belorussian publications in the 1970s, Nationalities Papers, 81; A History of the Byelorussians in Canada, 81. *Mailing Add:* Dept of Russ Queen's Univ Kingston ON K7L 3N6 Can

SAENZ, GERARDO, b Ballinger, Tex, July 12, 21; m 46; c 3. SPANISH. *Educ:* Sul Ross State Col, BA, 49, MA, 50; Univ Tex, PhD, 59. *Prof Exp:* Teacher Span, Edinburg High Sch, Tex, 50-54; lectr Span, Univ Puebla, Mex, 59; instr Span, Agr & Mech Col Tex, 59-60; lectr Span, Nat Inst Fine Arts, Mex 62; asst prof Span, Univ Ark, 60-67; assoc prof Span, 67-76, PROF ROMANCE LANG, UNIV KY, 76- *Mem:* Am Asn Teachers Span & Port; MLA. *Res:* Mexican poetry Spanish-American drama and novel. *Publ:* Auth, Luis G Urbina, Inst Naclla Artes, Mex, 63; En Torno a los Poemas Crueles de Luis G Urbina, El Nac, Mex 63. *Mailing Add:* Dept of Lang Univ of Ky Lexington KY 40506

SAENZ, PILAR G, b Madrid, Spain, Aug 18, 27; m 57; US citizen. SPANISH. *Educ:* Univ Madrid, Lic, 53; Bryn Mawr Col, MA, 57; Univ Md, PhD(Span), 66. *Prof Exp:* Instr Span, Trinity Col, DC, 57-61 & Univ Md, 61-67; asst prof, Am Univ, DC, 68-70; ASSOC PROF SPAN LIT, GEORGE WASHINGTON UNIV, 70- *Concurrent Pos:* Fel, Bryn Mawr Col, 54-57; prof lectr, Am Univ, DC, 67-68; Am Philos Soc res grant, 76. *Honors & Awards:* Am Asn Univ Women Grad Prize, 66. *Mem:* Am Asn Teachers Span & Port; MLA; Asn Int Hispanistas; Asoc de Licenciados y Doctores Espanoles en Estados Unidos. *Res:* Twentieth century Spanish literature; aesthetic theory; Eugenio d'Ors and Novecentism. *Publ:* Auth, El teatro universitario espanol en los ultimos treinta anos, Bol Inst Caro y Cuervo, 64; En torno al ultimo poema de Pedro Salinas, Insula, 2/67; Morfologia y tectonica: Principio de la estetica orsiana, Papeles Son Armadans, 6/67; Eugenio d'Ors: Su mundo de valores esteticos, Plenitud, Madrid, 69. *Mailing Add:* Dept of Romance Lang George Washington Univ Washington DC 20006

SAG, IVAN ANDREW, b Alliance, Ohio, Nov 9, 49. THEORETICAL & COMPUTATIONAL LINGUISTICS. *Educ:* Univ Rochester, BA, 71; Univ Pa, MA, 73; Mass Inst Technol, PhD(ling), 76. *Prof Exp:* Asst prof ling, Univ Pa, 76-79; ASST PROF LING, STANFORD UNIV, 79- *Concurrent Pos:* A Mellon fel, Stanford Univ, 78-79; vist asst prof, Univ Tex, Austin, 79, Univ Calif, Berkeley, 80 & Ling Inst, Univ Md, 82; consult, Hewlett-Packard Labs, 81- *Mem:* Ling Soc Am; Asn Comput Ling. *Res:* Natural language syntax and semantics; natural language processing. *Publ:* Auth, Pseudosolutions to the Pseudoparadox: Sanskrit Diaspirates Revisited, 76 & Deep and surface anaphora, 76, Ling Inquiry; Deletion and Logical Form, Garland, 80; co-ed, Elements of Discourse Understanding, Cambridge Univ Press, 80; auth, Coordination, extraction and generalized phase structure grammar, 82 & Coordination and transformational grammar (in press), Ling Inquiry; coauth, Auxiliaries and related phenomena in a restrictive theory of grammar, Language, 82; Referential and quantificational indefinites, Ling & Philos, 82. *Mailing Add:* Dept of Ling Stanford Univ Stanford CA 97305

SAHA, PROSANTA KUMAR, b Calcutta, India, Dec 4, 32; US citizen; m 58; c 2. ENGLISH, LINGUISTICS. *Educ:* Univ Calcutta, BA, 56; Oberlin Col, MA 57; Western Reserve Univ, PhD(English), 66. *Prof Exp:* Teacher, Hawken Sch, 57-62; instr English, 62-64, asst prof English & ling, 66-72, ASSOC PROF ENGLISH & LING & CHMN LING & UNDERGRAD HUMANITIES PROG, CASE WESTERN RESERVE UNIV, 72- *Honors & Awards:* Carl F Wittke Award, Case Western Reserve Univ, 71. *Mem:* Ling Soc Am. *Res:* English literature and linguistics; computer analysis of literature, especially stylistics; Bengali literature and linguistics. *Publ:* Auth, The dialectics of the Cuchulain theme in Yeat's works, Vol XV, No 24 & Shaftesbury--a significant thinker, Vol XVI, No 46, Thought; A linguistic approach to style, Style, winter 68; A modern view of language, Case Western Reserve Law Rev, winter 72; Blue Magic and other Poems, Writers Workshop, Calcutta, 74; Style, stylistic transformations and incorporators, Style winter 78. *Mailing Add:* Dept of English Clark Hall Rm 103 Case Western Reserve Univ Cleveland OH 44106

SAINE, THOMAS PRICE, b Brooklyn, NY, Mar 8, 41. GERMAN LITERATURE. *Educ:* Yale Univ, BA, 62, MPh, 67, PhD(Ger), 68. *Prof Exp:* From instr to assoc prof Ger, Yale Univ, 68-75; assoc prof, 75-76, PROF GER, UNIV CALIF, IRVINE, 76- *Concurrent Pos:* Vis prof Ger, Univ Cincinnati, 73-74; assoc ed, Ger Quart, 78-81; ed, Goethe Yearbk, 82-; Am Coun Learned Soc fel, 82-83; Guggenheim fel, 83. *Mem:* MLA; Lessing Soc; Am Asn Teachers Ger; Am Soc 18th Century Studies; Goethe Soc NAm. *Res:* German 18th century literature; 18th century European intellectual history; Goethe and German classicism. *Publ:* Auth, Wilhelm Meister's homecoming, J English & Ger Philol, 70; Die ästhetische Theodizee: Karl Philipp Moritz und die Philosophie des 18 Jahrhunderts, William Fink Verlag, Munich, 71; Georg Forster, Twayne (World Auth Ser 215), 72; Natural science and the ideology of nature in the German enlightenment, Lessing Yearbk, 76; Was ist Aufklärung?, Kulturgeschichtliche Überlegungen zu neuer Beschäftigung mit der deutschen Aufklärung, Zeitschrift für deutsche Philol, 74; contribr, Christian Ludwig Liscow and Georg Forster, Deutsche Dichter des 18 Jahrhunderts, Erich Schmidt Verlag, 77; Passion and Aggression: The Meaning of Werther's Last Letter, Orbis Litterarum, 80; The portrayal of Lotte in the two versions of Goethe's Werther, J English & Ger Philol, 81. *Mailing Add:* Dept of Ger Univ of Calif Irvine CA 92717

ST AUBYN, FREDERIC CHASE, b Russell, Kans, Sept 30, 21. FRENCH. *Educ:* Southwest Mo State Univ, BA, 42; Yale Univ, MA, 47, PhD, 52. *Prof Exp:* Asst instr French, Yale Univ, 47-49; instr, Harpur Col, 50-53, asst prof, 53-54; Univ Del, 54-61; assoc prof, Elmira Col, 61-64, prof mod lang & chmn div lang & lit, 64-71, dir, Jr Year Abroad Prog, 71-72; chmn dept French & Ital, 72-76, PROF FRENCH, UNIV PITTSBURGH, 76- *Concurrent Pos:* Mem comt for construction of proficiency test, NDEA-MLA, 58-60; Am Coun Learned Soc fel, 67-68. *Mem:* MLA; Am Asn Teachers Fr; Int Asn Fr Studies. *Res:* Contemporary French literature. *Publ:* Co-ed, Jean-Paul Sartre's Les Mouches, Harper, 63; Trois Pieces Surrealistes, Appleton, 69; auth, Stephane Mallarme, 69, Arthur Rimbaud, 75 & Charles Peguy, 77, Twayne. *Mailing Add:* Dept of Fr & Ital Univ of Pittsburgh Pittsburgh PA 15260

ST CLAIR, ROBERT NEAL, b Honolulu, Hawaii, Apr 24, 34; m. LINGUISTICS. *Educ:* Univ Hawaii, BA, 63; Univ Wash, MA, 67; Univ Calif, San Diego, MA, 70; Univ Kans, PhD(ling), 74. *Prof Exp:* Asst prof English, Calif State Univ, Los Angeles, 67-68; ASSOC PROF ENGLISH & LING, UNIV LOUISVILLE, 73- *Concurrent Pos:* Distinguished vis prof, NMex State Univ, 77; adj prof ethnic studies, Cent Wash Univ, 78. *Mem:* Int Reading Asn; MLA. *Res:* Sociolinguistics; bilingual education; interdisciplinary linguistics. *Publ:* Auth, Bilingual Education for Asian Americans, Bunka Hyoron Publ, 80; Language Renewal among Native American Indian Tribes, Nat Clearinghouse Biblingal Educ, 80; co-ed, Approaches to Language Acquisition, Tuebingen Beitrage Ling, 81; auth, Social and Educational Issues in Bilingualism and Biculturalism, Univ Press Am, 81; Developmental Kinesics, Univ Park Press, 82; Cognition and Developmental Linguistics, Charles Thomas Publ, 82; Developing Bilingual Literacy among Native American Indians in the Pacific Northwest, Advocates Pub Educ Press, 82; Bilingual and Bicultural Experiences of Asian-Americans, Nat Clearinghouse Bilingual Educ, 82. *Mailing Add:* Dept of English Univ of Louisville Louisville KY 40208

ST JACQUES, BERNARD, b Montreal, Que, Apr 26, 28; m 66. LINGUISTICS, ASIAN STUDIES. *Educ:* Univ Montreal, BA, 49, lic philos, 54; Sophia Univ, Japan, MA, 62; Georgetown Univ, MS, 64; Univ Paris, PhD(ling, Asian studies), 66, D es L, 75. *Prof Exp:* Asst prof French & ling, Sophia Univ, 56-67; assoc prof, 68-78, PROF LING & ASIAN STUDIES, UNIV BC, 78- *Concurrent Pos:* Can Coun res grant, 67-68 & 76-79; fac grad studies res grant, Univ BC, 67-68; Dept External Affairs Can grant, 67; vis fac mem, Simon Fraser Univ, 76; Japan Found prof fel, 81. *Mem:* Phonetic Soc Japan; Ling Soc Am; Ling Soc Japan; Int Sociol Asn; Ling Asn Can & US. *Res:* Japanese linguistics; transformational analysis and earlier linguistics; relationships of language and culture in sociolinguistics. *Publ:* Auth, Analyse structurale de la syntaxe du Japonais moderne, Klincksieck, Paris, 66; Some observations about transformational grammar, Ling, 67; Review of a review, Fouda Lang, 67; Festschrift Martinet, Ling Circle NY, 68; Aspects sociolinguistiques du bilinguisme canadien, Int Ctr Res Bilingualism, 76; co-ed (with Howard Giles), Language and Ethnic Relations, Pergamon Press, Oxford, 79; auth, Les tendances fonctionnelles des theories syntaxiques post-transformationnelles, Ling, Paris, Vol 17, 81. *Mailing Add:* Dept of Ling Univ of BC Vancouver BC V6T 1W5 Can

SAINT-LEON, CLAIRE BRANDICOURT, b Paris, France, Nov 20, 27; US citizen; c 2. FRENCH, THEATER ARTS. *Educ:* Sorbonne, Licence es Lett, 51; Univ Wash, MA, 53; Univ Calif, Los Angeles, PhD(French), 66. *Prof Exp:* Sub-ed, Etudes, 47-51; assoc French, Univ Calif, Los Angeles, 58-65, asst prof, 66-68; assoc prof, Fisk Univ, 68-70; PROF FRENCH, TENN TECHNOL UNIV, 70- *Honors & Awards:* Chevalier De L'Ordre Des Palmes Academiques, 76. *Mem:* MLA; AAUP. *Res:* French theatre; pronunciation and diction. *Publ:* Auth, L'Aventure des Theophiliens, Univ Microfilms 66; Technology and the medieval theater, Sci Fiction Res Asn, 72; Les bonnes de Jean Genet: quelle version faut-il jouer?, Proc Mountain Interstate Conf, 74; French Pronunciation, Tenn Technol Univ, 74. *Mailing Add:* 426 Loweland Rd Cookeville TN 38501

ST MARTIN, ADELE CORNAY, b Lafayette, La, Aug 13, 27; m 59; c 2. ROMANCE LANGUAGES. *Educ:* Univ Southwestern La, BA, 46; La State Univ, MA, 49; Tulane Univ, PhD(French), 57. *Prof Exp:* Instr French, Lake Erie Col, 55-56 & Newcomb Col, Tulane Univ, 57-60; PROF FRENCH, UNIV SOUTHWESTERN LA, 61- *Concurrent Pos:* Ed, Revue de Louisiane/La Rev, 74- *Mem:* MLA; Am Coun Teaching Foreign Lang; SCent Mod Lang Asn. *Mailing Add:* Box 4-0040 Univ of Southwestern La Lafayette LA 70504

ST MARTIN, GERARD LABARRE, b La Place, La, Oct 26, 29; m 59; c 2. FRENCH LANGUAGE & LITERATURE. *Educ:* Univ Southwestern La, BA, 56; Tulane Univ, MA, 60, PhD(French, Span), 69. *Prof Exp:* PROF FRENCH, UNIV SOUTHWESTERN LA, 60- *Concurrent Pos:* Scholar, Tulane Univ, 56-57; Fulbright scholar, Sorbonne, 57-58. *Mem:* MLA; SCent Mod Lang Asn; Am Asn Teachers Fr. *Res:* Translation of materials pertaining to literature of Louisiana; hagiography of Middles Ages; bilingual education. *Publ:* Coauth, Ecrits Louisianais, La State Univ, fall 78; Les materiaux ethniqnes et l'enseignement du francais, l'experience Louisianaise, Fr Rev, Vol LII, 5/79; auth, La presence francaise en Louisiane, Ville de Namur, Belgique, 82. *Mailing Add:* Dept of French Univ of Southwestern La Box 4-0040 Lafayette LA 70504

SAINTONGE, PAUL FREDERIC, b Ware, Mass, Feb 7, 04. FRENCH. *Educ:* Harvard Univ, AB, 24, AM 27, PhD, 30. *Prof Exp:* Instr, Univ NC, 24-25 & Harvard Univ, 25-28; from asst prof to prof French, 29-66, Mary Lyon prof, 66-69, chmn dept, 45-51, 54-69, EMER PROF, MT HOLYOKE COL, 69- *Concurrent Pos:* Sheldon traveling fel, Paris, 28-29; Am Coun Learned Soc fel, 33-34; Euurop observer, Save Children Fedn, 46, dir cult rels, 46-53; Fr-Am Cult Serv & Educ Aid grant, 66. *Honors & Awards:* Officier d'Acad, 48; Chevalier, Legion d'honneur, 48; Officier, Palmes Academiques, 62; key, New Eng Mod Lang Asn, 67; citation, Save Children Fedn, 67. *Mem:* MLA; Am Asn Teachers Fr. *Res:* Eighteenth century racketeering; influence of Horace on Ronsard and Montaigne; the memoirs of the Bishop of Beauvais. *Publ:* Auth, Fifty years of Moliere studies, 42; Anthologie de la poesie francaise, 57; La prononciation du francais, 58; Moliere, a critical bibliography 62; French vowel sounds, 67; coauth, Du francais oral au francais ecrit, 67; auth, Thirty years of Moliere studies, 1943-1973, Univ Southern Miss, 74. *Mailing Add:* 20 Ashfield Lane Hadley MA 01075

ST SURE, DONALD FRANCIS, b San Francisco, Calif, June 27, 12. CLASSICS, MUSIC. *Educ:* Gonzaga Univ, AB, 35, MA 36; Alma Col, Calif, STL 40, Univ Montreal, BMus, 48. *Prof Exp:* Instr theol, Univ Santa Clara, 41-42, instr philos, 42-43, prof classics, 43-51; chmn dept, Loyola Univ, Calif, 51-58, acad dean, Ryan Prep Col, 58-70, assoc prof Latin & assoc dean arts & sci, 64-70; RESIDENT CHAPLAIN, ST VINCENT'S SCH FOR BOYS, 70- *Concurrent Pos:* Teacher Bible, Old Testament, St Anthony's Parish, South Novato, Calif, 77- *Mem:* Class Asn Pac States (vpres, 62-63, pres, 63-64). *Res:* Vergil; Horace; Catullus. *Publ:* Auth, Selections, notes and commentary in Latin, Bks 7 & 8, In: Vergil's Aeneid, Loyola Univ, Calif, 52; Vernacular Mass in honor of St Aloysius for congregation, Ryan Prep Col, 66; composer for operetta, Comstock, John A. Lennon Co, 74; composer, The Music Box, John A Lennon Co, 80. *Mailing Add:* St Vincent's Sch for Boys Box M Civic Ctr Br San Rafael CA 94903

SAISSELIN, REMY G, b Moutier, Switz, Aug 17, 25; US citizen; m 55; c 3. FRENCH LITERATURE, ART HISTORY. *Educ:* Queens Col, NY, BA, 51; Univ Wis, MA, 52, MA, 53, PhD(French), 57. *Prof Exp:* Asst prof French, Western Reserve Univ, 56-59; asst cur publ, Cleveland Mus Art, 59-65; prof French lit, 65-68, PROF FRENCH LIT & FINE ARTS, UNIV ROCHESTER, 68- *Concurrent Pos:* Guggenheim fel, 72-73. *Mem:* MLA; Am Soc Aesthet; Col Art Asn Am; Am Soc 18th Century Studies. *Res:* French painting; aesthetics. *Publ:* Auth, Taste in Eighteenth Century France, Syracuse Univ, 65; Rococo muddle, 66 & Rouseau and portraiture, 68, Studies Voltaire; Room at the top of the eighteenth century, J Aesthet, 68; The Rule of Reason and the Ruses of the Heart, Case Western Reserve Univ, 79; Le Dix-huitieme Siecle, Prentice-Hall, 73; Still life in a consumer society, Leonardo, 76; The Literary Enterprise in Eighteenth Century France, Wayne State Univ, 79. *Mailing Add:* Dept of Fine Arts Univ of Rochester River Campus Rochester NY 14627

SAITZ, ROBERT LEONARD, b Boston, Mass, July 9, 28; m 62. ENGLISH AS SECOND LANGUAGE, LINGUISTICS. *Educ:* Boston Univ, BA, 49; Univ Iowa, MA, 50; Univ Wis, PhD(English ling), 55. *Prof Exp:* Instr English, Univ Wis, 57-59; asst prof, Southern Ill Univ, 59-60; coord, English as second lang, Fulbright grant, Colombia Univ, 60-62; from asst prof to assoc prof, 62-72, PROF LING & ENGLISH AS SECOND LANG, BOSTON UNIV, 72- *Concurrent Pos:* Consult English as second lang, Boston & New Bedford schs, 67; Fulbright lectr, Univ Seville, 69-70. *Mem:* Ling Soc Am; Nat Asn Foreign Student Affairs; Teachers English to Speakers Other Langs. *Res:* Old English syntax; second language learning; kinesics. *Publ:* Coauth, Selected Readings in English, Winthrop, 72; Handbook of Gestures, Mouton, The Hague, 72; Ideas in English, Winthrop, 74; Advanced Reading & Writing, Holt, 78; Challenge, Winthrop, 78. *Mailing Add:* Dept of English Boston Univ 236 Bay State Rd Boston MA 02215

SAJKOVIC, VLADIMIR I, b Pavlovsk, Russia, Jan 25, 12; m 37, 56; c 3. SLAVIC STUDIES. *Educ:* Russkoe Realnoe Uchilishche, Finland, BA, 32; Univ Pa, MA, 49, PhD(Slavic studies), 53. *Prof Exp:* Asst instr Slavic studies & Russ lang & lit, Univ Pa, 49-51, instr Slavic studies, 53-57, assoc Russ lang & lit, 57-59; instr Russ lang & lit & Ger, Univ Kans, 51-52; from asst prof to prof Russ lang & lit, 59-77, chmn dept, 59-70, EMER PROF RUSS LANG & LIT, MT HOLYOKE COL, 77- *Concurrent Pos:* Instr, Bryn Mawr Col, 54-57; vis prof, Middlebury Col, summer, 60 & Univ Pa, summer, 66. *Mem:* Am Asn Teachers Slavic & EEurop Lang; MLA; Am Asn Advan Slavic Studies; Soc Sci Studies Relig; Int Dostoevsky Soc. *Res:* Slavic languages and literature; philosophy; religion. *Mailing Add:* 101 College St South Hadley MA 01075

SAKHAROFF, MICHELINE, b Paris, France, June 7, 23; US citizen; m 46; c 1. FRENCH. *Educ:* Univ Calif, Los Angeles, BA, 58, MA, 60, PhD(French), 65. *Prof Exp:* Instr French, Whittier Col, 60-62; instr French, Univ Calif, Los Angeles, 62-63; from instr to assoc prof, 62-71, chmn dept foreign lang, 71-76, PROF FRENCH, CALIF STATE UNIV, NORTHRIDGE, 71- *Mem:* Am Asn Teachers Fr (vpres, 66-67); MLA. *Publ:* Auth, Le heros, sa liberte et son efficacite de Garnier a Rotrou, Nizet, Paris, 67; L'etourdi de Moliere, ou l'ecole des innocents, Fr Rev 12/69; Des grieux: Un cas de double identite, Rev Sci Humaines, 7-9/71; La poesie du langage theatral dans Huis clos, Mod Drama, 9/73. *Mailing Add:* Dept of Foreign Lang & Lit Calif State Univ Northridge CA 91324

SAKRAWA, GERTRUD M, b Austria, Jan 7, 24. MODERN LANGUAGES. *Educ:* Univ Vienna, PhD, 47; Columbia Univ, MA, 50, PhD, 62. *Prof Exp:* From instr to asst prof, 54-69, assoc prof, 70-82, PROF GER, BARNARD COL, COLUMBIA UNIV, 80- *Mem:* Am Coun Study Austrian Lit. *Res:* Georg Trakl; Theodor Fontane; 19th century realists. *Publ:* Auth, Scharmanter Egoismus-Theodor Fontanes Unwiederbringlich, Monatshefte, Vol LXI, No 1; Georg Trakls An die Verstummten, In: Untersuchungen zum Brenner, Salzburg, 82. *Mailing Add:* Dept of German Barnard Col Columbia Univ New York NY 10027

SALAS, TERESA CAJIAO, b Iquique, Chile, May 16, 27; US citizen; m 52; c 2. SPANISH AMERICAN LITERATURE. *Educ:* Inst Pedagog, Tech Univ Chile, Professor de Estado, 57; Kent State Univ, MEd, 60; Case Western Reserve Univ, MA, 65, PhD(Romance lang), 69. *Prof Exp:* Elem teacher pub schs, Iquique, Chile, 48-49; consult elem educ, Ministry Educ, Chile, 50-52; elem teacher pub schs, Santiago, 52-53; prof educ & English, Teachers Training Inst, Santiago, 54-60; asst, UNESCO Latin Am Ctr Training Specialists Educ, Santiago, 58-59; comp educ, Kent State Univ, 59-60; prof English, Inst Pedagog Tech, Univ Tech Chile, 60-63; instr Span, Kent State Univ, 63-65; from asst prof to assoc prof, 65-70, PROF SPAN, STATE UNIV NY COL, BUFFALO, 70- *Concurrent Pos:* Hon Chilean consul, Buffalo, 67-71. *Mem:* Am Asn Teachers Span & Port; MLA; Comp Educ Soc. *Res:* Latin American theater and narrative; foreign language teaching; international education. *Publ:* Auth, Temas y simbolos en la obra de Luis Alberto Heiremans, Ed Univ Chile, 69; coauth, La funcion del marco y la armonia simetrica en el Fausto de Estanislao del Campo, Ky Romance Quart, 70; auth, La angustia existencial en la obra del L A Heinemans, El Mercurio, 4/7/71; Balance de la temporada teatral 1972 en Buenos Aires, Latin Am Theater Rev, fall 73; coauth, Antologia critica del teatro costarricense contemporaneo, Ed Costa Rica, San Jose, 74; auth, Balance del ano teatral 1972 en Lima, Latin Am Theatre Rev, fall 74; coauth, Nicomedes Santa Cruz y la poesia de su conciencia de negri tud, Cuadernos Am, 9-10/75. *Mailing Add:* Dept of Foreign Lang State Univ of NY Col Buffalo NY 14222

SALDIVAR, RAMON, English & Comparative Literature. See Vol II

SALDIVAR, SAMUEL G, b Jerez, Mex, Mar 5, 37. SPANISH & HISPANIC AMERICAN LITERATURES. *Educ:* Fla State Univ, BA, 62, MA, 64; NY Univ, PhD(Span & Latin Am lit), 78. *Prof Exp:* Instr Span & foreign lang teaching methods, Fla State Univ, 64-66; PROF SPAN LANG & LIT, US MIL ACAD, 66- *Mem:* Nat Hispanic Soc. *Res:* Foreign language teaching methods; Spanish & Latin American literatures. *Mailing Add:* Dept of Foreign Lang West Point NY 10996

SALE, WILLIAM MERRITT, III, b New Haven, Conn, Nov 27, 29; m 53, 68; c 3. CLASSICS. *Educ:* Cornell Univ, AB, 51, MA, 54, PhD, 58. *Prof Exp:* Instr classics, Yale Univ, 57-58; from instr to assoc prof, 58-75, PROF CLASSICS & COMP LIT, WASHINGTON UNIV, 75- *Mem:* Am Philol Asn. *Res:* Greek religion, literature and philosphy. *Publ:* Auth, Aphrodite in the Theogony, Trans Am Philol Soc, 61; Hesiod and the myth of Callisto, 62 & The virginity of Artemis, 65, Rheinishces Mus; The dual vision of the Theogony, Arion, 66; Transl, commentary & introd, Sophocles' Electra, Prentice-Hall, 73; Temple legends of the Arkteia, Rheinishces Mus, 75; Review Edwards' Language of Hesiod, Am J Philol, 75; Existentialism & Euripides, Ramus Monograph, 77. *Mailing Add:* Dept of Classics Washington Univ St Louis MO 63130

SALGADO, MARIA ANTONIA, b Canary Islands, Spain, Jan 15, 33; US citizen; m 54; c 2. ROMANCE LANGUAGES. *Educ:* Fla State Univ, BA, 58; Univ NC, MA, 60; Univ Md, PhD(Span), 66. *Prof Exp:* Asst Span, Univ Md, 62, instr, 63-67; from asst prof to assoc prof, 67-77, PROF SPAN AM LIT, UNIV NC, CHAPEL HILL, 77- *Mem:* MLA; Am Asn Teachers Span & Port; Asn Int Hispanistas; Inst Int Lit Iberoam. *Res:* The art of caricature in literature; contemporary Spanish and Spanish-American poetry; literary portrait and autobiography. *Publ:* Auth, El arte polifacetico de las caricaturas liricas Juan Ramonianas, Insula, 68; Hablemos!, Harper, 75; El alma de la Sonatina, anales de Lit Hispanoamericana, 75; Civilizacion y barbarie o imaginacion o barbarie?, In: Explicacion de dien amos de soledad, Explicacion de Textol Literarios, 76; El Cepilla de dientes and El Apartamento: Two opposing views of alientated man, Romance Notes, 77; Trends of Spanish American fiction since 1950, SAtlantic Bull, 78; Rafael Arevalo Martinez, G K Hall, 79; Rio-mar-desierto: Plasmacion dinamica del revivir juanramoniano, Hispania, 82. *Mailing Add:* Dept of Romance Lang Univ of NC Chapel Hill NC 27514

SALIEN, JEAN-MARIE, b Port-au-Prince, Haiti, Jan 9, 45; US citizen; m 72; c 1. EIGHTEENTH CENTURY FRENCH LITERATURE, FRANCOPHONE LITERATURES. *Educ:* Univ Montreal, BA, 67; Columbia Univ, MA(foreign lang), 71; Univ Strasbourg, MA(French lit), 75; Univ Kans, PhD(French lit), 77. *Prof Exp:* Vis lectr, Univ Kans, 71-72; ASST

PROF FRENCH LIT, FORT HAYS STATE UNIV, 77-, CHMN FOREIGN LANG DEPT, 79- *Concurrent Pos:* Direct exchange scholar, Univ Strasbourg, 74-75; Nat Endowment for Humanities scholar, Wellesley Col, 82. *Mem:* MLA; Am Asn Teachers French. *Res:* Eighteenth century French literature; Jean-Jacques Rousseau; problems in Francophone literatures. *Publ:* Passions et raison dans la pensee de Jean-Jacques Rousseau, Int Studies Philos, 81; Who cares for foreign language education?, Univ Forum, spring 81; Francophonie et sous-developpement, Contemp Fr Civilization, winter 81; Negritude et luttle des classes dans le Roi Christophe d Aime Cesaire, Mod Lang Asn Conv, 12/81. *Mailing Add:* Fort Hays State Univ Hays KS 67601

SALINERO, FERNANDO GARCIA, b Vigo, Spain, Sept 30, 15; m 46. SPANISH, HISTORY OF THE LANGUAGE. *Educ:* Univ Madrid, MA, 45, PhD(Span lexicon), 63. *Prof Exp:* Vis prof Span lit, Purdue Univ, 64-65; asst prof, 65-70, ASSOC PROF SPAN LANG & LIT, UNIV WASH, 70. *Concurrent Pos:* Fulbright fel, 63-64; Premio Extraordinario de Doctorado, 64; premio Real Acad Espanola, 67. *Mem:* Am Asn Teachers Span & Port. *Res:* Spanish novel in the 16th century; lexicon of artists of the Spanish Golden Age; novela espanola del siglo XVI. *Publ:* Auth, Contribucion al estudio del vocabulario de arquitectura, Summary, Madrid, Span, 66; Alonso de Ledesma, autor del falso Quijote, Hispania, 67; Lexico de Alarifes del Siglo de Oro, Real Acad Espanola, 68; Teoria literaria de la cuidad, Papeles Armadans, 68; Lexico del ingeniero espanol del siglo XVI, Hispania, 69; ed, Don Quijote de Avellaneda, Castalia, Madrid, 72. *Mailing Add:* 7102 58th Ave NE Seattle WA 98115

SALINGER, HERMAN, b St Louis, Mo, Dec 23, 05; m 41; c 3. GERMAN & COMPARATIVE LITERATURE. *Educ:* Princeton Univ, AB, '27; Stanford Univ, AM, 29; Yale Univ, PhD, 37. *Prof Exp:* Asst instr, Stanford Univ, 27-29; instr Ger, Princeton Univ, 32-35 & Univ Wis, 37-42; asst prof, Univ Kans City, 46-47; assoc prof, Grinnell Col, 47-50, prof mod foreign lang, 50-55; prof Ger lang & lit, Duke Univ, 55-75, chmn comp lit prog, 56-70, 72-75; RETIRED. *Concurrent Pos:* Alex von Humboldt Found fel, 29, 71 & 74. *Mem:* MLA; Am Asn Teachers Ger; Int Arthur Schnitzler Res Asn (secy-treas, 61-72); Southern Comp Lit Asn; Am Comp Lit Asn. *Res:* Comparative literature; poetry; art of translation. *Publ:* Auth, Angel of Our Thirst (poems), 50-51; Twentieth Century German Verse, Princeton Univ, 52; coauth, The Creative Vision: European Writers on Their Art, Grove, 60; transl, Rudolf Hagelstange's Ballad of the Buried Life, 62; co-ed, Studies in Arthur Schnitzler, 63; auth, A Sigh is the Sword (poems), 63; transl, Karl Krolow's Poems Against Death, 69 & Hamlet, Poems and Fables, 80, Charioteer. *Mailing Add:* 3444 Rugby Rd Hope Valley Durham NC 27707

SALLESE, NICHOLAS F, b Whitestone, NY, Oct 30, 22; m 51; c 2. SPANISH. *Educ:* St John's Univ, NY, BS, 42; Niagara Univ, MA, 45; Columbia Univ, MA, 46, prof dipl, 47, EdD, 48; Univ Madrid, hon dipl, 60. *Prof Exp:* PROF SPAN, ST JOHN'S UNIV, NY, 46-, DIR LANG LAB & MEM ACAD SENATE, 63-, CHMN COMT FAC AFFAIRS, 67- *Concurrent Pos:* Mem Sign Sem, Havana, Cuba, 42; US Dept State exchange grant, Peru, 48; hon prof, Univ San Marcos, 48. *Mem:* Am Asn Teachers Span & Port. *Res:* Modern foreign languages. *Publ:* Auth, Literaturea y Civilizacion Espanola, Univ San Marcos, Peru, 48; Gramatica Moderna, 68, Audio Lingual Spanish, 68 & Espana: vida y Literatura, 69, Am Bk Co. *Mailing Add:* Dept of Span St John's Univ Jamaica NY 11432

SALLUSTIO, ANTHONY THOMAS, b Flushing, NY, June 26, 36; m 60. FRENCH, SPANISH LITERATURE. *Educ:* Iona Col, AB, 58; St John's Univ, MA, 60; Fordham Univ, PhD, 73. *Prof Exp:* Instr Mod lang, Iona Col, 60-63; from asst prof to assoc prof, 63-78, PROF FOREIGN LANG, PACE UNIV, NY, 78-, CHMN DEPT, 68- *Mem:* MLA; Am Asn Teachers of French; Am Asn Teachers Span & Port. *Res:* The works of Jean-Pierre Camus; early 17th century fictional prose in France; Hispanic and Italian literary influences on 17th century French letters. *Mailing Add:* Dept of Foreign Lang Pace Univ New York NY 10038

SALM, PETER, b Hameln, Ger, Aug 23, 19; m 57; c 1. GERMAN, COMPARATIVE LITERATURE. *Educ:* Univ Calif, Los Angeles, BA, 51; Yale Univ, PhD, 59. *Prof Exp:* Asst, Univ Calif, Los Angeles, 51-52; asst instr, Yale Univ, 56-57; instr Ger, Wesleyan Univ, 57-59, asst prof, 59-62; assoc prof, 63-65, chmn dept Ger & comp lit, 65-68, PROF GER & COMP LIT, CASE WESTERN RESERVE UNIV, 65-, DIR COMP LIT, 68-, CHMN DIV MOD LANG & LIT, 71- *Mem:* Am Asn Teachers Ger; MLA; Am Soc 18th Century Studies. *Res:* Goethe; European romanticism; the condensation of time and space in literature. *Publ:* Transl, Goethe's Faust I, Bantam, 62; auth, Three Modes of Criticism: The Literary Theories of Scherer, Walzel and Staiger, 68 & The Poem as Plant: A biological View of Goethe's Faust, 71, Case Western Reserve Univ; Pinpoint of eternity: The sufficient moment in literature, In: Vol III, Proceedings of the American Society for 18th Century Studies, Case Western Reserve Univ, 73; Wether and the sensibility of estrangement, Ger Quart, 1/73. *Mailing Add:* Dept of Comp Lit Case Western Reserve Univ Cleveland OH 44106

SALMON, EDWARD TOGO, Ancient History. See Vol I

SALMON, RUSSELL OWEN, b Port Jervis, NY, Dec 10, 33; m 56; c 3. SPANISH LITERATURE. *Educ:* Williams Col, BA, 56; Middlebury Col, MA, 62; Columbia Univ, PhD(Span), 69. *Prof Exp:* Teacher Span, Holderness Sch, 56-62; from instr to asst prof, 67-75, ASSOC PROF SPAN, IND UNIV, 75- *Mem:* MLA; Am Asn Teachers Span & Port; Latin Am Studies Asn; Midwest Mod Lang Asn; Midwest Asn Latin Am Studies. *Publ:* Auth, Alberto Blest Gana Como Retratista del Roto, Cahier Monde Hisp & Luso-Bresilien (Caravelle), 5/73; coed, Homenaje a Andres Iduarte, Clear Creek, 76; auth, Sarmiento y Jotabeche: Contrastes Literarios, In: Homenaje a Andres Iduarte, Am Hispanist, 76; The tango: Its origins and meaning, J Popular Cult, spring 77; coauth, Stones and birds: Consistency and change in the poetry of Pablo Neruda, Hispania, 5/77; auth, Jotabeche: Chile's First View of the Pueblo, Ibero-Am Pragensia (in press). *Mailing Add:* Dept of Span & Port Ind Univ Bloomington IN 47401

SALOMON, HERMAN PRINS, b Amsterdam, Netherlands, Mar 1, 30; US citizen. LITERATURE. *Educ:* NY Univ, AM, 52, PhD(French), 61. *Prof Exp:* From instr to asst prof French, Rutgers Univ, 61-65; asst prof French, Queens Col, NY, 65-68; asst prof French, 68-76, ASSOC PROF ROMANCE LANG, STATE UNIV NY, ALBANY, 76- *Mem:* Am Asn Teachers Fr; MLA; Ned Ver Leraren in Levende Talen; Int Asn Fr Studies. *Res:* Seventeenth century French literature; literature of the Netherlands; history of Spanish and Portuguese Judaism. *Publ:* Auth, Tartuffe Devant L'opinion Francaise, Presses Univs, France, 62; ed, Moliere's Tartuffe, 66; Racine's Phedre, 67 & Racine's Athalie, 68, Didier; auth, The Jews in New Spain, Am Jewish Hist Quart, 12/72; Was there a traditional Spanish translation of Sephardi prayers before 1552? & coauth, Nahmanides' approach to Midrash in the disputation at Barcelona, winter 73, Am Sephardi. *Mailing Add:* Dept of Romance Lang State Univ of New York Albany NY 12203

SALOMON, RICHARD GEOFFREY, b New York, NY, July 12, 48; m 70; c 1. SANSKRIT LANGUAGE & LITERATURE. *Educ:* Columbia Univ, BA, 70; Univ Pa, PhD(Sanskrit), 75. *Prof Exp:* Lectr Sanskrit, Univ Pa, 75-76; asst prof, Univ Wash, 78-79 & Univ Minn, 80-81; ASST PROF SANSKRIT, UNIV WASH, 81- *Concurrent Pos:* Res assoc, Univ Chicago, 77-78. *Mem:* Am Orient Soc; Asn Asian Studies; Am Numis Soc; Royal Asiatic Soc; Epigraphical Soc India. *Res:* Decipherment of sankhalipi (shell character) inscriptions; history and dialectology of Sanskrit; literary and cultural studies of the Saundaranandakavya of Asvaghosa. *Publ:* Auth, The Ksatrapas and Mahaksatrapas of India, Wiener A Kunde Süasiens; Western Ksatrapa and related coins, Am Numis Soc Mus Notes, 77; Shell Inscriptions, Calcutta Univ Press, 80; A linguistic analysis of the Mundaka Upanisad, Wiener A Kunde Süasiens, 81; The Spinwan (North Waziristan) Kharoshthi Inscription, Studien Indologie & Iranistik, 81; The Ukti-vyakti-prakarana as a manual of spoken Sanskrit Indo-Iranian J, 82; The Avaca Inscription and the origin of the Vikrama Era, J Am Orient Soc, 82; The Bridge to Three Holy Cities, Motilal Banarsidass (in prep). *Mailing Add:* Dept of Asian Lang & Lit Univ of Wash Seattle WA 98195

SALTARELLI, MARIO D, b Cisterna, Italy, Nov 26, 34; US citizen. GENERAL LINGUISTICS, ROMANCE LANGUAGES. *Educ:* niv Ill, BA, 61, MA, 62, PhD(ling), 66. *Prof Exp:* Asst prof ling, Cornell Univ, 64-70; assoc prof, 70-76, PROF SPAN & LING, UNIV ILL, URBANA, 76- *Mem:* Ling Soc Am; Ling Soc Ital (secy, 67-); MLA. *Res:* Grammatical theory; Italian grammar. *Publ:* Auth, A Phonology of Italian in a Generative Grammar, 70 & co-ed, Diachronic Studies in Romance Linguistics, 75, Mouton, The Hague; auth, A propostional theory of grammar, Proc IX Cong Ling, 72; Italian qua neo-Latin, In: Generative Studies in Romance Languages, 73; Semantica dei comparativi, Soc Ling Ital, 73. *Mailing Add:* 1405 Perkins RT 4 Urbana IL 61801

SALUDES, ESPERANZA G, b Cuba, Feb 5, 34; US citizen; c 4. SPANISH PENINSULAR LITERATURE. *Educ:* Univ Villanueva, Dr filos, 58; St Johns Univ, MA, 70; City Univ New York, PhD(Spanish lit), 80. *Prof Exp:* Asst prof Spanish, Manhattan City Col, 69-76; ASSOC PROF SPANISH LIT, ST JOHNS UNIV, 76- *Mem:* MLA; Asn Int Hispanists; Am Asn Teachers Spanish & Portuguese; Nat Asn Bilingual Educ. *Res:* Spanish literature 19th and 20th centuries; literature and psychology; literature of exile. *Publ:* Auth, La narrativa de Luis Martin-Santos a la luz de la psicologia, Ediciones Univ, 80; Como gaviota sobre el mar, Ediciones Ahora, 81; Presencia de Ortega y Gasset en Martin-Santos, Hisp J Pa Univ, 12/82. *Mailing Add:* 75-71 178th St Fresh Meadows NY 11366

SALUS, PETER HENRY, b Vienna, Austria, May 13, 38; US citizen; m 67. LINGUISTICS. *Educ:* NY Univ, BS, 60, MA, 61, PhD(ling), 63. *Prof Exp:* Instr Ger, Manhattan Sch Music, 61-62; instr, Queens Col, NY, 63-65, asst prof ling, 65-67; assoc prof & chmn prog ling, Univ Mass, Amherst, 67-69; assoc prof, 69-72, chmn div, 69-74, prof humanities, Scarborough Col, Univ Toronto, 72-80; DEAN ARTS & SCI, UNIV NORTH FLA, 80- *Concurrent Pos:* Fulbright grant, Univ Iceland, 62-63; Am Philos Soc res grant, 64; lectr Hittite, NY Univ, 64-65; Nat Transl Ctr, Ford Found Grant, 66-67; assoc acad dean, Scarborough Col, 76-77; dir, Connaught Development Group, 77-79. *Mem:* Ling Soc Am; Am Orient Soc; Am Psychiat Soc; Semiotic Soc Am. *Res:* History of linguistics; neurolingusitics; paedolinguistics. *Publ:* Auth, The types of nominal compound of Indo-European, Orbis, 65; coauth, Völuspa-Song of the Sybil, Windhover, 68; The Poetic Edda: A Selection, 68 & co-ed, For W H Auden, 72, Random; auth, On Language: Plato to von Humboldt, Holt, 69; Introduction to Linguistics, Bobbs, 69; Panini to postal, Ling Res, 71; coauth, Rule ordering in child phonology, Can J Ling, 74; Developmental neurophysiology and phonological acquistion order, Lang, 74; What is evidence evidence of?, Semiotics, 80. *Mailing Add:* Col Arts & Sci Univ NFla Jacksonville FL 32216

SALVAN, ALBERT JACQUES, b St Jean d'Angely, France, Aug 5, 04. FRENCH. *Educ:* Univ Poiiers, BLitt, 23; Sorbonne, Lic-es-Lett, 28, dipl, 29; Columbia Univ, PhD, 42. *Prof Exp:* Instr French, Wash Univ, 29-37; civilian instr, US Mil Acad, 37-39; from instr to prof, 39-72, EMER PROF FRENCH STUDIES, BROWN UNIV, 72- *Concurrent Pos:* Mem prog res & study on naturalism & Zola, Univ Toronto, 71- *Res:* Comparative literature; realism and naturalism; critical edition of Zola's Correspondence. *Publ:* Auth, Zola aux Etats-Unis, Brown Univ Studies, 43; L'Essence du realisme francais, Comp Lit, 51; Lettres inedites (d'Emile Zola) a Henry Ceard, Brown Univ, 59. *Mailing Add:* Dept of French Brown Univ Providence RI 02912

SALZMANN, ZDENEK, b Prague, Czech, Oct 18, 25; US citizen; m 49; c 3. LINGUISTIC ANTHROPOLOGY, CZECH & SLOVAK STUDIES. *Educ:* Charles Univ, Prague, Absolutorium, 48; Ind Univ, Bloomington, MA, 49, PhD(ling), 63. *Prof Exp:* Exec dir, Verde Valley Sch, Sedona, Ariz, 63-66; head prog anthrop, Phillips Exeter Acad, NH, 66-68; assoc prof, 68-74, PROF ANTHROP, UNIV MASS, AMHERST, 74- *Concurrent Pos:* Am Philos Soc grants, 50, 52, 61-63, 66 & 77; Nat Inst Ment Health grant, 69; Int Res & Exchanges Bd grant, 70, 72 & 75; Univ Mass vis prof, Univ Freiburg, 70; consult, Nat Bilingual Materials Develop Ctr, Univ Alaska, Anchorage, 79;

leader, Arapaho Lang and Cult Workshops, Wind River Reservation, Wyoming, 79, 80 & 81; sr Fulbright Hays scholar, 80; Nat Endowment for Humanities grant, 81; vis prof, Semester at Sea, 82. *Mem:* Int Ling Asn; Ling Soc Am; Am Folklore Soc. *Res:* American Indian linguistics; Czech and Slovak languages and cultures; Czech speaking settlements in Romania. *Publ:* Auth, Arapaho I-VII, Int J Am Ling, 56-67; Anthropology, Harcourt, 69 & 73; A contribution to the study of value orientations among the Czechs and Slovaks, Dept Anthrop Res Report, Univ Mass, 70; coauth, Komarov: A Czech Farming Village, Holt, 74; Humanity and Culture: An Introduction to Anthropology, Houghton, 78; compiler & ed, Arapaho stories, Nat Bilingual Materials Develop Ctr, 80; Analytical bibliography of sources concerning the Arapaho Indians, Arapaho Lang and Cult Instruct Materials, Wind River Reservation, Wyoming, 81. *Mailing Add:* Dept of Anthrop Univ of Mass Amherst MA 01003

SAMAN, PAUL ANTONIUS, b Istanbul, Turkey, Dec 7, 28; US citizen; m 62. FOREIGN LANGUAGES. *Educ:* Charles Univ, Prague, PhD(Turkish & Persian), 54. *Prof Exp:* Instr Turkish, Orient Inst, Czech Acad Sci, Prague, 51-54, prof, 54-61; from asst prof to assoc prof French, 63-73, PROF FRENCH & RUSS, UNIV NC, CHARLOTTE, 73- *Concurrent Pos:* Prof French, State Lang Inst, Prague, 54-61. *Mem:* SAtlantic Mod Lang Asn; Am Asn Teachers Fr. *Res:* Czech language, Turkish, modern Persian and French; Turkish, Persian and Arabic themes in sub-saharan Black African oral literature. *Publ:* Auth, Intermediate Readings in Turkish Prose, Czech Acad Sci, 54; coauth, Turkish Grammar, State Lang Inst, Prague, 55; auth, Nasreddin Hoca, State Belletristic Publ House, Prague, 56; Keloghlan in Turkish folklore, 57, Selected proverbs from Central Asia, 58 & Azerbaijan and Turkish fairy-tales, 58, New Orient; French Business Correspondence, Univ NC, 75 & 78. *Mailing Add:* Dept of Foreign Lang Univ NC PO Box 12665 Charlotte NC 28205

SAMARIN, WILLIAM J, b Los Angeles, Calif, Feb 7, 26; m 47; c 2. LINGUISTICS, ANTHROPOLOGY. *Educ:* Bible Theol Sem Los Angeles, BTh, 48; Univ Calif, Berkeley, BA, 50, PhD(ling), 62. *Prof Exp:* Missionary linguist, Foreign Missionary Soc, Brethren Church, 51-60; from asst prof to prof ling, Hartford Sem Found, 61-68, dir Sango grammar & dict proj, US Dept Health, Educ & Welfare, 62-68; assoc prof, 68-71, PROF ANTHROP & LING, UNIV TORONTO, 71- *Concurrent Pos:* Nat Sci Found travel gant, WAfrican Lang Surv Congr, Dakar, Senegal, 62; Am Coun Learned Soc travel grant, int colloquium on multilingualism in Africa, Brazzaville, Congo Repub, 62; consult, Africa educ, studies-math proj, Educ Serv Inc, 62; NCTE proj sec sch textbooks for teaching English as a second lang, Africa ed, 62-64; consult nat literacy prog, Repub of Mali, Agency Int Develop, 63; travel grant, chair ling session, African Studies Asn, San Francisco, Calif, 63; vis prof, Univ Leiden, 66-67; res grants, Can Coun, lang alternation among new Canadians, 70-71, Am Philos Soc, emergence of Sango as lingua franca, 72-73; mem ed bd, Lang in Soc, 72- *Mem:* Can Ling Asn; Ling Soc Am; African Studies Asn; Am Anthrop Asn; WAfrican Ling Soc. *Res:* African languages; sociolinguistics; marginal linguistic phenomena. *Publ:* Auth, The Gbeya Language: Grammar, texts, vocabularies, Univ Calif, 66; A Grammar of Sango, Mouton, The Hague, 67; Field Linguistics, Holt, 67; Basic Course in Sango (2 vols), US Dept Health, Educ & Welfare, 68; The art of Gbeya insults, Int J Am Ling, 69; Sango, Langue de L'Afrique Centrale, Brill, Leiden, 70; Salient and substantive pidginization, In: Pidginization and Creolization of Languages, Cambridge Univ, 71; Tongues of Men and Angels: The religious language of Pentecostalism, Macmillan, 72. *Mailing Add:* 24 Candleigh Ave Toronto ON M4R 1T2 Can

SAMELSON, WILLIAM, b Sosnowiec, Poland, Sept 21, 28; US citizen; m 54; c 4. GERMANIC & ROMANCE LANGUAGES. *Educ:* Univ Heidelberg, BS, 48; Western Reserve Univ, BA, 50: Kent State Univ, MA, 54: Univ Tex, PhD(philos & lit), 60. *Prof Exp:* PROF FOREIGN LANG, SAN ANTONIO COL, 56- *Concurrent Pos:* Piper prof, San Antonio Col, 82. *Mem:* MLA; Am Teachers Asn. *Publ:* Auth, A series of short stories, Jewish Forum, 59-60; Herrmann Mostar: A Critical Profile, Mouton, 66; Der Sinn des Lesens (anthology), Odyssey, 68; All Lie in Wait, Prentice-Hall, 69; Romances and songs of the Sephardim, In: The Sephardi Heritage, Vallentine, Mitchell, London, 71; English as a Second Language, Phase One: Let's Converse, 74, English as a Second Language, Phase Two: Let's Read, 75 & English as a Second Language, Phase Three: Let's Write, 76, Reston. *Mailing Add:* Dept Foreign Lang San Antonio Col San Antonio TX 78284

SAMMONS, JEFFREY LEONARD, b Cleveland, Ohio, Nov 9, 36. GERMANIC LANGUAGES & LITERATURES. *Educ:* Yale Univ, BA, 58, PhD(Ger), 62. *Prof Exp:* Instr Ger, Brown Univ, 61-62, asst prof, 63-64; from instr to assoc prof, 64-69, PROF GER, YALE UNIV, 69- *Concurrent Pos:* Guggenheim fel, 72-73: Am Coun Learned Socs fel, 77-78. *Mem:* MLA; Am Asn Teachers Ger; Lessing Soc; Heinrich-Heine-Gesellschaft, North Am Goethe Soc. *Res:* Nineteenth century German literature; literary sociology. *Publ:* Auth, The Nachtwachen von Bonaventura, Mouton, The Hague, 65: Angelus Silesius, Twayne, 67; Heinrich Heine, The Elusive Poet, Yale Univ, 69; co-ed, Lebendige Form: Festschrift für Heinrich E K Henel, Fink, Munich, 70; auth, Six Essays on the Young German Novel, Univ NC, 72; Literary Sociology and Practical Criticism: An Inquiry, Ind Univ, 77; Heinrich Heine: A Modern biography, Princeton Univ, 79; A Selected Critical Bibliography 1956-1980, Garland, 82. *Mailing Add:* Dept of German Yale Univ New Haven CT 06520

SAMPSON, EARL DELOS, b Rifle, Colo, Jan 26, 35; m 65. SLAVIC LANGUAGES. *Educ:* Univ Colo, BA, 60; Harvard Univ, MA, 61, PhD(Slavic), 68. *Prof Exp:* Asst prof, 64-72, ASSOC PROF RUSS, UNIV COLO, BOULDER, 72- *Mem:* Am Asn Teachers Slavic & EEurop Lang; Western Slavic Asn; MLA; Am Coun Teachers Russ. *Res:* Modern Russian literature. *Publ:* Auth, Maria Pawlikowska's lyrical miniatures, In: Studies Presented to Roman Jakobson by His Students, 68; Nikolay Gumilev: Toward a revaluation, Russ Rev, 7/70; In the middle of the journey of life: Gumilev's Pillar of fire, Russ Lit Triquart, 10/71; The Madman and the Monk: Two Types of Narrative Construction in Leskov, Mnemozina, Studia Litteraria Russica, Munich, 74; Dol'niks in Gumilev's Poetry, Toward a Definition of Acmeism, Nikolay Gumilev, Twayne Publ, 79. *Mailing Add:* 922 12th St Boulder CO 80302

SANCHEZ, ROBERTO GARZA, b San Antonio, Tex, Sept 24, 22. SPANISH LITERATURE & LANGUAGE. *Educ:* Univ Tex, BA, 43, MA, 44; Univ Wis, PhD(Span), 49. *Prof Exp:* Markham traveling fel, 49-50, from asst prof to assoc prof, 50-53, PROF SPAN, UNIV WIS, MADISON, 63- *Mem:* Am Asn Teachers Span & Port; Acad Norteamericana de la Lengua. *Res:* Spanish literature of the 19th century; 20th century theater; problems of dramatic criticism. *Publ:* Auth, Garcia Lorca: Estudio sobre su teatro, Ed Jura, Madrid, 50; co-ed, Galdos' Miau, Oxford Univ, 70; auth, Garcia Lorca y la literatura del XIX: Apuntes sobre Dona Rosita la soltera, Insula, 71; Lorca and the conflict of generations, Ky Romance Quart, 72; Cara y cruz de la teatralidad romantica, 73 & El teatro en la novela: Galdos y Clarin, 74, Insula; Between Macias and Don Juan: Spanish romantic drama and the mythology of love, Hisp Rev, 76; Gordon Craig and Valle Inclan, Revista de Occidente, 76. *Mailing Add:* Dept of Span & Port Univ of Wis Madison WI 53706

SANCHEZ-ARCE, NELLIE E, b Manati, PR, Dec 25, 21; US citizen. SPANISH. *Educ:* Univ PR, BA, 42; Mt Holyoke Col, MA, 44; Univ Pa, PhD, 53. *Prof Exp:* Instr Span, Mt Holyoke Col, 43-47; instr Span, Bryn Mawr Col, 51-56; from asst prof to assoc prof Span, Wells Col, 57-67; ASSOC PROF SPAN, UNIV MASS, BOSTON, 67- *Concurrent Pos:* Jusserand traveling fel, 54. *Mem:* MLA. *Res:* Spanish poetry of the 16th century; Spanish drama of the Golden Age. *Publ:* Auth, Los Glosas a las Coplas de Jorge Manrique, Ed Sancha, Madrid, 56: A critical edition of La Segunda de Don Alvaro, de Mira de Amescua, 60 & A critical edition of Comedia famosa de Ruy Lopez de Aralos, de Mira de Amescua, 65, Ed Jus, Mex. *Mailing Add:* Dept of Span Univ of Mass 100 Arlington St Boston MA 02116

SANCHEZ-BARBUDO, ANTONIO, b Madrid, Spain, Apr 18, 10; US citizen; m 38; c 2. MODERN SPANISH LITERATURE. *Educ:* Univ Madrid, 31-35. *Prof Exp:* Instr Span, Univ Tex, 45-46; from lectr to prof, 46-65, VILAS RES PROF, UNIV WIS-MADISON, 65- *Concurrent Pos:* Guggenheim fels, 48-49, 61-62. *Mem:* Hisp Soc Am. *Publ:* Auth, Estudios sobre Unamuno y Machado, Ed Guadarrama, Spain, 59; La segunda epoca de J R Jimenez, 62 & Cincuenta poemas comentados, 63, Ed Gredos, Spain; ed, Dios deseado y deseante of Juan Ramon Jimenez, Aguilar, Madrid, 65; Los poemas de Antonio Machado, Lumen, Barcelona, 67; ed, Diario de un poeta reciencasado, Labor, Barcelona, 70. *Mailing Add:* Dept of Span & Port Univ of Wis Madison WI 53706

SANCHEZ-BOUDY, JOSE, b Havana, Cuba, Oct 17, 28; m 50: c 3. LINGUISTICS, LATIN AMERICAN LITERATURE. *Educ:* Univ Havana, MA(diplomatic law) & MA(admin law), 51, PhD(law), & PhD(soc sci), 53, Univ Madrid, PhD(humanities), 76. *Prof Exp:* ASST PROF SPAN, UNIV NC, GREENSBORO, 65- *Honors & Awards:* Gonzalez Lanuza Nat Award, Univ Havana, 53. *Mem:* MLA: Am Asn Teachers Span & Port; Circulo Cultura Pan-Am; Soc Cubana Filosofia. *Res:* Dialectology; Cuban folklore: Black studies literature. *Publ:* Auth, Los Cruzados de la Aurora, 71, Orbus Terrarum, 71, Ache, Babalu, Aye, 75, El Corredor Kresto, 76, Los Sarracenos del Ocaso, 78, Diccionario de Cubanismos, 78, Lilayando Pal Tu, 78 & Lilayando, Editora Universal. *Mailing Add:* Dept of Romance Lang Univ NC Greensboro NC 27412

SANCHEZ-ROMERALO, ANTONIO, b Madrid, Spain, July 8, 24: m 60. SPANISH LITERATURE. *Educ:* Univ Madrid, Bachiller, 41, lic, 47; Univ Wis, PhD, 61. *Prof Exp:* Asst prof Span lang & lit, Univ Wis, Madison, 61-65, from assoc prof to prof, 65-71; PROF SPAN, UNIV CALIF, DAVIS, 71-, CHMN DEPT SPAN & CLASSICS, 76- *Mem:* MLA. *Res:* Spanish Renaissance and Golden Age literature; Spanish contemporary literature. *Publ:* Auth, Juan Ramon Jimenez en su fondo de aire, Revista Hisp Moderna, 61; El villacico Estudios sobre la lirica popular en los siglos xv y xvi, Gredos, 69; coauth, Antologia de Autores Espanoles (Antiguos), Macmillan, 72; El Romancero en la tradicion oral moderna, 72, auth, Mis amorese, In: Studia Hispanica in Honorem R Lapesa, 74 & Romancero rustico, 78, Gredos; La realidad invisible (by Juan Ramon Jimenez), Tamesis, 78: Leyenda (1896-1956) (by Juan Ramon Jimenez), Cupsa, 78. *Mailing Add:* Dept of Span Univ of Calif Davis CA 95616

SANDBERG, KARL C, b Salt Lake City, Utah, Mar 7, 31; m 54; c 4. FRENCH LITERATURE, LINGUISTICS. *Educ:* Brigham Young Univ, BA, 54, MA, 57; Univ Wis, PhD, 60. *Prof Exp:* Instr French, Duke Univ, 59-61; from asst prof to assoc prof, Univ Ariz, 61-68; PROF FRENCH & CHMN DEPT, MACALESTER COL, 68-, CHMN LING DEPT, 77- *Concurrent Pos:* Lectr, Ariz English Lang Ctr, 62, dir, 63. *Mem:* Am Asn Teachers Fr; Am Coun Teaching Foreign Lang; Teachers English to Speakers Other Lang. *Res:* French 17th century literature; applied linguistics; English as a second language. *Publ:* Coauth, French for Reading, Appleton, 68; auth, Conversational English, Blaisdell, 69; Lectures et conversations, 70 & coauth, Le nouveau passe-muraille: Manuel de lecture, 70, New Century; poems, In: Carleton Miscellany & Dialogue, Sunstone, 72, German for Reading, Appleton, 75; Reading as thought and dialogue: A cognitive approach, In: Proc of Am Coun of Teachers of Foreign Lang meetings, 73; Creative English (2 vols), Prentice-Hall, 80. *Mailing Add:* Dept of Ling Macalester Col St Paul MN 55105

SANDER, MARGARET M, b Frankfurt, Ger, Oct 14, 24; m 56. GERMAN, COMPARATIVE LITERATURE. *Educ:* Univ Mainz, PhD, 51. *Prof Exp:* Dir, English Lang Prog, US Info Ctr, Frankfurt, 52-57; asst prof English, Fla Southern Col, 57-58; assoc prof & asst head dept, Dutchess Community Col, 58-63; chmn dept, 65-73, assoc prof, 63-77, PROF GER, NY UNIV, 77- *Concurrent Pos:* Brit Coun fel, Univ Leicester, 51-52. *Publ:* Translr, Gopal Mittal, March of a Conspiracy, Aktueller Osten, Bonn, 56 & Reynolds Price: A Long and Happy Life, Suhrkamp, Frankfurt, 63; ed, Wedekind: Fruhlings Erwachen, Blaisdell, 69; Keller's Das Fahnlein der Sieben Aufrechten, Ginn, 70. *Mailing Add:* Dept of Ger NY Univ New York NY 10003

SANDER, VOLKMAR, b Frankurt am Main, Ger, Oct 20, 29; m 56. FOREIGN LANGUAGES. *Educ:* Univ Frankfurt, MA, 54, MEd, 56, PhD, 57. *Prof Exp:* Assessor English, Mustersch, Ger, 54-56; asst prof English, Fla Southern Col, 57-58; asst prof Ger, Vassar Col, 58-63; assoc prof, 63-68, all univ head Ger, 66-73, PROF GER, NY UNIV, 68-, CHMN DEPT, 78- *Concurrent Pos:* Ed, Ottendorfer Ser Ger Monogr, 70-; dir, Deutsches Haus, NY Univ, 77-; ed, Ger Libr, 82- *Mem:* MLA; Am Asn Teachers Ger. *Res:* German 19th and 20th century comparative literature. *Publ:* Auth, Ambrose Bierce Short Stories, Moritz Diesterweg, 55; B Brecht: Mutter Courage, Oxford Univ, 64; Form und Groteske, Ger-Romanische Monatsschr, 7/64; Realitat und Bewusstsein bei E T A Hoffmann, In: Studies in Germanic Language and Literature, Hutzler, 67; Die Faszination des Bosen, 68 & Wilhelm Raabes Alterswerk, In: Poetik des Romans, 68, Athenaum; ed, Tragik und Tragodie, Wiss Buchgemeinschaft, 71; F Durrenmatt, Continuum, 82. *Mailing Add:* Dept of Ger Lang & Lit NY Univ New York NY 10003

SANDERS, GERALD ALBERT, b Chicago, Ill, Jan 27, 31; wid. LINGUISTICS. *Educ:* Univ Chicago, AB, 50; Northwestern Univ, MA, 52; Ind Univ, PhD(ling), 67. *Prof Exp:* Instr English, Wilson Jr Col, Ill, 53-56; Fulbright teacher, Col Educ, Bangkok, 56-58; instr, Wayne State Univ, 59-61; lectr ling & English, Univ Mich English Proj, Bangkok, Thailand & Saigon, Vietnam, 61-63; lectr, Ind Univ, Bloomington, 65-67, asst prof, 67-70; vis lectr, 70-72, assoc prof, 72-76, PROF LING, UNIV MINN, MINNEAPOLIS, 76- *Concurrent Pos:* Fac grant-in-aid of res, Ind Univ, Bloomington, 67-68; fac assoc grant, Nat Sci Found Sci Develop Prog Ling & Behav, Univ Tex, Austin, 68-70; res assoc, Lang Universals Proj, Stanford Univ, 71. *Mem:* Ling Soc Am. *Res:* Syntax; linguistic theory; English grammar. *Publ:* Auth, On the natural domain of grammar, Lings, 70; Equational Grammar, Mouton, 72; Issues of explanation in linguistics, In: Explaining Linguistic Phenomena, Winston, 74; The simplex-feature hypothesis, Glossa, 74; Invariant Ordering, Mouton, 75; On the explanation of constituent-order universals, In: Word Order and Word Order Change, Univ Tex, 75; Functional constraints on grammars, In: Linguistic Studies Offered to J Greenberg, Anma Libr, 77; A functional typology of elliptical coordinations, In: Current Themes in Linguistics, Halsted, 77. *Mailing Add:* Dept of Ling Univ of Minn Minneapolis MN 55455

SANDERS, IVAN, b Budapest, Hungary, Jan 24, 44; US citizen; m 68; c 2. COMPARATIVE LITERATURE, EAST EUROPEAN FICTION. *Educ:* Brooklyn Col, BA, 65, MA, 67; NY Univ, PhD(comp lit), 72. *Prof Exp:* PROF ENGLISH, SUFFOLK COUNTY COMMUNITY COL, 68- *Concurrent Pos:* Vis assoc prof, Sch Continuing Educ, Columbia Univ, 78-79; Irex fel, Hungarian Acad Sci, Inst Lit Res, Budapest, 79; sr fel, Inst ECent Europe, Columbia Univ, 82. *Mem:* MLA; Am Hungarian Educ Asn; Am Fed Teachers. *Res:* Contemporary American fiction; contemporary East European fiction and film; Hungarian literature. *Publ:* Auth, Engaol'd tongue?: Notes on the language of Hungarian Americans, Valosag, Budapest, Vol XVI, No 5; The gifts of strangeness: Alienation and creation in Jerzy Kosinski's fiction, Polish Rev, Vol XIX, No 3-4; Human dialogues are born, Nation, 4/23/77; transl, George Konrad's The City Builder, Harcourt Brace Jovanavich, 77; auth, Simple elements and violent combinations: Reflections on the fiction of Amos Oz, Judaism, Vol XXVII, No 1; The possibilities of fiction: On recent American novels, Valosag, Vol XXI, No 1, 78; transl, George Konrad's The Loser, Harcourt Brace Jovanavich, 82; co-ed, Essays on World War I: Total War and Peacemaking, A Case Study on Trianon, Columbia Univ Press, 82. *Mailing Add:* 4 Coed Lane Stony Brook NY 11790

SANDERS, JAMES BERNARD, b Winnipeg, Man, May 28, 24: m 48: c 2. FRENCH. *Educ:* Univ Man, BA, 46, MA, 49; Univ Paris, DUniv, 52. *Prof Exp:* Lectr French, Univ Man, 48-51; from asst prof to assoc prof, Romance lang, Waterloo Col, Univ Western Ont, 54-61; from asst prof to assoc prof, 61-66, PROF FRENCH, UNIV WESTERN ONT, 66- *Concurrent Pos:* Humanities Res Coun Can grant, 55-59. *Mem:* MLA; Am Asn Teachers Fr; Humanities Asn Can (secy-treas, 64-66, exec mem, 64-68); Asn Can Univ Teachers Fr. *Res:* French theatre. *Publ:* Coauth, Contes de nos jours, la Communale, Appleton, 59; Contes d'aujourd'hui, Holt, 63; auth, Ibsen's introduction into France: Ghosts, Fr Studies, 10/64; coauth, A travers les siecles (anthology), Macmillan, 67; auth, Le Tartuffe d'Antoine (1907): Essai de mise en scene naturaliste, In: Moliere and the Commonwealth of Letters Univ Southern Miss, 75; Emile Zola, le transplante et l'arbre, In: From Naturalism to the New Novel, Ed France-Quebec, 76; Antoine a l'Odeon: Derniere etape d'une odyssee, Lettres mod, 77. *Mailing Add:* Univ of Western Ont London ON N6A 5B8 Can

SANDLER, SAMUEL, b Lodz, Poland, Oct 25, 25; Israeli citizen; m 48; c 1. POLISH LITERATURE. *Educ:* Wroclaw Univ, MA, 50, PhD(Polish philol), 51. *Prof Exp:* Instr Polish lit, Wroclaw Univ, 50-51; asst prof, Inst Lit Res, Polish Acad Sci, 51-57, 62-69; asst prof, Univ Warsaw, 54-57 & Univ Lodz, 55-62; assoc prof, Tel-Aviv Univ, 69-72; PROF POLISH LIT, UNIV CHICAGO, 72- *Concurrent Pos:* Co-ed & co-dir, Ed Polish & For Lit Classics Ser, Nat Libr, Ossolineum, 51-69; mem comt lit, Polish Acad Sci, 60-69; vis prof Polish lit, Univ Lodz, 64-69; vis assoc prof, Univ Ill, Chicago Circle, 70-72. *Mem:* Polish Inst Arts & Sci Am; MLA; Am Asn Teachers Slavic & E Europ Lang. *Res:* Polish literature of the 19th and 20th century; literary criticism; sociology of literature. *Publ:* Auth, Around Henryk Sienkiewicz's Trilogy, 52 & Bronislaw Biatobtocki, The Beginnings of Marxist Criticism in Poland, 54, Ossolineum, Wroclaw; Mickiewicz's Reduta Ordona in real life and in poetry, 56 & Andrzej Strug among the underground people, 59, Czytelnik, Warsaw; Studies on Swietochowski, 57 & Henry Sienkiewicz's Indian adventure, 67, ed, Ignacy Matuszewski, Criticism Vols I-III, 65 & Aleksander Swietochowski Liberum Veto (2 vols), 76, Pan Inst Wydawniczy, Warsaw. *Mailing Add:* 1465 E 55th Place Chicago IL 60637

SANDRO, PAUL DENNEY, b Marshfield, Wis, Nov 10, 44; m 67; c 1. FRENCH LANGUAGE & LITERATURE. *Educ:* Beloit Col, BA, 66; Univ Wis-Madison, MA, 67; Cornell Univ, PhD(romance studies), 74. *Prof Exp:* Asst prof, 74-80, ASSOC PROF FRENCH, MIAMI UNIV, OHIO, 80- *Res:* Film theory and criticism; 20th century French literature. *Publ:* Auth, Signification in the cinema, Diacritics, fall 74; The space of desire in An Andalusian Dog, 1977 Purdue Film Studies Ann (Part III), summer 78; Textuality of the subject in Belle de Jour, Sub-stance, No 26, 80; The management of destiny in narrative form, Cine-tracts, spring 81. *Mailing Add:* Dept of French & Ital Miami Univ Oxford OH 45056

SANDROCK, JAMES P, b Waterloo, Iowa, Mar 5, 29. GERMAN. *Educ:* Univ Iowa, BA, 51, MA, 58, PhD(Ger), 61; Ger Univ, Frankfurt, dipl, 59. *Prof Exp:* From instr to asst prof 60-67, chmn dept, 66-69, asst dean, Col Lib Arts, 67-70, assoc prof, 67-79, PROF GER, UNIV IOWA, 79- *Mem:* MLA; Am Asn Teachers Ger. *Res:* Ludwig Thomas as a regional German writer; Mark Twain and his relationship, both direct and indirect, to German literature; regional literature of Germany and Austria. *Publ:* Auth, Die Luther-Bibel als literarischer und kultureller Bruckenschlag, Z Kulturaustausch, 72; Languages and the Humanities; our roots and responsibilities, Bull Asn Depts Foreign Lang. *Mailing Add:* Dept of Ger Univ of Iowa Iowa City IA 52242

SANDY, GERALD NEIL, b Oct 15, 37; US citizen; m 61; c 4. CLASSICS, LATIN LITERATURE. *Educ:* Ohio State Univ, BA, 62, MA, 64, PhD(classics), 68. *Prof Exp:* Instr classics, Ohio State Univ, 65-66; asst prof, 67-72, ASSOC PROF CLASSICS, UNIV BC, 72- *Mem:* Am Philol Asn; Class Asn Can; Am Inst Archaeol; Soc Prom Roman Studies. *Res:* Ancient novel; Catullus. *Publ:* Auth, The imagery of Catullus 63, 68 & Petronius and the tradition of the interpolated narrative, 70, Trans & Proc Am Philol Asn; Catullus 63 and the theme of marriage, Am J Philol, 71. *Mailing Add:* 3887 W 14th Vancouver BC V6R 2X1 Can

SANGER, CURT, b Vienna, Austria; US citizen. GERMAN LANGUAGE, MODERN GERMAN LITERATURE. *Educ:* Univ Akron, BA, 50; Western Reserve Univ, MA, 52; Univ Cincinnati, PhD(Ger), 66. *Prof Exp:* Lectr Ger & English, Univ Akron, 50; teacher, Ellet High Sch, Akron, 52-53; teacher & chmn dept foreign lang, Woodward High Sch, Cincinnati, 53-62; instr Ger, Univ Cincinnati, 62-63; from instr to asst prof, 63-72, ASSOC PROF GER, MIAMI UNIV, 72- *Mem:* MLA; Am Asn Teachers Ger; AAUP. *Res:* Literature of the Weimar Republic; German exile literature; German post-World War II literature in East and West Germany. *Publ:* Auth, The figure of the non-hero in the novels of Joseph Roth, In: Modern Austrian Literature, State Univ NY, Binghamton, 69; Realitat und Realitatstransformation in der Exilliteratur, dargestellt am Beispiel Joseph Roths, In: Probleme der Deutschen Literatur im Exil Seit 1933, Europa Verlag, Vienna, 72; In the Avantgarde of Bertolt Brecht: Marieluise Fleisser's Pioniere in Ingolstadt, Univ Eastern Ky, 74. *Mailing Add:* Dept of Ger Russ & Far Eastern Lang Miami Univ Oxford OH 45056

SANGSTER, RODNEY BLAIR, b Albany, NY, Oct 8, 42. SLAVIC & GENERAL LINGUISTICS. *Educ:* Hamilton Col, AB, 64; Ind Univ, Bloomington, PhD(ling), 70. *Prof Exp:* US-USSR Cult Exchange res fel Slavic ling, Moscow State Univ, 70-71; res assoc, Cornell Univ, 71-72; asst prof, 72-80, asst chmn dept, 73-75, dir Slavic lang & area ctr, 75-79, ASSOC PROF SLAVIC LING, IND UNIV, BLOOMINGTON, 80- *Mem:* MLA; Ling Soc Am; Am Asn Advan Slavic Studies; Am Asn Teachers Slavic & East Europ Lang. *Res:* Russian language; linguistic theory; structural semantics. *Publ:* Coauth, The semantics of syntax, In: Memorial Volume for Ruth H Weir & Language as a System of Signs, Mouton. *Mailing Add:* Dept of Slavic Lang & Lit Ballantine Hall 502 Ind Univ Bloomington IN 47401

SANJIAN, AVEDIS KRIKOR, b Marash, Turkey, Feb 24, 21; US citizen; m 50; c 1. ARMENIAN STUDIES, NEAR EASTERN STUDIES. *Educ:* Am Univ Beirut, BA, 49; Univ Mich, MA, 50, PhD(Near Eastern studies), 56. *Prof Exp:* Res fel Armenian, Harvard Univ, 57-61, asst prof, 61-65; assoc prof, 65-68, chmn Near Eastern lang, 70-74, PROF ARMENIAN, UNIV CALIF, LOS ANGELES, 68- *Concurrent Pos:* Chmn, Armenian studies, Univ Calif, Los Angeles, 69. *Mem:* Am Orient Soc; Mid E Inst; Mid E Studies Asn NAm. *Res:* Armenian and Middle Eastern history. *Publ:* Auth, The Armenian Communities in Syria Under Ottoman Dominion, 65 & Colophons of Armenian Manuscripts, 1301-1480: A Source for Middle Eastern History, 69, Harvard Univ; The Historical Significance of Colophons of Armenian Manuscripts, 68 & Anastas Vardapet's List of Armenian Monasteries in Seventh-century Jerusalem, 69, Museon, Louvain: Two Contemporary Armenian Elegies on the Fall of Constantinople, 1453, Viator, 70; A Catalogue of Medieval Armenian Manuscripts in the United States, Univ Calif, 76. *Mailing Add:* Dept of Near Eastern Lang Univ of Calif Los Angeles CA 90024

SANKOVITCH, TILDE ANNA, b Antwerp, Belgium, Apr, 25, 35; m 57; c 3. MEDIEVAL & RENAISSANCE LITERATURE. *Educ:* Univ Louvain, Belgium, lic, 56; Northwestern Univ, PhD(French lit), 73. *Prof Exp:* Instr, 72-73, asst prof, 73-78, ASSOC PROF FRENCH, NORTHWESTERN UNIV, 78- *Concurrent Pos:* Panel mem, Nat Endowment for Humanities, 78-81. *Mem:* MLA; Medieval Acad; Renaissance Soc Am; Am Asn Teachers French; AAUP. *Res:* Provencal lyrics; Rabelais; Renaissance women authors. *Publ:* Auth, The romance of Flamenca: The puppetmaster and the play, Neophilologus, 76; Ronsard and the new iconograhy of death, Fr Lit, 78; Structure and unity in the poems of Peire Vidal, Neophilologus, 78; Etienne Jodelle and the mystic-erotic experience, Bibliotheque Humanisme & Renaissance, 78; Jodelle et la creation du masque, Fr Lit Publ, 79; Death of the mole: Two fifteenth century dances of death, 15th Century Studies, 79; Religious and erotic elements in Flamenca: The uneasy alliance, Romance Philol, 81; coauth, The Poetry of Bertran de Born, Critical Edition and Translation, Univ Calif Press (in press). *Mailing Add:* Dept Fr & Ital Northwestern Univ Evanston IL 60201

SANSONE, DAVID, b New York, NY, Sept 23, 46; m 69. CLASSICS. *Educ:* Hamilton Col, AB, 68; Univ Wis, MA, 69, PhD(classics), 72. *Prof Exp:* Asst prof classics, Univ Hawaii, 72-74; asst prof, 74-80, ASSOC PROF CLASSICS, UNIV ILL, 80- *Mem:* Am Philol Asn. *Res:* Greek drama; ancient biography. *Publ:* Auth, Aeschylean Metaphors for Intellectual Activity, F

Steiner Verlag, 75; The third stasimon of the Oedipus Tyrannos, Class Philol, 75; The Sacrifice-Motif in Euripides' Iphigenia in Tauris, Trans Am Philol Asn, 75; A Problem in Euripides' Iphigenia in Tauris, Rheinisches Mus, 78; The Bacchae as satyr-play?, Ill Class Studies, 78; Plutarch, Alexander and the discovery of Naphtha, Greek, Roman & Byzantine Studies, 80; Lysander and Dionysius, Class Philol, 81; ed, Euripidis Iphigenia in Tauris, Teubner Verlag, 81. *Mailing Add:* Dept of Classics Univ Ill Urbana IL 61801

SANTAMARINA, LEONARDO, b Fonsagrada, Spain, Mar 6, 12. SPANISH. *Educ:* Univ Havana, PhD, 46. *Prof Exp:* Instr schs, Spain, 31-36: from instr to asst prof, 45-61, chmn Dept Romance lang, 61-76, PROF SPAN LANG & LIT, DOUGLASS COL, RUTGERS UNIV, NEW BRUNSWICK, 61- *Mem:* MLA. *Res:* Spanish civilization; thought and poetry of Antonio Machado; problems of the plurilingual countries. *Mailing Add:* Dept of Romance Lang Douglass Col of Rutgers Univ New Brunswick NJ 08903

SANTANA, JORGE ARMANDO, b Rosarito, Baja California, Mex, Nov 21, 44; US citizen: m 69; c 1. LATIN AMERICAN LITERATURE, CHICANO STUDIES. *Educ:* San Diego Univ, AB, 67, MA, 70; Univ Madrid, PhD(Span), 72. *Prof Exp:* Instr Span, San Diego State Univ, 69-70; chmn dept Span & Port, 76-79, ASSOC PROF, CALIF STATE UNIV, SACRAMENTO, 72- *Concurrent Pos:* Ed, Explicacion Textos Literarios. *Res:* The Mexican revolution novel; Chicano literature and culture. *Publ:* Auth, Las influencias de A Trueba en Unamuno, Bol R S Vascongada, 12/70: ed, Lecturas espanolas, Plaza Mayo, 72; auth, Roots of Chicano literature, Progreso, 2/73; El oportunista en la narrativa de Azuela Cuadernos Hispanoam, 5/73; Antologia comentada del modernismo, Explicacion de Textos Literarios, 74. *Mailing Add:* Dept of Span & Port Calif State Univ Sacramento CA 95819

SANTI, ENRICO MARIO, b Santiago de Cuba, Cuba, July 1, 50; US citizen; m 72; c 2. LATIN AMERICAN LITERATURE. *Educ:* Vanderbilt Univ, BA, 72; Yale Univ, MA, 74, MPhil, 75, PhD(Span), 76. *Prof Exp:* Actg instr Span, Yale Univ, 75-76; instr, Duke Univ, 76-77; ASST PROF ROMANCE STUDIES, CORNELL UNIV, 77- *Concurrent Pos:* Danforth Found Kent fel, 74-76. *Mem:* MLA; Am Asn Teachers Span & Port. *Res:* Modern Hispanic poetry; Latin American narrative; literary theory. *Publ:* Auth, Escritura y tradicion: El Martin Fierro en dos cuentos de Borges, 74 & Lezama, Vitier y la critica de la razon reminiscente, 75, Revista Iberoam; Rereading the unknown Neruda, Latin Am Res Rev, 77; Neruda: La modalidad apocaliptica, Hisp Rev, 78; Canto General: The politics of the book, Symposium, 78; co-ed, Pablo Neruda, Taurus, 78; Parridiso, Mod Lang Notes, 79. *Mailing Add:* Dept of Romance Studies Cornell Univ Ithaca NY 14853

SANTI, VICTOR AMERIGO, b Pievepelago, Italy, Mar 10, 48. ITALIAN LANGUAGE AND LITERATURE. *Educ:* Univ Wis-Madison, BA, 70; Univ Calif, Los Angeles, MA, 72, Phd(Ital), 75. *Prof Exp:* Asst prof, Tulane Univ, 74-80; ASST PROF ITAL, UNIV NEW ORLEANS, LAKEFRONT, 80- *Concurrent Pos:* Reviewer of Italian, Nat Endowment for Humanities, 77- *Mem:* MLA; Renaissance Soc Am; SAtlantic Mod Lang Asn; SCent Mod Lang Asn. *Res:* Italian literature of the Renaissance; 20th century Italian poetry. *Publ:* Ed, L'Ottocentro, in the Bookshelf section of the Italian Quart, Italian Quart, 72; auth, Parole di Machiavelli: Gloria, Lingua Nostra, 12/73; Baldassar Castiglione in una lettera inedita di Felice da Sora al Duca di Urbino, Italianistica, 8/77; Fama e laude distinte da gloria in Machiavelli, Forum Italicum, 6/78; La Gloria Nelle Opere del Machiavelli, Longo Editore, 80; A few considerations on the aristodemo of Carlo de'Dottori, Romance Notes, 82; Torquato Tasso, Twayne, (in press). *Mailing Add:* Dept For Lang Univ New Orleans, Lakefront New Orleans LA 70148

SANTINI, VICTOR HUGO, b Chicago, Ill, Feb 17, 21; m 58; c 6. FRENCH, ITALIAN. *Educ:* Univ Florence, PhD(foreign lang & lit), 47. *Prof Exp:* Instr, 58-61, ASST PROF FRENCH & ITALIAN, COLO STATE UNIV, 61- *Mem:* Am Asn Teachers Fr; Am Asn Teachers Ital. *Res:* Language and sociology; arts and culture. *Mailing Add:* Dept of Lang Colo State Univ Ft Collins CO 80521

SANTIROCCO, MATTHEW STEPHEN, b New York, NY, July 11, 50. CLASSICS. *Educ:* Columbia Univ, BA, 71, MPhil, 76, PhD, 79; Cambridge Univ, BA, 73, MA, 77. *Prof Exp:* Asst prof, Univ Pittsburgh, 77-79; ASST PROF CLASSICS, COLUMBIA UNIV, 79-, HARTLEY HALL RES PROF, 81- *Concurrent Pos:* Am Numismatic Soc grant, 74; Vogelstein Found res grant, 76; mem, Nat Bd Bicentennial Lectr, Am Philol Asn, 76-77. *Mem:* Am Philol Asn; Soc Study Class Humanities Am; Class Asn Atlantic States. *Res:* Latin prose and poetry; Greek poetry, especially Hellenistic and tragedy; comparative literature-mythology. *Publ:* Auth, Metamorphosis in Ovid's Amores, Class Bull, 69; Sulpicia reconsidered, Class J, 79; Horace's Odes and the ancient poetry book, Arethusa, 80; Strategy and Structure in Horace's Odes, Collection Latomus, 80; Justice in Sophocles' Antigone, Philos & Lit, 80; Poet and patron in ancient Rome, Bk Forum, 82; The Two Voices of Horace, Archaeologica Transatlantica (in prep). *Mailing Add:* Columbia Univ 614 Hamilton Hall New York NY 10027

SAPORTA, SOL, b New York, NY, Mar 12, 25; m 52; c 3. SPANISH, LINGUISTICS. *Educ:* Brooklyn Col, BA, 44; Univ Ill, MA, 52, PhD, 55. *Prof Exp:* Asst prof Span & ling, Ind Univ, 55-60; chmn dept ling, 62-77, assoc prof, 60-79, PROF ROMANCE LANG & LING, UNIV WASH, 80- *Mem:* Am Asn Teachers Span & Port; Ling Soc Am. *Res:* Structural linguistics; psycholinguistics; Spanish linguistics. *Publ:* Auth, Psycholinguistics: A Book of Readings, Holt, 61; coauth, Stylistics, linguistics, and literary criticism, Hisp Inst, 62; A Phonological Grammar of Spanish, Univ Wash, 62. *Mailing Add:* Dept of Ling Univ of Wash Seattle WA 98105

SARA, SOLOMON ISHU, b May 1, 30; US citizen. THEORETICAL LINGUISTICS & PHONOLOGY. *Educ:* Boston Col, BA, 56, MA, 57; Weston Col, STB, 64; Georgetown Univ, PhD(ling), 69; Cleveland Inst Electronics, dipl, 76. *Prof Exp:* Asst prof, 69-80, ASSOC PROF LING, GEORGETOWN UNIV, 80- *Mem:* Ling Soc Am; Int Ling Asn; Int Phonetic Asn; Am Asn Adv Sci. *Res:* Instrumental phonetics; linguistic theory; comparative semitics. *Publ:* Auth, Modern Standard Arabic (19 vols), 71 & Spoken Iraqi Arabic (4 vols), 71, Monterey Lang Sch; A Grammar of Modern Chaldean, Mouton, 74; Vocalic Variability in Palatographic Impressions, Benjamins B V, 79. *Mailing Add:* Sch of Lang & Ling Georgetown Univ Washington DC 20057

SARAYDAR, ALMA COLLINS, b Los Angeles, Calif, Aug 10, 23; m 58. ROMANCE LANGUAGES & LITERATURES. *Educ:* Univ Calif, Los Angeles, BA, 45; Univ Paris, cert, French, 52; Univ Chicago, MA, 56; Univ Calif, Berkeley, PhD(Romance lang & lit), 65. *Prof Exp:* Instr French, Hobbart & William Smith Cols, 58-60; asst prof French, Univ Hawaii, 65-67; asst prof, 67-79, ASSOC PROF FRENCH, UNIV WESTERN ONT, 79- *Mem:* MLA; Am Asn Teachers Fr; Soc Amis Marcel Proust; Asn Amis Andre Gide. *Res:* Marcel Proust, especially A la recherche du temps perdu; modern and contemporary French novel, 1900-1970; Andre Gide as novelist, moralist and critic. *Publ:* Auth, Proust Disciple de Stendhal, Editions Leatres Modernes, Paris, 80. *Mailing Add:* Dept of French Univ of Western Ont London ON N6A 3K7 Can

SARGENT-BAUR, BARBARA NELSON, b Oshkosh, Wis, Jan 8, 28. FRENCH LITERATURE. *Educ:* Ind Univ, PhD, 60. *Prof Exp:* From instr to assoc prof, 60-71, PROF FRENCH, UNIV PITTSBURGH, 71- *Concurrent Pos:* Mem adv coun, Romance Philol. *Mem:* Mediaeval Acad Am; Int Arthurian Soc (vpres, NAm Br); Soc Rencesvals; Int Courtly Lit Soc. *Res:* Medieval French literature; Arthurian literature; comparative literature. *Publ:* Auth, Le livre du Roy Rambaux de Frise, Fries Inst, State Univ Groningen, 63 & Univ NC, 67; Francois Villon: Le Testament et poesies diverses, Appleton, 67; L'Autre chez Chretien de Troyes, Cahiers de Civilisation Medievale, 67; A medieval commentary on Andreas Capellanus, Romania, 73; Medieval ris, risus: A laughing matter?, Medium Aevum, 74; Erec's Enide: Sa fame ou s'amie? Romance Philol, 80; Personnages bibliques, personnages villoniens, In: Etudes ... Jules Horrent, Univ de Liege, 80; coauth (with Robert F Cook), Aucassin et Nicolete: A Critical Bibliography, Grant & Cutler, 81. *Mailing Add:* Dept of Fr & Ital Univ of Pittsburgh Pittsburgh PA 15260

SARKANY, STEPHANE, b June 1, 25; Can citizen; m 53, c 2. FRENCH, LITERARY THEORY. *Educ:* Lutheran Col Budapest, BA, 43; Univ Budapest, lic, 46; Univ Paris, MA, 50; Univ Strasbourg, DUniv, 65. *Prof Exp:* Asst prof French, Univ NB, 66-67; assoc prof, Univ Moncton, 67-69; assoc prof, 69-78, PROF FRENCH & COMP LIT, CARLETON UNIV, OTTAWA, 79- *Concurrent Pos:* Fels, Can Coun, 69, 74-75 & 78, Soc Sci & Humanities Res Coun Can, 79-81 & French Govt, 81 & 82. *Honors & Awards:* Nat Lit Award, Asn Can Univ Teachers Fr, 79. *Mem:* Can Asn Semiotic Res; Can Asn Comp Lit; Asn Can Univ Teachers Fr. *Res:* Sociological approaches in literary studies; 20th century short fiction in European languages; internationalist and cosmopolitan ideologies in literature . *Publ:* Auth, Paul Morand et le cosmopolitisme litteraire, Clinksieck, Paris, 68; Essai sur la sociologie de la litterature, Rev Lit Comp, 71; Histoire litteraire traditionnelle et sociologie de la lecture, Neohelicon, 1/74; auth, Le Point de vue social dans les e'tudes litteraires, Carleton Univ, Ottawa, 76; co-ed, La Prose Romanesque du XXe siecle, F-M Place, Paris, 77; Les Publics du recit court moderne, Beitr z Rom, Philologie, 79; ed, Lectures et lecteurs de l'ecrit moderne, Carleton Univ, Ottawa, 80; coauth (with Valery Larbaud), Bibliographie analytique annotee et critique, Asn Can Univ Teachers Fr, 82. *Mailing Add:* Dept of French Carleton Univ Ottawa ON K1S 5B6 Can

SARLES, HARVEY BURTON, b Buffalo, NY, July 12, 33; m 56; c 2. LINGUISTICS. *Educ:* Univ Buffalo, BA, 54, MA, 59; Univ Chicago, PhD(anthrop) 66. *Prof Exp:* Mathematician, Cornell Aeronaut Lab, 55-56; res asst ling, Univ Chicago, 60-61; asst prof anthrop & ling, Sch Med, Univ Pittsburgh, 62-66; assoc prof, 66-80, PROF ANTHROP, UNIV MINN, MINNEAPOLIS, 80- *Concurrent Pos:* Leverhulme vis fel ethnoling, Univ Sussex, 70-71; consult, Allegheny County Ment Health/Ment Retardation, 73-74; vis prof ling, State Univ NY, Buffalo, 74. *Mem:* Am Anthrop Asn; Animal Behav Soc; Ling Soc Am. *Res:* Behavioral linguistics; human ethology; non-verbal communication. *Publ:* Auth, The study of intelligiblity, Linguistics, 8/67; The study of language and communication across species, Current Anthrop, 4-6/69; Facial expression and body movement, In: Current Trends in Linguistics, Mouton, The Hague, 74; After Metaphysics, Peter de Ridder, 78. *Mailing Add:* Dept of Anthrop Univ of Minn Minneapolis MN 55455

SAROLLI, GIAN ROBERTO, b Voghera, Italy, Jan 10, 23. ROMANCE LANGUAGES & LITERATURE. *Educ:* Univ Pavia, LittD, 47; Univ Rome, Lib Doc(Ital lit), 69. *Prof Exp:* Asst dept Romance philol, Univ Pavia, 49-51; asst dept Romance philol, Univ Milan, 52-55; assoc prof Ital & hist, Int Inst Montana, Zugerberg, 56-57; attache, cult div, Ital Foreign Affairs Ministry, Buenos Aires, 57-59; prof Ital lit, Cath Univ Buenos Aires, 60; vis lectr Ital, Univ Pa & Johns Hopkins Univ, 60-61; assoc prof Romance lang & lit, Univ Cincinnati, 62-64; assoc prof Ital & Hisp studies, Univ Toronto, 64-65; prof Romance philol & Ital lit, Univ Calif, San Diego, 65-69; vis prof, 69-70, PROF ITAL & COMP LIT, HUNTER COL & GRAD CTR, CITY UNIV NEW YORK, 70- *Concurrent Pos:* Fel & grant, Inst Advan Medieval Studies, Spoleto, Ital, 53; Taft grant, 63; Can Coun grant, 65; Am Philos Soc grant, 67; City Univ New York Res Found grants, 71-73. *Honors & Awards:* Dante Soc Italy Gold Medal, 68. *Mem:* MLA; Mod Humanities Res Asn; Am Asn Teachers Ital; Dante Soc Am; Renaissance Soc Am. *Res:* History of the Italian, French and Spanish languages; medieval Italian, French and Spanish literatures; Dante and Machiavelli. *Publ:* Auth, El Italiano, Lengua Romance, Ed Nova, Buenos Aires, 62; Dante Scriba Dei, Convivium, Bologna, 63; Autoescegesi Dantesca e Tradizione Esegetica Medievale, Convivium, 65; Un dichirografor indeito del Machiavelli dictante e scribente, Mod Lang Notes, 65; Dante's katabasis and mission, In: The World of Dante, Univ Toronto, 67; Prolegomena alla Divina Commedia, BAR, Olschki, Florence, 69; Machiavelli: Inediti di Cancellaria e teatro, Adriatica, Bari, 73. *Mailing Add:* Dept of Ital & Comp Lit Hunter Col City Univ New York New York NY 10021

SARRE, ALICIA, b Mexico City, Mex, Oct 31, 16; US citizen. ROMANCE LANGUAGES. *Educ:* Barat Col, BA, 35; Marquette Univ, MA, 37; Stanford Univ, PhD(Span), 45. *Prof Exp:* Instr French & Span, Barat Col, 37-40; instr Span, Duchesne Col, 40-43; instr Span & French, San Francisco Col Women, 45-47; instr Span, Barat Col, 47-51; asst prof Span, Col Women, Univ San Diego, 52-60; asst prof Span & French, San Francisco Col Women, 60-64; PROF SPAN, COL WOMEN, UNIV SAN DIEGO, 64- *Res:* Mexican literature. *Publ:* Auth, Fuente liturgica de los villancicos de Sor Juana, 51 & Conceptismo y Gongorismo en la poesia de Sor Juana, 51, Rev Iberoam. *Mailing Add:* Dept of Foreign Lang Univ of San Diego Alcala Park San Diego CA 92110

SASSON, JACK MURAD, b Aleppo, Syria, Oct 1, 41; US citizen. FOREIGN LANGUAGES, HISTORY. *Educ:* Brooklyn Col, BA, 62; Brandeis Univ, MA, 63, PhD, 66. *Prof Exp:* From asst prof to assoc prof, 66-77, PROF RELIG, UNIV NC, CHAPEL HILL, 77- *Concurrent Pos:* Soc Relig Higher Educ fel, 69-70; assoc ed, J Am Orient Soc, 77. *Mem:* Soc Bibl Lit; Am Orient Soc; Israel Explor Soc; Dutch Orient Soc. *Res:* Ancient Near Eastern societies. *Publ:* Auth, Circumcision in the ancient Near East, J Bibl Lit, 66; The Military Establishments at Mari, 69 & contribr, Hebrew-Ugaritic Studies, 71, Pontif Bibl Inst; Archive keeping at Mari, Iraq, 72; Literary motif in . . . Gilgamesh epic, Studies Philol, 72; Commentary to Ruth, Johns Hopkins Univ, 78. *Mailing Add:* Dept of Relig Univ of NC Chapel Hill NC 27514

SATO, ESTHER MASAKO TATEISHI, b Paia, Maui, Hawaii, Dec 5, 15; m 43; c 3. FOREIGN LANGUAGE METHODOLOGY. *Educ:* William Jewell Col, BA, 38; Columbia Univ, MA, 39; Univ Hawaii, MA, 64. *Prof Exp:* Teacher, Hawaii Dept Educ, 39-44 & 57-64; instr Japanese, Univ Lab Sch, 64-66, asst prof Japanese, Col Educ, 66-71, assoc prof foreign lang methods, 71-76, PROF EDUC, COL EDUC, UNIV HAWAII, MANOA, 76- *Concurrent Pos:* Prof dir, Develop Instruct Materials for Japanese in Elem & Sec Schs, NDEA, 66-71, prof dir, Japanese Curric Materials Develop, 80- *Honors & Awards:* Achievement Award, William Jewell Col, 75. *Mem:* NEA; MLA; Am Coun Teaching Foreign Lang; Asn Supv & Curric Develop; Asn Teachers Japanese. *Res:* Methods in teaching foreign languages; Japanese language; Japansese culture. *Publ:* Ed, Hiragana Workbook-Text, 71, Test Booklet-Suppl to Teacher's Manual Learn-Japanese Ser, Elem & Sec, 71 & Learn Japanese-Elem Text, Student Ed, Bk I & Bk II, 72, Tongg Publ; auth, Japanese Language Instruction in Hawaii Public Schools, Educ Perspectives, 3/74; Japanese Now Text, Vol I, 82, Teacher's Manual, 82 & Exercise Sheets, 82, Univ Hawaii Press. *Mailing Add:* 2128 Oahu Ave Honolulu HI 96822

SATO, TOSHIHIKO, Comparative Literature. See Vol II

SAUER, ALFRED VON ROHR, b Winona, Minn, Dec 6, 08; m 38; c 6. THEOLOGY, SEMITIC PHILOLOGY. *Educ:* Northwestern Col, AB, 29; Univ Bonn, PhD, 39. *Prof Exp:* Res asst, Orient Inst, Univ Chicago, 36-38, instr Arabic & Syriac, 38-39; Lutheran pastor, 39-48; prof Old Testament theol, Concordia Sem, 48-74, chmn dept exeg theol, 67-74; PROF BIBL STUDIES, CHRIST SEM-SEMINEX, 74- *Concurrent Pos:* Mem standard Bible comt, Nat Coun Churches, 60; assoc dir, Joint Concordia- Am Sch Orient Res Excavation, Taanach, Jordan, 63, 66 & 68. *Mem:* Soc Bibl Lit; Nat Asn Prof Hebrew. *Res:* Field archaeology; modern Arabic; Hebrew prophets. *Publ:* Auth, Des Abu Dulaf Reisebericht, Scheur, Bonn, 39; coauth, Sex and the church, 62 & auth, The lure of the Palestine wilderness, 62, Concordia; Man as steward of creation, St Louis Univ Mag, 70; The meaning of archaeology for the exegetical task, 70 & Wisdom and law in Old Testament wisdom literature, 72, Concordia; When God comes, Currents at Seminex, 77. *Mailing Add:* Christ Sem-Seminex 607 N Grand Blvd St Louis MO 63103

SAUER, THOMAS G, b Indianapolis, Ind, Jan 24, 45; m 81. GERMAN & COMPARATIVE LITERATURE. *Educ:* Univ Notre Dame, BA, 67; Ind Univ, MA, 72, PhD(comp lit), 79. *Prof Exp:* Asst prof Ger, Col Fredonia, State Univ NY, 80-81; ASST PROF GERMAN, UNIV VA, 81- *Mem:* MLA; Am Comp Lit Asn; Int Comp Lit Asn; Am Asn Teachers Ger. *Res:* Anglo-German literary relations; German and European romanticism; German and European drama. *Publ:* Auth, Translation as a reflection of the receiving tradition: A W Schlegel's Vienna lectures in French and English, In: Literary Communication and Reception, Vol II, Proc IXth ICLA Cong, 80; A W Schlegel's Shakespearean Criticism in England, 1811-1846, Bouvier, 81. *Mailing Add:* Dept of Ger Cocke Hall Univ Va Charlottesville VA 22903

SAUNDERS, E DALE, Japanese. See Vol IV

SAUVE, MADELEINE, b St Timothee, Que, Sept 19, 24. THEOLOGY, LINGUISTICS. *Educ:* Col Jesus-Marie, BA, 55; Univ Montreal, Lic-en-pedag, 56, BSci Relig, 57, MA Sci Relig, 59, PhD(relig sci), 62; Laval Univ, MA, 66; Inst Cath Paris, Hab Dr, 70. *Prof Exp:* Prof philos, Norm Sch Valleyfield, 57-60; prof philos & relig, Col Jesus-Marie, 60-62, directress, 63-65; prof theol, 65-74, secy fac theol, 69-73, GRAMMARIAN, UNIV MONTREAL, 72- *Mem:* Can Philos Soc; Am Comp Lit Asn. *Res:* Woman in the Bible; the problem of language in the phenomenology of the spirit of Hegel and its implications; theological discourse. *Publ:* Auth, Questions de terminologies relatives aux operations de production de microfilm, 9/76 & Du trait d'union dans les noms designant les fonds prives, 6/77, Archives; L'ordre du jour ou les ordres du jour?, Metrop Educ TV Asn, 12/77; Line et staff, Vols, 6-7, 8-9/77 & Au niveau de, Sur le plan de et Dans le cadre de, Vol 11, 2/78, L'actualite terminol; Qui dit mieux?, Polytec, Bull d'info, Vol 2, 4/78; Expressions employees dans les formulaires: En majuscules, En capitales, etc, L'actualite terminol, Vol 12, 3/79; La documentation de base en matiere de langue francaise, Metrop Educ TV Asn, J des traducteurs, Vol 25, 3/80. *Mailing Add:* Secretariat Gen Univ Montreal PO Box 6128 Montreal 101 PQ H3C 3J7 Can

SAVACOOL, JOHN KENNETH, b Los Angeles, Calif, July 16, 17; m 64. FRENCH. *Educ:* Williams Col, BA, 39. *Prof Exp:* Instr, 45-46, lectr, 50, from asst prof to assoc prof, 52-64, PROF FRENCH, WILLIAMS COL, 64- *Honors & Awards:* Legion of Merit. *Mem:* Am Asn Teachers Fr; MLA. *Res:* Contemporary theatre. *Publ:* Coauth, Voix du siecle, Harcourt, Vols I & II, 60 & 66; transl, American Shakers, 71 & Jacob and The Angel, 73, Univ Mass. *Mailing Add:* Dept of Romanic Lang Williams Col Williamstown MA 01267

SAVAN, DAVID, Philosophy. See Vol IV

SAVET, GABRIELLE, b Cluj, Rumania, Nov 13, 11; US citizen; m 47; c 1. FRENCH. *Educ:* Univ Paris, Lic es Let, 32; Columbia Univ, PhD(French lit), 57. *Prof Exp:* Lectr, sch gen studies, Columbia Univ, 50-53; from instr to asst prof French, 55-64, assoc prof French & comp lit, 64-70, prof French, 70-74, EMER PROF FRENCH, HOFSTRA UNIV, 74- *Concurrent Pos:* Dir intensive summer prog, Hofstra Univ, 60-65, dept re French, 63-68. *Mem:* MLA; Am Asn Teachers Fr; Soc Fr Prof Am. *Publ:* Auth, Andre Suares, critique, Didier, Paris, 59. *Mailing Add:* Dept of French Hofstra Univ Hempstead NY 11550

SAVIGNON, SANDRA JOY, b Highland Park, Ill, Dec 30, 39. SECOND LANGUAGE ACQUISITION, PSYCHOLINGUISTICS. *Educ:* Univ Ill Urbana-Champaign, AB, 61, AM, 62, PhD(educ), 71. *Prof Exp:* Asst prof, 71-74, ASSOC PROF FRENCH, UNIV ILL URBANA-CHAMPAIGN, 74- *Concurrent Pos:* examr, Teachers English Foreign Lang Comt, Educ Testing Serv, 74-76. *Mem:* Teachers English Speakers Other Lang; Am Coun Teachers Foreign Lang; Am Asn Teachers Fr. *Res:* Bilingualism and second language acquisition; language pedagogy; language testing. *Publ:* Auth, Communicative Competence: An Experiment in Foreign Language Teaching, Ctr Curric Develop, 72; coauth, Language assessment: Where, what and how?, Anthrop & Educ, VIII: 83-91; auth, Teaching for communication, In: Developing Communication Skills, Newbury House, 78; Three Americans in Paris: A look at natural second language acquisition, Mod Lang J, 65: 241-247; Dictation as a measure of communicative competence in French as a second language, Lang Learning, Vol 32, 82; Communicative Competence: Theory and Classroom Practice, Addison-Wesley, 82. *Mailing Add:* Dept of French Univ of Ill Urbana IL 61801

SAVILLE-TROIKE, MURIEL RENEE, b Sacramento, Calif, Aug 8, 36; m 72. AMERICAN INDIAN LANGUAGES, ENGLISH AS A SECOND LANGUAGE. *Educ:* Fresno State Col, BA, 61, MA, 64; Univ Tex, Austin, PhD(ling), 68. *Prof Exp:* Asst prof ling, Tex A&M Univ, 68-70; asst prof appl ling, Univ Tex, Austin, 70-72; asst prof ling, Georgetown Univ, 72-81; ASSOC PROF ELEM EDUC & ENGLISH SECOND LANG, UNIV ILL, URBANA, 81- *Mem:* Teachers English to Speakers Other Lang (vpres, 73-74, pres, 74-75); NCTE; Ling Soc Am; Am Anthrop Asn. *Res:* Apachean dialectology; comparative athabaskan; second language acquisition. *Publ:* Coauth, A handbook of bilingual education, Teachers English to Speakers Other Lang, 71; auth, Diversity in southwestern Athabaskan: A historical perspective, Navajo Lang Rev, 74; Bilingual Children, Ctr Appl Lings, 75; Foundations for Teaching English as a Second Language, Prentice-Hall, 76; ed, GURT 77: Linguistics and Anthropology, Georgetown Univ, 77; Teaching Culture in the Bilingual Classroom, Nat Clearing house Bilingual Educ, 78; Ethnography of Communication, Basil Blackwells, 82; Language development, Encycl Educ Res, 82. *Mailing Add:* Dept of Elem Educ Univ of Ill Urbana IL 61801

SAVITT, JOAN NEUBURGER, b New York, NY, Oct 28, 46; m 68. LINGUISTICS, FRENCH. *Educ:* Russell Sage Col, BA, 67; State Univ NY Buffalo, MA, 70 & 73, PhD(ling), 75. *Prof Exp:* ASST PROF FRENCH & LING, STATE UNIV NY ALBANY, 75- *Mem:* Ling Asn of Can & US; Ling Soc Am; Am Asn Teachers Fr; MLA. *Res:* French linguistics; Franco-Canadian sociolinguistics; dialectology. *Publ:* Auth, Reconstitution and restructuring, Studies in Ling, 75; Cognate recognition across dialects, Phonetica, 75; Say AE, New Eng J Med, 76; Where do feature hierarchies come from?, Third Lacus Forum, 77; Les habitudes articulatoires maternelles (dans l'etude d'une langue seconde), Fourth Lacus Forum, 78. *Mailing Add:* Dept of French State Univ NY HU 235 Albany NY 12222

SAVVAS, MINAS, b Athens, Greece, Apr 2, 39; US citizen. COMPARATIVE LITERATURE, CREATIVE WRITING. *Educ:* Univ Ill, BA, 64, MA, 65; Univ Calif, Santa Barbara, PhD(English), 71. *Prof Exp:* Asst prof English, Univ Calif, Santa Barbara, 65-68; assoc prof, 68-74, PROF ENGLISH, SAN DIEGO STATE UNIV, 74- *Mem:* MLA; Mod Greek Studies Asn; Hellenic Cult Soc. *Res:* Modern Greek literature; continental novel; translation. *Publ:* Auth, Chekov's tragicomedy, Lang Quart, fall 70; Kazantzakis and Marxism, J Mod Lit, winter 72; Greece today, Colo Quart, summer 73; Scars and Smiles (poems), Athens, 75; Chronicle of Exile, Wire, 77; Samuel G Howe: Philhellene, Greek World, 78; The Subterranean Horses, Ohio Univ Press, 81; more than 100 poems in various journals. *Mailing Add:* Sch of Lit San Diego State Univ San Diego CA 92115

SAWYER, JANET B, b Madison, Wis, Mar 24, 21; wid; c 2. LINGUISTICS. *Educ:* Univ Minn, BA, 41; Univ Tex, MA & PhD, 57. *Prof Exp:* Assoc prof, 57-67, PROF LING, CALIF STATE UNIV, LONG BEACH, 67-, DIR MA IN LING, 76- *Concurrent Pos:* Consult, Los Angeles Standard Oral English Prog Blacks & Mexican-Am, 63-65. *Mem:* Ling Soc Am; Int Ling Asn; Am Dialect Soc. *Res:* Dialect geography and bilingualism; Spanish dialects; English grammar for foreign students and natives. *Publ:* Coauth, From Speech to Writing: An Applied Grammar, Holt, 66; auth, Aloofness from Spanish influence in Texas Spanish, Word, 8/59; Social aspects of bilingualism in San Antonio, Texas, Publ Am Dialect Soc, 4/64; Spanish-English bilingualism in San Antonio, In: Texas Studies in Bilingualism, de Gruyter, Berlin, 70; Existential sentences: A linguistic universal?, Am Speech, fall/winter 73; Passive & covert bilingualism, Swallow VI, 78. *Mailing Add:* Dept of English Calif State Univ Long Beach CA 90840

SAWYER, JESSE O, b Earlville, Ill, Feb 9, 18. LINGUISTICS. *Educ:* St Olaf Col, AB, 39; Univ Calif, Berkeley, PhD. *Prof Exp:* Asst prof speech & dir English prog foreign students, 60-62, asst prof ling, 62-65, DIR LANG LAB, UNIV CALIF, BERKELEY, 62-, LECTR LING, 65- *Mem:* Ling Soc Am; Norweg-Am Hist Asn; Nat Asn Lang Lab Dir. *Res:* American Indian languages; Yukian languages; language learning. *Publ:* Auth, Dictation in language learning, Lang Learning, 61; coauth, The Utility of Translation and Written Symbols During the First Thirty Hours of Language Study, US Off Educ, 62; auth, The implications of Spanish /r/ and /rr/ in Wappo history, Romance Philol, 11/64; ed, Studies in American Indian Languages, Vol 65, In: Univ Calif Publ Ling, 71. *Mailing Add:* Lang Lab B-40 Dwinelle Hall Univ of Calif Berkeley CA 94720

SAYERS, RAYMOND S, b New York, NY, Aug 29, 12. ROMANCE LANGUAGES. *Educ:* City Col New York, AB, 33; Columbia Univ, MA, 35, PhD(Span & Port), 52. *Prof Exp:* Teacher high sch, 36-46; asst dir courses, Brazil-US Inst, Rio de Janeiro, 46-47; exchange teacher English, Dept Educ, PR, 55-56; from asst prof to assoc prof Romance lang, City Col New York 59-66; assoc prof, 66-69, prof Romance lang, 69-80, prof comp lit, Grad Sch, 71-80, EMER PROF ROMANCE LANG, QUEENS COL, NY, 80- *Concurrent Pos:* Lectr Span & Port, grad fac, Columbia Univ, 50-71; vis asst prof, NY Univ, 63-64; Soc Sci Res Coun grant, 64; Fulbright res grant, Portugal, 68-69. *Mem:* MLA; Am Asn Teachers Span & Port; corresp mem Hisp Soc Am; Hisp Inst US; Am Port Cult Soc. *Res:* Brazilian and Portuguese literature, 19th and 20th centuries; the Negro in Brazilian literature. *Publ:* Auth, The Negro in Brazilian Literature, Hisp Inst, 56; O negro na literatura brasileira, O Cruzeiro, Brazil, 58; Portuguese literature, New Int Year Bk, 59-64; coauth, Portugal and Brazil in Transition, Univ Minn, 68. *Mailing Add:* 549 W 123rd St New York NY 10027

SAYLES, BARBARA, b Berlin, Ger, Dec 11, 29; US citizen. GERMAN & COMPARATIVE LITERATURE. *Educ:* MacMurray Col, BA, 52; Univ Calif, Los Angeles, MA, 56, PhD(Ger lang), 60. *Prof Exp:* Instr Ger, Pomona Col, 61-62; from asst prof to assoc prof Humanities, 62-76, ASSOC PROF MOD LANG, RAYMOND COL, UNIV OF THE PAC, 76- *Concurrent Pos:* Res, comp lit, Univ Cambridge, 68-69. *Res:* Thomas Mann; expressionism; 18th century German and English literature. *Mailing Add:* Dept of Humanities, Raymond Col Univ of the Pac Stockton CA 95204

SAYLOR, CHARLES FREDERICK, b San Pedro, Calif, Apr 6, 36; m 58; c 1. CLASSICS. *Educ:* Univ Wash, BA, 58, MA, 60; Univ Calif, Berkeley, PhD(classics), 68. *Prof Exp:* Instr classics, St Mary's Col, Calif, 65-66; lectr, Univ Calif, Davis, 66-67; asst prof, San Diego State Col, 67-68; asst prof, 68-72, assoc prof, 72-79, PROF CLASSICS, UNIV MO-COLUMBIA, 80- *Mem:* Am Philol Asn. *Res:* Latin love elegy. *Mailing Add:* Dept of Class Lang Univ of Mo Columbia MO 65201

SCAGLIONE, ALDO DOMENICO, b Torino, Italy, Jan 10, 25; m 52. ITALIAN & COMPARATIVE LITERATURE. *Educ:* Univ Torino, DLitt(French), 48. *Prof Exp:* Instr English, Tech Sch, Torino, 48-49; lectr Ital, Univ Toulouse, 49-51; instr, Univ Chicago, 51-52; instr, Univ Calif, Berkeley, 52, from asst prof to prof, 53-68, chmn dept, 63-65; WILLIAM RAND KENAN PROF ITAL & COMP LIT, UNIV NC, CHAPEL HILL, 68- *Concurrent Pos:* Fulbright fel, 51; Guggenheim fel, 58; sr resident fel, Newberry Libr, 64-65; vis prof, Yale Univ, 65-66; sr fel, Southeastern Inst Medieval & Renaissance Studies, 68; gen ed, Romance Notes, Studies Romance Lang, , 70-75; vis prof comp lit, grad ctr, City Univ New York, 71-72; ed, Series L'Interprete, Longo: Ravena, Italy, 75-; vis prof, Inst Res Humanities, Univ Wis-Madison, 81-82. *Honors & Awards:* Knight Order of Merit, President Repub Italy, 75. *Mem:* Am Asn Teachers Ital; MLA; Renaissance Soc Am; Dante Soc; Mediaeval Acad Am. *Res:* Latin humanism; medieval and Renaissance Italian and French literature; history of rhetoric and language sciences. *Publ:* Ed, M M Boiardo Opere, UTET, Torino, 2 vols, 51, reprint, 63, 67; auth, Nature and Love in the Late Middle Ages, Univ Calif, 63; Periodic Syntax in the Divina Commedia, Romance Philol, 67; Ars grammatica, Mouton, The Hague, 70; The Classical Theory of Composition, 72 & ed, Francis Petrarch, Six Centuries Later, 75, Univ NC, Chapel Hill; Ariosto 1974 in America, Longo, Ravenna, Italy, 76; Henri Weil, The Order of Words, John Benjamins, Amsterdam, 78; The Theory of German Word Order, Univ Minn Press, 81; Kimponierte Prosa, (2 vols), Klett, Stuttgart, 81. *Mailing Add:* Rte 4 Box 539 Chapel Hill NC 27514

SCANLAN, RICHARD T, b St Paul, Minn, May 30, 28; m 51; c 5. CLASSICS. *Educ:* Univ Minn, BS, 51, MA, 52. *Prof Exp:* Teacher Latin, Edina High Sch, Minn, 55-67; assoc prof, 67-80, PROF CLASSICS, UNIV ILL, URBANA, 80- *Concurrent Pos:* Mem Latin achievement test comt, Col Entrance Exam Bd, 60-65, chmn Latin advan placement exam comt, 67-72, chief examr, classics prog, 73-77. *Mem:* Am Philol Asn; Am Class League; Class Asn midwest & S; Am Coun Teaching Foreign Lang; Archives Asn Am. *Res:* The teaching of Latin; computer applications to the teaching of Latin; teaching of classical humanities. *Publ:* Auth, A survey of Latin textbooks, Class J, 76; A computer-assisted instruction course in vocabulary building, Foreign Lang Ann, 76; Suggestions for a course in ancient and modern tragedy, Class Outlook, 77; Beginning Latin, 77, Word Power, 77 & Latin Composition, 77, Control Data Co; Some criteria for the evaluation of Latin textbooks, 78 & The grading of the 1977 advanced placement examination, 78, Class J. *Mailing Add:* Dept of Classic Univ of Ill Urbana IL 61801

SCANLAN, TIMOTHY MICHAEL, b Akron, Ohio, Aug 31, 46; m 69; c 1. FRENCH LITERATURE. *Educ:* Univ Akron, BA, 66; Case Western Reserve Univ, MA, 68, PhD(French), 71. *Prof Exp:* From instr to asst prof, 70-75, assoc prof, 75-80, PROF FRENCH, UNIV TOLEDO, 80- *Mem:* MLA; Am Asn Teachers Fr; Am Soc 18th Century Studies; Am Coun Teaching Foreign Lang; NAm Soc 17th Century Fr Lit. *Res:* Foreign language pedagogy; 17th and 18th century French literature. *Publ:* Auth, Maternal mask and literary craft in La Princesse de Cleves, Rev du Pacifique, spring, 76; Rousseau and silence, Mod Lang Studies, fall 77; Racine's Bajazet: Noeuds and Denouement, SAtlantic Bull, 11/77; The dynamics of separation and communication in Rousseau's Julie, Esprit Createur, winter 77; Jean-Jacques Rousseau et le vin, Studia Neophilologica, fall 78; Another foreign language skill: Analyzing photographs, Foreign Lang Annals, 9/78; French mail-order catalogues as teaching tools: Vocabulary, culture and conversation, Fr Rev, 12/78; Aspects of figurative language in Rousseau's Dialogues, Essays in Fr Lit, fall 78. *Mailing Add:* Dept of Foreign Lang Univ of Toledo 2801 W Bancroft St Toledo OH 43606

SCANLON, THOMAS FRANCIS, b Pittsburgh, Pa, Sept 26, 51. CLASSICAL LANGUAGES. *Educ:* Duquesne Univ, BA, 72; Ohio State Univ, MA, 75, PhD(classics), 78. *Prof Exp:* Asst prof classics, Univ Md, College Park, 79-80 & Univ Calif, Los Angeles, 80-81; ASST PROF CLASSICS, UNIV CALIF, RIVERSIDE, 81- *Concurrent Pos:* Scholar, Univ Vienna, Austria, 78-79; Fulbright fel, Austrian Fulbright-Hays Prog, 78-79. *Mem:* Am Philol Asn. *Res:* Greek and Roman historical writing, athletics and linguistics. *Publ:* Auth, The Influence of Thucydides on Sallust, Carl Winter Press, Heidelberg, Ger, 80; The ancient Olympics mini-lessons, G Lawall, 80. *Mailing Add:* Dept of Lit & Lang Univ of Calif Riverside CA 92521

SCARATO, GIACOMO RINALDO, b Cosio d'Arroscia, Imperia, Italy, Mar 30, 37. ROMANCE LANGUAGES. *Educ:* Col del Monte, Italy, Lic in Classics, 57; St Bonaventure Univ, BA, 67, MSEd, 70; State Univ NY Buffalo, MAH, 78; Rensselaer Polytechnic Inst, PhD(commun & rhetoric), 78. *Prof Exp:* Teacher Span & French, Belfast Cent Sch Dist, 66-67; teacher French, Salamanca High Sch, 67-68; teaching asst foreign lang lab, St Bonaventure Univ, 68-70; teaching fel French, Rensselaer Polytechnic Inst, 70-71; teacher Span & French, Gen McArthur Mil Acad, 71-72; ASST PROF ITAL, BERGEN COMMUNITY COL, 72- *Concurrent Pos:* Travel consult, Romanda Tours, 73-78; ed consult, La Follia Di New York, 74-78; lang consult Ital & Span, Int Med Educ Inst, 76-; mem adv comt, World-wide Med Educ Inst, 76-78. *Mem:* Dante Soc Am; Am Class League; Am Ital Hist Asn; Am Asn Teachers Ital; MLA. *Res:* Mystical experience and literary creation; Dante studies; Italian dialectology. *Mailing Add:* Dept of Romance Lang Bergen Community Col 400 Paramus Rd Paramus NJ 07652

SCATTON, ERNEST ALDEN, b Hazleton, Pa, Sept 4, 42; m 64; c 2. SLAVIC LINGUISTICS. *Educ:* Univ Pa, BA, 64; Harvard Univ, MA, 67, PhD(Slavic lang & lit), 70. *Prof Exp:* From lectr to asst prof Slavic lang, Ind Univ, 70-72; asst prof, Univ Va, 72-76; assoc dean, Humanities & Fine Arts, 77-79, ASSOC PROF SLAVIC LANG, STATE UNIV NY ALBANY, 76-, CHMN SLAVIC LANG & LIT, 80- *Concurrent Pos:* Assoc dir, Slavic Workshop, Ind Univ, 71. *Mem:* Bulgarian Studies Asn (secy-treas, 72-78 & 79-); Am Asn Teachers Slavic & East Europ Lang; Asn Humanities Comput. *Res:* Phonology of Slavic languages, especially Russian, Bulgarian & Serbo-Croatian; Balkan linguistics; general phonology. *Publ:* Auth, The alternation e/a in modern Bulgarian, Slavic & East Europ J, 73; Bulgarian Phonology, Slavica, 75; Forms such as cal/cali in Bulgarian dialects, In: Bulgaria: Past and Present, Am Asn Advan Slavic Studies, 76; How Bulgarian treats its vowels, Folia Slavica, 77; A Bulgarian Reference Grammar, OE/DHEW, 78; co-ed, A Festschrift for Horace G Lunt, Slavica, 78; coauth, Towards a typology of vowel reduction, Lingua, 78; auth, Old Church Slavonic tj/dj, Linguistics, 78. *Mailing Add:* Dept Slavic Ling State Univ NY Albany NY 12222

SCAVNICKY, GARY EUGENE, b Youngstown, Ohio, Mar 9, 40; m 64; c 3. MESO-AMERICAN AND GENERAL LINGUISTICS. *Educ:* Youngstown State Univ, AB, 62; Univ Ill, Urbana, MA, 64, PhD(Span Ling), 69. *Prof Exp:* Instr Span, Univ Ill, 66-67; from instr to asst prof Span & ling, Univ Wis-Madison, 67-69; asst prof, 69-75, ASSOC PROF SPAN & GEN LING, WAYNE STATE UNIV, 75- *Mem:* Am Asn Teachers Span & Port; AAUP; Ling Soc Am. *Res:* Central-American Spanish linguistics; Andean-Spanish linguistics. *Publ:* Coauth, El sufijo -al en el espanol centro-americano, Espanol Acual, Spain, 12/74; Successful language laboratory performance, NALLD J, winter 76; contribr, Extent and use of indigenous vocabulary in Guatemalan Spanish, In: 1975 Colloquium on Hispanic Ling, Georgetown Univ, summer 76; Review of Wallace Lambert et al, Tu, Vous, Usted: A Social-Psychological Study of Address Patterns, 3/78 & Review of Virginia Zuniga Tristan's El anglicismo en el habla costarricense, vol LXI, 5/78, Hispania; Sobre algunos gentilicios nuevos en el espanol colombiano, Bol de Acad Norteamericana de Lengua Espanola, 79; ed, Dialectologia hispanoamericana: estudios actuales, Georgetown Univ Press; auth, The Suffix -oso in Central-American Spanish, Hispania, vol LXV, 3/82. *Mailing Add:* 487 Manoogian Hall Wayne State Univ Detroit MI 48202

SCHAARSCHMIDT, GUNTER HERBERT, b Zwickau, Ger, Dec 29, 38; Can citizen; m 64. SLAVIC & GENERAL LINGUISTICS. *Educ:* Univ Alta, MA, 63; Ind Univ, Bloomington, PhD(Slavic ling), 68. *Prof Exp:* From lectr to asst prof Slavic lang, Univ Alta, 63-69; asst prof ling, Ind Univ, 68-69; assoc prof & chmn dept, Univ Alta, 69-74, prof Slavic lang, 74-79; PROF SLAVIC STUDIES, UNIV VICTORIA, 79-, CHMN DEPT, 80- *Concurrent Pos:* Can Coun res fel, Inst Russ Lang, USSR Acad Sci, Moscow, 75. *Mem:* Can Asn Slavists (vpres, 72-73); Can Ling Asn; Ling Soc Am; Int Ling Asn; Am Asn Teachers Slavic & East Europ Langs. *Res:* Russian syntax; historical Slavic phonology, specifically Sorbian; linguistic theory. *Publ:* Auth, Subordinate subject deletion in Russian, Can J Ling, 70; Passive and pseudo-passive constructions in Russian, Scando-Slavica, 71; Invariant and variable ordering in Slavic syntax, Can Contrib to VII Int Cong Slavists, The Hague, 73; Stylistic processes and the grammatical structure of Slavic languages, In: Poetyka i stylistika slowianska, Ossolineum, Warsaw, 73; Some aspects of pronominal reference in contemporary Russian prose, In: Struktura i semantika literaturnogo teksta, Akademiai Kiado, Budapest, 77; Aspirated stops in Sorbian and German Germano-Slavica, 78; On the typological variability of argument regrouping in the Slavic languages, In: Canadian Contributions to the VIIIth International Congress of Slavists, Can Asn Slavists, 78; co-ed & contribr, Poetica Slavica: Studies in Honour of Zbigniew Folejewski, Ottawa, 81. *Mailing Add:* Dept of Slavonic Studies Univ of Victoria Victoria BC V8W 2Y2 Can

SCHABACKER, JOHN MONTGOMERY, b Erie, Pa, Jan 21, 17; m 41; c 3. GERMAN LITERATURE. *Educ:* Drew Univ, AB, 38; Montclair State Col, MA, 39; Univ NY, PhD(Ger), 52. *Prof Exp:* From instr to assoc prof mod lang, 39-59, chmn dept Ger, 54-65, chmn dept Ger & Russ 65-76, PROF GER, DREW UNIV, 59- *Concurrent Pos:* Mem, nat adv coun, jr year in Munich & Freiburg, 62-, resident dir,jr year in Freiburg, Wayne State Univ, 63-64; mem, nat adv coun, Europ studies prog, Cent Univ Iowa, 64-; resident dir, year abroad prog, Assoc Mid-Fla Cols, Freiburg, 70-71. *Mem:* Am Asn Teachers Ger; Mid States Asn Mod Lang Teachers. *Res:* French symbolism in its impact on German literature. *Mailing Add:* Dept of Ger Drew Univ Madison NJ 07940

SCHABER, STEVEN CONRAD, b San Diego, Calif, June 11, 41. GERMANIC LANGUAGES & LITERATURE. *Educ:* San Diego State Col, BA, 63; Princeton Univ, MA, & PhD, 67. *Prof Exp:* From asst prof to prof Ger, 67-76, PROF GER & CLASSICS, SAN DIEGO STATE UNIV, 76- *Mem:* MLA; AAUP; Philol Asn Pac Coast; Am Asn Teachers Ger. *Res:* German Romanticism and neo-Romanticism. *Publ:* Auth, The Lord Chandos letter in the light of Hofmannsthal's lyric decade, 1/70 & Novalis and the work of art as hieroglyph, 1/73, Ger Rev. *Mailing Add:* Dept of Ger San Diego State Univ San Diego CA 92115

SCHACH, PAUL, b Tremont, Pa, Oct 30, 15; m 40; c 3. GERMANIC PHILOLOGY. *Educ:* Albright Col, AB, 38; Univ Pa, AM, 41, PhD, 49. *Prof Exp:* From instr to asst prof Ger, Albright Col, 38-45; asst prof, NCent Col, 45-46, prof & head dept, 46-51; from assoc prof to prof, 51-66, chmn dept, 63-66, CHARLES J MACH PROF GERMANIC LANG, UNIV NEBR-LINCOLN, 66- *Concurrent Pos:* Guest lectr ling, Univ Colo, 60-64 & Univ Pa, 65 & 76; Am Philos Soc grant, 65-66; Woods humanities fel, 65-66; assoc ed, Scand Studies, 69-73, ed, 77- *Mem:* MLA; Am Asn Teachers Ger; Ling Soc Am; Mediaeval Acad Am; Soc Advan Scand Studies (secy-treas, 53-55, vpres, 55, pres, 56). *Res:* Medieval literature; applied linguistics; Old Norse. *Publ:* Auth, Some forms of writer intrusion in the Islendingasögur, Scand Studies, 70; Symbolic dreams in Old Icelandic literature, Mosaic, 71; transl, Einar Ol Sveinson, Njals Saga: A Literary Masterpiece, Univ Nebr, 71; auth, Some Observations on the Helgafell Episode in Eyrbyggja Saga and Gisla Saga, Vol II, Hollander, 72; transl, The Saga of Tristram and Isönd, 73 & Peter Hallberg, Old Icelandic Poetry, 75, Univ Nebr; auth, Antipagan sentiment in the sagas of Icelanders, Gripla, 75; Languages in Conflict: Linguistic Acculturation on the Great Plains, 80. *Mailing Add:* Dept of Mod Lang Univ of Nebr Lincoln NE 68588

SCHACHTER, ALBERT, b Winnipeg, Man, Aug 23, 32; m 60. CLASSICS. *Educ:* McGill Univ, BA, 55; Oxford Univ, DPhil(classics), 68. *Prof Exp:* From lectr to assoc prof, 59-72, chmn dept, 70-74, PROF CLASSICS MCGILL UNIV, 72- *Concurrent Pos:* Ford Found grant, 68-70; gen ed, Teiresias: Rev & Cont Bibliog of Boiotian Antiq, 71-; vis fel, Wolfson Col, Oxford, 82-83. *Mem:* Am Philol Asn; Hellenic Soc; Class Asn Can; Joint Asn Class Teachers; Soc Des Etudes Anciennes du Que. *Res:* Greek cults; Greek language teaching. *Publ:* Auth, The Re-organization of the Thespian Museia, Numis Chronicle, 61; A Boeotian cult type, Bull Inst Class Studies; The Theban Wars, Phoenix, 67; coauth, Ancient Greek: A Structural Programme, McGill-Queens Univ, 73; Cults of Boiotia, Vols 1 & 4, Inst Class Studies, London, 81. *Mailing Add:* Dept of Classics McGill Univ 855 Sherbrooke St W Montreal PQ H3A 2T7 Can

SCHACHTER, JACQUELYN ELIZABETH, b Honolulu, Hawaii, Sept 21, 36; m 67; c 1. LINGUISTICS. *Educ:* Univ Calif Los Angeles, BA, 59, MA, 65, PhD(ling), 71. *Prof Exp:* Asst prof, 71-78, ASSOC PROF ENGLISH AS SECOND LANG, AM LANG INST, UNIV SOUTHERN CALIF, 78- *Concurrent Pos:* AID/Nat Asn Foreign Student Affairs liaison comt res grant, 75; ed, Teachers of English to Speakers of Other Lang Quart, 78- *Mem:* Ling Soc Am; AAUP; Nat Asn Foreign Student Affairs; Teachers of English to Speakers Other Lang; Am asn Appl Ling. *Res:* Second language acquisition; semantics; syntax. *Publ:* Auth, Counterfactual conditionals, Papers in Montague Grammar, 71; An error in error analysis, Lang Learning, 74; Some semantic prerequisites for a model of language, Brain & Lang, 76; coauth, Learner intuitions of grammaticality, Lang Learning, 76; Research in interlanguage: Syntax, Teachers English Speakers Other Lang, 77; Some reservations concerning error analysis, Teachers English Speakers Other Lang Quart, 77; auth, Interrelationships between total production and error production in the syntax of adult learners, Papers in English as Second Lang, 78; coauth, An Analysis of Learner Production of English Structures, Georgetown Univ (in prep). *Mailing Add:* Am Lang Inst Univ of Southern Calif Los Angeles CA 90007

SCHACHTER, PAUL MORRIS, b New York, NY, May 22, 29; m 67. LINGUISTICS. *Educ:* Columbia Univ, BA, 50; Univ Calif, Los Angeles, MA, 57, PhD(English), 60. *Prof Exp:* Vis lectr, Univ Ghana, Legon, 59-60; asst prof English, 61-64, from asst prof to assoc prof Near East & African lang, 64-66, assoc prof, 66-69, PROF LING, UNIV CALIF, LOS ANGELES, 69- *Concurrent Pos:* Vis lectr, Univ Ibadan, 63-64 & Tel-Aviv Univ, 68-69. *Mem:* Ling Soc Am. *Res:* English syntax; Philippine languages; African languages. *Publ:* Coauth, A Phonology of Akan, 68 & co-ed, Critiques of Syntactic Studies, Vols I & II, 72 & 73, Univ Calif, Los Angeles; coauth, A Tagalog Reference Grammar, Univ Calif, Berkeley, 72; Major Syntactic Structures of English, Holt, 73; auth, Focus and relativization, Language, 3/73; A nontransformational account of gerundive nominals in English, Ling Inquiry, spring 76; The subject of Philippine languages, In: Subject and Topic, Acad Press, 76; Constraints on coördination, Language, 3/77. *Mailing Add:* Dept of Ling Univ of Calif Los Angeles CA 90024

SCHADE, GEORGE D, b Portland, Ore, July 16, 23. SPANISH, ROMANCE LANGUAGES. *Educ:* Univ Ore, BA, 45, MA, 47; Univ Calif, Berkeley, PhD(Romance lit), 53. *Prof Exp:* Instr Romance lang, Univ Ore, 46-47; lectr Span, Univ Calif, 53-54; instr, Univ NMex, 54-55; from instr to assoc prof, 55-66, PROF SPAN, UNIV TEX, AUSTIN, 66- *Concurrent Pos:* Fulbright-Hays Advan Res grant, 67-68. *Mem:* MLA; Am Asn Teachers Span & Port Chile, Mexico, and Argentina. *Publ:* Auth, Augury in Al filo del agua, Tex Studies in Lit & Lang, spring 60; Juan Jose Arreola, Confabulario and Other Inventions, translated with critical introd, 64, Juan Rulfo, The Burning Plain and Other Stories, transl with critical introd, 67, co-ed, Ruben Dario Centennial Studies, 70 & contrib, Introduction to The Decapitated Chicken and Other Stories by Horacio Quiroga, 76, Univ Tex, Austin; co-ed, Literatura espanola contemporanea, Antologia, Introduccion, notas, Charles Scribner's Sons, 65; Notas sobre Martin Rivas: Evaluacion y vigencia, La lit ibero-americana del siglo xix, Univ Ariz, 74; El arte narrativo de Garcia Marquez en su novela corta La increible y triste historia de la candida Erendira y de su abuela desalmada, Thesaurus, Mayoagosto, 77. *Mailing Add:* Dept of Span & Port Drawer C Univ of Tex Austin TX 78712

SCHAECHTER, MORDKHE, b Cernauti, Rumania, Dec 1, 27; US citizen; m 55; c 4. YIDDISH LINGUISTICS & FOLKLORE. *Educ:* Univ Vienna, PhD(comp ling), 51. *Prof Exp:* Instr Yiddish, Sem Sch Jewish Studies, 60-62; res asst, Lang & Cult Atlas of Ashkenazic Jewry, 62-72, LECTR YIDDISH, COLUMBIA UNIV, 72- *Concurrent Pos:* Chmn, ling circle, Yivo Inst Jewish Res, 60-67; assoc prof Yiddish, Jewish Teachers Sem, 62-72; pres, Benyumen Shekhter Found Advan Standard Yiddish, 68-; vis asst prof, Yeshiva Univ, 68-70; ed, Yidishe shprakh, 71-; consult Yiddish ling, Max Weinreich Ctr Advan Jewish Studies, 73- *Mem:* Am Asn Prof Yiddish; Ling Soc Am; PEN Club. *Res:* Yiddish language planning, especially terminological standardization. *Publ:* Auth, On the use of geographic names, Yidishe Shprakh, 57; coauth, Guide to Standardized Yiddish Orthography, Comt Implementation Standardized Yiddish Orthography, 61; auth, Dr S Birnbaum's contribution to standardization of the Yiddish language, Yidishe Shprakh, 62; Eliakum Zunser's Works: Critical Edition, Yivo Inst Jewish Res, 64; Names of trees and shrubs, Yidishe Shprakh, 66; Yiddish Orthography: An Outline for a Course, Comt Implementation Standardization Yiddish Orthography, 73; Food: A Yiddish terminology, J Zelitch Found, 76; Four schools of thought in Yiddish language planning, Mich Ger Studies, fall 77. *Mailing Add:* Room 406 Philos Hall Columbia Univ Broadway & 116th St New York NY 10027

SCHAEFER, JACQUELINE THIBAULT, b Caen, France, Apr 5, 30; m 60; c 1. FRENCH & COMPARATIVE LITERATURE. *Educ:* Univ Caen, Lic es Lett, 52, DES, 53; Sorbonne, Agregation, 62. *Prof Exp:* Asst French, Univ Edinburgh, Scotland, 54-55; instr, Middlebury Col, Vermont, 56-59; lectr, Mt Allison Univ, Can, 59-60; asst prof, Carleton Col, Minn, 62-67; assoc prof, 67-77, PROF FRENCH, UNIV OF THE SOUTH, 73-, ASST ED, TRISTANIA, 78- *Mem:* Int Comp Lit Asn; Int Arthurian Soc; Int Courtly Lit Soc; Am Comp Lit Asn; Renceval Soc. *Res:* Mediaeval literature, particularly Tristan studies. *Publ:* Auth, Tristan's folly: feigned or real?, Tristania, 11/77; review, Olifant, 5/77. *Mailing Add:* Univ of the South Sewanee TN 37375

SCHAEFFER, PETER MORITZ-FRIEDRICH, b Breslau, Ger, May 14, 30; US citizen; m 68. GERMANIC STUDIES, COMPARATIVE LITERATURE. *Educ:* Univ Ottawa, Lic Theol, 59; Princeton Univ, PhD(Germanic studies), 71. *Prof Exp:* From lectr to asst prof Germanic studies, Princeton Univ, 70-74; vis lectr Ger & comp lit, Univ Calif, Berkeley, 74-76; ASSOC PROF GER, UNIV CALIF, DAVIS, 76-, V CHMN, DEPT GER & RUSS, 78- *Mem:* MLA; Renaissance Soc Am; Soc Values Higher Educ. *Res:* Renaissance; Neo-Latin literature; German Democratic Republic literature. *Publ:* Auth, Joachim Vadianus, De poetica, Text, Translation & Commentary, Wilhelm Fink, Munich, 73; The emergence of the concept medieval in central European humanism, 16th Century J, 10/76; contrib, Letters of obscure men, In: The Renaissance and Reformation in Germany, Frederick Ungar, 77. *Mailing Add:* 1101 Alice St Davis CA 95616

SCHAFER, EDWARD HETZEL, b Seattle, Wash, Aug 23, 13; m 42, 71; c 3. EAST ASIATIC PHILOLOGY. *Educ:* Univ Calif, AB, 38, PhD, 47; Univ Hawaii, AM, 40. *Prof Exp:* From lectr to assoc prof, 47-58, PROF ORIENT LANG, UNIV CALIF, BERKELEY, 58- *Concurrent Pos:* Guggenheim fels, 53-54 & 68; assoc ed, Am Orient Soc J, 55-58, ed, 58-68; Am Coun Learned Soc grant, 60-61. *Mem:* Am Orient Soc (vpres, 74-75, pres, 75-76); Mediaeval Acad Am; Soc Medieval Archaeol. *Res:* Literature and civilization of T'ang dynasty China; man and nature in mediaeval China. *Publ:* Auth, The Stone Catalogue of Cloudy Forest: A Commentary and Synopsis, 61, The Golden Peaches of Samarkand: A Study of T'ang Exotics, 63, The Vermilion Bird: T'ang Images of the South, 67, coauth, Ancient Chain, Time-Life, 67, auth, Shore of Pearls: Hainan Island in Early Times, 70, The Divine Woman: Dragon Ladies and Rain Maidens in T'ang Literature, 73 & Pacing the Void: T'ang Approaches to the Stars, 77, Univ Calif; Mao Shan in T'ang Times, Univ Colo, 80. *Mailing Add:* 60 Avis Rd Berkeley CA 94707

SCHAFFER, MARTHA ELIZABETH, US citizen. ROMANCE PHILOLOGY, MEDIEVAL LITERATURE. *Educ:* Univ Calif, Berkeley, AB, 72, PhD(Romance philol), 80. *Prof Exp:* Actg instr Span & Port lang, Univ Calif, Berkeley, 78-79; ASST PROF SPAN LANG & LIT, BROWN UNIV, 80- *Mem:* MLA; Philol Asn Pac Coast; Mediaeval Acad Am; Asn Int Hisp; NAm Catalan Soc. *Res:* Romance historical linguistics (word formation by derivation); medieval lyric of the Iberian peninsula; Spanish of America. *Publ:* Auth, Portuguese -idao, Spanish -(e)dumbre, and their Romance cognates, A critical survey of a century of philological gropings, Romance Philol, 8/81; The learned transmission of the Latin Suffix -tudo/-tundine in English and Romance, Romance Philol (in prep). *Mailing Add:* Dept of Hisp & Italian Studies Brown Univ Providence RI 02912

SCHAMSCHULA, WALTER, b Prague, Czech, Dec 23, 29; WGer citizen; m 58; c 1. SLAVIC LANGUAGES & LITERATURES. *Educ:* Univ Frankfurt, PhD(Slavic lang & lit), 60, Habil, 70. *Prof Exp:* Asst Slavic lang & lit, Univ Frankfurt, 58-60, lectr Czech, 60-70, privatdocent Slavic lang & lit, 70-72; PROF SLAVIC LANG & LIT, UNIV CALIF, BERKELEY, 72- *Concurrent Pos:* Vis lectr, Univ Calif, Berkeley, 70-71; Univ Calif humanities res fel, 76. *Mem:* Asn Slavicists Fed Repub Ger. *Res:* Russian historical novel; Pushkin; Czech literature. *Publ:* Auth, Russian Historical Novel from Neoclassicism to Romanticism, A Hain, Meisenheim/Glan, 61; The sacral style and its function in the work of Karel Capek, Opera Slavica IV, Goettingen, 63; ed, Jan Hus, Essays and Letters, Insel, Frankfurt, 69; auth, The sources of Lomonosov's cosmological lyrics, Z fuer Slavische Philol, Heidelberg, 69; Beginnings of Czech National Revival and German Intellectual Life (1749-1800), W Fink, Munich, 73. *Mailing Add:* Dept of Slavic Lang & Lit Univ of Calif Berkeley CA 94720

SCHANE, SANFORD A, b Detroit, Mich, Aug 8, 37; m 60; c 2. LINGUISTICS. *Educ:* Wayne State Univ, BA, 58; Univ Mich, MA, 61; Mass Inst Technol, PhD(ling), 65. *Prof Exp:* Assoc prof, 65-70-, PROF LING, UNIV CALIF, SAN DIEGO, 70, DIR FOREIGN LANG INSTR, 71- *Concurrent Pos:* Ed, Found Mod Ling ser, Prentice-Hall, Inc, 70- *Mem:* Ling Soc Am. *Res:* Phonological theory; French phonology; orthography. *Publ:*

Auth, French Phonology and Morphology, Mass Inst Technol, 68; co-ed, Modern Studies in English, 69 & auth, Generative Phonology, 73, Prentice-Hall. *Mailing Add:* Dept of Ling Univ of Calif San Diego La Jolla CA 92093

SCHANZER, GEORGE O, b Vienna, Austria, Oct 26, 14; US citizen; m 44; c 4. SPANISH. *Educ:* Univ Vienna, DJr, 38; Univ Mo, MA, 46; State Univ Iowa, PhD(Span), 50. *Prof Exp:* Instr Span, Univ Mo, 45-46; asst, State Univ Iowa, 46-47; from instr to asst prof, Univ Kans, 48-52; from assoc prof to prof, St John's Univ, NY, 52-64; dir grad studies Span, 64-69 & 71-74, actg chmn dept Span, Ital & Port, 69-70, PROF SPAN AM LIT, STATE UNIV NY BUFFALO, 64- *Concurrent Pos:* Buenos Aires Convention res fel, Montevideo, Uruguay, 47-48; lectr, Queens Col NY, 59-64; vis prof, Hofstra Col, 59-60; Fulbright res grant, Madrid, Spain, 62-63; assoc ed, Hispania, 65-68; Orgn Am States res grant, Buenos Aires, 76. *Mem:* Am Asn Teachers Span & Port; MLA; Inst Int Lit Iberoam; Latin Am Studies Asn; Asoc Int Hispanistas. *Res:* Spanish American literature, fiction, theatre; Hispanic-Russian literary relations; La Plata literature. *Publ:* Auth, Rodo's notes on Tolstoi's What is Art?, Symposium, 51; La vida errante de Ernesto Herrera, Rev Nacional, Montevideo, 61; Ruben Dario, traductor de Gorki, Rev iberoam, 67; Russian Literature in the Hispanic World, Univ Toronto, 72; The four hundred years of myths and melancholies of Mujica Lainez, Latin Am Lit Rev, 73; Lo Mod Del Modernismo: De sobremesa, In: La literatura iberoamericana del siglo XIX, Univ Ariz, 74; On the problem of Ruben Dario's connection with Russian literature, In: The Comparative Study of Literature, Akad Nauk, Leningrad, 76; El teatro vanguardista de Eduardo Pavlovsky, Eduardo Pavlovsky, Madrid, 80. *Mailing Add:* Dept of Mod Lang & Lit State Univ NY Buffalo NY 14260

SCHARFE, HARTMUT E F, b Koethen, Ger, June 14, 30; m 62; c 3. INDIC STUDIES. *Educ:* Univ Halle, Dipl Indology, 52; Univ Berlin, Dr Phil(Indology), 56. *Prof Exp:* Asst Indology, Inst Orientforsch, Deut Akad Wiss, Berlin, 56-59; lectr Ger, Univ Kerala, 60-62; Deut Forschungsgemeinschaft res fel Indology, Univ Tübingen, 62-65; from asst prof to assoc prof, 65-70, PROF INDIC STUDIES, UNIV CALIF, LOS ANGELES, 70- *Concurrent Pos:* Am Inst Indian Studies res fel, India, 67-68. *Mem:* Deut Morgenländische Ges; Am Orient Soc; Asn Asian Studies. *Res:* Indian grammarians and linguistics; ancient Indian state craft. *Publ:* Auth, Die Logik im Mahabhasya, Akademie, Berlin, 61; Untersuchungen zur Staatsrechtslehre des Kautalya, Harrassowitz, Wiesbaden, 68; Panini's Metalanguage, Memoir Am Philos Soc, 71; The Maurya Dynasty and the Selecucids, 71 & The Sacred Water of the Ganges and the Styx-Water, 72, Z Vergleichende Sprachforsch; Grammatical literature, In: History of Indian Literature, Harrassowitz, Wiesbaden, 77. *Mailing Add:* Dept of Orient Lang Univ of Calif Los Angeles CA 90024

SCHATKIN, MARGARET AMY, b New York, NY, Apr 29, 44. PATRISTICS, CLASSICS. *Educ:* Queens Col, BA, 64; Fordham Univ, MA, 66, PhD(classics), 67, ThD, 82. *Prof Exp:* Asst prof, 69-75, ASSOC PROF THEOL, BOSTON COL, 75- *Concurrent Pos:* Princeton Univ fel, 67-68; Nat Endowment for Humanities sr fel, 76-77; Mellon grant, 81. *Honors & Awards:* Award, Marian & Jasper Whiting Found, 74. *Mem:* Asn Int Etudes Patristiques; Soc Ovidianis Studies; NAm Patristic Soc; Am Philol Asn. *Res:* Greek patristic literature; Greek palaeography; history of Christian thought. *Publ:* Auth, Cramer's Catena and Origen, Traditio, 70; The influence of Origen upon St Jerome's commentary on Galatians, Vigilae Christianae, 70; ed, The Heritage of the Early Church: Essays in Honor of Georges V Florovsky, Pontif Orient Inst, Rome, 73; auth, The Maccabean martyrs, Vigiliae Christianae, 74; Byzantine Greek manuscripts in Leningrad: The Granstrem catalog, In: Festschrift Marcel Richard, Berlin, 77; Idiophones of the Ancient World, Jahrbuch für Antike und Christentum, 78; ed, Bibliographia Patristica, De Gruyter, 81. *Mailing Add:* 215-05 39th Ave Bayside NY 11361

SCHATZBERG, WALTER, b Vienna, Austria, Aug 25, 30; US citizen. GERMAN LANGUAGE & LITERATURE. *Educ:* St John's Col, Md, BA, 54; Johns Hopkins Univ, PhD(Ger lit), 66. *Prof Exp:* Asst prof Ger, Washington Col, 59-66; from asst prof to assoc prof Ger, 66-76, chmn dept foreign lang, 71-76, PROF GER & CHMN DEPT FOREIGN LANG & LIT, CLARK UNIV, 76- *Mem:* MLA; Am Asn Teachers Ger; Am Coun Teaching Foreign Lang. *Res:* German Enlightenment; age of Goethe; literature and science. *Publ:* Auth, Gottsched as a popularizer of science, Mod Lang Notes, 10/68; Scientific themes in the popular literature and the poetry of the German Enlightenment, 1720-1760, Herbert Lang, 73. *Mailing Add:* Dept of Foreign Lang Clark Univ Worcester MA 01610

SCHAUM, G THEODORE, b Ger, July 9, 34; US citizen; m 59; c 3. GERMANIC LANGUAGES. *Educ:* Princeton Univ, AB, 57; Ind Univ, MA, 60, PhD(Ger), 64. *Prof Exp:* Teacher Ger & French, Choate Sch, Conn, 57-58; from lectr to asst prof Ger, Ind Univ, Bloomington, 62-69; assoc prof, 69-77, chmn dept, 70-77, PROF FOREIGN LANG & LIT, MOORHEAD STATE UNIV, 77- *Mem:* Am Coun Teachers Foreign Lang; Am Asn Teachers Ger. *Res:* German romanticism and poetic realism; German novel and novelle; foreign language teaching methodology. *Mailing Add:* Dept of Lang Moorhead State Univ Moorhead MN 56560

SCHAUM, KONRAD JOHANNES, b Sirgwitz, Ger, Sept 14, 24; US citizen; m 51; c 2. GERMAN LITERATURE. *Educ:* Univ Heidelberg, State Bd Cert Ger lit, 51; Queen's Univ, MA, 53; Princeton Univ, PhD(Ger lit), 55. *Prof Exp:* From instr to assoc prof Ger lit, Princeton Univ, 55-71; prof foreign lang & lit & chmn dept, Univ Denver, 71-74; PROF MOD & CLASS LANG & CHMN DEPT, UNIV NOTRE DAME, 74- *Concurrent Pos:* R Stockton Preceptorship, 60-63; assoc ed, Die Unterrichtspraxis, 68-71; chmn examr comt, Educ Testing Serv grad sch foreign lang test, 69-75; consult & panelist, Nat Found Arts & Humanities, 73-74; mem nat bd consult, Nat Endowment for Humanities, 74- *Honors & Awards:* Grillparzer-Ring, 80. *Mem:* MLA; Am Asn Teachers Ger; Cath Comn Intellectual & Cult Affairs; Asn Dept Foreign Lang; Grillparzer-Gesellschaft. *Res:* Nineteenth and 20th century German literature; German and European civilization; comparative literature. *Publ:* Auth, Die Grillparzer-forschung in Amerika im 20 Jahchundert, In: Festschrift der Osterreichischen Akad der Wissenschaften zum 100, Todestage von Franz Grillparzer, Wien, 72; Grillparzers Vliess-Trilogie als Welttheater, In: Grillparzer-Forum Forchtenstein, 74 & 75; Grillparzers Des Meeres und der Liebe Wellen: Seelendrama und Kulturkritik, In: Jahrbuch der Grillparzer-Gesellschaft, 74; Zum Verhaltnis von Drama und Geschichte im 19 Jahrhundert, In: Jahrbuch fur Int Germanistik, 75 & 76; Der Historische Aspekt in Goethes Iphigenie, In: Versuche zu Goethe, 76; Grillparzers Kloster bei Sendomir und Hauptmanns Elga-Ein Vergleich, In: Grillparzer-Forum Forchtenstein, 76 & 77; Universale und Zeitlose Aspekte in Grillparzers Goldenem Vliess, In: Colloquia Germania, 79; Ideologie und Kulturkritik in Grillparzers Dramen, In: Jahrbuch fur Internationale Germanistick, 80. *Mailing Add:* Dept of Mod & Class Univ of Notre Dame Notre Dame IN 46556

SCHEINDLIN, RAYMOND PAUL, b Philadelphia, Pa, May 13, 40; m 69; c 2. ARABIC & HEBREW LITERATURE. *Educ:* Gratz Col, Cert, 59; Univ Pa, BA, 61; Jewish Theol Sem Am, MHL, 63, Rabbi, 65; Columbia Univ, PhD(Arabic lit), 71. *Prof Exp:* Asst prof Hebrew, McGill Univ, 69-72; asst prof Hebrew & Arabic, Cornell Univ, 72-74; ASSOC PROF MEDIEVAL HEBREW LIT, JEWISH THEOL SEM AM, 74- *Mem:* Asn Jewish Studies; Rabbinical Assembly Am. *Res:* Medieval Arabic and Hebrew poetry; Judeo-Arabic literature and civilization. *Publ:* Transl, Mendele Mocher Seforim, Of bygone days, In: A Stetl and Other Yiddish Novellas, 73; auth, Form in Arabic poetry: Three poems by Al-Mu'tamid Ibn 'Abbad, Humanora Islamica, 73; Form and Structure in the Poetry of Al Mu'Tamid Ibn 'Abbad, De Goeje Fund, 74; Rabbi Moshe Ibn Ezra on the legitimacy of poetry, Medievalia et Humanistica, 76; 201 Arabic Verbs, Barron's Educ Ser, 78. *Mailing Add:* Jewish Theol Sem 3080 Broadway New York NY 10027

SCHELLE, HANSJOERG REINHOLD, b Ravensburg, Ger, Oct 22, 30; US citizen; m 66. GERMANICS, COMPARATIVE LITERATURE. *Educ:* Sorbonne, Paris, dipl, 56; Univ Zurich, Liz phil, 66, Dr phil, 67. *Prof Exp:* Vis lectr, Univ Cincinnati, 66-67; Vis asst prof, 67-68, asst prof, 68-73, assoc prof, 73-80, PROF GERMAN & FAC ASSOC, PROG COMP LIT, UNIV MICH, 80- *Mem:* MLA; Lessing Soc; Am Asn Teachers German. *Res:* German literature since 1500; theatre research, 18th century Southern Germany. *Publ:* Auth, Ernst Jüngers Marmorklippen: Eine kritische interpretation, E J Brill, Leiden, 70; Der junge Johann Friedrich von Meyer im Briefwechsel mit Wieland 1787 bis 1792, Johrbuch der Deutschen Schiller-Gesellschaft, 71; Christoph Martin Wielands Briefwechsel mit Friedrich Wilmans, Johrbuch des Freien Deutschen Hochstifts, 74; Wielands Beziehungen zu seinen Leipziger Verlegern, part 1-3, Lessing Yearbook 7, 75, 8, 76 & 9, 77; ed, Christoph Martin Wieland, Wissenschaftliche Buchgesellschaft, Darmstadt, 81; contribr, Wielands Märchendichtung zwischen Aufklärung und Romantik, In: Fairy Tales as Ways of Knowing, German Studies in Am, 81; auth, Totengespräch, 81 & Verserzählung, 82, Reallexikon der deutschen Literaturgeschichte. *Mailing Add:* 1235 Ravenwood Ann Arbor MI 48103

SCHENCK, DAVID PETER, b Chicago, Ill, Dec 6, 42; m 68; c 1. MEDIEVAL FRENCH LANGUAGE & LITERATURE. *Educ:* Ripon Col, BA, 64; Univ NC, Chapel Hill, MA, 68; Pa State Univ, PhD(French), 71. *Prof Exp:* Asst prof French, St Andrews Presby Col, 71-74; asst prof, 74-76, ASSOC PROF FRENCH, UNIV S FLA, 76- *Mem:* Mediaeval Acad Am; Societe Rencesvals; MLA; SEastern Medieval Asn; Int Courtly Lit Soc. *Res:* Old French epics of the William of Orange Cycle; poetics and narratology in medieval French literature. *Publ:* Auth, The finite world of the Chanson de Guillaume, Olifant, 73; The refrains of the Chanson de Guillaume: A spatial parameter, Romance Notes, 77; Le mythe, la semiotique et le Cycle de Guillaume, In: Charlemagne et l'epopee romane, Univ Liege, 78; Le Coronement Loois: A mythic approach to unity, Romanic Rev, 78; Des vues sur le temps et l'espace chez Chretien de Troyes, In: Oeuvres et Critiques, 81; Les relations spatio-temporelles dans la chanson de geste, In: Congreso de la societe Rencesvals, Vol VIII, Pamplona, 81. *Mailing Add:* Univ of SFla Tampa FL 33620

SCHENCK, MARY JANE STEARNS, Medieval Literature, Composition. See Vol II

SCHENKER, ALEXANDER MARIAN, b Cracow, Poland, Dec 20, 24; nat US. LINGUISTICS. *Educ:* Yale Univ, PhD(ling), 53. *Prof Exp:* From instr to asst prof Russ & Polish, 51-62, assoc prof, 62-67, PROF SLAVIC LING, YALE UNIV, 67- *Concurrent Pos:* Vis prof Slavic ling, Univ Calif, Berkeley, 69-70. *Mem:* Int Ling Asn; Ling Soc Am; MLA; Am Asn Teachers Slavic & East Europ Lang; Am Asn Advan Slavic Studies; Polish Inst Arts & Sci Am. *Res:* Slavic linguistics and philology. *Publ:* Auth, Polish Declension, Mouton, The Hague, 64; Beginning Polish, Vol I, 66 & Vol II, 67; ed, Fifteen Modern Polish Short Stories, Yale Univ, 70; co-ed, The Slavic Literary Languages, Yale Russian & East Europ Publ, 80; auth articles in Language, Word, Slavic & East Europ J, Biuletyn Pol Tow Jezykozn, Studia z filologii polskiej i slowianskiej & Voprosy Jazykoznanija. *Mailing Add:* 145 Deepwood Dr Hamden CT 06517

SCHER, HELENE LENZ, b New York, NY, Dec 26, 35. GERMAN LANGUAGE & LITERATURE. *Educ:* Univ Mich, AB, 56; Yale Univ, MA, 59, PhD(Ger), 67. *Prof Exp:* Actg instr Ger, Yale Univ, 62-63; instr, Southern Conn State Col, 63-64; lectr, City Col New York, 65-67; asst prof, Fairfield Univ, 67-75; ASSOC PROF GER, AMHERST COL, 75. *Concurrent Pos:* Fulbright grant & summer sem, Ger cult studies, 81. *Mem:* MLA; Am Asn Teachers Ger; Northeast Mod Lang Asn; Int Brecht Soc. *Res:* Twentieth century German literature; German Romanticism; literature of the German Democratic Republic. *Publ:* Ed, Friedrich Dürrenmatt, Die Ehe des Herrn Mississippi, Holt, Rinehart & Winston, 73; auth, British Queens in German Drama: Elizabeth and Mary in Plays by Schiller, Bruckner and Hildesheimer, In: Theatrum mundi: Studies in German Drama, Fink, Munich, (in print); auth, Silence in the poetry of Peter Huchel, Germanic Rev, 51: 52-61; Teaching foreign literatures in college: Premises, problems, proposals, Die

Unterrichtspraxis, 9: 55-61; Helga M Novak: Ballade von der reisenden Anna, In: Geschichte im Gedicht Text und Interpretationen, Suhrkamp, Frankfurt/Main, 79; Peter Huchel, In: Columbia Dict of Modern European Literature, Columbia Univ Press, 2nd ed, 80; British Queens in German drama: Elizabeth and Mary in plays by Schiller, Bruckner and Hildesheimer, In: Theatrum Mundi: Essays on German Drama and German Literature, Fink, München, 80; Heinrich Böll, Max Frisch, Rolf Hochhuth & Günter Kunert, In: Encycl of World Literature in the Twentieth Century, Ungar, rev ed (in press). *Mailing Add:* Dept Ger Amherst Col Amherst MA 01002

SCHER, STEVEN PAUL, b Budapest, Hungary, Mar 2, 36; US citizen. GERMAN & COMPARATIVE LITERATURE. *Educ:* Yale Univ, BA, 60, MA, 63, PhD(Ger), 65; Dartmouth Col, MA, 77. *Prof Exp:* Instr Ger, Columbia Univ, 65-67; from asst to assoc prof Yale Univ, 67-74; chmn Ger dept, 74-80, PROF GER, DARTMOUTH COL, 74- *Concurrent Pos:* Morse fel, 69-70; Humboldt fel, 72-73. *Mem:* MLA; Am Comp Lit Asn; Am Asn Teachers Ger. *Res:* Romanticism; 19th and 20th century literature; literature and music. *Publ:* Auth, Verbal Music in German Literature, Yale Univ, 68; Notes toward a theory of verbal music, Comp Lit, 70; Brecht's Die sieben Todsünden der Kleinbürger: Emblematic structure as epic spectacle, Silz-Festschrift, 74; co-ed, Postwar German Culture: An Anthology, Dutton, 74; auth, Der realismusbegriff in der musik, In: Realismustheorien in Literatur, Malerei, Musik u Politik, 75 & Kreativität als Selbstüberwindung: Thomas Mann's permanente Wagner-Krise, In: Rezeption der deutschen Gegenwartsliteratur im Ausland, 76, Kohlhammer, Stuttgart; Hoffmann and Sterne: unmediated parallels in narrative method, Comp Lit, 76; ed, E T A Hoffmann--Interpretationen, Klett, Stuttgart, 81. *Mailing Add:* Dept of Ger Dartmouth Col Hanover NH 03755

SCHERER, WILLIAM F, b Eureka, Ill, Aug 5, 39; m 68. GERMAN LITERATURE. *Educ:* Univ Colo, AB, 61; Univ Southern Calif, MA, 62, PhD(Ger), 67. *Prof Exp:* Asst prof Ger, Univ Calif, Berkeley, 65-68; asst prof, 68-72, curric develop grant, 69-70, chmn Ger div, 75-77, ASSOC PROF GER & EUROP LIT, UNIV HAWAII, MANOA, 72-, GRAD CHMN GER STUDIES, 75- *Concurrent Pos:* Consult, Am Coun Educ, 69; Univ Hawaii Found grant, Wash, 70; guest lectr, Mich State Univ, 72; 15th Congr Australasian Univs Lang & Lit Asn, Univ New South Wales, 73; Am Philos Soc res fel, Stuttgart, Ger, 74-75. *Mem:* Am Asn Teachers Ger; Philol Asn Pac Coast; Rocky Mtn Mod Lang Asn; Pac Northwest Conf Foreign Lang; Australasian Univs Lang & Lit Asn. *Res:* Sixteenth and 17th century German literature; medieval European lyric; history of Western consciousness and European civilization. *Publ:* Auth, Abraham a Sancta Clara's Franenspiegel, Univ Dayton Rev, 71; Exemplary riddles from the baroque sermon, Proc Pac Northwest Conf Foreign Lang, 4/71; Temporal and eternal realities in German baroque homiletics, Mod Lang Quart, 6/71; Der enzyklopädische Impuls und die Tendenz zur Heilpraktik bei Abraham a Sancta Clara, In: Europäische Tradition und deutscher Literaturbarock, Franke, Bern, 73; A living baroque exemplum of dying, Bull Rocky Mtn Mod Lang Asn, 73; Teaching European culture and literature in translation as humanities, Educ Perspectives, 73. *Mailing Add:* Dept Europ Lang & Lit Univ of Hawaii Manoa Honolulu HI 96822

SCHERR, BARRY PAUL, b Hartford, Conn, May 20, 45; m 74; c 1. RUSSIAN LANGUAGE & LITERATURE. *Educ:* Harvard Univ, AB, 66; Univ Chicago, AM, 67, PhD(Slavic lang & lit), 73. *Prof Exp:* Actg asst prof Russ, Univ Wash, 70-73, asst prof, 73-74; asst prof, 74-80, ASSOC PROF RUSSIAN, DARTMOUTH COL, 80-, CHMN, 81- *Mem:* MLA; Am Asn Advan Slavic Studies; Am Asn Teachers Slavic & EEurop Lang. *Res:* Twentieth century Russian prose; Russian versification. *Publ:* Coauth, Russian verse theory since 1960: A commentary and bibliography, Int J Slavic Ling & Poetics, 76; auth, Aleksandr Grin's Scarlet Sails and the fairy tale, Slavic & East Europ J, 76; Notes on literary life in Petrograd, 1918-1922: A tale of three houses, Slavic Rev, 77; co-transl, Alexander Grin, The Seeker of Adventure, Progress Publishers, Moscow, 78; auth, Gor'kij's Childhood: The Autobiography as Fiction, Slavic & East Europ J, 79; Russian and English Versification: Similarities, Differences, Analysis, Style, 80. *Mailing Add:* Dept of Russian Dartmouth Col Hanover NH 03755

SCHEUB, HAROLD, b Gary, Ind, Aug 26, 31. AFRICAN ORAL TRADITIONS & LITERATURE. *Educ:* Univ Mich, Ann Arbor, BA, 58, MA, 60; Univ Wis-Madison, PhD(African lang & lit) & cert African studies, 69. *Prof Exp:* Assoc prof, 70-76, PROF AFRICAN LIT & ORAL TRADITIONS, UNIV WIS-MADISON, 76- *Concurrent Pos:* Instr English, Valparaiso Univ; Nat Endowment for the Humanities fel, Southern Africa, 72-73, Social Sci Res Coun fel, 72-73, Rockefeller Found Humanities fel, 75-76; Fulbright lectr, Nat Univ of Lesotho, 77. *Mem:* MLA; Am Soc Aesthet; Am Comp Lit Asn; Am Folklore Soc. *Res:* Oral traditions of Africa; written literary traditions of Africa; general oral traditions. *Publ:* Auth, Translation of African oral narrative performances to the written work, Yearbk Comp & Gen Lit, 71; Fixed and nonfixed symbols in Xhosa and Zulu oral narrative tradition, J Am Folklore, 7-7/72; ed, A C Jordan, Tales from Southern Africa, introd & commentaries, Berkeley, 73; auth, The Xhosa Ntsomi, Oxford, 75; Oral narrative process and the use of models, 75 & Body and image in oral narrative tradition, 77, New Lit Hist; Performance of oral narrative, In: Frontiers of Folklore, Wash, 77; African Oral Narratives, Proverbs, Riddles, Poetry and Song: An Annotated Bibliography, Boston, 77. *Mailing Add:* Dept of Foreign Lang Univ of Wis Madison WI 53706

SCHEVILL, ISABEL MAGANA (MRS RUDOLPH SCHEVILL), b Mexico City, Mex, Sept 27, 06; US citizen; wid. SPANISH LITERATURE. *Educ:* Univ Calif, Berkeley, BA ,28, MA, 30; Stanford Univ, PhD, 52. *Prof Exp:* From asst to asst prof Span, Mills Col, 30-48; from lectr & instr to asst prof educ & Span, 48-56, asst prof Span lang & lit, 56-61, from assoc prof to prof Span lit, 61-72, univ rep, Int Conf Univ Prof English, Paris, France, 53, dir, Span Theatre, 52-67, actg chmn dept Span & Port, 71-72, EMER PROF SPAN & PORT, STANFORD UNIV, 72-; PROF PASTORAL SPAN, ST PATRICK'S SEM, 76- *Concurrent Pos:* From asst to instr, Univ Calif, Berkeley, 32-38; instr, Sarah Dix Hamlin, San Francisco, 39-43; life mem staff & contribr, Hispania, 50- *Mem:* MLA. *Res:* Modern and contemporary peninsular Spanish literature; modern language methodology; music. *Publ:* Auth, A day in Gerona with Gironella, Hispania, 5/59; Lo tragico en el teatro de Buero Vallejo, Hispanofila, 9/59; Juego de ninos, Prentice-Hall, 64; ed, Dos dramas de Buero Vallejo, 67 & coauth, Alfonso Sastre's La mordaza, 72, Appleton. *Mailing Add:* 801 San Francisco Ct Stanford CA 94305

SCHIAVO, LEDA BRIGIDA, b Buenos Aires, Arg, Dec 26, 35. CONTEMPORARY SPANISH & LATIN-AMERICAN LITERATURE. *Educ:* Univ Buenos Aires, Licenciado, 66; Univ Madrid, PhD(romance lang), 77. *Prof Exp:* Vis prof Span lit, Univ Catolica de Mar del Plata, 66-73; ASSOC PROF SPAN LIT, UNIV ILL, CHICAGO CIRCLE, 76- *Concurrent Pos:* Res asst prof Span lit, Inst de Filologia, Univ Buenos Aires, 69-73. *Mem:* Asn Int Hisp; MLA; Am Asn Teachers Span & Port. *Res:* Life and works of Valle Inclan; Spanish and Latin-American literature and history; 19th century. *Publ:* Ed, La Mujer Espanola y otros Articulos Feministas de Emilia Pardo Bazan, Editora Nacional, Madrid, 76; coauth, La Prosa Argentina del Siglo XIX, La Muralla, Madrid, 78; auth, Historia y Novela en Valle-Inclan-Para leer, Elrueds Serico, Madrid, Castalia, 80. *Mailing Add:* Dept of Span Univ of Ill at Chicago Circle Box 6368 Chicago IL 60680

SCHICK, EDGAR BREHOB, b Philadelphia, Pa, June 28, 34; m 59; c 2. GERMAN, PEDAGOGY. *Educ:* Muhlenberg Col, AB, 55; Rutgers Univ, MA, 62, PhD(Ger lit), 65. *Prof Exp:* Asst instr Ger, Rutgers Univ, 59-62; from instr to asst prof Ger, State Univ NY, Binghamton, 63-68; asst prof Ger & asst to pres, State Univ NY, Albany, 69-72; assoc prof Ger, vpres acad affairs & dean, St John Fisher Col, 72-80; PRES, NASSON COL & UNIV NEW ENGLAND FEDN, 80- *Concurrent Pos:* Consult, IBM Corp, 67, Univ Assocs, 70-72 & Fed Repub Ger Govt, 71-73. *Mem:* Am Asn Teachers Ger; MLA; Am Coun Teaching Foreign Lang; Am Asn Higher Educ; Am Asn Univ Adminr. *Res:* J G Herder and 18th century thought; modern German drama; higher education administration and issues. *Publ:* Auth, Metaphorical organisicm in the early Herder, Monton, 71; Campus fervent and tranquility, Sch & Soc, 2/72; Allen Collegiate Center: An option for liberal education, Intellect, 11/72; Youth, 1972, In: Grolier Encycl Yearbk. *Mailing Add:* Off of the Pres Nasson Col Springvale ME 04083

SCHIER, DONALD STEPHEN, b Ft Madison, Iowa, Sept 10, 14. ROMANCE LANGUAGES. *Educ:* State Univ Iowa, AB, 36; Columbia Univ, AM, 37, PhD, 41. *Prof Exp:* Instr, Minn State Teachers Col, Bemidji, 39-41 & Ill Inst Technol, 41-42 & 46; from asst prof to assoc prof, 46-53, prof, 53-80, EMER PROF ROMANCE LANG, CARLETON COL, 80- *Concurrent Pos:* Vis prof, Univ Wis, 64-65; mem selection comt younger scholar fel awards, Nat Found Art & Humanities, 66 & 67; Brown tutor French, Univ of the South, Sewanee, 80-81. *Mem:* MLA; Am Asn Teachers Fr; Midwest Mod Lang Asn; Am Soc 18th Century Studies. *Res:* French literature of the 18th and 20th centuries; Louis-Bertrand Castel. *Publ:* Co-ed, The Continental Model: Selected French Critical Essays of the Seventeenth Century in English Translation, Carleton Col & Univ Minn, 60 & rev ed, Cornell Univ, 70; ed, Nouveaux dialogues des morts, Univ NC, 65; transl & auth notes, Ch de Brosses, Letter on Italian Music, privately publ, 78. *Mailing Add:* 717 E 2nd St Northfield MN 55057

SCHIER, RUDOLF DIRK, b Amsterdam, Neth, Mar 4, 37; m 62; c 3. COMPARATIVE LITERATURE. *Educ:* Amherst Col, BA, 59; Cornell Univ, MA, 60, PhD(comp lit), 65. *Prof Exp:* From instr to asst prof Ger, Univ Ill, Urbana, 63-67, assoc prof, 67-79, dir, Austria-Ill Exchange Prog, 71-79; DIR, INST EUROP STUDIES, VIENNA, 80- *Concurrent Pos:* Prof English, Paed Acad, Austria. *Honors & Awards:* Exchange Prog Award, Ministry Educ & Art, Austria, 77; Develop Award, Nat Asn Foreign Student Affairs, 78. *Res:* Nineteenth and 20th century literature; Georg Trakl. *Publ:* Auth, Die Sprache Georg Trakls, Carl Winter, 70; Trakl und Buechner, PMLA, 10/72; The experience of the noumenal in Wordsworth and Goethe, Comp Lit, 2/73; Robert Musils Tonka als Vorlauefer des Noveau Roman, Etudes Ger, 1/77; Das Lenaubild Amerikas, das Amerikabild Lenaus, Lenau Forum, 82. *Mailing Add:* Inst of Europ Studies Johannesgasse 7 Vienna A-1010 Austria

SCHIFF, TIMOTHY HERBERT, b Los Angeles, Calif, Dec 24, 43; m 69; c 2. COMPARATIVE & SCANDINAVIAN LITERATURE. *Educ:* Univ Calif, Los Agneles, BA, 67; Univ Wis-Madison, MA, 69; Univ Calif, Berkeley, PhD(comp lit), 77. *Prof Exp:* asst prof, 75-81, ASSOC PROF GER LANG & LIT, UNIV CHICAGO, 81- *Concurrent Pos:* Nat Defense Foreign Lang fel, 68-69, 70-71 & 71-72. *Mem:* Soc Advan Scand Study; MLA; Am Scand Found; Norwegian-Am Hist Asn; Am Comp Lit Asn. *Res:* Henrik Ibsen; nineteenth century Scandinavian literature; modernism. *Publ:* Transl, Tarjei Vesaas, In the Fish's Golden Youth, Scand Rev, 68; Öystein Lönn, Accident, Lit Rev, 68-69; auth, Tryggve Andersen's novel Mot kvaeld and its motto, 76, Moral equivocality in the works of Tryggve Andersen, 78, Providence and dispensation in Henrik Ibsen's Peer Gynt, 79 & Social Value and the etiology of forkommenhet: Towards an understanding of Tryggve Andersen's concept of human nature, 81, Scand Studies; transl, Jens Bojörneboe's The bird Lovers (play), 82-83. *Mailing Add:* Dept of Ger Lang & Lit Univ of Chicago 1050 E 59th St Chicago IL 60637

SCHIFFER, EVA, b Vienna, Austria, Feb 7, 25; US citizen. GERMAN & COMPARATIVE LITERATURE. *Educ:* Univ Mass, BZS, 46; Radcliffe Col, MA, 47, PhD, 62. *Prof Exp:* Instr English, Ohio State Univ, 47-50; from instr to asst prof Ger, Univ Mass, 55-67; assoc prof Ger & comp lit, Univ Colo, 67-68; assoc prof, 68-78, PROF GER, UNIV MASS, AMHERST, 78- *Concurrent Pos:* Fel, Alex von Humboldt-Stifting (Bonn), 45-55 & 74-75; res grants, Univ Mass, Amherst, 62, 66, & 67; res, Thomas Mann Arch, Zurich, 64-65 & 74-75. *Mem:* MLA; Am Asn Teachers Ger; Am Comp Lit Asn; Int Comp Lit Asn; Int Asn Germanists. *Res:* Thomas Mann; narrative technique in the novel. *Publ:* Coauth, Island and star: Interpretation of Rilke's Insel: Nordsee, Ger Rev, 52; auth, Manolescu's Memoirs: The beginnings of Felix Krull?, 60 & Illusion und Wirklichkeit in T Mann's Felix Krull und Joseph, 63, Monatshefte; Irritierende Repräsentanz: Noch eine Bestandsaufnahme zu Thomas Manns 100, Geburtstag, In: Rezeption der deutschen

Gegenwartsliteratur im Ausland, Int Forschungen zur neueren deutschen Lit, 76; Politisches Engagement oder Resignation? Weiteres zu Uwe Johnsons Jahrestagen, In: Der duetsche Roman und seine historischen und politischen Bedingungen, 77; ed, Thomas Mann--Karl Loewenstein, Briefwechsel, Part 1, Blätter der Thomas--Mann--Gesellschaft Zürich, No 18, 81. *Mailing Add:* Dept Ger Lang & Lit Univ of Mass Amherst MA 01002

SCHIFFMAN, LAWRENCE H, Hebrew & Judaic Studies. See Vol IV

SCHIKORA, ROSEMARY GARBARINO, b Detroit, Mich, Dec 12, 47. AFRICAN LITERATURE IN FRENCH. *Educ:* Marygrove Col, BA, 70; Wayne State Univ, MA, 74, PhD(mod lang), 79. *Prof Exp:* Lectr, Wayne State Univ, 80-81, INSTR FRENCH, OAKLAND COMMUNITY COL, WAYNE STATE UNIV, 81- *Concurrent Pos:* Lectr African & Latin Am studies, Marygrove Col, 80-81. *Mem:* MLA; African Lit Asn; Am Asn Teachers French; Am Coun Teaching Foreign Lang. *Res:* African fiction in French; narrative techniques. *Publ:* Auth, Outfoxing the fox: Game strategy in Ouologuem's Le Devoir de violence, Perspectives on Contemporary Lit, Vol 6, 80; Narrative voice in Kourouma's Les Soleils des independances, French Rev, 5/82. *Mailing Add:* 16151 Stahelin Detroit MI 48219

SCHILLER, ANDREW, b Czech, Feb 1, 19; nat US; m 44; c 2. LINGUISTICS. *Educ:* City Col New York, BSS, 42; State Univ Iowa, MA, 47, PhD(English), 52. *Prof Exp:* Instr English, Univ Rochester, 47-48, Ohio State Univ, 48-49 & Wayne State Univ, 52-55; assoc prof English, 55-64, PROF ENGLISH & LING, UNIV ILL, CHICAGO CIRCLE, 64-, CHMN DEPT LING, 73- *Honors & Awards:* Standard Oil Found Award, 66. *Mem:* MLA; Ling Soc Am; Am Asn Appl Ling. *Res:* Morphology; applied linguistics; metrics. *Publ:* Auth, The Coming Revolution in Teaching English, Harper, 10/64; coauth, The Open Highways Series, Scott, 67; auth, The Gawain Rhythm, Lang & Style, 68; Grammar in the Grammar Schools? In: The Language Arts in the Elementary School, NCTE, 73; coauth, Language and How To Use It, Scott, 73; In Other Words, Scott, Foresman, Vols I & II, 3rd ed, 82. *Mailing Add:* Dept Ling Univ Ill Chicago IL 60680

SCHILLINGER, JOHN ARTHUR, b Aledo, Ill, Jan 13, 42; m 65; c 3. RUSSIAN LITERATURE. *Educ:* Monmouth Col, BA, 63; Univ Ill, Urbana-Champaign, MA, 66; Univ Wis-Madison, MA, 69; PhD(Russ lit), 73. *Prof Exp:* Instr Russ lang & lit, Saginaw Valley Col, 70-73; asst prof Russ lang & lit & asst head, Dept Mod Lang, Purdue Univ, West Lafayette, 73-79; assoc prof, 79-82, PROF RUSS LANG & LIT & HEAD, DEPT LANG, OKLA STATE UNIV, STILLWATER, 82- *Mem:* MLA; Am Asn Teachers Slavic & EEurop Lang (vpres, 82-). *Res:* Soviet literature; 19th century novel and criticism. *Publ:* Auth, Gogol's The Overcoat as a travesty of hagiography, Slavic & East Europ J, spring 72; A survey of materials used in undergraduate Russian instruction in the United States and Canada, Russ Lang J, winter 76; An analysis of college-level Russian textbooks, Mod Lang J, 11/76; ed, Solzhenitsyn, Mod Fiction Studies, 77; auth, The function of love in Solzhenitsyn's The First Circle, Studies 20th Century Lit, 1/78; Irony and the influence of the Potemkin facade in V Kruge Pervom, Russ Lang J, fall 78; Informing and informers during the Stalin era: From One Day in the Life of Ivan Denisovich to The First Circle, Topic, fall 79. *Mailing Add:* Dept of Foreign Lang Okla State Univ Stillwater OK 74074

SCHIMMELPFENNIG, PAUL ROBERT, b Dec 1, 40; US citizen; m 66. GERMAN LITERATURE, LITERARY CRITICISM. *Educ:* Univ Vt, BA, 62; Princeton, Univ, MA, 64, PhD(Ger), 68. *Prof Exp:* Asst prof Ger, Univ Calif, Irvine, 66-72; RES & WRITING, 72- *Mem:* MLA; Am Asn Teachers Ger. *Res:* Literary sociology; modern German literature; literature and psychology. *Publ:* Co-ed, Wahrheit und Sprache, Kummerle, 72; auth, Unwillkurliche Moralitat: zur Geschichte der literatur als Spiel, Goppingen Arbeiten zur Germanistik, 72; CF Meyers, religion of the heart, Ger Rev, 72; CF Meyers, Rhetoric of Fiction, Lothar Stiehm, 74. *Mailing Add:* 758 Manzanita Laguna Beach CA 92651

SCHINDLER, MARVIN SAMUEL, b Boston, Mass, Jan 2, 32; m 54; c 3. GERMAN, BAROQUE LITERATURE. *Educ:* Univ Mass, BA, 53; Ohio State Univ, MA, 55, PhD(Ger), 65. *Prof Exp:* Instr Ger, Pa State Univ, 55-59; from instr to asst prof, Ohio State Univ, 62-67; from asst prof to assoc prof, Univ Va, 67-71, from asst dean to assoc dean grad sch arts & sci, 69-71; prof Ger & chmn dept foreign lang & lit, Northern Ill Univ, 71-74; PROF GER & CHMN DEPT ROMANCE & GER LANG & LIT, WAYNE STATE UNIV, 74-, PROG DIR, JR YEAR IN FREIBURG/MUNICH PROG, 75- *Concurrent Pos:* Assoc ed, Ger Quart, 70-78; Am Coun Learned Soc grant, 81; Ger Acad Exchange Serv grant, 81. *Mem:* MLA; Am Asn Teachers Ger; Asn Dept Foreign Lang (pres, 81); Midwest Mod Lang Asn. *Res:* German baroque and comparative literature; lyric poetry. *Publ:* Auth, Interpretations of Es ist alles eitel: The changing face of Gryphius criticism, Mod Lang Quart, 6/67; Gryphius' religious poetry: The Biblical word as the poetic word Ger Rev, 70; The Sonnets of Andreas Gryphius, Univ Fla, 71; Structure and allegory in Der wilde Alexander's Hie vor do wir dinder waren, Ger Quart, 1/73 Petrarch's Sonnet no 132 to Laura and the German Petrarchists: Mastery of form or formal mastery?, Semasia, 75; Faust and his time: The Reformation, the Renaissance and humanism in Germany, In: Lives of Dr Faust, Univ Studies & Weekend Col, Wayne State Univ, 76; Historia von Dr Faustus, In: Italian Renaissance and Northern Humanism: A Guide to the Cultural and Literary Crosscurrents, Intermediaries, and Masterpieces of the Age, Ungar, 77; A Note on Paul Fleming's Grahschrife, Wege der Worte, 78. *Mailing Add:* Dept of Foreign Lang Wayne State Univ Detroit MI 48202

SCHLAM, CARL C, b New York, NY, Oct 23, 36; m 67. CLASSICS. *Educ:* Columbia Univ, BA, 56, MA, 58, PhD(Greek & Latin), 68. *Prof Exp:* Instr classics, Rutgers Univ, 64-66; preceptor Greek & Latin, Columbia Col, 66-67; asst prof, 67-73, ASSOC PROF CLASSICS, OHIO STATE UNIV, 73- *Mem:* Am Philol Asn. *Res:* Ancient literature; neo-Latin; paleography. *Publ:* Auth, The curiosity of the golden ass, Class J, 12/68; Platonica in the Metamorphoses of Apuleius, TAPA, 70; Scholarship on Apuleius since 1938, Class World, 5/71; Cupid and Psyche: Apuleius and the Monuments, Am

Philol Asn, 76; Graduation speeches of Gentile da Foligno, Medieval studies, 78; Sex and Sanctity, In: Aspects of Apuleius' Golden Ass, Groningen, 78; coauth (with John B Gabel), Thomas Chaloner's in Laudem Henrici Octavi, Coronado Press, 79. *Mailing Add:* Dept of Classics Ohio State Univ Columbus OH 43210

SCHLANT, ERNESTINE, b Passau, Ger, Aug 14, 35; US citizen; m; c 2. GERMAN, COMPARATIVE LITERATURE. *Educ:* Emory Univ, PhD(compt lit), 65. *Prof Exp:* Instr French, Spelman Col, 63-65; asst prof Ger, State Univ NY Stony Brook, 65-69; asst producer films, Cinema Arts Inc, 69-71; assoc prof, 71-80, PROF GER, MONTCLAIR STATE COL, 81- *Mem:* AAUP; MLA. *Publ:* Coauth, various Ger textbks for Holt, 69, 71 & 73; auth, Die Philosophie Hermann Brochs, Francke, Bern, 71; Hermann Broch, Twayne, 78. *Mailing Add:* Dept of Ger Montclair State Col Upper Montclair NJ 07043

SCHLATTER, FREDRIC WILLIAM, b Tacoma, Wash, June 16, 26. CLASSICAL LANGUAGES, HISTORY. *Educ:* Gonzaga Univ, AB, 49, MA, 50; Alma Col, Calif, STL, 57; Princeton Univ, PhD(classics), 60. *Prof Exp:* Instr classics, Gonzaga Prep, 50-52; instr, St Francis Xavier Div, 52-53, from asst prof to assoc prof, 61-74, dean, 62-65, PROF CLASSICS, GONZAGA UNIV, 74-, CHMN DEPT CLASS LANG, 68-, PROF HIST, 76- *Mem:* Am Philol Asn; Archaeol Inst Am; Asn Ancient Historians. *Res:* Justin's Epitome of Pompeius Trogus. *Publ:* Auth, The problem of John 1:3b-4a, Cath Bibl Quart, 1/72; Isocrates, against the Sophists, Am J Philol, Vol 16, 10/72. *Mailing Add:* Dept of Class Lang Gonzaga Univ Spokane WA 99258

SCHLEPP, WAYNE ALLEN, b Mobridge, SDak, July 8, 31; m 55; c 1. CHINESE LANGUAGE & LITERATURE. *Educ:* Northern State Teachers Col, BSc, 54; Univ London, BA, 61, PhD(Chinese lit), 64. *Prof Exp:* From asst prof to assoc prof Chinese, Univ Wis-Madison, 64-73, chmn dept EAsian lang & lit, 68-73, grad sch res grant, 65 & 68; PROF CHINESE, UNIV TORONTO, 73- *Concurrent Pos:* Nat Endowment for Humanities grant, 67-68; Am Coun Learned Soc study fel, 67-68; comt mem, Am Coun Learned Soc, 70-73; bk rev ed, Can-Mongolia Rev, 78-79. *Mem:* Am Orient Soc; Mongolia Soc; Conf Chinese Oral & Performing Lit. *Res:* Chinese poetics; Mongolian language and grammar. *Publ:* Auth, Translating Chinese, P Ward, Middlesex & North Harrow, 64; Metrics in Yüan San-ch'ü, Wen-lin, Studies Chinese Humanities, spring 68; Technique and Imagery of Yüan San-ch'ü, Univ Wis, 69; Yeh-lü Ch'u-ts'ai in Samarkand, Can-Mongolia Rev, 75; Tentative remarks on Chinese metrics, J Chinese Ling, 80. *Mailing Add:* Dept of EAsian Studies Univ of Toronto Toronto ON M5S 1A1 Can

SCHLUETTER, HANS J, b Hanover, Ger, Feb 25, 30; Can citizen. GERMAN LANGUAGE & LITERATURE. *Educ:* Univ Kiel, Dr phil, 61. *Prof Exp:* Lang asst Ger lang & lit, Queen Mary Col, Univ London, 62-63; asst prof, Univ Ill, 65-69; assoc prof, 69-78, PROF GER LANG & LIT, UNIV WESTERN ONT, 78- *Mem:* Can Asn Univ Teachers Ger; Int Asn Ger Studies; Goethe Soc NAm; Northeast Mod Lang Asn. *Res:* Modern German literature; metrics; the sonnet. *Publ:* Auth, Der rhythmus im strengen Knittelvers des 16. Jahruhunderts, Euphorion, 66; Goethes Sonette, Gehlen, 69; ed, Lyrik - 25 Jahre Bibliographie der deutschsparchigen Lyrikpublikationen 1945-1970, Olms, Vol I, 74 & Vol II (in prep); auth, Das engagierte Sonett der Sechziger Jahre, Jahrbuch Int Ger, 76; . . . als ob die Wahrheit Münze wäre, In: Nathan der Weise, Lessing Yearbook, Vol III, No 6; coauth, Sonett, Metzler, 79; auth, Fünf Thesen zu Prinz Friedrich von Homburg, Heinrich von Kleist-Studies, 80; Formdispens im sonett der gegenwart, Jahrbuch Int Ger. *Mailing Add:* Dept of Ger Univ Col Univ of Western Ont London ON N6A 3K7 Can

SCHLUNK, JUERGEN ECKART, b Marburg, Ger, May 26, 44. GERMAN LANGUAGE & LITERATURE. *Educ:* Univ NH, MA, 68; Philipps-Univ Marburg, PhD(Am drama), 70. *Prof Exp:* Dir & resident adv Ger, Jr Year Abroad Prog, Davidson Col, 72-73; asst prof, Franklin & Marshall Col, 73-74; asst prof, 74-80, ASSOC PROF GER, WVA UNIV, 80- *Concurrent Pos:* Dramatist, Theater tri-buehne, Stuttgart, Ger, 76-77 & 80-81. *Mem:* Am Asn Teachers Ger; MLA. *Res:* Theater; film. *Publ:* Auth, Foreign language exposure beyond the classroom: How to import theater, Die Unterrichtspraxis, 78; The image of America in German literature and in the new German cinema: Wim Wenders' The American Friend, Lit/Film Quart, Vol 7, No 3. *Mailing Add:* Dept of Foreign Lang WVa Univ Morgantown WV 26506

SCHMALSTIEG, WILLIAM RIEGEL, b Sayre, Pa, Oct 3, 29; m 52; c 2. SLAVIC LINGUISTICS. *Educ:* Univ Minn, BA, 50; Univ Pa, MA, 51, PhD(Balto-Slavic ling), 56. *Prof Exp:* Asst prof Russ, Univ Ky, 56-59; asst prof Russ & French, Lafayette Col, 59-63; assoc prof Slavic ling, Univ Minn, 63-64; assoc prof, 64-67, PROF SLAVIC LANG, PA STATE UNIV, UNIVERSITY PARK, 67-, HEAD DEPT, 69- *Concurrent Pos:* Ed, Gen Ling, 71-; consult, ling div, MLA Bibliog, 72-73; Nat Endowment for Humanities fel, 78. *Mem:* Am Asn Teachers Slavic & EEurop Lang; Ling Soc Am. *Res:* Historical linguistics; comparative Balto-Slavic linguistics. *Publ:* Coauth, Introduction to Modern Lithuanian, 66 & Lithuanian Reader for Self-Instruction, 67, Franciscan Fathers Press; Janis Endzelins' Comparative Phonology and Morphology of the Baltic Languages, Mouton, The Hague, 71; auth, Die Entwicklung der a-Deklination im Slavischen, Z Slavische Philol, 72; An Old Prussian Grammar, 74 & Studies in Old Prussian, 76, Pa State Univ; An Introduction to Old Church Slavic, Slavica, 76. *Mailing Add:* Dept of Slavic Lang Pa State Univ University Park PA 16802

SCHMANDT-BESSERAT, DENISE, Archeology, Art. See Vol I

SCHMELING, GARETH LON, b Algoma, Wis, May 28, 40; m 63. GREEK & LATIN LITERATURE. *Educ:* Northwestern Col, Wis, BA, 63; Univ Wis, MA, 64, PhD(Greek & Latin), 68. *Prof Exp:* Asst prof Greek & Latin, Univ Va, 68-70; assoc prof, 70-75, PROF & CHMN DEPT CLASSICS, UNIV FLA, 75-, DIR, HUMANITIES CTR, 78- *Concurrent Pos:* Am Philos Soc fel, 70-78; Univ Fla fel, 71-74; Nat Endowment for Humanities fel, 73-74; Am Coun Learned Soc grant-in-aid, 74; Rome prize, Am Acad, Rome, 77-78. *Mem:* Am Philos Asn; Am Class League; Class Asn Mid W & S; Vergilian Soc; Soc Studies Classics, France. *Res:* Ancient prose fiction; Petronius; Apuleius, Chariton, Xenophon. *Publ:* Contribr, Exclusus Amator Motif in Petronius, Baccola & Gili, Turin, 71; ed, Cornelius Nepos: Lives of Famous Mem, Coronado, 71; auth, Chariton, Twayne, 74; coauth, TS Eliot and Petronius, Comp Lit Ser, 75; coauth, Bibliography of Petronius, Brill, Leiden, 77; auth, The satyricon: Forms in search of a genre, Class Bull, 71; Humanities perspectives on the professions, Lib Educ, 77; Xenophon of Ephesus, Twayne, 80; Authority of the Author: From Muse to Aesthetics, MCSN, 81. *Mailing Add:* Dept of Classics Univ of Fla Gainesville FL 32611

SCHMIDT, GERARD F, b Bad Ems, Ger, Jan 20, 19; US citizen; m 62. GERMAN, MEDIEVAL LITERATURE. *Educ:* Sorbonne & Univ Algiers, Certs, 38-41; Harvard Univ, MA, 49, PhD, 53. *Prof Exp:* Instr Ger, Bryn Mawr Col, 52-54; asst prof, Harvard Univ, 54-59; from asst prof to assoc prof, Univ Ill, 59-63; assoc prof, 63-66, chmn dept, 65-68 & 73-77, PROF GER, STATE UNIV NY BINGHAMTON, 66- *Mem:* Am Asn Teachers Ger; MLA; Mediaeval Acad Am. *Res:* Late medieval German prose writings. *Publ:* Auth, Das Schachzabelbuch des Jacobus de Cessolis, OP, in mittelhochdeutscher Prosa-Übersetzung: nach den Handschriften herausgegeben, Erich Schmidt, Berlin, 61; Hör gut zu!, Macmillan, 64; co-ed, Der Hofmeister und die Gouvernante, De Gruyter, Berlin, 69; Spass und Spannung, Macmillan, 79. *Mailing Add:* Dept of Ger Libr Tower State Univ of NY Binghamton NY 13901

SCHMIDT, HANNS-PETER, b Berlin, Ger, July 30, 30. INDO-IRANIAN STUDIES. *Educ:* Univ Hamburg, PhD(Indo-Iranian studies), 57. *Prof Exp:* Asst prof Indo-Iranian studies, Univ Saugar, 59-61; asst Indology, Univ Tübingen, 61-64, dozent, 65-67; from asst prof to assoc prof, 67-70, PROF INDO-IRANIAN STUDIES, UNIV CALIF, LOS ANGELES, 70- *Concurrent Pos:* Res fel, Deccan Col Post-Grad & Res Inst, Poona, India, 57-59 & Ger Res Asn, 61; prof Sanskrit, Rijksuniversiteit te Leiden, Netherlands, 74-76. *Mem:* Am Orient Soc; Ger Orient Soc. *Res:* Sanskrit; Avesta; Middle Persian. *Publ:* Auth, Vedisch vrata und awestisch urvata, Cram de Gruyter, Hamburg, 58; The origin of ahimsa, Melanges Indianisme Mem Louis Renou, 68; Brhaspati und Indra, Harrassowitz, Wiesbaden, 68; Zarathustra's Religion and His Pastoral Imagery, Univ Pers, Leiden, 75; co-ed & contribr, Some Aspects of Indo-Iranian Literary and Cultural Traditions, Ajanta, Delhi, 77; auth, Indo-Iranian Mitra studies: The state of the central problem, Acta Iranica, 78; Ancient Iranian animal classification, Studien zur Indologie und Iranistik, 5-6/80; The senmurw--Of birds and dogs and bats, Persica, 9/80. *Mailing Add:* Dept of Near Eastern Lang & Cult Univ of Calif Los Angeles CA 90024

SCHMIDT, HENRY JACQUES, b Boston, Mass, Jan 1, 43; m 77. GERMAN LITERATURE. *Educ:* Queens Col, NY, BA, 63; Middlebury Col, MA, 64; Stanford Univ, PhD(Ger), 68. *Prof Exp:* Instr Ger, Stanford Overseas Campus, Beutelsbach, Ger, 66; asst prof, Univ Wis-Madison, 67-69; assoc prof, 69-79, PROF GER, OHIO STATE UNIV, 79- *Concurrent Pos:* Ed, Communications, Int Brecht Soc newslett; vis prof, Univ Cincinnati, 70; contrib ed, New German Critique, 79-; exec comt, MLA Div 19th & Early 20th Century Ger Lit, 78-83. *Mem:* MLA; Am Asn Teachers Ger; Lessing Soc; Georg Büchner Soc; Int Brecht Soc. *Res:* Georg Büchner; German drama; 18th century German literature. *Publ:* Auth, Georg Büchner, Woyzeck, Avon, 69; Satire, Caricature and Perspectivism in the Works of Georg Büchner, Mouton, The Hague, 70; co-ed, Brecht Fibel, Harper, 70; auth, Georg Büchner: Danton's Death, Avon, 71; co-ed, German Literature: Texts and Contexts, McGraw, 73; auth, Georg Büchner: The Complete Collected Works, Avon, 77; The Language of Confinement: Gerstenberg's Ugolino and Klinger's Sturm and Drang, Lessing Yearbk XI, 79; Brecht's Turandot: Tuis and Cultural Politics, Theatre J, 10/80. *Mailing Add:* Dept of Ger Ohio State Univ Columbus OH 43210

SCHMIDT, HUGO, b Vienna, Austria, Jan 24, 29; nat US; m 52; c 2. GERMAN LANGUAGES. *Educ:* Columbia Univ, AM, 54, PhD, 59. *Prof Exp:* Instr Ger, Columbia Col, Columbia Univ, 54-59; from asst prof to assoc prof, Bryn Mawr Col, 59-67; chmn dept, 68-72, PROF GER, UNIV COLO, 67- *Concurrent Pos:* Chief examr, Ger listening comprehension test, Col Entrance Exam Bd, 64-70 & Grad Rec Exam Bd, 69-76; rev ed, Mod Lang J, 71-79; Nat Endowment for Humanities sem dir, summer, 78. *Mem:* Am Asn Teachers Ger (vpres, 79-81); MLA. *Res:* German Romanticism; Austrain literature; Bertolt Brecht. *Publ:* Auth, Religious issues and images in Lenau's works, Ger Rev, 64; Eishoehle und Steinhaeuschen: Zur Weihnachtssymbolik in Stifters Bergkristall, Monatshefte, 64; coauth, Brecht: Manual of Piety, Grove, 66; auth, Nikolaus Lenau, Twayne, 71; Realms of action in Crillparzer's Bruderzwist, In: Walter Silz Festschrift, NC Univ, 74; Zum Symbolgehalt der Reitergeschichte Hofmannsthals, In: Klarmann Festschrift, Munich, 74. *Mailing Add:* Dept of Ger Univ of Colo Boulder CO 80302

SCHMIDT, JOSEF H K, b Zurich, Switz, Feb 26, 40; Can & Swiss citizen; m 67; c 1. GERMAN & COMPARATIVE LITERATURE. *Educ:* Univ Zurich, DPhil(Ger, Greek & English), 66. *Prof Exp:* Fel, Ctr Cult & Technol, Univ Toronto, 67-68; asst prof Ger, Queen's Univ, Ont, 68-70; asst prof, 70-73, ASSOC PROF GER, McGILL UNIV, 73- *Concurrent Pos:* Lectr, Univ Montreal, 73-74; vis prof, Hebrew Univ, Jerusalem, 78-79. *Mem:* Can Asn Univ Teachers Ger; Am Comp Lit Asn. *Res:* Reanissance; modern literature; paraliterature. *Publ:* Auth, Aegyptian Joseph in Baroque Literature, Keller, Zurich, 67; ed, Two Reformation Plays, 68, auth, Documents on Schiller's Tell, 70, Documents on Goethe's Hermann and Dorothea, 71, Documents on Keller's Faehnlein, 73 & Anthology: Renaissance/Reformation, 76, Reclam, Stuttgart; Reformation Satire, Lang, Bern & Las Vegas, 77; co-ed (with A Arnold), Reclams Kriminalromanführer, 78; Mosche Y Ben-gavriel, Bouvier, Bonn, 79. *Mailing Add:* Dept of Ger McGill Univ PO Box 6070 Montreal PQ H3C 1G5 Can

SCHMIDT, MAX L, b Maron, Papua, New Guinea, Sept 1, 07; nat US; m 39; c 2. GERMAN LANGUAGE & LITERATURE. *Educ:* St Francis Sem, AB, 32; Univ Bonn, PhD (Ger), 37. *Prof Exp:* Prof Ger, Col St Thomas, 39-47; assoc prof mod lang, Iowa State Univ, 47-51; prof, 51-78, chmn dept foreign lang, 73-78, EMER PROF GER, COL ST THOMAS, 78- *Mem:* MLA; Am Asn Teachers Ger. *Publ:* Auth, Amerikanismen bei Charles Sealsfield, Konrad Triltsch, Wützburg; coauth, Introduction to German, Holt. *Mailing Add:* 2216 Bayard Ave St Paul MN 55116

SCHMIDT, MICHAEL FRED, Philosophy. See Vol IV

SCHMIDT, PAUL FRANCIS, b Brooklyn, NY, Jan 29, 34; div. RUSSIAN LITERATURE, DRAMA. *Educ:* Colgate Univ, BA, 55; Harvard Univ, MA, 58, PhD(Russ), 74. *Prof Exp:* Assoc prof Russ, Univ Tex, Austin, 67-78; Davis prof Russ, Wellesley Col, 78-79; DIR, ART FOUND, NEW YORK, 80- *Mem:* PEN Club; Soc Cinema Studies; Univ Film Asn; Am Asn Advan Slavic Studies. *Res:* Film theory; Soviet film history; Nabokov. *Publ:* Translr, Bonnefoy, Yves, In: Rimbaud, Harper & Row, 73; auth, A chronicle of death in Russia, New York Rev Bks, 5/73; Arthur Rimbaud: Complete Works in Translation, Harper & Row, 75; First speculations: Russian formalist film criticism, Tex Studies Lang & Lit, 75; Constructivism and film, Soviet Union, 76; Meyerhold and Mayakovsky: A director works with a playwright, Educ Theater J, 5/77; coauth, The Sea Gull: A New Translation with Introduction and Textual Notes, Harper & Row, 77; Meyerhold at Work, Univ Tex Press, 80. *Mailing Add:* Slavic Dept Univ of Tex Austin TX 78712

SCHMIDT, RUTH ANN, b Mt Lake, Minn, Sept 16, 30. SPANISH LANGUAGE & LITERATURE. *Educ:* Augsburg Col, BA, 52; Univ Mo, MA, 55; Univ Ill, PhD(Span), 62. *Prof Exp:* Teacher English & Span, high sch, Detroit Lakes, Minn, 52-54; asst prof Span, Mary Baldwin Col, 55-58; asst, Univ Ill, 61-62; asst prof, 62-67, from assoc dean to dean humanities, State Univ NY Albany, 71-76, assoc prof Span, 67-80; PROF SPAN & PROVOST, WHEATON COL, 80- *Mem:* MLA; AAUP; Am Asn Teachers Span & Port; Am Asn Univ Women; Soc Values Higher Educ. *Res:* Nineteenth century Spanish novel; Galdos; Emelia Pardo Bazan. *Publ:* Auth, Manuel Tolosa Latour: Prototype of Augusto Miquis, Anales Galdosianos, 68; Cartas entre dos amigos del teatro: Manuel Tolosa Latour y Benito Perez Galdos, Cabildo Insular de Gran Canaria, Las Palmas, 69; Jose Ortega Munilla: Friend, critic, and disciple of Galdos, Anales Galdosianos, 71; Ortega Munilla y sus novelas, Rev Occidente, Madrid, 73; Woman's place in the sun: Feminism in Insolacion, Rev Estud Hisp, 74; Tristana or the importance of opportunity, Anales Galdosianos, 74; Role and reality: Amparo and esclavitud according to Pardo Bazan, Am Hispanist, 78. *Mailing Add:* Dept of Span Wheaton Col Norton MA 02766

SCHMIDT, VERNE, b San Antonio, Tex, Apr 4, 37; m 64; c 1. GERMANIC LANGUAGES. *Educ:* Univ Tex, BA, 58, MA, 61, PhD(Ger), 66. *Prof Exp:* From instr to asst prof Ger, Univ Ill, 65-67; asst prof, 67-72, ASSOC PROF GER, TRINITY UNIV, 72- *Mem:* MLA. *Res:* Modern German literature; Swedish. *Mailing Add:* Dept of Foreign Lang Trinity Univ San Antonio TX 78212

SCHMIEDEL, DONALD EMERSON, b Kent, Ohio, Nov 21, 39; m 65. SPANISH. *Educ:* Kent State Univ, AB, 61; Univ Southern Calif, AM, 63, PhD(Span), 66. *Prof Exp:* From lectr to asst prof, 65-73, ASSOC PROF SPAN, UNIV NEV, LAS VEGAS, 73- *Mem:* Asn Teachers Span & Port. *Res:* Spanish Golden Age drama. *Publ:* Auth, El Conde de Sex (Antonio Coello), a critical edition and study, Plaza Mayor, 72; Coello's debt to Gongora, Bull Comediantes, fall 73. *Mailing Add:* Dept of Span Univ of Nev Las Vegas NV 89154

SCHMIEL, ROBERT CHARLES, b Cedarburg, Wis, Aug 29, 35; m 62; c 1. CLASSICS. *Educ:* Northwestern Col, BA, 57; Univ Wash, MA, 63, PhD, 68. *Prof Exp:* From instr to assoc prof classics, Goucher Col, 63-76; ASSOC PROF CLASSICS, UNIV CALGARY, 76- *Mem:* Class Asn Atlantic States; Am Philol Asn; Class Asn Can; Class Asn Pack Northwest. *Res:* Greek poetry, especially Euripides and Homer. *Publ:* Auth, The recognition duo in Euripides' Helen, Hermes, 72; Telemachus in Sparta, Trans & Proc Am Philol Asn, 73; Youth and age: Mimnermus 1 & 2, Rivista di Filol, 74; Theocritus II: the purblind poet, Class J, 75; The impossible in Pope's The Rape of the Lock, Humanities Asn Rev, 78; A Vergilian formula?, Vergilius, 78; Moschus' Europa, Classical Philol, 81; Rhythm and Accent: Texture in Greek Epic Poetry, Quantitative Ling, 81. *Mailing Add:* Dept of Classics Univ of Calgary Calgary AB T2N 1N4 Can

SCHMITT, ALBERT RICHARD, b Mannheim, Ger, Oct 17, 29; US citizen; m 54; c 3. GERMAN LANGUAGE & LITERATURE. *Educ:* Colby Col, BA, 55; Univ Pa, MA, 57, PhD(Ger), 62. *Hon Degrees:* MA, Brown Univ, 70. *Prof Exp:* From instr to asst prof Ger, Univ Pa, 61-66; assoc prof, Univ Colo, Boulder, 66-69; assoc prof, 69-73, chmn dept, 77-80, PROF GER, BROWN UNIV, 73- *Concurrent Pos:* Vis prof, Yale Univ, 81; foreign lang ed, Mod Lang Studies. *Mem:* MLA; Am Asn Teachers Ger; Lessing Soc; Goethe Soc; Am Soc 18th Century Studies. *Res:* Eighteenth century German literature; German-American literary relations. *Publ:* Auth, Wielands Urteil über Goethes Wahlverwandtschaften, Schiller-Jahrbuch, 67; ed, Des Melchior Adam Pastorius Leben und Reisebeschreibungen, 68 & Festschrift für Detlev W Schumann, 70, Delp, Munich; auth, Schuld im Werke von Siegfried Lenz, Schumann-Festschrift, 70; ed, Johann Carl Wezel: Kritische Schriften (3 vols), Metzler, Stuttgart, 71-75; coauth, CM Wieland: Theorie und Geschichte der Red-Kunst und Dicht-Kunst Anno 1757, Lessing Yearbk, 73; auth, U Plenzdorfs Die neuen Leiden des jungen W, A D Klarmann-Festschrift, 74; Neues zum dt Amerikabild 1775-1777, Mod Lang Notes, 76. *Mailing Add:* Dept of Ger Brown Univ Providence RI 02912

SCHMITT, JAMES JOSEPH, b Evanston, Ill, Feb 1, 38; m 70; c 1. GERMAN LANGUAGE & LITERATURE. *Educ:* St Mary's Col, Ill, BA, 61; Georgetown Univ, MS, 67; Univ Iowa, PhD(Ger), 73. *Prof Exp:* Instr Ger, Divine Word Col, Iowa, 66-69; teaching asst, Univ Iowa, 69-72; ASSOC

PROF MOD LANG, ROCKFORD COL, 72- *Mem:* Am Asn Teachers Ger. *Res:* Fritz Hochwälder, modern Austrian dramatist; modern German drama; 18th century German literature. *Publ:* Auth, The theater of Fritz Hochwälder, 78 & Fritz Hochwälder bibliography, 78, Mod Austrian Lit. *Mailing Add:* Dept of Mod Lang Rockford Col Rockford IL 61101

SCHNAITER, SAMUEL ELLSWORTH, b Martinsville, Ind, Feb 11, 42; m 68; c 4. KOINE GREEK, NEW TESTAMENT LITERATURE. *Educ:* Bob Jones Univ, BA, 66, MA, 68, PhD(New Testament text), 80. *Prof Exp:* Grad asst instr ancient lang, 66-68, prof relig, 71-74, asst prof Bible & New Testament lang, 75-80, PROF BIBLE & NEW TESTAMENT LANG & CHMN, GREEK DEPT, BOB JONES UNIV, 80- *Res:* The attitudes of the ante-Nicene fathers to the copyists errors of the New Testament manuscripts. *Publ:* Auth, The King takes possession (Rev 11), 4/82, Textual criticism and the modern English version controversy, 4/82 & Epilogue (Rev 22), 11/82, Bibl Viewpoint. *Mailing Add:* 1555 Wade Hampton Blvd Greenville SC 29609

SCHNAUBER, CORNELIUS, b Freital, Ger, Apr 18, 39; m 66; c 2. GERMAN LITERATURE, LANGUAGE PSYCHOLOGY. *Educ:* Univ Hamburg, PhD(Ger lit, phonetics & polit sci), 69. *Prof Exp:* Teaching asst phonetics, Univ Hamburg, 62-66; lectr rhetoric, Res Inst Hamburg-Bergedorf, 65-66; asst prof Ger, Univ NDak, 66-67; asst prof, 68-72, ASSOC PROF GER LIT, UNIV SOUTHERN CALIF, 72-, CHMN DEPT, 75- *Honors & Awards:* Distinction of Honor in Gold for Serv to Repub of Austria, 79. *Mem:* MLA; Am Asn Teachers Ger; Philol Asn Pac Coast; Int Richard Wagner Soc. *Res:* German literature since 1700; language psychology; philosophy. *Publ:* Contribr, Gegenwarts Literatur und Drittes Reich, Reclam, 77; auth, Schritte in die Zukunft, Verlag, Georg Heintz, 78; contribr, Festschrift für Otto von Essen, Hbg Phonet Beiträge, 78; Festschrift für Friedrich Torberg, Langen-Müller, 78; auth, Pragmatische Humanismus, Verlag Georg Heintz, 79; contribr, Jahrbuch für Int Germanistik, Peter Lang Verlag, 81; Diedeutsche Lyrik, 1945-1975, August Bagel Verlag, 81; Welt im Wort, Schweiz Schriftstelleiverb, 81. *Mailing Add:* Dept of Ger Univ of Southern Calif University Park Los Angeles CA 90027

SCHNEER, RICHARD JAMES, b New York, NY, Oct 18, 27; m 50; c 2. SPANISH, PORTUGUESE. *Educ:* City Col New York, BSc, 48; NY Univ, MA, 49, PhD(Span), 61. *Prof Exp:* Instr mod lang, Univ Colo, 49-55; asst prof Span, Fisk Univ, 55-59; assoc prof, 59-66, chmn dept foreign lang, 67-72, PROF SPAN, CEDAR CREST COL, 66-, CHMN DEPT, 80- *Concurrent Pos:* Danforth assoc, 68- *Mem:* MLA; Am Asn Teachers Span & Port. *Res:* Golden Age drama; generation of 1898; teaching techniques. *Publ:* Auth, Object pronouns in French-a teaching technique, Fr Rev, 54; Let's Live a Little, Cedar Crest Col Bull, 62. *Mailing Add:* Dept of Foreign Lang Cedar Crest Col Allentown PA 18104

SCHNEEWIND, JEROME B, Philosophy. See Vol IV

SCHNEIDER, CHRISTIAN IMMO, b Dresden, Ger, Jan 27, 35; m 64; c 1. MODERN GERMAN LITERATURE. *Educ:* Univ Calif, Santa Barbara, MA, 65; PhD, 68; Cent Wash State Univ, MA, 78. *Prof Exp:* Asst Ger, Antioch Univ, 64-65; assoc, Univ Calif, Santa Barbara, 65-68; asst prof, 68-71, assoc prof, 72-80, PROF GER, CENT WASH STATE UNIV, 80- *Mem:* Am Asn Teachers Ger; AAUP; Am Guild Organists. *Res:* German literature of the 20th century; Hermann Hesse research; methods of literary criticism. *Publ:* Contribr, Hesse Companion, Suhrkamp, Frankfurt, 70; auth, Das Todesproblem bei Hermann Hesse, NG Elwert, Marlburg, 73; contribr, Materialien zu Hermann Hesses Das Glasperlenspiel, Suhrkamp, Frankfurt, 74; Hermann Hesse's Musik-kirtik, Bouvier, Bonn, 80. *Mailing Add:* Dept of Foreign Lang Cent Wash State Univ Ellensburg WA 98926

SCHNEIDER, GERD KLAUS, b Berlin, Ger, Apr 1, 31; Can citizen; m 67; c 1. GERMAN, LINGUISTICS. *Educ:* Univ BC, BA, 62; Univ Wash, MA, 63, PhD(Ger), 68. *Prof Exp:* Asst prof, 66-71, chmn dept Ger, 74-77, dir doctor of arts prog foreign lang, 77-80, ASSOC PROF GER LIT, SYRACUSE UNIV, 71- *Concurrent Pos:* Deutsche Sommerschule, Middlebury Col, 73. *Mem:* Am Asn Teachers Ger; MLA; Int Arthur Schnitzler Res Asn; Am Coun Studies Austrian Lit; Am Coun Teaching Foreign Lang. *Res:* Modern German literature; applied German linguistics. *Publ:* Auth, Tonund Schriftsprache in Schnitzler's Fräulein Else and Schumann's Carnaval, Mod Austrian Lit, 2/69; Das Vogelbild in Eichendorff's Taugenichts, Univ Dayton Rev, 7/71; Topical Bibliography in Theoretical and Applied German Linguistics, MLA/ERIC, 72; ed, Nietzsche's impact on Western thought, Symposium, 74; The place of foreign language in gerontology, Northeast Conf Teaching Foreign Lang, Vol 9, 81. *Mailing Add:* Dept of Ger Syracuse Univ Syracuse NY 13210

SCHNEIDER, GILBERT DONALD, b Dallas, Ore, 20; m 44; c 2. LINGUISTICS & ANTHROPOLOGY. *Educ:* Univ Rochester, BA, 45; Hartford Sem Found, MA, 46, PhD(ling), 64. *Prof Exp:* Missionary & adminr, NAm Baptist Mission, WAfrica, 47-51; adminr, Bamenda Highlands leprosy control prog, 52-61; dir Peace Corps lang training prog, 63-64; ed & res assoc, Ctr Int Studies, 64-68, assoc prof English, 68-69, chmn dept ling, 71-73, ASSOC PROF LING, OHIO UNIV, 69- *Concurrent Pos:* Consult, Cameroonian Dig, 72- *Mem:* Ling Soc Am. *Res:* Pidgins and Creoles; African anthropology; language and culture. *Publ:* Auth: GO: A graphic portrayal of a mission at work, Roger Williams, 57; A preliminary glossary of Pidgin to Pidgin-English, 65 & West African Pidgin-English: A descriptive linguistic analysis, 66, Ctr Int Studies; Pidgin-English proverbs, African Studies Ctr, 65; Focus on black, I, Schneiders, Athens, 70; Language and Culture: An informal student-teacher approach, Ohio Univ, 71; coauth, Our kind of afo-a-kom, Columbia J Rev, 3-4/74. *Mailing Add:* Dept of Ling Ohio Univ Athens OH 45701

SCHNEIDER, HENRY, III, b Newark, NJ, Apr 8, 16; m 66; c 4. GERMANIC LANGUAGES & LITERATURE. *Educ:* Princeton Univ, AB, 37, AM, 40, PhD(Ger lang & lit), 48. *Prof Exp:* Instr Ger, Princeton Univ, 38-41, 46-49; from assoc prof to prof, Ripon Col, 49-64, chmn dept, 49-64; Franklin prof & chmn dept Ger & Russ, 64-81, EMER FRANKLIN PROF, GETTYSBURG COL, 81- *Concurrent Pos:* Consult, Britannica World Lang Dict, 54. *Mem:* MLA; Am Asn Teachers Ger; AAUP. *Res:* Eighteenth century German literature. *Mailing Add:* Dept of Ger Gettysburg Col Gettysburg PA 17325

SCHNEIDER, MARILYN, b New York, NY, Jan 21, 33; m 59; c 3. ITALIAN. *Educ:* Brooklyn Col, BA, 54; Univ Wis, MA, 56, PhD(Ital), 68. *Prof Exp:* Instr Ital, Univ Wis-Madison, 64-69; asst prof Ital, 69-73, chmn dept French & Ital, 74-77, assoc prof, 73-79, assoc dean lib arts, 79-82, PROF ITAL & COMP LIT, UNIV MINN, 79- *Concurrent Pos:* Consult, Univ Minn Press, Nat Endowment for Humanities & MLA; reviewer, Libr Jour. *Mem:* MLA; Midwest Mod Lang Asn; Am Asn Teachers Ital. *Res:* Contemporary Italian literature; myth criticism; narrative structure. *Publ:* Auth, Circularity as mode and meaning in Conversazione in Sicilia, Mod Lang Notes, 1/75; Afterward, In: Il Giardino dei Finzi-Contini, Mondadori, 76; Introduction, In: L'airone, Mondadori, 78; To know is to eat: A reading of Malerba's Il serpente, Yale Ital Studies, winter 78; A conversion to death: Giorgio Bassani's L'airone, Can J Ital Studies, winter 78; Il pataffio, or how to feed on laughter, Contemp Lit, fall 79; Calvino at a crossroads: Il castello dei destini incrociati, Publ Mod Lang Asn Am, 1/80; Calvino's erotic metaphor and the hermaphroditic solution, Stanford Ital Rev, spring 81. *Mailing Add:* Dept of French & Ital Univ of Minn 200 Folwell Hall 9 Pleasant St SE Minneapolis MN 55455

SCHNEIDER, MARSHALL JERROLD, b Bronx, NY, Sept 21, 42. SPANISH LITERATURE, APPLIED LINGUISTICS. *Educ:* City Col New York, BA, 62; Univ Conn, MA, 67, PhD(Span), 69. *Prof Exp:* Asst prof, 67-74, ASSOC PROF SPAN, BARUCH COL, 74- *Concurrent Pos:* Consult, Holt, Rinehart & Winston & Harper & Row, 70-75, Encycl World Lit 20th Century, 79- & Al-Anon, 81- *Mem:* Am Asn Teachers Span & Port; AAUP; MLA. *Res:* Novels of Ramon J Sender; studies in literary structure and theory. *Publ:* Auth, La familia Marin, 71, Un amigo del norte, 71 & De vacaciones, 71, Holt; articles on Blasco Ibanez, Buero Vallejo, Casona, Garcia Lorca, Jimenez, In: Encycl of World Literature in the 20th Century, Vols I & II, 81-82. *Mailing Add:* Dept of Mod Lang Baruch Col New York NY 10010

SCHNEIDER, ROBERT JAMES, b Saginaw, Mich, Feb 28, 39. CLASSICAL LANGUAGES, MEDIEVAL STUDIES. *Educ:* Univ of the South, BA, 61; Univ Notre Dame, MSM, 63, DSM, 65. *Prof Exp:* Asst prof classics, Univ Southern Calif, 65-68; asst prof, 68-72, chmn dept, 68-74, assoc, 72-81, PROF CLASSICS, BEREA COL, 81- *Mem:* Mediaeval Acad Am; Am Class League; Am Philol Asn; Class Asn of Midwest & South; Vergilian Soc. *Res:* Western intellectual history; history of science; Vicent of Beauvais. *Publ:* Co-ed & contribr, Studium generale: Studies offered to Astrick L Gabriel . . ., Notre Dame, 67. *Mailing Add:* Dept of Foreign Lang Berea Col Berea KY 40404

SCHNEIDER-HALVORSON, BRIGITTE LINA, b Chemnitz, Ger, Mar 4, 35; nat US; c 2. MODERN GERMAN LITERATURE. *Educ:* San Diego State Univ, BA, 67, MA, 69; Univ Calif, Riverside, PhD(Ger), 78. *Prof Exp:* Teaching asst Ger, San Diego State Univ, 67-69; instr, Univ San Diego, fall, 69 & San Diego Evening Col, 69-81; ASSOC PROF GER, UNIV SAN DIEGO, 71- *Concurrent Pos:* Staff ed, Mod Austrian Lit J, 81- *Mem:* Asn Am Teachers Ger; AAUP; MLA; Int Arthur Schnitzler Res Asn; Int Asn Ger Studies. *Res:* Modern German and Austrian literature; exile literature. *Publ:* Auth, The Late Dramatic Works of Arthur Schnitzler, Peter Lang Verlag, Bern Switz, 82. *Mailing Add:* 3925 Rogers Rd Spring Valley CA 92077

SCHNERR, WALTER JOHNSON, b Blakely, Pa, Dec 17, 14. ROMANCE PHILOLOGY. *Educ:* Univ Pa, AB, 35, AM, 38, PhD, 49; Univ Perugia, dipl, 35; Univ Strasbourg, cert, 37. *Prof Exp:* Instr, 39-42, asst prof mod lang, Grinnell Col, 44-45; instr romance lang, Univ Pa, 45-46; from instr to prof romance lang, 46-76, PROF HISP & ITAL STUDIES, BROWN UNIV, 76- *Mem:* MLA; Am Asn Teachers Ital; Ling Soc Am; New England Mod Lang Asn. *Res:* Romance philology; European literature. *Mailing Add:* Dept of Hisp & Ital Studies Brown Univ Providence RI 02912

SCHODER, RAYMOND VICTOR, b Battle Creek, Mich, Apr 11, 16. GREEK, LATIN. *Educ:* Xavier Univ, Ohio, AB, 38; Loyola Univ, Ill, MA, 40; St Louis Univ, PhD, 44; West Baden Col, Ind, STL, 48. *Prof Exp:* Instr Latin, Greek & English, high sch, Univ Detroit, 43-44; asst prof Latin & Greek, West Baden Col, Ind, 51-59; PROF GREEK & LATIN LIT & ART, LOYOLA UNIV, ILL, 60- *Concurrent Pos:* Mem managing comt, Am Sch Class Studies, Athens, 53-, annual prof, 61-62; lectr, Archaeol Inst Am, 53, 54, 60-61, 67, 81 & 82; Fulbright prof Greek art & archaeol, Univ Nijmegen, 56-57; lectr art prog, Asn Am Cols, 58-60; Rojtman Found lectr class art, Milwaukee, Wis, 62-63. *Mem:* Am Philol Asn; Archaeol Inst Am; Class Asn Midwest & South; Vergilian Soc (vpres, 57-63); Manresa Educ Corp (pres, 77-). *Res:* Greek and Latin language, literature and art; classical and Near Eastern archaeology. *Publ:* Transl, Philippians and Galatians, In: New American Bible, 70; auth, Ancient Greece From the Air, Thames & Hudson, London, 73; Greco-Roman Antipolis, Antipolis, 74; Landscape and Inscape in Poetry of Hopkins, Paul Elek, London, 75; contribr, Princeton Encyclopedia of Classical Sites, 76; auth, The carrier-witted heart: The Ignatian quality of the Wreck of the Deutschland, In: Readings in the Wreck, Loyola Univ, 76; Genesis and goals of Cardinal Newman College, Homiletic & Pastoral Rev, 78. *Mailing Add:* Dept of Class Studies Loyola Univ Chicago IL 60626

SCHOECK, RICHARD J, English & Renaissance Humanism. See Vol II

SCHOENBOHM, GERTRUDE K, b Bonn, Ger, May 16, 16; US citizen; m 37; c 3. FOREIGN LANGUAGES & LITERATURES. *Educ:* Univ Iowa, BA, 50, MA, 52, PhD, 55. *Prof Exp:* Instr Ger & French, Jamestown Col, 46-48; instr French, Univ Iowa, 55-56; asst prof foreign lang & head dept French, Augustant Col, Ill, 56-61; ASSOC PROF FOREIGN LANG, NORTHERN ILL UNIV, 61- *Concurrent Pos:* Consult, foreign lang, Davenport High Sch, Iowa, 57-60; consult, foreign lang, St Katherine Sch, Davenport, 57-61; Lilly Found fel, 60; teacher, mod Ger lit, Berlin Sem, 64; teacher, mod Ger lit, NDEA Inst, Colo Univ, 65. *Mem:* MLA; Am Asn Teachers Fr; Am Asn Teachers Ger. *Res:* Comparative literature; Franco-German literary relations. *Publ:* Auth, Gide as translator of Rainer Maria Rilke, L'Esprit Createur, 61; co-auth, Oedipus, myth and drama, 68 & translr, Oedipus und die Sphynx von Hofmannsthal, 68, Odyssey. *Mailing Add:* Dept of Foreign Lang & Lit Northern Ill Univ De Kalb IL 60115

SCHOENHEIM, URSULA, b Leipzig, Ger, June 9, 29; US citizen. CLASSICS. *Educ:* Hunter Col, BA, 55; Cornell Univ, MA, 56, PhD(Latin, Greek & ancient hist), 58. *Prof Exp:* Teacher Latin, Fox Lane High Sch, Bedford, NY, 58-60; lectr classics, Hunter Col, 60-61; instr classics, 61-65, from asst prof to assoc prof, 66-75, PROF CLASS LANG, QUEENS COL, NY, 76-, CHMN DEPT, 80- *Concurrent Pos:* Fels, Cornell Univ, 55-58; bk rev ed, Class World, 58-70; lectr, Hunter Col, 58-60; asst prof, Montclair State Col, 61-62, vis prof, 70; consult, New Am Libr World Lit, Inc, 62 & Bobbs-Merrill Co, Inc, 63-67; co-ed, Am Class Rev, 71-73; contribr, Encycl Americana. *Mem:* Am Philol Asn; Am Class League; Class Asn Atlantic States. *Res:* Classical mythology; Greek and Roman drama; Roman satire. *Publ:* Auth, The place of Tactus in Lucretius, Philologus, 66; 39 radio lect on Greek civilization, with study guide, 66; contrib, Encycl Americana. *Mailing Add:* 45-31 171st Pl Flushing NY 11358

SCHOEPS, KARL H, b Dinslaken, W Ger, Dec 8, 35; m 65. GERMAN, COMPARATIVE LITERATURE. *Educ:* Bonn Univ, Staatsexam, 62; Univ Wis-Madison, PhD(Ger), 71. *Prof Exp:* Teacher English, Gymnasium Wipperfurth & Wuppertal, Ger, 64-67; teaching asst Ger, Univ Kans, 63-64 & Univ Wis, 67-71; asst prof, Univ Ill, 71-76 & Mt Holyoke Col, 77; ASSOC PROF GER, UNIV ILL, 77- *Mem:* MLA; Am Asn Teachers Ger; Int Brecht Soc. *Res:* Modern German drama; East German literature; Anglo-American and German literary relations. *Publ:* Auth, Bertolt Brecht und George Bernard Shaw, Brecht Heute/Brecht Today, 73; Bertolt Brecht und Bernard Shaw, Bouvier, 74; Epic structures in the plays of Bernard Shaw and Bertolt Brecht, Essays Brecht, 74; Zwei moderne Lenz-Bearbeitungen, Monatshefte, 75; Bertolt Brecht, Ungar, 78; Wandel und Erinnerung: Christa Wolfs Erzahlung Blickwechsel'als Paradigma ihrer Erzahlstruktur, Ger Quart, 79; Der DDR-Roman, In: Handbuch des deufschen Romans, Dusseldorf: Bagel, 82. *Mailing Add:* Dept of Ger Lang & Lit Univ of Ill Urbana IL 61801

SCHOGT, HENRY GILIUS, b Amsterdam, Neth, May 24, 27; m 55; c 3. ROMANCE & SLAVIC LANGUAGES. *Educ:* Univ Amsterdam, MA, 51 & 52; Univ Utrecht, PhD(French), 60. *Prof Exp:* Sr asst Old & Mod French & ling, Univ Utrecht, 54-63; sr asst ling, Sorbonne, 63-64; lectr French & Russ, Princeton Univ, 64-66; assoc prof, 66-69, chmn dept French, grad sch, 72-77, PROF FRENCH, UNIV COL, UNIV TORONTO, 69- *Concurrent Pos:* Lectr, Univ Groningen, 53-63. *Mem:* Ling Soc Paris; Can Ling Asn; fel Royal Soc Can. *Res:* General linguistics; structural descriptive methods; semantics. *Publ:* Transl, De palm die door het dak breekt, 66, Van Oorschot, Amsterdam; auth, Le systeme verbal du francais contemporain, Mouton, The Hague, 68; La dynamique du langage, 68; Quatre fois enseignement, Word, Vol 24, Nos 1, 2 & 3; Synonymie et signe linguistique, Linguistique, Vol 8, No 2; Semantique synchronique synonymie, homonymie, polysemie, Univ Toronto, 76; coauth, La Phonologie, Klincksieck, 77; Encycl de la Plecade: Le Langage, Gallemard, Paris. *Mailing Add:* 47 Turner Rd Toronto ON M6G 3H7 Can

SCHOLES, ROBERT, English, Comparative Literature. See Vol II

SCHOLES, ROBERT JAMES, b Ft Wayne, Ind, Aug 15, 32; m 62; c 2. LINGUISTICS. *Educ:* Ind Univ, AB, 57, PhD(ling), 64. *Prof Exp:* Teacher high sch, Ind, 57-59; from instr to asst prof ling, Ind Univ, 61-66; from asst prof speech to assoc prof speech & ling, 67-76, PROF SPEECH & LING, UNIV FLA, 76- *Concurrent Pos:* Mem res staff speech synthesis, Int Bus Machines Res Lab, Calif, 63-65. *Mem:* Ling Soc Am; Ling Circle NY; Asn Machine Transl & Computational Ling. *Res:* Language production and perception in children and adults; psycholinguistics. *Publ:* Coauth, Spoken Tunisian Arabic, Peace Corps, 66; auth, Phonotactic Grammaticality, Mouton, 67; The categorization of synthetic speech sounds as a predictive device in language teaching, J Eng Second Lang, 2/67; Categorial responses to synthetic vocalic stimuli by speakers of various languages, Lang & Speech, 10/67; Syllable segmentation and identification, Linguistics. *Mailing Add:* Dept of Speech & Ling Univ of Fla Gainesville FL 32611

SCHOLLER, HARALD, b Ger, Oct 8, 24; m 67; c 2. MEDIEVAL GERMAN LITERATURE, PHILOLOGY. *Educ:* Univ Marburg, DrPhil(Romance lang & lit), 56. *Prof Exp:* Res fel Franco-Can lang & lit, Univs Toronto & Marburg, 56-57; instr Ger, Waterloo Univ Col, 57-58; asst prof French & Ger, Univ SDak, Vermillion, 58-60; instr Ger, 60-62, from asst prof to prof Ger & comp lit, 62-76, PROF GER LANG & LIT, UNIV MICH, ANN ARBOR, 76- *Mem:* MLA; Am Asn Teachers Ger. *Res:* Medieval European literature; computer-aided lexicography of Middle High German literature; applied linguistics. *Publ:* Auth, Studien im semantischen Bereich des Schmerzes . . . im Renart le Contrefait, E Droz, Geneva, 59; A word index to the Nibelungenklage, Univ Mich, Ann Arbor, 66; Förderung der Nibelungen Forschung durch Elektronenrechner, Zfda, 66; Das Proömium des Helmbrecht: Inhalt, Form, Entstehung, Beitr, Tübingen, 67; co-ed, Lexicography and dialect geography, F Steiner, Wiesbaden, 73; ed, The epic in medieval society: Aesthetic and moral values, M Niemeyer, Tübingen, 74. *Mailing Add:* Dept of Ger Lang & Lit Univ Mich Ann Arbor MI 48109

SCHONS, PAUL ALLEN, b Tracy, Minn, Sept 12, 40; m 63; c 3. GERMAN LANGUAGE, LITERATURE & CULTURE. *Educ:* Col St Thomas, BA, 62; Univ Colo, MA, 67; Univ Minn, PhD(Ger), 74. *Prof Exp:* Teacher Ger & Latin, Gaylord High Sch, 62-64 & Ger, Palmer High Sch, Colorado Springs, 65-67; PROF GER, COL OF ST THOMAS, 67-, CHMN, DEPT FOR LANG, 78- *Concurrent Pos:* Dir, Study Abroad Prog, Col of St Thomas, 75- *Mem:* Am Asn Teachers Ger; NAm Nietzsche Soc; Asn Departments of For Lang. *Res:* American Nietzsche scholarship; foreign language curricular development. *Publ:* Auth, Minnesota AATG Resources Directory, Minn Am Assoc Teachers Ger, 78; The German opera, Options for the Teaching For Lang & Lit, 78; Influential ideas in non-fictional German, 82 & Modern Germany and current events, 82, Dir Teaching Innovation in For Lang; Minnesota AATG Resources Directory, Minn Am Asn Teaching Ger, 82. *Mailing Add:* Box 5027 Col of St Thomas St Paul MN 55105

SCHOOLFIELD, GEORGE C, b Charleston, WVa, Aug 14, 25; m 49. GERMANIC LANGUAGES & LITERATURES. *Educ:* Univ Cincinnati, BA, 46, MA, 47; Princeton Univ, PhD(Ger), 49. *Prof Exp:* Instr Ger, 49-52, tutor hist & lit, Harvard Univ, 50-52; from asst prof to assoc prof Ger lang, Univ Buffalo, 52-59; assoc prof Ger, Duke Univ, 59-61; prof Ger & Scand & head dept, Univ Cincinnati, 61-64; prof Ger lang & lit, Univ Pa, 64-69; PROF GER & SCAND LIT, YALE UNIV, 69- *Concurrent Pos:* Fulbright res fel, Austria, 52-53, Finland, 67-68, US Educ Found, Finland, 72; Guggenheim fel, Sweden, 55-56; managing ed, Scand Studies, 69-73, rev ed, 73-; vis prof Ger lit, Univ Fla, 71; grad ctr, City Univ New York, 71-72. *Mem:* Rilke Soc; Acad Lit Studies; Am Coun Studies Austrian Lit; MLA; Am Asn Teachers Ger. *Res:* German Scandinavian literary relations; recent German and Scandinavian literature. *Publ:* Auth, The musician in German literature, 56, The German lyric of the Baroque, 61 & co-ed, Studies in German drama; a festschrift in honor of Walter Silz, In: Studies in the Germanic languages and literatures, 73, Univ NC; translr, Fredrik Book's Hans Christian Andersen, Univ Okla, 62 & Hagar Olsson's The woodcarver and death, Univ Wis, 65; auth, Rilke's last year, Univ Kans Libr, 69. *Mailing Add:* Dept of Ger Lang & Lit Yale Univ New Haven CT 06520

SCHOR, NAOMI ANN, b New York, NY, Oct 10, 43. FRENCH. *Educ:* Barnard Col, BA, 63; Yale Univ, PhD(French), 69. *Prof Exp:* Actg instr French, Yale Univ, 68-69; from instr to asst prof, Columbia Univ, 69-78; ASSOC PROF FRENCH, BROWN UNIV, 78- *Concurrent Pos:* Am Coun Learned Soc study fel, 76-77; Nat Endowment for Humanities rel fel, 81. *Mem:* MLA. *Res:* Nineteenth century French prose fiction; literature and psychoanalysis; feminist criticism. *Publ:* Ed, Zola, Yale Fr Studies, spring 69; auth, Pour une thematique restreinte: ecriture, parole et difference dans Madame Bovary, Litterature, 5/76; Le Sourire du sphinx: Zola et l'enigme de la feminite, Romantisme, 12/76; Dali's freud, Dada/Surrealism, 76; Une vie/Des vides, ou le Nom de la Mere, Litterature, 5/77; Zola's Crowds, Johns Hopkins Univ, fall 78; Le ditail chez Freud, Litturature, Vol 37, 80; Truth in sculpture: Duane Hanson, New York Literary Forum, Vol 8, No 9, 81; Female Paranoia: The Case for Pshchoanalistic Feminist Criticism, Yale Fr Studies, Vol 62, 81. *Mailing Add:* Dept of French Studies Brown Univ Providence RI 02912

SCHORK, RUDOLPH JOSEPH, JR, b Baltimore, Md, Apr 17, 33; m 56; c 1. CLASSICAL PHILOLOGY, BYZANTINE STUDIES. *Educ:* Col of the Holy Cross, AB, 55; Oxford Univ, DPhil(Byzantine Greek), 57. *Prof Exp:* From instr to asst prof classics, John Carroll Univ, 57-60; from asst prof to assoc prof & chmn dept, Georgetown Univ, 60-66; from assoc prof to prof, Univ Minn, Minneapolis, 66-73; dir, Nat Humanities Ser, Princeton Univ, NJ, 72-73; vis prof classics, Univ Cincinnati, 73-74; vis prof & chmn Brooklyn Col, 74-75; PROF CLASSICS, UNIV MASS, BOSTON, 75- *Concurrent Pos:* Consult, Nat Humanities Fac, 69- *Mem:* Am Philol Asn. *Res:* Latin literature; Byzantine liturgical poetry; ancient epic poetry. *Publ:* Auth, Aemulos Reges: Allusion and Theme in Horace 3.16, Trans Am Philol Asn, 71; Allusion, Theme and Characterization in Cymbeline, Studies Renaissance, 72; Romanos: On Joseph I, stanza a: text and type, Byzantion, 75; Basic mythology courses: two suggestions, Class J, 76-77; A graphic exercise of mnemotechnic, James Joyce Quart, 79; Kennst Du Das Haus Citrons, Bloom?, James Joyce Quart, 80. *Mailing Add:* Dept of Classics Harbor Campus Univ of Mass Boston MA 02125

SCHOVILLE, KEITH NORMAN, b Soldiers Grove, Wis, Mar 3, 28; c 5. HEBREW, BIBLICAL STUDIES. *Educ:* Milligan Col, BA, 56; Univ Wis-Madison, MA, 66, PhD(Hebrew & Semitic studies), 69. *Prof Exp:* From instr to asst prof, 68-74, assoc prof, 74-81, chmn dept, 77-82, PROF HEBREW & SEMITIC STUDIES, UNIV WIS-MADISON, 81- *Concurrent Pos:* Ed, Hebrew Studies. *Mem:* Am Orient Soc; Soc Biblical Lit; Am Schs Orient Res; Nat Asn Prof Hebrew (secy); Archaeol Inst Am. *Res:* The human factor in archaeology; literary and historical illumination of biblical literature; the Intertestamental Period. *Publ:* Auth, The Song of Songs, entry 13108, In: Encyclopedia Judaica, 71; A note on the Oracles of Amos Against Gaza, Tyre, and Edom, Suppl Vetus Testamentum, 74; Two views of Death: 1 Shall He Live Again?, Wis Alumnus, 75; The problem of relevancy, Newslett, The American, Schs Orient Res, 76; The sins of Aram in Amos I, Proc Sixth World Cong Jewish Studies, 77; Biblical Archaeology in Focus, Baker Bk House, 78. *Mailing Add:* Hebrew & Semitic Studies Univ Wis Madison WI 53706

SCHRADER, DOROTHY LYNNE, b Pensacola, Fla, Aug 13, 47. FRENCH. *Educ:* Agnes Scott Col, BA, 69; Middlebury Col, MA, 71; Univ Paris III, lic es lett, 74; Fla State Univ, PhD(Fr), 76. *Prof Exp:* Asst prof French, Southern Ill Univ, Edwardsville, 76-77; asst prof, 77-82, ASSOC PROF FRENCH, OKLA STATE UNIV, 82- *Concurrent Pos:* Lectr English, Ecole Nat Admin, Paris & Inst Nat Agronomique, Paris, 72-74. *Mem:* MLA; Soc Rencesvals; Medieval Asn Midwest; Southeastern Medieval Asn. *Res:* Women protagonists in the French Medieval epics; Parise la Duchesse, critical edition; Le Dit de l'Unicorne, critical edition. *Publ:* Coauth, Teaching the Basics in the Foreign Language Classroom: Options and Strategies, Nat Textbk Co, 79. *Mailing Add:* Dept of Foreign Lang Okla State Univ Stillwater OK 74078

SCHRADER, RICHARD JAMES, Medieval English Literature. See Vol II

SCHRAIBMAN, JOSEPH, b Havana, Cuba, Sept 29, 35; US citizen; m 63. FOREIGN LANGUAGES & LITERATURES. *Educ:* Brooklyn Col, BA, 55; Univ Ill, MA, 56, PhD, 59. *Prof Exp:* From instr to asst prof Romance lang, Princeton Univ, 59-65, bicentennial preceptor, 63-65; assoc prof Span & Port, Ind Univ, Bloomington, 65-69; chmn dept, 72-78, PROF ROMANCE LANG, WASH UNIV, 69- *Concurrent Pos:* Am Coun Learned Soc grant-in-aid, 62-63; Fulbright res grant, Spain 62-63; consult, Educ Testing Serv Advan Placement Exam; chmn, Comt Advan Placement & consult ed, Xerox Publ Co, 65-; Danforth teaching assoc, 68; mem exec comt, Bks Abroad, 71-74; Mellon fel, Univ Pittsburgh, 75- *Mem:* MLA; Am Asn Teachers Span & Port; Am Asn Teachers Fr. *Res:* Stylistics; Galdos; Clarin. *Publ:* Auth, Dreams in the Novels of Galdos, Hisp Inst, 60; coauth, Cartas del archivo de Galdos, 67 & Cartas a Galdos, 68, Taurus, Madrid; ed & contrib, Homenaje a Sherman H Eoff, Castalia, 70; auth, Las citas biblicas en Misericordia de Galdos, Cuadernos Hispanoam, 10/70-1/71; coauth, Estructura simbolica de El jarama, Homenaje a Edmundo de Chasca, Philol Quart, 72; auth, Espacio historico literario en Espacio Gerona, Am Hisp, 11/76; Tiempo de silencio y la cura siquiatrica de un pueblo, Insula, 3/77; Tiempo de destruccion, Revista Ibero Americana, 7-12/81; Benito Perez Galdos, Los articulos politicos en la Revista de Espana, 1871-1872, 82. *Mailing Add:* 10 Pricewoods Lane St Louis MO 63132

SCHRAMM, GENE MOSHE, b New York, NY, Sept 15, 29. FOREIGN LANGUAGES. *Educ:* Univ Calif, AB, 48, MA, 50; Dropsie Col, PhD(Arabic), 56. *Prof Exp:* Asst prof semitic lang, Univ Calif, Berkeley, 57-67; assoc prof, 67-70, PROF NEAR EASTERN LANG & LIT, UNIV MICH, ANN ARBOR, 70- *Concurrent Pos:* Training officer, foreign lang, Nat Security Agency, US Defense Dept, 51. *Mem:* Am Orient Soc. *Res:* Arabic dialectology; comparative Semitics. *Publ:* Course in the Amharic language; coauth, Handbook of written Arabic & Course in written Arabic. *Mailing Add:* Dept of Near Eastern Lang Univ of Mich Ann Arbor MI 48104

SCHREIBER, FRED, b Berlin, Ger, Nov 24, 35; US citizen; m 64; c 1. CLASSICS. *Educ:* Queens Col, NY, BA, 64; Harvard Univ, MA, 66, PhD(class philol), 70. *Prof Exp:* Asst prof, 70-76, ASSOC PROF CLASSICS, LEHMAN COL, CITY UNIV NEW YORK, 76- *Concurrent Pos:* City Univ New York fac res award, bibliog aristophanes, 73-74; Am Coun Learned Soc fel, 76-77. *Mem:* Bibliog Soc Am; Renaissance Soc Am; Am Philol Asn. *Res:* Aristophanes; textual criticism; history of classical scholarship. *Publ:* Auth, Juvenal 14, 265-9, Hermes, 71; A double-barreled joke: Aristophanes, Birds, 38, Am J Philol, 73; The etiology of a misinterpretation: Aristophanes, Birds, 30, Class Philol, 74; Unpublished Renaissance Emendations of Aristophanes, Trans Am Philol Asn, 75. *Mailing Add:* 3140 Netherland Ave Bronx NY 10463

SCHREIBER, WILLIAM ILDEPHONSE, b Bonn, Ger, Sept 15, 06; m 34; c 4. FOREIGN LANGUAGES. *Educ:* Conception Col, AB, 26; Univ Wis, AM, 29; Univ Ill, PhD, 33. *Prof Exp:* Asst Ger, Univ Ill, 29-33; head dept foreign lang, Parsons Col, 33-37; asst prof, 37-47, actg head dept, 40-47, Gingrich prof & head dept, 47-76, EMER GINGRICH PROF GER, COL WOOSTER, 76- *Concurrent Pos:* Lectr Ger, US Ctr Info, 51-52; contract interpreter, State Dept, 58-76; dir Ger, Wooster in Vienna, Ger, summer, 60- *Mem:* Nat Carl Schurz Found; Midwestern Folklore Asn; MLA; Am Asn Teachers Ger; Am Folklore Soc. *Res:* Renaissance; Humanism; social elements of the humanistic school dialogues of the 15th and 16th centuries. *Publ:* Auth, Wie der Weihnachtsbaum nach Amerika kam, 60; The hymns of the Amish Ausbund in philological and literary perspective, 62; Our Amish Neighbors, Univ Chicago, 62; The fate of the Prussian Mennonites; The proverbs in Gottfried Keller's works; co-ed, Anton Macku Festschrift, 72. *Mailing Add:* Dept of Ger Col of Wooster Wooster OH 44691

SCHREINER, MARTHA E, b Kewanee, Ill, June 28, 14. FRENCH LITERATURE & LANGUAGE. *Educ:* Northern Ill State Teachers Col, BA, 36; Northwestern Univ, MA, 37; Univ Paris, PhD(French lit), 53. *Prof Exp:* Instr French, Ger & Span, Eureka Col, 37-43; asst prof French, Ger & Span, Delta State Col, 43-46; from asst prof French & Ger to assoc prof French, 46-56; dir div French & Ital, 69-72, PROF FRENCH, NORTHERN ILL UNIV, 56- *Concurrent Pos:* Consult, evaluating original French prog, Midwestern Prog Airborne TV Instr, 60. *Mem:* MLA; Am Asn Teachers Fr; Am Coun Teaching Foreign Lang; NEA. *Res:* Nineteenth century French literature, especially Parnassian and symbolist periods; Mark Twain in France; the teaching of French. *Mailing Add:* Dept of Foreign Lang & Lit Northern Ill Univ De Kalb IL 60115

SCHRERO, ELLIOT MITCHELL, English Language & Literature. See Vol II

SCHROEDER, ADOLF ERNST, b Covington, Va, Feb 1, 16; m 42; c 2. GERMAN. *Educ:* La State Univ, MA, 47; Ohio State Univ, PhD(Ger lang & lit), 50. *Prof Exp:* Instr Ger, Univ Mo, 46-47 & Ohio State Univ, 47-52; from asst prof to assoc prof, Univ Mass, 52-56; prof Ger & head dept foreign lang, Kent State Univ, 56-64; prof, La State Univ, 64-69; chmn dept Ger & Slavic Lang, 69-72, PROF GER, UNIV MO-COLUMBIA, 69- *Concurrent Pos:* Vis asst prof, Amherst Col, 52-53 & Ohio State, summers 53, 54, 56 & 59. *Honors & Awards:* Cross of Merit, 1st Class, Fed Repub Ger, 62. *Mem:* MLA; Am Asn Teachers Ger; Am Folklore Soc; AAUP ; Int Vereinigung fur germanische Sprach- und Literaturwissenschaft. *Res:* Nineteenth and 20th century German literature; American ballads and folk songs. *Publ:* Coauth, Interpretations of German poetry, 1939-1956, Monatschefte, 10/57; auth, A century of Sealsfield scholarship, Report Soc Hist Ger Md, 66; ed, Charles Sealsfield's Gesammelte Werke, Vols 13 & 14 (Pflanzerleben I & II), Georg Olms, Hildescheim, 75; auth, Nineteenth century folksong collectors in the Rhineland, Semasia, 7/75; The survival of German traditions in Missouri, In: The German Contribution to the Building of the Americas, Clark Univ, 77; Der Stand der deutschen Sprache in Missouri, Deutsch als Muttersprache in den Vereinigten Staaten, I, Fran Steiner, Wiesbaden, 78; The contexts of continuity: German Folklore in Missouri, Kansas Quart, spring 81; co-ed & transl, Gottfried Duden, Report on a Journey to the Western States of North America, Univ Mo Press, 80. *Mailing Add:* Dept of Ger & Slavic Studies Univ of Mo Columbia MO 65211

SCHUB, LOUISE RYPKO, b Paris, France, Oct 8, 22; US citizen; m 51; c 2. FRENCH LANGUAGE & LITERATURE. *Educ:* Brooklyn Col, BA, 43; Columbia Univ, MA, 48; Univ Paris, DUniv (French lit), 52. *Prof Exp:* Teaching asst French, Columbia Univ, 45; instr French, Span & Russ & dir Maison Francaise, Skidmore Col, 45-47; mem fac French & Span, Brooklyn Col, 47-48; teacher French, Lafayette High Sch, Brooklyn, NY, 58-62; from instr to assoc prof, 62-75, PROF FRENCH LANG & LIT, BROOKLYN COL, 75- *Concurrent Pos:* Consult, Bur Foreign Lang, Bd Educ, New York, 65-; exam asst, Bd Exam, New York, 72- *Honors & Awards:* Chevalier, Palmes Academiques, French Govt, 69-76, Officier, 76. *Mem:* Am Asn Teachers Fr; MLA; Asn Int Etudes Fr; Asn Int Amis Valery Larbaud; Soc Prof Fr Am. *Res:* Contemporary French literature; French poetry; language teaching methodology. *Publ:* Auth, Leon-Paul Fargue, Droz, Geneva, 73; La Chanson naturaliste: Aristide Bruant, ou le revers de la Belle Epoque, Cahiers l'Assoc Int des Etudes Francaises, 5/76; Fargue-Larbaud: Nouvelles lumieres (grace a des lettres inedites), sur une amitie orageuse, In: Valery Larbaud et la litterature de son temps, Klincksieck, Paris, 78; Charles-Louis Philippe & Leon-Paul Fargue, In: Columbia Dictionary of Modern European Literature, Columbia Univ, 80; Leon-Paul Fargue, In: A Critical Bibliography of French Literature--XXth Century, Syracuse Univ, 80. *Mailing Add:* Dept of Mod Lang & Lit Brooklyn Col Brooklyn NY 11210

SCHUBERT, VIRGINIA ANN, b St Paul, Minn, Oct 15, 35. FRENCH LANGUAGE & LITERATURE. *Educ:* Col St Catherine, St Paul, Minn, BA, 57; Univ Minn, Minneapolis, MA, 63, PhD(French), 74. *Prof Exp:* Instr French, Col St Catherine, 58-60; teacher, Alexander Ramsey High Sch, Roseville, 61-65; ASSOC PROF FRENCH, MACALESTER COL, 65- *Honors & Awards:* Chevalier Ordre des Palmes Academiques, French govt, 75. *Mem:* MLA; Am Asn Teachers French; Am Coun Teachers Foreign Lang. *Res:* Nineteenth century French literature; humanities, especially nineteenth century France. *Publ:* Coauth, Le Nouveau Passe-Muraille, Prentice-Hall, 70. *Mailing Add:* Dept of French Macalester Col St Paul MN 55105

SCHUELER, HEINZ JUERGEN, b Mbeya, Tanzania, July 15, 33; Can citizen; m 57; c 2. GERMAN LANGUAGE & LITERATURE. *Educ:* Univ Toronto, BA, 59, MA, 61, PhD(Ger), 65. *Prof Exp:* Lectr & asst prof Ger, Univ Western Ont, 64-66; asst prof, Univ Guelph, 66-68; asst prof, 68-70, assoc prof, 70-78, PROF GER, YORK UNIV, 78- *Concurrent Pos:* Can Coun res grants & fels, 68, 69, 73-74, 77 & 79-80. *Mem:* Internationale Vereinigung für Germanische Sprach- und Literaturwissenschaft; Am Asn Teachers Ger; MLA; Can Asn Univ Teachers Ger. *Res:* Late 18th, 19th and 20th century German literature; archetypal criticism; genre criticsm. *Publ:* Auth, The German Verse Epic in the 19th and 20th Centuries, Martinus Nijhoff, 67; Hans Fallada: Humanist and Social Critic, Mouton, 70; Initiatory patterns and symbols in A Döblins Manas and H Kasack's Die Stadt hinter dem Strom, Ger Life & Lett, 71; Cosmology and quest in Novalis' Klingsohrs Märchen, Ger Rev, 74; Figurative language and its relation to Pestalozzi's pedagogic intentions in Lienhard und Gertrud, Ger Life & Lett, 76; Johann Heinrich Pestalozzi's Poetry and the dialectic between heaven and earth, In: Analecta Helvetica et Germanica Eine Festschrift Zu Ehren von Hermann Boeschenstein, Bouvier, 79; Gotthelf and Pestalozzi reconsidered, Mich Germanic Studies, 81; The polar identity of descent and ascent in Goethe's Faust, Ger Life & Lett, 82. *Mailing Add:* Dept of Lang Lit & Ling York Univ 4700 Keele St Downsview ON M3J 1P3 Can

SCHUESSLER, AXEL HARTMUT, b Potsdam, Ger, 40. CHINESE PHILOLOGY. *Educ:* Univ Munich, PhD(Chinese philol), 66. *Prof Exp:* Instr Ger, Wayne State Univ, 65-69; asst prof, 69-80, ASSOC PROF HIST, WARTBURG COL, 80- *Mem:* Asn Asian Studies; Soc Study Pre-Han China. *Res:* Chinese historical linguistics. *Publ:* Auth, The Yüeh Chüeh Shu, an early text about South China, J Am Orient Soc, Mid W Br, 69; Final-1 in archaic Chinese, J Chinese Ling, 74; Prefixes in archaic Chinese, Zeitschrift Deutschen Morgenländischen Gessellschaft, 74; Prefixes in Proto-Chinese, Wiesbaden, 76; On word order in early Zhour Chinese, J Chinese Ling, 82. *Mailing Add:* Dept of Hist Wartburg Col Waverly IA 50677

SCHULAK, HELEN S, b Donetsk, Russia, Apr 3, 37; US citizen; m 59; c 1. SLAVIC LANGUAGES & LITERATURES. *Educ:* Univ Toledo, BA, 58; Univ Mich, MA, 60; Univ Calif, Berkeley, PhD(Slavic), 67. *Prof Exp:* Assoc Russ, Univ Calif, Berkeley, 64-67; asst prof, 67-69, assoc prof, 69-80, PROF RUSS, CALIF STATE UNIV, HAYWARD, 80- *Mem:* Am Asn Advan Slavic Studies; MLA; Western Slavic Conf. *Mailing Add:* Dept of Foreign Lang & Lit Calif State Univ Hayward CA 94542

SCHULER, MARILYN VERENA, b Columbus Ohio. FRENCH LANGUAGE & LITERATURE. *Educ:* Ursuline Col, BA, 54; Univ Laval, MA, 67; Univ Ky, Lexington, PhD(French lang & lit), 74. *Prof Exp:* ASST PROF MOD LANG, UNIV LOUISVILLE, 76- *Concurrent Pos:* Ed, Perspectives Contemp Lit, 76 & 77; chairperson conf twentieth-century lit, 77, 78, 79. *Mem:* Am Asn Teachers Fr; Am Coun Teaching Foreign Lang; AAUP; MLA; Alliance Francaise. *Res:* French language and literature of SVIIth, XIXth and XXth centuries. *Publ:* Auth, La Guerre de Trois a eu lieu au XVIIe siecle, Papers Fr XVIIth-Century Lit, winter 77. *Mailing Add:* Dept of Mod Lang Univ of Louisville Louisville KY 40208

SCHULMAN, IVAN ALBERT, b Brooklyn, NY, Oct 4, 31; m 56; c 3. ROMANCE LANGUAGES & LITERATURE. *Educ:* Brooklyn Col, BA, 53; Univ Calif, Los Angeles, MA, 54, PhD(Hisp lang & lit), 59. *Prof Exp:* From asst prof to prof Romance lang, Wash Univ, 59-68, chmn dept, 65-68, prof Span-Am lit, 68-70; prof Span-Am lit & chmn dept Hisp lang & lit, State Univ NY Stony Brook, 70-73; grad res prof Latin Am lit, Univ Fla, 73-80; PROF SPAN, WAYNE STATE UNIV, 80- *Concurrent Pos:* Res grant-in-aid, Joint Comt Latin Am Studies, Soc Sci Res Coun, 60; vis asst prof, Univ Ore, 61-62; Guggenheim fel, 68-69; consult Educ Testing Serv, Grad Foreign Reading Exam Comt; chmn comt scholarly rels with Cuba, Latin Am Studies Asn; vpres & secy, Jose Marti Found; external examiner, Latin American Literature, Univ West Indies, Mona, 76-77; vis lectr, Univ Fed de Rio de Janeiro, 77; consult, Woodrow Wilson Found, Latin Am fel, 77 & 78; dir, Ctr

Latin Am Studies, Univ Fla, 77-80, actg dir, Int Studies & Prog, 77-78; co-dir, Nat Endowment for Humanities summer sem, Wayne State Univ, 82. *Mem:* Am Asn Teachers Span & Port; MLA; Midwest Mod Lang Asn; Inst Int Lit Iberoam (pres, 75-77, vpres, 77-79). *Res:* Modernism; stylistics; Cuban and Spanish American novel. *Publ:* Ed, Latin America in Its Literature, (transl, America Latina en su lieratura), Holmes & Meler, 80; Texto, lenguaje, sistema social, Viaje hacia lo desconocido, INTI, nos 10-11, 80; Cecilia Valdes, Biblioteca Ayacucho Caracas, 81; Una vision del modernismo, nota de lectura, Insula, 5/81; (with Evelyn Picon Garfield), Modernismo/Mondernida: Apostillas a la teoria de la Edad Moderna, In honor of Boyd G Carter, Univ Wyo Press, 81; Ismaelillo, Versos libres, sencillos de Jose Marti (in press); Un centenario y cuatro decadas: Dos revistas, Cuadernos Americanos (in prep); El arte de la Sangre nueva' y el Ismaelillo, Insula (in prep). *Mailing Add:* Wayne State Univ Detroit MI 48202

SCHULTE, HANS HERBERT, b Hannover, Ger, Feb 18, 35; m 63; c 2. GERMAN. *Educ:* Univ Munich, Staatsexamen, 63; Kultusministerium, Bayern, Assessor, 66; DrPhil, Augsburg, 78. *Prof Exp:* Asst prof Ger, Univ New Brunswick, 62-63; asst prof, 65-77, ASSOC PROF GER, MCMASTER UNIV, 77- *Concurrent Pos:* Co-ed, Mod Ger Studies, 78-; councillor, Ont Goethe Soc, 74-, prog chmn, 82-; ed, The McMaster Colloquium on Ger Lit, 80- *Mem:* MLA; Ont Goethe Soc; Deutsche Schillergesellschaft. *Res:* Eighteenth century literature, German and comparative; twentieth century German literature; hermeneutics. *Publ:* Auth, Zur Geschichte des Enthusiasmus im 18 Jahrhundert, Publ English Goethe Soc, 69; Kinderlieder bei Bertolt Brecht, Wirkendes Wort, 3/77; Fiktionales Denken und poetische Fiktion, Psychobiologie, 78; Ist Thomas Mann noch lebendig? Verständigungsschwierigk eines klass Autors mit s Publikum, Thomas Mass: ein Kolloquium, 78; ed, Intro to Thomas Mann, 78; Werke der Begeisterung: Das Schaffen F Schillers--Ursprung und Eigenaart, Bouvier, Bonn, 80; co-ed, Krit Diskussionsber, The Turn of the Century, 81; ed, Introd to The Art of Literary Translation, 82. *Mailing Add:* Dept of Ger McMaster Univ Hamilton ON L8S 4M1 Can

SCHULTE-SASSE, JOCHEN, b Salzgitter-Bad, Ger, July 12, 40; m 76; c 2. GERMAN, COMPARATIVE LITERATURE. *Educ:* Ruhr-Univ Bochum, Staatsexamen & Dr phil(Ger, medieval studies & philos), 68, Habilitation, 76. *Prof Exp:* Asst prof Ger, Univ Minn, Minneapolis, 68-69; Wiss asst Ger, Ruhr-Univ Bochum, 69-76, priv-dozent, 76-77; vis prof, Univ Siegen, 77-78 & 79-80; ASSOC PROF GER & COMP LIT, UNIV MINN, MINNEAPOLIS, 78- *Concurrent Pos:* Co-ed, Theory & Hist Lit & Hefte für kritische Literaturwissenschaft. *Mem:* MLA; Lessing Soc. *Res:* Eighteenth century; theory of literature; popular literature. *Publ:* Auth, Die Kritik an der Trivialliteratur seit der Aufklärung, Fink, Munich, 71 & 77; Literarische Wertung, Metzler, Stuttgart, 71 & 76; Lessing/Mendelssohn/Nicolai-Briefwechsel über das Trauerspiel, Winkler, Munich, 72; Literarische Struktur und historisch-sozialer Kontext, Schoeningh, Paderborn, 75; Karl Mays Amerika-Exotik und deutsche Wirklichkeit, In: Literatur für viele 2, Vandenhoeck, Göttingen, 76; coauth, Einführung in die Literaturwissenschaft, UTB, Stuttgart, 77; auth, Friedrich Nicolai, In: Deutsche Dichter des 18 Jahrhundert, Schmidt, Berlin, 77; Drama, In: Hansers Sozialgeschichte der deutschen Literatur 3, Hanser, Munich, 80. *Mailing Add:* Dept of Ger Univ of Minn Minneapolis MN 55455

SCHULTZ, WILLIAM RUDOLPH, b Kalispell, Mont, Dec 25, 23; m 49; c 2. CHINESE LANGUAGE & LITERATURE. *Educ:* Univ Wash, BA, 47; China Inst Am PhD(Chinese lang & lit), 55. *Prof Exp:* Asst prof Chinese lang & lit, 61-63; assoc prof orient studies, 63-68, head dept, 72-76, dir orient lang & area studies ctr, 68-76, PROF ORIENT STUDIES, UNIV ARIZ, 68-, DIR, 76- *Concurrent Pos:* Res supvr Chinese hist, Mod Chinese Res Proj, Univ Wash, 50-53; asst rep, Asian Found, Taiwan , 55-58, Singapore, 59-61; vis lectr, Taiwan Prov Norm Univ, 57-58; mem ed bd, Lit E & W, 67-71, bk rev ed, 71-; consult, US Off Educ, 69-71; Soc Sci Res Coun res fel, 70-71. *Honors & Awards:* Pollard Mem Prize, Univ Wash, 53. *Mem:* Am Orient Soc; Asn Asian Studies; MLA; Am Coun Teaching Foreign Lang; Chinese Lang Teachers Asn. *Res:* Classical and modern Chinese literature and history. *Publ:* Contribr, Encycl Britannica, 61, Biographical dictionary of Republican China (4 vols), Columbia Univ, 67-71 & The Taiping Rebellion (3 vols), Univ Wash, 71; ed, China sect, Twayne World Auth Ser, 71- *Mailing Add:* Dept of Orient Studies Univ of Ariz Tucson AZ 85721

SCHULTZE, SYDNEY PATTERSON, b Louisville, Ky, Jan 20, 43; m 74; c 2. RUSSIAN LANGUAGE & LITERATURE. *Educ:* Univ Louisville, BA, 65; Ind Univ, MA, 68, PhD (Slavic lang & lit), 74. *Prof Exp:* ASSOC PROF RUSS, UNIV LOUISVILLE, 70- *Mem:* Am Asn Advan Salvic Studies; Am Asn Teachers Slavic & EEurop Lang. *Res:* Leo Tolstoy; 19th century Russian prose; early 20th century Russian prose. *Publ:* Auth, Notes on imagery and motifs in Anna Karenina, 71, Sexism in Russian grammars, 74, The chapter in Anna Karenina, 74 & The epigraphs in White Guard, 78, Russ Lit Triquart; Katayev, Korolenko & Slonimsky, In: Columbia Dictionary of Modern European Literature, 80; ed, Rudnitsky's Meyerhold the Director, 81 & auth, The Structure of Anna Karenina, 82, Ardis. *Mailing Add:* Dept of Mod Lang Univ of Louisville Louisville KY 40292

SCHULZ, MURIEL RIPLEY, b Pittsburgh, Pa, Nov 26, 28; m 52; c 3. ENGLISH, LINGUISTICS. *Educ:* Tulane Univ, BA, 59, MA, 61; Univ Southern Calif, MA, 67, PhD(ling), 73. *Prof Exp:* Lectr English, Calif State Univ, Los Angeles, 72-73; asst prof, 73-75, assoc prof, 75-80, PROF ENGLISH, CALIF STATE UNIV, FULLERTON, 81- *Concurrent Pos:* Co-chairperson sex and language prog, Ninth World Cong Ling, Uppsala, Sweden, 78; Nat Endowment for Humanities fel, 80-81; Rockefeller Found Scholar-in-Residence. *Mem:* MLA; Ling Soc Am; Am Dialect Soc. *Publ:* Auth, How sexist is Webster's Third?, Vis a Vis, 12/74; The Semantic derogation of woman, sex and language, In: Difference & Dominance, Newbury, 75; How serious is sex bias in English, Col Compos & Commun, 5/75; Rape is a four-letter word, 6/75 & Language is nobody's enemy, 10/75, ETC; A syle of one's own, women's language and style, Lang & Style, 78; Mother tongue, Osnabrucker Beitrage zur Sprachtheorie, 79. *Mailing Add:* Dept of English Calif State Univ Fullerton CA 92634

SCHULZ, RENATE ADELE-WOLF, b Lohr Main, Ger, Feb 24, 40; US citizen. FOREIGN LANGUAGE EDUCATION, GERMAN. *Educ:* Mankato State Col, BS, 62; Univ Colo, MA, 67; Ohio State Univ, PhD(foreign lang educ), 74. *Prof Exp:* Asst prof Ger, Otterbein Col, 74-76; asst prof French & Ger, State Univ NY Col Buffalo, 76-77; asst prof, Univ Ark, Fayetteville, 77-79; assoc prof, 79-82, PROF GER, UNIV ARIZ, 82- *Mem:* Am Coun Teaching Foreign Lang; MLA; Am Asn Teachers Ger; Am Asn Teachers Fr; Am Asn Appl Ling. *Res:* Foreign language testing, methodology and psycholinguistics. *Publ:* Auth, The Newspaper: A Reflection of Life-Styles in the French-Speaking World, 75, coauth, Evaluating cultural learnings, In: The Culture Revolution, 75, Free to communicate, In: Perspective: A New Freedom, 75, ed, Teaching for Communication in the Foreign Language Classroom, 76 & Personalizing Foreign Language Instruction: Learning Styles and Teaching Options, 77, Nat Textbk; auth, Discrete-point versus simulated communication testing in foreign languages, Mod Lang J, 3/77; coauth, Lesen, Lachen, Lernen, Holt, 78; auth, Back to basics in the foreign language classroom?, Foreign Lang Annals, 10/78. *Mailing Add:* Dept of German Univ of Az Tucson AZ 85721

SCHULZ, SIEGRIED A, b Lengainen, Ger, Feb 15, 25. GERMAN, COMPARATIVE PHILOLOGY. *Educ:* Univ Berne, PhD(compt philol), 51. *Prof Exp:* Lectr Ger, Ministry Defence, New Delhi, India, 52-55; instr Ger & French, Univ Md, 55-56; from instr to assoc prof Ger lang & lit, 56-71; chmn dept, 69-73, PROF GER & COMP PHILOL, CATH UNIV AM, 71- *Concurrent Pos:* Fac res fel, Am Inst Indian Studies, India, 64-65. *Mem:* MLA; Am Orient Soc; Am Asn Teachers Ger. *Res:* German philology; comparative philology and literature. *Publ:* Auth, Die Wurzel peith-(pith) im Ält Griech, Paulus, Freiburg, 52; Ein feste Burg ist unser Gott: Luther's treatment of the 46th Psalm, Colloquia Germanica, 69; A Hindu classic retold: Aubrey Menen's Ramayana satire, Lit East & West, 71; Premchand's novel Godan: Echoes of Charles Dickens in an Indian setting, In: Studies in Honor of Tatiana Fotitch, Cath Univ Am, 72. *Mailing Add:* Dept of Mod Lang & Lit Cath Univ of Am Washington DC 20064

SCHULZ-BEHREND, GEORGE, b Greifswald, Ger, Feb 12, 13; m; c 2. GERMANIC LANGUAGES. *Educ:* Univ Colo, AB, 35, AM, 36; State Univ Iowa, PhD, 44. *Prof Exp:* Instr English & Ger, Elkader Jr Col, 38-42; instr Ger, State Univ Iowa, 43-44, instr English, 44-46; from instr to assoc prof, 46-64, PROF GERMANIC LANG, UNIV TEX, AUSTIN, 64- *Concurrent Pos:* Res fel & guest prof, Free Univ Berlin, 63; guest prof, Univ Marburg, 66; W Germany govt grant, 57. *Mem:* MLA; Am Asn Teachers Ger; S Cent Mod Lang Asn; Renaissance Soc Am; Am Soc Ger Lit 16th & 17th Centuries. *Res:* German literature of the 17th century; modern German literature; Texana Germanica. *Publ:* Auth, John Barclay and Martin Opitz, PMLA, 55; Kafka's Ein Bericht für eine Akademie: An interpretation, Monatshefte, 63; transl, Simplicius Simplicissimus, Bobbs, 64; ed, Martin Opitz, Gesammelte Werke (5 vols), Hiersemann, Stuttgart, Vol I, 68, Vol III, 70 & Vol II, 74; The German Baroque, Univ Tex, 72; auth, Der englisch-redende Simplicissimus, Argenis, 77; co-ed, Vistas and Vectors, Rehder Mem, Univ Tex, 79. *Mailing Add:* Dept German Lang Univ of Tex Austin TX 78712

SCHULZE, LEONARD GENE, b Schulenburg, Tex, Jan 24, 47; m 68. COMPARATIVE LITERATURE, GERMAN. *Educ:* Univ Tex, Austin, BA, 69; Johns Hopkins Univ, MA, 72; Yale Univ, MPhil, 74, PhD(compt lit), 77. *Prof Exp:* Asst prof Ger, US Mil Acad, 74-78; ASST PROF GER, UNIV TEX, AUSTIN, 78- *Mem:* MLA; SCent Mod Lang Asn; SCent Soc 18th Century Studies; Am Coun Teaching Foreign Lang; NAm Nietzsche Soc. *Res:* Literary theory and hermeneutics; rhetoric and semiotics; European romanticism, especially German, English and French. *Publ:* Alkemene's Ominous Ach! On Bastards, Beautiful Souls, and the Spirit in Heinrich von Kleist, Studies in Roamnticism, summer 80; Andreas-Salome, Lou, In: Columbia Dict Mod Europ Lit, Columbia Univ Press, 80; The Romantic Movement: A Selective and Critical Bibliography for 1979, Garland, 80. *Mailing Add:* Dept of Ger Lang Univ of Tex Austin TX 78712

SCHUMAN, VERNE BRINSON, b Rolla, Mo, July 14, 02; m 33; c 1. GREEK PAPYRI. *Educ:* William Jewell Col, AB, 24; Ind Univ, AM, 26; Univ Mich, PhD(Greek), 37. *Prof Exp:* Instr Latin & Greek, Ind Univ, 26-27; mem staff, Near East Res, Fayoum, Egypt, Univ Mich, 27-31; asst prof Latin & Greek, 35-42, assoc prof Latin, 42-52, prof, 52-67, EMER PROF, IND UNIV, 67- *Mem:* Am Philos Asn; Am Asn Papyrologists; Asn Int Papyrologues; Fondation Egyptologique Reine Elisabeth. *Res:* Egyptian coinage in Ptolemaic and Roman Periods. *Publ:* Coauth, Tax Rolls from Karanis, Univ Mich Press, 36; contribr, Two unpublished inscriptions from the South Temple area of Karanis, Hesperia, Vol 16, 47; The basis of accounting practices in the Karanis tax rolls, Aegyptus, 12/52; A second century treatise on Egyptian priests and temples, Harvard Theol Rev, 7/60; Light on taxes in kind in Roman Egypt, Proc IX Int Cong Papyrology, 61; A Greek inscription from Karanis, Chronique d'Egypte, No 73, 62; Papyri Gen inventory 108 and Papyri Oslo 111, Rech Papyrologie, Vol XXXVI, 67; Washington University Papyri, Scholars Press, 80. *Mailing Add:* 1304 E Second Bloomington IN 47401

SCHÜRER, ERNST IGNATZ, b Löningen, Ger, Sept 13, 33; US citizen; m 64; c 3. GERMANIC LANGUAGES & LITERATURES. *Educ:* Univ Tex, Austin, BA, 60; Yale Univ, MA, 62, PhD(Ger), 65. *Prof Exp:* From instr to assoc prof Ger lang & lit, Yale Univ, 65-73, from dir under grad studies to dir grad studies, 69-73; prof Ger, Univ Fla, 73-78, chmn dept Ger & Slavic lang & lit, 77-78; PROF GER & HEAD DEPT, PA STATE UNIV, 78- *Concurrent Pos:* Morse fel, Yale Univ, 68-69; Alexander von Humboldt fels, 73, 76-77. *Mem:* MLA; Am Coun Teaching Foreign Lang; Asn Teachers Ger; Int Ver für Ger Sprach-und Literaturwissenschaft; Int Brecht Soc. *Res:* German expressionism; German and European drama; literature in exile. *Publ:* Auth, Die nachexpressionistische Komödie, In: Die deutsche Literatur der Weimarer Republik, 74, Georg Kaiser, Von morgens bis mitternachts, Erläuterungen und Dokumente, 75, ed, Georg Kaiser, Nebeneinander Volksstück 1923 in fünf Akten, 78, Carl Sternheim Tabula rasa Ein Schauspiel, 78 & Ernst Toller Hoppla, wir leben, Ein Vorspiel und fünf Akte,

80, Philipp Reclam jun Stuttgart; auth, Brochs Die Entsühnung und das Drama der Neuen Sachlichkeit, In: Modern Austrian Literature, Vol 13, No 4 & George Kaiser und die Neue Sachlichkeit (1922-1932): Themen, Tendenzen und Formen, In: George Kaiser Symposium, 80, Agora Verlag, Berlin; Die Gas-Dramen, In: George Kaiser, Ernst Klett, Stuttgart, 80. *Mailing Add:* Dept of Ger Pa State Univ S 323 Burrowes Building University Park PA 16802

SCHURFRANZ, ROBERT LEWIS, b Hamilton, Ohio, Apr 5, 29; m 55. PHILOLOGY. *Educ:* Miami Univ, BA, 50; Univ NC, MA, 54, PhD, 60. *Prof Exp:* Asst prof French, Univ Ark, 57-68; ASSOC PROF FRENCH & ITAL, LA STATE UNIV, BATON ROUGE, 68- *Mem:* MLA; Am Asn Teachers Fr. *Mailing Add:* Dept of French La State Univ Baton Rouge LA 70803

SCHUSTER, EDWARD JAMES, b Milwaukee, Wis, Mar 25, 08; m 35; c 2. MODERN FOREIGN LANGUAGES, HISTORY. *Educ:* Univ Mich, AB, 31; Univ Minn, PhD, 50. *Prof Exp:* Asst prof Span & Ger, St Thomas Col, 46-51 & St Louis Univ, 51-55; prof mod foreign lang & head dept, Iowa Wesleyan Col, 55-56; prof Span & Ger, 56-73, chmn div humanities, 72-73, EMER PROF MOD FOREIGN LANG, LORAS COL, 74- *Concurrent Pos:* Contrib ed, Social Justice Rev, 60-; assoc mem, Ctr Latin Am Studies, Univ Wis-Milwaukee, 72-73; lectr mod foreign lang, Northern Ariz Univ, 74-77. *Mem:* NCent Coun Latin Americanists (pres, 68-69); MLA. *Res:* Latin American culture and civilization; Spanish and German literatures; human rights in today's world. *Publ:* Auth, Spanish Literature in Today's World, Iowa English Yearbk, 60; Meister Eckhart as Christian Existentialist, Ky Foreign Lang Rev, fall 63; A Time of Change: Impacts of Science and Technology, 64-67, Law and the New Barbarians, 7-8/67, The Church and Social Revolution in Mexico, 7-8/70, The Liberal Arts Today, 71-72 & Energy, Ecology, and the Full Life, 5/74, Social Justice Rev; Human Rights Today: Evolution or Revolution?, Philos Libr, 81. *Mailing Add:* 1415 Parkway Dubuque IA 52001

SCHUSTER, INGRID HANNA, b Munich, Ger, Apr 17, 40. GERMAN & COMPARATIVE LITERATURE. *Educ:* Univ Munich, PhD(Japanology), 65. *Prof Exp:* Res fel Japanology, Univ Munich, 65-66 & Univ Bochum, 66-67; asst prof, 67-72, ASSOC PROF GER, McGILL UNIV, 72- *Concurrent Pos:* Can Coun leave fel, 75-76; leave fel, Social Sci & Humanities Res Coun Can, 80-81. *Mem:* Am Asn Teachers Ger; Can Asn Univ Teachers Ger; Can Comp Lit Asn; Theodor-Storm-Gesellschaft; MLA. *Res:* German literature in the 19th and 20th century; Japanese literature; comparative literature. *Publ:* Auth, Kamada Ryuko und seine Stellung in der Shingaku, Otto Harrassowitz, 67; Theodor Storm Die zeitkritische Dimension seiner Novellen, Bouvier, 71; Die ersten Wirkungen des Japanischen Theaters in Deutschland, Arcadia, 72; co-ed, Alfred Doeblin im Spiegel der zeitgenoessischen Kritik, 73 & China und Japan in der deutschen Literatur 1890-1925, 77, Francke; auth, Akribie und Symbolik in den Romananfängen Fontanes, In: Formen realistischer Erzählkunst, Sherwood Press Agencies, 79; ed, Zu Alfred Doeblin, Interpretationen, Klett, 80; auth, Die Schlangenfrau: Variationen eines chinesischen Motivs bei Herman Grimm und Gottfried Keller, Seminar, 82. *Mailing Add:* Dept of Ger McGill Univ 1001 Sherbrooke W Montreal PQ H3A 1G5 Can

SCHUSTER, MARILYN RUTH, b Washington, DC, Sept 23, 43. FRENCH, WOMEN'S STUDIES. *Educ:* Mills Col, BA, 65; Yale Univ, MPhil, 68, PhD(French), 73. *Prof Exp:* Instr French, Fordham Univ, 70-71; asst prof, 71-78, ASSOC PROF LANG & LIT & FRENCH, SMITH COL, 78- *Concurrent Pos:* Reader, Advan Placement Exam, Educ Testing Serv, 77- *Mem:* MLA; NE Mod Lang Asn. *Res:* Contemporary fiction by women in France, England, USA and Canada. *Publ:* Auth, Blind spots, New Current, 2/77; contribr, Fiction et folie dans l'oeuvre de Marguerite Duras, In: Ehrique et Esthetique dans la Litterature Francaise du XX siecle, Stanford Univ, spring 78; translr, var chaps in: Homosexualities and French Literature, Cornell Univ, 79; auth, L'Ironie dans les Illuminations: voix empruntces et codes litteraires, Nineteenth Century Fr Studies, Vol VIII, No 3-4, 80. *Mailing Add:* Smith Col Wright Hall Northampton MA 01063

SCHUTTE, LILITH EVA, b Berlin, Ger; US citizen. GERMAN. *Educ:* Ariz State Univ, BA, 67, MA, 69; Univ Ore, PhD(Ger), 73. *Prof Exp:* PROF GER, AM GRAD SCH INT MGT, 71- *Mem:* MLA; Am Asn Teachers Ger; Western Asn Ger Studies. *Res:* German culture and civilization. *Mailing Add:* Am Grad Sch of Int Mgt Glendale AZ 85306

SCHUTZ, ALBERT J, b Mishawaka, Ind, Aug 9, 36. LINGUISTICS. *Educ:* Purdue Univ, BS, 58; Cornell Univ, PhD, 62. *Prof Exp:* From asst prof to assoc prof, 62-72, PROF LING, UNIV HAWAII, MANOA, 72- *Concurrent Pos:* Prin investr, NSF grant, Nguna, New Hebrides lexicography, 69-70; dir, Fijian dictionary proj, 71-79; prin investr, Nat Endowment for Humanities res grant, 78-80. *Mem:* Ling Soc Am; Polynesian Soc. *Res:* Malayo-Polynesian linguistics; lexicography. *Publ:* Coauth, Spoken Fijian, Univ Hawaii, 71; auth, The Languages of Fiji, Clarendon, Oxford, 72; Say it in Fijian, Pac Publ, Sydney, 72; ed, The Diaries and Correspondence of David Cargill, 1832-1843, Australian Nat Univ, 77; auth, Suva: A History and Guide, Pac Publ, 78; ed, Fijian Language Studies: Borrowing and Pidginization, Fiji Mus, 78; auth, Fijian Grammar for Teachers of Fijian, Univ SPac, Suva, 79; co-ed, David Cargill's Fijian Grammar, Fiji Mus, 80. *Mailing Add:* Dept of Ling Univ of Hawaii Manoa 1890 East-West Rd Honolulu HI 96822

SCHUTZ, HERBERT, b Feb 25, 37; Can citizen. GERMAN LANGUAGE & LITERATURE. *Educ:* Univ Toronto, BA, MA, 65, PhD(Ger), 68. *Prof Exp:* Teacher sec sch French, Ger, hist & music, Toronto Bd of Educ, 61-65; asst head dept moderns, 65-66; asst prof, 68-71, ASSOC PROF GER, BROCK UNIV, 71- *Mem:* Can Asn Teachers Ger; Am Asn Teachers Ger; Lessing Soc; Am Soc Eighteenth Century Studies. *Res:* Eighteenth century German literature and thought; German cultural history; language teaching methodology. *Publ:* Auth, The theme of anonymity in the work of Hermann Kasack, Revue des Langues Vivantes, 71; coauth, Deutsch für Kanadier Pts I and II, Brock Univ, 71 & rev ed, 73; auth, The Role of the Critical Intellect in the Creative Writer's Work, H Lang Bern/Frankfurt-M, 72; Friedrich Gerstäcker's image of the German immigrant in Amerika, Ger Am Studies, 72; Eighteenth century German pedagogy and Lessing, Revue des Langues Vivantes, 73-74; The need for diversification in the teaching of German, Ont Mod Lang Rev, 74; coauth, transl of J Fernau, Genies der Deutschen as Farewell to Genius, Brock Univ, 74 & rev ed, 76. *Mailing Add:* Dept of Germanic & Slavic Studies Brock Univ St Catharines ON L2S 3A1 Can

SCHWARTZ, ARTHUR M, b New York, NY, Aug 31, 30; m 52; c 4. LINGUISTICS. *Educ:* City Col New York, BSS, 51; Lehigh Univ, MA, 58; Univ Wis, PhD(English), 61. *Prof Exp:* Asst prof English, Univ Mo, 61-65; PROF LING, UNIV CALIF, SANTA BARBARA, 67- *Concurrent Pos:* Nat Inst Ment Health res training fel, Mass Inst Technol, 65-67. *Mem:* Int Ling Asn; Ling Soc Am. *Res:* Syntactic theory; history of English. *Publ:* Auth, General aspects of relative clause formation, In: Working Papers in Linguistic Universals, Stanford Univ, 71; Constraints on movement transformations, J Ling, 72; The VP-constituent of SVO languages, In: Syntax and Semantics, Seminar Press, 72. *Mailing Add:* Dept of Ling Univ of Calif Santa Barbara CA 93106

SCHWARTZ, GARY STEPHEN, b Atlanta, Ga, Jan 11, 43; m 68. CLASSICS, ENGLISH. *Educ:* Columbia Univ, AB, 65, PhD(class philol), 72; Cambridge Univ, BA, 67, MA, 70. *Prof Exp:* Lectr classics, 69-72, asst prof, 72-76, ASSOC PROF CLASSICS & ENGLISH, HERBERT H LEHMAN COL, 76- *Concurrent Pos:* Lectr lit & compos, Sch Continuing Educ, New York Univ, 78-; coordr, Lehman Scholars Prog, Herbert H Lehman Col, 80- *Mem:* Am Philol Asn. *Res:* Homeric poetry; the ancient novel; modern American and English poetry. *Publ:* Auth, The Kopros motif: Variations on a theme in The Odyssey, Rev Studi Classici, Turin, Italy, 75; ed, Eight Essays in Classical Humanities, Am Univ Press, 75; auth, Apulei metamorphoseon 1.2: Desultoriae scientiae, Latomus, Belgium, 80; Hesiod Theogony 175: Harpein karcharodonta--why a sickle, Rev Studi Classici, Turin, Italy, 80; coauth, Index Locurim zu Kühner-Stegmann Grammatik der Lateinischen Sprache, Wiss Buchges, Darmstadt, Ger, 80. *Mailing Add:* Dept of Class, Orient, Ger & Slavic Lang Herbert H Lehman Col Bronx NY 10468

SCHWARTZ, HENRY CHARLES, b Toledo, Ohio, July 6, 15. ROMANCE LANGUAGES. *Educ:* Univ Toledo, AB, 37; Univ Mich, AM, 38, PhD(Romance lang), 54. *Prof Exp:* Prof English, Lycee Petion, Port-au-Prince, Haiti, 43-44; teacher, US Bi-Nat Ctrs, Lima, Peru, 44-45; dir courses, Santiago, Chile, 46 & Bahia, Brazil, 47-48; fel & lectr French & Span, Univ Mich, 49-51; prof mod lang & world lit, Ark Col, 54-59; prof mod lang, Marietta Col, 59-80; RETIRED. *Concurrent Pos:* Fulbright exchange teacher, France, 56-57; reviewer Choice; interpreter, State Dept Lang Serv; mem screening comt nat awards, Fulbright-Hays Found, Am Repubs, 74 & 77; lit transl, 80- *Mem:* MLA; Am Asn Teachers Fr; Am Asn Teachers Span & Port. *Res:* Mexican popular speech; the secular works of Gabriel Miro. *Mailing Add:* Dept of Mod Lang Marietta Col Marietta OH 45750

SCHWARTZ, JEROME, b New York, NY, Feb 10, 35; m 59; c 2. FRENCH LITERATURE. *Educ:* Columbia Univ, BA, 56, MA, 60, PhD(French), 65. *Prof Exp:* Asst English, Lycee Henri IV, Paris, 56-57; instr French, Columbia Col, Columbia Univ, 60-65; asst prof, 65-68, dir, Univ Prog in France, 70-71, ASSOC PROF FRENCH, UNIV PITTSBURGH, 68- *Mem:* MLA. *Res:* Sixteenth and 18th century French literature. *Publ:* Auth, Diderot and Montaigne: The Essais and the shaping of Diderot's humanism, Librairie Droz, 66; The ambiguous augury in Ronsard's sonnet Avant le temp . . ., L'Esprit Createur, 70; Gargantua's device and the Abbey of Theleme: A study in Rabelais's iconography, Yale Fr Studies, 73; Panurge's impact on Pantagruel, Romanic Rev, 76; contribr, La conscience d'un homme . . ., Donald Frame Festschrift (French Forum), 77; auth, Scatology and Eschatology in Gargantua's androgyne device, Etudes Rabelaisiennes, 78. *Mailing Add:* Dept of French & Ital Univ of Pittsburgh Pittsburgh PA 15260

SCHWARTZ, KESSEL, b Kansas City, Mo, Mar 19, 20; m 47; c 4. SPANISH. *Educ:* Univ Mo, BA, 40, MA, 41; Columbia Univ, PhD(Span Am lit), 53. *Prof Exp:* Dir cult ctr, US Dept State, Quito, Ecuador, 46-48; instr Span, Hofstra Col, 48-49 & Hamilton Col, 49-51; instr Span & Span lit, Colby Col, 51-53; asst prof Romance lang, Univ Vt, 53-57; prof Span & chmn dept, Univ Ark, 57-62; chmn dept, 62-64, PROF MOD LANG, UNIV MIAMI, 62-, CHMN DEPT, 74- *Concurrent Pos:* Assoc ed, Hispania, 66-; vis prof, Univ NC, Chapel Hill, 66. *Honors & Awards:* Outstanding Acad Bk Award, Am Asn Cols & Res Lebr, 72. *Mem:* Am Asn Teachers Span & Port; Asn Int Hispanistas; Asn Pensamiento Hisp. *Res:* Spanish American literature; contemporary Spanish literature, comparative Romance literature. *Publ:* Coauth, A New Anthology of Spanish Literature, La State Univ, 67; auth, Introduction to Modern Spanish Literature, 68, Juan Goytisolo, 70 & Vicente Aleixandre, 70, Twayne; The Meaning of Existence in Contemporary Hispanic Literature, 70 & A New History of Spanish American Fiction (2 vols), 72, Univ Miami; chap, In: The Cry of Home, Univ Tenn, 72;; The Poetry of Vicente Aleixandre, In: New Critical Approaches, New York, 81. *Mailing Add:* Dept Foreign Lang & Lit Univ of Miami Coral Gables FL 33124

SCHWARTZ, LEON, b Boston, Mass, Aug 22, 22; m 49; c 2. FRENCH LITERATURE & LANGUAGE. *Educ:* Univ Calif, Los Angeles, AB, 48; Inst Phonetique, Univ Paris, Dipl, 49; Univ Southern Calif, MA, 50, PhD, 62. *Prof Exp:* Teacher Span, jr & sr high sch, Redlands Calif, 51-59; from asst prof to assoc prof foreign lang, 59-68, chmn dept foreign lang & lit, 70-73, PROF FRENCH LIT & LANG, CALIF STATE UNIV, LOS ANGELES, 68- *Concurrent Pos:* NDEA consult, Calif State Dept Elem Educ, 62-63; ed comt, guide teaching Span - grade 6, Calif State Dept Educ, 64. *Honors & Awards:* Outstanding prof award, Calif State Univ, Los Angeles, 75-76. *Mem:* Am Asn Teachers Fr; Am Soc 18th Century Studies; West Soc 18th century studies. *Res:* Eighteenth century French literature; modern methods of teaching foreign language. *Publ:* Auth, Melchior Grimm on War and Peace, 5/67 & The other M's: manipulation and mastery, 10/69, Fr Rev; Jacques le fataliste and Diderot's equine symbolism, Diderot Studies, 73; L'Image de L'araignee dans Le Reve de d'Alembert de Diderot, Romance Notes, winter 73; Restif de la Bretonne and Nerval's Artemis, Romance Notes, winter 80; Diedrot and the Jews, Fairleigh Dickinson Univ Press, 81. *Mailing Add:* 3022 N Santa Rosa Altadena CA 91001

SCHWARTZ, LUCY MCCALLUM, b Birmingham, Ala, Aug 14, 44; m 69. MODERN FRENCH LITERATURE. *Educ:* Salem Col, NC, BA, 66; Harvard Univ, MA, 67, PhD(French), 72. *Prof Exp:* Teacher French, St Margaret's Sch, Waterbury, Conn, 70-71; asst prof, 72-77, ASSOC PROF FRENCH, UNIV NDAK, 77- *Concurrent Pos:* Nat Endowment for Humanities summer sem grant, 77; develop leave grant, Univ NDak, 78-79. *Mem:* MLA; Am Asn Teachers Fr; Am Coun Teachers Foreign Lang; AAUP. *Res:* Female French novelists; 20th century French novel and 19th century French poetry; women's studies. *Publ:* Auth, Sainte-Beuve's concept of the elegy, Proc Ling Circle Man & NDak, 73; A low budget FLES experiment, Mod Lang J, 3/74; Image of women in novels of Mme de Souza, Mich Papers Women's Studies, 6/74; Female characters of Francois Mauriac, ERIC, 10/74; Social revolt in the novels of Mme de Duras, NDak Quart, 9/75; Encore heureux qu'on va vers l'ete by Christiane Rochefort, Int Fiction Rev, 7/76; Persausion and resistance: Human relations in George Sand's novels Indiana and Lelia, George Sand Studies II, 82; George Sand, Critical Survey of Long Fiction, 82. *Mailing Add:* Dept of Mod & Class Lang Univ of NDak Grand Forks ND 58202

SCHWARTZ, PAUL JACOB, b Stamford, Conn, Apr 11, 45; m 69. FRENCH LITERATURE. *Educ:* Harvard Univ, BA, 67; Yale Univ, PhD(Fr), 71. *Prof Exp:* Asst prof, 71-75, assoc prof, 75-82, PROF FRENCH, UNIV NDAK, 82-, CHMN DEPT MOD & CLASS LANG, 74- *Concurrent Pos:* Resident dir, Sweet Briar Jr year in France prog, 78-79. *Mem:* MLA; Am Asn Teachers Fr. *Res:* Nineteenth century French poetry and French novel: 20th century French novel. *Publ:* Auth, Mallarme's Les noces d'herodiade, 19th Century Fr Studies, 11/72; Life and death in the mud: A study of Beckett's Comment C'est, Int Fiction Rev, 1/75; The triumph of parody and pun over San-Antonio's literary aspirations, Int Fiction Rev, 6/80; Why students drop: A first-hand report, Foreign Lang Ann, 5/81. *Mailing Add:* Dept of Mod & Class Lang Univ of NDak Grand Forks ND 58202

SCHWARTZ, STUART B, Colonial Latin America. See Vol I

SCHWARZ, EGON, b Vienna, Austria, Aug 8, 22; nat US; m 50; c 2. GERMAN. *Educ:* Ohio State Univ, BA, 50, MA, 51; Univ Wash, PhD, 54. *Prof Exp:* Instr Ger, Otterbein Col, 49-51; instr, Univ Washington, 51-54; from instr to asst prof, Harvard Univ, 54-61; assoc prof Ger, Wash Univ, 61-62; guest prof, Univ Hamburg, 62-63; prof Ger, 63-76, ROSA MAY DISTINGUISHED UNIV PROF HUMANITIES, WASHINGTON UNIV, 76- *Concurrent Pos:* Guggenheim fel, 57-58; Fulbright & Am Coun Learned Soc fels, 62-63; vis prof Ger, Univ Calif, Berkeley, 64-65; Nat Endowment for Humanities fel, 70-71; vis prof, Univ Calif, Irvine, 77; fel, Coun Humanities, Princeton Univ, 79. *Mem:* MLA; Am Asn Teachers Ger. *Res:* Modern German and comparative literature; German literature of the 19th and 20th centuries; literature and society. *Publ:* Coauth, On Four Modern Humanists, Princeton Univ, 70; auth, Joseph von Eichendorff, Twayne, 72; ed, Das verschluckte Schluchzen, 72, co-ed, Exil und innere Emigration, 73, auth, Keine Zeit für Eichendorff, An Autobiography, 79, ed, Hermann Heses Steppenwolf, Wirkungsgeschichtliche Zeugnisse & co-ed, Deutsche Literatur in der Bundesrepublik seit 1965, 80, Athenäum; Poetry and Politics in the Works of Rainer Maria Rilke, Ungar, 81. *Mailing Add:* 1036 Oakland Ave St Louis MO 63122

SCHWARZ, HANS-GÜNTHER, b Ger, Aug 13, 45. GERMAN & COMPARATIVE LITERATURE. *Educ:* Univ Munich, MA, 69; McGill Univ, PhD, 72. *Prof Exp:* asst prof, 72-78, ASSOC PROF GER, DALHOUSIE UNIV, 78- *Mem:* Can Asn Univ Teachers Ger; Can Comp Lit Asn; Deutsch Shakespeare Ges W; Deutsch Ges für Theatergeschichte. *Res:* Drama; German-English literary relations; literature and visual arts. *Publ:* Auth, Lenz und Shakespare, In: Deutsch Shakespeare Ges Jahrbuch, 71 & Shakespeare Jahrbuch, 72; Das stumme Zeichen, Bouvier, Bonn, 74; Lenz Shakespeare-Arbeiten, Reclam, Stuttgart, 74; Die metapher im drama, In: Kommunikative Metaphorik, Hrsg vonHolger Pausch, Bouvier, Bonn, 75; Lenz, Herder und die ästhetisch-poetologischen Folgen, In: Festschrift Rolf Badenhausen, Nohl, Munich, 77; Carpets from the Orient, Dalhousie Art Gallery, 77; Dumb significants, In: English and American Studies in German, A Suppl to Anglia, Niemeyer, Tübingen, 76; Die Ästhetik des Persischen Teppichs, Vol 3, No 2. *Mailing Add:* Dept of Ger Dalhousie Univ Halifax NS B3H 3J5 Can

SCHWARZ, MARTIN, b Halle, Ger, June 17, 31; US citizen. ROMANCE LANGUAGES, FRENCH LITERATURE. *Educ:* Univ Louisville, BA, 55; Washington Univ, MA, 57; Univ Mich, PhD, 63. *Prof Exp:* From instr to asst prof French, Univ Mich, Ann Arbor, 62-69; assoc prof, Rice Univ, 69-71; prof French & head dept, Univ Tulsa, 71-81; PROF FRENCH & CHMN DEPT, EAST CAROLINA UNIV, 81- *Concurrent Pos:* Horace H Rackham grant, 66. *Honors & Awards:* Chevalier, Palmes Academiques, 78. *Mem:* MLA; Am Asn Teachers Fr. *Res:* French 19th and 20th century literature. *Publ:* Auth, O Mirbeau et l'affaire Dreyfus, Fr Rev, 12/65; Octave Mirbeau: vie et oeuvre, Mouton, The Hague, 66; ed, Variete du conte francais, Holt, 71; auth, Prosper Merimee: Nouvelliste ou conteur?, Rice Univ Studies, 71. *Mailing Add:* Fac of Lett Univ of Tulsa Tulsa OK 74104

SCHWARZ, WILHELM JOHANNES, b Iba, Ger, Dec 25, 29; Can citizen. GERMAN LITERATURE. *Educ:* Univ Western Ont, BA, 62, MA, 63; McGill Univ, PhD(Ger lit), 65. *Prof Exp:* Asst prof, Mem Univ, 65-67; asst prof, 67-69, assoc prof, 69-75, dir, 71-73, PROF GER LIT, UNIV LAVAL, 75-, DIR, SUMMER SCH, 80- *Concurrent Pos:* Dir, Ger Can Acad Exchange Asn, 70-76; vis prof, Univ Denver, 76-77. *Res:* The German novel after 1945. *Publ:* Auth, Der Erazähler Heinrich Böll, Francke Verlag, Bern & Munich, 67; Heinrich Böll, In: Christliche Dichter der Gegenwart, Francke Verlag, 68; Der Erzähler Günter Grass, 69 & Der Erzähler Uwe Johnson, 70, Francke Verlag, Bern & Munich; Mensch und Welt, Blaisdell Publ Co, 70; Der Erzähler Martin Walser, 71 & Der Erzähler Siegfried Lenz, 74, Francke Verlag, Bern & Munich; War and the Mind of Germany, Herbert Lang Verlag, Bern, 75. *Mailing Add:* Dept of Foreign Lit Univ of Laval Quebec PQ G1K 7P4 Can

SCHWEITZER, CHRISTOPH EUGEN, b Berlin, Ger, July 11, 22; nat US; m 49. GERMAN. *Educ:* Univ Wis, MA(Span), 49, MA(Ger), 50; Yale Univ, PhD(Ger), 54. *Prof Exp:* From instr to asst prof Ger, Yale Univ, 53-59; from assoc prof to prof, Bryn Mawr Col, 59-70; chmn dept, 70-75, PROF GER LANG, UNIV NC, CHAPEL HILL, 70- *Concurrent Pos:* Vis prof, Yale Univ, spring 80. *Mem:* MLA; Am Asn Teachers Ger; Goethe Ges; Lessing Soc; Soc for Ger-Am Studies. *Res:* German baroque and classical literature; early German-American literature. *Publ:* Auth, Die Erziehung Nathans, Monatshefte, 61; German literature, In: Collier's Encyclopedia, Collier-Macmillan, 62-; ed, A Goes' Das Löffelchen, Appleton, 68 & Lessing's Nathan der Weise, McGraw, 70; auth, Goethes Egmont in heutiger Sicht, Unterrichtspraxis, 71; coauth, The Present Status of Conrad Beissel-Ephrata Research, Monatschefte, 76; Geben und Annehmen, Parabolische Varianten in der deutschen Literatur, Fs W Naumann, 81; ed, Francis Daniel Pastorius' Deliciae Hortenses, Camden House, 81. *Mailing Add:* Dept of Ger Lang Univ of NC Chapel Hill NC 27514

SCHWEITZER, JEROME WILLIAM, b Tuscaloosa, Ala, Dec 28, 08; m 31. ROMANCE LANGUAGES. *Educ:* Univ Ala, AB, 30, AM, 32; Johns Hopkins Univ, PhD, 40. *Prof Exp:* From instr to prof, 30-76, EMER PROF ROMANCE LANG, UNIV ALA, 76- *Concurrent Pos:* Jr instr, Johns Hopkins Univ, 35-39. *Mem:* MLA; Am Asn Teachers Span & Port; SAtlantic MLA; Comediantes; corres, Cahievs Tristan l'Hermite. *Res:* Classical French; Spanish Golden Age. *Publ:* Auth, Almahide: Authorship, Analysis, Sources and Structure, Johns Hopkins, 39 & 73; coauth, The Parisian Stage, 1831-1850, Univ Ala, 61; Contemporaries of Corneille, In: Critical Bibliography of French Literature, Vol III, Syracuse Univ, 61; The Scuderys revisited, In: Renaissance & Other Studies in Honor of W L Wiley, Univ NC, 68; Theatre Complet de Tristan l'Hermite, Univ Ala, 75. *Mailing Add:* Box 3195 Eastside Sta Tuscaloosa AL 35401

SCHWEITZER, JOHN LOUIS, b Lakewood, Ohio, May 20, 22; m 43, 53; c 4. FRENCH, LINGUISTICS. *Educ:* Univ Ariz, MA, 52; Univ Mich, MA, 57. *Prof Exp:* Head, Dept Foreign Lang, 78-81, ASSOC PROF FRENCH, OKLA STATE UNIV, 59- *Mem:* Am Asn Teachers Fr. *Res:* Linguistic analysis of modern French; French culture. *Mailing Add:* Dept of Foreign Lang Okla State Univ Stillwater OK 74074

SCHWEIZER, EVA JULIA (MRS WALTER J VOGEL), b Cologne, Ger, Apr 13, 35; US citizen; m 69; c 2. GERMANIC LANGUAGES. *Educ:* Univ Calif, Los Angeles, BA, 57, MA, 59; Yale Univ, PhD(Germanics), 65. *Prof Exp:* Asst Ger, Univ Calif, Los Angeles, 57-59; asst, Yale Univ & summer lang insts, 61-62; lectr, City Col New York, 62-65; from instr to asst prof Ger lang, 66-72. *Concurrent Pos:* Fulbright scholar, Denmark, 65-66; lectr Swed, Univ Pittsburgh, 71-72. *Mem:* Am-Scand Found; Am Asn Teachers Ger. *Res:* Modern German and Danish literature; medieval Germanic literature; Old Norse. *Publ:* Transl, Hans Lyngby Jepsen, Jezebel and the shoemaker, Am-Scand Rev, 9/69. *Mailing Add:* 5452 Bartlett St Pittsburgh PA 15217

SCHWEIZER, NIKLAUS R, b Zurich, Switz, Aug 24, 39. GERMAN. *Educ:* Univ Calif, Davis, MA, 66, PhD(English-Ger), 68. *Prof Exp:* Teacher Ger, Punahou Sch, Honolulu, 68-70; PROF GER, UNIV HAWAII, 70- *Mem:* AAUP; Am Asn Teachers Ger. *Res:* Eighteenth century German literature; Germans in the Pacific. *Publ:* Auth, The Ut Pictura Poesis Controversy in Eighteenth-Century England and Germany, Lang, 72; The Germans in old Hawaii, Ethnologische Zeitschrift Zürich, 72; A Poet among Explorers: Chamisso in the South Seas, Lang, 73; Introduction to Hildebrand Jacob of the sister arts: An essay, London, 1734, Augustan Reprint Soc, 74; The Swiss in Hawaii, Newslett Swiss Am Hist Soc, 76; Hawaii two centuries later, Swiss Rev World Affairs, 78; Hawai'i und die deutschsprachigen Völker, Lang, 82; Hawai'i and the German Speaking Peoples, Topgallant, 82. *Mailing Add:* Dept of Europ Lang & Lit Univ of Hawaii Honolulu HI 96822

SCHYFTER, SARA ETHEL, b San Jose, Costa Rica, Dec 26, 38; US citizen. SPANISH LITERATURE. *Educ:* Columbia Univ, BA, 62, MA, 63; State Univ NY Buffalo, MA & PhD(Span), 73. *Prof Exp:* Asst prof, 73-80, ASSOC PROF SPAN, STATE UNIV NY ALBANY, 80- *Mem:* MLA; Northeast Mod Lang Asn; Asn Teachers Span & Port. *Res:* Nineteenth century Spanish novel; Galdos; 20th century Spanish women writers. *Publ:* Auth, Almudena and the Jewish theme in Misericordia, Anales Galdosianos, 73; Christian Jews and Moors: Galdos' search for values in Aita Tellauen and Carlos VI, en la Rapita, Symposium, 75; The Judaism of Galdos' Daniel Morton, Hispania, 76; The fragmented family in the fiction of contemporary Spanish women writers, Perspectives Contemp Lit, 78; contribr, The male mistique and its victims in Nada by Carmen Laforet, In: Novelistas Femeninas de la Postguerra Espanola, Madrid, 78; auth, The Jew in the Novels of Glados, Tamesis Bks, London, 78; contribr, Rites without passage: The adolescent world of Ana Maria Moix, In: Contemporary Analysis of Literature, Bilingual Press, 79. *Mailing Add:* Dept of Hisp & Ital Studies State Univ of NY Albany NY 12222

SCOLLON, RONALD THOMAS, b Detroit, Mich, May 13, 39; m 69; c 2. LINGUISTICS, ANTHROPOLOGY. *Educ:* Univ Hawaii, BA, 71, MA, 72, PhD(ling), 74. *Prof Exp:* Vis asst prof English as second lang, Univ Hawaii, 76; res contract ling, Nat Mus Can, Can Ethnol Serv, 76-77; vis asst prof ling, Univ Hawaii, 78; mem staff, Alaska Native Lang Ctr, 78-81, ASSOC PROF, CTR CROSS-CULT STUDIES, UNIV ALASKA, FAIRBANKS, 81- *Mem:* Am Anthrop Asn. *Res:* Ethnography of speaking; Athabaskan (Chipewyan) linguistics; children's language. *Publ:* Auth, Conversations with a One Year Old, Univ Hawaii, 76; coauth (with Suzanne B K Scollon), Linguistic Convergence: An Ethnography of Speaking at Fort Chipewyan, Alberta, Acad Press, 79; Narrative Literacy and Face in Interethnic Communication, Ablex, 81. *Mailing Add:* Alaska Native Lang Ctr Univ of Alaska Fairbanks AK 99701

SCOTT, ANN MARTIN, Linguistics, Composition. See Vol II

SCOTT, CHARLES THOMAS, b New York, NY, Oct 21, 32; m 57; c 4. LINGUISTICS. *Educ:* St John's Univ, NY, BA, 54; NY Univ, MA, 58; Univ Tex, PhD(ling), 63. *Prof Exp:* Specialist comp lit, Teachers Col, Columbia Univ-Int Coop Admin, Afghanistan Proj, 58-60; from asst prof to assoc prof English, 63-68, chmn dept, 70-74, PROF ENGLISH, UNIV WIS-MADISON, 68- *Concurrent Pos:* Consult for Japan Soc, Inc to English lang Educ Coun, Tokyo, 65-66; mem, US Info Agency English Teaching Adv Panel, 67-73; Nat Adv Coun on Teaching English as Foreign Lang, 67-70; chmn, Comt on Inst Coop Panel in English Lang Teaching, 68-70; Comt Int Exchange Persons Screening Panel, Ling & Teaching English as Foreign Lang, 73-76. *Mem:* Ling Soc Am; NCTE; MLA; AAUP. *Res:* Formal criteria for definition of literary folkloristic genres; contemporary English linguistics; application of linguistics to literary theory. *Publ:* Auth, Persian and Arabic Riddles: A Language-Centered Approach to Genre Definition, Ind Univ, 65; Preliminaries to English Teaching, English Lang Educ Coun, Tokyo, 66; Linguistics basis for development of reading skill, Mod Lang J, 66; co-ed, Approaches in Linguistic Methodology, Univ Wis, 67; Readings for the History of the English Language, Allyn & Bacon, 68; auth, Transformational grammar and English as a second language/dialect, Georgetown Monogr Ser, 68; Literary history at Wisconsin, New Lit Hist, 73. *Mailing Add:* Dept of English Univ of Wis Madison WI 53706

SCOTT, JOSEPH REID, b Winslow, Ariz, Mar 10, 26; m 50; c 3. SPANISH. *Educ:* San Diego State Univ, BA, 50; Univ Calif, Berkeley, MA, 52, PhD, 62. *Prof Exp:* From instr to assoc prof, 55-66, PROF SPAN, SAN JOSE STATE UNIV, 66- *Concurrent Pos:* Assoc prof Span, Univ Hawaii, 63-64; resident dir Spain, Calif State Univ, Cols Int Prog, 65-66 & 75-76. *Honors & Awards:* Outstanding Teacher Award, Calif Foreign Lang Teachers Asn, 77. *Mem:* MLA; Am Asn Teachers Span & Port. *Res:* Phonetics; composition; Hispanic culture. *Publ:* Auth, Can NDEA institutes repay their debt to institutions?, Hispania, 65; La Pronunciacion del Espanol, His Bks, 71; Understanding Spanish-Speaking Cultures, Alameda County Sch Dept, 72. *Mailing Add:* Dept of Foreign Lang San Jose State Univ San Jose CA 95114

SCOTT, JOYCE ALAINE, b Long Beach, Calif, May 21, 43; m 72. FRENCH LITERATURE. *Educ:* Univ Conn, BA, 64; Univ Va, MA, 66; Duke Univ, PhD(French), 73. *Prof Exp:* Instr French, Patrick Henry Col, Univ Va, Martinsville, 66-67; asst prof, Madison Col, Va, 67-68; instr, 71-73, asst dean arts & sci, 74-78, ASST PROF FRENCH, UNIV WYO, 73-, ASST VPRES ACAD AFFAIRS, 76- *Mem:* Am Asn Teachers Fr; MLA; Rocky Mountain MLA. *Res:* Seventeenth century French literature, theater and novel. *Mailing Add:* Dept of Mod Lang Univ of Wyo Box 3603 Univ Sta Laramie WY 82071

SCOTT, NINA MARGARET, b Hamburg, Ger, Sept 4, 37; US citizen; m 61; c 3. MODERN SPANISH LITERATURE, SPANISH CIVILIZATION. *Educ:* Wellesley Col, BA, 59; Stanford Univ, MA, 61, PhD(Span), 68. *Prof Exp:* Teachers Ger, Am Sch in Switz, 63-64; asst prof, 68-74, ASSOC PROF SPAN & PORT, UNIV MASS, AMHERST, 74- *Concurrent Pos:* Fac Growth grant for teaching, Univ Mass, Amherst, 75; Mary Elvira Stevens Travelling fel, Wellesley Col, 76-77. *Mem:* Am Asn Univ Women; Am Asn Teachers Span & Port; MLA; Northeast Mod Lang Asn; Int Inst, Spain. *Res:* Contemporary Spanish literature; comparative North/South American literature; art and literature. *Publ:* Auth, Sight and insight in La casa de Bernarda Alba, Rev Estud Hisp, 10/75; Unamuno y el Cristo de Velazquez, Rev de lit, 70; Unamuno and Painting, Hispanofila, 75; Honors and the Family in La fuerza de la sangre, Studies in Honor of Ruth Lee Kennedy, 77; James Fenimore Cooper y Juan Leon Mera: Progenitoreo del mito del indio, El Tiempo, 77; The Tenth Muse, America, 78. *Mailing Add:* Dept of Span & Port 421 Herter Hall Univ of Mass Amherst MA 01003

SCOTT, RUSSELL T, JR, b Lewiston, Idaho, Dec 9, 38; m 67. LATIN, ITALIAN ARCHEOLOGY. *Educ:* Stanford Univ, BA, 60; Yale Univ, MA, 61, PhD(classics), 64. *Prof Exp:* Asst prof, 66-71, assoc prof, 71-80, PROF LATIN, BRYN MAWR COL, 80- *Concurrent Pos:* Fel, Am Acad Rome, 64-66; Am Coun Learned Soc grant, 68. *Mem:* Archaeol Inst Am; Am Philol Asn; Am Soc Papyrologists. *Res:* Roman religion, history and archaeology. *Publ:* Auth, Religion and philosophy in the histories of Tacitus, Am Acad Rome Papers & Monogr, 68. *Mailing Add:* Dept of Latin Bryn Mawr Col Bryn Mawr PA 19010

SCOTT, WILDER PATTILLO, b Atlanta, Ga, Feb 7, 35; m 60; c 1. SPANISH AMERICAN LITERATURE. *Educ:* Emory Univ, BA, 57, MA, 58; Univ Ga, PhD(Romance lang), 68. *Prof Exp:* Instr Romance lang, Westminster Schs, 59-61; asst prof Romance lang, Ga State Col, 61-64; instr, 67-68, ASST PROF SPAN, UNIV GA, 68- *Concurrent Pos:* Outstanding Honors Prof, Univ Ga, 82; prof-in-chg, Studies Abroad Programs, Spain, 71 & 75, Mexico, 77. *Mem:* Am Asn Teachers Span & Port; Latin Am Studies Asn; SAtlantic MLA; Southeastern Conf Latin Am Studies; MLA. *Res:* Spanish American drama, short story & essay. *Publ:* Auth, Rodolfo Usigli and contemporary dramatic theory, Romance Notes, spring 73; Toward an Usigli bibliography (1931-1971), Latin Am Theatre Rev, fall 72; A note on Rodolfo Usigli and the nickname Visconde, Romance Notes, spring 73; translr, Mexico in the Theater, Romance Monogr, 76. *Mailing Add:* Dept of Romance Lang Univ of Ga Athens GA 30602

SCOTT, WILLIAM CLYDE, b Oklahoma City, Okla, Sept 14, 37; m 64; c 3. CLASSICS. *Educ:* Princeton Univ, AB, 59, MA, 62, PhD(classics), 64. *Prof Exp:* Instr classics, Phillips Acad, Andover, 59-60; asst prof, Haverford Col, 64-66; asst prof classics, 66-70, assoc prof classics & drama, 70-75, assoc dean fac, 70-72, chmn dept, 70-76, PROF CLASSICS & DRAMA, DARTMOUTH COL, 75- *Concurrent Pos:* Dartmouth fac fel, 67-68; mem managing comt, Am Sch Class Studies Athens. *Mem:* Am Philol Asn; Am Inst Archaeol. *Res:* Oral epic; Greek drama; Roman lyric. *Publ:* Auth, The confused chorus (Agamemnon 975-1034), Phoenix, 69; Catullus and Caesar (c 29), Class Philol, 71; A repeated episode at Odyssey 1 125-48, TAPhA, 71; The Oral Nature of the Homeric Simile, Leiden, 74; Lines for Clytemnestra (Ag 489-502), 78 & Non-Strophic Elements in the Oresteia, 82, TAPhA. *Mailing Add:* Dept of Classics Dartmouth Col Hanover NH 03755

SCOTT-JONES, MARILYN ANN, b Long Beach, Calif, May 8, 46; m 69. MODERN GERMAN LITERATURE, GERMAN LYRIC. *Educ:* Pomona Col, BA, 67; Univ Ore, MA, 69, PhD(Ger), 75. *Prof Exp:* ASST PROF GER, UNIV NC, CHAPEL HILL, 76- *Mem:* MLA; SAtlantic Mod Lang Asn; Am Asn Teachers Ger. *Res:* Modern German poetry; literature and art; German women authors of nineteenth and twentieth centuries. *Mailing Add:* Dept of Ger Univ of NC Chapel Hill NC 27514

SCRASE, DAVID ANTHONY, b Bere Regis, England, Nov 27, 39; m 73. GERMAN & COMPARATIVE LITERATURE. *Educ:* Bristol Univ, Gt Brit, BA, 62; Ind Univ, Bloomington, PhD(Ger), 72. *Prof Exp:* Asst teacher English, Hermann-Boese Gymnasium, Bremen, Ger, 62-63; lektor, Univ Zurich, 64-68; asst prof Ger, Oxford Polytech, Eng, 68-69; from instr to asst prof, 71-77, ASSOC PROF GER, UNIV VT, BURLINGTON, 77- *Concurrent Pos:* Ger Acad Exchange Coun res grant, 73; Alexander von Humboldt Found res grant, 74; Brit Acad res fel, 74. *Mem:* MLA; Am Asn Teachers Ger; Deutsche Schiller-Gesellschaft; Arthur Schnitzler Soc. *Res:* Twentieth century German Literature; lyric poetry; East German literature. *Publ:* Auth, Essay on Wilhelm Lehmann, In: Essays on Contemporary German Literature, Brian Keith-Smith, London, 66; Wilhelm Lehmannas translator, Texte und Kontexte, Francke Verlag, 74; Translation of Sophokles by Siegfried Melchinger, F Ungar, 74; Point counterpoint: Variations on the Fest theme in Johannes Bobrowski's Levins Mühle, Ger Life & Lett, England (in press). *Mailing Add:* Dept of Ger & Russ Univ of Vt Burlington VT 05401

SCRIABINE, HELENE, b Dvinsk, Russia, Feb 13, 06; US citizen; m 24; c 1. LINGUISTICS. *Educ:* Leningrad Pedag Inst Foreign Lang, Russia, M, 41; Syracuse Univ, PhD(French), 62. *Prof Exp:* Dep Chief instr Russ, Air Force Lang Sch, Syracuse, NY, 51-53; from asst prof to prof, 60-74, EMER PROF RUSS, UNIV IOWA, 74- *Honors & Awards:* Key to City of Bendorf, WGer, in honor of Leningrader Tagebuch, 73. *Mem:* MLA; Am Asn Teachers Slavic & EEurop Lang. *Res:* Russian and French humour; Russian folklore. *Publ:* Auth, New trends in Soviet literature, Renaissance, 11/65; History of Russian Literature, 65 & coauth, Grammar Workbook, 65, Lucas; ed, Short Stories by Pushkin, Lermontov and Dostoevsky, Harper, 65; Auth, Siege and Survival, Southern Ill Univ, 71, Pinnacle, 73; Leningrader Tagebuch, Biederstein, Munich, 72; The Humor of M Zoshchenko, Coronado, 73; After Leningrad, Southern Ill Univ, 78. *Mailing Add:* Dept of Russ Univ of Iowa Iowa City IA 52240

SCROGGINS, DANIEL COY, b Compton, Ark, June 19, 37; m 61; c 1. HISPANIC LITERATURE. *Educ:* Univ Ark, BA, 58, MA, 61; Univ Mich, PhD(Span), 66. *Prof Exp:* Asst prof Span, Univ Miami, 63-65, Ind Univ, Bloomington, 66-69; asst prof, 69-71, ASSOC PROF SPAN, UNIV MO-COLUMBIA, 71- *Mem:* MLA; Am Asn Teachers Span & Port; Latin Am Studies Asn. *Res:* Argentine literature; colonial Latin American literature; the essay. *Publ:* Auth, A Concordance of Jose Hernandez Martin Fierro, Univ Mo, 71; Los poetas de una revista olvidada, Rev Univ Nac Autonoma Mex, 72; Vengeance with a Stickpin: Barreto, Quiroga, Garcia Calderon, Romance Notes, 73; Martin Fierro: Personal circumspection and public militancy, 75 & Roberto Arlt in the Aguafuertes portenas, 76, Am Hispanist; Leopoldo Lugones' defense of the Monroe Doctrine in the Revue Sudamericaine, Rev Int-Am Bibliog, 78; The crisis of 1930 in the Aguafuertes portenas of Roberto Arlt, Ky Romance Quart, 79; Las Aguafuertes portenas de Roberto Arlt, Ediciones Culturales Argentinas, Buenos Aires, 81. *Mailing Add:* Dept of Romance Lang Univ of Mo Columbia MO 65201

SCRUGGS, CHARLES EUGENE, b Cullman, Ala, Nov 16, 37; m 59; c 2. FRENCH LITERATURE, LINGUISTICS. *Educ:* Transylvania Col, BA, 59; Univ Ky, MA, 62, PhD(French & ling), 68. *Prof Exp:* Instr French, Appalachian State Univ, 62-65; asst prof Eastern Ky Univ, 67-72; ASSOC PROF FRENCH, UNIV S FLA, TAMPA, 72- *Mem:* Am Asn Teachers Fr; Am Coun Teaching Foreign Lang; SAtlantic MLA. *Res:* Seventeenth century literature; contemporary French society. *Publ:* auth, A baroque spirit in a classical age: Charles Coypeau Dassoucy, Ky Romance Quart, 77. *Mailing Add:* Dept of Mod Lang Box 131 Univ of SFla Tampa FL 33620

SCRUGGS, EMMA GUERRA, b Matanzas, Cuba; US citizen; m 63. ROMANCE LANGUAGES. *Educ:* Univ Havana, Dr Philos, 51, Dr Educ, 57. *Prof Exp:* Teacher, 48-57, dir English, Spec Ctr English, Havana, 57-61; teacher high sch, Ill, 61-62; instr, 62-64, ASST PROF SPAN, UNIV TEX, EL PASO, 64- *Mem:* Am Asn Teachers Span & Port. *Res:* Spanish; psychology; education. *Mailing Add:* Dept of Mod Lang Univ of Tex El Paso TX 79999

SCULLY, TERENCE PETER, b Toronto, Ont, Mar 17, 35; m 63; c 2. FRENCH & SPANISH LANGUAGE & LITERATURE. *Educ:* Victoria Col, Univ Toronto, BA, 57, Univ Toronto, MA, 58, PhD(Romance lang), 66. *Prof Exp:* From lectr to asst prof, 61-67, ASSOC PROF ROMANCE LANG, WILFRID LAURIER UNIV, 67- *Mem:* Asn Prof Francais Univ Can; Can Asn Univ Teachers; Int Courtly Lit Soc; Soc Rencesvals. *Res:* Courtly love in mediaeval literature; mediaeval French lyric poetry; mediaeval food and culinary practice. *Publ:* Co-ed, Correspondence of Iu Samarin and the Baroness Rahden, Wilfrid Laurier Univ, 74; auth, Le Court d'Amours de Mahieu le Poirier, Wilfred Laurier, 76; The two Yseults, Mediaevalia III (1977), 77; contribr, Expansion and Transformations of Courtly Literature, Univ Ga, 78; The Ordeal at Rencesvalles, Olifant, 81; Late 14th century qualifications of the Lady, Medioevo Romanzo, 80; Polyphonic Music of the 14th Century: French Secular Music (5 vols), Oiseau Lyre, 81. *Mailing Add:* Dept of Romance Lang Wilfred Laurier Univ Waterloo ON N2L 3C5 Can

SEAGRAVES, RICHARD WAYNE ALEXANDER, b Macon, Ga, Dec 25, 32. CLASSICAL PHILOLOGY, RENAISSANCE STUDIES. *Educ:* Loyola Univ, Chicago, AB, 53; Oxford Univ, BA, 63, MA, 66; Columbia Univ, MA, 72, MPh, 75, PhD(Greek & Latin), 76. *Prof Exp:* Asst prof classics, Ga State Univ, 76-78, Univ Pa, 79-80 & Loyola Col, 81-82; PROF CLASSICS, SOUTHWESTERN UNIV, 82- *Concurrent Pos:* Nat Endowment for Humanities fel, 78 & 80. *Mem:* Am Philol Asn; Int Asn Neo-Latin Studies;

Int Asn Greek & Latin Epigraphy; Medieval Acad Am; Renaissance Soc Am. *Res:* Latin epic poetry; Roman law. *Publ:* Auth, NILO--The Naval Intelligence Officer in Vietnam, US Naval Inst Proc, 12/68; A note on I M 115, Zeitschrift für Papyrologie und Epigraphik, 4/75; The moral virtues and Petrarch's Africa, ACTA Fourth Int Cong neo-Latin, 9/76; Neo-Latin in the undergraduate curriculum, New England Class Newslett, 12/77; The riddle of R Festus: C I L VI 563, ACTA VII Int Cong Greek & Latin Epigraphy, 79; The Municeps in Catullus 17, Latomus, Vol 164, 79; A Concordance to Petrarch's Africa, Fink Verlag, Munich (in prep). *Mailing Add:* Dept of Classics Southwestern Univ Georgetown TX 78626

SEALY, ROBERT J, b New York, NY, June 6, 18. FRENCH LANGUAGE & LITERATURE. *Educ:* Fordham Univ, AB, 39, MA, 49; Woodstock Col, PhD, 44; Weston Col, Theol L, 52; Univ Paris, DUniv, 56. *Prof Exp:* Instr philos, Le Moyne Col, NY, 57; asst prof French, 57-68, assoc prof, 68-82, dir jr year abroad & asst dir honors prog, 62-67, chmn dept mod lang, 67-73, PROF ROMANCE LANG, FORDHAM UNIV, 82- *Mem:* MLA; Am Asn Teachers Fr; Asn Int des Docteurs d l'Univ de Paris. *Res:* The Parisian Academy of Marquerite de Valois (1605-1615); the role of Francois de Valois in French renaissance thought. *Publ:* Auth Pieree Olivant, 64 & Eugene Sue, 64, In: New Catholic Encyclopedia, McGraw; Brunetiere, Montegut and George Eliot, Mod Lang Rev, 1/71; The palace academy of Henry III, Bibliotheque d'Humanisme et Renaissance, 78; The Palace Academy of Henry III (1576-1579), Droz, 81. *Mailing Add:* Dept of Mod Lang Fordham Univ New York NY 10458

SEAMAN, DAVID WILLIAM, b Alma, Mich, Jan 1, 40; m 62; c 2. FRENCH, HUMANITIES. *Educ:* Col Wooster, BA, 62; Stanford Univ, MA, 64, PhD(French), 70. *Hon Degrees:* MHL, Davis & Elkins Col. *Prof Exp:* From instr to asst prof French, Lake Forest Col, 66-72; assoc prof, 72-80, PROF LANG & CHAIRPERSON HUMANITIES, DAVIS & ELKINS COL, 80- *Concurrent Pos:* Dir, Int Awareness Prog, Davis & Elkins Col, 76-78, fel world cult & Kellogg Found grant, 77-78; reviewer, Film and the Arts, Elkins Intermountain Newspaper, 76- *Mem:* MLA; Am Asn Teachers Fr; NA NAm Mycol Asn; Am Film Inst; NCent Women's Studies Asn. *Res:* Visual literature; French literature and civilization; comparative literature and arts. *Publ:* Auth, Tennis match, Hiram Poetry Rev, 74; Poetry, painting, and science, Eric Abstr, 78; Critical problems with concrete poetry, Point of Contact/Punto de Contacto, 78; Korean Ciphers, Dada/Surrealism, 78; Maurice Lemaitre at the Salon de la Lettre et du Signe, LaLettre, 79; Human Values in Abstract Art, WVa Arts News, 80; Concrete Poetry in France, UMI Res Press, 81. *Mailing Add:* Dept of Lang Davis & Elkins Col Elkins WV 26241

SEAMAN, PAUL DAVID, b Connellsville, Pa, Jan 31, 32; m 58; c 3. LINGUISTICS, ANTHROPOLOGY. *Educ:* Asbury Col, AB, 57; Univ Ky, MA, 58; Ind Univ, Bloomington, PhD(ling), 65. *Prof Exp:* Prof lang, Asbury Col, 57-67, chmn div, 65-67; assoc prof, 67-70, PROF LING, NORTHERN ARIZ UNIV, 70-, CHMN COMT LING, 67- *Concurrent Pos:* Fulbright sr lectr, US Educ Found, Greece, 69-70; ling consult, Zuni Biling-bicult Proj, Gallup-McKinley County Schs, 71-73. *Mem:* Ling Soc Am; MLA; Teachers English to Speakers Other Lang. *Res:* Bilingualism; Amerindian languages; socio-linguistics. *Publ:* Auth, Modern Greek and American English in Contact, Mouton, The Hague, 72; Themistocles, ancient master of the diplomatic triple-cross, Ky Foreign Lang Quart. *Mailing Add:* Comt on Ling Box 15200 Northern Ariz Univ Flagstaff AZ 86001

SEAMAN, WILLIAM MILLARD, b Wheeling, WVa, Dec 26, 07; m 32; c 4. CLASSICAL PHILOLOGY. *Educ:* Col Wooster, AB, 30; Univ Ill, AM, 31, PhD, 39. *Prof Exp:* Instr, Knoxville Col, 31-35; asst prof, Alma Col, 36-42; res analyst, US Army Security Agency, 42-47; assoc prof, 47-59; prof, 59-74, EMER PROF CLASS PHILOL, MICH STATE UNIV, 74- *Concurrent Pos:* Assoc ed, Class Outlook, 62-67; Fulbright lectr, Trinity Col, Dublin, 67-68. *Mem:* Am Philol Asn; Archaeol Inst Am; Am Class League (pres, 69-72). *Res:* The appropriate name in Plautus; Roman comedy; visual aids in Latin teaching. *Publ:* Auth, A catalogue of audio-visual aids for classical studies; coauth, Forum Romanum, Am Class League, 72. *Mailing Add:* Forest Hills Wheeling WV 26003

SEARS, DONALD ALBERT, b Portland, Maine, May 25, 23; m 45, 64; c 4. LITERATURE, LANGUAGE. *Educ:* Bowdoin Col, BA, 44; Harvard Univ, MA, 47, PhD(English), 52. *Prof Exp:* Instr English, Dartmouth Col, 48-52; from asst prof to prof, Upsala Col, 52-62, dir freshman English, 53-58; prof English & chmn dept, Skidmore Col, 62-64; staff assoc comn plan & objectives higher educ, Am Coun Educ, 64-65; prof English, Howard Univ, 65-66; prof lang, Ahmadu Bello Univ, Nigeria, 66-67; prof English, 67-77, PROF ENGLISH & LING, CALIF STATE UNIV, FULLERTON, 77-, CHMN LING, 79- *Concurrent Pos:* Ed, CEA Critic, 60-70; dir, Book-of-the-Month Club Writing Fel Prog, 66-70. *Honors & Awards:* Lindback Found Award, 61; Outstanding Prof, Calif State Univ, Fullerton, 81. *Mem:* English Asn; Ling Soc Am; Milton Soc Am; MLA; Philol Asn Pac Coast. *Res:* English language; linguistics. *Publ:* Auth, The Harbrace Guide to the Library and the Research Paper, 56, 60, 73, The Discipline of English, 63, 74 & coauth, The Sentence in Context, 60, Harcourt; John Neal, Hall, 78; coauth, Aspects of Language, 3rd ed, Harcourt, 81; The Magella Heart (poetry), Harian, 82. *Mailing Add:* Dept of Ling Calif State Univ Fullerton CA 92634

SEATOR, LYNETTE HUBBARD, b Chicago, Ill, Mar 23, 29; m 50; c 4. SPANISH, COMPARATIVE LITERATURE. *Educ:* Western Ill Univ, BS, 64; Univ Ill, MA, 66, PhD(Span), 72. *Prof Exp:* Instr Span, Western Ill Univ, 66-67; PROF SPAN, ILL COL, 67- *Honors & Awards:* Distinguished Prof Harry J Dunbaugh Award, Ill Col, 76. *Mem:* MLA; AAUP; Am Asn Teachers Span & Port. *Res:* Modern theatre; modern novel. *Publ:* Auth, La creacion del ensueno en La ultima niebla, Armas y Letras, 65; Larra and Daumier, Romance Notes, 66; An existential view of man in three plays by Calderon, Hispanofila, 73; Alfonso Sastre's Homenaje a Kierkegaard, Romance Notes, 74; The antisocial humanism of Cela and Hemingway, 75 & The traditional nature of Sastre's Revolutionary Women, 78, Revista de Estudios Hispanicos; Alfonso Sastre, commited dramatist, Papers on Lang & Lit, 78; Women and men in the novels of Unamuno, Ky Romance Quart, 80. *Mailing Add:* Ill Col Jacksonville IL 62650

SEBEOK, THOMAS ALBERT, b Budapest, Hungary, Nov 9, 20; US citizen; m 47; c 1. LINGUISTICS, ANTHROPOLOGY. *Educ:* Univ Chicago, BA, 41; Princeton Univ, MA, 43, PhD(orient lang & civilizations), 45. *Prof Exp:* Mem fac, 43-65, dir human relat area files, 65-69, PROF URALIC & ALTAIC STUDIES, UNIV IND, BLOOMINGTON, 63-, PROF ANTHROP & DISTINGUISHED PROF LING, 67-, CHMN RES CTR LANG SCI, 56- *Concurrent Pos:* Guggenheim Found fel, 58-59; fel, Ctr Advan Studies Behav Sci, 60-61; ed, Current Trends in Linguistics, (14 Vols), 63-; Nat Sci Found fel, 66-67; Fulbright grants, Ger, 66 & 71, Italy, 69-71; Biog Dict Ling, ser, 71-; Nat Acad Sci exchange prof, Acad Socialist Repub Romania, 67, 69 & Acad Sci USSR, 73; consult, Ford Found, Guggenheim Found, Wenner-Gren Found Anthrop Res, US Off Educ, Fel Div, Nat Acad Sci, Can Coun & Nat Sci Found; sr fel, Cult Learning Inst, East-West Ctr, 73 & Nat Endowment for the Humanities, 73-74; fel Netherlands Inst Advan Study, 73-74; Johns Hopkins Centennial Scholar, 75; grantee, Nat Sci Found Off Int Progs, 76; consult, Peirce Museum Proj, 77-78; mem curric adv bd, Nat Endowment for Humanities, 77-79. *Mem:* Ling Soc Am (secy-treas, 69-); Am Anthrop Asn; Int Asn Semiotic Studies. *Res:* Ethnology; stylistics; semiotics. *Publ:* Coauth, Psycholinguistics, 54 & ed & contribr, Animal Communication, 69, Ind Univ; auth, Perspectives in Zoosemiotics, 72, Structure & Texture: Selected Essays in Cheremis Verbal Art, 74 & Zoosemiotics: At the Intersection of Nature & Culture, 77, Mouton, Hague; How Animals Communicate, Ind Univ, 77; The Play of Musement, Ind Univ Press, 81. *Mailing Add:* Res Ctr for Lang Sci Ind Univ Bloomington IN 47401

SEBESTA, JUDITH LYNN, b Chicago, Ill. CLASSICAL LANGUAGES & LITERATURE, ANCIENT HISTORY. *Educ:* Univ Chicago, AB, 68; Stanford Univ, PhD(classics), 72. *Prof Exp:* From instr to asst prof, 72-77, ASSOC PROF CLASSICS, UNIV S DAK, 77- *Concurrent Pos:* Dir, Integrated Humanities Prof, Univ SDak, 81 & dir classics, 81. *Mem:* Am Philol Asn; Vergilian Soc; Class Asn Midwest & South; Archaeol Inst Am; Am Classical League. *Res:* The Roman army; provinces of the Roman empire; classical philology. *Publ:* Auth, Dine With US as an Equal, Class Bull, 76; On Stilicho's consulship: Variations on a theme by Claudian, Class Bull, 78; The energy-efficient Roman house, Proc Helios, From Myth to Solar Energy, 78; Textbooks in Greek and Latin: Annual surveys, Class World, 79; Claudian's Credo: The de salvatore, Class Bull, 80. *Mailing Add:* Dept of Classics Univ of SDak Vermillion SD 57069

SEBOLD, RUSSELL PERRY, b Dayton, Ohio, Aug 20, 28; m 55; c 2. SPANISH. *Educ:* Ind Univ, BA, 49; Princeton Univ, MA, 51, PhD, 53. *Prof Exp:* Instr Span, Duke Univ, 55-56; from instr to assoc prof, Univ Wis, Madison, 56-66; prof foreign lang & chmn dept, Univ Md, 66-68; chmn dept, 68-78, PROF ROMANCE LANG, UNIV PA, 68- *Concurrent Pos:* Guggenheim fel, 62-63; co-ed, Hisp Rev, 68-73, gen ed, 73-; Am Philos Soc grant-in-aid, 71, 76 & 82; Am Coun Learned Soc fel, 79-80. *Mem:* MLA; Am Asn Teachers Span & Port; Hisp Soc Am; Centro de Estudios del Siglo XVIII (Oviedo, Spain). *Res:* Eighteenth century Spanish literature; Spanish Romanticism; aesthetics and poetics. *Publ:* Auth, El Rapto de la Mente, Poetica y Poesia Diechiochescas, Prensa Espanola, Madrid, 70; Colonel Don Jose Cadalso, Twayne, 71; ed, Ignacio Lopez de Ayala, Numancia Destruida, Ed Anaya, Salamanca-Madrid, 71; Cadalso: El Primer Romantico Europeo de Espana, Ed Gredos, Madrid, 74; Novela Y Autobiografia en la Vida de Torres Villarroel, Ed Ariel, Barcelona, 75; ed, Ignacio de Luzan, La Poetica, Ed Labor, Barcelona, 77; Tomas de iriarte, El Senorito Mimado (y) La Senorita Malcriada, Ed Castalia, Madrid, 78; auth, Becquer y la lima de Horacio, Insula, 1/82. *Mailing Add:* Dept of Romance Lang Univ of Pa Philadelphia PA 19104

SECOR, HARRY RENNELL, b Chicago, Ill, Nov 11, 24; m 51; c 3. FOREIGN LANGUAGES. *Educ:* Yale Univ, BA, 48, PhD(Fr), 57. *Prof Exp:* From instr to asst prof French, Vassar Col, 53-62; asst prof, 62-66, ASSOC PROF FRENCH, VICTORIA COL, UNIV TORONTO, 66-; ASSOC DIR CENTRE REFORMATION & RENAISSANCE STUDIES, VICTORIA UNIV, ONT, 76- *Mem:* MLA; Renaissance Soc Am; Can Soc Renaissance Studies. *Res:* French literature and language, especially medieval, Renaissance and 17th century; humanism and the Renaissance. *Publ:* Rabelais, In: Biographical Register, Collected Works of Erasmus, Univ Toronto Press (in press). *Mailing Add:* Dept of French Univ Toronto Toronto ON M5S 1K7 Can

SECRIST, ROBERT HEROLD, II, b Blawnox, Pa, Feb 26, 35. ENGLISH LINGUISTICS. *Educ:* Harvard Univ, AB, 57; NY Univ, MA, 59, PhD(English ling), 65. *Prof Exp:* Chmn dept foreign lang, E Rockaway High Sch, NY, 59-64; from asst prof to assoc prof mod lang, Kingsborough Community Col, 64-68, coordr French, 66-67, chmn dept mod lang, 67-68; assoc prof, 68-78, PROF ENGLISH & LING, YOUNGSTOWN STATE UNIV, 78- *Concurrent Pos:* Consult, Gov Comt Dict Am English, 72-; consult to ed-in-chief, Random House Dict of English Lang, 76; vis assoc prof English Ling, Univ Vt, 78. *Mem:* MLA; Ling Soc Am; Int Ling Asn; Am Name Soc; Dict Soc NAm. *Res:* Orthographic systems; international English; pronunciation in lexicography. *Publ:* Auth, Quand Pleurent les Dieux, Penguin Rev, spring 71; The not-so-wonderful world of pet shops, Natural World, fall 71; Internalization of English orthographic patterns, Visible Lang, 8/76; Pronunciation keys: Principles, practices, performance, Papers Dict Soc NAm, 77; Whither pronunciation? Past, present and future practices in English dictionaries, Studies Lexicography, 12/78; Respelling: Necessity or boondoggle?, Papers Dict Soc NAm, 79. *Mailing Add:* Dept of English Youngstown State Univ Youngstown OH 44555

SEDELOW, SALLY YEATES, b Greenfield, Iowa, Aug 10, 31; m 58. LINGUISTICS, INFORMATION SCIENCE. *Educ:* Univ Iowa, BA, 53; Mt Holyoke Col, MA, 56; Bryn Mawr Col, PhD(Anglo-Saxon & English lit), 60. *Prof Exp:* Asst pub rels, Sweet Briar Col, 53-54; instr English lang & lit, Smith Col, 59-60; asst prof English, Parsons Col, 60-61 & Rockford Col, 61-62; human factors scientist artificial intel & nat lang, res directorate, Syst Develop Corp, 62-64; asst prof English, St Louis Univ, 64-66; assoc prof English & computer & info sci, Univ NC, Chapel Hill, 66-70; PROF LING & COMPUT

SCI, UNIV KANS, 70-, ASSOC DEAN COL ARTS & SCI, 80- *Concurrent Pos:* Columnist, feature writer & reporter-photographer, Adair County Free Press, Iowa, 48-51; Mt Holyoke Col News Bur intern, Springfield Republican, Mass, 54-56; consult, Syst Develop Corp, 64-67; prin investr stylistic anal proj, US Off Naval Res, 64-74; consult, T Y Crowell Co, 66-67; field reader, US Off Educ, 67-; ed, Comput Studies in Humanities & Verbal Behav, 67-74; mem instnl comput serv adv panel, Nat Sci Found, 68-72, prin investr, Network Computational Res Lang, 71-73, comput adv panel, 72-73; mem, Comt Info Technol, Am Coun Learned Socs, 69; mem res adv panel, Nat Endowment for Humanities, 73-75 & 77; mem comput sci eval panel, Fulbright-Hays Sr Prog, 73-77; dir, Tech & Systs Progs & Intel Systs Prog, Nat Sci Found, 74-77. *Mem:* MLA; Asn Comput Mach; Ling Soc Am; Asn Comput Ling; Midwest Mod Lang Asn. *Res:* Mediaeval and Renaissance prose and poetry; computational linguistics; discourse analysis. *Publ:* Auth, The Narrative Method of Paradise Lost, Edwards Bros, 60; coauth, Language Research and the Computer, Univ Kans, 72; auth, Shakespeare studies and the computer, Proc World Shakespeare Cong, 72; language analysis in the humanities, Commun Asn Comput Mach, 72; coauth, Models, computing and stylistics, In: Current Trends in Stylistics, Ling Res, Inc, 72; auth, Analysis of natural language discourse, Am Fedn Info Processing Socs Conf Proc, 76; Computers on the fine arts & Computers on the humanities, In: Encyclopedia of Computer Science, Petrocelli, 76; coauth, Formalized historiography: The structure at scientific and literary texts, J Hist Behav Sci, 78. *Mailing Add:* Dept of Ling Blake Hall Univ of Kans Lawrence KS 66045

SEDELOW, WALTER ALFRED, JR, History of Science, Sociolinguistics. See Vol I

SEDURO, VLADIMIR ILYICH, b Minsk, Byelorussia, Dec 24, 10; US citizen; m 46; c 1. FOREIGN LANGUAGES & LITERATURE. *Educ:* State Univ, Leningrad, MA, 39; Acad Sci, Minsk, PhD, 41. *Prof Exp:* Instr Russ, Educ Courses, Leningrad, 36-41; prof lang & lit, Teachers Training Sch, Minsk, 41-44; prof Int Refugee Orgn Voc Training Sch, Ingolstadt, Ger, 45-51; sr fel, Res Prog USSR, Columbia Univ, 51-57; from asst prof to prof Russ, 59-76, EMER PROF RUSS, RENSSELAER POLYTECH INST, 76- *Concurrent Pos:* Free-lance writer, Radio Liberation, NY, 55-59; vis prof Russ lit Middlebury Col, 59-63; vis prof Russ lang & lit, Inst Critical Lang, Windham Col, 67; vis prof Soviet lit, Univ Ill, 69; mem, Byeloruss-Am Sci & Lit Club (pres, 64-); NAm Dostoevsky Soc (vpres, 70-75); Int Dostoevsky Soc; Asn Russ-Am Scholars USA. *Res:* Dostoevski and world theater; history of Byelorussian art; recent literary criticism of Dostoevski. *Publ:* Auth, The fate of Stavrogin's confession, Russ Rev, 10/66; The controversy over Dostoevsky in the 1960's, 71 & Dramatic musical versions of Dostoevski: Sergei Prokofiev's The Gambler, 75, Trans Asn Russ-Am Scholars in USA; In the Holy Land, On God's Highway, London, 72; Dostoevski's Image in Russia Today, 75 & Dostoevski in Russian Emigre Criticism, 75, Nordland Publ Co, Belmont, Mass; Solzhenitsyn and the Dostoevskian tradition of the Polyphonic Novel, Contemporary, Toronto, 76-78; Dostoevsky in Russian and World Theatre, Christopher, North Quincy, Mass 77. *Mailing Add:* 29 Mellon Ave Troy NY 12180

SEDWICK, FRANK, b Baltimore, Md, Apr 7, 24; m 49; c 4. SPANISH. *Educ:* Duke Univ, BA, 45; Stanford Univ, MA, 47; Univ Southern Calif, PhD, 53. *Prof Exp:* Instr Span, Univ Md, 47-49, Ital & Span, US Naval Acad, 51-53; asst prof Span & chmn dept, Univ Wis-Milwaukee, 53-58; assoc prof Span & Ital & chmn dept, Ohio Wesleyan Univ, 58-61, prof, 61-63; prof foreign lang & head dept, Rollins Col, 63-80. *Mem:* MLA; Am Asn Teachers Span & Port. *Res:* Twentieth century Spanish literature and history. *Publ:* Coauth, La Forja de los Suenos, Houghton, 63, La Gloria de don Ramiro, Heath, 66 & Selecciones de Madariaga, Prentice-Hall, 68; auth, Spanish Conversation: Points of Departure, 68, 2nd ed, 76 & Conversaciones con Madrilenos, 74, Van Nostrand; Conversation in Spanish, 3rd ed, 81, coauth French, Ital, English & Ger editions; Spanish for Careers, 80, coauth French & Ger editions; The Gold Coinage of Gran Colombia, 81. *Mailing Add:* 2033 Cove Trail Maitland FL 32751

SEEBA, HINRICH CLAASSEN, b Hannover, Ger, Feb 5, 40. GERMAN LITERATURE. *Educ:* Univ Tübingen, DPhil(Ger & Greek), 67. *Prof Exp:* From instr to assoc prof, 68-76, chmn dept, 77-81, PROF GER, UNIV CALIF, BERKELEY, 76- *Concurrent Pos:* Studienstiftung des deutschen Volkes fel, 63-68; Guggenheim Found fel, 70-71. *Mem:* MLA; Am Asn Teachers Ger; Philol Asn Pac Coast; Am Lessing Soc; Am Asn Advan Humanities. *Res:* Eighteenth to 20th century German literature; hermeneutics; methods of literary criticism. *Publ:* Auth, Die Liebe zur Sache, Offentliches und privates Interesse in Lessings Dramen, 73 & co-ed, Austriaca: Studien zur osterreichischen Literatur, 75, Niemeyer, Tubingen; auth, Die Kinder des Pygmalion: Die Bildlichkeit des Kunstbegriffs bei Heine, Beobachtungen zur Tendenzwende der Asthetik, In: Deutsche Vierteljahrsschrift fur Literaturwissenschaft und Geistesgeschichte, 76; co-ed, Literaturwissenschaft und Geistesgeschichte, Niemeyer, Tubingen, 81; auth, Literatur und Geschichte: Hermeneutische Ansatze zu einer Poetik der Geschichtsschreibung, In: Akten des VI, Int Germanisten-Kongresses Basel 1980, Peter Lang, Bern, 81; Personliches Engagement: Zur Autorenpoetik der siebziger Jahre, In: Monatshefte, 81; Historiographischer Idealismus? Fragen zu Schillers Geschichtsbild, In: Kunst, Humanitat und Politik in der spaten Aufklarung, Niemeyer, Tubingen, 82; Lessings Geschichtsbild: Zur asthetischen Evidenz historischer Wahrheit, In: Humanitat und Dialog: Lessing und Mendelssohn in neuer Sicht, Wayne State Univ Press, 82. *Mailing Add:* Dept of Ger Univ of Calif Berkeley CA 94720

SEELEY, FRANK FRIEDEBERG, b London, England, Jan 17, 12; m 62. SLAVIC & COMPARATIVE LITERATURE. *Educ:* Oxford Univ, BA, 33, MA, 37. *Prof Exp:* Lectr Ital lit, Oxford Univ, 35-36; asst lectr Russ, Sch Slavonic & East Europ Studies, Univ London, 43-45, lectr, 45-57; head dept Slavonic studies, Univ Nottingham, 57-67; prof Russ lit, Univ Pa, 67-71; prof Russ & comp lit & chmn dept Russ lang & lit, 71-76, PROF RUSS & COMP LIT, STATE UNIV NY BINGHAMTON, 76- *Concurrent Pos:* Sr fel Russ Inst, Columbia Univ, 49-50, vis prof Russ lit, Columbia Univ, 63-64. *Mem:* Int Dostoevsky Soc. *Res:* Russian 19th century literature; 19th century European literature, especially French and Italian; psychology and the social sciences. *Publ:* Co-transl, Leone Ebreo, The Philosophy of Love, Soncino, London, 37; co-auth, Russian Prose Reader I:XIX Century Authors, Blackwell, Oxford Univ, 45; auth, La nemesi di Anna Karenina, Annali Ist Univ Orient, Naples, 59; Dostoyevsky's women, 61 & The problem of Kamennyy Gost', 63, Slavonic & EEurope Rev; coauth, The Gateway Russian Course, Bk I, 63 & Bk II, 64, Methuen, London; auth, On Interpersonal relations in Chekhov's fiction, Annali Ist Univ Orient, Naples, 72; Tolstoy's philosophy of history, In: New Tolstoy Essays, Cambridge Univ, 78. *Mailing Add:* Dept of Russ Lang & Lit State Univ of NY Binghamton NY 13901

SEELIG, HARRY E, b New York, NY, Mar 13, 37; m 67; c 2. GERMAN LITERATURE, MUSIC. *Educ:* Oberlin Col, AB, 59, Conserv, BM, 61; Univ Kans, MA, 64, PhD(German), 69. *Prof Exp:* Instr, Univ Kans, 66-67; instr, 67-69, asst prof, 69-80, ASSOC PROF GERMAN, UNIV MASS, 80- *Concurrent Pos:* Vis lectr, Univ Kent, 78-79. *Mem:* MLA; Am Asn Teachers German. *Res:* German literature since Goethe; poetry and music; translation of contemporary German poetry. *Publ:* Transl, Rolf Bongs, Insel-Ile-Island, Guido Hildebrandt Verlag Duisburg, WGermany, 73; Rolf Bongs, Aufstieg zum Kilimandscharo, The Literary Rev, 74; auth, Schuberts Beitrag zu besserem Verständnis' von Goethes Suleika-Gestalt: Eine literarischmuskalische studie der Suleika-Lieder, Beiträge zur Musikwissenschaft, 75; transl, Rolf Bongs, Oberwelt, 76 & Ralph Glöckler's, Ich Sehe Dichnoch und andere lyrik, 76, Dimension. *Mailing Add:* German Dept Univ of Mass Amherst MA 01003

SEGAL, CHARLES PAUL, b Boston, Mass, Mar 19, 36; m 61; c 2. CLASSICS. *Educ:* Harvard Univ, AB, 57, PhD(class philol), 61. *Hon Degrees:* AM, Brown Univ, 69. *Prof Exp:* Instr classics, Harvad Univ, 63-64; from asst to assoc prof classic studies, Univ Pa, 64-67, assoc prof, 68-70, prof classics, 70-80, chmn dept, 78-81, DAVID BENEDICT PROF CLASSICS & COMP LIT, BROWN UNIV, 80- *Concurrent Pos:* Fel, Am Acad Rome, 61-63; jr fel, Ctr Hellenic Studies, Washington, DC, 67-68; Nat Endowment for Humanities & Am Coun Learned Soc travel grant, 69, 77 & 80; Marc Gutwirth mem class lectr, Colgate Univ, 70; vis prof, Intercol Ctr Class Studies Rome, 70-71, prof-in-chg, 71-72; mem class jury, Am Acad Rome, 72-74; vis prof, Brandeis Univ, 74; Am Coun Learned Soc fel, 74-75; dir d'Etiudes Associe, Ecole des Hautes Etudes, VI Section, Paris, 75-76; Nat Endowment for Humanities grant, 77; chmn, Am Philol Asn Comt Placement, 78-79; Fulbright vis prof, Univ Melbourne, Australia, 78; vis prof, Columbia Univ, 79; Guggenheim fel, 81-82. *Mem:* Vergilian Soc; Int Ovid Soc; Am Philol Asn; Class Asn New England. *Res:* Greek literature; Latin poetry; comparative literature. *Publ:* Auth, Landscape in Ovid's Metamorphoses; a Study in the Transformations of a Literary Symbol, Franz Steiner, Wiesbaden, 69; The Theme of the Mutilation of the Corpse in the Iliad, Brill, Leiden, 71; Tragedy and civilization: An interpretation of Sophocles, In: Martin Class Lectures, Harvard, Vol 26, 81; Poetry and Myth in Ancient Pastoral: Essays on Theocritus and Virgil, 81 & Dionysiac Poetics and Euripides' Bacchae, 82, Princeton; Griechische Tragödie und Gesellschaft, In: Vol 1, Propyläen Geschichte der Literatur, Propylen Verlag, Berlin, 81; ed, C H Whitman, The Heroic Paradox: Essays on Homer, Sophocles, and Aristophanes, Cornell, 82; auth, Archaic Choral Lyric and Choral Lyric in the Fifth Century, In: Vol 1, Cambridge History of Classical Literature, Cambridge Univ Press, UK, 82-83. *Mailing Add:* Dept of Classics Brown Univ Providence RI 02912

SEGAL, ERICH, b Brooklyn, NY, June 16, 37; m 75; c 1. CLASSICS, COMPARATIVE LITERATURE. *Educ:* Harvard Univ, AB, 58, AM, 59, PhD(comp lit), 65. *Prof Exp:* Vis lectr classics, Yale Univ, 64-65, asst prof, 65-68, assoc prof classics & comp lit, 68-73; vis prof class philol, Univ Munich, 73-74, classics, Princeton Univ, 74-75 ; vis prof classics & comp lit, Dartmouth Col, 75-78; PROF CLASSICS, YALE UNIV, 81- *Concurrent Pos:* Guggenheim fel, 68; mem Nat Adv Coun, Peace Corps, 70; vis fel classics, Wolfson Col, Oxford Univ, 78 & 80; commentator, Masterpiece Theatre, Mourning Becomes Electra, PBS, 78. *Honors & Awards:* Presidential Commendation, 72; Humboldt Stiftung Award, WGer, 73. *Mem:* Acad Lit Studies; Am Philol Asn; Am Comp Lit Asn. *Res:* Roman comedy; Greek tragedy; Latin poetry. *Publ:* Ed, Euripides: A Collection of Critical Essays, Prentice-Hall, 68; Roman Laughter: the Comedy of Plautus, Harvard Univ, 68; ed & transl, Plautus: Three Comedies, Harper, 69; The Ancient Games, Doc film for ABC-TV, 72 & 76; Scholarship on Plautus, 1965-76, Class World Survey, 81; ed, Oxford Readings in Greek Tragedy, Oxford Univ Press (in press); co-ed, Caesar August: Seven Essays, Oxford (in press). *Mailing Add:* Dept of Classics Yale Univ New Haven CT 06520

SEGAL, HOWARD PAUL, American History. See Vol I

SEGEL, HAROLD BERNARD, b Boston, Mass, Sept 13, 30. SLAVIC LANGUAGES & LITERATURES. *Educ:* Boston Col, BS, 51; Harvard Univ, PhD, 55. *Prof Exp:* Asst prof Slavic lang & lit, Univ Fla, 55-59; from asst prof to assoc prof Slavic Lit, Columbia Univ, 59-69, prof, 69-80. *Honors & Awards:* Polish Ministry of Cult Award, 75. *Mem:* Am Asn Advan Slavic Studies; Am Soc 18th Century Studies. *Res:* Slavic literatures; drama and theatre; Polish literature. *Publ:* Auth, The Literature of 18th Century Russia (2 vols), 67 & The Trilogy of Alexander Sukhovo-Kobylin, 69, Dutton; The Major Comedies of Alexander Fredro, Princeton Univ, 69; contribr, The Eighteenth Century in Russia, Oxford Univ, 73; The Baroque Poem, Dutton, 74; ed, Polish Romantic Drama, Cornell Univ, 77. *Mailing Add:* 700 Columbus Ave New York NY 10025

SEGERT, STANISLAV, b Prague, Czech, May 4, 21; m 57; c 2. SEMITIC PHILOLOGY, BIBLICAL STUDIES. *Educ:* John Huss Evangel Theol Fac, Prague, ThB, 45; Charles Univ, PhDr, 47; Orient Inst Czech Acad, Cand Sci, 58. *Prof Exp:* Asst & lectr Greek & Latin, Comenius Evangel Theol Fac, Prague, 45-52; researcher, Orient Inst Czech Acad, 52-70; vis assoc prof, Univ Chicago, 66; vis prof, Johns Hopkins Univ, 68-69; vis prof, 69-71, PROF

BIBL STUDIES & NORTHWEST SEMITICS, UNIV CALIF, LOS ANGELES, 71- *Concurrent Pos:* External teacher, Charles Univ, Prague, 51-57; Guggenheim fel, 76. *Honors & Awards:* Czech Acad Awards, 54 & 61; Fulbright Award, 82-83. *Mem:* Czech Soc Arts & Sci Am; Am Orient Soc; Soc Bibl Lit; Archaeol Inst Am; Am Schs Orient Res. *Res:* Canaanite and Aramaic philology; Bible; contacts between Semitic and Graeco-Roman civilizations. *Publ:* Auth, Vorabeiten zur hebräischen Metrik I-III, 53 & 56 & Zur Sprache der moabitischen Königsinschrift, 61 Archiv Orientalni; auth, Ugaritskiy Yazyk, Nauka, 65; coauth, Orientalistik an der Prager Universität, 1348-1848, Univ Karlova, 67; auth, Synove svetla a synove tmy, Orbis, 70; Altaramäische Grammatik, Verlag Enzyklopädie, 75; A Grammar of Phoenician and Punic, Beck, 76. *Mailing Add:* Dept of Near Eastern Lang & Cult Univ of Calif Los Angeles CA 90024

SEHMSKORF, HENNING, b Königsberg, Ger, Mar 16, 37; US citizen. SCANDINAVIAN. *Educ:* Univ Rochester, BS, 60; Univ Chicago, MA, 64, PhD(comp lit), 68. *Prof Exp:* Instr Ger, Wabash Col, 64; ASST PROF SCAND LANG & LIT, UNIV WASH, 67-, CHMN DEPT SCAND LANG & LIT, 79- *Mem:* Soc Advan Scand Studies. *Res:* German And Scandinavian Romanticism; folk literature, especially German and Scandinavian; Bjornstjerne Bjornson. *Publ:* Auth, A Strindberg's Swanwhite and Scandinavian folk poetry, barat Rev, 66; Two legends about St Olaf, the master builder: A clue to the dramatic structure of Ibsen's Bygmester Solness, Edda, 67; Bjornson's Trond and popular tradition, Scand Studies, 68. *Mailing Add:* 6272 19th NE Seattle WA 98115

SEIDENSTICKER, EDWARD G, b Castle Rock, Colo, Feb 11, 21. JAPANESE. *Educ:* Univ Colo, BA, 42; Columbia Univ, MA, 47. *Prof Exp:* From assoc prof to prof Japanese, Stanford Univ, 62-66; prof, Univ Mich, Ann Arbor, 66-77; PROF JAPANESE, COLUMBIA UNIV, 77- *Honors & Awards:* Nat Bk Award, Nat Bk Comt, NY, 70; Order of Rising Sun Award, Japanese Govt, 75; Kikuchi Kan Prize, Buugei Shuuju, Tokyo, 77. *Mem:* Asn Asian Studies; Am Orient Soc. *Res:* Modern Japanese literature; Heian literature. *Publ:* Auth, Japan, Life, 61; Kafu the Scribbler, Stanford Univ, 65; The Gossamer Years, Tuttle, 65; The image, In: The United States and Japan, Prentice-Hall, 66; Tanizaki Jun-ichiro, 1886-1965, Monumenta Nipponica, 66; The pure and the in-between in the modern Japanese novel, Harvard J Asiatic Studies, 66; transl, The Tale of Geuji, Knorf, 76. *Mailing Add:* Dept of East-Asian Lang & Cult 407 Kent Hall Columbia Univ New York NY 10027

SEIDLER, INGO, b Graz, Austria, Oct 8, 28; m 58; c 3. GERMAN & COMPARATIVE LITERATURE. *Educ:* Cornell Univ, BA 51; Univ Vienna, Dr Phil, 53. *Prof Exp:* From instr to assoc prof, 57-68, PROF GER, UNIV MICH, ANN ARBOR, 68- *Concurrent Pos:* H Rackham res fel, 60, 66 & 77; Am Coun Learned Soc travel grant, 65; vis prof, Washington Univ, 69, Univ Freidburg & res dir, jr year, 71-72 & Northwestern Univ, 82; res grant, Deutscher Akademisher Austauschdienst, 77; reader, Adv Placement Prog, 78; mem, Nat Endowment for Humanities transl proj, 79. *Mem:* Brecht Soc; Int Ver Germanisten; Am Nietzsche Soc; MLA. *Res:* Nineteenth and 20th century literature, especially poetry and drama; criticism; theory of literature. *Publ:* Auth, Kafkas Urteil, Psychol in Lit Wiss, Stiehm, 71; Peter Huchel, Uber P H Suhrkamp, 73; co-ed, W A Reichart Festschrift, 75, auth, Amerikaperspektive Nietzsches, Am in Deutsch Lit, Reclam, 75; Art and Power: G Benn, Mich Ger Studies, 76 ?; Rilke in English, Can Rev of Comp Lit, 79; Theater in West Germany, Col Germmanica, 81; Who is E Canetti?, Cross Currents, 82. *Mailing Add:* Dept of Ger Univ Mich Ann Arbor MI 48109

SEIDLIN, OSKAR, b Ger, Feb 17, 11. GERMAN LITERATURE. *Educ:* Univ Basel, PhD, 35. *Hon Degrees:* DHL, Univ Mich, 69. *Prof Exp:* Asst prof, Smith Col, 39-46; from asst prof to prof Ger, Ohio State Univ, 46-66, regents prof, 66-72; prof, Ind Univ, Bloomington, 72-74; distinguished prof, 74-79, EMER REGENTS PROF GER, OHIO STATE UNIV, 72-; EMER DISTINGUISHED PROF IND UNIV, 79- *Concurrent Pos:* Vis prof, Univ Wash, 49; Ford Found vis prof, Free Univ Berlin, 59; assoc ed, Ger Quart, 60-65; mem adv comn, Princeton Univ, 62-74; Guggenheim fel, 62-63 & 77-78; co-ed, Arcadia, 66-73; Ger Acad Lang & Lit prize, Ger Studies Abroad, 68; cor mem Acad Sci, Göttingen, Ger, 73- *Honors & Awards:* Distinguished Lectr Award, Germanistic Soc Am, 74; Eichendorff Medal, Eichendorff Gesellschaft, 74; Kulturpreis Award, State of Nordrhein-Westfalen, Ger, 75. *Mem:* Am Asn Teachers Ger; Int Humanities Res Asn. *Res:* Age of Goethe; Eichendorff; modern German literature. *Publ:* Coauth, Outline History of German Literature, Barnes & Noble, 48, 61; auth, Essays in German and Comparative Literature, Univ NC, 61 & 66; Von Goethe zu Thomas Mann, 63 & 69, Versuche Über Eichendorff, 65 & 68 & Klassische und Moderne Klassiker, 72, Vandenhoeck & Ruprecht; Der Briefwechsel Schnitzler-Brahm, 75 & Festschrift: Herkommen und Erneuerung, Essays fur Oskar Seidlin, 76, Niemeyer; Der Theaterkritiker Otto Brahm, Bouvier, 78; Von erwachendem Bewubtsein und vom Sündenfall, Klett-Cotta, 79. *Mailing Add:* Dept of Ger Ind Univ Bloomington IN 47401

SEIF, MORTON PHILIP VAN MOPPES, b Brooklyn, NY, Feb 19, 28. COMPARATIVE LITERATURE. *Educ:* Univ NC, BA, 48; Univ Aix-Marseille, Cert Fr, 49; NY UNiv, MA, 50; Univ London, Cert Brit Studies, 51; Univ Calif, Berkeley, MA, 58; Univ Amsterdam, Drlet(lit), 67; Pratt Inst, MLS, 74. *Prof Exp:* Teaching asst English & creative writing, Unliv Calif, Berkeley, 56-58; instr English & Am lit, State Univ NY Buffalo, 58-59; instr English, Univ Ariz, 59-60; lectr Am lit, Scand Univ, 60-62; asst prof English & world lit, Cent Mo State Univ, 67-68; assoc prof English & core curric, Baker Univ, 68-69; adj assoc prof classics & comp lit, lectr libr, regents scholar law & educ, City Univ New York, 70-75; INTERDISCIPLINARY SCHOLAR AM STUDIES, UNIV CALIF, BERKELEY, 80- *Concurrent Pos:* Ed, Photo Arts & TV Digest, 50-51; exec dir, Mag Info Bur, 52-55; arts critic, Saturday Rev, 55-66; ed staff, Times Lit Suppl, 62-65; publ & ed, Europ Bk News, 62-65; vis prof, Nassau Community Col, 71 & Univ DC, 72; John Adams prof, Am Col, Amsterdam, 72-82; consult, Nat Proj Ctr Film & Humanities, 74 & Libr Cong, 76-78; Western Europe adv, US Dept State, 78-80. *Mem:* MLA; Am Studies Asn; Am Lit Asn; AHA. *Res:* Modern literature and society; American-Dutch relations; bibliography. *Publ:* Auth, The Broken World, Beachcomber Press, 49; ed & transl, Verlaine, Ed Soleil Blond, 52; auth, The impact of T S Eliot on W H Auden and Stephen Spender, SAtlantic Quart, 54; ed & transl, A Mexican Sestet, Ed Mundo, 58; Sea and Star, North Lands Press, 62; New Writing from the Netherlands, 64 & New Dutch Writing and Art, 65, De Bezige Bij; Mark Twain's America, In: American Literature: Written Word and Visual Image, NEH, 74. *Mailing Add:* Dept of English Univ of Calif Berkeley CA 94704

SEIFERT, LESTER W J, b Juneau, Wis, Aug 15, 15; m 45; c 1. GERMAN, LINGUISTICS. *Educ:* Northwestern Col, Wis, Ab, 37; Univ Wis, AM, 38; Brown Univ, PhD(German ling), 41. *Prof Exp:* Instr Ger, Brown Univ, 41-42; from instr to assoc prof, 46-56, PROF GER, UNIV WIS-MADISON, 56- *Mem:* Am Asn Teachers Ger; MLA; Ling Soc Am. *Res:* Wisconsin German and Pennsylvania German; dialectology; bilingualism. *Publ:* Contribr, A contrastive discription of Pennsylvania German and standard German stops and fricatives, In: Approaches in Linguistic Methodology, Univ Wis, 67; The word geography of Pennsylvania German: extent & causes, In: The German Language in America, Univ Tex, 71; coauth, Otfrid von Weipenburg's Evangehinbuch, Allegorica, 77; auth, Methods and aims of the survey of German spoken in Wisconsin; collabr, A Linguistic Atlas of Pennsylvania German & Spoken German. *Mailing Add:* Dept of Ger Univ of Wis-Madison Madison WI 53706

SEIGNEURET, JEAN-CHARLES, b Lisieux, France, Mar 17, 37; Can citizen; m 58; c 3. FRENCH LITERATURE. *Educ:* Univ BC, BA, 58; Univ Calif, Los Angeles, MA, 60, PhD, 63. *Prof Exp:* Asst, Univ Calif, Los Angeles, 58-61; instr French, Western Wash State Col, 61-63, asst prof French & dir lang lab, 63-66; assoc prof, 66-71, chmn dept foreign lang & lit, 71-81, PROF FRENCH, WASH STATE UNIV, 71- *Concurrent Pos:* Educ consult, Film Assocs Calif, 60-61; Radio Corp Am res grant, 61; Nat Endowment for Humanities res grant, 77-78; consult bd regents, State La, 82. *Honors & Awards:* Chevalier dans l'Ordre des Palmes Academiques, French Govt, 76; Wash Asn Foreign Lang Teachers Pro-Lingua Award, 76. *Mem:* Am Asn Teachers Fr (vpres, 73-78); MLA; Am Coun Teaching Foreign Lang; Pac Northwest Coun Foreign Lang (pres, 79-80). *Res:* Old French; language and literature. *Publ:* Ed, Le Roman du Comte d'Artois, Droz, Paris-Geneva, 66; auth, Adulare to Aller, Romance Notes, fall 67; Teaching French in the 70's ?, Fr Rev, 71; Ici Paris, Office de la Radio-television Francaise, French Rev, Vol 46, 72; Le Dialogue Eugene Ionesco-Jean-Louis Barrault, French Rev, spring 78; transl & auth introd & notes, The spirits, In: Four Renaissance French Plays, Wash State Univ, 78; auth, Survey of research tool needs in French language and literature, Fr Rev, spring 79; ed, La Vie Francaise en Mutation, Newbury House, 79. *Mailing Add:* Dept of Foreign Lang & Lit Wash State Univ Pullman WA 99163

SEITTELMAN, ELIZABETH EDITH, b New York, NY, Dec 22, 22. CLASSICAL LANGUAGES & LITERATURE. *Educ:* Hunter Col, AB, 43; Fordham Univ, AM, 44, Phd(classics), 52. *Prof Exp:* Asst, Fordham Univ, 45-47; teacher, James Monroe High Sch, 49-50, Acad Mt St Ursula, 47-49, Washington Irving Eve High Sch, 54-55, Roosevelt High Sch, 55-56 & Nathan Hale Sch, 50-59; asst prin, Jr High Sch, 104, Man, 59-69; from asst prof to assoc prof, 69-73, PROF CLASSICS, YORK COL NY, 73-, CHMN DEPT TEACHER PREP, 72- *Concurrent Pos:* Columbia Univ grant classics, 44-45; lectr English, Bronx Community Col, 61-68; consult, task force, bd educ, New York, 66; classics bibliographer, Am Coun Teaching Foreign Lang, 66-71; lectr, Brooklyn Col, 67-69, ed, Epitome, 72-; educ expert, Evaluation Team Accreditation Comn, Nat Assoc Trade & Tech Schs, 76-; chmn, Am Class Leagues Comt, Study Class Humanities in Elm Schs, 77-81; vpres, Elem Sch Sect, NY State English Coun, 82-83. *Mem:* Class Asn Atlantic States; Am Philol Asn; Am Class League; Am Educ Res Assoc. *Res:* Aristophanes; Seneca and Roman Stoicism; Neoplatonic philosophy. *Publ:* Auth, Some contributions of Jewish Women to education in the US, The Principal, 9/75, 11/75 & 12/75; Developing positive values thru the study of the humanities, Humanities J, 9/76; Some future trends in administration, The Principal, 9/77; 1982 Supplementary Survey of Audio-Visual Materials in the Classics, Classical World, 3/82. *Mailing Add:* Dept of Teacher Prep York Col 150-14 Jamaica Ave New York NY 11451

SELBY, TALBOT RAYL, b Goldsboro, NC, Apr 1, 27; m 50; c 2. CLASSICAL LANGUAGES, BIBLICAL LITERATURE. *Educ:* Univ NC, PhD(classics), 56. *Prof Exp:* Asst prof Greek & Bible, Univ of the South, 56-58; assoc prof Ancient lang, Col William & Mary, 58-61; assoc prof, Col Charleston, 61-62; PROF ANCIENT LANG, UNIV RICHMOND, 62- *Mem:* Am Philol Asn; Class Asn Mid W & S; Vergilian Soc Am; Renaissance Soc Am; Am-Italy Soc. *Res:* Fourteenth century Italy; neo-Latin revival. *Publ:* Auth, Filippo Villani and his vita of Guido Bonatti, Renaissance News, 59; Pragmatism in Aeneid IV, Eleusis, 60. *Mailing Add:* Box 237 Univ Richmond Richmond VA 23173

SELIG, KARL-LUDWIG, b Wiesbaden, Ger, Aug 14, 26. ROMANCE LANGUAGES & LITERATURE. *Educ:* Ohio State Univ, BA, 46, MA, 47; Univ Tex, PhD, 55. *Prof Exp:* Asst prof, Johns Hopkins Univ, 54-58; assoc prof Romance lang & lit, Univ NC, 58-61; assoc prof Romance lang & comp lit, Univ Minn, 61-63; vis prof, Univ Tex, 63-64, prof Romance lang, 64-65; Hinchliff prof Span lit, Cornell Univ, 65-69, dir grad studies dept Romance studies, 66-69; PROF SPAN LIT, COLUMBIA UNIV, 69- *Concurrent Pos:* Am Philos Soc res grants, 55 & 61; assoc ed, Mod Lang Notes, 55-58; lectr, Goucher Col, 57; Newberry Libr fel, 58; Fulbright res scholar, Univ Utrecht, 58-59; Folger Shakespeare Libr fel, 59 & 63; managing ed, Romance Notes, 59-61; ed, Bull Comediantes, 59-64, assoc ed, 78-; ed, Univ NC Studies Comp Lit, 59-61, co-ed, Yearbk Comp Lit, Vol IX; spec fel, Belgian Am Educ Found, 60 & 61; vis prof, Univ Munich, 63 & 64 & Univ Berlin, 67; consult, Ohio State Univ, 67-69; vis lectr, Univ Zulia, 68; assoc ed, Hispania, 69-74; gen ed, Rev Hisp Mod, Columbia Univ Hisp studies, 71-; assoc ed, Ky Romance Quart, 74- & Teaching Lang Through Lit, 78-; vis scholar, Ga Univ Syst, 77-; sr fel, Medieval and Renaissance Inst, Duke Univ, 78; vis scholar,

Herzog August Bibliothek, 79- *Honors & Awards:* Mark van Doren Award, Columbia, 74. *Mem:* Col Art Asn Am; MLA; Acad Lit Studies; Am Asn Teachers Span & Port; Am Asn Teachers Ital. *Res:* Comparative literature. *Publ:* Co-ed, Studia philologica et litteraria in honorem L Spitzer, Francke, Bern, 58; auth, The library of cincencio Juan de Lastanosa, patron of Gracian, Droz, Switz, 60; ed, Thomas Blundeville, Of councils and counsellors, Scholars Facs, 63; co-ed, Essays in honor of N B Adams, Univ NC, Chapel Hill, 66. *Mailing Add:* Hamilton Hall 704 Columbia Univ New York NY 10027

SELIGER, HELFRIED WERNER, b Vienna, Austria, Aug 9, 39; Can citizen. GERMAN LITERATURE. *Educ:* Univ Alta, BA, 62; McGill Univ, MA, 64, PhD(Ger), 72. *Prof Exp:* Asst prof, 72-75, ASSOC PROF GER, VICTORIA COL, UNIV TORONTO, 75- *Mem:* MLA; Am Asn Teachers Ger; Can Asn Univ Teachers Ger (secy-treas, 73-75); Int Brecht Soc; Can Comp Int Asn. *Res:* German Romanticism; German-Spanish literary relations; 20th century German literature. *Publ:* Auth, Das Amerikabild Bertolt Brechts, Bouvier, Bonn, 74. *Mailing Add:* Dept of Ger Univ Toronto Toronto ON M5S 1A1 Can

SELIGSON, GERDA, b Freiburg, Ger, Mar 23, 09; Brit citizen; m 35; c 1. CLASSICAL STUDIES, LINGUISTICS. *Educ:* Univ London, AB, 45; Columbia Univ, MA, 55. *Prof Exp:* Assoc prof, 56-65, prof, 65-79, EMER PROF CLASS STUDIES, UNIV MICH, ANN ARBOR, 79- *Concurrent Pos:* Vis prof, Lawrence Univ, 79-82, Univ Iowa, 82-83. *Res:* The Roman stage. *Publ:* Translr, The Art of Bergil, Ann Arbor Press, 62; auth, The Structural approach the first decade, Class World, 12/65; coauth, Latin a Structural Approach, Ann Arbor Press, 67; On reading Latin, Class Outlook 1/74; auth, Reading Latin, a progress report, Strategies Teaching Greek & Latin, 81; coauth, Latin for Reading, Ann Arbor Press, 82. *Mailing Add:* 1037 Olivia Ann Arbor MI 48104

SELLIN, ERIC, b Philadelphia, Pa, Nov 7, 33; m 58; c 2. FRENCH, COMPARATIVE LITERATURE. *Educ:* Univ Pa, BA, 55, MA, 58, PhD(French), 65. *Prof Exp:* Asst instr French, Univ Pa, 55-56, 57-58, 59-62; lectr Am lit, Univ Bordeaux, 56-57; instr French, Clark Univ, 58-59; from instr to assoc prof, 62-70, PROF FRENCH, TEMPLE UNIV, 70- *Concurrent Pos:* Fulbright-Hays lectr Am lit, Univ Algiers, 68-69 & Univ Dakar, 78-79; Nat Endowment for Humanities sr fel, 73-74; founder & dir, Centre d'Etudes sur La Litterature Francophone de L'Afrique du Nord, 81-; ed, Celfan Rev, 81- & Celfan Eds, 82- *Mem:* Am Asn Teachers Fr; MLA; AAUP; African Lit Asn. *Res:* Modern French poetry; aesthetic theory; African literature of French expression. *Publ:* Auth, The Dramatic Concepts of Antonin Artaud, Univ Chicago, 68; Negritude: Status or dynamics?, L'Esprit Createur, fall 70; Alienation in the novels of Camara Laye, Pan-African J, Fall, 71; Simultaneity: Driving force of the surrealist aesthetic, Twentieth Century Lit, 2/75; Valery, Stevens and the Cartesian dilemma, Folio, Brockport, 75; The Unknown Voice of Yambo Ouologuem, Yale Fr Studies, 76; Literary Aftershocks of the Revolution: Recent Developments in Algerian Literature, Studies 20th Centuries Lit, spring 80; Nightfall over Lubumbashi, Celfan Eds, 82. *Mailing Add:* 312 Kent Rd Bala-Cynwyd PA 19004

SELLSTROM, ALBERT DONALD, b Sept 25, 26. FRENCH. *Educ:* Univ Tex, BA, 47, MA, 49; Princeton Univ, 53, PhD(French), 56. *Prof Exp:* Instr English, Univ Tex, 50-51; instr French, Princeton Univ, 54-58; from asst prof to assoc prof, 58-67, chmn dept French & Ital, 72-78, PROF FRENCH, UNIV TEX, AUSTIN, 67- *Honors & Awards:* Palmes Academiques, French Govt, 75. *Mem:* MLA; Am Asn Teachers Fr. *Res:* Seventeenth century French drama; Corneille; devotional poetry of the Counter-Reformation. *Publ:* Auth, The structure of Corneille's masterpieces, Romanic Rev, 12/58; The role of Corneille's Infante, Fr Rev, 11/65; ed, Le Cid, Prentice-Hall, 67; auth, Signatures de Corneille dans son theatre, L'Esprit Createur, summer 71; Comedy in Theodore and Beyond, Biblio 17, 82. *Mailing Add:* Dept of French & Ital Univ of Tex Austin TX 78712

SEMANN, KHALIL I H, b Safita, Syria, Mar 6, 20; US citizen; m 60; c 3. ARABIC. *Educ:* Georgetown Univ, BSceL, 54; Columbia Univ, MA, 55, PhD, 59. *Prof Exp:* Assoc Arabic, Georgetown Univ, 51-54; lectr Semitic lang, NY Univ, 55-56 & Arabic, Columbia Univ, 57; from res historian I to actg asst prof Orient lang, Univ Calif, Los Angeles, 57-59; reference librn Near E sect, Libr Congr, 60-62; researcher, Europe & Near East, 63-64; vis scholar, Teachers Col, Columbia Univ, 64-65; from asst prof to assoc prof Arabic, State Univ NY, Binghamton, 65-70, dir Arabic studies prog, 65-75; resident dir, Mediterranean studies prog, Univ of Malta, 75-76; PROF ARABIC, STATE UNIV NY, 70- *Mem:* Am Asn Teachers Arabic; Am Orient Soc; Mideast Studies Asn NAm. *Res:* Arabic & Islamic Studies. *Publ:* Auth, Arabic poetry, the old and the new, Etudes Arabes et Islamiques, Paris, 75; Genesis of Arabic Linguistics, Akad Wissen Göttingen, 76; Sibawaihi and the Christian West, Al-Lisan al-Arabi Rabat, XIII; Ash-Shafi'i's Risalah, Ibn Sina's Risalah, Linguisitcs in the Middle Ages & Murder in Baghdad, Islam & Medieval West, 80. *Mailing Add:* Dept of Class & Near Eastern Studies State Univ of New York Binghamton NY 13901

SENA, JORGE DE, b Lisbon, Portugal, Nov 2, 19; m 49; c 9. PORTUGUESE & BRAZILIAN LITERATURE. *Educ:* Univ Porto, MSc, 44; Univ Sao Paulo, PhD(lett) & Livre-docente, 64. *Prof Exp:* Prof theory of lit, Univ Sao Paulo, 59-61, Port lit, 61-65; prof Port & Brazilian lit, Univ Wis-Madison, 65-70; PROF PORT & COMP LIT, UNIV CALIF, SANTA BARBARA, 70-, CHMN DEPT COMP LIT, 72-, DEPT SPAN & PORT, 75- *Honors & Awards:* Great Int Poetry Prize, Etna- Thormina, 77. *Mem:* Hisp Soc Am; MLA; Port Acad Sci; Renaissance Soc Am. *Res:* Comparative literature; Renaissance and baroque literature; modern literature and poetry. *Publ:* Auth, A literatura inglesa, Ed Cultrix, Sao Paulo, 63; Uma cancao de Cameos, 66, Os sonetos de Camoes e o Soneto quinhentista peninsular, 69 & A estrutura de Os Lusiadas e outros estodos camonianos, 70, Portugalia Ed, Lisbon; Poemas Ingleses de Fernando Pessoa, critical ed, bilingual text, Atica, Lisbon, 76; Dialecticas Teoricas de Literatura, 77 & Dialecticas Aplicadas da Literatura, 77, Ed 70, Lisbon, 77; Complete Poetry, Moraes, Libon, 3 Vols, 77-78. *Mailing Add:* 939 Randolph Rd Santa Barbara CA 93111

SENIFF, DENNIS PAUL, b Columbus, Ohio, Mar 5, 49; m 72; c 2. SPANISH MEDIEVAL LITERATURE. *Educ:* Univ of the South, BA, 71; Univ Wis-Madison, MA, 73; PhD(Span), 78. *Prof Exp:* Vis instr Span, Washington Univ, St Louis, 77-78; ASST PROF SPAN, MICH STATE UNIV, EAST LANSING, 78- *Concurrent Pos:* Vis asst prof Span, Dartmouth Col, 80 & 82; consult Span, Rassias Found, Wyndmoor, Pa, 80-; All Univ Res Grants fel, Span & law, Mich State Univ Found, 81; Nat Endowment for Humanities grant, Span & philos, summer, 82. *Honors & Awards:* Excellence in teaching citation, Dartmouth Col, 80. *Mem:* MLA; Am Asn Teachers Span & Port; Midwest Mod Lang Asn; Medieval Acad Am. *Res:* Didactic, scientific and legal treatises of the Iberian Peninsula; editing of medieval manuscripts and related problems; philosophical currents in medieval Spanish prose treatises. *Publ:* Auth, Self-doubt in Clarice Lispector's Lacos de Familia, Luso-Brazilian Rev, winter 77; Bangue: ensaio Interpretivo de Caraterizacao, Estudios Ibero-Am, Porto Alegre, Brazil, 80; All the king's men and all the king's lands: The nobility and geography of the Libro de la Monteria, Proc 2nd La Conf Hispanic Lang & Lit, 81; coauth (with John Alford), A Bibliography for Legal Influences in Medieval Literature, Garland Press, 82; ed, An Edition of the Libro de la Monteria based on Escorial MS Y.II.19, 82 & Aragonese Plutarco, In: Texts & Concordances of Juan Fernandes de Heredia, 5/82, Hispanic Sem Ltd; auth, New views on drama in the foreign language and literature classroom, Ram's Horn, spring 82. *Mailing Add:* Dept of Romance & Class Lang Michigan State Univ East Lansing MI 48824

SENN, HARRY ANTHONY, b Minneapolis, Minn, May 22, 39; m 64; c 2. FRENCH, FOLKLORE. *Educ:* Univ Minn, BA, 61, MA, 64; Univ Calif, Berkeley, PhD(French), 72. *Prof Exp:* Instr French, 70-72, asst prof, 73-78, ASSOC PROF FRENCH & FOLKLORE, PITZER COL, 79- *Concurrent Pos:* Fulbright-Hays res fel, 75; Int Res & Exchanges Bd res fel, Am Coun Learned Socs, 77. *Mem:* Am Folklore Soc; MLA. *Res:* French society and civilization; folk mythology; folk legends in French literature. *Publ:* Auth, Arnold van Gennep: Structuralist and apologist for the study of folklore in France, Folklore, England, winter 74; Gaston Paris as folklorist (1867-1895): The rise and decline of French folklore studies, J Folklore Inst, winter 75; Some werewolf legends and the Calusari ritual in Romania, E Europ Quart, winter 76; Some werewolf legends and the Calusari ritual in Romania: Dracula doesn't live here anymore, Participant, fall 76. *Mailing Add:* Pitzer Col 1050 N Mills Ave Claremont CA 91711

SERIGHT, ORIN DALE, b Boulder, Colo, Nov 23, 32. ENGLISH, LINGUISTICS. *Educ:* Univ Col, BA, 55; Univ Ark, MA, 57; Ind Univ, PhD(English lang), 64. *Prof Exp:* Asst prof English & ling, Univ Southern Calif, 60-67; chmn dept ling, 67-76, ASSOC PROF ENGLISH & LING, SAN DIEGO STATE UNIV, 67- *Mem:* MLA; Ling Soc Am. *Res:* English language; 19th century romantic literature; linguistics. *Publ:* Auth, Keats' syntas: A Study in Style, Mouton, The Hague; On defining the appositive, Col Compos & Commun, 5/66; Double negatives in standard modern English, 5/66 & The negative-constrastive construction in standard modern English, 5/67, Am Speech. *Mailing Add:* Dept of Ling San Diego State Univ San Diego CA 92115

SERNA-MAYTORENA, MANUEL ANTONIO, b Empalme, Mex, Oct 23, 32; m 64; c 2. SPANISH, LATIN AMERICAN LITERATURE. *Educ:* Univ Guadelajara, BA, 52, MA, 63; Univ Mo, PhD(Span), 67. *Prof Exp:* From instr to asst prof Latin Am lit, 66-68, asst prof Latin Am lit & stylistics theory lit, 68-71, assoc prof, 71-76, PROF SPAN, OHIO UNIV, 76- *Concurrent Pos:* Res grant, 68-69 & Baker Award 73-74, Ohio Univ. *Mem:* MLA; Midwest Mod Lang Asn. *Res:* Mexican literature; Latin American novel; poetry and poetics of the post modernism. *Publ:* Auth, Silencio Desnudo, (poetry), Univ Guadalajara, 68; ed, La multiple, Etcaetera, Mex, 70; auth, El hombre y el paisaje del campo jalisciense en La cuesta de la comadres, 71 & Santa: Mexico, 72, Cucadernos Am; Notas en torno a la estructura de El Hombre, Etcaetera, 72; La Exacta Pasion, Cajica, Mex, 73. *Mailing Add:* Dept of Mod Lang Ohio Univ Athens OH 45701

SERRA-LIMA, FEDERICO, b Buenos Aires, Arg, July 17, 29; US citizen. SPANISH LITERATURE. *Educ:* Columbia Univ, BS, 63; New York Univ, MA, 65, PhD(Span), 71. *Prof Exp:* From lectr to instr Span, Columbia Univ, 63-70; asst prof, 70-71, assoc prof, 71-80, PROF SPAN, HARTWICK COL, 79-, CHMN, DEPT MOD & CLASS LANG, 78- *Concurrent Pos:* Nat Endowment for Humanities fel, 80. *Mem:* AAUP; Am Asn Teachers Span & Port; MLA; Inst Int Lit Iberoamericana; Hisp Inst. *Res:* Spanish poetry; Latin American Literature; Miguel de Unamuno. *Publ:* Auth, Ruben Dario y Gerard de Nerval, 1-4/66, Alberto Oscar Blasi, Los fundadores, 1-4/67 & F Fernandez Turienzo, Unamuno, ansia de Dios y creacion literaria, 1-4/69, Rev Hisp Mod. *Mailing Add:* Dept of Mod & Class Lang Hartwick Col Oneonta NY 13820

SERRANO-PLAJA, ARTURO, b Escorial, Spain, Dec 23, 09. ROMANCE LANGUAGES. *Educ:* Univ Madrid, Lic en lett, 34. *Prof Exp:* Vis prof Span & Port, Univ Wis, Madison, 61-63; assoc prof to prof Romance lang, Univ Minn, Minneapolis, 63-68; prof Span & Port, 68-76, EMER PROF SPAN, UNIV CALIF, SANTA BARBARA, 76- *Res:* Spanish literature of the Golden Age; contemporary Spanish literature. *Publ:* Auth, Galop de la Destinee, Seghers, Paris, 54; Galope del Destino, Losada, Buenos Aires, 58; Le Mano de Dios Pasa por Este Perro, Rialp, Madrid, 65; El absurdo en Camus y en Calderon de la Barca, In: Melanges a la Memoire de J Sarrailh, Paris, 66; Realismo Magico en Cervantes, Gredos, Madrid, 67; Magic Realism in Cervantes, Univ Calif, 70; Los alamos oscuros (poetry), Papeles Son Armadans, Palma de Mallorca, Spain, 70; Sera le religion el opio del pueblo?, Cuadernos Am, Mex, 73. *Mailing Add:* 2911 Kenmore Pl Santa Barbara CA 93105

SETCHKAREV, VSEVOLOD, b Charkov, Apr 8, 14; US citizen; m 44; c 1. SLAVIC LANGUAGES & LITERATURE. *Educ:* Univ Berlin, DPhil, 38, DPhil Habil, 48. *Hon Degrees:* Harvard Univ, MA, 57. *Prof Exp:* Dozent Slavic philol, Univ Bonn, 47-50, assoc prof, 50-53; prof, Univ Hamburg, 53-

57; prof, 57-63; CURT HUGO REISINGER PROF SLAVIC LANG & LIT, HARVARD UNIV, 63- *Res:* Russian literature; South Slavic literatures. *Publ:* Auth, Laodamia in Polen & Russlang, Z Slavische Philos, 58; NS Leskov, sein Leben und sein Werk, Harrassowitz, 59; The narrative prose of Brjusov, Int J Slavic Ling & Poetics, 59; Geschichte der Russishen Literatur, Reclam, Stuttgart, 62; A Puschkin, sein Leben und Werk, Harrassowitz, 63; Studies in the Life and Work of I Annenskij, Mouton, The Hauge, 63; Gogol, his Life and Work, NY Univ, 65; I A Goncharov, his Life and Work, JAL, Würzburg, 74. *Mailing Add:* 72 Scott Rd Belmont MA 02178

SETTLE, JAMES NORWOOD, b Lexington, NC, Oct 6, 29; m 57; c 1. CLASSICAL LANGUAGES. *Educ:* Wake Forest Col, AB, 50; Univ NC, PhD, 62. *Prof Exp:* Instr classics, Univ NC, 59-62; asst prof class lang, Duke Univ, 62-66; exec assoc, Am Coun Learned Soc, 66-81; DEAN HUMANITIES & ARTS, HUNTER COL, 81- *Mem:* Am Philos Asn. *Res:* Cicero, orations and letters. *Publ:* Auth, The trial of Milo and the other pro Milane, Trans Am Philol Asn. *Mailing Add:* 6 D North 2 Tudor City Pl New York NY 10017

SEVERINO, ALEXANDRINO EUSEBIO, b Olhao, Port, July 17, 31; US citizen; m 61; c 4. ROMANCE LANGUAGES. *Educ:* Univ RI, BA, 58; Univ Sao Paulo, Dr Lett(Port), 66. *Prof Exp:* Prof Am lit, Faculdade Marilia, Univ Sao Paulo, 60-66, English lit, 64-66; asst prof Port, Univ Tex, Austin, 66-68; assoc prof, 68-75, pres, 75-80, PROF PORT, CHMN DEPT SPAN & PORT, VANDERBILT UNIV, 75- *Concurrent Pos:* Ford Found fel, grad ctr Latin Am studies, 70-71. *Mem:* MLA; Mid-Atlantic Mod Lang Asn; Northeast Mod Lang Asn; Am Asn Teachers Span & Port; Latin Am Studies Asn. *Res:* Modern Portuguese poetry; contemporary Brazilian prose fiction; Camoes and Melville, Portuguese-American literary relations. *Publ:* Auth, Fernando Pessoana Africa do sul: Contribuicao ao estudo de sua formacao artistica, Fac Philos, Sci & Lett Marilia, Brazil, 69; co-ed, A presenca de Milton em uma Ode de Alvaro de Campos, Luso-Brazilian Rev, 70; Studies in short fiction: Contemporary Latin America, Newberry Col, 71; contribr, Brazil in the Sixties, Vanderbilt Univ, 72. *Mailing Add:* Dept of Span & Portuguese Vanderbilt Univ Nashville TN 37235

SEVIN, DIETER H, b Mühlanger, Ger, Nov 5, 38; US citizen; m 63; c 2. GERMAN LITERATURE. *Educ:* Calif State Univ, San Jose, BA, 63; Univ Wash, MA, 64, PhD(Ger & hist), 67. *Prof Exp:* Asst prof Ger Lang & lit, Pac Lutheran Univ, 67-68; asst prof, 68-73, dir Vanderbilt-in-Ger, Regensburg, 73-75, ASSOC PROF GER LANG & LIT, VANDERBILT UNIV, 73- *Concurrent Pos:* Am Coun Learned Soc grant, 81-82. *Mem:* MLA; Am Asn Teachers Ger; AAUP; Soc Exile Lit; Am Goethe Soc. *Res:* Nineteenth and 20th century German literature; German exile literature; East German literature. *Publ:* Coauth, Zur Diskussion, Harper, 72; auth, Theodor Plievier's Double Exile in Russia, Colloquia Germanica, 76/77; Die existentielle Krise im Büchners Lenz, Seminar spring 79; coauth, Wie geht's? An Introductory German Course, Holt, Rinchart and Winston, 80; auth, Joachim Maass: Exil ohne Enole, Colloguia Germanicca, 81; The Plea for Artistic Freedom in Christa Wolf's Nachdenden über Christa T & Lesen und Schreiben: Fiction and Essay a Mutually Supportive Gengre Forms, Studies in 6 DR Culture and Society, Univ Press, 82 ; Christa Wolf: Der geteilte Himmel Nach denken über Christa T Interpretationen: Olden Gourg, 82. *Mailing Add:* Dept of Ger Lang & Lit Vanderbilt Univ Nashville TN 37235

SEYMOUR, RICHARD KELLOGG, b Hinsdale, Ill, June 21, 30; m 51; c 2. GERMAN. *Educ:* Univ Mich, BA, 51, MA, 52; Univ Pa, PhD(Ger philol), 56. *Prof Exp:* Asst instr Ger, Univ Pa, 52-54; instr Ger & ling, Princeton Univ, 54-58; asst prof, Duke Univ, 58-63, assoc prof, 63-67; prof Ger & chmn dept Europ lang, Univ Hawaii, Manoa, 67-75; vis prof English, Univ Cologne, Ger, 75; prof Ger, Pennsylvania State Univ, 75-77; PROF GER, UNIV HAWAII, 77-, ACTG DEAN, LANG, LING & LIT, ARTS & SCI, 81- *Concurrent Pos:* Assoc ed, Unterrichtspraxis, 69-80; Fulbright travel grant, 81. *Mem:* Am Asn Teachers Ger; Ling Soc Am; Int Ling Asn; SAtlantic Mod Lang Asn (secy-treas, 62-67); Nat Ger Hon Soc (secy-treas, 68-). *Res:* German dialectology; German word formation; collegiate slang. *Publ:* Auth, A Bibliography of Word Formation in the Germanic Languages, Duke Univ, 68; Reflexes of French mecanique in German dialects, 7-9/60 & Old High German -ata, -at in Middle High German and in present-day German dialects, 4-6/63, Language; contribr, The Teaching of German: Problems and Methods, Nat Carl Schurz Asn, 70; ed, H Die thueringisch-saichsische Kanzleisprache bis 1325, Johnson Reprint, 72; auth, Collegiate slang: Aspects of word formation and semantic change, In, Introduction to Language, St Martin's Press, 72; Linguistic changes: Examples from the Westfalian dialect of Nienberge (near Muenster), Word, 26: 32-46. *Mailing Add:* Dept of German Univ Hawaii at Manoa Honolulu HI 96822

SHA, SHUNG-TSE, Far Eastern History, United States Diplomacy. See Vol I

SHACKLETON BAILEY, DAVID ROY, b Lancaster, England, Dec 10, 17; m 67. LATIN. *Educ:* Cambridge Univ, BA, 39, MA, 42, LittD, 58. *Prof Exp:* Lectr Tibetan, Cambridge Univ, 48-68; lectr classics, Jesus Col, 55-64; prof Latin, Univ Mich, Ann Arbor, 68-74; prof Greek and Latin, 75-82, POPE PROF LATIN LANG & LIT, HARVARD UNIV, 82- *Concurrent Pos:* Mem int jury, Prix Franqui, 53; vis lectr, Harvard Univ, 63; Andrew V V Raymond vis prof, State Univ NY, Buffalo, 73-74; fel, Caius Col, Cambridge, 44-55 & Jesus Col, 55-64, fel, Caius Col, 64-68, dep bursar, 64-65, sr bursar, 65-68; vis fel, Peterhouse, 80-81. *Honors & Awards:* Charles J Goodwin Award of Merit, 78. *Mem:* Fel Brit Acad; Am Philos Soc; Am Acad Arts & Sci. *Res:* Buddhist Sanskrit and Tibetan texts; textual criticism of classical Latin authors; letters of Cicero. *Publ:* Auth, Cicero, Duckworth, London, 72, Scribner's, 72; Two studies in Roman Nomenclature, Am Class Studies, 76; Cicero Epistulae ad Familiares (2 Vols), Cambridge Univ, 77; Cicero's Letters to Atticus, Penguin Classics, 78; Cicero's letters to his friends: Towards a text of anthologia Latina, Cambridge Philos Soc, 79; Cicero Epistulae ad Quintum Fratrem et M Brutum, 80 & Cicero Select Letters, 80, Cambridge Univ; Profile of Horace, Duckworth, London, 82, Harvard Univ, 82. *Mailing Add:* Dept of Classics Harvard Univ Cambridge MA 02138

SHADI, DOROTHY CLOTELLE CLARKE, b Los Angeles, Calif, July 16, 08; m 34; c 3. SPANISH LITERATURE. *Educ:* Univ Calif, Los Angeles, AB, 29; Univ Calif, AM, 30, PhD(Romance lit), 34. *Prof Exp:* Prof Span, Dominican Col San Rafael, 35-37; lectr Span & Port, 45-48, from asst prof to prof Span, 48-76, asst dean col lett & sci, 63-66, EMER PROF SPAN, UNIV CALIF BERKELEY, 76- *Honors & Awards:* Berkeley Citation, Univ Calif, Berkeley, 76. *Mem:* MLA; Mod Humanities Res Asn; Medieval Acad Am; Hisp Soc Am; Int Courtly Lyric Soc. *Res:* Spanish versification; medieval Spanish literature. *Publ:* Auth, Morphology of Fifteenth Century Castilian Verse, Duquesne Univ, 64; Early Spanish Lyric Poetry: Essays and Selections, Las Americas, 67; Allegory, Decalogue, and Deadly Sins in La Celestina, Univ Calif, 68; Agudiecism, Thematics, and the Newest Novel: A study of Juan Ventura Agudiez's heuristic novel Las Tardes de Thereze Lamarck, Exposition, 69; Juan de Mena's Laberinto de Fortuna: Classic epic and mester de clerecia, Romance Monogr, 73; Garcilaso's First Eclogue: Perspective, Geometric Figure, Epic Structure, Shadi, Tirso's Don Juan and Juan Ruiz's Don Amor, Folio: Essays on Foreign Lang & Lit, No 12, 80. *Mailing Add:* Dept of Span Univ of Calif Berkeley CA 94720

SHADICK, HAROLD, b London, Eng, Sept 30, 02; US citizen; m 27. CHINESE LANGUAGE & LITERATURE. *Educ:* Univ Toronto, BA, 25, MA, 51. *Prof Exp:* From instr humanities to prof hist & Western lit & chmn dept Western lang & lit, Yenching Univ, China, 25-46; prof Chinese lit, 46-71, dir China prog, 50-66, dir EAsian ctr, 60-66, EMER PROF CHINESE LIT, CORNELL UNIV, 71- *Concurrent Pos:* Dir, Inter- Univ Fel Field Training in Chinese, Ford Found, 56-62; mem Comt Studies Chinese Civilization & chmn comt Chinese lit, Am Coun Learned Soc, 62-68; ed, Chinoperl Papers. *Mem:* Asn Asian Studies; Conf Chinese Oral & Performing Lit; WLang Asn China (pres, 36). *Res:* Classical Chinese grammar and literature. *Publ:* Ed & transl, Liu Tieh-yün, The travels of Lao Ts'an, 52, 66 & auth, A First Course in Literary Chinese, 68, 70, 74 & 79, Cornell Univ. *Mailing Add:* China-Japan Prog Cornell Univ Ithaca NY 14853

SHALVEY, THOMAS JOSEPH, Philosophy. See Vol IV

SHAMMAS, JACOB YOUSIF, b Baghdad, Iraq, US citizen; m 49; c 4. ARABIC LANGUAGE, MIDDLE EAST STUDIES. *Educ:* Franklin & Marshal Col, BA, 49. *Prof Exp:* Teacher Arabic, 48-52, sr instr, 52-54, assoc prof Arabic course material, 56-62, coordr & proj off develop self-paced courses in Arabic dialects, 76, PROF ARABIC COURSE MATERIAL, DEFENSE LANG INST, 62- *Honors & Awards:* Outstanding Performance Award, 77 & Spec Act Award, 78, Defense Lang Inst. *Mem:* Am Coun Teaching Foreign Lang; Am Asn Teachers Arabic. *Res:* Contrastive Arabic-English studies; self-paced technique in preparing text for language learning. *Publ:* Auth, Modern Standard Arabic, Vols I-VIII, Defense Lang Inst, 64-65; coauth, Phonology and Script of Literary Arabic, 67 & A Basic Course of Literary Arabic, 69, McGill Univ; auth, Structural and vocabulary control in text writing, Newslett Am Asn Teachers Arabic, 71; coauth, Egyptian Dialect, 77, Syrian Dialect, 77 & Saudi Cultural Orientation, 78, Defense Lang Inst. *Mailing Add:* 460 Beaumont Ave Pacific Grove CA 93950

SHAND, MICHAEL ARTHUR, b New York, NY, Jan 19, 50. LINGUISTICS, LANGUAGE PEDAGOGY. *Educ:* State Univ NY Stony Brook, BA, 72; Univ Calif, San Diego, MA, 76, PhD(ling), 80. *Prof Exp:* Asst prof ling & teaching English second lang, Inter-Am Univ PR, 77-79; res assoc, Salk Inst Biol Studies, 79-82; ASST PROF PSYCHOLING & TEACHING ENGLISH SECOND LANG, UNIV PR MAYAGUEZ, 82- *Concurrent Pos:* Lectr psycholing & teaching English second lang, San Diego State Univ, 80-82. *Mem:* Ling Soc Am; Teachers English Speakers Other Lang. *Res:* Psycholinguistics; theory and practice of language teaching; biological foundations of language. *Publ:* Auth, Syllable vs segmental perception: On the inability to ignore irrelevant stimulus parameters, Perception & Psychophysics, 20: 430-432; coauth, Experimental English Textbook: English 113, 78 & Developing Reading Skills in English as a Second Language: English 113, 79, Inter-Am Univ Press; Nonauditory suffix effects in congenitally deaf signers of American Sign Language, J Exp Psychol: Human Learning & Memory, Vol 7, No 4; Role of initial and terminal similarity and Pig Latin presentation on serial recall of numbers, Bell Lab Tech Memorandum, No 82-11225-1, 82. *Mailing Add:* Dept of Ling Univ of PR Mayaguez PR

SHANE, ALEX MICHAEL, b San Francisco, Calif, July 16, 33; m 57; c 2. SLAVIC LANGUAGES & LITERATURES. *Educ:* Univ Chicago, BA, 53, MA, 55; Univ Calif, Berkeley, PhD(Slavic lang & lit), 65. *Prof Exp:* Instr Russ, Princeton Univ, 58-60; from asst prof to assoc prof, Univ Calif, Davis, 63-71; chmn dept, 71-80, PROF SLAVIC LANG & LIT, STATE UNIV NY ALBANY, 71-, DIR OFF INT PROG, 81- *Concurrent Pos:* Am Coun Learned Soc grant- in-aid, 66; Humanities Inst grant, Univ Calif, 67; vis assoc prof Russ lit, Stanford Univ, 69-70; fel, Nat Endowment for Humanities Independent Study & Res, 77-78; State Univ NY-Moscow State Univ exchange scholar, 81. *Mem:* Am Asn Teachers Slavic & East Europ Lang (pres, 77, 78); Am Asn Advan Slavic Studies. *Res:* Nineteenth and 20th century Russian prose fiction. *Publ:* Auth, The Life and Works of Evgenij Zamjatin, Univ Calif, 68; Russian literary periodicals (1901-1916) at the Helsinki University Library, Slavic Rev, 3/69; An evaluation of the existing college norms for the MLA-Cooperative Russian Test, Mod Lang J, 2/71; A prisoner of fate: Remizov's short fiction, Russ Lit Triquart, 5/72; An introduction to Alexei Remizov, Triquart, spring 73; American and Canadian doctoral disserations in Slavic and East European Languages and literatures, 1961-1972, Slavic and EEurop J, summer 73; The slavic workforce in the United States and Canada: Survey and commentary, Slavic & EEurop J, fall 78; Individualized, self-paced instruction: Alternative to the traditional classroom? ADFL Bull, 4/81. *Mailing Add:* Dept Slavic Lang & Lit State Univ of NY Albany NY 12222

SHANKOVSKY, IGOR, b Stryj, Ukraine, May 15, 31; US citizen; m 73. SLAVONIC PHILOLOGY, COMPARATIVE LITERATURES. *Educ:* Univ Pa, BA, 58; Univ Alta, MA, 66; Free Ukrainian Univ, Munich, PhD(Slavonic philol), 69. *Prof Exp:* Instr Ukrainian & Russ, Univ Alta, 66-67; lectr Russ, McMaster Univ, 67-68; from instr to asst prof Russ lang & lit Southern Ill Univ, 68-74; independent res, Venice, 74-79; ASSOC PROF RUSS LANG & LIT, UNIV TRIESTE, ITALY, 79- *Concurrent Pos:* Consult, Nat Adv Bd, Am Security Coun, 71-79; res grant, Univ Trieste, Italy, 82. *Honors & Awards:* Xi Columbian Trophy, Pugnold Verde, Campobasso, Italy, 77. *Mem:* MLA. *Res:* Russian-English scientific dictionary; comparative styles in Slavonic literatures; analysis of works by Vasyl Symonenko. *Publ:* Auth, The Gift of April, Munich, 58; Dissonances, 60; Hundred poets-hundred songs, Munich, 66; A Short Summer, Ukrainian Bookstore, Edmonton, 70; Literary monologues, 1/69, 1/70 & 4/76, Liberation Path, London; Symonenko, A Study in Semantics, in Ukrainian, 75 & English, 77, London, Eng; Il Russo in Aula, Cluet Trieste, 81; Fly Robin Fly, Campanotto, Udine, 82; Mostly Black on White, Campanotto, Voine, 82. *Mailing Add:* Via Zanotto 5 Mestre Venezia Italy

SHANNON, RICHARD STOLL, III, b New York, NY, Mar 22, 43; m 65; c 3. CLASSICAL PHILOLOGY. *Educ:* Stanford Univ, BA, 66, MA, 69; Harvard Univ, PhD(class philol), 73. *Prof Exp:* Asst prof class studies, Univ Mich, Ann Arbor, 73-78. *Mem:* Am Inst Archaeol; Am Philol Asn. *Res:* Homer; Lucretius; Greek linguistics and metrics. *Publ:* Auth, The Arms of Achilles and Homeric Compositional Technique, E J Brill, 75; co-ed, Oral Literature and the Formula, Univ Mich, 76. *Mailing Add:* Suite 220 155 S Madison Denver CO 80209

SHAPIRA, ELLIOTT KING, b Boston, Mass, Apr 11, 12; m 46. COMPARATIVE ROMANCE PHILOLOGY. *Educ:* Harvard Univ, AB, 35, AM, 39, PhD, 41. *Prof Exp:* From instr to prof, 45-77, EMER PROF ROMANCE LANG, TUFTS UNIV, 77- *Res:* Camus and North Africa; Romain Gary and the picaresque novel; Robbe-Grillet, an art form. *Mailing Add:* 100 Memorial Dr Apt 2-7 B Cambridge MA 02142

SHAPIRO, MICHAEL, b Yokohama, Japan, Nov 29, 39; US citizen; m 67; c 1. SLAVIC LANGUAGES & LITERATURES. *Educ:* Univ Calif, Los Angeles, AB, 61; Harvard Univ, AM, 62, PhD (Slavic lang), 65. *Prof Exp:* Acting instr, 63-64, from asst prof to assoc prof, 66-74, PROF RUSS LING & POETICS, UNIV CALIF, LOS ANGELES, 74- *Concurrent Pos:* Res fel, Harvard Univ, 65-66; Nat Sci Found fel, Univ Tokyo, 65-66, grant, fac assoc Russ derivational morphol proj, 68-71; Am Coun Learned Soc grant, 68-69, 72; Am Philos Soc grant, 71; dir, Nat Endowment for Humanities summer sem, 79, fel, 81; vis sr fel, Princeton Univ, 82-83. *Mem:* Charles S Peirce Soc. *Res:* Russian linguistics and poetics; general linguistics and semiotics; Slavic and Indo-European antiquities. *Publ:* Auth, Russian Phonetic Variants and Phonostylistics, Univ Calif, 68; Aspects of Russian Morphology: A Semiotic Investigation, Slavica, 69; Explorations into Markedness, Lang, 72; Morphophonemics as Semiotic, Acta Ling Hafniensa, 74; Tenues and mediae in Japanese: A reinterpretation, Lingua, 74; Asymmetry: An Inquiry into the Linguistic Structure of Poetry, North Holland, 76; coauth, Hierarchy and the Structure of Tropee, Ind Univ, 76; Russian Conjugation: Theory and Hermeneutic, Lang, 80. *Mailing Add:* Dept of Slavic Lang & Lit Univ of Calif Los Angeles CA 90024

SHAPLEY, CHARLES S, b Los Angeles, Calif, Aug 17, 25. FRENCH LANGUAGE & LITERATURE. *Educ:* Univ Calif, Berkeley, BA, 49, MA, 53, PhD, 62; Univ Paris, Dipl, 50. *Prof Exp:* Instr French, Univ Ariz, 57-61; from asst prof to assoc prof, 62-72, PROF FRENCH LANG & LIT, CALIF STATE UNIV, FULLERTON, 72- *Mem:* MLA. *Res:* Late medieval literature; fantastic literature; French film. *Publ:* Auth, Studies in French Poetry of the 15th Century, Martinus Nijhof, The Hague, 70. *Mailing Add:* Dept of Foreign Lang Calif State Univ Fullerton CA 92634

SHARP, FRANCIS MICHAEL, b Troy, Kans, Feb 10, 41; m 68; c 1. GERMAN LITERATURE. *Educ:* Univ Mo, BA, 64; Univ Calif, Berkeley, MA, 69, PhD(German lang & lit), 74. *Prof Exp:* Asst prof German lang & lit, Princeton Univ, 73-79; ASST PROF GERMAN LANG & LIT, UNIV OF THE PAC, 79- *Mem:* MLA; Am Asn Teachers German. *Res:* Modern German poetry; contemporary German prose; literature and psychology. *Publ:* Auth, Georg Heym and the aesthetics of traumatization, Rev of Nat Lit, 78; Expressionism and psychoanalysis, Pac Coast Philol, 10/78; Georg Buchner's Lenz: A futile madness, Wissenschaftliche Buchgesellschaft, 81; The Poet's Madness: A Reading of Georg Trakl, Cornell Univ Press, 81; Literature as self-reflection: Thomas Bernhard and Peter Handke, World Lit Today, autumn 81; Georg Trakl: Poetry and psychopathology, Bouvier Verlag (in prep). *Mailing Add:* Dept of Mod Lang & Lit Univ of the Pacific Stockton CA 95211

SHARPE, ALFREDO M, b Washington, DC, Oct 18, 27. FOREIGN LANGUAGES. *Educ:* Howard Univ, AB, 49; Nat Univ Mex, MA, 53, PhD, 55. *Prof Exp:* Clerk, War Manpower Comn, Washington, DC, 44-45 & US Employment Serv, 45-47; teacher several insts, Mex, 49-53; assoc prof Romance lang & chmn dept, Albany State Col, 53-57, chmn deps art & music, 55-57; US Off Educ grant, teacher French, Cambodia, 60; teacher Span, Turner Air Force Base, Albany, Ga, 61-62; PROF MOD FOREIGN LANG & CHMN DEPT, SC STATE COL, 62- *Concurrent Pos:* Teacher & chmn div, Humanities, Palmer Mem Inst, Sedalia, NC, 53-57; mem bd regents, Ga Off Educ, Univ Syst Ga, 61-; Int Adv Comt, Brazil, 63- *Mem:* CLA; Inst Int Lit Iberoam; MLA. *Res:* Poetry; literature; languages. *Publ:* Auth, El origen y el progreso de la peseia & Una critica de los elementos literarios de la novela revolucionaria mejicana que se encuentran en las obras de Azuela, CLA J. *Mailing Add:* Dept of Mod Foreign Lang SC State Col Orangeburg SC 29115

SHARPE, LAWRENCE A, b Burlington, NC, July 22, 20; w; c 6. ROMANCE LANGUAGES. *Educ:* Univ NC, AB, 40, PhD(Romance lang), 56; Univ Havana, cert, 41. *Prof Exp:* Transl Ger & Span, US Dept Justice, 42-44; dir English courses, Inst Brazil-EE UU, Fortaleza, 51-53; lectr Span & Port, 53-

56, from asst prof to assoc prof Romance lang, 56-75, dir lang lab, 57-62, 73-74, 77-78, instr English as foreign lang, 57-63, PROF ROMANCE LANG, UNIV NC, CHAPEL HILL, 75- *Concurrent Pos:* Instr lab methods, NDEA lang insts, 61-63. *Mem:* Am Asn Teachers Span & Port; MLA; SAtlantic Mod Lang Asn; Soc Lingua Port. *Res:* Twentieth century Portuguese novel; Camilo Castelo Branco; Hispanic philology. *Publ:* Ed, The Old Portuguese Vida de Sam Bernardo, Univ NC, 71. *Mailing Add:* 101 Virginia Dr Chapel Hill NC 27514

SHARRER, HARVEY LEO, b Oakland, Calif, May 26, 40. MEDIEVAL HISPANIC LANGUAGES & LITERATURES. *Educ:* Univ Calif, Berkeley, BA, 63, MA, 65; Univ Calif, Los Angeles, PhD(Hisp lang & lit), 70. *Prof Exp:* From actg asst prof to asst prof Span & Port, 68-77, assoc prof, 77-81, PROF SPAN & PORT, UNIV CALIF, SANTA BARBARA, 81- *Concurrent Pos:* Am Philos Soc grant, 72-73; vis lectr, Univ Wis-Madison, 75. *Mem:* MLA; Mediaeval Acad Am; Am Comp Lit Asn; Am Asn Teachers Span & Port. *Res:* Hispanic Arthurian materials; medieval Hispanic literatures; chivalric literature. *Publ:* Auth, Evidence of a fifteenth-century Libro del Infante don Pedro de Portugal and its relationship to the Alexander cycle, J Hisp Philol, winter 77; A Critical Bibliography of Hispanic Arthurian Materials, In: The Prose Romance Cycles, Grant & Cutler, London, 78; Two eighteenth-century chapbook romances of chivalry by Antonio da Silva, Mestre de Gramatica, Hispanic Rev, spring 78; The Legendary History of Britian in Lope Garcia de Saalazar's Libro de las biendandanzas e fortunas, Univ Penn Press, 79; co-ed (with Frederick G Williams), Studies on Jorge de Sena by his Colleagues and Friends, Jorge de Sena Ctr Port Studies, Univ Calif, 81. *Mailing Add:* Dept of Span & Port Univ of Calif Santa Barbara CA 93106

SHATTUCK, ROGER WHITNEY, b New York, NY, Aug 20, 23; m 49; c 4. FRENCH LITERATURE. *Educ:* Yale Univ, BA, 47. *Prof Exp:* Instr French, Harvard Univ, 53-56; from asst prof to prof, Univ Tex, 56-68, prof English & French & chmn dept French & Ital, 68-71; COMMONWEALTH PROF FRENCH LIT, UNIV VA, 74- *Concurrent Pos:* Provediteur general, Col Pataphysique, Paris, 55-; Guggenheim fel & Fulbright res fel, 58-59; chmn adv bd, Nat Transl Ctr, 66-70; Am Coun Learned Soc res grant, 69-70. *Honors & Awards:* Nat Bk Award, Arts & Letters, 75. *Mem:* MLA. *Res:* Modern French literature; literature and the arts; history and theory of education. *Publ:* Auth, The Banquet Years, Harcourt, 58; Proust's Binoculars, Random, 63; Half Tame, Univ Tex, 64; co-ed, The Craft & Context of Translation, Anchor Bks, 64; translr, Occasions by Paul Valery, Princeton Univ, 70; auth, The D-S Expedition, NY Rev Bks, 72; The humanities in higher education, In: Content and Context, Essays on College Education, McGraw, 73; Marcel Proust, Viking, 74; The Forbidden Experiment: The Story of the Wild Boy of Aveyron, Farrar-Straus, 80. *Mailing Add:* Dept of French Cabell Hall Univ of Va Charlottesville VA 22903

SHAW, ALVIN JOHN, b Owen Sound, Ont, Aug 30, 21. SPANISH. *Educ:* Univ Toronto, BA, 50; Univ Mich, MA, 55. *Prof Exp:* From lectr to prof Span, 50-70, actg head dept, 67-70, head, 70-72, PROF SPAN, UNIV NB, FREDERICTON, 70-, ASSOC DEAN FAC ARTS, 71- *Concurrent Pos:* Drama dir, Theatre Prod Prog, Univ NB; artistic dir, Theatre Fredericton, NB. *Honors & Awards:* Can Drama Award, Queen Elizabeth II Jubilee Medal. *Mem:* Can Asn Hispanists; Humanities Asn Can; Am Asn Teachers Span & Port; Can Actors' Equity Asn. *Res:* Nineteenth century Spanish literature, especially the generation of 1898. *Mailing Add:* Dean of Arts Univ of New Brunswick Fredericton NB E3B 5A3 Can

SHAW, ARACELIS GOBERNA, b Pinar del Rio, Cuba, June 22, 22; US citizen; m 52. SPANISH. *Educ:* Inst Pinar del Rio, BS & BL, 41; Univ Havana, PhD, 48; Univ Fla, MA, 57. *Prof Exp:* Instr Span, Berlitz Sch Lang, 49-53; res asst dept hist, Univ Fla, 55-57; from instr to assoc prof Span, 57-63, dir lang lab, 61-63, PROF SPAN & CHMN DEPT MOD LANG, COLUMBIA COL, SC, 63-, HEAD INTERCULTURAL & LANG CTR, 77- *Concurrent Pos:* Lang workshop dir, Va, NC, & SC, 59-63; lang consult, Educ Electronics, Inc, 60-62; teacher Span, SC Educ TV, Lang consult, 72- *Honors & Awards:* Cervantes Award, Am Asn Teachers Span and Port, 76; Bicentennial Award Revolution Bicentennial Comn, 76. *Mem:* Am Asn Teachers Span & Port; MLA; Southeastern Conf Latin Am Studies; SAtlantic Mod Lang Asn; AAUP. *Res:* Literary studies; linguistics; methods of teaching languages. *Publ:* Auth, The structural approach for teaching basic Spanish, SAtlantic Mod Lang Asn Bull, 1/61; El Espanol, paso a paso, W C Brown, 63, Books I & II, SC Educ TV Network; The importance of foreign languages today, spring 64 & Audio-visuals: Key to the development of linguistic skill, summer 70, Search. *Mailing Add:* Dept of Mod Lang Columbia Col Columbia SC 29203

SHAW, BRADLEY ALAN, b Tremonton, Utah, Dec 23, 45; m 69; c 2. SPANISH LANGUAGE, HISPANIC LITERATURES. *Educ:* Lewis & Clark Col, BA, 68; Northwestern Univ, Evanston, MA, 69; Univ NMex, PhD, 74. *Prof Exp:* From instr to asst prof Span, Va Commonwealth Univ, 72-74; asst prof, 74-80, ASSOC PROF SPAN & DIR, SECONDARY MAJ PROG LATIN AM STUDIES, KANS STATE UNIV, 80- *Concurrent Pos:* Assoc Dir, Tri-Univ Ctr Latin Am Studies, 76-; assoc ed, Studies in Twentieth Century Lit. *Mem:* MLA; Am Asn Teachers Span & Port; Latin Am Studies Asn. *Res:* Contemporary Peruvian literature; Latin American novel; Latin American theater. *Publ:* Auth, Latin American Literature in English Translation: An Annotated Bibliography, New York Univ, 76; coauth, Hispanic Writers in French Journals: An Annotated Bibliography, Soc of Span & Span-Am Studies, 78; The new Spanish American narrative, Pac Quart, 78; auth, Latin American Literature in English: 1975-1978, suppl to Rev, 4/79; coauth, Luis Romero, Twayne, 79; translr, Mogollon (transl, Augusto Higa Oshiro, El equipito de Mogollon, In: Between Fire and Love: Contemporary Peruvian Writing, Miss Mud Press, 80; The Indigenista Novel in Peru After Arguedas: The Case of Mauel Scorza, Selecta, (in prep). *Mailing Add:* Dept of Mod Lang Kans State Univ Manhattan KS 66506

SHAW, EDWARD PEASE, b Lowell, Mass, Dec, 18, 11; m 36; c 2. FRENCH LITERATURE. *Educ:* Harvard Univ, AB, 33, AM, 34, PhD, 37. *Prof Exp:* Instr French, Univ Ill, 38-42; assoc prof Romance lang, Miami Univ, 46-47; prof French, 47-73, EMER PROF FRENCH, STATE UNIV NY ALBANY, 73- *Concurrent Pos:* Harvard Sheldon travel fel, 37-38; State Univ NY Res Found res grant, 55-56. *Honors & Awards:* Chevalier, Palmes Academiques, 62, Officier, 73. *Mem:* MLA; Am Asn Teachers Fr. *Res:* French literature of the 18th century. *Publ:* Auth, Jacques Cazotte, Harvard Univ, 42; The case of the Abbe de Moncrif, 53 & Paradis de Moncrif, 58, Bookman Assoc; coauth, French Civilization through Fiction, 56; auth, Problems and policies of Malesherbes, Antioch, 66; coauth, Selected Literary References in the Manuscript Journal (1750-1769) of Joseph d'Hemery, State Univ NY, 73; Malesherbes, PMLA & Philol Quart. *Mailing Add:* 21 Rosewood Circle Unit 11 Kennebunk ME 04043

SHAW, JOSEPH THOMAS, b Ashland City, Tenn, May 13, 19; m 42; c 3. SLAVIC LANGUAGES. *Educ:* Univ Tenn, AB, 40, AM(English), 41; Harvard Univ, AM(compt lit), 47, PhD(Russ & English), 50. *Prof Exp:* From asst prof to assoc prof Slavic lang, Ind Univ, 49-61, actg chmn dept, 53-54; chmn dept, 62-68, chmn fac div humanities, 64-65, 72-73, 75-78, assoc dean grad sch, 65-68, PROF SLAVIC LANG, UNIV WIS-MADISON, 61-, CHMN DEPT, 77- *Concurrent Pos:* Vis prof, Inst Res Humanities, 68-69. *Honors & Awards:* Outstanding Achievement Award, Am Asn Teachers Slavic & EEurop Lang, 70. *Mem:* Am Asn Teachers Slavic & EEurop Lang (pres, 73-74); Am Asn Advan Slavic Studies; Am Coun Teaching Foreign Lang; MLA. *Res:* Russian literature of the 19th and 20th centuries; comparative literature, especially English and Russian; Russian language. *Publ:* Co-ed, Indiana Slavic studies; ed & translr, The Letters of Alexander Pushkin, Univ Pa & Ind Univ, 63 & Univ Wis, 67; The transliteration of modern Russian, Univ Wis, 67; auth, Pushkin's Rhymes: A Dictionary, 74, Batiushkov: A Dictionary of the Rhymes and a Concordance to the Poetry, 75 & Baratynskii: A Dictionary of the Rhymes and a Concordance to the Poetry, 75, Univ of Wis. *Mailing Add:* Dept of Slavic Lang Univ of Wis Madison WI 53706

SHAW, LEROY ROBERT, b Medicine Hat, Alta, Can, Jan 15, 23; nat US. GERMAN. *Educ:* Univ Calif, AB, 46, MA, 48, PhD(Ger), 54. *Prof Exp:* Instr Ger & Humanities, Reed Col, 51-53; from instr to assoc prof Ger lang, Univ Tex, 53-65; prof Ger, Univ Wis-Milwaukee, 65-68; PROF GER, UNIV ILL, CHICAGO, 68- *Concurrent Pos:* Alexander von Humboldt fel, Munich, 62-64; vis Fulbright prof Ger, Trinity Col, Dublin, 67-68; Ger Acad Exhange Serv, 75; Nat Endowment for Humanities fel, 79-80. *Mem:* Am Asn Teachers Ger; MLA; Midwest Mod Lang Asn. *Res:* German drama; expressionism; biography. *Publ:* Auth, Witness of Deceit: Gerhart Hauptmann, Univ Calif, 57; ed, The German Theater Today, Univ Tex, 62; auth, The Playwright and Historical Change, Univ Wis, 70. *Mailing Add:* 1137 N Euclid Ave Oak Park IL 60302

SHAW-MAZLISH, CONSTANCE, b Whitinsville, Mass; div; c 2. SPANISH LITERATURE. *Educ:* Smith Col, BA, 45; Columbia Univ, PhD(Span), 57. *Prof Exp:* Instr Span, Simmons Col, 56-58; asst prof, Bates Col, 60-62 & Smith Col, 62-66; ASSOC PROF SPAN, AGNES SCOTT COL, 66-, CHMN DEPT, 74- *Concurrent Pos:* Secy-treas, Int Inst Spain, 53-54; instr Span, Boston Univ, 56-58. *Mem:* MLA; Am Asn Teachers Span & Port; AAUP. *Publ:* Transl, Jose Ferrater Mora, On a radical form of thinking, Tex Quart; auth, Ortega y la circunstancia espanola, Insula, 10/65; Ortega y Gasset: Circumstantial thinker, In: Filologia y critica hispanica, Madrid, 69. *Mailing Add:* Dept of Span Agnes Scott Col Decatur GA 30030

SHAY, JAMES RODNEY, b Denver, Colo, Aug 26, 42; m 68; c 3. ENGLISH, LINGUISTICS. *Educ:* Univ Notre Dame, BA, 64; Univ Calif, Berkeley, MA, 70, PhD(English), 77. *Prof Exp:* Lectr English, Univ San Francisco, 75-76; instr, Univ NMex, 76-77; ASST PROF ENGLISH, UNIV TEX, 77- *Mem:* MLA; Medieval Acad Am; Ling Soc Am. *Res:* History of grammar; history and structure of English; linguistics and literary analysis. *Mailing Add:* Dept of English Univ of Tex Austin TX 78712

SHEA, GEORGE W, b Paterson, NJ, Oct 7, 34; m 56; c 3. CLASSICAL LANGUAGES. *Educ:* Fordham Univ, BA, 56; Columbia Univ, MA, 60, PhD(classics), 66. *Prof Exp:* Asst prof Latin & Greek, St John's Univ, NY, 61-65; asst prof classics, asst dean, Fordham Col & dir jr year abroad prog, 67-70, ASSOC PROF CLASSICS & DEAN COL AT LINCOLN CTR, FORDHAM UNIV, 70- *Mem:* Am Philol Asn; Am Conf Acad Deans. *Res:* Latin epic poetry and Roman history; Johannis of Flavius Cresconius Corippus. *Mailing Add:* Off Dean Col Lib Arts Fordham Univ New York NY 10023

SHECHTER, STANLEY JACOB, b Pittsburgh, Pa, Dec 25, 32. CLASSICAL PHILOLOGY. *Educ:* Univ Chicago, BA, 55, MA, 59; Harvard Univ, PhD(class philol), 63. *Prof Exp:* Instr classics, Brown Univ, 63-65; from instr to asst prof, Yale Univ, 65-68; asst prof, Hunter Col, 68-73; ASST PROF SPEECH & THEATRE, JOHN JAY COL CRIMINAL JUSTICE, 73- *Mem:* Am Philol Asn; Asn Int Papyrologues. *Res:* Virgil's Georgics. *Publ:* Auth, Thucydides 5.83.4, Class Philol, 63; Theocritus 17.2 once again, Rheinisches Mus, 65; Two emendations, Am J Philol, 65. *Mailing Add:* 430 E 63rd St New York NY 10021

SHEEHAN, ROBERT LOUIS, b Boston, Mass, May 3, 23; m 54. FOREIGN LANGUAGES. *Educ:* Boston Col, BS, 49; Boston Univ, AM, 50, PhD, 62. *Prof Exp:* Dir courses, Centro Cult Paraguayo-Am, 50-52, instr English lang, Georgetown Univ English Lang Prog in Yugoslavia, 53-54, asst prof, Turkey, 54-55; lectr Span, Boston Univ, 58-62; asst prof, 62-67; ASSOC PROF MOD LANG, BOSTON COL, 67- *Concurrent Pos:* Mem, Mass Educ Commun Comn, 72- *Mem:* Am Asn Teachers Span & Port. *Res:* Modern Spanish theatre. *Publ:* Auth, Moralda, Benevente's urban dimension to the generation of '98, In: Spanish Thought and Letters in the Twentieth Century, Vanderbilt Univ, 66; Un NorteAmericano en la Alcarria, Papeles de Son Armadians, 2 & 3/69; Buero Vallejo as el'Medico de su obra, Estreno, spring, 75; Benevente and the Spanish Panorama: 1894-1954, Estudios de Hispanifila, 76. *Mailing Add:* Dept of Romance Lang Boston Col Chestnut Hill MA 02167

SHEERIN, DANIEL JOSEPH, b St Louis, Mo, Dec 26, 43. MEDIEVAL LATIN, PATRISTICS. *Educ:* St Louis Univ, BA, 65; Univ NC, Chapel Hill, PhD(classics), 69. *Prof Exp:* Asst prof classics, Univ Del, 69-70; asst prof Latin & hist, Cath Univ Am, 70-74; asst prof, 74-76, ASSOC PROF MEDIEVAL LATIN, UNIV NC, CHAPEL HILL, 76-, ASSOC DEAN GRAD SCH, 80- *Mem:* Am Philol Asn; Mediaeval Acad Am; NAm Patristics Soc. *Res:* Medieval Latin; Latin patristics; liturgical history. *Publ:* Auth, An anonymous verse epitome of the life of St Anselm, Analecta Bollandiana, 74; Gilbert of Airvau's Verses on the Holy Eucharist, Rev Etudes Augustiniennes, 74; Some observations on the date of Lanfranc's Decreta, Studia Monastica, 75; Masses for Sts Dunstan and Elphege from the Queen of Sweden's Collection . . ., Rev benedictine, 75; St John the Baptist in the lower world, Vigiliae Christianae, 76; Gervase of Chichester and Thomas Becket, Mediaeval Studies, 76; John Leland and Milred of Worcester, Manuscripta, 77. *Mailing Add:* Dept of Classics Univ of NC Chapel Hill NC 27514

SHEETS, GEORGE ARCHIBALD, b Buenos Aires, Arg, Aug 18, 47; US citizen; m 69; c 2. CLASSICAL LANGUAGES, HISTORICAL LINGUISTICS. *Educ:* Univ NC, BA, 70; Duke Univ, PhD(class studies), 74. *Prof Exp:* Instr classics, Univ Tex, Austin, 74-75; Mellon fel classics, Bryn Mawr Col, 76-77; asst prof, 77-82, ASSOC PROF CLASSICS, UNIV MINN, MINNEAPOLIS, 82- *Mem:* Am Philol Asn; Class Asn Mid West & South. *Res:* Italic dialects; Greek dialects; Roman literature. *Publ:* Auth, Palatalization in Greek, Indoger Forsch, 75; Secondary midvowels in Greek, 79, The dialect gloss, Hellenistic poetics and Livius Andronicus, 81, Am J Philol; Grammatical commentary to Book I of the Histories of Herodotus, Bryn Mawr Commentaries, 81; Ennius Lyricus, Plautus and early Roman Tragedy, Ill Class Studies (in press). *Mailing Add:* Dept of Classics Univ of Minn Minneapolis MN 55455

SHEIN, LOUIS JULIUS, Philosophy, Foreign Languages. See Vol IV

SHEIRICH, RICHARD M, b Erie, Pa, Oct 9, 27; m 62; c 2. GERMANIC LANGUAGE & LITERATURE. *Educ:* Colgate Univ, BA, 49; Northwestern Univ, MA, 50; Harvard Univ, PhD(Ger lang & lit,) 65. *Prof Exp:* Instr Ger, Colgate Univ, 53-54; actg instr, Univ Calif, Berkeley, 60-62, lectr Ger & actg dir lang lab, 63-65; asst prof, 65-69, assoc prof, 69-80, PROF GER, POMONA COL, 80- *Mem:* MLA; Am Asn Teachers Ger; Philol Asn Pac Coast; Int Arthur Schnitzler Res Asn. *Res:* German medieval literature; edition of manuscripts, particularly those of Richard Beer-Hofmann, Viennese poet and dramatist. *Publ:* Auth: Beer-Hofmann and the Arabian nights, Harvard Lebr Bull, 60; Richard Beer-Hofmann on the centenary of his birth, J Int Arthur Schnitzler Res Asn, fall 66. *Mailing Add:* Dept of Ger Pomona Col Claremont CA 91711

SHELDON, AMY LOUISE, b New York, NY. PSYCHOLINGUISTICS, LANGUAGE ACQUISITION. *Educ:* Ind Univ, BA, 64, MA, 65; Univ Tex, PhD(ling), 72. *Prof Exp:* Instr Engligh, Anatolia Col, Greece, 65-66; instr English & math, Anti-poverty Prog, New York, 66-67; English lang preceptor & instr, Columbia Univ & NY Univ, 67; instr urban educ, Univ Hartford, 70-71; asst prof, 72-77, ASSOC PROF LING, UNIV MINN, MINNEAPOLIS, 77- *Concurrent Pos:* Consult, Lang Res Found, Mass, 70-71; researcher, Univ Que, Rimouski, 75; faculty affiliate, Ctr Res Human Learning, Univ Minn, 77-; researcher, Univ du Que, Rimouski, 80-81. *Mem:* Ling Soc Am; Teachers English Speakers Other Lang. *Res:* Child language acquisition; second language acquisition; psycholinguistics. *Publ:* Auth, The role of parallel function in the acquisition of relative clauses in English, J Verbal Learning & Verbal Behav, 74; Speakers' intuitions about the complexity of relative clauses in Japanese and English, Papers 12th Ann Meeting Chicago Ling Soc, 76; On strategies for processing relative clauses: A comparison of children and adults, J Psycholing Res, 77; The acquisition of relative clauses in French and English: Implications for language learning universales, Current Themes in Linguistics: Language Typologies, Bilingualism, Experimental Linguistics, 77; The acquisition of relative clauses in French, Etudes Linguistiques sur les Langues Romanes, 78; Response to Walter Loban, language and literacy, Minnesota Perspectives in Literacy, 78; Assumptions, methods and goals of language acquisition research, Studies in First and Second Language Acquisition, 78; coauth (with W Strange), The acquisition of /r/ and /l/ by Japanese learners of English: Evidence that speech production can precede speech perception, Applied Psycholinguistics, 82. *Mailing Add:* Dept of Ling Univ of Minn 320 16th Ave SE Minneapolis MN 55455

SHELDON, RICHARD ROBERT, b Kansas City, Kans, July 12, 32; m 64; c 4. RUSSIAN LANGUAGE & LITERATURE. *Educ:* Univ Kans, BA, 54; Univ Mich, LLB, 60, PhD(Slavic lang & lit), 66. *Prof Exp:* Asst prof Russ lang & lit, Grinnell Col, 65-66; asst prof, 66-70, chmn dept Russ, 70-81, dir foreign studies prog, 71-73; assoc prof, 70-75, PROF RUSS LANG & LIT, DARTMOUTH COL, 80- *Concurrent Pos:* Fac fel, Dartmouth Col, 69-70 & Ctr Advan Studies Urbana, Ill, 69-70; Am Coun Learned Soc fel, 70-; vis assoc prof, Stanford Univ, 74. *Mem:* Am Asn Teachers Slavic & EEurop Lang; Am Asn Advan Slavic Studies. *Res:* Soviet literature; 19th century Russian literature. *Publ:* Auth, Gorky, Shklovsky and the Serapion brothers, Slavic & EEurop J, spring 68; ed & translr, Viktor Shklovsky's A Sentimental Journey, 70 & Zoo, or Letters Not About Love, 71, Cornell Univ; The formalist poetics of Viktor Shklovsky, Russ Tri-Quart, winter 72; Viktor Shklovsky & the device of ostensible surrender, Slavic Rev, 3/75; Shklovsky and Mandelstam, In: Russ & Slavic Lit, Slavic, 76; ed & translr, Third Factory, 77 & Shklovsky Bibliography, 77, Ardis. *Mailing Add:* Dept of Russ Dartmouth Col Hanover NH 03755

SHELMERDINE, CYNTHIA WRIGHT, b Boston, Mass, Jan 7, 49. CLASSICS, CLASSICAL ARCHEOLOGY. *Educ:* Bryn Mawr Col, AB, 70; Cambridge Univ, BA, 72, MA, 80; Harvard Univ, AM, 76, PhD(class philol), 77. *Prof Exp:* ASST PROF CLASSICS, UNIV TEX, AUSTIN, 77- *Mem:* Archaeol Inst Am; Am Philol Asn; Am Sch Class Studies Athens Alumni Asn; Cambridge Philol Soc, Eng; Class Asn Middle West & South. *Res:* Greek tragedy; Homer and epic; Bronze Age studies. *Publ:* Auth, The Pylos Ma tables reconsidered, Am J Archaeol, 73; contribr, Excavations at Nichoria (vol II), Univ Minn, (in press); Nichoria in context, Am J Archaeol, 81. *Mailing Add:* Dept of Classics Univ of Tex Austin TX 78712

SHELTON, JAMES EDWARD, b Memphis, Tenn, Dec 13, 43. GREEK, LATIN. *Educ:* Southwestern at Memphis, BA, 65; Vanderbilt Univ, MA, 70, PhD(classics), 71. *Prof Exp:* From instr to asst prof classics, 69-76, ASSOC PROF CLASSICS, UNIV OF TENN, KNOXVILLE, 76- *Mem:* Class Asn MidW & S; Mediaeval Acad Am. *Res:* Ancient philosophy, early Christian literature, Mediaeval Latin. *Publ:* Auth, Achilles on Scyros, Proc Mountain Interstate Conf, 10/73; The storm scene in Valerius Flaccus, Class J, 1/75. *Mailing Add:* 2404 Woodson Dr Knoxville TN 37920

SHELTON, RICHARD WILLIAM, English, Creative Writing. See Vol II

SHEN, YAO, b Chekiang, China, Apr 29, 12; US citizen. LINGUISTICS, ENGLISH. *Educ:* Yenching Univ, China, BA, 35; Mills Col, MA, 38; Univ Mich, EdD(English), 44. *Prof Exp:* Teacher High Sch, China, 35-36; res asst English, Univ Mich, 44-46, res assoc, 46-47, instr Mandarin, 47-52 & English, 48-52, from asst prof to prof Mandarin & English, 52-77, EMER PROF, UNIV HAWAII, MANOA, 77- *Concurrent Pos:* Rackham res grant, 57-58, publ proj, 61-62; Univ Mich fac res grant, 60-61. *Mem:* NCTE; MLA; Ling Soc Am; Int Asn Phonetic Sci. *Res:* Contrastive analysis. *Publ:* Auth, Spectrographic light in Mandarin, Study of Sounds, Japan, IX: 265-314; English phonetics, Braun & Brumfield, 62, enlarged & rev ed, 66; Selected References of English Pronunciation for Teachers of English as a Second Language, Am Lang Inst, Georgetown Univ, 64; coauth, Teaching English as a Second Language, a Classified Bibliography, Univ Hawaii, 65; auth, Dialect and grammar, Bull English Lang Ctr, Thailand, Vol III, No 1; Surface grammar and deep grammar-a development in modern English, Philippine J Lang Teaching, 73; Modal need and verb need, Applied Ling, Korea, IX, I: 85-103; A note on Browning's Eagle-feather, Studies in Browning, V: 2, 7-16. *Mailing Add:* Dept of English Univ of Hawaii at Manoa Honolulu HI 96822

SHEPARD, JOE WILLWERTH, b Indianapolis, Ind, Sept 20, 30; m 62; c 2. RUSSIAN LITERATURE & LANGUAGE. *Educ:* Harvard Univ, AB, 58; Ind Univ, Bloomington, MA, 63, PhD(Russ lit & lang), 73. *Prof Exp:* Instr Russ lang, Purdue Univ, 59-60; lectr ling, Intensive Lang Training Ctr, Ind Univ, 62-63, asst dir ctr, 63-67; from instr to asst prof Russ, 67-75, ASSOC PROF RUSS, CARLETON COL, 75-, CHMN DEPT MOD LANG, 78- *Mem:* Am Asn Teachers Slavic & EEurop Lang. *Res:* The Soviet Writer Andrey Platonov, 1899-1951; early Soviet literature; Russian historical legends. *Mailing Add:* Dept of Mod Lang Carlton Col Northfield MN 55057

SHEPARD, SANFORD, b Pittsburgh, Pa, Mar 24, 28; m 52; c 2. SPANISH. *Educ:* Univ Pittsburgh, AB, 50; Pa State Univ, MA, 52; NY Univ, PhD, 60. *Prof Exp:* Lectr Span & French, Hunter Col, 55-56 & Spanish, Queens Col, NY, 56; instr, Univ Conn, 56-57; instr, Smith Col, 57-61, dir jr year in Spain, 59-61; from asst prof to assoc prof, 61-75, PROF SPAN, OBERLIN COL, 75-, CHMN HUMANITIES PROG, 71- *Mem:* MLA; Mediaeval Acad Am; Archaeol Inst Am. *Res:* Medieval-Renaissance literature; Classical tradition; Hispano-Hebrew poetry. *Publ:* Auth, E Pinciano y las teorias literarias del Siglo de Ore, Gredos, Madrid, 62, 2nd ed, 71; Shem Tov: His World and His Words, Ediciones Universal, 77; Lost lexicon: Secret meanings in the vocabulary and Spanish literature during the Inquisition, Ediciones Universal, 82. *Mailing Add:* Dept of Romance Lang Oberlin Col Oberlin OH 44074

SHEPPARD, DOUGLAS CLAIRE, b Fairfield, Idaho, May 12, 22; m 49; c 3. FOREIGN LANGUAGES. *Educ:* Mont State Univ, BA, 48; Univ Wis, MA, 49, PhD, 55. *Prof Exp:* Instr Span, Univ Conn, 53-57; from asst prof to assoc prof, Mont State Univ, 58-62; specialist, lang insts, US Off Educ, 62-63; chmn dept foreign lang, Mont State Univ, 63-65; assoc prof Span & foreign lang educ, State Univ NY, Buffalo, 65-69; prof Span & dir foreign lang teaching, WVa Univ, 69-71; chmn dept foreign lang, 71-75, PROF SPAN, ARIZ STATE UNIV, 75- *Concurrent Pos:* Albert Markham traveling fel, Spain & Port, 56-57; prof ling, NDEA Lang Inst, Mont State Univ, 60-61; rev ed appl ling & lang learning, Mod Lang J, 69- *Mem:* Northeast Conf Teaching Foreign Lang; Asn Dept Foreign Lang; Am Asn Teachers Span & Port; MLA; Am Coun Teaching Foreign Lang;. *Res:* Spanish language and literature; linguistics; teacher education. *Publ:* Auth, Certifying teachers of modern foreign languages for American public schools, 1969, Foreign Lang Ann, 5/70; Professional standards for teachers of foreign languages, Asn Dept Foreign Lang Bull, 12/72; The California foreign language framework, Mod Lang J, 12/72. *Mailing Add:* Dept of Foreign lang Ariz State Univ Tempe AZ 85281

SHERESHEVSKY, ESRA, b Königsberg, Ger, US citizen. HEBREW LANGUAGE & LITERATURE. *Educ:* Teachers' Col, Jerusalem, Dipl educ, 40; Dropsie Univ, PhD(post-Bible & rabbinical lit), 57. *Prof Exp:* Prin, NBondi Hebrew Day Sch, Sydney, Australia, 46-49; dir Hebrew studies, Carmel Col, England, 49-53; asst prof Hebrew lit & rabbinical lit, Gratz Col, 55-59; co-dir edpt educ, Am Joint Distribution Comt, Geneva & Paris, 59-61; chmn dept Hebrew, 67-80, ASSOC PROF HEBREW LANG & LIT, TEMPLE UNIV, 62- *Concurrent Pos:* Ed, Jewish Quart Rev, 70-; prof Hebrew lit, Univ Cape Town, SAfrica, 75. *Mem:* Nat Coun Jewish Educ; Hebrew Cult Coun; MLA; Mediaeval Acad Am; Asn Jewish Studies. *Res:* Mediaeval Bible exegesis; history and religion of the Jews. *Publ:* Auth, Use of prepositions in Rashi's communication, 1/67; Rashi and Christian interpretations, Jewish Quart Rev, 7/70; Inversions in Rashi's commentary, In: Gratz Col anniversary vol, 71; The accents in Rashi's commentary, 4/72; Life in Rashi's times, Jewish Quart Rev, 7/74; The generation gap in the Hebrew Language, Barkai, SAfrica, 9/75; Hebrew Studies versus Jewish studies, Jewish Affairs, SAfrica, 10/75. *Mailing Add:* Dept of Hebrew Lang & Lit Temple Univ Philadelphia PA 19122

SHERK, ROBERT KENNETH, b Buffalo, NY, Dec 12, 20; m. GREEK, LATIN. *Educ:* Univ Buffalo, BA, 47; Johns Hopkins Univ, PhD, 50. *Prof Exp:* From asst prof to prof classics, Univ Maine, 50-62; assoc prof, 62-66, PROF GREEK & LATIN, STATE UNIV NY, BUFFALO, 66- *Mem:* Am Philol Asn; Archaeol Inst Am. *Res:* Roman army and provinces; Greek and Roman history; Greek and Latin epigraphy. *Publ:* Auth, Legates of Galatia, 51 & Roman Documents From the Greek East, 69, Johns Hopkins; Municipal Decrees of the Roman West, State Univ NY, 70; The Inermes Provinciae of Asia Minor, Am J Philol; Roman Galatia, Berlin, 81. *Mailing Add:* Dept of Classics State Univ of NY Buffalo NY 14214

SHERMAN, CAROL LYNN, b Fairfield, Iowa. EIGHTEENTH-CENTURY FRENCH LITERATURE. *Educ:* Parsons Col, BS, 61; Northwestern Univ, Evanston, MA, 68; Univ Chicago, PhD(French), 72. *Prof Exp:* Asst prof, 72-77, ASSOC PROF FRENCH LIT, UNIV NC, CHAPEL HILL, 77- *Concurrent Pos:* Ed, Romance Notes. *Mem:* Am Soc 18th Century Studies; Soc Int 18th Century Studies; SAtlantic Mod Lang Asn; MLA. *Res:* Denis Diderot; rococo structures; Voltaire and narratology. *Publ:* Auth, In defense of the dialogue: Diderot, Shaftesbury and Galiani, Vol XV, No 2 & The Neveu de Rameau and the Grotesque, Vol VI, No 1, Romance Notes; Diderot and the Art of Dialogue, Droz, Geneva, 76; Response criticism: Do readers make meaning?, Romance Notes, 77; Diderot et la rhetorique du rococo, Saggi e Ricerche di Letteratura Francese, 78; Passing symmetry: Space and time in eighteenth-century esthetics, Stanford Fr Rev, 79; Diderot's speech acts: Essay, letter, and dialogue, Fr Lit Ser, 81. *Mailing Add:* Dept of Romance Lang Univ of NC Chapel Hill NC 27514

SHERVILL, ROBERT NEWTON, b London, Ont, Jan 21, 20; m 42; c 4. LITERATURE, LINGUISTICS. *Educ:* Univ Western Ont, BA, 42; Univ NC, MA, 48, PhD(Span), 51. *Prof Exp:* Instr French & Span, 46-47, lectr, 48-56, from asst prof to assoc prof, 56-62, PROF SPAN & ITAL, UNIV WESTERN ONT, 62-, EXEC ASST TO PRES, 68- *Concurrent Pos:* Dept Veterans' scholar, 51-52; asst prin, Middlesex Col, 63-65, dean, 65-68; chmn dept of Span & Ital, Univ Western Ont, 76-82. *Mem:* MLA; Humanities Asn Can; Am Asn Teachers Span & Port; Can Asn Hispanists. *Res:* Golden Age Spanish drama; Romance linguistics; 19th century Spanish drama. *Publ:* Auth, Panorama Economico e Industrial de Latinoamerica, 52, Old Spanish Morphology and Phonology, 53 & Old French Morphology and Phonology, 55, Univ Western Ont; Lope's Ways With Women, Comediantes Bul, spring 62; Spanish Literature, In: Merit Students' Encyclopedia, Vol XVII, Crowell-Collier Press, 67; ed & compiler, They Passed This Way, Univ Western Ont Centennial Publ, 78. *Mailing Add:* Stevenson Hall Univ Western Ont London ON N6A 3K7 Can

SHETTER, WILLIAM ZEIDERS, b Allentown, Pa, Aug 17, 27. GERMANIC LANGUAGES & LINGUISTICS. *Educ:* Univ Pa, AB, 51; Univ Calif, MA, 53, PhD(Ger), 55. *Prof Exp:* Teaching asst, Univ Calif, 51-55; instr Ger, Univ Wis, 56-59, asst prof, 59-61; from asst prof to assoc prof Ger, Bryn Mawr Col, 62-65, assoc prof Ger lang, 65-71, PROF GER LANG, IND UNIV, 71- *Concurrent Pos:* Fulbright fel, State Univ Leiden, 55-56; res grant ling, State Univ Groningen, 61-62. *Mem:* Ling Soc Am; MLA; Maatschappij der Nederlandse Taal - en Letterkunde; Int Vereniging voor Nederlandistiek. *Res:* Linguistics; civilization of the Netherlands; medieval literature. *Publ:* Auth, The Pillars of Society: Six Centuries of Civilization in the Netherlands, Martinus Nijhoff, The Hague, 71. *Mailing Add:* Dept Ger Lang Ind Univ Bloomington IN 47401

SHEVELOV, GEORGE YURY, b Lomza, Poland, Dec 17, 08. SLAVIC PHILOLOGY. *Educ:* Univ Kharkov, PhD, 39; Ukrainian Free Univ, PhD, 49. *Prof Exp:* Docent Ukrainian lang, Inst Jour, Kharkov, 33-41; Slavic philol, Univ Kharkov, 38-43; assoc prof, Free Ukrainian Univ, 45-49; lectr Russ & Ukrainian, Lund, 50-52; vis lectr, Harvard Univ, 52-54; from assoc prof to prof, 54-77, EMER PROF SLAVIC PHILOL, COLUMBIA UNIV, 77- *Concurrent Pos:* Guggenheim Mem Found fel, 58-59; Am Coun Learned Soc grant comt mem, 61-63, grant, 67-68; grant, Nat Endowment for Humanities, 74. *Mem:* Ling Soc Am; Polish Inst Arts & Sci Am; Ukrainian Acad United States (pres, 80-). *Res:* Slavic comparative studies; history of the Slavic languages; historical phonology and syntax. *Publ:* Auth, An Outline of Modern Ukrainian, Sevcenko Sci Soc, Munich, 51; Probleme der Bildung des Zahlwortes in den Slavischen Sprachen, Univ Lund, 52; Problems in the formation of Belorussian, Ling Circle NY, 53; A Pre-hisotry of Slavic, Winter, 64, Columbia Univ, 65; Dir Ukrainische Schriftsprache 1798-1965, Harrassowitz, 66; Teasers and Appeasers: Essays and Studies on Themes of Slavic Philology, Fink, Munich, 71; Historical Phonology of the Ukrainian Language, Heidelberg, winter 79. *Mailing Add:* 39 Claremont Ave New York NY 10027

SHEY, HOWARD JAMES, b July 21, 35; US citizen; m 62; c 2. CLASSICS. *Educ:* Creighton Univ, BA, 62; Ind Univ, Bloomington, MA, 63, Univ Iowa, PhD(classics), 68. *Prof Exp:* From instr to asst prof classics, 66-72, ASSOC PROF CLASSICS, UNIV WIS-MILWAUKEE, 72- *Concurrent Pos:* Bk rev ed, Class J, 68-73. *Mem:* Am Philol Asn; Class Asn Mid W & S. *Res:* Latin and Greek lyric poetry; Latin epic. *Publ:* Auth, Petronius and Plato's Gorgias, Class Bull, 5/71; The poet's progress: Horace Ode 1 1, 9/71 & Tyrtaeus and the art of propaganda, 5/76, Arethusa. *Mailing Add:* Dept of Classics Univ of Wis Milwaukee WI 53201

SHIBATANI, MASAYOSHI, b Shanghai, China, Feb 1, 44; Japan citizen. LINGUISTICS. *Educ:* Univ Calif, Berkeley, BA, 70, PhD(ling), 73. *Prof Exp:* ASST PROF LING, UNIV SOUTHERN CALIF, 73-; ASSOC PROF, KOBE UNIV, 82- *Concurrent Pos:* Vis asst prof Japanese ling, Univ Hawaii, 77. *Mem:* Ling Soc Am; Ling Soc Japan. *Res:* Grammatical theory; phonological theory; Japanese linguistics. *Publ:* Auth, Semantics of Japanese causativization, Foundations of Lang, 73; The role of surface phonetic constraints in generative phonology, Language, 73; Lexical vs periphrastic causatives in Korean, J Ling, 73; ed, Japanese Generative Grammar, 76 & The Grammar of Causative Constructions, 76, Academic; auth, Grammatical relations and surface cases, Language, 77; Analysis of Japanese, Taishukan, Tokyo, 79; coauth, The Japanese and Korean Languages, Cambridge Univ (in press). *Mailing Add:* Faculty of Letters Kobe Univ Nada Kobe 657 Japan

SHIDELER, ROSS PATRICK, b Denver, Colo, Apr 12, 36; m 69; c 2. SCANDINAVIAN, COMPARATIVE LITERATURE. *Educ:* San Francisco State Col, BA, 58; Univ Stockholm, MA, 63; Univ Calif, Berkeley, PhD, 68. *Prof Exp:* Asst prof English, Hunter Col, 68-69; from asst prof to PROF COMP LIT & SCAND, UNIV CALIF, LOS ANGELES, 69-, CHMN PROG COMP LIT, 80- *Mem:* Soc Advan Scand Studies; Am Comp Lit Asn; Dramatists Guild; MLA. *Res:* Nineteenth and 20th century Swedish literature; 19th and 20th century English and French literature--poetry;

literature and psychology. *Publ:* Auth, Voices Under the Ground: Themes and Images in the Early Poetry of Gunnar Ekelof, Univ Calif Publ Mod Philol, Berkeley, 73; translr & auth introd, Per Olov Enquist, The Night of the Tribades (play), Hill & Wang, 77; auth, The glassclear eye of dreams in twentieth-century Swedish poetry, World Lit Today, 77; A functional theory of literature applied to poems by Paul Valery and Gunnar Ekelof, PsychoCult Rev, summer 78; contribr, Ungar's Encycl of 20th Century World Literature, 82; auth, Per Olov Enquist, Twayne World Author Series/G K Hall (in press). *Mailing Add:* Dept of Scand & Ger Lang Univ of Calif 405 Hilgard Ave Los Angeles CA 90024

SHIH, CHUNG WEN, b China. ENGLISH, CHINESE. *Educ:* St John's Univ, China, BA, 45; Duke Univ, MA, 49, PhD(English), 55. *Prof Exp:* Asst prof English, Univ Bridgeport, 56-60; fel East Esian studies, Harvard, 60-61; asst prof Chinese, Stanford Univ, 61-64; Am Asn Univ Women fel, 64-65; assoc prof Chinese, 66-71, PROF CHINESE, GEORGE WASHINGTON UNIV, 71- *Concurrent Pos:* Soc Sci Res Coun fel, 77; Nat Endowment for Humanities, 79-80; Nat Acad Sci sr vis scholar, China, 80. *Mem:* Am Antiquarian Soc; MLA; Chinese Lang Teachers Asn. *Publ:* Auth, Cooperatives and communes in Chinese communist fiction, China Quart, 1-3/63; Injustice to Tou O (Tou O Yuan), Cambridge Univ, 72; The Golden Age of Chinese Drama: Yuan Tsachu, Princeton Univ, 76; The poetic images in Yuan drama, Actes du XXIX Congres int des Orientalistes, Paris Juillet 1973, Paris, 77; Dominant themes and values in Chinese films, China Film Wk, Am Film Inst, 81- *Mailing Add:* Dept of East Asian Lang & Lit George Washington Univ Washington DC 20052

SHILAEFF, ARIADNE, b Blagoveshchensk, USSR, Oct 1, 20; US citizen; m 66; c 1. RUSSIAN LANGUAGE & LITERATURE. *Educ:* YMCA Col, China, BA, 40; NY Univ, MA, 65, PhD(lit), 69. *Prof Exp:* Lectr Russ, Tech Inst, Kalgan, China, 49-50 & Nan-Kai Univ, Tientsin, 51-53; instr Russ lang & lit, univ col arts & sci, NY Univ, 62-66; asst prof Russ, Wash Sq Col, 67-70; assoc prof, 70-80, PROF RUSS LANG & LIT & CHMN DEPT RUSS, WHEATON COL, MASS, 80- *Concurrent Pos:* Lectr Russ, Tsin-Ku Pedag Inst, Tientsin, 51-53; lectr Russ lang & lit, Univ Mass, Amherst, 66-67; mem bd dirs, Northeast Conf Teaching Foreign Lang, 77- *Mem:* Am Asn Teachers Slavic & East Europ Lang; Am Asn Advan Slavic Studies; Asn Russ-Am Scholars in USA; AAUP. *Res:* Russian Soviet literature; Russian emigre literature. *Publ:* Ed, Reference Russian Grammar, Conversa-Phone, 69; Boris Zaitsev and his Fictionalized Biographies, Volga Publ, 71; Life and Work of B K Zaitsev, Translr Asn Russ-Am Scholars in USA, 70. *Mailing Add:* Dept of Russ Wheaton Col Norton MA 02766

SHIMER, DOROTHY BLAIR, English, Asian Literature. See Vol II

SHIPLEY, GEORGE A, b Alamogordo, NMex, Mar 5, 37; m 66; c 1. SPANISH LITERATURE. *Educ:* Dartmouth Col, AB, 59; Harvard Univ, AM, 62, PhD(Romance lang & lit), 68. *Prof Exp:* Acting asst prof & lectr Span, Univ Calif, Berkeley, 64-67; asst prof, 67-76, ASSOC PROF SPAN, UNIV WASH, 76- *Mem:* MLA; Asoc Int Hispanistas. *Res:* LaCelestina: 16th & early 17th century Spanish literature; psycho-social functions of literature. *Publ:* Auth, Non erat hic locus: The disconcerted reader in Melibea's Garden, Romance Philol, 74; El natural de la raposa: Un proverbio estrategico de La Celestina, Nueva Revista de Filol Hisp, 75; Qual dolor puede ser tal . . .?: A rhetorical strategy for containing pain in La Celestina, Mod Lang Notes, 75; Concerting through conceit: Unconventional uses of conventional sickness images, in La Celestina, Mod Lang Rev, 4/75; Usos y abusos de la autoridad de los refranes en La Celestina, In: La Celestina y su contorno Social: Actas del I Congreso Internacional Sobre La Celestina, Hisp, 77; La obra literaria como monumento historico: El caso de El Abencerraje, J Hisp Philol, 78; The critic as witness for the prosecution: Making the case against Lazaro de Tormes, Publ Mod Lang Asn Am, 97: 179-194; A case of functional obscurity: The master tambourine-painter of Lazarille, Tratado VI, Mod Lang Notes, 97: 225-253. *Mailing Add:* Dept of Romance Lang & Lit Univ of Wash Seattle WA 98195

SHIVELY, DONALD HOWARD, Japanese History & Literature. See Vol I

SHIVERS, GEORGE ROBERT, b Salisbury, Md, Sept 9, 43. SPANISH LANGUAGE & LITERATURE. *Educ:* Am Univ, BA, 65; Univ Md, MA, 69, PhD(Span), 72. *Prof Exp:* Asst prof, 69-74, ASSOC PROF SPAN, WASHINGTON COL, 74- *Mem:* MLA; Am Asn Teachers Span & Port; Span Heritage Asn. *Res:* Nineteenth century Spanish literature; contemporary Spanish American literature. *Publ:* Auth, La historicidad de El Cerco de Numancia de Milguel de Cervantes Saavedra, Hispanofila, 70; La vision magico-mesianica en tres relatos de Garcia Marquez, 6/75, El tema del hombre y su destino en Borges y Cortazar, 12/76 & La dualidad y unidad en La Casa Verde de Vargas Llosa, 6/77, Arbor; contribr, La unidad dramatica en la Cisma de Inglaterra de Calderon de la Barca, In: Perspectivas de la Comedia, Estudios de Hispanofila, 78. *Mailing Add:* Dept of Mod Lang Washington Col Chestertown MD 21620

SHOAF, RICHARD ALLEN, Medieval Literature, Literary Theory. See Vol II

SHOEMAKER, RICHARD LEE, b New York, NY, Oct 21, 15; m 44. FRENCH. *Educ:* Colgate Univ, AB, 38; Syracuse Univ, AM, 40; Univ Va, PhD, 46. *Prof Exp:* Asst, Syracuse Univ, 38-40; instr French, Span & Latin, Cook Acad, 40-41; asst, Univ Va, 41-45, instr French & Span, 45-47; instr & tutor Romance lang, Harvard Univ, 47-50; from asst prof to assoc prof, 50-64, PROF ROMANCE LANG, WAKE FOREST UNIV, 64- *Mem:* MLA; Am Asn Teachers Fr. *Res:* French theater, poetry and Romanticism. *Publ:* Auth, The France of Henry Adams, Fr Rev; The Enigma of Arvers, Symposium. *Mailing Add:* Dept Romance Lang Wake Forest Univ Winston-Salem NC 27109

SHOEMAKER, THEODORE HARVEY, b Denver, Colo, Aug 11, 15; m 42; c 2. MODERN LANGUAGES. *Educ:* Mont State Univ, AB, 36; Univ Calif, AM, 38; Univ Wis, PhD, 41. *Prof Exp:* From asst prof to assoc prof, 46-59, prof, 59-79, EMER PROF MOD LANG, UNIV MONT, 80- *Mem:* Am Asm Teachers Span & Port. *Res:* Spanish literature. *Mailing Add:* Dept Foreign Lang Univ Mont Missoula MT 59801

SHOLOD, BARTON, b Brooklyn, NY, May 10, 32; m 72. ROMANCE LANGUAGES, MEDIEVAL STUDIES. *Educ:* Brooklyn Col, AB, 53; Columbia Univ, AM, 54, PhD, 63. *Prof Exp:* Lectr Span, Columbia Univ, 54-63; from lectr to asst prof Romance lang, 63-67, ASSOC PROF ROMANCE LANG, QUEENS COL NY, 67- *Concurrent Pos:* Mem, Hisp Inst US; Nat Endowment Arts & Humanities res grant for study abroad, 68; res grant, Prof Staff Congr Bd Higher Educ, 80-81. *Honors & Awards:* Res Award, PSC-BHE, 81. *Mem:* MLA; Am Asn Teachers Span & Port; Soc Rencesvals; AAUP; Medieval Acad Am. *Res:* Medieval Epic and Chivalaic Literature; the comparative novel; medieval Jewish studies. *Publ:* Coauth, Studies in Honor & M J Benardete, Las Americas, 65; auth, Charlemagne in Spain: The Cultural Legacy of Roncesvalles, Droz, 66. *Mailing Add:* 142 Shoreview Rd Manhasset NY 11030

SHORES, DAVID LEE, English, Linguistics. See Vol II

SHOWALTER, ENGLISH, JR, b Roanoke, Va, May 14, 35; m 62; c 2. FRENCH & COMPARATIVE LITERATURE. *Educ:* Yale Univ, BA, 57, PhD(French), 64. *Prof Exp:* Asst prof French, Haverford Col, 61-64 & Univ Calif, Davis, 64-66; asst prof Princeton Univ, 66-74; assoc prof, 74-78, PROF FRENCH, RUTGERS UNIV, CAMDEN, 78- *Concurrent Pos:* Nat Endowment for Humanities res fel, 77-78; Guggenheim fel, 82-83. *Mem:* MLA; Am Asn Teachers Fr; Am Soc 18th Century Studies; Fr Soc 18th Century Studies. *Res:* French fiction; social history of 17th & 18th century France. *Publ:* Auth, The Evolution of the French Novel, 1641-1782, Princeton, 72; Voltaire et ses Amis, D'apres la Correspondance de Mme De Graffigny, 75 & Rousseau and Mme De Graffigny, 78, Voltaire Found; Exiles and Strangers: A Reading of Camus's Exile and the Kingdom, Ohio State Univ Press (in prep). *Mailing Add:* Dept of French Rutgers Univ Camden NJ 08102

SHREEVE, LYMAN SIDNEY, b Eagar, Ariz, Mar 28, 15; m 36; c 3. SPANISH & PORTUGUESE. *Educ:* Brigham Young Univ, BA, 48, MA, 50; Inter-Am Univ, Mex, PhD(Latin Am lit), 70. *Prof Exp:* Prof Span, Eastern Ariz Jr Col, 50-51; asst prof, Brigham Young Univ, 55-56; exec dir, Utah Soc Crippled Children & Adults, 56-59; dir, US Info Agency Binational Ctr, Chile, Mex & Uruguay, 59-65; assoc prof Span & Latin Am studies, 65-74, prof, 75-80, EMER PROF SPAN, BRIGHAM YOUNG UNIV, 80- *Concurrent Pos:* Pres, Church of Jesus Christ of Latter-day Saints Relig Mission, Uruguay-Paraguay, 51-55. *Honors & Awards:* Distinguished Serv Award, US Info Agency, 60. *Mem:* Rocky Mountain Coun Latin Am Studies (vpres, 68-70, pres, 70-71); Am Asn Teachers Span & Port. *Publ:* Auth, Gaucho, Uruguayan Publ Co, Montevideo, 55; El gaucho, Asn Estudiantes Arquitectura del Technol, Monterrey, 63 & Brigham Young Univ, 72. *Mailing Add:* Dept of Span & Port Brigham Young Univ Provo UT 84602

SHRODER, MAURICE ZORENSKY, b St Louis, Mo, June 6, 33. FRENCH & COMPARATIVE LITERATURE. *Educ:* Northwestern Univ, SB, 54; Harvard Univ, AM, 55, PhD, 59. *Prof Exp:* Instr Romance lang & lit, Harvard, 59-62, asst prof, 62-63; asst prof foreign & comp lit, Univ Rochester, 63-65; assoc prof French, Barnard Col, Columbia Univ, 65-69, prof, 69-80. *Concurrent Pos:* Samuel S Fels study fel, 57-58. *Mem:* MLA. *Res:* French Romanticism; theory of the novel. *Publ:* Auth, Icarus: The Image of the Artist in French Romanticism, Harvard, 61; ed, The novels as a genre, Mass Res, winter 63; auth, Poetes francais du dix-neuvieme siecle, Integral, 64; ed, On reading Salammbo, L'Esprit Createur, spring 70; France, In: Romantic and its Cognates, Toronto, 72; Le dix-neuvieme siecle, Prentice-Hall, 73. *Mailing Add:* 235 West 102nd St New York NY 10027

SHTOHRYN, DMYTRO MICHAEL, b Zvyniach, Ukraine, Nov 9, 23; US citizen; m 55; c 2. UKRAINIAN MODERN LITERATURE. *Educ:* Univ Ottawa, MA, 58, BLS, 59, PhD(Slavic studies), 70. *Prof Exp:* Cataloger, Libr, Nat Res Coun Can, 59-60; Slavic cataloger, Libr, Univ Ill, Urbana-Champaign, 60-64, asst prof Libr admin, 64-70, assoc prof Libr admin, 70-80, head Slavic cataloging, Libr, 64-80, instr Ukrainian lit, Univ, 69-80. *Concurrent Pos:* Assoc, Russ & East Europ Ctr, Univ Ill, 61-, grant, 69, instr hist Slavic printing, Grad Sch Libr Sci, 67-70, Sen, Univ, 73-75; vis prof Ukrainian lit, Univ Ottawa, 74; assoc prof Ukrainian lit, Ukrainian Cath Univ, Rome, Italy, 76- *Honors & Awards:* Silver Medal, Libr of Parliament of Can, 59; Award, Grolier Soc Can, 59. *Mem:* Am Asn Advan Slavic Studies; Ukrainian Libr Asn Am (vpres, 63-70, pres, 70-74); Asn Advan Ukrainian Studies (secy-treas, 75-); Int Ivan Franko Soc (pres, 77-); Ukrainian-Am Asn Univ Prof (vpres, 77-). *Res:* Bibliography of Ukrainian literary criticism; Ukrainian Soviet literature of the 1920's; biography of noteworthy Ukrainians in diaspora. *Publ:* Auth, Literary Analysis of Taras Shevchenko's David's Psalms, Liberation Path, 61; Scientific Work of O Kandyba-Ol'zhych, Phoenix, Munich, 62; Ukrainica in the Library of Congress, Horizon, Chicago, 66; ed, Catalog of Publications of the Ukrainian Academy of Sciences, 1918-1930, Ukrainian Libr Asn Am, 66; auth, Lights and Shadows of Ukrainian Studies in Harvard, Tusm, 73; ed, Ukrainians in North America: A Biographical Directory, Asn Advan Ukrainian Studies, 75; contribr, Contributor to Encyclopaedia of Ukraine, Shevchenko Sci Soc, 77-; auth, Ukrainian literature in the United States: Trends, influences, achievements, Nineth Comp Lit Symp, Tex Tech Univ, 78. *Mailing Add:* 403 Park Ln Dr C Champaign IL 61820

SHUFORD, WILLIAM HARRIS, b Lincolnton, NC, Oct 28, 32. ROMANCE LANGUAGES. *Educ:* Lenoir-Rhyne Col, AB, 54; Univ Fla, MA, 56; Univ NC, PhD(Romance lang), 63. *Prof Exp:* Asst prof Span, Lenoir-Rhyne Col, 61-64, assoc prof, 64-67; assoc prof, Furman Univ, 67-69; chmn dept mod & class lang, 69-80, PROF SPAN, LENOIR-RHYNE COL, 69- *Mem:* MLA; SAtlantic Mod Lang Asn; Am Asn Teachers Span & Port. *Mailing Add:* Dept of Mod & Class Lang Lenoir-Rhyne Col Hickory NC 28601

SHUKLA, SHALIGRAM, b Madhawapur, Uttar Pradesh, India, Mar 20, 40; m 58; c 2. LINGUISTICS, ANTHROPOLOGY. *Educ:* Banaras Hindu Univ, BA, 60; Gorakhpur Univ, MA, 62; Cornell Univ, MA, 65, PhD(ling), 68. *Prof Exp:* Teaching asst Hindi, Cornell Univ, 63-68; ASSOC PROF LING, GEORGETOWN UNIV, 68- *Mem:* Ling Soc Am; Am Anthrop Asn. *Res:* Comparative Indo-European phonology; syntactic, semantic, and phonological study of Indo-Aryan languages; linguistics and literature. *Publ:* Coauth, Palanwuin symbolism, J Am Folklore, 68; auth, Kinship system in Panini's Astadhyayi, 70 & Underlying representation and phonological change, 70, Lang & Ling; co-ed, Languages and Linguistics, Georgetown Univ, 70-74; auth, Phonological change and dialect variation, Proc First Int Cong Hist Ling, 74; Phonological rules and old Indo-Ayran isoglosses, Proc 2nd Int Cong Hist Ling, 76; Culture and historical semantics, Papers Anthrop, 77; Bhojpuri Grammar, 81. *Mailing Add:* Sch of Lang & Ling Georgetown Univ Washington DC 20057

SHUMAKER, JOHN WILLIAM, b Pittsburgh, Pa, Aug 21, 42. CLASSICAL LANGUAGES. *Educ:* Univ Pittsburgh, BA, 64; Univ Pa, MA, 66, PhD(classics), 69. *Prof Exp:* Asst prof classics, Ohio State Univ, 69-73, actg chmn dept, 72-73, assoc prof classics, 73-80, assoc dean humanities, 74-80; MEM FAC, DEPT CLASSICS, STATE UNIV NY, ALBANY, 80- *Concurrent Pos:* Vis asst prof class studies, Univ Pa, 69; secy, Ohio Class Conf, 71-73; assoc res prof, Thesaurus Linguae Graecae, Univ Calif, Irvine, 73. *Mem:* Am Philol Asn; Class Asn Mid West & South; Am Soc Papyrologists; Asn Int Papyrologues. *Res:* Hellenistic poetry; papyrology. *Publ:* Auth, A New fragment of a Homeric lexicon, 70, Two papyri from McCormick Theological Seminary, 70 & Two papyri from Vassar College, 70, Bull Am Soc Papyrologists; ed, A Cumulative Index to the Berichtigungsliste, Thesaurus Linguae Greacae, 74. *Mailing Add:* 4 Sagbrook Dr Glenmont NY 12077

SHUPP, ROBERT PETE, b Los Angeles, Calif, Dec 7, 42; m 66; c 3. FRENCH LITERATURE & LANGUAGE. *Educ:* Univ Calif, Santa Barbara, BA, 65, MA, 67, PhD(French), 71; Univ Bordeaux, Cert d'Etudes, 74. *Prof Exp:* Lab asst phonemics, Speech Synthesis Proj, Univ Calif, Santa Barbara, 65-66; from instr to asst prof French, Dartmouth Col, 69-77, assoc prof, 77-79; ASSOC PROF FRENCH, UNIV HOUSTON, 79- *Mem:* MLA; Am Asn Teachers French. *Res:* Seventeenth century; French language and civilization; pedagogical methodology. *Publ:* Coauth, Debuts Culturels, Holt, 77; Chere Francoise, 78 & LeMonde Francais, 78, Rand McNally; Student Workbook for Rassias: Le Francais: Depart-Arrivee, Harper & Row, 81. *Mailing Add:* Dept of French Univ Houston, Central Campus Houston TX 77004

SHURR, GEORGIA GREY HOOKS, b Columbus City, NC, Aug 5, 42; m 68; c 1. FRENCH, COMPARATIVE LITERATURE. *Educ:* E Carolina Univ, BS, 64; Univ NC, Chapel Hill, MA, 67, PhD (French & Romance Lang), 71. *Prof Exp:* Asst prof French, Univ Tenn, Chattanooga, 71-72; asst prof French, Univ Idaho, 72, assoc prof, 75-79, prof, 79-81; ADJ PROF CULT STUDIES, UNIV TENN, 81- *Honors & Awards:* Comite francais du Bicentenaire de l'Independence des Etats-Unis, Am Asn Teachers French, 76; Most outstanding teacher of foreign lang, Idaho Foreign Lang Teachers Asn, 79. *Mem:* MLA; Am Asn Teachers French; Claudel Soc Am (secy 80-82); SAm Mod Lang Asn. *Res:* Medieval and modern French literature; Claudel, Peguy; Rilke's French poetry. *Publ:* Auth, Artistic Creativity and Paralysis: Valery and LeConte de Lisle, Proc of PNCFL, 74; Claudel's religion: His critics and some conclusions, 75 & Claudel's Nouveau Guignol, L'Echange, 75, Claudel Studies; Thomas Jefferson et la revolution francaise, Annales Hist de Revolution Francaise, 78; The Jefferson and the French Revolution, Am Soc Legion of Hon Mag, winter 79-80; The significance of Rilke's French poetry, In: Papers in Romance, Univ Wash, winter 80; Marguerite Yourcenar, de l'Academie Fraucaise, Laurels of Am Soc French Legion of Hon, fall 81; The heavens and a conscious experience of immortality, Planetarian, summer 80. *Mailing Add:* Dept of Cult Studies Univ Tenn Knoxville TN 37916

SHUY, ROGER W, b Akron, Ohio, Jan 5, 31; m 52; c 2. LINGUISTICS. *Educ:* Wheaton Col, Ill, AB, 52; Kent State Univ, MA, 54; Western Reserve Univ, PhD, 62. *Prof Exp:* Teacher lang arts, Kenmore Jr & Sr High Sch, Akron, Ohio, 56-58; from instr to asst prof English & ling, Wheaton Col, Ill, 58-64; assoc prof, Mich State Univ, 64-67; dir sociolinguistics prog, Ctr Appl Ling, 67-70; dir Nat Sci Found grant to estabish prog in socioling, 70-73, PROF LING & DIR SOCIOLING PROG, GEORGETOWN UNIV, 70- *Concurrent Pos:* Am Coun Learned Soc grant, 57; Univ Chicago res grant, 62; dir, Detroit Dialect Study, 66-67; Carnegie Corp NY & Nat Inst Ment Health grants, Ctr Appl Ling, 67-; ling adv, Xerox Intermediate Dictionary, 72; mem eval panel, early childhood educ, Nat Inst Educ, 72; comt socioling, Soc Sci Res Coun, 72-; assoc dir, Ctr Appl Ling, 74-; res award on acquistion of children's use of lang functions, Carnegie Corp of NY, 75. *Mem:* Int Reading Asn; Ling Soc Am; AAAS; Am Asn Appl Ling (pres, 78); NCTE. *Res:* Linguistics and education; sociolinguistics; the English language. *Publ:* Auth, Discovering American Dialects, NCTE, 67; Field Techniques in an Urban Language Study, Ctr Appl Ling, 68; co-ed, New Ways of Analyzing Variation in Englihs, 73; Language Attitudes, 73 & ed, Sociolinguistics: Current Trends and Prospects, 73, Georgetown Univ; co-ed, Dialect Differences: Do They Interfere?, Int Reading Asn, 73; ed, Linguistic Theory: What Does it Have to Say About Reading, Int Reading Asn, 77; Studies in Language Variation, Georgetown Univ, 77. *Mailing Add:* Socioling Prog Georgetown Univ Washington DC 20057

SICES, DAVID, b New York, NY, June 10, 33; m 56, 63; c 4. FRENCH LANGUAGE & LITERATURE. *Educ:* Dartmouth Col, BA, 54; Yale Univ, PhD(French lit), 62. *Hon Degrees:* MA, Dartmouth Col, 71. *Prof Exp:* From instr to asst prof French, 57-66, assoc prof French & Ital, 66-71, chmn dept Romance lang & lit, 70-79, PROF FRENCH & ITAL, DARTMOUTH COL, 71- *Concurrent Pos:* Am Coun Learned Soc fel, Paris, 69-70; asst ed, French Rev, 80-; Nat Screening Comt, Inst Int Educ, 80- *Mem:* MLA; Am Asn Teachers Fr; Am Asn Teachers Ital; Am Asn Univ Professors Ital. *Res:* Theater of Musset and the Romantics; 19th century French poetry and novel; translation of French and Italian drama. *Publ:* Auth, Music and the Musician in Jean-Christopher, Yale Univ, 68; Theater of Solitude: The Drama of Alfred de Musset, New England Univ, 74; 2001 French and English Idioms, Barrow's, 82. *Mailing Add:* Dept of Romance Lang & Lit Dartmouth Col Hanover NH 03755

SICHA, JEFFREY FRANKLIN, Philosophy. See Vol IV

SICILIANO, ERNEST ALEXANDER, b East Boston, Mass, Jan 24, 16; m 40; c 6. ROMANCE PHILOLOGY. *Educ:* Boston Col, AB, 37, AM, 39; Harvard Univ, PhD, 46. *Prof Exp:* Teaching fel Romance lang, 37-39, from instr to assoc prof, 39-47, PROF ROMANCE LANG, BOSTON COL, 47- *Honors & Awards:* Medal, Acad Francaise, 37. *Mem:* Am Asn Teachers Span & Port; Am Asn Teachers Fr; Am Asn Teachers Ital; New Eng Mod Lang Asn (vpres, 50). *Res:* The Spanish legend. *Publ:* Auth, Preguntas sobre los metodos estilisticos de Damaso Alonso, Hispanofila, 5/67; Conscience in the Quijote, Romance Notes, spring 70; The absent hermit of the Quijote, Romance Notes, spring 71; La verdaderz Azucena en El Trovador, Nueva Revista de Filologia Hispanica, 71; Don Quijote's Housekeeper: Algebrista?, J Am Folklore, 10-12/73; The Jesuits in the Quijote and Other Essays, Hispam, Barcelona, 74; Absenteeism and language learning, Hispania, 3/78; Satire in the inversion of roles in the Quijote, Romance Notes, 81. *Mailing Add:* Dept of Romance Lang Boston Col Chestnut Hill MA 02167

SICROFF, ALBERT ABRAHAM, b New York, NY, Dec 7, 18; m 47; c 3. SPANISH LITERATURE. *Educ:* Brooklyn Col, BA, 40; Univ Paris, DUniv, 55. *Prof Exp:* Instr Span, Syracuse Univ, 46-47; from instr to asst prof, Princeton Univ, 50-61; assoc prof, Vanderbilt Univ, 61-64; PROF ROMANCE LANG, QUEENS COL, NY, 64- *Concurrent Pos:* Vis prof Span, Columbia Univ, 66. *Mem:* MLA; Am Asn Teachers Span & Port. *Res:* Jews and Judeo-Spaniards in Spain the the 15th and 17th centuries; the Order of St Jerome in Spain during the 15th century; the picaresque novel. *Publ:* Auth, Les Controverses sur les Statuts de Purete de Sang en Espange, Didier, Paris, 60; Clandestine Judaism in the Hieronymite Monastery of Nuestra Senora de Guadalupe, In: Studies in Honor of M J Benardete, Las Americas, 65; The Jeronymite Monastery of Guadalupe in 14th and 15th century Spain, In: Collected Studies in Honour of Americo Castro's 80th Year, Lincombe Lodge Res Libr, Oxford, England, 65. *Mailing Add:* Dept of Romance Lang Queens Col Flushing NY 11367

SIDDIQI, MOHAMMED MOAZZAM, b Hyderabad, India, Feb 20, 41; US citizen. INDO-PERSIAN LITERATURE. *Educ:* Osmania Univ, India, BSc, 61; Univ Calif, Berkeley, MA, 72, PhD(Near Eastern studies), 75. *Prof Exp:* Asst prof Persian, Univ Va, 76-77; ASST PROF URDU & PERSIAN, DUKE UNIV, 77- *Res:* Indo-Persian poetry; Urdu literature; Islamic mysticism. *Publ:* Auth, Bedil and his influence on the Indo-Persian literary tradition, Mir Ghulam Ali Azad Bilgrami, Abu'l Faraj Runi, the first Indo-Persian poet, In: Encycl Persica, Columbia Univ, 78. *Mailing Add:* Dept of Class Studies Duke Univ Durham NC 27706

SIDER, DAVID, b Bronx, NY, July 21, 40. CLASSICAL LANGUAGES. *Educ:* City Col New York, BA, 61; Columbia Univ, MA, 63, PhD(Greek), 70. *Prof Exp:* Mem staff, Univ NC, Chapel Hill, 67-75, Univ Ky, 75-76 & Univ Ill, Urbana, 76-77; ADJ ASSOC PROF CLASS, QUEENS COL, 80- *Mem:* Am Philol Asn; Soc Ancient Greek Philos; Soc Ancient Med. *Res:* Philosophy, especially Presocratics and Plato; poetry; medicine. *Publ:* Auth, The structure of Plato, Republic VI, Rivista di Studi Class 24, 76; Stagecraft in the Oresteia, Am J Philol 99, 78; Galen, on tremor, rigor, palpitation, and spasm, Transactions and Studies of the Col of Physicians of Philadelphia, 79; Confirmation of two conjectures in the presocratics: Parmenides B 12 and Anaxagoras B 15, Phoenix 33, 79; Did Plato write dialogues before the death of Socrates?, Apeiron 14, 80; Plato's Symposium as Dionysian festival, Quaderni Urbinati di Cultura Class 4, 80; The Fragments of Anaxagoras, Hain Verlag, Meisenheim, 81; Empedocles B 96 and the poetry of adhesion, Mnemosyne (in prep). *Mailing Add:* 3873 Orloff Ave Bronx NY 10463

SIDER, ROBERT DICK, b Cheapside, Ont, Mar 10, 32; m 59; c 3. CLASSICS, RELIGION. *Educ:* Univ Sask, BA, 55, MA, 56; Oxford Univ, BA(Hons), 58, MA, 64, PhD(patristics), 65. *Prof Exp:* Assoc prof class lit, Messiah Col, 62-68; from asst prof to assoc prof, 68-77, prof class studies, 77-81, DANA PROF CLASS LANG, DICKINSON COL, 81- *Concurrent Pos:* Am Coun Learned Soc fel, 74-75; vis prof Greek & Latin, Cath Univ Am, 78-79; gen ed, New Testament Scholarship of Erasmus for Collected Works of Erasmus, Univ Toronto Press. *Mem:* Can Asn Am Studies; Am Philol Asn; Archaeol Inst Am; NAm Patristic Soc (vpres, 72, pres, 73). *Res:* Classical rhetoric; early Christian literature; Renaissance humanism. *Publ:* Auth, Structure and design in the De resurrectione mortuorum of Tertullian, Vigilae Christianae, 69; Ancient Rhetoric and the Art of Tertullian, Oxford Univ, 71; On symmetrical composition in Tertullian, 73 & Tertullian's De Spectaculis: An analysis, 78, J Theol Studies; Credo Quia Absurdum?, Class World, 80. *Mailing Add:* Dept of Class Lang Dickinson Col Carlisle PA 17013

SIEBER, HARRY CHARLES, b Oklahoma City, Okla, Oct 4, 41; m 63; c 1. ROMANCE LANGUAGES. *Educ:* Baylor Univ, BA, 63; Duke Univ, PhD(Span lit), 67. *Prof Exp:* Asst prof Romance lang, 67-73, assoc prof Span lit, 73-77, PROF ROMANCE LANG, JOHNS HOPKINS UNIV, 77- *Concurrent Pos:* Ed, Mod Lang Newsletter, 67-; Am Coun Learned Soc travel grant, 71; Nat Endowment for Humanities younger humanist fel, 74; Guggenheim fel, John Simon Guggenheim Mem Found, 78-79. *Mem:* MLA; Asoc Int Hispanistas; Am Asn Teachers Span & Port; SAtlantic Mod Lang Asn; Northeast Mod Lang Asn. *Res:* Picaresque novel; Cervantes; Spanish comedia. *Publ:* Auth, Dramatic symmetry in Gomez Manrique's La representacion del nacimiento de nuestro senor, Hisp Rev, 65; Apostrophes in the Buscon: An approach to Quevedo's narrative art, Mod Lang Notes, 68; On Juan Huarte de San Juan and Anselmo's Locura in El curioso impertinente, Rev Hisp Mod, 73; The Picaresque, Methuen, London, 77; Language and Society in La vida de Lazarillo de Tormes, Johns Hopkins Univ, 78; ed, Novelas ejemplares, 2 volls, M de Cervantes, Madrid, 80. *Mailing Add:* Dept of Romance Lang Johns Hopkins Univ Baltimore MD 21218

SIEGWART, JOHN THOMAS, b Memphis, Tenn, Nov 12, 30; m 53; c 2. SPANISH LITERATURE. *Educ:* Memphis State Col, BS, 52; Univ Miss, MA, 52; Tulane Univ, PhD(Romance lang), 59. *Prof Exp:* Asst prof Span & French, Butler Univ, 55-62; prof Span & chmn dept foreign lang, Montevallo Col, 62-63; prof Span & French & chmn, Dept Mod Foreign Lang, Birmingham-Southern Col, 63-80. *Mem:* SAtlantic Mod Lang Asn; Asn Dept Foreign Lang; Am Asn Teachers Span & Port; Am Asn Teachers Fr. *Res:* History of Spanish literary criticism; 18th century Spanish literature; Spanish literary criticism, 18th and 19th centuries. *Mailing Add:* 1237 Greensboro Rd Birmingham AL 35208

SIEMENS, WILLIAM LEE, b Shafter, Calif, Mar 13, 37. SPANISH AMERICAN PROSE FICTION. *Educ:* Wheaton Col, Ill, AB, 58; Gordon-Conwell Theol Sem, MDiv, 61; Univ Mass, MA, 67; Univ Kans, PhD(Span), 71. *Prof Exp:* Instr Span & French, Fresno Pac Col, 66-68; asst prof, Va Intermont Col, 71-73; ASSOC PROF SPAN & HUMANITIES, WVA UNIV, 73- *Mem:* Am Asn Teachers Span & Port; MLA; Caribbean Studies Asn. *Res:* Recent Cuban novel; hero theme in 20th century Spanish American novel; language in 20th century Spanish American novel. *Publ:* Auth, The devouring female in four Latin American novels, Essays Lit, spring 74; Assault on the schizoid wasteland, Latin Am Theatre Rev, spring 74; Heilsgeschichte and the structure of Tres Tristes Tigres, Ky Romance Quart, 75; contribr, Explications of two sonnets of Enrique Gonzalez Martinez, In: Antologia Comentada del Modernismo, Explicaciones, Medellin, 75; Tiempo, entropia y la estructura de Cien Anos de Soledad, In: Explicacion de Cien Anos de Soledad, Texto, San Jose, 76; auth, Los Juglares de Tulua: Don Pedro Uribe, Biblioteca Munic, Tulua, 77; contribr, Tiempo y poder en El Bazar de los Idiotas, In: Aproximaciones a Gustavo Alvarez Gardeazabal, Plaza y Janes, Bogota, 77; Apollo's metamorphosis in Pantaleon y las Visitadora, In: Mario Vargas Llosa, Univ Tex, Austin, 78. *Mailing Add:* Dept of Foreign Lang WVa Univ Morgantown WV 26506

SIENKEWICZ, THOMAS J, b Hoboken, NJ, Apr 29, 50; m 72; c 2. CLASSICAL LITERATURES. *Educ:* Col of the Holy Cross, BA, 71; Johns Hopkins Univ, MA, 73, PhD (classics), 75. *Prof Exp:* asst prof, 75-81, ASSOC PROF CLASSICS, HOWARD UNIV, 81- *Concurrent Pos:* Honorary fel, Inst Advan Studies Humanities, Univ Edinburgh, 82. *Mem:* Am Philol Asn; Am Inst Archaeol; Class Asn Atlantic States; Am Class League. *Res:* The chorus in Greek tragedy; the fifth-century tragic tetralogy. *Publ:* Auth, Sophocles' Telepheia, Zeitschrift fur papyrologie und epigraphik, 76; Euripides' Trojan Women: An interpretation, Helios, 78; Helen-Scapegoat or Siren?, 56 & Catullus: Another Attis, 57, Class Bull; On Euripioes' Trojan Women, Class Outlook, 57. *Mailing Add:* Dept of Classics Howard Univ Washington DC 20059

SIEV, ASHER, b Jerusalem, Israel, Nov 15, 13; US citizen; m 40; c 3. HEBREW LITERATURE. *Educ:* Yeshiva Univ, BA, 37, DHL(Hebrew lit), 43. *Prof Exp:* Teacher Talmud, teachers inst, 38-63, instr Bible & Hebrew, Yeshiva Col, 38-63, assoc prof Hebrew lit, 63-68, PROF HEBREW LIT, YESHIVA UNIV, 68- *Honors & Awards:* Rabbi Kook Award, Tel-Aviv Munic, Israel, 73. *Res:* Jewish law, its development and codification. *Publ:* Auth, Life and Works of Rabbi Moses Isserles, Mosad Harav Kook, Jerusalem, 58, 2nd ed, 61; Responsa of Rabbi Moses Isserles, 70 & Rabbi Isserles and his Contemporaries, 72, Yeshiva Univ; Complete bibliography on the Rema, Talpiot, 9:314-342; The Maharam of Padua, Hadarom, 28:160-195; Maharshik, Hadarom, 34: 177-210. *Mailing Add:* 1505 Waring Ave Bronx NY 10469

SIGSBEE, DAVID LEE, b Detroit, Mich, Mar 6, 39. CLASSICAL STUDIES. *Educ:* Concordia Col, Ind, BA, 60; Univ Mich, MA, 61, PhD(class studies), 68. *Prof Exp:* Instr Grek & Latin, Univ SDak, 62-64; from lectr to asst prof, Ind Univ, Bloomington, 67-75; asst prof classics, Ball State Univ, 75-76; ASSOC PROF CLASSICS & SECT HEAD, MEMPHIS STATE UNIV, 76- *Mem:* Am Philol Asn; Ling Soc Am; Am Class League. *Res:* Satire and Menippean satire; Roman stoicism; classical linguistics. *Publ:* Auth, Varro and Menippean satire, The disciplined satires of Horace & Epilogue, In: Roman Satirists and Their Satire, Noyes, 74; Paradoxa Stoicorum in Varro's Menippeans, Class Philol, 75. *Mailing Add:* WD 361 Foreign Lang Memphis State Univ Memphis TN 38152

SIHLER, ANDREW L, b Seattle, Wash, Feb 25, 41. LINGUISTICS. *Educ:* Harvard Univ, BA, 62; Yale Univ, MA, 65, PhD(ling), 67. *Prof Exp:* From asst prof to assoc prof ling, 67-78, PROF LING, UNIV WIS-MADISON, 78- *Concurrent Pos:* Adv ed, Indo-Europ Studies, 72- *Mem:* Am Orient Soc; Ling Soc Am. *Res:* Auth, Proto-Indo-European post-consonantal resonants in word-initial sequences, Univ Microfilms, 67; Sievers-Edgerton phenomena and Rigvedic meter, 69, Word-initial semivowel alternation in the Rigveda, 71 & Review of Greek dialects and the transformation of an Indo-European process, by Gregory Nagy, 73, Language; Loss of w and y in Vedic Sanskirt, Indo-Iranian J, 77; The Proto-Indo-European Origins of the Germanic femina nomina agentis in -stri(o)n, Die Sprache, 77; Morphologically conditoned sound change and OE past participles in -en, Gen Ling, 77. *Publ:* Auth, Sievers-Edgerton phenomena and Rigvedic meter, 69, Word-initial semivowel alternation in the Rigveda, 71 & Review of Greek dialects and the transformation of an Indo-European process, by Gregory Nagy, 73, Language; Loss of w and y in Vedic Sanskrit, Indo-Iranian J, 77; The Proto-Indo-European Origins of the Germanic femina nomina agentis in -stri(o)n, Die Sprache, 77; Morphologically conditioned sound change and OE past participles in -en, Gen Ling, 77. *Mailing Add:* Dept of Ling Univ of Wis Madison WI 53706

SILBAJORIS, FRANK R, b Kretinga, Lithuania, Jan 6, 26; US citizen; m 55; c 2. RUSSIAN LANGUAGE & LITERATURE. *Educ:* Antioch Col, BA, 53; Columbia Univ, cert Russ & MA, 55, PhD, 62. *Prof Exp:* From instr to asst prof Ger & Russ, Oberlin Col, 57-63; assoc prof Slavic lang & lit, 63-67, PROF SLAVIC LANG & LIT, OHIO STATE UNIV, 67- *Concurrent Pos:* John Hay Whitney Opportunity fel, 53-55; Ford Found fel, 53-55; Ford Found Overseas Area studies fel, 54-56. *Honors & Awards:* Lithuanian Community Orgn Award, 82. *Mem:* Asn Advan Baltic Studies (pres, 73-74); Am Asn Teachers Slavic & EEurop Lang; Am Asn Advan Slavic Lang; Inst Lithuanian Studies (pres, 79-). *Res:* Russian versification of the 18th century; Lithuanian literature; creative work of Leo Tolstoy. *Publ:* Auth, The Poetic Texture of Dr Zhivago, spring 65 & Pasternak and Tolstoj: Some Comparisons, winter 67, Slavic & EEurop J; Dynamic Elements in the Lyrics of Fet, Slavic Rev, 6/67; Russian Versification: The Theories of Trediakovskij, Lomonosov and Kantemir, Columbia Univ, 68; Perfection of Exile: Fourteen Contemporary Lithuanian Writers, Okla Univ, 70; ed, The Architecture of Reading, Ohio State Univ Slavic Papers, 76; Lithuanian Literature, In: Columbia Dict Modern Literature. *Mailing Add:* Dept Slavic Lang Ohio State Univ Columbus OH 43210

SILBER, GORDON RUTLEDGE, b New York, NY, Nov 6, 09; m; c 2. FRENCH & ITALIAN LITERATURE. *Educ:* Princeton Univ, AB, 31, PhD, 35. *Prof Exp:* Instr classics, Princeton Univ, 31-32, instr French, 35-36; from instr to prof French & Ital, Union Col, NY, 36-60, chmn dept mod lang, 46-59, chmn div humanities, 52-55; chmn dept mod lang & lit, 60-67, chmn dept French, 68, prof, 60-80, EMER PROF ROMANCE LANG & FRENCH, STATE UNIV NY BUFFALO, 80- *Concurrent Pos:* Dir Europ off, Inst Int Educ, Paris, 51-52; consult foreign lang prog, Schenectady Pub Schs, 53-60; dir, Mod Lang Proj, Boston, 59; prof-in-charge, Sweet Briar Jr Year in France, 63-64; mem exec comt, Nat Fedn Mod Lang Teachers Asn, 65-77, secy-treas, 69-77. *Honors & Awards:* Officier d'Academie, 55; Officier Palmes Academiques, 69. *Mem:* MLA; Am Asn Teachers Fr; Am Asn Teachers Ital (vpres, 42); Dante Soc; Am Soc 18th Century Studies. *Res:* French 18th century; 18th century Masonic literature; 18th century Franco-American culture contacts. *Publ:* Auth, Poemes et chansons maconniques du XVIIIe siecle, Rev Sci Humaines, 72; In Search of Helvetius' Early Career as a Freemason, 18th Century Studies, 82. *Mailing Add:* 124 Brookedge Dr Williamsville NY 14221

SILBERMAN, MARC DAVID, b Minneapolis, Minn, Apr 8, 48. GERMAN, HUMANITIES. *Educ:* Univ Minn, BA, 69; Ind Univ,AM, 72, PhD(ger), 75. *Prof Exp:* Vis asst prof Ger, Ind Univ, 75-76; ASST PROF GER, UNIV TEX, SAN ANTONIO, 76- *Concurrent Pos:* Nat Endowment for Humanities grant, 81; Alexander von Humboldt-Stiftung, 82. *Mem:* MLA; Am Asn Teachers Ger; Int Brecht Soc. *Res:* Literature of the German Democratic Republic; film theory and history of German film; aesthetics. *Publ:* Auth, Literature of the Working World: A Study of the Industrial Novel in East Germany, Bern/Frankfurt, Herbert Lang, 76; Heiner Mueller, Forschungsbericht, Rodopi, Amsterdam, 80; ed, Interpretationen zum Roman in der DDR, Reclam, Stuttgart, 80; auth, Brecht Reception in the GDR, Theatre J, 3/80; Cine-Feminists in West Berlin, Quart Rev Film Studie, spring 80; Soll und Haben: Ueberlegungen zum Roman der DDR, in Deutsche Gegenwartsliteratur, Reclam, Stuttgart, 81; Industry, Text and Ideology in Expressionist Film, in Passion and Rebellion: The Expressionist Heritage, Bergin, New York, 82; The Ideology of Form: The Film As Narrative, Proc 13th Amherst Colloquim, Francke, Bern (in press). *Mailing Add:* Div Foreign Lang Univ of Tex San Antonio TX 48285

SILBERSCHLAG, EISIG, b Stryj, Austria, Jan 8, 03; nat US; m 38;. MODERN HEBREW LITERATURE. *Educ:* Univ Vienna, PhD, 26. *Hon Degrees:* Golden Doctorate for extraordinary sci contrib, Univ Vienna, 76; LHD, Hebrew Union Col, Jewish Inst, 77. *Prof Exp:* Instr Jewish hist, Teachers Inst, Jewish Theol Sem Am, 30-31; instr Biblical hist, Hebrew Union Col, 31-32; instr Hebrew lit & Jewish hist, Hebrew Teachers Col, 32-44, prof lit, 44-70, dean 47-68, pres, 68-70; vis prof Judiac studies, Emmanuel Col, 70-72; Gale prof, 73-77, prof comparative studies, 77-78, ASSOC, CTR MID EASTERN STUDIES, UNIV TEX, AUSTIN, 79- *Honors & Awards:* Lamed Prize, 43; Tschernichowsky Prize, 51; Abraham Friedman Prize, 80. *Mem:* Fel Am Acad Jewish Res; Nat Asn Professors Hebrew (pres); AAUP; fel MidE Studies Asn. *Res:* Hebrew literature; comparative literature. *Publ:* Auth, Kimron Yamai (poems), 59; Paulus Silentiarius, Poems of Love, Mahbarot le-Sifrut, 62; Saul Tschernichowsky--Poet of Revolt, Cornell Univ, 68; Iggerotai El Dorot Aherim (poems), 71; Bialik at the centenary, In: Jewish Book Annual, Nat Bk Coun, 72; From Renaissance to Renaissance, II & III, KTAV, 73, 77; Yesh Reshit lekol Aharit (poems-Hebrew), Kiryat Sefer, Jerusalem, 76; Ben Allimut, u-ben Adighut, Jerusalem, 81. *Mailing Add:* Ctr Mid Eastern Studies Univ Tex Austin TX 78712

SILENIEKS, JURIS, b Riga, Latvia, May 29, 25; US citizen; m 52; c 2. FRENCH LITERATURE. *Educ:* Univ Nebr, BA, 55, MA, 57, PhD, 63. *Prof Exp:* Instr French, Univ Nebr, 57-60; from instr to assoc prof, 61-71, head dept, 68-79, PROF MOD LANG, CARNEGIE-MELLON UNIV, 71-, DIR PROG MOD LANG, 79- *Mem:* MLA; Am Asn Teachers Fr; Asn Advan Baltic Studies. *Res:* Black writers of French expression; contemporary French theater; Latvian literature. *Publ:* Auth, Themes and Dramatic Forms in the Plays of Armand Salacrou, Univ Nebr, 67; The image of the United States in the writings of French-speaking Black authors, Africa Today, summer 72; Latvian literature in exile, Lituanus, 72; contribr, The middle passage in Francophone literature (festschrift), Soc Span Am Studies, 78; Glissant's prophetic vision of the past, African Lit, Today, 80; ed, Monsieur Toussaint (play by Glissant), Three Continents Press, 82. *Mailing Add:* Dept of Mod Lang Carnegie-Mellon Univ Schenley Park Pittsburgh PA 15213

SILVA, MOISES, Biblical Studies, Linguistics. See Vol IV

SILVA-CORVALAN, CARMEM M, b Chile. LINGUISTICS. *Educ:* Univ Chile, BA, 70; Univ London, MA, 73; Univ Calif, Los Angeles, MA, 77, PhD(ling), 79. *Prof Exp:* Assoc prof appl ling, Univ Chile, 73-75; ASST PROF SPAN LING, UNIV SOUTHERN CALIF, 79- *Mem:* Ling Soc Am; MLA; Am Asn Teachers Span & Port. *Res:* Sociolinguistics; language change; syntax and semantics. *Publ:* Auth, Semantics in foreign language teaching, English Lang J, 74; The application of a universal definition of passive to Spanish, Boletin Filologia, Vol XXIX, 78; The Ilokano causative in universal grammar, BLS, 78; La funcion pragmatica de la duplicacion de pronombres cliticos, Boletin Filologia, Vol XXXI, 80; contribr, Variation omnibus, Ling Res, 81; auth, The diffusion of object verb agreement in Spanish, Papers in Romance, 12/81; contribr, Spanish in the United States: Sociolinguistics Aspects, Cambridge Univ Press, 82; On the interaction of word order and intonation, In: Discourse Perspectives on Syntax, Acad Press, 82. *Mailing Add:* Dept of Span & Port Univ of Southern Calif Los Angeles CA 90089

SILVER, ISIDORE, b New York, NY, Aug 13, 06. FRENCH RENAISSANCE LITERATURE. *Educ:* City Col New York, AB, 29; Columbia Univ, PhD, 38. *Prof Exp:* Mem fac, City Col New York & Townsend Harris Prep Sch, 35-36; instr, high schs, New York, NY, 37-43; asst prof mod lang, Brown Univ, 45-48; Guggenheim fel, 48-49; from asst prof to prof foreign lang, Univ Conn, 49-57; prof Romance lang, 57-75, EMER ROSA MAY DISTINGUSHED UNIV PROF HUMANITIES, WASHINGTON UNIV, ST LOUIS, 75- *Concurrent Pos:* Am Philos Soc grants, 50, 51, 61; Fulbright fel, France, 55-56; Am Coun Learned Soc grant-in-aid, 60-61. *Mem:* MLA; Soc Textes Fr Mod; Am Asn Teachers Fr; Int Comp Lit Asn; Int Asn Fr Studies. *Publ:* Auth, Ronsard and The Greek Epic, Vol I, Washington Univ, 61 & Ronsard and the Grecian Lyre (Part I), Vol II, Droz, Geneva, 81, In: Ronsard and the Hellenic Renaissance in France; ed, Oeuvres de P de Ronsard--1587 text, Vols I & II, 66, Vols III & IV, 67, Vol V & VI, 68, Vols VII & VIII, 70, Didier & Washington Univ; Ronsard's Ethical Thought, Bibliot Humanisme et Renaissance, 62; Ronsard's Reflections On Cosmogony and Nature, 64 & Ronsard's Reflections on the Heavens and Time, 65, PMLA; auth, The Intellectual Evolution of Ronsard, Vol I: The Formative Influences, 69 & Vol II: Ronsard's General Theory of Poetry, 73, Washington Univ; Three Ronsard Studies, Droz, Geneva, 78. *Mailing Add:* Dept Romance Lang Washington Univ St Louis MO 63130

SILVER, PHILIP WARNOCK, b Bryn Mawr, Pa, Nov 12, 32; m 58; c 3. ROMANCE LANGUAGES. *Educ:* Haverford Col, BA, 54; Middlebury Col, MA, 55; Princeton Univ, MA, 60, PhD, 63. *Prof Exp:* Instr Span, Rutgers Univ, 61-63; asst prof, Oberlin Col, 63-66, assoc prof, 67-71; vis prof, 71-72, chmn dept, 73-76, PROF SPAN & PORT, COLUMBIA UNIV, 72- *Concurrent Pos:* Guggenheim fel, 66; Nat Endowment for Humanities fel, 76. *Mem:* MLA; Am Transl Am. *Res:* Modern Spanish poetry & novel; philosophy and esthetics of Oretga y Gasset. *Publ:* Transl, Unamuno: A Philosphy of Tragedy, Univ Calif, 62; auth, Luis Cernuda: el poeta en su legenda, Alfaguara, 65; transl, Ortega y Gasset, Phenomenology and Art, Norton, 75; auth, Ortega as Phenomenologist: The Genesis of Meditations on Quixote, Columbia Univ Press, 78; transl, Martinez Bonati, Fictive Discourse and the Structures of Literature, Cornell Univ, 81. *Mailing Add:* Dept Span & Port Columbia Univ New York NY 10027

SILVERBERG, JOANN CLAIRE, b New York, NY, May 19, 40. CLASSICAL PHILOLOGY. *Educ:* Columbia Univ, AB, 60; Radcliffe Col, AM, 62; Harvard Univ, PhD, 67. *Prof Exp:* Instr classics, Sweet Briar Col, 64-65; teaching asst, Harvard, 65-67; asst prof, 67-75, ASSOC PROF CLASSICS, CONN COL, 75- *Mem:* Am Philol Asn; Am Class League. *Res:* Ancient Roman historiography, especially commentary on Velleius Paterculus; Augustan poetry; Greek drama. *Mailing Add:* 101 Nameaug Ave New London CT 03620

SILVERMAN, HUGH J, Philosophy, Comparative Literature. See Vol IV

SILVERMAN, JOSEPH HERMAN, b New York, NY, Oct 15, 24; m 51; c 3. SPANISH LITERATURE. *Educ:* City Col New York, BSS, 46; Univ Southern Calif, MA, 50, PhD(Hisp lang & lit), 55. *Prof Exp:* Instr Span, Univ Southern Calif, 52-54; prof, Univ Calif, Los Angeles, 54-68; fac res lectr, 71, provost, Adlai E Stevenson Col, 74-81, PROF SPAN LIT, UNIV CALIF, SANTA CRUZ, 68- *Concurrent Pos:* Del Amo Found grant, Spain, 61-62; Am Coun Learned Soc grant-in-aid, Morocco, 62; mem bd dir, Inst Estud Sefardies, Madrid, 64-; Ford Found grant, 66-67; Nat Endowment for Humanities, sr fel, 71-72; Guggenheim Found fel, 77-78; Nat Endowment for Humanities res grant, 81-82. *Mem:* MLA; Am Asn Teachers Span & Port. *Res:* Spanish Golden Age drama; picaresque novel; Cervantes, Sephardic folk literature. *Publ:* Coauth, Siglo Veinte, Holt, 68; Judeo-Spanish Ballads from Bosnia, Univ Pa, 71; The Judeo-Spanish Ballad Chapbooks of Yacob A Yona, Univ Calif, 71; Auth, Los hidalgos cansados de Lope de Vega, Homenaje a W L Fichter, 71; Some aspects of literature and life in The Golden Age of Spain, Estudios ofrecidos a M A Morinigo, 71; The Spanish Jews: early references and later effects, Americo Castro and the The Meaning of Spanish Civilization, 76; coauth, Romances Judeo-Espanoles de Tanger, 77 & Tres Calas en el Romancero Sefardi, 78, Catedra-Seminario, Menendez Pidal; Judeo-Spanish Ballads From New York, Univ Calif, 81. *Mailing Add:* Span Lit Dept Univ of Calif Santa Cruz CA 95064

SILVERMAN, MALCOLM NOEL, b New York, NY, Apr 18, 46; m 74; c 1. PORTUGUESE & SPANISH LANGUAGES. *Educ:* Queens Col, NY, BA, 67: Univ Ill, MA, 68, PhD(Port), 71. *Prof Exp:* Asst prof Port & Span, Univ Kans, 70-73, dir jr year abroad, Costa Rica, 73; sr lectr Port, Univ Witwatersrand, 74-75; lectr, 75-77, asst prof, 77-79, assoc prof, 79-82, PROF SPAN & PORT, SAN DIEGO STATE UNIV, 82- *Concurrent Pos:* Vis prof Port, Univ Costa Rica, 73. *Mem:* Am Asn Teachers Span & Port. *Res:* Contemporary Brazilian prose fiction; Luso-Brazilian literature; 20th Century Portuguese novel. *Publ:* Auth, Moderna Ficcao Brasileira, Vol I, 78 & Vol II, 81, Civilizacao Brasileira/MEC; O Novo Conto Brasileiro, Nova Fronteira (in press); A Satira na Prosa Brasileira Pos-1964, Codecri (in press). *Mailing Add:* Dept of Span & Port San Diego State Univ San Diego CA 92182

SILVERMAN, MICHAEL H, b Boston, Mass, June 5, 40; m 68; c 1. HEBREW & JUDAIC STUDIES. *Educ:* Hebrew Teachers Col, Mass, BJewish Educ, 60; Harvard Univ, BA, 62; Brandeis Univ, MA, 63, PhD(Near Eastern & Judaic studies), 67. *Prof Exp:* Asst prof ling & Hebrew, Univ Tex, Austin, 67-72; asst prof Judaic studies, State Univ NY Buffalo, 72-77; sr res assoc, Inst for Study Human Issues, Philadelphia, 77-78; RES GRANT ANTHROP, NSF, 78- *Mem:* Asn Jewish Studies; Am Orient Soc; Soc Bibl Lit. *Res:* Bible; Northwest-Semitic epigraphy; ancient Jewish and Near Eastern history. *Publ:* Auth, Aramean nametypes in the Elephantine documents, J Am Orient Soc, 69; Onomastic notes to Aramaica Dubiosa, J Near Eastern Studies, 69; Hebrew nametypes in the Elephantine documents, Orientalia, 70; contribr, chap In: Essays in Honor of C H Gordon, Alter Orient und Altes Testament, 83; auth, Egyptian Aramaic texts, Chronique d'Egypte, 73; contribr, Proceedings of the Six World Congress of Jewish Studies in Jerusalem, 78. *Mailing Add:* 3 Cindy Dr Williamsville NY 14221

SILVERSTEIN, MICHAEL, b Brooklyn, NY, Sept 12, 45. LINGUISTICS, ANTHROPOLOGY. *Educ:* Harvard Univ, AB, 65, PhD(ling), 72. *Prof Exp:* Vis asst prof, Univ Chicago, 70, assoc prof ling & anthrop, 72-77; vis assoc prof anthrop, Temple Univ, 77-78, PROF ANTHROP, LING & BEHAV SCI, UNIV CHICAGO, 78- *Mem:* Ling Soc Am; Am Asn Advan Sci; fel, Am Anthrop Asn. *Res:* Linguistic theory in anthropological perspective; American Indians and Australian Aboriginals; linguistics and ethnography. *Publ:* Ed, Whitney on Language, Selected Writings of William Dwight Whitney, Mass Inst Technol, 71; auth, Chinook jargon: Language contact and the problem of multi-level generative systems, Language, 72; coauth, Linguistic theory: Syntax, semantics, pragmatics, In: Annual Review of Anthropology, Vol I, 72; Linguistik und Anthropologie, In: Lingvistik und die Nachbarwissenschaten, Skriptor, 73; auth, Dialectal Developments in Chinookan Tense-Aspect Systems, IJAL Monograph, Univ Chicago, 74; contribr, Shifters, Linguistic categories and cultural description, In: Meaning in Anthropology, Univ NMex, 76; Hierarchy of features and ergativity in: Grammatical Categories in Australian Languages, Humanities Press, 77. *Mailing Add:* Dept of Anthrop Univ of Chicago Chicago IL 60637

SILZ, WALTER, b Cleveland, Ohio, Sept 27, 94; m 22, 39. GERMAN LITERATURE. *Educ:* Harvard Univ, AB, 17, AM, 18, PhD, 22. *Prof Exp:* From instr to asst prof, Harvard Univ, 22-36; prof Ger & head dept, Washington Univ, 36-39, Swarthmore Col, 39-48 & Princeton Univ, 48-54; Gebhard prof Germanic lang & lit, 54-63, spec lectr, 63-66, EMER GEBHARD PROF GERMANIC LANG & LIT, COLUMBIA UNIV, 63- *Concurrent Pos:* Guggenheim fels, 26-27, 60-61; asst prof, Radcliffe Col, 28-36: Harvard exchange prof, Grinnell, Carleton & Pomona Cols, 29-30; vis prof, Ind Univ & Brown Univ, 65-66 & Queens Col, NY, 68-69. *Mem:* Int Asn Germanic Studies; MLA; Am Asn Teachers Ger; Mod Humanities Res Asn; Heinrich von Kleist Ges. *Res:* German literature of the 18th and 19th centuries. *Publ:* Auth, Early German Romanticism and German Romantic Lyrics, Harvard; Realism and Reality, Univ NC; Heinrich von Kleist, 61 & Hölderlin's Hyperion, 69, Univ Pa. *Mailing Add:* 60 Laurel Rd Princeton NJ 08540

SIMARD, JEAN CLAUDE, b Montreal, Que, May 12, 44; m 69; c 1. LATIN AMERICAN LITERATURE, THEORY OF LITERATURE. *Educ:* Univ Montreal, BA, 65; Laval Univ, Lic es Lett, 68; Univ Paris, Dr(Mex lit), 74. *Prof Exp:* From asst prof to assoc prof, 70-77, PROF LATIN AM LIT, LAVAL UNIV, 77- *Mem:* Can Asn Hispanists; Can Asn Latin Am Studies. *Res:* Latin American short story; Latin American novel; theory of narrative. *Publ:* Auth, Une Icongraphie du Clerge Francaise au XVIIe Siecles: Les Devotins de L'Ecole Francaise et les Sourses de L'imagerie religieuse en France, Int Scholarly Bk Serv, 77. *Mailing Add:* Dept of Lit Laval Univ Quebec PQ G1K 7P4 Can

SIMCHES, SEYMOUR O, b Boston, Sept 22, 19: m 53; c 2. ROMANCE LANGUAGES & LITERATURES. *Educ:* Boston Univ, AB, 41; Harvard Univ, MA, 42, PhD, 50. *Prof Exp:* Instr Romance lang, Harvard Univ, 50-53; asst prof, Amherst Col, 53-54; from asst prof to assoc prof, 54-62, chmn dept romance lang, 58-72, res grant, 63, dir, Col Within, 71-76, JONATHAN WADE PROF MOD LANG, TUFTS UNIV, 62- *Concurrent Pos:* Dir NDEA Foreign Lang Inst, 60-62, 66-67; mem bd dir, Northeast Conf Teaching Foreign Lang, 61-63, vchmn, 65-66; Am Philos Soc grant, 63; consult Foreign Lang Prog, US Off Educ, 63-65; mem exam comt, Advan Placement Bd, 68-72; Mass Adv Bd Nontraditional Educ, 73-; dir, Europ Ctr, Tufts Univ, Talloires, France, 79- *Honors & Awards:* Medaille Aeronautique, French Govt, 44, Palmes Academiques, 62. *Mem:* Am Asn Teachers Fr; MLA; New Eng Mod Lang Asn. *Res:* Relationship of art and literature in France in the 18th and 19th century: psycholinguistics: foreign language teaching. *Publ:* Auth, Modern French Literature and Language: A Bibliography of Homage Studies, Harvard Univ, 58; Le Romantisme et le Gout Esthetique du XVIIIe Siecle, Presses Universitaires, 64; coauth, Psycholinguistic Seminar, Tufts Univ, 65; A psycholinguistic rationale for FLES, Fr Rev, 2/66 & The classroom revisited, 68, Northeast Conf Report; auth, The theatre of Jacinto Grau, Waxman Studies, 69; Beckett's Godot: A symphony on the theme of waiting, Tufts Prologue, spring 82. *Mailing Add:* Dept of Romance Lang Tufts Univ Medford MA 02155

SIMMONS, DOUGLAS J, b Indianapolis, Ind, Aug 18, 29; m 53; c 3. FRENCH. *Educ:* Wabash Col, BA, 51; Harvard Univ, MAT, 56; Sorbonne, cert, 57. *Prof Exp:* Instr French, Bucknell Univ, 57-59; grad asst, Ind Univ, 59-63; ASST PROF FRENCH, ARIZ STATE UNIV, 63- *Mem:* MLA. *Res:* Application of linguistics to language teaching. *Mailing Add:* Dept of Foreign Lang Ariz State Univ Tempe AZ 85287

SIMMONS, MERLE EDWIN, b Kansas City, Kans, Sept 27, 18; m 48; c 2. SPANISH. *Educ:* Univ Kans, AB, 39, AM, 41; Univ Mich, PhD(Romance lang), 52. *Prof Exp:* Asst instr Span, Univ Kans, 39-42; from instr to assoc prof, 41-62, chmn prog for jr years in Peru, 61-66, chmn dept Span & Port, 76-81, PROF SPAN, IND UNIV, BLOOMINGTON, 62-, DIR GRAD STUDIES, DEPT SPAN & PORT, 66- *Concurrent Pos:* Am Philos Soc res grants, 55 & 76; Am Coun Learned Soc res grant-in-aid, 62. *Mem:* MLA; Am Asn Teachers Span & Port; Am Folklore Soc; Conf Latin Am Hist; AAUP. *Res:* Latin American literature and folklore; the Mexican corrido and related forms in other Latin American countries; history of ideas in Latin American. *Publ:* Auth, The Mexican corrido as a Source for Interpretive Study of Modern Mexico, 1870-1950, 57 & A Bibliography of the Romance and Related Forms in Spanish America, 63, Ind Univ; Folklore bibliography, Southern Folklore Quart, annually, 64-73; Folklore Bibliography for 1973, 75, for 1974, 77, for 1975, 79 & for 1976, 81, Ind Univ Folklore Inst Monography; US political ideas in Spanish America before 1830: A bibliographical study, Ind Univ Hispanic Lit Studies, Vol 2, 77; Santiago F Puglia, An early Philadelphia propagandist for Spanish American independence, Univ NC Studies Romance Lang & Lit, No 195, 77. *Mailing Add:* Dept of Span & Port Ind Univ Bloomington IN 47401

SIMON, ARTHUR, b Brooklyn, NY, Jan 17, 14; m 63. ROMANCE LANGUAGES. *Educ:* Brooklyn Col, BA, 35; Columbia Univ, MA, 37, PhD(French), 55. *Prof Exp:* From instr to asst prof French & Ital, 47-73, assoc prof, 73-81, PROF MOD LANG, BROOKLYN COL, 81- *Concurrent Pos:* Instr French, Barnard Col, Columbia Univ, 55-56 & Rutgers Univ, Newark, 56-58; mem, Nat Fedn Mod Foreign Lang Teachers Asn, 61-; consult, bur AV instr, Bd Educ, 61-63; educ dir, Coun Int Educ Exchange, summers, 67- *Honors & Awards:* Chevalier Ordre Palmes Academiques, French Ministry Univs, 78. *Mem:* MLA; Am Asn Teachers French; AAUP; Nat Fed Mod Lang Teachers Asn. *Res:* French theater; audio-visual and computer language instruction. *Publ:* Auth, The literary critic Charles Maurras, Georgetown Univ Fr Rev, 3/38; Le BRCA: Service secret de la France libre, J de France, 11/71; Gaston Baty: Theoricien du theatre, Ed Klincksieck, Paris, 72; La presence francaise a New York (film), Brooklyn Col, 76; De l'inedit sur Gastou Baty et Jacques Hebertot, Revue d'histoire du theatre, 80-81. *Mailing Add:* Dept of Mod Lang Brooklyn Col Brooklyn NY 11210

SIMON, ECKEHARD, b Schneidemühl, Ger, Jan 5, 39; US citizen; m 59: c 4. MEDIEVAL GERMAN LITERATURE & PHILOLOGY. *Educ:* Columbia Col, AB, 60; Harvard Univ, AM, 61, PhD(Medieval Ger), 64. *Prof Exp:* From instr to assoc prof Ger, 64-71, PROF GER, HARVARD UNIV, 71-, CHMN DEPT GER LANG & LIT, 76- *Concurrent Pos:* Nat Endowment for Humanities younger scholar fel, 69; Guggenheim Mem Found fel, 69; Nat Endowment for Humanities fel for Independent study and res, 77; asst ed, Speculum, J Medieval Studies; Fulbright sr res grant, Cologne, 83. *Mem:* Mediaeval Acad Am; MLA; Am Asn Teachers Ger. *Res:* Middle High German song poetry; Medieval German drama; Editing. *Publ:* Auth, Neidhart von Reuental: Geschichte der Forschung und Bibliographie, Harvard, 68; The origin of Neidhart plays: A reappraisal, J English & Ger Philol, Vol 68; Neidharte and Neidhartianer: Notes on the history of a song corpus, Beiträge Geschichte Deut Spr u Lit, 72: Eine neuaufgefundene Sammelhandschrift mit Rosenplüt Dichtungen aus dem 15 Jahrhundert, Z Deut Altertum u Deut Lit, 73; Neidhart von Reuental, Twayne's World Authors ser, 364, Twayne, G K Hall, 75; ed, Das Schwäbische Weihnachtsspiel, Zeitschrift für deutsche Philol, 75; Four unpublished Meisterlieder on the Legend of Adam's Death and the Holy Rood, J English & Ger Philol, 76; auth, Neidhart plays as shrovetide plays: Twelve additional documented performances, Ger Rev, 77; The home town of the Schaväbische Weihnuchtsspiel, 1420, and its original setting, Euphonon, 79. *Mailing Add:* Boylston Hall 420 Harvard Univ Cambridge MA 02138

SIMON, ERNEST, b Ger, Dec 23, 32; US citizen; m 56. FRENCH & COMPARATIVE LITERATURE. *Educ:* Columbia Univ, BA, 54, MA, 58, PhD(French), 63. *Prof Exp:* From instr to asst prof French, Columbia Col, Columbia Univ, 58-66; assoc prof, Yeshiva Univ, 66-73; ASSOC PROF COMP LIT, RAMAPO COL NJ, 73- *Concurrent Pos:* Danforth Assoc, 76. *Res:* History and theory of the novel. *Publ:* Auth, Descriptive and analytical techniques in Maupassant's Pierre et Jean, Romanic Rev, 2/60: The function of the Spanish stories in Scarron's Roman comique, L'Esprit Createur, fall 63; Fatalism, the hobby-horse and the esthetics of the novel, Diderot Studies XVI, 73. *Mailing Add:* Sch of Intercult Studies Ramapo Col of NJ Mahwah NJ 07430

SIMON, JOHN KENNETH, b New York, NY, Dec 23, 35; m 57: c 2. ENGLISH, FRENCH. *Educ:* Yale Univ, BA, 56, PhD(comp lit), 53. *Prof Exp:* Asst in instr, Yale Univ, 57-59, instr French lang & lit, 59-61, 62-63: asst prof French & English, Univ Ill, Urbana, 63-66, assoc prof English & French, 66-69: chmn dept French, 69-75, PROF FRENCH, STATE UNIV NY BUFFALO, 69- *Concurrent Pos:* French Ministry Foreign Affairs grant, 67; consult, Nat Humanities Fac, 78- *Mem:* MLA. *Res:* Development of modern fiction and modern drama in Europe and America: film: nineteenth and early twentieth century American painting. *Publ:* Auth, Perception and metaphor in the new novel: Notes on Robbe-Grillet, Claude Simon, Butor, Tri-Quart, fall 65; The scene and the imagery of metamorphosis in As I Lay Dying, Criticism, winter 65; A study of classical gesture: Henry James and Madame de La Fayette, Comp Lit Studies, fall 66: Modern French Criticism, Univ Chicago, 72; contribr ser, Bibliography of the Arts in the United States, Smithsonian Inst (in press). *Mailing Add:* 217 High Park Blvd Eggertsville NY 14226

SIMON, JOSE GREGORIO, b Santiago de Cuba, Cuba, May 9, 20; US citizen; m 46; c 4. PHILOLOGY. *Educ:* Univ Havana, LLD, 41: Univ Miami, MA, 66; Emory Univ, PhD(Span & Span Am lit), 69. *Prof Exp:* Instr Span, Univ Miami, 65-66; instr Span lang & lit, Emory Univ, 66-69; ASSOC PROF SPAN LANG & LIT, OLD DOMINION UNIV, 69- *Mem:* MLA; Am Asn Teachers Span & Port. *Res:* History and phonics of the Spanish language; medieval literature; Golden Age theatre. *Publ:* Auth, Apuntes de fonologia historica de la lengua espanola, Ed Plaza Mayor, 71; Desarrollo de la prosa medieval en los siglos XII y XIII, Bol Hist Acad Hist de Cartagenas, Colombia, 71; Temas y simbolos en los Entremeses de Cervantes, Cuadernos Am, Mex, 72. *Mailing Add:* Dept of Foreign Lang Old Dominion Univ Norfolk VA 23508

SIMON, ROLAND HENRI, b Haiphong, N Vietnam, Oct 7, 40; French citizen. LITERARY SEMIOTICS, FRENCH CIVILIZATION. *Educ:* Univ Wis, MA, 67 Stanford Univ, PhD(French & humanities), 76. *Prof Exp:* Instr French, Middlebury Col, 72-75, dean French sch, 73-76, asst prof, 75-76; ASST PROF FRENCH, UNIV VA, 76- *Mem:* MLA; Am Asn Teachers French; NEastern Mod Lang Asn; SAtlantic Mod Lang Asn. *Res:* Theory of literature; autobiography; French civilization. *Publ:* Auth, Le role de l'ecriture dans La Chute de Camus et Quelqu'un de Pinget, 74 & Les Prologues du Quart Livre de Rabelais, 74, French Rev; Langage et authenticite dans Biffures de Michel Leiris, Stanford French Rev, 78; Pour une nouvelle pedagogie du theatre classique, Australian J French Studies, 78. *Mailing Add:* Dept of French & Gen Ling Univ of Va Charlottesville VA 22903

SIMON, THOMAS WILLIAM, Philosophy, Linguistics. See Vol IV

SIMONELLI, MARIA, b Florence, Italy, May 16, 21. ROMANCE LANGUAGES, ITALIAN LITERATURE. *Educ:* Liceo Michelangelo, Florence, Maturita, 40; Univ Florence, Dr Humanities, 47; Univ Rome, Libera docenza, 66. *Prof Exp:* Asst prof Romance philol, Univ Florence, 48-56, actg prof Fulbright courses, 50-60; vis prof, Ital lit, Univ Calif, Los Angeles, 61-62; asst prof Romance lang, Univ Rome, 64-67; vis prof, 67-69, PROF ROMANCE LANG & LIT, BOSTON COL, 69- *Concurrent Pos:* Co-ed, Studi Danteschi, 52-56; vis prof Ital lit, Harvard Univ, 66-67. *Mem:* Dante Soc, Italy (secy, 52-56); Mediaeval Acad Am. *Res:* Romance philology; comparative medieval studies. *Publ:* Auth, Il Decameron--problemi e discussioni di critica testuale, Annali S N S, Pisa, 50; La parafrasi francese antico del salmo Eructavit, Adamo di Perseigne, Chretien de Troyes e Dante, 64 & Due note rudelliane, 65, Cult Neolatina; Il Convivio di Dante, ed critica, Patron, 66. *Mailing Add:* Dept of Mod Lang Boston Col Chestnut Hill MA 02167

SIMONS, GARY FRANCIS, b Oakland, Calif, Feb 26, 54; m 75; c 2. LINGUISTICS, COMPUTATIONAL LINGUISTICS. *Educ:* Seattle Pac Col, BA, 74; Cornell Univ, MA, 76, PhD(ling), 79. *Prof Exp:* TRANSL ADV MALAITAN LANG, SUMMER INST LING, 79-, INT LING CONSULT, 82- *Concurrent Pos:* Ed, Lang in Solomon Islands, 81- *Mem:* Asn Comput Ling; Asn Comput Mach. *Res:* Comparative study of oceanic languages; computational approaches to linguistic field method; design of programming languages for text processing. *Publ:* Co-ed, Language Variation and Survey Techniques, Summer Inst Ling, Papua New Guines Br, 77; auth, Language Variation and Limits to Communication, 79 & coauth, Microcomputer Design for Field Linguistics, 79, Cornell Univ; The PTP Programmer's Reference Manual, Summer Inst Ling, 79; auth, A survey of reading abilities among the To'abaita speakers, J Solomon Islands Studies, 80; The impact of on-site computing on field linguistics, 80 & coauth, PTP--A text processing language for personal computers, 82, Notes Ling; auth, Word taboo and comparative Austronesian linguistics, Pac Ling, 82. *Mailing Add:* 610 E 20th St The Dalles OR 97058

SIMONS, JOHN DONALD, b Lone Oak, Tex, Oct 5, 35; m 62. GERMAN & COMPARATIVE LITERATURE. *Educ:* Univ Tex, BA, 59, MA, 61; Rice Univ PhD(Ger), 66. *Prof Exp:* Instr English, Berlitz Sch Lang, Paris, 59-61; instr Ger, Tex Southern Univ, 62-66; asst prof, Univ Iowa, 66-70; ASSOC PROF GER & COMP LIT, FLA STATE UNIV, 70- *Mem:* MLA; Am Asn Teachers Ger; AAUP; Int Dostoevsky Soc. *Res:* Eighteenth and 20th century German literature. *Publ:* Auth, The nature of oppression in Don Carlos, Mod Lang Notes, 4/69; Myth of progress in Schiller and Dostoevsky, Comp lit, 4/72; Hermann Hesse's Steppenwolf: A Critical Commentary, 72, Günter Grass' The Tin Drum, 73, Thomas Mann's Death in Venice, 74, Dostoevsky's Crime and Punishment, 76 & The Brothers Karamazov, 76, Simon & Schuster; Friedrich Schiller, Twayne, 81. *Mailing Add:* Dept of Mod Lang Fla State Univ Tallahassee FL 32306

SIMONS, MADELEINE ANJUBAULT, b Alencon, France; US citizen; c 2. LITERATURE, FRENCH. *Educ:* Univ Paris, Licence, 44; Miami Univ, MA, 46; Johns Hopkins Univ, PhD(French), 72. *Prof Exp:* Teaching fel, Miami Univ, 45-46; instr French, Rosary Col, 46-47: teacher, Yorktown High Sch, 64-70; lectr, George Mason Univ, 74-75; asst prof, 75-80, ASSOC PROF FRENCH, GEORGETOWN UNIV, 80- *Mem:* MLA; Am Asn Teachers Fr; 19th Century Fr Studies; Stendhal Club. *Res:* Autobiography; literature and the arts; semiological studies. *Publ:* Auth, Rousseau's natural diet, Romanic Rev, winter 54; contribr, Rousseau's Oeuvres Completes, NRF, Pleiade, Vol I, 59; auth, Les regards dans A la recherche du temps perdu, 3/68 & Vellini, femme ou sorciere, 10/70, Fr Rev; Amitie et Passion, Rousseau et Sauttersheim, Librairie Droz, Geneva, 72; Le roman pedagogique d'Emile a Lamiel, Annales Rousseau, 78; Stendhal, Rousseau et la musique, Stendhal Club, 78; Semiotisme de Stendhal, Droz, 80. *Mailing Add:* 5205 Yorktown Blvd Arlington VA 22207

SIMPSON, HAROLD LESTER, b Mullins, SC, Oct 14, 25. FOREIGN LANGUAGES & LITERATURES. *Educ:* Col Charleston, BS, 51; Princeton Univ, MA, 53, PhD, 57. *Prof Exp:* Reader, Col Charleston, 50; teaching asst, Princeton Univ, 52; from instr French & Ger grammar to assoc prof French lit, Va Mil Inst, 54-62; from assoc prof to prof French & French lit, Tex

Technol Col 62-69; chmn dept foreign lang, 69-72, PROF FRENCH, E TEX STATE UNIV, 69-, EXEC ASST DEPT LIT & LANG, 72- *Mem:* Am Asn Teachers Fr; MLA; Am Coun Teaching Foreign Lang; Southern Conf Lang Teachers. *Res:* Soldier in French literature of the 19th century naturalist novel. *Publ:* Auth, Antimilitarism in the French naturalist novel, LEsprit Createur, summer 64; The poetic image of the soldier from Baudelaire to the First World War, SCent Bull, winter 67. *Mailing Add:* Dept of Lit & Lang E Tex State Univ Commerce TX 75248

SIMPSON, J ALLEN, b Burbank, Calif, Jan 18, 34; m 58; c 2. SCANDINAVIAN LITERATURE. *Educ:* Univ Minn, BA, 58; Univ Calif, Berkeley, MA, 61, PhD(Scand), 68. *Prof Exp:* From instr to assoc prof, 64-77, PROF SCAND, UNIV MINN, MINNEAPOLIS, 77- *Mem:* Soc Advan Scand Studies. *Res:* Knut Hamsuns novels; Scandinavian prose fiction. *Publ:* Auth, Knut Hamsuns Landstrykere, Gyldendal, Norway, 73; Hamsun and Camus: Consciousness in Markens grøde and The Myth of Sisyphus, Scand Studies, 76; Knut Hamsun's Antisemitism, Edda, 77. *Mailing Add:* Dept of Scand Folwell Hall 210 Univ of Minn Minneapolis MN 55455

SIMPSON, WILLIAM KELLY, b New York, NY, Jan 3, 28; m 53; c 2. EGYPTOLOGY. *Educ:* Yale Univ, BA, 47, MA, 48, PhD, 54. *Prof Exp:* Asst Egyptian art, Metropolitan Mus, 48-54; Fulbright grants, Egypt, 54-56; res fel, Ctr Mid Eastern Studies, Harvard Univ, 57-58; from asst prof to assoc prof, 58-65, chmn dept Near Eastern lang & lit, 66-69, PROF EGYPTOLOGY, YALE UNIV, 65- *Concurrent Pos:* Trustee, Mus Primitive Art, 56-, Sleep Hollow Restorations, 63; Am Res Ctr, Egypt, 60-68; Am Sch Class Studies, Athens & Am Univ Cairo; cur, dept Egyptian & ancient Near Eastern art, Mus Fine Arts, Boston, 70- *Mem:* Ger Archaeol Inst; Am Orient Soc; Archaeol Inst Am; Fr Soc Egyptology; Soc Coptic Archaeol. *Res:* Egyptian archaeology, language, and literature. *Publ:* Auth, Papyrus Reisner I: The Records of a Building Project, Boston Mus Fine Arts, 63; Heka-Nefer and the Dynastic Material from Toshka and Arminna, Univ Pa-Yale Exped, 63; coauth, The Ancient Near East: A History, Harcourt, 71; auth, The Terrace of the Great God at Abydos, Peabody Museum, Yale Univ, 74; The Mastabas of Qar and Idu, Giza Masatabas, 76 & The Offering Chapel of Sekhem-ankh-ptah, 76, Boston Mus Fine Arts; The Face of Egypt: Permanence and Change, Katonah Gallery, 77; ed, The Literature of Ancient Egypt, Yale Univ, 3rd ed, 77. *Mailing Add:* Katonah's Wood Rd Katonah NY 10536

SIMS, EDNA N, b Joliet, Ill. ROMANCE LANGUAGES. *Educ:* Univ Ill, Urbana, BAT, 62, MA, 63; Cath Univ Am, PhD(Romance Lang), 70. *Prof Exp:* Instr Span & French, Howard Univ, 63-69; PROF SPAN & FRENCH, DC TEACHERS COL, 70- *Concurrent Pos:* Vis prof Span, Inter-Am Univ PR, San German, 70; mem foreign lang comt, US Dept Agr Grad Sch, 70-; vis prof Span, Univ Panama, 71. *Mem:* Am Coun Teachers Foreign Lang; Am Asn Teachers Span & Port; Hisp Rev Soc; Col Lang Asn. *Res:* Spanish language; Spanish literature. *Publ:* Auth, La novela sentimental, Cult Libr Panama, 71; La mujer en Fray Luis de Leon, Loteria Mag, Panama, 71; contribr, The absent one (poem), In: Anthology of New Poets, 72; La misoginia en tres autores espanola, 72 & El antifeminismo en la literatura espanola, 73, Ed Andes, Bogota, Columbia. *Mailing Add:* Dept of Foreign Lang Univ of DC Washington DC 20009

SIMS, ROBERT LEWIS, b Petoskey, Mich, Oct 26, 43. FRENCH & SPANISH. *Educ:* Univ Mich, BA, 66; Univ Wis, MA, 68, PhD(French), 73. *Prof Exp:* Asst prof French & Span, Colby Col, 73-74; asst prof, Pa State Univ, 74-76; ASST PROF FRENCH & SPAN, VA COMMONWEALTH UNIV, 76- *Honors & Awards:* Best Article Award, Am Asn Teachers Span & Port, 77. *Mem:* Am Asn Teachers Fr; Am Asn Teachers Span & Port. *Res:* Twentieth century French literature; myth and novel; modern Latin American novel. *Publ:* Auth, L'influence du cinema et ses techniques sur quelques romans de Claude Simon, fall 75 & Memory, structure and time in La Route des Flandres, spring 76, Bonnes Feuilles; Garcia Marquez' La hojarasca: Paradigm of time and search for myth, 12/76 & The creation of myth in Garcia Marquez' Los funerales de la Mama Grande, 3/78, Hispania; The myths of war and the hero in Drieu LaRochelle's La Comedie de Charleroi, Bonnes Feuilles, fall 78; Myth and historico-primordial memory in Claude Simon's La Route des Flandres, Nottingham Fr Studies, 10/78; The banana massacre in Cien anos de soledad: A micro structural example of myth, history and bricolage, Chasque, VIII: 3-23; The Evolution of Myth in Gabriel Garcia Marquez from La hojarasca to Cien anos de soledad, Ediciones Universal, 82. *Mailing Add:* Dept of Foreign Lang Va Commonwealth Univ Richmond VA 23284

SINGER, ARMAND EDWARDS, b Detroit, Mich, Nov 30, 14; m 40; c 1. ROMANCE LANGUAGE & LITERATURE. *Educ:* Amherst Col, AB, 35, Duke Univ, AM, 39, PhD, 44, Univ Paris, Dipl, 39. *Prof Exp:* Inst French & Span, Duke Univ, 38-40; teaching fel Romance lang, 40-41, from instr to assoc prof, 41-60, chmn humanities, 63-72, actg chmn dept relig & prog humanities, 73, prof, 60-80, EMER PROF ROMANCE LANG, WVA UNIV, 80- *Concurrent Pos:* Ed, WVa Univ Philol Papers, 48-50, 52-54, ed-in-chief, 50-52, 54-; mem exec comt, SAtlantic Mod Lang Asn, 72-74; dir mod lit, WVa Univ, 76-80. *Mem:* MLA; Am Asn Teachers Span & Port; Am Asn Teachers Fr; SAtlantic Mod Lang Asn. *Res:* Cervantes; 19th century French and Spanish literature; Don Juan. *Publ:* Auth, The Don Juan Theme, Versions and Criticism: A Bibliography, 65; coauth, Humanities I Anthology of Readings, 66 & Humanities II Anthology of Readings, 67, WVa Univ; auth, Third supplement to the Don Juan theme (1965), WVa Univ Philol Papers, 73: Fourth Supplement to the Don Juan Theme, WVa Univ Philol Papers, 22: 70-140; Paul Bourget, Twayne, 76; Fifth Supplement to the Don Juan Theme, WVa Univ Philol Papers, 80; ed, West Virginia George Sand Conference Papers, 81 & Essays on the Literature of Mountaineering, 82, WVa Univ. *Mailing Add:* Dept of Foreign Lang WVa Univ Morgantown WV 26506

SINICROPI, GIOVANNI ANDREA, b Reggio Calabria, Italy, Dec 6, 24; US citizen; m 53; c 5. ITALIAN LITERATURE. *Educ:* Univ Messina, Dr, 49, Univ Toronto, PhD(Romance lang), 63. *Prof Exp:* Instr Ital lit, Univ Toronto, 57-69, lectr 59-63; from asst prof to assoc prof, Rutgers Univ, 64-70; PROF ITAL LIT, UNIV CONN, 70- *Concurrent Pos:* Am Philos Soc grant, 66, 71 & 76. *Mem:* MLA; Am Asn Teachers Ital; Dante Soc Am. *Res:* Aesthetics and literary criticism; Italian contemporary theatre; Structural semiotics. *Publ:* Critical ed, La natura nelle opere di G Verga, Italica, 60; El arte nuevo y la tecnica dramatica de Lope de Vega, Mapocho, Chile, 63; The later phase: Towards myth, In: Pirandello, Prentice-Hall, 67; Le novelle di G Sercambi, Laterza, Bari, 72; Saggio sulle Soledades di Gongora, Bologna, Cappelli, 76; Il Segno linguistico del Decamecon, Studi Sul Boccaccio, Venice, 77; The metaphysical dimension and Pirandello's theatre, Mod Drama, 77. *Mailing Add:* Dept of Romance Lang Univ of Conn Storrs CT 06268

SINKA, MARGIT M, b Debrecen, Hungary; US citizen. GERMAN LITERATURE & LANGUAGE. *Educ:* Baldwin-Wallace Col, BA, 64; Middlebury Col, MA, 65; Univ NC, PhD(German), 74. *Prof Exp:* Jr instr German, Univ Va, 65-66 & Univ NC, 67-71; instr, Ill State Univ, 66-67; asst prof German & Span, Mars Hill Col, 71-74; asst prof, 74-79, ASSOC PROF GERMAN & SPAN, CLEMSON UNIV, 79- *Concurrent Pos:* Nat Endowment for Humanities grant, Ind Univ, summer 77 & Fordham Univ, summer 81; Fulbright grant modern cult, Germany, summer 78; Clemson Univ grant medieval lit, summer 79. *Mem:* Am Asn Ger Teachers; SAtlantic Mod Lang Asn; MLA. *Res:* German medieval literature, epics and mysticism; 19th and 20th century German prose, genre studies and symbolism; pedagogy. *Publ:* Auth, Wound imagery in Gottfried von StraBburg's Tristan, SAtlantic Bull, 5/77; German conversation with focus and meaning: New approaches, Die Unterrichtspraxis, Vol XII, spring 79; Composition in German: Why can they write?, Schatzkammer, Vol V, 79; Der höveschste man: An analysis of Gawein's role in Hartmann von Aue's Iwein, Mod Lang Notes, 81; Heinrich Bll's Bie verlorene Ehre der Katharina Blum as Novelle, Colloquia Ger, 8 1; The flight motif in Martin Walser's Ein Fliehendes Pferd, Monatshefte, 82; Unappreciated symbol: The Unglücksäule in Stifter's Bergkristall, Mod Austrian Lit (in press). *Mailing Add:* Lang Dept Clemson Univ Clemson SC 29631

SINNEMA, JOHN RALPH, b Cleveland, Ohio, Apr 14, 11; m 43. GERMAN. *Educ:* Baldwin-Wallace Col, AB, 33; Western Reserve Univ, AM, 38; Univ Cincinnati, PhD, 49. *Prof Exp:* Teacher pub schs, Ohio, 34-36; from instr to prof, 36-75, head dept, 52-75, dean men, 47-52, EMER PROF GER & DIR AM-GER INST, BALDWIN-WALLACE COL, 75- *Concurrent Pos:* Ed consult, Britannica World Lang Dict, 59. *Honors & Awards:* Strosacker Excellence in Teaching Award, 61; Ficken Award for Outstanding Contrib to Teaching Mod Lang, Baldwin-Wallace Col, 75. *Mem:* MLA; Am Asn Teachers Ger; Mod Humanities Res Asn; Renaissance Soc Am; Soc Ger-Am Studies (treas, 76-). *Res:* Dutch and German literature, 12th to 16th centuries; German element in Greater Cleveland; Historical Linguistics. *Publ:* Auth, The German Source of the Middle Dutch Der zotten ende der narren scip, In: On Romanticism and the Art of Translation, Princeton, 56; Cartoons in conversation classes, Mod Lang J, 57, English Teaching Forum, 63 & In: The Teaching of German: Problems and Methods, Nat Carl Schurz Asn, 70; The Dutch origin of Play Hookey, Am Speech, fall-winter 70; Rotation drills in teaching conversation, Mod Lang J, 71; Hendrik van Veldeke, Twayne, 72; German Methodism's Ohio roots, Ger-Am Studies, fall 74. *Mailing Add:* 204 Franklin Dr Berea OH 44017

SIRACUSA, JOSEPH, b Siculiana, Italy, July 30, 29; US citizen. ROMANCE LINGUISTICS. *Educ:* Univ Rochester, AB, 58; Univ Ill, MA, 59, PhD, 62. *Prof Exp:* Asst prof Span & Ital, Rice Univ, 62-65; assoc prof, Del Mar Col, 65-67; PROF SPAN & ITAL, STATE UNIV NY COL, BROCKPORT, 67- *Concurrent Pos:* NDEA lang inst, vis prof Ital ling, Cent Conn State Col, 60 & Span ling, Knox Col, 61, 62; prof, Univ NC, 63; assoc dir & prof Span ling, Rice Univ, 64, 65, vis prof, San Lorenzo de El Escorial, Spain, 67; mem test develop comt, Am Asn Teachers Span & Port Nat Span Exam, 66-76. *Res:* Spanish and Italian historical linguistics; literary relations between Italy and the Hispanic world; Italian dialectology. *Publ:* Coauth, Relaciones literarias entre Espana e Italia (ensayo de una bibliografia de literatura comparada), G K Hall, 72; Federico Garcia Lorca y su mundo (Ensayo de una bibliografia general), Scarecrow Press, Inc, 74. *Mailing Add:* Dept of Foreign Lang State Univ of NY Brockport NY 14420

SIROIS, ANTOINE, b Sherbrooke, PQ, Sept 28, 25. COMPARATIVE LITERATURE. *Educ:* Univ Montreal, BA, 45; lic es lett, 60; Univ Paris, DUniv, 67. *Prof Exp:* Prin high sch, Quebec, 52-58; secy gen, 60-65, chmn dept French, 68-74, vdean, 75-83, PROF FRENCH-CAN & COMP LIT, UNIV SHERBROOKE, 67- *Concurrent Pos:* Exec, Can Res Coun Humanities, 70- *Mem:* Can Comp Lit Asn (pres, 75-77); Asn Can & Quebec Lit. *Res:* French Canadian literature; comparative English and French Canadian literature. *Publ:* Le mythe du nord chez Gabrielle Roy, Revue de l'Univ de Sherbrooke, 10/63; Montreal dan le Roman Candien, Didier, Paris & Montreal, 69; Gove et Ringuet, Can Lit, summer 71; L'image de la ville dans le roman du terroir d'expression francaises et d'expression anglaise, Can Rev Comp Lit, autumn 76; Conquete horizontale et verticale de la ville, Can Lit, spring 77; Bonheur d'occasion de Gabrielle Roy, Dict des oeuvres litterarieres du Quebec, Montreal, Fides, 82; Delegues du Pantheon au Plateau Mont-Royal: Sur deux romans de Michel Tremblay, In: Voic et Images, Hiver 82. *Mailing Add:* Dept of French Fac of Arts Univ Sherbrooke Sherbrooke PQ J1K 2R1 Can

SISTO, DAVID THEODORE, b Kans, Apr 5, 10; m 42; c 1. SPANISH, PORTUGUESE. *Educ:* Uni- Tex, BA, 30, MA, 33; State Univ Iowa, PhD, 52. *Prof Exp:* Teacher high sch, Tex, 30-41, 45-46; censor, US Off Censorship, 42-45; instr Span & Port, State Univ Iowa, 46-54; from asst prof to assoc prof Romance lang, Univ Tex, Austin, 54-75; RETIRED. *Mem:* MLA; Am Asn Teachers Span & Port. *Res:* Spanish American literature; Gaucho honor code; methods of teaching foreign languages. *Publ:* Auth, Perez Galdos Dona Perfecta and Louis Bromfield's A Good Woman, Symposium, fall 57, The string in the conjurations of La Celestina and Dona Barbara, Romance Notes, 59; Louis Bromfield, In: Encyclopedia of World Literature in the 20th Century, Ungar, 67. *Mailing Add:* 3212 Oakmont Blvd Austin TX 78703

SIZEMORE, MARGARET DAVIDSON, b Birmingham, Ala; m 37; c 2. MODERN LANGUAGES. *Educ:* Samford Univ, AB, 28, AM, 30; Sorbonne, dipl. *Hon Degrees:* LLD, Jacksonville State Univ, 80. *Prof Exp:* Teacher French & sci, 30-37; head dept social studies, High Sch, Fla, 37-38; 39-41; teacher French, Roney Plaza Patio & Mannheimer Tutorial Sch, Miami Beach, 38-39; teacher, Raphael Semmes Sch, Mobile, Ala, 41-42; from instr to asst prof French, 47-52, dean women, 50-70, ASSOC PROF FRENCH, SAMFORD UNIV, 52-, ASST TO PRES COMMUNITY AFFAIRS & DIR ADULT EDUC, 70- *Concurrent Pos:* Founder, Le Cercle Francais, 47; mem bd visitors, Monterrey Inst Technol, Mex, 57-; chmn, Brimingham Festival Arts, 61, Ala Women's Comn, 72- & Tannehill State Park Comn, 78-80; consult, Defense Adv Comt Women in Serv, 65-68 & Air Univ, 68. *Mem:* Am Asn Teachers Fr; Am Col Personnel Asn; Nat Asn Women Deans & Counr; Nat League Am Pen Women; Forney Hist Soc (pres, 76-79). *Res:* Eighteenth century, porcelain, silver, furniture; oriental rugs; early American folklore. *Publ:* Coauth, The Amazing Marriage of Marie Eustis and Josef Hofmann, Univ SC, 65; auth, Let's take stock, Eleusis, 9/67; Eighteenth century French porcelina, Antique Monthly, 3/73; La porcelaine de France, Visual Arts Bull, Birmingham Mus Art, 73; Collecting Antiques, Samford Univ Res, 12/77; Shades Valley Sun, Birmingham, weekly column in Down the Antiques Trail, 81- *Mailing Add:* Dept of French Samford Univ 800 Lakeshore Dr Birmingham AL 35209

SJAVIK, JAN IVAR, b Jektvik, Norway, July 16, 48; m 72; c 4. SCANDINAVIAN LITERATURE, LITERARY THEORY. *Educ:* Brigham Young Univ, BA, 74; Harvard Univ, AM, 76, PhD(Germanics), 79. *Prof Exp:* Instr, 78-79, ASST PROF SCAND, UNIV WASH, SEATTLE, 79- *Mem:* Soc Advan Scand Study; Norwegian-Am Hist Asn. *Res:* Scandinavian literature of the 1880's and 1890's; contemporary Norwegian novel; post-neocritical American literary theory. *Publ:* Auth, Intensjon og genre i Arne Garborgs Bondestudentar, Edda, 78; Form and Theme in Arne Garborg's Mannfolk and Hjaa ho Mor, Selecta, 80; Alfred Hauge's Utstein Monastery Cycle, World Lit Today, 82; Arne Garborg's Traette Maend: En retorisk og genetisk analyse, Edda, 82. *Mailing Add:* Scand Dept Univ of Wash Seattle WA 98195

SJOBERG, ANDREE FRANCES, b Jamaica, NY, Jan 19, 24; m 47. LINGUISTICS. *Educ:* Univ NMex, BS, 47; Univ Tex, MA, 51, PhD, 57. *Prof Exp:* Spec instr, 60-63, asst prof ling, 63-76, ASSOC PROF ORIENT & AFRICAN LANG & LIT, CTR ASIAN STUDIES, UNIV TEX, AUSTIN, 76- *Concurrent Pos:* Grants, US Off Educ & Am Coun Learned Soc, 60-62; Ctr Appl Ling, Washington, DC, fall 62; assoc, Current Anthrop; NDEA-Fulbright-Hays res award, SIndia, 65-66; US Off Educ, 68-69. *Mem:* Ling Soc Am; Am Anthrop Asn; Am Orient Soc; Ling Soc India; Asn Asian Studies. *Res:* Structure of Dravidian languages, especially Telugu; structure of Turkic languages, especially Uzbek; writing systems and literacy. *Publ:* Coauth, Culture as a significant variable in lexical change, Am Anthrop, 4/56; auth, Coexistent phonemic systems in Telugu: A socio-cultural perspective, Word, 12/62; Uzbek Structural Grammar, Uralic & Altaic Series, Ind Univ, 63; Sociocultural and linguistic factors in the development of writing systems for preliterate peoples, In: Sociolinguistics, Mouton, The Hague, 66. *Mailing Add:* Ctr for Asian Studies Univ Tex Austin TX 78712

SJÖBERG, LEIF, b Boden, Sweden, Dec 15, 25; m 59. SCANDINAVIAN LANGUAGES & LITERATURES. *Educ:* Univ Uppsala, BA, 52, MA, 54, PhD(comp lit), 68. *Hon Degrees:* Fil Dr hic, Univ Upprala, 80. *Prof Exp:* EO adj, Swed & English, Realskolan, Vindeln, 54-56; lectr Swed, Kings Col, Univ Newcastle, Eng, 56-58; lectr Scand lang & lit, Columbia Univ, 58-69; assoc prof Ger, 68-72, PROF GER & SCAND STUDIES & COMP LIT, STATE UNIV NY, STONY BROOK, 72- *Concurrent Pos:* Trustee Scand sem, NY, 65-; ed Scand sect, Twayne World Authors ser, 68-; Ida Bäckmann stipendium, Swed Acad, 76. *Honors & Awards:* Translr Award, Swed Acad, 66. *Mem:* Soc Advan Scand Study; Am Scand Found; Am Comp Lit Asn. *Res:* Modern Swedish literature; Icelandic literature; Biederman's structurism. *Publ:* Co-transl, Gunnar Ekelöf: Selected Poems, Penguin, 71, Pantheon, 72; Tomas Transtroömer: Windows and Stones, Univ Pittsburgh, 72; auth, A Reader's Guide to Gunnar Ekelöf's A Mölna elegy Twayne, 73; co-transl, Pär Lagerkvist: Evening Land, Wayne State Univ, 75 & Souvenir, London, 77; auth, Pär Lagerkvist, Columbia Univ, 76; co-translr, Artur Lundkvist: Agadir, Int Poetry Forum, Pittsburgh, 78; Gunnar Ekelöf: A Mölna Elegy, Cambridge Univ, 79. *Mailing Add:* Dept of Ger & Slavics State Univ of NY Stony Brook NY 11794

SJOGREN, CHRISTINE OERTEL, b Ger, Nov 1, 23; US citizen; m 50; c 6. LANGUAGE, LITERATURE. *Educ:* Mills Col, BA, 45; Johns Hopkins Univ, PHD, 50. *Prof Exp:* Instr Ger, Univ Kans, 49-51 & Portland State Col, 59-60; from asst prof to assoc prof, 60-68, head sect, 73, PROF GER, ORE STATE UNIV, 68- *Concurrent Pos:* Fulbright Hayes teaching award, 74-75; Col Lib Arts res grant, 77. *Mem:* Hugo von Hofmannsthal Ges; Lessing Soc; Am Soc 18th Century Studies; MLA; Goethe Soc NAm. *Res:* Modern German literature; 19th century German literature; Eighteenth century Goethe and Lessing. *Publ:* Auth, Isolation and death in Stifter's Nachsommer, 6/65 & Mathilde and the roses in Stifter's Nachsommer, 10/66, PMLA; The human Gestalten and the fools in A Stifter's Der Nachsommer, J English & Ger Philol, 1/71; The Marble Statue as Idea: Collected Essays on A Stifter's Der Nachsommer, Univ NC, Chapel Hill, 72; The enigma of Musil's Tonka, Mod Austrian Lit, 76; Wendelin and the theme of transformation in Thomas Mann's Wälsungenblut, Comparative Lit Studies, 77; The status of women in Lessing's dramas, Studies in Eighteenth Century Culture, 77; Piety, Pathology or Pragmatism in Goethe's Bekentnisse einer schönen Seele, Studies in Voltaire, 81. *Mailing Add:* Dept of Foreign Lang & Lit Ore State Univ Corvallis OR 97330

SKALITZKY, RACHEL IRENE, b Waterloo, Wis, Feb 7, 37. COMPARATIVE LITERATURE, MEDIEVAL STUDIES. *Educ:* Mt Mary Col, BA, 62; Fordham Univ, MA, 66, PhD(class lang & lit), 68. *Prof Exp:* Teacher 6th grade, St Boniface Sch, Milwaukee, 58-62; teacher Latin & music, St Anthony High Sch, Detroit, 62-63; instr classics, Mt Mary Col, 68-69, asst prof & chmn, 69-72; lectr classics, 72-73, asst prof, 73-76, ASSOC PROF COMP LIT, UNIV WIS-MILWAUKEE, 76-, COORDR WOMEN'S STUDIES, 75- *Mem:* Am Comp Lit Asn; Am Philol Asn; Nat Women's Studies Asn; MLA; Am Asn Univ Women. *Res:* Classical philology; literary criticism; patristic literature. *Publ:* Auth, Good wine in a new vase, Horace, Epistles 1.2, Trans & Proc Am Philol Asn, 68; Annianus of Celeda: His Text of Chrysostom's Homilies on Matthew, Aevum, 71; Horace on travel, Epistles 1.11, Class J, 73; Plotinian Echoes in Peri Hypsous 7.2 and 9.7-10, Class Bull, 2/77. *Mailing Add:* Curtin Hall 809 Dept of Comp Lit Univ of Wis Milwaukee WI 53201

SKEHAN, PATRICK WILLIAM, b New York, NY, Sept 30, 09. SEMITICS. *Educ:* Fordham Univ, AB, 29; Cath Univ Am, STD, 38. *Hon Degrees:* LLD, Boston Col, 57, Manhattan Col, 62. *Prof Exp:* From instr to assoc prof, 38-51, prof, 51-79, EMER PROF SEMITIC LANG & LIT, CATH UNIV AM, 79- *Concurrent Pos:* Vis prof, Johns Hopkins Univ; annual ; prof, Am Sch Orient Res, Jerusalem, Palestine, 54-55, dir, 55-56; vis prof, Pontif Bibl Inst, Rome, 69-70. *Mem:* Am Orient Soc; Cath Bibl Asn Am (pres, 46). *Res:* Semitic languages and literatures; Old Testament; Dead Sea scrolls. *Publ:* Auth, Studies in Israellite Poetry and Wisdom Cath Bibl Asn, 71. *Mailing Add:* Curley Hall Cath Univ of Am Washington DC 20064

SKELTON, ROBERT BEATTIE, b Auburn, Mich, Apr 23, 13; m 40; c 4. FOREIGN LANGUAGES. *Educ:* Eastern Mich Univ, AB, 37; Univ Mich, AM, 38, PhD, 50. *Prof Exp:* From instr to assoc prof Romance philol, Auburn Univ, 39-54, head prof foreign 54-67, res prof comp ling, 67-76; RETIRED. *Concurrent Pos:* Instr, Mich State Norm Col, 48-49; student Univ Paris & Univ Salamanca, 72. *Mem:* Ling Soc Am; Am Asn Teachers Span & Port. *Res:* Indo-European and Germanic philology; Romance philology; spectrographic analysis. *Publ:* Auth, Spanish Baldio and the settled village organization, Folia Ling, 71; Spanish Baldar and Islamic pen Romance Philol Quart, 71; La locucion adverbial de/en bald y la fusion fonematica, Bol Read Acad Espanola, 71. *Mailing Add:* 426 Scott St Auburn AL 36830

SKENDI, STAVRO, Balkan Languages. See Vol I

SKINNER, DANIEL T, b Boston, Mass, May 1, 16; m 44; c 2. MODERN LANGUAGES. *Educ:* Harvard Univ, AB, 38, PhD(Romance lang & lit), 53; Boston Col, MA, 39. *Prof Exp:* Instr French, Va State Col, 39-40; instr mod lang, Dillard Univ, 40-42; prof, Morgan State Col, 46-81; RES & WRITING, 81- *Concurrent Pos:* Vis lect Brandeis Univ, 48-49; vis prof, Tex Southern Univ, 53-56; US Dept State research & lectr, US Embassy, Paris, France, 56-57; vis lectr, Negro hist, Baltimore Fel House, 66-67; vis prof, Towson State Col, 69; chmn fac res, Morgan State Univ, 74-78; vis prof, Sojourner-Douglass Col, 81-82; instr, Balto Free Univ, 81-82. *Honors & Awards:* Cert Merit, Dictionary Int Biog, 73. *Mem:* MLA; Am Asn Teachers Fr. *Res:* French and French-Canadian literature of the 19th century; modern language teaching; black French literature in Haiti, Martinque and Africa. *Publ:* Auth, The United States Teacher-Training Program for France, 59 & coauth, Petit Album Francais (brochure), 65, Morgan State Col; auth, The poetic influence of Victor Hugo on Louis Frechette, Edwards Bros, 73; Foreign lang teaching at Morgan State Univ, Morgan J Educ Res, spring 77. *Mailing Add:* 2033 Wheeler Ave Baltimore MD 21216

SKITTER, HANS GUNTER, b Bad Kreuznach, WGer, July 26, 36; m 70; c 2. GERMAN & AMERICAN LITERATURE. *Educ:* Univ Freiburg, PhD(English & Ger), 68. *Prof Exp:* Asst teacher Ger, Queen Elizabeth's Sch Girls, London, 59-60; asst English, Univ Freiburg, 64-67; asst prof Ger, Shippensburg State Col, 68-69; asst prof, 69-71, dir jr yr abroad, 70-72, ASSOC PROF GER, MILLERSVILLE STATE COL, 71-, DIR JR YR ABROAD, MARBURG, 73- *Mem:* Am Asn Teachers Ger; MLA; Deut Shakespeare Ges; Nat His Soc. *Res:* Twentieth century German and American literature; language teaching. *Publ:* Auth, Die drie Letzten Romane F Scott Fitzgeralds, Gouvier, Bonn, 68. *Mailing Add:* Dept of Foreign Lang Millersville State Col Millersville PA 17551

SKOUSEN, ROYAL JON, b Cleveland, Ohio, Aug 5, 45; m 68; c 5. LINGUISTICS. *Educ:* Brigham Young Univ, BA, 69; Univ Ill, Urbana, MA, 71, PhD(ling), 72. *Prof Exp:* Asst prof ling, Univ Tex, Austin, 72-79; ASSOC PROF ENGLISH, BRIGHAM YOUNG UNIV, 79- *Concurrent Pos:* Vis prof, Univ Calif, San Diego, 81; Fulbright lectr, Univ Tampere, Finland, 82. *Res:* Probabilistic linguistics; morphology; Finnish language. *Publ:* Auth, On capturing regularities, Papers Eighth Regional Meeting Chicago Ling Soc, 72; On limiting the number of phonological descriptions, Glossa (vol 7), 73; An explanatory theory of morphology, Papers Chicago Ling Soc, 74; Substantive Evidence in Phonology, Mouton, 75; On the nature of morphophoemic alternation, TG Paradigm & Mod Ling Theory, John Benjamins, 75; Empirical restrictions on the power of transformational grammars, In: Formal Aspects of Cognitive Processes, Springer, 75; Analogical sources of abstractness, Phonology in the 1970's, Story-Scientia, 81; English spelling and phonemic representation, Visible Language, 82. *Mailing Add:* Dept of English Brigham Young Univ Provo UT 84602

SKRUPSKELIS, VIKTORIA, b Kaunas, Lithuania, Dec 1, 35; US citizen. ROMANCE LANGUAGES, FRENCH. *Educ:* St Joseph Col, Conn, BA, 55; Fordham Univ, MA, 59; Univ Ill, PhD(French), 66. *Prof Exp:* Instr French, Univ Ill, 62-63; asst prof, Univ Chicago, 63-67; asst prof, 67-76, ASSOC PROF FRENCH, OBERLIN COL, 76- *Mailing Add:* Dept of Romance Lang Oberlin Col Oberlin OH 44074

SKYRME, RAYMOND, b Blackmill, UK, May 2, 37; Can citizen; m 66; c 2. SPANISH, COMPARATIVE LITERATURE. *Educ:* Univ Bristol, BA, 55, MLitt, 67; Univ Mich, MA, 66, PhD(comp lit), 69. *Prof Exp:* Lectr Span & French, Univ Waterloo, 61-63; from lectr to asst prof, 68-73, ASSOC PROF SPAN & HUMANITIES, SCARBOROUGH COL, UNIV OF TORONTO, 73- *Mem:* Can Asn Hispanists. *Res:* Modern Latin American literature; 19th century Spanish and French literature. *Publ:* Auth, Dario's Azul . . ., A note on the derivation of the title, Romance Notes, 68; The Pythagorean vision of Ruben Dario in La tortuga de oro, Comp Lit Studies, 74; Ruben Dario and the Pythagorean Tradition, Univ Fla, 75; El caracter pictorico del Palimpsesto de Dario, Explicacion de textos literarios, 76; The death of the Empress of China, Contemp Lit in Trans, 78; The literary pictorialism of Dario's Palimpsesto, Romance Notes, 78; The divided self: The language of Scission in El tajo of Francisco Ayala, Rev Can Estud Hisp, Vol VI, No 1, 81. *Mailing Add:* Div of Humanities Scarborough Col Univ Toronto West Hill ON M1C 1A4 Can

SLADE, CAROLE, b Calif. COMPARATIVE LITERATURE, ENGLISH. *Educ:* Pomona Col, BA, 65; Univ Wis, MA, 66; New York Univ, PhD(comp lit), 73. *Prof Exp:* Lectr English, Bronx Community Col, City Univ New York, 71-74, asst prof, 74-78; asst prof, Baylor Univ, 78-80; ASST PROF ENGLISH & COMP LIT, COLUMBIA UNIV, 80- *Mem:* MLA; Northeast Mod Lang Asn; Am Comp Lit Asn; Dante Soc Am; NCTE. *Publ:* Auth, Unamuno's Abel Sanchez: L'ombre dolenti nella ghiaccia, Symposium, winter 74; Under the volcano and Dante's Inferno I, Univ Windsor Rev, spring 75; The Hell of Bernarda's house, Garcia Lorca Rev, fall 75; The Dantean journey through Dublin, Mod Lang Studies, spring 76; coauth, Writing the Research Paper, Houghton Mifflin, 78; The character of Yvonne in Under the Volcano, Can Lit, 79; coauth, Form and Style, 6th ed, Houghton Mifflin, 82. *Mailing Add:* Dept of English Columiba Univ New York NY 10027

SLAGER, WILLIAM R, b Butte, Mont, Nov 8, 25; m 57; c 3. APPLIED LINGUISTICS. *Educ:* Univ Minn, BS, 46; Mont State Univ, MA, 47; Univ Utah, PhD, 51. *Prof Exp:* From asst prof to assoc prof English, 51-66, chmn dept, 75-78, PROF ENGLISH, UNIV UTAH, 66- *Concurrent Pos:* Fulbright lectr, Cairo Univ & Ain Shams Univ, Cairo, 52-54; Smith-Mundt lectr, Am Univ Cairo, 58-59; Cult Exchange prof, Mex, 67-68; mem, Nat Adv Coun Teaching English as Foreign Lang, 69-73. *Mem:* NCTE; Ling Soc Am; Nat Asn Foreign Studies Affairs; Am Asn Teachers English as Second Lang; Am Dialect Soc. *Res:* English as a foreign language; grammar of contemporary English. *Publ:* Coauth, Learning English: A Review Grammar for Speakers of Arabic, Am Univ Cairo, 59 & Core English, Ginn, 71; gen ed, English for Today Series, McGraw. *Mailing Add:* Dept of English Univ of Utah Salt Lake City UT 84112

SLAUGHTER, MARY MARTINA, Intellectual History. See Vol II

SLAVOV, EUGENIA MARGARET HINTZE, b Reims, France, Feb 18, 25; US citizen; m 51. SLAVIC & GERMANIC LANGUAGES & LITERATURES. *Educ:* Univ Rome, Dr Lett, 54; Univ Del, cert comp lit, 63, French Romanticism, 65, 20th century Ger lit, 69 & 70; Univ Paris, cert French lang & civilization, 64. *Prof Exp:* Corresp accountant, Ger Naval Weapons Arsenal, Linz-Ebelsberg, Austria, 44-45; reporter, Radio Free Europe, Rome, Italy, 52-56; free lance corresp, Radio Liberty, Munich, Ger, 55-56; teacher, Tower Hill Sch, Del, 57-64; instr Russ, Ger, Ital & French, 64-65, ASST PROF FOREIGN LANG, UNIV DEL, 65- *Concurrent Pos:* Ger & Slavic lang ed, Del Coun Int Visitors. *Honors & Awards:* Excellence Teaching Award, Univ Del, 82. *Mem:* Am Asn Advan Slavic Studies; Am Asn Teachers Slavic & EEurop Lang; Am Class League; MLA; Am Coun Teaching Foreign Lang. *Res:* Comparative literature; music; science. *Publ:* Auth, La chiusura delle scuole straniere in Bulgaria dope l'avvento dei communisti, Bulgaria Libera ed Indipendente, 4/51; Il linguaggio universale della musica, Foreign Lang Del, spring 82. *Mailing Add:* Dept of Lang & Lit Univ of Del Newark DE 19711

SLAVUTYCH, YAR, b Blahodatne, Ukraine, Jan 11, 18; US citizen; m 48; c 2. SLAVIC LANGUAGES, LINGUISTICS. *Educ:* Pedag Inst Zaporizhja, Dipl, 40; Univ Pa, AM, 54, PHD, 55. *Prof Exp:* Instr Ukrainian, Army Lang Sch, 55-60; asst prof Slavic lang, 60-65, assoc prof, 66-79, PROF SLAVIC LANG & LIT, UNIV ALTA, 79- *Concurrent Pos:* Res grant-in-aid, 61, 63, 66, Univ Alta, Can Coun grant, 68. *Honors & Awards:* Gold Medal, Shevchenko Found, Can, 74; Bk Award, Shevchenko Sci Soc, 78. *Mem:* MLA; Am Name Soc; Can Asn Slavists; Shevchenko Sci Soc; Ukrainian Acad Sci Can. *Res:* Ukrainian literature and language; Onomastics; comparative literature. *Publ:* Ed, Collected Papers on Ukrainian Settlers, Vol 1, 73, & Vol 2, 75, Shevchenko Sci Soc; auth, Conversational Ukrainian, Gateway, 4th ed, 73; ed, Antolohija ukrajins'koji poeziji v Kanadi, Slovo, 75; auth, Trynadciata pisnia H Skovorody, Jubilee Collection of UVAN, 76; Ukrajins'ka poezija v Kanadi, Slavuta, 76; Frankovi sonety, Collected Papers Shevchenko Sci Soc, 77; Collected Works, 1938-1978, Slavuta, 78; Metafora utvorchosti L Ukrajinky, Lesia Ukrajinka, 1871-1970, 80. *Mailing Add:* Dept of Slavic Lang Univ of Alta Edmonton AB T6G 2E6 Can

SLAYMAKER, WILLIAM EARL, b Wolf Lake, Ind, Apr 9, 45. COMPARATIVE LITERATURE, GERMAN. *Educ:* Western Mich Univ, BA, 68; Ind Univ, MA, 73, PhD(comp lit), 75. *Prof Exp:* Instr Ger & English, Vigo County Sch Corp, 68-71; lectr Ger, Univ Mich, Dearborn, 74-75; adj asst prof humanities, Univ Louisville, 75-78; CHMN LIT & LANG, MIDWAY COL, 78- *Concurrent Pos:* Fulbright-Hays fel, Germany, 70; Nat Endowment for Humanities fel, Univ Minn, 77; Mellon fel, Vanderbilt Uninv, 82. *Mem:* Am Asn Teachers Ger; MLA; Am Comp Lit Asn. *Res:* Philosophy and literature; 20th century comparative literature, European and American. *Publ:* Auth, Tragic freedoms: Milton's Samson and Sartre's Orestes, Studies in Humanities, 4/78; Who cooks, winds up: The concept of freedom in Grass, Blechtrommel and Hundejahre, Collquia Germanica, 14: 48-68. *Mailing Add:* Dept of English Midway Col Midway KY 40347

SLESSAREV, HELGA, b Hamburg, Ger, Aug 29, 27; US citizen. GERMAN LITERATURE. *Educ:* Univ Cincinnati, PHD, 55. *Prof Exp:* Instr Ger, Univ Wis, 55-56; from instr to asst prof, Univ Minn, 57-61; from asst prof to assoc prof, 61-70, head dept Ger lang & lit, 74-80, PROF GER, UNIV CINCINNATI, 70-, DIR NAT WORK-STUDIES PROG, 67- *Mem:* MLA; Midwest Mod Lang Asn; Schiller Ges; Am Asn Teachers Ger; Lessing Soc. *Res:* Lessing Romanticism; literary criticism. *Publ:* Auth, Abgrund der Betrachtung Uber die schöpferische Einbildungskraft E Mörikes, 61 & Ironie in der Idylle über den Müssiggang von Friedrich Schlegel, 65, Ger Quart; E T A Hoffmanns Prinzessin Brambilla, Studies in Romanticism, 70; Eduard Mörike, Twayne, 70; Bedeytungsanreicherung des Wortes: Auge Betrachtungen zum Werke E T A Hoffmanns, Monatshefte, 71; Comprehensive Career Education Program at Univ Cincinnati, Unterrichtspraxis 2, 77; Divine and Human Justice in Works of H V Kleist, Coloquia Germanica, 77; Lessing und Hamburg Wechselbeziehungen zweier Persönlichkeiten, Lessing Yearbk XIII, 81. *Mailing Add:* Dept of Ger Lang & Lit Univ of Cincinnati Cincinnati OH 45221

SLICK, SAM L, b Oelwein, Iowa, Sept 7, 43; m 82; c 1. LATIN AMERICAN LITERATURE. *Educ:* Ill State Univ, BA, 65, MA, 66; Univ Iowa, PhD(Spanish), 74. *Prof Exp:* Asst prof, Simpson Col, 74-76; ASSOC PROF SPANISH, SAM HOUSTON STATE UNIV, 76- *Concurrent Pos:* Dir, Int Archives of Latin Am Polit Posters, 78- *Mem:* MLA; Am Asn Spanish & Portuguese Teachers; Southwestern Coun Latin Am Studies. *Res:* Mexican literature; Latin American political art. *Publ:* Auth, Performance objectives teaching, Bull Asn Dept Foreign Lang, 5/72; The Chicano in Los motivos de Cain, Rev Chicano-Riquena, 75; Spanish & law enforcement, Hispania, 12/75; Natividad as positive hero in El luto humano, The Anal Hisp Texts Current Trends Methodol, 76; Jose Ruben Romero, In: Encycl of World Literature in the 20th Century, 82; Jose Revueltas: His Life and Works, Twayne Publ (in prep). *Mailing Add:* Off of Foreign Lang Sam Houston State Univ Huntsville TX 77341

SLJIVIC-SIMSIC, BILJANA, b Belgrade, Yugoslavia, Jan 20, 33; div; c 1. SLAVIC LANGUAGES. *Educ:* Univ Belgrade, Dipl, 55; Harvard Univ, AM, 63, PhD(Slavic lang & lit), 66. *Prof Exp:* Asst contemporary Serbo-Croatian, Univ Belgrade, 57-62; asst Serbo-Croatian & Russ, Univ Calif, Los Angeles, 64-65, actg asst prof, 65-66; asst prof Russ, Univ Ky, 66-67; asst prof Serbo-Croatian, Yugoslav lit, Old Church Slavonic & hist Russ lang, Univ Pa, 67-73; ASSOC PROF SERBO-CROATIAN LANG & SLAVIC LING, UNIV ILL, CHICAGO CIRCLE, 73-, HEAD, DEPT SLAVIC LANG & LIT, 81- *Concurrent Pos:* Exchange lectr, Univ Clermont-Ferrand, 59-61; vis lectr Old Church Slavonic, Princeton Univ, 68. *Mem:* MLA; Am Asn Teachers Slavic & East Europ Lang; Am Asn Advan Slavic Studies; NAm Soc Serbian Studies(secy-treas, 78-). *Res:* Serbo-Croatian, Yugoslav literature and Slavic linguisitics. *Publ:* Auth, Genitive plural in the Serbocroatian Pashtrovichi dialect 16th-18th centuries, Int J Slavic Ling & Poetics, 68; coauth, Serbocroatian-English Dictionary, Univ Pa & Prosveta, Belgrade, 71 & Judeo-Spanish Ballads from Bosnia, Univ Pa, 71; transl, Mihailo Lalic's The snow is melting, Lit Rev, Vol XI, No 2; auth, Notes on the history of possessive pronoun-adjectives in Serbocroatian, J Slavic Ling & Poetics, 75; On Feminine Nouns in Zero, In: Serbo-Croatian, Floia Slavica, Vol 2, No 1-3; The Woman in Serbian folk Proverbs, Serbian Studies, Vol 1, 80. *Mailing Add:* Dept of Slavic Lang & Lit Univ of Ill at Chicago Circle Chicago IL 60680

SLOAT, CLARENCE, b Wasco, Ore, Apr 22, 36; m 56; c 3. LINGUISTICS, ENGLISH AS A SECOND LANGUAGE. *Educ:* Idaho State Univ, BA, 58, MA, 60; Univ Washington, PhD (ling), 66. *Prof Exp:* From asst prof to assoc prof English, Univ Ore, 69-75, chmn ling, 67-79, dir grad studies English, 74-75, prof ling & English, 74-80; DIR, INTENSIVE ENGLISH INST, LEWIS-CLARK STATE COL, 80- *Concurrent Pos:* Consult ling, Lang Materials Comt, Ore Curriculum Studies Ctr, 64-67; Nat Endowment for Humanities younger humanist fel, 72-73. *Mem:* Ling Soc Am. *Res:* American Indian and English linguistics; English language pedagogy. *Publ:* Auth, Vowel harmony in Coeur d'Alene, Int J Am Ling, 72; coauth, English irregular verbs, Language, 73; Isolating semantic units, Proc of the First Ann Meeting Berkeley Ling Soc, 75; coauth, Introd to Phonology, Prentice-Hall, 78. *Mailing Add:* Intensive English Inst Lewis Clark State Col Lewiston ID 83501

SLOBIN, DAN ISAAC, b Detroit, Mich, May 7, 39; m 69; c 2. PSYCHOLINGUISTICS. *Educ:* Univ Mich, Ann Arbor, BA, 60; Harvard Univ, MA, 62, PhD(social psychol), 64. *Prof Exp:* From asst prof to assoc prof, 64-72, PROF PSYCHOL, UNIV CALIF, BERKELEY, 72- *Concurrent Pos:* Ed, Soviet Psychol, 62-70; mem comt on cognition, Soc Sci Res Coun, 71-75. *Mem:* Soc Res Child Develop; Ling Soc Am; Int Asn Cross-Cult Psychol; Soc Cross-Cult Res; Int Soc Study Child Lang. *Res:* Language and cognitive development in the child; linguistics; cross-cultural psychology. *Publ:* Auth, Grammatical transformations and sentence comprehension in childhood and adulthood, J Verbal Learning & Verbal Behav, 66; Psycholinguistics, Scott, 71, 2nd ed, 79; ed, The Ontogenesis of Grammar, Acad Press, 71; co-ed, Psychology in the USSR, Int Arts & Sci, 72; ed, Bibliography of Child Language, Ind Univ, 72; co-ed, Studies of Child Language Development, Holt, 73; Cognitive prerequisites for the development of grammar, In: Studies of Child Language Development, Holt, 73; Universal and particular in the acquisition of language, In: Language Acquisition, Cambridge Univ Press, 82. *Mailing Add:* Dept of Psychol Univ of Calif Berkeley CA 94720

SLOTE, DANIEL CARL, b Windsor, Ont, Jan 27, 31. LINGUISTICS, TRANSLATION. *Educ:* Univ Western Ont, BA, 53; Univ de Paris, doctorate, 62. *Prof Exp:* Prof translation, Int Superieur di Interpretariat et de Traduction, 55-69; ASSOC PROF TRANSLATION, UNIV DE MONTREAL, 711- *Concurrent Pos:* Lectr, Inst Cath de Paris, 57-62, assoc prof English lit, 62-69; guest prof, Univ de Montreal, 69-71. *Mem:* Am Transl Soc. *Res:* Translation theory and practice; semiotics. *Publ:* Auth, Proceedings of Saint-Cloud, Coun Europe, 68; Illuminations, Editions Maisonneuve, Montreal, 71; coauth, Strange pedantry of William Rowley, Rev Hist Theatre, 71; auth, Translating Rimbaud, 78 & Comment traduire Rimbaud, 82, Transl J, Meta; Rimbaud et sa Vision de L'etre de Beaute, Rimbaud Vivant, Paris, 82. *Mailing Add:* 5390 Aue Decelles apt 2 Montreal PQ H3T 1V9 Can

SLOTKIN, ALAN ROBERT, b Brooklyn, NY, NOv 7, 43. ENGLISH LINGUISTICS, AMERICAN LITERATURE. *Educ:* Univ Miami, AB, 65; Univ SC, MA, 70, PhD(English), 71. *Prof Exp:* Asst prof, 70-80, ASSOC PROF ENGLISH, TENN TECHNOL UNIV, 80- *Concurrent Pos:* Ed, Tenn

Ling. *Mem:* Am Dialect Soc; Ling Soc Am; Southeastern Conf Ling; SAtlantic Mod Lang Asn. *Res:* American dialects; American dialect literature; modern drama. *Publ:* Coauth, Shakespeare's use of verse form as social dialect to stratify characters in A Midsummer Night's Dream, Tenn Philol Asn Bull, 7/73; auth, The negative aspect of Hono Faber: A reading of E E Cummings' pity this busy monster, manunkind, not, In: The Language of Poems, Univ SC, 73; Bungstarter, Mightish Well, and cultrual confusion, Am Speech, spring 79; Dialect manipulation in An Experiment in Misery, Am Lit Realism, autumn 81. *Mailing Add:* Dept English Tenn Technol Univ Cookville TN 38501

SLOTKIN, EDGAR MORRIS, b Buffalo, NY. CELTIC LITERATURES. *Educ:* Harvard Univ, BA, 65, MA, 67, PhD(Celtic lang & lit), 77. *Prof Exp:* Asst prof, 72-78, ASSOC PROF ENGLISH & COMP LIT, UNIV CINCINNATI, 78- *Mem:* Am Folklore Soc; Celtic Studies Asn NAm; Medieval Acad Am; MLA; Asn Scottish Lit Studies. *Res:* Medieval Irish saga; oral narrative; rhetorical theory. *Publ:* Ed, Celtic Literature, MLA Int Bibliog, 76-82; The structure of Fled Bricrenn before and after the Lebor na huidre Interpolations, Erin, 78; Medieval Irish scribes and fixed texts, Eigse, 78-79; co-transl, Group, A General Rhetoric, Johns Hopkins Univ Press, 81; auth, The formulaic nature of the Harlaw Brosnchadh?, Proceedings of the Third Int Conf of Scottish Lang and Lit, 81. *Mailing Add:* Dept of English & Comparative Lit Univ of Cincinnati Cincinnati OH 45221

SLUSSER, MICHAEL, Theology. See Vol IV

SMALL, JOCELYN PENNY, b New York, NY, May 21, 45. CLASSICAL ARCHEOLOGY. *Educ:* Bryn Mawr Col, BA, 67; Princeton Univ, MA, 70, PhD(class archaeol), 72. *Prof Exp:* Asst prof classics, Fla State Univ, 72-73 & Dartmouth Col, 73-76; DIR, US CTR, LEXICON ICONOGRAPHICUM MYTHOLOGIAE CLASSICAE, RUTGERS UNIV, 76- *Mem:* Archaeol Inst Am. *Res:* Etruscan and Roman archaeology; iconography. *Publ:* Auth, The Banquet Frieze from Poggio Civitate, Murlo, Studi Etruschi, 39: 25-61; Aeneas and Turnus on Late Etruscan Funerary Urns, Am J Archaeol, 74; The Death of Lucretia, Am J Archaeol, 76; The Matricide of Alcmaeon, Römische Mitteilungen, 76; Plautus and the three princes of Serendip, Renaissance Quart, 76; Studies Related to the Theban Cycle on Late Etruscan Urns, Giorgio Bretschneider, 81; Cacus and Marsyas in Etrusco-Roman Legend, Princeton Univ Press, 82. *Mailing Add:* LIMC Lang Bldg Rutgers Univ New Brunswick NJ 08903

SMALL, RICHARD B, b Toronto, Ont, Aug 13, 18; m 55. FRENCH LANGUAGE & LITERATURE. *Educ:* Park Col, AB, 41; Cornell Univ, MA, 46; Univ Paris, cert, 49 & 55; Univ San Carlos, Guatemala, cert, 52. *Prof Exp:* Instr French & Span, Endicott Jr Col, 42-43; master, Manlius Sch, 43-44; teaching asst Romance lang, Cornell Univ, 44-46; from instr to assoc prof French & Span, Fenn Col, 46-65, chmn dept mod lang, 60-65; chmn dept, 65-70, ASSOC PROF MOD LANG, CLEVELAND STATE UNIV, 65- *Concurrent Pos:* Mem eval team Orange High Sch, NCent Asn Cols & Sec Schs, 74. *Mem:* Am Asn Teachers Fr; MLA; Am Coun Teaching Foreign Lang; Am Translr Asn. *Res:* Nineteenth century literature; French civilization. *Mailing Add:* Dept of Mod Lang Cleveland State Univ Cleveland OH 44115

SMALL, STUART GERARD PAUL, b New York, NY, June 22, 16; m 42; c 3. CLASSICS. *Educ:* Bowdoin Col, BA, 38; Univ Cincinnati, PhD(classics), 42. *Prof Exp:* Instr classics, Marietta Col, 45-47; from instr to asst prof, Yale Univ, 47-55; ASSOC PROF CLASSICS, NORTHWESTERN UNIV, 55- *Mem:* Am Philol Asn. *Res:* Greek and Latin Literature. *Mailing Add:* 1840 Sheridan Rd Evanston IL 60201

SMALLEY, WILLIAM ALLEN, b Jerusalem, Apr 4, 23; US citizen; m 46; c 3. LINGUISTICS, ANTHROPOLOGY. *Educ:* Houghton Col, AB, 45; Columbia Univ, PhD(anthrop), 56. *Prof Exp:* Instr English, Missionary Training Inst, 46-49; missionary, Laos, 50-54; assoc secy for transl, Am Bible Soc, 56-62; ling & transl consult, Bible Soc Southeast Asia, 62-69; transl coordr, United Bible Soc, 69-72, res consult, 72-77; PROF LING, BETHEL COL, 78- *Concurrent Pos:* Asst prof anthrop, Nyack Missionary Col, 56-62; prin, Toronto Inst Ling, 55-62; Wenner-Gren Found Anthrop res grant, 62; res fel anthrop, Yale Univ, 67-69; res fel, Yale Divinity Sch, 74-75. *Mem:* Ling Asn Can & US; Am Asn Appl Ling; Siam Soc; Ling Soc Am; Am Anthrop Asn. *Res:* Linguistics and ethnology of Southeast Asia; discourse and semantics; translation theory. *Publ:* Coauth, Introducing animism, Friendship, 59; auth, Outline of Khmu? Structure, Am Orient Soc, 61; Manual of Articulatory Phonetics, William Carey Libr, 61; coauth, Orthography studies: Articles on new writing systems, United Bible Soc, 64; Becoming Bilingual: A Guide to Language Learning, William Carey Libr, 72; Phonemes and Orthography: Language Planning in Ten Minority Languages of Thailand, Australian Nat Univ, 76; ed, Readings in Missionary Anthropology II, William Carey Libr, 78; coauth, Translators Handbook on Amos, United Bible Soc, 79. *Mailing Add:* Dept of Ling Bethel Col St Paul MN 55112

SMART, IAN ISIDORE, b Trinidad, West Indies; Apr 4, 44; m 78; c 1. SPANISH AMERICAN LITERATURE. *Educ:* Univ Col, Dublin, BA, 68; Nat Autonomous Univ, Mexico, MA, 70; Univ Calif, Los Angeles, PhD, 75. *Prof Exp:* Instr English, Nat Autonomous Univ, Mex, 70; teacher Span & Fr, St James Sch, 70-71; teaching asst Span, Univ Calif, Los Angeles, 71-74, instr, 75-76; asst prof, Univ Ark, Fayetteville, 76-77; asst prof, 77-81, ASSOC PROF SPAN, HOWARD UNIV, 81- *Mem:* Afro-Hisp Inst; Col Lang Asn; Am Coun Teaching For Lang; Asn Caribbean Studies. *Res:* Calypso and Son: Towards a definition of Caribbean poetics; the poetry of Nicolas Guillen. *Publ:* Auth, Big rage and big romance: Discovering a New Panamanian author, Caribbean Rev, 79; The tremendismo negrista in Cuentos del negro Cubena, Studies in Afro-Hisp Lit, 79; Nicolas Guillen's Son poem: An African contribution to contemporary Caribbean poetics, Col Lang Asn J, 80; The African heritage in Spanish Caribbean literature, Western J Black Studies, 81; Discovering the Caribbean: Two important research tools, Caribbean Review, 81; A new Panamanian poet's promising quest for identity: The case of Gerardo Maloney, Plantation Soc in the Americas, 81; Religious Elements in the narrative of Quince Duncan, Afro-Hisp Rev, 82; Mulatez and the image of the Black Mujer Nueva in Guillen's poetry, Ky Romance Quart, 82. *Mailing Add:* Dept of Romance Lang Howard Univ Washington DC 20059

SMEATON, B HUNTER, b Oakland, Calif, Apr 29, 15; Can citizen; m 51; c 2. LINGUISTICS. *Educ:* Univ Calif, Berkeley, AB, 38, MA, 41; Columbia Univ, PhD, 59. *Prof Exp:* Teaching asst Ger, Univ Calif, Berkeley, 38-41; dir Arabic studies, Arabian Am Oil Co, Saudi Arabia, 45-49; instr Ger & Span, Polytech Inst Brooklyn, 54-60; asst prof English, Los Angeles State Col, 60-63; assoc prof English, Univ Calgary, 63-68, assoc prof ling, 68-70, chmn ling prog, 67-70, prof, 70-80. *Concurrent Pos:* Lectr ling, Columbia Univ, 53-60; consult, Can Dict, Univ Montreal, 59, Univ Victoria, 74; lectr ling, Summer Sch, Univ Alta, 61 & 63; ed, Can J Ling, 67-70; ed consult, Winston Dict Can English, 68-69. *Mem:* Int Ling Asn; Can Ling Asn (pres, 75-78); Philol Asn Pac Coast. *Res:* Bi- and multi-lingual lexicography; Scandinavian and Arabic studies; semantics. *Publ:* Auth, Arabic Work Vocabulary for Americans in Saudi Arabia, Elias Mod Press, Cairo, 45 & 47; Problems in the Analysis of the Modern English Operators, Word, 68; Concerning the restoration of Old Norse-Icelandic, Mediaeval Scand, 68; Lexical Expansion Due to Technical Change, as Illustrated by the Arabic of Al Hasa, Saudi Arabia, Ind Univ, 73. *Mailing Add:* 24 Brown Circle NW Calgary AB T2L 1N5 Can

SMETHURST, MAE J, b Houghton, Mich, May 28, 35; m 56. CLASSICS. *Educ:* Dickinson Col, BA, 57; Univ Mich, MA, 60, PhD(classics), 68. *Prof Exp:* Instr classics, Univ Mich, 66-67; from instr to asst prof, 67-76, ASSOC PROF CLASSICS, UNIV PITTSBURGH, 76- *Mem:* Am Philol Asn. *Res:* Aeschylus; tragedy; Oresteia. *Mailing Add:* Dept of Classic Univ of Pittsburgh Pittsburgh PA 15260

SMETHURST, STANLEY ERIC, b Manchester, England, Jan 19, 15; m 36; c 2. CLASSICS. *Educ:* Cambridge Univ, BA, 37, MA, 41. *Prof Exp:* Prof classics, Univ NB, 38-47; PROF CLASSICS, QUEEN'S UNIV, ONT, 47-, HEAD DEPT, 61- *Concurrent Pos:* Can Coun fel, 68-69. *Mem:* Am Philol Asn; Class Asn Can (vpres, 68-70, pres, 76-78); Humanities Res Coun Can. *Res:* Ancient history and literature. *Mailing Add:* Dept of Classics Queen's Univ Kingston ON K7L 4V8 Can

SMIEJA, FLORIAN LUDWIK, b Zabrze, Poland, Aug 22, 25; Brit citizen; m 54; c 4. SPANISH & LATIN AMERICAN LITERATURE. *Educ:* Nat Univ Ireland, BA, 50: Univ London, MA, 55, PhD(Span lit), 62. *Prof Exp:* Asst Polish, Sch Slavonic & East Europ Studies, Univ London, 50-54, from asst lectr to lectr Span, London Sch-Econ, 58-63; lectr, Univ Nottingham, 62-69; vis assoc prof, 69-70, PROF SPAN & ITAL, UNIV WESTERN ONT, 70- *Concurrent Pos:* Instr, Univ Md, Overseas Prog, 53-63. *Mem:* Am Asn Teachers Span & Port; MLA; Can Asn Hispanists. *Res:* Spanish Golden Age theatre; pastoral novel; Latin American novel. *Publ:* Auth, G Fiamma and P de Padilla, Philol Quart, 55; A de Ledesma y su poesia a lo divino, Estud Segovianos, 63; An alternative ending of La Fontana de Oro, Mod Lang Rev, 66; Ed, A Moreto, El lego del Carmen, Anaya, Madrid, 70; M Cervantes, El rufian dichiso, Ebro, Saragossa, 77. *Mailing Add:* Dept of Span & Ital Univ Col Univ of Western Ont London ON N6A 3K7 Can

SMITH, ALBERT B, b Jonesboro, Ga, Nov 17, 30; m 55; c 4. FOREIGN LANGUAGES. *Educ:* Emory Univ, AB, 51, MA, 52; Univ NC, PhD, 61. *Prof Exp:* Instr foreign lang, Union Col, Ky, 55-56; instr French, Col, Univ Chicago, 61-63; from asst prof to assoc prof, 63-77, PROF ROMANCE LANG, UNIV FLA, 77- *Concurrent Pos:* Contribr annual bibliog, The Romantic Movement. *Mem:* S Atlantic Mod Lang Asn; Am Asn Teachers French; Soc Theophile Gautier. *Res:* French Romanticism; Theophile Gautier; 19th century French theatre. *Publ:* Auth, Ideal and Reality in Fictional Narratives of Theophile Gautier, Univ Fla, 69; Vigny's Le cor: The tragedy of service, Studies Romanticism, spring 68; Gautier's Mademoiselle de Maupin: The quest for happiness, Mod Lang Quart, 71; Theophile Gautier and the Fantastic, Romance Monographs, Inc, 77; Mlle de Maupin Chap XI: Plot, character, literary theory, Ky Romance Quart, 78; Variations on a Mythical Theme: Hoffmann, Gautier, Queneau, Neophil, 79. *Mailing Add:* Dept of Romance Lang & Lit Univ of Fla Gainesville FL 32611

SMITH, ANDRE, b Montreal, Que, Feb 13, 43. FRENCH & CANADIAN LITERATURE. *Educ:* Univ Montreal, BCom, 64, BA, 65; McGill Univ, MA, 67; Univ Paris, Doctorat, 70. *Prof Exp:* ASSOC PROF FRENCH & CATH LIT, MCGILL UNIV, 70- *Res:* Quebec theatre, Michel Tremblay; Celine, Sartre, Camus. *Publ:* Auth, Celine et la notion de complot, Etudes francaises, 5/71; Ni catholique ni revolutionaire: Celine nihilste, Le Devoir, 9/71; La vie imaginaire de Charles Swann, In: Litterature, Montreal, 72; La nuit de Louis-Ferdinand Celine, Grasset, Paris, 73; Les romans de Jacques Godbout, Univ Montreal, 74; Le'univers romanesque de Jacques Godbout, Aquila, Montreal, 76. *Mailing Add:* Dept French McGill Univ Montreal PQ H3A 1X9 Can

SMITH, ANNETTE JACQUELINE, b Algiers, Algeria, Dec 8 24; Fr citizen; m 51; c 3. FRENCH LITERATURE, INTELLECTUAL HISTORY. *Educ:* Fac des Lett, Paris, BA, 46, MA, 50, Dr Fr lang & lit, 70. *Prof Exp:* Asst lectr French, Univ Wales, Swansea, 48-50; lectr, Scripps Col, 55-62; lectr, Claremont Men's Col, 58-62, asst prof, 64-70, lectr, 70-82, ASSOC PROF FRENCH, CALIF INST TECHNOL, 82- *Honors & Awards:* Wittler-Benner Award, Poetry Soc Am, 80. *Mem:* MLA. *Res:* Nineteenth century French literature and intellectual history; literature and natural sciences; Black writers in French. *Publ:* Auth, Mother Earth and mother country: Les Canaques, an anti-colonial play, AUMLA, 73; Un Bestiaire de Gobineau, Etudes gobiniennes, 76-78; L'Agression et le lien: Une lecture ethologique de Gobineau, Nouvelle, Ecole, 79; Playing with play: A textcase of ethocriticism, J Social & Biol Struct, 79; contribr, The Random House Anthology of 20th Century French Poetry, Random House, 82; auth, Gobineau et l'histoire naturelle, Droz (in press); co-ed & transl, The Collected Poetry of Aime Cesaire, Univ Calif Press (in press); co-transl, Return to My Native Land, Presence Africaine (in press). *Mailing Add:* Dept of French Calif Inst of Technol Pasadena CA 91125

SMITH, BEVERLY MOULTON ALLEN, b Jackson, Mich, May 13, 23; m 45; c 3. SPANISH LANGUAGE & LITERATURE. *Educ:* Univ Mich, BA, 45, MA, 62, PhD(Spanish), 73. *Prof Exp:* From instr to asst prof, 62-73, assoc prof, 73-77, PROF SPANISH, ADRIAN COL, 77- *Mem:* Am Asn Teachers Spanish & Portuguese; Nat Educ Asn. *Res:* Golden Age religious theater in Spain; individualized study for first-year college students in beginning Spanish; bilingual education. *Mailing Add:* Dept of Mod Lang Adrian Col Adrian MI 49221

SMITH, CARLOTA S, b New York, NY, May 21, 34; div; c 2. LINGUISTICS, PSYCHOLINGUISTICS. *Educ:* Radcliffe Col, BA, 55; Univ Pa, MA, 62; PhD(ling), 67. *Prof Exp:* Res asst ling, Univ Pa, 59-60 & 61-63 & Mass Inst Technol, 60-61; asst prof English, Univ Pa, 67-69; fac assoc ling, 69-71, asst prof, 71-72, assoc prof, 73-80, PROF & CHMN LING, UNIV TEX, AUSTIN, 80- *Mem:* Ling Soc Am; Int Ling Asn. *Res:* Syntax and semantics; language acquisition; text structure. *Publ:* Auth, Determiners and Relative Clauses in a Generative Grammar, Language, 65; An Experimental Approach to Children's Linguistic Competence, Proc Carnegie Symp Cognition, 68; coauth, Children's Responses to Commands, Language, 70; auth, Sentence in Discourse, J Ling, 71; Syntax and Interpretation of Temporal Expressions in English, Ling & Philos, 78. *Mailing Add:* Dept Ling Univ Tex Austin TX 78712

SMITH, CHARLES LAVAUGHN, b Indianapolis, Ind, Aug 25, 15; m 43; c 2. SEMITIC LANGUAGES & LITERATURE. *Educ:* Butler Univ, AB, 37, AM, 38; Yale Univ, BD, 40, PhD, 47. *Prof Exp:* Horowitz Found fel, Hebrew Union Col, 47-48; prof philos & relig, Rocky Mountain Col, 48-50; prof divinity sch, 50-68, PROF SEMITIC LANG & LIT, COL LIB ARTS, DRAKE UNIV, 68-, CHMN DEPT, 80- *Concurrent Pos:* Lectr, Jewish Chatauqua Soc; Inst Judaism. *Mem:* Am Acad Relig; Soc Bibl Lit; Am Schs Orient Res; Am Orient Soc. *Res:* Near Eastern studies; Biblical archaeology; Judaica. *Mailing Add:* 7125 Meredith Dr Des Moines IA 50324

SMITH, CLYDE CURRY, Ancient History, Ancient Religions. See Vol I

SMITH, DAVID RICHARD, b Jersey City, NJ, Apr 24, 42; m 61; c 1. CLASSICAL STUDIES. *Educ:* David Lipscomb Col, BA, 64; Vanderbilt Univ, MA, 66; Univ Pa, PhD(class studies), 68. *Prof Exp:* Asst prof classics, Univ Calif, Riverside, 68-70; asst prof, 70-75, assoc prof, 75-80, PROF HIST, CALIF STATE POLYTECH UNIV POMONA, 80- *Concurrent Pos:* Assoc ed, Helios J Class Asn Southwest, 75-77. *Mem:* Class Asn Southwest; Am Philol Asn; AHA. *Res:* Greek history, religion and philosophy of history. *Publ:* Auth, Hieropoioi and Hierothytai on Rhodes, L'Antiquite Classique, 72; The Hieropoioi on Kos, Numen, 73; The Coan Festival of Zeus Polieus, Class J, 10/73; Review of G S Kirk, Myth: Its meaning and function in ancient and other cultures, Helios, 5/76; The poetic focus in Horace, Odes 3.13, Latomus, 76; Xenophon as Historian: The Historiography of the Hellenica, Tex Tech Univ Press (in prep). *Mailing Add:* Dept of Hist Calif State Polytech Univ 3801 W Temple Ave Pomona CA 91768

SMITH, DAVID WARNER, b Loughborough, Eng, Nov 14, 32; m 63; c 2. FOREIGN LANGUAGES. *Educ:* Univ Leeds, BA, 53, PhD, 60. *Prof Exp:* Asst prof French, Mem Univ Nfld, 60-63; assoc prof, 63-71, chmn dept, 75-80, PROF FRENCH, VICTORIA COL, UNIV TORONTO, 71- *Res:* French 18th century philosophy. *Publ:* Auth, Helvetius: A Study in Persecution, Oxford Univ, 65; ed, Correspondance generale d'Helvetius, Univ Toronto Press, Vol I, 81. *Mailing Add:* Dept of French Univ Toronto Toronto ON M5S 1A1 Can

SMITH, DUNCAN, b Providence, RI, July 18, 40; m 61; c 3. GERMAN LITERATURE, MEDIEVAL STUDIES. *Educ:* Brown Univ, AB, 61, AM, 63, PhD(Ger), 67. *Prof Exp:* From instr to asst prof, 65-72, ASSOC PROF GER, BROWN UNIV, 72- *Concurrent Pos:* Consult to pres, Tempel Steel Co, Chicago, Ill, 65-; Int res exchange bd grants, Ger Dem Repub, 72, 73. *Mem:* MLA; Am Asn Teachers Ger. *Res:* German medieval drama; German Democratic Republic literature; 16th Century Studies. *Publ:* Auth, The role of the priest in the Redentiner Osterspiel, J English & Ger Philol; Konfrontation: (Adv Ger Text), Van Nostrand, 72; The education to despair: Thomas Mann's Death in Venice, Praxis, 73; The German image of America in the 16th century, In: Festschrift Für Karl Arnd, 76; Reaction and Revolution: Anti Humanism and the Reform Movements, Ungar, 77; translr, The metacritique of espistemology, Telos, 78. *Mailing Add:* Dept of Ger Brown Univ Providence RI 02912

SMITH, EDWARD LYMAN, JR, English Language & Linguistics. See Vol II

SMITH, EDWIN BURROWS, b Mar 11, 19; m 47; c 2. FRENCH. *Educ:* Swarthmore Col, AB, 38; Brown Univ, MA, 39, PhD(Romance lang), 50. *Prof Exp:* Lectr, Sorbonne, 39-40; instr French, Brown Univ, 47-50; from instr to assoc prof, 50-64, asst to vpres, 58-64, assoc dean col lib arts, 71-72, PROF FRENCH & CHMN DEPT, WAYNE STATE UNIV, 64-, ASSOC PROVOST ACAD ADMIN, 72- *Mem:* MLA; Am Coun Teaching Foreign Lang. *Res:* Eighteenth century French studies. *Publ:* Auth, Jean-Sylvain Bailly, astronomer, mystic, revolutionary, 1736-1793, Trans Am Philos Soc. *Mailing Add:* Assoc Provost Wayne State Univ Detroit MI 48202

SMITH, ELSDON COLES, b Virginia, Ill, Jan 25, 03; m 33; c 1. ONOMASTICS. *Educ:* Univ Ill, BS, 25; Harvard Univ, LLB, 30. *Prof Exp:* Instr, Chicago Law Sch, 33-35; mem, Int Comt Onomastic Sci, 51- *Concurrent Pos:* Pvt law pract, 30- *Mem:* Am Name Soc (pres, 51-54); Am Dialect Soc; Am Folklore Soc; MLA; English Place Name Soc. *Res:* Personal names. *Publ:* Auth, Bibliography of Personal Names, NY Pub Libr, 50; The Story of Our Names, 50 & Dictionary of American Family Names, 56, Harper & Bros; Treasury of Name Lore, 67 & New Dictionary of American Family Names, 72, Harper; American Surnames, Chilton, 69; The Book of Smith, Nellen, 78. *Mailing Add:* 8001 Lockwood Ave Skokie IL 60077

SMITH, EUNICE CLARK, b Flushing, NY, Oct 29, 12; m 57. FRENCH. *Educ:* Radcliffe Col, AB, 34; Univ Wis, MA, 35, PhD(French), 45. *Prof Exp:* Instr French & Span, Lawrence Col, 41-43; teaching asst French, Bryn Mawr Col, 44-46; relief worker, Quaker Serv, Paris, 46-47; asst prof French & Span, Beloit Col, 47-49; prof French & dean, Milwaukee-Downer Col, 49-52; prof Romance lang & chmn dept, Skidmore Col, 52-58; assoc prof French, State Univ NY, Albany, 58-66; Directrice cours premier cycle, 66-78, EMER PROF FRENCH, WILLIAMS COL, 78- *Mem:* MLA; Am Asn Teachers Fr; Am Coun Teaching Foreign Lang. *Res:* Late 19th century literary movements, especially the work of Jules Renard; 20th century literature; French civilization. *Publ:* Coauth, Voix du siecle, 60 & Voix du siecle 2, 66, Harcourt. *Mailing Add:* 10 Mary Dyer Lane North Easton MA 02356

SMITH, GILBERT GRAVES, b Anson, Tex, Sept 13, 37; m 59; c 4. SPANISH LANGUAGE & LITERATURE. *Educ:* Baylor Univ, AB, 59; Tulane Univ, MA, 62; Brown Univ, PhD(Span), 71. *Prof Exp:* Instr Span, Wake Forest Univ, 62-65 & Brown Univ, 67-68; instr, Vanderbilt Univ, 68-70, asst prof, 70-72; asst prof, 72-75, asst head dept, 75-78, ASSOC PROF SPAN, NC STATE UNIV, 75-, DIR EVENING HUMANITIES PROG, 78- *Mem:* MLA; Am Asn Teachers Span & Port; SAtlantic Mod Lang Asn; Asoc Int De Hispanistas; Asn Int De Galdositas. *Res:* Galdos; Novel since 1700; film. *Publ:* Auth, Christian attitudes toward the Jews in Spanish literature, Judaism, fall 70; Problems of testing in lower-level reading courses, Hispania, 9/72; Unamuno, Ortega, and the otro, Rev Estudios Hisp, 10/72; Galdos, Tristana and letters from Concha-Ruth Morell, Anales Galdosianos, 75; Juan Pablo Forner, Twayne, 76; Prometeo en Las Novelas de Torquemana, Actas Galdos, 80; Galdos y La Hermeticidad De La Novela, Actas AIH, 82. *Mailing Add:* Dept of Foreign Lang 126A 1911 Bldg NC State Univ Raleigh NC 27650

SMITH, GORDON WINSLOW, b June 22, 07; m 36. FRENCH. *Educ:* Univ Nancy, Dipl, 28; Boston Univ, AB, 29; Harvard Univ, AM, 30. *Prof Exp:* From instr to prof, 30-72, EMER PROF MOD LANG, COLBY COL, 72- *Concurrent Pos:* Instr math, Air Force Col Training Detachment, 43-44. *Res:* French 19th century drama; the contemporary theater. *Publ:* Auth, Handbook for students of French; Manual of phonetics and conversation; Letters from Paul Bourget to Vernon Lee, 8/54 & Une vie d'Ambassadrice, 6/62, Colby Libr Quart. *Mailing Add:* 56 Burleigh St Waterville ME 04901

SMITH, HARLIE LAWRENCE, JR, b Lexington, Ky, Mar 7, 27. LINGUISTICS. *Educ:* Westminister Col, Mo, BA, 48; Univ Minn, MA, 51, PhD, 53. *Prof Exp:* Asst prof French, Tex Christian Univ, 53-55; Smith-Mundt teaching grant, Ecole Normale Superieure, Port-au-Prince, Haiti, 55-58; regional lang supvr, Foreign Serv Inst, Mex, 58-60, asst chief, field oper br, Washington, DC, 60-61, regional lang supvr, Benghazi, 61-62, Tangier, 62-63, dir, Arabic lang & area sch, Tangier, 63-66, Beirut, 66-71, CHMN DEPT NEAR EAST & AFRICAN LANG, FOREIGN SERV INST, WASHINGTON, DC, 71- *Mem:* Royal Cent Asian Soc. *Res:* Arabic; Haitian Creole. *Publ:* Coauth, Spoken Egyptian Arabic, Foreign Serv Inst, 62; Moroccan Arabic, Foreign Serv Inst, Tangier, 66; ed, Modern Written Arabic, Vol I, Foreign Serv Inst, 69; FSI Modern Written Arabic, 10.75x (ISBN-0-686-10753-5), 144.00x (ISBN 0-686-10754-3). *Mailing Add:* Int Learning Systs Inc 1715 Connecticut Ave NW Washington DC 20009

SMITH, LAWRENCE RICHARD, b Charleston, WVa, July 3, 45; m 66; c 2. GENERATIVE & COMPUTATIONAL LINGUISTICS. *Educ:* Univ Conn, BA, 67; Univ Mich, MA, 68. *Prof Exp:* ASSOC PROF LING, MEM UNIV NFLD, CAN, 68- *Concurrent Pos:* Res assoc, Inst Social & Econ Res, Mem Univ Nfld, 80 & 82. *Mem:* Ling Soc Am; Asn Comput Ling; Asn Ling & Lit Comput. *Res:* Labador Eskimo language, descriptive, computational and theoretical analysis; sociolinguistic analysis of Newfoundland, Anglo-Irish dialects; computerization of linguistic and bibliographic database. *Publ:* Auth, Some Grammatical Aspects of Labrador Inutlut (Eskimo), 77 & A Survey of the Serivational Postbases of Labrador Inutlut Eskimo, 78, Nat Mus Can; Labrador Inutlut inverted number marking exchange rules and morphological markedness, Linguistics, 79; Some categories and types of Labrador Inutlut word Derivation, Int J Am Ling, 81; Propositional nominalization in Labrador Inutlut, Linguistics, 81; coauth, A Bibliovect Guide to the Literature in English Theoretical Syntax, Info Reduction Res, 81; auth, Affixal verbal derivation and complementation in Labrador Inutlut, Ling Analysis, 82; Labrador Inutlut and the theory of morphology, Studies in Lang, 82. *Mailing Add:* Ling Dept Mem Univ Nfld St Johns's NF A1B 3X9 Can

SMITH, LOUIS FRANCIS, b Tiffin, Ohio, Nov 2, 07. FRENCH LANGUAGE & LITERATURE. *Educ:* Univ Scranton, AB, 36; Laval Univ, MA, 49; Cath Inst Paris, dipl, 67. *Prof Exp:* Instr French, Latin & Greek, Maryknoll Sem, 32-42; asst prof French, French lit & Greek, St Gregory Sem, Athenaeum of Ohio, 42-47, assoc prof French lang & lit, 47-81; RETIRED. *Mem:* MLA; Am Asn Teachers Fr. *Res:* Nineteenth century French-Canadian literature. *Mailing Add:* 6616 Beechmont Ave Cincinnati OH 45230

SMITH, MARK ISRAEL, b Washington, DC, May 29, 48; m 82. MODERN LATIN AMERICAN LITERATURE. *Educ:* Univ Md, BA, 70; Univ Calif, Berkeley, MA, 72, PhD(comp lit), 75. *Prof Exp:* Teaching asst, Univ Calif, Berkeley, 74; instr, 75-76, asst prof, 76-80, ASSOC PROF SPAN, UNIV NC, GREENSBORO, 81- *Mem:* MLA. *Res:* Latin American modernista poetry; Latin American Romanticism. *Publ:* Auth, Julian del Casal y la violencia literaria, Mod Lang Studies, 80; Jose Asuncion Silva: Contexto y estructura de su obra, Ed Tercer Mundo, 81. *Mailing Add:* Dept of Mod Lang Univ of NC Greensboro NC 27412

SMITH, MURRAY FRANCIS, b Los Angeles, Calif, Apr 27, 31; m 53; c 3. GERMANIC LANGUAGES. *Educ:* Univ Utah, BA, 56; Univ Southern Calif, MA, 61, PhD(Ger), 68. *Prof Exp:* Instr Ger, Pomona Col, 60-61; asst prof, Los Angeles State Col, 61-62; from asst prof to assoc prof, 62-76, PROF GER, BRIGHAM YOUNG UNIV, 76- *Mem:* Am Asn Teachers Ger. *Res:* German-English translation bibliographical research. *Publ:* Auth, Bibliography of German-English Translations, 1956-1960, Scarecrow, 69. *Mailing Add:* Dept of Ger Brigham Young Univ Provo UT 84601

SMITH, NATHANIEL BELKNAP, b Boston, Mass, Oct 26, 43; m 72; c 1. ROMANCE LANGUAGES, MEDIEVAL STUDIES. *Educ:* Harvard Univ, BA, 64; Yale Univ, PhD(medieval studies), 72. *Prof Exp:* Lectr & asst prof French, Smith Col, 70-72; asst prof Romance lang, Univ Ga, 73-78; ASST PROF MOD FOREIGN LANG & LIT, BOSTON UNIV, 78- *Concurrent Pos:* Sarah Moss fel, Univ Ga, 74; asst ed, Tristania, 77- & Speculum, 79- *Mem:* Int Courtly Lit Soc (secy-treas, 77-80); North Am Catalan Soc (secy, 78-82); Tristania Soc; Guilhem IX Soc Occitan & Provencal Studies. *Res:* Old French literature; Old Provencal language and literature; Catalan. *Publ:* Co-ed, Anthology of the Provencal Troubadours, Yale Univ Press, 2nd ed, 73; auth, Figures of Repetition in the Old Provencal Lyric, Univ NC Press, 76; Nature comparisons in the Roman de la Rose, Res Publica Litterarum, 79; co-ed, The Expansion and Transformations of Courtly Literature, Univ Ga Press, 80; auth, In search of the ideal landscape in the Roman de la Rose, Viator, 80; Aucassin et Nicolette as stylistic comedy, Ky Romance Quart, 80; Medieval and Renaissance in Catalan courtly literature, In: Court and Poet, Francis Cairns, Liverpool, 81. *Mailing Add:* Dept of Mod Foreign Lang & Lit Boston Univ Boston MA 02215

SMITH, PETER LAWSON, b Victoria, BC, Mar 31, 33; m 57; c 3. CLASSICS. *Educ:* Univ BC, BA, 53; Yale Univ, MA, 55, PhD, 58. *Prof Exp:* Instr classics, Univ BC, 55-56 & Yale Univ, 58-59; lectr, Carleton Univ, 59-60; from asst prof to assoc prof, 60-75, chmn dept, 63-69, assoc dean arts & sci, 70-71, dean fine arts, 72-80, PROF CLASSICS, UNIV VICTORIA, 75- *Mem:* Am Philol Asn; Class Asn Can; Class Asn Pac Northwest; Cambridge Philol Soc: Vergil Soc Am. *Res:* Latin lyric poetry; Vergil; Roman drama. *Publ:* Auth, A symbolic pattern in Vergil's Eclogues, Phoenix, winter 65; Poetic tensions in the Horatian Recusatio, Am J Philol, 1/68; Vergil's Avena and the pipes of pastoral poetry, Trans Am Philol Asn, 70; Resonance in Vergil's Eclogues, Humanities Asn Rev, 77. *Mailing Add:* Dept of Classics Univ of Victoria Victoria BC V8W 2Y2 Can

SMITH, PETER MULLEN, b Trenton, NJ, May 27, 41; m 70; c 2. GREEK LITERATURE & PHILOSOPHY. *Educ:* Harvard Univ, AB, 61, AM, 63, PhD(classics), 70. *Prof Exp:* Lectr classics, Ind Univ, 67-69; asst prof, Columbia Univ, 69-74; vis lectr, Bryn Mawr Col, 74-77; ASST PROF CLASSICS, UNIV NC, CHAPEL HILL, 77- *Mem:* Am Philol Asn; Soc Ancient Greek Philos; Am Inst Archaeol; Mod Greek Studies Asn; Class Asn Midwest & South. *Res:* Early Greek intellectual history; Homer; presocratic philosophers. *Publ:* Auth, On the hymn to Zeus in Aeschylus' Agamemnon, Am Class Studies 5 & Am Philol Asn, 80; Nursling of mortality: A study of the Homer in hymn to Aphrodite, Studien Klass Philos, P Lang, Frankfort, Bern, 81. *Mailing Add:* Dept of Classics Univ NC Chapel Hill NC 27514

SMITH, PHILIP HILLYER, JR, b New York, NY, Feb 18, 27; m 53; c 3. LINGUISTICS, COMPUTER APPLICATIONS. *Educ:* Harvard Col, BA, 47; Univ Pa, PhD(ling), 60. *Prof Exp:* Instr English as foreign lang, Georgetown Univ, 57-59; mem staff, machine transl res, 58-59, Int Bus Machines, 60-66; mem staff, lang data processing Inst Computer Res Humanities, NY Univ, 67-69; assoc prof & comput fel, comput in humanities, 69-77, PROF ARTS, UNIV WATERLOO, 77-, DIR ARTS COMPUT OFF, 74- *Concurrent Pos:* Vis prof English, Univ Andes, 57-58; Fulbright lect grant, Univ Bonn, 66-67; chmn comt comput & math ling, Inter-Am Prog Ling & Lang Teaching, 71- *Mem:* Ling Soc Am; Ont Coop Prog Latin Am & Caribean Studies; Am Dialect Soc; Asn Comput Ling. *Res:* Applications of computers to processing language data; computer-aided humanistic research. *Publ:* Coauth, A Concordance to Beowulf, Cornell Univ 69, IBM, 71; A Concordance to The Waves by Virginia Woolf, Oxford, 82. *Mailing Add:* 20 John St E Waterloo ON N2J 1E7 Can

SMITH, RAOUL NORMAND, b West Warwick, RI, May 15, 38; m 66; c 2. LINGUISTICS. *Educ:* Brown Univ, AB, 63, AM, 64, PhD(ling), 68. *Prof Exp:* Asst prof ling, Northwestern Univ, Evanston, 67-69, assoc prof, 69-81; SR MEM TECH STAFF, GEN TEL & ELECTRONICS CORP LAB, 81- *Concurrent Pos:* Consult, Stenographic Machines, Inc, 73-74; grants-in-aid, Am Coun Learned Socs & Am Philos Soc, 74; res grants, Nat Endowment for Humanities, 75 & 76-77; vis prof, Univ Maine, 78. *Mem:* Ling Soc Am; Asn Comput Ling; Asn Comput Mach; Am Dialect Soc; MLA. *Res:* Computational linguistics; mathematical linguistics; text structure. *Publ:* Auth, Interactive lexicon updating, Comput & Humanities, 72; Probabilistic Performance Models of Language, Mouton, The Hague, 73; Automatic steno translation, Proc Asn Comput Mach, 73; coauth, A Computerized lexicon of English, In: Computers in the Humanities, Edinburgh Univ, 74; auth, The philosophical alphabet of Jonathan Fisher, Am Speech, 75; A bibliography of books on language and languages printed in the United States through the year 1800, Historiographia Ling, 77; coauth, Lexical-Semantic Relations: A Comparative Survey, Ling Res Inc, 80; The Language of Jonathan Fisher 1768-1847, Publ Am Dialect Soc, 82. *Mailing Add:* GTE Lab Inc 40 Sylvan Rd Waltham MA 02254

SMITH, RICHARD LEE, Philosophy. See Vol IV

SMITH, RILEY BLAKE, b Mexico, Mo, July 7, 30. ENGLISH, LINGUISTICS. *Educ:* Univ Tex, Austin, BA, 58, PhD(English lang), 73. *Prof Exp:* Asst prof English, Tex A&M Univ, 68-70; actg asst prof, Univ Calif, Los Angeles, 70-72; lectr Anglistics, Univ Duisburg, Ger, 74-76 & Univ Wuppertal, Ger, 76-77; asst prof, 77-81, ASSOC PROF ENGLISH, BLOOMSBURG STATE COL, 81- *Concurrent Pos:* Fulbright lectr, Leningrad Polytech Inst, USSR, 81; Nat Endowment for Humanities fel, summer sem, Univ Pa, 80; Fulbright Grantee, USSR, 81. *Mem:* Ling Soc Am; Am Dialect Soc; Teachers English to Speakers Other Lang; Ling Asn Can & US; Int Sociol Asn. *Res:* American dialects; language attitudes; language policy. *Publ:* Auth, Interrelatedness of certain deviant grammatical structures of Negro nonstandard dialects, 3/69 & Hyperformation and basilect reconstruction, 3/74, J English Ling; Black English: Books for English education, English educ, 4-5/75; Research perspectives on American Black English: A brief historical sketch, Am Speech, 76; Interference in phonological research in nonstandard dialects: its implication for teaching, In:

Soziolinguistik, Hochschulverlag, Stuttgart, 78; coauth, Standard and disparate varieties of English in the United States: Educational and socio-political implications, Int J Sociol Lang, 79. *Mailing Add:* Dept of English Bloomsburg State Col Bloomsburg PA 17815

SMITH, ROBERT LESTER, b New York, NY, Nov 30, 30; m 65. HISPANIC LANGUAGES & LITERATURES. *Educ:* Univ Calif, Los Angeles, BA, 52, MA, 54, PhD(Span), 68. *Prof Exp:* Instr Span, Univ Ore, 59-65; lectr, City Univ New York, 66-68; asst prof, Queens Col, 69-76; ASSOC PROF SPAN, STETSON UNIV, DeLAND, FLA, 77- *Mem:* MLA; Am Asn Teachers Span & Port; Latin Am Studies Asn; Inst Int Lit Iberoamericana. *Res:* Spanish American literature. *Publ:* Coauth, Lecturas Intermedias, Harper, 65. *Mailing Add:* Dept of Foreign Lang Stetson Univ De Land FL 32720

SMITH, ROBERT PETER, JR, b New Orleans, La, Oct 12, 23; m 54; c 2. FRENCH LANGUAGE & LITERATURE. *Educ:* Howard Univ, AB, 48; Univ Chicago, MA, 50; Univ Pa, PhD(French), 69. *Prof Exp:* Instr French, Span & Ger, Talladega Col, 53-54; asst prof French & Span, Fisk Univ, 54-58; actg assoc dean, Col Arts & Sci, 73-74, ASSOC PROF FRENCH, RUTGERS UNIV, CAMDEN, 65-, ASSOC DEAN ACAD AFFAIRS, 74- *Concurrent Pos:* Fac acad study res award, Rutgers Univ, Cadmen, 79-80. *Mem:* Am Asn Teachers French; Int Arthurian Soc; MLA; Col Lang Asn; Fulbright Alumni Asn. *Res:* French literature of the Middle Ages; black literature of French expression. *Publ:* Auth, Aime Cesaire playwright portrays Patrice Lumumba man of Africa, 71 & The misunderstood and rejected black hero in the theatre of Aime Cesaire, 72, Col Lang Asn J; Michele Lacrosil: Novelist with a color complex, Fr Rev, 74. *Mailing Add:* Col of Arts & Sci Rutgers Univ Camden NJ 08102

SMITH, ROCH CHARLES, b Sturgeon Falls, Ont, Apr 1, 41; US citizen; m 62; c 3. FRENCH LITERATURE, SPANISH. *Educ:* Univ Fla, AB, 62, MAT, 65; Emory Univ, MA, 70, PhD(French), 71. *Prof Exp:* Instr French & Span, Palm Beach Jr Col, 65-67; teaching assoc French, Emory Univ, 69-70; from lectr to assoc prof Romance lang, 70-82, ASSOC PROF ROMANCE LANG, UNIV NC, GREENSBORO, 82- *Concurrent Pos:* Actg head, Dept Romance Lang, Univ NC, Greensboro, 81- *Mem:* MLA; Am Asn Teachers Fr; SAtlantic Mod Lang Asn; Malraux Soc. *Res:* Andre Malraux; Gaston Bachelard; Literature and philosophy. *Publ:* Auth, Le Meurtrier et la vision tragique: Essai sur les romans d'Andre Malraux, Didier, 75; Orphic Motifs in Malraux's last novels, 76 & Gaston Bachelard and the power of poetic being, 77, Fr Lit Ser; Malranx's Miroir des Limbes and the Orphic Temptation, Symp, 78; French Canadian Literature: A Not-So-Anonymous Impertinence, Sci, Technol & Humanities, 79; Gaston Bachelard, Critical Bibliog Fr Lit, 80; Gaston Bachelard and critical discourse: The philosopher of science as reader, Stanford Fr Rev, 81; Gaston Bachelard, Twayne, 82. *Mailing Add:* Dept of Romance Lang Univ of NC Greensboro NC 27412

SMITH, SIDNEY RUFUS, JR, b Greensboro, NC, Sept 18, 31. GERMANIC LANGUAGES. *Educ:* Duke Univ, AB, 53; Univ NC, Chapel Hill, PhD(Ger lang), 65. *Prof Exp:* Instr Ger, Univ NC, Chapel Hill, 62-65; asst prof Ger Philol, Univ Conn, 65-66; asst prof, 66-71, actg chmn dept Ger lang, 75-76, assoc prof, 71-79, PROF GER PHILOL, UNIV NC, CHAPEL HILL, 79-, CHMN DEPT GER LANG, 79-, CHMN LING CURRICULUM, 81- *Honors & Awards:* Stephen Freeman Award, Northeast Conf Teaching Foreign Lang, 69. *Mem:* MLA; Ling Soc Am; Am Asn Teachers Ger; Soc Advan Scand Studies. *Res:* Icelandic orthography; comparative Germanic grammar. *Publ:* Auth, Historical linguistics and the teaching of German, Ger Quart, 3/68; Orthographical criteria in Eggert Olafsson, Scand Studies, 8/69; Genealogy and urtext of Icelandic manuscripts, SAtlantic Bull, 3/71; Grammatical and lexical materials for modern Icelandic, Scand Studies, 12/78. *Mailing Add:* Dept of Ger Lang Univ of NC Chapel Hill NC 27514

SMITH, STEPHEN LAWRENCE, b Fitzgerald, Ga. FRENCH LITERATURE. *Educ:* Univ Ga, BA, 58, MA, 61; Univ Pa, PhD(French), 68. *Prof Exp:* Instr French, Univ Ga, 60-61; lectr Am hist, sociol, Univ Lyons, 64-65; from asst prof to assoc prof French, Spelman Col, 65-68; from asst prof to assoc prof, 68-76, PROF FRENCH, CENT CONN STATE COL, 76- *Mem:* Am Asn Teachers Fr; MLA; Northeast Mod Lang Asn. *Res:* Contemporary French prose. *Publ:* Coauth, Le vocabulaire de l'architecture en France de 1500 a 1550, Cahiers de lexicologie, Vols I & II, 71; J M G LeClezio: Fiction's double bind, In: Surfiction: Fiction Now and Tomorrow, Swallow, 74; LeClezio's Taoist vision, Fr Rev, 74; Martin: A portrait of the artist as a young hydrocephalic, Int Fiction Rev, 75; Mors et Anima, La Dialectique du Paradoxe plausible, Rev Pacifique, 75; auth, Fragments of landscape, scraps of decor: Maurice Roche's Compact, Yale French Studies, 78. *Mailing Add:* Dept of Mod Lang Cent Conn State Col New Britain CT 06050

SMITH, WARREN SALE, JR, b Huntington, NY, Mar 7, 41; m 64; c 2. CLASSICAL LANGUAGES. *Educ:* Wesleyan Univ, BA, 62; Ind Univ, MA, 64; Yale Univ, PhD(classics), 68. *Prof Exp:* From instr to asst prof classics, Trinity Col, Conn, 67-68; asst prof, Luther Col, 69-71; asst prof, 71-74, ASSOC PROF MOD & CLASS LANG, UNIV NMEX, 74- *Mem:* Am Philol Asn. *Res:* Greek and Latin Romance, especially Apuleius' Metamorphoses. *Publ:* Auth, Speakers in the Third satire of Persius, Class J, 69; The narrative voice in Apuleius' Metamorphoses, Trans & Proc Am Philol Asn, 72. *Mailing Add:* Dept of Mod & Class Lang Ortega Hall Univ NMex Albuquerque NM 87113

SMITH, WESLEY DALE, b Ely, Nev, Mar 26, 30. CLASSICAL PHILOLOGY. *Educ:* Univ Wash, BA, 51; Harvard Univ, MA, 53, PhD, 55. *Prof Exp:* Instr classics, Princeton Univ, 57-61; asst prof class studies, 61-66, ASSOC PROF CLASS STUDIES, UNIV PA, 66- *Concurrent Pos:* Fel, Ctr Hellenic Studies, Washington, DC, 68-69; fel, Inst Hist Med, Baltimore, 72-73; Guggenheim fel, 73. *Mem:* Am Philol Asn; Class Asn Atlantic States. *Res:* Greek and Latin literature; ancient medicine. *Publ:* Auth, The ironic plot in

Euripides' Alcestis, Phoenix, 60; So-called posession in pre-Christian Greece, Am Philol Asn Trans, 65; Disease in Euripides Orestes, Hermes, 7/67; The Hippocratic Tradition, Cornell Univ Press, 79. *Mailing Add:* Dept of Class Studies Univ of Pa Philadelphia PA 19174

SMITHER, WILLIAM JONATHAN, b Pittsburg, Kans, Dec 10, 16; m 40; c 2. SPANISH & PORTUGUESE LANGUAGE & LITERATURE. *Educ:* Univ Wichita, Kans, BA, 39; Univ Kans, MA, 40; Tulane Univ, PhD(Span), 52. *Prof Exp:* From instr to assoc prof, 47-65, dir lang lab, 59-69, chmn dept, 69-78, PROF SPAN & PORT, NEWCOMB COL, TULANE UNIV, 65- *Concurrent Pos:* Ed, Dissertations in the Hispanic languages and literatures, Hispania ann, 51-64; actg Dean, Newcomb Col, 78-79. *Mem:* MLA; SCentral Mod Lang Asn; Am Asn Teachers Span & Port; Am Coun Teaching For Lang; Nat Asn Lang Lab Dirs. *Res:* Applied linguistics, language laboratory application; twentieth century Spanish literature, Valle-Inclan. *Publ:* Coauth, An Experimental Restructuring of the Undergraduate Foreign Language Curriculum, ERIC, 66; auth, Recorded Speaking Tests in the Language Laboratory, Proc Fifth Southern Conf Lang Teaching, 70. *Mailing Add:* Newcomb Col Tulane Univ 1229 Broadway New Orleans LA 70118

SMITHERMAN, GENEVA, b Brownsville, Tenn, Dec 10, 40; div; c 1. ENGLISH LINGUISTICS, AFRO-AMERICAN LANGUAGE & LITERATURE. *Educ:* Wayne State Univ, BA, 60, MA, 62; Univ Mich, PhD, 69. *Prof Exp:* Teacher English & Latin, Detroit Pub Schs, 60-65; instr English, Eastern Mich Univ, 65-66; instr English, Wayne State Univ, 66-69, asst prof English, 69-71; lectr Afro-Am studies, Harvard Univ, 71-73; prog coordr & inst dir, Ctr Black Studies, 73-77, dir, Ctr Black Studies & assoc prof speech, dept commun, 77-80, SR RES ASSOC & PROF SPEECH, WAYNE STATE UNIV, 81- *Concurrent Pos:* Consult, Detroit Dialect Studies, 68. *Honors & Awards:* Richard Wright-Woodie King Award for Drama Criticism, Black World Mag, 75; Excellence Award in Educ Jour, Educ Press Asn, 75. *Mem:* Conf Col Compos & Commun; Col Lang Asn; Speech Commun Asn; Inst Black World. *Res:* Black cognitive and communication styles; sociolinguistics; language and speech education. *Publ:* Auth, The power of the rap: The Black idiom and the new Black poetry, Twentieth Century Lit, 10/73; Soul 'n style, monthly column, English J, 74-76; Black Language and Culture: Sounds of Soul, Paperbook Press, 75; Linguistic diversity in the classroom, In: Cultural Revolution in Foreign Language Teaching, Nat Textbk, 75; How I got over: Communication dynamics in the Black community, Quart J Speech, 2/76; Talkin & Testifyin: The Language of Black America, Houghton, Mifflin, 77; Sociolinguistic conflict in the schools, J Non-White Concerns, Wayne State Univ, 1/78; ed, Black English and the Education of Black Children & Youth, Ctr Black Studies, 81. *Mailing Add:* Ctr Black Studies Wayne State Univ Detroit MI 48202

SMITHNER, ERIC W, b Cincinnati, Ohio, Dec 27, 19; m 48; c 2. FRENCH & CLASSICS. *Educ:* Muskingum Col, AM, 42; NY Univ, MA, 53, PhD(French) 67; Univ Lordeaux, dipl, 69. *Prof Exp:* Instr French & Latin, St Mary's Col, Ind, 59-61; asst prof French, Ill State Univ, 61-63; assoc prof, State Univ NY Col Geneseo, 63-67; chmn dept foreign lang, 67-69, PROF FRENCH & LATIN, BLOOMSBURG STATE COL, 67- *Mem:* ASUP; MLA; NEA; Am Asn Teachers Fr. *Res:* Seventeenth and 18th century literature; M Proust; Proust and Krishnamurti on the literary uses of Retrouvaille. *Publ:* Auth, Les poupees interieures de Marcel Proust, Fr Rev, 9/59; Rousseau and Auguste Comte on education, J John Dewey Soc, 1/68; Descartes & Auguste Comte, Fr Rev, 3/68. *Mailing Add:* Dept of Foreign Lang Bloomsburg State Col Bloomsburg PA 17815

SMITHSON, RULON NEPHI, b Neola, Utah, Mar 8, 27; m 55; c 7. FRENCH. *Educ:* Brigham Young Univ, BA, 54, MA, 55; Columbia Univ, PhD(French), 70. *Prof Exp:* Instr French & Latin, Brigham Young Univ, 55-57; lectr French, Columbia Univ, 57-60, instr, 60-61; from instr to asst prof, Brigham Young Univ, 61-70; assoc prof, 70-73, PROF FRENCH, WESTERN ILL UNIV, 73- *Concurrent Pos:* Assoc ed, Essays in Lit, spring 74. *Mem:* MLA; Am Asn Teachers Fr; Am Coun Teaching Foreign Lang. *Res:* French historiography and literature, 19th century. *Publ:* Auth, French culture and civilization for American high school students, In: French Language Education: Culture, 71; Augustin Thierry-Social and Political Consciousness in the Evolution of a Historical Method, Droz, Geneva, 73; contribr, A Critical Bibliography of French Literature-The Nineteenth Century, 75. *Mailing Add:* 2036 W Adams Rd Macomb IL 61455

SMUTNY, ROBERT JAROSLAV, b New York, NY, Mar 21, 19; m 47. CLASSICAL PHILOLOGY. *Educ:* City Col New York, AB, 40; Columbia Univ, AM, 49; Univ Calif, PhD(classics), 53. *Prof Exp:* Instr Latin, Manlius Sch, 42, 46-49; teaching asst, Univ Calif, 51-52; asst prof class lang, Univ NMex, 53-55; assoc prof classics, 55-59, PROF CLASSICS, UNIV PAC, 59-, CHMN DEPT, 55- *Mem:* Am Philol Asn; Archaeol Inst Am. *Res:* Classical literature; text history and criticism; Latin epigraphy Publ; Auth, The text history of the epigrams of Theocritus, Univ Calif Publ Class Philol; Greek and Latin inscriptions at Berkeley, Univ Calif Publ Class Studies, 66. *Mailing Add:* 1545 W Mendocino Ave Stockton CA 95204

SMYTH, PHILIP, b Moiese, Mont, Aug 17, 19; m 47; c 2. SPANISH LANGUAGE & LITERATURE. *Educ:* Univ Wash, BA, 49, MA, 50; Univ Madrid, PhD(Romance philol), 53. *Prof Exp:* From asst prof to assoc prof mod lang, High Point Col, 54-57; dir dept foreign lang, 57-74, PROF FOREIGN LANG, N TEX STATE UNIV, 57- *Mem:* Am Asn Teachers Span & Port. *Mailing Add:* 1831 Panhandle Denton TX 76201

SNAPPER, JOHAN PIETER, b Naaldwijk, Neth, June 4, 35; US citizen; m 59; c 3. GERMANIC LANGUAGES. *Educ:* Calvin Col, BA, 58; Univ Chicago, MA, 62; Univ Calif, Los Angeles, PhD(Ger), 67. *Prof Exp:* Instr Ger, Univ Calif, Los Angeles, 64-66; asst prof Ger & Dutch, 66-73, Princess Beatrix prof Dutch lang, lit & cult, 71, assoc prof, 73-82, QUEEN BEATRIX PROF GER & DUTCH, UNIV CALIF, BERKELEY, 82-, DIR DUTCH STUDIES, 73- *Mem:* MLA; Philol Asn Pac Coast; Am Asn Teachers Ger; Int Asn Netherlandists. *Res:* German literature, Aufklärung, Sturm und Drang, classicism; 20th century Dutch literature. *Publ:* Auth, Evenbeeld en tegenbeeld: de fata morgana in Heeresma's Dagje naar het strand, Raster, spring 70; The solitary player in Klinger's dramas, Ger Rev, 3/70; Post War Dutch Literature: A Harp Full of Nails, Delta, 71; G K van het Reve en de re vistische heterokliet, Raster, fall 72; Nederlands in het buitenland: heeft het nog zin?, Ons Erfdeel, 1/77; Teeth on edge: The child in the modern Dutch short story, Rev Nat Lit, 77; From Cronus to Janus: The problem of time in the works of G K Reve, Dutch Studies, 77. *Mailing Add:* Dept of Ger Univ of Calif Berkeley CA 94720

SNEED, EDWARD, b Cambridge, Md, Aug 9, 10; m 41; c 1. FOREIGN LANGUAGES. *Educ:* Fisk Univ, BA, 41, MA, 52; Sorbonne, dipl, 53; Univ Caen, cert, 53. *Prof Exp:* Prof foreign lang & educ & dean men, Butler Col, 53-54; prof foreign lang, Ala State Col, 55-63; assoc prof French, Span & Ger, Grambling Col, 64-77; PROF FOREIGN LANG & MUSIC, SELMA UNIV 77- *Concurrent Pos:* Lectr, Drug Awareness Prog, Univ Md, East Shore & mem selection comt study in Ger, Inst Int Educ, 72; ed, Coun Develop French in La, 72-74. *Mem:* MLA; Am Fed Musicians; Am Asn Teachers Ger. *Res:* Education; music. *Publ:* Contribr, The languages and the ideas too, Americas, 62; With my banjo on my knee, Am-Ger Rev, 65; An anthology of Eastern Shore prose and poetry, Tidewater, 74. *Mailing Add:* Dept Foreign Lang Selma Univ Selma AL 36701

SNIDER, FRANK PARMER, b Palo Alto, Calif, Sept 23, 40. MODERN COMPARATIVE LITERATURE. *Educ:* Moravian Col, BA, 72; Univ Ill, MA, 75, PhD(comp lit & French), 80. *Prof Exp:* Lectr English, Univ Dakar, Senegal, 76-77; lectr French & English, Allentown Col, 80-81; vis prof comp lit, Nagoya Univ, 81-82; ACTG HEAD, DEPT COMP LIT, NOUVEL INST FR NAGOYA, JAPAN, 82- *Concurrent Pos:* Ed, Mod Lang Bull, 77- *Mem:* Educrs Africa Asn; Am Transl Asn. *Res:* Modern Japanese literature; modern Senegalese Francophone literature; American and West African literature. *Publ:* Auth, English Creative Writing for the Modern Japanese Student, Chikusa Press, Nagoya, Japan, 81; Colonialism-leadership of Senegalese writers/politicians, In: First National Africanists Symposium, Univ Ind Press, 81; English teachers in Japan as remnants of the occupation force, Mod Lang Bull Japan, 4/82. *Mailing Add:* RD 1 Box 61 Riegelsville PA 18077

SNIDER, GEORGE LOUIS, JR, b Boston, Mass, Mar 13, 33; m 62; c 3. CLASSICAL PHILOLOGY. *Educ:* Boston Col, AB, 55; Harvard Univ, MA, 57, PhD(class philol), 70. *Prof Exp:* Lectr, 61-65, asst prof, 65-77, chmn dept, 75-81, ASSOC PROF CLASSICS, McGILL UNIV, 77- *Mem:* Am Philol Asn; Archaeol Inst Am; Class Asn Can; Am Class League. *Res:* Classical mythology and religion. *Publ:* Auth, Xenophon, In: The American People's Encyclopedia, 67; Two folklore parallels to Hesiod's Prometheus-Pandora myth, Cahier Etudes Anciennes, 73; coauth, The Archaic Age of Greece, McGill, Univ Bkstore, 73. *Mailing Add:* Dept of Classics McGill Univ 855 Sherbrooke St Montreal PQ H3A 2T7 Can

SNIPES, HAMPTON KENNETH, b Rock Hill, SC, Nov 4, 42. BYZANTINE LITERATURE & HISTORY. *Educ:* Univ Mich, BA, 65; Yale Univ, MPhil, 68; Cambridge Univ, BA, 71, MA, 76; Oxford Univ, DPhil, 78. *Prof Exp:* Instr, 76-77, ASST PROF CLASSICS, UNIV NC, CHAPEL HILL, 78- *Concurrent Pos:* Nat Endowment for Humanities fel, 81. *Mem:* Am Philol Asn; AHA; Mod Greek Studies Asn; Medieval Acad Am. *Res:* Byzantine historical writing; classical scholarship in Byzantium; Greek palaeography. *Publ:* Auth, A letter of Michael Psellos to Constantine the nephew of Michael Cerularios, Greek, Roman & Byzantine Studies, 81; A newly discovered history of the Roman emperors by Michael Psellos, Jahrbuch Osterreichischen Byzantinistik, 82; Ed, Pselli Historia brevis, Teubner, Leipzig (in press). *Mailing Add:* Dept of Classics Univ of NC Chapel Hill NC 27514

SNOW, JOSEPH T, b Atlantic City, NJ, Sept 21, 41. SPANISH & PORTUGUESE LANGUAGE & LITERATURE. *Educ:* Montclair State Col, BA, 63; Univ Iowa, MA, 65; Univ Wis, PhD(Span & Port), 72. *Prof Exp:* Instr Span, Univ Wis, 69-70; from instr to asst prof Span & Port, Univ Minn, 70-72; asst prof, 73-79, ASSOC PROF SPAN & PORT, UNIV GA, 79- *Concurrent Pos:* Fel Span, Inst Res in Humanities, Univ Wis, 78-79; vis prof, Univ Calif, Davis, 78; Mellon prof Span, Univ of South, 81. *Mem:* Medieval Acad Am; Int Asn Hispanistas; Am Asn Teachers Span & Port; MLA; Mod Humanities Res Asn. *Res:* Medieval lyric; Alfonso X; La Celestina. *Publ:* Auth, Alfonso X y la Cantiga 409; un nexo posible con la Danca de la Muerte, In: Studies in Honor of Lloyd A Kasten, Univ Wis, 75; coauth, Un cuarto de siglo de interes en La Celestina: 1949-75, Hispania, 76; auth, The poetry of Alfonso X: A Critical Bibliography, Grant & Cutler, London, 77; coauth, Romancero tradicional: La Dama y el Pastor (romance, villancico, glosas), Gredos-CSMP, Madrid, 77-78; auth, The central role of the troubadour persona of Alfonso X in the Cantigas, Bull Hisp Studies, 79; co-ed, The Expansions and Tranformations of Courtly Literature, Univ Ga Press, 80; auth, An additional attestation to the popularity of Rojas character creations from an early Seventeenth century manuscript, Hispanic Rev, 80; Self conscious references and the organic narr pattern of the Cantigas de Santa Maria, In: Studies in Honor of John Keller, J de la Cuesta, 81. *Mailing Add:* Dept of Romance Lang Univ of Ga Athens GA 30602

SNOWDEN, FRANK MARTIN, JR, b York Co, Va, July 17, 11; 35; c 2. CLASSICAL PHILOLOGY. *Educ:* Harvard Univ, AB, 32, AM, 33, PhD(class philol), 44. *Hon Degrees:* LLD, Bard Col, 57; LittD, Union Col, 79. *Prof Exp:* Instr Latin & French, Va State Col, 33-36; instr classics, Spelman Col & Atlanta Univ, 36-40; from instr to assoc prof, 40-45, chmn dept, 42-77, dean col lib arts, 56-68, PROF CLASSICS, HOWARD UNIV, 45- *Concurrent Pos:* Fulbright res grant, Italy, 49-50; leader & specialist lectr, US Dept State, WAfrica, Libya, Italy, Greece & Austria, 53, India, 57, Brazil, 60; cult attache, US Embassy, Rome, 54-56; vis lectr, Foreign Serv Inst, 56-62, 66-68; mem US deleg, 10th Gen Conf, UNESCO, Paris, 58, 11th Gen Cong, 60 & mem US Nat Comn, 61; secy-ed, Am Conf Acad Deans, 59-62, chmn, 63-; Am Coun Learned Soc fel, 62-63; lectr, Archaeol Inst Am, 70-79; Nat Endowment for Humanities grant res NAfrica, 70-; vis scholar, Univ Ctr,

Va, 71-72; fel selection jury, classics, Am Acad Rome, 71-73; Woodrow Wilson Int Ctr Scholars fels, 77 & 78-79. *Honors & Awards:* Medaglia d'Oro Outstanding Work Ital Cult & Educ, Italy, 58; Charles J Goodwin Award, Am Philol Asn, 73. *Mem:* Archaeol Inst Am; Am Philol Asn; Class Soc Am Acad Rome; Vergilian Soc Am. *Publ:* Auth, The Negro in classical Italy, Am J Philol, 7/47; The Negro in ancient Greece, Am Anthrop, 1-3/48; Some Greek and Roman observations on the Ethiopian, Tradition, 60; Blacks in Antiquity: Ethiopians in the Greco-Roman Experience, Harvard Univ, 70 & 71; coauth, L'Image du Noir dans l'Art Occidental I: Des Pharaons a la Chute de l'Empire Romain, Off du Livre, 76, English transl, William Morrow, 76; contribr, Blacks, Early Christianity and . . . , In: The Interpreter's Dictionary of the Bible: Supplementary Volume, Abingdon, 76; Ethiopians and the Graeco-Roman World, In: The African Diaspora: Interpretive Essays, Harvard Univ, 76. *Mailing Add:* Dept Classics Howard Univ Washington DC 20059

SNYDER, CAROLINE GROTE, b Berlin, Ger, Dec 10, 32; US citizen; m 59; c 2. GERMAN LITERATURE, ENGLISH. *Educ:* Radcliffe Col, BA, 54, MA, 56; Harvard Univ, PhD(Ger lang & lit), 66. *Prof Exp:* Instr Ger, Luther Col, iowa, 63-65; asst prof, Wilkes Col, 66-69; asst prof, 69-73, assoc prof, 72-81, PROF ENGLISH, ROCHESTER INST TECHNOL, 81- *Mem:* MLA; Am Asn Teachers Ger; Am Soc 18th Century Studies. *Res:* Goethe; 18th century literature; history of biology. *Publ:* Auth, The helmsman-rescue motif in Goethe's Die Wahlverwandtschaften, Monatsh, spring 71; Goethes loom poem Antepirrhema, Goethezeit, Bern & Munich, 82. *Mailing Add:* Col of Gen Studies Rochester Inst Technol Rochester NY 14623

SNYDER, EMILE, b Paris, France, Aug 22, 25; US citizen. FRENCH & COMPARATIVE LITERATURE. *Educ:* Adelphi Univ, BA, 49; Harvard Univ, MA, 52; Univ Calif, Los Angeles, PhD(French), 62. *Prof Exp:* Instr French, Dartmouth Col, 59-61; asst prof French, comp lit & African lit, Univ Wash, 61-65; chmn dept African lang & lit, Univ Wis, 65-67; PROF FRENCH, COMP LIT & AFRICAN STUDIES, IND UNIV, 69- *Concurrent Pos:* Ford Area fel, wAfrica, 63-64; Rockefeller grant & vis prof, Univ Col, Dar-es-Salaam, Tanzania, 67-69; consult, Can Coun Arts, 76-; consult- reader, Nat Endowment for Humanities, 77- *Mem:* MLA; African Lit Asn. *Res:* Twentieth century French poetry; politics and literature in 20th century European literature; modern Francophone and Anglophone African literature. *Publ:* Auth, The problem of Negritude in modern French literature, Comp Lit Studies, fall 63; Aime Cesaire: Return to my Native Land, Presence Africaine, 68; coauth, French neo-African literature, In: Encycl World Lit 20th Century, Vol 2, 69; auth, A reading of Aime Cesaire's Return to my Native Land, L'Esprit Createur, fall 70; co-transl, Aime Cesaire, Cadastre, Third Press, 73; auth, Aime Cesaire: The reclaiming of the land, Dalhousie Rev, winter 73; Le malaise des independances: Apercus du nouveau roman africain d'expression francaise, Presence Francophone, spring 76; African literature, In: Africa, Ind Univ, 77. *Mailing Add:* Dept of French Ital Ind Univ Bloomington IN 47401

SNYDER, JANE MCINTOSH, b Champaign, Ill, July 25, 43. GREEK & LATIN LITERATURE. *Educ:* Wellesley Col, 65; Univ NC, Chapel Hill, PhD(classics), 69. *Prof Exp:* Asst prof, 68-73, ASSOC PROF CLASSICS, OHIO STATE UNIV, 73- *Concurrent Pos:* Am Coun Learned Soc grant-in-aid, 72. *Mem:* Am Philol Asn; Am Inst Archaeol. *Res:* Lucretius; Greek lyric poetry; Greek musical instruments. *Publ:* Auth, The Barbitos in the classical period, Class J, 4-5/72; The meaning of musaeo contingens cuncta lepore, Lucretius i 934, Class World, 3/73; The poetry of Philodemus the Epicurean, Class J, 73; Aristophanes' Agathon as Anacreon, Hermes, 74; Aigisthos and the Barbitos, Am J Archaeol, 76; Lucretius and the status of women, Class Bull, 76; Puns and Poetry in Lucretius' De Rerum Natura, B R Grüner, Amsterdam, 80; The web of song: Weaving as a metaphor in Homer and the Lyric Poets, Class J, 2-3/81. *Mailing Add:* Dept of Classics Ohio State Univ Columbus OH 43210

SNYDER, WILLIAM H, b Osborn, Ohio, Oct 3, 27; m 53; c 5. COMPARATIVE LINGUISTICS, GERMAN PHILOLOGY. *Educ:* Ohio State Univ, BA, 53; Univ Tübingen, PhD(comp ling), 64. *Prof Exp:* Asst prof Ger, Univ Pittsburgh, 64-66; assoc prof, 66-73, PROF GER & LING, STATE UNIV NY BINGHAMTON, 73- *Honors & Awards:* Pro Meritis Silver Medal, Graz Univ, 72. *Mem:* Am Asn Teachers Ger; Int Arthur Schnitzler Res Asn (secy-treas, 72-76). *Res:* Place name research; Indo-European. *Publ:* Auth, Die Rechten Nebenflüsse der Donau von der Quelle bis zur Einmündung des Inn Hydronymia Germaniae Reihe A, Lieferung 3, Franz Steiner, Wiesbaden, 64; Zur ältesten Namensschicht der rechten Nebenflüsse der Donau, 66, Zur Aeugnis der Flussnamen dür die Früh und Vorgeschiecte, Beitrage Namenforsch Neue Folge, 67; Zur Gemination in der dritten Ablautsreihe der starken Verben, In: Z für Vergleichende Sprachforschung, 71; Das st-Verbalsuffix im Baltischen und Germanischen, In: Sprachwissen schaft, 81. *Mailing Add:* Prog of Ling State Univ NY Binghamton NY 13901

SO, FRANCIS KEI-HONG, b Canton, China, Sept 15, 48; m 78; c 1. CHINESE LANGUAGE & LITERATURE. *Educ:* Nat Taiwan Univ, BA, 70; Univ Wash, MA, 74, PhD(comp lit), 79. *Prof Exp:* CHINESE ED, ASIAN AM BILINGUAL CTR, BERKELEY UNIF SCH DIST, 77- *Concurrent Pos:* Adj asst prof Chinese, Monterey Inst Int Studies, 79- *Mem:* Am Comp Lit Asn; Asn Asian Studies; Nat Asn Asian & Pac Am Educ; Philol Asn Pac Coast. *Res:* Genre theory; Chinese Islamic European relations in the middle ages. *Publ:* Auth, A brief comparative study of some English and French translations of a Chinese poem, Tamkang Rev, 4/75; Desiderata in Chinese-Western comparative studies of literature, Chung-wai wen-hsueh, 10/77; Some rhetorical conventions of the verse sections of Hsi-yu chi, In: China and the West: Comparative Literature Studies, Chinese Univ Press, 80; On science fiction and the historical context of this genre, Chung-wai wen-hsueh, 9/81; The narrator's role in early Chinese and English fiction, In: The Chinese Text: Studies in Comparative Lit, Chinese Univ Press (in press); Sir Orfeo and Pai yuan chuan: A tale in two countries, In: Essays in Commemoration of the Golden Jubilee of the Fung Ping Shan Library, Univ Hong Kong Press (in press). *Mailing Add:* 953 Dolphin Ct Rodeo CA 94572

SOADY, ANA VICTORIA, b Atlanta, Ga, June 10, 50; m 73. CLASSICAL LANGUAGES. *Educ:* Ga State Univ, AB, 71; McMaster Univ, MA, 73, PhD(Roman studies), 80. *Prof Exp:* Lectr, McMaster Univ, 74-76; ASST PROF CLASS, BROCK UNIV, 76- *Mem:* Class Asn Can; Inst Mediterranean Studies; Am Philol Asn; Am Inst Archaeol. *Res:* Roman wall paintings; ancient satire; ancient drama. *Publ:* Auth, Romance elements in Vergil's Aencid Books I-IV, Trans of the Int Conf on the Ancient Novel, 76; Primigenius, crede mihi, quicquid discis, tibi discis, Newsletter of Women's Caucus, 77. *Mailing Add:* Dept of Class Brock Univ St Catharines ON L2S 3A1 Can

SOBEJANO, GONZALO, b Murcia, Spain, Jan 10, 28; m 55. SPANISH LITERATURE. *Educ:* Univ Madrid, Lic, 50, PhD(Romance philol), 55. *Prof Exp:* Teacher Span lit, Inst Islamic Studies, Madrid, 50-51; lectr Span, Univ Heidelberg, 51-54; lectr, Univ Mainz, 54-55; lectr, Univ Cologne, 56-62, vis lectr, 62-63; from assoc prof to prof Span lit, Columbia Univ, 63-70; prof, State Univ NY Stony Brook, 70-71; A W Mellon prof, Univ Pittsburgh, 71-73; PROF SPAN LIT, UNIV PA, 73- *Concurrent Pos:* Vis prof, Queens Col, NY, 64, Univ Cologne, 78 & Univ Md, 79; vis lectr, Univ Pa, 68 & 70; Guggenheim fel, 69; redactor, Anales Galdosianos, 69- *Honors & Awards:* Premio Nacional de Literatura, 71; Lindback Award, Univ Pa, 80. *Mem:* MLA; Hisp Soc Am; Am Asn Teachers Span & Port; Asn Int Hispanistas. *Res:* Spanish literature from 1880 to the present; Spanish literature of the Golden Age, 17th century. *Publ:* Auth, Forma literaria y sensibilidad social, 67 & Nietzsche en Espana, 67, Gredos, Madrid; Novela espanola de nuestro tiempo, Prensa Espanola, Madrid, 70 & 75; Razon y suceso de la dramatica galdosiana, Anales Galdosianos, 70; En los claustros de l'alma, apuntaciones sobre la lengua de Quevedo, Sprache und Geschichte, Festschrift H Meier, Munich, 71; co-ed & contribr, Homenaje a Casalduero, Gredos, Madrid, 72; ed, Leopoldo Alas, La Regenta, Clasicos Noguer, Barcelona, 76 & Castalia, Madrid, 81; M Delibes, Cinco horas con Mario, Espasa-Calpe, Madrid, 81. *Mailing Add:* Dept of Romance Lang Univ of Pa Philadelphia PA 19174

SOBEL, ELI, b New York, NY, Jan 17, 15; m 44; c 1. GERMAN LANGUAGE & LITERATURE. *Educ:* Univ Ala, AB, 37, AM, 38; Univ Calif, PhD, 47. *Prof Exp:* Instr Ger, Univ Ala, 38-39; teaching asst, Univ Calif, 39-42, 45-46; lectr, 46-47, instr, 47-48, asst prof Ger lang, 48-56, assoc prof Ger, 56-61, PROF GER, UNIV CALIF, LOS ANGELES, 61-, ASSOC DEAN COL LETT & SCI, 58-, CHMN DEPT GER LANG, 64- *Concurrent Pos:* Guggenheim fel, 59-60; mem sr accrediting comn, Western Asn Schs & Cols, 65-; foreign lang consult, Coun Grad Schs US, 66-; referee & consult, Can Coun, 70-; selection, Nat Endowment for Humanities, 71-; chmn fac, Col Lett & Sci, Univ Calif, Los Angeles, 74- *Mem:* MLA; Am Asn Teachers Ger; Philol Asn Pac Coast (secy-treas, 48-50, vpres, 52, pres, 74-75); Renaissance and Reformation; Georg Rollenhagnen; folklore and popular literature. *Publ:* Auth, Observations on MS Berlin 414, Ger Rev, 10/48; Sebastian Brant, Ovid, and Classical Allusions in the Narrenschiff, Univ Calif, 52; Georg Rollenhagen, sixteenth-century playwright, pedagogue, and publicist, PMLA, 9/55; Alte Neue Zeitung: A Sixteenth-Century Collection of Fables, 58 & The Tristan Romance in the Meisterlieder of Hans Sachs, 63, Univ Calif; Two Meisterlieder on the seven liberal arts in MS Berlin German Quarterly 414, In: Fachliteratur des Mittelalters, Metzler, Stuttgart, 68; coauth, Liebesspiele, Oxford Univ, 70. *Mailing Add:* Dept of Ger Lang Univ of Calif Los Angeles CA 90024

SOBIN, NICHOLAS JOHN, b Clovis, NMex, July 8, 45; m 67; c 2. LINGUISTICS. *Educ:* Univ Mo-Columbia, AB, 67, AM, 69; Univ Tex Austin, PhD(ling), 74. *Prof Exp:* Res asst socioling, Ctr Res Social Behav, Univ Mo, 69; ASST PROF LING, PAN AM UNIV, 74- *Mem:* Ling Soc Am. *Res:* Syntax-semantics; bilingualism; language acquisition. *Publ:* Coauth, On the inadequacy of some recent syntactic proposals, Papers Ling, 71; Auxiliary structures and time adverbs in Black American English, Am Speech, 73; auth, On the study of syntax and bilingualism, Swallow V Proc, 76; Pragmatics of lurking, Ling Inquiry, 76; Texas Spanish and Lexical borrowing, Papers Ling, 76; On echo questions in English, Mid-Am Conf on Ling Proc, 77; Notes on the acquisition of interrogative-word questions, Eric, 77; co-auth, Describing Languages, Pan Am Univ, 77. *Mailing Add:* Dept of Ling Pan Am Univ Edinburg TX 78539

SOGA, MATSUO, b Natori-shi, Japan, Mar 2, 31; m 56; c 4. LINGUISTICS, JAPANESE. *Educ:* Tohuku Univ, BEd, 55; Eastern Mennonite Col, BA, 56; Univ Mich, MA, 58; Ind Univ, Bloomington, PhD(ling), 66. *Prof Exp:* Asst English & Ling, Int Christian Univ, Tokyo, 60-62, instr, 63-67, asst prof English & ling, 67-68; asst prof Japanese & ling, Univ Utah, 68-69; from asst prof to assoc prof, Univ Iowa, 69-71; ASSOC PROF JAPANESE, UNIV BC, 71- *Concurrent Pos:* Lectr Japanese, Ind Univ, 65-66. *Mem:* Ling Soc Am; Asn Teachers Japanese; English Lit Soc Japan. *Res:* Theoretical linguistics; language teaching; Japanese syntax. *Publ:* Auth, Similarities between Japanese and English verb derivations, Lingua, 70; Negative transportation and cross-linguistic negative evidence, 72 & Yes-no reconsidered, 73, Papers Japanese Ling. *Mailing Add:* Dept of Asian Studies Univ BC Vancouver BC V6T 1W5 Can

SOHN, HO-MIN, b Sungjoo, Korea, Oct 5, 33; m 58; c 4. KOREAN & OCEANIC LINGUISTICS. *Educ:* Seoul Nat Univ, Korea, BA, 56, MA, 65; Univ Hawaii, PhD(ling), 69. *Prof Exp:* Instr English, Duksung Women's Sr Col, Seoul, 63-65; asst prof ling, Dongguk Univ, Seoul, 69-71; asst researcher, Pac & Asian Ling Inst, 71-72, asst prof Korean, 72-76, ASSOC PROF KOREAN, UNIV HAWAII, 76- *Concurrent Pos:* Univ Auckland fel ling, 70-71; ed, Int Circle of Korean Ling, 75-77. *Mem:* Ling Soc Am; Asn Asian Studies; MLA; Int Circle Korean Ling. *Res:* Korean syntax and semantics; Micronesian languages; syntactic and semantic theory. *Publ:* Coauth, A Ulithian Grammar, Australian Nat Univ, 73; auth, Relative clause formation in Micronesian languages, Oceanic Ling, 73; Modals and speaker- hearer perspectives in Korean, Papers in Ling, 74; Retrospection in Korean, Lang Res, 75; ed, The Korean Language: Its Structure and Social Projection, Univ Hawaii, 75; auth, Woleaian Reference Grammar, 75 & coauth, Woleaian-English Dictionary, 76, Univ Press Hawaii; auth, Goal and source in Korean locatives with reference to Japanese, Eoneohag, 77. *Mailing Add:* Dept of EAsian Lang Univ Hawaii East-West Rd Honolulu HI 96822

SOKEL, WALTER H, b Vienna, Austria, Dec 17, 17; nat US; m 61. GERMAN LANGUAGE & LITERATURE. *Educ:* Rutgers Univ, AB, 41, MA, 44; Columbia Univ, PhD(Ger), 53. *Prof Exp:* Instr Ger, Ohio State Univ, 46-47; instr, Temple Univ, 47-53; from instr to assoc prof Ger & humanities, Columbia Univ, 53-64; prof Ger, Stanford Univ, 64-73; COMMONWEALTH PROF GER & ENGLISH LIT, CTR ADVAN STUDIES, UNIV VA, 73- *Concurrent Pos:* Am Coun Learned Soc grant-in-aid, 62; exchange prof, Univ Hamburg, 65; Nat Endowment for Humanities sr fel, 71-72; vis prof Ger, Harvard Univ, 78-79. *Honors & Awards:* Alex von Humboldt Res Prize, Fed Repub Ger, 82. *Mem:* Int Brecht Soc (vpres, 74-); MLA; Am Asn Teachers Ger; Am Comp Lit Asn. *Res:* Modern German literature; the existentialist tradition; intellectual history and literature. *Publ:* Auth, The Writer in Extremis, Stanford Univ, 59; ed, An Anthology of German Expressionist Drama, Anchor Bks, 63; auth, Franz Kafka: Tragik und Ironie, Langen-Müller, Munich, 64; Franz Kafka, Columbia Univ, 66; Brecht's concept of character, Comp Drama, 71; Demaskierung und Untergang wilh Reprasentaz, In: Herkomen und Erneuerung, Max Niemeyer Verlag, 76; Perspectives and truth in The Judgment, In: The Problem of The Judgment, 77 & The three endings of Josef K, In: The Kafka Debate, 77, Gordian. *Mailing Add:* Dept of Ger Cocke Hall Univ of Va Charlottesville VA 22903

SOLA, DONALD FREDERICK, b Herkimer, NY, Feb 24, 22; m 46; c 3. GENERAL LINGUISTICS. *Educ:* Cornell Univ, AB, 52, PhD, 58. *Prof Exp:* From instr to asst prof Span ling, 53-68, assoc prof, 68-80, PROF MOD LANG & LING, CORNELL UNIV, 80- *Concurrent Pos:* Mem exec comt, Inter-Am Prog Ling & Lang Teaching, 63- *Mem:* Ling Soc Am; MLA; AAAS. *Res:* Sociolinguistics; language policy; South American Indian languages. *Mailing Add:* Div of Mod Lang Cornell Univ Ithaca NY 14850

SOLAN, LAWRENCE M, b New York, NY, May 7, 52. LINGUISTICS, LAW. *Educ:* Brandeis Univ, BA, 74; Univ Mass, Amherst, PhD(ling), 78; Harvard Univ, JD, 82. *Prof Exp:* Lectr legal studies, Brandeis Univ, 81-82; RES & WRITING, 82- *Concurrent Pos:* Consult, Cornell Univ, 79-82; instr, Harvard Exten Sch, 81-82. *Mem:* Ling Soc Am. *Res:* Child language and the theory of grammar; syntactic theory; linguistics and law. *Publ:* Contribr, University of Massachusetts Occasional Papers in Linguistics, Vol III & co-ed, Papers in the Structure and Development of Child Language, Univ Mass Dept Ling, 78; contribr, Studies in First and Second Language Acquisition, Newbury House, 79; coauth, A reevaluation of the basic operations hypothesis, Cognition, 79; auth, Contrastive stress and children's interpretation of pronouns, J Speech & Hearing Res, 80; contribr, Language Acquisition and Linguistic Theory, Mass Inst Technol Press, 81; Linguistic Symposium on Romance Languages: 9, Georgetown Univ Press, 81; auth, Pronominal Reference: Child Language and the Theory of Grammar, D Reidel (in press). *Mailing Add:* 594 Ramapo Rd Teaneck NJ 07666

SOLA-SOLE, JOSEP M, b Igualda, Spain, July 18, 24; m 59; c 2. PHILOLOGY, MEDIEVAL SPANISH LITERATURE. *Educ:* Univ Barcelona, Lic, 48, PhD, 59; Ecole Pratique Hautes Etudes, Sorbonne, dip, 55. *Prof Exp:* Asst Semitic philol, Centre Nat Rech Sci French, 50-52; lectr Span philol & lit, Univ Tübingen, 52-61; assoc prof Span philol & lit & Semitic philol, 61-65, chmn Span sect, 65-74, PROF SPAN PHILOL & LIT & SEMITIC PHILOL, CATH UNIV AM, 65-, DIR SUMMER SCH SPAIN, 68-, CHMN MOD LANG DEPT, 78- *Concurrent Pos:* Hon mem, Peruvian Inst Advan Islamic Studies, 60; Am Philos Soc fel, 64; Oppenheimer fel, 67-68 & 74-75; Am Coun Learned Soc grant-in-aid, 69; ed, Hispam, 73-; dir consult, Can Res Coun & Nat Endowment for Humanities, 76-; ed, Puvill, 77- *Honors & Awards:* Span Coun Sci Res Prize, 59. *Mem:* Am Orient Soc; MLA; Cath Bibl Asn; SAtlantic Mod Lang Asn; Acad Norteamericana de la Lengua Espanola; corresp mem Hisp Soc Am. *Res:* Spanish and Semitic philology; impact of the Semitic world in Spanish culture. *Publ:* Ed, Estudios literarios . . . dedicados A H Hatzfeld, 74, auth, Llibre de doctrina by Jaume D'Arago, 78 & coauth, Catalan studies, 78, Hispam, Barcelona; Los Sonetos l Italico Mddo Del Marques de Shatillana, 80, La Danca General Del muerte, 81, El Alfabeto Monetario de la Cecas Llibo Fenices, 81, ed, Hispania Judaica I and II, 81-82 & Sobre Arabes, Judios y Marranos, 82, Puvill, Barcelona. *Mailing Add:* Dept of Mod Lang Cath Univ of Am Washington DC 20064

SOLBRIG, INGEBORG HILDEGARD, b Weissenfels, Ger, July 31, 23; US citizen. GERMAN LANGUAGE & LITERATURE. *Educ:* State Sci Col, Halle, Ger, dipl chem, 48; San Francisco State Col, BA, 64; Stanford Univ, MA, 66, PhD(Ger & humanities), 69. *Prof Exp:* Asst prof Ger, Univ RI, 69-70, Univ Tenn, Chattanooga, 70-72 & Univ Ky, 72-75; assoc prof, 75-81, PROF GER, UNIV IOWA, 81- *Concurrent Pos:* Old Gold fel, Univ Iowa, 77; Grant-in-aid, Am Coun Learned Soc, 79; German Acad Exchange Serv grant, 80. *Honors & Awards:* Gold Medal, Hammer-Purgstall Soc, Austria, 74. *Mem:* MLA; Int Asn Ger Studies; Am Asn Teachers Ger; Am Soc 18th-Century Studies; Am Goethe Soc. *Res:* Goethe period and earlier 20th century; influence of Near-Eastern literature on German literature; women's studies. *Publ:* Auth, Hammer-Purgstall und Goethe, Herbert Lang, Bern, 73; ed, Rilke Heute, Frankfurt, 75; ed & transl, Reinh Goering/Seeschlacht/ Seabattle, Stuttgart, 77; numerous articles in int journals. *Mailing Add:* Dept of Ger Univ of Iowa Iowa City IA 52242

SOLE, CARLOS ALBERTO, b Panama, Sept 9, 39; m 64; c 1. SPANISH LANGUAGE. *Educ:* Georgetown Univ, BSL, 60, PhD(Span ling), 66. *Prof Exp:* Instr Span, Georgetown Univ, 64-66; asst prof Romance lang & lit, Harvard Univ, 66-70; ASSOC PROF SPAN & COORDR LOWER DIV PROG, UNIV TEX, AUSTIN, 70- *Concurrent Pos:* Gen ed Span ser, Charles Scribners Sons, Publ, NY, 73- *Mem:* MLA; Am Asn Teachers Span & Port; Latin Am Asn Ling & Philol; Am Coun Teaching Foreign Lang. *Res:* Spanish American dialectology; Spanish linguistics. *Publ:* Auth, Morfologia del adjetivo con -al, -ero, -ico, -oso, 66 & Bibliografia del espanol en America, 1920-1967, 69, Georgetown Univ; Bibliografia sobre el espanol en America, 1967-1971, Anuario de Letras, 72; coauth, Modern Spanish Syntax: A Study in Contrast, 77 & Foundation Course in Spanish, 4th ed, 78, Heath; Espanol: Ampliacion y repaso, Scribners, 82. *Mailing Add:* 7304 Lamplight Lane Austin TX 78731

SOLE, YOLANDA RUSSINOVICH, b Zagreb, Yugoslavia, Feb 4, 39; US citizen; m 64; c 1. SPANISH LINGUISTICS, SOCIOLINGUISTICS. *Educ:* Georgetown Univ, BS, 61, PhD(Span ling), 66. *Prof Exp:* Asst prof Span & ling, Tufts Univ, 66-70; asst prof, 70-76, ASSOC PROF LING, UNIV TEX, AUSTIN, 77- *Concurrent Pos:* Assoc ed, Hispania, 77- *Mem:* MLA; Am Asn Teachers of Span & Port; Am Coun Teaching Foreign Lang; Nat Asn Bilingual Educ; Latin Am Asn Ling & Philol. *Res:* Spanish syntax; Latin American and United States-Spanish language; language attitudes. *Publ:* Auth, Hacer: Verbo Funcional y Lexical, Georgetown Univ, 66; Correlaciones socioculturales del uso de tu, vos y used en Argentina, Peru y Puerto Rico, 70 & El elemento mitico-simbolico en el Amadis de Gaula, 74, Thesaurus; Language maintenance and language shift among Mexican-American college students, J of Southwest Ling Asn, 75; Sociocultural and sociopsychological factors in differential language retentiveness by sex, In: The Sociology of Language of American Women, Trinity, 76; Morphosyntactic variants in Texas Spanish, In: Lektos, 76; Language attitudes towards Spanish among Mexican American college students, J of Southwest Ling Asn, 77; coauth, Modern Spanish Syntax: A Study in Contrasts, Heath, 77. *Mailing Add:* Dept Span & Port Univ Tex Austin TX 78712

SOLECKI, JAN JOZEF, b Mar 23, 19; Can citizen; m 53; c 4. RUSSIAN LANGUAGE, ECONOMICS. *Educ:* London Sch Econ, BCommun, 48; Univ BC, MA, 61; Univ Wash, MA, 63. *Prof Exp:* From instr to asst prof, 64-71, ASSOC PROF RUSS LANG, UNIV BC, 71-, DIR SUMMER WORKSHOP, 69- *Mem:* Can Asn Slavists (secy-treas, 67-68); Am Econ Asn; Am Asn Teachers Slavic & E Europ Lang; Am Asn Asian Studies; Can Inst Int Affairs. *Res:* Forest resources and industries in Communist countries; Sino- Soviet economic and politcal relations; methods of teaching Russian and Polish. *Publ:* Auth, Forest resources and their utilization in the USSR, Vol 39, No 2 & Forest resources and their utilization in Communist China, 6/64, Forestry Chronicle; Economic Aspects of Fishing Industry in Mainland China, 66 & Russia, China, Japan: Economic Growth Resources, Forest Industries, 67, Univ BC; The reasons for and the methods of teaching Russian to scientists, Russ Lang J, 10/67; A Review of the USSR Fishing Industry Ocean Management, 5: 97-123; coauth (with Robert N North), The Soviet Forest Products Industry: Its Present and Potential Exports, Can Salvonic Papers, 9/77. *Mailing Add:* Dept of Slavonic Studies Univ BC Vancouver BC V6T 1W5 Can

SOLERA, RODRIGO, b San Jose, Costa Rica, Oct 20, 28; m; c 1. ROMANCE LANGUAGES. *Educ:* Cent Mo State Col, AB, 53; Univ Kans, MA, 58, PhD(Span & French), 64. *Prof Exp:* Instr Span, Univ Kans, 63-64; asst prof, Pa State Univ, University Park, 64-72; ASSOC PROF SPAN, MILLERSVILLE STATE COL, 72- *Mem:* MLA; Am Asn Teachers Span & Port. *Res:* Spanish American literature, history and culture. *Mailing Add:* Dept of Foreign Lang Millersville State Col Millersville PA 17551

SOLES, DEBORAH HANSEN, b Erie, Pa, Dec 24, 47; m 71. PHILOSOPHY. *Educ:* George Washington Univ, AB, 69; Johns Hopkins Univ, MA, 73, PhD(philos), 75. *Prof Exp:* ASST PROF PHILOS, WICHITA STATE UNIV, 73- *Concurrent Pos:* Kellog Found Admin intern, Off of the Pres, Wichita State Univ, 77-78. *Mem:* Am Philos Asn; AAUP; Southwestern Philos Soc. *Res:* Theory of knowledge; philosophy of language. *Publ:* Auth, Manufacturing and merchandising: The new pedagogy, J of Thought, winter 80; Russell's casual theory of meaning, Russell, summer 81; Some ways of going wrong: On mistakes, In: On Certainty, Philos & Phenomenol Res, 6/82; Hume, Language and God, Philos Topics, summer 81. *Mailing Add:* Dept of Philos Box 74 Wichita State Univ Wichita KS 67208

SOLETSKY, ALBERT Z, b New York, NY, Apr 25, 37. SPANISH LANGUAGE & LITERATURE. *Educ:* Columbia Univ, AB, 58, MA, 61, PhD(Span), 68. *Prof Exp:* Asst prof, 68-74, ASSOC PROF SPAN, FAIRLEIGH DICKINSON UNIV, TEANECK, 74- *Mem:* MLA; AAUP. *Res:* Hispanic linguistics; Spanish American literature; 19th and 20th century Spanish literature. *Publ:* Contribr, Articles to professional journals. *Mailing Add:* 124 W 79th St New York NY 10024

SOLLENBERGER, HOWARD E, b North Manchester, Ind, Apr 28, 17; m 45; c 3. LINGUISTICS, SOCIAL SCIENCE. *Educ:* Manchester Col, BA, 41. *Hon Degrees:* LLD, Manchester Col, 63. *Prof Exp:* Dir foreign serv inst, Chinese Lang Sch, 47-50; asst dean sch lang, 55-56, dean sch lang & area studies, 56-62, dean sch lang studies, 62-65, actg dir inst, 65-66, assoc dir, 66-71, ASSOC PROF CHINESE STUDIES, FOREIGN SERV INST, US DEPT STATE, 51-, DIR FOREIGN SERV INST, 71- *Concurrent Pos:* Mem, Adv Comt Lang Develop, 62; adv comt, Georgetown Sch Lang, 64-; adv comt, Int Affairs Sem of Washington, DC, 66- *Honors & Awards:* US Dept State Superior Honor Award, 61. *Res:* Descriptive linguistics, especially Chinese; China area studies. *Mailing Add:* 1287 Berry Pl McLean VA 22101

SOLLORS, WERNER, American Studies, Comparative Literature. See Vol II

SOLMSEN, FRIEDRICH (HEINRICH RUDOLF), b Bonn, Ger, Feb 4, 04; nat US; m 32. CLASSICAL PHILOLOGY. *Educ:* Univ Berlin, PhD, 28; Cambridge Univ, PhD, 36. *Hon Degrees:* PhD, Univ Kiel, 65, PhD, Univ Bonn, 68. *Prof Exp:* Privatdocent, Berlin, 29-33; prof, Olivet Col, Mich, 37-40; from acting asst prof to prof classics, Cornell Univ, 40-62, chmn dept, 53-62; prof, Inst Res Humanities & dept classics, 62-64, Moses Slaughter prof class studies, 64-74, MOSES SLAUGHTER EMER PROF CLASS STUDIS, UNIV WIS-MADISON, 74- *Concurrent Pos:* Guggenheim fel, 47-48; Fulbright prof, Univs Frankfort & Kiel, 58-59; Herbert F Johnson vis prof, Univ Wis, 60-61; Fulbright prof, St Andrew's Univ, 65; vis prof, Swarthmore Col, 70 & Yale Univ 72. *Honors & Awards:* Charles J Goodwin Award of Merit. *Mem:* Am Philol Asn; Am Philos Soc; British Acad; hon mem, Soc Promotion Hellenic Studies. *Res:* Ancient philosophy and rhetoric; Greek and Latin poetry. *Publ:* Auth, Antiphonstudien, Weidmann, Ger, 31; Plato's Theology, 42, Hesiod and Aeschylus, 49 & Aristotle's System of the Physical

World, 60, Cornell Univ; Electra and Orestes, three recognitions in Greek tragedy, Trans Netherlands Acad, 67; Kleine Schriften (3 vols), Olms, Hildesheim, 68 & 82; Hesiodi, Theogonia opera et dies Scutum, Oxford Class Texts, 70; Intellectual Experiments of the Greek Enlightenment, Princeton Univ, 75; Isis among the Greeks and Romans, Harvard Univ Press, 79. *Mailing Add:* 810 Old Mill Rd Chapel Hill NC 27514

SOLOMON, BERNARD SIMON, b New York, NY, June 10, 24. CHINESE LANGUAGE & THOUGHT. *Educ:* City Col New York, BS, 46; Harvard Univ, MA, 49, PhD(Chinese historiography), 52. *Prof Exp:* Res asst Chinese-English dict proj, Harvard Univ, 52-58; asst prof humanities, State Univ NY Col New Paltz, 59-62; from asst prof to assoc prof, 62-70, PROF CHINESE, QUEENS COL, NY, 70- *Concurrent Pos:* Fulbright award, Italy, 55-56; Nat Found for Humanities sr fel, 67-68; Am Coun Learned Socs fel, 77-78. *Res:* Chinese historiography. *Publ:* Auth, One is no number in China and the West, Harvard J Asiatic Studies, 6/54; The Shun-tsung Shih-lu: The Veritable Record of the T'ang Emperor Shun-tsung, Harvard Univ, 55; The assumptions of Hui-Tzu, Monumenta Serica, 69. *Mailing Add:* Dept of Class & Orient Lang Queens Col Flushing NY 11367

SOLOMON, JANIS VIRGINIA LITTLE, b Ranger, Tex, June 9, 38; m 78. GERMAN LITERATURE. *Educ:* Univ Tex, Austin, BA, 60; Yale Univ, MA, 64, PhD(Ger lit), 65. *Prof Exp:* From instr to assoc prof, 65-78, actg chmn dept, 67-71, chmn dept Ger, 71-79 & 81-82, dir mod Europ studies, 74-79, PROF GER, CONN COL, 81- *Concurrent Pos:* Alexander von Humboldt-Stiftung fel, 72-73; Yale fac fel, 75. *Mem:* MLA; Am Asn Teachers Ger. *Res:* Baroque lyric; modern drama; expressionism. *Publ:* Auth, Liebesgedichte & Lebensgeschichte bei Martin Opitz, Deut Vierteljahrsschrift für Literaturgeschichte, Vol 42, 161-181; contribr, Lebendige Form (Henelfestschrift), Fink, Munich, 70; Europäische Tradition & deutsche Barockliteratur, Francke, Bern, 73; auth, Die weltliche Lyrik des Martin Opitz, Francke, Bern & Munich, 73; Büchner's Dantons Tod: History as theatre, Ger Rev, Vol 54, 9-19; Further Dutch Sources Used by Martin Opitz, Neophilologus, Vol 53, 157-175; contribr, Arbeit als Thema in der deutschen Literatur vom Mittelalter bis zur Gegenwart, Athenäum, Königstein, 79; auth, Die Kriegsdramen Reinhard Goerings, Francke, Bern & Munich (in press). *Mailing Add:* Dept of Ger Conn Col New London CT 06320

SOLZBACHER, WILLIAM ALOYSIUS, b Honnef, Ger, Feb 1, 07; US citizen; m 31; c 4. LINGUISTICS, HISTORY. *Educ:* Univ Cologne, MA, 30, PhD(sociol), 32. *Prof Exp:* Foreign rel secy, Kolping Soc, Cologne, 31-33; freelance writer & lectr, US & Europe, 33-41; traveling secy, World Student Serv Fund, NY, 41-42; assoc ed, Cath Intercontinental Press, 42-50; asst prof hist & polit sci, Col Mt St Vincent, 50-51; chief prog schedule sect, Voice of Am, US Dept State, 51-53; educ dir, Student Tours, Affil Schs & Sem Int Studies & Training, 53-54; chief monitoring staff, Voice of Am, US Inform Agency, 54-67, off policy appl, 67-77. *Concurrent Pos:* Chmn, Int Comn Esperanto & Sociol, 52- *Mem:* Ling Soc Am; MLA; Am Asn Advan Slavic Studies; Polynesian Soc; Esperanto Asn North Am (pres, 48-53). *Res:* Language problems in international communications; history of Esperanto; the polynesian languages. *Publ:* Coauth, Esperanto: The World Interlanguage, Yoseloff, 48, 59 & 66; Say it in Esperanto, Dover, 57; contribr, Enciklopedio de Esperanto, Lit Mondo, Budapest, 33 & 34; contribr to various encycl & yearbks. *Mailing Add:* 6030 Broad St Bethesda MD 20816

SOMMERS, MARGARET PAULA, b Cheyenne, Wyo, May 23, 42. FRENCH LITERATURE. *Educ:* Univ Calif, Berkeley, BA, 60; Stanford Univ, MA, 66, PhD(French), 71. *Prof Exp:* Asst prof, 71-77, ASSOC PROF FRENCH, UNIV MO-COLUMBIA, 77- *Mem:* MLA; Am Asn Teachers Fr; Renaissance Soc Am. *Res:* French Renaissance literature. *Publ:* Auth, Jacques Tahureau's Art of Satire, Fr Rev, 3/74; Montaigne's Etiquette: The indispensable vanity, Romance Notes, autumn 74; D'Aubigne's Baron de Faeneste: Courtier, Matamore, Picaro, Fr Rev, 1/76. *Mailing Add:* Dept of Romance Lang Univ of Mo Columbia MO 65201

SOMMERVILLE, MARIE-THERESE, b Versailles, France, Jan 27, 21; US citizen; m 47. ROMANCE LANGUAGES. *Educ:* Univ Paris, Lic en droit, 41, Lic es lett, 43; Inst Etudes Polit, Paris, dipl, 41. *Prof Exp:* Instr French, Pomona Col, 46-47; instr, George Washington, Univ, 47-49; from asst prof to prof, US Naval Intel Sch, Washington, DC, 49-63; br chief, Defense Lang Inst, Washington, DC, 63-65; PROF FRENCH, SWEET BRIAR COL, 65- *Mem:* Am Asn Teachers Fr. *Res:* French linguistics. *Publ:* Auth, Montherlant: Dramaturge de la nuit, SAtlantic Mod Lang Bull, 5/74. *Mailing Add:* Dept of Mod Lang Sweet Briar Col Sweet Briar VA 24595

SONDRUP, STEVEN PREECE, b Salt Lake City, Utah, May 27, 44. COMPARATIVE & GERMANIC LITERATURE. *Educ:* Univ Utah, BA, 68; Harvard Univ, AM, 69, PhD(Ger), 74. *Prof Exp:* Assoc prof, 73-80, PROF COMP LIT, BRIGHAM YOUNG UNIV, 80- *Mem:* MLA; Am Comp Lit Asn; Soc Advan Scand Studies; Hofmannsthal-Gesellschaft. *Res:* Hugo von Hofmannsthal; linguistic and computational stylistics; turn-of-the-century literary relations. *Publ:* Auth, Hofmannsthal and the French Symbolist Tradition, Herbert Lang Verlag, 76; ed, Konkordanz zu den Gedichten Hugo von Hofmannsthals, Brigham Young Univ, 77; Arts and Inspiration, Brigham Young Univ, 80; Konkordunz zu den Gedichten Conrad Ferdinand Meyers, Niemeyer Verlag, 82. *Mailing Add:* 1346 S 18th E Salt Lake City UT 84108

SONG, SEOK CHOONG, b Seoul, Korea, Oct 2, 27; m 58; c 4. LINGUISTICS. *Educ:* Yonsei Univ, BA, 56, MA, 58; Ind Univ, PhD(ling), 67. *Prof Exp:* Instr English, Yonsei Univ, 59-61; from instr to asst prof, Sogang Col, Korea, 61-62; lectr Korean, Ind Univ, 64-65; asst prof ling, 65-74, assoc prof, 74-80, PROF LING, ORIENT & AFRICAN LANG, MICH STATE UNIV, 80- *Mem:* Ling Soc Am; Int Ling Asn. *Res:* Theoretical and Far Eastern linguistics. *Publ:* Coauth, An Intensive Course in English, Tong-myung, 58. *Mailing Add:* Dept of Ling Mich State Univ East Lansing MI 48823

SONKOWSKY, ROBERT PAUL, b Appleton, Wis, Sept 16, 31; m 56; c 3. CLASSICS. *Educ:* Lawrence Col, AB, 54; Univ NC, PhD, 58. *Prof Exp:* Teaching asst, Univ NC, 55-56, teaching fel, 57-58; from instr to asst prof classics, Univ Tex, 58-61; assoc prof, Univ Mo, 62-63; chmn dept, 64-78, ASSOC PROF CLASSICS, SPEECH & THEATRE ARTS, UNIV MINN, MINNEAPOLIS, 63- *Concurrent Pos:* Johnson fel, Inst Res Humanities, 61-62; selection juror, Am Acad Rome Fels, 70. *Mem:* Am Philol Asn: Class Asn Mid W & S; Speech Commun Asn; Am Theatre Asn; Int Soc Chronobiol. *Res:* Ancient rhetoric and drama; Latin literature. *Publ:* Auth, An aspect of delivery in ancient rhetorical theory, Trans & Proc Am Philol Asn, 59; Scholarship and showmanship, 61 & Greek euphony and oral performance, 67, Arion; A fifteenth century rhetorical opusculum, Class Medieval & Renaissance Studies for B L Ullman, 69; Euphantastik Memory and Delivery in the Classical Rhetorical Tradition, Rhetoric, Brown & Steinmann, 79. *Mailing Add:* Dept of Classics Univ of Minn Minneapolis MN 55455

SONNENFELD, ALBERT, b Berlin, Ger, July 22, 34; US citizen; m 55; c 2. FRENCH & COMPARATIVE LITERATURES. *Educ:* Oberlin Col, AB, 55; Princeton Univ, AM, 57, PhD, 58. *Prof Exp:* Instr French, 58-60, from asst prof to prof French & Europ lit, 60-76, PROF FRENCH & COMP LIT, PRINCETON UNIV, 76-, CHMN DEPT ROMANCE LANG, 78- *Concurrent Pos:* Humanities Res Coun grants, Princeton Univ, 59, 62, 63, 81 & 82; lectr, Adult Sch, 61-, Philip Freneau preceptorship, 62-65; vis lectr, Westminster Choir Col, 61-62; Am Philos Soc grant, 63; ed consult, Ed Bd, Idioma, 63-67; vis prof, Rutgers Univ, 66; vis prof, Univ Reading & Fulbright sr lectr, Eng, 67-68; assoc ed, Fr Rev, 68-71; master, Princeton Inn Col, 70-73; adv ed, J Europ Studies, 70-; vis prof, Dartmouth Col, 71-82; adv ed, Nineteenth Century Fr Studies, 72-; consult, Linguaphone Inst London, 75-; Nat Endowment for Humanities sr fel, 77-78; dir, Nat Endowment for Humanities summer seminar, 76 & 80; Am Philos Soc grant, 82. *Honors & Awards:* Chevalier des Palmes Academiques, French Govt, 77. *Mem:* Athenaeum, London; MLA; Am Asn Teachers Fr; Soc Fr Prof Am; Am Comp Lit Asn. *Res:* Erotic phantasm and poetic creation; 20th century European fiction and theater; modern Catholic novel, especially the novels of Georges Bernanos. *Publ:* Auth, L'Oeuvre poetique de Tristan Corbiere, Presses Univ France, 60; Thirty-six French Poems, Houghton, 60; coauth, Temoins de l'homme, Schribner, 65; contribr, Graham Greene, In: The Vision Obscured, Fordham Univ, 70; La Guerre, In: L'Esprit Moderne dans la Litterature Francaise, 72 & Mallarme's disappearing visions, In: Festrschift for C A Hackett, 73, Oxford Univ; Crossroads: Studies in the Catholic Novel, Fr Lit Publ, 82. *Mailing Add:* 1 Westcott Rd Princeton NJ 08540

SONNENFELD, MARION WILMA, b Berlin, Ger, Feb 13, 28. GERMAN. *Educ:* Swarthmore Col, BA, 50; Yale Univ, MA, 51, PhD, 56. *Prof Exp:* From instr to asst prof Ger, Smith Col, 54-62; assoc prof, Wells Col, 62-67, chmn dept, 65-67; from assoc prof to prof, 67-77, DISTINGUISHED TEACHING PROF GER, STATE UNIV NY COL FREDONIA, 77- *Concurrent Pos:* Mem fac, Middlebury Col Ger Sch, 61-; asst dir, Wells Col Summer Sch Ger, 64, dir, 65-67; actg dean arts & humanities, 80-81; actg dir, Int Educ, 80-81; coordr, Stefan Zweig Symp, Fredonia, 81. *Honors & Awards:* State Univ NY Summer Award, 80. *Mem:* MLA; Int Germanisten Ver; Am Asn Teachers Ger. *Res:* Novelle; Kafka; the German drama. *Publ:* Auth, An etymological interpretation of the Hagen figure, Neophilologus, 57; Paralleles in Novelle und Verwandlung, Symp, 59; Amerika und Prozess als Bildungsromanfragmente, Ger Quart, 62; transl, Kleist's Amphitryon, Ungar, 62; ed, Wert und Wort, Wells Col, 65; ed, Gepragte Form, Fredonia, 75; transl, Three Plays by Hebbel, 74 & co-transl, The Narrative Prose of C F Meyer, 76, Bucknell Univ. *Mailing Add:* Dept of Foreign Lang & Lit State Univ NY Fredonia NY 14063

SOONS, C ALAN, b Grantham, Eng, Feb 9, 25; m; c 3. SPANISH LITERATURE. *Educ:* Univ Sheffield, BA, 51, MA, 53; Harvard Univ, PhD(Romance lang & lit), 71. *Prof Exp:* Asst lectr Span, Univ St Andrews, 55-57; from lectr to sr lectr, Univ W Indies, Jamaica, Barbados & Trinidad, 57-68; vis assoc prof Romance lang, Univ Mass, Amherst, 68-70; vis assoc prof Span, Rice Univ, 71-72; assoc prof, 72-81, PROF SPAN, STATE UNIV NY BUFFALO, 81- *Concurrent Pos:* Vis fel, St Catherine's Col, Oxford, 80. *Mem:* Asoc Int Hispanistas; Soc Saint-Simon. *Res:* Late medieval and Renaissance literature; Spanish-American literature of the colonial period; folk-narrative. *Publ:* Auth, Ficcion y comedia en el Siglo de Oro, Madrid, 67; The patterning of La gitanilla, Romanistisches Jahrbuch, 75; Alonso Ramirez in an enchanted and a disenchanted world, Bull Hisp Studies, 76; Haz y enves del cuento risible en el Siglo de Oro, Tamesis, London, 76; contribr, Enxyklopädie des Märchens, Göttingen, 76; ed, Esteban Terralla Landa Lima por dentro y fuera, Exeter: Exeter Hisp Texts, 78; auth, Alonso de Castillo Solorzano, Twayne, 78; Juan de Mariana, Twayne, 82. *Mailing Add:* Dept Mod Lang State Univ of NY Buffalo NY 14260

SOONS, ROSALIE HUMPHREY, b San Diego, Calif, Nov 8, 24; m 48, 72; c 2. HISPANIC & COMPARATIVE LITERATURE. *Educ:* Bryn Mawr Col, AB, 47; Univ Conn, MA, 65, PhD(Romance lang), 67. *Prof Exp:* Jr ed, Yale Univ Press, 47-48; instr English & humanities, Dillard Univ, 56-57; instr Span, Sophie Newcomb Col & Univ Col, Tulane Univ, 58-59; instr French, Coventry Day Sch, Conn, 61-62; from instr to asst prof Span, 64-78, ASSOC PROF SPAN, UNIV MASS, AMHERST, 78- *Mem:* Am Asn Teachers Span & Port; Am Asn Univ Women; Les Amis de Marcel Proust. *Res:* Hispanic and modern European poetry; modern Spanish prose fiction. *Mailing Add:* Dept of Hisp Lang & Lit Univ of Mass Amherst MA 01002

SOPER, CHERRIE L, b Philadelphia, Pa, Nov 29, 37. ROMANCE LANGUAGES. *Educ:* Ursinus Col, AB, 59; Univ Madrid, dipl, 58; Univ Kans, MA, 61, PhD, 67. *Prof Exp:* Asst instr Span, Univ Kans, 59-61, 62-64, instr, 64-67; asst prof, Univ Mass, Amherst, 67-69; asst prof Span lit, Boston Univ, 69-73; asst prof, 73-79, ASSOC PROF SPAN LIT, IND STATE UNIV, TERRE HAUTE, 79- *Mem:* MLA; Mediaeval Acad Am. *Res:* Medieval chronicles in the Iberian peninsula; Spain and the Spaniard in United States literature. *Publ:* Coauth, La Mancha, land of Don Quijote, Americas, 10/73. *Mailing Add:* Dept of Foreign Lang Ind State Univ Terre Haute IN 47808

SOREN, EDGAR GREENE, b Brazil, Dec 18, 13; m; c 1. LANGUAGES. *Educ:* Rio de Janeiro Baptist Col, BS, 33; Sem Teologico Batista Sul Brasil, ThB, 37; Southern Baptist Theol Sem, ThM, 40. *Prof Exp:* Instr lang, gen hist & hist Brazil, Rio de Janeiro Baptist Col, 36-54, dir woman's dept, 42-43, admin dir col, 44, pres, 46-52; instr English, Getulio Vargas Found Col, Rio de Janeiro, 54-57; instr Span, medieval & mod hist & introd to philos, Linda Vista Baptist Col, San Diego, 57-60; assoc prof Span & chmn dept foreign lang, Limestone Col, 60-65, mem fac exec comt & col self-studies comt, 62-63; assoc prof, E coast br, 64-69, interim br chief Port sect, 65, PROF PORT, DEFENSE LANG INST, W COAST BR, 69- *Concurrent Pos:* Broadcast weekly English lessons, Radio Div US Embassy, Rio de Janeiro, 43-44; instr English, spec classes for Brazilian Army Officers, Brazilian Army Hq, 46-50; vpres representing Brazil, Baptist World Alliance, 47; mgt analyst, Morris & Van Wormer do Brasil Ltda, 56-57; instr Port, Johns Hopkins Univ Sch Advan Int Studies, 65. *Publ:* Auth, Vamos aprender ingles, Radio Div Am Embassy, Rio de Janeiro; Portuguese pattern drills, Port Br, Defense Lang Inst. *Mailing Add:* 305 Carmel Ave Pacific Grove CA 93950

SORIA, MARIO T, b La Paz, Bolivia, Aug 22, 27; US citizen; m 52; c 4. ROMANCE LANGUAGES. *Educ:* Baldwin Wallace Fol, BA, 50; Western Reserve Univ, MA, 57, PhD (Span), 62. *Prof Exp:* Instr Span, Western Reserve Univ, 57-59; prof Span Am lit, Hiram Col, 59-69; PROF FOREIGN LANG & CHMN DEPT, DRAKE UNIV, 69- *Concurrent Pos:* Lectr, Cuyahoga Community Col, 62-63 & Cleveland Pub Libr, 63-64. *Mem:* Latin Am Studies Asn. *Res:* Latin American drama and novel; Bolivian literature. *Publ:* Auth, Armando Chirveches, Novelista Boliviano, Univ La Paz, 63; cotranslr, The Other Shore, privately publ, 65; The Hands of God, Superior, 68; co-ed, translr of M Vilalta's Number 9, In: Best Plays of 1973, Chilton, 73. *Mailing Add:* Dept of Foreign Lang Drake Univ Des Moines IA 50311

SORIA, REGINA, b Rome, Italy, May 17, 11; US citizen; m 36. ROMANCE LANGUAGES, AMERICAN ART. *Educ:* Univ Rome, LittD, 33. *Prof Exp:* From instr to assoc prof foreign lang, 42-61, prof Ital, 61-76, EMER PROF MOD LANG, COL NOTRE DAME, MD, 76. *Concurrent Pos:* Instr Span, McCoy Col, 50-52; field researcher, Arch Am Art, 60-63, archivist, Rome Off, 63-64. *Mem:* MLA; Am Studies Asn; Am Asn Teachers Ital; AAUP. *Res:* Biography and catalogue of the works of Elihu Vedder-American painter; American artists in Italy, 1760-1914; Italian participation in the visual arts of 18th and 19th century America. *Publ:* Auth, Washington Allston's lectures on art, the first American art treatise, J Aesthet & Art Criticism, 3/60; Some background for Elihu Vedder's Cumean Sibyl and Young Marysays, spring 60 & Elihu Vedder's mythical creatures, summer 63; Art Quart; Mark Twain and Vedder's Medusa, Am Quart, winter 64; Life of Elihu Vedder & spring, 76; Elihu Vedder, American Old Master, Ga Mus Art Bull, spring 76. *Mailing Add:* 1609 Ramblewood Rd Baltimore MD 21239

SOSNOWSKI, SAUL, b Buenos Aires, Argentina, June 20, 45. CONTEMPORARY LATIN AMERICAN LITERATURE. *Educ:* Univ Scranton, BA, 67; Univ, Va, MA, 68, PhD(Span), 70. *Prof Exp:* From asst prof to assoc prof, 70-76, PROF LATIN AM LIT, UNIV MD, COLLEGE PARK, 76-, CHMN SPAN & PORT, 79- *Concurrent Pos:* Founder & ed, Hispamerica, 72- *Mem:* Am Asn Teachers Span & Port; AAUP; SAtlantic Mod Lang Asn; Latin Am Studies Asn; World Union Jewish Studies. *Res:* Contemporary Argentine narrative; 20th century Latin American literature; history-fiction relations in Latin America. *Publ:* Auth, The god's script-a Kabbalistic quest, Mod Fiction Studies, 73; Julio Cortazar: Una Busqueda Mitica, Ed Noe, Buenos Aires, 73; Los duenos de la tierra de David Vinas: Cuestionamiento e impugnacion del liberalismo, Cahiers du Monde Hispanique et Luso-Bresilien, 75; Borges y la Cabala: La busqueda del Verbo, Ediciones Hispamerica, 76; German Rozenmacher: Tradiciones rupturas y desencuentros, Revista de critica literaria latinoamericana, 77; Contemporary Jewish-Argentine Writers: Tradition and Politics, Latin Am Lit Rev, 78; Apuntes pobre lecturos miticos de textos hispanoamericanos Contemporaneos, Escritura, 81; Lectura pobre la Marcha de une obre in Marcha, In: Mas alls del boom, Lit y Mercado, 81. *Mailing Add:* 5 Pueblo Court Gaithersburg MD 20878

SOTOMAYER MILETTI, AUREA MARIA, b Santurce, PR, Apr 25, 51; US citizen. SPANISH AMERICAN LITERATURE. *Educ:* Univ PR, BA, 72; Ind Univ, Bloomington, MA, 76; Stanford Univ, PhD(Span-Am Lit), 80. *Prof Exp:* ASST PROF SPAN, UNIV INTERAM, PR, 80- *Concurrent Pos:* Curric consult, Caribbean Univ, 81-82. *Mem:* MLA; Consejo Puertorriqueno de Fotografia. *Res:* Argentinian literature; women's studies; Puerto Rican literature. *Publ:* Contribr, Poesiaoi, Antologia de la Sospecha, 78; co-ed, Victoc, Vol 2, No 2-3; auth, El hipogeo secreto: La escritura como palindromo y copula, Rev Iberoam, No 112-113, 80; Velando mi sueno madera, 80 & Sitios de la memoria, 82 (poetry), Inst de Cult Puertorriquena; Apuntes de un cronista: La llegada de J L Gonzalez, Vol 1, No 3, Mas herejes, meos mitificadores, Vol 2, No 1-2 & co-transl T S Eliot's East Coker, Vol 2, No 1-2, Reintegro. *Mailing Add:* 14 C Condominio Torrecielo Martin Travieso St #1481 Santurce PR 00907

SOUDEK, LEV I, b Brno, Czech, Dec 1, 29; m 53; c 1. ENGLISH & APPLIED LINGUISTICS. *Educ:* Masaryk Univ, MA, 53, Charles Univ, Prague, cand sci, 64, PhD(ling), 66. *Prof Exp:* From instr to asst prof ling, Univ Bratislava, 54-66, chmn dept English & Am studies, 63-66, assoc prof ling, 68-69; vis prof Am studies, Ind Univ, 66-67; vis fel ling, Princeton Univ, 67-68; assoc prof, 69-71, PROF ENGLISH, NORTHERN ILL UNIV, 71- *Concurrent Pos:* Co-dir & consult English as foreign lang, TV ser, Bratislava, 63-65; vpres Philol Soc, Slovak Acad Sci, 68-69; Am Coun Learned Soc res fel ling, Princeton Univ, 69. *Mem:* Ling Soc Am; Am Dialect Soc; Midwest Mod Lang Asn; Teachers English Speakers Other Langs. *Res:* British and American English; English morphology and word formation; theories and methods of teaching English to speakers of other languages. *Publ:* Coauth, English Textbook for Advanced Students, 63 & Selected English Texts, 64, Slovak Pedagog; auth, Structure of Substandard Words in British and American English, Acad Sci Bratislava, 68; The development and use of the morpheme burger in American English, 71 & Semantic and morphological aspects of in Nominalizations, 74, Ling; Error analysis and the system of English consonants: an application of contrastive phonology, in TESOL, English Lang Teaching J, 77; The Relation of Blending to English Word-Formation: Theory, Structure and Typological Attempts, Proc 12th Int Cong Ling, 78; Two Languages in One Brain: Recent Work in Neurolinguistics, English Lang Teaching J, 81. *Mailing Add:* Dept of English Northern Ill Univ De Kalb IL 60115

SOUFAS, CHARLES CHRISTOPHER, JR, b Wilson, NC, July 18, 48; m 70. CONTEMPORARY SPANISH LITERATURE. *Educ:* Emory Univ, BA, 70; Univ SC, MA, 75; Duke Univ, PhD(Span), 79. *Prof Exp:* Lectr Span, NC State Univ, 79-81; ASST PROF SPAN, WEST CHESTER STATE COL, 81- *Mem:* MLA; Am Asn Teachers Span & Port; Northeast Mod Lang Asn; AAUP. *Res:* Contemporary Spanish poetry and fiction; golden age drama and poetry; contemporary criticism. *Publ:* Auth, Velazquez en sus mundos, El Cafe Lit, 11/81; On the discrimination of contemporary criticisms: An annotated introductory bibliography & co-ed, The newest criticisms: A special issue, Col Lit, fall 82; auth, Et in Arcadia Ego: Luis Cernuda, ekphrasis and the reader, Anales Lit Espanola Contemporanea (in press); Cernuda and daimonic powere, Hispania (in press); Lope's Elegy to Gungora and the Culteranismo debate, Hispanofila (in press); contribr, Carlos Bousono, In: Twentieth Century Spanish Poets (in press). *Mailing Add:* Dept of Foreign Lang West Chester State Col West Chester PA 19380

SOURIAN, EVE, b New York, NY, June 9, 32; m 71; c 1. ROMANCE LANGUAGES. *Educ:* Sorbonne, Lic es Lett, 60; Bucknell Univ, MA, 62; Univ Colo, PhD(French), 71. *Prof Exp:* Instr French, Fairleigh Dickinson Univ, 63-65; lectr, 65-71, asst prof, 71-81, ASSOC PROF FRENCH, CITY COL NEW YORK, 81- *Concurrent Pos:* Assoc prof, French Summer Grad Sch, Millersville State Col, 67-71; City Univ New York Res Found grant, 79; Nat Endowment for Humanities Summer Inst French Contemp Cult, 82. *Mem:* MLA; Soc Fr Prof Am; Friends George Sand. *Res:* French Romanticism; European Romanticism; Mme de Stael. *Publ:* Auth, Les deux allemagnes: Mme de Stael et Henri Heine, Marcel Didier, Paris, 74; Diderot Retrouve, Diderot Studies, Vol XVIII, 75. *Mailing Add:* 30 E 70th St New York NY 10021

SOUSA, THOMAS FREDERICK, b Mansfield, Ohio, Apr 29, 26; m 60; c 1. PORTUGUESE, SPANISH. *Educ:* Univ Wis, BA, 50, MA, 51, PhD(Span & Port, 63. *Prof Exp:* From instr to asst prof Span, Univ Wash, 57-64; asst prof, Elmira Col, 64-65; asst prof, Univ Mass, Amherst, 65-73; CONSULT TEACHER TRAINING, NH STATE DEPT EDUC, 73- *Concurrent Pos:* Fulbright scholar, Port, 62-63. *Mem:* MLA; Am Asn Teachers Span & Port. *Res:* Portuguese dialectology; teacher training and education in foreign languages; General Education Manual. *Publ:* Coauth, Learning & Teaching Sound Letter Relationships, Northwest Regional Lab, 78. *Mailing Add:* NH State Dept of Educ 64 N Main St Concord NH 03301

SOUTHARD, GORDON DOUGLAS, b Toledo, Ohio, Sept 18, 17; m 39; c 2. ROMANCE LANGUAGES. *Educ:* Col Wooster, AB, 39; State Univ Iowa, AM, 40; Univ Chicago, PhD, 59. *Prof Exp:* Instr Romance lang, Lehigh Univ, 41-42; instr Span, Cranbrook Sch, 42-43; from asst prof to assoc prof, 46-60, PROF ROMANCE LANG, SOUTHWESTERN AT MEMPHIS, 60. *Mem:* MLA; Am Asn Teachers Span & Port. *Res:* Spanish American novel; American novel; modernism. *Mailing Add:* Dept of Romance Lang Southwestern at Memphis Memphis TN 38221

SOUTHARD, OSCAR BRUCE, II, b Lubbock, Tex, July 3, 43; m 71; c 2. ENGLISH & GENERAL LINGUISTICS. *Educ:* Tex Tech Univ, BA, 65; Purdue Univ, MA, 69; PhD(English ling), 72. *Prof Exp:* Asst prof English, Col William & Mary, 72-78; asst prof, 78-81, ASSOC PROF ENGLISH, OKLA STATE UNIV, 81- *Mem:* Ling Soc Am; Am Dialect Soc; MLA; SAtlantic Mod Lang Asn; Dict Soc Am. *Res:* History of language study in America; linguistic approaches to literary analysis; dialects of American English. *Publ:* Auth, Tagalog, English, and topicalization, In: Working Papers in Linguistics, Ohio State Univ, 71; Noah Webster: America's forgotten linguist, Am Speech, 79; Will Rogers and the Language of the Southwest: A Centennial Perspective, Chronicles Okla, 79; Syntax and time in Faulkner's Go Down, Moses, Lang & Style, 81; The Linguistic Atlas of England, J English Ling, 81; Defining the language of the Southwest, J Regional Cult, 81; The language of science-fiction fan magazines, Am Speech, 82; The linguistic atlas of Oklahoma and computer cartography, J English Ling (in press). *Mailing Add:* Dept of English Okla State Univ Stillwater OK 74074

SOUTHERLAND, RONALD HAMILTON, b Wilmington, NC, Mar 7, 42. LINGUISTICS, GERMAN. *Educ:* Univ NC, AB, 65, MA, 67; Univ Pa, PhD(ling), 70. *Prof Exp:* Asst prof ling & Ger, Duquesne Univ, 70-71; asst prof ling, 71-76, ASSOC PROF LING, UNIV CALGARY, 76- *Mem:* Ling Soc Am; Ling Soc Europe. *Res:* Sociolinguistics; social and situational differentiation of speech; historical linguistics. *Publ:* Ed, Readings on Language in Canada, 73 & auth, The linguistic mix in French Canada, In: Readings on Language in Canada, 73, Univ Calgary; Comparative and typological perspectives on the reconstruction of the PIE Gutturals, Calgary Working Papers Ling, 78. *Mailing Add:* Dept of Ling Univ of Calgary Calgary AB T2N 1N4 Can

SOUTHWORTH, FRANKLIN C, b Framingham, Mass, June 28, 29; m 66; c 3. LINGUISTICS. *Educ:* Harvard Univ, BA, 51; Yale Univ, MA, 56, PhD(ling), 58. *Prof Exp:* From asst prof to assoc prof SAsia regional studies, 59-76, PROF LING, UNIV PA, 76- *Concurrent Pos:* Rockefeller Found grant jr ling fel, Deccan Col, India, 58-59; prin investr & dir proj to produce English-Marathi dictionary, US Off Educ grant, 62-65; fac res fel, Am Inst Indian Studies, Poona, India, 66-67; vis assoc prof dept Mid East lang & cult, Columbia Univ, 67-68; prin investr, Nat Sci Found grant studies comp socioling SAsian semantic structures, 70-73. *Mem:* Ling Soc Am; Ling Soc India; Am Anthropol Asn. *Res:* Modern Indo-Aryan and Dravidian languages; lexicography; structural semantics sociolinguistics. *Publ:* Auth, The Marathi verbal sequences, Language, 61; coauth, Spoken Marathi, Univ Pa, 64; auth,

Transformational Structure of Nepali, Deccan Col, India, 67; A model of semantic structure, Language, 67; Student's Hini-Urdu Reference Manaual, Univ Ariz, 71; contribr, Pidginization & Creolization of Languages, Cambridge Univ, 71; coauth, Foundations of Linguistics, Free Press, 74; co-ed, Contact and convergence in South Asian languages(spec issue), Int J Dravidian Ling, Vol III, No 1. *Mailing Add:* Dept of Ling Univ Pa Philadelphia PA 19104

SOUZA, RAYMOND D, b Attleboro, Mass, Mar 11, 36; m 66; c 2. SPANISH. *Educ:* Drury Col, BA, 58; Univ Mo, MA, 60, PhD(Span), 64. *Prof Exp:* Teacher high sch, Mo, 58-59; instr Span, Kent State Univ, 61-62; from asst prof to assoc prof, 63-73, chmn dept Span & Port, 68-74, PROF SPAN, UNIV KANS, 73- *Concurrent Pos:* Am Philos Soc Johnson Fund fel, 68; Exxon inter-univ vis prof ling & philos, 81-82; Tinker Found fel, Costa Rica, 82. *Mem:* Am Asn Teachers Span & Port; Inst Int Lit Iberoam; MLA. *Res:* Spanish American prose fiction and poetry; Cuban literature; Argentine literature. *Publ:* Auth, Language vs structure in the contemporary Spanish American novel, Hispania, 12/69; Two early works of Augustin Yanez, Romance Notes, spring 70; Fernando as hero in Sabato's Sobre heroes y tumbas, Hispania, 5/72; Time and terror in the stories of Lino Novas Calvo, Symposium, winter 75; Time and space configurations in two poems of Octavio Paz, J Span Studies: Twentieth Century, fall 76; La imagen del circulo en Paradiso de Lezama Lima, Caribe, 76; Major Cuban Novelists: Innovation & Tradition, Univ Mo, Columbia 76, London 76; ; Lino Novas Calvo, G K Hall, 81. *Mailing Add:* Dept of Span & Port Univ of Kans Lawrence KS 66045

SPACAGNA, ANTOINE ERNEST, b Paris, France, Dec 2, 28; m 64; c 2. FRENCH LITERATURE & LINGUISTICS. *Educ:* Emory Univ, MA, 62; Ohio State Univ, PhD (French), 73. *Prof Exp:* Brit Ministry Educ asst French, Oldham Sec Sch, Eng, 49-50; teacher French & English, Paris English Sch, France, 50-52; community rels adv, French & US Govt, 54-59; instr French & Int House scholar, Jacksonville State Univ, 59-60; instr & lectr, Ohio State Univ, 62-70; asst prof, 70-78, ASSOC PROF FRENCH, FLA STATE UNIV, 78- *Concurrent Pos:* US Info Agency-Am Consulate Gen Strasbourg, France, scholar, Salzburg Sem Am Studies, 54. *Honors & Awards:* Chevalier des Palmes Acad, 79. *Mem:* Fr Asn Pub Rels; MLA; Soc Fr Prof Am; Am Asn Teachers Fr. *Res:* Semiotics and structuralism as methods of criticism; structure of Marivaux's theatre; French poetry and theatre after 1660. *Publ:* Auth, Several articles in French newspapers and magazines and TV broadcasts on American life and civilization, 54-59; Entre le oui et le non: Essai sur la structure profonde du Theatre do Marivaux, Peter Lang, Bern, 78. *Mailing Add:* Dept of Mod Lang Fla State Univ Tallahassee FL 32306

SPACCARELLI, THOMAS DEAN, b Chicago, Ill, Sept 25, 47; m 70. SPANISH LINGUISTICS, MEDIEVAL SPANISH LITERATURE. *Educ:* Univ Ill, Chicago Circle, AB, 69; Univ Wis-Madison, MA, 71, PhD(Span), 75. *Prof Exp:* Lectr Span, Univ Ill Chicago Circle, 73-74; instr, 74-75, ASST PROF SPAN, UNIV OF THE SOUTH, 75- *Concurrent Pos:* Mem, Span Joint Comt, Educ & Cult Affairs, 80-81. *Mem:* Am Asn Teachers of Span & Port; MLA; Mediaeval Acad Am. *Res:* Spanish lexicography; medieval romance. *Publ:* Ed, Complete Concordances and Texts of the Fourteenth-Century Aragonese Manuscripts of Jaun Fernandez de heredia, Hisp Sem of Medieval Studies, Ltd, 82. *Mailing Add:* Dept of Span Univ of the South Sewanee TN 37375

SPAETHLING, ROBERT HERBERT, b Weissenstadt, Ger, July 30, 27; US citizen; m; c 3. GERMAN. *Educ:* Univ Calif, Berkeley, PhD, 59. *Hon Degrees:* AM, Harvard Univ, 66. *Prof Exp:* Lectr Ger, Harvard, 59, from instr to asst prof, 59-65; assoc prof, Williams Col, 65-66; assoc prof, Harvard Univ, 66-68; prof, Univ Mass, Boston, 68-69; prof, Univ Calif, San Diego, 69-71; chmn dept Ger, 71-73, dean grad studies, 76-78, vchancellor acad affairs, 74-76, chmn dept Ger, 78-80, PROF GER, UNIV MASS, BOSTON, 71- *Concurrent Pos:* Harvard Joseph H Clark grant, 63; mem advan placement comt Ger, Col Entrance Exam Bd, 66-71, chmn, 77-80; Danforth Assoc, 74; Nat Endowment for Humanities fel, 82-83. *Mem:* Am Soc 18th Century Studies; MLA; Am Asn Teachers Ger; Am Lessing Soc; Goethe Soc NAm. *Res:* German literature and music of 18th century; German culture; contemporary literature. *Publ:* Co-ed, A Reader in German Literature, Oxford Univ, 69; auth, Günter Grass: Cat and Mouse, Monatshefte, 70; On Christin Thomasius and the German Enlightenment, Lessing Yearbk, 71; co-ed, Literatur eins, Oxford Univ, 72; auth, Folklore and enlightenment in the Libretto of Mozart's Magic Flute, Eighteenth-Century Studies, 75; The Germanist as educator, In: German Studies in the US, Univ Wis, 76; The Unwritten Masterpiece of German Classicism: Mozart's Music for Goethe's Faust, Forum, 76; Goethe and Mozart: The Abduction in Weimar, In: Essays in Honor of James Walsh, Goethe Inst Boston (in press). *Mailing Add:* 101 Washington Ave Cambridge MA 02140

SPAHN, RAYMOND J, b Lawton, Iowa, Sept 15, 09; m 55; c 2. GERMAN. *Educ:* State Univ Iowa, BA; 31; Northwestern Univ, MA, 32, PhD, 38. *Prof Exp:* Chmn, Dept Foreign Lang, Maine Twp High Sch & Jr Col, Ill; dir, Am Hauser in Bavaria, US Dept State, 45-49; dir foreign lang, Am Col Bur, 49-57; from assoc prof to prof, 57-77, chmn, Dept Foreign Lang, 75-77, EMER PROF GER, SOUTHERN ILL UNIV, EDWARDSVILLE, 77- *Res:* Nineteenth century German manuscripts in America. *Publ:* Ed, History of the Settling of Highland, 70 & co-ed, New Switzerland in Illinois, 77, Lovejoy Libr, Southern Ill Univ. *Mailing Add:* 429 Buena Vista Dr Edwardsville IL 62025

SPAHR, BLAKE LEE, b Carlisle, Pa, July 11, 24; m 57; c 1. GERMAN & COMPARATIVE LITERATURE. *Educ:* Dickinson Col, BA, 47; Yale Univ, MA, 48, PhD, 51. *Prof Exp:* Instr Ger, Dickinson Col, 46-47; instr, Yale Univ, 50-53; from asst prof to assoc prof, 54-64, chmn dept Ger, 65-70; chmn dept comp lit, 72-80, PROF GER & COMP LIT, UNIV CALIF, BERKELEY, 64- *Concurrent Pos:* Morse res fel, Yale Univ, 52-53; Guggenheim fel, 62. *Mem:* Mediaeval Acad Am; MLA; Int Arthurian Soc; Pegnesischer Blumenorden. *Res:* German literature of the Middle Ages and the 17th century; comparative Arthurian literature. *Publ:* Auth, The Archives of the Pegnesischer Blumenorden, 60 & Anton Ulrich and Aramena, 66, Univ Calif; Baroque and mannerism, Colloquia Germanica, 67. *Mailing Add:* Dept of Ger Univ of Calif Berkeley CA 94720

SPALATIN, CHRISTOPHER, b Ston, Yugoslavia, Oct 15, 09; nat US; m 37; c 3. ROMANCE PHILOLOGY. *Educ:* Univ Zagreb, MA, 32, PhD, 34. *Prof Exp:* Lectr French, Univ Zagreb, 35-41; Croatian & Serbian, Univ Rome, 41-48; prof Romance lang, Iowa Wesleyan Col, 48-52, head dept foreign lang, 48-52; from asst prof to prof mod lang, 52-76, EMER PROF MOD LANG, MARQUETTE UNIV, 76- *Concurrent Pos:* Prof, Orient Inst Naples, 47-48. *Mem:* MLA. *Res:* Comparative semantics; Croatian culture; editing the oldest Croatian-Italian dictionary. *Publ:* Auth, French influence on Croatian language, Annales l'Inst Fr, Zagreb, 41; A brief survey of French literature, In: Wisdom and Joy, Zagreb, 42-43; Do Croats and Serbs speak the same language?, In: Person and Spirit, Madrid, 51; co-ed & contribr, Croatia: Lang, People, Culture, Univ Toronto, Vols I & II, 64 & 70. *Mailing Add:* Dept of Foreign Lang & Lit Marquette Univ 526 N 14th St Milwaukee WI 53233

SPALEK, JOHN M, b Warsaw, Poland, July 28, 28; US citizen; m 57; c 2. GERMAN. *Educ:* Stanford Univ, PhD, 61. *Prof Exp:* From asst prof to prof Ger, Univ Southern Calif, 60-70; chmn dept Ger lang & lit, 70-76, PROF GER, STATE UNIV NY ALBANY, 70- *Mem:* MLA; Am Asn Teachers Ger; Brecht Soc; Int Arthur Schnitzler Res Asn. *Res:* German literature in exile, 1933-; German expressionism; contemporary German literature. *Publ:* Auth, Ernst Toller and His Critics: A Bibliography, Va Bibliog Soc, 68, Haskell, 73; ed, Lion Feuchtwanger: The Man, His Ideas and His Work, Hennessey, 72. *Mailing Add:* Dept of Ger Lang & Lit HU 209 State Univ NY Albany NY 12222

SPANGLER, CARL DAVID, b Bellevue, Pa, May 29, 36. FRENCH. *Educ:* Grove City Col, AB, 58; Pa State Univ, MA, 61. *Prof Exp:* Instr French & Span, Pac Lutheran Univ, 61-62; asst prof, Grove City Col, 62-63; asst prof French & Span, 63-76, ASSOC PROF MOD & CLASS LANG, PAC LUTHERAN UNIV, 76- *Mem:* MLA; Am Asn Teachers Fr; Am Coun Teaching Foreign Lang. *Res:* French syntax; structural analysis. *Mailing Add:* Dept of Foreign Lang Pac Lutheran Univ Tacoma WA 98447

SPANN, MENO HANS, b Koblenz, Ger, Mar 23, 03. GERMAN. *Educ:* Univ Marburg, PhD, 28. *Prof Exp:* Instr Ger, Cornell Univ, 28-30, Univ Ore, 30-31 & Univ NC, 31-35; asst prof, Univ Md, 35-36; asst prof, State Univ Iowa, 36-43; from asst prof to prof, 43-71, EMER PROF GER, NORTHWESTERN UNIV, EVANSTON, 71- *Concurrent Pos:* Vis porf Ger lit, Mich State Univ, 71-72. *Mem:* MLA; Am Asn Teachers Ger. *Res:* Modern German literature; Thomas Mann; Franz Kafka. *Publ:* Coauth, Deutsche Denker und Forscher, Appleton, 54; Franz Kafka, In: Einfuhrung in die deutsche Literatur, Holt, 64; auth, 5 Cultural Graded Readers, Am Bd Co, 65-67; Heine, Hillary, 66; Werther revisited, In: New Views of the European Novel, Univ Manitoba, 72; Schiller-Heine-Brecht, Appleton, 73; auth, Deutsch für Amerikaner, Am Bk Co, 73; Franz Kafka, Twayne, 76. *Mailing Add:* Dept of Ger Northwestern Univ Evanston IL 60201

SPARKS, JACKSON GILLEN, b Warrenton, Ga, Jan 19, 32; m 56. ROMANCE LANGUAGES. *Educ:* Univ NC, AB, 53, MA, 64, PhD(Romance lang), 67. *Prof Exp:* Instr French, Univ NC, 64-66; from asst prof to assoc prof, 66-73, chmn dept mod lang, 67-76, PROF FRENCH, UNIV NC, WILMINGTON, 73- *Mem:* MLA; Am Asn Teachers Fr. *Res:* French literature of the 18th century; 20th century French novel. *Mailing Add:* Dept Mod Lang Univ NC Wilmington NC 28401

SPARKS, KIMBERLY, b Baltimore, Md, Oct 2, 30; m 52; c 3. GERMANIC LANGUAGES. *Educ:* Princeton Univ, AB, 56, MA, 59, PhD(Ger), 63. *Prof Exp:* From instr to foreign lang, 66-71, chmn comt, 73-76, CHARLES A DANA PROF GER, MIDDLEBURY COL, 71- *Concurrent Pos:* Chmn exam comt, Ger Achievement Test, 66-68; dir, Northeast Conf Teaching Foreign Lang, 68-72; mem nat bd consults, Nat Endowment for Humanities, 77- *Mem:* MLA. *Res:* Novels of Hermann Broch; language teaching. *Publ:* Auth, Korfs Uhr, In: Perspective der Forschung; Drei Schwarze Kaninchen Z Deut Philol, 65; coauth, Der Web zum Lesen, 67, German in Review, 67, Modern German, 71, S ist es, 71 & Thomas Manns Tonio Kröger als Weg zur Literatur, 74, Harcout; auth, The radicalization of space in Kafka, In: On Kafka, Elek, London, 77. *Mailing Add:* Dept of Ger Middlebury Col Middlebury VT 05753

SPATZ, LOIS S, b Baltimore, Md, Mar 28, 40; m 62. ENGLISH, CLASSICS. *Educ:* Goucher Col, BA, 60; Johns Hopkins Univ, MAT, 61; Ind Univ, MA, 64, PhD(classics), 68. *Prof Exp:* Teaching asst Greek, Ind Univ, 61-62; lectr classics in transl Latin, Brooklyn Col, 65-66; assoc prof Western heritage, Park Col, 68-73; ASSOC PROF ENGLISH, UNIV MO-KANSAS CITY, 73- *Mem:* Am Philol Asn; Class Asn Midwest & South; Soc Bibl Lit. *Res:* Greek drama; mythology; bible as literature. *Publ:* Auth, Metrical motivs in Aristophanes' Clouds, Quad Urbinati, 72; Aristophanes (Twayne World Author Series), G K Hall, 6/78; Aeschylus, Twayne World Author Series/G K Hall (in press). *Mailing Add:* Dept of English Univ of Mo 5315 Holmes Kansas City MO 64110

SPEAR, FREDERICK AUGUSTUS, b Methuen, Mass, Dec 26, 23; m 47; c 2. FRENCH. *Educ:* Bowdoin Col, AB, 47; Harvard Univ, AM, 48; Columbia Univ, PhD, 57. *Prof Exp:* Instr French & Span, Union Col, NY, 48-50; instr, Wesleyan Univ, 51-53; instr French, Columbia Univ, 53-57; from instr to asst prof, Brown Univ, 57-61; from asst prof to assoc prof, 61-69, PROF FRENCH, SKIDMORE COL, 69- *Mem:* MLA; Am Asn Teachers Fr; Am Soc 18th Century Studies; Soc Fr Etude XVIIIe Siecle; Am Friends Lafayette (treas, 64-74, 2nd vpres, 75-). *Res:* Voltaire and Diderot bibliography; bibliography on the relations of literature and science. *Publ:* Auth, An inquiry concerning Ronsard and the sonnet form, Mod Lang Notes, 59; coauth, Relations of literature and science: Selected bibliography for 1965-66, Symposium, 67; Quarante annees d'etudes Voltairiennes, A Colin, 68; ed, Lettre inedite de Voltaire a Louis-Francois Prault, Rev Hist Lit France, 71; Discussion in The Reve de d'Alembert; studies . . ., Diderot Studies, 73; auth, Bibliographie de Diderot: Repertoire analytique international, Droz, 80. *Mailing Add:* 45 Webster St Saratoga Springs NY 12866

SPEAR, RICHARD LANSMON, b Passaic, NJ, Dec 20, 29; m 55; c 2. JAPANESE LANGUAGE & LITERATURE. *Educ:* Lafayette Col, AB, 52; Univ Mich, Ann Arbor, MA, 60, PhD (Far Eastern lang & lit), 66. *Prof Exp:* Educ adv, Dept of Army, 54-58; lectr Japanese, Univ Mich, 64-66; asst prof, Univ Wis, 66-68, actg chmn dept EAsian lang & lit, 67-68; chmn dept Orient lang & lit, 68-72, assoc prof Japanese, Univ Kans, 68-80. *Mem:* Asn Asian Studies. *Res:* Medieval Japanese linguistics. *Publ:* Auth, Research on the 1593 Jesuit Mission press edition of Aesop's Fables, Monumental Nipponica, 64; co-ed, Readings in Eastern Civilization, Univ Kans, 69; auth, Takaboku, su poesia y la sociedad, Estudios Orientales, 70; five items, In: Encycl of World Literature in the 20th Century, 70-72; Takaboku: The poet as social critic, Let E & W, 78; Collado's Grammar of Japanese, Univ Kans, 78. *Mailing Add:* 2003 W Fifth St Lawrence KS 66044

SPEARS, RICHARD ALAN, b Kansas City, Mo, Oct 28, 39; m 61; c 4. LINGUISTICS, AMERICAN CULTURE. *Educ:* Tex Christian Univ, BA, 61; Ind Univ, PhD(ling), 65. *Prof Exp:* Asst prof, 65-71, ASSOC PROF LING, NORTHWESTERN UNIV, EVANSTON, 71- *Mem:* Am Dialect Soc; Soc Caribbean Ling; Teachers English Speakers Other Languages. *Res:* Non-standardized English; Lexicography; standardization and codificatioin. *Publ:* Auth, Tonal Dissimilation in Maninka, J African Lang, 68; Basic Course in Mende, 68 & Elementary Maninka-kan, 73, Northwestern Univ; Toward a Mende Lexicon, J WAfrica Lang, 70; Mende, Loko, and Maninka Tonal Correspondences, Studies African Lang & Ling, 71; Slang and Euphemism: A dictionary of oaths, curses, insultss, sexual slang and metaphor, racial slurs, drug talk, homosexual lingo, and related matters, Jonathan David Publ, 81; Slang and Euphemism, New Am Libr, 82. *Mailing Add:* Dept Ling Northwestern Univ Evanston IL 60201

SPECTOR, NORMAN BERNARD, b Philadelphia, Pa, Jan 2, 21. FRENCH. *Educ:* Univ Pa, PhD, 50. *Prof Exp:* Instr Romance lang, Univ Pa, 47-50; from instr to asst prof, Northwestern Univ, 52-59; from asst prof to assoc prof French, Univ Chicago, 59-66; prof French & chmn, Dept Romance Lang, Oberlin Col, 66-68; chmn, Dept French & Ital, 68-78, PROF FRENCH, NORTHWESTERN UNIV, 68- *Concurrent Pos:* Univ Pa Jusserand traveling fel & Fulbright scholar, France, 50-51; mem, selection comt, Region IX, Woodrow Wilson Nat Fel Found, 62-64 & 65-66, Region II, 64-65; vis assoc prof, Yale Univ, 64-65. *Mem:* MLA; Am Asn Teachers Fr. *Res:* French Renaissance and Medieval literature; French linguistics. *Publ:* Auth, The procuress and religious hypocrisy, Italica; Odet de Turnebe's Les Contens and the Italian comedy, Fr Studies, 59; Edition critique, Odet de Turnebe: Les Contens, Soc Textes Fr Mod, 61, 2nd ed, 64; The Romance of Tristan and Isolt, Northwestern Univ, 73. *Mailing Add:* Dept of French & Ital Northwestern Univ Evanston IL 60201

SPECTOR, STEPHEN J, Medieval English, Philology. See Vol II

SPEER, DAVID GORDON, b Oak Park, Ill, Nov 16, 13; m 45; c 1. FRENCH LANGUAGE & LITERATURE. *Educ:* Univ Chicago, BA, 37, MA, 39; Univ Montpellier, DUniv, 53. *Prof Exp:* Asst headmaster, Pistakee Bay Sch, 39-41; instr French, Ger & Span, Miss State Col, 41-42; asst prof & chmn dept mod lang, St Helena exten, Col William & Mary, 47-48; from instr to asst prof, Purdue Univ, 48-58, asst head dept French, 58-59, assoc prof, 58-66, chmn, Dept French & Ital, 59-66; head dept foreign lang & lit, 66-72, prof foreign lang & lit, 66-72, prof French, 72-79, EMER PROF FRENCH, UNIV SC, 79- *Concurrent Pos:* Dir French, NDEA Inst, Purdue Univ, 60-61, 63-64. *Honors & Awards:* Chevalier des Palmes Acad, 80. *Mem:* Am Asn Teachers Fr; Am Name Soc; MLA; SAtlantic Mod Lang Asn. *Res:* Contemporary French literature; linguistics; Camus. *Publ:* Auth, Given names in Strasbourg, Names, 6/57; Anticipation and French vowels, Mod Lang J, 12/62; Meursault's newsclipping, 8/68 & More about Meursault's newsclipping, summer 70, Mod Fiction Studies; coauth, A la belle Etoile, McGraw, 70; ; auth, Camus' Fait divers, Mod Fiction Studies, 71; Edith Piaf and Alfred de Vigny, Lang Quart, summer 74. *Mailing Add:* Dept of Foreign Lang & Lit Univ of SC Columbia SC 29208

SPEHAR, ELIZABETH MARIE, English, Slavistics. See Vol II

SPEIDEL, WALTER HANS, b Stuttgart, Ger, Dec 5, 22; US citizen. GERMAN LANGUAGE & LITERATURE. *Educ:* Univ Utah, MA, 60; Univ Kans, PhD(Ger lit), 63. *Prof Exp:* Asst instr Ger, Univ Utah, 58-60; asst instr, Univ Kans, 60-63; from asst prof to assoc prof, 63-70, PROF GER, BRIGHAM YOUNG UNIV, 70- *Mem:* AAUP; MLA; Am Asn Teachers Ger; Asn Lit & Ling Comput; Am Translr Asn; Western Asn Ger Studies. *Res:* German idealism; computer applications in literature and linguistics; German literature after 1920. *Publ:* Coauth, Reviewing German, Dodd, 69; auth, Kafka Concordance, Comput & Humanities, 70; Themengebundene Horverstchensubungen, Mod Lang J, 3/78; coauth, Scenes from German Drama, Harper, 78; Structures and Themes--Categories and Ideas in Die Lehrlnge zu Sais by Novalis, Lang, 81; Existential Conflicts in the Exile Dramas of Ferdinand Bruckner, Mod Austrian Lit, 82; Das Amerikabild in Werfels Roman Stern der Ungeborenen, Das Exilerlebnis, 82; Franz Kafka: Beschreibung eines Kampfes--A Comparative Computer Concordance, Maney (in press). *Mailing Add:* 2147 N Oaks Lane Provo UT 84601

SPENCER, HANNA, b Kladno, Czech, Dec 16, 13; Can citizen; m 42; c 2. GERMAN LANGUAGE & LITERATURE. *Educ:* German Univ, Prague, DPhil(Germanistics), 37. *Prof Exp:* lectr, 59-67, from asst prof to assoc prof, 67-77, prof, 77-79, EMER PROF GER, UNIV WESTERN ONT, 79- *Concurrent Pos:* Can Coun fel, 75-76. *Mem:* Can Asn Univ Teachers Ger; Humanities Asn Can; Heine Soc; Internationaler Germanisten Verein. *Res:* European community-trends in cultural integration; Heinrich Heine. *Publ:* Auth, Dichter, Denker, Journalist, Versuche zum Werk Heinrich Heines, Verlag Peter Lang, Bern, 77; co-ed, Heinrich Heine, Dimensionen seines Wirkens, Bouvier Bonn, 79; Heinrich Heine, Thayne World Authors, G K Hall, 82. *Mailing Add:* Dept of Ger Univ of Western Ont London ON N6A 3K7 Can

SPENCER, SAMIA ISKANDER, b Alexandria, Egypt, July 4, 43; US citizen; m 69; c 2. FRENCH. *Educ:* Alexandria Univ, Egypt, BA, 64; Univ Ill, Urbana, MA, 69, PhD(French), 75. *Prof Exp:* Secy & gen asst, US Info Serv, Egypt, 65-67; secy, World Health Orgn, Egypt, 67 & UN Develop Prog, NY, 68; teaching asst French, Univ Ill, Urbana, 68-72; instr, 72-75, asst prof, 75-80, ASSOC PROF FRENCH, AUBURN UNIV, 80- *Concurrent Pos:* Res grant-in-aid, Auburn Univ, 75; Ala Comt Humanities & Pub Policy grant, 76; grant, Govt of Quebec, 82. *Mem:* Am Asn Teachers Fr (secy-treas, 81-); Am Soc 18th Century Studies; MLA. *Res:* The eighteenth century French novel; women in eighteenth century French literature; the teaching of foreign languages. *Publ:* Coauth, Testing: A hurdle or a means of learning, In: Changing Patterns in Foreign Language Programs, Newberry House, 72; auth, Testing to improve learning, Iowa Foreign Lang Bull, 2/76; coauth, Let's get the high school foreign language teachers back in the university, Can Mod Lang Rev, 3/77; auth, La femme dans l'oeuvre romanesque de Marivaux, USF Lang Quart, spring-summer 77; The rights of women, Fr-Am Rev, winter-spring 78; coauth, French and American Women in the Feminine Press: A Cross Cultural Look, Contemp Fr Civilization, winter 81. *Mailing Add:* Dept of Foreign Lang Auburn Univ Auburn AL 36830

SPENCER, SONIA BERON, b Medellin, Colombia, Feb 17, 42; US citizen; m 66; c 1. MEDIEVAL FRENCH LITERATURE & LANGUAGE. *Educ:* Hunter Col, BA, 63; Pa State Univ, MA, 65; Duke Univ, PhD, 74. *Prof Exp:* Instr French, Portsmouth Abbey Sch, 69-70; asst prof French, Span & methodology, State Univ NY Col, Cortland, 75-77; Rosemont Col, Rosemont, Pa, 80-81; lectr, Fr methodology, Chestnut Hill Col, Philadelphia, Pa, 77, 79-80. *Concurrent Pos:* Free-lance translator. *Mem:* MLA; Soc Rencesvals Am-Can Br. *Res:* The epic in relation to the romance; methodology of teaching foreign languages; twentieth century theatre. *Publ:* Auth, The Aliscans: A Focal Point of Late Epic Themes, Univ Microfilms, 74; The Song of William and the Aliscans: Comedy and the epic Bienseances, 10/77 & contribr, Discussion session on the Old French William Cycle, 3/78, Olifant. *Mailing Add:* 67-25 Harrow St Forest Hills NY 11375

SPERANZA, ERNEST VINCENT, b NY, May 25, 17; m 45; c 2. SPANISH. *Educ:* City Col New York, BS, 39; Columbia Univ, AM, 47, MPh(Span), 54. *Prof Exp:* Teacher, Harris High Sch, 40-42; asst prof Span, 45-73, ASSOC PROF SPAN, MANHATTAN COL, 73-, ASST DEAN SCH ARTS & SCI, 71- *Mem:* Am Asn Teachers Span & Port. *Res:* History of Spanish orthography. *Publ:* Auth, Spanish verbs at a glance; French verbs at a glance; Reading skill builder in Spanish. *Mailing Add:* Dept of Span Manhattan Col Bronx NY 10471

SPERATTI-PINERO, EMMA SUSANA, b Buenos Aires, Arg, Oct 31, 19. SPANISH & LATIN AMERICAN LITERATURE. *Educ:* Inst Sec Prof, Buenos Aires, MA, 48; Univ Mex, DLett, 55. *Prof Exp:* Prof humanities, Univ San Luis Potosi, 59-62; prof sch advan studies, Univ Sonora, 64-65; assoc prof Span, 65-68, PROF SPAN, WHEATON COL, MASS, 68- *Concurrent Pos:* Span Govt foreign rels grant, 51-52; Ford Found grant, 69-70; John Simon Guggenheim Mem Found fel, 71-72. *Mem:* Int Asn Hispanists. *Res:* Valle-Inclan; Julio Cortazar; Jorge Luis Borges; Alejo Carpentier. *Publ:* Coauth, Literatura fantastica en Argentina, Univ Mex, 57; auth, Elaboracion artistica en Tirano Banderas, Col Mex, 57; De Sonata de Otono al Esperpento, 68 & El ocultismo en Valle-Inclan, 74, Tamesis, London; Judas en laobra de Borges, Homenaje al Inst de Filol, Buenos Aires, 75; Cortazar y tres pintores belgas: Ensor, Delvaux, Magritte, Nueva Revista de Filol Hispanica, Mex, 75; Pasos hallados en El reino de este mundo, El Colegio de Mex, 81. *Mailing Add:* P O Box 463 Norton MA 02766

SPERONI, CHARLES, b Santa Fiora, Italy, Nov 2, 11; nat US; m 38. FOLKLORE. *Educ:* Univ Calif, Berkeley, AB, 33, PhD, 38. *Prof Exp:* Assoc Ital, 35-38, from instr to assoc prof, 38-53, chmn dept col fine arts, 49-56, dir summer sessions, 56-68, dean col fine arts, 68-80, prof, 53-80, EMER PROF ITAL, UNIV CALIF, LOS ANGELES, 80- *Concurrent Pos:* From asst ed to ed, Mod Lang Forum, 43-49; ed consult, World Lang Dict, Encycl Britannica, 54; assoc ed, Ital Quart, 57- *Honors & Awards:* Star of Solidarity, Cavaliere Ufficiale & Commendatore, Italy; Palmes Academiques, France. *Mem:* MLA; Philol Asn Pac Coast; Am Asn Teachers Ital(pres, 49). *Publ:* Auth, Proverbs and proverbial phrases in Basile's Pentameron, 41; The Italian Wellerism to the end of the seventeenth century, 53; Wit and Wisdom of the Italian Renaissance, Univ Calif, 64; The aphorisms of Orazio Rinaldi, Robert Greene, and Lucas Gracian Dantisco, 68. *Mailing Add:* Off Dean Col Fine Arts Univ of Calif Los Angeles CA 90024

SPICEHANDLER, EZRA ZEVI, b Brooklyn, NY, Apr 6, 20; m 44; c 2. MODERN HEBREW LITERATURE. *Educ:* Hebrew Union Col, Rabbi & MHL, 46, Phd(Talmud), 52. *Prof Exp:* Instr Hebrew lit, 51-55, asst prof, 55-59, assoc prof 59-63, prof, 63-80, DISTINGUISHED SERV PROF, JEWISH INST RELIG, HEBREW UNION COL, 80- *Concurrent Pos:* Teheran Fulbright res prof, 62-63; div ed, Mod Hebrew Lit, Encycl Judaka, 68-72; dean, Jewish Inst Relig, Sch of Hebrew Union Col, Jerusalem, 72-80; vis prof, Hebrew Univ, Jerusalem, 74-77; Oxford Ctr Hebrew Studies fel, 76-78. *Mem:* Cent Conf Am Rabbis; Asn Jewish Studies; World Union Jewish Studies. *Res:* Judeo Persian Studies. *Publ:* Auth, Notes on Gentile Courts in Talmudic Babylon, Hebrew Union Col Annal, 55; coauth, Chapters in Judaism, H Neuman Press, Tel Aviv, 60; Modern Hebrew Poem Itself, Holt, Reinhart & Winston, 65; auth, The Jews of Iran, Circle Study Contemp Jewry, 68; ed, Modern Hebrew Short Stories, Bantam, 70; auth, Joshua Heschel Schoir, Mosad Bialik, Jerusalem, 70; The persecution of the Jews of Isfahan, Hebrew Union Col Annal, 75; ed, New Writing in Israel, Schocken, 76. *Mailing Add:* Hebrew Lit Dept Hebrew Union Col Cincinnati OH 45220

SPIELMANN, EDDA, b Hildesheim, Ger, Jan 3, 43; US citizen. GERMAN, MEDIEVAL LITERATURE. *Educ:* Univ Calif, Santa Barbara, BA, 64; Univ Calif, Los Angeles, MA, 66, PhD(Ger), 71. *Prof Exp:* Teaching asst Ger, Univ Calif, Los Angeles, 64-67; lectr, Univ Calif, Riverside, 67-69; from instr to asst prof, 69-75, assoc prof, 75-80, PROF GER, CALIF STATE UNIV, NORTHRIDGE, 80- *Mem:* MLA; Mediaeval Asn Pac Coast; Medieval Acad

Am. *Res:* German medieval literature; Arthurian epic. *Publ:* Auth, Chretien's and Hartmann's treatment of the conquest of Laudine, Comp Lit, 66; coauth, From illiteracy to literacy: Prolegomena to a study of the Nibelungenlied, Forum Mod Lang Studies, 74. *Mailing Add:* Dept of Foreign Lang Calif State Univ Northridge CA 91330

SPINAS, JANET MALONEY, b Jackson, Ohio, Jan 2, 34; m 62; c 1. SPANISH LANGUAGE & LITERATURE. *Educ:* Ohio Univ, AB, 56; Northwestern Univ, MA, 57, PhD(Span), 62. *Prof Exp:* Instr Span, Valparaiso Univ, 57-58; from instr to assoc prof, 61-73, chmn dept foreign lang, 67-80, PROF SPAN, HUMBOLDT STATE UNIV, 73- *Mem:* Am Asn Teachers Span & Port; Am Coun Teaching Foreign Lang; MLA. *Res:* Argentine theater; contemporary Spanish novel; contemporary Spanish theater. *Mailing Add:* Dept of Foreign Lang Humboldt State Univ Arcata CA 95521

SPINELLI, DONALD CARMEN, b Rochester, NY, Dec 9, 42; m 71; c 1. FRENCH LITERATURE. *Educ:* State Univ NY, Buffalo, BA, 64, MA, 66; Ohio State Univ, PhD(Romance lang), 71. *Prof Exp:* Teaching asst French & Ital, Ohio State Univ, 66-70, lectr French, 71-72; asst prof, 72-80, ASSOC PROF FRENCH, WAYNE STATE UNIV, 80- *Mem:* MLA; Am Asn Teachers Fr; Am Soc 18th Century Studies. *Res:* Eighteenth century French literature: Marivaux and Beaumarchais. *Publ:* Coauth, An Annotated Bibliography of French Language and Literature, Garland, 76; auth, The search for truth in Marivaux's island plays, Mich Academician, summer 77; coauth, Beaumarchais Correspondance, Nizet, 78; Beaumarchais's Reading Public in 1809, Publ Hist, IX: 37-79. *Mailing Add:* Dept of Romance Lang Wayne State Univ Detroit MI 48202

SPINGLER, MICHAEL K, b Cambridge, Mass, May 27, 38; m 67. ROMANCE LANGUAGES, FRENCH THEATRE. *Educ:* Dartmouth Col, AB, 59; Univ Pittsburgh, MA, 61, PhD(French), 66. *Prof Exp:* Asst prof French Theatre, Univ Mich, Ann Arbor, 66-72; ASSOC PROF, FRENCH THEATRE, CLARK UNIV, 72- *Res:* Contemporary French theatre--mise en scene; Jarry, Ghelderode and Genet. *Publ:* Auth, Acphaville comes to Paris, Village Voice, 12/71; From the actor to ubu: Jarry's theatre of the double, Mod Drama, 6/73; Anouilh's little Antigone: Tragedy, theatricalism, and the romantic self, Comp Drama, fall 74. *Mailing Add:* Dept of Foreign Lang & Lit Clark Univ Worcester MA 01610

SPININGER, DENNIS JOSEPH, b New York, NY, Mar 18, 40. COMPARATIVE LITERATURE, ROMANTICISM. *Educ:* Brooklyn Col, BA, 63; Univ Wis, MA, 65, PhD(comp lit), 68. *Prof Exp:* Teaching asst comp lit, Univ Wis, 66-67; from asst prof to assoc prof, 68-77, chmn, Dept Classics, 72-73, PROF COMP LIT, BROOKLYN COL, 77-, CHMN DEPT, 72- *Mem:* Am Comp Lit Asn; MLA; Amis Proust. *Res:* European prose fiction; German literature. *Publ:* Auth, Thomas Mann's Thamar story in Joseph und seine Brüder, Monatsh, 69; Paradise setting in Chateaubriand's Atala, Publ Mod Lang Asn, 5/74; Complex generic mode of Andre Gide's Paludes, In: Festschrift for Germaine Bree, 74; Profiles and Principles: The Sense of the Absurd in O Wilde's Importance of Being Earnest, Papers Lang & Lit, winter 76. *Mailing Add:* Dept of Comp Lit Brooklyn Col New York NY 11210

SPIRES, ROBERT CECIL, b Missouri Valley, Iowa, Dec 1, 36; m 63; c 2. CONTEMPORARY SPANISH LITERATURE. *Educ:* Univ Iowa, BA, 59, MA, 63, PhD(Span), 68. *Prof Exp:* From instr to asst prof Span, Ohio Univ, 67-69; asst prof, 69-74, assoc prof, 74-78, PROF SPAN, UNIV KANS, 78- *Honors & Awards:* Univ Kans Mortar Bd Award, 77. *Mem:* MLA; Am Asn Teachers Span & Port. *Res:* Contemporary Hispanic novel; contemporary Spanish drama; contemporary Spanish poetry. *Publ:* Auth, Tecnica y tema en La familia de Pascual Duarte, Insula, 9/71; Systematic doubt: The moral art of La familia de Pascual Duarte, Hisp Rev, summer 72; Cela's La colmena: The creative process as message, Hispania, 12/72; contribr, Novelistas Epanoles de Postguerra, Taurus, Madrid, 76; auth, Linguistic codes and dramatic action in La casa de Bernarda Alba, Am Hispanist, 1/78; La Novela Espanola de Postguerra: Creacion Artistica y Experiencia Personal, Editorial Planeta/Universidad, Madrid, 78; Latrines, whirlpools and voids: The metafictional mode of Juan sin Tierra, Hisp Rev, spring 80; La colera de Aguiles: Un texto producto del lector, Revista Iberoamericana, Julio-Dic, 81. *Mailing Add:* Dept of Span & Port Univ of Kans Lawrence KS 66045

SPIVAKOVSKY, ERIKA, Renaissance History. See Vol I

SPRINGER, OTTO, b Aalen, WGer, Mar 18, 05; US citizen; 59; c 3. GERMANIC LANGUAGES & LITERATURES. *Educ:* Univ Tuebingen, PhD(Ger ling), 27. *Prof Exp:* Prof Ger, Wheaton Col, 32-36 & Univ Kans, 36-40; prof, 40-75, lectr Old Norse, 75-78, EMER PROF GER, UNIV PA, 75- *Concurrent Pos:* Dean col, Univ Pa, 59-68, vprovost, 63-68, actg dir univ libr, 72. *Honors & Awards:* Philos Fac Prize, Univ Tuebingen, 27. *Mem:* Fel Medieval Acad Am; Ling Soc Am (vpres, 54); MLA; corresp mem Inst Für Duet Sprache. *Res:* Old Germanic languages and literatures; medieval studies; dialectology. *Publ:* Auth, Die Flussnamen Wuerttembergs und Badens, Kohlhammer, Stuttgart, 30; Die Nordische Renaissance in Skandinavien, Kohlhammer, Stuttgart/Berlin, 36; A German Conscript with Napoleon, Univ Kans, 38; German and West Germanic, Ger Rev, 41; Medieval pilgrim routes from Scandinavia to Rome, Medieval Studies, 50; Wolfram's Parzival, In: Arthurian Literature in the Middle Ages, 59; Langenscheidts Enzykl Wörterbuch d engl u dt Sprache: English-Deutsch (2 vols), 62-63, Deutsch-English (2 vols), 74-75; Arbeiten zur Germanischen Philologie und zur Literatur des Mittelalters, W Fink, München, 75. *Mailing Add:* 737 Williams Hall Univ of Pa Philadelphia PA 19104

SPRINGER-STRAND, INGEBORG, b Salzburg, Austria, Nov 20, 35; US citizen. SEVENTEENTH CENTURY STUDIES. *Educ:* State Univ NY Albany, BA, 68, MA, 69; Univ Mass Amherst, PhD(Ger lit), 74. *Prof Exp:* Asst prof Ger lit & lang, Univ Cincinnati, 74-75; asst prof Ger lit, 75-80, ASSOC PROF GER LIT, UNIV SOUTHERN CALIF, 80- *Mem:* MLA; Am Asn Teachers Ger; Lessing Soc; Int Arbeiterkreis Barock Lit; Am Soc Ger Lit 16th & 17th Century. *Res:* Editions of 17th century novels and dramas; foreign literature in 17th century Germany: French novels with classical authors. *Publ:* Coauth, De Gerzan-Zesen Afrikanische Sofonisbe als Beispiel zur Funktion der Geschichte im höfisch historischem Roman, Daphnis, 73; auth, Barockroman und Erbauungsliterature: Studien zum Herkules Roman von Andreas H Buchholz, Herbert Lang, Bern, 75; Der Übersetzer als Ausleger zu HH Buchholz Übertragungen der Oden des Horaz, Johns Hopkins Press, 77; Einige Nachrichten zur Biographie JJ Beck's mit einer Biblographic seiner Werke, Wolfenbüttler Barock, Nachrichen, 77; co-ed, J G Schnabel, Insel Felsenburg, Reclam, Stuttgart, 79; auth, Von der schönen Ariana: Ein sehr anmüthige Historj, 1643-, Zur ersten Übersetzung von Desmarets Ariana, 80; Die Ballade von den Königskinder & Der Kriegsmann wil ein Schäfer werden oder: Krieg, Frieden und Poisic in Harsdörffers Friedenshoffnung, In: Renaissance Barock, Gedichte und Interpretation, Vol I, Reclam, Stuttgart, 81-82. *Mailing Add:* Dept of Ger Univ of Southern Calif Los Angeles CA 90007

SPRUELL, SHELBY OUTLAW, b Kingsport, Tenn, Aug 19, 36; div; c 3. FRENCH LITERATURE. *Educ:* Univ Tenn, Knoxville, BA, 58, MA, 63; Emory Univ, PhD(French), 80. *Prof Exp:* Instr French, Univ Tenn, 59-61, admin asst methods, NDEA Inst, 61-65; instr French & educ, 67-71, instr French lit, 76-80, ASST PROF FRENCH LIT, EMORY UNIV, 80- *Mem:* MLA; Western Soc Fr Hist; SAtlantic Mod Lang Asn; Am Soc 18th Century Studies. *Res:* Montesquieu and power relationships; the erotic novel in the 18th century. *Publ:* Auth, The metaphorical use of sexual repression to represent political oppression in Montesquieu's Persian Letters, 80 & Sade: Pornography or political protest, 81, Proc Western Soc Fr Hist. *Mailing Add:* 1192 Oakdale Rd NE Atlanta GA 30307

SPULER, RICHARD CARL, b Spokane, Wash, Aug 7, 53; m 74; c 2. MODERN GERMAN LITERATURE. *Educ:* Wash State Univ, BA, 75, MA, 76; Ohio State Univ, PhD(German), 80. *Prof Exp:* ASST PROF GERMAN, UNIV HOUSTON, 80- *Mem:* Am Asn Teachers of German; MLA; Am Coun Teaching of Foreign Lang; Western Asn German Studies. *Res:* Modern German poetry; literary theory and criticism; history of Germanistik. *Publ:* Auth, Concrete poetry and elementary language study, Teaching Lang Through Lit, 81; Mediating German culture: American Germanistik at the turn of the century, Yearbook of the German Am Soc, 81; Bertolt Brecht, 82 & Gottfried Benn, 82, Critical Survey of Poetry, Salem Press; American Germanistik and German Classicism: A 19th century exchange, In: Germans in America: Aspects of German-American Relations in the 19th Century, 82; Criticism in the wilderness? literary scholarship in American Germanistik, Univ Forum, summer 82; Germanistik in America: The Reception of German Classicism, 1870-1905, Stuttgarter Arbeiten zur Germanistik, Stuttgart, H D Heinz, fall 82. *Mailing Add:* 7700 Creekbend Apt 30 Houston TX 77071

SPURLOCK, JOHN HOWARD, Linguistics, American Literature. See Vol II

SPYRIDAKIS, STYLIANOS V, Ancient History. See Vol I

SQUIRE, DONALD HOVMAND, b Grand Island, Nebr, Dec 23, 37; m 63; c 1. MODERN LANGUAGES & LITERATURES. *Educ:* Univ Nebr-Lincoln, BA, 62; Univ Fla, PhD(Romance lang), 72. *Prof Exp:* Asst prof Romance lang, Col William & Mary, 66-69; assoc prof English, Univ PR, Mayaguez, 70-76, chmn dept, 73-76; ASSOC DEAN STUDENTS, TOWSON STATE UNIV, 76- *Concurrent Pos:* Mem & chmn comt examr in English, Col Entrance Exam Bd, PR, 71-75; Nat Endowment for Humanities fel, Johns Hopkins Univ, 75-76. *Mem:* MLA; Renaissance Soc Am; Am Asn Teachers Span & Port; Teachers English to Speakers Other Lang; Nat Asn Student Personnel Adminr. *Res:* Renaissance prose fiction; Cervantes; the lost generation. *Publ:* Auth, La novela de Ignacio Aldecoa, Isla Lit, 12-1/70-71; Cervantes y Hoffmann ante un tema similar, Atenea, 70. *Mailing Add:* Off of Dean of Student Serv Towson State Univ Baltimore MD 21204

SRIDHAR, S N, b Shimoga, Karnataka, India, May 26, 50; m 74. LINGUISTICS, FOREIGN LANGUAGES & LITERATURES. *Educ:* Bangalore Univ, India, BA Hons, 69, MA, 71; Univ Ill, MA, 75, PhD(ling), 80. *Prof Exp:* Res assoc, Teachers English to Speakers Other Lang, Cent Inst English & Lang, Hyderabad, India, 71-72, lectr ling, 72-73; res asst ling, Univ, Ill, Urbana,, 73-79; ASST PROF LING, STATE UNIV NY, STONY BROOK, 80- *Concurrent Pos:* Consult, Dict Int Varieties of English, 78- & Univ Wash, Seattle, 79; secy, NY State Coun Ling, 81-82. *Mem:* Ling Soc Am; Teachers English to Speakers Other Lang; Ling Soc India; Dravidian Ling Asn; Am Asn Applied Ling. *Res:* Dravidian linguistics; psycholinguistic aspects of sentence production, bilingualism and second language acquisition; teaching English as a second language. *Publ:* Co-ed, Language Through Literature, Vol II, Oxford Univ Press, 75; coauth, Clause-union and relational grammar, Ling Inquiry, 77; co-ed, Aspects of sociolinguistics in South Asia, Int J Sociol Lang, 78; auth, Dative subjects and the notion of subjective, Lingua, 79; Contrastive analysis, error analysis and interlanguage, In: Readings in English as a Second Language, Winthrop, 2nd ed, 80; coauth, Syntax & psycholinguistics of bilingual code mixing, Can J Psychol, 80; auth, Kannada: A Descriptive Grammar, North Holland Publ Co, 82; Language teaching and litercy in South Asia, In: Annual Review of Applied Linguistics, Newbury House, 82. *Mailing Add:* Prog in Ling State Univ NY Stony Brook NY 11794

STAAL, ARIE, American & Netherlandic Literature. See Vol II

STABB, MARTIN SANFORD, b New York, NY, Apr 5, 28; m 49; c 3. SPANISH. *Educ:* Rutgers Univ, BA, 49; Univ Calif, Los Angeles, MA, 51, PhD(Hisp lang & lit), 56. *Prof Exp:* Instr Span, Colgate Univ, 53-55; from instr to prof, Univ Mo-Columbia, 55-70, chmn dept Romance lang, 65-68; PROF SPAN, ITAL & PORT & HEAD DEPT, PA STATE UNIV, UNIVERSITY PARK, 70- *Concurrent Pos:* Consult lang inst, US Off Educ, 62; Soc Sci Res Coun joint comt Latin Am studies grant, 68-69; mem nat adv screening comt in Latin Am lit for Fulbright-Hays awards, 79-82. *Mem:* Am Asn Teachers Span & Port; MLA; Inst Int Lit Iberoam; Latin Am Studies Asn. *Res:* Spanish-American literature; essay; Argentine literature. *Publ:* Auth, La bella dormida: An interpretation of the image in selected Spanish-American poets, Hispania, 5/63; Martinez Estrada frente a la critica, Rev Iberoam, 1-6/66; In Quest of Identity: Patterns of the Spanish American Essay of Ideas, 1890-1960, Univ NC, 67; Jorge Luis Borges, Twayne, 70; Argentine letters and the Peronato: An overview, J Inter-Am Studies & World Affairs, 7-10/71; The new murena and the new novel, Ky Romance Quart, spring 75; The erotic mask: Notes on Donoso and the new novel, Symposium, summer 76; Utopia and anti-utopia: The theme in selected essayistic writings of Spanish America, Rev Estudios Hispanicos, 10/81. *Mailing Add:* 1351 Penrose Circle State College PA 16801

STABLEIN, PATRICIA HARRIS, b Chicago, Ill, June 29, 46; m 70. MEDIEVAL FRENCH & PROVENCIAL LITERATURE. *Educ:* Northwestern Univ, BA, 68, PhD(French lang & lit), 74. *Prof Exp:* Instr French lit, Barat Col, 70-72; adj prof French, Mesa Col, Colo, 79-81. *Mem:* Medieval Acad; MLA; Soc Rencesvals-Am-Can Br; Am Asn Teachers Fr; Int Courtly Lit Soc. *Res:* Old Provencal and Old French literature; structuralist and post-structuralist literary theories; classical and medieval comparative literature. *Publ:* Auth, The structure of the hero in the Chanson de Roland: Heroic being and becoming, Olifant, 5/78; The rotten and the burned: Normative and nutritive structures in the poetry of Bertran de Born, L'Esprit Createur, winter 79; The structure of the Planh, Romance Philol, 81; La structuration lyrique de Ronsasvals, Actes du VIII Congres de la Soc Int Rencesvals, Pamplona, 81; La Semiologie de la Chasse dans la Poesie de Bertran de Born, In: La Chasse au Moyen Age, Univ Nice, 81; Catastrophe theory in genre analysis: Figuring out Raoul de Cambrai and its role in the lyrics of Bertran de Born, Olifant (in press); The form in the mirror: Graven images and the reality of medieval song, Romance Philol (in press); coauth (with William D Paden & Tilde A Sankovitch), The Complete Poetry of Bertran de Born, Univ Calif Press (in press). *Mailing Add:* c/o Mr & Mrs George C Harris 2032 Lake Ave Wilmette IL 60091

STABLER, ARTHUR PHILLIPS, b Sandy Spring, Md, Apr 23, 19; m 43; c 2. FRENCH & COMPARATIVE LITERATURE. *Educ:* Univ Pa, BA, 41, MA, 47; Univ Va, PhD, 59. *Prof Exp:* Assoc prof French & dir lang skills, Lake Erie Col, 59-62; assoc prof French, Univ Mass, 62-63; assoc prof, 63-67, prof French, Wash State Univ, 67-82; RETIRED. *Concurrent Pos:* Contrib ed, Shakespeare Newslett, 73-; mem, Western Shakespeare Sem. *Mem:* Renaissance Soc Am; Am Asn Teachers Fr; MLA; Shakespeare Asn Am; Philol Asn Pac Coast. *Res:* Renaissance French literature; Renaissance comparative literature; Shakespeare. *Publ:* Auth, Melancholy, ambition, and revenge in Belleforest's Hamlet, PMLA, 6/66; The source of the German Hamlet, Shakespeare Studies, 69; The Legend of Marguerite de Roberval, Wash State Univ, 72; Rabelais, Thevet, I'Ile des demons, et les paroles gelees, Etudes Rabelaisiennes, 73; ed & coauth, Four French Renaissance Plays, Wash State Univ, 78. *Mailing Add:* Dept of Foreign Lang & Lit Wash State Univ Pullman WA 99164

STACK, EDWARD MACGREGOR, b Warren, Pa, Nov 7, 19. FRENCH LANGUAGE & LITERATURE. *Educ:* Princeton Univ, AB, 41, AM, 49, PhD(mod lang), 50. *Prof Exp:* Asst prof Romance lang, La State Univ, 50-51; instr, Univ Va, 51-52; asst prof mod lang, Agr & Mech Col Tex, 52-54; asst prof Romance lang, Univ Tex, 54-57; prof mod lang & chmn dept, Whittier Col, 57-60; prof, Villanova Univ, 60-61; dir educ mat, Electronic Teaching Lab, 61-63; PROF MOD LANG, NC STATE UNIV, 63- *Concurrent Pos:* Chmn, State of NC Lang Lab Consult Comt, 63- *Mem:* MLA; AAUP. *Res:* French 17th century literature; scientific literature; typography and printing. *Publ:* Auth, Reading French in the Arts and Sciences, Houghton, 57, 3rd ed, 79; Elementary Oral and Written French, 59 & The Language Laboratory and Modern Language Teaching, rev ed, 66, 3rd ed, 71, Oxford, New York; Le Pont Neuf--A Structural Review Grammar, Prentice, 66, 3rd ed, 78; Das Sprachlabor im Unterricht, Cornelsen, Berlin, 66; Language and language Learning, Ser 26, Oxford Univ, London, 69; co-ed, Pattern Practice in The Teaching of German: Problems & Methods, Karl Shurz Asn, 70; Laboratorio Linguistico e Insegnamento Moderno delle lingue, Le Monnier, 75. *Mailing Add:* Dept of Mod Lang NC State Univ Raleigh NC 27650

STACY, ROBERT HAROLD, b New York, NY, Dec 22, 19. SLAVIC LANGUAGES & LITERATURES. *Educ:* Univ Mich, BA, 46, MA, 47; Syracuse Univ, PhD(humanities), 65. *Prof Exp:* From instr to assoc prof, 64-78, PROF RUSS LIT, SYRACUSE UNIV, 78- *Res:* Russian literature. *Publ:* Auth, The Russian Ghazal, Symposium, winter 64; Types of charactonyms in Russian fiction, Can Slavic Studies, fall 68; Russian Literary Criticism: A Short History, 74 & Defamiliarization in Language & Literature, 77, Syracuse Univ. *Mailing Add:* 7267 Mott Rd Fayetteville NY 13066

STADLER, EVA MARIA (MRS RICHARD BROOKS), b Prague, Czech, Mar 28, 31; US citizen; m 57. FRENCH, COMPARATIVE LITERATURE. *Educ:* Barnard Col, AB, 52; Columbia Univ, PhD(French), 67. *Prof Exp:* Lectr French, Columbia Univ, 53-57; instr French & Ger, Wash Col, 57-58; instr French, Douglass Col, Rutgers Univ, 58-64; asst prof French & Ger, Manhattan Community Col, 65-66, assoc prof French & dir lang lab, 66-68; chmn dept mod & class lang, 69-73, ASSOC PROF COMP LIT & FRENCH, FORDHAM UNIV, 68-, CHMN DIV HUMANITIES, 73- *Mem:* MLA; Am Asn Teachers Fr; Am Comp Lit Asn. *Res:* Literature of the 18th century; the novel and theory of narration; prose fiction and film. *Publ:* Coauth, Premiers textes litteraires, Blaisdell, 66; auth, Salons, In: Critical Bibliography of French Literature: The Eighteenth Century, Syracuse Univ, 68. *Mailing Add:* Div of Humanities Fordham Univ Col at Lincoln Ctr New York NY 10023

STADT, BESSIE WINIFRED, b Rochester, NY, Aug 7, 14; m 58. SPANISH LANGUAGE & LITERATURE. *Educ:* Univ Rochester, BA, 38, MA, 39; Univ Ariz, PhD(Span), 69. *Prof Exp:* Asst prof Span, Simpson Col, 65-66; from asst prof to assoc prof, 66-75, head dept foreign lang, 74-77, prof Span, 75-80, EMER PROF FOREIGN LANG, ROLLINS COL, 80- *Concurrent*

Pos: Res grants, Rollins Col, 70 & 72. *Mem:* MLA; Am Asn Teachers Span & Port; SAtlantic Mod Lang Asn. *Res:* Poets of Extremadura; 19th century writers (women novelists) of Spain. *Mailing Add:* Dept of Foreign Lang Rollins Col Winter Park FL 32789

STADTER, PHILIP AUSTIN, b Cleveland, Ohio, Nov 29, 36; m 63; c 3. CLASSICAL LITERATURE. *Educ:* Princeton Univ, AB, 58; Harvard Univ, MA, 59, PhD(class philol), 63. *Prof Exp:* From instr to assoc prof, 62-71, PROF CLASSICS, UNIV NC, CHAPEL HILL, 71-, CHMN DEPT, 76- *Concurrent Pos:* Guggenheim fel, 67-68; Nat Endowment for Humanities sr fel, 74-75; Am Coun Learned Soc fel, 82-83. *Mem:* Am Philol Asn; Class Asn Midwest & South; Asn Ancient Historians. *Res:* Plutarch, Arrian, Greek in Renaissance; Greek historiography. *Publ:* Auth, Plutarch's Historical Methods, Harvard Univ, 65; Flavius Arrianus: The new Xenophon, Greek, Roman & Byzantine Studies, 67; The structure of Livy's history, Historia, 72; coauth, The Public Library of Renaissance Florence, Antenore, Italy, 72; ed, The Speeches of Thucydides, Univ NC, 73; auth, Pace, Planudes, and Plutarch, Ital Medioevale e Umanistica, 73; Arrianus, Flavius, In: Catalogus Translationum et Commentariorum, Vol III, Cath Univ Am, 76; Arrian of Nicomedia, Univ NC, 80. *Mailing Add:* Dept of Classics Univ of NC Chapel Hill NC 27514

STAGG, GEOFFREY (LEONARD), b Birmingham, Eng, May 10, 13; m 48; c 3. ROMANCE LANGUAGES. *Educ:* Cambridge Univ, BA, 34, MA, 46; Harvard Univ, AM, 35. *Prof Exp:* Master mod lang, King Edward's Sch, Birmingham, Eng, 39-40, 46-47; lectr Span & Ital, Nottingham Univ, 47-53, head dept Span, 54-56; chmn dept Ital & Hisp, 56-66, 69-77, PROF ITAL & HISP STUDIES, UNIV TORONTO, 56- *Concurrent Pos:* Sr fel, Massey Col & fel, New Col, Univ Toronto, 65; Can Coun sr fel, 67-68. *Mem:* Am Asn Teachers Span & Port; Asn Teachers Span & Port Gt Brit & Ireland (vpres, 50-); Asn Hispanists Gt Brit & Ireland (secy-treas, 55-56); Can Asn Hispanists (pres, 64-66 & 72); Asn Int de Hispanistas (vpres, 77-). *Res:* Cervantes; Hispano-Italian literary relations; Spanish Golden Age novel. *Mailing Add:* Dept of Span & Port Univ of Toronto Toronto ON M5S 1A1 Can

STAGG, LOUIS CHARLES, English. See Vol II

STAHL, VERLAN H, b Bakersfield, Calif, June 6, 25. SPANISH. *Educ:* Col of the Pac, AB, 50; Fla State Univ, MA, 55; Univ Madrid, PhD(Span), 69. *Prof Exp:* Instr Span & French, Wake Forest Col, 58-60; lectr, 68-69, from asst prof to assoc prof, 69-76, PROF SPAN, CALIF POLYTECH STATE UNIV, SAN LUIS OBISPO, 76-, DEPT HEAD, 75- *Concurrent Pos:* Am prog officer, Fulbright Comn Educ Exchange US-Spain, Madrid, 62-68. *Mem:* Am Asn Prof Span & Port. *Mailing Add:* Dept of Foreign Lang Calif Polytech State Univ San Luis Obispo CA 93407

STAHLBERGER, LAWRENCE L, b Rochester, NY, Mar 3, 16; m 49. SLAVIC LANGUAGES & LITERATURES. *Educ:* Harvard Univ, AB, 50, AM, 51, PhD(Russ lit), 56. *Prof Exp:* Asst prof Russ, Boston Univ, 56-62; asst prof, 62-65, ASSOC PROF SLAVIC LIT, STANFORD UNIV, 65- *Mem:* Am Asn Advan Slavic Studies. *Res:* Russian 20th century poetry; Russian romanticism; Old Russian literature. *Publ:* Auth, The Symbolic System of Mujukovskij, Mouton, 65. *Mailing Add:* Dept of Slavic Lang & Lit Stanford Univ Stanford CA 94305

STAHLKE, HERBERT FREDERIC WALTER, b Monroe, Mich, Mar 20, 42; m 68; c 2. LINGUISTICS, AFRICAN STUDIES. *Educ:* Concordia Sr Col, BA, 63; Univ Calif, Los Angeles, MA, 68, PhD(ling), 71. *Prof Exp:* Vol Peace Corps, Anglican Grammar Sch, Otan-Aiyegbaju, Nigeria, Ogoja, Nigeria, 65-68; asst Yoruba, Univ Calif, Los Angeles, 68-69, asst phonetics & hist ling, 69; from instr to asst prof ling, Univ Ill, Urbana, 69-74; asst prof, Ga State Univ, 74-77, assoc prof, 77-80; MEM FAC, DEPT ENGLISH, BALL STATE UNIV, 80- *Concurrent Pos:* Assoc ed, Studies African Ling, 70-; collab scientist, Yerkes Regional Primate Res Ctr, Emory Univ, 76- *Mem:* Ling Soc Am; Semiotic Soc Am. *Res:* African linguistics; linguistic theory; language training of non-human primates. *Publ:* Auth, Serial verbs, Studies African Ling, 70; co-ed, Papers in African Linguistics, 71 & Current Trends in Stylistics, 72, Ling Res, Edmonton; auth, Pronouns and Islands in Yoruba, 74 & Segment sequences and segmental fusion, 76, Studies African Ling; Some problems with binary features for tone, Int J Am Ling, 76; Which that, Lang, 76; On asking the question: Can apes learn language, In: Child Language, Gardner, 78. *Mailing Add:* Dept of English Ball State Univ Muncie IN 47306

STALEY, CONSTANCE MARIE, Speech Communication, Linguistics. See Vol II

STALEY, GREGORY ALLAN, b Hagerstown, Md, Aug 12, 48; m; c 1. CLASSICS. *Educ:* Dickinson Col, BA, 70; Princeton Univ, MA, 73, PhD(classics), 75. *Prof Exp:* Instr classics, Dickinson Col, 74-75; asst prof, Fordham Univ, Lincoln Ctr, 75-76; lectr, Univ Alta, 76-78; asst prof, Dickinson Col, 78-79; ASST PROF CLASSICS, UNIV MD, COLLEGE PARK, 79- *Mem:* Am Philol Asn; Vergilian Soc; Class Asn Atlantic States. *Res:* Senecan tragedy; Greek drama; ancient philosophy. *Publ:* Speculum Iratis: Philosophy and rhetoric in Senecan tragedy, In: Vol II, Univ of Florida Comparative Drama Conference Papers (in prep). *Mailing Add:* Dept of Classics Univ of Md College Park MD 20742

STAM, JAMES HENRY, Philosophy, Classical Languages. See Vol IV

STAMBAUGH, RIA, b Aachen, Ger, Mar 13, 18; US citizen; m 48; c 1. GERMANIC LANGUAGE & LITERATURE. *Educ:* Piedmont Col, BA, 57; Univ NC, Chapel Hill, PhD, 63. *Prof Exp:* From instr to assoc prof Ger lang, 61-72, chmn div humanities, 77-80, PROF LATE MEDIEVAL & REFORMATION FOLKLORE, UNIV NC, CHAPEL HILL, 72-, PROF GERMAN, 80- *Mem:* Am Asn Teachers Ger; SAtlantic Mod Lang Asn; Int Ver ger Sprach- & Lit Wiss. *Res:* Late medieval and Reformation era literature; critical editions of 16th century prints-devilbooks; folklore-proverbs and jests, narrative research. *Publ:* Auth, Proverbial material in sixteenth century German jestbooks, Proverbium, 68; auth & ed, Teufelbücher i Ausw Ludw Millichius: Zauberteufel Schrapteufel, Vol I, 70, Teufelbücher i Ausw Strauss, Daul, Hoppenrod, Schubart, Schmidt, Vol II, 72, Teufelbücher i Ausw Joach Westphal: Hoffartsteufel, Vol III, 73 & Teufelbucher i Ausw Andreas Musculus: Hosenteufel, Vol IV, 78, Gruyter, Berlin & New York. *Mailing Add:* Dept of Ger Univ of NC Chapel Hill NC 27514

STAMELMAN, RICHARD HOWARD, b Newark, NJ, Mar 7, 42; m 65; c 2. FRENCH LITERATURE, MODERN POETRY. *Educ:* Hamilton Col, AB, 63; Duke Univ, PhD(French lit), 67. *Prof Exp:* Asst prof Romance lang, 67-74, coordr, Wesleyan in Paris Prog, 73-75, assoc prof, 74-79, PROF ROMANCE LANG, WESLEYAN UNIV, 79-, DIR, CTR FOR HUMANITIES, 76- *Concurrent Pos:* Nat Endowment for Humanities Younger Humanists fel, 72. *Mem:* MLA; Am Asn Teachers French; Asn Study Dada & Surrealism; Northeast Mod Lang Asn; Am Asn Advan of Humanities. *Res:* Nineteenth and twentieth century French poetry; comparative modern poetry; relationships between painting and poetry. *Publ:* Auth, From muteness to speech: The drama of expression in Francis Ponge's Poetry, Bks Abroad, autumn 74; Andre Breton and the poetry of intimate presence, 75 & The relational structure of surrealist poetry, 76, Dada/Surrealism; The Drama of Self in Guillaume Apollinaire's Alcools, Univ NC, 76; The object in poetry and painting: Ponge and Picasso, Contemp Lit, fall 78; The allegory of loss and exile in the poetry of Yucs Bonnefoy, World Lit Today, summer 79; Landscape and loss in Yucs Bonnefoy and Philippe Jaccottet, Fr Forum, 1/80; The syntax of the ephemeral, Dalhousie Fr Studies, 10/80. *Mailing Add:* Ctr for the Humanities Wesleyan Univ Middletown CT 06457

STAMM, JAMES RUSSELL, b Shelbyville, Ind, Nov 5, 24; m 54. SPANISH LANGUAGE & LITERATURE. *Educ:* Columbia Univ, BS, 49; Mex City Col, BA & MA, 50; Stanford Univ, PhD(Span lang & lit), 59. *Prof Exp:* Instr philos, Mex City Col, 50-52; teaching asst Span, Stanford Univ, 54; instr, Lehigh Univ, 56-58; asst prof humanities, Mich State Univ, 58-63; resident dir, NY Univ in Spain, 65-71, chmn dept Span & Port, 75-78, ASSOC PROF SPAN & PORT, NY UNIV, 63- *Concurrent Pos:* Fulbright res scholar, Madrid, 61-63. *Mem:* MLA; Am Asn Teachers Span & Port. *Res:* Spanish Golden Age literature and history; generation of '98; contemporary Spanish and Portuguese literature. *Publ:* Coauth, Unamuno: Dos novelas cortas, Ginn, 61; auth, A Short History of Spanish Literature, Doubleday, 67, rev ed, NY Univ Press, 79. *Mailing Add:* Dept of Span & Port NY Univ New York NY 10003

STAMMLER, HEINRICH A, b Jena, Ger, Dec 15, 12. SLAVIC LANGUAGES & LITERATURE. *Educ:* Univ Munich, PhD(Slavic philol & lit). *Prof Exp:* Instr & lectr foreign lang, Bus Col Svishtov, Bulgaria, 37-40; first asst & lectr Am lit & civilization, Univ Munich, 49-53; asst prof Ger & Russ, Northwestern Univ, 53-60; assoc prof, 60-61, PROF SLAVIC LANG & LIT, UNIV KANS, 62- *Concurrent Pos:* Vis prof, Vanderbilt Univ, 70. *Mem:* Am Asn Teachers Ger; Am Asn Teachers Slavic & E Europ Lang; Am Comp Lit Asn; Am Asn Advan Slavic Studies. *Res:* Russian literature and philosophy; Polish civilization and intellectual history; Balkan studies. *Publ:* Auth, Die Russische Geistliche Volksdichtung, 39; J A Boratynskij, 48; W W Rosanow: Ausgewählte Schriften, 63 & ed, Fürst Wladimir F Odojewskij: Russische Nächte, 70; Stanislaw Przybyszerski and Antoni Choloniewski: Two interpreters of the meaning of Polish history, J Geschichte Osteuropas, 72; Wandlungen des deutschen Geschichtbildes von Polen, In: Ost West Polarität, Wissenschaft & Politik, Cologne, 72; Metamorphoses of the will: Schopenhauer and Feth, Western Philos Systs Russ Lit, 80. *Mailing Add:* Dept of Slavic Lang & Lit Univ Kans Lawrence KS 66045

STANDRING, ENID MARY, b Egerton, England; US citizen. FRENCH, COMPARATIVE LITERATURE. *Educ:* Univ Manchester, BA Hons, 35, MA, 41; Univ Poitiers & Besancon, LesL, 39; NY Univ, PhD(Romance lang), 57. *Prof Exp:* Spec lectr French & Ger, Hofstra Col, 57; vis lectr, State Col Educ, NY, 58-59; assoc prof, Chadron State Col, 59-60; asst prof French & Ger, 60-63, asst prof, 63-67, ASSOC PROF FRENCH, MONTCLAIR STATE COL, 67- *Mem:* MLA; NE Mod Lang Asn. *Res:* Berlioz; George Sand; Stendhal. *Publ:* Auth, articles on Copland, Persichetti and Sanders, Dict Musique, 69; The Lelios of Berlioz and George Sand, Commemorative Vol George Sand Conf 1976, Hofstra, 78. *Mailing Add:* Dept of French Montclair State Col Upper Montclair NJ 07043

STANISLAWCZYK, IRENE ELEANOR, b New Britain, Conn. SPANISH FOREIGN LANGUAGE METHODOLOGY. *Educ:* St Joseph Col, BA, 48; Wesleyan Univ, MALS, 59. *Prof Exp:* Teacher Span & Latin, Mt St Joseph Acad, 50-56; teacher Latin, East Hartford High, Conn, 56-57; teacher Span & Latin Windsor High, 57-64; ASSOC PROF SPAN METHODOLOGY, CENT CONN STATE COL, 64- *Concurrent Pos:* Distinguished vis prof Span, Univ of Mont, 70 & 71; vis prof Span, Fairfield Univ, Spain, 71-82; Nat Endowment for Humanities grant, Stanford Univ, 78. *Mem:* Am Asn Teachers Span & Port (secy, 67-73, vpres, 82-); Am Asn Univ Women; New England Mod Lang Asn; AAUP; Class Asn New England. *Publ:* Auth, Discovering South America, Conn Teacher, 3/66; coauth, Tierras, Costumbres y Tipos Hispanicos, Bobbs, 70; auth, Teaching here and abroad, 2/74 & Using parameters in preparing learning packets, 2/76, Foreign Lang News Exchange; coauth, Creativity in the Language Classroom, Newbury House, 76; contribr, Bringing Culture to Language Classroom, 76 & Goals, 77, Conn Coun of Lang Teachers; ed, Warsaw's restitution, Madrid's destitution, Perspectives, 1-2/78. *Mailing Add:* Cent Conn State Col 1615 Stanley St New Britain CT 06053

STANKIEWICZ, EDWARD, b Poland, Nov 14, 20; nat US; m 50; c 2. SLAVIC LANGUAGES & LITERATURES & LINGUISTICS. *Educ:* Univ Chicago, MA, 51; Harvard Univ, PhD, 54. *Prof Exp:* Asst prof Slavic ling, Ind Univ, 54-55, 56-59, assoc prof, 59-62; from assoc prof to prof, Univ Chicago, 62-71; PROF SLAVIC LING, YALE UNIV, 71- *Concurrent Pos:* Ford fel, 55-56; Am Coun Learned Soc res grant, Yugoslavia, 62-63; NSF grant, 66-71; Guggenheim fel, 77. *Mem:* Ling Soc Am. *Res:* History of linguistics; poetic and expressive language; Slavic accentology. *Publ:* Auth, Phonemic patterns of Polish dialects, 56; Interdependence of paradigmatic & derivational patterns, Word, 62; Problems of emotive language, In: Approaches to Semiotics, Humanities, 64; coauth, Selected Bibliography of Slavic Linguistics, Mouton, The Hague, 66; auth, Opposition & hierarchy in morphophonemics, In: To Honor R Jakobson, 67; Declension & Gradation of Russian Substantives, Mouton, The Hague, 68; transl & ed, Baudouin de Courtenay Anthology, Ind Univ, 72; Studies in Slavic Accentology, 79. *Mailing Add:* Dept of Slavic Lang & Lit Yale Univ New Haven CT 06520

STANLEY, DENIS KEITH, JR, b Gainesville, Fla, Aug 9, 34. CLASSICAL LANGUAGES. *Educ:* Univ Fla, BA, 57; Johns Hopkins Univ, PhD(classics), 61. *Prof Exp:* From instr to asst prof Greek, 61-67, ASSOC PROF CLASS STUDIES, DUKE UNIV, 67-, ASST CUR UNIV MUS, 73- *Concurrent Pos:* Greek and Roman epic; ancient literary criticism. *Mailing Add:* 324 Carr Duke Univ Durham NC 27708

STANLEY, DOROTHY EVELYN, b Nurenberg, Ger, Sept 18, 09; US citizen; m 32; c 2. FOREIGN LANGUAGES. *Educ:* Hunter Col, MA, 51. *Prof Exp:* Head of proofroom, George Grady Press, New York, 39-42; asst head monitoring sect, Overseas Radio Div, US Dept State, 42-45; prof English & French, Lycee French, New York, 45-46; prof Latin & French, Acad Sacred Heart, NY, 46-49; prof French & Ger, Acad Lang, 49-52; transl & interpreter, First Nat City Bank NY, 52-59; asst prof Ger & French, Old Dominion Univ, 60-75; RETIRED. *Concurrent Pos:* Lectr & exhibitor art galleries, New York, 54-59 & Va, 59-75. *Honors & Awards:* Recipient Grand Nat Finalist Award, Am Artists Professional League, 56 & 57. *Mem:* Am Asn Retired Persons. *Res:* Foreign languages and linguistics, especially semantics; metaphysics and philosophy; music and art, especially painting. *Publ:* Auth, Die Kunterbunte Spielkiste, 29 & coauth, Das Lustige Kinderbuch, 31, Levy & Muller, Stuttgart; auth, They Call it Courage, Vantage, 68; How to Live Creatively, Donning, 80. *Mailing Add:* 330 W Brambleton Ave Norfolk VA 23510

STANLEY, GEORGE EDWARD, b Memphis, Tex, July 15, 42. LINGUISTICS, GERMAN. *Educ:* Tex Tech Univ, BA, 65, MA, 67; Univ Port Elizabeth, DLitt(ling), 74. *Prof Exp:* Instr ling, East Tex State Univ, 67-69; instr English as foreign lang, Univ Kans, 69-70; ASSOC PROF LING & GER, CAMERON UNIV, 70- *Concurrent Pos:* Fulbright prof, Univ Chad, 73. *Mem:* Philol Soc England; Crime Writers' Asn Gr Brit; Soc Children's Bk Writers. *Res:* Sociolinguistic problems in South Africa. *Publ:* Auth, Semantics and elementary education, English Studies Africa, 9/69; Phonoaesthetics and West Texas (Lubbock) dialect, Linguistics, 7/71; Linguistic relativity and the EFL teacher in South Africa, English Lang Teaching, 6/71; Mini Mysteries, Sat Eve Post Co, 79; The toxic tuber, 6/79, The vacuum victim, 4/80, The rhubarb revenge, 4/81 & The deadly dosage, 1/82, Child Life. *Mailing Add:* Dept of Lang Arts Cameron Univ Lawton OK 73505

STANLEY, PATRICIA HAAS, b New Bedford, Mass. GERMAN HUMANITIES. *Educ:* Univ Louisville, AB, 64, MA, 69; Univ Va, PhD(Ger), 75. *Prof Exp:* Asst prof Ger, Univ Va, 76-77; asst prof, 77-80, PROF GER, FLA STATE UNIV, 80- *Mem:* Am Asn Teachers Ger; MLA; SAtlantic Mod Lang Asn; Am Lit Translators Asn; Kafka Soc Am. *Res:* Literature of the absurd. *Publ:* Auth, Verbal music in theory and practice, Ger Rev, 5/77; Wolfgang Hildesheimers Tynset, Scriptor Verlag, WGer, fall 78; The structure of Wolfgang Hildesheimer's Tynset, Monatshefte, spring 79; Wolfgang Hildesheimer's Mary Stuart: Language Run Riot, Ger Rev, summer 79; Ilse Aichinger's Absurd I, Ger Studies Rev, 10/79; An examination of Walter Kempowski's Ein Kapitel für sich, SAtlantic Rev, 1/82; transl, Wolfgang Hildesheimer, Dimension, Vol VIII, No 3, Gargoyle, Vol 6, 77-79, Lit Rev, Vol 24, No 1, Denver Quart, fall 80. *Mailing Add:* Dept of Mod Lang Fla State Univ Tallahassee FL 32306

STANTON, EDWARD F, b Colorado Springs, Colo, Oct 29, 42; m 70; c 1. HISPANIC LANGUAGE & LITERATURE. *Educ:* Univ Calif, Los Angeles, BA, 64, MA, 69, PhD(Hisp lang & lit), 72. *Prof Exp:* Asst prof, 72-78, ASSOC PROF SPAN & ITAL, UNIV KY, 78- *Concurrent Pos:* Nat Endowment for Humanities summer fel, 81. *Mem:* MLA; Am Asn Teachers Span & Port; Hemingway Soc. *Res:* Modern Spanish poetry; Spanish and Latin American literature; comparative literature. *Publ:* Auth, Cervantes and Cinthio . . . Persiles y Segismunda, Hisp-Ital Studies, 76; The origins of the saeta, Romanische Forschungen, 76; Antonioni's The Passenger: A parabola of light, Lit/Film Quart, winter 77; Machado and Dante . . ., Mod Lang Notes, 3/78; The Tragic Myth: Lorca and Cante Jondo, Univ Ky, 78; A Model for Lorca's Poetic World, Garci Lorca Rev, spring 78; The Correspondent and the Doctor, Hemingway Rev, fall 81; Basilio da Gama, The Uruguay, Univ Calif, 82. *Mailing Add:* Dept of Span & Ital Univ of Ky Lexington KY 40506

STARK, BRUCE RODERICK, b Chicago, Ill, July 9, 31. ENGLISH, LINGUISTICS. *Educ:* Beloit Col, BA, 53; Columbia Univ, MA, 61, PhD(ling & English), 70. *Prof Exp:* Asst English, Lycee Michel Montaigne, Bordeaux, France, 53-54; teaching asst English as second lang, Columbia Univ, 55-63; instr ling, Cornell Univ, 63-65; instr English ling, Univ Wis, Madison, 65-68; asst prof, 68-73, ASSOC PROF ENGLISH LING, UNIV WIS, MILWAUKEE, 74- *Concurrent Pos:* Teacher French, US Air Froce Inst, Okinawa, Rinkin Islands, 55. *Mem:* Ling Soc Am; MLA Conrad Soc. *Res:* Stylistics; criticism. *Publ:* Auth, The Bloomfieldian model, Lingua, 30: 385-421; The intricate pattern in The Great Gatsby, Hemingway/Fitzgerald Ann, 74; Kurtz's intended: The heart of Heart of Darkness, Tex Studies Lit & Lang, 74. *Mailing Add:* Dept of English Univ Wis Milwaukee WI 53212

STAROSTA, STANLEY, b Oconomowoc, Wis, Nov 28, 39; m 70. LINGUISTICS. *Educ:* Univ Wis, BA, 61, PhD(ling), 67. *Prof Exp:* From asst prof to assoc prof, 67-75, PROF LING, UNIV HAWAII, MANOA, 75- *Concurrent Pos:* Vis asst prof ling, Cornell Univ, 69; vis lectr, Monash Univ,

Australia, 73; vis res fel, Inst Advan Studies Humanities, Univ Edinburgh, 73-74; vis res fel, Inst deutsche Sprache, Mannheim, 79. *Mem:* Ling Soc Am; Ling Soc India; Ling Asn Gt Brit; Asn Comput Ling; Deutsche Gesellschaft fur Sprachwissenschaft. *Res:* Syntactic theory, especially lexicase; Asian and Pacific languages, especially Munda and Formosan languages. *Publ:* Auth, Some lexical redundancy rules for English nouns, Glossa, 71; The faces of Case, Lang Sci, 73; Causative verbs in Formosan languages, Oceanic Ling, 74; A place for Case, Lang Learning, 6/76; Affix hobbling, Working Papers Ling, 77; The one per Sent solution, In: Valence, Semantic Case and Grammatical Relations, John Benjamins, Amsterdam, 78; The derivation of combining forms and nominal pseudocompounds in Sora, In: Proceedings of the symposium on Austroasiatic languages, Scandinavian Inst Asian Studies, Lund; coauth, The evolution of focus in Austronesian, In: Selected Papers from the Third International Conference on Austronesian Linguistics, Australian Nat Univ, Canberra. *Mailing Add:* 1607 Ruth Pl Honolulu HI 96816

STARR, RAYMOND JAMES, b Grand Rapids, Mich, May 17, 52; m 75. CLASSICAL LANGUAGES. *Educ:* Univ Mich, BA, 74; Princeton Univ, MA, 76, PhD(class), 78. *Prof Exp:* Lectr class, Princeton Univ, 78-79; ASST PROF GREEK & LATIN, WELLESLEY COL, 79- *Concurrent Pos:* Fel, Am Coun Learned Soc, 82-83. *Mem:* Am Philol Asn; Class Asn Can; Class Asn New England. *Res:* Social context of ancient literature; Roman historiography; comedy. *Publ:* Auth, Velleius' literary techniques in the organization of his history, Trans of the Am Philol Asn, 80; The scope and genre of Velleius' history, Class Quart, 81; Cross-references in Roman prose, Am J of Philol, 81. *Mailing Add:* Dept of Greek & Latin Wellesley Col Wellesley MA 02181

STARR, WILLIAM THOMAS, b Kirksville, Mo, Mar 11, 10; m 34; c 2. FRENCH LITERATURE. *Educ:* Northeast Mo State Teachers Col, BS, 31; Univ Ore, AM, 32, PhD, 38. *Prof Exp:* Instr French, Univ Ariz, 36-38; instr mod lang, Phoenix Jr Col, Ariz, 38-39; asst prof Romance lang, Gettysburg Col, 40-41, asst prof Ger, 41-45; from instr to prof Romance lang, 45-78, EMER PROF FRENCH & ITAL, NORTHWESTERN UNIV, EVANSTON, 78- *Concurrent Pos:* Gen ed, French 6 Bibliog Studies 19th Century Fr Lit, Fr Inst, 56-67; mem adv bd, 19th Century Fr Studies, 72-; lit ed, Fr Rev, 73- *Mem:* MLA; Am Asn Teachers Fr; Am Asn Teachers Ital; Asn Amis Romain Rolland. *Res:* Nineteenth century and contemporary French literature; Romain Rolland. *Publ:* Auth, A Critical Bibliography of the Published Works of Romain Rolland, 50 & Romain Rolland and a World at War, 56, Northwestern Univ; The Romantic movement; a bibliography, Italian, Philol Quart, 61-63 & English Lang Notes, 65-67; Rolland and Schiller, Annali Inst Univ Orientale, 71; Romain: One Against All, a Biography, Mouton, The Hague, 71; Water symbols in the novels of Romain Rolland, Neophilologus, 72. *Mailing Add:* 3121 Grande Vista Pl NW Albuquerque NM 87120

STARY, SONJA GALE, b Minneapolis, Minn. FRENCH LANGUAGE & LITERATURE. *Educ:* Univ Minn, Minneapolis, BS(French) & BA(Span), 63; Univ Cincinnati, MA, 67, PhD(French), 71. *Prof Exp:* ASST PROF FRENCH, UNIV MO-ST LOUIS, 72- *Mem:* Am Asn Teachers Fr; AAUP; MLA: Malraux Soc. *Res:* Balzac; 19th and 20th century novel. *Publ:* Coauth, Mask and vision in Malraux's L'Espoir, Fr Rev, spring 74; Cyclic time in Malraux's La Voie Royale, Neophilologus, 1/76; Recollections of Dante's Inferno in Malraux's La Voie Royale, Symposium, summer 76; auth, Providential justice in Balzac's Comedie humane, Romanic Rev, 11/77; The animal identities of Malraux's characters in La Condition humaine, French Forum, 5/79; The artist and the monkey in Butor's Portrait de l'artiste en jeunne singe, Symposium, spring 80. *Mailing Add:* Dept of Mod Foreign Lang Univ of Mo St Louis MO 63121

STATHATOS, CONSTANTINE CHRISTOPHER, b Athens, Greece, Apr 12, 39. SPANISH. *Educ:* Eastern Ore Col, BA, 63; Univ Ore, MA, 66, PhD(Span), 70. *Prof Exp:* Asst prof, 70-75, ASSOC PROF SPAN, UNIV WIS-PARKSIDE, 75- *Res:* Spanish drama of the Siglo de Oro; Gil Vicente; translation. *Publ:* Ed, A Critical Edition with Introduction and Notes of Gil Vicente's Floresta de Enganos, Univ NC, 72; auth, Antecendents of Gil Vicente's Floresta de Enganos, Luso-Brazilian Rev, 72; co-ed, En onda, Norton, 75; A bibliography of translations of Gil Vicente's works since 1940, Vortice, 75; French contributions to the study of Gil Vicente (1942-1975), Luso-Brazilian Rev, 78; Another Look at Mira de Amescua's Don Alvaro de Luna, Segismundo, 78-80; A Gil Vicente Bibliography (1940-1975), Grant & Cutler, 80; Lazarillo de Tormes in Current English: Two Notes, Hispanofila, 82. *Mailing Add:* Div of Humanistic Studies Univ of Wis-Parkside Kenosha WI 53141

STAUBACH, CHARLES NEFF, b Yonkers, NY, Mar 15, 06; m 37; c 2. ROMANCE LANGUAGES & LITERATURES. *Educ:* Univ Mich, AB, 28, AM, 30, PhD, 37. *Prof Exp:* Instr Span, La State Univ, 29-30; instr, Univ Mich, 30-33, 34-43, from asst prof to prof, 43-65, chmn dept Romance lang, 51-59; prof, Univ Ariz, 65-68; res & writing, 68-80; RETIRED. *Concurrent Pos:* Vis prof, Nat Univ Colombia, 44-45; vis prof appl ling, Univ NMex, 63-65; ed, Ariz Foreign Lang Teachers Forum, 66-69. *Mem:* MLA; Am Asn Teachers Span & Port. *Res:* Applied linguistics; 18th century Hispanic literature; language pedagogy. *Publ:* Coauth, Teaching Spanish: A Linguistic Orientation, Ginn, 61, Blaisdell, 65; First Year Spanish, Second Year Spanish & Lengua Activa (2vols), Ginn, 70. *Mailing Add:* 10625 White Mountain Rd Sun City AZ 85351

STAVAN, HENRY-ANTHONY, b Ostrava, Czech, June 13, 25; US citizen. FRENCH. *Educ:* San Francisco State Col, BA, 56; Univ Calif, Berkeley, MA, 60, PhD(Romance lit), 63. *Prof Exp:* Instr Span, Sacramento State Col, 61-62; asst prof French, Univ Wyo, 63-64; asst prof, Univ Minn, 64-66; assoc prof, 66-75, PROF FRENCH, UNIV COLO, BOULDER, 75- *Concurrent Pos:* Foe fel, Colo Univ, 69-70 & 74-75; vis prof, Univ of Tubingen, Ger, 78-79. *Mem:* Fr Soc 18th Century Studies. *Res:* Eighteenth century French literature. *Publ:* Auth, Un roman sentimental entre Rousseau et Bernardin de Saint-Pierre, Rev Univ Ottawa, 72; Quelques aspects de lyrisme dans la poesie du XVIIIe siecle, Rev Sci Huamaines, 73; coauth, Editing The Complete Works of Voltaire, Voltaire Found, Banbury, Oxfordshire, UK, 73-75; auth, Le lyrisme dans la poesie francaise de 1760 a 1820, Mouton, The Hague, 76; The Ugly Americans of 1780, Stanford Fr Studies, 78; Voltaire und Kurfürst Karl Theodor von der Pfalz, Gesellschaft der Freunde Mannheims, 78; Voltaire et la Duchesse de Gotha, Studies Voltaire, 80; Herzogin Louise Dorothee von Sachsen-Gotha und Voltaire, Jahrbuch Coburger Landesstiftung, 80. *Mailing Add:* Dept of French Univ of Colo Boulder CO 80302

STAVENHAGEN, LEE, b Galveston, Tex, Mar 12, 33; m 57; c 3. GERMAN & MEDIEVAL LITERATURE. *Educ:* Univ Tex, BA, 58, MA, 60; Univ Calif, Berkeley, PhD(Ger), 64. *Prof Exp:* Asst prof Ger, Rice Univ, 64-72; asst prof, Brandeis Univ, 72-76; ASSOC PROF MOD LANG, TEX A&M UNIV 76- *Concurrent Pos:* Folger Libr fel, 75. *Mem:* Fel Mediaeval Acad Am; Soc Hist Alchemy & Chem Res. *Res:* Medieval and Renaissance German literature; German Romanticism; history and literature of alchemy. *Publ:* Auth, Das Petruslied, Wirkendes Wort, 67; A legendary backdrop for Gahmuret, Rice Univ Studies, 67; The original text of the Latin Morienus, Ambix, 3/70; A Testament of Alchemy, Brandeis Univ, 74; Narrative Illustration Techniques and the Mute Books of Alchemy, Explor Renaissance Cult, 79. *Mailing Add:* Dept of Mod Lang Tex A&M Univ College Station TX 77843

STEEDMAN, DAVID WILSON, b Grand Falls, Nfld; Can citizen. FRENCH LANGUAGE & LITERATURE. *Educ:* Univ Toronto, BA, 62; Yale Univ, PhD(French lit), 66. *Prof Exp:* Assoc dean, fac arts, McGill Univ, 71-73, asst to acad vprin, 73-76, actg chmn, Dept French Lang, 74-76; ACAD DIR, HUMANITIES RES COUN CAN, 76- *Mem:* MLA. *Publ:* Auth, La Morale de Daphne, Melanges, 71. *Mailing Add:* 54 Reid Ave Ottawa ON K1Y 1S6 Can

STEELE, CHARLES W, b Manchester, Conn, May 1, 18; m 43; c 4. LANGUAGES. *Educ:* Univ Mo, AB, 42; Univ Calif, Berkeley, MA, 48; Ohio State Univ, PhD, 57. *Prof Exp:* Asst prof Span, Westminster Col, Mo, 48-49; from instr to assoc prof mod lang, 49-64, chmn dept, 64-70, PROF MOD LANG, DENISON UNIV, 64- *Concurrent Pos:* Vis prof English, Univ Valle, Columbia, 70-71. *Mem:* Am Asn Teachers Span & Port; MLA; Midwest Mod Lang Asn. *Res:* Nineteenth and 20th century Spanish and Latin American literature. *Publ:* Auth, The Krausist educator as depicted by Galdos, Ky Foreign Lang Quart, 58; Poe's The Cask of Amontillado, Explicator, 4/60; Functions of the Grisostomo-Marcela episode in Don Quijote: Symbolism, drama, parody, Revista De Estudios Hispanicos, 1: 3-17. *Mailing Add:* Dept of Mod Lang Denison Univ Granville OH 43023

STEELE, CYNTHIA, b Colusa, Calif, Aug 7, 51. LATIN AMERICAN & SPANISH LITERATURE. *Educ:* Calif State Univ, Chico, BA, 73; Univ Calif, San Diego, MA, 79, PhD(Spanish lit), 80. *Prof Exp:* ASST PROF SPANISH, OHIO STATE UNIV, 80- *Mem:* Int Comparative Lit Asn; MLA. *Res:* Mexican literature; modern and contemporary Latin American novel; Latin American women writers. *Publ:* Auth, Con las armas que el traia: Closure and thematic structure in Romance de una fatal ocasion, Part II: Changing characterization in the evolution of a tragic ending in El Romancero hoy: Poetica, Madrid, 79; Literature and national formation: Indigenista fiction in the United States, 1820-1860 and in Mexico, 1920-1960, Proceedings of the Pac Coast Coun on Latin Am Studies, Campanile Press, 82; Ideology in Mexican mass literature: The case of Sangre India: Chamula, Studies in Latin Am Popular Culture (in prep). *Mailing Add:* Dept of Romance Lang & Lit Ohio State Univ Columbus OH 43210

STEER, ALFRED GILBERT, JR, b Lansdowne, Pa, May 30, 13; m 47; c 2. GERMAN LANGUAGE & LITERATURE. *Educ:* Haverford Col, BA, 35; Duke Univ, MA, 38; Univ Pa, PhD(Ger lit), 54. *Prof Exp:* Instr Ger & French, Washington & Lee Univ, 37-41; instr Ger, Haverford Col, 47-55; asst prof, Harpur Col, 55-59; assoc prof & dept rep, Columbia Univ, 59-67; PROF GER & SLAVIC LANG & HEAD DEPT, UNIV GA, 67- *Concurrent Pos:* Instr, Univ Pa, 48-55; co-ed, Ger Rev, 60; treas, Northeast Lang Conf, 61; Am Philos Soc grant, 65; Columbia Coun Res Humanities grants, 65, 67. *Mem:* MLA; Am Asn Teachers Ger. *Res:* Goethe; Sophocles. *Publ:* Coauth, Readings in Military German, Heath, 42; auth, Goethe's Social Philosophy, Univ NC, 55; The diary of Johann Conrad Wagner, 1737-1802, and Goethe's Campagne in Frankreich, Ger Rev, 1/62; Goethe's St Rochus--Fest zu Bingen, Jahrbuch Freien Deutschen Hochstifts, Frankfurt, 65; The wound and the physician in Goethe's Wilhelm Meister, In: Studies in German Literature of the Nineteenth and Twentieth Centuries, Univ NC, Chapel Hill, 70; Goethe's Novelle as a document of its time, Deutsche Vierteljahrsschrift, fall 76; Science in the Structure of Goethe's Wander jahre, Univ Ga (in prep). *Mailing Add:* 215 Bishop Dr Athens GA 30606

STEGEMEIER, HENRI, b Indianapolis, Ind, Aug 23, 12; m 48; c 2. GERMANIC LITERATURES. *Educ:* Ind Univ, AB, 33; Univ Chicago, PhD, 39. *Prof Exp:* Instr, Univ Chicago, 33-35, 37-38, 40; instr Ger, Mt Holyoke Col, 40-42; assoc prof, 42-73, prof Ger, Univ Ill, Urbana, 73-80. *Mem:* MLA; Am Asn Teachers Ger. *Publ:* Auth, Dance of death in folksong; Problems in emblem literature, J English & Ger Philol. *Mailing Add:* 604 Hessel Blvd Champaign IL 61820

STEIGERWALD, JACOB, US citizen. GERMAN LANGUAGE & LITERATURE. *Educ:* Columbia Col, Chicago, BA, 58; Univ Ill, Urbana, BA, 65, MA, 67; Univ Cincinnati, PhD(Ger), 75. *Prof Exp:* Teacher Ger, Edison Jr High Sch, 65-66; asst prof, 71-78, ASSOC PROF GER, WINONA STATE UNIV, 78- *Mem:* Soc Ger-Am Studies. *Res:* The Danube Swabians; German place names in Minnesota; proverbial sayings. *Publ:* Auth, The Emigrants, Donauschwäbische Lehrerblätter, Vol 14, No 1; Contingency in foreign language study in the US, Donauschwäbische Lehrerblätter, Vol 21, No 2 & Nachrichten der Donauschwaben in Chicago, 3 & 4/75; German language use in the Federal Republic and in the US: Crisis or Renewal?, Südostdeutsche

Vierteljahresblätter, Vol 24, No 4; Saluting the Danube Swabian Society of Chicago upon its 25th anniversary, Nachrichten der Donauschwaben in Chicago, 8/78; The Danube Swabians Today, Donauschwäbische Lehrerblätter, Vol 15, No 2; Bibliography of pre-1956 publications of works by Adam Müller-Guttenbrunn, 1852-1923, that are available at American and Canadianlibraries, Donauschwäbische Forschungs u Lehrerblätter, Vol 25, No 3; Observations concerning the background of the Danube Swabians, Nachrichten der Donauschwaben in Chicago, 2/81; The problems of US immigrants in maintaining native language fluency, In: Entwicklung und Erbe des Donauschwäbischen Volksstammes, Donauschwäbisches Arch, Munich, 82. *Mailing Add:* 355 W Fourth St Winona MN 55987

STEIN, JESS, b New York, NY, June 23, 14; m 43; c 2. ENGLISH, LINGUISTICS. *Educ:* Wayne State Univ, AB, 33; Univ Chicago, MA, 34. *Prof Exp:* Ed, Scott Foresman & Co, Chicago, 34-42; chief, ref & rev units, Off Censorship, Washington, DC, 42-45; ed ref, 45-50, head col & ref depts, 50-59, mem bd dirs, 66-74, VPRES, RANDOM HOUSE, INC, 60- *Concurrent Pos:* Managing ed, American College Dict, 47-, ed, American Everyday Dict, 49-, Basic Everyday Encyclopedia, 54- & ed dir, Random House Encycl, Random House, 77; chmn, Col Publ Group, 60-61; vchmn col sect, Am Textbk Publ Inst, 61-62, mem bd dirs, 62-66, treas, 64-65, chmn statist comn, 68; mem, Govt Adv Comt Int Bk Prog, 64-66; vpres, Alfred A Knopf, Inc, 69-74; pres, Jess Stein Assocs, 73-; consult, Univ Mass Press, 75- & Int Reading Asn, 76- *Mem:* MLA; Ling Soc Am; Am Dialect Soc; Col English Asn; Dict Soc Am. *Res:* Lexicography; educational publishing. *Publ:* Ed, American Vest Pocket Dict of Rhymes, 60, Random House Dict of the English Language, 66 & Great Russian Stories & ed & translr, Tolstoy's Kreutzer Sonata, Random; ed, Washington Irving, Life of Washington, Sleepy Hollow Restorations, 75; Random House College Dict (rev ed), Random House, 75. *Mailing Add:* Random House Inc 201 E 50th St New York NY 10022

STEINER, CARL, b Vienna, Austria, Aug 5, 27; US citizen; m 54; c 3. GERMAN LANGUAGE & LITERATURE. *Educ:* George Washington Univ, BA, 58, MA, 62, PhD(Ger), 66. *Prof Exp:* From instr to asst prof, 64-68, assoc prof, 68-78, chmn dept Ger lang & lit, 70-82, PROF GER, GEORGE WASHINGTON UNIV, 78- *Concurrent Pos:* Recording secy, Am Goethe Soc, 67; consult, Can Coun, 76-77. *Mem:* SAtlantic Mod Lang Asn; Am Asn Teachers Ger; Am Goethe Soc (pres, 81-). *Res:* German emigre literature; 19th century German realism; 20th century German literature; German socio-critical literature. *Publ:* Auth, Über Gottfried Kellers Verhältnis zur Demokratie, Vol LX, No 4 & Die Goethe- Geselschaft von Washington, Vol LX, No 4, Monatsh, Univ Wis; Frankreichbild und Katholizismus bei Joseph Roth, Ger Quart, 1/73; Moliere und die Kleistische Komödie Versuch einer Deutung, In: Moliere and the Commonwealth of Letters, Univ Miss, 75; Kafkas Amerika Illusion oder Wirklichkeit?, In: Franz Kafka-Symposium, Agora Verlag, Berlin, 78; Georg Kaiser, Ein Moderner Mythenmacher, In: Georg Kaiser, Agora Verlag, Berlin, 80. *Mailing Add:* Dept of Ger Lang & Lit George Washington Univ Washington DC 20052

STEINER, GRUNDY, b Plainfield, Ill, Mar 20, 16; m 46; c 3. CLASSICAL PHILOLOGY. *Educ:* Univ Ill, AB, 37, AM, 38, PhD, 40. *Prof Exp:* Res asst classics, Univ Ill, 40-42, asst, 46; prof Greek & Latin, Westminster Col, Mo, 46-47; from instr to asst prof class lang, 47-71, ASSOC PROF CLASS LANG, NORTHWESTERN UNIV, EVANSTON, 71- *Concurrent Pos:* Asst ed, Class J, 50-55. *Mem:* Am Philol Asn; Archaeol Inst Am; Class Asn Mid W & S. *Res:* Renaissance editions of Ovid; Roman agriculture; myth and folklore. *Publ:* Auth, Source-Editions of Ovid's Metamorphoses, 1471- 1500, Trans Am Philol Asn; The skepticism of the elder Pliny, Class Weekly; Cicero as a mythologist, Class J, 2/68. *Mailing Add:* Dept of Class Lang Northwestern Univ Evanston IL 60201

STEINER, PETER, b Prague, Czech, May 7, 46; US citizen; m 73. RUSSIAN & CZECH LANGUAGE & LITERATURE. *Educ:* Yale Univ, MPhil, 73, PhD(Slavic lang & lit), 76. *Prof Exp:* Vis asst prof Slavic, Univ Mich, 76-77; asst prof, Harvard Univ, 77-78; ASST PROF SLAVIC, UNIV PA, 78- *Concurrent Pos:* Vis prof comp lit, Univ NC, Chapel Hill, spring, 81; Nat Endowment for Humanities fel, 82. *Mem:* MLA; Semiotic Soc Am; Comp Lit Asn. *Res:* Modern Slavic literatures; theory of literature; semiotics. *Publ:* Auth, The conceptual basis of Prague structuralism, In: Sound, Sign and Meaning, Univ Mich, 76; ed, The Word and Verbal Art: Selected Essays by Jan Mukarovsky, 77 & Structure, Sign and Function: Selected Essays by Jan Mukarovsky, 78, Yale Univ; auth, Poem as manifesto: Mendel Stam's Notre Dame, Russ Lit, 77; Jan Mukarovsky's structural esthetics, Intro to Structure, Sign and Function, Yale Univ, 78; Three metaphors of Russia formalism, Poetics Today, 81; In defense of semiotics, New Lit Hist; ed, The Prague School: Selected Writings, 1929-1948, Univ Tex Press, 82. *Mailing Add:* Dept of Slavic Lang & Lit Univ Pa Philadelphia PA 19104

STEINER, ROGER JACOB, b South Byron, Wis, Mar 27, 24; m 54; c 2. ROMANCE LANGUAGES, LINGUISTICS. *Educ:* Franklin & Marshall Col, AB, 45; Union Theol Sem, NY, MDiv, 47; Univ Pa, MA, 58, PhD(Romance ling), 63. *Prof Exp:* Lectr Am civilization & lang, Univ Bordeaux, 61-63; from instr to asst prof, 63-71, assoc prof French, 71-80, PROF LANG & LIT, UNIV DEL, 80- *Mem:* MLA; Am Asn Teachers Fr; Am Asn Teachers Span & Port; Mediaeval Acad Am; Dictionary Soc NAm. *Res:* Lexicography; Romance linguistics; medieval literature. *Publ:* Auth, Domaa/demanda and the priority of the Portugese demands, Mod Philol, 8/66; Two Centuries of Spanish and English Bilingual Lexicography (1590-1800), Mouton, The Hague, 70; La technica narrativa de 'entrelazamiento' en La Demanda del Sancto Grial, Rev Lit, Madrid, 7-12/70; A cardinal principle of lexicography: Equivalency, Tijdschrift voor Toegepaste Ling, 71; The New College French and English Dictionary, Amsco Sch Publ, 72; The Bantam New College French and English Dictionary, Bantam, 72; Monodirectional bilingual dictionaries (a lexicographical innovation), Babel, Munich, 8/75; Neologisms and scientific words in bilingual lexicography: Ten problems, Lebende Sprachen, Budapest, 12/76. *Mailing Add:* Dept of Lang & Lit Univ of Del Newark DE 19711

STEINER, WENDY LOIS, English Literature, Critical Theory. See Vol II

STEINHAUER, HARRY, b Cracow, Poland, June 11, 05; m; c 2. FRENCH & GERMAN LITERATURE. *Educ:* Univ Toronto, AB, 27, MA, 28, PhD, 37. *Prof Exp:* From instr to asst prof Ger, Univ Sask, 29-36, prof Ger & French, 36-43; prof Ger & head dept, Univ Man, 43-50; vis prof, Ohio State Univ, 50-51; prof, Antioch Col, 51-62; prof & chmn dept, Western Reserve Univ, 62-64; chmn dept, 64-69, prof, 64-71, EMER PROF GER, UNIV CALIF, SANTA BARBARA, 71- *Honors & Awards:* Order of Merit, First Class, Rebup Ger, 62. *Mem:* MLA; Am Asn Teachers Ger. *Res:* World literature; humanities. *Publ:* Auth, Omnibus of French Literature, Macmillan; German Literature, 1830-1950, Houghton; ed, Ten German Novellas, Anchor-Doubleday, 69; auth, Goethe's Werther, Norton, 70; Twelve German Novellas, Univ Calif, 77. *Mailing Add:* Dept of Ger Univ of Calif Santa Barbara CA 93106

STEINIGER, ERICH WILHELM, b Meuselwitz, Ger, July 19, 13. GERMANIC PHILOLOGY. *Educ:* Univ Idaho, aB, 36; Ohio State Univ, AM, 37, PhD, 47. *Prof Exp:* Instr, Ala Polytech Inst, 39-42; instr, Ohio State Univ, 46-47; asst prof, Ala Polytech Inst, 47-48; from asst prof to prof Ger, 48-76, EMER PROF GER & RUSS, MIAMI UNIV, 76- *Res:* Metaphors in German in the 18th century. *Mailing Add:* Dept of Ger Miami Univ Oxford OH 45056

STEINLE, GISELA BERTA, b Ulm, Donau, Ger, June 17, 47. MEDIEVAL GERMAN LANGUAGE & LITERATURE. *Educ:* Univ Munich, WGer, BA, 68; Univ Aachen, WGer, MA, 71; McGill Univ, PhD(Ger), 75. *Prof Exp:* Lectr Ger, Ger Acad Exchange Serv, Bonn, WGer at McGill Univ, 71-76; vis asst prof, McGill Univ & Concordia Univ, 76-78; DEP PROF GER, UNIV MONTREAL, 78- *Mem:* Can Asn Univ Teachers Ger; Can-Fr Asn Advan Sci. *Res:* Mediaeval German literature; structural linguistics; descriptive grammar. *Publ:* Auth, Das Defensorium inviolatae virginitatis Mariae als Vorläufer der Emblematik, 73 & Heinrich Mann et ses romans de l' Empire, 75, Annales l'Acfas; Kennzeichen durch Bezeichnen: Studien zur Verwendung der Personenbezeichnungen in den Epen Hartmanns von Aue, Bouvier, Bonn, 78. *Mailing Add:* Dept of Ger McGill Univ PO Box 6070 Station A Montreal PQ H3C 3G1 Can

STEINMAN, ROBERT MORRIS, b Newburgh, NY, July 14, 46. PHILOSOPHY. *Educ:* Franklin & Marshall Col, BA, 72; Mich State Univ, MA, 75, PhD(philos), 81. *Prof Exp:* Instr philos, Univ Mich, Flint, 80-81; VIS ASST PROF PHILOS, UNIV TEX, SAN ANTONIO, 81- *Mem:* Am Philos Asn. *Res:* Philosophy of language and epistemology. *Publ:* Auth, Naming and evidence, Philos Studies, Vol 41, 82. *Mailing Add:* 515 W Agarita San Antonio TX 78212

STEISEL, MARIE-GEORGETTE, b Langon, France, Aug 3, 20; US citizen; m 49; c 2. FRENCH LITERATURE. *Educ:* Univ Rennes, Lic es Let, 41, dipl, 42; State Univ Iowa, MA, 46, PhD, 52. *Prof Exp:* Instr French, State Univ Iowa, 46-49; assoc prof, Rosemont Col, 58-60; from asst prof to assoc prof, 60-72, PROF FRENCH, TEMPLE UNIV, 72- *Concurrent Pos:* Traveling fel from Sorbonne, France, 46; French Resistance traveling fel, 47; teacher French, Pub Schs, Seattle, Wash, 49-57. *Mem:* Am Asn Teachers Fr. *Res:* French poetry for children. *Publ:* Coauth, Cultural Commentary of French Poems, 64 & Filmed Recitations of French Literature: An Evaluation, 64, US Off Educ; auth, Etude des couleurs dan La Jalousie de Robbe-Grillet, Fr Rev, 2/65; Robert Pinget's method in L'Inquisitoire, Bks Abroad, summer 66; Paroles de Robert Pinget, Pa State Mod Lang Asn Bull, 12/66; coauth, Background Data for the Teaching of French, US Off Educ, 67. *Mailing Add:* 730 Conshohocken State Rd Philadelphia PA 19103

STELTEN, LEO FREDERICK, b Minneapolis, Minn, Aug 11, 25. CLASSICAL LANGUAGES. *Educ:* Saint Paul Sem, BA, 46; Saint Louis Univ, MA, 57, PhD(Latin & Greek), 70. *Prof Exp:* Teacher Latin & relig, Shanley High Sch, 50-62, Cardinal Muench Sem, 62-66; asst prof, NDak State Univ, 67-77; ASSOC PROF LATIN & GREEK, PONTIFICAL COL JOSEPHINUM, 78- *Concurrent Pos:* Prof class civilization, Seton Hill Summer Study in Greece, 69-74. *Mem:* Am Class League; The Vergilian Soc; Class Asn Middle West & South. *Res:* Palaeography; military institutions of the Romans. *Publ:* Auth, New excerpts from Gregory the Great, In: Codex Vaticanus Reginensis Latinus 140, Manuscripta, 59; Royal wisdom or royal offspring, 66 & Vegetius and the military, 68, The Class Bull; Archaeological impressions, The Class Outlook, 69. *Mailing Add:* Pontifical Col Josephinum 7625 N High St Columbus OH 43085

STELZMANN, RAINULF ALEXANDER, b New Orleans, La, Sept 30, 24; m 57; c 5. GERMAN, PHILOSOPHY. *Educ:* Univ Freiburg, PhD(English, Ger, philos), 53. *Prof Exp:* Instr English & Ger, Aloisius Kolleg, Bad Godesberg, Ger, 54-55; lectr, Loyola Univ, Tulane Univ, Univ Notre Dame & Columbia Univ, 56; from asst prof to assoc prof English, Xavier Univ, La, 57-63; from asst prof to assoc prof Ger, 63-70, res prof, 66-67, PROF GER, UNIV S FLA, TAMPA, 70- *Concurrent Pos:* Lectr, Asn Cath Univ Alumni Ger, 56-61; co-ed, Aegidius Albertinus Proj; ed consult, Thought: A Rev Cult & Idea. *Mem:* MLA. *Res:* Theological aspects in literature; German idealism and Romanticism; German existentialism. *Publ:* Auth, Religious yearning in the American novel, Stimmen der Zeit, 12/61; Goethe, F Schlegel and Schleiermacher, Arch für das Studium der neueren Sprachen, 12/66; Kant and academic freedom, Thought, 6/68; Kantian faith in Musil's Tonka, Ger Rev, 11/75; Paul Celan's Argumentum e Silentio, Monatshefte, 75; Albertinus Lucifer, Daphnis, 75; Das Schwert Christi: Zwei Versuche Walker Percys, Stimmen der Zeith, 77; Major Themes in Recent American Novels, Thought, 80. *Mailing Add:* Dept of Foreign Lang Univ of SFla Tampa FL 33620

STENBERG, PETER ALVIN, b Brooklyn, NY, May 28, 42. GERMAN & SCANDINAVIAN LITERATURE. *Educ:* Wesleyan Univ, BA, 64; Univ Calif, Berkeley, MA, 66, PhD(Ger), 69. *Prof Exp:* Asst prof, 69-75, ASSOC PROF GER, UNIV BC, 75- *Mem:* Can Asn Univ Teachers; Humanities Asn Can; Comp Lit Asn Can. *Res:* Modern Austrian literature; modern Swedish literature; German drama. *Publ:* Auth, Der Rosenkavalier: Hofmannsthal's

Marchen of time, Ger Life & Lett, 10/72; Strindberg and Grillparzer: Contrasting approaches to the battle of the sexes, Can Romance Comp Lit, 11/74; The move from the tower, Hofmannsthal's Der Turm Monatshefte, spring 75; The last of the magicians--Horvath's Zauberkoenig and his predecessors, Ger Life & Lett, 7/75; Servants to two masters: Strindberg and Hofmannsthal, Mod Lang Rev, 10/75; Silence, ceremony and song in Hofmannsthal's Libretti, Seminar, spring 76; Moving into the Eighties: The German Theatre a Decade after the Breakthrough, Mod Drama, 1/81; Remembering Times Past: Canetti, Sperber, and a World That is no More, Seminar, 11/81. *Mailing Add:* Dept of Ger Studies Univ of BC Vancouver BC V6T 1W5 Can

STENBOCK-FERMOR, ELISABETH, b Paris, France, Jan 19, 00; US citizen; m 33. RUSSIAN, FRENCH. *Educ:* Radcliffe Col, MA, 50, PhD, 55. *Prof Exp:* Teaching fel, Radcliffe Col, 51-53; lectr Russ, Wellesley Col, 54-55; asst cataloguer, Houghton Libr, Harvard Univ, 55-56, lectr Russ, 56-57; asst prof Russ lang & Lit, 59-66, EMER ASST PROF SLAVIC LANG & LIT, STANFORD UNIV, 66- *Concurrent Pos:* Chmn dept Russ, Monterey Inst Foreign Studies, 66-70. *Mem:* Am Asn Teachers Slavic & East Europ Lang; Am Asn Advan Slavic Studies. *Res:* Russian folklore; Russian 18th and 19th century literature; French medieval literature. *Publ:* Auth, Neglected features of the epigraphs in the Captain's Daughter, Int J Slavic Ling & Poetics, 64; Bulgakov's The Master and Margarita and Goethe's Faust, Slavic & East Europ J, 69; Russian literature from 1890 to 1917, In: Russia Enters the 20th Century, Temple Smith Ltd, London, 71; The Architecture of Anna Karenina, Ridder, Lisse, 75; French medieval poetry as a source of inspiration for Puskin, In: Alexander Puskin: A Symposium, NY Univ, 76. *Mailing Add:* 2315 Columbia St Palo Alto CA 94306

STENSON, NANCY JEAN, b San Mateo, Calif, Aug 7, 45; m 76. LINGUISTICS. *Educ:* Pomona Col, BA, 67; Univ Calif, San Diego, MA, 70, PhD(ling), 76. *Prof Exp:* English as second lang specialist, Lang Res Found, 71-72; ASST PROF LING, UNIV MINN, MINNEAPOLIS, 78- *Concurrent Pos:* Dublin Inst for Advan Studies scholar, 76-77; consult, Havasupai & Hualapai Bilingual Ed Prog, 75-76. *Mem:* Ling Soc Am; Teachers of English to Speakers of Other Lang; MLA; Am Asn Applied Ling. *Res:* Syntax; Irish language; second language acquisition. *Publ:* Contribr, Let's Talk Iipay Aa: An Introduction to Mesa Grande Diegueno, Malki Mus, 75; co-ed, New Frontiers in Second Language Learning, Newbery House, 75; coauth, Literacy and linguistics: the Havasupai writing system, Proc 76 Hokan-Yuman Lang Workshop, 77; auth, Overlapping systems in the Irish comparative construction, Word, 77: Plural formation in Rath Cairn Eigse: J Irish Studies, 78; Questions on the accessibility heirarchy, Elements, Chicago Ling Soc, 79; Studies in Irish syntax, Gunter Narr Verlag, 81; On short term language change: Developments in Irish Morphology, Proc 5th Int Cong Hist Ling, 82. *Mailing Add:* Dept of Ling Univ Minn 320 16th St SE Minneapolis MN 55455

STENZEL, JOACHIM ALBRECHT, b Breslau, Ger, Apr 8, 15; US citizen; m 46; c 5. CLASSICS, GERMAN. *Educ:* Univ Florence, DLet, 38. *Prof Exp:* Instr Latin & Ger, Hastings Col, 39-41, assoc prof Latin & Greek, 41-42; assoc prof Ger, Ill Col, 46-47, prof Greek & Latin, 47-50, prof classics, 53-54; assoc prof, DePauw Univ, 50-51; chief Europ monitoring, Radio Free Europe, Munich, 51-53; tech dir telecommun, Am Nat Red Cross, Richmond, Va 54-59; from asst prof to assoc prof Latin & Ger, 59-65, prof classics, 65-77, chmn dept foreign lang, 69-75, EMER PROF CLASSICS, SAN JOSE STATE UNIV, 77- *Concurrent Pos:* Resident dir Ger, Calif State Col Int Progs, 65-66. *Mem:* Am Philol Asn. *Res:* Early Greek literature; foreign language teaching techniques. *Mailing Add:* Dept of Foreign Lang San Jose State Univ San Jose CA 95192

STEPHAN, ALEXANDER F, b Ludenscheid, Ger, Aug 16, 46; m 69; c 1. GERMAN LITERATURE. *Educ:* Freie Univ Berlin, BA, 68; Univ Mich, MA, 69; Princeton Univ, PhD(Ger lit), 73. *Prof Exp:* Instr Ger lang & lit, Princeton Univ, 72-73; asst prof, 73-77, ASSOC PROF GER LIT, UNIV CALIF, LOS ANGELES, 77- *Mem:* Am Asn Teachers Ger; Int Ver Ger Sprach & Literaturwissenschaft; Soc Exile Studies. *Res:* Twentieth century German literature; exile literature; literature and area studies of the German Democratic Republic. *Publ:* Georg Lukacs erst Bitrage zur marxistischen Literaturtheorie, Brecht-Jahrbuch, 75; Christa Wolf, C H Beck, 76 & 2nd ed, 79; Plane fur ein neues Deutschland: Die Kulturpolitic der Exil-KPD vor 1945, Jahrbuch deut Gegenswartslit, 77; Zwischn Verburgerung und Plitisierung: Arbeiterliteratur in der Weimarer Republic, Handbuch deut Arbeiterlit, 77; Die wissenschaftlich-technische Revolution in der Literatur der DDR, Deutschunterricht, 2/78; Die deutsche Exilliteratur 1933-1945, C H Beck, 79; Christa Wolf: Forschungsbericht, Rodopi, 80; Max Frisch, Fritisches Lexikon deutschsprachigen Gegenswartslit, 82. *Mailing Add:* Dept of Germanic Lang Univ of Calif Los Angeles CA 90024

STEPHAN, HALINA, b Lwow, Poland, Aug 24, 43; US citizen; m 69; c 1. RUSSIAN & POLISH LITERATURE. *Educ:* Mundelein Col, BA, 66; Univ Mich, MA, 69, cert Russ area studies, 69, PhD(Russ lit), 75. *Prof Exp:* Asst prof, 75-81, ASSOC PROF RUSS LIT, UNIV SOUTHERN CALIF, 81- *Mem:* Am Asn Teachers Slavic & East Europ Lang; Am Asn Advan Slavic Studies. *Res:* Twentieth century Russian literature; avant-garde art and literature; Polish literature. *Publ:* Auth, Cement: From Gladkov's monumental epos to Muller's avant-garde drama, Germano-Slavica, 2/79; The rediscovery of the left front of the arts in the 1960s and 1970s, Can-Am Slavic Studies, 3/79; Wisseschaftliche Fantastik und fantastische Parabel in der sowjetischen Gegenwartsliteratur, Osteuropa, 11/79; The changing protagonist of Soviet science fiction, Proc Int Conf Fiction & Drama Eastern Europe, 80; Majakovskij's post-revolutionary poetics and the Lef concept of art, Russ Lang J, 80; Lef and the development of early Soviet prose, Slavic & East Europ J, 4/80; Lef and the Left Front of the Arts, Sagner, 81; Ivan Antonovich Efremov, Mod Encycl Russ & Soviet Lit, 82. *Mailing Add:* Dept of Slavic Lang & Lit Univ of Southern Calif Los Angeles CA 90089

STEPHAN, PHILIP H, b Philadelphia, Pa, Aug 9, 26; m 51. FRENCH LITERATURE. *Educ:* Yale Univ, BA, 49, MA, 51; Univ Calif, Berkeley, PhD(Romance lit), 59. *Prof Exp:* Asst French, Univ Calif, Berkeley, 50-54; instr, Univ Ariz, 56-57; underwriter, Gen Accident Fire & Life Assurance, 57-58; teacher, Menlo Sch, Calif, 58-59; asst prof French, Univ Mont, 59-61, Univ Ill, Urbana, 61-63 & Bowling Green State Univ, 63-67; ASSOC PROF FRENCH, NORTHEASTERN UNIV, 67- *Mem:* AAUP; Am Asn Teachers Fr; Northeast Mod Lang Asn. *Res:* French literature of the 19th century; cubist influences in French poetry, 1907-1918; Verlaine and decadence. *Publ:* Auth, Verlaine's distant emotions, Romanic Rev, 10/61; Problems of structure in the poetry of Tristan Corbiere, 12/61 & Decadent poetry in Le Chat Noir before Verlaine's Langueur, 12/69, Mod Lang Quart; Naturalist influences on symbolist poetry, 1882-1886, Fr Rev, 12/72; Paul Verlaine and the Decadence, 1892-90, Machester Univ, 74. *Mailing Add:* Dept of Mod Lang Northeastern Univ Boston MA 02115

STEPHENSON, BUFORD STUART, b Richmond, Va, Nov 28, 22. GERMAN. *Educ:* Washington & Lee Univ, AB, 42; Univ Minn, AM, 49. *Prof Exp:* From instr to assoc prof, 46-77, PROF GER, WASHINGTON & LEE UNIV, 77- *Res:* Modern German lyric; Rilke. *Mailing Add:* Dept of Ger Washington & Lee Univ Lexington VA 24450

STEPHENSON, EDWARD A, English. See Vol II

STEPHENSON, MARY ELLEN, b Richmond, Va, Sept 16, 15. ROMANCE LANGUAGES. *Educ:* Univ Richmond, BA, 36; Middlebury Col, MA, 41; Univ Chicago, PhD(Romance lang), 51. *Prof Exp:* Teacher, Richmond Pub Schs, Va, 36-48; from asst prof to assoc prof Span, 48-64, chmn dept mod foreign lang, 67-73, dir Latin Am studies, 70-76, acad adv, 73-75, PROF SPAN, MARY WASHINGTON COL, UNIV VA, 64-, CHMN DEPT MOD FOREIGN LANG, 75- *Mem:* Am Asn Teachers Span & Port; MLA. *Mailing Add:* Dept of Mod Foreign Lang Mary Washington Col Fredericksburg VA 22401

STERN, ANNE WELLNER, b New York, NY, Mar 17, 41. FRENCH LITERATURE. *Educ:* Bard Col, BA, 62; Columbia Univ, MA, 64, PhD(French Lit), 77. *Prof Exp:* Instr French lang & lit, Columbia Univ, 67-71; teacher French, Little Red Sch House & Elis Irwin High Sch, 71-72; instr French lit & Lang, Middlebury Col, 72-75; instr, Harvard Univ, 75-77, asst prof French, 77-80. *Mem:* MLA; Am Coun Teaching Foreign Lang. *Res:* Nineteenth century French literature, structuralism and stylistics; foreign language teaching. *Mailing Add:* 133 W 74 St No 3 New York NY 10023

STERN, CHARLOTTE DANIELS, b Philadelphia, Pa, Dec 22, 29; m 52; c 2. SPANISH. *Educ:* Temple Univ, AB, 51; Univ Pa, AM, 54, PhD(Span), 60. *Prof Exp:* Teaching asst, Univ Pa, 52-53; asst prof Span, Lynchburg Col, 53-61, Randolph-Macon Woman's Col, 61-62 & Lynchburg Col, 62-68; assoc prof, 68-75, prof, 75-80, CHARLES A DANA PROF ROMANCE LANG, RANDOLPH-MACON WOMAN'S COL, 80- *Concurrent Pos:* Am Coun Leanred Soc grant-in-aid, 63. *Mem:* MLA; Am Asn Teachers Span & Port; Renaissance Soc Am; SAtlantic Mod Lang Asn; Ling Soc Am. *Res:* Early Spanish drama; Spanish stylistics; Golden Age comedia. *Publ:* Auth, Fray Inigo de Mendoza & medieval dramatic ritual, Hisp Rev, 65; Juan del Enzina's Carnival Eclogues and the Spanish drama of the Renaissance, 65 & The early Spanish drama: From Medieval ritual to Renaissance art, 74, Renaissance Drama; The Coplas de Mingo Revulgo and the early Spanish drama, Hisp Rev, 76; The comic spirit in Diego de Avila's Egloga interlocutoria, Bull Comediantes, 77; A kaleidoscopic view of the Lazarillo, Romance Philol, 81; Lope de Vega, propagandist?, Bull Comediantes, 82. *Mailing Add:* Dept of Mod Lang Randolph-Macon Woman's Col Lynchburg VA 24503

STERN, CINDY DEBRA, b Amityville, NY, June 15, 52. METAPHYSICS, PHILOSOPHY OF LANGUAGE. *Educ:* Col William & Mary, BA, 74; Syracuse Univ, MLS, 75, PhD(philos), 80. *Prof Exp:* Asst prof philos, Univ NC, Chapel Hill, 80-81; ASST PROF PHILOS, UNIV NOTRE DAME, 81. *Mem:* Am Philos Asn. *Res:* Causation, modality, ontology, Montague grammar. *Publ:* Auth, On the alleged extensionality of causal explanatory contexts, Philos Sci, 78; coauth, Natural kind terms and standards of membership, Ling Philos, 79; auth, Lewis' counterfactual analysis of causation, Synthese, 81; Logical features of reference to facts in causal contexts, Philos Studies, 82. *Mailing Add:* Dept of Philos Univ of Notre Dame Notre Dame IN 46556

STERN, GUY, b Ger, Jan 14, 22; nat US; m 78. GERMAN, COMPARATIVE LITERATURE. *Educ:* Hofstra Col, BA, 48; Columbia Univ, MA, 50, PhD, 54. *Prof Exp:* Instr Ger, Columbia Univ, 48-54; assoc prof mod lang, Denison Univ, 54-64; prof Ger lang & lit & chmn dept Ger, Univ Cincinnati, 64-75, univ dean grad educ & res, 73-75; prof Ger & Slavic lang & lit & chmn dept, Univ Md, College Park, 75-78; provost & sr vpres, 78-81, DISTINGUISHED PROF ROMANCE LANG & GER, WAYNE STATE UNIV, 81-; DIR, INT EXCHANGE, DIV ARTS & HUMANITIES, 78- *Concurrent Pos:* Adv ed, Dover Publ, 58-; Fulbright res grant, 61-62; Leo Baeck fel, 61-; Bollingen res fel, 62-63; chmn, Fulbright Screening Comt Germanistics, 67-72; consult, Col Entrance Exam Bd, 68-72; secy, Am Coun Ger Studies, 68-; Ger Acad Exchange Serv res fel, 81. *Mem:* SAtlantic Mod Lang Asn; Am Asn Teachers Ger (pres, 70-72); Lessing Soc (pres, 74-76); MLA. *Res:* Classical and modern German literature; English-German comparative literature. *Publ:* Auth, Saint or hypocrite: A study of Wieland's Jacinte episode, Ger Rev, 53; Hugo v Hofmannsthal and the Speiers, PMLA, 1/57; Konstellationen, 1914/25, Deut Verlangs-Anstalt, Stuttgart, 64; Efraim Frisch: Zum Verständnis des Geistigen, Lambert Schneider, Heidelberg, 64; Prolegomena zu einer Geschichte der deutschen Nachkriegsprose, Colloquia Germanica, 11/67; War, Weimar and Literature: The Story of the Neue Merkur, Pa State Univ, 71; Exile literature: Designation or misnomer, Colloquia Germanica, 1/72; Science and literature: Arno Reinfrank as a poet of facts, In: Festschrift Andre von Gronicka, Bouvier, Bonn, 78; ed, Alfred Neumann, Steiner, Wiesbaden, 79. *Mailing Add:* Dept of Foreign Lang Wayne State Univ Detroit MI 48202

STERN, IRWIN, b Brooklyn, NY, July 28, 46. LUSO-BRAZILIAN LANGUAGE & LITERATURE. *Educ:* Queens Col, NY, BA, 67, MA, 69; City Univ New York, PhD(Port), 72. *Prof Exp:* Instr Romance lang, Univ Nebr-Lincoln, 69-71; adj lectr, City Col New York, 71-72, asst prof Port & Span, 72-76. *Concurrent Pos:* Grad fac comp lit, City Univ New York, 75-76; adj asst prof Span & Port, New York Univ, 77-; lectr Port, Columbia Univ, 79-; vis asst prof, Adelphi Univ, spring, 76; vis prof, Univ Pittsburgh, 78; vis asst prof, Queens Col, 79. *Honors & Awards:* PEN Club Transl Prize, 81. *Mem:* Am Asn Teachers Span & Port; MLA; Am-Port Soc; Int Conf Group Mod Port. *Res:* Nineteenth century Portuguese literature; 19th and 20th centuries Luso-Brazilian fiction; Spanish fiction. *Publ:* Auth, Julio Dinis e o romance portugues, Porto: Lello & Irmao, Editores, 72; Suppressed Portuguese Fiction: 1926-1974, Bks Abroad, winter 76; Jane Austen e Julio Dinis, 3/76 & Ecade Queiroz e Pinhero Chagas, 5/80, Coloquio/Letras; Luandino Vieira's Short Fiction: Decolonization in the Third Register, When the Drumbeat Changes, Three Continents, 81; Continuing the Marvelous Journes, Review, 1-4/81; co-ed, Modern Iberian Literature, Ungar (in press). *Mailing Add:* 380 Riverside Dr Apt 5-M New York NY 10025

STERN, JACOB HOWARD, b Portland, Ore, Apr 9, 40; m 64; c 2. CLASSICS. *Educ:* Reed Col, BA, 61; Columbia Univ, MA, 63, PhD(Classics), 65. *Prof Exp:* Lectr, 64-65, from instr to asst prof, 65-71, assoc prof, 71-81, PROF CLASSICS, CITY COL NEW YORK, 81- *Mem:* Am Philol Asn. *Res:* Greek lyric and hellenistic poetry. *Publ:* Auth, The imagery of Bacchylides Ode 5, Greek, Roman & Byzantine Studies, 67; The structure of Bacchylides Ode 17, Rev Belge Philol Hist, 67; The myth of Pindar's Olympian 6, Am J Philol, 70; co-ed, Pindaros und Bakchylides, Wissenschaftliche Buchgesellschaft, 70; auth, The structure of Pindar's Nemean 5, Class Philol, 71; Theocritus' Idyll 14, Greek, Roman & Byzantine Studies, 75; Herodas' Mimiamb 6, Greek, Roman & Byzantine Studies, 79. *Mailing Add:* Dept of Classics City Col of New York New York NY 10031

STERNGLASS, MARILYN SEINER, Rhetorical Theory. See Vol II

STEVENS, CJ, b Kirksville, Mo, Nov 23, 14; m 36; c 2. SPEECH. *Educ:* L La State Univ, BA, 51, MA, 52, PhD, 54. *Prof Exp:* Instr speech, La State Univ, 51, instr English lang & orientation, 51-54; chmn radio & speech, Shepherd State Col, 54-55; asst prof speech & dir radio-TV, Univ Kansas City, 55-57, actg dean even div, 56-57, dir div continued educ, 57-59; human factors scientist res & develop, Syst Develop Corp, 59-61; dir intensive English lang prog, Georgetown Univ, Ankara, 62-65; assoc prof speech & theatre, 65-73, PROF SPEECH & THEATRE, LEHMAN COL, 73-, CHMN DEPT, 68- *Concurrent Pos:* Smith-Mundt vis prof, State Univ Mex, 61. *Mem:* Speech Commun Asn. *Res:* Phonetics; English linguistic. *Mailing Add:* 178 Vernon Ave Yonkers NY 10704

STEVENS, HENRY JOSEPH, JR, b Hagerstown, Md, Feb 5, 46; m 69; c 2. CLASSICS. *Educ:* Brown Univ, BA, 68; Bryn Mawr Col, MA, 69, PhD(Latin & Greek), 73. *Prof Exp:* MASTER CLASSICS, PORTSMOUTH ABBEY SCH, 71- *Concurrent Pos:* Chmn develop comt classics, Advan Placement Prog, 77-; reader, Advan Placement Exam, 78 & 81. *Mem:* Am Philol Asn; Class Asn New End. *Res:* Latin and Greek literature; history of classical scholarship. *Publ:* Auth, Lorenzo Valla and Isidore of Seville, Traditio, 75. *Mailing Add:* Portsmouth Abbey Portsmouth RI 02871

STEWART, DAVID D, b Can citizen. GERMAN. *Educ:* Univ Toronto, BA, 54, MA, 56, PhD(Ger), 60. *Prof Exp:* Can Coun res grants, 66-67; assoc prof Ger, 67-76, PROF GER & ASSOC CHMN DEPT, TRENT UNIV, 76- *Mem:* MLA; Asn Can Univ Teachers Ger. *Res:* Literature and religion, especially German; aspects of Classicism and Romanticism in modern German literature. *Publ:* Auth, Schiller's Die Kraniche des Ibykus, Can Mod Lang Rev, 64; German Poetry from Luther to Brecht, Ryerson, 64. *Mailing Add:* Dept of Ger Trent Univ Peterborough ON K9J 7B8 Can

STEWART, DOUGLAS JAMES, b Los Angeles, Calif, Dec 31, 33; m 61; c 3. CLASSICS. *Educ:* Loyola Univ, Los Angeles, AB, 55; Cornell Univ, MA, 59, PhD, 63. *Prof Exp:* Lectr Latin, St Michael's Col, Can, 61-62; instr classics, Reed Col, 62-64; asst prof, Emory Univ, 64-66; from asst prof to assoc prof, 66-74, chmn dept, 73-79, PROF CLASSICS, BRANDEIS UNIV, 74- *Concurrent Pos:* Southeastern Inst Medieval & Renaissance Study fel, 66; vis prof class lit, Univ Calif, San Diego, 70. *Mem:* Am Philos Asn. *Res:* Greek philosophy and comedy; historiography; mythology. *Publ:* Auth, Hesiod and history, Bucknell Rev, spring 76; Socrates' last bath, J Hist Philos, summer 71; Falstaff the centaur, Shakespeare Quart, 72; The Disguised Guest: Rank, Role and Identity in the Odyssey, Bucknell Univ Press, 76. *Mailing Add:* Dept of Classics Brandeis Univ Waltham MA 02154

STEWART, HARRY EUGENE, b Indianapolis, Ind, Mar 24, 31; m 54; c 2. FRENCH LANGUAGE & LITERATURE. *Educ:* DePauw Univ, BA, 53; Ind Univ, MA, 56, PhD, 61. *Prof Exp:* Instr French & Ger, Univ Richmond, 58-61; asst prof French, Kent State Univ, 61-69; prof & head dept mod lang, Univ Tulsa, 69-71; PROF FRENCH & HEAD DEPT LANG, CLEMSON UNIV, 71. *Mem:* MLA. *Res:* Medieval French literature. *Publ:* Auth, Jean Genet's saintly preoccupation in Le Balcon, Drama Surv, II: 24-30; A note on verbal play in Genet's Le Balcon, Wis Studies Contemp Lit, summer 69; Ionesco in search of Ionesco, Univ Tulsa Monogr Ser, spring 71; The case of the lilac murders: Genet's Haute Surveillance, 10/71, In Defense of Lefranc as a hero of Haute Surveillance, 12/71 & Jean Genet: Bogus Count of Tillancourt, 4/77, Fr Rev. *Mailing Add:* Dept of Lang Clemson Univ Clemson SC 29631

STEWART, JOAN HINDE, b New York, NY; m 70; c 2. FRENCH LITERATURE. *Educ:* St Joseph's Col, BA, 65; Yale Univ, PhD(romance lang), 70. *Prof Exp:* From instr to asst prof French, Wellesley Col, 70-72; asst prof, 73-77, assoc prof, 77-81, PROF FRENCH, NC STATE UNIV, 81- *Concurrent Pos:* Fel, Nat Humanities Ctr, 82-83. *Honors & Awards:* NC State Univ Outstanding Teacher Award, 77. *Mem:* MLA; SAtlantic Mod Lang Asn; Southeast Am Soc for 18th Century Studies; Southern Comp Lit Asn; Am Asn Teachers of Fr. *Res:* Eighteenth-century fiction; women wirters; Colette. *Publ:* Auth, The Novels of Madame Riccoboni, NC Studies Romance Lang & Lit, 76; Some aspects of verb use in Aucassin et Nicolette, Fr Rev, 77; Sensibility with irony: Mme de Montolieu at the end of an era, Ky Romance Quart, 78; Colette: The Mirror Image, Fr Forum, 78; Colette and the hallowing of age, Romance Notes, 79-80; Colette's Gynaeceum: Regression and Renewal, Fr Rev, 80; The School and the Home, Women's Studies, 81; Colette, G K Hall (in prep). *Mailing Add:* 6 Logging Trial Durham NC 27707

STEWART, JOHN G, b Vienna, Austria, May 17, 18; US citizen; m 48. GERMAN. *Educ:* Col Pac, BA, 41; Columbia Univ, MA, 46. *Prof Exp:* Instr, Highland Manor Sch, NJ, 46-51; teacher high sch, Va, 51-57; asst prof French & Latin, 57-67, ASSOC PROF GER, MADISON COL, VA, 67- *Concurrent Pos:* Madison Col res grants, 64-72. *Mem:* Am Asn Teachers Ger. *Res:* Folklore of the Shenandoah Valley of Virginia; teaching foreign languages. *Publ:* Coatuh, The Pennsylvania Germans of the Shenandoah Valley, Pa Ger Folklore Soc, 62; The mill as a preventative of whooping cough, J Am Folklore, 1-3/64; auth, Shanghaiing in the valley of Virginia, 2/66 & Ambrose Henkel of New Market, Va: A brief analysis of his German primers, 2/67, Madison Col Studies 7 Res. *Mailing Add:* Dept of Foreign Lang Madison Co Harrisonburg VA 22801

STEWART, PAMELA DAWES, b Montreal, Que, Jan 23, 34. ITALIAN, COMPARATIVE LITERATURE. *Educ:* Univ Montreal, BA, 59; McGill Univ, MA, 61. *Prof Exp:* Lectr, 63-65, asst prof, 65-69, assoc prof, 69-80, PROF ITAL STUDIES, McGILL UNIV, 80-, CHMN DEPT ITAL, 77- *Concurrent Pos:* Assoc dir, McGill Ctr for Continuing Educ, 68-; mem comt aid to publ, Can Fedn for Humanities, 77- *Mem:* MLA; Can Soc Ital Studies; Am Asn Ital; Can Soc Renaissance Studies. *Res:* Boccaccio; Italian Renaissance theatre; the reception of Machiavelli in France. *Publ:* Auth, Innocent Gentillet e la sua Polemica Antimachiavellica, La Nuova Italia, Firenze, 69; contribr, Dizionario Critico Della Letteratura Francese, UTET, Torino, 72; auth, An unknown edition of the Praxis aurea by J P De Ferrariis, Yearbk Ital Studies 1971, 72; co-ed, Discours contre Machiavel, Casalini Libri, Firenze, 74; auth, La novella di Madonna Oretta e le due parti del Decameron, Yearbk Ital Studies 1973-75, 77; Boccaccio e lat tradizione retoriaca: La definizione della novella come genere letterario, Stanford Ital Rev, Vol I, No 1, 79; Il testo teatrale e la questione del doppio destinatario: L'eoempio della Calandria, Quaderri d'i'talianistica, Vol I, 80. *Mailing Add:* Dept of Ital McGill Univ Montreal PQ H3A 1G5 Can

STEWART, PHILIP ROBERT, b Kansas City, Mo, May 21, 40; m 70; c 2. FRENCH LITERATURE. *Educ:* Yale Univ, BA, 62, PhD(French), 67. *Prof Exp:* Instr French, Yale Univ, 66-68; asst prof, Harvard Univ, 68-72; assoc prof, 72-80, PROF FRENCH, DUKE UNIV, 80- *Concurrent Pos:* Mem comt examrs, Col Bd Advan Placement Prog French, 72-74; managing ed, Fr Rev, 74-77; Nat Endowment for Humanities fel, 78-79; vpres, Am Asn Teachers Fr, 79-84. *Mem:* MLA; Am Asn Teachers Fr; Fr Soc 18th Century Studies; Am Soc 18th Century Studies. *Res:* Theory of narrative; 17th and 18th century French literature; history of novel. *Publ:* Auth, Imitation and Illusion in the French Memoir-Novel, 1700-1750, Yale Univ, 69; Cometes et lumieres, Rev Humaines Sci, 70; Le masque et la parole: Le language de l'amour au XVIIIe siecle, Jose Corti, Paris, 73; Prevost et son Cleveland: Essai de mise au point historique, Dix-Huitieme Siecle, 75; ed, Prevost: Cleveland, Presses Universitaires de Grenoble, 77; Decent eroticism: Representations of love in the French eighteenth century, Studies in Iconography, 78; Vox naturae: A reading of prevost, Romanic Rev, 80; Les Signes du comique, Saggi e Ricerche di Litteratura Francese, 82. *Mailing Add:* Dept of Romance Lang Duke Univ Durham NC 27706

STEWART, WALTER K, b Los Angeles, Calif. GERMAN LITERATURE. *Educ:* Calif State Univ, Northridge, BA, 68; Univ Calif, Los Angeles, MA, 70, PhD(Ger lit), 75. *Prof Exp:* Scholar Ger, Univ Calif, Los Angeles, 78-79; ASST PROF GER & CHMN DEPT, CALIF LUTHERAN COL, 79- *Mem:* MLA; Am Asn Teachers Ger; Philol Asn Pac Coast. *Res:* Goethe period literature; dramatic theory; Thomas Mann. *Publ:* Auth, Hans Carossa, In: Encycl Hebraica, 77; Der Tod in Venedig: The path to insight, Ger Rev, (in press); Time Structure in Drama: Goethe's Sturm und Drang Plays, Amsterdamer Publikationen Rodopi Verlag (in press). *Mailing Add:* Dept of German Calif Lutheran Col Thousand Oaks CA 91360

STEWART, ZEPH, b Jackson, Mich, Jan 1, 21. CLASSICS. *Educ:* Yale Univ, AB, 42. *Hon Degrees:* Am, Harvard Univ, 55. *Prof Exp:* From asst prof to assoc prof, 53-62, master Lowe ll House, 63-75, Burr Sr Tutor, Adams House, 55-60, acting master, 61-62, PROF GREEK & LATIN, HARVARD UNIV, 62-, CHMN DEPT CLASSICS, 77- *Concurrent Pos:* Forum lectr, Univ Colo, 62; trustee, Hotchkiss Sch, 64-; Guggenheim Found fel, 65-66; affil mem fac divinity, Harvard Univ, 70-; mem adv coun classics dept, PRINCETON Univ, 70-; trustee, Radcliffe Col, 72-76; trustee, Loeb Class Libr, 73-; mem, Yale Univ Coun, 76- *Mem:* Class Asn New England; Am Philol Asn; Soc Promot Roman Studies; fel, Am Acad Arts & Sci; Brit Class Asn. *Res:* Latin literature; Greek philosophy; ancient religion. *Publ:* Auth, Sejanus, Gaetulicus and Seneca, Am J Philol, 53; Democritus and the cynics, Harvard Studies Class Philol, 58; The god Nocturnus in Plautus' Amphitruo, J Roman Studies, 60; The ancient World, Prentice, 66; ed, Essays on Religion and the Ancient World, Clarendon, 72, Harvard Univ, 72; contribr, La religione, In: La societa ellenistica, Bompiani, Italy, 77. *Mailing Add:* Dept of the Classics Boylson Hall 319 Harvard Univ Cambridge MA 02138

STEWART-ROBINSON, JAMES, b Edinburgh, Scotland, Mar 3, 28; m 57; c 3. ISLAMICS. *Educ:* Univ Edinburgh, MA, 54, PhD, 59. *Prof Exp:* Instr Turkish, 56-59, from asst prof to assoc prof Turkish studies, 59-70, PROF TURKISH STUDIES, UNIV MICH, ANN ARBOR, 70- *Concurrent Pos:* M M Treasury grant, 54; mem, Soc Sci Res Coun, 62; mem bd gov, Am Res Inst Turkey, 67- *Mem:* Inst Soc Orient Res(Am treas, 56); Am Orient Soc; Royal Cent Asian Soc; MidE Studies Asn NAm. *Res:* Ottoman literature and history; Turkish language; Islamic biographies of poets. *Publ:* Auth, The

Tezkere genre in Islam, 64 & The Ottoman biographies of poets, 65, J Near Eastern Studies; The Traditional Near East, Prentice-Hall, 66. *Mailing Add:* Dept of Near Eastern Studies Univ of Mich 3074 Frieze Bldg Ann Arbor MI 48104

STICCA, SANDRO, b Italy, Nov 23, 31; US citizen; m; c 1. MIDDLE AGES & RENAISSANCE. *Educ:* Syracuse Univ, BA, 57, MA, 59; Columbia Univ, PhD(French), 67. *Prof Exp:* Asst French, Columbia Univ, 63-64; from instr to asst prof, 64-67, assoc prof French & comp lit, 68-76, PROF FRENCH & COMP LIT, STATE UNIV NY BINGHAMTON, 76- *Concurrent Pos:* Ed assoc, Mod Austrian Lit, 66-; NY State fac fel, 67, fel, 68; Nat Found Arts & Humanities fel, 67. *Mem:* MLA; Mediaeval Acad Am. *Res:* Middle Ages, Renaissance. *Publ:* Auth, The Medieval Latin Passion Play, Its Origins and Development, 70 & ed & contribr, Medieval Drama, 72, NY State Univ; auth, Christian ethics and courtly doctrine in Beroul's Tristan et Iseut, Classica et Mediavalia, 72; Dramatic texts and Ars Dictaminis in medieval Italy, In: Festschrift Mario Pei, NC, 72; Drama and spriituality in the Middle Ages, Mediaevalia et Humanistica, fall 73. *Mailing Add:* Dept of French State Univ NY Binghamton NY 13901

STIEHM, BRUCE GILBERT, b Milwaukee, Wis, Jan 31, 37; m 62; c 5. SPANISH, LINGUISTICS. *Educ:* Marquette Univ, BS, 59; Univ Wis-Madison, MA, 66, PhD(Span), 72. *Prof Exp:* From instr to asst prof Span, Univ Wis-Parkside, 69-76; ASST PROF SPAN, UNIV PITTSBURGH, 76- *Mem:* Am Asn Teachers Span & Port; MLA; Am Coun Teaching Foreign Lang; AAUP; Ling Soc Am. *Res:* Spanish descriptive linguistics; Spanish semantics. *Publ:* Auth, Spanish word order in non-sentence constructions, Language, Vol 51, No 1; Information value of Spanish phonotactic occurrence, Studies Ling, 75; The order of sentence elements in eighteenth-century Western Romance, Lektos, 76; Cultural values and lexical features in Spanish grammar, In, Approaches to the Romance Lexicon, Georgetown Univ, 78; Element order in the Spanish word, Word, 78; Teaching Spanish word order, Hispania, 78. *Mailing Add:* Dept of Hisp Lang & Lit Univ of Pittsburgh Pittsburgh PA 15260

STILLMAN, YEDIDA KALFON, b Fez, Morocco, Apr 8, 46; US citizen; m 67; c 2. MIDDLE EASTERN ETHNOGRAPHY & LITERATURE. *Educ:* Univ Pa, MA, 68, PhD(Oriental studies), 72. *Prof Exp:* Asst prof, 73-79, ASSOC PROF CLASS & NEAR EASTERN STUDIES, STATE UNIV NY, BINGHAMTON, 79- *Concurrent Pos:* Consult, Int Folk Art Found, 72-, Cult Res & Commun, Inc, 78-79 & Irth Cult Heritage Found, 80-; vis sr lectr, Haifa Univ, 79-80. *Honors & Awards:* Chancellor's Award for Excellence in Teaching, State Univ NY, 78. *Mem:* Am Oriental Soc; Asn Jewish Studies. *Res:* Middle Eastern costume history; middle Eastern folk literature. *Publ:* Auth, The three magic objects: A Yemanite folktale: (Analysis and parallels), Fabula, Vol XIV, 73; The importance of the Cairo Geniza manuscripts for the history of medieval female attire, Int J Middle East Studies, Vol VII, 76 ; coauth, The art of a Moroccan folk poetess, Zeitschrift der Deutschen Morganla6ndischen Gesellschaft, Vol 128, 78; auth, New data on Islamic textiles from the Geniza, Textile Hist, Vol X, 79; Palestinian Costume and Jewelry, Univ NMex Pres, 79; The costume of the Moroccan Jewish woman, Studies in Jewish Folklore, 80; Attitudes toward women in traditional Near Eastern societies, Studies in Judaism & Islam, Magnes Press, Jerusalem, 81; From Southern Morocco to Northern Israel: Material Culture in Shelomi, Haifa Univ Press, Haifa, 82. *Mailing Add:* Dept Class & Near Eastern Studies State Univ NY Binghamton NY 13901

STILWELL, ROBERT, b San Benito, Tex, Nov 17, 10; m 40; c 2. GERMANIC PHILOLOGY. *Educ:* Univ Tex, AB, 34, AM, 36, PhD, 47. *Prof Exp:* Instr Span & Ger, Brownsville Jr Col, 34-43; from instr to prof Ger, 47-73, dir NDEA summer lang inst, 61-67, chmn dept foreign lang, 63-73, EMER PROF GER, WVA UNIV, 73- *Mem:* Am Asn Teachers Ger; Ling Soc Am; Advan Scand Studies. *Res:* Old Norse language and literature; descriptive linguistics; Old English language and literature. *Publ:* Auth, Herbert von Hoerner as poet, 56 & The narrative prose of Herbert von Hoerner, 58, Philol Papers, WVa Univ. *Mailing Add:* Dept of Foreign Lang WVa Univ Morgantown WV 26506

STIMSON, FREDERICK SPARKS, b Newark, Ohio, Jan 1, 19. SPANISH. *Educ:* Ohio State Univ, BA, 40; Univ Mich, MA, 48, PhD(Span), 52. *Prof Exp:* Dir, Cult Ctr for US Dept State, Medellin, 44-46; asst pub affairs officer, Am Embassy, San Salvador, 47; teaching fel Span, Univ Mich, 47-51; assoc prof, Franklin Col, 52-54; from instr to assoc prof, Northwestern Univ, Evanston, 54-67, chmn dept, 76-81, prof, 67-79; RETIRED. *Concurrent Pos:* From instr to vis prof, Univ Antioquia, Colombia, 43. *Mem:* MLA. *Res:* Latin American literature. *Publ:* Auth, Yo y el ladron, 57 & Moctezuma, el de la silla de oro, 58, Oxford Univ; Origenes del hispanismo norteamericano, Coleccion Studium No 29, 61; Cuba's Romantic Poet, the Story of Placido, Univ NC, 64; The New Schools of Spanish American Poetry, Hispanofila, 70; coauth, Literatura de la America Hispanica (3 vols), Dodd, 71-75; Los poemas mas representativos de Placido, Hispanofila, 76. *Mailing Add:* Dept of Span Northwestern Univ Evanston IL 60201

STIMSON, HUGH MCBIRNEY, b Port Chester, NY, Dec 5, 31. LINGUISTICS, PHILOLOGY. *Educ:* Yale Univ, BA, 53, MA, 57, PhD, 59. *Prof Exp:* Sci linguist, Foreign Serv Inst, US Dept State, 59; suprvy instr Chinese, Chinese Lang Sch, China, 59-60; from asst prof to assoc prof, 60-69, assoc prof Chinese lang & ling, 69-74, PROF CHINESE LING, YALE UNIV, 74- *Mem:* MLA; Ling Soc Am; Am Orient Soc(secy-treas, 69-76); Asn Asian Studies. *Res:* Chinese historical phonology; Chinese grammar especially classical and modern; Chinese poetics. *Publ:* Auth, The Jong-yuan in yunn: A Study of Early Mandarin Phonology, Far Eastern Publ, 66; The sound of a Tarng poem: Grieving about Green Slope by Duh-Fuu, 69 & Sheir, Shwu 'who? whom?' and moh 'none' in old Chinese, 71, J Am Orient Soc; More on Peking archaisms, T'oung Pao, 72; T'ang Poetic Vocabulary, 76, Fifty-Five T'ang Poems, 76 & coauth, Spoken Standard Chinese Vols 1 & 2, 76 & 78 & Written Standard Chinese, Vol I, 80, Far Eastern Publ. *Mailing Add:* Dept of East Asian Lang & Lit Yale Univ New Haven CT 06520

STIVERS, WILLIAM NEAL, b Amarillo, Tex, Aug 18, 18; m 48; c 3. SPANISH, FRENCH. *Educ:* Pepperdine Col, BA, 41; Univ Southern Calif, MA, 48; Cent Univ Ecuador, PhD(Span), 61. *Prof Exp:* Instr Span, Pepperdine Col, 46-52; chief dep, County Supvr, Los Angeles County, 52-62; assoc prof foreign lang, 62-67, PROF FOREIGN LANG, PEPPERDINE UNIV, MALIBU, 67- *Mem:* MLA. *Res:* Linguistics; etymology; foreign language instruction. *Mailing Add:* Dept of Lang Pepperdine Univ Malibu CA 90265

STIXRUDE, DAVID LAWRENCE, b Seattle, Wash, Nov 29, 35; m 62; c 3. SPANISH LITERATURE. *Educ:* Princeton Univ, AB, 57, MA, 60, PhD(Span lit), 67. *Prof Exp:* From instr to asst prof Span, 60-78, asst chmn dept lang, 70-77, ASSOC PROF SPAN, UNIV DEL, 78- *Mem:* MLA Am Asn Teachers Span & Port. *Res:* Contemporary Spanish poetry. *Publ:* Auth, The Early Poetry of Pedro Salinas, Castalia, 75; El Largo Lamento de Pedro Salinas, Papeles Son Armadans, 7/75; Glosando a Ronsard: El alba inoportuna de Antonio Machado, Explicacion Textos Lit, 76; La espontaneidad en los poemas de Ancia, Papeles Son Armadans, 6/77; The final lament of Pedro Salinas, Revista Can Estudios Hisp, 78; Pedro Salinas: Aventura Poetica, Catedra, 80. *Mailing Add:* Dept of Lang Univ of Del Newark DE 19711

STOCKER, ARTHUR FREDERICK, b Bethlehem, Pa, Jan 24, 14; m 68. CLASSICAL PHILOLOGY, MEDIEVAL STUDIES. *Educ:* Williams Col, AB, 34; Harvard Univ, AM, 35, PhD(class philol), 39. *Prof Exp:* Sheldon traveling fel class philol, Harvard Univ, 40-41; instr Greek, Bates Col, 41-42; asst prof ancient lang, 46-52, assoc prof classics, 52-60, chmn dept, 56-63, assoc dean grad sch arts & sci, 62-66, chmn dept, 68-78, PROF CLASSICS, UNIV VA, 60- *Concurrent Pos:* Assoc ed, Classical Outlook, 80- *Mem:* Am Philol Asn; Archaeol Inst Am; Mediaeval Acad Am; Class Asn Mid W & S (pres, 70-71); Am Class League. *Res:* Servius, fourth century commentator on Vergil; Latin palaeography; Augustan Latin literature. *Publ:* Co-ed, Servius' commentary on Vergil; Servianorum in Vergilii Carmina Commentariorum Editio Harvardiana, Vol II, 46 & ed, Vol III, 65, Am Philol Asn. *Mailing Add:* Box 3331 Univ Sta Charlottesville VA 22903

STOCKIN, FRANK GORDON, JR, b Dobbs Ferry, NY, Nov 23, 15; m 41; c 4. CLASSICAL PHILOLOGY. *Educ:* Houghton Col, AB, 37; Univ Cincinnati, AM, 38; Univ Ill, PhD, 54. *Prof Exp:* Instr Latin, 38-45, from asst prof to assoc prof class lang, 45-54, prof, 54-81, EMER PROF CLASSICS, HOUGHTON COL, 81- *Concurrent Pos:* Vis instr, Ohio Wesleyan Univ, 41; prin, Houghton Sem, NY, 43-46. *Honors & Awards:* First Prize Medal, French Govt, 37. *Mem:* Am Philol Asn; Class Asn Atlantic States(secy-treas, 54-60, vpres, 62-64). *Res:* Poetical vocabulary of Seneca; motivation in Apuleius' Metamorphoses. *Mailing Add:* Div of Foreign Lang Houghton Col Houghton NY 14744

STOCKWELL, ROBERT PAUL, b Okla, June 12, 25; m 46; c 1. ENGLISH LANGUAGE & LINGUISTICS. *Educ:* Univ VA, BA, 46, MA, 49, PhD(English philol & ling), 52. *Prof Exp:* Instr English, Univ Okla City, 46-48; dir English for foreigners proj Nashville Auto-Diesel Col, 52; from instr to assoc prof ling, Foreign Serv Inst, US Dept State, 52-56, chmn Latin-Am lang & area prog, 53-56; asst prof English, 56-58, from assoc prof to prof, 58-66, chmn dept, 66-73, PROF LING, UNIV CALIF, LOS ANGELES, 66-, CHMN DEPT, 79- *Concurrent Pos:* Vis prof, Philippines, 59 & 60 & Ling Inst, Univ Tex, 61; Am Coun Learned Soc fel, 63-64; vis prof, Univ Mich, 65. *Honors & Awards:* Distinguished Teaching Award, Univ Calif, Los Angeles, 68. *Mem:* MLA; Ling Soc Am; Philol Soc, England. *Res:* English and Spanish language; history of English phonology and syntax; general linguistic theory. *Publ:* Coauth, Patterns of Spanish Pronunciation, 60, Sounds of English and Spanish, 65 & Grammatical Structure of English and Spanish, 65, Univ Chicago; co-ed, Linguistic Change and Generative Theory, Ind Univ 72; coauth, Major Syntactic Structures of English, Holt, 73; auth, Foundations of Syntactic Theory, Prentice-Hall, 77. *Mailing Add:* Dept of Ling Univ of Calif Los Angeles CA 90024

STODDARD, DONALD RICHARD, American & English Literature. See Vol II

STOEKL, ALLAN INLOW, b Milwaukee, Wis, Oct 31, 51. COMPARATIVE LITERATURE. *Educ:* Univ Wis-Madison, BA, 73, MA, 77; State Univ NY Buffalo, PhD(comp lit), 80. *Prof Exp:* ASST PROF FRENCH & ENGLISH, WILKES COL, 80- *Mem:* MLA. *Res:* French fiction, 1920-1950; contemporary critical theory; theory of photography and film. *Publ:* Auth, Nietzsche in the text of Bataille, Glyph, 79; The photographs of Robert Frank, Enclitic, 82; Politics, mutilation, writing, Raritan Rev, 82. *Mailing Add:* Dept of Lang & Lit Wilkes Col Wilkes-Barre PA 18766

STOFFERS, MARIA EDLINGER, b Austria, May 17, 29; nat US. GERMANIC LANGUAGE & LINGUISTICS. *Educ:* Teacher's Training Col Vienna, cert, 53; Univ Innsbruck, PhD(Europ hist), 58, MA, 59. *Prof Exp:* Lectr hist, Marquette Univ-Milwaukee, 60-61; lectr Ger, Univ Calif, Davis, 61-62; prof English & psychol, State Teacher's Col Innsbruck, 62-64; lectr Ger, Univ Calif, Davis, 64-66; lectr Mod lang, Kans State Col, 66-67; PROF GER LANG & LIT, QUEENSBOROUGH COL & GRAD SCH, CITY UNIV NEW YORK, 67- *Concurrent Pos:* Fulbright scholar, US Govt for Marquette Univ & Univ Calif, 60-62; consult media lang, NY State Educ Dept, 69-71; chairperson, Comn on Instr, NY State Asn Jr Cols, 76-78, secy, 78-79 & pres, 79-80; ed, Educ Dimensions, 80-82 & Nat Info Exchange Newslett, 80- *Mem:* Am Asn Teachers Ger; MLA; Am Asn Univ Women. *Res:* Applied linguistics; 19th century literature and European history. *Publ:* Coauth, Price fixing and public policy, Marquette Bus Rev, 62; auth, Comparative Linguistics: The Passive Voice in English and in German, Paedagogische Inst, Innsbruck, 63; coauth, Beginning German II, Study Text and Assignments, State Univ NY Albany, 70; auth, Heteronomous vs autonomous, Psychother, spring 71; The changing role of the junior college professor, 76 & Motivation-is it our responsibility?, 77, J NY State Asn Jr Cols; Grillpaizers Koenig Ottokar-ein tragischer held?, Jahrbuch Grillpaizer Gesellschaft, Vienna, 78. *Mailing Add:* Dept of Ger Lang City Univ NY Grad Sch 33 W 42nd St New York NY 10036

STOKKER, KATHLEEN MARIE, b St Paul, Minn, Oct 10, 46. NORWEGIAN LANGUAGE & LITERATURE. *Educ:* St Olaf Col, Minn, BA, 68; Univ Wis-Madison, MA, 71, PhD(Scand), 78. *Prof Exp:* Instr Norweg, Moorhead State Univ, 73-77 & St Olaf Col, 77-78; asst prof, 78-82, ASSOC PROF NORWEG, LUTHER COL, IOWA, 82- *Concurrent Pos:* Res fel, Am Scand Found, 72-73 & Nat Endowment for Humanities, 81-82; trustee Norweg-Am Cult Inst, 78- *Mem:* Soc Advan Scand Study; Norweg Am Hist Asn; Am Scand Found; Norweg Am Cult Inst; Ibsen Soc Am. *Res:* Norwegian folklore, folkbelief and legends, study of cultural historical background and function of folktales; Norwegian literary and cultural periodicals pre-1900; foreign language pedagogy. *Publ:* Auth, J E Sars and Nyt Norsk Tidsskrift: Their Influence on the Modern Breakthrough in Norway, Norweg Scholarly Res Asn, 78; coauth, Norsk, Nordmann og Norge, Univ Wis Press, 81. *Mailing Add:* Dept of Norweg Luther Col Decorah IA 52101

STOKOE, WILLIAM CLARENCE, b Lancaster, NH, July 21, 19; m 42; c 2. LINGUISTICS. *Educ:* Cornell Univ, AB, 42, PhD, 46. *Prof Exp:* From asst to actg instr, Cornell Univ, 43-46; from asst prof to assoc prof, Wells Col, 46-55, chmn dept, 50-52; prof English & chmn dept, 55-68, prof ling & English, 68-81, LING RES PROF, GALLAUDET COL, 57- & DIR, LING RES LAB, 71- *Concurrent Pos:* Assoc ed, Am Ann Deaf, 56-57; adj prof ling, Gallaudet Col, 81-; NSF grants, 60-63, 71-78; ed, Sign Lang Studies, 72- & Linstok Press, Inc, 78-; vis fel Claire Hall, Univ Cambridge, 77. *Mem:* MLA; fel Am Anthrop Asn; fel AAAS. *Res:* Sign language of the American deaf; linguistics theory and structure; language origins. *Publ:* Coauth, A Dictionary of American Sign Language, 65, 76 & Generating English Sentences, 68, Gallaudet Col; Sign Language Diglossia, Studies Ling, 69-70; The Study of Sign Language, CAL/ERIC, 70, 2nd ed, Nat Asn Deaf, 72; Semiotics and Human Sign Languages, 72 & Classification and Description of Sign Language, In: Current Trends in Linguistics, 74, Mouton, The Hague; auth, Sign Language Autonomy, Ann NY Acad Sci, 76; Sign Languages, McGraw-Hill Yearbk Sci & Tech, 82. *Mailing Add:* Ling Res Lab Gallaudet Col Washington DC 20002

STOLL, ANITA KAY, b Beaver, Ohio; m 73. SPANISH LANGUAGE & LITERATURE. *Educ:* Wilmington Col, BA, 61; Ind Univ, MA, 63; Case Western Reserve Univ, PhD(Span), 72. *Prof Exp:* Instr Span, Otterbein Col, 63-64; teaching asst, Univ Wis, 64-66; from instr to asst prof, 66-72, ASSOC PROF SPAN, CLEVELAND STATE UNIV, 72- *Mem:* MLA; Am Asn Teachers Span & Port. *Res:* Spanish Golden Age literature; Spanish linguistics. *Mailing Add:* Dept of Span Cleveland State Univ Cleveland OH 44115

STOLTZFUS, BEN F, b Sofia, Bulgaria, Sept 15, 27; US citizen; m 55; c 3. FRENCH LITERATURE. *Educ:* Amherst Col, BA, 49; Middlebury Col, MA, 54; Univ Wis, PhD, 59. *Hon Degrees:* LittD, Amherst Col, 74. *Prof Exp:* Instr French, Loomis Inst, 51-53; instr, Choate Sch, 54-55; asst, Univ Wis, 56-58; instr French lit, Smith Col, 58-60; asst prof, 60-68, assoc prof, 68-73, chmn, Humanities Interdisciplinary Prog, 72-75, PROF FRENCH LIT, UNIV CALIF, RIVERSIDE, 73- *Concurrent Pos:* Fulbright grant, Univ Paris, 55-56, res grant, 63-64; Creative Arts Inst fel, Univ Calif, 67-68 & 69, Humanities Inst fel, 72 & 75; dir, French Prog, 79-82. *Mem:* MLA; Asn Amis d'Andre Gide. *Res:* Contemporary French and American novelists. *Publ:* Auth, Georges Chenneviere et l'unanimisme Minard, Paris, 65; The Eye of the Needle, Viking, 67, Faber & Faber, 67; Gide's Eagles, Southern Ill Univ, 69; contribr, Dos Passos, the Critics and the Writer's Intention, Southern Ill Univ, 71; Andre Gide, Lettres Mod, 72; auth, Black Lazarus, Winter House, 72; Gide and Hemingway: Rebels Against God, Kennikat, 78; Robbe-Grillet's labyrinths, Contemp Lit, 81. *Mailing Add:* 2040 Arroyo Dr Riverside CA 92506

STOLZ, BENJAMIN ARMOND, b Lansing, Mich, Mar 28, 34; m 62; c 2. SLAVIC LANGUAGES. *Educ:* Univ Mich, AB, 55; Univ Brussels, cert Polish, 56; Harvard Univ, AM, 57, PhD(Slavic), 65. *Prof Exp:* Lectr, 63, from asst prof to assoc prof, 64-73, PROF SLAVIC LANG & LIT, UNIV MICH, ANN ARBOR, 73-, CHMN DEPT, 71- *Concurrent Pos:* Fulbright-Hays fel, Eng & Yugoslavia, 70-71. *Mem:* Am Asn Advan Slavic Studies; Am Asn Teachers Slavic & EEurop Lang; Ling Soc Am; MLA; Midwest Mod Lang Asn (pres, 76-77). *Res:* Slavic linguistics and folklore. *Publ:* Auth, Nikac and Hamza: multiformity in the Serbo-Croatian heroic epic, J Folklore Inst, 69; On the history of the Serbo-Croatian diplomatic language and its role in the formation of the contemporary standard, In: American Contributions to the Seventh International Congress of Slavists, Vol I, 73 & Serbo-Croatian in the works of Bartholomaeus Georgievits (Bartol Durdevic): a reappraisal, In: Konstantin Mihailovic, Memoirs of a Janissary, 75 & ed, Papers in Slavic Philology, Vol I & IV, 77, Mich Slavic Publ; co-ed, Oral Literature and the Formula, Ctr Coord Ancient & Mod Studies, 77; On the language of Kanstantin Mihailovic's Kronilca turecka, Am Contribr 8th Int Congr Slavists, Vol I, 78; Kopitar and Vuk: An assessment of their roles in the rise of the new Serbian literary language, Vol II, 82. *Mailing Add:* Dept of Slavic Lang & Lit 3040 Mod Lang Bldg Univ of Mich Ann Arbor MI 48109

STONE, DONALD ADELBERT, JR, b Hackensack, NJ, June 29, 37. FRENCH LITERATURE. *Educ:* Haverford Col, AB, 59; Yale Univ, PhD(French), 63. *Hon Degrees:* AM, Harvard Univ, 69. *Prof Exp:* Instr French, Yale Univ, 62-63; from instr to asst prof, 63-69, PROF FRENCH, HARVARD UNIV, 69- *Concurrent Pos:* Guggenheim fel, 68-69. *Mem:* Am Asn Teachers Fr; Renaissance Soc Am; MLA. *Res:* Medieval literature; the 16th and 17th centuries. *Publ:* Auth, Ronsard's Sonnet Cycles, Yale Univ, 66; ed, Four Renaissance Tragedies, Harvard, 66; ed & translr, Tristan et Iseut, 66 & auth, France in the Sixteenth Century, 69, Prentice-Hall; From Tales to Truths: Essays on French Fiction in the Sixteenth Century, V Klostermann, 73; French Humanist Tragedy, Manchester, 74; ed, Nicolas de Montreux, La Sophonisbe, Droz, 76; Pierre de Larivey, Les Esprits, Harvard Univ, 78. *Mailing Add:* 201 Boylston Hall Harvard Univ Cambridge MA 02138

STONE, H REYNOLDS, b San Jose, Calif, Apr 4, 28; m 68; c 3. ROMANCE LANGUAGES & PHILOLOGY. *Educ:* San Jose State Col, BA, 49; Univ NC, Chapel Hill, MA, 62, PhD(Romance lang), 65. *Prof Exp:* Asst prof, 65-61, ASSOC PROF SPAN, UNIV ARIZ, 71- *Concurrent Pos:* Founder & first acad, dir Estudios Hispanicos en Segovia, 79; fel, Ford Found Fund for Advan Educ, 53-4. *Mem:* Mediaeval Acad Am; Am Asn Teachers Span & Port; MLA. *Res:* Renaissance theatre; mediaeval philology; Spanish civilization. *Mailing Add:* Dept of Span & Port Univ of Ariz Tucson AZ 85721

STONE-BARNARD, LAURA MARJORIE, b Boston, Mass, Apr 1, 49; m 77; c 2. CLASSICAL LANGUAGES. *Educ:* Smith Col, AB, 71; Univ NC, MA, 73, PhD(classics), 77. *Prof Exp:* Teaching asst, Univ NC, 72-76; asst prof, Oberlin Col, 76-77, Wake Forest Univ, 77-80 & Duke Univ, 81; ASST PROF CLASSICS, UNIV WIS-MILWAUKEE, 82- *Mem:* Am Philol Asn; Class Asn Midwest & South. *Res:* Aristophanes; Greek drama; Roman drama. *Publ:* The obscene of use ΜΕΓΑΣ in Aristophanes, Am J Philol, 78; A note on Clouds 1104-1105, Class Philol, 80; Costume in Aristophanic Comedy, Arno Press, 81. *Mailing Add:* 9070B N 95th St Milwaukee WI 53224

STONG-JENSEN, MARGARET TELLER, b Elmira, NY, Mar 21, 44; m 72. LINGUISTICS. *Educ:* Sarah Lawrence Col, BA, 68; Syracuse Univ, MA, 72; Univ Colo, PhD(ling), 80. *Prof Exp:* Instr ling, Univ Ottawa, 76-77; INSTR HIST ENGLISH, UNIV COLO, 79- *Concurrent Pos:* Fel ling, Univ Ottawa, 81-83. *Mem:* NE Ling Soc; Can Ling Soc. *Res:* Morphology and structure of the lexicon; phonology; syntax of case systems. *Publ:* Coauth, Ordering and directionality of iterative rules, In: The Application and Ordering of Grammatical Rules, Mouton, 76; auth, The syntax of es-relatives in Old Icelandic, Cahiers Ling Ottawa, 77; coauth, The relevancy condition and variables in phonology, Ling Anal, 79. *Mailing Add:* Dept of English Univ of Colo Boulder CO

STORVICK, OLIN JOHN, b Chicago, Ill, July 12, 25; m 49; c 5. CLASSICAL STUDIES. *Educ:* Luther Col, AB, 49; Univ Mich, AM, 50, PhD(classics), 68. *Prof Exp:* From instr to assoc prof, 55-67, head dept, 62-76, PROF CLASS LANG, CONCORDIA COL, MOORHEAD, MINN, 67-, ACAD DEAN, 79- *Concurrent Pos:* Fulbright scholar, Am Sch Class Studies, Athens, 54-55; Danforth teacher study grant, Univ Mich, 61-62. *Mem:* Am Philol Asn; Class Asn Mid W & S; Archaeol Inst Am; Am Sch Orient. *Res:* Palestine archaeology; atticism in the Theophrastus of Aeneas of Gaza. *Mailing Add:* 1310 S Sixth St Moorhead MN 56560

STORY, GEORGE MORLEY, English. See Vol II

STOUDEMIRE, STERLING AUBREY, b Concord, NC, Sept 4, 02; m 25, 46; c 2. SPANISH. *Educ:* Univ NC, AB, 23, AM, 24, PhD(Romance lang), 30. *Prof Exp:* From instr to prof span, Univ NC, 24-72, chmn dept Romance lang, 49-64; RETIRED. *Mem:* MLA; Am Asn Teachers Span & Port; Am Name Soc; S Atlantic Mod Lang Asn(pres, 62). *Res:* Spanish drama of the 19th century; literature of exploration of the 15th and 16th centuries. *Publ:* Auth, Cuentos de Espana y de America; Critical Edition of Fernandez de Oviedo, De la natural historia de las Indias, Univ NC, 59; coauth, Tesoro de lecturas, Spanish Anthology, Holt, 59; translr & auth, Pedro de Cordoba's Christian Doctrine, Univ Miami, 70; auth, Ramon Carnicer y Batlle 1789-1855): Composer, conductor, director, In: Studies in Honor of Alfred G Engstrom, Univ NC, 72; Ramon Carnicer and the Italian opera in Madrid, Hispanofila, 73; Ramon Carnicer aids Rossini, Donizetti and Bellini, In: Estudis sobre el Catala, Hispam, Barcelona, 77; Santiago, Guadalupe, Pilar: Spanish shrines, Spanish names, Names, 3/78. *Mailing Add:* 712 Gimghoul Rd Chapel Hill NC 27514

STOUT, HARRY L, b Windfall, Ind, Feb 18, 23; m 51. COMPARATIVE LITERATURE. *Educ:* Ball State Teachers Col, AB, 50, MA, 52; Ind Univ, PhD, 59. *Prof Exp:* Teacher English, Ger & Span, New Albany High Sch, Ind, 51-55; instr Ger & Span, 57-60, ASST PROF GER, PURDUE UNIV, WEST LAFAYETTE, 60- *Concurrent Pos:* Res Found travel res grant, France & Ger, Purdue Univ, West Lafayette, 61. *Mem:* Am Asn Teachers Ger; MLA; Am Comp Lit Asn; Int Comp Lit Asn; Mod Humanities Res Asn. *Res:* Franco-German literary relations; French Faust translations. *Publ:* Auth, French translations of Faust II, Ky Foreign Lang Quart, 12/61; Lessing's Riccaut and Thomas Mann's Fitelberg, Ger Quart, 1/63. *Mailing Add:* Stanley Coulter Hall Purdue Univ West Lafayette IN 47907

STOW, HENRY LLOYD, b Park Ridge, Ill, July 31, 09; m 37; c 2. CLASSICAL PHILOLOGY. *Educ:* Univ Chicago, AB, 30, PhD, 36. *Prof Exp:* Res asst, Univ Chicago, 33-37; from assoc prof to prof Greek, Univ Okla, 37-52, chmn dept, 41-52; prof class lang & chmn dept, 52-66, EMER PROF CLASS LANG, VANDERBILT UNIV, 66- *Concurrent Pos:* Vis prof, Am Sch Class Studies, Athens, 59-60, mem exec bd managing comt, 60. *Mem:* Am Philol Asn; Class Asn Mid West & South; Archaeol Inst Am. *Res:* Greek comedy; the violation of the dramatic illusion in the comedies of Aristophanes. *Mailing Add:* 2004 Castleman Dr Nashville TN 37215

STOWE, RICHARD S, b Milwaukee, Wis, Jan 2, 25; m 62; c 2. FRENCH LANGUAGE & LITERATURE. *Educ:* Univ Wis, BA, 49, PhD, 64; Univ Calif, Los Angeles, MA, 51. *Prof Exp:* Asst French, Univ Calif, Los Angeles, 49-52; from instr to asst prof mod lang, Park Col, 52-56; from instr to assoc prof French, 57-76, PROF FRENCH, LAWRENCE UNIV, 76- *Mem:* Am Asn Teachers Fr. *Res:* French Romanticism; 19th century fiction. *Publ:* Auth, Alexandre Dumas, Pere, Twayne, 76. *Mailing Add:* Dept of French Lawrence Univ P O Box 599 Appleton WI 54912

STOWELL, ERNEST, b Spokane, Wash, Nov 5, 16; m 39; c 3. SPANISH, MODERN LANGUAGE EDUCATION. *Educ:* Univ Wash, BA, 39, MA, 40; Univ of the Americas, PhD, 49. *Prof Exp:* Instr Span, Wash State Univ, 42-43; asst prof, Whitman Col, 43-46; asst prof, Kent State Univ, 46-47; prof, Ill Col, 47-53; from assoc prof to prof, Wis State Univ, Eau Claire, 53-65; PRES, AMITY INST, 65- *Concurrent Pos:* Fund Advan Educ fac fel, Spain, 54-55; supvr mod foreign lang, State Dept Pub Instr, Wis, 60; pres, Wis Lang

Ctrs Abroad, 61-63; res grant, Wis State Col Bd of Regents of State Cols, 62-63, 63-64; deleg, Nat Fedn Mod Lang Teachers Asn, 62-64; dir, Nat Foreign Lang Teachers Aide Prog, 62-63. *Mem:* Am Asn Teachers Span & Port; MLA. *Res:* Philosophy of language structure; comparative linguistics; Latin American literature. *Mailing Add:* Amity Inst Box 118 Del Mar CA 92014

STRAIGHT, H STEPHEN, b Ann Arbor, Mich, May 15, 43; m 65; c 2. LINGUISTICS, ANTHROPOLOGY. *Educ:* Univ Mich, Ann Arbor, AB, 65; Univ Chicago, AM, 70, PhD(ling), 72. *Prof Exp:* From instr to asst prof anthrop, 70-78, ASSOC PROF ANTHROP, STATE UNIV NY BINGHAMTON, 78-, DIR GRAD STUDIES ANTHROP, 80- *Concurrent Pos:* Vis asst prof ling, Ling Soc Am summer inst, State Univ NY, Oswege, 76; dir ling, State Univ NY, Binghamton, 76-81; Fulbright lectr psychol & ling theory, Univ Bucharest, Romania, 79-80. *Mem:* Ling Soc Am; Am Anthrop Asn; Am Asn Advan Sci; Int Ast Study Child Lang. *Res:* Linguistic theory and description; theoretical and developmental psycholinguistics; Mayan ethnolinguistics and sociolinguistics. *Publ:* Auth, On representing the encoding/decoding dichotomy in a theory of idealized linguistic performance, Papers Seventh Regional Meeting, Chicago Ling Soc, 71; Decompositional structure in Yucatec verbs, In: Mayan Linguistics (Vol I), Univ Calif, Los Angeles, 76; The Acquisition of Maya Phonology: Variation in Yucatec Child Language, Garland, 76; The transformational-generative grammar of American English kinship terminology: A revision of Bock's 1968 analysis, Anthrop Ling, 76; Comprehension versus production in linguistic theory, Foundations of Lang, 76; Psycholinguistics: A review essay, Can J of Ling, 77; Auditory versus articulatory phonological processes and their development in children, In: Child Phonology, Vol I, Academic, 80; Cognitive development and communicate interaction as determinants of the emerging language abilities of children, Int J of Psycholing, 80. *Mailing Add:* Dept of Anthrop State Univ of NY Binghamton NY 13901

STRAND, GISELA GALLMEISTER, b Hannover, Ger; m 61; c 2. GERMAN, HISTORY. *Educ:* Univ Chicago, MA, 62; Vanderbilt Univ, PhD(Ger), 73. *Prof Exp:* Instr Ger, Vanderbilt Univ, 67; instr, 69-73, asst prof, 73-79, ASSOC PROF GER, HOPE COL, 79- *Concurrent Pos:* Consult & panelist Ger, Nat Endowment for Humanities, 76-78; Fulbright summer grant, 76; Nat Endowment for Humanities grant, 78-79. *Mem:* Am Asn Teachers Ger; MLA; Women in Ger. *Res:* Contemporary German women writers; relationship between history and literature. *Publ:* Auth, Gabriele Wohmann, Mich Acad, 76; The return of the White God, Americas, 78; Mothers and Daughters in the Contemporary German Novel, Mich Acad, 79. *Mailing Add:* Dept of Ger Hope Col Holland MI 49423

STRANGE, JOHN OLEN, Old Testament, Hebrew. See Vol IV

STRATFORD, PHILIP C, English, Comparative Literature. See Vol II

STRAUSS, WALTER ADOLF, b Mannheim, Ger, May 14, 23; m; c 5. ROMANCE LANGUAGES. *Educ:* Emory Univ, BA, 44; Harvard Univ, MA, 48, PhD, 51. *Prof Exp:* Instr Romance lang & gen educ, Harvard Univ, 51-54; from asst prof to prof Romance lang, Emory Univ, 54-70, dir div humanities prog, 65-70; TREUHAFT PROF HUMANITIES, CASE WESTERN RESERVE UNIV, 70-, CHMN DEPT MOD LANG, 79- *Concurrent Pos:* Guggenheim & Bollingen fels, 62-63; NDEA summer fel, 77. *Mem:* MLA; Dante Soc; Midwest Mod Lang Asn; Kafka Soc; Beckett Soc. *Res:* Contemporary French literature; comparative literature, 19th and 20th centuries. *Publ:* Auth, Proust and literature: The novelist as a critic; Twelve unpublished letters of Marcel Proust, Harvard Libr Bull; Dante's Belacqua and Beckett's tramps, Comp Lit, 59; Descent and Return: The Orphic Theme in Modern Literature, Harvard Univ, 71. *Mailing Add:* Dept of Mod Lang & Lit Case Western Reserve Univ Cleveland OH 44106

STRAWN, RICHARD R, b Independence, Kans, June 19, 23; m 44; c 2. FRENCH LITERATURE. *Educ:* Univ Wyo, AB, 44; Univ Kans, AM, 46; Yale Univ, PhD, 51. *Prof Exp:* From asst prof to assoc prof French lit & head dept Romance lang, 51-70, head librn, 78-80, PROF FRENCH, WABASH COL, 60- *Concurrent Pos:* Fulbright res grant, France, 55-56; Lilly Endowment Fac open fel, 76-77. *Mem:* Am Asn Teachers Fr; Am Lit Transl Asn. *Res:* Stylistics; translating; opera. *Publ:* Auth, Seven poems of Francis Ponge, In: New Directions 17, New Directions, 61; First-Year French, Wabash Col, 68; auth & transl, Pierre Gascar, Le Presage, Carolina Quart, winter 75; Rimsky-Korsakov, Christmas Eve (libretto), performed at Ind Univ Opera Theater, 77; auth, Massenet, Manon, Ind Univ, 80. *Mailing Add:* Dept of Modern Lang Wabash Col Crawfordsville IN 47933

STREADBECK, ARVAL LOUIS, b Salt Lake City, Utah, Apr 6, 16; m 42; c 5. GERMAN. *Educ:* Univ Utah, BA, 41, MA, 46; Stanford Univ, PhD, 52. *Prof Exp:* Instr, Latter Day Saints Sem, 41-42, 45-46; from instr to assoc prof Ger, 45-58, foreign studies adv, 58-72, PROF GER, UNIV UTAH, 68- *Mem:* Am Asn Teachers Ger; Am Name Soc. *Res:* Germanic philology; American place names. *Publ:* Auth, A short introduction to Germanic philology; Ueben Sie Deutsch; Teaching and Learning German, Univ Utah, 62. *Mailing Add:* Dept of Lang Univ of Utah Salt Lake City UT 84112

STREEBING, CECILIAN M, b Detroit, Mich, July 31, 12. ROMANCE LANGUAGES. *Educ:* Cath Univ Am, BA, 34, PhD(French), 55; Canisius Col, MA, 40, MA, 43. *Prof Exp:* Instr French & Span, De La Salle Col, Cath Univ Am, 45-52; asst prof, Hillside Hall Col, 54-58, assoc prof, 59-62; ASSOC PROF FRENCH & SPAN, MANHATTAN COL, 62- *Mem:* MLA; Col Theol Soc. *Res:* French stylistics; French literature of the 17th century. *Publ:* Auth, Devout Humanism as a Style: St Francois De Sales' Introduction a la vie devote, Cath Univ Am, 54. *Mailing Add:* Manhattan Col Bronx NY 10471

STREET, JACK DAVID, b Lafayette, Ala, Apr 17, 29; m 55; c 2. FOREIGN LANGUAGES. *Educ:* Jacksonville State Col, AB & BS, 50; Univ Ala, MA, 52; State Univ Iowa, PhD(French), 64 Univ of Florence, dipl(Ital lang, lit & cult), 75; Scuola Dante Alighieri, dipl(Ital lang, lit & cult), 77. *Prof Exp:* Teacher French & English, Tuscaloosa High Sch, 51-52; asst prof mod lang, NCent Col, 58-61; from asst prof to assoc prof, 61-72, PROF MOD LANG, BELOIT COL, 72-, CHMN DEPT OF MOD LANG & LIT, 75- *Mem:* Am Asn Teachers Fr; Am Coun Teaching Foreign Lang; AAUP. *Res:* Marcel Proust; Chateaubriand; Montherlant. *Publ:* Auth, Seminar in France, 1959: An appraisal, 2/60 & A statistical study of the vocabulary of Les aventures du dernier Abencerage by Chateaubriand, 10/68, Fr Rev. *Mailing Add:* Dept of Mod Lang Beloit Col Beloit WI 53511

STREET, JOHN CHARLES, b Chicago, Ill, Apr 3, 30; m 75. LINGUISTICS. *Educ:* Yale Univ, BA, 51, MA, 52, PhD(ling), 55. *Prof Exp:* Asst prof English & ling, Mich State Univ, 57-59; asst prof ling, Columbia Univ, 59-62; vis asst prof, Univ Wash, 62-63; assoc prof, 63-67, PROF LING, UNIV WISMADISON, 67- *Concurrent Pos:* Res assoc, Am Coun Learned Soc, 59-62. *Mem:* Ling Soc Am; Am Orient Soc; Soc Uralo-Altaica; Mongolia Soc. *Res:* General linguistics; Mongolian languages; Altaic linguistics. *Publ:* Auth, The Language of the Secret History of the Mongols, Am Orient Soc, 57; Khalkha Structure, Ind Univ, 63. *Mailing Add:* Dept of Ling Univ of Wis Madison WI 53706

STRELKA, JOSEPH PETER, b Wiener Neustadt, Austria, May 3, 27; m 63; c 1. GERMAN LITERATURE, THEORY OF LITERATURE. *Educ:* Univ Vienna, PhD(Ger lit), 50. *Prof Exp:* Assoc prof Ger lit, Univ Southern Calif, 64, dir Vienna prog, Univ Vienna, 65; prof Ger, Pa State Univ, University Park, 66-71; PROF GER & COMP LIT, STATE UNIV NY ALBANY, 71- *Concurrent Pos:* Theodor Koerner Found award, 55-57; City of Vienna award, 58; Austrian Govt res fel, Austrian Inst Cult Affairs Paris, 58-59; ed, Yearbook of Comparative Criticism Ser, 68 & Penn State Series in German literature, 71-; exchange scholar, State Univ NY, 75; Inst Humanistic Studies fel, 77; New Yorker Beitrage zur Vergleichenden Literaturwissenschaft, 82-; New Yorker Studien zur Neueren Deutschen Literaturgeschichte, 82- *Honors & Awards:* Austrian Cross of Honor for the Arts and Sci First Class, Republic of Austria, 78. *Mem:* PEN Club; Int Asn Ger Studies, Int Comp Lit Asn; MLA; Humboldt-Gesellschaft. *Res:* LIterary theory; literature of the Renaissance; German literature of the 20th century. *Publ:* Brücke u vielen Ufern, Europa, Vienna, Frankfurt, Zurich, 66; Vergleichende Literaturkritik, Francke, Bern, 70; Die gelenkten Musen, Europa, Vienna, Frankfurt, Zurich, 71; Auf der Suche nach dem verlorenen Selbst, Francke, Bern, 77; Werk, Werkverständnin, Wertung, Francke, Bern, 78; Methodologie der Literaturwissenschaft, Nimeyer, Tübingen, 78; Esoterik bei Goethe, Niemeyer Tübingen, 80; Stefan Zweig, Österreichischer Bundesverlag, Vienna, 81. *Mailing Add:* Dept of Ger State Univ of NY Albany NY 12222

STRICKLAND, WILLIAM EMILE, b Greensboro, Ala, July 31, 20; m 48; c 2. MODERN LANGUAGES. *Educ:* Fla Southern Col, AB, 40; Univ NC, MA, 42, PhD, 50. *Prof Exp:* From asst prof to assoc prof, 51-60, dir, Univ Summer Sch in France, 53-69, PROF MOD LANG & CHMN DEPT, UNIV MISS, 60- *Concurrent Pos:* Res, Univ Paris, 50-51. *Honors & Awards:* Palmes Academiques, 57, Officer, 66. *Mem:* MLA; Am Asn Teachers Fr; S Cent Mod Lang Asn; S Atlantic Mod Lang Asn. *Res:* French dialectology of Central France; French literature of the seventeenth and eighteenth centuries. *Publ:* Auth, The classroom that stretched 3,6000 miles, Miss Educ Advan; Social and literary satire in Furetiere's Roman bourgeois, Fr Rev; coauth, Mme Juliette Adam and George Sand: An unpublished souvenir, Romance Notes, spring 67. *Mailing Add:* PO Box 213 University MS 38677

STROMECKY, OSTAP, b Kolomya, Ukraine, Feb 2, 30; US citizen; m 56; c 2. SLAVIC LANGUAGE & LITERATURES. *Educ:* Vanderbilt Univ, BA, 66, MA, 68; Ukrainian Free Univ, PhD(Slavic lit & ling), 70. *Prof Exp:* ASST PROF SLAVIC LANG & LIT, UNIV ALA, HUNTSVILLE, 67-, CHMN MOD FOREIGN LANG DEPT, 80- *Concurrent Pos:* Fel, Vanderbilt Univ, 66-68; area consult NASA, Hayes Int Corp, 71-72. *Mem:* MLA; Am Asn Advan Slavic Studies; Ukrainian Acad Arts & Sci. *Res:* Nickolai Gogol's linguistics and philosophy; Anton Chekov's philosophy of art. *Publ:* Auth, Ukrainian elements in Nikolai Gogol's Taras Bulba, Ukrainian Quart, winter 69; contribr, Chekov and Ukraine, Ukrainian Free Univ, Munich, 73. *Mailing Add:* Dept of Mod Foreign Lang Univ of Ala Huntsville AL 35807

STROUD, MATTHEW DAVID, b Hillsboro, Tex, Oct 4, 50. SPANISH. *Educ:* Univ Tex, Austin, BA, 71; Univ Southern Calif, MA, 74, PhD(Span), 77. *Prof Exp:* ASST PROF SPAN, TRINITY UNIV, 77- *Mem:* MLA; SCent Mod Lang Asn; Am Asn Teachers Span & Port; AAUP; Asoc Int Hisp; Cervantes Soc Am. *Res:* Seventeenth century Spanish dramas de honor; principles of dramatic irony and stagecraft; poetics. *Publ:* Auth, Social-comic Anagnorisis in La dama duende, Bull Comediantes, fall 77; La Numancia comoauto secular, Actas del Primer Congreso Int Sobre Cervantes, 80; Los comendadores de Cordoba: Realidad, manierismo y el barroco, Actas del Primer Congreso Int Sobre Lope de Vega, 81; ed & transl, Pedro Calderon de la Barca, Celosaun del aire matan, Trinity Univ Press, 81; auth, Stylistic considerations of Calderon's opera Librettos, Critica Hisp, 82; The resocializaiton of the Muher Varonil in three plays by Velez, In: Antiguidad y actualidad de Luis Velez de Guevara: Estudios Criticos, Purdue Univ Press, 82. *Mailing Add:* Dept of Span Trinity Univ San Antonio TX 78284

STROUD, RONALD SIDNEY, b Toronto, Can, July 8, 33; Can citizen; m 63; c 2. CLASSICS. *Educ:* Univ Toronto, BA, 57; Univ Calif, Berkeley, PhD(classics), 65. *Prof Exp:* Secy, Am Sch Class Studies Athens, 60-63; from asst prof to assoc prof, 65-72, PROF CLASSICS, UNIV CALIF, BERKELEY, 72- *Concurrent Pos:* Am Philos Soc, Am Coun Learned Socs & Guggenheim fels, 77-78. *Res:* Greek history; Greek epigraphy; classical archaeology. *Publ:* Auth, Tribal Boundary Markers from Corinth, Calif Studies Class Antiq, 68; Drakon's Law on Homicide, Univ Calif, 68; An Ancient Fort on Mt Oneion, 71 & Inscriptions from the North Slope of the Acropolis, 71 & 72, Hesperia; Thucydides and the Battle of Solygeia, Calif Studies Class Antiq, 71; An Athenian Law on Silver Coinage, Hesperia, 74; The Axones and Kyrbeis of Drakon and Solon, Univ Calif, 79; co-ed, Supplementum Epigraphieum Graecum, Vol 26, 79, Vol 27, 80 & Vol 28, 82. *Mailing Add:* Dept Classics Univ Calif Berkeley CA 94720

STROUT, LILIA DAPAZ, b Mendoza, Arg, July 26, 30; m 62; c 3. SPANISH DRAMA, SPANISH AMERICAN LITERATURE. *Educ:* Nat Univ Cuyo, Prof lit, 54; Univ, NC, Chapel Hill, MA, 64; Univ Ky, PhD(Span), 73. *Prof Exp:* Prof Greek, Sch Philos & Lit, Nat Univ Cuyo, 54-64; teacher Latin, Greek, Span & lit, Nat Univ Cuyo, Ministry Educ, normal & sec schs, Prov Mendoza, Arg, 63-67; lectr Span lang & lit, Mem Univ Newf, 68-71; asst prof Span, Univ SC, 73-74; ASST PROF LIT, UNIV PR, MAYAGUEZ, 74- *Concurrent Pos:* Inst Hisp Cult grant, Univ Madrid, 58-59. *Mem:* MLA; Int Asn Hispanists; Int Inst Iberoam Lit. *Res:* Spanish drama, Golden Age; Spanish American literature; psychology and literature. *Publ:* Auth, El cambio de la realidad social y politica en Hispanoamerica y la actitud de sus novelistas, In: Revista de Literaturas Modernas, Nat Univ Cuyo, 71; Mito, realidad y superrealidad en Sobre Heroes y Tumbas, In: Homenaje a Sabato, Las Americas, 73; Casamiento ritual y el mito del hermafrodita en Omnibus de Cortazar, In: Anales Lit Hispanamericana, 2-3, Univ Madrid, 73-74; Nuevos cantos de vida y esperanza: Salmos de Ernesto Cardenal y la nueva etica, In: Ernesto Cardenal, Poeta de la Liberacion Latinoamericana, Cambeiro, 75; Viaje al ser de un Silenciero, Megafon, 76; Sobre heroes y tumbas: Misterio ritual de purificacion; La resurreccion de la carne, In: Novelistas Hispanoamericanos de hoy, Taurus, 76; El misterio de El Caballero de Olmedo, In: Studies on Golden Age, Miami Univ, 77; Un espacio sagrads en Prosas profavas, XVIII Cong Inst Int Lit Iberoam, Univ Fla, 77. *Mailing Add:* PO Box 5608 Univ Puerto Rico Mayaguez PR 00708

STRUC, ROMAN SVIATOSLAV, b Ukraine, Oct 18, 27; US citizen. GERMAN & SLAVIC LITERATURE. *Educ:* Univ Wash, MA, 57, PhD(comp lit, Ger, Russ), 62. *Prof Exp:* Teaching asst Ger, Univ Washington, 58-60, instr, 60-62; from asst prof to assoc prof Ger & Russ, Washington Univ, 62-66; assoc prof Ger & comp lit, Univ Wash, 66-70; prof Ger & Russ & head, Dept Ger & Slavic Studies, 70-80, PROF GER, UNIV CALGARY, 80- *Concurrent Pos:* Can Coun res grant, 74. *Mem:* MLA; Ukrainian Acad Arts & Sci in US; Can Asn Slavists. *Res:* Modern German literature; 19th century German-Slavic literary relations. *Publ:* Coauth, Dialogue on Poetry and Literary Aphorisms, Pa State Univ, 68; Zwei Erzählungen von E T A Hoffmann und Franz Kafka, Rev Langues Vivantes, 68; Categories of the grotesque: Gogol and Kafka, Comp Lit Symp, 70; Petty demons and beauty: Gogol, Dostoevsky, Sologub, In: Essays on European Literature, Washington Univ, 72; contribr, Die Slawische Welt im Werke Joseph Roths, In: Joseph Roth und die Tradition, Agora, Darmstadt, 75; Zu einigen Gestalten in Effi Briest und Buddenbrooks, 81. *Mailing Add:* Dept of Ger & Slavic Studies Univ of Calgary Calgary AB T2N 1N4 Can

STRUEBIG, PATRICIA ANN, b Gary, Ind, Oct 28, 43. FRENCH & SPANISH LANGUAGE & LITERATURE. *Educ:* Northwestern Univ, AB, 65; Univ Miami, MA, 69; Fla State Univ, Tallahassee, PhD(French & Span), 79. *Prof Exp:* Serv rep, Chicago Sale Off, US Steel Corp, 65-67; jr financial planning exec, Corp Planning Dept, Int Hq, Philip Morris, Inc, 69-70; transl to commerical secy, Embassy Pakistan, Paris, 75-76; independent transl & interpreter, Embassy Pakistan, UNESCO & Lab Biocodex, 76-77; prof French, Columbia Col, 73-75 & Ind Univ Northwest, 79-80; PROF FRENCH & SPAN, BALL STATE UNIV, 80- *Mem:* MLA; SAtlantic Mod Lang Asn; Am Comp Lit Asn. *Res:* Contemporary French literature; structuralism; interdisciplinary approaches to literary criticism. *Publ:* Auth, The structure of transformation in Michel Butor's La Modification, J Comp Lit Circle Fla State Univ, 82; Michel Butor's Volis: The creation of the mythic domain, French Rev (in prep). *Mailing Add:* 439 S Court St Crown Point IN 46307

STRUTYNSKI, UDO, b Vienna, Austria, Sept 21, 42; US citizen. MEDIEVAL LITERATURE. *Educ:* Loyola Univ Los Angeles, AB, 63; Univ Calif, Los Angeles, MA, 66, PhD(Germanic lang), 75. *Prof Exp:* Assoc ed, Univ Calif Press, 75-78; asst prof anthrop, Occidental Col, 79-80; ASST PROF COMP LIT & GER, NORTHWESTERN UNIV, 80- *Mem:* MLA. *Res:* Comparative Indo-European mythology; epic and heroic literature; Germanic and comparative European folklore. *Publ:* Contribr, Myth and Law among the Indo-Europeans, 70, Gods of the Ancient Northmen, 73 & Myth in Indo-European Antiquity, 74, Univ Calif Press; auth, Germanic divinities in weekday names, 75 & Philippson Contra Dumezil: An answer to the attack, 77, J Indo-Europ Studies; ed, Camillus: A Study of Indo-European Religion as Roman History, Univ Calif Press, 80; auth, Ares: A reflex of the Indo-European war god?, Arethusa, 80; contribr, Georges Dumezil, Centre Goerges Pompidou/Pandora Editions, 81. *Mailing Add:* Dept of German Northwestern Univ Evanston IL 60201

STUART, DOUGLAS KEITH, Old Testament, Near Eastern Languages. See Vol IV

STUDERUS, LENARD HENRY, b Guttenberg, NJ, June 23, 40. SPANISH, LINGUISTICS. *Educ:* Univ Wash, BA, 64; San Diego State Univ, MA, 67; Univ Colo, PhD(Span), 74. *Prof Exp:* Instr English, Cath Univ Puerto Rico, 67-68; asst prof Span, Mo Southern State Col, 70-73; lectr, Regis Col, 73-74; asst prof, 74-80, ASSOC PROF SPAN, UNIV TEX, ARLINGTON, 80- *Mem:* Asn Teachers Span & Port; Ling Asn Southwest; SCent Mod Lang Asn; Ling Asn Can & US. *Res:* Spanish language. *Publ:* Auth, Spanish Imperatives and the Notion of Imperativity, 9/75, Obliqueness in Spanish Imperative Utterances, 3/78, A Model of Temporal Reference in Spanish, 9/79, Guarda Words: Interpretation and Usage, 12/78 & A Spanish Twilight Zone: Mood, Syntax, and Past Temporal Reference, 3/81, Hispania; Regional, universal, and popular aspects of Chicano Spanish grammar, Bilingual Rev, 12/80; A national feature map to Spanish aspect, 7th Lat Am Can & US Forum 1980, 3/81. *Mailing Add:* Dept Foreign Lang & Ling Univ Tex Arlington TX 76019

STURCKEN, HENRY TRACY, b Charleston, SC, Apr 2, 28; m 51; c 2. SPANISH LITERATURE, ROMANCE LINGUISTICS. *Educ:* Col Charleston, AB, 47; Univ NC, MA, 50, PhD(Romance lang), 53. *Prof Exp:* Instr Span, Univ NC, 47-53; instr, Amherst Col, 53-55; from asst prof to assoc prof Romance lang, 55-64, PROF ROMANCE LANG, PA STATE UNIV, 64- *Mem:* Am Asn Teachers Span & Port; Mediaeval Acad Am; Am Acad Res Historians Medieval Spain. *Res:* Romance philology; medieval Spanish literature. *Publ:* Coauth, Oral Spanish Review, Holt, 64; auth, Don Juan Manuel, Twayne, 73; Spanish in Review, Wiley, 79. *Mailing Add:* Dept of Span Pa State Univ University Park PA 16802

STURGES, ROBERT STUART, Middle English Literature. See Vol II

STURM, HARLAN GARY, b Libby, Mont, Feb 24, 41; m 65; c 1. ROMANCE LANGUAGES. *Educ:* Univ Minn, BA, 63, MA, 65; Univ NC, PhD(Romance lang), 67. *Prof Exp:* Asst prof lang Queens Col, NC, 66-67; asst prof Span, Univ Ky, 67-69; asst prof Romance lang, 69-72, actg chmn dept Span & Port, 77-78, assoc prof, 72-80, PROF SPAN, UNIV MASS, AMHERST, 80-, DEPT CHMN, 79- *Res:* Medieval Spanish literature. *Publ:* Auth, The Conde Lucanor: The first ejemplo, Mod Lang Notes, 69; coauth, The two Sanchos in La estrella de Sevilla, Romantisches Jahrbuch, 70; auth, The Libro de los buenos proverbios: A Critical Edition, Univ Ky, 71; Repaso Revised, Norton, 71; Author and authority in El Conde Lucanor, Hispanofila, 74; From Plato's Cave to Segismundo's Prison: The four levels of reality and experience, Mod Lang Notes, 74; The concept of the individual in El Conde Lucanor, In: Don Juan Manuel Studies, Tamesis, London, 77; Epic Imagery in The Laberinto de Fortuna: Some Notes on Juan de Mena and Homer, In: Medieval, Renaissance and Folklore Studies in Honor of John Erten Ketter, 80. *Mailing Add:* Dept of Span & Port Univ of Mass Amherst MA 01002

STURM, RUDOLF, b Doubravice, Czech, Apr 15, 12; US citizen; m 54; c 3. FOREIGN LANGUAGES & LITERATURES. *Educ:* Charles Univ, Prague, Absolutorium, 37; Harvard Univ, PhD, 56. *Prof Exp:* Instr French & Ital, Boston Col, 49-51; res assoc Slavic studies, Mid-Europ Studies Ctr, New York, NY, 51-53; head dept foreign lang, Hershey Jr Col, 56-58; assoc prof Ital & Russ, 58-73, fac res grants, 62, 63, 65, 67, PROF ITAL & SLAVIC LIT, SKIDMORE COL, 73- *Concurrent Pos:* Danforth Found grants, 59, 61; consult, Libr Cong, 64-65; assoc bibliogr, MLA, 66-; Ford Found grant, 69. *Mem:* MLA; Am Asn Teachers Slavic & EEurop Lang; Czech Soc Arts & Sci in US(secy-gen, 59-60, 62-66, vpres, 68-). *Res:* Czechoslovak and Italian literature. *Publ:* Coauth, Czechoslovakia: An Area Manual, Johns Hopkins Univ, Vols I & II, 55; auth, Czechoslovakia: A Bibliographic Guide, Libr Cong, 67; contribr, Slavonic Encycl: Bks Abroad & World Yearbk Educ. *Mailing Add:* Dept of Mod Lang & Lit Skidmore Col Saratoga Springs NY 12866

STURM-MADDOX, SARA, b Nashville, Tenn, Dec 22, 38. ROMANCE LANGUAGES; MEDIEVAL LITERATURE. *Educ:* Univ Minn, BA, 63, MA, 65; Univ NC, PhD(Romance philol), 67. *Prof Exp:* Asst prof French, Queens Col, NC, 66-67; asst prof Ital, Univ Ky, 67-69; PROF FRENCH & ITAL, UNIV MASS, AMHERST, 75- *Concurrent Pos:* Am Coun Learned Soc. *Mem:* Dante Soc Am; Int Arthurian Soc; Soc Rencesvals; Am Asn Teachers Fr; Int Courtly Lit Soc. *Res:* Medieval French romance, epic and lyric; Dante; Renaissance Italian. *Publ:* Auth, The Lay of Guingamor: A Study, Univ NC, 68; Magic in Le Bel Inconnu, L'Esprit Createur, 72; The stature of Charlemagne in the Pelerinage, Studies Philol, 74; Lorenzo de'Medici, Twayne, 74; Structure and meaning in Inferno XXVI, Dante Studies, 74; contribr, The poet-persona in the Canzoniere, In: Francis Petrarch, Six Centuries Later: A Symposium, Univ NC, 75; auth, The pattern of witness: Narrative design in the Vita Nuova, Forum Italicum, 78; contribr, La pianta piu gradita in cielo: Petrarch's Laurel and Jove, In: Dante, Petrarch, and others: Studies in the Italian Trecento, SUNY, 82. *Mailing Add:* Dept of French & Ital Univ of Mass Amherst MA 01003

STUYVESANT, PHILLIP WAYNE, b Greenville, Pa, Nov 29, 40; m 62; c 2. NINETEENTH CENTURY SPANISH LITERATURE. *Educ:* Thiel Col, AB, 62; Western Reserve Univ, MA, 64, Case Western Reserve Univ, PhD(Romance lang), 70; Inst Hisp Cult, Madrid, Spain, dipl, 66. *Prof Exp:* Instr, 66-70, asst prof, 70-80, ASSOC PROF SPAN, UNIV AKRON, 80- *Mem:* Am Asn Teachers Span & Port; AAUP; Midwest Mod Lang Asn. *Res:* Life and works of Gustavo Adolfo Becquer; archetypal patterns in literature; contemporary Spanish drama. *Publ:* Auth, La busqueda como simbolo de unidad en las obras imaginativas de G A Becquer, Rev Estudios Hisp, 1/74; El teatro social de Alfonso Sastre, 3/75; Realidades convergentes: Hacia un drama metafisico, 1/76, Una sintesis ontologica: una perspectiva estetico-existencial, 9/76, La distancia como guia a la vision dramatica de Victor Ruiz Iriarte, 9/77, El determinismo en los dramas de Jaime Salom, 12/78 & La mentira en el teatro de Juan Jose Alonso Millan, 8/80, Presencia literaria. *Mailing Add:* Dept of Mod Lang Olin Hall Univ of Akron Akron OH 44325

SUAREZ, BERNARDO, b Havana, Cuba, May 29, 20; US citizen; m 47; c 2. SPANISH & SPANISH AMERICAN LITERATURE. *Educ:* Univ Havana, LLD, 42; Univ Ga, MA, 65; Univ Fla, PhD(Span & Port), 69. *Prof Exp:* Lawyer, Havana, Cuba, 42-60; instr Span, Univ Ga, 62-65; asst prof Span & Port, 68-78, ASSOC PROF SPAN & PORT, UNIV ALA, 78- *Mem:* Am Asn Teachers Span & Port; SAtlantic Mod Lang Asn; Southeastern Coun Latin Am Studies. *Res:* Spanish-American literature; XIX century Peninsular Spanish literature; Brazilian literature. *Publ:* Auth, El impresionismo en la prosa de Ramon Lopez Velarde, Cuadernos Americanos, 74; Facetas en la estetica de Ramon Lopez Velarde, Cuadernos Hispanoamericanos, 76; La renovacion de la poesia brasilena en los ultimos veinte anos, Anales de Lit Hispanoam, 76; En torno a siete cuentos de Gabriel Garcia Marquez: Estructura y estilo, Explicacion de Textos Literarios, 77; Tecnicas impresionistas en las novelas valencianas de Blasco Ibanex, Selected Proc 27th Annual MIFLC, 77; La modalidad negra en seleccionados escritores brasilenos, Homenaje a Lydia Cabrera, 78; La creacion artistica en La barraca, de Blasco Ibanez, Cuadernos Hispanoamericanos, 81. *Mailing Add:* Dept of Romance Lang Univ of Ala P O Box 1963 University AL 35486

SUAREZ, MANUEL LAURENTINO, b Havana, Cuba, Nov 8, 45; US citizen; m 70; c 2. ROMANCE LANGUAGES. *Educ:* Bloomfield Col, BA, 67; Univ Iowa, MA, 69; Univ Ga, PhD(Romance lang), 73. *Prof Exp:* Asst mgr, Int Div, Am Hosp Supply Corp, 69-70; chmn dept lang, Tift Col, 72-73; chmn dept foreign lang, Wesleyan Col, 73-74; ASSOC PROF ROMANCE LANG, E TENN STATE UNIV, 74- *Concurrent Pos:* Res grant, E Tenn State Univ, 75; Nat Endowment Humanities grant, 77. *Mem:* MLA; SAtlantic Mod Lang Asn; AAUP; Mountain Interstate Foreign Lang Conf (vpres, 76, pres, 77); Asn Int Hisp. *Res:* Spanish and Latin American literature (poetry and drama); Galician poetry. *Publ:* Auth, La Espana de Erasmo, Ediciones

Univ, 73; El teatro en verso del XX, Universal, 75; Female characters in Benavente and Lorea, Ariel, 75; La poesia de Celso Emilio Ferreiro, Proc Mountain Interstate Foreign Lang Conf, 77; Desarrollo de un personaje en Carpentier, Estudos Ibero-Americanos, 77; coauth, De aqui y de alla, Heath, 78; co-ed, Selected Proceedings Mountain Interstate Foreign Lang Conf, E Tenn State Univ, 78; auth, Brief comparison between Benavente and Lorca, Idem, 78; Cervantes en Cadalso, Estudos Ibero-Americanos, 80; San Juan de la Cruz, Poeta Contemplativo, La Chispa, Tulane Univ, 82. *Mailing Add:* Dept of Romance Lang ETenn State Univ Johnson City TN 37601

SUAREZ-TORRES, J DAVID, b Cucuta, Santander, Colombia, Oct, 22, 19; US citizen; m 64; c 2. LATIN AMERICAN LITERATURE. *Educ:* Univ Cent, Caracas, Ven, BPhil, 44; Middlebury Col, MA, 66; Boston Univ, PhD(contemp lit), 72. *Prof Exp:* Instr Span & French, Boston Col, 63-67; asst prof Span, Boston State Col, 67-69; assoc prof Span & French, Stratford Col, 69-71; PROF SPAN, GEORGETOWN UNIV, 71- *Concurrent Pos:* Dir Quito summer prog, 73-, dir Latin Am studies, 75-76, acad adv Quito, Georgetown Univ, 75- *Mem:* MLA; Am Asn Teachers Span & Port. *Res:* Commitment in Spanish-American literature; humor in the novels of Jose Maria Gironella. *Publ:* Auth, Y de nuevo Don Quijote, Logos, Cali, Colombia, 1/74; Cabrera Infante, Bustrofedon y la retorica, de la Narrat H Am Memorias del IV Congreso, 8/74; Prespectiva humoristica en la trilogia de Gironella, Torres Lib Lit Studies, 11/75. *Mailing Add:* 2713 Welcome Dr Falls Church VA 22046

SUH, DOO SOO, b Korea, Mar 11, 07; m 30; c 5. KOREAN & JAPANESE LITERATURES. *Educ:* Keijo Imp Univ, MA, 30; Columbia Univ, PhD, 53. *Prof Exp:* Res asst Korean lang, Keijo Imp Univ, 30-34; dean & prof Japanese lit, Ewha Woman's Col, 34-43; dean & prof Korean lit, Chosun Christian Univ, 45-49; dean & prof, Seoul Nat Univ, Korea, 49; vis lectr Far Eastern lang, Harvard Univ, 52-55; from vis lectr to asst prof Korean studies, 55-73, assoc prof, Korean Lang & Lit, 73-77, EMER PROF KOREAN STUDIES, GRAD SCH, UNIV WASH, 77- *Concurrent Pos:* Pres, Sung Kyun Kwan Univ, 62-63. *Res:* Comparative study of Oriental literature; Korean history; education. *Publ:* Auth, Korean Literary Reader-With a Short History of Korean Literature, Tonga, Seoul, 63; Struggle for academic freedom in Japanese universities before 1945, Libr Cong, A53-385, Univ Microfilm, Ann Arbor, Mich. *Mailing Add:* Dept of Asian Lang & Lit Univ of Wash Seattle WA 98195

SUHADOLC, JOSEPH, b Yugoslavia, Mar 26, 14; US citizen. RUSSIAN LANGUAGE & LITERATURE. *Educ:* Univ Zagreb, MS, 38; Univ Ljubljana, DJur, 42; Univ Venice, PhD, 54; Middlebury Col, MA, 61. *Prof Exp:* Instr Russ & Ger, Kent State Univ, 56-59; assoc prof Russ, 59-73, PROF RUSS, NORTHERN ILL UNIV, 73- *Mem:* NEA; Am Asn Advan Slavic Studies; Am Asn Teachers Slavic & East Europ Lang; Midwest Mod Lang Asn. *Publ:* Transl, N Mikhailov & Z Kosenko's Those Americans, Regnery, 62; auth,The strain within the frame of Sholokhov's Virgin Soil Upturned, Slavic & EEurop J, fall 62; Pushkin and serfdom, In: Literature and Society, Univ Nebr, 63. *Mailing Add:* Dept of Foreign Lang Northern Ill Univ De Kalb IL 60115

SUITS, THOMAS ALLAN, b Milwaukee, Wis, Apr 5, 33; m 55; c 2. CLASSICAL PHILOLOGY. *Educ:* Yale Univ, AB, 55, MA, 56, PhD(classics), 58. *Prof Exp:* From instr to asst prof Greek & Latin, Columbia Univ, 58-66; assoc prof classics, 66-72, PROF CLASSICS, UNIV CONN, 72- *Concurrent Pos:* Mem class jury, Am Acad in Rome, 77-79. *Mem:* Am Philol Asn; Class Asn New England (pres, 80-81). *Res:* Latin literature, especially Elegy; Propertius. *Publ:* Coauth, Latin Selections, Bantam, 61; auth, Mythology, address, and structure in Propertius 2.8, 65 & The Vertumnus elegy of Propertius, 69, Trans & Proc Am Philol Asn; ed, Macrobius: The Saturnalia, Columbia Univ, 69; auth, The structure of Livy's 32nd book, Philologus, 74; The knee and the shin: Seneca, Apocolocyntosis 10.3, Class Philol, 75; The iambic character of Propertius 1.4, Philologus, 76. *Mailing Add:* 12 Hillyndale Rd Storrs CT 06268

SULEIMAN, SUSAN RUBIN, b Budapest, Hungary; US citizen; m 66; c 2. FRENCH & COMPARATIVE LITERATURE. *Educ:* Columbia Univ, BA, 60; Harvard Univ, MA, 64, PhD(Romance lang & lit), 69. *Prof Exp:* Asst prof French, Columbia Univ, 69-76; from asst prof to assoc prof, Occidental Col, 76-81; ASSOC PROF ROMANCE LANG & LIT, HARVARD UNIV, 81- *Concurrent Pos:* Vis asst prof, Univ Calif, Los Angeles, 76. *Mem:* MLA; Am Asn Teachers French; Am Comp Lit Asn. *Res:* Twentieth century French fiction; theory of narrative; feminist theory. *Publ:* Auth, The Parenthetical Function in A la recherche du temps perdu, PMLA, 5/76; Interpreting ironies, Diacritics, summer 76; Reading Robbe-Grillet: Sadism and text in Projet pour une revolution a New York, Romanic Rev, 1/77; Le recit exemplaire: Parabole, fable, roman a these, Poetique, 11/77; co-ed & contribr, The Reader in the Text: Essays on Audience and Interpretation, Princeton Univ Press, 80; contribr, What is Criticism?, Ind Univ Press, 81; The question of readability in Avant-Garde fiction, Studies in Twentieth Century Lit, 82; Authoritarian Fictions: The Ideological Novel as a Literary Genre, Columbia Univ Press (in press). *Mailing Add:* Dept of Romance Lang & Lit Harvard Univ Cambridge MA 02138

SULLENS, IDELLE, English, Humanities. See Vol II

SULLIVAN, DENNIS GEORGE, b Chicago, Ill, Nov 24, 41; m 63 c 1. ROMANCE LANGUAGES. *Educ:* DePaul Univ, BA, 63; Johns Hopkins Univ, PhD(Romance lang), 68. *Prof Exp:* Asst prof Romance lang, Johns Hopkins Univ, 67-73, assoc prof, 73-80. *Mem:* MLA. *Res:* French novel of the 19th and 20th centuries; existentialism; modern criticism. *Publ:* Auth, The function of the theater in the work of Nerval, 12/65, On vision in Proust: The icon and the voyeur, 69 & On theatricality in Proust: Desire and the actress, 71, Mod Lang Notes. *Mailing Add:* 2828 Beechland Ave Baltimore MD 21214

SULLIVAN, EDWARD DANIEL, b Boston, Mass, Dec 9, 13; m 40; c 2. FRENCH LITERATURE. *Educ:* Harvard Univ, AB, 36, AM, 38, PhD, 41. *Prof Exp:* Instr French, Harvard Univ, 38-42; from instr to assoc prof, 46-72, chmn dept Romance lang & lit, 58-66, dean col, 66-72, PROF COMP LIT, PRINCETON UNIV, 75-, AVALON PROF HUMANITIES, 72-, CHMN COUN HUMANITIES, 74- *Concurrent Pos:* Fulbright res fel, Paris, 56-57; gen ed, Scribner's French Ser, 60-74; chmn univ adv coun, Inst Life Insurance, 67-; consult, Nat Endowment for Humanities, 74- *Honors & Awards:* Palmes Academiques, 60; Legion d'Honneur, 67; Officier, Palmes Academiques, French Govt, 78. *Mem:* Int Asn Fr Studies; MLA: Am Asn Teachers Fr; Soc Fr Prof Am. *Res:* Nineteenth century French novel; Maupassant; short fiction. *Publ:* Auth, Maupassant the Novelist, Princeton Univ, 54; Maupassant: The Short Stories, Edward Arnold, London, 62, Barron's 63; coauth, Temoins de l'homme, Nouvelles et Recits, Scribner, 65; auth, The relevance of fiction, Va Quart, summer 70; The meaning of literature, Bull Pa State MLA, fall 73; 5/75; Alternative careers, Asn Dept Foreign Lang Bull, 9/77. *Mailing Add:* 122 E Pyne Princeton Univ Princeton NJ 08540

SULLIVAN, HENRY WELLS, b London, England, Dec 8, 42. SPANISH & COMPARATIVE LITERATURE. *Educ:* Oxford Univ, BA, 66, MA, 68; Harvard Univ, PhD(Span), 70. *Prof Exp:* Asst prof Span, NY Univ, 69-71; asst prof, Univ Ill, Chicago Circle, 72-77; asst prof Span, Northwestern Univ, 77-80; ASSOC PROF & CHMN, DEPT MOD LANG, UNIV OTTAWA, 80- *Concurrent Pos:* Nat Endowment for Humanities fel, 76; Humboldt Found fel, 78-79. *Mem:* Asoc Int de Hispanistas; Renaissance Soc Am; MLA; AAUP. *Res:* Spanish 17th century theater; Hispano-German literary relations. *Publ:* Coauth, The unholy martyr: Don Juan's misuse of intelligence, Romanische Forsche, 69; auth, George Henry Lewes: Critic of Calderon, Iberoromania, 71; Was Gaspar Lucas Hidalgo the godfather of Tirso de Molina?, Bull Comediantes, 74; Lord Macaulay and Calderon, Romance Notes, 75; Juan del Encina, Twayne World Auth Ser, 76; Tirso de Molina, the Arias Davila family, Bull Comediantes, 76; Tirso de Molina and the Drama of the Counter Reformation, Rodopi, Amsterdam, 76; Towards a new chronology for the dramatic eclogues of Juan del Encina, Studies Bibliog, 77. *Mailing Add:* Dept of Mod Lang Univ of Ottawa Ottawa ON K1N 6N5 Can

SULLIVAN, JOHN P, b Liverpool, England, July 13, 30. FOREIGN LANGUAGES. *Educ:* Cambridge Univ, BA, 53, MA, 57; Ozford Univ, MA, 57. *Prof Exp:* Teacher classics, Clare & Magdalene Cols, Cambridge Univ, 52-53; teacher philos & classics, Hertford & Lincoln Cols, Oxford Univ & Queens' Col, Cambridge Univ, 53-55; fel & tutor classics, Lincoln Col, Oxford Univ, 55-62, dean, 60-61; vis prof class lang, Univ Tex, Austin, 61-62, assoc prof, 62-63, prof class lang, 63-69, actg chmn dept classics, 62-63, chmn dept, 63-65, Univ Res Inst grants, 61, 62, Bromberg award, 62; provost, State Univ NY, Buffalo, 72-75, fac prof arts & lett, 69-78; PROF CLASSICS, UNIV CALIF, SANTA BARBARA, 78- *Concurrent Pos:* Lectr, Oxford Univ, 56-60; co-ed, Arion, 61-69; Am Coun Learned Soc grant, 63; Nat Endowment Humanities sr fel, 67-68; ed, Arethusa, 71-; vis fel classics, Clare Hall, Cambridge Univ, 75-76; Martin lectr Neronian lit, Oberlin Col, 76; vis prof classics, Univ Hawaii, Manoa, 77; Gray lectr Martial, Cambridge Univ, 78; vis fel, Wolfson Col, Oxford Univ, 81; vis Hill prof, Univ Minn, 82. *Mem:* Am Philol Asn; Hellenic Soc. *Res:* Latin literature; comparative literature. *Publ:* Coauth, Critical Essays in Roman Literature (2 vols), Routledge & Kegan Paul, 62 & 63; auth, The Satyricon of Petronius: A Literary Study, Faber, 68; ed,Ezra Pound: A Critical Anthology, Penguin, 72; Politics and literature in the Augustan Age, 72, Women in classical antiquity, 72 & Psychoanalysis and the classics, 74, Arethusa; auth, Propertius: A Critical Introduction, Cambridge Univ, 76; auth, & translr, Petronius: The Satyricon & Seneca: The Apocolocyntosis, Penguin, rev ed, 77. *Mailing Add:* Classics Dept Univ of Calif Santa Barbara CA 93010

SULLIVAN, SHIRLEY DARCUS, b Vancouver, BC. CLASSICAL LANGUAGES, EARLY GREEK PHILOSOPHY. *Educ:* Univ BC, BA, 66, MA, 68; Univ Toronto, PhD(class), 73. *Prof Exp:* ASSOC PROF CLASS, UNIV BC, 72- *Mem:* Am Philol Asn; Class Asn Can; Soc Ancient Greek Philos; Class Asn Pac NW; Class Asn Can West. *Res:* Presocratic philosophers; Greek lyric poets; Homer. *Publ:* Auth, Daimon parallels the Holy Phren in Empedocles, Phronesis, 77; Noos precedes Phren in Greek lyric poetry, L'Antiquite Classique, 77; Thumos and Psyche in Heraclitus B 85, Rivista di Studi Classici, 77; The Phren of the Noos in Xenophane's God, Symbolae Osloenses, 78; What death brings in Heraclitus, Gymnasium, 78; A Person's Relation to Psyche in Homer, Hesiod and the Greek Lyric Poets, 79 & How a Person Relates to Noos in Homer, Hesiod and the Greek Lyric Poets, 80, Glotta; A Strand of Thought in Pindar, Olympians 7, TAPA, 82. *Mailing Add:* Dept of Class Univ of BC Vancouver BC V6T 1W5 Can

SULLIVAN, WILLIAM JOSEPH, b Hartford, Conn. SLAVIC LANGUAGES, LINGUISTICS. *Educ:* Yale Univ, AB, 63, MPhil, 68, PhD(Slavic ling), 69. *Prof Exp:* Instr Slavic lang, Yale Univ, 69-70, res assoc ling automation proj, 69-70; asst prof Slavic & ling, 70-75, ASSOC PROF SLAVIC & LING UNIV FLA, 75- *Concurrent Pos:* Bk rev ed, Forum Linguisticum, 76- *Mem:* Southeastern Conf Ling; Ling Asn Can & US; Ling Soc Am; Am Asn Teachers Slavic & EEurop Lang. *Res:* Slavic languages; stratificational theory; logic and language. *Publ:* Auth, The archiphoneme in stratificational phonology, Proc XI Int Cong Ling, 74; Alternation, transformation, realization, and stratification revisited, First Ling Asn Can & US Forum, 75; Abstractness, the syllable, and the fleeting vowel in Russian, Second Ling Asn Can & US Forum, 76; Toward a logical definition of linguistic theory, Third Ling Asn Can & US Forum, 77; Active and passive sentences in English and Polish, Studies Contrastive Ling, 77; The archiphonemes of Russian: A stratificational view, In: Linguistics at the Crossroads, Jupiter, 77; A stratificational view of the lexicon, Lang Sci, 77; Raising: A stratificational description and some methatheoretical considerations, Proc Second Mich State Univ Ling Metatheory Conf, 78. *Mailing Add:* Dept of Ger & Slavic Lang Univ of Fla Gainesville FL 32611

SULLIVANT, RAYMOND L, b Topeka, Kans, June 1, 25. FRENCH, SPANISH. *Educ:* Sorbonne, dipl French, 52; Washington Univ, St Louis, PhD(French), 59. *Prof Exp:* Instr French & Span, Purdue Univ, 52-53; from instr to assoc prof, St Louis Univ, 53-59; research, France & Spain, 63-69; assoc prof, 70-76, PROF SPAN, ST LOUIS UNIV IN SPAIN, 76-, DIR SPAN, 68- . *Mem:* Am Asn Teachers Span & Port; Regional Conf Am Progs Spain. *Publ:* Auth, Antecendents for Balzac's character Sir Arthur Ormond, Lord Grenville, Ky Foreign Lang Quart, 63; Dating Balzac's Rendez-Vous, Manuscripta, 64; Aspectos de la Novelistica de Camilo Jose Cela, Resenas, autumn, 64; In Gerona with Gironella, St Louis Rev, 65; transl, The Church's Holiness and Religious Life, Waverly, 66; auth, Garcia Lorca: The ghost of a genius won't let Spain rest, St Louis Post-Dispatch, 8/67. *Mailing Add:* St Louis Univ in Madrid Calle de la Vina 3 Madrid 3 Spain

SUMBERG, LEWIS ARTHUR MATTHEW, b Schenectady, NY, Jan 29, 24; m 56; c 2. FRENCH LITERATURE, MEDIEVAL HISTORY. *Educ:* State Univ NY Albany, BA, 48; Univ Paris, DUniv, 54. *Prof Exp:* Instr French, Yale Univ, 54-56; asst prof, Boston Col, 56-65; prof foreign lang & chmn dept, Lake Forest Col, 65-67; prof French, State Univ NY Col Oswego, 67-69; prof & chmn dept, Univ Ky, 69-72; UNIV PROF HUMANITIES, UNIV TENN, CHATTANOOGA, 72- *Concurrent Pos:* Fac res fels, Boston Col, 63 & State Univ NY, 68 & 69; consult, Tenn Comt Humanities, Nat Endowment for Humanities, 73-76; co-dir, Off Educ Planning, Univ Tenn, Chattanooga, 74-76; ed, Tristania, Univ Tenn Press, 75- *Mem:* MLA; Soc Rencesvals; Mediaeval Acad Am; Int Arthurian Soc; Acad Polit Sci. *Res:* Symbolism; medieval history; esoteric political systems. *Publ:* Auth, The Tafurs and the first crusade, Medieval Studies, 59; coauth, Les Grands Ecrivains Francais, Holt, 65; auth, The Folie Tristan in the romance lyric, Ky Romance Quart, 67; La chanson d'Antioche, Picard, Paris, 68; Art et artifices dans le Testament de Villon, In: Melanges Pierre Le Gentil, Paris, 73; transl, The Occult and the Third Reich, Macmillan, 74; ed, Tristania Monogr, Church Publ, 78. *Mailing Add:* Div of Humanities Univ of Tenn Chattanooga TN 37403

SUMMERFIELD, ELLEN BETH, b Hyattsville, Md, Dec 28, 49. GERMAN LITERATURE & LANGUAGE. *Educ:* Univ Pa, BA, 70; Univ Conn, MA, 73, PhD(Ger), 75. *Prof Exp:* Asst prof Ger, Middlebury Col, 75-80; ASST DIR FOREIGN STUDY & ASST PROF GER, KALAMAZOO COL, 81-, DIR, SCH IN MAINZ, 77- *Mem:* MLA; Am Asn Teachers Ger. *Res:* Twentieth century German literature; the German novel. *Publ:* Auth, Ingeborg Bachmann: Die Auflösung der Figur in ihrem Roman Malina, Bouvier, 76; Inborg Bachmanns Sprachverständnis, Neophilologus, 1/78; Die Kamera als literarisches Mittel: Zu Peter Handkes Die Angst des Tormanns beim Elfmeter, Mod Austrian Lit, Vol 12, No 1, 79; Verzicht auf den Mann: Zu Ingeborg Bachmanns Erzählungen Simultan, In: Die Frau als Heldin und Autorin, Francke Verlag, Bern, 79. *Mailing Add:* Office of Foreign Study Kalamazoo Col Kalamazoo MI 49007

SUMNER, GRAHAM VINCENT, b Manchester, UK, Sept 28, 24; Can citizen; m 54. CLASSICS, HISTORY. *Educ:* Oxford Univ, BA, 49, MA, 49. *Prof Exp:* Asst keeper manuscripts, Brit Mus, 49-50; lectr classics, Rhodes Univ SAfrica, 50-53; master, Sedbergh Sch & Cardiff High Sch, UK, 54-56; lectr, Univ Newcastle, NSW, 56-58; sr lectr classics & ancient hist, Univ Canterbury, 58-63; assoc prof, 64-66, chmn, Dept Classics, 68-73, PROF CLASSICS & ANCIENT HIST, UNIV TORONTO, 66-, ASSOC CHMN GRAD STUDIES, DEPT CLASSICS, 77- *Mem:* Am Philol Asn; Class Asn Can; Soc Prom Hellenic Studies; Soc Prom Roman Studies; Asn Ancient Historians. *Res:* Roman history and historiography; ancient and medieval Spanish history and historiography. *Publ:* Auth, Notes on chronological problems in the Aristotelian Athenaion Politeia, Class Quart, 61; Curtius Rufus and the historiae Alexandri, AUMLA (Australia), 61; The chronology of the outbreak of the Second Punic War, Proc African Class Asn, 66; The legion and the centuriate organization, J Roman Studies, 70; The truth about Velleins Paterculus: Prolegomena, Harvard Studies Class Philol, 70; The orators in Cicero's Brutus: Proseopography and Chronology, Univ Toronto, 73; Philippicus, Anastasius II and Theodosius III, Greek, roman & Byzantine Studies, 76; Notes on Provinciae in Spain (197-133 BC), Class Philol, 77. *Mailing Add:* Dept of Classics Univ of Toronto Toronto ON M5S 1A1 Can

SUMNER, LAURA VOELKEL, b Brooklyn, NY, Sept 5, 21; m 53; c 1. CLASSICAL ARCHEOLOGY. *Educ:* Vassar Col, AB, 42; Johns Hopkins Univ, AM, 43, PhD, 45. *Prof Exp:* From asst prof to assoc prof Latin & hist or aft, Wesleyan Col, 45-58; asst prof Greek & Latin, 48-56, assoc prof classics, 56-63, PROF CLASSICS, MARY WASHINGTON COL, 63- *Concurrent Pos:* Vis asst prof, Univ Wis, 54. *Mem:* Archaeol Inst Am; Am Philol soc; Am Numis Soc; fel Royal Numis Soc. *Res:* Roman coins, theater and religion. *Publ:* Auth, Sonnets, Holly Hill, 62; co-ed, Mostellaria, Univ Mich, 2nd ed, 63; Latin Coloring Book, 63 & Bennett Ballads, 73 Fredericksburh. *Mailing Add:* Box 1275 Col Sta Mary Washington Col Fredericksburg VA 22401

SUNER, MARGARITA, b Buenos Aires, Argentina; US citizen. SYNTAX, HISPANIC LINGUISTICS. *Educ:* Univ del Salvador, EFL, 65; Univ Kans, MA, 68; Ind Univ, MA, 70, PhD(Span ling), 73. *Prof Exp:* Asst prof, 73-79, ASSOC PROF LING & HISP LING, CORNELL UNIV, 79- *Mem:* Ling Soc Am; Am Asn Teachers Span & Port; Asn Linguistica y Filologia de America Latina. *Res:* Spanish syntax; properties of gaps; relative clauses. *Publ:* Auth, Spanish adverbs: Support for the phonological cycle?, Linguistic Inquiry, 75; Looking down the tree in Spanish, Lingua, 76; Perception verb complements in Spanish: Same or different?, Can J Ling, 78; ed, Contemporary Studies in Romance Linguistics, Georgetown Univ Press, 78; coauth, Para a Frente: An intermediate course in Portuguese, Cabrilho Press, 81; Syntax and Semantics of Spanish Presentational Sentence-Types, Georgetown Univ Press, 82; On null subjects, Ling Analysis, 82; contribr, Spanish haber and English There-be: Their co-occurrence with definite modification, Readings in Span-English Contrastive Ling, III, 82. *Mailing Add:* Mod Lang & Ling Morrill Hall Cornell Univ Ithaca NY 14853

SUNG, MARGARET MIAN YAN, b Amoy, China, Sept 11, 38; US citizen; m 64; c 1. CHINESE & ANTHROPOLOGICAL LINGUISTICS. *Educ:* Nat Taiwan Univ, BA, 62; Cornell Univ, MA, 69; Stanford Univ, PhD(ling), 74. *Prof Exp:* Asst prof Chinese I & II, Univ San Francisco, 73-74; lectr Mandarin & Cantonese, Calif State Univ, Hayward, 73-75; asst prof, 75-81, ASSOC PROF, CHINESE LANG & LING, IND UNIV, BLOOMINGTON, 81- *Mem:* Ling Soc Am; Asn for Asian Studies; Chinese Lang Teachers Asn; Chinese Lang Comput Soc. *Res:* Chinese historical linguistics; Chinese dialectology; Chinese anthropological linguistics. *Publ:* Auth, Language of the Kanakanavu and La?alua: A preliminary comparison, Vol XXXV, 135-154 & Phonetic and phonemic system of the Kanakanavu language Formosa, Vol XXXVI, 783-800, Bull Inst Hist & Philos Acad Sinica; A study of literary and colloquial Amoy Chinese, 9/73 & Chinese language and culture: A study of homonyms, lucky words and taboos, 1/79, J Chinese Ling; Morphology of the Kanakanavu language Formosa, Bibliog Quart, 9/80; Chinese personal naming, J Chinese Lang Teachers Asn, 5/81. *Mailing Add:* Dept of East Asian Lang & Cult Ind Univ Bloomington IN 47405

SUNGOLOWSKY, JOSEPH, b Charleroi, Belg, Dec 21, 31; US citizen; m 67; c 2. FRENCH LITERATURE. *Educ:* Yeshiva Univ, BA, 55; NY Univ, MA, 58; Yale Univ, PhD, 63. *Prof Exp:* Asst instr French, Yale Univ, 57-59, instr, 59-62; from instr to asst prof, Vassar Col, 62-65; asst prof, 65-72, ASSOC PROF FRENCH LIT, QUEENS COL, NY, 72- *Mem:* MLA; Am Asn Teachers Fr; Soc Professors Fr Am. *Res:* Beaumarchais; contemporary French Jewish literature; 18th and 19th centuries in France. *Publ:* Auth, Alfred de Vigny et le dix-huitieme siecle, Nizet, Paris, 68; Vue sur Germinal apres une lecture de La peste, Cahiers Naturalistes, 70; Du cote de Beaumarchais, Les Nouveaux Cahiers, 71: Beaumarchais, Twayne, 74. *Mailing Add:* Dept of Romance Lang Queens Col Flushing NY 11367

SURLES, ROBERT LEO, b Los Angeles, Calif, May 12, 39. MEDIEVAL LITERATURE, SPANISH LINGUISTICS. *Educ:* San Diego State Univ, BA, 67, MA, 68; Univ Southern Calif, PhD(Span), 74. *Prof Exp:* Instr Span & Ger, Int Lang Acad, 67-68 & Los Angeles City Schs, 70-72; ASSOC PROF SPAN, UNIV IDAHO, 72- *Concurrent Pos:* Instr Span & Ger, Chadwick High Sch, 71-72; vis prof Chicano lit, San Diego City Col, 74 & Univ San Diego, 79-80. *Mem:* Medieval Asn Pac; Am Asn Teachers Span & Port; Soc Rencesvals; Philol Asn Pac Coast; MLA. *Res:* Medieval Romance lit as influenced by Germanic Sage; early Spanish humanism; lyric poetry of courtly love. *Publ:* Auth, El ciclo de Gaiferos: Herencia de la epica germanica, Publ Pac Northwest Coun Foreign Lang, 74; Herido esta don Tristan: Distance, point of view and piggy-back poetics, Tristania, 82; Genesis and progeny: The course of a legend, Hispanofila (in prep); A homocentristic view of superbia in the Spanish Celestina, Fifteenth Century Studies (in prep); Germanic Epic/Spanish Legend: Roots and Branches, Univ Press Am (in prep). *Mailing Add:* Foreign Lang Dept Univ of Idaho Moscow ID 83843

SUSSKIND, NATHAN, b Stropkov, Czech, Sept 10, 06; m 33; c 2. GERMAN. *Educ:* City Col New York, AB, 29, MS, 30; NY Univ, PhD, 42. *Prof Exp:* Tutor Ger, 32-35, from instr to assoc prof, 35-70, prof, 71-72, sub-chmn dept, 41-45, 46-61, dir Inst Yiddish Lexicology, 64-72, EMER PROF GER, CITY COL NEW YORK, 73- *Concurrent Pos:* Chmn educ, E Concourse Hebrew Ctr, 32-42; prin, Mt Eden Ctr Hebrew Sch, 36-37; consult, Great Yiddish Dict, 51-, co-ed, 70-; guest prof Yiddish, Yeshiva Univ, 55-62; mem, Acad Coun Jewish Teachers Sem, 61-, lectr grad div, 62-; mem, Yivo Inst Jewish Res. *Mem:* Ling Soc Am; Am Asn Teachers Ger; Col Yiddish Asn(treas, 61-); World Cong Jewish Studies. *Res:* Germanic, Indo-Germanic and Semitic philology; Yiddish; Jews and the New Testament. *Publ:* Auth, Judah A Joffe's work, Goldene Keyt, 68; Yiddish in Israel, Hadoar, 69; Introduction to Old and Midldle Yiddish, Yiddishe Shprakh, 69, 70; Reply to many questions (about Yiddish), Bnai-Yiddish, 70; Tov Sheba-Goyim, Cent Conf Am Rabbis J, spring 76; coauth, The Language of Herz's Esther, a Study in Judeo-German Dialectology, Univ of Ala, 76; plus articles in Bitzaron, Bnai-Yiddish, Ger Quart, Zukunft, Unzer Tzait, Am Zionist, Yivo-Bleter. *Mailing Add:* 82-15 Britton Ave Elmhurst NY 11373

SUSSKIND, NORMAN, b New York, NY, July 24, 29; m 52; c 3. FRENCH. *Educ:* Adelphi Col, BA, 51; Yale Univ, PhD, 57. *Prof Exp:* Instr French, Ohio State Univ, 57-60; chmn dept mod lang & lit, 72-76, PROF FRENCH, OAKLAND UNIV, 60- *Mem:* MLA. *Res:* Old French language and literature. *Publ:* Auth, Guerri's leg of venison, Romance Notes, 59; Humor in the Chanson de Geste, Symposium, 61; Love and laughter in the Romans Courtois, Fr Rev, 5/64. *Mailing Add:* Dept of Mod Lang & Lit Oakland Univ Rochester RI 48063

SUSSMAN, LEWIS ARTHUR, b New York, NY, June 26, 41; m 65. CLASSICS. *Educ:* Princeton Univ, AB, 64; Univ NC, Chapel Hill, PhD(classics), 69. *Prof Exp:* Asst prof classics, Univ Calif, Irvine, 69-76, chmn dept, 72-75; ASSOC PROF CLASSICS, UNIV FLA, 76- *Concurrent Pos:* Univ Fla Humanities Coun grant, 77; Nat Endowment for Humanities summer sem, Rome, 79. *Mem:* Am Philol Asn; Class Asn Mid West & South (secy-treas, 77-78). *Res:* Ancient rhetoric; Ovid; Roman literature of the Augustan Age. *Publ:* Auth, Early imperial declamation: A translation of the elder Seneca's prefaces, Speech Monogr, 6/70; The artistic unity of the elder Seneca's first preface & Controversiae as a whole, Am J Philol, 4/71; The elder Seneca's discussion of the decline of Roman eloquence, Calif Studies Class Antiq, 72; The Elder Seneca, E J Brill, 78; Latin and Basic skills, Class J, 78; Arellius Fuscus and the unity of Seneca's Suasorial, Rheinisches Mus, 78. *Mailing Add:* Dept of Classics Univ of Fla Gainesville FL 32611

SUTHER, JUDITH D, b Lawton, Okla, Feb 18, 40. FRENCH & COMPARATIVE LITERATURE. *Educ:* Univ Mo-Columbia, BA, 60, PhD(French), 67; Univ Mich, MA, 61; Univ Grenoble, CAPES, 62. *Prof Exp:* Instr French, Randolph-Macon Woman's Col, 62-64; asst prof French & hon humanities, Univ Mo-Columbia, 67-68; from asst prof to prof French, Tex Christian Univ, 68-78, chmn mod lang, 72-74; prof French & chmn dept foreign lang, 78-82, PROF FRENCH, UNIV NC, CHARLOTTE, 82- *Concurrent Pos:* Elizabeth Stanton Michaels Fel, Am Asn Univ Women, 75;

co-ed, Fr-Am Rev, 76-; Am Philos Soc Res grant, 78; French Cult Serv grants, 79 & 81. *Mem:* Am Asn Teachers Fr; MLA; Am Lit Translators Asn; Inst Jacques Maritain. *Res:* French literature, 20th century; French-American comparative literature; translation theory and practice. *Publ:* Co-tbordel,ansl, Three Plays of Andre Obey: One for the Wind, Noah, and the Phoenix, Tex Christian Univ, 72; auth, Marquerite de Navarre's quiet victory over misogyny, Explorations Renaissance Cult, winter 75; Ionesco's symbiotic pair: Le Solitaire and Ce formidable bordell, Fr Rev, 4/76; Raissa Maritain in America, Res Studies, 6/77; co-transl, Three More Plays of Andre Obey: The Reunion, Moses and the Mountain, and The Window, Tex Christian Univ, 77; auth, Thomas Merton's French background, Fr-Am Rev, spring 78; Dante's use of the Gorgon Medusa in Inferno IX, Ky Romance Quart, winter 80; ed, Essays on Camus's Exile and the Kingdom, Romance Monographs, 80. *Mailing Add:* Dept of Foreign Lang Univ of NC Charlotte NC 28223

SUTHERLAND, ROBERT DONALD, b Blytheville, Ark, Nov 4, 37; m 59; c 2. LINGUISTICS, ENGLISH LANGUAGE. *Educ:* Univ Wichita, BA, 59; State Univ Iowa, MA, 61, PhD(English), 64. *Prof Exp:* From asst prof to assoc prof, 64-73, PROF ENGLISH, ILL STATE UNIV, 73- *Concurrent Pos:* Lectr NDEA Inst Teachers Cult Disadvantaged, Ill State Univ, 64. *Honors & Awards:* Juvenile Bk Merit Award, Friends Am Writers, 81. *Mem:* Ling S c Am. *Res:* The nature of metaphor; general linguistics; semantic theory. *Puvl:* Auth, Education through freedom, In: Readings for Rhetoric, Wadsworth, 69; Language and Lewis Carroll, Mouton, The Hague, 70; Letting students be: Report on a continuing experiment in education, Col English, 4/71; auth & illusr, Sticklewort and Feverfew (novel), Pikestaff Press, 80. *Mailing Add:* Dept of English Ill State Univ Normal IL 61761

SUTHERLAND, RONALD, English, Comparative Literature. See Vol II

SUTTON, DANA FERRIN, b White Plains, NY, Oct 10, 42; m 75. CLASSICAL SCHOLARSHIP. *Educ:* New Sch Soc Res, BA, 65; Univ Wis, MA, 66, PhD(Greek, Latin), 70. *Prof Exp:* Lectr classics, Lehmann Col, 69-72; sr mem, Darwin Col, Cambridge Univ, 72-73; res fel classics, Univ Auckland, 74-75; asst prof, Univ Ill, Urbana, 75-79; ASSOC PROF CLASSICS, UNIV CALIF, IRVINE, 79- *Concurrent Pos:* Guggenheim fel, 75-76. *Mem:* Am Philol Asn; Class Asn Atlantic & Midwestern States. *Res:* Classical literature, especially drama. *Publ:* Auth, A handlist of satyr plays, Harvard Studies Class Philol, 74; The date of Euripides' Cyclops, Univ Microfilm Monogr Ser, 74; Sophocles' Inachus, 79 & The Greek satyr play, 80, Beiträge Klass Philol; Self and Society in Aristophanes, Univ Press Am, 80; A concordance to the Greek satyr play, Am Philol Asn, 81; A Concordance to the Anonymous Constitution of Athens, Bolchazy-Carducci, 81; contribr, The satyr play, Cambridge Hist Ancient Lit (in press). *Mailing Add:* Dept of Classics Univ of Calif Irvine CA 92717

SUTTON, LEWIS F, b Goldsboro, NC, Jan 25, 36; m 61; c 2. FRENCH. *Educ:* Univ NC, Chapel Hill, AB, 58, MA, 62, PhD(Romance lang), 66. *Prof Exp:* From instr to asst prof French, Univ Va, 64-69; assoc prof, 69-70, head dept mod lang, 69-81, PROF FRENCH, WESTERN CAROLINA UNIV, 70- *Mem:* Am Asn Teachers Fr; SAtlantic Mod Lang Asn. *Res:* French 19th century theatre. *Mailing Add:* Dept of Mod Foreign Lang Western Carolina Univ Cullowhee NC 28723

SUTTON, LOIS MARIE, b Ft Worth, Tex, July 5, 25. FOREIGN LANGUAGES. *Educ:* Univ Tex, BA, 45, PhD, 56; Baylor Univ, MA, 46. *Prof Exp:* Instr French & Span, 45-49, from asst prof to assoc prof French, 49-58, PROF FRENCH, BAYLOR UNIV, 58-, CHMN DEPT MOD FOREIGN LANG, 76- *Concurrent Pos:* Fulbright lectr, Univ Ceara, 63. *Mem:* SCent Mod Lang Asn; Am Asn Teachers Fr; AAUP; Am Coun Teachers Foreign Lang; Nat Asn Lang Lab Dirs. *Res:* Romance philology; French and Spanish language and literature. *Mailing Add:* Dept of Mod Foreign Lang Baylor Univ Waco TX 76703

SVEJKOVSKY, FRANTISEK, b Suchdol n Luznici, Czech, Nov 3, 23; m 51; c 1. CZECH & SLOVAK LITERATURE. *Educ:* Charles Univ, Prague, MD(Czech philol), 48, PhD(Slavic lit, aesthet), 49, MD(libr sci), 50. *Prof Exp:* Res Czech lit, Acad Sci, Prague, 50-57; from assoc prof to prof Old Czech lit, Charles Univ, Prague, 57-70; PROF CZECH & SLOVAK LIT, UNIV CHICAGO, 71- *Mem:* AAUP; Mediaeval Acad Am. *Res:* Slavic literatures; comparative literatures; history of the theatre. *Publ:* Auth, History of the Humanistic Literature in Bohemia Moravia, 59 & Czech Poetry of the Hussite Period, 63, Czech Acad Sci, Prague; History of Old Czech Drama: Latin and Latin-Czech Plays about Three Maries, Charles Univ, Prague, 66; History of the Theatre in Bohemia: From Beginnings to the 16th Century, Czech Acad Sci, Prague, 68; plus over 50 papers published in Europe and the US. *Mailing Add:* Dept of Slavic Lang & Lit Univ of Chicago Chicago IL 60637

SVENDSEN, JAMES THOMAS, b St Paul, Minn, Apr 30, 42; m 67; c 1. CLASSICS, DRAMA. *Educ:* St Paul Sem, Minn, AB, 64; Univ Minn, Minneapolis, MA, 66, PhD(classics), 71. *Prof Exp:* ASSOC PROF CLASSICS, UNIV UTAH, 69- *Mem:* Am Philol Asn; Philol Asn Pac Coast; Rocky Mountain Mod Lang Asn. *Res:* Greek and Roman comedy; ancient novel; Greek and Roman tragedy. *Publ:* Auth, Apuleius' The Golden Ass: The demands on the reader, Pac Coast Philol, Vol 13. *Mailing Add:* Dept of Lang Univ of Utah Salt Lake City UT 84112

SVOBODA, GEORGE JIRI, Central European History, Slavic Languages. See Vol I

SWAFFAR, JANET KING, b Minneapolis, Minn, Apr 28, 35; m 64; c 2. GERMAN LITERATURE, FOREIGN LANGUAGE PEDAGOGY. *Educ:* Mankato State Teachers Col, BA, 56; Univ Wis, MA, 59, PhD(Ger), 65. *Prof Exp:* From instr to asst prof, 65-71, assoc prof, 71-82, PROF GER, UNIV TEX, AUSTIN, 82- *Concurrent Pos:* Dir, Nat Endowment for Humanities Prog grant, Univ Tex, 77-80. *Honors & Awards:* Paul Pimsleur Award, Am Coun Teaching Foreign Lang, 80. *Mem:* MLA; Am Asn Teachers Ger; Am Coun Teaching Foreign Lang. *Res:* Modern Germany (east-west), foreign language acquistion, reading history. *Publ:* Coauth, Imitation and correction in foreign language learning, Mod Lang J, 12/71 & Educ Digest, 72; Literarische Zeitschriften 1945-70, Sammlung, Stuttgart, 74; Lenz viewed sane, Ger Rev, 74; The Ethics of Exploitation: Brecht's Der gute Mensch von Sezuan, University of Dayton Review, spring 79; (with Don Stephens), What comprehension-based classes look and feel like in theory and in practice, Newbury House, 81; Foreign Languages in the University: The Case for a Content Orientation for the Discipline, Monatshefte, Vol 73, 271-288; Reading in the Foreign Language Classroom: Focus on Process, Unterrichtaspraxis, Vol 14, 176-194; (with Arens & Morgan), Teacher classroom practices: Redefining method as task hierarchy, Mod Lang J, Vol 66, 24-33. *Mailing Add:* Dept of Ger Lang Univ of Tex Austin TX 78712

SWAIN, JAMES OBED, b Greenfield, Ind, Dec 31, 96; m 23; c 2. SPANISH LITERATURE. *Educ:* Ind Univ, AB, 21, AM, 23; Univ Ill, PhD, 32. *Prof Exp:* Instr Romance lang, Mich State Col, 31-33, asst prof, 34-37; prof, Univ Tenn, 37-64; RES & WRITING, 65- *Concurrent Pos:* Assoc ed, Hispania, 36-42; mem cult mission to France, 46; Pan-Am Airways travel grant, Chile, 51-52. *Mem:* MLA; Am Asn Teachers Span & Port; Am Asn Teachers Fr; Am Asn Teachers Ital; SAtlantic Mod Lang Asn (pres, 47). *Res:* Jose Santos Gonzalez Vera, Chilean socialistic novelist, his life and writings; Latin-American novel; Costa Rican mystics and literature. *Publ:* Coauth, Latin American creative writers & Spain's contribution to world literature, In: Compton's Pictured Encyclopedia, Encycl Britannica Educ Corp; Funcion y Alcance de la Escuela de Temporada, Univ Chile, 53; auth, Vicente Blasco Ibanez--exponent of realism: general study with emphasis on realistic techniques, 59; coauth, Life and Works of Juan Marin, Juan Marin-Chilean, the Man and His Writings, Pathway, 71; Typical Chilean novels of social impact, Ann Southeastern Conf Latin Am Studies, 73. *Mailing Add:* 414 Forest Park Blvd Knoxville TN 37919

SWAIN, VIRGINIA EDITH, b Waterville, Maine. FRENCH LITERATURE. *Educ:* Middlebury Col, BA, 64, MA, 65; Yale Univ, PhD(French), 79. *Prof Exp:* ASST PROF FRENCH, DARTMOUTH COL, 78- *Mem:* MLA; Am Soc 18th Century Studies; Northeast Modern Lang Asn. *Res:* Eighteenth and 19th century French and comparative literature; Diderot, Rousseau and Baudelaire. *Publ:* Auth, Diderot's Paradoxe sur le Comedien: The Paradox of Reading, Studies in Voltaire, England, fall 82. *Mailing Add:* Dept of Fr & Italian Dartmouth Col Hanover NH 03755

SWANSON, ROY ARTHUR, b St Paul, Minn, Apr 7, 25; m 46; c 4. CLASSICS, COMPARATIVE LITERATURE. *Educ:* Univ Minn, BA, 48, BS, 49, MA, 51; Univ Ill, PhD, 54. *Prof Exp:* Instr educ, Univ Ill, 52-53; instr classics, Ind Univ, 54-57; from asst prof to prof classics & humanities, Univ Minn, 57-65, chmn dept comp lit, 64-65; prof English, Macalester Col, 65-67, coordr humanities, 66-67; chmn dept classics, 67-70, grad sch res grant, 68-69, 74 & 81, chmn dept comp lit, 69-73, PROF CLASSICS & COMP LIT, UNIV WIS-MILWAUKEE, 67-, CHMN DEPT COMP LIT, 76- *Concurrent Pos:* Fulbright scholar, Rome, 53; fel, Univ ill, 54; ed, Minn Rev, 64-67; Lilly Found fel, Stockholm, 65-66; ed, Class J, 68-73. *Honors & Awards:* Distinguished Teacher Award, Univ Minn, 62 & Univ Wis- Milwaukee, 74. *Mem:* Am Philol Asn; MLA; Am Comp Lit Asn; Int Comp Lit Asn. *Res:* Lyric poetry, especially Greek and Roman; mediaeval studies; literary criticism. *Publ:* Auth, Odi et Amo: the complete poetry of Catullus, Lib Arts Press, 59; Heart of reason: Introductory essays in modern-world humanities, Denison, 63; The humor of Don Quixote, Romanic Rev, 10/63; Evil and love in Lagerkvist's crucifixion cycle, Scand Studies, 11/66; Pindar's odes, Bobbs, 74; Love is the function of death: Forster, Lagerkvist, and Zamyatin, Can Rev Comp Lit, 76; Deceptive symmetry: Classical echoes in the poetry of Richard Emil Braun, Mod Poetry Studies, 76; Ionesco's classical absurdity, In: The Two Faces of Ionesco, Whitston, 78. *Mailing Add:* Dept of Classics Univ of Wis Milwaukee WI 53201

SWAYZE, ERNEST HAROLD, b Portland, Ore, Dec 22, 30. SLAVIC LITERATURE, POLITICAL SCIENCE. *Educ:* Reed Col, BA, 52; Harvard Univ, MA, 54, PhD(polit sci), 59. *Prof Exp:* Instr polit sci, Smith Col, 57-58; from instr to asst prof, Univ Mich, 59-62; asst prof Russ lit, 63-71, ASSOC PROF RUSS LIT, UNIV WASH, 71- *Concurrent Pos:* Am Coun Learned Soc study fel, 66-67. *Mem:* Am Asn Advan Slavic Studies; Far Western Slavic Conf. *Publ:* Auth, Political Control of Literature in the USSR, 1946-1959, Harvard Univ, 62. *Mailing Add:* 4548 47th NE Seattle WA 98105

SWEENEY, ROBERT DALE, b Fayetteville, Tenn, Jan 9, 39. CLASSICS. *Educ:* Univ of the South, BA, 59; Harvard Univ, PhD(classics), 65. *Prof Exp:* Instr Greek & Latin lang & lit, Wayne State Univ, 65; from instr to asst prof classics, Dartmouth Col, 65-69; ASSOC PROF CLASSICS, VANDERBILT UNIV, 69- *Concurrent Pos:* Dartmouth Col fac fel, 67-68; Guggenheim fel, 74-75. *Mem:* Am Philol Asn; Mediaeval Acad Am; Class Asn Mid W & S; Vergilian Soc Am. *Res:* Latin textual criticism and palaeography; Latin poetry; Mediaeval Latin. *Publ:* Auth, Sacra in the philosophic works of Cicero, Orpheus, 65; The Catalogus Codicum Classicorum Latinorum: Proposal and progress report, Italia Medioevale e Umanistica, 68; Prolegomena to an Edition of the Scholia to Statius, Supplementary Volume VIII to Mnemosyne, E J Brill, Leiden, 69; Vanishing and unavailable evidence: Latin Manuscripts in the Middle Ages and today, In: Classical Influences on European Culture AD 500-1500, Cambridge Univ, 71. *Mailing Add:* Dept of Class Studies Vanderbilt Univ Nashville TN 37235

SWEET, DENIS MARSHALL, b Pasadena, Calif, Dec 9, 43. GERMAN LITERATURE, GERMAN INTELLECTUAL HISTORY. *Educ:* Stanford Univ, BA, 65, MA, 70, PhD(Ger thought), 78. *Prof Exp:* Instr English, Schuyler Acad, 66-67; teach asst, Hildegard-Wegscheider Gym, 68-69, Ger, Stanford Univ, 71-72; lectr, Volkshochschule Spandau, Berlin, 75-77; ASST PROF GER, UNIV NH, 79- *Honors & Awards:* Transl Award, Int Nationes, 79. *Mem:* Winckelmann-Gesellschaft; Am Soc Aesthetics; NAm Nietzsche Soc; MLA. *Res:* German Enlightenment aesthetics; German Classical literature and thought; literary criticism. *Publ:* Transl, Outsiders: A Study in Life and Letters, Hans Mayer, Aussenseiter, Mass Inst Technol, 82. *Mailing Add:* AMLL-Murkland Hall Univ NH Durham NH 03824

SWEET, PHILIP DALE, b Gloversville, NY, Dec 29, 48; m 74; c 1. GERMAN LITERATURE. *Educ:* Univ Richmond, BA, 70; Univ Mich, MA, 72, PhD(German), 80. *Prof Exp:* Instr German & French, Univ Cent Ark, 79-80, asst prof, 80-81; RES & WRITING, 81- *Mem:* Am Asn Teachers German; South Cent Mod Lang Asn. *Res:* Modern German poetry; man and nature in German literature; German Democratic Republic literature. *Publ:* Transl, Nibelungenklage, Sources for the Study of High Medieval Culture, Univ Mich, 76; A farewell to childhood: Lyrical discourse in Peter Huchel's Von Nacht Übergraut, Germanic Notes, 81; The prophet in Peter Huchel's poetry, Germanic Rev, 82. *Mailing Add:* 5 Woodlawn Conway AR 72032

SWEET, RONALD FRANK GARFIELD, b Bristol, England, Mar 9, 30. ASSYRIOLOGY. *Educ:* Univ Manchester, BA, 54, MA, 57; Univ Chicago, PhD(Assyriol), 58. *Prof Exp:* Lectr, 59-64, asst prof, 64-67, chmn dept, 72-75, ASSOC PROF NEAR EASTERN STUDIES, UNIV TORONTO, 67- *Concurrent Pos:* Assoc dir, Grad Ctr Religious Studies, Univ Toronto, 77-78 & 81- *Mem:* Am Orient Soc; Soc Bibl Lit. *Res:* Babylonian social institutions. *Publ:* Coauth, The Assyrian Dictionary of the Oriental Institute of the University of Chicago, Vols XVII, II & VIII, 62, 65 & 71. *Mailing Add:* Dept of Near Eastern Studies Univ of Toronto Toronto ON M5S 1A1 Can

SWEET, WALDO EARLE, b Hartford, Conn, Apr 26, 12; m 43; c 2. CLASSICAL STUDIES. *Educ:* Amherst Col, AB, 34; Columbia Univ, MA, 35; Princeton Univ, AM & PhD, 43. *Prof Exp:* Teacher, Eaglebrook Sch, Mass, 35-37, Millbrook Sch, NY, 37-40 & Phillips Acad, Mass, 42-43; classics master, William Penn Charter Sch, Pa, 46-53; assoc prof Latin & teaching of Latin, 53-61, PROF LATIN & TEACHING OF LATIN, UNIV MICH, ANN ARBOR, 61- *Concurrent Pos:* Mem vis fac, State Univ Iowa, 51 & Univ Wash, 61. *Honors & Awards:* Ovatio, Class Asn Mid W & S, 75. *Mem:* Am Philol Asn; Am Class League. *Res:* Application of descriptive linguistics to teaching and learning of Latin; programmed learning; Greek and Roman sport and recreation. *Publ:* Auth, Latin: A Structural Approach, 57, Vergil's Aeneid: A Structural Approach, 60 & Clozes and Vocabulary Exercises for Books I & II of the Aeneid, 61, Univ Mich; Artes Latinae (multi-media prog course including Latin: levels one and two), Lectiones Primae, and Lectiones Secundae, Encycl Britannica Educ Corp, 66-71 & Bolchazy-Carducci, 82; The continued development of the structural approach, Didaskalos, 67; The teacher and programmed learning, Class Outlook 71; A Study of Poetical Ambiguity, Classical Bull, 81; A Course on Words, Harcourt Brace Jovanovich, 82. *Mailing Add:* 1905 Pontiac Trail Ann Arbor MI 48105

SWEETSER, FRANKLIN P, b Newton, Mass, May 7, 20; m 55. ROMANCE LANGUAGES. *Educ:* Haverford Col, BA, 42; Univ Pa, MA, 49, PhD(French lang & lit), 56. *Prof Exp:* Asst prof Span, Cedar Crest Col, 55-57; asst prof French, Mills Col, 57-60; assoc prof, C W Post Col, Long Island Univ, 60-67; asst prof, Brooklyn Col, 67-69; assoc prof, 69-76, PROF FRENCH, UNIV ILL, CHICAGO CIRCLE, 76- *Mem:* MLA; Int Arthurian Soc; Mediaeval Acad Am; Am Asn Teachers Fr. *Res:* Medieval French literature. *Publ:* Ed, Blancandin et L'Orgueilleuse d'amour: Nouvelle edition critique, 64, Les cent nouvelles nouvelles, 66 & L'escoufle--roman d'aventure, 74, Textes litteraires francais, Droz, Geneva. *Mailing Add:* Dept of French Univ of Ill at Chicago Circle Chicago IL 60680

SWEETSER, MARIE-ODILE, b Verdun, France, Dec 28, 25; US citizen; m 55; c 1. FRENCH LANGUAGE & LITERATURE. *Educ:* Univ Nancy, Lic es Let, 44, dipl, 45; Bryn Mawr Col, MA, 50; Univ Pa, PhD, 56. *Prof Exp:* Lectr French, McGill Univ, 50-52; asst instr, Univ Pa, 52-56; instr, Cedar Crest Col, 56-57 & Mills Col, 57-60; from instr to asst prof, City Col New York, 60-69; assoc prof, 69-79, PROF FRENCH, UNIV ILL, CHICAGO CIRCLE, 79- *Concurrent Pos:* Chmn, Fourth Conf 17th Century French Lit, Corneille Symp, 72; exec comt MLA div French 17th century lit, 71-78; Nat Endowment for Humanities panelist, 80 & 81; consult, La Bd of Regents, 82. *Mem:* MLA; Am Asn Teachers Fr; Soc Prof Fr Am; Int Asn Fr Studies. *Res:* French literature of the 17th century; theater, novel, literary criticism poetry; classical tradition in French literature. *Publ:* Auth, Corneille et nouvelle critique, Fr Lit Ser, fall 77; La Dramaturgie de Corneille, Droz, Geneva, 77; La Femme abandonnee: Esquisse d'une typologie, PFSCL, 79; Neron et Titus vus par Racine, Fr Lit Series, Vol 8, 81; Madame de Sevigne et Saint-Simon, artistes et aristocrates: Deux proces sous l'ancien regime, Cahiers St-Simon, 81; Domaines de la critique molieresque, Oeuvres et critiques, Vol VI, No 1, 81; De la comedie a la tragedie: Le 'change et la conversion de melite a Polyeucte, Corneille comique, Paris, Seattle, Tuebingen, 82; Adonis, poeme d'amour, Conventions et creation poetiques, L'Esprit createur, Vol 21, No 4, 82. *Mailing Add:* Dept French Univ Ill Chicago IL 60680

SWENSON, BIRGIT EWERTS, b Vestervik, Sweden, Oct 30, 16; m 50. FRENCH LITERATURE. *Educ:* Columbia Univ, MA, 47, PhD, 57. *Prof Exp:* Mem staff, UN, 46-62; from asst prof to assoc prof French, Skidmore Col, 62-77; RETIRED. *Mem:* MLA; Int House Asn. *Res:* French and German literature; creative writing. *Publ:* Auth Charles Du Bos and the riddle of poetic inspiration, Romanic Rev, 12/67; An Anthology of Modern French Poetry--From Baudelaire to Bonnefoy, 73 & The Eagle and the Flower, Poems by Birgit Swenson, 76, Astra Bks. *Mailing Add:* Dept of Mod Lang Skidmore Col Saratoga Springs NY 12866

SWENSON, RODNEY NEWCOMB, b Crookston, Minn, July 31, 30; m 57; c 2. GERMAN. *Educ:* Bemidji State Col, BS, 52; Univ Minn, MA, 56, PhD(Ger), 67. *Prof Exp:* Instr Ger, St Olaf Col, 59-61; instr, Hamline Univ, 61-66, asst prof, 67-68; ASSOC PROF GER, PAC LUTHERAN UNIV, 68- *Concurrent Pos:* Fulbright-Hays res & study grant, 67-68. *Mem:* Am Asn Teachers Ger; AAUP; Am Coun Teaching Foreign Lang. *Res:* Vocabulary frequency studies; teacher training; English as a foreign language. *Mailing Add:* Dept of Mod & Class Lang Pac Lutheran Univ Tacoma WA 98447

SWETMAN, GLENN ROBERT, English, Languages. See Vol II

SWIECICKA-ZIEMIANEK, MARIA A J, b Wilno, Poland; US citizen; m. SLAVIC LANGUAGES & LITERATURES. *Educ:* Univ Pa, PhD(Slavic lit), 71. *Prof Exp:* Asst prof, 71-76, ASSOC PROF RUSS & GER, TEMPLE UNIV, 76- *Concurrent Pos:* Recorded a ser of radio progs on Poles in Philadelphia & the Temple University Philadelphia Stories; lectr var orgn & insts. *Honors & Awards:* Kosciuszko Found Award, 73. *Mem:* Coun Polish Inst Arts & Sci (secy); Polish Am Hist Asn. *Publ:* Auth, The Memoirs of Jan Chryzostom z Goslanic Pasek, The Kescinszko Found, 78; Chapt In: Polish Civilization: Essays and Studies, New York, Univ Press, 79; co-translr, Stanislau Lem's Memoirs of a Space Traveler, Harcourt Brace Jovanovich, New York, 81. *Mailing Add:* Dept of Ger & Slavic Lang Temple Univ Philadelphia PA 19122

SWIETEK, FRANCIS ROY, Medieval History, Latin. See Vol I

SWIFT, LOUIS JOSEPH, b Scranton, Pa, Aug 1, 32; m 64; c 3. CLASSICS. *Educ:* St Mary's Univ, Md, AB, 54; Pontif Gregorian Univ, STB, 56; Johns Hopkins Univ, MAT, 58, PhD(classics), 63. *Prof Exp:* From asst prof to assoc prof classics, State Univ NY Buffalo, 63-70; assoc prof, 70-76, PROF CLASSICS & CHMN DEPT, UNIV KY, 82- *Concurrent Pos:* Am Philos Soc grant-in-aid, 64; State Univ NY Res Found fac fel, 68. *Mem:* Am Philol Asn; Arch Archaeol Inst Am; Class Asn Mid West & South; NAm Patristic Soc; AAUP. *Res:* Latin literature; pastristics; ancient rhetoric. *Publ:* Auth, Augustine on war and killing, Harvard Theol Rev, 66; Constantine to Augustine, In: Aufstieg und Niedergang der Römischen Welt, De Gruyter; coauth, Classical rhetoric in the psychology of Vives, J Hist Behav Sci, 1/74; Basil & Ambrose on the Six Days of Creation, Augustinianum, 81. *Mailing Add:* Dept of Classics 1127 Office Tower Univ of Ky Lexington KY 40506

SWIGGER, RONALD T, Comparative Literature. See Vol II

SWINDELL, KIMI MUSHIAKI, b Okayama, Japan. JAPANESE LANGUAGE. *Educ:* Tsuda Univ, Tokyo, BA, 36; San Francisco State Univ, MA, 54; Stanford Univ, PhD(ling), 68. *Prof Exp:* Asst prof English, Int Christian Univ, Tokyo, 57-63; prof Japanese, San Jose State Univ, 63-75; PROF JAPANESE, SAN JOSE CITY COL, 75- *Res:* Linguistics; American English usage. *Publ:* Auth, Usage in Today's American English, 70 & A Linguistic Approach to Conversational Japanese, Vols I & II, 72 & 73, Kairyudo, Tokyo. *Mailing Add:* 101 N Sixth St San Jose CA 95112

SWITALA, WILLIAM J, b Pittsburgh, Pa, Mar 30, 39; m 66; c 7. CLASSICS, HISTORY. *Educ:* St Vincent's Col, BA, 63; Duguesne Univ, MA, 68; Univ Pittsburgh, PhD(Classics), 77. *Prof Exp:* Teacher hist, Epiphany Elem Sch, 65-66; teacher Latin & social studies, 66-73, SUPVR SOCIAL STUDIES, BETHEL PARK SCH DIST, 73- *Concurrent Pos:* Asst instr classics & humanities, Pa State Univ, 70-; asst instr classics, Univ Pittsburgh, 73-; mem, Class Lang Task Force Pa Dept Educ, 73-74. *Honors & Awards:* Outstanding Sec Sch Educr, Sec Sch Educr Am, 74. *Mem:* Am Class League; Asn Subv & Curric Develop; Nat Coun Social Studies. *Res:* Latin poetry; Greek and Roman history; social studies curriculum development. *Publ:* Auth, Reincarnation Reexamined, Carlton, 72; A program for the classics, Class Outlook, 3/73; An elective program in the social studies, Social Studies J, spring 74; translr, Cheerful old age (Bergk: Poeta Lyrici Graeci), Classical Outlook, 2/74; A portrait of the effects of politcal corruption: Tacitius Histories II: 62-90, Class Bull, fall 78; A practical experience in civic education: the Bethel Park Student Government, fall 78 & A reexamination of an elective program in the social studies, spring 78, Social Studies J. *Mailing Add:* 5306 Greenridge Dr Pittsburgh PA 15236

SWITTEN, MARGARET L, US Citizen; m 50. FRENCH & PROVENCIAL LANGUAGE & LITERATURE. *Educ:* Westminster Choir Col, BMus, 47; Barnard Col, BA, 48; Bryn Mawr Col, MA, 49, PhD(Fr), 52. *Prof Exp:* From asst prof to assoc prof music & French, Hampton Inst, 52-62, prof French, 62-63; from asst prof to assoc prof, chmn dept, 69-76 & 82-83, PROF FRENCH, MT HOLYOKE COL, 63-, CHMN DEPT, 82- *Concurrent Pos:* Lectr, Smith Col, 66 & 68. *Mem:* Am Asn Teachers Fr; Medieval Acad Am; MLA; Mod Humanities Res Am; Int Courtly Lit Asn. *Res:* The poetry and the music of the Old Provencal troubadours; literature and society in 12th century France; medieval music. *Publ:* Auth, Diderot's theory of language as the medium of literature, 44: 185-196, L'Histoire and La Poesie in Diderot's writings on the novel, 47: 259-269 & Metrical and musical structure in the Songs of Peirol, 51: 241-255, Romanic Rev; Text and melody in Peirol's Cansos, Publ Mod Lang Asn, 86: 320-325; Raimon de Miraval's Be m'agrada and the unrhymed refrain in troubadour poetry, Romance Philol, 11: 432-448; The Cantos of Raimon de Miraval: A Study of Poems and Melodies, Med Acad Am (in press). *Mailing Add:* 16 W Sycamore Knolls South Hadley MA 01075

SWITZER, PERRY RICHARD, b Cedar Rapids, Iowa, July 30, 25. FRENCH LITERATURE. *Educ:* Univ Chicago, AB, 47, AM, 48; Univ Calif, Berkeley, PhD, 55. *Prof Exp:* From instr to asst prof French, Northwestern Univ, 55-62; assoc prof, Univ Wis-Madison, 62-66, prof French & Ital & chmn dept, 66-70; dean humanities, 70-79, PROF FRENCH, CALIF STATE COL, SAN BERNARDINO, 70- *Mem:* Am Asn Teachers Fr; MLA; Soc Chateaubriand. *Res:* French literature of the 17th, 18th and 19th centuries. *Publ:* Auth, Chateaubriand: Voyage en Amerique, Edition Critique, Soc Textes Fr Mod, 63; America in the encyclopedie, Studies Voltaire, 67; Chateaubriand's sources, Rev Lit Comp, 68; Chateaubriand and the foreign office, Fr Rev, 68; transl & ed, Chateaubriand: Travels in America, Univ Ky, 69; ed, Chateaubriand Today, Univ Wis, 70; Pensee et litterature francaises, McGraw, 71; auth, Chateaubriand, 71, coauth, Eugene Scribe, 81, Twayne. *Mailing Add:* Sch of Humanities Calif State Col San Bernardino CA 92407

SYBEN, ISOLDE, b Austria; US citizen. FOREIGN LANGUAGES. *Educ:* Ger Univ, Prague, PhD(philol), 39. *Prof Exp:* Assoc prof Ger, St Cloud State Col, Univ SAla & Chapman Col, 62-68; assoc prof, 68-78, prof, 78-80, EMER PROF GER, KUTZTOWN STATE COL, 81- *Res:* Modern German literature. *Mailing Add:* 2248 Hamilton St Allentown PA 18104

SYMINGTON, RODNEY TERENCE, b Southport, England, May 3, 41; Can citizen. GERMAN & COMPARATIVE LITERATURE. *Educ:* Leeds Univ, BA, 63, DiplEd, 64; McGill Univ, PhD(Ger), 68. *Prof Exp:* From instr to asst prof, 67-70, ASSOC PROF GER, UNIV VICTORIA, BC, 70- *Mem:* Can Asn Univ Teachers Ger (secy-treas, 71-73). *Res:* Brecht; modern drama. *Publ:* Coauth, When the War Was Over and Other Modern German Short Stories (transl), 67 & German Humanist Reader (transl), 69, H Erdmann, Tübingen; auth, Brecht und Shakespeare, Bouvier, Bonn, 70. *Mailing Add:* Dept of Ger Univ of Victoria Victoria BC V8W 2Y2 Can

SYNDERGAARD, LARRY EDWARD, English Literature, Scandinavian Studies. See Vol II

SZANTO, GEORGE HERBERT, Comparative Literature, Sociology of Literature. See Vol II

SZEMLER, GEORGE JOHN, History, Classics. See Vol I

SZKLARCZYK, LILLIAN, b New York, NY, Dec 28, 30; m 54. ROMANCE LANGUAGES. *Educ:* Hunter Col, BA, 51; Middlebury Col, MA, 52; Inst de Phonetique, Univ Paris, dipl, 52; Univ Pa, PhD(Romance lang), 61. *Prof Exp:* From asst prof to assoc prof, 59-76, PROF FRENCH, MONTCLAIR STATE COL, 76-, DIR LANG LAB, 67- *Mem:* MLA; Am Asn Teachers Fr; Fr Inst-Alliance Francaise; Popular Cult Asn. *Res:* French phonetics and phonology; contemporary French poetry; contemporary French theater. *Publ:* Contribr, Ethique et esthetique dans la litterature francaise du 20e siecle, In: Studies in French and Italian Series, Stanford Univ, (in press). *Mailing Add:* Dept of French Montclair State Col Upper Montclair NJ 07043

SZOGYI, ALEXANDER W, b New York, NY, Jan 27, 29. ROMANCE LANGUAGES. *Educ:* Brooklyn Col, AB, 50; Yale Univ, MA, 54, PhD, 58. *Prof Exp:* From instr to asst prof Romance lang, Wesleyan Univ, 56-61; asst prof, 61-70, chmn dept, 70-77, PROF FRENCH LIT, HUNTER COL, 70- *Concurrent Pos:* Fels from Yaddo Writers Found 56, Danforth Found 59, Guggenheim Found, 62-63 & Hunter Col, 64; adaptor Chekhov's & Giraudoux's plays performed in professional theatres, Bermuda & Vancouver, summer stock & Chekhov's A Country Scandal, 60, The Sea Gull, 62 & Maxim Gorki's The Lower Depths, 64 & 72, New York; grant for res on & performance of Corneille's Tite et Berenice, City Univ New York & Hunter Col, 70-71; mem exec bd, Fr Doctoral Prog, City Univ New York, 70, mem comp lit doctoral prog, 74; chmn distinguished prof comt, Hunter Col, 73- *Honors & Awards:* Chevalier, Palmes Academiques, French Govt & Distinguished Alumnus, Brooklyn Col, 74. *Mem:* MLA; Am Asn Teachers Fr; Am Soc Theatre Res; Am Comp Lit Asn; PEN Club. *Res:* Seventeenth century French writers, theatre, literature & cuisine. *Publ:* Auth, Truth-telling and truth-suggesting in Moliere's theatre, Ky Romance Quart, 70; Sartre and the Greeks: A vicious magic circle, In: The Persistent Voice: Hellenism in French literature since the Eighteenth Century, NY Univ & Droz, Geneva, 71; Racine: L'image obsedante, Buff Soc Fr Prof Am, 72; adaptor, Gorki's The Lower Depths, French, 72; transl, Raymonde Temkine's Grotowski, Avon, 73; Anouilh's Antigone, Winthrop, 74; co-ed, George Sand Studies & auth, High analytical Romanticism: George Sand's narrative voice in Lucrezia Floriani, In: George Sand Studies, Hofstra Univ, 78; Esthetic Structures: Checkhov and Miliere Talk given in Budapest: 1976, Int Comp Lit Asn, 78. *Mailing Add:* Dept of Romance Lang Hunter Col 695 Park Ave New York NY 10021

SZÖVERFFY, JOSEPH, b Clausenbourgh, Transylvania, June 19, 20; US citizen. COMPARATIVE LITERATURE, MEDIEVAL LITERATURE. *Educ:* State Col High Sch Teachers, Budapest, MA, 44; Budapest Univ, PhD, 43; Univ Fribourg, Dr Phil Habil, 50. *Prof Exp:* Prof foreign lang, Glenstal Col, Ireland, 50-52; archivist, Irish Folklore Comn, Dublin, 52-57; spec prof classics & mediaeval Latin, Univ Ottawa, 57-58, asst prof, 58-59; from asst prof to assoc prof Ger philol, Univ Alta, 59-62; assoc prof mediaeval Ger lit, Yale Univ, 62-65; prof Ger & medieval lit, Boston Col, 65-70, acting chmn Ger studies & dir grad studies, 68-70; prof comp lit, State Univ NY Albany, 70-77, chmn dept, 72-75; vis prof Byzantine studies, Dumbarton Oaks Ctr Byzantine Studies, Washington, DC, 77-78; prof medieval lit, Sch Hist Studies, Inst Advan Study, 78-79; RICHARD MERTON VIS PROF, INST MEDIEVAL STUDIES, FREIE UNIVERSITAT, BERLIN, GER, 80- *Concurrent Pos:* Guggenheim fel, 61, 69-70, publ grants, 63, 71, 75; Am Philos Soc fels, 65, 72; res grants, Port & Ger Govt, 69-70; co-ed, Mittellateinisches Jahrbuch, Ger, 71-; fel, Ctr Medieval & Early Renaissance Studies, State Univ NY, 73-; Life time fac exchange scholar, State Univ NY, 74-; hon res assoc, Harvard Ukrainian Res Inst, Harvard Univ, 75-; Nat Endowment for Humanities fel, 78-79; proj dir & fel, Dumbarton Oaks Ctr Byzantine Studies, 79- *Honors & Awards:* Chicago Folklore Prize, Univ Chicago, 54. *Mem:* Mediaeval Acad Am; MLA; Am Comp Lit Asn. *Res:* Medieval literature; Byzantine studies; German literature. *Publ:* Auth, Der hl Christophorus und sein Kult, Budapest Univ, 43; Irisches Erzählgut im Abendland, 57, Annalen der lateinischen Hymnendichtung I-II, 64-65 & Weltliche Dichtungen des lateinischen Mittelaters, 70, E Schmidt, Berlin; Iberian Hymnody: Survey and problems, Mass Class Folia Ed, 71; Peter Abelard's Hymnarius Paraclitensis, Vol I-II, 75, Bermanistische Abhandlugen, 77, A Guide to Byzantine Hymnography, Vol I-II, 79-80 & Repertorium Novum Hymnorum Medii Aevi, Vol I-IV, Leyden, Berlin, 82, Brill. *Mailing Add:* Dept of Classics & Medieval Latin Freie Univ D 1000 Berlin 33 Germany, Federal Republic of

SZTACHO, JIRINA ANNA, b Hradec Kralove, Czech; US citizen; m. FRENCH LANGUAGE & LITERATURE. *Educ:* Charles Univ, Prague, PhD, 36; Univ Grenoble, dipl, 33; Univ Paris, dipl, 49; Columbia Univ, MA, 65. *Prof Exp:* From instr to prof French, State Cols, Czech, 37-48; prof philos, Course Bergson, Paris, 48-49; dir & ed-in-chief, Int Bibliog Hist Sci, Int Comt Hist Sci, Zurich, 49-52; res worker, Mid-Europ Studies Ctr, NY, 52-55; instr French, Queens Col, NY, 57-64; asst prof, Bronx Community Col, 60-64, head dept, 64-71, prof French, 65-77. *Concurrent Pos:* French Govt fel, Univ Paris, 45-46; hon secy bibliog comt, Int Comt Hist Sci & rep to Int Comt

Philos & Humanistic Studies, UNESCO, Paris, 50-52; instr mod Europ hist, Mills Col Educ, 58-60; lectr, St John's Univ, NY, 59-60. *Mem:* MLA. *Res:* Modern French literature; philosophy, ethics and morals. *Publ:* Auth, Mid-Europe, Free Europe Comt, 53; ed, International Bibliography of Historical Sciences, Int Comt Hist Sci, Vols 17 & 18. *Mailing Add:* 99-54 65th Ave Flushing NY 11374

SZUBIN, ZVI HENRI, Comparative Jewish Law & Religion. See Vol IV

SZYMANSKI, LADISLAS ISIDORE, b Ford City, Pa, Dec 29, 17. CLASSICS. *Educ:* Duns Scotus Col, BA, 41; Cath Univ Am, MA, 55, PhD, 63. *Prof Exp:* Instr Greek & Latin, St Francis Sem, Cincinnati, Ohio, 45-53, 56-59; instr, 59-63, prof Greek & Latin, Duns Scotus Col, 63-80. *Concurrent Pos:* Vis prof Latin, Univ Detroit, 70-71; vis prof Greek & Latin, Wayne State Univ, 72- *Mem:* Am Class League; Am Philol Asn; Class Asn Mid W & S. *Res:* Patristic and medieval Greek and Latin; classical mythology. *Publ:* Auth, The Translation Procedure of Cassiodorus-Epiphanius in the Historia Tripartita, Bks I & II, Cath Univ Am, 63. *Mailing Add:* 24602 Lincoln Ct Apt 192 Farmington MI 48018

T

TABBERT, RUSSELL DEAN, b Osage, Iowa, July 8, 38; m 64; c 2. ENGLISH LINGUISTICS. *Educ:* Univ Iowa, BA, 63, PhD(English lit & ling), 69. *Prof Exp:* Asst prof English, Bowling Green State Univ, 67-72; asst prof, 72-75, head dept, 75-78, ASSOC PROF ENGLISH, UNIV ALASKA, FAIRBANKS, 75- *Mem:* Long Soc Am; Am Dialect Soc; MLA; NCTE; Dict Soc NAm. *Res:* English dialects; English lexicography. *Publ:* Auth, Dialect differences and the teaching of reading and spelling, Elem English, 11-12/74; Grammar as fact and fiction, Lang Arts, 10/76. *Mailing Add:* Dept of English Univ of Alaska Fairbanks AK 99701

TAFOYA, FRANCIS PINARD, b Brillant, NMex, Dec 24; m 47; c 2. FRENCH. *Educ:* Univ Colo, BA, 48, MA, 51; Yale Univ, PhD, 59. *Prof Exp:* Instr French, Yale Univ, 53-57; asst prof, Goucher Col, 57-59; assoc prof, Oakland Univ, 59-62, prof French & chmn dept mod lang & lit, 62-65; chmn dept, 65-72, PROF FRENCH & SPAN, SWARTHMORE COL, 65-, CHMN DEPT MOD LANG & LIT, 80- *Mem:* MLA; Am Asn Teachers Fr. *Res:* Nineteenth century French literature; comtemporary French leftist novelists and critics; Franco-Latin-American literary relationships. *Mailing Add:* Dept of Mod Lang & Lit Swarthmore Col Swarthmore PA 19081

TAGGART, GILBERT CHARLES, b Colorado Springs, Colo, July 23, 34; m 64; c 2. FRENCH LANGUAGE & LINGUISTICS. *Educ:* Univ Colo, BA, 56, MA, 60; Univ Lille, dipl, 58; Univ Montreal, PhD(ling), 69. *Prof Exp:* Lectr, 62-64; from asst prof to assoc prof, 64-77, PROF FRENCH, CONCORDIA UNIV, 77- *Mem:* Can Asn Appl Ling (pres, 75-77). *Res:* Applied linguistics. *Publ:* Co-ed, Language Laboratory Learning: New Directions, 71, coauth, Panorama de la grammaire Francaise, 72 & auth, Le Francaise parle contemporain, 72, Aquila; Obtaining lexical information in conversation: strategies for advanced language learners, 73 & Pictures in second language learning, 74, Can Mod Lang Rev; L'utilisation de l'image dans les exercices structuraux, Langue Francaise, 74; coauth, Je reponds au telephone, Aquila, 79. *Mailing Add:* Dept Fr Concordia Univ Montreal PQ H3G 1M8 Can

TAGORE, AMITENDRANATH, b Calcutta, India, Oct 9, 22; m 53; c 1. CHINESE & INDIAN LANGUAGES & LITERATURES. *Educ:* Univ Calcutta, BCom, 42; Yale Col Chinese Studies, Peiping, dipl, 47; Nat Peking Univ, MA, 50; Visva-Bharati Univ, PhD, 62. *Prof Exp:* Lectr Chinese, Visva-Bharati Univ, 50-63; from asst prof to assoc prof, 63-68, actg chmn area studies prog & actg dir lang & area ctr for EAsia, 69-70, coord Asian lang, 72-73, PROF CHINESE, OAKLAND UNIV, 68- *Concurrent Pos:* Lectr, Nat Defense Acad, India, 52-57; Fulbright vis lectr Orient studies, Univ Pa, 61-62; secy, EAsian Sect, XXVI Int Cong Orientalists, New Delhi, 63; Fulbright alumni res grant, India, 63-64. *Mem:* Am Coun Teaching Foreign Lang; Am Orient Soc; Asn Asian Studies; Asia Soc; Chinese Lang Teachers Asn Am. *Res:* Chinese literature and art; Sino-Indian cultural diffusion; Sung dynasty landscape poetry. *Publ:* Auth, Wartime literature of China--its trends and tendencies, 50 & Early decades of modern Chinese literature (1918-1937), 62, Visva-Bharati Quart; Translr, Tao-te-ching, 60 & Lun-yü, 64, Sahitya Akad, New Delhi; coauth, Cheena-mati, Rupa, Calcutta, 61 & Sapta sindhu dasha diganta, New Lit House, Calcutta, 62; auth, Literary Debates in Modern China (1918-1937), Centre EAsian Cult Studies, Tokyo, 67; Moments of Rising Mist: A Collection of Sung Landscape Poetry, Grossman/Mushinsha, 73; The Luminous Landscape: Chinese Art & Poetry, Doubleday, 81. *Mailing Add:* Dept of Mod Lang & Lit Oakland Univ Rochester MI 48063

TAHARA, MILDRED MACHIKO, b Hilo, Hawaii, May 15, 41. CLASSICAL & MODERN JAPANESE LITERATURE. *Educ:* Univ Hawaii, Manoa, BA, 63, MA, 65; Columbia Univ, PhD(Japanese lit), 69. *Prof Exp:* Asst prof, 69-76, ASSOC PROF JAPANESE LIT, UNIV HAWAII, MANOA, 76- *Mem:* Asn Asian Studies; Asn Teachers Japanese; Japan Soc. *Res:* Heian literature; modern and contemporary novels and short stories; classical poetry. *Publ:* Auth, Heichu, As Seen in Yamato Monogatari, 71 & Yamato Monogatari: A Poem-tale of Heian Japan, 72, Monumenta Nopponica; Genji monogatari: Heian loves, Orientations, 12/72; The ink stick (short story), Japan Quart, Vol 22, No 4; Fujiwara Michinaga, In: Great Historical Figures of Japan, Japan Cult Inst, 78; auth & transl, Tales of Yamato, Univ Hawaii Press, 80; transl, Ariyoshi Sawako, The River Ki, Kodansha Int, 80. *Mailing Add:* Dept of EAsain Lit Univ of Hawaii Honolulu HI 96822

TAKACS, ZOLTON, b Kendilona, Hungary, July 16, 14; US citizen. LANGUAGES & LINGUISTICS. *Educ:* Univ Pecs, PhD, 39. *Prof Exp:* Asst French, Univ Pecs, 37-39; asst prof French, Ger & English, Budapest Commercial Col, 39-40; asst prof Span, Curry Col, 59-61; asst prof French & Ger, 61-67, PROF FRENCH, MISS STATE UNIV, 67- *Mem:* MLA; Am Asn Teachers Fr; SAtlantic Mod Lang Asn; SCent Mod Lang Asn. *Res:* Comparative literature, especially French-Hungarian and French-German; 20th century French literature; 20th century French literature. *Publ:* Auth, Un ecrivain hongrois francophile: Paul Jambor, Univ Pecs, 39; co-ed, Erasmus, Int Bull Contemp Scholar, Wiesbaden, Ger. *Mailing Add:* Box 153 Miss State Univ Mississippi State MS 39762

TAKAHASHI, GEORGE, b Twin Falls, Idaho, Sept 17, 31. JAPANESE. *Educ:* Univ Calif, Los Angeles, MA, 61. *Prof Exp:* Assoc, 62-66, LECTR JAPANESE, UNIV CALIF, LOS ANGELES, 66- *Mem:* Asn Teachers Japanese; Am Orient Soc. *Publ:* Auth, New classification for Japanese verb, 3/67 & Psychological approach to Japanese particles, ga, ni, and o, 11/68, J Newslett Asn Teachers Japanese. *Mailing Add:* Dept of Orient Lang Univ of Calif Los Angeles CA 90024

TALAMANTES, FLORENCE WILLIAMS, b Alliance, Ohio; m 70. SPANISH LANGUAGE & LITERATURE. *Educ:* Mt Union Col, BA, 54; Univ Cincinnati, MA, 56, PhD(Span), 61. *Prof Exp:* Teacher Span & English, Windham High Sch, Ohio, 54-55; teacher, Hughes High Sch, Cincinnati, Ohio, 56-57; teaching asst Span, Ind Univ, Bloomington, 57-58; teaching asst, Univ Cincinnati, 58-61, part-time instr, 60-61; asst prof, Lake Forest Col, 61-62; asst prof, 62-67, ASSOC PROF SPAN, SAN DIEGO STATE UNIV, 67- *Res:* Nineteenth century Spanish novel and short story; Jose Maria de Pereda; Joseph Conrad. *Publ:* Conrad and Balzac: A Trio of Balzacian Interrelationships: The Sisters, The Tremolino, and The Arrow of Gold, Polish Rev, Proceedings & Twayne Publ, 75; Alfonsina Storni: Argentina's Feminist Poet, San Marcos Press, 75; transll, Women Poets and Suicide, (trans, Poetisas suicidas), J Comp Study Int Lit, Art & Ideas, 9-10/76; auth, Alfonsina Storni: Poemas de Amor, B Costa-Amic, 77; Jose Maria de Pereda: Selections from Sotileza and Penas Arriba, Univ Press Am, 78; Ramon Sender: Selections de Poesia Lirica y Aforistica, El Sol de Calif, Mex, 79; Editor's Note & selection from Libro Armilar de Poesia y Memorias Bisiestas, J Comp Study Int Lit, Art & Ideas, 1-2/80. *Mailing Add:* Dept of Span San Diego State Univ San Diego CA 92115

TALBOT, EMILE JOSEPH, b Brunswick, Maine, Apr 12, 41; m 66; c 2. FRENCH. *Educ:* St Francis Col, BA, 63; Brown Univ, MA, 65, PhD(French), 68. *Prof Exp:* From instr to asst prof, 67-73, ASSOC PROF FRENCH, UNIV ILL, URBANA, 73- *Concurrent Pos:* Fel, Ctr Advan Studies, Univ Ill, 73; Nat Endowment for Humanities younger humanist fel, 73-74; Camargo Found fel, 77; distinguished vis prof, Eastern Ill Univ, summer, 81. *Mem:* MLA; Am Asn Teachers Fr; Midwest Mod Lang Asn; Asn for Can Studies US. *Res:* French Romanticism; criticism; French Canadian literature. *Publ:* Auth, Considerations sur la definition stendhalienne du romantisme, 69, Remarques sur la mort de Madame de Renal, 73 & Stendhal, le beau et le laid: Autour de quelques problemes esthetiques, 78, Stendhal-Club; Style and the Self: Some Notes on La Chartreuse de Parme, Lang & Style, 72; Stendhal, the Artist, and Society, Studies in Romanticism, 74; Author and Audience: A Perspective on Stendhal's Concept of Literature, Nineteenth-Century Fr Studies, 74; La crituque Stendhalienne de Balzac a Zola, Fr Lit Publ, 79; Les Incarnations d'un texte nationaliste: Hemon, Savard, Carrier, Presence Francophone, 80. *Mailing Add:* Dept of French Univ of Ill Urbana IL 61801

TALL, EMILY, b New York, NY, May 22, 40. RUSSIAN. *Educ:* Cornell Univ, BA, 61; Middlebury Col, MA, 67; Brown Univ, PhD(Slavic lang & lit), 74. *Prof Exp:* asst prof, 73-80, ASSOC PROF RUSS, STATE UNIV NY BUFFALO, 80- *Mem:* Am Asn Teachers Slavic & EEurop Lang; Am Asn Advan Slavic Studies; Am Coun Teachers Russ. *Res:* Russian language teaching; Soviet literary criticism; Soviet literature. *Publ:* Auth, Who's afraid of Franz Kafka?: Kafka criticism in the Soviet Union, Slavic Rev, 9/76; Camus in the Soviet Union: Some Recent Emigres Speak, Comp Lit Studies, 9/79; Letters of Camus and Pasternak, Partisan Rev, 80; Soviet Responses to Albert Camus: 1956-1976, Can Slavonic Papers, 80; James Joyce Returns to the Soviet Union, James Joyce Quart, summer 80. *Mailing Add:* State Unif of NY Buffalo NY 14261

TAMARGO, MARIA ISABEL, b Baton Rouge, La, Sept 18, 50; c 2. SPANISH AMERICAN LITERATURE. *Educ:* Int Am Univ, BA, 72; Johns Hopkins Univ, MA, 72, PhD(Span & Span Am lit), 75. *Prof Exp:* ASST PROF SPAN LANG & LIT, UNIV TEX, AUSTIN, 75- *Mem:* MLA; Am Asn Teachers Span & Port; Latin Am Studies Asn; SCent Mod Lang Asn; SCent Orgn Latin Am Studies. *Res:* Twentieth century Latin American narrative; literary theory and criticism. *Publ:* Auth, La Invencion de Morel: Lectura y lectores, Rev Iberoam, 7-12/76; Celestino Antes del Alba: La Violencia y el Lenguaje infantil, Hisp Lit, 78; La disqluciondel sujeto y el discurso de Adolfo Bloy Caseres, 1980 Proc Rocky Mountain Coun Latin Am Studies, 80; Parodia e intertextualidad en un cuerto de Borges y Bloy Casares, Am Hispanist, 5/80; Amistad Funesta: Una teoria del personaje novelesco, Explicacion de Textos Literarios, 81; Plan to escape: The loss of Referentiality, Hisp J, 82; El texto como escritura-lectura: A propositio del discurso de Adolfo Bloy Casares, Ed Playor, Madrid, 82. *Mailing Add:* 5810 Marilyn Dr Austin TX 78731

TANAKA, YOSHIO, b Covina, Calif, May 12, 19; m 48. GERMANIC & INDO-EUROPEAN LINGUISTICS. *Educ:* Univ Tokyo, LLB, 50; Univ Calif, Los Angeles, BA, 62, MA, 63, PhD(Ger ling & philol), 65. *Prof Exp:* From asst prof to assoc prof, 65-76, PROF GER, SAN DIEGO STATE UNIV, 76- *Mem:* Ling Soc Am; Philol Asn Pac Coast. *Res:* Historical Germanic linguistics; German dialects; Lappish phonology. *Publ:* Auth, The syllable shape in phonetic analysis, Orbis, Vol XV, No 2. *Mailing Add:* Dept of Foreign Lang San Diego State Univ San Diego CA 92182

TANNER, ROY LYNN, b Provo, Utah, Apr 27, 47; m 68; c 6. LATIN AMERICAN LITERATURE, SPANISH. *Educ:* Brigham Young Univ, BA, 71, MA, 73; Univ Ill, Urbana, PhD(Latin Am lit), 76. *Prof Exp:* Asst prof Span, Grinnell Col, 76-77; ASST PROF SPAN & LATIN AM LIT, UNIV VA, 77- *Mem:* Am Asn Teachers Span & Port; MLA. *Res:* Colonial and nineteenth-century Spanish American literature. *Publ:* Auth, La influencia de la emblematica en El cisne de Apolo, Cuadernos Hispanoamericanos, 10/77; Literary portraiture in Ricardo Palma's Tradiciones peruanas, Am Hispanist, 5/78; El arte de la caracterizacion en 'Don Dimas de la Tijereta' de Ricardo Palma, Explicacion de Textos Literarios, 7/79; Las expresiones alternativas y perifrasticas en la prosa de Ricardo Palma: una clave estilistica, Cuadernos Hispanoamericanos, 82; Ricardo Palma and Francisco de Quevedo: A case of rhetorical affinity and debt, Ky Romance Quart; Ricardo Palma's rhetorical debt to Miguel de Cervantes, Revista de Estudios Hispanicos (in press). *Mailing Add:* Dept of Span Ital & Port 301 Cabell Hall Univ Va Charlottesville VA 22903

TAPP, HENRY L, b Pasadena, Calif, May 14, 18; m 52; c 2. LINGUISTICS, PHILOLOGY. *Educ:* Univ Calif, Los Angeles, AB, 39, MA, 40; Yale Univ, MA, 42, PhD, 54. *Prof Exp:* From instr to asst prof Ger, Amherst Col, 53-57; asst prof, 57-60, assoc prof Ger & Slavic lang, 60-77, PROF GER, KENT STATE UNIV, 76-, CHMN DEPT, 80- *Mem:* MLA; Am Asn Teachers Ger. *Res:* Middle High German; Old Norse. *Publ:* Auth, Hinn almattki Ass-Thor or Odin?, J English & Ger Philol, 1/56. *Mailing Add:* Dept of Ger & Slavic Lang Kent State Univ Kent OH 44240

TAPPAN, DONALD WILLARD, b Syracuse, NY, Feb 24, 32. FRENCH LANGUAGE & LITERATURE. *Educ:* Hamilton Col, AB, 53; Rice Inst, MA, 56; Yale Univ, PhD(French), 64. *Prof Exp:* Instr French, Hamilton Col, 56-58; from instr to asst prof, Rice Univ, 61-70; prof, Northern Ill Univ, 70-71; chmn dept foreign lang, 71-77, PROF FRENCH, UNIV NEW ORLEANS, 71- *Mem:* Am Asn Teachers Fr. *Res:* Medieval French language and literature; 17th century French literature. *Publ:* Auth, Two chroniclers of Louis IX, Rice Univ Studies, fall 67; coauth, Deux pieces comiques inedites du manuscrit B N fr 904, Romania, 70; auth, The MSS of the Recits d'un menestrel de Reims, Symposium, 71; Musset's murderous rose, Romance Notes, 74. *Mailing Add:* Dept of Foreign Lang Univ of New Orleans Lake Front New Orleans LA 70148

TAPSCOTT, BANGS L, b Riverside, Calif, May 31, 35; m 59; c 2. PHILOSOPHY. *Educ:* Univ Ore, BA, 61; Univ Wash, MA, 63, PhD(philos), 68. *Prof Exp:* From instr to assoc prof, 66-76, PROF PHILOS, UNIV UTAH, 76- *Concurrent Pos:* Gardner fel, Univ Utah, 75 & 79. *Mem:* Am Philos Asn; AAUP. *Res:* Philosophy of logic; philosophy of language; metaphysics. *Publ:* Auth, Elementary Applied Symbolic Logic, Prentice-Hall, 76. *Mailing Add:* Dept of Philos Univ of Utah Salt Lake City UT 84112

TARABA, ANNE-SOPHIE, b Malmö, Sweden, July 22, 30; US citizen; m 81; c 1. SCANDANAVIAN & COMPARATIVE LITERATURE. *Educ:* Univ Minn, BA, 66, MA, 69, PhD(Scand), 78. *Prof Exp:* Instr Swedish & Scand Lit, Univ Minn, 66-69; RES & WRITING, 80- *Concurrent Pos:* Instr cult heritage, Minneapolis Pub Schs, 77-78. *Publ:* Auth, Our pen in Hollywood, weekly column in Femina Mag, 59-60; Ludvig Holberg and Moliere, In: Moliere and the Commonwealth of Letters, Univ Miss Press, 75; Journey through Poland, Sun Newpapers, 81; Sailing from Byzantium, Bra Böcker, Sweden, 82; Something like silver, This Week Mag, Sweden, 82. *Mailing Add:* 8339 139th Ct Minneapolis MN 55124

TARABA, WOLFGANG F, b Buddenbrock, Ger, July 15, 27; US citizen; m 54; c 2. GERMAN, HUMANITIES. *Educ:* Univ Munster, Dr Phil (Ger, English & philos), 53. *Prof Exp:* Instr Ger, Princeton Univ, 54-56; asst prof, Duke Univ, 56-59; asst prof Ger & humanities, Wesleyan Univ, 59-63; assoc prof, 63-66, PROF GER & HUMANITIES, UNIV MINN, MINNEAPOLIS, 66- *Concurrent Pos:* Ed-in-chief, Classics in Ger Lit & Philos, Johnson Reprint Corp, NY, 64- *Mem:* MLA; Am Asn Teachers Ger. *Res:* German lyric poetry and the novelle from Goethe to the present; the infludence of Friedrich Nietzsche's thought on later writers and philosophers. *Publ:* Auth, Chapters on Eduard Morike, Friedrich Nietzsche and Agnes Miegel, In: Die deutsche Lyrik, Bagel, Dusseldorf, 56; Der Schopferische Einzelne und die Gesellschaft in Nietzsches Zarathustra, In: Literatur und Gesellschaft, Bouvier, Bonn, 63; coauth, Structural German, Gilbert, 65; auth, Friedrich Nietzsche, In: Deutsche Dichter der Moderne, Erich Schmidt, Berlin, 66. *Mailing Add:* Dept of Ger Univ of Minn Minneapolis MN 55455

TARAN, LEONARDO, b Galarza, Arg, FEb 22, 33; nat US; m 71; c 1. CLASSICS, ANCIENT PHILOSOPHY. *Educ:* Princeton Univ, PhD(classics), 62. *Prof Exp:* Fel res, Inst Res Humanities, Univ Wis, 62-63; jr fel res, Ctr Hellenic Studies, 63-64; asst prof classics, Univ Calif, Los Angeles, 64-67; assoc prof, 67-71, chmn dept, 76-79, PROF GREEK & LATIN, COLUMBIA UNIV, 71- *Concurrent Pos:* Am Philos Soc grant, 63, 71 & 75; fel Am Coun Learned Soc, 66-67, 71-72; Guggenheim Found fel, 75; mem Inst Advan Study, Princeton, 66-67 & 78-79. *Mem:* Am Philol Asn; Soc Ancient Greek Philos. *Res:* Ancient philosophy; Greek literatue. *Publ:* Auth, Parmenides, Princeton Univ, 65; Asclepius of Tralles: Commentary to Nicomachus' introduction to arithmetic, Am Philos Soc, 69; The creation myth in Plato's Timaeus, In: Essays in Greek Philosophy, State Univ NY, 71; coauth, Eraclito, testimonianze e imitazioni, La Nuova Italia Editrice, 72; auth, Academica: Plato, Philip of Opus and the Pseudo-Platonic Epinomis, Am Philos Soc Memoirs, 75; Anonymous Commentary on Aristotle's de Interpretatione, Anton Hain, 78; Speusippus and Aristotle on homonymy and synonymy, Herme, 106: 73-99; Speusippus of Athens, Leiden, Brill, 81. *Mailing Add:* Dept of Greek & Latin Columbia Univ New York NY 10027

TARANOVSKY, KIRIL, b Tartu, Estonia, Mar 19, 11; m 40, 58; c 2. SLAVIC LANGUAGES & LITERATURES. *Educ:* Univ Belgrade, LLB, 33, MA, 36, PhD, 41. *Hon Degrees:* MA, Harvard Univ, 63. *Prof Exp:* From asst to prof Slavic lang & lit, Univ Belgrade, 37-59; prof, Univ Calif, Los Angeles, 59-62; vis lectr, 58-59, prof, 63-80, EMER PROF SLAVIC LANG & LIT,

HARVARD UNIV, 80- *Mem:* Asn Teachers Slavic & EEurop Lang. *Res:* Slavic poetics and metrics; Russian and Yugoslav literature. *Publ:* Auth, Ruski Dvodelni Ritmovi, Serbian Acad Sci, Belgrade, 53; Essays on Mandelstam, Harvard Univ, 76. *Mailing Add:* Boylston Hall 301 Harvard Univ Cambridge MA 02138

TARAS, ANTHONY F, b Dicson City, Pa, Nov 13, 27; m 56. FRENCH, SPANISH. *Educ:* Univ Scranton, BA, 48; Kent State Univ, MA, 50; Fordham Univ, PhD, 61. *Prof Exp:* From instr to assoc prof foreign lang, Idaho State Col, 50-63, chmn dept, 52-63; assoc prof mod lang, 63-65, chmn dept, 63-73, PROF MOD LANG, ITHACA COL, 65- *Concurrent Pos:* Ed consult, Britannica World Lang Dict, 55. *Mem:* Am Asn Teachers Fr; MLA; Am Coun Teaching Foreign Lang; Nat Asn Lang Lab Dir. *Res:* Eighteenth century French literature; modern language laboratories research and development. *Mailing Add:* Dept of Foreign Lang Ithaca Col Ithaca NY 14850

TARICA, RALPH, b Atlanta, Ga, Sept 9, 32; m 64; c 2. FRENCH LITERATURE. *Educ:* Emory Univ, BA, 54, MA, 58; Harvard Univ, PhD(Romance lang), 66. *Prof Exp:* Instr mod lang, Ga Inst Technol, 58-60; from instr to asst prof French, Brandeis Univ, 63-69; ASSOC PROF FRENCH, UNIV MD, COLLEGE PARK, 69- *Mem:* MLA; SAtlantic Mod Lang Asn; Malraux Soc; Am Asn Teachers Fr. *Res:* Modern French literature; the novel; stylistics. *Publ:* Contrib, Image and Theme in Modern French Fiction, Harvard Univ, 69; Imagery in the Novels of Andre Malraux, Fairleigh Dickinson, 80. *Mailing Add:* Dept of French and Ital Univ of Md College Park MD 20742

TARKOW, THEODORE A, b Madison, Wis, 1944; m 70. CLASSICAL LANGUAGES. *Educ:* Oberlin Col, BA, 66; Univ Mich, PhD(classics), 71. *Prof Exp:* Asst prof classics, 70-76, assoc prof, 76-81, dir, Hon Col, 77-78, PROF CLASSICS, UNIV MO-COLUMBIA, 81-, DIR, HON COL, 79- *Honors & Awards:* Award for Excellence in Undergrad Teaching, Amoco Found, 75; Award for Excellence in Teaching Classics, Am Philos Asn, 80. *Mem:* Am Philol Asn; Class Asn Midwest & South; Vergilian Soc Am. *Res:* Greek tragedy, comedy and lyric poetry. *Publ:* Auth, The dilemma of Pelasgus and the nautical imagery of Aeschylus' Suppliants, Class Mediaevalia, No 31, 76; The glorification of Athens in Euripides' Heracles, Helios, No 5, 77; Theognis 237-254: A reexamination, Quaderni Urbinati di Cultura Classica, No 26, 77; Dependence on externals: The role of animals in Bacchylides Ode 5, Rivista di Studi Classici, No 26, 78; Electra's role in the opening scene of the Choephori, Eranos, No 77, 79; The Scar of Orestes: Observations on a Euripidean innovation, Rheinisches Museum for Philologie, 81; Thematic implications of costuming in the Oresteia, Maia, No 32, 81; Achilles and the Ghost of Aeschylus in Aristophanes' Frogs, Traditio, No 32, 82. *Mailing Add:* Dept of Class Studies Univ of Mo Columbia MO 65211

TARNAWECKY, IRAIDA IRENE, b Ukraine; Can citizen. EAST SLAVIC LANGUAGES. *Educ:* Univ Goettngen, Ger, BSc, 49; Univ Man, MA, 64; Ukrainian Free Univ, Ger, PhD(Slavic philol), 66, Doct habil Slavic philol, 69. *Prof Exp:* Lectr Slavic studies, 66-68, asst prof, 68-75, ASSOC PROF SLAVIC STUDIES, UNIV MAN, 75. *Concurrent Pos:* Ed, Can Inst Onomastic Sci, 70-73; mem, Can Comt Int Cong Slavists, 70- *Mem:* Can Asn Slavists; Can Soc Study Names (vpres, 70-73 & 79-82); Am Name Soc; Ukrainian Acad Sci Can; Can Inst Ukrainian Studies. *Res:* New trends in North American Ukrainian language; Cyrillica Canadiana; stylistic function of proper names. *Publ:* Auth, Anthroponymy in the Pominayk of Horodysce of 1484, Ukrainian Acad Sci, 65; Names in Poetry, Unkrainian Free Univ, Ger, 66; contribr, Literary onomastics, Names, 68; Reducible Vowels & Xomonija in Toronto Krjuki-Manuscript, Mouton Publ, 73; Recent Trends in North American Ukrainian, Can Asn Slavists, 78; The Pomianyk in a historical perspective, Analecta OSBM, 79; Slavic manuscripts & their study in Canada, Polata knigopis'naja, 80; auth, East Slavic Cyrillica in Canandian Repositories, Res Inst Volyn, 81. *Mailing Add:* Dept of Slavic Studies Univ of Man Winnipeg MB R3T 2N2 Can

TARONE, ELAINE E, b Modesto,, Calif, Feb 13, 45. APPLIED LINGUISTICS, PHONETICS. *Educ:* Univ Calif, Berkeley, AB, 66; Univ Edinburgh, dipl(appl ling), 69; Univ Wash, MA, 70, PhD(speech), 72. *Prof Exp:* Teacher English & Span, Encinal High Sch, Alameda, Calif, 67-68; teaching asst speech, Univ Wash, 69-72; dir develop skills, Roxbury Community Col, 73-74; instr speech & English, Seattle Cent Community Col, 74-76; dir English as second lang Ctr, Univ Wash, 76-80; MEM FAC, DEPT LING, UNIV MINN, 80- *Concurrent Pos:* Lectr dept spec educ, Boston Univ, 73-74. *Mem:* Teachers English to Speakers Other Lang; Am Asn Applied Linguists. *Res:* Second language acquisition; psycholinguistics; sociolinguistics. *Publ:* Auth, A suggested unit for interlingual identification in pronunciation, TESOL Quart, 12/72; Speech perception in Second Language acquisition, Lang Learning, 74; Some influences on interlanguage phonology, Working Papers Bilingualism, 76 & IRAL, 78; coauth, Some limitations to classroom applications, TESOL Quart, 76; Closer look at some interlanguage terminology, Working Papers Bilingualism, 76; auth, Conscious communication strategies, In: Teaching and Learning ESL, 77, Phonology, In: Understanding Second Language Learning,78 & English for Academic and Technical Purposes, 78, Newbury House. *Mailing Add:* Dept of Ling Univ of Minn Minneapolis MN 53455

TARPLEY, FRED ANDERSON, b Leonard, Tex, Jan 27, 32. LINGUISTICS, ENGLISH. *Educ:* ETex State Univ, BA, 51, MA, 54; La State Univ, PhD(ling), 60. *Prof Exp:* Fac res grant, 66-67, 77-78, PROF LING & ENGLISH, ETEX STATE UNIV, 57-. HEAD DEPT LANG & LIT, 73- *Concurrent Pos:* Ling consult, Tex Educ Agency, 64-; nat dir, Place Name Surv US, Am Name Soc, 73- *Mem:* Ling Soc Am; MLA; NCTE; Am Name Soc; Ling Asn Southwest(pres, 77-78). *Res:* American regional and social dialects; place names; teaching composition. *Publ:* Auth, Historical aspects of linguistic research in East Texas, ETex Hist Asn J, 2/64; Pseudo-syllabification in Written English, Tex Joint Coun Teachers English Anthology, 66; Place Names of Northeast Texas, ETex State Univ, 68; From Blinky to Blue John: A Word Atlas of Northeast Texas, Univ, Wolfe City, Tex, 70; co-ed, Of Edsels and Marauders, 71 & ed, Love and Wrestling, Butch and O K, 73, They Had to Call It Something, 75, Naughty Names, 76, SCent Names Inst. *Mailing Add:* Dept of Lit & Lang ETex State Univ Commerce TX 75428

TARRANT, PATRICK, b County Cork, Ireland, Oct 25, 16; US citizen; m 51; c 4. FRENCH. *Educ:* Univ Col, Dublin, BA, 47; Nat Univ Ireland, MA, 49; Columbia Univ, MA, 57, EdD(French), 60; Sorbonne, dipl, 62. *Prof Exp:* Teacher French, La Salle Sec Leix, Ireland, 40-44, Teacher's Training Col, Waterford, Ireland, 47-48 & Clarke's Col, Leicester, 49-50; prin lower sch, Eastern Mil Acad, NY, 50-53; head foreign lang dept high sch, WBabylon NY, 55-63; assoc prof French, 63-66. chmn dept, 65-76, PROF FRENCH, ILL STATE UNIV, 66- *Mem:* NEA. *Publ:* Auth, Les Auteurs Francais, Wood Publ Works , Dublin, 63. *Mailing Add:* Dept of French Ill State Univ Normal IL 61761

TARRANT, RICHARD JOHN, b New York, NY, Apr 4, 45; m 68. CLASSICS. *Educ:* Fordham Univ, BA, 66; Oxford Univ, DPhil, 72. *Prof Exp:* From lectr to prof classics, Univ Toronto, 70-82; PROF GREEK & LATIN, HARVARD UNIV, 82- *Concurrent Pos:* Rev ed, Phoenix, Class Asn Can, 75-78, ed, 78-82. *Mem:* Am Philol Asn; Class Asn; Class Asn Can. *Res:* Greek and Latin drama; Latin poetry; textual criticism. *Publ:* Auth, Greek and Latin Lyric Poetry in Translation, Am Philol Asn, 72; ed & auth, Seneca, Agamemnon, Cambridge Univ, 76; auth, Senecan drama and its antecedents, 78, The addressee of Virgil's eighth eclogue, 78 & Aeneas and the gates of sleep, 82, Harvard Studies Class Philol. *Mailing Add:* Dept of Greek & Latin Harvard Univ Cambridge MA 02138

TASSIE, JAMES STEWARD, b Winnipeg, Man, June 6, 17; m 45; c 1. FRENCH-CANADIAN LANGUAGE & LITERATURE. *Educ:* McMaster Univ, BA, 41; Univ Toronto, MA, 47, PhD(Romance lang), 57. *Prof Exp:* From lectr to assoc prof French, Carleton Univ, 48-64, chmn dept, 52-62 & 65-71, actg chmn, Dept Ger, 64-65, chmn, Dept Span, 64-67, prof, 64-80. *Concurrent Pos:* Vis asst prof humanities, Mass Inst Technol, 55-56; Can Coun sr res fel, France, 59-60; mem bd examr, Ont Dept Educ, 60-65. *Mem:* Humanities Asn Can; Can Asn Univ Teachers; Asn Can Univ Teachers Fr; Can Ling Asn. *Res:* French-Canadian novel; French language. *Publ:* Auth, French Canadian Literature, Encycl Britannica, 59-; The Use of Sacrilege in the Speech of French Canada, Am Speech, 61; Le conditionnel, tiroir uniquement modal, Can J Ling, 63; La societe canadienne a travers le Roman Canadien-Francais, Arch Lett Can, 64. *Mailing Add:* 527 Eccho Dr Ottawa ON K1S 1N7 Can

TATAR, MARIA, b May 13, 45. GERMAN LITERATURE. *Educ:* Denison Univ, BA, 67; Princeton Univ, MA, 69, PhD(Ger), 71. *Prof Exp:* Asst prof, 71-77, assoc prof, 77-79, PROF GER, HARVARD UNIV, 79- *Concurrent Pos:* Res fel lit, Nat Endowment for Humanities, 74-75 & Radcliffe Inst Independent Study, 77-79. *Mem:* MLA; Am Asn Teachers Ger. *Res:* German romanticism; literature and psychology; comparative literature. *Publ:* Auth, Mesmerism, madness, and death in E T A Hoffmann's Der goldne Topf, Studies Romanticism, 75; Spellbound: Studies on Mesmerism and Literature, Princeton Univ, 78; Deracination and alienation in Ludwig Tieck's Der Runenberg, Ger Quart, 78; Reflections and romantic irony: E T A Hoffmann's Der Sandmann, Mod Lang Notes, 80; The art of biography in Wackenroder's Herzensergiessungen eines kunstliebenden Klosterbruders and phantasien über die kunst, Studies Romanticism, 80; The houses of fiction: Toward a definition of the uncanny, Comp Lit, 81; Folkloristic phantasies: Grimms' fairy tales and Freud's family romance, In: Fairy Tales as Ways of Knowing, 81. *Mailing Add:* Dept of Ger Harvard Univ Cambridge MA 02138

TATE, GEORGE SHELDON, b Santa Monica, Calif, Sept 7, 44; m 69; c 2. MEDIEVAL LITERATURE. *Educ:* Brigham Young Univ, BA, 69; MA, 70; Cornell Univ, PhD(Medieval studies), 74. *Prof Exp:* Asst prof, 74-78, ASSOC PROF COMP LIT, BRIGHAM YOUNG UNIV, 79- *Concurrent Pos:* Chmn dept, Humanities, Class & Comp Lit, 81- *Mem:* Mediaeval Acad Am; Soc Advan Scand Studies; Viking Soc Northern Res; Rocky Mountain Medieval & Renaissance Asn; Asn Mormon Letters. *Res:* Old Norse literature, especially Christian skaldic poetry; Old English literature; Middle High German literature. *Publ:* Ed, Liknarbraut: A Skaldic Drapa on the Cross, Univ Microfilms, 74; auth, Good Friday Liturgy and the Structure of Liknarbraut, Scand Studies, 78; Chiasmus as Metaphor: The Figura Crucis Tradition and The Dream of the Rood, Neuphilologische Mitteilungen, 78; The Cross as Ladder: Geisli 15-16 and Liknarbraut 34, Mediaeval Scand, 78; Halldor Laxness, the Mormons, and the Promised Land, Dialogue, 78. *Mailing Add:* Dept of Comp Lit 253 JKBA Brigham Young Univ Provo UT 84602

TATE, ROBERT STUART, JR, b Cincinnati, Ohio, June 24, 39; c 2. FRENCH. *Educ:* Duke Univ, BA, 61; Ind Univ, MA, 63, PhD(French), 67. *Prof Exp:* From instr to asst prof Romance lang, Duke Univ, 65-70; asst prof French, Univ Iowa, 71-73; ASSOC PROF FRENCH, UNIV SC, 73- *Concurrent Pos:* Leverhulme Trust vis fel, Univ Exeter, 70-71; Am Philos Soc grant-in-aid, 73. *Mem:* Am Soc 18th Century Study; Brit Soc 18th Century Study; Soc Fr Etudes SVIIIe Siecle; MLA; Am Asn Teachers Fr. *Res:* French 18th century literature; comparative literature; bibliography. *Publ:* Auth, Petit de Bachaumont: His circle and the Memoires secrets, Inst & Mus Voltaire, 68; Bachaumont revisited: Some unpublished papers and correspondence, 71 & Voltaire and the parlements: A reconsideration, 72, Studies Voltaire & 18th Century; Voltaire and the question of law and order in the eihteenth century: Locke against Hobbes, In: Studies in Eithteenth-Century French Literature Presented to Robert Niklaus, 75. *Mailing Add:* 4214 Bethel Church Rd Columbia SC 29206

TATUM, JAMES CARL, b Litchfield, Nebr, Jan 25, 39; m 61; c 2. LATIN AMERICAN & SPANISH LITERATURE. *Educ:* Nebr State Col, Kearney, BA, 60; Tulane Univ, MA, 62, PhD(Span), 68. *Prof Exp:* From instr to asst prof, 63-70, ASSOC PROF SPAN, UNIV SOUTH FLA, 70- *Concurrent Pos:*

Fulbright-Hays scholar, 68. *Mem:* SAtlantic Mod Lang Asn; Am Asn Teachers Span & Port. *Res:* Nineteenth century Mexican literature; history of Mexican independence; Latin American literature. *Publ:* Auth, Viaje de Perico Ligero al Pais de los Moros, Mid Am Res Inst, 72; Veracruz en 1816-1817: Fragmento del diario de Antonio Lopez Matoso, Hist Mexicana, Vol 19, No 1; The Legends of Luis Rosado Vega, Lang Quart, Vol 3, No 2. *Mailing Add:* Dept of Foreign Lang Univ of SFla Tampa FL 33620

TATUM, JAMES HARVEY, b Longview, Tex, Dec 3, 42. CLASSICAL PHILOLOGY. *Educ:* Univ Tex, Austin, BA, 63, Princeton Univ, PhD(classics), 69. *Prof Exp:* Asst prof, 69-75, assoc prof, 75-80, PROF CLASSICS, DARTMOUTH COL, 80- *Concurrent Pos:* Fac fel, Dartmouth Col, 72-73; jr fel, Ctr Hellenic Studies, Washington, DC, 78-79. *Mem:* Am Philol Asn; Soc Prom Roman Studies; Soc Prom Hellenic Studies; Class Asn New England. *Res:* Latin and Greek literature; narrative technique in Greek and Latin prose; Plautus. *Publ:* Auth, The Tales in Apuleius Metamorphoses, Trans & Proc Am Philol Asn, 69; Apuleius and metamorphosis, 72 & Non usitata nec tenui ferar, 73, Am J Philol; Apuleius and the Golden Ass, Cornell Univ, 78. *Mailing Add:* Dept of Classics Dartmouth Col Hanover NH 03755

TAUSSIG, ANNA, b Austria, May 18, 11; US citizen; m 33; c 2. LANGUAGES & LINGUISTICS. *Educ:* Hofstra Col, BA, 44; Univ Colo, MA, 62. *Prof Exp:* From instr to asst prof French & Ger, 60-64, assoc prof French, Ger & Russ, 64-66, prof foreign lang, 66-77, chmn dept, 60-71, EMER PROF FOREIGN LANG, UNIV SOUTHERN COLO, 77- *Mem:* NEA; AAUP; Am Asn Teachers Fr; Am Asn Teachers Ger; Nat Asn Teachers Slavic Eastern Europ Lang. *Res:* Methods of teaching foreign languages; French civilization; English as a foreign language. *Mailing Add:* 110 Marian Dr Pueblo CO 81004

TAX, PETRUS W, b Nijmegen, Netherlands, June 12, 31; m 59; c 5. GERMANIC LANGUAGES & LITERATURES. *Educ:* Keizer Karel Univ, Drs, 57; Univ Saarlandes, PhD(Ger), 59. *Prof Exp:* Asst Ger, Univ Saarlandes, 58-62; lectr, Johns Hopkins Univ, 62-65, assoc prof, 65-68; assoc prof, 68-70, PROF GER, UNIV NC, CHAPEL HILL, 70- *Mem:* Am Asn Teachers Ger; SATlantic Mod Lang Asn; Mediaeval Acad Am; Swiss-AM Hist Soc. *Res:* Medieval German literature; folklore; Dutch. *Publ:* Auth, Wort, Sinnbild, Zahl im Tristanroman: Studien zum Denken und Werten Gottfrieds von Strassburg, 61, 2nd ed, 71 & Trevrizent, Die Verhüllungstechnik des Erzählers, In: Festschrift Hugo Moser, 74, Erich Schmidt, Berlin; ed, Notker latinus, Die Quellen zu den Psalmen (3 vols), 72-75 & Notker der Deutsche, Der Psalter (3 vols), Niemeyer, Tübingen; auth, Gahmuret zwischen Aneas und Parzival, zur Struktur der Vorgeschichte von Wolframs Parzival, Z Deut Phil, 73; Wolfram von Eschenbach's Parzival in the Light of Biblical Typology, Seminar, 73; The Grail Kingdom and Parzival's First Visit: Intrigue, Minne, Despair, In: Medieval and Renaissance Studies, Chapel Hill, 78. *Mailing Add:* Dept of Ger Univ of NC Chapel Hill NC 27514

TAY, WILLIAM S, b Amoy, China. COMPARATIVE & CHINESE LITERATURE. *Educ:* Univ Calif, San Diego, PhD(comp lit), 77. *Prof Exp:* Lectr, Chinese Univ, Hong Kong, 77-79; ASST PROF COMP LIT, UNIV CALIF, SAN DIEGO, 80- *Concurrent Pos:* Ed, Pa-feng Literary J, Hong Kong, 78-81. *Mem:* Int Comp Lit Asn; Am Comp Lit Asn; Hong Kong Comp Lit Asn; Am Studies Res Ctr; Ezra Pound Soc Nat Poetry Found. *Res:* Chinese-Western literary relations; critical theory; contemporary Chinese literature. *Publ:* Co-ed, Chinese Women Writers Today, Contemp Asian Studies, 79; auth, Orphic Variations: Essays in Comparative Literature, Su-yeh Books, 79; co-ed, China & the West: Comparative Literature Studies, Chinese Univ Press & Univ Wash Press, 80; Chinese-Western Comparative Literature, China Times Books, 80; Structuralism: Theory & Practice, Li-min Books, 80; auth, Literary Theory & Comparative Literature, China Times Books (in prep); ed, The Short Stories of Lo Hung, Yuan-Ch'in Press (in prep). *Mailing Add:* Dept of Lit Univ of Calif San Diego La Jolla CA 92093

TAYLER, NEALE HAMILTON, b Windsor, Ont, June 18, 17; m 49; c 2. ROMANCE LANGUAGES. *Educ:* Univ Toronto, BA, 39, MA, 41, PhD(Romance lang), 48. *Prof Exp:* Lectr Span, Univ Toronto, 41-46; asst prof Romance lang, Univ Western Ont, 46-47; asst prof Span & Ital, Univ Toronto, 48-62; dean fac arts & sci, 68-72, acad pres, 72-78, PROF ROMANCE LANG, WILFRID LAURIER UNIV, 62-, PRES & VCHANCELLOR, 78- *Concurrent Pos:* Humanities Res Coun Can grant, 58-59. *Mem:* Asn Can Univ Teachers Fr; Am Asn Teachers Span & Port; MLA Pub: Coauth, Lecturas iberoanmericanas, Heath, 48 & La vida espanola, 55, Appleton; auth, Has Spain a future?, Univ Toronto Quart, 52; Manuel Tamayo Y Baus: Some Early Romantic Influences, Hispania, 52; Las fuentes del teatro de Tamayo y Baus, Gredos, Madrid, 59; Quelques idees sur les Confessions de Rousseau, Asn Can Univ Teachers Fr, 66. *Mailing Add:* Wilfrid Laurier Univ Waterloo ON N2L 3C5 Can

TAYLOR, ALLAN ROSS, b Palisade, Colo, Dec 24, 31; m 58; c 5. LINGUISTICS. *Educ:* Univ Colo, Boulder, BA, 53; Univ Calif, Berkeley, PhD(ling), 69. *Prof Exp:* Teaching assoc Russ, Univ Calif, Berkeley, 58-61, lectr, 61-62; from instr to assoc prof ling, 64-77, PROF LING, UNIV COLO, BOULDER, 77- *Concurrent Pos:* Consult, MLA, 65-66; mem Russ listening comprehension comt, Col Entrance Exam Bd, Educ Testing Serv, Princeton, NJ, 66-71; dir Lakhota proj, Nat Endowment for Humanities grant, 72-75; asst dir, Siouan Lang Archives, Nat Endowment for the Humanities, 78; dir, Gros Ventre Dict, Nat Endowment for Humanities grants, 80. *Mem:* Ling Soc Am; Am Anthrop Asn. *Res:* American Indian languages; applied linguistics. *Publ:* Auth, The Classification of the Caddoan Languages, Proc Am Philos Soc, 63; Comparative Caddoan, 63 & On verbs of motion in Siouan languages, 76, Int J Am Ling; Nonverbal Communications Systems in Native North America, Semiotica, 74; Nonverbal Communication in Aboriginal North America: The Plains Sign Language, Plenum, 78; co-auth, Languages of the plains & A grammar of Lakhota, In: Handbook of North American Indians, Smithsonian Inst, (in press). *Mailing Add:* Dept of Ling Univ of Colo Boulder CO 80309

TAYLOR, DANIEL JENNINGS, b Covington, Ky, Sept 1, 41; m 66; c 2. CLASSICS, LINGUISTICS. *Educ:* Lawrence Col, BA, 63; Univ Wash, MA, 65, PhD(classics), 70. *Prof Exp:* From instr to asst prof classics, Univ Ill, Urbana, 68-74; asst prof, 74-78, ASSOC PROF CLASSICS, LAWRENCE UNIV, 78-, CHMN DEPT, 75- *Concurrent Pos:* Actg vpres & dean for Campus life, Lawrence Univ, 77-78, 79-80; Nat Endowment for Humanities fel, 80-81. *Mem:* Am Philol Asn; Am Class League; Archaeological Inst Am. *Res:* Syntax of Greek and Latin; history of linguistics; Varro. *Publ:* Auth, Rationalism in language learning, Asn Dept Foreign Lang Bull, 72; Aspects of negation in classical Greek, Studies Ling Sci, 72; Declinatio: A Study of the Linguistic Theory of M T Varro, Amsterdam: John Benjamins, 74; Varro, De Lingua Latina, 76 & Two notes on Varro, 77, Am J of Philol; Varro's mathematical models of inflection, Trans & Proc Am Philol Asn, 77; Ordo in book ten of Varro's De Lingua Latina, Melanges Collart, 78; Palaemon's Pig, Historiographia Linguistica, 81. *Mailing Add:* 2 Winona Ct Appleton WI 54911

TAYLOR, HARLEY USTUS, JR, b Weston, WVa, July 19, 25; m 51; c 2. FOREIGN LANGUAGES, GERMAN. *Educ:* WVa Univ, AB, 49, MA, 51; Ind Univ, PhD(Ger), 63. *Prof Exp:* From instr to assoc prof, 51-74, assoc chmn dept foreign lang, 68-77, acting chmn, 77-78, PROF GER, WVA UNIV, 74- *Concurrent Pos:* Cur Erich Maria Remarque Arch, WVa Univ, 76- *Mem:* Am Asn Teachers of Ger. *Res:* Erich Maria Remarque, Hermann Hesse and Ernst Weiss. *Publ:* Auth, Ernst Weiss: Fortune's Stepchild, 66, Homoerotic elements in the novels of Hermann Hesse, 67, Autobiographical elements in the novels of Erich Maria Remarque, 68, Hermann Hesse's Berthold: probable source of Narziss und Goldmund, 73, Friendship in the life of Hermann Hesse, 74, The dramas of August von Kotzebue on the New York and Philadelphia states from 1798 to 1805, 77, Erich Maria Remarque's In Western Nights Neues & The Movie All Quiet on the Western Front: Genesis, Execution, and Reception, 80, WVa Univ Philol Papers. *Mailing Add:* Dept of Foreign Lang WVa Univ 205-A Chitwood Hall Morgantown WV 26506

TAYLOR, HARVEY MARTIN, b Moline, Ill, Feb 25, 31; m 56; c 4. JAPANESE LINGUISTICS, SECOND LANGUAGE ACQUISITION. *Educ:* Seattle Pac Col, BA, 57; Univ Hawaii, Manoa, MA(ling) & MA(teaching English as second lang), 69, PhD(ling), 71. *Prof Exp:* Teacher, Harkins Sch, Mont, 54-55; ling investr, Summer Inst Ling, SVietnam, 59-62; missionary educ, Hirosaki Univ, 62-67; asst prof Janapese lang & ling, Univ Hawaii, Manoa, 71-74; asst prof ling, English Lang Inst, Univ Mich, 74-77; DIR, AM LANG ACAD, UNIV TAMPA, 77- *Concurrent Pos:* Japan Found fel, 73. *Mem:* Asn Teachers English to Speakers Other Lang; Am Coun Teaching Foreign Lang; Nat Asn Foreign Student Affairs; Soc Intercult Educ, Training & Res. *Res:* Japanese non-verbal communication, kinesics; Japanese grammar; second language teaching. *Publ:* Auth, Case in Japanese, Seton Hall Univ, 71; Japanese Potentials, Pseudo-Potentials, and Case, Papers Japanese Ling, 6/72; coauth, Japanese language situations (13 videotaped language teaching prog), GBC Closed Circuit TV Corp, 72; auth, Japanese kinetics, J Asn Teachers Japanese, 3/74; coauth, Developing Fluency in English, Prentice, 74; auth, Beyond Words: Nonverbal Communication in English as a Foreign Language, In: New Directions in Secondary Language Learning, TESOL, 75; coauth, Michigan Action English, World Times Japan, 75, 76 & 77; ed, English and Japanese in Contrast, Regents, 78. *Mailing Add:* Am Lang Acad Univ Tampa Tampa FL 33606

TAYLOR, JAMES SCOTT, b Provo, Utah, Mar 10, 30; m 59; c 7. ROMANCE & GERMANIC LANGUAGES. *Educ:* Brigham Young Univ, BA, 57, MA, 60; Ohio State Univ, PhD(foreign lang educ), 67. *Prof Exp:* Teacher, Polytech High Sch, Calif, 60-62; instr mod lang, Brigham Young Univ, 62-64; teaching assoc Span & Ger, Ohio State Univ, 64-66; from asst prof to assoc prof Span, 66-76, PROF SPAN, BRIGHAM YOUNG UNIV, 76- *Mem:* MLA; Am Coun Teaching Foreign Lang; Am Asn Teachers Span & Port; Rocky Mountain Mod Lang Asn. *Res:* Language learning and teaching; foreign language testing; teacher training. *Mailing Add:* Dept of Span & Port Brigham Young Univ Provo UT 84602

TAYLOR, M FRANCES, b Bloomington, Ind, July 21, 34;. SPANISH. *Educ:* Ind Univ Bloomington, AB, 56; Middlebury Col, BA, 61; Univ Minn, Minneapolis, PhD(foreign lang educ), 72. *Prof Exp:* Teacher Span & English, Columbus Sr High Sch, Ind, 56-63; TV teacher-consult Span, Indianapolis Pub Schs, 63-67; instr Span & on-campus supvr student teachers, High Sch, Univ Minn, Minneapolis, 67-68, teaching assoc Span, instr foreign lang educ & off-campus supvr student teachers, univ, 68-70; asst prof Span & foreign lang educ, State Univ NY Col Buffalo, 70-72; asst prof Span & foreign lang educ, 72-80, ASSOC PROF SPAN & SECONDARY LANG EDUC, RI COL, 80- *Mem:* Am Asn Teachers Span & Port; Am Coun Teaching Foreign Lang. *Res:* Foreign language education; Spanish linguistics. *Mailing Add:* 12 Hazard Ave Providence RI 02906

TAYLOR, ORLANDO LEROY, b Chattanooga, Tenn, Aug 9, 36; m 57; c 2. LINGUISTICS, SPEECH. *Educ:* Hampton Inst, BS, 57; Ind Univ, AM, 60; Univ Mich, PhD(speech path), 66. *Prof Exp:* Speech & hearing clinician, Ft Wayne State Sch, Ind, 57-58, dir speech & hearing dept, 60-62; speech therapist, Ind Univ, 58-59; asst, Univ Mich, 62, instr speech, 65; asst prof, Ind Univ, Bloomington, 65-69; vis assoc prof, Howard Univ, 69-70; assoc dir lang in educ prog, 69-70, SR RES FEL LING, CTR APPL LING, WASHINGTON, DC, 70-; PROF SPEECH PATH, HOWARD UNIV, 73- *Concurrent Pos:* Consult subcomt on compensatory educ, Soc Sci Res Coun, 69-71; consult model pre-sch prog for socially disadvantaged deaf children, Mt Carmel Guild, 69-; vis assoc prof, Univ Pittsburgh, 69-; prof commun sci, Fed City Col, 70-73; consult, Ford Found Urban Educ Prog, 72-74 & Dayton Pub Schs Minority Lang Prog, 73-74. *Mem:* Fel Am Speech & Hearing Asn; Acad Aphasia; Am Psychol Asn. *Res:* Sociolinguistics; psycholinguistics; language pathology. *Publ:* Coauth, The onset of language, In: Principles of Childhood Language Disabilities, Appleton, 72 & Language behavior and disorders associated with brain injruy, In: Current Trends in Linguistics, Mouton, The Hague, 74; co-ed, Blacks and Their Words, Ind Univ, 74. *Mailing Add:* Dept of Speech Howard Univ Washington DC 20001

TAYLOR, RANSOM THEODORE, b Munich, Ger, Dec 14, 13; US citizen; m 41; c 1. GERMAN. *Educ:* Handelschochschule St Gallen, Switz, Lic Oec, 39; Univ Calif, Los Angeles, MA, 49; Univ Calif, PhD(Ger), 56. *Prof Exp:* Master Ger, Fountain Valley Sch Boys, Colorado Springs, 42-43; lectr, Univ Calif, Santa Barbara, 50-51; instr, Yale Univ, 54-56; from asst prof to assoc prof, Univ NC, 56-66; assoc prof, Univ Nebr, Lincoln, 66-70; prof, 70-80, EMER PROF GER & COMP LIT, MARQUETTTE UNIV, 80- *Honors & Awards:* Tanner Award, 62. *Mem:* MLA; SAtlantic Mod Lang Asn (secy-treas, 59-62); Thomas Mann Ges. *Res:* Contemporary German literature; the age of Goethe. *Publ:* Auth, Eine Zeit steht Modell, F Bruckmann, Munich, 68. *Mailing Add:* Dept of Ger Marquette Univ Milwaukee WI 53233

TAYLOR, ROBERT ALLEN, b Toronto, Ont, Apr 8, 37; m 60; c 4. FRENCH LANGUAGE & LITERATURE. *Educ:* Univ Toronto, BA, 59, MA, 61, PhD(Romance philol), 65; Univ Strasbourg, dipl phonetics, 60. *Prof Exp:* Lectr French, Univ Calif, Berkeley, 62-64; asst prof, 64-69, assoc prof, 69-81, PROF FRENCH, VICTORIA COL, UNIV TORONTO, 81- *Mem:* Soc Ling Romane; MLA; Medieval Acad Am; Int Courtly Lit Soc. *Res:* Medieval translations from Latin to French; Provencal lyric poetry; Medieval French sermons and saints' lives. *Publ:* Auth, Les neologismes chez Nicole Oresme, traducteur de XIVe siecle, In: Actes Xe Congres Ling et Philol Romanes, Klincksieck, Paris, 65; Sermon anonyme sur Sainte Agnes, Travaux Ling et Lit, 69; Les prefixes de negation non- et nient- en ancien francais, In: Actes XIIIe Congres Ling et Philol Romanes, Univ Laval; La litterature occitane du moyen age, bibliograhie selective et critique, Univ Toronto, 77; Les images allegoriques d'animaux dans les poemes de Rigaut de Berbexilh, Cult Neolatina, 78; The figure of AMOR in the Old Provencal Narrative Allegories, Court & Poet, Liverpool, 81. *Mailing Add:* Dept of French Univ Toronto Toronto ON M5S 1K7 Can

TAYLOR, ROBERT EDWARD, b Portland, Ore, Nov 22, 19; m 43; c 1. FRENCH LANGUAGE & LITERATURE. *Educ:* Reed Col, AB, 43; Columbia Univ, AM, 47, PhD, 51. *Prof Exp:* From lectr to instr French, Columbia Univ, 47-50; from instr to prof, NY Univ, 50-63, asst head dept Romance & Slavic lang & lit, 59-61, actg head, 60-61, grad French adv, 61-63; head dept Romance lang, 63-71, actg chmn dept French & Ital, 78-79, PROF FRENCH, UNIV MASS, AMHERST, 63- *Concurrent Pos:* Sem assoc, Columbia Univ, 59-; chmn, Nat Fulbright Comt France, 63; ling consult 3rd ed, Webster's Int Dict. *Honors & Awards:* Chevalier, Palmes Academiques, 68. *Mem:* MLA; Renaissance Soc Am; Am Asn Teachers Fr; Asn Francaise Prof Langues Vivantes. *Res:* Bibliography; Marquis de Sade; libertinage and enlightenment in 17th and 18th centuries. *Mailing Add:* Dept of French Univ of Mass Amherst MA 01003

TAYLOR, ROBERT H, b Adrian, Minn, June 13, 30. CLASSICS HISTORY. *Educ:* St Mary's Col, BA, 53; Gregorian Univ, STL, 57; Cath Univ Am, MA, 63. *Prof Exp:* Instr, 61-65, ASSOC PROF CLASSICS, ST MARY'S COL, MINN, 65-, CHMN DEPT, 66- *Mem:* Am Philol Asn; Archeol Inst Am. *Res:* Latin methods and techniques; early Christian writers. *Mailing Add:* Dept of Classics St Mary's Col Winona MN 55987

TAYLOR, STEVEN MILLEN, b Detroit, Mich, June 13, 41; m 73; c 1. FRENCH MEDIEVAL LITERATURE. *Educ:* Wayne State Univ, PhD(French), 76. *Prof Exp:* Asst prof French & Russian, Univ Tex, El Paso, 77-78; ASST PROF MEDIEVAL FRENCH, MARQUETTE UNIV, 78- *Mem:* MLA; Am Asn Teachers Fr; Medieval Acad Am; Soc Rencesvals; Soc Prof Francais en Am. *Res:* French didactic literature of the 13th-15th centuries; French comic literature of the 13th-15th centuries; 19th century French and Russian literature. *Publ:* Auth, Heavenly humility: The Holy family as a role model for parents and children in Medieval French literature, Cahiers de Josephologie, 80; Helios and Hegemeny: The sun as a symbol for authority in Medieval French literature, Proc PMR Conf Villanova Uiv, 80; Portraits of pestilence: The plague in the works of Machaut and Boccaccio, Allegorica, 80; Constantine the Great: Folk hero of the fourth crusade, 80 & In defense of larceny: A fourteenth-century French ironic encomium, 81, Neophilologus; The virtues and vices in court: A fourteenth-century Psychomachia, Ball State Univ Forum, 81; Monsters of Misogyny: The Medieval French Dit de Chincheface and Dit de Bigorne, Allegorica, 82; coauth, Eschatological Christianity in Dostoevsky and Silone, Renascence, 82. *Mailing Add:* Dept For Lang & Lit Marquette Univ Milwaukee WI 53233

TEBBEN, JOSEPH RICHARD, b Columbus, Ohio, Nov 26, 43; m 68; c 4. CLASSICS. *Educ:* Duquesne Univ, BA, 65; Univ Pittsburgh, MA, 66; Ohio State Univ, PhD(classics), 71. *Prof Exp:* From instr to asst prof, 70-77, ASSOC PROF CLASSICS, OHIO STATE UNIV, 77- *Mem:* Am Philol Asn. *Res:* Homeric hymns; Greek epic. *Publ:* Auth, A Course Guide for Medical and Technical Terminology, Collegiate, 73; Verba: A computer-assisted course in terminology, Class World, 75; Hesiod Konkordanz, 77 & Homer Konkordanz, 77, Georg Olms; Computer resotration of Greek diacritical symbols, RELO Rev, 77. *Mailing Add:* Dept of Classics Ohio State Univ Newark OH 43055

TEDDER, JAMES D, b High Point, NC, July 14, 38. FRENCH, ITALIAN. *Educ:* Univ NC, AB, 60, PhD(Romance lang), 67; Univ Wis, MA, 61. *Prof Exp:* Asst prof French & Ger, NC Wesleyan Col, 62-64; asst prof French, Univ Tex, Austin, 67-72; ASSOC PROF FRENCH, GEORGE MASON UNIV, 72- *Mem:* Soc Exchange Ethnic & Cult Affairs; Am Asn Teachers Fr; MLA; Dante Soc Am. *Publ:* Coauth, Liberation in suicide: Meursault in the light of Dante, Fr Rev, 2/68; On the palingenetic aesthetic: A suggested term for critical inquiry, J Aesthet & Art Criticism, 72. *Mailing Add:* Dept of French George Mason Univ Fairfax VA 22030

TEDLOCK, DENNIS, American Indian Languages & Literature. See Vol IV

TEELE, ROY EARL, b Albia, Iowa, June 29, 15; wid; c 3. COMPARATIVE LITERATURE. *Educ:* Cornell Col, BA, 38; Columbia Univ, MA, 40, PhD(English & comp lit), 49. *Prof Exp:* Instr English, Ohio State Univ, 42-44; prof English & chmn dept foreign lang, Nanking Univ, 47-48; prof English, Kwansei Gakuin Univ, Japan, 50-55, 56-60; assoc prof, Southwestern Univ, 60-61; vis assoc prof English, Chinese, Japanese, Univ Tex, 61-63; prof English & chmn dept, Southwestern Univ, 63-66; vis prof English, ling & Asian studies, 66-67, vis prof ling & Asian studies, 67-68, prof, 68-71, PROF JAPANESE-CHINESE COMP LIT, UNIV TEX, AUSTIN, 71- *Concurrent Pos:* Am Coun Learned Soc res grant, 65; Japanese ed, Twayne Publ World Authors Ser, 65-81; ed, Lit East & West, 69- *Mem:* MLA; Asn Asian Studies; Asn Chinese Teachers; Asn Teachers Japanese; Am Orient Soc. *Res:* Arthurian studies; Chinese and Japanese literature and language; Noh plays and eary Heian lyric poetry. *Publ:* Auth, Through a glass darkly: A study of English translations of Chinese poetry, 49; Kyogen essential part of the world, Lit East & West, 67; Introduction to Ikkaku Sennin in four classical Asian plays, Pelican, 72; contribr, Chinese and Japanese Music-Dramas, Univ Mich, 75; Speculations on the critical principles underlying the editing of the Manyoshu, Tamkang Rev, 10/76. *Mailing Add:* 1708 McCoy Pl Georgetown TX 78626

TEELING, JOHN PAUL, English. See Vol II

TEETER, KARL VAN DUYN, b Berkeley, Calif, Mar 2, 29; m 51; c 4. LINGUISTICS. *Educ:* Univ Calif, Berkeley, AB, 56, PhD, 62. *Hon Degrees:* AM, Harvard Univ, 66. *Prof Exp:* Teaching asst Orient lang, Univ Calif, Berkeley, 56-68, grad res linguist, Thai Dict Proj & fieldworker, Surv Calif Indian Lang, 56-59; jr fel, Harvard Soc Fels, 59-62; from instr to assoc prof ling, 62-69, actg chmn dept, 66-67, chmn dept, 67-69, 70-71 & 77-78, PROF LING, HARVARD UNIV, 69- *Mem:* Ling Soc Am; Sigma Xi. *Res:* Nature of linguistic change; description and history of Algonquian. *Publ:* Auth, The Wiyot Language: Grammar and Texts, Univ Calif, 64; Descriptive linguistics in America: Triviality vs irrelevance, Word, 20: 197-206; American Indian linguistics, Ann Rev Anthrop, 72; Linguistics and anthropology, Daedalus, summer 73. *Mailing Add:* Dept of Ling Sci Harvard Univ Cambridge MA 02138

TENENBAUM, LOUIS, b Chelsea, Mass, Aug 23, 22; m 44; c 5. ITALIAN. *Educ:* Univ Wis, AB, 47, AM, 48, PhD(French), 53. *Prof Exp:* Instr French & Ital, Univ Wis, 53-54; instr, Univ Mich, 54-57; from asst prof to assoc prof Romance lang, 57-65, PROF ROMANCE LANG & CHMN DEPT ITAL LANG & LIT, UNIV COLO, BOULDER, 65- *Honors & Awards:* Cavaliere, Order of Merit, Italy, 66. *Mem:* Am Asn Teachers Ital; Dante Soc Am. *Res:* Modern Italian literature. *Publ:* Auth, Vitaliano Brancati and Sicilian eroticism, Bks Abroad, summer 57; Character treatment in Pavese's fiction, Symposium, summer 61; The Italian novel: Traditions and new paths, In: Contemporary European Novelists, Southern Ill Univ, 68. *Mailing Add:* Dept of Ital Lang & Lit Univ of Colo Boulder CO 80302

TERAKURA, HIROKO, b Osaka, Japan, May 8, 36. JAPANESE LINGUISTICS. *Educ:* Osaka Kyooiku Daigaku, BA, 59; Univ Wis-Madison, MA, 76, PhD(Japanese ling), 80. *Prof Exp:* Vis asst prof Japanese, Univ BC, 79-80; vis asst prof, 80-82, ASST PROF JAPANESE, UNIV ALTA, 82- *Mem:* Ling Soc Am; Asn Teachers Japanese; Can Asn Asian Studies; Pac Northwest Conf Foreign Lang. *Res:* Japanese linguistics, syntax, semantics and pragmatics; applied linguistics, teaching English or Japanese as a foreign language. *Publ:* Coauth, On the assertive predicate no desu in Japanese, Papers from 14th Regional Meeting Chicago Ling Soc, 78. *Mailing Add:* #706-11145 87 Ave Edmonton AB T6G 0Y1 Can

TERASAKI, ETSUKO TAKEMOTO, US citizen; m 61; c 1. JAPANESE LANGUAGE & LITERATURE. *Educ:* New Sch Soc Res, BA, 60; Yale Univ, MA, 61; Columbia Univ, PhD(Japanese lang & lit), 69. *Prof Exp:* Asst prof lang & lit, Cornell Univ, 67-73, res assoc, 73-76, vis assoc prof Japanese lit, 75-76, sr res assoc, 76-77. *Mem:* Asn Asian Sudies; Japan Soc. *Res:* No theatre; life and works of Lady Ise; Matsuo Basho. *Publ:* Auth, The saga diary by Matsuo Basho, Lit East & West, 6/72; transl, Hori Tatsuo, The holy family, Japan Quart, 74; Naka Kansuke, The Silver Spoon, Chicago Rev Press, 76; auth, Hatsushigure: A linked verse series by Basho and his disciples, Harvard J Asiatic Studies, 76; The representation of reality in the No Theatre: Hachi no ki, J Assoc Teachers of Japanese, 11/78; transl, Lady Ise's poems, In: Women Poets from Antiquity to Now, Schocken Bks, 80; Basho's The Summer Moon, Cut Bank 14, spring-summer, 80. *Mailing Add:* 115 Ellis Hollow Creek Rd Ithaca NY 14850

TERDIMAN, RICHARD, b New Rochelle, NY, Oct 18, 41. NARRATIVE LITERATURE & LITERARY THEORY. *Educ:* Amherst Col, BA, 63; Yale Univ, PhD(French), 68. *Prof Exp:* From instr to asst prof French, Swarthmore Col, 67-72; vis asst prof French & comp lit, Univ Calif, Berkeley, 72-74; assoc prof French, Mills Col, 74-76; ASSOC PROF FRENCH LIT & HEAD FRENCH SECT, UNIV CALIF, SAN DIEGO, 76- *Concurrent Pos:* Vis lectr philos of criticism, San Francisco State Univ, 71. *Mem:* MLA; Proust Res Asn. *Res:* Nineteenth century fiction; Proust; dialectial criticism. *Publ:* Auth, The structure of Villon's Testament, Publ Mod Lang Asn Am, 12/67; Flaubert formaliste, Rev Sci Humaines, 10-12/70; Problematical virtuosity: Dante's depiction of the thieves (Inferno XXIV-XXV), Dante Studies, 73; The Dialectics of Isolation, Yale Univ, 76; Counter-humorists: Strategies of ideological critique in Mary and Flaubert, Diacritics, fall 79; Materialist imagination: Notes toward a theory of literary strategies, Helios, winter 79; Structures of initiation: On semiotic education and its contradictions in Balzac, Yale Fr Studies, 6/82; Discours et contre-discours: D'une des-orientation flaubertienne, In: L'Orient de Flaubert: Constituents d'une ecriture d'avant-garde, Presses Universitaires de France, 82. *Mailing Add:* Dept of Lit C-005 Univ of Calif San Diego La Jolla CA 92093

TER HORST, ROBERT, b Paterson, NJ, July 15, 29; m 61; c 2. SPANISH LITERATURE. *Educ:* Princeton Univ, AB, 52; Johns Hopkins Univ, MA, 61, PhD(Span), 63. *Prof Exp:* Asst prof Span, Univ Wis-Madison, 63-64; asst prof, Duke Univ, 64-66; from asst prof to assoc prof Span lit, Univ Rochester, 66-69; PROF SPAN LIT, UNIV ARIZ, 69- *Concurrent Pos:* Vis prof Span, Universite de Lille III, 76-77; sr fel, Nat Humanities Ctr, 82- *Res:* Spanish and comparative literature. *Publ:* Auth, Calderon: The Secular Plays, Ky Univ Press, 82. *Mailing Add:* Dept of Romance Lang Univ of Ariz Tucson AZ 85721

TERLECKI, TYMON TADEUSZ J, b Przemysl, Poland, Aug 10, 05; m 47. POLISH LITERATURE. *Educ:* King John Casimir Univ, PhD(Polish lit), 32. *Prof Exp:* Prof world drama, State Inst Dramatic Art, Warsaw, 34-39; sr lectr Polish lit, Polish Univ Abroad, London, 48-52; vis prof, Univ Chicago, 64-65, prof, 65-72; vis prof, Univ Ill, Chicago Circle, 72-77; EMER PROF POLISH LIT, UNIV CHICAGO, 72-; PROF POLISH LIT, POLISH UNIV ABROAD, LONDON, 78- *Concurrent Pos:* Fr Govt study grant, Sorbonne & Col France, 33-34; mem, Bd Lit Adv Munic Theaters, Warsaw, 35-39; mem, Philol Comn Polish Acad Arts & Sci, Cracow, 35-39; vis res scholar, Univ Tex, Austin, 78. *Honors & Awards:* Awards, Soc Polish Arts & Lett, Chicago, 71 & Alfred Jurzykowski Found, 72; Polonia Restituta, 78. *Mem:* Polish Soc Arts & Sci Abroad; Polish Inst Arts & Sci Am; Polish Lit & Hit Soc, Paris; PEN Club; Am Asn Teachers Slavic & East Europ Lang. *Res:* History of Polish literature; relationships between Polish and European theatre; Edward Gordon Craig Archives, Paris, Los Angeles and Austin. *Publ:* Coauth & ed, Straty kultury polskiej (2 vols), Ksiaznica Polska, Glasgow, 45; auth, Le theatre 1919-1939, In: Pologne 1919-1939, Vol III, Ed Baconniere, 47; Krytyka personalistyczna, Oficyna Poetowi Malarzy, London, 57; Ludzie, ksiazki i kulisy, B Swiderski, London, 62; Pani Helena, Veritas, London, 62; coauth & ed, Literatura polska na obczyznie 1940-1960 (2 vols), B Swiderski, London, 64-65; Stanislaw Wyspianski and the Poetics of Symbolist Drama, NY, 70; The Greatness and Ill Fortune of Stanislaw Wyspianski, Rome, 70. *Mailing Add:* 84 Hazlewell Rd London SW England United Kingdom

TERNES, HANS, b Kogolniceanu, Romania, Sept 10, 37; US citizen; m 62; c 2. GERMAN LITERATURE, AESTHETICS. *Educ:* Univ Ill, BA, 61, MA, 63; Univ Pa, PhD(Ger), 68. *Prof Exp:* Lectr English, Univ Freiburg, Ger, 65-66; instr Ger, Univ Pa, 66-68; asst prof, 68-75, ASSOC PROF GER, LAWRENCE UNIV, 76- *Mem:* Am Asn Teachers Ger; MLA. *Res:* Twentieth century German literature, primarily Thomas Mann, Friedrich Dürrenmatt, Franz Kafka; problems in aesthetics, the grotesque; genre studies, nature poetry. *Publ:* Auth, Das problem der gerechtigkeit in Dürenmatts Die Panne, Germanic Notes, 75; Das Groteske in den Werken Thomas Manns, Stuttgarter Arbeiten zur Germanistik, 75; Anmerkungen zur Zeitblomgestalt, Germanic Notes, 76; co-ed, Probleme der Komparatistik & Interpretation, Festschrift for Prof Andre von Gronicka, Bouvier Vlg, Bonn, 78; contribr, Franz Kafka's Hunter Gracchus: an interpretation, In: Festschrift for Prof Andre von Gronicka, 78; The fantastic in the works of Franz Kafha, In: The Scope of the Fantastic, Greenwood Press, Inc, 82. *Mailing Add:* Dept of Ger Lawrence Univ College Ave Appleton WI 54911

TERRAS, RITA, b Ger; US citizen; m 51; c 1. GERMAN LANGUAGE & LITERATURE. *Educ:* Univ Ill, Urbana, BA, 61, MA, 66; Univ Wis-Madison, PhD(Ger), 69. *Prof Exp:* Lectr Ger, Univ Wis, 69-70; asst prof, Univ RI, 71-72; asst prof, 72-76, ASSOC PROF GER, CONN COL, 76- *Concurrent Pos:* Vis fac fel, Yale Univ, 78-79; vis assoc prof Ger, Brown Univ, 81-82. *Mem:* MLA; Am Asn Teachers Ger; Lessing Soc; Am Soc 18th Century Studies. *Res:* German Classicism & Romanticism; the contemporary German novel; contemporary poetry. *Publ:* Auth, Wilhelm Heinses Asthetik, Fink, Munich, 72; Heinse und Lessing, In: Vol II, 70 & Friedrich Justus Riedel, In: Vol IV, 72, Lessing Yearbk; Goethe's use of the mirror image, 12/75, & The development of the three faculties from Leibniz to Kant, 78, Monatshefte; The Doppelgänger in German Romantic literature, In: Symposium on Romanticism, Conn Col, 77; Juvenal und die satirische Struktur der Nachwachen von Bonaventura, Ger Quart, 1/79; Ein unbekannter Brief Gottfried Benns an Ina Seidel, In: Jahrbuch der deutschen Schillergesellschaft, Kröner, Stuttgart, 79. *Mailing Add:* Dept of Ger Box 1586 Conn Col New London CT 06320

TERRAS, VICTOR, b Estonia, Jan 21, 21; US citizen; m 51; c 1. SLAVIC LANGUAGES & LITERATURE. *Educ:* Univ Estonia, Cand Phil, 41, Mag Phil, 42; Univ Chicago, PhD(Russ lit), 63. *Prof Exp:* From instr to assoc prof Russ, Univ Ill, 59-65, prof Slavic lang & lit, 65-66; prof Slavic lang, Univ Wis-Madison, 66-70; chmn dept, 72-76, PROF SLAVIC LANG, BROWN UNIV, 70- *Res:* Comparative Slavic linguistics; Russian literature. *Publ:* Auth, The Young Dostoevsky, 1846-1849: A Critical Study, Mouton, The Hague & Paris, 69; Belinskij and Russian Literary Criticism, Univ Wis-Madison, 73; A Karamazov Companion: Commentary on the Genesis, Language, and Style of Dostoevsky's Novel, Univ Wis-Madison, 81; Aleksis Rannit: Lühimonograafia, Lund, 75. *Mailing Add:* Dept of Slavic Lang Brown Univ Providence RI 02912

TERRASSE, JEAN, b Belgium, Mar 8, 40; m 67; c 1. FRENCH LITERATURE. *Educ:* Free Univ Brussels, Cand Phil, 60, lic phil, 62, DPhil, 68. *Prof Exp:* From vis asst prof to asst prof, 68-71, assoc prof, 71-82, PROF FRENCH, MCGILL UNIV, 82- *Honors & Awards:* Award, Acad Royale Lang et Lit Fr, Belg, 74. *Mem:* Soc Can Etude 18th Siecle; Am Soc 18th Century Studies; NAm Asn Study J J Rousseau; Soc Francaise D'etude du XVIII' Siecle. *Res:* French literature of the 18th century; modern French poetry. *Publ:* Auth, Jean Jacques Rousseau et la quete de l'age d'or, Palais des Acad, Brussels, 70; Le mal du siecle et l'ordre immuable, Andre de Rache, 73; Rhetorique de l'essai litteraire, Univ Que, 77; Jean-Jacques Rousseau et la societe du XVIII' siecle, Univ Ottawa Quart, 1-3/81. *Mailing Add:* Dept of Fr Lang & Lit McGill Univ Montreal PQ H3A 1X9 Can

TERRELL, TRACY D, b Huntington, WVa, June 23, 43. LINGUISTICS. *Educ:* Marshall Univ, BA, 65; Univ Tex, Austin, PhD(ling), 69. *Prof Exp:* Asst prof, 70-80, ASSOC PROF SPAN & LING, UNIV CALIF, IRVINE, 80- *Concurrent Pos:* Shoptalk ed, Hispania, Am Asn Teachers Span & Port; Am Coun Teaching Foreign Lang. *Res:* Applied linguistics; Spanish syntax and phonology. *Mailing Add:* Dept of Span & Port Univ of Calif Irvine CA 92664

TERRIZZI, ANTHONY R, b New Brunswick, NJ, Oct 4, 39; m 64; c 3. TWENTIETH CENTURY ITALIAN FICTION. *Educ:* Rutgers Univ, PhD(Ital), 72. *Prof Exp:* asst prof, 67-80, ASSOC PROF ITAL, UNIV MASS, AMHERST, 81- *Mem:* Am Asn Teachers Ital; Am Coun Teaching Foreign Lang; Am Asn Teachers Ital (sec-treas, 77-80). *Res:* Twentieth century Italian fiction. *Publ:* Auth, Another look at Corrado Alvaro's L'uomo nel labirinto, Forum Italicum, 3/73; Notes on Alrano's Gente in Aspromonte, Romance Notes, Vol XXII, No 2, 81; Gioranni Arpino, Columbia Dict of Modern European Literature, 80. *Mailing Add:* 61 Pondview Dr Amherst MA 01002

TERRY, EDWARD DAVIS, b Eclectic, Ala, May 19, 27. SPANISH AMERICAN. *Educ:* Univ Ala, BS(com) & BS(bus admin), 49, MA, 53; Univ NC, PhD(Romance lang), 58. *Prof Exp:* Grad asst, Univ Ala, 50 & 53; instr Span, Sullins Col, 53-55; part-time instr, Univ NC, 57-58; asst prof, Southern Methodist Univ, 58-62; asst prof Spanish, Univ Tenn, Knoxville, 62-64; assoc prof, 64-70, dir Latin Am studies prog, 66-72, PROF SPANISH, UNIV ALA, 70- *Concurrent Pos:* Ed, SEastern Latin Americanist, 70-73. *Mem:* Am Asn Teachers Span & Port; SAtlantic Mod Lang Asn; Latin Am Studies Asn; Southeastern Coun Latin Am Studies (secy-treas, 70-73, pres, 76-77). *Res:* Contemporary Spanish American literature; Spanish language academies; Yucatan, Mexico. *Publ:* Ed, Artists and Writers in the Evolution of Latin America, Univ Ala, 69; Literature: A key to understanding Spanish America, Ann Southeastern Conf Latin Am Studies, 3/71; The humanities-social science linkage in the interdisciplinary course, Southeastern Latin Americanist, 6/73; Spanish lexicography and the Real Academia Espanola: A sketch, Hisp, 12/74; auth, La defensa y difusion del idioma y el estado actual de la ensenanza del espanol en los Estados Unidos de America, In: Memoria del Sexto Congreso de la Asociacion de Academias de la Lengua Espanola, Caracas, Venezuela, Acad Venezolana, 74. *Mailing Add:* PO Box 1422 University AL 35486

TERRY, ROBERT MEREDITH, b Danville, VA, Dec 16, 39; m 65; c 3. ROMANCE LANGUAGES. *Educ:* Randolph-Macon Col, BA, 62; Duke Univ, PhD(Romance lang), 66. *Prof Exp:* Instr French, Duke Univ, 63-64, 65-66; asst prof, Univ Fla, 66-68; ASSOC PROF FRENCH, UNIV RICHMOND, 68- *Concurrent Pos:* Ed, Les Nouvelles. *Mem:* Am Asn Teachers Fr; Am Coun Teaching For Lang. *Res:* Contemporary French language; foreign language methodology. *Publ:* Auth, The frequency of use of the interrogative formula est-ce que, 5/67 & Faut-il or Est-ce qu'il faut: Inversion vs est-ce que, 2/70, Fr Rev; Contemporary French Interrogative Structures, Ed Cosmos, 70; Students work with Monique and learn French, Foreign Lang Ann, 4/77; En Bref . . . Enfin, Univ Richmond, 77; Let Cinderella & Luke Skywalker help you teach the passe compose & imperfect, Am Coun Teaching Foreign Lang, 78; Open syllabification and diphthongization of e and o in preliterary Spanish, Word, 7/80; Concepts of pastness: The passe compose and the imperfect, For Lang Annual, 4/81. *Mailing Add:* Dept of Mod Foreign Lang Univ Richmond Richmond VA 23173

TESCHNER, RICHARD VINCENT, b Madison, Wis, July 19, 42. SPANISH, LINGUISTICS. *Educ:* Stanford Univ, AB, 65; Middlebury Col, MA, 66; Univ Wis-Madison, PhD(Span), 72. *Prof Exp:* From instr to asst prof Span, Univ Wis-Parkside, 70-74; asst prof, Univ Iowa, 74-76; asst prof, 76-82, ASSOC PROF SPAN, UNIV TEX, EL PASO, 82- *Concurrent Pos:* Dir, Nat Endowment for the Humanities sponsored Surv of Res Tool Needs in the Hisp Lang and Lit, 77-78. *Mem:* Ling Soc Am; MLA; Am Asn Teachers Span & Port; Ling Asn Southwest; Am Asn Applied Ling. *Res:* Spanish lexicography; bilingualism; Hispanic bibliography. *Publ:* Coauth, En onda: An Intermediate-level Spanish Reader, Norton, 74; auth, A critical, annotated bibliography of Anglicisms in Spanish, Hisp, 10/74; Southwest Spanish lexicography: problems and solutions, Int J Socioling, 74; coauth, Spanish and English of United States Hispanos: A Critical, Annotated, Linguistic Bibliography, Ctr Appl Ling, 75; El diccionario del espanol chicano, The Dictionary of Chicano Spanish, Inst Mod Lang, 77; Espanol escrito: curso para hispano-hablantes bilingües, Charles Scribner's Sons, 78; Festschrift for Jacob Ornstein, Newbury House, 80; Historical-psychological portraits as complements to sociolinguistic studies in relational bilingualism, Bilingual Review, 81. *Mailing Add:* Dept of Mod Lang Univ of Tex El Paso TX 79968

TESTA, DANIEL PHILIP, b St Paul, Minn, June 22, 27; m 63; c 2. SPANISH LITERATURE. *Educ:* Univ Minn, BA, 52, MA, 55; Univ Mich, PhD, 62. *Prof Exp:* Instr Span, Univ Mich, 57-59; from instr to asst prof, Univ Ill, 59-65; resident chmn, Syracuse Univ in Spain, 75-76 & 78; asst prof, 65-70, chmn dept, 74-81, ASSOC PROF SPAN, SYRACUSE UNIV, 70- *Mem:* MLA; Am Asn Teachers Span & Port. *Res:* Sixteenth and 17th century Spanish literature; Critical theory; Chicano literature; Cervantes. *Publ:* Auth, Botelho de Carvalho's Fabula de Piramo y Tisbe, Rev Estudios Hisp, 11/68; co-ed, The Spanish generation of 1936, Symp, summer 68; Spanish Writers of 1936: Crisis and Commitment in the Poetry of the Thirties and the Forties, Tamesis Bks, 73; co-ed & transl, Luigi Pirandello, On Humor, Studies Comp Lit, 74; auth, Love in Alurista's poetry, Revista Chicano-Riquena, 1/76; Anaya's Bless Me, Ultima, Latin Am Res Rev, 1/78; Don Quijote y la intertextualidad, Cerantes: Su obra y su mundo, Madrid, 81; Cervantes Don Quijote: The Ego Divided and Doubled, Actas, State Univ NY, Albany. *Mailing Add:* Dept of Foreign Lang Span & Port Syracuse Univ Syracuse NY 13210

TETEL, MARCEL, b Paris, France, Oct 11, 32; US citizen; m 57; c 1. ROMANCE LANGUAGES. *Educ:* Univ Chattanooga, BA, 54; Emory Univ, MA, 56; Univ Wis, PhD, 62. *Prof Exp:* From asst prof to assoc prof, 60-68, PROF ROMANCE LANG, DUKE UNIV, 68- *Concurrent Pos:* Am Coun Learned Soc grant-in-aid, 63; Fulbright res grant, Florence, 66-67; Guggenheim fel, 70; Am Philos Soc grant, 73. *Mem:* Int Asn Fr Studies; Am Asn Teachers Fr; Am Asn Teachers Ital; MLA; SAtlantic Mod Lang Asn. *Res:* French and Italian Renaissance. *Publ:* Auth, Rabelais et L'Italie, 69, Olschki, Florence; Rabelais, 67 & Montaigne, 74, Twayne; ed, Pirandello: Enrico IV, Appleton, 71; auth, Marguerite de Navarre's Heptameron: Themes, Language and Structure, 73 & ed, Symbolism and Modern Literature, 78, Duke Univ; auth, Lectures sceviennes: L'embleme et les mots, Klincksieck, Paris (in press); ed, Colloque Montaigne: Duke-UNC, Nizet, Paris (in press). *Mailing Add:* Dept of Romance Lang Duke Univ Durham NC 27706

TETZLAFF, OTTO WALTER, b Noerenberg, Ger, Aug 26, 30; US citizen; m 58; c 3. GERMANIC LANGUAGES & LITERATURE. *Educ:* Northern Ill Univ, BA, 62; Univ Ill, MA, 63; Univ Tex, PhD(Ger lang), 68. *Prof Exp:* Instr Ger & Latin, Northern Ill Univ, 63-68; asst prof Ger, Va Polytech Inst, 68-69; assoc prof, 69-71, PROF GER & CHMN DEPT, ANGELO STATE UNIV, 71- *Mem:* MLA; Am Asn Teachers Ger; Am Class League. *Res:* Eighteenth century German Literature; Gottsched and his age; Gottsched's Weltweisheit edited. *Publ:* Auth & transl, Handbook for German Immigrants, 72; auth, Effi Briests Hollaendische Nachfolgerin, Fontaneblaetter, Vol II, No 2; Neo-Latin Drama of the Netherlands and its influence upon German Literature, Amsterdamer Beitraege aelteren Germanistik, 72; Das Gemeinsame, Die Götter lesen nicht, Bonn, 75; A Guide for German Immigrants, Rice Univ Studies, 77. *Mailing Add:* Dept of Mod Lang Angelo State Univ San Angelo TX 76901

THANIEL, GEORGE, b Messinia, Greece, Feb 23, 38; Can citizen. CLASSICS, MODERN GREEK. *Educ:* Univ Athens, BA, 62; McMaster Univ, MA, 68, PhD(classics), 71. *Prof Exp:* From lectr to asst prof, 72-78, ASSOC PROF GREEK, UNIV TORONTO, 78- *Concurrent Pos:* Univ of Toronto travelling awards, 72, 74, Norwood travelling award, 78-79. *Mem:* Am Philol Asn; Class Asn Can; Mod Greek Studies Asn; Can Comp Lit Asn; Soc Mediter Studies. *Res:* Modern Greek; comparative literature; classics. *Publ:* Auth, Vergil's leaf and bird-similes of ghosts, Phoenix, 71; Le scepticisme et le refus de croyance touchant l'au-dela dans la Rome du 1er siecle avant J-C, Antiq Class, 73; George Seferis's Thrush and the poetry of Ezra Pound, Comp Lit Studies, 74; George Seferis's Thrush: A modern descent to the underworld, Can Rev Comp Lit, 76; George Seferis's Thrush and T S Eliot's Four Quartets, Neohelicon, 77; Odysseus and Deatz: A Study of Kagantgakis' Odyssey, Neo-Hallenika, 78; A Landmark Book on Seferis, Neo-Hallenies, 81; The Lepidopterist of Anguish Nikos Kachtitisis, Athens, 81. *Mailing Add:* Dept of Classics Univ Toronto Toronto ON M5S 1A1 Can

THATCHER, DAVID S, English. See Vol II

THAYER, TERENCE KELSO, b Indianapolis, Ind, Oct 9, 40; m 62; c 2. GERMAN. *Educ:* Oberlin Col, BA, 62; Harvard Univ, PhD(Ger lang & lit), 67. *Prof Exp:* Asst prof, 67-72, ASSOC PROF GER LANG, IND UNIV, BLOOMINGTON, 72- *Concurrent Pos:* Res fel, Alexander von Humboldt-Found, Bonn, 76. *Mem:* MLA; Am Asn Teachers Ger; Am Soc 18th Century Studies. *Res:* Eighteenth-century German literature; German poetry; Kleist. *Publ:* Auth, Klopstock's Occasional Poetry, Lessing Yearbk II, 70; Hans Castorp's hermetic adventures, Ger Rev, 11/71; Knowing and being: Mörike's Denk'es, o Seele!, Ger Quart, 5/72; Klopstock and the literary afterlife, Literaturwissenschaftliches Jahrbuch, 73; Kleist's Don Fernando and Das Erdbeben in Chili, Colloquia Germanica, 11/78; Rhetoric and the rhetorical in Klopstock's odes, Euphorion, 80; From topos to mythos: The poet as immortalizer in Klopstock's works, J English & Germanic Philol, 80-81; Intimations of immortality: Klopstock's ode Der Eislauf, In: Goethezeit, Festschrift Stuart Atkins, Francke Verlag, Bern, 81. *Mailing Add:* Dept of Ger Lang Ind Univ Bloomington IN 47401

THELANDER, DOROTHY RAMONA, b Brooklyn, NY, Jan 21, 27; m 65. FRENCH. *Educ:* Columbia Univ, BA, 48, MA, 50, PhD(French), 60. *Prof Exp:* Lectr French, Sch Gen Studies, Columbia Univ, 54-57; instr, Univ Chicago, 60-63; asst prof, Univ Kans, 63-65; ASSOC PROF FRENCH, UNIV ILL, CHICAGO CIRCLE, 68- *Mem:* MLA; Am Soc 18th Century Studies. *Res:* Eighteenth century French novel; epistolary fiction. *Publ:* Auth, The oak and the thinking reed, Studies Voltaire & 18th Century, Vol CII; Laclos and the Epistolary Novel, Droz, Geneva, 63. *Mailing Add:* Dept of French Univ of Ill at Chicago Circle Chicago IL 60680

THELEN, LYNN MARSHA, b Providence, RI, May 13, 49; m 74; c 1. MEDIEVAL LITERATURE. *Educ:* Pa State Univ, BA, 71; Univ Pa, MA, 73, PhD(Ger), 79. *Prof Exp:* Lectr Ger, Univ Pa, 76-79; vis lectr & prof, Bryn Mawr Col, 79-80; ASST PROF GERMAN, URSINUS COL, PA, 80- *Mem:* Am Asn Teachers of Ger; MLA; NEastern Mod Lang Asn. *Res:* Medieval German literature, nineteenth century novella, specifically the medieval epic and Minnesang. *Publ:* Auth, The Internal Source and Function of King Gunther's Bridal Quest, Monatshefte (in prep). *Mailing Add:* Dept of Ger 021 Corson Hall Ursinus Col Collegeville PA 19426

THERRIEN, MADELEINE B, b Fribourg, Switz, Mar 27, 31. FRENCH LITERATURE. *Educ:* Univ Fribourg, cert English, 52; Nat Univ Athens, cert French, 56; Univ Paris, lic, 60; Mich State Univ, PhD(French), 66. *Prof Exp:* Instr Latin, French & Ger, Ctr Pedag, Paris, 58-59; instr, Lycee Buffon, Paris, 60; asst French, Mich State Univ, 61-62; lectr, Univ Calif, Riverside, 62-64; asst prof, Mich State Univ, 64-67; from asst prof to assoc prof, Emory Univ, 67-76; PROF FRENCH & CHMN DEPT, UNIV MD, 76- *Concurrent Pos:* Exec bd, Soc francaise d'etude du 18th siecle, 74-79; Elections comt, Parker Prize comt & Delegate assembly, MLA, 77-79; exec bd, Int Soc 18th Century Studies & Soc Roucher-Chenier, 80-82; chmn comt res activ, MLA, 81-84. *Mem:* MLA; Am Asn Teachers Fr; Am Soc 18th Century Studies (first vpres, 78-79, pres, 79-80); Soc Fr Etude 18th Siecle; SAtlantic Mod Lang Asn (pres, 81-82). *Res:* Eighteenth century literature; Rousseau. *Publ:* Auth, Les liaisons dangereuses: Une interpretation psychologique, Soc d'edition d'ensignement superieus Paris, 73; Morale sociale et ethique personnelle dans La nouvelle Heloïse, Rev Sci Humaines, 76; Rousseau: Lucidite et sincerite, Trans Fourth Int Cong Enlightenment, 76; Rousseau: Le vocabulaire de l'autoestimation, Crocker Festschrift, 79; Aspects de texture verbale dans les liensons dangereuses, Rev Hist Lit France, 4/82. *Mailing Add:* Dept of French & Ital Lang & Lit Univ of Md College Park MD 20742

THIBAULT, JOHN CROWELL, b Spalding, Mich, Apr 27, 22; m 61; c 1. CLASSICAL PHILOLOGY. *Educ:* Xavier Univ, LittB, 44; Loyola Univ, Ill, MA, 47; Univ Ill, MA, 56, PhD, 60. *Prof Exp:* Asst prof Latin, Greek & English, Univ Calif, Santa Barbara, 61-65; assoc prof Class lang, 65-70, chmn dept, 67-81, PROF CLASS LANG, UNIV MO-COLUMBIA, 70- *Mem:* Am Philol Asn; Archaeol Inst Am. *Res:* Philosophy; ancient history; Latin and Greek literature. *Publ:* Auth, Ovid's Exile, Univ Calif, 64. *Mailing Add:* Dept of Class Studies Univ of Mo Columbia MO 65201

THIELEMANN, LELAND JAMES, b Portland, Ore, June 12, 15; m 40; c 3. FRENCH LITERATURE. *Educ:* Univ Ore, BA, 36; Columbia Univ, MA, 39, PhD, 50. *Prof Exp:* Lectr French, Univ Calif, Los Angeles, 47-50, from asst prof to assoc prof, 50-64; PROF FRENCH, UNIV TEX, AUSTIN, 64- *Concurrent Pos:* Teaching asst French & Greek, Univ Ore, 36-38; consult panelist, Nat Endowment for Humanities, 70-73. *Mem:* Fr Soc Studies 18th Century. *Res:* Eighteenth century French literature; the tradition of Hobbes in 18th century France; Rousseau and Mme Dupin. *Publ:* Auth, Thomas Hobbes dans l'Encyclopedie, Rev Hist Lit France, 7/51; Voltaire and Hobbism, In: Studies on Voltaire and the 18th Century, Vol X, 59; Diderot's encyclopedic article Juste: Its sources and significance, In: Diderot Studies, Vol IV, 63. *Mailing Add:* 2401 Camino Alto Austin TX 78746

THIESSEN, JACK, b De Salaberry, Man, Apr 14, 31; m 61; c 2. GERMAN LANGUAGE & LITERATURE. *Educ:* Univ Marburg, PhD, 61. *Prof Exp:* Assoc prof Ger, 61-73, sabbatical grant, 68-69, PROF GER, UNIV WINNIPEG, 73-, HEAD DEPT, 61- *Concurrent Pos:* Vis prof, Strasbourg, 68-69. *Mem:* Asn Can Univ Teachers Ger; Ger-Can Acad Exchange Asn (pres, 71-). *Res:* Mennonite dialectology and folklore; study of Yiddish. *Publ:* Auth, Studien zum deutschsprachigen Wortschatz der kanadischen Mennoniten, Elwert, Marburg, 63; Es war einmal--Once Upon a Time, Friesen, Altona, 67; Mennonite proverbs and sayings, Jahrbuch Niederdeutsch, 68; Arnold Dyck--the Mennonite artist, Mennonite Live Rev, 69; Canadian-Mennonite literature, Can Lit, spring 72; Yiddish in Canada, Schuster, 73. *Mailing Add:* Dept of Ger Univ of Winnipeg Winnipeg MB R3B 2E9 Can

THIHER, O ALLEN, b Ft Worth, Tex, Apr 4, 41. MODERN FRENCH & COMPARATIVE LITERATURE. *Educ:* Univ Tex, BA, 63; Univ Wis, PhD(French), 68. *Prof Exp:* Asst prof French, Duke Univ, 67-69 & Middlebury Col, 69-76; ASSOC PROF FRENCH, UNIV MO-COLUMBIA, 76- *Concurrent Pos:* Guggenheim Found fel, 76-77. *Mem:* MLA; Am Asn Teachers Fr; Societe des Etudes Celiniennes. *Res:* Modern comparative fiction; film criticism and theory. *Publ:* Auth, Celine and Sartre, Philol Quart, 71; Celine: The Novel as Delirium, Rutgers Univ, 72; Le feu follet . . ., PMLA, 73; Post-modern dilemmas . . ., Boundary 2, 76; Man Ray and the limits of metaphor, Dada/Surrealism, 76; Bunuel's Un Chien andalou, Film/Lit, 77; Montherlant's tragic vision, Ky Quart Romance Studies, 78; The Cinematic Muse, Univ Mo Press, 79. *Mailing Add:* Dept of Romance Lang Univ of Mo Columbia MO 65201

THILL, RICHARD SIMMONS, b Alexandria, La, Nov 2, 35; m 59; c 2. GERMAN LANGUAGE & LITERATURE, FOLKLORE. *Educ:* Univ of Calif, Riverside, BA, 61; Univ Calif, Los Angeles, MA, 65, PhD(Ger lang), 73. *Prof Exp:* Instr, Pitzer Col, 66-67; ASSOC PROF GER, UNIV NEBR, OMAHA, 67-, CHAIR, DEPT FOR LANG, 82- *Concurrent Pos:* Bus mgr, Mod Lang J, 76-79; Mid Am State Univ Asn hon lectr, 81-82; fel, Univ Nebr Grad Col, 79- *Mem:* MLA; Am Coun Teaching Foreign Lang; Nat Asn Teacher Ger; Am Folklore Soc; Am Folklore Soc. *Publ:* Auth, A manual and selective bibliography for fieldworkers in the Omaha Folklore Project, Part I: Omaha area library resources for the study of folklore, Nebr Asn Teachers For Lang & Univ Nebr Senate Res Comt, 75; Users' Manual for the Computerized German Drills on the UNO KRONOS 2 1 Timesharing System, Univ Nebr, 75, rev ed, 76; A rose by any other name: computers, traditions and the folklorist, Tenn Folklore Soc Bull, 3/74; coauth, An open-ended application of information processing techniques in the humanities, SIGLASH Newslett, 4/75; GRAREP and GRPSTD: automated, individualized grade reports, Univ Nebr, 12/75; History and purpose of the Omaha Folklore Project: A synopsis prepared for the membership of the Nebraska Association of Teachers of German, Tenn Folklore Soc Bull, 12/75; auth, The monster machine: A modern topos in scholarship, literature and oral tradition essays on the history of myths and legends, 77. *Mailing Add:* Dept of Foreign Lang Univ of Nebr Omaha NE 68182

THOENELT, KLAUS, b Estrella, Brazil, July 8, 26; m 61; c 1. GERMAN, FRENCH. *Educ:* Univ Freiburg, PhD(Ger & French), 61. *Prof Exp:* Studienrat, Gym Säckingen, Ger, 58-61; instr Ger & French, Bates Col, 61-62; from asst prof to assoc prof Ger, 62-75, PROF GER, GEORGE WASHINGTON UNIV, 75-, DIR GER LANG WORKSHOP, 70- *Concurrent Pos:* Nat Endowment for Humanities grant, 73-74. *Mem:* Am Asn Teachers Ger; MLA; Am Soc 18th Century Studies; NAm Goethe Soc. *Res:* Literatures impact on society; literature as the maker of history, and the creator of patterns of thought and behavior; applied literature. *Publ:* Auth, Heinrich Mann's Psychologie des Faschismus, Monatshefte, fall 71; Sebbstentfremdung aes deutsches Phanomen, Sahbuch fes Internatochle Gesmanistik, 77. *Mailing Add:* Dept of Ger George Washington Univ Washington DC 20052

THOGMARTIN, CLYDE ORVILLE, b Spickard, Mo, June 15, 40. ROMANCE LINGUISTICS. *Educ:* Univ Kans, AB, 62, MA, 64; Univ Mich, MA, 66, PhD(Romance ling), 70. *Prof Exp:* Asst prof, 68-74, ASSOC PROF FOREIGN LANG, IOWA STATE UNIV, 74- *Concurrent Pos:* Fel, Edinburgh Univ, 76-77. *Mem:* Am Asn Teachers Fr. *Res:* Dialectology; text linguistics; acquisition of second language. *Publ:* Auth, A survey of attitudes toward foreign language education among first-year students, Bull Asn Dept Foreign Lang, 71; The phonology of three dialects of Manitoba French, Orbis, Rev Int de Doc Ling, 74; Prosper Jacotot: A french worker looks at Kansas in 1876-77, Kans Hist Quart, 75; A Bibliography of Empirical Investigations of Certain Aspects of Foreign Language Teaching and Learning, 1925-1975, 76 & Age, Musical Talent, and Certain Psycholinguistic Abilities in Relation to Achievement in a FLES Course in Chinese, 77, Eric Report; Old Mines, Missouri et la survivance de la langue francaise dans la haute vallee du Mississippi, Le francais hors de France, Paris, 79; Age, Individual Differences in Musical and Verbal Aptitude & Pronunciation Achievement by Elementary School Children Learning a Foreign Language, IRAL, 82; Mr Dooley's Brogue: The literary dialect of Finley Peter Dunne, Visible Lang, 82. *Mailing Add:* Dept of Foreign Lang Iowa State Univ Ames IA 50010

THOMANN, DONALDO J, b Entre Rios, Arg, Nov 11, 13; US citizen; m 39; c 3. LANGUAGES. *Educ:* Pac Union Col, BA, 39; Univ Ore, MEd, 53; Stanford Univ, PhD(Span), 68. *Prof Exp:* Missionary, Nicaragua Seventh Day Adventist Mission, 39-42; teacher relig & hist, Cent Am Vocational Col, 42-46, pres, 47-49; dept secy, Mex Union of Seventh Day Adventists, 49-52, chmn-dir, Mex Sem of Seventh Day Adventists, 52-56; dir, Dominican Col, Dominican Repub, 56-58; prof Span & chmn dept mod lang, Pac Union Col, 58-74; acad dean, Inst Colombia, Venezuela, 74, pres, 74-76; bilingual expediter, Pomona Unified Sch Dist, 76-77; CONSULT BILINGUAL EDUC, CALIF STATE DEPT EDUC, 77- *Concurrent Pos:* Consult lang arts, Calexico sch dist, Calif, 69-73; researcher biling educ, Calif State Dept Educ, 72-73. *Mem:* MLA; Am Asn Teachers Span & Port; Nat Asn Lang Lab Dir; Int Ling Asn; Adventist Lang Teachers Asn. *Res:* Secondary school programs in Hispanic-America; linguistic study of the Spanish language. *Publ:* Coauth, Principios de musica, 54 & Solfeo e historia de la musica, 56, Col Voc y Prof Montemorelos, Mex; auth, Dictionary of Spanish Syllables, Mouton, The Hague. *Mailing Add:* Bilingual Bicult Educ Sect State Dept of Educ 721 Capitol Mall Sacramento CA 95814

THOMAS, EARL WESLEY, b Sumner, Ill, Jan 22, 15; c 5. ROMANCE LANGUAGE. *Educ:* Univ Ill, AB, 36, AM, 37; Univ Mich, PhD, 47. *Prof Exp:* From asst prof to assoc prof Romance lang, 47-62, assoc prof, 62-64, prof Span & Port, Vanderbilt Univ, 64-80; RETIRED. *Concurrent Pos:* Ford fel advan teaching, Spain & Port, 54-55; Soc Sci Res Coun grant, Brazil, 65-66. *Mem:* SAtlantic Mod Lang Asn; Am Asn Teachers Span & Port. *Res:* Brazilian literature; Portuguese language; Romance philology. *Publ:* Auth, Emerging patterns of the Brazilian language, In: New Perspectives of Brazil, 66, The Syntax of Spoken Brazilian Portuguese, 69 & Protest in the ovel and theater, In: Brazil in the Sixties, 72, Vanderbilt Univ; The changing Brazilian language, Ky Foreign Lang Quart, Vol 8, No 1. *Mailing Add:* Box 1558 Sta B Nashville TN 37235

THOMAS, GARY CRAIG, b Long Beach, Calif, Nov 20, 44. GERMAN LITERATURE, MUSICOLOGY. *Educ:* Univ Calif, Los Angeles, AB, 66; Harvard Univ, MA, 70, PhD(Ger lang & lit), 73. *Prof Exp:* ASST PROF HUMANITIES & GER, UNIV MINN, MINNEAPOLIS, 71- *Mem:* MLA; Am Soc Study 16th & 17th Century Ger Lit; Renaissance Soc Am; Am Guild Organists. *Res:* German baroque literature; musical-literary relations; interdisciplinary theory of rhetoric. *Publ:* Auth, Philipp von Zesen's German Madrigals, Argenis, 78; Zesen, Rinckart and the Musical Origins of the Dactyl, Argenis, 78. *Mailing Add:* Dept of Humanities Univ of Minn Minneapolis MN 55455

THOMAS, GEORGE, b Romford, England, Aug 14, 45. RUSSIAN LANGUAGE HISTORY. *Educ:* Univ London, BA, 66, PhD(Russ), 69. *Prof Exp:* Asst prof, 69-75, ASSOC PROF RUSS, McMASTER UNIV, 75-, CHMN DEPT, 77- *Mem:* Hansischer Ger; Can Asn Slavists. *Res:* Loanwards in Russian; typology of Slavic vocabularies; language purism. *Publ:* Auth, The role of calqnes in the early Czech language renewal, 56 & Russian naval terms from Low German, 71, Slavonic & East Europ Rev; Woher Kommen Russisch master und mester?, Zeitschrift für slavische Philologie, 71; Sprachliche Belege für die im Mittelalter nach Russland eingeführten Gewürzarten, Hansische Geschichtblätter, 71; Some theories concerning the unification of the endings of the dative, instrumental and locative plural of Russian nouns, Can Contriv VII Int Cong Slavists, 73; The calqne--an international trend in lexical development of the literary languages of eighteenth century Europe, Germanoslavica, 75; Srednenizhnenemetskie zaimstvovanija Tusskom jazyke, Russ Ling, 76; Middle Low German Loanwords in Russian Munich, 78. *Mailing Add:* Dept of Russ McMaster Univ Hamilton ON L8S 4M4 Can

THOMAS, GERALD, b Porthcawl, UK, Dec 29, 40; Can citizen; m 81; c 5. FOLKLORE, FRENCH. *Educ:* Univ Wales, BA, 63; Mem Univ Nfld, MA, 70, PhD(folklore), 77. *Prof Exp:* Lectr Fr, 64-67, asst prof, 67-74, assoc prof, 74-77, ASSOC PROF FR & FOLKLORE, MEM UNIV NFLD, 78-, DIR, CENTRE D'ETUDES FRANCO-TERRENEUVIENNES, 75- *Concurrent Pos:* Mem, Fel Comt, Social Sci & Humanities Res Coun Can, 79-81. *Mem:* Folklore Studies Asn Can (pres, 78-79); Am Folklore Soc; Can Folk Music Soc. *Res:* Folk narrative; folklore of French cultures, especially Newfoundland French; traditional aesthetics. *Publ:* Auth, The Tall Tale and Philippe D'Alcripe, 77 & Songs Sung by French Newfoundlanders: A Catalogue, 78, Mem Univ Nfld; The folktale and folktale style in the tradition of French Newfoundlanders, Can Folklore Can, 79; contribr, Folklore Studies in Honour of Herbert Halpert (The Folktale & Soap Opera in Newfoundland's French Tradition), 80; auth, Effects Reciproques Entre Conteur Et Assistance Dans un Contexte Narratif Franco-Terreneuvien, Cult & Tradition, 80; Contemporary traditional music in Newfoundland, Bull Can Folk Music Soc, 81; Cornelius Rouzes (1926-1981), violoneux, chanteur, raconiteur Franco-Terreneuvien, The Livyere, 82. *Mailing Add:* Dept of French Mem Univ Nfld St John's NF A1B 3X9 Can

THOMAS, JOHN WESLEY, b Thomas, Okla, May 24, 16; m 48; c 3. GERMAN. *Educ:* Houghton Col, AB, 37; Pa State Col, AM, 39, PhD, 42. *Prof Exp:* Instr, Cent Jr Col, 37-38, Roberts Col, 41-42, Washington & Jefferson Col, 42-44 & Univ Mich, 46-47; from assoc prof to prof Ger, Univ Ark, 47-69; PROF GER, UNIV KY, 69- *Concurrent Pos:* Fulbright res scholar, Luxembourg, 49-50; guest prof, Univ Hamburg, 55-56 & Univ Tübingen, 59-60. *Mem:* MLA; SAtlantic Mod Lang Asn. *Res:* German. *Publ:* Coauth, Ullrich von Liechtenstein's Service of Ladies, 69, Univ NC; The Songs and Tales of Herrand von Wildonie, Univ Ky, 72; Tannhäuser: Poet and Legend, Univ NC, 73; Wirnt von Grafenberg's Wigalois, 77, Eilhart von Oberge's Tristrant, 78, Hartmann von Aue's Iwein, 79, The Legend of Duke Ernst, 80 & Hartmann von Aue's Erec, 81, Univ Nebr. *Mailing Add:* Dept of Ger Univ of Ky Lexington KY 40506

THOMAS, LAWRENCE LESLIE, b Butte, NDak, Mar 15, 24. SLAVIC LANGUAGES & LITERATURES. *Educ:* Univ Calif, PhD, 54. *Prof Exp:* Lectr Slavic lang, Univ Calif, Berkeley, 50-53, instr, 53-56, from asst prof to assoc prof Slavic lang & lit, 56-65; chmn dept Slavic lang, 68-74, chmn Russ area studies prog, 69-72, PROF SLAVIC LANG, UNIV WIS-MADISON, 65- *Concurrent Pos:* Inter-Univ Comt Travel Grants fel, Poland, 56; Soc Sci Res Coun & Humanities Fund grants, Poland & USSR, 60; vis lectr, Univ Wis, 63-64. *Mem:* Ling Soc Am. *Res:* Slavic linguistics; modern Polish literature. *Publ:* Auth, Linguistic Theories of N Ja Marr, Univ Calif, 57; coauth, Kosciuszko Foundation English-Polish, Polish-English Dictionary, Mouton, The Hague, 61; ed & translr, Vinogradov: History of the Russian Literary Language from the Seventeenth Century to the Nineteenth, Univ Wis, 69. *Mailing Add:* Dept Slavic Lang Univ Wis Madison WI 53706

THOMAS, LINDSAY, JR, b Waynesboro, Ga, Jan 28, 29; m 59; c 1. FRENCH. *Educ:* Sem Adventiste, France, AB, 55; Boston Univ, AB, 56, AM, 57; Univ Calif, Los Angeles, PhD(French), 63. *Prof Exp:* Teaching asst French, Univ Calif, Los Angeles, 58-61; asst prof, Calif State Col, Long Beach, 61-64; prof French & hist, Col Mod, Ivory Coast, 64-66; assoc prof French, 66-73, chmn dept French & Ital, 71-76, PROF FRENCH, CALIF STATE UNIV, LONG BEACH, 73- *Concurrent Pos:* NDEA title VI fels, 63, 67, 68. *Mem:* Am Asn Teachers Fr. *Res:* Miracles of Middle Ages; languages of West Africa. *Mailing Add:* Dept of Foreign Lang Calif State Univ Long Beach CA 90840

THOMAS, OWEN PAUL, English, Linguistics. See Vol II

THOMAS, P ALOYSIUS, b New York, NY, Mar 16, 36. FRENCH. *Educ:* Manhattan Col, BS, 59; St John's Univ, MA, 61; State Univ NY Buffalo, PhD(French), 71. *Prof Exp:* Asst prof French, Niagara Univ, 63-67; asst prof, Thiel Col, 67-68; asst prof, Ball State Univ, 68-72; assoc prof, Univ Louisville, 72-78. *Mem:* Int Soc Courtly Lit; MLA; Am Asn Teachers Fr; Int Arthurian Soc; Medieval Acad Am. *Res:* Courtly love tradition; 20th century French literature; 17th century French literature. *Publ:* Ed, L'oeuvre poetique de Jacques de Baisieux, Mouton, The Hague, 73; auth, Translation of Des trois chevaliers et del chainse, Allegorica, 76; Ideal involvement: The Camusian hero, USF Lang Quart, 77. *Mailing Add:* 1362 Clay Ave Bronx NY 10456

THOMAS, ROSEMARY HYDE, b Central Falls, RI, Jan 4, 39; m 65; c 1. PSYCHOLINGUISTICS, FOLKLORE. *Educ:* Newport Col-Salve Regina, BA, 61; Ind Univ, MA, 66; St Louis Univ, PhD(psycholing), 78. *Prof Exp:* Instr French, Lindenwood Col, 66-67; from instr to prof French & ling, St Louis Community Col Forest Part, 67-79; PROF ENGLISH, ST LOUIS COMMUNITY COL MERAMEC, 79- *Concurrent Pos:* Mem, Comn Teaching Foreign Lang & Lit, MLA, 77-78; proj dir, PsychoSocial Study of Old Mines Fr Cult, Nat Endowment for Humanities, 78-82. *Mem:* MLA; Asn Dept Foreign Lang (pres, 78-79); Am Folklore Soc. *Res:* Folklore in Missouri; psychological coordinates of bilingualism; the effects of language death on the development of a cultural community. *Publ:* Auth, The foreign language requirement: Some reflections, Midwest Mod Lang Asn Bull, 71; A resource approach to foreign language department planning, Asn Dept Foreign Lang Bull, 72; The Guillonnee: A traditional New Year's Eve celebration, Mid-South Folklore, 79; Naming practices among people of French descent in Washington County, Mo, Midwest Folklore Soc J, 81; It's Good to Tell You: French Folk Tales from Missouri, Univ Mo Press, 81. *Mailing Add:* 488 W Lockwood Webster Groves MO 63119

THOMAS, RUTH PAULA, b New York, NY, Nov 9, 35; m 74; c 2. FRENCH. *Educ:* Bryn Mawr Col, BA, 57; Yale Univ, MA, 58, PhD(French), 64. *Prof Exp:* Instr French, Simmons Col, 61-63; asst prof, 64-73, ASSOC PROF FRENCH, TEMPLE UNIV, 73- *Mem:* Am Asn Teachers Fr; MLA; Am Soc Eighteenth Century Studies. *Res:* Eighteenth and 17th century French novel. *Publ:* Auth, The critical narrators of Marivaux's unfinished novels, Forum Mod Lang Studies, 10/73; Jacques le fataliste, Les Liaisons dangereuses and the autonomy of the novel, 74 & Les Bijoux indiscrets as a laboratory for Diderot's later fiction, 75, Studies Voltaire & Eighteenth Century; The modern hero of Manon Lescaut: DesGrieux as a prototype of Adolphe, Mod Lang Studies, fall 75; Diderot and Rousseau as literary critics: A comparison of the Entretiens sur le Fils naturel and the Entretien sur les romans, Mod Lang Rev, 1/78; Montesquieu's Harem and Diderot's Convent: The Woman as Prisoner, Fr Rev, 10/78; Light and darkness in La Princesse de Cleves, Ky Romance Quart, Vol 28, No 1; Chess as metaphor in Le Neveu de Rameau, Forum Mod Lang Studies, Vol 18, No 1. *Mailing Add:* 1530 Locust St Apt 5F Philadelphia PA 19012

THOMAS, URSULA MAY, b Klemme, Iowa, May 13, 16. GERMAN, EDUCATION. *Educ:* State Univ Iowa, BA, 39, MA, 40; Univ Wis, PhD(Ger), 57. *Prof Exp:* Teacher high sch, Ill, 42-45; instr Ger & Span, Blackburn Col, Ill, 45-46 & Lake Forest Col, 46-50; from instr to asst prof Ger, 57-64; assoc prof, 64-76, PROF GER & EDUC, UNIV WIS-MADISON, 76- *Mem:* Am Coun Teaching Foreign Lang; Am Asn Teachers Ger. *Res:* Improvement of language teaching at the intermediate level; teacher training. *Publ:* Coauth, Verstehen und Sprechen, 62, rev ed, 70, Sprechen und Lesen, 63, rev ed, 71, Lesen und Denken, 64 & Denken, Wissen und Kennen, 66, Holt; Lesestoff nach Wahl: Einführung, Literatur, Mensch und Gesellschaft, Biologie, Physik und Chemie, Teacher's Manual, Univ Wis, 77. *Mailing Add:* Dept of Ger Univ of Wis 814 Van Hise Madison WI 53706

THOMAS, WILLIAM WILFRID, b Buffalo, NY, Dec 5, 40; m 65; c 2. FRENCH LITERATURE. *Educ:* Hamilton Col, AB, 62; State Univ NY, Buffalo, PhD(French), 70. *Prof Exp:* Instr French, State Univ NY, Buffalo, 65-68; lectr English Fac Lett, Tours, France, 68-69; asst prof, 69-73, ASSOC PROF FRENCH, UNION COL, NY, 73- *Mem:* MLA; Am Asn Teachers Fr. *Res:* Realism and naturalism; the modern novel; modern intellectual history. *Mailing Add:* Dept of Mod Lang Union Col Schenectady NY 12308

THOMPSON, B BUSSELL, b Kingsport, Tenn, Nov 23, 42. SPANISH MEDIEVAL LITERATURE. *Educ:* Carson-Newman Col, AB, 64; Univ Tenn, AM, 65; Univ Va, PhD(Span), 70. *Prof Exp:* Instr French & Span, Ga Southern Col, 65-67; asst prof Span, Univ Idaho, 70-71; asst prof Span, 71-80, MEM FAC, COLUMBIA COL, COLUMBIA UNIV, 80- *Concurrent Pos:* Chamberlain fel humanities, Columbia Col, 75. *Mem:* MLA; Mediaeval Acad

Am; Am Asn Teachers Span & Port. *Res:* Hagiography; paremiology; theater. *Publ:* Ed, Dr Francisco del Rosel: La razon de algunos refranes, Tamesis Bks, 75; co-ed, Vida de Santa Marie Egipciaca, Univ Exeter, 77; auth, Libros de caballeria, or -ias?, Anothersourcesford 77 & coauth, Poema de mio Cid, Line 508: The Cid as a Rebellious Vassal?, 77, La Coronica; auth, Another source for Lucena's Repeticion de amores, Hisp Rev, 77; Misogyny and misprint in La Celestina, Act I, Celestinesca, 77. *Mailing Add:* Five E 67th St New York NY 10021

THOMPSON, BOZENA HENISZ-DOSTERT, b Warsaw, Poland; US citizen. LINGUISTICS, COMPUTATIONAL LINGUISTICS. *Educ:* Univ Warsaw, MA, 56; Georgetown Univ, MS, 62, PhD(ling), 65. *Prof Exp:* Instr English, Univ Warsaw, 56-58; res assoc comp ling, Georgetown Univ, 61-64, assoc scientist ling, 67-69; sr res fel, 69-73, res assoc, 73-80, SR RES ASSOC LING, CALIF INST TECHNOL, 81- *Concurrent Pos:* Consult, Univ Tex, 64, 65 & 73, Rand Corp, 65-71 & Hewlett-Packard Corp, 78; Nat Acad Sci Foreign Exchange fel, 73. *Mem:* Ling Soc Am; Asn Computational Ling; AAUP. *Res:* Psycholinguistics; sociolinguistics; human factors in communication with computers. *Publ:* Coauth, Do You Speak English?, Wiedza Powszechna, Warsaw, 59; auth, Morphological analysis of Polish nouns, Georgetown Univ, 6/62; contribr, Experimental machine translation, In: Papers in Linguistics for Leon Dostert, Mouton, 67; How features resolve syntactic ambiguity, In: Proc Nat Symposium Info Storage & Retrieval, Univ Md, 71; auth, Users' evaluation of machine translation, 1963-1973, RADC Report, 6/73; coauth, Practical natural language processing: The REL system as prototype, In: Advances in Computers, Vol 13, Academic, 75; Machine Translation, Mouton, 79; auth, Linguistic analysis of natural language communication with computers, In: Proc Conf Ling 80, 8th Int Conf Comput Ling, Tokyo, 80. *Mailing Add:* Calif Inst of Technol Pasadena CA 91125

THOMPSON, CLAIBORNE WATKINS, b Little Rock, Ark, Sept 19, 40; m 66; c 2. MEDIEVAL SCANDINAVIAN LANGUAGE & LITERATURE. *Educ:* Princeton Univ, BA, 63; Harvard Univ, PhD(Scand), 69. *Prof Exp:* Asst prof, 69-75, ASSOC PROF GER LANG, UNIV MICH, ANN ARBOR, 75-, CHMN DEPT, 76- *Concurrent Pos:* Am Coun Learned Soc fel, 73-74. *Mem:* Soc Advan Scand Studies; MLA; Mediaeval Acad Am. *Res:* Icelandic sagas; Norse myth and legend; runology. *Publ:* Auth, A Swedish runographer and a headless bishop, Mediaeval Scandinavica, 70; Gisla saga: The identity of Vestein's slayer, Arkiv for Nordisk Filologi, 73; Inscriptions: Runes and runic, Encycl of Libr & Info Sci, 74; Studies in Upplandic Runography, Univ Tex, 75; Moral values in the Icelandic sagas, Epic in Medieval Soc, 77; Rune and runic, Scandinavica, 77; The Runes in Bosa saga ok Herrauds, Scand Studies, 78. *Mailing Add:* Dept of Ger Lang Univ of Mich Ann Arbor MI 48109

THOMPSON, DAVID BRADFORD, Intellectual History. See Vol I

THOMPSON, ELIZABETH LONG, b Crowley, La, July 20, 38. ROMANCE PHILOLOGY, SPANISH. *Educ:* La State Univ, Baton Rouge, BA, 58, MA, 60; Univ NC, Chapel Hill, PhD(Span & Romance philol), 64. *Prof Exp:* Asst prof Span, La State Univ, New Orleans, 65-66; asst prof, Univ NC, Asheville, 69-70; ASST PROF SPAN & ROMANCE PHILOL, LA STATE UNIV, BATON ROUGE, 70- *Res:* Celtic folklore. *Mailing Add:* Dept of Foreign Lang La State Univ Baton Rouge LA 70803

THOMPSON, EWA M, b Kovno, Lithuania; nat US; m 67. COMPARATIVE & SLAVIC LITERATURES. *Educ:* Univ Warsaw, BA, 63; Sopot Conserv Music, Poland, MFA, 63; Ohio Univ, MA, 64; Vanderbilt Univ, PhD(comp lit), 67. *Prof Exp:* Teaching asst, Ohio Univ, 63-64; instr, Vanderbilt Univ, 64-67; asst prof mod lang, Ind State Univ, 67-68; asst prof Slavic lang & comp lit, Ind Univ, Bloomington, 68-70; asst prof Russ, Rice Univ, 70-73; assoc prof Slavic lang & lit, Univ Va, 73-74; assoc prof Russ & Ger, 74-78, PROF GER & RUSS, RICE UNIV, 79- *Concurrent Pos:* Consult-panelist, Nat Endowment for Humanities, 73-79 & Int Res & Exchanges Bd, 76-79; vis univ fel, Princeton Univ, 77; vis prof Russ, Univ Warsaw, 78; sr coordr, Mellon Sem Col Teachers, summer, 82. *Mem:* MLA; Am Asn Advan Slavic Studies; Am Comp Lit Asn; Am Asn Teachers Slavic & East Europ Lang. *Res:* Russia literature. *Publ:* Auth, Russian Formalism and Anglo-American New Criticism: A Comparative Study, Mouton, The Hague, 71; Il Folle sacro e le sue trasformazioni nella letteratura russa, Strumenti Critici, 75; Witold Gombrowicz, G K Hall, 79; The archetype of the fool in Russian literature, Can Slavonic Papers, XV: 245-273; The artistic world of Mixail Bulgakov, Russ Lit, V: 54-64; Russian holy fools and shamanism, In: American Contributions to the Eighth International Congress of Slavonists, 2: 691-706; D S Likhachev and the study of Old Russian literature, In: American Contributions to the Second World Congress of Soviet and East European Studies. *Mailing Add:* Dept of Russ Rice Univ Houston TX 77001

THOMPSON, GRAVES HAYDON, b Charleston, WVa, May 4, 07; m 38; c 2. CLASSICAL PHILOLOGY. *Educ:* Hampden-Sydney Col, AB, 27; Harvard Univ, AM, 28, PhD, 31. *Hon Degrees:* DLitt, Hampden-Sydney Col, 79. *Prof Exp:* Prof class lang, Cumberland Univ, 31-39; Blair prof, 39-78; EMER BLAIR PROF LATIN, HAMPDEN-SYDNEY COL, 78- *Mem:* Am Philol Asn; Am Class League; Class Asn Mid West & South. *Publ:* Auth, For an international auxiliary language, Class Weekly, 4/49; The literary sources of Titian's Bacchus and Ariadne, Class J, 3/56; To what extent did Jesus use Greek?, Relig in Life, winter 62-63; Selections from the Ars Amatoria & Remedia Amoris of Ovid, Edward Bros; A History of the Southern Section of the Classical Association of the Middle West and South, Univ Ga, 80. *Mailing Add:* Penshurst Hampden-Sydney VA 23943

THOMPSON, HENRY SWIFT, b Abington, Pa, July 1, 50. COMPUTATIONAL LINGUISTICS. *Educ:* Univ Calif, Berkeley, BA, 72, MSc, 74, MA, 77, PhD(ling), 80. *Prof Exp:* Sr programmer, Comput Systems Res Proj, Univ Calif, Berkeley, 73-74; res intern & consult, Xerox, Palo Alto, 75-80; LECTR ARTIFICIAL INTELLIGENCE & COMPUT LING, DEPT ARTIFICIAL INTELLIGENCE, UNIV EDINBURGH, 80- *Concurrent Pos:* Contract consult, Xerox, Palo Alto Res Ctr, 81- *Mem:* Asn Comput Mach; Asn Comput Ling. *Res:* Computational methods for parsing and generating natural language; the human sentence processing mechanism; knowledge representation. *Publ:* Auth, On the other hand, Academic Press, 76; coauth, A frame-based dialog system, Artificial Intelligence, Vol 8, 77; auth, A model for language production, Papers 13th Annual Mtg Chicago Ling Soc, 77; coauth, KRL-O, A retrospective, Papers 5th Joint Conf Artificial Intelligence, 77; auth, Chart parsing and rule schemata in GPSG, Proc 19th Annual Mtg Asn Comput Ling, 81; Natural language processing: A critical analysis of the structure of the field with some implications for parsing, Proc Workshop, Univ Essex Cognitive Studies, 82; Handling metarules in a parser for GPSG, Proc 9th Int Conf Comput Ling, 82. *Mailing Add:* Dept Artificial Intelligence Univ Edinburgh Edinburgh EH8 9NW Scotland United Kingdom

THOMPSON, JOHN A, b Milton, NC, Jan 28; 06; m 36; c 2. SPANISH, LITERATURE. *Educ:* Davidson Col, AB, 25; Univ NC, PhD, 37. *Prof Exp:* Instr Span, Wake Forest Col, 26-28, asst prof Romance lang, 28-29; from instr to prof Span, 30-73, dir div Latin Am relat, 42-5 42-53, chmn dept foreign lang, 53-71, EMER PROF SPAN, LA STATE UNIV, BATON ROUGE, 73- *Concurrent Pos:* Mem, Nat Adv Comt Adjustment Foreign Studies in US, 44-47; field secy, Inst Int Educ & dir Wash bur, 45; exec dir, Brazilian Am Cult Inst, Rio de Janeiro, 50-52. *Mem:* SCent Mod Lang Asn (pres, 69); Am Asn Teachers Span & Port. *Res:* Spanish literature. *Publ:* Auth, Alexandere Dumas in Spanish Romantic Drama, La State Univ, 38; coauth, Practicing Spanish, 62 & 67 & Speaking and Understanding Spanish, 4th ed, 73, Holt. *Mailing Add:* 4245 Highland Rd Baton Rouge LA 70808

THOMPSON, LAURENCE CASSIUS, JR, b Manchester, NH, Mar 11, 26. LINGUISTICS. *Educ:* Middlebury Col, AB, 49; Yale Univ, MA, 50, PhD(ling), 54. *Prof Exp:* Asst Vietnamese, Yale Univ, 53-54; asst dean, Army Lang Sch, Monterey, Calif, 54-56; instr English, Univ Wash, 57-59, supvr English for foreign students, 58-59, from asst prof to assoc prof ling & Russ, 59-67, coordr Russ lang prog, 59-65; vis prof, 66-67, PROF LING, UNIV HAWAII, MANOA, 67- *Concurrent Pos:* Am Coun Learned Soc fel, 57-59; consult res Southeast Asian & Slavic lang, US Off Educ, 60-67, res contract, 60-62, res grant, 63-65; Nat Endowment for Humanities grant, 79-82, John Simon Guggenheim Mem fel, 79-80. *Mem:* Int Ling Asn; Ling Soc Am; Am Orient Soc; Am Anthrop Asn; Soc Study Indigenous Lang Am. *Res:* Southeast Asia studies; American Indian linguistics; general linguistics. *Publ:* Coauth, A Vietnamese Reader, 61 & auth, A Vietnamese Grammar, 65, Univ Wash; coauth, Ballada o Soldate, Harcourt, 66; Clallam: A preview, In: Studies in American Indian Languages, Univ Calif, 71; Language universals, nasals, and the Northwest Coast, In: Studies in Linguistics in Honor of George L Trager, Mouton, The Hague, 72; co-ed, Austroasiatic Studies, 76 & auth, Proto-Viet-Muong phonology, In: Austroasiatic Studies, 76, Univ Hawaii; Salishan and the Northwest, In: The Languages of Native America, Univ Tex, 79. *Mailing Add:* Dept of Ling Univ of Hawaii at Manoa Honolulu HI 96822

THOMPSON, LAWRENCE SIDNEY, b Wake Co, NC, Dec 21, 16; m 50, 68; c 3. CLASSICS, SCANDINAVIAN LITERATURE. *Educ:* Univ NC, AB, 34, PhD(Ger lang), 38. *Prof Exp:* Asst to librn, Iowa State Col, 40-42; spec agent, Fed Bur Invest, 42-45; librn, Western Mich Col, 46-48; librn, 48-64, PROF CLASSICS, UNIV KY, 48- *Concurrent Pos:* Consult, Ministry Educ, Ankara, 51-52 & Caribbean Comn, Port-of-Spain, 54. *Mem:* Am Philol Asn; hon mem counc Bibliog Soc Am; Archaeol Inst Am; hon mem Southeastern Libr Asn, 80. *Res:* History of printing; book collecting; bibliography. *Publ:* Coauth, The Kentucky Novel, Univ Ky, 52; auth, Kentucky Tradition, Shoestring, 56; Bibliography of Hispanic Drama in Microform, Archon Bks, 68; The New Sabin (8 vols), 74, coauth, History of Printing in Colonial Spanish America, 77 & Medical Terminology from Greek and Latin, 78, 2nd ed, 82, Whitston. *Mailing Add:* Dept of Classics Univ of Ky Lexington KY 40506

THOMPSON, MITTIE LYNETTE, b Gretna, Fla, Feb 27, 19. LATIN, GREEK. *Educ:* Fla State Col Women, AB, 40; Oberlin Col, AM, 41; Univ Chicago, PhD(Latin), 56. *Prof Exp:* Teacher, High Sch, Fla, 41-42; from instr to assoc prof classics, 42-62, chmn dept, 61-80, PROF CLASSICS, FLA STATE UNIV, 62- *Mem:* Am Philol Asn; Archaeol Inst Am; Class Asn Midwest & S (pres, 78-79). *Res:* Lucan and Seneca, philosopher and tragedian. *Publ:* Auth, Lucan's apotheosis of Nero, 7/64, coauth, Lucan's use of Virgilian reminiscences, 1/68 & The Virgilian background of Lucan's Fourth Book, 7/70, Class Philol. *Mailing Add:* Dept of Classics Fla State Univ Tallahassee FL 32306

THOMPSON, ROGER MARK, b Oakland, Calif, July 15, 42; m 67; c 7. LINGUISTICS, SOCIOLINGUISTICS. *Educ:* Brigham Young Univ, BA, 66, MA, 68; Univ Tex, Austin, PhD(ling), 71. *Prof Exp:* Prog specialist teaching English as foreign lang, Int Off, Univ Tex, Austin, 68-71; asst prof, 71-76, ASSOC PROF ENGLISH & LING, UNIV FLA, 76- *Concurrent Pos:* Ed, Southern Folklore Quart, 72-75. *Mem:* Ling Soc Am; Am Dialect Soc; Teachers of English to Speakers of Other Lang; Am Asn Applied Ling. *Res:* Bilingualism; second language acquisition; English as a second language. *Publ:* Coauth, Cakchiquel Basic Course, Brigham Young Univ, Vol I, 69; auth, Mexican American language loyalty and the validity of the 1970 census, Int J Sociol Lang, 74; The decline of Cedar Key: Mormon stories in North Florida and their social function, Southern Folklore Quart, 75; Mexican-American English: Social correlates of regional pronunciation, Am Speech, 75; Language planning in frontier America, Lang Problems & Lang Planning, 82. *Mailing Add:* Dept of English Univ of Fla Gainesville FL 32611

THOMPSON, WESLEY E, b Washington, DC, Apr 22, 38; m 65; c 1. CLASSICS. *Educ:* Univ Cincinnati, AB, 59; Princeton Univ, PhD(classics), 63. *Prof Exp:* Instr classics, Haverford Col, 63; from asst prof to assoc prof, 63-71, PROF CLASSICS, UNIV CALIF, DAVIS, 71- *Mem:* Am Philol Asn; Asn of Ancient Historians. *Res:* Greek epigraphy and history. *Publ:* Auth, De Hagniae Hereditate, Brill, Leiden, 76; contribr, Inscriptiones Graecae, Berlin, Vol I, 3rd ed, 81. *Mailing Add:* Dept of Classics Univ of Calif Davis CA 95616

THOMSON, DOUGLAS FERGUSON SCOTT, b Bridge of Weir, Scotland, Oct 13, 19; Can citizen; m 53; c 3. CLASSICS, LATIN. *Educ:* Oxford Univ, BA & MA, 46. *Prof Exp:* Lectr, 48-54, from asst prof to assoc prof, 54-69, PROF CLASSICS, UNIV COL, UNIV TORONTO, 69- *Concurrent Pos:* Nuffield traveling fel, London, Oxford & Italy, 59-60; vis prof, Univ NC, Chapel Hill, 67-68; Can Coun fel, Oxford, 70-71; Soc Sci & Humanities Res Coun Can fel, London, 82-83. *Mem:* Class Asn Can. *Res:* Latin poetry, especially Catullus and Augustan elegy; Renaissance Latin prose and poetry. *Publ:* Coauth, Erasmus and Cambridge: The Cambridge Letters of Erasmus, Univ Toronto, 63; auth, The Latinity of Erasmus, In: Erasmus, vol in ser: Studies in Latin Literature and Its Influence, Routledge & Kegan Paul, London, 69; auth, The Codex Romanus of Catullus, Rheinisches Mus, Vol 113, Nos 2-3, 70; coauth, Poggio's earliest manuscript?, Italia Medioevale e Umanistica, 73; contribr, Yale Classical Studies 23, Cambridge Univ, 73; contribr, Linacre Studies, Clarendon, 77; auth, Catullus: A Critical Edition, Univ NC, 78; transl, Collected Works of Erasmus in English, Univ Toronto, Vols I-VI, 74-82. *Mailing Add:* 116 Manor Rd E Toronto ON M4S 1P8 Can

THOMSON, IAN, b Dundee, Scotland, Mar 1, 33. CLASSICAL STUDIES. *Educ:* Univ St Andrews, MA, 55, Dipl Ed, 59, PhD(Guarino da Verona), 69. *Prof Exp:* Asst prof classics, Univ Okla, 63-66; lectr, 67-68, asst prof, 69-70, ASSOC PROF CLASSICS, IND UNIV, BLOOMINGTON, 71- *Mem:* Am Philol Asn; Renaissance Soc Am. *Res:* Medieval studies; Renaissance humanism. *Mailing Add:* Dept of Class Studies Ind Univ Bloomington IN 47401

THOMSON, ROBERT WILLIAM, b Cheam, England, Mar 24, 34; m 63. NEAR EASTERN LANGUAGES. *Educ:* Cambridge Univ, BA, 55, dipl Orient lang, 57, MA, 59, PhD(theol), 62; Univ Louvain, lic Orient Lang, 62. *Hon Degrees:* MA, Harvard Univ, 69. *Prof Exp:* Instr class Armenian, 63-65, asst prof, 65-69, chmn, Dept Near Eastern Lang, 73-78, PROF ARMENIAN STUDIES, HARVARD UNIV, 69- *Res:* Armenian; patristic studies. *Publ:* Coauth, Biblical and Patristic Studies in Memory of R P Casey, Herder, 63; auth, Athanasiana Syriac, Part 1, 65, Part 2, 67, Part 3, 72 & Par 4, 77, Corpus SCO, Louvain; Athanasius: Contra Gentes and De Incarnatione, Oxford Univ, 71; The Teaching of Saint Gregory, Harvard Univ, 71; Introduction to Classical Armenian, 75 & coauth, Testbook of Modern Western Armenian, 77, Caravan; Auth, Agathangelos, History of the Armenians, State Univ NY Albany, 77; Moses Khorenatsi, History of the Armenians, Harvard Univ, 78. *Mailing Add:* Dept of Near Eastern Lang Harvard Univ 6 Divinity Ave Cambridge MA 02138

THOMSON, WILLIAM GREGORY, b Detroit, Mich, May 25, 18; m 43; c 3. CLASSICS, HUMANITIES. *Educ:* Olivet Col, BA, 42; Cornell Univ, MA, 47; Univ Mich, EdD, 61. *Prof Exp:* Master Latin, Lower Can Col, 47-49; from instr to asst prof classics, Wayne State Univ, 49-56; assoc prof lit & fine arts, Heidelberg Col, 57-62; from assoc prof to prof classics, Eckerd Col, 62-73, dir summer sch, 63-67, dir upward bound proj, 66-73, dir continuing educ, 66-67, fac leader, London Studies Ctr, 73; PROF CLASSICS & LIT, OLIVET COL, 73- *Concurrent Pos:* Consult, Educ Assoc, Inc, DC, 66-72; assoc mem, Inst Class Studies, Univ London, 73. *Mem:* Class Asn Midwest & South; Am Philol Asn; Archaeol Inst Am. *Res:* College curriculum and administration; programmed learning of Latin; teaching of humanities. *Publ:* Auth, Study of General Education at Heidelberg College, Heidelberg Col, 59. *Mailing Add:* Dept of English Olivet Col Olivet MI 49706

THORMANN, WOLFGANG E, b Augsburg, Ger, Nov 28, 24; US citizen; m 53; c 3. FRENCH LANGUAGE & LITERATURE. *Educ:* Columbia Univ BA, 49, MA, 50, PhD(French), 55. *Prof Exp:* Lectr French, Columbia Univ, 50-52, instr, 52-55; instr, Williams Col, 55-56; asst prof, Johns Hopkins Univ, 56-60; assoc prof, 60-63, chmn dept mod lang, 60-72, PROF FRENCH, GOUCHER COL, 63- *Concurrent Pos:* Managing asst ed, Mod Lang Notes, 58-60; mem, French Grad Rec Exam Comt & Advan French Col Entrance Exam Bd Comt, 66- *Mem:* MLA; Am Asn Teachers Fr; Soc Fr Hist Studies. *Res:* French literature of the 17th and 20th centuries; Franco-German relations. *Publ:* Auth, Again the Je ne sais quoi, Mod Lang Notes, 5/58; coauth, Travel literature, In: Critical Bibliography of French Literature, Vol III, Syracuse Univ, 61. *Mailing Add:* Dept of Mod Lang Goucher Col Towson MD 21204

THORN, ARLINE ROUSH, Comparative & English Literature. See Vol II

THORN, ERIC P, English, Comparative Literature. See Vol II

THORNTON, MARY ELIZABETH KELLY, b Mar, 2, 20; US citizen; m 41; c 4. CLASSICS, HUMANITIES. *Educ:* Goucher Col, AB, 41; Univ Mich, Ann Arbor, AM, 51, AM, 67; Fla State Univ, PhD(humanities), 72. *Prof Exp:* ASST PROF CLASSICS, MIAMI UNIV, 75- *Mem:* Am Philol Asn: Am Int Archaeol; Royal Numis Soc; Am Class League. *Res:* Numismatics; Roman history. *Publ:* Auth, Nero's New Deal, Trans & Proc Am Philol Asn, 71; The Enigma of Nero's Quinquennium, Historia, 73; The Round Temple, Archaeol News, 73; Augustan Tradition & Neronian Economics & Hadrian & His Reign, In: Aufstieg und Niedergang der Roemischen Welt, Temporini, 75; The Roman Lead Tesserae, Archaeol News, 76; The Roman lead Tesserae: Observations on two historical problems, Historia, 29:335-355. *Mailing Add:* Dept Classics Miami Univ Oxford OH 45056

THREATTE, LESLIE LEE, b Miami, Fla, Feb 1, 43. CLASSICAL PHILOLOGY. *Educ:* Oberlin Col, BA Harvard Univ, PhD(class philol), 69. *Prof Exp:* Asst prof class, Cornell Univ, 68-70; asst prof 70-75; ASSOC PROF CLASS, UNIV CALIF, BERKELEY, 75- *Mem:* Am Philol Asn; Mod Greek Studies Asn; Class Asn Can; Class Asn GB; Soc Promotion Hellenic Studies. *Publ:* Auth, The Grammar of Attic Inscriptions I, de Gruyter, Berlin, 79. *Mailing Add:* Dept of Class Univ of Calif Berkeley CA 94720

THURMAN, WILLIAM SIMS, b Paris, France, Mar 17, 31; US citizen; m 54; c 5. ROMAN HISTORY, GRECO-ROMAN LAW. *Educ:* David Lipscomb Col, BA, 51; Univ Tex, MA, 59, PhD(class lang), 64. *Prof Exp:* Asst prof Latin, Winthrop Col, 60-62; asst prof class lang & ancient hist, 64-66, assoc prof classics & ancient hist, 66-73, PROF CLASSICS & ANCIENT HIST, UNIV NC, ASHEVILLE, 73-, HEAD DEPT CLASSICS, 68- *Mem:* Am Philol Asn; Am Soc Polit & Legal Philos. *Res:* Roman law; Byzantine law; Biblical interpretation. *Publ:* Auth, How Justinian I sought to handle the problem of religious dissent, Greek Orthodox Theol Rev, spring 68; The application of subjecti to citizens in the imperial laws of the later Roman Empire, Klio, 70; A juridical and theological concept in the sixth century AD, Byzantino-slavica, 71; Thurman's Primer of Roman Law for Common Lawyers, Allied, 73. *Mailing Add:* Dept of Classics Univ of NC Asheville NC 28804

TICHOVSKIS, HERONIMS, b Latvia, Sept 22, 07; US citizen; m 49. LITERATURE & LINGUISTICS. *Educ:* Univ Latvia, MA, 33; Univ Bonn, Dr Phil, 49. *Prof Exp:* Instr Russ & Latvian, Commercial Insts, Rezekne & Ludsa, 30-39; supvr schs, Latvian Ministry Educ, 39-46; adv mod lang teaching, Ont Dept Educ, 55-60; instr Russ, Univ Conn, 60-61, asst prof, 62-67; from assoc prof to prof, 67-76, EMER PROF MOD LANG, NC A&T STATE UNIV, 76- *Concurrent Pos:* Comt Krisjanis Barons res award, 37; Latvian Found Cult res awards, 39 & 40; instr Russ, Univ Latvia & Inst Lang Riga, 40-41; ed-in-chief, Latvian Educ J, 42-44; chmn, Latvian Press Soc, 54-60; lit adv, Am Latvian Assoc, 65-71; transl mod lang, US Dept Com, DC, 67- *Honors & Awards:* Latrian Cult Award, 78. *Mem:* MLA; Am Asn Advan Slavic Studies; Am-Latvian Humanitarian Asn; Asn Advan Baltic Studies. *Res:* Relationship between the Baltic and Slavic languages and literature; German and Russian literature of the eighteenth and nineteenth centuries; Latvian literature. *Publ:* Auth, Wedding Customs in Latgale, Inst Folklore, 39; Ten Years of the Latvian exile, 54, ed, Ave Maria: An Anthology 58 & coauth & ed, Bishop Joseph Rancans: His Life and Work, 73, Astra Publ; auth, Lomonosov's view on the relation between Baltic and Slavic languages, In: Baltic Literatures and Linguistics, 73; ed, Selected Writings of Bishop Joseph Rancans, 77 & coauth & ed, Appreciation to Dr Zenta Maurina, 77, Astra. *Mailing Add:* Postal Sta D PO Box 365 Toronto ON M6P 3J9 Can

TIDWELL, JULIA BRUMBELOE, b Roanoke, Ala, Jan 4, 30; m 50; c 1. ROMANCE LANGUAGES. *Educ:* Birmingham-Southern Col, BA, 51; Univ Ala, MA, 55, PhD, 69. *Prof Exp:* Teacher, Shades Valley High Sch, 51-54 & Tuscaloosa Sr High Sch, 55-57; from asst prof to assoc prof, 58-73, PROF FRENCH & CHMN DIV HUMANITIES, STILLMAN COL, 73- *Concurrent Pos:* Gen consult, Southern Asn Cols & Schs, 70- *Mem:* MLA; SAtlantic Mod Lang Asn; Am Asn Teachers Fr; Am Asn Teachers Span & Port; Am Coun Teaching Foreign Lang. *Res:* Twentieth century French literature, especially Colette. *Mailing Add:* PO Box 4920 Stillman Col Tuscaloosa AL 35401

TIEE, HENRY HUNG-YEH, b Honan, China, Sept 20, 22; m 48; c 3. ENGLISH EDUCATION, LINGUISTICS. *Educ:* Peking Univ, BE, 45; Univ Nebr, MA, 63; Univ Tex, PhD, 67. *Prof Exp:* Dean & prin, Nat Northwestern Norm Sch, 45-48; dean & teacher high sch, Taiwan, 48-50; instr Chinese hist, Taipei Med Col, Taiwan, 50-52; assoc prof guid & coun, Taiwan Prov Norm Univ, 52-57; supvr teachers educ, Ministry Educ, Repub China, 56-60, sect chief, 60-63; asst educ admin, Univ Nebr, 63-64; res asst curric & instr, Univ Tex, Austin, 64-67; asst prof, 67-73, ASSOC PROF CHINESE LANG & LING, UNIV SOUTHERN CALIF, 73-, CHMN, DEPT EAST ASIAN LANG & CULT, 81- *Concurrent Pos:* Consult, Int Training Consult, Inc, Burbank, 71- *Mem:* Ling Soc Am; Am Coun Teaching Foreign Lang; MLA; Chinese Lang Teachers Asn; Asn Asian Studies. *Res:* Chinese phonology and syntax; teaching Chinese as a second language; foreign language teaching. *Publ:* Auth, Focus on Change, Guide to Better Schools, 63 & Curriculum Planning for Better Teaching & Learning, 63, Nat Educ Ctr; English Phonology for Speakers of Chinese, Univ Tex, 67; Contrastive analysis of the monosyllable structure of American English & Mandarin Chinese, Lang Learning, 69; An Approach for Teaching American English to Chinese Speakers Based on a Contrastive Syllabic & Prosodic Analysis, Ctr Appl Ling, 70; A Dict of 1800 High-Frequency Chinese Characters, Burbank, Calif, 73; Recent psycholinguistic development and the teaching Mandarin Chinese, J Chinese Teachers Asn, 75; The Profuctive Affixes in Modern Chinese Morphology, WORD, 79. *Mailing Add:* Dept of East Asian Lang & Cult Univ of Southern Calif Los Angeles CA 90007

TIEFENBRUN, SUSAN WANDA, b New York, NY, Sept 14, 43; m 67; c 3. FRENCH LITERATURE. *Educ:* Univ Wis, BS, 65, MS, 66; Columbia Univ, PhD(French), 71. *Prof Exp:* Lectr French, Brooklyn Col. 67-71; instr, Westchester Community Col, 71-72; ASST PROF FRENCH, COLUMBIA UNIV, 72- *Concurrent Pos:* Reader, Nat Endowment for Humanities, 78- *Honors & Awards:* Justin O'Brien Award, Columbia Univ, 73. *Mem:* MLA; Am Asn Teachers Fr; Northeast Mod Lang Asn; Ann Conf 17th Century Fr Lit. *Res:* Seventeenth century French literature; stylistics; semiotics. *Publ:* Auth, The art of repetition in La Princesse de Cleves, Mod Lang Rev, 1/73; A Structural Stylistic Analysis of La Princesse de Cleves, Mouton, 76; auth, Mathurin Regnier's Macette: A semiotic study in satire, Semiotica, 76; Boileau and his friendly enemy: A poetics of satiric criticism, Mod Lang Notes, 76; Computational stylistics and the French classical novel, Lang & Style, 78; Francois Maynard: La Belle Vieille: Une lecture semiotique, Cahier de l'Assoction des Amis de Maynard, fall 78; Semiotics, the arts and the sciences, Puncto de Contacto, fall 78; Signs of the Hidden: Semiotic Studies in XVIIth Century French Literature, Peter de Ridder, 78. *Mailing Add:* Dept of French & Romance Philol Columbia Univ New York NY 10027

TIFFOU, ETIENNE DESIRE, b Oran, Algeria, Sept 15, 35; Can Citizen; m 60; c 4. CLASSICS, LINGUISTICS. *Educ:* Sorbonne, Lic, 57, Dipl Etudes Super, 58, Agrege, 61, Dr es Lett, 71. *Prof Exp:* Prof, Oran Lycee, 60-62, Mourenx Lycee, 62-63; teaching asst, Univ Sherbrooke, 63-64; from asst prof to assoc prof, 64-77, PROF LING, UNIV MONTREAL, 77- *Mem:* Soc Etudes Latines; Class Asn Can; Can Ling Asn; Am Ling Asn; Soc Asiatique.

Res: History of Roman thought; Historical grammar of ancient languages; Burushaski. *Publ:* Auth, La discorde chez Ennius, Rev Et Lat, 68; Essai sur la pensec morale de Salluste a la lumiere de ses prologues, Paris, Klincksieck, 75; L'effacement de l'erfatif en bourouchaski, Studia Ling 78; Essai sur l'imparfait en latin et en francais, Rev Can Ling, 78; Note sur le personnage de Romulus, Melanges Heurgon P Ecole de Rome, 78; Salluste et la fortuna, Phoenix, 78; coauth, Pour une plus grande adepuation de traits phoentiques, Phonetica, 78; A note on split ergativity in Burushaski, Bull Sch Orient & African Studies, 82. *Mailing Add:* Dept of Ling Univ of Montreal Montreal PQ H3C 3J7 Can

TIGAY, JEFFREY HOWARD, b Detroit, Mich, Dec 25, 41; m 65; c 4. BIBLICAL STUDIES, ANCIENT NEAR EASTERN LITERATURE. *Educ:* Columbia Col, BA, 63; Jewish Theol Sem, Am, MHL, 66; Yale Univ, PhD(comp Blbl & ancient Near East studies), 71. *Prof Exp:* Ellis asst prof, 71-77, ABRAHAM M ELLIS ASSOC PROF HEBREW & SEMITIC LANG & LIT, UNIV PA, 77- *Concurrent Pos:* Grantee, Nat Sci Found, 72; assoc, Univ Sem on Studies Hebrew Bible, Columbia Univ, 72; Am Coun Learned Soc fel, 75-76; fel, Inst Advan Studies, Hebrew Univ, Jerusalem, 78-79; grant, Am Philos Soc, 80 & Am Coun Learned Soc, 80-81; Nat Endowment for Humanties summer res fel, 80; Mem Fedn Jewish Cult fel, 81-82; vis assoc prof, Bible Jewish Theol Sem Am. *Mem:* Asn Jewish Studies; Am Orient Soc; World Union Jewish Studies; Soc Bibl Lit; Am Schs Orient Res. *Res:* Biblical literature; comparative Biblical and ancient Near Eastern studies; ancient Judaism. *Publ:* Contribr, Encycl Judaica, MacMillan, 72; auth, An empirical basis for the documentary hypothesis, J Bibl Lit, 75; On Some Aspect of Prayer in the Bible, Asn Jewish Studies Rev, 76; On the Word Phylacteries, Matthew 23:5, Harvard Theol Rev, 79; the Evolution of the Gilgamesh Epic, Univ Pa Press, 82; Notes on the Development of the Jewish Week, In: H L Ginsberg Festschrift (in press); The Stylistic Criteria of Source Criticism in the Light of Ancient Near Eastern Literature, In: I L Seeligmann Festchrift (in press). *Mailing Add:* Dept Orient Studies Univ of PA Philadelphia PA 19104

TIKKU, GIRDHARI LAL, b Kashmir, India, Aug 18, 25; m 63; c 2. PERSIAN. *Educ:* Panjab Univ, India, BA, 43; Univ Panjab, WPakistan, MA, 45; Univ Tehran, MLit, 56, PhD(persian lang & lit), 61. *Prof Exp:* Res historian & lectr Persian & Urdu, Univ Calif, Los Angeles, 61-64, vis lectr Persian, Berkeley, 64-65; assoc prof Near Eastern lang & lit, Ind Univ, 65-68; prof Persian lit & assoc dir Asian ctr, 68-74, PROF COMP LIT & LING, UNIV ILL, URBANA, 74- *Concurrent Pos:* Indian Coun Cult Rels prof Indian Studies, Univ Tehran, 63; assoc dir, Ctr Asian Studies, Univ Ill, 68-71, campus coordr, Tehran Res Unit, 68-71; vis prof, Michigan State Univ, 69; adj prof, Univ Tehran, 71-72; res grant for proj, Mod Persian Soc: Lit as Index of Change, Midwest Univs Consortium for Int Activities, 71-72. *Mem:* Asiatic Soc, India; PEN Club; MLA; Mid Eastern Studies Asn. *Res:* Social change and value system; Persian literature; philosophy. *Publ:* Ed, Parsisarayan-i-Kashmir, 63 & Divani-i-Fani, 63, Indo-Iranian, Tehran; auth & ed, Furugh-i Farrukhzad, Studies Islamica, spring 67; Satinama of Varasta, Hist Relig, 11/67; translr, The School Principal, 69; auth, Persian Poetry in Kashmir, Univ Calif, 71; auth & ed, Islam and Its Cultural Divergence, Univ Ill, 71; Poems: Nineteen and Ten, 75. *Mailing Add:* Prog in Comp Lit Univ of Ill Urbana IL 61801

TILLES, SOLOMON H, b New York, NY, July 19, 32; m; c 3. SPANISH AMERICAN LITERATURE. *Educ:* Rutgers Univ, BA, 53; Columbia Univ MA, 58; Univ Mich, PhD(Span), 69. *Prof Exp:* Mem fac Span, Grinnell Col, 61-63; mem fac Span, 63-80, ASSOC PROF ROMANCE & CLASS LANG, UNIV CONN, 80- *Mem:* AAUP. *Res:* Spanish American theatre; language teaching. *Publ:* Auth, Some examples of zeitgeist in the Spanish American novel. Romance Notes, 65; A revised Spanish Major, 65 & Ruben Dario's Emelina, 66, Hispania; Rudolfo Usigli's concept of dramatic art, Latin Am Theatre Rev, 70; An experimental approach to the Spanish American theatre, Mod Lang J, 72; La importancia de la palabra en Rosalba y los Llaveros, Latin Am Theatre Rev, 75; coauth, Voces y Vistas, 75 & auth, Puntos de Vista, 77, Harper & Row. *Mailing Add:* Dept of Lit & Lang Univ Conn Storrs CT 06268

TILLETT, ANNE SMITH, b Norton, Va, Sept 15. MODERN FOREIGN LANGUAGES. *Educ:* Carson-Newman Col, AB, 35; Vanderbilt Univ, AM, 36; Northwestern Univ, PhD, 43. *Prof Exp:* From asst to prof mod foreign lang, Carson-Newman Col, 37-56, head dept, 45-51; asst prof Romance lang, 56-66, assoc prof Romance lang & Russ, 66-76, PROF RUSS & FRENCH, WAKE FOREST UNIV, 75-CHMN DEPT ROMANCE LANG, 74- *Mem:* Am Asn Teachers Fr; SAtlantic Mod Lang Asn; MLA; Am Asn Advan Slavic Studies. *Res:* Franco-American literary relations; criticism of American life and letters. *Publ:* Auth, Washington Irving in the Revue encyclopedique, Rev Lit Comp, 7-9/60; Some Sait-Simonian criticism of the United States before 1835, Romantic Rev, 2/61; coauth, Grammar in the Cold War, New Repub, 9/65. *Mailing Add:* Dept of Romance Lang Wake Forest Univ Winston-Salem NC 27109

TILLONA, ZINA, b Catania, Italy, Sept 3, 29; US citizen. ITALIAN. *Educ:* Hunter Col, BA, 50; Wellesley Col, MA, 51; Middlebury Col, DML, 60. *Prof Exp:* Instr Ital & Span, Univ Mass, 51-60; lectr Ital, Wellesley Col, 60-61, asst prof, 61-64; asst prof, Boston Univ, 64-66; assoc prof, 66-72, assoc chmn dept French & Ital, 69-73, actg assoc provost, 72-73, spec asst to chancellor, 73-78, asst chancellor, 78-80, PROF ITAL, UNIV MASS, AMHERST, 72- *Concurrent Pos:* Teacher English as foreign lang, Ctr Am Studies, Rome, 55-57; lectr, Hunter Col, 59-60; consult, Nat Broadcasting Found, 60; chmn comt exam Ital listening comprehension, Col Entrance Exam Bd, 68, chmn Ital exam comt, 68-72; mem, Fulbright Nat Screening Comt, 71-74, chmn Northeast sect, 72 & 74. *Mem:* MLA; Dante Soc Am; Am Asn Teachers Ital; Northeast Conf Teaching Foreign Lang. *Res:* Nineteenth and 20th century Italian literature; modern theater; Luigi Pirandello. *Publ:* Auth, Neo-realism revisited: La ragazza di Bube, 1/67 & La morte nelle novelle de Pirandello, 12/67, Forum Italicum; Bonaventura Tecchi, In: Encyclopedia of World Literature in the Twentieth Century, 71; Pirandello's Liola: A variation on a theme by Verga, Italica, 75; Francesco Jovine, In: Columbia Dictionary of Modern European Literature, 80. *Mailing Add:* 52 Chapel Rd Amherst MA 01002

TIMBIE, JANET ANN, History of Christianity, Coptic Language. See Vol IV

TIMPE, EUGENE FRANK, b Tacoma, Wash, Sept 24, 26; m 50; c 3. COMPARATIVE LITERATURE. *Educ:* Occidental Col, BA, 48; Univ Southern Calif, MA, 52, PhD(comp lit), 60. *Prof Exp:* Instr English, El Camino Col, 53-66; assoc prof Ger & comp lit, Pa State Univ, University Park, 66-72; chmn dept foreign lang & lit, 72-81, PROF GER & COMP LIT, SOUTHERN ILL UNIV, CARBONDALE, 72- *Concurrent Pos:* Fulbirght grants, Vienna, 58-59, Rome 60-61; lectr, Univ Md, Munich, 63-64; vis prof, Univ Neuchatel, Switz, 70-71. *Mem:* MLA; Am Comp Lit Asn; Int Ver Ger Sprach-u Literaturwiss; Am Lessing Soc; Asn Dept Foreign Lang (pres, 77). *Res:* 18th century; literary theory. *Publ:* Auth, American literature in Germany, 1861-1872, Chapel Hill, 64; Hesse's Siddhartha and the Bhagavad Gita, Comp lit, 70; The spatial dimension: A stylistic typology, In: Yearbook of Comparative Criticism, Vol III, 71; ed & contribr, Thoreau Abroad, Archon Bks, 71; auth, Infernal space: Structure and context, Ital Quart, 72; Wieland's Singspiele and the rebirth of German opera, Seminar, 77; Memory and literary structures, J Mind & Behav, 81. *Mailing Add:* Dept of Foreign Lang & Lit Southern Ill Univ Carbondale IL 62901

TINKLER, JOHN DOUGLAS, English, Philology. See Vol II

TINNELL, ROGER DALE, b Lynchburg, Va, Aug 18, 44. SPANISH, COMPARATIVE LITERATURE. *Educ:* Univ Va, BA, 66, MA, 68, PhD(Span), 73. *Prof Exp:* Asst prof Span, The Citadel, 70-72; instr, Univ Va, 72-73; asst prof, 73-76, assoc prof, 76-80, PROF SPAN, PLYMOUTH STATE COL, 80- *Mem:* MLA, Am Asn Teachers Span & Port; SAtlantic Mod Lang Asn; Northeastern Mod Lang Asn; Southern Comp Lit Asn. *Res:* Medieval Spanish literature and music; modern spanish literature; Jungian criticism. *Publ:* Auth, Role playing and motherhood in La Familia de Pascual Duarte, Int Fiction Rev, 76; An annotated discography of recordings of music from the Middle Ages in Spain, 76-77 & A discography of recordings of Las Cantigas de Santa Maria of Alfonso X, el Sabio, 77, La Coronica; Carl Jung Pascual Duarte, secret stones and the individuation process, Papers Lang & Lit, 78; An Annotated Discography of Music in Spain Before 1650, Hisp Sem Medieval Studies, 80; Authorship and composition: Music and Poetry in the Cantigas de Santa Maria, Ky Romance Quart, 81; Conversation with Eugenio Florit, Mod Lang Studies (in prep). *Mailing Add:* Plymouth State Col Plymouth NH 03264

TINNIN, ALVIS LEE, b Graham, NC, May 7, 22. FRENCH LITERATURE. *Educ:* Carleton Col, BA, 49; Yale Univ, MA, 54, PhD(French lit), 61. *Prof Exp:* Instr French, Yale Univ, 54-57; admin asst metals, Olin Mathieson Chem Corp, 59-6l; spec rep pharmaceuticals, E R Squibb & Sons, WAfrica, 61-63, export sales mgr, 63-64; dir int mkt, Doyle Dane Bernback, Inc, 64-66; cult attache, US Inform Agency, Turkey, 67-69; fel, Johnston Col, 69-71, assoc prof, 71-73, PROF FRENCH LIT, UNIV REDLANDS, 73-, CHMN DEPT, 77- *Mem:* Am Coun Teaching For Lang; Western Soc Fr Hist. *Res:* Nineteenth century French antislavery writers; techniques of translation. *Mailing Add:* Dept of French Univ of Redlands Redlands CA 92373

TINSLEY, ROYAL LILBURN, JR, b Houston, Tex, July 26, 25; m 52; c l. GERMANIC LANGUAGES & LITERATURE. *Educ:* Univ Houston, BA, 60; Tulane Univ, PhD(Ger), 65. *Prof Exp:* Lectr Ger & Russ, 63-66, asst prof, 66-68, assoc prof, 68-80, PROF GER, UNIV ARIZ, 80- *Concurrent Pos:* Mem Am foreign students resl comt & US students abroad comt, Nat Asn Foreign Students Affairs, 67-70. *Mem:* Am Coun Teaching Foreign Lang; Am Asn Teachers Ger; MLA; Am Translr Asn (pres-elect, 73-75, pres, 75-77). *Res:* Foreign language teacher training and teaching methods; cross-cultural communication, especially American-foreign student relations; translator training. *Publ:* Auth, Guidelines for college and university programs in translator training, Bull Asn Depts Foreign Lang, 5/73; coauth, Approaching German culture: A tentative analysis & auth, An alternate major in German, Die Unterrichtspraxis, spring 74; coauth, Translation: American doctoral dissertation, 1970-74, Mod Lang J, 3/77; contribr, International Encyclopedia of Higher Education, Jossey-Bass, 77; co-translr, The Mongoloid Child, Univ Ariz, 77. *Mailing Add:* Dept of Ger Univ of Ariz Tucson AZ 85721

TIPTON, GARY PRIOR, b Springville, Utah, Apr 5, 38; m 62; c 4. CHINESE LANGUAGE & LITERATURE. *Educ:* Ind Univ, PhD(Chinese), 74. *Prof Exp:* ASST PROF CHINESE, ARIZ STATE UNIV, 69- *Mem:* Asn Asian Studies; Chinese Lang Teacher's Asn. *Res:* Chinese language pedagogy; Chinese linguistics; Chinese-American history. *Publ:* Auth, Non-cognate consonants of Mandarin and Cantonese, J Chinese Lang Teachers Asn, 75; Men out of China, J Ariz Hist, autumn 77. *Mailing Add:* Dept of Foreign Lang Ariz State Univ Tempe AZ 85281

TITCHE, LEON L, JR, b Monroe, La, Jan 14, 39; m 60 c 3. GERMAN LANGUAGE & LITERATURE. *Educ:* Tulane Univ, BA, 61, PhD(Ger), 64. *Prof Exp:* PROF GER, PURDUE UNIV, WEST LAFAYETTE, 64-, ASST HEAD DEPT, 80- *Mem:* MLA: Mod Humanities Res Asn. *Res:* The Austrian writer Adalbert Stifter; the works of Robert Musil; the application of myth to literary analysis. *Publ:* Auth, The concept of the hermaphrodite: Agathe and Ulrich in Musil's novel Der Mann ohne Eigenschaften, Ger Life & Lett, 69; Döblin and Dos Passos: aspects of the city novel, Mod Fiction Studies, 71; Into the millenium: Robert Musil's Der Mann ohne Eigenschaften, Oxford Ger Studies, 73; Robert Musil's die portugiesin: Psychology of the modern fairy tale, Univ Dayton Rev, 80. *Mailing Add:* Dept of Foreign Lang & Lit Grad Sch Purdue Univ West Lafayette IN 47907

TITTLER, JONATHAN PAUL, b Brooklyn, NY, Apr 19, 45; m 78. LATIN AMERICAN NOVEL, CONTEMPORARY LITERARY CRITICISM. *Educ:* Hamilton Col, AB, 67; Cornell Univ, PhD(Span lit), 74. *Prof Exp:* Asst prof Span, Hamilton Col, 74-75; Bates Col, 75-76; vis asst prof, Hamilton Col, 76-77; vis asst prof, 77-78, asst prof, 78-82, ASSOC PROF SPAN, CORNELL UNIV, 82- *Concurrent Pos:* Juror Premico Novela Jorge Isaacs,

Calif, Columbia, 82. *Mem:* MLA: Am Asn Teachers Span & Port; Northeast Mod Lang Asn. *Res:* Afro-Latin-American novel; popular culture; semiotics. *Publ:* Auth, Intratextual distance in Tres tristes tigres, Mod Lang Notes, 3/78; Interview with Carlos Fuentes, Diacritics, 9/80; Interview with Gustavo Alvarez Gardeazabal, Chasqui, 11/81; Latia Julia (historia) y el escribidor (ficcion), Actas en honeuaje a Slejo Carpentier, Monte Avila, 6/82; The Esthetics of Fragmentation in La Vida a Plazos de don Jacobo Lerner, Taller Literario, 6/82; transl, Abalberto Ortiz, Juyungo, Three Continents Press, 6/82; auth, Order, Chaos, and Re-order: The Novels of Manuel Prig, Ky Romance Quart (in press); Approximately Irony, Mod Lang Studies (in press). *Mailing Add:* Dept of Romance Studieses Cornell Univ Ithaca NY 14853

TJART, PETER, b Crimea, Russia, Nov 27, 16; US citizen; m 51; c 2. GERMAN & RUSSIAN LANGUAGE & LITERATURE. *Educ:* Anderson Col, BA, 49; Ind Univ, MA, 52. *Prof Exp:* From instr to asst prof, 56-65, ASSOC PROF GER, ANDERSON COL, IND, 65- *Mem:* Am Asn Teachers Ger; Am Coun Teaching Foreign Lang; Am Asn Advan Slavic Studies; Am Hist Soc Ger from Russia. *Res:* Schiller, the dramatist and philosopher; the process of learning a foreign language; the history and literature of the Soviet Union. *Mailing Add:* 1317 Rainike Dr Anderson IN 46012

TOBIN, FRANK JUDE, b Omaha, Nebr, July 13, 35; m 66; c 2. GERMAN LITERATURE. *Educ:* Berchmanskolleg, Pullach, Ger, PhL, 60; Marquette Univ, MA, 64; Stanford Univ, PhD(Ger), 67. *Prof Exp:* Asst prof, Univ Calif, Santa Barbara, 67-75; assoc prof Ger, 75-80; PROF FOREIGN LANG & LIT, UNIV NEV, RENO, 80- *Mem:* MLA; Asn Teachers of Ger; Medieval Acad Am. *Res:* Medieval German narrative literature; medieval German mystical thought. *Publ:* Auth, Eckhart's mystical use of language: The contexts of eigenschaft, Seminar, 72; Gregorius and Der arme Heinrich, In: Hartmann's Dualistic and Gradualistic View of Reality, Stanford Univ, 73; Legality and formality in the Nibelungenlied, Monatschefte, 74; Gregorius and fallen man, Ger Rev, 75; Style in Eckhart's German sermons, Semasia, 76; translr with introd, Der arme Heinrich Allegorica, 76; Hartmann's Erec: The perils of young love, Seminar, 78; Final irony in Der Zauberberg, German Life and Lett, 77. *Mailing Add:* Dept of Foreign Lang & Lit Univ Nev Reno NV 89557

TOBIN, RONALD WILLIAM FRANCIS, b New York, NY, June 19, 36; m 60; c 1. FRENCH LANGUAGE & LITERATURE. *Educ:* St Peter's Col, AB, 57; Princeton Univ, MA, 59, PhD(Romance lang), 62. *Prof Exp:* Instr French lang & lit, Williams Col, 62-63; from asst prof to assoc prof French, Univ Kans, 63-69, chmn dept French & Ital, 67-69; chmn dept French & Ital, 69-71, chmn dept French & Ital, 75-80, PROF FRENCH, UNIV CALIF, SANTA BARBARA, 69- *Concurrent Pos:* Asst, Princeton Univ, 60-61; Am Philos Soc res grant, 63; mem univ adv coun, Am Coun Life Insurance, 70-; mem bd trustees, Baudry Franco-Am Found, 77-; Am Coun Learned Soc grant, 78 & 80. *Honors & Awards:* Chevalier, Palmes Academiques, 72. *Mem:* Mod Humanities Res Asn; MLA; Am Asn Teachers Fr; Soc Etude XVIIe Siecle. *Res:* Seventeenth century French tragedy; Racine; Mythology in literature. *Publ:* Auth, Racine and Seneca, Univ NC, 71; coauth, Paths to Freedom: Studies in French Classicism in Honor of E B O Borgerhoff, L'Esprit Createur, 71; auth, Trends in Racinian Criticism, Fr Rev, 72; ed, Myth and Mythology in 17th Century French Literature, L'Esprit Createur, 76; Esthetique et Societe au 17e Siecle, Papers on French 17th Century Literature, No 6, 76; Theme et Thematique de la Tragedia, Papers French 17th Century Lit, 79. *Mailing Add:* Dept French Univ Calif Santa Barbara CA 93106

TOCONITA, MICHAEL J, b Philadelphia, Pa, Dec 8, 21. MODERN LANGUAGES. *Educ:* Univ Pa, BS, 48, MS, 51, PhD, 64. *Prof Exp:* Instr mod lang, Drexel Inst Technol, 48; from asst prof to assoc prof, 48-67, dir lang lab, 61-73, PROF MOD LANG, ST JOSEPH'S UNIV, PA, 67-, CHMN DEPT, 79- *Concurrent Pos:* Fulbright award, 54; lectr, Grad Sch, Villanova Univ, 56-73; consult, Pa Dept Educ Lang Labs, 64; Am Philos Soc res grant, 65-66; vis comt bd trustees, Lehigh Univ, 78-81. *Mem:* MLA; Am Asn Teachers Fr; NEA. *Res:* French literature; applied linguistics; lexicography. *Publ:* Auth, Three Problems in Contemporary French Monolingual Lexicography, Univ Pa, 64; Abbreviations, words formed by literation and acronyms, Ling, 6/65; Lexicographical treatment of inflected forms of irregular verbs, Fr Rev, 11/65; The defining of transitive verbs, Int Rev Appl ling, 12/65. *Mailing Add:* Dept of Mod Lang St Joseph's Univ Philadelphia PA 19131

TODD, EVELYN MARY, b Hamilton, Ont, Sept 22, 39. LINGUISTICS, CULTURAL ANTHROPOLOGY. *Educ:* Univ Toronto, BA, 60; Univ NC, Chapel Hill, PhD(anthrop), 70. *Prof Exp:* Asst prof anthrop & ling, Univ Toronto, 63-68; assoc prof, 68-80, PROF OF ANTHROP AND LING, TRENT UNIV, 80- *Concurrent Pos:* Vis prof, Univ Sask, Saskatoon, 67. *Mem:* Ling Soc Am; fel Am Anthrop Asn; Can Ling Asn; Am Orient Soc. *Res:* Oceanic linguistics; Pacific ethnography; Algonquian linguistics. *Publ:* Auth, Ojibwa syllabic writing and its implications for a standard Ojibwa alphabet, Anthrop Ling, 12/72. *Mailing Add:* Dept of Anthrop Trent Univ Peterborough ON K9J 7B8 Can

TODD, WILLIAM MILLS, III, b Newport News, Va, Aug 15, 44; m 68; c 1. RUSSIAN & COMPARATIVE LITERATURE. *Educ:* Dartmouth Col, AB, 66; Oxford Univ, BA & MA, 68; Columbia Univ, PhD(Russ & comp lit), 73. *Prof Exp:* Asst prof Slavic, 72-77, ASSOC PROF SLAVIC & COMP LIT, STANFORD UNIV, 77-, CHMN DEPT, 80- *Concurrent Pos:* Fel, Fulbright Hays Found, 76, Int Res & Exchanges, 76 & Nat Endowment Humanities, 78; vis asst prof Slavic, Yale Univ, 77; US rep, Int Dostoevsky Soc, 77- *Honors & Awards:* Dean's Award Superior Teaching Stanford Univ, 76. *Mem:* MLA; Am Asn Advan Slavic Studies; Int Dostoevsky Soc. *Res:* Eighteenth and nineteenth century Russian and European literature; theory of literature; literature and society. *Publ:* Auth, Gogol's epistolary writing, Columbia Essays Int Affairs, 70; The anti-hero with a thousand faces: Saltykov-Shchedrin's Porfiry Golovlev, Studies Lit Imagination, 76; The Familiar Letter as a Literary Genre in the Age of Pushkin, Princeton Univ, 76; Eugene

Onegin: Life's novel, In: Literature and Society in Imperial Russia: 1800-1914, 78; ed, Literature and Society in Imperial Russia: 1800-1914, Stanford Univ, 78. *Mailing Add:* Dept of Slavic Lang & Lit Stanford Univ Stanford CA 94305

TOELKEN, JOHN BARRE, Medieval Literature. See Vol II

TOLIVER, HAZEL MAY, b Fayetteville, Ark, Mar 20, 09. LATIN. *Educ:* Univ Ark, AB, 29, AM, 33; State Univ Iowa, PhD(class lang), 45. *Prof Exp:* Teacher high schs, Ark, 29-32, 34-42; teacher Latin, Univ High Sch, State Univ Iowa, 42-43, asst classics, 43-45; instr class lang & lit, Ind Univ, 45-50, mem staff res & transl class lit, 50-52; asst prof classics & hist, Univ Kansas City, 52-55; assoc prof Latin, Northeast Mo State Teachers Col, 55-57; prof classics, Lindenwood Col, 57-74, chmn dept, 60-74, chmn humanities div, 71-73; RETIRED. *Mem:* Am Philol Asn; Am Class League; Class Asn Mid West & South. *Res:* Classical languages, literature and civilization; social influence of the ancient Roman theater; activities and status of Roman women. *Publ:* Auth, The Terentian doctrine of education, 3/50, Oved's attitude toward the Roman Theater, 1/51, Class Weekly; Plautus and the state Gods of Rome, 11/52 & The Fabulae Palliatae and the spread of Hellenism, 4/54, Class J; The Roman theatre: Breeder of cosmopolites, Ky Foreign Lang Quart, 58; The Roman matinee-goes, 1/58, Reincarnation of the Gods, 10/61, Elementary Latin: Preparation or entertainment, 3/65, Class Outlook. *Mailing Add:* Rte 3 Box 221 Pocahontas AR 72455

TOLLERSON, MARIE SHERROD, b New Haven, Conn, Jan 1, 34; div. AFRICAN FRANCOPHONE LITERTURE. *Educ:* St Augustine's Col, BA, 55; Univ Conn, Storrs, MA, 58; Univ Ariz, PhD(French), 78. *Prof Exp:* Chmn, Dept Mod Lang, Southern Univ, Shreveport, 67-68; supvr secondary practice teachers, Univ Hartford, 69-70; COORDR FOREIGN LANG, LEMOYNE-OWEN COL, 77- *Mem:* MLA; African Lit Asn; Am Asn Teachers French; Am Asn Teachers Span & Port. *Res:* African folktale; West African novel; French theater. *Publ:* Auth, Mythology and Cosmology in the Narratives of B Dadie and B Diop: A Structural Approach, Three Continents Press, 82. *Mailing Add:* Apt 6 802 Walker Ave Memphis TN 38126

TOLTON, CAMERON DAVID EDWARD, b Toronto, Ont, Aug 15, 36. ROMANCE LANGUAGES & LITERATURES, CINEMA. *Educ:* Univ Toronto, BA, 58; Harvard Univ, AM, 59, PhD(Romance lang & lit), 65. *Prof Exp:* From lectr to asst prof, 64-69, ASSOC PROF FRENCH, VICTORIA COL, UNIV TORONTO, 69- *Concurrent Pos:* Mem adv acad panel, Soc Sci & Humanities Res Coun of Can, 79- *Mem:* MLA; Asn Can Univ Teachers Fr; Can Comp Lit Asn; Film Studies Asn Can. *Res:* Andre Gide; the French novel, 1800-1950; French autobiography. *Publ:* Auth, Image-conveying abstractions in the works of Andre Gide, In: Image and Theme: Studies in Modern French Fiction, Harvard Univ, 69; Andre Gide and the Art of Autobiography, Macmillan, Can, 75; The revirement: A structural key to the novels of Francois Mauriac, Australian J of Fr Studies, 1-4/75; Andre Gide and Christopher Isherwood: Two worlds of counterfeiters, Comp Lit, spring 78; Le Mottheme Attente et l'Ironie Gidienne, Bull Des Amis D'Andre Gide, 1/82. *Mailing Add:* Dept of French Victoria Col Univ of Toronto Toronto ON M5S 1K7 Can

TOMANEK, THOMAS J, b Hodonin, Czech, June 5, 31; m 68. SPANISH AMERICAN LITERATURE, SPANISH LANGUAGE. *Educ:* Charles Univ, Prague, PhD(Romance lang & lit), 55. *Prof Exp:* Instr Span, Univ Victoria, BC, 65-66; asst prof Span Am lit, Univ Ore, 66-71; assoc prof, 71-80, PROF FOREIGN LANG, CALIF STATE UNIV, HAYWARD, 80- *Concurrent Pos:* Orgn Am States res grant, 76. *Mem:* Inter-Am Soc; Int Invention Development Asn. *Res:* The modern novelists, the Modernista movement and the early chroniclers in Spanish America. *Publ:* Auth, Gottfried Keller, Literarni Noviny, Prague, 57; Padaji s nebe kvety (anthology), Ceskoslovensky Spisovatel, Prague, 58; The estranged man--Kafka's influence on Arreola, Rev des Lang Vivantes, 71; El mito y el lenguaje en la nueva novela hispanoamericana, Rev des lang romanes, 72; Barrenechea's Restauracion de la Imperial y conversion de almas infieles, Rev des lang vivantes, 74. *Mailing Add:* Dept of Foreign Lang & Lit Calif State Univ Hayward CA 94952

TOMARKEN, ANNETTE HERDMAN, b Faversham, England, Aug 31, 38; m 66; c 1. FRENCH. *Educ:* Univ London, England, BA, 60, PhD(French), 66. *Prof Exp:* Asst lectr French, Univ Leeds, England, 62-63; from asst lectr to lectr, Birkbeck Col, London Univ, 64-66; asst prof, NY Univ, 69-72; VIS ASST PROF FRENCH, MIAMI UNIV, OHIO, 76- *Concurrent Pos:* Lang programme coordr, Miami Univ Europ Ctr, Luxembourg, 80-82. *Mem:* MLA; Midwestern Mod Lang Asn Am; Int Soc Hist Rhet; Soc Study Medievalism (secy, 77-). *Res:* Renaissance French poetry and satire; late medieval poetry and rhetoric; French women writers. *Publ:* Coauth, The rise and fall of the sixteenth-century French Blason, Symposium, 75; co-transl, Autobiography in the third person, New Lit Hist, 77; auth, Clement Marot and the grands rhetoriqueurs, Symposium, 78; co-transl, The great game of rhetoric, New Lit Hist, 79; auth, The Bernesque writers capitoli on disease, 15th Century Studies, 80; transl, Reflexivity and reading, New Lit Hist, 80; Marguerite Dural, The King's Garden, Univ Va Press, 82; auth, Mock-epideictic literature of the Renaissance, Acta of Int Soc Hist Rhet, 82. *Mailing Add:* 326 W Vine St Oxford OH 45056

TOMAYKO, JAMES EDWARD, b Charleroi, Pa, July 8, 49; m 72. CHINESE LANGUAGE, HISTORY OF TECHNOLOGY. *Educ:* Carnegie-Mellon Univ, BA, 71, DA, 80; Univ Pittsburgh, MA, 72. *Prof Exp:* Headmaster, Self-Directed Learning Ctr, 75-80; instr hist, Garden City Community Col, 80-81; tech pub specialist, NCR Corp, 81; ASST PROF COMP SCI, HIST & CHINESE, WICHITA STATE UNIV, 82- *Mem:* Soc for the Hist of Technol; Asn Comput Mach; Chinese Lang Teachers Asn; Am Asn Artificial Intelligence; Asn Comput Ling. *Res:* History of computing; Chinese natural language processing. *Publ:* Auth, The ditch irrigation boom in Southwest Kansas, J of the West, fall 82; A simple, comprehensive input/output system for Chinese natural language processing, Comp Sci Dept, Wichita State Univ, 5/82; The relationship between the N-BU-N and V-BU-V constructions in Chinese, Proc of the Mid-Am Ling Conf, 82. *Mailing Add:* 828 S Holyoke Wichita KS 67218

TOMKIW, BOHDAN STEPHEN, b Podvolochyska, Sept 20, 13; US citizen; m 50; c 1. GERMAN, POLITICAL SCIENCE. *Educ:* Univ Lvov, PhD(Ger lit), 33; Univ Warsaw, PhD(math), 37. *Hon Degrees:* LLD, Innsbruck Univ, 47. *Prof Exp:* Instr Ger lit, Univ Warsaw, 33-37; asst prof math, Univ Lvov, 37-39; Ger tutor, 39-60; PROF GER, ST BONAVENTURE UNIV, 60- *Concurrent Pos:* Consult, Cong Comt of Am, 60- *Mem:* Am Acad Polit & Soc Sci; Coun Foreign Relat; Acad Polit Sci; Nat Affairs Asn. *Res:* East-European problems; Soviet-economy; socialist legality. *Publ:* Auth, Free or planned Economy (in Ger), 47, The Political Parties and the Democracy, 49, Revolution in Russia, 1917, 61, New Policy in Soviet Economy, 64, Religious Consciousness in SSSR, 66 & The Intellectual Climate of the Russian Revolution, 72, Wagn Univ Buchdruckerei. *Mailing Add:* Dept Mod Lang St Bonaventure Univ St Bonaventure NY 14778

TOMLINS, JACK EDWARD, b El Reno, Okla, Jan 21, 29. FOREIGN LANGUAGES. *Educ:* Univ NMex, AB, 51, MA, 53; Princeton Univ, MA, 56, PhD, 57. *Prof Exp:* Instr Span & Port, Princeton Univ, 56-59; asst prof Span, Wake Forest Col, 59-60; asst prof Span & Port, Rutgers Univ, 60-64; assoc prof, Chatham Col, 64-67, chmn dept mod lang, 65-67; assoc prof, 67-71, PROF PORT, UNIV NMEX, 71- *Concurrent Pos:* US Dept State res grant, Rio de Janeiro, Brazil, 54. *Mem:* MLA; Rocky Mountain Mod Lang Asn (pres, 76-77); Am Asn Teachers Span & Port; SCent Mod Lang Asn; SAtlantic Mod Lang Asn. *Res:* Brazilian literature of the 20th century; Portuguese literature of the 20th century; medieval Spanish literature. *Publ:* Auth, Machado's Cock and Bull story: Tristram Shandy and Braz Cubas, In: The Brazilian Novel, Luso-Brazilian Lit Ser No 1, Ind Univ, 76; Mario de Andrade, In: Modern Latin American Literature, Frederick Ungar, 75; Selected translations, In: The Borzoi Anthology of Latin American Literature, Alfred A Knopf, 77; Selected translations, In: The Literary Review, Fairleigh Dickinson Univ, Vol 21, No 2; Selected translation, In: The Poetry of Jorge de Sena, Mudborn Press, 80; Jorge de Sena: Miniaturista Lirico, In: Studies on Jorge de Sena, Jorge de Sena Ctr for Port Studies & Bandanna Bks, 81; coauth, A likely contemporary source for The Damned be the First Builder of Boats, Bull Comediantes, 33: 63-65; auth, Character and structure in Almeida Faria's A Paixao, Selected Proc of the 2nd La Conf on Hispanic Langs & Lits, La Chispa, 81. *Mailing Add:* Dept of Mod & Classical Lang Univ of NMex Albuquerque NM 87131

TONELLI, FRANCO, b Modena, Italy, Nov 25, 34. FRENCH LITERATURE. *Educ:* Univ Rome, Laurea law, 58; Univ Lausanne, cert French, 61; La State Univ, PhD(French), 66. *Prof Exp:* Instr French & Span, McNeese State Col, 62-63; instr French & Ital, La State Univ, 64-66; asst prof, 66-71, ASSOC PROF FRENCH & ITAL, UNIV CALIF, IRVINE, 71-, CHMN DEPT, 73-, DIR, FILM STUDIES PROG, 80- *Mem:* MLA. *Res:* Contemporary French theatre; 16th century French literature. *Publ:* Auth, When theatre becomes cruelty: Artaud and Sade, Comp Drama, 6/69; L'Esthetique de la cruaute, Nizet, Paris, 72; Le rite et le mythe dans le theatre de M de Ghelderode, Fr Rev. *Mailing Add:* Dept of French & Ital Univ of Calif Irvine CA 92650

TONOLO, ALFRED E, b Mestre-Venice, Italy, Dec 30, 20; US citizen; m 49; c 1. SPANISH. *Educ:* Ca'Foscari Univ, BEd, 40; Colgate Univ, MA, 65; Univ Madrid, DR(Span), 66. *Prof Exp:* Teacher Ital, Liceo Venice, 45-55; teacher Span & French, Farragut Acad, NJ, 56-59; teacher Span, Binghamton Sch Dist, 59-67; assoc prof, 67-70, dir Span lit symp, 69, PROF SPAN, BLOOMSBURG STATE COL, 70-, DIR FOREIGN STUDY ABROAD, 67- *Concurrent Pos:* Foreign lang consult, Wyoming Valley Sch Dist, Kingston, Pa, 68- *Honors & Awards:* Civil Merit Cross of Comendador, Gen Francisco Franco, Spain, 72. *Mem:* Am Asn Teachers Span & Port; MLA. *Res:* Italian. *Publ:* Auth, Angel Ganivet, 110 anniversary, 75 & Teaching La Vida Es Sueno in H S, 76, Ind Univ Pa. *Mailing Add:* 928 Bel Air Dr Berwick PA 18603

TOON, THOMAS EDWARD, b Ann Arbor, Mich, Mar 24, 42; m 69; c 1. ENGLISH LINGUISTICS. *Educ:* Univ Mich, BA, 70, PhD(English lang), 75; Eastern Mich Univ, MA, 72. *Prof Exp:* Asst prof English & ling, Univ Utah, 75-78; ASST PROF ENGLISH LANG & LIT, UNIV MICH, 78- *Mem:* Ling Soc Am; MLA; Medieval Acad Am; Am Dialect Soc; Ling Asn Can & US. *Res:* English historical syntax and phonology; American social and regional dialects; Old English manuscripts and dialects. *Publ:* Auth, The actuation and implementation of an Old English sound change, Third LACUS Forum, 76; The variationist analysis of Early Old English manuscript data, Current Progress in Hist Ling, 76; Dialect mixture and language change, Proc XII Int Cong Linguists, 78; Lexical diffusion in Old English, CLA XIV, 78; Old English dialects: Methodology reconsidered, Int Conf Methods in Dialectol, 78. *Mailing Add:* Dept of English Univ of Mich 7607 Haven Hall Ann Arbor MI 48109

TOPAZIO, VIRGIL WILLIAM, b Middletown, Conn, Mar 27, 15; m 41; c 1. FRENCH LITERATURE. *Educ:* Wesleyan Univ, BA, 43; Columbia Univ, MA, 47, PhD(French), 51. *Prof Exp:* Lectr, Columbia Univ, 47-48; from instr to assoc prof French, Univ Rochester, 48-60, prof, 60-64; Fulbright vis prof, Univ Rennes, 64-65; chmn dept French, 65-67, vpres of univ, 68-70, PROF FRENCH, RICE UNIV, 65-, DEAN DIV HUMANITIES & SOC SCI, 67- *Honors & Awards:* Chevalier des Palmes Academiques, 66 & Officier des Palmes Academiques, 77, French Govt. *Mem:* MLA; Am Asn Teachers Fr. *Res:* Eighteenth and 19th century French literature; Italian literature. *Publ:* Auth, D'Holbach's Moral Philosophy: Its Background and Development, Inst Musee Voltaire, Geneva, 56; Voltaire: A Critical Study of His Major Works, Random, 67; Emma vs Madame Bovary, Rice Univ Studies, spring 71; Voltaire, the poet revisited, Symposium, summer 72; D'Holbach's moral code: Social and humanistic, Studies Voltaire, 72. *Mailing Add:* Div of Humanities & Soc Sci Rice Univ Houston TX 77001

TOPPING, DONALD M, b Huntington, WVa, Nov 1, 29; c 5. LINGUISTICS. *Educ:* Univ Ky, BA, 54, MA, 56; Mich State Univ, PhD(English ling), 63. *Prof Exp:* Asst prof English, Col of Guam, 56-58; instr English, Mich State Univ, 59-60; asst prof English lang, Col of Guam, 60-62;

instr English lang, 62-64, from asst prof to assoc prof, 64-73, PROF LING, UNIV HAWAII, MANOA, 73-, DIR, SOCIAL SCI RES INST, 74- *Concurrent Pos:* Ling consult, off int prog, Univ Hawaii, 63-67, Asia Training Ctr, 66-68; coordr US Peace Corps, Materials Prep Micronesian Lang, 66-67; Nat Sci Found res award, 68-69; consult, Regional English Lang Ctr, Singapore, 68-69; dir, Pac & Asian Ling Inst, 69- *Mem:* Ling Soc Am; Int Ling Asn. *Res:* Micronesian linguistics; Land Dayak languages; Political and economic development in Pacific Islands and attendant social change. *Publ:* Auth, Restatement of Chamorro phonology, Anthrop Ling, 69; Spoken Chamorro, 69, Chamorro Reference Grammar, 73 & Chamorro-English Dictionary, 74, Univ Hawaii; The Pacific Islands: Polynesia, Vol 25, No 2, Melanesia, Vol 25, No 3, & Micronesia, Vol 25, No 3, Am Univ Field Staff, Field Reports, 3/77. *Mailing Add:* Social Sci Res Inst 2424 Maile Way Honolulu HI 96822

TOPPING, EVA CATAFYGIOTU, b Fredericksburg, Va, Aug 23, 20; m 51; c 1. MEDIEVAL LITERATURE. *Educ:* Mary Washington Col, BA, 41; Radcliffe Col, MA, 43. *Prof Exp:* Instr class, Wheaton Col, 44-45; instr Latin, Buckingham Sch, 47-48; lectr mod Greek, Univ Cincinnati, 66-69 & 76-78; RES & WRITING, 78- *Res:* Byzantine literature, particularly hymnography; Byzantine hagiography; Greek-American history. *Publ:* Auth, A Byzantine Song for Symeon, Traditio, 68; The Apostle Peter, Jusinian..., Byzantine & Mod Greek Studies, 76; Sacred Stories from Byzantium, Holy Cross Orthodox Press, 77; Romanos, On the Entry into Jerusalem, Byzantion, 77; Mary at the Cross, Byzantine Studies, 77; On Earthquakes and Fires, Byzantinische Zectschuft, 78; Three Byzantine Sacred Poetry Hymnography, Holy Cross Orthodox Press, 79; A Guide to Byzantine, Class Folia Ed, 79. *Mailing Add:* 1823 Rupert St McLean VA 22101

TORRES, DAVID, b Laredo, Tex, Oct 30, 34. SPANISH LANGUAGE & LITERATURE. *Educ:* Univ Tex, Austin, BA, 58, MA, 62; Univ Ill, PhD(Span), 69. *Prof Exp:* Asst prof Span, Eastern Wash State Col, 69-71, Ind State Univ, 71-73 & WVa Univ, 73-79; ASSOC PROF SPAN, ANGELO STATE UNIV. *Mem:* Am Asn Teachers Span & Port; SCent Mod Lang Asn. *Res:* Nineteenth century Spanish literature; culture and civilization of Spain; Hispanic culture and civilization. *Publ:* Auth, La fantasia y sus consecuencias en La desheredada, Boletin Bibliot Menendez Pelayo, 76; Las comedias moratinianas de Martinez de la Rosa, Cuadernos Hispanoam, 78; Trece cartas ineditas de Pereda, Boletin Bibliot Menendez Pelayo, 80; Estudio de un personaje galdosiano, Cuadernos Am, 81; Del archivo epistolar de Palacio Valdes, Rev Lit, 81; Clarin y Las virgenes locas: Doce autores en busca de una novela, Cuadernos Hispanoam, 82; Los prologos de Leopoldo Alas, Rodopi, Amsterdam, 82. *Mailing Add:* Dept of Mod Lang Angelo State Univ San Angelo TX 76909

TORRES, SIXTO E, b Comerio, PR, Oct 16, 44; m 71; c 2. SPANISH LITERATURE & DRAMA. *Educ:* Kent State Univ, BS, 69, MA, 72; Fla State Univ, PhD(Span lit), 80. *Prof Exp:* Teacher Span & Math, Ohio Sch, 68-72 & Fla Sch, 72-80; ASST PROF SPAN LIT, UNIV LOUISVILLE, 81- *Concurrent Pos:* Instr Span, Pasco Community Col, 72-74; consult, Dept Educ, Fla State Testing, Curriculum & Testing, 79-80, Ky Testing Comn & Nat Span Examinations, 82-; adv Grad Teachers, Univ Louisville, 81-, lang coordr, 81- & asst ed, Perspectives, 82- *Mem:* MLA; Am Asn Teachers Span & Port; SAtlantic Mod Lang Asn; AAUP. *Res:* Twentieth century drama--theater of Eduardo Quiles; 20th century Afro-antillian poetry; theater of the avant-garde. *Publ:* Auth, Jose Martin Recuerda's El enganao, Lang Q, 80-81; ed, Jose M Recuerda, El teatrito de don Ramon, Scribner's & Sons, 82. *Mailing Add:* Dept Class & Mod Langs Univ Louisville Louisville KY 40292

TORRES-DELGADO, RENE, b New York, NY, June 10, 47. FOREIGN LANGUAGES, FINE ARTS. *Educ:* Univ PR, Rio Piedras, BA, 69; Middlebury Col, MA, 70; Pac Southern Univ, PhD(Span), 77. *Prof Exp:* Instr classics, Ponce Col, 71-72; instr fine arts, 73-77, ASST PROF FINE ARTS, UNIV PR, RIO PIEDRAS, 77- *Concurrent Pos:* Dep dir, Inst Puerto Rican Cult, 80-81. *Honors & Awards:* Cavaliere di Grazia Magistrale, Ordine di S Giorgio ex-Carinthia, 77. *Mem:* Am Asn Teachers Span & Port. *Res:* Art appreciation; historical subjects and literary criticism. *Publ:* Auth, Apuntes Historico-literarios, 76, Voz de Jose de Diego, 77 & Retratos galdosianos, 78, Florentia; Del Interregno, 1868, a la Restauracion, 1874, Clio, 78. *Mailing Add:* Fine Arts Dept Col of Humanities Univ of PR Ponce de Leon Ave Rio Piedras PR 00931

TORRIELLI, ANDREW JOSEPH, b Boston, Mass, Dec 18, 12; m 38; c 1. ROMANCE LANGUAGES. *Educ:* Harvard Univ, AB, 33, AM, 34, PhD(Romance philol), 39. *Prof Exp:* From instr to asst prof Romance lang, Fordham Univ, 37-41; pres, Eaton Press, Inc, 46-64; assoc prof mod lang, Mass State Col Lowell, 64-67; chmn dept, 67-72, prof, 67-80, EMER PROF MOD LANG, LOYOLA UNIV, ILL, 80- *Mem:* MLA; Am Asn Teachers Ital. *Res:* European-American cultural relations. *Publ:* Auth, Italian Opinion on America, 1860-1900, Harvard Univ, 41; Order of Battle, Italian Army, 42, coauth, Military Phrase Books, 42 & Military Dictionary, 42, US Army; The French Presence in Illinois, Am Bicentennial Comn, 77; Guerra d'America, an unpublished manuscript on the American Revolution, Prco 1st Int Cong Am Hist, 78; Americana Italiana, 1600-1940, Univ Florence, 78. *Mailing Add:* 655 W Irving Park Rd Apt 1610 Chicago IL 60613

TOSCANI, BERNARD MICHAEL, b Philadelphia, Pa, Apr 7, 26. ITALIAN, FRENCH. *Educ:* Bowdoin Col, AB, 47; Harvard Univ, AM, 48; Columbia Univ, MA, 58; Univ Pa, PhD, 61; Univ Rome, Dr Lett, 72. *Prof Exp:* From instr to asst prof Ital & French, Bryn Mawr Col, 60-66, lectr Ital, 66-68; dean, Am Col Monaco, 68-69; from asst prof to assoc prof, 69-78, PROF ITAL & FRENCH, BROOKLYN COL, 78- *Concurrent Pos:* City Univ New York fac res award, 75-76. *Mem:* Mediaeval Acad Am; Am Asn Teachers Ital; Renaissance Soc Am; Am Asn Teachers Fr; Dante Soc Am. *Res:* Renaissance Italian and French, especially the Italian lauda of the 15th century. *Publ:* Translr, Daius Milhaud's L'amour chante poems of Ronsard, Dubellay, Labe, Verlain & Rimbaud), Presser, 65; Pirandello, Se trouver, Ed Denöel, Paris, 68; auth, Jean Meschinot: Les lunettes des Princes, une edition critique, Minard, Paris, 71; L'indice dei capoversi del Codice Vaticano Chigiano L VII, 266, 76 & Una nota sul cpaitolo Madre de Cristo, 76, Aevum; Una inedita lauda quattro centista in onore di S Domenic, La Nuova Rivista Ascetica e Mistica, 76; Le laude dei Bianchi contenute nel Codice Vaticano Chigiano L VII 266: edizione critica, Diorentina, Florence, 78. *Mailing Add:* Dept of Mod Lang & Lit Brooklyn Col Brooklyn NY 11210

TOSH, L WAYNE, b Rusk, Tex, Apr 2, 33; m 67; c 3. COMPUTATIONAL LINGUISTICS, GERMANIC LANGUAGES. *Educ:* Univ Tex, Austin, BA, 55, MA, 57, PhD(Ger philol), 62. *Prof Exp:* Res assoc machine transl, Univ Tex, Austin, 60-67, spec res assoc machine transl & comput ling & asst prof ling, 67-68; from asst prof to assoc prof, 69-75, PROF LING, ST CLOUD STATE UNIV, 75- *Mem:* Ling Soc Europe; Asn Comput Ling. *Res:* Computer-aided instruction. *Publ:* Auth, Syntactic Translation, Mouton, The Hague, 65; Initial results of syntactic translation at the Linguistics Research Center, 68 & Translation model with semantic capability, 69, Linguistics; chap, In: Stratificational Grammar and Interlingual Mapping, Proc 10th Int Congr Linguists, 69. *Mailing Add:* Dept of English St Cloud State Univ St Cloud MN 56301

TOTTEN, CHRISTINE M, b Frankfurt, Ger, Aug 12, 20; US citizen; m 50; c 3. GERMAN LITERATURE, CULTURAL HISTORY. *Educ:* Univ Heidelberg, PhD(Ger & English philol), 44. *Prof Exp:* Asst lectr, Univ Heidelberg, 46-51; lectr Ger hist, Univ Md Overseas, 53-65; PROF GER, CLARION STATE COL, 65- *Res:* History of American-German relations. *Publ:* Auth, Matthias Claudius, Stahlberg, Karlsruhe, 49; Deutschlang-Soll und Haben: Amerikas Deutschlandbild, Rütten & Loening, Munich, 64. *Mailing Add:* Dept of Ger Clarion State Col Clarion PA 16214

TOTTEN, MONIKA M, b Krefeld, Ger. GERMAN LITERATURE. *Educ:* Univ Mass, Boston, BA, 71; Harvard Univ, MA, 75, PhD(Ger lit), 77. *Prof Exp:* ASST PROF GER LIT & LANG, DARTMOUTH COL, 77- *Mem:* MLA; Am Asn Teachers Ger; Northeast Mod Lang Asn. *Res:* Literary theory; narrative technique; literary criticism. *Mailing Add:* Dept of Ger Dartmouth Col Hanover NH 03755

TOUGAS, GERARD RAYMOND, b Edmonton, Alta, Aug 5, 21; m 48; c 2. FRENCH. *Educ:* Univ Alta, BA, 43; McGill Univ, MA, 46; Stanford Univ, PhD(French), 53. *Prof Exp:* Interpreter French-English, World Health Orgn, Geneva, 48-50; instr French, Stanford Univ, 51-53; PROF FRENCH, UNIV BC, 63- *Concurrent Pos:* Carnegie Corp fel, 63-64; Can Coun fel, 70-71. *Mem:* Royal Soc Can. *Res:* Literatures of French-speaking countries. *Publ:* Auth, Litterature romande et culture francaise, Ed Seghers, Paris, 63; La francophonie en peril, Cercle Livre France, Montreal, 67; Litterature canadienne-francaise contemporaine, Oxford Univ, Toronto, 69; Litterature canadienne-francaise, Presses Univ France, Paris, 5th ed, 73; Les ecrivains d'expression francaise et la France, Ed Denoel, Paris, 73. *Mailing Add:* Dept of French Univ of BC Vancouver BC V6T 1W5 Can

TOWNSEND, CHARLES EDWARD, b New Rochelle, NY, Sept 29, 32; m 57; c 3. SLAVIC LANGUAGES & LINGUISTICS. *Educ:* Yale Univ, AB, 54; Harvard Univ, MA, 60, PhD, 62. *Prof Exp:* Instr Slavic lang & lit, Harvard Univ, 62-65, asst prof Slavic lang, 65-66; asst prof Slavic lang, 66-68, assoc prof Slavic Lang & Lit, 68-71, bicentennial preceptor, 66-68, dir, Critical Lang Prog, 68-70, PROF SLAVIC LANG & LIT, PRINCETON UNIV, 71-, CHMN DEPT, 70- *Concurrent Pos:* Clark Fund grant, Harvard Found Advan Studies & Res, 63, 65; Inter-Univ Comt travel grant, Czech & res fel, Inst Lang & Lit, Czech Acad Sci, 68, Int Res & Exchanges Bd res fel, Czech Lang Inst, 71; mem adv bd, Russ Lang J, 73- & ed bd, Folia Slavica, 77- *Mem:* Am Asn Teachers Slavic & East Europ Lang; Ling Soc Am; Am Coun Teachers Russ. *Res:* Russian language and linguistics; Czech language and linguistics; Slavic linguistics. *Publ:* Auth, Russian Word-formation, McGraw, 68; Part of speech in roots and the zero-suffix in Russian, In: Studies Presented to Roman Jacobson by his students, Slavica, 68; Continuing with Russian, McGraw, 70; On small words that can be big problems, Russ Lang J, 72; coauth, Toward a new classification of Czech verbs, 72 & auth, Semantic shifts: an approach to difficult vocabulary, Slavic & East Europ J; On i-verbs in Russian and Czech; transitivization and factitives, Folia Slavica, 77; The Memoirs of Princess Natal'ja Borisovna Dolgorukaja, 77 & Czech Through Russian, 81, Slavica. *Mailing Add:* 145 Hickory Ct Princeton NJ 08540

TRACY, GORDON, b Winnipeg, Man, Sept, 18, 24; m 47; c 4. GERMAN. *Educ:* Queen's Univ, Ont, BA, 48; Univ Strasbourg, cert, 49; Univ Wis, MA, 50, PhD, 55. *Prof Exp:* Instr Ger, Grinnell Col, 52-53; from instr to asst prof, Victoria Col, 53-58, assoc prof, 59-61; assoc prof, 61-64, chmn dept, 67-70, PROF GERMAN, UNIV WESTERN ONT, 64- *Mem:* Humanities Asn Can (Secy-treas, 62-64); Can Ling Asn; Am Asn Teachers Ger; MLA; Asn Can Univ Teachers Ger. *Res:* Modern German literature. *Publ:* Co-ed, Deutsche Gedichte, Am Bk Co, 63; coauth, Dauer im Wechsel: An Antology of German Literature, Heath, 68; auth, Das Gestische and the poetry of Brecht, In: Essays on German Literature, Univ Toronto, 68. *Mailing Add:* Dept of Ger Univ of Western Ont London ON N6A 5B8 Can

TRACY, STEPHEN VICTOR, b Brockton, Mass, Apr 6, 41; m 59; c 2. CLASSICAL PHILOLOGY. *Educ:* Brown Univ, BA, 63; Harvard Univ, MA, 65, PhD(Class philol), 68. *Prof Exp:* From instr to asst prof, Greek & Lating, Wellesley Col, 67-71; from asst prof to assoc prof, 71-77, PROF CLASSICS, OHIO STATE UNIV, 77- *Concurrent Pos:* Am Coun Learned Soc fel, 70-71; Nat Endowment for Humanities res fel, 72-73. *Mem:* Am Philol Asn; Archaeol Inst Am; Vergilian Soc; Am Sch Class Studies, Athens. *Res:* Greek and Latin literature; Greek epigraphy. *Publ:* Auth, Identifying epigraphical hands, Greek Roman & Byzantine Studies, winter 70; Prometheus bound 114-117, Harvard Studies Class Philol, 71; The lettering of an Athenian Mason, Hesperia Suppl, Vol 15, 74; Notes on the Pythais inscriptions, Bull de Corresp Hellenique, 75; The Marcellus passage and Aeneid 9-12, Class J, 75; Greek Inscriptions from the Athenian Agora, Hesperia, 76; Catullan echoes: Aeneid 6, 333-336, Am J Philol, 77. *Mailing Add:* Dept of Class 414 Univ Hall Ohio State Univ Columbus OH 43210

TRACY, THEODORE JAMES, b Chicago, Ill, Jan 2, 16. CLASSICS, PHILOSOPHY. *Educ:* Loyola Univ, Ill, AB, 38, MA, 42; West Baden Col, Ind, STL, 51; Princeton Univ, MA, 55, PhD, 62. *Prof Exp:* Instr classics, Xavier Univ, Ill, 55-56; instr classics & ancient philos & researcher, Loyola Univ, Ill, 56-58, asst prof class studies, 58-68, chmn dept, 60-68, assoc prof, 68-70; assoc prof, 70-82, EMER ASSOC PROF CLASS STUDIES, UNIV ILL, CHICAGO CIRCLE, 82- *Concurrent Pos:* Trustee, Loyola Univ, 59-61, 72-81 & Jesuit Sch Theol, Chicago, 74-80. *Honors & Awards:* Distinguished Prof of the Year, Loyola Univ, Chicago, 70. *Mem:* Am Class League; Am Philol Asn; Archaeol Inst Am; Class Asn Midwest & S; Soc Ancient Greek Philos. *Res:* Classical languages and literature; Greek philosophy; Greek science and medicine. *Publ:* Auth, Physiological Theory and the Doctrine of the Mean in Plato and Aristotle, Mouton, The Hague, 70, Loyola Univ, 70; Plato, Galen, and the center of consciousness, 76 & Perfect friendship in Aristotle's Nicomachean Ethics, 79, Ill Class Studies; The soul as boatman of the body: Presocratics to Descartes, Diotima, 79; The soul/boatman analogy in De Anima, Class Philol, 82. *Mailing Add:* 6525 Sheridan Rd Chicago IL 60626

TRAGER-JOHNSON, EDITH CROWELL, b New York, NY, Oct 13, 24; m 51, 69; c 3. LINGUISTICS. *Educ:* Wilson Col, AB, 44; Hunter Col, AM, 46; Univ Pa, PhD, 60. *Prof Exp:* Sci linguist, Bd Geog Names, US Dept Interior, 49-53; asst prof ling, Am Univ, 54-56; res assoc ling, Walter Reed Army Inst Res, 60-61; res assoc, Stanford Univ, 61-62; assoc prof English & ling, San Jose State Univ, 62-68, prof ling, 68-70; vis prof English, Univ Calif, Santa Barbara, 70-72; prof & chmn ling prog, 72-79, EMER PROF ENGLISH, SAN JOSE STATE UNIV, 79- *Concurrent Pos:* Fulbright lectr ling, Tel-Aviv Univ, 67-68; consult, Speech Commun Res Lab, Santa Barbara, Calif, 73-75; consult, Univ Calif, Santa Barbara & Speech Technol Lab, Santa Barbara, Calif, 79- *Mem:* Fel Am Anthrop Asn; Ling Soc Am; Am Dialect Soc. *Res:* Linguistic theory; automatic speech recognition; psycholinguistics. *Publ:* Coauth, Pronunciation drills, English for Foreigners, English Lang Serv, 62 & 75; Linguistics and the design of psycholinguistic experiments, In: Papers in Honor of Leon Dostert, Mouton, 67; Kiowa and English pronouns, In: Studies in Linguistics in Honor of Raven I McDavid, Univ Ala, 72; Black on Black: An Interview Analyzed, Mid Am Ling Conf, 76; The Interface between Linguistics and Speech Recognition, Speech Technology (in prep). *Mailing Add:* 951 Cocopah Dr Santa Barbara CA 93110

TRAHAN, ELIZABETH WELT, b Ger, US citizen. GERMAN & COMPARATIVE LITERATURE. *Educ:* Sarah Lawrence Col, BA, 51; Cornell Univ, MA, 53; Yale Univ, PhD, 57. *Prof Exp:* Instr Ger & Russ, Univ Mass, 56-60; from asst prof to assoc prof Russ, Univ Pittsburgh, 60-66; assoc prof comp lit & chmn dept transl & interpretation, 68-74, interim acad dean, 77, PROF HUMANITIES, MONTEREY INST INT STUDIES, 75-, COORDR PROG HUMANITIES & GER, 77- *Concurrent Pos:* Asst, Dramaturg Vienna Burgtheater, 45-47. *Mem:* MLA; Am Asn Teachers Slavic & EEurop Lang; Am Translr Asn; Am Asn Teachers Ger; Am Comp Lit Asn. *Res:* Comparative & German literature of the 19th and 20th centuries; Tolstoy; translation and interpretation techniques. *Publ:* Auth, A common confusion: A basic approach to Franz Kafka's world, Ger Quart, 5/63; Clamence vs Dostoevsky: An approach to La Chute, Comp Lit, fall 66; ed, Gruppe 47: Ein Querschnitt, Blaisdell, 69; co-translr, Gogol, Russ Lit Triquart, fall 72, reprinted, Twentieth Century Russian Literary Criticism, Yale Univ, 75; Vasily Gippius: A company of freaks, Criticism in Translation, spring 76; The Literary Translator as Involuntary Critic, Pac Quart, 80; ed, Gogol's Overcoat: An Anthology of Critical Essays, Ardis, 82. *Mailing Add:* 79 Via Ventura Monterey CA 93940

TRAILL, DAVID ANGUS, b Helensburgh, Scotland, Jan 28, 42. LATIN, GREEK. *Educ:* Univ St Andrews, MA, 64; Univ Calif, Berkeley, PhD(classics), 71. *Prof Exp:* Asst prof, 70-78, ASSOC PROF CLASSICS, UNIV CALIF, DAVIS, 78- *Mem:* Am Philol Asn; Medieval Asn Pac; Am Inst Archaeol. *Res:* Classical and medieval Latin poetry; Schliemann. *Publ:* Auth, The addressee and interpretation of Walahfrid Strabo's Metrum Saphicum, Medievalia et Humanistica, 71; contribr, Vol XLI, The Oxyrhynchus papyri, Egypt Explor Soc, 72; auth, Walahfrid Strabo's Wettini, Lang, 74; Schliemann's mendacity: Fire and fever in California, Class J, 74; Horace, Odes 1.14: Genealogy, courtesans and cyclades, Studies Latin Lit, 1: 266-270; Ring-composition in Catullus 64, Class J, 76: 232-241; Catullus 63: Rings around the sun, Class Philol, 76: 211-214; Schliemann's Discovery of Priam's Treasure, Antiquity, 82. *Mailing Add:* Dept Classics Univ of Calif Davis CA 95616

TRAILL, JOHN STEWART, b Ottawa, Ont, May 24, 39; m 68; c 2. CLASSICAL PHILOLOGY. *Educ:* Univ Toronto, BA, 61; Harvard Univ, MA, 62, PhD(class philol), 67. *Prof Exp:* Instr classics, Colby Col, 64-65; asst prof, Victoria Col, Univ Toronto, 68-69; Can Coun & Edward Capps res fels, Am Sch Class Study, Athens, 69-70; res assoc Greek epigraphy, Inst Advan Study, Princeton, 70-72; asst prof, 72-76, ASSOC PROF CLASSICS, VICTORIA COL, UNIV TORONTO, 76- *Concurrent Pos:* Can Coun Leave fel, Am Sch Class Studies, Athens, 78-79. *Mem:* Am Philol Asn; Clas Asn Can; Can Mediterranean Int. *Res:* Greek epigraphy; Greek and Latin literature; Athenian topography. *Publ:* Auth, Athenian inscriptions honoring Prytaneis, Hesperia, 71; coauth, The Athenian councillors, Vol XV, In: Athenian Agora, 74; auth, The political organization of Attica, suppl XIV, 75, Revision of A New Ephebic inscription from the Athenian Agora, 76, Diakris, the inland Trittys of Leontis, 78 & Greek inscriptions for the Athenian Agora, Addenda to Athenian Agora, Vol XV, 78, Hesperia; Athenian Bouleutre Alternate, In: Studies in Honour of M F McGregor, 81; Interpretation of Six Rock-Cut Inscriptions from the Attre Demes of Lamptrai, Heperia, Suppl 19, 82; Prytary and Ephebic Incriptions from the Athenan Agora, Hesperia, 82. *Mailing Add:* Dept of Classics Victoria Col Univ of Toronto Toronto ON M5S 1K7 Can

TRAKAS, PEDRO NICHOLAS, b Spartanburg, SC, May 19, 23; m 46; c 5. SPANISH. *Educ:* Wofford Col, AB, 44; Nat Univ Mex, MA, 45; Univ NC, PhD, 54. *Hon Degrees:* LittD, Wofford Col, 72. *Prof Exp:* Asst prof Span, Davidson Col, 47-49, 51-54, assoc prof, 54-60; PROF SPAN LANG & LIT, ECKERD COL, 60- *Concurrent Pos:* Dir jr yr abroad, Assoc Mid-Fla Cols in Spain, 72-73. *Mem:* Am Asn Teachers Span & Port; SAtlantic Mod Lang Asn. *Res:* Spanish American literature; Spanish language and literature. *Publ:* Ed, A Buero Vallejo's Concierto de San Ovidio, Scribner, 65. *Mailing Add:* 5048 43rd St S St Petersburg FL 33711

TRAPNELL, WILLIAM HOLMES, b Richmond, Va, Sept 16, 31; m 58. FRENCH LITERATURE. *Educ:* Hampden-Sydney Col, BA, 54; Middlebury Col, MA, 62; Univ Pittsburgh, PhD (French lit), 67. *Prof Exp:* Instr French, Hampden-Sydney Col, 59-60; instr, Rollins Col, 60-63; asst instr, Univ Pittsburgh, 66-67; asst prof, Brown Univ, 67-69; asst prof, 69-73, ASSOC PROF FRENCH, IND UNIV, BLOOMINGTON, 73- *Mem:* Am Soc Eighteenth Century Studies; Mod Humanities Res Asn. *Res:* Eighteenth century French literature; Marivaux; Voltaire. *Publ:* Auth, The philosophical implications of Marivaux's Dispute & Voltaire's manuscripts and collective edition, In: Studies on Voltaire and the Eighteenth Century, 70; Marivaux's unfinished novels, Fr Studies, 7/70; Voltaire and his portable dictionary, Analecta Romanica, 72; Voltaire and the Eucharist, In: Studies on Voltaire and the Eighteenth Century, 81; Christ and his associates in Voltairian polemic, In: Stanford French and Italian Studies, 82. *Mailing Add:* Dept of French & Ital Ind Univ Bloomington IN 47401

TRAPP, RICHARD L, b Rockford, Ill, Sept 3, 23; m 50; c 4. CLASSICS. *Educ:* Univ Calif, Berkeley, AB, 49, MA, 52, PhD(classics), 59. *Prof Exp:* Instr classics, Univ Ariz, 49-51; assoc, Univ Calif, Berkeley, 55-56; instr, Stanford Univ, 56-60; asst prof, Univ Southern Calif, 60-65; ASSOC PROF CLASSICS & WORLD LIT, SAN FRANCISCO STATE UNIV, 65-, CHMN DEPT & ASSOC DEAN SCH HUMANITIES, 70- *Concurrent Pos:* Consult, Am Class League, 66-68. *Mem:* Am Comp Lit Asn; Am Class League; Archaeol Inst Am; Am Philol Asn. *Res:* Greek epic; Greek and Roman drama; Greek and Latin lyric poetry. *Publ:* Auth, Ajax in the Iliad, Class J, 3/61; Aspects of imagery in Catullus, Horace and Ovid, Class Bull, 3/65; Renaissance of Latin, NCalif Foreign Lang, 12/67. *Mailing Add:* Dept of Classics San Francisco State Univ San Francisco CA 94132

TRAUGOTT, ELIZABETH CLOSS, b Bristol, England, Apr 9, 39; m 67. LINGUISTICS. *Educ:* Oxford Univ, BA, 60, MA, 64; Univ Calif, Berkeley, PhD(English lang), 64. *Prof Exp:* Asst prof English, Univ Calif, Berkeley, 64-68; lectr ling, 68-71, assoc prof, 71-76, PROF LING & ENGLISH, STANFORD UNIV, 76- *Concurrent Pos:* Mem, Joint Inst/Ministry Educ Lang & Lit Panel, Dar es Salaam, Tanzania, 65-66; vis lectr ling, Univ EAfrica, 65-66 & Univ York, England, 66-67; Am Coun Learned Soc fel, 75-76. *Mem:* Ling Soc Am; Int Ling Asn; Ling Asn Gt Brit; Am Asn Univ Women. *Res:* Language change; structure and history of the English language; linguistics and literature. *Publ:* Auth, Diachronic syntax and generative grammar, Language, 65; A History of English Syntax, Holt, 72; Pidgins, Creoles, and the origins of Vernacular Black English, In: Black English: A Seminar, 76; Natural Semantax: Its role in the study of second language acquisition, In: Actes du 5eme colloque linguistique appliquee de Neuchatel, Libr, Droz, Geneva, 76; Pidginization, creolization and language, In: Pidgin and Creole Linguistics, Ind Univ, 77; On the expression of spatio-temporal relations in language, Universals Human Lang, Vol III, 78; Meaning-change in the development of grammatical markers, Lang Sci, 80; coauth (with Mary L Pratt), Linguistics for Students of Literature, Harcourt, 81. *Mailing Add:* Dept of Ling Stanford Univ Stanford CA 94305

TRAUPMAN, JOHN CHARLES, b Nazareth, Pa, Jan 2, 23; m 49; c 1. CLASSICAL LANGUAGES. *Educ:* Moravian Col, BA, 48; Princeton Univ, MA, 51, PhD(classics), 56. *Prof Exp:* From instr to assoc prof, 51-61, PROF CLASSICS, ST JOSEPH'S UNIV, 61-, CHMN DEPT, 56- *Concurrent Pos:* Assoc ed, Scribner Bantam English Dictionary, 77. *Mem:* Am Philol Asn; Archaeol Inst Am; Am Class League. *Res:* Archaeology; Latin lexicography. *Publ:* Auth, New Collegiate Latin and English Dictionary, Bantam, 66; The New College Latin and English Dictionary, Amsco, 68. *Mailing Add:* Dept of Classics St Joseph's Univ Philadelphia PA 19131

TRAVERSA, VINCENZO PAOLO, b Venezia, Italy, Apr 8, 23; US citizen; m 57. ITALIAN LANGUAGE & LITERATURE. *Educ:* Orient Inst, Naples, DLett, 49; Univ Calif, Los Angeles, MA, 59, PhD(Romance lang & lit), 63. *Prof Exp:* Instr Ital, Allied Forces Southern Europ, Naples, 53-57; from instr to asst prof, Stanford Univ, 60-67; assoc prof, Univ Kans, 67-70; PROF FOREIGN LANG & LIT & CHMN DEPT, CALIF STATE UNIV, HAYWARD, 70- *Mem:* MLA; AAUP; Am Asn Teachers Ital. *Res:* Modern English novel; the Verista school in Italian literature. *Publ:* Auth, Quaderno di esercizi, 67 & Parola e pensiero del professore, 67, Harper; Racconti di Alberto Moravia, Appleton, 68; Luigi Capuana: A Critic and Novelist, Mouton, The Hague, 68; Idioma in prospettiva, 69, Idioma in prospettiva del professore, 69 & Programma di laboratorio, 69, Harper ; coauth, Frequency Dictionary of Italian Words, Mouton, The Hague, 73. *Mailing Add:* Dept of Foreign Lang & Lit Calif State Univ Hayward CA 94542

TRAVIS, ALBERT HARTMAN, b Los Angeles, Calif, Dec 22, 13; m 57; c 1. CLASSICAL PHILOLOGY. *Educ:* Univ Southern Calif, AB, 36; Harvard Univ, AM, 38, PhD, 40. *Prof Exp:* Instr Greek & Latin, Harvard Univ & Radcliffe Col, 40-42; asst prof, Univ Southern Calif, 46-47; from asst prof to prof classics, 47-76, chmn dept, 54-62, 65-68, actg chmn dept, 75-76, EMER PROF CLASSICS, UNIV CALIF, LOS ANGELES, 76- *Mem:* Am Philol Asn; Archaeol Inst Am; Philol Asn Pac Coast(pres, 60); Mediaeval Acad Am. *Res:* Virgil; Greek drama. *Publ:* Auth, Donatus and the Scholia Danielis, Harvard Studies Class Philol, 42; co-ed, Editio Harvardiana of Servius, Am Philol Asn, Vols III & IV, 65-80; sr co-ed, California Studies in Classical Antiquity, Univ Calif, Vols IV & V, 71 & 72. *Mailing Add:* 1166 Mill Lane San Marino CA 91108

TREGGIARI, SUSAN MARY, Ancient History, Classics. See Vol I

TREICHLER, PAULA ANTONIA, Language, Medicine. See Vol II

TREMBLEY, GEORGE R, b Ridgewood, NJ, Dec 10, 24; Swiss citizen; m 50. FRENCH. *Educ:* Univ Montpellier, Lic es Let, 49; Yale Univ, PhD, 60. *Prof Exp:* Instr French, Yale Univ, 54-58; asst prof, Smith Col, 58-65; assoc prof, 65-76, PROF FRENCH, UNIV TORONTO, 76- *Mem:* MLA; Am Asn Teachers Fr. *Res:* Seventeenth, eighteenth and nineteenth century French literature. *Mailing Add:* Dept of French Scarsboro Col Univ of Toronto Toronto ON M5S 1A1 Can

TREUSCH, PAUL E, b Chicago, Ill; c 1. LAW. *Educ:* Univ Chicago, PhB, 32, JD, 35. *Prof Exp:* Atty, pvt practice, 35-37; law fac legal res & writing, Law Sch, La State Univ, 37-38; asst chief coun, Off Chief Coun, Internal Revenue Serv, 38-70; prof law, Law Sch, Howard Univ, 65-73 & 76-79 & Sch of Law, Boston Univ, 73-76; PROF LAW, SCH OF LAW, SOUTHWESTERN UNIV, 79- *Concurrent Pos:* Prof lectr law, Law ctr, George Washington Univ, 66-72; prof lectr law, Law Ctr, George Washington, 66-72; nat pres Feb Bar Asn, 69-70; mem, House of Deligates, Am Bar Asn, 70-72; Fed Bar Found Bd, 70-; head, law firm of Winston & Strawn, 70-72; tax adv comt, Am Law Inst, 79- *Mem:* Am Law Inst; Am Judicature Soc; Asn Am Law Sch. *Publ:* Auth, Tax Exempt Charitable Organizations, Am Law Inst, 79. *Mailing Add:* 675 S Westmoreland Ave Los Angeles CA 90005

TREVES, NICOLE, b Cairo, Egypt, Feb 15, 36; US citizen; m 72; c 1. FRENCH LITERATURE, CINEMA. *Educ:* Am Univ Cairo, BSc, 56; Rice Univ, PhD (French), 71. *Prof Exp:* Actg asst prof French, Univ Calif, Los Angeles, 68-70, asst prof, 70-76; asst prof French, San Diego State Univ, 76-80. *Concurrent Pos:* Newspaper reporter, J d'Eqypte & Images, 53- 57; ed, Corrosion Abstracts, Nat Asn Corrosion Engrs, 58-62. *Mem:* MLA; Am Asn Teachers Fr; Popular Cult Asn; Ctr Study Dem Inst; Mensa. *Res:* Sixteenth century French literature; contemporary thought; women studies. *Publ:* Auth, numerous articles in Images & J d'Egypte, 53-57; ed, Bibliographic Survey of Corrosion, Nat Asn Corrosion Engrs, Vols 1958 & 1959, 60 & 62; auth, The slapsticks of politics: Protagonists in French and American films, Can Rev Am Studies, fall 74; Le livre des ressemblances d'Edmond Jabes, Fr Rev, 12/77; Le moi vulnerable de Montaigne, Synthesis, 12/77. *Mailing Add:* 19201 Schoenborn St Northridge CA 91324

TRIFILO, S SAMUEL, b Italy, Mar 8, 17; US citizen; m 48; c 3. SPANISH LANGUAGE & LITERATURE. *Educ:* Cornell Univ, BS, 40; Univ Buffalo, MA, 51; Univ Mich, PhD, 57. *Prof Exp:* Instr, Univ Mich, 55-57; from asst prof to assoc prof, 57-65, resident dir, Madrid studies ctr, 67-68, chmn dept foreign lang, 72-78, PROF SPAN, MARQUETTE UNIV, 65- *Concurrent Pos:* Am Philos Soc grant, 61; Soc Sci Res Coun grant, 63. *Mem:* MLA; Midwest Mod Lang Asn; Am Asn Teachers Span & Port; Am Coun Teaching Foreign Lang. *Res:* British travelers in 19th century South America; Mexican theater. *Publ:* Auth, La Argentina vista por viajeros ingleses, 1810-1860, Ed Gure, Buenos Aires, 59; co-ed, Nosotros somos dios, Harper, 66; El color de nuestra piel, Macmillan, 66; coauth & transl, Corostiza's The Color of our Skin, Drama & Theatre, fall 71; auth, The theater of Wilberto Canton, Hispania, 12/71; coauth & transl, Canton's We Are God, Drama & Theatre, spring 72; auth, Maximilian and Carlota in Mexican drama, Univ Wis-Milwaukee, Ctr Latin Am, 80. *Mailing Add:* Dept of Foreign Lang & Lit Marquette Univ Milwaukee WI 53233

TRIMBLE, LOUIS P, b Seattle, Wash, Mar 2, 17; m 38; c 1. ENGLISH, LINGUISTICS. *Educ:* Eastern Wash State Col, BA, 50, EdM, 52. *Prof Exp:* Instr English & Span, Eastern Wash State Col, 50-54; teaching fel Span, Univ Pa, 55-56; from instr to assoc prof humanities & social studies, 56-75, prof sci & tech commun, 75-79, PROF HUMANISTIC SOCIAL STUDIES, UNIV WASH, 79- *Concurrent Pos:* Tech consult, Fed Civil Serv Comn, 67-; consult, Int Commun Agency, 72- & Pac Am Inst Inc, 77-; AmSpec, US Dept of State, 77. *Mem:* Teachers English to Speakers Other Lang; Int Asn Teachers English as Foreign Language; Asoc Mexicana de Maestros de Ingles; MEXTESOL. *Res:* Rhetoric and grammar of scientific languages; rhetoric and grammar of occupational English; teaching technical English to foreign students. *Publ:* Coauth, Grammar and technical English, In: English as a Second Language, Chilton, 70; Working Papers in English for Science and Technology, Off English Res, Univ Wash, 72; Technical rhetorical principles and grammatical choice, Teachers English to Speakers Other Lang Quart, 73; New Horizons: A Reader in Scientific and Technical English, skolska Knjiga, Zagreb, Yugoslavia; Presuppositional rhetorical information in EST discourse, TESOL Quart, 76; Literary training and the teaching of scientific and technical English, English Teaching Forum, 76; The development of English as a foreign language materials for occupational English: the technical manual, In: English for Specific Purposes, EST, Ore State Univ, 78; co-ed, English for Specific Purposes: English for Science and Technology, Ore State Univ, 78. *Mailing Add:* Dept of Humanistic-Social Sci FH-40 Univ of Wash Seattle WA 98195

TRIMBLE, ROBERT GENE, b Carlisle, Ind, Jan 10, 30; m 54; c 2. SPANISH LANGUAGE & LITERATURE. *Educ:* Ind Univ, AB, 52, AM, 58, PhD, 68. *Prof Exp:* Instr Span, Purdue Univ, 58-60; from asst prof to assoc prof, 61-70, PROF SPAN, HANOVER COL, 70- *Mem:* Am Asn Teachers Span & Port; Am Coun Teaching Foreign Lang. *Res:* Latin American history; Brazilian literature; 19th century Spanish novel. *Mailing Add:* Dept of Spanish Hanover College Hanover IN 47243

TRIMPI, WILLIAM WESLEY, JR, English. See Vol II

TRIWEDI, MITCHELL D, b New York, NY, Dec 7, 26. SPANISH LITERATURE. *Educ:* City Col New York, AB, 47; Nat Univ Mex, AM, 48; Univ Southern Calif, PhD, 58. *Prof Exp:* From instr to asst prof foreign lang, Univ Bridgeport, 52-58; from instr to asst prof Span, Univ Ill, Urbana, 58-64; asst prof, 64-66, ASSOC PROF SPAN, RUTGERS UNIV, NEW BRUNSWICK, 66- *Mem:* Renaissance Soc Am; MLA; Am Asn Teachers Span & Port. *Res:* Spanish poetry and drama of the 16th and 17th centuries. *Publ:* Ed, Jeronimo Bermudez: Primeras Tragedias Espanolas, Castalia, 75. *Mailing Add:* Dept of Spanish & Portuguese Rutgers University New Brunswick NJ 08903

TROIANO, JAMES J, b Elizabeth, NJ, Dec 17, 44; m 72. SPANISH. *Educ:* Rutgers Col, AB, 66; State Univ NY, Buffalo, AM, 68, PhD(Span), 73. *Prof Exp:* From instr to asst prof Span, Canisius Col, 70-75; instr, 75-76, asst prof, 76-80, ASSOC PROF SPAN, UNIV MAINE, ORONO, 80- *Concurrent Pos:* Consult, Libr J, 73-; ed, Revista Entre Nosotros, 75-76; Seville Ctr Policy Comt, Coun Int Educ Exchange, 78- *Mem:* MLA; Am Asn Teachers Span & Port; Nat Educ Asn. *Res:* Contemporary Latin American theater and short story. *Publ:* Auth, Pirandellism in the theater of Roberto Arlt, Latin Am Theatre Rev, fall 74; The grotesque tradition and the interplay of fantasy and reality in the theater of Roberto Arlt, Latin Am Lit Rev, spring-summer 76; The grotesque tradition in Medusa by Emilio Carballido, Inti: Revista de Lit Hispanica, spring-autumn 77; Cervantinism in two plays by Roberto Arlt, Am Hisp, 10/78; Social criticism and the fantastic in Robert Arlt's La Fiesta Del Hierro, Latin Am Theater Rev, fall 79. *Mailing Add:* Dept of Foreign Lang & Classics Univ of Maine Orono ME 04473

TROIKE, RUDOLPH C, b Brownsville, Tex, Jan 11, 33. LINGUISTICS, AMERICAN ANTHROPOLOGY. *Educ:* Univ Tex, BA, 54, MA, 57, PhD, 59. *Prof Exp:* Instr English, Georgetown Univ English Lang Prog, Ankara, Turkey, 59-60, asst prof, 60-62; from asst prof to prof English & ling, Univ Tex, Austin, 62-73; dir, Ctr Applied Ling, Washington, DC, 72-78 ; PROF EDUC POLICY STUDIES & DIR, OFF MULTCULT BILINGUAL EDUC, INT PROG EDUC & EDUC POLICY RES, UNIV ILL, URBANA-CHAMPAIGN, 80- *Concurrent Pos:* Sr Fulbright lectr, Nat Taiwan Norm Univ, 70-71; mem, Nat Adv Panel Res Bilingual Educ, 76-78; dep dir, Nat Clearinghouse Bilingual Educ, 77-79; vis prof, Dept Anthrop, Johns Hopkins Univ, 78 & Univ Md, 79-80. *Mem:* Ling Soc Am; Am Anthrop Asn; NCTE; Soc Mex Anthrop; Nat Asn Bilingual Educ. *Res:* Anthropological linguistics of North America; sociolinguistics; English linguistics. *Publ:* Auth, Anthropological theory and plains archeology, Bull Tex Archeol Soc, 55; The origins of Plains Mescalism, Am Anthropologist, 62; A structural comparison of Tonkawa and Coahuilteco, In: Studies in Southwestern Ethnolinguistics, Mouton, The Hague, 67; coauth, An Introduction to Spoken Bolivian Quechua, Univ Tex, 69; auth, Overall pattern and generative phonology, In: Readings in American Dialectology, Appleton, 70; co-ed, Proceedings of the First Inter-American Conference on Bilingual Education, Ctr Appl Ling, 75; auth, Subject-Object Concord in Coahwilteco, Lang, 81; A linguistic sketch of Coahuilteco (Pajalate), In: Handbook of North American Indians, Vol II, Languages, Smithsonian Inst (in press). *Mailing Add:* Dept Ed Policy Univ Ill Urbana IL 61801

TROMMLER, FRANK ALFRED, b Zwickau, Ger, May 11, 39. GERMAN LITERATURE. *Educ:* Univ Munich, Dr phil (Ger lit), 64. *Prof Exp:* Vis lectr Ger lit, Harvard Univ, 67-69; PROF GER LIT, UNIV PA, 70- *Concurrent Pos:* Vis prof, Princeton Univ, 72, Johns Hopkins Univ, 80. *Mem:* MLA. *Res:* German literature of the 19th and 20th centuries; modern social history. *Publ:* Auth, Roman und Wirklichkeit, Kohlhammer, 66; Der 'Nullpunkt 1945', Basis 1, 70; Der zocgernde Nachwuchs: Entwicklungsprobleme der Nachkriegsliteratur, Tendenzen der deutschen Literatur seit 1945, Kröner, 71; Sozialistische Literatur in Deutschland, Kröner, 76; coauth, die Kultur der Weimarer Republik, Nymphenburger, 78; co-ed, Jahrhundertwende Deutsche Literatur VIII, Rowohlt, 82; Literatur und sozialismus Neues Handbuch 20, Athenaioh, 82; Kulturpolitik der Nachkmegszeit Kulturpolitisches Woerterbuch, Metzler, 82. *Mailing Add:* Dept German CU Univ of Pa Philadelphia PA 19104

TRUEBLOOD, ALAN STUBBS, b Haverford, Pa, May 3, 17. SPANISH COMPARATIVE LITERATURE. *Educ:* Harvard Univ, BA, 38, MA, 41, PhD, 51; Brown Univ, MA, 57. *Prof Exp:* Educ dir, Chile-Us Cult Inst, Santiago, Chile, 42-43; instr English, Inter-Am Meteorol Sch, 43; from instr to assoc prof Span, 47-63, chmn dept Span & Ital, 67-72, chmn dept comp lit, 73-76, PROF SPAN, BROWN UNIV, 63- *Concurrent Pos:* Guggenheim fel, 55-56; Fulbright res scholar, Chile, 58; sr Fulbright lectr, Inst Caro y Cuervo, Bogota, Colombia, 72; vis res scholar, Merton Col, Oxford Univ, 73. *Mem:* MLA; Am Soc Aesthet; Renaissance Soc Am; Dante Soc Am; Assoc Int Hispanistas. *Res:* Sixteenth and 17the century literature; modern poetry; literary translation. *Publ:* Auth, Silence in Don Quixote, Nueva Rev Filol Hisp, 58; Role-playing and the sense of illusion in Lope de Vega, Hisp Rev, 64; Ruben Dario: The sea and the jungle, Comp Lit Studies, 67; Experience and Artistic Expression in Lope de Vega: The Making of La Dorotea, Harvard Univ, 74; Antonia Machado, Selected Poems, Harvard Univ, 82. *Mailing Add:* Dept of Comp Lit Brown Univ Providence RI 02912

TRUKA, MARY CHRYSOSTOM, b Berlin, NH, June 28, 08. FRENCH. *Educ:* Marygrove Col, BA, 33; Univ Detroit, MA, 36; Univ Montreal, lic es Lett, 66; Wayne State Univ, PhD, 73. *Prof Exp:* Teacher, I H M Parachial Sch Syst, 38-49 & St Mary Acad, Monroe, 49-53; instr French & theol, Marygrove Col, 53-56, asst prof French, 56-62, assoc prof French & Span, 62-73, head dept, 58-64; TEACHER, ST MARY ACAD, MONROE, 73- *Concurrent Pos:* Marygrove Col Dads Club award fac studies abroad, 62; res grant, Asn Independent Cols & Univs Mich sem, 71-72. *Mem:* Am Coun Teaching Foreign Lang; Am Asn Teachers Fr; Nat Audubon Soc; Am Asn Teacher Span & Port. *Res:* Unpublished medieval manuscript of Romance of Athis and Prophilias, Sweden; teaching English as a foreign language. *Mailing Add:* Dept of Foreign Languages St Mary Academy 502 W Elm Ave Monroe MI 48161

TRUSCOTT, JAMES GEORGE, b New York, NY, Jan 6, 42; m 60; c 2. RENAISSANCE & ITALIAN COMPARATIVE LITERATURE. *Educ:* Johns Hopkins Univ, BA, 62, MA, 63, PhD(Romance lang & lit), 70. *Prof Exp:* Instr Ital, Brandeis Univ, 66-68; lectr Romance lang & lit, 68-70, asst prof, 70-73, fac fel, Ctr Humanities, 73, ASSOC PROF ROMANCE LANG & LIT, WESLEYAN UNIV, 73- *Mem:* Dante Soc Am. *Res:* Dante; Italian lyric poetry of the Renaissance, specifically, Petrarca, Lorenzo de' Medici. *Publ:* Auth, Ulysses and Guido: Inferno XXVI and XXVII, Dante Studies, 73. *Mailing Add:* Dept of Romance Lang & Lit Wesleyan Univ 300 High St Middletown CT 06457

TSEVAT, MATITIAHU, b Kattowitz, Ger, July 15, 13; US citizen; m 49; c 3. BIBLE, SEMITIC LANGUAGES. *Educ:* Hebrew Univ, MA, 49; Hebrew Union Col-Jewish Inst Relig, PhD(Bible), 53. *Prof Exp:* Acquisitions librn & lectr Bible, 53-58, from asst prof to assoc prof Bible, 58-66, ed, Hebrew Union Col Ann, 68-70, PROF BIBLE, HEBREW UNION COL-JEWISH INST RELIG, 66- *Concurrent Pos:* Dir Jewish studies, Hebrew Union Col-Bibl & Archaeol Sch, Jerusalem, 64-66; mem coun, World Cong Jewish Studies, Jerusalem, 65-; mem-in-residence, Inst for Advan Studies, Hebrew Univ, Jerusalem, 78-79; Julian Morgenstein Prof Bible, Hebrew Union Col, 79. *Honors & Awards:* Bialik Prize, Hebrew Univ, 43. *Mem:* Soc Bibl Lit; Am Orient Soc; Cath Bibl Asn. *Res:* Old Testament; ancient Near Eastern languages and civilizations; music history and theory. *Publ:* Auth, A Study of the Language of the Biblical Psalms, Soc Bibl Lit, 55; Studies in the Book of Samuel, Hebrew Union Col Ann, 61 & 75; A reference to Gudea in an Old Mari text, Oriens Antiquus, 62; The meaning of the Book of Job and other Biblical Studies, Ktav Publ House, 80; An index to the Religious poetry of Judah Haleir, Studies Biblog & Booklore, 80. *Mailing Add:* 764 Red Bud Ave Cincinnati OH 45229

TSIAPERA, MARIA, b Cyprus, July 26, 32; US citizen. LINGUISTICS, ARABIC. *Educ:* Univ Tex, BA, 57, MA, 58, PhD(ling), 63. *Prof Exp:* Asst prof ling, Fresno State Col, 64-66; from asst prof to assoc prof, 66-68, from actg chmn dept to chmn dept, 67-73, PROF LING, UNIV NC, CHAPEL HILL, 72- *Concurrent Pos:* Fel, Univ Tex, 63-64; NSF travel grant, 77; res grant, Univ NC, 77. *Mem:* Ling Soc Am; Southeastern Conf Ling (vpres, 70-71, pres, 71-72); SAlantic Mod Lang Asn; Am Orient Soc; Am Asn Teachers Arabic. *Res:* History and philosophy of linguistics; Greek historical dialectology; Arabic dialectology. *Publ:* Ed, Greek borrowings in the Arabic dialect of Cyprus, J Am Orient Soc, 4-6/64; auth, A Descriptive Analysis of Cypriot Maronite Arabic, Mouton, The Hague, 69; ed, Palatalization in Cretan and Cypriot Greek, Papers Ling, 12/69; The phonology of a Cypriot dialect, 10th Int Cong Ling, 70; Generative Studies in Historical Linguistics, Ling Res Inc, 71. *Mailing Add:* Dept of Linguistics Univ of North Carolina Chapel Hill NC 27514

TSIEN, TSUEN-HSUIN, b Kiangsu, China, Dec 1, 09; US citizen; m 36; c 3. CHINESE LITERATURE & HISTORY. *Educ:* Nanking Univ, BA, 32; Univ Chicago, MA, 52, PhD, 57. *Prof Exp:* Ed, Nat Libr Peking, 37-47; prof lectr, 49-58, assc prof Chinese, 58-64, prof Chinese lit & libr sci, 64-79, cur, Far Eastern Libr, 49-78, dir, Inst Far Eastern Librarianship, 69-78, EMER PROF & CUR, UNIV CHICAGO, 78- *Concurrent Pos:* Chmn Comt EAsian Libr, Asn Asian Studies, 67-69; adv ed, Tsing Hua J Chinese Studies; adv, Int Asn Orient Libr, 67-72; Am Coun Learned Socs grant, 68-69; consult, Pahlavi Nat Libr, Iran, 74-; res grants, Nat Sci Found, 77-82; Nat Endowment for Humanities, 78-81. *Honors & Awards:* Ministry of Educ Award, 43; Distinguished Serv Award, Comt on EAsian Libr, Asn Asian Studies, 78. *Mem:* Am Orient Soc; Asn Asian Studies; Am Libr Asn. *Res:* Chinese book history; Chinese-Western literary relations; Chinese paper and printing. *Publ:* Auth, Western impact on China through translation, Far Eastern Quart, 5/54; Written on Bamboo and Silk, Univ Chicago, 62; First Chinese-American exhcange of publications, Harvard J Asiatic Studies, 64-65; co-ed, Area Studies and the Library, Univ Chicago, 66; China: True birthplace of paper, printing and movable type, Unesco Courier, 12/72; History of Writing and Writing Materials in Ancient China, 75 & Ancient China: Studies of Early Civilization, 78, Chinese Univ Honk Kong; China: An Annotated Bibliography of Bibliographies, Hall, 78; Paper and Printing in Chinese Civilization, Cambridge Univ Press, 82. *Mailing Add:* 1408 E Rochdale Pl Chicago IL 60615

TSUBAKI, ANDREW TAKAHISA, Speech & Drama. See Vol II

TSUKIMURA, REIKO, b Tokyo, Japan, Feb 13, 30. JAPANESE LITERATURE, COMPARATIVE LITERATURE. *Educ:* Japan Women's Univ, BA, 51; Univ Sask, MA, 62; Ind Univ, PhD(comp lit), 67. *Prof Exp:* Instr English, Japan Women's Univ, 59-60; instr Japanese, Univ BC, 62-63; from instr to assoc prof, Univ Minn, Minneapolis, 66-74; assoc prof, 74-79, PROF JAPANESE LIT, UNIV TORONTO, 79- *Concurrent Pos:* Vis lectr, Harvard Univ, 68-69; Soc Sci Res Coun/Am Coun Learned Soc res grant Japanese studies, 73-74; Japan Found prof fel, 80-81. *Mem:* Asn Teachers Japanese; Can Asian Studies Asn. *Res:* Japanese literature, especially poetry; comparative literature, especially Western and Oriental literary relationships. *Publ:* Auth, A comparison of W B Yeats' At the Hawk's Well and its Noh Adaptation, Taka no izumi, Lit E & W, 12/67; A thematic study of the works of Kawabata Yasunari, J-Newslett Asn Teachers Japanese, 7/68; Theme and technique in Mizuumi by Kawabata Yasunari, In: Studies on Japanese Culture, Japan PEN Club, 73; A Japanese adaptation of The Raven: Hagiwara Sakutaro and Edgar Allan Poe, Hikakubungaku, 73; The Lake (transl of Mizuumi, a novel by Kawabata Yasunari), Kodansha Int, Tokyo, 74; The sense of loss in The Makioka Sisters, In: Approaches to Modern Japanese Novel, Sophia Univ, Tokyo, 76; ed, Life, Death, and Age in Modern Japanese Fiction, Univ Toronto-York Univ Joint Ctr Mod EAsian, 78; Hagiwara Sakutaro no shi, Gakuto, Tokyo, 5/79-12/80. *Mailing Add:* Dept of EAsian Studies Univ of Toronto Toronto ON M5S 1A5 Can

TSUZAKI, STANLEY MAMORU, b Mountain View, Hawaii, Oct 10, 30; m 58; c 1. APPLIED LINGUISTICS. *Educ:* Univ Hawaii, BA, 52; Colo State Col, MA, 54; Univ Mich, MS, 61, PhD(ling), 63. *Prof Exp:* Instr English, Army Educ Ctr, Schofield, 54-56; teacher, Kuhuku High & Elem Sch, 56 & Waimea High & Elem Sch, 56-58; from asst prof to assoc prof, 63-77, PROF LING, UNIV HAWAII, MANOA, 77- *Concurrent Pos:* Res assoc & consult, descriptive studies Hawaiian pidgin, 65-67; publ subsidy award, Hawaii Curric Ctr, 66, lang consult, 67; Nat Endowment for Humanities res grants, 70-71 & 72-73. *Mem:* Ling Soc Am; Am Asn Teachers Span & Port; AASP; Teachers English to Speakers Other Lang; Am Dialect Soc. *Res:* Language contact, including pidgin and creole languages; Hawaiian English; sociolinguistics. *Publ:* Coauth, English in Hawaii, Pac & Asian Ling Inst, 66; Hawaiian loanwords in Hawaiian English of the 1930's, Oceanic Ling, winter 67; auth, English Influences on Mexican Spanish in Detroit, Mouton, The

Hague, 70; contribr art, In: Pidginization and Creolization of Languages, Cambridge Univ, 71; ed, Language and Dialect in Hawaii, 69 & Japanese Pidgin English in Hawaii, 72, Univ Hawaii; auth, Hawaiian English, Am Speech, 73; coauth, A Bibliography of Pidgin and Creole Languages, Univ Hawaii, 75. *Mailing Add:* Dept of Ling Univ of Hawaii at Manoa Honolulu HI 96822

TU, CHING-I, b Nanking, China, May 13, 35; US citizen; m; c 2. CHINESE LANGUAGE & LITERATURE. *Educ:* Nat Taiwan Univ, BA, 58; Univ Wash, PhD, 67. *Prof Exp:* Res fel, Univ Wash, 61-64, teaching asst, 64-66; lectr, 66-67, asst prof, 67-71, assoc prof, 71-75, chmn, Dept Comp Lit & Orient Lang, 80-81, PROF, RUTGERS UNIV, 75-, CHMN, DEPT CHINESE, COMP LIT & SLAVIC STUDIES, 81- *Concurrent Pos:* Res fels & grants, Rutgers Univ, 68-81; vis assoc prof, Univ Hawaii, 71-72; vis prof, Nat Taiwan Univ, 74-75; res grant, Nat Comn Sci, Taiwan, 74-75; dir, Chinese Prog, Rutgers Univ, 71-77 & 78-, Comt Asian Studies, 79- *Mem:* MLA; Asn Asian Studies; Am Asn Chinese Studies; Chinese Lang Teachers Asn; Chinese Comp Lit Asn. *Res:* Chinese literary criticism; intellectual history; East-West literary study. *Publ:* Auth, Poetic Remarks in the Human World, Chung Hwa, Taipei, 70; Chung-Kuo Wen-Hsueh Hsuan, Kwang Wen, Taipei, 72; Modern Chinese literary criticism: Hung-Lou-Meng P'ing-Lun, Literature East & West, Vol XVIII, 73; The concept of evaluation in Chinese literary criticism, Rec 30th Int Cong Human Sci in Asia & NAm, Mexico City, 78; The study of classical Chinese literary criticism in the West, J Chinese Lang Teachers Asn, Vol XIV, No 3; Readings in Classical Chinese Literature, Vol 1, New Brunswick, 81; The Chinese examination essay, Monumenta Serica, 31: 74-75; A biography of T'ang Shun-chih 1507-1560, In: Companion to Traditional Chinese Literature, Ind Univ Press (in press). *Mailing Add:* Dept of Comp Lit & Orient Lang Rutgers Univ New Brunswick NJ 08903

TU, KUO-CH'ING, b Taiwan, China, July 19, 41; m 71; c 1. CHINESE & JAPANESE LITERATURE. *Educ:* Nat Taiwan Univ, BM, 63; Kwansei Gakuin Univ, Japan, MA, 70; Stanford Univ, PhD(Chinese lit), 74. *Prof Exp:* Lectr, 74-75, asst prof, 75-80, ASSOC PROF CHINESE, UNIV CALIF, SANTA BARBARA, 81- *Res:* Chinese poetry; literary theories; comparative studies of modern Chinese and Japanese literatures. *Publ:* Transl, Ai Lüeh-t'e wen-hsüeh p'ing-lun hsüan-chi, (T S Eliot's Essays on Literature), T'ien-yuan Publ, Taipei, 69; auth, Hsüeh-peng, (Avalanche, collected creative poems in Chinese), Li Poetry Mag, Taipei, 10/72; transl, E Chih Hua (C Baudelaire's Les Fleurs du Mal), Ch'un-wen-hsüeh Publ, Taipei, 77; auth, Li Ho, Twayne, 79; contribr, The introduction of French symbolism into modern Chinese and Japanese poetry, Tamkang Rev, spring-summer 80. *Mailing Add:* Dept of Eastern Lang Univ of Calif Santa Barbara CA 93106

TUBACH, FREDERIC C, b San Francisco, Calif, Nov 9, 30; m 59; c 3. GERMAN LITERATURE, MEDIEVAL STUDIES. *Educ:* Univ Calif, Berkeley, BA, 53, MA, 55, PhD(Ger), 57. *Prof Exp:* Instr Ger, Univ Mich, 57-58; from asst prof to assoc prof, 58-68, dir educ abroad prog, Göttingen, 70-72, PROF GER, UNIV CALIF, BERKELEY, 68- *Concurrent Pos:* Alexander von Humboldt fel, 64-65, 72-73; Univ Calif humanities res grant, 67-68. *Mem:* MLA; Int Folknarrative Soc; Philol Asn Pac Coast. *Res:* Medieval German literature; literary theory and methodology; folklore. *Publ:* Auth, An Essay on medieval symbolic structures, Deut Vierteljahrschrift, 68; Strukturanalytische probleme: Das Mittelalterliche Exemplum, Hessische Blätter für Volkskunde, 68; Index exemplorum: A handbook of medieval tales, Folklore Fel Commun, 69; Postulates for an approach to medieval German lyric poetry, J English & Ger Philol, 7/71; Struktur im Widerspruch: Studien zum minnesang, MaxNiemeyer, Tübingen, 77. *Mailing Add:* Dept of German Univ of Calif Berkeley CA 94720

TUCKER, HARRY, JR, b Raleigh, NC, Sept 5, 21; m 55; c 5. GERMAN LITERATURE. *Educ:* Univ NC, BA, 42, MA, 48; Ohio State Univ, PhD, 50. *Prof Exp:* Instr Ger, WVa Univ, 50-51; asst prof, Univ Va, 52-62; from assoc prof to prof, Parsons Col, 62-67; ASSOC PROF GER, NC STATE UNIV, 67- *Mem:* Am Asn Teachers Ger; MLA; SAtlantic Mod Lang Asn. *Res:* The lyric; the Novelle; literature and psychology. *Publ:* Auth, Clemens Brentano: The imagery of despair and salvation, Mod Lang Quart; Joseph, the musician in Stifter's Nachsommer, Montshefte, 1/58; Theodor Storm, Schlaflos, Ger Quart, 1/68; transl & ed, Otto Rank, The Double, Univ NC, 71; auth, Post-traumatic psychosis in Romeo und Julia auf dem Dorfe, Ger Life & Lett, 12/72; The importance of Otto Rank's Theory of the Double, J Otto Rank Asn, 1/78. *Mailing Add:* Dept of Foreign Lang & Lit NC State Univ Raleigh NC 27650

TUCKER, ROBERT ASKEW, b Atlanta, Ga, Mar 23, 30. LATIN, GREEK. *Educ:* Emory Univ, BBA, 51, MAT, 62; Johns Hopkins Univ, PhD(classics), 67. *Prof Exp:* Teacher Latin, Cross Keys High Sch, DeKalb County, Ga, 62-65; asst prof classics, 67-72, ASSOC PROF CLASSICS, UNIV GA, 72- *Mem:* Class Asn Mid W & S (secy-treas, 71-73); Am Philol Asn; Vergilian Soc Am; Am Archaeol Inst; Am Class League. *Res:* Roman epic, especially Lucan. *Publ:* Auth, Sententiae in the Bellum Civile of Lucan and earlier Latin epics, Univ Microfilms, 67; The speech-action-simile formula in Lucan's Bellum Civile, Class J, 5/69; Lucan and the French Revolution: the Bellum Civile as a political mirror, Class Philol, 1/71; Caesar's escape from the Egyptians: variant conclusions to Lucan's Bellum Civile, Class Bull, 3/72. *Mailing Add:* Dept of Classics Univ of Georgia Athens GA 30602

TUCKER, ROBERT WHITNEY, b Chicago, Ill, Mar 29, 06; m 30; c 2. LINGUISTICS, CLASSICS. *Educ:* Cornell Univ, AB, 26, PhD(ling), 29. *Prof Exp:* Instr classics, Cornell Univ, 29-30; prof Latin, Susquehanna Univ, 30-33; instr Ger, Latin & French, Emergency Col Ctr, Alfred Univ, 34-36; prof foreign lang, Pa Mil Col, 36-46; ed work, writing, translating, Fed Govt, 45-68; teacher Latin, Charlotte Country Day Sch, NC, 68-69; RETIRED. *Concurrent Pos:* Lectr classics, George Washington Univ, 67-68; lectr Ger, Univ NC, Charlotte, 68-69. *Mem:* Am Philol Asn; Ling Soc Am; Archaeol Inst Am; Mod Greek Studies Asn. *Res:* Phonology of Latin and Greek; American dialects; genealogy. *Publ:* Auth, The Roumanian vocatives, Language, 44; On the dual pronunciation of Eta, 62 & Accentuation before enclitics in Latin, 65, Trans Am Philol Asn; Chronology of Greek sound changes, Am J Philol, 69; The Descendants of the Presidents, Delmar Publ, 75. *Mailing Add:* 1839 Wendover Rd Charlotte NC 28211

TUDISCO, ANTHONY, b Brooklyn, NY, Aug 5, 15; m 39; c 1. SPANISH. *Educ:* Brooklyn Col, BA, 36; Columbia Univ, MA, 37, PhD(Span), 50. *Prof Exp:* Instr Span, Long Island Univ, 38-41; tutor, Queens Col, 43-47; from instr to assoc prof, 47-64, spec asst to dir bicentennial, Dept Rep Latin-Am Studies, Sch Gen Studies, PROF SPAN, COLUMBIA UNIV, 64- *Concurrent Pos:* Mem, Hisp Inst US. *Mem:* Am Asn Teachers Span & Port; Conf Latin Am Hist; corresp mem Hisp Soc Am. *Res:* Spanish and Latin-American literature; 18th century Spanish literature. *Publ:* Auth, El agua en la poesia de Juan Ramon Jimenez; Hipotesis espanolas en el siglo XVIII sobre el origen de los indios; co-ed, Cerilo Villaverde: Cecilia Valdes, 64 & Marti, antologia critica, 68, Las Americas; auth, Espana y America: apuntes, Ed Mensaje, 73. *Mailing Add:* 402 Casa Hispanica Columbia Univ New York NY 10027

TUMINS, VALERIE AGNES, b Vologda, Russia, Mar 1, 22; US citizen. PHILOLOGY. *Educ:* Univ Freiburg, BA, 48; Radcliffe Col, MA, 53; Harvard Univ, PhD, 59. *Prof Exp:* From instr to asst prof Russ lang, Regis Col, Mass, 54-59; asst prof Russ & Mediaeval Russ lit, Brown Univ, 59-65; assoc prof, 65-70, PROF RUSS & MEDIEVAL RUSS LIT, UNIV CALIF, DAVIS, 70- *Concurrent Pos:* Am Coun Learned Soc grant-in-aid, 61; chmn writing comt Russ, Educ Testing Serv, Princeton, NJ, 61-63. *Mem:* MLA; Am Asn Teachers Slavic & East Europ Lang; Mediaeval Acad Am; Renaissance Soc Am; Am Asn Advan Slavic Studies. *Res:* Russian mediaeval literature and culture; Russian literature in the 18th century. *Publ:* Co-ed, Quelques remarques sur le caractere oratoire des lettres du price Andre Kurbsky au Tsar Ivan le Terrible, Can Slavonic Papers, fall 63; Voltaire and the rise of the Russian drama, Proc Int Cong Enlightenment, 63; Enlightenment and mysticism in 18th century Russia, Studies Voltaire & 18th Century, Geneva, 67; auth, Tsar Ivan IV's Reply to Jan Rokyta, 71 & co-ed, Patriarch Nikon on Church and State: Nikon's Refutation, 82, Walter de Gruyter & Co, Berlin. *Mailing Add:* Dept of Russian Univ of Calif Davis CA 95616

TUNKS, ALICE G, b Versailles, France, July 15, 33; m 61; c 2. FRENCH, ENGLISH. *Educ:* Northwest Mo State Col, BA, 55; Univ Mo-Kansas City, MA, 61; Univ Kans, MA, 67, PhD(Frenchlit), 70. *Prof Exp:* Instr English & French, NKansas City High Sch, 55-61; instr, Metrop Jr Col, Kansas City, 61-68, asst prof French, Univ Mo-Kansas City, 68-69; asst prof, 69-73, assoc prof, 73-80, PROF FRENCH & CHMN DEPT LANG, ROCKHURST COL, 80- *Mem:* Am Asn Teachers Fr; Midwest Mod Lang Asn; MLA. *Res:* Contemporary theatre; surrealist poetry; poetic language and the innovations of Antonin Artaud. *Mailing Add:* Dept of Modern Languages Rockhurst College 5225 Troost Kansas City MO 64110

TUNSTALL, GEORGE CHARLES, b Columbia, SC, Apr 29, 42; m 68. GERMAN LITERATURE & PHILOSOPHY. *Educ:* Hamilton Col, AB, 64; Princeton Univ, MA, 66, PhD(Ger), 68. *Prof Exp:* Asst prof Ger, Williams Col, 68-69 & Univ Fla, 69-73; asst prof, 73-81, ASSOC PROF, KANS STATE UNIV, 81- *Concurrent Pos:* Ed, Studies in Twentieth Century Lit, 76-78. *Mem:* MLA: Am Asn Teachers Ger; Schopenhauer-Ges; Int Asn Philos & Lit. *Res:* Nineteenth and 20th century German literature and philosophy. *Publ:* Auth, Light symbolism in Georg Kaiser's Die Burger von Calais, J English & Germanic Philol, 79; Nietzsche and Georg Kaiser's Schellenkonig, Mod Lang Notes, 81; Hebbel and Georg Kaiser: Reflections of Judith in Die Burger von Calais, Colloquia Germanica, 81; The turning point in Georg Kaiser's attitude toward Friedrich Nietzsche, Nietzsche-Studien, 82; Autobiography and mythogenesis: The case of Georg Kaiser and Nietzsche's Ecce homo, GLL (in prep); ed, Richard Dehmel: Gedichte, Philipp Reclam jun, Stuttgart (in press). *Mailing Add:* Dept of Mod Lang Kans State Univ Manhattan KS 66506

TURK, EDWARD BARON, b New York, NY, Sept 29, 46. FRENCH LITERATURE AND FILM. *Educ:* Brooklyn Col, BA, 67; Yale Univ, MPh, 71, PhD(French), 73. *Prof Exp:* Asst prof & dir undergrad studies, Yale Univ, 72-78; ASSOC PROF FRENCH & HUMANITIES, MASS INST TECHNOL, 78- *Concurrent Pos:* Morse fel humanities, Yale Univ, 75-76; Nat Endowment for Humanities grant, 81. *Mem:* MLA; Am Asn Teachers Fr; NAm Soc Seventeenth-Century French Lit; Am Film Inst. *Res:* Seventeenth century French literature; French film history. *Publ:* Auth, La Fontaine: Mythologue et mythologicien, French Lit Ser, 76; Nature and women: Jean Renoir's une partie de campagne, French Rev, 2/78; Baroque fiction-making: A study of Gomberville's Polexandre, NC Studies Romance Lang & Lit, 6/78; Scarron's Dom Japhet d'Armenie: Metaphor, burlesque, and comic language, Papers in French Seventeenth Century Lit, 3/79; Marcel Carne, Twayne (in press); Film treasures of the Palais de Chaillot, Am Film, 6/80. *Mailing Add:* Dept of Humanities Mass Inst Technol Cambridge MA 02139

TURKEVICH, LUDMILLA BUKETOFF, b New Britain, Conn, Sept 14, 09; m 34; c 2. MODERN LANGUAGES & LITERATURES. *Educ:* NY Univ, BA, 31; Univ Kans, MA, 32; Columbia Univ, PhD(Russ, Span & comp lit), 48. *Prof Exp:* Instr Span, Univ Kans, 31-32, NJ Col, Rutgers Univ, 41-42, Wash Sq Col, NY Univ, 42-44 & Princeton Univ, 44-45; lectr Russ, Rutgers Univ, 45-46 & Princeton Univ, 46-61; prof Russ & chmn dept, Douglass Col, Rutgers Univ, 60-80. *Concurrent Pos:* Consult, Rand Corp, 53-54; mem sch hist studies, Inst Advan Studies, 55-56. *Mem:* Am Asn Teachers Slavic & EEurop Lang (pres, 65); Am Asn Teachers Span & Port; Am Asn Advan Slavic Studies; MLA. *Res:* Soviet literature and intellectual scene; Russian and Soviet literature and culture; comparative literature. *Publ:* Auth, Masterpieces of Russian literature, 64 & coauth & ed, Materials and Methods of Teaching Russian, 66, Van Nostrand; auth, Spanich Literature in Russia and the Soviet Union, 1735-1964, Scarecrow, 67; coauth, The Prominent Men of Science: Continental Europe, Am Elsevier, 68; auth, Culture under Lenin and Stalin, Problems of Communism, 3-4/73; Andreev and the mask, Russ Lit Triquart, 6/73; Cervantes in Russia, Univ Press, 50 & Gordian Press, 75; Russian literature in modern Japan, Russ Lang J, 31: 69-90; Tolstoj and Galdos: Affinites and coincidences reviewed, Proc 8th Int Congr Slavists, fall 78. *Mailing Add:* 109 Rollingmead Princeton NJ 08540

TURNER, ELBERT DAYMOND, JR, b Gainesville, Fla, Nov 15, 15; m 45; c 5. SPANISH. *Educ:* Davidson Col, AB, 37; Univ NC, AM, 39; PhD, 49. *Prof Exp:* Instr, Univ NC, 38-39; instr, Ga Teachers Col, 39-41; instr, Univ NC, 45-49; asst prof mod lang, Univ Del, 49-58, assoc prof Span, 58-60, prof mod lang & lit, 60-66, dir lang lab, 55-66; chmn dept foreign lang, 66-71, dir grad studies, 70-80, prof, 66-81, res prof, 81, EMER PROF SPANISH, UNIV NC, CHARLOTTE, 81- *Concurrent Pos:* Consult, Pub Schs, Del, 51-52, Del Dept Pub Instr, 59, Memphis State Univ, 67-70 & Prof Child Care Ctr, Inc, 69-73; secy, Charlotte Area Educ Consortium, 71-72; Huntington Libr fel, 82; res grant, Nat Endowment for Humanities, 80-82 & comt Conjunto Hisp-NorteAmericano Para Asuntos Educativos y Culturales, 81. *Mem:* Am Asn Teachers Span & Port; Renaissance Soc Am; Am Coun Teaching Foreign Lang; SAtlantic Mod Lang Asn; Latin Am Studies Asn. *Res:* Literature of exploration; improved methods of teaching modern languages; graduate and undergraduate foreign language curricula. *Publ:* Auth, Gonzalo Fernandez de Oviedo y Valdes, An Annotated Bibliography, Univ NC, 66; Correlation of language class and language laboratory, ERIC Focus Reports, No 13, MLA, 69; Los libros del alcaide: la biblioteca de Gonzalo Fernandez de Oviedo y Valdes, Rev India, Madrid, 71; ed & translr, The Conquest and Settlement of the Island of Puerto Rico, Ltd Ed Club, 75. *Mailing Add:* 233 Fenton Place Univ of NC University Station Charlotte NC 28207

TURNER, JAMES HILTON, b Woodville, Ont, Apr 19, 18; nat citizen; m 45; c 3. CLASSICAL LANGUAGES. *Educ:* Univ Toronto, BA, 40; Univ Cincinnati, PhD, 44. *Prof Exp:* Mem fac, Bishop's Col Sch, 44-45 McCallie Sch, 45-47; from instr to asst prof class lang, Univ Vt, 47-51; asst prof, Heidelberg Col, 51-52; from asst prof to assoc prof, 52-57, chmn dept lang, 53-62, PROF CLASS LANG, WESTMINSTER COL, 57- *Concurrent Pos:* Assoc ed, Class World, 57-60. *Mem:* Class Asn Atlantic States; Am Class League (vpres, 58-59); AAUP. *Res:* Aristophanes. *Publ:* Auth, Epicurus and friendship & Roman elementary mathematics: The operations, Class J; Audio-visual materials for the teaching of the classics, Class World; ed, Aristophanes, Lysistrata, Bryn Mawr Col, 82. *Mailing Add:* Dept of Foreign Languages Westminster Col New Wilmington PA 16142

TURNER, PAUL RAYMOND, b Peoria, Ill, June 4, 29; m 50; c 2. ANTHROPOLOGICAL LINGUISTICS. *Educ:* Wheaton Col, Ill, BA, 52; Univ Chicago, MA, 64, PhD(anthrop), 66. *Prof Exp:* Asst prof anthrop, Univ Nebr-Lincoln, 66-67; assoc prof, 67-74, PROF ANTHROP, UNIV ARIZ, 74- *Concurrent Pos:* Chmn comt ling, Univ Ariz, 71-77. *Mem:* Fel Am Anthrop Asn; fel Soc Applied Anthrop. *Res:* Urban anthropology; psychological anthropology; bilingualism. *Publ:* Auth, The Highland Chontal, Holt, 72; Self-Guide for Linguistic Fieldwork, Impresora Sahuaro, 72; ed, Bilingualism in the Southwest, Univ Ariz, 73. *Mailing Add:* Dept of Anthrop Univ of Arizona Tucson AZ 85721

TUSIANI, JOSEPH, b San Marco in Lamis, Italy, Jan 14, 24; US citizen. ITALIAN LANGUAGE & LITERATURE. *Educ:* Univ Naples, Dott in Lettere, 47. *Hon Degrees:* LittD, Col Mt St Vincent, 71. *Prof Exp:* Instr Ital, Col New Rochelle, 48-51; asst prof Ital, 51-60; from assoc prof to prof, Col Mt St Vincent, 60-71; PROF, LEHMAN COL CITY UNIV, NEW YORK, 71- *Concurrent Pos:* Vis prof, New York Univ, 58-63, Cent Conn State Col, 64, Fairleigh Dickinson Univ, 68, Rutgers Univ, 70 & Fordham Univ, 80. *Honors & Awards:* Greenwood Prize, Poetry Soc England, 56; Di Castagnola Award, Poetry Soc Am, 68; Spirit Gold Medal, Cath Poetry Soc Am, 69. *Mem:* Dante Soc Am; Am Asn Teachers Ital; Poetry Soc Am (vpres, 57-69); Am PEN. *Res:* Verse translation of Pulci's Morgante. *Publ:* Ed, trans, The Complete Poems of Michelangelo, Farrar & Straus, 60; The Poems of Machiavelli, Obolensky, 63; auth, Tasso's Jerusalem Delivered, 70 & Boccaccio's Nymphs of Fiesole, 71, Fairleigh Dickinson Univ Press; The Age of Dante, 72, Italian Poets of the Renaissance, 74 & From Marino to Marinetti, 75, Baroque Press; Tasso's Creation of the World, State Univ NY Press, 82. *Mailing Add:* 2140 Tomlinson Ave Bronx NY 10461

TUSKEN, LEWIS WILLIAM, b Chippewa Falls, Wis, Sept 3, 31; m 59; c 1. GERMAN LANGUAGE & LITERATURE. *Educ:* Univ Wis, BA, 59; Univ Colo, MA, 61, PhD(Ger), 66. *Prof Exp:* From lectr to asst prof Ger, Univ Victoria, BC, 64-66; PROF GER, UNIV WIS-OSHKOSH, 66- *Honors & Awards:* Ethnic Prog Award, Nat Endowment for Humanities, 77. *Mem:* Am Lit Asn; Am Asn Teachers Ger. *Res:* The German novella; 19th century German literature; 19th and 20th century German prose. *Publ:* Auth, Annette von Droste-Hülshoff's Die Judenbuche: A Study of Its Background, Univ Colo, 68; C F Meyer's Der Heilige: The problem of Becket's conversion, Seminar, 10/71; The question of perspective in Hesse's Steppenwold, In: Festschrift for Gerhart Loose, Francke, 73. *Mailing Add:* Dept of Foreign Languages Univ of Wisconsin Oshkosh WI 54901

TUSO, JOSEPH FREDERICK, English Literature, History of English Language. See Vol II

TUSSING, MARJORIE O, b Waterville, Maine, May, 40; m 64. GERMAN LANGUAGE & LITERATURE. *Educ:* Whittier Col, AB, 62; Univ Mainz & Middlebury Col, MA, 64; Univ Southern Calif, PhD(Ger), 71. *Prof Exp:* assoc prof, 65-80, PROF GER, CALIF STATE UNIV, FULLERTON, 80- *Mem:* Am Asn Teachers Ger (treas, 72-76); MLA :Comt Advan Studies Austrian Lit; Am Coun Teaching Foreign Lang. *Res:* The modern narrative; German literature in Film. *Publ:* Auth, Vocabulary in first year German texts, Die Unterrichtspraxis, 77. *Mailing Add:* Dept of Foreign Lang & Lit Calif State Univ Fullerton CA 92634

TUTTLE, EDWARD FOWLER, b Los Angeles, Calif, Mar 8, 42; m 62; c 2. ROMANCE LINGUISTICS. *Educ:* Univ Calif, Los Angeles, BA, 65, MA, 67; Univ Calif, Berkeley, PhD(Romance philol), 72. *Prof Exp:* assoc prof Ital & chmn Romance ling, 71-81, PROF ITAL & ROMANCE LING, UNIV CALIF, LOS ANGELES, 81- *Mem:* Ling Soc Am; Mediaeval Acad Am. *Res:* Comparative Romance linguistics; Italian dialectology and philology. *Publ:* Auth, Sviluppo delle palatali stridule dell'italiano, Atti XIV Cong Int di Linguistica e Filologia Romanza, 74; Distinctive features and Geolinguistic patterns, Revue de Linguistique Romane, 75; Borrowing versus semantic shift: New World nomenclature in Europe, First Images of Am, Berkeley, 76; Analogy and language change in the notes of a Renaissance Florentine, Bibliot d'Humanisme et Renaissance, 77; Apocope in Upper Veneto, RID, 82; Plurali in-n, VR, 82; Oda rusticale, Misc-Pellegrim, 82; Snaturalite & s-pavana, SMVL, 82; Sardinian, Current Trends: Romano, 82. *Mailing Add:* Dept of Italian Univ of Calif Los Angeles CA 90024

TWAROG, LEON IGNACE, b New Bedford, Mass, May 20, 19; m 63; c 2. SLAVIC LANGUAGES & LITERATURES. *Educ:* Harvard Univ, AB, 47, MA, 49, PhD(Slavic), 52; Middlebury Col, AM, 48. *Hon Degrees:* DHL, Alliance Col, 69. *Prof Exp:* Instr Russ, Kent State Univ, 52-53; from instr to assoc prof Slavic lang & lit, Boston Univ, 53-60; chmn dept Slavic lang & lit, 62-72, assoc dean col arts & sci, 63-64, assoc dean fac int prog, 66-70, actg dean, Col of Humanities, 77-78, dir, Individualized Instr Foreign Lang, Col of Humanities, 79-82, PROF SLAVIC LANG & LIT, OHIO STATE UNIV, 60-, DIR SLAVIC & E EUROP PROG, 63-, CHMN DEPT, 78- *Concurrent Pos:* Mem gov-acad interface comt, Am Coun Educ, 73-78; chmn task force less commonly taught langs, MLA-Am Coun Learned Soc, 77-79; consult, NEH; chmn, lang comt, Am Asn Advan Slavic Studies, 81- *Mem:* MLA; Am Asn Teachers Slavic & East Europ Lang (vpres, 58, pres, 59 & 60); Am Asn Advan Slavic Studies (exec secy, 72-73). *Res:* Russian historical novel; modern Russian literature. *Publ:* Auth, A novel in flux: V Kostylev's Ivan Groznyj, Am Slavic & East Europ Rev; Arithmetic and the Soviet historical novel, Studies on Soviet Union, 71; Literary censorship in Russia and the Soviet Union, In: Essays on Russian Intellectual History, Univ Tex, 71; A National Ten Year Plan for Teaching and Training in the Less Commonly Taught Languages, Language Study for the 1980's, MLA, 80; Foreign language recommendations of the president's commission and the JNCL resolutions on language in American education: An analysis, autumn 80 & coauth (with E Garrison Walters), Mastery-Based, self-paced instruction in foreign languages at the Ohio State University: A report to the profession on a four year experiment in individualized instruction in six foreign languages, spring 81, Mod Lang Jour. *Mailing Add:* Dept of Slavic Lang & Lit Ohio State Univ Columbus OH 43210

TWEDDELL, COLIN ELLIDGE, b Melbourne, Australia, Mar 19, 99; c 3. ANTHROPOLOGY, LINGUISTICS. *Educ:* Univ Wash, BA, 45, MA, 48, PhD(ling), 58; Bible Col Victoria, dipl theol, 48; Vancouver Bible Col, Assoc relig studies, 78. *Prof Exp:* Instr Chinese, Univ Wash, 42-45; assoc prof anthrop, 65-66, lectr anthrop & ling, 67-78, EMER PROF ANTHROP, WESTERN WASH UNIV, 78- *Concurrent Pos:* Consult, Puyallup Indian Tribal Coun, 69; vis prof anthrop, Trinity Western Col, 75-76, Vancouver Bible Col, 75-76. *Mem:* Ling Soc Am; Am Ethnol Soc. *Res:* Ethnology and languages of Southwest China and Philippines; Indians of the Pacific Northwest Coast; culture contact theory. *Publ:* Auth, The Snoqualmie-Duwamish Dialects of Pugent Sound Coast Salish: Phonemics and Morphology, Univ Wash, 50; Youth and society: Harry's web of life, The Science Teacher, 69; contribr, Contributions and Annotations to Philippine Ethnography: A Critical . . . Bibliography, Univ Hawaii, 72; coauth, Iraya Mangyan phonology and Philippine orthography, Anthrop Ling, 74; Historical and ethnological study of the Snohomish Indian People, In: American Indian Ethnohistory, Garland, 74; The Tuli-Chinese Balk Line: Minimal group identity, In: Perspectives on Ethnicity, Mouton, 78; coauth, Peoples and Cultures of Asia, Prentice-Hall (in press). *Mailing Add:* Dept of Anthrop Western Wash Univ Bellingham WA 98225

TYLER, JOSEPH V, b Culiacan, Sinaloa, Mex, Nov 18, 39; US citizen; c 2. SPANISH AMERICAN LITERATURE. *Educ:* San Diego State Univ, BA, 67, MA, 69; Univ Calif, San Diego, PhD(Span Am lit), 78. *Prof Exp:* Instr Span, San Diego State Univ, 67-69; teaching asst, Univ Calif, San Diego, 69-74; ASST PROF SPAN, UNIV MICH, FLINT, 75- *Concurrent Pos:* Instr Span, San Diego Eve Col, 69-74 & Grossmont Community Col, 72-74; assoc Univ Calif, SAnta Cruz, 72-78. *Mem:* Am Asn Span & Port; MLA. *Res:* The Spanish American novel; Spanish dialects in the United States; literature and film. *Publ:* Auth, The Fall of Santiago desde San Diego (poem), Helicon, Univ Calif San Diego, 75 & in Season of Somber J, 76. *Mailing Add:* Dept Foreign Lang Univ of Mich 1321 E Court St Flint MI 48503

TYLER, RICHARD WILLIS, b West Willington, Conn, Jan 7, 17; m 46; c 2. ROMANCE LANGUAGES. *Educ:* Univ Conn, AB, 38; Brown Univ, PhD, 46. *Prof Exp:* Asst, Brown Univ, 42-43; vis lectr, State Univ Iowa, 44-46; from asst prof to assoc prof Romance lang, Univ Tex, 46-65; prof Romance lang, 65-71, PROF MODERN LANG & LIT, UNIV NEBR-LINCOLN, 72- *Mem:* MLA; Comediantes; Asociacion Int de Hispanistas; AAUP; Am Asn Teachers Span & Port. *Res:* Spanish drama of the Golden Age; false accusations in Spanish literature; other Spanish Golden Age literature. *Publ:* Coauth, Los Nombres de Personajes en las Comedias de Lope de Vega (2 vols), Univ Calif, 61; auth, Algunos aspectos tecnicos de la acusacion falsa en Lope de Vega, In: Homenaje a William L Fichter, Castalia, Madrid, 71; A Critical Edition of Lope de Vega's La Corona de Hungria, In: Estudios de Hispanofila, No 20, Castalia, Madrid, 72; coauth, Beginning Spanish Course, Heath, 3rd ed, 76; auth, The New World in Some Spanish Golden Age Plays, In: Studies in Honor of Reino Virtanen, Ann Arbor, 78; Celestina in the comedia, Celestinesca, 81; coauth, The Characters, Plots and Settings of Calderon's comedias, Soc Span & Span Am Studies, 81. *Mailing Add:* Dept Modern Lang & Lit Univ Neb Lincoln NE 68588

TYLER, ROYALL, b London, Eng, Dec 10, 36. JAPANESE LITERATURE. *Educ:* Harvard Univ, BA, 57; Columbia Univ, MA, 66, PhD(Japanese lit), 77. *Prof Exp:* Vis lectr Japanese, Univ Toronto, 72-73; vis lectr, 75-77, asst prof, Ohio State Univ, 77-80; PROF JAPANESE, UNIV WIS-MADISON, 80- *Concurrent Pos:* Japan Found res fel, 78-79; Fulbright fac res fel, 82-82. *Res:* No Theater; medieval poetry and religion. *Publ:* Co-ed, Twenty Plays of the No Theatre, Columbia Univ, 70; auth, Selected Writings of Suzuki Shosan, 77, Pining Wind: A Cycle of No Plays, 78, Cornell EAsia Papers. *Mailing Add:* Univ Wis Madison WI 53706

TZITSIKAS, HELENE, b Athens, Greece, Apr 2, 26; US citizen. ROMANCE LANGUAGES. *Educ:* Lake Forest Col, BA, 52; Northwestern Univ, MA, 54, PhD(Span), 63. *Prof Exp:* From instr to asst prof Span lit, Rockford Col, 62-65; assoc prof, 65-71, PROF HISP LIT, MICH STATE UNIV, 71- *Mem:* MLA: Am Asn Teachers Span & Port; Midwest Mod Lang Asn: AAUP. *Res:* Spanish American literature; 19th and 20th century Spanish literature. *Publ:* Auth, Santiago Ramon y Cajal-obra literaria, 65 & El pensamiento espanol-1898-1899, 67, De Andrea, Mex; Fernando Santivan-humanista y literato, 71 & Dos revistas chilenas-Los Diez y Artes y letras, 73, Ed Nascimento, Chile; El sentimiento ecologico en la Generacion del 98, Hispam, Spain, 77; La supervivencia existencial de la mujer en las obras de Benavente, Biblioteca Universitaria Puvill, Spain, 82. *Mailing Add:* Dept of Romance Lang Mich State Univ East Lansing MI 48823

U

UBER, DAVID MERRILL, b New York, NY, Aug 8, 48; m 72. FRENCH LITERATURE & THEATER. *Educ:* Hamilton Col, AB, 70; Rice Univ, MA, 75, PhD(French), 76. *Prof Exp:* Teaching asst French, Rice Univ, 71-74; lectr Am theatre, Univ Gt Brit & France, 74-75; lectr French, 76-80, asst prof-at-large, 80-82, ASST PROF FRENCH, BAYLOR UNIV, 82-, DIR FRENCH & ITAL DIV, 82- *Concurrent Pos:* NDEA fel, Rice Univ, 71-74; dir int prog, Baylor Univ, 79- *Mem:* MLA; SCent MLA; Am Asn Teachers French. *Res:* Family structure in Moliere's theater. *Mailing Add:* Dept of Mod Foreign Lang Baylor Univ Waco TX 76703

UCELAY, MARGARITA, b Madrid, Spain, May 5, 16; nat citizen; div; c 1. SPANISH. *Educ:* Inst Escuela, Madrid, BA, 33; Columbia Univ, MA, 42, PhD(Span), 50. *Prof Exp:* Instr Span, Vassar Col, 40-42; lectr, Hunter Col, 42-43; from instr to assoc prof, 43-64, chmn dept, 62-70, PROF SPAN, BARNARD COL, COLUMBIA UNIV, 65-, CHMN DEPT, 73- *Honors & Awards:* Hisp Medal, Am Asn Teachers Span, 42. *Res:* Spanish theater and drama; 19th century Spanish prose. *Publ:* Auth, Los espanoles pintados por si mismos, Col Mex, 51; coauth, Literatura del siglo XX, Holt, 55, rev ed, 68; auth, Spanish language and literature, In: Book of Knowledge, Groliers, 64; Luis Velez de Guevara, 67 & Espinel, Vicente Martinez, 67, In: European Authors (1000-1900), Wilson; coauth, Vision de Espana, Holt, 68. *Mailing Add:* Dept of Spanish Barnard College Columbia Univ New York NY 10027

UDELL, GERALD R, Enlgish, Linguistics. See Vol II

UDRIS, ZANE, b Würzburg, Ger, Aug 24, 49; US citizen. CLASSICAL PHILOLOGY. *Educ:* Barnard Col, BA, 71; Yale Univ, PhD(class philol), 76. *Prof Exp:* Vis asst prof, 76-77, ASST PROF CLASS PHILOL, UNIV MICH, ANN ARBOR, 77- *Mem:* Am Philol Asn. *Res:* Latin Augustan poetry. *Mailing Add:* Dept of Class Studies Univ Mich Ann Arbor MI 48109

UEDA, MAKOTO, b Ono, Japan, May 20, 31; Can citizen; m 62; c 2. LITERATURE, AESTHETICS. *Educ:* Kobe Univ, BLitt, 54; Univ Nebr, MA, 56; Univ Wash, PhD(comp lit), 61. *Prof Exp:* Lectr Japanese, Univ Toronto, 61-62; from asst prof to prof, 62-71; PROF JAPANESE, STANFORD UNIV, 71- *Res:* Japanese literature, including theatre; comparative literature, especially Japanese and Western; literary theory and criticism. *Publ:* Auth, The Old Pine Tree and Other Noh Plays, Univ Nebr, 62; Zeami, Basho, Yeats, Pound, Mouton, The Hague, 65; Literary and Art Theories in Japan, Western Reserve Univ, 67; Matsuo Basho, Twayne, 70; Modern Japanese Writers and the Nature of Literature, Stanford Univ, 76; Modern Japanese Haiku: An Anthology, Univ Toronto, 76. *Mailing Add:* Dept of Asian Languages Stanford Univ Stanford CA 94305

UEHARA, TOYOAKI, Comparative Religion, Japanese. See Vol IV

UFFENBECK, LORIN ARTHUR, b Fond du Lac, Wis, Sept 25, 24. FRENCH. *Educ:* Univ Wis, BA, 49, PhD, 57; Univ Grenoble, cert, 50; Middlebury Col, MA, 52. *Prof Exp:* Asst prof French, Hamilton Col, 57-64; lectr, Univ Minn, 64-65; assoc prof, 65-69, PROF FRENCH, UNIV WIS-MADISON, 69- *Mem:* Am Asn Teachers Fr; MLA; Soc Chateaubriand; Soc 19th Century Fr Studies; Groupe Etudes Balzaciennes. *Res:* Chateaubriand studies; Balzac studies; Sainte-Beuve studies. *Publ:* Auth, Charles Didier and Chateaubriand, Rev Lit Comp, 10-12/63; George Sand and the Memoires d'Outre-Tombe, Fr Rev, 1/64; ed, Hortense Allart, Nouvelles lettres a Sainte-Beuve, 1832-1864, Droz, 65; co-auth, A la Recherche de Paris, Oxford Univ, 66; auth, Balzac a-t-il connu Goriot?, L'Annee Balzacienne, 70; Sainte-Beuve, Chateaubriand et son groupe litteraire: index alphabetique et analytique, Univ NC, 73. *Mailing Add:* Dept of French & Italian 618 Van Hise Hall Univ of Wis Madison WI 53706

UHLFELDER, MYRA L, b Cincinnati, Ohio, Sept 16, 23. CLASSICS. *Educ:* Univ Cincinnati, AB, 45, MA, 46; Bryn Mawr Col, PhD, 52. *Prof Exp:* Instr classics, Sweet Briar Col, 50-52; from instr to asst prof, State Univ Iowa, 52-63; assoc prof Latin, 63-72, PROF LATIN, BRYN MAWR COL, 72- *Concurrent Pos:* Guggenheim fel, 58-59. *Mem:* Am Philol Asn; Mediaeval Acad Am. *Res:* Ancient and Mediaeval Latin literature; Roman linguistic theory. *Publ:* Auth, De Proprietate sermonum vel rerum, Am Acad Rome 54; Nature in Roman linguistic texts, Trans Am Philol Asn, 66; transl, The Dialogues of Gregory the Great, Book Two, Bobbs-Merrill, 77. *Mailing Add:* Dept of Latin Bryn Mawr College Bryn Mawr PA 19010

UHLIG, LUDWIG, b Dresden, Ger, June 2, 31; m 59. GERMAN LITERATURE. *Educ:* Univ Tübingen, PhD(Ger), 65. *Prof Exp:* PROF GER, UNIV CONN, 66- *Mem:* MLA. *Res:* German literature of the 18th, 19th and 20th centuries. *Publ:* Auth, Georg Forster, Niemeyer, 65; coauth, Hermann Hettner: Schriften zur Literatur und Philosophie, Insel, 67; ed, Winckelmann: Gedanken über die Nachahmung, Reclam, 69; auth, Ein Brief George Forsters, Monatshefte, 72; Der Todesgenius in der deutschen Literatur von Winckelmann bis Thomas Mann, Niemeyer, 75; Goethes Römisches Carneval im Wandel seines Kontexts, Euphorion, 78; Kunst und Dichtung bei Winckelmann, Zeitschrift für deutsche Philol, 79; Klassik und Geschichtsbewusstsein in Goethes Winckelmannschrift, Germanisch Romanische Monatsschrift, 81. *Mailing Add:* Dept of Germanic & Slavic Lang Univ of Conn Storrs CT 06268

UITTI, KARL DAVID, b Calumet, Mich, Dec 10, 33; m 74; c 1. FRENCH LITERATURE & PHILOLOGY. *Educ:* Univ Calif, Berkeley, BA & MA, 52, PhD, 59. *Prof Exp:* From instr to assoc prof, 59-68, preceptor, 63-66, chmn dept, 72-78, PROF ROMANCE LANG, PRINCETON UNIV, 68- *Concurrent Pos:* Guggenheim Mem fel, 63-64; consult, Nat Endowment for Humanities, 76-78. *Mem:* Mediaeval Acad Am; MLA. *Res:* Old French and Romance philology; Medieval poetics; linguistics and literary theory. *Publ:* Auth, The Concept of Self in the Symbolist Novel, Mouton, The Hague, 61; La Passion Litteraire de Remy de Gourmont, Presses Universitaires, 62; Linguistics and Literary Theory, Prentice-Hall, 69; Story, Myth and Celebration in Old French Narrative, Princeton Univ, 73. *Mailing Add:* Dept of Romance Lang Princeton Univ Princeton NJ 08540

ULATOWSKA, HANNA K, b Krynica-Zdroj, Poland, Mar 14, 33; US citizen. LINGUISTICS. *Educ:* Univ Warsaw, MA, 55; Univ Edinburgh, dipl, 59, PhD(ling), 61. *Prof Exp:* Lectr English, Univ Warsaw, 55-58; res scientist ling, Georgetown Univ, 62-63; lectr, Witwatersrand Univ, 63-65; res scientist, Ling Res Ctr, Univ Tex, Austin, 65-67; comput syst analyst, Div Comput Res & Technol, NIH, 67-70; sr staff fel, 70-71; assoc prof, Univ Tex, Arlington, 71; vis prof, Southern Methodist Univ, 71-72; ASSOC PROF OF LING, UNIV TEX, DALLAS, 73- *Concurrent Pos:* Assoc prof dept neurol, Univ Tex Health Sci Ctr, Dallas, 71. *Mem:* Acad Aphasia; Soc Neurosci; Ling Soc Am; MLA. *Res:* Neurolinguistics. *Publ:* Auth, Preliminary observations on the behavior of some aphasics in a sentence construction task, Proc Conf Clinical Aphasio, 3/72; Cognitive and linguistic strategies in processing of sentences, Trans Am Neurol Asn, 73; A longitudinal study of an adult with aphasia: Considerations for research and therapy, Brain & Lang. *Mailing Add:* 4422 Wildwood Rd Dallas TX 75208

ULERY, ROBERT WARREN, JR, b Goshen, Ind, Apr 2, 44. CLASSICAL LANGUAGES & LITERATURES. *Educ:* Yale Univ, BA, 66, MA, 68, PhD(class lang & lit), 71. *Prof Exp:* Asst prof, 71-78, ASSOC PROF CLASS LANG & LIT, WAKE FOREST UNIV, 78- *Mem:* Am Philol Asn; AAUP; Mediaeval Acad Am. *Res:* Manuscript tradition of Cornelius Tacitus; influence of Cornelius Tacitus in the Renaissance; Renaissance studies. *Mailing Add:* Box 7343 Reynolda Station Winston-Salem NC 27109

ULIBARRI, SABINE REYES, b Santa Fe, NMex, Sept 21, 19; m 42; c 1. SPANISH LITERATURE. *Educ:* Univ NMex, BA, 47, MA, 49; Univ Calif, Los Angeles, PhD(Span, Span Am lang & lit), 59. *Prof Exp:* Teacher pub schs, NMex, 38-42; assoc prof mod lang, 47-68, PROF SPAN, UNIV NMEX, 68-, CHMN DEPT MOD & CLASS LANG, 73- *Concurrent Pos:* Consult, DC Heath-Louis de Rochemont Proj, 62. *Mem:* MLA; Rocky Mountain Mod Lang Asn; Am Asn Teachers Span & Port (vpres, 68, pres, 69); Inst Int Lit Iberoam. *Res:* Modern Spanish poetry; methods of teaching Spanish in the elementary, secondary and university levels. *Publ:* Auth, Al cielo se sube a pie, Impresora Medina, Mex, 61; coauth, Fun Learning Elementary Spanish, Univ NMex, 61; auth, El mundo poetico de Juan Ramon, Edhigar, SL, Madrid, 62; Tierra Amarilla (short stories), Casa Cult Quito, 64; Amor y Ecuador (poems), Alfaguara, Madrid, 66; Tierra Amarilla, bilingual ed, 71 & El alma de mi raza, 71, Univ NMex. *Mailing Add:* Dept of Modern & Classical Lang Univ of New Mexico Albuquerque NM 87131

ULLMAN, PIERRE LIONI, b Nice, France, Oct 31, 29; US citizen; m 56; c 2. SPANISH. *Educ:* Yale Univ, BA, 52; Columbia Univ, MA, 56; Princeton Univ, PhD, 62. *Prof Exp:* Master French & Span, Choate Sch, Wallingford, Conn, 56-57; master French, Latin & Span, St Bernard's Sch, Gladstone, NJ, 57-58; asst French & Span, Princeton Univ, 58-61; instr, Rutgers Univ, 61-63; asst prof Span, Univ Calif, Davis, 63-65; assoc prof, chmn dept, 66-67, PROF SPAN, UNIV WIS-MILWAUKEE, 68- *Concurrent Pos:* Adv ed, Papers on Lang & Lit, 66-; vis prof Span, Univ Minn, Minneapolis, 70-71; adv ed, Estudos Ibero-Americanos, Brazil, 75-; vis prof, Univ Mich, summer 75; adv ed, Los Ensayistas, 77- *Mem:* Am Asn Teachers Span & Port; MLA; Am Asn Teachers Esperanto; Midwest Mod Lang Asn; Universal Esperanto Asn; Esperanto League NAm. *Res:* Spanish literature; contemporary Esperanto poetry. *Publ:* Auth, Mariano de Larra and Spanish Political Rhetoric, Univ Wis, 71; An emblematic interpretation of Sanson Carrasco's Disguises, Estudios Literarios de Hispanistas Norteamericanos dedicados a Helmut Hatzfeld, 74; The antifeminist premises of Clarin's Su unico hijo, Estudos Ibero-Americanos, 4/75; Clarin's Androcratic Ethic and the Antiapocalyptic Structure of Adios, Cordera, The Analysis of Hispanic Texts: Second York Col Colloquium, 76; Torquemada, San Eloy o Dagoberto, Anales Galdosianos, Vol 13, 78; Schizoschematic rhyme in Esparanto, Vol 16, 80 & Romanticism and Irony in Don Quixote, Vol 17, 81, Papers on Lang & Lit; Rectificacion del Espejo Emblematico, In: San Camilo, 1936, Neophilologus (in press). *Mailing Add:* Dept of Spanish & Portuguese Univ of Wisconsin Milwaukee WI 53201

ULMER, BERNHARD, b Saranac Lake, NY, Aug 5, 07. GERMAN LITERATURE. *Educ:* Hamilton Col, AB, 29; Harvard Univ, AM, 30; Yale Univ, PhD, 37. *Prof Exp:* Instr, Conn State Col, 30-31 & Trinity Col, Conn, 31-36; from instr to prof Ger, 36-76, EMER PROF GER, PRINCETON UNIV, 76- *Concurrent Pos:* Bk consult; vic prof, Wash Univ, St Louis, 60-61. *Mem:* MLA; Am Asn Teachers Ger. *Res:* Eichendorff, one-act drama in Germany; Lessing and Mann; baroque. *Publ:* Auth, Martin Opitz, Twayne, 71; coauth, Traditions and Transitions, Delp, 72. *Mailing Add:* 22 Hamilton Ave Princeton NJ 08540

UMBACH, WILLIAM ECKHARD, b Racine, Wis, Aug 31, 12. GERMAN LITERATURE & PHILOLOGY. *Educ:* Denison Univ, AB, 34; Univ Mich, AM, 35, PhD, 50. *Prof Exp:* Instr Ger, Case Inst Technol, 36-46, asst prof lang & lit, 46-50, assoc prof Ger, 50-52; dir summer session, Univ Redlands, 63-68, vpres admin, 68-70, prof Ger, 52-80, dean grad studies, 61-80. *Concurrent Pos:* Etymology ed, Webster's New World Dict, 42-; mem sr fac, Univ Phoenix, 79- *Mem:* Am Asn Teachers Ger; Philol Asn Pac Coast. *Res:* Influence of science on German Literature in the 19th century; reflection of natural science in German literature from 1830-1859. *Publ:* Co-ed, Webster's New World Dictionary, World Publ, 70. *Mailing Add:* Grad Studies Off Univ of Redlands Redlands CA 92373

UMPIERRE, LUZ MARIA, b San Juan, PR, Oct 15, 47. CARIBBEAN LITERATURE & CULTURE. *Educ:* Univ Sagrado Corazon, BA, 70; Bryn Mawr Col, MA, 76, PhD(Latin Am lit), 78. *Prof Exp:* Chmn, Acad Maria Reina, PR, 71-74; instr, Haverford Col, 75-76; teaching asst, Bryn Mawr Col, 76-77; ASST PROF SPAN, RUTGERS UNIV, 78- *Concurrent Pos:* Lectr, Int Classroom, Univ Pa, 74-78; vis prof, Immaculata Col, Pa, 78-; consult, Nat Endowment for Humanities, 80-; Minority Res Coun fac fel, Rutgers Univ, 81; vis scholar, Univ Kans, 81-82; guest ed, Third Woman, Indiana Univ, 82. *Honors & Awards:* First Prize Poetry, Int Publ, Calif, 78; Nat Res Coun fel, 81-82. *Mem:* MLA; Am Asn Teachers Span. *Res:* Latin American literature and culture; women writers. *Publ:* Auth, Entrevista con Pedro Juan Soto, Revista Chicano-Riquena, 79; Corrientes ideologicas en Usmail de P J Soto, Bilingual Rev, 1-4/81; coauth, Ecriture de ambiguedad en La lluvia de A Uslar-Pietri, Hisp J, 82; auth, Introduccion al Taetro de Myrna Casas, Third Woman, 82; Un manifiesto literario: Papeles de Pandora de R Ferre, Revista Bilingue, 82; Inversion de valores y efectos en el lector en Oracion de Gloria Fuertes, Plaza, 82; Pedro Juan Soto, In: Encycl of World Literature 20th Century, 82; En el Pais de las maravillas (poetry), Third Woman Press, 82. *Mailing Add:* PO Box 1703 New Brunswick NJ 08903

UNDANK, JACK, b New York, NY, June 18, 28. FRENCH LANGUAGE & LITERATURE. *Educ:* City Col New York, AB, 49; Rutgers Univ, MA, 50; Harvard Univ, PhD, 56. *Prof Exp:* Teaching fel French, Harvard Univ, 51-52, 53-56; from instr to assoc prof, 56-71, dir French Grad Prog, 76-79, PROF FRENCH, RUTGERS UNIV, 80- *Concurrent Pos:* Vis assoc prof, Williams Col, Mass, 62-63; collabr, Int Ed for complete works of Diderot; bk rev ed, Degre Second. *Mem:* MLA; Am Soc 18th-Century Studies. *Res:* French literature; the Enlightenment; philosophy and aesthetics. *Publ:* Auth, A new date for Jacques le Fataliste, MLN, 59; Diderot's Est-il bon? Est-il mechant?, Inst Voltaire, 61; Vauvenarques and the whole truth, PMLA, 70; Sighting and signifying metaphors: The example of Diderot, Substance, 79; Diderot, Inside, Outside, and In-Between, Coda Press, 79; Diderot's Egg: Life, Death and other Things in Pieces, New York Lit Forum, 81; The Open and Shut Case of Est-ie bon?, Diderot Studies, 81; ed, Diderot, Ocuvres Completes, Hermann, Vol 23, 81. *Mailing Add:* Dept of French Rutgers Univ New Brunswick NJ 08903

UNDERHILL, ROBERT, b Newton, Mass, Sept 24, 36; m 64; c 2. LINGUISTICS. *Educ:* Harvard Univ, AB, 58, PhD(ling), 64. *Prof Exp:* From instr to asst prof ling, Harvard Univ, 64-72; asst prof, 72-77, ASSOC PROF LING, SAN DIEGO STATE UNIV, 77-, CHMN DEPT, 79- *Mem:* Ling Soc Am; Am Anthrop Asn; Soc Uralo-Altaica; Turkish Studies Asn; Soc Study Indigenous Langs of Am. *Res:* Theoretical and descriptive linguisitics; grammar and structure of the Turkish language; Eskimo linguistics. *Publ:* Auth, Turkish participles, Ling Inquiry, 72; Turkish Grammar, Mass Inst Technol, 76. *Mailing Add:* Dept of Linguistics San Diego State Univ San Diego CA 92182

UNDERWOOD, GARY NEAL, b Piggott, Ark, Oct 20, 40; div; c 2. ENGLISH LINGUISTICS. *Educ:* Tex A&M Univ, BA, 62, MA, 64; Univ Minn, Minneapolis, PhD(English), 70. *Prof Exp:* Teaching asst English, Tex & A&M Univ, 62-64; instr, San Antonio Col, 64-65; teaching assoc, Univ Minn, Minneapolis, 65-66, res fel & asst ed, Ling Atlas Upper Midwest, 66-70; asst prof English, Univ Ark, Fayetteville, 70-72; asst prof, 72-78, ASSOC PROF ENGLISH, UNIV TEX, AUSTIN, 78- *Concurrent Pos:* Vis sr lectr English, Univ Queensland, Brisbane, Australia, 81. *Mem:* NCTE; MLA; Conf Col Compos & Commun; Am Dialect Soc; Ling Soc Am. *Res:* Linguistic variation; American English; Australian English. *Publ:* Auth, Linguistic realism in Roderick Random, J English & Ger Philol, 70; co-ed, Readings in American Dialectology, Appleton, 71; auth, American English dialectology: Alternatives for the Southwest, Int J Sociol Lang, 74; Bidialectal freshman handbooks--the next film-flam, Fla FL Reporter, 74; Towards a reassessment of Edward Eggleston's literary dialects, Bull Rocky Mountain Mod Lang Asn, 74; Subjective reactions of Ozarkers to their own English and the English of other Americans, J Ling Asn Southwest, 75; The dialect of the Mesahi range, Publ Am Dialect Soc, 81; Arkansawyer postvocalic r, Am Speech, 82. *Mailing Add:* Dept of English Univ of Tex Austin TX 78712

UNGAR, STEVEN RONALD, b Chicago, Ill, Sept 8, 45; m 68; c 2. FRENCH LITERATURE. *Educ:* Univ Wis-Madison, BA, 66, MA, 68; Cornell Univ, PhD(French), 73. *Prof Exp:* Asst prof French, Case Western Reserve Univ, 72-76; asst prof, 76-79, ASSOC PROF FRENCH, UNIV IOWA, 79- *Concurrent Pos:* Lectr English, Lycee Technique d'Etat, Rennes, France, 68-69; res fel, Camargo Found, Cassis, France, 81. *Mem:* MLA; Asn Study of Dada & Surrealism. *Res:* Modern literature and philosophical disciplines; literary criticism; applied and theoretical. *Publ:* Auth, Ponge, Sartre, and the ghost of Husserl, Sub-stance, 4/74; Waiting for Blanchot, Diacritics, 5/75; Parts and holes: Heraclitus, Nietzsche, Blanchot, Sub-stance, 9/76; RB: the third degree, Diacritics, 3/77; Night Moves: Spatial Perception & the Place of Blanchot's Early Fiction, 4/79 & The Professor of Desire, 6/82, Yale Fr Studies; Roland Barthes: The Professor of Desire, Univ Nebr Press (in press). *Mailing Add:* Dept of French & Ital Univ of Iowa Iowa City IA 52242

UNGER, JAMES MARSHALL, b Cleveland, Ohio, May 28, 47. JAPANESE LANGUAGE, LINGUISTICS. *Educ:* Univ Chicago, BA, 69, MA, 71; Yale Univ, MA, 73, PhD(ling), 75. *Prof Exp:* Sr lectr Japanese, Univ Canterbury, NZ, 75-76; ASST PROF JAPANESE, UNIV HAWAII, MANOA, 77- *Mem:* Ling Soc Am; Asn Asian Studies; Kokugo Gakkai, Japan; Asn Teachers Japanese. *Res:* Historical linguistics. *Publ:* Coauth, Evidence of a consonant shift in seventh century Japanese, Papers in Japanese Ling, 72; auth, Review of Lange: Phonology of eighth century Japanese, Can J Ling, 74; Studies in Early Japanese Morphophonemics, Ind Univ, 77; Intuition and rigor: More on ko-type o-ending syllables in Old Japanese, Papers in Japanese Ling, 78. *Mailing Add:* Dept of East Asian Lang Univ of Hawaii Manoa Honolulu HI 96822

URBAIN, HENRI, b Hanoi, Indochina, May 24, 27; US citizen; m 62. FRENCH LITERATURE. *Educ:* Univ Calif, Berkeley, AB, 56, MA, 57, PhD(Romance lit), 71. *Prof Exp:* Teaching asst, Univ Calif, Berkeley, 57-61; assoc, Univ Calif, Santa Barbara, 61-63; asst prof French, San Diego State Col, 63-64 & Mills Col, 65-66; PROF FRENCH, SALEM STATE COL, 68- *Mem:* MLA; Soc Detude Du IVIIeme Siecle. *Res:* Seventeenth century French literature; Franco-Spanish literary relations in the 17th century. *Mailing Add:* Dept of Foreign Lang Salem State College Salem MA 01970

URBANO, VICTORIA EUGENIA, b San Jose, Costa Rica, June 4, 26; US citizen. LITERATURE OF SPAIN & SPANISH AMERICA. *Educ:* Royal Sch Dramatic Arts, Madrid, dipl drama, 54; Univ Madrid, MA, 62, PhD(lit hist), 65. *Hon Degrees:* Dr, Col Maria Immaculada, Madrid, 72. *Prof Exp:* From asst prof to assoc prof Span, 66-74, Regents' prof, 73 & 74, PROF SPAN, LAMAR UNIV, 74- *Concurrent Pos:* Lamar Res Ctr res awards, Lamar Univ Leon Felipe Award, Pres of Mex, 69; vconsul of Costa Rica at Houston, Tex, Govt Costa Rica, 71; founder & dir, Asoc de Literatura Feminina Hispanica, 74- & jour, Letra Femeninas, 75- *Mem:* Am Asn Teachers Span & Port; SCent Mod Lang Asn. *Res:* Chaucer and the Spanish picaresque; the contemporary Spanish theater; feminine literature of Spain and Spanish America. *Publ:* Auth, Juan Vazquez de Coronado y su etica en la conquista de Costa Rica, Ed Cult Hisp, Madrid, 68; Una escritora costarricense: Yolanda Oreamuno, 68 & Los nueve circulos, 70, Ed Castilla de Oro, Madrid; El teatro Espanol y sus directrices contemporaneas, Ed Nacional, vadrid, 72; Antologia de cuentos premio Leon Felipe, Ed Finisterre, Mex, 72; Un amor en Gandia, In: Voces de Manana, Harper, 73; auth & ed, Five Women Writers of Costa Rica, Asociacion de Literatura Feminina Hispanica, 78; contribr, La Nacion, Costa Rica, 11-12/65 & 1-2/66. *Mailing Add:* Dept of Modern Language Box 10049 Lamar Univ Beaumont TX 77710

URBANSKI, EDMUND STEPHEN, b Poland, July 6, 09; US citizen; c 2. SPANISH & LATIN AMERICAN LITERATURE. *Educ:* Class State Col, Poland, AB, 30; Univ Lund, dipl, 39; Nat Univ Mex, MA, 43, PhD, 46; Univ Barcelona, dipl, 55; Univ San Marcos, cert, 59. *Prof Exp:* Lectr hist, Tech Inst, Poland, 31-33; prof Slavic ling, Nat Univ Mex, 42-45; asst prof Span lang & Span Am lit, Marquette Univ, 46, Univ San Francisco, 48-50, Idaho State Univ, 50-55, Univ Notre Dame, 55-56 & John Carroll Univ, 56-59; vis assoc prof, Univ Buffalo, 60-62; assoc prof, Western Ill Univ, 62-65 & Western Mich Univ, 65-67; prof, Howard Univ, 67-76; vis prof, Univ Warsaw, Poland, 76-78 & Fed Univ Parana, Brazil, 79; RES & WRITING, 80- *Concurrent Pos:* Res asst, Ola Apenes archaeol exped, Mex, 40-41; Polish-Brit studies grant, Mex, 43-45; res dir Latin Am collection, Prof Adv Comt, 47-48; Orgn Am States res fel, Colombia, Ecuador, Peru & Bolivia, 59-60; foreign mem, Acad Hist Santander, Colombia, 68; mem, Int Cong Americanists. *Honors & Awards:* Gold Medal & hon dipl, Inst Estudios Humanos, Lima, 66. *Mem:* Am Asn Teachers Span & Port; MLA; Asn Latin Am Studies; fel Anthrop Asn Can; Asoc Int Hispanistas. *Res:* Modern and indigenous novel in Spanish America; comparative Anglo-American and Spanish American civilizations; social and cultural structure of Mexico. *Publ:* Auth, Studies in Spanish American Literature and Civilization, Western Ill Univ, 64; Angloamerica e Hispanoamerica, Ed Studium, Madrid, 65; El revisionismo en la valoracion de las letras y cultura contemporanea de Espana, Hispania, 65; Two different cultural orientations in the Western Hemisphere, Anthrop J Can, 67; Hispanoamerica, sus razas y civilizaciones, E Torres, 72; Hispanic America and Its Civilizations, Univ Okla Press, 78 & 80; Hispanoameryka i jej cywilizacje, PWN, Warsaw, 81; Poles in Latin America, Charaszkiewicz Found, 82. *Mailing Add:* 8625 Piney Branch Rd Silver Spring MD 20901

URIA-SANTOS, MARIA ROSA, b Ferrol, Spain, Dec 13, 35. ROMANCE LANGUAGES, SPANISH AMERICAN LITERATURE. *Educ:* Univ Madrid, MA, 58; Univ Fla, MA, 62, PhD(Inter-Am studies), 65. *Prof Exp:* Instr Span, Stephen F Austin State Col, 64-65; asst prof, Ind Univ Pa, 65-67, Univ Wis-Milwaukee, 67-71 & William Paterson Col, 71-76; ASST PROF ROMANCE LANG, DOUGLASS COL, RUTGERS UNIV, 76- *Mem:* Am Asn Teachers Span & Port. *Res:* Hispanic civilization and culture; literary criticism. *Publ:* Auth, El simbolismo de'Dona Beatiz: Primera obra de Carlos Solorzano, Rev Studies Hispanicos, Vol VI, No 1; The relationship of audio-visuals: Application from Spanish civilization, Nat Asn Lang Lab Dirs J, 12/71; O antiteismo do teatro de Carlos Solorzano, Grial, spring 73. *Mailing Add:* Dept of Romance Lang Douglass Col Rutgers Univ New Brunswick NJ 08903

URRUTIBEHEITY, HECTOR NORBERT, b Magdelena, Arg, Oct 23, 31; US citizen; m 60; c 3. APPLIED & ROMANCE LINGUISTICS. *Educ:* La Plata Nat Univ, BA, 56; Stanford Univ, PhD(ling), 68. *Prof Exp:* Instr English, Arg Naval Acad, 58-60; teacher French, Willis High Sch, Delaware, Ohio, 60-61; instr French & Span, univ sch, Ohio State Univ, 61-63; asst prof, San Jose State Col, 63-67; ASSOC PROF SPAN & CHMN DEPT SPAN, PORT & CLASSICS, RICE UNIV, 67- *Mem:* Am Asn Teachers Span & Port; Am Coun Teaching Foreign Lang. *Res:* Applied linguistics. *Publ:* Coauth, Echelons, C E Merrill, 67; Peldanos, Xerox, 72; auth, The statistical properties of the Spanish lexicon, Cahiers Lexicologie, 72; coauth, The Lexical Structure of Spanish, Mouton, The Hague, 73. *Mailing Add:* Dept of Span & Port & Classics Rice Univ Houston TX 77001

URTIAGA, ALFONSO, b Madrid, Spain, May 20, 23. ROMANCE LANGUAGES, SPANISH LITERATURE. *Educ:* Univ Madrid, BA, 41, LLM, 55; Faculta Filos, SJ, Madrid, MA, 49; Columbia Univ, MComp Law, 56; La State Univ, PhD, 63. *Prof Exp:* Adv, Inst Cult Hisp, Madrid, 57; instr Span, La State Univ, 57-61 & Oakland Univ, 61-63; asst prof, Univ Windsor, 63-66; assoc prof, Univ Iowa, 66-67, Univ Cincinnati, 67-69 & Kalamazoo Col, 69-76; ASSOC PROF SPAN & FRENCH, NMEX HIGHLAND UNIV, 76- *Mem:* Am Asn Teachers Span & Port; MLA. *Res:* Biography of Tirso de Molina; Spanish myths in literature; folkloric drama in Spain. *Publ:* Auth, Semblanza humana de Suarez, Razon y Fe, Medarid, 48; El indiano en la dramatica de Tirso de Molina, Estudios, Madrid, 65; Documentos notariales firmados por Tirso de Molina en Trujillo, Estudios, 4-6/70; Matices Misticos en el Tema de Don Juan, Hispanofila, 9/72. *Mailing Add:* Dept of Spanish New Mexico Highland Univ Las Vegas NM 87701

URY, MARIAN BLOOM, b Chicago, Ill, Oct 5, 32; m 55. JAPANESE LITERATURE. *Educ:* Univ Calif, Berkeley, BA, 55, MA, 65, PhD(Orient lang), 70. *Prof Exp:* Lectr Japanese, Stanford Univ, 67-68; lectr, 69-70, asst prof orient lang, 70-74, asst prof comp lit, 74-77, ASSOC PROF COMP LIT, UNIV CALIF, DAVIS, 77- *Concurrent Pos:* Soc Sci Res Coun grant, 76 & 79-80; Japan Found grant, 78-79; Nat Endowment for Humanities grant, 79-80. *Mem:* Asn Asian Studies; Asn Teachers Japanese; MLA. *Res:* Japanese literature in Chinese and its practitioners; setsuwa and other tale literature; Genji monogatari. *Publ:* Auth, Recluses and eccentric Monks: Tales from the Hosshinshu, Monumenta Nipponica, 72; The imaginary kingdom and the translator's art: Notes on re-reading Waley's Genji, J Japanese Studies, 76; The complete Genji, Harvard J Asiatic Studies, 77; Poems of the Five Mountains: An Introduction to the Literature of the Zen Monasteries, Mushinsha, Serendipity, 77; Tales of Times Now Past: 62 Stories from a Medieval Japanese Collection, Univ Calif Press, 79. *Mailing Add:* Comp Lit Prog Univ of Calif Davis CA 95616

USCHALD, WILLI ANDREAS, b Holzhammer, Ger, Mar 18, 26; US citizen. ROMANCE LANGUAGES, ENGLISH. *Educ:* Mich State Univ, MA, 52, PhD(English), 57. *Prof Exp:* Dir lang training, KAW-Siemens & Verein Merkur Ger, 47-51; from instr to asst prof foreign lang, Mich State Univ, 53-58; asst prof French & Ger, Harpur Col, 58-63; chmn dept foreign lang, 63-67, PROF FOREIGN LANG, STATE UNIV NY COL CORTLAND, 63-, DIR INT PROG, 67- *Concurrent Pos:* Dir, Cortland-Harpur Studies Abroad Prog, 64- *Mem:* Renaissance Soc Am; Mod Humanities Res Asn; MLA; Am Asn Teachers Fr; Am Asn Teachers Ger. *Res:* Renaissance literature, Italian, French, English. *Mailing Add:* For Lang Dept State Univ NY Cortland NY 13045

V

VAGO, ROBERT MICHAEL, b Hungary, Feb 15, 48; US citizen. LINGUISTICS. *Educ:* Univ Calif, Los Angeles, BA, 70; Harvard Univ, MA, 73, PhD(ling), 74. *Prof Exp:* Asst prof, 74-79, ASSOC PROF LING, QUEENS COL, 79- *Concurrent Pos:* Ed, CUNY Forum, 76- *Mem:* Ling Soc Am. *Res:* Phonological theory; Hungarian linguistics. *Publ:* Auth, Abstract vowel harmony systems in Uralic and Altaic languages, Lang, 73; Theoretical implications of Hungarian vowel harmony, Ling Inquiry, 76; In support of extrinsic ordering, J Ling, 77; Some controversial questions concerning the description of vowel harmony, Ling Inquiry, 78; The lengthening of final low vowels in Hungarian, Ural-Altaische Jahrbücher, 78; The Sound Pattern of Hungarian, Georgetown Univ Press, 80; ed, Issues in Vowel Harmony, John Benjamins BV, 80; coauth, The non-evidence for the cycle in Klamath, In: Phonology in the 1980s, Story-Scientia, 81. *Mailing Add:* Dept of Ling Queens Col Flushing NY 11367

VAHAMAKI, KURT BORJE, b Vaasa, Finland, Mar 28, 44; m 67; c 2. FINNISH LANGUAGE & LINGUISTICS. *Educ:* Abo Acad, Turku, Finland, Cand Hum, 66, Fil Cand, 69 & Fil Lic(Finnish lang & lit), 75. *Prof Exp:* Lectr Scand philol, Univ Oulu, Finland, 74-75; vis asst prof, 75-77, ASST PROF FINNISH, UNIV MINN, 77- *Mem:* Soc Advan Scand Studies; MLA; Ling Soc Am. *Res:* Finnish linguistics, syntax and semantics; Finnish literature; American-Finnish language. *Publ:* Auth, On the function of existential sentences in Finnish, Tex Ling Forum V, 76; Aleksis Kivi's Kullervo: A historical drama of ideas, Scand Studies, Fall 78; Deixis, Place and Entity, The Nordic Languages and Modern Linguistics, Oslo, Norway, 80. *Mailing Add:* Dept of Scand Studies 9 Pleasant St SE Univ Minn Minneapolis MN 55455

VAIL, VAN HORN, b Buffalo, NY, Dec 23, 34; m 61. GERMANIC LANGUAGES. *Educ:* Univ Wash, BA, 56; Princeton Univ, MA, 61, PhD(Ger), 64. *Prof Exp:* From instr to asst prof Ger, Princeton Univ, 62-66; from asst prof to assoc prof, 66-75, dir studies, Grad Sch in Ger, 67-68, 70-71 & 74-75, chmn dept Ger, 70-73, PROF GER, MIDDLEBURY COL, 75- *Concurrent Pos:* Mem nat screening comt for Fulbright scholarships, 79-81. *Mem:* MLA. *Res:* Romanticism; poetic realism; methods of language instruction. *Publ:* Coauth, Der Weg zum Lesen, 67, rev ed, 74, German in Review, 67, Modern German, 71, Thomas Mann's Tonio Kröger als Weg zur Literatur, 74 & Modern German, rev 2nd ed, 78, Harcourt. *Mailing Add:* Dept of German Middlebury College Middlebury VT 05753

VAIO, JOHN, b Oakland, Calif, Nov 7, 39. GREEK, LATIN. *Educ:* Columbia Col, AB, 61; Oxford Univ, BA, 63, MA, 67; Columbia Univ, PhD(classics), 66. *Prof Exp:* From instr to asst prof classics, Columbia Univ, 64-71; from asst prof to assoc prof, Hunter Col, 71-75; ASSOC PROF CLASSICS, UNIV ILL, CHICAGO CIRCLE, 75- *Concurrent Pos:* Jr fel, Ctr Hellenic Studies, 69-70; distinguished vis, Haverford Col, 72. *Mem:* Am Philol Asn: Soc Promotion of Hellenic Studies Class Asn, UK. *Res:* Attic Old Comedy; Babrius and Greek fable. *Publ:* Auth, The Unity and Historical Occasion of Horace's Ode 1.7, 66 & Four Notes on the Text of Babrius, 69, Class Philol; Aristophanes' Wasps: The relevance of the final scenes, 71 & Manipulation of theme and action in Aristophanes' Lysistrata, 73, Greek, Roman & Byzantine Studies; A new Ms of Babrius: Fact or fable?, Ill Class Studies, 76. *Mailing Add:* Dept of Classics Univ Ill at Chicago Circle Chicago IL 60680

VALBUENA-BRIONES, ANGEL JULIAN, b Madrid, Spain, Jan 11, 28; nat citizen; m 57; c 2. HISPANIC LITERATURE. *Educ:* Univ Murcia, MA, 49; Univ Madrid, PhD, 52. *Prof Exp:* Lectr Span & Span-Am lit, Oxford Univ, 53-55; asst prof Span lit, Univ Madrid, 55-56; vis lectr Span-Am lit, Univ Wis, 56-58; asst prof Span lit, Yale Univ, 58-60; ELIAS AHUJA PROF SPAN LIT, UNIV DEL, 60- *Concurrent Pos:* Mem Int Fedn Mod Lang & Lit Am; Consejo Super Invest Ciient fel, Madrid, 70-71; vis prof, Univ Madrid, 70-71; consult, Found Int Del, 72-78; vis prof, Inst Caro y Cuervo, Columbia, summer 80; Nat Screening bd, Fulbright-Hays Comt, Spain & Port, 81-82; chmn, div 16th & 17th century Span Lit, MLA, 77. *Mem:* Asn Teachers Span & Port; MLA; Renaissance Soc Am; Am Asn Univ Prof; Int Asn Hispanist. *Res:* Spanish Golden Age literature; Latin American literary currents; history of the Spanish languague; history of the Spanish language. *Publ:* Auth, Obras completas de Calderon, Aguilar, Madrid, Vols I & II, 56, 59; Literatura Hispanoamericana, Gustavo Gili, Barcelona, 62, 4th ed, 69; Perspectiva critica de los dramas de Calderon, Rialp, Madrid, 65; Ideas y palabras, Eliseo Torres, 68; ed, Calderon's El alcalde de Zalamea, Anaya, Madrid, 71; Primera parte de las comedias de Calderon, Vol I, 74, Vol II, 81, Consejo Superior de Investigaciones Cientificas, Madrid; La dama duende de Calderon, 76 & El alcalde de Zalamea, Calderon, 77 Catedra, 77; auth, Calderon y la comedia nueva, Espasa-Calpe, 77. *Mailing Add:* 203 Nottingham Rd Newark DE 19711

VALDES, GUADALUPE, b El Paso, Tex. APPLIED LINGUISTICS, SPANISH. *Educ:* Univ WFla, BA, 68; Fla State Univ, MA, 70, PhD(Span), 72. *Prof Exp:* Asst prof Span, Western NMex Univ, 72-73; asst prof, 73-76, assoc prof, 76-82, PROF SPAN, N MEX STATE UNIV, 82- *Mem:* Am Asn Teachers of Span & Port; Ling Soc Am; MLA; Am Coun Teaching Foreign Lang. *Res:* Spanish-English language contact in the American Southwest; teaching Spanish to the Spanish-speaking. *Publ:* coauth, Teaching Spanish to the Spanish-Speaking: An Annotated Bibliography, Nat Educ Lab, 77; Toward a probabilistic automata model of some aspects of code-switching, Lang & Soc, 77; auth, A comprehensive approach to the teaching of Spanish to bilingual Spanish-speaking students, Mod Lang J, 78; coauth, Individualized instructional program for Foundation Course in Spanish, Heath, 78; auth, Code-switching and the classroom teacher, CAL/Eric-C11 Ser Appl Ling, 78; coauth, Espanol Escrito: Primer Curso para Estudiantes Hispanohablantes, Scribners, 78; Muy a tus ordenes: Compliment responses among Mexican American bilinguals, Lang & Soc, 81; co-ed, Teaching Spanish to the Hispanic Bilingual: Issues, Aims & Methods, Teachers Col Press, 81. *Mailing Add:* Dept of Foreign Lang Box 3-L NMexico State Univ Las Cruces NM 88003

VALDES, JORGE HORACIO, b Havana, Cuba, Sept 12, 50; US citizen. SPANISH & SPANISH AMERICAN LITERATURE. *Educ:* Fla State Univ, BA, 71; Univ Conn, MA, 72, PhD(Span), 75. *Prof Exp:* Asst prof, Union Col, Schenectady, 75-80; ASST PROF SPAN LANG & LIT, COL HOLY CROSS, 80- *Mem:* Am Asn Teachers Span & Port. *Res:* Contemporary Spanish-American poetry; 20th century Spanish poetry; theory of literary criticism. *Publ:* Auth, Perfil del aire: dos etapas de la evolucion poetica de Luis Cernuda, Am Hisp, 1-2/79; La aportacion de Egloga, Elegia Oda a la evolucion poetica de Luis Cernuda, Soc Span & Span-Am Studies (in press). *Mailing Add:* 23 Dockerel Rd Tolland CT 06084

VALDES, MARIO JAMES, b Chicago, Ill, Jan 28, 34; m 55; c 2. SPANISH LITERATURE. *Educ:* Univ Ill, BA, 57, MA, 59, PhD(Span), 62. *Prof Exp:* Instr Span, Univ Mich, 62-63; from asst prof to assoc prof, 63-70, PROF SPAN & COMP LIT, UNIV TORONTO, 70-, DIR COMP LIT, 78- *Concurrent Pos:* Can Coun fels, 65, 66, 67 & grant, 72-73; Victoria Col, Univ Toronto sr fel, 75; head dept Span, Ital & Port, Univ Ill, Chicago Circle, 76-78; ed, Revista Canadiense Estud Hisp, 76-; co-ed, Monogr Ser Comp Lit, 78- *Mem:* MLA; Asn Int Hispanistas; Int Asn Comp Lit; Can Asn Comp Lit. *Res:* Theory of literature; literary and philosophical studies of Unamuno; 20th century Spanish novel. *Publ:* Auth, Toward a structure of criticism, New Lit Hist, winter 72; Metaphysics and the novel in Unamuno's last decade: 1926-1936, Hispanofila, 72; coauth, An Unamuno Source Book Univ Toronto, 73; auth, Le texte narratif, Etud Litteraires, 75; The real and realism in the novels of Benito Perez Galdos, Hispanofila, 77; The reader's Cervantes in Don Quixote, Int Fiction Rev, 77; ed, Interpretation of Narrative, Univ Toronto, 78; Shadows in the Cave: A Phenomenological Approach to Literary Criticism based on Hispanic Texts, Univ Toronto, 82. *Mailing Add:* Dept of Comp Lit Univ of Toronto Toronto ON M5S 1A1 Can

VALDESPINO, LUIS CESAR, b Havana, Cuba, Apr 30, 14; US citizen; m 47; c 4. LAW, FOREIGN LANGUAGE. *Educ:* Havana Univ, DCL, 39; Pac Univ, BA, 65, MA(Span), 67. *Hon Degrees:* Dipl de Honor, Havana Bar Asn, 50. *Prof Exp:* Atty, Sanguily & Valdespino, Havana, Cuba, 39-60; from lectr to asst prof, 65-77, ASSOC PROF SPAN, CENT WASH UNIV, 77- *Concurrent Pos:* Coord Span prog, Cent Wash Univ, 66-67. *Mem:* Circulo de Cultura Panamericano; Cruzada Edu Cubana. *Res:* Law and Spanish American and Spanish literature. *Publ:* Auth, La accion de nulidad en el Derecho Marcario, Havana Bar Asn J, 42; Biografia literaria de Carlos Manuel de Cespedes, Revista El Habanero, 74; Monstruo de naturaleza: a research on Cervantes, 74 & Huella bibliografica de un Diario de Marti, 76, Diario Las Americas; El poema apocrifo de Heredia, Proceedings, 77; Nuevo ensayo de Lavin sobre Miranda, Diario Las Americas, 81; Sanguily intimo, Academia Hondurena de la Lengua, Tegucigalpa, Honduras, 82; Prologue-writer, Manuel Sanguily, Nobles Memorias, Int Press, 82. *Mailing Add:* Dept of Foreign Lang Cent Wash Univ Ellensburg WA 98926

VALDMAN, ALBERT, b Paris, France, Feb 15, 31; US citizen; m 60; c 1. FRENCH, ITALIAN, LINGUISTICS. *Educ:* Univ Pa, AB, 53; Cornell Univ, MA, 55, PhD(French ling), 60. *Prof Exp:* Ling scientist, Foreign Serv Inst, US Dept State, 57-59, acting head French, 59; asst prof Romance lang, Pa State Univ, 59-60; from asst prof to assoc prof French & Ital, 60-66, chmn dept ling, 63-68, PROF FRENCH & ITAL, IND UNIV, BLOOMINGTON, 66- *Concurrent Pos:* Coordr, Univ Ore NDEA Inst, 61-62; vis lectr, Univ W Indies, 65-66; Guggenheim fel, 67-68; Fulbright lectr, Univ Nice, 71-72 & vis prof ling, 75-76. *Mem:* Ling Soc Am; MLA; Am Asn Teachers Fr; Am Asn Appl Ling; Cent States Foreign Lang Conf. *Res:* French language and linguistics, including Creole; language acquisition; phonology. *Publ:* Co-ed, Identite Culturelle et Francophonie dans les Ameriques, Laval Univ, Vol I, 77; Identite Culturelle et Francophonie dans les Ameriques, Res Ctr in Lang Sci, Ind Univ, Vol II, 77; coauth, Promenades et Perspectives, 3rd Level HS French, Scott, Foresman, 78; auth, Le Creole: Structure, statut et origine, Klincksieck, Paris, 78; ed, Le francais hors de France, Champion, Paris, 79; co-ed, Theoretical Orientations in Creole Studies, NY Acad Press, 80; Historicity and Variation in Creole Studies, Ann Arbor, Karowa, 81; Issues in Bilingual Education, Plenum, 82. *Mailing Add:* Dept of Ling Ind Univ Bloomington IN 47401

VALENCIA, JUAN OCTAVIO, b Zamora, Mex, June 24, 25; US citizen. SPANISH POETRY OF THE GOLDEN AGE. *Educ:* Temple Theol Sem, BD, 57; Tenn Temple Col, BA, 60; Univ Tenn, MA, 62; Univ Southern Calif, PhD(Span), 66; Univ Cincinnati, cert mental retardation, 74. *Prof Exp:* Instr philos & Span, Knoxville Col, 60-62; teaching asst Span, Univ Ill, 62-63; teaching asst, Univ Southern Calif, 63-65; lectr Span, Mt St Mary's Col, 65-77; instr, Peace Corps, Calif State Col, Los Angeles, 66-67; asst prof Span, San Francisco State Col, 68-69, PROF SPAN, UNIV CINCINNATI, 69- *Concurrent Pos:* Ed, Fontana, 69- *Mem:* Am Asn Univ Prof; Asn for Poetry Therapy. *Res:* Origin and evolution of Spanish lyric poetry. *Publ:* Auth, Carmel (poems), Univ Cincinnati, 70; coauth, Antologia y estudio de teatro espanol anterior a Lope de Vega, Alcala, Colombia, 71; Bibliografia critica de Octavio Paz, Univ Mex, 73; auth, El simbolismo en La venganza de Tamar, In: Estudios sobre la comedia del Siglo de Oro, Comediantes, 74; coauth, Homenaje a Octavio Paz, Univ Sal Luis Potosi, 74; auth, Signo y sentimiento (concrete poetry), Univ Cincinnati, 76; Espacios vacios (poems), Escuela Super del Profesorado, Tegucigalpa, Honduras, 77; Pathos y tabu en el teatro biblico del Signlo de Oro, Ed Isla, Madrid, 77. *Mailing Add:* Dept of Romance Lang & Lit Univ of Cincinnati Cincinnati OH 45221

VALENCIA, PABLO, b Bogota, Colombia, July 14, 30; US citizen; m 57; c 3. ROMANCE LINGUISTICS. *Educ:* Univ Mich, BA, 58, MA, 60, PhD(Romance ling), 66. *Prof Exp:* PROF SPAN & ITAL, COL WOOSTER, 61-, CHAIRPERSON DEPT SPAN, 77- *Concurrent Pos:* Fulbright lectr, Inst Caro y Cuervo, Bogota, Colombia, 68. *Mem:* Am Asn Teachers Span & Port; Am Asn Teachers Ital; Am Coun Teaching Foreign Lang. *Res:* Applied linguistics; language and culture. *Publ:* Contribr, Spanish Oral Approach (bks 1, 2 & 3), Ginn, 65, 66 & 68; coauth, Calidoscopio de las Americas, Ginn-Xerox, 71; auth annotated ed, Oggi in Italia, Houghton. *Mailing Add:* Dept of Span & Ital Col of Wooster Wooster OH 44691

VALENTINE, ROBERT YOUNG, b May 21, 42; US citizen. ROMANCE LANGUAGES, LATIN AMERICAN LITERATURE. *Educ:* Brigham Young Univ, BA, 68, MA, 69; Duke Univ, PhD, 76. *Prof Exp:* Asst prof Span, Univ Nebr-Lincoln, 76-80. *Publ:* Auth, Use of light to depict the transformation of Montenegro in Valle-Inclan's Romance de Lobos, Perspective, spring 72; The artistic quest for freedom in Libro de Manuel, Chasqui, 2/74; The artistic personality in Cortazar's El perseguidor, J of Span Studies: 20th Century, 74; Contazar's rhetoric of reader participation, In: The Analysis of Hispanic Texts: Current Trends in Methodology, Bilingual, 78; Horacio's mental voyage in Rayuela, In: Travel, Quest, and Pilgrimage as a Literary Theme: Studies in Honor of Reino Virtanen, Soc Span & Span-Am Studies, 78. *Mailing Add:* 2660 Park Ave Lincoln NE 68502

VALENZUELA, VICTOR MANUEL, b Chillan, Chile, Oct 23, 19; US citizen; m 56; c 1. ROMANCE LANGUAGES. *Educ:* San Francisco State Col, BA, 51; Columbia Univ, MA, 52, PhD(lit), 65. *Prof Exp:* Instr Latin Am lit, Univ Conn, 52-54; instr, Columbia Univ, 54-57; assoc prof, 57-69, PROF LATIN AM LIT, LEHIGH UNIV, 69- *Concurrent Pos:* Lectr, Univ Chile, Santiago, 64, Chillan, 67; Inst Res grant, Lehigh Univ, 66. *Mem:* Am Asn Teachers Span & Port; AAUP; Mid Atlantic Coun Latin Am Studies. *Res:* The literature of Spain and Latin America. *Publ:* Auth, Latin America: Notes and Essays, Las Americas, 65; Ensayos Sobre literatura espanola, Arancibia, Chile, 67; Contemporary Latin American Writers, Las Americas, 71; Chilean Society as Seen Through the Novelistic World of Alberto Blest Gana, 71 & Grandes Escritoras Hispanoamericanas, 74, Arancibia, Chile; Siete Comedografas Hispanoamericanas, Bethlehem, Pa, 76; Anti United States Sentiment in Latin American Literature, 82. *Mailing Add:* Dept of Mod Foreign Lang Lehigh Univ Bethlehem PA 18015

VALESIO, PAOLO, b Bologna, Italy, Oct 14, 39; m 63; c 1. RHETORICS, LITERARY THEORY. *Educ:* Univ Bologna, Dr Lett, 61, libero docente, 69. *Prof Exp:* Asst, Inst Glottology, Univ Bologna, 61-62, 66-68; lectr Romance lang & lit, Harvard Univ, 68-70, assoc prof, 70-73; assoc prof Ital & dir prog, NY Univ, 73-74, prof, 74-76; PROF ITAL, YALE UNIV, 76- *Concurrent Pos:* Fel, Harvard Univ, 65-66. *Mem:* Ling Soc Italy; AAUP; Dante Soc Am. *Res:* Religion and literature. *Publ:* Auth, Strutture dell' allitterazione: Grammatica, retorica e folklore verbale, Zanichelli, Bologna, 68; The language of madness in the Renaissance, In: Yearbook of Italian Studies, Vol I, 71; The virtues of traducement: Sketch of a theory of translation, In: Semiotica, 76; Between Italian and French: The Fine Semantics of Active Versus Passive, Peter de Ridder, Lisse, 76; The lion and the ass: The case for D'Annunzio's novels, In: Yale Italian Studies, Vol I, winter 77; L'ospedale di Manhattan, Editori Riuniti, Roma, 78; The practice of literary semiotics, Point of Contact/Punto de Contacto, 4-5/78; Novantiqua: Rhetorics as a Contemporary Theory, Univ Press, 80. *Mailing Add:* Dept of Ital Yale Univ 80 Wall St New Haven CT 06520

VALETTE, JEAN-PAUL, b Paris, France, Oct 21, 37; US citizen; m 59; c 3. FRENCH, ECONOMICS. *Educ:* Sch Advan Bus Studies, Paris, dipl, 59; Univ Colo, PhD(econ), 62. *Prof Exp:* Acct, Arthur Anderson & Co, 64-66; res economist, Charles River Assoc, Boston, 67-71; RES & WRITING, 71- *Mem:* Am Asn Teachers Span & Port; Am Asn Teachers Fr; Am Coun Teaching For Lang. *Res:* Transportation; French pedagogy; Spanish pedagogy. *Publ:* Coauth, The Role of Transportation in Regional Economic Development, Heath Lexington Bks, 72; France: A Cultural Review Grammar, Harcourt, 73; French for Mastery, Heath, 75, rev ed, 81; Contacts: Langue et Culture Francaises, Houghton, 76, rev ed, 81; C'est comme ca, 78 & Spanish for Mastery, 80, Heath; Con Mucho Gusto, Holt, 81; Panorama: Lectures faciles, Heath, 82. *Mailing Add:* 16 Mt Alvernia Rd Chestnut Hill MA 02167

VALETTE, REBECCA MARIANNE, b New York, NY, Dec 21, 38; m 59; c 3. FRENCH, FOREIGN LANGUAGE EDUCATION. *Educ:* Mt Holyoke Col, BA, 59; Univ Colo, PhD(French), 63. *Hon Degrees:* LHD, Mt Holyoke Col, 74. *Prof Exp:* Instr & examr French & Ger, Univ SFla, 61-63; res assoc phonetics, Supreme Hq Allied Powers Europe Educ Off, Paris, 63-64; instr French, Wellesley Col, 64-65; from asst prof to assoc prof French, 65-73, PROF FRENCH, BOSTON COL, 73-, DIR LANG LAB, 65- *Concurrent Pos:* Fulbright Comn sr lectr, Ger, 73-74; fel acad admin, Am Coun Educ, 76-77; mem, MLA Task Force on Commonly Taught Languages. *Mem:* Am Coun Teaching Foreign Lang; MLA; Am Asn Teachers Fr (vpres, 80-82); Am Asn Teachers Ger; Am Asn Teachers Span & Port. *Res:* Modern language testing and methodology. *Publ:* Coauth, French for Mastery, Heath, 75, rev ed, 81; Contacts: Langue et Culture Francaise, Houghton, 76, rev ed, 81; auth, Modern Language Testing, rev ed, 77 & coauth, Classroom Techniques: Foreign Languages and English as a Second Language, 77, Harcourt; C'est comme ca, 78 & Spanish for Mastery, 80, Heath; Con Mucho Gusto, Holt, 81; auth, Nouvelles Lectures Libres, 82. *Mailing Add:* 16 Mt Alvernia Rd Chestnut Hill MA 02167

VALIN, ROCH, b Jonquiere, Que, June 25, 18; m 49; c 1. LINGUISTICS. *Educ:* Laval Univ, Lic es Let, MA, 45. *Prof Exp:* Teacher ancient Greek & Latin, Col St Jean Etudes, 45-47; teacher French as foreign lang, 46-48, assoc prof gen ling & dir French summer sch, 51-57, PROF GEN LING & DIR DEPT LANG & LING, LAVAL UNIV, 57- *Concurrent Pos:* Lectr, Univs Strasbourg, Lyons & Angers, 54-55; Univ Nancy vic prof, Cath Inst, Paris, 62-; vis prof, Univ Strasbourg, 67. *Mem:* Can Ling Asn; Ling Soc Paris; Soc Ling Romane. *Publ:* Auth, Petite Introduction a la Psychomecanique du Langage; ed, Gustave Guillaume's Unpublished Works; auth, La Methode Comparative en Linguistique Historique et en Psychomecanique de Langage, Laval Univ, 64; ed, Lecons de linguistique 1948-49, A: Structure semiologique et structure psychique de la langue francaise I, 71, B: Psycho-systematique du langue, principes, methodes et applications I, 71 & C: Grammaire particuliere du francais et grammaire generale IV, 73 & Principes de linguistique theorique de Gustave Guillaume, 73, Laval Univ & Libr Klincksieck, Paris. *Mailing Add:* Fonds Gustave Guillaume Dept of Lang & Ling Laval Univ Quebec PQ G1K 7P4 Can

VALIS, NÖEL MAUREEN, b Lakewood, NJ, Dec 24, 45. SPANISH & FRENCH LITERATURE. *Educ:* Douglass Col, BA, 68; Bryn Mawr Col, MA, 70, PhD(Span-French), 75. *Prof Exp:* Lectr Span, Rosemont Col, 71-72 & 76-77; asst prof, 77-81, ASSOC PROF SPAN, UNIV GA, 81- *Concurrent Pos:* Asst & res librn, Privacy Protection Study Comn, 75-76; assoc ed, J Los Ensayistas, 78-81, co-ed, 81-; Nat Endowment for Humanities summer fel, 81. *Honors & Awards:* Creative Res Medal, Univ Ga, 82. *Mem:* MLA; SAtlantic Mod Lang Asn; Northeast Mod Lang Asn; Am Asn of Teachers Span & Port; Asoc Int de Hispanistas. *Res:* Leopoldo Alas/Clarin; 19th century Spanish literature; modern Spanish and Latin American novel and fiction. *Publ:* Auth, The voices of solitude: The modern Latin American novel, Am Spectator, 12/78; Rotrou and Lope de Vega: Two approaches to Saint-Genest, Can Rev Comp Lit, fall 79; Pereda's Penas arriba: A reexamination, Romanistisches Jahrbuch, 79; Romantic reverberation in Clarin's La Regenta, Comparatist, 5/79; The landscape of the soul in Clarin and Baudelaire, Revue de Lit Comparee, 80; Directory of publication sources in the fields of Hispanic language and literature, Hispania, 5/81; The use of deceit in Valera's Juanita la larga, Hisp Rev, 81; The Decadent Vision in Leopoldo Alas, La State Univ press, 81. *Mailing Add:* Dept of Romance Lang Univ of Ga Athens GA 30602

VALLBONA, RIMA-GRETEL ROTHE, b San Jose, Costa Rica, Mar 15, 31; m 56; c 4. LATIN AMERICAN & SPANISH LITERATURE. *Educ:* Colegio superior de Senoritas, BA & BS, 48; Univ Paris, Dipl, 53; Univ Salamanca, Dipl, 54; Univ Costa Rica, MA, 62; Middlebury Col, DML, 80. *Prof Exp:* Teacher Fr & Hisp lit, Liceo J J Vargas Calvo, Costa Rica, 55-56; chmn, Span Dept, 66-71, Mod Lang Dept, 79-80, PROF SPAN & HISP LIT, UNIV ST THOMAS, 64- *Concurrent Pos:* Vis prof, Univ Houston, 75-76 & Rice Univ, 80-83. *Honors & Awards:* Aquileo J Echeverria, Nat Novel Prize, Costa Rica, 68; Jorge Luis Borges, Short Story Award, 77; Agripina Montes del Valle, Latin Am Novel Prize, Colombia, 78. *Mem:* Am Asn Teachers Span & Port. *Res:* Colonial Latin American literature; contemporary Latin American literature; Latin American women writers. *Publ:* Auth, Editorial del Ministerio de Cultura, San Jose, Costa Rica, 72; Yolanda Oreamuno: El estigma del escritor, Cuadernos Hispanoamericanos, 12/72; El tiempo en siete relatos de Alejo Carpentier, In: Troquel II, Part 1, 8/77 & Part 2, 9/77; Eunice Odio, a Homeless Writer, In: Five Women Writers of Costa Rica, Lamar Univ Printing Press, 78; Trayectoria actual de la poesia femenina en Costa Rica, Kanina-Revista de la Univ de Costa Rica, 7-12/78; Eunice Odio: Rescate de un poeta, Int-Am Rev Bibliog, Vol 31, 199-214; La obra en prosa de Eunice Odio, Editorial Costa Rica, 81. *Mailing Add:* 3002 Ann Arbor Houston TX 77063

VALLERIE, JOSEPHINE E, b Norwalk, Conn, July 10, 06. MEDIEVAL LITERATURE & PHILOLOGY. *Educ:* Col New Rochelle, AB, 27; Columbia Univ, AM, 30, PhD, 45; Univ Grenoble, dipl, 32. *Prof Exp:* Teacher jr high sch, Conn, 27-31; PROF FRENCH, COL NEW ROCHELLE, 32-,

CHMN DEPT, 35- *Honors & Awards:* Angela Merici Medal, Col New Rochelle, 59; Palmes Academiques, 59. *Mem:* Am Asn Teachers Fr; MLA; Soc Fr Prof Am; AAUP. *Res:* Garin le Loheren. *Mailing Add:* 19 Briar St Rowayton CT 06854

VALVERDE, JOSE ANTONIO, b Madrid, Spain, Dec 26, 29; Can citizen; m 65; c 3. SPANISH LANGUAGE & LITERATURE. *Educ:* Univ Zaragoza, Titulo Bachiller, 47; Cambridge Univ, BA, 54, MA, 60; Univ Alta, MA, 66; Univ Zaragoza, Dr Cert, 69. *Prof Exp:* Instr Span, Univ Alta, 64-65; asst prof, Univ Man, 65-71; ASSOC PROF SPAN & HEAD DEPT, ACADIA UNIV, 71- *Concurrent Pos:* Mem Span curric comt, Dept Educ, Winnipeg, 69-71. *Mem:* Can Asn Hispanists (secy-treas, 70-72); Can Asn Latin Am Studies; MLA; Am Asn Teachers Span & Port. *Res:* Peninsular literature; contemporary Spanish American novel; computer-aided linguistic and literary research. *Publ:* Auth, Fases poeticas de Damaso Alonso, Las artes y las letras, 3/67; translr, Miguel Angel Asturia's Legend of the Dean Bell, 1/68; auth, Fragmented man, fragmented words, fragmented reality, 2/68, Mosaic; ed, A new and Total Alonso Concordance on a CDC 6400 System, Dalhousie Univ Comput Ctr, 72. *Mailing Add:* Dept of Spanish Acadia Univ Wolfville NS B0P 1X0 Can

VALVERDE ZABALETA, LUIS JAIME, ROMANCE LANGUAGES & LITERATURE. *Educ:* Mankato State Col, BA, 51; Southern Ill Univ, Carbondale, BS, 52; Univ Ill, Champaign, MA, 55; Univ Calif, Los Angeles, PhD(English), 60. *Prof Exp:* PROF ROMANCE LANG & LIT, BOISE STATE UNIV, 65- *Concurrent Pos:* Fels, Ling Inst, Univ Calif, Los Angeles, 66 & 76, Ling Inst, Univ Ill, 69 & Ling Inst, Univ Madrid, 77. *Mem:* Ling Soc Am; MLA; Am Asn Span & Port; AAUP. *Res:* Spanish and English as second languages; psycholinguistics; sociolinguistics. *Publ:* Auth, Psycholinguistics Applied to Language Teaching-Learning, 67, Socio-Psycholinguistics in Syntheses, 68, Espana y los Espanoles en Sintesis, 72, Morfologia Espanola, 73, Hispanoamerica: Sintesis de sus Gentes y Culturas, 73, Plurivalencias de una Minoria Etnica en los Estados Unidos, 77, La Mujer Hispana: Ayer, Hoy y Manana, 81 & Teaching and Learning a Second Language for Communication, 82, Boise State Univ Press. *Mailing Add:* Dept of Foreign Lang Boise State Univ Boise ID 83725

VAMOS, MARA, b Kishineff, Roumania, Oct 30, 27; US citizen; m 48; c 1. FRENCH, COMPARATIVE LITERATURE. *Educ:* Hebrew Univ, Israel, MA, 48; Brown Univ, PhD(French), 61. *Prof Exp:* Press analyst, Am Embassy, Tel Aviv, 49-52; asst ed textbks, Ginn & Co, Chicago, 52-53; res assoc teaching foreign lang, MLA, 58-61; from asst prof to assoc prof foreign lang, 61-68, chmn dept, 65-68, dir, Ctr Women's Advan, 74-77, PROF LANG & LIT, FAIRLEIGH DICKINSON UNIV, 68- *Concurrent Pos:* Fulbright fel, 64; ed & contribr, From the Center, Fairleigh Dickenson Univ, 76 & 77. *Mem:* Northeast Mod Lang Asn; Am Asn Teachers Fr; Am Soc 18th Century Studies; Comp Lit Asn; AAUP. *Res:* Franco-English intellectual crosscurrents in the 17th and 18th centuries; phenomenology and existentialism; women's issues. *Publ:* Transl, Brissot de Warville's New Travels to the United States, 1788, Harvard Univ, 64; auth, The forgotten book of Pascal's Pensees, Romanic Rev, 12/71; Pascal's Pensees and the Enlightenment, Studies Voltaire, 12/72; The literary treatment of women, Female Studies IX, 75; transl, The quality of witness: A Romanian diary, Jewish Publ Soc Am, fall 82. *Mailing Add:* Dept of Foreign Lang Fairleigh Dickinson Univ Madison NJ 07940

VAN BAELEN, JACQUELINE, b Belgium, Sept 27, 30; US citizen. FRENCH. *Educ:* Vassar Col, BA, 52; Univ Geneva, Lic es Sci Morales, 54, dipl, 54; Univ Calif, Los Angeles, PhD, 62. *Prof Exp:* Instr Span & Ger, Keuka Col, 55-57; asst French, Univ Calif, Los Angeles, 57-60, 61-62, assoc, 60-61, lectr, Riverside, 62-63, asst prof, Santa Barbara, 63-65; assoc prof comp lit & French, Emory Univ, 65-68; assoc prof, 68-76, PROF ROMANCE LANG, STATE UNIV NY COL, BINGHAMTON, 76- *Concurrent Pos:* Off asst, NY Times, Geneva, 54; interpreter, Black Gold Studios, 60; Radio Corp Am donation for res, 61. *Mem:* MLA; Am Asn Teachers French. *Res:* French drama, especially 17th century and contemporary; film and literature. *Publ:* Auth, Rotrou: Le heros tragique et la revolte, Nizet, 65; Cyrano de Bergerac: The narrative voyage, Yale French Studies, 6/73; co-ed, Theatre Complet de Tristan L'Hermite, Univ Ala, 74. *Mailing Add:* Dept of Romance Lang State Univ of New York Col Binghamton NY 13901

VAN BEYSTERVELDT, ANTONY A, b Netherlands, Apr 22, 23; m 59; c 4. SPANISH LANGUAGE & LITERATURE. *Educ:* Univ Tilburg, BA & MA, 52; Univ Utrecht, BA & MA, 59; Univ Amsterdam, PhD(Span), 66. *Prof Exp:* Lectr Span, Netherlands Sch Bus, 64-68; assoc prof, York Univ, 68-69; assoc prof, 69-72, PROF SPAN, BOWLING GREEN STATE UNIV, 72- *Res:* Spanish theater of the 16th and 17th centuries; Spanish courtly love in 15th and 16th centuries; French language. *Publ:* Auth, Repercussions du souci de la purete de sang sur la conception de l'honneur dans la Comedia nueva espagnole, E J Brill, Leiden, 66; Nueva interpretacion de los Comentarios Reales de Garcilaso el Inca, Cuadernos Hispanoam, 2/69; contribr, Estudios sobre la obra de Americo Castro, Taurus, Madrid, 71; auth, La poesia amatoria del siglo XV y el teatro profano de Juan del Encina, Insula, Madrid, 72; La inversion del amor cortes en Moreto, Cuadernos Hispanoam, 1/74; Nueva interpretacion de La Celestina, Segismundo, 75; contribr, Americo Castro and the Meaning of Spanish Civilization, Univ Calif, Los Angeles, 76; Revision de los debates feministas del siglo XV y las novelas de Juan de Flores, Hispania, Vol 64, 81. *Mailing Add:* Dept of Romance Lang Bowling Green State Univ Bowling Green OH 43403

VAN CAMPEN, JOSEPH ALFRED, b Trucksville, Pa, June 14, 33; m 63. LINGUISTICS. *Educ:* Univ Chicago, BA, 53, MA, 55; Harvard Univ, PhD(Slavic lang), 61. *Prof Exp:* Instr Slavic lang, Harvard Univ, 60-61, res fel, 61-62, asst prof, 62-68; assoc prof Slavic lang & lit, 68-72, PROF SLAVIC LANG & LIT, STANFORD UNIV, 72-, CHMN DEPT, 76- *Mem:* Am Asn Teachers Slavic & EEurop Lang; Ling Soc Am. *Res:* Linguistics; Slavic languages; Germanic languages. *Publ:* Coauth, The Bulgarian nonsyllabic phonemes, Language, 59; auth, Alternative solutions to a problem in Bulgarian morphology, Slavic & EEurop J, 6/62; Old Church Slavic vowel alternations, Int J Slavic Ling, 5/63. *Mailing Add:* Dept of Languages Stanford Univ Stanford CA 94305

VANCE, SYLVIA PHILLIPS, b New Britain, Conn, Dec 24, 25; m 48; c 3. FRENCH LITERATURE & HISTORY. *Educ:* Otterbein Col, BA, 47; Ohio State Univ, MA, 48, PhD(French lit), 80. *Prof Exp:* Instr French, 61-69, asst prof, 69-81, ASSOC PROF FRENCH & HIST & CHMN DEPT INTEGRATIVE STUDIES, OTTERBEIN COL, 81- *Mem:* MLA; Am Asn Teachers Fr; Soc Fr Hist Studies; Am Soc 18th Century Studies; Soc Etude XVII Siecle. *Res:* The intendant Nicolas de Lamoignon de Basville; the cardinal de Retz. *Publ:* Auth, History as dramatic reinforcement: Voltaire's Use of history in four tragedies set in the Middle Ages, Studies on Voltaire & the 18th Century, 76. *Mailing Add:* 223 Knox St Westerville OH 43081

VANCE, TIMOTHY JOHN, b Minneapolis, Minn, Aug 25, 51; m 81. LINGUISTICS, JAPANESE LANGUAGE. *Educ:* Washington Univ, BA, 73, Univ Chicago, MA, 76, PhD(ling), 79. *Prof Exp:* Asst prof, Univ Ill, Chicago Circle, 79-80; ASST PROF LING & JAPANESE, UNIV FLA, 81- *Mem:* Ling Soc Am; Asn Teachers Japanese. *Res:* Phonological theory; experimental phonetics; Japanese phonology. *Publ:* Co-ed, Papers from the Eleventh Regional Meeting of the Chicago Linguistic Society & Papers from the Parasession on Functionalism, Chicago Ling Soc, 75; auth, An experimental investigation of tone and intonation in Cantonese, 76 & Tonal distinction in Cantonese, 77, Phonetica; The psychological status of a constraint on Japanese consonant alternation, Ling, 80. *Mailing Add:* 701 NW 24th Ave Gainesville FL 32601

VAN COETSEM, FRANS C, b Grammont, Belgium, Apr 14, 19; m 47; c 2. GERMANIC LINGUISTICS. *Educ:* Univ Louvain, Cand, 43, Lic, 46, PhD(Ger philol), 52, Agrege, 56. *Prof Exp:* Collabr, Official Dutch Dictionary, Leiden, 63-68, co-ed, 52-57; prof Ger ling, Univ Louvain, 57-67; PROF GER LING, CORNELL UNIV, 68- *Concurrent Pos:* Prof extraordinarius, Ger ling, Univ Leiden, 63-68; vis prof, Cornell Univ, 65-66; Fulbright vis prof, Univ Vienna, spring 76. *Mem:* Royal Neth Acad Sci; Ling Soc Am. *Res:* Germanic comparative linguistics; Dutch linguistics; Frisian linguistics. *Publ:* Auth, Das System der starken Verba, North-Holland Publ, Amsterdam, 56; A syntagmatic structure in development, Lingua, 68; contribr, In: Vorschläge für eine strukturale Grammatik des Deutschen, Wiss Buchges, Darmstadt, 70; coauth, Kurzer Grundriss der Germ Philologie, de Gruyter, Berlin, Vol I, 70; Toward a Grammar of Proto-Germanic, Niemeyer, Tübingen, 72; Woordenboek der Nederl, Taal Nijhoff-Sijthoff, The Hague & Leiden, Vol 12, 72; contribr, Historical linguistics, Brill, Leiden, 80. *Mailing Add:* Dept of Mod Lang & Ling Cornell Univ Ithaca NY 14853

VAN D'ELDEN, KARL HERBERT, b Frankfurt am Main, Ger, Sept 9, 23; US citizen; m 61. GERMANIC LANGUAGES & LITERATURES. *Educ:* Pa State Col, AB, 47; Harvard Univ, AM, 48; Western Reserve Univ, PhD, 50; William Mitchell Col, JD, 79. *Prof Exp:* Mem US Foreign Serv, Am Consulate Gen, Frankfurt, Ger, 39-40; instr Ger, Tufts Univ, 47; asst prof mod lang, Fenn Col, 48-50; lectr Ger, Univ Calif, Japan, 54-56; lectr Ger & French, Univ Md, Japan, 56-57; lectr Ger & English, Univ Md, Munich, Ger, 62-63; asst prof Ger, US Mil Acad, 57-61; dir instr, Defense Lang Inst, 64; prof mod lang & head dept, The Citadel, 65-68; chmn dept mod lang & lit, 68-75, PROF GER, HAMLINE UNIV, 68-, PROF LEGAL STUDIES, 81- *Concurrent Pos:* Pvt pract law, 80-; supv ed, Speciality Law Dig: Educ, Bur Nat Affairs, 80-81. *Mem:* MLA; AAUP. *Res:* Contemporary Austrian poetry; medieval law; law and literature. *Publ:* Transl, Instruction pro confessariis, Bruce 50; ed, German Military Readings, US Mil Acad, 60; auth, The blue flower--the symbol of early German romanticism?, Hamline Rev, 69; coauth, Was Deutsche Lesen, McGraw, 73; auth, West German Poets on Society and Politics, Wayne State Univ, 79. *Mailing Add:* Dept of Mod Lang & Lit Hamline Univ St Paul MN 55104

VAN D'ELDEN, STEPHANIE CAIN, b Galveston, Tex, June 16, 40; m 61. MEDIEVAL LITERATURE & CULTURE. *Educ:* Univ Minn, BA, 61-PhD(Ger philol), 74; Univ Heidelberg, Ger, cert Ger, 62; San Jose State Col, MA, 65; Unic SC, MA, 68. *Prof Exp:* Teacher Ger, Am High Sch, Heidelberg, Ger, 61-62; from teaching asst to teaching assoc & res asst Ger & art hist, Univ Minn, 68-74; asst prof, 75-79, PROF GER, HAMLINE UNIV, 79- *Mem:* AAUP; Medieval Acad Am; Int Courtly Lit Soc; Int Arthurian Soc; MLA. *Res:* Medieval German literature; heraldry and heralds; medieval drama. *Publ:* Auth, The ehrenreden of Peter Suchenwirt and Gelre, Beiträge zur Geschichte der deutschen Sprache und Literatur, 75; Peter Suchenwirt als herald, Adler Zeitschrift für Genealogie und Heraldik, 76; Peter Suchenwirt and Heraldic Poetry, K M Halosar, 76; In a blazon of glory: Three tournament and siege poems, Coat of Arms, 78; Seifried Helbling's ein maer ist guot ze schriben an-a reevaluation, Amsterdamer Beiträge zur älteren Germanistik, 78; From shield to emblem: Changing fashions in heraldry, Euphorion Zeitschrift für Literaturgeschichte, 79. *Mailing Add:* Hamline Univ St Paul MN 55104

VAN DELFT, LOUIS, b Amsterdam, Neth, Mar 24, 38; c 2. FRENCH & COMPARATIVE LITERATURE. *Educ:* Univ France, Agregation, 65; Univ Provence, Doctorat(French lit), 71. *Prof Exp:* Asst prof French lit, Eastern Mich Univ, 66-67 & Yale Univ, 67-68; asst prof, 68-70, ASSOC PROF FRENCH LIT, McGILL UNIV, 70- *Concurrent Pos:* Can Coun leave fel, 74-75; Alexander von Humboldt-Stiftung res fel comp lit, 78-79. *Mem:* Asn Can Comp Lit; N Am Asn 17th Century Fr Lit. *Res:* French and European moralists of classical era; foreign influences on French classical literature; modern Jewish writers of French expression. *Publ:* Auth, Eyes and words in Britannicus, Yale Fr Studies; La Bruyere moraliste, Droz, Geneva, 71; Andre Schwarz-Bart, peintre de la negritude, Actes du Colloque sur la negritudes, 73; contribr, La litterature de l'Exode: une lecture d'Andre Schwarz-Bart, Mosaic, 75; Racine: mythese et realites, Soc d'Etude du XVIIe siecle, 76; auth, Qu'est-ce qu'un moraliste?, Caief, 78; Tradition et innovation dans l'Examen de ingenios de J Huarte, Actes du VIIIe Cong Int Lit compt, 79. *Mailing Add:* 4095 Corte des Neiges Montreal PQ H3H 1W9 Can

VAN DEN BERGHE, CHRISTIAN LOUIS, b Brussels, Belgium, May 17, 38; US citizen; m 61; c 2. FRENCH LINGUISTICS & LITERATURE. *Educ:* Stanford Univ, BA, 61, MA, 63, PhD(French ling & lit), 71. *Prof Exp:* Instr French & Span, Ripon Col, 63-66; asst prof French ling & educ, 69-74; dir MAT in French, 70-73, ASSOC PROF FRENCH & LING, UNIV SANTA CLARA, 74- *Mem:* Am Coun Teaching Foreign Lang. *Res:* Phonostylistics; French applied linguistics; style and idea in French literature. *Publ:* Auth, Dictionnaire des Idees dans l'Oeuvre de Simo de Beauvoir, Mouton, The Hague, 66; co-ed, Linguistic Studies Presented to Andre Martinet, Vol I: General Linguistics, 69, Vol II: Indo-European Linguistics, 70 & Vol III: Non-Indo-European Linguistics, 71, Ling Circle NY & Word, Vols XXIII, XXIV & XXV; auth, La Phonostylistique du francais, Col De Proprietatibus Litterarum, Mouton, The Hague, 76. *Mailing Add:* Dept of Mod Lang & Lit Univ of Santa Clara Santa Clara CA 95053

VAN DEN BOSSCHE, EDMOND C, b Antwerp, Belgium, Apr 15, 23. FRENCH & COMPARATIVE LITERATURE. *Educ:* Fordham Univ, MA, 61, PhD(Romance lang), 68. *Prof Exp:* From instr to asst prof, 61-72, ASSOC PROF FRENCH, MANHATTAN COL, 72-, DIR, INT STUDIES PROG, 76- *Concurrent Pos:* Dir, NDEA Inst French, 66. *Res:* Early Renaissance in Netherlands; Belgian theater, 19th-20th century; symbolism. *Publ:* Ed, Encycl Philos, Philos Libr, 73; auth, Margareta of Austria: Princess of the Renaissance?, Handelingen of Koninklijke Kring voor Oudheidkunde, Lett en Kunst, 73. *Mailing Add:* Dept of Mod Lang Manhattan Col Riverdale NY 10471

VANDERFORD, KENNETH H(ALE), b Columbia City, Ind, Sept 30, 08. ROMANCE LANGUAGES. *Educ:* Wittenberg Univ, AB, 30; Wash State Univ, MA, 32; Univ Chicago, PhD(Span), 40. *Prof Exp:* Instr Span, Allen Acad, Tex, 35-36, Lon Morris Col, Tex, 36-37 & Univ Miami, 37-38; mem staff off coord inter-Am affairs, Wash, DC, 41; exec dir, Coord Comt for Ecuador, 42; mem staff, US Govt, Bolivia, 43-44, Argentina, 45, Venezuela, 46; mem pub rel dept, Creole Petroleum Corp & Creole Found, Venezuela, 46-58; from asst prof to assoc prof Span, 67-74, EMER ASSOC PROF SPAN, RIPON COL, 74- *Mem:* MLA; Am Name Soc. *Res:* Old Spanish language and literature; Spanish personal names, specifically Venezuelan. *Publ:* Ed, Macias in legend and literature, Mod Philol, 33; El setenario y su relacion con las Siete partidas, Rev Filol Hisp, 41; Alfonso el Sabio's Setenario, Univ Buenos Aires, 45. *Mailing Add:* RR 3 Columbia City IN 46725

VANDER MEULEN, ROSS, b South Bend, Ind, Nov 13, 35; m 60; c 2. GERMAN LITERATURE. *Educ:* Northwestern Univ, BA, 58; Univ Mich, Ann Arbor, MA, 61, MA, 62, PhD(Ger lit), 72. *Prof Exp:* Lectr Am studies, Univ Maine, 64-65; instr Ger, Univ Mich, 66-68; from instr to asst prof, 68-77, ASSOC PROF GER, KNOX COL, ILL, 77-, ASSOC DEAN COL, 79- *Mem:* Am Asn Teachers Ger; MLA; Am Soc 18th Century Studies. *Res:* Goethe; Schiller; 18th century German literature. *Publ:* Auth, The Fables of Erasmus Alberus, Univ Microfilms, 72; How to succeed in a foreign language without really crying, Knox Now, 73; Luther's Betriegen zur Warheit and the Fables of Erasmus Alberus, Ger Rev, 1/77; The theological texture of Schiller's Wilhelm Tell, German Rev, 2/78. *Mailing Add:* Dept of Modern Foreign Lang Knox Col Galesburg IL 61401

VANDERSALL, STANLEY TALBOTT, b Columbus, Ohio, Sept 13, 17; m 40; c 3. CLASSICS. *Educ:* Col Wooster, BA, 39; Ohio State Univ, MA, 40, PhD(classics), 47. *Prof Exp:* Instr class lang & lit, Ohio State Univ, 47-48; from instr to assoc prof classics, 48-70, PROF CLASSICS, UNIV NEBR-LINCOLN, 70- *Mem:* Am Philol Asn; Class Asn Mid W&S. *Res:* Greek comedy; Augustan poetry. *Publ:* Auth, Line omissions in Homeric papyri since 1932, Class Philol, Vol XXXVII, 7/42; co-ed, Ovid's Metamorphosis Englished..., Univ Nebr, 70. *Mailing Add:* Dept Classics Univ of Nebr Lincoln NE 68508

VAN DUSEN, ROBERT LABRANCHE, b New York, NY, May 5, 29. GERMAN. *Educ:* Harvard Univ, BA, 51; Univ Tex, MA, 59, PhD(Ger), 64. *Prof Exp:* From lectr to asst prof, 60-68, ASSOC PROF GER, McMASTER UNIV, 68- *Concurrent Pos:* Can Coun grant, 67-68. *Mem:* MLA; Am Soc 18th Century Studies; Can Soc 18th Century Studies. *Res:* Popularphilosophic; essay; Klopotock. *Publ:* Auth, Christian Garve and the English Belles-Lettres, 70 & The Literary Ambitions and Achievements of Alexander von Hunboldt, 72, Lang, Bern; Goethe's Dichtung und Wahrheit, In: The Triumph of Culture, Hakkert, Toronto, 73; Freedom and constraint in Zacharaes' satire The Braggart, In: Satire in the 18th Century, Garland, 82. *Mailing Add:* Dept of Ger McMaster Univ Hamilton ON L8S 4M2 Can

VAN EERDE, JOHN ANDREWS, b Paterson, NJ, Oct 2, 16; m 46. ROMANCE LANGUAGES. *Educ:* Harvard Univ, AB, 38, MA, 39; Johns Hopkins Univ, PhD(Romance lang), 53. *Prof Exp:* Instr French, Amherst Col, 46-47; instr, Smith Col, 47-48; instr Romance lang, Johns Hopkins Univ, 48-53; asst prof French, Univ RI, 54-60; assoc prof Romance lang, 60-63, chmn dept, 68-72, PROF ROMANCE LANG, LEHIGH UNIV, 63. *Honors & Awards:* Chevalier, Palmes Academiques, 73. *Mem:* MLA; Am Asn Teachers Fr; Am Soc 18th Century Studies; Renaissance Soc Am; Am Name Soc. *Res:* French theatre of the 17th and 18th centuries; Rousseau. *Publ:* Auth, The imagery in Gautier's Dantesque nightmare, Studies Romanticism, summer, 62; Quinault, the court and kingship, Romanc Rev, 10/62; Curzio Malaparte, In: Encyclopedia of World Literature, 69. *Mailing Add:* Dept of Mod Foreign Lang & Lit Lehigh Univ Bethlehem PA 18015

VAN GINNEKEN, EVA, b Budapest, Hungary, Oct 13, 32; US citizen; m 59. FRENCH LANGUAGE & LITERATURE. *Educ:* Wayne Univ, BA, 53, MA, 54; Brown Univ, PhD, 63. *Prof Exp:* Instr French, Hofstra Col, 61-62; from instr to asst prof, Colo State Univ, 62-64; from asst prof to assoc prof French lang & lit, 64-73, PROF FRENCH LANG & LIT, CALIF STATE UNIV, FULLERTON, 73- *Mem:* MLA; Am Asn Teachers Fr. *Res:* Seventeenth and twentieth century French literature. *Publ:* Ed, Nouvelle Allegorique, Droz, 67. *Mailing Add:* Dept of French Calif State Univ Fullerton CA 92631

VAN-HUY, PIERRE NGUYEN, b Quang-binh, Vietnam, Sept 25, 29; US citizen; m 67; c 2. FRENCH LITERATURE, PSYCHOLOGY. *Educ:* Univ Fribourg, Switz, MA, 59, PhD(French lit), 62, dipl spec educ, 64. *Prof Exp:* Vis asst prof French lit, La State Univ, Baton Rouge, 67-68; asst prof, Univ Miss, 68-69; assoc prof, 69-75 PROF FRENCH LIT, ST JOHN'S UNIV, NY, 75- *Concurrent Pos:* Speaker's Bur, St John's Univ. *Mem:* MLA; Am Asn Teacher Fr. *Res:* Twentieth century French literature; literary philosophy; psychology and mythology. *Publ:* Auth, La Metaphysique du Bonjeur chez A Camus, La Baconniere, Neuchatel, 62; L'Etranger ou le conflit des Valeurs Maternelles et paternelles, 73 & A propos du theatre d'Ionesco, 73, Lang Quart; coauth, La Chute de Camus, Le Dernier Testament, La Baconniere, Neuchatel, 74; auth, Camus et la responsabilite, 75, Clamence ou le grand messager camusien, 75, La Lecon selon le langage oublie, 76 & The Gap by Ionesco and the Sartrian psychoanalysis, 77, Lang Quart; Pilote de guerre ou la Conscience cosmique de St Ex, 81 & Sartre and Teilhard or the ontological proof, 81, Lang Quart. *Mailing Add:* St John's Univ Grand Central & Utopia Pkwy New York NY 11439

VAN LENT, PETER COSBY, b Boston, Mass, Sept, 14, 41; m 66; c 2. FRENCH LITERATURE. *Educ:* Dartmouth Col, BA, 63; Stanford Univ, PhD(French), 72. *Prof Exp:* Instr, Phillips Acad Andover, 63-64; ASSOC PROF FRENCH, ST LAWRENCE UNIV, 70- *Mem:* Am Asn Teachers Fr; Asn Can Studies US. *Res:* French literature of Africa and the Caribbean; French literature of Canada; stained glass. *Publ:* Auth, Hantu and the theme of self-realization in Laye's L'Enfant noir, Col Lang Asn J, 6/75; Ten projects to involve your students directly in French, Fr Rev, 12/81. *Mailing Add:* Dept of Mod Lang & Lit St Lawrence Univ Canton NY 13617

VANN, ROBERTA JEANNE, Teaching English as a Foreign Language, Applied Linguistics. See Vol II

VAN NOOTEN, BAREND ADRIAN, b Larantuka, Indonesia, Sept 21, 32; Can citizen; m 60; c 2. SANSKRIT, INDOLOGY. *Educ:* Univ Toronto, BSc, 58; Univ Calif, PhD (Sanskrit), 63. *Prof Exp:* Jr fel Sanskrit, Am Inst Indian Studies, 64-66; asst prof Sanskrit & ling, 66-72, ASSOC PROF SANSKRIT, UNIV CALIF, BERKELEY, 72- *Mem:* Am Orient Soc; Ling Soc Am. *Res:* Sanskrit grammar; Indian epics. *Publ:* Auth, Panini's theory of meaning, Found Lang, 70; Mahabharata, Twayne, 72. *Mailing Add:* Dept of South & Southeast Asian Studies Univ of Calif Berkeley CA 94720

VAN NORTWICK, THOMAS, b Geneva, Ill, Oct 10, 46; m 69. CLASSICAL LANGUAGES & LITERATURE. *Educ:* Stanford Univ, BA, 69; Yale Univ, MA, 72; Stanford Univ, PhD(classics), 75. *Prof Exp:* Instr, 74-75, ASST PROF CLASSICS, OBERLIN COL, 75- *Mem:* Am Philol Asn; Archeol Inst Am; Am Sch Class Studies at Athens. *Res:* Early Greek poetry; Augustan Latin poetry. *Publ:* Coauth, Enjambment in Greek Hexameter Poetry, Trans & Proc Am Philol Asn, 78. *Mailing Add:* Dept of Classics Oberlin Col Oberlin OH 44074

VAN OLPHEN, HERMAN HENDRIK, b Amsterdam, Neth, Apr 1, 40; US citizen; m 62; c 2. HINDI, LINGUISTICS. *Educ:* Rice Univ, BA, 63; Univ Tex, Austin, PhD (ling), 70. *Prof Exp:* Res asst Russ & Ger ling, Ling Res Ctr, 63-65, instr teaching English as foreign lang, Peace Corps Iran Training Prof, 66, asst prof ling & Asian studies, 68-70, ASST PROF ORIENT & AFRICAN LANG & LIT & ASIAN STUDIES, UNIV TEX, AUSTIN, 70- *Mem:* Ling Soc Am; Asn Asian Studies; Am Orient Soc; Am Coun Teachers Uncommon Asian Lang (vpres, 77-); Am Coun Teaching Foreign Lang. *Res:* Hindi syntax; modern Hindi literature: sociolinguistics. *Publ:* Auth, Elementary Hindi Grammar and Exercises, Univ Tex, Austin, 72; Functional and non-functional conjuncts in Hindi, Indian Ling, 1/74; Guidelines for teaching first and second-year South Asian languages, Asian Prof Rev, spring 74; ed, Linguistic Borrowing, Univ Tex, Austin, 74; auth, Aspect, tense, and mood in the Hindi verb, Indo-Iranian J, 75; Ergative and causative in Hindi, Orbis, 75; The hindi verb in indirect constructions, Int J Dravidian Ling, 6/76; First-Year Hindi Course, Univ Tex-Austin, 80. *Mailing Add:* Dept of Orient & African Lang & Lit Univ of Tex 2601 University Ave Austin TX 78712

VAN RUTTEN, PIERRE M, b Brussels, Belgium, July 3, 20; Can citizen; m 70; c 1. FRENCH LITERATURE, LINGUISTICS. *Educ:* Sorbonne, dipl French lit & lang, 60; Univ Ottawa, PhD(French lit), 70. *Prof Exp:* Teacher Latin, Greek & French, Col Albert I Kinshasha, Zaire, 60-62; teacher, Col Brebeuf, Montreal, 62-65; asst prof French lit, Univ Ottawa, 65-70; assoc prof & chmn dept, Laurentian Univ, 70-71; assoc prof, 71-77, PROF FRENCH LIT, CARLETON UNIV, 77- *Honors & Awards:* Prix Christophe Plantin, Belgium, 81. *Mem:* Can Ling Soc; MLA; Soc Can Semiotique; Asn Can Univ Teachers Fr. *Res:* Saint-John Perse; literary stylistics; use of computers in literary research. *Publ:* Auth, Ce que dit la bouche d'ombre de Victor Hugo, etude stylistique, 4-6/68 & La condition humaine ou la difficulte d'etre communiste, 7-9/69, Rev Univ Ottawa; La torsade des images dans le XXIIeme chant du paradis de la Divine comedie de Dante, Syntheses, Brussels, 6/69; Le Langage Poetique de Saint-John Perse, Mouton, The Hague; Eloges de Saint-John Perse, Collection Lire aujourd'hui, Hachette, Paris. *Mailing Add:* Dept of French Carleton Univ Ottawa ON K1S 5B6 Can

VAN SCHOONEVELD, CORNELIS HENDRIK, b The Hague, Netherlands, Jan 19, 21; US citizen; m 67; c 3. SLAVIC LINGUISTICS. *Educ:* Univ Leiden, Drs, 46; Columbia Univ, PhD(Slavic), 49. *Prof Exp:* Instr Slavics, Okla Univ, 49-51; prof, Univ Leiden, 52-59; prof, Stanford Univ, 59-66; PROF SLAVICS, IND UNIV, BLOOMINGTON, 66- *Concurrent Pos:* Vis lectr, Harvard Univ, 51; Inter-Univ Comt Travel Grants fel, Bulgaria, 68. *Mem:* MLA; Am Asn Teachers Slavic & East Europ Lang; Ling Soc Am. *Res:* Comparative analysis of the semantic structures of Slavic languages; description and analysis of comtemporary Standard Russian. *Publ:* Ed, Janua Linguarum Ser, 54-, Slavistic Printings & Reprintings, 54-, auth, A Semantic Analysis of the Old Russian Finite Preterite System, 59, coauth, The Sentence Intonation of Contemporary Standard Russian as a Linguistic Structure, 61, ed, De Proprietatibus Litterarum, 66- & auth, Semantic Transmutations I, 78, Mouton, Berlin. *Mailing Add:* PO Box 1314 Bloomington IN 47401

VAN SICKLE, JOHN BABCOCK, b Freeport, Ill, Sept 30, 36; m 65. CLASSICAL & COMPARATIVE LITERATURE. *Educ:* Harvard Univ, AB, 58, PhD(class philol), 66; Univ Ill, AM, 59. *Prof Exp:* PROF CLASSICS & COMP LIT, CITY UNIV NEW YORK, 76- *Concurrent Pos:* Corresp ed, Quaderni Urbinati di Cultura classica, 77-; regional ed, Class J, 78-; Guggenheim fel, 78-79; ed secy, Instrumentum Litterarum, 81-; Fulbright prof, Virgil Bimillennium, Univ Rome, 82. *Mem:* Am Philol Soc; Soc Promotion Roman Studies; Virgilian Soc Am. *Res:* Latin literature and its traditions; the poetic sequence and the poetry book. *Publ:* Ed, The New Archilochus, Arethusa, 76; auth, The Design of Virgil's Bucolics, Ateneo, Rome, 78; ed, Augustan Poetry Books, 80, auth, The Book Roll and Some Conventions of the Poetic Book, 80, Commentaria in Maroneum Commenticia: A Case History of Bucolics Missread, 81, Arethusa; Dawn and dusk as motifs of opening and closure in heroic and bucolic epos, Virgilian Acad Mantua, 82. *Mailing Add:* 380 Riverside Dr 6T New York NY 10025

VAN, STRAALEN JOHANNES, Modern History. See Vol I

VANSWORD, ROBERT C, b Przemysl, Poland, Sept 16, 21; US citizen; m 67. COMPARATIVE LITERATURE & PHILOLOGY. *Educ:* J Slowacki Col, Poland, BA, 39; State Teachers Col, Poland, BS, 40; Univ Lvov, MA, 41, PhD(comp lit), 44; City Col New York, BA, 56. *Prof Exp:* From instr Polish hist to asst prof ling jr cols, Poland, 39-43; vis prof comp lit, UNRRA, Univ Munich, 45-46; supt Dist Tuttlingen, State Dept Educ, 48-50; instr Latin, Russ & French, Ukrainian Tech Inst New York, 58-60; teacher high sch , NY, 60-61; instr Ger lang, Utica Col, Syracuse Univ, 61-62; asst prof French, Ital, Russ, Ger & Polish, State Univ NY Col Potsdam, 62-65; assoc prof Russ & Ger lang & lit, Samford Univ, 65-67; assoc prof, Univ Ala, Birmingham, 67-80. *Concurrent Pos:* Consult educ affairs, Polish Govt, 45-61; grants, Koscuiszko Found, 57, Paderewski Found , 58, Polish Sociol Soc, 58, 67, 69, Univ Ala, 68, 69 & Univ Ala, Birmingham, 73 & 74; hon dean, Am Acad Parapsychology, 77- *Mem:* Polish Inst Arts & Sci Am; Am Asn Advan Slavic Studies; Am Asn Teachers Ger; Am Asn Teachers Slavic & East Europ Lang; Am Asn Advan Polish Studies. *Res:* Comparative culturology. *Publ:* Auth, White and Red, Polish Sociol Soc, 58; September 1939, Vol I, In: The War, E S Press, 78. *Mailing Add:* 1319 Chester St Birmingham AL 35226

VAN SYOC, WAYLAND BRYCE, b Ackworth, Iowa, May 8, 16; m 43; c 3. LINGUISTICS. *Educ:* Simpson Col, BA, 37; Univ Mich, MA, 50, PhD, 59. *Prof Exp:* Teacher high schs, Iowa, 37-43; instr English, Univ Mich, 47-53, head, Ford Found English Teacher Proj for Indonesia, 53-56, lectr methods of teaching English as foreign lang, English Lang Inst, 56-59, asst prof methods of teaching English as foreign lang & ling, Southeast Asian Regional English Proj, 59-63; assoc prof English, 63-67, PROF ENGLISH, SOUTHERN ILL UNIV, EDWARDSVILLE, 67- *Concurrent Pos:* Teaching English as a foreign language. *Publ:* Auth, Teaching English inThailand, Chulalongkorn Univ Bangkok, 63; coauth, Let's Learn English, Am Bk Co, Vols IV-VI, 67-72. *Mailing Add:* Dept of English Southern Illinois Univ Edwardsville IL 62025

VAN TREESE, GILBERTE (GREINER), b France, Apr 6, 27; US citizen; m 53; c 1. FRENCH LITERATURE & CIVILIZATION. *Educ:* Bowling Green State Univ, BA, 50; Univ Paris, cert Am lit & civilization, 51; Ind Univ Bloomington, MA, 61, PhD(French), 64. *Prof Exp:* Instr Span, Univ Md Overseas Prog, England, 54; from instr to asst prof French, 63-71, assoc prof, 71-79, PROF FRENCH, SWEET BRIAR COL, 79- *Mem:* AAUP; Am Asn Teachers Fr; MLA; Am Asn Univ Women. *Res:* French contemporary novel; French civilization and culture. *Mailing Add:* Dept of Mod Lang Sweet Briar Col Sweet Briar VA 24595

VAN TREESE, GLENN JOSEPH, b Indianapolis, Ind, May 18, 29; m 53; c 1. FRENCH LITERATURE & LANGUAGE. *Educ:* Ind Univ, Bloomington, AB, 51, MA(French lit) & MA(French lang), 62, PhD(French lit), 68; Sorbonne, cert French lang & civilization, 55, cert French lit, 60, cert French pronunciation, 60. *Prof Exp:* From instr to assoc prof French, 63-81, dir lang lab, 66-78, chmn dept mod lang, 71-75, PROF FRENCH, SWEET BRIAR COL, 81- *Concurrent Pos:* Andrew W Mellon Found fac grant humanities, 72; Nat Endowment for Humanities challenge grant, 81; Mednick Mem Fund grant, 81. *Mem:* MLA; Am Asn Teachers Fr; Am Coun Teaching Foreign Lang; Am Soc 18th Century Studies; Soc Francaise d'Etude du XVIIIe Siecle. *Res:* The Enlightenment in France; 18th century French literature; contemporary socio-economic France. *Publ:* Auth, D'Alembert and Frederick the Great: A Study of their Relationship, Nauwelaerts, Louvain, Belgium, 74. *Mailing Add:* Dept of Mod Lang Sweet Briar Col Sweet Briar VA 24595

VAN TUYL, CHARLES DON, b Tulsa, Okal, July 5, 42; m 65; c 4. TIBETAN LANGUAGE & LITERATURE. *Educ:* Yale Univ, BA, 64; Ind Univ, MA, 70, PhD(Uralic-Altaic studies), 71. *Prof Exp:* Instr hist, Univ Dayton, 70-71; fel relig studies, Yale Univ, 72-74; assoc prof social sci, Bacone Col, 75-82. *Concurrent Pos:* Ed, Ind Univ Press; Nat Endowment for Humanities grant, 82. *Mem:* Tibet Soc. *Res:* Tibetan studies; Native American studies. *Publ:* Auth, Love songs by the Sixth Dalai Lama, 68 & Account of the Jesuit Fathers Dorville and Grueber Journey in 1661 through Tibet, 70, Tibet Soc Newslett; Milarepa, Tibetan Buddhist poet and saint, Vesak Ann, Ceylon, 74; The Tshe rin ma account - an old document incorporated into the mi la ras pa'i mgur 'bum, Zentralasiatische Studien, 75; The Natchez People and Language, Okla Hist Soc, 77; Evaluating the variant readings in the mi las ras pa': rnam thar, Zentralasiatische Studien, 77; Milarepa and the gCod ritual, J Tibetan Studies, 78; Milarepa and the Eighteen Great Demons, Zentralasiatische Studient, 78. *Mailing Add:* Social Sci Dept Bacone Col Muskogee OK 74401

VAN ZWOLL, CORNELIUS, b Rochester, NY, Nov 12, 16; m 46; c 3. GERMANIC LANGUAGES & LITERATURES. *Educ:* Calvin Col, BA, 38; Univ Mich, MA, 47; Mich State Univ, PhD, 65. *Prof Exp:* Instr Ger & Latin, Eastern Acad, 38-41; asst prof Ger, Carroll Col, Wis, 47-50; crypto-linguist, Nat Security Agency, US Dept Defense, 52-53; prin & instr, Eastern Acad, 53-56; asst prof mod lang, Calvin Col, 56-59; asst prof Ger & Russ, Albion Col, 59-63; assoc prof mod lang, Alma Col, Mich, 63-65, prof Ger & Russ & chmn dept, 65-68; PROF GER & RUSS & HEAD DEPT, DEPAUW UNIV, 68- *Concurrent Pos:* WGer Govt studies award, 61; Nat Endowment for Humanities award, 75. *Mem:* Am Asn Teachers Ger; MLA; Midwest Mod Lang Asn. *Res:* German literature of the 20th century; the modern Russian novel. *Mailing Add:* Dept of Ger & Russ DePauw Univ Greencastle IN 46135

VARDAMAN, HAZEL CLARE, b Utica, NY, Sept 12, 13; m 40. GERMAN. *Educ:* Smith Col, AB, 35; Univ Minn, MA, 37; Northwestern Univ, PhD, 41. *Prof Exp:* Teacher Ger & English, high sch, Jeffersonville, NY, 37-39; asst prof Ger & French, Doane Col, 41-42; instr Ger, Smith Col, 42-46; from asst prof to assoc prof, 46-59, prof, 59-79, EMER PROF GER, UNIV ILL, CHICAGO CIRCLE, 79- *Concurrent Pos:* Guest prof, Fed Repub Ger, 61 & 75. *Mem:* Am Asn Teachers Ger; MLA; AAUP; Am Coun Teaching Foreign Lang. *Res:* Teacher training; methodology of language teaching. *Publ:* Auth, Language and general education, Ger Quart, 1/53; coauth, Materials for teaching and testing German sounds, Unterrichtspraxis, spring 71. *Mailing Add:* Dept of Ger Univ of Ill Chicago IL 60680

VARDY, AGNES HUSZAR, b Debrecen, Hungary; US citizen; c 2. COMPARATIVE LITERATURE, ENGLISH. *Educ:* Ohio State Univ, BS, 63; Univ Pittsburgh, MA, 68; Univ Budapest, PhD(comp lit, Ger lang & lit), 70. *Prof Exp:* asst prof, 71-79, ASSOC PROF COMP LIT & ENGLISH, ROBERT MORRIS COL, 79- *Concurrent Pos:* Pub grant, Hungarian Cult Found,, 74; Uralic & Ultaic res grant, Ind Univ, Bloomington, summer, 78; Ford Found travel grant, summer, 79. *Mem:* Am Comp Lit Asn; MLA; Am Asn Advan Slavic Studies; Am Hungarian Educr Asn; Am Asn Study Hungarian Hist. *Res:* Modern German and Austrian literature; Central and East European literature; ethnic literature. *Publ:* Auth, A Study in Austrian Romanticism: Hungarian Influences in Lenau's Poetry, State Univ NY Col Buffalo, 74; Hungarian studies on the elementary and secondary level in North America, In: Kronika, Arpad Publ, 74; The image of the Turks in Jokai's historical novels and short stories, Duquesne Univ Studies in Hist, 79; (with S B Vardy), Research in Hungarian-American culture: Achievements and prospects, In: The Folk Arts of Hungary, 81 & ed (with Walter W K Kolar), The Folk Arts of Hungary, 81, Duquesne Univ Tamburitza Press; (with S B Vardy), Society in Change: Studies in Social and Military History, 82 & auth, Trianon in transylvanian Hungarian literature: Sandor Remenyik's Vegvari poems, In: War and Society in East Central Europe, 82, Columbia Univ Press; Karl Beck, Hungarian Acad Sci (in press). *Mailing Add:* 5740 Aylesboro Ave Pittsburgh PA 15217

VARI, VICTOR B, b San Francisco, Calif, Feb 22, 20; m 52. PHILOLOGY, LITERATURE. *Educ:* San Francisco State Col, AB, 42; Stanford Univ, MA, 52; Univ Madrid, PhD, 61. *Prof Exp:* News announcer, foreign lang, Radio Sta KRE, 41-42; assoc prof Romance lang, 46-64, dir div mod & class lang, 49-59, chmn dept, 64-73, PROF MOD LANG & LIT, UNIV SANTA CLARA, 49- *Concurrent Pos:* Lectr, Col Notre Dame, 53-62; res grant, Span Govt, 60-61; Fulbright grant, 64; Harold J Toso prof Ital Studies, Univ Santa Clara, 82-83. *Honors & Awards:* Cavaliere nell'Ordine Al Merito dell Repubblica Italiana, 82. *Mem:* MLA; Int Asn Study Ital Lang & Lit; Int Asn Hisp Studies. *Res:* Comparative literature. *Publ:* Auth, Carducci y Espana, Gredos, Spain, 63; Appunti su Carducci, Rivista Lett Mod e Comparata, 64. *Mailing Add:* Dept of Mod Lang & Lit Unit of Santa Clara Santa Clara CA 95053

VARONA, ALBERTO JORGE, b La Habana, Cuba, Apr 19, 21; US citizen; m 46; c 2. SPANISH AMERICAN LITERATURE, LATIN AMERICAN HISTORY. *Educ:* Univ Havana, Doctor en Leyes, 42; Univ Miami, MA, 66, PhD(Span & Span-Am lit), 70. *Prof Exp:* Prof criminol, Univ Oriente, Cuba, 48-49, prof penal law, 49-52; dir labor soc law, Ministery Labor, Cuba, 52-54; instr Span lang & lit, Hamilton Col, 65-66; from instr to asst prof, 66-72, assoc prof Span lang & lit, Wells Col, 72-78; RES & WRITING, 78- *Concurrent Pos:* Fel, Univ Miami, 62-65. *Mem:* MLA; Am Asn Teachers Span & Port. *Res:* The essay in Latin America; Cuban literature; women of America. *Publ:* Auth, Francisco Bilbao, Revolucionario de America, Ed Excelsior, Arg, 73; Cuba ante el mundo, 1960, Francisco Bilbao, Revolucionario de America, Excelsior, 73; ed, Jose Marti, Ismaelillo, Versus sencillos y Versus libres, Ahora Printing, 81. *Mailing Add:* 106 Zamora Ave Coral Gables FL 33134

VASLEF, NICHOLAS P, b Seattle, Wash, July 8, 30; m 56; c 2. SLAVIC LANGUAGES & LITERATURES. *Educ:* Univ Wash, BA, 52; Stanford Univ, MA, 60; Harvard Univ, MA, 63, PhD(Slavic lang & lit), 66. *Prof Exp:* Instr Russ lang & lit, US Air Force Acad, 68-72, chmn Russ & chmn Soviet area studies prog, 69-72; dep chief res & anal, Directorate of Mgt Anal, HQ, 73-74, chief analyst, Foreign Mil Doctrine & Strategy, HQ, 74-76, CHIEF, SOVIET/WARSAW PACT DIV, DEFENSE INTEL AGENCY, US AIR FORCE, 76- *Concurrent Pos:* Res grant, Inst Studies USSR, Munich, 67-68. *Mem:* Col Am Asn Teachers Slavic & EEurop Lang; AAUP; Am Asn Advan Slavic Studies. *Res:* Soviet doctrine and strategy; Soviet affaires. *Publ:* Ed, Alexander Pushkin, 70, A K Tolstoy, 71, Anna Akhamtova, 72, Evgeny Baratynsky, 72, Ivan Goncharov, 72, Gleb Uspensky, 72, Boris Pasternak, 72 & Ivan Krylov, 73, Twayne. *Mailing Add:* 1405 Grady Randall Ct McLean VA 22101

VASQUEZ, MARY SEALE, b Bronxville, NY, Oct 16, 42; m 76; c 1. HISPANIC LITERATURE, SPANISH LANGUAGE. *Educ:* Fla State Univ, BA, 64; Univ Wash, MA, 66, PhD(Romance lang & lit), 72. *Prof Exp:* Teacher Span, Newport High Sch, Bellevue, Wash, 66-68; instr, Kendall Col, 70-71; asst prof, Fla State Univ, 73-75; asst prof, 75-81, ASSOC PROF SPAN, ARIZ STATE UNIV, 81- *Concurrent Pos:* Ariz State Univ fac grant-in-aid, 76 & 82; Am Philos Soc grant, 81. *Mem:* MLA; Am Asn Teachers Span & Port; AAUP. *Res:* Contemporary novel of Spain and Mexico; 19th Century novel; contemporary Hispanic poetry. *Publ:* Transl, The friend who bought a Picasso, Tex Quart, 76; auth, Two views of contemporary urban Mexico, SAtlantic Bull, 76; Nota preliminar, Teresa Maria Rojas Compos Oscuro, Ediciones Unversal, 76; The creative task: Existential self-invention in

Benet's Una meditacion, Selecta, 80; Sender's Iman: Narrative Focus in a Portrayal of Horror, La Chispa II, 81; The definition of the individual in Sender's Hipogrifo Violento, Hispanofila, 81. *Mailing Add:* Dept of Foreign Lang Ariz State Univ Tempe AZ 85281

VAZQUEZ, WASHINGTON RAMPA, b Rivera, Uruguay, June 15, 22; US citizen; m 56; c 4. HISPANIC LANGUAGES & LITERATURE. *Educ:* Univ London, cert ling & pedag, 47; Nat Univ Brazil, cert philol, 51; Univ of the Repub, Uruguay, PDO(ling, soc sci), 59. *Prof Exp:* Mem fac foreign lang & ethics, Tech Univ Uruguay, 48-62; assoc prof Span & Port, 63-76, PROF SPAN & PORT, MIAMI UNIV, 76- *Concurrent Pos:* Mem fac foreign lang, Naval Acad Uruguay, 52-62; mem fac philol, Brazilian Cult Ctr, Uruguay, 52-62; insternship soc sci, Col Law & Soc Sci, Uruguay, 60-62; Fulbright vis prof Latin Am civilization, 62-64. *Mem:* Latin Am Asn Ling & Philol; Am Asn Teachers Span & Port; AAUP; AM Soc 18th Century Studies. *Res:* Folklore of the Hispanic peoples; Amerindian languages of Latin America. *Publ:* Auth, El Fonema /s/ en el Espanol del Uruguay, Univ Uruguay, 53; Los Karaya: Una Sociedad Agrafa, Univ Uruguay, 59; Literature as reference for a philosophy of man-and-time as given in Latin America, Univ Parana, Brazil, 69. *Mailing Add:* Dept of Span & Port Miami Univ Oxford OH 45056

VAZQUEZ-BIGI, ANGEL MANUEL, b Cordoba, Arg, July 2, 18; m 43; c 5. ROMANCE LANGUAGES. *Educ:* Nat Univ Cordoba, LLD, 42; Univ Minn, PhD, 62. *Prof Exp:* From asst prof to prof Romance lang, Northern Ill Univ, 58-69; PROF ROMANCE LANG, UNIV TENN, KNOXVILLE, 69- *Concurrent Pos:* Head dept romance lang, Univ Tenn, Knoxville, 69-71. *Mem:* MLA; Am Acad Polit & Soc Sci; Inst Lit Iberoam; World Inst Advan Phenomenol Res & Learning; Vergilian Soc. *Res:* Comparative literature; Spanish American and Spanish literature. *Publ:* Ed & auth introd, El arbol de la ciencia, Las Americas, 69; auth, Los conflictos psiquicos y religiosos de El hermano asno, 3-4/68 & Introduccion al estudio de la influencia barojiana en Hemingway y Dos Passos, 72, Cuadernos Hispanoam; El pesimismo filosofico europeo y la Generacion del Noventa y Ocho, Rev Occidente, 72; Lungarians and Lunatics from Aphra Behn to Goldoni-Haydn, In: Travel, Quest, and Pilgrimage as a Literary Theme, Imprint Series, 78; Abbadon: Ascendencia cervantina para una tematica apocaliptica, Texto Critico, Vol V, No 15, 79; Temperamento y polaridad en los personajes de Julio Cortazar--Excurso sobre la vision caracterologica en la filosofia y el arte, Cuadernos Hispanoam, 80; The Present Tide of Pessimism in Philosophy and Letters--Agonistic Literature and Cervantes' Message, Analecta Husserliana, Vol XVII, 82. *Mailing Add:* Dept of Romance Lang Univ of Tenn Knoxville TN 37916

VEDVIK, JERRY DONALD, b Madison, Wis, Nov 4, 36; m 69; c 2. ROMANCE LANGUAGES. *Educ:* Univ Wis, BA, 58; Univ Mo, MA, 62, PhD(French), 65. *Prof Exp:* Asst prof French & Ital, Ind Univ, Bloomington, 65-69; assoc prof French, George Washington Univ, 69-72; ASSOC PROF FRENCH, COLO STATE UNIV, 72- *Concurrent Pos:* Ed, An Annual Descriptive Bibliography of French 17th Century Studies, Colo State Univ. *Mem:* MLA; Am Asn Teachers Fr; AAUP. *Res:* Seventeenth century French literature; 18th century French literature; drama. *Mailing Add:* Dept of Foreign Lang Colo State Univ Ft Collins CO 80521

VEGAS-GARCIA, IRENE, b Valparaiso, Chile; Peru citizen. CONTEMPORARY LATIN AMERICAN POETRY. *Educ:* Inst Tecnol y de Estudios Super, Lic, 73; Univ Calif, Berkeley, PhD(Romance lang & lit), 78. *Prof Exp:* Asst prof Span & Span Am Lit, Univ Monterrey, Mex, 71-73; from teaching asst to teaching assoc, Span lang, Univ Calif, Berkeley, 73-77; lectr, Span Am lit & Span lang, Univ Calif, Los Angeles, 77-79; ASST PROF SPAN AM LIT & SPAN LANG, DARTMOUTH COL, 79- *Mem:* MLA; Circulo de Cult Cubana; Asn Caribbean Studies; Asoc Int Hisp. *Res:* Post-revolutionary Cuban poetry; Cesar Vallejo. *Publ:* Auth, Trilce: Estructura de un Nuevo Lenguaje, Pontif Univ Catolica del Peru, Lima, Peru, 82. *Mailing Add:* Spam & Am Lit & Lang Dept Dartmouth Col Hanover NH 03755

VEIT, PHILIPP F, b Goddelau, Ger, Jan 22, 20; US citizen; m 47; c 2. GERMAN LITERATURE. *Educ:* Univ Toronto, BA, 47, MA, 49, PhD(Ger), 52. *Prof Exp:* Lectr Ger, Univ Toronto, 48-52; instr, Univ Pa, 56-59; asst prof, Marquette Univ, 69-63; assoc prof, 63-73, PROF GER, STATE UNIV NY, BUFFALO, 73- *Mem:* MLA. *Res:* The poetry and prose of Heinrich Heine. *Publ:* Auth, Heine's imperfect Muses in Atta Troll, 11/64 & Heine and his cousins, a reconsideration, 1/72, Ger Rev; Moritz Spiegelberg: Eine Charakterstudie zu Schillers Die Räuber, Deut Schillerges, 73; Heine: The Marrano pose, Monatshefte, 5/74; Fichtenbaum und Palme, Ger Rev, 1/76; Lore-Ley and Apollogott, Analecta Helvetica et Germanica, 79; Heine's Polemics, In: Die Bäder von Lucca, Germanic Rev, 8/80. *Mailing Add:* Dept Mod Lang & Lit State Univ of NY Buffalo NY 14214

VELEZ, JOSEPH FRANCISCO, b Puebla, Mex, Jan 29, 28; US citizen; m 69; c 6. ROMANCE LANGUAGES, THEOLOGY. *Educ:* Howard Payne Univ, BA, 62; Univ Okla, MA, 68, PhD(romance lang), 69. *Prof Exp:* Instr Span, Univ Okla, 65-68; from asst prof to assoc prof Span & French, Western Ky Univ, 68-71; co-chmn dept Span, 76-77, ASSOC PROF SPAN, BAYLOR UNIV, 71-, DIR LATIN AM STUDIES, 77- *Concurrent Pos:* Interim pastor for Span speaking congregation, First Baptist Church, Marlin, Tex, 81. *Mem:* MLA; SCent Mod Lang Asn; Nat Asn Chicano Studies; Am Asn Teachers Span & Port; AAUP. *Res:* Latin American literature. *Publ:* Auth, La llave vieja & La condenacion del libro, Antologia Comentada del Modernismo, Calif State Univ, 74; La Biblia y la literatura castellana, Introd to Biblia de Estudio Mundo Hispanico, 77; El Arbusto Junto al Camino (short story), 8/77 & Entre perro y gato (short story), 9/78, Caracol; Humor en La guerra de las gordas, un drama precortesiano de Salvador Novo, Explicacion de Textos Literarios, 7/79; Entrevista con Wilberto Canton, Latin Am Theatre Rev, fall 79; Essays: Understanding bilingual-bicultural education in the eighties, Baylor Educator, spring 81; Entrevistas: Entrevista a Jesus Romero Flores, La Semana de Bellas Artes, 8/81. *Mailing Add:* Dept of Spanish Baylor Univ Waco TX 76798

VELILLA, ANA ALMONA, b Ranchuelo, Cuba, July 1, 25; US citizen; m 51; c 2. ROMANCE LANGUAGES. *Educ:* Univ Havana, Dr Philos & Lett, 60. *Prof Exp:* Teacher Span, Lincoln-Sudbury Regional High Sch, 65-66; tech asst, Mass Inst Technol, 64-65; instr Span, Boston Univ, 66-71; asst prof, 71-77, ASSOC PROF SPAN, REGIS COL, 77-, CHMN DEPT, 78- *Mem:* MLA; AAUP; Am Asn Teachers Span & Port. *Res:* Spanish and Latin American literature; history; philosophy. *Publ:* Auth, Versos claros como el agua, Ciupiak-Cantarelli, Buenos Aires, 62; Una luz en el camino (in a volume of short stories), Ed Universal, 76. *Mailing Add:* Dept of Span Regis Col Weston MA 02193

VELLEK, GARY FRANKLIN, b West Grove, Pa, July 16, 43. CLASSICS. *Educ:* Univ Del, BA, 65; Johns Hopkins Univ, PhD(classics), 69. *Prof Exp:* From asst prof to assoc prof, 69-78, JOHN W BARSS PROF CLASSICS, ACADIA UNIV, 79-, HEAD DEPT, 78- *Mem:* Class Asn Can; Am Philol Asn; Am Inst Archaeol; Class Asn Atlantic Prov; Am Class League. *Res:* Hellenistic and Roman art; Greek history 86 BC-267 AD; Athenian priesthoods. *Mailing Add:* Dept of Classics Acadia Univ Wolfville NS B0P 1X0 Can

VELTMAN, FREDERICK, b St Petersburg, Fla, June 25, 27; m 49; c 2. NEW TESTAMENT THEOLOGY, BIBLICAL LANGUAGES. *Educ:* Southern Missionary Col, BTh, 51; Andrews Univ, BD, 62; Pac Sch of Relig & Grad Theol Union, ThD, 75. *Prof Exp:* Instr relig, Mid East Col, Lebanon, 56-57; from instr to assoc prof, 62-75, chmn dept gen studies, 76-78, PROF RELIG, PAC UNION COL,, 75-, CHMN DEPT, 78- *Concurrent Pos:* Vchmn, Rhetorical Criticism Sem, Pac Coast Sect Soc Biblical Lit, 78. *Mem:* Soc Bibl Lang; Am Acad Relig; Soc Bibl Lit. *Res:* Luke-Acts; Hellenistic Greek; Hermeneutics. *Publ:* Auth, The Defense Speeches of Paul in Acts, Soc Bibl Lit Papers, 12/77. *Mailing Add:* Dept of Relig Pac Union Col Angwin CA 94508

VENA, MICHAEL, b Jelsi, Italy, July 4, 41; US citizen. FOREIGN LANGUAGES. *Educ:* Univ Bridgeport, BA, 65; Yale Univ, MA, 67, PhD(Ital), 72; Univ Rome, dipl Ital, 72. *Prof Exp:* Lectr Ital, Yale Univ, 69-70; assoc prof, 70-80, PROF ITAL, SOUTHERN CONN STATE COL, 80-, CHMN DEPT FOREIGN LANG, 76- *Mem:* MLA; Am Asn Teachers Ital. *Res:* Renaissance literature and language; modern theatre. *Publ:* Auth, Alcune retrodatazioni e aggiunte lessicali dal de Iciarchia dell'Alberti, Lingua Nostra, 6/70; Luigi Chiarelli, 75; Alberti's Linguistic Innovations, Yale Univ, 76. *Mailing Add:* Dept of Ital Southern Conn State Col New Haven CT 06515

VENCLOVA, TOMAS ANDRIUS, b Klaipeda, Lithuania, Sept 11, 37; Stateless; m 73; c 2. SLAVIC & LITHUANIAN LITERATURES. *Educ:* Univ Vilnius, dipl(philol), 60. *Prof Exp:* Lectr lit, Univ Vilnius, 66-73; jr fel semiotics, Acad Sci, Lithuania, 74-76; Regents prof semiotics art, Univ Calif, Berkeley, 77; lectr semiotics art, Univ Calif, Los Angeles, 77-80; LECTR RUSS LIT, YALE UNIV, 80- *Concurrent Pos:* Lit consult, Siauliai Drama Theater, Lithuania, 74-76. *Mem:* Semiotic Soc Am; Int Soc Comp Study Civilizations; PEN Club; Am Asn Advan Slavic Studies; MLA. *Res:* Slavic literatures; Lithuanian literature; semiotics of art. *Publ:* Auth, The myth of beginning, Teksty, 74; Czeslaw Milosz: Despair and grace, World Lit Today, 78; Viacheslav Iuanov--translator of Kristijonas Donelaitis, J Baltic Studies, 78; Prison as communicative phenomenon: The literature of Gula, Comp Civilizations Rev, 79; Towards the zero prototext: Notes on Pushkin's Ballad Budrys and his sons, Alexander Pushkin, Symposium, Vol 2, 80; Lithuanian divertissement of Joseph Brodsky, Russ Lit in Emigration (in press); On Russian mythological tragedy: Viacheslav Iuanov and Marina Tsuetaeva, New York Univ Slavic Papers (in press); Soviet semiotics on Destoevsky, Am J Semiotics (in press). *Mailing Add:* Dept of Slavic Lang & Lit Yale Univ New Haven CT 06520

VENDLER, ZENO, Philosophy. See Vol IV

VENEZKY, RICHARD L, b Pittsburgh, Pa, Apr 16, 38; m 64; c 2. EDUCATIONAL PSYCHOLOGY, LINGUISTICS. *Educ:* Cornell Univ, BEE, 61, MA, 62; Stanford Univ, PhD(ling), 65. *Prof Exp:* Tech writer & syst analyst comput software, Control Data Corp, 63-65; asst prof English & comput sci, Univ Wis-Madison, 65-69, from assoc prof to prof comput sci, 69-77, chmn dept, 75-77; UNIDEL PROF OF EDUC STUDIES, UNIV DEL, 77- *Concurrent Pos:* Adv data proc, Dictionary of Old English, 72-; res fel educ sci, Tel-Aviv Univ, 73-; consult, Oxford English dictionary suppl, 73-; mem adv bd, Visible Lang, 76- *Mem:* Asn Comput Mach; Int Reading Asn; Am Psychol Asn; Am Educ Res Asn. *Res:* Literacy; effective schools; use of computers in education. *Publ:* Auth, The Structure of English Orthography, Mouton, 70; Reading Assessment and Instructional Decision Making, NCTE, 74; Research on reading processes: A historical perspective, Am Psychologist, 77; coauth, Man-machine integration in a lexical processing system, Cahiers de Lexicologie, 77; A Microfiche Concordance to Old English, Ctr Medieval Studies, Toronto, 80; co-ed, Orthography, Reading, and Dyslexia, Univ Park Press, 80; coauth, Letter and Word Perception, North-Holland, 80; The Ginn Reading Program, Ginn & Co, 82. *Mailing Add:* Dept of Educ Studies Univ of Del Newark DE 19711

VENKATACHARYA, TUPPIL, b Tirupati, India, Jan 1, 24; m 61. SANSKRIT LANGUAGE & LITERATURE. *Educ:* Univ Madras, BOL, 49; Univ Calcutta, MA, 52. *Prof Exp:* Prof Sanskrit publ, Ital Inst Mid & Far East, Rome & Univ Rome, 61-64; from asst prof to assoc prof Sanskrit, 64-71, PROF SANSKRIT, UNIV TORONTO, 71- *Mem:* Am Orient Soc. *Res:* Sanskrit grammar and literature including dramaturgy and poetics. *Publ:* Coauth, Buddhacarita & co-translr, Nepalese Inscriptions, Ital Inst Mid & Far East, Rome; auth, critique on Dr Agrawala's India as known to Panini, 59 & An appraisal of the Hindi Dasarupaka, 60, J Univ Gauhati; Some names and etymologies inthe anonymous Buddhacarita, East & West, 12/65; coauth, THe Ubhyabhisarika, V Sambamurty, Madras, 67; ed, Dasarupaka-Paddhati, 68 & Sriharicarita-mahakavya, 72, Adyar Libr & Res Ctr, Madras. *Mailing Add:* Dept of Sanskrit & Indian Studies Univ of Toronto Toronto ON M5S 1A1 Can

VENTO, ARNOLD, b Edinburg, Tex, Feb 19, 39. LATIN AMERICAN LITERATURE. *Educ:* Univ Tex-Austin, BA, 60; NMex Highlands Univ, MA, 62; Univ Mo-Columbia, PhD (Latin-Am lit), 72. *Prof Exp:* Fac Span, Ball State Univ, 67-69 & Calif State Univ, Los Angeles, 69-71; coordr, Chicano Studies, Univ Mich-Flint, 72-75; dir, Outreach Inst, Univ Wis-Milwaukee, 75-78; DIR CTR MEX-AM STUDIES, UNIV TEX, AUSTIN, 78-, ASSOC PROF, 78- *Mem:* Am Asn Univ Prof; MLA; Am Asn Teachers Span & Port; Nat Asn Interdisciplinary Studies; North Cent Coun Latin-Am. *Res:* Mexican literature; Chicano art and literature; Axtec thought and philosophy. *Publ:* Auth, El Periquillo y el Quijote, Rev Univ Mex, 8/65; Niebla, laberinto a traves de la estructura, Cuadernos Hisp Am, 66; ed, Alonzo S Perales: His Struggles for the Rights of Mexican-Americans, Artes Graficas, 77; coauth, Mestizo Voices: Readings in Contemporary Chicano Thought, 77 & Canto Al Pueblo: An Anthology of Chicano Art and Literature, 77, Tonatiuh; Canto Al Pueblo: An Anthology of Experiences, Penca, 78; Milhuas Blues y Gritos Nortenos, Univ Wis, 78; El Hijo Prodigo: A Critical Index of XX Century Thought, Pajarito, 78. *Mailing Add:* Dept of Lit Univ Tex Austin TX 78710

VENUTI, LAWRENCE M, Renaissance & Contemporary Italian Literature. See Vol II

VERA, CATHERINE ANNE, b Oklahoma City, Okla, Dec 31, 42; c 2. SPANISH AMERICAN LITERATURE. *Educ:* Univ Mo-Kansas City, BA, 65; Univ Mo-Columbia, MA, 69, PhD(Span), 75. *Prof Exp:* Instr Span, William Woods Col, 69 & 71-72; instr, 74-75, ASST PROF SPAN, WILLIAM JEWELL COL, 75-, CHMN DEPT MOD LANG, 77- *Mem:* Am Asn Teachers Span & Port; MLA. *Res:* Modernism in Spanish America; Mexican literature; modernism in Mexican literature. *Publ:* Contribr, El dilema del hombre moderno en Sobre heroes y tumbas, In: Homenaje a Ernesto Sabato, Las Am, 73; auth, Paul Verlaine en dos poemas de Efren Rebolledo, Revista Communidad Latinam Escritores, 76; Dolora: Poema inedito de Luis G Urbina, Abside, Revista de Cult Mejicana, 76; Chocano y Heredia: La primera dedicatoria de Alma America, Anales Lit Hispanoam, 76; El Cuento de las tres reinas y Las tres reinas matas de Ruben Dario, Explicacion Textos Literarios, 77; contribr, La comida ye el hambre en El Buscon, In: Studies in Honor of Ruth Lee Kennedy, Atlee, Estudios de Hispanofila, 77; auth, Francois Coppee en tres cuentos de Manuel Gutierrez Najera, Am Hispanist, 1/78. *Mailing Add:* Dept of Mod Lang William Jewell Col Liberty MO 64068

VERANI, HUGO JUAN, b Montevideo, Uruguay, Apr 4, 41; US citizen; m 64; c 2. LATIN AMERICAN LITERATURE. *Educ:* Phillips Univ, AB, 66; Univ Wis-Madison, MA, 67, PhD(Span), 73. *Prof Exp:* From instr to asst prof, Mt Holyoke Col, 70-74; asst prof, 74-78, assoc prof, 78-82, PROF SPAN, UNIV CALIF, DAVIS, 82- *Mem:* MLA; Am Asn Teachers Span & Port; Inst Int Lit Iberam; Asn Int Hispanistas; Philol Asn Pac Coast. *Res:* Contemporary Spanish American literature; 20th century fiction; literary theory. *Publ:* Narrativa contemporanea, La Muralla, Madrid, 80; Onetti: el ritual de la impostura, Monte Avila, Caracas, 81; Las vanguardias literarias en America Latina, Mexico, Centroamerica, Caribe, 82 & auth intro & ed, Maria Eugenia Vaz Ferreira, In: Poesias completas, 82, Arca, Montevideo; auth, Octavio Paz: Bibliografia critica, UNAM, Mexico, 82. *Mailing Add:* Dept of Spanish Univ of Calif Davis CA 95616

VERGANI, GIANANGELO, b Milan, Italy, July 8, 31; m 60; c 3. ITALIAN. *Educ:* Univ Pavia, Dr Latin, 54. *Prof Exp:* Instr, Univ Munich, 54-55 & Univ Calif, Berkeley, 60-62; instr Ital, Univ Colo, 62-63; assoc prof, 63-76, PROF ITAL, SAN DIEGO STATE UNIV, 76- *Mem:* Am Asn Teachers Ital. *Res:* Language teaching; philological criticism of the text of Divine Comedy. *Publ:* Auth, Italiano Moderno, Pruett, 63; Reading in Italian Civilization, Atzec Shops, 67; Notes about teaching Italian in Italian, Italica, 6/67; A 14th century unpublished manuscript of the Divine Comedy, Studies Guisleriana, 67; Reconstructing the Divine Comedy, Romanic Rev, 12/67. *Mailing Add:* Dept of Italian San Diego State Univ San Diego CA 92115

VERGANI, LUISA, b Verona, Italy, June 21, 31; US citizen; m 60; c 3. ITALIAN. *Educ:* Univ Milan, Dr(Ital), 56. *Prof Exp:* Teacher schs, Italy, 56-60; assoc Ital, Univ Colo, 62-63; asst prof, Univ San Diego, 65-69; asst prof, 69-76, assoc prof, 76-80, PROF ITAL, SAN DIEGO STATE UNIV, 80- *Mem:* Am Asn Teachers Ital. *Res:* Italian teaching methodology; Italian Renaissance; Dante. *Publ:* Coauth, Italiano moderno, Pruett, 64; auth, Dante e Verona, Italica, 66; The Prince (critical outline), 67 & Inferno (critical outline), 68. *Mailing Add:* Dept of Italian San Diego State Uiv San Diego CA 92115

VERMETTE, ROSALIE ANN, b Lewiston, Maine, May 10, 46; m 82. FRENCH LANGUAGE & LITERATURE. *Educ:* Univ Maine, Orono, AB, 68; Univ Iowa, MA, 70, PhD(French), 75. *Prof Exp:* Lectr English, Univ Poitiers, France, 72-73; from instr to asst prof French, Univ Iowa, 74-76; ASSOC PROF FRENCH, IND UNIV/PURDUE UNIV, INDIANAPOLIS, 76- *Mem:* Mediaeval Acad Am; Int Arthurian Soc; MLA; Am Asn Teachers Fr; Midwest Mod Lang Asn. *Res:* Medieval French hagiographic textual studies; medieval French romance studies; textual criticism. *Publ:* Auth, The Huit Beatitudes in old French prose, Manuscripta, 74; coauth, Un manuscit inconnu de Bartolomeo Visconti: les Dialogi de Gregoire le grand, Scriptorium, 78; auth, An Unrecorded Fragment of Richart d'Irlande's Propheties dde Merlin, Romance Philol, 81. *Mailing Add:* Dept of French Ind Univ Purdue Univ Indianapolis IN 46202

VERNIER, RICHARD, b Clermont-Ferrand, France, Feb 1, 29; US citizen; m 62; c 3. FRENCH LITERATURE. *Educ:* Univ Calif, Berkeley, AB, 58, PhD(Romance lang), 65. *Prof Exp:* Lectr French, City Col New York, 62-63; asst prof, San Diego State Col, 63-66 & Univ Wash, 66-72; assoc prof, State Univ NY Fredonia, 72-73; ASSOC PROF FRENCH, WAYNE STATE UNIV, DETROIT, 73- *Concurrent Pos:* Vis assoc prof, Scripps Col, 75-76. *Honors & Awards:* Palmes Academiques, Fr Govt, 81. *Mem:* MLA; Am Asn Teachers Fr. *Res:* Modern poetry and poetics; French culture and civilization; Swiss-French literature. *Publ:* Auth, Poesie ininterrompue et la poetique de Paul Eluard, Mouton & Co, 71; Lettres de l'interieur, poemes, Subervie, 71; Prosodie et silence dans un recueil d'Yves Bonnefoy, Studia Neophilol, 73; Poeta ludens: Le rire de Saint-John Perse, Pac Coast Philol, 76; Locus patriae, L'Arc, 76; Words like the sky: The accomplishment of Yves Bonnefoy, World Lit Today, 79; La Voix de Gustave Roud, Swiss-French Studies, 80; Le Feu parmi les arbres, poemes, Solaire, 81. *Mailing Add:* 1706 Oxford Berkley MI 48072

VERY, FRANCIS GEORGE, b San Francisco, Calif, July 7, 22. ROMANCE LANGUAGES. *Educ:* Univ Calif, Berkeley, AB, 47, MA, 50, PhD, 56. *Prof Exp:* Instr Span, Univ Wis, 57-60; asst prof, 60-63, ASSOC PROF SPAN, NORTHWESTERN UNIV, 63- *Mem:* MLA; Am Asn Teachers Span & Port; Int Arthurian Soc. *Res:* Mediaeval Spanish literature; folklore, especially Hispanic; Golden Age comedia. *Publ:* Co-ed, Castillo Solorzano: Sala de Recreacion, Estudios de Hispanofila, Chapel Hill, NC, 77. *Mailing Add:* 135 Centennial Hall Northwestern Univ Evanston IL 60201

VESCE, THOMAS EUGENE, b Mt Vernon, NY, Mar 24, 34; m 59; c 3. FRENCH, ITALIAN. *Educ:* Manhattan Col, BA, 54; Fordham Univ, MA, 56; PhD(Romance philol), 67; Western Conn State Col, MA, 77. *Hon Degrees:* Accademico, Accademia Artistica Internazionale de Napoli, 75. *Prof Exp:* Instr French & Span, St Simon Stock High Sch, Bronx, 56-57; instr French grammar & lit, King's Col, Pa, 59-61; asst prof French & Ital, Briarcliff Col, 61-67; assoc prof, Fairfield Univ, 67-68; PROF OF FRENCH & ITAL, DIR INST MEDIEVAL & RENAISSANCE STUDIES & CHMN DIV MOD LANG, MERCY COL, 68- *Concurrent Pos:* Lectr Ital, Marymount Col, NY, 64-67; consult Romance lit, Choice, 64-; lectr Ital, Sch Adult Educ, Elizabeth Seton Jr Col, 65-66; co-dir & founder, Mid-Hudson Medieval Circle, 69-; adj prof educ & ling, Long Island Univ, 76-; dean acad affairs, Univ Int Coluccio Salutati, Pescia, Italy, 76-; Nat Endowment for Humanities fel, Yale Univ, 77; Nat Endowment for Humanities fel, Univ Calif, Los Angeles, 82. *Honors & Awards:* Knight, Sovereign Order St John of Jerusalem, Malta, 77. *Mem:* Mediaeval Acad Am; Int Arthurian Soc; Am Asn Teachers Ital. *Res:* Arthurian literature; comparison of the early romances and late epics of France and Italy; Antoine de la Sale. *Publ:* Ed, Ci commence Doctrinal de Latin en Roumanz, Nemarest, 68; auth, Chivalric virtue and the Histoire du Seigneur de Bayart, Romance Notes, 70; On identifying the Popelican(t), 70 & Reflections on the epic quality of Ami et Amile: Chanson de geste, 73, Mediaeval Studies; Antoine de la Sale's fabulous trip to the Lipari Isles, Jean Misrahi Mem Vol, 76; The sin of Brunetto Latini: False Rhetoric, NE Mod Lang Asn, 80; Towards an appreciation of Arthur's persona, In: Spenser's Faerie Queene, MHLS, 81. *Mailing Add:* Dept of Mod Lang Mercy College Dobbs Ferry NY 10522

VESSELY, THOMAS RICHARD, b San Marcos, Tex, Nov 6, 44; m 78; c 1. FRENCH LITERATURE. *Educ:* Ind Univ, PhD(French), 79. *Prof Exp:* ASST PROF FRENCH, UNIV TEX, AUSTIN, 79- *Mem:* MLA; Am Asn Teachers Fr; Soc 18th Century Studies. *Res:* The French fairy tale; short prose fiction. *Publ:* Auth, Innocence and impotence: The scenario of initiation in L'Ecumoire and in the literary fairy tale, 18th Century Life, 82. *Mailing Add:* Dept Fr & Ital Univ Tex Austin TX 78712

VETRANO, ANTHONY JOSEPH, b Endicott, NY, Feb 3, 31; m 64; c 2. ROMANCE LANGUAGES. *Educ:* State Univ NY Binghamton, BA, 55; Univ Rochester, MA, 56; Syracuse Univ, PhD(Romance lang), 66. *Prof Exp:* From instr to assoc prof, 59-74, PROF MOD LANG, LE MOYNE COL, 74-, CHMN DEPT, 62- *Concurrent Pos:* Fac res grants, Le Moyne Col, 67-68 & 73-74. *Mem:* AAUP; MLA; Am Asn Teachers Span & Port. *Res:* Twentieth century Spanish American novel, especially the Ecuadorian novel of social protest; modern Spanish Peninsular literature; Italian Trecento. *Publ:* Auth, Imagery in two of Jorge Icaza's novels: Huasipungo and Huairapamushcas, Rev Estudios Hisp, 5/72; La problematica Psico-social y su correlacion linguistica en las novelas de Jorge Icaza, Ed Universal, 74; Jorge Icaza and the Spanish-American Indianist Novel: Some Observations on Huasipungo, In: Studies in Romance Languages and Literature, State Univ NY Binghamton, 79. *Mailing Add:* Dept of For Lang & Lit Le Moyne Col Syracuse NY 13214

VICKERY, WALTER, b London, England, Sept 14, 21; US citizen; m; c 6. SLAVIC LANGUAGE & LITERATURE. *Educ:* Oxford Univ, BA, 48, MA, 52; Harvard Univ, PhD, 58. *Prof Exp:* Lectr Russ, Oxford Univ, 48-53; from asst prof to assoc prof Slavic lang & lit, Ind Univ, Bloomington, 58-64; prof, Univ Colo, 64-69; PROF SLAVIC LANG & LIT, UNIV NC, CHAPEL HILL, 69- *Concurrent Pos:* Ind Univ fac fel, Oxford Univ, 63; Fulbright-Hays fel, Italy, 65; Am Coun Learned Soc fel, Leningrad, 67-68; Univ Colo fac fel, Italy, 68; mem screening comt, Int Asn Exchange of Persons, 72-; vis prof Yale Univ, 75; exchange scholar, Am Coun Learned Soc, Soviet Acad, 1-6/76. *Mem:* Am Asn Advan Slavic Studies. *Res:* Soviet literary problems; Pushkin; Russian versification. *Publ:* Coauth, The Year of Protest: 1956, Vintage, 61; auth, The Cult of Optimism, Ind Univ, 63; co-ed, V Zhirmunsky's Introduction to Metrics, Mouton, The Hague, 66; auth, Pushkin: Death of a Poet, Ind Univ, 68; Alexander Pushkin, Twayne, 70. *Mailing Add:* Dept of Slavic Lang Univ of NC Chapel Hill NC 27514

VICTOR-ROOD, JULIETTE ANN, b Minneapolis, Minn. GERMAN & COMPARATIVE LITERATURE. *Educ:* Univ Minn, BA & BS, 66; Univ Colo, MA, 69, PhD(Ger lit), 75. *Prof Exp:* Lectr Ger & methodology, Univ Colo, Boulder, 79-80, asst prof Ger lang & lit, 80-81; asst prof Ger lang, ling, comp lit & methodology, Pa State Univ, University Park, 81-82; RES & WRITING, 82- *Concurrent Pos:* Vis prof, Portland State Univ, 80; consult, Holt, Rinehart & Winston & Harper & Row, 82- *Mem:* MLA; Am Asn Teachers Ger; Am Asn Teachers Slavic & East Europ Lang; Am Coun Teaching Foreign Lang; Hugo von Hofmannsthal Soc. *Res:* Austrian literature; comparative literature: Middle Ages and 19th century; Hungarian literature: 20th century. *Publ:* Auth, A Key-Word-in-Line Concordance to the Poems of Hugo von Hofmannsthal, Xerox Res Publ, 76; A critical survey of published computer-generated concordances to modern German literature,

Asn Lit & Ling Comput Bull, 81; transl, 4 poems by Johannes Bobrowski, Denver Quart, 81; auth, Travels through prepositionland, 81 & Survival German for travelers: An evening course for adults, 82, Die Unterrichtspraxis; Say It in Hungarian, Dover, 82; transl & contribr, 2 poems by Anna Hajnal, In: Contemporary East European Poetry: An Anthology, 82. *Mailing Add:* 1350 Knox Dr Boulder CO 80303

VIDAL, ELIE R, b Beni Saf, Algeria, June 3, 25; US citizen. FRENCH LITERATURE. *Educ:* Univ Mich, BA, 53, MA, 54, PhD, 57. *Prof Exp:* Instr French & Span, Phillips Exeter Acad, 55-56; instr, French, Univ Mich, 56-57; from instr to asst prof, Univ Calif, Berkeley, 57-62; asst prof, San Francisco State Col, 62-65; chmn dept, 65-67, PROF FRENCH, CALIF STATE UNIV, HAYWARD, 65- *Concurrent Pos:* Prof, Univ Hawaii, 61; ed, Far-Western Forum, 73- *Mem:* Mediaeval Acad Am; MLA; Philol Asn Pac Coast; Medieval Asn Pac (secy-treas, 67, 1st vpres, 68). *Res:* Villon; Montaigne, Camus. *Publ:* Auth, Lelegs de Villon a son pere adoptif, In: Romance Studies in Memory of Edward Billings Ham, 67; contribr, Romance Philol, Studies Philol, Encycl Americana, Grolier, 68, MLQ, 76 & Speculum, 80. *Mailing Add:* Dept of Foreign Lang Calif State Univ Hayward CA 94542

VIDAL, HERNAN, b Villa Alemana, Chile, Apr 18, 37; m 62; c 3. SPANISH AMERICAN LITERATURE. *Educ:* Univ Iowa, PhD(Span), 67. *Prof Exp:* Instr English, Univ Chile, Temuco, 62-64; instr Span, Univ Iowa, 66-67; asst prof, Univ Va, 67-72; assoc prof, 72-80, PROF SPAN & PORT & DIR GRAD STUDIES, UNIV MINN, MINNEAPOLIS, 80- *Mem:* Am Asn Teachers Span & Port; MLA. *Res:* Spanish American novel and drama. *Publ:* Auth, El modo narrativo en El Hermano Asno de Eduardo Barrios, Rev Hisp Mod, 7-10/67. *Mailing Add:* Dept of Span & Port Univ of Minn Minneapolis MN 55455

VIDRINE, DONALD RAY, b Palmetto, La, Aug 13, 32. ROMANCE LANGUAGES. *Educ:* La State Univ, BS, 54, MA, 62, PhD(Romance philol), 68. *Prof Exp:* Instr French & Span, Nicholls State Col, 60-63; instr French, La State Univ, 64-68; ASST PROF FRENCH, N TEX STATE UNIV, 68- *Mem:* Am Asn Teachers Fr. *Res:* French symbolist poetry; French theatre of entre-deux-guerres; 20th century French poetry. *Mailing Add:* Dept of Foreign Lang North Texas State Univ Denton TX 76201

VIEHMEYER, L ALLEN, b Peoria, Ill, July 30, 42; m 67; c 1. GERMAN LITERATURE & LINGUISTICS. *Educ:* Western Ill Univ, BSEd, 64; Univ Ill, Urbana- Champaign, AM, 67, PhD(Ger), 71. *Prof Exp:* Instr Ger, Wartburg Col, 69-71; asst prof, 71-78, ASSOC PROF GER, YOUNGSTOWN STATE UNIV, 78- *Mem:* Am Asn Teachers Ger. *Res:* Pennsylvania German literature 1683-1830; German-American hymnology 1683-1830; use of computers in foreign language teaching. *Publ:* Auth, Gothic letterforms and codex vindobonensis, Visible Lang, 73; Anna of Ephrata, Hist Schaefferstown Rec, 74; Umlaut, B, and learning German verb conjugation by computer, Proc 1977 Conf on Computers in Undergraduate Curric, 77; auth & transl, The Tumultuous Years: Schwenkfelder Chronicles 1580-1750, The Reports of Martin John Jr & Balthazar Hoffmann, Schwenkfelder Libr, 80. *Mailing Add:* Dept Foreign Lang & Lit Youngstown State Univ Youngstown OH 44555

VIENS, CLAUDE PAUL, b Pawtucket, RI, Jan 31, 12; m 37; c 2. FRENCH LITERATURE. *Educ:* Brown Univ, AB, 32, AM, 33, PhD, 37. *Prof Exp:* Asst, Brown Univ, 36-38; from instr to prof, 38-72, asst dean grad col, 53-58, asst dean, col lib arts & sci, 62-65, EMER PROF FRENCH, UNIV ILL, URBANA, 72- *Res:* French literary criticism; French 19th century literature; contemporary French theatre. *Mailing Add:* Box 117 Cedar Mountain NC 28718

VIERA, DAVID JOHN, b Providence, RI, June 9, 43; m 80. MEDIEVAL HISPANIC LITERATURE. *Educ:* Providence Col, BA, 65; Cath Univ of Am, MA, 69, PhD(Iberian studies), 72. *Prof Exp:* Asst prof, State Univ Col Geneseo, NY, 75-77; ASSOC PROF SPANISH, TENN TECH UNIV, 77- *Concurrent Pos:* Asst prof Spanish, Tenn Tech Univ, 72-74. *Honors & Awards:* Ferran Soldevila Award, Fundacio Salvador Vives Casajuana, 79. *Mem:* Medieval Acad Am; MLA; South Atlantic Mod Lang Asn; Am Asn Teachers Spanish & Portuguese; NAm Catalan Soc. *Res:* Francesc Eiximenis; Antero de Quental. *Publ:* Auth, Mas sobre Vives y el Carro de las donas, Rev valenciana de filologia, 75; The presence of Francesc Eiximenis in 15th and 16th century Castilian literature, Hispanofila, 76; An annotated bibliography on the life and works of Alfonso Martinez de Toledo, Ky Romance Quart, 77; La obra de Francesc Eiximenis en los siglos XV a XVII, Archivo Ibero-Am, 79; El corcel negro en la obra de Antero de Quental y Federico Garcia Lorca, Thesaurus, 81; Luis de Sttau Monteiro's As Maos de Abraao Zacut, Rev de Estudios Hispanicos, 81; O Conceito da Idade Media na Prosa de Antero de Quental, Estudos Ibero-Am, 81; Bibliografia anotada de la vida i obra de Francesc Eiximenis, Dalmau, Barcelona, 81. *Mailing Add:* Dept of Foreign Lang Tenn Technol Univ Cookeville TN 38501

VIGGIANI, CARL ALBERT, b West New York, NJ, May 8, 22; m 45; c 3. ROMANCE LANGUAGES. *Educ:* Columbia Col, AB, 43; Harvard Univ, AM, 47; Columbia Univ, PhD(French), 52. *Prof Exp:* From instr to asst prof French, Columbia Col, 47-54; from asst prof to assoc prof Romance lang, 54-62, PROF ROMANCE LANG & LIT, WESLEYAN UNIV, 62- *Concurrent Pos:* Managing ed, Romanic Rev, 52-54; Guggenheim fel, 57-58. *Mem:* MLA; AAUP; Am Asn Teachers Fr. *Res:* Contemporary French literature; Paris school of existentialism; avant-gardism. *Publ:* Auth, camus' L'Etranger, PMLA; Camus and the fall from innocence, Yale Fr Studies, 60; Albert Camus' first publications, Mod Lang Notes, 60. *Mailing Add:* Dept of Romance Lang & Lit Wesleyan Univ Middletown CT 06457

VIGNEAULT, ROBERT, b Toronto, Ont, June 10, 27; m 70; c 2. FRENCH & FRENCH-CANADIAN LITERATURE. *Educ:* Univ Laval, BA, 46, Lic, 55; Jesuit Col Immaculate Conception, Montreal, Lic(philos), 52, Lic(theol), 59; Univ Aix- Marseille, PhD(French lit), 66. *Prof Exp:* Asst prof French Lit, Laurentian Univ, 66-67; asst prof French & French-Can lit, Carleton Univ, 67-69; vis prof French-Can lit, Laval Univ, 69-70; assoc prof French & French-Can lit, McGill Univ, 70-76; PROF FRENCH & FRENCH-CAN LIT, UNIV OTTAWA, 76- *Concurrent Pos:* Vis prof French-Can lit, Univ Strasbourg, 73-75; mem lit comt, Art Coun Ottawa. *Honors & Awards:* First Prize, Lit Competetion of PQ, 68. *Mem:* Can Asn Univ Teachers; Asn Can Univ Teachers Fr. *Res:* Twentieth century French literature; literature of Quebec; the essay as a literary form. *Publ:* Auth, L'Univers Feminin dans l'Oeuvre de Charles Peguy, Desclee de Brouwer, 68; ed, Claire Martin, Avec ou sans amour, Ed Renouveau Pedag, 69; contribr, Litteratures, Hurtubise, HMH, 71; auth, L'essai quebecois: La naissance d'une pensee, Etudes Lit, 72; La critique et l'essai, Etudes Fr, 73; Saint-Denys Garneau a travers Regards et Jeux dans l'Espace, Univ Montreal, 73; Claire Martin, son oeuvre, les reactions de la critique, Pierre Tisseyre, 75; ed, Langue, Litterature, culture au Canada Francais, Univ Ottawa, 77. *Mailing Add:* Dept of Lettres Francaises Univ of Ottawa Ottawa ON K1N 6N5 Can

VILAS, SANTIAGO, b Vigo, Spain, Aug 15, 31; US citizen. FOREIGN LANGUAGES, CIVILIZATION. *Educ:* Univ Santiago, dipl, 52; La State Univ, Baton Rouge, MA & PhD(Romance lang & lit), 66. *Prof Exp:* Teacher & writer Span, Int House, New Orleans, 61; teacher, Spartanburg High Sch, SC, 61-62; instr, Univ NC, Charlotte, 62-64; assoc prof, La State Univ, Baton Rouge, 66-81. *Concurrent Pos:* Spec lectr, Davidson Col, 63, Univ SC, 63, Univ Mediter Studies, Rome 70 & Southwestern at Memphis, 71. *Mem:* Nat Asn Teachers Span & Port; MLA; Soc Gen Autores, Spain; hon mem, Asn Periodistica Iberoam. *Res:* Spanish literature; philosophy. *Publ:* Contribr, Medicina magica en Galicia, Zunzunegui, Spain, 58; Nuevos horizontes para el estudiante de espanol, Mangiafico, Spain, 58; Nuevos horizontes para el estudiante de espanol, Mangiafico, 58 & 63; auth, El humor y la novela espanola contemporanea, Guadarrama, Madrid, 68; Espana: Cultura y civilizacion, Regents, 73; Tres Sombreros de Copa, 74; Louisiana Professional Real Estate Manual, 74. *Mailing Add:* 814 W Lakeview Dr Baton Rouge LA 70810

VILLEGAS, FRANCISCO, b Costa Rica, Nov 25, 17. SPANISH, SPANISH AMERICAN LITERATURE. *Educ:* Univ Costa Rica, cert, 41; Univ Mich, MA, 43 & 45, PhD, 52. *Prof Exp:* Teaching fel Span, Univ Mich, 43-50; asst prof, Eastern Mich Univ, 50- 59, assoc prof Span & Span Am lit, 59-62; assoc prof, Univ Houston, 62-63; assoc prof, 63-73, prof, 73-79, EMER PROF SPAN & SPAN AM LIT, EASTERN MICH UNIV, 79- *Concurrent Pos:* Assoc prof, Univ Calif, Los Angeles, 61. *Mem:* Am Asn Teachers Span & Port. *Res:* Linguistics; Spanish literature; Spanish-American literature. *Publ:* Auth, El Argor costarricense, 53 & The Voseo in Costa Rican Spanish, 63, Hispania. *Mailing Add:* Dept of Foreign Lang & Lit Eastern Mich Univ Ypsilanti MI 48179

VINAY, JEAN-PAUL, b Paris, France, July 18, 10; m 40; c 4. LINGUISTICS. *Educ:* Sorbonne, Lic es Let, 31, dipl, 32; Univ London, MA, 37; Univ Paris, Agrege, 41. *Hon Degrees:* DLitt, Univ Ottawa, 75. *Prof Exp:* Asst lectr, Univ Col, London, 37-39; prof agrege d'anglais, Lycee de Chartres, 41-42; chief inspector foreign lang schs, Paris, 42-46; prof ling & head dept, Univ Montreal, 46-66; dean fac arts & sci, Univ Victoria, 68-75, dir res machine transl, prof ling & head dept, 66-75. *Concurrent Pos:* Res fel, Ctr Nat Rech Sci, 41-42; lectr, Ecole du Louvre, Paris, 41-44; consult, Int Civil Aviation Orgn, Montreal, 46-48; ed-in-chief, Can Bilingual Dict, 55-59; ed, J Traducteurs, 56; vis prof, fac lett, Univ Strasbourg, 64-65; Int Coun French Lang fel, 67. *Mem:* Fel Royal Soc Can; fel Soc Gens de Lett, Paris; Ling Soc Am; Can Ling Asn (pres, 65-). *Res:* Phonetics; theory of translation; lexicography. *Publ:* Auth, A Basis and Essentials Welsh Grammar; Stylistique Comparee du francais et de l'anglais, Chilton, 58; The Canadian Dict--dict Canadien, McClelland & Stewart, Toronto, 62 & 78; Le Francais International, Ctr Educ & Cult, Montreal, 66. *Mailing Add:* 2659 Currie Rd Victoria BC V8S 3B9 Can

VINCENT, JON S, b Denver, Colo, Feb 28, 38; m 62; c 2. BRAZILIAN LITERATURE, PORTUGUESE. *Educ:* Univ NMex, BA, 61, PhD(Ibero-Am studies), 70. *Prof Exp:* Instr, Univ NMex, 63-64; asst prof, 67-74, assoc prof Span & Port & assoc chmn dept, 74-78, PROF & CHMN DEPT, UNIV KANS, 79- *Concurrent Pos:* Encargado de Catedra Port, Univ Costa Rica, 72. *Mem:* MLA; Latin Am Studies Asn; Am Asn Teachers of Span & Port. *Res:* Modern Brazilian prose fiction, Brazilian poetry, Spanish-American fiction. *Publ:* Auth, The Brazilian novel: Some paradoxes of popularity, J Interam Studies & World Affairs, 72; Graciliano Ramos: The dialectics of defeat, Ind Univ, 76; Corpo de Baile, Luso-Brazilian Rev, 77; Jose Marti: Surrealist or seer?, Latin Am Res Rev, 78; Jorge Amado, Jorge Desprezado, Luso Brazilian Rev, summer 78; Gran Serton: El imperativo critico, Texto Critico, summer 78; Joao Guimaraes Rosa, Twayne, 78. *Mailing Add:* Dept of Span & Port Univ Kans Lawrence KS 66045

VINCENT, PATRICK RUSSELL, b Dursley, England, Nov 16, 18; m 46; c 3. FRENCH LITERATURE. *Educ:* Univ Hull, BA, 48; Johns Hopkins Univ, PhD(Romance lang), 52. *Prof Exp:* Instr humanities, Johns Hopkins Univ, 52-54; asst prof, Duke Univ, 54-62, assoc prof French, 62-82; RETIRED. *Mem:* MLA; Am Asn Teachers Fr. *Res:* Medieval French literature. *Publ:* Auth, The Jeu de Saint Nicolas of Jean Bodel of Arras, Johns Hopkins, 54; coauth, Contes a lire et a raconter, Ronald, 60. *Mailing Add:* Dept of Romance Lang Duke Univ Durham NC 27706

VINCI, JOSEPH, b Serradifalco, Italy, Mar 26, 19; nat US; m 49; c 3. ROMANCE LANGUAGES & LITERATURE. *Educ:* City Col New York, BA, 42; Stanford Univ, BA, 44; Columbia Univ, MA, 49; Univ Madrid, cert, 54; Middlebury Col, DML(Span, Ital & French), 55. *Prof Exp:* Instr mod lang, Champlain Col, Plattsburgh, 46-48; asst prof Romance lang & lit, St Michael's Col, Vt, 48-58; Assoc prof, Bellarmine Col, 58-62 & Frostburg State Col, 62-66; PROF MOD LANG & CHMN DEPT, SOUTHEASTERN MASS UNIV, 66- *Mem:* MLA; Am Asn Teachers Ital; Am Asn Teachers Span & Port; Renaissance Soc Am. *Res:* Neoplatonism, mysticism and Spanish Italian cultural relations in the Renaissance. *Publ:* Auth, The Neoplatonic influence of Marsilio Ficino Pedro Malon de Chaide, Hisp Rev, 10/61; Robert Bellarmine, Renaissance News, winter 61; Petrarchan source of Jorge Manrique's Las Coplas, Italica, Vol 45, No 3. *Mailing Add:* 31 Old Westport Rd North Dartmouth MA 02747

VINES, MURRAY, b New York, NY; m 73. FRENCH LITERATURE, SPANISH GRAMMAR. *Educ:* City Col NY, BA, 63; Duke Univ, PhD(Romance lang), 70. *Prof Exp:* Asst prof French, 67-72, assoc prof, 72-79, PROF FRENCH & SPAN GRAMMAR, VA MIL INST, 80- *Mem:* Am Asn Teachers Fr; AAUP: SAtlantic Mod Lang Asn; Southern Comp Lit Asn. *Res:* Baudelaire's plagiarisms; relationship of Baudelaire to Gautier; comparative literature. *Publ:* Auth, Baudelaire's Recueillement and the Greek Cycle, The Comparatist, inaugural issue; Baudelaire's Le guignon: Hippocrates or Longfellow, Romance Notes, Vol 18, No 2. *Mailing Add:* Dept of Mod Lang Va Mil Inst Lexington VA 24450

VIRGILLO, CARMELO, b Sept 4, 34; US citizen; m 65; c 1. SPANISH, PORTUGUESE. *Educ:* State Univ NY, Albany, AB, 56; Ind Univ, Bloomington, MA, 58, PhD(Am lit & lang), 63. *Prof Exp:* From instr to asst prof Span, Port & Ital, Univ Notre Dame, 62-65; asst prof, 63-76, PROF ROMANCE LANG & FOREIGN LANG, ARIZ STATE UNIV, 76- *Mem:* Am Asn Teachers Span & Port; Am Asn Teachers Ital. *Res:* Latin American literature; Italian literature and language. *Publ:* Auth, Methodology of studying middle class Ucatan families, In: Annual Report to the III, Social Psychol Lab Univ Chicago, 65; The French Influence on Machado de Assis, Univ Ga, 66; ed, Correspondencia de Machado de Assis com Carlos Magalhaes de Azaredo, Ministerio Educ Cult, Inst Nac Livro, Rio de Janeiro, Vol I, 68; auth, Discussion of Professor Mercedes Valdivieso's paper, Dos approximaciones literarias al problema de la existencia: El extranjero de Albert Camus y El Tunel de Ernesto Sabato, In: Papers on Fr-Span, Luso-Brazilian, Span-Am Lit Rel, State Univ NY, 70; Primitivism in Latin American fiction, In: The Ibero-American Enlightenment, Univ Ill, 71. *Mailing Add:* Dept of Foreign Lang Arizona State Univ Tempe AZ 85281

VIRTANEN, REINO, b Ishpeming, Mich, June 26, 10; m 37; c 2. FRENCH LITERATURE & PHILOSOPHY. *Educ:* Univ Wis, AB, 32, AM, 33, PhD, 37. *Prof Exp:* Markham traveling fel, Univ Wis, France, 37-38, instr French, 38-42, asst prof, 46-48; from asst prof to assoc prof Romance lang, Univ Tenn, 48-54; assoc prof, 54-57, prof, 57-78, EMER PROF FRENCH, UNIV NEBR-LINCOLN, 78- *Concurrent Pos:* Vis prof French, Univ Minn, 52-53 & Univ Calif, Los Angeles, 70; Woods fel, 59-60 & 73. *Honors & Awards:* Festschrift, Univ Nebr-Lincoln, 78; Camargo Found, 80. *Mem:* MLA. *Res:* Relations of literature and science. *Publ:* Auth, Claude Bernard and his Place in the History of Edeas, Univ Nebr, 60; Marcelin Berthelot, Univ Nebr Studies, 65; French national character in the 20th century, Ann Am Acad Polit & Soc Sci, 3/67; Anatole France, Twayne, 68; L'Imagerie scientifique de Paul Valery, Vrin, Paris, 75; Conversations on Dialogue, Univ Nebr, 78. *Mailing Add:* Dept of Mod Lang Univ of Nebr Lincoln NE 68508

VISSON, LYNN, b New York, NY, Apr 26, 45. RUSSIAN LANGUAGE & LITERATURE. *Educ:* Radcliffe Col, BA, 66; Columbia Univ, MA, 67; Harvard Univ, PhD(Slavic lang & lit), 72. *Prof Exp:* Instr & assoc Russ, Barnard Col, Columbia Univ, 69-70, from instr to asst prof, 71-76; asst prof, Bryn Mawr Col, 76-78; asst prof Russ, Hunter Col, 78-79; INTERPRETER, UN, 81- *Concurrent Pos:* Mem fac exchange with Soviet Union, Moscow State Univ, 70-71; Am Coun Learned Soc grant in Soviet Studies, 76. *Mem:* Am Asn Teachers Slavic & East Europ Lang; Am Coun Teachers Russ. *Res:* Soviet poetry; Esenin; Russian language. *Publ:* Coauth, Bellini's casta diva and Goncharov's Oblomov, In: Studia Russica in Honorem V Setchkarev, 74 & The Moscow Gourment: Dining Out in the Capital of the USSR, Ardis, 74; Esenin's literary reworking of The Riddle, Vol 18, No 1 & Problems of teaching stylistics, Vol 19, No 1, Slavic & East Europ Lang J; Sergel Esenin: Poet of the Crossroads, JAL, 80. *Mailing Add:* 60 Riverside Dr Apt 7H New York NY 10024

VISWANATHAN, JACQUELINE J, Can citizen. GENERAL LITERATURE, CONTEMPORARY FICTION. *Educ:* Univ Liege, Belg, Lic es Lett, 62, Agrege, 63, D es Lett, 72; Univ Ill, MA, 65. *Prof Exp:* From instr to asst prof, 65-77, ASSOC PROF FRENCH, SIMON FRASER UNIV, 77- *Res:* Narrative techniques in contemporary fiction; French-Canadian literature. *Publ:* Auth, In between two worlds: Wuthering Heights, Under Western Eyes, Faustus, Orbis Litterarum, 74; The innocent bystander, H Lit Stud, 75; Narrateurs chez Provst e Butor, PNCFL, 76; Mai 68, introd to culture, Fr Rev, 76; Neige noire: etude temporelle, Voix et Images, 77; Prochain episode: etude Temporelle, Presence Francophone, 77; La Chanson Quebecoise, Francia, 78. *Mailing Add:* Dept of Lang Lit & Ling Simon Fraser Univ Burnaby BC V5A 1S6 Can

VITELLO, RALPH MICHAEL, b Buffalo, NY, Dec 26, 49. FRENCH RENAISSANCE LITERATURE. *Educ:* State Univ NY Buffalo, BA, 71; Yale Univ, MPhil, 77, PhD(French), 78. *Prof Exp:* Actg instr French, Yale Univ, 75-77; lectr, Univ Calif, Los Angeles, 77-78; ASST PROF FRENCH, YALE UNIV, 78- *Mem:* Soc Amis Montaigne; MLA; Am Asn Teachers Fr. *Res:* Literature of ideas in the Renaissance; French and American modern poetry. *Publ:* Transl, Hemingway a la lumiere de Hegel, Semiotext(e), 76. *Mailing Add:* Dept of French Yale Univ New Haven CT 06520

VITZ, EVELYN BIRGE, b Indianapolis, Ind, Oct 16, 41; m 69; c 3. FRENCH MEDIEVAL & FRENCH RENAISSANCE LITERATURE. *Educ:* Smith Col, BA, 63; Yale Univ, PhD(French), 68. *Prof Exp:* From instr to asst prof, 68-74, ASSOC PROF FRENCH, DEPT FRENCH & ITAL, NEW YORK UNIV, 74- *Concurrent Pos:* Nat Endowment for Humanities younger humanist fel, 74-75. *Mem:* MLA; Medieval Acad Am. *Res:* Medieval narrative; modern narrative theory; medieval and Renaissance lyric poetry. *Publ:* Auth, Symbolic contamination in the Testament of Francois Villon, Mod Lan Notes, 71; The I of the Roman de la Rose, Genre, 3/73; Type et individu dans l'autobiographie medievale, Poetique, 75; Ronsard's Sonnets pour Helene: Narrative structures and poetic language, Romanic Rev, 11/76; Narrative analysis of medieval texts: La Fille du Comte de Pontieu, Mod Lang Notes, 77; La Vie de Saint Alexis: Narrative analysis and the quest for the sacred subject, PMLA, 78. *Mailing Add:* Dept of French New York Univ New York NY 10003

VIVANTE, PAOLO, b Rome, Italy, Sept 30, 21. CLASSICS. *Educ:* Oxford Univ, BA, 47; Univ Florence, PhD(classic philol), 48. *Prof Exp:* Vis lectr Greek lit, Hebrew Univ, Israel, 58-60; asst prof classics, Univ Tex, 63-66; asst prof, 67-69, assoc prof, 69-82, PROF CLASSICS, McGILL UNIV, 82- *Res:* Literature, especially Greek. *Publ:* Auth, The Homeric Imagination, Ind Univ, 70; On myth and action in Pindar, fall 71 & On time in Pindar, fall 72, Arethusa; On poetry and language in Homer, Ramus, 73; On Homer's winged words, Classical Quart, 5/75; Rose-fingered dawn and the idea of time, Ramus, 79; Homer's epithets of men, a study in poetic syntax, 80 & The syntax of Homer's epithets of wine (in press), Glotta; The Epithets in Homer, A Study in Poetic Values, Yale Univ Press (in press). *Mailing Add:* Dept Classics McGill Univ Montreal PQ H3A 2T7 Can

VOGE, WILFRIED MICHAEL, b Lauenburg Ger, Nov 17, 43; US citizen. LINGUISTICS, GERMAN PHILOLOGY. *Educ:* Brigham Young Univ, BA, 68; Univ Calif, Berkeley, MA, 70, PhD(Ger ling), 76. *Prof Exp:* Actg instr Ger, Univ Calif, Berkeley, 73-74; ASST PROF GER & LING, UNIV CALIF, IRVINE, 74- *Honors & Awards:* Innovative Proj in Univ Teaching Award, Regents, Univ of Calif, 75-76. *Mem:* Ling Soc Am; MLA; Am Coun Teaching Foreign Lang; Am Asn Teachers Ger. *Res:* German phonetics; second language acquisition; applied linguistics. *Publ:* Coauth, Individualized German instruction at the college level, Foreign Lang Ann, 10/72; An artificial intelligence approach to language instruction, Artificial Intelligence, 78; auth, The Pronunciation of German in the 18th Century, In: Hamburger Phonetische Beitraege Ser, Buske Verlag, 4/78; coauth, The Contemporary Pronunciation of Long(ä) in Modern Standard German: A Data-Based, Computer-Assisted Analysis, Hamburger Phonetische Beiträge, XXX: 125-179. *Mailing Add:* Dept of Ger Univ of Calif Irvine CA 92717

VOGEL, LUCY ELAINE, b Kiev, Russia; US citizen. RUSSIAN LANGUAGE & LITERATURE. *Educ:* Brooklyn Col, BA, 60; Fordham Univ, MA, 62; NY Univ, PhD(Russ), 68. *Prof Exp:* Instr Russ & Ital, Queen's Col NY, 61-67; asst prof, 67-72, ASSOC PROF RUSS, STATE UNIV NY, STONY BROOK, 73-, DIR SLAVIC STUDIES, 74- *Mem:* Am Asn Teachers Slavic & EEurop Lang; Am Asn Univ Women. *Res:* Symbolism in Russian literature. *Publ:* Auth, Alexander Blok: A Journey to Italy, Cornell Univ, 73; Gogol's Rome, Slavic & EEurop J, summer 67; A symbolist's inferno: Blok and Dante, Russ Rev, 1/70. *Mailing Add:* Dept of Ger & Slavic Lang State Univ of NY Stony Brook NY 11794

VOGELEY, NANCY JEANNE, b San Pedro, Calif, June 19, 37. LATIN AMERICAN & SPANISH LITERATURE. *Educ:* Pa State Univ, BA, 58, MA, 62; Univ Madrid, dipl Span, 60; Stanford Univ, PhD(Span), 80. *Prof Exp:* Instr Span, Allegheny Col, 62-63; Ithaca Col, 63-64 & Col San Mateo, 65-66; instr, 66-70, asst prof, 70-81, ASSOC PROF SPAN, UNIV SAN FRANCISCO, 81- *Concurrent Pos:* Instr Span, Univ San Francisco, Valencia, Spain, summer, 69. *Mem:* Am Asn Teachers Span & Port; MLA; Philol Asn Pac Coast; Am Soc 18th Century Studies; Latin Am Studies Asn. *Res:* Jose Joaquin Fernandez de Lizardi and the period of Mexican Independence; Alfonso Sastre and contemporary Spanish theater. *Publ:* Auth, Jose Joaquin Fernandez Lizardi and the Inquisition, Dieciocho, fall 80; Alfonso Sastre on Alfonso Sastre (interview), Hispania, 9/81; Blacks in Peru: The poetry of Nicomedes Santa Cruz, Phylon (in press); The figure of the Black Payador in Martin Fierro, CLA J (in press). *Mailing Add:* Dept of Mod Lang Univ of San Francisco San Francisco CA 94117

VOGLER, FREDERICK WRIGHT, b Burlington, Vt, May 27, 31; m 65. ROMANCE LANGUAGES. *Educ:* Univ NC, Chapel Hill, AB, 53, MA, 55, PhD(Romance lang), 61. *Prof Exp:* Instr French, Univ NC, Chapel Hill, 61-62; asst prof, Univ Iowa, 62-63; from asst prof to assoc prof, 63-78, PROF FRENCH, UNIV NC, CHAPEL HILL, 78-, ASSOC DEAN COL ARTS & SCI, 76- *Concurrent Pos:* Mem French achievement comt, Col Entrance Exam Bd, 67-70. *Mem:* MLA; SAtlantic Mod Lang Asn; Am Asn Teachers French. *Res:* Early 17th century French novel; French classical doctrine and practice. *Publ:* Auth, Vital d'Audiguier and the Early 17th Century French Novel, Univ NC, 64; La premier apparition en France du Peregrino de Lope de Vega, (1614), Bull Hisp, 64; Hippolyte: The woman scorned, Symposium, 64; ed, Moliere Mocked: Three Contemporary Hostile Comedies, Univ NC, 73; Moliere and the comical teuton, In: Moliere and the Commonwealth of Letters, Univ Miss, 75. *Mailing Add:* Dept of Romance Lang Univ of NC Chapel Hill NC 27514

VOLEK, BRONISLAVA, b Decin, Czech, May 15, 46; US citizen. SLAVIC LANGUAGES, LINGUISTICS. *Educ:* Charles Univ, PromPhil, 69, PhD(Slavic lang), 70. *Prof Exp:* Internal sci aspirant Russ ling, Charles Univ, Prague, 69-73; asst prof, Univ 17th of Nov, 73-74; asst prof Slavic ling, Univ Cologne, 74-75; assoc prof, Philipps-Univ Marburg, 76; Mellon fac fel, Harvard Univ, 77-78; vis prof Slavic lang & lit, Ind Univ, Bloomington, 78-80; asst prof, Univ Va, Charlottesville, 80-82; ASST PROF SLAVIC LANG & LIT, IND UNIV, BLOOMINGTON, 82- *Concurrent Pos:* Fel, Moscow State Univ, 72; Mellon fac fel, Harvard, 77. *Honors & Awards:* Res Award, Univ Va, 81. *Mem:* Soc Ling Europ; Am Asn Teachers Slavic & E Europ Lang; Am Advan Slavic Studies; Semiotic Soc Am. *Res:* Slavic linguistics & literatures; general linguistics. *Publ:* Auth, Abgeleitete benennungen mit emotionalen bedeutungen: Methodologishe ausgangspunkte, In: Marburger Abhandlungen zur Geschichte und Kultur Osteuropas, Theoretische und praktische Linguistik des Russischen, Beitrage zum VIII Int Slawisten Kongress, 81; co-transl (with W Barnstone), three poems in Nimrod, Vol 25, No 1; auth, ten poems in Promeny, 81; co-transl (with W Barnstone), Between the crossing of the legs, Artful Dodge, 81; auth, The semantic structure of derived substantives with an emotive component in Russian--a comparative study, SEEJ; Guinea pigs and the Czech novel Under Padlock in the 1970s: From the modern absolutism to the postmodernist absolute, Rocky Mountain Rev; The guinea pigs of Ludvik Vaculik: Interrelation of areas of reference, SSA Proc, 81; co-transl (with A Durkin), Vladimir Holan, At Mother's After Many Years, The Cave of Words & Memory II (3 poems), In: Contemporary East European Poetry: An Anthology, Ardis (in press). *Mailing Add:* Dept of Slavic Lang & Lit Ind Univ Bloomington IN 47401

VOLEK, EMIL, b Roznov, Czech, Mar 22, 44; US citizen. SPANISH AMERICAN & SPANISH LITERATURE. *Educ:* Charles Univ, Prague, Prom Phil, 67, PhD(Span & Span-Am lit), 70. *Prof Exp:* From asst prof to assoc prof Ibero-Am lit, Czech Acad Sci, 69-74; vis prof Span & Span-Am lit, Romanisches Sem, Univ Cologne, 74-76; asst prof, 76-78, ASSOC PROF SPAN, ARIZ STATE UNIV, 78- *Mem:* Instituto Internacional de Literatura Iberoamerican; MLA. *Res:* Theory of literature. *Publ:* Auth, Analisis de las estructuras musicales de El acoso de Alejo Carpentier, Philologica Pragensia, 69; Oktosylabus romanci-brana k autochtonnimu spanelskemu versi, Casopis pro moderni filologii, 70; Algunas reflexiones sobre El siglo de las luces de Alejo Carpentier, Casa de las Americas, 72; Alejo Carpentier y la narrativa lationamericana actual, Cuadernos Hispanoamericanos, 75; Die begriffe fabel und sujet in der modernen literaturwissenschaft, Poetica, 77; Aquiles y la tortuga: arte, imaginacion y la realidad en J L Borges, Revista Iberoamericana, 77; Un soneto de Sor Juana Ines de la Cruz, Cuadernos Americanos, 79; Colloquial language in narrative structure: Towards a nomothetic typology of styles and of narrative discourse, Dispositio, 80-81. *Mailing Add:* Dept of Foreign Lang Ariz State Univ Tempe AZ 85281

VOLPE, GERALD CARMINE, b Fitchburg, Mass, May 27, 31. ROMANCE LANGUAGES. *Educ:* Holy Cross Col, BA, 54; Fordham Univ, MA, 56; Princeton Univ, PhD(Romance lang), 63. *Prof Exp:* From instr to asst prof French & Ital, Brandeis Univ, 60-66; asst prof, 66-72, acting chmn dept Ital, 73-74, chmn dept, 74-75, ASSOC PROF FRENCH & ITAL, UNIV MASS, BOSTON, 72- *Mem:* MLA; AAUP; Am Asn Teachers Fr; Am Asn Teachers Ital; Dante Soc. *Res:* French Renaissance; Dante; Ethnic studies. *Mailing Add:* Dept of French & Ital Univ of Mass Boston MA 02116

VON GODANY, URSULA BACH, b West Ger, Feb 15, 24; m 46; c 2. GERMAN LANGUAGE & LITERATURE. *Educ:* Univ Munich, MA, 52; Case Western Reverve Univ, MSLS, 59, PhD(Ger lang & lit), 76. *Prof Exp:* Ref librn & asst dept head, Cleveland Pub Libr, 59-65; teaching asst Ger, Case Western Reserve Univ, 68-71; HUMANITIES BIBLIOGR, IOWA STATE UNIV, 73-, ASSOC PROF, 77- *Mem:* MLA; AAUP. *Res:* Eighteenth century German literature; alchemy in literature; Thomas Mann. *Mailing Add:* Iowa State Univ Ames IA 50011

VON HOFE, HAROLD, b Plainfield, NJ, Apr 23, 12; m 47; c 2. GERMAN LITERATURE. *Educ:* NY Univ, BS, 36; Northwestern Univ, PhD, 39. *Prof Exp:* Asst, Northwestern Univ, 38-39; from instr to assoc prof, 39-45, chmn div humanities, 58-62, dean grad sch, 74-77, chmn, Dept Comp Lit, 77-78, PROF GER & CHMN DEPT, UNIV SOUTHERN CALIF, 45-, DIR, FERCHTWANGER INST EXILE STUDIES, 78- *Concurrent Pos:* Fulbright res fel, Univ Munich, 55-56; chmn, Nat Fulbright Selection Comt for Ger, 57-59; managing ed, Ger Quart, 58-63; vis prof, Univ Calif, Berkeley, 59; Ger adv ed, Charles Scribner's Sons, 61-; Fulbright res fel, Austria, 62-63. *Mem:* MLA; Am Asn Teachers Ger (1st vpres); Philol Asn Pac Coast. *Res:* American motifs in German literature; parallel cultural patterns in German and American civilization; German literature in exile. *Publ:* Coauth, A German Sketchbook, Houghton, 50; auth, Im Wandel der Jahre, Holt, 55, 6th ed, 78; Die Kultur der Vereinigten Staaten von Amerika, Akad Verlagsges Athenaion, 63, 2nd ed, 72; Kultur und Alltag, Scribner, 73; Briefe von und an Ludwig Marcuse, 76; Der Briefwechsel Feuchtwanger, Annold Zweig (in press). *Mailing Add:* 12733 Vulholland Dr Beverly Hills CA 90210

VON KRIES, FRIEDRICH WILHELM, b Berlin, Ger, Nov 4, 27; m 60; c 2. GERMAN LITERATURE, PHILOLOGY. *Educ:* Univ BC, BA, 61; Univ Wash, MA, 62, PhD, 65. *Prof Exp:* From instr to asst prof Ger, Bibliog & medieval lit, Univ Wash, 65-69; ASSOC PROF GER, BIBLIOG & MEDIEVAL LIT, UNIV MASS, AMHERST, 69- *Mem:* Mediaeval Acad Am; MLA. *Res:* Mediaeval German literature; palaeography; bibliography. *Publ:* Auth,Textkritische Studien zum Welschen Gast Thomasins von Zerclaere, De Gruyter, Berlin, 67; Bemerkungen zur Datierung von Walthers von der Vogelweide König Friedrichton, Archiv, 74. *Mailing Add:* Dept of Ger Lang & Lit Univ of Mass Amherst MA 01003

VON MOLNAR, GEZA WALTER ELEMER, b Leipzig, Ger, Aug 5, 32; US citizen; m 57; c 2. GERMAN LANGUAGE & LITERATURE, PHILOSOPHY. *Educ:* Hunter Col, BA, 58; Stanford Univ, MA, 60, PhD(Ger), 66. *Prof Exp:* From instr to asst prof, 63-69, chmn dept, 71-75, ASSOC PROF GER, NORTHWESTERN UNIV, 69- *Concurrent Pos:* Am Coun Learned Soc res fel, 73-74. *Mem:* MLA; Am Soc 18th Century Studies. *Res:* Early German Romanticism, in particular the contributions of Friedrich von Hardenberg known by the pen name Novalis; Kantian philosophy; Goethe and Schiller. *Publ:* Auth, Novalis' Fichte Studies: The Foundations of His Aesthetics, Stanford Studies Germanics & Slavics, Mouton, The Hague, 69; co-ed, Versuche zu Goethe: Festschrift für Erich Heller, Heidelberg: Lothar Stiehm Verlag, 76; Die Fragwürdigkeit des Frageszeichens: Einige Überlegungen zur Pakstzene, Goethe Jahrubuch, 79; The Conditions of Faust's Wager and its Resolution in the Light of Kantian Ethics, Publ of the English Goethe Soc, 82; Goethe's Reading of Kant's Critique of Aesthetic Judgment: A Referential Guide for Wilhelm Meister's Aesthetic Education, 18th Century Studies, 82; Conceptual Affinities Between Kant's Critique of Judgment and Goethe's Faust, Lessing Yearbk (in press). *Mailing Add:* Dept of German Northwestern Univ 1859 Sheridan Rd Evanston IL 60201

VON OHLEN, HENRY BRUCE, b Mankato, Minn, Dec 8, 46; m 73. FRENCH. *Educ:* Stanford Univ, AB, 68; Univ Chicago, MA, 69; Cornell Univ, PhD(French), 76. *Prof Exp:* ASST PROF FRENCH, OHIO STATE UNIVG 76- *Mem:* MLA; Am Asn Fr. *Res:* French Renaissance poetry; poetics; discourse analysis. *Publ:* Translr, Michel Serres, Peter-Stephen isomorphisms, 2, Diacritics, fall 75; coauth, Si doulx and attrayant subiect: Sceve's Delie and four modern critics, Romanic Rev, 3/77. *Mailing Add:* Dept of Romance Lang Ohio State Univ Columbus OH 43210

VON RICHTHOFEN, ERICH, b Hirschberg, Ger, May 8, 13; m 50; c 1. PHILOLOGY. *Educ:* Univ Frankfurt, Dr Phil, 40, Dr Phil Habil, 43. *Prof Exp:* Privatdozent Romance philol, Univ Frankfurt, 43-51, assoc prof, 51-56; assoc prof French & Romance philol, Univ Alta, 56-61, prof Romance philol, 62; prof, Boston Col, 62-64, prof Medieval Span & Ital lit, 64; prof Medieval Span & Ital lit, 64-79, EMER PROF ROMANCE LANG, UNIV TORONTO, 79- *Concurrent Pos:* Vis prof, Univ Chicago, 54; dir, Int Summer Sch, Frankfurt, 52-56. *Mem:* Mediaeval Acad Am; Renaissance Soc Am; MLA; Asn Int Hispanistas; Royal Soc Can. *Res:* Toponymy; mediaeval epics; Romanic stylistics and semantics. *Publ:* Auth, Veltro und Diana, Dantes mittelaterliche und antike Gleichnisse, Max Niemeyer, Tübingen, 56; Commentaire sur Mon Faust de Paul Valery, Univ France, Paris, 61; Vier altfranzösische Lais: Chievrefueil, Austic, Bisclavret, Guingamor, 3rd ed, Max Niemeyer, Tübingen, 68; Nuevos estudios epicos medievals, Ed Gredos, Madrid, 70; Dante Apollinian, Annali ist Univ Orient, Naples, 70; Analogias historico-legendarias en las tradiciones epicas medievales, Prohemio, 72; Tradicionalismo epiconovelesco, 72 & Limites de la critica litteraria, 76, Ed Planeta, Barcelona. *Mailing Add:* Dept of Ital & Hisp Studies Univ of Toronto Toronto ON M5S 1A1 Can

VON SCHNEIDEMESSER, LUANNE H, b San Diego, Calif, Feb 28, 45; m 72; c 1. AMERICAN ENGLISH, LEXICOGRAPHY. *Educ:* Kans State Univ, BA, 68; Univ Wis-Madison, MA, 70, PhD(Ger ling & philol), 79. *Prof Exp:* Teaching asst Ger & English as second lang, 69-76, asst ed, Dict of American Regional English, 78-81, PROD ED, DICT OF AMERICAN REGIONAL ENGLISH, UNIV WIS-MADISON, 81- *Mem:* Am Dialect Soc; Am Asn Teachers Ger; Ling Soc Am. *Res:* American English; influence of German on English; sociolinguistics. *Publ:* Coauth, German loanwords in American English, A bibliography of studies, 1872-1978, 79 & auth, Purse and its synonymns, 80, Am Speech; Report on the Dict of American Regional English, Ling Reporter & Inc Ling, 81. *Mailing Add:* Dict of American Regional English Univ of Wis Madison WI 53706

VON WIREN-GARCZYNSKI, VERA, b Nov-Sad, Yugoslavia, July 6, 31; US citizen; m 48; c 4. SLAVIC LANGUAGES & LITERATURE. *Educ:* Brooklyn Col, BA, 58; Columbia Univ, MA, 61; NY Univ, PhD(Slavic lang), 64. *Prof Exp:* Lectr Russ, Queens Col, NY, 62-64; from instr to asst prof Slavic lang & lit, 64-72, ASSOC PROF SLAVIC LANG & LIT, CITY COL NEW YORK, 72- *Mem:* MLA; Am Asn Advan Slavic Studies; Am Asn Teachers Slavic & EEurop Lang; Polish Inst Arts & Sci Am. *Res:* Old Russian and Soviet literature; Polish language and literature; psychology in literature. *Publ:* Auth, Zoshchenko in retrospect, Russ Rev, 10/62; coauth, Seven Russian Short Novel Masterpieces, Popular Libr, 67; Pered Voskhodom Solntsa, M Zoshchenko, Interlang Lit Assoc, 67; auth, Zoshchenko's psychological interests, Slavic & EEurop J, spring 67; Language and the revolution: Russian experience of the 1920's, Can Slavic Studies, 6/68. *Mailing Add:* Dept of Slavic Lang City Col of New York New York NY 10031

VOORHIS, PAUL H, b Indianapolis, Ind, Jan 27, 37; m 61; c 1. LINGUISTICS. *Educ:* Yale Univ, PhD(ling), 67. *Prof Exp:* Linguist, Smithsonian Inst, 67-70; consult ling, Nishnawbe Inst, 70-71; PROF LING, BRANDON UNIV, 71- *Concurrent Pos:* Adj prof, Univ Man, 73-76. *Mem:* Ling Soc Am; Am Anthrop Asn; Can Ling Asn. *Res:* North American Indian languages; teaching of languages. *Publ:* Auth, New notes on the Mesquakie (fox) language, 4/71 & Notes on Kickapoo whistle speech, 10/71, Int J Am Ling; Introduction to the Kickapoo Language, Lang Sci Monogr, 74. *Mailing Add:* 10 Westcott Bay Brandon MB R7B 2V6 Can

VOS, MORRIS, b Mahaska Co, Iowa, Dec 10, 44; m 66; c 2. GERMAN LITERATURE & LANGUAGE. *Educ:* Calvin Col, BA, 66; Ind Univ, Bloomington, MA, 67, PhD(Ger), 75. *Prof Exp:* Assoc instr Ger, Ind Univ, Bloomington, 70-71; asst prof, 71-79, ASSOC PROF GER, WESTERN ILL UNIV, 79- *Concurrent Pos:* Western Ill Univ Res Coun award, 78; Ger Acad Exchange Serv study visit, 80. *Mem:* Midwest Mod Lang Asn; Am Asn Teachers Ger; Am Coun Teaching Foreign Lang; Conf Christianity & Lit. *Res:* German narration theory of the 18th century; religion and literature; foreign language pedagogy. *Publ:* Auth, The concept of dramatic narration, In: Jahrbuch für Internationale Germanistik, Band 4, 79. *Mailing Add:* Foreign Lang & Lit Western Ill Univ Macomb IL 61455

VOWLES, RICHARD BECKMAN, b Fargo, NDak, Oct 5, 17; div; c 2. SCANDINAVIAN LITERATURE. *Educ:* Davidson Col, BS, 38; Yale Univ, AM, 42, PhD, 50. *Prof Exp:* Chem eng, Hercules Powder Co, 41-42; econ consult, US Dept War, 43-44; Am vconsul, US Foreign Serv, 44-46; asst prof English, Southwestern at Memphis, 48-50 & Queens Col, NY, 50-51; from asst prof to assoc prof, Univ Fla, 51-61; chmn dept comp lit, 63-67 & 71-72, chmn dept Scand studies, 77-80, PROF COMP LIT & SCAND STUDIES, UNIV WIS-MADISON, 61- *Concurrent Pos:* Res fel, Yale Univ, 55; Fulbright fel, 55-56; gen ed, Nordic Transl Ser, 62-; vis res prof, Univ Helsinki, 68; Fulbright lectr, England, 68; Norwegian & Swedish govt awards, 78. *Mem:* Am-Scand Found; Soc Advan Scand Studies; Strindberg Soc; MLA. *Res:* Modern Scandinavian literature; comparative drama; dramatic theory. *Publ:* Ed, Paer Lagerkvist's Collected Fiction, Dramatic Theory: A Bibliography & August Strindberg: A Survery and a Fragment; ed & translr, Peder Sjögren, Bread of Love, Univ Wis, 65; ed, Two Novels by Ausust Strindberg, Bantam, 68; co-ed, comparatists at Work, Blaisdell, 68; auth, Expressionism in Scandinavia, Hungarian Acad Papers, 74; Myth in Sweden, World Lit Today, 74; Boganis, Father of Osceola, Scand Studies, 76. *Mailing Add:* 1115 Oak Way Madison WI 53705

VOYLES, JOSEPH BARTLE, b New Albany, Ind, Aug 20, 38. GERMANIC LANGUAGES, LINGUISTICS. *Educ:* Ind Univ, BA, 60, MA, 62, PhD(Ger & ling), 65. *Prof Exp:* From asst prof to assoc prof, 65-75, PROF GERMANICS & LING, UNIV WASH, 75- *Mem:* Ling Soc Am. *Res:* Historical linguistics; computational linguistics. *Publ:* Auth,German noun and adjective compounds, Lang Learning, 5/67; Simplicity, ordered rules, and the first sound shift, 9/67 & Gothic and Germanic, 69, Language. *Mailing Add:* Dept of Ger Lang & Lit Univ of Wash Seattle WA 98195

VRANICH, STANKO B, b Yugoslavia, Oct 10, 32; US citizen; m 61; c 2. SPANISH LITERATURE. *Educ:* Tulane Univ, BA, 55; Univ Iowa, MA, 57; Univ Calif, Berkeley, PhD(Romance lang), 65. *Prof Exp:* Assoc prof Span, Univ Wis-Madison, 65-71; ASSOC PROF SPAN, LEHMAN COL, 72- *Concurrent Pos:* Am Philos Soc grant-in-aid, 71; Nat Endowment Humanities fel, 77; Guggenehim fel, 78. *Mem:* MLA; Int Asn Hisp Res. *Res:* Golden age poetry; history of Seville, 16th and 17th centuries; semantics. *Publ:* Auth, Gaspar de Arguijo y el comercio de negros, In: Homenaje a Rodriguez Monino, 66; Carta de un ciudadano de Sevilla, 66 & Escandalo en la catedral, 72, Archivo Hispalense; ed, Juan de Arguijo: Obra poetica, Castalia, Madrid, 72; Sigmund Freud and the case history of Berganza, Psychoanalytic Rev, spring 76; Un poema inedito de Francisco de Medina, Revista de Filologia Espanola, 75; Don Juan de Espinosa: Poeta sevillano del XVII, Archive Hispalense, 76; Un soneto inedito atribuido a Arguijo, Romance Notes, 77. *Mailing Add:* Dept of Romance Lang Lehman Col Bronx NY 10468

VROOMAN, JACK ROCHFORD, b Toledo, Ohio, Feb 27, 29. FRENCH LITERATURE. *Educ:* Princeton Univ, BA, 51, PhD(Romance lang), 65; Columbia Univ, MAG 52. *Prof Exp:* Master French & English, St Andrew's Sch, Middletown, 54-60; teaching asst French, Princeton Univ, 61-62; asst prof, Univ Calif, Berkeley, 62-70; ASSOC PROF FRENCH & CHMN DEPT, UNIV NH, 71- *Concurrent Pos:* Mem Examining Comt, Advan Prog in Fr, 67-69; chief reader, Col Bd Advan Placement Prog in French, 69-72. *Mem:* Am Soc 18th Century Studies; MLA; Am Soc Aesthet; Soc Fr Etude XVIIIe Siecle. *Res:* Voltaire; 18th century French theatre; aesthetics. *Publ:* Auth, Rene Descartes-A Biography, Putman, 70; Voltaire's Theatre: The Cycle from OEdipe to Merope, Inst & Musee Voltaire, Geneva, 70; Voltaire's aesthetic pragmatism, J Aesthet & Art Criticism, fall 72. *Mailing Add:* 114 Mechanic St Portsmouth NH 03801

W

WACHAL, ROBERT STANLEY, b Omaha, Nebr, Mar 13, 29; m 68. NEUROLINGUISTICS, APPLIED LINGUISTICS. *Educ:* Univ Minn, Minneapolis, BA, 52; Univ Wis-Madison, MS, 59, PhD(English, ling), 66. *Prof Exp:* From asst prof to assoc prof, 70-75, PROF LING, UNIV IOWA, 75- *Concurrent Pos:* Coordr English lang prog, US Educ Found, Greece, 66-67. *Mem:* Ling Soc Am; Acad Aphasia; Teachers of English to Speakers of Other Lang. *Res:* Language pathology; style and statistics; sociolinguistics. *Publ:* Auth, The machine in the garden: Computers and literary scholarship, Comput & Humanities, 9/70; coauth, Psycholinguistic analysis of apasic languages, summer 73 & Some measures of lexical diversity, summer 73, Lang & Speech. *Mailing Add:* Dept of Ling Univ of Iowa Iowa City IA 52242

WADE, CLAIRE LYNCH, b Chattanooga, Tenn, Dec 26, 15; m 38. FRENCH. *Educ:* Sorbonne, dipl, 37; George Peabody Col, BA, 38, MA, 40; Vanderbilt Univ, MA, 68; Open Univ, St Louis, PhD, 78. *Prof Exp:* Teacher English, Montgomery Bell Acad, 42-43; teacher French, Ward-Belmont Col, 43-44; teaching asst, Vanderbilt Univ, 59-61; asst prof, Belmont Col, 61-62; instr, Watkins Inst, 62-63; ASSOC PROF FRENCH & ITAL, BELMONT COL, 63- *Mem:* SAtlantic Mod Lang Asn; Am Asn Teachers Fr. *Res:* French literature; creative writing; Italian. *Publ:* Auth, Albert Camus et le Christianisme, Tenn Philol Bull, 4/64; Second bloom, Lyric, summer 73. *Mailing Add:* PO Box 12044 Nashville TN 37212

WADE, LUTHER IRWIN, III, Drama, Speech. See Vol II

WADEPUHL, WALTER, b Berlin, Ger, Dec 29, 95. GERMAN LITERATURE. *Educ:* City Col New York, AB, 18; Columbia Univ, AM, 19; Univ Wis, PhD, 21. *Prof Exp:* Instr, Univ Pittsburgh, 21-22; assoc, Univ Ill, 22-26; from asst prof to assoc prof, WVa Univ, 26-38; prof, 46-65, EMER PROF GER, ELMHURST COL, 65- *Concurrent Pos:* Am Coun Learned Soc res fel, 30-31, 33 & 35, travel grant, 73; guest prof, City Col New York, 35 & 38; fel, Nat Forsch und Gedenkstatten klassischen deutschen Lit, Weimar, Ger, 65; distinguished vis prof Ger, Fla Atlantic Univ, 65-66. *Mem:* MLA; Goethe Soc; Am Asn Teachers Ger; fel Inst Int Arts & Lett. *Res:* German literature of the 18th and 19th centuries; Goethe and Heine; archaeology. *Publ:* Auth, Goethe's interest in the New World, Heine-Studien, Weimar, 56; Die alten Maya und ihre Kultur, Seemann, Leipzig, 63; Basic German Grammar and Vocabulary, Fla Atlantic Univ, 66; Heinrich Heine, Sein Leben und Seine Werke, Bohlau, Cologne, 73. *Mailing Add:* 3884 Carnation Circle N West Palm Beach FL 33410

WAELTI-WALTERS, JENNIFER ROSE, b Wolverhampton, Eng, Mar 13, 42; m 72. MODERN FRENCH LITERATURE. *Educ:* Univ Col, Univ London, BA, 64, PhD(French), 68; Univ Lille, lic, 66. *Prof Exp:* Asst prof, 68-74, assoc prof, 74-80, PROF FRENCH & CHMN DEPT, UNIV VICTORIA, 80- *Concurrent Pos:* Can Coun res grants & fels, 69-78; Soc Sci & Humanities Res Coun Can res grants, 79-82. *Mem:* Asn Prof Fr Can Univ; Can Comp Lit Asn; Asn Amis Ctr Cult Pontigny-Cerisy; Asn Can & Quebec Lit; Humanities Asn Can; Can Humanities Asn. *Res:* Twentieth century French novel; Women's writing; 20th century Quebec novel. *Publ:* Auth, Alchimie et Litterature: Etude de Portrait de l'Artiste en Juene Singe, Denoel, Paris, 75; Michel Butor, Sono Nis, Victoria, 77; J M G Le Clezio, Twayne, 77; Icare ou l'evasion, the food of love: Plato's banquet and Bersianik's picnic, Atlantis 6, 80; Guilt: The prison of this world (Blais: L'execution), Can Lit, Vol 88, 81; The Mirror Cracked: Fairytales and the Female Imagination, Eden Press, Montreal, 82. *Mailing Add:* Dept of French Univ of Victoria Victoria BC M5S 1K7 Can

WAGENER, HANS, b Lage, WGer, July 27, 40. GERMAN LITERATURE. *Educ:* Univ Freiburg, BA, 63; Univ Calif, Los Angeles, MA, 65, PhD(Ger), 67. *Prof Exp:* Asst prof Ger, Univ Southern Calif, 67-68; from asst prof to assoc prof, 68-75, chmn dept, 77-81, PROF GER, UNIV CALIF, LOS ANGELES, 75- *Mem:* MLA; Am Asn Teachers Ger. *Res:* Modern German literature; 17th and 18th century German literature. *Publ:* Coauth, Die Anredeformen in den Dramen des Andreas Gryphius, Wilhelm Fink, Munich, 70; auth, The German Baroque Novel, Twayne, 73; Erich Kästner, 73; Stefan Andres, 74 & Frank Wedekind, 79, Colloquium, Berlin; ed, Zeitkritische Romane Des 20 Jahrhunderts, Reclam, Stuttgart, 75; auth, Siegfried Lenz, C H Beck, Munich, 76; ed, Gegenwarts-literatur und Drittes Reich, Reclam, Stuttgart, 77. *Mailing Add:* Dept of Ger Lang Univ of Calif Los Angeles CA 90024

WAGGONER, LAWRENCE W, b Sidney, Ohio, July 2, 37; m 63; c 2. LAW. *Educ:* Univ Cincinnati, BBA, 60; Univ Mich, JD, 63; Oxford Univ, DPhil, 66. *Prof Exp:* Atty, Cravath, Swaine & Moore, 63; prof, Col of Law, Univ Ill, 68-72 & Sch of Law, Univ Va, 72-73; PROF LAW, LAW SCH, UNIV MICH, 73- *Mem:* Am Law Inst; Acad fel, Am Col Probate Coun. *Res:* Property law; federal taxation; estate planning. *Publ:* Auth, Reformulating the structure of estates, Harvard Law Rev, 85: 729; coauth, Trust and Succession, Found Press, 3rd ed, 78; Family Property Transactions, Michie & Bobbs-Merrill, 3rd ed, 80; auth, Future Interests in a Nutshell, West Publ Co, 81; coauth, Federal Taxation of Gifts, Trusts, and Estates, Little, Brown & Co, 2nd ed, 82; Reformation of wills on the ground of mistake: Change of direction in American law?, Univ Pa Law Rev, 130: 521. *Mailing Add:* Law Sch Univ Mich Ann Arbor MI 48109

WAHLGREN, ERIK, b Chicago, Ill, Nov 2, 11; m 39, 52, 71; c 4. SCANDINAVIAN PHILOLOGY. *Educ:* Univ Chicago, PhB, 33, PhD(Germanic lang), 38; Univ Nebr, AM, 36. *Prof Exp:* Asst Swedish & Ger, Univ Nebr, 34-36; asst Germanics, Univ Chicago, 36-38; from instr to prof Scand & Ger, 38-77, sr prof, Army Specialized Training Prog, 43-44, vchmn dept Germanic lang, 63-69, dir Scand Studies Ctr, Univ Lund, 72-74, EMER PROF SCAND & GERMANIC LANG, UNIV CALIF, LOS ANGELES, 77- *Concurrent Pos:* Am Scand Found fel, Sweden, 46-47; lectr, Univ Uppsala, 47-48; spec lectr, Univ Stockholm & Stockholm Sch Econ, 47-48; assoc ed, Scand Studies, 47-58 & 69-73, assoc managing ed, 57-69; Am Philos Soc grant, Sweden & Denmark, 54-55; Guggenheim fel, Scandinavia, 61-62; vis prof, Univ Calif, Berkeley, 68, Univ Wash, 70 & Portland State Univ, 79-80; Am mem, Comn Educ Exchange Between US & Sweden, 73-; sr fel & consult, Monterey Inst Foreign Studies, 77-; adv, Nat Endowment for Humanities, 78- & Gov Comm Int Study & Foreign Lang, 80- *Honors & Awards:* Knight, Order of the Polar Star, Sweden; Knight, Order of the Lion of Finland; Knight, Icelandic Order of the Falcon; Int Gold Medal, The Am-Scand Found, 75. *Mem:* MLA; Soc Advan Scand Studies; fel Int Inst Arts & Lett; Swed Pioneer Hist Soc. *Res:* Scandinavian literature and philology; runology. *Publ:* Transl, Education of an Historian, Speller, 57; auth, The Kensington Stone, A Mystery Solved, Univ Wis, 58; Fact and fancy in the Vinland sagas, In: Old Norse Literature and Mythology, Univ Tex, 69; Ordet och begreppet Vinland, Gardar, 74; American Runes: From Kensington to Spirit Pond, J English & Germanic Philol, Vol 81, 82. *Mailing Add:* 1501 NW 12th St Corvallis OR 97330

WAILES, STEPHEN L, b Summit, NJ, May 28, 37; m 64. GERMANIC LANGUAGES. *Educ:* Harvard Univ, AB, 60, PhD(Ger), 68. *Prof Exp:* Asst prof, 68-72, assoc prof, 72-80, PROF GER, IND UNIV, BLOOMINGTON, 80-, ASSOC DEAN FAC, 78- *Concurrent Pos:* Soc for Values in Higher Educ fel, 72; Alexander von Humboldt-Stiftung fel, 76. *Res:* Medieval theological and didactic literature. *Mailing Add:* 1710 Devon Lane Bloomington IN 47401

WAINMAN, ALEXANDER WHEELER, b Otterington, England, Mar 11, 13. RUSSIAN LANGUAGE & LITERATURE, SERBO-CROATIAN LANGUAGE. *Educ:* Oxford Univ, MA, 47. *Prof Exp:* Asst prof, 47-54, assoc prof, 54-78, EMER ASSOC PROF SLAVONIC STUDIES, UNIV BC, 78- *Concurrent Pos:* Can Coun res fel, 65-66. *Res:* The Croatian dialect of the Molise, Italy. *Mailing Add:* 1849 Allison Vancouver BC V6T 1T1 Can

WAITE, STEPHEN VAN FLEET, b Hartford, Conn, July 5, 40. CLASSICAL STUDIES, COMPUTER APPLICATIONS. *Educ:* Haverford Col, BA, 62; Harvard Univ, AM, 63, PhD(class philol), 69. *Prof Exp:* From instr to asst prof classics, 65-70, fac appl resource adv, Kiewit Comput Ctr, Dartmouth Col, 70-78; OWNER, LOGOI SYSTS, 78- *Concurrent Pos:* Ed, Calculi, 67-79; supvr repository of Greek & Latin texts in machine-readable form, Am Philol Asn, 69-; ed, Annual Bibliog, Comput & Humanities, 73-77. *Mem:* Am Philol Asn. *Res:* Ancient metrics; computer applications in literary studies; computerized typesetting. *Publ:* Co-ed, Basic, Univ Press New England, 6th ed, 71; auth, The contest of Vergil's Seventh Eclogue, Class Philol, 72; contribr, Approaches to metrical research in Plautus, In: The Computer and Literary Studies, Univ Edinburgh, 73; Homer and IMPRESS: Application to Greek metrics of a social-science analysis package, In: Computing in the Humanities, Proc 3rd Int Conf Comput in Humanities, Univ Waterloo, 8/77; Application of a vocabulary variety index to Homer and Vergil, Cahiers Lexicologie, 77; Hephaistos and the Muses: Effects of computers on literary studies, In: Humanismo y Technologia en el Mundo Actual, Actes Invest Humanistica, Madrid, 4/77 & 79. *Mailing Add:* 27 School St Hanover NH 03755

WAKEFIELD, RAY MILAN, b Fremont, Mich, Jan 30, 42; m 64; c 2. PHILOLOGY, NETHERLANDIC LITERATURE. *Educ:* Dartmouth Col, BA, 64; Ind Univ, Bloomington, MA, 66, PhD(Ger, dutch & Scand), 72. *Prof Exp:* Instr, 69-72, ASST PROF GER & DUTCH, UNIV MINN, MINNEAPOLIS, 72- *Mem:* MLA; Am Asn Teachers Ger; Int Ver Ned. *Res:* Comparative Germanic prosody; courtly Romance; third language learning. *Publ:* Auth, Nibelungen Prosody, Mouton, 76; Hadewijch: A Formalist's Dream, Dutch Crossings, 79; The Early Dutch-German Poetic Tradition, Amsterdammer, Berträgezur Älteren Germanistik, 79. *Mailing Add:* Dept of Ger Univ of Minnesota 303a Folwell Hall Minneapolis MN 55455

WALDAUER, JOSEPH L, b Memphis, Tenn, Nov 7, 26; m 62; c 2. FRENCH. *Educ:* Swarthmore Col, BA, 48; Columbia Univ, MA, 55, PhD, 62. *Prof Exp:* Instr French, Columbia Univ, 57-62; asst prof, Goucher Col, 62-63 & Amherst Col, 63-65; assoc prof, 65-69, PROF FRENCH, UNIV MINN, MINNEAPOLIS, 69- *Mem:* MLA; Am Soc 18th Century Studies; Soc Fr Etude XVIIIe Siecle. *Res:* Diderot; the novel; Rousseau. *Publ:* Auth, Society and the Freedom of the Creative Man in Diderot's Thought, Droz, 63. *Mailing Add:* Dept of French & Ital Univ of Minn Minneapolis MN 55455

WALDECK, PETER B, b Wyandotte, Mich, Apr 6, 40; m 66. GERMAN. *Educ:* Oberlin Col, BA, 62; Univ Conn, MA, 66, PhD(Ger), 67. *Prof Exp:* Asst prof Ger, Univ Mass, Amherst, 67-70; assoc prof, 70-80, PROF GER, SUSQUEHANNA UNIV, 80- *Mem:* MLA. *Res:* Hermann Broch; anxiety in literature. *Publ:* Auth, Kafka's Die Verwandlung and Ein Hungerkünstler as influenced by Leopold von Sacher-Masoch, Monatshefte, 72; Georg Büchner's Dantons Tod: Tragic structure and individual necessity, Susquehanna Studies, 74; Anxiety, tragedy and Hamlet's delay, In: Perspectives on Hamlet, Bucknell Univ, 74; The Split Self from Goethe to Broch, Bucknell Univ, 79. *Mailing Add:* Dept of Mod Lang Susquehanna Univ Selinsgrove PA 17870

WALDINGER, RENEE, b Aug 26, 27; US citizen; m 48; c 2. FRENCH LANGUAGE & LITERATURE. *Educ:* Hunter Col, BA, 48; Columbia Univ, MA, PhD(French), 53. *Prof Exp:* Lectr French, Queens Col, NY, 54-55; from instr to assoc prof, 57-70, chmn dept Romance lang, 70-76, PROF FRENCH, GRAD SCH & UNIV CTR, CITY UNIV OF NEW YORK, 72-, EXEC OFF, 81- *Concurrent Pos:* Nat Endowment for Humanities grant, Inst Contemp Cult, 82. *Honors & Awards:* Chevalier, Ordre Palmes Acad, 80. *Mem:* MLA; Am Asn Teachers Fr; Am Asn 18th Century Studies; AAUP. *Res:* French literature of the 18th century; pedagogy; French contemporary culture. *Publ:* Auth, Voltaire and reform in the light of the French Revolution, Droz, Geneva, 59; coauth, Promenades litteraires et grammaticales, Heath, 66; Lamartine and Voltaire, Fr Rev, 66; Voltaire and medicine, Studies Voltair & 18th Century, 67; Etapes litteraires, Am Bk, Vols I-III, 67-69; America: Another link in Voltaire's philosophic campaign, Ky Romance Quart, 69. *Mailing Add:* Romance Lang Dept Grad Sch & Univ Ctr New York NY 10036

WALDMAN, GLENYS A, b Philadelphia, Pa, March 24, 45. GERMANIC LANGUAGES, PENNSYLVANIA GERMAN. *Educ:* Oberlin Col, BA, 67; Univ Pa, MA, 70, PhD(Germanic lang), 75; Drexel Univ, MSLS, 78. *Prof Exp:* Ed asst for lang, Chilton Bks, Philadelphia, 67-68; lectr German & Fr, Cheyney State Col, 73-74, Rutgers Univ, 74-75 & Univ Pa, 75-76; LIBRN, HIST SOC PA, 77- *Mem:* MLA; Medieval Acad Am; Am Asn Teachers Ger. *Res:* Germanic philology, language and literature to 1500. *Publ:* Auth, Excerpts from a little encyclopaedia: The Wessobrunn Prayer Manuscript Clm 22053, Allegorica, Vol 2, No 2; trans, The Study of Incunables: Problems and aims, Philobiblon Club, 77; auth, The German and geographical glosses of the Wessobrunn Prayer Manuscript, Beitrage zur Namenforschung, NF, Bd 13, nr 3; The Scriptorium of the Wessobrunn Prayer Manuscript, Scriptorium, 32: 259-250; ed, Three letters of Thomas Mann to Franz Werfel and Alma Mahler-Werfel, Blätter der Thomas Mann Gesellschaft Zürich, 17: 5-8; A note on Horen, Hear, Germanic Notes, Vol 11, No 3; co-transl, Letters from our Palatine Ancestors, 1671-1709, The Eby Report, 82. *Mailing Add:* 100 Raynham Rd Merion Station PA 19066

WALKER, CHERYL L, b Elgin, Ill, Feb 17, 52. CLASSICAL LANGUAGES, ANCIENT HISTORY. *Educ:* Univ Chicago, BA, 73, Univ NC, MA, 76, PhD(classics), 80. *Prof Exp:* Teaching asst Latin, classics in transl, Univ NC, Chapel Hill, 74-79; instr Latin, Greek hist, Brandeis Univ, 79-80; ASST PROF ANCIENT HIST, CLASSICS IN TRANSL, LATIN & GREEK, BRANDEIS UNIV, 80- *Mem:* Class Asn New England. *Res:* Hostages in antiquity; Spartan women. *Publ:* Co-ed, Ancient History, Recently Publ Articles, Vols 6 & 7; contribr, Encyclopedia of Military Biography, T N Dupuy Assocs (in prep). *Mailing Add:* Dept of Class & Orient Studies Brandeis Univ Waltham MA 02254

WALKER, CLAIRE, b Oakland, Calif, Mar 24, 11; m 40; c 2. FOREIGN LANGUAGES. *Educ:* Mt Holyoke Col, BA, 31; Univ Buffalo, MA, 37. *Prof Exp:* Teacher, high sch, 33-37; teaching fel, Univ Minn, 38-40; teacher for lang, Friends Sch, Baltimore, Md, 47-75. *Concurrent Pos:* Soc Sci Res Coun grant, 41-44; founder, ed & chmn Russ comt, Nat Asn Independent Schs, 59-63, auth, Newsletter, 59-67, auth, Packet Serv, 60-; Am Friends Serv Comt exchange teacher, USSR, High Schs, 68; bd trustees, Friends Sch, 74-81. *Mem:* Am Asn Teachers Slavic & East Europ Lang (vpres, 61-64); Am Coun Teachers Russ (secy-treas, 75-81). *Res:* History, especially non-Western; Russian; theosophy. *Publ:* Ed, The Little House in the Swamp, 70 & Djel'somino in Liars Land, 74, Russian Packet, Friends Sch; auth, It doesn't have to end badly, Slavic & EEurop J, Vol X, No 3; Hear and understand, A T R Jour, Eng, No 17, 68. *Mailing Add:* Friends Sch 5114 N Charles St Baltimore MD 21210

WALKER, HALLAM, b Newark, NJ, May 23, 21; m 49; c 2. ROMANCE LANGUAGES. *Educ:* Princeton Univ, AB, 43, MA, 50, PhD(Romance lang), 52. *Prof Exp:* Instr French, Pa State Univ, 49-51; instr, Washington & Lee Univ, 53-54; asst prof, Duke Univ, 54-65; assoc prof, 65-72, PROF FRENCH & CHMN DEPT, DAVIDSON COL, 72- *Mem:* MLA; Am Asn Teachers Fr; SAtlantic Mod Lang Asn. *Res:* Classical French theater; nineteenth and twentieth centuries French novel and poetry. *Publ:* Auth, Moliere's Tartuffe, Prentice, 68; Moliere, Twayne, 71; Strength and style in Le bourgeois gentilhomme, Fr Rev, 1-64; Lex facheux and Moliere's use of games, L'Esprit Createur, summer 71; Visual and spatial imagery in Verlaine's Fetes galantes, PMLA, 10/72; Music and meaning in Baudelaire: The Thyrse image, French Lit Series, Univ SC, 77; Cyrano de Bergerac's solar science and fantasy, Helios Conf, State Univ New York Albany, 78. *Mailing Add:* Dept of French Davidson Col Davidson NC 28036

WALKER, JANET ANDERSON, b Milwaukee, Wis; m 67. COMPARATIVE & ASIAN LITERATURE. *Educ:* Univ Wis, Madison, BA, 65; Harvard Univ, AM, 68, PhD(comp lit), 74. *Prof Exp:* Asst prof, 71-77, ASSOC PROF COMP LIT, RUTGERS UNIV, 77- *Concurrent Pos:* Japan Found Short-term fel, 82-83. *Mem:* Am Comp Lit Asn; Int Comp Lit Asn; Int Courtly Lit Soc; Asn Asian Studies; Asn Teachers Japanese. *Res:* Japanese-Western literary relations; narrative East and West; courtly literature in Japan and Western Europe. *Publ:* Auth, Poetic ideal and fictional reality in the Izumi Shikibu Nikki, Harvard J Asiatic Studies, 6/77; The Japanese Novel of the Meiji Period and the Ideal of Individualism, Princeton Univ, 79; Conventions of Love Poetry in Japan and the West, J Asn Teachers of Japanese, 79. *Mailing Add:* Dept of Com Lit Rutgers Univ New Brunswick NJ 08903

WALKER, JOHN, b Dumbarton, Scotland, Aug 8, 33; m 60; c 3. HISPANIC & ENGLISH LITERATURE. *Educ:* Univ Glasgow, MA, 62; Univ London, BA, 70, PLD, 75. *Prof Exp:* Lectr Span, Brock Univ, 67-69; from asst prof to assoc prof, 69-77, PROF SPAN, QUEEN'S UNIV ONT, 77-, HEAD DEPT, 81- *Mem:* MLA; Asn Int Hispanistas; Inst Int Lit Iberoam; Am Asn Teachers Span & Port; Can Asn Hispanists. *Res:* Twentieth century novel in Latin America: Chile & Argentina; British writers of the River Plate region; the work of R B Cunninghame Graham. *Publ:* Auth, Gran Snor y Rajadiablos: A shift in sensibility, Bull Hisp Studies, 7/72; Bernard Shaw and Don Roberto, Sahw Rev, 9/72; Tamarugal: Barrios' neglected link novel, Rev Estudios Hisp, 10/74; Paginas de un pobre diablo: The light in the darkness, Ibero-Am Arch, 1/77; Schopenhauer and Nietzsche in the work of Eduardo Barrios, Rev Can Estudios Hisp, autumn 77; Los hombres del hombre: Barrios' final comment, Am Hispanist, 10/77; The South American Sketches of R B Cunninghame Graham, Univ Okla, 78; Anacronismo y novedad en Ednardo Barrios, Anaderaos Americanos, 6/81; The Scottish sketches of R B Cunningham Graham, Scottish Acad Press, 82. *Mailing Add:* Dept of Span & Ital Queen's Univ Kingston ON K7L 3N6 Can

WALKER, LARRY L, b Ft Wayne, Ind, July 11, 32; m 57; c 5. OLD TESTAMENT, SEMITICS. *Educ:* Bob Jones Univ, BA, 55; Northern Baptist Theol Sem, BD, 58; Wheaton Col, MA, 59; Dropsie Univ, PhD(Assyriol), 67. *Prof Exp:* Asst prof, 66-71, ASSOC PROF OLD TESTAMENT, SOUTHWESTERN BAPTIST THEOL SEM, 71- *Res:* Old Testament; Assyriology; ancient languages. *Mailing Add:* Old Testament Dept Southwestern Baptist Theol Seminary Ft Worth TX 76122

WALKER, PHILIP DOOLITTLE, b Newburyport, Mass, Oct 10, 24; m 52; c 3. FRENCH. *Educ:* Yale Univ, BA, 47, MA, 51, PhD, 56. *Prof Exp:* Asst instr French, Yale Univ, 53-54; instr, Lawrence Col, 54-57; from instr to assoc prof, 57-70, assoc dir univ studies ctr, Bordeaux, France, 62-63, chmn dept French & Ital, 71-75, PROF FRENCH, UNIV CALIF, SANTA BARBARA, 70- *Concurrent Pos:* Guggenheim Mem Found fel, 67-68. *Mem:* Am Asn Teachers Fr; MLA. *Res:* Nineteenth century French literature; the art of fiction; literature and religion. *Publ:* Auth, Prophetic myths in Zola, 9/59, The Ebauche of Germinal, 65, PMLA; Emile Zola, Routledge & Kegan Paul, 68; The mirror, the window, and the eye in Zola's fiction, 69 & Zola, myth and the birth of the modern world, 69, Yale Fr Studies; Zola's Hellenism, The Persistent Voice, NY Univ, 71; Zola et la lutte avec L'ange, 71 & Germinal et la pensee religieuse de Zola, 76, Cahiers Naturalistes. *Mailing Add:* Dept of French & Ital Univ of Calif Santa Barbara CA 93106

WALKER, STEVEN FRIEMEL, b Washington, DC, Mar 28, 44; m 66. COMPARATIVE LITERATURE. *Educ:* Univ Wis-Madison, BA, 65; Harvard Univ, MA, 66, PhD(comp lit), 73. *Prof Exp:* Asst prof, 71-79, ASSOC PROF COMP LIT, RUTGERS UNIV, 79- *Mem:* Am Comp Lit Asn; MLA; Asn Asian Studies. *Res:* Renaissance love poetry; 19th century literature; pastoral poetry. *Publ:* Auth, Pastoral and Kalidasa's Cloud Messenger, Lit East & West, 77; Mallarme's symbolist eclogue, PMLA, 1/78; The conflict of Theocritean and Petrarchan Topoi in the Shepheardes Calender, Studies in Philol, fall 79; Marvell's To His Coy Mistress, Explicator, fall 79; The orribile and the pastorale in literature and music from Poliziano to Berlioz, Proc 9th Cong Int Comp Lit Asn, 79; Theocritus: A Critical Introduction, Twayne Publ, 80; Gongora's Soledad Primera, Ky Romance Quart, 81; Vivekananda in America, In: The Occult Experience in America, Univ Ill Press, 82. *Mailing Add:* 77 Lincoln Ave Highland Park NJ 08904

WALKER, WILLARD, b Boston, Mass, July 29, 26; m 52; c 2. ANTHROPOLOGY, LINGUISTICS. *Educ:* Harvard Univ, AB, 50; Univ Ariz, MA, 53; Cornell Univ, PhD(gen ling), 64. *Prof Exp:* Res assoc, Univ Chicago Carnegie Cross-Cult Educ Proj, Tahlequah, Okla, 64-66; from asst prof to assoc prof anthrop, 66-77, PROF ANTHROP, WESLEYAN UNIV, 77- *Mem:* Am Anthrop Asn; Ling Soc Am; Soc Appl Anthrop; Am Ethnol Soc; Am Soc Ethnohist. *Res:* North American Indian languages; ethnology of North America; native writing systems. *Publ:* Auth, Toward the sound pattern of Zuni, Int J Am Ling, 72; The Proto-Algonquians, Peter Ridder, Lisse, 75; Cherokee in Studies in Southeastern Indian Languages, Univ Ga, 75; Zuni semantic categories, In: Handbook of North American Indians, Vol 9, Smithsonian Inst, 79; coauth, A chronological account of the Wabanaki Confederacy, In: Political Organization of Native North Americans, Univ Press Am, 80; auth, Native American writing systems, In: Language in the USA, Cambridge Univ Press, 81; Cherokee curing and conjuring, identity, and the southeastern co-tradition, In: Persistent Peoples, Univ Az, 81. *Mailing Add:* Dept of Anthrop Wesleyan Univ Middletown CT 06457

WALL, ROBERT EUGENE, b Mulberry Grove, Ill, Oct 20, 36. LINGUISTICS. *Educ:* Univ Ill, BS, 57; Harvard Univ, MA, 58, PhD(chem), 61. *Prof Exp:* Mem res staff ling, Int Bus Machines Res Lab, 63-65; asst prof, Ind Univ, 65-67; fac assoc, 67-69, ASSOC PROF LING, UNIV TEX, AUSTIN, 69- *Concurrent Pos:* Nat Sci Found fel, Harvard Univ, 61-63; managing ed, Ling & Philos, 76- *Mem:* Ling Soc Am. *Res:* Syntax; semantics. *Publ:* Auth, Introduction to Mathematical Linguistics, Prentice-Hall, 72. *Mailing Add:* Dept of Ling Univ of Tex Austin TX 78712

WALLACE, KRISTINE GILMARTIN, b Detroit, Mich, Feb 14, 41; m. CLASSICS. *Educ:* Bryn Mawr Col, BA, 63; Stanford Univ, MA, 65, PhD(classics), 67. *Prof Exp:* Instr classics, Rice Univ, 66-67; asst prof, Vassar Col, 67-69; asst prof, 69-74, ASSOC PROF CLASSICS, RICE UNIV, 74- *Mem:* Am Philol Asn; Archaeol Inst Am. *Res:* Roman poetry; Tacitus. *Publ:* Auth, Talthybius in the Trojan Women, Am J Philol, 70; Corbulo's campaigns in the East, Historia, 73; Tacitean evidence for Tacitean style, Classical J, 74; A rhetorical figure in Latin historical style: The imaginary second person singular, Trans Am Philol Asn, 75; The Thraso-Gnatho subplot in Terence's Eunuchus, Classical World, 75/76. *Mailing Add:* Dept of Classics Rice Univ Houston TX 77001

WALLACE, MALCOLM VINCENT TIMOTHY, b Pittsfield, Mass, Oct 3, 15; m 43; c 3. CLASSICS. *Educ:* St Bonaventure Col, AB, 36; Univ Buffalo, EdM, 47; Harvard Univ, AM, 49, PhD, 55. *Prof Exp:* Instr classics, 50-51, prof, 51-81, EMER PROF CLASSICS, ST BONAVENTURE UNIV, 81- *Concurrent Pos:* Ed, Cithara, 61-63. *Mem:* Am Philol Asn; Vergilian Soc; Classical Asn Atlantic States. *Res:* Greek historiography; Latin epigraphy; Greek and Latin literature. *Publ:* Architecture of the Punica: A hypothesis, Classical Philol, 4/58; Some aspects of Time in the Punica of Silius Italicus, Classical World, 11/68; The Wodehouse world I: Classical echoes, Cithara, 5/73. *Mailing Add:* 3276 West State Rd Olean NY 14760

WALLACE, NATHANIEL OWEN, Comparative Literature, Classical Languages. See Vol II

WALLACE, PAUL WALTER, b Washington, Ind, May 25, 38; c 2. GREEK ARCHEOLOGY & HISTORY. *Educ:* David Lipscomb Col, BA, 62; Ind Univ, Bloomington, MA, 63, PhD(classics), 69. *Prof Exp:* Asst prof classics, Dartmouth Col, 68-72; ASSOC PROF CLASSICS, STATE UNIV NY ALBANY, 73- *Mem:* Asn Ancient Hist; Archaeol Inst Am. *Res:* Greek topography and archaeology; Cypriot archaeology. *Publ:* Auth, Psyttaleia and the trophies of the Battle of Salamis, Am J Archaeol, 69; Strabo on Acrocorinth, 69 & The Tomb of Themistokles in the Piraeus, 72, Hesperia; Hesiod and the valley of the muses, Greek, Roman & Byzantine Studies, 74; The route of the Dorian Invasion, Athens Ann Archaeol, 78; Strabo's Description of Boiotia: A Commentary, Heidelberg, 79; The Anopaia path at Thermopylai, Am J Archaeol, 80; The final battle at Plataia, Suppl 19, Hesperia, 82. *Mailing Add:* Dept of Classics State Univ NY Albany NY 12222

WALLACH, BARBARA PRICE, b Roanoke, Va, Aug 31, 46; m 70. CLASSICAL PHILOLOGY, HUMANITIES. *Educ:* Mary Washington Col, BA, 68; Univ Ill, Urbana, AM, 70, PhD(class philol), 74. *Prof Exp:* Vis lectr Latin, Univ Ill, Urbana, 77; ASST PROF CLASS STUDIES, UNIV MO-COLUMBIA, 77- *Mem:* Am Philol Asn; Women's Caucus Am Philol Asn; Soc Ancient Greek Philols: Class Asn Midwest & South. *Res:* Latin literature; ancient rhetoric and literary criticism; Hellenistic Greek literature. *Publ:* Auth, Lucretius and the Diatribe, De Rerum Natura, II, Beitrage L Wallach Gewidmet, 75; Lucretius and the Diatribe Against the Fear of Death, De Rerum Natura, II, Brill, 76; Response to George Kustas, Diatribe in ancient rhetorical theory, Protocol 22nd Colloquy, Ctr Hermeneutical Studies, 76; Deiphilus of Polydorus: The ghost in Pacuvius' Iliona, Mnemosyne, 78. *Mailing Add:* Dept of Class Studies Univ of Mo Columbia MO 65201

WALLACH, LUITPOLD, b Munich, Bavaria, Ger, Feb 6, 10; US citizen; m 70. CLASSICS, MEDIEVAL LATIN. *Educ:* Univ Tuebingen, DPhil(hist), 32; Cornell Univ, PhD(classics), 47. *Prof Exp:* Asst prof classics, Hamilton Col, 51-52; asst prof hist, Univ Ore, 53; asst prof classics, Cornell Univ, 53-55; asst prof, Univ Okla, 55-57; asst prof, Harpur Col, 57-62; prof, Marquette Univ, 62-67; prof, 67-78, EMER PROF CLASSICS, UNIV ILL, URBANA, 78- *Concurrent Pos:* Fund Advan Educ fel, 52; Am Coun Learned Soc grant, 60; mem bd, Grad Sch, Marquette Univ, 63-67; fac fel, 67; Leo Baeck Inst fel, 67; assoc, Ctr Advan Studies, Univ Ill, 69-70. *Honors & Awards:* Festschrift: Beitraege Luitpold Wallach Gewidmet, Hiersemann, Stuttgart, 75. *Mem:* Am Philol Asn; AHA; Mediaeval Acad Am. *Res:* Philology; mediaeval Latin and history. *Publ:* Auth, Berthold of Zwiefalten's Chronicle, Fordham Univ, 58; Liberty and Letters, E & W Libr, London, 59; Alcuin and Charlemagne, Cornell Univ, 59, Johnson reprint, 2nd ed, 68; auth & ed, The Classical Tradition, 66 & Diplomatic Studies in Carolingian Documents, 77, Cornell Univ; auth, Die Zwiefalter Chroniken, Thorbecke, Sigmaringen, Ger, 2nd ed, 78; The Roman Synod of December 800, Harvard Theol Rev, 49: 123-144; The Greek and Latin versions of II Nicea, Traditio, XXII: 103-125. *Mailing Add:* Dept of Classics Univ of Ill Urbana IL 61801

WALLACKER, BENJAMIN E, b San Francisco, Calif, Nov 27, 26. EAST ASIAN PHILOLOGY. *Educ:* Univ Calif, Berkeley, AB, 50, MA, 54, PhD (Orient lang), 60. *Prof Exp:* Instr Chinese, Univ Kans, 59-60, from asst prof to assoc prof Orient lang, 60-64; assoc prof, 64-69, PROF ORIENT LANG, UNIV CALIF, DAVIS, 70- *Mem:* Am Orient Soc; Asn Asian Studies. *Res:* The art of war in traditional China; the growth of imperial institutions in Former Han; the development of law in early China. *Publ:* Coauth, Local tribe products of the T'ang dynasty, J Orient Studies, 57-58; auth, The Huai-nantzu, Book Eleven: Behavior, Culture, and the Cosmos, Am Orient Soc, 62; Studies in medieval Chinese siegecraft, J Asian Studies & J Asian Hist, 70-71; Liu An, second king of Huai-nan, J Am Orient Soc, 72; contribr, The Dict of Ming Biography, Columbia Univ, 76; Han confucianism and confucius in Han, In: Ancient China: Studies in Early Civilization & co-ed, Chinese Walled Cities, 79, Chinese Univ Hong Kong; The poet as jurist: Po Chü-i and a case of conjugal homicide, Harvard J Asiatic Studies, 81. *Mailing Add:* Dept of Anthrop Univ of Calif Davis CA 95616

WALLIS, RICHARD TYRRELL, b Woburn, England, Aug 12, 41. CLASSICS, ANCIENT PHILOSOPHY. *Educ:* Cambridge Univ, BA, 62, MA, 66, PhD(classics), 67. *Prof Exp:* Jr res fel classics, Churchill Col, Cambridge Univ, 65-69; asst prof, 70-80, ASSOC PROF CLASSICS, UNIV OKLA, 80- *Mem:* Am Philol Asn. *Res:* Neoplatonic philosophy. *Publ:* Auth, Neoplatonism, Duckworth, UK & Scribners, US, 72. *Mailing Add:* Dept of Classics Univ of Oklahoma Norman OK 73069

WALPOLE, RONALD NOEL, b Monmouthshire, England, Dec 24, 03; m 34; c 1. ROMANCE PHILOLOGY & LITERATURE. *Educ:* Univ Col, Cardiff, BA, 25; Univ Wales, MA, 36; Univ Calif, PhD, 39. *Prof Exp:* From instr to prof, 39-71, chmn dept, 57-63, EMER PROF FRENCH, UNIV CALIF, BERKELEY, 71- *Concurrent Pos:* Guggenheim traveling fel, 49-50. *Honors & Awards:* Chevalier, Legion d'honneur, 62. *Mem:* Mediaeval Acad Am; Philol Asn Pac Coast; fel Am Acad Arts & Sci. *Res:* The Old French translations of the Pseudo-Turpin Chronicle; Carolingian legend and early French historiography. *Publ:* Auth, Charlemagne and Roland, A Study of Two Middle English Metrical Romances, Roland and Vernagu-Otuel and Roland & Philip Mouskes and the Pseudo-Turpin Chronicle, Univ Calif Publ Mod Philol; Sur la Chronique du Pseudo-Turpin, 65 & Le sens moral de la Chanson de Roland, In: Travaux de Linguistique it de litterature, Ctr Philol & Roman Lit, Univ Strasbourg, 66; The Old French Johannes Translation of the Pseudo-Turpin Chronicle, A Critical Edition, Univ of Calif, 76; An Anonymous Old French Translation of the Pseudo-Turpin Chronicle, Mediaeval Acad Am, 79. *Mailing Add:* 1680 La Loma Ave Berkeley CA 94709

WALSH, JOHN KEVIN, b New York, NY, Aug 10, 39. MEDIEVAL SPANISH LITERATURE, SPANISH LINGUISTICS. *Educ:* Univ Notre Dame, AB, 61; Univ Madrid, dipl, 62; Columbia Univ, MA, 64; Univ Va, PhD(Span), 67. *Prof Exp:* From instr to asst prof Span, Univ Va, 66-69; asst prof, 69-75, assoc prof, 75-78, PROF SPAN, UNIV CALIF, BERKELEY, 78- *Mem:* MLA; Am Asn Teachers Span & Port. *Res:* Hispanic linguistics; Garcia Lorca. *Publ:* Auth, The Hispano-Oriental derivational suffix-i, Romance Philol, 72; ed, El Libro de Los Doze Sabios, Madrid, Real Academia Espanola, 75; co-ed, Vida de Santa Maria Egipciaca, Univ Exeter, 77; auth, The chivalric dragon, Bull Hisp Studies, 77; Versiones peninsulares del Kitab Adab AlFalasifa, Al-Andalus, 76. *Mailing Add:* Dept of Span & Port Univ of Calif Berkeley CA 94720

WALTER, RENEE, b Senta, Yugoslavia, Jan 15, 30. SPANISH & HISPANO-AMERICAN LITERATURE. *Educ:* Univ of the Repub, Uruguay, BABS, 56; Brooklyn Col, BA, 62; Univ Poitiers, dipl, 65; NY Univ, MA, 65, PhD(Span lang & lit), 69. *Prof Exp:* Instr Span lang & lit, Brooklyn Col, 63-65; Fulbright scholar, Spain, 66-68; asst prof, 68-73, ASSOC PROF SPAN & HISP AM LIT, GUSTAVUS ADOLPHUS COL, 73- *Mem:* MLA; Asn Span Writers. *Res:* Spanish Golden Age; 16th century European history; Reformation and counterreformation. *Publ:* Auth, Cristobal de Castillejo, hombre del renacimiento, Ed Planeta, Barcelona; Poems, Castillos Espana, Spain, 67 & 68; La tumba de Cristobal de Castillejo, ABC, 7/69; Pertenece Orlando Lasso a la familia de Petro Lasso?, Annuario Musical, 70; Un cuarto siglo de silencio, Urogallo, 8-9/70; Relaciones Italianas de Cristobal de Castillejo, 70. *Mailing Add:* Dept of Spanish Gustavus Adolphus Col St Peter MN 56082

WALTERS, ROBERT LOWELL, b Canton, Ohio, Nov 20, 21; m 62; c 1. FRENCH. *Educ:* Oberlin Col, BA, 43; Princeton Univ, AM, 47, PhD(mod lang), 55. *Prof Exp:* Instr French, Ind Univ, 46-48 & Princeton Univ, 50-51; asst prof, Univ Man, 51-63; asst prof, 63-64, assoc prof, 64-78, PROF FRENCH, UNIV WESTERN ONT, 78- *Res:* Voltaire; science and literature, 18th century French literature. *Publ:* Auth, Chemistry at Cirey, Studies Voltaire & 18th Century, 67; Voltaire, Newton & the reading public, In: The Triumph of Culture: 18th Century Perspectives, Hakkert, Amsterdam, 72. *Mailing Add:* Dept of French Univ of Western Ontario London ON N6A 5B8 Can

WALTERS, STANLEY DAVID, Religion, Ancient Languages. See Vol IV

WALTHER, DON H, b Shandon, Ohio, Mar 30, 16; m 37; c 2. SPANISH, PORTUGUESE. *Educ:* Miami Univ, AB, 38; Univ NC, MA, 40, PhD, 48. *Prof Exp:* Spec agent, FBI, 42-46; from instr to asst prof Span & Port, Univ NC, 46-50; with CIA, 50-52; attache, US Embassy, Madrid, Spain, 52-56; chief training, Armed Forces Exp Training Activity, 56-57; assoc prof Span & Port, 57-60, head dept mod lang, 62-78, PROF SPAN & PORT, PURDUE UNIV, 60- *Mem:* MLA; Am Asn Teachers Span & Port. *Res:* Brazilian and Portuguese literature; Spanish contemporary novel. *Publ:* Auth, The critics and O Missionario, In: Romance Studies Presented to William Morton Dey, Univ NC, 50. *Mailing Add:* Dept of Mod Lang Purdue Univ West Lafayette IN 47907

WALTHER, JAMES ARTHUR, New Testament. See Vol IV

WALTHER, MAUD SUSIE, b France, Sept 16, 35; c 2. FRENCH LITERATURE & CINEMA. *Educ:* Sorbonne, Dr(comp lit), 72. *Prof Exp:* Teacher French, French High Schs, 59-65; vis instr, 65-67, from instr to asst prof, 68-75, chairperson French & Ital, 77-79, asst, Equal Employ Opportunity, 79-81, ASSOC PROF FRENCH, PURDUE UNIV, 75- *Concurrent Pos:* Fullbright scholar, 65-67. *Honors & Awards:* Palmes Academiques, 79. *Mem:* MLA; Int Comp Lit Asn; Am Asn Teachers Fr:. *Res:* French literature; French cinema; French civilization. *Publ:* Auth, La Presence de Stendhal aux Etats-Unis 1818-1920, Le Grand-Chene, Aran, Switz, 74; co-ed, Purdue Film Studies Annual, Purdue Res Found, 76. *Mailing Add:* Dept of Foreign Lang & Lit Purdue Univ West Lafayette IN 47907

WALTMAN, FRANKLIN MCCLURE, b Clearfield, Pa, Sept 5, 38; m 66; c 2. SPANISH. *Educ:* Lycoming Col, BA, 66; Pa State Univ, MA, 67, PhD(Span), 71. *Prof Exp:* From asst prof to assoc prof, 70-76, PROF SPAN INT COMMUN & CULT, STATE UNIV NY COL CORTLAND, 77- *Honors & Awards:* Hisp Award for Best Article, Am Asn Teachers of Span & Port, 73; State Univ NY Chancellor Award, 74. *Mem:* Am Asn Teachers of Span & Port; Societe Rencesvals. *Res:* Medieval Spanish epic; Juan Fernandez de Heredia; literary research through computers. *Publ:* Auth, Formulaic expression and unity of authorship in the Poema de Mio Cid, 73 & Synonym choice in the Cantar de Mio Cid, 74, Hispania; Divided heroic vision or dual-authorship in the CMC, Romance Notes, 75; Similarities in the three cantares of CMC, Hispania, 76; CLAS and the cantar de Mio Cid, Comput in Humanities, 76; Verb tenses in the CMC, Ky Romance Quart, 77; Parallel expressions in the CMC, Bull Hisp Studies, 78; ed, Concordance to Flor de las ystorias de orient, Part 3, 82 & Grant cronica de Espanya, Part 3, 82, Hisp Sem Medieval Studies. *Mailing Add:* 163 Madison St Cortland NY 13045

WALTON, GERALD WAYNE, English. See Vol II

WALTON, JOHN HARVEY, Old Testament, Semitic Languages. See Vol IV

WALTON, SARAH LUVERNE, b Nash, Okla, Jan 13, 21. GERMAN. *Educ:* Univ Okla, BS, 46; Columbia Univ, MA, 49; Ind Univ, Bloomington, MA, 64, PhD (Ger), 66. *Prof Exp:* Asst prof educ & assoc dean students, Southwestern Tex State Col, 52-62; teaching asst Ger, Ind Univ, Bloomington, 62-64; instr, DePauw Univ, 64-65; asst prof, 66-68, chmn dept Germanic & Slavic lang, 68-69 & 72-76, ASSOC PROF GER, UNIV MO-COLUMBIA, 68- *Concurrent Pos:* Univ Mo-Columbia res grants, 68 & 72; Ger Acad Exchange Serv stipend, 72. *Mem:* MLA; Am Asn Teachers Ger; Int Arthur Schnitzler Res Asn; Am Asn Univ Women. *Res:* Modern German drama; Arthur Schnitzler; 20th century German literature. *Publ:* Auth, Anatol on the New York stage, Mod Austrian Lit, 69; Theatre research in New York, Mo Libr Asn Quart, 69. *Mailing Add:* Dept of Ger & Slavic Lang Univ of Missouri Columbia MO 65201

WANAMAKER, MURRAY GORHAM, b St John, NB, Aug 17, 20; m 51; c 2. ENGLISH, LINGUISTICS. *Educ:* Acadia Univ, BA, 41, BEd, 42; Queen's Univ, Ont, MA, 49; Univ Mich, EdD(English), 65. *Prof Exp:* Lectr English, Acadia Univ, 52-54, from asst prof to prof, 54-66; assoc prof, 66-73, PROF ENGLISH, UNITED COL, UNIV WINNIPEG, 73- *Concurrent Pos:* Mem bd dirs, Can Fedn of Humanities, 77. *Mem:* Can Coun Teachers English; Asn Can Univ Teachers English; Can Ling Asn; NCTE; Am Dialect Soc. *Res:* History of English; dialectology; American literature. *Publ:* Auth, Canadian English: Whence? Whither?, J Educ, 11/59; Your dialect is showing, In: Looking at Language, W J Gage, Toronto, 66; Dialectology, In: Introductory Essays in Linguistics, Univ Victoria, 67; coauth, A revised phonetic alphabet proposed by the Maritime Dialect Survey, J Int Phonetic Asn, 73; auth, Who controls writing standards, Eng Quart, winter 76-77; The Language of Kings County, Nova Scotia, J Atlantic Provinces Ling Asn, 80. *Mailing Add:* Dept of English Univ of Winnipeg Winnipeg MB R3B 2E9 Can

WANDEL, JOSEPH, b Duisburg, Ger, Jan 4, 18; US citizen; m 52; c 4. GERMAN. *Educ:* Marquette Univ, MA, 58; Northwestern Univ, PhD(Ger), 65. *Prof Exp:* Instr, 58-65, asst prof, 65-79, ASSOC PROF GER, LOYOLA UNIV, ILL, 79- *Mem:* MLA; Am Asn Teachers Ger. *Res:* Modern German literature; the role of the German in American history and in present-day American society. *Publ:* Auth, Brecht and his A effect, Drama Critique, spring 67; The German Dimension of American History, Nelson-Hall, Chicago, 79. *Mailing Add:* Dept of Mod Lang Loyola Univ Chicago IL 60611

WANG, FRED FANGYU, b Peiping, China, Feb 2, 13; US citizen; m 56; c 1. FAR EASTERN LANGUAGES. *Educ:* Cath Univ, BA, 36; Columbia Univ, MA, 46. *Hon Degrees:* LLD, SChina Univ, Macao, 69. *Prof Exp:* Instr Chinese, Yale Univ, 45-65; res prof, Steton Hall Univ 66-67, assoc prof, 68-69, chmn dept Asian Studies & non-western civilization, 69-76, prof, Chinese lang & cult, 69-80. *Concurrent Pos:* Consult Chinese-English mach transl, Int Bus Mach Corp, 62-64; consult Chinese-Japanese-Korean, three lang photo-composing mach, Radio Corp Am, 63-68 & Appleton-Century-Crofts, 67. *Mem:* Chinese Lang Teachers Asn; Am Asn Teachers Chinese Lang & Cult. *Res:* Chinese linguistics and language teaching; history of Chinese art; Chinese literature and performing art. *Publ:* Auth, Chinese Dialogues, 51, Read Chinese, Vol I, 53, Vol II, 61 & Chinese Cursive Script, 58, Yale Far East; Mandarin Chinese Dictionary, Seton Hall Univ, 67; Mandarin Chinese Dictionary, Chinese to English, 69 & English to Chinese, 71; Introduction to Literary Chinese, 72. *Mailing Add:* 12 Farmstead Rd Short Hills NJ 07078

WANG, JOHN B, b Shantung, China, OCt 18, 28. SPANISH, LAW. *Educ:* Univ Zaragoza, PhB, 50; Pontif Lateran Univ, LLD, 59; Univ Fla, MAT, 63; Univ Md, PhD(Span), 67. *Prof Exp:* Prof philos, St Leo Col, 60-64, prof theol & law, 60-64; teacher, Priory Sch, Washington, DC, 64-65; asst Span, Univ Md, 65-66, instr, 66-67; asst prof, 67-73, assoc prof Span & Chinese, 73-78, PROF CHINESE LANG & LIT, UNIV MONT, 79- *Concurrent Pos:* Exec comt, Pac Northwest Coun Foreign Lang, 76-78. *Mem:* Canon Law Soc Am; Am Asn Teachers Span & Port; MLA; AAUP; Chinese Lang Teachers Asn. *Res:* Comparative literature; East-West cultural relations; cultural history. *Publ:* Auth, De Vita Seminariorum Sinensium, La Editorial, Zaragoza, 60; La poetica de fray Luis de Leon, Revista de Estudios Hispanicos, 4/70; Intermision O Paraxismo, Pueblos del Tercer Mundo, 11/71; Un decaconio espanol, MFLTA Bull, 12/71; La Estetica Rimadora de fray Luis, 72 & Don Juan disparatado, 73, Proc Pac Northwest Conf Foreign Lang; Religious Vacuum on Mainland China, Christianity Today, 11/77. *Mailing Add:* Dept of Foreign Lang & Lit Univ of Mont Missoula MT 59801

WANG, JOHN CHING-YU, b Honan, China, Nov 20, 34; m 64; c 2. CHINESE LANGUAGE & LITERATURE. *Educ:* Nat Taiwan Univ, BA, 57; Univ Minn, MA, 62; Cornell Univ, PhD (Chinese & English), 68. *Prof Exp:* Instr Chinese, Univ Iowa, 62-63; from lectr to asst prof, Univ Mich, 66-69; asst prof, 69-72, assoc prof, 72-82, PROF CHINESE, STANFORD UNIV, 82- *Concurrent Pos:* Fulbright-Hays Fac Res Abroad fel, 75-76; Am Coun Learned Soc fel, 75-76. *Mem:* MLA; Asn Asian Studies; Chinese Lang Teachers Asn. *Res:* Chinese literature and literary criticism; general literary criticism; myth. *Publ:* Auth, Chin Sheng-t'an, Twayne, 72; Fiction criticism in traditional China, Lit East & West, 72; coauth, The Lin-ch'i dialect and its relation to Mandarin, J Am Orient Soc, 73; auth, The nature of Chinese narrative: A preliminary statement on methodology, Tamkang Rev, 75-76; The cyclical view of life and meaning in the traditional Chinese novel, Etudies D'Hist & Lit Chinoises, 76; The Chih-yen Chai commentary and the Dream of the Red Chamber: A literary study, In: Chinese Approaches to Literature, 77; Early Chinese narrative: The Tso-chuan as example, In: Chinese Narrative, 77. *Mailing Add:* Dept of Asian Lang Stanford Univ Stanford CA 94305

WANG, LEONARD JUDAH, b New York, NY, Mar 9, 26; m 49; c 3. FRENCH. *Educ:* City Col New York, BA, 47; Columbia Univ, MA, 48, PhD(French), 55. *Prof Exp:* Lectr French, Columbia Univ, 48-53, instr, 53-55, 57-58; instr, Queens Col, NY, 55-57; from instr to assoc prof Romance lang, 58-70, PROF ROMANCE LANG, NEWARK COL, RUTGERS UNIV, 70- *Mem:* MLA; Soc Etude XVII Siecle. *Res:* History of ideas in seventeenth century France; seventeenth century French theatre ecclesiastical history; old Provencal literature. *Publ:* Auth, A controversial biography--Baillet's La Vie de Monsieur Des-Cartes, Romanische Forsch, 3rd quarter, 63; Une compilaton controversee--Les Vies des Saints de Baillet, 66 & La querelle des jugemens des Scavans d'Adrien Baillet (1685-1691), 69, XVIIe Siecle; coauth, Le Voyage Imaginaire, Macmillan, 70. *Mailing Add:* 1064 E 27th St Brooklyn NY 11210

WANG, STEPHEN S, b Nanking, China, June 30, 34; US citizen; m 58; c 1. SINO-TIBETAN LINGUISTICS. *Educ:* Fresno State Col, BA, 55; Univ Calif, Berkeley, MA, 63; Univ Wash, PhD(Far Eastern lang), 66. *Prof Exp:* From asst prof to assoc prof, 65-74, PROF E ASIAN LANG, UNIV MINN, MINNEAPOLIS, 74- *Mem:* Ling Soc Am; Am Orient Soc. *Res:* Tibetan linguistics; Chinese linguistics. *Mailing Add:* Dept of East Asian Lang Univ of Minn Minneapolis MN 55455

WANG, WILLIAM S Y, b Shanghai, China, Aug 14, 33; US citizen; m 73; c 4. LINGUISTICS. *Educ:* Columbia Col, AB, 55; Univ Mich, MA, 56, PhD(ling), 60. *Prof Exp:* Mem staff, Res Lab Electronics, Mass Inst Technol, 60; instr commun sci & res assoc, Commun Sci Lab, Univ Mich, 60-61; mem staff, Int Bus Machines Res Ctr, 61; asst prof ling & chmn dept Eastern Asian lang & lit, Ohio State Univ, 61-63, assoc prof ling, 62-65, chmn div, 62-65; PROF LING, UNIV CALIF, BERKELEY, 65- *Concurrent Pos:* Nat Sci Found res grant, 61; Ohio State Univ grant to establish ling res lab, 62; fel ling, Ctr Advan Studies Behav Sci, 69-70; Fulbright prof ling, Sweden, 71-72; ed, J Chinese Ling, 73-; Guggenheim fel, 78. *Mem:* Charter mem Am Asn Phonetic Sci; Ling Soc Am; MLA; Acoust Soc Am. *Res:* Languages; speech. *Publ:* Over 80 publications in various Journals. *Mailing Add:* Dept of Ling Univ of Calif Berkeley CA 94720

WANNER, DIETER, b Bern, Switzerland, Aug 8, 43. ROMANCE & GENERAL LINGUISTICS. *Educ:* Univ Zürich, DPhil(Romance ling), 68. *Prof Exp:* Asst pro, 70-75, ASSOC PROF SPAN, ITAL & LING, UNIV ILL, URBANA-CHAMPAIGN, 75- *Mem:* Ling Soc Am; MLA. *Res:* Italian linguistics; Romance linguistics; historical linguistics. *Publ:* Auth, The derivation of inflectional paradigms in Italian, In: Generative Studies in Romance Languages, Newbury House, 72; The evolution of Romance clitic order, In: Linguistic Studies in Romance Languages, Georgetown Univ, 74; Die historische Motivierung der Endungiamo im Italienischen, ZrPh, 75; co-ed, Diachronic Studies in Romance Linguistics, Mouton, The Hague, 75; On the order of clitics in Italian, Lingua, 77; Die Bewahrung der lateinischen Hauptton stelle im Romanischen, Vox Romanica, Vol 37, 79; Surface complementizes deletion: Italian che-o, J of Ital Ling, Vol 6, 81; A history of Spanish clitic movement, Berkeley Linguistics Soc, Vol 8, 82. *Mailing Add:* Dept of Span Ital & Port 4080 FLB Univ of Ill Urbana IL 61801

WARD, ALLEN MASON, Ancient History, Classics. See Vol I

WARD, DONALD JAMES, b Petaluma, Calif, Mar 16, 30; m 58; c 2. GERMANIC LANGUAGES, FOLKLORE. *Educ:* San Francisco State Col, AB, 59; Univ Calif, Los Angeles, MA, 61, PhD(Ger), 65. *Prof Exp:* Instr Ger, Univ Calif, Riverside, 63-65; from asst prof to assoc prof, 65-73, dir, Ctr Study Comp Folklore & Mythol, 74-78, PROF GER, UNIV CALIF, LOS ANGELES, 73- *Concurrent Pos:* Assoc dir, Univ Calif Study Ctr, Univ Göttingen, 69-71; Alexander von Humboldt Found fel, 71-72; assoc ed, Fabula, 75-; Fulbright research scholar, Freiburg, WGer, 78-79. *Mem:* Am Folklore Soc; Int Soc Folk Narrative Res; Int Soc Ethnol & Folklore; Am Asn Teachers Ger. *Publ:* Auth, The Divine Twins, Univ Calif, 68; The fiddler and the beast, Fabula, 72; Nochmals Kudrun: Ballade und Epos, Jahrbuch für Volkslied Forsch, 72; Scherz und Spottlieder, Handbuch des Volklieds, 73; American and European narratives as socio-psychological indicators, VI Cong Int Soc Folk Narrative Res; The little man who wasn't there: Encounters with the supranormal, Fabula, 77; contribr, Enzyklopädie des Märchens, 77-; transl & ed, The German Legends of the Brothers Grimm, 2 vols, ISHI, 81. *Mailing Add:* Ger Dept Univ of Calif Los Angeles CA 90024

WARD, DOROTHY COX, b Birmingham, Ala, June 14, 25; m 49; c 4. GERMANISTICS. *Educ:* Birmingham-Southern Col, AB, 45, BM, 50; Columbia Univ, MA, 54, PhD, 76. *Prof Exp:* Instr Ger & French, Birmingham-Southern Col, 46-49; instr Ger, Univ Ala, 49-50; instr Ger & French, Birmingham-Southern Col, 50-52; instr Ger, Sch Gen Studies, Columbia Univ, 52-54; asst prof Ger & French, Birmingham-Southern Col, 54-56; instr English & French, Walddörfer Schule, Hamburg, Ger, 56-57; from asst prof to assoc prof Ger & French, 57-76, PROF GER & FRENCH & CHMN DEPT MOD FOREIGN LANG, BIRMINGHAM-SOUTHERN COL, 76-, CHAIRPERSON DIV HUMANITIES, 80- *Mem:* Am Asn Teachers Ger; SAtlantic Mod Lang Asn, Southern Conf on Foreign Lang Teaching. *Res:* Modern German literature; Hermann Hesse. *Mailing Add:* Dept of Mod Foreign Lang Birmingham-Southern Col Birmingham AL 35204

WARD, JACK HAVEN, b Topeka, Kans, July 26, 29; m 61; c 3. LANGUAGE TEACHING, LINGUISTICS. *Educ:* Univ Kans, BA, 51; Univ Hawaii, MA, 62; Cornell Univ, PhD(gen ling), 73. *Prof Exp:* Fulbright lectr ling, Ateneo Univ Manila & Philippine Norm Univ, 65-66; lectr Indonesian Tagalog, Cornell Univ, 66-68; actg dir, Hawaiian Studies Prog, 71-77, asst prof Polynesian lang, 68-77, ASSOC PROF POLYNESIAN LANG, UNIV HAWAII, MANOA, 77- *Concurrent Pos:* Vis prof, Kanazawa Univ, Japan Soc for the Promotion of Sci, 77. *Mem:* Ling Soc Am; Asn Asian Studies; Polynesian Soc; Soc Etudes Oceaniennes. *Res:* Descriptive and comparative linguistics of islands of Southeast Asia and the Polynesian languages; linguistic history; prehistory in eastern Polynesia. *Publ:* Auth, Some background for a linguistic of the Lesser Sunda Islands, In: Working Papers in Linguistics, Univ Hawaii, 69; Philippine linguistic studies, Philippine J Ling, 70; A Bibliography of Philippine Linguistics and Minor Languages, Cornell Univ, 71; I Watu Gunung: A Balinese Calendrical Myth, Bishop Mus, 76. *Mailing Add:* Dept Indo-Pac Lang Univ Hawaii Manoa Honolulu HI 96822

WARD, MARGARET ELLEN, b Philadelphia, Pa, Feb 22, 44; m 75. GERMAN LANGUAGE & LITERATURE. *Educ:* Wilson Col, BA, 65; Ind Univ, MA, 67, PhD(Ger), 73. *Prof Exp:* Instr, 71-73, asst prof, 73-78, ASSOC PROF GER, WELLESLEY COL, 78- *Concurrent Pos:* Early leave grant Ger drama, Wellesley Col, 76-77. *Honors & Awards:* Huber Award, Wellesley Col, 73. *Mem:* MLA; Northeast Mod Lang Asn; Am Asn Teachers Ger; Goethe Soc New Eng. *Res:* Contemporary German literature, East and West; politics and literature; English, French and German comparative drama. *Publ:* Auth, Rolf Hochhuth, In: Twaynes World Authors Ser, G K Hall, 77; Gatti, Brecht und die Lehre von der Einfühlung, Brecht-Jahrbuch, 77; Volker Braun's Tinka: Two views, Dayton Univ Rev, 78. *Mailing Add:* Dept of Ger Wellesley Col Wellesley MA 02181

WARD, PATRICIA ANN, b Warren, Pa, Aug 26, 40. COMPARATIVE LITERATURE & FRENCH. *Educ:* Eastern Nazarene Col, BA, 62; Univ Wis, MA, 64, PhD(comp lit), 68. *Prof Exp:* Asst prof comp lit, State Univ NY Albany, 68-72; asst prof, 72-75, actg head, dept French, 80-81, assoc prof, 75-82, PROF FRENCH & COMP LIT, PA STATE UNIV, UNIVERSITY PARK, 82- *Concurrent Pos:* State Univ NY Res Found grant-in-aid, 71; res initiation grant, Pa State Univ, 73-74; fel Inst Arts & Humanistic Studies, Pa State Univ, 79; assoc ed, Christian Scholar's Rev, 81-; vis prof comp lit, Baylor Univ, 82. *Mem:* MLA; Am Comp Lit Asn; Conf Christianity & Lit (treas, 72-74, vpres, 78-80); Am Asn Teachers Fr; Alliance Fr. *Res:* Literary criticism; 19th-century French literature; European Romanticism. *Publ:* Auth, Victor Hugo's creative process in Saison des Semailles, Fr Studies, 72; The Medievalism of Victor Hugo, Pa State Univ, 75; Simone Weil, or radical Sainthood, Christianity Today, 76; Joseph Joubert on language and style, Symposium, 77; Great Spiritual Autobiographies and the Modern Reader, Christianity Today, 78; Joseph Joubert and the Critical Tradition: Platonism and Romanticism, Ed Droz, 80; Encoding in the Texts of Literary Movements: Late European Romanticism, Comp Lit Studies, 81; Christian Women at Work, Zondervan Publ House, 81. *Mailing Add:* Dept of French Pa State Univ University Park PA 16802

WARD, RALPH LAWRENCE, b Orange, NJ, Oct 23, 10; m 39; c 3. CLASSICAL LINGUISTICS. *Educ:* Rutgers Univ, AB, 31; Yale Univ, PhD, 35. *Prof Exp:* Instr classics, Yale Univ, 35-40; from instr to asst prof, Cornell Univ, 40-46; from asst prof to assoc prof, Yale Univ, 46-62; prof classics, Hunter Col, 62-81; RETIRED. *Concurrent Pos:* Dir instr mod Greek, UNRRA Training Ctr, Univ Md, 44; mem, Am Coun Learned Soc, 44-46; mem fac, Ling Inst, Univ Mich, 49; consult, Clarence L Barnhart, Bronxville, NY, 50-55; Fulbright res grant, Greece, 59-60. *Mem:* Ling Soc Am; Am Philol Asn; Int Ling Asn. *Res:* Modern Greek; classical and Indo-European linguistics. *Publ:* Coauth, Spoken Greek. *Mailing Add:* 5 Locust Ave Shelter Island Hts New York NY 11965

WARDEN, JOHN RICHARD, b London, Eng, Mar 2, 36; m 60; c 4. CLASSICS. *Educ:* Cambridge Univ, BA, 59, MA, 63. *Prof Exp:* Asst master classics, Marlborough Col, England, 59-63; lectr, Univ Ghana, 64-66; asst prof, 66-68, assoc dean acad, 77-80, ASSOC PROF CLASSICS, SCARBOROUGH COL, UNIV TORONTO, 68- *Mem:* Am Philol Asn; Classics Asn Can. *Res:* Latin elegiac poets; Orpheus; Ficino. *Publ:* Auth, ΙΦΘΙΜΟΣ: a semantic analysis, 69 & ΨΥΧΗ in Homeric death descriptions, 71, Phoenix; The mind of Zeus, J Hist Ideas, 71; The Poems of Propertius, Bobbs, 72; Another would-be Amazon, Hermes, 78; Fallax Opus: Poet and Reader in the Elegies of Propertius, Univ Toronto Press, 80. *Mailing Add:* Div of Humanities Scarborough Col Univ of Toronto 1265 Military Trail West Hill ON M5S 1A1 Can

WARDHAUGH, RONALD, b Widdrington, England, May 17, 32; Can citizen. APPLIED ENGLISH LINGUISTICS. *Educ:* Univ Durham, BA, 55; Univ Alta, BEd, 59, PhD(English educ), 64; Univ Mich, MA, 61. *Prof Exp:* Asst prof ling, Univ Alta, 65-66; from asst prof to prof, Univ Mich, Ann Arbor, 66-75, dir, English Lang Inst, 68-74; PROF LING & CHMN DEPT, UNIV TORONTO, 75- *Mem:* Ling Soc Am; Can Ling Asn. *Res:* Second language teaching; linguistics and reading; applied linguistics. *Publ:* Auth, Reading: A Linguistic Perspective, Harcourt, 69; Topics in Applied Linguistics, 74 & Contexts of Language, 76, Newbury House; coauth, Survey of Applied Linguisitics, Univ Mich, 76; auth, Introduction to Linguistics, McGraw, 77. *Mailing Add:* Dept of Ling Univ of Toronto Toronto ON M5S 1A1 Can

WARDROPPER, BRUCE WEAR, b Edinburgh, Scotland, Feb 2, 19; m 42, 60; c 1. ROMANCE LANGUAGES. *Educ:* Cambridge Univ, BA, 39, MA, 42; Univ Pa, PhD, 49. *Prof Exp:* Head dept mod lang, Wolmer's Sch, Kingston, Jamaica, West Indies, 40-45; instr, Univ Pa, 45-49; from asst prof to assoc prof Span lit, Johns Hopkins Univ, 49-55, chmn dept Romance lang, 54-55; prof Span, Ohio State Univ, 55-59; prof, Johns Hopkins Univ, 59-62; WILLIAM H WANNAMAKER PROF ROMANCE LANG, DUKE UNIV, 62- *Concurrent Pos:* Guggenheim fels, 52-53, 59; Am Philos Soc res grant, 56; Am Coun Learned Soc grant, 59, fels, 68 & 69-70; gen ed, Mod Lang Notes, 61-62; mem comt grants-in-aid, Am Coun Learned Soc, 64-67, 80-; consult, Bur Higher Educ, div grad acad facilities, Off Educ, 65-; vis prof, Univ NC, Chapel Hill, 67-68; dir, Nat Endowment for Humanities Fellowships in Residence for Col Teachers, 77-78. *Mem:* MLA; Renaissance Soc Am; Asn Int Hispanistas; Cervantes Soc Am; Mod Humanities Res Asn; Asn Hispanists Gt Brit & Ireland. *Res:* Spanish Golden Age and twentieth century literature; Spanish elegiac and folk poetry. *Publ:* Auth, Cancionero espiritual, Castalia, 54; Historia de la poesia lirica a lo divino, Rev Occidente, 58; Critical Essays on the Theatre of Calderon, NY Univ, 65; Poesia elegiaca espanola, Bibliot Anaya, 67; auth, Spanish literature, In: Modern Literature, III, Prentice, 68; ed, Teatro espanol del Siglo de Oro, Scribner, 69; Spanish Poetry of the Golden Age, Appleton, 72; coauth, Teoria de la Comedia, Aniel, 78. *Mailing Add:* 3443 Rugby Rd Durham NC 27707

WARNER, NICHOLAS OLIVER, b San Francisco, Calif, Feb 11, 50. COMPARATIVE & ENGLISH LITERATURE. *Educ:* Stanford Univ, BA, 72; Univ Calif, Berkeley, PhD(English), 77. *Prof Exp:* Assoc freshman English, Univ Calif, Berkeley, 76-77; asst prof lit, Oberlin Col, 78-80; ASST PROF LIT, CLAREMONT MCKENNA COL, 80- *Mem:* MLA; Am Asn Advan Slavic Studies; Am Asn Teachers Slavic & East Europ Lang. *Res:* Literature and visual arts; Russian literature; literary theory. *Publ:* Auth, Blakes Moon-Ark symbolism, Blake Quart, fall 80; The theme of travel in Russian and English romanticism, Russian Lit Triquart (in press); In search of literary science! The Russian formalist tradition, Pac Coast Philol (in press); The iconic mode of William Blake, Rocky Mountain Rev (in prep). *Mailing Add:* Dept of Lit Claremont McKenna Col Claremont CA 91711

WARNOCK, ROBERT GLENN, b Dodge City, Kans, June 21, 31; m 56; c 4. GERMAN LITERATURE. *Educ:* Univ Kans, AB, 58, MA, 60; Stanford Univ, PhD(Ger), 65. *Prof Exp:* Instr Ger, Univ Va, 63-66; asst prof, 66-70, assoc prof, 70-80, PROF GER, BROWN UNIV, 81- *Concurrent Pos:* Alexander von Humboldt-Stiftung res grant, 72-73 & 76; Ger Acad Exchange Serv res grant, summer, 80; Am Philos Soc grant, 80 & 81. *Mem:* Int Arthurian Soc; Am Asn Teachers Ger; MLA; Am Asn Teachers Yiddish; Medieval Acad Am. *Res:* Medieval German and old Yiddish language and literature; German prose literature of the 14th-16th centuries; Arthurian literature. *Publ:* Auth, Die Predigten Johannes Paulis, C H Beck, 70; The German pattern poem: A study in mannerism of the seventeenth century, In: Festschrift für Detlev W Schumann, Delp, 70; coauth, Der Traktat Heinrichs von Friemar über die Unterscheidung der Geister, Lateinisch-mittelhochdeutsche Textausgabe mit Untersuchungen, Augustinus-Verlag, 77; auth, Johannes Pauli's thirty types of hypocrites: A study of sources, Res Publica Litterarum, 2: 327-345; Heinrich von Friemar der Altere, In: Die deutsche Literatur des Mittelalters: Verfasserlexikon, de Gruyter, 81; Wirkungsabsicht und Bearbeitungstechnik im altjiddischen Artushof, Zeitschrift fur deutsche Philologie, 82; Some problems in working with old Yiddish literary texts, Yiddish, Queens Col Press, 82. *Mailing Add:* Dept of Ger Brown Univ Providence RI 02912

WARRIN, DONALD OGDEN, b Montclair, NJ, Apr 17, 33; div; c 4. PORTUGUESE. *Educ:* Univ Southern Calif, BA, 60; NY Univ, MA, 66, PhD(Port), 73. *Prof Exp:* ASSOC PROF PORT, CALIF STATE UNIV, HAYWARD, 69- *Mem:* Am Asn Teachers Span & Port; Philol Asn Pac Coast; Pac Coast Coun Latin Am Studies. *Res:* Portuguese immigrant literature in California; Brazilian literature. *Publ:* Coauth, Bibliography of Instructional Materials for the Teaching of Portuguese, Calif Dept Educ, 76; auth, A literatura do imigrante portugues na California, Horizontes, 3-4/77; On the function of the poetic sign in Alvares de Azevedo, Luso-Brazilian Rev, summer 1980; Alfred Lewis--Romance e poesia em dois idiamas, Arquipelago, 1/81. *Mailing Add:* Dept of Foreign Lang Calif State Univ 25800 Carlos Bee Blvd Hayward CA 94542

WARRINER, HELEN PAGE, b Amelia Co, Va, July 7, 35. FOREIGN LANGUAGE EDUCATION. *Educ:* Longwood Col, BA, 56; Nat Univ Mex, MA, 58; Ohio State Univ, PhD(foreign lang educ), 71. *Prof Exp:* Teacher English & gen lang, Albert H Hill Jr High Sch, Richmond, Va, 56-57; teacher Spanish & French, Newport News High Sch, Newport News, Va, 58-61; asst supvr, 61-63, SUPVR, FOREIGN LANG, VA STATE DEPT EDUC, 63- *Honors & Awards:* Va Cult Laureate & Peer Eminent, Va Cult Laureate Comt, 77. *Mem:* Am Asn Teachers Span & Port; Nat Coun State & Supvrs Foreign Lang (vpres, 71-72, pres, 72-73); Am Coun Teaching Foreign Lang (pres, 76); Teaching English to Speakers Other Lang. *Publ:* The Language Laboratory in Virginia: A Survey Report, 67 & The Effectiveness of the Use of Foreign Languages in Teaching Academic Subjects, 68, Va State Dept Educ; The status of research in foreign languages, Bull Mod Foreign Lang Asn Va, 10/69; Foreign language interdisciplinary programs and activities, In: Vol III, Britannica Review of Foreign Language Education, Encycl Britannica, 71; Individualized instruction in the teaching of foreign languages: A broad view, Oklahoma in World, 72. *Mailing Add:* 4700 W Franklin St Richmond VA 23226

WARTENBERG, DOROTHY M, b Leeds, Eng, Sept 16, 21; m 45; c 2. GERMAN, COMPARATIVE LITERATURE. *Educ:* Oxford Univ, Eng, BA, 43, MA, 47; Univ Cincinnati, MA, 68, PhD(Ger), 75. *Prof Exp:* From instr to asst prof French & Ger, Raymond Walters Col, Univ Cincinnati, 68-76, chmn, Dept Foreign Lang, 73-76; humanities adminr, 76-78, PROG OFFICER, FEL DIV, NAT ENDOWMENT FOR HUMANITIES, 78- *Mem:* Am Asn Teachers Ger; Brecht Soc; MLA. *Res:* Twentieth century German literature; 19th and 20th century French-German literary relations. *Publ:* Contribr, The Teaching of German: Problems and Methods, Carl Schurz Found, 70; auth, The bird of paradise and the sparrow: Brecht & George in poetic confrontation, Colloquia Ger, 74; coauth, Flucht und Exil: Werkhematik und Autorenkommentare, In: Gegenwartsliteratur und Drittes Reich, Reclam, Stuttgart, 77. *Mailing Add:* Nat Endowment for Humanities 806 15th St NW Washington DC 20506

WARWICK, JACK, b Huddersfield, England, Sept 9, 30; m 54; c 3. ROMANCE LANGUAGES. *Educ:* Oxford Univ, BA, 53, MA, 59; Univ Western Ont, PhD(French), 63. *Prof Exp:* Instr French, Huron Col, 59-60; from instr to asst prof French & Span, Univ Western Ont, 60-68; assoc prof French, McMaster Univ, 68-70; ASSOC PROF FRENCH LIT & SOC SCI, YORK UNIV, 70- *Concurrent Pos:* Can Coun sr fel, 66-67; vis prof, Laval Univ, 72. *Mem:* Int Asn Fr Studies; Asn Can Univ Teachers Fr; MLA; Asn Prof de Francais des Univ Can (pres, 76-78). *Res:* French-Canadian literature; seventeenth century French nature concepts particularly early happy savages; sociological methodology in literature. *Publ:* Auth, The Long Journey, Univ Toronto, 68 & French transl, HMH, Montreal, 72; Un cas type d'application de la methode sociologique: les ecrivains canadiens-francais, Rev Inst Sociol, Brussels, 69; Humanisme chretien et bons sauvages (Gabriel Sagard, 1623-1636), XVIIe siecle, 72; Le Civilise devant le defi du sauvage, Marseille, 77; Litterature de la Nouvelle-France, Etudes Francaises, 78. *Mailing Add:* Atkinson Col York Univ 4700 Keele St Toronto ON M3J 1P3 Can

WASEEM, GERTRUD SPRENGER, b Nagold, Ger, Sept 16, 27; m 52; c 1. GERMAN. *Educ:* McGill Univ, PhD, 74. *Prof Exp:* Mem fac Ger, Univ Dacca, 53-55; mem fac, Auburn Univ, 56-57; instr, Sir George Williams Univ, 57-60; from asst prof to assoc prof, 60-75, PROF GER, ACADIA UNIV, 75- *Concurrent Pos:* Teaching asst, McGill Univ, 58-60. *Mem:* Can Asn Univ Teachers Ger; MLA. *Res:* Modern novel, Heinrich Heine; Germans in Nova Scotia. *Mailing Add:* Dept of Ger Acadia Univ Wolfville NS B0P 1X0 Can

WASHINGTON, IDA HARRISON, b Port Washington, NY, Nov 19, 24; m 48; c 6. GERMAN LITERATURE. *Educ:* Wellesley Col, AB, 46; Middlebury Col, AM, 50; Columbia Univ, PhD, 62. *Prof Exp:* Instr Ger, Univ Minn, 61-62; instr, Drew Univ, 64; instr, NY Univ, 64-65; lectr, Seton Hall Univ, 65-66; asst prof, 66-72, assoc prof mod lang, 72-77, PROF MOD LANG, SOUTHEASTERN MASS UNIV, 77- *Concurrent Pos:* Exec secy, Northeast Mod Lang Asn, 80- *Mem:* Am Asn Teachers Ger; MLA; Northeast Mod Lang Asn; Soc Ger-Am Studies. *Res:* Poetic realism. *Publ:* Coauth, Preview of German Literature, Holt, 69; Carleton's Raid, Phoenix, 77; auth, Otto Ludwigs komische Oper Die Kohlerin, Bouvier Verlag Herbert Grundmann, Bonn, 79; Dorothy Canfield Fisher, a Biography, New England Press, 82. *Mailing Add:* Dept of Mod Lang Southeastern Mass Univ North Dartmouth MA 02747

WASHINGTON, LAWRENCE MOORE, b Manchester, Conn, Nov 5, 25; m 48; c 6. GERMAN. *Educ:* Middlebury Col, AB, 49, AM, 50; Brown Univ, PhD, 58. *Prof Exp:* Instr Ger, King's Col, Pa, 50-51; instr, Gettysburg Col, 51-53; instr, Bowdoin Col, 54-56; from instr to asst prof, Rensselaer Polytech Inst, 56-61; assoc prof, Hamline Univ, 61-62; assoc prof, Upsala Col, 62-66; assoc prof, 66-72 PROF GER, SOUTHEASTERN MASS UNIV, 72- *Concurrent Pos:* Vis prof, Drew Univ, 63-64. *Mem:* MLA; Am Asn Teachers Ger; Ling Soc Am; Northeast Mod Lang Asn. *Res:* Nineteenth century German prose; comparative linguisitics; methods in language teaching. *Publ:* Coauth, The several aspects of fire in Achim von Arnim's Der tolle Invalide, Ger Quart, 11/64; A Preview of German Literature, Holt, 69; auth, Perspectives on People: Five Stories by Gottfried Keller, Banner Int, 77. *Mailing Add:* Dept of Foreign Lit & Lang Southeastern Mass Univ North Dartmouth MA 02747

WASIOLEK, EDWARD, b Camden, NJ, Apr 27, 24; m 48; c 3. COMPARATIVE LITERATURE. *Educ:* Rutgers Univ, BA, 49; Harvard Univ, MA, 50, PhD, 55. *Prof Exp:* Res assoc, Russ Res Ctr, Harvard Univ, 51-53, teaching fel English, 53-54; instr English & humanities, Ohio Wesleyan Univ, 54-55; asst prof English, 55-59, assoc prof English, Slavic lang & lit, 59-64, chmn dept, 70-76, PROF COMP LIT, ENGLISH & SLAVIC LANG & LIT, UNIV CHICAGO, 64-, CHMN DEPT COMP LIT, 65- *Concurrent Pos:* Mem adv bd, Encycl Brittanica, 73. *Res:* Modern novel; especially technique and comparative aspects; theory of criticism. *Publ:* Coauth, Nine Soviet Portraits, Mass Inst Technol, 55; Croce and contextualist criticism, Mod Philol, 8-59; Tolstoy's The Death of Ivan Ilych, and James' fictional imperatives, Mod Fiction Studies, winter 61; ed, Crime and Punishment and the Critics, Wadsworth, 61; Aut Caesar, aut Nihil, a study of Dostoevsky's moral dialectic, PMLA, 3/63; auth, Dostoevsky: The Major Fiction, Mass Inst Technol, 64; The Brothers Karamazov and the Critics, Wadsworth, 67; The Notebooks for Crime and Punishment, 67, The Notebooks for the Idiot, 68, The Notebooks for the Possessed, 68, ed & transl, The Notebooks for the Brothers Karamazov, 71 & ed, The Gambler and Paulina Suslova's diary, 72, Univ Chicago; auth, Tolstoy's Major Fiction, Univ Chicago, 78. *Mailing Add:* Dept of Slavic Lang & Lit Foster 404 Univ of Chicago Chicago IL 60637

WASKIE, ANTHONY JOSEPH, b Bloomsburg, Pa, Dec 22, 46; m 64; c 3. GERMANIC & SLAVIC PHILOLOGY. *Educ:* Bloomsburg State Col, BS, 68; New York Univ, MA, 71, PhD(Ger-Slavic philol), 78. *Prof Exp:* Teacher lang, 68-73, ADMINR LANG CURRIC, PENNSBURY SCHS, 73- *Mem:* Am Asn Teachers Ger; Nat Educ Asn; MLA. *Res:* Comparative studies of linguistic contact of Germanic and Slavic languages; studies of foreign language teaching strategies. *Publ:* Auth, Germano-Polabica: A phonological analysis of the adaptation of German loan words in Polabian, Dissertation Abstr, 5/78. *Mailing Add:* 12 Margin Turn Rd Levittown PA 19056

WASOW, THOMAS ALEXANDER, b New Rochelle, NY, Dec 14, 45; m 71; c 2. THEORETICAL LINGUISTICS. *Educ:* Reed Col, BA, 67; Mass Inst Technol, PhD(ling), 72. *Prof Exp:* Asst prof ling, Hampshire Col, 72-73; asst prof, 74-78, ASSOC PROF LING & PHILOS, STANFORD UNIV, 78- *Concurrent Pos:* Vis prof, Ling Soc Am Summer Inst, 79; co-ed, Squibs & Discussion Sect, Ling Inquiry, 79-81; consult, Hewlett-Packard Corp, 81- *Mem:* Ling Soc Am; Asn Comput Ling. *Res:* Syntactic theory; computational and mathematical linguistics; mental representation of linguistic knowledge. *Publ:* Coauth, On the subject of Gerunds, Found of Lang, 72; auth, Anaphoric pronouns & bound variables, Lang, 75; co-ed, Formal Syntax, 77 & auth, Transformations and the Lexicon, 77, Acad Press; On constraining the class of transformational languages, Synthese, 78; coauth, The category aux in universal grammer, Ling Inquiry, 79; auth, Anaphora in generative grammer story, Scientia, 79; The Aux in German & the History of English, Mass Inst Technol Press, 81. *Mailing Add:* Dept of Ling Stanford Univ Stanford CA 94305

WATERMAN, JOHN THOMAS, b Council Bluffs, Iowa, Aug 1, 18; m 42; c 2. GERMANIC PHILOLOGY. *Educ:* Concordia Theol Sem, AB, 40; Wash Univ, AM, 45; Univ Calif, Los Angeles, PhD, 49. *Prof Exp:* From asst prof Ger to prof Ger & ling & head dept Ger, Univ Southern Calif, 48-67, chmn dept ling, 60-67; vis prof ling, Univ BC, 67-68; prof, 68-80, EMER PROF GER & CHMN DEPT GER & RUSS, UNIV CALIF, SANTA BARBARA, 80- *Concurrent Pos:* Am Philos Soc grant, 67-68. *Mem:* Ling Soc Am; MLA. *Res:* History of linguistics; historical and comparative linguistics. *Publ:* Auth, Perspectives in Linguistics, Univ Chicago, 63; Die Linguistik und ihre perspektiven, Max Hueber, Munich, 66; A History of the German Language, Univ Wash, 66; Perspectives in Linguistic, Univ Calif, 2nd ed, 70; History of the German Language, Univ Wash, 2nd rev ed, 75; Leibniz and Ludolf on Things Linguistic, Univ Calif, 78; The preterite and perfect tenses in German: A study in functional determinants, Ger Rev; Benjamin Lee Whorf and linguistic field-theory, Southwestern J Anthrop. *Mailing Add:* Dept of Ger & Russ Univ of Calif Santa Barbara CA 93106

WATERS, HAROLD A, b Wilmington, NC, Nov 8, 26; m 52; c 3. FRENCH. *Educ:* Harvard Univ, AB, 49; Univ Paris, dipl & cert, 51; Univ Wash, MA, 54, PhD(Romance lang), 56. *Prof Exp:* From instr to asst prof mod lang, Col William & Mary, 55-60; asst prof Romance lang, Carleton Col, 60-62; from asst prof to assoc prof French, 62-69, PROF FRENCH, UNIV RI, 69- *Concurrent Pos:* Founder & coordr, Claudel Newslett, 68-72; assoc ed, Claudel Studies, 72- *Mem:* Am Asn Teachers Fr; AAUP; Northeast Mod Lang Asn. *Res:* Black French literature; French social theater; Claudel. *Publ:* Auth, Philosophic progression in Anouilh's plays, Symposium, summer 62; A propos de la seconde version de l'Echange, Rev Lett Mod annual Paul Claudel issue, 65; Paul Claudel, Twayne, 70; The heroic years of French Social Theater, Mod Lang Studies, spring 75; Black Theater in French: A Guide, Editions Naaman, 78; coauth, Today's English, Hatier-Nouvelles Editions Africaines, 79. *Mailing Add:* Box 233 Saunderstown RI 02874

WATERS, LINDSAY E, English & Comparative Literature. See Vol II

WATKINS, ARTHUR RICH, b Salt Lake City, Utah, July 31, 16; m 41; c 7. GERMAN. *Educ:* Brigham Young Univ, BA, 41, MA, 42; Stanford Univ, PhD, 48. *Prof Exp:* Instr Ger, Stanford Univ, 46-48; asst prof mod lang, Brigham Young Univ, 48-50; instr lang, Weber State Col, 50-52; assoc prof mod lang, 52-55, actg chmn dept lang, 53-54, chmn dept lang, 54-76, chmn dept Germanic & Slavic lang, 69-71, chmn dept Germanic lang, 71-74, PROF MOD LANG, BRIGHAM YOUNG UNIV, 55- *Res:* Comparative Germanic philology; teaching of modern languages. *Publ:* Coauth, German Through Conversational Patterns, 65 & Reviewing German, 69, Dodd; German Through Conversational Patterns, 3rd ed, 81. *Mailing Add:* Dept of Germanic Languages 326 McKay Bldg Brigham Young Univ Provo UT 84601

WATKINS, CALVERT WARD, b Pittsburgh, Pa, Mar 13, 33; m 80; c 4. LINGUISTICS. *Educ:* Harvard Univ, BA, 54, PhD(ling), 59. *Prof Exp:* From instr to assoc prof, 59-66, chmn dept ling, 63-66, 69-70 & 71 72, PROF LING & CLASSICS, HARVARD UNIV, 66- *Concurrent Pos:* Vis prof, Sch Celtic Studies, Dublin Inst Advan Studies, 61-62 & 81; Ctr Advan Study Behav Sci fel, 66-67; overseas fel, Churchill Col, Cambridge, 70-71; Am Acad Arts & Sci fel, 73. *Mem:* Ling Soc Am; Am Orient Soc; Philol Soc; hon mem Royal Irish Acad; Am Philol Soc; Soc Ling Paris. *Res:* Indo-European; linguistics and poetics; Hittite. *Publ:* Auth, Indo-European Origins of the Celtic Verb I, The Sigmatic Aorist, Dublin Inst Advan Study, 62; Geschichte der indogermanischen verbalflexion, Carl Winter, 69; Indo-European Studies, NSF Spec Report, 72; coauth & ed, Indo-European Studies II, 75, Indo-European Studies III, 77 & Indo-European Studies, IV, 81, Harvard Univ. *Mailing Add:* Dept of Ling Sci Ctr 223 Harvard Univ Cambridge MA 02138

WATSON, HAROLD MARK, b Andale, Kans, Oct 29, 24. ROMANCE LANGUAGES. *Educ:* St Benedict's Col, BA, 46; Laval Univ, MA, 56; Univ Lyon, dipl lang & lit, 57; Univ Colo, PhD, 65. *Prof Exp:* Teacher, Maur Hill High Sch, 50-56; instr French & Latin, St Benedict's Col, Kans, 57-61, from asst prof to assoc prof French, 64-70, chmn dept mod lang, 66-70; assoc prof, 70-73, head French sect, 76, PROF FRENCH, MEMPHIS STATE UNIV, 73-, HEAD, GRAD COUN, ARTS & SCI, 76- *Concurrent Pos:* Assoc ed, Claudel Studies, 76- *Mem:* MLA; AAUP; Am Asn Teachers Fr; Claudel Soc (pres, 74-76); Soc Paul Claudel, France. *Res:* Contemporary French literature, especially Claudel. *Publ:* Auth, Claudel's Immortal Heroes: A Choice of Deaths, Rutgers Univ, 71; Fire and water, love and death in Le soulier de satin, Fr Rev, 4/72; Bauderlairian realism in early Claudelian drama, L'Esprit Createur, spring 73; contribr, Critical Bibliography of French Literature, twentieth century, Syracuse Univ; auth, Les etats-Unis que Claudel a connus, In: Actes des Journees Claudel a Brangues, Grenoble Univ, 77. *Mailing Add:* Dept of Foreign Lang Memphis State Univ Memphis TN 38152

WATSON, JOHN A, b Greenville, SC, July 8, 20; div; c 2. ROMANCE LANGUAGES. *Educ:* Howard Univ, AB, 42; Univ Paris, cert French, 46; Columbia Univ, MA, 50; Cath Univ Am, PhD, 76. *Prof Exp:* Instr Span & French, Va Union Univ, 48-50; instr, Howard Univ, 53; asst prof, 54-57, assoc prof, 59-76, PROF SPAN & FRENCH, VA UNION UNIV, 76- *Concurrent Pos:* Danforth spec award, 57-58; assoc prof Span & French, Va State Col, 59-61. *Mem:* NEA; MLA; Am Asn Teachers Span & Port; Nat Asn Lang Lab Dir. *Res:* Gongorism: Luis de Gongora, sixteenth century Spanish poet; metaphorical procedure of Gongora and Calderon. *Mailing Add:* Dept of Mod Lang Va Union Univ Richmond VA 23220

WATSON, JOHN W, b Blacksburg, Va, Nov 9, 17; m 41, 62; c 3. LINGUISTICS, STATISTICS. *Educ:* Va Polytech Inst, BS, 37; Univ Va, MA, 39, PhD(English philol), 41. *Prof Exp:* Asst prof English, Tulane Univ, 45-46; analyst, US Dept Navy, 46-49; analyst, Armed Forces Security Agency, Nat Security Agency, 49-61; staff engr & scientist, Radio Corp Am, 61-64; MEM TECH STAFF, MITRE CORP, 64- *Concurrent Pos:* Lectr, George Washington Univ, 46-58; consult, Govt Employees Ins Co, 52-54; mem, Architectural Bd Rev, Alexandria, Va, 54-57; lectr, Univ Va Ext, 54-60. *Res:* Old English phonology; statistical inference; computer simulation. *Publ:* Auth, Northumbrian Old English EA and EO, 46 & Noninitial K in the North of England, 47, Language; An operational model of crisis decision-making, 67 & Scenario generator: A cybernetic model, 74, Mitre Tech. *Mailing Add:* 8131 Saxony Dr Annandale VA 22003

WATT, WILLIAM CARNELL, b Philadelphia, Pa, Apr 23, 32; m 80; c 4. SEMIOTICS, LINGUISTICS. *Educ:* Univ NC, AB, 54; Georgetown Univ, MSL, 59; Univ Pa, PhD(ling), 67. *Prof Exp:* Systems analysis, Nat Bureau of Standards, 63-66; asst prof comput sci, Carnegie-Mellon Univ, 67-70; assoc prof, 70-80, PROF LING & SEMIOTICS, UNIV CALIF, IRVINE, 80- *Concurrent Pos:* Consult, Bunker-Ramo Corp, 69-70, Nat Bureau of Standards, 69- & Tech Operations Res, 70-72. *Mem:* Semiotic Soc Am; AAAS; Soc Archit Historians. *Res:* Cognitive semiotics; cognitive linguistics. *Publ:* Auth, Competing economy critera, Prob actuels en psycholinguistique, CNRS, Paris, 74; The indiscreteness with which impenetrables are penetrated, Lingua, 75; What is the proper characterization of the alphabet?, I: Desiderata, Visible Lang, 75; Iconic perspectives on linguistic explanation,

Perspectives on Experimental Ling, John Benjamins BV, 79; Against evolution, Ling & Philos, 79; Iconic equilibrium, Semiotica, 79; What is the proper characterization of the alphabet?, II: Composition, 80 & What is the proper characterization of the alphabet?, III: Appearance, 81, Ars Semiotica. *Mailing Add:* Sch Social Sci Univ Calif Irvine CA 92717

WATTS, LEE BARNETT, b Indiana, Pa; m. ROMANCE LANGUAGES, ENGLISH LITERATURE. *Educ:* Pa State Univ, BA & MA; Univ Conn, PhD(Romance lang), 67. *Prof Exp:* Instr Span, Manchester Community Col, 66-67; asst prof, 67-69, PROF SPAN & ENGLISH, EASTERN CONN STATE COL, 69-, CHMN DEPT MOD LANG, 72- *Mem:* MLA; Am Asn Teachers Span & Port; Am Coun Teaching Foreign Lang. *Res:* Comparative studies between the Siglo de Oro, especially The Comedia and the Elizabethan Period, especially Shakespeare. *Mailing Add:* Dept of Mod Lang Eastern Conn State Col Windham St Willimantic CT 06226

WATTS, ROBERT JOHNSON, b La Grange, Ky, Nov 26, 24. GERMANIC PHILOLOGY & COMPARATIVE LINGUISTICS. *Educ:* Duke Univ, AB, 46, AM, 49. *Prof Exp:* Instr Ger & Span, Wake Forest Col, 48-52; instr Ger, Univ Kans, 58-61; vis instr, Univ Wis, 61-62; instr, Univ Kans, 62-64; asst prof, Lamar Univ, 64-65; asst prof, 65-72, chmn dept foreign lang, 72-78, ASSOC PROF GER, CENTENARY COL LA, 72-, REGISTR, 78- *Mem:* Am Asn Teachers Ger; AAUP. *Res:* German-American bilingualism; methodology; foreign language teaching. *Mailing Add:* Dept of Foreign Lang Centenary Col of La Shreveport LA 71104

WAUGH, LINDA RUTH, b Boston, Mass, Nov 2, 42. LINGUISTICS, FRENCH. *Educ:* Tufts Univ, BA, 64; Stanford Univ, MA, 65; Ind Univ, PhD(ling), 70. *Prof Exp:* Asst prof, 71-76, assoc prof, 76-82, PROF LING, CORNELL UNIV, 82- *Concurrent Pos:* Ford Found fel, 77; vis assoc prof ling, Yale Univ, 78; Nat Endowment for Humanities fel, 79-80. *Mem:* Ling Soc Am; Am Asn Teachers French; Semiotic Soc Am; Int Ling Asn. *Res:* Semantics; structure of French; semiotics. *Publ:* Auth, Lexical meaning: The prepositions en and dans in French, Lingua, 76; Roman Jakobson's Science of Language, Peter de Ridder, 76; A Semantic Analysis of Word Order: Adjective Position in French, Brill, Leiden, Holland, 77; coauth, Basic Course in Susu/Susu: Cours de base, Ind Univ (in press); The context-sensitive meaning of the French subjunctive, In: Cornell Linguistic Contributions, Grammatical Studies, 79; coauth, The Sound Shape of Language, Ind Univ, 79; co-ed, The Melody of Language, Univ Pk Press, 80; Contributions to Historical Linguistics, Brill, 80; Marks Sign's Poems: Semiotics, Linguistics, Poetics, Toronto Semiotic Circle, 82. *Mailing Add:* Dept of Mod Lang & Lit Cornell Univ Ithaca NY 14853

WEBB, BENJIMAN DANIEL, b Childersburg, Ala, Feb 5, 42; m 66. GERMAN LITERATURE & EXPRESSIONISTIC DRAMA. *Educ:* Memphis State Univ, BS, 64; Univ Southern Calif, MA, 66, PhD(Ger), 68. *Prof Exp:* Teaching asst Ger, Univ Southern Calif, 64-68; ASSOC PROF GER, UNIV MIAMI, 68- *Concurrent Pos:* Fulbright fel, 79. *Mem:* MLA, Am Asn Teachers Ger. *Res:* German exile literature. *Publ:* Auth, The demise of the new man: An analysis of ten plays from late German expressionism, Kummerle, W Ger, 73; coauth, Common course designation and numbering: A method, Col & Univ, spring 74; Heinrich Eduard Jacob, Exilliteratur II, 82. *Mailing Add:* Dept of Foreign Lang Univ of Miami Coral Gables FL 33124

WEBB, KAREN SCHUSTER, b Richmond, Va, Nov 11, 46; c 2. APPLIED LINGUISTICS. *Educ:* Ind Univ, Bloomington, AB, 68, MS, 73, PhD(appl ling & English educ), 80. *Prof Exp:* Teacher, Merriman Sch, Waterbury, Conn, 68-69; teacher Span & English as second lang, T C Williams High Sch, Alexandria, Va, 69-72; assoc instr appl ling, Indiana Univ, Bloomington, 72-73; prof Span, ling, English & English as second lang, Coppin State Col, 73-76; PROF LANG EDUC, CURRIC & INSTR, IND UNIV, BLOOMINGTON, 78- *Concurrent Pos:* Consult English, Inst Serv Educ, Washington, DC, 73-76; Int Develop Comt, Phelps-Stokes Fund, Coppin State Col, 74-76, coordr freshman English, 75-76; assoc instr, Mid East Proj, Ind Univ, Bloomington, 76-78; consult, Ind Dept Pub Inst, 79; asst dir, Title VII Haitian Creole Inst, Ind Univ, summer, 80; consult lang educ, Indianapolis Pub Schs, summer, 82. *Mem:* Teachers English to Speakers Other Lang; Am Educ Res Asn; Nat Asn Bilingual Educ. *Res:* Language acquisition and memory systems; language attrition; effective teaching strategies in multicultrual settings. *Publ:* Auth, The case for Black English revisited, Viewpoints Teaching & Learning, winter, 80; Language and you & Communication, In: Ideas and Their Expression, Vol I, Inst Serv Educ, 76; A study of cognitive processing strategies for the encoding of English idioms into long-term memory: A study of native, advanced nonnative, and low intermediate nonnative speakers of English, 80. *Mailing Add:* Sch of Educ Ind Univ Bloomington IN 47405

WEBB, KARL EUGENE, b Lehi, Utah, Mar 12, 38; c 4. GERMAN LITERATURE, ART HISTORY. *Educ:* Brigham Young Univ, BA, 62; Univ Pa, MA, 65, PhD(Ger lit), 69. *Prof Exp:* From instr to assoc prof Ger, Univ Houston, 65-78, prof, 78-79, assoc dean, Col Humanities & Fine Arts, 76-79; Actg dean, Col Humanities & Fine Arts, Univ Houston, 78-79, PROF GER & DEAN, COL ARTS & SCI, UNIV MAINE, ORONO, 79- *Mem:* MLA; SCent Mod Lang Asn; Am Asn Teachers Ger; Northeast Mod Lang Asn; Am Asn Advan Humanities. *Res:* Modern German literature; modern poetry; relationship between literature and art. *Publ:* Auth, Themes in transition: girls and love in Rilke's Buch der Bilder, Ger Quart, 70; R M Rilke's Das Lied des Aussatzigen, Seminar, 72; Rilke's Poetic Art Nouveau: from art to literature, Centennial Rev, 72; Rilke, Rodin and Jugendstil, Orbis Litterarum, 72; Von Kunst zur Literatur: R M Rilkes literarischer Jugendstil, Rilke Heute, Beziehungen & Wirkungen, 75; Rainer Maria Rilke and Jugendstil: Affinities, Influences, Adaptation, Univ NC, Chapel Hill, 78; Else Lasker-Schüler and Franz Marc: A comparison, Orbis Littererum, summer 78; Gerhart Hauptmann and Jugendstil, Festschrift Harold Lenz, 78; R M Rilke and Paul Cezanne: A stylistic comparison, In: Festschrift for Andre von Greniche, Bouvier Verlag, Bonn, 77; co-ed (with Gertrud Pickar), German Expressionism: Literature and the Arts, Proc Univ Houston Symposium Ger Expressionism, Fink Verlag, Munich, 79; Rilke and Russia: Influences of the visual arts upon the young poet, Mod Austrian Lit (in press). *Mailing Add:* Col Arts & Sci Univ Maine Orono ME 04469

WEBB, KENNETH, b Woodlawn, Pa, Mar 19, 18; m 51; c 1. SPANISH, FRENCH. *Educ:* Univ Pittsburgh, BA, 39, PhD, 51. *Prof Exp:* From asst prof to assoc prof, 46-61, PROF ROMANCE LANG, MUHLENBERG COL, 61- *Mem:* MLA; Am Asn Teachers Span & Port. *Res:* Latin American prose. *Mailing Add:* Dept or Romance Languages Muhlenberg College Allentown PA 18104

WEBBER, EDWIN JACK, b Grand Blanc, Mich, Oct 29, 18; m 48. ROMANCE LANGUAGES & LITERATURE. *Educ:* Mich State Univ, AB, 43; Univ Calif, MA, 45, PhD(Romance lit), 49. *Prof Exp:* From instr to asst prof Span, Univ Calif, 49-56; assoc prof Romance lang, 56-66, PROF SPAN, NORTHWESTERN UNIV, 66- *Concurrent Pos:* Guggenheim fel, 53-54. *Mem:* Am Asn Teachers Span & Port; MLA; Mediaeval Acad Am; Renaissance Soc Am; fel Am Philos Soc. *Res:* Mediaeval literature and language; Renaissance drama. *Publ:* Auth, The literary reputation of Terence and Plautus in mediaeval and pre-Renaissance Spain, Hisp Rev; A Spanish linguistic treatise of the fifteenth century, Romance Philol, 8/62; A lexical note on afortunado, Hisp Rev, 65; Disappearance of albardan, Hom a Rodriguez-Monino, 66; Figura autonoma del arcipreste, Actas del I Cong, 73; Ancestry of the Gracioso, Renaissance Drama, 73; La Comedia . . . como arte de amor, Actas del I Cong, 77; La Romeria De Dona Cuaresma, VIII Congreso Soc Rencesvals, 81. *Mailing Add:* Dept of Span Northwestern Univ Evanston IL 60201

WEBBER, PHILIP ELLSWORTH, b Akron, Ohio, Dec 2, 44; m 66; c 3. GERMANIC PHILOLOGY. *Educ:* Earlham Col, AB, 67; Univ Chicago, MA, 68; Bryn Mawr Col, PhD(Ger philol), 72. *Prof Exp:* Instr English community col, Reutlingen, Ger, 70-71; asst prof Ger, ling & educ, Widener Col, 72-76; asst prof, 76-80, ASSOC PROF GER, LING & DUTCH, CENTRAL COL, IOWA, 80- *Concurrent Pos:* Res counr, Shipley Sch, Bryn Mawr, 71-72, prog coordr Ger, Alternative Schs Proj, 71-72; instr Ger, Bryn Mawr Col, 72. *Mem:* Int Ver Ned; Am Asn Teachers Ger. *Res:* Mediaeval Netherlandic manuscripts; ethnic sociolinguistics. *Publ:* Auth, The need for a closer description of Medieval Netherlandic Manuscripts in American libraries: Specific cases in point, Vol XLVI, 75 & Medieval Netherlandic Manuscripts in Greater Philadelphia libraries, Vol XLVII, 76, Archief- en Bibliotheekwezen in Belgie; A Medieval Netherlandic Prayer Cycle on the life of Christ: Princeton University Library, Garrett Ms 63, Ons Geestelijk Erf, Vol LII, 78; Pella Dutch: Mogelijkheden voor Sociolinguïstisch Onderzoek, Taal en Tongval, Vol XXXI, 79; Testing organizational models for vernacular (Dutch) initia indices, Vol XXIV, No 2, 80 & Evidence for the planned integration of literary and visual imagery in Medieval Netherlandic Life of Christ Manuscripts, 82, Manuscripta; A report on ethnic heritage and language education in Pella, Iowa, Am Folklife Ctr of Libr Cong, 82; An ethno-sociolinguistic study of Pella Dutch, Proc Third Conf Asn for Advan Dutch-Am Studies, Cent Col (in prep). *Mailing Add:* Dept of Ger Cent Col Pella IA 50219

WEBBER, RUTH HOUSE, b Sept 27, 18; m 48. ROMANCE LITERATURE & LANGUAGE. *Educ:* State Univ Iowa, BA, 40, MA, 41; Univ Calif, PhD(Romance lit), 48. *Prof Exp:* Instr Span, Albion Col, 41-43; teaching asst, Univ Calif, 43-47, assoc, 47-48, lectr, 48-51; teacher, Pub Schs, 51-53; instr Span & French, Oakland Jr Col, 55-56; from asst prof to assoc prof Span, 58-78, Willett fel, 63-64, PROF SPAN, UNIV CHICAGO, 78- *Concurrent Pos:* Mem MLA Exec Coun, 79-82. *Mem:* Renaissance Soc Am; Asn Int Hisp; Soc Roncesvales; Mediaeval Acad Am. *Res:* Mediaeval literature of Spain, especially epic and ballad; the generation of '98 in Spain. *Publ:* Auth, Formulistic Diction in the Spanish Ballad, Univ Calif, 51; coauth, Brief Course in Spanish, Ginn, 55; Kierkegaard and the elaboration of Unamuno's Niebla, Hisp Rev, 4/64; Un aspecto estilistico del Cantar de mio Cid, Anuario Estudios Medievales, 65; The diction of the Roncesvales fragment, In: Homenaje al profesor Rodrigues-Monino, Vol II, 66; auth, Narrative organization of the Cantar de Mio Cid, Olifant, 73; Pedro Manuel de Urrea y La Celestina, In: Actas del I Congreso Internacional sobre La Celestina, 78; Formulaic language in the Mocedades De Rodrigo, Hisp rev, 2/80. *Mailing Add:* Univ Chicago Chicago Ill

WEBER, BERTA M, b Hollabrunn, Austria, May 19, 21; US citizen. FOREIGN LANGUAGES. *Educ:* Univ Vienna, PhD, 45. *Prof Exp:* Lectr Ital, Adult Continued Educ Sch, Vienna, 43-44; prof English & Ger, Gymnasium, Austria, 44-45; asst prof Ger, 47-52, from lectr to assoc prof, 61-69, PROF GER, GANNON COL, 69-, CHMN DEPT FOREIGN LANG, 77- *Honors & Awards:* Am Asn Teachers Ger Merit Award, 81. *Mem:* Am Asn Teachers Ger; MLA; Am Coun Teching Foreign Lang; Am Ger Soc. *Res:* Methodology of foreign language teaching; business German; German literature. *Mailing Add:* Gannon Col Erie PA 16501

WEBER, CHARLES EDGAR, b Cincinnati, Ohio, Oct 22, 22; m 56. GERMAN. *Educ:* Univ Cincinnati, BA, 49, MA, 50, PhD, 54. *Prof Exp:* From instr to asst prof Ger, Univ Mo, 53-56; asst prof, Univ Tulsa, 56-62; assoc prof, La State Univ, 62-66; assoc prof, 66-67, PROF GERMAN, UNIV TULSA, 67- *Mem:* MLA; Am Asn Teachers Ger; Am Numis Asn. *Res:* History of German language; numismatics. *Publ:* Co-ed, Selections From the Numismatist, Whitman, 61; auth, Johannes von Tepl and Sebastin Brant, SCent Bull, 61; Perils of a Debased Coinage, Am Numis Asn, 65; A numismatist's note on Russia, Numismatist, 7/71; A closer look at gold, Freeman, 9/72. *Mailing Add:* Dept of Modern Languages Univ of Tulsa Tulsa OK 74104

WEBER, CLIFFORD WHITBECK, b Scranton, Pa, Apr 22, 43; m 67. CLASSICS. *Educ:* Harvard Univ, AB, 65; Univ Calif, Berkeley, PhD(classics), 75. *Prof Exp:* Asst prof, 69-78, ASSOC PROF CLASSICS, KENYON COL, 78- *Mem:* Am Philol Asn. *Res:* Latin poetry. *Publ:* Auth, The diction for death in Latin epic, Agon, 69; Gallus' Grynium and Virgil's Cumae, Mediterraneus, 78. *Mailing Add:* 319 Ascension Hall Kenyon Col Gambier OH 43022

WEBER, EUGENE MATHEW, b Vassar, Mich, July 21, 39. GERMAN LITERATURE. *Educ:* Williams Col, BA, 61; Harvard Univ, MA, 63, PhD(Ger), 66. *Prof Exp:* From instr to asst prof Ger, Harvard Univ, 66-73; assoc prof, 73-80, PROF GER, SWARTHMORE COL, 80- *Concurrent Pos:* Am Coun Learned Soc fel, 71-72; mem, Comt Examr, Advan Placement in Ger, Col Entrance Exam Bd, 71- *Mem:* MLA; Am Asn Teachers Ger; Hofmannsthal Ges. *Res:* Eithteenth century and modern German literature. *Publ:* Coauth, Vievvan: 1888-1938, Harvard Univ, 67; co-ed, A Reader in German Literature, S Fischer, 69; auth, A chronology of Hofmannsthal's poems, Euphorion, 69; Die Hofmannsthal-Sammlung im Besitz der Harvard Universität, Hofmannsthal Blätter, 69; Hofmannsthal und Oscar Wilde, Hofmannsthal Forsch I, 71; ed, Literatur I, Oxford Univ, 72 & Briefe Richard Beer-Hofmanns aus dem Exil, Neue Zurcher Zeitung, 73; auth, Hofmannsthal, His Publications and His Publishers, Hofmannsthal Collection, Houghton Libr, Lothar Stiehm, Heidelbert, 74; Zur Uraufführung von Büchners Wozzeck, Festschrift für Rudolf Hirsch, 75. *Mailing Add:* Dept of Mod Lang Swarthmore PA 19081

WEBER, HARRY BUTLER, b Pocatello, Idaho, May 4, 28; m 61; c 2. RUSSIAN LANGUAGE & LITERATURE. *Educ:* Princeton Univ, BA, 50; Ind Univ, MA, 58, PhD(comp lit), 69. *Prof Exp:* Teacher English & foreign lang, Hobson High Sch, Mont, 59-62; from instr to asst prof Russ, 66-75, ASSOC PROF RUSS, UNIV IOWA, 76- *Mem:* Am Asn Teachers Slavic & E Europ Lang; Am Asn Advan Slavic Studies. *Res:* Russian Romanticism; Russian prose of the Soviet period. *Publ:* Auth, Pikovaja drama: A case for freemasonry in Russian literature, 68 & Belinskij and the aesthetics of utopian socialism, 71, Slavic & East Europ J; coauth, Zamyatin's We, the Proletarian Poets, and Bogdanov's Red Star, Russ Lit Triquart, spring 75; ed, The Modern Encyclopedia of Russian and Soviet Literatures, Acad Int, Vols 1-6, 77-82; transl, B M Eikhenbaum, Lermontor, Ardis, 81. *Mailing Add:* Dept of Russ Univ of Iowa Iowa City IA 52242

WEBER, J B, b Barberton, Ohio, Nov 5, 31; m 65; c 2. FRENCH, ROMANCE LANGUAGES. *Educ:* Princeton Univ, AB, 53; Univ Ill, MA, 57, PhD, 63. *Prof Exp:* Asst French, Univ Ill, 55-60; from instr to asst prof, Northwestern Univ, 60-65; asst prof, Tufts Univ, 66-70; chmn dept, 74-76, ASSOC PROF FRENCH, SYRACUSE UNIV, 70. *Concurrent Pos:* Resident chmn Syracuse semester in France, 71-72; res grant, Kittredge Fund, 73 & 77; consult reader, PMLA, 73; mem, Conf on French Seventeenth Century Lit, 74; consult & prog evaluator, Can Coun Arts, 77-; Syracuse Univ res grant, 78. *Mem:* MLA; Annuaire XVII Siecle; Am Asn Teachers Fr; AAUP; N Am Soc Seventeenth Century Fr Lit. *Res:* Moralist literature of the French seventeenth century; French literature and history of the seventeenth and nineteenth centuries; comparative literature. *Publ:* Auth, The hero in France, Commonweal, 10/58; Pascal's Formation in Persuasive Art, French Rev, 11/66; coauth, Avatara in the West, Lit E & W, 66; auth, Jules Monchanin: An introduction, Cross Currents, 1/69; Person as figure of ambiguity and resolution, PMLA, 3/69; The Persone in La Rochefoucauld's Maximes, PMLA, 74; Pascal and music, Symposium, spring 76; In Quest of the Absolute, Mowbray/Cistercian, 77. *Mailing Add:* Dept French Syracuse Univ Syracuse NY 13210

WEBER, JEAN-PAUL, b Paris, France, Dec 3, 12; div; c 1. ROMANCE LANGUAGES, AESTHETICS. *Educ:* Sorbonne, Agrege, 39, DLett(Fr lit), 61. *Prof Exp:* Prof philos, var cols & univs, Paris, India, 45-61; instr of French lit, Bryn Mawr Col, 61-62; assoc prof, City Col New York, 62-67; prof, 67-80, EMER PROF FRENCH LIT, CITY COL NEW YORK & GRAD CTR, CITY UNIV NEW YORK, 80- *Concurrent Pos:* Lectr, univs, Am, 61-68 & Univ Montreal, 66. *Mem:* Am Acad Polit & Soc Sci. *Res:* History of French philosophy; aesthetics; French literature. *Publ:* Auth, La psychologie de l'art, PUF, Paris, 58, 4th ed, 72, Span transl, Paidos, Buenos Aires, 67, English transl, Dell, NY, 69; Genese de l'oeuvre poetique, 61 & Domaines Thematiques, 63, Gallimard, Paris; La constitution de texte des Reguiae, 64 & Stendhal, 69, Sedes, Paris; Contre Picard, Pauvert, Paris, 66; contribr, Nouvelle Rev Fr, Figaro Litteraire, Mod Lang Notes. *Mailing Add:* 8200-8 Blvd East North Bergen NJ 07047

WEBER, ROSE-MARIE, b New York, NY, June 22, 38. GENERAL LINGUISTICS. *Educ:* Queens Col, BA, 60; Cornell Univ, MA, 61, PhD(ling), 65. *Prof Exp:* Res assoc ling, Cornell Univ, 64-68, asst prof, 67-68; from asst prof to assoc prof, McGill Univ, 68-75; sr res assoc ling, Cornell Univ, 76-78. *Concurrent Pos:* Fulbright lectr, Bogota, Colombia, 62-63; vis assoc prof educ, Univ Mass, Amherst, fall, 79; vis assoc prof ling, Cornell Univ, summer, 81. *Mem:* Ling Soc Am; Am Anthrop Asn. *Res:* Linguistics applied to reading; sociolinguistics. *Publ:* Auth, First graders' use of grammatical context in reading, In: Basic Research on Reading, Harper, 69; Linguistics and reading, In: Psychological Factors in the Teaching of Reading, Merrill, 73; Adult illiteracy in the United States, In Toward a Literate Society, McGraw-Hill, 75; coauth, The emergence of sentence modalities in the English of Japanese-speaking children, Lang Learning, 76; auth, Reading (survey of applied linguistics), Univ Mich, 76. *Mailing Add:* 108 Northway Rd Ithaca NY 14850

WEDBERG, LLOYD WARREN, b Fremont, Nebr, Feb 29, 24; m 45; c 2. FOREIGN LANGUAGES & LITERATURE. *Educ:* Univ Mich, AB, 54, MA, 55, PhD(Ger lang & lit), 62. *Prof Exp:* From instr to assoc prof, 61-71, chmn dept lang & ling, 65-81, prof Ger, 71-81, dir Dartmouth Intensive Lang Model, 77-81, DIR DIV CONTINUING PROF EDUC, UNIV DETROIT, 82- *Concurrent Pos:* Chmn dept mod lang, Univ Detroit, 65-70; consult, Mich Foreign Lang Innovative Curricula Studies, 65-66; consult, Rassias Found, 80-, Mich reg dir, 80-82. *Mem:* Am Asn Teachers Ger; MLA; Am Coun Teachers Foreign Lang; Rassias Found. *Res:* Nineteenth century German prose fiction; innovative curricula development in foreign languages; adult and corporate application of Dartmouth Intensive Language Method. *Publ:* Auth, The Theme of Loneliness in the Novellen of Theodor Storm, Mouton, The Hague, 63; Expanding the Dartmouth Intensive Language Model, The Ram's Horn, Rassias Found, 81. *Mailing Add:* Dir Div Continuing Educ Univ of Detroit Detroit MI 48221

WEDECK, HARRY EZEKIEL, b Sheffield, England, Jan 11, 94; m 37; c 2. CLASSICAL & MEDIEVAL LITERATURE. *Educ:* Univ Edinburgh, MA, 16; Inst Int Caen & Univ Caen, dipl, 19; Sorbonne, dipl, 20. *Prof Exp:* Chmn dept class lang, Erasmus Hall High Sch, Brooklyn, NY, 35-50; lectr classics, Brooklyn Col, 50-68; LECTR CLASSICS, NEW SCH SOCIAL RES, 68- *Mem:* Am Philol Asn; Medieval Acad Am; Am Class League; Renaissance Soc Am. *Res:* Metaphysics; English literature; cultural history. *Publ:* Contribr, Aristotle Dictionary, 62; Classics in Logic, 62; transl, I B N Gabirol, Fons Vitae, 62; auth, Dictionary of Erotic Literature, 62; Pictorial History of Morals, 63; Love Potions Through the Ages, 63; Dictionary of Medieval History, 64; transl, Late Latin Writers and Their Greek Sources, Harvard Univ, 69; contribr, Exorcism Through the Ages, 74; Roman Morals, Coronado Press, 80. *Mailing Add:* 425 E 79th St New York NY 10021

WEDEL, ALFRED R, b Sevilla, Spain, Oct 31, 34; US citizen; m 61; c 2. GERMAN & SPANISH PHILOLOGY. *Educ:* Univ Madrid, BA, 60; Univ Pa, MA, 65, PhD(Ger philol), 70. *Prof Exp:* Instr Ger & English, Mangold Inst, Madrid, 60-61; instr Ger, Span & French, Marple Newtown High Schs, Pa, 61-65; asst prof, 65-74, ASSOC PROF GER & SPAN, UNIV DEL, 74-, ASSOC CHMN, 80- *Concurrent Pos:* Res grant, 76; fac adv, Medieval Soc, Univ Del. *Honors & Awards:* Excellence in Teaching Award, Univ Del, 75. *Mem:* MLA; Am Asn Teachers Ger. *Res:* German literature; Germanic philology; comparative literature. *Publ:* Auth, Ortega y Gassett y su concepto de una facultad de cultura, Rev Occidente, 73; The verbal aspects of the prefixed and unprefixed verbal forms: Stantan, sizzan, sezzan, lickan, leckan in the Old High German Benedictine rule, J English & Ger Philol, 74; Subjective and objective aspect: The preterit in the Old High German Isidor, Linguistics, 74; Der Konflikt von Aspekt/Zeitstufe und Aktionsart in der althochdeutschen Übersetzung der Benediktinerregel, Neuphilologische Mitteilungen, 76; Die Gauchfigur und er Cornuto in Moscheroschs Bearbeitung der Traumvisionen des Spaniers Quevedo, In: Problemeer Komparatistik und der Interpretation, Festschrift für A von Gronicka, 77. *Mailing Add:* Dept of Lang & Lit Univ of Del Newark DE 19711

WEED, PATRICIA, b Newton, Mass, Mar 31, 32. FRENCH LITERATURE. *Educ:* Smith Col, BA, 53; Middlebury Col, MA, 54; Yale Univ PhD(French), 64. *Prof Exp:* From instr to asst prof, 62-71, chmn dept, 71-76, assoc prof, 71-80, PROF FRENCH, SMITH COL, 80- *Mailing Add:* Dept of French Smith College Northampton MA 01060

WEGENER, ADOLPH HERMAN, b Philadelphia, Pa, Oct 19, 27; m 53; c 3. GERMAN LANGUAGE & LITERATURE. *Educ:* Muhlenbert, Col, BA, 48; Univ Pa, MA, 51, PhD(Ger), 56. *Prof Exp:* Asst instr Ger, Univ Pa, 48-51, instr, 51-56; from asst prof to assoc prof, 56-66, PROF GER, MUHLENBERG COL, 66- *Concurrent Pos:* Guest lectr, Beaver Col, 55-63; res travel grant, Europe, 63; res grant, 67; mem nat adv coun, Vienna Studies Abroad Prog, 66-; nat selection comt, Intensive Overseas Prog for Prospective Teachers Ger, 67- *Honors & Awards:* Lindback Distinguished Teaching Award, 72. *Mem:* MLA; Am Asn Teachers Ger. *Res:* Modern German and comparative literature. *Publ:* Auth, Zur Lyrik und Graphik von Günter Grass, Philobiblon, 6/66; The absurd in modern literature, Bks Abroad, spring 67; Günter Grass, der realistische Zauberlehrling, In: Helen Adolf Festschrift, Ungar, 68; coauth, Modern College German, Harper, 71; Fussnoten zuden Welten Peter Handkes, In: Views and Reviews of Modern German Literature, Delp'she Verlag, Bad Windsheim, 74; Mehr Tragik als Komik in den Kunstnovellen E T A Hoffamnns, In: Studies in Nineteenth Century and Early Twentieth Century German Literature, Germanistische Forschungsketten No 3, Lexington, Ky, 74. *Mailing Add:* Dept of Ger Muhlenberg Col Allentown PA 18104

WEGNER, HART, b Breslau, Silesia, Ger, Oct 7, 31; US citizen. MODERN GERMAN, COMPARATIVE LITERATURE. *Educ:* Univ Utah, BA, 60, MA, 63; Harvard Univ, PhD(Ger), 70. *Prof Exp:* Lectr Ger, Univ Utah, 66-67, asst prof, 67-68; asst prof Ger & comp lit, 68-71, ASSOC PROF GER & COMP LIT, UNIV NEV, LAS VEGAS, 71- *Concurrent Pos:* Host weekly film prog, Old Flicks for Old Fans, KUED-TV, Salt Lake City; host & creator, Hartbeat, KLVX-TV, Las Vegas, 70-71, host & exec producer, Window on the Arts, 72-73; consult educ satellite proj, Fed of Stated, 73. *Mem:* Am Asn Teachers Ger; Am Film Inst; Int Brecht Soc; MLA; Philol Asn Pac Coast. *Res:* Literature of German expressionism; international documentary theater, film and literature relations. *Mailing Add:* Dept of Foreign Lang & Lit Univ of Nevada Las Vegas NV 89109

WEHNER, JAMES VINCENT, b Cleveland, Ohio, May 29, 43; m 70; c 2. GERMAN & COMPARATIVE LITERATURE. *Educ:* Thiel Col, BA, 65; Vanderbilt Univ, MA, 69, PhD(Ger lit), 74. *Prof Exp:* Teacher Ger & English, Conneaut Valley High Sch, Pa, 65-66; instr Ger, Millsaps Col, 70-71; guest teacher English, Humboldt Gymnasium, Ger, 71-72; instr, 73-74, asst prof Ger, Carnegie-Mellon Univ, 74-78; ASST PROF GER, MANCHESTER COL, 78- *Mem:* MLA; Am Asn Teachers Ger; NEA. *Res:* Late 19th and 20th century German; contemporary American and English literature. *Publ:* Auth, A comparison of the characterizations of Christ and Mary in the Eisenacher Zehnjungfrauenspiel and in Schernberg's Schön Spil von Frau Jutten, South Cent Bull: Studies Mem South Cent Mod Lang Asn, winter 71; Confrontation of a Negative Myth in Ralph Ellison's Invisible Man and in Günter Grass' Hundejahre, Verlag Herbert Lang, Bern, fall 78; Evil and innocence in Herman Melville's Billy Budd and Thomas Mann's Mario und der Zauberer, In: The Comparatist, Southern Comp Lit Asn, 80. *Mailing Add:* 709 N Mill St North Manchester IN 46962

WEHRINGER, HELEN MAXWELL, b Philadelphia, Pa; c 2. COMPARATIVE LITERATURE, FRENCH. *Educ:* Oxford Univ, England, BA, 45; Harvard Univ, MA, 48; City Univ New York, PhD(comp lit), 79. *Prof Exp:* Adj lectr English, Hunter Col, City Univ New York, 73-74, adj lectr French, 76-77; instr French & Span, Keene State Col, 79-80; asst prof humanities, 80-81, ASSOC PROF HUMANITIES, HAWTHORNE COL, 81- *Mem:* MLA. *Res:* Post-modernism; contemporary novel: American and European; French surrealism. *Publ:* Auth, Krapp: Anti-Proust, In: Theatre Wookbook, Vol I, Brutus Bks, London, 80. *Mailing Add:* PO Box 376 North Branch Antrim NH 03440

WEIGAND, HERMANN JOHN, b Philadelphia, Pa, Nov 17, 92; m 61. GERMANIC LITERATURE. *Educ:* Univ Mich, AB, 13, PhD, 16. *Hon Degrees:* AM, Yale Univ, 19; DHL, Univ Colo, 68. *Prof Exp:* Teaching asst, Univ Mich, 13-14, instr, 14-18; from instr to asst prof, Univ Pa, 19-28, prof, 28-29; prof Ger, 29-55, dir grad studies in Ger, 38-61, Sterling prof, 55-61, EMER STERLING PROF GER LIT, YALE UNIV, 61- *Concurrent Pos:* Lectr, Curtis Inst Music, 23-29 & Bryn Mawr Col, 28-29; vis prof, Univ Calif, 47-48, 55 & Harvard Univ, 52; Festschrift, Wächter & Hüter, 57; vis prof Ger, Univ Mass, 61-69. *Honors & Awards:* Alumni Medal, Univ Mich, 67; Knight Comdr Cross, Order of Merit, Fed Ger Repub, 67. *Mem:* MLA (2nd vpres, 63, pres, 66). *Res:* Comparative literature; recitation. *Publ:* Auth, The Modern Ibsen, Holt, 25; Thomas Mann's Novel, Der Zauberberg, Appleton, 33; transl, Goethe's Wisdom and Experience, Pantheon, 49; auth, Three Chapters on Courtly Love in Arthurian France and Germany, Univ NC, 57; Surveys and Soundings in European Literature, Princeton Univ, 65; Fährten und Funde, Francke, Berne, 67; Studies in Wolfram von Eschenbach's Parzival, Cornell Univ, 69; Critical Probings, Lang, Berne, 82; publ on Goethe, Rilke, Kafka, Nietzsche, Thomas Mann and Wolfram von Eschenback. *Mailing Add:* 40 Trumbull St New Haven CT 06510

WEIGER, JOHN GEORGE, b Dresden, Ger, Feb 6, 33; US citizen; m 55; c 3. ROMANCE LANGUAGES. *Educ:* Middlebury Col, BA, 55; Univ Colo, MA, 57; Ind Univ, PhD(Span), 66. *Prof Exp:* Instr Span, Univ Colo, 55-57 & Lawrence Col, 57-58; from instr to assoc prof, 58-73, from asst dean to dean, Col Arts & Sci, 68-76, PROF SPAN, UNIV VT, 73- *Concurrent Pos:* Consult, Eirikk Borue, Inc; vis lectr, Univ Bologna, Italy, 78. *Mem:* Renaissance Soc Am; MLA; Am Asn Teachers Span & Port; Comediantes; Asoc Int Hisp. *Res:* Spanish comedia; Cervantes; linguistics. *Publ:* Auth, The Valencian Dramatists of Spain's Golden Age, 76 & Cristobal de Virues, 78, Twayne; Initial and extended speech in the theater of Guillen de Castro, In: Studies in Honor of Gerald E Wade, 78; La supercheria esta descubierta: Don Quijote and Gines de Pasamonte, Philol Quart, spring 78; The Individuated Self: Cervantes and the Emergence of the Individual, Univ Ohio, 79; Hacia la comedia: De los valencianos a lope, Cupsa, Madrid, 78; Las Hazanas del cid, Puvill, Barcelona, 80; The curious pertinence of Eugenio's tale in Don Quijote, Mod Lang Notes, 81. *Mailing Add:* Dept of Romance Lang Univ of Vermont Burlington VT 05405

WEIL, HELEN HARMASH, b Russia, Feb 5, 33; US citizen; c 2. RUSSIAN LANGUAGE & LITERATURE. *Educ:* San Diego State Univ, BA, 68; Univ Calif, Los Angeles, MA, 71. *Prof Exp:* From actg dir to dir, Prog in Russ, 75-78, LECTR RUSS LANG & LIT, UNIV CALIF, IRVINE, 74- *Concurrent Pos:* Consult Russ, Satra Corp, 75-; prin investr, 1st-yr Russ prof grant, Univ Calif, 75-76 & 2nd-yr, 76-77. *Mem:* MLA; Foreign Lang Asn Am; Am Asn Advan Slavic Studies; Am Asn Teachers Slavic & E European Lang. *Res:* Methodology of language teaching; development of innovative instructional programs in language and literature. *Mailing Add:* Russ Inst Univ of Calif Irvine CA 92717

WEIL, IRWIN, b Cincinnati, Ohio, Apr 16, 28; m 50; c 3. RUSSIAN LITERATURE. *Educ:* Univ Chicago, AB, 48, MA, 51; Harvard Univ, PhD, 60. *Prof Exp:* Instr Russ, Boston Univ, 55; lectr Russ & comp lit, Brandeis Univ, 59-60, asst prof, 60- 65; assoc prof Russ & Russ lit, 66-70, PROF RUSS & COMP LIT, NORTHWESTERN UNIV, EVANSTON, 70- *Concurrent Pos:* Inter-Univ Comt grant, Moscow Inst World Lit & Moscow State Univ, 60, 63 & 68; Am Coun Learned Soc traveling grant, 67; vis US sr scholar, Moscow State Univ, 68; master, Willard Residential Col, 72-76, dept chmn, 76-82; vis US scholar, USSR Acad Sci. *Mem:* Am Asn Teachers Slavic & EEurop Lang (exec secy, 62-67); MLA; Am Coun Teachers Russ (pres, 80-). *Res:* Russian and comparative literature. *Publ:* Auth, Gorky: His Literary Development and Influence on Soviet Intellectual Life, Random, 66; Soviet literary tradition in a revolutionary context, Proc Pac Foreign Lang Conf, 67; On Soviet and American translating Murther, In--Razboi, Tri-Quart Rev, winter 67; Soviet cultural life, In: Colliers Encycl, Collier-Macmillan, 68. *Mailing Add:* Slavic Dept Northwestern Univ Evanston IL 60201

WEIMAR, KARL SIEGRRIED, b Philadelphia, Pa, Dec 1, 16; m 43; c 3. GERMAN. *Educ:* Univ Pa, AB, 37, AM, 38, PhD, 44; Univ Heidelberg, dipl, 37. *Prof Exp:* Instr Ger, Univ Del, 40-41, Univ Ill, 42-43, Army Specialized Training Prog, Univ Pa, 44-45 & Temple Univ, 45-46; from instr to assoc prof, 46-66, chmn dept, 67-73, PROF GER, BROWN UNIV, 66- *Concurrent Pos:* Ed, Ger Ser, Prentice-Hall, Inc, 64-76. *Mem:* MLA; Am Asn Teachers Ger. *Res:* Translations of German poetry; concept of love in the works of Hermann Stephr; a study of Wolfgang Borchert, J P Sartre, Hauptmann and Thomas Mann. *Publ:* Coauth, Practice and Progress, Review Grammar, Blaisdell, 63, 2nd rev ed, 70; ed & contribr, German Language and Literature: Seven Essays, Prentice-Hall, 74; Paul Celan's Todesfuge: Translation and interpretation, Publ Mod Lang Asn, 1/74. *Mailing Add:* Dept of Ger Box E Brown Univ Providence RI 02912

WEINBERG, FLORENCE MAY, b Alamogordo, NMex, Dec 3, 33; m 55. ROMANCE LANGUAGES. *Educ:* Park Col, AB, 54; Univ BC, MA, 63; Univ Rochester, PhD(French), 68. *Prof Exp:* From asst prof to assoc prof, 67-75, chmn dept mod lang & class studies, 72-79, PROF FRENCH & SPAN LIT, ST JOHN FISHER COL, 75- *Concurrent Pos:* Am Coun Learned Soc grant-in-aid, 74; consult-panelist, Nat Found Arts & Humanities & Nat Endowment for Humanities, 77-; Nat Endowment for Humanities sr fel, 79-80. *Mem:* MLA; Am Comp Lit Asn; Northeast Mod Lang Asn; Am Asn Teachers Fr. *Res:* French humanism; Francois Rabelais and Christian hermetism; iconography of the French and Spanish Renaissance. *Publ:* Auth, Frere Jean, Evangelique: His function in the Rabelaisian world, Mod Lang Rev, 71; Aspects of symbolism in La Celestina, Mod Lang Notes, 71; The Wine and the Will: Rabelais's Bacchic Christianity, Wayne State Univ, 72; Francesco Colonna and Rabelais's Tribute to Guillaume du Bellay, Romance Notes, 74; La Parolle faict le jeu: Mercury in the Cymbalum Mundi of Bonaventure des Periers, L'Esprit Createur, 76; Chess, a literary archetype, in Colonna's Hypnerotomachia and in Rabelais' Cinquiesme Livre, Romanic Rev, 79; Comic and Religious Elements in Rabelais, Tempete en Mer, Etudes Rabelaisiennes, 80; Fischart's Geschichtklitterung: A questionable reception of Gargantua, 16th Century J (in press). *Mailing Add:* 290 Forest Hills Rd Rochester NY 14625

WEINBERG, KURT, b Hannover, Ger, Feb, 24, 12; nat US; m 55. COMPARATIVE LITERATURE. *Educ:* Trinity Col, Conn, MA, 49; Yale Univ, PhD(French), 53. *Prof Exp:* Asst prof mod lang, Hillyer Col, 46-50; asst instr French, Yale Univ, 50-53; instr Romance lang, Hunter Col, 53-54; vis prof French, State Univ Iowa, 54-55; vis prof, Univ BC, 55-57; asst prof French lang & lit, 57-61; prof foreign & comp lit, 62-68, prof French, Ger & comp lit, 68-77, EMER PROF FRENCH, GER & COMP LIT, UNIV ROCHESTER, 77- *Concurrent Pos:* Guggenheim fel, 60; Nat Endowment for Humanities sr fel, 74-75; vis prof, Univ Konstanz, 79-80. *Mem:* MLA; Am Comp Lit Asn. *Res:* French and comparative literature of the 19th and 20th centuries; philosophy of language; aesthetics. *Publ:* Auth, Henri Heine, Romantique defroque, Heraut du Symbolisme francais, Yale Univ & Univ France, 53; Kafkas Dichtungen, Die Travestien des Mythos, Francke, Bern, 63; Sprache und Realität, Sprache im technischen Zeitalter, 68-69; Andre Gide: Le Promethee mal enchaine, In: Der moderne französische Roman, 68 & Zu Valerys Dialogue de l'arbre, das Gedicht von den Antipoden Valery und Gide, In: Interpretation und Vergleich, 72, Erich Schmidt; On Gide's Prometheе, Private Myth and Public Mystification, Princeton Univ, 72; The Figure of Faust in Valery and Goethe: An Exegesis of Mon Faust, Princeton Univ, 76; The Lady and the Unicorn, or M de Nemours a Coulommiers, Euphorion, 4/77; Baudelaires Une Charogne: Paradigma Einer Asthetik des Unbehagens in der Natur, Poetica, 1/80. *Mailing Add:* 290 Forest Hills Rd Rochester NY 14625

WEINBERG, WERNER, b Rheda, Ger, May 30, 15; US citizen; m 38; c 1. HEBREW. *Educ:* Hebrew Teachers Sem, Würzburg, Ger, Grad, 36; Univ Louisville, MA, 53; Hebrew Union Col, PhD, 61. *Prof Exp:* From instr to assoc prof, 61-70, PROF HEBREW LANG & LIT, HEBREW UNION COL, OHIO, 70- *Concurrent Pos:* Fulbright scholar grammar spoken Hebrew, 69-70; mem, Subcomt Conversion Hebrew & Yiddish, Am Nat Standard Inst, 71- *Mem:* Nat Asn Prof Hebrew; Soc Bibl Lit; Israel Ling Soc. *Res:* The emerging new grammar of spoken Hebrew; Hebrew linguistics; Judaeo-German. *Publ:* Auth, Spoken Israeli Hebrew, J Semitic Studies, spring 66; Die Reste des Jüdischdeutschen, Kohlhammer, Stuttgart, 69, 2nd en, 73; Transliteration and transcription of Hebrew, Hebrew Union Col Ann, 70; The way of the language improvers, In: Studies on Jewish themes by contemporary American scholars, Jerusalem, 72; The reform of Hebrew orthography, Hebrew Univ, Juerusalem, 72; How Do You Spell Chanukah?, Ktav, 76; The Tale of a Torah Scroll, Hebrew Union Col, 76; the history of Hebrew Plene spelling: part 1: From antiquity to Haskalah, Hebrew Union Col Ann, 76. *Mailing Add:* Hebrew Union Col 3101 Clifton Ave Cincinnati OH 45220

WEINBERGER, LEON JUDAH, Philosophy, Religion. See Vol IV

WEINBERGER, MARVIN ELMER, b Cleveland, Ohio, June 6, 30. FRENCH. *Educ:* Western Reserve Univ, BA, 51; Cornell Univ, MA, 52, PhD, 56. *Prof Exp:* Teaching asst French, Cornell Univ, 51-56; instr, Brown Univ, 56-58; asst prof, Reed Col, 58-60; from asst prof to assoc prof, 60-71, PROF FRENCH, SAN FRANCISCO STATE UNIV, 71- *Mem:* Am Asn Teachers Fr. *Res:* The aesthetics of symbolist poetry; theory of the linguistic sing in literature. *Mailing Add:* Dept of Lang San Francisco State Univ San Francisco CA 94132

WEINER, JACK, b Baltimore, Md, Jan 13, 34; m 68; c 1. SPANISH, RUSSIAN. *Educ:* Univ Md, BA, 56; Middlebury Col, MA, 59 & 63; Ind Univ, PhD(Span, Russ), 68. *Prof Exp:* Asst prof Span, Univ Kans, 66-70; assoc prof, 70-77, PROF SPAN, NORTHERN ILL UNIV, 77- *Mem:* Am Asn Teachers Span & Port; MLA; Int Asn Hispanists; Renaissance Soc Am. *Res:* Spanish Golden Age literature, especially the comedia and prose; Hispano-Russian literary and cultural relations. *Publ:* Auth, Mantillas in Moscovy: The Spanish Golden Age Theater in Tsarist Russia: 1672-1917, Humanities Ser, Univ Kans, 70; El Diario Espanol de Alexander Veselovskii, Cuadernos Hispanoamericanos, 70; Cancionero de Sebastian de Horozco, Utah Studies in Lit & Ling, 75; El escudero y las prostitutas: Lazaro y el escuder en el rio, Rev Signos, Vol IV, No 2 & Romance Notes, Vol XIII, No 2; coauth, Turgenev's Fathers and Sons and Galdos' Dona Perfecta, PMLA, LXXXVI: 19-23. *Mailing Add:* Dept of Foreign Lang & Lit Northern Ill Univ De Kalb IL 60115

WEINER, SEYMOUR SIDNEY, b New York, NY, Sept 4, 17; m 41; c 3. ROMANCE LANGUAGES. *Educ:* City Col New York, AB, 40; Univ Calif, MA, 41; Columbia Univ, PhD(French), 50, MSLS, 52. *Prof Exp:* Lectr & instr French, Columbia Univ, 46- 50; head photog reproduction div & acquisitions asst, Univ Ill Libr, 52-53; vis lectr Romance lang & librarianship, Univ Wash, 53-54, from asst prof to assoc prof Romance lang & lit, 54-63; assoc prof French, State Univ NY Col, Stony Brook, 63-64; PROF FRENCH, UNIV MASS, AMHERST, 64- *Concurrent Pos:* Instr, Brooklyn Col, 46-47; managing ed, Fr Rev, 65-68; gen ed, Critical Biblio Fr Lit, till 71. *Honors & Awards:* Chevalier, Palmes Academiques, 67. *Mem:* MLA; Am Asn Teachers Fr; Am Soc Aesthet; Renaissance Soc Am; Am Comp Lit Asn. *Res:* Contemporary French literature; bibliography and methodology of research in the humanities; the French little magazine. *Publ:* Auth, Francis Carco, The Career of a Literary Bohemian, Columbia Univ; contribr, European Authors 1000-1900, Wilson, 67; contribr, Mod Lang Forum, Mod Lang Quart & Pac Coast Philol. *Mailing Add:* Dept of French & Italian Univ of Massachusetts Amherst MA 01002

WEINGARTNER, RUSSELL, b Newport, Ky, June 23, 21; m 48; c 3. FRENCH LITERATURE & LINGUISTICS. *Educ:* Univ Cincinnati, AB, 48; Princeton Univ, MA, 51, PhD(French lit), 68. *Prof Exp:* Instr ling, Cornell Univ, 51-56; instr Romance lang, Northwestern Univ, 56-66; asst prof French lit, Carleton Col, 66-70; dir, Semester in Paris, 73, ASSOC PROF MOD LANG, UNIV AKRON, 70- *Mem:* MLA; Am Asn Teachers Fr; Int Arthurian Soc. *Res:* Short stories of Guy de Maupassant; Old French language and literature; linguistics applied to language teaching. *Publ:* Auth, Stylistic analysis of an anonymous work: The Old French Lai Guingamor, Mod Philol, 8/71. *Mailing Add:* 61 Sand Run Rd Akron OH 44313

WEINKAUF, ARNOLD LEWIS, b Wausau, Wis, May 17, 24. GERMAN. *Educ:* Northwestern Univ, BS, 47, MA, 48, PhD(Ger), 51. *Prof Exp:* Instr Ger, Col of Wooster, 52-53 & Univ Mich, 53-54; from instr to asst prof, 54-72, ASSOC PROF FOREIGN LANG, MICH TECHNOL UNIV, 72- *Concurrent Pos:* Fulbright scholar, Austria, 51-52; adv, Fulbright Comt, 69. *Mem:* Am Asn Teachers Ger; MLA; Can Ling Asn; Nat Asn Lang Lab Dirs. *Res:* Baroque literature; linguistics; scientific German. *Mailing Add:* Dept of Humanities Mich Technol Univ Houghton MI 49931

WEINREICH, BEATRICE, b New York, NY, May 14, 28; m 49; c 2. ANTHROPOLOGY. *Educ:* Brooklyn Col, BA, 49; Columbia Univ, MA, 55. *Prof Exp:* From res asst to res dir, 47-49, res assoc, Yiddish Lang & Cult Atlas, 59-72, RES ASSOC YIDDISH FOLKLORE, YIVO INST JEWISH RES, 72- *Concurrent Pos:* Co-ed, Yidisher Folklor, 55-; consult Yiddish lang prog, Columbia Univ, 68-; consult folklore, Max Weinreich Ctr Advan Jewish Studies, Yivo Inst & Columbia Univ, 70- *Mem:* Am Folklore Soc. *Res:* Yiddish folktales, proverbs and riddles; acculturation and its effects on old world customs. *Publ:* Coauth, Yiddish Language & Folklore: A Selective Bibliography for Research, Mouton, The Hague, 59; auth, The Americanization of Passover, In: Studies in Biblical and Jewish Folklore, Ind Univ, 60; A structural analysis of Yiddish proverbs, In: Studies in Honor of Max Weinreich, Mouton, The Hague, 64; Kinship Terminology in a Modern Fusion Language, Yivo Inst, 75; co-ed, On Semantics, Univ Pa Press, 81; Language and Culture Atlas of Ashkenazic Jewry, Ishi (in press). *Mailing Add:* Yivo Inst for Jewish Res 1048 Fifth Ave New York NY 10028

WEINSTEIN, ALLEN ISAAC, b Brooklyn, NY, Feb 7, 33; m 54; c 2. APPLIED LINGUISTICS, ANTHROPOLOGY. *Educ:* Columbia Univ, BA, 55, MA, 56; State Univ NY, Buffalo, PhD(anthrop), 66. *Prof Exp:* Instr German, State Univ NY, Buffalo, 59-64, lectr, 64-65, asst prof, 65-66; sci ling Vietnamese, 66-71, sci ling Germanic lang, 71-81, CHMN DEPT OF RESOURCES & SUPPORT, SCH LANG STUDIES, FOREIGN SERV INST, 81- *Mem:* Am Anthrop Asn; AAAS; Ling Soc Am; AAUP; Soc Applied Anthrop. *Res:* Cultural awareness as a factor in second language acquisition; impact of foreign language competence on United States government affairs. *Publ:* Coauth, Deutsche Stunden, Scribner's, 64; auth, Foreign language majors: The Washington perspective, Asn Dept For Lang Bull, 5/75; coauth, FSI Dutch Reader, Govt Printing Off, 76; ed, FSI Swedish Basic Course, Nat AV Ctr (in press). *Mailing Add:* Foreign Serv Inst US Dept of State Arlington VA 22209

WEINSTEIN, ARNOLD LOUIS, b Memphis, Tenn, July 8, 40; m 62; c 2. COMPARATIVE LITERATURE, FRENCH STUDIES. *Educ:* Princeton Univ, BA, 62; Harvard Univ, MA, 64, PhD(comp lit), 68. *Prof Exp:* Asst prof French, 68-73, assoc prof French & comp lit, 73-77, PROF COMP LIT, BROWN UNIV, 77- *Concurrent Pos:* Nat Endowment for Humanities jr humanist fel, 71-72; Fulbright prof Am Lit, Stockholm Univ, 83. *Res:* Modern American, English, French and German fiction; early English and European fiction. *Publ:* Auth, Vision and Response in Modern Fiction, Cornell Univ, 74; Character as Lost Cause, Novel 78; Kafka's writing machine: Metamorphosis in the Penal Colony, Studies in 20th century Lit, 80; Literature as home, Brown Alumni Monthly, 80; Freedom and control in the erotic novel: The classical and the surrealist model: Les Liaisons dangereuses and Naked Lunch, Dada/Surrealism, 80; The Fiction of Relationship, Novel, 81; Fictions of the Self: 1550-1800, Princeton Univ Press, 81; Does individualism have a future, Reflections on Oneness and Other Things, Brown Univ, 81. *Mailing Add:* Dept of French Studies & Comp Lit Brown Univ Providence RI 02912

WEINSTEIN, LEO, b Rustringen-Wilhelmshaven, Ger, May 15, 21; US citizen. FRENCH. *Educ:* Fla Southern Col, AB, 47; Stanford Univ, AM, 48, PhD, 51. *Prof Exp:* From inst to assoc prof, 51-65, PROF FRENCH, STANFORD UNIV, 65- *Res:* Comparative literature; 17th and 19th century French literature. *Publ:* Coauth, Ernest Chausson: The Composer's Life and Works, Univ Okla, 55; auth, The Metamorphoses of Don Juan, Stanford Univ, 59; Kafka's ape: Heel or hero?, Mod Fiction Studies, spring 62; ed, The Age of Reason, Braziller, 65; auth, Stendhal's Count Mosca as a statesman, PMLA, 6/65; Hippolyte Taine, Twayne, 72; Die beiden Don-Juan Typen, Don Juan, Darmstadt, 76; Altered states of consciousness in Flaubert's Madame Bovary and Kafka's A Country Doctor, In: Voices of Conscience, Temple Univ, 77. *Mailing Add:* Dept of French & Ital Stanford Univ Stanford CA 94305

WEINSTEIN, STANLEY, Buddhist & East Asian Studies. See Vol IV

WEINTRAUB, WIKTOR, b Zawiercie, Poland, Apr 10, 08; nat US; m 34. POLISH. *Educ:* Jagiellonian Univ, MA, 29, PhD(philos), 30. *Prof Exp:* Researcher, Parish, 37-39; mem press off, Polish Embassy, Moscow, 41-42; ed, Polish Fortnightly, Jerusalem, 43-45; mem, Polish Ministry Inform, London, 45; writer & lectr, London, 45-50; vis lectr, 50-54, from assoc prof to prof Slavic lang & lit, 54-71, Jurzykowski prof, 71-78, EMER JURZYKOWSKI PROF POLISH LANG & LIT, HARVARD UNIV, 78- *Concurrent Pos:* Guggenheim fel, 53. *Honors & Awards:* Alfred Jurzykowski Found Award, 77. *Mem:* Am Compt Lit Asn; Am Asn Teachers Slavic Lang & Lit. *Res:* Polish literature, modern Renaissance, baroque and Romantic periods. *Publ:* Auth, The Style of J Kochanowski, Kasa im Mianowskiego, Warsaw, 32; The Poetry of Adam Michiewicz, 54 & Literature as Prophecy, 59, Mouton, The Hague; Prophecy and Professorship: Michiewicz, Michelet and Quinet, 75 & From Rej to Boy, 77, Panstwowy Inst Wydawniczy, Warsaw; Jan Kochanowski, Wydawnictwo Literackie, Cracow, 77. *Mailing Add:* 383 Broadway Cambridge MA 02139

WEISBERG, DAVID B, b New York, NY, Nov 15, 38; M 58; c 4. ASSYRIOLOGY. *Educ:* Columbia Col, AB, 60; Jewish Theol Sem Am, BHL, 60; Yale Univ, PhD, 65. *Prof Exp:* Res Assoc Assyriol, Orient Inst, Univ Chicago, 65-67; from asst prof to assoc prof, 67-71, PROF BIBLE & SEMITIC LANG, HEBREW UNION COL, OHIO, 71- *Mem:* Am Orient Soc; Soc Bibl Lit. *Res:* Bible; Assyriology. *Publ:* Auth, Guild Structure and Political Allegiance in Early Achaemenid Mesopotamia, Near Eastern Res, No. 1, Yale Univ, 67; A neo-Babylonian temple report, J Am Orient Soc, 67; Rare accents of the 21 books, Jewish Quart Rev, 67; Texts from the Time of Nebuchadnezzar, Yale, Vol 17, 80. *Mailing Add:* Dept of Bible & Semitic Lang Hebrew Union Col Cincinnati OH 45220

WEISER, ERNEST L, b Buffalo, NY, Oct 17, 30; m 67; c 2. GERMAN LANGUAGE & LITERATURE. *Educ:* Univ Buffalo, BA, 52; Syracuse Univ, AM, 54; Univ Calif, Los Angeles, PhD(Ger), 66. *Prof Exp:* From instr to asst prof Ger, Reed Col, 58-63, asst prof humanities, 62-63; asst prof Ger, Univ Miami, 63-66; from asst prof to assoc prof, 63-77, actg chmn dept lang & ling, 68-69, PROF GER, FLA ATLANTIC UNIV, 77-, CHMN DEPT LANG & LING, 69- *Concurrent Pos:* WGer Govt travel & study grant, 61. *Mem:* MLA; SAtlantic Mod Lang Asn; Am Asn Teachers Ger; Asn Dept Foreign Lang; Am Coun Teachers Foreign Lang. *Res:* Friedrich Schiller and Friedrich Dürrenmatt; 18th century German literature; modern German poetry. *Publ:* Auth, The inner form of Schiller's Die Braut von Messina, SAtlantic Bull, 11/69; The language and linguistics program at Florida Atlantic University, Asn Dept Foreign Lang, 12/73; Dürrenmatt's Dialogue with Schiller, Ger Quart, 5/75; Dürrenmatt's Akki: An Actor's Life for Me! An interpretation, Monatshefte, winter 76. *Mailing Add:* Dept of Lang & Ling Col of Humanities Fla Atlantic Univ Boca Raton FL 33432

WEISERT, JOHN JACOB, b Louisville, Ky, Dec 18, 14; m 62. GERMANICS. *Educ:* Univ Louisville, AB, 36; Columbia Univ, AM, 38, PhD, 47. *Prof Exp:* Lectr Ger, Barnard Col, Columbia Univ, 40-42; instr, Univ Tenn, 47-48; asst prof mod lang, Univ Louisville, 48-51 & Pa State Univ, 51-53; assoc prof, 56-62, head dept, 63-72, PROF MOD LANG, UNIV LOUISVILLE, 62- *Concurrent Pos:* Carnegie intern, Univ Chicago, 55-56; ed, Univ Louisville Libr Rev, 67-74. *Mem:* MLA. *Res:* German literature; American theatre. *Mailing Add:* Dept of Mod Lang Univ of Louisville Louisville KY 40208

WEISINGER, KENNETH DEAN, b Blanco Co, Tex, Dec 8, 42. GERMAN, COMPARATIVE LITERATURE. *Educ:* Stanford Univ, BA, 64; Univ Calif, Berkeley, MA, 67, PhD(comp lit), 71. *Prof Exp:* ASSOC PROF GER & COMP LIT, UNIV CALIF, BERKELEY, 71- *Mem:* MLA; Am Philol Asn. *Res:* Greek and Latin literature; German literature. *Publ:* Auth, Irony and moderation in Juvenal XI, Calif Studies Class Antiq, 72; Goethe's Phaethon, Deut Vierteljahrsschrift, 73; The structure of Rilke's Seventh Duino Elegy, Germanic Rev, 74. *Mailing Add:* Dept of Comp Lit Univ Calif Berkeley CA 94720

WEISS, ARNOLD HENRY, b Cleveland, Ohio, Aug 19, 15. SPANISH. *Educ:* Western Reserve Univ, AB, 43; Univ Wis, MA, 48, PhD(Span), 52. *Prof Exp:* Instr Span & acting chmn dept, exten, Univ Wis, 52-53; asst prof, 56-61, ASSOC PROF SPAN, UNIV KANS, 61-, ASST DEAN GRAD SCH, 64- *Mem:* Am Asn Teachers Span & Port; MLA; Archaeol Inst Am. *Res:* Hispano-Roman archaeology; international programs; foreign language and area studies. *Publ:* Auth, The Roman walls of Barcelona, Archaeology, autumn 61. *Mailing Add:* Grad Sch Univ of Kans Lawrence KS 66045

WEISS, BENO, b Fiume, Italy, Aug 7, 33; US citizen; m; c 1. ITALIAN LITERATURE. *Educ:* NY Univ, BA, 63, MA, 65, PhD(Ital), 71. *Prof Exp:* Instr Ital, NY Univ, 66-69; asst prof, 69-76, ASSOC PROF ITAL, PA STATE UNIV, UNIVERSITY PARK, 76- *Concurrent Pos:* Inst Arts & Humanistic Studies res fel, Italy, 72; Am Philos Soc fel, 78. *Honors & Awards:* Teaching Award, Col Lib Arts, Pa State Univ, 77. *Mem:* MLA; Am Names Soc; Am Asn Teachers Ital; Am Ital Hist Asn; Am Soc Sephardic Studies. *Res:* The theater of Italo Svevo. *Publ:* Auth, Svevo's Inferiorita, Mod Fiction Studies, spring 72; Translation of a husband: a play in three acts by Italo Svevo, Mod Int Drama, fall 72; An Annotated Bibliography on the Theater of Italo Svevo, Pa State Univ, 74; Federico Garcia Lorca in Italy, Garcia Lorca Rev, spring-fall, 75. *Mailing Add:* Dept of Span, Ital & Port N-352 Burrowes Pa State Univ University Park PA 16802

WEISS, GERHARD HANS, b Berlin, Ger, Aug 6, 26; nat US; m 53. GERMAN. *Educ:* Wash Univ, AB, 50, MA, 52; Univ Wis, PhD(Ger), 56. *Prof Exp:* From instr to asst prof Ger, 56-64, assoc prof Ger & comp lit, 64-66, assoc dean humanities & fine arts, 67-71, chmn dept comp lit, 67-72, PROF GER & COMP LIT, UNIV MINN, MINNEAPOLIS, 66- *Concurrent Pos:* Ed, Unterrichtspraxis, 75-80. *Honors & Awards:* Mores Award, AMOCO, 81. *Mem:* MLA; Am Asn Teachers Ger (pres, 82-83); Am Coun Teaching Foreign Lang; Am Comp Lit Asn. *Res:* Cultural contrasts; 17th century literature; 20th century literature. *Publ:* Auth, Das Haus des Schicksals, Monatshefte, 61; An interpretation of the miner's scene in Goethe's Wilhelm Meisters Lehrajahre, In: Lebendige Form, Wilhelm Fink, Munich, 70; coauth, Begegnung mit Deutschland, Dodd, 70; auth, Rolf Hochhuth, In: Deutsche Dichter der Gegenwart, Erich Schmidt, Berlin, 73; Die Prosawerke Werner Bergengruens. *Mailing Add:* Dept of Ger Univ of Minn Minneapolis MN 55455

WEISS, GERSHON, b Haifa, Israel, Feb 11, 35; US citizen; m 58; c 3. ORIENTAL STUDIES, HEBREW LANGUAGE. *Educ:* Hebrew Univ Jerusalem, BA, 61, dipl, 62; Univ Pa, MA, 67, PhD(Orient studies, Hebrew-Arabic), 70. *Prof Exp:* Asst prof Hebrew-Arabic, Temple Univ, 72-73; asst prof, Hebrew-Bible, Gratz Col, 73-76; ASST PROF HEBREW, TEMPLE UNIV, 76- *Concurrent Pos:* Res asst Geniza proj, Univ Pa, 70-71 & Inst Advan Studies, 71- *Mem:* MidE Studies Asn; Am Orient Soc; Asn Jewish Studies. *Res:* Documentary fragments from the Cairo geniza; Hebrew language; history of the Muslim world. *Publ:* Auth, Financial arrangement for a widow in a Cairo geniza document, In: Gratz Col Anniversary Vol, 71; Mortgage procedures and interest rates as reflected in the Cairo geniza documents at the first quarter of the twelfth century, 72, Formularies reconstructed from the Cairo geniza, 73, Formularies, Vol II & III, 74-75 & Herem-excommunication Formulary, 77, Gratz Col Ann Jewish Studies, 77; Testimony from the Cairo geniza, JQR, 77. *Mailing Add:* 470 Woodhaven Rd Philadelphia PA 19116

WEISS, HERMANN FRIEDRICH, b Beuel, Ger, June 17, 37; m 66. GERMAN LANGUAGE & LITERATURE. *Educ:* Univ Bonn, Staatsexamen, 63; Princeton Univ, MA, 67, PhD(Ger lit), 68. *Prof Exp:* Lektor Ger, Univ St Andrews, 63-64; instr, Univ Ore, 64-65; asst prof, 68-75, PROF GER, UNIV MICH, ANN ARBOR, 75- *Mem:* MLA; Am Asn Teachers Ger; AAUP. *Res:* Achim von Arnim; fiction from the 18th to the 20th century; 18th and 19th century drama. *Publ:* Auth, Achim von Arnims Metamorphosen der Gesellschaft, Zeitschrift für Deut Philol, 72; Image structures in Goethe's Iphigenie auf Tauris, Mod Lang Notes, 72; The reader as spectator: the direct speech opening in eighteenth and nineteenth century German fiction, Neophilologus, 73; A von Arnim's Kirchenordnung, Orbis Lit, 76; The labyrinth of crime A reinterpretation of Hoffmann's Fräulein von Scuderi, Ger Rev, 76; Unveröffentlichte prosaentwürfe A von Arnim's zur Zeitkritik (um 1810), Jahrbuch des Hochstifts, 77; Die bewertung der demut in den vierziger Jahren des 19 Jahrhunderts, Zeitschrift für Deut Philol, 78; Ein unbekannter brief Heinrichs von Kleist an Marie von Kleist, Jahrbuch der Deutschen Schillergesellschaft, 78. *Mailing Add:* Dept of Ger Univ of Mich Ann Arbor MI 48109

WEISS, RICHARD AUGUST, b Staten Island, NY, Dec 23, 32. GERMAN. *Educ:* Wash Sq Col, NY Univ, BA, 53, MA, 58; NY Univ, PhD(Ger), 68. *Prof Exp:* Instr, 58-60, PROF GER & CHMN DEPT, WESLEYAN COL, 64-, LIBR BIBLIOGRAPHER, 74- *Mem:* MLA; Am Asn Teachers Ger; Southeast Mod Lang Asn; AAUP. *Res:* German literature; American history: German influence; Kentucky Methodist history. *Publ:* Translr, Hermann Zagel, An Excursion to the Mammoth Care of Kentucky, Register Ky Hist Soc, 7/73; Hermann Zagel's Gretna-Algiers Railroad, La Hist, fall 76. *Mailing Add:* 2311 S York Dr Owensboro KY 42301

WEISS, ROBERT OTTO, b Berlin, Ger, Sept 25, 18; nat US; m 55; c 4. GERMAN LANGUAGE & LITERATURE. *Educ:* Univ Mo, MA, 51; Stanford Univ, PhD(Ger & Span), 55. *Prof Exp:* Chief, educ rehabil, Army Serv Forces Regional Hospital, Camp Crowder, Mo. 46; instr Ger, Southwestern Mo State Col, 48-49; instr, Drury Col, 49-50; instr, Univ Mo, 50-51; instr Ger & Span, Stanford Univ, 52-55; instr Ger, Army Lang Sch, 55-56; assoc prof & head dept, WVa State Col, 56-58; assoc prof, Univ Ky, 59-64; PROF GER, STATE UNIV NY BINGHAMTON, 64-, SR CONSULT GERMANIC LANG, DEPT COMP LIT & SUPVR GER SECTOR TRANSL CTR, 73- *Concurrent Pos:* Mem, Am Comt Studies Austrian Lit, 67- *Mem:* Am Acad Polit & Soc Sci. *Res:* Philosophical and social developments in contemporary German literature; psychopathology; Arthur Schnitzler and his works. *Publ:* Auth, The levelling effect of the masses in the view of Kierkegaard and Ortega y Gasset, Ky Foreign Lang Quart, 60; ed, Arthur Schnitzler, Aphorismen und Betrachtunger, Vol V, In: Gesammelte Werke, S Fischer, Frankfurt/Main, 67; auth, The psychoses in the works of Arthur Schnitzler, Ger Quart, 5/68; ed & translr, Arthur Schnitzler, The Mind in Words and Actions, 72 & Someday Peace Will Return, 72, Ungar. *Mailing Add:* Dept of Ger Lang & Lit State Univ of New York Binghamton NY 13901

WEISS, SYDNA STERN, US citizen. GERMAN LANGUAGE & LITERATURE. *Educ:* Vassar Col, AB, 64; Middlebury Col, AM, 66; Princeton Univ, PhD(Ger), 75. *Prof Exp:* Instr in Ger, Manhattanville Col, 66-69; asst prof, 74-80, ASSOC PROF GER, HAMILTON COL, 80- *Concurrent Pos:* Teaching assoc, Danforth Found, 78-84. *Mem:* MLA; Am Asn Teachers Ger; AAUP. *Res:* Relations of science and literature; portrayals of scientists in German fiction. *Publ:* Auth, The non-euclidean idea in the conclusion of Kleist's Marionettentheater Essay, Hofstra Univ, 80; Dürrenmatt's The Physicists: The Möbius Strip as Structural Analogue, STTH, 80. *Mailing Add:* Dept of Ger Hamilton Col Clinton NY 13323

WEISS, WINFRIED FERDINAND, b Ger, Nov 10, 37; US citizen. COMPARATIVE LITERATURE. *Educ:* Univ NC, Chapel Hill, BA, 61; Harvard Univ, MA, 63, PhD(comp lit), 70. *Prof Exp:* From asst prof to assoc prof, 66-77, PROF FOREIGN LANG, CALIF STATE UNIV, HAYWARD, 77- *Mem:* MLA; Am Fedn Teachers, Am Asn Ger Teachers. *Publ:* Auth, England, Hofmannsthal's insular mirage, Comp Lit, winter 73; Ruskin, pater and Hofmannsthal, 73 & Hofmannsthal's Early Essay Uber moderne Englische malere, 75, Colloquia Ger. *Mailing Add:* Dept of Foreign Lang Calif State Univ Hayward CA 94542

WEISSBORT, DANIEL JACK, b London, Eng, Apr 30, 35; Brit citizen. TRANSLATION, MODERN EUROPEAN POETRY. *Educ:* Cambridge Univ, BA, 56, MA, 81. *Prof Exp:* ED, MOD POETRY IN TRANSL J, 65-; ED DIR, PERSEA BKS, INC, 78- *Concurrent Pos:* Adv dir, Poetry Int, 70-73; Arts Coun Gr Brit grants, 71, 72 & 80; dir transl workshop, Univ Iowa, 76-; mem int comt, Columbia Univ Transl Ctr, 76-; Nat Educ Asn transl fel, 81. *Mem:* MLA; Poetry Soc Gr Brit; Soc Authors, UK; PEN Club; Am Lit Transl Asn; Mid West Mod Lang Asn. *Res:* History and theory of translation; contemporary Russian poetry. *Publ:* Ed, Post-War Russian Poetry, Penguin, 74; coauth, The War is Over, Selected Poems of Evgeny Vinokurov, 76 & auth, Soundings (poems), 77, Carcanet, UK & Dufour, US; co-ed, Russian Poetry, the Modern Period, Univ Iowa, 78; ed, Lev Mak, From The Night & Other Poems, Ardis, 78; coauth, Russian Poetry: The Modern Period, Univ Iowa Press, 78; auth, Yevgeny Yeviushenko, Ivan the Terrible and Ivan the Fool, Gollancz, UK & Marek, 79; Patrick Modiano, Missing Person, Cape, UK, 80. *Mailing Add:* Dept of Comp Lit Univ of Iowa Iowa City IA 52242

WEISSENBERGER, KLAUS, b Sydney, Australia, Nov 15, 39; m 74. GERMAN LITERATURE. *Educ:* Univ Hamburg, Staatsexamen, 65; Univ Southern Calif, PhD(Ger), 67. *Prof Exp:* From asst prof to assoc prof, 67-77, chmn dept, 72-79, PROF GER, RICE UNIV, 77- *Mem:* Am Asn Teachers Ger; MLA; Int Asn Ger Studies; SCent Mod Lang Asn. *Res:* Lyric poetry as a genre; German exile literature; development of lyric poetry from Rilke to Celan. *Publ:* Auth, Formen der Elegie von Goethe bis Celan, 69, Die Elegie bei Paul Celan, 69 & Zwischen Stein und Stern, Mystische Formgebung in der Dichtung von Else Lasker-Schuler, Nelly Sachs und Paul Celan, 74, Franke, Bern; Dissonanzen und neugestimmte Saiten--eine Typologie der Exillyrik,

Literaturwissenschaftliches Jahrbuch, Vol 17, 76; Mythopoesis in German literary criticism, Lit & Myth, Vol 9, 79; Eine systematische Stiltypologie als Antwort auf einen dichtungsfrmeden Systemzwang, Jahrbuch fur Int Germanistik, Vol 12, 80; ed, Die deutsche Lyrik von 1945 bis 1975, Zwischen Botschaft und Spiel, 81. *Mailing Add:* Dept of Ger Rice Univ Houston TX 77001

WEISSMAN, HOPE PHYLLIS, English Literature, Medieval Studies. See Vol II

WEISSTEIN, ULRICH (WERNER), b Breslau, Ger, Nov 14, 25; m 52 c 4. COMPARATIVE LITERATURE, GERMAN. *Educ:* Ind Univ, MA, 53, PhD(comp lit), 54. *Prof Exp:* From instr to asst prof Ger & fine arts, Lehigh Univ, 54-58; from asst prof to assoc prof English & comp lit, 59-66, PROF GER & COMP LIT, IND UNIV, BLOOMINGTON, 66- *Concurrent Pos:* Vis prof comp lit, Univ Wis-Madison, 66, Univ Vienna, 76 & Stanford Univ, 78, vis prof Ger, Deut Sommerschule, Middlebury Col, 70, Univ Hamburg, 71 & 82; Guggenheim Found fel, 73; dir, Ind Purdue Studienprogramm, Hamburg, 81-82. *Mem:* Am Asn Teachers Ger; MLA; Am Comp Lit Asn; Int Comp Lit Asn. *Res:* Anglo-German and Franco-German relations; literature and the arts; German literature, especially since 1870. *Publ:* Auth, The Essence of Opera, Free Press, 64; Max Frisch, Twayne, 67; Einführung in die vergleichende Literaturwissenschaft, Kohlhammer, Stuttgart, 68; ed, Expressionism as an International Literary Phenomenon, Akad Kiado, Budapest & Didier, Paris, 73; co-ed, Texte and Kontexte: Festschrift für Norbert fuerst zum 65 Geburstag, Francke, Bern, 73; auth, Comparative Literature and Literary Theory: Survey and Introduction, Ind Univ, Bloomington, 73; ed, Literature and the other arts, Vol III, Proc IXth ICLA Cong, Innsbruck, 81; Vergleichende Literaturwissenschaft: Ein Forschungsbericht 1968-1977, Lang, Berne, 82. *Mailing Add:* 2204 Queens Way Bloomington IN 47401

WEISZ, PIERRE, b Lisieux, France, May 17, 30; m 56; c 3. FRENCH & AMERICAN LITERATURE. *Educ:* Univ Paris, Lic es Let, 55, DES, 56, CAPES, 59, Dr, 65. *Prof Exp:* Asst prof French, Dalhousie Univ, 61-63; asst prof, Reed Col, 63-67; assoc prof, Scripps Col, 67-69; resident dir, Ill Year Abroad Prog in France, 69-71, fel, Inst Advan Studies, 74, vis assoc prof, 71-80, ASSOC PROF FRENCH, UNIV ILL, URBANA, 80- *Mem:* Am Asn Teachers Fr; Soc Fr Prof Am. *Res:* French prose fiction; 17th century French literature; structuralism. *Publ:* Auth, Langage et imagerie chez Jacques Prevert, Fr Rev, Spec Issue No 1, winter 70; Incarnations du Roman, Mallier, 73; Classicisme et verite romanesque, L'Esprit Createur, fall 74. *Mailing Add:* Dept of French Univ of Ill Urbana IL 61801

WEITZMAN, RAYMOND STANLEY, b Los Angeles, Calif, June 23, 38; c 1. LINGUISTICS, JAPANESE LANGUAGE. *Educ:* Univ Calif, Los Angeles, AB, 64; Univ Southern Calif, MA, 66, PhD(ling), 69. *Prof Exp:* From asst prof to assoc prof, 71-76, chmn dept, 79-82, PROF LING, CALIF STATE UNIV, FRESNO, 77- *Concurrent Pos:* Proj dir grant, Nat Sci Found Instr Sci Equip Prog, 70-72. *Mem:* Ling Soc Am; Asn Comput Ling; Phonetic Soc Japan; Acoust Soc Am. *Res:* Acoustic phonetic properties of speech; the structure of the Japanese language; phonological theory. *Publ:* Auth, Lacuna in generative phonology: Contrast and free variation, Papers Ling, 72; coauth, Devoiced and whispered vowels in Japanese, Ann Bull Res Inst Logopedics & Phoniatrics, 76; Rehabilitation of a patient with complete mandibulectomy and partial glossectomy, Am J of Otolaryngology, 80. *Mailing Add:* Dept of Ling Calif State Univ Fresno CA 93740

WELCH, LILIANE, b Esch-Alzette, Luxembourg, Oct 20, 37; Can citizen; m 63; c 1. FRENCH LITERATURE, AESTHETICS. *Educ:* Univ Mont, BA, 60, MA, 61; Pa State Univ, PhD(French), 64. *Prof Exp:* Instr French, Univ Mont, 60-61; teaching fel, Pa State Univ, 61-64; asst prof, East Carolina Univ, 65-66, Antioch Col, 66-67; asst prof, 67-71, assoc prof, 71-77, PROF FRENCH, MOUNT ALLISON UNIV, 77- *Concurrent Pos:* Chmn, Int Cong of Aesthetics in Bucharest, 72. *Mem:* League of Can Poets. *Res:* Twentieth century French literature; nineteenth century French literature. *Publ:* Coauth, Emergence: Baudelaire, Mallarme, Rimbaud, Bald Eagle Press, 73; auth, Winter Songs, Killally Press, 77; coauth, Address: Rimbaud, Mallarme Butor, Sono Nis Press, 79; auth, Syntax of Ferment, Fiddlehead Poetry Bks, 79; Assailing Beats, Borealis Press, 79; October Winds, 80 & Brush and Trunks, 81, Fiddlehead Poetry Bks. *Mailing Add:* PO Box 246 Sackville NB E0A 3C0 Can

WELDEN, ALICIA GALAZ-VIVAR, b Valparaiso, Chile, Dec 4, 31; US citizen. SPANISH LITERATURE, LATIN AMERICAN POETRY. *Educ:* Univ Chile, prof, 55; Univ Ala, PhD(Spanish), 80. *Prof Exp:* Prof, Univ Chile, 66-76; LECTR SPANISH LIT, APPALACHIAN STATE UNIV, 82- *Res:* Spanish Peninsular poetry of the Golden Age; contemporary Spanish Latin American poetry; Spanish medieval and Renaissance literature. *Publ:* Auth, Anologia de Luis de Gongora, Ed Univ, Santiago, 61; Chile, poesia actual, Mundo Nuevo, Paris, 70; Notas para un acercamiento a Polifemo, Norte, Mex, 73; Retrato de Piramo de Luis de Gongora, Estudios Filologicos, IX, Univ Austral, Chile, 74; Galatea y Tisbe de Luis de Gongora, Univ Chile, 74; Luis de Gongora: Antologia clave, Ed Nascimento, Santiago, 74; Algunos escorzos comparativos de la poetica de Gongora y Lorca, Cuadernos Hispanoamericanos, Madrid, 82. *Mailing Add:* Dept of Spanish Lit Appalachian State Univ Boone NC 28608

WELKER, JOHN W, b Clarksville, Tenn, Jan 16, 21; m 45; c 2. ROMANCE LANGUAGES, LINGUISTICS. *Educ:* Austin Peay State Univ, BS, 47; Middlebury Col, MA, 51. *Prof Exp:* Asst prof French, Presby Jr Col, 51-54; asst prof, Austin Peay State Univ, 55-64; asst, Vanderbilt Univ, 64-66; ASSOC PROF FRENCH, AUSTIN PEAY STATE UNIV, 66- *Concurrent Pos:* Dir & lectr, Lang Workshop, 67-68; consult, Mod Lang Teachers, 68; educ leader, Exp Inter-Nat Living, Putney, Vt, 68. *Mem:* MLA; Am Asn Teachers Fr; Ling Soc Am. *Res:* Colette--an atypical novelist of the 20th century; role of foreign residence in language education. *Mailing Add:* Dept of French Austin Peay State Univ Clarksville TN 37040

WELLEK, RENE, b Vienna, Austria, Aug 22, 03; nat citizen; m 32, 68; c 1. ENGLISH & COMPARATIVE LITERATURE. *Educ:* Charles Univ, Prague,, PhD, 26. *Hon Degrees:* DHL, Lawrence Col, 58; DLitt, Oxford Univ, 60, Harvard Univ, 60, Univ Rome, 61, Univ Md, 64, Boston Col, 65, Columbia Univ, 68, Univ Mich, 72, Univ Munich, 72 & Univ EAnglia, Eng, 75; D es Lett, Univ Montreal, 70, Univ Louvain, 70. *Prof Exp:* Procter fel English, Princeton Univ, 27-28, instr, 29-30; instr, Smith Col, 28-29; docent, Univ Prague, 32-35; lectr, Sch Slavonic Studies, London, 35-39; lectr, State Univ Iowa, 39-41, from assoc prof to prof English, 41-46; prof Slavic & comp lit, 46-52, Sterling prof comp lit, 52-72, chmn dept comp lit, 59-72, chmn dept Slavics & dir grad studies comp lit, 47-59, STERLING EMER PROF COMP LIT, YALE UNIV, 72- *Concurrent Pos:* Assoc ed, Philol Quart, 41-46; vis prof, Harvard Univ, 50, 53-54; vis prof sem lit criticism, Princeton Univ, 50; Guggenheim fel, 51-52, 56-57 & 66-67; fel, Silliman Col; Fulbright res prof, Univs Florence & Rome, 59-60, prof, Mainz, Ger, 69; Nat Endowment for Humanities sr fel, 72-73; vis prof, Princeton Univ, 73; Patton prof comp lit, Ind Univ, 74; Cornell Univ Inst Humanities fel, 77; Walker-Ames prof, Univ Washington, 79; vis prof, Univ Calif, San Diego, 79, State Univ NY, Albany, 80 & Univ Calif, Riverside, 82. *Honors & Awards:* Am Coun Learned Soc Distinguished Scholar Humanities Award, 59; Bolligen Found Award, 63; Mary Peabody Waite Award, Nat Inst Arts & Lett, 76. *Mem:* MLA (vpres, 64); Int Comp Lit Asn (pres, 61); Am CompLit Asn (pres, 62); Czech Soc Arts & Sci in US (pres, 62); Mod Humanities Res Asn (pres, 74). *Res:* History of criticism; theory of literature; Slavic literatures. *Publ:* Auth, Theory of Literature, Harcourt Brace, 48; A History of Modern Criticism (4 vols), 55-65 & Concepts of Criticism, 63, Yale Univ; Dostoevsky, Prentice-Hall, 62; Essays on Czech Literature, Mouton, The Hague, 63; Irving Babbitt, Paul More, In: Transcendentalism, Mich Univ, 66; Discriminations, Yale Univ, 70; Four Critics: Croce, Valery, Lukacs, Ingarden, Univ Washington Press, 81; The Attack on Literature and Other Essays, Univ NC Press, 82. *Mailing Add:* 45 Fairgrounds Rd Woodbridge CT 06525

WELLER, HUBERT P, b Holland, Mich, Feb 27, 34. SPANISH. *Educ:* Univ Mich, BA, 56; Ind Univ, MA, 58, PhD(Span), 65. *Prof Exp:* Instr Span, Ohio Univ, 61-62; from instr to assoc prof, 62-70, prof & chmn dept foreign lang & lit, 70-76, PROF SPAN, HOPE COL, 76- *Mem:* MLA; Am Asn Teachers Span & Port. *Res:* Contemporary Latin American poetry; computer-assisted instruction in languages. *Publ:* Auth, La casa de carton de Martin Adan, y el mar como elemento metaforico, Letras, Univ San Marcos, 61; Bibliografia anotada y analitica de y sobre Martin Adan (Rafael de la Fuente Benavides) (1927-1974), Inst Nac de Cult, Lima, Peru, 75; An experiment in CAI in Spanish, Proc CCUC, 76; SPANCOM: Computer-Assisted Instruction for Spanish (Software and Manuals), Conduit, 79. *Mailing Add:* Dept of Foreign Lang & Lit Hope College Holland MI 49423

WELLES, MARCIA LOUISE, b Bridgeport, Conn, June 17, 43; m 67; c 2. SPANISH LITERATURE. *Educ:* Columbia Univ, AB, 65, PhD(Span), 71; Middlebury Col, MA, 66. *Prof Exp:* ASST PROF SPAN, BARNARD COL, COLUMBIA UNIV, 70- *Mem:* MLA; Am Asn Teachers Span & Port. *Res:* Seventeenth century Spanish prose; feminist studies in Spain and Latin America. *Mailing Add:* Dept of Span Barnard Col Columbia Univ New York NY 10028

WELLINGTON, MARIE ADELE ZEILSTRA, b Chicago Heights, Ill, Aug 11, 24; m 48; c 1. ROMANCE LANGUAGES. *Educ:* St Mary-of-the-Woods Col, BA, 46; Northwestern Univ, MA, 49, PhD(Romance lang), 51. *Prof Exp:* Instr Span, Univ Ill, 46-47, Mundelein Col, 48-49 & Seabury-Western Theol Sem, 54; from asst prof to assoc prof Span & Ital, Elmhurst Col, 54-62, chmn dept, 62-76, dir lang lab, 62-64, prof, 62-78; RES & WRITING, 78- *Concurrent Pos:* Fulbright award, Italy, 51-52; ed, Papers on Romance Lit Rel, 68 & 75. *Mem:* Am Asn Teachers Span & Port; MLA; Midwest Mod Lang Asn. *Res:* Galdos; Spanish pastoral novel; Romance literary relations. *Publ:* Auth, La Arcadia de Sannazaro y la Galatea de Cervantes, Hispanofila, 59; Marianela: Nuevas Dimensiones, 3/68 & The Awakening of Galdos Lazaro, 72, Hispania; Marianela de Galdos y Diderot, cuadernos Hispanoamericanos, 6/77; Marianela and La Symphonie pastorale, In: Romance Literary Studies: Homage to Harvey L Johnson, 79; ed, Romance Literary Studies: Homage to Harvey L Johnson, 79; auth, Galdos Gloria and Manzoni's I promessi sposi, Festschrift Jose Cid Perez, 81; A Symbolism Linking Marianela and the Torquemada Series, Hispanofila, 9/81. *Mailing Add:* 130 Cottage Hill Ave Elmhurst IL 60126

WELLIVER, GLENN EDWIN, b Baltimore, Md, Feb 20, 33; m 58; c 1. GERMAN LANGUAGE & LITERATURE. *Educ:* Dickinson Col, AB, 55; Northwestern Univ, Evanston, MA, 56, PhD(Ger), 64. *Prof Exp:* From instr to assoc prof Ger, 61-76, PROF GER, DePAUW UNIV, 76- *Mem:* MLA; Midwest Mod Lang Asn. *Res:* Modern drama; German cultural history. *Mailing Add:* 430 Anderson St Greencastle IN 46135

WELLS, COLIN MICHAEL, Roman History, Classical Archeology. See Vol I

WELLS, JOHN CORSON, b Cambridge, Mass, Feb 3, 18; m; c 1. GERMAN. *Educ:* Harvard Univ, AB, 40, AM, 42, PhD, 52. *Prof Exp:* From instr to asst prof, 47-68, assoc prof, 68-80, PROF GER, TUFTS UNIV, 81- *Concurrent Pos:* Nat Found Arts & Humanities grant, 67-78; res scholar, Mellon grant, Tufts Univ, 82-83; auth, Althochdeutsches Glossenworterbuch, 72-83. *Honors & Awards:* Verdienstkreuz I Klasse, Fed Repub Ger, 61. *Mem:* MLA; Am Asn Teachers Ger; Mediaeval Acad Am; Ling Soc Am. *Res:* Old High German; lexicography; literary data processing. *Publ:* Auth, Meanings of Mediaeval Latin 'propositum' as reflected in Old High German, Mod Lang Notes; The origin of the German suffix -heit, In: Festschrift Taylor Starck, 64; The -heit compounds and derivatives in Notker's works, In: Festschrift E H Sehrt, 68. *Mailing Add:* Dept of German Tufts Univ Medford MA 02155

WELLS, LAWRENCE DAVID, b Seattle, Wash, Nov 3, 40; m 70; c 1. GERMAN LANGUAGE & LITERATURE. *Educ:* Univ Wash, BA, 61; Ohio State Univ, MA, 64, PhD(Ger), 69. *Prof Exp:* From instr to asst prof Ger, Ohio State Univ, 68-70; asst prof, 70-78, ASSOC PROF GER, STATE UNIV NY COL BINGHAMTON, 78-, CHMN DEPT, 80- *Mem:* MLA; Am Asn Teachers Ger; Adalbert Stifter Inst. *Res:* German novelle; 18th and 19th century German literature. *Publ:* Auth, Aldalbert Stifter's Bergkistall, Adalbert Stifter Vierteljahrsschrift, 70; Zeit und Zeitalter in Gottfried Keller's Verlornem Lachen, Ger Quart, 5/73; An von Droste-Hulshoff's Johannes Niemand: Much Ado About Nobody, Germanic Rev, 2/77; Words of music: Hauptmann's composition Bahnwarter Thiel, Wege der Worte, Fleischhauer Festschrift, 78; Sacred and profane: a spatial archetype in the early tales of Ludwig Tieck, Monateshefte, 1/78; Indeterminacy as provocation: The reader's role in Annette von Droste-Hulshoff's Die Judenbuche, Mod Lang Notes, German Issue, 79; Organic structure in Goethe's Novelle, German Quart, 11/80. *Mailing Add:* 704 Keenan Dr Vestal NY 13850

WELLS, MAURICE BURTON, b Salt Lake City, Utah, Jan 27, 39; m 64; c 2. GERMAN. *Educ:* Univ Utah, BA, 64, PhD(Ger), 70; Northwestern Univ, MA, 65. *Prof Exp:* Instr Ger & English, Westminster Col, Utah, 65-66; asst prof Ger, E Carolina Univ, 70-73, actg asst dean, Div Continuing Educ, 73; TRAINING SPECIALIST, UTAH DIV FAMILY SERV, 74- *Res:* The writings of Swiss playwright Friedrich Dürrenmatt; the teaching of German to American students. *Publ:* Auth, The ripening of a dramatist: Friedrich Dürrenmatt, NC Foreign Lang Teacher, fall 72. *Mailing Add:* 361 Jackson Midvale UT 84037

WELLWARTH, GEORGE, Dramatic Literature. See Vol II

WELMERS, WILLIAM EVERT, b Orange City, Iowa, Apr 4, 16; m 40; c 3. AFRICAN LANGUAGES. *Educ:* Hope Col, AB, 36; Westminster Theol Sem, ThB & ThM, 39; Univ Pa, PhD, 43. *Hon Degrees:* LittD, Hope Col, 67. *Prof Exp:* Instr Army specialized training prog, Univ Pa, 43-44 & 45-46; mem, Lutheran Mission, Liberia, 46-48, 54-55; ling tech, Am Coun Learned Soc fel, Africa, 48-50; vis asst prof ling, Cornell Univ, 50-51, actg assoc prof, 51-54; assoc prof, Kennedy Sch Missions, Hartford Sem Found, 55-60; PROF AFRICAN LANG, UNIV CALIF, LOS ANGELES, 60- *Concurrent Pos:* Pastor, Knox Orthodox Presby Church, Philadelphia, Pa, 43-46; consult, US Off Educ, 59- *Mem:* Ling Soc Am; Int African Inst; African Music Soc; African Studies Asn. *Res:* Descriptive linguistics; African languages; foreign language teaching. *Publ:* Auth, Notes on the structure of two languages in the Senufo group, Language, 50; The phonology of Kpelle, J African Lang, 62; Efik, 68 & Jukun of Wukari and Jukun of Takum, 68, Univ Ibadan; coauth, Igbo: A Learner's Manual, privately publ, 68; Igbo: A Learner's Dictionary, Univ Calif, 68; Mathematics and Logic in the Kpelle Language, Univ Ibadan, 71; auth, African Language Structures, Univ Calif, 73. *Mailing Add:* 2272 Overland Ave Los Angeles CA 90064

WELSH, ANDREW, English Literature. See Vol II

WELSH, DAVID JOHN, b London, England, Sept 15, 20. SLAVIC LANGUAGES & LITERATURES. *Educ:* Univ London, BA, 56, PhD(Polish lit), 67; Univ Liverpool, MA, 62. *Prof Exp:* Lectr Polish lang & lit, 61-62, from asst prof to assoc prof, 64-71, fac res fel, Rackham Grad Sch, 65, PROF POLISH LANG & LIT, UNIV MICH, ANN ARBOR, 71- *Mem:* MLA; Am Asn Advan Slavic Studies; Am Asn Teachers Slavic & EEurop Lang. *Res:* Polish Renaissance; Slavic baroque. *Publ:* Auth, Sienkiewicz as narrator, Slavonic & EEurop Rev, 65; Russian Comedy, 1765-1823, Mouton, The Hague, 66; Adam Mickiewicz, Twayne, 66; Sienkiewicz versus Kraszewski, Ind Slavic Studies, 67; Sienkiewicz and the historical novel, Polish Rev, 68; Ignacy Krasicki, Twayne, 69; Jan Kochanowski, Twayne, 74. *Mailing Add:* 3206 Modern Languages Univ of Michigan Ann Arbor MI 48109

WELSH, MICHAEL EDWARD, b Cape Town, SAfrica, Apr 16, 34; m 62; c 2. CLASSICS. *Educ:* Rhodes Univ, SAfrica, BA, 54; Univ Cape Town, BA, 63; Univ London, PhD(Latin), 66. *Prof Exp:* Asst teacher, Potchefstroom Boys' High Sch, 55 & Rondebosch Boys' High Sch, 55-64; lectr classics, Rhodes Univ, SAfrica, 67; asst prof, Brock Univ, 67-68; asst prof, 68-70, ASSOC PROF CLASSICS, CARLETON UNIV, 70- *Res:* Latin rhetoric; Latin drama; Horace. *Publ:* Auth, The transmission of Aquila Romanus, Classica et Mediaevalia, 69. *Mailing Add:* 2071 Niagara Dr Ottawa ON K1H 6G9 Can

WELTON, ARCHIBALD JAMES, b Petersburg, WVa, July 19, 27. ROMANCE LANGUAGES. *Educ:* WVa Univ, AB, 48; Middlebury Col, MA, 49; Inst Phonetique, Paris, cert Fr, 61; Columbia Univ, PhD(French), 66; Sorbonne, cert French lang, 67. *Prof Exp:* Instr Romance Lang, WVa Univ, 49-52; instr French, Upsala Col, 60-64, asst prof, 64-67; ASSOC PROF FRENCH, STATEN ISLAND COMMUNITY COL, 67- *Concurrent Pos:* Reviewer, Choice, 63- *Mem:* Am Asn Teachers Fr; MLA. *Res:* Contemporary French theater and novel. *Mailing Add:* 14 W Ninth St Apt 6 New York NY 10011

WEN, VICTOR YEN-HSIUNG, b Peiping, China, May 23, 25; US citizen; m 52; c 3. CHINESE LANGUAGE, POLITICAL SCIENCE. *Educ:* St John's Univ, China, BA, 45; Ind Univ, Bloomington, MA, 49. *Prof Exp:* Ass ed, Cent News Agency, Shanghai, China, 45-47; from instr to assoc prof, 51-66, supvry prof & chmn dept Air Force Chinese, 66-68, SUPVRY PROF CHINESE LANG & CHMN DEPT CHINESE-MANDARIN, DEFENSE LANG INST, W COAST BR, 68- *Mem:* Ling Soc Am; Am Coun Teaching Foreign Lang; Chinese Lang Teachers Asn. *Mailing Add:* PO Box CF Pacific Grove CA 93950

WENDEL, JOHN RICHARD, b Salt Lake City, Utah, July 25, 35. GERMAN LANGUAGE & LITERATURE. *Educ:* Univ Utah, BA, 60; Univ Conn, MA, 64, PhD(Ger), 66. *Prof Exp:* From instr to asst prof Ger, Univ Mass, 64-67; asst prof, 67-73, LECTR GER, UNIV ARIZ, 73- *Concurrent Pos:* Fulbright-Hays exchange prog teacher, Graz, Austria, 70-71. *Res:* The drama; the lyric; the humanities. *Publ:* Coauth, German for Reading, Prentice-Hall, 73. *Mailing Add:* Dept of Ger Univ of Ariz Tucson AZ 85721

WENDELL, CHARLES, b New York, NY, May 5, 19. NEAR EASTERN LANGUAGES & LITERATURES. *Educ:* New Sch Soc Res, BA, 53; Univ Calif, Los Angeles, PhD(Near Eastern lang & lit), 67. *Prof Exp:* Assoc Arabic, Univ Calif, Los Angeles, 60-64, actg asst prof, 66-67; asst prof, 67-75, lectr relig studies, 73-75, ASSOC PROF ARABIC & RELIG STUDIES, UNIV CALIF, SANTA BARBARA, 75- *Concurrent Pos:* Sr fel Am Res Ctr Egypt, 64-66. *Mem:* Am Orient Soc; Am Asn Teachers Arabic; fel Mid E Studies Asn. *Res:* Arabic language and literature; Islamic history; Islamic relgion. *Publ:* Transl, Osman Amin, Muhammad 'Abduh, Am Coun Learned Soc, 53; co-transl, The Hashemite Kingdom of Jordan, Human Rels Area Files, 56; auth, Ahmad Lutfi Al-Sayyid: In memoriam, Mid Eastern Affairs, 63; Baghdad: Imago mundi, and other foundation-lore, Int J Mid East Studies, 4/71; The pre-Islamic period of Sirat Al-Nabi, Muslim World, 1/72; The Evolution of the Egyptian National Image, Univ Calif, 72; The denizens of paradise, Humaniora Islamica, 74. *Mailing Add:* Dept of Eastern Lang & Lit Univ Calif Santa Barbara CA 93106

WENDELL, CHARLES WARNER, b Schenectady, NY, Feb 11, 30; m 55; c 1. COMPARATIVE LITERATURE. *Educ:* Cath Univ Am, AB, 51, MA, 52; Yale Univ, PhD(comp lit), 64. *Prof Exp:* Asst, Cath Univ Am, 51-52; from instr to asst prof French, St John's Univ NY, 60-66; asst prof, Rutgers Univ, 66-69; chmn dept foreign lang, 72-75, ASSOC PROF FRENCH, KEAN COL, NJ, 69- *Mem:* MLA; Am Comp Lit Asn. *Res:* French and English style and criticism; the novel; satire. *Mailing Add:* 205 W Ninth St Plainfield NJ 07060

WENDER, DOROTHEA SCHMIDT, b Dayton, Ohio, Aug 28, 34; div; c 3. CLASSICS. *Educ:* Radcliffe Col, BA, 56; Univ Minn, MA, 59; Harvard Univ, PhD(classics), 64. *Prof Exp:* Asst prof classics & chmn dept, Trinity Col, DC, 67-70; A Howard Meneeley res chair, 74-75, PROF & CHMN DEPT CLASSICS, WHEATON COL, 70- *Mem:* Am Philol Asn; AAUP; Class Asn New England; Am Lit Transl Asn. *Publ:* Auth, The Will of the Beast: Sexual Imagery in the Trachiniae, Ramus, 74; Plain in diction, plain in thought: Some criteria for translating the Iliad, Am J Philol, 75; The Myth of Washington, Arion, 76; Homer, Ardo Medovic and The Elephant's Child, Am J Philol, 77; Imagery on Symbolic Naming in Plato's Lysis, Ramus, 78; The Last Scenes of the Odyssey, E J Brill, Leiden, 78; The Literary Sources of the Georgics, Ramus, 79; Classical Roman Poetry from the Republic to the Silver Age, Southern Ill Univ Press, 80. *Mailing Add:* Dept of Classics Wheaton College Norton MA 02166

WENDLAND, ERNST RICHARD, b Washington, Iowa, Oct 14, 44; m 71; c 4. BANTU LANGUAGES & LITERATURE. *Educ:* Northwestern Col, BA, 68; Summer Inst Ling, cert, 72; Univ Wis-Madison, MA, 76, PhD(African lang & lit), 79. *Prof Exp:* INSTR ENGLISH, BIBLE GREEK, COMMUN & TRANSL, LUTHERAN BIBLE INST & SEM, 68- *Concurrent Pos:* Lang coordr, Lutheran Church of Cent Africa, 71-; lectr semantics & transl, Summer Inst Ling, 74; transl adv, United Bibl Soc, 76-; hon lectr African lang, Univ Zambia, 82; mem, Zambian Lang Curric Comt, Ministry of Educ, Republic of Zambia, 82. *Mem:* Zambia Lang Group (vchmn & treas, 81-). *Res:* Stylistics and discourse structure of Chewa and Tonga literature (oral and written); stylistics and discourse structure of Biblical Hebrew and Greek; idiomatic and figurative language in Chewa. *Publ:* Auth, Lexical recycling in Chewa discourse, Summer Inst Ling, Univ NDak, 75; ed, Nthano Za Kwa Kawaza, Folktales from Kawaza-Land, Zambia Lang Group, 76; auth, Receptor language style and Bible translation, Bible Transl, 81-82; A Characteristic African Folktale Pattern reconsidered, 81 & A sketch of English borrowings in the Nyanja narratives of Julius Chongo, 82, Bull Zambia Lang Group; A communications model for the measurement of fidelity and naturalness in Bible translation, In: Essays in Memory of John Beekman, Summer Inst Ling (in press). *Mailing Add:* PO Box CH-91 Lusaka Zambia

WENNBERG, BENKT, b Nykoeping, Sweden, Nov 21, 20; US citizen; m 50; c 3. FRENCH, COMPARATIVE LITERATURE. *Educ:* Univ Uppsala, Fil Kand, 51; Bryn Mawr Col, MA, 53; Univ Pa, PhD, 56. *Prof Exp:* Asst instr French, Univ Pa, 53-54, res asst, 55-56; asst prof French, Univ Fla, 56-62 & State Univ NY Stony Brook, 62-67; prof foreign lang & chmn dept, Beaver Col, 67-76; asst prof French, Pa State Univ Ogontz Campus, 76-80; MEM FAC, DEPT FRENCH, DREXEL UNIV, 80- *Concurrent Pos:* Consult computer assisted instr French, Holt, Rinehart & Winston, 67-68. *Honors & Awards:* Lindback Distinguished Teaching Award, 68. *Mem:* MLA; Am Asn Teachers Fr; Int Arthurian Soc; Mod Humanities Res Asn. *Res:* Anglo-Norman literature; Arthurian Romances; history of ideas. *Mailing Add:* Dept of French Drexel Univ Philadelphia PA 19104

WENSINGER, ARTHUR STEVENS, b Grosse Pointe, Mich, Mar 9, 26. GERMAN LITERATURE & LANGUAGE. *Educ:* Dartmouth Col, AB, 48; Univ Mich, AM, 50, PhD, 58. *Prof Exp:* From instr to prof, 55-77, MARCUS TAFT PROF GER & HUMANITIES, WESLEYAN UNIV, 77-, SR TUTOR, COL LETT, 63-, CHMN DEPT GER, 70-73, 77- *Concurrent Pos:* Danforth grant, 59; Ford Found fel, 70-71; Wesleyan Ctr Humanities fel, 74; Int Nationes grantee, 79. *Mem:* MLA; Am Asn Teachers Ger; Heinrich von Kleist Ges; Am Translr Asn; Kafka Soc Am. *Res:* Heinrich von Kleist; translations from German; Thomas Mann & Franz Kafka. *Publ:* Transl, Ger sect, Language of Love (short story anthology), 64 & ed, Ger & Austrian sect, Modern European Poetry, 66, Bantam; co-transl & co-ed, Chapliande, Mass Rev, Vol VI, No 3, Methusalem or the Eternal Bouregois, In: Plays for a New Theater, New Directions, 66; The Immortals, Malahat Rev, Univ Victoria, 10/67; ed & transl, Hogarth on High Life, The Lichtenberg Commentaries, Wesleyan Univ Press, 71; ed & coauth, Peter et amicorum: Memorial Anthology for Novelist P S Boynton, Gehenna, 72; ed, Stone Island, Harcourt, 73; ed & transl, Paula Modersohn-Becker in Letters and Journals, Taplinger Publ Co, 82. *Mailing Add:* Dept Ger Lang & Lit Wesleyan Univ Middletown CT 06457

WENTE, EDWARD FRANK, b New York, NY, Oct 7, 30; m 70. EGYPTOLOGY. *Educ:* Univ Chicago, AB, 51, PhD(Egyptol), 59. *Prof Exp:* Dir Egyptol, Am Res Ctr Egypt, 57-58; res assoc, 59-63, from asst prof to assoc prof, 63-70, chmn, Dept Near Eastern Lang & Civilization, 75-79, PROF EGYPTOL, ORIENT INST, UNIV CHICAGO, 70- *Concurrent Pos:* Mem, Am Res Ctr Egypt, 57-; field dir epigraphic surv, Orient Inst, Luxor, Egypt, 72-73; mem archeol adv coun, Smithsonian Inst, 79-82. *Res:* Epigraphy; Egyptian philology; history of the Egyptian New Kingdom. *Publ:* Coauth, Medinet Habu, Vol VI, 63, Vol VII, 64; auth, Late Ramesside Letters, 67 & coauth, The Beit el-Wali Temple of Ramesses II, 67, Univ Chicago; The Literature of Ancient Egypt, Yale Univ, 72; A chronology of the New Kingdom, In: Studies in Honor of George R Hughes, Univ Chicago, 76; The Temple of Khonsu, Vol I, 79, Vol II, 81; The Tomb of Kheruef, 80; co-ed, An X-Ray Atlas of the Royal Mummies, Univ Chicago, 80. *Mailing Add:* Orient Inst Univ of Chicago 1155 E 58th St Chicago IL 60637

WENTZ, DEBRA LINOWITZ, b Cape May Court House, NJ, 52. FRENCH LITERATURE & LANGUAGE. *Educ:* Goucher Col, BA, 73; Univ Conn, MA, 75; Univ Paris, PhD(mod lit expression), 78; Univ Conn, PhD(Fr lang & lit), 80. *Prof Exp:* Sr copywriter & dir pub rels, Berry & Wittey Assocs, 73-74; dir & coordr, For Lang Lab, Univ Conn, 74-77; admin dir & mkt coordr, Cabinet Joncour, Brunoy, France, 77-79; coordr spec proj, James C Giuffre Med Ctr, Philadelphia, 79-81; PUB INFO OFFICER, EWING TOWNSHIP PUB SCHS, TRENTON, 81- *Concurrent Pos:* Proj specialist, NJ Div Gaming Enforcement, NJ Dept Law & Pub Safety, 77; contribr ed, Asn pour l'etude et la diffusionde l'aeuvre de George Sand, France, 79-81; standard develop specialist, NJ State Health Dept, 79-80; contribr ed, Amis de George Sand, France, 76- *Mem:* Nat Sch Pub Rels Asn; Amis de George Sand, France; Am Med Writers Asn. *Res:* George Sandis later life; nineteenth century French literature; Gustave Flaulaert's literary works. *Publ:* Les Grandes Possibilites d'un theatre in time, Bull de l'Asn des Amis de George Sand, 10/77; Les Profils du Theatre de Nohant de George Sand, Nizet, Paris, 78; Daguerrotypes Nocturnes, Kineloisirs, 6/78; Le Projet d'Independance: Robinson Crusoe et les Contes d'une grand'mere, Bull del'Asn des Amis de George Sand, 78; Autour d'und Nuit de Don Juan et de Madame Bovary de Flaubert, Bull des Amis de Flaubert, 79; Sur les pas de George Sand a Majorque, Bull de l'Asn des Amis de George Sand, 79; Fait et Fiction: Les Formules pedagogiques des Contes d'une grandmere de George Sand, Nizet, Paris, 81; George Sand's Contes d'une grandmere as an Educational Device, Newsletter of the Friends of George Sand, Hofstra Univ, summer-fall 81. *Mailing Add:* 7 Aberfeldy Dr Trenton NJ 08618

WENTZLER, MARILYN LOUISE, b Rochester, Minn. CLASSICAL LANGUAGES & LITERATURE. *Educ:* Pa State Univ, MA, 75, PhD(Teutonic studies & ling), 80. *Prof Exp:* INSTR ENGLISH COMPOS, WILLIAMSPORT AREA COMMUNITY COL, 81- *Res:* Germanic languages and literatures; Latin language and literature; Spanish language and literature. *Publ:* Coauth (with E Ebbinghaus), The Gothic E-type alphabet of Cod Vindob 795, Vol 17, 77 & auth, The Gothic text of Nehemiah 6:16, Vol 21, 81, Gen Ling. *Mailing Add:* PO Box 118 Muncy PA 17756

WERBOW, STANLEY NEWMAN, b Philadelphia, Pa, Apr 19, 22; m 52; c 3. GERMANIC LANGUAGES & LITERATURE. *Educ:* George Washington Univ, AB, 46; Johns Hopkins Univ, PhD(Ger), 53. *Prof Exp:* Inst Germanic lang, McCoy Col, Johns Hopkins Univ; from asst prof to assoc prof, 53-65, chmn dept Ger, 69-71, dean Col Humanities, 71-78, actg dean, Col Fine Arts, 80-81, PROF GERMANIC LANG, UNIV TEX, AUSTIN, 65-,. *Concurrent Pos:* Fulbright grant to Ger & Guggenheim fel, 60-61; vis prof Germanic ling, Univ Marburg, 63. *Honors & Awards:* Bundesverdienstkreuz Erstens Klasse, 79. *Mem:* MLA; Ling Soc Am, Medieval Acad Am; Int Asn Ger Lang & Lit. *Res:* Medieval German literature; early new High German. *Publ:* Auth, Martin von Amberg: Der Gewissensspiegel, Erich Schmidt, Berlin, 57; auth, Die Gemeine Teutsch: Ausdruck und Begriff, Z Deut Philol, 63; ed, Formal Aspects of Medieval German Poetry, 70; auth, The establishment of standard modern literary German, In: The Challenge of German Literature, Wayne State Univ, 71. *Mailing Add:* Dept of German Lang Univ of Tex Austin TX 78712

WERNER, JOHN ROLAND, b Philadelphia, Pa, Sept 28, 30; m 58; c 2. CLASSICAL LANGUAGES. *Educ:* Shelton Col, BA, 51; Faith Theol Sem, BD, 54; Univ Pa, MA, 56, PhD, 62. *Prof Exp:* Teacher Latin, Am Acad, Athens, 58-59; asst prof Greek, Latin & Ancient hist, Trinity Christian Col, 62-68, assoc prof Greek, Latin & ling, 68-70, prof Greek & ling, 70-72; INT CONSULT TRANSLATION, WYCLIFFE BIBLE TRANSLATORS, 75- *Mem:* Evangel Theol Soc; Near East Archaeol Soc. *Res:* Programmed instruction; discourse analysis. *Publ:* Auth, Greek: A Programed Primer, Presbyterian & Reformed, 69. *Mailing Add:* 2127 Northmoor Dr Carrollton TX 75006

WERTH, RONALD NICHOLAS, b Smederevo, Yogoslavia, Apr 26, 38; US citizen; m 63; c 5. GERMANIC LINGUISTICS & PHILOLOGY. *Educ:* Fordham Univ, BA, 61; Cornell Univ, PhD(Germanic ling), 65. *Prof Exp:* Asst prof Ger, Univ Calif, Riverside, 65-67; from asst prof to assoc prof Ger & ling, Univ Rochester, 67-77; PROF GER & LING & CHMN DEPT FOREIGN LANG & LING, UNIV TEX, ARLINGTON, 77- *Concurrent Pos:* Am Coun Learned Soc ling grant, 72. *Mem:* MLA; Ling Soc Am. *Res:* Germanic syntax and semantics, specially Gothic; historical linguistics. *Publ:* Auth, The problem of Germanic sentence prototype, Lingua, 70; Die gotischen Bezeichnungen für Hoherpriester, ZVS, 73; A methodology for reconstructing patterns of cross-cultural semantic contact, In: Proc of 11th Int Cong Linguists, 75; co-ed, Readings In Historical Phonology, Pa State Univ, 78. *Mailing Add:* Dept of Foreign Lang & Ling Univ of Texas Arlington TX 76019

WERTZ, CHRISTOPHER ALLEN, b Lakewood, Ohio, June 13, 41. SLAVIC & GENERAL LINGUISTICS. *Educ:* Columbia Univ, BA, 63; Univ Michigan, Ann Arbor, PhD(Slavic), 71. *Prof Exp:* Asst prof Russ & ling, Washington Univ, St Louis, 71-75 & Univ Wyo, Laramie, 75-77; asst prof, 77-

80, ASSOC PROF RUSSIAN, UNIV IOWA, IOWA CITY, 81- *Res:* Russian morphology; Polish morphology; interlinguistics. *Publ:* Auth, The number of genders in Polish, Can Slavonic Papers, Vol 19, No 1; entry on Baudouin de Courtenay, Mod Encycl Russ & Soviet Lit, Vol 2, 78; An alternate way of teaching verbs of motion in Russian, Russ Lang J, Vol 32, No 116; coauth, entry on Ferdinand de Saussure, Mod Encycl Russ & Soviet Lit, Vol 5, 81; auth, Some proposals regarding the creation of an international auxiliary language, Brit J Lang Teaching, Vol 19, No 3. *Mailing Add:* Dept of Russ Univ of Iowa Iowa City IA 52242

WESCOTT, ROGER WILLIAMS, b Philadelphia. Pa, Apr 28, 25; m; c 2. LINGUISTIC ANTHROPOLOGY. *Educ:* Princeton Univ, AB, 44 & 45, MA, 47, PhD(ling sci), 48; Oxford Univ, BLitt, 52. *Prof Exp:* Ed & interviewer, Gallup Poll, 52; asst prof hist & human rels, Mass Inst Technol & Boston Univ, 53-57; assoc prof English & soc sci, Mich State Univ, 57-62, dir African lang prog, 59-62; prof anthrop & hist & chmn, Div Soc Sci, Southern Conn State Col, 62-63; lectr sociol & anthrop, Wilson Col, 64-66; co-dir behav studies prog, 73-76, PROF ANTHROP & LING & CHMN DEPT ANTHROP, DREW UNIV, 66- *Concurrent Pos:* Ford fel, Univ Ibadan, Nigeria, 55-56; foreign lang consult, US Off Educ, 61; West African Ling Surv grant, Ibadan, 61-62; consult ed, J African Lang, 62-; poetry ed, The Interpreter, 62-; ling fieldworker, Sierra Leone, 63; linguist, Bur Appl Social Res, Columbia Univ, 63-64; rev ed, Int Soc Studies Comp Civilizations, 73-; pres prof humanities & soc sci, Colo Sch Mines, 80-81. *Mem:* Fel African Studies Asn; fel Am Anthrop Asn; fel AAAS; Int Ling Asn; Int Soc Comp Study of Civilizations. *Publ:* Auth, The Divine Animal: An Exploration of Human Potentiality, Funk, 69; coauth, A Pre-Conference Volume on Cultural Futurology, Am Anthrop Asn, 70; Human Futuristics, Univ Hawaii, 71; The Experimental Symposium on Comparative Futurology, Univ Minn, 71; auth, Traditional Greek conceptions of the future, In: The Experimental Symposium on Comparative Futurology, Univ Minn, 71; coauth, The Highest State of Consciousness, Anchor Bks, 72; auth, Seven Bini charms, Folklore Forum, 10/72; Metaphones in Bini and English, In: Studies in Linguistics in Honor of George L Trager, Mouton, The Hague, 73; Sound and Sense, Jupiter Press, 80. *Mailing Add:* Dept of Anthropology Drew Univ Madison NJ 07940

WEST, DENNIS DEFOREST, b Akron, Ohio, Mar 20, 42; m 67. LATIN AMERICAN & SPANISH CINEMA. *Educ:* Ohio Univ, BA, 64; Univ Ill, AM, 66, PhD(Span-Am lit), 71. *Prof Exp:* Teaching asst Span, Univ Ill, 64-66; lectr Span, Ind Univ, 69-71, asst prof, 72-79; ASSOC PROF SPAN-AM LIT, DEPT FOREIGN LANG & LIT, UNIV IDAHO, 81- *Concurrent Pos:* Instr English, Centro-Colombo-Americano, 65; guest prof Span-Am lit, Pontificia Univ Catolica del Peru, 73; ed, Am Hisp, 79-; consult, Choice, 81- *Mem:* Am Asn Teachers Span & Port; Soc Cinema Studies; Latin Am Studies Asn; MLA. *Publ:* Auth, Documenting the end of the Chilean road to socialism, Am Hisp, 2/78; Slavery and cinema in Cuba: The case of Gutierrez Alea's The Last Supper, Western J Black Studies, summer 79; Film and revolution: A Cuban perspective, Inti: Revista de Lit hisp, 79; Highlights first international festival of new Latin American cinema, Review, 1-4/81; Revolution in Central America: A survey of recent documentaries, Cineaste, Vol 12, No 1. *Mailing Add:* Dept of Foreign Lang & Lit Univ of Idaho Moscow ID 83843

WEST, JAMES DENISON, b Ceylon, May 3, 39; Brit citizen. RUSSIAN & COMPARATIVE LITERATURE. *Educ:* Cambridge Univ, BA, 62, MA, 66, PhD(Russ lit), 70. *Prof Exp:* Mem permanent overseas staff, Brit Coun, 62-66; lector Russ for scientists, Cambridge Univ, 66-67; lect Russ & Soviet studies, Univ Lancaster, 69-72; ASSOC PROF RUSS LIT, UNIV WASH, 72- *Mem:* MLA; Brit Univs Asn Slavists; Am Asn Advanc Slavic Studies. *Res:* Intellectual history as reflected in European literature, especially 1750-1830 and 1890-1920; modern literary theory. *Publ:* Ed, Pjataja Jazva, 69 & V rozovom bleske, 70, Bradda; auth, Russian Symbolism, Methuen, 70; ed, Borozdy i mezhi, Po zvezdam, Dradda, 71; auth, Neo-Romanticism in the Russian symbolist aesthetic, Slavonic & EEruop Rev, 7/73; The poetic landscape of the Russian symbolists, Forum Mod Lang Sutides, 75. *Mailing Add:* Dept of Slavic Languages Univ of Washington Seattle WA 98195

WEST, PAUL NODEN, English, Comparative Literature. See Vol II

WEST, REBECCA J, b Butler, Pa, Dec 14, 46; m 75. ITALIAN LANGUAGE AND LITERATURE. *Educ:* Univ Pittsburgh, BA, 68; Yale Univ, MPhil, 71, PhD(Ital), 74. *Prof Exp:* Instr, 73-74, asst prof, 74-81, ASSOC PROF ITAL, UNIV CHICAGO, 81-, DEAN STUDENTS, HUMANITIES DIV, UNIV CHICAGO, 81- *Concurrent Pos:* Fel Ital, Am Acad Rome, 78-79. *Mem:* MLA; Midwest Mod Lang Asn; Am Asn Univ Prof Ital; Am Asn Teachers of Ital; Am Acad Rome Soc Fel. *Res:* Modern Italian poetry; contemporary Italian fiction; criticism. *Publ:* Auth, On Montale, Chicago Rev, winter 75-76; Montale's latest voice: Readings in Satura and Diario, Ital Quart, winter-spring, 76; The marginal concept in Ossi di seppia, Italica, winter 78; Montale's Forse: The poetics of doubt, summer 79 & A long fioclity: The critical edition of Montale's poetry, spring 81, Forum Italicum; Eugenio Montale: Poet on the Edge, Harvard Univ Press, 81. *Mailing Add:* Ital Dept Univ Chicago Chicago IL 60637

WEST, WILLIAM CUSTIS, III, b Onancock, Va, Aug 20, 36; m 64; c 2. CLASSICS. *Educ:* Yale Univ, BA, 58; Univ NC, PhD(classics), 66. *Prof Exp:* From instr to asst prof, 66-73, assoc prof, 73-81, PROF CLASSICS, UNIV NC, CHAPEL HILL, 82- *Concurrent Pos:* Collabr, Annee Philol, 68; Nat Endowment for Humanities younger humanist fel, 73-74; co-ed, L'Annee Philologique, 74- *Mem:* Am Philol Asn; Archaeol Inst Am; Class Asn Midwest & South. *Res:* Herodotus; Greek history and archaeology. *Publ:* Auth, The trophies of the Persian wars, Class Philol, 1/69; Saviors of Greece, Greek, Roman & Byzantine Studies, 70; A bibliography of scholarship on speeches in Thucydides, 1873-1974 & The speeches in Thucydides description and listing, In: The Speeches in Thucydides, Univ NC, 73; Hellenic Homonoia and the new decree from Plataea, Greek, Roman and Byzantine Studies, 77. *Mailing Add:* Dept Classics Univ NC Chapel Hill NC 27514

WESTERINK, LEENDERT G, b Rheden, Neth, Nov 2, 13; m 45; c 4. LATIN, GREEK. *Educ:* Univ Nijmegen, Drs, 39, Drs, 45, LittD(classics), 48. *Prof Exp:* Teacher, Munic Lyceum, Emmen, Neth, 45-65; prof classics, 65-74, DISTINGUISHED PROF CLASSICS, STATE UNIV NY, BUFFALO, 74- *Concurrent Pos:* Correspondent, Royal Neth Acad Sci, 66; vis scholar, Dumbarton Oaks, 71; researcher, Nat Ctr Sci Res, Ministry Educ, France, 73-74. *Honors & Awards:* Charles J Goodwin Award of Merit, Am Philol Asn, 79. *Res:* Neoplatonism; Byzantine literature. *Publ:* Auth, Damascius, Lectures on the Philebus, 59 & Anonymous Prolegomena to Platonic Philosophy, 62, NHolland Publ Co, Amsterdam; co-ed, Proclus, Theologie Platonicienne, Vol I-IV, Bude, Paris, 68-81; auth, Arethae Archiepiscopi Caesariensis scripta minora, Vols I & II, 68-72 & Olympiodorus, In Platonis Gorgiam commentaria, 70, Teubner, Leipzig; ed, Nicetas Magistros, Lettres d'un exile (928-946), Nat Ctr Sci Res, Paris, 73; co-ed, Nicholas I, Patriarch of Constantinople, Letters, Dumbarton Oaks, 74; auth, The Greek Commentaries on Plato's Phaedo, Vols I & II, NHolland Publ, 76-77. *Mailing Add:* Dept of Classics State Univ of NY Buffalo NY 14214

WETTSTEIN, HOWARD K, Philosophy. See Vol IV

WETZEL, HEINZ, b Ziesar, Ger, May 11, 35; m 57; c 3. GERMAN LANGUAGE & LITERATURE. *Educ:* Univ Gottingen, DrPhil, 67. *Prof Exp:* Lectr Ger lang & lit, Univ Lille, 60-64; vis instr, Univ Wis-Madison, 64-65; asst prof, Queen's Univ, Ont, 65-69; assoc prof, 69-72, PROF GER LANG & LIT, UNIV TORONTO, 72- *Concurrent Pos:* Vis prof, Univ Calif, San Diego, spring 73 & Technische Univ Braunschweig, Ger, fall 73; ed, Seminar: A Journal of Germanic Studies, 80. *Mem:* MLA; Can Asn Univ Teachers. *Res:* German literature of the 19th and 20th centuries; comparative literature. *Publ:* Auth, Klang und Bild inden dichtungen Georg Trakls, Vandenhoeck & Ruprecht, Fottingen, 68, 2nd rev & enlarged ed, 72; Konkordanz zu den Dichtungen Georg Trakis, Otto Muller, Salburg, 72; Banale Vitalitat and lahmenes Erkennen, Drei vergleichende Studien u T S Eliiots The Waste Land, Herbert Lang, Bern & Frankfurt, 74; Dantons Tod und das Erwachen von Buechners sozialem Selbstverstandis, Deut Vierteljahrsschritt, 76; Bildungsprivileg und Vereinsamung in Buchners Lenz und Dostojewskis Damonen, Arcadia 78; ElektrasKult der Tat - freilich mit Ironie behandelt, Jahrbuch des Freien Deutschen Hochstifts 80; Die Entwicklung Woyecks in Buchners Entwurfen, Euphorion 80; Georg Buchner und ein polnischer General: Zwischen politischem Engagement und ironischer Distan, Jahrbuch der Deutschen Schillergesellschaft, 81. *Mailing Add:* Dept of Ger Univ Col Univ of Toronto Toronto ON M5S 1A1 Can

WETZLER, DUANE LEWIS, b Ft Collins, Colo, June 16, 21; m 61; c 2. SPANISH LANGUAGE & LITERATURE. *Educ:* Univ Calif, Berkeley, AB, 47; San Diego State Univ, MA, 57; Tulane Univ, PhD(Span & Port), 70. *Prof Exp:* Assoc prof, 62-80, PROF SPAN, BIOLA UNIV, 80- *Mem:* Am Asn Teachers Span & Port. *Res:* Bible translation; colonial Brazil. *Mailing Add:* Dept of Span Biola Univ La Mirada CA 90639

WEVERS, JOHN WILLIAM, b Baldwin, Wis, June 4, 19; Can citizen; m 42; c 4. SEMITIC LANGUAGES, HELLENISTIC GREEK. *Educ:* Calvin Col, BA, 40; Princeton Theol Sem, ThB, 43; Princeton Theol Sem & Princeton Univ, ThD, 45. *Hon Degrees:* DD, Knox Col, Ont, 73. *Prof Exp:* Teaching fel, Bibl lang, Princeton Theol Sem, 44-46, lectr Old Testament & Semitic lang, 46-48; asst prof, 48-51; asst prof Orient lang, Univ Col, 51-57, assoc prof Near Eastern Studies, 57-63, chmn, Grad Dept Near Eastern Studies, 72-75, chmn dept, 75-80, PROF NEAR EASTERN STUDIES, UNIV TORONTO, 63- *Mem:* Corresp mem Akad Wiss Göttingen, Philol Hist Klasse; fel Royal Soc Can; Soc Bibl Lit; Int Orgn Septuagint & Cognate Studies(pres, 72-80). *Res:* Septuagint; Classical Hebrew studies; Semitic linguistics. *Publ:* Coauth, R H Robinson and D Theall, Let's Speak English, 4 Vols, Gage, 61-62; auth, The Way of the Righteous, Philadelphia, Westminster, 61; Commentary on the Book of Ezekiel, Nelsons, London, 69; ed, Genesis, SEPTUAGINTA, Göttingen, 73, auth, Text History of the Greek Genesis, 74, ed, Deuteronomium, SEPTUAGINTA, 77, auth, Text History of the Greek Deuteronomy, 78 & Numeri SEPTUAGINTO, 82, Vandenhoect & Ruprecht. *Mailing Add:* Dept of Near Eastern Studies Univ of Toronto 280 Huron St Toronto ON M5S 1A1 Can

WEVERS, RICHARD FRANKLIN, b Baldwin, Wis, Mar 23, 33; m 56; c 4. CLASSICAL LANGUAGES. *Educ:* Calvin Col, BA, 56; Univ Wis, MA, 59, PhD, 62. *Prof Exp:* From instr to assoc prof, 61-69; PROF CLASS LANG, CALVIN COL, 69-, CHMN DEPT, 75- *Mem:* Am Philol Asn; Class Asn Mid W & S. *Res:* Greek oratory; computer stylometry. *Publ:* Auth, Isaeus: Chronology, Prosopography and Social History, Mouton, The Hague, 68. *Mailing Add:* 1237 Franklin SE Grand Rapids MI 49506

WEXLER, SIDNEY FREDERICK, b Brooklyn, NY, Oct 16, 12; m 37; c 1. SPANISH. *Educ:* NY Univ, BS, 32, PhD(Romance lang), 52; Univ Colo, MA, 33. *Prof Exp:* Export mgr, United Naval Stores Co, NY, 34-36; teacher high schs, 36-42; sr transl & censor, US Off Censorship, 42-43; training specialist, Veterans Admin, 46-49; from instr to assoc prof, 49-69, prof, 69-78, EMER PROF ROMANCE LANG, UNIV MASS, AMHERST, 78- *Concurrent Pos:* Sr supvr adult educ, State Dept Educ, NY; sr transl, US Civil Serv Comn; Span lang coordr, Peace Corps Proj, Springfield Col, 63. *Mem:* MLA; Am Asn Teachers Span & Port; Am Coun Teaching Foreign Lang. *Res:* Spanish drama of the Golden Age; Cervantes; Spanish romanticism and modernism. *Publ:* Auth, Rights for Spanish Protestants?, Christian Century, 7/65; Franco's peace: Spain thirty years after the insurrection, Yale Rev, fall 66; Changing status of Jews in Spain, Jewish Digest, 11/66; La devocion de la cruz de D Pedro Calderon de la Barca, Bibliot Anaya, Salamanca, Madrid & Barcelona, 66. *Mailing Add:* 43 Fearing St Amherst MA 01002

WHALEN, ROBERT GEORGE, b Boiestown, NB, Oct 17, 31; m 60; c 5. FRENCH, ENGLISH AS SECOND LANGUAGES. *Educ:* Univ NB, BA, 52; Inst Phonetique, Paris, cert, 57; Univ Paris, dipl contemp lit, 60. *Prof Exp:* From lectr to assoc prof French, 58-76, dir English as second lang, summer prog, 57-67, PROF FRENCH, UNIV NB, 76-, CHMN DEPT, 77-

Concurrent Pos: Researcher, Royal Comn Bilingualism & Biculturalism, 65; mem, comt teaching second lang in Can, Asn Univs & Cols Can, 67- *Mem:* Asn Can Univ Teachers Fr; Am Asn Teachers Fr; Asn Can & Quebec Lit. *Res:* Contemporary theatre, especailly French; comparative literature, English and French; literature of Quebec and Acadia. *Publ:* Auth, The NDEA Act-an American Model for Canada, Royal Comn Bilingualism & Biculturalism, 66; ed, The Teaching of English & French as Second Languages in Canada-a Symposium, Asn Univs & Cols Can, 68. *Mailing Add:* Dept of French Univ of NB Fredericton NB E3B 6E5 Can

WHALLON, WILLIAM, b Richmond, Ind, Sept 24, 28; m 57. COMPARATIVE LITERATURE. *Educ:* McGill Univ, BA, 50; Yale Univ, PhD, 57. *Prof Exp:* From instr to asst prof, Reed Col, 57-62; Ctr Hellenic Studies fel, Washington, DC, 62-63; from asst prof to assoc prof, 63-75,, PROF COMP LIT, MICH STATE UNIV, 73- *Publ:* Auth, Formula, Character, and Context, Ctr Hellenic Studies & Harvard Univ; Problem and Spectacle: Studies in the Oresteia, Carl Winter, Heidelberg, 80. *Mailing Add:* 1532 Parkvale Ave East Lansing MI 48823

WHEELOCK, FREDERIC MELVIN, b Lawrence, Mass, Sept 19, 02; m 37; c 2. CLASSICAL PHILOLOGY. *Educ:* Harvard Univ, AB, 25, AM, 26, PhD(class philol), 33. *Prof Exp:* Instr Latin, Haverford Col, 26-29; instr & tutor, Harvard Univ, 29-30; instr, City Col New York, 35-38; from instr to asst prof, Brooklyn Col, 38-52; prof humanities, Cazenovia Jr Col, 54-58, dean, 57-58; master Latin, Darrow Sch Boys, 58-60; from assoc prof to prof classics, 60-68, EMER PROF CLASSICS, UNIV TOLEDO, 68- *Concurrent Pos:* Vis prof classics, Eckert Col, 69-70. *Mem:* Am Philol Asn; Am Class League; Class Asn New Eng. *Res:* Textual criticism; paleography; teaching of Latin. *Publ:* Auth, The Manuscript Tradition of Probus, Leto's Hand and Tasso's Horace, Latin-An Introductory Course Based on Latin Authors, 3rd ed, 63 & Latin Literature, A Book of Readings, 67, Harper & Row; ed, Quintilian as Educator, Twayne, 74. *Mailing Add:* 112 Mack Hill Rd Amherst NH 03031

WHEELOCK, KINCH CARTER, b Amarillo, Tex, July 6, 24; m 45; c 2. SPANISH AMERICAN LITERATURE. *Educ:* Tex Tech Univ, BA, 49, MA, 50; Univ Tex, Austin, PhD(Span), 66. *Prof Exp:* Instr Span, 59-60 & 64-66, asst prof, 66-69, assoc dean col humanities, 74-77, ASSOC PROF SPAN, UNIV TEX, AUSTIN, 69- *Concurrent Pos:* Head dept mod lang, Univ del Valle, Colombia, 62-64. *Mem:* MLA; SCent Mod Lang Asn; Am Asn Teachers Span & Port. *Res:* Fantastic literature. *Publ:* Auth The mythmaker: A study of motif and symbol in the short stories of Jorge Luis Borges, Univ Tex, 69; Borges' new porse, TriQuart, fall 72; The committed side of Borges, Mod Fiction Studies, autumn 73; Spanish American fantasy and the believable, autonomous world, 1/74 & Borges, courage and will, 7/75, Int Fiction Rev; The subversive Borges, Tex Quart, spring 75; Fantastic symbolism in the Spanish American short story, Hisp Rev, autumn 80. *Mailing Add:* Dept of Span & Port Univ of Texas Austin TX 78712

WHELAN, DENNIS, b New York, NY, Mar 12, 42. LITERATURE, LAW. *Educ:* Roosevelt Univ, BA, 64; Univ Chicago, PhD(Slavic lang & lit), 70; Vt Law Sch, JD, 82. *Prof Exp:* Instr Russ lit, Univ Ill, Chicago Circle, 67-69; from instr to assoc prof, Russ lit & chmn dept Russ, Grinnell Col, 69-73; visitor, Russ Res Ctr, Harvard Univ, 73-74; VIS SCHOLAR RUSS LIT, DARTMOUTH COL, 74- *Res:* Dostoevsky; legal history; legal history. *Publ:* transl, Before the Dawn (play), produced on Broadway, 82. *Mailing Add:* Dept of Russ Lang & Lit Dartmouth Col Hanover NH 03755

WHITAKER, PAUL KNOWLTON, b Galeton, Pa, Apr 8, 07; m 34; c 1. GERMAN. *Educ:* Ohio State Univ, PhD(Ger), 42. *Prof Exp:* Prof Ger, 32-74, EMER PROF GER, UNIV KY, 74- *Mem:* MLA; SAtlantic Mod Lang Asn; Am Asn Teachers Ger; Int Ver Ger Sprch-u Literaturforsch. *Res:* Hermann Sudermann; 19th century German literature; the German novelle. *Publ:* Auth, The Inferiority Complex in Hermann Sudermann's Life and Works & The Concept of Sammlung in Grillparzer's Works, Monatshefte; assoc ed, Standard German & English Dictionary, Vol II, G G Haarap, Ltd, London, 67; Penthesilea and the Problem of Bad Faith, Cooloquia Germanica, 72. *Mailing Add:* Dept German Univ of Ky Lexington KY 40506

WHITAKER, SHIRLEY BLUE, b Lumberton, NC, Sept 19, 28; div; c 1. SPANISH. *Educ:* Duke Univ, AB, 49, AM, 52; Univ NC, Chapel Hill, PhD(Romance lang), 65. *Prof Exp:* Instr Span, Duke Univ, 50-51 & 54-55 & Meredith Col, 53-54; asst prof, Mary Baldwin Col, 55-57; from instr to asst prof, 60-72, ASSOC PROF SPAN, UNIV NC, GREENSBORO, 72- *Mem:* MLA; Am Asn Teachers Span & Port; Renaissance Soc Am. *Res:* Spanish Golden Age literature. *Publ:* Auth, Schoolboy Actors in El Gran Duque de Gandia, Bull Comediantes, 70; The Dramatic Works of Alvaro Cubillo de Aragon, Univ NC, 75; Wallenstein as a Character in Seventeen-Century Spanish Literature, Studies in Lang & Lit, Eastern Ky Univ, 76. *Mailing Add:* Dept Romance Lang Univ NC Greensboro NC 27412

WHITBY, WILLIAM MELCHER, b Philadelphia, Pa, Apr 1, 20; m 46; c 2. SPANISH. *Educ:* Haverford Col, BA, 48; Yale Univ, PhD(Span), 54. *Prof Exp:* From asst instr to instr Span,Yale Univ, 48-54; from instr Span & Ital to asst prof Span, Univ Southern Calif, 54-60; from asst prof to prof, Univ Ariz, 60-68; PROF SPAN, PURDUE UNIV, WEST LAFAYETTE, 68- *Concurrent Pos:* Ed, Bull of the Comediantes, 64-66; Fulbright-Hays res award, Spain, 66-67; assoc ed, Hispania, 72-74; ed Span, Purdue Univ Monogr Romance Lang, 77-79, gen ed, 79- *Mem:* MLA; Am Asn Teachers Span & Port; Asoc Int Hispanistas; Comediantes. *Res:* Spanish Golden Age literature. *Publ:* Co-ed, La Fianza Satisfecha, Cambridge Univ, 71; Metamorphoses, Transfigurations and Transmogrifications in Sannazaro, Garcilaso and Cervantes, In: Papers on Romance Literary Relations, MLA, 77; Luis Velez y 'la verdad desnuda': A lo que obliga el ser rey, In: Actas del VI Congr, Int Hisp, Univ Toronto, 80; Calderon's El principe constante: Structure and Ending, Approaches to the Theater of Calderon, Univ Press Am, 82. *Mailing Add:* Dept of Foreign Lang & Lit Purdue Univ West Lafayette IN 47907

WHITCOMB, RICHARD OWENS, b Waltham, Mass, Aug 16, 26; m 57; c 2. GERMAN LANGUAGE & LITERATURE. *Educ:* Bowdoin Col, BA, 50; Harvard Univ, MA, 51; Stanford Univ PhD(Ger), 64. *Prof Exp:* Instr Ger & French, Tabor Acad, Marion, Mass, 51-53 & Hobart Col, 57-59; asst prof Ger, Lawrence Univ, 60-64, assoc prof, 64-65; prof, State Univ NY Albany, 65-68; prof Ger & chmn dept foreign lang, Eastern Wash State Col, 68-74; PROF GER & CHMN DEPT FOREIGN LANG, ILL STATE UNIV, 74- *Concurrent Pos:* Dir students, Middlebury Grad Sch Ger, Univ Mainz, 64; State Univ NY fac res fel, 67-68; mem exec bd, Nat Fedn Mod Lang Teachers Asn, 73-74; dir foreign lang, Inland Empire Cult Insts, Wash, 73- *Mem:* Am Asn Teachers Ger; AAUP; Am Coun Teaching Foreign Lang; MLA; Pac Northwest Conf Foreign Lang (pres, 73-74). *Res:* Modern German drama; modern German prose; foreign language methodology. *Publ:* Auth, The enrollment crisis: Exploiting our untapped markets, Asn Dept Foreign Lang Bull, 12/72; Max Frisch's Andorra: national bias and critical reception, Proc Pac Northwest Conf Foreign Lang, 3/73; Heinrich Böll and the mirror-image tech technique, Univ Dayton Rev, 10/73. *Mailing Add:* 104 Ellis Ave Normal IL 61761

WHITE, DIANE VIRGINIA, b Birmingham, Ala, Oct 12, 53. GERMAN LANGUAGE & LITERATURE. *Educ:* Bryn Mawr Col, AB, 75; Yale Univ, PhD(German), 79. *Prof Exp:* Asst prof, Haverford Col, 79-80 & Grinnell Col, 80-81; ASST PROF GERMAN, UNIV NC, ASHEVILLE, 81- *Mem:* Soc Ger-Am Studies (secy, 81-83); MLA; Am Asn Teacher Ger; SAtlantic Mod Lang Asn; NEast Mod Lang Asn. *Res:* Nineteenth century German literature; German-Americana; popular literature. *Publ:* Auth, Sauerbraten, Rotkäppchen und Goethe: The quiz show as and introduction to German studies, Die Unterichtspraxis, 80 & 82. *Mailing Add:* Dept For Lang Univ NC Asheville NC 28804

WHITE, DONALD OWEN, b Lewiston, Maine, Mar 2, 32; m 54; c 4. GERMAN LANGUAGES & LITERATURE. *Educ:* Yale Univ, BA, 53, MA, 56, PhD, 63. *Hon Degrees:* MA, Amherst Col, 70. *Prof Exp:* From instr to prof, 57-76, assoc prof, 76-80, PROF GER, AMHERST COL, 80-, CHMN DEPT, 80- *Concurrent Pos:* Alexander von Humboldt-Stiftung res fel, Univ Bonn, 64-65. *Mem:* Am Asn Teachers Ger; MLA. *Res:* Twentieth century German literature; music and letters; translation. *Publ:* Translr, Oswald Spengler, Selected Essays, Regnery, 66 & Paul Celan, Fugue of Death, In: Modern European Poetry, Bantam, 66. *Mailing Add:* Dept of Ger Amherst Col Amherst MA 01002

WHITE, JOHN LEE, Early Christian Literature, Hellenistic Culture. See Vol IV

WHITE, JOSEPH SENTER, b West Palm Beach, Fla, Feb 15, 32; c 2. CLASSICS. *Educ:* Univ NC, Chapel Hill, AB, 56, PhD(Latin), 68. *Prof Exp:* Part-time instr Latin, Univ NC, 58-61; instr, Duke Univ, 61-62; instr class lang, La State Univ, 62-67; asst prof, 67-72, ASSOC PROF CLASS LANG, UNIV RICHMOND, 72-, CHMN DEPT CLASS STUDIES, 73- *Mem:* Class Asn Mid W & S; Am Philol Asn. *Mailing Add:* Dept of Classical Studies Univ of Richmond Richmond VA 23173

WHITE, JULIAN EUGENE, JR, b Hanover, Co, Va, Dec 21, 32; m 53; c 3. CLASSICAL LANGUAGES & LITERATURE. *Educ:* Randolph-Macon Col, BA, 52; Univ NC, MA, 54, PhD, 62. *Prof Exp:* Asst prof French & comp lit, Mary Baldwin Col, 60-64; asst prof mod lang, 64-66, assoc prof mod & class lang, 66-71, asst chmn dept, 74-76, PROF MOD & CLASS LANG, UNIV NMEX, 71-, ASSOC DEAN COL ARTS & LETT, 76- *Mem:* Mediaeval Acad Am; Am Asn Teachers Fr; Am Comp Lit Asn; Renaissance Soc Am; MLA. *Res:* Romance philology; mediaeval literature; 17th century French literature. *Publ:* Auth, A chanson de Roland: Secular or religious inspriation?, Romania, 63; ed, Three Philosophical Voyages, Dell, 64; auth, Racine's Phedre: A Sophoclean and Senecan tragedy, Rev Lit Comp, 65; The conflict of generations in the Debat Patriotique, Fr Rev, 11/65; Phedre is not incestuous, Romance Notes, 67; ed, Villehardouin, La Conqueste de Constantinople, Appleton, 68; auth, Nicolas Boileau, Twayne, 69. *Mailing Add:* Dept of Modern & Classical Lang Univ of New Mexico Albuquerque NM 87131

WHITE, KENNETH STEELE, b State College, Pa, Nov 19, 22; div; c 2. FRENCH. *Educ:* Pa State Univ, BA, 44; Johns Hopkins Univ, MA, 48; Stanford Univ, PhD, 58. *Prof Exp:* From instr to asst prof French, Univ Mich, 57-65; assoc prof, 65-70, dir int theatre studies ctr, 68-71, PROF FRENCH, UNIV KANS, 70- *Concurrent Pos:* Rackham res grant, 60; lectr French lit, Inst Am Univ, Aix-en-Provence, 61-62; rev ed French, Mod Lang J, 71-79; grad fel, Univ Kans, 78. *Mem:* MLA; Am Asn Teachers French; Am Comp Lit Asn; Mid West Mod Lang Asn. *Res:* French dramatic literature of the 20th century; comparative drama and international theatre; drama and physics. *Publ:* Auth, Savage Comedy Since King Ubu, Univ Press of Am, 77; Scientists' dilemmas: Prophetic metaphors in 20th century drama, Proc Int Comp Lit Asn, 78; Montale after the Nobel Prize, Stone Country, winter 78; ed, Savage Comedy: Structures of Humor, Rodopi, 78; auth, Centers of a Universe, Lawton, 78; Man's New Shapes, Univ Press Am, 79; Les Centres dramatiques Nationaux de Province, 1945-1965, Peter Lang, 79; Like Morning, Dorrance, 81. *Mailing Add:* Dept of Fr & Ital Univ of Kans Lawrence KS 66045

WHITE, PETER, b Washington, DC, Sept 24, 41; m 68; c 2. CLASSICAL PHILOLOGY. *Educ:* Boston Col, BA, 63; Harvard Univ, PhD(class philol), 72. *Prof Exp:* Asst prof, 68-74, chmn dept classics, 80-83, ASSOC PROF CLASSICS, UNIV CHICAGO, 74- *Concurrent Pos:* Ed, Classical Philology, 74-78; Am Coun Learned Soc fel, 78-79; chmn comt publ, Am Philol Asn, 82-84. *Mem:* Am Philol Asn. *Res:* Latin literature of the early Empire; Greek and Roman historiography. *Publ:* Auth, The authorship of the Historia Augusta, J Roman Studies, 67; Vibius Maximus the friend of Statius, Historia, 73; The presentation and dedication of the Silvae and the Epigrams, J Roman Studies, 74; The friends of Martial, Statius and Pliny, Harvard Studies in Class Philol, 75; Amicitia and the profession of poetry in early Imperial Rome, J Roman Studies, 78. *Mailing Add:* Dept of Classics Univ of Chicago Chicago IL 60637

WHITE, ROBERT HENRY, b Columbia, SC, Aug 28, 39; m 68; c 2. FRENCH LANGUAGE & LITERATURE. *Educ:* Rollins Col, BA, 62; Sorbonne, dipl, comtemp Fr lit, 63; Univ Colo, Boulder, PhD(French), 70; Ecole Norm Musique, Paris, Lic d'Enseignement, 73. *Prof Exp:* PROF FRENCH, LYNCHBURG COL, 66-, CHMN DEPT FOREIGN LANG, 80- *Concurrent Pos:* Fulbright jr lectr grant, Univ Strasbourg, 72-73. *Mem:* Am Asn Teachers Fr; Am Coun Teachers Foreign Lang. *Res:* Alain; Proust; Brahms. *Mailing Add:* 3 Adele St Lynchburg VA 24503

WHITENACK, JUDITH A, b Milwaukee, Wis, Oct 29, 44. SPANISH LITERATURE. *Educ:* Univ Wis, BS, 66, MA, 70, PhD(Span), 80. *Prof Exp:* Lectr, Univ Wis, 78-79; ASST PROF SPAN, UNIV NEV, RENO, 79- *Mem:* MLA; Medieval Asn Pac; Philol Asn Pac Coast; Rocky Mountain Mod Lang Asn; Am Asn Teachers of Span & Port. *Res:* Goldn age Spanish prose and poetry; Medieval Spanish poetry; Judaeo-Spanish poetry. *Publ:* Auth, The destruction of confession in Guzman de Alfarache, Revista de Estudios Hispanicos (in press); Cada dia notables afientas: Time and the protagonist in Guzman de Alfarache, Am Hispanis (in press); A new look at autobiography and confession, Forum (in press). *Mailing Add:* 1530 Hillside Dr Reno NV 89503

WHITESELL, FREDERICK RHODES, b Ann Arbor, Mich, May 7, 11; m 35; c 2. GERMAN LITERATURE. *Educ:* Univ Mich, AB, 34, AM, 35; Univ Calif, PhD, 42. *Prof Exp:* Instr Ger, Mich State Col, 37-40; teaching asst, Univ Calif, 40-43; from instr to asst prof, Univ Wis, 46-52; assoc prof, 52-54, prof, 54-76, EMER PROF GER, UNIV OF THE SOUTH, 76- *Mem:* MLA; AAUP; SAtlantic Mod Lang Asn; Am Asn Teachers Ger. *Res:* Mediaeval German literary history; history of Middle High German philology. *Publ:* Coauth, A Middle High German Courtly Reader. *Mailing Add:* Dept of German Univ of the South Sewanee TN 37375

WHITESIDE, ANNA, b Caterham, England, June 2, 42; Can citizen. FRENCH & COMPARATIVE LITERATURE. *Educ:* Nottingham Univ, England, BA Hons, 68; Univ BC, PhD(French), 72. *Prof Exp:* Lectr French, McGill Univ, 72-75; ASST PROF FRENCH, McMASTER UNIV, 75-, HEAD SECT, 77- *Mem:* Asn Int Etudes Francaises; MLA; Northeast Mod Lang Asn; Am Asn Teachers Fr; Asn Professerus Francais Univ Can. *Res:* Twentieth century French poetry and fiction; literary theory. *Publ:* Auth, La dialectique du noi dans (Zone) d'Apollinaire, Bull Assocation Professeurs Francais Universites Canadiennes, 77. *Mailing Add:* Dept of Romance Lang McMaster Univ Hamilton ON L8S 4M2 Can

WHITFIELD, FRANCIS JAMES, b Springfield, Mass, Mar 25, 16; m 50. SLAVIC LANGUAGES & LITERATURES. *Educ:* Harvard Univ, AB, 36, AM, 37, PhD, 44. *Prof Exp:* Asst prof, Univ Chicago, 45-48, actg chmn dept ling, 47-48; from actg assoc prof to assoc prof Slavic lang & lit, 48-58, actg chmn Slavic dept, 57, chmn dept Slavic lang & lit, 58-64, 69-70 & 72-74, PROF SLAVIC LANG & LIT, UNIV CALIF, BERKELEY, 58- *Concurrent Pos:* Vis assoc prof, Columbia Univ, 51-52 & Univ Mich, 55; co-ed, Int J Slavic Ling & Poetics, 59-; Guggenheim Found fel, 64-65. *Honors & Awards:* Kosciuszko Found Medal, 62. *Mem:* Ling Soc Am; Ling Soc Paris; Lingvistkredsen, Denmark. *Res:* Slavic linguistics; general linguistics; Polish literature. *Publ:* Auth, Beast in View: A Study of the Earl of Rochester's Poetry; A Russian Reference Grammar, Harvard Univ, 44; coauth, The Kosciuszko Foundation Dictionary, Mouton, The Hague, 59 & 61; ed, Pzolegomen to a Theory of Language, 61 & Language, 70, Univ Wis; Resume of a Theory of Language, Univ Wis & Nordisk Sprog-og Kulturforlag, Copenhagen, 75. *Mailing Add:* Dept of Slavic Lang & Lit Univ of Calif Berkeley CA 94720

WHITING, CHARLES G, b Boston, Mass, Sept 26, 22; m 54; c 4. FRENCH. *Educ:* Yale Univ, AB, 43, PhD, 51; Harvard Univ, AM, 48. *Prof Exp:* Instr French, Lawrence Col, 51-53; asst prof, Brown Univ, 57-62; assoc prof, State Univ NY, 62-63; assoc prof, 63-71, PROF FRENCH, NORTHWESTERN UNIV, EVANSTON, 71- *Concurrent Pos:* Mem adv comt, Sweet Briar Jr Year in France. *Mem:* MLA; Am Asn Teachers Fr. *Res:* Modern theatre; 19th century French poetry; 20th century French theatre and poetry. *Publ:* Auth, Valery Jeune Poete, Yale Univ, 60; Profusion du soir & Le cimetiere marin, Publ Mod Lang Asn Am, 3/62; Preciosite in La jeune parque and Charmes, Publ Mod Lang Asn Am, 10/71; ed, Chamres ou poemes de Paul Valery, Univ London, 73; auth, Paul Valery, Univ London, 78. *Mailing Add:* Dept of French & Italian Northwestern Univ Evanston IL 60201

WHITLEY, MELVIN STANLEY, b Concord, NC, Apr 14, 48; m 72. LINGUISTICS, SPANISH. *Educ:* Wake Forest Univ, BA, 70; Cornell Univ, MA, 73, PhD(ling), 74. *Prof Exp:* Asst prof, 74-79, ASSOC PROF LING & SPAN, WVA UNIV, 79- *Honors & Awards:* Outstanding Teacher Award, WVa Univ, 77. *Mem:* Ling Soc Am; Am Dialect Soc; Am Coun Teaching Foreign Lang; Am Asn Teachers Span & Port; Southeastern Coun Ling. *Res:* Contrastive linguistics; language variation; phonology. *Publ:* Auth, Dialectal syntax: Plurals and modals in Southern American, Linguistics, 75; Stress in Spanish--two approaches, Lingua, 76; Workbook in Generative Phonology, Univ Wis, 78; Person and number in the use of we, you, they, Am Speech, 78; Rule reordering in the phonological history of Spanish, In: Seventh Annual Linguistic Symposium on the Romance Languages, Georgetown, 80; Chirping birds and budging beads: Diagnosis of a Japanese problem in learning English, J Japanese Asn Language Teachers, 80. *Mailing Add:* Dept of Foreign Lang WVa Univ Morgantown WV 26506

WHITMAN, CEDRIC HUBBELL, b Providence, RI, Dec 1, 16; m 59; c 2. CLASSICAL PHILOLOGY. *Educ:* Harvard Univ, AB, 43, PhD, 47. *Prof Exp:* From instr to prof Greek & Latin, 47-66, chmn dept classics, 60-66, Francis R Jones prof class Greek lit, 66-74, ELIOT PROF GREEK LIT, HARVARD UNIV, 74- *Concurrent Pos:* Charles Beebe Martin class lectr, Oberlin Col, 61; Guggenheim fel, 61-62. *Honors & Awards:* Christian Gauss Award, 58; Award of Merit, Am Philol Asn, 52. *Mem:* Am Philol Asn; Am Acad Arts & Sci. *Res:* Ancient Greek poetry and drama; modern Greek literature; general poetry. *Publ:* Auth, Orpheus and the Moon Craters, Middlebury Col, 41; Sophocles: A Study of Heroic Humanism, 51, Homer and the Heroic Tradition, 58, Aristophanes and the Comic Hero, 64, Abelanrd (narrative poem), 65 & Euripides and the Full Circle of Myth, 74, Harvard Univ; translr, Musaus: Hero and Leader, Loeb Libr, 75. *Mailing Add:* 3 Shady Hill Sq Cambridge MA 01238

WHITMAN, ROBERT HENRY, b Sapporo, Japan, July 27, 29; US citizen; m 53; c 1. SLAVIC LINGUISTICS. *Educ:* Hamilton Col, AB, 51; Univ Calif, Berkeley, MA, 56; Harvard Univ, PhD(Slavic lang & lit), 64. *Prof Exp:* Asst prof Russ lang & lit, Wesleyan Univ, 59-64; asst prof Slavic lang & lit, Cornell Univ, 64-65; asst prof, Ind Univ, 65-66; vis asst prof, Univ Calif, Berkeley, 66-67, asst prof, 67-68, acting assoc prof, 68-70; chmn dept, 70-76, ASSOC PROF RUSS LANG & LIT, WESLEYAN UNIV, 70-, CHMN LING PROG, 70- *Concurrent Pos:* Mem screening comt, foreign area fel prog, Ford Found, 60-63, consult, int studies in undergrad educ, 62-63. *Mem:* Ling Soc Paris. *Res:* Slavic and general linguistics; philosophy of language; work of R G Collingwood. *Publ:* Auth, The 1073 Izbornik: The manuscript and its sources, Ind Slavic Studies, 67; Une interpolation tardive de l'Izbornik de 1073, Rev Etudes Slaves, 67; On generative semantics, In: Studies Present to Professor Roman Jakobson by His Students, Slavica, 68. *Mailing Add:* Dept of Russ Lang & Lit Wesleyan Univ Middletown CT 06457

WHITMORE, DONNELL RAY, b Houston, Tex, Apr 18, 33; m 55; c 4. IBERO-AMERICAN LANGUAGES. *Educ:* NTex State Col, BA, 55; Univ NMex, MA, 63, PhD(Ibero-Am studies), 72. *Prof Exp:* Teacher English & Span, Katy Independent Sch Dist, Tex, 55-60; teacher Span, Rockdale Pub Sch, Tex, 60-65; instr, Temple Jr Col, 65-69; prof Span & head dept of foreign lang, Hardin-Simmons Univ, 72-75; PROF BILING EDUC, TEX WOMAN'S UNIV, 75- *Mem:* Teachers English to Speakers Other Lang Int; Southwestern Coun Latin Am Studies. *Res:* English as a second language; Chicano literature; dictionary of North Texas Spanish. *Publ:* Auth, Brazilian Positivism and the Military Republic, Religion in Latin America, Markham, 78; Musical references of Joao Cruz e Souza, Luso-Brazilian Rev, 78; coauth, Teaching English in Texas as a second language, English in Tex, winter 78; Training ESL teachers, Tex Foreign Lang Asn Bull, 4/80; transl, Manual para padres de los ninos incapacitados pre-escolares, ESC Region 9, 81; coauth, ESL: Now it's the law in Texas, Teachers English to Speakers Other Lang Newslett, 4/82; Perspectives on bilingual teacher education, Doctorate Asn New York Educators, 82; Conventional curricula and bilingual curricula, R&E Assoc, 82. *Mailing Add:* Box 23029 Tex Woman's Univ Denton TX 76204

WHITNEY, MARK STEWART, b Philadelphia, Pa, Oct 12, 30; m 52; c 3. FOREIGN LANGUAGES. *Educ:* Rutgers Univ, AB, 52; Univ Pa, MA, 61, PhD, 62. *Prof Exp:* Teaching asst, Univ Pa, 56-62; from asst prof to assoc prof French, Brown Univ, 62-71; chmn dept French & Ital, 71-73, PROF FRENCH, STATE UNIV NY COL, STONY BROOK, 71- *Concurrent Pos:* Lectr, Univ Bordeaux, 55-56. *Mem:* Am Asn Teachers Fr; Mod Humanities Res Asn; MLA (chmn, 65-66); Renaissance Soc Am. *Res:* French Renaissance; prose and poetry of the French Renaissance. *Publ:* Ed, Les odes amoureuses d'Olivier de Magny, Droz, Geneva, 64; auth, Petrarch's influence on Olivier de Magny's Amatory odes of 1559, Studies Philol, 1/69; Olivier de Magny: Les amours de 1553, Droz, Geneva, 70; Critical reactions and the Christian element in the poetry of Pierre de Ronsard, NC Studies Romance Lang & Lit, 71; Choice and ambiguity in Ronsard, Romance Notes, 71; Du Bellay in April 1549: Continuum and change, Fr Rev, 4/71. *Mailing Add:* Dept of French & Italian State University of NY Stony Brook NY 11790

WHITON, JOHN NELSON, b Glencoe, Minn, Dec 11, 33; m 56; c 2. GERMAN LITERATURE. *Educ:* Univ Minn, BA, 58, MA, 59, PhD, 67. *Prof Exp:* Instr Ger, Col St Catherine, 60-62 & Univ Minn, 62-67; asst prof, Univ Alta, 67-69; asst prof, 69-72, ASSOC PROF GER, UNIV WATERLOO, 72- *Mem:* Am Asn Teachers Ger; Asn Can Univ Teachers Ger; MLA. *Res:* Modern German literature. *Publ:* Auth, Sacrifice and society in Wieland's Abderiten, Lessing Yearbk II, 70; Symbols of social renewal in Stifter's Bergkristall, Germanic Rev, Vol 47 (1972); Grillparzer-Forschung in Kanada, Öster Akad der Wissenschaften, 72; Hermann Hesse's Demian, Simon & Schuster Monarch Notes, 73; Aspects of reason and emotion in Lessing's Nathan der Weise, Lessing Yearbk IX, 78. *Mailing Add:* Dept of Ger & Slavic Lang & Lit Univ of Waterloo Waterloo ON N2L 3G1 Can

WHITTED, JOSEPH WILLARD, b Chadbourne, NC, Dec 13, 10; m 44; c 1. SPANISH LITERATURE. *Educ:* Davidson Col, BS, 33; Univ NC, AM, 41, PhD(Romance lang), 63. *Prof Exp:* Instr, Riverside Mil Acad, 35-39; instr, Univ NC, 40-41 & 46-49; from asst prof to assoc prof Span lit, 41-42 & 49-64, Hampden-Sydney Col, prof Span, 63-81, chmn dept mod lang, 70-79; RETIRED. *Mem:* SAtlantic Mod Lang Asn; Am Asn Teachers Span & Port; MLA; AAUP. *Res:* Classification of folk motifs in various works in Spanish literature. *Mailing Add:* 741 Masonboro Sound Rd Wilmington NC 28403

WHITWORTH, KERNAN BRADLEY, JR, b Lakewood, Ohio, Mar 9, 23; m 47; c 2. ROMANCE LANGUAGES. *Educ:* Oberlin Col, AB, 43; Princeton Univ, MA, 47, PhD(French), 51. *Prof Exp:* Instr French, Princeton Univ, 45-46 & Bryn Mawr Col, 47-49; lectr, Univ Calif, Los Angeles, 50-51, from instr to asst prof, 51-57; from asst prof to assoc prof, 57-68, chmn dept Romance lang, 68-72, PROF FRENCH, UNIV MO-COLUMBIA, 68- *Concurrent Pos:* Ed, Mod Lang Forum, 54-57. *Mem:* MLA; Midwest Mod Lang Asn; Am Asn Teachers Fr; Am Soc 18th Century Studies; Soc Fr Etude XVIII Siecle. *Res:* Eighteenth century French literature, especially the novel. *Publ:* Coauth, Anthology of Critical Prefaces to the Nineteenth Century French Novel, Univ Mo, 62. *Mailing Add:* Dept of Romance Lang Univ of Mo Columbia MO 65211

WICKENS, GEORGE MICHAEL, b London, Eng, Aug 7, 18; Can citizen; m 40; c 8. ISLAMIC LITERATURES & HISTORY. *Educ:* Cambridge Univ, BA, 39, MA, 46. *Prof Exp:* Lectr Arabic & Persian, Univ London, 46-49 & Cambridge Univ, 49-57; from assoc prof to prof Near Eastern Studies, 57-61, chmn dept Islamic studies, 61-68, prof, 61-80, UNIV PROF ISLAMIC

STUDIES, UNIV TORONT0, 80- *Concurrent Pos:* Mem East-West maj proj comt, Can Nat Comn UNESCO, 60-; mem prog appraisals comt, Ont Coun Grad Studies, 71-73; adv acad panel, Can Coun, 73-76. *Mem:* Fel Royal Soc Can; Am Orient Soc. *Res:* Persian poetic structures; Islamic and comparative literature; translation theory as it concerns Islamic literatures. *Publ:* Auth, Religion, In: Legacy of Persia, Oxford Univ, 53; Poetry in modern Persia, Univ Toronto Quart, 1/60; The Nasirean Ethics, Allen & Unwin, London, 64; auth, The Imperial epic of Iran: A literary approach, In: Iranian Civilization and Culture, McGill Univ, 72; Morals Pointed and Tales Adorned: The Bustan of Sa'di, Univ Toronto, 74; Haji Agha, Tex Univ Press, 79; Arabic Grammar, Cambridge Univ Press, 80. *Mailing Add:* Dept of Middle E & Islamic Studies Univ of Toronto Toronto ON M5S 1A1 Can

WICKERSHAM, JOHN MOORE, b Philadelphia, Pa, Aug 12, 43. CLASSICAL STUDIES, ANCIENT HISTORY. *Educ:* Univ Pa, AB, 64, MA, 65; Princeton Univ, MA, 68, PhD (class philol), 72 Oxford Univ, BA & MA, 72. *Prof Exp:* Instr class studies, Univ Pa, 69-72; asst prof, 72-80, ASSOC PROF CLASS STUDIES, URSINUS COL, 80-, CHMN DEPT, 72- *Concurrent Pos:* Nat Endowment for Humanities fel-in-residence, 76-77. *Mem:* Am Philol Asn; Class Asn Can; Soc Prom Hellenic Studies; Soc Prom Roman Studies. *Res:* Ancient historical writers; classical Greek history; teaching of Greek and Latin. *Publ:* Auth, The financial prospects of Ptolemaic oilmen, Bull Am Soc Papyrol, 70; coauth, Greek Historical Documents: The Fourth Century BC, Hakkert, Toronto, 73. *Mailing Add:* Dept of Class Studies Ursinus Col Collegeville PA 19426

WICKS, CHARLES BEAUMONT, b Port Washington, NY, Oct 21, 07; m 29; c 3. MODERN FRENCH LITERATURE. *Educ:* Wesleyan Univ, AB, 29; Johns Hopkins Univ, PhD, 35. *Prof Exp:* Instr Romance lang, Wesleyan Univ, 32-34; jr instr French, Johns Hopkins Univ, 34-35; from instr to prof Romance lang, 35-75, head dept, 51-72, EMER PROF ROMANCE LANG, UNIV ALA, 75- *Concurrent Pos:* Fulbright res grant, France, 61-62. *Honors & Awards:* Officier, Palmes Academiques; Croix de Guerre with Palm, Belg. *Mem:* MLA; Am Asn Teachers Fr; SAtlantic Mod Lang Asn (vpres, 51, pres, 54). *Res:* French novel; 19th century French drama. *Publ:* Auth, Charles-Guillaume Etienne, Johns Hopkins Univ, 40; The Parisian Stage, Univ Ala, Vols I-IV, 50-67, Vol V, 79. *Mailing Add:* 2510 20th St Northport AL 35476

WIDDOWS, PAUL F, b London, Eng, Aug 5, 18; m 57. CLASSICS. *Educ:* Oxford Univ, BA, 39, MA, 46; Univ Chicago, PhD(classics), 67. *Prof Exp:* From asst prof to assoc prof, 57-69, PROF CLASSICS, CONCORDIA UNIV, 69- *Mem:* Class Asn Can. *Res:* Latin poetry. *Mailing Add:* Dept of Classics Concordia Univ Montreal PQ H3Q 1M8 Can

WIEDEN, FRITZ, b Komotau, Czech, Sept 2, 26; Can citizen; m 65. GERMANIC STUDIES, ENGLISH. *Educ:* Univ Western Ont, BA, 58, MA, 59; Univ Toronto, PhD (Germanic lang & lit), 63. *Prof Exp:* Asst prof English & chmn dept, King's Col, Univ Western Ont, 61-68; assoc prof Germanic studies, 68-70, head dept Germanic & Slavic studies, 70-76, PROF GERMANIC & SLAVIC STUDIES, UNIV WINDSOR, 70- *Concurrent Pos:* Exec secy, Can-Ger Acad Exchange Asn, 66-76; vis prof Ger studies, State Univ NY, Buffalo, 68; chmn, Ont Soc Can & Ger Exchanges, 69-76; vis prof, McMaster Univ, 73-74. *Mem:* Can-Ger Acad Exchange Asn; Can Asn Univ Teachers. *Res:* Anglo-German literary relations; Canadiana Germanica; Austrian literature. *Publ:* Auth, A Canadian Study Guide to German Civilisation, Univ Windsor, 75; Die deutschkanadische Presse seit dem Ende des 2. Weltkriegs, Deutschsprachige Rundfunk- und Fernsehsendungen in Kanada, Deutschkanadische, Literatur: Ein Überblick & Der muttersprachliche Deutschunterricht, Überörtliche weltliche Vereine, Deutsch als Muttersprache in Kanada, Wiesbaden, 77; A Canadian Study Guide to German Civilisation, 2nd ed rev, Univ Windsor, 77. *Mailing Add:* Dept of Germanic & Slavic Studies Univ of Windsor Windsor ON N9B 3P4 Can

WIEHR, JOSEF HENRY, b Northampton, Mass, Mar 3, 25; m 52; c 2. GERMAN. *Educ:* Univ SC, AB, 49; Univ Mich, MA, 51, MA, 53. *Prof Exp:* Teacher high sch, Mich, 52-54; asst prof Ger & registr, Upper Iowa Univ, 55-56; instr Ger, Westminster Col, Pa, 56-59; asst prof, Valparaiso Univ, 61-68; prof, Jackson Community Col, 68-69; PROF GER, OAKLAND COMMUNITY COL, 69- *Mem:* MLA; Am Asn Teachers Ger; NEA. *Res:* German drama of the 19th century; the German novelle; modern German literature. *Mailing Add:* 2321 Delaware Drive Ann Arbor MI 48103

WIENCKE, MATTHEW IMMANUEL, b Grand Island, Nebr, Jan 18, 20; m 58; c 4. CLASSICAL ARCHEOLOGY. *Educ:* Wittenberg Univ, AB, 42; Lutheran Theol Sem, Philadelphia, Pa, BD, 45; Johns Hopkins Univ, PhD(art & archaeol), 47. *Hon Degrees:* Dartmouth Col, MA, 68. *Prof Exp:* Instr classics, Yale Univ, 47-52, asst prof, 52-55; vis asst prof, Univ Va, 55-56; assoc archaeol, Am Sch Class Studies, Athens, 56-58; vis asst prof classics & archaeol, Univ Mo, 58-59; asst prof, 59-63, assoc prof, 63-67, chmn dept, 63-67, PROF CLASSICS, DARTMOUTH COL, 67- *Concurrent Pos:* Yale fel, 51-52; Guggenheim fel, 56-57; Am Philos Soc grant, 57-58, 63-64; lectr, Archaeol Inst Am, 58-; Am Coun Learned Soc fel, 63-64; res assoc, Inst Advan Studies, 68-69; mem adv coun, Am Acad Rome. *Mem:* Archaeol Inst Am; Am Philol Asn. *Res:* Classical languages; Greek art and archaeology. *Publ:* Auth, An epic theme in Greek art, Am J Archaeol, 54; Studies in the frieze of the Parthenon in Athens, Yrbk Am Philos Soc, 58; biog articles, In: Encycl Britannica, 68. *Mailing Add:* Dept of Classics Dartmouth Col Hanover NH 03755

WIERSCHIN, MARTIN WERNER, b Namslau, Ger, Dec 15, 33; m 62. GERMAN LITERATURE & PHILOLOGY. *Educ:* Univ Munich, PhD(Ger philol & lit), 63. *Prof Exp:* Lectr medieval Ger lit & philol, Univ Munich, 64-66; cur Germanic lang publ, Stanford Univ Libr, 66-67; from asst prof to assoc prof, 67-73, PROF GER LIT & PHILOL, UNIV CALIF, SAN DIEGO, 73- *Concurrent Pos:* Appointee of res, medieval manuscripts of Deut Forschungsgemeinschaft, 63-65; mem adv bd Ger & English medieval lit, Kindlers Lit Lexikon, Munich, 64-; consult, Univ Calif Press, 70-, Comite Int Paleographie, Paris, 71- & Ger Quart, 71- *Mem:* Mediaeval Acad Am; MLA; Int Vereinigung fuer Germanische Sprach-und Literaturwissenschaft; Wolfram von Eschenbach-Gesellschaft; Oswald von Wolkenstein-Gesellschaft. *Res:* Medieval German literature and philology. *Publ:* Auth, Meister Johann Liechtenauers Kunst des Fechtens, C H Beck, Munich, 65; contribr, Kindlers Lit Lexikon, 65-68; auth, Johann Hartliebs Mantische Schriften, Beitraege, Tuebingen, 68; Handschriften der Ratsbuecherei Lueneburg, Harrassowitz, Wiesbaden, 69; Einfache Formen Beim Sticker?, In: Werk-Typ-Situation, Metzler, Stuttgart, 69; Introd & Bibliog & ed, Eckenlied, Fassung L, Niemeyer, Tuebingen, 74; auth, Das Ambraser Heldenbuch Maximilians I: Parts I-III, Der Schlern 50, 76; Artus und Alexander im Mosaik der Kathedrale von Otranto, Colloquia Germanica, 80. *Mailing Add:* Dept of Lit Univ Calif San Diego La Jolla CA 92093

WIESE, HERBERT FRANK, b Ogden, Utah, Aug 4, 24; m 47; c 1. GERMAN. *Educ:* Univ Utah, BA, 48; Univ Wash, MA, 50, PhD(Germanics), 55. *Prof Exp:* Instr, Univ Wash, 49-51 & Purdue Univ, 51-52; from asst prof to assoc prof, 52-67, PROF GER & CHMN DEPT FOREIGN LANG, COE COL, 67- *Concurrent Pos:* Vis prof Ger lit, Schiller Col, 65. *Mem:* MLA; Am Coun Teaching Foreign Lang. *Res:* Franz Werfel; 20th century German literature. *Publ:* Coauth, Moderne deutsche Sprachlehre, Random, 75. *Mailing Add:* 3821 Bever Ave SE Cedar Rapids IA 52403

WIESEN, DAVID S, b New York, NY, May 27, 36; m 63. CLASSICS. *Educ:* Harvard Univ, AB, 57, PhD(classics), 61. *Prof Exp:* Instr classics, Cornell Univ, 61-63; asst prof, Swarthmore Col, 63-66; from assoc prof to prof, Brandeis Univ, 66-75; PROF CLASSICS, UNIV SOUTHERN CALIF, 75-, DEAN HUMANITIES, 81- *Concurrent Pos:* Nat Endowment for Humanities fel, 71. *Mem:* Am Philol Asn. *Res:* Latin church fathers; Roman satiric poetry; the classical influence on the American slavery debate. *Publ:* Auth, St Jerome as a Satirist, Cornell Univ, 64; translr, St Augustine, City of God, Books 8-11, Harvard Univ, 68; Juvenal's Moral Character, Latomus, 63; Vergil Minucius Felix, and the Bible, Hermes, 71; Herodotus and the modern debate over race and slavery, The Ancient World, 80; The great priestess of the tree, Classical J, 80. *Mailing Add:* Dept of Classics Founders Hall 307 Univ Southern Calif Los Angeles CA 90007

WIESHOFER, INGRID, b Vienna, Austria, Sept 22, 38. GERMAN. *Educ:* Univ Vienna, PhD(English), 64. *Prof Exp:* Asst prof Ger, Idaho State Univ, 67-68; assassoc prof, Mankato State Col, 68-70; ASSOC PROF GER, AGNES SCOTT COL, 70- *Mem:* MLA; Am Asn Teachers Ger; Am Coun Study Austrian Lit. *Res:* Nineteenth century prose writing; current Austrian literature. *Mailing Add:* Dept of German Agnes Scott College Decatur GA 30030

WIFALL, WALTER R, JR, Theology, Old Testament Studies. See Vol IV

WIGODSKY, MICHAEL, b Houston, Tex, May 23, 35. CLASSICS. *Educ:* Univ Tex, Austin, BA, 57; Princeton Univ, MA, 59, PhD(classics), 64. *Prof Exp:* Instr, Fla State Univ, 61-62; from instr to asst prof, 62-69, ASSOC PROF CLASSICS, STANFORD UNIV, 69- *Mem:* AAUP; Am Philol Asn; Vergilian Soc; Soc Ancient Greek Philos. *Res:* Latin poetry; Hellenistic philosophy. *Publ:* Auth, The Salvation of Ajax, Hermes, 62; The arming of Aeneas, Classica & Mediaevalia, 65; Vergil and Early Latin Poetry, Hermes Einzelschriften, Steiner, Vol 24, 72; A pattern of Argument in Lucretius, Pac Coast Philol, 74; Nacqui sub Iulio, Dante Studies, 75; Horace's Miser and Aristotelian self-love, Symbolae Osloenses, 80. *Mailing Add:* Dept of Classics Stanford Univ Stanford CA 94305

WIGTIL, DAVID NORVAL, b Thief River Falls, Minn, Oct 10, 51; c 2. CLASSICAL LANGUAGES. *Educ:* Concordia Col, Moorhead, Minn, BA, 72; Univ Minn, Minneapolis, BA, 75, PhD(ancient Greek relig studies), 80. *Prof Exp:* Teaching assoc Class Greek, Univ Minn, 74-77; instr class lang, Concordia Col, Moorhead, Minn, 77-81; ASST PROF CLASS LANG, OKLA STATE UNIV, 81- *Mem:* Class Asn Mid West & South; Am Philol Asn; Soc Bibl Lit. *Res:* Ideological variation as shown in translations of religious texts, ancient and modern; ancient writing and perceptions of writing; computer-assisted language instruction. *Publ:* Auth, Toward a date for the Greek Fourth Eclogue, Class J, Vol 76, No 4; The ideology of the Greek Res Gestae, Part II, Vol 30.1 & Incorrect apocalyptic: The Hermetic Asclepius as an improvement on the Greek original, In: Augstieg und Niedergang der Römischen Welt, Part II, Vol 17.3, Walter de Gruyter, Berlin (in prep); Improving on the original Greek New Testament: English translation as correction, Southwest Cult Heritage Festival, Okla State Univ, (in prep); The translator of the Greek Res Gestae of Augustus, Am J Philol, Vol 103 (in prep). *Mailing Add:* Dept of Foreign Lang Okla State Univ Stillwater OK 74078

WIJSEN, LOUK M P T, b 's-Hertogenbosch, Neth, July 27, 35; US citizen. GERMAN LITERATURE. *Educ:* Monterey Inst Foreign Studies, BA, 70, MA, 71; Univ Calif, Berkeley, PhD(Ger), 77. *Prof Exp:* Instr, 75-77, LECTR GER LIT & DUTCH LANG, LIT & CULT, UNIV CALIF, BERKELEY, 77- *Res:* Literature; psychology of literature; cognitive psychoanalysis. *Publ:* Auth, De synthetische tekst, Forum Letteren, 78; From text to symbol: The cognitive and affective response to literature, Psychocult Rev, summer 78; contribr, Psychoanalytische und Psychopathologische Literaturinterpretation, Wissenschaftliche Buchgesellschaft, Darmstadt, 78; auth, Cognition and Image Formation in Literature, Van Gorcum Assen, 79. *Mailing Add:* Dept of Ger Univ of Calif Berkeley CA 94720

WIKE, VICTORIA SHANOWER, b Wooster, Ohio. CONTINENTAL PHILOSOPHY. *Educ:* MacMurray Col, BA, 74; Univ Paris, licence, 75; Pa State Univ, MA, 77, PhD(philos), 79. *Prof Exp:* ASST PROF PHILOS, LOYOLA UNIV, 79- *Mem:* Am Philos Asn; Metaphys Soc Am; Am Cath Philos Asn. *Res:* Kant; ethics; medical ethics. *Publ:* Auth, History or philosophy? An account of the origin of Kant's antinomies, Acten des 5, Int Kant-Kongresses, 4/81; Kant's Antinomies of Reason: Their Origin and Their Resolution, Univ Press of Am, 82. *Mailing Add:* Dept of Philos Loyola Univ Chicago IL 60626

WILBERGER, CAROLYN HOPE, b Corvallis, Ore, Nov 11, 48. FRENCH LANGUAGE & LITERATURE. *Educ:* Ore State Univ, BA, 69; Cornell Univ, PhD(French), 72. *Prof Exp:* From instr to asst prof, 72-77, ASSOC PROF FRENCH, PORTLAND STATE UNIV, 77- *Mem:* MLA; Pac Northwest Conf Foreign Lang; Am Soc 18th Century Studies. *Res:* Voltaire; 18th century France and Russia; 18th century France and America. *Publ:* Auth, Eighteenth-century French scholarship on Russian literature, 18th Century Studies, 72; Peter the Great: An 18th-Century Hero of Our Times?, 72 & Voltaire's Russia: Window on the East, 76, Studies on Voltaire & the 18th Century; Benjamin Franklin: The good Quaker at King Louis' court, 76, A tale of four travelers: American and Russian views of 18th-century France, 77 & From Manon to Virginie: The search for the American Golden Age, 78, Proc Pac Northwest Conf Foreign Lang. *Mailing Add:* Dept of Foreing Lang Portland State Univ PO Box 751 Portland OR 97207

WILBUR, TERENCE H, b Oakland, Calif, Apr 8, 24. GERMAN. *Educ:* Univ Calif, PhD(Ger), 54. *Prof Exp:* Instr Ger, Univ Mass, 52-53; asst prof, 53-71, ASSOC PROF, GER, UNIV CALIF, LOS ANGELES, 71 & ASSOC PROF PHILOL, 76- *Mem:* MLA; Ling Soc Am; Am Asn Teachers Ger; Soc Advan Scand Studies. *Res:* Germanic linguistics; Basque linguistics; general linguistics. *Mailing Add:* Dept of Ger Lang 310 Royce Hall Univ of Calif Los Angeles CA 90024

WILCOX, JOHN CHAPMAN, b Liverpool, England, Apr 20, 43; m 67. SPANISH LITERATURE, POETRY. *Educ:* Univ Bristol, BA, 65; Univ Tex Austin, PhD(Span), 76. *Prof Exp:* Teaching asst, Univ Tex Austin, 66-70; lectr, Queens Col, 70-75; fel, Univ Cincinnati, 77-78, asst prof, 78-79; ASST PROF SPAN, UNIV ILL-URBANA, 79- *Mem:* MLA; Am Asn Teachers Span & Port. *Res:* The poetry of Juan Ramon Jimenez; Spanish poetry of the 1920s; contemporary critical theories. *Publ:* Auth, Algunas configuraciones espaciales en la poesia de Juan Ramon Jimenez, In: La Estructura y el Espacio en la Novela y la Poesia, Hisp Press, 80; William Butler Yeats: Ma lirico del notre en la poesia de Juan Ramon Jimenez, Insula, 81; Juan Ramon Jimenez: Transformacion y evolucion poetica de 4 temas Fundamentales en su obra, Cuadernos Hispanoam, 81; co-ed, Spanish Poetry of the 1920s: A Collection of Critical Essays, Soc Span & Span-Am Studies (in prep); auth, The evolution of la poesia desnuda in Juan Ramon Jimenez: Remarks on the Yeatsian influx, Hisparia (in prep). *Mailing Add:* Dept of Span, Ital & Port Univ of Ill Urbana IL 61801

WILDER, WILLIAM RUSSELL, b Crystal City, Mo, Oct 27, 22. ROMANCE LANGUAGES. *Educ:* Univ Dayton, BA, 43; St Louis Univ, PhD(Latin Am area studies), 66. *Prof Exp:* Assoc prof, 64-76, chmn dept, 64-73, PROF LANG, ST MARY'S UNIV, TEX, 77- *Concurrent Pos:* Consult Peruvian affairs, US Govt, 66-70; lang consult, Scholatic Testing Co, 66-70. *Mem:* MLA; Am Asn Teachers Span & Port. *Res:* Ricardo Palma, stylistic development of his prose. *Mailing Add:* Dept of Lang St Mary's Univ San Antonio TX 78284

WILEY, RAYMOND A, b New York, NY, Oct 30, 23; m 58; c 8. GERMAN MYTHOLOGY & CLASSICAL LITERATURE. *Educ:* Fordham Univ, AB, 46, MA, 48; Goethe Inst, Munich, cert, 56; Syracuse Univ, PhD(humanities), 66. *Prof Exp:* Instr Ger & English, Boston Col, 47-48; from instr to asst prof, 48-66, assoc prof Ger, 66-71, dir lang lab, 70-77, actg chmn dept mod lang, 76, actg chmn dept classics, 76-78, PROF FOREIGN LANG & LIT, LE MOYNE COL, 71- *Concurrent Pos:* Fordham Univ Encaenia award, 56. *Mem:* Am Asn Teachers Ger. *Res:* The correspondence between John Mitchell Kemble and Jakob Grimm, 1832-52; 19th century German-English literary relations; Teutonic mythology. *Publ:* Four unpublished letters of Jacob Grimm to John Mitchell Kemble, 1832-40, J English & Ger Philol, 7/68; ed, John Mitchell Kemble and Jacob Grimm, a Correspondence: 1832-1852, Brill, Leiden, 71; auth, From letters to life, Heights Mag, Le Moyne Col, fall 71; The German-American verse of Dr Franz Lahmeyer, Ger-Am Studies, spring 74; ed, Austausch, Cent NY Chap Am Asn Teachers Ger Newslett, Vols 1-5, 70-74; auth, Dear Harriet: Fanny Kemble's View of Centennial America, Pa Gazette, 7/76; Anglo-Saxon Kemble, The Life and Works of John Mitchell Kemble 1807-57: Philologist, Historian, Archaeologist, Brit Archaeol Rec, No 72: Anglo-Saxon Studies Archaeol & Hist, 1: 165-273; ed, John Mitchell Kemble's Review of Jacob Grimm's Deutsche Grammatik, State Univ NY Ctr Medieval & Early Renaissance Studies, 81. *Mailing Add:* Dept of Foreign Lang Le Moyne College Syracuse NY 13214

WILEY, WILLIAM LEON, b Tate, Ga, Mar 14, 03; m 27; c 1. FRENCH LITERATURE. *Educ:* Univ Chattanooga, AB, 21; Harvard Univ, AM, 25, PhD, 30. *Hon Degrees:* DLitt, Univ Chattanooga, 61. *Prof Exp:* Prin, High Sch, Ga, 21-23; instr French, Univ NC, 25-28; instr Span, Harvard Univ, 28-30, Sheldon traveling fel, 30-31; from asst prof to prof French, 31-55, Kenan prof, 55-69, EMER KENAN PROF FRENCH, UNIV NC, CHAPEL HILL, 69- *Concurrent Pos:* Asst ed, Studies Philol, 42-; Folger traveling fel, 51; mem operations reserve, US Info Agency, 58-; vis prof, Brown Univ, 64-65; chmn Southern regional comt, Nat Found Humanities, 66-67. *Honors & Awards:* Thomas Jefferson Award, Univ NC, 66; Chevalier, Palmes Academiques, 68. *Mem:* MLA; Am Asn Teachers Fr; SAtlantic Mod Lang Asn; Renaissance Soc Am; Soc Amis Montaigne. *Res:* French literature of the 16th and 17th centuries; French Renaissance; French drama. *Publ:* Auth, The Gentleman of Renaissance France, 54, The Early Public Theatre in France, 60 & The Formal French, 67, Harvard Univ; coauth, Literature of the French Renaissance: a blbiography, Studies Philol; auth, The Hotel de Bourgogne, Univ NC, 73; Mary, Queen of Scots, in France, In: John L Lievsay Festschrift Volume, Duke Univ, 77; Madame Bovary et le Theatre des Arts a Rouen, Rev d'Hist du Theatre, 79. *Mailing Add:* 132 Dey Hall Univ of NC Chapel Hill NC 27514

WILHELM, JAMES JEROME, Comparative Literature. See Vol II

WILHELM, ROBERT MCKAY, b Stratford, Ont, Mar 30, 44; m 70. CLASSICS. *Educ:* McMaster Univ, BA, 67; Ohio State Univ, MA, 69, PhD(classics), 71. *Prof Exp:* Asst prof, 72-80, ASSOC PROF CLASSICS, MIAMI UNIV, 80- *Concurrent Pos:* Ed, Auxilia Magistris Oblata, Am Class League, Humanitas, Ohio Class Conf; assoc ed, Class Outlook, dir placement serv, assoc dir, Teaching Materials & Resource Ctr, Am Class League; dir, Am Class League Placement Serv. *Mem:* Am Class League; Class Asn Mid West & South; Am Philol Asn; Vergilian Soc Am; Archaeol Inst Am. *Res:* Ancient epic and Vergilian studies; Greek and Roman art, archaeology (ancient solar technology); classical mythology. *Publ:* Vergil and Pliny, Class Outlook, 53: 40-41; Vergil's dido and Petrarch's sophonisba, Studies Lang & Lit, 76; Vergil, In: Georgic II: The sowing of a republic, Ziva Antika, 26: 63-72; Sol, Caesar and Apollo: Triumvirate of order in Vergil's Georgics, Proc Helios: From myth to solar energy, 1: 148-157; The plough-chariot: Symbol of order in the Georgics, Class J, 77: 213-230. *Mailing Add:* Dept of Classics Miami Univ Oxford OH 45056

WILHELSMEN, ALEXANDRA LEONORE, Spanish History. See Vol I

WILHITE, JOHN F, b McMinnville, Tenn, Nov 6, 47; m 71; c 2. SPANISH LANGUAGE & LITERATURE. *Educ:* Univ Tenn, BA, 69, MA, 74, PhD(Span), 76. *Prof Exp:* Asst prof Span, Univ Tenn, 76-77; ASST PROF SPAN & LATIN AM LIT & CULT, UNIV CINCINNATI, 77- *Concurrent Pos:* Ed, Hisp Enlightenment Asn, 80- *Mem:* MLA; Am Asn Teachers Span & Port; Am Coun Teachers Foreign Lang; Hisp Enlightenment Asn (pres, 81-82). *Res:* Contemporary Latin American literature; Latin American history and culture; Spanish language methods. *Publ:* Auth, Charros y chocolate, Scott, Foresman & Co, 78; Borges and Chesterton: View of the universe, God and man, In: Proceedings, Ind Univ Pa Press, 78; The Inter-American enlightenment, Rev Interam Bibliog, 80; Mitologia India en la poesia de Barba-Jacob, Rev del Convenio Andres Bello, 80; The enlightenment in New Granada, Americas, 80; La alienacion en la literatura Argentina, Mich State Univ, 80; Cambios: La cultura hispanic (in prep) & coauth, Encuentros: Lengua y cultura del mundo hispanico (in prep), Heinle & Heinle Publ. *Mailing Add:* Dept of Romance Lang & Lit Univ of Cincinnati Cincinnati OH 45221

WILKIE, BRIAN, English, Comparative Literature. See Vol II

WILKIE, NANCY C, b Milwaukee, Wis, Dec 27, 42. GREEK ARCHEOLOGY, CLASSICS. *Educ:* Stanford Univ, AB, 64; Univ Minn, MA, 67, PhD(Greek), 75. *Prof Exp:* Instr classics, Macalester Col, 72-75; adj instr, 74-75, adj asst prof classics, 75-79, ASST PROF CLASSICS & SOCIOANTHROP, CARLETON COL, 79- *Concurrent Pos:* Field dir, Phocis-Doris Exped, Loyola Univ, Chicago, 77-80. *Mem:* Archaeol Inst Am; Am Philol Asn; Soc Prof Archaeologists; Asn Field Archaeol; Soc Am Archaeol. *Res:* Prehistoric Greek archaeology; archeological sampling. *Publ:* Auth, The Nichoria Tholos & Area-IV-6, Hesperia, 75; Area I, Excauations at Nichoria in Southwest Greece, Vol I, Minn, 78; Early Helladic Pottery from Phokis and Doris, Teiresias, 79; Shaft Graves at Nichoria, Temple Univ Aegean Symp, 81. *Mailing Add:* Carleton Col Northfield MN 55057

WILKINS, GEORGE WESLEY, JR, b Memphis, Tenn, June 5, 31; m 57; c 4. SPANISH, APPLIED LINGUISTICS. *Educ:* Tulane Univ, BA, 53, PhD(Span), 61; Stanford Univ, MA, 55. *Prof Exp:* TV instr Span, Sta WYES-TV, New Orleans, 59-60; from instr to asst prof, 60-67, asst dir lang lab, 67-69, ASSOC PROF SPAN, TULANE UNIV, 67-, DIR LANG LAB, 69- *Concurrent Pos:* NDEA res contract, 60-63; consult, MLA, 62, mem comt teacher prep, 63, comt eval advan tests, 64. *Mem:* Nat Asn Lang Lab Dir (pres, 71-73); Southern Conf Lang Teaching (exec secy, 73); Am Coun Teaching Foreign Lang. *Res:* Spanish linguistics; linguistics applied to foreign language teaching and testing; the preparation of modern foreign language teachers. *Publ:* Auth, The use of cognates in testing pronunciation, Lang Learning, 12/59; Language laboratory techniques via televised language instruction, Hispania, 3/60; ed, Dimension: Languages '69, 69 & Dimension: Languages '71, 71, Southern Conf Lang Teachers; auth, What can we expect from audio in the 1970's?, Defense Lang Inst Workshop, 70. *Mailing Add:* 4113 Napoli Dr Metairie LA 70002

WILKINS, KATHLEEN SONIA, b Conon Bridge, Scotland, Dec 28, 41. FRENCH LITERATURE, HISTORY OF IDEAS. *Educ:* Univ Southampton, BA, 63, PhD(French), 67. *Prof Exp:* Asst prof French, State Univ NY, Stony Brook, 67-71; col lectr, Univ Col, Dublin, 71-72; ASSOC PROF FRENCH, MONTCLAIR STATE COL, 72- *Concurrent Pos:* Am Philos Soc grant-in-aid, 73 & 76. *Mem:* MLA; Am Soc 18th Century Studies; Am Asn Teachers Fr; North East Mod Lang Asn. *Res:* Irrational in 18th century France; French women authors in the 17th and 18th centuries; women's education in the USA, critical bibliography. *Publ:* Auth, A study of the works of Claude Buffier, Inst Voltaire, 69; The treatment of the supernatural in the encyclopedie, Studies Voltaire & 18th Century, 72; Witchcraft and demonic possession in 18th century France, J Europ Studies, 73; Women in two eighteenth century French periodicals, Studies in 18th Century Cult, 76. *Mailing Add:* Dept of French Montclaire State Col Upper Montclair NJ 07043

WILL, ELIZABETH LYDING, b Oak Park, Ill, Apr 27, 24; m 51; c 2. CLASSICS. *Educ:* Miami Univ, AB, 44; Bryn Mawr Col, MA, 45, PhD(Greek & Latin), 49. *Prof Exp:* Instr Greek & Latin, Sweet Briar Col, 48-50 & Dartmouth Col, 53-54; instr classics, Univ Tex, Austin, 63-64; asst prof, 71-76, ASSOC PROF CLASSICS, UNIV MASS, AMHERST, 76- *Concurrent Pos:* Seymour fel Greek, Am Sch Class Studies, Athens, 50-51; Am Philos Soc res grant, 61; fac res grant, Univ Mass, Amherst, 74. *Mem:* Archaeol Inst Am; Am Philol Asn; Rei Cretariae Romanae Fautores; Class Asn New Eng. *Res:* Roman amphoras; Roman economic and social history. *Publ:* Auth, Les amphores de Sestius, Revue archeol l'est centre'est, 56; coauth, L'ilot de la maison des comediens (Exploration archeologique de Delox, XXVII), 70; auth, The ancient commercial amphora, Archaeol, 77; coauth, Underwater excavations at the Etruscan Port of Populonia, J Field

Archaeol, 77; auth, Women in Pompeii, Archaeol, 79; The sestius amphoras: A reappraisal, J Field Archaeol, 79; Ambiguity in Horace, Odes, Class Philol, 82; Greco-Italic Amphoras, Hesperia, 82. *Mailing Add:* Dept of Classics Herter Hall Univ of Mass Amherst MA 01003

WILLARD, CHARITY CANNON, b Eureka, Ill, Aug 9, 14; m 44. FRENCH HISTORY & LITERATURE. *Educ:* Hiram Col, AB, 34; Smith Col, MA, 36; Radcliffe Col, PhD, 40. *Prof Exp:* Instr French, Lake Erie Col, 40-41; chmn dept French & Span, Westbrook Jr Col, 42-45; lectr, Bennington Col, 49-50; vis prof, St Lawrence Univ, 50-51; instr French, Emma Willard Sch, 52-55; lectr, French & Span, Ladycliff Col, 61-65, assoc prof, 65-74, chmn dept, 72-80, prof, 74-80. *Concurrent Pos:* Ann Radcliffe fel, Radcliffe Col, 51-54; scholar, Radcliffe Inst Independent Study, 62-64; dir, Int Inst for Girls in Spain, 60- *Mem:* MLA; Mediaeval Acad Am; Renaissance Soc Am; Soc Hist Discoveries. *Res:* Mediaeval French language, literature and history; Mediaeval Portuguese history and literature. *Publ:* Ed, Le livre de la paix, Mouton, The Hague, 58; auth, Christine de Pisan's Treatise of the art of warfare, In: Essays in Honor of Louis F Solano, Univ NC, 70; A fifteenth-century Burgundian version of the Roman de Florimont, Medievalia et Humanistica, 71. *Mailing Add:* 11 Prospect St Cornwall-on-Hudson NY 10928

WILLARD, SUMNER, b Arlington, Mass, July 18, 16; m 44. ROMANCE PHILOLOGY. *Educ:* Harvard Univ, AB, 37, AM, 38, PhD, 43. *Prof Exp:* Instr French, Longwood Day Sch, Brookline, Mass, 37-39; tutor, Harvard Univ, 39-42; instr mod lang, US Mil Acad, 43-47; asst prof Romance lang, Univ Vt, 47-51; instr mod lang, US Mil Acad, US Army, 51-57, from asst prof to assoc prof foreign lang, 57-64, actg chmn dept, 72-73, prof, 64-80, chmn dept, 77-80; RETIRED. *Concurrent Pos:* Mem, Int Inst, Spain. *Mem:* MLA; Renaissance Soc Am. *Res:* The non-dramatic works of Paul Hervieu. *Publ:* Co-translr, Art of Warfare in Western Europe from the 9th to 14th Centuries, NAmsterdam Publ, Holland, 77. *Mailing Add:* 11 Prospect St Cornwall-on-Hudson NY 12520

WILLECKE, FREDERICK HENRY, b Bremen, Ger, Dec 14, 17; US citizen; m 42; c 3. GERMAN LITERATURE. *Educ:* Wagner Col, AB, 40; Columbia Univ, AM, 41; NY Univ, PhD, 60. *Prof Exp:* Lectr Ger, Columbia Univ, 41 & Polytech Inst Brooklyn, 42; from asst prof to assoc prof, 46-61, dir pub rel, 46-48, PROF GER, WAGNER COL, 61-, CHMN DEPT FOREIGN LANG, 62- *Concurrent Pos:* Lectr, Hunter Col, 61-63. *Mem:* MLA; Am Asn Teachers Ger. *Publ:* Auth, Hebbel's Conception of Woman; Thomas Mann und Luther, 10/58 & Style and form in Hermann Hesse's Unterm Rad, 10/61, Ky Foreign Lang Quart; Foreign languages, Can Open New Horizons, 10/79. *Mailing Add:* Dept of German Wagner College Staten Island NY 10301

WILLGING, HERBERT M, b Dubuque, Iowa, Apr 20, 12; m 38; c 10. FOREIGN LANGUAGES. *Educ:* Loras Col, BA, 33; State Univ Iowa, MA, 34, PhD, 37. *Prof Exp:* Instr French, Rockhurst Col, 36-37; instr French & Span, Creighton Univ, 37-39; assoc prof French, Col New Rochelle, 39-43; assoc prof, 46-73, PROF FRENCH, COL ST THOMAS, 73- *Mem:* Am Asn Teachers Ger. *Res:* Audio-lingual techniques in elementary French and Spanish; English for foreign students. *Publ:* Auth, Henri Gheon . . . , Cath Libr World, 2/42; A new approach to the reading objective, Mod Lang J, 2/48; On phonetic spelling, J Teacher Educ, 12/56; English by Ear, 60, coauth, Spanish in Slow Motion, 62-67 & auth, French in Slow Motion, 63-68, privately publ. *Mailing Add:* Dept of Foreign Lang Col of St Thomas St Paul MN 55105

WILLIAMS, CHARLES GARFIELD SINGER, b Mt Vernon, Ohio, May 17, 39. FRENCH LITERATURE, COMPARATIVE LITERATURE. *Educ:* Kenyon Col, AB, 63; Oxford Univ, BA, 65; Yale Univ, MPhil, 69; Oxford Univ, MA, 70; Yale Univ, PhD(Fr), 70. *Prof Exp:* From instr to asst prof, 68-74, ASSOC PROF FRENCH, OHIO STATE UNIV, 74- *Concurrent Pos:* Contrib ed, French 17, 79- *Mem:* MLA; Mod Humanities Res Asn; Am Asn Teacher Fr; Am Soc 18th Century Studies; Fr Hist Soc. *Res:* Sevigne; Valincour; 17th century French prose and academic eloquence. *Publ:* Auth, Valincour's life of guise, In: Literature and History in the Age of Ideas, Ohio State Univ, 75; ed, Literature and History in the Age of Ideas, Ohio State Univ, 75; Madame de Sevigne, G K Hall, 81; Memorialists, Historiography & History of science and medicine, In: Cabeen Bibliography, Suppl III, 82. *Mailing Add:* Dept of French Ohio State Univ Columbus OH 43210

WILLIAMS, DANIEL ANTHONY, b Frederick, Md, May 8, 42; m 63; c 2. SPANISH LANGUAGE & LITERATURE. *Educ:* Univ Md, College Park, AB, 64; Johns Hopkins Univ, MA, 67, PhD(Romance lang), 72. *Prof Exp:* Instr Span, Villa Julie Col, 66-67 & Sweet Briar Col, 67-71; asst prof, Va Wesleyan Col, 69; asst prof, 72-79, ASSOC PROF & CHMN, WESTERN MD COL, 79- *Res:* Contemporary Latin American narrative; comparative studies; 20th century Spanish poetry. *Publ:* Auth, Phantoms of the Afternoon (poem), Delta, 5/60; translr, War (poem), Brambler, 5/68 & Numbers (poem), Inlet, 5/72. *Mailing Add:* Dept of Foreign Langs Western Maryland College Westminster MD 21157

WILLIAMS, EDWARD BAKER, b Taunton, Mass, July 20, 11; m 51. ROMANCE LANGUAGES. *Educ:* Tufts Univ, AB, 33; Brown Univ, AM, 52, PhD(French), 60. *Prof Exp:* Instr French, Trinity Col, Conn, 57-60; from instr to asst prof, Univ Conn, 60-64; from asst prof to assoc prof, Northeastern Univ, 64-72; Hollis prof Romance lang & lit, Wesleyan Univ, 72-76; assoc prof Mod lang, Northeastern Univ, 76-80; RETIRED. *Mem:* Renaissance Soc Am; Am Asn Teachers Fr; MLA; Am Guild Organists. *Res:* French language and literature, especially Renaissance and classical; relationships of French literature and music. *Publ:* Auth, The observations of Epistemon and condign punishment, Esprit Createur, summer 63. *Mailing Add:* Dept of Mod Lang Northeastern Univ Boston MA 02115

WILLIAMS, FREDERICK GRANGER, b Buenos Aires, Arg, Mar 31, 40; US citizen; m 64; c 6. PORTUGUESE, SPANISH. *Educ:* Brigham Young Univ, BA, 65; Univ Wis, MA, 67, PhD(Luso-Brazilian lit), 71. *Prof Exp:* Dir Port, Lang Training Mission, Brigham Young Univ, 64-66; lectr, Univ Wis, 70-71; asst prof Span & Port, Univ Calif, Los Angeles, 71-73; curric consult Port, Fed Bilingual Proj, Artesia, Calif, 73-74; asst prof, 74-79, ASSOC PROF SPAN & PORT, UNIV CALIF, SANTA BARBARA, 79- *Concurrent Pos:* Dir, LDS Inst Relig, 70-71; contrib ed, Chasqui: Revista de Literatura, 76-; dir, Summer Inst Port, Univ Calif, Santa Barbara, 76-; Calouste Gulbenkian Found fel, 77 & 80; dir, Jorge de Sena Ctr Port Studies, Univ Calif, Santa Barbara; mem, Nat Comn Inter-Univ Study, Brazil, 79- *Honors & Awards:* Merit of Timbira Medal, Gov State of Maranhao, Brazil, 76. *Mem:* Corresp mem Maranhao State Acad Lett; Asn of Teachers Span & Port; MLA; Pac NW Coun Foreign Lang; Pac Coast Coun Latin Am Studies. *Res:* Brazilian literature; Portuguese literature; Luso-American community. *Publ:* Auth, Breve estudo do Orto do Esposo, Ocidente, 5/68; co-ed, Sousandrade: Ineditos, Dept de Cultura do Estado do Maranhao, 70; auth, Sousandrade: Vida e Obra, Sioge, 76; Portuguese tiles in the great American mosaic: An overview of 500 years, Proc Pac Nat Conf Foreign Lang, 4/76; co-ed, Sousandrade: Prosa, Sioge, 78; ed, The Poetry of Jorge de Sena, Mudborn Press, 80; auth, Port bilingualism among Azoreans in California, Hispania, 12/80; Elementos estilisticos no poesia de Jorge de Sena, Studies on Jorge de Sena, Bandanna, 81. *Mailing Add:* Dept of Span & Portuguese Univ of Calif Santa Barbara CA 93106

WILLIAMS, GERHILD SCHOLZ, b Perleberg, Ger, Sept 18, 42; US citizen; m 74; c 1. MEDIEVAL STUDIES, LINGUISTICS. *Educ:* Univ Wash, BA, 69, MA, 71, PhD(comp lit), 74. *Prof Exp:* Asst prof, 75-81, ASSOC PROF GER, WASHINGTON UNIV 81- *Mem:* Medieval Acad Am; MLA, Am Asn Teachers Ger; Foreign Lang Teachers Asn; Midwestern Mod Lang Asn. *Res:* French, German, Latin literature of the early and later Middle Ages. *Publ:* Auth, The vision of death, A study of the memento mori expressions in some Latin, German and French Didactic texts of the 11th and 12th centuries, Kummerle Göppingen W Ger, 10/76; Against court and school: Heinrich of Melk and Helinant of Froidmont as critics of Twelfth Century Society, Neophilolgus, 7/78; Against church and state: Heinrich von Melk und Helinant de Froidmont as critics of 12th century society, Neophilologus, 62: 513-526; Sozio-Semiotik als rekonstruktion, Zur interpretation mittelalterlicher literatur, Germanistiche Linguistik, 1-2: 217-236; coauth (with Alexander Schwarz), Das Uberetzen aus dem mittelalterlichen Deutsch, Sprachspiegel, 9/80; auth, The arthurian model in Emperor Maximilian's autobiographic writings Weisskunig & Theuerdannk, Sixteenth Century J, 11, 4: 2-23; Es war einmal, ist und wird einmal sein: Geschichte und Geschichten in Günter Grass Der Butt, In: deutsche Literatur in der Bundesrepuseit 1965, Königstein/Ts Athenäum, 80; Annotated Bibliography of Maximilian I, his literary activities and the impact on the culture of his day, Sixteenth Century Bibliog, Vol 21, 82. *Mailing Add:* Dept of Ger Washington Univ St Louis MO 63130

WILLIAMS, HARRY FRANKLIN, b Chester Co, Pa, Sept 10, 11; m. MEDIEVAL FRENCH & SPANISH. *Educ:* Univ Nancy, Dipl, 31; Univ Del, AB, 33; Middlebury Col, AM, 38; Univ Mich, PhD, 42. *Prof Exp:* Prof mod lang & head dept, Lincoln Mem Univ, 42-44; mem fac Span, Univ Wis, 44-46; mem fac French, Univ Calif, Los Angeles, 46-63; prof Romance lang, Univ Minn, Minneapolis, 63-66; PROF ROMANCE LANG, FLA STATE UNIV, 66- *Mem:* MLA; Int Arthurian Soc; Mediaeval Acad Am. *Res:* Provencal. *Publ:* Auth, Floriant et Florete, Univ Mich, 47; Lazarillo de Tormes, Univ Wis, 48, 62; Index of Mediaeval Studies in Festschriften, Univ Calif, 51. *Mailing Add:* Dept of Mod Lang Fla State Univ Tallahassee FL 32306

WILLIAMS, JAMES EDWARD, b Youngstown, Ohio, Nov 11, 23. ROMANCE LANGUAGES. *Educ:* Ohio State Univ, BS, 48, MA, 51; Univ Wis, MA, 58; Univ Colo, PhD(Span), 69. *Prof Exp:* Teacher pub schs, Okla, 48-51; instr French, WVa State Col, 52-53; instr Span & French, St Philip's Col, 54-57; assoc prof Span, Jackson State Univ, 58-62, head dept mod foreign lang, 65-68; assoc prof Span, Tenn State Univ, 68-80. *Mem:* Am Asn Teachers Span & Port; MLA. *Res:* Spanish American literature. *Mailing Add:* 204 Cunniff Pkwy Nashville TN 37217

WILLIAMS, JOHN BRINDLEY, American Literature, Stylistics. See Vol II

WILLIAMS, JOHN CARTER, b Hartford, Conn, July 12, 27; m 55; c 2. CLASSICS. *Educ:* Trinity Col, Conn, BA, 49; Yale Univ, MA, 51, PhD, 62. *Prof Exp:* Tutor Latin, Loomis Prep Sch, 49-50; asst English, Trinity Col, Conn, 49-50; asst classics, Yale Univ, 52-53; from asst prof to assoc prof classics & chmn dept, Goucher Col, 54-68; assoc prof class lang, 68-70, chmn dept classics, 70-78, prof, 70-80, HOBART PROF CLASSICS, TRINITY COL, 80- *Concurrent Pos:* Consult, Nat Endowment for Humanities, 74- *Mem:* Am Philol Asn; Archaeol Inst Am; Class Asn Atlantic States; Am Studies Asn; Class Asn New England. *Res:* Greek/Latin metrics; Horace. *Mailing Add:* Dept of Classics Trinity College Hartford CT 06106

WILLIAMS, JOHN HOWARD, b Louisville, Ky, Nov 19, 46; m 69; c 2. FRENCH LANGUAGE & LITERATURE, CLASSICS. *Educ:* David Lipscomb Col, BA, 67; Univ Wis-Madison, MA, 68, PhD(French), 72. *Prof Exp:* Instr French, Tenn Technol Univ, 68-69; Fulbright advan teaching fel Am lit, Univ Besancon, 71-72; asst prof French, Eastern Ky Univ, 72-74; asst prof, 74-76, assoc prof, 76-82, PROF FRENCH & CHMN DEPT, ABILENE CHRISTIAN UNIV, 82- *Mem:* MLA; Am Asn Teachers Fr. *Res:* Contemporary French culture; 16th century French Poetry. *Mailing Add:* Abilene Christian Univ Station Box 8248 Abilene TX 79601

WILLIAMS, JOHN R, b Malone, NY, Jan 24, 30. FRENCH. *Educ:* Col Wooster, BA, 53; Middlebury Col, MA, 57; Univ Colo, PhD(French), 68. *Prof Exp:* Instr French, Col Wooster, 59-60; from instr to asst prof, 63-71, ASSOC PROF FRENCH, UNIV KANS, 71- *Mem:* Am Asn Teachers French. *Res:* Nineteenth century French literature; especially Romanticism.

Publ: Auth, Flaubert and the religion of art, French Rev, 10/67; Jules Michelet and the notion of literary commitment, Fr Rev, 2/73; Jules Michelet--critic of Rousseau, In: French Literary Criticism, Univ SC Fr Lit Serv IV, 77. *Mailing Add:* Dept of French & Italian Univ of Kans Lawrence KS 66405

WILLIAMS, LOIS VIRGINIA, b Philadelphia, Pa, June 29, 13. CLASSICS. *Educ:* Beaver Col, AB, 35; Univ Pa, MA, 39; Johns Hopkins Univ, PhD(Latin), 46. *Prof Exp:* Instr classics, Juniata Col, 43-47; from instr to assoc prof, 48-64, prof, 64-79, EMER PROF CLASSICS, STATE UNIV NY ALBANY, 79- *Concurrent Pos:* Fel, Am Acad Rome, 47-48. *Mem:* Am Philol Asn; Archaeol Inst Am. *Res:* Roman religion; Latin literature. *Mailing Add:* 48 Providence St McKownville Albany NY 12203

WILLIAMS, LORNA VALERIE, b Hanover, Jamaica, Aug 26, 40. SPANISH. *Educ:* Univ WI, BA, 63; Ind Univ, MA, 67, PhD(Span), 74. *Prof Exp:* Asst prof Span, Dartmouth Col, 72-78; ASST PROF SPAN, UNIV MO, ST LOUIS, 78- *Concurrent Pos:* Vis fel hist, Johns Hopkins Univ, 78-79; fel Span, Tinker Found, 78-79; res grant Span, Soc Sci Res Coun, 78-79. *Mem:* MLA; Col Lang Asn; Am Asn Teachers Span & Port; Inst Int Lit Iberoamericana; Asn Int Hispanistas. *Res:* Latin American literature; Caribbean literature; comparative literature. *Publ:* Auth, Perspective in the Memorias Posthumas de Braz Cubas, 75, The image of King Christophe, 77 & The utopian vision in Carpentier's El Reino de Este Mundo, 78, Col Lang Asn J; The black woman and revolution in Cuba, Revista Rev Interam, 78; coauth, Africa and The Caribbean: Legacies of The Link, Johns Hopkins, 79. *Mailing Add:* Dept of Hist Johns Hopkins Univ Baltimore MD 21218

WILLIAMS, LOUISE LYLE GIVENS, Literature, Linguistics. See Vol II

WILLIAMS, MILLER, English, Spanish Translations. See Vol II

WILLIAMS, RAYMOND LESIE, b Oregon City, Ore, Mar 9, 50; m 72. LATIN AMERICAN LITERATURE. *Educ:* Wash State Univ, BA, 72; Univ Kans, MA, 74, PhD(Span), 77. *Prof Exp:* Asst prof Span, Univ Chicago, 77-79; ASST PROF SPAN, WASH UNIV, 80- *Mem:* MLA; Inst Int Lit Iberoamericana; Am Asn Teachers Span & Port; Ctr Inter-Am Rels. *Res:* Contemporary Latin American fiction; 20th century Latin American literature; Colombian literature. *Publ:* Ed, Aproximaciones a Gustavo Alvarez Gardeazabal, Plaza y Janes, 77; auth, The narrative art of Mario Vargas Llosa: Two organizing principles in Pantaleon y las Visitadoras, Tex Studies Lit & Lang, winter, 77; The dynamic structure of Garcia Marquez's El Otono del Patriarca, Symposium, spring 78; Structure and transformation of reality in Alvarez Gardeazabal, Ky Romance Quart, No 2, 80; Una decada de la novela colombiana, Plaza y Janes, 81. *Mailing Add:* Dept of Romance Lang & Lit Washington Univ St Louis MO 63130

WILLIAMS, RONALD JAMES, b Dublin, Ireland, May 9, 17; m 40; c 2. NEAR EASTERN LANGUAGES. *Educ:* Univ Toronto, BA, 40, MA, 43; Univ Chicago, PhD, 48; Victoria Univ, BD, 43. *Prof Exp:* Spec lectr, 43-44, from lectr to assoc prof 44-57, PROF ORIENT LANG, UNIV TORONTO, 57- *Concurrent Pos:* Res assoc & asst prof, Univ Chicago, 47-48; Nuffield fel, Oxford Univ, 53-54. *Mem:* Am Orient Soc; Soc Bibl Lit; Soc Old Testament Studies; Can Soc Bible Studies (vpres, 51, pres, 52); Egypt Explor Soc. *Res:* Egyptology; Near Eastern wisdom literature; the fable in the Near East. *Publ:* Coauth, The fable in the ancient Near East, In: A Stubborn Faith, Southern Methodist Univ, 56; Documents from Old Testament Times, Nelson, 58 & Challenge and Response: Modern Ideas and Religion, Ryerson, 59; auth, Hebrew Syntax: An Outline, Univ Toronto, 67. *Mailing Add:* Dept of Near Eastern Studies Univ Col Univ of Toronto Toronto ON M5S 1A1 Can

WILLIAMS, SIDNEY JAMES, JR, b Bellamy, Ala, Aug 21, 38. ROMANCE LANGUAGES, SPANISH. *Educ:* Davidson Col, AB, 60; Univ NC, MA, 63, PhD, 66. *Prof Exp:* Instr Span, Univ NC, 60-66; from asst to assoc prof, 66-76, PROF ROMANCE LANG, WASHINGTON & LEE UNIV, 77- *Mem:* Am Asn Teachers Span & Port. *Res:* Modern Spanish theatre; the Spanish Pastoral novel. *Mailing Add:* Dept of Romance Lang Washington & Lee Univ Lexington VA 24450

WILLIAMSEN, VERN G, b San Jose, Calif, June 11, 26; m 59; c 2. SPANISH. *Educ:* San Jose State Col, AB, 48; Univ Ariz, MA, 64; Univ Mo-Columbia, PhD(Span), 68. *Prof Exp:* Teacher Span & music, Ft Jones High Sch, Calif, 48-49 & Camptonville High Sch, Calif, 50-53; teacher 6th grade, San Francisco Pub Schs, 53-59; teacher Span & music, Pleasanton Pub Schs, 59-62 & Tucson Pub Schs, Ariz, 62-65; asst prof Span, Westminster Col, 65-68; assoc prof, 68, PROF SPAN, UNIV MO-COLUMBIA, 68- *Mem:* MLA; Asn Teachers Span & Port; Asoc Int de Hispanistas. *Res:* Golden Age drama; Golden Age poetry. *Publ:* Ed, Mira de Amescua: No hay dicha ni desdicha hasta la muerte, Univ Mo, 71; auth, The dramatic function of Cuentecillos in some plays by Mira de Amescua, Hispania, 71; ed, Mira de Amescua: La Casa del Tahur, Castalia, 73; coauth, A study of reading lists for graduate degrees in Spanish, Hispania, 73; coauth, Annual bibliography of publications on the comedian, Bull Comediantes, 73-78; ed, Juan Ruiz de Alarcon: Don Domingo de Don Blas, Est Hispanofila, 75; An Annotated Analytical Bibliography of Tirso de Molina Studies, Univ Mo, 79; auth, Forma simetrica en las comedias barroca de Sor Juana Ines, Cuadernos Am, 79; The Minor Dramatists of Seventeenth-Century Spain, Twayne, 82. *Mailing Add:* Dept of Romance Languages Univ of Missouri Columbia MO 65201

WILLIAMSON, JUANITA VIRGINIA, b Shelby, Miss, Jan 18, 17. ENGLISH. *Educ:* Le Moyne Col, BA, 38; Atlanta Univ, MA, 40; Univ Mich, PhD(ling), 61. *Prof Exp:* Prof English, 46-80, DISTINGUISHED SERV PROF ENGLISH & LING, LE MOYNE-OWEN COL, TENN, 80-, CHMN HUMANITIES, 76- *Concurrent Pos:* Vis prof, Ball State Univ, 62-63; consult, English NDEA Inst, SC State Col, 65; consult, Ball State Univ, 65, Guidance Inst, Memphis State Univ, 68, Southeastern Educ Lab, 68, Ford Found spec proj, 68, NDEA Proj, Univ Miss, 69, Oral Lang Proj, Tupelo Schs, Miss, 69 & Univ Nebr, 69; vis scholar, NC Col Durham, 69, Southeastern Jr

Col Orgn, 71, Memphis State Univ Reading Conf, spring 72 & Tenn Speech Asn, 71. *Mem:* MLA; NCTE; AAUP; Conf Col Compos & Commun; Am Dialect Soc. *Res:* Speech of the South; speech of Black Americans; linguistics. *Publ:* Auth, Speech of Negro high school students of Memphis, ERIC, 68; A note on It Is/there is, Word Study, 10/69; A phonological and morphological study of the speech of the Negro of Memphis, Tennessee, Am Dialect Soc, 70; Selected features of speech: black and white, CLA J, 6/70; co-ed, A Various Language, Holt, 71; A look at Black English, Crisis, 8/71. *Mailing Add:* Dept of English LeMoyne-Owen Col Memphis TN 38126

WILLIAMSON, RICHARD COLT, b Tuxedo, NY, Aug 29, 44; m 65; c 2. FRENCH LANGUAGE & LITERATURE. *Educ:* Yale Col, BA, 66; Yale Univ, MA, 67; Ind Univ, PhD(French), 75. *Prof Exp:* Assoc instr French, Ind Univ, 70-75; asst prof, 75-80, PROF FRENCH, BATES COL, 80- *Concurrent Pos:* Mellon fel French, Bates Col, 78-79; dir, Northeast Conf, 82- *Mem:* Am Coun Teaching Foreign Lang; MLA; Am Asn Teachers French. *Res:* Contemporary French-Canadian literature; the decadent movement; 19th century novel in France. *Publ:* Auth, Taking advantage of the study abroad program: Before and after Foreign Lang Ann, 2/78; Language on the rebound, Bates Col Bull, 4/78; Toward an international dimension in higher education, Northeast Conf Reports, 81. *Mailing Add:* 307 Hathom Hall Bates College Lewiston ME 04240

WILLIMAN, JOSEPH P, b Roselle, NJ, Aug 26, 42; m 64. ROMANCE LANGUAGES. *Educ:* Univ NC, Chapel Hill, AB, 63, PhD(Romance philol), 67 Columbia Univ, MA, 64. *Prof Exp:* Asst prof French, 67-71, ASSOC PROF MOD LANG, CATH UNIV AM, 71- *Concurrent Pos:* Assoc, Danforth Found, 69-; mem Forum on Psychiat & Humanities, Washington Sch Psychiat, 72- *Mem:* MLA; Mediaeval Acad Am. *Res:* Medieval humanism and translations; the development of vernacular allegory. *Publ:* Auth, Dante and Durandus: The liturgical cincture, Ky Romance Quart, 71; The sources and composition of Marie's Tristan episode, In: Studies in Honor of Tatiana Fotitch, 72; The hidden proeme in verse of the Vie de St Alexis, Romance Notes, 73. *Mailing Add:* Dept of Mod Lang Catholic Univ of Am Washington DC 20064

WILLIS, DONALD S, b Astoria, Ore, June 16, 17; m 42; c 3. FOREIGN LANGUAGES. *Educ:* Univ Wash, AB, 43, PhD, 51. *Prof Exp:* From asst prof to assoc prof Orient lang & lit, Univ Ore, 48-62; prof Slavic & Eastern lang & chmn dept, 62-65, dir lang & area Ctr EAsian Studies, 67-71 & 72-77, prof & chmn dept orient lang & lit, 68-80, EMER PROF CHINESE & JAPANESE, UNIV COLO, 80- *Concurrent Pos:* Ford res fel, Japan, 55-56; prof Asian lang & head dept, Univ Canterbury, NZ, 70-72. *Mem:* Asn Asian Studies; Chinese Lang Teachers Asn; Asn Teachers Japanese. *Res:* Chinese and Japanese languages and literatures; translations; writing systems. *Mailing Add:* Dept of Orient Univ of Colo Boulder CO 80309

WILLIS, RAYMOND SMITH, b Orizaba, Mex, Dec 10, 06; m 32. SPANISH, PORTUGUESE. *Educ:* Princeton Univ, AB, 28, PhD, 33. *Prof Exp:* Instr Latin & French, Storm King Sch, NY, 28-29; from instr to prof Span, 32-56, asst to dean col, 41-42, Ford prof, 56-75, EMER FORD PROF SPAN, PRINCETON UNIV, 75- *Concurrent Pos:* Vis prof, Rutgers Univ, 60-61, Univ Pa, 67-68 & Bryn Mawr Col, 71-72. *Mem:* MLA; Am Asn Teachers Span & Port; Soc Brasileira Folklore; Hisp Soc Am; Acad Lit Studies. *Res:* Spanish and Portuguese language and literature. *Publ:* Auth, The Phantom Chapters of the Quijote, 53; Studies of the Libro de Alexandre, 34 & 35; Libro de Alexandre, 34 & coauth, Spanish From Thought to Word, 44, Princeton Univ; Iberoamerica, Dryden, 54; auth, Mester de clerecia: A definition of the libro de Alexandre, Romance Philol, 57; Juan Ruiz: Libro de Buen Amor, Princeton, 72. *Mailing Add:* 10 Campbelton Cir Princeton NJ 08540

WILLIS, ROBERT M, b Pittsburgh, Pa, July 25, 18. ENGLISH, LINGUISTICS. *Educ:* Columbia Univ, MA, 52; NY Univ, EdD. *Prof Exp:* Supvr English, Dept of Educ, San Juan, PR, 48-53; instr, Univ Mich, 53-54 & Tohoku Univ, Japan, 54-56; instr, 56-59, PROF ENGLISH & DIR LANG LAB, NY UNIV, 59- *Concurrent Pos:* US Dept State grants, Peru, Bolivia & Panama, 62, Brazil & Venezuela, 63, lectr English as foreign lang, Poxman, Poland, 68; consult teaching English as second lang, Nat Asn Foreign Studies Affairs, 71- *Mem:* Nat Asn Foreign student affairs; Nat Asn Lang Lab Dir; Teachers English to Speakers Other Lang. *Res:* English as a foreign language; language laboratories. *Publ:* Coauth, American English in twenty lessons, RD Cortina, 65. *Mailing Add:* New York Univ Washington Square Shimkin Hall New York NY 10003

WILLIS, WILLIAM HAILEY, b Meridian, Miss, Apr 29, 16; m 43; c 4. CLASSICAL PHILOLOGY. *Educ:* Miss Col, AB, 36; Columbia Univ, AM, 37; Yale Univ, PhD(Greek), 40. *Prof Exp:* Instr classics, Yale Univ, 40-42; assoc prof Greek & Latin, Univ Miss, 46-47; prof Greek & Latin & chmn dept classics, 47-63; PROF GREEK, DUKE UNIV, 63- *Concurrent Pos:* Fund Advan Educ fac fel, Harvard Univ, 52-53; mem managing comt, Am Sch Class Studies Athens, 53-, vchmn, 79-81; vis prof class lang, Univ Tex, 57-58; vis prof classics, Univ NC, 59, 63-64, 66; fac fel theol, Church Divinity Sch Pac, 59; sr ed, Greek, Roman & Byzantine Studies, 59-79; vis scholar, Fac of Relig, Oxford Univ, 61-62, vis mem, Brasenose & Queen's Cols, 61-62; Am Philos Soc Penrose Fund res grant, 62; Am Coun Learned Soc fac res grant, 62; corresp mem, Inst Antiquity & Christianity, 68-; Guggenheim fel, 80-81. *Mem:* Archaeol Inst Am; Am Philol Asn (pres, 72-73); Southern Class Asn (pres, 58-60); Southern Humanities Conf (secy, 56-58); Class Asn Mid W & S (pres, 66-67). *Res:* Greek philology; papyrology; Coptic studies. *Publ:* Auth, A Parchment Palimpsest of Plato, Archiv fur Papyrusforschung, 74; Cession of Catoecic Land, Collectanea Papyrologica I, Bonn, 76; Recent Papyrological Work in North America, Studia Papyrologica, 76; Two Literary Papyri in an Archive from Panopolis, Ill Class Studies, 78; The Letter of Ammon of Panopolis to his Mother, Papyrologica Bruxellensia, 79; Three Robinson Papyri, Bull Am Soc Papyrologists, 79. *Mailing Add:* Box 4715 Duke Station Durham NC 27706

WILLIS, WILLIAM S, b Gordonsville, Va, Nov 29, 21; m 53; c 2. ROMANCE LANGUAGES. *Educ:* Univ Va, BA, 42, MA, 47; Inst de Phonetique, Univ Paris, dipl, 49, Dr Univ, Paris, 51. *Prof Exp:* Commun asst, Econ Coop Admin, Paris, 50; admin asst, Tech Asst Admin, UN, 51-52; dir col dept, Coop Bur Teachers, NY, 52-53; from instr to asst prof French, NY Univ, 53-68, asst to dean, Wash Sq Col, 53-57, asst dean univ grad sch arts & sci, 61-65, dir int student ctr, 65-68; assoc prof French, Univ Va, 68-72, dean grad sch, 72-78, PROF FRENCH, GEORGE MASON UNIV, 72- *Concurrent Pos:* Army spcialized training prog, Lafayette Col, 43-44; secy-gen, Fed French Alliances in US, 54-57, mem adv comt, 59-; mem, French Inst in US, 59-; Am Philos Soc res grant, France, 64-65; secy, Am Comt Centennial of Romain Rolland, 66-67; mem exec comt, Conf Southern Grad Schs, 76-78. *Honors & Awards:* Grande Medaille, Alliance Francaise, 58; Chevalier, Palmes Academiques, 65. *Mem:* Am Asn Teachers French; Nat Asn Foreign Studies Affairs; MLA. *Res:* Contemporary French literature; French culture and civilization; international educational exchange. *Publ:* Coauth, Points de Vue, Appleton, 59; ed, Women and Education: A Mutual Responsibility, NY Univ, 59; auth, Henry Ford, Romain Rolland et les Pelerins de la paix, Rev Deux Mondes, 63; Foreign Student Credentials Guide, NY Univ, 68; Graduate Faculty Adviser's Handbook, George Mason Univ, 77. *Mailing Add:* Dept of French George Mason Univ Fairfax VA 22030

WILLNER, ERNEST STEVEN, b Vienna, Austria, Feb 11, 10; nat US; m 48; c 2. FOREIGN LANGUAGES. *Educ:* Univ Vienna, PhD, 35. *Prof Exp:* Prof foreign lang, Col Mt St Joseph-on-the-Ohio, 39-46; assoc prof humanities, 46-76, ASSOC PROF GER, UNIV ILL, CHICAGO CIRCLE, 76- *Mem:* Am Asn Teachers Ital; MLA; NEA. *Res:* Comparative, 16th century French and modern German literature. *Publ:* Contribr, Yearbook of Comparative and General Literature, 63; auth, Veterans in foreign language classes, Fr Rev; Muenchhausen Ohnegleichen textbook, Nat Textbk Co, 71. *Mailing Add:* Dept of Ger Univ of Ill Chicago Circle Chicago IL 60680

WILLSON, AMOS LESLIE, b Texhoma, Oklahoma, June 14, 23; m 50; c 3. GERMANIC LANGUAGES & LITERATURE. *Educ:* Univ Tex, Austin, BJ, 47, BA, 49, MA, 50; Yale Univ, PhD(Ger), 54. *Prof Exp:* Vis instr Ger, Wesleyan Univ, 52-53; instr, 53-54; instr, Northwestern Univ, 54-55; from instr to asst prof, Univ Tex, Austin, 55-61; assoc prof, Duke Univ, 61-65; prof, Pa State Univ, 65-66; PROF GER, UNIV TEX, AUSTIN, 66-, CHMN DEPT, 72- *Concurrent Pos:* Fulbright sr res scholar, 62-63. *Honors & Awards:* Bundesverdienstkreuz, Govt of the Fed Repub of Ger, 76. *Mem:* Corresp mem, Mainzer Akademie der Wiss und Lit; MLA; Am Asn Teachers Ger; Am Lit Translr Asn; Am Translr Asn. *Res:* German romanticism; contemporary German writing; literary translation. *Publ:* Ed, A Schiller Symposium, Univ Tex, Austin, 60; A Mythical Image: The Ideal of India in German Romanticism, Duke Univ, 64; Surveys and Soundings in European Literature, Princeton Univ, 66; translr, Günter Grass' The Wicked Cooks, In: Four Plays, Harcourt, 67; ed, A Günter Grass Symposium, Univ Tex, Austin, 71, 2nd printing, 73; co-translr, Günter Grass' Max, Harcourt, 72; auth, Beckmann, der Ertrinkende Zu Wolfgang Borcherts DrauBen vor der Tür, 72, Alte und neue Fenster oder wie man deutsche Literatur in den USA vermittelt, 22: 113-120, Akzente. *Mailing Add:* Dept of Ger Lang Univ of Tex PO Box 7939 Austin TX 78712

WILSHERE, A D, b Norwich, Eng, Feb 18, 18; m 57; c 3. FRENCH, ROMANCE PHILOLOGY. *Educ:* Univ London, BA, 50, PhD(medieval French), 64. *Prof Exp:* Lectr English, Univ EAfrica, 51-54; tutor, Univ Bristol, 55-57; assoc prof French, Mem Univ Nfld, 57-62; lectr, Univ Col Rhodesia, 62-65 & Univ St Andrews, 65-67; assoc prof, 67-69, PROF FRENCH, UNIV GUELPH, 69-, JOINT APP, DEPT ENGLISH, 77- *Concurrent Pos:* Can Coun res grant, 68, 70-72, 73 & 78. *Res:* Medieval French and English; medieval Latin. *Publ:* Auth, Conflict and conciliation in Graham Greene, In: Essays and Studies 1966, 66; Sermo vulgaris or sermo urbanus?, Forum Mod Lang Studies, 4/73; co-ed, Fouke le Fitz Waryn, Anglo-Norman Text Soc, 75; auth, The Latin Primacy of St Edmund's Mirror of Holy Church, Mod Lang Rev, 76; Mirour de Seynte Eglise, Anglo-Norman Text Soc, 82. *Mailing Add:* Dept of Languages Univ of Guelph Guelph ON N1G 2W1 Can

WILSON, ALICE S, b NY; m 51; c 1. COMPARATIVE LITERATURE, CLASSICS. *Educ:* Ladycliff-on-Hudson Col, BA; Cornell Univ, MA, PhD(comp lit), 47. *Prof Exp:* Instr English, Cornell Univ, 45-46; instr classics & humanities, Univ Mo, 47-48; asst prof classics & humanities, Smith Col, 48-52; lectr, Univ NC, Chapel Hill, 54-55; vis asst prof, Barnard Col, Columbia Univ, 55-56; lectr English, Univ Colo, 58; asst prof English, Univ Calif, San Jose, 61-64; ASSOC PROF ENGLISH & COMP LIT, STATE UNIV NY STONY BROOK, 64- *Concurrent Pos:* Guggenheim Found fel, 52-53. *Mem:* Am Philol Asn; MLA; Mediaeval & Renaissance Soc; Mediaeval Acad Am; Am Boccaccio Soc. *Res:* Classical literature; mythology; Mediaeval and Early Renaissance in England and the continent. *Publ:* Auth, Concept of divine inspiration in antiquity, Tapha, 50; coauth, Selections from Petrarch's Africa, Forum Italicum, fall 74; Petrarch's Africa--Translation and Commentary, Yale Univ, 77. *Mailing Add:* Humanities Bldg State Univ NY Stony Brook NY 11794

WILSON, BAXTER DOUGLAS, b Charlotte, NC, Sept 19, 23; m 47; c 2. ENGLISH PHILOLOGY. *Educ:* Univ Va, PhD, 52. *Prof Exp:* Asst ed, G & C Merriam Co, 52-55; asst prof, The Citadel, 55-62; assoc prof, Madison Col, Va, 62-65; asst prof, 65-71, PROF ENGLISH, PORTLAND STATE UNIV, 71- *Mem:* Mediaeval Acad Am. *Res:* Germanic philolgy; medieval literature. *Publ:* Auth, The astrolabe and medieval English life, Popular Astron; The Jefferson polygraph in the University of Virginia Library, Am Doc. *Mailing Add:* Dept of English Portland State Univ PO Box 751 Portland OR 97207

WILSON, CLOTILDE M, b Seattle, Wash, May 19, 06. ROMANCE LANGUAGES & LITERATURE. *Educ:* Univ Wash, BA, 26, MA, 27, PhD(Romance lang), 31. *Prof Exp:* From asst prof Romance lang to assoc prof, Univ Wash, 37-74, prof, 74-76; RETIRED. *Publ:* Transl, Machado de Assis, Philosopher or Dog?, Noonday, 54, Gustavo Corcao, My Neighbour as Myself, Longman, Green, 58; auth, Nausee and Mort de quelqu'un, Fr Rev, 65; transl, Gustavo Corcao, Who if I Cry Out?, Univ Tex, 67; auth, Rilke and Corcao, Lux-Brazilian Rev, 70; transl, Story in New Directions, 72. *Mailing Add:* Dept of Romance Lang Univ of Washington Seattle WA 98105

WILSON, GRAHAM CUNNINGHAM, English, Linguistics. See Vol II

WILSON, HARRY REX, b Halifax, NS, Mar 13, 20; m 45; c 4. ENGLISH LINGUISTICS. *Educ:* Univ Toronto, BA, 43, MA, 48; Univ Mich, PhD, 59. *Prof Exp:* Reporter, Globe & Mail, Toronto, 44-46; instr English, Univ NB, 46-47 & Brown Univ, 47-49; asst prof, Augustana Col, Ill, 49-58; from asst prof to assoc prof, Royal Mil Col Can, 58-67; ASSOC PROF ENGLISH, UNIV WESTERN ONT, 67- *Mem:* Can Ling Asn; Am Dialect Soc. *Res:* Applied linguistics; historical phonology; dialect of Lunenburg County, Nova Scotia. *Mailing Add:* Dept of English Univ of Western Ont London ON N6A 3K7 Can

WILSON, JOHN RICHARD, b Leeds, England, June 16, 31; US citizen; m; c 2. CLASSICS. *Educ:* Oxford Univ, BA, 53, MA, 58; Univ Calif, Berkeley, PhD(classics), 65. *Prof Exp:* Lectr classics, Ind Univ, Bloomington, 63-65, asst prof, 65-70; vis assoc prof, Cornell Univ, 70-71; asst prof, 71-72, assoc prof, 72-79, PROF CLASSICS, UNIV ALTA, 79-, CHMN, 82- *Mem:* Am Philol Asn. *Res:* Greek tragedy. *Publ:* ed, 20th Century Interpretations of Euripides' Alcestis, Prentice-Hall, 68; Action and emotion in Aeneas, Greece & Rome, 69; Tolma and the meaning of talas, Am J Philol, 71; auth, The Wedding Gifts of Peleus, Phoenix, 74; Kairos as Due Measure, Glotta, 80. *Mailing Add:* Dept of Classics Univ of Alberta Edmonton AB T6G 2E9 Can

WILSON, JOSEPH BENJAMIN, b Houston, Tex, Oct 11, 28; m 47; c 4. GERMANIC LANGUAGES & LITERATURE. *Educ:* Rice Univ, BA, 50, MA, 53; Stanford Univ, PhD, 60. *Prof Exp:* From instr to asst prof, 54-63, ASSOC PROF GER, RICE UNIV, 63- *Concurrent Pos:* Humboldt Found fel, Univ Kiel, 65-66 & Univ Marburg, 79. *Mem:* MLA; AAUP; Am Asn Teachers Ger; Soc Advan Scand Studies; Soc Am Archaeol. *Res:* Germanic philology; computerized lexicography; Paleo-Indian archaeology. *Publ:* Auth, A conjecture on the second Merseburg charm, Rice Univ Studies, 69; Unusual German lexical items from Lee-Fayette County, In: Texas Studies in Bilingualism, de Gruyter, Berlin, 70; Probleme der Wortindexarbeit, In: Literatur und Datenverarbeitung, Niemeyer, Tubingen, 72; Extended Rime in Otfrid, Rice Univ Studies, 76; ed, Texas and Germany: Crosscurrents, Rice Univ, 77; English of German Americans in Texas, In: Languages in Conflict, Univ Nebr Press, 81; A prelim report on a Clovis-Plainview site, Bull Tex Archeol Soc, 80; Earliest Anglicisms in Texas German, Yearbk Ger-Am Studies, 81. *Mailing Add:* Dept of German Rice Univ Houston TX 77001

WILSON, LESLIE NELSON, b Bridgeton, NJ, Jan 29, 23; c 3. LITERATURE, LINGUISTICS. *Educ:* Temple Univ, BS, 50; NY Univ, MA, 60; Inter-Am Univ, Mex, PhD(Span lang & lit), 70. *Prof Exp:* Teacher English, Adjuntas Jr-Sr High Sch, PR, 53-54; zone supvr, Camuy-Hatillo Sch Dist, PR, 54-55 & Humacao Sch Dist, PR, 55-64; from asst prof to assoc prof Span & French, Fla A&M Univ, 64-74, dir Peace Corps minority intern prog, 72-74; assoc prof, 74-81, PROF SPAN, FLA STATE UNIV, 81- *Concurrent Pos:* Instr English & methods, Humacao Extramural Ctr, Univ PR, Humacao, 58-60, adult educ, Humacao Sch Dist, 60. *Mem:* NEA; Am Asn Teachers Span & Port; MLA; Col Lang Asn; SAtlantic Mod Lang Asn. *Res:* Contemporary Spanish literature; contemporary Spanish American literature. *Publ:* Auth, Literature as a Tool for Social Change, Fla Col English Asn; El negro en la poesia hispanoamerica, 6/70 & La poesia dominicana contemporanea, 6/73, Col Lang Asn Jour; Federico Garcia Lorca and Afro-Cuban poetry, Oelschlager Festschrift, 76; La Poesia Negra: Its background themes and significance, In: Blacks in Hispanic Literature, Kennikat, 77; La Poesia afroantillana, Ediciones Universal, Miami, 79. *Mailing Add:* Dept of Mod Lang & Ling Fla State Univ Tallahassee FL 32307

WILSON, LOIS MAYFIELD, b Berea, Ky, Jan 28, 24; m 48; c 1. LINGUISTICS. *Educ:* Bowling Green State Univ, BS, 43; Univ Mich, MA, 44; Stanford Univ, PhD, 54. *Prof Exp:* Teaching asst English, Univ Ill, 44-46; actg instr, Stanford Univ, 56-58; from asst prof to assoc prof, 49-64, PROF ENGLISH, SAN FRANCISCO STATE UNIV, 64- *Concurrent Pos:* Inst Int Educ studies fel, Chile, 47; Fulbright lectr ling & teaching English as foreign lang, Univ Rome, 56-57. *Mem:* Nat Asn Foreign Studies Affairs; Teachers English to Speakers Other Lang. *Res:* English as a foreign language; Shakespeare; higher education. *Mailing Add:* Dept of English San Francisco State Univ San Francisco CA 94132

WILSON, WILLIAM RITCHIE, b Chicago, Ill, Jan 8, 11; m 46. JAPANESE LITERATURE. *Educ:* US Naval Acad, BS, 32; Univ Wash, MA, 64, PhD(Japanese lit), 67. *Prof Exp:* Asst prof Asian studies, Univ Southern Calif, 67-71, asst prof hist & Asian studies, 70-71; RETIRED. *Honors & Awards:* Letter of Merit, Shuppan Bunka Kokusai Koryukai, Tokyo, 72. *Mem:* Asn Asian Studies; Am Orient Soc. *Res:* Medieval Japanese literature, especially military chronicles; the Noh drama and poetry. *Publ:* Auth, UNESCO collection of representative works: Japan ser; The sea battle of Dannoura, Am Neptune, 7/68; Nihon Bungaku ni Okeru Eiyuzo, In: Koten to Gendai, Shimizu Kobundo, Osaka, 70; Hogen Monogatari, Tale of the Rebellion in Hogen, Sophia, Monumenta Nipponica monogra, 71; The way of the bow and the arrow: The Japanese warrior in Konjaku monogatari, Monumenta Nipponica, summer 73; Okitsu Yagoemon no Isho, In: The Incident at Sakai and Other Stories, Vol I, Univ Press of Hawaii, 77; Saiki Koi, In: Saiki Koi and Other Stories, Vol II, Univ Press of Hawaii, 77; contribr, Encyl of Japan (in press). *Mailing Add:* 16102 41st Ave NE Seattle WA 98155

WILTROUT, ANN ELIZABETH, b Elkhart, Ind, Aug 3, 39. SPANISH. *Educ:* Hanover Col, BA, 61; Ind Univ, MA, 64, PhD(Span), 68. *Prof Exp:* Vis asst prof Span, Ind Univ, Bloomington, 68-69; asst prof foreign lang, 69-71, ASSOC PROF FOREIGN LANG, MISS STATE UNIV, 71- *Concurrent Pos:* Nat Endowment for Humanities fel-in-residence for col teachers, 77-78.

Honors & Awards: Distinguished Alumni, Hanover College, 74. *Mem:* MLA; Am Asn Teachers Span & Port; SCent Mod Lang Asn; SAtlantic Mod Lang Asn; AAUP. *Res:* Spanish Renaissance and Golden Age literature. *Publ:* Auth, The Lazarillo de Tormes and Erasmus Opulentia Sordida, Romanische Forschungen, Vol 69; Hacia algunas interpretaciones dramaticas de la leyenda de Santa Barbara, Filologia, Vol 15; Women in the Works of Antonio de Gueriara, Neophilologus, Vol 60; Quien espere desespera: El suicidio en el teatro de Juan del Encina, Hispanofila, Vol 72; Gines de Pasamonte: The Picaro and his Art, Anales Cervantinos, Vol 17; Gomez Suarez de Figueroa, Patron od Diego Sanchez de Badajoz's Recopilacion en metro, Bull Comediantes, Vol 31; Role Playing and Rites of Passage: La ilustre fregona and La gitanilla, Hispania, Vol 64; El Villano del Danubio: Foreign Policy and Literary Structure, Critica Hispanica, Vol 3. *Mailing Add:* Dept of Foreign Languages Drawer FL Miss State Univ Mississippi State MS 39762

WIMSATT, JAMES I, English. See Vol II

WINBERY, CARLTON LOYD, b Urania, La, Feb 15, 37; m 57; c 2. HELLENISTIC GREEK. *Educ:* La Col, BA, 59; New Orleans Baptist Theol Sem, ThM, 68, ThD, 73. *Prof Exp:* Asst prof relig & lang, Baptist Col, Charleston, 73-76; ASSOC PROF, NEW TESTAMENT & GREEK, NEW ORLEANS BAPTIST THEOL SEM, 76. *Concurrent Pos:* Lectr New Testament, New Orleans Baptist Theol Sem, 70-73. *Mem:* Soc Bibl Lit; Bibl Archaeol Soc. *Res:* Greek language; textual criticism; translation, linguistics. *Publ:* Auth, Exodus in the New Testament, 77, Sharing in Christ: Fellowship in the Church, 78, Discipleship in Mark, 78 & Introduction to Philippians, 80, Theol Educator; Introductgion to I Peter, Southwestern J Theol, 82; Coauth, Syntax of New Testament Greek, Univ Press Am, 78. *Mailing Add:* 3939 Gentilly Blvd New Orleans LA 70126

WINBURNE, JOHN NEWTON, b Morrilton, Ark, Feb 28, 11. ENGLISH. *Educ:* Univ Colo, AB, 34, AM, 38; Mich State Univ, PhD, 51. *Prof Exp:* Teacher & prin, Pub Sch, Colo, 34-36; dist dir, Nat Youth Admin, 36-37; teacher & dramatics coach, High Sch, 37-43; field dir, Am Red Cross, Africa & Italy, 43-45; asst prof & asst to dean basic col, 45-72, asst dean student affairs, 45-72, assoc dean, 72-76, prof, 72-80, EMER PROF AM THOUGHT & LANG, MICH STATE UNIV, 80-, EMER ASSOC DEAN, UNIV COL, 76- *Concurrent Pos:* Mem comn XIV, Am Col Personnel Asn, 64-65. *Mem:* Am Personnel & Guidance Asn; Ling Soc Am; Am Dialect Soc. *Res:* American English; linguistics; the current American English idiom. *Publ:* Auth, Sentence attachment in expository discourse, IX Int Cong Ling, 59; Dictionary of Agricultural and Allied Terminology, Mich State Univ, 62. *Mailing Add:* Univ Col Mich State Univ East Lansing MI 48823

WIND, ROBERT LEWIS, b Hartford, Conn, Aug 13, 33; m 59; c 2. CLASSICS. *Educ:* Wesleyan Univ, BA, 55; Univ Wis, MA, 57; State Univ Iowa, PhD(classics), 64. *Prof Exp:* From instr to asst prof classics, Univ Tex, Austin, 64-71; assoc prof, Emory Univ, 71-75; HEAD DEPT CLASSICS, MUHLENBERG COL, 75- *Res:* Greek lyric poetry and drama. *Publ:* Transl, Bacchylides and Pindar: A question of imitation, Class J, 11-12/71; Myth and history in Bacchylides Ode 18, Hermes, 72; Pseudo-Xenophon, The Old Oligarch, Dunwoody, 72; Handbook for an Election Campaign, Dunwoody 78. *Mailing Add:* Dept of Classics Muhlenberg Col Allentown PA 18104

WINDFUHR, GERNOT LUDWIG, b Essen, Ger, Aug 2, 38; m 65; c 2. IRANISTICS. *Educ:* Univ Hamburg, Dr Phil, 65. *Prof Exp:* Acad asst ling, Univ Kiel, 65-66; from asst prof to assoc prof, 66-73, PROF IRANIAN LANG & LING, UNIV MICH, ANN ARBOR, 73-, CHMN DEPT NEAR EASTERN STUDIES, 77- *Mem:* Ling Soc Am; Ling Soc Europe; MidE Studies Asn NAm; Am Orient Soc. *Res:* Linguistics; literary theory; Zoroastrianism. *Publ:* Auth, Verbalmorpheme in Sangesari, privately publ, 65; Diacritic and Distinctive Features in Avestan: Some Avestan Rules and Their Signs, J Am Orient Soc, 71 & 72; coauth, A Dictionary of Sangesari with a Grammatical Outline, Franklin BK, Tehran, 72; A Linguist's Criticism of Persian Literature, In: Neue Methodologia in der Iranistik, Harrassowitz, Wiesbaden, 74; Isoglosses: A Sketch on Persians and Parthians, Kurds and Medes, Acta Iranica, V, 75; Vohu Manah: A Key to the Zoroastrain World Formula, Studies in Honor of GG Cameron, Ann Arbor, 76; Linguistics: The Study of the Middle East: Research and Scholarship in the Humanities and Social Sciences, John Wiley, NY, 76; Auth, Persian Grammar: History and State of Research, In: Jauna Linguarum Series Critica, Mouton, The Hague, 79. *Mailing Add:* Dept of Near Eastern Studies Univ of Mich Ann Arbor MI 48109

WING, BARBARA HAMMANN, b Plainfield, NJ, July 27, 33; m 56; c 2. SPANISH. *Educ:* Middlebury Col, BA, 55; Harvard Grad Sch Educ, MAT, 56; Middlebury Col, MA, 71; Ohio State Univ, PhD(foreign lang educ), 80. *Prof Exp:* Instr Spanish, Colby Jr Col, 61-67; instr Spanish & methodology, Elmira Col, 67-68; teacher Spanish & French, Horseheads Jr & Sr High Sch, 68-70; lectr, 70-81, ASST PROF SPANISH, UNIV NH, 81- *Concurrent Pos:* Co-ed, POLYGLOT, Newsletter of NH Asn for Teaching of Foreign Lang, 74-78; mem, Bd Exam, Off Teacher Educ, 80-; coordr, ACTFL Alert Network, 80- *Mem:* Am Coun Teaching Foreign Lang; Am Asn Teaching Spanish & Portuguese; AAUP. *Res:* Foreign language learning and acquisition; foreign language teaching; curriculum and materials development. *Publ:* Auth, Free to become: Preservice education, Perspective: A New Freedom, Nat Textbook Co, 75; Increasing the ratio of student talk to teacher talk in the foreign language classroom, Defense Lang Inst, 82. *Mailing Add:* 31 Oyster River Rd Durham NH 03824

WING, NATHANIEL, b Mineola, NY, June 23, 38; m 59; c 3. FRENCH LITERATURE. *Educ:* Haverford Col, BA, 59; Columbia Univ, MA, 62, PhD(French), 68. *Prof Exp:* From instr to asst prof, Univ Pa, 65-73; assoc prof, 73-77, PROF FRENCH, MIAMI UNIV, 77-, CHMN DEPT, 73- *Concurrent Pos:* Fel, Univ Pa, 69; vis prof Romance lang, Univ Mich, spring 79. *Mem:* Am Asn Teachers Fr; AAUP; Int Asn Fr Studies; MLA; Midwest Mod Lang Asn. *Res:* Nineteenth century French literature; poetics; post-structuralist theory. *Publ:* Auth, Metaphor and ambiguity in Rimbaud's Memoire, Romanic Rev, 10/72; The stylistic functions of rhetoric in Baudelaire's Au Lecteur, Ky Romance Quart, 10/72; Rimbaud's Les Ponts, Parade, Scenes: The poem as performance, Fr Rev, 2/73; Present Appearances: Aspects of Poetic Structure in Rimbaud's Illuminations, Romance Monogr, 74; Semiotics of poetry: The meaning of form, Diacritics, fall 74; The poetics of irony in Baudelaire's La Fanfarlo, Neophilologus, 4/75; Effects and affects of theory: Reading Bersani on Baudelaire and Freud, Diacritics, 12/79; The Danaide's Vessel: On reading Baudelaire's allegories, In: Pre-Text/Text/Context: Essays in 19th Century French Literature, Ohio State Univ Press, 80. *Mailing Add:* Dept of French & Ital 101 Irvin Hall Miami Univ Oxford OH 45056

WINGET, LYNN WARREN, b Garden City, Kans, July 28, 26. SPANISH LANGUAGE & LITERATURE. *Educ:* Univ Wichita, AB, 48; Univ Wis, MA, 49, PhD(Span), 60. *Prof Exp:* Prof Span, Murray State Col, 54-61; PROF SPAN, WICHITA STATE UNIV, 61- *Mem:* Am Asn Teachers Span & Port; Mediaeval Acad Am; MLA. *Res:* Old Spanish language; medieval Spanish literature. *Publ:* Coauth, Dictionary of Spanish & English Idioms, Barron's Educ Ser, 76. *Mailing Add:* Wichita State Univ 1845 Fairmount Wichita KS 67208

WINGO, E OTHA, b Booneville, Miss, Sept 17, 34; m 61; c 3. CLASSICAL LANGUAGES. *Educ:* Miss Col, BA, 55; Univ Ill, MA, 56, PhD, 63. *Prof Exp:* Asst, Univ Ill, 56-57, 60-62; asst instr, Univ Mo, 57-58; asst prof Latin, William Jewell Col, 58-60; from asst prof to assoc prof, 62-74, PROF CLASS LANG, SOUTHEAST MO STATE UNIV, 75- *Concurrent Pos:* Vis lectr Latin, St Mary's Sem, Perryville, Mo, 64-65; res ed, Huna Res Inc, 72-; ed, The Huna Work, Quart Periodical. *Mem:* Am Philol Asn. *Res:* Latin epigraphy; mythology; Hawaiian antiquities. *Publ:* Latin Punctuation in the Classical Age, Mouton, The Hague, 72; ed, Tarot Card Symbology, 72 & auth, Letters on Huna Psychology, 73, Huna Res Inc. *Mailing Add:* Dept of Class Lang Southeast Mo State Univ Cape Girardeau MO 63701

WINKELMAN, JOHN, b New York, NY, May 8, 11; m 39; c 3. GERMAN. *Educ:* City Col New York, AB, 33, MS, 38; Univ Mich, PhD, 52. *Prof Exp:* Instr Ger, Massanutten Acad, 35-38, Montclair Acad, 38-40 & Univ Mo, 45-53; from asst prof to assoc prof, Univ Nebr, 53-63; prof, Univ Waterloo, 63-66; chmn dept Germanic & Slavic lang, 66-70, prof, 66-80, EMER PROF GER, STATE UNIV NY ALBANY, 66- *Concurrent Pos:* Civilian lang expert, US Strategic Bombing Surv, 45. *Mem:* MLA; Am Asn Teachers Ger; Nat Fedn Mod Lang Teachers Asn. *Res:* Modern German literature. *Publ:* Auth, Social criticism in the early works of Erich Kästner & The poetic style of Erich Kästner, Univ Mo Studies; An Interpretation of Kafka's Das Schloss, Monatshefte, 72; contribr, Felice Bauer and Kafka's The Trial, In: The Kafka Debate, Gordian, 77. *Mailing Add:* 33 Broadleaf Dr Clifton Park NY 12065

WINKLER, JULIUS S, b Lenoir, NC, July 22, 32; m 54; c 2. FOREIGN LANGUAGES. *Educ:* Ohio Wesleyan Univ, BA, 54; Princeton Univ, MA, 57, PhD, 63. *Prof Exp:* Instr Ger, Univ Miss, 57-59; asst prof, Winthrop Col, 59-61; asst prof, 61-67, ASSOC PROF GER, DAVIDSON COL, 67- *Mem:* MLA; Am Asn Teachers Ger. *Res:* Seventeenth century German literature. *Mailing Add:* Dept of Ger Davidson Col Davidson NC 28036

WINN, COLETTE HENRIETTE, b La Grand-Combe, France, Dec 10, 51; m 74. FRENCH LITERATURE & LANGUAGE. *Educ:* Universite Paul Valery Montpellier, Fr, Lic D'Anglais, 73; Univ Mo, MA, 76, PhD(Fr lang & lit), 80. *Prof Exp:* Teaching asst Fr, Winslow Pub Sch, England, 71-72 & Univ Mo-Columbia, 75-79; ASST PROF FRENCH, WASHINGTON UNIV, ST LOUIS, 80- *Concurrent Pos:* Instr Fr, Univ Mo-Columbia, 78-79. *Mem:* MLA; Am Asn Teachers Fr. *Res:* French poetry, particularly sixteenth and twentieth centuries; women poets and writers of the sixteenth century; Marguerite de Navarre. *Publ:* Auth, Sponde's Sonnet de la Mort II: A Semantic analysis, Lang & Style (in press); Le symbolisme des mains dans la poesi de Paul Eluard, Romanische Forschungen (in press). *Mailing Add:* 15975 Deer Trail Chesterfield MO 63017

WINN, CONCHITA HASSELL, b Santurce, PR, May 11, 23; US citizen; m 45; c 5. SPANISH & LATIN AMERICAN LITERATURE. *Educ:* Columbia Univ, BA, 44, MA, 45, PhD(Span), 53. *Prof Exp:* From asst prof to assoc prof Span, 60-72, PROF SPAN, SOUTHERN METHODIST UNIV, 72- *Concurrent Pos:* Grad Coun Humanities fel, Southern Methodist Univ, 64-65; consult, McGraw-Hill Bk Co, 71-72; chmn civil serv bd, Dallas, Tex, 73-75; Inst Latin Am Studies Asn; Am Asn Teachers Span & Port; AAUP. *Res:* Spanish-American literature; Ricardo Palma; Spanish language newspapers of Texas. *Publ:* Auth, Mas sobre las fuentes y documentos de informacion de que se sirvio Ricardo Palma: Sus lecturas en lenguas foraneas, Rev Hisp Mod, Vol 34, No 3-4; Four centuries of writing in Mexico, Southwest Rev, winter 70. *Mailing Add:* Dept of Foreign Lang & Lit Southern Methodist Univ Dallas TX 75275

WINNER, THOMAS GUSTAV, b Prague, Czech, May 4, 17; nat US; m 42; c 2. RUSSIAN LANGUAGE & LITERATURE. *Educ:* Harvard Univ, BA, 42, MA, 43; Columbia Univ, PhD(Slavic lang & lit), 50. *Hon Degrees:* MA, Brown Univ, 67. *Prof Exp:* Vis fel Cent Asian studies, Johns Hopkins Univ, 47-48; from instr to assoc prof of Russ lang & lit, Duke Univ, 48-57; from assoc prof to prof Slavic lang & lit, Univ Mich, 58-66; prof Slavic lang, 66-76, chmn dept, 68-72, PROF SLAVIC LANG & COMP LIT, BROWN UNIV, 76-, ED, SLAVIC REPRINTS, 66-, DIR CTR RES SEMIOTICS, 77- *Concurrent Pos:* Ford Found fac fel, 51-52; Fulbright lectr, Sorbonne, 56-57; mem, Am Comt Slavists, 61-; sr fel, Nat Endowment for Humanities, 72-73; US Off Educ fac res abroad grant, 73; Rockefeller humanities grant, 77; ed, Am J Semiotics, 79- *Mem:* Am Asn Teachers Slavic & East Europ Lang; MLA; Mod Humanities Res Asn; Am Asn Advan Slavic Studies, Semiotic Soc of Am (vpres, 76-77, pres, 77-78). *Res:* Russian literature of the 19th century; literary theory; semiotic theory. *Publ:* Auth, The Literature and Oral Art of the Kazakhs of Russian Central Asia, Duke Univ, 58; Cexov v Soedinennys Statax Ameriki, Literaturnoe Nasledstvo, 60; Style and structure in Chekhov's The Betrothed, Ind Slavic Studies, 63; Speech levels in Chekhov's Ivanov and Capek's Loupeznik, In: American Contributions to Fifth Congress of Slavists, Mouton, The Hague, 63; Chekhov and His Prose, Holt, 66; The aesthetics of the Prague Linguistic Circle, Poetics, 73. *Mailing Add:* 19 Garden St Cambridge MA 02138

WINNETT, FREDERICK VICTOR, b Oil Springs, Ont, May 25, 03; m 28; c 2. NEAR EASTERN STUDIES. *Educ:* Univ Toronto, BA, 23, MA, 24, PhD(Orient), 28. *Prof Exp:* Lectr Near Eastern studies, 29-34, from asst prof to assoc prof, 36-52, prof & head dept, 52-67, vprin, Univ Col, 66-69, EMER PROF NEAR EASTERN STUDIES, UNIV TORONTO, 71- *Concurrent Pos:* Dir, Am Sch Orient Res, Jerusalem, Jordan, 50-51 & 58-59; trustee, Am Schs Orient Res, 57-58 & 64-65; mem archaeol & epigraphical surv exped, NArabia, 62 & 67. *Mem:* Fel Royal Soc Can; Am Orient Soc; Soc Bibl Lit (pres, 64). *Res:* Pre-Islamic Arabic; Old Testament. *Publ:* Auth, A study of the Lihyanite and Thamudic Inscriptions, Univ Toronto, 37; The place of the Minaeans in the history of pre-Islamic Arabic, Bull Am Sch Orient Res, 39; The Mosaic Tradition, 49 & Safaitic Inscriptions from Jordan, 57, Univ Toronto; The excavations at Dibon (Dhiban) in Moab, 1950-51, Am Schs Orient Res, 64; coauth, Ancient Records from North Arabia, 70 & Inscriptions from Fifty Safaitic Cairns, 78, Univ Toronto. *Mailing Add:* 56 Otter Crescent Toronto ON M5N 2W5 Can

WINOGRAD, TERRY ALLEN, b Takoma Park, Md, Feb 24, 46; m 68; c 1. LINGUISTICS, COMPUTER SCIENCES. *Educ:* Colo Col, BA, 66; Mass Inst Tech, PhD(appl math), 70. *Prof Exp:* Instr math, Mass Inst Tech, 70-71, asst prof elec eng, 71-73; asst prof ling & comput sci, 73-79, ASSOC PROF LING & COMPUT SCI, STANFORD UNIV, 79- *Concurrent Pos:* Consult, Xerox Palo Alto Res Ctr, 72- *Mem:* Ling Soc Am. *Res:* Computational linguistics; cognitive science. *Publ:* Auth, Understanding Natural Language, Cognitive Psychol, Vol 3, No 1 & Acad Press, 72 & 76, Russ transl, MIR, 76, Japanese transl, 76; Towards a procedural understanding of semantics, Rev Int Philos, 3:117-118; coauth (with D Bobrow), An overview of KRL: A knowledge representation language, Cognitive Sci, 1/77; auth, A framework for understanding discourse, In: Cognitive Processes in Comprehension, Lawrence Erlbaum Assoc, 77; On some contested suppositions of generative linguistics about the scientific study of language, Cognition, 5: 151-179; Towards convivial computing, In: Future Impact of Computers: The Next Twenty Years, Mass Inst Technol Press, 79; What does it mean to undestand language, Cognitive Sci, 7-9/80 & In: Perspectives on Cognitive Science, Ablex & Erlbaum Assoc, 81; Syntax, Vol I, In: Language as a Cognitive Process, Addison Wesley, 82. *Mailing Add:* Dept of Ling Stanford Univ Stanford CA 94305

WINSLOW, RICHARD WALTER, b Minneapolis, Minn, June 16, 30; m 53; c 2. SPANISH. *Educ:* Univ Minn, BA, 51, MA, 54, PhD, 61. *Prof Exp:* Asst prof Span & English, Northern State Teachers Col, 57-58; from instr to asst prof, 58-68, ASSOC PROF SPAN, LAWRENCE UNIV, 68- *Concurrent Pos:* Fulbright res fel, Madrid, 62-63. *Mem:* MLA; Am Asn Teachers Span & Port. *Res:* Spanish 19th century prose fiction. *Mailing Add:* Dept of Foreign Lang Lawrence Univ Appleton WI 54911

WINSTON, KRISHNA RICARDA, b Greenfield, Mass, June 7, 44; m 66; c 1. GERMAN LANGUAGE & LITERATURE. *Educ:* Smith Col, BA, 65; Yale Univ, MPhil, 69, PhD(Ger), 74. *Prof Exp:* Teaching assoc Ger, Yale Univ, 68-70; from instr to asst prof, 70-77, ASSOC PROF GER, WESLEYAN UNIV, 77- *Concurrent Pos:* Freelance translr, 68- *Mem:* Am Asn Teachers of Ger (vpres, 76-78); NE Mod Lang Asn; MLA. *Res:* German literature of 1920's; tradition of Austrian literature; Ödön von Horvath. *Publ:* Transl, Gunilla Bergsten, Thomas Mann's Doctor Faustus, Univ Chicago, 69; The Letters and Diaries of Oskar Schlemmer, Wesleyan Univ, 72; auth, The Hermann Hesse phenomenon: Four new translations, Am PEN, winter 74; transl, Manes Sperber, Masks of Loneliness, Macmillan, 74; Heike Dontine, German Requiem, Scribner's 75; auth, The old lady's day of judgment: Notes on a mysterious relationship between Ödön von Horvath and Friedrich Dürrenmatt, Germanic Rev, 76; Ödön von Horvath: A man for this season, Mass Rev, 78; transl, Aniela Jaffe, C G Jung in Word and Image, Princeton Univ, 78. *Mailing Add:* Dept of German Lang & Lit Wesleyan Univ Middletown CT 06457

WINSTON, MORTON EMANUEL, Philosophy, Linguistics. See Vol IV

WINTER, IAN JAMES, b Penang, Malaya, May 21, 27; m 58. FRENCH LANGUAGE & LITERATURE. *Educ:* Univ Lyon, dipl, 50; Univ Edinburgh, MA, 51, dipl educ, 54; Wash Univ, PhD(French), 70. *Prof Exp:* Instr French, Moray House Teachers Col, Edinburgh, 56-58; instr French & Span, Fettes Col, Edinburgh, 58-63 & Principia Col, 63-66; asst prof French, Millikin Univ, 67-70; asst prof, 70-76, ASSOC PROF FRENCH, UNIV WIS-MILWAUKEE, 76-, CHMN DEPT FRENCH & ITAL, 77- *Mem:* Am Asn Teachers French; Mod Humanities Res Asn; La Societe des amis de Montaigne; Bibliog Soc, Renaissance Soc Am. *Res:* Montaigne; 16th century French literature. *Publ:* Auth, Mon livre et moi: Montaigne's deepening evaluation of his own work, Renaissance Quart, 3/72; From self-concept to self-knowledge: Death and nature in Montaigne's de la phisionomie, In: French Renaissance Studies in Honor of Isidore Silver & Ky Romance Quart, Vol 21, 74; Montaigne's self-portrait and its influences in France, 1580-1630, French Forum, Lexington, 76; Montaigne's self-portraiture: Contemporary and societal reaction, Ky Romance Quart, Vol 23, 76; Concordances to Montaigne's Journal De Voyage, Lettres and Ephemerides, Hist Sem Medieval Studies, 81. *Mailing Add:* Dept of French & Italian Univ of Wisconsin Downer & Kenwood Milwaukee WI 53201

WINTER, JOHN F, b Piestany, Czech, July 30, 13; nat US; m 46; c 2. FRENCH LITERATURE. *Educ:* Lafayette Col, AB, 41; Princeton Univ, AM, 46, PhD, 50. *Prof Exp:* Teacher French & Span, Stuyvesant Sch, Warrenton, Va, 41-42 & Lawrenceville Sch, NJ, 42-43; instr French, Princeton Univ, 45-46; from instr to assoc prof, Fordham Univ, 46-67, vchmn dept mod lang, 66-67; PROF FRENCH & DIR GRAD STUDENTS FRENCH, UNIV CINCINNATI, 67- *Concurrent Pos:* Lectr French, Span & Ger, Fairleigh Dickinson Univ, 52-67; Am Philos Soc grants, 61, 65 & 69; vis prof French, Grad Sch, NY Univ 63-64. *Mem:* MLA; Am Asn Teachers Fr; Soc Fr Prof Am; Hist Sci Soc; Renaissance Soc Am. *Res:* Transition from the 16th to the 17th century; Rabelais; literature and the arts. *Publ:* Auth, A forerunner of Moliere's Misanthrope, Mod Lang Notes, 6/59; Visual variety and spatial grandeur in Rabelais, Romantic Rev, 4/65; Visual variety and spatial grandeur in Ronsard's Ode a Michel de l'Hospital, Symposium, winter 67; co-ed, Directions of Literary Criticism in the Seventies, Univ Cincinnati, 72; Literature, The Visual Arts & Music, Univ Cincinnati, 74; auth, Consideration on the Medieval and Renaissance concept of space, Jean Misrahi Mem Vol, 77. *Mailing Add:* Dept of Romance Lang Univ of Cincinnati Cincinnati OH 45221

WINTER, THOMAS NELSON, b Lansing, Mich, Jan 27, 44; m 64; c 2. CLASSICS, ANCIENT SCIENCE. *Educ:* Mich State Univ, BA, 64; Northwestern Univ, MA, 65, PhD(classics), 68. *Prof Exp:* Lectr astronomy, Adler Planetarium, 66; asst prof classics, Univ Hawaii, 68-70; asst prof, 70-76, ASSOC PROF CLASSICS, UNIV NEBR-LINCOLN, 76- *Mem:* Am Class League; Am Philol Asn; Class Asn Mid W & S. *Res:* Ancient novels; Greek science and technology; Attic orators. *Publ:* Auth, On the Publication of Apuleius' Apology, Trans Am Philol Asn, 69; Catullus purified, Arethusa, 73; On the Corpus of Lysias, Class J, 73; Cincinnatus and the disbanding of Washington's army, 75 & The strategy that gave Independence to the United States, 76, Class Bull; Did the Romans really talk like that?, Class Outlook, 77; The direction of Vergil's weather, Class Bull, 79; Roman concrete: The ascent, summit and decline of an art, Trans & Proc Nebr Acad Sci, 79. *Mailing Add:* Dept Classics Univ Nebr Lincoln NE 68508

WINTER, WERNER, b Haselau, Ger, Oct 25, 23; US citizen; m 52; c 1. LINGUISTICS. *Educ:* Univ Berne, PhD, 49. *Prof Exp:* Instr ling, Univ Hamburg, 50-53; asst prof Russ & Ger, Univ Kans, 53-57; from assoc prof to prof ling, Ger & Russ, Univ Tex, Austin, 57-65; PROF LING, UNIV KIEL, 64- *Concurrent Pos:* Res grants, Univs Kans & Tex, 54-63; vis prof, Univ Kiel, 58; res sci & consult mech transl prof, Austin, 59-63; Am Coun Learned Soc fel, 60-61, deleg to USSR, 63; vis prof, Univ Hamburg, 63-64; Collitz prof, Ling Inst, Univ Calif, Los Angeles, 66; vis prof, Univ Copenhagen 66, Yale Univ, 67, Univ Calif, Berkeley, 69, Stanford Univ, 73 & Poznan, 77, 80, 81; Rose Morgan vis prof ling, Univ Kans, 73; ed, Ars Linguistica, Tuebingen, 78-; dir, Linguistic Survey of Nepal, 81- *Honors & Awards:* Medal of Merit, Univ Poznan, 82. *Mem:* Ling Soc Am; Am Orient Soc; Ling Soc Paris; Ling Soc India; Ling Soc Europe (secy, 66-). *Res:* Indo-European linguistics; Central Asian studies; American Indian languages. *Publ:* Auth, Studien zum Prothetischen Vokal im Griechischen, Gildenverlag, Hamburg, 50; Coauth, Tuerkische Turfantexte IX, German Acad, Berlin, 58 & Evidence for Laryngeals, Univ Tex, 60 & Mouton, The Hague, 65; ed, Series Critica, Janua Linguarum, 70-76; co-ed, Current Trends in Linguistics IX, Mouton, The Hague, 73; Trends in Linguistics, 77- *Mailing Add:* Von Liliencronstr 2 D 2308 Preetz Germany, Federal Republic of

WISE, DAVID OAKLEY, b Ottawa, Ill, June 8, 49. LATIN AMERICAN LITERATURE. *Educ:* Western Ill Univ, BA, 71; Univ Ill, AM, 73; PhD(Span Am lit), 78. *Prof Exp:* Teaching asst Spanish, Univ Ill, 72 & 74-77, res asst, 77-78; Andrew Mellon fel, Washington Univ, 78-79; ASST PROF FOREIGN LANG, TEXAS WOMAN'S UNIV, 79- *Mem:* Latin Am Studies Asn; SCent Mod Lang Asn; Southwest Coun Latin Am Studies; Am Asn Teachers Span & Port. *Res:* Intellectual and cultural history of Latin America; literary journals; 19th and 20th century Peru. *Publ:* Auth, Mariategui's Amauta (1926-1930), a source for Peruvian cultural history, Inter-Am Rev Bibliog, 79; Un acercamiento a la narrativa de Alvaro Menen Desleal, Ky Romance Quart, 79; Andreas Capellanus: A source for Medieval Spanish antifeminism, Hispania, 9/80; A Peruvian indigenista forum of the 1920s: Jose Carlos Mariategui's Amauta, Ideologies & Lit, 6-8/80; Writing for fewer and fewer: Peruvian fiction, 1979-1980, Latin Am Res Rev (in press). *Mailing Add:* Dept of Lang & Lit Texas Woman's Univ Denton TX 76204

WISE, SHELDON, b Brooklyn, NY, Oct 12, 23. ENGLISH AS A FOREIGN LANGUAGE, LINGUISTICS. *Educ:* Yale Univ, PhD(ling), 53. *Prof Exp:* Linguist, Am Coun Learned Soc, 52-53; instr English, Ford Found, Inst Int Educ, Indonesia, 53-55; assoc prof & dir mil English prog, Robert Col, Istanbul, 56-58, prof English & dir English lang div, 58-77; DIR ENGLISH FOR SPEC PURPOSES, AM LANG ACAD, WASHINGTON, DC, 77- *Mem:* Ling Soc Am; Teachers English to Speakers Other Lang; Nat Asn Foreign Student Affairs. *Res:* Structure of English; teaching of English to foreigners; Russian language. *Publ:* Coauth, Kurs Govornog Engleskog Jezika, Am Coun Learned Soc, 54; auth, Common Mistakes in English: As Used in Indonesia, Pustaka Rakjat, Indonesia, 55; Spoken English, English Acad, Japan, Vol IV, 62; coauth & ed, Spoken English for Turks, Robert Col, Istanbul, Vols I-XVIII, 64-77; Essentials of Management, 79 & coauth, The ALA TOEFL Course: Preparation for the Test of English as a Foreign Language, 2nd & 3rd ed, 80, 81, Am Lang Acad. *Mailing Add:* Am Lang Acad Cath Univ Am Washington DC 20064

WISE, VALERIE MERRIAM, Renaissance & Classical Literature. See Vol II

WISEMAN, JAMES RICHARD, b North Little Rock, Ark, Aug 29, 34; m 54; c 2. CLASSICAL LANGUAGES & ARCHEOLOGY. *Educ:* Univ Mo, AB, 57; Univ Chicago, MA, 60, PhD(Greek hist & archaeol), 66. *Prof Exp:* From instr to assoc prof classics & archaeol, Univ Tex, Austin 60-70, prof classics, 70-73, dir univ excavations, ancient Corinth, Greece, 65-72, chmn archaeol studies, 71-73; prof art hist & chmn dept class studies, 74-82, PROF CLASSICS, BOSTON UNIV, 73-, PROF & CHMN DEPT ARCHEOL, 82- *Concurrent Pos:* Am Coun Learned Soc fels, 67-68 & 78-79; Ford Found & Nat Endowment for Humanities grants, 68-69 & 77-80; lectr, Archaeol Inst Am, 68-, mem exec comt, 73-78, vpres, 80-; Smithsonian grants co-dir Stobi excavations, Yugoslavia, 70-75; Guggenheim fel, 71-72; mem exec comt, Am Sch Class Studies, Athens, 72-76; ed, J Field Archaeol, 74-; mem admin & prog comts, Ctr Mat Res Archaeol & Ethnol, 77- *Mem:* Archaeol Inst Am;

Am Philol Asn; Asn Field Archaeol; Soc Am Archaeol. *Res:* History, archaeology and topography of ancient Greece; archaeological procedures and theory; Greek historiography. *Publ:* Auth, Epaminondas and the Theban invasions, Klio, 69; The gymnasium area at Corinth, 1969-1970, Hesperia, 72; Stobi: A Guide to the Excavations, 73 & ed & auth, Gods, war and plague in the time of the Antonines, In: Vol I, Studies in the Antiquities of Stobi, Vol II, Boston Univ & Nat Mus Titov Veles, 75, co-ed, Vol III, Skopje, 81; auth, The Land of the Ancient Corinthians, P Astroms Forlag, Gøteborg, Sweden, 78; Archaeology in the future: An evolving discipline, Am J Archaeol, 84: 279-285. *Mailing Add:* 60 Browne St Apt 4 Brookline MA 02146

WISEMAN, MARY BITTNER, b Philadelphia, Pa, Aug 21, 36; m 60; c 1. PHILOSOPHY, LITERARY THEORY. *Educ:* St John's Col, Md, AB, 59; Harvard Univ, AM, 63; Columbia Univ, PhD(philos), 74. *Prof Exp:* Instr, 72-81, ASSOC PROF PHILOS, BROOKLYN COL, 81- *Concurrent Pos:* Dep exec officer, Humanities Inst, Brooklyn Col, 81- *Mem:* Am Philos Asn; Am Soc Aesthet; Soc Philos & Pub Affairs; Soc Women Philos. *Res:* Moral philosophy; philosophy of art. *Publ:* Auth, Empathetic identification, Am Philos Quart, 4/78; Practical principles, Ethics, 10/79; Action consistency, Tulane Studies Philos, 79; Identifying with characters in literature, J Comp Lit & Aesthet, 82; Identifying subjects, Am Philos Quart, 10/82. *Mailing Add:* Dept of Philos Brooklyn Col Brooklyn NY 11210

WISHARD, ARMIN, b Gmunden, Austria, June 7, 41; US citizen. GERMAN LANGUAGE & LITERATURE. *Educ:* Univ Calif, Riverside, BA, 65, MA, 67; Univ Ore, PhD(Ger), 70. *Prof Exp:* Asst prof of Ger, Wash State Univ, 69-70; asst prof, 70-76, ASSOC PROF GER, COLO COL, 76-, CHMN DEPT GER & RUSS, 79- *Concurrent Pos:* NDEA fel, 77-78. *Mem:* MLA; AAUP; Am Asn Teachers Ger; Pac Northwest Conf Foreign Lang. *Res:* East German literature; medieval epics; teaching of foreign languages. *Publ:* Contribr, Meisterwerke der deutschen Sprache, Random House, 71; auth, Spielmannsepik: Oral Formulaic Composition in a Middle High German Genre, Mouton, The Hague, 74; co-ed, Cuentos y Juegos, 75 & Tout a' fait Francais, 78, Norton. *Mailing Add:* Dept of German & Russian Colorado Col Colorado Springs CO 80903

WISSE, RUTH, b Cernauti, Rumania, May 13, 36; Can citizen; m 57; c 3. YIDDISH & AMERICAN JEWISH LITERATURE. *Educ:* McGill Univ, BA, 57, PhD(English), 69; Columbia Univ, MA, 61. *Prof Exp:* Asst prof English & Yiddish, McGill Univ, 69-71; sr lectr Yiddish lit, Tel-Aviv Univ, 71-73 & Hebrew Univ, 71-72; assoc prof, 74-78, PROF YIDDISH LIT, MCGILL UNIV, 78- *Concurrent Pos:* Consult, Yivo Inst Jewish Res, 71-; Killam Found fel, 75-76. *Mem:* Asn Jewish Studies. *Res:* Modern Jewish literature; modern Yiddish literature. *Publ:* Auth, The Schlemiel as Modern Hero, Univ Chicago, 71; ed, A Shtetl and Other Yiddish Novellas, Behrman House, 73; contribr, The prose of Abraham Sutzkever, Introduction, In: Green Aquartium, Hebrew Univ, 75; co-ed (with Irving Howe), The Best of Shelen Aleichen, New Repub Bks, 79; Singer's Paradoxical Progress, 2/79, Reading About Jews, 3/80 & Philip Roth Then and Now, 9/82, Commentary; Di Yurge: Immigrants or Exiles?, Prooftexts, 1/81. *Mailing Add:* Jewish Studies Prog McGill Univ 3511 Peel St Montreal PQ H3A 1W7 Can

WISWALL, DOROTHY ROLLER, b Alpirsbach, WGer, Aug 6, 47; US citizen, m 76; c 1. GERMANIC LANGUAGES & LITERATURES. *Educ:* Cornell Univ, AB, 71; Univ Mich, AM, 72, PhD(Ger lang & lit), 79. *Prof Exp:* Fel, Vico Col, State Univ NY Buffalo, 79-80; LECTR GER, NIAGARA UNIV, 80- *Mem:* MLA; Am Asn Teachers Ger. *Res:* Albrecht von Haller (1708-1777); 18th century German literature; literature and science. *Publ:* Auth, A Comparison of Selected Poetic and Scientific Works of Albrecht von Haller, Peter Lang, Berne, 81. *Mailing Add:* 1421 West River Rd Grand Island NY 14072

WITHERELL, JULIAN WOOD, African History. See Vol I

WITHERS, SARA COOK, b Birmingham, Ala, June 30, 24; m 62; c 1. LINGUISTICS. *Educ:* Ala Col, AB, 45; Univ NC, MA, 47. *Prof Exp:* Instr English for foreigners, Am Lang Ctr, Am Univ, 52-56; ASSOC PROF ENGLISH, GALLAUDET COL, 56- *Mem:* MLA; SAtlantic Mod Lang Asn; Am Instr Deal. *Res:* Renaissance; 18th century; linguistics, especially as applied to teaching English to non-native speakers. *Publ:* Coauth, Pronunciation Drills for Non-Native Speakers of English, English Lang Serv, 62; auth, A Guide to Improved English, Bobbs, 64; Stories of the American West, Prentice-Hall, 65; The United Nations in Action: A Structured Reader, Crowell, 69; coauth, A note on Browning's Statue and the Bust, Browning Newslett, 72; auth, Helen Keller, In: First Person Female American: A Selected and Annotated Bibliography of Autobiographical Writings by Contemporary American Women & Am Notes & Queries, 9/77. *Mailing Add:* Dept of English Gallaudet Col Washington DC 20002

WITKE, CHARLES, b Los Angeles, Calif, Sept 22, 31; m 75; c 1. CLASSICAL PHILOLOGY, MEDIEVAL LATIN LITERATURE. *Educ:* Univ Calif, Los Angeles, BA, 53; Harvard Univ, AM, 57, PhD, 62. *Prof Exp:* Asst prof classics, Univ Chicago, 62-63; asst prof, Univ Calif, Berkeley, 63-68, assoc prof classics & comp lit, 68-70; prof, State Univ NY, Binghamton, 70-71; assoc dean, 71-74, dir prog comp lit, 71-78, PROF GREEK & LATIN, UNIV MICH, ANN ARBOR, 71- *Concurrent Pos:* Lectr, Kyoto Univ, 66; prof, Class Civilization Sem, Columbia Univ, 71; grant, Nat Endowment for Humanities, 82. *Mem:* Am Philol Asn, Mediaeval Acad Am; Dante Soc Am; Soc Prom of Roman Studies. *Res:* Classical and mediaeval Latin poetry; late antique and early mediaeval poetics; classical tradition in the Middle Ages. *Publ:* Auth, Enarratio Catulliana, 68 & Latin Satire: The Structure of Persuasion, 70, Brill, Leiden; Numen Litterarum: The old and the new in Latin poetry from Constantine to Gregory the Great, Mittellateinische Studien und Texte, Leiden, Cologne, 71; Horace's Roman Odes, Leiden, Brill (in prep). *Mailing Add:* Dept of Class Studies Univ of Mich Ann Arbor MI 48109

WITTKOWSKI, WOLFGANG, b Halle, Ger, Aug 15, 25; m 54 c 4. GERMAN LITERATURE. *Educ:* Univ Frankfurt, PhD(Ger), 54. *Prof Exp:* Asst Ger, Univ Frankfurt, 50-53; studienrat, gymnasium, Bad Nauheim, Ger, 56-63; from assoc prof to prof, Ohio State Univ, 63-77; PROF GER, STATE UNIV NY, ALBANY, 78- *Concurrent Pos:* Vis prof Ger, State Univ NY, Albany, 77-78. *Mem:* MLA; Am Asn Teachers Ger. *Res:* Classical and 19th century German literature; Kleist; ETA Hoffmann. *Publ:* Auth, Der junge Hebbel, Walter de Gruyter, Berlin, 68; Kleist's Amphitryon, de Gruyter, Berlin, 78; Georg Buechner, Heidelberg, winter 78; ed, Friedrich Schiller Kunst, Humanität und Politik in der späten Aufklärung Ein Symposium Niemeyer, Tübingen, 82. *Mailing Add:* State Univ NY Hu 209 1400 Washington Ave Albany NY 12222

WITTLIN, CURT J, b Basel, Switz, Apr 13, 41; m 66. ROMANCE LANGUAGES. *Educ:* Basel Latin Col, BA, 60; Univ Basel, MA & PhD(Romance lang), 65. *Prof Exp:* Instr Span, Basel State Bus Col, 63-65; asst prof French, Union Col, Ky, 66-67; asst prof Old French, 67-70, assoc prof Old French & hist ling, 70-74, PROF FRENCH & SPAN, UNIV SASK, 74- *Concurrent Pos:* Can Coun grant, 68-69; Swiss Nat Res Fund grant, 72-73. *Mem:* MLA: Asn Can Hispanists (vpres, 78-81); Asn Int Catalan; NAm Catalan Soc. *Res:* Medieval translations; Catalan; Eiximenis. *Publ:* Auth, La trad cat de les histories Romanes, Estudis Romanics, 67 & 68; Brunetto Latini, Tresor, Trad Cat, Barcelona, 71, 76 & 82; Nicolau Quilis traduint Cicero, Bol Acad Barcelona, 73; Un inventario turolense de 1484, Arch Filol Arag, 76; Commentaires et traductions medievaux de la Cite de Dien, Tralili, 78; Un nuevo tipo de siglas: Acronimos lexemas contextuales, Ling Esp Actual, 81; Eiximenis, Lo libre de les dones, Barcelona, 81; Pero Lopez de Ayala, Las Decadas de Tito Livio, Barcelona, 82. *Mailing Add:* Dept of Fr & Span Univ of Sask Saskatoon SK S7N 0W0 Can

WITTMANN, HORST H, b Bleicherode, Ger, May 17, 35; US citizen; m 60; c 3. GERMAN & COMPARATIVE LITERATURE. *Educ:* Amherst Col, dipl Am lit, 60; Univ Mass, Amherst, PhD(Ger lit), 69. *Prof Exp:* Instr Ger, Univ Mass, Amherst, 60-61, from instr to asst prof, 63-69; asst prof, 69-75, ASSOC PROF GER, SCARBOROUGH COL, UNIV TORONTO, 75- *Concurrent Pos:* Fulbright scholar, Amherst Col, 59-60; Can Coun leave fel, 75-76. *Mem:* Can Asn Univ Teachers Ger; Can Fedn for Humanities. *Res:* European literature of turn of 19th to 20th century; H v Hofmannsthal. *Publ:* Auth, Die Potentialität des Leichten, Hofmannsthals Der Schwierige, Seminar, 10/74. *Mailing Add:* Scarborough Col Univ of Toronto West Hill ON M1C 1A4 Can

WITTMANN, RICHARD GERARD, b St Louis, Mo, Aug 6, 33. CLASSICAL LANGUAGES, WORLD LITERATURE. *Educ:* St Louis Univ, AB, 55, MA, 57, PhD(Latin & Greek), 69. *Prof Exp:* Instr Latin & English, St Benedict's Col, 59-62, asst prof, 62-67, assoc prof Latin, Greek & English, 68-70; asst dean, 71-72, assoc prof, 73-77, PROF CLASS & ENGLISH, BENEDICTINE COL, 78- *Res:* Renaissance Latin drama; ancient history; Greek mythology. *Publ:* Auth, A Renaissance pictogram, Class Bull, 2/57; Flying saucers or flying shields, Class J, 2/68. *Mailing Add:* RR 2 Box 34A Atchison KS 66002

WITUCKI, JEANNETTE RENNER, b Omaha, Nebr, Feb 28, 30; m 49; c 2. ANTHROPOLOGY, LINGUISTICS. *Educ:* Univ Calif, Los Angeles, BA, 60, PhD(anthrop), 66. *Prof Exp:* Assoc prof, 67-80, PROF ANTHROP & LING, CALIF STATE UNIV, LOS ANGELES, 80- *Concurrent Pos:* Calif State Univ Found res grant, 68-69. *Mem:* Am Anthrop Asn; Ling Soc Am; Int Ling Asn. *Res:* Ethnolinguistics; linguistics; Chamorro. *Publ:* Auth, A language pattern co-occurring with violence-permissiveness, Behav Sci, 11/71; Alternative analyses of Chamorro vowels, Anthrop Ling, 11/73; A lexicostatistical evaluation of Tagalog-Chamorro relations, 74, The vowels of Chamorro, 75, The consonants of Chamorro, 76 & Chamorro infixes, 78, Pac Linguistics. *Mailing Add:* Dept of Anthrop Calif State Univ Los Angeles CA 90032

WIVELL, CHARLES JOSEPH, b Pittsburgh, Pa, Aug 11, 31; m 68; c 2. CHINESE LITERATURE & LANGUAGE. *Educ:* Univ Pittsburgh, AB, 55; Univ Wash, PhD(Chinese lang & lit), 68. *Prof Exp:* Asst prof Chinese, Univ Hawaii, Manoa, 66-67; asst prof, 67-71, ASSOC PROF CHINESE, UNIV ROCHESTER, 71- *Concurrent Pos:* Fulbright fac grant, Kyoto Univ, 71. *Mem:* Asn Asian Studies. *Res:* Chinese fiction; the Chinese oral narrative tradition; Chinese myth, legend and folklore. *Publ:* Auth, Modes of coherence in the Second West Lake Collection, Lit East & West, 71; Myth and ritual patterns in King Wu's campaign against King Chou, J Asian Folklore, 72; contribr, Transition and Permanence: Chinese History and Culture, Cathay Press, Hong Kong, 72. *Mailing Add:* Dept of Foreign Lang Lit & Ling Univ of Rochester Rochester NY 14627

WIXTED, JOHN TIMOTHY, b Chicago, Ill, Aug 4, 42. CHINESE & JAPANESE LITERATURE. *Educ:* Univ Toronto, BA, 65; Stanford Univ, AM, 66; Univ Oxford, DPhil(Chinese lit), 77. *Prof Exp:* Vis asst prof Chinese & Japanese, Univ Mich, 77-78; ASST PROF ASIAN LANG, ARIZ STATE UNIV, 78- *Mem:* Am Orient Soc; Asn Asian Studies; Japanese Lang Teachers Asn; Chinese Lang Teachers Asn. *Res:* Chinese poetry and poetics; modern Japanese literature. *Publ:* Auth, The Song-Poetry of Wei Chuang (836-910 AD), Ctr Asian Studies, Ariz State Univ, 79. *Mailing Add:* Dept of Foreign Lang Ariz State Univ Tempe AZ 85281

WLASSICS, TIBOR, b Budapest, Hungary, Sept 8, 36; US citizen; m 61; c 1. ITALIAN LITERATURE. *Educ:* Columbia Univ, MA, 65, PhD(Ital lit), 68. *Prof Exp:* From asst prof to assoc prof, 67-76, PROF FRENCH & ITAL LIT, UNIV PITTSBURGH, 77- *Honors & Awards:* XI Tasso Award for Lit Criticism, 71. *Mem:* Dante Soc Am; Northeastern Mod Lang Asn. *Res:* Dante; 20th century Italian literature; comparative literature. *Publ:* Auth, Interpretazioni ki prosodia dantesca, Signorelli, Rome, 72; Da Verga a Sanguineti Giannotta, Catania, 73; Galilei Critico Letterario, Longo, Ravenna, 74; Dante Narratore, Olschki, Firenze, 75. *Mailing Add:* Dept of French & Italian Univ of Pittsburgh Pittsburgh PA 15260

WOEHR, RICHARD ARTHUR, b Portchester, NY, May 1, 42. SPANISH. *Educ:* St Lawrence Univ, BA, 64; Middlebury Col, MA, 65; Stanford Univ, PhD(Span lit), 71. *Prof Exp:* Assoc prof English as second lang, Col Notre Dame, 71-73; ASSOC PROF SPAN, CALIF STATE UNIV, HAYWARD, 73- *Mem:* Am Asn Teachers Span & Port; Pedagog Sem Romance Philol. *Res:* Syntax of the subjunctive in Spanish; reflective verbs in Spanish. *Publ:* Coauth, Espanol esencial, Holt, 74; auth, Grammar of the factive nominal in Spanish, Lang Sci, 8/75; Syntactic atrophy and the indirect interrogative in Spanish, Studia Neophilol, 77; Coauth, Pasaporte, Wiley, 80. *Mailing Add:* Dept of Foreign Lang Calif State Univ Hayward CA 94542

WOLCK, WOLFGANG, b Koenigsberg, Ger, Sept 19, 32; m 66. LINGUISTICS. *Educ:* Univ Frankfurt, DPhil(English ling), 63. *Prof Exp:* Wiss asst English, Univ Frankfurt, 60-63 & Univ Freiburg, 64-65; vis asst prof ling, Ind Univ, Bloomington, 65-66, asst prof, 66-70; assoc prof, 70-75, dir Latin Am Studies, 72-76, PROF LING, STATE UNIV NY BUFFALO, 75-, CHMN DEPT, 77- *Concurrent Pos:* Res asst, Ind Univ, Ling Res Proj & Fulbright travel award, 63-64; field reader ling, US Off Educ, 66-; dir, Ind Univ Prog Undergrad Study in Peru, 68; vis prof ling, Univ Nac Mayor de San Marcos, Peru, 68-69, hon prof, 72-; mem policy adv coun, Ctr Appl Ling, 72-; mem exec comt, Interam Prog Ling & Lang Teaching, 74-78; vis res fel, Studies Inst Peru, Lima, 76-77. *Honors & Awards:* Bronze Medal, Univ Brno, Czech, 71. *Mem:* Ling Soc Am; Am Dialect Soc; Int Sociol Asn; Latin Am Studies Asn; Ling Asn Can & US. *Res:* Bilingualism; dialectology; English and Quechua. *Publ:* Auth, Phonematische Analyse der Sprache von Buchan, Carl Winter, Heidelberg, 65; A computerized dictionary of Andean languages, Lang Sci, 69; contribr chaps, In: El reto del multilinguismo en el Peru, Inst Estudios Peruanos, 72 & In: Language Attitudes: Current Trends and Prospects, Georgetown Univ, 73; co-ed, The Social Dimension of Dialectology, Mouton, The Hague, 76; auth, Community profiles, Int J Sociol Lang, 76; Sociolinguistics: Revolution of interdiscipline?, Am Behav Sci, 77; contribr, Aspects of Bilingualism, Hornbeam, 78. *Mailing Add:* Dept of Ling Amherst Campus State Univ NY Buffalo NY 14261

WOLD, RUTH, b Gordon, Tex, Aug 31, 23; m 59. SPANISH. *Educ:* NTex State Col, BA, 45; Univ Tex, MA, 48, PhD(Span, econ), 56. *Prof Exp:* Asst Span & English, Univ Tex, 46-48, 54-56; instr, Ark Agr & Mech Col, 48-50; instr Span, Univ Ariz, 56-50; from asst prof to assoc prof foreign lang, 60-72, chmn dept, 65-67, PROF FOREIGN LANG, CALIF STATE UNIV, NORTHRIDGE, 72-, HEAD SPAN DEPT, 80- *Mem:* MLA; Am Asn Teachers Span & Port. *Res:* Latin American literature. *Publ:* Auth, Diario de Mexico, Rev Iberoam Bibliog, 64; The Mexican Arcadia, Hispania, 69; Diario de Mexico, Gredos, Madrid, 70. *Mailing Add:* Dept of Foreign Lang Calif State Univ Northridge CA 91326

WOLF, ERNEST MICHAEL, b Dortmund, Ger, Jan 6, 09; nat US; m 37; c 1. ROMANCE LANGUAGES, GERMAN. *Educ:* Univ Bonn, PhD(Romance lang, Ger), 34. *Prof Exp:* Teacher, Herrlingen, Ger, 35-37; prin, Kristinehov, Sweden, 37-40; teacher high sch, Calif, 45-47; from instr to prof, 47-76, EMER PROF GER & ROMANCE LANG, SAN DIEGO STATE UNIV, 76- *Concurrent Pos:* Fac Res Comt res grants, 66-68. *Mem:* MLA; Am Asn Teachers Ger; Philol Asn Pac Coast; Am Asn Teachers Fr; Thomas Mann Ges. *Res:* European civilization; R M Rilke; Thomas Mann. *Publ:* Auth, Rilke's L'Angedu Meridien: A thematic analysis, PMLA, 3/65; Blick auf Deutschland, Scribner's, 66; Notre-Dame of Chartres and Notre-Dame of Paris in Rilke's Die Kathedrale, Etudes Germaniques, 4-6/69; The sculpting surf: An interpretation of Rilke's Das Portal I, Seminar, fall 69; Savonarola in Muenchen-Eine Analyse von Thomas Mann's Gladius Dei, Euphorion, 3/70; A case of slighty mistaken identity: Gustav Mahler and Gustav Aschenbach, Twentieth Century Lit, 1/73; Stone into Poetry; the Cathedral Cycle in Rainer Maria Rilke's Neue Gedichte, Bouvier, 78; Hagenstroems: The rival family in Thomas Mann's Buddenbrooks, Ger Studies Rev, 1/82. *Mailing Add:* Box 983 La Mesa CA 92041

WOLF, HERBERT MARTIN, b Springfield, Mass, July 15, 38; m 61; c 3. HEBREW, OLD TESTAMENT STUDIES. *Educ:* Wheaton Col, Ill, AB, 60; Dallas Theol Sem, ThM, 64; Brandeis Univ, MA, 65, PhD(Mediter studies), 67. *Prof Exp:* From instr to asst prof, 67-75, ASSOC PROF OLD TESTAMENT, WHEATON COL, 75- *Mem:* Evangel Theol Soc. *Res:* Hittite and Biblical studies; comparative Semitic languages. *Publ:* Auth, A solution to the Immanuel Prophecy in Isiah 7: 14-8: 22, J Bibl Lit, 72; The desire of all nations in Haggai's 2: 7: Messianic or not?, J Evangel Theol Soc, 76; Haggai-Malachi: Rededication and Renewal, Moody, 76. *Mailing Add:* Grad Sch Wheaton College Wheaton IL 60187

WOLF, MEYER L, b Minneapolis, Minn, Jan 9, 37; m; c 3. LINGUISTICS. *Educ:* Columbia Univ, PhD(ling), 68. *Prof Exp:* From instr to asst prof ling, Mich State Univ, 66-71; LECTR, HEBREW UNIV JERUSALEM, 71- *Concurrent Pos:* NSF fel computational ling, 65-66; asst ed, Great Dictionary of the Yiddish Language, 76- *Mem:* Ling Soc Am. *Res:* Yiddish linguistics; dialect geography; transformational grammar. *Publ:* Auth, The geography of Yiddish case & gender variation, In: Field of Yiddish, 3rd collection; Did R Benjamin of Tudela really cite Slavic words?, Tarbiz, 76; The language of the Seyfer Shivkhey baal shem tov, Yidishe Shprakh, 76; Phonological processes in plural formation, Sefer Dov Sadan, Hakibbutz Hameuhad, 77. *Mailing Add:* Rehov Rav Yehuda Petaya 3/12 Sanhedria Hamurhevet Jerusalem Israel

WOLFE, ETHYLE RENEE, b Burlington, Vt, Mar 14, 19; m 54. CLASSICAL LANGUAGES & LITERATURE. *Educ:* Univ Vt, BA, 40, MA, 42; NY Univ, PhD, 50. *Prof Exp:* Lectr classics, eve session, 47-49, from instr to assoc prof, 49-67, acting chmn dept classics & comp lit, 62-63, chmn, 67-72, PROF CLASSICS, BROOKLYN COL, 68-, DEAN SCH HUMANITIES, 71- *Concurrent Pos:* Assoc ed, Class World, 65-70; co-ed, Am Class Rev, 70- *Mem:* Am Philol Asn; Archaeol Inst Am; Am Soc Papyrologists. *Res:* Latin poetry; Greek tragedy; papyrology. *Publ:* Auth, Transportation in Augustan Egypt, Trans Am Philol Asn, 53; Contract of Loan with Mortgage, Am Soc Papyrologists, Bicentennial comt, Festschrift Vol, 76. *Mailing Add:* Apt 15E 360 W 22nd St New York NY 10011

WOLFE, GERARD RAYMOND, b Brooklyn, NY, Apr 2, 26. FOREIGN LANGUAGES. *Educ:* City Col New York, BBA, 48; NY Univ, MA, 49; Sorbonne, cert French lang, 54; Union Grad Sch, Ohio, PhD(jour, hist), 78. *Prof Exp:* Teacher Span & French, Franklin K Lane High Sch, New York, 49-51 & Sewanhaka High Sch, Floral Park, NY, 51-58; lectr, 58-71, assoc prof Span & French, 71-77, PROF CONTINUING EDUC, NEW YORK UNIV, 77-, DIR FOREIGN LANG PROG, COL PREP PROG & GRAD ENGLISH PROFICIENCY PROG, 58- *Concurrent Pos:* Researcher, Am Mus Nat Hist, 59-64; proj dir, Peace Corps Training Prog Turkey, 66; mem, Nat Trust Hist Preserv, 69-; assoc prof, Sch Continuing Educ, New York Univ, 69-77; consult, New York Landmarks Preserv Comn, 70-; guest lectr, Jewish Mus, 71-; sen, NY Univ Senate, 73-75; lectr, Hofstra Univ, 75- *Mem:* MLA; Am Coun Teaching Foreign Lang; Nat Univ Exten Asn; Am Scand Found; Nat Trust Hist Preserv. *Res:* New York City history and architecture; foreign language teaching methods; book publishing history. *Publ:* Auth, How to Pass Spanish, Youth Educ Syst, 59; ed, A New Functional French, 59 & Les du Pont, 60, Am Bk Co; auth, Read, Write, Speak French, Bantam, 63; The Peace Corps in Turkey, A Training Manual for Volunteers, 66, New York: A Guide to the Metropolis, 75 & The Synagogues of New York's Lower East Side, 78, New York Univ. *Mailing Add:* Foreign Lang Prog New York Univ New York NY 10003

WOLFE, MANSELL WAYNE, b Monessen, Pa, Aug 5, 18; m 43; c 4. SPANISH AMERICAN LITERATURE & CULTURE. *Educ:* DePauw Univ, AB, 49; Ind Univ, Bloomington, MA, 50, PhD(Latin Am area studies), 64. *Prof Exp:* Inst jour, Wis State Col-River Falls, 50-53 & Ind Univ, 53-55; from asst prof to prof, 55-70, asst to pres, 58-64, admin vpres, 64-72, PROF MOD LANG, UNIV WIS-RIVER FALLS, 70-, ASST CHANCELLOR, 72- *Concurrent Pos:* Fulbright prof, Inst Mass Commun, Univ W Indies, Kingston, Jamaica, 76-77. *Mem:* NEA; Am Asn Higher Educ; Asn Educ Jour. *Res:* Latin American literature, journalism and history. *Publ:* Translr, Usigli, Another Springtime, Samuel French, 61; ed, Search for a mission, Mexico, 7/69; Earl Chapin's Tales of Wisconsin, Univ Wis-River Falls, 73. *Mailing Add:* Univ of Wis River Falls WI 54022

WOLFE, PHILLIP JERROLD, b Greencastle, Ind, Dec 8, 47; m 72; c 1. FRENCH LITERATURE. *Educ:* Hamilton Col, AB, 70; Princeton Univ, MA, 72, PhD(romance lang), 74. *Prof Exp:* Instr, 74-75, asst prof, Univ Ga, 75-81; ASST PROF FRENCH, ALLEGHENY COL, 81- *Mem:* MLA; Am Asn Teachers Fr; Asn des professeurs de francais a l'etranger; NAm Soc 17th Century Fr Lit. *Res:* Seventeenth century French prose; the genre of the dialogue; free thought. *Publ:* Ed, Choix de Conversations de Mlle de Scudery, Longo, Ravenna, 77; Lettres de Gabriel Naude a Jacques Dupuy, Alta, Edmonton, 82. *Mailing Add:* Dept of Lit Allegheny Col Meadville PA 16335

WOLFE, WARREN JERROLD, b Monessen, Pa, Feb 20, 24; m 46; c 2. FRENCH. *Educ:* DePauw Univ, AB, 48; Ind Univ, MA, 49; PhD(French), 53. *Prof Exp:* Assoc prof mod lang, Ky Wesleyan Col, 51-53; assoc prof lang & chmn dept, Univ Idaho, 53-61; from asst prof to prof Romance lang, 61-71, actg chmn dept, 67-68, PROF ROMANCE LANG, BOWLING GREEN STATE UNIV, 71- *Mem:* MLA; Am Asn Teachers Fr; Am Soc 18th Century Studies; Societe des Professeurs Francais en Amerique. *Res:* Comparative literature; applied linguistics; 18th century French literature. *Publ:* Auth, Humanitarianism in 18th century French literature; Foreign language entrance and degree requirements for the BS degree, PMLA, 9/59; The Fevret de Saint-Memin Journal, Am Soc Legion of Honor Mag, summer 77. *Mailing Add:* 709 Birch St Bowling Green OH 43402

WOLFF, CHRISTIAN, b Nice, France, Mar 8, 34; US citizen; m 65. CLASSICS, MUSIC. *Educ:* Harvard Univ, AB, 55, MA, 57, PhD(comp lit), 63. *Prof Exp:* Instr classics, Harvard Univ, 62-65, asst prof, 65-71; assoc prof classics, comp lit & music, 71-78, prof classics & music, 78-80, STRAUSS PROF MUSIC & CLASSICS, DARTMOUTH COL, 80- *Concurrent Pos:* Loeb bequest grant, Harvard Univ, 67-68; fel Ctr Hellenic Studies, Washington, DC, 70-71; vis composer, Deutscher Akademischer Austauschdienst, Berlin, 74; vis prof classics, Harvard Univ, 80. *Honors & Awards:* Music Award, Am Acad & Nat Inst of Arts & Letts, 74. *Mem:* Soc Ethnomusicol; Soc for Hellenic Studies. *Res:* Greek literature and philosophy, especially drama, Thucydides and Plato; music, especially contemporary. *Publ:* Auth, Ueber form, Reihe, 60; Myth and design in Euripides' Ion, Harvard Studies Class Philol, 65; Orestes, In: Euripides, A Collection of Critical Essays, Prentice, 68; On Euripides' Helen, Harvard Studies Class Philol, 73; On Political Texts and New Music, SONUS, 80; Euripides, In: Ancient Writers: Greece and Rome, Scribners', 82. *Mailing Add:* Dept of Classics Darthmouth Col Hanover NH 03755

WOLFF, JOHN ULRICH, b Berlin, Ger, Nov 1, 32; US citizen; m 63; c 4. GENERAL & MALAYOPOLYNESIAN LINGUISTICS. *Educ:* Cornell Univ, BA, 54, MA, 55; Yale Univ, PhD(ling), 64. *Prof Exp:* Assoc prof, 63-80, PROF MOD LANG & LING, CORNELL UNIV, 80- *Mem:* Ling Soc Am; Am Orient Soc; Asn Asian Studies. *Publ:* Auth, Beginning Cebuano, Yale Univ, 66 & 68; History of the Camotes dialect, Oceanic Ling, 68; Beginning Indonesian, 72 & Dictionary of Cebuano Visayan, 72, SEA Prog, Cornell Univ. *Mailing Add:* SEA Prog Uris Hall Cornell Univ Ithaca NY 14853

WOLFGANG, LENORA D PODEN, b Philadelphia, Pa; m 57; c 2. ROMANCE LANGUAGES, MEDIEVAL FRENCH LITERATURE. *Educ:* Univ Pa, BA, 56, MA, 65, PhD(Romance lang), 73. *Prof Exp:* Teaching asst French, Univ Pa, 58-60; teacher, Swarthmore-Routledge Sch Union, 64; instr Temple Univ, 64-66; teacher, Ravenhill Acad, 71; co-adjutant, Rutgers Univ, 75-76; lectr, Univ Pa, 76-77; ASST PROF FRENCH, LEHIGH UNIV, 80- *Concurrent Pos:* Travel grant, Am Coun Learned Soc, 78; Woodrow Wilson fel, Fulbright Scholar & res grant, Am Philos Soc, 81. *Mem:* Mediaeval Acad Am; MLA; Soc Int Arthurienne; Am Asn Teachers French; Soc Int Rencesvals. *Res:* Medieval French literature; Arthurian and the epic; Old French philology. *Publ:* Auth, Bliocadran: A Prologue to the Perceval of Chretien de Troyes, Edition and Critical Study, Max Niemeyer, Tübingen, 76; Prologues to the Perceval of Chretien de Troyes, Oeuvres et Critiques, 2:

81-90; Perceval's Father: Problems in Medieval narrative art, Romance Philol, XXXIV: 28-47; The Song of Roland: After 1200 Years, Vol III, Proc PMR Conf, 1978, The Augustinian Hist Inst Villanova Univ, 80. *Mailing Add:* 4106 Locust St Philadelphia PA 19104

WOLF-ROTTKAY, WOLF HELMUT, b Berlin, Ger, Jan 25, 08; m 38; c 2. GERMANIC LANGUAGES. *Educ:* Univ Greifswald, PhD(Scand & English), 39. *Prof Exp:* Instr Ger, Univ Iceland, 38-39; lectr Gothic, Old Norse & mod Scand, Univ Munich, 48-66; lectr Swed & Ger, Univ Calif, Los Angeles, 66-67; asst prof Ger, Univ Scranton, 67-68; assoc prof Ger & ling, 68-73, EMER PROF GER, UNIV SOUTHERN CALIF, 73- *Concurrent Pos:* Vis prof, Univ Salamanca, 52-56. *Honors & Awards:* Schiller Mem Medal, Ger Fed Govt, 55. *Mem:* MLA; Am Asn Teachers Ger; Am-Scand Found. *Res:* Germanic word study; semantics; Icelandic linguistic traditionalism. *Publ:* Auth, Das Bewusstsein der undurchbrochenen sprachlichen Uberlieferung, Wolf & Sohn, Munich, 43; Review of Friedrich Kluge, Etym Woerterbuch der deutschen Sprache, 19th ed, 64; Altnordisch-isländisches Lesebuch, Hueber, Munich, 67; Aspects of Icelandic linguistic traditionalism, In: Dichtung, Sprache und Gesellschaft, Athenaeum, 71; Some onomastic and toponomastic aspects of Icelandic traditionalism, Names, 71; Tongue in cheek--a recent harvest of punny language from Los Angeles, Neusprachliche Mitt, 72. *Mailing Add:* 12915 Venice Blvd 37 Los Angeles CA 90066

WOLMAN, HOWARD BENNETT, b Baltimore, Md, Aug 10, 36. CLASSICAL LANGUAGES, ANCIENT HISTORY. *Educ:* Amherst Col, BA, 58; Johns Hopkins Univ, MA, 61, PhD(classics), 66. *Prof Exp:* Asst prof classics, Dartmouth Col, 66-67; asst prof, 67-76, assoc prof, 76-80, PROF CLASSICS, BROOKLYN COL, 80- *Mem:* Am Philol Asn; Archaeol Inst Am. *Res:* Plutarch; ancient historiography; Herodotus. *Mailing Add:* 127 E 10th St New York NY 10003

WOLOCH, GEORGE MICHAEL, Classics. See Vol I

WOLOSHIN, DAVID JORDAN, b Lawrence, Mass, Jan 8, 30. GERMAN, FOREIGN LANGUAGE PEDAGOGY. *Educ:* Tufts Col, BA, 51; Univ Mich, MA, 52; Univ Ariz, PhD(sec educ), 68. *Prof Exp:* Instr Ger, 57-62, lectr, 62-65, from asst prof to assoc prof, 65-71, PROF GER, UNIV ARIZ, 71-, HEAD DEPT, 78- *Concurrent Pos:* Bibliogr, Am Coun Teaching of Foreign Lang, 74-75; Danforth Found assoc, 76. *Honors & Awards:* Univ Ariz Found Award, 75. *Mem:* MLA; Am Coun Teaching Foreign Lang; Am Asn Teachers Ger. *Res:* Cross-cultural analysis. *Publ:* Coauth, Approaching German culture, Die Unterrichtspraxis, 5/74; auth, Foreign language as a weapon, Ariz Mag, 3/75; translr, Karl Jasper, Strindberg and Van Gogh, Univ Ariz, 77; Where are we today? A survey, Die Unterrichtspraxis, 5/82. *Mailing Add:* Dept of German Univ of Arizona Tucson AZ 85721

WOLSEY, MARY LOU MORRIS, b Baltimore, Md, Feb 21, 36; m 65; c 2. MEDIEVAL FRENCH LANGUAGE & LITERATURE. *Educ:* Mary Washington Col, BA, 58; Univ Kans, MA, 61; Univ Besancon, cert etudes super, 64; Univ Minn, PhD(French), 72. *Prof Exp:* Asst instr French, Univ Kans, 58-61; instr, Mary Washington Col, 61-63; asst English, Teachers Col, Besancon, France, 63-64; teaching assoc French, Univ Pa, 64-65 & Univ Minn, 65-67; instr, Macalester Col, 67-68, adj prof, 72-78; part-time asst prof, 76-81, ASST PROF FRENCH, COL ST THOMAS, 81- *Concurrent Pos:* Vis prof, Univ Bristol, England, 78-79. *Mem:* Am Asn Teachers French; Am Coun Teaching Foreign Lang; Mediaeval Acad Am; Alliance Francaise; Midwest Mod Lang Asn Am. *Res:* Medieval French romance; the French novel; computer research in French. *Publ:* Auth, The Eracle of Gautier d'Arras: A critical study, Diss Abstr Int, 10/72. *Mailing Add:* 2197 Berkeley Ave St Paul MN 55105

WOLVERTON, ROBERT E, b Indianapolis, Ind, Aug 4, 25; m 52; c 4. CLASSICS. *Educ:* Hanover Col, AB, 48; Univ Mich, MA, 49; Univ NC, PhD(Latin, Greek & ancient hist), 54. *Hon Degrees:* LittD, Col of Mt St Joseph on the Ohio, 77. *Prof Exp:* Asst prof classics, Univ Ga, 54-59; from asst to assoc prof classics & hist, Tufts Univ, 59-62; assoc prof classics & dir hon prog, Fla State Univ, 62-67; assoc dean grad col, Univ Ill, 67-69; dean grad sch, Miami Univ, Ohio, 69-72; prof classics & pres, Col of Mt St Josephs on the Ohio, 72-77; PROF CLASSICS & EDUC LEADERSHIP & VPRES ACAD AFFAIRS, MISS STATE UNIV, 77- *Concurrent Pos:* Title IV consult-reader of langs, NDEA, 67-72; consult-reviewer admin, NCent Asn Cols & Schs, 67-77; instr personnel mgt, Main Event Mgt Inc, 76-; mem exec comt, Nat Coun Chief Acad Officers, 81- *Honors & Awards:* Alumni Achievement Award, Hanover Col, 71; hon life pres, Am Class League, 77. *Mem:* Am Class League (pres, 72-76); Am Philol Asn; Class Asn Mid West & South; Am Asn Higher Educ . *Res:* Administration in higher education; classical mythology; etymology. *Publ:* Auth, Classical Elements in English Words, 66 & An Outline of Classical Mythology, 67, Littlefield; contribr, Graduate Programs and Admission Manual, 4 vols, Grad Record & Exam Bd & Coun Grad Schs USA, 71 & 72; auth, The future of classics, Class Outlook, 76; contrib auth & translr, A Life of George Washington, in Latin Prose, George Washington Univ, 76; The future of graduate studies in the humanities, Nat Forum, 79; contribr, Mythological References, Arete Publ, 80. *Mailing Add:* Off of VPres for Academic Affairs PO Drawer BQ Miss State Univ Mississippi State MS 39762

WOLZ, HENRY GEORGE, b Kornwestheim, Ger, Sept 10, 05; nat US; m 55; c 1. PHILOSOPHY. *Educ:* Fordham Univ, BS, 36, AM, 38, PhD, 46. *Prof Exp:* Asst prof philos, Wagner Col, 47-51; from asst prof to assoc prof, 51-64, supvr philos, sch gen studies, 61-68, PROF PHILOS, QUEENS COL, NY, 65- *Concurrent Pos:* Asst, eve session, Brooklyn Col, 47, Hunter Col, 47-49. *Mem:* Am Philos Asn; Metaphys Soc Am. *Res:* Ancient philosophy; phenomenology. *Publ:* Auth, The Protagoras Myth and the Philosopher Kings, Rev Metaphys, 12/63; Extrapolation: Its Use and Abuse in Plato, Augustine and Dante, Southern J Philos, fall 64; Plato's Discourse on Love in the Phaedrus, The Personalist, spring 65; Plato's Doctrine of Truth: Orthotes or Aletheia?, Philos & Phenomenol Res, 10/66; Hedonism in the Protagoras, J hist Philos, 7/67; Philosophy as Drama: An Approach to Plato's Symposium, Philos & Phenomenol Res, 3/70; The Paradox of Piety in Plato's Euthyphro in the Light of Heidegger's Conception of Authenticity, Southern J Philos, winter 74; Plato and Heidegger: In Search of Selfhood, Bucknell Univ Press, 81. *Mailing Add:* Dept of Philos Queens Col Flushing NY 11367

WOMACK, THURSTON, b Woodburn, Ky, Apr 2, 20; m 46; c 3. LINGUISTICS. *Educ:* Humboldt State Col, AB, 46; Stanford Univ, MA, 49; Columbia Univ, PhD, 57. *Prof Exp:* Asst prof English, Humboldt State Col, 46-51; assoc prof, State Univ Teachers Col, Geneseo, NY, 53-54; PROF ENGLISH, SAN FRANCISCO STATE UNIV, 54- *Concurrent Pos:* Vis Fulbright lectr ling & English as foreign lang, Tokyo Univ Educ, 60-62; US Agency Int Develop consult, India, 66. *Mem:* Ling Soc Am; Conf Col Compos & Commun; Nat Asn Foreign Student Affairs; Teachers English to Speakers Other Lang; NCTE. *Res:* English linguistics; teaching English as a foreign langauges language. *Publ:* Coauth, Processes in Writing, Wadsworth, 59; a Linguistic Approach to English, Kaibunsha, Japan, 59; Style and Usage in Written English, Kenkyusha, Japan, 62. *Mailing Add:* Dept of English San Francisco State Univ San Francisco CA 94132

WONDER, JOHN P, b Long Beach, Calif, July 29, 21; m 46; c 2. SPANISH LANGUAGE & LITERATURE. *Educ:* Stanford Univ, AB, 43, MA, 48, PhD(Romance lang), 52. *Prof Exp:* From instr to asst prof Span, Univ Ariz, 50-55; dir binationalional ctr, Belo Horizonte, Brazil, 56-58; dir courses and activities, Binational Ctr, Rio de Janeiro, 58-60; dir, Binational Ctr, Port-au-Prince, Haiti, 60-62; asst prof Span, Los Angeles State Col, 62-63; assoc prof, 63-67, chmn dept mod lang, 67-75, dir, Ctr Int Prog, 79-82, PROF SPAN, UNIV OF THE PAC, 67- *Concurrent Pos:* Assoc ed, Language and Linguistics, Hispania, 79- *Mem:* Am Asn Teachers Span & Port; Ling Soc Am. *Res:* Latin American language and literature; Portuguese language; linguistics, especially Spanish. *Publ:* Auth, Angel Ganivet and the study of language, Romance Notes, spring 69; Ambiguity and the English gerund, Lingua, 70; Complementos de adjectivo del genitivo, Hispania, 71; coauth, Gramatica Analitica, DC Heath, 76; The determiner & adjective phrase in Spanish, Hispania, 81. *Mailing Add:* Dept of Modern Lang & Lit Univ of the Pacific Stockton CA 95211

WONG, SHIRLEEN SAO-WAN, b Macao, July 14, 40. CHINESE LANGUAGE & LITERATURE. *Educ:* Skidmore Col, BA, 61; Columbia Univ, MA, 63; Univ Wash, PhD(Chinese lit), 70. *Prof Exp:* Asst prof, 70-75, ASSOC PROF ORIENT LANG, UNIV CALIF, LOS ANGELES, 75- *Mem:* Asn Asian Studies. *Res:* Classical Chinese poetry. *Publ:* Auth, The quatrains of Tu Fu, Monumenta Serica, 70-71; Kung Tzu-chen, Twayne's World Auth Ser, 75. *Mailing Add:* Dept of Oriental Languages Univ of Calif Los Angeles CA 90024

WOO, CATHERINE YI-YU CHO, b Peking, China, May 23, 35; US citizen; m 57; c 2. CHINESE LANGUAGE & LITERATURE. *Educ:* San Diego State Univ, BA, 68, MA, 72; SChina Univ, LLD, 78. *Hon Degrees:* EdD, Univ San Francisco, 81. *Prof Exp:* ASSOC PROF CHINESE LANG & LIT, SAN DIEGO STATE UNIV, 70- *Concurrent Pos:* Bilingual educ teacher trainer fel Chinese, HEW, 78. *Mem:* Chinese Lang Teachers Asn; Asn Asian Studies. *Res:* Chinese poetry; Chinese painting; Chinese calligraphy. *Publ:* Auth, Stroke Order Chat, Calif State Univ, San Diego, 73; contribr, Our Own Thing--Contemporary Thought in Poetry, Prentice-Hall, 73; auth, Thousand Year Pine, For All the Tender Hearts Under Heaven, Dah Chung, Taipei, 74; four poems, Chinese Pen, Taipei Chinese Ctr Int PEN, autumn 76; Man-nature relationship in Chinese poetry, 2/78 & The beauty of the non-descriptive in Chinese painting and calligraphy, 2/79, J Chinese Lang Teachers Asn; coauth, Magic of the Brush, Art Bk Co Ltd, Taipei, 81; auth, Chinese poetry and painting--some observations on their interrelationship, Monumenta Serica (in prep). *Mailing Add:* Dept of Class & Orient Lang & Lit San Diego State Univ San Diego CA 92182

WOOD, ALLEN GEORGE, b Cedar Falls, Iowa, May 13, 50; m 72; c 2. FRENCH & COMPARATIVE LITERATURE. *Educ:* Univ Northern Iowa, BA, 72; Univ Mich, Ann Arbor, MA, 73, PhD(comp lit), 78. *Prof Exp:* Instr French, Ohio State Univ, 78-80; ASST PROF FRENCH, MARQUETTE UNIV, 80- *Mem:* MLA; Am Asn Teacher French; Am Comp Lit Asn; NAm Soc Seventeenth Century French Lit; Midwest Mod Lang Asn. *Res:* Satire; neoclassical drama; francophonic literature. *Publ:* Co-ed, A Conversation with Stanley Fish & ed, Rackham Literary Studies, spring 78; The Regent du Parnasse and Vraisemblance, French Forum, 9/78; Murder in the Seraglio: Orientalism in 17th century tragedy, 1/80 & Les noms places dans les niches: Satires and sermons, 1/82, Papers on French Seventeenth Century Lit; The end of dawn: Poetic closure in the Baroque Belle Matineuse, Esprit Createur, winter 80. *Mailing Add:* Dept of Foreign Lang Marquette Univ Milwaukee WI 53218

WOOD, CAROL JEAN LLOYD, Medieval Literature, Linguistics. See Vol II

WOOD, FRANK BOARDMAN, b Bangor, Maine, Nov 5, 22; m 48; c 5. ROMANCE LANGUAGES. *Educ:* Univ Maine, AB, 48; Univ Iowa, MA, 50, PhD(Romance lang), 53. *Prof Exp:* Teaching asst French, Univ Iowa, 48-53; from asst prof French, Span & Ger to assoc prof French & Ital, 53-63, chmn dept foreign lang, 53-66, 74-76, coordr, 66-79, PROF FRENCH, HUMBOLDT STATE UNIV, 63- *Mem:* Am Asn Teachers Fr; AAUP. *Res:* Baudelaire and the symbolists; 17th century dramatists. *Mailing Add:* Dept of Foreign Lang Humboldt State Univ Arcata CA 95521

WOOD, JOHN SINCLAIR, b Hastings, Eng, Oct 27, 08; m 50; c 2. FRENCH. *Educ:* Univ London, BA, 31, dipl, 32; Univ Paris, DUniv, 34. *Prof Exp:* Lectr French, London Sch Econ, 35-39 & Univ Birmingham, 46-49; vis prof, 49-50, prof, 50-67, chmn dept French, 50-52, Gooderham prof, 67-77, EMER PROF FRENCH, VICTORIA COL, UNIV TORONTO, 77- *Concurrent Pos:* Nuffield res fel, 52; traducteur agree French-English, Fed Transl Bur, Secy of State, Ottawa, 77- *Mem:* Humanities Asn Can; Asn Can

Univ Teachers Fr. *Res:* Nineteenth century French novel. *Publ:* Auth, Un aspect du mouvement traditionaliste et social dans la litterature francaise contemporaine: Rene Bazin, sa vie et son oeuvre; transl, Dictionary of Canadian Biography, Univ Toronto; auth, Les Goncourt et le realisme, Romanic Rev; Sondages dans le roman francais au point de vue social, Rev hist Litteraire France; Sondages 1830-48: Romanciers francais secondaires, Univ Toronto, 65; Hector Malot, La Guerre de 1870, et la commune, Soc Hist Litteraire France, 72; La Mythologie sociale dans Les Mystere de Paris, d'Eugene Sue, In: Lecture socioeritique du texte romanesque, Hakkert and Co, Toronto, 75; La Correspondance Josephy Reinach-Emile Zola, Cahiers naturalistes, 77. *Mailing Add:* Dept of French Victoria Col Univ of Toronto Toronto ON M5S 1V4 Can

WOOD, MARY ELIZABETH, b Washington Court House, Ohio, Sept 7, 16. FOREIGN LANGUAGES. *Educ:* Denison Univ, AB, 38; Tex Woman's Univ, MA, 45; Univ d'Aix-Marseille, cert French lang & lit, 50. *Prof Exp:* Instr Span, English & sci, Washington High Sch, Washington Court House, 38-45; assoc prof, 45-79, EMER ASSOC PROF FOREIGN LANG, BALL STATE UNIV, 79- *Honors & Awards:* Recipient, McClintock Award, Ball State Univ, 71. *Mem:* Nat League Am Pen Women; Am Friends of Lafayette. *Res:* French influence in Indiana and the Ohio Valley. *Publ:* Auth, Indiana's fascinating French heritage, Ind Teacher, 71; French Imprint on the Heart of America, Unigraphic, 76 & Bookmark, 77. *Mailing Add:* Dept of Foreign Lang Ball State Univ Muncie IN 47306

WOOD, PAUL WILLIAM, b Cincinnati, Ohio, Mar 24, 33; m 60; c 4. FRENCH LANGUAGE & LITERATURE. *Educ:* Athenaeum of Ohio, BA, 54; Univ of Cincinnati, MA, 60; Northwestern Univ, Evanston, PhD(French), 70. *Prof Exp:* High sch teacher French & Latin, Forest Hills Sch Dist, Ohio, 60-62; instr French, Loyola Univ Chicago, 62-67; asst prof, Univ Akron, 67-71; asst prof, 71-76, ASSOC PROF FRENCH, ST BONAVENTURE UNIV, 76-, CHMN DEPT MOD LANG & LIT, 77- *Mem:* MLA; Am Asn Teachers Fr; Am Coun Teaching Foreign Lang; AAUP. *Res:* Modern French theatre; Moliere. *Publ:* Auth, How to Conduct a Language Fair (Filmstrip), NY State Asn Foreign Lang Teachers, 77; coauth, Student motivation: Try a foreign language day, Foreign Lang Annals/Accent on Am Coun Teachers For Lang, 2/78. *Mailing Add:* Dept of Modern Lang & Lit St Bonaventure Univ St Bonaventure NY 14778

WOODALL, NATALIE JOY, b Adams, NY, Jan 5, 46. CLASSICS. *Educ:* State Univ NY, Albany, BA, 68, MA, 69, PhD(classics), 72. *Prof Exp:* INSTR LATIN, FAIRPORT CENT SCH, 72- *Concurrent Pos:* Panelist, Nat Endowment for Humanities, 78-79; Newspaper Fund Jour fel, 82. *Mem:* Am Philol Asn; Vergilian Soc; Petronian Soc; Am Class League. *Res:* Roman history; mythology. *Publ:* Auth, Trimalchio's limping pentameters, Class J, 71; Review of Petronian poetry, 72 & Lucretian motifs in Petronius Satyricon, 76, Petronian Newslett; coauth, a Latin record of the opening of a Roman will, Herbert W Youtie Festschrift, 76; The King of the Phaeacians, Class Outlook, 1/77. *Mailing Add:* Fairport High Sch 1358 Ayrault Rd Fairport NY 14450

WOODBRIDGE, HENSLEY CHARLES, b Champaign, Ill, Feb 6, 23; m 53; c 1. SPANISH. *Educ:* Col William & Mary, AB, 43; Harvard Univ, MA, 46; Univ Ill, PhD(Span), 50, MSLS, 51; Lincoln Mem Univ, Tenn, DA, 76. *Prof Exp:* Instr French & Span, Univ Richmond, 46-47; teaching asst Span, Univ Ill, 48-50; ref librn, Ala Polytech Inst, 51-53; head librn, Murray State Col, 53-63; assoc prof foreign lang, 65-71; bibliogr Latin Am, 65-74, PROF FOREIGN LANG, SOUTHERN ILL UNIV, CARBONDALE, 71- *Concurrent Pos:* Assoc ed, Hispania, 67-81; contrib ed, Am Bk Collector; ed, Jack London Newslett. *Mem:* Am Asn Teachers Span & Port; MLA; Medieval Acad Am. *Res:* Spanish nautical terms; Jack London; Ruben Dario. *Publ:* Auth, Jesse Stuart: A Bibliography, Lincoln Mem Univ, 60; coauth, Ruben Dario y el cojo illustrado, Hisp Inst, Columbia Univ, 64; Jack London: A Bibliography, Talisman, 66 & Kraus, 73; Jesse & Jane Stuart: A Bibliography, 69 & 79; auth, Ruben Dario, 75 & Benito Perez Galdos, 75, Scarecrow; coauth, Printing in Colonial Spanish America, Whitston, 76. *Mailing Add:* Dept of Foreign Lang Southern Ill Univ Carbondale IL 62901

WOODBURY, LEONARD (ERNEST), b Regina, Sask, Aug 30, 18; m 44; c 2. CLASSICAL PHILOLOGY. *Educ:* Univ Man, BA, 40; Harvard Univ, AM, 42, PhD, 44. *Prof Exp:* Lectr classics, 45-48, from asst prof to assoc prof Greek, 48-59, head dept, 58-66, PROF CLASSICS, UNIV COL, UNIV TORONTO, 59- *Concurrent Pos:* Guggenheim fel, 56-57; Can Coun Leave fel, 73-74. *Mem:* Fel Royal Soc Can; Class Asn Can (pres, 74-76); Am Philol Asn; Brit Class Asn; Soc Ancient Greek Philos (pres, 64-66). *Res:* Early Greek poetry; Greek philosophy. *Publ:* Auth, The seal of Theognis, Studies Honour Gilbert Norwood Phoenix, Suppl I: 20-41; Parmenides on names, Harvard Studies Class Philol, 63; Equinox at Acragas: Pindar, OL 2 61-62, Trans Am Philol Asn, 79. *Mailing Add:* Univ Col Univ ot Toronto Toronto ON M5S 1A1 Can

WOODHOUSE, WILLIAM WALTON, III, b Raleigh, NC, Feb 8, 39; m 63; c 2. SPANISH LITERATURE. *Educ:* Univ NC, Chapel Hill, AB, 61; Univ Wis-Madison, MA, 63, PhD(Span), 76. *Prof Exp:* Instr Span, Univ Wis-Madison, 67-69 & Univ Minn, 69-75; asst prof, 76-81, ASSOC PROF SPAN, UNIV NC, WILMINGTON, 81- *Mem:* Am Asn Teachers Span & Port; SAtlantic Mod Lang Asn; Asoc Int de Hispanistas; Cervantes Soc Am. *Res:* Quevedo; 17th century Spanish poetry; satire. *Publ:* Auth, El soneto de Quevedo, 'Mientras que fui tabiques y desvanes,' sobre la Plaza Mayor de Madrid, Villa de Madrid, 12/75; Una sala de viuda: An interpretational and editorial problem in a quevedo sonnet, Romance Notes, 20: 376-380. *Mailing Add:* 6238 Trowbridge Dr Wilmington NC 28403

WOODMANSEE, MARTHA ANN, b Kansas City, Mo. GERMAN & COMPARATIVE LITERATURE. *Educ:* Northwestern Univ, BA, 68; Stanford Univ, MA, 69, PhD(Ger), 77. *Prof Exp:* Inst Ger, Univ Pittsburgh, 74-77; ASST PROF COMP LIT, NORTHWESTERN UNIV, EVANSTON, 77- *Concurrent Pos:* Fel, Ger Acad Exchange, 77; Andrew W Mellon Fel, Univ Pittsburgh, 79-80; fel Nat Humanities Ctr, 82-83; coordr, Sch Criticism

& Theory, 80-82. *Mem:* MLA; Am Studies Asn; Am Soc 18th Century Studies; Am Comp Lit Asn. *Res:* Aesthetics; theory of literature; history of criticism. *Publ:* Auth, Melville's Confidence Man, In: Der amerikanische Roman, Erich Schmidt Verlag, 74; The role and value of literature, In: Proceedings of the 42nd Annual Meeting of the American Association of Teachers of German, 75; Toward a coherent undergraduate curriculum, Monatshefte, 78; Speech Act Theory and the Perpetuation of the Dogma of Literary Autonomy, Centrum, 78; Deconstructing Deconstruction: Toward a History of Modern Criticism, In: Erkennen und Deuten, 82 & ed, Erkennen und Deuten, 82, Erich Schmidt Verlag. *Mailing Add:* Comp Lit Prog Northwestern Univ Evanston IL 60201

WOODS, JEAN MUIR, b Osceola, Iowa, Aug 1, 26; m 54. GERMAN. *Educ:* Wellesley Col, BA, 48; Univ Ore, MA, 65, PhD(Ger), 68. *Prof Exp:* Instr Ger, 67-69, asst prof, 69-79, ASSOC PROF GER, UNIV ORE, 79- *Concurrent Pos:* Wolfenbüttler Stipendium, 80. *Mem:* Am Asn Teachers Ger; Int Arbeitskreis Barockliteratur; Western Asn Ger Studies. *Res:* Seventeenth century German literature; German women writers; bibliography. *Publ:* Auth, Variation and expansion in the German lyric of the 17th century, Proc Pac Northwest Conf Foreign Lang, 69; Günter Grass: A selected bibliography, WCoast Rev, 71; Weckherlin's Ebenbild on Gustavus Adolphus and the Swedish intelligencer, Daphnis, 74; Memory and inspiration in Morike's Mozart auf des Reise nach Prag, Rev Lang Vivantes, 75; A rhythmic theme in Schiller's Die Jungfrau von Orleans, Ger Studies Rev, 78; Die Pflicht befihlet mir/zu schreiben und zu tichten: Drei literarisch tätige Frauen aus dem Hause Baden-Durlach, In: Die Frau von der Reformation zur Romantik, Bouvier, Bonn, 80. *Mailing Add:* Dept of Ger Univ of Ore Eugene OR 97403

WOODS, MARJORIE CURRY, Medieval & English Literature. See Vol II

WOODYARD, GEORGE W, b Charleston, Ill, Nov 18, 34; m 60; c 4. SPANISH. *Educ:* Eastern Ill Univ, BS in Ed, 54; NMex State Univ, MA, 55; Univ Ill, PhD(Span), 66. *Prof Exp:* Teacher, Palatine High Sch, 55-57 & Riverside-Brookfield High Sch, 59-61; instr Span, Eastern Ill Univ, 61-63 & Univ Ill, 65-66; from asst prof to assoc prof, 66-76, PROF SPAN, UNIV KANS, 76-, CHMN DEPT SPAN & PORT, 74-, ASSOC DEAN GRAD SCH, 80- *Concurrent Pos:* Ed, Latin Am Theatre Rev. *Mem:* MLA; Am Asn Teachers Span & Port. *Res:* Latin American theatre. *Publ:* Auth, The theatre of the absurd in Spanish America, Comp Drama, 69; ed, The Modern Stage in Latin America: Six Plays, Dutton, 71; auth, Toward a radical theatre in Spanish America, Contemp Latin Am Lit, 73; A metaphor for repression: Two Portuguese inquisition plays, Luso-Brazilian Rev, 73; El teatro de Oscar Villegas, Texto Critico, 78; Language and tensions in Jose Agustin's theatre, Hispania, 80. *Mailing Add:* Dept of Span & Port Univ of Kansas Lawrence KS 66045

WOOLEY, ALLAN D, b Rumford, Maine, Jan 2, 24, 36. CLASSICAL PHILOLOGY. *Educ:* Princeton Univ, PhD, 62. *Prof Exp:* Asst instr, Princeton Univ, 59-61; from instr to instr classics, Duke Univ, 62-67; asst prof Latin, Gould Acad, Bethel, Maine, 67-68; INSTR CLASSICS, PHILLIPS EXETER ACAD, 68- *Mem:* Am Philol Asn. *Res:* Plato; Vergil; ancient philosophy, mythology. *Mailing Add:* Dept of Class Studies Ewald Hall Phillips Exeter Acad Exeter NH 03833

WOOLLEY, DALE EDWARD, b Decatur, Ill, Dec 20, 36. LINGUISTICS, SPEECH SCIENCE. *Educ:* Wash Univ, AB, 58; Univ Ill, AM, 60, PhD(speech sci & ling), 68. *Prof Exp:* Educ consult & lectr space sci, Nat Aeronautics & Space Admin, 64-65; instr English, Northwestern Univ, 65-66; asst prof ling, 66-76, ASSOC PROF LING, UNIV ILL, CHICAGO, 76- *Concurrent Pos:* USPHS fel, 68-69. *Mem:* Ling Soc Am. *Res:* Phonetics; speech perception; English phonology. *Mailing Add:* Dept of Ling Univ Illinois Chicago IL 60680

WOOLSEY, WALLACE, b Yoakum, Tex, May 1, 06; m 33; c 1. FOREIGN LANGUAGES. *Educ:* Univ Tex, AB, 29, AM, 30, PhD, 45. *Prof Exp:* Prof, Harding Col, 31-33; instr high sch, Tex, 34-41; teaching fel, Univ Tex, 41-42; prof foreign lang, Tex Woman's Univ, 44-74, chmn dept, 53-74; RETIRED. *Mem:* MLA; Am Asn Teachers Span & Port; SCent Mod Lang Asn; Am Coun Teaching Foreign Lang; Am Transl Asn. *Res:* Spanish drama; el mundo Espanol; actividades hispanicas. *Publ:* Auth, Cultural Mission No 53, San Pablo Huixtepec, Oaxaca, Mod Lang J, 1/64; transl, The Witch of Trazmoz (tales & poems from Becquer), Olympic, 65; auth, Buero Vallejo: Versatile Spanish dramatist, SCent Bull, winter 66; transl, La Celestia, Las Americas, 68; auth, Man's tryst with death as an element of Sastre's dramatic art, SCent Bull, winter 69; transl, Dreams from Quevedo, Barron's Educ Ser, 76; Zavala, Journey to the United States of America, Shoal Creek Publ, 80. *Mailing Add:* 619 Grove St Denton TX 76201

WOOTEN, CECIL WILLIAM, b Kinston, NC, July 21, 45. FRENCH, CLASSICS. *Educ:* Davidson Col, AB, 67; Univ NC, Chapel Hill, MA, 68; Middlebury Col, MA, 73; Univ NC, Chapel Hill, PhD(classics), 72. *Prof Exp:* Instr Latin, Col William & Mary, 69-70, instr French, 70-71; instr classics, Univ NC, Chapel Hill, 73-74; asst prof class studies, Ind Univ, Bloomington, 74-80; ASSOC PROF CLASSICS, UNIV NC, CHAPEL HILL, 81- *Mem:* Am Philol Asn; Int Soc Study of Hist Rhet. *Res:* Latin and Greek rhetoric and oratory; grammar. *Publ:* Auth, The ambassador's· speech: A particularly Hellenistic genre of oratory, Quart J Speech, 73; The speeches in Polybius: An insight into the nature of Hellenistic oratory, Am J Philol, 74; Le developpement du style oratoire asiatique pendant la periode Hellenistique, Revue des Etudes Grecques, 75; Petronius, the mime, and rhetorical education, Helios, 76; Cicero's reactions to Demosthenes: A clarification, Class J, 77; A few observations on form and content in Demosthenes, Phoenix, 77; Qualche osservazione intorno all'uso di metafore e di similitudini nelle orazioni di Demostene, Quaderni Urbinati (in press). *Mailing Add:* Dept Class Studies Univ NC Chapel Hill NC 27514

WORKMAN, JOHN ROWE, b Lancaster, Pa, June 3, 18. CLASSICAL PHILOLOGY. *Educ:* Princeton Univ, AB, 40, PhD, 44. *Prof Exp:* Instr, Princeton Univ, 43; master Greek & Latin, St Mark's Sch, Southborough, Mass, 44-47; from instr to assoc prof classics, 47-66, asst dean col, 51-52, chmn dept classics, 59-66, PROF CLASSICS, BROWN UNIV, 66- *Concurrent Pos:* Carnegie vis asst prof, Columbia Univ, 52-53; Fulbright fel, Univ Edinburgh, 53-54. *Mem:* Am Philol Asn; Am Sch Class Studies, Athens. *Res:* Ancient philosophical terminology; economic history; comparative literature. *Publ:* Auth, Arx Antiqua; A Term of College Latin; New Horizons of Higher Education, Pub Affairs, 59. *Mailing Add:* Dept of Classics Brown University Providence RI 02912

WORMHOUDT, ARTHUR LOUIS, b Pella, Iowa, June 17, 17; m 48; c 1. FOREIGN LANGUAGE, ENGLISH. *Educ:* State Univ Iowa, BR, 39, PhD(English), 42; Harvard Univ, MA, 40. *Prof Exp:* Assoc prof English, St Cloud State Col, 49-57, prof lang & lit, 58-74, Eltse prof, 74-79, ELTSE EMER PROF ENGLISH, WILLIAM PENN COL, 79- *Mem:* MLA; Am Asn Teachers Arabic. *Res:* Theory of literature; translation of classical Arabic literature. *Publ:* Auth, Newton and William law, J Hist Ideas, 49; The identification of words-milk, 49 & Five layer structure of sublimation, 56, Am Imago; Hamlet's Mousetrap, Philos Libr, 56; The Five Books as Literature: Shakespeare Head, 61; Poems of Al Mutanabbi, Basil Blackwell, 68. *Mailing Add:* Dept of Language & Literature William Penn Col Oskaloosa IA 52577

WORTH, DEAN STODDARD, b Brooklyn, NY, Sept 30, 27; m 53; c 1. SLAVIC LINGUISTICS. *Educ:* Dartmouth Col, AB, 49; Ecole Langues Orient, Paris, dipl, 52; Sorbonne, cert, 52; Harvard Univ, AM, 53, PhD, 56. *Prof Exp:* Res fel, Russ Res Ctr, Harvard Univ, 56-57; from asst prof to assoc prof Slavic lang, 57-65, PROF SLAVIC LANG, UNIV CALIF, LOS ANGELES, 65- *Concurrent Pos:* Secy, Am Comt Slavists, 60-, chmn, 78-; Guggenheim fel, 63-64; fel, Konnan Inst Advan Russ Studies (Wilson Ctr), 78-79. *Mem:* Am Asn Advan Slavic Studies; Ling Soc Am; Medieval Acad Am; Am Asn Teachers Slavic & East Europ Lang; Ling Soc Europe. *Res:* Paleosiberian languages; Old Russian literature. *Publ:* Ed, Kamchadal Texts Collected by W Jochelson, 61, coauth, Sofonija's Tale of the Russian-Tatar Battle on the Kulikovo Field, 63 & Selected Bibliography of Slavic Linguistics, Vol I, 66, Vol II, 68, Mouton, The Hague; Russian Derivational Dictionary, Am Elsevier, 72; auth, Dictionary of Western Kamchadal, Univ Calif, 72; A Bibliography of Russian Word-Formation, Slavica, 77; On the Structure and History of Russian, Selected Essays, Sagner, 77. *Mailing Add:* 300 Bellino Dr Pacific Palisades CA 90272

WORTH, FABIENNE ANDRE, b Lyon, France, May 24, 44, m 67; c 2. FRENCH LITERATURE, CINEMA. *Educ:* Univ NC, Chapel Hill, BA, 70, MA, 73, PhD(comp lit), 79. *Prof Exp:* Vis lectr, 78-79, VIS LECTR FRENCH LIT, DUKE UNIV, 80- *Concurrent Pos:* Instr, French Cinema Arts Sch, Carrboro, NC, 80. *Mem:* MLA; Am Asn Teachers Fr; Am Comp Lit Asn. *Res:* History and the novel; authorship in the cinema. *Publ:* Auth, Importer la France dans votre salle de classe: Telefrance USA, Am Asn Teachers Fr Bull, 11/81; Report on the 1981 MLA sessions on film, Quart Rev Film Studies, winter 82. *Mailing Add:* 209 Pritchard Ave Chapel Hill NC 27514

WORTHEN, THOMAS DE VOE, b Salt Lake City, Utah, Aug 18, 37; c 2. CLASSICS. *Educ:* Univ Utah, BA, 59; Univ Wash, MA, 63, PhD(classics), 68. *Prof Exp:* Lectr, 65-68, asst prof, 68-72, ASSOC PROF GREEK, UNIV ARIZ, 72- *Mem:* Am Philol Asn; Rocky Mountain Lang Asn. *Res:* Greek drama; Greek ethnoastronomy. *Publ:* Auth, Pneumatic action in the Klepsydra and Empedocles' account of breathing, Isis, 70; Note on Ajax 494-5, Class Philol, 72. *Mailing Add:* Dept of Classics Univ Ariz Tucson AZ 85721

WORTLEY, W VICTOR, b Portadown, Northern Ireland, Aug 29, 29; div; c 2. ROMANCE LANGUAGES. *Educ:* Univ Ore, BA, 59, MA, 61, PhD(Romance lang), 64. *Prof Exp:* Asst prof French, Whitman Col, 63-65; asst prof, 65-77, PROF FRENCH, UNIV WASH, 77- *Mem:* Am Asn Teachers Fr; Philol Asn Pac Coast. *Res:* French 17th century prose and drama; French 16th century prose. *Publ:* Auth, Tallemant des Reaux: The Man Through His Style, Mouton, The Hague, 69; From Pantagruel to Gargantua: the development of an action scene, 68 & Horace's Crime Passionnel, Vol 14, Romance Notes; Moliere's Henriette: An Imbalance Between Raison and Coeur, Romance Notes, Vol 19, 79; Soon It would be June (novelette), 5/78, The Baby (story), 5/79 & Land (story), 5/81, J Irish Lit; Perceptions and Misperceptions: A European Cleric's View of the American Indian, Pac Northwest Quart, 10/81. *Mailing Add:* 122 N 59th St Seattle WA 98108

WOSHINSKY, BARBARA REISMAN, b Los Angeles, Calif, Jan 21, 42. FRENCH LITERATURE. *Educ:* Oberlin Col, BA, 63; Univ Paris, dipl, 62; Yale Univ, PhD(French), 68. *Prof Exp:* Asst prof French, Edinboro State Col, 70-71, Colby Col, 73-74 & Boston Univ, 75-79; ASST PROF FRENCH, UNIV MIAMI, 81- *Concurrent Pos:* Vis asst prof, Kenyon Col, 69-70; fel, Bunting Inst of Radcliffe Col, 79-80; vis asst prof, Clark Univ, 80-81. *Mem:* MLA; NAm Soc for 17th Century French Lit; Int Asn Philos & Lit. *Res:* Epistemology of French classical literature; textual history of La Biuyeneo Caraeteres; French classical drama. *Publ:* Auth, La Princesse de Cleves: The Tension of Elegance, Mouton, 73; Rhetorical vision in Le Cid, French Forum, 5/79; Truth in literature: The little man who wasn't there, Radcliffe Col Bunting Inst Working Papers, 80; Pascal's Penseco and the discourse of the inexpressible, 81 & Shattered speech: La Bruyere, De Lacour, 81, Papers on French 17th Century Lit; Biblical discourse: Reading the unreadable, Esprit Createur, summer 81; The discourse of disbelief in Moliere's Dom Juan, Romanic Rev, 11/81; coauth, La France et la Francophonie, Random House, 82. *Mailing Add:* Dept of Foreign Lang Box 248093 Univ of Miami Coral Gables FL 33176

WRAGE, MARIE-CLAIRE CONNES, b Dijon, France, Dec 31, 33; m 59; c 2. FRENCH RENAISSANCE LITERATURE. *Educ:* Acad Dijon, Baccalaureat, 53; Univ Dijon, lic, 57; Univ Wis-Madison, MA, 62, PhD(French), 68. *Prof Exp:* From instr to asst prof French, Western Col, Miami Univ, 63-68; lectr French, 69-70, asst prof, 70-75, ASSOC PROF FRENCH, OHIO UNIV, 75- *Concurrent Pos:* Lectrice French, Univ Sheffield, 57-58; asst, Univ Wis-Madison, 58-63. *Mem:* Am Asn Teachers Fr. *Res:* French stylistics; 16th century French literature; regional literature. *Publ:* Contribr, Introductory French Reader, Macmillan, 63; auth, Sceve's Delie, Explicator, 66; L'enseignement du Francais aux Etats-Unis, Bull Lycee Dijon, 72. *Mailing Add:* Dept of Modern Lang Ohio Univ Athens OH 65701

WRAGE, WILLIAM, b Lincoln, Ill, Jan 10, 36; m 59; c 2. FRENCH. *Educ:* Wash Univ, BA, 57; Univ Wis-Madison, MA, 60, PhD(French), 64. *Prof Exp:* From instr to asst prof French, Miami Univ, 63-69, adv studies abroad, 66-69; assoc prof, 69-73, grad chmn mod lang, 70-72 & 77-80, chmn dept mod lang, 72-77, grad chmn mod lang, 77-80, PROF FRENCH, OHIO UNIV, 73- *Mem:* Am Asn Teachers Fr. *Res:* French civilization; 18th century French literature. *Mailing Add:* Dept of Mod Lang Ohio Univ Athens OH 45701

WRENN, JAMES JOSEPH, b New Haven, Conn, July 7, 26; m 53; c 4. CHINESE LANGUAGE & LITERATURE. *Educ:* Yale Univ, BA, 53, PhD(Chinese lang & lit), 64. *Prof Exp:* Dir Chinese studies, Inter-Univ Fel Prog, 59-60; lectr Chinese, Yale Univ, 60-62; lectr, 62-64, asst prof, 64-67, assoc prof ling, 67-73, PROF LING, BROWN UNIV, 73- *Concurrent Pos:* Occasional consult, Ctr Applied Ling, Am Math Soc & Responsive Environments Corp; dir, Inter-Univ Prog Chinese Lang Training, Taipe, 70-71; mem planning coun, Chinese Core Curric Proj, Foreign Serv Inst, 74- *Mem:* MLA; Am Coun Teaching Foreign Lang; Chinese Lang Teachers Asn (secy-treas, 60-63); Asn Asian Studies. *Res:* Textual criticism; programmed learning; computer assisted instruction. *Publ:* Auth, Textual method in Chinese with illustrative examples, Tsing Hua J Chinese Studies, 12/67; The dialogue in the classroom, J Chinese Lang Teachers Asn, 2/68; Chinese language teaching in the United States: The state of the art, Educ Resources Inform Ctr Ling, 9/68. *Mailing Add:* Box E Brown Station Providence RI 02912

WRIGHT, ALFRED JOHN, JR, b Lakewood, Ohio, Sept 6, 15; m 46; c 4. ROMANCE LANGUAGES. *Educ:* Western Reserve Univ, AB, 37, AM, 38; Columbia Univ, PhD(French), 50. *Prof Exp:* Master French, Span & Latin, Roosevelt Mil Acad, 39-40 & Los Alamos Rance Sch, 40-42; master Span & Ger, Trinity Pawling Sch, 47-48; asst prof Romance lang, Trinity Col, Conn, 49-56; PROF FRENCH & CHMN DEPT FOREIGN LANG & LIT, BATES COL, 58- *Concurrent Pos:* Instr, Hartt Col Music, 50-51; lectr, Hartford Br, Univ Conn, 55-56; vis fel Romance lang, Harvard Univ, 73. *Mem:* AAUP; MLA; Am Asn Teachers French. *Res:* Contemporary French literature; 19th century French poetry; foreign language teaching techniques. *Publ:* Auth, Translation of Hugo's Les Djinns, Poet Lore; Verlaine's Art Poetique reexamined, PMLA; auth, Verlaine and Debussy: Fetes Galantes, Fr Rev, 4/67; Paroles et Musique-Verlaine's Composers, 19th Century Fr Studies, spring-summer 77; contribr, French XX Bibliography, Fr Inst-Alliance Francaise & Camargo Found, 54-56 & 58-77. *Mailing Add:* Bates College Lewiston ME 04240

WRIGHT, CHAD CARLYLE, b Hinckley, Utah. SPANISH LITERATURE. *Educ:* Brigham Young Univ, BA, 64, MA, 66; Harvard Univ, PhD(Span lit), 76. *Prof Exp:* Instr Span, Univ Mass, Boston, 70-73 & 74-75; ASST PROF SPAN UNIV VA, 76- *Concurrent Pos:* Res comp lit, Oxford Univ, 73-74 & 75-76 Mem MLA; SAtlantic Mod Lang Asn; Harvard Mellon fac fel, 80-81. *Res:* The novel; comparative literature; 19th century Spanish literature. *Publ:* Auth, The symbolism of Isidora de Rufete's house and her son Riquin in La Desheredada, Romanische Forschungen, 70; Imagery of light and darkness in Galdos' La de Bringas, 78 & Artifacts and effigies: The Porreno household revisited, 79, Anales Galdosianos; Secret space, In: Galdos La de Bringas, Hisp Rev, Vol 58, 82; Lo prohibido: Las cuatro paredes de la Restauracion, MLN, Vol 97, 82. *Mailing Add:* Dept of Spanish, Italian & Port Univ of Virginia 301 Cabell Hall Charlottesville VA 22903

WRIGHT, DONALD EDWARD, b Crystal City, Mo, Oct 20, 37; m 61; c 2. LINGUISTICS, MEDIEVAL LITERATURE. *Educ:* St Louis Univ, BS, 59, AM, 66. *Prof Exp:* Instr English, Monticello Col, 63-65 & Bradley Univ, 65-67; asst prof, 67-71, ASSOC PROF ENGLISH, ST XAVIER COL, 71- *Concurrent Pos:* Mem bibliog comt, MLA, 70- *Mem:* MLA; Ling Soc Am. *Res:* Indo-European, Celtic and Germanic linguistics. *Publ:* Contribr, bibliog entries in Celtic ling, Albanian ling & comp & hist ling sect, MLA int bibliog of bks and articles on the mod lang & lit, 70- *Mailing Add:* Dept of English Xavier Col Chicago IL 60655

WRIGHT, ELIZABETH CATHERINE, b Washington, DC, Sept 8, 43. FRENCH LANGUAGE & LITERATURE. *Educ:* Sarah Lawrence Col, BA, 65; Hunter Col, MA, 67; NY Univ, PhD(French lang & lit), 75. *Prof Exp:* Asst prof, 73-80, ASSOC PROF FRENCH, SAN FRANCISCO STATE UNIV, 80- *Concurrent Pos:* Camargo Found fel, 82. *Mem:* MLA; Women's Caucus Mod Lang; Renaissance Soc Am. *Res:* French Renaissance literature; French medieval literature; French women writers. *Mailing Add:* Dept of Foreign Lang San Francisco State Univ San Francisco CA 94132

WRIGHT, JAMES RICHARD, b Cleveland, Ohio, Dec 15, 34; m 61. LINGUISTICS, SPANISH. *Educ:* Northwestern Univ, BA, 56; Middlebury Col, MA, 60; Ind Univ, MA, 68, PhD(ling), 72. *Prof Exp:* Instr Span, Rollins Col, 60-62; lectr English & foreign lang, Univ of Andes & Univ Bogota, Colombia, 62-64; asst prof ling, 69-76, ASSOC PROF LING, E CAROLINA UNIV: 76- *Concurrent Pos:* NDEA fel ling, Ind Univ, 65-68. *Mem:* Ling Soc Am; Mountain Interstate Foreign Lang Conf; Southeast Conf Ling. *Res:* Linguistic theory; generative semantics; computational linguistics. *Publ:* Contribr, Avoiding ambiguity and doublespeak in technical writing, Teaching English in the Two-Year College (vol 2), fall 75; Linguistics in the teaching of Standard English, Teaching English in the Two-Year College (vol 3), fall 76; Linguistic theory applied to dialect reshaping, 11/77 & Computer-based linguistic analysis, 1/78, ERIC Clearinghouse for Lang & Ling. *Mailing Add:* Dept of English E Carolina Univ Greenville NC 27834

WRIGHT, JOHN (HENRY), b New York, NY, Mar 9, 41; m 62; c 2. CLASSICS, MEDIEVAL LITERATURE. *Educ:* Swarthmore Col, BA, 62; Ind Univ, Bloomington, MA, 64, PhD(classics), 71. *Prof Exp:* From instr to asst prof classic, Univ Rochester, 68-75; assoc prof, 75-77, PROF CLASSICS, NORTHWESTERN UNIV, 77-, CHMN DEPT, 78- *Concurrent Pos:* Fel Am Acad in Rome, 68; Nat Endowment for Humanities younger humanist fel, 73-74; dir, Lang of the Masters Freshman Sem Prof, Nat Endowment for Humanities grant, 78-79. *Mem:* Am Philol Asn. *Res:* Roman comedy; Medieval Latin; Medieval Italian. *Publ:* Auth, The play of Antichrist, Pontif Inst Mediaeval Studies, 67; Homer and elementary Greek, Class J, 72; Dancing in Chains: The Stylistic Unity of the Comoedia Palliata, Am Acad Rome, 74; The transformations of Pseudolus, Trans Am Philol Asn, 75; The Life of Cola di Rienzo, Pontif Inst Mediaeval Studies, 75; Publishing in North American classical periodicals: a survey, Class J, 77; Essays on the Iliad: Selected Modern Criticism, Ind Univ, 78; Plautus, Curculio: Introduction and Notes, Scholars Press, 81. *Mailing Add:* Dept of Classics Northwestern Univ Evanston IL 60201

WRIGHT, ROCHELLE ANN, b Lansing, Mich, Oct 31, 50. SCANDINAVIAN & COMPARATIVE LITERATURE. *Educ:* Univ Wash, BA(Ger) & BA(Swed), 70, MA, 71, PhD(Scand), 75. *Prof Exp:* Teaching asst Swed, Univ Wash, 72; teacher English, Kursverksamheten vid Stockholms Univ, 74; vis lectr, Swed & Scand lit, Univ Va, 75; asst prof, 75-82, ASSOC PROF SWED & SCAND LIT, UNIV ILL, 82- *Mem:* Soc Advan Scand Study; Am-Scand Found; Swed Pioneer Hist Soc. *Res:* The image of America and the Scandinavian emigrant and immigrant in Scandinavian and Scandinavian-American literature; Swedish proletarian writers; comparative literature, Scandinavian-German literary relations. *Publ:* Auth, Stuart Engstrand & Bishop Hill, Swed Pioneer Hist Quart, 7/77; auth, Bergman's Wild Strawberries and Söderberg's Doctor Glas, Purdue Film Studies Ann, 78; Kerstin Ekman: Voice of the vulnerable, World Lit Today, spring 81; From Farm to Factory: Walter Dickson's Urban Immigrants, Edda, 81; Strindberg's Ett drömspel and Hofmannsthal's Die Frau ohne Schatten, In: Structures of Influence: A Comparative Approach to August Strindberg, Univ NC Press, 81; coauth (with Robert L Wright), Danish Emigrant Ballads and Songs, Southern Ill Univ Press, 82; auth, Pär Lagerkvist & Vilhelm Moberg, In: Encycl of World Literature in the Twentieth Century (in prep). *Mailing Add:* Dept of Ger Lang & Lit Univ of Ill Urbana IL 61801

WRUCK, ERICH-OSKAR JOACHIM SIEGFRIED, b Ger, Oct 29, 28; US citizen; m 53; c 3. GERMAN. *Educ:* Rutgers Univ, BA, 59, MA, 61, PhD(Ger lit), 69. *Prof Exp:* Asst instr Ger, Rutgers Univ, 59-62; asst prof, 62-69, dir jr yr prog, Marburg, 66-67, 71-72, ASSOC PROF GER, DAVIDSON COL, 69- *Concurrent Pos:* Mem consult fac, US Army Command & Gen Staff Col, 74- *Mem:* Am Asn Teachers Ger; Freies Deut Hochstift; Goethe Ges; Schiller Ges; Hebbel Ges. *Res:* German classical and romantic period; Goethe, Moerike. *Mailing Add:* 501 Pine Rd Davidson NC 28036

WU, PEI-YI, b Nanking, China, Dec 3, 27; US citizen. CHINESE LITERATURE, INTELLECTUAL HISTORY. *Educ:* Nat Cent Univ, Nanking, AB, 50; Boston Univ, MA, 52; Columbia Univ, PhD(Chinese lit), 69. *Prof Exp:* Ibstr Chinese, Army Lang Sch, 53-58; res linguist, Univ Calif, Berkeley, 58-59; preceptor, Columbia Univ, 62-63; instr, 63-66, lectr, 66-67; vis assoc prof, 67-69, ASSOC PROF CHINESE, QUEENS COL, 69- *Concurrent Pos:* Mem univ fac senate, City Univ New York, 71-74; vis assoc prof, Columbia Univ, 72-; Nat Endowment for Humanities fel, 74. *Mem:* Am Orient Soc; Asn Asian Studies. *Res:* Chinese autobiography and myth. *Publ:* Auth,Biography of Ho Hsin-yin, In: Draft Ming Biographies, 70; Rhetorical devices in a Ming short story, Studies Short Fiction, spring 73; The spiritual autobiography of Te-Ch'ing, In: The Unfolding of Neo-Confucianism, Columbia Univ, 74. *Mailing Add:* Dept of Class & Orient Lang Queens Col Flushing NY 11367

WULBERN, JULIAN H, b Shanghai, China; US citizen; m 67; c 1. GERMAN, COMPARATIVE LITERATURE. *Educ:* Univ Calif, Berkeley, AB, 50; Univ Colo, MA, 62; Northwestern Univ, PhD(Ger), 67. *Prof Exp:* Teacher English,Grossmont High Sch, 53-54; teacher English & Ger, Covina High Sch, 54-58, 59-61; Fulbright exchange teacher English,Bundesstaatliche Frauenoberschule, Graz, 58-59; instr Ger & English, Foothill Col, 62-64; from asst prof to assoc prof, 66-73, PROF GER, SAN DIEGO STATE UNIV, 73- *Concurrent Pos:* Fulbright-Hays sr res grant, Univ Cologne, 73-74; resident dir, Calif State Univ & Col Syst Int Prog, Univ Heidelberg, 74-75. *Mem:* MLA; Am Asn Teachers Ger. *Res:* Modern European drama. *Publ:* Auth, Brecht and Ionesco: Commitment in Context, Univ Ill, 71, Scholar's Libr selection, fall 71; Theory and ideology in context, In: Brecht Heute: Erstes Jahrbuch der Internationallen Brecht-Gesellschaft, Athenäum, 71. *Mailing Add:* Dept of Ger & Slavic Lang & Lit San Diego State Univ San Diego CA 92182

WYATT, JAMES LARKIN, b Enid, Okla, Mar 7, 23; m 48; c 1. ROMANCE LANGUAGES, LINGUISTICS. *Educ:* Univ Tex, Austin, BA, 44, PhD(ling), 65; Nat Univ Mex, MA, 48, PhD(Span), 50. *Prof Exp:* Staff corresp, United Press Int, 44-47; asst prof Span, Univ Tex, Arlington, 48-51; asst cult attache, US Embassy, Rio de Janeiro, 51-53; coordr Latin Am rel & foreign studies adv, La State Univ, 53-57; prof Span & Port, Univ Tex, Arlington, 57-74, head dept foreign lang & lit, 57-69, assoc vpres acad affairs, 69-74; PROF ROMANCE LANG & LING & CHMN DEPT MOD LANG, FLA STATE UNIV, 74- *Mem:* Ling Soc Am; Am Asn Teachers Span & Port. *Res:* Spanish; Portuguese; English contrastive linguistics. *Publ:* Auth, Some general techniques for the structural analysis of Portuguese and Spanish, Comput Studies Humanities & Verbal Behav, 1/68; coauth, Modern Portuguese, A Project of the Modern Language Association, Knopf, 70; auth, Deep structure in a contrastive transformational grammar, In: Papers in Contrastive Linguistics, Cambridge Univ, 71; A Computer, Validated Portuguese to English Transformational Grammar, Mouton, The Hague, 72; Nominalized clauses in English and contrastive linguistics, In: Applied Contrastive Linguistics, Vol I, Proc 3rd Cong Int Asn Appl Ling, Copenhagen, 1972, Heidelberg, 74; SNOBOL 4 applications in natural language research, SIGLASH Newslett, 8/75; A contrastive sketch of some patterns of ellipsis, Contrastive Ling, Stuttgart, 77; Can function word distribution indicate authorship?, SIGLASH Newslett, Vol 13, 80. *Mailing Add:* Dept of Modern Languages Florida State Univ Tallahassee FL 32306

WYATT, JEAN MURDY, Comparative Literature. See Vol II

WYATT, WILLIAM F, JR, b Medford, Mass, July 14, 32; m 59; c 3. CLASSICS, LINGUISTICS. *Educ:* Bowdoin Col, Ab, 53; Harvard Univ, MA, 57, PhD(classics), 62. *Prof Exp:* Teaching asst, Tufts Univ, 59; from asst prof to assoc prof classics & ling, Univ Wash, 60-67; assoc prof classics, 67-70, chmn dept, 72-76, assoc dean fac & acad affairs, 76-78, PROF CLASSICS, BROWN UNIV, 70-, CHMN DEPT, 81- *Concurrent Pos:* Fel, Inst Res in Humanities, Univ Wis, 65-66; mem, RI Comn on Humanities, 72-79; vis prof, Col Yr in Athens, Greece, 73-74; dir, Am Philol Asn, 79-82. *Mem:* Am Philol Asn; Ling Soc Am; Mod Greek Studies Asn (vpres, 80); Am Sch Class Studies, Athens (secy, 75-80); Class Asn New England (pres, 83). *Res:* Anthropology; classical linguistics and philology. *Publ:* Auth, Metrical Lengthening in Homer, Ateneo, 69; Indo-European /a/, Univ Pa, 70; The Greek Prothetic Vowel, Case-Western Reserve Univ, 72; Anthropology and the Classics, Am Philol Asn, 77. *Mailing Add:* Dept of Classics Brown Univ Providence RI 02912

WYCZYNSKI, PAWEL, b Zelgoszcz, Poland, June 29, 21; nat US; m 51; c 1. FRENCH LITERATURE, SLAVIC STUDIES. *Educ:* Univ Lille, Lic es Lett, 49, dipl, 50; Univ Ottawa, PhD, 57. *Prof Exp:* Lectr Slavic civilization, Polish lit & lang, 51-53, lectr, French lit, 53-56; fromlectr to assoc prof, 56-63, PROF FRENCH CAN LIT, UNIV OTTAWA, 63- *Concurrent Pos:* Dir French Can Lit Res Ctr, Ottawa, 58-; chief ed, Arch Let Can, 60-; mem Royal Comn Bilingualism & Biculturalism, Can, 63- *Mem:* Asn Can Univ Teachers Er; Can Asn Slavists; Asn Can Authors; Roayl Soc Can; Soc Fr Hist Outre-Mer. *Publ:* Auth, Histoire et critique litteraire au Canada francais, In: Recherches sociographiques, Univ Laval, 64; coauth, Le roman canadian-grancais: Evolution, temoignages, bibliographie, Ed Fides, Montreal, 65; auth, Poesie et symbole, In: Collection Horizons, Libr Deom, Montreal, 65; coauth, Francois-Xavier Garneau: Aspects litteraire de son oeuvre, 66, auth, Edition critique du Voyage en Angleterre et en France dans les annees 1831, 1832, 1933 par Francois-Xavier Garneau, Univ Ottawa, 68; Emile Nelligan, In: Ecrivains canadiens d'aujoud'hui, Fides, Montreal & Paris, 68; Nelligan et la musique, 70 & Bibliographie descriptive et critique d'Emile Nelligan, 73, Univ Ottawa. *Mailing Add:* Dept of French Univ of Ottawa 550 Cumberland St Ottawa ON K1N 6N5 Can

WYERS, FRANCES, b Chicago, Ill, May 5, 31; m 50; c 2. ROMANCE LANGUAGES. *Educ:* Univ Chicago, BA, 50; Univ Mich, MA, 57, PhD(Span), 62. *Prof Exp:* From instr to assoc prof, Univ Mich, Ann Arbor, 63-73, prof, 73-81; PROF SPAN & CHMN DEPT SPAN & PORT, IND UNIV, BLOOMINGTON, 81- *Concurrent Pos:* Publ grant, Horace H Rackham Sch Grad Studies, Univ Mich, 65, Rackham fac res fel, 67. *Honors & Awards:* Distinguished Serv Award, Univ Mich, 66. *Mem:* MLA. *Res:* Nineteenth century Spanish literature; 20th century Spanish literature and thought; 20th century Latin American literature. *Publ:* Auth, The Literary Perspectivism of Ramon Perez de Avala, Univ NC, 66; Borges's stories: Fiction and philosophy, Hisp Studies, 4/68; Unamuno's nibela: From novel to dream, PMLA, 3/73; Cortazar: Doubles, figures and others, In: Narradores Hispanoamericanos de Hoy, Univ NC, Chapel Hill, 73; Miguel de Unamuno, The Contrary Self, Tamesis, London, 76; The contexts of Alejo Carpentier's El Recurso del Metodo, Entretiens, Paris. *Mailing Add:* Dept Span & Port Indiana Univ Bloomington IN 47405

WYLIE, HAL, b New York, NY, Sept 16, 35; m 56, 71; c 5. FRENCH LITERATURE. *Educ:* Univ Ariz, BA, 57; Stanford Univ, MA, 61, PhD(French & humanities), 65. *Prof Exp:* Asst ed, Agr Experiment Station, Univ Ariz, 57-59; ASST PROF FRENCH, UNIV TEX, AUSTIN, 64- *Mem:* African Lit Asn; South Cent Mod Lang Asn; Am Asn Teachers Fr. *Res:* Caribbean and African literature. *Publ:* Auth, The reality-game of Robbe-Grillet, Fr Rev, 5/67; Breton, schizophrenia and Nadja, Fr Rev, winter 70; Dennis Brutus talks of exile and commitment, 2/75, Toward a socialist art, 3/77 & Rene Depestre speaks of Negritude, Cuba, Socialist Writing & Communist Eros, 2/79, The Gar; auth & ed, Creative Exile: Dennis Brutus and Rene Depestre, In: When the Drumbeat Changes, Three Continents Press, 81; Joseph Zobel's use of Negritude and Social Realism, World Lit Today, winter 82. *Mailing Add:* Dept of French Univ of Tex Austin TX 78712

WYLIE, TURRELL VERL, b Durango, Colo, Aug 20, 27. PHILOLOGY & HISTORY. *Educ:* Univ Wash, BA, 52, PhD, 58. *Prof Exp:* Instr Tibetan lang, 58-59, asst prof Tibetan lang & hist, 59-64, exec chmn inner Asia res proj, 62-70, asst prof Tibetan lang & civilization, 64-68, prof, 68-72, chmn, Dept Asia Lang & Lit, 69-72, PROF TIBETAN STUDIES, UNIV WASH, 72- *Mem:* Am Orient Soc; Asn Asian Studies; Tibet Soc. *Res:* Tibetan Buddhism, history, language and literature. *Publ:* Auth, Geography of Tibet according to the Dzam-Gling-rgyas-bshad, Serie Orient Roma, 62; Ro-langs: The Tibetan Zombie, Hist Relig J, 64; Mortuary Customs at Sa-skya, Tibet, Harvard J Asiatic Studies, 65; ed, Tibet: A Political History, Yale Univ, 67; auth, Tibet: A Study in Chinese chauvinism, Orient-West, 67. *Mailing Add:* Dept Asian Languages & Lit Univ Washington Seattle WA 98195

Y

YACKLE, LARRY W, b Ottawa, Kans, Oct 10, 46. CONSTITUTIONAL LAW. *Educ:* Univ Kans, Lawrence, BA, 68, JD, 73; Harvard Univ, LLM, 74. *Prof Exp:* Instr, Boston Univ, 73-74; asst prof, 74-77, assoc prof, 77-80, PROF LAW, UNIV ALA, 80- *Concurrent Pos:* Vis prof, Univ Tex, Austin, 80-81. *Mem:* Soc Am Law Teachers. *Res:* Criminal procedure; federal jurisdiction. *Publ:* Auth, The Burger Court and the fourth amendment, 26: 335 & Confessions of a horizontalist: A dialogue on the first amendment, 27: 541, Kans Law Rev; Postconviction Remedies, 81. *Mailing Add:* Sch of Law Univ Ala University AL 35486

YAKOBSON, HELEN BATES, b St Petersburg, Russia, May 21, 13; US citizen; m 51; c 2. RUSSIAN LANGUAGE. *Educ:* Univ Harbin, Manchuria, BS, 34. *Prof Exp:* Teacher Russ lang & lit, Tientsin Russ Sch, China, 36-38; researcher & pvt tutor Russ lang, 39-46; info specialist, script writer & announcer polit & cult commentary to Russia, US Dept State, 47-50; lectr Russ lang, 51-53, from asst prof to assoc prof Slavic lang & lit & exec off dept, 53-64, chmn dept, 60-69, PROF SLAVIC LANG & LIT, GEORGE WASHINGTON UNIV, 65- *Concurrent Pos:* Consult foreign lang textbooks, McGraw-Hill Bk Co, Inc, 59; mem exec comt, Studies Ctr Sec Schs, Choate Sch, 62- *Honors & Awards:* Nat Foreign Lang Achievement Award, Nat Fed Mod Lang Teachers Asn, 65. *Mem:* Am Asn Teachers Slavic & East Europ Lang (pres, 61-63); Nat Slavic Hon Soc (pres, 68-73); Am Asn Advan Slavic Studies; MLA; hon mem SAtlantic Mod Lang Asn. *Res:* Educational television; foreign language teaching methodology; language and culture. *Publ:* Auth, TV Study Guide for Beginning Russian: Parts I & II, 58-59 & Beginner's Book in Russian, 59, Educ Serv; New Russian Reader, George Washington Univ, 60; coauth, Essentials of Russian, Prentice-Hall, 4th ed, 64; auth, Conversational Russian--Intermediate Course, Heath, 65; Russian Readings: Past and Present, Appleton, 66; contribr to methods of Teaching Russian, Van Nostrand. *Mailing Add:* Dept of Slavic Lang & Lit George Washington Univ Washington DC 20052

YALDEN, JANICE MACKENZIE, b Kingston, Jamaica, Dec 12, 31; Can citizen; m 52; c 2. LINGUISTICS, SPANISH LANGUAGE. *Educ:* Univ Toronto, BA, 52; Univ Mich, MA, 56. *Prof Exp:* Lectr Span, 69-71, asst prof, 71-76, ASSOC PROF LING, CARLETON UNIV, 76-, DIR CTR FOR APPL LANG STUDIES, 82- *Mem:* Teachers of English to Speakers of Other Lang; Can Asn Ling; Ling Soc Am; Ont Mod Lang Teachers Asn (pres, 76-77); Can Asn Teachers of English as a Second Lang. *Res:* Second language teaching and learning; error analysis; Spanish-English contrastive analysis. *Publ:* Auth, Approaches to TESL in the UK, 10: 58-62 & The functional approach to curriculum design, Conf Proc 78, X: 175-187, TESL Talk; Second languages at the universities: A look into the future, XXXV: 431-442 & Form and function: The design of a six-phase syllabus in English for academic purposes, 36: 452-460, CMLR; Current approaches to second language teaching in the UK, System, 8: 151-156; The teacher's role: A new conception, In: Bulletin de L'Association Canadienne de Linguistique Appliquee, Automne, 80; Communicative language teaching: Principles and practice, In: OISE Handbook Series in Language and Literacy in Canadian Education, Toronto: Ont Inst for Studies in Educ Press. *Mailing Add:* Dept of Ling Carleton Univ Ottawa ON K1S 5B6 Can

YALOM, MARILYN K, b Chicago, Ill, Mar 10, 32; m 54; c 3. FOREIGN LANGUAGES. *Educ:* Wellesley Col, BA, 54; Harvard Univ, MAT, 56; Johns Hopkins Univ, PhD(comp lit), 63. *Prof Exp:* Lectr French, Univ Hawaii, 61-62; from asst prof to prof foreign lang, Calif State Univ, Hayward, 63-76; ASSOC DIR, CTR RES WOMEN, STANFORD UNIV, 76- *Publ:* Auth, Prophet within his own language, Adam Int Rev, 67; coauth, Ernest Hemingway: A psychiatric view, Arch Gen Psychiat, 6/71; auth, A note on Stendhal and Proust, Adam Int Rev, fall 72; Triangles and prisons: A psychological study of Stendhalian love, Hartford Studies in Lit, 76. *Mailing Add:* 951 Matadero Palo Alto CA 94306

YAMAUCHI, EDWIN MASAO, Ancient History, Semitic Languages. See Vol I

YANG, PAUL FU-MIEN, b Poating, China, Oct 16, 25; US citizen. CHINESE LINGUISTICS. *Educ:* San Jose Sem, Manila, BA, 53; Bellarmine Col, Philippines, STL, 59; Univ Tokyo, MA, 64; Georgetown Univ, PhD, 67. *Prof Exp:* Lectr Chinese, Chabanel Lang Sch, Philippines, 54-55; bibliogr Chinese & Japanese, Ling Bibliog, 58-68; asst prof Chinese, 67-72, ASSOC PROF CHINESE, GEORGETOWN UNIV, 72- *Concurrent Pos:* NSF grant, 66-67; Am Philos Soc grant, 68-69. *Mem:* Chinese Lang Teachers Asn; Am Asn Chinese Studies; Chinese Lang Soc Japan; Inst of Eastern Cult Japan. *Res:* History of Chinese language; Chinese dialectology; Chinese linguistic bibliography. *Publ:* Auth, The Catholic Missionary Contributions to the Study of Chinese Dialects, 60 & Chinese Dialectology, 1955-1965, 66, Orbis; Elements of Hakka dialectology, Monumenta Serica, 67; Chinese Linguistics: A Selected and Classified Bibliography, 74 & Chinese Dialectology: A Selected and Classified Bibliography, 81, Chinese Univ, Hong Kong. *Mailing Add:* Dept of Chinese & Japanese Sch of Lang & Ling Georgetown Univ Washington DC 20057

YANG, RICHARD F S, b Peiping, China, Apr 23, 18; US citizen; m 47; c 2. FOREIGN LANGUAGES. *Educ:* Yenching Univ, China, BA, 43; Univ Wash, MA, 50, PhD, 55. *Prof Exp:* Assoc Chinese, Univ Wash, 48-49, from instr to asst prof, 50-60; vis assoc prof, Univ Southern Calif, 60-63, assoc prof, 63-67; chmn dept, 67-70, PROF E ASIAN LANG & LIT, UNIV PITTSBURGH, 67- *Mem:* MLA; Asn Asian Studies. *Res:* Chinese literature and drama. *Publ:* Auth, Tales from Chinese Drama (in Chinese), Vols I, II, III, IV & V, 66, 67, 68, 69 & 72 College Chinese, Vols I-III, 67, Eastern Publ, Taipei, China; coauth, Fifty Songs of the Yüan, Poetry of 13th Century China, Allen & Unwin, London, 67; Four Plays of the Yüan Drama, 72 & Eight Colloquial Tales of the Sung, 72, China Post, Taipei. *Mailing Add:* Dept of EAsian Lang & Lit Univ of Pittsburgh Pittsburgh PA 15260

YANG, WINSTON LIH-YEU, b China, June 1, 33; US citizen. CHINESE & COMPARATIVE LITERATURE. *Educ:* Nat Taiwan Univ, BA, 57; Stanford Univ, AM, 67, PhD(Chinese lit), 71. *Prof Exp:* Instr Chinese, Winthrop Col, 63-66, asst prof Asian studies, 67-68, assoc prof & chmn dept, 69-70; lectr Chinese lit, Calif State Univ, San Francisco, 68-69; assoc prof Asian studies, 70-71, chmn dept, 71-72, dir educ prof develop assistance grad prog Chinese & Japanese, 73-78, PROF CHINESE, SETON HALL UNIV, 73-, DIR ASIAN BILINGUAL EDUC FEL PROG, 78- *Mem:* MLA; Asn Asian Studies; Am Orient Soc; Am Coun Teaching Foreign Lang; Chinese Lang Teachers Asn (secy-treas, 70-73). *Res:* Classical Chinese fiction; modern Chinese fiction. *Publ:* Auth, Classical Chinese Fiction, G K Hall, 78; Critical Essays on Chinese Fiction, Chinese Univ Hong Kong Press, 80; Stories of Contemporary China, Paragon, 80; Modern Chinese Fiction, G K Hall, 81. *Mailing Add:* Dept of Asian Studies Seton Hall Univ South Orange NJ 07079

YAO, TAO-CHUNG, b Wuchin, Kiangsu, China, Sept 2, 46; m 71; c 1. CHINESE LANGUAGE & HISTORY. *Educ:* Soochow Univ, BA, 68; Seton Hall Univ, MA, 73; Univ Ariz, PhD(Oriental studies), 80. *Prof Exp:* Instr Chinese Lang, Adult Sch Montclair, 72-73; teaching asst, Univ Ariz, 73-77, teaching assoc, 77-79, instr, 79-80, vis asst prof, 80-81; vis asst prof Chinese lang, Univ Mass, 81-82; VIS ASST ASIAN STUDIES, MT HOLYOKE COL, 82- *Mem:* Asn Asian Studies. *Res:* Taoism. *Publ:* Auth, The historical value of Ch'uan-Chen sources in the Tao-Tsang, Sung Studies Newsletter, 77; coauth, A comparative analysis of selected passages from the Tzu-I, Meng Tzu and Mo Tau, 77, Ch'uan-Chen Taoism and Yuan drama, 80 & Mery-Go-Round: A group of Chinese classroom games, 80, J Chinese Lang Teachers Asn; coauth, The Character Book: A Workbook to Accompany Read Chinese I, Far Eastern Publ (in press). *Mailing Add:* Dept of Asian Studies Mt Holyoke Col South Hadley MA 01075

YARRILL, ERIC HERBERT, b Heston Hounslow, England, Dec 28, 14. MODERN COMPARATIVE LITERATURE. *Educ:* Univ Toronto, BA, 37, MA, 38; Sorbonne, cert, 38. *Prof Exp:* Lectr French, 38-45, prof, 45-77, EMER PROF MOD LANG, BISHOP'S UNIV, 77- *Concurrent Pos:* Contribr, Erasmus Speculum Scientiarum, 55-; br vpres, Alliance Francaise; mem ed bd, Erasmus Speculum Scientiarum, 70- *Honors & Awards:* Centennial Medal, Can, 67. *Mem:* MLA; Humanities Asn Can; Asn Can Univ Teachers Fr; fel Int Inst Arts & Lett; Asn Can Univ Teachers Ger. *Res:* Voltaire's uncollected letters; synesthesia in literature. *Publ:* Auth, Browning's Roman murder story as recorded in a hitherto unknown Italian contemporary manuscript, Baylor Bull, 39; French in school and college: Questions of continuity, Fr Rev, 54. *Mailing Add:* 11 High St Lennoxville PQ J1M 1E6 Can

YAR-SHATER, EHSAN, b Hamadan, Iran, Apr 3, 20; m 61. LITERATURE, HISTORY. *Educ:* Univ Tehran, Dr Lit, 47; Univ London, MA, 51, PhD(Old & Mid Iranian), 60. *Prof Exp:* Assoc prof Iranian philol, Univ Tehran, 53-58; vis assoc prof Indo-Iranian, Columbia Univ, 58-60; prof Iranian philol, Univ Tehran, 60-61; chmn dept, Mid E Lang & Cult, 68-73, HAGOP KEVORKIAN PROF IRANIAN STUDIES, 61-, DIR IRANIAN STUDIES, 68- *Concurrent Pos:* Ed, Persian Texts Ser, BTNK, Tehran, 55-79, Rahnema-ye Ketab, 57-79, Persian Studies Ser, 68-, Bibliotheque des oeuvres classiques persanes, 68-, Encycl Iranica, 75- & Mod Persian Lit Ser, 78-; secy gen, Iranian Comt Int Coun Philos & Humanistic Sci, 56-61; mem exec coun, Corpus Inscriptionum Iranicum, 57-; ed, Persian Heritage Ser, Univ Chicago, Univ Toronto, Columbia Univ, Routledge & Kegan Paul & Caravan, 65- *Mem:* Am Soc Studies Islamic Philos & Sci; Book Soc Persia (pres, 56-79); Am Orient Soc; Mid E Studies Asn NAm; Am Inst Iranian Studies. *Res:* Iranian linguistics; Persian cultural history; Iranian dialects of central and northwestern Persia. *Publ:* Auth & ed, Iran Faces the Seventies, Praeger 71; auth, Development of Persian drama in the context of Cultural conffontation, In: Iran: Continuity and Variety, Ctr Near Eastern Studies, New York Univ, 71; Current trends in linguistics: Iran and Afghanistan, In: Current Trends in Linguistics, Vol 6, 71; Persian modern literary idiom, In: Iran Faces the Seventies, Praeger, 71; co-ed (with D Bivar), Persian Inscriptions of East Mazandaran, 78; co-ed & auth (with R Ettinghansen), Highlights of Persian Art, 81; auth & ed, Cambridge History of Iran III, 82; Problems of Iranian History in the Seleuaid, Parthian, and Sasanian Periods, Iranian National History, Madakism, In: Cambridge History of Iran III, 82. *Mailing Add:* Dept of Mid E Lang & Cult 604 Kent Hall Columbia Univ New York NY 10027

YASHINSKY, JACK, b Detroit, Mich, June 14, 26; m 48; c 1. FRENCH LITERATURE & LINGUISTICS. *Educ:* Wayne State Univ, BA, 64, MA, 66; Univ Calif, Santa Barbara, PhD(French), 70. *Prof Exp:* ASSOC PROF FRENCH, UNIV TORONTO, 68- *Mem:* Am Asn Teachers French; Can Asn Univ Teachers; Asn Prof Fr of Can Univs; MLA; Fr Soc Studies 18th Century. *Res:* Semiology in Moliere's comedies; Voltaire's comedies; 18th century French theater. *Publ:* Auth, Les comedies de Voltaire: Popularite et influence, 74 & Voltaire's enfant prodigue, 76, Studies Voltaire & 18th Century; Voltaire's L'Ecossaise: Background, structure, originality, Studies Voltaire and 18th Century, Vol 182, 79; Metaphore, langage et mouvement dramatique dans le Misanthrope, Les Lettres Romanes, Tome 34, 80; Options Nouvelles en Didactique du Francais Langue Etrangere, 81 & L'Enseignement du francais aux adultes: Bilan d'une experience, Options Nouvelles en Didactique du Francais Langue Etrangere, 81, Didier. *Mailing Add:* Dept of French Univ Col Univ of Toronto Toronto ON M5S 1V4 Can

YASUDA, KENNETH KENICHIRO, b Auburn, Calif, June 23, 14; m 49; c 3. JAPANESE LITERATURE. *Educ:* Univ Wash, BA, 45; Univ Tokyo, DLitt(Japanese lit), 56. *Prof Exp:* Ct interpreter & Textbook specialist, US Dept State, 46-49; asst rep, Asia Found, Tokyo Off, 51-60; from asst prof to assoc prof Japanese, Univ Hawaii, 60-67; assoc prof, 67-73, PROF JAPANESE LANG & LIT, IND UNIV, BLOOMINGTON, 73- *Concurrent Pos:* Lectr comp lit, Tokyo Women's Col, 53-54 & Japan Women's Col, 58-59; mem bd dir, Meguro Parasitological Mus, Tokyo, 58-; Fulbright-Hays sr res fel, 66-67. *Honors & Awards:* Third Order Sacred Treasure, Japanese Govt, 74. *Res:* Japanese poetry; the theater of Noh; Japanese landscape architecture. *Publ:* Auth, Pepper Pod, Knopf, 47; Minase Sangin Hyakuin,

Kogakusha, Tokyo, 56; The Japanese Haiku, Charles Tuttle, 57, 2nd ed, 72; translr, Forms in Japan, E-W Ctr, 65; auth, Six Noh Plays, Kofusha, Tokyo, 67-68; The Land of the Reed Planes, Charles Tuttle, 72; The dramatic structure of Ataka, a Noh play, Monumenta Nipponica, Tokyo, 72; The structure of Hagoromo, a Noh play, Harvard J Asiatic Studies, 73. *Mailing Add:* Dept of East Asian Lang & Lit Indiana Univ Bloomington IN 47401

YATES, DONALD ALFRED, b Ayer, Mass, Apr 11, 30; m 51; c 3. FOREIGN LANGUAGES. *Educ:* Univ Mich, BA, 51, MA, 54, PhD(Span), 61. *Prof Exp:* Teaching asst Span, Univ Mich, 53-57; all-univ res grant to Mex, 58 & 61, PROF SPAN, MICH STATE UNIV, 57- *Concurrent Pos:* Fulbright res award, Arg 62-63; gen ed, Macmillan Mod Span Am Lit Ser, 62-; Fulbright lectr, Arg, 67-68 & 70; lectr Am lit, Univ Buenos Aires & Univ La Plata; vis prof, Ctr 20th Century Studies, Univ Wis-Milwaukee, 74; vis prof, San Francisco State Univ, 81. *Honors & Awards:* Silver Medallion for Contrib to Field of Latin Am Lit, Instituto de Cultura Hisp, Madrid, Spain, 75. *Mem:* Am Asn Teachers Span & Port; MLA; Inst Int Lit Iberoam; Latin Am Studies Asn; Asoc Int Hispanistas. *Res:* Spanish American literature of fantasy and imagination; Argentine literature; writings of Jorge Luis Borges. *Publ:* Ed, Rosaura a las diez, Scribners, 64; ed & transl, Latin Blood: Best Crime Stories of Spanish America, 72 & transl, Thunder of the Roses, 72, Herder & Herder; ed, Otros mundos, otros fuegos: fantasia y realismo magico en Iberoamerica, Mich State Univ, 75; Espejos: doce relatos hispanoamericanos de nuestro tiempo, Holt, Rinehart & Winston, 80. *Mailing Add:* 537 Wells Hall Michigan State Univ East Lansing MI 48824

YATES, LAWRENCE EDWARD, b Eng, July 23, 12; nat US; m 43; c 2. GREEK, PHILOSOPHY. *Educ:* McGill Univ, BA, 40; Univ Toronto, MA, 45; Presby Col, Can, BD, 45; Princeton Theol Sem, ThD, 61. *Prof Exp:* Assoc prof, 61-64, PROF GREEK & PHILOS, WHITWORTH COL, 64- *Mailing Add:* Dept of Philos & Greek Whitworth Col Spokane WA 99218

YEAGER, CHARLES H, b Evansville, Ind, Oct 3, 31. FOREIGN LANGUAGES. *Educ:* Ind Univ, BA, 56, MA, 57. *Prof Exp:* Lectr Russ, Evansville Col, 58-59; asst prof Ger & Rus, 60-66, ASSOC PROF RUSS, GALLAUDET COL, 66-, CHMN DEPT, 67- *Concurrent Pos:* Teaching assoc, Ind Univ, 60 & 62-63. *Mem:* Am Asn Advan Slavic Studies; MLA; Am Instr Deaf. *Res:* Russian 19th century literature. *Mailing Add:* Dept Russ Gallaudet Col Washington DC 20002

YEAGER, ROBERT FREDERICK, Medieval English Literature. See Vol II

YEDLICKA, JOSEPH W, b St Joseph, Mo, Apr 6, 11; m 55; c 2. LITERATURE & LINGUISTICS. *Educ:* DePaul Univ, AB, 31, MA, 33; Univ Montreal, Lic es Let, 40; Cath Univ Am, PhD, 44. *Prof Exp:* Prof class lang, St Mary's Col, Minn, 35-39, prof Romance lang, 45-52; prof English, Col Mont-Saint-Louis, Montreal, 39-40; prof Romance lang, Univ Detroit, 52-53; from assoc prof to prof, 55-80, EMER PROF ROMANCE LANG, DEPAUL UNIV, 80- *Honors & Awards:* Officier, Palmes Academiques, 62. *Mem:* MLA; Am Asn Teachers Fr. *Res:* Old French semantics and philology; Spanish and French literature. *Publ:* Auth, Expressions of the Linguistic Area of Repentance and Remorse in Old French, Cath Univ Am, 45; Old French synderesis as remorse of conscience, New Scholasticism, 4/63; La question d'Argent of Dumas fils, Fr Rev, 5/63; Speculation in Second Empire, Empire. *Mailing Add:* Dept of Foreign Lang DePaul Univ Chicago IL 60614

YEN, ISABELLA YIYUN, b Peking, China, July 16, 12; nat; m. LINGUISTICS. *Educ:* Nat Peking Univ, BA, 38; Univ Mich, AM, 51; Cornell Univ, PhD(ling), 56. *Prof Exp:* From asst instr to asst prof educ, Southwest Assoc Univ, 38-46; asst prof English & educ, Nat Peking Univ, 46-47; isntr critic teaching, State Univ NY Teachers Col Oneonta, 47-50; res assoc ling, Cornell Univ, 52-54, instr, 55-56; asst prof Asiatic studies, Univ Southern Calif, 56-60; assoc prof, 60-76, PROF CHINESE LANG, UNIV WASH, 76- *Concurrent Pos:* Lectr French, Univ Franco-Chinoise, 42-45; Fulbright-Hays fel, 68-69. *Mem:* Am Orient Soc; Philol Asn Pac Coast. *Res:* Chinese language and linguistics; teaching of English to foreign stiudents; teaching of foreign languages in elementary schools. *Publ:* Auth, English for speakers of Mandarin Chinese; The Chinese abacus, Math Teacher. *Mailing Add:* 215 NE 47th Seattle WA 98105

YEN, SIAN LIN, b Keelung, Taiwan, Jan 12, 33; m 64; c 3. LINGUISTICS, ORIENTAL LANGUAGES. *Educ:* Nat Taiwan Univ, BA, 56; Univ Ill, MA, 61, PhD(ling), 65. *Prof Exp:* Instr ling, Univ Ill, Urbana, 64-65; asst prof, 65-72, ASSOC PROF LING & ORIENT LANG, UNIV TEX, AUSTIN, 72- *Mem:* Ling Soc Am; Am Orient Soc. *Res:* Linguistic theory; history of the Chinese language; structures of Chinese and Japanese. *Publ:* Auth, Notes on the Initials Ying and Yü in Ancient Chinese, T'oung Pao, 66; On negation with fei in classical Chinese, J Am Orient Soc, 7/71; On the negative Wei in Classical Chinese, J Am Orient Soc, 10/77. *Mailing Add:* Dept of Ling Univ of Tex Austin TX 78712

YERKES, DAVID M, English, Linguistics. See Vol II

YETIV, ISAAC, b Nabeul, Tunisia, Mar 13, 29; US citizen; m 53; c 3. FRENCH & HEBREW LANGUAGE & LITERATURE. *Educ:* Hebrew Univ Jerusalem, BA, 67; Univ Wis- Madison, PhD(French lit, Hebrew), 70. *Prof Exp:* Teacher math, physics & lang, Safed High Sch, Israel, 50-54; teacher math & physics, Reali Lyceum, Haifa, 54-67; teaching asst Hebrew, Univ Wis-Madison, 67-69; from asst prof to assoc prof French & Hebrew, Univ Hartford, 69-75; PROF FRENCH & HEBREW & HEAD DEPT MOD LANG, UNIV AKRON, 75-, DIR ENGLISH LANG INST, 76- *Concurrent Pos:* Lectr Hebrew, Univ Conn, 70-71. *Mem:* MLA; Nat Asn Prof Hebrew. *Res:* Twentieth century French and Hebrew literature; Black African and North African literature in French; alienation of the marginal man in world literature. *Publ:* Auth, The three thematic phases of the Maghrebian novel in French, Presence Francophone, 70; The literary technique of Mouloud Mammeri in his novel The Sleep of the Just, Le Roman Contemporain d'Expression Francaise, CELEF, 71; A by-product of French colonization in the Maghreb: The elite, L'Esprit Createur, 72; The Theme of Alienation in the North-African Novel in French (1952-1956), CELEF, Univ Sherbrooke, 72; L'mad Ivrit, Learn Hebrew, a Comprehensive Course for United States Universities, Shilo, 73; Djihada, a Novel, Alef, Tel Aviv, Israel, 74; Alientation in the modern novel of French North-Africa before independence, In: Exile and Tradition, Longman, London, 76; Iconoclasts in Maghrebian literature, Fr Rev, 77. *Mailing Add:* 2078 Wyndham Rd Akron OH 44313

YNGVE, VICTOR H, b Niagara Falls, NY, July 5, 20; m 43; c 3. LINGUISTICS, MECHANICAL TRANSLATION. *Educ:* Antioch Col, BS, 43; Univ Chicago, SM, 50, PhD(physics), 53. *Prof Exp:* Mem staff, res lab electronics, Mass Inst Technol, 53-54, asst prof mod lang, 54-61, res assoc, Dept Elec Engineering, 61-65; PROF INFO SCI, UNIV CHICAGO, 65-, PROF LING, 76- *Mem:* Asn Comput Ling(pres, 62); Ling Soc Am. *Res:* Linguistic theory; communicative interaction; cognitive processes. *Publ:* Auth, A model and an hypothesis for language structure, Proc Am Philos Soc, 10/60; Computer Programming with COMIT II, Mass Inst Technol, 72; I forget what I was going to say, Papers 9th Regional Meeting Chicago Ling Soc; 73; Human linguistics and face-to-face interaction, In: The Organization of Behavior in Copresent Interaction, Mouton, The Hague (in press). *Mailing Add:* Dept of Ling Univ of Chicago Chicago IL 60637

YODER, LAUREN WAYNE, b Newport News, Va, Mar 9, 43; m 64; c 2. FRENCH LANGUAGE & LITERATURE. *Educ:* Eastern Mennonite Col, BA, 64; Univ Iowa, MA, 69, PhD(French), 73. *Prof Exp:* Teacher physics, Ecole Pedag Protestante, Kikwit, Zaire, 66-68; vis asst prof English, Univ Paris, 71-72; asst prof, 73-80, ASSOC PROF FRENCH, DAVIDSON COL, 80- *Mem:* MLA; Am Asn Teachers Fr; African Lit Asn; Southern Asn Africanists. *Res:* Medieval French tale; African novel. *Publ:* Auth, L'aventure ambigue, Bull Southern Asn Africanists, 9/74; Les quatre elements dans L'Enfant Noir, Fer de Lance, 9/77 & spring 78. *Mailing Add:* Davidson Col Davidson NC 28036

YOKEN, MELVIN BARTON, b Fall River, Mass, June 25, 39; m 76; c 3. FRENCH LANGUAGE & LITERATURE. *Educ:* Univ Mass, Amherst, BA, 60; Brown Univ, MAT, 61; Five-Col Prog, Univ Mass, Amherst Col, Smith Col, Mt Holyoke Col & Hampshire Col, PhD(French), 72. *Prof Exp:* From instr to asst prof, 66-76, assoc prof, 76-81, PROF FRENCH, SOUTHEASTERN MASS UNIV, 82- *Concurrent Pos:* Res fel, Quebec Studies, 81. *Mem:* MLA; Am Asn Teachers Fr; Am Coun Teaching Foreign Lang; New England Foreign Lang Asn. *Res:* The French novel; French literature of the 19th century; French literature of the 20th century. *Publ:* Auth, Paleneo, Mass Foreign Lang Bull, fall 73; Wise guy Solomon, Outlook 3/74; Claude Tillier, Twayne, 76; Speech is Plurality, Univ Press of Am, 78; Claude Tillier: Fame and fortune in his novelistic work, Fairleigh Dickinson Univ, 78; France's Shakespeare: Moliere, Cambridge Univ Press. *Mailing Add:* Dept of Mod Lang Southeastern Mass Univ North Dartmouth MA 02747

YON, ANDRE FRANCOIS, b Paris, France, Mar 19, 30; US citizen; m 54; c 3. FRENCH LANGUAGE & LITERATURE. *Educ:* Pa State Univ, MA, 53, PhD, 59. *Prof Exp:* Instr French, Harvard Univ, 59-62; asst prof Wesleyan Univ, 62-67; asst prof, Oberlin Col, 67-69, assoc prof, 69-70; PROF FRENCH & CHMN DEPT MOD LANG, WASHINGTON COL, 70- *Concurrent Pos:* Palmes Academiques, 74. *Mem:* MLA; AAUP; Am Asn Teachers Fr; Soc Fr Prof Am. *Res:* Contemporary French literary criticism; contemporary French novel. *Publ:* Coauth, Dictionnaire des critiques litteraires, Pa State Univ, 69. *Mailing Add:* Dept of Mod Lang Washington Col Chestertown MD 21620

YORK, ANTHONY DELANO, b Winston-Salem, NC, Aug 23, 34; m 57; c 4. BIBLICAL LITERATURE, SEMITIC LANGUAGES. *Educ:* Cornell Univ, PhD(Semitic lang), 73. *Prof Exp:* Fel Hebrew, Oxford Ctr for Post-Grad Hebrew, 73-75; lectr Hebrew, Leeds Univ, 75-78; asst prof, 78-81, ASSOC PROF BIBLE, UNIV CINCINNATI, 81- *Mem:* Soc Old Testament Study. *Res:* Targum; Book of Job; ancient versions of the bible. *Publ:* Auth of articles in J Study Judaism, 73 & 78, J Bibl Lit, 74, Rev de Qumran, 75, Bibliotheca Orientalis, 75 & Vetus Testamentum 76. *Mailing Add:* 3343 Sherlock Ave Cincinnati OH 45220

YORK, ERNEST CHARLES, English. See Vol II

YORK, RUTH BEATRICE, b Boston, Mass, June 20, 24. FRENCH. *Educ:* State Univ Iowa, BA, 45, MA, 47; Columbia Univ, PhD(French), 64. *Prof Exp:* Mem staff French & Span, Graceland Col, 47-56; asst prof French, Ill Col, 56-59; lectr, Columbia Univ, 60-63, from instr to asst prof, 63-65; asst prof, 65-71, LECTR FRENCH, UNIV CALIF, DAVIS, 71-, CHMN DEPT, 80- *Mem:* MLA; Philol Asn Pac Coast; Am Asn Teachers Fr; Asn Amis Valery Larbaud. *Res:* Valery Larbaud; 20th century French literature and theatre. *Publ:* Auth, Circular patterns in Gide's Soties, 2/61 & Ubu revisited: The reprise of 1922, 2/62, Fr Rev; Selected works of Alfred Jarry and Shattuck Taylor, eds, Mod Lang J, 4/66. *Mailing Add:* Dept of French & Ital Univ of Calif Davis CA 95616

YOTSUKURA, SAYO, b Tokyo, Japan, Apr 23, 21; m 49; c 2. LINGUISTICS, JAPANESE. *Educ:* Univ Tokyo, BA, 50; Univ Mich, MA, 55, PhD(ling), 63. *Prof Exp:* Asst prof Japanese & head div, Georgetown Univ, 63-70; assoc prof, Dag Hammarskjold Col, 72-73; res assoc & consult, Futuremics, Inc, Washington, DC, 73-75; coordr Lang Serv Prog, Ketron, Inc, 76-79; DIR FAC RESOURCES, INST RES & DEVELOPMENT, WASHINGTON INT COL, WASHINGTON, DC, 80- *Concurrent Pos:* Lectr, Univ Pa, 72-73; vis lectr, Mary Washington Col, 73-74; bd mem & dir multilingual prog, Multilingual/Polycult Found, 75- *Mem:* Ling Soc Am; Int Ling Asn; Asn Teachers Japanese. *Res:* Theoretical linguistics; theory of communication; Japanese structure. *Publ:* Auth, English noun classification, In: Linguistic Studies in Memory of R S Harell, 67; The Japanese tone and intonation systems, 9/67 & Beginning Japanese: A review essay, 11/67, Linguistics; The articles in English, Ser Janua Linguarum, Mouton, The Hague, 70; Tagmemics as wave grammar, Proc XIth Int Cong Linguists, 74; Ethnolinguistic introduction to Japanese literature, Lang & Thought: Anthrop Issues, 77; Ethnolinguistic Contributions to Global Understanding Converging Trend, World Univ, Puerto Rico, 1:94-109. *Mailing Add:* 3711 N Vernon St Arlington VA 22207

YOUMAN, ALFRED ELIOT, b Miami, Fla, Mar 3, 33; m 56; c 2. CLASSICS. *Educ:* Yale Univ, BA, 55, PhD, 59. *Prof Exp:* Chmn classics, Hopkins Grammar Sch, 59-61; asst prof, Union Col, NY, 61-64; asst prof, 64-73, assoc prof, 73-76, PROF CLASSICS, MERCER UNIV, 76- *Concurrent Pos:* Mellon regional fac grant, 81. *Mem:* Archaeol Inst Am; Class Asn Midwestern & Southern States. *Res:* Homer; tragedy; Plato's Gorgias. *Publ:* Auth, How Many Homers to Make a Masterpiece?, Union Col Symp, 64; Climactic themes in the Iliad, Class J, 2/66; Santayana's attachements, New Eng Quart, 9/69; Aristophanes: Country boy or city?, Class Bull, 4/74. *Mailing Add:* Dept of Class Lang Mercer Univ Macon GA 31207

YOUNG, DAVID CHARLES, b Lincoln, Nebr, Dec 9, 37; m 58; c 3. CLASSICS. *Educ:* Univ Nebr, BA, 59; Univ Iowa, MA, 60, PhD(classics), 63. *Prof Exp:* From asst prof to assoc prof, 63-72, chmn dept, 68-72, PROF CLASSICS, UNIV CALIF, SANTA BARBARA, 72- *Mem:* Am Philol Asn. *Res:* Greek poetry, especially choral lyric. *Publ:* Auth, Three odes of Pindar, Vol IX, In: Mnemosyne: Supplementa, Brill, 68; Pindaric criticism 2, Vol 134, In: Pindaros und Bakchylides, Wege d Forschung, Wiss Buchges, 70; Pindar Isthmian 7, Myth and Exempla, Brill, Leiden, 71. *Mailing Add:* Dept of Classics Univ of Calif Santa Barbara CA 93106

YOUNG, DWIGHT WAYNE, b Lambert, Okla, Dec 15, 25; m 46; c 2. SEMITIC PHILOLOGY. *Educ:* Hardin Simmons Univ, BA, 49, ThM(Semitics), 56; Dropsie Col, PhD(Egyptol), 55. *Prof Exp:* Asst prof Semitic lang, Dallas Theol Sem, 54-58; asst prof, Brandeis Univ, 58-63, assoc prof Mediterranean studies, 63-67; vis prof Coptic, Hebrew Univ, Israel, 65; vis prof Semitic lang, Cornell Univ, 67-69; assoc prof Semitic lang, 69-72, PROF ANCIENT NEAR EAST CIVILIZATION, BRANDEIS UNIV, 72- *Concurrent Pos:* NDEA fel, 60; mem, Am Res Ctr Egypt. *Honors & Awards:* Solomon Award, Dallas Theol Sem, 51. *Mem:* Am Orient Soc; Soc Bibl Lit; Am Res Ctr Egypt. *Res:* Comparative Semitic grammar; ancient history; Egyptology. *Publ:* Auth, On Shenoute's use of present I, 4/61 & Esope and the conditional conjugation, 7/62, J Near Eastern Studies; Unfulfilled conditions in Shenoute's dialect, J Am Orient Soc, 4/69; The milieu of Nag Hammadi: Some historical considerations, Vigiliae Christianae, 70; With snakes and dates: A sacred marriage drama at Ugarit, 77 & The Ugaritic Myth of the god Horan and the mare, 79, Ugarit Forschungen; A ghost word in the Testament of Jacob (Gen 49:5)?, J Bibl Lit, 81; ed, Studies presented to Hans Jakob Polotsky, 81. *Mailing Add:* Dept of Near East Studies Brandeis Univ Waltham MA 02154

YOUNG, HOWARD THOMAS, b Cumberland, Md, Mar 24, 26. SPANISH, FRENCH. *Educ:* Columbia Univ, BS, 50, MA, 52, PhD(Span), 56. *Prof Exp:* Lectr, Columbia Col, Columbia Univ, 53-54; PROF ROMANCE LANG, POMONA COL, 54-, CHMN DEPT MOD LANG, 77- *Concurrent Pos:* Fulbright lectr, Spain, 67-68; independent study & res, Nat Endowment for Humanities, 75-76; chmn Span lang develop comt, Educ Testing Serv, Princeton, NJ, 77-81. *Mem:* MLA; Am Asn Teachers Span & Port; Am Comp Lit Asn; Asn Dept For Lang. *Res:* Contemporary Spanish poetry; comparative study of modern Spanish and English poetry. *Publ:* Auth, Mexico-a revolution gone bankrupt, New Repub, 4/60; Pedro Salinas y los Estados Unidos, Cuadernos Hispanoam, 62; The Victorious Expression, Univ Wis, 64; Juan Ramon Jimenez, Columbia Univ, 67; Anglo-American poetry in the correspondence of Luisa and Juan Ramon Jimenez, Hispanic Rev, 76; On using foreign service institute tests and standards on campuses, In: Measuring Spoken Language Proficiency, Georgetown Univ, 80; The Line in the Margin: Juan Ramon Jimenez and His Readings in Blake, Shelley, and Yeats, Univ Wis, 80; The exact names, Modern Lang Notes, 81. *Mailing Add:* Mason 205 C Pomona Col Claremont CA 91711

YOUNG, JOHN, b Tientsin, China, Mar 6, 20; US citizen; m 49; c 3. HISTORY, LINGUISTICS. *Educ:* Tokyo Imp Univ, BA, 42; Georgetown Univ, BS, 49, MS, 51; Johns Hopkins Univ, PhD, 55. *Prof Exp:* Lectr hist & Far East lang, Georgetown Univ, 51-56, from asst prof to assoc prof, 56-62; prof & lang supvr, Univ Md, 62-64; chmn dept Asian & Pac lang, Univ Hawaii, Manoa, 64-70, prof, 64-74; PROF ASIAN STUDIES & CHMN DEPT, SETON HALL UNIV, 74- *Concurrent Pos:* Ford Found grant, 58 & 59-60; US Off Educ grant as co-dir Japanese instr materials compilation proj, 66-71; ed, Hawaii Lang Teacher, 69-71; Nat Endowment for Humanities grant as prin investr, Japanese Cult Text Proj, 71-72; Asian bks rev ed, Mod Lang J, 71-; co-dir, Chinese/Japanese-English Bilingual Inst, 74-77; dir, Asian Bilingual Curric Develop Ctr, 76-78 dor. Asian Bilingual Inst, Title VII, Bilingual Teachers Training Prog, 77- *Mem:* Asn Asian Studies; MLA; Chinese Lang Teachers Asn (pres, 69-70); Nat Asn Bilingual Educ; Nat Asn Social Studies. *Res:* Far East history and languages. *Publ:* Auth, The Research Activities of the South Manchurian Railroad Co, E Asian Inst, Columbia Univ, 67; coauth, Learn Japanese, East-West Ctr, 67; Nihon No Dento-Cha No Yu, Tankosha, 68; Learn Japanese-Secondary School Text, 69-71 & Learn Japanese-Elementary School Text, 69-71, Tongg; auth, Cultural Materials for College Text, Univ Hawaii, 72; Essential considerations in compiling Asian bilingual curriculum developmental materials, J Chinese Lang Teachers Asn, 2/76; Analysis of bilingual/bicultural/bilerate curriculum development in connection with equal educational opportunity in Title VI, Southwest Educ Develop Lab, 6/77. *Mailing Add:* Dept of Asian Studies Seton Hall Univ South Orange NJ 07079

YOUNG, MYRNA GOODE, b Hartsburg, Ill, July 24, 14; m 40; c 2. CLASSICAL LANGUAGES. *Educ:* Eureka Col, AB, 35; Univ Ill, MA, 36, PhD(class lang), 38. *Prof Exp:* Asst prof class lang, Millikin Univ, 38-42; vis instr, Agnes Scott Col, 55-56; high sch teacher sr English, Westminster Schs, Atlanta, Ga, 56-57; from asst prof to assoc prof, 57-74, PROF CLASS LANG,

AGNES SCOTT COL, 74- *Mem:* Archaeol Inst Am; Class Asn Mid West & South; Vergilian Soc. *Publ:* Auth, The Appropriate Name in Petronius' Satyricon, Univ Ill, 41. *Mailing Add:* Dept of Class Lang Agnes Scott Col Decatur GA 30030

YOUNG, RICHARD E, English Literature, Rhetoric. See Vol II

YOUNG, ROBERT F, b Philadelphia, Pa, Nov 2, 26. CLASSICAL LANGUAGES. *Educ:* St Louis Univ, AB, 50, AM & PhL, 52; Woodstock Col, ThL, 59. *Prof Exp:* From instr to asst prof classics, Col, Georgetown Univ, 52-55 & 60-65; asst prof classics, 65-79, chmn dept foreign lang & fine arts, 78-81, ASSOC PROF FOREIGN LANG, UNIV SCRANTON, 79- *Concurrent Pos:* Fulbright-Hays fel, Italy, summer, 78. *Mem:* Am Philol Asn; Class Asn Atlantic States; Am Class League; Vergilian Soc. *Res:* Vergil; Sophocles; Seneca. *Publ:* Auth, Milton in Latin: A version of To Cyriack Skinner, 9/74 & transl, Horace: Carmina I 38, 5/77, Classical Outlook; John Milton, Samson Agonistas (373-381, into Latin verse), Class Outlook, 3/80. *Mailing Add:* Dept of Foreign Lang & Fine Arts Univ of Scranton Scranton PA 18510

YOUNG, ROBERT VAUGHAN, Renaissance English, Comparative Literature. See Vol II

YOUNG, ROBERT WENDELL, b Chicago, Ill, May 18, 12; m 39; c 1. HISTORY, LINGUISTICS. *Educ:* Univ Ill, BA, 35. *Hon Degrees:* LLD, Univ NMex, 69. *Prof Exp:* Specialist Indian lang, Bur Indian Affairs, from asst to area dir to area tribal oper officer, Albuquerque Area Off; prof Navajo ling, 73-78, EMER PROF & DIR NAVAJO DICTIONARY PROJ, UNIV NMEX, 74- *Concurrent Pos:* Lectr Navajo lang, Univ NMex, 71-72, Nat Endowment for Humanities grant, Nat Dictionary Proj, 74-77. *Honors & Awards:* Distinguished Service Award, US Dept Interior, 72. *Res:* Navajo language, ethnology and history; lexicography; grammar. *Publ:* Auth, English as a Second Language for Navajos, Bur Indian Affairs, 67; contribr, Reading for the Disadvantaged, Harcourt, 70; Language and Cultural Diversity in American education, Prentice-Hall, 72; Plural Society in the Southwest, Arkville, 72; auth, Political History of the Navajo Tribe, Navajo Community Col, Ford Found, 78; The Navajo Language, Grammar and Dictionary; Selections from Navajo History; The Navajo Yearbook. *Mailing Add:* 2929 Indiana NE Albuquerque NM 87110

YOUNG, RONALD ROBERT, b Chippewa Falls, Wis, Nov 14, 44; m 65; c 2. SPANISH LINGUISTICS. *Educ:* Univ Wis, BA, 65; Univ Ill, MA, 67, PhD(Span & ling), 72. *Prof Exp:* Instr Span, Univ Ill, Urbana, 70-71; asst prof, 71-80, ASSOC PROF SPAN, SAN DIEGO STATE UNIV, 80- *Mem:* Am Asn Teachers Span & Port; Am Coun Teaching Foreign Lang; Am Transl Asn. *Res:* Hispanic dialectology; applied linguistics. *Publ:* Auth, Alto Lucero: Estudios Linguisticos, Ed Playor, Madrid, 74; Rehilamiento of /y/ in Spanish, Hispania, 5/77; An Introduction to Spanish Linguistics, 81 & Self Paced Spanish, 82, Campanile Press. *Mailing Add:* Dept of Span & Port San Diego State Univ San Diego CA 92182

YU, ANTHONY C, Religion, Western & Chinese Literature. See Vol IV

YU, PAULINE RUTH, b Rochester, NY, Mar 5, 49; m 75. COMPARATIVE LITERATURE, CHINESE POETRY. *Educ:* Radcliffe Col, BA, 71; Stanford Univ, MA, 73, PhD(comp lit), 76. *Prof Exp:* Asst prof, 76-80, ASSOC PROF HUMANITIES, UNIV MINN, MINNEAPOLIS, 80- *Concurrent Pos:* Am Asn Univ Women fel, 75-76; Stanford Univ fel humanities, 79; Nat Endowment for Humanities grant, 81. *Mem:* MLA; Asn Asian Studies; Am Comp Lit Asn; Am Orient Soc; Chinese Lang Teachers Asn. *Res:* Chinese poetry; modern Western poetry; Chinese and Western literary criticism. *Publ:* Contribr, Ssu-k'ung T'u's shih-p'in, In: Studies in Chinese Poetry and Poetics, Vol I, CMC, Taipei, 78; Chinese and symbolist poetic theories, Comp Lit, fall 78; The poetics of discontinuity: East-West correspondences in lyric poetry, PMLA, 3/79; Wang Wei: Recent studies and translations, CLEAR, 7/79; The Poetry of Wang Wei: New Translations and Commentary, Ind, 80; Metaphor and Chinese poetry, CLEAR, 7/81; Li Ch'ing-chao and Else Lasker-Schuler: Two Shattered Worlds, Comp Lit Studies, 82; contribr, Formal distinctions in Chinese literary theory, In: Theories of the Arts in China, Princeton (in press). *Mailing Add:* Humanities Prog Univ of Minn Minneapolis MN 55455

YUDIN, FLORENCE L, b Brooklyn, NY, Jan 26, 37. SPANISH LITERATURE. *Educ:* Brooklyn Col, BA, 58; Univ Ill, Urbana, MA, 60, PhD(Span), 64. *Prof Exp:* From instr to asst prof Span, Univ Mich, Ann Arbor, 64-69; asst prof, Dartmouth Col, 69-71; assoc prof, 71-74, chmn dept mod lang, 71-76, PROF SPAN, FLA INT UNIV, 74- *Concurrent Pos:* Publ subsidy, Fla Int Univ Found, 74. *Mem:* MLA; Midwest Mod Lang Asn. *Res:* Contemporary Spanish poetry; contemporary English poetry; 17th & 20th century Spanish literature. *Publ:* Auth, The novela corta as comedia: Lope's Las Fortunas de Diana, Bull Hisp Studies, 68; Theory and practice of the novela comdiesca, Romanishche Forsch, 69; Earth words, 74 & Whose House of books, 74, Caribbean Rev; The Vibrant Silence in Jorge Guillen's Aire Nuestro, Univ NC, 74; The dark silence in Lorca's poetry, Garcia Lorca Rev, 78; The Yes and the No of Lorca's Ocean, The World of Nature in the Works of Federico Garcia Lorca, 80. *Mailing Add:* Dept of Mod Lang Fla Int Univ Tamiami Campus Miami FL 33199

YURIEFF, ZOYA I, b Siemiatycze, Poland, Aug 24, 22; US citizen; m 52; c 2. RUSSIAN LITERATURE. *Educ:* Barnard Col, BA, 49; Radcliffe Col, MA, 50, PhD, 56. *Prof Exp:* Tech asst Slavonic div, New York Pub Libr, 59; instr Russ, 59-62, asst prof Russ lit, 62-66, ASSOC PROF SLAVIC LIT, WASH SQ COL ARTS & SCI, NY UNIV, 66- *Concurrent Pos:* Russ-English translr for Sol Hurok, 56-; instr, Queens Col, NY, 60-61; mem ed bd, Novyj Zhurnal/New Rev. *Mem:* Am Transl Asn; Asm Asn Advan Salvic Studies; PEN Club; MLA; AAUP. *Res:* Modern Russian literature; comparative Slavic literature; literary translations. *Publ:* Auth, introd, Lug zelenyj, Johnson Reprint, 68; On Julian Tuwin's Overcoat, Orbis Scriptus, Dmitrij Tschizewskij zum 70, Geburtstag, 68; An eclipse of the moon metaphor and death, New Rev, 72. *Mailing Add:* Dept of Slavic Lang & Lit New York Univ New York NY 10003

Z

ZABKAR, LOUIS VICO, b Lagosta, Italy, Dec 7, 14; US citizen. EGYPTOLOGY, ANCIENT HISTORY. *Educ:* Univ Zagreb, STL, 42; Pontif Bibl Inst, Rome, SSL, 43, Lic orient lang, 45; Univ Chicago, PhD(Egyptol), 58. *Prof Exp:* From asst prof to prof hist, Loyola Univ, Ill, 54-69; chmn dept Mediterranean Studies, 73-77, prof Egyptol, 69-80, FOSTER PROF CLASS & ORIENTAL STUDIES, BRANDEIS UNIV, 80-, DIR GRAD STUDIES, 77- *Concurrent Pos:* Mem, Queen Elizabeth Egypt Found, Belgium, 50- & Am Res Ctr Cairo, Egypt, 58-; mem staff, Nubian Exped, Orient Inst, Univ Chicago, 61-63, field dir, 66-68; Nat Found Arts & Humanities sr fel, 68-69. *Mem:* Egypt Explor Soc. *Res:* Egyptian mortuary texts; Ptolemaic and Roman period in Egypt; Nubian studies. *Publ:* Auth, Herodotus and the Egyptian idea of immortality, J Near Eastern Studies, 63; A Study of the Ba in Ancient Egyptian Texts, 68 & coauth, Ausgrabungen von Khor-Dehmit Bis Bet El-Wali, 68, Univ Chicago; auth, The Egyptian name of the fortress of Semna South, J Egyptian Archaeol, 72; A hieracocephalous deity from Naqa, Qustul, and Philae, Z Agyptische Sprache und Altertumskunde, 74; Apedemak, Lion-god of Meroe, A Study in Egyptian-Meroitic Syncretism, Aris & Phillips, Warminster, Eng, 75. *Mailing Add:* Dept of Class & Orient Studies Brandeis Univ Waltham MA 02154

ZACHAU, REINHARD KONRAD, b Lübeck, Ger, May 4, 48; m 75; c 1. GERMAN LITERATURE. *Educ:* Univ Hamburg, Staatsexamen, 74; Univ Pittsburgh, PhD(Ger lit), 78. *Prof Exp:* Instr Ger for foreigners, Christian-Albrechts Univ, 77; ASST PROF GER, UNIV OF THE SOUTH, 78- *Mem:* MLA; Am Asn Teacher's German; SAtlantic Mod Lang Asn; Northeast Mod Lang Asn. *Res:* East German literature; exile literature; modern West German literature. *Publ:* Auth, Stefan Heym, C H Beck, 82; Das New Yorker Deutsche Volksecho-Akten d IV Exilliteraturkonferenz 1937-1939, Symp Univ Calif Camden House, 82. *Mailing Add:* SPO 1199 Sewanee TN 37375

ZAENKER, KARL A, b Waldenburg, Ger, Sept 19, 41; Can citizen. MEDIEVAL GERMAN LITERATURE. *Educ:* Goettingen Univ, Ger, Staatsexamen Ger & Fr, 66; Univ BC, PhD(Ger), 74. *Prof Exp:* ASST PROF GER, UNIV BC, 74- *Mem:* Can Asn Univ Teachers; Can Comp Lit Asn. *Res:* Late medieval travel literature; relationship between literature and music. *Publ:* Auth, The cult of the Holy Blood in late medieval Germany, Mosaic X, Vol 4, 77; Homage to Roswitha, Humanities Asn Rev, 78; Zur Arzt-Szene in Wittenwilers Ring, Seminar Vol XV, 79; String quartets in prose, Can Rev Comp Lit, 81; Hrotsvits von Gandersheim Abraham, Mittellatein Jahrbuch, 81. *Mailing Add:* Dept of Germanic Studies Univ of BC Vancouver BC V6T 1W5 Can

ZAETTA, ROBERT, b LaSeyne, France, Oct 6, 32; US citizen; m 64; c 1. ROMANCE LANGUAGES. *Educ:* Pa State Univ, BA, 54, MA, 59, PhD(Span), 68. *Prof Exp:* Teacher, Springfield Sch Syst, 59-62; instr Span, Allegheny Col, 64-68; genfac grant, 68-69, ASST PROF SPAN & ITAL, UNIV DEL, 68-; STATE SUPVR MOD FOREIGN LANG, DEL STATE DEPT PUB INSTR, 74- *Mem:* MLA; Am Asn Teachers Span & Port. *Res:* Twentieth century Spanish novel, especially comic devices. *Publ:* Auth, Wenceslao Fernandez Florez: The evolution of his technique in his novels, Ky Romance Quart, 70; The burla in the novels of W Fernandez Florez, Rev Estudies Hisp, 5/72. *Mailing Add:* Mod For Lang Dept Dept Pub Instr Dover DE 19901

ZAHAREAS, ANTHONY NICHOLAS, b Chios, Greece, Aug 2, 30; US citizen; m 53; c 1. HISPANIC & COMPARATIVE LITERATURES. *Educ:* Ohio State Univ, BA, 56, MA, 58, PhD(romance lang & lit), 62. *Prof Exp:* Instr comp lit, Ohio State Univ, 61-62; asst prof Span & comp lit, Smith Col, 62-65; assoc prof romance lang, Univ Pa, 65-67; prof Span & Port & comp lit, NY Univ, 68-71, head dept, 69-71; chmn dept Span & Port, Univ Minn, Minneapolis, 72-76, dir res, Col Lib Arts, 77-82. *Concurrent Pos:* Andrew Mellon res fel, Univ Pittsburgh, 64-65; Guggenheim fel, Spain, 67-68; vis prof, Univ Calif, Los Angeles, winter, 79; Nat Endowment for Humanities res grant, 81-82. *Honors & Awards:* Nat Award, Am Acad Poets, 80. *Mem:* MLA; Midwestern Mod Lang Asn; Inst for Study Ideologies & Lit; Asoc Int de Hispanistas; Am Asn Teachers Span & Port. *Res:* Medieval, Golden Age and modern Hispanic literatures; structure and ideology of fictional texts; comparative literature and social history. *Publ:* Auth, The Art of Juan Ruiz, Archpriest of Hita, Estudios de Literatura Espanola, 65; coauth, Vision del Esperpento, Ed Castalia, Madrid, 70; transl & ed, Bohemian Lights by Ramon del Valle-Inclan, Univ Edinburgh, 75; auth, Galdos' Dona Perfecta: Fiction, history and ideology, Anales Galdosianos, 76; Quevedo's Buscon: Structure and ideology, Homenaje a Julio Caro Baroja, Madrid, 78; coauth, Vida y hechos de Estebanillo Gonzalez (2 vols), Ed Castalia, Madrid, 78; Book of True Love, Pa State Univ Press, 78; Structure and ideology in the LBA, Coronica, spring 79. *Mailing Add:* 1920 S First St, #409 Minneapolis MN 55454

ZAHN, LOUIS J, b Atlanta, Ga, Nov 24, 22. ROMANCE LANGUAGES & LITERATURES. *Educ:* Emory Univ, AB, 47, AM, 49; Univ NC, PhD, 57. *Prof Exp:* Instr Romance lang, Emory Univ, 50-57; from asst prof to assoc prof, 57-65, PROF SPAN LANG & LIT, GA INST TECHNOL, 65-, HEAD DEPT MOD LANG, 76-, ACAD ADMIN SPEC COURSES ENGLISH FOR INT STUDENTS, 58- *Mem:* Am Asn Teachers Span & Port; SAtlantic Mod Lang Asn; Teachers English to Speakers of Other Lang. *Res:* Spanish medieval literature and linguistics; phonology of medieval Spanish; dictionary of medieval Spanish. *Publ:* Auth, Libro de los Exenplos por a b c Vocabulario Etimologico, Consejo Super Invest Cient, Madrid, 62; History of St John's Lutheran Church, 1869-1969, Atlanta, Ga, 69; Teoria y Ejercicios Sobre la Fonologia y la Morfologia de la Lengua espanola, Atlanta, Ga, 74; Juan Ruiz, Arcipreste de Hita, Libro de buen Amor, Parts I & II, 75 & 76. *Mailing Add:* Dept of Mod Lang La Inst of Technol Atlanta GA 30332

ZAÏTZEFF, SERGE IVAN, b Versailles, France, Nov 14, 40; Can citizen; m 72. LATIN AMERICAN LITERATURE. *Educ:* Ind Univ, Bloomington, AB, 62, AM, 63, PhD(Span), 70. *Prof Exp:* Lectr French & Span, 63-64, from asst prof to assoc prof, 67-78, PROF SPAN, UNIV CALGARY, 78- *Concurrent Pos:* Univ Calgary res grant, 72-73; Can Coun leave fel, 73-74, res grant, 77-78; mem exec comt, Can Asn Hisp, 75-77; Killam res fel, 80; Soc Sci & Humanities Res Coun Can fel, 81. *Mem:* Am Asn Teachers Span & Port; Inst Int Lit Ibero-Am; Can Asn Hispanists; Can Asn Latin Am Studies; Can Asn Univ Teachers. *Res:* Twentieth century Latin American literature; modernism in Mexico; the generation of the Areneo de la Juventud. *Publ:* Auth, Rafael Lopez, Poeta y Prosista, Inst Nac Bellas Artes, 72; La Venus de la Alameda, Antologia de Rafael Lopez, Sep/Septentas, 73; Fuerza y Dolor Antologia Poetica de Roberta Argüelles Bringas, Sep/Setentas, 75; Mas sobre la novela modernista: Claudio Oronoz de Ruben M Campos, Anales de Lit Hispanoam, 76; Textos desconocidos de Efren Rebolledo (1877-1929), Text Critico, 77; Julio Torri, dialogo de los libros, Fondo de Cultura Economica, 80; Julio Torri y la critica, Univ Nac Autonoma de Mex, 81; Ricardo Gomez Robelo y Carlos Diaz Dufoo Jr, Obras, Fondo de Cultura Economica, 81. *Mailing Add:* Dept of Romance Studies Univ Calgary Calgary AB T2N 1N4 Can

ZAKARIAN, RICHARD HACHADOOR, b Lawrence, Mass, July 25, 25. FOREIGN LANGUAGES. *Educ:* Bates Col, AB, 49; Middlebury Col, MA, 50; Northwestern Univ, PhD, 60. *Prof Exp:* Asst, Northwestern Univ, 51-53 & 59-60; instr French, NY Univ, 54; from instr to asst prof French & Span, State Univ SDak, 54-56 & 57-58; asst prof, Bates Col, 58-59; from asst prof to assoc prof mod lang, 61-72, PROF FOREIGN LANG, CALIF STATE UNIV, NORTHRIDGE, 72- *Concurrent Pos:* Smith-Mundt fel, Cambodia, 60-61; res dir, Calif State Univ Int Prog, Aix-en-Provence, France, 68-70. *Mem:* MLA. *Res:* Novels and plays of Emile Zola. *Publ:* Auth, Zola's Germinal: A Critical Study of Its Primary Sources, Libr Droz, Geneva, 72. *Mailing Add:* Dept of Foreign Lang Calif State Univ Northridge CA 91324

ZALACAIN, DANIEL, b Havana, Cuba, Dec 15, 48; US citizen; m 76; c 1. LATIN AMERICAN LITERATURE & THEATRE. *Educ:* Wake Forrest Univ, BA, 71; Univ NC, Chapel Hill, MA, 72, PhD(Latin Am lit), 76. *Prof Exp:* Asst prof Span lang & lit & bus Span, Northern Ill Univ, 77-80; ASST PROF SPAN LANG & LIT & BUS SPAN, SETON HALL UNIV, 80- *Mem:* Am Asn Teachers Span & Port; MLA. *Res:* Latin American theatre of the absurd; Spanish for business careers; Latin American myths. *Publ:* Auth, Rene Marques, del absurdo a la realidad, Latin Am Theatre Rev, fall 78; El arte dramatico en Cuculcan, Explicacion textos lit, 78; Calabar: O elogio da traicao, Chasqui: Rev Lit Latinoam, 2/79; Falsa alarma: Vanguardia del absurdo, Romance Notes, 80; El tiempo, tema fundamental en la obra de Rene Marques, Ky Romance Quart, 80; El personaje fuera del juego en el teatro de Griselda Gambaro, Rev Estudios Hispanicos, 5/80; Los recursos dramaticos en Soluna, Latin Am Theatre Rev, spring 81; La Antigona de Sanchez: Recreacion puertorriquena del mito, Explicacion Textos Lit, 81. *Mailing Add:* Dept of Mod Lang Seton Hall Univ South Orange NJ 07079

ZAMORA, JUAN C, b New York, NY, May 14, 30; m 53; c 2. HISPANIC LINGUISTICS & DIALECTOLOGY. *Educ:* Univ Havana, D Derecho, 52, lic ciencias soc, 60; State Univ NY Buffalo, MA, 66, PhD(Span), 71. *Prof Exp:* Prof law, Univ Popular, Havana, 47-57; adv, Ministry Educ & chief of chancellery, Ministry Foreign Affairs, Cuba, 59-60; teacher English, Dade County pub schs, 62-63; from instr to lectr Span, State Univ NY Buffalo, 63-70; asst prof, Cent Conn State Col, 70-71; asst prof, 71-77, ASSOC PROF SPAN, UNIV MASS, AMHERST, 77- *Concurrent Pos:* Grad prog dir, dept Span & Port & dir, summer prog, Spain, Univ Mass, Amherst. *Mem:* MLA; Am Asn Teachers Span & Port; Ling Soc Am; Int Ling Asn; Asn Int Hispanistas. *Res:* Spanish American dialectology and lexicology; bilingualism; Cuban literature. *Publ:* Auth, Early loan-words in the spanish of Mexico and the Caribbean, Buffalo Studies, 8/68; Lexicologia indianorromaiva: Chingar y singar, Romance Notes, 12/72; Morfologia bilingue: lA ASIGNACION DE GENERO A LOS ; Indigenismos en la lengua de los conquistadores, Univ of PR, 76; Perspectiva historica de la educacion bilingue en los Estados Unidos, Hispania, 5/78; Interferencia reciproca: Receptividad y productividad, Word, 8/78; The impact of the New World on Spanish, Revista Interamericana, 9/80; coauth, Dialectologia hispanoamericana, Almar Spain, 82. *Mailing Add:* Dept of Span & Port Univ of Mass Amherst MA 01003

ZAMORA, MARGARITA MOUNTSERRAT, b Havana, Cuba; US citizen. LATIN AMERICAN & COMPARATIVE LITERATURE. *Educ:* Univ Mass, BA, 76; Yale Univ, MA, 78, PhD(Latin Am lit), 82. *Prof Exp:* ASST PROF LATIN AM LIT, UNIV WIS-MADISON, 82- *Mem:* MLA. *Res:* Colonial Latin American literature; translation; comparative literature. *Publ:* Auth, Language instruction for bilinguals at the college level: Strategies for self correction, Bilingual Rev, 1/81; Language and history in the Comentarios reales, Mod Lang Quart, 9/82. *Mailing Add:* Dept of Span & Port Univ of Wis Madison WI 53406

ZANETEAS, PETER C, b Greece, May 21, 26; US citizen; m; c 3. GREEK, LATIN. *Educ:* Columbia Col, BA, 52; Columbia Univ, MA, 54, PhD, 72. *Prof Exp:* Lectr classics, Brooklyn Col, 56-62; instr, NY Univ, 60-63; from instr to asst prof, 63-75, ASSOC PROF CLASSICS, BROOKLYN COL, 75-, ASST DEAN, 72- *Mem:* Am Philol Asn; AAUP; Class League. *Res:* Greek Sophists; Stocis of the Roman Empire period; Greek cynics. *Mailing Add:* 926 75th St Brooklyn NY 11228

ZANTS, EMILY, b Tulsa, Okla, Aug 3, 37. FRENCH LITERATURE. *Educ:* Stanford Univ, BA, 58; Columbia Univ, MA, 61, PhD(French), 65. *Prof Exp:* Instr French, Brooklyn Col, 65-67; asst prof, Univ Calif, Davis, 67-72; assoc prof, 72-80, PROF FRENCH LANG & LIT, UNIV HAWAII, MANOA, 80- *Honors & Awards:* Mabelle McLeod Lewis Award, Stanford Univ, 72. *Mem:* MLA; Am Soc 18th Century Studies; Am Asn Teachers Fr; Am Inst Architects. *Res:* The novel; Flaubert; Proust. *Publ:* Auth, The Aesthetics of the New Novel in France, Univ Colo, 68; Dialogue, Diderot and the new novel in France, 18th Century Studies, winter 68; The relation of Epiphany to description in the modern French novel, Comp Lit Studies, winter 69; Proust and the new novel in France, PMLA, 1/73. *Mailing Add:* Dept of Europ Lang Univ of Hawaii at Manoa Honolulu HI 96822

ZAPATA, CELIA CORREAS, b Mendoza, Arg, Oct 9, 35; US citizen; m 55; c 2. LATIN AMERICAN LITERATURE & CULTURE. *Educ:* Nat Univ Cuyo, Profesora, 56; Univ Calif, Irvine, PhD(Span lit), 71. *Prof Exp:* Instr Span, Santa Ana Jr Col, 64-65; assoc, Univ Calif, Irvine, 65-68; assoc prof Span, 69-79, PROF FOREIGN LANG, SAN JOSE STATE UNIV, 79- *Res:* Contemporary period of Latin American literature. *Publ:* Auth, Cantos de evocacion y ensueno, Troquel Publ, Buenos Aires, 68; Por aqui pasaron los ninos Cantores de Mendoza, Los Andes, Mendoza, 3/71; Lirismo del lenguaje en el cuento hispanoamericano, Rev Interam Bibliog, Washington, DC, 5/73; Juegos de ninos: La magia en dos cuentos de Julia Cortazar, Anales de Lit Hispanoam, Madrid, Spain, 6/74. *Mailing Add:* Dept of Foreign Lang San Jose State Univ San Jose CA 95192

ZARECHNAK, MICHAEL, b Vydran, Nov 18, 20; m 43; c 2. SLAVIC LANGUAGES & LINGUISTICS. *Educ:* Czech Acad Sci, MA, 44; Harvard Univ, PhD(Slavic lang & ling), 67. *Prof Exp:* Instr Russ, Commercial Acad, Slovakia, 42; instr, High Sch, Salzburg, 46-48; instr, Army Lang Sch, Monterey, Calif, 50-51; asst prof Slavic Lang, Georgetown Univ, 51-54; instr Russ lang, Assumption Col, 54-56; asst prof Slavic ling, 56-68, ASSOC PROF LING, GEORGETOWN UNIV, 68- *Concurrent Pos:* Programming specialist automatic processing ling data, Nuclear Div, Union Carbide Co, 66-67. *Mem:* Ling Soc Am; Am Asn Teachers Slavic & East Europ Lang; Am Asn Advan Slavic Studies. *Res:* Syntactic patterns; mechanical translations; computational semantics. *Publ:* Coauth, Mechanical Translation, Trends in Linguistics, The Hague, 74; Reflections on Cook's Case Grammar Matrix, GU Working Papers on Lang & Ling, No 8, 75; Machine Translation, The Hague, Mouton, 79; Outline of Semantic Research for Future Machine Translation Development, Int Forum on Info & Documentation, Vol 5, No 2. *Mailing Add:* 1308 Farragut St Washington DC 20011

ZARKER, JOHN WILLIAM, b Lancaster, Pa, Oct 25, 28; m 51; c 5. CLASSICS. *Educ:* Franklin & Marshall Col, AB, 50; Univ NC, MA, 52; Princeton Univ, PhD, 58. *Prof Exp:* Instr classics, Univ Tex, 58-59; from instr to assoc prof, Dartmouth Col, 60-66, assoc prof, Vanderbilt Univ, 66-71; actg chmn dept fine arts, 72-74, ASSOC PROF CLASSICS & CHMN DEPT, TUFTS UNIV, 71- *Concurrent Pos:* Prix de Rome fel, Am Acad Rome, 59-60. *Mem:* Am Philol Asn; Class Asn New England; Vergilian Soc. *Res:* Latin literature and epigraphy. *Publ:* Auth, Catullus 18-20, Trans Am Philol Asn, 62; Acrostic Carmina Latina Epigraphica, Orpheus, 67; Amata: Vergil's other tragic queen, Vergilius, 69. *Mailing Add:* Dept of Classics Tufts Univ Medford MA 02155

ZATLIN-BORING, PHYLLIS, b Green Bay, Wis, Dec 31, 38; m 62; c 2. SPANISH, PORTUGUESE. *Educ:* Rollins Col, BA, 60; Univ Fla, MA, 62, PhD(Span), 65. *Prof Exp:* Instr Romance lang, 63, assoc prof, 71-79, assoc dean affirmative action, 74-80, PROF SPAN, RUTGERS UNIV, 79-; DEPT CHMN, 80- *Mem:* MLA; AAUP; Am Asn Teachers Span & Port; Women's Equity Action League; Am Coun Teachers Foreign Lang. *Res:* Contemporary Spanish theater; women writers of 19th and 20th century Spain. *Publ:* Coauth, Lengua y Lectura, 70 & ed, El Rapto, 71, Harcourt; auth, Elena Quiroga, 77 & Victor Ruiz Iriarte, Twayne, 80; ed, El lando de seis caballas, 79 & La pel del limon, 80, Almar; Noviembre y un poco de yerba & Petra Regalada, Catedra, 81; Jaime Salom, Twayne, 82. *Mailing Add:* Dept of Span & Port Rutgers Univ New Brunswick NJ 08903

ZAVALA, IRIS M, b Ponce, PR, Dec 27, 36; US citizen. ROMANCE LANGUAGES, SPANISH HISTORY. *Educ:* Univ PR, BA, 57; Univ Salamanca, MA, 60, PhD(Span lit) 62. *Prof Exp:* Instr Span, Univ PR, 62-64; lectr, Queens Col, NY, 65; asst prof, Hunter Col, 67-68; assoc prof, 68-71, dir, Grad Studies, 75-79, PROF SPAN, STATE UNIV NY STONY BROOK, 71-, CHMN DEPT HISP LANG & LIT, 73- *Concurrent Pos:* Res fel, Col Mex, 64; Orgn Am States res fel, 65; Guggenheim Found fel, 66 & 67; Soc Sci Res Coun-Am Coun Learned Soc res fel, 72-73; mem, Selection Comt, Grad Fel Prog, 77-78. *Honors & Awards:* Nat Lit Prize, PR, 72, 74, 75 & 78. *Mem:* MLA; Soc Span & Port Hist Studies; Am Asn Teachers Span & Port. *Res:* Nineteenth century Spanish political thought; 18th-20th century Spanish intellectual history and literature; Spanish American novel. *Publ:* Auth, Clandestinidad y Libertinaje Erudito en los Albores de la Ilustracion, Ariel, Barcelona, 78; coauth, Historia Social de la Literature Espanola (3 vols), Castalia, 79-80; auth, Kiliagonia (novel), Mex, 80; ed, Intellectual Roots of Puerto Rican Independence: An Anthology of Puerto Rican Political Essay, Monthly Rev Press, 80; auth, El Texto en la Historia, Madrid, 81; Que Nadie Muera Sin Amar el Mar (poems), Madrid, 82; Historia Critica de la Literature Espanola, Romanticismo y Realismo, Critica, Barcelona, 82; Genetica de Los Cisnes de Ruben Dario, 82. *Mailing Add:* Dept of Hisp Lang State Univ NY Stony Brook NY 11794

ZAYAS-BAZAN, EDUARDO, b Camagüay, Cuba, Nov 17, 35; US citizen; m 59; c 2. HISPANIC CULTURE & LITERATURE. *Educ:* Nat Univ Jose Marti, Havana, JD, 58; Kans State Teachers Col, MA, 66. *Prof Exp:* Teacher Span, Plattsmouth High Sch, Nebr, 64-65 & Topeka West High Sch, Kans, 65-66; instr, Appalachian State Univ, 66-68; asst prof, 68-73, assoc prof, 73-79, PROF SPAN FOREIGN LANG DEPT, EAST TENN STATE UNIV, 79-, CHMN DEPT, 73- *Mem:* Am Asn Teachers Span & Port; MLA. *Res:* Bilingual education. *Publ:* Co-ed, Del amor a la revolucion, Norton, 75; auth, Hemingway: His Cuban friends remember, Fitzgerald/Hemingway Ann, 75; co-ed, MIFC Selected Proceedings; coauth, De aqui y de alla, D C Heath & Co, 80; Secret Report on the Cuban Revolution, Trans, 81. *Mailing Add:* Dept of Foreign Lang East Tenn State Univ Johnson City TN 37614

ZAYED, GEORGES H, b Cario, Egypt, June 14, 16; m 40; c 2. FRENCH LITERATURE, SYMBOLIST MOVEMENT. *Educ:* Cairo Univ, Lic es Let, 39, Mag es Let, 41, Dr es Let, 45; Sorbonne DEtat, 56. *Prof Exp:* Teacher sec schs, Egypt, 39-42; from asst master to prof, Univ Alexandria, 42-65; PROF MOD LANG, BOSTON COL, 65- *Honors & Awards:* Commandeur, Palmes Academiques, France, 76. *Mem:* MLA. *Res:* French literature of the 19th century; the evolution of the poetry of Romanticism and symbolism. *Publ:* Auth, La formation litteraire de Veriaine, Droz, Geneva & Minard, Paris, 62, 2nd ed, Nizet Paris, 70; Lettres inedites de Verlaine a Charles Morice, Droz & Minard, 64, 2nd ed, Nizet, 69; Variantes d'Amumone et hermetisme de Mallarme, Rev Hit Lit France, 1/71; Un Salon d'avant-garde: Nina de Villard et ses hotes, Aquila, 73; Paul Verlaine (1844-1896), In: Encyclopedia Universalis, 73; Les Romances sans Paroles ou la Nostalgie Du Paradis Perdu, Avant-siecle, 75; Verlaine: Lettres Inedites a Divers Correspondants, Droz, Geneve, 76; Le Genie D'Edgar Poe et le Gout Francais, Aquila, 76. *Mailing Add:* 21 Linda Lane Newton MA 02161

ZDENEK, JOSEPH WILLIAM, b Chicago, Ill, Aug 30, 31; m 58; c 2. SPANISH. *Educ:* Northern Ill Univ, BS, 53; NMex State Univ, MA, 54; Univ Madrid, D Filos y Let, 65. *Prof Exp:* Teacher high sch, Ill, 54-63; teacher Span & French, Lyons Twp Jr Col, 64-66; assoc prof Span, 66-70, PROF SPAN & CHMN DEPT MOD & CLASS LANG, WINTHROP COL, 70- *Honors & Awards:* Cervantes Award, SC Am Asn Teachers Span & Port, 79. *Mem:* Am Asn Teachers Fr; SAtlantic Mod Lang Asn; Am Asn Teachers Span & Port; Asn Dept Foreign Lang; Asn Int Hisp. *Res:* Spanish chroniclers of the 16th and 17th centuries, especially cronistas de Indias; Garcia Lorca; 20th century Spanish drama. *Publ:* Auth, Two neglected stories of Azorin, Studies Short Fiction, summer 78; Psychical conflicts in Benavente's La Malquerida, Romance Notes, winter 78; Introd & notes, Teatro espanol contemporaneo, Porrua, Mex, Vol I, 79; History and Ethos in the Romancero of Rodrigo, Critica Hisp, No 1, 80; Twenty-five pointers on foreign languages testing, For Lang Annuals, 10/80; Dos escritos de Jose Marti, SEastern Latin Am, 12/80; ed, The world of nature in the works of Federico Garcia Lorca, Winthrop Studies Maj Mod Writers, 80; coauth (with L D Joiner), Art, renunciation and religious imagery on Proust and Azorin, Mod Fiction Studies, summer 81. *Mailing Add:* Dept of Mod & Class Lang Winthrop Col Rock Hill SC 29733

ZEBOUNI, SELMA ASSIR, b Beirut, Lebanon, Oct 26, 30; m 55; c 2. FRENCH. *Educ:* Univ Lyon, BA, 52; Sorbonne Univ, MA, 55; La State Univ, Baton Rouge, PhD(English lit), 63. *Prof Exp:* Asst prof, 63-72, ASSOC PROF FRENCH, LA STATE UNIV, BATON ROUGE, 72- *Res:* History of ideas; Moliere; French classicism. *Publ:* Auth, Dryden, a Study in Heroic Characterization, La State Univ, 65; Classicis me et vraisemblance, Papers Fr 17th Century Lit, winter 77-78. *Mailing Add:* 264 Stanford Ave Baton Rouge LA 70808

ZEINZ, JOSEPH HENRY, b New York, NY, July 1, 17. CLASSICAL LANGUAGES & LITERATURE. *Educ:* Col Holy Cross, AB, 38; Cath Univ Am, MA, 41; Ohio State Univ, PhD(classics), 65. *Prof Exp:* Teacher, Cathedral Latin Sch, Ohio, 41-42 & 47-55; teacher high sch, Calif, 42-44; instr math, St Joseph Col, Japan, 55-61; teaching asst comp lit, Ohio State Univ, 63-64; from instr to asst prof classics, Univ Dayton, 64-70, assoc prof, 70-81, educ res & develop off, 67-70; RETIRED. *Concurrent Pos:* Assoc ed, Class Outlook, 67-72. *Mem:* Am Philol Asn; Am Class League; Am Conf Teaching Foreign Lang. *Res:* Textual studies in the prose writings of Lucius Annaeus Seneca; computer analysis of stylistic and metric characteristics in Latin literature; utilization of computers in learning and instruction. *Mailing Add:* 300 College Park Ave Dayton OH 45469

ZEITLIN, FROMA I, b New York, NY, May 9, 33; m 53; c 3. CLASSICS. *Educ:* Radcliffe Col, BA, 54; Cath Univ Am, MA, 65; Columbia Univ, PhD(classics), 70. *Prof Exp:* Instr classics, Brooklyn Col, 69-70; from asst prof to assoc prof, Douglas Col, Rutgers Univ, 70-77; vis assoc prof, 76-77, ASSOC PROF CLASSICS, PRINCETON UNIV, 77- *Concurrent Pos:* Mem adv comt, Iconographical Lexicon of Class Mythology, 73; Nat Endowment for the Humanities fel for res, 75-76; dir, Am Philol Asn, 78-80. *Mem:* Am Philol Asn; Am Class League; Vergilian Soc; Petronian Soc. *Res:* Greek tragedy; ancient religion and mythology; women studies. *Publ:* Auth, The Argive Festival of Hera and Euripides' Electra, 70 & Petronius as Paradox: Anarchy and Artistic Integrity, 71, Trans Am Philol Asn; The Dynamics of Misogyny: Myth & Myth Making in the Oresteia, Arethusa, 78; Travesties of Gender and Genre in Aristophanes' Theshisphoriazousae, Critical Inquiry, 81. *Mailing Add:* Dept of Classics Princeton Univ Princeton NJ 08540

ZEKULIN, NICHOLAS GLEB, b Prague, Czech, Jan 23, 46; Can citizen; m 68; c 3. RUSSIAN LITERATURE. *Educ:* McGill Univ, BA, 66; Yale Univ, MPhil, 69, PhD(Slavic), 74. *Prof Exp:* Asst prof, 71-79, ASSOC PROF RUSS LANG & LIT, UNIV CALGARY, 79- *Mem:* Can Asn Slavists (secy-treas, 79-82, vpres, 82-83); Am Asn Advan Slavic Studies; Asn des Amis d'Ivan Tourgueniev, Pauline Viardot, Maria Malibran. *Res:* Ivan Turgenev and era; A I Solzhenitsyn; literature and music links. *Publ:* Auth, Two unpublished letters of Ivan Turgenev, 10/75 & Turgenev in Scotland, 1871, 7/76, Slavonic & East Europ Rev; The Russian translation of The Clockmaker, ARIEL, Vol XI, 80; Pavel Annenkov et les archives d'Ivan Tourgueniev, Vol 4, 80 & Ernest Charriere, critique de Tourgueniev, Vol 5, 81, Cahiers Tourgueniev--Pauline Viardot--Maria Malibran. *Mailing Add:* Dept of Ger & Slavic Studies Univ of Calgary Calgary AB T2N 1N4 Can

ZELDIN, JESSE, b New York, NY, Apr 8, 23; m 48; c 1. COMPARATIVE LITERATURE. *Educ:* New York Univ, AB, 47; Columbia Univ, MA, 48, PhD, 53. *Prof Exp:* From instr to asst prof English, 53-62, assoc prof comp lit, 62-70, PROF COMP LIT, HOLLINS COL, 70- *Concurrent Pos:* Sr Fulbright lectr, Chinese Univ Hong Kong, 65-66; Am Philos Soc grant, 69-70; vis scholar, Hokkaido Univ, Japan, 82-83. *Mem:* Am Asn Advan Slavic Studies; Southern Conf Slavic Studies (pres, 71-72). *Res:* Russian literature; French Renaissance. *Publ:* Auth, The Abbey and the Bottle, Esprit Createur, summer 63; The Place of Socialist Realism in Marxist Communist Ideology, SAtlantic Quart, winter 69; translr & introd, Nikolai Gogol's Selected

Passages from Correspondence with Friends, Vanderbilt Univ, 69; coauth, Literature and National Identity, Nebr Univ, 70; auth, Poems and Political Letters of F.I. Tyutchev, Univ Tenn, 74; Nikolai Gogol's Quest for Beauty, Univ Kans, 78. *Mailing Add:* Dept Lit Hollins Col Hollins VA 24020

ZELLJADT, IGOR, b Riga, Latvia, Aug 31, 29; US citizen. LINGUISTICS. *Educ:* Univ Wurzburg, Cand Phil, 52; Yale Univ, MA, 54. *Prof Exp:* Instr Russ & Ger, Brown Univ, 54-56; instr Russ, Ger & ling, Univ Conn, 56-59; from asst prof to assoc prof, 59-76, PROF RUSS, SMITH COL, 76-, CHMN DEPT, 63- *Concurrent Pos:* Asst ling, Ind Univ, 52; asst in instr, Yale Univ, 53-54; vis lectr, Univ RI, 59, Mt Holyoke Col, 60, Univ Mass, 61, Amherst Col, 64-71 & Univ Hamburg, 72-73; vis asst prof, Hartford Col, 62. *Mem:* Am Asn Teachers Slavic & EEurop Lang; MLA. *Res:* Slavic and Germanic philology; Russian literature. *Mailing Add:* Dept of Russ Smith Col Northampton MA 01063

ZENKOVSKY, BETTY JEAN BUBBERS, b Mankato, Minn, Mar 6, 27; m 52. FOREIGN LANGUAGES. *Educ:* Univ Mich, AB, 50; Ind Univ, MA, 54. *Prof Exp:* Reader, Russ lit, Harvard Univ, 57; instr Russ, Stetson Univ, 58-60; instr, Univ Colo, 60-62; asst prof Russ lang & lit, Stetson Univ, 62-65; vis lectr Russ, Vanderbilt Univ, 67-68; RES ASSOC NIKONIAN CODEX, NAT ENDOWMENT FOR HUMANITIES, 78- *Concurrent Pos:* Fac res grant, Stetson Univ, 62. *Mem:* Am Asn Advan Slavic Studies; Am Asn Teachers Slavic & East Europ Lang; AAUW. *Res:* Russian literature. *Publ:* Co-transl, Nikonian Chronicle, Vol I & II, Kingston Press, 82. *Mailing Add:* 126 Interlake Ave De Land FL 32720

ZENKOVSKY, SERGE A, b Kiev, Russia, June 16, 07; US citizen; m 52. SLAVIC CIVILIZATION & LITERATURE. *Educ:* Inst Econ, Prague, Czech, dipl, 27; Univ Paris, Lic Let, 30; Charles Univ, Prague, PhD, 42. *Prof Exp:* Instr Slavic studies, Ind Univ, 50-54; lectr, Dept Slavic Lang & Lit, Harvard Univ, 54-56, res fel, Russ Res Ctr, 56-58; from asst prof to assoc prof hist, Stetson Univ, 58-60; from assoc prof to prof Slavic lang & lit, Univ Colo, 60-62; prof hist & dir Russ studies, Stetson Univ, 62-67; prof, 67-77, EMER PROF SLAVIC CIVILIZATION & LIT, VANDERBILT UNIV, 77-; RES PROF HIST, STETSON UNIV, 77- *Concurrent Pos:* Vis lectr, Conn Col Women, 57-58; Soc Sci Res Coun res grant, 60; Am Philos Soc res grant, 63; vis prof, Univ Heidelberg, 65-66; Guggenheim Mem Found res fel, 65-66; ed, Russ Rev; Fulbright-Hays Res fel, Yugoslavia, 73, Int Res & Exchange Bd, 77-78; Nat Endowment for Humanities grant, Research in Russia & On Nikonian Codex, 78-79. *Mem:* AHA; MLA; Am Asn Teachers Slavic & E Europ Lang; Southern Conf Slavic Studies (pres, 63-64); NAm Dostoevsky Soc (vpres, 74-). *Res:* Russian history; Russian literature. *Publ:* Auth, Medieval Russia's Epics, Chronicles and Tales, Dutton, 63, rev ed, 74; Aus dem alten Russland, C Hansen, München, 68; Russia's Old Believers, Wilhelm Fink, 69; coauth, A Guide to the Bibliography of Russian Literature, 70 & ed, Comparative History of Slavic Literatures, 71, Vanderbilt Univ; auth, Islam ve Turkilez (in Turkish), Ipak Mattbassi, Ankara, 71; ed, History of Russian Nineteenth Century Literature (Romanticism), 74 & History of Russian Nineteenth Century Literature (Realism), 74, Vanderbilt Univ; ed & co-transl, Nikonian Chronicle, Kingston Press, Vol I-II, 82. *Mailing Add:* 126 Interlake Ave De Land FL 32720

ZENN, ELIZABETH GOULD, b McKeesport, Pa, July 14, 22. CLASSICAL LANGUAGES & LITERATURE. *Educ:* Allegheny Col, AB, 43; Univ Pa, AM, 45, PhD, 47. *Prof Exp:* From instr to assoc prof, 47-58, PROF CLASS LANG & LIT, AGNES SCOTT COL, 58-, CHMN DEPT, 80- *Mem:* Am Philol Asn; Ling Soc Am; Archaeol Inst Am. *Res:* The neuter plural in Latin lyric verse. *Mailing Add:* Dept of Class Lang & Lit Agnes Scott Col Decatur GA 30030

ZEPHIR, JACQUES JOSEPH, b Brooklyn, NY, Oct 15, 25; m 54, 74; c 1. FRENCH LANGUAGE & LITERATURE. *Educ:* Univ Haiti, B es L, 45; St Eugene's Col, BA, 48; Laval Univ, MA, 53, PhD, 57; Univ Paris, dipl, 58. *Prof Exp:* Instr philos, Lycee Toussaint Louverture, 49-52; asst prof French Lang & Lit, Assumption Col, Mass, 54-58; from assoc prof to prof, Newton Col Sacred Heart, 59-66; assoc prof, 66-74, PROF FRENCH LANG & LIT, CITY COL NEW YORK, 74- *Concurrent Pos:* Vis asst prof, Col Holy Cross, 57-58; mem fac, grad sch & univ ctr, City Univ New York, 68. *Mem:* MLA; Am Asn Teachers Fr; Soc Fr Prof Am. *Res:* Literary psychology; French literature of the 20th century; French language and literature of Haiti. *Publ:* Auth, La psychologie de Salavin, 54 & Situation de la langue francaise en 'laiti, 4/65, Rev Univ Laval; La personnalite humaine dans l'oeuvre de Marcel Proust; Essai de psychologie litteraire, 60 & Duhamel devant la critique contemporaine, 71, Ed Lett Mod, Paris; La psychologie de Salavin, Ed Univ, Paris, 70; Bibliographie des etudes en francais consacrees a Georges Duhamel 1907-1951, Ed Nizet, Paris, 72. *Mailing Add:* Dept of Romance Lang City Col of New York New York NY 10031

ZEPS, VALDIS JURIS, b Daugavpils, Latvia, May 29, 32; US citizen; m 57; c 4. LINGUISTICS. *Educ:* Miami Univ, AB, 53; Ind Univ, PhD, 61. *Prof Exp:* Sci linguist, Off Geog, US Dept Interior, 61-62; vis asst prof Slavic lang, 62, from asst prof to assoc prof ling, 63-68, PROF LING, UNIV WIS-MADISON, 68- *Concurrent Pos:* Nat Sci Found fel, Ctr Advan Studies Behav Sci, 60-61; Soc Sci Res Coun- Am Coun Learned Soc, Univ Wis, 63; managing ed, Slavic & EEurop Lang; Asn Advan Baltic Studies. *Res:* Linguistic theory; East European languages; East Latvian History. *Publ:* Coauth, Con-cordance and Thesaurus of Cheremis Poetic Language, Mouton, The Hague, 61; auth, Latvian and Finnic Linguistic Convergences, Uralic & Altaic Ser, Ind Univ & Mouton, The Hague, 62; coauth, The meter of the so-called trochaic Latvian folksongs, Int J Slavic Ling & Poetics, 63; auth, Optional rules in the formation of the Old Church Slavonic aorist, Lang, 64; The meter of the Latvian folk dactyl, Celi, 69; Latvian folk meters and styles, In: A Festschrift for Morris Halle, Holt, 73; coauth, The Basel Epigram--A newley discovered test of Old Prussian, Gen Ling, 75; auth, The Placenames of Latgola, Univ Wis-Madison, 78. *Mailing Add:* Dept of Ling Univ of Wis Madison WI 53706

ZERNICKOW, OSKAR HANS, b Ossining, NY, Sept 22, 19. SPANISH, GERMAN. *Educ:* Tulane Univ, BA, 49, MA, 56, PhD(Span), 66. *Prof Exp:* Asst prof, 60-66, ASSOC PROF SPAN & GER, MISS STATE UNIV, 66- *Mem:* Am Asn Teachers Span & Port; Am Asn Teachers Ger. *Res:* Spanish literature, 1800-1936; German literature, 1750-1930. *Mailing Add:* Dept of Foreign Lang Miss State Univ Mississippi State MS 39762

ZETZEL, JAMES E G, b London, England; US citizen. CLASSICAL LITERATURE. *Educ:* Harvard Univ, BA, 68, MA, 70, PhD(class philol), 73. *Prof Exp:* Vis asst prof, Brown Univ, 74-75; asst prof, 75-81, ASSOC PROF CLASS, PRINCETON UNIV, 81- *Concurrent Pos:* Fel, Am Coun of Learned Soc, 77-78; vis assoc prof, Harvard Univ, 82; ed, Transactions of the Am Philol Asn, 82- *Res:* Latin literature; ancient intellectual history; history of classical scholarship. *Publ:* Auth, Emendavi ad Tironem, Harvard Studies in Class Philol, 73; Statilius Maximus and Ciceronian studies in the Antonine Age, Bull Inst Class Studies, Univ London, 74; On the history of Latin scholla, Harvard Studies in Class Philol, 75; The subscriptsions in the manuscript of Livy and Fronto and the meaning of Emendatio, Class Philol, 80; Horace's Lifer Sermonism: The structure of Amgiguity, Arethusa, 80; Latin textual criticism in Antiquity, Arno Press, 81; contribr, Catullue, In: Ancient Writer's, Scribners, 82. *Mailing Add:* Dept of Class Princeton Univ Princeton NJ 08544

ZEVIT, ZIONY, b Winnipeg, Man, Feb 13, 42; nat US; m 66; c 2. SEMITIC LANGUAGES & LITERATURE. *Educ:* Univ Southern Calif, BA, 64; Univ Calif, Berkeley, MA, 67, PhD(Near Eastern studies), 73. *Prof Exp:* Assoc Hebrew, Univ Calif, Berkeley, 69-71; instr biblical lit, Univ Negev, 71-72; lectr, Haifa Univ, 72-74; ASSOC PROF BIBLICAL LIT, UNIV JUDAISM, 74- *Mem:* Am Orient Soc; Am Schs Orient Res; Soc Biblical Lit; Asn Jewish Studies; Int Orgn Old Testament Scholars. *Res:* Hebrew orthography of the First Temple Period; Phoenician poetry; redaction criticism of the Old Testament. *Publ:* Auth, The use of Cebed as a diplomatic term in Jeremiah, J Biblical Lit, 69; A misunderstanding at Bethel--Amos VII, 12-17, Vetus Testementum, 75; The so-called interchangeability of the prepositions b, l, and m(n) in Northwest Semitic, J Ancient Near Eastern Soc, 75; The Eglah Ritual of Deuteronomy 21: 1-9, J Biblical Lit, 76; The linguistic and contextual arguments in support of a Hebrew 3 m s suffic -y, Ugarit Forschung, 77; A Phoenician inscription and Israelite covenant theology, Israel Exploration J, 77. *Mailing Add:* Univ of Judaism 15600 Mulholland Dr Los Angeles CA 90024

ZGUSTA, LADISLAV, b Libochovice, Czech, Mar 20, 24; m 48; c 2. LINGUISTICS. *Educ:* Caroline Univ, Prague, PhD(class philol & indology), 49. *Hon Degrees:* DSc, Czech Acad Sci, 64. *Prof Exp:* Vis prof ling, Cornell Univ, 70; PROF LING, UNIV ILL, URBANA-CHAMPAIGN, 71- *Concurrent Pos:* Res grants, Int Coun Philos & Sci, Paris, 65, 69 & Deut Forschungsgemeinschaft, 69-73; consult, Mod Greek-English Dict, 69 & Ger-English mach transl proj, Ling Res Ctr, Univ Tex, Austin, 70-72; vis mem, Ctr Advan Studies, Univ Ill, 70-71; Am Coun Learned Soc grant, 73; Nat Endowment for Humanities fel, 74; Guggenheim fel, 77. *Honors & Awards:* Prize, Czech Acad, 55 & 64. *Mem:* Am Ling Soc; Am Name Soc; Soc Ling Ital; Indoger Ges; Dict Soc North Am. *Res:* Asia Minor; onomastics; lexicology. *Publ:* Auth, Die Personennamen griechischer Städte der nördlichen Schwarzemeerküste, 55, Kleinasiatische Personennamen, 64, Anatolische Personennamensippen, 64, Neue Beiträge zur kleinasiatischen Anthroponymie, 70, Prague; Frankish and Allemanic trifles, 70 & Trifles from the USA, 70, Zpravodaj; Die Entwicklung der Lexikographie als sprachwissenschaftliche Disziplin, In: Probleme der Lexikographie, Berlin, 70; Manual of Lexicography, Prague & The Hague, 71. *Mailing Add:* 4096 Foreign Lang Bldg Univ of Ill at Urbana-Champaign Urbana IL 61801

ZHOLKOVSKY, ALEXANDER K, b Moscow, USSR, Sept 8, 37; m 73. RUSSIAN LITERATURE & POETICS. *Educ:* Moscow Univ, Dipl, 59, PhD(African studies), 69. *Prof Exp:* Res fel machine transp, Inst For Lang, Moscow, 59-70 & sr res fel comput ling, 70-74; sr res fel, Informelectro, Moscow, 76-78; vis prof gen lang studies, Univ Amsterdam, 79; vis prof Russ lit, 80-81, PROF RUSS LIT, CORNELL UNIV, 81-, CHMN DEPT, 82- *Concurrent Pos:* Vis prof Somali lang, Inst Orient Lang, Moscow Univ, 63-65; fel, Cornell Univ, 80; mem, Soviet Acad Sci Comn Semantics Cult, 77-79. *Mem:* Am Asn Advan Slavic Studies; Asn Comput Ling. *Res:* Russian and comparative literature; theoretical linguistics and poetics; Somali studies. *Publ:* Auth, Sintaksis Somali (The Somali Syntax in Russian), Nauka, 71; coauth, Towards a functioning meaning-text, model of language, Ling, Vol 57, 70; auth, Articles on lexical semantics in a collection of translations from Russian: Essays on Lexical Semantics, Vol 1 & 2, Stockholm, 76; Articles on Puskin and Pasternak, New Lit Hist, Vol IX, 78; How to show things with words: On the iconic representation of themes, Poetics, Vol 8, 79; coauth, Poetika Vyrazitelnosti (The Poetics of Expressiveness in Russian), Wiener Slawistischer Almanach, Sonderband, Vol II, 80; Articles on Pushkin and Sergey Eisenstein, In: Russian Poetics in Translation, Essex Univ & Holdan Bks, Ltd, Vol 8, 81; Themes & Texts: Essays in a Poetics of Expressiveness, Cornell Univ Press (in prep). *Mailing Add:* Dept of Russ Lit Smith Hall 185 Goldwin Cornell Univ Ithaca NY 14853

ZIADEH, FARHAT JACOB, b Palestine, Apr 8, 17; nat US; m 49; c 5. ARABIC, ISLAMICS. *Educ:* Am Univ Beirut, BA, 37; Univ London, LLB, 40. *Prof Exp:* Magistrate, Govt of Palestine, 47-48; from lectr to assoc prof Orient studies, Princeton Univ, 48-66; PROF NEAR EASTERN STUDIES, UNIV WASH, 66- *Concurrent Pos:* Gov Am Res Ctr, Egypt, 70-78, fel, 71-72 & 77. *Mem:* Am Orient Soc; Mid East Studies Asn NAm (pres, 80). *Res:* Arabic language and literature; Islamic law; Islamic institutions. *Publ:* Coauth, Introduction to Modern Arabic, 57, Princeton Univ; auth, Reader in Modern Literary Arabic, Princeton Univ, 63, Univ Wash, 81; ed & transl, Philosophy of Jurisprudence in Islam, Brill, Leiden, 61; auth, Lawyers, the Rule of Law, and Liberalism in Modern Egypt, Hoover Inst, Stanford Univ, 68; Law of Property in the Arab World: Real Rights in Egypt, Iraq, Jordan, Lebanon, Libya, Syria, Graham & Trotman, Ltd, 79; al-Khassaf's Adab al-Qadi (The Discipline of the Judge, edition with introduction and notes), Am Univ Cairo, 79. *Mailing Add:* Dept of Near Eastern Lang & Lit Univ of Wash Seattle WA 98195

ZIDE, NORMAN H, b Brooklyn, NY, May 30, 28; m 63; c 2. LINGUISTICS, INDOLOGY. *Educ:* NY Univ, BA, 47; Columbia Univ, MA, 48; Univ Pa, PhD(SAsia studies, ling), 60. *Prof Exp:* Asst prof ling, 60-66, assoc prof ling & SAsian lang & civilizations, 66-69, PROF S ASIAN LANG & CIVILIZATIONS, UNIV CHICAGO, 69- *Concurrent Pos:* Sr fel, Am Inst Indian Studies, India, 66-67; Nat Sci Found res grant, 66-69; res fel, India, Univ Chicago, 70-72. *Mem:* Ling Soc Am; Am Orient Soc; Asn Asian Studies; Am Anthrop Asn; Soc Ethnomusicol. *Res:* Historical linguistics; Munda languages and cultures; Indian literature. *Publ:* Coauth, A Premchand Reader, East-West Ctr, 65; ed & contribr, Studies in Comparative Austroasiatic Linguistics, Mouton, The Hague, 66; auth, The love songs of Vidyapati, J Am Orient Soc, 65; Graphemic system in the Ol Cemed script, Papers IV Regional Metting Chicago Ling Soc, 68; Munda, Current Trends Ling V, 69; co-ed, Austroasiatic numeral systems, Mouton, 74; Studies in the Munda Numerals Central, Inst Indian Lang, 78. *Mailing Add:* Dept of Ling Univ of Chicago Chicago IL 60637

ZIEFLE, HELMUT WILHELM, b Heilbronn-Sontheim, Ger, Apr 2, 39; US citizen; m 65; c 2. GERMAN LITERATURE, MODERN GERMAN HISTORY. *Educ:* State Univ NY Albany, BA, 64, MA, 66; Univ Ill, PhD(17th century Ger lit), 73. *Prof Exp:* Teacher Ger, Bethlehem Cent High, 65-67; instr, 67-72, asst prof, 72-77, assoc prof, 77-82, PROF GER, WHEATON COL, 82- *Concurrent Pos:* Dir, Wheaton in Ger, 77-; pres, Ger Evening Sch, Wheaton, 78-80; scholar in residence, Ger Dept, Circle Campus, fall, 79. *Mem:* Am Asn Teachers Ger; Czech Soc Arts & Sci. *Res:* Early German baroque literature; modern German literature: Hesse, Mann and postwar German literature; history of the Third Reich especially German opposition to Hitler. *Publ:* Auth, Sibylle Schwarz: Life and work, In: Studies in German, English and Comparative Literature, Bouvier, Bonn, 75; Opitz' influence on poetry of Sibylle Schwarz, Vol 4, 76 & Occupation of Greifswald during Thirty Years War, Vol 2, 77, Pommern; A Christian family resists Hitler, Christianity Today, Vol 6, 78; The long shadow of Hitler, The Christian Reader, 79, 2-5; ed, Sibylle Schwarz: German poetic poems, In: Middle German Literature, Lang, Bern, 80; auth, One Woman Against the Reich, Bethany House Publ, 81; Dict of Modern Theological German, Baker Bk House, 82. *Mailing Add:* ON 460 Fanchon St Wheaton IL 60187

ZIEGFELD, RICHARD EVAN, Comparative Literature, Modern Fiction. See Vol II

ZIEGLER, CARL H, b West Bend, Wis, July 19, 40. GERMAN, COMPARATIVE LITERATURE. *Educ:* Valparaiso Univ, AB, 62; Vanderbilt Univ, PhD, 66. *Prof Exp:* Asst prof, 66-72, ASSOC PROF GER, IND UNIV, BLOOMINGTON, 72- *Mem:* MLA; Midwest Mod Lang Asn. *Res:* Programmed visual instruction of German; the use of computers and German translators. *Mailing Add:* Dept of Ger Lang Ind Univ Bloomington IN 47401

ZIEGLER, VICKIE LYNNE, b Rock Island, Ill. GERMAN. *Educ:* MacMurray Col, BA, 64; Yale Univ, PhD(Ger), 70. *Prof Exp:* Asst prof, 70-76, ASSOC PROF GER, PA STATE UNIV, UNIVERSITY PARK, 76- *Mem:* Mediaeval Acad Am; Int Vereinigung fü germanische Sprachen und Literaturwissenschaft. *Res:* Medieval German lyric; Medieval German romance; romantic Rahmennovelle. *Publ:* Auth, The Leitword in Minnesang, Ger ser, Pa State Univ, 74; Justice in Brentano's 'Die Schactel mit der Friedenspuppe', Ger Rev, fall 78. *Mailing Add:* Dept of German Pa State Univ University Park PA 16802

ZIMANYI, RUDOLPH FRANCIS, b Hodoscsepany, Hungary, May 13, 23; US citizen. ROMANCE LANGUAGES. *Educ:* St Bernard Gym, Eger, Hungary, BA, 42; Canisius Col, MA, 54; Marquette Univ, MA, 56; Northwestern Univ, PhD(French), 63. *Prof Exp:* From instr to asst prof, 59-67, ASSOC PROF FRENCH, UNIV DALLAS, 67- *Mem:* MLA; Am Asn Teachers Fr; SCent Mod Lang Asn; Soc Amis Francois Mauriac. *Res:* Pascal and Francois Mauriac; Baudelaire; French symbolism. *Publ:* Auth, A regi körben, versek, Katolikus Szemle, Rome, 68; Pascal dans l'oeuvre de Francois Mauriac, Diss Abstr, Vol XXIV, No 2; Szomjusag, versek (1969-1972), Sovereign, Toronto, 73. *Mailing Add:* Dept of Foreign Lang Univ of Dallas Irving TX 75061

ZIMMER, KARL ERNST, b Berlin, Ger, Sept 17, 27, US citizen; m 56, 80; c 2. LINGUISTICS. *Educ:* Univ Chicago, BA, 51; Columbia Univ, MA, 54, PhD(ling), 63; Univ Mich, MA, 58. *Prof Exp:* Instr English, Brit Coun, Ankara, Turkey, 55; adv & instr, English Lang Training Ctr, Turkish Ground Forces Command, Ankara, 55-57; programmer Ger, Ctr Programmed instr, NY, 60-62; actg asst prof ling, Univ NC, Chapel Hill, 63-65; from asst prof to assoc prof, 65-75, PROF LING, UNIV CALIF, BERKELEY, 75- *Mem:* Ling Soc Am. *Res:* Structure of Turkish; word formation. *Publ:* Auth, Affixal Negation in English and Other Languages, Ling Circle NY, 64; Psychological correlates of some Turkish morpheme structure conditions, Lang, 6/69; Some general observations about nominal compounds, In: Wortbildung, Wissenschaftliche Buchgesellschaft, Darmstadf, 81. *Mailing Add:* Dept of Ling Univ of Calif Berkeley CA 84720

ZIMMERMAN, EUGENIA NOIK, b New York, NY, Sept 12, 36; div. ROMANCE LANGUAGES. *Educ:* Columbia Univ, BA, 57; Univ Wis, MA, 60, PhD(French), 65. *Prof Exp:* Instr foreign lang, D'Youville Col, 66-67, asst prof, 67-68; asst prof, 68-73, ASSOC PROF FRENCH, CARLETON UNIV, 73- *Mem:* MLA; Asn Can Univ Teachers Fr. *Res:* Proust, Sartre; 20th century intellectual history. *Publ:* Auth, Some of these days: Sartre's petite phrase, Contemporary Lit, summer 70; La nausee and the avatars of being, spring 72 & Death and transfiguration in Proust and Tolstoy winter 73, Mosaic. *Mailing Add:* Dept of French Carleton Univ Ottawa ON K1S 5B6 Can

ZIMMERMAN, MELVIN, b New York, NY, Dec 14, 26; m 54; c 2. FRENCH, COMPARATIVE LITERATURE. *Educ:* Sorbonne, dipl, 48; Univ Md, master foreign studies, 58; City Col NY, BSS, 50; Univ Wis-Madison, PhD(French), 64. *Prof Exp:* Teacher high sch, NY, 58-59; lectr Romance lang, City Col NY, 59; instr French, Univ Wis-Madison, 61-64; asst prof, Univ Md, 64-69; prof interdisciplinary studies, Fac Grad Studies, 74-76, ASSOC PROF FRENCH STUDIES, YORK UNIV, 69- *Concurrent Pos:* Minor res grant, York Univ, 71-72; reader, Univ Toronto Press, 71; reader, Humanities Res Coun Can, 71; proj assessor, Can Coun, 77. *Mem:* Int Asn Lit Critics, Asn Int Critiques Litteraires; Soc d'Etudes Romantiques. *Res:* Baudelaire and modern poetry; comparative literature, France, England and America; art history. *Publ:* Auth, Baudelaire et Montaigne, les themes Carpe diem et Vita brevis, Romance Notes, spring 67; Controversies on Le Jeu de la Feuillee, Studia Neophilol, 67; Baudelaire's studies of Guys and Meryon, In: Hommage a Baudelaire, 68; Scholarly edition of Charles Baudelaire, Petits poemes en prose, In: Fr Classics Ser, Manchester Univ, 68; coauth, Foreign influences & relations, In: A Critical Bibliography of French Literature, Vol 4, suppl, Syracuse Univ, 68; auth, L'Homme et la nature dans Germinal, Cahiers Naturalistes, 72; Problemes d'annotation de textes baudelairiens, Regards sur Baudelaire, 74; Trois Etudes sur Baudelaire et Roussean, In: Boudelaire, Roussean et Hugo, Etudes Bundelairiennes, Vol 9, Neuchatel, 81. *Mailing Add:* Dept of French Studies York Univ 4700 Keele St Downsview ON M3J 1P3 Can

ZIMMERMANN, ELEONORE M, US citizen. FRENCH, COMPARATIVE LITERATURE. *Educ:* Swarthmore Col, BA, 51; Yale Univ, MA, 53, PhD(comp lit), 56. *Prof Exp:* Instr French, Wellesley Col, 56-59; from lectr to asst prof French, Ger & comp lit, Brandeis Univ, 59-66; assoc prof, Univ Rochester, 66-71; prof French, 71-72; PROF FRENCH & COMP LIT, STATE UNIV NY STONY BROOK, 72- *Concurrent Pos:* Am Coun Learned Soc fel, 63-64; Guggenheim fel, 71-72. *Mem:* MLA; Am Asn Teachers Fr; Am Comp Lit Asn; Int Asn Fr Studies. *Res:* Romanticism, especially French, German and English; 19th century lyricism, especially French and German; 17th century French theatre. *Publ:* Auth, Magies de Verlaine, Corti, Paris, 67, Slatkine, Geneva, 81; Vision in poetry, In: Disciplines of criticism, Yale Univ, 68; Le role de Swann et dela societe dans l acte de creation proustien, Studi Frandesi, 9/71; Audela d Athalie, French Forum, 1/80; La Liberte et le destin dans le theatre de Racine, Anma Libri, Stanford, 82. *Mailing Add:* Dept of French & Ital State Univ of NY Stony Brook NY 11790

ZIMMERMANN, FRANK, b US, Apr 17, 07; m 32, 80; c 1. BIBLICAL LITERATURE, SEMITIC LANGUAGES. *Educ:* City Col, New York, BA, 29; Dropsie Col, PhD, 35; Jewish Theol Sem, DHL, 36. *Prof Exp:* PROF BIBL LIT, DROPSIE UNIV, 59- *Concurrent Pos:* Cur, Jewish Mus, 35-36; assoc trustee, Am Sch Orient Res, 61-63. *Mem:* Soc Bibl Lit; World Bible Soc, Jerusalem. *Res:* Semitic philology; Biblical exegesis; Aramaic-Greek studies. *Publ:* Auth, Book of Tobit, Harper, 58; Inner World of Qohelet, 72, Biblical Books Translated from the Aramaic, 72 & Aramaic Origin of the Four Gospels, 79, Ktav. *Mailing Add:* 112-20 72nd Dr Forest Hills NY 11375

ZIMNAVODA, HELEN FEINSTEIN URY, b St Petersburg, Russia, May 31, 08; US citizen; wid; c 3. RUSSIAN LANGUAGE & CULTURE. *Educ:* Univ Chicago, BS, 30; Univ Southern Calif, MS, 39. *Prof Exp:* Assoc prof educ & sci, 57-60, assoc prof Russ lang, lit & civilization, 60-75, EMER ASSOC PROF RUSS LANG, LIT & CIVILIZATION, CALIF STATE UNIV, LOS ANGELES, 75- *Honors & Awards:* Medal, Lomonosav Inst & Mendeleev Chemistry Inst, USSR, 71. *Mem:* Am Asn Teachers Slavic & EEurop Lang; Comp & Int Educ Soc; Nat Sci Teachers Asn; MLA. *Res:* Russian linguistics and literature. *Mailing Add:* 4605 Los Feliz Blvd Apt 1 Los Angeles CA 90027

ZIMRA, CLARISSE, b France, Jan 4, 44; m 74. COMPARATIVE LITERATURE, FRENCH. *Educ:* Univ Aix-en-Provence, Lic es Let, 65; Univ Wash, MA, 68, PhD(comp lit), 74. *Prof Exp:* Vis prof Am studies, HoaHao Budhist Univ VietNam, 71-72; ASST PROF FRENCH & FRANCOPHONE STUDIES, UNIV VA, 74- *Concurrent Pos:* Mem exec comt, MLA, 78- *Honors & Awards:* Prix Inst Francais de Washington, 76. *Mem:* MLA; Am Asn Teachers Fr; African Studies Asn; African Lit Asn; Ctr d'Etudes Lit En'dehors France. *Res:* Women writiers of the Francophone world; Franco-American relations; the image of Blacks in French Romanticism. *Publ:* Auth, Un Francais au desert, Buffl Fedn Int Prof Francais, 76; La vision du nouveau monde, Fr Rev, 76; Patterns of liberation, Esprit Createur, 77; Cross-cultural encounters, Folio, 78; contribr, Ecrivaines de Langue Francaise, Stok Paris, 78. *Mailing Add:* Dept of French Cabell Hall Univ Va Charlottesville VA 22901

ZINKAND, JOHN M, b Hempstead, NY, Mar 8, 27; m 49; c 5. CLASSICAL LANGUAGES. *Educ:* Wheaton Col, Ill, AB, 50; Johns Hopkins Univ, AM, 51; Westminster Theol Sem, BD, 54, ThM, 55; Brandeis Univ, PhD, 58. *Prof Exp:* Teacher lang, Dordt Col, 58-62, from assoc prof to prof class lang, 62-66; spec lectr Old Testament, Westminster Theol Sem, 65-66, assoc prof, 66-69; PROF CLASS LANG, DORDT COL, 69- *Concurrent Pos:* Consult & transl, New Int Version of the Bible. *Mem:* Am Philol Asn; Am Class League; Class Asn Midwest & South; Evangel Theol Soc. *Res:* Greek and Hebrew language; Biblical translation. *Publ:* Auth, articles in Pro Rege, Westminster Theol J & Class World. *Mailing Add:* Dept of Foreign Lang Dordt Col Sioux Center IA 51250

ZINNI, HANNAH CASE, b Cincinnati, Ohio, Oct 1, 44; m 77. FRENCH LANGUAGE & LITERATURE. *Educ:* Oberlin Col, BA, 66; Northwestern Univ, MA, 67, Phd(French lit), 71. *Prof Exp:* Asst prof, 70-75, assoc prof, 75-81, PROF FRENCH, SLIPPERY ROCK STATE COL, 81- *Mem:* Am Asn Teachers French; MLA; Northeastern Mod Lang Asn. *Res:* Art and the artist in the works of Samuel Beckett; the couple in Samuel Beckett's works; the Louisiana French. *Publ:* Auth, Art and the Artist in the Works of Samuel Beckett, Mouton, 75; The couples in Comment C'est, In: Samuel Beckett: The Art of Rhetoric, Univ NC, 76; bibliog for Andre DuBouchet, Andre Frenaud & Philippe Soupault, In: Critical Bibliography of French Literature of the Twentieth Century, 80. *Mailing Add:* Dept of Mod Lang & Cult Slippery Rock State Col Slippery Rock PA 16057

ZINTL, CARRIE-MAY KURRELMEYER, b Baltimore, Md, Sept 26, 04; wid; c 1. GERMAN & CLASSICS. *Educ:* Goucher Col, AB, 24; Johns Hopkins Univ, PhD(classics), 29. *Prof Exp:* Asst prof classics, Wilson Col, 28-29; prof, Mt St Agnes Col, 46-71, EMER PROF GER & CLASSICS, LOYOLA COL, MD, 71- *Concurrent Pos:* Lectr class mythology, Johns Hopkins Univ, 71- *Mem:* Am Asn Teachers Ger; MLA; Archaeol Inst Am; Am Philol Asn. *Res:* Teaching of German and classical mythology. *Mailing Add:* 3601 Greenway Baltimore MD 21218

ZIOBRO, WILLIAM JEROME, b Kingston, Pa, Dec 28, 44; m 66; c 2. CLASSICS. *Educ:* Col Holy Cross, AB, 66; John Hopkins Univ, PhD(classics), 69. *Prof Exp:* ASSOC PROF CLASSICS, COL HOLY CROSS, 69-, ASST DEAN, 71- *Mem:* Am Philol Asn; Class Asn New England. *Res:* Greek tragedy; classics in Colonial and post-Revolutionary America. *Publ:* Auth, Where was Antigone: Antigone v 766-833?, Am J Philol, 71; The Entrance and Exit of Athena in the Ajax, Class Folia, 72. *Mailing Add:* Off of the Asst Dean Col of the Holy Cross Worcester MA 01610

ZIOLKOWSKI, JOHN EDMUND, b Montevallo, Ala, June 19, 38; m 58; 71; c 2. CLASSICAL LANGUAGES. *Educ:* Duke Univ, AB, 58; Univ NC, PhD(classics), 63. *Prof Exp:* Instr Latin, Univ NC, 62-64; asst prof classics, Randolph-Macon Woman's Col, 64-67; asst prof, 67-72, ASSOC PROF CLASSICS, GEORGE WASHINGTON UNIV, 72-, CHMN DEPT, 71- *Mem:* Am Philol Asn; Am Inst Archeol. *Res:* Greek and Roman literature; Renaissance Latin; Classical influence on Washington DC. *Publ:* Auth, Thueydides and the Tradition of Funeral Speeches at Athens, Arno, 81. *Mailing Add:* Dept of Classics George Washington Univ Washington DC 20052

ZIOLKOWSKI, THEODORE J, b Birmingham, Ala, Sept 30, 32; m 51; c 3. GERMAN, COMPARATIVE LITERATURE. *Educ:* Duke Univ, AB, 51, AM, 52; Yale Univ, PhD, 57. *Prof Exp:* From instr to asst prof Ger, Yale Univ, 56-62; assoc prof, Columbia Univ, 62-64; prof Ger lit, 64-69, CLASS OF 1900 PROF MOD LANG, PRINCETON UNIV, 69-, CHMN, DEPT GER, 73-, PROF COMP LIT, 75-, DEAN, GRAD SCH, 79- *Concurrent Pos:* Fulbright res grant, Ger, 58-59; Am Philos Soc grant, 59; Guggenheim fel, 65-66; vis prof, Rutgers Univ, 66, Yale Univ, 67 & 75 & City Univ New York, 71; vis scholar, Piedmont Univ Ctr NC, 71 & Univ Ctr Va, 71; Am Coun Learned Soc fel, 72; chmn, Doctoral Eval Prog in Ger, NY State, 74-76; Nat Endowment for Humanities fel, summer, 78. *Honors & Awards:* James Russell Lowell Award Criticism, MLA, 73; Howard T Behrman Award Humanities, 78; Dancy lectr, Univ Montevallo, 79; Patton Found lectr, Ind Univ, 81. *Mem:* MLA; Auth Guild; Am Asn Teachers Ger; Int Ver Germanisten. *Res:* German and comparative literature of the 19th and 20th centuries; history of genre and themes. *Publ:* Auth, Novels of Hermann Hesse, 65, Dimensions of the Modern Novel, 69 & Fictional Transfigurations of Jesus, 72, Princeton Univ; ed, Hermann Hesse: Autobiographical Writings, 72 & Stories of Five Decades, 72 & My Belief: Essays on Life and Art, 74, Farrar, Straus; auth, Disenchanted Images: A Literary Iconology, 77 & The Classical German Elegy, 1795-1950, 80, Princeton Univ. *Mailing Add:* Dept of Ger Princeton Univ Princeton NJ 08540

ZIOMEK, HENRYK, b Druzbin, Poland, Jan 8, 22; US citizen; m 56; c 3. SPANISH GOLDEN AGE LITERATURE. *Educ:* Ind State Univ, BA, 55; Ind Univ, MA, 56; Univ Minn, PhD, 61. *Prof Exp:* Teaching asst, Ind Univ, 55-56; teaching asst, Univ Minn, 58-59; from instr to asst prof Span, French & Latin, Wis State Univ, 56-60; asst prof Span & French, Butler Univ, 60-62; assoc prof, Colo State Univ, 62-64; assoc prof Span Golden Age Lit, Ohio Univ, 64-66; assoc prof, 66-71, PROF SPAN GOLDEN AGE LIT, UNIV GA, 71- *Concurrent Pos:* Contrib, Abstr English Studies, 66-; Am Coun Learned Soc grant, 81. *Mem:* Am Asn Teachers Span & Port; MLA; SAtlantic Mod Lang Asn; Asn Int Hispanistas; Polish Inst Arts & Sci Am. *Publ:* Auth, Reflexiones del Quijote, 71 & A critical edition of Lope de Vega's autograph play El poder en el discreto, 71, Ed M Molina; ed, An edition with notes and an introduction of Lope de Vega's La batalla del honor, 72, An edition with notes and an introduction of Lope de Vega's La prueba de los amigos, 73 & A critical edition of Luis Velez de Guevara's play La creacion del mundo, 74, Univ Ga; El Amor en Vizcaino y El Principe Vinador de Luis Velez de Guevara: Edicion critica de dos somedias, 75, Mas Pesa el Rey Que la Sangre, y Blason de los Guzmanes de Luis Velez de Guevara: Edicion critica con introduccion y notas, 76, Ed Ebro, Zaragoza, Spain; auth, Impresiones de lo grotesco en la literatura del siglo de oro, Ed Alcala, S Am, 82. *Mailing Add:* Dept of Romance Lang Univ of Ga Athens GA 30602

ZIPES, JACK DAVID, b New York, NY, June 7, 37. GERMAN, COMPARATIVE LITERATURE. *Educ:* Dartmouth Col, BA, 59; Columbia Univ, MA, 60, PhD(English & comp lit), 65. *Prof Exp:* Admin asst English, Inst Teachers English at Columbia, 64-65; instr Am lit, Univ Munich, 66-67; asst prof, Ger, NY Univ, 67-72; ASSOC PROF GER, UNIV WIS-MILWAUKEE, 72- *Concurrent Pos:* Ed, New Ger Critique, 73-; contrib ed, Theater, Yale Univ, 77- *Mem:* MLA; Brecht Soc. *Res:* Drama. *Publ:* Auth, The Great Refusal: Studies of the Romantic Hero in German and American Literature, Athenaeum, Frankfurt, 70; transl & introd, Steppenwolf and Everyman, 71 & coauth, Crowell's Handbook of Contemporary Drama, 71, Crowell; ed & introd, Romantik in Kritischer Perspektive, Stiehm, Heidelberg, 73; Die Funtkion der Frau in den Komodien der DDR, Noch einmal: Brecht und die Folgen, In: Die Deutsche Komödie im 20, Jahrhundert, Heidelberg, 73; Talking children seriously: The recent popularity of children's theatre in East and West Germany, In: Children's Literature: The Great Excluded, 73; auth, The Revolutionary Rise of the Romantic Fairy Tale in Germany, Studies in Romanticism, fall 77. *Mailing Add:* Dept of Ger Univ of Wis-Milwaukee Milwaukee WI 53201

ZIPSER, RICHARD ALFRED, b Baltimore, Md, Jan 23, 43; m 81. GERMAN LITERATURE. *Educ:* Colby Col, BA, 64; Middlebury Col, MA, 65; Johns Hopkins Univ, PhD(Ger), 72. *Prof Exp:* Asst prof, 69-76, ASSOC PROF GER, OBERLIN COL, 76- *Concurrent Pos:* IREX exchange scholar fel, 77-78; Nat fel, Hoover Inst, 80-81. *Mem:* Am Asn Teachers Ger; New England Mod Lang Asn; Am Lit Transl Asn. *Res:* Contemporary East German literature; German literature and society in the mid-19th century. *Publ:* Auth, Bulwer-Lytton and Goethe's Mignon, Mod Lang Notes, 4/74; Edward Bulwer-Lytton and Germany, German Studies in America, Vol XVI, Herbert Lang, 74; ed, Die neuen Leiden des jungen W,Wiley, 78; ed, Contemporary East German Poetry, Field, 80; co-ed, From Kafka and Dada to Brecht and Beyond, Univ Wis Press, 82. *Mailing Add:* Dept of Ger & Russ Oberlin Col Oberlin OH 44074

ZIRIN, RONALD ANDREW, b New York, NY, May 14, 40; m 62; c 3. CLASSICAL LINGUISTICS. *Educ:* Queens Col, BA, 62; Princeton Univ, MA, 65, PhD(ling), 66. *Prof Exp:* Asst prof, 66-72, actg chmn dept, 72-73, ASSOC PROF CLASSICS, STATE UNIV NY BUFFALO, 72- *Concurrent Pos:* Jr fel, Ctr Hellenic Studies, Washington, DC, 73-74; Nat Endowment for Humanities younger humanist fel, 73-74. *Mem:* Am Philol Asn; Ling Soc Am. *Res:* Greek and Latin prosody; early history of linguistic thought; historical linguistics. *Publ:* Auth, The Phonological Basis of Latin Prosody, Mouton, The Hague, 70. *Mailing Add:* Dept of Classics State Univ of NY Buffalo NY 14214

ZITZELSBERGER, OTTO JOSEPH, b New York, NY. GERMANIC LANGUAGES. *Educ:* City Col New York, BA, 56; Columbia Univ, MA, 60, PhD(Ger), 67. *Prof Exp:* Instr Ger, Columbia Univ, 57-58; instr, 60-62, asst prof, 64-68, ASSOC PROF GER, RUTGERS UNIV, NEWARK, 69- *Concurrent Pos:* Germanistic Soc Am fel, Univ Kiel, 62-63; co-adj assoc prof Icelandic, NY Univ, 76-81. *Mem:* MLA; Soc Advan Scand Studies; Am Asn Teachers Ger; Am-Scand Found; Dict Soc North Am. *Res:* Germanic philology; paleography. *Publ:* Auth, The Two Versions of Sturlaugs Saga Starfsama: A Decipherment, Edition, and Translation of a Fourteenth Century Icelandic Mythical-Herioc Saga, M Triltsch, Dusseldorf, 69; Medieval physiology encoded: An Icelandic Samtal, In: Mediaeval Scandinavia, Odense Univ Denmark, 78; Etymological Dictionaries for Icelandic: Some Critical Comments, 2: 3-8 & transl, Konrads saga keisarasonar, 3: 38-67, Yearbk, Sem Germanic Philol; AM 567, 4 to, XVI, IV: An Instance of Conflation?, Arkiv för nordisk filologi, Vol XCV, 183-188; The Filiation of the Manuscripts of Konrads saga keisarasonar, Amsterdamer Beitrage zur alteren Germanistik 16: 145-176. *Mailing Add:* Dept of Foreign Lang & Lit Rutgers Univ Newark NJ 07102

ZLOTCHEW, CLARK M, b Jersey City, NJ, Oct 14, 32. SPANISH LANGUAGE, HISPANIC LITERATURE. *Educ:* New York Univ, BS, 57; Middlebury Col, MA, 66; State Univ NY Binghamton, PhD(Romance lang & lit), 74. *Prof Exp:* Mem staff sales/prod, Schenley Int Corp, New York, 57-62; teacher Span, Dumont High Sch, NJ, 62-66; asst prof Span, Norwich Univ, 66-68; instr, State Univ NY Geneseo, 70-74; proj coordr migrant educ, Genesee-Wyo Bd of Coop Educ Serv, 75; asst prof, 75-78, assoc prof, 78-82, PROF SPAN & LING, STATE UNIV NY FREDONIA, 82- *Concurrent Pos:* Nat Endowment for Humanities grant, 78. *Mem:* Am Asn Teachers Span & Port; Northeastern Mod Lang Asn; MLA. *Res:* Nineteenth-century Peninsular literature; comtemporary Latin-American literature; Hispanic linguistics. *Publ:* Auth, Recurrent phonetic developments in the Spanish consonant, Orbis, 12/71; Tlön, Llhuros, N Daly, J L Borges, Mod Fiction Studies, autumn 73; On the origins of ole!, Orbis, 76; Galdos and mass psychology, Anales Galdosianos, 77; Galdos's Gloria: A new annunciation, Hispania, 79; La experiencia directa de la obsesiva en Borges y Robbe-Grillet, Kanina, 80; The collaboration of the reader in Borges and Robbe-Grillet, Mich Acad, 81; transl, Seven Conversations with Jorge Luis Borges, Whitston Publ Co, 82. *Mailing Add:* Dept of Foreign Lang State Univ of NY Fredonia NY 14063

ZOHN, HARRY, b Vienna, Austria, Nov 21, 23; nat US; m 62; c 2. GERMAN. *Educ:* Suffolk Univ, BA, 46; Clark Univ, MA Ed, 47; Harvard Univ, AM, 49, PhD(Ger lang & lit), 52. *Hon Degrees:* LittD, Suffolk Univ, 76. *Prof Exp:* From instr to assoc prof, 51-67, PROF GER, BRANDEIS UNIV, 67- *Concurrent Pos:* Trustee, Suffolk Univ, 78-81; chmn grad prog lit studies, 81- *Mem:* Am Transl Asn; Am Asn Teachers Ger; MLA; PEN Club; Int Arthur Schnitzler Res Asn (vpres, 77-). *Res:* Problems of translation; Austrian literature; German-Jewish writers. *Publ:* Transl & ed, Kurt Tucholsky, The World is a Comedy, Sci-Art, 57; Theodor Herzl, Complete Zionist Writings, 60; ed, Der farbenvolle Untergang, 71 & Friderike Zweig's Greatness Revisited, Deutschland ueber alles, 72; auth, Participation in German Literature, In: Jews of Czechoslovakia, Karl Kraus, 71; transl & ed, Marianne Weber: Max Weber, A Biography, Wiley, 75; Karl Kraus: Half-Truths and One-and-a-Half Truths & In These Great Times, Engendra, 76; transl, Greshorn Scholem: Walter Benjamin, The Story of a Friendship, JPS, 81. *Mailing Add:* Dept of Ger Brandeis Univ Waltham MA 02154

ZOLBROD, PAUL GEYER, Literary Criticism, Linguistics. See Vol II

ZOLDESTER, PHILIP H, b Vienna, Austria, Oct 29, 23; US citizen. GERMAN. *Educ:* Univ Vienna, D rer pol, 48; Univ Minn, PhD(Ger, French), 68. *Prof Exp:* Instr Ger, Mt Holyoke Col, 59-62; instr, Univ Minn, 62-65; asst prof Ger & humanities, Reed Col, 65-67; asst prof Ger, Univ Va, 67-72; ASSOC PROF GER, NORTHERN ILL UNIV, 72- *Mem:* Am Asn Teachers Ger; Mod Austrian Lit; Adalbert Stifter Ges. *Res:* Stifter; Novalis; Goethe. *Publ:* Auth, Adalbert Stifters Weltanschauund, Lang, Bern, 70; Stifter und Novalis, Vierteljahrschrift Adalbert Stifter Inst, Austria, 5/73. *Mailing Add:* Dept of Foreign Lang North Ill Univ De Kalb IL 60115

ZOLLITSCH, REINHARD, b Kiel, Ger, May 14, 39; m 64; c 3. GERMAN LANGUAGE & LITERATURE. *Educ:* Kiel Univ, BA, 62; Univ Maine, Orono, MA, 64; Univ Mass, Amherst, MA, 69, PhD(Ger), 71. *Prof Exp:* Instr, 64-66, asst prof, 69-74, ASSOC PROF GER, UNIV MAINE, ORONO, 74- *Mem:* Am Asn Teachers Ger. *Res:* Heinrich von Kleist, 1777-1811; 19th and 20th century German literature. *Mailing Add:* Dept of Foreign Lang Univ of Maine Orono ME 04473

ZORITA, CELESTINO ANGEL, b Valladolid, Spain, Aug 2, 25; m 71; c 2. SPANISH LITERATURE, CLASSICAL LANGUAGES. *Educ:* Gregorian Univ, Rome, MA, 49, dipl Latin, 50; Univ Seville, PhD(philos, lett), 74. *Prof Exp:* Teacher Span, Sem Madrid, 52-66 & Cathedral Latin High Sch, Cleveland, Ohio, 66-67; asst prof, WVa State Col, 67-71; ASSOC PROF SPAN, CLEVELAND STATE UNIV, 71- *Concurrent Pos:* Lectr relig, Univ Madrid, 55-64. *Mem:* Am Asn Teachers Span & Port. *Res:* Twentieth century Spanish peninsular poetry; Spanish humanists of the Renaissance. *Publ:* Auth, Las inscripciones del Arco de la Victoria, Razon y Fe, 4/62; El anticlericalismo de Silverio Lanza, Papeles de Son Armadans, 7/64; Este otro Damaso Alonso: Pervivencia soterrana del poeta Puro, Boletin Fernan Gonzalez, 1/75; contribr, La poesia de D Alonso y Unamuno, In: Studies in Language and Literature, Eastern Ky Univ, 76; auth, Damaso Alonso, Epesa, Madrid, 76. *Mailing Add:* Dept of Mod Lang Cleveland State Univ Cleveland OH 44115

ZRIMC, RUDOLF, b Yugoslavia, Apr 14, 23; US citizen; m 58; c 2. LINGUISTICS. *Educ:* Western Reserve Univ, BA, 54; Harvard Univ, MA, 56, PhD, 61. *Prof Exp:* Asst prof Slavic, Ohio State Univ, 61-62; asst prof ling, Univ Southern Calif, 63-68; from asst prof to assoc prof foreign lang, 68-75, PROF FOREIGN LANG, CALIF STATE POLYTECH UNIV, POMONA, 75- *Mem:* MLA; Am Asn Teachers Slavic & EEurop Lang. *Res:* Russian; South Slavic languages. *Mailing Add:* Dept of English & Mod Lang Calif State Polytech Univ Pomona CA 91766

ZUCK, OUTI VIRPI, b Tampere, Finland, Nov 23, 39; m 62; c 2. SCANDINAVIAN LITERATURE. *Educ:* Univ Helsinki, BA, 64, MA, 65, Ind Univ, MLS, 68; Univ Wis-Madison, PhD(Scand lit), 77. *Prof Exp:* Vis asst prof, 74-76, asst prof, 76-80, ASSOC PROF SCAND, UNIV ORE, 80- *Mem:* Soc Advan Scand Study. *Res:* Finno-Swedish prose; Swedish novel; Scandinavian women writers. *Publ:* Auth, Runar Schildt, Scand Studies, 77; Cora Sandel, A Norwegian feminist, Edda, 81. *Mailing Add:* Dept of Ger & Russ Univ Ore Eugene OR 97403

ZUCKER, GEORGE KENNETH, b New York, NY, Oct 5, 39; m 60; c 4. SPANISH PHILOLOGY, MEDIEVAL LITERATURE. *Educ:* Queens Col, NY, BA, 60; State Univ Iowa, MA, 61, PhD(Span), 64. *Prof Exp:* Asst prof Span, Ind Univ, Bloomington, 64-68; assoc prof, 68-74, PROF SPAN, UNIV NORTHERN IOWA, 74- *Mem:* MLA; Am Asn Teachers Span & Port; Asn Study Jewish Lang. *Res:* Medieval and Renaissance Spanish linguistics; literary criticism; Judeospanish. *Publ:* Auth, Indice de materias citadas en el Dialogo de la lengua de Juan de Valdes, Univ Iowa, 62; La prevaricacion idiomatica: Un recurso comico en el Quijote, Thesaurus, 73. *Mailing Add:* Dept of Mod Lang Univ of Northern Iowa Cedar Falls IA 50614

ZUJEWSKYJ, OLEH, b Khomutets, Ukraine, Feb 16, 20; US citizen; m 39; c 2. SLAVONIC LANGUAGES & LITERATURES. *Educ:* Univ Pa, MA, 58, PhD(Russ lang & lit), 62. *Prof Exp:* Instr Russ, Fordham Univ, 60-63; asst prof, Rutgers Univ, 63-66; from asst prof to assoc prof, 66-77, PROF RUSS, UNIV ALTA, 77- *Res:* The art of translation; Chekhov; West-European and Russian literary relations, especially 19th century and modernism. *Publ:* Auth, The Golden Gate, a collection of poems in Ukrainian, Munich, 47; Under the Sign of Phoenix, a collection of poems in Ukrainian, 58 & coauth, Stefan George, Selected poems in Ukrainian and in other, mainly Slavic languages, 68-71, Na hori, Munich; auth, The principle of absolutization in E Kostetzky's translations, In: Eaghor G Kostetzky: On the Occasion of the 50th birthday of the Ukrainian Writer E G Kostetzky, Munich, 63-64; articles on N Gogol, N Leskov, D Merezhkovski & V Rozanov, In: New Cath Encycl, McGraw, 66; Elements of Biographical Conception in I Franko's Translations of Shakespeare's Sonnets, Symbolae in Honorem Georgii Y Shevelov, Munich, 71. *Mailing Add:* Dept of Slavic Lang Univ of Alta Edmonton AB T6G 2G2 Can

ZWART, MARTIN, b Rotterdam, Neth, July 18, 08; US citizen. FOREIGN LANGUAGES & LITERATURE. *Educ:* Univ Leyden, BA, 28; Univ Amsterdam, MA, 33, PhD, 37. *Prof Exp:* Instr Ger, Hiram Col, 49-50, prof Ger, French & Span, Iowa Wesleyn Col, 52-54; prof, Olivet Col, 56-62; prof Ger, 62-73, EMER PROF GER, N CENT COL, ILL, 74- *Concurrent Pos:* Dir, Ill Educ Foregn Lang and Art Libr. *Mem:* Am Soc Geoling. *Res:* Literary and cultural history of France, Netherlands and German speaking nations; Dutch language; anthology of modern world poetry in English translation. *Publ:* Contribr, Mod Lang J, 11/54 & Int Lang Rev; translr & coauth, Anthology of German poetry, Ungar, 64. *Mailing Add:* 122 S Brainard Naperville IL 60540

ZWEERS, ALEXANDER FREDERIK, b Amsterdam, Holland, June 11, 31; Can citizen; m 63; c 2. RUSSIAN LITERATURE. *Educ:* Univ Amsterdam, Drs, 59; Univ Groningen, Holland, PhD(Russ lit), 71. *Prof Exp:* Instr, Univ BC, 62-67; asst prof, 67-73, ASSOC PROF RUSS & CHURCH SLAVONIC, UNIV WATERLOO, 73- *Concurrent Pos:* Can Coun res grants, 71, 72, 74 & 77; partic, Exchange Prog Can & Soviet Scholars, 74. *Mem:* Can Asn Slavists; Can Asn Advan Netherlandic Studies. *Res:* L N Tolstoy; I A Bunin; Russian-Dutch literary relations. *Publ:* Auth, Is there only one Anna Karenina?, Can Slav Papers, 69; Grown-up Narrator and Childlike Hero, Mouton, The Hague, 71; The narrator's position in Dostoevskij's Netocka Nezvanova and Malen'kij Geroj, Tijdschrift voor Slavische Taal-en Letterkunde, 73; ed, Pis'ma I Bunina k G Adamovicu, 73, Pis'ma I A Bunina k N A Teffi, 74, Pis'ma I A Bunina k F A Stepunu, 75 & Dva pis'ma I A Bunina k A G Bloku, 75, Novyj Zurnal; auth, Herman Heijermans' Second Play Ahasverus, Germano-Slavica, 75. *Mailing Add:* 116 Keats Way Pl Waterloo ON N2L 5H3 Can

ZWICKY, ARNOLD MELCHIOR, b Allentown, Pa, Sept 6, 40; m 62; c 1. LINGUISTICS. *Educ:* Princeton Univ, AB, 62; Mass Inst Technol, PhD(ling), 65. *Prof Exp:* Mem res staff, Mitre Corp, Bedford, Mass, 63-65; asst prof ling, Univ Ill, Urbana, 65-69, actg head dept, 66-67; asst prof, Ling Inst, Univ Ill, 68; assoc prof, 69-71, PROF LING, OHIO STATE UNIV, 71- *Concurrent Pos:* Prof & assoc dir, Ling Inst, Univ NC, 72; Guggenheim Mem Found fel, 72-73; vis prof theoret psychol, Univ Edinburgh, 73; prof, Ling Inst, Univ Mass, 74; vis prof exp psychol, Univ Sussex, 76 & Fulbright res prof, 77; fel, Ctr Adv Study Behav Sci, 81-82; prof & assoc dir, Ling Inst, Univ Md, 82; Nat Endowment for Humanities grants, 77-78; NSF res grant, 77-78; Nat Endowment for Humanities summer sem Col Teachers, 79; Alfred P Sloan Found grant, 80-82, trustee, Ctr Applied Ling, 79- *Mem:* Ling Soc Am; Ling Asn Can & US; Soc Ling Europ; Asn Comp Ling; Am Dial Soc. *Res:* Methodology and argumentation in generative grammar; linguistic theory; syntax-phonology interactions. *Publ:* Auth, On casual speech, Papers 8th Regional Meeting, Chicago Ling Soc, 72; The strategy of generative phonology, In: Phonological 1972, Wilhelm Fink, 75; coauth, Ambiguity Tests and How to Fail Them, In: Syntax and Semantics IV, Acad, 75; auth, On Clitics, Ind Univ Ling Club, 77; Mistakes, Advocate, 80; An expanded view of morphology in the syntax-phonology interface, 13th Int Cong Ling, 82. *Mailing Add:* 63 W Beaumont Rd Columbus OH 43214

ZYLA, WOLODYMYR T, b Zbaraz, Ukraine, June 25, 19; US citizen; m 45; c 3. SLAVIC PHILOLOGY. *Educ:* Univ Man, BS, 59, MA, 62; Ukrainian Free Univ, Munich, PhD(Slavic philol), 67. *Prof Exp:* Assoc prof Russ & Ger lang & Russ lit, 63-74, PROF SLAVIC LANG & LIT, TEX TECH UNIV, 74- *Concurrent Pos:* Ed, Proc Comp Lit Symp, Vol I-IV, 68-71, coed, Vol V-X, 72-77; chmn, Interdept Comt Comp Lit, Tex Tech Univ, 69-76; Nat Endowment for Humanities grant, 75. *Honors & Awards:* Lett & Cert, Am Revolution Bicentennial Admin, 76. *Mem:* Multi-Ethnic Lit US; Am Asn Teachers Slavic & East Europ Lang; Am Name Soc; Shevcheko Sci Soc; Am Comp Lit Asn. *Res:* Ukrainian literature, 16th and 17th centuries; literary criticism of modern literature; comparative literature. *Publ:* Auth, Contribution to the History of Ukrainian and Other Slavic Studies in Canada, Ukrainian Free Acad Sci, 61; A Ukrainian Version of Scotland's Liberator Bruce, Studies in Scottish Lit, 73; Mova i styl' Panasa Nyrnoho, Ukrainian Free Univ, 74; Obraz Alhapja Honcharenka, Zaxidn' okanads' kyj zbirnyk, 75; Manifestions of Ukrainian Poetry and Prose in Exile, Bks Abroad, 76; The Ukrainian Isolt, SCent Bull, 76; Yar Slavutych: Spiritual Aristocrat, 78 & Tvorcist' Yara Slavutycha, 78, Juvilejnyj Komitet. *Mailing Add:* 5220 29th St Lubbock TX 79407

GEOGRAPHIC INDEX

ALABAMA

Auburn

DiOrio, Dorothy May, Foreign Languages
Posniak, Alexander Richard, French & Italian
Rivas, Daniel Eusebio, French, Spanish
Skelton, Robert Beattie, Foreign Languages
Spencer, Samia Iskander, French

Auburn University

Helmke, Henry Conrad, German Language & Literature
Peak, John Hunter, Nineteenth Century Spanish Drama

Birmingham

Baxter, William, III, General & Chinese Linguistics
Carter, William Causey, French Language & Literature
Harper, Hubert Hill, Jr, Classical Languages, English
Hawley, Wheeler, Modern Languages
Hines, Thomas Moore, French Literature
Lehmeyer, Frederick Robert, German Literature
McLaughlin, Blandine Laflamme, Romance Languages
Martin, Dellita Lillian, Spanish Literature, Comparative Literature
Pezzillo, Samuel Joseph, Classical Languages & Literatures
Siegwart, John Thomas, Spanish Literature
Sizemore, Margaret Davidson, Modern Languages
Vansword, Robert C, Comparative Literature & Philology
Ward, Dorothy Cox, Germanistics

Huntsville

Penot, Dominique Marie, Romance Philology, French Literature
Stromecky, Ostap, Slavic Language & Literatures

Marion

Davis, Joe Edward, Jr, Spanish, Latin American Studies

Mobile

Kargleder, Charles Leonard, Spanish & Latin-American Literature

Montevallo

DiOrio, Joseph Frederick, II, French, Latin
Mayfield, Milton Ray, Spanish, Latin-American History

Northport

Wicks, Charles Beaumont, Modern French Literature

Selma

Sneed, Edward, Foreign Languages

Tuscaloosa

Schweitzer, Jerome William, Romance Languages
Tidwell, Julia Brumbeloe, Romance Languages

University

Bell, Robert Fred, German Language & Literature
Cargo, Robert T, Romance Languages
Dobson, Eugene, German, Comparative Literature
Frost, Edgar Lee, Russian Language; Russian Literature
Glenn, Richard Foster, Romance Languages
Nelson, Jan Alan, Romance Languages
Parker, Samuel Emmett, French Language & Literature
Pickett, Terry H, German Literature & History
Porter, Mary Gray, German
Ruiz-Fornells, Enrique, Foreign Languages
Suarez, Bernardo, Spanish & Spanish American Literature
Terry, Edward Davis, Spanish American
Yackle, Larry W, Constitutional Law

ALASKA

Anchorage

Loflin, Marvin D, Linguistics, Anthropology

Fairbanks

Brenckle, Joseph John, Jr, Russian & Slavic Linguistics
Hollerbach, Wolf, Romance Languages
Krauss, Michael E, Linguistics
Scollon, Ronald Thomas, Linguistics, Anthropology
Tabbert, Russell Dean, English Linguistics

ARIZONA

Flagstaff

Atkin, Dennis H, Japanese Literature & Asian Cultures
Giauque, Gerald S, Medieval & Seventeenth Century French
Harvey, Gina Cantoni, Linguistics, Language Pedagogy
Kyte, Elinor Clemons, Linguistics, English
Seaman, Paul David, Linguistics, Anthropology

Glendale

Jackle, Frank Robert, Spanish, Portuguese
Peters, Issa, Arabic, Middle East History
Schutte, Lilith Eva, German

Prescott

Bartelt, Hans Guillermo, Linguistics

Sun City

Staubach, Charles Neff, Romance Languages & Literatures

Tempe

Ahern, Maureen Veronica, Latin American Literature, Literary Translation
Baldini, Pier Raimondo, Italian
Barkin, Florence, Sociolinguistics, Spanish
Bowman, Russell Keith, French, Spanish
Brink, Daniel Theodore, English Historical Linguistics
Carver, George L, Classical Languages
Croft, Lee B, Slavic Linguistics, Russian Literature
Curran, Mark Joseph, Spanish, Portuguese
Ekmanis, Rolf, Slavic Linguistics & Literatures
Faltz, Leonard M, Linguistics
Flys, Michael Jaroslaw, Spanish
Foster, David William, Romance Languages, Linguistics
Friedman, Edward Herbert, Spanish Literature
Gruzinska, Aleksandra, French Language & Literature
Guntermann, Gail, Spanish, Foreign Language Education
Hendrickson, William Lee, French, Medieval Literature
Horwath, Peter, Nineteenth Century German Literature, Austrian Literature
Lamberts, Jacob J, English, Linguistics
Losse, Deborah Nichols, French Literature
Luenow, Paul Ferdinand, Jr, Foreign Languages
Ney, James Walter, English, Linguistics
Nilsen, Don Lee Fred, English Linguistics
Rodd, Laurel Rasplica, Japanese Language & Literature
Sheppard, Douglas Claire, Foreign Languages
Simmons, Douglas J, French
Tipton, Gary Prior, Chinese Language & Literature
Vasquez, Mary Seale, Hispanic Literature, Spanish Language
Virgillo, Carmelo, Spanish, Portuguese
Volek, Emil, Spanish American & Spanish Literature
Wixted, John Timothy, Chinese & Japanese Literature

ARIZONA (cont)

Tucson

Akmajian, Adrian, Theoretical Linguistics
Austin, John Norman, Classical Languages
Beck, Jean Robert, German
Brown, Edward Guillen, Jr, Romance Languages
Carnes, Pack, Germanic Languages & Literatures
Chambers, Frank McMinn, Romance Philology
Chandola, Anoop Chandra, Linguistics
Chisholm, David, German Language & Literature
Cook, Mary Jane, Linguistics
Davis, Jack Emory, Spanish
Demers, Richard Arthur, Linguistics
Demorest, Jean Jacques, French
Elson, Benjamin F, Linguistics
Evans, Gilbert Edward, Spanish
Flemming, Leslie Abel, South Asian Languages & Literature
Gamal, Adel Sulaiman, Classical Arabic Literature, Arabic Language
Gryting, Loyal Ansel Theodore, Romance Languages
Gyurko, Lanin Andrew, Latin American & Comparative Literature
Iventosch, Herman, Spanish
Jensen, Richard Carl, Classics
Kennedy, Ruth Lee, Spanish Literature
Kinkade, Richard Paisley, Romance Languages
Kitagawa, Chisato, Linguistics
Kohn, Ingeborg Margaret, French Literature
Lehrer, Adrienne Joyce, Linguistics
Malik, Joe, Jr, Slavonic Languages
Martin, John Watson, Spanish Language & Literature, Portuguese Language
Miao, Ronald Clendinen, Chinese Language & Literature
Nelson, Dana A, Spanish Language & Literature
Putzar, Edward David, Foreign Languages, Japanese
Qafisheh, Hamdi Ahmad, Linguistics, Language Teaching
Rivero, Eliana Suarez, Spanish, Latin American Literature
Roche, Alphonse Victor, French & Modern Provencal Language & Literature
Rosaldo, Renato Ignacio, Latin American Literature
Rosenberg, Charles Ira, French
Schultz, William Rudolph, Chinese Language & Literature
Schulz, Renate Adele-Wolf, Foreign Language Education, German
Stone, H Reynolds, Romance Languages & Philology
Ter Horst, Robert, Spanish Literature
Tinsley, Royal Lilburn, Jr, Germanic Languages & Literature
Turner, Paul Raymond, Anthropological Linguistics
Wendel, John Richard, German Language & Literature
Woloshin, David Jordan, German, Foreign Language Pedagogy
Worthen, Thomas De Voe, Classics

ARKANSAS

Arkadelphia

Ramirez, Manuel, Foreign Languages

Conway

Paulson, Michael George, Jr, French & Spanish Language & Literature
Sweet, Philip Dale, German Literature

Fayetteville

Clark, Margaret Louise, French Language & Culture
Cross, Robert Brandt, Classical Language
Eichmann, Raymond, French Medieval Literature
Falke, Rita, Romance Languages & Literatures
Ford, James Francis, Foreign Language Education, Spanish
Guinn, Lawrence, Linguistics, Philology
Hanlin, Todd Campbell, Germanic Languages & Literature
Hassel, Jon Brian, French
Jarvis, Barbara Meacham, Spanish Literature
Levine, Daniel Blank, Classical Language & Literature
Ricker-Abderhalden, Judith, German & French Literature

Magnolia

Blue, Betty A, Linguistics

Marshall

De La Pena, Carlos Hector, Spanish & Spanish-American Culture

Pocahontas

Toliver, Hazel May, Latin

CALIFORNIA

Altadena

Schwartz, Leon, French Literature & Language

Angwin

Escandon, Ralph, Spanish
Veltman, Frederick, New Testament Theology, Biblical Languages

Arcata

Cornejo, Rafael Esteban, Spanish Linguistics & Literature
Pence, Ellsworth Dean, French Language & Literature, Latin
Richter, Glenda Roberta, German
Spinas, Janet Maloney, Spanish Language & Literature
Wood, Frank Boardman, Romance Languages

Atherton

Aguzzi-Barbagli, Danilo, Italian

Bakersfield

Corral, Helia Maria, Hispanic Language & Literatures
Lozano, Carlos, Romance Literatures

Belmont

LoCoco, Veronica Gonzalez-Mena, Second Language Learning, Psycholinguistics
Naughton, Helen Thomas, French Language & Literature

Berkeley

Amyx, Darrell Arlynn, Classical Archaeology
Anderson, William Scovil, Classics
Aoki, Haruo, Linguistics
Askins, Arthur L, Spanish & Portuguese Literature
Augst, Bertrand P, French
Azevedo, Milton Mariano, Ibero-Romance & Applied Linguistics
Beck, Jonathan, French, Medieval Literature
Beeler, Madison Scott, Linguistics
Bersani, Leo, French, Critical Theory
Birch, Cyril, Chinese Language & Literature
Bloch, Ariel Alfred Karl, Semitic Languages, Linguistics
Block, Ralph Howard, French
Bonwit, Marianne, Literature
Boyd, Julian, English Language
Brinkmann, Richard A, German Literature
Brinner, William Michael, Philology, Islamic History
Cascardi, Anthony Joseph, Comparative Literature
Chafe, Wallace L, Linguistics
Chang, Kun, Chinese Language & Literature
Chapman, George Arnold, Spanish American Literature
Clubb, Louise George, Comparative Literature
Costa, Gustavo, Italian, History
Craddock, Jerry Russell, Romance Philology, Medieval Hispanic Literature
Duggan, Joseph John, Medieval Literature, Philology
Emeneau, Murray Barnson, Sanskrit, Linguistics
Eustis, Alvin Allen, Jr, French Literature
Faulhaber, Charles Bailey, Medieval Spanish Literature
Fleischman, Suzanne, Romance Linguistics, Medieval Literature
Fontenrose, Joseph, Classical Philology
Freidin, Gregory, Russian Literature & Intellectual History
Goodwin, Reason Alva, Linguistics
Grossman, Joan Delaney, Slavic Languages
Gumperz, John J, Linguistics, Anthropology
Guy, Basil James, French

Haas, Mary Rosamond, Linguistics
Hillen, Gerd, German Literature
Holub, Robert C, German Literature, Literary Theory
Huet, Marie-Helene Jacqueline, French Literature
Jaini, Padmanabh S, Linguistics, South & Southeast Asian Religions
Jamieson, John Charles, Chinese Literature, Medieval Civilization
Jaszi, Andrew Oscar, German
Johnson, Leonard Wilkie, Foreign Languages
Judovitz, Dalia, French Literature
Kaes, Anton J, German Literature, Comparative Literature
Karlinsky, Simon, Slavic Languages & Literatures
Kassatkin, Serge, Oriental Languages, Russian Language
Khouri, Mounah, Arabic Literature
Kilmer, Anne Draffkorn, Ancient Near Eastern History & Literature
Knapp, Robert Carlyle, Ancient History, Classics
Kudszus, Winfried, German Literature
Lakoff, Robin Tolmach, Linguistics
Lindow, John Frederick, Germanic & Scandinavian Linguistics
McCullough, William H, Japanese Literature
McKnight, Christina Soderhjelm, Scandinavian Literature
McLean, Hugh, Slavic Languages & Literatures
Madsen, Borge Gedso, Foreign Languages
Malkiel, Yakov, Romance Philology
Mastronarde, Donald John, Classical Philology
Matisoff, James Alan, Linguistics, Southeast Asian Studies
Melia, Daniel Frederick, Celtic Languages & Literature
Mileck, Joseph, German
Miller, James Whipple, Comparative & Chinese Literature
Miller, Stephen Gaylord, Classics, Classical Archeology
Milosz, Czeslaw, Polish Literature
Monguio, Luis, Spanish, Spanish American Literature
Monroe, James T, Arabic & Comparative Literature
Moses, Gavriel, Italian & Comparative Literature
Mueller, Klaus Andrew, Foreign Languages, Linguistics
Murgia, Charles Edward, Classics
Murillo, Louis Andrew, Spanish Literature
Nagler, Michael Nicholas, Classical Literature and Society
Ohala, John Jerome, Linguistics
Penzl, Herbert, Linguistics
Perella, Nicolas J, Romance Languages & Literature, Comparative Literature
Polt, John H R, Foreign Languages
Pritchett, William Kendrick, Greek Philology
Putter, Irving, French Literature
Rabinowitz, Wilson Gerson, Greek
Rejhon, Annalee Claire, Medieval Literature, Philology
Rex, Walter Edwin, French Literature
Rosenmeyer, Thomas Gustav, Classics, Comparative Literature
Sawyer, Jesse O, Linguistics
Schafer, Edward Hetzel, East Asiatic Philology
Schamschula, Walter, Slavic Languages & Literatures
Seeba, Hinrich Claassen, German Literature
Seif, Morton Philip van Moppes, Comparative Literature
Shadi, Dorothy Clotelle Clarke, Spanish Literature
Slobin, Dan Isaac, Psycholinguistics
Snapper, Johan Pieter, Germanic Languages
Spahr, Blake Lee, German & Comparative Literature
Stroud, Ronald Sidney, Classics
Threatte, Leslie Lee, Classical Philology
Tubach, Frederic C, German Literature, Medieval Studies
Van Nooten, Barend Adrian, Sanskrit, Indology
Walpole, Ronald Noel, Romance Philology & Literature
Walsh, John Kevin, Medieval Spanish Literature, Spanish Linguistics
Wang, William S Y, Linguistics
Webber, Ruth House, Romance Literature & Language
Weisinger, Kenneth Dean, German, Comparative Literature
Whitfield, Francis James, Slavic Languages & Literatures
Wijsen, Louk M P T, German Literature
Zimmer, Karl Ernst, Linguistics

Beverly Hills

Von Hofe, Harold, German Literature

Camarillo

Jasper, Susan D Penfield, Applied Linguistics, Anthropology

Campbell

Nichols, Patricia Causey, English, Linguistics

Carmel

Loya, Arieh R, Middle Eastern Languages & Literatures

Carson

Elliott, Dale Eugene, Linguistics
Garber, Marilyn, History, Law

Chico

Brown, James Lorin, French
Haynes, Maria Schnee, English, German

Claremont

Adler, Sara Maria, Italian Language & Literature
Brueckner, Hans-Dieter, German
Goodrich, Norma Lorre, French, Comparative Literature
Johnson, Phyllis Anne, Medieval & Modern French Literature
Johnson, Roberta Lee, Peninsular Spanish & Comparative Literature
Jones, Stanleigh Hopkins, Jr, Japanese Language & Literature
Koldewyn, Phillip, Latin American Literature & Intellectual History
Lamb, Ruth Stanton, Spanish Literature
Lindstrom, Thais S, Russian Language & Literature
McGaha, Michael Dennis, Spanish Language & Penninsular Literature
McKirahan, Richard Duncan, Jr, Classics, Philosophy
Potter, Edith Geyler, Germanic Languages
Poynter, John Durward, Older German Literature
Rinkus, Jerome Joseph, Russian Literature
Ruyter, Hans C, Languages
Senn, Harry Anthony, French, Folklore
Sheirich, Richard M, Germanic Language & Literature
Warner, Nicholas Oliver, Comparative & English Literature
Young, Howard Thomas, Spanish, French

Davis

Abraham, Claude Kurt, French
Allen, David Harding, Jr, Spanish, Portuguese
Armistead, Samuel Gordon, Spanish Literature & Language
Bach, Max, French
Benward, Wilbur Alan, German, Linguistics
Bernd, Clifford Albrecht, German Literature
Bloomberg, Edward M, French Literature
Castanien, Donald Garner, Hispanic Languages & Literatures
Dutschke, Dennis John, Italian Literature
Fetzer, John F, German
Grimm, Richard E, Classics
Harsh, Wayne C, English, Linguistics
Herman, Gerald, French, Medieval Literature
Hoermann, Roland, Modern German Literature, Comparative Literature
Jaen, Didier Tisdel, Spanish Literature
Keller, Daniel Schneck, Spanish-American Literature
Kusch, Manfred, French Literature, Comparative Literature
Lindsay, Marshall, Foreign Languages
McConnell, Winder, German Medieval Literature
Motley, Michael Tilden, Speech Communication, Linguistics
Nerjes, Herbert Guenther, German
Redfield, Robert Lowell, Medieval Literature
Rojas, Guillermo, Mexican & Chicano Literature
Sanchez-Romeralo, Antonio, Spanish Literature
Schaeffer, Peter Moritz-Friedrich, Germanic Studies, Comparative Literature
Thompson, Wesley E, Classics
Traill, David Angus, Latin, Greek
Tumins, Valerie Agnes, Philology
Ury, Marian Bloom, Japanese Literature
Verani, Hugo Juan, Latin American Literature

Wallacker, Benjamin E, East Asian Philology
York, Ruth Beatrice, French

Del Mar

Stowell, Ernest, Spanish, Modern Language Education

El Cerrito

Carr, Denzel (Raybourne), Linguistics

Fair Oaks

Blatchford, Charles H, English as a Second Language

Fresno

Bowen, Wayne Scott, Romance Languages
Brengelman, Frederick Henry, Linguistics, English Language Studies
Clough, Carmen Pella, Romance Linguistics
Ensslin, Walter, German
Gammon, Edward Roy, Psycholinguistics, Linguistics
Gendron, Maurice C, French Literature
Mistry, Purushottam J, Linguistics
Nagy, Elemer Joseph, Foreign Languages
Pronin, Alexander, Russian Language & Literature
Raney, George William, Linguistics, English as a Second Language
Weitzman, Raymond Stanley, Linguistics, Japanese Language

Fullerton

Andersen-Fiala, Linda Ruth, Medieval & Modern French Literature
Arana, Oswaldo, Spanish, Spanish American Literature
Baden, Nancy Tucker, Spanish-American Literature & Language
Boarino, Gerald L, Romance Languages
Cartledge, Samuel J, French Linguistics
Kaye, Alan Stewart, Linguistics, Near Eastern Studies
Kline, Walter Duane, Romance Languages
Merrifield, Doris Fulda, Germanic Languages
Pena, Ervie, Spanish Literature & Linguistics
Prado, Marcial, Spanish Linguistics
Schulz, Muriel Ripley, English, Linguistics
Sears, Donald Albert, Literature, Language
Shapley, Charles S, French Language & Literature
Tussing, Marjorie O, German Language & Literature
Van Ginneken, Eva, French Language & Literature

Goleta

Leal, Luis, Spanish

Guerneville

Dinsmore, John David, Theoretical Linguistics

Hayward

Gries, Frauke, German Language & Literature
Ham, Galia M, French
Mecke, Gunter Adolf, Germanic & Classical Philology
Ponce de Leon, Luis Sierra, Spanish Language & Literature
Schulak, Helen S, Slavic Languages & Literatures
Tomanek, Thomas J, Spanish American Literature, Spanish Language
Traversa, Vincenzo Paolo, Italian Language & Literature
Vidal, Elie R, French Literature
Warrin, Donald Ogden, Portuguese
Weiss, Winfried Ferdinand, Comparative Literature
Woehr, Richard Arthur, Spanish

Inverness

Gordon, Arthur E, Latin

Irvine

Berkowitz, Luci, Classics
Brunner, Theodore Friederich, Classics
Crowley, Ruth, German, Comparative Literature
De Mallac, Guy, Comparative & Russian Literature
Hubert, Judd David, French Literature
Hubert, Renee Riese, French, Comparative Literature

Key, Mary Ritchie (Mrs Audley E Patton), Linguistics
Lee, Meredith Ann, German Literature, German Language
Lehnert, Herbert Hermann, German
Lillyman, William J, German Comparative Literature
McDonald, Marianne, Classics
Nagel, Bert, German
Orjuela, Hector Hugo, Spanish American Literature, Hispanic Poetry
Palley, Julian, Romance Languages
Reardon, Bryan Peter, Classics
Regosin, Richard Lloyd, Romance Languages
Saine, Thomas Price, German Literature
Sutton, Dana Ferrin, Classical Scholarship
Terrell, Tracy D, Linguistics
Tonelli, Franco, French Literature
Voge, Wilfried Michael, Linguistics, German Philology
Watt, William Carnell, Semiotics, Linguistics
Weil, Helen Harmash, Russian Language & Literature

Kensington

Oswalt, Robert L, Linguistics

Laguna Beach

Mathieu, Gustave Bording, German Literature
Schimmelpfennig, Paul Robert, German Literature, Literary Criticism

Laguna Hills

Coulter, Mary Welles, Foreign Languages

La Jolla

Bellugi-Klima, Ursula, Linguistics, Cognitive Psychology
Blanco-Aguinaga, Carlos, Romance Languages, Spanish Literature
Cancel, Robert, African Literature
Catalan, Diego Menendez-Pidal, Romance Languages, Linguistics
Chen, Matthew Y, Linguistics, Chinese Linguistics
Chung, Sandra Lynn, Linguistics
Crowne, David K, Comparative Literature, English
Klima, Edward Stephen, Linguistics, Theory of Language
Kuroda, Sige-Yuki, Linguistics
Langacker, Ronald Wayne, Linguistics
Langdon, Margaret Hoffmann, Linguistics, American Indian Languages
Lettau, Reinhard, Germanic Literatures
Lyon, James Karl, Germanic Languages & Literatures
Newmark, Leonard, Linguistics
Schane, Sanford A, Linguistics
Shand, Michael Arthur, Linguistics, Language Pedagogy
Tay, William S, Comparative & Chinese Literature
Terdiman, Richard, Narrative Literature & Literary Theory
Wierschin, Martin Werner, German Literature & Philology

La Mesa

Wolf, Ernest Michael, Romance Languages, German

La Mirada

Mayers, Marvin Keene, Anthropology, Linguistics
Morris, J Vincent, Greek
Wetzler, Duane Lewis, Spanish Language & Literature

La Verne

Arias, Joan Zonderman, Spanish Literature & Language

Long Beach

Burne, Kevin George, English, Linguistics
Cardenas, Daniel Negrete, Spanish
Creel, Bryant Lawrence, Spanish Literature & Language
DeLong-Tonelli, Beverly Jean, Spanish Literature, Translation
Donahue, Francis J, Spanish Modern American Literature
Hubble, Thomas N, Comparative Literature

Oakland

Asturias, Rosario Maria, Spanish
Charney, Ben Louis, Classical Philology
Cottam, Martha Lemaire, French Literature,
Philosophy of Education

Orange

Alderson, Edwin Graham, Modern Foreign
Languages
Bergel, Alice R, Foreign Languages
Bergel, Kurt, German Literature & History
Mills, Dorothy Hurst, Linguistics, Spanish

Orangevale

Perfler, Olaf Karl, German & Austrian Literature

Oxnard

Guyer, Leland Robert, Portuguese & Brazilian
Literature

Pacific Grove

Hulanicki, Leo Sergius, Russian Linguistics &
Literature
Hutchinson, Joseph Candler, Romance
Languages
Shammas, Jacob Yousif, Arabic Language,
Middle East Studies
Soren, Edgar Greene, Languages
Wen, Victor Yen-Hsiung, Chinese Language,
Political Science

Pacific Palisades

Worth, Dean Stoddard, Slavic Linguistics

Palo Alto

Bolinger, Dwight LeMerton, English & Spanish
Linguistics
Mueller-Vollmer, Kurt, German, Humanities
Nordmeyer, George, Germanic Linguistics
Petersen, Phillip Burns, Foreign Languages
Raubitschek, Antony Erich, Classics
Stenbock-Fermor, Elisabeth, Russian, French
Yalom, Marilyn K, Foreign Languages

Pasadena

Ghattas-Soliman, Sonia Rezk, French Language
& Literature
Martin, Nicholas O, French
Smith, Annette Jacqueline, French Literature,
Intellectual History
Thompson, Bozena Henisz-Dostert, Linguistics,
Computational Linguistics

Pomona

Smith, David Richard, Classical Studies
Zrimc, Rudolf, Linguistics

Port Hueneme

Reissner, Arthur J, Foreign Languages

Presidio of Monterey

Cartier, Francis Arthur, Speech Science,
Communication

Rancho Mirage

Kreuter, Katherine Elizabeth, French Literature

Redlands

Aparicio-Laurencio, Angel, Foreign Languages,
Law
Brigola, Alfredo, Romance Languages
Tinnin, Alvis Lee, French Literature
Umbach, William Eckhard, German Literature &
Philology

Redondo Beach

Ayres, Glenn Thompson, Linguistics

Riverside

Ayllon, Candido, Spanish
Barricelli, Jean-Pierre, Romance Languages,
Comparative Literature
Borg, Sam Joseph, French
Carilla, Emilio, Romance Languages
Daviau, Donald G, German
Decker, Henry Wallace, French
Fagundo, Ana Maria, Comparative Literature,
Spanish & English Literature

Garbutt-Parrales, Ernestina Florencia, Hispanic
Philology, Medieval Spanish Literature
Gericke, Philip Otto, Romance Languages &
Literature
Griffin, Robert Berry, Romance Languages &
Literatures
Hilts, Margarete Ambs, French Language &
Literature
Kern, Gary Wooward, Russian Literature
Levin, Jules Fred, Linguistics
MacFarlane, Keith H, Romance Languages
Mead, William Curtis, French, Comparative
Literature
Megenney, William Wilber, Latin American
Linguistics
Pedrotti, Louis A, Slavic Languages &
Literatures
Radoyce, Lubomir, Slavic & Comparative
Literature
Rimbach, Guenther C, German & Comparative
Literature
Rivera, Tomas, Romance Literatures, English
Rodriguez-Alcala, Hugo, Spanish
Scanlon, Thomas Francis, Classical Languages
Stoltzfus, Ben F, French Literature

Rodeo

So, Francis Kei-hong, Chinese Language &
Literature

Rohnert Park

Cord, William Owen, Spanish American
Literature
Fallandy, Yvette Marie, French Language &
Literature
Friedman, Adele Charlene, French Language &
Literature
Katz, Eli, Germanic Linguistics
Previtali, Giovanni, Romance Languages &
Literature

Rolling Hill Estates

Beym, Richard, Language Training &
Administration

Sacramento

Dennis, Harry Joe, Spanish & Portuguese
Languages & Literatures
Eisner, Robert Allen, Medieval & Comparative
Literature
Giles, Mary E, Spanish Literature, Humanities
Jenkins-Blanco, Jacinto, Spanish
Klucas, Joseph Arthur, Spanish & Portuguese
Languages
Lo Verso, Rosabianca, French & Italian
Lieterature
Porrata, Francisco Eduardo, Foreign Languages
Reveley, Betty Brown, English Linguistics
Santana, Jorge Armando, Latin American
Literature, Chicano Studies
Thomann, Donaldo J, Languages

San Bernardino

Bas, Joe, Spanish
Galbis, Ignacio Ricardo Maria, Hispanic
Literatures & Language
Rydell, Mireille Guillet, Foreign Language
Switzer, Perry Richard, French Literature

San Bruno

Liedtke, Kurt Ernst Heinrich, German

San Clemente

Davis, J Cary, Romance Languages

San Diego

Baker, Clifford Henry, Spanish Literature
Boney, Elaine Emesette, German Literature
Case, Thomas Edward, Spanish
Cassedy, Steven Dennis, Comparative Literature
Dukas, Vytas, Slavic Languages
Dunkle, Harvey I, German
Fetzer, Leland, Russian Literature
Genovese, Edgar Nicholas, Classics
Glasgow, Janis M, French
Head, Gerald L, Spanish, Portuguese
Jackson, Elizabeth R, French Literature
Jonsson-Devillers, Edith, French, Spanish &
Comparative Literature
Lemus, George, Spanish, Latin American Studies
Mapa, Marina Vargas, Spanish Languages &
Literature
Max, Stefan Leopold, French Language &
Literature

Messier, Leonard Norbert, French
Moore, Joachim Michael, Foreign Language
Education
Pacheco, Manuel Trinidad, Linguistics
Paulin, Harry Walter, German Literature
Piffard, Guerard, French Philology, Romance
Languages
Rigsby, Jeanne Brink, French Language &
Literature
Sarre, Alicia, Romance Languages
Savvas, Minas, Comparative Literature, Creative
Writing
Schaber, Steven Conrad, Germanic Languages &
Literature
Seright, Orin Dale, English, Linguistics
Silverman, Malcolm Noel, Portuguese & Spanish
Languages
Talamantes, Florence Williams, Spanish
Language & Literature
Tanaka, Yoshio, Germanic & Indo-European
Linguistics
Underhill, Robert, Linguistics
Vergani, Gianangelo, Italian
Vergani, Luisa, Italian
Woo, Catherine Yi-Yu Cho, Chinese Language &
Literature
Wulbern, Julian H, German, Comparative
Literature
Young, Ronald Robert, Spanish Linguistics

San Francisco

Axelrod, Joseph, Comparative Literature,
Humanities
Costa-Zalessow, Natalia, Italian
Croft, Kenneth, Linguistics, English as a Second
Language
Dorwick, Thalia, Spanish Literature
Goldblatt, Howard Charles, Chinese Literature &
Language
Hsu, Kai-Yu, Literature, Humanities
Iaccarino, Pietro Luigi, Romance Languages &
Literatures
Ianni, Lawrence Albert, English Linguistics,
Literary Criticism
Kolbert, Jack, Romance Languages
Law, Howard W, Linguistics, Anthropology
Matteucig, Giacinto, Classical Archeology
Trapp, Richard L, Classics
Vogeley, Nancy Jeanne, Latin American &
Spanish Literature
Weinberger, Marvin Elmer, French
Wilson, Lois Mayfield, Linguistics
Womack, Thurston, Linguistics
Wright, Elizabeth Catherine, French Language &
Literature

San Jose

Borovski, Conrad, Foreign Languages
Cassarino, Sebastian, Italian
Da Silva, Heraldo Gregorio, Portuguese
Language & Literature
Dietiker, Simone Renaud, French
Goddard, Wesley (Rawdon), French
Gustafson, Donna J, Spanish Literature
Isaacson, Lanae, Scandinavian Literature,
Folklore
Leung, Kai-cheong, Chinese Language & Culture
Lin, Chaote, Japanese
Noble, Gladwyn Kingsley, Jr, Anthropology,
Linguistics
Pereyra-Suarez, Esther, Romance Languages
Pimentel, Raul (Ray), German
Radke, Werner J, German Language &
Literature
Scott, Joseph Reid, Spanish
Stenzel, Joachim Albrecht, Classics, German
Swindell, Kimi Mushiaki, Japanese Language
Zapata, Celia Correas, Latin American Literature
& Culture

San Luis Obispo

Johnson, Van Loran, Classical Philology
Lint, Robert Glen, English Linguistics, Stylistics
Stahl, Verlan H, Spanish

San Marino

Travis, Albert Hartman, Classical Philology

San Rafael

Bundy, Barbara Korpan, Comparative Literature,
German
St Sure, Donald Francis, Classics, Music

CALIFORNIA (cont)

Santa Ana

Cowan, George McKillop, Theology, Linguistics

Santa Barbara

Ashby, William James, Romance Linguistics, French
Athanassakis, Apostolos N, Philology
Atkins, Stuart, German & Comparative Literature
Backus, Robert Lee, Japanese Studies
Barron, Carlos Garcia, Romance Languages, Spanish Literature
Bary, David A, Hispanic Literature
Bennett, Alva W, Classics
Billigmeier, Jon-Christian, Philology & Linguistics, Ancient History
Bonadeo, Alfredo A, Italian Literature
Caldwell, Helen F, Classics
Clarke, Howard W, Comparative Literature
Cushing, Anne Hyde Greet, French
Delattre, Genevieve, French
Exner, Richard, German & Comparative Literature
Fuentes, Victor Floreal, Literature
Goodrich, Chauncey Shafter, Chinese Language & Literature
Gottschalk, Gunther H, German Language & Literature
Greene, Naomi, French
Hetzron, Robert, General Linguistics, Afro-Asiatic Languages
Hoffmeister, Gerhart, German & Comparative Literature
Jantzen, John Benjamin, French, Higher Education
Johnson, Donald Barton, Russian Literature
Li, Charles N, Linguistics
Linn, Rolf Norbert, German
Lundell, Torborg Lovisa, Comparative Literature, Folktale
Mahlendorf, Ursula R, German Literature
Malecot, Andre, Linguistics
Martinez-Lopez, Enrique, Spanish
Murray, Jack, French
Perissinotto, Giorgio, Hispanic Linguistics
Phillips, Allen Whitmarsh, Spanish, Spanish American Literature
Pigeon, Gerard Georges, Literature, Linguistics
Renehan, Robert, Classical Philology
Reynolds, Winston Allin, Spanish
Rossi, Patrizio, Romance Languages
Schwartz, Arthur M, Linguistics
Sena, Jorge De, Portuguese & Brazilian Literature
Serrano-Plaja, Arturo, Romance Languages
Sharrer, Harvey Leo, Medieval Hispanic Languages & Literatures
Steinhauer, Harry, French & German Literature
Sullivan, John P, Foreign Languages
Tobin, Ronald William Francis, French Language & Literature
Trager-Johnson, Edith Crowell, Linguistics
Tu, Kuo-Ch'ing, Chinese & Japanese Literature
Walker, Philip Doolittle, French
Waterman, John Thomas, Germanic Philology
Wendell, Charles, Near Eastern Languages & Literatures
Williams, Frederick Granger, Portuguese, Spanish
Young, David Charles, Classics

Santa Clara

Howard, Catherine Montfort, French Literature
Jimenez, Francisco, Latin American Literature
Rematore, Andrew Irving, Spanish, Linguistics
Van Den Berghe, Christian Louis, French Linguistics & Literature
Vari, Victor B, Philology, Literature

Santa Cruz

Brown, Norman Oliver, Classical Philology, History
Ellis, John Martin, German Literature, Language Theory
Hankamer, Jorge, Linguistics
Hummel, John Hull, French, Comparative Literature
Lynch, John Patrick, Classics
Metcalf, George J(oseph), Germanic Philology
Orlandi, Mary-Kay Gamel, Classics, Comparative Literature
Puknat, Siegfried Berthold, German & Comparative Literature
Silverman, Joseph Herman, Spanish Literature

Santa Monica

Nieman, Nancy Dale, Romance Languages

Sherman Oaks

Benitez, Ruben A, Spanish Literature
Bodroglegeti, Andras J E, Turkic & Iranian Philology

Spring Valley

Schneider-Halvorson, Brigitte Lina, Modern German Literature

Stanford

Alegria, Fernando, Spanish American Literature
Berman, Russell, Alexander, German Literature
Bertrand, Marc Andre, French Literature
Brown, Edward James, Russian Language & Literature
Cavallari, Hector Mario, Latin American Literature, Literary Theory
Cazelles, Brigitte Jacqueline, Medieval French Literature
Clark, Eve Vivienne, Linguistics, Psycholinguistics
Cohn, Robert G, French
Dien, Albert E, Chinese Language
Edwards, Mark William, Classical Philology
Ferguson, Charles Albert, Linguistics
Franco, Jean, Literature
Gicovate, Bernard, Romance Languages
Girard, Rene Noel, French
Giraud, Raymond Dorner, French
Greenberg, Joseph Harold, Anthropology, Linguistics
Hester, Ralph M, Romance Languages & Literature
Jameson, Michael Hamilton, Classical Studies, Ancient History
Liu, James Jo-Yu, Chinese & Comparative Literature
Lohnes, Walter F W, German
McCall, Marsh Howard, Jr, Classics
Mommsen, Katharina, German Literature
Newman-Gordon, Pauline, French Literature
Pick, Mary Maritza, Comparative Literature
Politer, Robert Louis, Romance Linguistics
Pratt, Mary Louise, Comparative Literature
Sag, Ivan Andrew, Theoretical & Computational Linguistics
Schevill, Isabel Magana (Mrs Rudolph Schevill), Spanish Literature
Stahlberger, Lawrence L, Slavic Languages & Literatures
Todd, William Mills, III, Russian & Comparative Literature
Traugott, Elizabeth Closs, Linguistics
Ueda, Makoto, Literature, Aesthetics
Van Campen, Joseph Alfred, Linguistics
Wang, John Ching-Yu, Chinese Language & Literature
Wasow, Thomas Alexander, Theoretical Linguistics
Weinstein, Leo, French
Wigodsky, Michael, Classics
Winograd, Terry Allen, Linguistics, Computer Sciences

Stockton

Decker, Donald Milton, Foreign Languages
Sayles, Barbara, German & Comparative Literature
Sharp, Francis Michael, German Literature
Smutny, Robert Jaroslav, Classical Philology
Wonder, John P, Spanish Language & Literature

Sunnyvale

Biondi, Raymond Liberty, Romance Languages & Literature

Thousand Oaks

Fonseca, James Francis, Spanish
Stewart, Walter K, German Literature

Turlock

Mack, Gerhard Georg, German Literature

Tustin

Girard-Corkum, Jerria, Spanish Literature

Van Nuys

Kunzer, Ruth Goldschmidt, Germanic Languages, Jewish Studies

Woodland Hills

Plutschow, Herbert Eugen, Japanese Literature

COLORADO

Arvada

Manier, Martha Jane, Spanish

Boulder

Barchilon, Jacques, Romance Languages, The Fairy Tale
Brown, Jane Kurshan, Comparative Literature
Calder, William Musgrave, III, Classical Philology
Daugherty, Howard, Slavic Languages & Literatures
DeOnis, Jose, Modern Languages
Evjen, Harold Donald, Foreign Languages
Firestone, Robert T, German Linguistics
Frajzyngier, Zygmunt, Linguistics, African Languages & Linguistics
Fredricksmeyer, Ernst, Classical Philology
Frey, Julia Bloch, French Literature and Culture
Garcia-Moya, Rodolfo, Spanish
Geary, John Steven, Medieval Literature, Romance Philology
Goldsmith, Ulrich Karl, German Literature
Grupp, William John, Spanish Literature
Hall, Clifton D, Medieval German Literature
Heimann, David Francis, Latin, Greek
Hough, John Newbold, Classical Philology
Hulley, Karl Kelchner, Classical Philology
Jensen, Frede, French & Provencal Philology
Kail, Andree Fourcade, French
Kaschube, Dorothea Vedral, Anthropological Linguistics
Ketchum, Anne, Romance Languages
King, Charles Lester, Spanish
Kite, Ralph Beverly, Latin American Literature
Kopff, Edward Christian, Greek, Latin
Kroll, Paul William, Chinese Medieval Literature
Lazzarino, Graziana, Italian & French
Lee, Charles Nicholas, Russian Literature
Lewis, Brian Arthur, German Linguistics
Mayer, Edgar Nathan, Linguistics
Plank, Dale Lewin, Russian Literature
Rawlings, Hunter Ripley, III, Classical Philology, Ancient History
Romeo, Luigi, Romance Linguistics
Rood, David Stanley, General Linguistics
Sampson, Earl Delos, Slavic Languages
Schmidt, Hugo, German Languages
Stavan, Henry-Anthony, French
Taylor, Allan Ross, Linguistics
Tenenbaum, Louis, Italian
Victor-Rood, Juliette Ann, German & Comparative Literature
Willis, Donald S, Foreign Languages

Colorado Springs

Baay, Dirk, German & Comparative Literature
Bizzarro, Salvatore, Latin American Literature & Studies
Cramer, Owen Carver, Classics
Dobson, Marcia Dunbar-Soule, Classics, Humanities
Fernandez, Jose Benigno, Romance Languages, Social Sciences
McKay, Douglas Rich, Spanish
Peterson, Elmer Robert, French
Richardson, Horst Fuchs, German Language and Literature
Wishard, Armin, German Language & Literature

Denver

Brom, Libor, Slavic Languages & Literature
Cere, Ronald Carl, Eighteenth Century Spanish
Doerr, Richard Paul, Spanish Language, Latin American Literature
Gilroy, James Paul, French Literature, Romance Languages
Hieke, Adolf E F, Linguistics, English as a Second Language
Lug, Sieglinde, Comparative Medieval & Feminist Literature
Palleske, Siegwalt Odo, Modern Languages & Literature
Ranwez, Alain Daniel, French Literature
Rogers, Edith Randam, Spanish & Comparative Literature

Shannon, Richard Stoll, III, Classical Philology

Ft Collins

Bachmann, James Kevin, English as a Foreign Language, Linguistics
Boyer, Harriet P, Romance Languages
Echevarria, Evelio A, Spanish, Spanish American Literature
Evans, Joseph Clark, French Language & Literature
Jones, Tobin H, French Literature
McMurray, George Ray, Romance Language
Mah, Kai-Ho, French & Chinese Literature & Language
Moseley, William Whatley, Spanish
Otero, Jose, Hispanic American Literature
Santini, Victor Hugo, French, Italian
Vedvik, Jerry Donald, Romance Languages

Greeley

Graham, Robert Somerville, French
Owechko, Iwan, Russian Language & Literature
Rodriguez, Alfonso, Foreign Language

Pueblo

Taussig, Anna, Languages & Linguistics

CONNECTICUT

Bridgeport

Bloom, Leonard, Modern Languages & Literature
Daigle, Richard Joseph, Linguistics, Russian Literature

Bridgewater

Purdy, Strother Beeson, Comparative Philology

Fairfield

Fedorchek, Robert Marion, Romance Languages
Leeber, Victor F, Romance Languages
Levitt, Jesse, Romance Languages & Linguistics
Panico, Marie J, Spanish
Rosivach, Vincent John, Classical Philology

Farmington

Russell, Kristina Sandberg, German Literature

Greenwich

Flexner, Stuart Berg, American Language

Guilford

Porter, Howard Newton, Classical Philology

Hamden

Arrom, Jose Juan, Spanish American Literature
Correa, Gustavo, Spanish Linguistics & Literature
Knight, Elizabeth C, German Language & Literature
Quirk, Ronald Joseph, Spanish Language & Literature
Schenker, Alexander Marian, Linguistics

Hartford

Andrian, Gustave William, Romance Languages
Bradley, James Robert, Classics
Djaparidze, Justinia Besharov, Russian Language & Literature
Gomez-Gil, Alfredo, Poetry, Spanish & Latin American Literature
Hansen, Carl Victor, German
Hook, Donald Dwight, Linguistics, German
Kerson, Arnold Lewis, Spanish & Spanish American Literature
Lee, Sonia M, French Literature
Macro, Anthony David, Classical Philology, Ancient History
Perkins, Judith B, Classical Languages
Williams, John Carter, Classics

Madison

Bergin, Thomas Goddard, Romance Languages

Mansfield

Perez, Carlos Alberto, Romance Languages

Mansfield Center

Coy, Susanna Peters, Italian Literature

Middletown

Arnold, Herbert A, German, History
Briggs, Morton Winfield, Romance Languages & Literature
Dunn, Peter Norman, Romance Languages
Frenzel, Peter Michael Justinian, German Literature, Medieval Music
Gonzalez, Bernardo Antonio, Modern Spanish Literature
Konstan, Jay David, Greek, Latin
Lowrie, Joyce Oliver, Romance Languages
McMahon, Joseph H, French
Miel, Jan, French Literature, History of Ideas
Needler, Howard, Italian Literature
Stamelman, Richard Howard, French Literature, Modern Poetry
Truscott, James George, Renaissance & Italian Comparative Literature
Viggiani, Carl Albert, Romance Languages
Walker, Willard, Anthropology, Linguistics
Wensinger, Arthur Stevens, German Literature & Language
Whitman, Robert Henry, Slavic Linguistics
Winston, Krishna Ricarda, German Language & Literature

Mt Carmel

Lutz, Cora Elizabeth, Classical Philology

New Britain

Abel, Adeline, French
Force, Edward, German Language & Literature
Goodell, Ralph Jefferson, Linguistics
Iannace, Gaetano Antonio, Italian Language & Literature, Humanities
Jarlett, Francis Grenier, French
Kahn, Lothar, Foreign Languages
Kapetanopoulos, Elias, Classics, Greek & Roman History
Pomerantz, Donald, French Literature
Smith, Stephen Lawrence, French Literature
Stanislawczyk, Irene Eleanor, Spanish Foreign Language Methodology

New Haven

Auld, Louis Eugene, French Literature, Music
Batchelor, C Malcolm, Romance Languages
Brooks, Peter Preston, French & Comparative Literature
Bruce, Novoa John David, Mexican & Chicano Literature
Capretz, Pierre Jean, French
Chang, Kang-i Sun, Chinese Literature
Cole, Andrew Thomas, Jr, Classics
Cowgill, Warren Crawford, Linguistics
Demetz, Peter, German, Comparative Literature
Dumont, Jean-Louis, French, Spanish
Duran, Manual Emil, Spanish Language & Literature
Dworski, Sylvia, Modern Foreign Languages
Dyen, Isidore, Linguistics, Austronesian Comparative Grammar
Erlich, Victor, Slavic Languages & Literatures
Foster, Benjamin Read, Assyriology
Frankel, Hans Hermann, Chinese, Comparative Literature
Garey, Howard Burton, French, Linguistics
Geada, Rita, Spanish
Glier, Ingeborg Johanna, German Language & Literature
Gonzalez-Echevarria, Roberto, Spanish & Modern Latin American Literature
Goold, George Patrick, Classical Philology
Gould, Thomas Fauss, Classics, Philosophy
Greene, Thomas McLernon, English
Hadded, Elaine, Romance Languages
Halpern, Joseph David, French, Literature
Herington, Cecil John, Classics
Hubert, Marie Louise, French
Insler, Stanley, Indo-Iranian Linguistics
Jackson, Robert Louis, Slavic Languages & Literatures
Johnson, Barbara Ellen, French & Comparative Literature
McClellan, Edwin, Japanese Language & Literature

Magnarelli, Sharon Dishaw, Hispanic Literature
Martin, Samuel Elmo, Linguistics
May, Georges (Claude), French Literature
Nelson, Lowry, Jr, Comparative Literature
Picchio, Riccardo P, Slavic Literatures
Pollitt, Jermome J, History of Art, Classical Philology
Pope, Marvin Hoyle, Semitic Philology
Porter, Charles Allen, French Language & Literature
Rassner, Ronald Mark, African Oral & Written Literature
Rodgers, Gary Bruce, French Literature
Rosenthal, Franz, Arabic & Semitic Languages
Sammons, Jeffrey Leonard, Germanic Languages & Literatures
Schoolfield, George C, Germanic Languages & Literatures
Segal, Erich, Classics, Comparative Literature
Stankiewicz, Edward, Slavic Languages & Literatures & Linguistics
Stimson, Hugh McBirney, Linguistics, Philology
Valesio, Paolo, Rhetorics, Literary Theory
Vena, Michael, Foreign Languages
Venclova, Tomas Andrius, Slavic & Lithuanian Literatures
Vitello, Ralph Michael, French Renaissance Literature
Weigand, Hermann John, Germanic Literature

New London

Artinian, Robert Willard, French Language & Literature
Chu, Charles J, Chinese
Deguise, Pierre Emile, French
Deredita, John Frederick, Hispanic-American Literature
Halleran, Michael Ros, Classics
Jones, Malcolm Bancroft, Romance Philology
Murstein, Nelly Kashy, French
Proctor, Robert Emmet, III, Italian Literature, Renaissance History
Reeve, Helen, Slavic Languages
Rice, Argyll Pryor, Spanish
Silverberg, Joann Claire, Classical Philology
Solomon, Janis Virginia Little, German Literature
Terras, Rita, German Language & Literature

New Milford

Havelock, Eric Alfred, Ancient Philosophy

Old Lyme

Fehrer, Catherine, Romance Languages

Rowayton

Vallerie, Josephine E, Medieval Literature & Philology

Southbury

Avila, Lilian E, Modern Languages
Kurz, Edmund Paul, German Literature

Stamford

Borysiuk, Myroslav, Latin

Storrs

Abramson, Arthur Seymour, Linguistics
Andrews, Oliver, Jr, Foreign Language
Barberet, Gene Joseph, French Literature
Bilokur, Borys, Russian & East Slavic Literature
Bizziccari, Alvaro, Italian
Cambon, Glauco, Comparative Literature
Cirurgiao, Antonio Amaro, Portuguese, Spanish
Crosby, Donald H, Germanic Studies
Dombroski, Robert Stanley, Italian & Comparative Literature
Eyzaguirre, Luis B, Spanish, Spanish American Literatures & Language
Gilliam, B June, French Language & Literature
Goldsmith, Emanuel Sidney, Hebrew & Yiddish Literature
Guiney, Mortimer Martin, French, Comparative Literature
Kaplowitt, Stephen Joseph, Germanic Languages & Literature
Lederer, Herbert, German
McHugh, Michael P, Classical Philology, Patristic Studies
Maddox, Donald, French, Medieval Studies
Marrone, Nila Gutierrez, Spanish Linguistics, Spanish American Literature
Mattingly, Ignatius G, Linguistics
Mead, Robert G, Jr, Spanish

Storrs, CONNECTICUT (cont)

Meyer, Paul Hugo, French
Michaels, David, Linguistics
Naudin, Marie, Romance Languages
Obuchowski, Chester W, Foreign Languages
Orringer, Nelson Robert, Hispanic Philosophy & Literature
Perry, Theodore Anthony, Romance Languages
Reinhardt, George William, German & Comparative Literature
Sachs, Jacqueline S, Linguistics, Psychology of Language
Sinicropi, Giovanni Andrea, Italian Literature
Suits, Thomas Allan, Classical Philology
Tilles, Solomon H, Spanish American Literature
Uhlig, Ludwig, German Literature

Tolland

Valdes, Jorge Horacio, Spanish & Spanish American Literature

West Hartford

Clark, Charlotte, Germanic & Romance Languages
Danielson, J David, Hispanic Studies

Willimantic

Emmel, Hildegard, German Literature
Watts, Lee Barnett, Romance Languages, English Literature

Wilton

Gelson, Mary Aline, Literature, Linguistics

Woodbridge

Wellek, Rene, English & Comparative Literature

DELAWARE

Dover

Espadas, Elizabeth Anne, Spanish, Spanish American Literature
Zaetta, Robert, Romance Languages

Newark

Alvarez, Roman, Spanish & Comparative Literature
Bohning, Elizabeth Edrop, German Literature
Borton, Samuel Lippincott, Modern Languages & Literature
Braun, Theodore Edward Daniel, French Literature & Language
Culley, Gerald Ray, Classical Philology
Di Pietro, Robert J, Linguistics
Dominguez, Ivo, Spanish, Spanish American Literature
Donaldson-Evans, Mary Prudhomme, French Language & Literature
Frawley, William John, Linguistics
Kirch, Max Samuel, Modern Languages
Lantolf, James Paul, Linguistics, Spanish
McInnis, Judy Bredeson, Comparative Literature, Spanish
McLaren, James Clark, French
Pitou, Spire, Romance Literature
Slavov, Eugenia Margaret Hintze, Slavic & Germanic Languages & Literatures
Steiner, Roger Jacob, Romance Languages, Linguistics
Stixrude, David Lawrence, Spanish Literature
Valbuena-Briones, Angel Julian, Hispanic Literature
Venezky, Richard L, Educational Psychology, Linguistics
Wedel, Alfred R, German & Spanish Philology

DISTRICT OF COLUMBIA

Washington

Abreu, Maria Isabel, Portuguese
Alatis, James Efstathios, English, Linguistics
Allee, John Gage, Jr, Philology, English
Applegate, Joseph Roye, Descriptive Linguistics
Baugh, John, Linguistics, Sociolinguistics
Bensky, Roger Daniel, Avant-Garde & French Theatre
Blumenthal, Gerda Renee, French & Comparative Literature
Brown, John Lackey, Comparative Literature, French

Callahan, John Francis, Classical Philology, Ancient Philosophy
Carter, Marion Elizabeth, Foreign Languages & Linguistics
Chambers, Bettye Thomas, French Bibliography
Chapin, Paul Gipson, Linguistics
Cook, Walter Anthony, Linguistics, South Asian Languages
Cowherd, Carrie Elizabeth, Latin, Greek
Cressey, William Whitney, Spanish Linguistics
Cruz-Saenz, Michele S De, Romance Languages, Medieval Studies
Damiani, Bruno Mario, Spanish, Italian
Delaney, John Thomas, Romance Languages
Dimmick, Ralph Edward Ingalls, Romance Languages & Literature
Dinneen, Francis Patrick, Linguistics
Ebanks, Gerardo Mack, Romance Languages & Literature
Erwin, Wallace Moore, Linguistics, Arabic
Fasold, Ralph William August, Linguistics
Fink, Stefan Richard, Linguistics, German
Fitzgerald, Aloysius, Semitic Languages
Fitzmyer, Joseph Augustine, Biblical Literature & Languages
Fox, Robert Paul, Linguistics, English As Second Language
Frank, Richard MacDonough, Semitic Studies, Arabic
Frey, John Andrew, Romance Languages
Gage, William Whitney, Linguistics
Gary, Edward Norman, Applied & Theoretical Linguistics
Gerli, Edmondo Michael, Spanish Language & Literature
Gignac, Francis Thomas, Philology, Theology
Ginsberg, Ellen Sutor, French Language & Literature
Goddard, R H Ives, III, Linguistics, Ethnohistory
Golla, Victor Karl, Anthropological Linguistics
Guieu, Jean-Max, French Literature
Halton, Thomas, Greek, Latin
Hubbard, Louise Jones, Romance Languages
Jacobson, Leon Carl, Linguistics, African Languages
Jamme, Albert W F, English, French
Jankowsky, K R, Germanic Languages
King, James Cecil, German
Knox, Bernard MacGregor Walker, Classical Philology
Korn, David, Languages, Linguistics
Kreidler, Charles William, Linguistics
Latimer, John Francis, Classical Languages & Literatures
Levitine, Eda Mezer, French Literature
Logan, Paul Ellis, German Language & Literature
McCarthy, Mary Frances, Foreign Languages & Literature
Maubrey, Pierre Remi, French, Linguistics
Mazzeo, Guido Ettore, Spanish Language & Literature
Meyer, Robert T, Celtic & Comparative Philology
Moser, Charles A, Slavic Language & Literature
Mujica, Barbara Louise, Spanish Literature
Nemoianu, Virgil Petre, Comparative Literature, English
Nicolich, Robert Nicholas, French Literature
Norris, William Edward, Applied Linguistics, English As A Foreign Language
Nugent, Gregory, German
Nunez, Benjamin, Linguistics, Latin American Civilization
Racine, Daniel Leandre, Francophone & Comparative Literature
Rameh, Clea Abdon, Linguistics, Portuguese Language
Robb, James Willis, Romance Languages & Literature
Roberts, Aaron Hood, Linguistics
Rosenfield, Leonora Cohen, French Literature
Saenz, Pilar G, Spanish
Sara, Solomon Ishu, Theoretical Linguistics & Phonology
Schulz, Siegried A, German, Comparative Philology
Shih, Chung Wen, English, Chinese
Shukla, Shaligram, Linguistics, Anthropology
Shuy, Roger W, Linguistics
Sienkewicz, Thomas J, Classical Literatures
Sims, Edna N, Romance Languages
Skehan, Patrick William, Semitics
Smart, Ian Isidore, Spanish American Literature
Smith, Harlie Lawrence, Jr, Linguistics
Snowden, Frank Martin, Jr, Classical Philology
Sola-Sole, Josep M, Philology, Medieval Spanish Literature

Steiner, Carl, German Language & Literature
Stokoe, William Clarence, Linguistics
Taylor, Orlando LeRoy, Linguistics, Speech
Thoenelt, Klaus, German, French
Wartenberg, Dorothy M, German, Comparative Literature
Williman, Joseph P, Romance Languages
Wise, Sheldon, English as a Foreign Language, Linguistics
Withers, Sara Cook, Linguistics
Yakobson, Helen Bates, Russian Language
Yang, Paul Fu-Mien, Chinese Linguistics
Yeager, Charles H, Foreign Languages
Zarechnak, Michael, Slavic Languages & Linguistics
Ziolkowski, John Edmund, Classical Languages

FLORIDA

Boca Raton

Estarellas, Juan, Second Language Learning, Psycholinguistics
Hokenson, Jan Walsh, Modern European & French Literature
Resnick, Melvyn C, Spanish & Applied Linguistics
Weiser, Ernest L, German Language & Literature

Casselberry

Maurino, Ferdinando D, Comparative Romance Literature

Cocoa Beach

Ferrigno, James Moses, Romance Languages

Coral Gables

Abraham, Richard D, Foreign Languages, Linguistics & Philology
Boggs, Ralph Steele, Folklore, English for Foreigners
Dees, Joseph Benjamin, Russian Literature
Javens, Charles, Spanish, Portuguese
Kirsner, Robert, Romance Languages
Lanius, Edward W, Romance Languages
Norris, Frank Pelletier, Medieval Romance Literature
Randolph, Donald Allen, Spanish Language & Literature
Roy, Joaquin, Latin American Literature, Linguistics
Ruggerio, Michael John, Romance Languages & Literatures
Schwartz, Kessel, Spanish
Varona, Alberto Jorge, Spanish American Literature, Latin American History
Webb, Benjiman Daniel, German Literature & Expressionistic Drama
Woshinsky, Barbara Reisman, French Literature

De Land

Minter, Elsie Grey, Romance Languages, Comparative Literature
Smith, Robert Lester, Hispanic Languages & Literatures
Zenkovsky, Betty Jean Bubbers, Foreign Languages
Zenkovsky, Serge A, Slavic Civilization & Literature

Gainesville

Allen, John Jay, Spanish
Baker, Susan Read, French Literature
Barksdale, Ethelbert Courtland, Russian Literature
Bonneville, Douglas, Foreign Languages
Cailler, Bernadette Anne, African & Caribbean Literature
Casagrande, Jean, French Language & Linguistics
Chu, Chauncey Cheng-Hsi, Linguistics
Conner, John Wayne, Romance Languages
Der-Houssikian, Haig, Linguistics
Dickison, Sheila Kathryn, Classics, Ancient History
Diller, George Theodore, Medieval French
Gay-Crosier, Raymond, French Literature
Gellinek, Christian Johann, Germanic Languages & Literature
Hardman-De-Bautista, Martha James, Anthropological Linguistics, Andean Languages
Hartigan, Karelisa Voelker, Classics

Hayes, Francis Clement, Spanish, Folklore
Hower, Alfred, Romance Languages & Literature
Jimenez, Reynaldo Luis, Spanish American literature
Johnston, Otto William, Germanic Languages & Literatures, Philology
Lambert, Roy Eugene, Linguistics, Cybernetics
Lasley, Marion Murray, Spanish
Miller, D Gary, Linguistics, Classics
Popp, Daniel McVagh, Germanic Languages & Literatures
Rennert, Hal H, German & Comparative Literature
Schmeling, Gareth Lon, Greek & Latin Literature
Scholes, Robert James, Linguistics
Schulman, Ivan Albert, Romance Languages & Literature
Smith, Albert B, Foreign Languages
Sullivan, William Joseph, Slavic Languages, Linguistics
Sussman, Lewis Arthur, Classics
Thompson, Roger Mark, Linguistics, Sociolinguistics
Vance, Timothy John, Linguistics, Japanese Language

Hialeah

Funke, Francis Joseph, Spanish & French Literatures

Jacksonville

Godoy, Gustavo J, Spanish, French
Salus, Peter Henry, Linguistics

Lakeland

Martinez, Jose Ramon, Spanish, Comparative Literatures

Longboat Key

Pratt, Norman Twombly, Jr, Classics, Comparative Literature

Maitland

Sedwick, Frank, Spanish

Miami

Aid, Frances Mary, Spanish, Linguistics
Crosby, James O'Hea, Spanish Literature
Gorman, John, German
Guers-Villate, Yvonne, Romance Languages
Hammond, Robert M, Linguistics, Phonetics
Jensen, John Barry, Portuguese, Linguistics
Leeder, Ellen Lismore, Spanish & Spanish American Language & Literature
Mirabeau, Roch Lucien, French
Roberts, Gemma, Spanish Literature
Yudin, Florence L, Spanish Literature

Miami Shores

Lee, Joseph Patrick, French Language & Literature

Oviedo

Reinke, Edgar Carl, Greek, Latin

Palm Beach

Artinian, Artine, French Literature

Pensacola

Caballero, Juan A, Spanish
Josephs, Allen, Modern Spanish Literature, Modern Literatures
Kaufke, Pierre H G, English, Foreign Languages

Pompano Beach

Nelson, Richard John Andrew, Romance Linguistics & Literatures

St Petersburg

Genz, Henry Edward, French
Trakas, Pedro Nicholas, Spanish

Sanibel

Brown, Calvin Smith, Comparative Literature

Tallahassee

Allaire, Joseph Leo, Romance Languages, French
Bourgeois, Louis Clarence, Romance Languages
Braendlin, Hans Peter, German Language & Literature
Cancalon, Elaine Davis, French Literature
Carrabino, Victor, Twentieth Century French Literature
Darst, David High, Golden Age Spanish Literature
Davies, Michael Brent, Classics, Indo-European Linguistics
de Grummond, W W, Classics, Romance Languages
Eisenberg, Daniel Bruce, Spanish Literature
Eubanks, Melvin O, Foreign Languages
Forehand, Walter Eugene, Classics
Gerato, Erasmo Gabriele, Italian & French Language & Literature
Glenn, Justin Matthews, Greek & Latin Literature
Golden, Leon, Classical Languages
Hilary, Richard Boyd, Italian Literature
Leamon, Max Phillip, French
Leduc, Albert Louis, Modern Languages, French
Lu, John H-T, Theoretical Linguistics
Nantell, Judith Ann, Modern Language & Literature
Pribic, Elizabeth, Slavic Languages & Literatures, German Philology
Pribic, Nikola R, Slavic Literature & Philology
Simons, John Donald, German & Comparative Literature
Spacagna, Antoine Ernest, French Literature & Linguistics
Stanley, Patricia Haas, German Humanities
Thompson, Mittie Lynette, Latin, Greek
Williams, Harry Franklin, Medieval French & Spanish
Wilson, Leslie Nelson, Literature, Linguistics
Wyatt, James Larkin, Romance Languages, Linguistics

Tampa

Camp, John B, Linguistics
Capsas, Cleon Wade, Spanish & Portuguese
Cole, Roger William, Linguistics, English
Fernandez, Eustasio, Spanish
Gessman, Albert Miloslav, Linguistics
Grothmann, Wilhelm Heinrich, Modern German Literature
Hampton, Warren Reed, Spanish & Portuguese
McLean, Edward F, Spanish
Motto, Anna Lydia, Classics
Neugaard, Edward Joseph, Romance Languages
Schenck, David Peter, Medieval French Language & Literature
Scruggs, Charles Eugene, French Literature, Linguistics
Stelzmann, Rainulf Alexander, German, Philosophy
Tatum, James Carl, Latin American & Spanish Literature
Taylor, Harvey Martin, Japanese Linguistics, Second Language Acquisition

Temple Terrace

Cano, Carlos Jose, Spanish & Latin American Literature
Guinagh, Kevin Joseph, Classical Philology
Peppard, Victor Edwin, Russian Language & Literature

Tierra Verde

Keeton, Kenneth E, Germanic Languages & Literature

West Palm Beach

Wadepuhl, Walter, German Literature

Winter Park

Bonnell, Peter H, Foreign Languages
Lancaster, Patricia Anne, French, Modern French Theater
Stadt, Bessie Winifred, Spanish Language & Literature

GEORGIA

Athens

Alexander, James Wagner, Greek & Classical Civilization
Best, Edward Exum, Jr, Classics
Cocco, Mia (Maria), Italian & French Renaissance Literature
Davis, James Herbert, Jr, French Literature
de Gorog, Ralph Paul, Romance Philology, Old French
Dowling, John Clarkson, Spanish
Gantz, Timothy Nolan, Classics, Classical Archeology
Gomez-Martinez, Jose Luis, Spanish Literature, Hispanic Thought
Hassell, James Woodrow, Jr, Foreign Languages
Hellerstein, Nina Salant, Modern French Literature, French Civilization
Howard, John Anderson, Medieval German Language & Literature, Yiddish Language & Literature
Johnson, Julie Greer, Spanish American Literature
Jorgensen, Peter Alvin, Germanic Philology, German
Kalidova, Theodore B, Romance Languages, Education
Klein, Jared Stephen, Linguistics, Indo-European Philology
Krispyn, Egbert, German & Comparative Literature
LaFleur, Richard Allen, Classical Studies
Lewis, Ward Bevins, Jr, Modern German Literature
Mantero, Manuel, Modern Hispanic Poetry
Morain, Genelle Grant, Foreign Language
Nicolai, Ralf Rochus, German Literature & Philosophy
Piriou, Jean-Pierre Joseph, French Literature
Ramirez, Manuel D, Spanish, Spanish American Literature
Rogers, Lindsey Swanson, Jr, Germanic Languages
Rubin, Nancy Felson, Classics
Ruppersburg, Hugh Michael, American Literature, The Novel
Scott, Wilder Pattillo, Spanish American Literature
Snow, Joseph T, Spanish & Portuguese Language & Literature
Steer, Alfred Gilbert, Jr, German Language & Literature
Tucker, Robert Askew, Latin, Greek
Valis, Noel Maureen, Spanish & French Literature
Ziomek, Henryk, Spanish Golden Age Literature

Atlanta

Austin, John Southern, Jr, Germanic Linguistics, Danish Phonology
Ballard, William Lewis, General Linguistics, Chinese Language
Bauslaugh, Robert Alan, Classical Languages & History
Beasley, Shubael Treadwell, German Literature
Benario, Herbert W, Classics
Benario, Janice Martin, Classics
Braunrot, Bruno, French Literature
Bucsela, John, Russian Language & Literature
Celler, Morton Mark, French Language & Literature
Coleman, Ingrid Roberta Hoover, French Literature, Drama
Conant, Joseph M, Classical Languages & Literature
Dickerson, Harold Douglas, Jr, German Language & Literature
Dorsey, David Frederick, Jr, African Literature, Linguistics
Duarte, Julio M, Spanish Golden Age Literature
Duban, Jeffrey M, Classical Languages
Evans, Arthur R, Jr, Romance Languages
Fowler, Carolyn, Afro-French & Afro-American Literature
Frazier, Earlene Freeman, Foreign Languages, English
Hudson, Benjamin F, Romance Languages
Inal, Halimat, French Language & Literature
Jones, Edward Allen, French Literature
Kaiser, Grant E, Romance Languages
Kelley, Emilia Navarro, Spanish Poetry & Novel
Kelley, Kathleen Ann, Classics
Kuntz, Marion Leathers Daniels, Classics, Renaissance Studies
McMahon, James Vincent, German Literature & Language

Atlanta, GEORGIA (cont)

Murray, James Christopher, Medieval Spanish Language & Literature
Pederson, Lee A, English Linguistics & Philology
Richmond, Garland Campbell, German Literature
Rojas, Carlos, Spanish Literature, History
Spruell, Shelby Outlaw, French Literature
Zahn, Louis J, Romance Languages & Literatures

Carrollton

Corriere, Alex, French Language & Literature

Decatur

Allen, Mary Virginia, French
Bicknese, Gunther, Literature & Linguistics
Dunstan, Florene J, Foreign Languages & Literature
Hubert, Claire Marcom, Comparative Literature
Shaw-Mazlish, Constance, Spanish Literature
Wieshofer, Ingrid, German
Young, Myrna Goode, Classical Languages
Zenn, Elizabeth Gould, Classical Languages & Literature

Ft Valley

Douglas, Elaine Elizabeth, Linguistics

Macon

Davis, William Richard, Jr, Spanish Literature
Dunaway, John Marson, French Language & Literature
Youman, Alfred Eliot, Classics

Milledgeville

Gonzalez, Jaime Jose, Spanish & Portuguese Literatures
Guitton, Jean Marie, Foreign Languages

Statesboro

Bouma, Lowell, Germanic Linguistics
Krug, Clara Elizabeth, French Language & Literature

HAWAII

Hilo

Howell, Richard Wesley, Anthropology, Linguistics
Komenaka-Purcell, April R, Sociolinguistics, Writing
Rogers, Lawrence William, Japanese Literature and Language

Honolulu

Araki, James Tomomasa, Oriental Languages
Aspinwall, Dorothy Brown, French Language & Literature
Ball, Robert J, Classical Languages
Bender, Byron Wilbur, Linguistics
Benouis, Mustapha Kemal, French Language & Literature
Burns, Alfred, Classics, Greek Philosophy
Clark, Marybeth, Linguistics, English as a Second Language
Crean, John Edward, Jr, Germanic Languages
Dardjowidjojo, Soenjono, Indonesian Languages & Linguistics
Dauer, Dorothea W, Languages & Literature
DeFrancis, John, Chinese
Dias, Austin, Spanish Languages, Spanish Penninsular Literature
Dykstra, Gerald, Linguistics
Elbert, Samuel Hoyt, Linguistics
Ellsworth, James Dennis, Classical Philology
Fairbanks, Gordon Hubert, Indo-European Linguistics
Forman, Michael Lawrence, Linguistics, Anthropology
Gething, Thomas Wilson, Southeast Asian Linguistics
Grace, George William, Linguistics, Anthropology
Hadlich, Roger Lee, Linguistics
Heien, Larry G, Contemporary Russian & Foreign Language Pedagogy
Hinds, John Van, III, Linguistics, Japanese Language
Holton, James S, Foreign Languages
Howard, Irwin Jay, Linguistics
Hsieh, Hsin-I, Linguistics, Chinese

Ikeda, Hiroko, Japanese Folklore
Jackson, Ernest, French
Jackson, Kenneth Leroy, English as a Second Language
Jacobs, Roderick Arnold, Comparative & Diachronic Linguistics, Stylistics
Kato, Hiroki, Sociolinguistics, Political Science
Kleinjans, Everett, Linguistics, Educational Administration
Klimenko, Michael, Russian Literature & Church
Knowlton, Edgar Colby, Jr, Romance Languages
Krohn, Robert Karl, Linguistics, English as a Second Language
Lee, Gregory, Linguistics
Lee, Peter Hacksoo, Languages
Li, Fang Kuel, Linguistics
Liem, Nguyen Dang, Linguistics, Foreign Languages
Lo, Chin-Tang, Chinese
Lyovin, Anatole Vladimirovich, Chinese Linguistics, Phonology
Ma, Yau-Woon, Chinese Literature, Bibliography
McKaughan, Howard Paul, Linguistics
Mathias, Gerald Barton, Japanese Language & Literature, Linguistics
Maurer, Walter Harding, Sanskrit
Montes, Yara Gonzalez, Spanish Peninsular Literature
Montes-Huidobro, Matias, Spanish Peninsular & Caribbean Literature
Moody, Raymond Albert, Hispanic Languages & Literatures
Moore, Cornelia Niekus, German, Dutch
Niedzielski, Henri, English & French Linguistics
Niyekawa, Agnes Mitsue, Psycholinguistics, Japanese Linguistics
Peters, Ann Marie, Linguistics
Ramos, Teresita Villarica, Linguistics, Second Language Teaching
Reid, Lawrence Andrew, Linguistics
Rodgers, Theodore Stephen, English Linguistics, Education
Roop, D Haigh, Southeastern Asian Languages, Linguistics
Rosenthal, Charlotte Joy, Russian Literature & Language
Sato, Esther Masako Tateishi, Foreign Language Methodology
Scherer, Willaim F, German Literature
Schutz, Albert J, Linguistics
Schweizer, Niklaus R, German
Seymour, Richard Kellogg, German
Shen, Yao, Linguistics, English
Sohn, Ho-Min, Korean & Oceanic Linguistics
Starosta, Stanley, Linguistics
Tahara, Mildred Machiko, Classical & Modern Japanese Literature
Thompson, Laurence Cassius, Jr, Linguistics
Topping, Donald M, Linguistics
Tsuzaki, Stanley Mamoru, Applied Linguistics
Unger, James Marshall, Japanese Language, Linguistics
Ward, Jack Haven, Language Teaching, Linguistics
Zants, Emily, French Literature

Manoa

Bickerton, Derek, Linguistics

Pearl City

Michalski, John, Comparative Literature & Linguistics

IDAHO

Boise

Valverde Zabaleta, Luis Jaime, Romance Languages & Literature

Lewiston

Sloat, Clarence, Linguistics, English as a Second Language

Moscow

Koubourlis, Demetrius John, Slavic Linguistics
Moody, Michael Weston, Spanish, Latin American Literature
Rowe, Galen Otto, Classics, Comparative Literature
Surles, Robert Leo, Medieval Literature, Spanish Linguistics
West, Dennis DeForest, Latin American & Spanish Cinema

Rexburg

Maxwell, Harry J, Germanic Languages, Latin American Studies

ILLINOIS

Bloomington

Johnston, Mark David, Medieval & Renaissance Studies, Romance Languages & Literatures

Carbondale

Angelis, Paul J, Linguistics
Bender, Marvin Lionel, Linguistics, Anthropology
Betz, Frederick, German Language & Literature
Canfield, Delos Lincoln, Spanish Linguistics
Carrell, Patricia Lynn, Linguistics
Epro, Margaret Winters, Romance Linguistics, French Medieval Literature
Gilbert, Glenn G, Sociolinguistics
Gobert, David Lawrence, French Language & Literature
Hartman, Steven Lee, Spanish, Linguistics
Keller, Thomas Lawrence, Germanic Linguistics & Literature
Kilker, James Anthony, French Literature & History
Kupcek, Joseph R, Slavic Languages & Literatures
Liedloff, Helmut, German
Maring, Joel Marvyl, Anthropology, Linguistics
Meinhardt, Warren Lee, Latin American Literature
Nathan, Geoffrey Steven, Linguistics
Nguyen, Dinh-Hoa, Linguistics, Literature
O'Brien, Joan V, Classical Languages & Literature
Parish, Charles, Linguistics, English as Foreign Language
Perkins, Allan Kyle, Applied & Theoretical Linguistics
Redden, James Erskine, Linguistics, African Studies
Timpe, Eugene Frank, Comparative Literature
Woodbridge, Hensley Charles, Spanish

Champaign

Choldin, Marianna Tax, Russian & Soviet Studies
Haile, Harry G, German Literature
Klein, Kurt A, Russian Language
Myers, M Keith, Romance Languages
Omaggio, Alice Catherine, Foreign Languages
Shtohryn, Dmytro Michael, Ukrainian Modern Literature
Stegemeier, Henri, Germanic Literatures

Charleston

Carr, Gerald Francis, German, Linguistics
Kirby, Paul Francis, Classics
Miess, Martin Michael, German Literature & Philology
Orcharenko, Maria M, Slavic Philology

Chicago

Aronson, Howard Isaac, Linguistics
Baer, Klaus, Egyptology
Bahl, Kalicharan, Linguistics
Bassett, Edward Lewis, Classical Philology
Bergquist, Violet, Spanish
Betoret-Paris, Eduardo, Spanish
Bevington, Gary Loyd, Linguistics
Biggs, Robert Dale, Assyriology
Blanco-Gonzalez, Manuel, Contemporary Literature
Bofman, Theodora Helene, Southeast Asian Language & Literature
Bozon-Scalzitti, Yvette Pauline, French Literature
Bruce, James Charles, German
Burnett, Anne Pippin, Classics
Busse, Bonnie Beulah, Spanish Language & Linguistics
Callahan, Anne M, French & Comparative Literature
Cantrall, William Randolph, Linguistics, Rhetoric
Chamberlin, Wells Fenton, French
Cherchi, Paolo Agostino, Romance Languages
Civil, Miguel, Assyriology, Linguistics
Clark, Priscilla Parkhurst, French Literature, Sociology of Literature
Conroy, Peter Vincent, Jr, French Language & Literature

Crone, Anna Lisa, Russian Literature, Literary Theory
Davis, Alva Leroy, English Linguistics
De Costa, Rene, Spanish, Spanish-American Literature
Dee, James Howard, Classical Languages & Literature
Dembowski, Peter Florian, Romance Philology
Denning, Gertrude R, Philology
Dickie, Matthew Wallace, Classical Philology
Dimock, Edward Cameron, Jr, Modern Indian Languages, History of Religion
Ehre, Milton, Russian Literature, General Humanities
Eiler, Mary Ann, Linguistics
Elias-Olivares, Lucia E, Hispanic Sociolinguistics, Applied Linguistics
El Saffar, Ruth Snodgrass, Spanish Literature
Festle, John Edward, Classical Literature, Philosophy of Education
Friedrich, Paul, Linguistics, Anthropology
Galassi, Battista J, Spanish, Italian
Gebhard, Elizabeth Replogle, Classical Archeology
Gelb, Ignace J, Assyriology
Gerow, Edwin, Sanskrit
Gethner, Perry Jeffrey, French Literature, History of Drama
Golab, Zbigniew, Slavic Linguistics
Gragg, Gene Balford, Linguistics, Sumerology
Gullon, Ricardo, Spanish & Spanish American Literature
Haley, George, Spanish Literature
Hallowell, Robert Edward, French Literature
Hamp, Eric Pratt, Linguistics
Hartoch, Arnold J, German
Hathaway, Luise H, Germanic Linguistics
Heitner, Robert Richard, German
Helmbold, Nancy Pearce, Classics
Hoffner, Harry A, Jr, History, Ancient Near East Languages
Holdsworth, Carole A, Romance Languages
Hoppe, Manfred Karl Ernst, German Literature
Hughes, George Robert, Egyptology
Ingham, Norman William, Slavic Languages & Literatures
Jarvi, Raymond, Modern Swedish Literature, Swedish Theater
Jennings, Lee B, German
Johnson, Janet Helen, Egyptology
Judd, Elliot L, Linguistics, English as a Second Language
Kaiser, Leo Max, Classical Philology
Kaster, Robert Andrew, Classical Languages and Literatures
Kauf, Robert, German Language & Literature
Kazazis, Kostas, Balkan Linguistics
Killean, Carolyn Garver, Arabic Linguistics
Kochman, Thomas Michael, Anthropological Linguistics
Komai, Akira, Japanese Linguistics, Classical Japanese
Kouvel, Audrey Lumsden, Romance Literatures
Krance, Charles Andrew, French Language & Literature
Kurczaba, Alex, Slavic Languages & Literatures
Lee, Leo Ou-Fan, Modern Chinese Literature & History
Leighton, Lauren Gray, Russian Literature, Romanticism
Libhart, Byron R, Romance Languages
McCawley, James D, Linguistics
McCawley, Noriko Akatsuka, Linguistics
McCluney, Daniel C, Jr, German Literature
McDavid, Raven Ioor, Jr, Linguistics, Dialectology
MacGregor, Alexander Paul, Jr, Classics, Palaeography
McKenna, Andrew Joseph, French Literature
McNeill, David, Psycholinguistics
McQuown, Norman Anthony, Anthropological Linguistics
Maharg, James, Spanish American & Brazilian Literatures
Maher, John Peter, General & Historical Linguistics
Makkai, Adam, Linguistics
Makkai, Valerie June Becker, Linguistics
Martinez, Miguel Angel, Spanish & Spanish American Literature
Matlaw, Ralph E, Russian & Comparative Literature
Meltzer, Francoise Claire, Comparative Literature, French Literature
Mittman, Barbara G, Eighteenth Century French Theatre
Moayyad, Heshmat, Oriental Languages
Mollenhauer, Hans-Joachim Gunther, Modern Languages

Moravcevich, June, French Literature
Moravcevich, Nicholas, Comparative Literature, Slavic Studies
Morrissette, Bruce Archer, French Literature
Muller-Bergh, Klaus, Latin American & Comparative Literature
Naim, Choudhri Mohammed, Urdu Language & Literature
Najita, Tetsuo, Modern & Japanese History
Nebel, Sylvia Sue, German Literature
Nims, Charles Francis, Egyptian Archaeology & Philology
Noakes, Susan Jeanne, Medieval & Renaissance Literature
Northcott, Kenneth J, Older German Literature
O'Connell, David Joseph, French Literature
Otto, Karl Frederick, Jr, German Literature
Pardee, Dennis Graham, Semitic Philology
Pendergast, Joseph S, Classical Philology
Perry, Kenneth I, Romance Languages & Literatures
Pillet, Roger A, Romance Languages, Education
Playe, George Louis, French Language & Literature
Putzel, Max J, Germanic Languages & Literature
Ragland, Eloise, French Literature & Language
Ramanujan, Attipat Krishnaswami, Linguistics, Literature
Ramsey, John Tyler, Latin Literature, Roman History
Redfield, James M, Archaic & Classical Literature & History
Reiner, Erica, Assyriology
Reklaitis, Janine Konauka, Baltic Languages & Literature
Rodriguez-Florido, Jorge Julio, Latin American Literature, Stylistics
Rohlfing, Martha Mae, German Literature
Rohlich, Thomas Henry, Japanese Literature & Language
Ross, William Braxton, Jr, Medieval Latin, Latin Paleography
Roy, David Tod, History, Far Eastern Languages
Rudall, David Nicholas, Classics
Sandler, Samuel, Polish Literature
Schiavo, Leda Brigida, Contemporary Spanish & Latin-American Literature
Schiff, Timothy Herbert, Comparative & Scandinavian Literature
Schiller, Andrew, Linguistics
Schoder, Raymond Victor, Greek, Latin
Silverstein, Michael, Linguistics, Anthropology
Sljivic-Simsic, Biljana, Slavic Languages
Svejkovsky, Frantisek, Czech & Slovak Literature
Sweetser, Franklin P, Romance Languages
Sweetser, Marie-Odile, French Language & Literature
Thelander, Dorothy Ramona, French
Torrielli, Andrew Joseph, Romance Languages
Tracy, Theodore James, Classics, Philosophy
Tsien, Tsuen-Hsuin, Chinese Literature & History
Vaio, John, Greek, Latin
Vardaman, Hazel Clare, German
Wandel, Joseph, German
Wasiolek, Edward, Comparative Literature
Wente, Edward Frank, Egyptology
West, Rebecca J, Italian Language and Literature
White, Peter, Classical Philology
Wike, Victoria Shanower, Continental Philosophy
Willner, Ernest Steven, Foreign Languages
Woolley, Dale Edward, Linguistics, Speech Science
Wright, Donald Edward, Linguistics, Medieval Literature
Yedlicka, Joseph W, Literature & Linguistics
Yngve, Victor H, Linguistics, Mechanical Translation
Zide, Norman H, Linguistics, Indology

Decatur

Ferris, William N, French, Spanish

Deerfield

Ivy, Robert Henry, Jr, French

De Kalb

Gutsche, George J, Russian & Serbo-Croatian Literature
Heilbronn, Denise Martin, Italian Language & Literature, French
Jegers, Benjamin, Linguistics
Kerr, John Austin, Jr, Portuguese, History
Mahmoud, Parvine, French & Persian Literature
Mazzola, Michael Lee, Romance Linguistics

Mocega-Gonzales, Esther P, Spanish-American Literature
Murray, Frederic William, Ibero American Studies
Osterle, Heinz D, German Literature
Palmer, Joe Lerner, Spanish Literature
Rogan, Richard George, German Literature, Scandinavian Studies
Schoenbohm, Gertrude K, Foreign Languages & Literatures
Schreiner, Martha E, French Literature & Language
Soudek, Lev I, English & Applied Linguistics
Suhadolc, Joseph, Russian Language & Literature
Weiner, Jack, Spanish, Russian
Zoldester, Philip H, German

Edwardsville

Baltzell, James Henry, French
Drake, Gertrude Coyne, Comparative Study of Literature
Francis, Claude, French Literature
Goode, Helen D, Romance Languages
Griffen, Toby David, Linguistics, German
Guenther, Paul Felix, Comparative Literature
Osiek, Betty Tyree, Romance Languages
Spahn, Raymond J, German
Van Syoc, Wayland Bryce, Linguistics

Elmhurst

Wellington, Marie Adele Zeilstra, Romance Languages

Elsah

Bradley, Edward Drake, French

Evanston

Atkinson, Ross W, Bibliography, German Literature
Avins, Carol Joan, Russian & Comparative Literature
Bregoli-Russo, Mauda Rita, Italian Renaissance & Medieval Literature
Cooper, Henry Ronald, Jr, Slavic Literatures & Languages
DeCoster, Cyrus Cole, Spanish
Doney, Richard Jay, German
Fernandez-Morera, Dario Oscar, Comparative Literature, Spanish
Garrison, Daniel Hodges, Classics, Comparative Literature
Heller, Erich, German
Kantor, Marvin, Slavic Linguistics, Russian Literature
Levi, Judityh Naomi, Linguistics
Levine, Edwin Burton, Greek & Latin
Libertson, Joseph, French Literature, Critical Theory
Moses, Rae Arlene, Linguistics, African Languages
Nebel, Henry Martin, Jr, Russian Literature & Aesthetics
Paden, William Doremus, Jr, Medieval Literature, Romance Philology
Pickel, Frank Givens, Classical Philology
Reed, David Wooderson, English Language
Robles, Humberto E, Spanish American Literature
Romanowski, Sylvie, French Literature
Rudy, Peter, Russian Language & Literature
Rumold, Rainer Y, German Language & Literature
Sankovitch, Tilde Anna, Medieval & Renaissance Literature
Small, Stuart Gerard Paul, Classics
Spann, Meno Hans, German
Spears, Richard Alan, Linguistics, American Culture
Spector, Norman Bernard, French
Steiner, Grundy, Classical Philology
Stimson, Frederick Sparks, Spanish
Strutynski, Udo, Medieval Literature
Very, Francis George, Romance Languages
Von Molnar, Geza Walter Elemer, German Language & Literature, Philosophy
Webber, Edwin Jack, Romance Languages & Literature
Weil, Irwin, Russian Literature
Whiting, Charles G, French
Woodmansee, Martha Ann, German & Comparative Literature
Wright, John (Henry), Classics, Medieval Literature

ILLINOIS (cont)

Evansville

Felsher, William Munson, French Language &
Literature

Galesburg

Baacke, Margarita I, German, English
Fox, Edward Inman, Foreign Languages
Jeffries, Elna Louise, Romance Languages
Livosky, Isabel C, Spanish Language &
Literatures
Prats, Jorge, Spanish
Regenos, Graydon Wendell, Classical Philology,
Mediaeval Latin
Vander Meulen, Ross, German Literature

Jacksonville

Fuhrig, Anne Marie, German Language &
Literature
Gustafson, Marjorie Lillian, Foreign Language
Palmer, Richard E, Comparative European
Literature & Philosophy
Seator, Lynette Hubbard, Spanish, Comparative
Literature

Kenilworth

Markey, Constance, Italian Literature & Film

Lake Bluff

Dilkey, Marvin Charles, German

Macomb

Alsip, Barbara Wittman, French Language &
Literature
Grass, Roland Leo, Hispanic Language &
Literature
Helwig, Frank Scott, Spanish & Spanish-
American Literature
Kalwies, Howard H, French Renaissance
Literature & Civilization
Kurman, George, Comparative & Estonian
Literature
McKinney, James E, Modern Language
Risley, William Roy, Spanish Language &
Literature
Smithson, Rulon Nephi, French
Vos, Morris, German Literature & Language

Monmouth

Fox, Bernice Lee, Classical Languages &
Literature

Morton Grove

Johnson, Falk Simmons, English Linguistics

Mt Carmel

Carrell, Thelma Ruth, Romance Languages

Naperville

Lebeau, Bernard Pierre, French Language &
Literature
Zwart, Martin, Foreign Languages & Literature

Normal

Bohn, Williard, French & Comparative Literature
Comfort, Thomas Edwin, French
Dixon, Christa Klingbeil, German Language &
Literature, Folklore
Ferguson, Albert Gordon, Spanish, French
Kuhn, Brigitta Johanna, French
Laurenti, Joseph L, Foreign Languages
Olivier, Louis Antoine, French Literature,
Literary Translation
Parent, David J, German Language & Literature
Parker, Kelvin Michael, Romance Linguistics
Sutherland, Robert Donald, Linguistics, English
Language
Tarrant, Patrick, French
Whitcomb, Richard Owens, German Language &
Literature

Oak Park

Bras, Mary Benvenuta, French Language &
Literature
Rolfs, Daniel James, Italian Language &
Literature
Shaw, Leroy Robert, German

Peoria

Maier, Carol Smith, Hispanic Literature
Rastatter, Paul Henry, Romance Languages

Quincy

Dressler, Hermigild, Classical Philology

River Forest

Kreiss, Paul Theodore, French, German

Rockford

Den Adel, Raymond L, Ancient History,
Archeology
Schmitt, James Joseph, German Language &
Literature

Rock Island

Nations, Elisabeth S, German

Skokie

Smith, Elsdon Coles, Onomastics

Springfield

Bomhard, Allan R, Indo-European & Semitic
Linguistics

Urbana

Accad, Evelyne, Francophone Studies, African
Studies
Antonsen, Elmer H, Germanic Linguistics
Aston, Katharine O, English, Linguistics
Baldwin, Spurgeon Whitfield, Medieval Spanish
Literature, Philology
Bateman, John Jay, Classics, Speech
Blaylock, Curtis, Romance Philology
Bowen, Barbara C, French
Bowen, Vincent Eugene, French
Bright, David F, Classical Languages
Brown, H Douglas, Linguistics
Browne, Gerald Michael, Classics, Linguistics
Burkhard, Marianne, Modern German
Literature, Comparative Literature
Carreno, Antonio G, Spanish & Spanish-
American Literature
Cassell, Anthony K, Italian & Medieval
Literature
Chang, Richard I-Feng, Chinese, Law
Cheng, Chin-Chuan, Linguistics
Cole, Peter, Linguistics, Language Teaching
Davison, Alice Louise, Linguistics
Dawson, Clayton L, Slavic Languages &
Literature
De Ley, Herbert Clemone, Jr, French Language
& Literature
Dengate, James Andrew, Classical Archeology
Flores, Joseph S, Spanish
Friedberg, Maurice, Slavic Languages &
Literature
Gaeng, Paul A, Romance Linguistics & Philology
Gerlach, U Henry, German Literature
Gladney, Frank Y, Slavic Languages
Gotoff, Harold Charles, Classical Philology
Gray, Stanley Everts, French
Green, Georgia Marks, Linguistics
Haidu, Peter, French
Heller, John Lewis, Classical Philology
Hill, Steven Phillips, Slavic Languages &
Literatures
Hollerer, Walter Friedrich, German Language &
Literature
Jacobson, Howard, Classical Literature
Jenkins, Frederic Magill, Contemporary French,
Linguistics
Jost, Francois, Languages
Kachru, Braj Behari, Non-Native Englishes,
Sociolinguistics
Kachru, Yamuna, Linguistics
Kahane, Henry, General & Romance Linguistics
Kenstowicz, Michael John, Linguistics,
Phonology
Kim, Chin-Wu, Linguistics, Phonetics
Knust, Herbert, German, Comparative Literature
Kolb, Philip, Romance Languages
Lorbe, Ruth Elisabeth, Modern German
Literature
Lott, Robert Eugene, Spanish, Romance
Stylistics
McGlathery, James Melville, Germanic
Languages
Maggs, Barbara Widenor, Comparative
Literature, Slavic Literature
Mainous, Bruce Hale, French
Makino, Seiichi, Linguistics

Marchand, James Woodrow, Germanic
Languages
Marty, Fernand Lucien, French
Meehan, Thomas Clarke, Romance Languages
Mitchell, P M, Germanic Languages &
Literatures
Morgan, Jerry Lee, Linguistics
Mortimer, Armine Kotin, French Literature &
Criticism
Musumeci, Antonino, Italian, French
Nelson, Robert James, French
Newman, Frances Stickney, Classical Philology
Newman, John Kevin, Classical Philology,
Comparative Literature
Oliver, Revilo Pendleton, Classics, Spanish &
Italian
OsGood, Charles Egerton, Psycholinguistics,
International Relations
Pachmuss, Temira, Russian Literature &
Language
Palencia-Roth, Michael, Comparative Literature
Pasquariello, Anthony Michael, Romance
Languages
Philippson, Ernst Alfred, Germanic Philology
Porqueras-Mayo, Alberto, Spanish Literature
Preto-Rodas, Richard A, Romance Languages
Price, Larkin Burl, French Literature
Rauch, Irmengard, Germanic Linguistics
Saltarelli, Mario D, General Linguistics,
Romance Languages
Sansone, David, Classics
Savignon, Sandra Joy, Second Language
Acquisition, Psycholinguistics
Saville-Troike, Muriel Renee, American Indian
Languages, English as a Second Language
Scanlan, Richard T, Classics
Schoeps, Karl H, German, Comparative
Literature
Talbot, Emile Joseph, French
Tikku, Girdhari Lal, Persian
Troike, Rudolph C, Linguistics, American
Anthropology
Wallach, Luitpold, Classics, Mediaeval Latin
Wanner, Dieter, Romance & General Linguistics
Weisz, Pierre, French & American Literature
Wilcox, John Chapman, Spanish Literature,
Poetry
Wright, Rochelle Ann, Scandinavian &
Comparative Literature
Zgusta, Ladislav, Linguistics

Wheaton

DeVette, Robert Oscar, Spanish Language &
Literature
Henning, William Andrew, French Linguistics
Rupprecht, Arthur A, Classical Languages
Wolf, Herbert Martin, Hebrew, Old Testament
Studies
Ziefle, Helmut Wilhelm, German Literature,
Modern German History

Wilmette

Roberts, William, French Literature
Stablein, Patricia Harris, Medieval French &
Provencial Literature

INDIANA

Anderson

Tjart, Peter, German & Russian Language &
Literature

Bloomington

Al-Toma, Salih Jawad, Arabic, Linguistics
Banta, Frank Graham, German, Linguistics
Bareikis, Robert Paul, Germanic Languages &
Literature
Barnstone, Willis, Spanish & Comparative
Literature
Basgoz, Mehmet Ilhan, Folklore, Language
Beltran, Luis, Comparative Literature
Berkvam, Michael Leigh, French Literature
Bieder, Maryellen Wolfe, Spanish Literature
Bird, Charles Stephen, Linguistics, Folklore
Blaisdell, Foster Warren, Jr, German, Old Norse
Boerner, Peter, Comparative Literature, German
Literature
Bondanella, Julia Conaway, Comparative
Literature, Romance Languages
Bondanella, Peter Eugene, Italian & Comparative
Literature
Calinescu, Matei Alexe, Comparative Literature,
West European Studies
Carr, Richard Alan, French & Renaissance
Literature

Champigny, Robert Jean, French
Chih, Yu-Ju, Chinese Language, Political Science
Clark, Katerina, Soviet Literature & Society
Cluver, Claus, Comparative Literature
Decker, Frances Louise, Germanic Language &
  Literature, Medieval Studies
Decsy, Gyula Jozsef, Uralic Finno-Ugric
  Linguistics, Slavic Languages
Degh-Vazsonyi, Linda, Folklore, Anthropology
Draghi, Paul Alexander, Comparative Literature,
  Asian Studies
Durzak, Manfred Heinrich, German
Dyson, John Payne, Spanish, Portuguese
Edgerton, William Benbow, Slavic Languages
Eoyang, Eugene Chen, Comparative Literature,
  East Asian Languages & Cultures
Feldstein, Ronald Fred, Slavic Linguistics,
  Russian
Franklin, James Lee, Jr, Greek & Latin
  Literature
Fredericks, Sigmund Casey, Classical Studies,
  Comparative Literature
Gerrard, Charlotte Frankel, Romance Languages
Gradman, Harry Lee, Linguistics, English as a
  Foreign Language
Gravit, Francis West, French Literature
Guiragossian Carr, Diana, French Literature
Halporn, James Werner, Greek, Latin
Hangin, John Gombojab, Mongolian Language &
  Civilization
Hansen, William Freeman, Classical Studies,
  Folklore
Helbig, Louis Ferdinand, German Studies
Hodge, Carleton Taylor, Linguistics
Holquist, James Michael, Russian Literature
Holschuh, Albrecht, Germanic studies
Hope, Quentin Manning, French Literature
Householder, Fred Walter, Jr, Classics, General
  Linguistics
Houston, John Porter, French
Houston, Mona Tobin, French Literature
Hunt, Joel Andrews, French
Hyde, John Kenneth, French Language &
  Literature
Impey, Olga Tudorica, Spanish Medieval &
  Renaissance Literature
Iwamoto, Yoshio, Modern Japanese Literature
Jacobsen, Thomas Warren, Classical Archeology
  & Languages
Johnson, John William, Folklore, African
  Folklore
Johnson, Sidney Malcolm, German
Kadic, Ante, Slavic Languages & Literature
Kagan-Kans, Eva, Russian Literature
Kromer, Gretchen, Greek & Latin Literature
Krueger, John Richard, Linguistics
Leach, Eleanor Winsor, English, Latin
Leake, Roy Emmett, Jr, French
Lebano, Edoardo Antonio, Italian
Lo, Irving Yucheng, Comparative Literature,
  Chinese
Long, Timothy, Classics
Lopez-Morillas, Consuelo, Romance & Hispano-
  Arabic Literature
Martins, Heitor Miranda, Portuguese
Matsuda, Shizue, Chinese Literature, Japanese
  Bibliography
Mickel, Emanuel John, Jr, Romance Languages
Mitchell, Breon, Comparative Literature,
  German
Moody, Marvin Dale, French Language &
  Linguistics
Musa, Mark, Italian
Nagle, Betty Rose, Classical Studies
Najam, Edward William, French Language &
  Literature
Norbu, Thubten Jigme, Tibetan Language &
  Culture
Oinas, Felix Johannes, Slavic & Finno-Ugric
  Linguistics
Oviedo, Jose Miguel, Spanish American
  Literature
Piedmont, Ferdinand, German
Pizzini, Quentin A, Linguistic Theory,
  Portuguese Linguistics
Poesse, Walter, Spanish
Powell, Hugh, German Literature
Ramage, Edwin Stephen, Classical Languages
Raun, Alo, Uralic Linguistics
Reichmann, Eberhard, German
Remak, Henry Heymann Herman, German,
  Comparative Literature
Rollins, Jack Drake, Comparative Literature
Rosenberg, Samuel Nathan, Romance Philology,
  French Literature
Rushton, Peter Halliday, Chinese Language &
  Literature
Salmon, Russell Owen, Spanish Literature
Sangster, Rodney Blair, Slavic & General
  Linguistics

Schuman, Verne Brinson, Greek Papyri
Sebeok, Thomas Albert, Linguistics,
  Anthropology
Seidlin, Oskar, German Literature
Shetter, William Zeiders, Germanic Languages &
  Linguistics
Simmons, Merle Edwin, Spanish
Snyder, Emile, French & Comparative Literature
Sung, Margaret Mian Yan, Chinese &
  Anthropological Linguistics
Thayer, Terence Kelso, German
Thomson, Ian, Classical Studies
Trapnell, William Holmes, French Literature
Valdman, Albert, French, Italian, Linguistics
Van Schooneveld, Cornelis Hendrik, Slavic
  Linguistics
Volek, Bronislava, Slavic Languages, Linguistics
Wailes, Stephen L, Germanic Languages
Webb, Karen Schuster, Applied Linguistics
Weisstein, Ulrich (Werner), Comparative
  Literature, German
Wyers, Frances, Romance Languages
Yasuda, Kenneth Kenichiro, Japanese Literature
Ziegler, Carl H, German, Comparative Literature

Columbia City

Vanderford, Kenneth H(ale), Romance
  Languages

Crawfordsville

Bedrick, Theordore, Classical Languages
Charles, John Fredrick, Classical Philology
Kudlaty, John Michael, Spanish Language &
  Literature
Planitz, Karl-Heinz, German Language &
  Literature
Strawn, Richard R, French Literature

Crown Point

Struebig, Patricia Ann, French & Spanish
  Language & Literature

Evansville

Diaz, Lomberto, Spanish & Spanish American
  Literature

Franklin

Ashley, Gardner Pierce, French
Pianca, Alicia Margarita, Romance Languages

Ft Wayne

Beecher, Graciela Fernandez, Spanish, French
Craig, Virginia Robertson, Spanish Language &
  Literature
Fox, Linda Chodosh, Foreign Language

Goshen

Bender, Mary Eleanor, French, Germand
Davis, Judith Mary, Medieval French,
  Comparative Literature

Greencastle

Beaudry, Agnes Porter, French Literature
Carl, Ralph Fletcher, Romance Languages
Mecum, Kent Bruce, Spanish American
  Literature & Intellectual History
Minar, Edwin LeRoy, Jr, Classical Philology
Van Zwoll, Cornelius, Germanic Languages &
  Literatures
Welliver, Glenn Edwin, German Language &
  Literature

Hammond

Lamb, Anthony Joseph, Spanish Language &
  Literature

Hanover

Hill, Emma May, Spanish Literature
Mullett, Fred Maurice, Foreign Languages
Rothert, Elayne Larsen, Foreign Languages
Trimble, Robert Gene, Spanish Language &
  Literature

Huntington

Bealer, Ralph George, Biblical Languages &
  Literature

Indianapolis

Barlow, John Denison, German Literature, Film
Black, Margaretta, French Language &
  Literature
Hoyt, Giles Reid, German Literature
Jessup, Florence L Redding, Spanish Language &
  Literature
Kooreman, Thomas Edward, Spanish, Spanish
  American Literature
Meier, Marga, Languages
Vermette, Rosalie Ann, French Language &
  Literature

Kokomo

Miller, Herbert Cleo, Slavic Linguistics

Lafayette

Pasco, Allan Humphrey, Romance Languages

La Porte

Jones, Larry Bert, Linguistics

Muncie

Brown, James W, Spanish
Gardiol, Rita Mazzetti, Spanish Literature, Latin
  American Studies
Gilman, Donald, French, Comparative Literature
Kasparek, Jerry Lewis, Classics, Comparative
  Literature
Stahlke, Herbert Frederic Walter, Linguistics,
  African Studies
Wood, Mary Elizabeth, Foreign Languages

Munster

Ade, Walter Frank Charles, Foreign Languages,
  Education

New Albany

Mitsch, Ruthmarie H, Modern Languages

North Manchester

Glade, Henry, German, Russian
Wehner, James Vincent, German & Comparative
  Literature

Notre Dame

Banas, Leonard Norbert, Classical Languages
Bayhouse, Anna Teresa, Romance Languages,
  Linguistics
Berberi, Dilaver, Linguistics
Bosco, Paul Fred, Romance Philology
Carter, Henry Hare, Modern Languages
Cervigni, Dino Sigismondo, Italian Literature
Doering, Bernard, French Language & Literature
Klawiter, Randolph Jerome, German Language
  & Literature
Lacombe, Anne, French Language & Literature
Lazenby, Francis D, Classical Archaeology,
  Philology
O'Neal, John Coffee, French Literature
Parnell, Charles Ephraim, Modern French
  Literature
Profit, Vera Barbara, French & German
  Literature
Roedig, Charles Francis, French Language &
  Literature
Rubulis, Aleksis, East European Literature
Schaum, Konrad Johannes, German Literature
Stern, Cindy Debra, Metaphysics, Philosophy of
  Language

Rensselaer

Lang, Frederick Richard, Classical Studies
Luzay, Joseph Yusuph, Classical & Modern
  Languages

Richmond

Brewster, Robert Riggs, German
Heiny, Stephen Brooks, Classics
Hiatt, Mary Lane Charles, French Language &
  Literature
Matlack, Charles W, Spanish

St Mary-of-the-Woods

Knoerle, Jeanne, Comparative & Asian
  Literature

INDIANA (cont)

Schereville

Koch, Regina Marie, Germanic Languages & Literature

South Bend

Gessel, Van C, Japanese Literature & Language
Lanzinger, Klaus, American & German Literature
Renaldi, Thomas Wayne, Spanish American Literature

Terre Haute

Bruning, Peter, German
Carmony, Marvin Dale, Linguistics, English Language
Gates, John Edward, Lexicography
Ghurye, Charlotte Wolf, German Language & Literature
Grun, Ruth Dorothea, German Language, Romance Languages
Krause, Maureen Therese, German
Pound, Glen M, Linguistics, English
Soper, Cherrie L, Romance Languages

Upland

Heath, Dale E, Ancient Language & History

Valparaiso

Falkenstein, Henning, German Language & Literature
Moulton, Thora Mary, German Civilization & Language
Must, Gustav, Germanic Philology, Comparative Linguistics
Must, Hildegard, Linguistics
Peters, Howard Nevin, Spanish, Comparative Literature
Petersen, Carol Otto, German, French

Waveland

Hook, Julius N, English

West Lafayette

Barnett, Richard Lance, French Language & Literature
Beer, Jeanette Mary Ayres, Medieval French, Linguistics
Benhamou, Paul, French Literature
Blickenstaff, Channing B, Spanish Language & Education
Garfinkel, Alan, Spanish Education
Hughes, Shaun Francis Douglas, Medieval English Language & Literature
Kadir, Djelal, Latin American & Comparative Literature
Keck, Christiane Elisabeth, Germanic Language & Literatures
Kelly, Thomas Edward, Romance Languages
Kirby, Carol Lynn Bingham, Spanish Golden Age Literature
Kirby, Steven Darrell, Spanish Medieval Literature
Marti De Cid, Dolores, Romance Philology & Linguistics
Randall, Earle Stanley, German, French
Ruiz-Ramon, Francisco Jose, Spanish Drama & Literature
Stout, Harry L, Comparative Literature
Titche, Leon L, Jr, German Language & Literature
Walther, Don H, Spanish, Portuguese
Walther, Maud Susie, French Literature & Cinema
Whitby, William Melcher, Spanish

IOWA

Ames

Bernard, Robert William, French, Italian
Bruner, Charlotte Hughes, French, Comparative Literature
Courteau, Joanna, Spanish, Portuguese
Dial, Eleanore Maxwell, Spanish
Dow, James Raymond, German Folklore
Frink, Orrin, Slavic Languages & Literatures
Graupera, Arturo Agustin, Spanish
Lacasa, Jaime, Spanish Language & Literature
Lacasa, Judith Noble, Spanish Language & Literature
McVicker, Cecil D, Romance Languages

Morris, Walter D, Germanic Languages & Literatures
Nabrotzky, Ronald Heinz Dieter, German Language & Literature
Thogmartin, Clyde Orville, Romance Linguistics
Von Godany, Ursula Bach, German Language & Literature

Cedar Falls

Chabert, Henry L, French Civilization & Literature
Hawley, Donald C, Spanish
Oates, Michael David, French Linguistics & Methodology
Zucker, George Kenneth, Spanish Philology, Medieval Literature

Cedar Rapids

Almasov, Alexey, Russian, Spanish
Irving, Evelyn Uhrhan, Spanish
Irving, Thomas Ballantine, Contemporary Islamic World, Central American Culture
Larkin, James Brian, Spanish
Wiese, Herbert Frank, German

Davenport

Coussens, Prudent C, German
Farrell, Anthony Gorham, Classical Languages, Theology

Decorah

Bahe, Barbara Ann, Germanic Language & Literature
Caldwell, Ruth Louise, French Language & Literature
Fjelstad, Ruth Naomi, Romance Languages
Kurth, William Charles, Latin, Greek
Stokker, Kathleen Marie, Norwegian Language & Literature

Des Moines

Smith, Charles Lavaughn, Semitic Languages & Literature
Soria, Mario T, Romance Languages

Dubuque

Buller, Jeffrey Lynn, Classical Languages, Comparative Literature
Carton, Mary Josepha, Latin, Greek
Johannes, Wilfred Clemens, Philology
O'Connor, Mary Lucilda, Foreign Languages
Schuster, Edward James, Modern Foreign Languages, History

Grinnell

Brown, Francis Andrew, German
Kleinschmidt, John Rochester, French
Lalonde, Gerald Vincent, Classics, Ancient History
McKibben, William Torrey, Classics
Michaels, Jennifer Elizabeth, German & Comparative Literature
Noble, Beth Wilson, Modern Foreign Languages
Parslow, Morris, French
Percas de Ponseti, Helena, Modern Foreign Languages & Literatures
Perri, Denis Roy, Spanish

Indianola

Gieber, Robert L, French Language & Literature

Iowa City

Aikin, Judith Popovich, German Literature & Language
Altman, Charles Frederick, French Literature, Cinema
Cerreta, Florindo V, Romance Languages
Ch'eng, Hsi, Chinese Language & Literature
Coblin, Weldon South, Chinese & Sino-Tibetan Linguistics
Delaty, Simone, French Literature
Deutelbaum, Wendy, Comparative & French Literature
Diaz-Duque, Ozzie Francis, Romance Languages & Literatures
Douglass, R Thomas, Spanish, Linguistics
Duran-Cerda, Julio, Spanish American Literature
Dvoretzky, Edward, German Literature
Ertl, Wolfgang, Germanic Languages & Literature
Fernandez, Oscar, Romance Languages
Hahn, Oscar, Spanish American Poetry, Literary Theory

Holtsmark, Erling Bent, Classics
Hornsby, Jessie Gillespie, Romance Languages
Hornsby, Roger Allen, Classics
Iknayan, Marguerite, French Languages & Literature
Iverson, Gregory Keith, Linguistics, Germanic Languages
Jackson, Donald Francis, Classical Languages & Literature
Jeffers, Coleman Reynolds, Spanish
Koutsoudas, Andreas, Linguistics
Ladusaw, William Allen, Linguistics
Luxenburg, Norman, History, Russian
Nothnagle, John Thomas, French Language & Literature
O'Gorman, Richard F, French
Parkes, Ford Briton, German Medieval Literature
Parrott, Ray Jennings, Jr, Russian Language & Literature
Ringen, Catherine Oleson, Linguistics
Runge, Richard Martin, Germanic Linguistics
Ryan, Marleigh, Japanese Literature
Sandrock, James P, German
Scriabine, Helene, Linguistics
Solbrig, Ingeborg Hildegard, German Language & Literature
Ungar, Steven Ronald, French Literature
Wachal, Robert Stanley, Neurolinguistics, Applied Linguistics
Weber, Harry Butler, Russian Language & Literature
Weissbort, Daniel Jack, Translation, Modern European Poetry
Wertz, Christopher Allen, Slavic & General Linguistics

Mt Pleasant

Aspel, Paulene Violette, Foreign Languages

Mt Vernon

DuVal, Francis Alan, German

Orange City

Radandt, Friedhelm K, Germanic Languages

Oskaloosa

Wormhoudt, Arthur Louis, Foreign Language, English

Pella

Webber, Philip Ellsworth, Germanic Philology

Sioux Center

Zinkand, John M, Classical Languages

Sioux City

Baak, Leonhard E, German
Mazeika, Edward John, Developmental Psycholinguistics

Waverly

Schuessler, Axel Hartmut, Chinese Philology

KANSAS

Atchison

Wittmann, Richard Gerard, Classical Languages, World Literature

Emporia

Hernandez-Daniel, Oscar F, Spanish Literature, Applied Linguistics

Hays

Kuchar, Roman Volodymyr, German, Russian & Latin
Salien, Jean-Marie, Eighteenth Century French Literature, Francophone Literatures

Lawrence

Anderson, Robert Edward, French Literature, Foreign Language Pedagogy
Anderson, Sam Follett, Germanic & Slavic Languages
Asuncion-Lande, Nobleza Castro, Speech Communications, Sociolinguistics
Baron, Frank, German Literature, Renaissance History

Blue, William Robert, Spanish Literature
Booker, John T, French Literature
Boon, Jean-Pierre, French Language & Narrative Arts
Brushwood, John Stubbs, Spanish American Literature
Chamberlin, Vernon Addison, Spanish Literature
Conrad, Joseph Lawrence, Russian Language & Literature
Cook, Albert Baldwin, III, English, Linguistics
Craig, Barbara Mary St George, French
Debicki, Andrew Peter, Spanish
Dick, Ernst Siegfried, Germanic Literature & Philology
Dinneen, David Allen, French, Linguistics
Doudoroff, Michael John, Spanish Language & Literature
Erazmus, Edward T, Linguistics
Freeman, Bryant C, French Literature
Galton, Herbert, Slavic Languages
Hartman, James Walter, English Language, Linguistics
Herzfeld, Anita, Linguistics, English as a Second Language
Huelsbergen, Helmut Ernest, German, Comparative Literature
Ingemann, Frances, Linguistics
Johnson, John Theodore, Jr, Romance Languages
Kozma, Janice M, Italian Language & Literature
Lacy, Norris Joiner, Medieval French Literature
Lind, Levi Robert, Classical Philology
Mikkelson, Gerald, Slavic Languages
Parker, Stephen Jan, Russian & Comparative Literature
Percival, Walter Keith, Linguistics
Phillips, Oliver Clyde, Jr, Greek, Latin Language & Literature
Prete, Sesto, Classical Languages & Literatures
Rosen, Karl Meltzer Dresner, Linguistics, Classical Languages
Sedelow, Sally Yeates, Linguistics, Information Science
Souza, Raymond D, Spanish
Spear, Richard Lansmon, Japanese Language & Literature
Spires, Robert Cecil, Contemporary Spanish Literature
Stammler, Heinrich A, Slavic Languages & Literature
Vincent, Jon S, Brazilian Literature, Portuguese
Weiss, Arnold Henry, Spanish
White, Kenneth Steele, French
Williams, John R, French
Woodyard, George W, Spanish

Manhattan

Alexander, Loren Ray, German Language & Literature
Beeson, Margaret E, Spanish Language & Literature
Benson, Douglas Keith, Spanish Literature & Culture
Corum, Robert Tillman, Jr, French Literature
Dehon, Claire L, French
Kolonosky, Walter F, Russian Language & Literature
O'Connor, Thomas Austin, Spanish
Ossar, Michael Lee, German Literature
Shaw, Bradley Alan, Spanish Language, Hispanic Literatures
Tunstall, George Charles, German Literature & Philosophy

Pittsburg

Beerman, Hans, Romance & Slavic Languages, Philosophy
Freyburger, Henri, German, French

Salina

Riordan, Francis Ellen, French Literature

Wichita

Bennett-Kastor, Tina Lynne, Linguistics, Psycholinguistics
Bravo-Elizondo, Pedro Jose, Latin American Theater & Literature
Cardenas, Anthony John, Spanish
Froning, Dorothy Gardner, Foreign Languages
Gregg, Alvin Laner, English Language & Linguistics
Koppenhaver, John Holley, Contemporary Spanish Literature
Myers, Eunice Doman, Spanish Literature & Language
Ritchie, Gisela F, German & English Literature

Soles, Deborah Hansen, Philosophy
Tomayko, James Edward, Chinese Language, History of Technology
Winget, Lynn Warren, Spanish Language & Literature

KENTUCKY

Barbourville

Marigold, W Gordon, German Literature

Berea

Birznieks, Ilmars, German
Fuentevilla, Alberto, Spanish Language, Latin American History
Pauck, Charles E, German Literature
Schneider, Robert James, Classical Languages, Medieval Studies

Bowling Green

Babcock, James Christopher, French Language & Literature
Baldwin, Thomas Pratt, German Literature
Brown, Carol Paul, Romance Languages
Hatcher, Paul Gilliam, Spanish, French
Kibbee, Douglas Alan, French & Romance Linguistics
Miller, Jim Wayne, German Language & Literature, American Literature
Nolan, William Joseph, Romance Languages

Danville

Ciholas, Karin Nordenhaug, Comparative Literature, French
DiLillo, Leonard Michael, Spanish Language & Literature
Munoz, Willy Oscar, Latin-American & Spanish Literature

Lexington

Binger, Norman Henry, German
Charron, Jean Daniel, Romance Languages
Costich, Julia Field, Modern French Literature
Dendle, Brian John, Romance Languages
Duncan, Phillip Aaron, French
Fiedler, Theodore, German & Comparative Literature
Flowers, Mary Lynne, Seventeenth Century French Literature
Forand, Paul Glidden, Arabic Language, Islamic History
Hernandez, Juan Eduardo, Modern Languages
Jones, Joseph Ramon, Spanish
Jones, Margaret E W, Spanish
Keating, Louis Clark, French Literature, Spanish Translation
Keller, John Esten, Romance Languages
Kratz, Bernd, Germanic Linguistics, Medieval German Literature
La Charite, Raymond Camille, Romance Languages
La Charite, Virginia Anding, Romance Languages
Lihani, John, Spanish Language & Literature
McCrary, William Carlton, Spanish
Martin, Hubert M, Jr, Classics
Mueller, Theodore Henry, French
Phillips, Jane Ellen, Classics
Pickens, Rupert Tarpley, Romance Philology, Medieval French
Probst, Gerhard, German, Comparative Literature
Rabel, Robert Joseph, Classical Languages
Rea, Joanne Ewing, Comparative & French Literature
Rea, John A, Linguistics, Romance Philology
Reedy, Daniel R, Spanish
Saenz, Gerardo, Spanish
Stanton, Edward F, Hispanic Language & Literature
Swift, Louis Joseph, Classics
Thomas, John Wesley, German
Thompson, Lawrence Sidney, Classics, Scandinavian Literature
Whitaker, Paul Knowlton, German

Louisville

Akeroyd, Richard Hewson, Foreign Language, Religion
Altman, Howard Bruce, Foreign Language Education
Berrong, Richard Michael, Sixteenth Century French Literature

Cunningham, William Leonard, German
Ford, Gordon Buell, Jr, Linguistics, English
Hershberg, David Ralph, Spanish, Italian
Hume, David Raymond, Germanic Languages & Literatures
Mullen, Karen A, English, Linguistics
Nuessel, Frank Henry, Spanish & Applied Linguisitics
Petersen, Hans, Classical Philology
St Clair, Robert Neal, Linguistics
Schuler, Marilyn Verena, French Language & Literature
Schultze, Sydney Patterson, Russian Language & Literature
Torres, Sixto E, Spanish Literature & Drama
Weisert, John Jacob, Germanics

Midway

Slaymaker, William Earl, Comparative Literature, German

Murray

Ball, Bertrand Logan, Jr, French Language & Literature
Haws, Gary Lewis, Ibero-American Studies
Keller, Howard Hughes, Theoretical Linguistics, Russian Literature

Owensboro

Browne, Maureen, Foreign Languages
Mitchell, Katherine Blanc, Romance Languages
Weiss, Richard August, German

Richmond

Burkhart, Sylvia Davis, German Literature
Nelson, Charles L, Spanish

Wilmore

Corbitt, Roberta Day, Language
Kinlaw, Dennis F, Linguistics, Philology

LOUISIANA

Baton Rouge

Baglivi, Giuseppe, Medieval Literature
de Armas, Frederick A, Comparative Literature, Romance Languages
Del Caro, Adrian, German, Philosophy
Di Maio, Irene Stocksieker, German Studies
Di Napoli, Thomas John, Modern & Contemporary German Literature
Erickson, John David, Contemporary French & Comparative Literature
Hart, Pierre Romaine, Russian Literature
Hintze, S James, Old Germanic Philology
Humphries, John Jefferson, French & American Literature
Kirby, Harry Lee, Jr, Nineteenth Century Spanish Literature
Lewis, Earl Nicholas, Jr, German
Lozada, Alfredo Ruiz, Romance Literature
Parker, Frank Peyton, Linguistics
Parker, Margaret, Spanish
Ricapito, Joseph V, Romance Languages
Roubey, Lester Walter, French & Italian Languages & Literatures
Schurfranz, Robert Lewis, Philology
Thompson, Elizabeth Long, Romance Philology, Spanish
Thompson, John A, Spanish, Literature
Vilas, Santiago, Foreign Languages, Civilization
Zebouni, Selma Assir, French

Hammond

Gaines, James Frederick, French Literature

Lafayette

Allain, Mathe, French, History
Cain, Joan T, Romance Languages
Chandler, Richard Eugene, Modern Foreign Languages
Flowers, Frank C, Linguistics, Semantics
Koenig, Virginia Charlotte, French
St Martin, Adele Cornay, Romance Languages
St Martin, Gerard Labarre, French Language & Literature

LOUISIANA (cont)

Lake Charles

Novak, Richey Asbury, Foreign Languages
Novak, Sigrid Scholtz, European Literature,
Teaching English As A Second Language

Metairie

Wilkins, George Wesley, Jr, Spanish, Applied
Linguistics

New Orleans

Brosman, Catharine Hill Savage, French
Brosman, Paul William, Jr, Historical Linguistics
Brou, Marguerite, Romance Languages, French
Brumfield, William Craft, Russian Literature &
Art History
Buchanan, James Junkin, Classics
Carroll, Linda Louise, Italian, Linguistics
Claudel, Calvin Andre, Romance Languages &
Literatures
Cook, Robert Geiger, English, Medieval
Literature
Cortinez, Carlos, Spanish American Poetry,
Creative Writing
Donaldson, Weber David, Jr, French, Linguistics
Etheridge, Sanford Grant, Classical Philology
Fischer, Simonne Sanzenbach, French Literature
Frank, Elfrieda, Latin
Frazer, Richard McIlwaine, Jr, Classical
Philology
Gex, Robert Bernard, French Language &
Literature, Linguistics
Gotzkowsky, Bodo Karl, German Language &
Literature
Hallock, Ann Hayes, Italian Literature
Hasselbach, Ingrid Tiesler, German Literature
Hasselbach, Karl Heinz, German Language &
Literature
Heiple, Daniel L, Spanish Literature,
Comparative Literature
Horan, William David, Romance Languages,
German
Lawrence, Francis Leo, French & Italian
Lytle, Evelyn Pomroy, Spanish & Portuguese
Literature & Language
Mace, Carroll E, Spanish
McPheeters, Dean William, Romance Languages
Montgomery, Thomas (Andrew), Spanish
Monty, Jeanne Ruth, French Literature
Morphos, Panos Paul, Romance Languages
Nash, Jerry Carroll, French Language &
Literature
Olivera, Otto Hugo, Spanish
Paolini, Gilberto, Romance Languages &
Literature
Porter, Michael, Comparative & German
Literature
Reck, Rima Drell, Comparative Literature
Redman, Harry, Jr, French
Santi, Victor Amerigo, Italian Language and
Literature
Smither, William Jonathan, Spanish &
Portuguese Language & Literature
Tappan, Donald Willard, French Language &
Literature
Winbery, Carlton Loyd, Hellenistic Greek

Pineville

Alexandrenko, Nikolai Alexei, Classical & Slavic
Languages & Religion

Ruston

Ezell, Richard Lee, Spanish

Shreveport

Gottlob, Vickie Neely, French Literature
Penuel, Arnold McCoy, Spanish Language &
Literature
Watts, Robert Johnson, Germanic Philology &
Comparative Linguistics

Thibodaux

LeCompte, Nolan P, Jr, Linguistics, English

MAINE

Brunswick

Ambrose, John William, Jr, Latin & Greek
Classics
Cerf, Steven Roy, German, Comparative
Literature
Hodge, James Lee, German
Nunn, Robert Raymond, Romance Languages

Cape Elizabeth

O'Neill, Elmer Wesley, Jr, Romance Languages,
Methodology

Chebeaque Island

Bates, Blanchard Wesley, French Literature

Kennebunk

Shaw, Edward Pease, French Literature

Lewiston

Harrison, Regina L, Latin American Literature
Williamson, Richard Colt, French Language &
Literature
Wright, Alfred John, Jr, Romance Languages

New Vineyard

Bliss, Francis Royster, Latin, Greek

Orono

French, Paulette, Comparative Literature, French
Rioux, Robert N, Literature
Russell, Olga Wester, Foreign Languages
Troiano, James J, Spanish
Webb, Karl Eugene, German Literature, Art
History
Zollitsch, Reinhard, German Language &
Literature

Portland

Duclos, Gloria Shaw, Greek & Latin

South Berwick

Armstrong, James, Classics

South Harpswell

Locke, William Nash, Modern Languages

Springvale

Schick, Edgar Brehob, German, Pedagogy

Temple

Kimber, Rita Hausammann, German &
Comparative Literature

Waterville

Biron, Archille Henri, Modern Foreign
Languages
Bundy, Jean, French Language & Literature
Ferguson, Charles Anthony, Romance Languages
Holland, Henry, Spanish Literature
Smith, Gordon Winslow, French

MARYLAND

Adelphi

Fuegi, John B, Comparative Literature

Annapolis

Brent, Steven Tracy, French Language &
Literature

Baltimore

Anderson, Wilda Christine, French Literature
Cacossa, Anthony Alexander, Romance
Languages & Literatures
Cooper, Jerrold Stephen, Assyriology
DuVerlie, Claud A, French Language &
Literature
Ferrer, Olga Prjevalinskaya, Spanish, Russian
Fischetti, Renate Margarete, German Literature
Freese, Wolfgang F O, German Language &
Literature, Philosophy
Giro, Jorge Antonio, Spanish, Spanish Literature
Goedicke, Hans, Egyptology
Grundlehner, Philip, German

Harari, Josue V, French & Comparative
Literature
Henley, Norman, Russian Language & Literature
Hillers, Delbert Roy, Old Testament, Semitic
Languages
Homann, Holger, Medieval German Language &
Literature
Jeremiah, Milford Astor, Linguistics, Reading
Instruction
Jordan, Charles F, Foreign Languages
Kaltenbach, Philip Edward, Latin, Ancient
History
Krotkoff, Georg, Arabic Philology
Kurth, Lieselotte E, German Literature
Litzinger, Elizabeth, French
Lucente, Gregory L, Italian & Comparative
Literature
Luck, Georg H, Classics
McClain, William H, German Literature
McDermott, Madeleine Guenser, French
Literature & Civilization
Macksey, Richard Alan, Comparative Literature,
English
Musser, Frederic Omar, French
Nagele, Rainer, German Literature, Literary
Theory
Olson, Paul Richard, Romance Languages
Poirier, Roger Luc, French Literature, The
Novel
Poultney, James Wilson, Classical Philology
Rodriguez, Antonio Guillermo, Foreign
Language Literature & Linguistics
Rosenthal, Alan Stuart, French, Comparative
Literature
Roswell, May M, Foreign Languages
Sieber, Harry Charles, Romance Languages
Skinner, Daniel T, Modern Languages
Soria, Regina, Romance Languages, American
Art
Squire, Donald Hovmand, Modern Languages &
Literatures
Sullivan, Dennis George, Romance Languages
Walker, Claire, Foreign Languages
Williams, Lorna Valerie, Spanish
Zintl, Carrie-May Kurrelmeyer, German &
Classics

Bethesda

Bates, Margaret Jane, Spanish, Portuguese
Fink, Beatrice, French Literature, History of
Ideas
Mueller, Hugo Johannes, German Language &
Literature
Solzbacher, William Aloysius, Linguistics,
History

Bowie

Norton, Mary Elizabeth, Classical Languages

Catonsville

Field, Thomas Tilden, Romance & Theoretical
Linguistics

Chestertown

Shivers, George Robert, Spanish Language &
Literature
Yon, Andre Francois, French Language &
Literature

Chevy Chase

Bingham, Alfred Jepson, French Literature
La Follette, James E, French

College Park

Beicken, Peter U, German Literature & Culture
Berry, Thomas Edwin, Russian Language &
Literature
Best, Otto Ferdinand, German Literature
Beyl, David Windell, Linguistics, Portuguese
Brecht, Richard Domenick, Linguistics, Slavic
Language & Literatures
Demaitre, Ann, French, Comparative Literature
Dingwall, William Orr, Linguistics
Fleck, Jere, Germanic Linguistics
Goodwyn, Frank Eppse, Modern Languages
Hall, Thomas W, French, Italian
Herin, Christoph Abraham, German
Hitchcock, Donald Raymond, Slavic Languages
& Literatures
Hubbe, Rolf Oskar, Classics
Igel, Regina, Portuguese, Spanish
James, Edward Foster, Linguistics, English
Jones, George Fenwick, Medieval Literature,
German Language
Lee, Hugh Ming, Classics

Macbain, William, Medieval French Language & Literature
Mehl, Jane Rima, Germanic Language & Literature
Mendeloff, Henry, Foreign Languages
Miller, Mary Rita, Linguistics
Nemes, Graciela Palau de, Spanish
Rovner, Philip, Foreign Languages
Russell, Charles Coulter, Italian Language & Literature
Staley, Gregory Allan, Classics
Tarica, Ralph, French Literature
Therrien, Madeleine B, French Literature

Columbia

Levy, Howard S, Oriental Languages & Literatures

Elkton

Coulet Du Gard, Rene, Romance Languages

Emmitsburg

Marshall, Robert T, Foreign Languages, Linguistics

Essex

Allen, Richard John, German Language & Literature

Frederick

Daniels, William John, Slavic Languages, Linguistics
Guillermo, Edenia, Spanish & Spanish American Language & Literature
Hernandez, Juana Amelia, Spanish & Spanish American Literature
Leonard, Etta Louise, French

Frostburg

Adams, Howard Chauncey, Jr, French
Jablon, Kenneth, Spanish
O'Brien, MacGregor, Modern Languages & Literatures
Redick, Patricia C, Romance Languages

Gaithersburg

Sosnowski, Saul, Contemporary Latin American Literature

Greenbelt

Cor, M Antonia, Medieval French Literature

Hyattsville

Avery, William Turner, Classical Languages & Literature
Chaves, Teresa Labarta de, Spanish Language & Literature
Eichman, Thomas Lee, Linguistics, Information Science
Lipovsky, James Peter, Classical Languages & Literature
Pfister, Guenter Georg, German

Lanham

Bormanshinov, Arash, Slavic Linguistics

Laurel

Feinman, Roy, Slavic Linguistics

Reisterstown

Martin, Joan Mary, Germanic Languages & Linguistics

St Mary's City

Miller, Elinor Smith, French Language & Literature

Salisbury

Engler, Leo F, Linguistics

Silver Spring

Colton, Robert Edward, Classical Philology, Comparative Literature
Levy, Diane Wolfe, French Literature, Comparative Literature
Urbanski, Edmund Stephen, Spanish & Latin American Literature

Towson

Thormann, Wolfgang E, French Language & Literature

West Hyattsville

Cooper, Grace Charlotte Washington, Psycholinguistics, Sociolinguistics

Westminster

Cobb, Eulalia Benejam, French, Spanish
Palmer, Melvin Delmar, Comparative Literature, Sports Fiction
Williams, Daniel Anthony, Spanish Language & Literature

MASSACHUSETTS

Amherst

Anderson, Warren DeWitt, Comparative Literature, Classical Languages
Barreda, Pedro M, Latin American Literature
Basto, Ronald Gary, Classical Languages
Bauschinger, Sigrid Elisabeth, Modern German Literature
Beekman, Eric Montague, Germanic Languages, Comparative Literature
Boudreau, Harold Laverne, Modern Spanish Literature
Carre, Jeffrey James, Romance Languages
Cassirer, Thomas, French & African Literature
Cathey, James Ernest, Germanic Linguistics, Scandinavian Languages
Chen, Ursula F, Romance Philology & Linguistics
Cheng, Ching-Mao, Chinese & Japanese Literature
Cleary, Vincent John, Classics
Cohen, Alvin Philip, Chinese Philology & Cultural History
De Puy, Blanche, Spanish
Duckert, Audrey Rosalind, English Philology & Linguistics
Esformes, Maria, Spanish Language & Literature
Fernandez-Turienzo, Francisco, Spanish History of Ideas
Giordanetti, Elmo, Romance Languages
Greenfield, Sumner M, Spanish
Gugli, William V, Romance Languages
Hudson, Alfred Bacon, Anthropology, Linguistics
Johnson, Ernest Alfred, Romance Languages
Lawall, Gilbert Westcott, Classics
Lawall, Sarah Nesbit, Comparative Literature, French
Levin, Maurice Irwin, Slavic Linguistics
Mankin, Paul A, Romance Language & Literature
Margolis, Nadia, Medieval Literature, French Poetry
Marshall, Peter K, Classical Languages, Medieval Literature
Martin, Daniel, French Renaissance Literature
Meid, Volker, German Literature
Naff, William E, Japanese
Partee, Barbara Hall, Linguistics
Paulsen, Wolfgang, German Literature
Peter, Klaus, German Literature
Philippides, Marios, Greek, Latin
Phinney, Edward Sterl, Jr, Classics
Raymond, Agnes G (Mrs Marshall C Howard), Modern Languages
Reed, Carroll Edward, Germanic Linguistics
Reh, Albert M, German Language & Literature
Rothberg, Irving Paul, Romance Languages
Rountree, Benjamin C, French
Ryan, Lawrence, German
Salzmann, Zdenek, Linguistic Anthropology, Czech & Slovak Studies
Scher, Helene Lenz, German Language & Literature
Schiffer, Eva, German & Comparative Literature
Scott, Nina Margaret, Modern Spanish Literature, Spanish Civilization
Seelig, Harry E, German Literature, Music
Soons, Rosalie Humphrey, Hispanic & Comparative Literature
Sturm, Harlan Gary, Romance Languages
Sturm-Maddox, Sara, Romance Languages; Medieval Literature
Taylor, Robert Edward, French Language & Literature
Terrizzi, Anthony R, Twentieth Century Italian Fiction
Tillona, Zina, Italian
Von Kries, Friedrich Wilhelm, German Literature, Philology

Weiner, Seymour Sidney, Romance Languages
Wexler, Sidney Frederick, Spanish
White, Donald Owen, German Languages & Literature
Will, Elizabeth Lyding, Classics
Zamora, Juan C, Hispanic Linguistics & Dialectology

Barnstable

Huck, Georgina M, Germanic Studies, Archeology

Belmont

Arnaud, Daniel Leonard, Classics
Bloch, Herbert, Classics, History
Dalton, Margaret, Slavic Languages & Literatures
Fairley, Irene R, Linguistics, English
Haugen, Einar Ingvald, Scandinavian & General Linguistics
Moran, William Lambert, Assyriology
Setchkarev, Vsevolod, Slavic Languages & Literature

Boston

Ackermann, Paul Kurt, German
Beye, Charles Rowan, Classical Philology
Bowen, Charles Arthur, Jr, Celtic Literature, English
Bronner, Luise Helen, German
Burgin, Diana Lewis, Slavic Languages & Literatures
Cardona, Rodolfo, Spanish Literature
Chavous, Quentin, Romance Languages
Cioffari, Vincenzo, Romance Languages & Literatures
Collignon, Jean Henri, French
Cooperstein, Louis, Modern Language
Dayag, Joseph H, Foreign Languages
Elder, John Petersen, Classics
Fraser, James Bruce, Linguistics
Giustiniani, Vito Rocco, Italian Literature, Romance Philology
Golden, Herbert Hershel, Romance Languages & Literatures
Green, Eugene, English Linguistics
Green, James Ray, Jr, Medieval & Renaissance Spanish Literature
Hanawalt, Emily Albu, Medieval Literature & History
Hoddie, James Henry, Romance Languages
Hoelzel, Alfred, Germanic Languages
Horsley, Ritta Jo, German Language & Literature
Jaramillo, Samuel, Languages
Jones, Robert Emmet, French
Kelly, Dorothy Jean, French Literature, Literary Criticism
Kline, Thomas Jefferson, French Literature
Kostis, Nicholas, Contemporary French Literature
McKeen, Don Hayes, Romance Languages & Literatures
Mackey, Charles Ruyle, Romance Languages
Moylan, Paul A, French & Italian Literatures
Navas-Ruiz, Ricardo, Romance Languages
Newman, Richard William, Romance Languages
Nisetich, Frank Joseph, Classical Philology, Poetry
Ott, Friedrich Peter, Comparative Literature, German
Philip, Michel Henri, French Literature, Creative Writing
Proulx, Alfred Charles, Romance Languages
Quain, Estelle Eleanor, Spanish & Latin American Literature
Relyea, Suzanne Ladue, French Literature, Women's Studies
Rose, Constance Hubbard, Spanish & Comparative Literature
Rosser, Harry L Enrique, Latin American Literature
Ruck, Carl Anton Paul, Greek Language & Literature
Saitz, Robert Leonard, English As Second Language, Linguistics
Sanchez-Arce, Nellie E, Spanish
Schork, Rudolph Joseph, Jr, Classical Philology, Byzantine Studies
Smith, Nathaniel Belknap, Romance Languages, Medieval Studies
Stephan, Philip H, French Literature
Volpe, Gerald Carmine, Romance Languages
Williams, Edward Baker, Romance Languages

MASSACHUSETTS (cont)

Brookline

Lutcavage, Charles Patrick, German Language & Literature
Wiseman, James Richard, Classical Languages & Archeology

Cambridge

Alazraki, Jaime, Spanish & Spanish American Literature
Alexandrov, Vladimir, Russian & Comparative Literature
Baxter, Glen William, Far Eastern Languages
Berlin, Charles, Hebraic & Judaic Literature
Bishal, Wilson B, Semitics
Chomsky, Avram Noam, Linguistics
Chvany, Catherine Vakar, Slavic Languages & Literatures
Clausen, Wendell Vernon, Classical Languages
Cohn, Dorrit, German & Comparative Literature
Cranston, Edwin Augustus, Japanese Literature
Crecelius, Kathryn June, French Literature
Cross, Frank Moore, Jr, Biblical & Semitic Languages & Literature
Della Terza, Dante, Italian Literature
DeVito, Anthony J, Romance Philology
Dunn, Charles William, Medieval Literature
Dyck, Martin, German Literature, Literature & Mathematics
Edson, Laurie Dale, French Language & Literature
Fanger, Donald Lee, Russian & Comparative Literature
Finley, John Huston, Jr, Classics
Frohock, Wilbur Merrill, French Literature
Frye, Richard Nelson, Iranian
Gilman, Stephen, Spanish Literature
Goetchius, Eugene Van Ness, Biblical Languages, New Testament Philology
Guthke, Karl Siegfried, German Literature
Halle, Morris, Modern Languages, Linguistics
Halperin, David M, Classical & Comparative Literature
Hammond, Mason, Roman History, Latin Literature
Hanan, Patrick Dewes, Chinese Literature
Hatfield, Henry Caraway, German
Hibbett, Howard Scott, Japanese Literature
Hightower, James Robert, Chinese Literature
Ingalls, Daniel Henry Holmes, Sanskrit
Jakobson, Roman, Linguistics
Jasinski, Rene, French Literature
Ketchian, Sonia, Russian Literature & Language
Kuhn, Thomas Samuel, History & Philosophy of Science
Kuno, Susumu, Linguistics
Lichtenstadter, Ilse, Islam, Arabic Literature
Lord, Mary Louise, Classics
Lunt, Horace Gray, Slavic Linguistics
Mahdi, Muhsin Sayyid, Arabic, Islamic Philosphy & Religion
Marichal, Juan, Spanish
Marichal, Solita Salinas, Foreign Languages & Literatures
Marquez, Francisco, Spanish Language & Literature
Miller, Robin Feuer, Russian & Comparative Literature
Mitchell, Stephen Arthur, Scandinavian Literature, Folklore & Mythology
Nagy, Gregory John, Classics, Linguistics
Nash, Laura L, Classical Philology
Philippides, Dia Mary Laurette, Modern & Ancient Greek Philology
Pomorska, Krystyna, Russian
Reinhold, Meyer, Classical Language, Ancient History
Resnick, Margery, Hispanic Literature
Rivers, Wilga Marie, French, Foreign Language Education
Rogers, Francis Millet, Romance Languages & Literatures
Shackleton Bailey, David Roy, Latin
Shapira, Elliott King, Comparative Romance Philology
Simon, Eckehard, Medieval German Literature & Philology
Spaethling, Robert Herbert, German
Stewart, Zeph, Classics
Stone, Donald Adelbert, Jr, French Literature
Suleiman, Susan Rubin, French & Comparative Literature
Taranovsky, Kiril, Slavic Languages & Literatures
Tarrant, Richard John, Classics
Tatar, Maria, German Literature
Teeter, Karl Van Duyn, Linguistics

Thomson, Robert William, Near Eastern Languages
Turk, Edward Baron, French Literature and Film
Watkins, Calvert Ward, Linguistics
Weintraub, Wiktor, Polish
Whitman, Cedric Hubbell, Classical Philology
Winner, Thomas Gustav, Russian Language & Literature

Canton

Mahoney, Elizabeth Veronica, Spanish

Chestnut Hill

Araujo, Norman, Foreign Languages
Bluhm, Heinz, German Literature
Brenk, Frederick Eugene, Greek & Roman Classics
Bruhn, Gert Ernst, German Language & Literature
Bushala, Eugene Waldo, Classics
Cartier, Normand Raymond, Medieval Literature, Romance Languages
Eykman, Christoph Wolfgang, German Literature
Figurito, Joseph, Romance Languages, Philology
Jones, Lawrence Gaylord, Linguistics
Michalczyk, John Joseph, French Literature, Cinema
Rahv, Betty Thomas, French Literature
Resler, W Michael, Medieval German Language & Literature
Sheehan, Robert Louis, Foreign Languages
Siciliano, Ernest Alexander, Romance Philology
Simonelli, Maria, Romance Languages, Italian Literature
Valette, Jean-Paul, French, Economics
Valette, Rebecca Marianne, French, Foreign Language Education

Concord

Maxfield-Miller, Elizabeth, Romance, Moliere

Fitchburg

Burke, John Michael, Russian & German Language & Literature

Florence

Navarro, Joaquina, Foreign Languages & Literature

Gardner

O'Neill, Samuel J, Romance Languages

Hadley

Demay, Andree Jeanne, Romance Languages
Saintonge, Paul Frederic, French

Ipswich

Finkenthal, Stanley Melvin, Spanish Drama, Comparative Literature

Leicester

Back, Arthur William, History, Language

Lenox

Ehle, Carl Frederick, Jr, Biblical Languages, Modern Hebrew

Lexington

Gendzier, Stephen J, French Literature, History of Ideas

Lincoln

Iliescu, Nicolae, Languages

Lowell

Aste, Mario, Italian, Spanish
Bentas, Christos John, Classics, History

Malden

Bousquet, Robert Edward, French Novel, Linguistics

Medford

Ascher, Gloria Joyce, German Literature & Language
Clayton, Alan J, Modern French Literature
Corcoran, Thomas Henry, Classics
Gittleman, Sol, German, Comparative Literature
Maxwell, David Evans, Slavic Languages & Literatures
Ortega, Noel Guilherme, Portuguese
Phillips, Joanne Higgins, Classical Philology
Reid, Peter Lawrence Donald, Classics
Rosenberg, Joel William, Hebrew & Comparative Literature
Simches, Seymour O, Romance Languages & Literatures
Wells, John Corson, German
Zarker, John William, Classics

Milton

Evans, Mary Lee, History, French

Nahant

Butler, Thomas J, Slavic Languages & Literature

Natick

McSorley, Bonnie Shannon, Spanish, Italian

Needham

Bottiglia, William Filbert, French Literature, Humanities

Newton

Etmekjian, James, Romance Languages, Armenian Studies
Lee, Vera G, Romance Languages
Zayed, Georges H, French Literature, Symbolist Movement

Newton Centre

Maguire, Joseph Patrick, Classics, Philosophy

Northampton

Ball, David Raphael, French & Comparative Literature
Banerjee, Maria Nemcova, Russian & Comparative Literature
Berndt-Kelley, Erna, Romance Languages
Brooks, E Bruce, Chinese Literature
Clemente, Alice Rodrigues, Spanish & Portuguese
Dimock, George Edward, Jr, Classical Philology
Gasool, Anne, French Language & Literature
Gregory, Justina Winston, Classics
Henderson, Charles, Jr, Classics
Joseph, Lawrence Alexander, French Literature
Ryan, Judith Lyndal, German
Schuster, Marilyn Ruth, French, Women's Studies
Weed, Patricia, French Literature
Zelljadt, Igor, Linguistics

North Dartmouth

Panunzio, Wesley Constantine, Romance Language & Linguistics
Vinci, Joseph, Romance Languages & Literature
Washington, Ida Harrison, German Literature
Washington, Lawrence Moore, German
Yoken, Melvin Barton, French Language & Literature

North Easton

Smith, Eunice Clark, French

Norton

Bishop, John David, Classics
Hacthoun, Augusto, Spanish, Portuguese
Lepinis, Asta Helena, German & Scandinavian Literature
Letts, Janet Taylor, French Literature
Ruiz, Roberto, Spanish Language & Literature
Schmidt, Ruth Ann, Spanish Language & Literature
Shilaeff, Ariadne, Russian Language & Literature
Speratti-Pinero, Emma Susana, Spanish & Latin American Literature
Wender, Dorothea Schmidt, Classics

Salem

Urbain, Henri, French Literature

Sheffield

Gross, Charles J, Jr, Classical Languages

South Hadley

Ciruti, Joan Estelle, Foreign Languages
Erwin, John Francis, Jr, French Literature
Farrell, Mary MacLennan, French Language &
Literature
Gelfand, Elissa Deborah, French Studies,
Women's Studies
Giamatti, Valentine, Romance Languages &
Literatures
Mazzocco, Angelo, Romance Languages &
Literatures
Mihalchenko, Igor S, Russian Language &
Literature
Quinn, Betty Nye, Classics
Sajkovic, Vladimir I, Slavic Studies
Switten, Margaret L, French & Provencial
Language & Literature
Yao, Tao-Chung, Chinese Language & History

Springfield

Dragone, Olindo, Romance Languages
Racine, R Joseph, Humanities

Waltham

Brandwein, Naftali Chaim, Biblical & Modern
Hebrew Literature
Frey, Eberhard, German Language & Literature
Gill, M Rosenda, French, Italian
Hallett, Judith Peller, Classical Philology
Harth, Erica, French Literature
Jackendoff, Ray Saul, Linguistics
Johnston, Patricia Ann, Classical Languages
Joseph, George L, French
Kaplan, Edward Kivie, French Literature
Kasell, Walter, Comparative & French Literature
Lansing, Richard Hewson, Italian & Comparative
Literature
Lida, Denah Levy, Spanish
Sachs, Murray, French, Comparative Literature
Smith, Raoul Normand, Linguistics
Stewart, Douglas James, Classics
Walker, Cheryl L, Classical Languages, Ancient
History
Young, Dwight Wayne, Semitic Philology
Zabkar, Louis Vico, Egyptology, Ancient History
Zohn, Harry, German

Wareham

Kossoff, Ruth Horne, Spanish Literature

Watertown

Boulton, Maureen Barry McCann, Medieval &
French Literature

Wellesley

Agosin Halpern, Marjorie, Latin American &
Spanish Literature
Avitabile, Grazia, Italian
Ellerman, Mei-Mei Akwai, Italian
Francois, Carlo Roger, French Language &
Literature
Galand, Rene, French
Gascon-Vera, Elena, Spanish Language &
Literature
Geffcken, Katherine Allston, Classics
Gillain, Anne Therese, French Literature,
Cinema
Goth, Maja Julia, Foreign Languages
Grimaud, Michel Robert, Discourse Analysis
Hansen, Thomas Svend, German Language &
Literature
Hules, Virginia Thorndike, French Language &
Literature
Lefkowitz, Mary Rosenthal, Classics
Lin, Helen T, Chinese Language
Lovett, Gabriel H, Romance Languages
McCulloch, Florence, French
Mistacco, Vicki, French Language & Literature
Proussis, Costas Michael, Greek & Latin, History
Roses, Lorraine Elena, Spanish
Ruiz-De-Conde, Justina, Romance Philology
Starr, Raymond James, Classical Languages
Ward, Margaret Ellen, German Language &
Literature

Wellesley Hills

Molinsky, Steven J, Linguistics, English as a
Second Language

Wenham

Covey, Delvin, Classical Philology
Miller, Royce W, Romance Languages,
Linguistics

West Newton

Barrs, James Thomas, Philology
Fabrizi, Benedetto, Foreign Languages

Weston

Hamilton, Mary P, German Literature
Mahan, Mary Juan, French
Velilla, Ana Almona, Romance Languages

Williamstown

Bell-Villada, Gene Harold, Spanish, Comparative
Literature
Chick, Edson Marland, German
Dunn, Susan, French Literature
Fuqua, Charles, Classics, Ancient Drama
Katz, Michael Ray, Russian Language &
Literature
Kieffer, Bruce, German Literature
Piper, Anson Conant, Romance Languages
Pistorius, George, French
Savacool, John Kenneth, French

Worcester

Arndt, Karl John Richard, German Language &
Literature
Aubin, George Francis, French, Linguistics
Barbera, Raymond Edmond, Romance
Languages
Bernstein, Eckhard Richard, German &
Comparative Literature
Bernstein, Jutta, German Language & Literature
Burke, Paul Frederic, Jr, Classics
Carlson, Gregory Ivan, Latin & Greek Literature
D'lugo, Marvin Alan, Modern Spanish American
Literature
Fitzgerald, William Henry, Classical Languages
Hamilton, John Daniel Burgoyne, Classical
Languages, Greek Mythology & Religion
Healey, Robert Fisher, Classics
Kaiser, Hartmut Michael, German Language &
Literature
King, Jesse Fannin, Romance Languages &
Literatures
Lavery, Gerard B, Classical Languages
McKenna, John Francis, French
Macris, James, Linguistics, English
Quintal, Claire, French Culture & Literature
Reid, J Richard, General & Romance Linguistics
Schatzberg, Walter, German Language &
Literature
Spingler, Michael K, Romance Languages,
French Theatre
Ziobro, William Jerome, Classics

MICHIGAN

Adrian

Elardo, Ronald Joseph, German Language &
Literature
Smith, Beverly Moulton Allen, Spanish
Language & Literature

Albion

Baumgartner, Ingeborg Hogh, German Literature
Keller, Jean Paul, Spanish
Kragness, Sheila Ione, French Language &
Literature

Allendale

Franklin, Ursula, French Language & Literature

Alma

Hayward, Earl Franklin, French Language &
Literature
Kaiser, Gunda S, Foreign Languages

Ann Arbor

Abdel-Massih, Ernest Tawfik, Linguistics
Becker, Alton Lewis, Linguistics
Bellamy, James Andrew, Medieval Arabic
Literature, Arabic Papyrology
Billick, David Joseph, Spanish Literature
Bibliography
Braun, Frank Xavier, German
Budel, Oscar, Romance Languages & Literature
Burling, Robbins, Linguistics
Buttrey, Theodore V, Jr, Classical Languages
Cameron, Howard Don, Classics, Linguistics
Carduner, Jean R, French Language & Literature
Casa, Frank Paul, Romance Languages
Catford, John Cunnison, Linguistics
Chambers, Leigh Ross, French & Comparative
Literature
Coffin, Edna Amir, Hebrew Language &
Literature
Cottrell, Alan P, Germanic Languages
Cowen, Roy Chadwell, Jr, German Literature
Crichton, Mary Christina, German
Crump, James Irving, Jr, Chinese Language &
Literature
Danly, Robert Lyons, Japanese Literature
D'Arms, John Haughton, Classical Studies
Dew, James Erwin, Chinese Language &
Literature, Linguistics
Dunnhaupt, Gerhard, Germanic Languages &
Literatures
Dvorak, Trisha Robin, Applied Linguistics
Fabian, Hans Joachim, German
Frier, Bruce Woodward, Classical Studies,
History of Law
Gass, Susan Mary, Applied Linguistics
Gedney, William John, Linguistics
George, Emery Edward, Germanic Languages,
East European Studies
Goic, Cedomil, Spanish American & Chilean
Literature
Gray, Floyd Francis, French
Grilk, Werner Hans, German Literature
Hafter, Monroe Z, Spanish Literature
Hagiwara, Michio Peter, Romance Languages
Henderson, Jeffrey James, Classical Philology
Hill, Kenneth Cushman, Linguistics
Hofacker, Erich Paul, Jr, Germanic Languages
Hubbs, Valentine Charles, German
Humesky, Assya Alexandra, Russian & Ukranian
Literature & Language
Ilie, Paul, Romance Languages
Kiddle, Lawrence Bayard, Romance Languages
& Literatures
King, Harold Vosburgh, Linguistics
Koenen, Ludwig, Classical Philology, Papyrology
Krahmalkov, Charles R, Ancient Near East
History
Krieg, Martha Fessler, Romance Linguistics, Old
& Middle English
Kurath, Hans, Linguistics
Kyes, Robert Lange, German, Linguistics
Lawler, John Michael, Linguistics
Legassick, Trevor John, Arabic
Leonard, Clifford Shattuck, Jr, Romance
Linguistics
Li, Chi, Chinese & English Literature
Lopez-Grigera, Luisa, Spanish Philology
McCarren, Vincent Paul, Classical Studies,
Medieval Literature
McCarus, Ernest Nasseph, Linguistics
Markey, Thomas Lloyd, Linguistics, Germanic
Philology
Matejka, Ladislav, Slavic Languages &
Literatures
Mermier, Guy R, Romance Languages &
Literature
Mignolo, Walter D, Latin American Literature,
Semiotics
Mills, Harriet Cornelia, Chinese
Morgan, Raleigh, Jr, Linguistics
Morton, Brian Neville, French Literature,
French American Relations
Morton, Jacqueline, Twentieth Century French
Literature
Muller, Marcel, French
Nagara, Susumu, Linguistics, Japanese Language
Nelson, Roy Jay, French Literature
Ngate, Jonathan, African Literatures
O'Meara, Maureen Frances, French
O'Neill, James Calvin, French
Paslick, Robert H, German Literature
Pearl, Orsamus Merrill, Greek, Latin
Peters, Frederick George, German Humanities,
Comparative Literature
Pierssens, Michel J, French Literature,
Philosophy
Pike, Kenneth Lee, Linguistics
Proffer, Carl Ray, Slavic Languages &
Literatures

Ann Arbor, MICHIGAN (cont)

Proffer, Ellendea Catherine, Russian & Comparative Literature
Pulgram, Ernst, Romance & Classical Linguistics
Rammuny, Raji M, Applied Linguistics
Reichart, Walter Albert, German Language & Literature
Schelle, Hansjoerg Reinhold, Germanics, Comparative Literature
Scholler, Harald, Medieval German Literature, Philology
Schramm, Gene Moshe, Foreign Languages
Seidler, Ingo, German & Comparative Literature
Seligson, Gerda, Classical Studies, Linguistics
Stewart-Robinson, James, Islamics
Stolz, Benjamin Armond, Slavic Languages
Sweet, Waldo Earle, Classical Studies
Thompson, Claiborne Watkins, Medieval Scandinavian Language & Literature
Toon, Thomas Edward, English Linguistics
Udris, Zane, Classical Philology
Waggoner, Lawrence W, Law
Weiss, Hermann Friedrich, German Language & Literature
Welsh, David John, Slavic Languages & Literatures
Wiehr, Josef Henry, German
Windfuhr, Gernot Ludwig, Iranistics
Witke, Charles, Classical Philology, Medieval Latin Literature

Berkley

Vernier, Richard, French Literature

Berrien Springs

Economou, Elly Helen, Biblical & Modern Languages
Kunze, Wolfgang P F, German & German-American Literature
Running, Leona Glidden, Semitic Languages

Dearborn

Bruhn, Joachim, Germanic Languages & Literature
Nichols, James Mansfield, Spanish & Arabic Languages, Applied Linguistics

Detroit

Bershas, Henry Norton, Spanish
Bezdek, Valadimir, German
Cobbs, Alfred Leon, German Language & Literature
Dabringhaus, Erhard, German
Di Tommaso, Andrea, Italian Renaissance Literature, Cinema
DuBruck, Edelgard E, Foreign Languages
Eddington, Marilyn Lamond, Romance Languages, Spanish
Evans, Harry Birbeck, Classics
Ewald, Marie Liguori, Classical Philology
Garfield, Evelyn Picon, Latin American Contemporary Literature
Goff, Penrith Brien, German Literature
Gutierrez, Jesus, Spanish Language & Literature
Haase, Donald Paul, German & Comparative Literature
Hill, Jane Hassler, Linguistics, Anthropology
Kibler, Louis Wayne, Italian, French
Kovach, Edith M A, Classical Languages
Minadeo, Richard William, Classics
Ordon, Edmund, Polish, English
Romero, Hector R, Spanish Literature
Roth, Maria, German Language & Literature
Scavnicky, Gary Eugene, Meso-American and General Linguistics
Schikora, Rosemary Garbarino, African Literature in French
Schindler, Marvin Samuel, German, Baroque Literature
Smith, Edwin Burrows, French
Smitherman, Geneva, English Linguistics, Afro-American Language & Literature
Spinelli, Donald Carmen, French Literature
Stern, Guy, German, Comparative Literature
Wedberg, Lloyd Warren, Foreign Languages & Literature

Dexter

Mersereau, John, Jr, Slavic Languages & Literatures

East Lansing

Barrett, Ralph P, Linguistics, English Language
Belgardt, Raimund, German, Comparative Literature
Brend, Ruth Margaret, Linguistics
Brown, Frieda Starling, Romance Languages & Literature
Calvo, Juan Antonio, Spanish
Compitello, Malcolm Alan, Spanish Language & Literature
DeSua, William Joseph, Italian & Comparative Literature
Donohoe, Joseph Ignatius, Jr, Romance Languages & Literatures
Doty, Edith Aultman, Spanish
Dulai, Surjit Singh, Comparative Literature, South Asian Studies
Dynnik, Alexander George, Russian Language & Literature
Fairchild, William DeForest, Jr, Classical Languages
Falk, Julia Sableski, Linguistics, English
Falk, Thomas Heinrich, Contemporary German Literature
Fiore, Robert L, Romance Languages
Gray, Eugene Francis, French Literature
Hughes, William Nolin, German
Imamura, Shigeo, Linguistics, English as a Second Language
Ingram, Frank LeQuellec, Slavic Languages & Literatures
Josephs, Herbert, Romance Languages
Joyaux, Georges Jules, French Language & Literature, Comparative Literature
Juntune, Thomas William, Germanic Linguistics
Kistler, Mark Oliver, German
Koppisch, Michael Seibert, French
Kronegger, Maria Elisabeth, Modern Languages
Lockwood, David G, General & Slavic Linguistics
Mansour, George Phillip, Spanish Literature
Munsell, Paul Edwin, English as a Second Language
Porter, Laurence M, French & Comparative Literature
Seniff, Dennis Paul, Spanish Medieval Literature
Song, Seok Choong, Linguistics
Tzitsikas, Helene, Romance Languages
Whallon, William, Comparative Literature
Winburne, John Newton, English
Yates, Donald Alfred, Foreign Languages

Farmington

Szymanski, Ladislas Isidore, Classics

Flint

Drake, Glendon Frank, Linguistics, American Studies
Lynch, Theophilus S, Modern Languages
Richardson, Frank C, Foreign Languages, Comparative Literature
Tyler, Joseph V, Spanish American Literature

Grand Rapids

Lagerwey, Walter, Germanic Languages
Lamse, Mary Jane, German Language & Literature
Otten, Arthur James, French Language & Literature
Otten, Robert Theodore, Classics
Wevers, Richard Franklin, Classical Languages

Holland

McCarthy, Mary Susan, French Literature & Language
Megow, Gerhard F, Foreign Languages
Nyenhuis, Jacob Eugene, Classics
Pott, Clarence K, Germanic Literature
Strand, Gisela Gallmeister, German, History
Weller, Hubert P, Spanish

Houghton

Weinkauf, Arnold Lewis, German

Kalamazoo

Cohen, Henry David, Romance Languages
Cole, Roger L, Germanic Languages & Literatures
Collins, David Almon, French Language & Literature
Coutant, Victor Carlisle Barr, Foreign Languages
Dale, Marcelle Esther, Foreign Languages
Dwarikesh, Dwarika Prasad Sharma, Linguistics
Ebling, Benjamin, II, French, Applied Linguistics

Fugate

Fugate, Joe K, Foreign Languages
Hendriksen, Daniel P, Linguistics, English as a Second Language
Henkels, Robert MacAllister, Jr, French Literature
Lance, Betty Rita Gomez, Romance Language & Literature
Noble, Frances E, Foreign Languages
Osmun, George Feit, Greek, Latin
Palmatier, Robert Allen, Linguistics, English
Reish, Joseph George, French Language & Literature
Summerfield, Ellen Beth, German Literature & Language

Lansing

Harrison, Ann Tukey, Romance Languages, Linguistics

Marquette

Glenn, Robert Bruce, Linguistics
Hoff, Peter, Foreign Languages & Philology
Javor, George, Philology
Kreitz, Helmut, German
Prusok, Rudi, German Literature & Language

Milan

Holoka, James Paul, Classical Languages & Literatures

Monroe

Truka, Mary Chrysostom, French

Mt Pleasant

Etnire, Elizabeth Louise, Spanish
Evans, Charlotte Buff, German
Fries, Peter H, Linguistics, English Grammar
Kadler, Eric H, Foreign Languages
Lawton, David Lloyd, English, Creolized Languages
Librie, Gilles Raphel, Contemporary French & Quebec Literature
McManamon, James Edward, Modern Languages
Roberts, Edward Arthur, Foreign Languages, Linguistics

Olivet

Thomson, William Gregory, Classics, Humanities

Rochester

Blatt, Gloria Toby, English Literature, Education
Bryant, William C, Romance Languages & Literatures
Burdick, Dolores Mann, French
Coppola, Carlo, Comparative Literature, Linguistics
DuBruck, Alfred Joseph, French
Gerulitis, Renate, German Language & Literature
Hart-Gonzalez, Lucinda, Linguistics
Iodice, Don Robert, Foreign Languages
Moeller, Jack R, German
Rahman, Munibur, Persian & Urdu Literature
Tagore, Amitendranath, Chinese & Indian Languages & Literatures

Rogers City

Copley, Frank Olin, Latin

Sterling Heights

Lonchyna, Bohdan Ivan, Romance Philology

University Center

Herkstroeter, Lynn H, French, German

Ypsilanti

Gibson, Eugene M, Foreign Languages
Keller, Gary D, Spanish-English Bilingualism, Chicano Literature
Pillsbury, Paul Whipple, English
Villegas, Francisco, Spanish, Spanish American Literature

MINNESOTA

Bemidji

Day, Richard Merton, French Language & Literature

Bloomington

Allen, Harold Byron, English Language

Collegeville

Haile, Getatchew, Linguistics, Religion

Duluth

Conant, Jonathan Brendan, Germanic Philology, Pedagogy
Hols, Edith Jones, Linguistics, Medieval English Literature
Linn, Michael D, Linguistics, American English

Minneapolis

Achberger, Friedrich, German Literature
Akehurst, F Ronald P, French
Armes, Keith, Russian Literature
Barker, Muhammad Abd-Al-Rahman, South Asian Linguistics
Bashiri, Iraj, Modern Iranian Linguistics & Literature
Belfiore, Elizabeth Stafford, Classical Languages, Philosophy
Birkmaier, Emma Marie, Modern Languages
Brewer, Maria Minich, French Literature & Theory
Conley, Tom Clark, French Literature
Downing, Bruce Theodore, Linguistics
Duroche, Leonard LeRoy, German, Comparative Literature
Erickson, Gerald M, Classical Languages
Escure, Genevieve Jeanne, Linguistics, Sociolinguistics
Federico, Joseph A, German Literature, Drama & Theater
Firchow, Evelyn Scherabon, Germanic Languages & Literatures
Fullerton, Gerald Lee, German Linguistics
Godzich, Wladyslaw B, Comparative Literature, Semiotics
Hasselmo, Nils, Linguistics, Scandinavian
Hershbell, Jackson Paul, Philosophy, Classics
Hirschbach, Frank Donald, Foreign Languages
Holm, Lydia, Spanish, Latin
Houlihan, Kathleen, Linguistics, Hispanic Linguistics
Jahn, Gary Robert, Russian Literature
Joeres, Ruth-Ellen Boetcher, German Literature, Women's History
Kac, Michael Benedict, Linguistics
Keuls, Eva Clara, Classical Philology
Liberman, Anatoly, Linguistics, Old Germanic Literature
Lock, Peter William, French Literature
Loveless, Owen Robert, Linguistics, Japanese
MacLeish, Andrew, Linguistics, Philology
Mather, Richard B, Chinese Language & Literature
Miller, John Francis, Classical Languages
Miranda, Rocky, Linguistics
Narvaez, Ricardo Augusto, Spanish, Linguistics
Pinkerton, Sandra, Linguistics, Anthropology
Pipa, Arshi, Languages
Ramos-Gascon, Antonio, Spanish Literature
Renaud, Armand A, French & Comparative Literature
Robinett, Betty W, Linguistics
Robinson, Peter Holbrook, French Literature
Sanders, Gerald Albert, Linguistics
Sarles, Harvey Burton, Linguistics
Schneider, Marilyn, Italian
Schulte-Sasse, Jochen, German, Comparative Literature
Sheets, George Archibald, Classical Languages, Historical Linguistics
Sheldon, Amy Louise, Psycholinguistics, Language Acquisition
Simpson, J Allen, Scandinavian Literature
Sonkowsky, Robert Paul, Classics
Stenson, Nancy Jean, Linguistics
Taraba, Anne-Sophie, Scandanavian & Comparative Literature
Taraba, Wolfgang F, German, Humanities
Tarone, Elaine E, Applied Linguistics, Phonetics
Thomas, Gary Craig, German Literature, Musicology
Vahamaki, Kurt Borje, Finnish Language & Linguistics
Vidal, Hernan, Spanish American Literature

Wakefield, Ray Milan, Philology, Netherlandic Literature
Waldauer, Joseph L, French
Wang, Stephen S, Sino-Tibetan Linguistics
Weiss, Gerhard Hans, German
Yu, Pauline Ruth, Comparative Literature, Chinese Poetry
Zahareas, Anthony Nicholas, Hispanic & Comparative Literatures

Moorhead

Buttry, Dolores Jean, Scandinavian & Comparative Literature
Cavazos, Nelson Augusto, Spanish
Green, David Royle, French Literature & Language
Hwang, Hi Sook, French Language & Literature
Kaplan, James Maurice, French Literature
Schaum, G Theodore, Germanic Languages
Storvick, Olin John, Classical Studies

Morris

Blake, Elizabeth Stanton, French
Farrell, Clarence Frederick, Jr, French
Gumpel, Liselotte, Humanities, German

Northfield

Achberger, Karen Ripp, German Literature, Women's Studies
Anderson, Keith Owen, Applied Linguistics
Bodman, Richard Wainwright, Chinese Language, Literature & History
Brust, William Zoltan, German, Russian
Bryant, Lucie M, French Literature
Bryce, Frank Jackson, Jr, Classics
Cantwell, William Richard, German Language & Literature
Fink, Karl J, German Language & Literature
Gunderson, Lloyd L, Classical Languages, Ancient History
Hewitt, Leah Dianne, Contemporary French Literature
Knecht, Loring D, French Language & Literature
May, James Michael, Classical Philology
Messner, Charles A, Jr, French
Obaid, Antonio Hadad, Spanish Literature
Porter, David Hugh, Classics, Music
Rippley, La Vern J, German Romanticism & Immigration History
Schier, Donald Stephen, Romance Languages
Shepard, Joe Willwerth, Russian Literature & Language
Wilkie, Nancy C, Greek Archeology, Classics

St Cloud

Plante, Julian Gerard, Classical Philology, Medieval Latin
Tosh, L Wayne, Computational Linguistics, Germanic Languages

St Paul

Bieter, Frederic Arnold, Classical Philology
Clark, Richard C, Modern Language
Donovan, William P, Classics, Archeology
Dye, Robert Ellis, German Language & Literature
Engelhardt, Walter Henry, Latin, German
Fabian, Donald Leroy, Spanish
Larson, Donald Norman, Linguistics, Anthropology
McGhee, Dorothy Madeleine, Comparative Literature
Middendorf, Marvin Luther, Foreign Languages, Comparative Religion
Nachtsheim, Mary Henry, French, German
Root, Tamara Goldstein, French Literature
Sandberg, Karl C, French Literature, Linguistics
Schmidt, Max L, German Language & Literature
Schons, Paul Allen, German Language, Literature & Culture
Schubert, Virginia Ann, French Language & Literature
Smalley, William Allen, Linguistics, Anthropology
Van D'Elden, Karl Herbert, Germanic Languages & Literatures
Van D'Elden, Stephanie Cain, Medieval Literature & Culture
Willging, Herbert M, Foreign Languages
Wolsey, Mary Lou Morris, Medieval French Language & Literature

St Peter

Everett, Aaron B, Romance Languages
Flory, Stewart Gilman, Classical Languages & Literatures
Maione, Michael, French Language & Literature
Walter, Renee, Spanish & Hispano-American Literature

Wayzata

Hannah, Richard Warren, German Literature, Philosophy

Winona

Aynesworth, Janine Chery, French Language & Literature
Ochrymowycz, Orest Robert, Spanish, Russian
Raab, Mary Ricarda, Romance Languages, Latin American Studies
Steigerwald, Jacob, German Language & Literature
Taylor, Robert H, Classics History

MISSISSIPPI

Clinton

Martin, Charles Edward, Modern Languages

Columbia

Reindorp, Reginald Carl, Spanish

Hattiesburg

Brown, Marice Collins, Linguistics, English
Johnson, Roger Barton, Jr, Comparative Literature, German
Lott, Thomas Wesley, Spanish
Neumann, Editha Schlanstedt, German Language & Literature

Jackson

Banks, Sarah Jane, Spanish Literature
Guest, John LeMuel, German
Harvey, Maria-Luisa Alvarez, Twentieth Century Spanish Literature
Krabbe, Judith, Classical Languages

Mississippi State

Blaney, Benjamin, Germanic Linguistics
Chatham, James Ray, Spanish Philology
Emplaincourt, Edmond Arthur, Romance Philology
Lopez, Mariano, Spanish Language & Literature
McClendon, Carmen Chaves, Spanish Language & Literature
Robbins, Kittye Delle, French Language & Literature
Takacs, Zolton, Languages & Linguistics
Wiltrout, Ann Elizabeth, Spanish
Wolverton, Robert E, Classics
Zernickow, Oskar Hans, Spanish, German

Newton

Garner, Gary Neil, German & French Language & Literature

Oxford

Capps, Edward, III, Classical Philology & Linguistics

University

Brown, Jack Davis, French, Romance Philology
Dolin, Edwin, Classics, Comparative Literature
Moysey, Robert Allen, Classical Languages, Ancient History
Strickland, William Emile, Modern Languages

MISSOURI

Cape Girardeau

Crowley, Cornelius J, Linguistics
Crowley, Frances G, Modern Language
Wingo, E Otha, Classical Languages

Schmiedel, Donald Emerson, Spanish
Wegner, Hart, Modern German, Comparative
Literature

Reno

Aaron, M Audrey, Romance Languages
Grotegut, Eugene K, Germanic Language &
Literature
Jacobsen, William Horton, Jr, Linguistics
Petersen, Gerald Wegener, Spanish American
Literature
Tobin, Frank Jude, German Literature
Whitenack, Judith A, Spanish Literature

NEW HAMPSHIRE

Amherst

Wheelock, Frederic Melvin, Classical Philology

Antrim

Wehringer, Helen Maxwell, Comparative
Literature, French

Bradford

Jacobsen, Thorkild, Assyriology

Bristol

Barrett, Madie Ward, Linguistics, Romance
Languages

Concord

Sousa, Thomas Frederick, Portuguese, Spanish

Dover

Jacoby, Frank Rainer, Germanic Languages

Durham

Callan, Richard Jerome, Romance Languages
Casas, R Alberto, Romance Languages
Clark, Mary Morris, Linguistics, African
Languages
Diller, Karl Conrad, Linguistics, English as a
Second Language
Forbes, Francis William, Spanish Theater
Fort, Marron Curtis, Germanic Philology,
Netherlandic
Held, Warren Howard, Jr, Linguistics
Hudon, Louis Joffre, French Literature
Leighton, Charles Henry, Spanish
Marshall, Grover Edwin, French, Italian
Pfanner, Helmut Franz, German Language &
Literature
Rasico, Philip Donald, Hispanic & Romance
Linguistics
Rouman, John Christ, Classics, Linguistics
Sweet, Denis Marshall, German Literature,
German Intellectual History
Wing, Barbara Hammann, Spanish

Exeter

Coffin, David Douglas, Classical Languages
de Lancey, DeVaux, French
Easton, Howard Trevelyan, Classical Languages
Wooley, Allan D, Classical Philology

Hanover

Arndt, Walter Werner, Linguistics, Slavic
Languages & Literature
Bradley, Edward Mix, Classics
Castro-Klaren, Sara, Modern Latin American
Literature
Doenges, Norman Arthur, Ancient History,
Classics
Duncan, Bruce, German Literature, Germanic
Linguistics
Harman, Mark, German & Comparative
Literature
Harvey, Lawrence Elliot, Romance Languages
Higgins, Lynn Anthony, French Language &
Literature
Hirsch, Marianne, Comparative Literature,
French
Hoffmeister, Werner Georg, German Language
& Literature, Comparative Literature
Horne, Elinor Clark, Linguistics, English
Kenkel, Konrad O, German Literature & History
Kleinhardt, Werner Bernhard, Romance
Languages, German
Kogan, Vivian, Romance Languages
Loseff, Lev Lifschutz, Russian Literature

Luis, William, Spanish American Literature
Luplow, Carol Ann, Russian Language &
Literature
Lyons, John David, Romance Languages &
Literatures
Nichols, Stephen G, Jr, Romance Languages,
Comparative Literature
Oxenhandler, Neal, French
Pastor, Beatriz, Latin American & Spanish
Literature
Perkell, Christine Godfrey, Classical Philology
Rashkin, Esther Joan, French & Comparative
Literature
Reeder, Claudia Gene, French Language &
Literature
Russell, Robert Hilton, Spanish Literature
Scher, Steven Paul, German & Comparative
Literature
Scherr, Barry Paul, Russian Language &
Literature
Scott, William Clyde, Classics
Sheldon, Richard Robert, Russian Language &
Literature
Sices, David, French Language & Literature
Swain, Virginia Edith, French Literature
Tatum, James Harvey, Classical Philology
Totten, Monika M, German Literature
Vegas-Garcia, Irene, Contemporary Latin
American Poetry
Waite, Stephen Van Fleet, Classical Studies,
Computer Applications
Whelan, Dennis, Literature, Law
Wiencke, Matthew Immanuel, Classical
Archeology
Wolff, Christian, Classics, Music

Keene

Arkin, Alexander Habib, Spanish & Portuguese
Literature
Frink, Helen Hiller, German Literature

Manchester

Cordova, Jose Hernan, Spanish American
Literature
Oria, Tomas G, Spanish American Literature

Plymouth

Brook, Richard, English Linguistics
Tinnell, Roger Dale, Spanish, Comparative
Literature

Portsmouth

Vrooman, Jack Rochford, French Literature

NEW JERSEY

Barnegat Light

De Lacy, Phillip, Classics

Bloomfield

Fuller, Clarence, Foreign Languages

Caldwell

Bollettino, Vincenzo Zin, Foreign Language &
Literature

Camden

Horowitz, Louise Kahan, French Literature
Showalter, English, Jr, French & Comparative
Literature
Smith, Robert Peter, Jr, French Language &
Literature

Cherry Hill

Milstein, Barney M, German Languages &
Literature

Dover

Prisco, Carlo, Romance Languages

Eatontown

Craig, Charlotte Marie, German Language &
Literature

Edison

Ratych, Joanna Maria, German Language &
Literature

Fair Lawn

Rose, Ernst (Andreas Gottlieb), Literature

Hackettstown

Glaettle, Walter Eric, German, French

Highland Park

Benjamin, Anna Shaw, Classics, Archaeology
Pane, Remigio Ugo, Romance Languages
Walker, Steven Friemel, Comparative Literature

Hillside

Mills, Edgar, German

Jamesburg

Fitzell, John, German Literature

Jersey City

Condoyannis, George Edward, Modern
Languages
Finn, Margaret R, Classics
Jimenez, Onilda Angelica, Spanish American
Literature
Meadows, Gail Keith, Philology, Medieval
Literature

Lakewood

McCarthy, Mary Theresa, French Language &
Literature

Lawrenceville

Finello, Dominick Louis, Spanish Renaissance &
Baroque Literature
Gloeckner, Nydia Rivera, Spanish Medieval
Literature, Philology
Onyshkevych, Larissa M L, Slavic Literatures &
Languages
Rodriguez, Rodney Tapanes, Spanish Literature

Little Silver

Portuondo, Alicia Edelmira, Spanish

Livingston

Fenner, Rest, Jr, Romance Languages
Minc, Rose S, Latin American & Spanish
Literature

Madison

Becker, Lucille Frackman, French Language &
Literature
Coombs, Ilona C, French Literature
Huebner, Madelene Codina, Foreign Languages,
Spanish Language & Literature
Kopp, Richard L, Romance Languages
McMullen, Edwin Wallace, Jr, Linguistics,
English
Marchione, Margherita Frances, Romance
Languages; American History
Properzio, Paul Joseph, Classical Languages,
Ancient History
Schabacker, John Montgomery, German
Literature
Vamos, Mara, French, Comparative Literature
Wescott, Roger Williams, Linguistic
Anthropology

Mahwah

Simon, Ernest, French & Comparative Literature

Millburn

DeCarlo, Andrew, Spanish & Italian Literature

Moorestown

Robinson, Henry Schroder, Classics & Classical
Archeology

Morganville

Monahan, Patrick Joseph, Jr, Literature,
Linguistics

NEW JERSEY (cont)
Newark

Balbin, Julius Frederic, English, Foreign Languages & Literatures
Laguna-Diaz, Elpidio, Spanish Literature and Civilization
Plevich-Darretta, Mary, Spanish Language & Literature
Rodriuez-Seda de Laguna, Asela, Comparative Literature
Zitzelsberger, Otto Joseph, Germanic Languages

New Brunswick

Allen, Robert Franklin, French, Linguistics
Boros Azzi, Marie-Denise, Romance Languages
Bretz, Mary Lee, Spanish Literature, Literary Theory
Ciklamini, Marlene Hiedewohl, Languages
Derbyshire, William W, Russian & Slavic Linguistics
Fizer, John, Slavic & Comparative Literature
Fortenbaugh, William Wall, Classics
Guarino, Guido, Italian Literature
Laggini, Joseph Enrico, Italian Language & Literature
Ley, Ralph John, German
McCormick, John Owen, Comparative Literature
Mariani, Umberto Carlo, Italian
Misiego-Llagostera, Michaela, Modern Literature, Romance & Germanic Linguistics
Morrow, John Howard, French Literature
Nagy, Edward, Romance Languages
Naumann, Marina Turkevich, Russian Literature and Language, Comparative Literature
Neuse, Erna Kritsch, German Language & Literature
Perez-Stansfield, Maria Pilar, Spanish Literature
Pirog, Gerald, Slavic Languages and Literatures
Santamarina, Leonardo, Spanish
Small, Jocelyn Penny, Classical Archeology
Triwedi, Mitchell D, Spanish Literature
Tu, Ching-I, Chinese Language & Literature
Umpierre, Luz Maria, Caribbean Literature & Culture
Undank, Jack, French Language & Literature
Uria-Santos, Maria Rosa, Romance Languages, Spanish American Literature
Walker, Janet Anderson, Comparative & Asian Literature
Zatlin-Boring, Phyllis, Spanish, Portuguese

North Bergen

Weber, Jean-Paul, Romance Languages, Aesthetics

Paramus

Scarato, Giacomo Rinaldo, Romance Languages

Piscataway

Dauster, Frank Nicholas, Spanish
Macdonald, Antonina Hansell, Computational Linguistics

Plainfield

Wendell, Charles Warner, Comparative Literature

Princeton

Angress, Ruth K, Germanic Language & Literature
Atkins, Samuel DeCoster, Classical Philology
Bill, Valentine Tschebotarioff, Russian History & Literature
Bing, Janet Mueller, Linguistics
Bishop, George Reginald, Jr, Romance Languages & Literature
Brombert, Victor Henri, French Comparative Literature
Brown, Clarence Fleetwood, Jr, Comparative Literature
Champlin, Edward James, Ancient History
Cherniss, Harold Fredrick, Greek, Ancient Philosophy
Clinton, Jerome Wright, Persian Literature
Corngold, Stanley Alan, German & Comparative Literature
Curschmann, Michael Johann Hendrik, Germanic Languages
DeJean, Joan Elizabeth, French
Dunkel, George Eugene, Indo-European Linguistics, Sanskrit

Ermolaev, Herman, Soviet & Russian Literature
Forcione, Alban Keith, Romance Languages, Spanish
Frassica, Pietro, Italian Literature & Language
Furley, David John, Classics, History of Philosophy
Gehman, Henry Snyder, Old Testament
Gilliam, James Frank, Classics, Ancient History
Gossman, Jeffrey Lionel, French
Hanson, John Arthur, Classics
Hill, Claude, German
Hinderer, Walter Hermann, German Literature & Criticism
Hoffmann, Leon-Francois, French Literature
Hollander, Robert B, Jr, Literature
Irby, James East, Latin American Literature
Juhl, P D, Germanic Languages & Literatures, Literary Theory
Keaney, John Joseph, Classics
Kimmich, Flora Graham Horne, German Literature
King, Edmund Ludwig, Spanish Literature
Lange, Victor, German Literature
Luce, Torry James, Jr, Classics, Ancient History
Maman, Andre, French
Martin, Janet Marion, Classics
Molloy, Sylvia, Latin American & Comparative Literature
Most, Glenn Warren, Comparative Literature, Classical Languages
Moulton, William Gamwell, Linguistics
Nash, Suzanne Julie Crelly, French Literature
Negus, Kenneth George, German
Parente, James Andrew, Jr, German Literature
Parris, Jean Jacob, Romance Languages & Literature
Plaks, Andrew Henry, Chinese & Comparative Literature
Rigolot, Francois Paul, French Literature
Roberge, Paul Timothy, Germanic Languages, General Linguistics
Silz, Walter, German Literature
Sonnenfeld, Albert, French & Comparative Literatures
Sullivan, Edward Daniel, French Literature
Townsend, Charles Edward, Slavic Languages & Linguistics
Turkevich, Ludmilla Buketoff, Modern Languages & Literatures
Uitti, Karl David, French Literature & Philology
Ulmer, Bernhard, German Literature
Willis, Raymond Smith, Spanish, Portuguese
Zeitlin, Froma I, Classics
Zetzel, James E G, Classical Literature
Ziolkowski, Theodore J, German, Comparative Literature

Rutherford

Pincus, Michael Stern, Spanish, Romance Philology
Ryding, William Wellington, French

Short Hills

Wang, Fred Fangyu, Far Eastern Languages

Somerset

Gil, Ildefonso-Manuel, Romance Languages, Spanish Literature

South Orange

Jovicevich, Alexander, French Literature
O'Connor, David, Analytic Philosophy, Philosophy of Religion
Pastor, Leslie P, European History, German
Yang, Winston Lih-Yeu, Chinese & Comparative Literature
Young, John, History, Linguistics
Zalacain, Daniel, Latin American Literature & Theatre

Teaneck

Solan, Lawrence M, Linguistics, Law

Trenton

Calo, Jeanne Eugenie, French Language & Literature
Fritsch, Charles Theodore, Oriental Languages
Porter, Ellis Gibson, Foreign Languages
Wentz, Debra Linowitz, French Literature & Language

Union

Hacke, Robert E L, English, Linguistics

Upper Montclair

Cagnon, Maurice, Twentieth Century Francophone & French Literature
Frankenthaler, Marilyn Rosenbluth, Latin American Literature, Law
Fulton, Norman, Modern Philology, Spanish History
Gibson, Elsa Maria Peterson, Classical Philology, Greek Epigraphy
Heilbronner, Walter Leo, German
Kelly, David H, Classical Linguistics
Klein, Harriet Esther Manelis, Linguistics, Anthropology
Klibbe, Helene Foustanos, French Literature
Miller, Robert L, Linguistics
Moore, John Virgil, Jr, German Literature, Music
Rambaldo, Ana M, Spanish, Spanish Community Relations
Roederer, Louis J M, Languages
Schlant, Ernestine, German, Comparative Literature
Standring, Enid Mary, French, Comparative Literature
Szklarczyk, Lillian, Romance Languages
Wilkins, Kathleen Sonia, French Literature, History of Ideas

Wayne

Aguirre, Angela M, Modern Spanish Literature

West Long Branch

Ahrens, Frederick Christian, German Language & Literature

NEW MEXICO
Albuquerque

Bergen, John Joseph, Linguistics, Philology
Bills, Garland Dee, Linguistics
Book, E Truett, French Language & Literature
Calvert, Laura Merle, Romance Languages
Duncan, Robert Manly, Modern Languages
Fernandez, Pelayo Hipolito, Spanish Literature
Gerdes, Dick Charles, Latin American Literature
Guyler, Samuel Lerert, Spanish & Italian Literature
Holzapfel, Robert, Modern German Drama
Holzapfel, Tamara, Spanish
Jehenson, Yvonne Myriam, Comparative Literature, History of Ideas
Lindsey, Byron Trent, Russian Language & Literature
MacCurdy, Raymond Ralph, Spanish Literature
Murphy, Patricia, French
Nason, Marshall Rutherford, Romance Languages
Newman, Stanley Stewart, Anthropology, Linguistics
Oller, John William, Jr, Linguistics, Psychology
Peters, George Frederick, German Literature & Language
Roberts, William Holloway, Romance Languages
Rodriguez, Alfred, Romance Languages
Smith, Warren Sale, Jr, Classical Languages
Starr, William Thomas, French Literature
Tomlins, Jack Edward, Foreign Languages
Ulibarri, Sabine Reyes, Spanish Literature
White, Julian Eugene, Jr, Classical Languages & Literature
Young, Robert Wendell, History, Linguistics

Las Cruces

Ader, Kathleen M Joyce, Spanish
Comeau, Paul T, Romance Languages
Elizondo, Sergio (Danilo), Romance Languages
Haycock, Bevan Orlando, Spanish Language & Literature
Lamb, Eva K, Foreign Language, Fine Arts
Rundell, Richard Jason, German Literature & Linguistics
Valdes, Guadalupe, Applied Linguistics, Spanish

Las Vegas

Johnson, Jean (Lee), Comparative Indo-European Linguistics
Lopez-Gaston, Jose Romon, Foreign Languages, Spanish Literature
Urtiaga, Alfonso, Romance Languages, Spanish Literature

Portales

Fox, Eugene Jackson, Foreign Languages

Santa Fe

Halpern, Abraham Meyer, Anthropology, Linguistics
Oppenheimer, Max, Jr, Modern Languages & Literature

University Park

Dubois, Betty Lou, Applied Linguistics, English as Foreign Language

NEW YORK

Albany

Alexander, Douglas II, Romance Languages
Baker, Armand Fred, Spanish & Spanish American Literature
Barnard, Sylvia Evans, Classics
Beharriell, Frederick John, German & Comparative Literature
Bleiberg, German, Spanish Literature & History
Campbell, Lyle, Linguistics, Anthropology
Carlos, Alberto J, Hispanic & Italian Studies
Carrino, Frank G, Hispanic Studies
de Colombi-Monguio, Alicia, Medieval & Renaissance Poetry
Frank, Francine, Linguistics, Spanish
Grava, Arnolds, Romance Languages & Literature, Philosophy
Greene, Robert William, Romance Languages
Kanes, Martin, Romance Languages
Laroche, Roland Arthur, Classics
Mache, Ulrich, German Literature
Mithun, Marianne, Linguistics
Moore, Erna Marie, German Literature
Moore, Frederick Willard, French
Neat, (Sister) Charles Marie, German
Nepaulsingh, Colbert Ivor, Spanish Language & Literature
Ortali, Raymond, Romance Languages
Overbeck, John Clarence, Classical Archeology, Ancient Greek
Pohlsander, Hans Achim, Classics
Prakken, Donald Wilson, Classical Philology
Richtman, Jack, French Language & Literature
Salomon, Herman Prins, Literature
Savitt, Joan Neuburger, Linguistics, French
Scatton, Ernest Alden, Slavic Linguistics
Schyfter, Sara Ethel, Spanish Literature
Shane, Alex Michael, Slavic Languages & Literatures
Spalek, John M, German
Strelka, Joseph Peter, German Literature, Theory of Literature
Wallace, Paul Walter, Greek Archeology & History
Williams, Lois Virginia, Classics
Wittkowski, Wolfgang, German Literature

Amherst

Richards, Henry Joseph, Spanish Literature

Annandale-on-Hudson

Rosenberg, Justus, Applied Linguistics

Aurora

Barooshian, Vahan Dickran, Russian Art & Literature
Deinert, Waltraut, Comparative Literature, German
Kirtland, Lynn, Classical Languages

Baldwin

Chanover, Pierre E, French, Poetry

Bayside

Alfonsi, Sandra Resnick, Medieval French Language & Literature
Altabe, David Fintz, Spanish, Sephardic Studies
Schatkin, Margaret Amy, Patristics, Classics

Binghamton

Bernardo, Aldo Sisto, Romance Philology
Block, Haskell M, Comparative Literature
Coates, Carrol Franklin, French Literature
Cocozzella, Peter, Spanish Language & Literature
Cypess, Sandra Messinger, Spanish, Portuguese

Fischler, Alexander, Comparative Literature
Garber, Frederick Meyer, Comparative Literature, Romanticism
Gullace, Giovanni, French, Italian
Heyer, Elfriede Annemarie, German Literature & Language
Hopper, Paul John, Linguistics
Jasenas, Elaine Francine Charlotte, French
Kerr, Richard A, Romance Languages
Lakich, John J, Modern Languages
Levin, Saul, Classics
Mignani, Rigo, Romance Philology
Mittelstadt, Michael Charles, Classics
Norton, Roger C, German Language & Literature
Pavlovskis, Zoja, Classics
Pellegrini, Anthony Louis, Romance Languages & Literature
Ramsey, Jerome A, Romance Languages
Rodriguez-Luis, Julio, Spanish
Rose, Marilyn Gaddis, Comparative Literature
Schmidt, Gerard F, German, Medieval Literature
Seeley, Frank Friedeberg, Slavic & Comparative Literature
Semann, Khalil I H, Arabic
Snyder, William H, Comparative Linguistics, German Philology
Sticca, Sandro, Middle Ages & Renaissance
Stillman, Yedida Kalfon, Middle Eastern Ethnography & Literature
Straight, H Stephen, Linguistics, Anthropology
Van Baelen, Jacqueline, French
Weiss, Robert Otto, German Language & Literature

Brockport

Alvarez-Altman, Grace DeJesus, Linguistics, Spanish
Chorney, Stephen, Slavic Languages & Literatures
Kayser, H Christoph, German Language & Literature
Marti, Jorge Luis, Spanish
O'Nan, Martha (Birchette), Spanish, French
Rojas, Victor Julio, Spanish Language and Literature
Siracusa, Joseph, Romance Linguistics

Bronx

Alfonsi, Ferdinando Pietro, Comparative Literature, Italian
Altieri, Marcelle Billaudaz, French Language & Literature
Arbeitman, Yoel, Linguistic Archeology
Arias, Richardo, Spanish Literature & History
Bergman, Hannah Estermann, Spanish Literature
Braun, Sidney David, French Literature
Brodin, Dorothy R, Romance Languages, Linguistics
Bronznick, Norman Meyer, Hebraic Studies, Religion
Clark, John Richard, Classical Languages, Medieval Latin
Dimler, George Richard, German Language & Literature
Doyle, Richard Edward, Classical Languages
Gertner, Michael Howard, Linguistics, French Literature
Gottlieb, Marlene Diane, Contemporary Latin American Literature
Hill, Emita B, French Literature
Hoar, Leo Jerome, Jr, Romance Languages & Literatures
Hoffmann, Ursula F, German Literature
Kabakoff, Jacob, Hebrew Language & Literature
Lerner, Isaias, Spanish Literature
Macary, Jean Louis, French Literature
McCulloch, Donald F, Linguistics
McLaughlin, John Dennis, Classical Studies
Marzi, Alfeo Hugo, Italian, Spanish
Memmo, Paul Eugene, Jr, English & Comparative Studies
Mills, Judith Oloskey, Russian Literature & Language
Minton, William Warren, Classics
Murtaugh, Kristen Olson, Italian Renaissance Literature
Natella, Arthur A, Jr, Spanish & Latin American Language & Literature
Noble, Shlomo, Germanic & Yiddish Philology
Pappas, John Nicholas, French
Penella, Robert Joseph, Classics, Roman History
Schreiber, Fred, Classics
Schwartz, Gary Stephen, Classics, English
Sider, David, Classical Languages
Siev, Asher, Hebrew Literature
Speranza, Ernest Vincent, Spanish

Streebing, Cecilian M, Romance Languages
Thomas, P Aloysius, French
Tusiani, Joseph, Italian Language & Literature
Vranich, Stanko B, Spanish Literature

Bronxville

Gisolfi, Anthony M, Italian
Mish, John L, Chinese Philosophy

Brooklyn

Alba-Buffill, Elio, Spanish American Literature, Spanish Language & Grammar
Bobetsky, Victor, Foreign Languages
Brener, Bernard J, Modern Languages
Bryant, Margaret M, English Linguistics
Casey, Camillus, Philology
Clayman, Dee Lesser, Classical Philology
de Weever, Jacqueline Elinor, Middle English
Doron, Pinchas, Hebrew Language, Bible
Ferrari, Lena M, Foreign Languages
Filer, Malva Esther, Spanish American Literature
Fiorenza, Nicholas A, Foreign Languages, Fine Arts
Fogel, Herbert, Romance Languages
Gerber, Barbara Leslie, Comparative Literaure, French
Goldberg, Nathan, Hebrew Language & Literature
Hernandez-Miyares, Julio Enrique, Spanish, Hispanic Literatures
Hill, Charles Graves, French
Huffman, Claire, Italian, Comparative Literature
Hung, Ming Shui, Chinese Literature
Jofen, Jean, German Literature
Juszczak, Albert S, Slavic Languages & Literatures
Kahn, Arthur David, Classical Literatures, History
Kattan, Olga, Romance Languages
Kiremidjian, Garabed David, Comparative Literature
Koch, Ernst, Germanic Languages & Literatures
Lacosta, Frank, Spanish, French
Lichtman, Celia S, Romance Languages
Lipton, Wallace S, Romance Linguistics
Loy, John Robert, French Language & Literature
Mallia, Norma, French Literature
Matenko, Percy, Yiddish, German Romanticism
Mermall, Thomas, Romance Languages
Meyer, Doris L, Romance Languages
Moreland, Floyd Leonard, Classical Languages & Literatures
Moretta, Eugene Lawrence, Spanish-American Literature
Ochsenschlager, Edward Lloyd, Classical Languages, Archeology
Rechtschaffen, Bernard, German Language & Comparative Literature
Roberts, Spencer Eugene, Russian Language & Literature
Schub, Louise Rypko, French Language & Literature
Simon, Arthur, Romance Languages
Toscani, Bernard Michael, Italian, French
Wang, Leonard Judah, French
Wiseman, Mary Bittner, Philosophy, Literary Theory
Zaneteas, Peter C, Greek, Latin

Buffalo

Aubery, Pierre, French Language & Literature
Balowitz, Victor H, Philosophy of Language
Bandera, Cesareo, Spanish Literature, Comparative Literature
Benay, Jacques G, French, Italian
Bernal, Olga, Nineteenth & Twentieth Century French Literature
Bernheimer, Charles Clarence, Comparative Literature
Boyd-Bowman, Peter (Muschamp), Romance Linguistics
Burtniak, Michael, Slavic Philology
Camurati, Mireya Beatriz, Spanish American Literature
Clough, Raymond Joseph, French Language & Literature
Curran, Leo Christopher, Classical Literature
Dooling, Margaret, Modern Languages
Dudley, Edward J, Spanish, English
Feal, Carlos, Romance Languages, Spanish
Feal, Gisele C, Spanish, French
Feldman, Thalia Phillies, Classical Languages, Ancient Art
Fitzgerald, Marie Christine, Romance Languages
Garton, Charles, Classics
Garvin, Paul Lucian, Linguistics

Houghton

Paine, Stephen W, Classics
Stockin, Frank Gordon, Jr, Classical Philology

Huntington

Allentuch, Harriet R, French

Hyde Park

Norkeliunas, Casimir John, Slavic Literatures

Ithaca

Agard, Frederick Browning, Romance
   Linguistics
Ahl, Frederick Michael, Classics, Comparative
   Literature
Armstrong, Douglas Holcombe, Spanish
   Language & Literature
Babby, Leonard Harvey, Slavic & General
   Linguistics
Blackall, Eric Albert, German & Comparative
   Literature
Bodman, Nicholas Cleaveland, Linguistics
Caplan, Harry, Classics
Clinton, Kevin, Classics
Colby-Hall, Alice Mary, Medieval French
   Literature
Cowan, J Milton, General Linguistics
De Aguero, Eduardo, Comparative Literature,
   Romance Languages
Deinert, Herbert, German Literature
Echols, John Minor, Linguistics
Emerson, Caryl Geppert, Russian Literature &
   Music
Ezergailis, Inta Miske, German Literature
Gair, James Wells, Linguistics
Gibian, George, Russian, Comparative Literature
Gilman, Sander Lawrence, German Literary &
   Intellectual History
Grimes, Joseph Evans, Linguistics
Groos, Arthur Bernhard, Jr, German Literature
Grossvogel, David I, French, Romance Studies
Hall, Robert Anderson, Jr, Romance & General
   Linguistics
Hohendahl, Peter U, German
Holdheim, William Wolfgang, Comparative &
   French Literature
Huffman, Franklin Eugene, General Linguistics,
   Southeast Asian Languages
Jasanoff, Jay Harold, Linguistics, Germanic
   Philology
Jones, Robert Burton, Jr, Linguistics
Jorden, Eleanor Harz, Linguistics
Kaplan, Jane Payne, French Language &
   Literature, Linguistics
Kirkwood, Gordon Macdonald, Classical
   Philology
Kronik, John William, Spanish Language &
   Literature
Kufner, Herbert Leopold, Germanic Linguistics
Leed, Richard Leaman, Slavic Linguistics
Lewis, Philip Eugene, French Literature
McCann, David Richard, Korean & Japanese
   Literature
McCoy, John, Jr, Chinese & Japanese Linguistics
Mazzotta, Giuseppe F, Italian Language,
   Literature
Mei, Tsu-Lin, Chinese Linguistics, Philosophy
Messing, Gordon Myron, Indo-European
   Linguistics
Moron-Arroyo, Ciriaco, Spanish Literature,
   Philosophy
Noblitt, James Starkey, Romance Languages
Pelli, Moshe, Hebrew Literature & Language
Rabinowitz, Isaac, Semitic Languages &
   Literature
Santi, Enrico Mario, Latin American Literature
Shadick, Harold, Chinese Language & Literature
Sola, Donald Frederick, General Linguistics
Suner, Margarita, Syntax, Hispanic Linguistics
Taras, Anthony F, French, Spanish
Terasaki, Etsuko Takemoto, Japanese Language
   & Literature
Tittler, Jonathan Paul, Latin American Novel,
   Contemporary Literary Criticism
Van Coetsem, Frans C, Germanic Linguistics
Waugh, Linda Ruth, Linguistics, French
Weber, Rose-Marie, General Linguistics
Wolff, John Ulrich, General & Malayopolynesian
   Linguistics
Zholkovsky, Alexander K, Russian Literature &
   Poetics

Jamaica

Abrams, Fred, Romance Languages
Akielaszek, Stanislaus, Classical Philology
Astuto, Philip Louis, Spanish
Bieler, Arthur, French
Dominicis, Maria Canteli, Spanish
Gillespie, John Kinsey, Japanese Literature,
   Theatre
Hueppe, Frederick Ernst, Germanic Philology
Lang, Frederick Frank, Germanic Language &
   Literature
Martin, Lynn Simpson, English Philology
Nauss, Janine Rossard, French, English
Raitiere, Anna, French Language & Literature
Reynolds, John Joseph, Spanish
Sallese, Nicholas F, Spanish

Katonah

Simpson, William Kelly, Egyptology

Keuka Park

Riemschneider, Ernst Gunther, German
   Literature, History

Larchmont

Devlin, John Joseph, Jr, Modern Languages,
   Humanities

Little Neck

Bird, Thomas Edward, Slavic Languages &
   Literatures

Long Island City

Blaszczyk, Leon Thaddeus, Classics, Slavic
   Literature

Loudonville

Horgan, Daniel James, Modern Languages,
   History
Muller, Liguori, Greek, Latin
Ortal, America Yolanda, Spanish Language &
   Literature

McKnownville

Colman, Charles Wilson, French Literature

Manhasset

Glass, Elliot Steven, Latin American & Spanish
   Literature
Sholod, Barton, Romance Languages, Medieval
   Studies

New Paltz

Alphonso-Karkala, John B, Comparative
   Literature
Borenstein, Walter, Spanish
Faulkner, James Clement, French Language,
   Literature
Jones, Morgan Emory, Linguistics & English
   Language
Pap, Leo, Hispanics, Linguistics
Paz, Francis Xavier, Comparative Literature,
   Oriental Studies
Piluso, Robert Vincent, Romance Languages

New Rochelle

Colaneri, John Nunzio, Italian Languages &
   Literature
Collins, Patrick Joseph, Classics, Creative
   Writing
Raia-Colaneri, Ann Rose, Classical Languages &
   Literatures
Russo, Mary, Classical Languages & Literatures

New York

Abruzzi, Giovanna Ghetti, Modern Italian
   Literature
Affron, Charles M, Romance Languages
Agudiez, Juan Ventura, Spanish, French
Alcala, Angel, Romance Languages, Philosophy
Aldridge, Adriana Garcia De, Latin-American
   Literature & Criticism
Allen, Robert Livingston, Linguistics, English
Anderson, Helene Masslo, Latin American
   Literature
Anger, Alfred, Germanic Languages &
   Literatures
Austerlitz, Robert Paul, Linguistics
Bacon, Helen Hazard, Classical Languages &
   Literature

Bacon, Isaac, German Philology & Literature
Bagnall, Roger Shaler, Greek Papyrology,
   Ancient History
Balakian, Anna (Mrs Stephan Nalbantian),
   French Literature
Barrenechea, Ana Maria, Hispanic Literature,
   Theory of Literature
Bauke, Joseph P, Germanics
Beardsley, Theodore S, Jr, Spanish & French
   Language & Literature
Belknap, Robert Lamont, Russian Literature
Benardete, Seth Gabriel, Classics
Bendelac, Alegria, French Language & Literature
Benedict, Coleman Hamilton, Greek & Latin
   Literature
Berger, Marshall Daniel, Linguistics
Bishop, Thomas W, French & Comparative
   Literature
Blasi, Alberto O, Spanish American Literature,
   Comparative Literature
Bradley, Brigitte L, Germanic & Romance
   Languages
Brady, James F, Classics
Braun, Micheline Tison, Romance Languages
Braun, Shirley Worcester, Linguistics, English As
   A Second Language
Brause, Rita S, Linguistics
Breunig, LeRoy Clinton, French Literature
Brod, Richard Ira, Foreign Languages
Bronstein, Arthur J, Speech, Linguistics
Brush, Craig Balcombe, French
Cameron, Alan (Douglas Edward), Classical
   Philology, Byzantine Studies
Campbell, James Marshall, Greek
Carson, Katharine Whitman, French Literature
Castagnaro, R Anthony, Romance Languages &
   Literatures
Caws, Mary Ann, French Literature, Poetry
Chang-Rodriguez, Raquel, Spanish American
   Literature
Charney, Hanna Kurz, French
Chelkowski, Peter Jan, Near Eastern Languages
   & Literatures
Clements, Robert John, Literature
Coleman, John Alexander, Contemporary Latin
   American & Comparative Literature
Commager, Steele, Classics
Costello, John Robert, Linguistics
Coulter, James Albert, Classical Philology
Daitz, Stephen G, Classics
Damrosch, David N, Comparative & English
   Literature
Dean, Ruth Josephine, Medieval Literature
De La Campa, Antonio Radames, Spanish,
   Spanish-American Literature
De La Nuez, Manuel, Spanish Literature
Dellepiane, Angela B, Spanish American
   Literature
Demetrius, James Kleon, Greek, History of
   Grecian Scholarship
Dennis, Ward H, Spanish Language & Literature
Dilts, Mervin R, Classics
Dorenlot, Francoise, French Language &
   Literature
Doubrovsky, Serge, French
Dougherty, Ray Cordell, Linguistics, Philosophy
   of Language
Drabkin, Miriam F, Classical Languages, History
   of Science
Dunmore, Charles William, Classics
Falb, Lewis W, Romance Languages, Drama
Fanselow, John Frederick, Teaching English To
   Speakers of Other Languages
Feiman Waldman, Gloria Frances, Spanish
   Language, Women's Studies
Fellows, Otis Edward, French Literature
Feuerlicht, Ignace, German, Romance Languages
Fine, Ellen Sydney, French Literature &
   Language
Finocchiaro, Mary, Linguistics
Fishman, Joshua Aaron, Sociolinguistics
Flaxman, Seymour Lawrence, Germanics
Fox, Dian, Spanish Literature
Frame, Donald Murdoch, French Literature
Frankel, Margherita, Italian & French Literature
Freeman, Michelle Alice, French Literature,
   French Philology
Frydman, Anne, Russian & Comparative
   Literature
Fryscak, Milan, Slavic Linguistics, Czech
   Literature
Fulvi, Philip Anthony, French, Italian
Gavronsky, Serge, Romance Languages, French
   Civilization
Gearey, John E, German Language & Literature
Gille, Gisele Corbiere, Romance Languages
Goldin, Frederick, Medieval & Comparative
   Literature
Gonzalez, Emilio, Romance Languages

New York, NEW YORK (cont)

Gordon, Cyrus H, Near East Culture
Gorlin, Lalla E, Germanic Languages & Literature
Greene, Tatiana W, French Literature
Grenewitz, Rainer Vadim, Russian Literature & History
Grimaldi, William A, Classical Languages
Guedenet, Pierre, French
Guilloton, Doris Starr, German Language & Literature
Guss, Evelyn Grace, Classics
Gustafson, Richard Folke, Russian Language & Literature
Gutierrez de la Solana, Alberto, Spanish American & Spanish Literature
Gutierrez-Vega, Zenaida, Spanish, Spanish American Literature
Gutmann, Anni, German Language & Literature
Halpert, Inge D, Foreign Languages
Hamilton, Carlos D, Spanish Literature & History
Hampares, Katherine J, Spanish Language, Latin American Literature
Harkins, William E, Philology, Literary History & Criticism
Harris, Frederick John, French, Comparative Literature
Heinrich, Amy Vladeck, Japanese & Comparative Literature
Held, Moshe, Semitic Languages
Hoffmann, Ernst Fedor, German Language & Literature
Holm, John Alexander, Linguistics, English
Holtz, Avraham, Modern Hebrew Literature
Hoover, Marjorie Lawson, German & Russian Literature
Hornstein, Norbert R, Philosophy, Linguistics
Horvath, Violet M, French & Italian Literature
Hsia, Chih-Tsing, Chinese Literature
Imerti, Arthur D, Romance Languages
Jackson, William Thomas Hobdell, Medieval Literature
Javitch, Daniel Gilbert, English, Comparative Literature
Jimenez, Jose, Spanish & Spanish American Poetry
Jochnowitz, George, Linguistics, Romance Languages
Jungemann, Fredrick Henry, Spanish, Hispanic Linguistics
Kahn, Ludwig Werner, German & Comparative Literature
Kastner, George Ronald, Comparative Literature
Keene, Donald Lawrence, Japanese Literature
Kieser, Rolf, German Literature & History
Klibbe, Lawrence H, Romance Languages
Klimov, Alla, Russian Literature
Knapp, Bettina, French Literature
Kneller, John William, French Literature
Kodjak, Andrej, Russian Literature
Kohler, Lotte E, German Language & Literature
Kostka, Edmund K, Modern Languages, Comparative Literature
Kra, Pauline, French Literature
Lamont, Rosette C, French & Comparative Literature
Langendoen, Donald Terence, Linguistics, English
Lasry, Anita Benaim, Medieval Spanish Literature
LeClerc, Paul Omer, French
Ledyard, Gari Keith, East Asian Languages, History
Lencek, Rado L, Slavic Philology & Civilizations
Leo, Ernest John, German
Lerner, Lia Schwartz, Spanish & Comparative Literature
Lichtenstein, Aaron, Semitic Studies
Litman, Theodore Armand, French Literature
Logan, Marie-Rose Van Stijnvoort, French Literature & Thought
Lorch, Maristella De Panizza, Italian
Losada, Luis Antonio, Classics, Ancient History
Louria, Yvette, Romance & Slavic Languages
Lowin, Joseph Gerald, French Language & Literature
Lubetski, Meir, Judaica
McCormick, Edward Allen, German, Comparative Literature
Mades, Leonard, Spanish Literature
Maguire, Robert A, Language, Literature
Malone, Joseph Lawrence, Linguistics
Martin, Catherine-Rita, French
Martinez, H Salvador, Medieval Spanish Literature, Philosophy of History
Martinez-Bonati, Felix, Spanish Literature, Aesthetics

Martins, Wilson, Romance Languages
Mas-Lopez, Edita, Twentieth-Century Art & Literature, Spanish Literature & Civilization
May, Gita, French
Minkoff, Harvey, Linguistics, English
Mocha, Frank, Polish Language and Literature
Mora, Gabriela, Spanish, Hispanic American Literature
Mottola, Anthony C, Foreign Language
Muscarella, Grace Freed, Latin, Classical Philology
Naro, Anthony Julius, Linguistics
Nelson, John Charles, Italian
Nida, Eugene Albert, Linguistics, Anthropology
Nimetz, Michael Gerson, Romance Languages
Noakes, Warren David, French Language & Literature
Norman, Isabel H, Spanish, Portuguese
Orlinsky, Harry Meyer, Biblical Philology & History
Pitkin, Harvey, Linguistics, Anthropology
Plant, Richard, German Philology
Plottel, Jeanine Parisier, Languages
Pohoryles, Bernard Martin, French, German
Pomeroy, Sarah B Porges, Classical Philology
Popkin, Debra, French Language & Literature
Portner, Irving Alan, Italian, Comparative Literature
Purczinsky, Julius O, Medieval Philology, Structural Linguistics
Quintian, Andres Rogelio, Spanish Linguistics
Ragusa, Olga, Italian, Comparative Literature
Raphael, Robert, Germanic Languages & Literatures
Rebay, Luciano, Italian Literature
Regalado, Antonio, Spanish Literature
Regalado, Nancy F, Romance Languages
Rengstorf, Michael E, French Language & Literature
Rensky, Miroslav, English, Linguistics
Riccardi, Theodore, Jr, Modern South Asian Languages, Sanskrit
Riffaterre, Michael, French
Rosen, Robert Samuel, German Comparative Literature
Rosoff, Gary H, Romance Languages, Linguistics
Rothschild, Suzanne Arvedon, Romance Language & Literature
Roudiez, Leon Samuel, Twentieth Century French Literature
Roy, Paulette B, French
Rubin, Mordecai S, Foreign Languages
Rywkin, Michael, Foreign Languages, Political Science
Sacks, Richard, Comparative Literature, Indo-European Linguistics
Sakrawa, Gertrud M, Modern Languages
Sallustio, Anthony Thomas, French, Spanish
Sander, Margaret M, German, Comparative Literature
Sander, Volkmar, Foreign Languages
Santirocco, Matthew Stephen, Classics
Sarolli, Gian Roberto, Romance Languages & Literature
Sayers, Raymond S, Romance Languages
Schaechter, Mordkhe, Yiddish Linguistics & Folklore
Scheindlin, Raymond Paul, Arabic & Hebrew Literature
Schneider, Marshall Jerrold, Spanish Literature, Applied Linguistics
Sealy, Robert J, French Language & Literature
Segel, Harold Bernard, Slavic Languages & Literatures
Seidensticker, Edward G, Japanese
Seittelman, Elizabeth Edith, Classical Languages & Literature
Selig, Karl-Ludwig, Romance Languages & Literature
Settle, James Norwood, Classical Languages
Shea, George W, Classical Languages
Shechter, Stanley Jacob, Classical Philology
Shevelov, George Yury, Slavic Philology
Shroder, Maurice Zorensky, French & Comparative Literature
Silver, Philip Warnock, Romance Languages
Slade, Carole, Comparative Literature, English
Soletsky, Albert Z, Spanish Language & Literature
Sourian, Eve, Romance Languages
Spininger, Dennis Joseph, Comparative Literature, Romanticism
Stadler, Eva Maria (Mrs Richard Brooks), French, Comparative Literature
Stamm, James Russell, Spanish Language & Literature
Stein, Jess, English, Linguistics
Stern, Anne Wellner, French Literature

Stern, Irwin, Luso-Brazilian Language & Literature
Stern, Jacob Howard, Classics
Stoffers, Maria Edlinger, Germanic Language & Linguistics
Szogyi, Alexander W, Romance Languages
Taran, Leonardo, Classics, Ancient Philosophy
Thompson, B Bussell, Spanish Medieval Literature
Tiefenbrun, Susan Wanda, French Literature
Tudisco, Anthony, Spanish
Ucelay, Margarita, Spanish
Van-Huy, Pierre Nguyen, French Literature, Psychology
Van Sickle, John Babcock, Classical & Comparative Literature
Visson, Lynn, Russian Language & Literature
Vitz, Evelyn Birge, French Medieval & French Renaissance Literature
Von Wiren-Garczynski, Vera, Slavic Languages & Literature
Waldinger, Renee, French Language & Literature
Ward, Ralph Lawrence, Classical Linguistics
Wedeck, Harry Ezekiel, Classical & Medieval Literature
Weinreich, Beatrice, Anthropology
Welles, Marcia Louise, Spanish Literature
Welton, Archibald James, Romance Languages
Willis, Robert M, English, Linguistics
Wolfe, Ethyle Renee, Classical Languages & Literature
Wolfe, Gerard Raymond, Foreign Languages
Wolman, Howard Bennett, Classical Languages, Ancient History
Yar-Shater, Ehsan, Literature, History
Yurieff, Zoya I, Russian Literature
Zephir, Jacques Joseph, French Language & Literature

Oakdale

Forchheimer, Paul, Lingusitcs, German

Olean

Wallace, Malcolm Vincent Timothy, Classics

Oneonta

Anderson, David L, Romance Languages
Basdekis, Demetrios, Modern Spanish Literature
Frye, Wendell Whitney, German Language & Literature
Macris, Peter John, German Language & Literature
Serra-Lima, Federico, Spanish Literature

Orangeburg

Grossman, Edith Marian, Latin American & Spanish Literature

Oswego

Diez Del Rio, Peter, Romance Languages
Fisher, John C, Linguistics, Literature
Hertz-Ohmes, Peter Donald, German Literature, Philosophy
Kaminsky, Amy Katz, Latin American Literature
Marshall, Thomas Edward, Romance Languages
Sabatini, Arthur Vincent, French Literature

Palenville

Flores, Angel, Comparative Literature

Pittsford

Coulter, Geoffrey Restall, Linguistics

Plattsburgh

Braga, Thomas, Foreign Languages, Literature
Doyle, Raymond Harold, Spanish Language & Literature
Hamblet, Edwin Joseph, Romance Languages
Kyritz, Heinz Georg, German

Port Jefferson

Dunham, Vera S, Slavic Languages & Literature

Port Washington

Bergel, Lienhard, Comparative Literature

Potsdam

Rothrauff, Conrad M, Classics, English

Poughkeepsie

Corcoran, Mary B, German Literature &
Philology
Day, James H, Classical Languages
Gittleman, Anne Iker, French Medieval
Literature
Gregg, Richard Alexander, Russian Literature
Hytier, Adrienne Doris, French
Lipschutz, Ilse Hempel, French
McKenzie, Margaret, German
Pope, Randolph D, Spanish & Latin American
Literature

Purchase

De La Portilla, Marta Rosa, Spanish Literature

Riverdale

Coman, Colette M, French Literature
O'Connor, Basilides Andrew, French Literature
Van Den Bossche, Edmond C, French &
Comparative Literature

Rochester

Beck, Hamilton Hammond Hagy, German
Literature & Language
Braun, Wilhelm, German Literature
Clark, William Harrington, German
Debevec Henning, Sylvie Marie, French
Doolittle, James, Romance Languages &
Literatures
Harrington, Ronald Vern, Slavic Languages,
General Linguistics
Klimas, Antanas, Linguistics
Lecumberri-Cilveti, Angel, Spanish Literature &
Philosophy
Locke, Frederick William, Classics, Comparative
Literature
Marceau, William Charles, French Literature
Moutsos, Demetrius George, Linguistics
Otto, Virginia, Foreign Languages
Reiff, Donald Gene, Linguistics
Rosen, Nathan, Russian Literature
Saisselin, Remy G, French Literature, Art
History
Snyder, Caroline Grote, German Literature,
English
Weinberg, Florence May, Romance Languages
Weinberg, Kurt, Comparative Literature
Wivell, Charles Joseph, Chinese Literature &
Language

Rockville Centre

Amor, Rose Teresa, Spanish Language &
Literature

St Bonaventure

Tomkiw, Bohdan Stephen, German, Political
Science
Wood, Paul William, French Language &
Literature

St James

Aronoff, Mark H, Morphology, Orthography
Godfrey, Aaron W, Classics

Saratoga Springs

Gelber, Lynne Levick, French & Comparative
Literature
Hubbard, Thomas Kent, Classical Languages
Karsen, Sonja Petra, Spanish
Nazzaro, Anthony M, French
Spear, Frederick Augustus, French
Sturm, Rudolf, Foreign Languages & Literatures
Swenson, Birgit Ewerts, French Literature

Sayville

Marino, Nicholas Joseph, Romance Languages

Schenectady

Ginsberg, Judith Ellen, Spanish Literature
Klemm, Frederick Alvin, Germanics
Lindsay, Frank Whiteman, French
Roberts, Alan, French
Thomas, William Wilfrid, French Literature

Seaford

Patkowski, Mark S, Applied Linguistics

Seneca Falls

Petrizzi, Daniel Joseph, Romance Language &
Literature

Snyder

Hagspiel, Robert, Languages

Staten Island

Brooks, Richard A, Comparative Literature
Mezzacappa, Carmine Anthony, Italian
Language & Literature
Willecke, Frederick Henry, German Literature

Stony Brook

Bieber, Konrad Ferdinand, French
Blum, Carol Kathlyn, French Literature
Brown, Frederick, Foreign Languages
Brown, Russell E, German Literature
Brugmans, Linette F, Romance Languages
Czerwinski, Edward J, Slavic Drama & Theatre,
Comparative Literature
Elling, Barbara Elizabeth, German Literature
Fainberg, Louise Vasvari, Spanish Medieval
Literature
Giordano, Jaime Anibal, Spanish-American
Literature
Haac, Oscar Alfred, Romance Languages
Hathorn, Richmond Yancey, Classical Languages
McKenna, James Brian, Romance Languages
Mills, Leonard Russell, Romance Languages
Petrey, Donald Sandy, French & Italian
Radley, Philippe Daniel, Slavic Languages &
Literatures
Rivers, Elias Lynch, Spanish
Ruplin, Ferdinand, German, Linguistics
Russell, John R, German Language & Literature
Sabat-Rivers, Georgina, Spanish Literature,
French
Sanders, Ivan, Comparative Literature, East
European Fiction
Sjoberg, Leif, Scandinavian Languages &
Literatures
Sridhar, S N, Linguistics, Foreign Languages &
Literatures
Vogel, Lucy Elaine, Russian Language &
Literature
Whitney, Mark Stewart, Foreign Languages
Wilson, Alice S, Comparative Literature, Classics
Zavala, Iris M, Romance Languages, Spanish
History
Zimmermann, Eleonore M, French, Comparative
Literature

Syracuse

Adorno, Rolena, Spanish
Archambault, Paul Joseph, French, Latin
Ayerbe-Chaux, Reinaldo, Spanish Literature
Bhatia, Tej K, Linguistics, India Literature &
Linguistics
Boot, Christine, Medieval German, Dutch
Language & Literature
Cannon, Joann Charlene, Italian
Davis, Hugh Hamlin, Classical Languages,
History
Ferran, Jaime, Foreign Languages
Hart, Thomas Elwood, Germanic Literature &
Language
Harth, Dorothy Eve, Foreign Languages
Lichtblau, Myron I, Spanish
McCort, Dennis Peter, German Language &
Literature
Matthews, John H, French
O'Reilly, Robert Francis, French & Comparative
Literature
Pallotta, Augustus G, Italian Literature
Pia, John Joseph, Linguistics
Ritchie, William Craig, Linguistics, Adult Second
Language Acquisition
Roberts, Louis William, Classical Languages,
Ancient Philosophy
Schneider, Gerd Klaus, German, Linguistics
Testa, Daniel Philip, Spanish Literature
Vetrano, Anthony Joseph, Romance Languages
Weber, J B, French, Romance Languages
Wiley, Raymond A, German Mythology &
Classical Literature

Tarrytown

Henle, Jane Elizabeth, Archeology, Literature

Troy

Der-Ohannesian, Jeanine Nelly, French, Spanish
Rogers, Adrienne, French
Seduro, Vladimir Ilyich, Foreign Languages &
Literature

Vestal

Wells, Lawrence David, German Language &
Literature

Wappingers Falls

Boyd, Lola Elizabeth, Romance Languages

West Point

Garcia, Frederick Charles Hesse, Portuguese
Language & Literature
Saldivar, Samuel G, Spanish & Hispanic
American Literatures

Williamsville

De Capua, Angelo George, German Literature
Silber, Gordon Rutledge, French & Italian
Literature
Silverman, Michael H, Hebrew & Judaic Studies

Yonkers

Barros, Eduardo Enrique, Spanish
Bayerschmidt, Carl Frank, Germanic Philology
Fowkes, Robert Allen, Linguistics
Sacoto, Antonio, Spanish & Latin American
Literature
Stevens, Cj, Speech

NORTH CAROLINA

Asheville

Cranston, Philip Edward, Romance Languages &
Literatures
Renfroe, Walter Jackson, Jr, Foreign Languages
Thurman, William Sims, Roman History, Greco-
Roman Law
White, Diane Virginia, German Language &
Literature

Blowing Rock

Jordan, Emil Leopold, German Literature

Boiling Springs

Morgan, Robert Earle, French, Mathematics

Boone

Welden, Alicia Galaz-Vivar, Spanish Literature,
Latin American Poetry

Buies Creek

Burkot, Alexander Roman, Romance &
Germanic Languages

Cedar Mountain

Viens, Claude Paul, French Literature

Chapel Hill

Allen, Walter, Jr, Latin
Black, Joel Dana, Comparative Literature,
Cultural History
Brown, Edwin Louis, Classics
Casado, Pablo Gil, Spanish Literature
Clark, Fred M, Spanish Golden Age Literature
Cortes, Julio, Arabic Language
Daniel, George B, Jr, French Literature
Debreczeny, Paul, Russian Literature
Dessen, Cynthia Sheldon, Roman Literature
Duffey, Frank Marion, Spanish
Ebersole, Alva Vernon, Jr, Spanish Language &
Literature
Else, Gerald Frank, Classical Studies
Engstrom, Alfred Garvin, French
Falk, Eugene Hannes, French Language &
Literature
Flax, Neil M, Comparative Literature, German
Friederich, Werner Paul, German & Comparative
Literature
Ganz, David, Classical & Medieval Latin
Gates, Henry Phelps, Classical Linguistics
Haig, Irvine Reid Stirling, French

Chapel Hill, NORTH CAROLINA (cont)

Hardre, Jacques, French Literature
Henry, Eric Putnam, Chinese Literature & History
Houston, George Woodard, Latin Literature, Roman History
Howren, Robert, Linguistics
Illiano, Antonio, Romance Languages & Literatures
Immerwahr, Henry Rudolph, Classics
Kennedy, George Alexander, Classics
Lawson, Richard Henry, German
Linderski, Jerzy, Classical Languages, Ancient History
Lore, Anthony George, Romance Languages
Mack, Sara, Classical Philology
Maissen (della Casacrap), Augustin, Romance Languages, Minor Romance Philology
Maley, Catherine Anne, Romance Linguistics
Marti, Berthe Marie, Classical Philology
Masters, George Mallary, Romance Languages
Mews, Siegfried, German, Comparative Literature
Michels, Agnes Kirsopp Lake, Classics
Mihailovich, Vasa D, Slavic Languages & Literatures
Morot-Sir, Edouard B, History Of Ideas, Literary Criticism
Perez, Rosa Perelmuter, Colonial Spanish American Literature
Reckford, Kenneth J, Classics
Salgado, Maria Antonia, Romance Languages
Sasson, Jack Murad, Foreign Languages, History
Scaglione, Aldo Domenico, Italian & Comparative Literature
Schweitzer, Christoph Eugen, German
Scott-Jones, Marilyn Ann, Modern German Literature, German Lyric
Sharpe, Lawrence A, Romance Languages
Sheerin, Daniel Joseph, Medieval Latin, Patristics
Sherman, Carol Lynn, Eighteenth-Century French Literature
Smith, Peter Mullen, Greek Literature & Philosophy
Smith, Sidney Rufus, Jr, Germanic Languages
Snipes, Hampton Kenneth, Byzantine Literature & History
Solmsen, Friedrich (Heinrich Rudolf), Classical Philology
Stadter, Philip Austin, Classical Literature
Stambaugh, Ria, Germanic Language & Literature
Stoudemire, Sterling Aubrey, Spanish
Tax, Petrus W, Germanic Languages & Literatures
Tsiapera, Maria, Linguistics, Arabic
Vickery, Walter, Slavic Language & Literature
Vogler, Frederick Wright, Romance Languages
West, William Custis, III, Classics
Wiley, William Leon, French Literature
Wooten, Cecil William, French, Classics
Worth, Fabienne Andre, French Literature, Cinema

Charlotte

Bush, Newell Richard, Foreign Languages
Gabriel, Karl Michael, German, English
Gleaves, Robert Milnor, Spanish Language, Spanish American Literature
Hedges, James Stoy, Linguistics, American Literature
Hopper, Edward Warren, Spanish Language & Literature
Lassaletta, Manuel Claudio, Spanish Literature, Linguistics
Saman, Paul Antonius, Foreign Languages
Suther, Judith D, French & Comparative Literature
Tucker, Robert Whitney, Linguistics, Classics
Turner, Elbert Daymond, Jr, Spanish

Cullowhee

Haberland, Paul Mallory, German Literature & Language
Sutton, Lewis F, French

Davidson

Causey, James Young, Spanish Literature
Davies, Mark Ingraham, Classical Art & Literature
Ghigo, Francis, Romance Languages
Jacobus, Everett Franklin, Jr, French
Labban, George, Jr, Classical Languages & Literature
Walker, Hallam, Romance Languages

Winkler, Julius S, Foreign Languages
Wruck, Erich-Oskar Joachim Siegfried, German
Yoder, Lauren Wayne, French Language & Literature

Dunn

Britt, Claude Henry, Jr, Hispanic Language & Literature

Durham

Alt, Arthur Tilo, Germanic Languages
Andresen, Julie Tetel, History & Philosophy of Linguistics
Apte, Mahadev L, Linguistics & Anthropology
Avalle-Arce, Diane Pamp de, Spanish Literature
Avalle-Arce, Juan Bautista, Spanish
Borchardt, Frank L, German
Burian, Peter Hart, Classical Studies
Butters, Ronald Richard, Dialectology, Linguistic Theory
Caserta, Ernesto Giuseppe, Italian Literature
Cordle, Thomas Howard, French
Davis, Gifford, Romance Languages
Di Bona, Joseph, International & Comparative Studies
Fein, John Morton, Spanish
Fowlie, Wallace, French Literature
Garci-Gomez, Miguel, Spanish Language & Literature
Hedges, Inez Kathleen, Comparative Literature, French Literature
Horry, Ruth Naomi, French Literature
Hull, Alexander, French
Jackson, Irene Dobbs, French, Latin
Krynski, Magnus Jan, Slavic Languages
Newton, Francis Lanneau, Latin
Osuna, Rafael, Romance Languages
Perez-Firmat, Gustavo, Modern Hispanic Literature
Phelpa, Leland Richter, German
Predmore, Richard Lionel, Spanish
Richardson, Emeline Hill, Classical Archeology
Richardson, Lawrence, Jr, Latin Archeology
Rigsby, Kent Jefferson, Classical Languages, Ancient History
Rolleston, James Lancelot, Germanic Languages
Rosenberg, Donald Karl, Medieval German Language & Literature
Salinger, Herman, German & Comparative Literature
Siddiqi, Mohammed Moazzam, Indo-Persian Literature
Stanley, Denis Keith, Jr, Classical Languages
Stewart, Joan Hinde, French Literature
Stewart, Philip Robert, French Literature
Tetel, Marcel, Romance Languages
Vincent, Patrick Russell, French Literature
Wardropper, Bruce Wear, Romance Languages
Willis, William Hailey, Classical Philology

Elon College

Cepas, Kostas Vytautas, Foreign Languages

Greensboro

Almeida, Jose Agustin, Spanish Language & Literature
Archibald, Brigitte Edith, Germanic Language & Literature
Atkinson, James Carroll, Romance Languages
Baecker, Anne, German
Baer, Joachim Theodor, Foreign Languages
Bell, Sarah Fore, Romance Languages
Brewer, Jeutonne Patten, Linguistics, English
Fein, David Alan, French
Felt, William Norcross, Romance Languages
Gochberg, Herbert S, French
Goode, William Osborne, French Literature
Hoy, Camilla, French, Spanish
Kish, Kathleen Vera, Spanish Literature
Koenig, Jean-Paul Francois Xavier, French, African Literature
Lagos, Ramiro, Spanish & Spanish American Literature
McSpadden, George Elbert, Spanish Language & Literature
Newton, Robert Parr, Modern German Literature, Stylistics
Rener, Frederick M, German
Sanchez-Boudy, Jose, Linguistics, Latin American Literature
Smith, Mark Israel, Modern Latin American Literature
Smith, Roch Charles, French Literature, Spanish
Whitaker, Shirley Blue, Spanish

Greenville

Aronson, Nicole Habatjou, French Literature & Civilization
Bassman, Michael Frederic, Philology, Foreign Language
Fernandez, Joseph Anthony, Romance Languages
Malby, Maria Bozicevic, Russian & Serbo-Croatian Languages & Literatures
Mayberry, Nancy Kennington, Spanish Drama & Literature
Resnik, Bramy, German
Wright, James Richard, Linguistics, Spanish

Hickory

Blakey, John Mawson, Classics
Clayton, Laura Bland, Classics, English
Keller, Werner Oswin, German
Shuford, William Harris, Romance Languages

Mars Hill

Knapp, Richard Gilbert, French Literature & Language
Macoy, Katherine Wallis, Spanish & Latin American Literature
Obergfell, Sandra Cheshire, Medieval French Literature

Raleigh

Burnett, David Graham, French Literature, Humanities
Dahlin, Lois Ann, French Language & Literature
Duda, Sadik Tufan, Russian, German
Feeny, Thomas Paul, Spanish Language & Literature
Gonzalez, Alan Angel, Hispanic Languages & Literature
Holler, William McFall, Romance Philology, French Literature
Kaplan, Arthur, Greek & Latin Classics
Kelly, John Rivard, Spanish, Portuguese
Paschal, Mary, Romance Languages
Poland, George Waverly, Modern Languages
Rollins, Ernest William, Jr, German
Rollins, Yvonne Bargues, French Literature
Smith, Gilbert Graves, Spanish Language & Literature
Stack, Edward MacGregor, French Language & Literature
Tucker, Harry, Jr, German Literature

Salisbury

Reitz, Richard Allen, Spanish

Statesville

Hostettler, Agnes Freudenberg, German Language & Literature

Wilmington

Beeler, James Rush, Romance Languages
Randall, William Madison, Linguistics
Sparks, Jackson Gillen, Romance Languages
Whitted, Joseph Willard, Spanish Literature
Woodhouse, William Walton, III, Spanish Literature

Winston-Salem

Andronica, John Louis, Classical Languages
Bree, Germaine, French Literature
Bryant, Shasta M, Spanish Literature
Bueno, Julian Lopez, Medieval Spanish Literature
Cardwell, Walter Douglas, Jr, French Literature, French Language
Fraser, Ralph Sidney, German
Glenn, Kathleen Mary, Spanish Literature
Harris, Carl Vernon, Classical Languages & Literature
King, Harry Lee, Jr, Romance Languages
Margitic, Milorad R, French Literature
Martin, Gregorio Cervantes, Spanish Literature
Newton, Candelas Maria, Foreign Languages
O'Flaherty, James Carneal, German
Parker, John Ernest, Jr, Romance Languages
Shoemaker, Richard Lee, French
Tillett, Anne Smith, Modern Foreign Languages
Ulery, Robert Warren, Jr, Classical Languages & Literatures

NORTH DAKOTA

Fargo

Lacy, Gregg Farnsworth, French
Lacy, Margriet Bruyn, French, German

Grand Forks

Brekke, Arne, Germanic Philology
Georgacas, Demetrius John, Classics
Hildebrandt, Bruno Franz, Germanistics,
    Linguistics
Marshall, David Franklin, English Linguistics
Morgan, William Ingraham, German
Patterson, Channing Ford, Languages, Mexican
    Studies
Schwartz, Lucy McCallum, Modern French
    Literature
Schwartz, Paul Jacob, French Literature

OHIO

Ada

Davey, Donald William, Spanish, Portuguese

Akron

Lepke, Arno Karl, German, French
Lijeron, Hugo, Romance Languages, Spanish-
    Romanic Philology
Mackiw, Theodore, East European History,
    Russian
Maio, Eugene Anthony, Hispanic Language &
    Literature
Miller, William Irvin, Spanish Language &
    Literature
Stuyvesant, Phillip Wayne, Nineteenth Century
    Spanish Literature
Weingartner, Russell, French Literature &
    Linguistics
Yetiv, Isaac, French & Hebrew Language &
    Literature

Ashland

Bihari, Stephen T, French Literature

Athens

Bond, Zinny Sans, Linguistics
Burns, Joseph M, German Language &
    Literature
Cameron, Wallace John, Spanish Language &
    Literature
Carrier, Carl Edward, German Literature
Coady, James Martin, Linguistics
Dewees, Will, Linguistics, Writing
Flum, Philip Newton, Romance Philology,
    Linguistics
Franz, Thomas Rudy, Spanish Literature
Hinkle, Douglas Paddock, Spanish Literature,
    Romance Linguistics
LaJohn, Lawrence Anthony, Spanish
Lawson, Ursula D, German Literature &
    Philosophy
Murphy, Paul Robert, Latin
Parsons, Adelaide Heyde, Psycholinguistics
Schneider, Gilbert Donald, Linguistics &
    Anthropology
Serna-Maytorena, Manuel Antonio, Spanish,
    Latin American Literature
Wrage, Marie-Claire Connes, French
    Renaissance Literature
Wrage, William, French

Berea

Sinnema, John Ralph, German

Bowling Green

Bradford, Carole A, Spanish & French
Gray, Joseph LaRue, III, German Language &
    Literature
Pallister, Janis Louise, Romance Languages
Povsic, Boleslav Selic, Classics
Pretzer, Diana Goodrich, Romance Languages
Van Beysterveldt, Antony A, Spanish Language
    & Literature
Wolfe, Warren Jerrold, French

Cincinnati

Arden, Heather Marlene, Medieval & French
    Literature
Bleznick, Donald William, Romance Languages
Boulter, Cedric Gordon, Classical Archeology
Brichto, Herbert Chanan, Bible, Near Eastern
    Studies
Burrell, Paul Bakewell, French
Caskey, John Langdon, Archeology, Classics
Cohen, Getzel Mendelson, Classics
Coughlin, Edward V, Romance Languages
Fenik, Bernard Carl, Classics
Friedrichsmeyer, Erhard Martin, German
Galt, Alan Baker, German Language Pedagogy &
    Literature
Glenn, Jerry, German
Greenberg, Irwin L, Romance Languages
Greengus, Samuel, Semitic Philology
Hamilton, James Francis, French Literature &
    Language
Harkins, Paul William, Classical Languages
Harris, Edward Paxton, German Language &
    Literature
Huvos, Kornel, Romance Languages &
    Literatures
Jerusalmi, Isaac, Bible, Semitics
Knorre, Martha Lee, Spanish
Mahler, Annemarie Ettinger, Comparative
    Literature, History of Art
Merkel, Gottfried Felix, German
Mills, Carl Rhett, Linguistics, English Literacy
Murray, Robert J, Classical Languages
Muyskens, Judith Ann, Foreign Language
    Education, French Civilization
O'Connor, Patricia W, Romance Languages
Orvieto, Enzo Umberto, Italian Language &
    Literature
Paper, Herbert Harry, Linguistics
Pauls, John P, Russian Language & Literature
Rettig, John William, Classical Languages,
    Patrology
Richert, Hans-Georg, German Philology &
    Literature
Slessarev, Helga, German Literature
Slotkin, Edgar Morris, Celtic Literatures
Smith, Louis Francis, French Language &
    Literature
Spicehandler, Ezra Zevi, Modern Hebrew
    Literature
Tsevat, Matitiahu, Bible, Semitic Languages
Valencia, Juan Octavio, Spanish Poetry of the
    Golden Age
Weinberg, Werner, Hebrew
Weisberg, David B, Assyriology
Wilhite, John F, Spanish Language & Literature
Winter, John F, French Literature
York, Anthony Delano, Biblical Literature,
    Semitic Languages

Cleveland

Aube, Lucien Arthur, Seventeenth Century
    French Literature
Bartelemez, Erminnie Hollis, Germanic
    Philology
Beatie, Bruce A, Medieval & Folk Literature
Bynum, David Eliab, Eastern European Oral
    Literature
Diaconoff, Suellen, Eighteenth Century French
    Novel
Greppin, John Aird Coutts, Linguistics
Guralnik, David Bernard, Lexicography
Heiser, Mary Margaret, Linguistics, French
    Language
Hinze, Klaus-Peter Wilhelm, German &
    Comparative Literature
Koerner, Charlotte Wittkowski, German
    Literature & Language
Konrad, Alexander N, Russian & German
    Language, Literature
Kostoroski-Kadish, Emilie Pauline, French
    Language & Literature
Labrador, Jose Julian, Spanish Language &
    Literature
Laing, Donald Rankin, Jr, Classics, Ancient
    History
Lairet, Dolores Person, French Language &
    Literature
Long, Herbert Strainge, Classics, History of
    Ancient Philosophy
Luther, Gisela, German Literature & Language
Oberhelman, Steven Michael, Classical
    Languages, Byzantine History
Poduska, Donald Miles, Classical Languages
Purcell, John Marshall, Foreign Language
    Education, Spanish
Reeves, Charles Howell, Classical Philology
Saha, Prosanta Kumar, English, Linguistics
Salm, Peter, German, Comparative Literature

Small, Richard B, French Language & Literature
Stoll, Anita Kay, Spanish Language & Literature
Strauss, Walter Adolf, Romance Languages
Zorita, Celestino Angel, Spanish Literature,
    Classical Languages

Cleveland Heights

Hinze, Diana Orendi, German

Columbus

Abbott, Kenneth Morgan, Classical Philology
Allen, Edward David, Foreign Language
    Education
Astier, Pierre Arthur Georges, Romance
    Languages
Babb, Georgiana, German, Linguistics
Babcock, Charles Luther, Classics
Bekker, Hugo, German
Belkin, Johanna S, German, Philology
Bennett, John Michael, Spanish American
    Literature, Creative Writing
Benseler, David Price, German
Beynen, G(ijsbertus) Koolemans, Slavic
    Bibliography & Folklore
Bonin, Therese Marcelle, Foreign Language
Borker, David, Slavic Language & Literature
Bulatkin, Eleanor Webster, Romance Philology
Cadora, Frederick Joseph, Arabic Language &
    Linguistics
Caires, Valerie Anne, Comparative Literature,
    Greek
Callaghan, Catherine A, Linguistics
Carlut, Charles E, Romance Languages &
    Literatures
Castillo, Rafael Federico, Hispanic Poetry,
    Comparative Literature
Ching, Eugene, Chinese
Churma, Donald George, Linguistics, African
    Languages
Cottrell, Robert Duane, French Literature
Davis, John T, Classical Philology
DeStefano, Johanna Sue, Linguistics
Dowty, David R, Linguistics
Farina, Luciano Fernando, Italian,
    Computational Linguistics
Fleischhauer, Wolfgang, Germanic Philology
Forbes, Clarence Allen, Classical Philology
Garcia-Castaneda, Salvador, Spanish Literature
Garnica, Olga K, Linguistics
Gribble, Charles Edward, Slavic Languages
Griffin, David Alexander, Romance Languages
Haas, Werner, German, History
Haenicke, Diether Hans, German Literature &
    Philology
Hahm, David Edgar, Classical Languages,
    Intellectual History
Hatton, Robert Wayland, Romance Languages
Hoffmann, Charles Wesley, German Literature
Howden, Marcia S, French Linguistics,
    Structural Semantics
Hsueh, Feng-Sheng, Chinese
Iglesias, Mario, Spanish Language & Literature
Jarvis, Gilbert Andrew, Foreign Language
    Education
Jones, Lowanne Elizabeth, Old French Literature
    & Language
Joseph, Brian Daniel, Linguistics, Indo-European
    Studies
Kalbouss, George, Russian Language &
    Literature, Drama
Keller, Hans-Erich, Medieval French Literature,
    History of Romance Languages
Klopp, Charles, Italian Literature
Krzyzanowski, Jerzy Roman, Slavic Languages &
    Literature
Lao, Yan-Shuan, Chinese Language, Literature &
    History
Larson, Donald Roy, Spanish Literature
Lehiste, Ilse, Linguistics
Lenardon, Robert Joseph, Classics
Levisi, Margarita, Romance Languages
Light, Timothy, East Asian Languages &
    Literature
Lisko, Bonnie D, Foreign Languages
McElrath, Miles Kenneth, Jr, Japanese Language
    & Literature, Linguistics
Mancini, Albert Nicholas, Literary History
Matejic, Mateja, Slavic Languages & Literatures
Mayne, Judith, French, Film
Meiden, Walter, Romance Languages
Morford, Mark Percy Owen, Classics, Ancient
    History
Morita, James R, Japanese Literature
Nacci, Chris Natale, Modern Languages
Naylor, Kenneth Edwin, Slavic Languages,
    Linguistics
Nelson, Donald Frederick, German Literature &
    Linguistics

Columbus, OHIO (cont)

Newman, Lawrence W, Jr, Slavic Languages & Literature
Oulanoff, Hongor, Russian Literature & Language
Redenbarger, Wayne Jacob, Romance Linguistics, Portuguese
Rentschler, Eric, German Literature, Cinema
Robinson, David Franklin, Slavic & Baltic Linguistics
Rosbotton, Ronald Carlisle, French Literature
Rudavsky, Tamar, Medieval Philosophy
Rugaleva, Anelya Elizabeth, Slavic Languages, Linguistics
Schlam, Carl C, Classics
Schmidt, Henry Jacques, German Literature
Silbajoris, Frank R, Russian Language & Literature
Snyder, Jane McIntosh, Greek & Latin Literature
Steele, Cynthia, Latin American & Spanish Literature
Stelten, Leo Frederick, Classical Languages
Tracy, Stephen Victor, Classical Philology
Twarog, Leon Ignace, Slavic Languages & Literatures
Tyler, Royall, Japanese Literature
von Ohlen, Henry Bruce, French
Williams, Charles Garfield Singer, French Literature, Comparative Literature
Zwicky, Arnold Melchior, Linguistics

Dayton

Horn, Pierre Laurence, French, Comparative Literature
Hye, Allen Edward, German & Scandinavian Literature
Islam, A K M Aminul, Anthropology, Linguistics
Matual, David Michael, Russian
Racevskis, Karlis, French
Zeinz, Joseph Henry, Classical Languages & Literature

Delaware

Bauerle, Richard F, Linguistics
Blanchard, Homer Disbro, Linguistics
Courtney, Alice Kaaren, French Literature, Women's Studies
Guddat, Kurt Herbert, German
Harper, Sandra Nadine, Romance Languages
Harter, Hugh A, Foreign Languages
Lateiner, Donald, Classical Studies, Ancient History

Fairborn

Larkins, James Edward, Spanish

Findlay

Holzhauser, Emil K, Classical & Modern Languages, Philosophy
Nye, Jean C, Romance Languages

Gambier

Bennett, Robert Ernest, Ancient History, Greek & Latin
Fink, Robert Orwill, Latin, Ancient History
Goodhand, Robert, French
Harvey, John Edward, Jr, Romance Languages
Haywood, Bruce, German
McCulloh, William Ezra, Classical Languages & Literatures
Weber, Clifford Whitbeck, Classics

Granville

Alvarez, Nicolas Emilio, Latin American Studies & Literature
Armas, Joseph R de, Romance Languages, Latin American Area Studies
Emont, Milton D, Foreign Languages
Preston, Fred Lorenzo, French
Steele, Charles W, Languages

Hamersville

Friskney, Thomas Edwin, Classical Greek, New Testament

Hiram

Adams, Charles Lindsey, Romance Languages
Gauthier, George Joseph, Romance Languages

Kent

Kane, John Robert, Medieval French Literature
Manley, Timothy McLemore, Linguistics
Mellen, Philip Allan, German Literature, German Language
Muratore, Mary Jo, French Classical Literature
Parks, John H, Latin, Greek
Perez, Aquilino, Spanish
Radcliff-Umstead, Douglas, Romance Languages
Tapp, Henry L, Linguistics, Philology

Marietta

Amash, Paul J, Romance Languages
Kaminski, Edmund Joseph, Foreign Languages
Schwartz, Henry Charles, Romance Languages

Newark

Tebben, Joseph Richard, Classics

New Concord

Mitrovich, Mirco, Foreign Languages

Oberlin

Arrojo, Fernando, Spanish Culture & Civilization
Casson, Ronald William, Anthropology, Linguistics
Greenberg, Nathan Abraham, Classical Philology
Helm, James Joel, Classical Studies
Johnson, Dale Ralph, Chinese Poetry & Drama
Kryzytski, Serge, Russian Literature & Language
Kurtz, John William, German Literature
McNaughton, William F, Chinese Language & Literature
Nortwick, Thomas Van, Classical Languages & Literature
Reichard, Joseph Ruch, German
Rosenfeld, Sidney, German Literature
Rossi, Vinio, Romance Languages
Shepard, Sanford, Spanish
Skrupskelis, Viktoria, Romance Languages, French
Van Nortwick, Thomas, Classical Languages & Literature
Zipser, Richard Alfred, German Literature

Oxford

Bahr, Gisela Elise, Modern German Literature
Creech, James Narvin, French Literature
Dutra, John Anthony, Classical Languages
Fiber, Louise, French Language & Literature
Franzblau, Daniel, Foreign Language
Fuller, Helene R, Linguistics, English
Greenberg, Mitchell David, Romance Languages & Literature
Kamuf, Peggy, French Literature & Criticism
Leigh, James Anthony, French Literature, Comparative Literature
Listerman, Randall Wayne, Modern Languages
Luce, Stanford Leonard, French Language & Literature
Moloney, Raymond L, Spanish & Portuguese Language & Literature
Morenberg, Max, Linguistics, Composition
Phillips, Robert N, Jr, Phonetics, Phonology
Plater, Edward M V, German
Rose, Peter Wires, Classical Philology
Runyon, Randolph Paul, French Literature, American Studies
Sandro, Paul Denney, French Language & Literature
Sanger, Curt, German Language, Modern German Literature
Steiniger, Erich Wilhelm, Germanic Philology
Thornton, Mary Elizabeth Kelly, Classics, Humanities
Tomarken, Annette Herdman, French
Vazquez, Washington Rampa, Hispanic Languages & Literature
Wilhelm, Robert McKay, Classics
Wing, Nathaniel, French Literature

Painesville

Jones, Marilyn Scarantino, Spanish & Comparative Literature
Nugent, Robert L, French
Pick, Ernest, Romance Languages
Rubio, Susana Gonzales, Spanish Language & Literature

Parma

Mykyta, Larysa Ann, French Literature

Springfield

Fickert, Kurt Jon, German, Language & Literature

Stow

Crawford, Ronald Lee, German Literature

Tiffin

Horvay, Frank Dominic, Foreign Languages
Kramer, Frank Raymond, Classical History

Toledo

Abu-Absi, Samir, Linguistics
Feustle, Joseph A, Jr, Latin American Literature
Kuk, Zenon M, Slavic Languages & Literatures
Moreno, Ernesto Enrique, Spanish Language & Literature
Normand, Guessler, French Literature, Foreign Language Education
Pulleyn, John William, Jr, French
Scanlan, Timothy Michael, French Literature

Westerville

Vance, Sylvia Phillips, French Literature & History

Willoughby

Knight, Adele Irene, Classical Languages

Wooster

Day, Leslie Preston, Classical Archeology & Languages
Durham, Carolyn Ann, French Language & Literature
Holliday, Vivian Loyrea, Classics, Ancient History
Peyton, Myron Alvin, Hispanic Literature
Schreiber, William Ildephonse, Foreign Languages
Valencia, Pablo, Romance Linguistics

Xenia

Kingsbury, Edwin C, Old Testament, Semitic Languages

Yellow Springs

Otten, Anna Von Kutschig, French & German Language & Literature

Youngstown

Aliberti, Domenico Bernardino, Italian & Latin Languages & Literature
Dykema, Christine Rhoades, Foreign Languages
Ives, David Scott, Classics, Comparative Literature
Loud, Mary Beth, Spanish Literature & Language
Secrist, Robert Herold, II, English Linguistics
Viehmeyer, L Allen, German Literature & Linguistics

OKLAHOMA

Ada

Herman, Jack Chalmers, Spanish, French

Bethany

Huhnke, Geraldine Mae, Spanish German

Durant

Fouillade, Claude Jean, French, Romance Philology

Lawton

Stanley, George Edward, Linguistics, German

Muskogee

Van Tuyl, Charles Don, Tibetan Language & Literature

Norman

Abbott, James Hamilton, Spanish
Artman, Jim Paine, Spanish Literature
Catlin, John Stanley, Classics
Clement, Besse Alberta, French
Drechsel, Emanuel Johannes, Linguistics
Dunham, Lowell, Modern Languages
Eichholz, Erich Herbert, German Language & Literature
Feiler, Seymour, French
Fife, James David, French, Spanish
Horwitz, William James, Ancient Near Eastern Civilizations
Ivask, Ivar Vidrik, German, Comparative Literature
Madland, Helga Stipa, German Literature & Language
Nolan, Philip Jerome, Classics, Comparative Literature
Payne, Ancil Newton, Jr, Classical Philology
Wallis, Richard Tyrrell, Classics, Ancient Philosophy

Shawnee

Combe, Guy P, French

Stillwater

Deveny, John Joseph, Jr, Spanish Language
Garcia-Saez, Santiago, Spanish Literature, French
Joseph, John Earl, Linguistics & Literature
Lin, Paaul Puo-Yaun, Chinese Linguistics & Literature
Schillinger, John Arthur, Russian Literature
Schrader, Dorothy Lynne, French
Schweitzer, John Louis, French, Linguistics
Southard, Oscar Bruce, II, English & General Linguistics
Wigtil, David Norval, Classical Languages

Tulsa

Schwarz, Martin, Romance Languages, French Literature
Weber, Charles Edgar, German

OREGON

Ashland

Miller, John Louis, German, Music

Corvallis

Cadart-Ricard, Odette Marie-Helene, French, Education
Carroll, Carleton Warren, French Language
Carson, Jane Isabelle, French Novel
Kraft, Walter Carl, German, Spanish
Lusetti, Walter Italo, Spanish Education
Malueg, Sara Ellen, Romance Language, Comparative Literature
Rossbacher, Peter Georg, Russian Language & Literature
Sjogren, Christine Oertel, Language, Literature
Wahlgren, Erik, Scandinavian Philology

Eugene

Ayora, Jorge Rodrigo, Spanish-American Literature
Beall, Chandler Baker, Romance Languages
Beebe, John Fred, Slavic Linguistics
Bien, Gloria, Comparative Literature
Birn, Randi Marie, French & Scandinavian Literature
Calin, William Compaine, French
DeLancey, Scott Cameron, Linguistics
Desroches, Richard Henry, Romance Languages
Diller, Edward, German
Dougherty, David Mitchell, French Language & Literature
Epple, Juan Armando, Spanish American Literature
Gontrum, Peter B, German & Comparative Literature
Hahn, Walter Lucian, German Literature
Hart, Thomas Roy, Romance Languages & Literature
Hatzantonis, Emmanuel S, Romance Languages
Johnson, Carl Leonard, Romance Philology
Kohl, Stephen William, Japanese Language & Literature
Leppmann, Wolfgang A, German
Lowenstam, Steven, Classical Languages
McClain, Yoko Matsuoka, Japanese Language & Literature

McWilliams, James Robert, German
Marlow, Elisabeth A, Romance Languages
May, Barbara Dale, Spanish Literature, Literary Criticism
Nadar, Thomas Raymond, Twentieth Century German Drama & Cinema
Nicholls, Roger Archibald, German
Palandri, Angela Chih-Ying Jung, Chinese Language & Literature
Pascal, Cecil Bennett, Classical Philology
Plant, Helmut R, German
Powers, Perry John, Spanish Literature
Rendall, Steven Finlay, Romance & Comparative Literature
Woods, Jean Muir, German
Zuck, Outi Virpi, Scandinavian Literature

McMinnville

Richardson, Peter Nichols, Germanic Philology

Monmouth

Alva, Charles (Allen), Linguistics, Language

Portland

Andereggen, Anton Joseph, Romance Linguistics, French Literature
Danon, Samuel, Romance Languages
Engelhardt, Klaus Heinrich, French Literature
Ferrua, Pietro Michele Stefano, Romance Languages & Literatures
Flori, Monica Roy, Latin American & Spanish Literature
Greis, Naguib A F, English, Arabic
Lobo Filho, Blanca, Romance Languages
Locher, Kaspar Theodore, Comparative Literature, German
Macias, Manuel Jato, Spanish
Parshall, Linda Bryant, Medieval German Literature
Peachy, Frederic, Classics
Peters, H Frederick, German & Comparative Literature
Rudolf, Ottomar I, Germanic Languages, Humanities
Wilberger, Carolyn Hope, French Language & Literature
Wilson, Baxter Douglas, English Philology

The Dalles

Simons, Gary Francis, Linguistics, Computational Linguistics

PENNSYLVANIA

Aaronsburg

Buehne, Sheema Z, German Literature & Language

Abington

Cintas, Pierre Francois Diego, General & French Linguistics

Allentown

Brunner, John Wilson, German
Conner, William Boudinot, Romance Languages & Linguistics
Kipa, Albert Alexander, German & Slavic Literature
Schneer, Richard James, Spanish, Portuguese
Syben, Isolde, Foreign Languages
Webb, Kenneth, Spanish, French
Wegener, Adolph Herman, German Language & Literature
Wind, Robert Lewis, Classics

Annville

Piel, Sara Elizabeth, Modern Languages

Bala-Cynwyd

Sellin, Eric, French, Comparative Literature

Bellefonte

Ebbinghaus, Ernst A, Germanic Philology

Berwick

Tonolo, Alfred E, Spanish

Bethlehem

DeAngeli, Edna Sophia, Classical Languages
Feaver, Douglas David, Classical Languages & Archaeology
Fifer, Elizabeth, Comparative Literature, English
Gardner, Arthur Parcel, German Literature
Lewis, David Wilfrid Paul, Modern languages
O'Connor, John Joseph, Computational Linguistics
Pirscenok, Anna (Mrs Julius M Herz), Slavic & Baltic Studies
Rubenstein, Herbert, Psycholinguistics, Linguistics
Valenzuela, Victor Manuel, Romance Languages
Van Eerde, John Andrews, Romance Languages

Bloomsburg

Carpenter, Charles Whitney, II,, Germanic Philology
Murphy, Allen Forrest, Foreign Languages, Spanish
Neel, George Washington, IV, German & Romance Languages
Smith, Riley Blake, English, Linguistics
Smithner, Eric W, French & Classics

Blue Bell

Anderson, Charlotte M, German Literature

Bryn Mawr

Banziger, Hans, German Literature
Davidson, Dan E, Russian Language & Literature
Dersofi, Nancy, Italian, Comparative Literature
Dickerson, Gregory Weimer, Classical Languages & Literature
Dorian, Nancy Currier, Linguistics, Germanic & Celtic Languages
Flaherty, Marie Gloria, German Literature & Literary Criticism
Gaisser, Julia Haig, Classical Philology
Gonzalez-Muela, Joaquin, Spanish Language & Literature
Hamilton, Richard, Greek Literature
Jaeger, Charles Stephen, German Literature of the Middle Ages
King, Willard Fahrenkamp, Spanish Literature
Lafarge, Catherine, Romance Languages
Lang, Mabel Louise, Classical Philology
Langer, Ullrich Gert, French Literature
Lograsso, Angeline Helen, Romance Philology, History
Maurin, Mario, French
Pearce, Ruth Lilienthal, Comparative Linguistics
Scott, Russell T, Jr, Latin, Italian Archaeology
Uhlfelder, Myra L, Classics

California

Marsh, John Osborn, Romance Languages

Carlisle

Angiolillo, Paul Francis, Romance Languages
Bogojavlensky, Marianna, Russian Language
Henderson, John Stanton, French
Lockhart, Philip N, Classical Studies
Sider, Robert Dick, Classics, Religion

Chalfont

MacDonald, Gerald John, Spanish Philology & Medieval Literature

Chambersburg

Kellinger, Josef Michael, German

Chester

Goodale, Hope K, Spanish
Melzi, Robert C, Romance Languages

Cheyney

Applewhite, James V, Romance Languages

PENNSYLVANIA (cont)

Clarion

Bays, Gwendolyn M, French, German
Garcia, Jose G, Spanish
Junod, Alfred E, French
Nikoulin, Dilara, Russian Literature & History
Totten, Christine M, German Literature, Cultural History

Collegeville

Clouser, Robin A, German Literature
Lloyd, Danuta Swiecicka, German Literature
Thelen, Lynn Marsha, Medieval Literature
Wickersham, John Moore, Classical Studies, Ancient History

Easton

Arboleda, Joseph R, Modern Spanish Literature
Cap, Biruta, French Literature & Civilization
Cap, Jean-Pierre, French Languages & Literature
Gostautas, Stasys, Latin American Literature
Pribic, Rado, German & Russian Literatures

East Stroudsburg

Brooks, Blossom Sheila, Foreign Language Education
Oberlander, Barbara Joyce, Romance Languages

Edinboro

Hensley, Gordon, Romance Languages

Erie

Fin, Robert George, Slavic & East European Languages, French
Peterson, Paul W, Linguistics
Weber, Berta M, Foreign Languages

Fogelsville

Greenberg, Wendy, French, Comparative Literature

Ft Washington

McDonald, John Paul, French Literature & History

Gettysburg

Barriga, Guillermo, Linguistics
Held, Charles Robert, Philology
Kurth, Arthur Lincoln, French
Lenski, Branko Alan, Modern French & Yugoslav Literature
Pavlantos, Ruth Esther, Classics
Ritterson, Michael, German Language and Literature
Schneider, Henry, III, Germanic Languages & Literature

Glenside

Perfecky, George A, Russian, Slavic Philology

Greenville

Miller, Eugene Wesley, Classical Language & Literature
Mueller, Paul Eugene, German

Grove City

Hart, William Robert, Linguistics, English
Huebert, Catherine Muder, French, English

Haverford

Cary, John R, German
Cormier, Raymond Joseph, Medieval French Literature
Gillis, Daniel J, Classics
Gutwirth, Marcel Marc, French Literature
Russo, Joseph Anthony, Classics

Huntingdon

Frijters, Cornelis Joseph, Linguistics, Modern & Classical Languages

Immaculata

Bonfini, Marie Roseanne, French Language & Literature, Comparative Literature

Kennett Square

Comfort, Howard, Latin, Greek

Kimberton

Rice, Allan Lake, Languages

King of Prussia

Fernandez Y Fernandez, Enrique, Spanish Language & Literature

Kutztown

Fortune, Richard D, Russian Language & Literature
Matula, Anne Elizabeth, French, Spanish
Monroe, George Karl, Linguistics, German

Lancaster

Barnett, Robert John, Jr, Classics
DeCamp, Joseph E, Jr, Spanish Language & Literature
Englert, Donald M C, Semitic Philology
Farber, Jay Joel, Classical Languages & Literatures
Frey, John William, Modern Languages & Linguistics
Jeannet, Angela Maria, French
Kally, Konstantin Michael, Russian Language

Lansdowne

Roach, Eleanor (Ann), French & Latin Paleography

Levittown

Waskie, Anthony Joseph, Germanic & Slavic Philology

Lewisburg

Beard, Robert Earl, Slavic Linguistics
Coombs, Virginia M, Germanic Linguistics
Edgerton, Mills Fox, Jr, Romance Philology
Folkers, George Fulton, German Language & Literature
Grundstrom, Allan Wilbur, French Language & Linguistics
Heath, James Maguire, Classics
Huffines, Marion Lois, German, Sociolinguistics

Lincoln University

Rodgers, Joseph James, Jr, French, Spanish

Lock Haven

Carney, Edmund Jeremiah, Spanish American & Brazilian Literature

Meadville

Hanson, Blair, Romance Languages
Hogan, James Charles, Classics
Lotze, Dieter Paul, German Language & Literature
Wolfe, Phillip Jerrold, French Literature

Merion Station

Waldman, Glenys A, Germanic Languages, Pennsylvania German

Millersville

Beam, C Richard, German
Heesen, Philip T, Classical Languages, Latin & Greek
Oppenheimer, Fred E, German Language & Literature
Rupp, Theodore Hanna, Romance Languages
Skitter, Hans Gunter, German & American Literature
Solera, Rodrigo, Romance Languages

Muncy

Wentzler, Marilyn Louise, Classical Languages & Literature

Murrysville

Phillips, Betty Steedley, English Linguistics

Nazareth

Barthold, Allen Jennings, Romance Languages

New Kensington

Gonzalez-Cruz, Luis F, Hispanic Languages, Latin American Literature

Newtown

Doreste, Octavio Oscar, Spanish
Morneau, Kenneth Armand, French & Spanish Language & Literature

New Wilmington

Castro, Albert Dwight, Classics, Ancient History
Erhardt, Jacob, German
Turner, James Hilton, Classical Languages

Oil City

Masterson, Allene H, Romance Languages

Philadelphia

Adolf, Helen, Germanics
Allen, Roger Michael Ashley, Arabic Language & Literature
Alter, Jean Victor, French Literature
Aponte, Barbara Bockus, Romance Languages
Bandy, Anastasius Constantine, Greek & Latin Languages & Literatures
Bender, Ernest, Indology
Benson, Morton, Foreign Languages, Lexicography
Bernian, Daniel, French & Spanish
Block, Elizabeth, Classical Languages, Comparative Literature
Blumenthal, Bernhardt George, German
Bowman, Frank Paul, French
Brevart, Francis B, German Medieval Literature
Brooks, Maria Zagorska, Slavic Linguistics
Brown, Sylvia Grace, Classics
Caputo-Mayr, Maria Luise, German Literature
Cardona, George, Indoaryan & Indo-European Linguistics
Cherpack, Clifton (Cyril), Romance Languages
Conway, George Edward, Classics
Daemmrich, Horst, German Literature
DiBlasi, Sebastiano, Romance Linguistics, Lexicography
Donahue, Thomas John, French Literature, Theatre
Donaldson-Evans, Lancelot Knox, French Literature
Dresden, Mark J, Philology, History
Earle, Peter G, Spanish & Latin American Literature
Easby, Elizabeth Kennedy, Art & Archeology of Latin America
Edberg, George John, Spanish
Eichler, Barry Lee, Ancient Near Eastern Civilization
Espantoso-Foley, Augusta, Romance Languages
Evin, Ahmet O, Turkish Literature & Cultural History
Fought, John Guy, Linguistics, Mayan Studies
Frappier-Mazur, Lucienne, French Literature
Frey, Peter W, French Language & Literature
Gaeffke, Peter, Indology, Comparative Literature
Galanes, Adriana Lewis, Spanish & Spanish-American Colonial Literature
Garr, W Randall, Semitic Languages
Gaudiani, Claire Lynn, Seventeenth Century French Literature
Goldin, Judah, Oriental Studies
Gronicka, Andre Von, German
Gullon, German, Spanish & Spanish American Literature
Hanaway, William Lippincott, Jr, Persian Language & Literature
Harris, Zellig, Mathematical Linguistics
Herz, Julius Michael, German
Hoenigswald, Henry M, Linguistics
Humphrey, George, Comparative Literature
Hymes, Dell Hathaway, Folklore, Linguistics
Iannucci, James Emanuel, Romance Linguistics
Ihrie, Maureen E, Peninsular Spanish Literature
Kashuba, Irma Mercedes, French & Russian Language & Literature
Katsh, Abraham Issac, Hebrew & Islamic Studies
Kirkham, Victoria Eulalia, Italian Literature
Kleis, Charlotte Costa, French Renaissance Literature
Knauer, Georg Nicolaus, Classical Studies
Knauer, Georg Nicolaus, Classical Studies

Kuhn, Anna Katharina, German Literature
Langebartel, William Winter, Germanic Philology
LaVallee-Williams, Marthe, French Literature & Language
Lebofsky, Dennis Stanley, Linguistics, History & Structure of English
Leichty, Erle Verdun, Assyriology
Lieberman, Stephen Jacob, Assyriology, Linguistics
Lisker, Leigh, Linguistics
Lloyd, Albert L, Germanic Languages & Literatures
Lloyd, Paul M, Romance Philology
Loding, Darlene Marilyn, Assyriology, Ancient History
Long, Michael J, Classical Studies, Biblical Languages
McCarthy, John Aloysius, German
McDermott, William Coffman, Classical Studies
McDonough, James Thomas, Jr, Ancient Greek
McMahon, Kathryn Kristine, French
Mall, Rita Sparrow, French Literature
Means, John Barkley, Portuguese & Brazilian Literature
Menocal, Maria Rosa, Romance Philology, Italian Literature
Moenkemeyer, Heinz, Languages
Nemoy, Leon, Arabic Philology, Bibliography
O'Donnell, James Joseph, Classics, Patristics
Palmer, Robert Everett Allen, Classical Studies
Pillwein, Rudolf, Modern Languages, Philology
Prince, Gerald Joseph, French
Regueiro, Jose Miguel, Spanish Literature
Richman, Michele Helene, Twentieth Century French Literature
Rickett, Adele Austin, Chinese Languages & Literature
Roach, William (Joseph), Old French Literature, Textual Criticism
Rocher, Ludo, Sanskrit, Indic Studies
Rocher, Rosane Debels, Indology, Linguistics
Rodriguez-Peralta, Phyllis White, Spanish American Literature
Ruch, Barbara, Japanese Language & Literature
Rudnytzky, Leo Dennis, German & Slavic Literatures
Ruttkowski, Wolfgang, German, Comparative Literature
Sebold, Russell Perry, Spanish
Shereshevsky, Esra, Hebrew Language & Literature
Smith, Wesley Dale, Classical Philology
Sobejano, Gonzalo, Spanish Literature
Southworth, Franklin C, Linguistics
Springer, Otto, Germanic Languages & Literatures
Steiner, Peter, Russian & Czech Language & Literature
Steisel, Marie-Georgette, French Literature
Swiecicka-Ziemianek, Maria A J, Slavic Languages & Literatures
Thomas, Ruth Paula, French
Tigay, Jeffrey Howard, Biblical Studies, Ancient Near Eastern Literature
Toconita, Michael J, Modern Languages
Traupman, John Charles, Classical Languages
Trommler, Frank Alfred, German Literature
Weiss, Gershon, Oriental Studies, Hebrew Language
Wennberg, Benkt, French, Comparative Literature
Wolfgang, Lenora D Poden, Romance Languages, Medieval French Literature

Pittsburgh

Albert, Walter E, French
Anthony, Edward Mason, Linguistics
Ashliman, Dee L, German Language & Literature, Comparative Literature
Avery, Harry Costas, Classics
Bart, Benjamin Franklin, Romance Languages
Beverley, John R, Hispanic & Comparative Literature
Cano-Ballesta, Juan, Spanish Literature, Philology
Chu, Wen-Djang (John), Asian Studies
Clack, Jerry, Classics
Colecchia, Frances, Modern Languages
Dana, Marie Immaculee, French Language & Literature
Duffy, Kenneth J, Spanish
Floyd, Edwin Douglas, Classics
Frey, Herschel J, Spanish Linguistics, Applied Linguistics
Gaichas, Lawrence Edward, Classics
Greco, Joseph Vittorio, Languages
Harris, Jane Gary, Slavic Languages & Literatures

Harris-Schenz, Beverly, German Literature
Hauber, Rose Marie, Classical Languages
Hoffmeister, Donna L, German Literature
Jaszczun, Wasyl, Slavic Philology
Jonas, Ilsedore B, German
Jonas, Klaus Werner, German Language & Literature
Jones, Nicholas Francis, Ancient History, Classical Philology
Kaufman, Terrence Scott, Linguistics
Koch, Philip, Romance Languages
Koehler, Ludmila, Russian Literature
McClain, M Patrick, Romance Languages
McCulloch, James A, Classics
McDuffie, Keith A, Latin American Literature
Matas, Julio, Hispanic Languages & Literatures
Meriz, Diana Teresa, French & Provencal Linguistics
Miller, Yvette Espinosa, Spanish & Spanish American Literature
Mills, David Otis, Japanese Language & Literature, Linguistics & Language
Neubauer, John, Germanic & Comparative Literature
Neumarkt, Paul, German Language & Literature
Newmyer, Stephen Thomas, Classics
Parslow, Robert LaVerne, Linguistics, Liberal Arts
Paulston, Christina Bratt, Linguistics, Language Teaching
Poltoratzky, Nikolai Petrovich, Russian Literature & Civilization
Roggiano, Alfredo Angel, Spanish
Rudolph, Celesta, Modern German Literature, English
Russell, Daniel, Romance Languages
St Aubyn, Frederic Chase, French
Sargent-Baur, Barbara Nelson, French Literature
Schwartz, Jerome, French Literature
Schweizer, Eva Julia (Mrs Walter J Vogel), Germanic Languages
Silenieks, Juris, French Literature
Smethurst, Mae J, Classics
Stiehm, Bruce Gilbert, Spanish, Linguistics
Switala, William J, Classics, History
Vardy, Agnes Huszar, Comparative Literature, English
Wlassics, Tibor, Italian Literature
Yang, Richard F S, Foreign Languages

Pottstown

Groten, Frank John, Jr, Greek, Latin

Reading

Incledon, John S, Latin American Literature

Ridley Park

Daly, Lloyd William, Classical Studies

Riegelsville

Snider, Frank Parmer, Modern Comparative Literature

Rosemont

Conwell, Marilyn J, Linguistics, Romance Languages
Glass, Erlis, Germanic Languages & Literatures
Russell, Lois Ann, French Literature & Language

St Davids

Boehne, Patricia Jeanne, Medieval Hispano-Arabic & Catalan Literature
Coughanowr, Effie, Classics

Scranton

Brennan, M Josephine, Classical Patristic Languages & Literature
Cimini, Frank A, Spanish
Petrovic, Njegos M, Serbo-Croatian & French Language & Literature
Young, Robert F, Classical Languages

Selinsgrove

Abler, Lawrence Anthony, English, Comparative Literature
Barlow, Jane Fox, Classics
Gilbert, Russell Wieder, German
Waldeck, Peter B, German

Shippensburg

Barrick, Mac Eugene, Spanish Language & Literature

Slippery Rock

Zinni, Hannah Case, French Language & Literature

State College

Armitage, Isabelle, French Language & Literature
Grossman, Kathryn Marie, French Literature, Utopian Studies
Hyslop, Lois Boe, Romance Languages
Stabb, Martin Sanford, Spanish

Swarthmore

Avery, George Costas, German
Krugovoy, George G, Russian Philosophy & Literature
Mautner, Franz H, German, Comparative Literature
Metzidakis, Philip, Foreign Languages
Mitchell, Thomas N, Ancient Classics
Moskos, George, French Literature
North, Helen Florence, Classical Literature, Rhetoric
Ostwald, Martin, Classical Philology
Perkins, Jean Ashmead, French
Rose, Gilbert Paul, Greek & Latin Literature
Tafoya, Francis Pinard, French
Weber, Eugene Mathew, German Literature

University Park

Ariew, Robert A, French Language & Literature
Birkenmayer, Sigmund S, Slavic Languages & Literatures
Brault, Gerard Joseph, French
Browning, Barton W, German Literature
Carrubba, Robert William, Greek, Latin
Chapman, Hugh Harding, Jr, Romance Languages
Dalbor, John Bronislaw, Spanish
Danahy, Michael Charles, French Language & Literature
De Levie, Dagobert, German
Donlan, Walter, Classical Languages, Ancient History
Fitz, Earl Eugene, Luso-Brazilian Studies
Frautschi, Richard Lane, French
Hale, Thomas Albert, African & French Literature
Halsey, Martha T, Romance Languages
Kiffer, Theodore Edwin, English, Linguistics
Knight, Alan Edgar, French & Comparative Literature
Kopp, W LaMarr, German
Lima, Robert F, Jr, Spanish & Comparative Literatures
Lyday, Leon Faidherbee, III, Romance Languages
Magner, Thomas Freeman, Slavic Linguistics
Makward, Christiane Perrin, French Literature, Women's Studies
Moser, Gerald Max Joseph, Romance Languages
Norton, Glyn Peter, Romance Languages, French Renaissance
Paternost, Joseph, Languages
Peavler, Terry J, Latin American & Comparative Literature
Perez, Louis Celestino, Romance Languages
Preisner, Rio, German Literature
Schmalstieg, William Riegel, Slavic Linguistics
Schurer, Ernst Ignatz, Germanic Languages & Literatures
Sturcken, Henry Tracy, Spanish Literature, Romance Linguistics
Ward, Patricia Ann, Comparative Literature & French
Weiss, Beno, Italian Literature
Ziegler, Vickie Lynne, German

Villanova

Alter, Maria Pospischil, German, French
Di Vincenzo, Vito John, Modern Spanish
Frescoln, Wilson Lysle, French Literature
Gildea, Joseph James, Medieval French & Latin Literature
Goldberg, Harriet Alice, Medieval Spanish Literature, History of Language
Helmetag, Charles Hugh, German
McEnerney, John Ignatius, Classics
Mazur, Oleh, Romance Languages
Mulligan, John J, Foreign Languages

PENNSYLVANIA (cont)

Washington

Moreno, Antonio William, Foreign Languages
Quintana, Judith Terrie, French Language & Literature

Wayne

Hunt, John Mortimer, Jr, Classical Philology

West Chester

Frieman, Walter Edgar, Jr, Systematic Theology, Classical Languages
Gougher, Ronald Lee, Foreign Language, International Education
Gutwirth, Madelyn, French Literature, Women's Studies
Lombardi, Ronald Paul, Spanish, Italian
Roberts, Alfred D, Romance Languages
Soufas, Charles Christopher, Jr, Contemporary Spanish Literature

Wilkes-Barre

Corgan, Margaret M, French Language & Literature
DiBlasi, Daniel F, Romance Languages & Literatures
Krawczeniuk, Joseph V, German, Russian
LeBlanc, Herve A, Modern Languages
Stoekl, Allan Inlow, Comparative Literature

Williamsport

Flam, Bernard Paul, Spanish
Maples, Robert John Barrie, Romance Languages, French Literature

RHODE ISLAND

Kingston

Benesch, Marlene, German Studies
Capasso, Henry F, Italian
Dornberg, Otto, German
Hutton, Lewis J, Romance Languages, Religion
Kuhn, Ira Astride, French & Comparative Literature
Manteiga, Robert Charles, Spanish Letters
Navascues, Michael, Hispanic Studies
Rogers, Kenneth Hall, Romance Linguistics, French
Rothschild, Harriet Dorothy, French Literature

Newport

Lappin, John Eugene, French, English

Peace Dale

Hyland, Jean Scammon, Romance Languages

Portsmouth

Stevens, Henry Joseph, Jr, Classics

Providence

Ahearn, Edward J, French & Comparative Literature
Amor y Vazquez, Jose, Hispanic Studies
Arant, Patricia Mayher, Slavic Language & Literatures
Barnouw, Jeffrey, Comparative Literature, Intellectual History
Baron, Naomi Susan, Linguistics
Benson, Edward George, French
Blumstein, Sheila Ellen, Linguistics, Psycholinguistics
Boegehold, Alan Lindley, Classics
Caminos, Ricardo Augusto, Egyptology
Chaika, Elaine Ostrach, Linguistics
Coons, Dix Scott, Spanish; Latin American Literature
Crosman, Inge Karalus, French Literature
Crossgrove, William Charles, German, Medieval Studies
Donovan, Bruce E, Classics
Driver, Samuel Norman, Russian
Durand, Frank, Spanish Literature & Language
Echeverria, Durand, French Literature
Elliott, Alison Goddard, Classical Languages, Medieval Literature
Fido, Franco, Italian & Comparative Literature
Fornara, Charles William, Classics
Francis, Winthrop Nelson, Linguistics
Gallagher, Edward J(oseph), Medieval French Literature

Good, Robert McClive, Old Testament, Near Eastern Languages
Huntley, Martin Adrian, Linguistics, Philosophy
Kossoff, Aron David, Spanish
Kucera, Henry, Slavic Languages & Linguistics
Lesko, Leonard Henry, Egyptology
Lieberman, Philip, Linguistics
Love, Frederick Rutan, German Language & Literature
Millward, Celia McCullough, Linguistics, English
Oldcorn, Anthony, Italian Language and Literature
Putnam, Michael Courtney Jenkins, Classical Philology
Ridgely, Beverly Sellman, French Literature
Salvan, Albert Jacques, French
Schaffer, Martha Elizabeth, Romance Philology, Medieval Literature
Schmitt, Albert Richard, German Language & Literature
Schnerr, Walter Johnson, Romance Philology
Schor, Naomi Ann, French
Segal, Charles Paul, Classics
Smith, Duncan, German Literature, Medieval Studies
Taylor, M Frances, Spanish
Terras, Victor, Slavic Languages & Literature
Trueblood, Alan Stubbs, Spanish Comparative Literature
Warnock, Robert Glenn, German Literature
Weimar, Karl Siegrried, German
Weinstein, Arnold Louis, Comparative Literature, French Studies
Workman, John Rowe, Classical Philology
Wrenn, James Joseph, Chinese Language & Literature
Wyatt, William F, Jr, Classics, Linguistics

Rochester

Susskind, Norman, French

Saunderstown

Waters, Harold A, French

Tiverton

Kamm, Lewis Robert, French Literature & Language

SOUTH CAROLINA

Aiken

Rich, John Stanley, Dialectology

Bennettsville

Matthews, Hester Poole, Spanish & French Literature

Charleston

Byrd, Suzanne Wade, Spanish, Spanish Theater
Cook, Vernon, Foreign Languages
Griebsch, Heinz-Jurgen, Modern Languages
Johnson, David Donovan, Romance Languages
Miller, William Henry, Jr, French
Pappas, Luke Theodore, Modern Languages
Ralston, Zachary T, Romance Languages

Clemson

Calvez, Daniel Jean, Medieval French Literature
Cranston, Mechthild, Romance Languages & Literatures
Fernandez, Gaston J, Spanish, Spanish-American Literature
McGregor, Rob Roy, Jr, French Language & Literature, Latin
Rudowski, Victor Anthony, German Literature, Comparative Literature
Sinka, Margit M, German Literature & Language
Stewart, Harry Eugene, French Language & Literature

Columbia

Alber, Charles Julius, Chinese Language & Literature
Belasco, Simon, Romance Dialectology, French Syntax & Phonology
Briggs, Ward W, Jr, Classics
Dannerbeck, Francis J, German Education
de Oliveira, Celso Lemos, Portuguese, Spanish
Elfe, Wolfgang Dieter, Modern German Literature
Fryer, T Bruce, Foreign Languages
Hardee, A Maynor, French Language & Literature

Hardin, James Neal, German & Comparative Literature
Hatch, Mary Gies, Germanic Languages
Henry, Freeman George, French Literature
Jordan, Gerda Petersen, German, Comparative Literature
Lane, Nancy E, French Literature, Contemporary Drama
Levy, Isaac Jack, Romance Languages
Little, Greta D, Linguistics, English as a Foreign Language
Matsen, Patricia Paden, Classical Languages & Literatures
Moreno, Nestor A, Latin American Studies
Mould, William Anderson, French Language & Literature
Norman, George Buford, Jr, French Literature, Musicology
Pearson, Bruce L, Anthropological Linguistics
Reeves, George M, English & Comparative Literature
Shaw, Aracelis Goberna, Spanish
Speer, David Gordon, French Language & Literature
Tate, Robert Stuart, Jr, French

Due West

Horton, Margaret, Romance Languages

Florence

James, Joseph Alston, Romance Languages

Gaffney

Forgac, Albert, Romance Languages

Greenville

Cherry, Charles Maurice, Spanish Golden-Age Literature
Cox, Jerry Lynn, German, Applied Linguistics
Kocher, Myron Low, French
Lindahl, Roy Elwin, Jr, Classical Philology
Parsell, David Beatty, French Language & Literature
Reece, Benny Ramon, Classical Languages
Schnaiter, Samuel Ellsworth, Koine Greek, New Testament Literature

Newberry

Mature, Albert P, Romance Languages
Romeiser, John Beals, French Language & Literature

Orangeburg

Sharpe, Alfredo M, Foreign Languages

Rock Hill

Castillo-Feliu, Guillermo Ignacio, Spanish Language, Spanish American Literature
Delano, Lucile Kathryn, Spanish Literature
Exum, Frances Bell, Spanish Golden Age Literature
Medlin, Dorothy Moser, French
Zdenek, Joseph William, Spanish

Spartanburg

DeVelasco, Joaquin Fernandez, Spanish Language & Literature
Goldberg, Maxwell Henry, Modern Philology
Newell, Sanford, Romance Languages

SOUTH DAKOTA

Brookings

Barnes, Allen Ray, Spanish

Sioux Falls

Rusch, Frederick A, Classical Languages

Vermillion

Arana, Nelson G, Spanish & Latin American Literature
Bunge, Robert Pierce, Modern Languages
Froberg, Brent Malcolm, Classics
Hartman, Alexander Paul, French, German
Klein, Dennis Allan, Spanish
Sebesta, Judith Lynn, Classical Languages & Literature, Ancient History

TENNESSEE

Chattanooga

Banoun, Merilee, French, German
Byrum, C Stephen, Philosophy, Literature
Phillips, John Frederick, Classical Language, Philosophy
Sumberg, Lewis Arthur Matthew, French Literature, Medieval History

Clarksville

Welker, John W, Romance Languages, Linguistics

Collegedale

Morrison, Robert Reid, Spanish, French

Cookeville

Campana, Phillip Joseph, German
Saint-Leon, Claire Brandicourt, French, Theater Arts
Slotkin, Alan Robert, English Linguistics, American Literature
Viera, David John, Medieval Hispanic Literature

Johnson City

LeCroy, Anne Kingsbury, Classics, English
Suarez, Manuel Laurentino, Romance Languages
Zayas-Bazan, Eduardo, Hispanic Culture & Literature

Knoxville

Arrington, Teresa Ross, Spanish Linguistics
Barrette, Paul Edouard, Romance Languages
Campion, Edmund John, French Literature
Cobb, Carl Wesley, Spanish Literature
De Rycke, Robert M, Romance Languages
Dumas, Bethany Kay, Linguistics
Elliott, Jacqueline Cecile, French Language & Literature
Falen, James Edward, Russian Language & Literature, Soviet Area Studies
Fiene, Donald Mark, Slavic Languages & Literature
Fuller, Homer Woodrow, Modern German Literature
Gesell, Geraldine Cornelia, Classical Archeology & Literature
Handelsman, Michael H, Spanish
Hiller, Robert Ludwig, Germanic Languages & Literature
Kratz, Henry, Germanic Languages
Lee, David Elwood, German Language & Literatures
Leki, Ilona, French Literature, English as a Second Language
Lewald, Herald Ernest, Spanish
Mellor, Chauncey Jeffries, Germanic Philology
Petrovska, Marija, French Language and Literature, Comparative Literature
Ritzenhoff, Ursula Christa, German Language & Literature
Rutledge, Harry Carraci, Classics
Shelton, James Edward, Greek, Latin
Shurr, Georgia Grey Hooks, French, Comparative Literature
Swain, James Obed, Spanish Literature
Vazquez-Bigi, Angel Manuel, Romance Languages

McKenzie

Odom, William Lee, Greek Languages & Literature

Martin

Mohler, Stephen Charles, Spanish & Portuguese Languages

Maryville

Collins, Ralph Stokes, German Language & Literature, Russian

Memphis

Anderson, Emmett H, Jr, Modern Languages
Brantley, Franklin Oakes, Spanish
Brewer, William Benjamin, Spanish Language & Literature, Romance Philology
Burgos, Fernando, Spanish-American Literature
Freire, Jose Luis, Linguistics, Spanish

Harwood, Sharon Elizabeth, Foreign Languages
Jolly, William Thomas, Linguistics, Classical Languages
Lapuente, Felipe Antonio, Romance Languages, Philosophy
O'Connell, Richard B, German
Pell, Carroll Lee, Modern Languages
Ratiu, Basil, Romance Languages
Sigsbee, David Lee, Classical Studies
Southard, Gordon Douglas, Romance Languages
Tollerson, Marie Sherrod, African Francophone Literture
Watson, Harold Mark, Romance Languages
Williamson, Juanita Virginia, English

Murfreesboro

McCash, June Hall, Medieval French & Comparative Literature
Ordoubadian, Reza, Linguistics
Porter, Thaddeus Coy, Spanish

Nashville

Andrews, James Richard, Spanish, Portuguese
Bandy, William Thomas, French Literature
Bell, Wendolyn Y, Romance Languages
Bingham, John L, Spanish
Brooks, H Franklin, French
Chaney, Virginia M, Foreign Languages
Cheek, John H, Jr, Linguistics
Church, Dan McNeil, Twentieth-Century French Drama
Crispin, John, Spanish Language & Contemporary Literature
Crist, Larry S, French
Deschenes, Martin Ovila, Francophone Literature & Civilization
Drews, Robert Herman, Classics, Ancient History
Elliott, Joan Curl, German Literature, Linguistics
Engel, Walburga Von Raffler, Linguistics
Leblon, Jean Marcel Jules, French Literature, Romance Languages
Lowe, David Allan, Russian Literature & Language
Monga, Luigi, French Italian
Nyabongo, Virginia Simmons, French Literature
Patty, James Singleton, French
Philips, Frank Carter, Classical Studies
Pichois, Claude, French Literature, Comparative Literature
Poggenburg, Raymond Paul, French
Pupo-Walker, C Enrique, Romance Languages, Latin American Studies
Rhein, Phillip Henry, Comparative Literature, German
Rysan, Josef, Germanic & Slavic Languages
Severino, Alexandrino Eusebio, Romance Languages
Sevin, Dieter H, German Literature
Stow, Henry Lloyd, Classical Philology
Sweeney, Robert Dale, Classics
Thomas, Earl Wesley, Romance Language
Wade, Claire Lynch, French
Williams, James Edward, Romance Languages

Notre Dame

O'Healy, Anne-Marie, Italian, French

Sewanee

Bates, Scott, French, Film
Binnicker, Charles Mathews, Jr, Classical Languages & Literature
Davidheiser, James Charles, Foreign Language, Literature
Fort, Jane Benton, Spanish, Latin American Studies
Lockard, Thaddeus (Constantine), Jr, Modern Languages
Naylor, Eric Woodfin, Romance Languages
Schaefer, Jacqueline Thibault, French & Comparative Literature
Spaccarelli, Thomas Dean, Spanish Linguistics, Medieval Spanish Literature
Whitesell, Frederick Rhodes, German Literature
Zachau, Reinhard Konrad, German Literature

TEXAS

Abilene

Dowdey, David, German Language & Literature
Ellis, William Ray, Religion, Greek
Johnston, Robert T Lee, Jr, Classical Languages
Kearley, F Furman, Classical Hebrew & Greek
Miller, Leonard Haven, Modern Languages
Williams, John Howard, French Language & Literature, Classics

Arlington

Adams, Duane A, Romance Language & Philology
Frank, Luanne Thornton, Comparative Literature & German
Frank, Ted Earl, German Language & Literature
Keilstrup, Duane Victor, German, Old Norse
Longacre, Robert Edmondson, Linguistics
McDowell, Charles Taylor, Foreign Languages & Linguistics
McLean, Malcolm Dallas, History, Foreign Language
Ordonez, Elizabeth Jane, Spanish Literature
Reddick, Robert John, Linguistics
Studerus, Lenard Henry, Spanish, Linguistics
Werth, Ronald Nicholas, Germanic Linguistics & Philology

Austin

Abboud, Peter Fouad, Linguistics, Arabic Studies
Andersson, Theodore, Romance Languages
Baker, Mary Jordan, French Renaissance Literature
Bar-Adon, Aaron, Linguistics, Hebrew & Semitics
Becker-Cantarino, Barbara, German
Bennett, Winfield Scott, III, Germanic Languages, Linguistics
Bezirgan, Najm A, Philosophy, Linguistics
Biasin, Bian-Paolo, Romance Studies
Bordie, John George, Linguistics, Applied Linguistics
Boyer, Mildred (Vinson), Spanish
Brody, Robert, Spanish American Literature
Bulhof, Francis, Dutch & German Literature
Cauvin, Jean-Pierre Bernard, French Language & Literature
Currie, Eva Garcia-Carrillo, Speech, Sociolinguistics
Dabbs, Jack Autrey, Linguistics
Dailey, Virginia Flood, Linguistics, English
Dassonville, Michel, French Literature
Dawson, Robert Lewis, French Literature, Portuguese
Ellison, Fred P, Portuguese & Spanish
Faurot, Jeannette L, Chinese Literature, Chinese Language
Fontanella, Lee, Hispanic Studies, Comparative Literature
Forster, Merlin Henry, Spanish & Portuguese
Francis, Eric David, Classics, Linguistics
Gagarin, Michael, Classics
Galinsky, Gotthard Karl, Classics
Gold, Barbara Kirk, Classics
Gonzalez-Perez, Anibal, Latin American Literature
Grant, Richard Babson, French
Green, Peter Morris, Classics, History
Haden, Ernest Faber, Romance Linguistics
Harms, Robert Thomas, Linguistics
Heinen, Hubert, German Language & Literature
Hensey, Frederick Gerald, Linguistics, Romance Languages
Hewitt, Helen-Jo Jakusz, Applied Lingustics
Higginbotham, Virginia, Romance Languages, Contemporary Spanish Literature
Hill, Archibald Anderson, Linguistics
Hillmann, Michael Craig, Persian Literature, Middle Eastern Studies
Hitt, James Alfred, Classics
Jackson, Kenneth David, Luso-Brazilian Literature, Comparative Literature
Jackson, William Vernon, Spanish, Latin American Studies
Jazayery, Mohammad Ali, Linguistics
Kibler, William W, Medieval French, Romance Philology
King, Robert Desmond, Linguistics
Kolsti, John Sotter, Slavic Languages & Literature
Lariviere, Richard Wilfred, Sanskrit, Indology
Lehmann, Winfred Philipp, Linguistics & Germantic Philology
Lindstrom, Naomi E, Latin American Literature
Lippmann, Jane N, French

Austin, TEXAS (cont)

Lopez-Morillas, Juan, Spanish, Comparative Literature
Lujan, Marta Elida, Spanish Linguistics
Malti-Douoglas, Fedwa, Arabic Literature, Islamic Civilization
Matluck, Joseph H, Romance Languages
Merrim, Stephanie, Latin American & Brazilian Literature
Michael, Wolfgang Friedrich, German
Middleton, John Christopher, Germanic Languages
Moeller, Hans-Bernhard, German Literature, European Studies
Mollenauer, Robert Russell, Languages
Monas, Sidney, Russian Language & History
Morgan, Gareth, Renaissance Greek, Classical Languages
Nethercut, William Robert, Classics
O'Hare, Thomas Joseph, Linguistics, Germanic Languages
Ortega, Julio, Latin American Literature
Parker, Carolyn Ann, Swahili, Folklore
Pearcy, Lee Theron, Jr, Classics
Peters, Paul Stanley, Jr, Theoretical Linguistics
Polome, Edgar Charles, Linguistics
Potter, Joy Hambuechen, Italian & Comparative Literature
Priest, Nancy Elizabeth, Classical Studies, Greek Papyrology
Rappaport, Gilbert Charles, Slavic Languages, General Linguistics
Rogers, Andrew Daylon, Jr, Linguistics
Rogers, Douglass Marcel, Foreign Languages
Rovinsky, Robert Thomas, Scandinavian Languages & Literature
Rubino, Carl A, Classics, Comparative Literature
Schade, George D, Spanish, Romance Languages
Schmidt, Paul Francis, Russian Literature, Drama
Schulz-Behrend, George, Germanic Languages
Schulze, Leonard Gene, Comparative Literature, German
Sellstrom, Albert Donald, French
Shay, James Rodney, English, Linguistics
Shelmerdine, Cynthia Wright, Classics, Classical Archeology
Silberschlag, Eisig, Modern Hebrew Literature
Sisto, David Theodore, Spanish, Portuguese
Sjoberg, Andree Frances, Linguistics
Smith, Carlota S, Linguistics, Psycholinguistics
Sole, Carlos Alberto, Spanish Language
Sole, Yolanda Russinovich, Spanish Linguistics, Sociolinguistics
Swaffar, Janet King, German Literature, Foreign Language Pedagogy
Tamargo, Maria Isabel, Spanish American Literature
Thielemann, Leland James, French Literature
Underwood, Gary Neal, English Linguistics
Van Olphen, Herman Hendrik, Hindi, Linguistics
Vento, Arnold, Latin American Literature
Vessely, Thomas Richard, French Literature
Wall, Robert Eugene, Linguistics
Werbow, Stanley Newman, Germanic Languages & Literature
Wheelock, Kinch Carter, Spanish American Literature
Willson, Amos Leslie, Germanic Languages & Literature
Wylie, Hal, French Literature
Yen, Sian Lin, Linguistics, Oriental Languages

Beaumont

Ellis, Marion LeRoy, French
Urbano, Victoria Eugenia, Literature of Spain & Spanish America

Brackettville

Curcio, Louis Leroy, French, Spanish

Brownwood

Gottschalk, Martin E, German
Phillips, Ewart E, Romance Languages

Bryan

Breitenkamp, Edward Carlton, Germanics
Christian, Chester C, Jr, Spanish, Sociology
Naudeau, Olivier Leonce, Romance Philology, Medieval & Renaissance Literature

Canyon

Juniper, Walter Howard, Classics

Carrollton

Werner, John Roland, Classical Languages

Cedar Park

Hamilton, Thomas Earle, Spanish

Cleveland

Lewis, Hanna B, Germanics, Comparative Literature

College Station

Cannon, Garland H, Linguistics
Deudon, Eric Hollingsworth, French Literature
Dyer, Nancy Joe, Spanish Language & Literature
Elmquist, Anne Marie, Applied Linguistics, French
Esau, Helmut, Linguistics, Philology
Koepke, Wulf, German Language & Literature
Lewis, Bartie Lee, Jr, Latin American & Peninsular Spanish Literature
Puppe, Heinz W, German Literature
Richards, Katharine Coles, Spanish Language
Stavenhagen, Lee, German & Medieval Literature

Commerce

Gamez, Juan, Classical & Romance Languages
Hanak, Miroslav John, Romance Languages, Comparative Literature
Harvey, William Journeaux, Germanic Languages & Literatures
Simpson, Harold Lester, Foreign Languages & Literatures
Tarpley, Fred Anderson, Linguistics, English

Corpus Christi

Marrocco, Mary Anne Wilkinson, Spanish Linguistics

Cypress

Cimerhanzel-Nestlerode, Samye-Ruth Mott, Spanish Language & Culture

Dallas

Beauchamp, William Edward, French Literature, Semiotics
Burquest, Donald Arden, Linguistics, African Studies
Deschner, Margareta N, German
Furst, Lilian Renee, Comparative Literature, German
Jordan, Gilbert John, German Languagage & Literature
LaPrade, John Harry, Spanish
Merrifield, William R, Linguistics, Anthropology
Olchyk, Marta, Spanish, Latin American History
Pulte, William John, Linguistics
Ulatowska, Hanna K, Linguistics
Winn, Conchita Hassell, Spanish & Latin American Literature

Denton

Crowder, Robert Douglas, French
Gionet, Arthur Joseph, French, Latin
Griggs, Silas, Linguistics, English Language
Hardin, Robert Joseph, Romance Languages
Nahrgang, Wilbur Lee, Modern German Literature
Olsen, Solveig, German Language & Literature
Oonk, Gerrit Johan, Medieval German Literature, Linguistics
Rich, Carroll Young, Linguistics
Smyth, Philip, Spanish Language & Literature
Vidrine, Donald Ray, Romance Languages
Whitmore, Donnell Ray, Ibero-American Languages
Wise, David Oakley, Latin American Literature
Woolsey, Wallace, Foreign Languages

Duncanville

Greenlee, Jacob Harold, New Testament Greek

Edinburg

Dominguez, Sylvia Maida, Spanish & Latin American Literature
Maloney, James Charles, Hispanic Literature
Sobin, Nicholas John, Linguistics

El Paso

Amastae, Jon Edward, Linguistics
Anderson, Robert Floyd, Romance Languages & Literatures
Astiazaran, Gloria C, Spanish & Italian
Coltharp, Lurline Hughes, English, Linguistics
Ewton, Ralph Waldo, Jr, German Language & Literature
Natalicio, Diana, Linguistics, English as Second Language
Scruggs, Emma Guerra, Romance Languages
Teschner, Richard Vincent, Spanish, Linguistics

Friendswood

Raley, Harold C, Romance Languages

Ft Worth

Compton, Bita Hall, French, Italian
Hammond, John Hays, Romance Languages, Latin American Literature
Hildebrand, Janet Elizabeth, Foreign Language
Reed, William LaForest, Near Eastern Languages & Literature
Walker, Larry L, Old Testament, Semitics

Georgetown

Seagraves, Richard Wayne Alexander, Classical Philology, Renaissance Studies
Teele, Roy Earl, Comparative Literature

Houston

Alcover, Madeleine, Romance Languages
Aresu, Bernard Camille, French & Comparative Literature
Boorman, Joan Rea, Latin American & Comparative Literature
Bourgeois, Andre M, French Literature
Bourne, Marjorie Adele, Romance Languages
Brady, Patrick, French & Comparative Literature
Brady-Papadopoulou, Valentini, French
Carrington, Samuel Macon, Jr, Romance Languages
Castaneda, James Agustin, Spanish Literature
Clark, Susan Louise, Medieval Literature, Women's Studies
Copeland, James Everett, General & Germanic Linguistics
Davis, Philip Wayne, Linguistics, Russian
Decker, Eugene Moore, III, Romance Languages
Eifler, Margret Eva, German Literature
Fischer, Peter Alfred, Slavic Languages & Literatures
Fong, Eugene Allen, French & Italian Linguistics
Guenther, Peter, Art History
Haymes, Edward Randolph, German Comparative Literature
Jacquart, Emmanuel Claude, French Literature & Language, French Civilization
Johnson, Harvey Leroy, Spanish
Kahn, Lisa M, German
Kimbrough, Mary Alice, French
Konrad, Linn Bratteteig, French Literature
Lecuyer, Maurice Antoine Francois, French
Lenz, Harold F H, German Language & Literature
Levin, Donald Norman, Classics
McGaw, Jessie Brewer, English
McLendon, Will Loving, French
Malin, Jane Wofford, French Literature
Marino, Nancy Frances, Spanish Medieval Literature
Monsanto, Carlos Hugo, Spanish, French
Nelson, Deborah Hubbard, Medieval French & Provencal Language & Literature
Parle, Dennis Jerome, Spanish Language, Latin American Literature
Prier, Raymond Adolph, Jr, Comparative & Classical Literature
Raaphorst, Madeleine, French
Reschke, Claus, German Literature, Applied Linguistics
Shupp, Robert Pete, French Literature & Language
Spuler, Richard Carl, Modern German Literature
Thompson, Ewa M, Comparative & Slavic Literatures
Topazio, Virgil William, French Literature
Urrutibeheity, Hector Norbert, Applied & Romance Linguistics

Vallbona, Rima-Gretel Rothe, Latin American &
Spanish Literature
Wallace, Kristine Gilmartin, Classics
Weissenberger, Klaus, German Literature
Wilson, Joseph Benjamin, Germanic Languages
& Literature

Huntsville

Gutermuth, Mary Elizabeth, French
Meredith, Hugh Edwin, Germanic Languages &
Literature
Pierce, Vaudau, Foreign Languages
Price, Robert Harold, French
Richards, Donnie Dean, Spanish
Slick, Sam L, Latin American Literature

Irving

Nagy, Moses Melchior, Romance Languages
Zimanyi, Rudolph Francis, Romance Languages

Kingsville

Benitez, Mario Antonio, Romance Languages,
Philosophy
Callas, James Howard, Classics, English
Hinojosa-Smith, R R, English, Southwestern
Literature
Rovira, Rosalina Reinalda, Spanish Literature &
Linguistics

Lubbock

Alexander, Theodor Walter, German
Andrews, Norwood, Jr, Luso-Brazilian & Spanish
Literatures
Bacon, Thomas Ivey, German Language &
Literature, Scholarly & Literary Translations
Bumpass, Faye Laverne, English, Spanish
Christiansen, Peder George, Classics
Cismaru, Alfred, French Literature
Cooley, Marianne, English Language &
Linguistics
Diaz, Janet Winecoff, Romance Languages,
Contemporary Spanish Literature
Dietz, Donald T, Spanish
Finco, Aldo, Foreign Languages
Garcia-Giron, Edmundo, Latin American
Literature
George, Edward V, Classical Languages
Hammer, Carl, Jr, German
Jirgensons, Leonid Aurelijs, Classical Languages
Klein, Theodore Michael, Ancient Literature,
Comparative Literature
Morris, Robert Jeffry, Spanish & Portuguese
Language & Literature
Oberhelman, Harley Dean, Spanish Language &
Literature
Patterson, William Taylor, French, Romance
Linguistics
Zyla, Wolodymyr T, Slavic Philology

Marshall

Hunter, William Arthur, Spanish Language &
Literature

Nacogdoches

Bellamy, Sidney Eugene, Germanic Languages,
Linguistics
Gruber, Vivian M, Languages
Keul, Carl, German
Quinn, John Joseph, English Language, Medieval
Literature

Odessa

Rees, Thomas Matthew, Foreign Languages

Richardson

Kratz, Dennis Merle, Medieval Latin Literature
Mayes, Janis Alene, African Literature, French
Literature

San Angelo

Jenkins, Michael Frederick Owen, French
Language & Literature
Tetzlaff, Otto Walter, Germanic Languages &
Literature
Torres, David, Spanish Language & Literature

San Antonio

Benavides, Ricardo F, Romance Literature
Chittenden, Jean Stahl, Romance Languages
Duncan, Annelise Marie, Germanics
Gibbs, Beverly J, Spanish Language & Literature
Hayes, Curtis W, English, Linguistics
Holcomb, George L, Foreign Languages
Icaza, Rosa Maria, Spanish Culture & Linguistics
Jacobson, Rodolfo, Linguistics, Bilingual
Education
Kassier, Theodore Laurence, Medieval & Golden
Age Spanish Literature
Michel, Joseph, Foreign Language Education,
Spanish
Pino, Frank, Jr, Spanish, History
Rivas, Fernando, Romance Languages
Samelson, William, Germanic & Romance
Languages
Schmidt, Verne, Germanic Languages
Silberman, Marc David, German, Humanities
Steinman, Robert Morris, Philosophy
Stroud, Matthew David, Spanish
Wilder, William Russell, Romance Languages

San Marcos

Brister, Louis Edwin, German Language &
Literature
Fischer, Robert Allen, Linguistics, French
Galvan, Roberto A, Modern Languages
Reeves, Dona Batty, Germanic Language &
Literature

Seabrook

Neumann, Alfred Robert, German

Sherman

Cornette, James Clarke, Jr, German Language &
Literature

Stephenville

Peterson, Russell Warren, Spanish, French

Tyler

Payne, David Lawrence, Linguistics

Waco

Butler, Roy Francis, Classical Philology
Cutter, Charles Richard, III, Classics
Johnson, Phillip, Spanish American Fiction
Norden, Ernest Elwood, Romance Languages
Ortuno, Manuel Joseph, Spanish Literature
Ortuno, Marian Mikaylo, Spanish Literature
Potter, Edithe Jeanmonod, Foreign Language &
Literature
Rubio, Nieves del Rosario Marquez, Spanish
Language, Literature
Sutton, Lois Marie, Foreign Languages
Uber, David Merrill, French Literature &
Theater
Velez, Joseph Francisco, Romance Languages,
Theology

Wichita Falls

Klein, Rudolf Manfred, German Literature &
Linguistics

UTAH

Logan

Cantarovici, Jaime, Latin American Literature,
Culture & Civilization
Eliason, Lynn Russell, German Language &
Literature
Fife, Austin Edwin, French Language &
Literature
Pitkin, Willis Lloyd, Jr, Linguistics, Composition
Theory
Reese, Lowell Grant, Comparative Literature

Midvale

Wells, Maurice Burton, German

Ogden

Adams, Kenneth R, Germanic Languages &
Literature
Doman, Larry Wallace, Spanish Language &
Literature

Orem

Green, John Alden, Foreign Languages

Provo

Ashworth, Peter P, Spanish Literature
Baker, Joseph O, German Language & Literature
Blair, Robert Wallace, Linguistics, Applied
Linguistics
Brown, Thomas Harold, French Literature,
Foreign Language Methodology
Clark, Hoover W, French
Clegg, Joseph Halvor, Romance Philology &
Linguistics
Compton, Merlin David, Hispanic Languages &
Literature
Davis, Garold N, German & Comparative
Literature
Dowdle, Harold L, Spanish
Folsom, Marvin Hugh, Germanic Linguistics
Gibson, Moses Carl, Romance Languages &
Literature
Gubler, Donworth Vernon, Slavic Language &
Literature
Jackson, Kent Phillips, Ancient Near Eastern
Languages
Jarvis, Donald Karl, Foreign Language
Education
Jones, Randall Lee, Linguistics, Germanic
Languages
Keele, Alan Frank, German Language &
Literature
Kelling, Hans-Wilhelm L, German Language &
Literature
Kimball, Merl Douglas, Jr, French Literature &
Language
Lambert, L Gary, French Language & Literature
Lounsbury, Richard Cecil, Classical Languages,
American Intellectual History
Luthy, Melvin Joseph, Linguistics, English
Language
Lyon, Thomas Edgar, Jr, Romance Languages,
Latin American Literature
Lytle, Eldon Grey, Linguistics
Monson, Samuel Christian, English
Moon, Harold Kay, Spanish, French
Peer, Larry Howard, Comparative Literature
Perkins, George W, Japanese Literature &
Language
Quackenbush, Louis Howard, Latin American
Literature
Rogers, R Max, Modern German Literature
Rogers, Thomas Franklyn, Russian Literature
Roos, Keith L, German Renaissance Literature
Rosen, Harold Earl, Romance Languages
Shreeve, Lyman Sidney, Spanish & Portuguese
Skousen, Royal Jon, Linguistics
Smith, Murray Francis, Germanic Languages
Speidel, Walter Hans, German Language &
Literature
Tate, George Sheldon, Medieval Literature
Taylor, James Scott, Romance & Germanic
Languages
Watkins, Arthur Rich, German

Salt Lake City

Barnett, Andree M-L (Paheau), Romance
Philology
Chopyk, Dan Bohdan, Russian Language
Davison, Ned J, Hispanic Languages &
Literature
Gresseth, Gerald K, Classics, Mythology
Hanna, Sami A, Foreign Languages,
Comparative Education
Harvey, John Edmond, French, Drama
Helbling, Robert E, German & French Literature
Hess, William Huie, Classics
Jones, Clelland Evans, French
Kelly, James Michael, Turkic Linguistics, Arabic
Studies
Knapp, Gerhard Peter, Literary Criticism,
Linguistics
Knapp, Mona Linda, German & Modern British
Literature
Lenowitz, Harris, Linguistics, Jewish Studies
Lorenzo-Rivero, Luis, Spanish Language &
Literatuare
Miletich, John Steven, Spanish Medieval
Literature
Slager, William R, Applied Linguistics
Sondrup, Steven Preece, Comparative &
Germanic Literature
Streadbeck, Arval Louis, German
Svendsen, James Thomas, Classics, Drama
Tapscott, Bangs L, Philosophy

VERMONT

Bennington

Newman, Lea Bertani Vozar, American Literature

Burlington

Ambrose, Zuell Philip, Classical Languages
Davison, Jean Margaret, Classical Languages, Ancient History
Gilleland, Brady Blackford, Latin, Greek
Murad, Timothy, Spanish & Latin American Literature
Scrase, David Anthony, German & Comparative Literature
Weiger, John George, Romance Languages

Castleton

Hackel, Roberta Joyce, Eighteenth Century French Prose Fiction

Middlebury

Andreu, Alicia Graciela, Spanish Literature
Baker, Robert Lawrance, Slavic Languages & Literature
Beyer, Thomas R, Jr, Russian Literature & Language
Bourcier, Claude Louis, French Literature
Heibges, Ursula Margarete, Classics
Huber, Thomas, German Language & Literature
Knox, Edward Chapman, Romance Languages
Sparks, Kimberly, Germanic Languages
Vail, Van Horn, Germanic Languages

New Haven

Rodgers, Robert Howard, Classical Philology

Northfield

Lockhart, Donald M, Romance Languages & Literatures

Norwich

Milovsoroff, Basil, Language & Literature

Perkinsville

King, Donald Bernard, Classical Philology

Wolcott

Bertocci, Angelo Philip, Comparative Literature

VIRGINIA

Alexandria

Irizarry, Estelle Diane, Hispanic Literature

Annandale

Cannon, Harold Charles, Classics
Watson, John W, Linguistics, Statistics

Arlington

Eddy, Peter Armes, French Language, Applied Linguistics
Feagin, Louise Crawford, Sociolinguistics, English Linguistics
Robson, Roy Anthony, Theoretical & Applied Linguistics
Simons, Madeleine Anjubault, Literature, French
Weinstein, Allen Isaac, Applied Linguistics, Anthropology
Yotsukura, Sayo, Linguistics, Japanese

Ashland

Challis, David J, Modern & Contemporary Spanish Literature

Blacksburg

Bishop, Lloyd Ormond, French Language & Literature
Doswald, Herman K, German
Drake, Dana Blackmar, Romance Languages, Law
Kline, Galen Richard, Romance Languages
MacAdoo, Thomas Ozro, Classical Languages, German
Palermo, Joseph, Romance Philology

Boyce

Magill, Robert A, French

Bridgewater

Andes, Raymond Nelson, Modern Languages
Kyger, M Ellsworth, Comparative Linguistics

Charlottesville

Alden, Douglas William, French
Arnold, Albert James, Modern French & Comparative Literature
Beizer, Janet L, French Literature
Best, Thomas Waring, German Literature
Bjorklund, Berniel Beth, German Language & Literature
Blackwell, Marilyn Johns, Scandinavian Literature, Film
Chastain, Kenneth Duane, Spanish
Colker, Marvin Leonard, Latin
Connolly, Julian Welch, Slavic Languages & Literature
Cook, Robert Francis, Medieval French Language & Literature
Cozad, Mary Lee, Spanish Literature, Literary Theory
Crocker, Lester Gilbert, Romance Languages
Davidson, Hugh MacCullough, Romance Languages
Davisson, Mary Helen Thomsen, Classical Languages
Daydi-Tolson, Santiago, Spanish Literature
Del Greco, Arnold Armand, Hispanic & Italian Literature
Denomme, Robert T, French
Duisit, Lionel Roger, French Language & Literature
Elson, Mark Jeffrey, Slavic & General Linguistics
Follinus, Gabor J, Russian Literature
Garrard, John G, Soviet Studies
Ghanoonparvar, Mohammad Reza, Persian Language & Literature
Gies, David Thatcher, Spanish Literature
Guzzardo, John Joseph, Italian Language & Literature
Haberly, David T, Romance Languages
Harris, Marvyn Roy, Romance Philology & Linguistics
Herrero, Javier, Romance Languages
Hull, Alexander Pope, Jr, Germanic Languages
Jackson, William Edward, German Language & Literature
Kovacs, Paul David, Classical Language & Literature
Leiter, Sharon L, Russian Literature, Russian Language
Little, W A, German Literature
MacAdam, Alfred John, Latin American Literature, Comparative Literature
McDonald, William Cecil, Medieval German Literature & Language
McGrady, Donald Lee, Spanish
McKinley, Mary B, French Renaissance Literature
Mikalson, Jon Dennis, Greek Religion & Literature
Miles, David Holmes, German
Moyle, Natalie Kononenko, Folklore, Slavic Studies
Perkowski, Jan Louis, Slavic Languages
Reynolds, John Francis, German Literature
Rivkin, Laura Madelaine, Spanish Literature
Roberts, John Taylor, Indic Studies, Linguistics
Roy, Gilbert Wilfrid, Language, Linguistics
Rubin, David Lee, French Literature
Russo, Gloria Marion, Eighteenth Century Literature, Pedagogy
Ryder, Frank Glessner, Germanic Linguistics & Literature
Sauer, Thomas G, German & Comparative Literature
Shattuck, Roger Whitney, French Literature
Simon, Roland Henri, Literary Semiotics, French Civilization
Sokel, Walter H, German Language & Literature
Stocker, Arthur Frederick, Classical Philology, Mediaeval Studies
Tanner, Roy Lynn, Latin American Literature, Spanish
Wright, Chad Carlyle, Spanish Literature
Zimra, Clarisse, Comparative Literature, French

Fairfax

Adamson, Hugh Douglas, Linguistics, Teaching English as a Second Language
Aguera, Victorio Garcia, Spanish Literature
Elstun, Esther Nies, Germanic Languages & Literatures
Hazera, Lydia DeLeon, Spanish American Literature
Hecht, Leo, Russian Language & Literature
Hobson, Irmgard Wagner, German
Tedder, James D, French, Italian
Willis, William S, Romance Languages

Falls Church

Lowe, Pardee, Jr, Germanic Languages & Linguistics
Oney, Earnest Ralph, Indo-European Linguistics, Middle East Politics
Pham, Hai Van (Pham-Van-Hai), Vietnamese & Chinese Linguistics
Suarez-Torres, J David, Latin American Literature

Franklin

LeBlanc, Wilmer James, Linguistics

Fredericksburg

Ascari, Clavio Ferdinando, Modern Languages & Literatures
Breffort-Blessing, Juliette, French Language & Literature
Burns, Mary Ann T, Classics
Hofmann, Margaret Meader, French
Hoge, Miriam Eloise Bowes, Romance Languages
Jones, Edwin Harvie, French
Stephenson, Mary Ellen, Romance Languages
Sumner, Laura Voelkel, Classical Archeology

Hampden-Sydney

Arieti, James Alexander, Classics, History
Thompson, Graves Haydon, Classical Philology

Harrisonburg

Lisle, Robert, Classics
Neatrour, Elizabeth Baylor, Russian Language & Literature
Rauch, Margarete Woelfel, Linguistics
Stewart, John G, German

Hollins

Mitchell, Margarete Koch, German, Spanish
Zeldin, Jesse, Comparative Literature

Hollins College

Bossiere, Jacques P, French, Comparative Literature
Laidlaw, Laura Anne, Classics, Ancient Art
Reimers, Theresia Elizabeth, German
Ritter, William Willis, Jr, Romance Philology

Lexington

Barritt, Carlyle Westbrook, Linguistics, Spanish
Brown, John Madison, German
Hill, Harold Clinton, German, Chinese
Lancaster, Albert Lake, German Philology
Phillips, Klaus Peter, Germanic Languages and Literatures
Pusey, William Webb, III,, German
Stephenson, Buford Stuart, German
Vines, Murray, French Literature, Spanish Grammar
Williams, Sidney James, Jr, Romance Languages, Spanish

Lynchburg

Frank, Margot Kunze, Modern Languages
Hastings, Hester, Romance Languages
Kimball, Anne Spofford, French Language & Literature
Kreusler, Abraham Arthur, Russian Studies
Lloyd, Robert Bruce, Classical Philology
Stern, Charlotte Daniels, Spanish
White, Robert Henry, French Language & Literature

McLean

Donahue, Moraima De Semprun, Spanish &
Latin American Literature
Kim-Renaud, Young-Key, Linguistics
Rudd, Margaret T, Hispanic Literature
Sollenberger, Howard E, Linguistics, Social
Science
Topping, Eva Catafygiotu, Medieval Literature
Vaslef, Nicholas P, Slavic Languages &
Literatures

Newport News

Guthrie, John Richard, Jr, French, German
King, Norma R, Spanish

Norfolk

Moore, Woodrow Wilson, Spanish Language &
Literature
Riley, William Kent, Linguistics, Sociolinguistics
Simon, Jose Gregorio, Philology
Stanley, Dorothy Evelyn, Foreign Languages

Radford

Benjamin, Steven Michael, German Language &
Literature

Richmond

Beck, William John, French Theatre
Birmingham, John Calhoun, Jr, Spanish,
Romance Linguistics
Bowling, Townsend Whelen, French Language &
Literature
Brooke, Francis John, German Literature
Duckworth, James E, English
Duke, Elizabeth Ann Foster, English Linguistics
Dvorak, Paul Francis, German Language &
Literature
Larkin, Neil Matthew, Romance Languages &
Literatures
MacDonald, Robert Alan, Spanish
Marcone, Rose Marie, Spanish
Peischl, Margaret Theresa, German Language
and Literature
Reisler, Marsha Lynn, French Literature &
Language
Selby, Talbot Rayl, Classical Languages, Biblical
Literature
Sims, Robert Lewis, French & Spanish
Terry, Robert Meredith, Romance Languages
Warriner, Helen Page, Foreign Language
Education
Watson, John A, Romance Languages
White, Joseph Senter, Classics

Roanoke

Forte, Bettie Lucille, Classical Languages,
Ancient History

Salem

Favata, Martin Alfred, Spanish, Linguistics
Gathercole, Patricia May, Foreign Languages

Staunton

Evans, Martha Noel, French Literature
Hogsett, Charlotte, Romance Languages

Sweet Briar

Burrows, Reynold Z, Latin, Greek
Embeita, Maria, Spanish
Horwege, Ronald Eugene, Germanic Linguistics
Kirrmann, Ernest Nestor, German & French
Literature
Marshall, Robert G, Romance Languages
Sommerville, Marie-Therese, Romance
Languages
Van Treese, Gilberte (Greiner), French
Literature & Civilization
Van Treese, Glenn Joseph, French Literature &
Language

Williamsburg

Babenko-Woodbury, Victoria A, Russian
Literature & Language
Coke, James Wilson, French, Italian
Cox, Ralph Merritt, Romance Languages
Esler, Carol Clemeau, Classics
Fraser, Howard Michael, Spanish American
Literature
Martel, J Luke, Sr, French Literature
Monson, Don Alfred, Medieval French &
Provencal Literature
Moore, John Aiken, Spanish Literature

Reboussin, Marcel (A), French
Reed, Ann Murphy, Linguistics

WASHINGTON

Bellingham

Baird, Herbert LeRoy, Jr, Spanish
Bowman, Elizabeth, Linguistics, English
Brockhaus, Henrich, German Literature
Bryant, William Howell, French & French-
Canadian Literature
Hiraoka, Jesse, French Language & Literature,
Ethnic Studies
Kimmel, Arthur S, Romance Languages
Milicic, Vladimir, Slavic Languages, Linguistics
Param, Charles, Spanish American & Brazilian
Literature
Rangel-Guerrero, Daniel, Romance Languages
Robinson, Walter L, Languages
Tweddell, Colin Ellidge, Anthropology,
Linguistics

Cheney

Carey, Richard John, Medieval French
Literature
Gariepy, Robert Joseph, Jr, Classics,
Comparative Literature

Clinton

Johnson, Walter, Scandinavian Literature

College Place

Caviness, George Lewis, German Language &
Linguistics

Ellensburg

Bilyeu, Elbert E, Spanish Literature
Herum, John Maurice, Rhetoric, Applied English
Linguistics
Schneider, Christian Immo, Modern German
Literature
Valdespino, Luis Cesar, Law, Foreign Language

Pullman

Beamish, Robert LaLonde, German Literature,
Germanic Languages
Blackwell, Frederick Warn , South Asian
Culture, Literature
Brewer, John T, German
Chang, Aloysius, East Asian Languages &
History
Kappler, Richard G, Russian, Italian
Kim, Hack Chin, Classical Philology,
Comparative Literature
Knox, Robert Baker, Spanish
Lord, Elizabeth Grunbaum Sands, German
Language & Literature
Luchting, Wolfgang Alexander, German, Spanish
Matteson, Marianna Merritt, Spanish Language
& Literature
Seigneuret, Jean-Charles, French Literature
Stabler, Arthur Phillips, French & Comparative
Literature

San Juan Island

Miller, Charles Anthony, German

Seattle

Ammerlahn, Hellmut Hermann, German &
Comparative Literature
Andrews, Walter Guilford, Near East Literature,
Turkish
Armstrong, William, Romance Languages
Barrack, Charles Michael, Germanic Linguistics,
German Literature
Behler, Diana Ipsen, Germanics, Comparative
Literature
Behler, Ernst, Germanics, Comparative
Literature
Bliquez, Lawrence John, Classical Languages,
Ancient History
Buck, George Crawford, German Literature
Christofides, Constantine George, French, Art
History
Contreras, Heles, Spanish Linguistics & Syntactic
Theory
Cooke, Joseph Robinson, Linguistics
Creore, Alvin Emerson, French Language &
Literature
Dale, Robert Charles, French Literature
Dozer, Jane B, French Language & Literature
Eastman, Carol M, Linguistics, Anthropology

Ellrich, Robert John, French Literature
Field, William Hugh W, Romance Languages
Friedman, Lionel Joseph, Romance Languages
Gribanovsky, Paul V, Russian Language &
Literature
Grummel, William Charles, Classical Language
& Literature
Hanzeli, Victor Egon, French Linguistics,
History of Linguistics
Harmon, Daniel Patrick, Classical Languages &
Literature
Heer, Nicholas Lawson, Arabic & Islamic
Studies
Hertling, Gunter H, German
Hruby, Antonin, German
Immerwahr, Raymond Max, German &
Comparative Literature
Keller, Abraham Charles, French
Klausenburger, Jurgen, Romance Linguistics
Kramer, Karl D, Russian Language & Literature
Leiner, Jacqueline, French & Comparative
Literature
Leiner, Wolfgang, Romance Languages,
Comparative Literature
Loraine, Michael B, Islamic Studies, Persian
McDaniel, Gordon Lawrence, Slavic Philology,
Medieval Literature
McDiarmid, John Brodie, Classics
MacKay, Pierre A, Classics, Near Eastern
Studies
McLean, Sammy Kay, Comparative Literature,
Germanics
Micklesen, Lew R, Slavic Linguistics
Miller, Roy Andrew, Linguistics
Niwa, Tamako, Japanese Language
Norman, Jerry, Chinese Linguistics
Nostrand, Howard Lee, French Culture
Pace, Antonio, Romance Languages &
Literatures
Pascal, Paul, Classics, Medieval Latin
Peck, Jeffrey Marc, German & Comparative
Literature
Penuelas, Marcelino C, Spanish
Pool, Jonathan Robert, Sociolinguistics,
Language Planning
Predmore, Michael P, Spanish Language &
Literature
Rabura, Horst M, Germanic Language &
Literature
Read, William Merritt, Classics
Rey, William Henry, German Literature
Rieckmann, Jens, German Literature
Rossel, Sven Hakon, Scandinavian Languages &
Literature
Salinero, Fernando Garcia, Spanish, History of
the Language
Salomon, Richard Geoffrey, Sanskrit Language &
Literature
Saporta, Sol, Spanish, Linguistics
Sehmskorf, Henning, Scandinavian
Shipley, George A, Spanish Literature
Sjavik, Jan Ivar, Scandinavian Literature,
Literary Theory
Suh, Doo Soo, Korean & Japanese Literatures
Swayze, Ernest Harold, Slavic Literature,
Political Science
Trimble, Louis P, English, Linguistics
Voyles, Joseph Bartle, Germanic Languages,
Linguistics
West, James Denison, Russian & Comparative
Literature
Wilson, Clotilde M, Romance Languages &
Literature
Wilson, William Ritchie, Japanese Literature
Wortley, W Victor, Romance Languages
Wylie, Turrell Verl, Philology & History
Yen, Isabella Yiyun, Linguistics
Ziadeh, Farhat Jacob, Arabic, Islamics

Spokane

Schlatter, Fredric William, Classical Languages,
History
Yates, Lawrence Edward, Greek, Philosophy

Tacoma

Martin, Jacqueline, Romance Languages &
Literature
Spangler, Carl David, French
Swenson, Rodney Newcomb, German

Walla Walla

Cosper, D Dale, French Literature

WEST VIRGINIA

Elkins

Seaman, David William, French, Humanities

Huntington

Hoy, Louise Price, Foreign Languages

Morgantown

Borsay, Laszlo Aaron, Classical Languages, Linguistics
Buck, Arthur Charles, Comparative Literature of France & Asia
Claesges, Axel Walter, German Language & Literature
Conerly, Porter Patrick, Spanish & Italian Language
Cummins, Patricia Willett, French
Elkins, Robert Joseph, German, Education
Gonzalez, Pablo, Spanish & Latin American Literature & Culture
Herrera y Sanchez, Francisco, Romance Languages
Hinckley, Lois Vivian, Classical Languages & Literature
Lemke, Victor Jacob, Modern German Literature
Murphy, Joseph Anthony, Foreign Language Education, Romance Languages
Schlunk, Juergen Eckart, German Language & Literature
Siemens, William Lee, Spanish American Prose Fiction
Singer, Armand Edwards, Romance Language & Literature
Stilwell, Robert, Germanic Philology
Taylor, Harley Ustus, Jr, Foreign Languages, German
Whitley, Melvin Stanley, Linguistics, Spanish

Wheeling

Seaman, William Millard, Classical Philology

WISCONSIN

Appleton

Alfieri, Graciela Andrade, Spanish Language & Literature
Alfieri, John Joseph, Spanish Language & Literature
Cronmiller, Bruce, French
Gerlach, Hans Hartmut, German Language & Literature
Jones, Anne Prioleau, French Medieval Literature
McMahon, John Frederick, German
Reed, Gervais Eyer, French
Stowe, Richard S, French Language & Literature
Taylor, Daniel Jennings, Classics, Linguistics
Ternes, Hans, German Literature, Aesthetics
Winslow, Richard Walter, Spanish

Beloit

Black, Robert Greenough, Spanish Medieval Literature, Comparative Literature
Freeman, Thomas Parry, German Literature, Humanities
Paley, Nicholas Miroslav, Romance & Slavic Languages
Robson, Arthur George, Classics, Comparative Literature
Street, Jack David, Foreign Languages

Eau Claire

Gingerich, Vernon J, Modern Foreign Languages
Hoff, Roma B, Spanish Education
Poitzsch, Manfred, German, French

Greenfield

Gatti-Taylor, Marisa, Comparative Literature

Kenosha

Eger, Ernestina N, Spanish
Norwood, Eugene L, German
Ortega, Jose, Romance Languages
Stathatos, Constantine Christopher, Spanish

La Crosse

Nixon, Ruth A, Romance Languages, Education

Madison

Aldrich, Earl M, Spanish, Portuguese
Aragno, Piero, Italian Literature
Baeumer, Max Lorenz, German Literature & Humanities
Bailey, James O, Jr, Russian Literature
Bennett, Emmett Leslie, Jr, Classics
Berghahn, Klaus L, German Literature
Brancaforte, Benito, Spanish Literature of Golden Age, Literary Criticism
Brancaforte, Charlotte Lang, German Literature, German Studies
Brooks, Mary Elizabeth, Spanish & Luso-Brazilian Literature
Cassidy, Frederic Gomes, English & American Language
Caulkins, Janet Hillier, French Language & Literature
Chow, Tse-Tsung, Chinese Literature & Language
Ciplijauskaite, Birute, Romance Languages
Cooper, Robin Hayes, Linguistics
Cunliffe, William Gordon, German
Daniel, Mary L, Portuguese
Dunbar, Ronald William, Germanic Linguistics
Fowler, Barbara Hughes, Classics
Garofalo, Silvano, Italian & Spanish Literature
Gasiorowska, Xenia Z, Slavic Languages & Literatures
Geitz, Henry, Jr, German
Gentry, Francis Gerard, Medieval German Literature, Medieval Studies
Gertel, Zunilda Aimaretti, Spanish American Literature, Literary Criticism
Glauser, Alfred Charles, French Literature
Gras, Maurice Marc, Romance Languages
Grimm, Reinhold, German & Comparative Literature
Grittner, Frank Merton, Foreign Languages
Hanrez, Marc, Romance Languages
Harris, Julian Earle, Old French
Hermand, Jost, Modern German Literature
Howe, Evelyn Mitchell, English, Art History
Howe, Herbert Marshall, Classics
Ingwersen, Niels, Scandinavian Literature
Kasten, Lloyd (August William), Spanish
Kelly, Frederick Douglas, French
Kleinhenz, Christopher, Italian Literature, Philology
Knop, Constance Kay Petersen, French, Education
Kunst, Arthur Egon, Comparative Literature
Lau, Joseph Shiu-Ming, Chinese, Comparative Literature
LeMoine, Fannie John, Classics, Comparative Literature
Lokke, Kari Elise, Comparative Literature, European Romanticism
Loram, Ian Craig, German Literature
MacKendrick, Paul Lachlan, Classical Philology
Mansoor, Menahem, Biblical & Semitic Studies
Marks, Elaine, French Literature, Women's Studies
Marquess, Harlan Earl, Slavic Linguistics, Russian Language
Miller, Arnold, French
Mulvihill, Edward Robert, Spanish
Naess, Harald S, Scandinavian Studies
Nicholas, Robert Leon, Modern Spanish Literature
Nienhauser, William H, Jr, Chinese Literature
Nilsson, Kim G, Linguistics, Scandinavian Languages
Nilsson, Usha Saksena, Indian Language & Literature, English
Nitti, John Joseph, Spanish & Portuguese Language & Literature
Nollendorfs, Valters, German & Latvian Literature
Perkins, Merle Lester, French, Spanish
Plass, Paul Christian, Classical Languages
Read, Charles, Linguistics, Psycholinguistics
Rodini, Robert Joseph, Romance Languages
Rose, Theodore E, Spanish, Portuguese
Sacks, Norman Paul, Hispanic Linguistics & Civilization
Sanchez, Roberto Garza, Spanish Literature & Language
Sanchez-Barbudo, Antonio, Modern Spanish Literature
Scheub, Harold, African Oral Traditions & Literature
Schoville, Keith Norman, Hebrew, Biblical Studies
Scott, Charles Thomas, Linguistics

Seifert, Lester W J, German, Linguistics
Shaw, Joseph Thomas, Slavic Languages
Sihler, Andrew L, Linguistics
Street, John Charles, Linguistics
Thomas, Lawrence Leslie, Slavic Languages & Literatures
Thomas, Ursula May, German, Education
Uffenbeck, Lorin Arthur, French
von Schneidemesser, Luanne H, American English, Lexicography
Vowles, Richard Beckman, Scandinavian Literature
Zamora, Margarita Mountserrat, Latin American & Comparative Literature
Zeps, Valdis Juris, Linguistics

Manitowoc

Bjerke, Robert Alan, Germanic Languages

Milwaukee

Andrade, Leonor, Romance Languages
Arnold, Richard Eugene, Classics
Baldassaro, Lawrence A, Medieval & Modern Literature
Bartley, Diana Esther, Applied Linguistics
Benda, Gisela, German Language & Literature
Carozza, Davy Angelo, Comparative Literature, Romance Languages
Corre, Alan David, Semitic Studies, Linguistics
Cortina, Lynn Ellen Rice, Spanish Language & Literature
Cortina, Rodolfo Jose, Spanish Language & Literature
Coste, Brigitte Marie, French Literature, History of Ideas
De Lauretis, Teresa, Italian Language & Literature
Dial, John Elbert, Spanish
Filips-Juswigg, Katherina P, Russian Literature, European Literature
Flynn, Gerard Cox, Spanish
Grossfeld, Bernard, Hebrew Language & Literature
Harrigan, Renny K, German Language & Literature
Jones, Robert Alston, Modern German Literature
Manalich, Ramiro, Language, Law
Marquardt, Patricia Ann, Classical Languages & Philology
Marshall, James F, Modern Languages
Meyer, Martine Darmon, French
Mileham, James Warren, French Literature
Montante, Michela, Comparative Italian & Spanish Literature
Moravcsik, Edith Andrea, Linguistics
Myers, Oliver Tomlinson, Spanish
Pappanastos, Georgia, Spanish Language & Literature
Pinet, Christopher Paul, French Language & Literature
Rauscher, Gerhard, German
Roeming, Robert Frederick, French & Italian Literature
Ross, Robert Christopher, Classical Philology, Ancient History
Sable, Martin Howard, Latin American Studies, Library Science
Shey, Howard James, Classics
Skalitzky, Rachel Irene, Comparative Literature, Medieval Studies
Spalatin, Christopher, Romance Philology
Stark, Bruce Roderick, English, Linguistics
Stone-Barnard, Laura Marjorie, Classical Languages
Swanson, Roy Arthur, Classics, Comparative Literature
Taylor, Ransom Theodore, German
Taylor, Steven Millen, French Medieval Literature
Trifilo, S Samuel, Spanish Language & Literature
Ullman, Pierre Lioni, Spanish
Winter, Ian James, French Language & Literature
Wood, Allen George, French & Comparative Literature
Zipes, Jack David, German, Comparative Literature

New Berlin

Milham, Mary Ella, Classics

Oshkosh

Bedwell, Carol, German
Tusken, Lewis William, German Language & Literature

Ripon

Delakas, Daniel Liudviko, Romance Languages & Literatures
Hooker, Alexander Campbell, Jr, Romance Languages
Hyatte, Reginald L, Medieval French Literature
Hyde, James Franklin, German Literature

River Falls

Wolfe, Mansell Wayne, Spanish American Literature & Culture

Shorewood

Lacy, Kluenter Wesley, Jr, French Language and Literature

Stevens Point

Assardo, M Roberto, Spanish & Portuguese
Kaminska, Alexandra Barbara, French, Comparative Literature
Kroner, Peter Albert, Foreign Languages

Superior

Bahnick, Karen Kay, Historical Linguistics, Germanic Languages

Waukesha

Aman, Reinhold Albert, Germanic Languages
Jacobson, John Wesley, German

Whitewater

Busot, Adriana B, Spanish Language & Literature
Busot, Aldo J, Spanish
Durette, Roland, French Education

WYOMING

Laramie

Bagby, Lewis, Russian Literature
Bangerter, Lowell Allen, German Language & Literature
Godfrey, Robert G, Linguistics
Hanson, Klaus Dieter, German Literature & Theatre
Heck, Francis S, French
Landeira, Ricardo, Spanish Literature
Langlois, Walter G, Romance Languages
Mayer, Sigrid, German Language & Literature
Mellizo-Cuadrado, Carlos, Contemporary Spanish Literature
Picherit, Jean-Louis Georges, French Medieval Literature, Romance Philology
Scott, Joyce Alaine, French Literature

PUERTO RICO

Cayey

Escalera-Ortiz, Juan, Medieval Spanish Literature, Romance Linguistics

Hato Rey

Nash, Rose, Linguistics, English as Second Language

Mayaguez

Cordaro, Philip, Romance Languages, Philosophy
Ferracane, Gerardo, Romance Languages, Classical History
Figueroa-Chapel, Ramon Antonio, Comparative Literature, Modern Languages
Gonzalez-Mas, Ezequiel, Spanish Literature
Martinez-Tolentino, Jaime, French
Rivera De Alvarez, Josefina, Puerto Rican & Spanish American Literature
Strout, Lilia Dapaz, Spanish Drama, Spanish American Literature

Rio Piedras

Arroyo, Anita, Spanish American Literature, Communication
Azize, Yamila, Spanish & Latin American Literature
Forastieri Braschi, Eduardo J, Spanish Literature, Linguistics
Gonzalez, Rafael A, Spanish Language and Literature
Torres-Delgado, Rene, Foreign Languages, Fine Arts

San German

Martin, Jose Luis, Romance Languages
Muckley, Robert L, English as a Second Language
Saciuk, Bohdan, General & Ibero-Romance Linguistics

San Juan

Babin, Maria Teresa, Spanish Literature
Morris, Marshall, Translation, Social Anthropology

Santurce

Sotomayer Miletti, Aurea Maria, Spanish American Literature

VIRGIN ISLANDS

St Thomas

Cooper, Vincent O'Mahony, Linguistics, English

CANADA

ALBERTA

Calgary

Anderson, James Maxwell, Linguistics
Baker, John Arthur, Philosophy, Ethics
Bresky, Dushan, Modern French Literature, Comparative Literature
Breugelmans, Rene, Comparative Literature
Chadbourne, Richard McClain, French & French-Canadian Literature
Cook, Eung-Do, Linguistics
de Jubecourt, Gerard Stheme, Romance Languages, French
Donovan, Lewis Gary, Medieval French Literature
Gilby, William Reid, German Literature
Greaves, Anthony A, Romance Studies
Heinrich, Albert Carl, Anthropology, Linguistics
Izzo, Herbert John, Romance Linguistics
Laychuk, Julian Louis, Russian & Soviet Literature
McCormack, William Charles, Anthropology, Linguistics
Oyler, John Edward, Modern Foreign Languages
Schmiel, Robert Charles, Classics
Smeaton, B Hunter, Linguistics
Southerland, Ronald Hamilton, Linguistics, German
Struc, Roman Sviatoslav, German & Slavic Literature
Zaitzeff, Serge Ivan, Latin American Literature
Zekulin, Nicholas Gleb, Russian Literature

Edmonton

Blodgett, Edward Dickinson, Mediaeval & Canadian Literature
Braun, Richard Emil, Classics, Literature
Buck, Robert John, Classics
Busch, Robert Louis, Russian Literature & Language
Creore, Jo Ann Davis, Romance Languages, Linguistics
D'Alquen, Richard J E, Germanic Languages
Derwing, Bruce Lloyd, Linguistics
Dimic, Colette Anne Marie, French Language & Literature, Germanic Philology
Dimic, Milan Velimir, Comparative & German Literature
Dryer, Matthew S, Linguistics
Eckert, Lowell Edgar, Classical Languages, Biblical Studies
Egert, Eugene, Germanic Languages
Fishwick, Duncan, Classical Philology, Ancient History
Forcadas, Alberto M, Romance Languages

Garbrah, Kweku Arku, Classical Lingustics & Philology
Hardy, William George, Latin & Greek Literature
Hoffmann, Gisela Elise, German Language & Literature
Langdon, David Jeffrey, French Literature, Philosophy
Marahrens, Gerwin, German Language & Literature
Margolin, Uri, Comparative Literature, Poetics
Morcos, Gamila, French Literature
Mozejko, Edward, Comparative Literature
Nielson, Rosemary Mullin, Latin & Greek Languages & Literature
Ober, Kenneth Harlan, Comparative Literature, Foreign Languages
Pausch, Holger Arthur, Modern German Literature, Methodology
Prideaux, Gary Dean, Linguistics
Reinhold, Ernest, German
Slavutych, Yar, Slavic Languages, Linguistics
Terakura, Hiroko, Japanese Linguistics
Wilson, John Richard, Classics
Zujewskyj, Oleh, Slavonic Languages & Literatures

Lethbridge

Cormier, Louis-Philippe, Romance Languages

BRITISH COLUMBIA

Abbotsford

Loewen, Jacob Abram, Linguistics, Modern Languages

Burnaby

Bartlett, Barrie Everdell, General Linguistics, History of Linguistics
Bouton, Charles Pierre, Linguistics, History of Grammar
Bursill-Hall, Geoffrey Leslie, Linguistics
Colhoun, Edward Russell, Spanish, Linguistics
Foley, James Addison, Linguistics, Philosophy of Linguistics
Hammerly, Hector Marcel, Applied Linguistics, Second Language Teaching
Knowles, Donald Roland John, General Linguistics, Spanish
Merler, Grazia, French & French Canadian Literature
Newton, Brian Elliott, Linguistics, Modern Greek
Viswanathan, Jacqueline J, General Literature, Contemporary Fiction

Vancouver

Aklujkar, Ashok Narhar, Sanskrit Language & Literature
Barrett, Anthony Arthur, Classics
Batts, Michael S, German
Baudouin, Dominique, French Language & Literature
Bongie, Elizabeth Bryson, Classics
Bongie, Laurence Louis, French Literature
Boulby, Mark, German & Comparative Literature
Bouygues, Claude P, French Language & Literature
Bryans, John Victor, Spanish & Comparative Literature
Carden, Guy, Linguistics
Carr, Derek Cooper, Hispanic & Medieval Studies
Ciccone De Stafanis, Stefania, Italian Language & Literature
Coope, Marian Garrison Robinson, Spanish
Goetz-Stankiewicz, Marketa, German & Comparative Literature
Gregg, Robert John, Linguistics
Grover, Frederic John, French
Hamlin, Frank Rodway, Romance Linguistics
Highnam, David Ellis, French Literature
Hurvitz, Leon Nahum, Far Eastern Languages, Far Eastern Buddhism
Ingram, David, Linguistics
Kinkade, Marvin Dale, Anthropological Linguistics
Knutson, Harold Christian, French
Ma, Sen, Chinese Language & Literature
McGregor, Malcolm Francis, Classical Philology, Ancient History
MacKay, Alistair R, Romance Languages & Literatures
McNeely, James A, German

Vancouver, CANADA (cont)

Matte, Edward Joseph Francis, French
    Literature & Linguistics
Mornin, Edward, Modern German Literature
Niederauer, David John, French
O'Neill, Patrick James, German, Comparative
    Literature
Pacheco-Ransanz, Arsenio, Spanish Literature
Petersen, Klaus, German Literature
Podlecki, Anthony Joseph, Classics
Primeau, Marguerite A, French Literature &
    Language
Pronger, Lester James, French Literature
Pulleyblank, Edwin George, Chinese Language &
    History
Rochemont, Michael Shaun, Linguistics
Russell, James, Classical Archeology & Philology
St Jacques, Bernard, Linguistics, Asian Studies
Sandy, Gerald Neil, Classics, Latin Literature
Soga, Matsuo, Linguistics, Japanese
Solecki, Jan Jozef, Russian Language, Economics
Stenberg, Peter Alvin, German & Scandinavian
    Literature
Sullivan, Shirley Darcus, Classical Languages,
    Early Greek Philosophy
Tougas, Gerard Raymond, French
Wainman, Alexander Wheeler, Russian Language
    & Literature, Serbo-Croatian Language
Zaenker, Karl A, Medieval German Literature

Victoria

Abrioux, Olivier Marie, French Language &
    Literature
Archbold, Geoffrey John D E, Classics, Ancient
    History
Campbell, David Aitken, Classics
Donskov, Andrew, Russian Literature
Edwards, Prior Maximilian Hemsley, Linguistics,
    Music
Esling, John Henry, Linguistics, Phonetics
Folejewski, Zbigniew, Slavic Literature &
    Linguistics
Griffiths, David A, French Language &
    Literature
Hadley, Michael Llewellyn, German Language &
    Literature
Huxley, Herbert H, Greek & Latin Literature
Juricic, Zelimir Bob, Russian & Croato-Serbian
    Languages & Literature
Kess, Joseph Francis, Linguistics
Mordaunt, Jerrold L, Spanish Language &
    Literature
Moreau, Gerald E, French & Franco-Canadian
    Literature
Riedel, Walter Erwin, German
Schaarschmidt, Gunter Herbert, Slavic &
    General Linguistics
Smith, Peter Lawson, Classics
Symington, Rodney Terence, German &
    Comparative Literature
Vinay, Jean-Paul, Linguistics
Waelti-Walters, Jennifer Rose, Modern French
    Literature

MANITOBA

Brandon

Voorhis, Paul H, Linguistics

Winnipeg

Allen, John Robin, Romance Languages,
    Computational Linguistics
Balcaen, Hubert Louis, French Language &
    Literature
Beckers, Gustav Eugen, German Language &
    Literature
Bendor-Samuel, Brian Leslie, French Literature
Berry, Edmund Grindlay, Classical Philology
Bessason, Haraldur, Icelandic Language &
    Literature
Doerksen, Victor Gerard, German Literature &
    Criticism
Eagle, Edwin Douglas, Classics, Philosophy
Egan, Rory Bernard, Classics
Glendinning, Robert James, German Language &
    Literature
Golden, Mark, Classical Languages, Ancient
    History
Gordon, Alexander Lobban, French
Gordon, Donald Keith, Spanish American
    Literature
Harvey, Carol Josephine, French Language &
    Literature

Hofmann, Thomas Karl, German Baroque
    Literature
Ilnytzkyj, Oleh Stepan, Slavic Languages &
    Literatures
Jensen, Christian Andrew Edward, Romance
    Language & Literature
Jones, Cyril Meredith, Medieval Romance
    Literature
Joubert, Andre, French
Joubert, Ingrid, French, German
Marantz, Enid Goldstine, French
Rozumnyj, Jaroslav, Ukrainian & Russian
    Language & Literature
Tarnawecky, Iraida Irene, East Slavic Languages
Thiessen, Jack, German Language & Literature
Wanamaker, Murray Gorham, English,
    Linguistics

NEW BRUNSWICK

Anagance

Osborne, Robert Edward, Modern Spanish
    Literature

Fredericton

Elkhadem, Saad Eldin Amin, German &
    Comparative Literature
Kinloch, A Murray, English
Konishi, Haruo, Classics
London, J Dalton George, Second Language
    Didactics, French Literature
Lusher, Harold Edward, German Language &
    Literature
Moore, Roger, Spanish
Piquer, Mariano Julio, Spanish Language,
    History of Spanish Civilization
Poyatos, Fernando, Romance Languages
Pugh, Anthony Roy, French Literature
Shaw, Alvin John, Spanish
Whalen, Robert George, French, English as
    Second Languages

Sackville

Bour, Jean-Antoine, French Language &
    Literature
Welch, Liliane, French Literature, Aesthetics

NEWFOUNDLAND

St John's

Artiss, David Sturge, German Language &
    Literature
Ashley, John Benedict, Classics
Bruce, Iain Anthony Fyvie, Classical Languages,
    Ancient History
Bubenik, Vit Moric, Classics, Linguistics
Clark, Raymond John, Classics
Hewson, John, Linguistics
Jackson, Herbert Hugh, Modern Languages
Montoya, Emilio, Spanish Language & Literature
Muzychka, Stephan, Foreign Languages
Ratz, Alfred Egon, German Language and
    Literature
Smith, Lawrence Richard, Generative &
    Computational Linguistics
Thomas, Gerald, Folklore, French

NOVA SCOTIA

Antigonish

Fink, Robert J, French Renaissance, Cinema

Halifax

Aikens, Harry Forbes, French Linguistics
Aucoin, Gerald Edgar, French
Bishop, Michael, Modern French Literature
Brown, James W, Romance Languages,
    Semiotics
Chavy, Paul, French Language & Literature
Friedrich, Rainer Walter, Classics, Comparative
    Literature
Gaede, Friedrich Wolfgang, German Literature,
    Philosophy
Gesner, B Edward, Dialectology, Applied
    Linguistics
Holloway, James Edward, Jr, Spanish American
    Literature
Ingalls, Wayne Barritt, Classics

Kocourek, Rostislav, Terminology & Lexicology,
    Linguistics
Lawler, James Ronald, French Literature
Lawrence, Derek William, Modern French
    Literature
Runte, Hans R, French Literature
Runte, Roseann, French, Comparative Literature
Schwarz, Hans-Gunther, German & Comparative
    Literature

Wolfville

Northey, Anthony Droste, German
Roden, Lethem Sutcliffe, Romance Languages
Valverde, Jose Antonio, Spanish Language &
    Literature
Vellek, Gary Franklin, Classics
Waseem, Gertrud Sprenger, German

ONTARIO

Downsview

Corbett, Noel L, French Language & Linguistics
Cotnam, Jacques, French & French-Canadian
    Literature
Grabowski, Yvonne S, Russian, Slavic Studies
Priestley, John Edward, French Literature,
    Humanities
Rathe, Charles Edward, French
Schueler, Heinz Juergen, German Language &
    Literature
Zimmerman, Melvin, French, Comparative
    Literature

Guelph

Adams, Leonard, French Language & Literature
Andersen, M, Romance Languages, Comparative
    Literature
Barrell, Rex Arthur, Comparative Literature &
    Linguistics
Bartocci, Gianni, Romance Languages
Bell, John Marshall, Classical Languages
Benson, Renate, German & Comparative
    Literature
Matthews, Victor John, Classics
Mose, Kenrick Ewart, Spanish Language &
    Literature
Wilshere, A D, French, Romance Philology

Hamilton

Chapple, Clement Gerald, German &
    Comparative Literature
Colarusso, John J, Jr, Linguistics, Caucasian
    Languages
Conlon, Pierre Marie, French Language &
    Literature
Cro, Stelio, Italian, Spanish
Guite, Harold Frederick, Classics
Jeeves, William Norman, Romance Languages
McKay, Alexander Gordon, Classical Art &
    Architecture
Morgan, Owen Rees, French Language &
    Literature
Nardocchio, Elaine F, French-Canadian
Paul, George MacKay, Classics, Ancient History
Schulte, Hans Herbert, German
Thomas, George, Russian Language History
Van Dusen, Robert LaBranche, German
Whiteside, Anna, French & Comparative
    Literature

Kingston

Avis, Walter Spencer, English, Linguistics
Bastianutti, Diego Luigi, Foreign Languages &
    Literatures
Bessette, Gerard, French
Bly, Peter Anthony, Spanish Literature
Evans, Wilfred Hugo, French
Hope-Simpson, Richard, Ancient History &
    Archeology, Classical Languages
Hunter-Lougheed, Rosemarie, German &
    Comparative Literature
Kilpatrick, Ross Stuart, Classics
Krausse, Helmut K, Germanic Languages &
    Literature
Kushnir, Slava Maria, French
Loeb, Ernst, German Language & Literature
Marshall, Anthony John, Classics, Roman
    History
Parker, Charles Haldor, Linguistics, Religion
Reesor, Margaret E, Classics
Riley, Anthony William, German Language &
    Literature
Sadouski, John, Byelorussian Language &
    Literature

Smethurst, Stanley Eric, Classics
Walker, John, Hispanic & English Literature

Kitchener

Bongart, Klaus Herman, German Literature
Roller, Duane Williamson, Classical Archeology, Ancient History

London

Anderson, Alexander R, German Language & Literature
Baguley, David, French Literature
Brunet, Jean Paul, French, American Literature
Bush, William Shirley, French Literature
Creighton, Douglas George, French Language & Literature
de Fabry, Anne Srabian, French & Canadian Literature
Eramian, Gregory Michael, Russian Language, Slavic Linguistics
Flint, Weston, Romance Languages
Forsyth, Louise H, French
Gerber, Douglas Earl, Classics
Holmes, Glyn, French
Issacharoff, Michael, French Language & Literature
Kalbfleisch, Herbert Karl, German Language & Literature
Marti, Antonio M, Spanish
Raymond, Alfred Ernest, Classical Philology
Richmond, Ian McKenzie, French Literature & Language
Sanders, James Bernard, French
Saraydar, Alma Collins, Romance Languages & Literatures
Schluetter, Hans J, German Language & Literature
Shervill, Robert Newton, Literature, Linguistics
Smieja, Florian Ludwik, Spanish & Latin American Literature
Spencer, Hanna, German Language & Literature
Tracy, Gordon, German
Walters, Robert Lowell, French
Wilson, Harry Rex, English Linguistics

Mississauga

Beck, Roger Lyne, Classics
Hegyi, Ottmar, Spanish Language & Literature
Neglia, Erminio, Spanish American Literature, Italian & Spanish Theatre
Rubincam, Catherine Isobel Reid, Ancient Greek History & Literature

Ottawa

Arbour, Romeo, French Literature
Barratt, Glynn Richard, Russian Literature & History
Bida, Constantine, Slavic Linguistics & Literatures
Blockley, Roger Charles, Ancient History, Classics
Brearley, Denis George, Latin Paleography, Medieval Latin
Calve, Pierre Jean, French Language
Clayton, John Douglas, Russian Literature
Cousin, Florence Camille, Linguistics, French
Cowan, William George, Linguistics
Dallett, Joseph Birdsall, German Literature
Dennis, Nigel Robert, Contemporary Spanish Literature
Elbaz, Andre Elie, French & Comparative Literature
Fleischauer, Charles Paul, French
Galliani, Renato, French Literature
Gareau, Etienne, Latin
Giangrande, Lawrence, Classics
Goheen, Jutta, German
Grebenschikov, Vladimir, Linguistics, Literature
Hodge, A Trevor, Classics
Imbert, Patrick Louis, French Literature, Semiotics
Jensen, John T, Phonology, English Linguistics
Jurado, Jose, Spanish Literature
Kaye, Eldon Fenton, French
Kelly, Louis Gerard, Linguistics
Koerner, E F Konrad, General Linguistics
Kresic, Stephen, Classics
Kunstmann, Pierre Marie Francois, Medieval Literature, French Philology
Lapierre, Andre, French & French-Canadian Linguistics
Larson, Ross, Latin American Literature
Laurette, Pierre, French

Lize, Emile Jean-Claude, French Literature
Major, Jean-Louis, French & French Canadian Literature
Maurach, Bernhard, German Literature & Language
Mercie, Jean Luc, French Literature
Neufeld, Gerald G, Psycholinguistics
Nicholson, John Greer, Linguistics, Philology
Poplack, Shana, Linguistics
Renart, Juan Guillermo, Hispanic Literature
Rivero, Maria Luisa, Linguistics
Robidoux, Rejean, French & French Canadian Literature
Robinson, Terence Reginald, Ancient History, Classics
Sarkany, Stephane, French, Literary Theory
Steedman, David Wilson, French Language & Literature
Stong-Jensen, Margaret Teller, Linguistics
Sullivan, Henry Wells, Spanish & Comparative Literature
Tassie, James Steward, French-Canadian Language & Literature
Van Rutten, Pierre M, French Literature, Linguistics
Vigneault, Robert, French & French-Canadian Literature
Welsh, Michael Edward, Classics
Wyczynski, Pawel, French Literature, Slavic Studies
Yalden, Janice Mackenzie, Linguistics, Spanish Language
Zimmerman, Eugenia Noik, Romance Languages

Parry Sound

Brown, Harcourt, French Literature

Peterborough

Baumgaertel, Gerhard, Germanic Language & Literature
Gonzalez-Martin, Jeronimo Pablo, Spanish Language & Literatures
Kinzl, Konrad Heinrich, Classics
Noriega, Teobaldo Alberto, Spanish American & Latin American Literature
Orsten, Elisabeth M, Anglo Saxon & Middle English
Royle, Peter, French
Stewart, David D, German
Todd, Evelyn Mary, Linguistics, Cultural Anthropology

Richmond Hill

Magnotta, Michael, Foreign Languages & Literature

St Catharines

Bismuth, Rene, French Language & Literature
Bucknall, Barbara Jane, Romance Languages
Cardy, Michael John, French Language & Literature
Casler, Frederick Howard, Classical Languages, Indo-European Linguistics
Lehn, Walter, Linguistics, History
Owen, Claude Rudolph, Germanic Languages & Literature
Robertson, Noel D, Classics
Schutz, Herbert, German Language & Literature
Soady, Ana Victoria, Classical Languages

Sudbury

Arango, Manuel Antonio, Latinoamerican Literature, Spanish Philology
Gubern, Santiago, Spanish
Kitching, Laurence Patrick Anthony, Modern Language & Literature
Lewis, Gertrud Jaron, Medieval German Literature
Roque-Nunez, Horacio, Romance Languages, Philosophy
Sabourin, Pascal, French Modern Novel

Thornhill

Echard, Gwenda, French Renaissance Literature

Thunder Bay

Andrachuk, Gregory Peter, Mediaeval Hispanic Studies

Toronto

Amos, Ashley Crandell, Old English Philology
Bakker, Barend Hendrik, French Literature
Bar-Lewaw, Isaac, Spanish American Literature
Barnes, Timothy David, Classics, History
Bedford, Charles Harold, Russian Literature
Bisztray, George, Comparative Literature, Hungarian Studies
Bouraoui, Hedi E, French & Comparative Literature
Bowman, Herbert Eugene, Slavic & Comparative Literature
Brown, Virginia, Classics, Medieval Latin
Burke, James F, Medieval Spanish Language & Literature
Catholy, Eckehard Kurt, German, Drama
Chandler, Stanley Bernard, Romance Languages
Chew, John James, Jr, Linguistics
Chicoy-Daban, Jose Ignacio, Spanish Literature
Clivio, Gianrenzo Pietro, Linguistics, Literature
Cloutier, Cecile, French
Collet, Paulette F, Romance Languages
Conacher, Desmond John, Classical Philology
Curtis, Alexander Ross, Romance Languages
Dainard, James Alan, French
Dalzell, Alexander, Classics
Danesi, Marcel, Linguistics, Italian
De Montmollin, Daniel-Philippe, Classics
Dolezel, Lubomir, Slavic Languages & Literature
Dolezelova-Velingerova, Milena, Modern & Classical Chinese Fiction
Ducretet, Pierre Raymond, Romance Languages & Linguistics
Eichner, Hans, German Language & Literature
Falconer, Alexander Graham, French & Comparative Literature
Fantham, Rosamund Elaine, Classical Languages & Literature
Farquharson, Robert Howard, German Language & Literature
Field, George Wallis, German
Fitch, Brian Thomas, French
Fitzgerald, Wilma L, Latin, Greek
Flinn, John Ferguson, French Literature & Language
Genno, Charles Norman, German
Gordon, Alan Martin, Romance Languages
Graham, Victor Ernest, French Literature
Grant, John Neilson, Classics
Grant, John Ratcliffe, Classics
Grise, Catherine Margaret, French Language & Literature
Gulsoy, J, Romance Languages, Hispanic Linguistics
Hamlin, Cyrus, Comparative Literature
Hanley, Mary Esther, Classics
Harden, Arthur Robert, French Literature
Harris, Kathleen, German Studies
Hayes, Walter Martin, Classics, Byzantine Greek
Hayne, David Mackness, French
Heinemann, Edward Arthur, French
Iannucci, Amilcare Alfredo, Italian Literature
Jennings, L Chantal, French Literature & Language
Joliat, Eugene A, French & Comparative Literature
Jones, Christopher Prestige, Classical Literature, Ancient History
Joyce, Dougals A, Germanic Languages
Kerslake, Lawrence Carl, French Literature
Keyes, Gordon Lincoln, History, Classics
Kirkness, William John, French Language & Literature
Kuitunen, Maddalena Teresa, Italian Language, Literature
Laillou-Savona, Jeannette, French, English
Latta, Alan Dennis, German Language & Literature
Lee, M Owen, Classics
Lehouck, Emile, Romance Languages, French Literature
Le Huenen, Roland Jean, French Literature, Semiotics
Leon, Pedro, Phonetics, Linguistics
Leon, Pierre R, Phonetics, Linguistics
Lesley, Arthur Michael, Jr, Comparitive Literature, Hebrew Literature
Levy, Kurt Leopold, Spanish
Luckyj, George Stephen Nestor, Slavic Languages & Literature
McClelland, John A, French
McCready, Warren Thomas, Romance Languages
McLeod, Wallace Edmond, Classics
Marin, Diego, Spanish
Martin, Philippe Jean, Linguistics, Acoustics
Mason, Hugh John, Classics
Masson, Jeffery Lloyd, Sanskrit

Bernath, Peter, German Literature, European
    Civilization
Bonenfant, Joseph, Literature
Brodeur, Leo Arthur, French & Comparative
    Literatures
Forest, Jean, French Literature
Kom, Ambroise, Black Comparative Literature
Lacasse, Rodolphe Romeo, Contemporary
    French & Comparative Literature
Michon, Jacques, French, French Canadian
    Literature
Naaman, Antoine, French Literature
Sirois, Antoine, Comparative Literature

Sutton

Houpert, Jean, French

Trois-Rivieres

Legare, Clement, Semantics, Semiotics

Waterville

Giroux, Robert, French & French Canadian
    Literatures

Westmount

Elia, Maurice, French Language & Civilization

SASKATCHEWAN

Regina

Adrianow, Gennadij Y, Slavic Language &
    Literature
Belcher, Margaret, French
Kocks, Günter Hermann, German Language &
    Literature
McGoldrick, John Malcolm, French, French
    Literature

Saskatoon

Andrusyshen, Constantine Henry, Slavic
    Philology
Buyniak, Victor O, Slavic Languages
Genuist, Monique Suzanne, French Canadian
    Literature, French Language
Genuist, Paul Marcel, Romance Languages
Green, Maria, French & World Literature
Haderlein, Kuonrat Georg Josef, Comparative
    Literature, Contemporary German Theatre
Perez, Luis A, Spanish
Pritchet, Christopher Dixon, Classical Languages
    & Literatures
Ridgway, Ronald Sidney, French
Wittlin, Curt J, Romance Languages

OTHER COUNTRIES

ARGENTINA

Castagnino, Raul Hector, Spanish American
    Literature

AUSTRIA

Homberger, Conrad Paul, Modern Languages
Schier, Rudolf Dirk, Comparative Literature

BRAZIL

Lockett, Landon Johnson, Linguistics,
    Portuguese

CHINA, REPUBLIC OF

Cohen, William Howard, Comparative
    Literature, Philosophy

COSTA RICA

Hanks, Joyce Main, French Renaissance Poetry

EGYPT

MacCoull, Leslie Shaw Bailey, Classics,
    Papyrology

FRANCE

Atherton, John H, Comparative Literature,
    American Studies
Benichou, Paul, French Literature
Lightner, Theodore M, Linguistics, Slavic
    Languages
Lynes, Carlos, Jr, French Literature

GERMANY, FEDERAL REPUBLIC OF

Bailey, Charles-James Nice, Comparative
    Philology, Theology
Hopkins, Edwin Arnley, Germanic Languages,
    Linguistics
Lattey, Elsa Maria, Linguistics, English as a
    Second Language
Luzbetak, Louis Joseph, Linguistic Analysis,
    Cultural Anthropology
Maxwell, Daniel Newhall, Linguistics
Menzel, Peter, Linguistics
Szoverffy, Joseph, Comparative Literature,
    Medieval Literature
Winter, Werner, Linguistics

HONG KONG

Rudolph, Richard Casper, Chinese Culture

ISRAEL

Cohen, Andrew David, Language Testing &
    Education
Gershenson, Daniel Enoch, Greek & Latin
Goldman, Howard Allen, Russian Literature &
    Language
Greenberg, Moshe, Semitics
Greenfield, Jonas Carl, Hebrew & Semitic
    Languages
Lees, Robert B, Linguistics
Reif, Joseph A, Linguistics
Wolf, Meyer L, Linguistics

ITALY

Costelloe, M Joseph, Classical Languages
Galpin, Alfred, Romance Languages, Musical
    Composition
Shankovsky, Igor, Slavonic Philology,
    Comparative Literatures

JAPAN

Hofmann, Th R, Linguistics, Mathematics
Shibatani, Masayoshi, Linguistics

KENYA

Kanyoro, Rachel Angogo, Linguistics

MEXICO

Antaki, Vivian Jane, Comparative Literature

NETHERLANDS

Lightfoot, David William, Linguistics
Newman, Paul, African Linguistics

NEW GUINEA

Litteral, Robert Lee, Linguistics, Sociolinguistics

NEW ZEALAND

Biggs, Bruce Grandison, Linguistics

NIGERIA

Harris, Rodney Elton, French Literature

PORTUGAL

Da Cal, Ernesto Guerra, Spanish & Portuguese

SOUTH AFRICA

Gasinski, Thaddeus Zdzislaw, Slavic Linguistics

SPAIN

Ramos-Orea, Tomas, English Literature;
    Matrimonial Law
Sullivant, Raymond L, French, Spanish

SWITZERLAND

Hiebel, Frederick, German Language &
    Literature
Jost, Dominik, German Literature
Kilchenmann, Ruth Johanna, German &
    Comparative Literature
Mendels, Judica (Ignatia Hendrika), German,
    Dutch

UNITED KINGDOM

Dillon, John Myles, Classics
Hippisley, Anthony Richard, Russian Language
    & Literature
Lass, Roger, Linguistics
Terlecki, Tymon Tadeusz J, Polish Literature
Thompson, Henry Swift, Computational
    Linguistics

ZAMBIA

Wendland, Ernst Richard, Bantu Languages &
    Literature